BLACKSTONE'S

CRIMINAL
PRACTICE

BLACKSTONE'S
CRIMINAL PRACTICE
2015

GENERAL EDITOR

DAVID ORMEROD QC (HON)

LAW COMMISSIONER, BARRISTER, BENCHER OF MIDDLE TEMPLE,
PROFESSOR OF CRIMINAL JUSTICE, QUEEN MARY,
UNIVERSITY OF LONDON

FOUNDING EDITOR

HHJ PETER MURPHY

CONSULTANT EDITOR

HHJ JOHN PHILLIPS CBE

ADVISORY EDITORIAL BOARD

LORD JUSTICE LEVESON, THE HONOURABLE MR JUSTICE GLOBE,
HHJ ROBERT ATHERTON, HHJ PETER BEAUMONT QC,
HHJ SALLY CAHILL QC, HHJ RICHARD MARKS QC,
HHJ JEFFREY PEGDEN QC, HOWARD RIDDLE,
MICHAEL BOWES QC, ALISON LEVITT QC,
TIM OWEN QC, DAVID PERRY, ROBERT SMITH QC,
ADRIAN WATERMAN QC, HH ERIC STOCKDALE

CONTRIBUTORS

DUNCAN ATKINSON, ALEX BAILIN QC, DIANE BIRCH,
MICHELLE BREWER, ED CAPE, HHJ JOHANNAH CUTTS QC,
ANAND DOOBAY, ANTHONY EDWARDS, RUDI FORTSON QC,
MICHAEL HIRST, LAURA C. H. HOYANO, PETER HUNGERFORD-WELCH,
PAUL JARVIS, ADRIAN KEANE, MICHAEL LEREGO QC,
RICHARD MCMAHON QC, VALSAMIS MITSILEGAS, TIM MOLONEY QC,
STEPHEN PARKINSON, AMANDA PINTO QC, EDWARD REES QC,
HHJ PETER ROOK QC, RICHARD D. TAYLOR, MARK TOPPING,
MARTIN WASIK CBE

OXFORD
UNIVERSITY PRESS

OXFORD
UNIVERSITY PRESS

Great Clarendon Street, Oxford, OX2 6DP,
United Kingdom

Oxford University Press is a department of the University of Oxford.
It furthers the University's objective of excellence in research, scholarship,
and education by publishing worldwide. Oxford is a registered trade mark of
Oxford University Press in the UK and in certain other countries

Published in the United States of America by Oxford University Press
198 Madison Avenue, New York, NY 10016, United States of America

British Library Cataloguing in Publication Data

Data available

ISBN
978–0–19–871312–8 (Book with all supplements)
978–0–19–871313–5 (Book and eBook with all supplements)
978–0–19–871311–1 (Book)

Printed in Italy by
L.E.G.O. S.p.A.—Lavis TN

Preface

I am delighted to write the preface for this 25th edition of *Blackstone's Criminal Practice*. Since its inception in 1991 it has been the only practitioner text to offer a comprehensive manual meeting the criminal practitioner's need in every level of court.

In collaboration with Alistair McQueen and others at *Blackstone Press*, the Founding Editor Peter Murphy launched *Blackstone's Criminal Practice* to meet "the clear and widely recognized need for a new work . . . in a single volume, giving an up to date service, [with] writing of uncompromising and rigorous scholarly quality, [and] meticulous attention to detail [with] emphasis on the practice of the courts, [designed] to promote maximum utility and minimum confusion". It has achieved its aims. It is now trusted and regularly cited in the Supreme Court, the Court of Appeal, and the Divisional Court. It is found in every Crown Court and magistrates' court in the country. It has become the preferred text of many judges, advocates, and legal professionals attracted by its clear readable style and authoritative content.

There have of course been many changes over the last 25 years as the book has evolved, including changes to the editorial team. For the first 16 years, under Peter Murphy's editorship the book gained the respect of practitioners and the judiciary alike. In 2008 Sir Anthony Hooper and I began a joint editorship reflecting the core strengths underpinning the entire book: a unique blend of academic scholarship and comment with practical experience and insight. This year, Sir Anthony has stepped down following his retirement from the Court of Appeal in 2013. His decades of experience and expertise as an advocate, a judge, and as deputy chairman of Criminal Procedure Rule Committee have benefitted the book enormously. I would like to record my huge gratitude to him for the years of support and guidance on all aspects of the editorial work and beyond. I am delighted that in 2016 I will be joined by a new co-Editor in Chief: Mr David Perry QC, who is renowned as one of the greatest criminal advocates of our time. He will bring with him unrivalled experience from the criminal courts. Changes have also occurred to the membership of the Advisory Editorial Board. It has, throughout, been formed of a high calibre team bringing a wealth of experience from practice and the bench. The members offer guidance on the contents and structure of the book.

The author team has evolved too. Many of the team of original authors remain from 1991, and their commitment and dedication along with their vast experience has been vital to the success of the book. The team has also expanded as more specialists have been brought in to deal with individual subjects, and we have been successful in attracting many of the leading practitioners in the fields as contributors. This has ensured that *Blackstone's* users can retain their confidence that the text is focussed on meeting the needs of those in practice by providing authoritative treatment presented in an accessible manner. The entire team of authors deserves the highest praise for continuing to produce such high quality work. We will continue to work with leading practitioners to ensure that we have expert coverage of particular specialisms. Congratulations are also due to the editorial coordinator, Laurence Eastham, who has been with *Blackstone's* from the outset. It is difficult to overestimate the significance of the impact he has had in ensuring the continued quality of the book. His unique experience and intimate knowledge of the entire work has proved invaluable year after year. He continues to provide great inspiration to all those involved in each edition.

The original publishers—Blackstone Press—was acquired in 2001 but the commitment of Oxford University Press has been unstinting since taking over the work. Although the team working on the book has changed many times, the dedication of everyone at OUP to *Blackstone's Criminal Practice* and its objectives has been unfailing.

Changes in the presentation of the work have also occurred to meet the needs of our readers. Along with the main work, which is now available as an app, an e-book, and in print, there are three cumulative supplements. Although never envisaged at the time of our launch, the introduction of supplements has proved a huge success: access to these essential documents in a separate convenient volume is immensely popular with judges and practitioners alike. These incorporate the entire text of the Criminal Procedure Rules, the Crown Court Practice Directions, and the relevant sentencing guidelines. There are also online monthly updates and the popular Quarterly Update offering topical reviews. In short, *Blackstone's* offers a complete coverage of criminal practice materials in a range of formats to suit all readers' preferences.

Of course, some things never change: *Blackstone's Criminal Practice* continues to provide an affordable, high quality, comprehensive manual of everything the criminal practitioner will need in any level of court.

This edition

As ever, the work includes all the major developments in legislation and case law over the last 12 months. Once again we have been fortunate in not having a substantial criminal justice Act to incorporate, although there are numerous changes throughout the text resulting from the Anti-social Behaviour, Crime and Policing Act 2014; the Offender Rehabilitation Act 2014, and the Data Retention and Investigatory Powers Act 2014. We also analyse the many relevant statutory instruments, including those bringing into force provisions in the Legal Aid, Sentencing and Punishment of Offenders Act 2012, the Crime and Courts Act 2013, the Prevention of Social Housing Fraud Act 2013, Protection of Freedoms Act 2012, as well as the usual raft of orders amending the Misuse of Drugs Act 1971.

This year also saw revisions of the importance PACE Codes of Practice Codes A, B, C, E, F, and H, all of which are included in the main volume and analysed in Part D. The protocols on disclosure introduced in December 2013 and the revised Attorney General's disclosure guidelines are also included. The supplement to this edition also reproduces the latest Criminal Procedure Rules, the Criminal Practice Directions (with its latest revisions effective from 6 October) and sentencing guidelines, including that on Fraud, bribery and money laundering. Cumulative supplements will be produced to include developments in the law throughout 2014–15.

As one would expect, this edition also includes analysis by the expert team of contributors of all the important decisions from the appellate courts, including: *Robinson-Pierre* on causation and dangerous dogs; *Grant* on transferred malice; *Oye* and *Thompson and Press* on insanity, automatism and defences; *Montague* and *Bristow* on joint enterprise; *Dang* on conspiracy; *Pace* on attempts and *mens rea; Bunch, Brown* and *Golds* on diminished responsibility; *Workman* on loss of control; *R (Nicklinson) v Ministry of Justice* on assisting suicide; *Golding* on transmission of infection; a raft of decisions on sentencing in sexual cases including *Hall, Master, Wilson, Knight, Livesey; Sakalauskas* on possession or control of articles for use in fraud; *Gul, Miranda* and *Beghal* on terrorism; *Monteiro* on sentencing for knife possession; *Richardson v DPP* on aggravated trespass; *King, Bunyan, Mitchell* and *Shoyeju* on misconduct in public office; *Beeres v CPS West Midlands* on intoxication and interviews; *R (TD) v Metropolitan Police Commissioner* on biometric data retention; the many cases on the execution of search warrants including *Cheema v Nottingham and Newark Magistrates Court, R (Lees) v Solihull Magistrates' Court,* and *R (Chief Constable of South Yorkshire Police) v Sheffield Crown Court; Crawley* on abuse of process and legal representation; *Guardian News and Media Ltd v AB CD* on secret trials and *JC* on reporting restrictions of youth trials; *White* on defective indictments; *BH (A Child) v Llandudno Youth Court* on committal of youths for trial; *Achogbuo* on loss of time and frivolous appeals; *Bucnys v Ministry of Justice, Lithuania* on extradition; *Dyer on* sentencing council guidelines; *Vinter v UK* and *McLaughlin* on whole life tariffs; *Burinskas* on dangerous offenders under LASPO; *Ahmad* and *Fields, King* and *Mackie* on confiscation; *Khan* on exclusion of covert evidence; *Gjoni* on sexual history evidence; *Bowman Matthews* and *Lewis* on bad character; *Minchin, Harvey* and *Taylor* on hearsay; *Ogden* on DNA.

The team at Oxford University Press (Andy Redman, Fiona Sinclair, Briony Ryles, Sarah Randall, and Amy Jones) have worked efficiently and tirelessly as ever. I am grateful to them for ensuring that this edition maintains the excellence for which *Blackstone's* has become renowned.

Blackstone's welcomes constructive comments and suggestions from readers. These assist us in providing a publication that meets the needs of the users. Please continue to offer your feedback via the web site at <**http://www.oup.com/blackstones/criminal**>. Alternatively, you can send us your comments by email at **blackstonescriminal@oup.com**.

David Ormerod is the Criminal Law Commissioner for England and Wales, but nothing in this work should be taken as representing the views of the Law Commission unless expressly stated to do so.

We have endeavoured to state the law as at 1 August 2014.

Professor David Ormerod QC

Acknowledgements

Particular thanks are due to the editorial coordinator, Laurence Eastham. Thanks are also due to Moira Greenhalgh for the preparation of the original index and to Kim Harris for updating it for this edition, Nicola Freshwater for the copyediting, Margaret Humbert for the proofreading, and Deborah Harris for the tables.

The Code for Crown Prosecutors in appendix 3 is reproduced with the kind permission of the Crown Prosecution Service.

The publishers are grateful to readers for the suggestions (and corrections) which they provide throughout the year. They would like to invite subscribers to email (**blackstonescriminal@oup. com**) with any feedback or comments so that the service can continue to be developed and improved.

Abbreviations

The following abbreviations have been used in this edition:

ABCPA 2014	Anti-social Behaviour, Crime and Policing Act 2014
A-G	Attorney-General
A-G's Ref	Attorney-General's Reference
AJA 1999	Access to Justice Act 1999
ASBA 2003	Anti-social Behaviour Act 2003
ASBO	anti-social behaviour order
A-tCSA 2001	Anti-terrorism, Crime and Security Act 2001
BA 1976	Bail Act 1976
CAA 1981	Criminal Attempts Act 1981
CAJA 2009	Coroners and Justice Act 2009
CCA 2013	Crime and Courts Act 2013
CCRC	Criminal Cases Review Commission
CDA 1998	Crime and Disorder Act 1998
CJA	Criminal Justice Act (dates vary)
CJCSA 2000	Criminal Justice and Court Services Act 2000
CJEU	Court of Justice of the European Union
CJIA 2008	Criminal Justice and Immigration Act 2008
CJPA 2001	Criminal Justice and Police Act 2001
CJPO 1994	Criminal Justice and Public Order Act 1994
CLA	Criminal Law Act (dates vary)
CMCHA 2007	Corporate Manslaughter and Corporate Homicide Act 2007
CPD	Criminal Practice Directions
CPIA 1996	Criminal Procedure and Investigations Act 1996
CPS	Crown Prosecution Service
CrimPR	Criminal Procedure Rules 2014
C(S)A 1997	Crime (Sentences) Act 1997
CSO	community support officer
C-TA 2008	Counter-Terrorism Act 2008
CYPA	Children and Young Persons Act (dates vary)
DPP	Director of Public Prosecutions
DTTO	drug treatment and testing order
DVCVA 2004	Domestic Violence, Crime and Victims Act 2004
EAW	European Arrest Warrant
ECHR	European Convention on Human Rights
ECtHR	European Court of Human Rights
FA 1968	Firearms Act 1968
F(A)A	Firearms (Amendment) Act (dates vary)
FCA	Financial Conduct Authority
FSMA 2000	Financial Services and Markets Act 2000
HRA 1998	Human Rights Act 1998
IPP	imprisonment for public protection
LASPO 2012	Legal Aid, Sentencing and Punishment of Offenders Act 2012
MCA 1980	Magistrates' Courts Act 1980
MDA 1971	Misuse of Drugs Act 1971
NCA	National Crime Agency
OAPA 1861	Offences Against the Person Act 1861
ORA	Offender Rehabilitation Act

PACA 2009	Policing and Crime Act 2009
PACE 1984	Police and Criminal Evidence Act 1984
PCC(S)A 2000	Powers of Criminal Courts (Sentencing) Act 2000
POA	Public Order Act (dates vary)
POCA 2002	Proceeds of Crime Act 2002
PRSRA 2011	Police Reform and Social Responsibility Act 2011
RCPO	Revenue and Customs Prosecutions Office
RIPA 2000	Regulation of Investigatory Powers Act 2000
RTA	Road Traffic Act (dates vary)
RTOA 1988	Road Traffic Offenders Act 1988
RTRA	Road Traffic Regulation Act (dates vary)
SCA 2007	Serious Crime Act 2007
SCPO	serious crime prevention order
SFO	Serious Fraud Office
SGC	Sentencing Guidelines Council
SMD	special measures direction
SOA	Sexual Offences Act (dates vary)
SOCPA 2005	Serious Organised Crime and Police Act 2005
SOPO	sexual offences prevention order
TA 2000	Terrorism Act 2000
TA 2006	Terrorism Act 2006
UNCLOS	United Nations Convention on the Law of the Sea
VCRA 2006	Violent Crime Reduction Act 2006
VOO	violent offender order
YJCEA 1999	Youth Justice and Criminal Evidence Act 1999
YOT	youth offending team
YRO	youth rehabilitation order

Contributors

Duncan Atkinson, Barrister
6 King's Bench Walk, Junior Prosecuting Counsel for the Crown at the Central Criminal Court

Alex Bailin, QC, Barrister
Matrix Chambers, Recorder of the Crown Court, Deputy High Court Judge (Administrative Court)

Diane Birch, LLB
JC Smith Professor of Law, University of Nottingham

Michelle Brewer, LLB, Barrister
Garden Court Chambers

Ed Cape, LLM, Solicitor
Professor of Criminal Law and Practice, Bristol Law School, University of the West of England, Bristol

Her Honour Judge Johannah Cutts, QC
Aylesbury and Amersham Crown Courts

Anand Doobay, LLB, LLM, Solicitor
Consultant, Peters & Peters

Anthony Edwards, Solicitor
Senior Partner, TV Edwards

Rudi Fortson, QC, LLB, Barrister
25 Bedford Row, London
Visiting Professor of Law at Queen Mary, University of London

Michael Hirst, LLB, LLM, FRSA
Professor of Criminal Justice, Leicester De Montfort Law School

Laura C. H. Hoyano, BA, MA, JD, BCL
Hackney Fellow & Tutor in Law, Wadham College, University of Oxford and Fellow of the Middle Temple

Peter Hungerford-Welch, LLB, FHEA, Barrister
Assistant Dean (Professional Programmes), The City Law School, City University London

Paul Jarvis, MA, Barrister
6KBW College Hill

Adrian Keane, LLB, Barrister
Professor of Law, The City Law School, City University London

Michael Lerego, QC, MA, BCL, FCIArb, FHEA
Recorder of the Crown Court

Richard McMahon, QC, LLB, LLM
The Deputy Bailiff of Guernsey

Valsamis Mitsilegas, LLB, LLM, PhD
Head of the Department of Law, Professor of European Criminal Law and Director of the Criminal Justice Centre, Queen Mary, University of London

Contributors

Tim Moloney, QC, Barrister
Doughty Street Chambers

Stephen Parkinson, LLB, Solicitor
Partner and Head of Kingsley Napley's Criminal and Regulatory Group

Amanda Pinto, QC, MA, Barrister
33 Chancery Lane

Edward Rees, QC, LLB
Doughty Street Chambers, Honorary Fellow of Criminal Process at the University of Kent

His Honour Judge Peter Rook, QC
Central Criminal Court

Richard D. Taylor, MA, LLM, Barrister
Professor of English Law, Lancashire Law School, University of Central Lancashire

Mark Topping, LLB, RD, Solicitor
Crown Advocate, Special Crime and Counter Terrorism Division, Crown Prosecution Service

Martin Wasik, CBE, LLB, MA, FRSA, Barrister
Recorder of the Crown Court, Professor of Criminal Justice, Keele University

Summary of Contents

PART A CRIMINAL LAW

PART B OFFENCES

APPENDICES

Table of Cases

Table of Cases

Table of Cases

Table of Cases

Table of Cases

Table of Cases

Table of Cases

Table of Cases

Table of Cases

Table of Cases

Table of Cases

Table of Cases

Table of Statutes

Where a paragraph reference is underlined, this is the main entry for the relevant material, much of which is reproduced at that reference

s. 1(3) . . . . <u>B8.25</u>, B8.26,
   B8.27, B8.28, D6.5
s. 1(4) B8.27
s. 2 . . . . B5.53, B8.26,
   <u>B8.31</u>, B10.81, D6.5
s. 2(a) B7.32, B8.33, F4.16
s. 3 . . . . B4.155, <u>B8.36</u>, B8.38, D6.5
s. 3(a) B8.40
s. 3(b) B8.40
s. 4(1) B8.41
s. 4(2) B8.41
s. 5 . . . . <u>B8.12</u>, B8.13,
   B8.15, B8.19, B8.21,
   B8.24, B8.35, B8.40
s. 5(1) B8.35
s. 5(2) A3.18, B8.13, B8.14
s. 5(2)(a) B8.8, B8.15
s. 5(2)(b) B8.14
s. 5(2)(b)(i) B8.14
s. 5(2)(b)(ii) B8.14
s. 5(3) B8.14
s. 5(5) B8.13
s. 6 . . . . <u>B8.40</u>
s. 10 . . . . <u>B8.8</u>
s. 10(1) . . . . <u>B8.7</u>, B13.53
s. 10(2) . . . . <u>B8.8</u>

Criminal Evidence Act
   1898 . . . . F12.12, F12.77, F12.78,
   F12.81, F12.82, F12.84,
   F12.88, F12.89, F12.97
s. 1 . . . . F4.10
s. 1(1) D17.8, F4.10, F4.13
s. 1(2) F9.35
s. 1(3) F12.1, F12.14,
   F12.95, F12.96, F19.45
s. 1(3)(ii) F12.92
s. 1(3)(iii) F7.55, F12.77, F12.79
s. 1(4) D17.11, F4.11, F4.12
s. 1(b) F19.41
s. 1(g) F4.11
s. 2 . . . . D17.7, D17.9

Criminal Evidence Act
   1965 . . . . F16.31, F16.37

Criminal Evidence
   (Amendment) Act 1997
s. 1 . . . . D1.113
s. 2 . . . . D1.113

Criminal Evidence
   (Witness Anonymity)
   Act 2008 . . . . D14.3, D14.50
s. 7 . . . . D14.50
s. 11 . . . . D26.19

Criminal Justice Act 1925
s. 13(3) F1.39
s. 33 . . . . B15.21
s. 36 . . . . B14.25, D6.5
s. 41 . . . . B14.111
s. 41(1) B14.111
s. 41(2)(a) B14.111
s. 41(2)(c) B14.111
s. 47 . . . . A3.53

Criminal Justice Act 1948
s. 27 . . . . D7.136
s. 27(1) D7.130
s. 31(1) A8.19
s. 37 . . . . D7.88
s. 37(1)(b) D29.23
s. 37(1)(b)(i) D7.88
s. 37(1)(b)(ii) D7.88
s. 37(1)(d) D7.88, D29.36
s. 37(6) D29.17

Criminal Justice Act 1961
s. 22(2) . . . . <u>B14.75</u>

Criminal Justice
   Act 1967 . . . . D14.31, E6.2
s. 3 . . . . D1.7
s. 6(1)(c) D12.19
s. 6(2) D19.50
s. 6(3) D19.49
s. 8 . . . . <u>A2.34</u>, A5.12,
   <u>B1.12</u>, B1.13, F3.63
s. 9 . . . . B14.7, B14.20, C5.42,
   D16.19, D21.42, D22.13,
   D22.25, <u>D22.39</u>,
   F6.6, F16.87
s. 9(1) D15.42
s. 9(2)(a) D22.28
s. 9(2)(b) D22.28
s. 9(2)(d) D22.13
s. 9(3) D22.28
s. 10 . . . . C6.41, D12.71,
   D16.40, D21.41,
   D22.40, <u>F1.2</u>,
   F1.3, F10.27
s. 10(1) F1.1
s. 10(2)(b) F1.3
s. 10(2)(d) F1.3
s. 10(4) F1.3
s. 11 . . . . D17.14
s. 12 . . . . B14.20
s. 14(2) D19.50
s. 17 . . . . <u>D12.82</u>, D22.9
s. 22 . . . . D29.17
s. 22(1) D7.88
s. 22(1A) D31.9
s. 25 . . . . B18.16
s. 89 . . . . B14.7, <u>B14.20</u>
s. 91 . . . . . . B11.68, B11.205, D2.41
s. 91(1) B11.202
s. 91(4) B11.205

Criminal Justice Act 1972
s. 36 . . . D3.60, <u>D28.5</u>, D28.6, D32.2
s. 46(1) F16.88

Criminal Justice Act 1977
s. 36 . . . . D16.74

Criminal Justice Act 1982 . . . . . B14.70
s. 1(6) E7.2
s. 36 . . . . D26.1
s. 37(2) E15.9
s. 55 . . . . F4.12
s. 56 . . . . F4.12
s. 72 . . . . <u>F4.12</u>
s. 96(1) E7.2
sch. 16 . . . . D29.2

Criminal Justice Act 1987 . . . . . D3.62,
   D13.79, D13.81, D15.49,
   D15.51, D15.60
s. 1(2) D3.62
s. 1(3) D3.62
s. 1(5) D3.62
s. 1(7) D3.62
s. 1(8) D3.62
s. 2 . . . . D1.95, D1.146, F9.43
s. 2(8) D1.95
s. 2(8AA) D1.95
s. 4 . . . . D9.2, D10.2, D10.34,
   D10.49, D15.4, D15.9,
   D28.11, D32.10, D33.41
s. 4(2) D28.11
s. 6(1) D28.11
s. 7 . . . . D15.6, D15.59
s. 7(1) D13.79,
   D13.81, D15.61
s. 7(1)(a) D15.65
s. 7(1)(a)–(e) D15.62, D15.65
s. 7(2) D15.61

ss. 7–11 . . . . D15.65
s. 8 . . . . D15.11, D15.38,
   D15.45, D15.63
s. 9 . . . . D15.65, D30.2
s. 9(3) D15.65
s. 9(4) D15.65
s. 9(5) D15.65, D15.76
s. 9(10) D15.65
s. 9(11) D13.81, D15.67,
   D15.70, D27.34,
   D33.5, D33.41
s. 9(11)–(14) D26.1
s. 9(13) D15.67, D15.70
s. 9(14) D15.67, D15.70
s. 10(1) D15.66
s. 10(2) D15.66
s. 10(3) D15.66
s. 12 . . . . A5.39
s. 12(1) A5.62
s. 12(3) A5.63

Criminal Justice Act 1988 . . . . . A5.56,
   A7.92, B3.303, B3.324,
   B12.164, C6.44, D1.89,
   D6.36, D16.36, D26.42,
   D26.46, E19.1, F16.12,
   F16.21, F16.27, F16.31
pt. IV D26.3, D28.11, E16.9
s. 4(b) B5.48
s. 23 . . . . D16.36, F1.39, F3.56,
   F16.9, F16.18,
   F16.22, F16.47
s. 23(3)(b) F1.39
s. 24 . . . . D16.36, F1.39,
   F16.24, F16.26, F16.51
s. 24(1)(i) F1.39
s. 24(1)(ii) F1.39
s. 26 . . . . D16.36
s. 27 . . . . F8.7
s. 30 . . . . <u>F10.49</u>, F16.88
s. 30(1) F10.44
s. 32 . . . . B14.7, D15.97,
   <u>D15.98</u>, D16.31
s. 32(2)(a) F4.16
s. 32(3) B14.7
s. 32A F4.32
s. 34(2) F5.16
s. 35 . . . . D12.64, D26.1,
   <u>D28.7</u>, D28.8, D28.10
s. 35(3)(b)(i) D28.11
s. 35(6) D28.10
s. 36 . . . . D3.60, D26.1,
   <u>D28.7</u>, D28.11
s. 36(3A) D28.9, E3.6
s. 36(3B) D28.9
s. 36(5) D28.12
s. 39 . . . . B2.1, B2.2,
   B2.3, C3.54, D21.14
s. 40 . . . . . . A5.37, A5.69, B2.2,
   B4.118, B8.2, B8.19,
   C3.17, C6.44, D3.16,
   D6.2, D6.3, D6.40, D9.3,
   D10.29, D10.43, <u>D11.18</u>,
   D11.19, D11.20, D11.21,
   D16.70, D19.56, D19.57,
   D21.37, D26.26
s. 40(1) D11.17, D11.20
s. 40(2) D11.17, D11.19, E7.18
s. 40(3) D11.19
s. 41 . . . . C6.8, C6.61,
   D11.21, D26.43, D26.46
s. 41(7) D26.42, E7.18
s. 78 . . . . D8.36
ss. 93A–93C B21.1

Table of Statutes

Table of Statutes

Table of Statutory Instruments

Where a paragraph reference is underlined much of the relevant material is reproduced at that reference

Table of Statutory Instruments

Table of Practice Directions

Where a paragraph reference is underlined the relevant material is reproduced at that reference

Table of Codes of Conduct

Where a paragraph reference is underlined the relevant material is reproduced at that reference

Table of Guidelines

Where a paragraph reference is underlined the relevant material is reproduced at that reference

Table of Protocols and Circulars

Where a paragraph reference is underlined the relevant material is reproduced at that reference

Table of International Treaties and Conventions

Where a paragraph reference is underlined the relevant material is reproduced at that reference

Table of European Legislation

Where a paragraph reference is underlined the relevant material is reproduced at that reference

Section A1   *Actus Reus*: The External Elements of an Offence

INTRODUCTION

A1.1 It is customary to separate the essential elements of a crime into two main elements: (1) the prohibited act, omission, consequence or state-of-affairs (the *actus reus*); and (2) any fault element, such as intent or recklessness, required in respect of it (the *mens rea*). *Smith and Hogan Criminal Law* (13th edn, 2011, at p. 49) defines the *actus reus* as including 'all the elements in the definition of the crime except D's mental element'. It thus represents the external manifestation of the offence.

THE NATURE OF AN *ACTUS REUS*

Conduct Crimes and Result Crimes

A1.2 The *actus reus* of an offence may be defined in such a way that D's conduct must cause or result in specified consequences. Homicide, for example, requires proof that D's conduct caused the death of another; and no assault is committed if D's behaviour goes unnoticed by any victim. Such offences may be referred to as 'result crimes'. In contrast, many offences are defined in such a way that the consequences, if any, of D's behaviour are irrelevant to his liability. His behaviour may amount to the complete *actus reus* of the offence even if it fails to bring about the consequences he intends or indeed any consequences at all. The *actus reus* of blackmail, for example, is complete as soon as D makes an unwarranted demand with menaces. A demand is 'made' as soon as it is uttered, and does not require successful communication to the victim (or anyone else). The mere posting of a letter containing such a demand is sufficient (*Treacy v DPP* [1971] AC 537). Blackmail, therefore, is a 'conduct crime'.

The classification of offences into 'conduct crimes' and 'result crimes' may sometimes seem awkward and unhelpful. Nevertheless, it is always necessary to identify the constituent elements of an offence, and use of this classification sometimes highlights key differences between offences. Thus, the offence of indecent exposure formerly contained within the Town Police Clauses Act 1847, s. 28, was a result crime, because it required proof that D's conduct caused residents or 'passengers' to be 'annoyed, obstructed or endangered'. In contrast, the offence of genital exposure created by the SOA 2003, s. 66, is a conduct crime, because it requires proof only that D exposed himself and intended this to cause alarm or distress. Nobody need actually have suffered alarm or distress. In theory, nobody need even have seen the offending act.

A1.3 **Jurisdictional Importance of Classification**   The distinction between conduct crimes and result crimes was for many years crucial in determining jurisdiction over cross-frontier offences. Under the so-called 'terminatory' principle, jurisdiction over a conduct crime was held to depend on the relevant conduct occurring within England or Wales, whereas jurisdiction over a result crime ordinarily depended on at least some part of the proscribed result taking place there (see, e.g., *Secretary of State for Trade v Markus* [1976] AC 35, per Lord Diplock at p. 61 and *Harden* [1963] 1 QB 8); but a different rule now applies to any offences of fraud or dishonesty to which the CJA 1993, part I, applies (see **A8.5**), and in *Smith (Wallace Duncan) (No. 4)* [2004]

QB 1418 the Court of Appeal effectively rejected the terminatory principle in favour of what has subsequently been referred to as the 'substantial measure principle' (see *Sheppard* [2010] 2 All ER 850 and **A8.5**).

RELATIONSHIP BETWEEN *ACTUS REUS* AND *MENS REA*

General

A1.4   The general rule, expressed in the maxim, *actus non facit reum nisi mens sit rea*, is that an offence can be committed only where criminal conduct is accompanied by some element of fault, the precise fault element required depending upon the particular offence involved. There are nevertheless many offences of strict liability, where it is not necessary to establish fault in relation to every element or where, in some cases, no fault element need be proved (see **A2**). In such cases, one can therefore have an *actus reus* without any corresponding *mens rea*.

In theory, there can be no criminal liability based on *mens rea* alone, but if the *actus reus* element of a crime is defined very widely (as is sometimes the case) a 'guilty mind' may turn an objectively innocent act into the *actus reus* of that offence. Thus, a witness who tells the court something that he believes to be untrue is guilty of perjury, even if his evidence turns out, to his surprise, to be true after all (see **B14.11**); and a shopper who openly selects goods in a self-service store, whilst secretly nursing a dishonest intention to avoid paying for them, is regarded as committing theft at the moment he first selects them, even though he may have done nothing objectively wrong at that stage. The *actus reus* of perjury involves nothing more than giving material evidence in court; and the concept of appropriation, which lies at the heart of the *actus reus* of theft, has been defined so widely in cases such as *Gomez* [1993] AC 442 as to strip it of any special significance. Almost any form of dealing with another person's property, legitimate or otherwise, must now be regarded as an appropriation of it: the *actus reus* of theft (see generally **B4.34** *et seq.*).

A person can meanwhile be guilty of a criminal attempt by doing an entirely lawful thing in the mistaken belief that he is doing something different, which would indeed have been criminal. If, for example, D imports a harmless vegetable powder mistakenly believing it to be heroin, he may be guilty of attempting to import a controlled drug, contrary to s. 1 of the Criminal Attempts Act 1981. The objectively lawful importation of the powder becomes the *actus reus* of the criminal attempt (*Shivpuri* [1987] AC 1; see **A5.81**).

A Mental Element in the *Actus Reus*?

A1.5   The usual distinction between the mental element and the external manifestation of a crime can be difficult to apply in cases where the crime is one of 'possessing', 'permitting', 'keeping', 'appropriating', etc., because these terms simultaneously import both mental and physical elements. A person may, for example, possess a controlled drug without realising what it is that he possesses, but he does not possess something which, unknown to him, has become stuck to the sole of his shoe or the blade of his penknife (*Warner v Metropolitan Police Commissioner* [1969] 2 AC 256; *Marriott* [1971] 1 All ER 595). It might therefore be argued that there is a mental element implicit in the *actus reus* of any offence of unlawful possession. From a strictly theoretical viewpoint, this cannot be correct. The correct analysis must be that the legal concept of possession involves both the *actus reus* element of physical possession and a state of mind, the *animus possidendi*, which can only be a part of the requisite *mens rea*. Nevertheless, it may be convenient in practice to treat the *animus possidendi* as if it were an *actus reus* element, because it must always be proved by the prosecution, even where, as in drug possession cases, the burden of proof in respect of other *mens rea* elements is placed on the defence (see **B19.23** *et seq.*).

Contemporaneity of *Actus Reus* and *Mens Rea*

The general rule is that, to be guilty of a criminal offence requiring *mens rea*, an accused must   **A1.6**
possess that *mens rea* when performing the act or omission in question, and it must relate to that
particular act or omission. If, for example, D accidentally kills his wife in a car crash on Monday,
the fact that he was planning to cut her throat on Tuesday does not make him guilty of her murder, even if he was thinking about the planned murder at the time of the accident, and even if he
is subsequently delighted to find that his wife has died. The general rule as to contemporaneity
must nevertheless be qualified in certain respects.

Short-lived Mens Rea   D's *mens rea* need not last beyond the moment at which he causes the   **A1.7**
actus reus to occur. He will not be excused merely because he abandons the crime before that
actus reus is complete. After inflicting a fatal injury on V with murderous intent, D may repent
of his actions and may even do his utmost to save V's life; but if V dies he will be guilty of murder (*Jakeman* (1983) 76 Cr App R 223, per Wood J at p. 228). In *Jakeman*, J booked suitcases
containing drugs onto a series of flights terminating in London. She abandoned them in Paris,
allegedly because she no longer intended to import them, but the cases were sent on to London
where the drugs were discovered. The Court of Appeal held that J's loss of *mens rea* came too late
to prevent her being guilty of an importation offence.

Course of Conduct   The *actus reus* of a crime may consist of an extended or ongoing course of   **A1.8**
conduct, rather than one that occurs at one instant in time. The *actus reus* of rape, for example,
extends from the moment of initial non-consensual penetration to the moment at which the
penis is withdrawn (SOA 2003, s. 79(2)). If D has no *mens rea* at the moment of penetration,
but later becomes aware of the absence of consent, he may commit rape by not withdrawing
immediately thereafter (*Kaitamaki v The Queen* [1985] AC 147). Consent may even be withdrawn after initial penetration, and rape may therefore be committed if, for example, D pays no
heed when V protests that he should stop because he is hurting her.

A controversial example of the 'continuous act' principle can be found in *Fagan v Metropolitan
Police Commissioner* [1969] 1 QB 439, where F was directed by a police officer to park his
vehicle by the kerb, and drove it right onto the officer's foot. There was no proof that he did so
deliberately, but it was clear that he deliberately left it there after the officer told him what he
had done. His conviction for assaulting the officer was upheld by the Divisional Court on the
basis that there was on ongoing act, which became a criminal assault once F became aware of it.
James J said:

> It is not necessary that *mens rea* should be present at the inception of the *actus reus*; it can be super-
> imposed on an existing act. On the other hand, the subsequent inception of *mens rea* cannot convert
> an act which has been completed without *mens rea* into an assault.

Series of Actions   The courts may extend the above principle by treating a series of different   **A1.9**
actions culminating in the *actus reus* of a crime as if they were a single, extended or continuous
course of conduct. It will then be sufficient if D possessed the requisite *mens rea* at any point
during that course of conduct. If, for example, D attempts to murder V by beating him to death,
and believes that he has done so, but actually kills V by burying or dismembering what he
assumes to be his corpse, D will still be guilty of murder. As Lord Reid said in *Thabo Meli v The
Queen* [1954] 1 All ER 373:

> It is much too refined a ground of judgement to say that, because the appellants were under a misap-
> prehension at one stage and thought that their guilty purpose had been achieved before, in fact, it
> was achieved, therefore they are to escape the penalties of the law.

This principle has subsequently been applied, not only in cases where there was a prearranged
plan, of which disposal of the body was a part (as in *Moore* [1975] Crim LR 229), but also in
cases where there was no such plan. In *Church* [1966] 1 QB 59, C struck a woman and panicked because he mistakenly thought he had killed her. He threw her into a river, where she

drowned. Edmund-Davies J, giving the judgment of the Court of Criminal Appeal, held that, '…if a killing by the first act would have been manslaughter, a later destruction of the supposed corpse should also be manslaughter'. *Church* was followed in *Le Brun* [1992] QB 61, where B struck his wife in the course of an argument outside their house, after she had refused to enter it with him. The blow left her unconscious. He then tried to drag her into the house. As he did so, her head struck the pavement, fracturing her skull and killing her. The case differed from *Church* in that the fatal impact was accidental, whereas Church's disposal of the 'body' was deliberate, but the Court of Appeal upheld a conviction for manslaughter by identifying a course of unlawful conduct. In attempting to drag his unconscious wife indoors, B was either trying to conceal his initial assault on her, or forcing her to enter the house against her wishes (this being the original reason for the assault). The trial judge had directed the jury to acquit if they concluded that B had been trying to aid or assist his wife when he attempted to move her, and the Court of Appeal agreed that this would have broken the essential nexus between the two halves of the incident.

A further difficulty arose in *A-G's Ref (No. 4 of 1980)* [1981] 2 All ER 617 where, in the course of a struggle, D pushed his girlfriend V over a landing rail onto the floor below and then, believing her dead, cut her throat and dismembered her in the bath so as to dispose of her body. It was impossible to establish whether V died in the original fall or whether he killed her (as in *Church*) by his subsequent actions. The Court of Appeal held that a manslaughter conviction was possible, despite uncertainty as to the actual cause of death, but only if it could be proved that each of D's acts was performed with the requisite *mens rea* for that offence. Since the initial fall may well have killed V, it would not suffice to establish *mens rea* (such as gross negligence) only in the subsequent act of disposal: the prosecution also had to disprove D's claim that he had merely pushed her away in a 'reflex action' when she dug her nails into him in the struggle on the upstairs landing.

VOLUNTARY AND INVOLUNTARY CONDUCT

Introduction

A1.10 The vast majority of criminal offences require acts or omissions on D's part, and these acts or omissions must ordinarily be willed or 'voluntary'. D does not therefore commit criminal damage if his enemies throw him from an upstairs window onto the roof of a car below. Nor is this merely because he lacks the requisite *mens rea* for that offence. It is because involuntary movements cannot ordinarily constitute the *actus reus* of any offence, not even one of strict liability. Involuntary conduct or events of this kind can best be understood not as anything *done* by D, but as something that *happens* to him.

Physical compulsion is merely one possible cause of involuntary conduct. Such conduct may also be caused by uncontrollable reflex actions or by a physical collapse brought on by injury or illness. If, for example, D suffers a sudden and unforeseen stroke or blackout whilst driving his car, which then careers through a red traffic light and collides with another vehicle, no offence is committed by him. The same rule would apply if D loses control of his car when attacked by a swarm of bees (an example suggested by Devlin J in *Hill v Baxter* [1958] 1 QB 277).

'Involuntary' conduct in this context does not include acts done by reason of duress, necessity or coercion (as to which, see **A3.34** *et seq.*) because such acts are still conscious, willed and rational; but it may include reflex acts and acts 'committed' by D when in a state of automatism, i.e. when not consciously in control of his own mind or body. A condition of automatism can arise where D is suffering from concussion, where he is a diabetic who suffers an attack of hypoglycaemia (very low blood sugar) after taking insulin (*Quick* [1973] QB 910) or, arguably, where he commits the *actus reus* whilst in a somnambulistic trance induced by hypnotism.

Limitations on the Defence of Automatism

Although involuntariness or automatism is ordinarily a defence to any criminal charge, the use **A1.11**
of that defence is limited by a number of considerations. These are more fully explained at
A3.12 *et seq*. It must suffice to note at this point that the defence may be rendered invalid where
D was culpable for falling into such a condition, as for example by driving whilst suffering from
exhaustion (*Kay v Butterworth* (1945) 173 LT 191) or by abusing alcohol or drugs (*Lipman*
[1970] 1 QB 152; *Coley* [2013] EWCA Crim 223). It is also unavailable where the cause of the
condition is a 'defect of reason arising from a disease of the mind', because this amounts in law
to insanity. The term 'disease of the mind' embraces both organic and functional disorders of
the mind, but excludes external causes, such as drugs, hypnosis or concussion. Epilepsy is in this
sense a disease of the mind (*Sullivan* [1984] AC 156) as is a brain tumour (*Kemp* [1957] 1 QB
399) or even hyperglycaemia (excessive blood sugar) if this occurs naturally in a diabetic
(*Hennessy* [1989] 2 All ER 9). Sleepwalking was regarded in *Bratty v A-G for Northern Ireland*
[1963] AC 386 as a classic example of non-insane automatism, but sleep-associated automatism
may be caused by functional disorders of the mind and in *Burgess* [1991] 1 QB 92 the Court of
Appeal held that any such condition which manifests itself in violence must be treated as one of
insanity. Finally, the defence of automatism appears to be unavailable where D has some, albeit
impaired, control over his actions (*Broome v Perkins* [1987] Crim LR 272; *A-G's Ref (No. 2 of
1992)* [1994] QB 91; *Coley*); mere disinhibition is exactly *not* automatism (*Coley* at [46]).

The Burden of Proof

Where the defence raise a defence of non-insane automatism, this must be disproved by the **A1.12**
prosecution (in contrast to a defence of insanity, which must be proved by the defence) but there
is always an evidential burden on the defence, who must produce some evidence of automatism
before the prosecution can be required to address it (*Hill v Baxter* [1958] 1 QB 277; *Bratty v A-G
for Northern Ireland* [1963] AC 386). See further **F3.43**.

Situational Liability

Voluntary conduct need not always be proved where D is charged with a strict liability offence **A1.13**
in which the *actus reus* takes the form not of a prohibited act or omission but of a prohibited
state of affairs. Authority can be found in *Larsonneur* (1933) 24 Cr App R 74 and *Winzar v Chief
Constable of Kent* (1983) *The Times*, 28 March 1983. In the former case, L, a French citizen,
visited the UK for the purpose of entering into a marriage of convenience. The police prevented
this marriage and an order was served on her requiring her to leave and not re-enter the country.
Instead of returning to France, L travelled to Ireland, whence she was deported and handed over
to the British police in Holyhead. She was charged under the Aliens Order 1920 with 'being
found in the United Kingdom' in breach of the original order excluding her. The fact that she
had been returned to the UK under physical compulsion was held to be 'perfectly immaterial'.
All that mattered was that she was found in the UK on the occasion in question.

In *Winzar*, the charge was one of being 'found drunk on a highway', contrary to the Licensing
Act 1872, s. 12. W had been found drunk in a hospital and was asked to leave. When he failed to
do so, police officers removed him to their patrol car, which was parked on the highway outside,
and charged him with being found drunk there. Upholding his conviction, Goff LJ pointed out
that a distinction would otherwise have to be drawn between a drunk who leaves a restaurant
when asked to do so and one who is forcibly ejected after refusing to leave. If both are arrested
in the street shortly afterwards, it would be wrong to regard the former as guilty and the latter as
not; but the position would be different if the police were to drag a person from his own bed and
into the street before charging him with being found drunk on a highway, because that would
involve an abuse of process (see **D3.70**).

These cases were considered in *Robinson-Pierre* [2014] 1 Cr App R 305 (22), in which it was
accepted that 'the supremacy of Parliament embraces the power to create "state of affairs" offences

in which no causative link between the prohibited state of affairs and the defendant need be established'. The question in any given case will be 'whether in any particular enactment Parliament intended to create one'. This is likely to require clear words to that effect, or a context in which the provision would otherwise be ineffective. In *Robinson-Pierre*, the Court of Appeal rejected submissions that this must have been Parliament's intent in enacting the Dangerous Dogs Act 1991, s. 3 (see **B20.5**). That provision, as originally enacted, created a strict liability offence of owning or being in charge of a dog that is 'dangerously out of control in a public place' but it did not, said the Court, make such liability 'absolute in the sense that criminal liability may follow notwithstanding the absence of any act or omission of the defendant contributing to the prohibited state of affairs'.

OMISSION TO ACT

Introduction

A1.14   Most criminal offences require D to carry out some positive act before liability can be imposed. There can ordinarily be no liability for failure (or omission) to act, unless the law specifically imposes such a duty upon a particular person. The general rule is illustrated by this example from Stephen's *Digest of the Criminal Law* (3rd edn, 1887):

> A sees B drowning and is able to save him by holding out his hand. A abstains from doing so in order that B may be drowned, and B is drowned. A has committed no offence.

Although A may have failed to save B, he did no positive act to cause B's death. In some jurisdictions, A would always be under a duty to act in such a situation, at least where he does not have to put his own life in danger. Under English law, however, such a duty arises only in certain specific situations, and there are several offences which can be committed only through positive acts (see **A1.24**).

Where Statute Imposes a Specific Duty to Act

A1.15   There are many statutory provisions (mostly regulatory) which specifically impose duties on particular persons to act in particular ways and which impose criminal sanctions for failure or omission to act. A failure to keep proper accounts or business records, where these are required by law, may for example lead to criminal liability under the Companies Act 2006 or the Value Added Tax Act 1994. Road traffic law provides many further examples, including the offences of failing to stop after an accident and failing to provide a breath sample or a specimen for analysis.

Failure to Prevent or Report Criminal Conduct

A1.16   Failure to prevent or report the criminal activities of other persons is not ordinarily an offence. The offence of misprision of felony was abolished in 1967, but failure to report a known act of treason still amounts to misprision of treason and it also remains an offence at common law to refuse to assist a constable who calls for assistance in dealing with a breach of the peace (*Brown* (1841) Car & M 314; *Waugh* (1976) *The Times*, 1 October 1976). Modern legislation has added new offences of failure to disclose information relating to acts of terrorism or the funding of terrorism (see **B10.136** *et seq.*) and failure to disclose knowledge or suspicion of money laundering (see **B21.27**). As to the position of police officers who fail to act in accordance with their duty, see **A1.19**.

Duty Arising from Special Relationships

A1.17   **Care or Control of Children**   If persons are in a close or special relationship to one another, the law may impose on one a duty to act on behalf of the other. Under the CYPA 1933, s. 1 (see **B2.137** *et seq.*), a parent or any other person over the age of 16 years who has responsibility for a child under that age may incur liability for any wilful neglect of that child that was likely to cause unnecessary suffering or injury to health. This specifically includes failure by a parent etc. to provide or obtain adequate food, clothing or medical care but could also include other forms of neglect, such as failure to rescue from drowning in circumstances of the kind described at **A1.14** or failure by a carer towards an elderly client or patient. Neglect leading to death may lead to liability for manslaughter by gross negligence (*Downes* (1875) 13 Cox CC 111; *Lowe* [1973] QB 702). The wilful neglect of a child contrary to s. 1 of the 1933 Act does not automatically give rise to liability for manslaughter merely because death results (*Lowe*), but it may sometimes do so if, for example, there is proof of an intent to harm the child through such neglect. Indeed, a parent who deliberately starves a child to death may be guilty of murder (*Gibbins* (1918) 13 Cr App R 134). As to the offence of causing or allowing the death of a child or vulnerable adult, see **B1.73**.

Assumption of Care for Another   The CYPA 1933, s. 1, has no statutory counterpart in cases   **A1.18** where the person in need of care or assistance is over the age of 16 (but note the specific duties that may arise under the DVCVA 2004, as amended, in relation to both children and vulnerable adults: see **B1.86** and **B2.157**). In *Shepherd* (1862) 9 Cox CC 123 it was held that the parents of an 18-year-old and 'entirely emancipated' daughter were under no special duty to care for her. The common law nevertheless recognises that such a duty may arise in the context of a family relationship, as for example where a couple live together as husband and wife, or where a child continues to live with (and be dependent upon) his parents even after becoming an adult (*Chattaway* (1922) 17 Cr App R 7).

If D voluntarily undertakes to care for another who is unable to care for himself as a result of age, illness or other infirmity, he may thereby incur a duty to discharge that undertaking, at least until such time as he hands it over to someone else. In *Instan* [1893] 1 QB 450, D lived with her aunt, who was suddenly taken ill with gangrene in her leg and became unable either to feed herself or to call for help. D did not give her any food, nor did she call for medical help, even though she remained in the house and continued to eat her aunt's food. She was convicted of manslaughter. The principle laid down in *Instan* was applied and extended in *Stone* [1977] QB 354. Stone's sister, Fanny, came to live with him and his mistress, Dobinson. Fanny was suffering from anorexia, but was initially able to look after herself. Gradually, however, her condition deteriorated, until she became bed-ridden. She needed medical help, but none was summoned and she eventually died in squalor, covered in bed sores and filth. Stone and Dobinson were each convicted of her manslaughter and the Court of Appeal upheld their convictions. Because they had taken Fanny into their home, they had assumed a duty of care for her and had been grossly negligent in the performance of that duty. The fact that Fanny was Stone's sister was merely incidental to this.

Official, Contractual or Public Duties   A person may in some cases incur criminal liability   **A1.19** through failure to discharge his official duties or contractual obligations. A typical example is provided by *Pittwood* (1902) 19 TLR 37, in which P was employed to operate a level-crossing on a railway but omitted to close the crossing gates when a train was signalled. A cart was crossing when the train struck it and killed one of the carters. P was convicted of manslaughter. In one sense this was based on his breach of contractual duty, but the victim was not, of course, a party to the contract, and P's liability can more accurately be based on the breach of a duty of care to users of the crossing, which his employers paid him to discharge, and on which the users of the crossing relied. In the absence of such a duty, it is doubtful whether any criminal liability could have arisen, whatever his contractual position with his employers (cf. *Smith* (1869) 11 Cox CC 210).

Neglect of duty by a police officer was examined by the Court of Appeal in *Dytham* [1979] QB 722. D, whilst on duty, stood aside and watched as a man was beaten to death outside a nightclub. He then left the scene, without calling for assistance or summoning an ambulance. For this, he was convicted of the common-law offence of wilful misconduct in public office. Lord Widgery CJ said (at p. 727):

> The allegation was not one of mere non-feasance, but of deliberate failure and wilful neglect. This involves an element of culpability which is not restricted to corruption or dishonesty, but which must be of such a degree that the misconduct impugned is calculated to injure the public interest so as to call for condemnation and punishment.

Although D was not charged with manslaughter, it is submitted that a conviction for manslaughter might be possible on such facts, if it were proved that D's inaction was a factor contributing to the death of the deceased. It was not clear in *Dytham* that D could have saved the deceased even if he had tried to do so.

See also *A-G's Ref (No. 3 of 2003)* [2005] 1 QB 73 on misconduct in a public office at **B15.26**.

Duty to Avert a Danger of One's Own Making

A1.20 If D creates or contributes to the creation of a dangerous situation through his own fault, he may be under a duty to take reasonable steps to avert that danger, and may therefore incur criminal liability for the consequences of his failure to do so. In *Miller* [1983] 2 AC 161, D was 'sleeping rough' in a building, and fell asleep on his mattress while smoking a cigarette. When he awoke, he saw that his mattress was smouldering but, instead of calling for help, he simply moved into another room, thereby allowing the fire to flare up and spread. He was convicted of arson, not for starting the fire but for failing to do anything about it. Lord Diplock said (at p. 176):

> ...I see no rational ground for excluding from conduct capable of giving rise to criminal liability, conduct which consists of failing to take measures that lie within one's power to counteract a danger that one has oneself created, if at the time of such conduct one's state of mind is such as constitutes a necessary ingredient of the offence.

The *Miller* principle may also apply in cases of gross negligence manslaughter; as where D unlawfully supplies V with a dangerous drug and then fails to summon help when it is obvious that V has become dangerously ill as a result of ingesting it (*Evans* [2009] 1 All ER 13 at [21] and [31]). It must, however, be proved that this failure was a contributory cause of V's death. See also **B1.69**.

Failure to Provide Medical Treatment

A1.21 **Refusal of Consent to Treatment**   Doctors and other health care professionals have a duty to provide medical care for their patients, and an omission to discharge that duty may sometimes involve criminal liability (e.g., for manslaughter or, in the case of a patient under 16, for wilful neglect under the CYPA 1933, s. 1), although this duty may be terminated if the patient refuses to accept medical treatment. If, for example, an adult hospital patient refuses his consent to a life-saving amputation, the medical staff, far from being under a duty to provide that treatment, would ordinarily be acting unlawfully if they ignored his wishes (*Re C (Adult: Refusal of Treatment)* [1994] 1 All ER 819; *Re MB* [1997] 2 FLR 426).

Refusal of consent is not always decisive in such cases. Where children are concerned, the High Court may exercise its wardship jurisdiction and override parental refusal of consent (*Re B (A Minor) (Wardship: Medical Treatment)* [1981] 1 WLR 1421). In acute emergencies, health care professionals may need to act without consent.

Even in respect of adults, a refusal of consent to treatment may be vitiated by lack of capacity (within the meaning of the Mental Capacity Act 2005, s. 2) or by undue influence (*Re T (Adult: Refusal of Treatment)* [1993] Fam 95). Health care professionals must then provide appropriate treatment, in accordance with the patient's best interests. There is a presumption of capacity to choose, even if the patient's choice appears unwise. As to effect of advance directives or 'living wills', see the Mental Capacity Act 2005, s. 26.

A1.22 **Withholding Treatment in the Best Interests of the Patient**   If a patient is incapable of communicating his wishes, a health care professional's normal duty is to do everything that he reasonably can to keep the patient alive. In certain circumstances, however, a doctor may be absolved of this duty, as the House of Lords recognised in *Airedale National Health Service Trust v Bland* [1993] AC 789. The patient was left in a 'persistent vegetative state' after suffering irreversible brain damage. He continued to breathe normally, but was kept alive only by being fed through tubes. The Trust sought a declaration that it might lawfully discontinue this treatment and allow him to die with dignity and with minimum distress. The House of Lords held that treatment could properly be withdrawn, because the best interests of the patient did not involve him being kept alive at all costs. Lord Goff nevertheless drew a fundamental distinction between acts and omissions in this context (at p. 865):

> ...the law draws a crucial distinction between cases in which a doctor decides not to provide, or to continue to provide, for his patient treatment or care which could or might prolong his life, and those in which he decides, for example by administering a lethal drug, actively to bring his patient's life to an end... the former may be lawful, either because the doctor is giving effect to his patient's wishes... or even in certain circumstances in which... the patient is incapacitated from stating whether or not he gives his consent. But it is not lawful for a doctor to administer a drug to his patient to bring about his death, even though that course is prompted by a humanitarian desire to end his suffering, however great that suffering may be: see *Cox* (unreported) 18 September 1992.

See also *Frenchay Healthcare National Health Service Trust v S* [1994] 2 All ER 403. Similar issues can arise in respect of the very elderly or babies born with very severe mental or physical handicaps, especially where major (and possibly repeated) surgery would be needed to keep them alive (*Re J* [1991] 3 All ER 930). It may be good practice to seek a declaration as to the lawfulness of any proposed treatment (or its withdrawal) but this is not a legal requirement (*R (Burke) v General Medical Council* [2006] QB 273 at [67]–[80]).

Practical and Financial Considerations Even apart from the question of whether treatment   **A1.23**
would be in the patient's best interests, it is recognised that financial or manpower constraints on the health service must come into consideration. It is clearly not practicable for the NHS to provide intensive forms of medical care (such as major surgery) to every patient whose life might possibly be prolonged by it; nor does a patient have the right to demand treatment that his doctors consider to be clinically inappropriate (*R (Burke) v General Medical Council* [2006] QB 273 at [50]).

Offences for which Omissions cannot be the Basis of Liability

Some offences are capable of commission only by positive acts. The offence of acting with intent   **A1.24**
to prevent the apprehension of an offender, contrary to the Criminal Law Act 1967, s. 4, is an example (see **B14.54** *et seq.*). Crimes of assault or battery arguably come into this category. This was at least the view of the Divisional Court in *Fagan v Metropolitan Police Commissioner* [1969] 1 QB 439 (see **A1.8**) although F's conviction was upheld on the basis that his conduct amounted to a continuing act, rather than an innocent act followed by a deliberate omission to rectify it.

It has also been held that omissions cannot be the basis of liability for 'doing acts' likely to interfere with the peace and comfort of a residential occupier, contrary to the Protection from Eviction Act 1977 (*Ahmad* (1987) 84 Cr App R 64; and see **B13.17**) but the courts have not been consistent in interpreting references to 'acts' as necessarily excluding omissions. In *Speck* [1977] 2 All ER 859, for example, it was held that an omission could amount to an 'act' of gross indecency with a child, contrary to the Indecency with Children Act 1960, s. 1 (now repealed). See also *Yuthiwattana* (1984) 80 Cr App R 55, in which it was held that a landlord's omission to replace a lost key could be an 'act' of harassment against a tenant. As to constructive manslaughter, see *Lowe* [1973] QB 702 and **B1.52**.

CAUSATION

Introduction

Causation issues appear to feature most frequently in homicide cases, but they can arise in respect   **A1.25**
of any 'result crime'. In order to establish whether D can be guilty of a given result crime, one must first establish a factual link between his conduct and the result he is alleged to have caused. Once this has been established, a second and more difficult question must be considered, namely whether that conduct was a sufficient cause in law. This is a question of 'imputability' or 'legal causation'. It involves issues of value-judgment and the allocation of responsibility for what has occurred.

Factual Causation

A1.26 The importance of proving factual causation is illustrated by *White* [1910] 2 KB 124. W put potassium cyanide in his mother's bedtime drink. When she was found dead the next morning, he was charged with her murder, but it was eventually established that his mother had consumed very little of the poison. She had died, coincidentally, of natural causes. W's conduct had not in any sense contributed to this. He was therefore guilty only of attempting to murder her.

It may also be necessary to prove a link between the proscribed result and a particular aspect of D's conduct, such as his negligence. In *Dalloway* (1847) 2 Cox CC 273, D was charged with manslaughter when his cart struck and killed a girl who ran out in front of him. D was not holding the horse's reins at the time, but Erle J directed the jury that they could convict D of manslaughter only if they were satisfied that D could have avoided the accident had he been holding the reins correctly.

Factual causation is sometimes referred to as 'but for' (or *sine qua non*) causation, because it can be established only where the alleged result would not have occurred, or would not have occurred at the time or in the way it did, 'but for' D's act or culpable omission. The only qualification to this basic rule involves cases of complicity or joint venture, under which D may incur liability for encouraging or assisting the principal offender, even where it is proved that his conduct made no difference to the outcome. Procuring appears to be the only form of secondary participation that requires a causal link between the participation and the crime. See **A4.1**.

Legal or Imputable Causation

A1.27 Legal causation is a narrower and more subjective concept than factual causation. Not every cause in fact is a cause in law. To be so, it must be adjudged an 'operating and substantial' cause of the consequence in issue (*Smith* [1959] 2 QB 35) albeit that it does not have to be the only or even the principal such cause. The isolation of a legal cause from amongst a possible multitude of factual causes is a process involving subjective common sense rather than objectively measurable criteria, but when seeking to apportion possible criminal responsibility in this way, one must in practice look for some kind of abnormal and culpable behaviour. The logic behind such reasoning is explained by Hart and Honore, *Causation in the Law* (2nd edn, 1985):

> The notion that a cause is essentially something which interferes with or intervenes in the course of events which would normally take place, is central to our common-sense concept of cause...
>
> In distinguishing between causes and conditions, two contrasts are of prime importance. These are the contrasts between what is abnormal and what is normal in relation to any given thing or subject-matter, and between a free deliberate human action and all other conditions...
>
> In the case of a building destroyed by fire, 'mere conditions' will be factors such as the oxygen in the air, the presence of combustible material or the dryness of the building... which are present alike both... where such accidents occur and... where they do not... Such factors do not 'make the difference' between disaster and normal functioning, as... the dropping of a lighted cigarette does....

Multiple Causes and Multiple Blame

A1.28 D may be guilty of causing something to happen even if his conduct was not the only legal cause of it and even his conduct could not, on its own, have sufficed to make it happen (*Warburton* [2006] EWCA Crim 627). In *Hennigan* [1971] 3 All ER 133, H argued that he was not guilty of causing death by dangerous driving, because another driver was more to blame than him. The Court of Appeal replied that, as long as H's contribution was substantial, he could be held accountable. Without purporting to lay down any precise limits, the court suggested that, even if just 20 per cent of the blame could be attributed to H, that would suffice. *Hennigan* was followed in *Notman* [1994] Crim LR 518, where it was stated that anything more than a *de minimis* contribution could suffice. In cases of causing death by driving when uninsured, etc. (RTA 1988, s. 3ZB), the Supreme Court in *Hughes* [2013] 4 All ER 613 has held, reversing the Court of Appeal's ruling in *H* [2011] 4 All ER 761 and overruling *Williams* [2011] 3 All ER 969, that to be guilty D must be proved to have done something more than merely drive his vehicle on the road so that it was there to be involved in a fatal accident. It must be proved that D did or omitted to do something else that contributed in a more than minimal way to the death. There must in other words be something more than mere 'but for' causation (at [33]):

> Juries should thus be directed that it is not necessary for the Crown to prove careless or inconsiderate driving, but that there must be something open to proper criticism in the driving of the defendant, beyond the mere presence of the vehicle on the road, and which contributed in some more than minimal way to the death. How much this offence will in practice add to the other offences of causing death by driving will have to be worked out as factual scenarios present themselves; it may be that it will add relatively little.

Indirect Causation

Although legal causation must be 'operative and substantial', it need not necessarily be a direct cause of the proscribed result. In *McKechnie* (1992) 94 Cr App R 51, M inflicted serious head injuries on V. These were not in themselves fatal, but they prevented doctors from operating on V's duodenal ulcer, and V died when the ulcer burst. M was held to have caused his death. Not all indirect causes will be sufficiently proximate to the result; questions of fact and degree may be crucial, and it is therefore impossible to formulate any universal rule in such cases. Indirect causation may also be the basis of liability in cases involving crimes other than homicide. See, e.g., *Roberts* (1971) 56 Cr App R 95 (see **A1.35**) and *Miller* (1992) 95 Cr App R 421.

A1.29

The 'Eggshell Skull' Rule

D must ordinarily take his victim as he finds him. If, for example, the victim of his assault is unusually vulnerable to physical injury as a result of an existing medical condition or old age, D must accept liability for any unusually serious consequences which result. In *Hayward* (1908) 21 Cox CC 692, H chased his wife into the road, threatening her with violence. She then collapsed and died as a result of a long-standing heart condition and H was held liable for her manslaughter. This principle was extended in *Blaue* [1975] 3 All ER 446. B stabbed a woman. A blood transfusion would have saved her life, but as a Jehovah's Witness she refused it. B was convicted of manslaughter (on grounds of diminished responsibility) and this verdict was upheld on appeal. Lawton LJ said (at p. 1415):

A1.30

> It has long been the policy of the law that those who use violence on other people must take their victims as they find them. This in our judgment means the whole man, not just the physical man. It does not lie in the mouth of the assailant to say that the victim's religious beliefs which inhibited him from accepting certain kinds of treatment were unreasonable.

One possible qualification to this general rule may need to be noted. Where the victim of a crime dies of heart failure etc., resulting from stress or fright, the charge is likely to be one of manslaughter, and it must then be proved that D's unlawful conduct was obviously dangerous, in the sense of being likely to cause some injury. Where blows are struck, this is unlikely to be a problem, but what of cases in which the victim proved unusually vulnerable to injury caused by fear or stress? In *Dawson* (1985) 81 Cr App R 150 the Court of Appeal quashed D's conviction for the manslaughter of V, a 60-year-old petrol station attendant, who died of a heart attack after being threatened with a replica gun. The court held that the trial judge had misdirected the jury by inviting them to take account of V's heart condition when deciding whether D's conduct had been obviously dangerous. D could not have known of this condition at the time. At first sight, *Dawson* may seem inconsistent with the eggshell skull rule, but it merely decides that it was unfair to judge the dangerousness of D's conduct as if V's heart defect was already obvious to everyone concerned. It is submitted that the jury should instead have been directed to consider whether the act of threatening an elderly man (of unknown health) with a replica gun involved an obvious risk of harming him. The answer to that question would surely have been 'yes', and the eggshell skull rule would then have been applied. See also *Watson* [1989] 2 All ER 865, discussed at **B1.57**, *Carey* [2006] EWCA Crim 604 and *M (J)* [2013] 1 WLR 1083.

NOVUS ACTUS INTERVENIENS

Introduction

A1.31 D will not be regarded as having caused the consequence for which it is sought to make him liable if there was a *novus actus interveniens* (or new intervening act) sufficient to break the chain of causation between his original action and the consequence in question. Although his original act may remain a factual cause, but for which the consequence would never have occurred, the intervening act may supplant it as the imputable or legal cause for the purpose of criminal liability. This intervening act may be the act of a third party, an act of the victim or an unforeseeable natural event, sometimes called an 'act of God'. These three variants will be considered in turn, but one general point may be made at the outset: no intervening act can break the chain of causation if it merely complements or aggravates the effects of D's initial conduct. Suppose, for example, that D attacks V, inflicting grave injuries, and that V later suffers further injuries, caused by his own foolishness, by E's act, or by some natural disaster. If V dies of his *cumulative* injuries, there can be no question of the chain of causation being broken. The chain of causation is broken only where the effect of the intervening act is so overwhelming that any initial injuries are relegated to the status of mere background. The detailed application of this principle will be explored in the specific contexts within which it may arise, but the principle is the same in each case.

If the aggravation of injuries cannot break the chain of causation, then *a fortiori* an omission to treat those initial injuries cannot do so, even if such neglect results in relatively minor injuries becoming fatal (*Holland* (1841) 2 Mood & R 351). As Lawton LJ said in *Blaue* [1975] 3 All ER 446, where V refused a life-saving blood transfusion on religious grounds:

> The question for decision is what caused [V's] death. The answer is the stab wound. The fact that [V] refused to stop this end coming about did not break the causal connection between the act and death.

It can make no difference whether the omission is that of the victim (as in *Blaue*) or of a third party, such as a doctor. It may even be the result of an unforeseen natural event, such as a flood which prevents medical assistance from reaching V.

Acts of Third Parties

A1.32 **Deliberate and Informed Interventions**   The subsequent intervention of a third party will ordinarily break the chain of causation if it is free, deliberate and informed, and provides the immediate cause of the event in question (*Pagett* (1983) 76 Cr App R 279; *Latif* [1996] 1 All ER 353). Another way of stating this principle is that the voluntary act of the accused will usually be taken to be the cause of an act or omission where it was the last human conduct before the result that is said to have been caused. But even an accidental intervention may break the chain of causation if it was unforeseeable in the circumstances (*Girdler* [2009] EWCA Crim 2666).

In *Latif*, L and S were involved in a plan to smuggle heroin into Britain. The heroin was delivered by S to a supposed accomplice in Pakistan, who was in fact an undercover operative of the US Drug Enforcement Agency. It was then flown into Britain by a British customs officer, technically without lawful authority, whilst L and S were lured to a meeting in London, where they were arrested. It was held that the importation by the customs officer, whilst unlawful, was a deliberate third-party act for which S was not responsible, although S could still be convicted of being concerned in an *attempt* to import it, contrary to the Customs and Excise Management Act 1979, s. 170(2) (see **B16.38** *et seq.*). In contrast, the actions of an innocent agent, who is unaware of the true facts, cannot break the chain of causation. Had the case containing the heroin been forwarded by airline officials as lost luggage (as in *Jakeman* (1983) 76 Cr App R 223: see **A1.7**), S would have been held responsible for their actions.

In *Pagett*, P forcibly used his pregnant girlfriend, V, as a 'human shield' in a shoot-out with **A1.33** police officers. V was killed by bullets from officers returning his fire. He was convicted of her manslaughter. The Court of Appeal reasoned that the officers had acted 'involuntarily' in taking reasonable measures for the purpose of self-preservation and in the performance of their legal duty to apprehend P, and there was of course no suggestion that they shot V deliberately. Whether the police indeed acted 'reasonably' may be open to question; but this would make no difference to the outcome. Even if the police officers were at fault, their conduct was not free, deliberate and informed. P created a situation in which V's life was inevitably endangered, and what happened was a natural and foreseeable consequence of that behaviour.

In a controversial ruling that remains difficult to reconcile with *Latif*, the House of Lords held in *Environment Agency v Empress Car Co. (Abertillery) Ltd* [1999] 2 AC 22 that the operator of an installation from which diesel fuel escaped into a watercourse could be convicted of 'causing' that pollution, contrary to the Water Resources Act 1991, s. 85(1), even though the immediate cause of the disaster was an act of vandalism by an unknown third party, who had opened the tap on a fuel storage tank during the night. Significantly, the defendant company had no measures in place to prevent such vandalism, or to restrict the subsequent escape of any fuel leaking from the tap. Lord Hoffmann reasoned that, 'there may be different answers to questions about causation when attributing responsibility to different people under different rules' or even 'when attributing responsibility to different people under the same rule'. Looking at the policy behind the provision in question, he continued:

> Strict liability is imposed in the interests of protecting controlled waters from pollution. . . . Clearly, therefore, the fact that a deliberate act of a third party, caused the pollution does not in itself mean that the defendants' creation of a situation in which the third party could so act did not also cause the pollution for the purposes of section 85(1).

Lord Hoffmann added that it remained necessary to consider whether the third party's act was a 'normal fact of life or something extraordinary':

> If it was in the general run of things a matter of ordinary occurrence, it will not negative the causal effect of the defendant's acts, even if it was not foreseeable that it would happen to that particular defendant or take that particular form. . . . The distinction between ordinary and extraordinary is one of fact and degree to which the [court] must apply common sense and knowledge of what happens in the area.

The principles applied in *Empress* are not, however, of general application. In *Kennedy (No. 2)* [2008] 1 AC 269 the House of Lords explained that:

> It was not [in *Empress*] purporting to lay down general rules governing causation in criminal law. It was construing, with reference to the facts of the case before it, a statutory provision imposing strict criminal liability on those who cause pollution of controlled waters.

The company in *Empress* might reasonably have been expected to protect its tank against commonplace acts of vandalism, but liability did not turn on proof of default or neglect in that respect. See also *L* [2009] 1 All ER 786 and *National Rivers Authority v Yorkshire Water Services Ltd* [1995] 1 AC 444.

Medical Intervention   It is foreseeable that the victim of an attack or accident may require **A1.34** medical treatment, but it is also foreseeable that his injuries may be misdiagnosed or that treatment may not be performed correctly. This is one reason why incorrect medical treatment is hardly ever categorised by the courts as amounting to a *novus actus interveniens*. An equally valid reason, in many cases, is that failure to provide proper treatment for an initial injury rarely amounts to an independent cause of death or injury: it is far more likely that such failure will merely aggravate the original injury, or that it will allow the original injury to take its natural course. In particular, the 'switching off' of a life support system, even if wrongful, will never break the chain of causation flowing from the original injury (*Malcherek* [1981] 2 All ER 422). Even where incorrect treatment leads to death or more serious injury, it will only break the chain of causation if it is (a) unforeseeably bad, and (b) the sole significant cause of the death (or more serious injury) with which D is charged.

An exceptional case in which palpably wrong medical treatment was held to have broken the chain of causation was *Jordan* (1956) 40 Cr App R 152. J stabbed B, who was taken to hospital, where he died. J was initially convicted of his murder, but on appeal new evidence was admitted. This showed that at the time of B's death his wound had almost totally healed and that he had died as a result of a mix-up in which he was given antibiotics to which he had already proved highly allergic. The Court of Criminal Appeal concluded that, if the jury had heard this new evidence, they would have concluded that it was the medical treatment which had caused death and not the stab wound.

Smith [1959] 2 QB 35 is clearly distinguishable from *Jordan*. S stabbed his fellow soldier, C, with a bayonet during a brawl. Other soldiers carried C to a medical centre, dropping him twice on the way. An overworked doctor failed to notice that one of C's lungs had been pierced and the treatment C received 'might well have affected his chances of recovery'. This did not however break the chain of causation. According to the Courts-Martial Appeals Court:

> If at the time of death the original wound is still an operating cause and a substantial cause, then the death can properly be said to be the result of the wound, albeit that some other cause of death is also operating. Only if it can be said that the original wounding is merely the setting in which another cause operates can it be said that the death did not result from the wound ... only if the second cause is so overwhelming as to make the original wound merely part of the history can it be said that the death does not flow from the wound.

C's death could still be attributed to the wound inflicted by s. In contrast, the wound inflicted on B in *Jordan* had largely healed, and his mistreatment was in effect the sole cause of death. Furthermore, the mistreatment was so bizarre as to be unforeseeable. Had B died from the first dose of antibiotics, J's murder conviction would almost certainly have been upheld. This is apparent from the later case of *Cheshire* [1991] 3 All ER 670, in which C shot V, who later died as a result of medical complications arising from an tracheotomy he had undergone as part of his emergency treatment. The gunshot wounds had healed at the time of death, but C's conviction was upheld on the grounds that the complications were still a natural consequence of his acts. After careful consideration of existing authorities, including *Jordan, Smith* and *Malcherek*, Beldam LJ concluded (at pp. 851–2):

> ...when the victim of a criminal act is treated for wounds or injuries by a doctor or other medical staff attempting to repair the harm done, it will only be in the most extraordinary and unusual case that such treatment can be said to be so independent of the acts of the defendant that it could be regarded in law as a cause of the victim's death to the exclusion of the defendant's acts...

> Even though negligence in the treatment of the victim was the immediate cause of his death, the jury should not regard it as excluding the responsibility of the accused unless the negligent treatment was so independent of his acts, and in itself so potent in causing death, that they regard the contribution made by his acts as insignificant.

Cheshire was followed in *Mellor* [1996] 2 Cr App R 245; see also *Gowans* [2003] EWCA Crim 3935.

Conduct of the Victim

A1.35   In many cases, the *actus reus* of a crime is completed, not by an act of the offender, but by an act of his victim as where the victim of a criminal deception is tricked into making a payment into the deceiver's account. Another is where V injures himself in a fall whilst attempting to escape from an attack by D: the latter may be regarded as having caused that injury. In *Roberts* (1971)

56 Cr App R 95, R was convicted of an assault causing actual bodily harm to a young woman who was injured jumping from his moving car after he had assaulted her in that car. See also *DPP v Daley* [1980] AC 237, *Mackie* (1973) 57 Cr App R 453 and *Corbett* [1996] Crim LR 594. A clear direction on causation is essential in such cases. In *Williams* [1992] 2 All ER 183, it was held that the question is whether V's reaction was 'within a range of responses which might be anticipated from a victim in his situation', or whether it was 'so daft as to make it his own voluntary act which amounted to a *novus actus interveniens*'. The jury should not, in this context, be invited to make any allowance for D's youth or inexperience (*Marjoram* [2000] Crim LR 372). D's inability to foresee V's reaction may be relevant to the question of *mens rea*, but as far as causation is concerned, the only subjective element relates to V. As Stuart-Smith LJ pointed out in *Williams*, the jury must be directed 'to bear in mind any particular characteristic of the victim and the fact that, in the agony of the moment, a victim may act without thought and deliberation'.

Conversely, D cannot be held responsible for 'causing' the voluntary and deliberate acts of V, merely because they were foreseeable responses to his own actions. The supplier of a controlled drug does not ordinarily 'cause' his client to take or ingest that drug, even if such conduct is both foreseeable and expected (*Dalby* [1982] 1 All ER 916; *Armstrong* [1989] Crim LR 149; *Kennedy (No. 2)* [2008] 1 AC 269). The distinction between such cases and *Roberts* is that the drug supplier does not force his customers to do anything. They exercise informed free will and harm themselves by their own voluntary acts.

Drug-dealing Cases   This is not to suggest that a drug dealer can never be guilty of man-slaughter if his customer dies after taking the drugs supplied. Where D supplies contaminated drugs, or supplies a drug such as heroin to a child, who is unable to make an informed decision concerning the dangers involved, he may well be considered to have 'caused' any harm that then results, just as if he had left the child a loaded gun to play with. Liability may also arise under the *Miller* principle (*Miller* [1983] 2 AC 161: see **A1.20**) where D fails to summon help when it is obvious that V has become dangerously ill as a result of ingesting drugs that D has supplied. See also **B1.69**.   **A1.36**

There may also be cases in which D and V can each be said to have jointly administered the drug. If the drug is held to be a noxious substance (as for example heroin would be), this might suffice to make D guilty of an offence under the OAPA 1861, s. 23, and of manslaughter if death results. See *Burgess* [2008] EWCA Crim 516 and **B1.63**. In *Rogers* [2003] 1 WLR 1374 it was held to suffice that D applied a tourniquet to V's arm as V self-injected; but in *Kennedy (No. 2)* the House of Lords disagreed (at [20]):

> There is, clearly, a difficult borderline between contributory acts which may properly be regarded as administering a noxious thing and acts which may not. But the crucial question is not whether the defendant facilitated or contributed to administration of the noxious thing, but whether he went further and administered it. What matters . . . is whether the injection itself was the result of a voluntary and informed decision by the person injecting himself. In *R v Rogers*, as in the present case, it was. That case was, therefore, wrongly decided. . . .

The House of Lords also overruled *Finlay* [2003] EWCA Crim 3868 and reversed the Court of Appeal's ruling in *Kennedy (No. 2)* [2005] 4 All ER 1083.

Victim's Aggravation or Neglect   As explained at **A1.31**, a victim's aggravation or neglect of his   **A1.37** injuries is unlikely to affect the chain of causation. Thus, in *Wall* (1802) 28 St Tr 51, W was found guilty of murdering a soldier, S, whom he had subjected to an illegal flogging, notwithstanding that S aggravated his condition by drinking spirits to ease the pain. A victim's subsequent suicide is (or at least should be) another matter. In *Dear* [1996] Crim LR 595, D appealed against his conviction for murder, arguing that V, whom he had repeatedly slashed with a knife, subsequently aggravated his own wounds so that they reopened, with fatal results. D's conviction was nevertheless upheld.

A1.38 **Suicide and Manslaughter**   The Court of Appeal in *Dhaliwal* [2006] 2 Cr App R 348 held that, where D inflicts physical and/or psychological abuse on V and thereby causes her some kind of recognised psychiatric illness (i.e. injury amounting in law to actual or grievous bodily harm for the purposes of the OAPA 1861, s. 47 or s. 20) his conduct may give rise to liability for manslaughter (i.e. constructive manslaughter) should this illness in turn cause V to commit suicide. Conditions such as post-traumatic stress disorder, battered wife syndrome, or reactive depression were identified as potential causes. In *Dhaliwal*, however, the prosecution could not prove that V had suffered any such psychiatric injury. The infliction of mere psychological harm would not suffice.

The Court of Appeal left open the possibility that a manslaughter conviction might sometimes be supportable on a somewhat different basis, which had been suggested by the trial judge but disavowed by the prosecution, namely that: 'where a decision to commit suicide has been triggered by a physical assault which represents the culmination of a course of abusive conduct, it would be possible... to argue that the final assault played a significant part in causing the victim's death'.

Exceptional Natural Events

A1.39 An 'act of God' or other exceptional natural event may break the chain of causation leading from D's initial act, if it was the sole immediate cause of the consequence in question. Such an event must be 'of so powerful a nature that the conduct of the defendant was not a cause at all, but was merely a part of the surrounding circumstances' (*Southern Water Authority v Pegrum* [1989] Crim LR 442). If D attacks V and leaves him slowly dying of his injuries, the chain of causation may be broken if V is ultimately killed by a lightning bolt or a falling tree, rather than by the original injuries. In contrast, routine hazards, such as seasonal rain or cold winter nights, would not have such an effect (*Alphacell Ltd v Woodward* [1972] AC 824). Such things are more readily foreseeable, but as Lord Hoffmann said in *Environment Agency v Empress Car Co. (Abertillery) Ltd* [1999] 2 AC 22 at pp. 34–5 (see **A1.33**):

> The true common sense distinction is, in my view, between acts and events which, although not necessarily foreseeable in the particular case, are in the generality a normal and familiar fact of life, and acts or events which are abnormal and extraordinary....
>
> ...In the context of natural events, this distinction between normal and extraordinary events emerges in the decision of this House in *Alphacell Ltd v Woodward*.

Causation Issues and Alternative Explanations

A1.40 The court or jury must of course be satisfied that D caused the event which is the subject of the charge against him. If possible innocent explanations cannot be disproved D must be acquitted. Difficulties may arise where the evidence suggests that D might have caused the *actus reus* in one of two or more different ways. The court or jury must be able to agree, not just on their verdict but on the basis for it, and must be directed accordingly. As Otton LJ explained in *Boreman* [2000] 1 All ER 307, 'where the two possible means by which the [offence] is effected comprise completely different acts, happening at different times... the jury ought to be unanimous on which act leads them to the decision to convict'. See also *Brown* (1983) 79 Cr App R 115 at **D18.44**. This does not mean, however, that a court or jury must always be able to agree on how exactly D committed the crime. It will suffice if they can agree that he must, one way or another, have committed it. Thus, if six jurors believe that D committed murder by killing V himself (or, if not, by hiring an assassin to kill for him) and the other six believe that he committed that same murder by hiring an assassin (or, if not, by killing V himself) they may still be able to convict D of that offence, because they can all agree that he was implicated in one way or another (*Giannetto* [1997] 1 Cr App R 1). Alternatively, the jury may have no idea as to how or when D committed the offence, and yet be able to agree that he must have done so, in one way or another (*A-G's Ref (No. 4 of 1980)* [1981] 2 All ER 617: see **A1.9**). In *Boreman*, however, V was beaten up by the appellants and later died in a fire at his home. There was some evidence that the beating had contributed to his death. There was also some evidence that the appellants had started the fire; but it did not follow that they must have killed V in one way or the other. It would not therefore suffice if some jurors thought they were guilty only on the first basis and some only on the second.

Section A2   *Mens Rea*

THE MENTAL ELEMENT GENERALLY

A2.1   In addition to proving that the accused satisfied the definition of the *actus reus* of the particular crime charged, the prosecution must also prove *mens rea*, i.e. that the accused had the necessary mental state or degree of fault at the relevant time. Lord Hailsham of St Marylebone said in *DPP v Morgan* [1976] AC 182 at p. 213: 'The beginning of wisdom in all the "*mens rea*" cases . . . is, as was pointed out by Stephen J in *Tolson* (1889) 23 QBD 168 at p. 185, that "*mens rea*" means a number of quite different things in relation to different crimes'. Thus one must turn to the definition of particular crimes to ascertain the precise *mens rea* required for specific offences. Nevertheless, there are a number of recurrent concepts (such as intention, recklessness etc.) which can usefully be examined here. There are some general points which can be made which ought to be borne in mind when looking at the definition of any individual crime. Some of these general points (such as the question of transferred *mens rea*) are best looked at after examining the meaning of particular concepts such as intention etc. but by way of introduction it is useful to point out the varied ways in which the individual concepts may be used.

Criminal offences vary in that some may require intention as the *mens rea*, some require only recklessness or some other state of mind and some are even satisfied by negligence. The variety in fact goes considerably further than this in that not only do different offences make use of different types of mental element, but also they utilise those elements in different ways. Compare, for example, assault occasioning actual bodily harm (OAPA 1861, s. 47) and criminal damage contrary to the Criminal Damage Act 1971, s. 1(1). Both are in one sense crimes of recklessness (see *Venna* [1976] QB 421 for assault, and the Criminal Damage Act 1971, s. 1(1), itself for criminal damage) but the *extent* to which they apply this concept is quite different. It has been confirmed that the mental element in assault occasioning actual bodily harm only extends to the element of 'assault' and not to the element of 'occasioning actual bodily harm'. In *Roberts* (1971) 56 Cr App R 95, the accused was liable even though he did not intend or foresee any actual bodily harm and this case was approved by the House of Lords in *Savage* [1992] 1 AC 699. In contrast, in relation to damaging any property belonging to another; the mental element applies not only to the elements of 'damaging' and 'property' but also to the element of 'belonging to another'. So in *Smith* [1974] QB 354, the accused was not guilty because he intended to damage only his own property, not property belonging to another. Thus the *range of application* of the concept of recklessness has been wider in relation to criminal damage than in relation to assault occasioning actual bodily harm.

A2.2   This 'range of application' should be contrasted with the scope of meaning of recklessness which has recently undergone radical change. The House of Lords' decision in *Metropolitan Police Commissioner v Caldwell* [1982] AC 341 *formerly* gave recklessness a so-called objective interpretation in relation to offences of criminal damage so as to include those who had failed to consider an obvious risk. In contrast, in relation to offences against the person, recklessness was understood in a more subjective sense to include only those who were actually aware of the relevant risk (*Spratt* [1990] 1 WLR 1073). Thus recklessness differed in both its range (of application) and its scope (of meaning) as between assault and criminal damage. This led to further distinctions between the meaning of recklessness in the offence of criminal damage and its meaning in rape (*S (Satnam)* (1983) 78 Cr App R 149), including the notion or attitude of 'couldn't care less', although the SOA 2003 has since redefined rape.

Quite apart from the disappearance of recklessness from the definition of rape, much greater consistency of meaning as between criminal damage and offences against the person has now been restored (for the time being at least) by the decision of the House of Lords in *G* [2004] 1 AC 1034 which has overruled *Caldwell* and reasserted a subjective test requiring actual aware-ness of risk in cases of criminal damage. However it is clear from both Lord Bingham's opinion at [28] and from Lord Rodger's at [69] that it is still perfectly *possible* that recklessness could have different meanings in relation to different offences.

Lord Rodger, in agreeing that the subjective meaning of recklessness was the correct one under the Criminal Damage Act 1971, nevertheless recognised that:

> ...there is much to be said for the view that, if the law is to operate with the concept of recklessness, then it may properly treat as reckless the man who acts without even troubling to give his mind to a risk that would have been obvious to him if he had thought about it. This approach may be better suited to some offences than to others...the opposing view, that only advertent risk-taking should ever be included within the concept of recklessness in criminal law, seems to be based, at least in part, on the kind of thinking that the late Professor Hart demolished in his classic essay, 'Negligence, *Mens Rea* and Criminal Responsibility' (1961), reprinted in HLA Hart *Punishment and Responsibility* (1968), pp. 136–157.

It therefore remains true to say that, in considering the mental element of any particular crime one has to consider not only the *scope* (of meaning) of that element and its *range* (of application) but also the *context* of its use which may itself influence the scope of meaning to be adopted.

The position of the word expressly requiring the mental element may be significant, as can be seen in the House of Lords decision in *Wings Ltd v Ellis* [1985] AC 272, which turned on the interpretation of the Trade Descriptions Act 1968, s. 14(1) (now repealed): **A2.3**

> It shall be an offence for any person in the course of any trade or business—
>
> (a) to make a statement which he knows to be false; or
> (b) recklessly to make a statement which is false.

The House was concerned with s. 14(1)(a) and held that the requirement of knowledge applied only to the element of the falsity of the statement and not to the act of making the statement in the first place. Thus Wings Ltd was convicted in relation to a statement in a brochure which was initially made innocently and which the company attempted to withdraw as soon as its falsity was realised. The statement was regarded as being made when a customer read it and booked a holiday and Wings Ltd was liable since by then the statement was known to the company to be false even though it was not known that the statement was being made. The decision is not beyond criticism but the contrast in wording between paras. (a) and (b) of s. 14(1) and the respective positioning of the words requiring *mens rea* help to explain the decision. The adverb 'recklessly' is right at the start of para. (b) so that it can naturally refer to both the act of making a statement and the requirement of its falsity whereas para. (a), instead of referring to 'know-ingly making a false statement', which would be more consistent with para. (b), merely refers to making 'a statement which he knows to be false'. Thus the *range* of application of the concept of knowledge was restricted by the *position* of the word in the section.

INTENTION

'Intention' is a word that is usually used in relation to consequences. A person clearly intends a consequence if he wants that consequence to follow from his action. This is so whether the consequence is very likely or very unlikely to result. Thus an accused who shoots at another **A2.4** wanting to kill him, intends to kill whether the intended victim is 2 metres away and an easy target or whether he is 200 metres away and it would have taken an exceptionally good shot to hit him. In either case, even if the accused misses, he will be liable for a crime requiring intention to kill, such as attempted murder.

The meaning of 'intention' is not restricted to consequences which are wanted or desired (sometimes referred to as 'direct' intent) but includes consequences which an accused might not want to follow but which he knows are virtually certain to do so (sometimes referred to as 'oblique' or 'indirect' intent). At one point it seemed that there was support in the House of Lords for a very wide view of oblique intent, i.e. that it included a state of not wanting a consequence to occur while knowing that it was 'highly probable' or even just 'probable' or 'likely' (*Hyam v DPP* [1975] AC 55 and see also per Lord Diplock in *Lemon* [1979] AC 617 at p. 638). This was regarded as too wide by the Court of Appeal in *Mohan* [1976] QB 1 in relation to attempt and in *Belfon* [1976] 3 All ER 46 in relation to wounding with intent to cause grievous bodily harm under the OAPA 1861, s. 18. It seemed that intention might mean different things in different offences but much of the uncertainty appeared to have been resolved by the decisions of the House of Lords in *Moloney* [1985] AC 905 and *Hancock* [1986] AC 455, although further refinements have been added by another House of Lords case, *Woollin* [1999] AC 82.

A2.5   The most important principles to emerge from *Moloney* were that (a) intention should have the same meaning throughout the criminal law (see per Lord Bridge of Harwich at p. 920F), although Lord Steyn appears to have cast doubt upon this in *Woollin*, and (b) the foresight of the probability of a consequence does not of itself amount to intention but may be evidence of it. Unfortunately the guidelines laid down in that case for directing a jury on this issue (essentially that the jury could, but would not be obliged to, infer that a person intended a consequence if he foresaw it as a 'natural' consequence of his action) were subsequently found by the House of Lords in *Hancock* to be 'unsafe and misleading'. Lord Scarman said ([1986] AC 455 at p. 473):

> [The guidelines] require a reference to probability. They also require an explanation that the greater the probability of a consequence the more likely it is that the consequence was foreseen and that if that consequence was foreseen the greater the probability is that that consequence was also intended. But juries also require to be reminded that the decision is theirs to be reached upon a consideration of all the evidence.

The result seemed to be that:

(a)   Where there is clear evidence that the accused desired the consequence to occur, the question of whether the accused intended that consequence can be left to the jury without further elaboration.

(b)   Where the accused may not have desired the consequence but may have foreseen it as a by-product of his action, a more detailed direction may be necessary.

(c)   Such a direction would emphasise that 'the probability, however high, of a consequence is only a factor, though it may in some cases be a very significant factor, to be considered with all the other evidence in determining whether the accused intended to bring it about' (Lord Scarman in *Hancock* at p. 474).

The first two principles (paras. (a) and (b)) continue to apply following *Woollin*, whether the charge be murder or any other offence requiring intention. In the light of *Woollin*, para. (c) now seems potentially too broad, in relation to murder at least, since only foresight of a virtual certainty entitles a jury to find intention (in the absence of desire) on a murder charge (see further **B1.12** and **B1.14**). Given the statement of Lord Steyn in *Woollin* (at p. 96) that 'it does not follow that "intent" necessarily has precisely the same meaning in every context in the criminal law', it remains possible that lower levels of foresight could still be a sufficient basis for a legitimate inference in relation to other offences requiring intention. In either case, the effect of (c) seems to be that a discretion is conferred on the jury because the core notion of intention which they are inferring is left undefined (even after *Woollin*, in which Lord Steyn confirmed that 'the decision is for the jury upon a consideration of all the evidence in the case'). For more detail on intent in relation to murder, see **B1.12** and **B1.14**; in relation to wounding with intent to cause grievous bodily harm, see *Bowden* [1993] Crim LR 379, which reiterates that foresight of 'virtual certainty' or at least 'a very high degree of probability' is required.

RECKLESSNESS

Recklessness Generally

Essentially concerned with unjustified risk-taking, the precise meaning of the term 'reckless- **A2.6** ness' has been the subject of great controversy and will no doubt continue to be so. The reason for this is that recklessness has come to be the touchstone of criminal responsibility for a large number of criminal offences. For many offences, the precise boundaries of the concept of intention are not in themselves crucial as recklessness constitutes an alternative and sufficient *mens rea* and one which it is easier to prove. For example, under the Criminal Damage Act 1971, s. 1(1), a person has the requisite *mens rea* if he acts 'intending to destroy or damage any property or being reckless as to whether any property would be destroyed or damaged'. If an accused threw a stone which damaged X's window and is charged under s. 1(1), he may plausibly be able to say, for example, that he was aiming for the dog in front of the window and that he did not *intend* to damage the window. There would be little point here trying to argue that the accused realised that the probability was that he would miss the dog and break the window from which the jury should infer an intention to break the window. There would be a much greater chance of success in relying on recklessness which equally suffices for liability. The issue of foresight of probability as intention need only be explained in crimes such as murder or attempt where intention alone suffices for liability.

The relationship between intention and recklessness (in relation to consequences), and indeed the debate about the scope of recklessness itself, can be seen more clearly from the following list:

(a) Consequence aimed at (i.e. D acts in order to cause that consequence): intention.
(b) Consequence foreseen as virtually certain: intention *may* be found.
(c) Consequence foreseen as probable: typically (if risk unreasonable) recklessness (subjective).
(d) Consequence foreseen as possible: typically (if risk unreasonable) recklessness (subjective).
(e) Consequence not foreseen but ought to have been: negligence (objective recklessness).
(f) Consequence even reasonable man would not foresee: strict liability.

The central case of intention is situation (a) although the jury may still find intention in situation (b) and possibly, although not in murder cases, even in (c). However, (b) and (c) are more appropriately and easily dealt with as recklessness where this will suffice for liability. Situation (d) is also capable of being within recklessness as is category (e). The difference between (d) and (e) essentially represents the distinction between the narrower subjective '*Cunningham*' recklessness (*Cunningham* [1957] 2 QB 396) and the wider objective '*Caldwell*' recklessness (*Metropolitan Police Commissioner v Caldwell* [1982] AC 341) favoured for two decades by the House of Lords but rejected by them, for criminal damage at least, in *G* [2004] 1 AC 1034. Category (f), of course, is not a culpable state of mind and would not normally give rise to criminal responsibility except in relation to crimes of strict liability.

'Subjective' *Cunningham* Recklessness

Following the decision of the House of Lords in *G* [2004] 1 AC 1034, this type of reckless- **A2.7** ness can perhaps now be referred to as 'standard' recklessness, but it has in the past often been referred to as *Cunningham* recklessness (*Cunningham* [1957] 2 QB 396).

It covers categories (b), (c) and (d) (most typically the latter two) in the list at **A2.6**. These states of mind, of course, equally qualified as recklessness under the *Caldwell* test (*Metropolitan Police Commissioner v Caldwell* [1982] AC 341), *Caldwell* merely adding category (e) to the scope of recklessness. The spread over categories (b), (c) and (d) emphasises the point that the degree of foresight of risk that constitutes subjective recklessness is not fixed but variable.

As Lord Bingham formulated it in *G* in relation to criminal damage, adopting the Law Commission's Draft Criminal Code (Law Com. No. 177):

A person acts recklessly ... with respect to—

(i) a circumstance when he is aware of a risk that it exists or will exist;
(ii) a result when he is aware of a risk that it will occur;
and it is, in the circumstances known to him, unreasonable to take the risk.

The degree of foreseen risk which would make one reckless depends therefore on the reasonableness or otherwise of the risk. At one end of the scale, a surgeon operating on a critically ill patient may knowingly run a very high risk of his patient's death, but if the patient is even more likely to die if the operation is not attempted then it would be a reasonable risk to run and no one would describe the operation as reckless. There is a very strong justification which makes the operation reasonable. On the other hand, if one offers another a chocolate from a box containing 50, just one of which the offeror knows to contain arsenic, the offeror is clearly acting recklessly. The risk is a relatively low one (one in 50, or 2 per cent) but, since there is no justification for running the risk, it is an unreasonable one to take and the offeror is reckless. Thus in some circumstances, to run a very high risk may not be reckless and yet in others it may be reckless to run a relatively low risk. In the context of alleged criminal offences there will often be no plausible justification for running the risk (e.g., of wounding someone) and so often the foresight of *any* degree of risk, of the mere possibility of injury, may be sufficient. The greater the justification for running a risk, the higher the degree of *foreseen* risk which will be required to constitute recklessness.

Subjective Awareness of an Unreasonable Risk

A2.8 **Awareness of Risk** Following *G* [2004] 1 AC 1034, the emphasis is on the degree of risk that is actually foreseen by the accused or of which he is aware. It is to that extent that the test is subjective. The jury will perforce *normally* assess this by reference to what they themselves would have foreseen in the circumstances which is why in many cases there will be little difference in outcome whether they are directed to consider a test of what the accused actually appreciated or the alternative (under the previous test in *Metropolitan Police Commissioner v Caldwell* [1982] AC 341) of whether the risk would have been obvious to a reasonable person. Focusing on the actual awareness of the accused clearly may, however, make a difference where there is reason to suppose that the accused did not appreciate what the reasonable person would have appreciated. This is likely to be the case where the accused differs from the reasonable person in some relevant way, for example, because of age (the accused were 11 and 12 in *G*) or because of mental disorder (see *Stephenson* [1979] QB 695, one of a number of decisions which as a result of *G* must be regarded as rehabilitated, where the accused was incapable of appreciating the risk of lighting a small fire in a straw stack in order to keep warm). The list of situations where the jury will find a difference between the accused's appreciation of risk (or lack of it) and what the reasonable person would have realised is not closed. Any reason why the accused did not in fact appreciate the risk seems at first sight, in principle, to be admissible except for, it still seems clear, voluntary intoxication through drink or drugs — see Lord Bingham's reference in *G* at [32] to *Majewski* [1977] AC 443 (see **A3.17**).

On the other hand, as Lord Bingham stated in *G* at [39]:

There is no reason to doubt the common sense which tribunals of fact bring to their task. In a contested case based on intention, the defendant rarely admits intending the injurious result in question, but the tribunal of fact will readily infer such an intention, in a proper case, from all the circumstances and probabilities and evidence of what the defendant did and said at the time. Similarly with recklessness: it is not to be supposed that the tribunal of fact will accept a defendant's assertion that he never thought of a certain risk when all the circumstances and probabilities and evidence of what he did and said at the time show that he did or must have done.

Whilst this may be true, the question of what the accused was actually aware of must be left to the jury and, if it is not, any conviction may be quashed as happened in *Briggs* [1977] 1 All ER 475, a pre-*Caldwell* case where the appellant claimed that it did not occur to him that he might damage the handle of another person's car which he was trying forcibly to open in order to move the car out of the way of his garage door. If the correct question is left to the jury, it may well be that a jury will not be sympathetic to a claim that an appellant, acting in bad temper or for some other unattractive motive, did not appreciate an obvious risk and will conclude that he was in fact aware of it. Furthermore, Lord Bingham in *G* seemed quite happy (at [14]) with the approach in *Parker* [1977] 2 All ER 37 whereby, when a defendant is fully aware of all the circumstances, including the degree of force he is using, closing one's mind to an obvious risk is regarded as equivalent to conscious awareness of the risk and:

> . . . a man certainly cannot escape the consequences of his action in this particular set of circumstances by saying, 'I never directed my mind to the obvious consequences because I was in a self-induced state of temper.' (Geoffrey Lane LJ in *Parker* [1977] 1 WLR 600 at p. 604.)

One can explain this on the basis of the argument (referred to by Lord Bingham) that to close your mind to a risk you have first to realise that there is one (in which case it adds little to the requirement of awareness of risk) or alternatively on the basis that we all act in the light of a combination of explicit and implicit items of knowledge. I am aware in one sense (the implicit sense) that if I drive too fast I may cause an accident. I do not consciously think about this (at least most of the time) when driving as I am habituated to drive at a sensible speed. If I am late or angry or frustrated when driving, I may impulsively drive faster than is advisable. I may be aware of the risks in so doing but on occasions I may also truthfully be able to say I was so intent on getting to an appointment in time that the increased risk I ran did not consciously occur to me. But if I am aware of the speed I was doing, I do know (implicitly) of the increased risk even though my preoccupation with something else means I did not specifically think about it at the time. One can call this closing one's mind to the obvious or one can classify the case as one of implicit knowledge sufficient to satisfy a subjective test. In comparison, a child or mentally disordered person may lack even the implicit knowledge about the dangers of speed (or, as in *G*, about how fire can spread) and cannot in any sense be said to be aware of the risk. This was of no avail to the 'tipsy' defendant in *Booth v CPS* (2006) 170 JP 305, where the Divisional Court upheld a finding in effect that a pedestrian who steps out into the path of a car and is aware of the risk of a collision is implicitly aware of the risk of damaging the car. As Hallet LJ put it at [20]: 'The magistrates were entitled to find . . . that if he was aware of the risk of a collision, inherent in that risk of a collision was not only the risk of personal injury but the risk of damage to property'.

Reasonableness of Running that Risk Whatever the route to concluding that the accused is aware of a risk, which is the ultimate issue for the jury, even subjective recklessness then imposes an objective test of reasonableness as to whether it was reckless to run *that* risk (which is just one reason why labels of 'objective' or 'subjective' recklessness can be misleading or over simplistic). A very small risk may be unreasonable in many situations. For example, in *Chief Constable of Avon and Somerset Constabulary v Shimmen* (1986) 84 Cr App R 7 showing off one's martial arts skills to friends did not justify the small risk of which the accused was aware (despite his pride in his own skill) that he might misjudge matters and break the window he was shadow kicking. Nor would it avail the accused to say that personally he regarded the running of such a (low) risk to be justifiable or reasonable. The accused's awareness is only relevant as to the level of the risk, not as to its reasonableness. It is the court's assessment of reasonableness that counts (albeit looking at the level of risk perceived by the accused).

A2.9

In many other situations however, running certain levels of risk are an inherent and accepted part of ordinary life. Driving a car carries a risk of damaging other vehicles but the degree of risk involved in driving with due care and attention is reasonable in the light of the overall balance as perceived in the current social consensus. Lighting a bonfire on Bonfire Night on one's own land inevitably carries *some* risk of fire spreading to adjoining land but, if reasonable precautions are taken so that the risk is sufficiently and suitably low, it would not be regarded as reckless to run that low risk of damage to another's property. But in the context in which many prosecutions are brought, there will be very little if any arguable justification for taking a risk (or for taking the degree of risk which was in fact taken) and the question will simply be whether the accused was aware of that risk.

'Objective' *Caldwell* Recklessness

A2.10 The *Caldwell* test of recklessness (*Metropolitan Police Commissioner v Caldwell* [1982] AC 341), now abandoned even for offences under the Criminal Damage Act 1971, was encapsulated in the following model direction given by Lord Diplock in *Caldwell* at p. 354:

> ...a person charged with an offence under section 1(1) of the Criminal Damage Act 1971 is 'reckless as to whether any such property would be destroyed or damaged' if (1) he does an act which in fact creates an obvious risk that property will be destroyed or damaged and (2) when he does the act he either has not given any thought to the possibility of there being any such risk or has recognised that there was some risk involved and has nonetheless gone on to do it.

Although initially the same basic approach was simultaneously applied by the House of Lords' decision in *Lawrence* [1982] AC 510 to the now defunct offence of causing death by reckless driving and thereafter for a time to manslaughter (see **B1.66**), the Criminal Damage Act 1971 was the last remaining arena in which the *Caldwell* test held any real sway. It is difficult to see now that there are any remaining offences of any significance to which this version of recklessness applies, whereby a person may be 'reckless' on the basis that he has failed to consider an obvious risk if he cannot be said to be aware of the risk (even in the sense explained above of closing his mind to a risk).

It would be dangerous however to write off entirely this 'objective' version of recklessness. In *G* [2004] 1 AC 1034 at [70], Lord Rodger recognised that the decision in *Caldwell* involved:

> ... [a] legitimate choice between two legal policies, I was initially doubtful whether it would be appropriate for the House to overrule it. ... But, for the reasons that I have already indicated, I have come to share your lordships' view that we should indeed overrule *Caldwell* and set the law back on the track that Parliament originally intended it to follow. If Parliament now thinks it preferable for the 1971 Act to cover culpably inadvertent as well as advertent wrongdoers, it can so enact. The Law Commission recognised that, if codifying the law, Parliament might wish to adopt that approach: *A Criminal Code for England and Wales Vol 2 Commentary* (LC No. 177), paras. 8.21 and 17.6.

In *Caldwell* Lord Diplock took his wider view of recklessness encompassing both awareness of risk and failure to consider a risk because ([1982] AC 341 at p. 352):

> Neither state of mind seems to me to be less blameworthy than the other; but if the difference between the two constituted the distinction between what does and what does not in legal theory amount to a guilty state of mind for the purposes of a statutory offence of damage to property, it would not be a practicable distinction for use in a trial by jury.

A2.11 The House of Lords in *G* has now taken the view that it is a practicable distinction. Questionable assertions by apparently culpable defendants that they were not aware of the risks inherent in their conduct will be left to the jury to resolve in the light of common-sense inferences from the facts, aided perhaps by the response that closing one's mind to an obvious risk is equivalent to awareness of it. Judges will at least no longer have to tell juries to their own and the jury's obvious discomfort, as the trial judge was compelled to in *G*, that the accused can be guilty of an offence of recklessness where the risk is one that the accused would not have appreciated even if he had thought about it. This particular consequence of *Caldwell* was not explicitly spelled out in the decision itself but was, rightly or wrongly, regarded as implicit in it by the Divisional Court in

Elliot v C [1983] 2 All ER 1005. This was the aspect of *Caldwell* as interpreted that was most problematic — the rejection of the conditionally subjective test for determining whether a risk is obvious (i.e. the rejection of the idea that the risk had to be one which would have been obvious to the particular accused if he had actually stopped to think about it). Once that conditionally subjective test was rejected, it was not surprising that the law gradually withdrew from the *Caldwell* definition and that eventually the decision has been overruled in *G* even in relation to criminal damage. But, if the purely subjective approach to awareness of risk throws up its own problems (much will depend on how juries assess defences of 'it never occurred to me' and how problems of 'closing one's mind to the obvious' are dealt with), a modified form of *Caldwell* recklessness, where the risk must be one which the accused himself could have appreciated, may yet resurface at some time in the future, in relation to some offences at least. In truth there may be very little if any difference between a *Caldwell* test of recklessness moderated by a conditionally subjective test of 'obvious risk' and a 'subjective' awareness test of recklessness bolstered by a robust attitude to risks of which the accused is implicitly or subliminally aware or to which he may be regarded as having closed his mind. The idea that a purely subjective test of conscious awareness of risk at the time of acting can adequately deal with all the situations likely to arise has proved naïve in the past and a full reading of *G* reveals that the House of Lords was itself conscious of the risks of too simplistic an approach to complex issues.

MALICE

A2.12 Many provisions of the OAPA 1861, notably ss. 18, 20, 23 and 24, define offences in terms of 'maliciously' performing an act and it is now well established that this word is not to be understood in the sense of 'wickedly' or 'with ill will' but as requiring either actual intention to cause the relevant harm or at least foresight of the risk of causing the particular type of harm. The classic formulation was given by the Court of Appeal in *Cunningham* [1957] 2 QB 396 where it was said:

> ... malice must be taken ... as requiring either (1) An actual intention to do the ... harm ...; or (2) recklessness as to whether such harm should occur or not (i.e., the accused has foreseen that the particular type of harm might be done and yet has gone on to take the risk of it).

The case of *W (A Minor) v Dolbey* (1983) 88 Cr App R 1 made it clear (as had Lord Diplock himself in *Metropolitan Police Commissioner v Caldwell* [1982] AC 341) that this meaning of malice 'as a term of art' was unaffected by the *Caldwell* definition of recklessness. In *W (A Minor) v Dolbey*, the magistrates had convicted, of malicious wounding, a juvenile who had fired at his friend an air rifle, which he believed not to be loaded. This was on the basis of *Caldwell* recklessness (though arguably he was not even *Caldwell* reckless if he had consciously ruled out any risk of causing harm). The Divisional Court quashed the conviction since the juvenile did not foresee the risk of any harm to his friend. The Court of Appeal adopted a similar approach in quashing a conviction in *Morrison* (1988) 89 Cr App R 17, which was certainly not a case of ruling out the risk but of an accused not thinking about the risk to others in seeking to avoid arrest. The subjective meaning of malice was confirmed by the House of Lords in *Savage* [1992] 1 AC 699 (see B2.36). It is, however, sufficient for the accused to foresee that the harm 'might' or 'may' occur; it is not necessary that the accused foresees that it definitely would occur (*Rushworth* (1992) 95 Cr App R 252, and see more recently *DPP v A* [2001] Crim LR 140).

WILFULLY

A2.13 'Wilfully', which has some similarities with 'malice' since it dates from an earlier legislative vocabulary, should not be understood merely in its most obvious or literal sense of 'deliberately' or 'voluntarily'. It is now taken as a composite word to cover both intention and recklessness (and trial judges ought to give a direction as to its meaning: *JD* [2008] EWCA Crim 2360).

Until recently, it arguably differed from malice in that it may not have been restricted to subjective recklessness but appeared to include *Caldwell* recklessness or something very similar to it. The leading case is *Sheppard* [1981] AC 394, which in many ways was the precursor of the decision in *Metropolitan Police Commissioner v Caldwell* [1982] AC 341. In *Sheppard*, Lord Diplock provided a model direction as follows:

> ...on a charge of wilful neglect of a child under section 1 of the Children and Young Persons Act 1933 by failing to provide adequate medical aid, ... the jury must be satisfied (1) that the child did in fact need medical aid at the time at which the parent is charged with failing to provide it (the *actus reus*) and (2) either that the parent was aware at that time that the child's health might be at risk if it were not provided with medical aid, or that the parent's unawareness of this fact was due to his not caring whether his child's health were at risk or not (the *mens rea*).

As Lord Diplock himself commented, this last state of mind 'imports the concept of recklessness which is a common concept in *mens rea* in the criminal law' and the model direction, though not identical, is remarkably similar in structure and effect to that subsequently laid down for recklessness in *Caldwell*.

It now seems likely however that the meaning of recklessness imported by the term wilful will be the same subjective one adopted in *G* [2004] 1 AC 1034 in preference to the *Caldwell* test. In *A-G's Ref (No. 3 of 2003)* [2005] QB 73, Pill LJ said in relation to the offence of misconduct in a public office (at [26] and [27]):

> Whether *Sheppard*, which was not cited in *Caldwell* and in which Lord Edmund-Davies did not, as in *Caldwell* a few months later, dissent, is consistent with *Cunningham* (not cited in *Sheppard*) and *G*, may be arguable, though, for present purposes, we greatly doubt whether there is any material difference. Lord Diplock is likely to have taken the view that the expression 'wilful neglect', in section 1 of the 1933 Act, required a subjective element not required in his view in *Caldwell* but, with the demise of *Caldwell*, the distinction is immaterial.
>
> ...We do not accept the submission that *Sheppard* imposes a lower duty on the prosecution than does *G*. Indeed, we do not accept the submission that, in the present context, there is any material difference between them and, in our view, the approach to recklessness in *G* can be incorporated into a direction on wilfulness in relation to this offence.

Thus it would seem that wilfully now means intentionally or recklessly and the meaning of recklessness is the same subjective meaning which is discussed at **A2.7**. Any objective tendencies detectable in Lord Diplock's model direction in *Sheppard* can be regarded as having been discarded along with the rejection of his approach in *Caldwell*. The subjective aspect of the meaning of 'wilfully' can be seen to have been confirmed in *W* [2006] EWCA Crim 2723, although the case turned on knowledge rather than recklessness. Sir Igor Judge P (at [38]) quoted with approval Lord Keith's observation in *Sheppard* that '... a parent who has genuinely failed to appreciate that his child needs medical care, through personal inadequacy or stupidity or both, is not guilty'. The subjective nature of the test was also stressed in *Turbill* [2014] 1 Cr App R 62 (7). Although the trial judge had used the word recklessness, he had not made it clear to the jury that this imported a subjective test and had also used expressions such as 'grossly careless' and 'couldn't care less' which detracted from the essential subjective nature of the test for wilfulness.

KNOWLEDGE

A2.14   'Knowledge' can be seen in many ways as playing the same role in relation to circumstances as intention plays in relation to consequences. One knows something if one is absolutely sure that it is so although, unlike intention, it is of no relevance whether one wants or desires the thing to be so. Since it is difficult ever to be absolutely certain of anything, it has to be accepted that a person who feels 'virtually certain' about something can equally be regarded as knowing it. See *Dunne* (1998) 162 JP 399 for confirmation of this approach. On the other hand, one may feel entirely sure and yet be proved wrong, in which case it is difficult to say that one 'knew'. For example,

that negligence will suffice for all the other elements. To return to the example of the Trade Descriptions Act 1968, s. 14(1) (now repealed), and *Wings Ltd v Ellis* [1985] AC 272 discussed in **A2.3**, that offence expressly required knowledge as to the falsity of the statement but, as a result of the no-negligence defence in the Trade Descriptions Act 1968, s. 24 (on which the accused in *Wings Ltd v Ellis* chose not to rely), it was an offence satisfied by negligence in other respects, for example, as to whether a particular statement is being made.

STRICT LIABILITY

The point just made is particularly important in connection with offences of so-called strict   **A2.20** liability. The term 'strict liability' is sometimes loosely explained as meaning 'liability without fault' but this is misleading insofar as it suggests that no mental or fault element whatsoever is required. Strict liability offences are normally those where no fault element is required in relation to one (perhaps crucial) element of the *actus reus* but where *mens rea* is required in relation to other aspects. The classic example is *Prince* (1875) LR 2 CCR 154 where the accused was convicted of taking a girl under the age of 16 out of the possession and against the will of her father. The accused's reasonable belief that she was over 16 was no defence, so even negligence was not required in relation to the element of her being over the age of 16. However, *mens rea* was required in relation to other elements of the offence, e.g., in relation to whether the taking was against the will of the father. As Bramwell B put it: 'If the taker believed he had the father's consent, though wrongly, he would have no *mens rea*'. (See Brooke LJ in *B (A Minor) v DPP* [2000] 2 AC 428 for a critical analysis of the influence of the decision in *Prince*, an influence which will henceforth be drastically reduced following the House of Lords' decisions in that case and in *K* [2002] 1 AC 462.) The influence of these two House of Lords decisions (see **A3.6** for further discussion) was illustrated in the Court of Appeal decision in *Kumar* [2005] 1 WLR 1352 in which it was held that the offence of buggery under the SOA 1956, s. 12 (now replaced by the SOA 2003), was not a strict liability offence in respect of the other person's age. Thus an honest belief that the other person was over 16 was a valid defence Although, by virtue of the SOA 2003, equivalent beliefs in this particular context are now required to be reasonable, the principle stated by the House of Lords, that, in the absence of strict liability, the normal inference of *mens rea* involves that there is a defence of honest belief that an aspect of the *actus reus* was not present, was reaffirmed in *CPS v M* [2010] 4 All ER 51 (see **A2.23**).

Elements where Liability is Strict   Rather than talking of an offence as a whole being one of   **A2.21** strict liability, it is more accurate to speak of it being an offence of strict liability with respect to a particular element or elements. Of course, the element in respect of which liability is strict may be the only element which has any possible criminal connotation, the remaining elements as to which some mental element is required being by contrast mundane and, in themselves, non-criminal in character. For example, in *Parker v Alder* [1899] 1 QB 20, the defendant was convicted of selling adulterated milk when the adulteration took place after the milk had left his control and was en route by rail to the purchaser. The offence was therefore of strict liability as regards the milk being adulterated and the only element left was the act of selling. To say that the offence requires *mens rea* in respect of this element, that it requires 'an intention to sell milk', has a hollow ring about it since that is not an intention which is in any way culpable. By contrast with *Prince* then, this is an example of an offence where the imposition of strict liability in relation to the one significant aspect of the *actus reus* effectively means that the offence did indeed give rise to liability without fault. At the other end of the scale, assault occasioning actual bodily harm could be regarded as an offence of strict liability as far as relates to the requirement of actual bodily harm since the only *mens rea* required relates to the assault and not to the element of actual bodily harm. However, a person who intends to assault is clearly culpable and no one would describe this offence as giving rise to liability without fault, thus it is not normally thought of as an offence of strict liability but rather as an example of constructive liability (which amounts to much the same thing).

A2.22 **Traditional Attitude to Regulatory Offences** A large number of regulatory offences are traditionally referred to as strict liability offences since, as with the case of *Parker v Alder* discussed at A2.21, no fault or mental element is required in respect of those features of the *actus reus* which give the offence its criminal character. The circumstances under which the courts will impose strict liability in respect of a particular statutory offence are difficult to predict and regard must be had to the authority (if any) on the individual statutory provision in question.

The Imposition of Strict Liability

A2.23 As Lord Reid emphasised in *Sweet v Parsley* [1970] AC 132, in cases where Parliament has not made it clear that strict liability is intended, the courts, in construing criminal legislation, start from the presumption that Parliament did not intend to punish a blameless individual and therefore that words importing *mens rea* must be read into the statute. The force of this presumption and its status as a matter of 'constitutional principle', especially in cases of offences carrying potentially serious sentences of imprisonment, was powerfully reasserted in *CPS v M* [2010] 4 All ER 51 (bringing a prohibited article into prison under the Prison Act 1952, s. 40C(1)(a), not an offence of strict liability). Therefore, in line with the highly significant decisions of the House of Lords in *B (A Minor) v DPP* [2000] 2 AC 428 and *K* [2002] 1 AC 462, it was held in *CPS v M* that the prosecution had to be able to prove the absence of an honest belief on the part of the accused that he was not bringing the article in question with him when he entered the prison. On the other hand, strict liability is often applied to a so-called class of quasi-criminal offences, those referred to by Wright J in *Sherras v De Rutzen* [1895] 1 QB 918 as acts which are not criminal in the real sense but which are prohibited, by a penalty, in the public interest. The question even in this context is whether the danger to be guarded against is of such importance that strict liability is required (*Kirkland v Robinson* (1987) 151 JP 377) and whether the imposition of strict liability would promote the objects of the legislation (*Lim Chin Aik v The Queen* [1963] AC 160). Thus, in *Gammon (Hong Kong) Ltd v A-G of Hong Kong* [1985] AC 1, a case involving breaches of building regulations, the Privy Council stressed that the matter was one of social concern, and that strict liability could be shown to promote the objects of the statute and, in particular, greater vigilance in the carrying out of works. In *Matudi* [2003] EWCA Crim 697 the offence of importation of animal products contrary to the Products of Animal Origin (Import and Export) Regulations (SI 1996 No. 3124) was held to be one of strict liability; the Court of Appeal remarked that the unmonitored importation of animal products was of public concern because it posed hazards to human and animal health and possible economic consequences from an outbreak of, for example, foot and mouth disease. The social risk was great and the imposition of strict liability was likely to deter importers from acting improperly. Liability would also conduce to the use of reputable importers.

A2.24 **Significance of Penalty** The circumstance that the likely penalty is pecuniary is more compatible with the imposition of strict liability (*Customs and Excise Commissioners, ex parte Claus* (1987) 86 Cr App R 189). This applies even though the maximum fine may be heavy (*Gammon (Hong Kong) Ltd v A-G of Hong Kong*). This is not an absolute principle: some offences bearing a heavy pecuniary penalty and even in theory a penalty of imprisonment attract strict liability (*Pharmaceutical Society of Great Britain v Storkwain Ltd* [1986] 2 All ER 635; *Blake* [1997] 1 All ER 963; *Harrow London Borough Council v Shah* [1999] 3 All ER 302). Allied to this is the mode of trial: where, as in *Ex parte Claus*, the offence is triable only summarily, strict liability will be more readily inferred than if the offence is triable either way or on indictment. In regulatory offences courts continue to give weight to the nature of the social danger involved, the limited applicability and reach of the legislation as regulating a particular trade or business, and the exigencies of successful enforcement.

A2.25 **Absence or Use of Particular Words** The use of words importing *mens rea* elsewhere in a statute regulating a trade, profession or industry may be treated as an indication that an offence which uses no such words is intended to convey strict liability (*Pharmaceutical Society of Great Britain v Storkwain Ltd*; *Gammon (Hong Kong) Ltd v A-G (Hong Kong)*; *Kirkland v Robinson* (1987) 151 JP 377; *Jackson* [2007] 1 WLR 1035; *R (Thames Water Utilities Ltd) v Bromley*

Magistrates' Court (No. 2) [2013] 1 WLR 3641 (contrasting 'deposit' with 'knowingly cause or knowingly permit') — but contrast the approach in the non-regulatory context of *CPS v M* where such considerations were given little weight). In this context, it should be noted that whilst some words such as 'intentionally' always convey *mens rea*, other words, referable to knowledge rather than to purpose, sometimes do not do so. In general, such words as 'permitting' convey the need to prove *mens rea* (*Sweet v Parsley*; *Reynolds v G.H. Austin & Sons Ltd* [1951] 2 KB 135). On some occasions they have been held not to do so (*Browning v J.W.H. Watson (Rochester) Ltd* [1953] 2 All ER 775). The context in which a word is used may be significant and so too may be the use of the passive voice (*Cheshire County Council v Clegg* (1991) 89 LGR 600; *Cheshire County Council Trading Standards Department, ex parte Alan Helliwell & Sons (Bolton) Ltd* [1991] Crim LR 210). 'Causing' is relatively neutral as to whether *mens rea* is required and it was not so required in the leading case of *Alphacell Ltd v Woodward* [1972] AC 824 where the imperative of preventing pollution of rivers was a strong factor in the decision of the House of Lords that the company could be liable for causing polluted matter to enter a river irrespective of the lack of knowledge or negligence on the company's part.

Social Dangers   Dangerous drugs and offensive weapons are other areas where the social danger   **A2.26**
being guarded against has led to restrictive interpretations of *mens rea* and of the meaning of the term 'possession'. In relation to possession of drugs, in *Warner v Metropolitan Police Commissioner* [1969] 2 AC 256, Lords Pearce, Wilberforce and Reid (dissenting) sought a construction which would require the prosecution to prove some element of knowledge of the thing in possession, but not so particular a degree of knowledge as to stultify enforcement of the legislation. In the context of offensive weapons, this means that, in contrast to the introduction since *Warner* of a statutory defence under the Misuse of Drugs Act 1971, it is not a defence for an accused to show that he did not know and could not be expected to know that the article was an offensive weapon (*Bradish* [1990] 1 QB 981; now emphatically confirmed in *Deyemi* [2008] 1 Cr App R 345, which also confirmed that strict liability is not inconsistent with the ECHR, Article 6 or 7).

Statutory Defences   Where a statutory due-diligence or no-negligence defence is provided in   **A2.27**
relation to a prohibition otherwise apparently cast in absolute terms, the courts are likely to hold that the offence is, the statutory defence apart, one of strict liability (*Wings Ltd v Ellis* [1985] AC 272; *Kirkland v Robinson* (1987) 151 JP 377; *Bradish* [1990] 1 QB 981; *Harrow London Borough Council v Shah* [1999] 3 All ER 302). The absence of such a defence does not, however, necessarily imply that *mens rea* is to be presumed (*Alphacell Ltd v Woodward* [1972] AC 824).

In relation to such statutory defences, the accused may sometimes have to satisfy a legal burden but in other cases the provision will be interpreted only to impose an evidential burden. A legal burden makes inroads into the presumption of innocence protected by the ECHR, Article 6(2), and the HRA 1998 (see **F3.18**). Such a provision may, however, be valid provided that it is objectively justified and proportionate (*Johnstone* [2003] 3 All ER 884 at p. 1749 per Lord Nicholls; *Sheldrake v DPP* [2003] 2 All ER 497; *Matthews* [2003] Crim LR 553). If however a legal burden is found to be incompatible with Article 6(2), the provision may be 'read down' so as only to impose an evidential burden rendering it compatible with Article 6(2) (see *Lambert* [2002] 2 AC 545 at **F3.19**).

Human Rights Compatibility   Strict liability is not in itself incompatible with the HRA   **A2.28**
1998 (*Muhamad* [2003] QB 1031; *Barnfather v Islington Education Authority* [2003] 1 WLR 2318) and its imposition is not incompatible with the presumption of innocence enshrined in Article 6(2), even in relation to serious sexual offences such as the offence of rape of a child under 13 contrary to the SOA 2003, s. 5. That offence requires an intentional penetration with the penis but does not require knowledge that the child is under 13 and does not permit any defence of reasonable mistake as to age. The House of Lords in *G* [2009] 1 AC 92 (see also **B3.76**) confirmed this interpretation of the offence and also the more general proposition that Article 6(2) does not affect the substance of the matters which may be legitimately proscribed by the content of the criminal law (provided that the burden of proving the matters selected for proscription is

on the prosecution). The irony is that Article 6(2) can limit the nature of the burden put on an accused to establish a statutory defence but it has no impact on the more restrictive decision not to provide any such defence at all. The decision in *G* was approved in *G v UK* (2011) 53 EHRR 237 and the approach was further underlined in *Brown* [2013] 4 All ER 860, where the offence of unlawful carnal knowledge of a girl under the age of 14 years, contrary to the Criminal Law Amendment Acts (Northern Ireland) 1885–1923, s. 4, was also confirmed as an offence of strict liability in relation to which the presumption of *mens rea* was displaced.

A2.29   **General Defences**   As far as general defences to crime are concerned, it has to be remembered that liability is normally strict, not absolute, and that many general defences to crime will equally apply to strict liability offences. Thus strict-liability offences normally involve proof that the accused voluntarily acted or omitted to act. This requirement may exceptionally be displaced by the words of the statute. In *Larsonneur* (1933) 24 Cr App R 74, a French citizen who was deported from the Irish Free State to the UK against her will was convicted of being an alien 'found within' the UK in breach of immigration legislation. In *Winzar v Chief Constable of Kent* (1983) *The Times*, 28 March 1983, the accused was convicted of being found drunk on a highway even though his presence there was attributable to the police who took him from a hospital corridor to the highway. Although these instances may be explicable on the basis of some prior fault on the part of the accused, it is generally regarded as surprising that a requirement of voluntariness was not implied in the legislation in these cases.

A2.30   **Act of God**   It does, however, seem both from *Alphacell Ltd v Woodward* [1972] AC 824 and from *Southern Water Authority v Pegrum* [1989] Crim LR 442 that act of God can amount to a defence. So too will automatism, provided that the degree of impairment is virtually absolute (*A-G's Ref (No. 2 of 1992)* [1994] QB 91). Duress by threats and duress of circumstances should apply to offences of strict liability since they represent independent circumstances of excuse. Mistake on the other hand will not serve as a defence to the extent that its effect is to negate *mens rea* which, *ex hypothesi*, is not applicable here (contrast the House of Lords' decisions in *B (A Minor) v DPP* [2000] 2 AC 428 and *K* [2002] 1 AC 462 discussed at **A3.6**) where the availability of the defence of genuine mistake was the logical consequence of the presumption of *mens rea* and of the offence *not* being one of strict liability.

TRANSFERRED *MENS REA*

A2.31   Transferred mens rea (an expression now acknowledged as 'a better description' by the Supreme Court in *Gnango* [2012] 1 AC 827 (at [16])) has traditionally been referred to as 'transferred malice' since the principal illustration was to be found in the case of *Latimer* (1886) 17 QBD 359, which was concerned with malicious wounding under the OAPA 1861, s. 20. The accused struck with his belt at C but missed and accidentally cut open the face of R. The Court for Crown Cases Reserved upheld the conviction. Lord Coleridge CJ pointed out that the section referred to wounding 'any other person'. This underlines the point that it is a question of interpreting the particular mental element required for the particular offence. The identity of the victim is not a material detail as far as most offences against the person are concerned, and therefore the accused's intention to injure A can be transferred so as to make the accused liable for an injury accidentally inflicted on B. The principle was applied to the offence of manslaughter in *Mitchell* [1983] QB 741 where the accused assaulted A, aged 72, causing him to fall on to the even more elderly B (aged 89), ultimately causing her death. The Court of Appeal upheld the conviction for her manslaughter, Staughton J saying: 'We can see no reason of policy for holding that an act calculated to harm A cannot be manslaughter if it in fact kills B'.

A more restrictive approach to the doctrine of transferred malice was taken by the House of Lords in *A-G's Ref (No. 3 of 1994)* [1998] AC 245. Lord Mustill (at p. 261) recognised the doctrine only as a ' "arbitrary exception to general principles"… useful enough to yield rough justice in particular cases . . . [which] could sensibly be retained not withstanding its lack of any sound intellectual basis'. However, it could not be extended to create liability for murder from an intentional infliction of grievous bodily harm on a pregnant woman which later resulted in the death of the child *in utero* subsequent to it having been born alive. Such a situation could give rise to liability for manslaughter, apparently without the need of the doctrine of transferred malice, but it was not murder. The decision seems to be influenced as much by the desire not to build any further on the grievous bodily harm/murder rule as by any deficiency in the transferred *mens rea* rule explained above. The logic of the decision would not necessarily preclude liability for murder of the child where the initial attack on the mother was with intent to *kill* her. More difficult would be the case where the attack was done with intent to destroy the foetus which resulted in a live birth followed by death. This would appear to be attempted child destruction (and possibly manslaughter) rather than murder.

Transfer within the Same Offence

The last point is further exemplified by the rule that the *mens rea* for one offence cannot be **A2.32** transferred so as to make an accused liable for a different offence even if the two offences happen to share similar terminology in their definition. This is illustrated by the case of *Pembliton* (1874) LR 2 CCR 119 where the accused threw a stone at a crowd of people but missed and broke a glass window behind them. The jury found that he intended to hit the people but not the window. Although he could have been convicted of malicious wounding, had he injured someone, the Court for Crown Cases Reserved quashed his conviction for malicious damage since that was a separate offence with its own separate *mens rea* requiring foresight of damage to property rather than foresight of injury to a person. Lord Coleridge CJ observed that it would have been different if 'the jury had found that the prisoner had been guilty of throwing the stone recklessly, knowing that there was a window near which it might probably hit' for then he would have had the separate *mens rea* of the independent offence of malicious damage. If two separate offences have *precisely* the same *mens rea* then the problem disappears. Proof of the *mens rea* of one automatically involves proof of the *mens rea* of the other. This principle was applied in *Ellis* (1986) 84 Cr App R 235, in which it was held that an intention to import a prohibited substance is the *mens rea* sufficient both for importing a controlled drug of Class A and also for the separate offence (cf. *Courtie* [1984] AC 463) of importing a controlled drug of Class B. Thus if an accused believed he was importing a Class B drug but was in fact importing a Class A drug, he can be convicted of the latter offence since he had the necessary *mens rea* of an intention to import a prohibited substance. His mistake might be relevant in determining the sentence. Similarly, he could be convicted of importing a controlled drug even if he believed he was importing material prohibited under some other enactment, such as pornographic material.

Accessories

The issue ultimately hinges on precisely what is required by the *mens rea* of the particular **A2.33** offence charged. This is an important point in relation to the liability of accessories (see **A4.5**) for an accessory must know or at least contemplate what it is the principal is going to do, and if the principal does something outside the scope of that contemplation, the accessory will not be liable. Thus if the accessory encourages violence against a *particular* victim and the principal *deliberately* chooses another victim not contemplated by the accessory, the accessory will not be liable (*Saunders* (1573) 2 Plow 473). However, if the principal tries to carry out the agreed plan but it accidentally misfires and victim B rather than victim A is injured, then the doctrine of transferred intention applies to the accessory too and he will remain liable because the principal has at least tried to do what the accessory contemplated: the principal's acts, although perhaps not their consequences, are within the accessory's contemplation and *mens rea*. This is neatly illustrated by *Grant* [2014] EWCA Crim 143, where the Court of Appeal applied the transferred *mens rea* principle to the conviction of a principal and two accessories in an attempted murder by shooting which also resulted in grievous bodily harm to two innocent bystanders. A finding of an intent to kill a specific individual forming the basis of the conviction on the attempted murder count was found inevitably to encompass within it an intent to cause grievous bodily harm, which could be the basis also of a conviction or convictions for causing grievous bodily harm to the bystanders under the OAPA 1861, s. 18, using the transferred *mens rea* rule. The argument that the intent to kill for attempted murder and the intent to cause grievous bodily harm for s. 18 were mutually exclusive or inconsistent with one another was roundly rejected — the former included the latter and conviction for the attempted killing of A plus conviction for the grievous bodily harm caused to B and C when the plan miscarried was perfectly proper for all three defendants. The application of the principle of transferred *mens rea* to accessories is also starkly illustrated by the strikingly unusual facts of *Gnango* [2012] 1 AC 827, a judgment of the Supreme Court, where D took part in a shoot-out with P. D was found to have encouraged P to shoot at D with intent to kill and D was found liable, on the basis of transferred *mens rea*, for the death of the innocent passer-by who was shot by P in attempting to kill D himself.

PROOF OF *MENS REA*

A2.34 The various mental states discussed in this section undeniably present courts and juries with difficult practical problems since, even when one is clear about the precise meaning of the mental state to be proved, it is not easy to be sure whether that corresponds to what actually went on in the accused's mind. Even in apparently clear cases, the accused's denial may raise a doubt in the minds of the jury. If a man shoots at another at point-blank range with a revolver it may seem easy to infer that he intended to kill or at least injure that other but an accused may seek to deny this by asserting that he believed the revolver was not loaded or was merely a harmless imitation. In the absence of such an explanation, of course, a jury will doubtless infer that he intended the natural and probable result of his action, i.e. death or injury to the other. Apart from admissions from the accused, this is indeed the most obvious way to ascertain his state of mind. Thus juries will probably infer that the accused intended or at least foresaw the natural and probable consequences of his actions. This is unexceptionable as a purely factual inference. Problems have arisen, however, when courts have sought to elevate such an inference to the status of an irrebuttable presumption. In the light of one such decision, *DPP v Smith* [1961] AC 290, Parliament intervened to ensure that it remains open to the jury to find that the accused did not intend or foresee the consequences (see also *Frankland v The Queen* [1987] AC 576). The CJA 1967, s. 8, provides:

A court or jury, in determining whether a person has committed an offence,—

(a) shall not be bound in law to infer that he intended or foresaw a result of his actions by reason only of its being a natural and probable consequence of those actions; but

(b) shall decide whether he did intend or foresee that result by reference to all the evidence, drawing such inferences from the evidence as appear proper in the circumstances.

Although this section makes it clear that there is no irrebuttable presumption, the concluding words of para. (b) equally mean that a jury *may* infer that a person intended or foresaw the natural and probable consequences of his actions if this seems appropriate on all the evidence, e.g., in the absence of any evidence explaining why the accused did not intend or foresee that consequence. (For further discussion of s. 8 and the relationship between foresight and intention in murder, see **B1.12** and **B1.14**.)

The CJA 1967, s. 8, can apply only where the prosecution are seeking to prove that the accused intended or foresaw something. Therefore whilst it can apply to the proof of intention in murder or to the proof of foresight in, for example, crimes of malice or subjective recklessness, it cannot apply where the definition of the offence does not require intention or foresight. Thus it is of no relevance to the element of manslaughter that requires the accused's act to be likely to cause bodily harm since that is a purely objective element which does not require any intent or foresight on the part of the accused (*Lipman* [1970] 1 QB 152).

Section 8 is concerned with proof of intention and foresight in relation to consequences but **A2.35** a similar problem arises in relation to circumstances. Again, a reasonable prima facie rule is to assume that the accused was aware of facts of which the reasonable man would have been aware provided one is prepared to adjust that conclusion in the face of credible evidence from the accused as to why he was not actually aware of it. This will often take the form of a defence of mistake. The former requirement that such mistakes had always, as a matter of law, to be based on reasonable grounds was, in effect, an irrebuttable presumption that the accused was aware of facts of which the reasonable man would be aware. The House of Lords in *DPP v Morgan* [1976] AC 182, in abandoning this rule for crimes requiring subjective *mens rea*, performed a similar function in this area to that performed by the CJA 1967, s. 8, in relation to foresight of consequences. The reasonableness or otherwise of a mistake is certainly an important factor in deciding whether the accused actually made that mistake but the court must look at all the evidence in order to decide on the accused's actual state of mind.

The *Morgan* principle applies only to crimes for which a genuine mistake is inconsistent with the *mens rea* and does not apply to crimes which are in effect satisfied by negligence in this respect, e.g., bigamy (see the comments of the Law Lords on *Tolson* (1889) 23 QBD 168 in *DPP v Morgan* itself, but see also the approach now taken by the House of Lords in *B (A Minor) v DPP* [2000] 2 AC 428 and *K* [2002] 1 AC 462, which seems to make the *Tolson* approach much less likely). Paradoxically, the *Morgan* principle no longer applies to the offence of rape as the SOA 2003 now expressly requires a belief in consent to be reasonable.

Section A3   General Defences

CATEGORIES OF GENERAL DEFENCE

A3.1   This section deals with defences which are available in relation to a range of offences rather than those which are available only in relation to a particular crime. Particular defences to particular crimes (such as diminished responsibility in relation to murder) are dealt with in the section of this work dealing with the particular offence. The expression 'general defences' suggests something positive that must be put forward on behalf of the accused, but in truth it is more accurate to regard these defences as circumstances where the prosecution have been unable to prove all the requirements of liability beyond reasonable doubt. This is most obviously true of defences that consist of denying the existence of the mental element of the offence charged (as with the defence of mistake) but it is also true of defences such as duress where the burden is not on the accused to show affirmatively that he was acting under duress but rather on the prosecution (once there is evidence before the court capable of supporting duress) to prove that the accused was not acting under duress. Nevertheless, it is still possible and helpful to divide general defences into two categories:

(a) those which involve a denial of the basic requirements of *mens rea* and voluntary conduct (the defences of mistake and automatism are best regarded in this way), and

(b) those which do not deny these basic requirements but which rely on other circumstances of excuse or justification, as in the defences of duress and self-defence.

These two categories will be examined in turn.

DEFENCES DENYING BASIC ELEMENTS OF LIABILITY

Mistake and Inadvertence: Offences Requiring Intention or Foresight

A3.2   Because the defences of mistake and inadvertence consist of a denial of the *mens rea* of the particular crime charged, the nature and the availability of the defences will vary from offence to offence but it is possible to identify categories of offences for which consistent principles can be formulated. The first category consists of offences requiring subjective fault (e.g., crimes requiring intention or subjective recklessness). For this category of offences it is clear that either a mistake (i.e. a positive belief) that a particular ingredient of the offence charged is lacking or, alternatively, a simple failure to appreciate the presence of the same ingredient will operate as a defence. For example, A, out in open country, shoots V dead with a crossbow at a range of 200 metres. A has a defence if he thinks that V is a scarecrow (mistake) or, alternatively, if it has never occurred to him that V or anybody else might be so foolish as to traverse that part of the countryside selected by A to practise his archery (inadvertence). In either case A would lack the necessary *mens rea* for murder, the intention to kill or cause grievous bodily harm, although he may well be liable for other offences. Similarly, the offence of malicious wounding (OAPA 1861, s. 20) requires subjective awareness at least of the risk of wounding, and either mistake or inadvertence will suffice for a defence. See, e.g., *W (A Minor) v Dolbey* (1983) 88 Cr App R 1, in which the Divisional Court held that the accused's belief that his air rifle was unloaded was a defence to a charge under s. 20. (This case also illustrates the artificiality and difficulty in many cases of distinguishing between mistake and inadvertence since the accused was also described as ignoring the risk that the gun might be unloaded. Fortunately, at least in this category of offences, it is not a distinction which needs to be made, a defence of lack of *mens rea* being present in either case.) See also *Morrison* (1988) 89 Cr App R 17.

It should be stressed that, because this category of offences requires subjective fault, the test of mistake (and of inadvertence) is also a subjective one; there is no requirement that the mistake be one which a reasonable man would have made (or that a reasonable man would have failed to appreciate that which the accused failed to appreciate). The previously traditional requirement that, as a matter of law, mistakes have to be reasonable was emphatically refuted by the House of Lords in *DPP v Morgan* [1976] AC 182, although it will naturally be more difficult to persuade a jury to accept that an accused genuinely made an unreasonable mistake. (The House of Lords upheld the convictions in *DPP v Morgan* itself on the basis that the accused had not actually held any mistaken belief.)

The important point is that the courts regard the rule that mistakes do not have to be reasonable in this context as a logical one which flows from the nature of the mental element required for this category of offences (see especially the speech of Lord Hailsham of St Marylebone in *DPP v Morgan*). Thus one can generalise that wherever an offence requires subjective awareness of a particular element, a genuine mistake that such an element is absent will be a defence.

The logic of this rule is unassailable as applied to proof of intention. If a person believes he is **A3.3** shooting only at an inanimate object such as a scarecrow, he cannot at the same time by that very act intend to kill. The same is true where knowledge is required. A person who believes that the goods he buys are not stolen cannot at the same time know (or even believe) that the goods are stolen — the two states of mind are logically inconsistent with one another. However, with crimes satisfied by foresight or awareness of risk (i.e. crimes satisfied by malice or subjective recklessness) the logic is somewhat flawed. One can believe that the stone one throws in the open country is not going to injure someone whilst still recognising that there is a risk that someone lying out of sight might be injured. The point is that beliefs are not usually absolute and are not inconsistent with the recognition of the possibility of a contrary state of affairs (whereas a belief *is* inconsistent with *knowledge* of a contrary state of affairs). Of course, in most cases the belief will be sufficiently strong to leave only the faintest possibility (if any at all) in the believer's mind that he may be wrong and this small degree of possibility would not be sufficient to amount to recklessness or malice. It does, however, depend on what one means by 'belief' and also on what the jury understand by that term.

Mistake and Inadvertence: Implications of the Demise of Objective Recklessness

It is clear that inadvertence is no defence to an offence satisfied by objective recklessness even **A3.4** should that concept survive or resurface anywhere in the criminal law following the overruling of *Metropolitan Police Commissioner v Caldwell* [1982] AC 341. It ought to be equally clear that a positive mistake can be a defence even to objective recklessness. The question of mistake in relation to consequences came to be considered under the heading of 'ruling out the risk' and the leading case was *Chief Constable of Avon and Somerset Constabulary v Shimmen* (1986) 84 Cr App R 7, where the accused claimed to have ruled out the risk of causing damage to a window when he aimed a martial-art-style kick in its direction, basing his view on his faith in his own prowess as an exponent of the Korean art of self-defence. In other words, he claimed to believe that no damage would result from his action (the subsequent shattering of the window revealing this belief to be a sadly mistaken one). The Divisional Court remitted the case to the magistrates with a direction to convict since the evidence did not show that the accused had ruled out all the risk (hence he was still reckless in consciously running a small risk). But the court also expressly left open the possibility that an accused whose mistake in his mind rules out any risk would not be objectively reckless (since he has neither failed to consider the risk nor consciously run it). The interesting point is the requirement that the risk has to be totally ruled out, which is akin to saying that mistaken beliefs have to be held with a degree of conviction equal to certainty and admitting of no doubts. Logically the same argument should apply in a case like *Shimmen* even following the reversal of *Caldwell* as *Shimmen* was not based on D's failure to consider a risk but on his appreciation that there remained a small but unjustified risk.

The overall point to note is that the treatment of mistakes should not vary as between subjective and objective recklessness since the latter merely extended the former to include failure to think and the person who acts under a mistaken belief has not failed to think — the only question can be whether he is subjectively reckless. His mistake is either inconsistent with the required awareness of an unreasonable risk, in which case he is not subjectively reckless, or, despite his mistake, he is still aware of an unreasonable level of risk — in which case, in principle, he may still be reckless. In general though, cases such as *Shimmen* apart, the courts seem to assume that, where a person is treated as acting under a mistaken belief, that indicates that he is not at the same time conscious of any remaining risk that could be regarded as unreasonable.

Mistake and Inadvertence: Offences Satisfied by Negligence

A3.5 It is clear that inadvertence is no defence to a crime of negligence. (This assumes that the risk of which the accused was unaware was one of which a reasonable man would have been aware. Strictly speaking, of course, inadvertence is wide enough to cover failure to consider non-obvious risks but the normal context of the use of the word 'inadvertence' is one whereby it is assumed that the risk is one of which a reasonable man would have been aware.)

Equally clearly, mistake can be a defence to crimes of negligence subject to the important qualification that the mistake must be a reasonable one since an unreasonable mistake itself supplies the negligence which is the sufficient basis of liability. The House of Lords in *DPP v Morgan* [1976] AC 182 specifically stated that the old requirement of reasonableness still applies to offences not requiring full *mens rea* but deliberately refrained from overruling *Tolson* (1889) 23 QBD 168, which required a mistaken belief in the death of a spouse in the offence of bigamy to be based on reasonable grounds. As Lord Fraser of Tullybelton put it ([1976] AC 182 at p. 238):

> ...bigamy was an absolute offence, except for one defence set out in a proviso, and it is clear that the mental element in bigamy is quite different from that in rape. In particular, bigamy does not involve any intention except the intention to go through a marriage ceremony, unlike rape in which I have already considered the mental element. So, if a defendant charged with bigamy believes that his spouse is dead, his belief does not involve the absence of any intent which forms an essential ingredient in the offence.

Thus, the logical argument that even an unreasonable mistake must deny the mental element, and so be a defence, does not apply to bigamy, and the offence is in effect interpreted as one satisfied by negligence as to whether the spouse is still alive. The courts sometimes adopt this approach in relation to other statutory offences as, for example, in *Phekoo* [1981] 3 All ER 84 in relation to the offence of harassment of a residential occupier under the Protection from Eviction Act 1977, s. 1(3). The Court of Appeal held that a belief that a person was not a residential occupier had to be reasonable to afford a defence. This is entirely consistent with the House of Lords' comments on *Tolson* in *DPP v Morgan*.

A3.6 Treating the offence as one of negligence is at least a more sensitive approach than imposing strict liability (whereby even a reasonable mistake would be no defence) and again is in line with the sentiments expressed by Lord Diplock in *Sweet v Parsley* [1970] AC 132 where he said (at pp. 163–4):

> ...had the significance of *Tolson* been appreciated here, as it was in the High Court of Australia, our courts, too, would have been less ready to infer an intention of Parliament to create offences for which an honest and reasonable mistake was no excuse.

When the Court of Appeal considered the case of *B (A Minor) v DPP* [2000] 2 AC 428, Brooke LJ clearly felt uneasy in holding that the offence under the Indecency with Children Act 1961, s. 1(1) (inciting a girl under 14 to commit an act of gross indecency), was one of strict liability in respect of the age of the girl. However, the House of Lords overturned the decision (also at [2000] 2 AC 428), holding not only that the offence was not one of strict liability but that the accused's honest belief that the girl was over 14 need not be based on reasonable grounds. Lord Nicholls indicated that 'as a matter of principle, the honest belief approach must be preferable' and that Lord Diplock's dictum in *Sweet v Parsley* referring to 'the absence of a belief, held honestly and upon reasonable grounds in the existence of facts which if true would make the act innocent' had in future to be read as though the reference to reasonable grounds were omitted. In *K* [2002] 1 AC 462, the House of Lords held that K's honest belief that a girl was over 16 would be a defence to indecent assault under the Sexual Offences Act 1956, s. 14. Once again, as in *B (A Minor)*, their lordships held that the prosecution has to prove the absence of a belief in excusing circumstances and that such a defence of mistaken belief ought not to be tempered by a requirement that the belief be a reasonable one. Subjectivists welcomed these developments but it would be a pity if the courts regarded themselves as being confronted by a stark choice between full *mens rea* and strict liability and felt obliged to opt for strict liability in circumstances where the middle way of a defence of reasonable mistake and hence liability for negligence might better serve the social purposes of the legislation. The offences considered in these two House of Lords decisions have now been replaced by the SOA 2003 and, where the child has in fact reached the age of 13, the half-way house of a defence of reasonable belief in age of 16 or over, has been adopted.

The case of *Lamb* [1967] 2 QB 981 provides an unusual example of a defence of mistake suc- **A3.7**
ceeding in relation to an offence involving negligence (manslaughter). The accused had 'jokingly' pointed and fired a revolver containing two live bullets at his best friend, thereby killing him. His mistake was in believing that, because the bullets were not in the firing position, the gun could not fire when in fact, unknown to him, pulling the trigger caused the cylinder to rotate and, in this case, placed one of the bullets in the firing position. The trial judge in effect directed the jury that the accused's beliefs were irrelevant, as was the evidence called on his behalf to show that this was a mistake that the ordinary man might make. The Court of Appeal quashed the conviction commenting (at p. 990):

> ...it would, of course, have been fully open to a jury, if properly directed, to find the defendant guilty because they considered his view as to there being no danger was formed in a criminally negligent way. But he was entitled to a direction that the jury should take into account the fact that he had undisputedly formed that view and that there was expert evidence as to this being an understandable view.

Thus an 'understandable' (reasonable) mistake could be a defence but a criminally negligent (unreasonable) one would not be.

Mistake and Inadvertence: Offences of Strict Liability

Even a reasonable mistake is no defence to an offence of strict liability (see **A2.20**), although **A3.8**
many so-called offences of strict liability now have statutory defences available based on particular types of reasonable mistake, the burden of proof of such defences being put on the accused. Such provisions may need to be read, in the light of the ECHR, Article 6, as imposing only an evidential burden. See, e.g., the Misuse of Drugs Act 1971, s. 28, at **B19.96**. As to burden of proof generally, see **F3.1** *et seq*.

Mistake of Law and Similar Defences

Whilst the maxim 'Ignorance of the law is no excuse' generally holds good in English law, it is **A3.9**
no more than a broad generalisation and is subject to exceptions. These exceptions are really no more than an illustration of the general theme already expounded — that where the accused lacks the *mens rea* required for the offence charged, he has a defence. Since *mens rea* generally relates to facts, it is mistake or ignorance of facts that is usually the basis of a denial of *mens rea*. However, in some offences the requirement of *mens rea* includes legal concepts and a mistake

about that legal concept can mean that the accused lacks *mens rea*. Thus in *Smith* [1974] QB 354 the conviction of the accused for criminal damage was quashed on the basis of a mistaken belief that the property damaged was still his own property and was therefore not property 'belonging to another'. It was the accused's ignorance of the civil law on the question of when property belongs to another (in particular, the law relating to a landlord's fixtures) which caused him to believe mistakenly that the property did not belong to the landlord. He thus lacked the *mens rea* of the offence because of his ignorance of law, and this was relevant because the offence required *mens rea* in relation to the civil-law concept of ownership (belonging to another).

It should be stressed that the mistake must be one of civil law rather than about the ambit or meaning of a criminal provision. This precludes not only defences such as 'I didn't think burglary included breaking into houses during the day' but also, for example, a defence to theft of a wild creature based on a belief that a wild creature is not 'property'. The Theft Act 1968, s. 4(4), specifically states that wild creatures are property for the purpose of theft (although there are restrictions on the circumstances when they can be the subject of a charge of theft) and this is a matter of the criminal law rather than whether wild creatures are property in any other branch of the law. Similarly, on a charge of handling stolen goods, it would be no defence to say that one did not know that goods obtained by fraud count as 'stolen' since this too is a matter of criminal rather than civil law (Theft Act 1968, s. 24(4)). The point can be further illustrated by reference to *Johnson v Youden* [1950] 1 KB 544. It was an offence under the Building Materials and Housing Act 1945, s. 7, to sell a house in excess of the prescribed price. The defendant solicitor knew that an extra £250 was being paid to the builder in a separate account to be spent on possible future work which might be done to the house by the builder. Even if the solicitor genuinely believed that this was not part of the price under the Act, his mistake was merely one of criminal law since s. 7(5) specifically stated that associated transactions had to be included in calculating the price.

A3.10   Some offences expressly make the accused's beliefs about the legality of his action relevant and in these cases there can be no question that a mistake of law can be relevant. The most obvious example is the Theft Act 1968, s. 2(1), under which a person is not to be regarded as dishonest: '(a) if he appropriates the property in the belief that he has in law the right to deprive the other of it'. A less obvious example is provided by *Secretary of State for Trade and Industry v Hart* [1982] 1 All ER 817 which concerned the statutory offence of acting as auditor of a company 'at a time when he knows that he is disqualified'. As a director of the company Hart was disqualified but he did not know of the quite separate statutory provision which so provided. Thus, although he knew the facts (that he was a director of the company), he did not know that he was disqualified (as the offence specifically required). Contrast *A-G's Ref (No. 1 of 1995)* [1996] 4 All ER 21, where the offence did not require any specific knowledge that deposit-taking had to be licensed by the Bank of England. See also *Lee* [2001] 1 Cr App R 293 — mistake of law that arrest unlawful not capable of negating an intent to resist lawful arrest.

A3.11   By the Statutory Instruments Act 1946, s. 3, it is a defence to prove that a relevant statutory instrument had not been issued at the time of the alleged offence although it is open to the Crown to prove that reasonable steps had been taken to bring it to the attention of relevant persons. However, it should be remembered that the *ultra vires* and unlawful nature of subordinate legislation or administrative decisions may be raised as a defence to a criminal charge (*Boddington v British Transport Police* [1999] 2 AC 143).

It is a question of statutory interpretation for the trial judge whether a defence based on EU law is permitted (*Re Searby Ltd* [2003] EWCA Crim 1910, confirming the right of a citizen faced with a criminal charge to defend himself with any plea open to him, particularly the invalidity of the instrument under which he was charged). Provisions of UK criminal law, or its application in a particular instance, may be resisted on the ground of incompatibility with EU law, relying on either the general principles of EU law such as free movement rights (Case 34/79 *Henn and Darby* [1979] ECR 3795) or directly applicable legal instruments. See, e.g., the unsuccessful challenge to the ban on hunting under the Hunting Act 2004 as incompatible with specific provisions of the EC Treaty in *R (Countryside Alliance) v A-G* [2008] 1 AC 719; for a similarly unsuccessful preliminary reference to the ECJ, see *Ahokainen v Wirallinen Syyttaja* [2007] 1 CMLR 11. For a full discussion of EU law and its influence on criminal law, see **A9**.

Automatism

The defence of automatism arises where the accused's conduct lacks the basic requirement of being voluntary (see **A1.10** and **A1.11**).   **A3.12**

The defence is limited to cases where there is a total destruction of voluntary control; impaired or reduced control is not enough (*A-G's Ref (No. 2 of 1992)* [1994] QB 91, a view confirmed in *Coley* [2013] EWCA Crim 223 (at [22]), where it was said that the question is not whether the accused is acting consciously or not but whether there is a 'complete destruction of voluntary control'). Where the accused is conscious, automatism will be rare but possible (e.g., reflex actions when startled by a sudden loud noise or when stung by a swarm of bees while driving: see *Hill v Baxter* [1958] 1 QB 277 and *Burns v Bidder* [1967] 2 QB 227 at p. 240). Contrast the mistaken pressing of the accelerator rather than the brake in *A-G's Ref (No. 4 of 2000)* [2001] RTR 415, which was held not to be a case of automatism. Where the accused has acted in a state of total unconsciousness, it is easier to conclude that he could not have acted otherwise, and in principle he should have the defence of automatism. The law imposes serious restrictions on such a defence, however, through the rules on voluntary intoxication and insanity to be discussed in **A3.16 to A3.33**. The question which remains for discussion here is the extent to which, even where the automatism is not caused by insanity or voluntary intoxication, there is some further restriction or requirement that the automatism should not be self-induced.

Such a requirement was first suggested by the Court of Appeal in *Quick* [1973] QB 910 even though in that case it quashed the conviction of the appellant for assault. The alleged assault had taken place whilst the appellant (a diabetic) had been in a state of hypoglycaemia (low blood sugar) which the trial judge had (wrongly, in the view of the Court of Appeal) ruled amounted to insanity. The defence of (non-insane) automatism was thus never put to the jury, but Lawton LJ had the following to say (at pp. 922–3) about such a defence: **A3.13**

> A self-induced incapacity will not excuse... nor will one which could have been reasonably foreseen as a result of either doing, or omitting to do something, as, for example, taking alcohol against medical advice after using certain prescribed drugs, or failing to have regular meals while taking insulin...

> Had the defence of automatism been left to the jury, a number of questions of fact would have had to be answered... to what extent had he brought about his condition by not following his doctor's instructions about taking regular meals? Did he know that he was getting into a hypoglycaemic episode? If yes, why did he not use the antidote of eating a lump of sugar as he had been advised to do? On the evidence which was before the jury Quick might have had difficulty in answering these questions in a manner which would have relieved him of responsibility for his act.

It thus appeared after *Quick* that, even where automatism was not caught by the rules on insanity and intoxication, it was not available if it could be said to be self-induced. Thus in *Bailey* [1983] 2 All ER 503 a similar defence based on automatism caused by hypoglycaemia was held by the trial judge to be unavailable (on charges under the OAPA 1861, ss. 18 and 20) since it was self-induced. The Court of Appeal (whilst dismissing the appeal on the basis that no miscarriage of justice had actually occurred) held that this was too absolute a rule:

> In our judgment, self-induced automatism, other than that due to intoxication from alcohol or drugs, may provide a defence to crimes of basic intent. The question in each case will be whether the prosecution have provided the necessary element of recklessness. In cases of assault, if the accused knows that his actions or inaction are likely to make him aggressive, unpredictable or uncontrolled with the result that he may cause some injury to others and he persists in the action or takes no remedial action when he knows it is required, it will be open to the jury to find that he was reckless.

The result of these authorities would seem to be that the fact that automatism is self-induced is a bar to the defence only if the accused was at fault (to the degree required by the particular   **A3.14** offence charged). In *Bailey*, Griffiths LJ took the view that a diabetic falling into a state of hypo-glycaemia is not inevitably at fault since it is not common knowledge, even among diabetics, that a failure to take food after an insulin injection may lead to aggressive, unpredictable and uncontrolled conduct. What is more, the limitation on self-induced automatism as a defence could not apply at all to the offence under the OAPA 1861, s. 18, since even self-induced intoxi-cation by drink or drugs would be a defence to such a charge, the offence being one, as will be seen, of specific intent. (Another way of looking at this would be to say that since *intent* to cause grievous bodily harm is required for this offence, the accused would have to *intend* to become violent through failure to take food in order to be deprived of the defence of automatism, cf. the Dutch courage rule in relation to intoxication discussed in **A3.22**.)

Intoxication: General Rule

A3.15   Intoxication is not a defence as such. It is, for example, no defence to say (as is undoubtedly true in many cases) that the accused would not have acted as he did but for the fact that his inhibitions were reduced due to the effect of alcohol which he had consumed. On the contrary, intoxication operates so as to restrict what would otherwise be valid defences of mistake, inad-vertence or automatism. However, intoxication provides very credible evidence of the fact that the accused did in fact make the mistake he alleges or that he did in fact fail to foresee the obvi-ous risk he was running or that he was indeed in a state of automatism. The restrictions which the law imposes on defences caused by voluntary intoxication are a response to the evidential power of intoxication in supporting such defences and to the frequency and ease with which such defences could be put forward.

Intoxication: Voluntary and Involuntary

A3.16   The restrictive rules apply only where the accused's intoxication is voluntary. This is satisfied if the accused knowingly takes alcohol or other intoxicating drugs (save under medical supervi-sion or direction) and it is immaterial that the accused may have misjudged the degree to which he would become intoxicated (*Allen* [1988] Crim LR 698). On the other hand, a person who thought he was drinking only orange juice but who was in fact drinking orange juice spiked with quantities of vodka would not be regarded as being voluntarily intoxicated and would have any defence that his resultant state of mind warranted on ordinary principles (e.g., lack of *mens rea*). However, just as with voluntary intoxication, if despite or because of his involuntary intox-ication the accused forms the necessary *mens rea* for the crime, there is no separate defence of involuntary intoxication recognised by the law — see the fully reasoned decision of the House of Lords in *Kingston* [1995] 2 AC 355, which reversed the decision of the Court of Appeal and restored the trial judge's ruling that involuntary intoxication provided no defence where the accused (with the necessary *mens rea*) indecently assaulted a boy pursuant to an intent induced by the influence of drugs administered secretly to the accused by a third party. Thus, the only advantage of a finding that the intoxication was involuntary is that it avoids the application of the restrictive rules discussed at **A3.17**.

What counts as an intoxicating drug for the purposes of the restrictive rules governing volun-tary intoxication has been discussed by the courts in two cases, *Bailey* [1983] 2 All ER 503 and *Hardie* [1985] 3 All ER 848. In *Bailey*, the Court of Appeal talked about the intoxication rules being applicable to 'dangerous drugs', i.e. those where it is 'common knowledge' that the taker 'may become aggressive or do dangerous or unpredictable things' (amphetamines and LSD being obvious examples). In the second case the court had to consider an accused, charged with an offence under the Criminal Damage Act 1971, s. 1(2), who had taken a number of Valium tablets (which were prescribed for someone else) and held that this did not necessarily amount to voluntary intoxication.

> [Valium is] wholly different in kind from drugs which are liable to cause unpredictability or aggres-siveness... if the effect of a drug is merely soporific or sedative the taking of it, even in some

> excessive quantity, cannot in the ordinary way raise a *conclusive* presumption against the admission of proof of intoxication for the purpose of disproving *mens rea*...
>
> [The jury] should have been directed that if they came to the conclusion that, as a result of the Valium, the appellant was, at the time, unable to appreciate the risks to property and persons from his actions they should then consider whether the taking of the Valium was itself reckless.

Thus it would seem that there are two categories of drugs: 'dangerous' and 'non-dangerous', LSD being an obvious example of the former category and Valium being an example of the latter. Knowingly taking a 'dangerous' drug counts as voluntary intoxication whereas taking a 'non-dangerous' drug is governed by a similar rule to that discussed in relation to self-induced automatism (see **A3.12**) and depends on the subjective appreciation by the accused of the likely effects of the drug.

Intoxication: Specific and Basic Intent

The principal restriction imposed on defences based on intoxication is that voluntary intoxication can only give rise to a defence to crimes of specific rather than basic intent. The precise nature of the distinction between these two categories of offence has been shrouded in obscurity ever since Lord Birkenhead used the phrase 'specific intent' in *DPP v Beard* [1920] AC 479. Matters are a little clearer today, notwithstanding the *obiter* comments of the Court of Appeal in *Heard* [2008] QB 43. Prior to this decision, the view seemed to have emerged that any offence for which only intention will suffice as the mental element can be regarded as an offence of specific intent, whereas crimes satisfied by recklessness are to that extent crimes of basic intent (basic *mens rea* might be a better expression since the whole point is that intention as opposed to recklessness is *not* required). Thus murder, theft, robbery, wounding with intent, burglary under the Theft Act 1968, s. 9(1)(a), and any offence of attempt would all appear to be crimes requiring a specific intent and it is open to the accused to adduce evidence that he lacked the specific intent required by these offences due to voluntary intoxication. There is no doubt that these offences remain offences which require a specific intent.

However, the Court of Appeal in *Heard* took the view that the offence of sexual assault under the SOA 2003, s. 3, even though it required an intentional rather than reckless touching, was not in this respect an offence of specific intent, and evidence of intoxication could not be used to show that the touching was not intentional. (This was *obiter* since the Court of Appeal clearly indicated that the appeal could be dismissed on the basis that on the facts the intoxication did not negate the accused's intent.) Rather than a distinction between intention and recklessness, Hughes LJ (at [31]) preferred the distinction referred to by Lord Simon in *DPP v Majewski* [1977] AC 443 (who was quoting from Fauteux J in the Canadian case of *George* (1960) 128 CCC 289 at p. 301) 'between (i) intention as applied to acts considered in relation to their purposes and (ii) intention as applied to acts apart from their purposes'. It is the first category which is regarded as specific intent and this appears to include not only cases of so-called ulterior intent, i.e. an intent to do something beyond the *actus reus*, as with wounding with intent to cause grievous bodily harm, but also intent to cause a consequence in result crimes such as murder, the consequence being death (or grievous bodily harm). Intention to touch seems to be regarded as an example of the second category, i.e. intention as applied to acts apart from their purposes, and thus as not being a specific intent. The problem with this approach, however, is that it all depends how narrowly or broadly one describes the 'act'. If the act is described simply as moving one's hand with the result that it touches another, it would be an intentional act of moving with the specific intent (purpose) that it results in a touching. If, however, one describes it simply as an act of 'touching', as the Court of Appeal sees it, it is simply an intentional act of touching, the purpose of causing a touching having been subsumed within the description of the act as a 'touching' which requires only a basic and not a specific intent. Conversely, murder which looks like doing an act (e.g., stabbing) with a purpose (e.g., of causing a consequence — death) could equally be described as a 'killing' which term subsumes the purpose and could therefore be regarded simply as an intentional act of killing without any express reference to purpose and thus as not involving a specific intent but only a basic intent to do the act of killing, which is clearly not the law.

A3.18   Whatever the impact of the Court of Appeal's observations in *Heard* might turn out to be, certain other offences which do not specifically require intention but which require other special mental states, such as dishonesty, are clearly to be treated as offences of specific intent, e.g., handling stolen goods (*Durante* [1972] 3 All ER 962). So too with criminal damage where the indictment restricts the allegation against the accused to intention as opposed to recklessness (*Metropolitan Police Commissioner v Caldwell* [1982] AC 341 at p. 356). The view was previously taken in this work that aggravated criminal damage under s. 1(2) of the 1971 Act was not a crime requiring specific intent (unless restricted to an allegation of committing it intentionally) since it could be committed recklessly, but the Court of Appeal in *Heard* was of the view (clearly *obiter*, as expressly acknowledged by Hughes LJ himself in the more recent case of *Coley* [2013] EWCA Crim 223 at [57]) that the requirement of being reckless as to endangering life is a specific intent since it goes beyond the *actus reus* of causing damage and thus voluntary intoxication could be relevant to show that there was no recklessness as to the endangerment of life. This basis of specific intent is at least intelligible and does not depend on the narrowness or otherwise of the definition of the act, since it is based on the notion of ulterior intent, or rather ulterior *mens rea*, i.e. a *mens rea* going beyond the *actus reus* of the offence as defined. It also works well in policy terms since it allows the accused a possible defence to the more serious offence under s. 1(2) but liability would remain for the less serious basic intent offence under s. 1(1) of reckless criminal damage.

All offences other than those requiring specific intent can be regarded as crimes of basic intent and the accused will not be allowed to show that he lacked the *mens rea* or was in a state of automatism due to voluntary intoxication. Crimes requiring only basic intent clearly include manslaughter, malicious wounding, all forms of assault (except those requiring a specific intent such as assault with intent to rob), and taking a conveyance contrary to the Theft Act 1968, s. 12. Thus, in these cases, even the fact that the accused has 'completely blacked out', as was alleged in the House of Lords case of *DPP v Majewski*, will provide no defence, nor will the fact that he is hallucinating that he is fighting snakes at the centre of the earth, as was alleged in the Court of Appeal case of *Lipman* [1970] 1 QB 152. The rule applies not only to the person who is so intoxicated that he cannot remember anything of the offence (as in *Woods* (1981) 74 Cr App R 312) but also where the accused makes a mistake about a particular aspect of his actions as in *Fotheringham* (1988) 88 Cr App R 206. However, where a defence of honest mistake is specifically provided in a statute, then it appears that even an intoxicated mistake may sometimes suffice despite the offence being one of basic intent. In *Jaggard v Dickinson* [1981] QB 527, the Divisional Court held that the defence of honest belief in the owner's consent under the Criminal Damage Act 1971, s. 5(2), was still available even though the defendant was drunk. The decision is today regarded as anomalous and unlikely to be extended to other provisions. Certainly the Court of Appeal was not prepared to allow, in relation to self-defence, a drunken mistake by the accused that he was being attacked (*O'Grady* [1987] QB 995: see further **A3.60**).

A3.19   Various justifications for the basic intent rule have been put forward but not all have been persuasive and the Australian courts refused to adopt it (*O'Connor* (1980) 146 CLR 64). At root the rule seems to be one of legal policy — that an intoxicated offender should have a potential defence to the most serious offences such as murder or wounding with intent but should remain liable for an appropriate lesser offence of basic intent such as manslaughter or malicious wounding. Although a Law Commission Consultation Paper in 1993 proposed abolition of the basic intent rule, the subsequent report (No. 229, 1995) reverted to recommending the retention of the rule in codified form; somewhat less complex proposals for achieving a similar end were contained in the Commission's Report, *Intoxication and Criminal Liability* (Law Com No. 314, 2009) but these were rejected by the government.

A3.20   **Applying the Basic Intent Rule**   Although the policy behind the basic intent rule is clear, the precise manner of its application is less so. Early editions of this work, in common with many other commentators, followed the words of Lord Elwyn Jones in *DPP v Majewski* [1977] AC 443, which stated that evidence of intoxication 'supplies the evidence of *mens rea*, of guilty mind, certainly sufficiently for crimes of basic intent' and therefore suggested that to proffer such evidence would seem to discharge the prosecution from the burden of showing that the accused had the *mens rea* or was acting voluntarily in relation to basic intent crimes.

The alternative and better view is that evidence of intoxication is simply irrelevant and has to be ignored on the question of whether the accused has the *mens rea* of a basic intent crime but that the jury have to answer the hypothetical question of whether the accused would have had the *mens rea* if, contrary to the facts, he had not been intoxicated. This was the approach favoured by the Court of Appeal in *Richardson* [1999] 1 Cr App R 392 but it is an approach not without difficulties, especially in cases where the intoxication has reduced the accused to a state of automatism or something close to it. In most cases of course, either approach will yield the same result since, in the absence of any other special factor apart from intoxication, the jury will assume that the accused would have foreseen the natural and probable consequence of his actions if not intoxicated. The decision to quash the convictions in *Richardson* was perhaps a little generous since the only other factor mentioned by the Court of Appeal was the fact that the appellants 'were not hypothetical reasonable men, but university students' (who nevertheless are surely able to appreciate the natural and probable consequences of their actions, at least when sober) and the Court had previously stated that the 'reason they did not [appreciate the risk] was the amount of drink they had consumed'. Despite this, *Richardson* usefully suggests an opportunity for the defence to raise the issue that there was some exculpatory or innocent cause of the accused's mistake or inadvertence, other than voluntary intoxication, and the convictions were quashed on the facts because the jury had never been asked to consider this question.

In relation to specific intent crimes, where evidence of intoxication can be relevant, the degree **A3.21** of intoxication required can be an issue as a result of the somewhat remarkable decision of the Court of Appeal in *McKnight* (2000) *The Times*, 5 May 2000. Here it was decided that the trial judge was correct not to have given the standard direction, based on *Sheehan* [1975] 2 All ER 960, telling the jury to take into account the evidence of intoxication in deciding whether the accused had formed the specific intent to kill or cause grievous bodily harm. This was despite the fact that the accused had approximately 300 microgrammes of alcohol per 100 millilitres of blood at the time of the killing. The Court seems to have been unduly influenced by some dicta of the Privy Council in *Sooklal* [1999] 1 WLR 2011 where there was much weaker evidence of a much lower level of intoxication (see also *Porceddu* [2004] EWCA Crim 1043). Both the Privy Council and the Court of Appeal are in danger of reverting to the more demanding test of whether the accused was *incapable* of forming the intent as opposed to the question emphasised in *Sheehan* of whether the accused *actually* formed the intent. The decisions are very difficult to reconcile with a number of other Court of Appeal authorities, including *McKinley* [1994] Crim LR 944 and *Bennett* [1995] Crim LR 877.

Intoxication: the Dutch Courage Rule

The so-called Dutch courage rule is more important in principle than in practice. A person who **A3.22** deliberately makes himself intoxicated in order to commit a crime cannot raise a defence based on such intoxication, even to a crime of specific intent (*A-G for Northern Ireland v Gallagher* [1963] AC 349, per Lord Denning). The rule is eminently sensible but not necessarily applicable even to the facts of *A-G for Northern Ireland v Gallagher* itself and there seem to be no reported cases of it being applied since. The principle, however, is effectively the same as that laid down by the courts in relation to 'non-dangerous' drugs (see **A3.16**) — that if the accused has the fault element of the offence in becoming intoxicated, the lack of the fault element at the time of the offence due to such intoxication is irrelevant.

Insanity: General Principles: the M'Naghten Rules

A3.23　The defence of insanity is still governed by the M'Naghten rules (*M'Naghten's Case* (1843) 10 Cl & F 200), which today operate largely as a restriction on what might otherwise be a complete defence based on lack of *mens rea* or automatism. Only where the accused falls under that limb of the rules which requires him not to know that his act is 'wrong' do the rules provide any defence additional to that which would be available under the above general principles. The relationship between insanity and defences based not on lack of *mens rea* or voluntariness, such as self-defence, was discussed in *Oye* [2014] 1 All ER 902, where D suffered from insane delusions that he was being confronted by 'evil spirits' intent on harming him. On the facts it was not necessary to decide, and the question was left open, whether self-defence could be put to the jury before insanity even though the belief in the need for self-defence was based on an insane delusion. In principle, where the accused's lack of responsibility is caused by insanity rather than any other factor, it would seem logical that the defence should be confined to, and classified as, insanity irrespective of whether the lack of responsibility takes the form of no *mens rea*/automatism or a belief in a justifying defence.

The 'special verdict' of 'not guilty by reason of insanity' is provided for in the Trial of Lunatics Act 1883, s. 2, and is one that is required to be returned by a jury rather than simply as a result of the accused's plea (*Crown Court at Maidstone, ex parte Harrow London Borough Council* [1999] 3 All ER 542). However, the Court of Appeal has power to substitute special verdicts under the Criminal Appeal Act 1968, s. 6, as was done in *Oye*. Where a special verdict is returned, under the Criminal Procedure (Insanity) Act 1964, s. 5, the court has a range of orders from which to choose (see **D12.16**). These include an order for a hospital order (with or without a restriction order), a supervision order, and even an absolute discharge. The range of available orders does not apply where the offence to which the special verdict relates is murder or any other offence for which the sentence is fixed by law; in such a case the court must make a hospital order with a restriction order.

Whilst the burden of proving insanity is on the accused on the balance of probabilities (see **A3.26**), for a special verdict to be returned the prosecution must prove that the accused 'did the act or made the omission charged' (Trial of Lunatics Act 1883, s. 2(1)), otherwise the defendant is entitled to a complete acquittal on the ground of lack of an *actus reus*, despite any insanity. It was confirmed in *A-G's Ref (No. 3 of 1998)* [2000] QB 401 that this does not involve proving *mens rea* but did require proof of 'the ingredients which constitute the *actus reus* of the crime' which seems to include the circumstances (other than *mens rea*) whose presence or absence render the act or omission criminally unlawful (such as, for example, on appropriate facts, the absence of legitimate grounds for self-defence). For a creative interpretation of the concept of the 'act ... charged against him as the offence' in the context of unfitness to plead, see *MB* [2012] 3 All ER 1093, and see more generally **D12.11**.

Even though the disincentives to plead insanity were reduced in 1991 by expanding the range of possible disposals, the scope of the M'Naghten rules remains important. Once the defence puts the accused's state of mind in issue, it is open to the prosecution to argue (see Lord Denning in *Bratty v A-G for Northern Ireland* [1963] AC 386) and to the trial judge to rule (see, e.g., *Sullivan* [1984] AC 156) that the defence really amounts to insanity (see also the Criminal Procedure (Insanity) Act 1964, s. 6). The rules in effect mark out one boundary of the defences of automatism (as in *Sullivan*) or lack of *mens rea* (see, e.g., *Clarke* [1972] 1 All ER 219 where, however, the accused was found on appeal not to be within the M'Naghten rules and thus had a complete defence of lack of *mens rea*).

A3.24　It should be noted that the above discussion relates to trials on indictment and that s. 2 of the Trial of Lunatics Act 1883 is inapplicable to trial in magistrates' courts. That the defence of insanity is available in magistrates' courts and that it leads to a complete acquittal rather than the special verdict was confirmed by the Divisional Court in *Horseferry Road Magistrates' Court*, *ex parte K* [1997] QB 23 and reiterated in *R (Singh) v Stratford Magistrates' Court* [2007] 4 All ER 407. Whilst magistrates have a power to make a hospital order under the Mental Health Act 1983, s. 37(3), even though the accused is not convicted, there is no power to commit to the Crown Court for a restriction order to be made under s. 41 of that Act. The significance of the availability of the defence of insanity in the magistrates' court has been considerably reduced following *DPP v H* [1997] 1 WLR 1406 where the Divisional Court ruled that insanity could be a defence only in relation to crimes requiring *mens rea* or where *mens rea* was in issue. This decision may represent a pragmatic limitation on the availability of the insanity defence in summary trials (and in cases triable either way a plea of insanity is likely to result in the case being committed to the Crown Court as in *Ex parte K*). It is, however, open to criticism on the grounds that, as has already been pointed out, the defence of insanity can go beyond a mere denial of *mens rea*. This is true both in the sense that insanity may extend to automatism, i.e. a denial of voluntariness (which is normally a requirement even of crimes of strict liability) and also in that the defence may apply where the accused 'does not know that his act is wrong'.

The status of the M'Naghten rules in terms of the doctrine of precedent is somewhat anoma- **A3.25**
lous but they have long been treated as authoritative, a treatment confirmed by the House of Lords in *Sullivan* in 1983. In *M'Naghten's Case* (1843) 10 Cl & F 200, the crucial passage (at p. 210) in the response given by Tindal CJ (on behalf of all the other judges save Maule J) reads as follows:

> ... the jurors ought to be told in all cases that *every man is to be presumed to be sane*, and to possess a sufficient degree of reason to be responsible for his crimes, *until the contrary be proved to their satisfaction*; and that to establish a defence on the ground of insanity, it must be clearly proved that, *at the time of the committing of the act*, the party accused was labouring under such *a defect of reason, from disease of the mind, as not to know the nature and quality of the act he was doing; or,* if he did know it, *that he did not know he was doing what was wrong.*

The emphases have been added and each emphasised phrase will now be explained in turn.

'... every man is to be presumed to be sane ... until the contrary be proved to [the jury's] **A3.26**
satisfaction'   This is the basis on which, exceptionally, the burden of proof in establishing the defence is placed on the accused but it is established that the proof need only be on the balance of probabilities (*Sodeman v The King* [1936] 2 All ER 1138, and see **F3.8**). This exception to the general rule on burden of proof is particularly problematical where the accused puts forward both insanity and non-insane automatism as in *Bratty v A-G for Northern Ireland* [1963] AC 386. The solution seems to lie in remembering that, just as with intoxication, the principal utility of evidence of insanity to an accused is that the insanity is itself explanatory evidence of why the accused was not conscious of his actions (or of their obvious results). Other evidence of automatism, such as, for example, a blow on the head causing concussion, need only raise a doubt in the minds of the jury as to whether the accused's act was involuntary, but insofar as the evidence consists of evidence of insanity, the jury must be convinced on a balance of probabilities that the act was involuntary. The result may be, as was possibly the case in *Bratty*, that a jury convict even though they entertain some doubt as to whether the accused's act was voluntary because the only evidence causing that doubt is evidence of insanity and it is not sufficiently strong to convince them on a balance of probabilities. This may appear to be anomalous but it should be noted that in *Woolmington v DPP* [1935] AC 462, Lord Sankey said 'it is the duty of the prosecution to prove the prisoner's guilt *subject to what I have already said as to the defence of insanity*' (emphasis added).

'... at the time of the committing of the act'   The M'Naghten rules, in common with the **A3.27**
other defences discussed in this section, are concerned with the accused's state of mind at the time of the alleged offence. The sanity or otherwise of the accused at other times may be relevant in other ways, not by way of defence but, for example, in relation to whether he is fit to plead (see **D12.3** *et seq.*) or in relation to the type of sentence or order to be passed. Such issues relating to the sanity of the accused at the time of the trial or the time of sentencing can arise whether or not the accused was sane or not at the time of the alleged offence.

A3.28 '...**a defect of reason**' This is a central notion in the rules even though it is not the concept around which most of the case law turns. It is the basic reason why irresistible impulse and other emotional or volitional defects or disorders are not within the rules, since they are not defects of reason. Rationality is the litmus test of criminal responsibility, and defects of will are regarded either as non-existent or as irrelevant. In this respect, the defence of diminished responsibility is potentially much more liberal. However, given the way in which insanity can operate as a restriction on other defences, the requirement of a defect of reason may sometimes come to the defendant's aid. See *Clarke* [1972] 1 All ER 219 where the Court of Appeal held that even if the other elements of the rules were satisfied, there was no *defect* of reason but at most a mere absent-minded failure to use the powers of reasoning that the accused undoubtedly still possessed and thus the accused was entitled to have the simple defence of lack of *mens rea* considered by the jury rather than the defence of insanity.

A3.29 '...**from disease of the mind**' The defect of reason must be caused by a disease of the mind (rather than by, for example, intoxication, which is probably the best explanation for the decision in *Thomas* [1995] Crim LR 314). It is the meaning of this concept around which most of the recent case law turns as it is this which primarily distinguishes insane automatism (a defence of insanity leading to the special verdict) from non-insane automatism (a defence of simple automatism leading to a complete acquittal).

The meaning of 'disease of the mind' is a legal question for the judge to decide rather than a medical one, even though the evidence of medical experts is required by the Criminal Procedure (Insanity and Unfitness to Plead) Act 1991, s. 1. In *Sullivan* [1984] AC 156, two medical experts in the course of their testimony stated that they would not regard something as a disease of the mind unless it produced a disorder of brain functions for a prolonged period — in the case of one witness for more than a day and in the case of the other for more than a month. It was therefore argued that the relatively short period over which an epileptic seizure takes place meant that epilepsy was not a disease of the mind. Lord Diplock emphatically rejected this argument, noting (at p. 172) that:

> The nomenclature adopted by the medical profession may change from time to time...But the meaning of the expression 'disease of the mind' as the cause of 'a defect of reason' remains unchanged for the purposes of the application of the M'Naghten rules...'mind' in the M'Naghten rules is used in the ordinary sense of the mental faculties of reason, memory and understanding. If the effect of a disease is to impair these faculties so severely as to have either of the consequences referred to in the latter part of the rules, it matters not whether the aetiology of the impairment is organic, as in epilepsy, or functional, or whether the impairment itself is permanent or is transient and intermittent, provided that it subsisted at the time of commission of the act.

A3.30 The relevance of the medical evidence seems to be limited to showing that the impairment of the mental faculties did in fact take place and what in fact was the cause. The classification of that impairment and its cause (whether or not it is a defect of reason from disease of the mind), is then purely a matter of law for the judge. It can also be seen that to a large extent, whether something is a disease *of the mind* depends on the consequences it produces — impairment of the faculties of reason, memory and understanding. The disease certainly need not be one primarily located in the brain if it produces the relevant consequences there. Thus arteriosclerosis (hardening of the arteries) causing temporary loss of consciousness is a disease of the mind for these purposes even though it is of physical rather than mental origin (per Devlin J in *Kemp* [1957] 1 QB 399 at p. 408).

However, not every cause of an impairment of these mental faculties is a *disease* of the mind. A disease is something *internal* to the accused and so:

> A malfunctioning of the mind of transitory effect caused by the application to the body of some *external* factor such as violence, drugs, including anaesthetics, alcohol and hypnotic influences cannot fairly be said to be due to disease (per Lawton LJ in *Quick* [1973] QB 910 at p. 922, emphasis added).

Quick's condition of hypoglycaemia was held not to have been due to a disease of the mind since it was attributable to an external factor — his use of insulin prescribed by his doctor:

> Such malfunctioning of his mind as there was, was caused by an external factor and not by a bodily disorder in the nature of a disease which disturbed the working of his mind (ibid. at pp. 922–3).

Treating the insulin, rather than the diabetes which necessitated the insulin, as the cause of the malfunctioning enabled the court in *Quick* to keep the case outside the M'Naghten rules. However, this course was not available in *Hennessy* [1989] 2 All ER 9, which again concerned a diabetic, this time suffering from the opposite condition of hyperglycaemia (excessive blood sugar) which is directly caused by the diabetes when uncorrected by the administration of insulin. It was thus the *absence* of an external factor which allowed the disease of diabetes to produce the malfunctioning and, given this effect of the disease, the Court of Appeal felt constrained to classify it as a disease of the mind. See also *Bingham* [1991] Crim LR 433.

The Court of Appeal in *Hennessy* also rejected the argument that the accused's anxiety and depres-   **A3.31**
sion due to his marital problems constituted an external factor (even though there was medical evidence that anxiety and depression could contribute to an increased blood-sugar level). See also the Canadian case of *Rabey* (1977) 79 DLR (3d) 414, in which the Ontario Court of Appeal said (at p. 435) that 'the ordinary stresses and disappointments of life which are the common lot of mankind do not constitute an external cause'. This was subsequently approved by the English Court of Appeal in *Burgess* [1991] 1 QB 92. In this case, the court held that violence whilst sleepwalking or 'sleep associated automatism' was due to an internal factor and was therefore within the M'Naghten rules. Where there is a combination of internal and external factors, it would appear from *Roach* [2001] EWCA Crim 2698 that, if the jury might conclude that it is the external factors which are operative, a defence of non-insane automatism (which it is for the prosecution to disprove) should be left to them notwithstanding that the defence psychiatrists had described it as 'insane automatism' (where the burden is on the accused).

In *Coley* [2013] EWCA Crim 223 the accused, having taken quantities of cannabis, per-petrated a violent knife attack on a man in his neighbour's bedroom. His conviction for attempted murder was upheld; the Court of Appeal dismissed the argument that insanity should have been left to the jury on the grounds that there was a temporary defect of reason within the M'Naghten rules. To the extent that the accused was in a psychotic state, it was caused by an external factor, the cannabis, and was thus, applying *Quick* [1973] QB 910, not due to a disease of the mind but rather to voluntary intoxication. Neither was it necessary for (non-insane) automatism to be separately left to the jury since they had been told to consider whether D had the specific intent to kill and, having found against him on that score, there was no room on the facts for finding that he had acted with intent but involuntarily. The Court, however, was careful to say that in some cases, e.g., short-lived actions where intent may be inferred from the action, the question of automatism (i.e. whether the action was completely involuntary) ought to be separately put. For further observations on the internal/external distinction, see RD Mackay's discussion in [2007] Crim LR 782 at pp. 791–3. It should be remembered, however, that, once one is in the realm of non-insane automatism, the question of prior fault may become relevant and the defence might fail altogether, at least in relation to basic intent crimes, a restriction in *Bailey* [1983] 2 All ER 503 that certain comments in *Coley* appear to overlook (see **A3.13**).

'…as not to know the nature and quality of the act he was doing' This refers to the physical   **A3.32**
rather than moral quality of the act (per Lord Reading CJ in *Codere* (1916) 12 Cr App R 21) and according to Lord Diplock in *Sullivan* [1984] AC 156 at p. 173: 'Addressed to an audience of jurors in the 1980s it might more aptly be expressed as "He did not know what he was doing"'. Clearly this would be satisfied if the accused was unconscious at the time or, even if conscious, thought, to adopt an example quoted by Lord Denning in another context, that he was throwing a log rather than the baby on the fire. Equally clearly, the accused would have a defence of automatism or lack of *mens rea* respectively in these two situations, and this underlines the point

previously made that the M'Naghten rules generally merely qualify what would otherwise be a complete defence.

A3.33   '...or...that he did not know he was doing what was wrong'   This is an alternative to not knowing the nature and quality of the act and is the only sense in which an insane person is given a defence where none would be available to the sane (knowledge of moral or legal wrongness, as opposed to knowledge of the facts which render it wrong, being generally irrelevant to criminal responsibility). The major question debated here is whether 'wrong' means legally wrong or morally wrong. It is suggested that the key to a proper understanding of this question is to recognise that the question is a negative one. If the accused *does* know *either* that his act is *morally* wrong (according to the ordinary standard adopted by reasonable men, per Lord Reading in *Codere* (1916) 12 Cr App R 21) *or* that it is *legally* wrong then it cannot be said that he does *not* know he was doing what was wrong. In two leading decisions on the matter (*Codere* (1916) 12 Cr App R 21 and *Windle* [1952] 2 QB 826), it was only necessary to hold that it was correct to tell the jury that the accused could not rely on the defence if he knew that his act was legally wrong. Both were murder cases and it was not seriously suggested in either that the accused did not know his act was legally wrong and yet knew that it was morally wrong. (On the contrary, Windle thought he was morally right to kill his suicidal wife and yet knew it was legally wrong since he said, 'I suppose they will hang me for this'.) The ruling in *Windle* that ' "wrong" means contrary to law' has now also been applied in *Johnson* [2007] EWCA Crim 1978 to a case where there was some evidence that the accused did not know that his act was morally wrong; it was held that this could not avail him as it was agreed that he knew that it was legally wrong. A converse case would be that of an accused who does not appreciate that his act is legally wrong but who does realise that it is morally wrong, where arguably the defence would again not be made out.

DEFENCES INVOLVING OTHER EXCUSES AND JUSTIFICATIONS

Introduction

A3.34   To treat certain defences as excuses or justifications and to deal with them separately from defences which deny the basic elements of liability is in one sense artificial since it can be pointed out, for example, that no one commits any offence unless he acts unlawfully and, if the accused has a defence of justification available, then he has not acted unlawfully and one of the basic elements of liability is missing. Equally, it can be pointed out that the defences treated here as a denial of the elements of liability, such as mistake of fact, may be also properly classified as excuses. In the end all classifications are somewhat artificial and are really made for convenience and ease of understanding and exposition. On these grounds it seems sensible to separate out defences where the accused admits that he has voluntarily committed what is prima facie a crime with the state of mind normally sufficient for that offence but at the same time asserts some *special* circumstances which he claims excuse or justify his actions. As Lord Wilberforce said of duress in *DPP for Northern Ireland v Lynch* [1975] AC 653 (at pp. 679–80):

> [It] is something which is superimposed upon the other ingredients which by themselves would make up an offence, i.e., upon act and intention....the victim completes the act and knows that he is doing so; but the addition of the element of duress prevents the law from treating what he has done as a crime.

Duress by Threats: General Principles

A3.35   There has been a great deal of development since the 1960s in the defence of duress by threats. Its basis seems to be excuse rather than justification; an analysis confirmed by the House of Lords in *Hasan* [2005] 2 AC 467 at [18]. The details of the defence can conveniently be considered under three headings: the type of threat necessary, the required cogency of the threat, and the offences and persons excluded from the defence.

The Type of Threat Required   All the decisions recognising duress as a defence have concerned   **A3.36**
threats of death or grievous bodily harm although in *Steane* [1947] KB 997, Lord Goddard CJ,
obiter, included fear of imprisonment. While this has not been definitively ruled out by subsequent authorities, in *Dao* [2012] EWCA Crim 1717 the Court of Appeal *obiter* gave a number
of reasons for its provisional view that duress should be regarded as confined to threats of death
or serious injury and that a threat of false imprisonment should not of itself suffice. It would
seem from *Baker* [1997] Crim LR 497 that a threat of serious psychological injury will not suffice and in *Quayle* [2005] 1 All ER 988 it was said that an 'imminent danger of physical injury'
was required. Another question is whether the threat has to be directed at the accused or whether
threats to third parties, especially close relatives, can suffice. In principle threats to third parties
should be *capable* of constituting duress since even the bravest man may be prepared to risk his
own neck whilst flinching at subjecting his loved ones to serious peril. In *Ortiz* (1986) 83 Cr
App R 173 threats to the accused's wife or family appear to have been considered to be sufficient
and the suggestion in the 2003 Judicial Studies Board specimen direction (and preserved in the
Crown Court Bench Book, p. 306) that the threat can be directed to the accused or a member of his
immediate family or alternatively 'to a person for whose safety the defendant would reasonably
regard himself as responsible' commended itself to Lord Bingham in *Hasan* [2005] 2 AC 467 as
being 'if strictly applied . . . consistent with the rationale of the duress exception'.

The Cogency of the Threat   The fact that the accused believes that a threat of death or grievous bodily harm will be carried out if he does not commit the offence is not of itself sufficient   **A3.37**
'if a person of reasonable firmness sharing the characteristics of the defendant would not have
given way to the threats' (third certified question in *Howe* [1987] AC 417). In other words, the
threat is only sufficiently cogent, and the accused will only be excused, if a person of reasonable
firmness might have yielded to the threat. This objective approach was most clearly articulated
by Lord Lane CJ in *Graham* [1982] 1 All ER 801 in a suggested direction (at p. 300) later
approved by the House of Lords in *Howe*:

> (1) Was the defendant, or may he have been, impelled to act as he did because, as a result of what he
> reasonably believed [the threatener] had said or done, he had good cause to fear that if he did not so
> act [the threatener] would kill him or . . . cause him serious physical injury? (2) If so, have the prosecution made the jury sure that a sober person of reasonable firmness, sharing the characteristics of
> the defendant, would not have responded to whatever he reasonably believed [the threatener] said
> or did by taking part [in the offence].

Although the requirement of reasonableness, in relation to the accused's belief as to the facts,
has been questioned by, amongst others, the Law Commission (whose subjective approach in
its 1993 Report, *Legislating the Criminal Code*, continued to be preferred by Baroness Hale in
Hasan [2005] 2 AC 467 and has been the subject of some vacillation in the Court of Appeal
(*DPP v Rogers* [1998] Crim LR 202; *Cairns* [1999] 2 Cr App R 137; *Martin* [2000] 2 Cr App
R 42; *Safi* [2004] 1 Cr App R 157)), Lord Bingham, with whose speech the majority concurred
in *Hasan*, was clear that 'there is no warrant for relaxing the requirement that the belief must be
reasonable as well as genuine'.

Turning from reasonableness of belief to the reasonableness of the accused's response in committing the offence, the extent to which a person of reasonable firmness shares the characteristics of the accused is a moot point. In *Bowen* [1996] 4 All ER 837, Stuart-Smith LJ, in denying   **A3.38**
the relevance of low IQ, derived a number of principles from the case law of which the seventh
and last was as follows (at p. 380):

> In the absence of some direction from the judge as to what characteristics are capable of being
> regarded as relevant, we think that the direction approved in [*Graham*] without more will not be
> as helpful as it might be, since the jury may be tempted, especially if there is evidence, as there was
> in this case, relating to suggestibility and vulnerability, to think that these are relevant. *In most
> cases it is probably only the age and sex of the defendant that is capable of being relevant. If so, the judge
> should . . . confine the characteristics in question to these.* (emphasis added)

For the majority of cases, this is, it is respectfully suggested, a useful working rule, and confirms earlier cases such as *Horne* [1994] Crim LR 584 and *Hegarty* [1994] Crim LR 353, which excluded psychiatric or medical evidence to the effect that the accused was unusually pliable or vulnerable to pressure or emotionally unstable or in a 'grossly elevated neurotic state'. There remains the difficult question of what characteristics other than age and sex can exceptionally be relevant. In *Bowen* Stuart-Smith LJ gave some examples in his second principle (at p. 379) whereby:

> . . .the defendant may be in a category of persons who the jury may think less able to resist pressure than people not within that category. Obvious examples are age, where a young person may well not be so robust as a mature one; possibly sex, though many women would doubtless consider they had as much moral courage to resist pressure as men; pregnancy, where there is added fear for the unborn child; serious physical disability, which may inhibit self protection; recognised mental illness or psychiatric condition, such as post traumatic stress disorder leading to learned helplessness.

A3.39 Putting aside age, the true relevance of most of these, it is submitted, lies in the fact that they increase the gravity of the threat rather than reducing the courage or steadfastness of the accused. A threat of physical violence to a pregnant woman is much more serious because of the vulnerability of the child in the womb. Similarly, physical violence to a physically disabled person is more serious and likely to result in more serious harm if there is reduced ability to defend oneself or ward off blows. On this basis, the mention of 'recognised mental illness or psychiatric condition, such as post traumatic stress disorder', which seems to refer to conditions rendering sufferers 'more susceptible to pressure and threats' (see the fifth principle described in the judgment of Stuart-Smith LJ at p. 379) may be thought problematic since it conflicts with the basic premise of the objective test of a person of reasonable firmness. However, it is clear that the courts will accept post-traumatic stress disorder as a relevant characteristic (*Sewell* [2004] EWCA Crim 2322) and in *Antar* (2004) *The Times*, 4 November 2004 the evidence of a psychologist as to the appellant's level of suggestibility should, in the Court of Appeal's view, have been put before the jury since it was not merely put 'on the basis of the appellant's very low IQ, but on the basis of the psychologist's opinion that he functioned cognitively at a significantly impaired level; that he had a moderate (now a mild) learning disability; and importantly, that he had a level of suggestibility sufficiently higher than that of the general population'. The decision in *Antar* seems to be a fairly generous application of the fifth principle in *Bowen*, which is as follows ([1996] 4 All ER 837 at p. 844):

> Psychiatric evidence may be admissible to show that the defendant is suffering from some mental illness, mental impairment or recognised psychiatric condition provided persons generally suffering from such condition may be more susceptible to pressure and threats and thus to assist the jury in deciding whether a reasonable person suffering from such a condition might have been impelled to act as the defendant did. It is not admissible simply to show that in the doctor's opinion an accused, who is not suffering from such illness or condition, is especially timid, suggestible or vulnerable to pressure and threats. . . .

Vulnerability to pressure and threats is not of itself relevant unless, it seems, the accused belongs to a particular category of persons recognised as so vulnerable and this inevitably puts pressure on the criteria for recognising such a category, whether they be medical or otherwise.

The reference to a 'sober' person of reasonable firmness makes it plain that intoxication cannot be a relevant characteristic. Intoxication is of course normally self-induced (*quaere* whether involuntary intoxication might be relevant) and in *Flatt* [1996] Crim LR 576 it was held that other self-induced conditions, such as being a drug addict, are excluded.

A3.40 The immediacy of the threat and the possibility of seeking official protection are matters which the Court of Appeal said, in *Hurst* [1995] 1 Cr App R 82, require more attention to be paid to them. These matters had been considered in *Hudson* [1971] 2 QB 202 where the Court of Appeal (at p. 207) had taken what is now regarded as too liberal a view that:

> In the present case [of perjury] the threats. . .were likely to be no less compelling, because their execution could not be effected in the court room, if they could be carried out in the streets of Salford the same night.

Whether the accused could be expected to take any opportunity of rendering the threat ineffective in the meantime by, for example, seeking police protection was a matter for the jury and:

> In deciding whether such an opportunity was reasonably open to the accused the jury should have regard to his age and circumstances, and to any risks to him which may be involved.

In *Hasan* at [27], Lord Bingham attributed to the decision in *Hudson*:

> ...the unfortunate effect of weakening the requirement that execution of a threat must be reasonably believed to be imminent and immediate if it is to support a plea of duress...I can understand that the Court of Appeal [in *Hudson*] had sympathy with the predicament of the young appellants but I cannot, consistently with principle, accept that a witness testifying in the Crown Court at Manchester has no opportunity to avoid complying with a threat incapable of execution then or there.

For the future, Lord Bingham thought (at [28]) that it should:

> ...be made clear to juries that if the retribution threatened against the defendant or his family or a person for whom he reasonably feels responsible is not such as he reasonably expects to follow immediately or almost immediately on his failure to comply with the threat, there may be little if any room for doubt that he could have taken evasive action, whether by going to the police or in some other way, to avoid committing the crime with which he is charged.

Increasingly, the issue is resulting in the defence not even being put to the jury. In *Hammond* [2013] EWCA Crim 2709 the defence of duress was found to have been correctly withdrawn from the jury because the evidence could not satisfy the requirement that 'the threat must be imminent or immediate and have been operating on the actions which constituted the criminal conduct, namely the escape from prison'. Similarly, in *Batchelor* [2013] EWCA Crim 2638 the Court of Appeal relied heavily on Lord Bingham's views in *Hasan* and held that the defence was correctly withheld from the jury where D could have gone to the police at any time over a period of two and a half years and, notwithstanding the serious nature of the alleged threat, 'he could not reasonably believe that the execution of the threat was imminent and immediate'.

Although, as matter of logic, both the question of the immediacy of the threat and the question of any opportunity to render it ineffective could be subsumed under the question of whether, under the *Graham* test, a person of reasonable firmness would have responded to the threat by committing the offence, Lord Bingham specifically warned (in *Hasan* at [24]) against collapsing these questions together.

Duress by Threats: Excluded Offences and Persons

Although duress has now been recognised as available on a wide range of charges, including strict liability offences (*Eden District Council v Braid* [1999] RTR 329), and is available in contempt proceedings (*K* (1983) 78 Cr App R 82), and is to that extent a general defence, there have always been doubts about whether it extends to murder or certain types of treason.   **A3.41**

Murder   In *Howe* [1987] AC 417, the House of Lords unequivocally held that the defence of   **A3.42** duress is *not* available on a murder charge either to a principal offender or to a secondary party, and in so doing declined to follow its own previous decision in *DPP for Northern Ireland v Lynch* [1975] AC 653. Singling out murder in this way does itself raise some anomalies, particularly in that duress appears still to be a defence to wounding with intent under the OAPA 1861, whereas if the victim should die the intent to cause grievous bodily harm is sufficient to found a murder charge and the defence suddenly becomes unavailable. The exclusion of duress applies equally on a charge of attempted murder (*Gotts* [1992] 2 AC 412) but the exclusion would not appear to apply to conspiracy to murder (*Ness* [2011] Crim LR 645). There is thus no defence in law on a charge of murder available, even to a 13-year-old complying with instructions from his father which he was too frightened to disobey (*Wilson* [2007] 2 Cr App R 411).

The Law Commission has recommended in its Report, *Murder, Manslaughter and Infanticide* (Law Com No. 304, 2006), that duress should be a defence to murder but with the legal burden on the accused.

A3.43   **Treason**   Duress, or something akin to it, seems to have been recognised as a defence to certain forms of treason both as long ago as 1419 (*Oldcastle's Case* (1419) 1 Hale PC 50) and as relatively recently as 1945 in *Purdy* (1945) 10 JCL 182 (although see per Lord Goddard CJ in *Steane* [1947] KB 997 at p. 1005). Writers such as Hale and Stephen have doubted whether duress applies to the more serious forms of treason and the judges have traditionally reserved their opinion as to the extent to which duress is available (see, e.g., Lord Brandon in *Howe* [1987] AC 417 at p. 438). Given the decision in *Howe*, the courts may well be unwilling to allow a plea of duress where the particular act of treason would inevitably lead to the deaths of identifiable individuals, even if it would be difficult or impossible to bring a murder charge in relation to those deaths.

A3.44   **Excluded Persons**   It is now clear that a person cannot rely on the defence of duress if he has voluntarily by association with others exposed himself to the risk of such duress (e.g., by joining a criminal organisation or gang). One of the earlier illustrations of this principle was in the Northern Ireland case of *Fitzpatrick* [1977] NI 20 where the accused had voluntarily joined the IRA and was therefore unable to plead duress based on threats from that organisation as a defence to, *inter alia*, armed robbery carried out on its behalf. The restriction on the defence was supported by dicta of members of the House of Lords in *DPP for Northern Ireland v Lynch* [1975] AC 653 and by provisions of various Commonwealth codes and was then applied by the English Court of Appeal in *Sharp* [1987] QB 853. Sharp was a member of a gang which had carried out a series of armed robberies. He sought to plead duress as a defence to manslaughter when a sub-postmaster was shot dead by the gang leader during the course of the last robbery. Sharp alleged that he had sought to withdraw from this robbery when he saw the guns being put into the car but that a gun had then been pointed at him and a threat made 'to blow his head off' if he did not participate. Lord Lane CJ said (at p. 861):

> ...where a person has voluntarily, and with knowledge of its nature, joined a criminal organisation or gang which he knew might bring pressure on him to commit an offence and was an active member when he was put under such pressure, he cannot avail himself of the defence of duress.

It seemed clear from this statement that the organisation or gang had to be one likely to exercise duress and the accused had to be aware of this when he joined. In *Shepherd* (1987) 86 Cr App R 47, the accused, a member of a shoplifting gang, claimed that he found the experience unnerving and that he had only taken part in a subsequent burglary because of threats of violence to himself and his family. The Court of Appeal quashed the conviction for burglary as the trial judge had wrongly withdrawn the defence of duress from the jury purely on the basis that the accused had voluntarily joined a criminal organisation. Mustill LJ said (at p. 51):

> ...the concerted shoplifting enterprise did not involve violence to the victim either in anticipation or in the way it was actually put into effect. The members of the jury have had to ask themselves whether the appellant could be said to have taken the risk of P's violence simply by joining a shoplifting gang.

A3.45   The precise ambit of the accused's knowledge was at issue in a number of conflicting Court of Appeal cases between 1999 and 2003, most of them cases involving duress exercised in furtherance of debts run up for the illegal supply of drugs. The last of these cases, *Z* [2003] 1 WLR 1489 (although not in itself a drugs case) *appeared* to settle the conflict and held that the proper question related to the risk of compulsion to commit 'offences of the type charged'. Thus on the facts of *Z*, the accused's participation in a prostitution racket may not have been thought by the jury to lay him open to an offence as serious as aggravated burglary.

However *Z* went to the House of Lords under the name of *Hasan* [2005] 2 AC 467 and was reversed and the accused's conviction restored. The certified question was as follows:

Whether the defence of duress is excluded when as a result of the accused's voluntary association with others:
(i)   he foresaw (or possibly should have foreseen) the risk of being subjected to any compulsion by threats of violence, or
(ii) only when he foresaw (or should have foreseen) the risk of being subjected to compulsion to commit criminal offences, and, if the latter,
(iii) only if the offences foreseen (or which should have been foreseen) were of the same type (or possibly of the same type and gravity) as that ultimately committed.

In a speech, which generally took a deliberately restrictive approach to the ambit of the defence of duress (see **A3.40**), Lord Bingham effectively selected option (i), which is of course the widest possible limitation on the defence. Not only that, it was the wider more objective form of option (i) which was approved, whereby it was enough that the risk of compulsion *ought* to have been foreseen rather than that it must have been *actually* foreseen by the accused. Option (i) means that not only do the foreseeable consequences of the compulsion not need to include offences of the same type as those with which the accused has actually been charged but there is not even any *requirement* that the foreseeable compulsion be related to the commission of any offences at all. The implications of this can be illustrated by reference to *Heath* [2000] Crim LR 109, where it was enough that the accused knew that in the drugs world violence is used to enforce debts and therefore, when his debt was enforced by means of requiring him to commit offences, he could not rely on duress. This point has been reinforced by *Mullally* [2012] EWCA Crim 687, where the Court of Appeal indicated that not only will the defence of duress not be available but that the threats will not be likely to have any significant impact on sentence.

Although it was Lord Bingham's speech with which the majority agreed, Baroness Hale, in **A3.46** agreeing with the decision to allow the Crown's appeal, answered the certified question in a slightly different fashion and chose option (ii) (again with, it would seem, the objective variant of 'should have foreseen'). Baroness Hale also indicated a need to put a limitation on the exclusion of duress, by means of further explanation of the requirement of 'voluntary association' with the duressor, referring back also to the Law Commission's requirement that the exposure to the risk of duress should be 'without reasonable excuse', so as to cater for 'battered wives' or 'others in close personal or family relationships with their duressors and their associates, such as their mothers, brothers or children'. She prefaced this by saying (at [78]):

It is one thing to deny the defence to people who choose to become members of illegal organisations, join criminal gangs, or engage with others in drug-related criminality. It is another thing to deny it to someone who has a quite different reason for becoming associated with the duressor and then finds it difficult to escape.

See also *C (GA)* [2013] EWCA Crim 1472 as to the possibility of duress arising from Battered Woman's Syndrome. The width of the exclusion of duress on the grounds of voluntary association is further illustrated by *Ali* [2008] EWCA Crim 716, where it was said not to be essential (for the exclusion to apply) to be associating with persons engaged in criminal activity so long as they were persons from whom threats of violence could reasonably be foreseen.

Necessity

It has long been unclear whether a general defence of necessity exists in English law. The courts **A3.47** have now recognised a defence of duress of circumstances that achieves many of the same results. It is first necessary to examine the nature of, and the authorities concerning, necessity in order to appreciate the more recent cases on duress of circumstances.

Necessity differs from duress in that it is generally conceived of not as a concession to human frailty, i.e. as an excuse, but rather as a *justified* choice between two evils — the evil represented by committing the offence is outweighed by the greater evil which would ensue if the offence were not to be committed. This difference is often lost sight of because cases where necessity is raised also tend to be cases where there is an arguable case for excusing the accused.

A3.48   The leading case of *Dudley* (1884) 14 QBD 273 is a good example which is complicated by the fact that it was a murder charge (and involved cannibalism). (As with duress, the courts are reluctant to widen the range of available defences in such cases.) The two accused had found themselves adrift in a small boat on the high seas with another man and the young cabin boy. They had had virtually no food or water for 20 days and had been reduced, for example, to drinking their own urine. Finally they killed and ate the cabin-boy who was likely anyway to have been the first to die and without this deed they would probably themselves not have survived the further four days which elapsed before they were rescued. In rejecting any defence of necessity on these facts, Lord Coleridge CJ constantly switched from the language of justification to that of excuse, but it was the notion of justification which appears to have been dominant. On that basis, the defence was probably doomed on the facts since the jury had found that there was no greater necessity for killing the boy than any of the others. Although *Dudley* was distinguished by Brooke LJ in *Re A (Children) (conjoined twins: surgical separation)* [2001] Fam 147, ruling to be lawful an operation which would save one conjoined twin but kill the other; the earlier case set the tone whereby English courts have generally rejected a defence of necessity even where the balance of evils points much more clearly in favour of committing the offence. Thus in *Buckoke v Greater London Council* [1971] Ch 655 (a civil case concerning the legality of instructions issued to drivers of fire-engines), Lord Denning MR (at p. 668) accepted as correct the proposition that a driver would have no defence if he proceeded through a red light to save a man in imminent peril in a blaze 200 yards away (regulations passed since would now permit this), 'nevertheless such a man should not be prosecuted. He should be congratulated.'

The defence is denied in law but the realities are recognised in practice by exercising discretion in prosecuting or sentencing. (The two accused in *Dudley* were sentenced to death but their sentences were later commuted to six months' imprisonment.)

A3.49   So it seems that necessity as a justification is rarely recognised by English law (but see the dicta of Lord Brandon and Lord Goff in *F v West Berkshire Health Authority* [1990] 2 AC 1) as a general defence although *particular* offences may be defined in such a way as to make such a defence available. For example, the presence of the word 'unlawfully' in the OAPA 1861, s. 58, was used in *Bourne* [1939] 1 KB 687 to show that some abortions must be lawful and that that included one performed in good faith for the purpose of preserving the life of the mother (see now the Abortion Act 1967). Other statutes have more obvious specific defences such as that of lawful excuse in the Criminal Damage Act 1971 (see **B8.12**). The reluctance of the courts to recognise a *general* defence of necessity (as a justification) perhaps reflects sentiments similar to those expressed by Dickson J in the Supreme Court of Canada in *Perka* (1984) 13 DLR (4th) 1 where he said (at p. 14):

> It is still my opinion that, 'No system of positive law can recognise any principle which would entitle a person to violate the law because on his view the law conflicted with some higher social value' [*Morgentaler v The Queen* (1985) 53 DLR (3d) 161 at p. 209]. The Criminal Code has specified a number of identifiable situations in which an actor is justified in committing what would otherwise be a criminal offence. To go beyond that and hold that ostensibly illegal acts can be validated on the basis of their expediency, would import an undue subjectivity into the criminal law. It would invite the courts to second-guess the legislature and to assess the relative merits of social policies underlying criminal prohibitions.

Similar considerations influenced the Law Commission in once recommending (Law Com. No. 83 — but see now Law Com. No. 218, para. 35.7) that any general defence of necessity that might exist should be abolished. This proposal would have presented the apparent anomaly that a person who committed an offence in response to threats would have the defence of duress whereas if the pressure were created by some natural emergency or surrounding circumstances, no defence would be available. As will be seen in **A3.50**, the courts (and indeed the Law Commission — see Law Com. No. 218, para. 35.1) are now addressing this anomaly by recognising, as an excuse rather than as a justification, the defence of duress of circumstances which, again in the words of Dickson J in *Perka* is:

> ...much less open to criticism. It rests on a realistic assessment of human weakness, recognising that a liberal and humane criminal law cannot hold people to the strict obedience of laws in emergency situations where normal human instincts, whether of self-preservation or of altruism, overwhelmingly impel disobedience. The objectivity of the criminal law is preserved; such acts are still wrongful, but in the circumstances they are excusable. Praise is indeed not bestowed, but pardon is, when one does a wrongful act under pressure.

Duress of Circumstances

The early authorities on the defence of duress of circumstances were a series of cases dealing with road traffic offences, but in *Pommell* [1995] 2 Cr App R 607 the Court of Appeal confirmed that the defence applies to all crimes except murder, attempted murder and some forms of treason. The first case was *Willer* (1986) 83 Cr App R 225 where the accused drove his car on to the pavement and into (and back out of) a shopping precinct to escape from a gang of youths bent on attacking himself and his passengers. At his trial for reckless driving, the judge refused to put the defence of necessity to the jury, but the Court of Appeal thought that 'a very different defence', that of duress, should have been available. According to Watkins LJ (at p. 227, emphasis added) the question then would be:

> ...whether or not upon the outward or the return journey, or both, the appellant was wholly driven *by force of circumstance* into doing what he did and did not drive the car otherwise than under that form of compulsion.

It should be noted that although there were, in a sense, threats to the accused in this case, it was not a case of duress *by threats* as traditionally understood since in such a case the accused commits in order to *comply* with the threatener's demands rather than merely to *escape* from the threats. On the distinction between the two types of duress, see *Cole* [1994] Crim LR 582.

Willer was followed and applied in *Conway* [1989] QB 290, another reckless driving case, in which the Court of Appeal quashed the conviction, saying (at p. 297) 'it is still not clear whether there is a general defence of necessity' and 'necessity can only be a defence to a charge of reckless driving where the facts establish "duress of circumstances" '. See also *DPP v Harris* [1995] 1 Cr App R 170 for discussion of whether 'necessity of circumstances' can be a defence to a charge of driving without due care and attention for a police driver going through a red light. In *Backshall* [1998] 1 WLR 1506 the Court of Appeal confirmed that the defence is indeed available on a charge of driving without due care, a conclusion consistent with that in *Pommell* that the defence is of general application.

In *Martin* [1989] 1 All ER 652, duress of circumstances was recognised as a potential defence to driving while disqualified. According to Simon Brown J, it could arise from 'objective dangers threatening the accused or others' but 'the defence is available only if, from an objective standpoint, the accused can be said to be acting reasonably and proportionately in order to avoid a threat of death or serious injury'. The questions for the jury would then be virtually identical to that in relation to duress by threats (see **A3.35** to **A3.40**):

> ...first, was the accused, or may he have been, impelled to act as he did because as a result of what he reasonably believed to be the situation he had good cause to fear that otherwise death or serious physical injury would result; second, if so, would a sober person of reasonable firmness, sharing the characteristics of the accused, have responded to that situation by acting as the accused acted?

A3.50

A3.51

The reference to the sober person of reasonable firmness shows that, as with duress by threats, the crucial question is not so much whether the accused was justified as whether he can be excused on the grounds that a reasonable person would have felt impelled to act in the same way.

The circumstances impelling the accused to act must be external to himself, so that the suicidal thoughts of life sentence prisoners could not of themselves amount to relevant circumstances excusing the offence of prison breaking according to the Court of Appeal in *Rodger* [1998] 1 Cr App R 143. The suicidal thoughts were 'a purely subjective element' as is the pain from which the cultivators of cannabis may wish to seek relief (*Quayle* [2005] 1 All ER 988).

A3.52 Duress of circumstances has also been allowed by the Divisional Court on a charge of driving with excess alcohol in *DPP v Bell* [1992] RTR 335, where the accused, because of his terror of his pursuers, ran back to his car and drove off some distance down the road. The fact he did not continue to drive all the way home supported the finding that he was driving because of his fear and not because of any prior intention to use his car to get home even if intoxicated. This contrasted with the earlier case of *DPP v Jones* [1990] RTR 33 where a similar defence failed because the accused drove the two miles home without even bothering to check whether he was still being pursued. *DPP v Davis* [1994] Crim LR 600 was to similar effect and reflected an increasingly restrictive attitude to both types of duress, which has since been explicitly articulated in *Hasan* [2005] 2 AC 467 (discussed at **A3.40** and **A3.45**) and applied in *Quayle* to deny the defence in relation to the production etc. of cannabis. *Quayle* was followed in *Altham* [2006] 1 WLR 3287, where the ECHR, Article 3, was unsuccessfully invoked by the appellant. *Quayle* was also referred to in *S (C)* [2012] 1 All ER 793, where duress of circumstances (or necessity) was ruled not to be available in relation to the offence of removing a child from England and Wales contrary to the Child Abduction Act 1984. *DPP v Mullally* [2006] EWHC 3448 (Admin) further illustrates the increasingly restrictive attitude to duress and its failure in a motoring case; the accused continued to drive despite having been informed that the police had arrived to deal with the threat of violence. However, as to the difficulties in ruling out the defence at the stage of a preliminary hearing, see *S Ltd and L Ltd* [2009] 2 Cr App R 171. It should also be noted that there is no requirement that the threat being avoided should be 'life threatening', a threat of either death or serious injury being sufficient (*Pipe v DPP* [2012] EWHC 1821 (Admin)).

Coercion

A3.53 At common law there was a rebuttable presumption that a wife who committed an offence (except murder or treason) in the presence of her husband did so under coercion and that she should be acquitted. The presumption was abolished by the CJA 1925, s. 47, which nevertheless went on to provide that:

> ...on a charge against a wife for any offence other than treason or murder it shall be a good defence to prove that the offence was committed in the presence of, and under the coercion of, the husband.

Coercion is presumably wider than duress since otherwise the defence is otiose. It seems that it is wider in that there is no need for threats of death or serious injury, it being sufficient that the wife acted because of the dominating influence of her husband, her will being 'overborne by the wishes of her husband' so that 'she was forced unwillingly to participate' (*Shortland* [1996] 1 Cr App R 116, followed in *Cairns* [2003] 1 WLR 796 where a direction that 'coercion does not just mean physical force or the threat of physical force' was considered ambiguous and did not make clear that physical force or a threat of it was not actually required). The ABCPA 2014, s. 177, abolishes the defence in relation to offences committed on or after 13 May 2014.

An increasingly more relevant concept today, however, is the coercion to which victims of trafficking are subject. There is no separate defence of 'coercion' applicable to such victims but they may be entitled to a defence of duress on ordinary principles, whether it be as a defence to immigration offences or other offences which they are coerced into committing; see *O* [2008] EWCA Crim 2835, *N* [2013] QB 379 and *L* [2014] 1 All ER 113 for the protocols for dealing with offences committed by trafficked victims and other offences committed by young persons who may have been trafficked. See also the discussion at **B22.11**.

Self-defence, Prevention of Crime and Related Defences Generally

These defences are generally regarded as matters of justification rather than excuse. They are normally available only as defences to crimes committed by the use of force (*Renouf* [1986] 2 All ER 449, where reckless driving was regarded as involving force where the only relevant evidence of reckless driving was the 'forcing' of another car off the road). Nevertheless, they are undoubtedly available to a wide range of offences. Where there is evidence 'which if accepted could raise a prima facie case of self-defence, this should be left to the jury even if the accused has not formally relied upon self-defence' (*DPP (Jamaica) v Bailey* [1995] 1 Cr App R 257). See also *Hayes* [2011] EWCA Crim 2680 as to the importance of giving a full and careful direction on self-defence tailored to the circumstances of the case and, where relevant, tailored in relation to each count charged. Where self-defence is not available because the offence charged does not involve the use of force, duress of circumstances may equally be available (*Symonds* [1998] Crim LR 280).

Self-defence, defence of property and defence of another (sometimes referred to collectively as 'private defence') are still defences at common law (notwithstanding the impact of the CJIA 2008, s. 76: see **A3.57**) whereas the law on the use of force in the prevention of crime and in lawful arrest has for many years been statutory and is to be found in the CLA 1967, s. 3(1).

Criminal Law Act 1967, s. 3

(1) A person may use such force as is reasonable in the circumstances in the prevention of crime, or in effecting or assisting in the lawful arrest of offenders or suspected offenders or of persons unlawfully at large.

Prevention of Crime   Where an accused is relying on the prevention of crime, within the meaning of the Criminal Law Act 1967, s. 3, as the justification for the use of reasonable force, the crime being prevented must not already have been completed. This is illustrated by *Attwater* [2011] RTR 173 (dangerous driving to force another car to stop some time after an alleged accident could not be justified as preventing the crime of failing to stop after an accident since any offence of failure to stop was already by then complete: see **C6.53**). Contrast *Morris* [2014] 1 WLR 16 (see **B5.38**), where D may have honestly believed that an offence of making off was in the course of being committed.

The term 'crime' here means a crime in domestic law and this does not include a crime such as 'aggression', which is recognised only in customary international law (*Jones* [2007] 1 AC 136). More generally, in relation to 'direct action protesters' who claim 'to be justified in doing acts which would otherwise be criminal', Lord Hoffmann had the following to say (at [94]):

> In a case in which the defence requires that the acts of the defendant should in all the circumstances have been reasonable, his acts must be considered in the context of a functioning state in which legal disputes can be peacefully submitted to the courts and disputes over what should be law or government policy can be submitted to the arbitrament of the democratic process. In such circumstances, the apprehension, however honest or reasonable, of acts which are thought to be unlawful or contrary to the public interest, cannot justify the commission of criminal acts and the issue of justification should be withdrawn from the jury. Evidence to support the opinions of the protesters as to the legality of the acts in question is irrelevant and inadmissible, disclosure going to this issue should not be ordered and the services of international lawyers are not required.

Consistency of Defences based on Use of 'reasonable force'   The criterion in the CLA 1967, s. 3, of 'such force as is reasonable in the circumstances' differs slightly from traditional formulations of the common-law rule for self-defence, which usually also include some reference to necessity. See, e.g., per Lord Lane CJ in *Williams* [1987] 3 All ER 411 at p. 414: 'the exercise of any necessary and reasonable force to protect himself'.

Some of the restrictive rules that applied at common law could be attributed to this reference to necessity but the modern trend seems to be to adopt a more flexible approach (as with the former so-called duty to retreat which has now been abandoned as such). Given the fact that in most cases where the accused is acting in self-defence he will also be acting to prevent a crime being committed by his aggressor, it would seem sensible for the tests for self-defence and prevention of crime to be identical. Even though the courts have not always formulated the test for self-defence in the exact words used in the CLA 1967, s. 3, for prevention of crime, there is no evidence from any of the cases that any such differences are matters of substance. Indeed in *Beckford v The Queen* [1988] AC 130, Lord Griffiths said (at p. 145) that: 'the test to be applied for self-defence is that a person may use such force as is reasonable in the circumstances as he honestly believes them to be in the defence of himself or another'. Whilst his lordship was primarily concerned with the question of mistaken belief in this case, his dictum closely echoes s. 3 and supports the view that the common-law rules governing the use of force in self-defence and the rules applicable to prevention of crime are now identical (see also *Clegg* [1995] 1 AC 482). The same view underpins the 'clarificatory' provisions of the CJIA 2008, s. 76, which, subject to one exception changing the formulation of the law relating to householders, applies in identical terms to both defences. Accordingly, the law can in general terms be formulated quite simply and neatly along the following lines:

A person may use such force as is reasonable in the circumstances as he believes them to be for the purposes of:

(a) self-defence (and defence of another),
(b) defence of property,
(c) prevention of crime, or
(d) lawful arrest.

Although (a) and (b) above remain common-law defences, as distinct from (c) and (d) which are governed by the CLA 1967, s. 3, the meaning and interpretation of 'reasonable force' is now, for all of them, subject to statutory provision under the CJIA 2008, s. 76. Initially, this provision was intended to be solely 'to clarify' the operation of the common law but since the amendments to it made by the CCA 2013, s. 43, it now has to be seen as intending to change the law to some extent, but in relation to self-defence only, and only in 'householder cases'. It remains true, however, that even in such 'householder cases' the test is one of reasonable force and it is merely the interpretation of what force is 'not to be regarded as reasonable' which is subject to a different test (one of 'grossly disproportionate' as opposed to simply 'disproportionate' in the circumstances). It is convenient to set out s. 76 at this point, its various provisions are commented on further in subsequent paragraphs where appropriate.

A3.57   Criminal Justice and Immigration Act 2008, s. 76

(1) This section applies where in proceedings for an offence—
   (a) an issue arises as to whether a person charged with the offence ('D') is entitled to rely on a defence within subsection (2), and
   (b) the question arises whether the degree of force used by D against a person ('V') was reasonable in the circumstances.
(2) The defences are—
   (a)   the common law defence of self-defence;.
   (aa) the common law defence of defence of property; and
   (b)   the defences provided by section 3(1) of the Criminal Law Act 1967 or section 3(1) of the Criminal Law Act (Northern Ireland) 1967 (use of force in prevention of crime or making arrest).

(3)   The question whether the degree of force used by D was reasonable in the circumstances is to be decided by reference to the circumstances as D believed them to be, and subsections (4) to (8) also apply in connection with deciding that question.

(4)   If D claims to have held a particular belief as regards the existence of any circumstances—
   (a)   the reasonableness or otherwise of that belief is relevant to the question whether D genuinely held it; but
   (b)   if it is determined that D did genuinely hold it, D is entitled to rely on it for the purposes of subsection (3), whether or not—
       (i)   it was mistaken, or
       (ii)   (if it was mistaken) the mistake was a reasonable one to have made.

(5)   But subsection (4)(b) does not enable D to rely on any mistaken belief attributable to intoxication that was voluntarily induced.

(5A)   In a householder case, the degree of force used by D is not to be regarded as having been reasonable in the circumstances as D believed them to be if it was grossly disproportionate in those circumstances.

(6)   In a case other than a householder case, the degree of force used by D is not to be regarded as having been reasonable in the circumstances as D believed them to be if it was disproportionate in those circumstances.

(6A)   In deciding the question mentioned in subsection (3), a possibility that D could have retreated is to be considered (so far as relevant) as a factor to be taken into account, rather than as giving rise to a duty to retreat.

(7)   In deciding the question mentioned in subsection (3) the following considerations are to be taken into account (so far as relevant in the circumstances of the case)—
   (a)   that a person acting for a legitimate purpose may not be able to weigh to a nicety the exact measure of any necessary action; and
   (b)   that evidence of a person's having only done what the person honestly and instinctively thought was necessary for a legitimate purpose constitutes strong evidence that only reasonable action was taken by that person for that purpose.

(8)   Subsections (6A) and (7) are not to be read as preventing other matters from being taken into account where they are relevant to deciding the question mentioned in subsection (3).

(8A)   For the purposes of this section 'a householder case' is a case where—
   (a)   the defence concerned is the common law defence of self-defence,
   (b)   the force concerned is force used by D while in or partly in a building, or part of a building, that is a dwelling or is forces accommodation (or is both),
   (c)   D is not a trespasser at the time the force is used, and
   (d)   at that time D believed V to be in, or entering, the building or part as a trespasser.

(8B)   Where—
   (a)   a part of a building is a dwelling where D dwells,
   (b)   another part of the building is a place of work for D or another person who dwells in the first part, and
   (c)   that other part is internally accessible from the first part,
   that other part, and any internal means of access between the two parts, are each treated for the purposes of subsection (8A) as a part of a building that is a dwelling.

(8C)   Where—
   (a)   a part of a building is forces accommodation that is living or sleeping accommodation for D,
   (b)   another part of the building is a place of work for D or another person for whom the first part is living or sleeping accommodation, and
   (c)   that other part is internally accessible from the first part,
   that other part, and any internal means of access between the two parts, are each treated for the purposes of subsection (8A) as a part of a building that is forces accommodation.

(8D)   Subsections (4) and (5) apply for the purposes of subsection (8A)(d) as they apply for the purposes of subsection (3).

(8E)   The fact that a person derives title from a trespasser, or has the permission of a trespasser, does not prevent the person from being a trespasser for the purposes of subsection (8A).

(8F)   In subsections (8A) to (8C)—
   'building' includes a vehicle or vessel, and
   'forces accommodation' means service living accommodation for the purposes of Part 3 of the Armed Forces Act 2006 by virtue of section 96(1)(a) or (b) of that Act.

(9) This section, except so far as making different provision for householder cases, is intended to clarify the operation of the existing defences mentioned in subsection (2).

(10) In this section—

(a) 'legitimate purpose' means—

(i) the purpose of self-defence under the common law, . . .

[(ia) the purpose of defence of property under the common law, or]

(ii) the prevention of crime or effecting or assisting in the lawful arrest of persons mentioned in the provisions referred to in subsection (2)(b);

(b) references to self-defence include acting in defence of another person; and

(c) references to the degree of force used are to the type and amount of force used.

A3.58   **The Subjective Question and the Objective Question in Defences based on the Use of 'reasonable force'**   It has become axiomatic that there are two basic questions to be answered in relation to self-defence, prevention of crime and related defences. First, were the facts (as the accused believed them to be) such that the use of force was reasonably necessary (for the purpose claimed, e.g., for the purpose of self-defence). Secondly, was the degree of force used reasonable for that purpose in the light of those perceived facts. The first question is clearly, from the terms in which it is put, a subjective matter in that D is judged on the basis of the facts as he genuinely believed them to be. The second question is essentially an objective question in that how much force is reasonable in the perceived circumstances is ultimately a matter for the jury and not primarily dependent on D's own evaluation. These two basic questions will be examined in turn, starting with the subjective question.

A3.59   **The Subjective Question: The Circumstances as the Accused Believes them to be**   Although the previous common-law rule, that the accused's belief had to be reasonable, remains true for the purpose of defending civil law claims for battery (*Ashley v Chief Constable of Sussex Police (Sherwood intervening)* [2008] 1 AC 962), for the purposes of the criminal law, the Court of Appeal rescinded this requirement in the landmark decision in *Williams* [1987] 3 All ER 411, by analogy with the House of Lords' decision in *DPP v Morgan* [1976] AC 182. The Criminal Law Revision Committee's recommendation that a person may use such force as is reasonable in the circumstances *as he believes them to be* was adopted by Lord Lane CJ as representing the law. This approach was approved and followed by the Privy Council in *Beckford v The Queen* [1988] AC 130, where the appeal was allowed, as in *Williams*, because the trial judge had directed the jury that a reasonable belief was required. This subjective test for mistakes of fact is confirmed by the CJIA 2008, s. 76(3) and (4) (see **A3.57**).

It has been argued that, under the ECHR, Article 2, a more demanding standard of honest belief 'for good reasons' may be required — especially as far as trained law enforcement officers are concerned (*Andronicou v Cyprus* (1998) 25 EHRR 491). The controversy as to how far the subjective belief rule ought to be amended in the light of the HRA 1998 is discussed by Ashworth [2000] Crim LR 564 at p. 567 and by Leverick [2002] Crim LR 347. However, the CJIA 2008, s. 76 (3) and (4), effectively confirm that the subjective test still holds sway; in *Shaw v The Queen* [2001] 1 WLR 1519 the subjective test was interpreted to apply not only to the accused's belief as to the circumstances but also to his belief as to the danger involved in those circumstances, an approach also endorsed in *Harvey* [2009] EWCA Crim 469. Of course, as is pointed out in s. 76(4), the reasonableness of a belief can be a factor in whether a jury believes it is genuinely held, but if it is found to be so held, it can be relied on irrespective of whether or not it is reasonable.

Even where the main defence is that the accused was *actually* under attack, the judge may be under a duty to direct the jury on the possibility of a defence based on mistaken belief if there is evidence capable of supporting this (*Oatridge* (1991) 94 Cr App R 367). However, in *Keane* [2010] EWCA Crim 2514, Hughes LJ commented (at [39]) that there are many cases where the question of mistake is not relevant because there is no suggestion that, if the accused may be telling the truth, he was not actually under attack. In such cases, it is not necessary or desirable to direct the jury about mistaken belief and to do so may distract the jury from the real question of whether they are sure that he was not in fact under attack. See also *Mohammed Ibrahim* [2014] EWCA Crim 121, where late medical evidence about the state of D's mind was held to have been rightly excluded, *inter alia*, because the case essentially turned on the factual question of whether D had been the sole aggressor. In that case, the Court of Appeal also noted that the case before it was not a case:

> ... in which the defendant suffered from a psychiatric condition that caused him to believe in a state of affairs which did not exist. In such case, as the authorities show, expert medical evidence is admissible in relation to the first limb of the defence of self-defence in order to establish what state of affairs the defendant genuinely believed to exist.

The Subjective Question: Effect of Voluntary Intoxication on Mistaken Belief The sub-   **A3.60** jective approach to mistake does not apply where the accused's mistake was due to voluntary intoxication (*O'Grady* [1987] QB 995). Although the actual conviction in *O'Grady* was for manslaughter (a basic intent offence), the Court of Appeal seemed clear in the view that an intoxicated mistake could not be relied upon even in relation to a crime of specific intent such as murder. Lord Lane CJ said (at p. 999):

> We do not consider that any distinction should be drawn on this aspect of the matter between offences involving what is called specific intent, such as murder, and offences of so-called basic intent, such as manslaughter ... the question of mistake can and ought to be considered separately from the question of intent.

O'Grady was followed in *O'Connor* [1991] Crim LR 135, although in that case the conviction was reduced to manslaughter on the separate ground that the intoxication might have prevented the formation of the specific intention to cause grievous bodily harm. *O'Grady* and *O'Connor* have been reaffirmed by the Court of Appeal in *Hatton* [2006] 1 Cr App R 247 and now by the CJIA 2008, s. 76(5), which provides: 'subsection (4)(b) does not enable D to rely on any mistaken belief attributable to intoxication that was voluntarily induced'. Whether the offence is one of specific intent or not is therefore immaterial as far as defences of self-defence and prevention of crime are concerned and the accused cannot rely on a mistake about the existence or degree of an attack on himself which is due to self-induced intoxication.

The Objective Question: The Degree of Force Permitted It is for the jury to determine   **A3.61** whether the force was reasonable in the circumstances as the accused believed them to be, as is illustrated by *Owino* [1996] 2 Cr App R 128 and numerous other cases. However, the courts have generally applied the rule in a manner which attempts to take account of the motives and situation of the accused and which is not totally and unreservedly objective. Thus in *Palmer v The Queen* [1971] AC 814, Lord Morris of Borth-y-Gest said (at p. 832):

> ... it will be recognised that a person defending himself cannot weigh to a nicety the exact measure of his necessary defensive action. If a jury thought that in a moment of unexpected anguish a person attacked had only done what he honestly and instinctively thought was necessary that would be most potent evidence that only reasonable defensive action had been taken. A jury will be told that the defence of self-defence, where the evidence makes its raising possible, will only fail if the prosecution show beyond doubt that what the accused did was not by way of self-defence.

This passage is echoed and indeed quoted almost verbatim in the CJIA 2008, s. 76(7). Section 76(8) goes on to make it clear that other considerations may also be taken into account where relevant.

The approach in *Palmer* (now reiterated in s. 76(7)) was described by Ormrod LJ in *Shannon* (1980) 71 Cr App R 192 at p. 194 as:

> ... a bridge between what is sometimes referred to as 'the objective test', that is what is reasonable judged from the viewpoint of an outsider looking at a situation quite dispassionately, and 'the subjective test', that is the viewpoint of the accused himself with the intellectual capabilities of which he may in fact be possessed and with all the emotional strains and stresses to which at the moment he may be subjected.

The Court of Appeal in this case quashed the conviction because the judge had ignored the subjective aspect of the question and put the question to the jury purely as: 'Did the appellant use more force than was necessary in the circumstances?' whereas the real question, according to Ormrod LJ (at p. 197), was:

> Was this stabbing within the conception of necessary self-defence judged by the standards of common sense, bearing in mind the position of the appellant at the moment of the stabbing, or was it a case of angry retaliation or pure aggression on his part?

A3.62   It is nevertheless clear from *Owino* and *DPP v Armstrong-Brown* [1999] Crim LR 417 that the test of unreasonable force remains an essentially objective test. Furthermore, in *Martin* [2002] 2 WLR 1, a highly publicised case of a reclusive farmer using lethal and unreasonable force to defend his property, on appeal the accused tried to use the fact that, in relation to the objective condition in provocation, the House of Lords in *Smith* [2001] 1 AC 146 had, at that time, allowed evidence of the accused's subjective psychiatric condition to be considered relevant. The Court of Appeal in *Martin* however said that self-defence was a distinct and complete defence and subject to different considerations. Whilst the physical characteristics of the accused might be relevant (e.g., one presumes, to explain why a physically weaker individual used a weapon rather than physical force in self-defence), it would not be appropriate 'except in exceptional circumstances which would make the evidence especially probative, in deciding whether excessive force has been used to take into account whether the defendant is suffering from some psychiatric condition'.

This raises the question of what will count as 'exceptional circumstances' making such evidence 'especially probative'. In *Oye* [2014] 1 All ER 902 the Court of Appeal found it difficult to see in what circumstances, even exceptionally, a psychiatric condition could (or on policy grounds, ought to) be relevant to the question of excessive force (contrast its possible relevance to the question of subjective belief in the facts: see *Mohammed Ibrahim* [2014] EWCA Crim 121 and **A3.59**). Reference was made to the earlier case of *Canns* [2005] EWCA Crim 2264 where three highly experienced members of the Court of Appeal had also found it 'impossible to identify the sort of exceptional circumstances in which it would be appropriate to take a psychiatric condition from which a defendant is suffering into account'. However, in *Press and Thompson* [2013] EWCA Crim 1849 there was evidence that D's post-traumatic stress disorder (a consequence of military service in Afghanistan) may have caused him to react over-sensitively to perceived threats. The trial judge was found to have been correct to invite the jury to consider the psychiatric evidence when resolving the question whether D did only what he honestly believed was necessary in the circumstances, which under *Palmer v The Queen* [1971] AC 814, at common law, and now by statute under the CJIA 2008, s. 76(7)(b), 'constitutes strong evidence that only reasonable action was taken'. The jury nevertheless convicted and the conviction was upheld since 'strong evidence is not conclusive evidence and it was for the jury, not the defendant, to resolve the ultimate and objective question of whether the degree of force used was reasonable'.

A3.63   **The Objective Question: Force which is not Reasonable within the Meaning of the CJIA 2008, s. 76, and Householder Cases**   The CJIA 2008, s. 76 (see **A3.57**), in addressing the essentially objective meaning of reasonableness, somewhat impenetrably provides in s. 76(6) that '[t]he degree of force used by D is not to be regarded as having been reasonable in the circumstances as D believed them to be if it was disproportionate in those circumstances'. To bring in the concept of 'disproportionate' as a (negative) gloss to 'reasonable in the circumstances' is not helpful since it simply explains one open-textured evaluative question in terms of another. In *Keane* [2010] EWCA Crim 2514, Hughes LJ helpfully confirmed that the statutory formulation of some of the rules relating to self-defence and related defences in the CJIA 2008, s. 76, did not alter the law as it had been for many years and expressed the view that to ask whether force is *reasonable* in all the circumstances or whether it is *proportionate* in all the circumstances is to ask the same question, as these expressions mean the same thing. However, the explanation of what is not reasonable in terms of it being disproportionate has taken on a new significance as from 25 April 2013 and the coming into force of the CCA 2013, s. 43, which inserted the new s. 76(5A):

> In a householder case, the degree of force used by D is not to be regarded as having been reasonable in the circumstances as D believed them to be if it was grossly disproportionate in those circumstances.

By s. 76(8A) a case is 'a householder case' only where the defence concerned is the common law of self-defence (there are also requirements that the force is used by D while in a building or part of a building which is a dwelling or forces accommodation, that D is not a trespasser at the time and that D believed V to be a trespasser). Thus it seems now that a householder who uses what is in fact regarded as disproportionate (as opposed to grossly disproportionate) force in self-defence may be found nevertheless to have used reasonable force in the circumstances as he believed them to be. It should also be noted, however, that s. 76(5A) does not actually dictate this result in every case; it simply says that grossly disproportionate force is *not* reasonable, rather than saying that disproportionate force (falling short of grossly disproportionate) *is* automatically reasonable. The fundamental test still remains that in s. 76(1)(b), i.e. whether the force used was 'reasonable in the circumstances'. The new provision merely affects the interpretation of '(un)reasonable in the circumstances' so that force is not by law automatically unreasonable in householder cases simply because it is disproportionate, provided it is not grossly disproportionate. The extra leeway which this is designed to give to householders (and the public signal that they should not be afraid of, or at risk of, prosecution for using reasonable force in self-defence against burglars, arguably already signalled, e.g., by s. 76(7) and the honest and instinctive test) is at the cost of considerable and arguably unnecessary complexity. The complexity includes the fact that a householder whose use of force is sought to be justified on the separate grounds of self-defence and defence of property is subject to different statements (in s. 76(5A) and s. 76(6)) of what is unreasonable in relation to the two separate defences, which may not prove to be an easy matter to explain to a jury should a prosecution actually be brought. The provision is arguably unnecessary in that s. 76(7) (and the common law which it reproduces) already provided considerations which could be used to mitigate the objective nature of the test in the context of the dilemma faced by a householder confronted by a trespasser in his own home.

The Objective Question: Self-defence: Complete Defence which Succeeds or Fails in its   **A3.64**
Entirety   Where the charge is murder, there is no common-law rule whereby, if self-defence fails because of the use of excessive force, it can have the effect of reducing the conviction to manslaughter (*McInnes* [1971] 3 All ER 295, confirmed in *Clegg* [1995] 1 AC 482) unless, for example, as in *Martin* [2002] 2 WLR 1, the psychiatric evidence rejected as irrelevant to self-defence can be used as the basis for diminished responsibility. Perhaps a more significant example of how the use of excessive force in self-defence might nevertheless result in a manslaughter rather than murder conviction arises from the creation of the new partial defence of loss of control in the CAJA 2009, s. 54, which applies, *inter alia*, where D has lost self-control as a result of 'a fear of serious violence' (see B1.25).

Trespassers Outside the Home   Whilst it has long been recognised that an occupier is entitled   **A3.65**
to use reasonable force to remove a trespasser from his land or home (either as part of, or by analogy with, the right to defend one's property), this right does not apply so clearly to removing someone from one's car, especially when the person was originally invited into the car and has only subsequently become a trespasser and the trespass can be more appropriately ended by returning the person to the place where originally invited into the car (*Burns* [2010] 1 WLR 2694). See also *Francis* [2011] EWCA Crim 877, as to the right to eject passengers from a bus.

Self-defence and Pre-emptive Strikes   A person can use force to ward off an anticipated attack   **A3.66**
provided that it is anticipated as 'imminent' (*Chisam* (1963) 47 Cr App R 130). Any other rule would leave little room in which the mistaken belief rule could operate. In *Beckford v The Queen* [1988] AC 130, Lord Griffiths said (at p. 144) 'a man about to be attacked does not have to wait for his assailant to strike the first blow or fire the first shot; circumstances may justify a

pre-emptive strike'. However, if a threat of force may be expected to deter the attacker, it may be difficult to convince the jury that it was reasonable to use actual force (cf. *Cousins* [1982] QB 526).

A3.67 **Scope of Defence of Another** Given the overlap already referred to between, for example, self-defence and prevention of crime, the precise boundaries of the individual defences are not always clear. Thus it is unclear whether defence of another is restricted to defence of a relative (and if so, how close) or extends to anyone with a sufficient nexus with the defender (*Devlin v Armstrong* [1971] NI 13) or to anyone at all. In *Duffy* [1967] 1 QB 63 the Court of Appeal found it unnecessary to decide whether defence of another extended to defence of a sister since what was done could be justified on the alternative basis of prevention of crime. The only case where this might not be so would be where the defender knows that the attacker is, for example, insane or under age, so that it cannot be said that he is acting 'in the prevention of crime' (cf. the reasoning of Ward LJ in *Re A (Children) (conjoined twins: surgical separation)* [2001] Fam 147). In such a case one would need to determine whether the person being attacked has a sufficient nexus with the defender to be within the scope of defence of another. In order to prevent anomalies, the better view is surely that no such nexus should be required and that one can act in defence of any other person (as recommended by the Criminal Law Revision Committee (14th Report)) provided, as always, that the use of force is reasonable in the circumstances.

A3.68 **Scope of Defence of Property** As with defence of another, it is unclear to what extent defending property of other persons is a justification for committing a crime, but the arguments in favour of having no restrictions are the same. In *DPP v Bayer* [2004] 1 WLR 2856, it was emphasised that the accused must be acting to ward off an 'unlawful or criminal act'. Therefore defence of property did not arise in relation to opposing the lawful sowing of GM seed. In relation to defence of one's own home, it should be noted that the statement approved in *Hussey* (1924) 18 Cr App R 160 that: 'In defence of a man's house, the owner or his family may kill a trespasser who would forcibly dispossess him of it' is of debatable authority today. Forceful resistance would no doubt be in order (which might unintentionally cause death) but deliberate killing would normally be hard to justify. See also *Burns* [2010] 1 WLR 2694 at **A3.65**.

A3.69 **No Duty to Retreat *per se* and the Position of the Initial Aggressor** The statement approved in *Hussey* (1924) 18 Cr App R 160 and quoted in **A3.68** went on to say of the defender that '...in defending his home he need not retreat, as in other cases of self-defence, for that would be giving up his house to his adversary'. There is no longer any duty to retreat in any category of private defence. The duty was first watered down in *Julien* [1969] 2 All ER 856 where it was said (at p. 843) that 'what is necessary is that he should demonstrate by his actions that he does not want to fight'. Even this was subsequently held, in *Bird* [1985] 2 All ER 513, to be too restrictive. It is not 'necessary' to demonstrate by one's actions an unwillingness to fight. That is merely one way of negativing any suggestion that the defendant was the attacker or was acting out of motives of retaliation or revenge rather than self-defence, but it is by no means the only method of doing that. As Edmund-Davies LJ said in *McInnes* [1971] 3 All ER 295 at p. 1607: 'We prefer the view expressed by the Full Court of [South] Australia [in *Howe* [1958] SASR 95] that a failure to retreat is only an *element* in the consideration upon which the reasonableness of an accused's conduct is to be judged'. The CJIA 2008, s. 76(6A) (see **A3.57**), inserted by the LASPO 2012, s. 148, effectively confirms this approach by providing that 'a possibility that D could have retreated is to be considered (so far as relevant) as a factor to be taken into account, rather than as giving rise to a duty to retreat'.

A3.70 Similarly, there is no hard and fast rule that a person who initiates a confrontation cannot rely on self-defence (*Balogun* [1999] EWCA Crim 2120) nor that it cannot be used against an assailant who is known to be a police officer (*Burley* [2000] Crim LR 843). Although the appeal was dismissed on the facts, the Court of Appeal in *Rashford* [2005] EWCA Crim 3377 has re-emphasised that the fact that a person is the initial aggressor does not automatically mean that he cannot be acting in self-defence. Dyson LJ approved the Scottish decision in *Burns v HM Advocate* 1995 SLT 1090 as an important decision which should be more widely known wherein (at p. 1093H) it was said that the question:

> ...depends upon whether the violence offered by the victim was so out of proportion to the accused's own actings as to give rise to the reasonable apprehension that he was in an immediate danger from which he had no other means of escape, and whether the violence which he then used was no more than was necessary to preserve his own life or protect himself from serious injury.

The reference to 'reasonable' apprehension is not in line with English law in relation to the subjective approach to mistaken belief. *Rashford* was followed and considered in *Harvey* [2009] EWCA Crim 469, where it was however acknowledged that, in principle, it is not a question of reasonable apprehension of danger but of the accused's 'perception of the events and of the danger he believes he faces'. In *Keane* [2010] EWCA Crim 2514, Hughes LJ also followed *Rashford* and commented favourably on the decision in *Harvey*, including the use of the homely expression whether 'the tables had been turned' as being suitable for many cases subject to the following point. Just because the tables have been turned in the sense that the original aggressor finds himself getting the worst of it, merely because the original victim is defending himself reasonably, does not reverse the roles and turn the original victim into the aggressor and justify force used in response by the original aggressor. The Court of Appeal in *Keane* also rejected the argument that, if D succeeds in verbally provoking V into striking a blow at D which is not itself lawful, D is entitled to respond with force simply because of the fact that he is responding to unlawful force by V. D's use of force is not reasonable because the opportunity to use it has been unreasonably engineered by D and this would merely be one of many situations where the parties to voluntary fights are both using unlawful force. It would be different if D set out only to provoke a punch but V unexpectedly and disproportionately used a knife in response. In that case D could be entitled to use force to defend himself against the unexpected and disproportionate force confronting him, provided the force used was reasonable in all the circumstances.

Unknown Circumstances Justifying Force in Self-defence etc.

The converse of mistaken belief in the need for self-defence etc. is the use of force in circum-   **A3.71**
stances where, unknown to the accused, the facts would in fact justify the use of force. The case of *Dadson* (1850) 2 Den CC 35 has long been thought to hold that no defence is available in these circumstances. Dadson shot and wounded a fleeing thief, but this degree of force was only permissible, even at that time, in the prevention of crime if the offence being committed amounted to a felony. The particular form of theft involved was only a felony if the thief had two previous convictions for the offence. Although this condition was in fact satisfied in this case, Dadson was unaware of this fact when he shot. His conviction was upheld. Although this case may be taken to lay down the general principle, it may seem to be modified in relation to force used to effect an arrest by the PACE 1984, s. 24. It may be argued that since, under s. 24, an arrest of a person is lawful if *in fact* he is, for example, 'in the act of committing an offence' (s. 24(1)(b)), the use of force in such circumstances is also lawful under the CLA 1967, s. 3. This argument could apply only to force used in effecting arrest, not self-defence or prevention of crime. However, s. 3 itself only permits 'such force as is reasonable in the circumstances'. If the circumstances include the accused's state of mind (cf. *Williams* [1987] 3 All ER 411) it could be said that it is not *reasonable* to use force where the accused lacks any knowledge of the lawfulness of the arrest. Since an arrest can be effected without any force at all being used, the fact that the arrest itself is lawful under the PACE 1984 does not automatically validate the use of force, the reasonableness of which is a distinct question.

Infancy

Prior to the CDA 1998, s. 34, children fell into one of three age groups for the purposes of   **A3.72**
criminal responsibility. Once a child has reached the age of 14, no special defence based on his

age was or is available. Children aged under 10 were (and still are) irrebuttably presumed to be incapable of criminal responsibility (*doli incapax*) by virtue of the CYPA 1933, s. 50, but in relation to children aged ten, 11, 12 or 13 there was formerly a rebuttable presumption of *doli incapax* which could be rebutted if the prosecution proved that the child had 'mischievous discretion', i.e. knew that what he did was 'seriously' wrong, not just naughty or mischievous (*JM v Runeckles* (1984) 79 Cr App R 255). In *C (A Minor) v DPP* [1996] AC 1 the Divisional Court had boldly decided that the rebuttable presumption no longer formed part of English law since it had become outdated in the changed conditions of society; this decision had however been promptly reversed in the House of Lords (also [1996] AC 1), where it was held that such a change could only be made by statute. Section 34 of the CDA 1998 effected that change by declaring that the 'rebuttable presumption of criminal law that a child aged ten or over is incapable of committing an offence is hereby abolished'. It is only children under ten therefore who are now specifically exempted from the criminal law on account of their age, the irrebuttable presumption in their case being unaffected, thus producing a clear line with responsibility commencing at the relatively young age of ten.

As far as children between ten and 14 are concerned, s. 34 leaves them to be treated as equally responsible as adults since the *via media* of reversing rather than abolishing the presumption, which would have expressly permitted the defence to prove that the child did not understand that what he had done was seriously wrong, was argued for in Parliament but not accepted by the government. Although the brief wording of s. 34 only expressly abolishes the rebuttable presumption in favour of the child, any arguments that s. 34 should be treated as having merely reversed the burden of proof, or that the concept of *doli incapax* survives in any other way for those who have reached the age of ten, have now been finally laid to rest by the House of Lords in *JTB* [2009] 1 AC 1310. (The concept is of course still applicable to subsequent trials of offences alleged to have been committed prior to the coming into force of s. 34 (30 September 1998) by persons aged between ten and 14 at the time of the offence, as is illustrated by *H* [2010] EWCA Crim 312.)

A3.73   The age of the accused, whether over or under 14, is clearly a factor to be taken into account in assessing the reasonableness of the accused's conduct under the defences of provocation or its replacement, loss of control (see **B1.24**), duress (*Bowen* [1997] 4 All ER 837 at **A3.38**) and arguably self-defence (see **A3.61**). In crimes requiring subjective recklessness and *a fortiori* intention, the age of the accused may also be a relevant factor in assessing whether the accused did in fact foresee what might seem to be (to an adult) the obvious consequences of his actions or whether the accused was aware of the relevant circumstances. Such considerations were perhaps less acute under the old law since children who lacked an understanding of the likely consequences or full circumstances of their actions were likely to argue first that the prosecution had not discharged the burden of rebutting the presumption of *doli incapax* but, in the absence of the rebuttable presumption, arguments based on lack of *mens rea* may need to be pressed into service more often. Similarly, if a child can be shown by the defence not to be of normal development for his age (proving normal development was previously a common means for the prosecution to reverse the presumption of *doli incapax*), this might possibly be brought within the partial defence of diminished responsibility on a murder charge (but see the discussion of 'developmental immaturity' at **B1.19**). Arguments such as these will turn on the precise *mens rea* to be proved for the individual offence or the terms of a particular defence.

Section A4 Parties to Offences

LIABILITY OF PRINCIPALS AND ACCESSORIES GENERALLY

Responsibility for a criminal offence may be incurred either as a principal offender or as an **A4.1** accessory. Liability as an accessory applies to all offences (including statutory ones) unless it is expressly excluded by statute (*Jefferson* [1994] 1 All ER 270). See s. 73 of the SOA 2003 at **B3.69** for an example of partial exclusion. A principal offender is the actual perpetrator of the offence, the person whose individual conduct satisfied the definition of the particular offence in question, whilst an accessory is one who aids, abets, counsels or procures the commission of the offence. For indictable offences, the Accessories and Abettors Act 1861, s. 8, provides that such an accessory 'shall be liable to be tried, indicted, and punished as a principal offender'. The MCA 1980, s. 44(1), is of similar effect as far as summary offences are concerned.

The distinction between an accessory and a principal offender is thus in many cases of little importance. Indeed a person charged as a principal may be convicted even though the real case against him was that he was an accessory, although it is preferable that the particulars of the offence be drawn 'in such a way as to disclose with greater clarity the real nature of the case that the accused has to answer' (per Lord Hailsham of St Marylebone in *DPP for Northern Ireland v Maxwell* [1978] 3 All ER 1140 at p. 1357D). If this is not done and if the prosecution do not make plain in presenting the case to the jury that liability as an accessory is one of the alleged bases of liability, it may be a misdirection for the judge to introduce it in summing-up (*Taylor* [1998] Crim LR 582 — contrast *Montague* [2013] EWCA Crim 1781 where, on the particular facts of the case, such a misdirection was not significant). However, as *Giannetto* [1997] 1 Cr App R 1 demonstrates, if the jury are unsure as to whether D was an accessory or the principal, they can still convict (of murder) provided that they are all agreed that he was responsible on one basis or, if not, on the other (see also **A1.40** and *Morton* [2003] EWCA Crim 1501, but contrast *Banfield* [2013] EWCA Crim 1394 where it was not clear whether A or B was the perpetrator and whilst it was possible the other was an accessory it could not be ruled out that one of them was acting alone and therefore neither could be convicted of murder). See **B1.73** for how this problem is dealt with in the context of causing death or serious physical harm to children or vulnerable adults in a domestic context.

The phrase 'aid, abet, counsel and procure' may be, and generally is, used as a whole even **A4.2** though the accused's conduct may be properly described only by one of the four constituent words (*Re Smith* (1858) 3 H & N 227). Partly for this reason, the precise meaning of each constituent word has not been authoritatively determined, but putting procuring on one side for a moment, the modern approach is to say that assistance or encouragement is what is required to bring a person within the meaning of the ancient formula — see, e.g., the decision in *Stringer* [2012] QB 160. Individual words are occasionally the subject of judicial discussion, as in *A-G's Ref (No. 1 of 1975)* [1975] QB 773, where the accused had laced the drinks of a friend with alcohol knowing that he would soon be driving home. As a result the friend drove with an excess quantity of alcohol in his body and was convicted as principal. The accused was then charged with aiding, abetting, counselling and procuring that offence but the trial judge took the view that, since there was not the usual shared intention or meeting of minds between the principal and alleged accessory, the accused could not be said to be an accessory. The Court of Appeal took the view that, whilst that might be right for aiding, abetting and counselling, procuring did not require any sort of conspiracy or common purpose and therefore the accused could properly have been convicted. The Court said (at p. 779F): 'To procure means to produce by endeavour' and added at p. 780B: 'You cannot procure an offence unless there is a causal link between what you do and the commission of the offence'.

A4.3   The reference to causation can however be misleading and it is the element of endeavour, intentionally trying (successfully) to bring about the offence which is arguably more important even in procuring. Certainly, other modes of complicity such as counselling do not require such a clear causal link (*Calhaem* [1985] QB 808, followed in *Luffman* [2008] EWCA Crim 1739); as long as the advice or encouragement of the accessory comes to the attention of the principal offender, it does not matter that he would have committed the offence anyway, even if not encouraged by the accessory (*A-G v Able* [1984] QB 795 at p. 812). Similarly in relation to what have come to be known as joint ventures, comments by the Court of Appeal in *Mendez* [2010] EWCA Crim 516 suggesting a stronger role for causation were subsequently explained in *Stringer* [2012] QB 160 where it was reiterated that 'but-for' causation is not required although there must be a connection between the accessory's actions and the acts of the principal. 'Joint enterprise' grounding so-called 'parasitic liability' clearly falls outside procuring since the whole point of these cases is that the principal has done something slightly different from the initial common purpose but the accessory is nonetheless responsible for the actual offence committed if it was within his contemplation. The accessory cannot be said to have caused the offence (in the procuring sense of intentionally securing an outcome which he set out to achieve), but it is the common purpose and shared understanding which renders the accessory complicit in the act which the principal has committed following the accessory's assistance or encouragement. These issues were discussed by the Supreme Court in *Gnango* [2012] 1 AC 827, where their lordships agreed with the Court of Appeal that on the facts it was not a case of parasitic liability since there was no joint enterprise to commit a limited affray to which the actual offence of murder could parasitically be attached. Lords Phillips and Judge commented (at [41]) in their judgment (with which Lord Wilson agreed) that it would be 'undesirable...if a practice developed of relying on the doctrine of parasitic accessory liability to charge with murder parties to an affray who had not themselves intended that it would result in serious injury'. This comment may prove significant for the future in limiting the number of cases where joint enterprise/parasitic liability is relied upon (the DPP subsequently issued guidance in December 2012 on the use of joint enterprise when charging: see www.cps.gov.uk/legal/h_to_k/joint_enterprise/index.html).

However, on the facts Lords Phillips, Wilson and Judge considered that there was a more straightforward joint enterprise to shoot and be shot at which did involve an intent to kill or cause GBH. It followed that D had encouraged P to shoot back at him with murderous intent and thus, when the shot by P missed D but hit and killed an innocent passer-by, by means of the doctrine of transferred *mens rea*, D was liable for straightforward aiding and abetting (i.e. encouragement) of a murder which was intended (and attempted) to be of D himself but which turned out to be of C, the passer-by. The facts of the case were highly unusual and the conviction of the accessory does not fit easily into a single theory of liability as is shown by the fact that Lord Clarke and Lord Brown preferred to base the conviction of D on liability as a principal rather than as an accessory. On this point there is much force in the dissenting judgment of Lord Kerr who could not see how D's actions could be said to have been a cause of the death of C who was killed by a shot voluntarily fired by P whose free voluntary and informed action broke any chain of causation that could lead back to D. As Lord Kerr also pointed out, the approach of Lord Clarke and Lord Brown is difficult to reconcile with the approach of the House of Lords to causation in *Kennedy (No. 2)* [2008] 1 AC 269, discussed at **A4.4**.

A4.4   Before the abolition (by the CLA 1967, s. 1) of the distinction between felonies and misdemeanours, it was necessary to distinguish, as far as felonies were concerned, between principals in the first degree (now simply principals), principals in the second degree (roughly corresponding to aiders and abettors, now simply accessories) and accessories before the fact (roughly counsellors and procurers, again now simply accessories). Such distinctions are today otiose and the only distinction which should ever need to be made is between a principal offender and an accessory.

In the light of the Accessories and Abettors Act 1861, s. 8, even this distinction will not often be of significance, the accessory's liability being equal to that of the principal. The availability of duress on a murder charge used to depend on whether the accused was in truth a principal or merely an accessory, but that anomalous rule did not survive the House of Lords' decision in *Howe* [1987] AC 417. The distinction between conduct constituting that of a principal and that of (at most) an accessory has however more recently resurfaced in another, but somewhat different, context in homicide. An example is where D assists a drug abuser to inject himself resulting in fatal (but unintended) consequences — see the cases discussed at **B1.61** culminating in *Kennedy (No. 2)* [2008] 1 AC 269. If D's role (such as performing or taking part in the act of injection) can be classified as a cause of death, he is guilty of manslaughter as a principal; if he is merely assisting or encouraging the act causing death (as it is now recognised is all that is involved in preparing and supplying a loaded syringe), he will not be guilty of manslaughter. The fact that the voluntary and informed act of another normally breaks the chain of causation and prevents a previous actor from being the principal is one of the main reasons that accessory liability is so important and significant (and forensically useful) in treating those who assisted or encouraged the offence as being equally guilty of it as the principal. Thus it *often* does not matter or need to be proved whether a person is principal or accessory, but it does matter in the *Kennedy* type scenario where it is only an offence for D to do something to *another* (D negligently causes V's death, D guilty of manslaughter as principal) but not for that other to do it *to himself* (assisted or encouraged by D, V freely chooses to do an act which negligently causes his *own* death, V commits not even the *actus reus* of an offence and there is therefore no offence to which D can be accessory). Aside from relatively unusual situations such as that outlined above (and see *Ferguson v Weaving* [1951] 1 KB 814 for a difference between principals and accessories in the quite different context of vicarious liability), the most important general distinction which remains between accessories and principals lies in the mental element required of an accessory.

THE MENTAL ELEMENT FOR ACCESSORIES

The *actus reus* of an accessory involves two concepts: (a) aiding, abetting, counselling and pro-   **A4.5**
curing (b) an offence. The *mens rea* can also be expected to relate to these two concepts. The mental element for an accessory is generally considerably narrower and more demanding than that required for the principal offender in that intention or knowledge rather than recklessness or negligence or any other less culpable state of mind is required. The classic statement of the *mens rea* for an accessory is that of Lord Goddard CJ in *Johnson v Youden* [1950] 1 KB 544 at p. 546 that: 'Before a person can be convicted of aiding and abetting the commission of an offence, he must at least know the essential matters which constitute that offence'. As the facts of the case demonstrate, in accordance with general principles, it is knowledge of the facts that counts not knowledge of the law, as was reiterated in *O'Neil v Gale* [2013] EWCA Civ 1554, where knowledge of the legislation which renders those facts criminal was not required.

The Requirement of Knowledge

The requirement of knowledge of the facts applies even where the principal offence is one of strict   **A4.6**
liability as in *Callow v Tillstone* (1900) 83 LT 411 where a vet negligently certified meat as sound and fit for sale, and a butcher was convicted of the strict-liability offence of exposing for sale meat which was unsound and unfit for human consumption. The vet's conviction for aiding and abetting was quashed since negligence was not sufficient for this form of liability even though the butcher's liability as principal offender was not dependent on proof of any degree of fault whatsoever.

The importance of this principle can be further seen in *Smith v Mellors* (1987) 84 Cr App R 279 where Mellors and Soar were both charged under the Road Traffic Act 1972, s. 6(1)(a) (driving with excess alcohol, now Road Traffic Act 1988, s. 5(1)(a)). The prosecution were unable to prove who was the driver and who was the passenger. Nor could they prove that each defendant was aware that the other was over the limit. The magistrates ruled that there was no case to answer. The Divisional Court affirmed their decision whilst pointing out that, in the light of the MCA 1980, s. 44 (see **A4.1**), it was not always necessary to determine who was the accessory and who the principal. However, it was necessary where, as in this case, there was a material difference between the liability of the principal and the accessory. The Road Traffic Act 1972, s. 6(1)(a), created an offence of strict liability for the principal but the accessory could be liable only if he knew the facts. Only if both knew that the other was over the limit could both be convicted without proof of who was driving. Presumably, if it is proved that one party had the requisite knowledge, he, though not the other, could be convicted since in that case he would be liable whether or not he was the driver. Croom-Johnson LJ stated (at p. 284), 'It might be that an aider and abettor would be an aider and abettor if he was simply reckless as to whether or not the driver had the requisite amount of alcohol in his blood'. Whilst this statement might find some support in the earlier case of *Carter v Richardson* [1974] RTR 314, the better view seems to be that recklessness is not sufficient. In *Giorgianni v The Queen* (1985) 156 CLR 473, the Australian High Court, having discussed at length the English authorities, held that recklessness was not sufficient for an accessory to an offence of causing death by culpable (reckless) driving. The owner of a lorry involved in a fatal crash was not guilty as accessory unless he knew or was wilfully blind to the brake defect in the lorry. In *Blakely v DPP* [1991] Crim LR 763, which was more concerned with intention to aid (see **A4.7**) than with knowledge of circumstances, the Divisional Court was reluctant to countenance recklessness as sufficient *mens rea* for complicity, at least in relation to counselling or procuring.

Intention to Aid

A4.7   Lord Goddard's statement in *Johnson v Youden* [1950] 1 KB 544 (see **A4.5**) that the accessory 'must at least know the essential matters which constitute the offence' is not, and does not purport to be, a complete definition of the mental element because, *inter alia*, it relates only to part (b) of the *actus reus* as set out in **A4.5**, i.e. the principal offence. It says nothing about the intention to 'aid, abet, counsel and procure'. As Devlin J put it in *National Coal Board v Gamble* [1959] 1 QB 11 (at p. 20):

> ... aiding and abetting is a crime that requires proof of *mens rea*, that is to say, of intention to aid as well as of knowledge of the circumstances.

However, as Devlin J went on to point out, at p. 23, intention to aid does not require that the accused's purpose or motive must be that the principal offence should be committed:

> If one man deliberately sells to another a gun to be used for murdering a third, he may be indifferent about whether the third man lives or dies and interested only in the cash profit to be made out of the sale, but he can still be an aider and abettor. To hold otherwise would be to negative the rule that *mens rea* is a matter of intent only and does not depend on desire or motive.

A4.8   Thus in *DPP for Northern Ireland v Lynch* [1975] AC 653 the accused's alleged opposition to the principal offence did not preclude a finding that he intended to aid. It is submitted that the question of intention to aid is now governed by the decisions in *Moloney* [1985] AC 905 and *Hancock* [1986] AC 455 discussed in **A2.4** and that where the accused does not act in order to assist or encourage the commission of an offence, but knows that his actions are extremely likely or virtually certain to have that result, then the question is one for the jury to infer whether or not he has the requisite intent. If *Woollin* [1999] AC 82 were to be applied beyond the context of the meaning of intention for murder, only foresight of a virtual certainty would entitle the jury to find intention. *Gillick v West Norfolk and Wisbech Area Health Authority* [1986] AC 112 is an example of a type of case where the uncertainties of the precise meaning of intention effectively confer a perhaps welcome discretion on whether to impose responsibility. That case concerned, *inter alia*, the question of whether a doctor giving contraceptive advice or treatment to a girl under the age of 16 could be liable as accessory to a subsequent offence of unlawful sexual intercourse committed by the girl's sexual partner. The House of Lords held that generally this would not be the case (the action was a civil one for a declaration) since the doctor would lack the necessary intention (even though he realised that his actions would facilitate such intercourse). One rationale for the decision would be that a jury would not infer intention in such circumstances if they thought that the doctor was acting in what he considered to be the girl's best interests (such situations are now expressly catered for in the SOA 2003, s. 73).

Similar reasoning could be applied to a troublesome group of cases involving the supply of articles for use in crime which the recipient already has some sort of civil right to receive. The general position seems to be that this is not aiding and abetting (see, e.g., *Lomas* (1913) 9 Cr App R 220 concerning the return of a jemmy to its owner) because the alleged accessory does not intend to aid the offence but rather merely to comply with his supposed civil-law duties. Critics of this general position rightly point out that it can hardly apply to a person returning a revolver to its owner knowing that he is then going to use it to carry out a murder. But here a jury probably would infer intention to aid from the accused's knowledge of the effects of his action, and the flexibility of the notion of intention enables an appropriate solution to be found to situations for which it is difficult to formulate precise rules in advance.

It is particularly important to stress the need for an intention to aid where the accused may not **A4.9** personally appreciate the natural and probable consequences of his action as in *Clarkson* [1971] 3 All ER 344 where there was 'at least the possibility that a drunken man with his self-discipline loosened by drink…might not intend that his presence should offer encouragement to rapers;…he might not realise that he was giving encouragement' (at p. 1406). The reference to intoxication underlines the fact that complicity normally requires intention rather than recklessness (*Blakely v DPP* [1991] Crim LR 763) and that, for the purposes of the *Majewski* rule (*DPP v Majewski* [1977] AC 443: see **A3.17**), complicity can be regarded as requiring specific intent.

The foregoing discussion was quoted approvingly in *Bryce* [2004] 2 Cr App R 592 at [63] where the Court of Appeal confirmed that an intention to assist (in the sense explained above) is required (although in many cases, as on the facts of *Bryce*, such an intention may be readily inferred from the voluntary performance of acts which obviously do in fact assist the principal offender, in the absence of a credible explanation from the accused as to why this was not his intention — see *Bryce* at [101]). The decision of the Supreme Court in *Gnango* [2012] 1 AC 827 (see **A4.3**) provides a further example of an (indirect) intention to aid and abet being sufficient, notwithstanding it not being D's purpose that the offence should successfully be carried out. D's actions in shooting at P, in pursuance of an agreement to shoot and be shot at, had the foreseen (virtually certain) effect of encouraging P to attempt to kill D even though D had no wish to be killed. Therefore D was guilty of encouraging the shots fired at himself and could be liable as accessory to the murder by P of a passer-by who was accidentally shot by a bullet intended for D.

THE SCOPE OF THE JOINT VENTURE

The Contemplation Test

The test of 'knowledge of the essential matters constituting the offence' needs some further **A4.10** elucidation since a strict requirement of knowledge is inappropriate or unworkable in certain situations, notably where the offence is to be committed in the future or by a person of whose precise intentions the accused cannot be certain in advance. A relatively simple case is where the accused knows that, for example, a burglary is to be committed and provides equipment to be used in the burglary. He is guilty even if he does not know of the precise time, date or place of the proposed offence. Provided that he knows the type of crime, i.e. that it will be a burglary, it does not matter that he does not know the details of the particular crime in the sense of a particular date at particular premises (*Bainbridge* [1960] 1 QB 129 esp. at pp. 133–4). In some cases an accused may be convicted even though he is not sure whether the offence is to be burglary or some other type of crime such as handling or robbery. In *Maxwell* [1978] 1 WLR 1363, the accused had driven his car so as to guide a following car out to a remote public house into which a bomb was thrown from the second car. He argued that since he did not know exactly what type of offence was to be committed (it was obviously a terrorist attack of some sort but it was unclear whether it was to be a bombing or a shooting) he did not know the essential matters constituting the offences with which he was charged (under the Explosive Substances Act 1883). Nevertheless, Lowry CJ upheld the conviction of the accused in relation to the bombing, saying (at pp. 1374–5):

> His guilt springs from the fact that he contemplates the commission of one (or more) of a number of crimes by the principal and he intentionally lends his assistance in order that such a crime will be committed....

> The relevant crime must be within the contemplation of the accomplice and only exceptionally would evidence be found to support the allegation that the accomplice had given the principal a completely blank cheque.

> [He] must...have contemplated the bombing of the Crosskeys Inn as not the only possibility but one of the most obvious possibilities among the jobs which the principals were likely to be undertaking.

Thus the test in this sort of case is not so much knowledge (the accused cannot 'know' things in advance) as contemplation. It is capable of application in a wide range of situations including:

> ...that of two persons who agree to rob a bank on the understanding, either express or implied from conduct (such as the carrying of a loaded gun by one person with the knowledge of the other), that violence *may* be resorted to. The accomplice knows, not that the principal *will* shoot the cashier, but that he may do so; and if the principal does shoot him, the accomplice will be guilty of murder. (Ibid.)

A4.11 This type of case has been the subject of a long line of authorities including the leading case of *Anderson* [1966] 2 QB 110, where the principal (Anderson) armed himself with a knife unknown to the accessory (Morris) who was nevertheless convicted of manslaughter (Anderson was convicted of murder). A five-judge Court of Criminal Appeal quashed Morris's conviction, Lord Parker CJ (at p. 118F–G) accepting as correct the following principles put forward on his behalf:

> ...where two persons embark on a joint enterprise, each is liable for the acts done in pursuance of that joint enterprise, ... that includes liability for unusual consequences if they arise from the execution of the agreed joint enterprise.

Thus Morris would have been responsible for the sort of attack he had contemplated (i.e. one without a knife) and if death had happened to result he would have been liable for manslaughter: 'but...if one of the adventurers goes beyond what has been tacitly agreed as part of the common enterprise, his co-adventurer is not liable for the consequences of that unauthorised act' (p. 118G). See *Mahmood* [1995] RTR 48 for a case where the accessory contemplated reckless driving but not the unusual form of reckless driving concerned, and was therefore not responsible for that driving or the consequences. In contrast in *Bristow* [2013] EWCA Crim 1540 each defendant did contemplate that the burglary might involve a rapid vehicular escape and their convictions for unlawful act manslaughter were upheld on the basis that they did all contemplate an unlawful act of this nature which was dangerous in the relevant sense and which actually occurred and caused death. The fact that the driver might have intended to kill or cause grievous bodily harm did not matter as it did not render the unlawful *act* fundamentally different from what was contemplated (see further **A4.22**).

A4.12 Contemplation of the *Mens Rea* of Murder The principles described at **A4.10** have been further developed and applied in a series of decisions commencing with that of the Privy Council in *Chan Wing-Siu v The Queen* [1985] AC 168. In *Chan Wing-Siu*, the three appellants had broken into the victim's flat armed with knives to commit robbery. In the course of the robbery, the victim was stabbed to death. The trial judge directed the jury: 'You may convict...of murder if you come to the conclusion...that the accused contemplated that either of his companions might use a knife to cause serious bodily injury on any one or more of the occupants of that flat'. The Privy Council upheld the convictions for murder based upon this direction.

Although some difficulties were initially experienced (*Barr* (1986) 88 Cr App R 362) in reconciling this approach (based on contemplation) with the test for intention laid down in *Moloney* [1985] AC 905 and *Hancock* [1986] AC 455 (see **A2.4**), the Court of Appeal in *Slack* [1989] QB 775 subsequently adopted a similar, though logically distinguishable, approach. The Court (at p. 781E–G) made the important point that the *mens rea* required of the accessory is not necessarily the same as that of the principal offender:

> A [the principal offender] must be proved to have intended to kill or do serious harm at the time he killed. B [the accessory] may not be present at the killing; he may be a distance away, for example, waiting in the get-away car; he may be in another part of the house; he may not know that A has killed; he may have hoped, and probably did hope, that A would not kill or do serious injury. If however as part of their joint plan it was understood between them expressly or tacitly that if necessary one of them would kill or do serious harm as part of their common enterprise, then B is guilty of murder.

In *Hyde* [1991] 1 QB 134 it was made clear that foresight of what the principal may do is sufficient *mens rea* for the accessory even if there is not actual agreement between them. This point was confirmed by the Privy Council in *Hui Chi-ming* [1992] 1 AC 34 and has now been put beyond all doubt by the House of Lords in *Powell* [1997] 4 All ER 545 where the certified question was as follows (at p. 967):   **A4.13**

> Is it sufficient to found a conviction for murder for a secondary party to a killing to have realised that the primary party might kill with intent to do so or must the secondary party have held such an intention himself?

The House of Lords answered, in accordance with previous Court of Appeal authorities, that the first part of the certified question was sufficient, i.e. the secondary party need only realise that the primary party might kill with intent to do so and the secondary party did not himself need to have the intention to kill; hence *Moloney* and *Hancock* did not apply directly to the *mens rea* of the secondary party. This substantive rule has also survived a challenge under the ECHR, Article 6, in *Concannon* [2002] Crim LR 213. It applies whatever the form of participation of the secondary party, whether it amounts to actual assistance or simply encouragement; for example, provided that the accessory realises that the principal may use a knife with intent to kill or cause grievous bodily harm, his participation in whatever form renders him liable for murder (*Jogee* [2013] EWCA Crim 1433).

As to what degree of foresight counts as contemplation, Lord Hutton in *English* [1997] 4 All ER 545 agreed with the Privy Council in *Chan Wing-Siu v The Queen* [1985] AC 168 that the realisation by the accessory of a fleeting risk which is then dismissed as altogether negligible is not sufficient, although the Court of Appeal in *Roberts* [1993] 1 All ER 583 said that to distinguish expressly between this and the continuing realisation of a real risk will, in most cases, be unnecessary, and would only serve to complicate directions and lead to confusion. Contemplation or foresight of a real or serious risk is clearly sufficient (provided that the crime actually committed is an incident of, and is in the course of, the common purpose: see the observations of the Court of Appeal in *Gnango* [2011] 2 All ER 129 at [68]) and it is immaterial whether the secondary party is present at the scene of the crime or lends assistance or encouragement in advance (*Rook* [1993] 2 All ER 955).   **A4.14**

Departures from the Contemplated Method   Reference must also be made to the House of Lords judgment in *English* [1997] 4 All ER 545, where the first certified question (at p. 968) was identical with that in *Powell* except that it expressly included, crucially as will be seen, a contemplated intention to cause grievous bodily harm. The House of Lords' answer to the certified question, including this alternative state of mind contemplated by the accessory, was made subject to the qualification that, where the particular weapon used by the principal or the manner of its use was different from that contemplated by the accessory, that may take the killing outside the scope of the joint venture and the accessory may not be liable. In *English*, the accessory contemplated the intentional infliction of grievous bodily harm with a wooden post but the principal used a knife which on the evidence the jury could have found was unknown and unforeseen by the accessory. The trial judge had told the jury in effect that they could   **A4.15**

convict, even if the accessory did not know of the knife, if he nevertheless knew that there was a substantial risk that the principal might cause grievous bodily harm with the wooden post. This part of the direction was held to be defective and the conviction for murder quashed.

Lord Hutton was anxious to make it clear, however, that a difference in the weapon used would not always exempt the accessory 'if the weapon used by the principal is different to, but as dangerous as, the weapon which the secondary party contemplated he might use…for example, if he foresaw that the primary party might use a gun to kill and the latter used a knife to kill, or vice versa' (at p. 981). This observation is clearly correct although it is submitted that one aspect of the reason is that in such a case, as formulated, the accessory contemplates an act done with intent to kill and that is precisely what the principal does, the difference in weapon being relatively immaterial. The more difficult case is where the accessory's contemplation is of an act done with intent to cause grievous bodily harm. It is clear now that in this situation the test is whether *the act* done by the principal (including the weapon used) is of a 'fundamentally different nature' to that contemplated by the accessory.

A4.16   The correct approach to these cases was further considered by the House of Lords in *Rahman* [2009] 1 AC 129 where it was said that there was no prescriptive formula for directing juries. The following restatement by Lord Brown in the House of Lords (at [68]) did however gain the express approval of a number of their lordships:

> If B realises (without agreeing to such conduct being used) that A may kill or intentionally inflict serious injury, but nevertheless continues to participate with A in the venture, that will amount to a sufficient mental element for B to be guilty of murder if A, with the requisite intent, kills in the course of the venture *unless (i) A suddenly produces and uses a weapon of which B knows nothing and which is more lethal than any weapon which B contemplates that A or any other participant may be carrying and (ii) for that reason A's act is to be regarded as fundamentally different from anything foreseen by B.* (The italicised words are designed to reflect the *English* qualification.)

The defence argument that in considering whether the principal's *act* (stabbing in this case) was fundamentally different from what was contemplated, the jury had to consider the possibility that the principal's *intention* might actually have been to kill rather than, as contemplated by the appellant, to cause grievous bodily harm, was rejected both by the Court of Appeal and the House of Lords in *Rahman*. Although in one sense this intention might make the principal's act more dangerous than the one contemplated by the accessory, it would unduly complicate an already highly technical area of law and further enlarge, to an inappropriate extent, the escape route provided by the 'fundamentally different' test. That the important question is whether the accessory foresaw what the principal might do as a possibility, rather than what his precise intentions were, was confirmed by the Court of Appeal in *Badza* [2009] EWCA Crim 2695; the crucial point in that case being that the accused knew that the principal had a knife and that he might use it in the course of their joint enterprise with intent sufficient for murder, whether in the form of an intent to kill or an intent to cause grievous bodily harm. It must not be lost sight of that this latter intent is the minimum that must be foreseen even if the actual act (e.g., the use of a knife) is foreseen although, as noted in *A (Joint Enterprise)* [2010] 2 Cr App R 369, once the use of a weapon such as a knife is foreseen, finding that there was foresight of an intention to cause at least grievous bodily harm will not normally be a large additional step for the jury to take. However, the Court of Appeal in *Ellis* [2013] EWCA Crim 2554 has emphasised that this does not mean that this additional step or inference is inevitable in all cases where the use of the knife is contemplated or that directions to juries should not make clear that the accessory must have contemplated the murderous intent with which the knife might be used. Furthermore 'the failure to include the requisite knowledge of the stabber's intention, that is to say knowledge or realisation that the stabber intended to kill or cause really serious harm', constituted a defect in the direction to the jury, which on the facts of the case rendered the convictions for murder unsafe.

Notwithstanding the need to be satisfied that the accessory contemplated the principal acting with the *mens rea* for murder, if the *act* contemplated by the accessory is fundamentally different to that done by the principal, then in accordance with *English* there can be no conviction of the accessory. Thus in *Mendez* [2010] 3 All ER 231 the directions to the jury had unduly undermined the difference between the knife used by the principal and the weapons contemplated by the accessory, which were altogether less life-threatening. The accessory's conviction for murder had therefore to be quashed.

There was much discussion by their lordships in *Rahman* of the case of *Gamble* [1989] NI 268, **A4.17** where the use of a gun to knee-cap was contemplated but the actual cause of death was the use of a knife to cut the victim's throat. In *English*, Lord Hutton had regarded the acquittal of the accessories on murder charges to have been correct and appeared also to have been of the view that, for example, the use of a gun to shoot in the head would have been a fundamentally different act to shooting in the knee. A number of their lordships were uneasy about this (see the discussion by Lord Neuberger at [93]) and not all were convinced that even the use of the knife was sufficient to take the acts of the principal outside the type of act contemplated by the accessories. It would appear that the question of whether a weapon is 'more lethal than any weapon' contemplated, and whether an act is of a type which is fundamentally different to that contemplated by the accessory, will in practice fall to be decided by juries. However, in *Lewis* [2010] EWCA Crim 496, it was emphasised that there is no need to complicate a complex murder trial unduly with an *English* direction if there is only a theoretical possibility of fundamental difference, e.g., where all parties foresaw a severe beating with fists or kicking.

In *A (Joint Enterprise)* the point was made that it must not be lost sight of that for D to be guilty of murder on the basis of being an accessory to a joint venture the jury have to be satisfied that at least one other person in the joint venture, whether identified or not, was guilty of murder (i.e. caused the death with intent at least to cause grievous bodily harm). In some cases, e. g., where obviously lethal weapons have been used, this may not be difficult to prove, but in other cases (of which A was one) where the common purpose is to administer a beating, it may not be so obvious and the jury must be satisfied that there was a murder committed by someone as principal (i.e. that an act causing death was done by someone who at least intended to cause grievous bodily harm rather than any lesser harm). Otherwise manslaughter would be the only principal offence to which D could be an accessory.

Divergence of *Mens Rea*—Residual Liability for Manslaughter (or Lesser Offence) Difficult **A4.18** questions have arisen where the difference between the two parties lies not so much in the act or weapon contemplated but more in the type of *mens rea*, i.e. the accessory does not contemplate even the minimum degree of *mens rea* (e.g., intention to cause grievous bodily harm or to kill) with which the principal acts. The accessory is clearly not liable for the offence committed by the principal (e.g., murder), but does the accessory remain liable for the consequences of the principal's act by means of a lesser crime according to his own *mens rea* (e.g., manslaughter)? The fundamental question is whether what was done by the principal is within the scope of the joint venture contemplated by the accessory. The principal's *mens rea* will in some cases change the nature of his act and take it outside the joint venture just as much as if he had suddenly produced a weapon unforeseen by the accessory. However, in other cases, the fact that the principal does precisely the act contemplated by the accessory but with the *mens rea* for a more serious offence will not change the nature of the act nor take it outside the scope of the joint venture.

The above argument was accepted by the Court of Appeal in Northern Ireland in *Gilmour* [2000] 2 Cr App R 407, where the following hypothetical (posed in this work since the 1996 edition) was cited with approval by Sir Robert Carswell CJ:

> Suppose P and A agree that P will post a specific incendiary device to V, A contemplating only superficial injuries to V when he opens it but P foreseeing and hoping that the injuries will be serious or fatal. If V is killed as a result, P will clearly be guilty of murder, A is clearly not guilty of murder as an accessory but should be guilty of manslaughter because the act done by P is precisely what was envisaged. The fact that P happens also to have the *mens rea* of murder is irrelevant because it does not change the nature of the act that he does or the manner in which he does it.

The Court of Appeal decided that this was the correct principle to apply in *Gilmour*, where the accessory drove the principals to a housing estate where they threw a petrol bomb into a house causing a fierce fire in which three young boys died. Although the principals were guilty of murder as they had an intention to kill, unknown to the accessory who, in the view of the Court of Appeal, did not even contemplate an intention to cause grievous bodily harm, the accessory could nevertheless be guilty of manslaughter since he knew about the petrol bomb and the principals had 'carried out the very deed' contemplated by him.

A4.19   Whilst the Court of Appeal's endorsement of the hypothetical posed above is welcome, the facts of *Gilmour* are not necessarily completely analogous with the example which is of the agreed use of a 'specific' incendiary device. In *Gilmour* the petrol bomb was of an unusually large size which is why the principals could be inferred to have intended to kill. The accessory was not specifically aware of its unusually large size which is why the Court of Appeal inferred he contemplated only a blaze causing damage, fear and intimidation rather than serious injury. If this was so, was the throwing of an unusually large bomb the 'very deed' contemplated by the accessory? Possibly not, but as against that the accessory did see the bomb glistening in the hand of the principal after they arrived at the estate and, at least at that stage, contemplated the throwing of that particular bomb. It does not appear to have been so large that it was beyond the range of his contemplation despite the fact that his lack of specific or detailed knowledge of its size meant that one could not infer that he was aware of the principals' intention to kill (or to cause grievous bodily harm).

A4.20   **Fundamentally Different Acts**   Suppose now, in contrast to the incendiary device hypothetical, that P and A agree that P shall assault V with an iron bar, A contemplating that P will act only with intent to cause actual bodily harm as opposed to grievous bodily harm. If P uses the bar with intent to kill or cause grievous bodily harm, there must come a point where P's intent changes the nature of the assault on V and the manner in which he does it (e.g., in the number or severity of the blows) so as to take what he does outside the scope of the joint venture. *Stewart* [1995] 3 All ER 159 seems to be a case where the Court of Appeal, perhaps somewhat harshly, took the view that that particular line had not been crossed, that the accessory knew that an iron bar might be used and that the actual manner of its use was not beyond the scope of the joint venture. The point was not specifically put to the jury, but it is submitted that the best approach would be to ask the jury to consider whether the principal's act (causing death) *and the manner of its doing* was within the contemplation of the accessory and thus within the scope of the joint venture (cf. the reference to 'the manner in which a particular weapon is used' at the end of Lord Hutton's speech in *English*). Depending on the answer to this question, the accessory may or may not be liable for the consequences of the act even though the principal's *mens rea* makes him liable for a more serious offence such as murder. See *Roberts and Day* [2001] EWCA Crim 1594 for another example of the accessory being liable for manslaughter even though the principal did the act with sufficient *mens rea* for murder. *Roberts and Day* was discussed with approval in *A-G's Ref (No. 3 of 2004)* [2005] EWCA Crim 1882 (at [61]) as:

> ...authority for the proposition that the failure to 'foresee [that] a murderous state of mind would be harboured by his fellows' does not, of itself, mean that what the primary party did was outside the scope of the joint enterprise. However, as Laws LJ made clear, in his example, the participants all foresaw the same kind of violence being inflicted on their victim, let it be punching with the possibility of kicking to follow. One could put it another way. What happened was (so a jury would inevitably find) not fundamentally different from what [D] had foreseen might occur.

A4.21   *Gilmour* [2000] 2 Cr App R 407 (see **A4.18**) was not cited or discussed either in *Roberts and Day* or *A-G's Ref (No. 3 of 2004)* but the principle is the same — see further the discussion in the commentary to *Roberts and Day* at [2001] Crim LR 984. The principle was applied in *D* [2005] EWCA 1981 where the Court of Appeal stated (at [38]):

> It is clear from the Court's decision in *Attorney General's Reference No. 3* that *the critical issue* on the question of whether the actions of the principal in causing the death of the victim were outwith the

scope of the joint venture involving the secondary party, *is whether those actions were fundamentally different to what was contemplated.* (Emphasis added.)

The manslaughter verdict was, however, quashed on the separate issue of withdrawal from the joint enterprise. The difficult factual issue in all these cases will be whether, in the words of Gage LJ, the 'actions…contemplated were precisely the actions which caused death' or, as the same idea was put by Carswell CJ in *Gilmour*, whether the principals had 'carried out the very deed' contemplated by the accessory, as opposed to doing an act which was fundamentally different.

In *Yemoh* [2009] EWCA Crim 930, the Court of Appeal took a restrictive approach to this ques-   **A4.22**
tion and considered it to be implicit in the decision of the House of Lords in *Rahman* [2009] 1 AC
129 (see **A4.16**) that a less than murderous state of mind on the part of the accessory, in relation to
the type of injury to be inflicted with a knife which the accessory contemplated might be used by
the principal, did not mean that the act done with the knife was fundamentally different. Thus if P
killed with a knife intending to kill or cause grievous bodily harm (and was thus guilty of murder),
whereas D only contemplated the knife being used to cause a less than serious injury, D was properly convicted of manslaughter and the act was not fundamentally different on the grounds of the
difference in the mental states of P and D. In *Carpenter* [2012] QB 722 the Court of Appeal has
reiterated this approach and confirmed that the trial judge is right in such cases to leave the alternative verdict of manslaughter to the jury. Comments made in *Mendez* [2010] 3 All ER 231 about the
unavailability of a manslaughter verdict in certain cases did not affect this principle since *Mendez*
was 'directed to a case where use of a knife was not foreseen, rather than to a case where use of a
knife was foreseen but the secondary party did not share or foresee the intention with which it was
used'. Notwithstanding the decisions in *Yemoh* and *Carpenter* on their own facts, there surely must
come a point in principle where a contemplated intention (e.g., to use a knife only to scratch) is so
relatively trivial that the murderous use of the knife by P is quite outside what D contemplated and
for the consequences of which D should not be liable, (a jury might find), even in manslaughter.

LIABILITY OF ACCESSORY WHERE THERE IS NO PRINCIPAL

A person can be liable as an accessory even though the principal offender cannot be identified   **A4.23**
or has been acquitted in a previous trial (*Hui Chi-ming* [1992] 1 AC 34) or even earlier in the
same trial (*Hughes* (1860) Bell CC 242), although in this latter case such a result would only be
justified where there was evidence admissible against the accessory but not against the alleged
principal (*Humphreys* [1965] 3 All ER 689). See also *Petch* [2005] 2 Cr App R 657, where the
alleged principal was allowed to plead to a lesser offence in a subsequent trial. Where the same
evidence is admissible against both it would normally be inconsistent for the same jury to acquit
the principal and yet convict the accessory of a crime which it has already found has not been
committed by the principal.

Liability where Principal has Complete Defence

In a number of cases the Court of Appeal has upheld convictions of accessories whilst recognising   **A4.24**
that the principal offender would have a valid defence. Thus in *Bourne* (1952) 36 Cr App R 125,
a husband's conviction for aiding and abetting his wife to commit buggery with a dog was upheld
even though it was recognised that the wife could not have been convicted as principal (she was
not in fact charged) since she was acting under duress from her husband. In *Cogan* [1976] QB
217, Leak's terrified wife had intercourse with Cogan (who had allegedly been told by Leak that
she would consent) because of her fear of her husband. Cogan's conviction for rape was quashed
because the jury had been told, contrary to the law at the time, that his alleged belief that Mrs Leak
was consenting had to be reasonable whereas it was possible that his belief was genuinely held,
but Leak's conviction as accessory was upheld. The Court of Appeal pointed out (at p. 223) that:

> …one fact is clear — the wife had been raped. Cogan had had sexual intercourse with her without
> her consent. The fact that Cogan was innocent of rape because he believed that she was consenting
> does not affect the position that she was raped.

The court then pointed out (at pp. 223–4) that Leak could have been guilty as a principal acting through an innocent agent:

> Had Leak been indicted as a principal offender, the case against him would have been clear beyond argument. Should he be allowed to go free because he was charged with 'being aider and abettor to the same offence'? If we are right in our opinion that the wife had been raped (and no one outside a court of law would say that she had not been), then the particulars of offence accurately stated what Leak had done, namely, he had procured Cogan to commit the offence.

A4.25 There has been some debate over the precise principle involved in these cases but everyone agrees that the result is just. To say that the liability is really that of a principal acting through an innocent agent can cause problems where the accused lacks some characteristic essential for liability as a principal, e.g., if in *Cogan* it had been a woman, rather than Mrs Leak's husband, who had terrorised her into submitting to intercourse. The definition of rape, even in the SOA 2003, s. 1, still requires it in effect to be committed by a man, whereas there is no problem in convicting a person as accessory to an offence which he or she cannot commit as principal (see *Ram* (1893) 17 Cox CC 609, woman as accessory to rape). Thus it is probably preferable to adopt the principle that an accessory can be liable provided that there is the *actus reus* of the principal offence even if the principal offender is entitled to be acquitted because of some defence personal to himself.

It may well be, however, that this principle is limited to cases where the accessory has procured the *actus reus* (i.e. has caused it to be committed as was the case in both *Bourne* and *Cogan*). This would also be consistent with the position stated above (see **A4.1**) that procuring does not need a common intention between the accessory and the principal whereas other forms of aiding and abetting generally do. If the principal lacks the *mens rea* of the offence there can hardly be a common intention that it should be committed, but this is not required for procuring.

The above two paragraphs were specifically approved by the Court of Appeal in *Millward* [1994] Crim LR 527 as correctly stating the law. The accessory in that case was convicted on the basis of procuring the offence of causing death by reckless driving even though the actual driver (his employee) did not know of the defect in the vehicle and was not therefore personally reckless. The case is not an easy one in which to apply the current principles because of the peculiar difficulties in defining the *actus reus* of (causing death by) reckless driving which was nevertheless, in the view of the Court of Appeal, to be found in 'the taking of the vehicle in the defective condition on to the road so as to cause the death of the little boy'; the accessory, 'being aware of the defects, . . . had procured the offence by the giving of instructions to . . . his employee'. *Millward* was approved in *Wheelhouse* [1994] Crim LR 756 and was followed in *DPP v K and B* [1997] 1 Cr App R 36, where two girls were convicted of procuring the rape of another teenage girl by an unknown boy even though the boy may not have had the *mens rea* of rape and in any event had to be assumed not to be responsible under the rebuttable presumption of *doli incapax* (abolished by the CDA 1998, s. 34). It would apparently have been different if the boy had been shown to be under the age of ten, although the logic behind this last conclusion is not particularly compelling. For further support for the *Cogan* principle as being consistent with the principles now applicable to encouraging or assisting under the SCA 2007 (esp. s. 47(5)(a)(iii): see **A5.13**), see *Watkins* [2010] EWCA Crim 2349 where, however, the principle could not be applicable on the facts on any reasonable reading of the evidence.

A4.26 Of course, if not even the *actus reus* is committed there can be no liability. See *Kenning* [2009] QB 221 for a simple illustration and confirmation of this basic proposition and of the related rule that there can be no liability for attempting (or it seems, conspiring) to aid and abet. As regards *Millward*, the situation would now be governed by the offence of causing death by dangerous rather than reckless driving, as is illustrated by *Loukes* [1996] 1 Cr App R 444. Under the relevant version of the new offence the test of whether a person is driving dangerously is satisfied if 'it would be obvious to a competent and careful driver that driving the vehicle in its current state would be dangerous' (Road Traffic Act 1988, s. 2A(2)). If it would not be so obvious *to the driver*, and the driver is acquitted on that ground (as in *Loukes*) then, according to the Court of

Appeal in that case, there is not even the *actus reus* as no one has driven the vehicle dangerously. Therefore, the person responsible for maintaining the vehicle and sending it out on the road cannot be liable even as an accessory, a result described by the Court of Appeal as an 'injustice'.

The situation in *Thornton v Mitchell* [1940] 1 All ER 339, in which a bus driver was acquitted of driving without due care and attention, was somewhat simpler and clearer. The driver had had to rely on signals from his conductor in reversing the bus. Because of the conductor's negligence, two pedestrians were injured, one of them fatally. The conductor's conviction for aiding and abetting had to be quashed because clearly there was no principal offence of driving without due care to which he could be accessory. The driver had driven *with* due care rather than without it, so there was not even the *actus reus* of that offence. On the other hand, there was the *actus reus* of homicide (the causing of the death of the pedestrian). It may be that the conductor could have been liable for manslaughter if his negligence were sufficiently gross, though only on the basis that the conductor was the principal (whose own conduct caused the death) since liability as an accessory requires subjective fault rather than negligence (see **A4.6**).

Liability where Principal Liable Only for Lesser Offence

An analogous problem to that described in **A4.24** arises where there are two or more offences **A4.27** which share the same *actus reus*, e.g., murder and manslaughter, or the offences under the OAPA 1861, ss. 18 and 20. If the principal offender commits the *actus reus* but with only the *mens rea* for the less serious of the two possible offences, can the accessory nonetheless be convicted of the more serious offence if he has sufficient *mens rea*? The Court of Appeal in *Richards* [1974] QB 776 appeared to make the answer depend on whether the accessory was present at the scene of the crime or not. However, this case almost certainly no longer represents the law following the House of Lords' decision in *Howe* [1987] AC 417, where it was indicated that *Richards* should not be followed (see at pp. 436B and 457–8) and having regard to *Millward*, where it was immaterial that the procurer was not present. The issue cannot be regarded as finally settled as the question certified for the House in *Howe* was in the following terms:

> Can one who incites or procures by duress another to kill or to be a party to a killing be convicted of murder if that other is acquitted by reason of duress?

This differs from the *Richards* question in that (a) the alleged principal is not guilty of *any* crime and (b) his defence is duress rather than lack of *mens rea*. In fact the certified question in *Howe* really raises the same question as in *Bourne* (1952) 36 Cr App R 125 and the affirmative answer given by the House of Lords to the question can be regarded as confirmation of that decision. It would be extremely odd if an accessory could be convicted where the principal is acquitted altogether but could not be convicted if the principal happens to be guilty of some lesser offence. *Richards* can perhaps safely be regarded as no longer stating the law. However, just as with the principle following from *Bourne* and *Cogan*, it may be that the *mens rea* of the accessory can only be linked with the *actus reus* of the principal where the accessory can be said to have procured the *actus reus*.

Such a limitation, however, would not apply to the Homicide Act 1957, s. 2(4), whereby. 'The fact that one party to a killing is by virtue of this section [diminished responsibility] not liable to be convicted of murder shall not affect the question whether the killing amounted to murder in the case of any other party to it'. In other words, an accessory with sufficient *mens rea* can be convicted of murder even though the principal offender is convicted only of manslaughter because of diminished responsibility or, by virtue of the CAJA 2009, s. 54(8), because of loss of control.

MISCELLANEOUS ISSUES

Presence at the Scene of the Crime: Omissions

Neither mere presence at the scene of a crime nor a failure to prevent an offence will gener-   **A4.28** ally give rise to liability. However, presence at the scene of a crime is *capable* of constituting encouragement (see *Jefferson* [1994] 1 All ER 270 for an example and contrast *Coney* (1882) 8 QBD 534 — spectators at illegal prize fight, conviction quashed since jury directed that presence was *conclusive* evidence of encouragement and similarly see *L v CPS* [2013] EWHC 4127 (Admin)). If the accused is present in pursuance of a prior agreement with the principal, that will normally amount to aiding and abetting, but if the accused is present only accidentally then he must know that his presence is actually encouraging the principal(s) (see *Allan* [1965] 1 QB 130, in which it was held that a secret intention to join in if required was not of itself sufficient); there must be both actual encouragement and also awareness of that fact (*Allan* and *Tate* [1993] Crim LR 538). *Wilcox v Jeffery* [1951] 1 All ER 464 was a case where there was ample evidence to draw the inference of intentional encouragement from the presence of a spectator at an illegal saxophone performance (by an American forbidden to take employment in this country). The accused had not only paid for a ticket at the performance (thus his presence was not accidental) but had reported the arrival of the American at the airport in his magazine, *Jazz Illustrated*, and subsequently wrote a laudatory review of the concert. In contrast, in *Willett* [2010] EWCA Crim 1620, mere presence in a car which was deliberately driven over a person blocking its route was not of itself sufficient to constitute encouragement by the passenger of the murder committed by the driver. The Privy Council in *Robinson v The Queen* [2011] UKPC 3 reiterated (at [14]) the importance of making it clear to juries 'that mere approval of (ie "assent" to, or "concurrence" in) the offence by a bystander who gives no assistance, does not without more amount to aiding… [and] that the communication of willingness to give active assistance is a minimum requirement'.

A4.29 Where the accused is present and has both the right and ability to control the principal offender, his failure to exercise that right of control may make him liable as an accomplice. Thus in *Rubie v Faulkner* [1940] 1 KB 571 a learner driver was convicted of driving without due care and attention in that he overtook on a bend, and the defendant who was supervising him was convicted of aiding and abetting him by failing to exercise his right of control. Similarly, in *Tuck v Robson* [1970] 1 All ER 1171, a publican was held liable for aiding and abetting his customers to commit the offence of drinking after hours by failing to collect the customers' glasses or to eject them from the premises. See also *National Coal Board v Gamble* [1959] 1 QB 11, in which Slade J said: 'Mere passive acquiescence is sufficient only, I think, where the alleged aider and abettor has the power to control the offender *and is actually present when the offence is committed*' (emphasis added). Presence in this sort of case is arguably significant not only as evidence of encouragement but also as evidence that the accused has the knowledge that the offence is being committed and the opportunity to exercise control. In *J.F. Alford Transport Ltd* [1997] 2 Cr App R 326, the convictions of managers of a company for the offence of aiding and abetting the making of false tachograph records by the company's drivers were quashed because there was no evidence of knowledge in relation to any specific count. If such knowledge could have been proved, irrespective it was said of whether the accused was present when the offence was committed, the ability to control the action of the offender coupled with a decision to refrain from doing so would have been sufficient. Proof of encouragement and of knowledge of the facts may however be difficult to achieve where the accused is not present.

Withdrawal

A4.30 There is often an interval between the act of the accessory and the completion of the offence by the principal offender. In some circumstances, a change of heart by the accessory coupled with steps to withdraw from participation in the offence can remove his responsibility for the completed offence (although he may remain liable for inchoate offences). Precisely what is required for an effective withdrawal will vary from case to case. It may depend on how imminent the completed offence is at the time of the attempted withdrawal by the accomplice and also on the nature of assistance and encouragement already given by the accessory. Thus in *Becerra* (1975) 62 Cr App R 212, A1 gave A2 a knife to use if they were disturbed during the course of a burglary. When A1 heard the tenant coming he called to A2: 'There's a bloke coming. Let's go' and jumped out of a window and fled. A2, however, stabbed and killed the tenant. Both A1 and A2 were convicted of murder. A1's application for leave to appeal was refused since, according to Roskill LJ at p. 219 (emphasis added):

> ...if [he] wanted to withdraw *at that stage*, he would have to 'countermand', to use the word that is used in some of the cases or 'repent' to use another word so used, in some manner vastly different and vastly more effective than merely to say 'Come on, let's go' and go out through the window.

Similarly, leave to appeal against a conviction for murder was refused in *Baker* [1994] Crim LR 444, where D inflicted three knife wounds, passed the knife to another, saying 'I'm not doing it', moved a few feet away and turned his back whilst others inflicted further wounds: the Court of Appeal considered that this constituted far from unequivocal notice that D was wholly disassociating himself from the entire enterprise. The words were quite capable of meaning no more than 'I will not myself strike any more blows'.

In *Becerra*, the court left open the question whether it was necessary to take all reasonable steps to prevent the commission of the crime which he had agreed the others should commit. As a minimum however, the accessory must communicate his intention to withdraw to the other parties; it is not sufficient merely to fail to turn up as arranged (*Rook* [1993] 2 All ER 955). Such communication was found to be a sufficient withdrawal from a proposed burglary on the facts of *Whitefield* (1983) 79 Cr App R 36. The failure of the trial judge to put the defence of withdrawal to the jury was one of the grounds for the Court of Appeal quashing the conviction of Derek Bentley for murder, 45 years after he was hanged, following a reference by the Criminal Cases Review Commission (*Bentley* [1999] Crim LR 330).

In *Mitchell* (1999) 163 JP 75, the Court of Appeal drew a distinction between pre-planned and **A4.31** spontaneous violence. With the latter, the issue was not whether there had been communication of withdrawal but whether the original joint venture was still continuing at the time of the principal's act. *Mitchell* was followed in *O'Flaherty* [2004] 2 Cr App R 315, where the question was 'whether a particular defendant disengaged before the fatal injury or injuries were caused'. Further illustrations of these principles, whereby continuing participation in a joint enterprise is found not to have been curtailed and thus extends to subsequent fatal assaults committed by others, can be found in *Mitchell* [2009] 1 Cr App R 438 and *Campbell* [2009] EWCA Crim 50.

Victims Not Regarded as Accessories

Where a statutory offence is designed to protect a particular class of persons, a member of that **A4.32** class, i.e. a 'victim' of the offence, cannot be convicted as accessory even though the offence takes place with his voluntary assistance. The principle is most likely to arise in the context of sexual offences where the offence takes place despite the victim's consent. The classic illustration is *Tyrrell* [1894] 1 QB 710, in which it was held that a girl under 16 could not be guilty of aiding and abetting an offence of unlawful carnal knowledge of her since the offence was created for the protection of the girl (see now the SOA 2003, s. 9, for the modern offence). The principle can sometimes rebound so that it results in the acquittal of some other party who is not a victim, as in *Whitehouse* [1977] QB 868 where a father was acquitted of inciting his 15-year-old daughter to commit incest with him. The girl was regarded as within the class of persons the offence was designed to protect and if the girl herself could not be liable, even as an accessory, her father could not be liable for inciting her to do something which was not a crime. A special offence of incitement in these particular circumstances was subsequently created by the CLA 1977, s. 54 (see now the SOA 2003, s. 26, at **B3.155**). The exempted 'victim' rule is based on the implied intention of Parliament where legislation is designed for the protection of a particular class of persons. The Supreme Court in *Gnango* [2012] 1 AC 827 held that there was no warrant for a common-law extension of the rule so as to exempt victims in any wider sense and that the principle certainly had no application so as to exempt from accessory liability a putative 'victim' who had encouraged the principal offender to shoot at him where the bullet had hit and killed an innocent third party.

Section A5　Inchoate Offences

INCITEMENT

Abolition of the Common-law Offence

A5.1　The common-law offence of incitement was abolished by the SCA 2007, s. 59, with effect from 1 October 2008 (Serious Crime Act 2007 (Commencement No. 3) Order 2008 (SI 2008 No. 2504)) and is supplanted by inchoate offences created by that Act. These are examined at **A5.3** *et seq.* A number of statutory offences of incitement or solicitation nevertheless survive, notably under the OAPA 1861, s. 4 (solicitation of murder: see **B1.131**); the Official Secrets Act 1920, s. 7 (see **B9.18**, **B9.24**, **B9.30** and **B9.35**), and the Misuse of Drugs Act 1971, s. 19 (see **B19.95**). For detailed consideration of the common-law offence, see the 2009 edition of this work at **A5.1** *et seq.*, and see also *Jones* [2010] 3 All ER 1186.

References to offences of 'incitement' in a number of older statutes such as the CJA 1993 and the Sexual Offences (Conspiracy and Incitement) Act 1996 must now be construed as references to the new offences which have replaced it (SCA 2007, s. 63(1)), but this is true only if the statute in question is one of those listed in sch. 6, part 1. Further consequential amendments are contained in sch. 6, part 2. As to transitional provisions, see **A5.2**.

Transitional Arrangements

A5.2　Prosecutions may still be brought at common law in respect of any acts of incitement committed 'wholly or partly' before that date (SCA 2007, sch. 13, para. 5). Under para. 5(2):

> . . .an offence is partly committed before commencement if—
> (a)　a relevant event occurs before commencement; and
> (b)　another relevant event occurs on or after commencement.

A 'relevant event' is any act or other event (including any consequence of an act) proof of which is required for conviction of the offence (para. 5(3)).

Where it is impossible to prove whether conduct inciting or encouraging the commission of an offence occurred before or after 1 October 2008, sch. 13, para. 6 provides that it must be presumed to have occurred *before* that date.

ENCOURAGING OR ASSISTING CRIME: SERIOUS CRIME ACT 2007

General

A5.3　The SCA 2007, part 2, creates three inchoate offences that supplanted the common-law offence of incitement with effect from 1 October 2008. They overlap with, but do not supplant, some older statutory offences of incitement, such as solicitation of murder (see **B1.131**) and there is some further overlap with the rules governing secondary participation in substantive offences (see **A4**).

The most obvious difference between the new and old law is that it is now an offence to provide assistance to a potential offender, even if he does not go on to commit the anticipated offence, but there are many other differences. The new offences are supplemented by a 'reasonableness defence' (SCA 2007, s. 50) and by complex interpretative, evidential, procedural, limitational, jurisdictional, consequential and sentencing provisions, spread over 18 sections and two schedules.

The three new offences are: intentionally encouraging or assisting an offence (s. 44); encouraging or assisting an offence, believing it will be committed (s. 45); and encouraging or assisting offences, believing one or more will be committed (s. 46). These offences share certain common elements.

Actus Reus Elements Common to Offences under Part 2

In respect of each offence under the SCA 2007, part 2, D must merely do an act that is *capable*   **A5.4** of encouraging or assisting the commission of an offence (or in the case of s. 46, one or more offences) by another person or persons. It does not matter for this purpose whether any 'anticipated offence' is ever committed by the other person(s) (s. 49(1)) nor does it matter whether anyone was in fact assisted or encouraged by D's act. If the anticipated offence is indeed committed, a more appropriate charge against D may well be one of complicity in that offence (see **A4**).

By s. 65, D's act may take a number of different forms, including a course of conduct or a failure to discharge a duty; and it may also involve making threats (cf. *Race Relations Board v Applin* [1973] QB 815; *Evans* [1986] Crim LR 470). By s. 52 and sch. 4, an act committed abroad may suffice if certain jurisdictional requirements are satisfied, as may an act that is capable of encouraging or assisting the commission of an offence abroad (see **A5.33**); and a single act may give rise to liability under more than one of the three offence-creating provisions (s. 49(3)).

Serious Crime Act 2007, ss. 65 to 67   **A5.5**

65.—(1) A reference in this Part to a person's doing an act that is capable of encouraging the commission of an offence includes a reference to his doing so by threatening another person or otherwise putting pressure on another person to commit the offence.

(2) A reference in this Part to a person's doing an act that is capable of encouraging or assisting the commission of an offence includes a reference to his doing so by—

    (a) taking steps to reduce the possibility of criminal proceedings being brought in respect of that offence;

    (b) failing to take reasonable steps to discharge a duty.

(3) But a person is not to be regarded as doing an act that is capable of encouraging or assisting the commission of an offence merely because he fails to respond to a constable's request for assistance in preventing a breach of the peace.

66. If a person (D1) arranges for a person (D2) to do an act that is capable of encouraging or assisting the commission of an offence, and D2 does the act, D1 is also to be treated for the purposes of this Part as having done it.

67. A reference in this Part to an act includes a reference to a course of conduct, and a reference to doing an act is to be read accordingly.

Whether D's act was or was not 'capable' of encouraging or assisting E to commit a crime must   **A5.6** ordinarily be a question of fact for the court or jury. At common law D could not 'incite' E unless E was aware of D's words or acts (*Ransford* (1874) 13 Cox CC 9; *Krause* (1902) 66 JP 121), but there is no such requirement in respect of offences under ss. 44 to 46 (see s. 65). Many inadvertent acts or omissions are capable of encouraging or assisting the commission of an offence, but *mens rea* must also be proved. No offence will be committed by an employee who genuinely forgets to set a burglar alarm when he locks up for the night.

A5.7 **Impossibility** The 'impossibility defence', which in 1981 was expunged from the law relating to statutory conspiracy and attempt (see **A5.57** and **A5.81**), survived in respect of incitement and now survives in the SCA 2007. If D's act is incapable of providing encouragement or assistance to E, D cannot be guilty even if he intended to provide such encouragement, etc. If for example D provides E with the wrong keys to F's house, this cannot assist E to commit a planned burglary at F's house. D might however be guilty of *attempting* to do an act that would have been capable of assisting E (i.e. providing the right keys) because impossibility is no defence to a charge of criminal attempt. Similarly, if D encourages E to steal, thinking him to be ten years old, when E is in fact below the age of criminal responsibility, D's act is incapable of encouraging E to commit a crime, but D may once again be guilty of attempting to do such an act.

Impossibility is heavily fact dependent. If D mistakes a police officer for a drug dealer, and seeks to buy heroin from him, D could still be guilty of encouraging the officer to supply him with heroin, because it would not be impossible for the officer to do so (cf. *DPP v Armstrong* [2000] Crim LR 379).

INTENTIONALLY ENCOURAGING OR ASSISTING AN OFFENCE

A5.8 Serious Crime Act 2007, s. 44

(1) A person commits an offence if—
   (a) he does an act capable of encouraging or assisting the commission of an offence; and
   (b) he intends to encourage or assist its commission.
(2) But he is not to be taken to have intended to encourage or assist the commission of an offence merely because such encouragement or assistance was a foreseeable consequence of his act.

Jurisdiction and Procedure

A5.9 The mode of trial for an offence under the SCA 2007, s. 44, is to be determined as if D had been charged with committing the 'anticipated offence'. If this was an offence triable either way, the s. 44 offence is thus triable either way (s. 55(1)). If tried on indictment, it is a class 3 offence. As to restrictions on the institution of proceedings in certain cases, see **A5.35**. As to alternative verdicts, see **A5.37**. As to acts done wholly or partly abroad, or with a view to encouraging or assisting the commission of offences abroad, see **A5.33**.

Indictment

A5.10 *Statement of Offence*

Intentionally [encouraging or] assisting an offence, contrary to section 44(1) of the Serious Crime Act 2007.

Particulars of Offence

A on or about the … day of … supplied B with keys to a house belong to C with the intention of assisting B to commit a burglary of that house.

Sentencing

A5.11 The penalties for offences under the SCA 2007, ss. 44 to 46, are laid down by s. 58. See **A5.38**.

Elements

A5.12 Section 44 of the SCA 2007 appears to create a single offence, and not separate offences of assistance and encouragement. By s. 49(2), however, 'If a person's act is capable of encouraging or assisting the commission of a number of offences, section 44 applies separately in relation to each offence that he intends to encourage or assist to be committed'. As to the *actus reus*, see also A5.4 to A5.7.

The *mens rea* elements are more complex. The first (which distinguishes the s. 44 offence from that created by s. 45) is that D must specifically intend to encourage or assist in the commission of the 'anticipated offence'. That is not, however, the same thing as an intent that the offence should be committed by the person he encourages, etc. By s. 47, recklessness as to this may suffice: see A5.13. Section 44(2) states that a consequence is not intended merely because it was foreseeable; but that is trite law, since the CJA 1967, s. 8, has for many years laid down such a rule (see A2.34). The explanatory notes to s. 44 suggest that s. 44(2) (and s. 47(7)(b)) were meant to distinguish between direct intent (aim or purpose) on the one hand and oblique intent on the other, only the former sufficing for liability; but arguably they state a different rule. Some kind of oblique intent might therefore suffice; but if D's intent is unclear it would probably be easier to charge him under s. 45 or s. 46.

Proof of *Mens Rea*　　Sections 44 to 46 must be read in accordance with s. 47, which lays down　**A5.13** various rules as to proof of *mens rea*.

Serious Crime Act 2007, s. 47

(2) If it is alleged under section 44(1)(b) that a person (D) intended to encourage or assist the commission of an offence, it is sufficient to prove that he intended to encourage or assist the doing of an act which would amount to the commission of that offence.

(3) [See A5.22]

(4) [See A5.29]

(5) In proving for the purposes of this section whether an act is one which, if done, would amount to the commission of an offence—

    (a) if the offence is one requiring proof of fault, it must be proved that—

        (i) D believed that, were the act to be done, it would be done with that fault;

        (ii) D was reckless as to whether or not it would be done with that fault; or

        (iii) D's state of mind was such that, were he to do it, it would be done with that fault;

    and

    (b) if the offence is one requiring proof of particular circumstances or consequences (or both), it must be proved that—

        (i) D believed that, were the act to be done, it would be done in those circumstances or with those consequences; or

        (ii) D was reckless as to whether or not it would be done in those circumstances or with those consequences.

(6) For the purposes of subsection (5)(a)(iii), D is to be assumed to be able to do the act in question.

(7) In the case of an offence under section 44—

    (a) subsection (5)(b)(i) is to be read as if the reference to 'D believed' were a reference to 'D intended or believed'; but

    (b) D is not to be taken to have intended that an act would be done in particular circumstances or with particular consequences merely because its being done in those circumstances or with those consequences was a foreseeable consequence of his act of encouragement or assistance.

(8) Reference in this section to the doing of an act includes reference to—

    (a) a failure to act;

    (b) the continuation of an act that has already begun;

    (c) an attempt to do an act (except an act amounting to the commission of the offence of attempting to commit another offence).

By s. 47(2), D need not 'intend' that the act he encourages or assists should be committed in　**A5.14** circumstances that render it criminal, or that it should result in consequences that render it criminal; but to be guilty of any of the offences in part 2 he must believe or be reckless as to those matters (s. 47(5)(b)). D does not, for example, encourage E to rape V unless he is at least reckless as to the possibility that sex would occur without V's consent; and he cannot be guilty of assisting E to commit murder if it never occurs to him that E might unlawfully kill someone. But ignorance of the law cannot be a defence, so it does not matter whether D knew that the act encouraged by him was, in the circumstances, an offence.

Section 47(5)(a) represents a departure from the law governing incitement. At common law, D did not incite E to commit an offence if D's plan was merely to use E as his innocent agent (this was the point that the Court of Appeal intended to make in *Curr* [1968] 2 QB 944 under the old law) but under s. 47(5)(a)(iii) it may suffice that D has *mens rea*, even if he knows that E has none. Section 47(6) ensures that D's own capacity to commit the 'anticipated offence' is not an issue. If, for example, D encourages E, a company director, to publish a materially false statement on behalf of E's company, D may be guilty of encouraging the commission by E of an offence under the Theft Act 1968, s. 19 (see **B6.15**), if D knows the statement to be false and seeks to deceive company creditors, etc. It would not matter that E honestly believed the statement to be true or that D (not being an officer of the company) was himself incapable of committing the s. 19 offence.

The new law may apply less strictly to those who plan to commit an offence than to those who merely offer assistance or encouragement. If, for example, D1 declares that he is going to burn down V's house, and D2 hands him some matches for that purpose, D2 will at once become guilty of encouraging or assisting an offence; but in the absence of a conspiracy D1 will not at that stage be guilty of any offence; and if he changes his mind he may never incur criminal liability.

This statement must however be qualified in one respect. If D1 *intentionally* encourages D2 to assist or encourage him (e.g., by asking D2 for his help or support) he may himself commit an offence under s. 44 of the Act. As explained at **A5.32**, however, any 'doubly inchoate' offence must be committed with intent: such liability cannot arise under s. 45 or 46.

Defence of 'Acting Reasonably'

A5.15   Serious Crime Act 2007, s. 50
(1) A person is not guilty of an offence under this part if he proves—
    (a) that he knew certain circumstances existed; and
    (b) that it was reasonable for him to act as he did in those circumstances.
(2) A person is not guilty of an offence under this part if he proves—
    (a) that he believed certain circumstances to exist;
    (b) that his belief was reasonable; and
    (c) that it was reasonable for him to act as he did in the circumstances as he believed them to be.
(3) Factors to be considered in determining whether it was reasonable for a person to act as he did include—
    (a) the seriousness of the anticipated offence (or, in the case of an offence under section 46, the offences specified in the indictment);
    (b) any purpose for which he claims to have been acting;
    (c) any authority by which he claims to have been acting.

No indication is given in the Act or notes for guidance as to what conduct is likely to fit within the s. 50 defence. The Law Commission's original proposal was that the defence would not be open to those charged under s. 44, but only to those whose behaviour might unintentionally encourage others to break the law. For example, a TV crew covering a riot may become aware that their presence is encouraging some rioters to intensify their actions. The Commission proposed that the TV crew would avoid liability for this if they could prove that their actions were reasonable. As it is, it may be open to D to argue that it was 'reasonable' for him to encourage E to commit a serious crime with the intent that E should commit it. A possible beneficiary of this defence might be an undercover journalist or member of the security service engaged in entrapping and unmasking an offender, although s. 50 would not prevent such a person incurring liability as a secondary party to any crime actually committed by the person he entraps. See *Hardwicke* [2000] All ER (D) 1776; and in the context of corruption see also *Smith* [1960] 2 QB 423 (see **B15.36**).

There may be argument as to whether the reverse burden of proof imposed by s. 50 is compliant with the ECHR, Article 6. If there is no doubt that 'certain circumstances existed' and the court would be minded to consider D's actions wholly reasonable in those circumstances, ought there to be any risk of the defence failing merely because it is not clear whether D actually knew of those circumstances? Arguably D deserves the benefit of any reasonable doubt in such a case; but s. 50 denies him this.

Potential Victims of 'Protective Offences'

Serious Crime Act 2007, s. 51

A5.16

(1) In the case of protective offences, a person does not commit an offence under this part by reference to such an offence if—
  (a) he falls within the protected category; and
  (b) he is the person in respect of whom the protective offence was committed or would have been if it had been committed.
(2) 'Protective offence' means an offence that exists (wholly or in part) for the protection of a particular category of persons ('the protected category').

As the notes for guidance make clear, this provision is designed to give effect to the so-called 'Tyrell principle' which also applies in respect of conspiracy and secondary participation, although its exact limits in those contexts are not wholly clear (Gnango [2012] 1 AC 827 at [49]). Underage children clearly fall within a protected category in respect of sex offences that may be committed against them. Similarly, D commits no offence under s. 44 if he begs E to help him commit suicide, even though he is thereby encouraging E to commit an offence under the Suicide Act 1961, s. 2 (see **B1.136**).

ENCOURAGING OR ASSISTING AN OFFENCE BELIEVING IT WILL BE COMMITTED

Serious Crime Act 2007, s. 45

A5.17

A person commits an offence if—
(a) he does an act capable of encouraging or assisting the commission of an offence; and
(b) he believes—
  (i) that the offence will be committed; and
  (ii) that his act will encourage or assist its commission.

Jurisdiction and Procedure

The mode of trial for an offence under the SCA 2007, s. 45, is to be determined as if D had been charged with committing the 'anticipated offence'. If this was an offence triable either way, the s. 45 offence is triable either way (s. 55). If tried on indictment, it is a class 3 offence. As to restrictions on the institution of proceedings in certain cases, see **A5.35**. As to alternative verdicts, see **A5.37**. As to acts done wholly or partly abroad, or with a view to encouraging or assisting the commission of offences abroad, see **A5.33**.

A5.18

Indictment

Statement of Offence

A5.19

[Encouraging or] assisting an offence, believing it will be committed, contrary to section 45 of the Serious Crime Act 2007.

Particulars of Offence

A on or about the... day of... supplied B with keys to a house belong to C believing that B would commit a burglary of that house and that the keys would assist him to do so.

Sentencing

The penalties for offences under the SCA 2007, ss. 44 to 46, are laid down by s. 58. See **A5.38**.

A5.20

Elements

A5.21   Section 45 of the SCA 2007 apparently creates a single offence, not separate offences of assistance and encouragement. By s. 49(2)(b), however, s. 45 'applies separately in relation to each offence that [D] believes will be encouraged or assisted to be committed'. As to the *actus reus*, see **A5.4** to **A5.7**.

A5.22   *Mens Rea*   Section 47(5) and (6) of the SCA 2007 applies to offences under s. 45 as it applies to offences under s. 44 (see **A5.13**); but s. 47(3) applies in place of s. 47(2).

Serious Crime Act 2007, s. 47

(3)   If it is alleged under section 45(b) that a person (D) believed that an offence would be committed and that his act would encourage or assist its commission, it is sufficient to prove that he believed—
  (a)   that an act would be done which would amount to the commission of that offence; and
  (b)   that his act would encourage or assist the doing of that act.

Section 45 does not make it an offence for D to do something, fearing or suspecting that it may possibly assist or encourage another person (or persons) to commit an offence. To be guilty under s. 45, D must positively believe that the conduct in question will indeed be committed, or that it will be committed if certain conditions are met (s. 49(7)). If D has this positive belief and his own conduct is capable of providing such encouragement or assistance, it does not matter if he is mistaken and there is never any question of the offence being committed by the person he encourages or assists. But s. 47(5) applies as it does to a s. 44 offence, so recklessness on D's part as to the circumstances or consequences of the act in question, or of the fault element required for it, may still suffice (see **A5.13**).

Defences etc.

A5.23   The SCA 2007, s. 50, creates a defence of 'acting reasonably' (see **A5.15**) and the potential victims of 'protective offences' are also exempt from liability by virtue of s. 51 (see **A5.16**).

ENCOURAGING OR ASSISTING OFFENCES BELIEVING ONE OR MORE WILL BE COMMITTED

A5.24

Serious Crime Act 2007, s. 46

(1)   A person commits an offence if—
  (a)   he does an act capable of encouraging or assisting the commission of one or more of a number of offences; and
  (b)   he believes—
    (i)   that one or more of those offences will be committed (but has no belief as to which); and
    (ii)   that his act will encourage or assist the commission of one or more of them.
(2)   It is immaterial for the purposes of subsection (1)(b)(ii) whether the person has any belief as to which offence will be encouraged or assisted.
(3)   If a person is charged with an offence under subsection (1)—
  (a)   the indictment must specify the offences alleged to be the 'number of offences' mentioned in paragraph (a) of that subsection; but
  (b)   nothing in paragraph (a) requires all the offences potentially comprised in that number to be specified.
(4)   In relation to an offence under this section, reference in this Part to the offences specified in the indictment is to the offences specified by virtue of subsection (3)(a).

Jurisdiction and Procedure

A5.25   An offence under the SCA 2007, s. 46, is triable on indictment (s. 55(2)). It is a class 3 offence. As to restrictions on the institution of proceedings in certain cases, see **A5.35**. As to alternative verdicts, see **A5.37**. As to jurisdiction over acts done wholly or partly abroad, or with a view to encouraging or assisting the commission of offences abroad, see **A5.33**.

Indictment

Statement of Offence   **A5.26**

Intentionally assisting offences, believing one or more will be committed, contrary to section 46(1) of the Serious Crime Act 2007.

Particulars of Offence

A…between the…day of…and the…day of…, supplied an ex-army bayonet to X, such supply being capable of assisting two or more possible offences by X, namely robbery, assault with intent to rob, or malicious wounding, believing that at least one such offence would be committed by X and that the bayonet supplied would assist him in its commission.

The indictment above follows *Sadique* [2013] 4 All ER 924, in which the Court of Appeal revised its guidance as to the drafting of indictments for offences under the SCA 2007, s. 46(1). In particular, the Court accepted academic criticism of guidance previously given in *S* [2012] 2 All ER 793 (see the 2013 edition of this work). This called for separate counts for each allegedly contemplated offence to which s. 46 might apply. Separate counts were said to be necessary in order to avoid challenges based on uncertainty of scope that might otherwise be brought under the ECHR, Article 7, but this made it difficult to see what s. 46 usefully added to the offence created by s. 45 of the Act. Moreover, the guidance given in *S* was arguably in conflict with s. 46 itself, because a conviction on any one count was said to be possible only if D was proved to have believed that the offence in question *would* be committed, whereas an express element of the s. 46 offence is that D 'has no belief as to which' of the contemplated offences will actually be committed.

The Court in *Sadique* considered that the guidance in *S* was *obiter* and not strictly binding upon them. Lord Judge CJ noted that s. 46 was intended to cover the kind of scenario that featured in *DPP for Northern Ireland v Maxwell* [1978] 3 All ER 1140 (see **A4.1**) and added (at [34]):

In our judgment the ingredients of the s. 46 offence, and the ancillary provisions, and s. 58(4)–(7) in particular, underline that an indictment charging a s. 46 offence by reference to one or more offences is permissible, and covers the precise situation for which the legislation provides.

Such an indictment is not bad for duplicity, nor defective for uncertainty. It achieves the objective of every count in any indictment, i.e. to give sufficient indication to the accused of the criminal conduct alleged against him (*Sadique* at [36]).

Where there is an issue as to whether D believed that only one of the specified offences would be committed (e.g., the less serious of the two) it may be helpful to combine a count under s. 46 with two or more counts under s. 45 (*Sadique* at [39]).

Sentencing

The penalties for offences under the SCA 2007, ss. 44 to 46, are laid down by s. 58. See **A5.38**.   **A5.27**

Elements

As the Court of Appeal noted in *Sadique* [2013] 4 All ER 924, s. 46 provides for the 'relatively   **A5.28** common case' where D contemplates that one of a range of offences might be committed as a result of his encouragement or assistance. It apparently creates a single offence, not separate offences of assistance and encouragement. By s. 49(2)(b), however, s. 45 'applies separately in relation to each offence that [D] believes will be encouraged or assisted to be committed'. As to the *actus reus*, see **A5.4 to A5.7**. In *S* [2012] 2 All ER 793 and again in *Sadique* the Court of

Appeal rejected submissions that the offence created by s. 46 is too vague and uncertain to be compatible with the ECHR, Article 6 or 7.

A5.29 *Mens Rea*   Section 47(5) and (6) of the SCA 2007 applies to offences under s. 46 as it applies to offences under s. 44 (see **A5.13**); but s. 47(4) applies in place of s. 47(2); and s. 48 makes further provision as to what must be proved in order to establish a s. 46 offence.

Serious Crime Act 2007, ss. 47 and 48

47.—(4) If it is alleged under section 46(1)(b) that a person (D) believed that one or more of a number of offences would be committed and that his act would encourage or assist the commission of one or more of them, it is sufficient to prove that he believed—

    (a) that one or more of a number of acts would be done which would amount to the commission of one or more of those offences; and

    (b) that his act would encourage or assist the doing of one or more of those acts.

48.—(1) This section makes further provision about the application of section 47 to an offence under section 46.

  (2) It is sufficient to prove the matters mentioned in section 47(5) by reference to one offence only.

  (3) The offence or offences by reference to which those matters are proved must be one of the offences specified in the indictment.

  (4) Subsection (3) does not affect any enactment or rule of law under which a person charged with one offence may be convicted of another and is subject to section 57.

A5.30 The problem addressed in s. 46 is that of the person who knowingly provides assistance etc. to a potential offender, but without knowing (and perhaps without wanting to know) what the anticipated offence might be. By s. 46, if D positively believes that the gun he supplies to E will be used either to commit a robbery or to commit a murder, but is not sure which, then he can be convicted under that section, and is punishable on the same basis as if he was sure it would be the more (or most) serious one. It makes no difference if it transpires, to D's surprise, that E never had any intention of committing either offence.

Section 46 does not make it an offence for D to do something, merely fearing or suspecting that it may possibly encourage or assist another person (or persons) to commit offences. To be guilty under s. 46, D must positively (if perhaps wrongly) believe that some such offence will indeed be committed, or will be committed if certain conditions are met (s. 49(7)).

ENCOURAGING OR ASSISTING ANOTHER PERSON TO COMMIT AN INCHOATE OFFENCE

A5.31   **Serious Crime Act 2007, s. 49**

  (4) In reckoning whether—

    (a) for the purposes of section 45, an act is capable of encouraging or assisting the commission of an offence; or

    (b) for the purposes of section 46, an act is capable of encouraging or assisting the commission of one or more of a number of offences;

  offences under this Part and listed offences are to be disregarded.

  (5) 'Listed offence' means—

    (a) in England and Wales, an offence listed in Part 1, 2 or 3 of Schedule 3...

A5.32 Schedule 3 (which the Secretary of State is empowered to amend) contains a long list of statutory offences involving incitement, solicitation, conspiracy, attempt, assistance or encouragement. The offences listed in sch. 3, parts 1 to 3, include those under the OAPA 1861, s. 4; the Official Secrets Act 1920, s. 7; the MDA 1971, ss. 19 and 20; the Immigration Act 1971, ss. 25 and 25B; the Computer Misuse Act 1990, s. 3A(1), (2) and (3); the Terrorism Act 2000, s. 59; the Terrorism Act 2006, ss. 1(2), 2(1), 5, 6(1) and (2); the Perjury Act 1911, s. 7(2); the CLA 1967, ss. 4(1) and 5(1); the CLA 1977, ss. 1(1), 5(2) and (3); the CAA 1981, s. 1(1); the Public

Order Act 1986, ss. 12(6), 13(9) and 14(6) and the Cluster Munitions (Prohibitions) Act 2010, s. 2. Also covered are offences of attempt under special statutory provisions (see the CAA 1981, s. 3).

The SCA 2007, s. 49(4), ensures that it is not an offence to do an act that may encourage or assist another person to commit some other inchoate offence (whether under ss. 44 to 46 or under any other enactment) unless the original act is committed with the specific intention of encouraging or assisting its commission. To put it another way, encouraging or assisting the commission of an inchoate offence can be prosecuted under s. 44 (which requires proof of such intent) or not at all. It cannot be prosecuted under s. 45 or 46.

Under s. 44, D may incur liability by (for example) intentionally encouraging E to solicit F to commit murder (contrary to the OAPA 1861, s. 4) or by asking G to assist him in committing an offence. Inviting H to join a criminal conspiracy would also suffice.

JURISDICTION AND PROCEDURE

Offences with Foreign Elements

Serious Crime Act 2007, s. 52   A5.33

(1) If a person (D) knows or believes that what he anticipates might take place wholly or partly in England or Wales, he may be guilty of an offence under section 44, 45 or 46 no matter where he was at any relevant time.
(2) If it is not proved that D knows or believes that what he anticipates might take place wholly or partly in England or Wales, he is not guilty of an offence under section 44, 45 or 46 unless paragraph 1, 2 or 3 of schedule 4 applies.
(3) A reference in this section (and in any of those paragraphs) to what D anticipates is to be read as follows—
 (a) in relation to an offence under section 44 or 45, it refers to the act which would amount to the commission of the anticipated offence;
 (b) in relation to an offence under section 46, it refers to an act which would amount to the commission of any of the offences specified in the indictment.
(4) [Northern Ireland.]
(5) Nothing in this section or Schedule 4 restricts the operation of any enactment by virtue of which an act constituting an offence under this Part is triable under the law of England and Wales...

Where s. 52(1) applies, the position is relatively simple. D's conduct may amount to an offence under English law, wherever he acts, if he intends or believes that an act 'which would amount to the commission of the anticipated offence' (or offences) *will* be committed (as is required by ss. 44 to 46) and that it *might* be committed wholly or partly in England and Wales. In all other cases, s. 52(2) requires reference to be made to sch. 4.   A5.34

Schedule 4, para. 1, applies where D acts wholly or partly within England and Wales, and the act he anticipates would still be punishable as an offence under English law, even if committed abroad (e.g., he encourages E, a British citizen, to commit murder on land outside the UK: a murder punishable under English law by virtue of the OAPA 1861, s. 9). If para. 1 does not apply, para. 2 applies where D acts wholly or partly within England and Wales and, although what he anticipates might take place outside England and Wales, it would be an offence under the law applicable in that place. If the defence wish to argue that the anticipated offence was *not* punishable under local law, the defence must raise this issue for determination by the judge in accordance with the procedure set out in para. 2(2)–(4). Failing this, criminality will be presumed. Finally, sch. 4, para. 3, applies where there may be no proven connection with England and Wales, but D would himself be liable to prosecution under English law if he were to commit the anticipated offence in the place or country in question.

Where the offence is punishable only by virtue of sch. 4, proceedings may not be instituted except by or with the consent of the A-G (s. 53) but, since the Bribery Act 2010 came into force on 1 July 2011 (see **B15.1**), this does not apply to offences of encouraging or assisting bribery (as to which see the SCA 2007, s. 54(1) and (2) (see **A5.35**) and the Bribery Act 2010, sch. 1, para. 13).

Institution of Proceedings etc.

A5.35   Serious Crime Act 2007, s. 54

(1) Any provision to which this section applies has effect with respect to an offence under this Part as it has effect with respect to the anticipated offence.

(2) This section applies to provisions made by or under an enactment (whenever passed or made) that—

    (a) provide that proceedings may not be instituted or carried on otherwise than by, or on behalf or with the consent of, any person (including any provision which also makes exceptions to the prohibition);

    (b) confer power to institute proceedings;

    (c) confer power to seize and detain property;

    (d) confer a power of forfeiture, including any power to deal with anything liable to be forfeited.

(3) In relation to an offence under section 46—

    (a) the reference in subsection (1) to the anticipated offence is to be read as a reference to any offence specified in the indictment; and

    (b) each of the offences specified in the indictment must be an offence in respect of which the prosecutor has power to institute proceedings.

(4) Any consent to proceedings required as a result of this section is in addition to any consent required by section 53.

(5) No proceedings for an offence under this Part are to be instituted against a person providing information society services who is established in an EEA State other than the United Kingdom unless the derogation condition is satisfied.

(6) The derogation condition is satisfied where the institution of proceedings—

    (a) is necessary to pursue the public interest objective;

    (b) relates to an information society service that prejudices that objective or presents a serious and grave risk of prejudice to it; and

    (c) is proportionate to that objective.

(7) The public interest objective is public policy.

(8) In this section 'information society services' has the same meaning as in section 34, and subsection (7) of that section applies for the purposes of this section as it applies for the purposes of that section.

Section 54(5)–(8) gives effect to the EC E-Commerce Directive (2000/31/EC), which governs the circumstances in which an internet (or 'information society') service provider may exceptionally be prosecuted for offences in a state other than the one in which it is established.

Persons who may be Perpetrators or Encouragers etc.

A5.36   Serious Crime Act 2007, s. 56

(1) In proceedings for an offence under this Part ('the inchoate offence') the defendant may be convicted if—

    (a) it is proved that he must have committed the inchoate offence or the anticipated offence; but

    (b) it is not proved which of those offences he committed.

(2) For the purposes of this section, a person is not to be treated as having committed the anticipated offence merely because he aided, abetted, counselled or procured its commission.

(3) In relation to an offence under section 46, a reference in this section to the anticipated offence is to be read as a reference to an offence specified in the indictment.

This provision enables D to be convicted on a charge of committing an inchoate offence under ss. 44 to 46 even if it is not clear whether he assisted or encouraged the anticipated offence, on the one hand, or actually committed it, on the other. In contrast, D cannot be convicted of the full offence if it is possible that he committed only an inchoate offence. As to the position where

D must be guilty either of committing an offence or of aiding, abetting, counselling or procuring it, see *Giannetto* [1997] 1 Cr App R 1 and **A4.1**.

Alternative Verdicts and Guilty Pleas

Serious Crime Act 2007, s. 57 **A5.37**

(1) If in proceedings on indictment for an offence under section 44 or 45 a person is not found guilty of that offence by reference to the specified offence, he may be found guilty of that offence by reference to an alternative offence.

(2) If in proceedings for an offence under section 46 a person is not found guilty of that offence by reference to any specified offence, he may be found guilty of that offence by reference to one or more alternative offences.

(3) If in proceedings for an offence under section 46 a person is found guilty of the offence by reference to one or more specified offences, he may also be found guilty of it by reference to one or more other alternative offences.

(4) For the purposes of this section, an offence is an alternative offence if—
   (a) it is an offence of which, on a trial on indictment for the specified offence, an accused may be found guilty; or
   (b) it is an indictable offence, or one to which section 40 of the Criminal Justice Act 1988 applies (power to include count for common assault etc. in indictment), and the condition in subsection (5) is satisfied.

(5) The condition is that the allegations in the indictment charging the person with the offence under this Part amount to or include (expressly or by implication) an allegation of that offence by reference to it.

(6) Subsection (4)(b) does not apply if the specified offence, or any of the specified offences, is murder or treason.

(7) In the application of subsection (5) to proceedings for an offence under section 44, the allegations in the indictment are to be taken to include an allegation of that offence by reference to the offence of attempting to commit the specified offence.

(8) Section 49(4) applies to an offence which is an alternative offence in relation to a specified offence as it applies to that specified offence.

(9) In this section—
   (a) in relation to a person charged with an offence under section 44 or 45, 'the specified offence' means the offence specified in the indictment as the one alleged to be the anticipated offence;
   (b) in relation to a person charged with an offence under section 46, 'specified offence' means an offence specified in the indictment (within the meaning of subsection (4) of that section), and related expressions are to be read accordingly.

(10) A person arraigned on an indictment for an offence under this Part may plead guilty to an offence of which he could be found guilty under this section on that indictment.

(11) This section applies to an indictment containing more than one count as if each count were a separate indictment.

(12) This section is without prejudice to—
   (a) section 6(1)(b) and (3) of the Criminal Law Act 1967...

Section 57 makes similar provision in relation to alternative verdicts to that which would apply in respect of the anticipated offences (see generally **D19.41** *et seq*.), subject in the case of an alleged inchoate offence under s. 45 or s. 46 to the restriction imposed by s. 49(4) (as to which see **A5.31**). If for example D tells E where his enemy, V, is hiding, and D is charged under s. 45 with assisting or encouraging E, believing he would murder V, the jury may perhaps not be satisfied that D believed E would commit murder, but convict him instead of providing assistance in the belief that E would commit an offence of causing grievous bodily harm with intent.

Penalties and Sentencing

Serious Crime Act 2007, s. 58 **A5.38**

(1) Subsections (2) and (3) apply if—
   (a) a person is convicted of an offence under section 44 or 45; or
   (b) a person is convicted of an offence under section 46 by reference to only one offence ('the reference offence').

(2) If the anticipated or reference offence is murder, he is liable to imprisonment for life.

(3) In any other case he is liable to any penalty for which he would be liable on conviction of the anticipated or reference offence.

(4) Subsections (5) to (7) apply if a person is convicted of an offence under section 46 by reference to more than one offence ('the reference offences').

(5) If one of the reference offences is murder, he is liable to imprisonment for life.

(6) If none of the reference offences is murder but one or more of them is punishable with imprisonment, he is liable—

  (a) to imprisonment for a term not exceeding the maximum term provided for any one of those offences (taking the longer or the longest term as the limit for the purposes of this paragraph where the terms provided differ); or

  (b) to a fine.

(7) In any other case he is liable to a fine.

(8) Subsections (3), (6) and (7) are subject to any contrary provision made by or under—

  (a) an Act;...

(9) In the case of an offence triable either way, the reference in subsection (6) to the maximum term provided for that offence is a reference to the maximum term so provided on conviction on indictment.

Amongst the many sentencing appeals considered by the Court of Appeal in *Blackshaw* [2012] 1 WLR 1126 in the aftermath of the August 2011 riots were two arising out of inchoate offences under the SCA 2007. In the first, the offender (Blackshaw) pleaded guilty to a s. 46 offence after using Facebook to encourage or assist the commission of offences of riot, burglary and criminal damage. In the second, the offender pleaded guilty to a s. 44 offence in which he had used Facebook to invite 400 contacts to meet up for the purpose of starting public disorder. Sentences of four years' imprisonment were upheld in each case.

CONSPIRACY GENERALLY

Common Law and Statutory Conspiracies

A5.39 There are at least three distinct forms of conspiracy under English law, namely conspiracy to defraud at common law, conspiracy to commit a criminal offence contrary to the CLA 1977, s. 1, and conspiracy to commit abroad an offence under foreign law (to which the CLA 1977, s. 1, applies by virtue of s. 1A). The first two forms overlap because a conspiracy to defraud may also involve a statutory conspiracy, in which case the CJA 1987, s. 12, allows the prosecution to charge either offence (see **A5.62**). The Court of Appeal referred in *Dosanjh* [2013] EWCA Crim 2366 at [16] to a supposed '[c]ommon law conspiracy to cheat... the public revenue', but clearly meant by this a statutory conspiracy (under s. 1) to commit the substantive common-law offence of cheating the revenue.

Two other forms of common-law conspiracy require brief consideration, namely conspiracy to corrupt public morals and conspiracy to outrage public decency; but their survival as separate forms of conspiracy is extremely doubtful. Section 5(3) of the 1977 Act purports to preserve such conspiracies as common-law offences, but only:

...if and in so far as [they] may be committed by entering into an agreement to engage in conduct which—

  (a) tends to corrupt public morals or outrages public decency; but

  (b) would not amount to or involve the commission of an offence if carried out by a single person otherwise than in pursuance of an agreement.

If, in other words, a conspiracy to outrage public decency involves an agreement to commit a substantive criminal offence, it can be charged *only* as a conspiracy under s. 1 of the Act. No overlap with the common-law offence is possible. When the 1977 Act was drafted, it was considered unclear whether any substantive offences of outraging public decency or corrupting public morals existed, and s. 5(3) was intended to preserve the effect of the notorious decisions of the House of Lords in *Shaw v DPP* [1962] AC 220 and *Knuller (Publishing, Printing and Promotions) Ltd v DPP* [1973] AC 435, lest statutory conspiracy failed to cover conduct of the kind dealt with in those cases. It is now clear that outraging public decency is indeed a substantive offence at common law (see **B3.330** *et seq.*). Agreements to do acts amounting to that offence must accordingly be charged as statutory conspiracies.

Authority in respect of corrupting public morals is sparse, but the Court of Criminal Appeal in *Shaw* held that it did indeed exist as a substantive common-law offence, and the House of Lords did not reject that view (although it did not form part of their *ratio decidendi*). It seems probable, therefore, that this form of common-law conspiracy has also been subsumed within the statutory offence, and that nothing at all has been preserved by s. 5(3). In any event, there has been no reported prosecution for this form of conspiracy since the 1977 Act came into force, and it does not warrant further discussion.

Cartel Offences under the Enterprise Act 2002

An individual who agrees with others to make or implement, or cause to be made or implemented, a prohibited cartel arrangement relating to two or more undertakings concerning the supply of products or services in the UK may be prosecuted under the Enterprise Act 2002, s. 188, as amended by the Enterprise and Regulatory Reform Act 2013. Cartel arrangements are extensively defined in ss. 188(2)–(6) and 189 and involve price-fixing, 'bid-rigging' or agreements limiting or preventing supply or production by one of the parties, or dividing supply or production between them. **A5.40**

A prosecution under s. 188 may or may not relate to trade in the European Union (*IB* [2010] 2 All ER 728). From 1 April 2014 dishonesty is no longer a required element of the offence but the amended offence is subject to various balancing measures and defences, as provided by ss. 188A and 188B. See also **B7.36**. As to price-fixing agreements pre-dating the commencement of s. 188, see *Norris v Government of the USA* [2008] 1 AC 920 and *Goldshield Group plc* [2009] 2 All ER 738.

STATUTORY CONSPIRACY

Definition

Criminal Law Act 1977, s. 1   **A5.41**

(1) Subject to the following provisions of this part of this Act, if a person agrees with any other person or persons that a course of conduct will be pursued which, if the agreement is carried out in accordance with their intentions, either—
   (a) will necessarily amount to or involve the commission of any offence or offences by one or more of the parties to the agreement; or
   (b) would do so but for the existence of facts which render the commission of the offence or any of the offences impossible,
he is guilty of conspiracy to commit the offence or offences in question.
(2) Where liability for any offence may be incurred without knowledge on the part of the person committing it of any particular fact or circumstance necessary for the commission of the offence, a person shall nevertheless not be guilty of conspiracy to commit that offence by virtue of subsection (1) above unless he and at least one other party to the agreement intend or know that the fact or circumstance shall or will exist at the time when the conduct constituting the offence is to take place.
(3) [Repealed.]
(4) In this part of this Act 'offence' means an offence triable in England and Wales.

Agreements relating to acts involving summary offences not punishable by imprisonment must be disregarded if the acts are to be done in contemplation or furtherance of a trade dispute (Trade Union and Labour Relations (Consolidation) Act 1992, s. 242).

Indictment

Statement of Offence   **A5.42**

Conspiracy to commit criminal damage contrary to section 1(1) of the Criminal Law Act 1977.

Particulars of Offence

A [and B] on or about the…day of…conspired together [and/or with persons unknown] to damage the braking systems on two heavy goods vehicles belonging to V plc, with intent to endanger life, contrary to s. 1(2) of the Criminal Damage Act 1971.

A single agreement (and a single count of conspiracy) may embrace conduct involving several offences, without being bad for duplicity (*Roberts* [1998] 1 Cr App R 441; *Greenfield* [1973] 3 All ER 1050; *Taylor* [2002] Crim LR 205; see also **D11.35**). It was suggested in *Roberts* that, where a single count alleges an agreement to commit more than one offence, failure to prove the conspiracy in respect of any one of those offences would be fatal to the charge as a whole; but this must, with respect, be wrong (contrast *Fussell* [1997] Crim LR 812 and *Taylor*). It may nevertheless be good practice to charge such a conspiracy by means of two or more separate counts. As Lord Bridge said in *Cooke* [1986] AC 909:

A single agreement to pursue a course of conduct which involves the commission of two different specific offences could perfectly properly be charged in two counts alleging two different conspiracies, e.g. a conspiracy to steal a car and a conspiracy to obtain money by deception by selling the car with false registration plates and documents.

A5.43   In *Ali* [2011] 3 All ER 1071, the indictment at the initial trial of eight alleged Islamist terrorists was amended so as to include counts both for conspiracy to murder persons unknown and for conspiracy to commit such murders through the destruction of transatlantic airliners. This was because an issue arose as to whether some of the defendants might only have agreed to commit murder on a smaller scale and by different methods, albeit that the proposed substantive offence (murder of persons unknown) would be the same in each case. The Court of Appeal held (at [37]):

It is not permissible to put into an indictment an alternative factual basis which makes no difference to the offence committed whether it is for the purpose of enabling a jury to decide an issue of fact or for any other purpose. The judge must resolve the factual issues which are material to sentencing if the offences are the same; in limited circumstances, the judge may ask the jury a specific question.

The Court was nevertheless satisfied (at [52]) that the indictment in this case addressed two 'distinctly different agreements as to the method and scale of the murder to be carried out' which meant that the inclusion of multiple counts was entirely lawful, albeit not essential.

Whether an indictment for conspiracy alleges one ulterior offence or several, it is important that it properly identifies the individual offences in question, in accordance with the Indictments Act 1915, s. 3(1), and what is now the CrimPR, r. 14.2 (*Roberts* [1998] 1 Cr App R 441 at pp. 449–50). Where, for example, an indictment charges a conspiracy to commit criminal damage, it should make it clear whether this refers to the basic offence (contrary to the Criminal Damage Act 1971, s. 1(1)) or to the aggravated offence (contrary to s. 1(2)). See also *Booth* [1999] Crim LR 144 (arson). As to 'either/or' conspiracies, in which the parties agree to a course of conduct which will clearly involve the commission of some offence but cannot be certain which offence this will be, see *Hussain* [2002] Crim LR 407, *Singh* [2003] EWCA Crim 3712 (although *Singh* was overruled on other grounds in *Saik* [2007] 1 AC 18) and *Suchedina* [2007] 1 Cr App R 305.

A5.44   An indictment for conspiracy must not be misleading. An indictment alleging that the defendants conspired to supply drugs to 'another' cannot sensibly apply to a case in which the intended recipient was one of the conspirators (*Jackson* (1999) *The Times*, 13 May 1999; *Drew* [2000] 1 Cr App R 91).

A conspiracy count may be joined to substantive counts in an indictment where the facts warrant it and the interests of justice demand it, but as the Court of Appeal warned in *Shillam* [2013] EWCA Crim 160 (at [25]):

…the prosecution should always think carefully, before making use of the law of conspiracy, how to formulate the conspiracy charge or charges and whether a substantive offence or offences would be more appropriate.

As to the selection of charges generally, see Jarvis and Bisgrove, 'The use and abuse of conspiracy' [2014] Crim LR 261. See also CPD I, para. 14A.3 (see Supplement, **PD-19**), and **D11.96** generally.

Procedure and Sentencing

Conspiracy is triable only on indictment, even where it relates to a summary offence; but under **A5.45** the CLA 1977, s. 4(1), proceedings for conspiracy to commit summary offences may not be instituted except by or with the consent of the DPP. Where a prosecution for a substantive offence may only be brought by or with leave of the DPP or A-G, this is also required in respect of a charge of conspiracy to commit it (s. 4(2) and (3)). Where the time-limit for prosecuting a summary offence has expired, s. 4(4) provides that a prosecution for conspiracy is also barred, but this rule applies only where the substantive offence has been committed. As to the power of local authorities to prosecute for conspiracy (e.g., in trade descriptions cases), see *Jarrett* [1987] Crim LR 517 and *Richards* [1999] Crim LR 598.

By s. 3, a person guilty of conspiracy to commit murder, any offence for which the maximum penalty is life imprisonment, or any indictable offence punishable with imprisonment where no maximum term is specified is subject to a maximum penalty of life imprisonment. In particularly grave cases of revenue fraud, it may accordingly be proper to charge the alleged offenders with conspiracy to commit the common-law offence of cheating the revenue (for which the maximum penalty is at large) rather than with conspiracy to commit offences under the Fraud Act 2006 (*Dosanjh* [2013] EWCA Crim 2366).

For the relevant principles relating to the sentencing of conspiracy to commit murder see *McNee* [2008] 1 Cr App R (S) 108 and *Barot* [2008] 1 Cr App R (S) 156. The maximum for other statutory conspiracies is the same as the maximum provided for the completed offence.

Agreement

Agreement is the essence of conspiracy. There is no conspiracy if negotiations fail to result in **A5.46** agreement (*Walker* [1962] Crim LR 458) nor is there a conspiracy between A and B merely because each has conspired separately with C (*Griffiths* [1966] 1 QB 589). As Toulson LJ explained in *Shillam* [2013] EWCA Crim 160 (at [19]–[20]):

> ... for two or more persons to be convicted of a single conspiracy each of them must be proved to have a shared common purpose or design ... there must be a shared criminal purpose or design in which all have joined, rather than merely similar or parallel ones.

It is possible, however, to have conspiracies in which some parties never meet others. These include 'chain' and 'wheel' conspiracies. In a chain conspiracy, A agrees with B, B agrees with C, C agrees with D, etc. In a wheel conspiracy, A, at the 'hub', recruits B, C and D to his scheme (*Ardalan* [1972] 2 All ER 257). In either case, however, the alleged conspirators must each be shown to be party to a common design, and they must be aware that there is a larger scheme to which they are attaching themselves (*Meyrick* (1929) 21 Cr App R 94; *Chrastny* [1991] 1 All ER 189; *Barratt* [1996] Crim LR 495; *D* [2009] EWCA Crim 584). If B and C each believe they have their own individual agreements with A, there are two separate conspiracies, and a single count will not be valid, even if B and C are aware that A is making similar agreements with others (*Griffiths*).

Where a series of offences is committed by a group of persons over a long period, the prosecution may be tempted to proceed on the basis of a single conspiracy count, in preference to several substantive counts; but this tactic may be misconceived, because such offences are more likely to be the product of a series of agreements, and a single conspiracy may be impossible to prove (*Barratt*). As to the drafting of indictments in cases involving agreements within agreements, see *Ali* [2011] 3 All ER 1071 at **A5.43**.

Parties to Conspiracies and Acquittal of Other Alleged Conspirators

At least two persons must agree in order for there to be a conspiracy, although a single accused **A5.47** may be charged and convicted, even if the identities of his fellow conspirators remain unknown. Furthermore, the CLA 1977, s. 5(8), confirms the principle established in *DPP v Shannon* [1975]

AC 717, namely that acquittal of the only other alleged parties to a conspiracy (whether in the current trial or at a previous trial) need not prevent the conviction of the remaining accused, 'unless under all the circumstances of the case his conviction is inconsistent with the acquittal of the other person or persons in question'. Conviction of A and acquittal of B would be inconsistent if B is acquitted on the basis of a defence which, if true, must exonerate both, or if the evidence against each is the same (*Longman* (1980) 72 Cr App R 121); but it may be permissible to convict A on the basis of a pre-trial confession or other evidence which is not admissible against B or which does not incriminate him (cf. *Roberts* (1983) 78 Cr App R 41; *Testouri* [2004] 2 Cr App R 26; *Elkins* [2005] EWCA Crim 2711). It is likewise possible for A and B to be tried for conspiring with C, who has been acquitted at an earlier trial, even though it requires the prosecution to impugn or contradict the verdict at the earlier trial (*Austin* [2012] 1 Cr App R 320). But as to the position where only one conspirator actually intended the agreed crime to be committed, see **A5.54**.

A5.48   A corporation may be a party to a conspiracy (*ICR Haulage Ltd* [1944] KB 551), but a company and one of its directors cannot be the only parties to it because there can be no meeting of minds in such circumstances (*McDonnell* [1966] 1 QB 233). Certain other combinations are excluded under s. 2(2): a person cannot be convicted of statutory conspiracy if the only person(s) with whom he agrees (initially and during the currency of the agreement) are (a) his spouse; (b) children under the age of ten; and (c) intended victims of the relevant offences. If, however, a husband and wife conspire with a third person who does not fall within categories (b) or (c), all three may be guilty (*Chrastny* [1991] 1 All ER 189; cf. *Lovick* [1993] Crim LR 890).

Intended victims are exempt from liability for statutory conspiracy (s. 2(1)). This appears designed to apply the principle established in *Tyrell* [1894] QB 710 in respect of laws prohibiting intercourse with underaged girls, etc. (see **A4.32**), and may perhaps be confined (as in the SCA 2007, s. 51) to cases in which the 'victim' is one of a class that the relevant offence is intended to protect (*Gnango* [2012] 1 AC 827, *obiter* at [49]). But the fact that A may be incapable of committing the substantive offence does not prevent him incurring liability for conspiracy with B, if they agree that B will commit that offence (*Duguid* (1906) 21 Cox CC 200; *Burns* (1984) 79 Cr App R 173; *Sherry* [1993] Crim LR 536).

Agreement to Engage in Criminal Conduct

A5.49   To amount to a conspiracy under the CLA 1977, s. 1, an agreement must propose that a course of conduct be pursued which would necessarily involve the commission, by one or more of the parties, of a substantive offence which would itself be triable in England and Wales. Some substantive offences may be triable in England and Wales even if committed abroad, but conspiracies in England or Wales to commit acts abroad which are punishable *only* under the relevant foreign law must be dealt with by invoking s. 1A. See further **A5.58**.

To be the subject of a conspiracy, the course of conduct proposed must be something that will be done by one or more of the parties to the agreement. An agreement to procure the commission of a murder by a third party (e.g., to hire a 'hit man') is not a conspiracy to commit murder, even though anyone hiring such an assassin would become a secondary party to murder if the job is done. A conspiracy to aid, abet or procure an offence is not an offence under the CLA 1977. See the Court of Appeal's ruling in *Hollinshead* [1985] 1 All ER 850, which was followed in *Kenning* [2009] QB 221. The appellants in *Hollinshead* conspired to market devices for use by third parties, which would falsify electricity meter readings and enable users to avoid paying for electricity used. The court held that this could not amount to a conspiracy to commit offences under the Theft Act 1978, s. 2, even though any users would commit such offences. (Such conduct would now give rise to liability under the Fraud Act 2006, s. 7: see **B5.23**.) *Kenning* was distinguished in *Dang* [2014] EWCA Crim 348, where the defendants were held to have been properly convicted under the CLA 1977, s. 1, of conspiracy to be concerned in the production of a controlled drug in contravention of the MDA 1971, s. 4(2)(b), by agreeing to supply hydroponic and other products and equipment for the purpose of assisting others to grow cannabis plants. The defendants might not have been guilty of conspiracy actually to produce a controlled drug (the offence under the MDA 1971, s. 4(2)(a)) but the substantive offence under s. 4(2)(b) is much broader and does not require involvement in any particular process of production.

Conditional Agreements and Contingencies

Problems may also arise where agreements could be carried out without committing the alleged **A5.50** substantive offence, or where the parties recognise that it might not prove necessary to carry out the agreement itself. On the face of it, the first kind of agreement falls outside the definition of a conspiracy. In *Reed* [1982] Crim LR 819, the Court of Appeal stated that, if A and B agree to drive from London to Edinburgh in a time which might or might not be achievable without breaking speed limits, depending on the traffic conditions, they do not thereby agree that they will *necessarily* commit any offence and are not therefore guilty of conspiracy. The Court of Appeal subsequently approved this dictum in *Jackson* [1985] Crim LR 442, whilst purporting to distinguish it on the facts before them. The appellants in *Jackson* agreed with one W, who was on trial for burglary, that he would be shot in the leg so as to induce the court to treat him leniently, should he be convicted. They were charged with conspiracy to pervert the course of justice, but argued that, when the agreement was made, it was not known whether W would be convicted. Thus, the planned shooting would not necessarily have interfered with the course of justice. Rejecting this argument, the court replied that 'contingency planning' could amount to conspiracy:

> 'Necessarily' is not to be held to mean that there must inevitably be the carrying out of an offence, it means, if the agreement is carried out in accordance with the plan, there must be the commission of the offence referred to in the conspiracy count.

With respect, the agreed course of conduct (the shooting of W) was not contingent on the outcome of the trial: indeed, it was carried out before the trial ended. It was the effect of that conduct on the future course of justice that was uncertain. The convictions in *Jackson* can better be justified on the basis that the appellants conspired (unconditionally) to commit an act which was intended (conditionally on the outcome of the trial) to pervert the course of justice; and an act committed with such an intent is sufficient to amount to the substantive offence of perverting the course of justice (see **B14.34**). If, however, planning for a contingency may indeed amount to conspiracy (and *O'Hadhmaill* [1996] Crim LR 509 is clear authority that it may), motorists who agree to break speed limits, if necessary, in order to get to Edinburgh on time must after all be guilty, and robbers who agree to 'shoot to kill' if challenged must equally be guilty of conspiracy to murder. This was acknowledged by the House of Lords in *Saik* [2007] 1 AC 18; but their lordships distinguished such cases from that in which A and B agree to launder money or other property that they suspect may *possibly* represent the proceeds of crime. If they do not know or intend this to be the case (as is required by the CLA 1977, s. 1(2); see **A5.55**), they are not guilty of conspiracy, even though it may transpire that their suspicions are well founded (in which case they may end up committing a substantive money laundering offence).

Agreement is the basis of liability in conspiracy. Abandonment of the agreement cannot affect such liability once it has been incurred (*Bolton* (1991) 94 Cr App R 74).

Agreement Without Real Intent

If the *actus reus* of conspiracy is agreement, the *mens rea* is harder to identify. The concept of **A5.51** agreement does not necessarily import an intent by each party to carry out that agreement, but such an intent was (and still is) required in respect of conspiracy at common law (*Thomson* (1965) 50 Cr App R 1; *Yip Chieu-Chung v The Queen* [1995] 1 AC 111) whilst there are references in the CLA 1977, s. 1(1) and (4), to agreements being carried out in accordance with the intentions of the parties. The issue of intent may become problematic where one or more of the parties does not intend to keep his part of the agreement, as where a hired assassin agrees to commit a murder but intends only to make off with his advance fee, or where the supposed assassin is working undercover for the police, and intends only to collect evidence against those who hired him. Is the dishonest assassin or undercover officer guilty of conspiracy to murder. If not, where does that leave the other parties to the supposed agreement?

A5.52 The House of Lords touched upon such questions in *Anderson* [1986] AC 27. A was charged with conspiracy to effect a convicted prisoner's escape from jail. He had agreed to such a plan and had supplied the other conspirators with diamond cutting wire in furtherance of it, but claimed that he had never believed the jailbreak could succeed, and was concerned only to obtain the money he had been promised for the wire. The Court of Appeal held that this amounted to an admission of complicity in the conspiracy as a secondary party, but the House of Lords preferred to categorise A as a principal offender. Lord Bridge, with whom the other members of the House agreed, said:

> I ... reject any construction of the statutory language which would require the prosecution to prove an intention on the part of each conspirator that the criminal offence or offences ... should in fact be committed.
>
> ... [B]eyond the mere fact of agreement, the necessary *mens rea* ... is ... established if, and only if ... the accused ... intended to play some part in the agreed course of conduct in furtherance of the criminal purpose which the agreed course of conduct was intended to achieve. Nothing less will suffice; nothing more is required.

Lord Bridge went on to emphasise that an undercover agent, 'ostensibly agreeing [but] with the purpose of exposing and frustrating the purpose of the other parties' cannot be guilty of conspiracy. This must be correct, but the earlier excerpts from his speech are problematic, and much of what he said is now widely considered to have been wrong. In particular, his ruling that a conspirator need not intend the offence in question to be committed does violence to the wording of the CLA 1977, s. 1(1), and is difficult to reconcile with s. 1(2) (see **A5.55**). Elsewhere, however, Lord Bridge refers to 'the criminal purpose which the agreed course of conduct was *intended* to achieve', adding, '[it] is, of course, necessary that any party to the agreement shall have assented to play his part ... knowing that the part to be played by one or more of the others will amount to or involve the commission of an offence'.

On that basis, the fraudulent hit-man who intends only to make off with his advance fee cannot after all be guilty of conspiracy to murder, because he knows that without him the plan must fail. Similarly, fraudulent drug dealers who intend to supply their customers with harmless powder cannot be regarded as having conspired to supply drugs. Their plan is in fact to obtain property from the customers by deception. This interpretation makes far more sense and appears to have been accepted by the Court of Appeal in *Edwards* [1991] Crim LR 352 and by the Northern Ireland Court of Appeal in *McPhillips* (1990 unreported). See also *Yip Chieu-Chung v The Queen* [1995] 1 AC 111 (see **A5.54**).

Where an apparent agreement to commit an offence is nothing more than fantasy, in that none of the parties seriously intend to put it into execution, the position is clear: a shared fantasy is not a conspiracy; and if the prosecution evidence is so equivocal that no reasonable jury, properly directed, could be sure the agreement was anything more than mere fantasy, there can be no case to answer. There must in other words, be some credible evidence of 'executory intent'. See *Goddard* [2012] EWCA Crim 1756.

Active and Passive Conspirators

A5.53 A second problem with Lord Bridge's ruling in *Anderson* [1986] AC 27 is that it appears to require each conspirator to intend playing some active part in furtherance of the conspiracy. If so, it is a proposition for which there is no basis in the CLA 1977 or in any cases decided before or after it. In *Siracusa* (1989) 90 Cr App R 340, the court concluded that Lord Bridge could not have meant what he said. 'He cannot have been intending that the organiser of a crime, who recruited others to carry it out, would not himself be guilty of conspiracy ... Participation in a conspiracy is infinitely variable: it can be active or passive.'

Where Only One Conspirator is Genuine

A cannot be guilty of conspiracy if B (the only other party to the supposed agreement) intends **A5.54**
to frustrate or sabotage it. This issue did not arise in *Anderson* [1986] AC 27, but the Privy
Council were required to consider it in *Yip Chieu-Chung v The Queen* [1995] 1 AC 111, where
N, the appellant's only fellow conspirator in a plan to smuggle heroin out of Hong Kong, was
an undercover agent working with the knowledge of the authorities. The Privy Council held
that, if N's purpose had been to prevent the heroin being smuggled, no conspiracy would have
existed. Lord Griffiths said:

> The crime of conspiracy requires an agreement between two or more persons to commit an
> unlawful act with the intention of carrying it out. It is the intention to carry out the crime that
> constitutes the necessary *mens rea* for the offence. As Lord Bridge pointed out [in *Anderson*] an
> undercover agent who has no intention of committing the crime lacks the necessary *mens rea* to be a
> conspirator.

Conspiracy under Hong Kong law remains a common-law offence, but Lord Griffiths did not
seek to distinguish in this respect between common-law and statutory conspiracy. He was,
however, able to uphold the appellant's conviction on the basis that N had intended to smuggle
the heroin out of Hong Kong as agreed. The trap was to be sprung later, when the heroin arrived
in Australia. The fact that the Hong Kong authorities acquiesced in this plan did not prevent
it from being a criminal act. Both parties were therefore guilty, albeit that N would never be
prosecuted. But see *Rafiq* [2008] EWCA Crim 1518, in which the Court doubted whether in
such circumstances the undercover officer would be guilty of any offence in English law.

Mens Rea as to Circumstances

At common law, a person could be guilty of conspiracy only if he and at least one other conspira- **A5.55**
tor knew of any relevant circumstances necessary for the commission of the offence (*Churchill
v Walton* [1967] 2 AC 224). The CLA 1977, s. 1(2) (see **A5.41**), maintains this rule in relation
to statutory conspiracies. Thus, it was a strict liability offence for a trader to provide false or
misleading information when marketing his products to consumers but there could be no conspiracy to commit the offence if the parties were unaware that the information was either false or
likely to deceive. This rule applies to all conspiracies, and not merely to those concerning strict
liability offences. As the House of Lords noted in *Saik* [2007] 1 AC 18, any other interpretation
would be absurd. On the other hand, knowledge of the relevant law which makes the proposed
conduct illegal need not be proved, because ignorance of the law is no defence (*Broad* [1997]
Crim LR 666).

Despite s. 1(2), an indictment may properly charge conspiracy to commit criminal damage or
arson 'being reckless as to whether the life of another person would thereby be endangered',
because actual endangerment is not 'a fact or circumstance necessary for the commission of
the offence' under the Criminal Damage Act 1971, s. 1(2). It is necessary only that the conspirators realise that their plan *may*, if carried out, endanger life. See *Mir* (22 April 1994 unreported), *Browning* (6 November 1998 unreported), *Ryan* (1999) 163 JP 849, and *Saik*, per Lord
Nicholls at [4].

Difficulties have arisen as to the application of the CLA 1977, s. 1(2), to cases of conspiracy to **A5.56**
commit money laundering offences under the 'old' law (i.e. in cases not governed by the POCA
2002; see **B21**). These difficulties arose largely because of uncertainty as to the proper interpretation of the substantive money laundering offences under the Drug Trafficking Act 1994 or
the CJA 1988, but have now largely been resolved by decisions of the House of Lords in *Montila*
[2005] 1 All ER 113 and *Saik*, and by those of the Court of Appeal in *Harmer* [2005] 2 Cr App
R 23, *Ali* [2006] QB 322 and *Suchedina* [2007] 1 Cr App R 305.

Reliance may no longer be placed on cases such as *Rizvi* [2003] EWCA Crim 3575, *Singh*
[2003] EWCA Crim 3712 and *Sakavickas* [2005] 1 WLR 857 (examined in the 2006 edition

of this work), because these were based on an interpretation of the substantive money laundering law that was later rejected by the House of Lords in *Montila*, and *Saik* confirms that none of
those cases survives the ruling in *Montila*. See also *El-Kurd (No. 2)* [2007] 1 WLR 3190.

The true position in respect of such conspiracies was summarised in *Harmer* [2005] 2 Cr App
R 23, in which it was held that an agreement to convert or transfer property that is merely
suspected of being the proceeds of criminal conduct cannot amount to a criminal conspiracy
within the meaning of the CLA 1977, s. 1. As May LJ explained:

> A defendant is not to be guilty of conspiracy [to commit a money laundering offence under the
> CJA 1988] unless he and at least one other party to the agreement intend or know that the money
> will be the proceeds of crime when the agreed conduct takes place. This intention or knowledge is
> precisely what the prosecution in the present case accepted they could not prove when the words
> 'knew or' were omitted from the particulars of count 2. If the prosecution cannot prove that the
> money was the proceeds of crime, they cannot prove that the appellant knew that it was. So section
> 1(2) of the 1977 Act applies and is not satisfied.

This dictum was later approved in *Saik* (per Lord Hope at [72]). A similar approach would seem
to be called for in the context of conspiracies to commit offences under the POCA 2002, because,
with the possible exception of offences under s. 328 (see **B21.15** *et seq.*), the substantive money
laundering offences can be committed only in respect of property that is in fact 'criminal property'. See also *R* [2007] 1 Cr App R 150 and *Pace* [2014] EWCA Crim 186. It follows that the
CLA 1977, s. 1(2), seriously compromises the Crown's ability to use a single 'umbrella' conspiracy
count in preference to multiple charges alleging a series of substantive money laundering transactions. The price for using such a charge is the need to prove knowledge or intent as to the criminal
character of the property in question, where proof of well-founded suspicion would generally
suffice for the substantive offences. But *Saik* itself makes clear that where a conspiracy count looks
to future transactions there can be no question of having to prove that the property in question
is in fact of illicit origin, for *ex hypothesi* it is as yet unidentified. What matters is the intent of the
conspirators. See *Suchedina* at [18]–[20].

Impossibility

A5.57 At common law it was a defence to a charge of conspiracy that the object of the conspiracy was
impossible to achieve. One could not, for example, be guilty of a conspiracy to extract cocaine
from a substance which proved not to contain any cocaine (*DPP v Nock* [1978] AC 979). The
CLA 1977, s. 1(1), was amended by the Criminal Attempts Act 1981, so as largely to eliminate
defences based on impossibility. If A and B wrongly believe that cocaine can be extracted from a
given substance, they may now commit an indictable conspiracy or attempt to do so. They may
also enter into an indictable conspiracy to murder someone who turns out to be dead already or to
handle goods which they wrongly believe to have been stolen. On the other hand, an agreement
to pursue a course of conduct which the parties wrongly believe to be criminal, because they have
misunderstood the law, cannot be indictable as a conspiracy (cf. *Taaffe* [1984] AC 539).

Jurisdiction over Statutory Conspiracy

A5.58 Conspiracy under the CLA 1977, s. 1, must involve an agreement to commit an offence triable
under English law (s. 1(4)) and this usually means an offence which is to be committed within
England and Wales or aboard a British ship or aircraft. A number of offences can however be
tried under English law even if committed abroad (e.g., offences under the Aviation Security
Act 1982 (see **B10.214** *et seq.*) or murder/manslaughter committed by a British citizen on land
outside the UK). Persons who conspire anywhere to commit such crimes abroad are therefore
indictable under s. 1 (*Bow Street Metropolitan Stipendiary Magistrate, ex parte Pinochet Ugarte
(No. 3)* [2000] 1 AC 147).

Persons who conspire in England and Wales to commit acts outside England and Wales, which
are not offences under English law but are punishable under the law of the country or territory

in question and would be punishable under English law if committed in England or Wales, may be charged with conspiracy by virtue of the CLA 1977, s. 1A. In *Patel* [2009] EWCA Crim 67, the object of the agreement was illegal entry to the USA, contrary to US federal law. This fell within the ambit of s. 1A, the equivalent offence in English law being that under the Immigration Act 1971, s. 25 (see **B22.21**). In such a case, part I of the 1977 Act (ss. 1 to 5) 'has effect in relation to the agreement' on the same basis as it applies to conspiracies that fall within s. 1(1) itself (see s. 1A(1)). In other words, s. 1A is not a stand-alone provision, but operates as an extension to the s. 1 offence.

A s. 1A conspiracy is committed if a party to the agreement, or his agent, did anything in England and Wales in relation to the agreement before its formation, or if a party joined it there (in person or through an agent), or if a party (or his agent) did or omitted anything there in pursuance of the agreement (s. 1A(5)). Prior to 1 February 2010 (when amendments made by the CAJA 2009, s. 72, came into force), a s. 1A conspiracy had to involve an agreement to commit acts etc. outside the UK, thus excluding conspiracies to commit offences in Scotland or Northern Ireland.

A5.59 Conspiracy to commit a 'cross frontier' offence of fraud or dishonesty which would itself be triable in England and Wales as a Group A offence under part I of the CJA 1993 should be indicted under the CLA 1977, s. 1, without reference to s. 1A. A person may be guilty of conspiracy to commit such an offence whether or not any act or omission in relation to that offence occurred in England or Wales (CJA 1993, s. 3(2); and see further **A8.10** *et seq.*).

Even in cases not covered by the CJA 1993, conspirators who, whilst abroad, plot the commission of a crime within England or Wales, may be indicted under English law, even if none of them enter the jurisdiction or trigger any consequences here. See *Liangsiriprasert v USA* [1991] 1 AC 225; *Sansom* (1991) 92 Cr App R 115; *Manning* [1998] 2 Cr App R 461; *R (Al-Fawwaz) v Governor of Brixton Prison* [2002] 1 AC 556.

Evidential Issues

A5.60 There are no special evidential rules peculiar to conspiracy. In *Murphy* (1837) 8 C & P 297, proof of conspiracy was said to be generally 'a matter of inference deduced from certain criminal acts of the parties accused', but there is no actual need for any such acts, and conspiracies may also be proved, *inter alia*, by direct testimony, secret recordings or confessions, subject only to the proviso that A's pre-trial confession cannot ordinarily be evidence against B. The acts and statements of one conspirator may be given in evidence against both him and his fellow conspirators, provided they were done or said in furtherance of their common purpose, but that rule is not confined to conspiracies. See further **F16.72** *et seq.*

CONSPIRACY TO DEFRAUD

Definition

A5.61 The common-law offence of conspiracy to defraud was expressly preserved by the CLA 1977, s. 5(2). There are two principal variants of this offence, although these are not mutually exclusive. The first is defined in the leading case of *Scott v Metropolitan Police Commissioner* [1975] AC 819, where Viscount Dilhorne said:

> ...an agreement by two or more [persons] by dishonesty to deprive a person of something which is his or to which he is or would be or might be entitled [or] an agreement by two or more by dishonesty to injure some proprietary right of his suffices to constitute the offence...

There may or may not be an intent to deceive in such cases, and there may or may not be an intent to cause economic or financial loss to the proposed victim or victims, but it suffices if there is a dishonest agreement to expose the proposed victim to some form of economic risk or disadvantage to which he would not otherwise be exposed.

In the second variant there must be a dishonest agreement to deceive another person into acting contrary to his duty. There is some doubt as to the exact scope of this offence. It was suggested (*obiter*) in *DPP v Withers* [1975] AC 842 that the person deceived must be a public official, and this was also the view of Lord Diplock in *Scott*, but the opinion of the Privy Council in *Wai Yu-tsang v The Queen* [1992] AC 269 was that it suffices if any person is deceived into acting contrary to the duty he owes to his clients or employers. The Privy Council approved and adopted the concept of 'intent to defraud' previously expounded by Lord Denning and Lord Radcliffe in *Welham v DPP* [1961] AC 103, which is that to defraud means 'to practise a fraud' and this need not necessarily involve any form of economic loss or prejudice.

A5.62 Either variant of conspiracy to defraud is capable of overlapping with the offence of statutory conspiracy (see **A5.41** *et seq.*). Such overlap will occur wherever the course of action agreed on would necessarily involve the commission of any offence or offences by one or more of the parties to the conspiracy if carried out in accordance with their intentions and would also involve a fraud being practised on another person. In such circumstances, the prosecution has a choice as to which kind of charge to prefer (CJA 1987, s. 12(1)). Under guidelines issued by the A-G in 2007, however, a charge of statutory conspiracy (or a charge alleging a substantive offence) should be brought in preference to a charge of conspiracy to defraud unless there are good reasons for doing otherwise. A charge of conspiracy to defraud may be appropriate where no charge of statutory conspiracy (or of a substantive offence) could properly reflect the gravity of the offence, and/or where such charges might require a large number of separate counts, severed trials, etc. There may also be cases in which the identification of specific target offences would be problematic.

Prior to the commencement of the Enterprise Act 2002, a price-fixing or 'cartel' agreement could not amount to a conspiracy to defraud unless combined with other elements such as deliberate misrepresentation (*Norris v Government of the USA* [2008] 1 AC 920; *Goldshield Group plc* [2009] 2 All ER 738). A cartel agreement now constitutes a statutory offence and would be prosecuted under s. 188 of the 2002 Act.

Indictment and Procedure

A5.63 Conspiracy to defraud is triable only on indictment. It is punishable by up to ten years' imprisonment or a fine or both (CJA 1987, s. 12(3)). For trial purposes, it is a class 3 offence. An indictment for conspiracy to defraud should not lack particularity and should enable the defence and the judge to know precisely the nature of the prosecution's case (*Landy* [1981] 1 All ER 1172). This prevents the prosecution from shifting their ground during the trial, unless they obtain leave of the judge and amend the indictment itself (*Landy*). A single count of conspiracy to defraud may be founded on evidence of several fraudulent transactions if it can be shown that those transactions were each effected pursuant to a single agreement (*Mba* [2006] EWCA Crim 624).

In *K* [2005] 1 Cr App R 408, the Court of Appeal considered *Landy* and added this guidance as to the drafting of indictments for conspiracy to defraud:

> [The indictment] should identify the agreement alleged with the specificity necessary in the circumstances of each case; if the agreement alleged is complex, then details of that may be needed and those details will ... form part of what must be proved. If this course is followed, it should then be clear what the prosecution must prove and the matters on which the jury must be unanimous: see *Bennett* [1999] EWCA Crim 1486. Further particulars should be given where it is necessary for the defendants to have further general information as to the nature of the charge and for the other purposes identified by Lawton LJ in *Landy*. Such further particulars form no part of the ingredients of the offence and on these the jury do not have to be unanimous, as this court correctly decided in *Hancock*.

Statement of Offence

Conspiracy to defraud contrary to common law.

Particulars of Offence

A and B on divers days between ... and ... conspired together [and with ...] to defraud the C Bank plc and its existing and potential shareholders, creditors and depositors

(i) by dishonestly concealing in the accounts of the C Bank the dishonouring of cheques in the sum of £50 million drawn on the account of D Ltd with the E Bank Inc, such cheques having been purchased by the C Bank

(ii) [etc.]

As to the power of local authorities to prosecute for conspiracy to defraud (e.g., in consumer protection cases), see *Jarrett* [1997] Crim LR 517 and *Richards* [1999] Crim LR 598. As to the A-G's guidelines on prosecutions for conspiracy to defraud, see **A5.66** and **appendix 2**.

Sentence

The definitive sentencing guideline, *Fraud, Bribery and Money Laundering Offences* (see Supplement, **SG-288**) includes guidance on sentencing for conspiracy to defraud. The guideline applies to individual offenders aged 18 and over and organisations. It applies to all offenders sentenced on or after 1 October 2014 regardless of the date of the offence. There is a separate part of the guideline applicable to corporate offenders. **A5.64**

Actus Reus

As in cases of statutory conspiracy, there must always be an agreement. Two or more similar but separate agreements cannot be charged as a single conspiracy to defraud (see *Mehta* [2012] EWCA Crim 2824 and **A5.46**). The agreement may however be wider in certain respects than that required in respect of the statutory offence. It need not be an agreement that would necessarily involve the commission of a substantive offence if carried out (*Scott v Metropolitan Police Commissioner* [1975] AC 819; *Cooke* [1986] AC 909) and it need not necessarily be envisaged that the fraud will be perpetrated by the conspirators themselves. In *Hollinshead* [1985] AC 975, the appellants agreed to market devices designed to falsify gas or electricity meters, which would enable customers (who were not themselves party to the conspiracy) to defraud their gas and electricity suppliers. The appellants had no intention of using the devices themselves, but they were nevertheless guilty of conspiracy to defraud. In such circumstances a charge under the Fraud Act 2006, s. 7 (see **B5.23**), would now be more appropriate (see **A5.62** and the A-G's guidelines on prosecutions for conspiracy to defraud at **appendix 2**). **A5.65**

Other reported illustrations of agreements amounting to conspiracy to defraud include: agreement to conceal a bank's losses or liabilities from its shareholders, creditors and depositors (*Wai Yu-tsang v The Queen* [1992] AC 269); agreement by company directors to conceal secret profits from the company, where the company would be entitled to demand that the profits be accounted for (*Adams v The Queen* [1995] 1 WLR 52); agreement by British Rail catering staff to sell their own refreshments to customers whilst on duty, thereby depriving British Rail of profits from legitimate sales (*Cooke* [1986] AC 909); agreement to falsify hire-purchase or credit applications, so as to induce credit companies or other lenders to make loans they might not otherwise be willing to make (*Allsop* (1976) 64 Cr App R 29); and agreement to make pirate copies of films, etc., thereby depriving the makers and distributors of legitimate profits (*Scott v Metropolitan Police Commissioner*). As in cases of statutory conspiracy (see **A5.47**), it may be possible in some cases for one of two alleged conspirators to be convicted while the other is acquitted; but this would only be possible where there is evidence admissible against one but not the other (*Testouri* [2004] 2 Cr App R 26; *Elkins* [2005] EWCA Crim 2711).

As to the position where only one of the supposed conspirators really intends to proceed with or carry out the conduct agreed upon, see **A5.54**.

Mens Rea

A5.66 To be guilty of conspiracy to defraud, D must be dishonest (in the *Ghosh* sense, as to which see **B4.54**) and must intend to defraud the proposed victim, in one or other of the senses explained at **A5.61**; but an intent to deceive is necessary only in respect of the second of the two variants of the offence. In *A-G's Ref (No. 1 of 1982)* [1983] QB 751, it was held that there can be no conspiracy to defraud where the defrauding would be a mere side-effect (rather than the 'true object') of the scheme agreed to, but this is now generally thought to be wrong, and has not been followed in subsequent cases. The correct position must be that D intends to defraud V wherever he is aware that the successful implementation of his plan will result in V being defrauded (cf. *McPherson* [1985] Crim LR 508).

Jurisdiction over Conspiracy to Defraud

A5.67 In *Board of Trade v Owen* [1957] AC 602, the House of Lords held that jurisdiction over conspiracy to defraud was governed by the same principles as conspiracy to commit a crime. In other words, a conspiracy abroad to defraud a victim within England and Wales may be indictable here, but no indictment will lie where the victim is to be defrauded abroad. Lord Tucker said:

> A conspiracy to commit a crime abroad is not indictable in this country unless the contemplated crime is one for which an indictment would lie here...It necessarily follows that a conspiracy of the nature of that charged in count 3 [i.e. a conspiracy to defraud a West German government department] — which in my view was a conspiracy to attain a lawful object by unlawful means, rather than to commit a crime — is not triable in this country, since the unlawful means and the ultimate object were both outside the jurisdiction.

See also *A-G's Ref (No. 1 of 1982)* [1983] QB 751 and *Naini* [1999] 2 Cr App R 398, and **A8**. The position is now different in respect of things done on or after 1 June 1999. Section 5(3) of the CJA 1993 provides that various acts done or omitted within England and Wales, whether by a conspirator or by someone acting as his agent, may bring all the conspirators within English jurisdiction, even if the defrauding was intended to occur abroad. Conspirators may even be liable on the basis of acts previously done in England and Wales, before the conspiracy was formed.

Impossibility

A5.68 The abolition of the defence of impossibility in respect of attempts and statutory conspiracies has not affected the operation of that defence in the context of conspiracy to defraud nor did it affect the common-law offence of incitement. As to impossibility in offences under the SCA 2007, part 2, see **A5.7**.

ATTEMPT

Definition

A5.69 The law relating to attempts is primarily governed by the CAA 1981.

Criminal Attempts Act 1981, s. 1

(1) If, with intent to commit an offence to which this section applies, a person does an act which is more than merely preparatory to the commission of the offence, he is guilty of attempting to commit the offence.

[(1A) and (1B) deal with attempts in England or Wales to commit acts abroad which would amount to offences of computer misuse (see **B17.17**) if committed in England and Wales.]

(2) A person may be guilty of attempting to commit an offence to which this section applies even though the facts are such that the commission of the offence is impossible.

(3) In any case where—

    (a) apart from this subsection a person's intention would not be regarded as having amounted to an intent to commit an offence; but

(b) if the facts of the case had been as he believed them to be, his intention would be so regarded,

then for the purpose of subsection (1) above, he shall be regarded as having had an intent to commit that offence.

(4) This section applies to any offence which, if it were completed, would be triable in England and Wales as an indictable offence, other than—

(a) conspiracy (at common law or under section 1 of the Criminal Law Act 1977);

(b) aiding, abetting, counselling, procuring or suborning the commission of an offence;

(c) offences under section 4(1) (assisting offenders) or 5(1) (accepting or agreeing to accept consideration for not disclosing information about a relevant offence) of the Criminal Law Act 1967.

(5) This section also applies to low-value shoplifting (which is defined in, and is triable only summarily by virtue of, section 22A of the Magistrates' Courts Act 1980).

An offence such as common assault is not 'triable in England and Wales as an indictable offence' merely because it can be included in a wider indictment by virtue of the CJA 1988, s. 40. Dicta to the contrary in *Nelson* [2013] 1 Cr App R 405 (30) must be disregarded, because they overlook the Interpretation Act 1978, sch. 1, which is explicit on that point. As to low value shoplifting, see **D6.29**.

Where an offence is not 'triable as an indictable offence', it cannot be the object of a criminal attempt under the CAA 1981, s. 1, but provisions creating summary offences sometimes create matching offences of attempt: see, e.g., the Road Traffic Act 1988, ss. 4 and 5, which create summary offences of driving *or attempting to drive* when unfit through drink or drugs or when over the prescribed limit for alcohol (see **C5.35** and **C5.57**). The CAA 1981, s. 3, provides that 'attempts under special statutory provisions' shall be governed by rules which mirror those in s. 1(1)–(3).

Section 1(4)(b) does not preclude charges of attempt in relation to substantive offences of 'procuring'; nor does anything in s. 1(4) preclude a charge of attempting to incite the commission of a criminal offence, or of attempting to commit a preparatory offence such as that under the SOA 2003, s. 14 (*Robson* [2009] 1 WLR 713).

Indictment

Statement of Offence   A5.70

Attempted murder contrary to section 1(1) of the Criminal Attempts Act 1981.

Particulars of Offence

A on or about the... day of... attempted to murder V.

A person charged on indictment with an attempt to commit an offence can be convicted on that charge, notwithstanding any evidence proving that he has committed the substantive offence (CLA 1967, s. 6(4)). The same rule applies to summary trials. See *Webley v Buxton* [1977] QB 481. This rule is unaltered by the CAA 1981.

Evidence, Procedure and Sentencing

Criminal Attempts Act 1981, s. 2   A5.71

(1) Any provision to which this section applies shall have effect with respect to an offence under section 1 above of attempting to commit an offence as it has effect with respect to the offence attempted.

(2) This section applies to provisions of any of the following descriptions made by or under any enactment (whenever passed)—

(a) provisions whereby proceedings may not be instituted or carried on otherwise than by, or on behalf or with the consent of, any person (including any provisions which also make other exceptions to the prohibition);

(b) provisions conferring power to institute proceedings;

(c) provisions as to the venue of proceedings;

(d) provisions whereby proceedings may not be instituted after the expiration of a time limit;

(e) provisions conferring a power of arrest or search;

(f) provisions conferring a power of seizure and detention of property;

(g) provisions whereby a person may not be convicted or committed for trial on the uncorroborated evidence of one witness (including any provision requiring the evidence of not less than two credible witnesses);

(h) provisions conferring a power of forfeiture, including any power to deal with anything liable to be forfeited;

(i) provisions whereby, if an offence committed by a body corporate is proved to have been committed with the consent or connivance of another person, that person also is guilty of the offence.

An attempt to commit an offence which is triable only on indictment is itself triable only on indictment, whilst an attempt to commit an offence triable either way is triable either way (CAA 1981, s. 4(1)).

A5.72 By s. 4, the maximum penalty for attempted murder is life imprisonment. Other indictable offences are subject to the same maximum as applies on conviction on indictment for the offence attempted, and if the offence is triable either way (or is low value shoplifting as defined by the MCA 1980, s. 22A) the maximum penalty on summary conviction is the same as the maximum penalty available for that offence tried summarily. The Court of Appeal in *Robson* (1974) CSP A1–4B01 indicated that it would be 'at least unusual that an attempt should be visited with punishment to the maximum extent that the law permits in respect of a completed offence'. It is submitted that the sentence for a given attempt should almost always be less than the sentence which would have been imposed if that offence had been completed, but clearly much will depend on the stage at which the attempt failed, and the reason(s) for its non-completion. On the other hand, within an offence category, some examples of attempt may merit more severe punishment than some examples of the completed offence.

The proper approach to sentencing for attempted murder is set out in the definitive sentencing guideline, *Attempted Murder* (see Supplement, **SG-464**).

Actus Reus

A5.73 The CAA 1981, s. 1(1), requires D to have committed an act which is 'more than merely preparatory' to the offence attempted. A mere omission cannot suffice, even where accompanied by the requisite *mens rea*. A refusal to call an ambulance for a person who is gravely ill cannot, for example, amount to attempted murder; but in *Nevard* [2006] EWCA Crim 2896 the court arguably erred in ruling that the same was true of D's attempt to deceive and put off the emergency services following a 999 call made by V. This surely was a positive act, and would, if successful, have resulted in V's death. Where trial is on indictment, it is for the judge to determine whether there is evidence on which a jury could properly find that D's actions did go beyond mere preparation, but it is then for the jury to decide that question as one of fact (s. 4(3); and see also *DPP v Stonehouse* [1978] AC 55).

At common law, acts amounting to attempts were distinguished from mere preparatory acts by the concept of 'proximity'. An example of the proximity test was provided in *Robinson* [1915] 2 KB 342, in which a jeweller clumsily faked a robbery at his premises with a view to making a fraudulent insurance claim in respect of his supposed loss. It was held that his conviction for attempting to obtain money from his insurers by false pretences could not stand, because he had been arrested before he could send any claim to his insurers. As it was not a decision under the 1981 Act, *Robinson* cannot be a binding authority on its interpretation, but it is unlikely that such a case would be decided differently under the Act. Indeed, a similar approach was adopted in *Campbell* [1991] Crim LR 268, where the appellant armed himself with an imitation gun, approached to within a yard of a post office which he intended to rob, but never drew his weapon; it was held that there was no evidence on which the jury could properly have concluded that his acts went beyond mere preparation. See also *Widdowson* (1985) 82 Cr App R 314. In *Gullefer* [1990] 3 All ER 882, Lord Lane CJ stated that the crucial question was whether D had 'embarked upon the crime proper', but that it was not necessary, as some earlier cases had suggested, that D should have reached a 'point of no return' in respect of the full offence.

This view was echoed in *A-G's Ref (No.1 of 1992)* [1993] Crim LR 274, in which it was held that attempted rape may be committed without D having physically attempted to penetrate his victim. In practice, however, it may be difficult to prove attempted rape in the absence of either an attempt to penetrate or a confession by D. A conviction for sexual assault may be easier to secure (*Beaney* [2010] EWCA Crim 2551; *Ferriter* [2012] EWCA Crim 2211).

In *Jones* [1990] 3 All ER 886, D was charged with attempted murder. He climbed into V's car **A5.74** and drew a loaded gun with the intention of killing him, but was disarmed in a struggle that followed. The Court of Appeal held that it was open to the jury to regard this as attempted murder and in his judgment Taylor LJ provided useful guidance as to the distinction between preparation and attempts:

> The question for the judge in the present case was whether there was evidence from which a reasonable jury, properly directed, could conclude that [V] had done acts which were more than merely preparatory. Clearly his actions in obtaining the gun, in shortening it, in loading it, in putting on his disguise and going to the [ambush point] could only be regarded as preparatory acts. But … once he had got into the car, taken out the loaded gun and pointed it at [V] with the intention of killing him, there was sufficient evidence for the consideration of the jury on the charge of attempted murder. It was a matter for them to decide whether they were sure those acts were more than merely preparatory.

Similar reasoning was applied in *Geddes* [1996] Crim LR 894, in which D was found trespassing in the lavatory block of a school, armed with a large knife and lengths of rope and tape. It appears that he had intended to kidnap a child, but his conviction for attempted false imprisonment was quashed on appeal. Citing *Campbell* with approval, Lord Bingham CJ held that no jury could properly have concluded that D's acts had gone beyond the stage of mere preparation. He may have equipped himself, and put himself in a position to commit the crime when the opportunity arose, but it could not be said that he had actually tried or started to commit it. Similarly, in *Mason v DPP* [2010] RTR 120, it was held that D could not be said to have 'attempted to drive' when over the legal limit for alcohol since he was prevented from even getting into his vehicle; attempting to open the car door was not enough. But contrast *Moore v DPP* [2010] RTR 429 in which D started his car on private property and was stopped by an officer a few metres from the public road towards which he was heading; on those facts, it was held that a court was fully entitled to find that he had attempted to drive on a public road.

The question will often be one of fact and degree, and the answer may not always be obvious. In **A5.75** *Tosti* [1997] Crim LR 746 the appellants had provided themselves with cutting equipment, driven to the scene, concealed the cutting equipment nearby, and approached the door of the premises they intended to break into. They were disturbed as they examined the padlock, and were arrested shortly afterwards. On those facts, it was held that a jury *was* entitled to convict of attempted burglary. *Campbell* is perhaps distinguishable on those facts, but the contrast with *Geddes* is less obvious. See also *Toothill* [1998] Crim LR 876, *K* [2009] EWCA Crim 1931 and *R* [2009] 1 WLR 713.

It may be necessary to identify the essential elements of the crime allegedly attempted, in order to determine whether D got beyond mere preparation. In *Nash* [1999] Crim LR 308, the Court of Appeal construed 'attempting to procure an act of gross indecency' as if it meant '*inciting* an act of gross indecency'; but procuring requires the commission of the offence procured (*Johnson* [1964] 2 QB 404) and it would seem, with respect, that the wrong test was applied.

Mens Rea

Intent is the essence of any crime of attempt under the CAA 1981, as it was at common law **A5.76** (*Pearman* (1984) 80 Cr App R 259). The prosecution must ordinarily prove that D acted with a specific intent to commit the particular crime attempted, even if the full offence is one of strict liability, or one in which the *mens rea* required falls short of the *actus reus* (*Boyton* [2005] EWCA Crim 2979). Thus, although murder may be committed by someone who intends only to cause grievous bodily harm, attempted murder requires nothing less than an intent to kill (*Whybrow* (1951) 35 Cr App R 141).

'Intent' in this context bears the meaning laid down in *Moloney* [1985] AC 905 (see **A2.4**) and *Nedrick* [1986] 3 All ER 1. In most cases, however, a full *Nedrick* direction (see **B1.14**) would be unnecessary and potentially confusing. On a charge of attempted murder by shooting, for example, it may suffice to direct the jury to decide: (a) whether D shot V deliberately; and (b) if so, whether D was 'shooting to kill' (*Fallon* [1994] Crim LR 519).

In *Walker* (1989) 90 Cr App R 226, the defendants were convicted of attempted murder. They had hurled their victim from a third-floor balcony, but he somehow survived the fall. After correctly directing the jury to decide whether the defendants were 'trying to kill him', the trial judge elaborated by suggesting that such an intent may sometimes be inferred in cases where there is a 'very high degree of probability' that death will result. The Court of Appeal upheld the convictions, but doubted whether any such elaboration was called for on the facts of the case. There was a danger of confusing the jury into thinking that foresight of high probability could be equated with intention.

Mens Rea as to Circumstances

A5.77 Although the CAA 1981, s. 1(1), specifies that D must act 'with intent to commit an offence to which this section applies', there is authority to the effect that something less may suffice in respect of any relevant circumstances. In *Khan* [1990] 2 All ER 783, it was held that, since recklessness as to the victim's lack of consent sufficed in relation to the full offence of rape, the offence of attempted rape was committed where D intended (but failed) to have intercourse with a woman and was reckless as to her lack of consent. In *A-G's Ref (No. 3 of 1992)* [1994] 2 All ER 121, the court held that D is guilty of an attempt to commit a criminal offence if he is in one of the states of mind required for the full offence and he does his best, so far as he can, to supply what is missing from the completion of the full offence. If this is correct, then if D attempts to set fire to property, being reckless as to whether life would be endangered, he may be convicted of an attempt to commit an offence under the Criminal Damage Act 1971, s. 1(2).

In *Pace* [2014] EWCA Crim 186, however, the Court of Appeal rejected the argument that, on a charge of attempting to commit an offence of converting criminal property, contrary to the POCA 2002, s. 327(1)(c), it would be sufficient for the prosecution to prove that D merely suspected the property in question to be criminal property. Suspicion of this kind suffices for the substantive offence (as it does for all such offences under ss. 327 to 329) but it cannot, said the Court, suffice for an attempt.

The Court suggested that *Khan* and *A-G's Ref (No. 3 of 1992)* could be distinguished (it had no power to overrule either of those cases) but its preferred view appears to have been that the same intent or knowledge as to the circumstances should be required for attempt as it is (under the CLA 1977, s. 1(2)) for conspiracy (see **A5.55**). One problem with that view is that Parliament could easily have inserted a similar provision into the CAA 1981, but chose not to do so. *Pace* was a case on 'attempting the impossible' (see further **A5.81**). This may be the best way to understand it, and the best way to distinguish it from *Khan*.

Conditional Intent

A5.78 Problems of conditional intent in attempts seldom arise otherwise than in relation to theft and related offences. A would-be thief may not know what he will find when searching through another person's property, and may not even be sure what he is hoping to find. In *Husseyn* (1978) 67 Cr App R 131, H and G dishonestly opened the door of a van, but were challenged just as they were about to examine a holdall lying inside the van. The holdall contained valuable scuba-diving equipment, but it was held that they could not be convicted on an indictment alleging that they attempted to steal that equipment. They did not even know what the holdall contained. A properly drafted indictment would have avoided this problem. Had it merely alleged that they 'attempted to steal from' the holdall or van, it would not have mattered whether the holdall or van contained anything which they might actually want to steal, or indeed any property at all.

Attempts with a Foreign Element

The CAA 1981, s. 1(4) (see **A5.69**), restates the common-law rule that conduct cannot amount   **A5.79** to a criminal attempt under English law unless it is directed towards the commission of a substantive offence which would itself be indictable under English law. An attempt in England and Wales to publish an obscene article in Scotland is not, for example, indictable under English law, because the ulterior offence would not be. Attempts to commit offences of fraud or dishonesty are now covered by part I of the CJA 1993 (see **A8.10**). An attempt in England and Wales to commit a 'Group A' offence (such as theft, forgery, etc.) abroad would be triable under the CAA 1981, s. 1, because a Group A offence is triable under English law where any 'relevant event' concerning it takes place in England or Wales.

The CJA 1993 inserted s. 1A into the CAA 1981, supposedly to cover cases where D in England and Wales attempts to commit abroad something which *would* be a Group A offence, but for the fact that it is not triable under English law. This provision is fundamentally at odds with itself. If a Group A offence is instigated by conduct within England and Wales, that offence will inevitably be triable under English law.

Where an attempt to commit an offence within England and Wales is instigated from abroad, the general rule is that such conduct does amount to an offence under s. 1. This has long been true where the attempt is furthered by consequences occurring within the jurisdiction (*Baxter* [1972] 1 QB 1; *DPP v Stonehouse* [1978] AC 55); but it is now clear that (as in conspiracy) such consequences are unnecessary (*Latif* [1996] 1 All ER 353). As to attempts made abroad to commit Group A offences wholly or partly in England and Wales, see the CJA 1993, s. 3(3).

Withdrawal

There is no recognised defence of voluntary withdrawal in English law. If D has not progressed   **A5.80** beyond the stage of mere preparatory acts (see **A5.73**) he can avoid incurring liability by refraining from further acts but, once he has gone beyond that stage, withdrawal will be irrelevant as far as his liability for attempt is concerned.

Impossibility

At common law, no offence of attempt could be committed where it would have been impos-   **A5.81** sible (even in theory) for D to succeed in committing the substantive offence. D could not be guilty of attempting to steal from a bag or pocket which was empty, and could not be guilty of attempting to handle stolen goods if the goods in question had been recovered by the police and had accordingly ceased to be stolen (*Haughton v Smith* [1975] AC 476). This rule was abrogated by the CAA 1981, s. 1(2) and (3), but the precise effect of those provisions was for a time uncertain. In *Anderton v Ryan* [1985] AC 560, the House of Lords held that a distinction had to be drawn between the person who attempts to commit a crime but fails because the crime is impossible (the 'empty pocket' kind of case) and the person who succeeds in doing an 'objectively innocent' act but labours under a mistaken view of the facts or circumstances, and wrongly believes that he is committing an offence.

Anderton v Ryan was thought to be an example of the latter type of case. R bought a video recorder in suspicious circumstances, firmly believing it to be stolen. There was, however, no evidence to prove that it was stolen, and the House of Lords held she could not be guilty even of an attempt to handle stolen goods. The decision was much criticised, and in *Shivpuri* [1987] AC 1 the House of Lords acknowledged that their earlier decision was wrong. Lord Bridge said:

> I am satisfied . . . that the concept of 'objective innocence' is incapable of sensible application in relation to the law of criminal attempts . . . Any attempt to commit an offence which . . . for any reason

fails, so that in the event no offence is committed must, *ex hypothesi*, from the point of view of the criminal law, be objectively innocent. What turns what would otherwise...be an innocent act into a crime is the intent of the actor to commit an offence.

In *Shivpuri*, S was charged with an attempt to commit an offence under the Misuse of Drugs Act 1971, s. 3(1). He confessed to acting as a recipient and distributor of what he assumed to be an illegally imported drug. It transpired (to his surprise) that the substance was not a drug at all, but in accordance with the CAA 1981, s. 1(3), his liability for attempting to commit that offence was assessed on the basis of the facts as he believed them to be. See also *Jones* [2008] QB 460.

Section 1(3) does not enable D to be convicted of attempting to commit an offence where he merely suspects the existence of facts that (if true) would make him guilty of the substantive offence (*Pace* [2014] EWCA Crim 186 at [61]). The defendants in *Pace* could not therefore be convicted of attempting to convert criminal property that was not in fact criminal property at all, 'because the Crown's case had been put not on the basis of belief but on the basis of suspicion'.

If D is not mistaken as to the facts, but wrongly believes that his actions amount to a criminal offence (i.e. as a result of his mistaken view of the law), this mistake cannot make him guilty of any criminal attempt. Section 1(2) does not apply in such cases (cf. *Taaffe* [1984] AC 539).

Interfering with Vehicles

A5.82   Where D is seen interfering with a vehicle or trailer, it is often difficult to prove which of a number of possible offences he is trying to commit. A charge of attempt under the CAA 1981, s. 1, may therefore be impossible to prove, but see the specific offence of interference with vehicles created by s. 9 (see **B4.137** *et seq.*).

Section A6   Corporate Liability

LIABILITY OF COMPANY

Although in many ways a company enjoys the same rights and is bound by the same duties **A6.1** as an individual, there are also marked differences in the application of the criminal law to it. The essence of a limited liability company is that it has a separate legal personality distinct from its shareholders, and indeed its directors and officers, so it enjoys rights and is subject to duties in its own right like an individual person. It is a distinct legal entity, capable of owning and dealing with property, suing and being sued and contracting on its own behalf. It is equally capable of committing crimes. Who owns the shares and in what proportion is irrelevant. The company's acts are not the shareholders' acts, even if one of them also has sole control of its affairs (*Salomon v A Salomon & Co Ltd* [1897] AC 22). The way in which criminal liability attaches to a limited company depends on the appropriate rule of attribution as determined by the particular statutory provision and the interpretation of the courts; to establish whether a company is criminally liable, it is necessary to ascertain which rule of attribution applies.

A company can commit most offences. A requirement of *mens rea* is no bar to a company's guilt. The only crimes it cannot commit as a principal are murder and treason (because the punishment is necessarily incapable of being imposed on a company). Although a company could not factually be a principal offender in offences such as rape or bigamy, it could, just like a human person, be liable as an accessory (as indeed it could be to murder). For example, a company might procure girls for underage sex. Proof of *mens rea* is, of course, required for liability as an accessory but this is no bar to corporate liability; a company was convicted of aiding and abetting causing death by dangerous driving in *Robert Millar (Contractors) Ltd* [1970] 2 QB 54, the mental element being proved through a director with whom the company was identified.

RULES OF ATTRIBUTION: PRINCIPLE OF IDENTIFICATION

For most crimes which require proof of a mental element (such as 'dishonestly', 'wilfully' or **A6.2** 'recklessly') the identification principle will be the appropriate rule of attribution. A company is fixed with criminal liability through the acts or omissions of its 'directing mind'; a corporation can be convicted of a criminal offence requiring proof of *mens rea* if the natural person who committed the offence is identified with the company. The ambit of those who fall into this category is both limited and uncertain, save to say that the officers of the company and the main board are likely to be included. It is important to observe that the person identified with the company who commits the offence is acting *as* the company not *for* it.

A company can act only within the terms of its memorandum and articles of association. These two instruments are important so far as corporate criminal liability is concerned because they represent the starting point in determining whose acts may be identified as those of the corporation itself. Lord Diplock (in *Tesco Supermarkets Ltd v Nattrass* [1972] AC 153 at p. 199) regarded them as paramount:

> ...a corporation...owes its corporate personality and its powers to its constitution, the memorandum and articles of association. The obvious and the only place to discover by what natural persons its powers are exercisable, is in its constitution...
>
> In my view, therefore, the question: 'what natural persons are to be treated in law as being the company for the purposes of acts done in the course of its business'...is to be found by identifying those natural persons who by the memorandum and articles of association or as a result of action taken by the directors, or by the company in general meeting pursuant to the articles, are entrusted with the exercise of the powers of the company.

Lord Reid said (at p. 170) that:

> It must be a question of law whether, once the facts have been ascertained, a person in doing particular things is to be regarded as the company or merely as the company's servant or agent.

This principle was reaffirmed in *A-G's Ref (No. 2 of 1999)* [2000] QB 796. A prosecution for manslaughter was brought against Great Western Trains as a result of the Southall rail disaster. To the question the A-G referred to the Court of Appeal: 'Can a non-human defendant be convicted of the crime of manslaughter by gross negligence in the absence of evidence establishing the guilt of an identified human individual for the same crime?' the answer was 'No'. Rose LJ stated:

> In our judgment, unless an identified individual's conduct, characterisable as gross criminal negligence, can be attributed to the company, the company is not, in the present state of the common law, liable for manslaughter.

The 'identified individual' being referred to by the Court was a single person identified as the embodiment of the company itself.

Seniority and Identification

A6.3 The day-to-day management of a relatively substantial company will typically be delegated by the board to a managing director or directors. Whether a person is sufficiently senior to be identified with the company has been tested in court with apparently inconsistent results. In *Tesco Supermarkets Ltd v Nattrass* [1972] AC 153 a store manager was not sufficiently senior to be identified with the nationwide company, but was regarded as a third person (thus providing Tesco with a statutory defence to the charge); equally in *John Henshall (Quarries) Ltd v Harvey* [1965] 2 QB 233, a weighbridge operator was not identified with the company. In *Tesco v Nattrass*, Lord Reid said (at p. 175) that:

> ...the board never delegated any part of their functions. They set up a chain of command through regional and district supervisors, but they remained in control. The shop managers had to obey their general directions and also take orders from their superiors. The acts or omissions of shop managers were not acts of the company itself.

On the other hand, where the agreement and intention of the managing director were regarded as those of the company, even though the mental element is central to proof of the offence of conspiracy to defraud, the company was guilty (*ICR Haulage Ltd* [1944] KB 551). For a case at the other extreme, see *Redfern and Dunlop Ltd (Aircraft Division)* [1993] Crim LR 43.

Scope of Office

A6.4 Although there seems to be no decision directly in point, it is generally accepted that a company would only be identified with an act done by one of its officers within 'the scope of his office', to use the expression adopted in the Law Commission's Draft Criminal Code (Law Com No. 177), cl. 30(2). For example, if a director driving to a board meeting causes death by his dangerous driving, the company would not be liable for the statutory offence, or for manslaughter, since the director was not exercising his managerial functions whilst driving, even though he was on his way to a place where he would exercise those functions. On the other hand, if the acts done are within the scope of his office, as with the false purchase tax returns made by the company secretary in *Moore v I Bresler Ltd* [1944] 2 All ER 515, it does not matter that they are done to conceal a fraud on the company.

Conspiracy

A company cannot be guilty of a conspiracy with just its own director(s) as at least two separate **A6.5**
minds are required for a conspiracy (*McDonnell* [1966] 1 QB 233). (There were several other named conspirators in *ICR Haulage Ltd* [1944] KB 551.) It should be noted that under the doctrine of identification the acts or omissions of several persons who might be identified with the company cannot be aggregated to attribute the company with criminal conduct — there must be a sole person whose act or omission is criminal and who can be identified with the company for it to be liable.

SPECIAL RULES OF ATTRIBUTION: STATUTORY CONSTRUCTION

The practical result of the House of Lords' decision in *Tesco Supermarkets Ltd v Nattrass* [1972] **A6.6**
AC 153 (see **A6.2**) was a narrow interpretation of corporate criminal liability. As a result of difficulties in pinning criminal responsibility on a corporation for offences with a mental element, a further theory of liability was expounded, the so-called 'rules of attribution'.

According to Lord Hoffmann in *Meridian Global Funds Management Asia Ltd v Securities Commission* [1995] 2 AC 500, the articles of association provide only the 'primary rules of attribution'. Through the primary and general rules of attribution, the acts of an employee can count as the acts of the company. In the context of any particular criminal offence, it is necessary to determine whether the act of any particular agent of a company can be attributed to the company. In these circumstances:

> ... the court must fashion a *special* rule of attribution for the particular substantive rule ... By applying the usual canons of interpretation, taking into account the language of the statutory provision, its content and policy, it is possible for the court to ascertain whose act (or knowledge or state of mind) was for this purpose intended to count as the act etc. of the company (at p. 507).

Meridian decided that the policy behind legislation ought to determine who fixed a company with the *actus reus* and the *mens rea* of an offence. For offences involving consumer protection, the courts are likely to adopt a wide interpretation of the category of individuals through whom a company is saddled with liability. On trial on indictment it is for the judge to determine as a matter of law whether the criminal act and/or state of mind of the officer, servant or agent of the company is to be treated as that of the company itself.

The decisions in the following cases can be explained by reference to the public interest in the **A6.7**
objective of the legislation being achieved. In *Alphacell Ltd v Woodward* [1972] AC 824 a company had its conviction, for causing polluting matter to enter a stream contrary to the Rivers (Prevention of Pollution) Act 1951, upheld by the House of Lords. Similarly, in *Atkinson v Sir Alfred McAlpine & Son Ltd* (1974) 16 KIR 220, a company was held liable for failure to give written notice or provide protective clothing as required by the Asbestos Regulations 1969 (SI 1969 No. 690). In *Tesco Stores Ltd v Brent London Borough Council* [1993] 2 All ER 718 the knowledge of, and information available to, a sales assistant (as to whether a video purchaser was underage) was sufficient to prove the offence against the company and prevent it from relying on the defence in the Video Recordings Act 1984, s. 11(2), because to allow it to do so would have defeated the aim of the legislation.

The interaction between *Tesco* and *Meridian* was considered in *St Regis Paper Co. Ltd* [2012] 1 Cr App R 177. Moses LJ characterised the question of statutory construction in terms of whether the provision justified 'a departure from the normal rule of attribution of liability of a corporation' (i.e. the identification principle as set out in *Tesco*). It was held that where the regulatory scheme provided liability for some offences of strict liability and others requiring *mens rea*, the legislation was not emasculated by limiting corporate liability for the *mens rea* offences via that small category of persons who could properly be described as the directing mind or will of the company. Nonetheless, it was stated (at [20]) that 'the lesson to be learned from *Meridian* is the importance of construing the statute which creates the statutory offence in order to determine the rules of attribution applicable to the statutory offence in question'.

Companies may be liable for acts done by individual employees to the same extent as human employers where the definition of the offence is equally capable of applying to the employer as to the employee. See *Green v Burnett* [1955] 1 QB 78, where the employer limited company was convicted of 'using' a vehicle being driven by its employee.

It was the case that a company could be convicted of the common-law offence of manslaughter (*A-G's Ref (No. 2 of 1999)* [2000] QB 796 arising out of the Southall Rail crash). However, because it depended on the identification principle it was practically impossible to prove except in relation to the smallest companies (in effect one-man bands) such as the one in *Mark* [2004] EWCA Crim 2490.

Following the enactment of the Corporate Manslaughter and Corporate Homicide Act 2007, a company can no longer be convicted of involuntary manslaughter at common law. This Act provides another way, quite different from the identification doctrine, in which corporate liability for crime can be proved. See **B1.148** *et seq*.

As to the possibility of a company being liable for perjury, see the Court of Appeal (Civil Division) decision in *Odyssey Re (London) Ltd v OIC Run-Off Ltd* [2000] EWCA Civ 71.

Vicarious and Personal Liability

A6.8 'In general, criminal liability only results from personal fault. We do not punish people in criminal courts for the misdeeds of others' (per Lord Morris in *Tesco Supermarkets Ltd v Nattrass* [1972] AC 153 at p. 179). This basic tenet of English law applies to liability whether corporate or not, but vicarious liability must not be confused with personal liability. It is suggested that vicarious liability has no significant place in English criminal law, in contrast to English civil law or criminal law in the United States.

> Prima facie a master is not to be made criminally responsible for the acts of his servant to which the master is not party. But it may be the intention of the Legislature in order to guard against the happening of the forbidden thing, to impose a liability upon a principal even though he does not know of, and is not party to, the forbidden act done by his servant. Many statutes are passed with this object. (Viscount Reading CJ in *Mousell Bros v London & North West Railway Co.* [1917] 2 KB 836, at p. 844.)

It is necessary to distinguish this from liability for the acts of another (true vicarious liability). In personal liability, although the offending act may be committed by an employee, it is the employer's own failure to prevent the harm that renders him liable.

A6.9 Other than where the accused has aided, abetted, counselled or procured the act of another, the general principle is that one cannot be held criminally responsible as a result of the act of another. At common law, public nuisance and criminal libel (now abolished) were the only exceptions. An acknowledgement of this principle is *R (Craik, Chief Constable of Northumbria Police) v Newcastle upon Tyne Magistrates' Court* [2010] EWHC 935 (Admin). There are, however, two further exceptions to this principle in relation to statutory offences involving strict liability (see also **A2.20**):

(a) where the words of the statute are apt to describe not only the physical perpetrator of an act but also some other person, typically his employer;

(b) where the statute casts some special duty on a person, typically a licensee of a public house, which he delegates to another (the delegation principle: see **A6.14**).

There is a distinction between liability for the acts of another (true vicarious liability) and liability for breach of a personal duty. In the latter category, although the act may be committed by an employee, it is the employer's own failure to prevent the harm that renders him liable. The person committing the act does not himself commit the offence because it can only be committed by the person fixed with the duty. Such duties have been described as non-delegable, not because the person fixed with the duty must carry it out personally (impossible in the case of a corporation), but because the responsibility cannot be delegated.

An example of a personal duty is to be found in the Merchant Shipping Act 1995, s. 100(1), which imposes on the 'owner of a ship' a duty 'to take all reasonable steps to secure that the ship is operated in a safe manner'. The Divisional Court has held that although s. 31 excludes *mens rea* because of the public interest in protecting life and property at sea, it did not follow that ship owners are vicariously liable for the actions of all employees however lowly. A ship owner was criminally liable only in respect of the failure to take such steps as it was reasonable for him to take in the circumstances (*Seaboard Offshore Ltd v Secretary of State for Transport* [1994] 2 All ER 99).

Whether the duty imposed by statute is vicarious or personal depends upon 'the object of the statute, the words used, the nature of the duty laid down, the person upon whom it is imposed, the person by whom it would in ordinary circumstances be performed, and the person upon whom the penalty is imposed' (per Atkin J in *Mousell Bros Ltd v London and North-Western Railway Co* [1917] 2 KB 836 at p. 845).

A6.10 Not all offences of strict liability also involve vicarious liability (e.g., some driving offences may be strict in the sense that they require no *mens rea*, but do not invoke vicarious liability of the employer). On the other hand, where a statute imposes a strict duty, an employer or principal may well be liable for the acts of his employees or agents whether he has authorised them or not. See *Chisholm v Doulton* (1889) 22 QBD 736, per Cave J at p. 741:

> A master is not criminally responsible for a death caused by his servant's negligence, and still less for an offence depending on the servant's malice; nor can a master be held liable for the guilt of his servant in receiving goods knowing them to be stolen. And this principle of common law applies also to statutory offences, with this difference, that it is in the power of the Legislature, if it so pleases, to enact . . . that a man may be convicted and punished for an offence although there was no blameworthy condition of mind about him.

See also *Coppen v Moore (No. 2)* [1898] 2 QB 306. In these circumstances a corporation can properly be convicted for a breach of duty it did not encourage and may even have taken steps to prevent.

In *Coppen v Moore (No. 2)*, the shop owner, Mr Coppen had given a clear written order forbidding staff from misdescribing goods for sale; nonetheless Lord Russell CJ stated:

> . . . having regard to the language, scope, and object of those Acts, the Legislature intended to fix criminal responsibility upon the master for acts done by his servant in the course of his employment, although such acts were not authorized by the master, and might even have been expressly prohibited by him.

In effect, the courts have and will continue to interpret legislation to enable the desired result to follow in ordinary circumstances, much as propounded by Lord Hoffmann in *Meridian Global Funds Management Asia Ltd v Securities Commission* [1995] 2 AC 500.

A6.11 Although many offences which attract vicarious liability are strict, it is not true to say that vicarious liability attaches *only* to offences with no fault element. By way of example, the offence of selling videos to an underage person, where the person at the till has to consider the age of the purchaser before him, has been held to be an offence of vicarious liability for the company selling the video, despite the fact that those identified with the company had no part to play in the transaction. To interpret the requirement otherwise would have defeated the aim of the legislation (*Tesco Supermarkets Ltd v Brent London Borough Council* [1993] 2 All ER 718). Where a statutory provision would be inoperable without it, the courts will read in such an interpretation.

Strict Liability

A6.12   Given the presumption that some criminal state of mind, even in offences typically committed by a company, is required to prove a criminal offence (*Woolmington v DPP* [1935] AC 462 at p. 481), when considering whether an offence is one of strict liability, one must first determine whether it requires proof of *mens rea*. The court will presume that *mens rea* is an element of an offence unless Parliament has clearly indicated to the contrary either expressly or by necessary implication (see *B (A Minor) v DPP* [2000] 2 AC 428, *K* [2002] 1 AC 462 and **A2.20**). The presumption can be displaced by the wording of the offence-creating section and frequently is displaced in the case of the types of offences for which companies are most often prosecuted. As Lord Bingham CJ said in *Milford Haven Port Authority* [2000] 2 Cr App R (S) 423 at p. 432:

> Parliament creates an offence of strict liability because it regards the doing or not doing of a particular thing as itself so undesirable as to merit the imposition of criminal punishment on anyone who does or does not do that thing irrespective of that party's knowledge, state of mind, belief or intention. This involves a departure from the prevailing canons of the criminal law because of the importance which is attached to achieving the result which Parliament seeks to achieve.

This 'departure from the prevailing canons' is also necessary because without such liability many provisions are likely to be ineffective.

Strict liability offences do not offend the HRA 1988 unless disproportionate (see **A2.23**), but the courts have tended to distinguish between 'real' and 'quasi-crimes' in this regard. Clearly, the more serious the crime, the less likely it is, in the absence of powerful policy considerations, that an offence of strict liability will be proportionate.

A6.13   Where a statutory duty is expressed as requiring the achievement/prevention of a particular result, the prosecution have to prove only that the identified result was not achieved or prevented. They need not identify the acts or omissions by which the breach of duty is alleged. The Crown has to prove the breach of duty; how it proves the breach of duty will vary; the detail of the particulars need only be sufficient to give the defence proper notice of the breach alleged in the circumstances (*Chargot Ltd* [2009] 2 All ER 645). Where the prosecution can prove an essential ingredient of the offence, but in a variety of ways, the jury have to agree on at least one of them (see *Brown* (1983) 79 Cr App R 115 (fraudulently inducing the investment of money by false statements), discussed at **D18.44**). Where the prosecution have to prove the result (e.g., breach of duty), the jury need *not* be agreed on the way in which the Crown proves that result.

Delegation

A6.14   The principle of delegation imposes a duty on a particular class of person, making breach of that duty an offence. Again, this is a personal liability arising in particular areas of operation such as licensing, where the offences have an element of *mens rea*. The crime can be committed only by the office holder even if the act or omission is that of another person. The person under the duty can be convicted where he has delegated the duty to another and that other does the prohibited act and has the appropriate state of mind. The *mens rea* of the delegate will be imputed to the office holder. In *St Regis Paper Co. Ltd* [2012] 1 Cr App R 177 Moses LJ reiterated (at [28]–[29]) the very rare circumstances in which delegation arises, and the fact that it must not be confused with vicarious liability.

PARTNERSHIPS AND OTHER UNINCORPORATED BODIES

Partnerships

Unlike companies, partnerships and other unincorporated bodies cannot themselves be liable **A6.15** for common-law offences since such bodies are not legal persons at common law. In an ordinary partnership, each partner is personally liable for all debts of the firm, whereas the members of an incorporated company have no individual liability to the company's creditors; their liability is only to the company and it is satisfied if they pay the calls properly made upon them by the company or its liquidator. However, for statutory offences enacted since 1889, it appears that the effect of the Interpretation Act 1889, s. 19 (and sch. 1 to the Interpretation Act 1978), is that 'person' includes a body of persons 'unincorporate'. This applies 'unless the contrary intention appears' (s. 5 of the 1978 Act). Woolf J seemed to think that such a contrary intention applied to statutory offences when he commented in passing that there could be no question of the Voluntary Euthanasia Society being liable for aiding and abetting suicide under the Suicide Act 1961 in *A-G v Able* [1984] QB 795. In *W. Stevenson & Sons (a Partnership)* [2008] 2 Cr App R 187, Lord Phillips CJ stated (at [28]):

> ...whether or not the context permits one to read 'person' in a criminal statute as including a partnership may depend critically upon whether there is some restriction upon the assets that will properly be available to meet any penalty imposed.

His lordship had in mind the danger of an individual partner who was not personally at fault or responsible in any way for the offence becoming liable for his personal assets to be seized as a result of the conviction of the partnership. A number of statutes now provide expressly that an offence can be committed by a partnership or unincorporated body but generally this is not seen as problematic since, in most cases, the statute restricts recovery of any fine to partnership assets or funds (e.g., the Health Act 2006, s. 77(5) and (6); for other examples see those listed in *Stevenson*, to which can now be added the Corporate Manslaughter and Corporate Homicide Act 2007, s. 14(3)). The problem that arose in *Stevenson* was that the particular offence-creating provision (a Sea Fishing Order) did not expressly limit recovery to partnership assets, but Lord Phillips was clear that such a limitation was implicit in the overall design of the order which permitted liability of an individual for the offence committed by the partnership only if it was committed with his consent, connivance or due to his neglect. In the context of a solicitors firm being liable for breaches of rules made by the Financial Services Authority (prior to its replacement by the FCA) under the FSMA 2000, the Court of Appeal clearly considered the assets of the partnership to include one partner's hidden payments which, upon discovery, were accountable to the partnership to be properly taken into account when considering the profits of the firm (*Financial Services Authority v Fox Hayes (a firm)* [2009] EWCA Civ 76).

Although called partnerships, Limited Liability Partnerships or LLPs have more of the characteristics of corporations. They are creatures of statute, under the Limited Liability Partnerships Act 2000. Section 1(2) of that Act provides that an LLP is:

> ...a body corporate (with legal personality separate from that of its members) which is formed by being incorporated under this Act; and—
> (a) in the following provisions of this Act (except in the phrase 'oversea limited liability partnership'), and
> (b) in any other enactment (except where provision is made to the contrary or the context otherwise requires),
> references to a limited liability partnership are to such a body corporate.

An LLP explicitly has a separate legal personality from its members and it appears that criminal liability would attach for *mens rea* crimes in the same manner as to a corporation, principally via the doctrine of identification. Various provisions of the Companies Act 2006 specifically apply to an LLP through the Limited Liability Partnerships (Application of Companies Act 2006) Regulations 2009 (SI 2009 No. 1804), e.g., s. 993 on fraudulent trading.

Other Unincorporated Bodies

A6.16 The liability of unincorporated bodies other than partnerships was considered in *L* [2009] 1 All ER 786, a prosecution under the Water Resources Act 1991, s. 85, brought against the chairman and treasurer of the golf club whose oil heating pipe was the source of a polluting escape. The absence of any specific statutory procedural provisions governing any aspect of the alleged responsibility of the unincorporated body did not amount to a contrary intention against such responsibility arising. Accordingly, the trial judge had been correct in his ruling that the golf club itself could have been prosecuted. It was recognised that different considerations might well apply to statutory offences requiring *mens rea* as in *A-G v Able* [1984] QB 795. More worryingly perhaps, the absence of any officers' liability clause restricting the liability of members to offences in which they consented or connived etc. allowed for individual liability of all or any of the 900 members of the golf club, including the two defendants, and the trial judge had been wrong to rule they could not be prosecuted. (However, given that it was recognised that the club could itself be prosecuted and it was agreed that this was the appropriate choice to be made, the acquittal of the individual officers was directed.)

CORPORATIONS AND HUMAN RIGHTS

A6.17 Somewhat counter-intuitively, companies benefit from the ECHR and the HRA 1998, much as individual defendants do (see **A7** for human rights generally). A company is entitled to a fair trial under Article 6, and many other provisions, such as Article 10 (right to freedom of expression) and Protocol 1 (right to property), also apply. Although the right to a fair trial is absolute, the constituent rights are not; other rights are balanced against the rights of others and public interest considerations. One can glean a distinction perhaps between where the balance is struck for an individual as opposed to a corporation in the application of the concept of proportionality. In recent cases, the courts have consistently made decisions with reference to proportionality (e.g., *Bank Mellat v HM Treasury (No. 2)* [2012] QB 101 on Protocol 1, Article 1 and *Sinclair Collis Ltd v Secretary of State for Health* [2010] EWHC 3112 (Admin), determining that a ban on the sale of tobacco from automatic vending machines was a necessary and proportionate response to public health concerns). Strict liability offences do not offend the presumption of innocence (see **A2.20**), neither do reverse burdens in appropriate circumstances (see **F3.18** *et seq*.): the seriousness of the criminal charge, the risks to the public and the ability of the defendant to raise the defence are all matters considered relevant to Article 6 compliance.

DEFENCES TO CORPORATE CRIMES

A6.18 Many statutory provisions, especially those of strict liability, provide a statutory defence most of which incorporate a reverse burden. They mitigate against the severity of strict liability offences on the basis that normally a person should be guilty of a criminal offence only where there is some element of fault by the accused, not another person. These defences may be in terms of 'all reasonable steps', 'so far as reasonably practicable' or 'due diligence', proof of which usually lies with the accused. Even where the burden on a defendant is a legal and not merely an evidential one, it may be HRA compliant. This reverse burden has frequently been tested in the courts and generally found to be proportionate in cases with corporate defendants. The test is whether the modification or limitation on the right to a fair trial (under the ECHR, Article 6(2)) pursues a legitimate aim and whether it satisfies the principle of proportionality in *Ashingdane v UK* (1985) 7 EHRR 528. See further **F3.18** *et seq*.

'All reasonable steps'

This gives rise to a duty that cannot be delegated to a third party or independent contractor. In **A6.19** *DEFRA v Keam* [2005] EWHC 1582 (Admin) the principle was stated:

> In a case where the keeper defendant employs an independent contractor to take care of his animals and nothing more, whether in these circumstances he has taken all reasonable steps is a matter for the trial court. In many cases if not in most, one would expect the keeper (a) to have ensured his independent contractor was indeed competent and (b) to take steps to ensure that his independent contractor was doing that which ought to be done in caring for the animals. In many if not most cases, simply to appoint an independent contractor...to care for his animals may well not amount to the taking of all reasonable steps. Conversely the fact that an independent contractor fails to take all reasonable steps does not of itself involve criminal liability on the part of the person...who has employed the independent contractor, if that [person] has taken all reasonable steps to ensure that [the regulations are complied with], that is to say, there is no vicarious liability for the default of the independent contractor in circumstances in which the keeper can show that he himself did take all reasonable steps.

As the defence states, the accused must show that he took *all* reasonable steps and not just some; if he could have taken more, or other reasonable steps which objectively would have prevented the offence, he will not have proved the defence. On the other hand, he need not show that he has taken all steps possible, only those which are reasonable.

'So far as reasonably practicable'

Again, this is a personal duty. In *Associated Octel Co Ltd* [1996] 4 All ER 846 the House of Lords **A6.20** emphasised that engaging an independent contractor to do work and omitting to stipulate for 'whatever conditions are needed to avoid those [offending] risks and [which] are reasonably practicable' would not entitle an accused to rely on the defence. In *Gateway Foodmarkets Ltd* [1997] 3 All ER 78 the Court of Appeal indicated that:

> ...the duty...is broken if the specified consequences occur, but only if 'so far as is reasonably practicable' they have not been guarded against. So the company is in breach of duty unless all reasonable precautions have been taken and we would interpret this as meaning 'taken by the company or on its behalf'. In other words...the company is liable in the event that there is a failure to ensure the [duty is undertaken] unless all reasonable precautions have been taken...by the company or on its behalf.

If the event was wholly unknown or unexpected, it would be unreasonable to require the accused to take measures against it and thus the defence could pertain (*Austin Rover Group Ltd v Inspector of Factories* [1990] 1 AC 619). Latham LJ in *HTM Ltd* [2006] EWCA Crim 1156 stated (at [22]): 'Foreseeability is merely a tool with which to assess the likelihood of a risk eventuating. It is not a means of permitting a defendant to bring concepts of fault appropriate to civil proceedings into the equation by the back door.'

From a recent string of cases concerning the Health and Safety at Work etc. Act 1974, the following principles can be gleaned: health and safety offences are concerned primarily with exposure to risk; the law does not aim to create an environment which is risk-free, only one in which there is no material (as opposed to trivial, fanciful or hypothetical) risk to health and safety, i.e. risks 'which any reasonable person would appreciate and take steps to guard against' per Lord Hope in *Chargot Ltd* [2009] 2 All ER 645 at [27]. This has an impact on both the question of whether there was a risk of harm at all, and whether a defence of guarding against a risk so far as reasonably practicable had been raised or discharged; foreseeability of danger (and thus risk) is relevant to the question whether a risk to safety exists; but the principal relevance of foreseeability is to the defence of whether all reasonable precautions have been taken (*Tangerine Confectionery Ltd* (2012) 176 JP 349 at [36]; *Porter* [2008] EWCA Crim 1271; *EGS Ltd* [2009] EWCA Crim 1942). In *Baker v Quantum Group Ltd* [2011] 4 All ER 223 the Supreme Court, in a civil case relating to the Factories Act 1961, considered that compliance with acceptable standards at the time or 'recognized and established practice' was relevant to the issue of negligence. This reasoning was followed in the criminal case of *Tangerine Confectionery*.

'Due diligence'

A6.21 A number of permutations of the due diligence defence exist, with corresponding differences in application. Some offences require 'due diligence' whilst others require 'all due diligence' and yet others 'all due diligence and taken all reasonable steps'. They should not be considered to have identical effect; indeed, clearly the standard an accused has to meet is higher if 'all due diligence' is specified. What is sufficient to amount to due diligence is an objective fact and may not be based on ignorance of the law (*Renaissance Accountancy Services Ltd v Revenue and Customs Commissioners* [2012] UKFTT 83 (TC)). Acting in accordance with a relevant code of practice may be evidence of due diligence but need not be; the opposite will almost inevitably indicate a failure so to do. The phrase 'with all due diligence' consists of ordinary words; to add a further gloss such as negligence and a reprehensible state of mind to prove guilt runs the risk of importing a mental element which is inappropriate (*Croydon London Borough Council v Pinch a Pound (UK) Ltd* [2010] EWHC 3283 (Admin)). A company cannot rely on the defence if it has delegated its responsibilities to another because the defence, like the obligation, is personal (*Seaboard Offshore Ltd v Secretary of State for Transport* [1994] 2 All ER 99). But, as long as the company has put in place procedures, or relied upon another in such a manner that it amounts to evidence that it has done (all) due diligence, the defence will be available. In the seminal case of *Tesco Supermarkets Ltd v Nattrass* [1972] AC 153 the magistrates heard a considerable body of evidence and found as a fact that Tesco had fulfilled the defence of taking all reasonable precautions and had exercised all due diligence. It was emphasised in the Court of Appeal that such evidence is necessary if the defence is to be made out; if an accused calls no evidence whatsoever, the defence will inevitably fail (*Associated Octel Co Ltd* [1996] 4 All ER 846).

SENTENCING CORPORATE CRIMES

A6.22 Sentencing corporations convicted of crime brings its own specific challenges. Many of the guideline cases relate to health and safety and environmental legislation. The guideline case of *F Howe & Son (Engineers) Ltd* [1999] 2 All ER 249 (see **E15.20**) provides a number of factors relevant to sentence which the parties should address and the court should take into account. These factors are now largely replicated and enhanced in the guideline published by the Sentencing Council entitled *Corporate offenders: fraud bribery and money laundering* (see Supplement, **SG-504**). The guideline has effect from 1 October 2014.

A guideline for sentencing organisations for corporate manslaughter and health and safety offences has been in place since 15 February 2010 (see Supplement, **SG-528**).

DIRECTOR'S DUTIES AND CRIMES

Separate Identity of Company

A6.23 Because a company is a separate person from its officers, the officers will not necessarily be guilty of a crime just because the company is. Conversely, since a company may be fixed with criminal liability through the acts or omissions of its 'directing mind', the way for criminal liability to be proved may, depending on the relevant rule of attribution, be by identifying the criminal acts of one of its officers; in those circumstances both the individual officer and the company may be guilty. In appropriate circumstances, both the company and its officers may be charged with a criminal offence and/or with aiding and abetting an employee to commit a crime (*J.F. Alford Transport Ltd* [1997] 2 Cr App R 326). On the other hand, it is no defence to a charge properly brought, that a person was acting in the course of employment or committing crime on behalf of an employer (*Standard Chartered Bank v Pakistan National Shipping Corp (Nos. 2 and 4)* [2003] 1 AC 959). Despite the separate identity of the company, a director cannot conspire with his company alone, the essence of conspiracy being an agreement between at least two separate persons (see **A6.5**).

Consent, Connivance and Neglect

The liability of a company for an offence does not preclude the liability of an individual **A6.24** employee, but the fact that the company is liable may also have the effect of casting the net of individual responsibility more widely. This is due to the fact that many statutes now contain a section imposing liability on any 'director, manager, secretary or other similar officer' with whose 'consent or connivance' the offence has been committed or to whose 'neglect' it is attributable (see, e.g., the Trade Descriptions Act 1968, s. 20). In order for any person to be successfully prosecuted under these provisions, the prosecution must prove that the company is guilty of an offence, although it need not be convicted nor in the dock. In many cases such a person would be liable on normal principles as an accessory. However, the reference to 'neglect' means liability is wider than that for accessories for whom negligence is not normally sufficient (see A4.5). Neglect does not necessarily require actual knowledge if the circumstances were such that they should have put the officer on inquiry (see *P* [2007] EWCA Crim 1937, a case under the Health and Safety at Work etc. Act 1974, s. 37). The approach in *P* was subsequently approved in the House of Lords in *Chargot Ltd* [2009] 2 All ER 645, upholding a director's conviction for corporate offences under s. 37 arising from the death of a dumper-truck driver who had been working for the companies of which the appellant was a director. Lord Hope expressly referred to the issue of whether the officer 'should have been put on inquiry so as to have taken steps to determine whether or not the appropriate safety procedures were in place'. His lordship also commented that:

> ...no fixed rule can be laid down as to what the prosecution must identify and prove in order to establish that the officer's state of mind was such as to amount to consent, connivance or neglect. In some cases, as where the officer's place of activity was remote from the workplace or what was done there was not under his immediate direction and control, this may require the leading of quite detailed evidence of which fair notice may have to be given. In others, where the officer was in day to day contact with what was done there, very little more may be needed.

On the other hand, an officer of the company must hold a position of real authority with both the power and responsibility to decide corporate policy. He must perform a governing role in respect of the affairs of the company rather than merely a day-to-day management function (*Boal* [1992] 1 QB 591).

There is no need for the Crown to prove specific knowledge of each allegation. In *Hutchins* [2011] EWCA Crim 1056 Rix LJ stated (at [25]):

> ...the nature of these regulatory statutes with their provisions for secondary liability by directors and managers in accordance with their consent, connivance or neglect is to ensure that they are held to proper standards of supervision and that the size of the company and the distance of directors and managers from the coal face of individual acts should not, where there is consent, connivance or neglect, afford directors or managers with the necessary knowledge a defence.

In some statutes, the reference to 'neglect' is omitted (see, e.g., the Theft Act 1968, s. 18; Public **A6.25** Order Act 1986, s. 28; Copyright, Designs and Patents Act 1988, s. 110) and the prosecution must rely on connivance or consent, both of which would appear to require the same degree of knowledge as aiding and abetting. Even here, though, the liability is potentially wider than that of an accessory since a positive act of aiding and abetting is not necessarily required. A conscious failure to prevent or report a fellow director committing an offence would seem to be enough, even though there is not a sufficiently clear or immediate right of control over the fellow director to give rise to liability as an accessory.

Section A7   Human Rights

INTRODUCTION

A7.1   The European Convention for the Protection of Human Rights and Fundamental Freedoms (Cm. 8969) (the ECHR) is an international treaty of the Council of Europe. It was adopted in 1950, ratified by the UK in 1951 and entered into force in 1953. The unusual feature of the Convention, as an international human rights instrument, is that it provides a mechanism for individuals to enforce their Convention rights against States Parties.

The Convention has been amplified by a number of Protocols. One of the most important is Protocol 11, which abolished the European Commission of Human Rights. As a result, the Convention is now administered by two bodies: the European Court of Human Rights (ECtHR) and the Committee of Ministers of the Council of Europe. The great majority of the judgments of the Court are given by Chambers, but a Grand Chamber of the Court, composed of 17 judges, deals with cases that raise a serious question of interpretation or application of the Convention, or a serious issue of general importance.

The Human Rights Act 1998 is designed 'to give further effect to the rights and freedoms guaranteed under the European Convention on Human Rights' (see the long title). It is intended to 'give people in the United Kingdom opportunities to enforce their rights under the European Convention in British courts rather than having to incur the cost and delay of taking a case to the European Human Rights…Court in Strasbourg' (Prime Minister's preface to the White Paper, *Bringing Rights Home*, Cm. 3782).

Convention Rights

A7.2   The rights protected by the HRA 1998 are called 'Convention rights' (s. 1(1)). They are set out in sch. 1 to the HRA 1998.

In the HRA 1998, 'the Convention rights' means the rights and fundamental freedoms set out in: (a) Articles 2 to 12 of the ECHR, (b) Articles 1 to 3 of the First Protocol, and (c) Articles 1 and 2 of the Sixth Protocol (s. 1(1)).

The subject-matter of these rights is as follows:

Article 2:	The right to life
Article 3:	Prohibition on torture
Article 4:	Prohibition on slavery and forced labour
Article 5:	Right to liberty and security
Article 6:	Right to a fair trial
Article 7:	No punishment without law
Article 8:	Right to respect for private and family life
Article 9:	Freedom of thought, conscience and religion
Article 10:	Freedom of expression
Article 11:	Freedom of assembly and association

Article 12:	Right to marry
Article 14:	Prohibition on discrimination
Article 1, Protocol 1:	Protection of property
Article 2, Protocol 1:	Right to education
Article 3, Protocol 1:	Right to free elections
Article 1, Protocol 6:	Abolition of the death penalty
Article 2, Protocol 6:	Death penalty in times of war

These rights are to be read with Article 16 (restrictions on political activities of aliens), Article 17 (prohibition on abuse of rights) and Article 18 (limitation on use of restrictions on rights) (s. 1(1)).

Categories of Convention Rights

Convention rights are not all of equal status. The protection afforded under the ECHR and the **A7.3** HRA 1998 varies from right to right. Broadly speaking, the ECtHR recognises three categories of Convention rights:

Absolute Rights   Absolute rights are those rights that are strongly protected and that cannot **A7.4** be restricted even in times of war or other public emergency: Article 2 (the right to life), Article 3 (prohibition on torture), Article 4(1) (prohibition on slavery) and Article 7 (no punishment without law).

Although there are special provisions dealing with the death penalty and death caused by the use of force, in all other respects the public interest cannot justify any interference with absolute rights.

Special Rights   Special rights are those rights that are less strongly protected than absolute **A7.5** rights. They can be restricted in times of war or other public emergency: Article 4(2) and (3) (prohibition on forced labour), Article 5 (right to liberty and security), Article 6 (fair trial), Article 9(1) (freedom of thought, conscience and religion — but not freedom to manifest religion or belief, which is a qualified right), Article 12 (right to marry), Protocol 1, Article 2 (the right to education), Protocol 1, Article 3 (right to free elections) and Protocol 6, Article 1 (abolition of the death penalty).

The practical difference between these rights and absolute rights is that restriction in the public interest can be justified, but only on the grounds expressly provided for within the text of the provision itself: e.g., Article 4(2) prohibits forced labour, but Article 4(3) then sets out a number of exceptions; similarly, the first sentence of Article 5(1) provides for the right to liberty and security of person; the second sentence then lists (exhaustively) all the circumstances in which that right can be restricted. Unless a restriction is expressly provided for in the text of the provision, the public interest cannot justify any interference with special rights.

Strictly speaking, Article 6 (fair trial) probably falls into a category of its own. That is because the ECtHR has read a number of implied restrictions into Article 6; including restrictions designed to ensure the protection of victims and vulnerable witnesses within the trial process. Such restrictions are limited and must be strictly necessary and proportionate. In all other respects, the public interest cannot justify any interference with Article 6 rights.

In *Brown v Stott* [2003] 1 AC 681, Lord Bingham said:

> The jurisprudence of the European Court very clearly establishes that while the overall fairness of a criminal trial cannot be compromised, the constituent rights comprised, whether expressly or implicitly, within Article 6 are not themselves absolute. Limited qualification of these rights is acceptable if reasonably directed by national authorities towards a clear and proper public objective and if representing no greater qualification than the situation calls for.

But, overall, the trial must be fair. If an accused has not had a fair trial, the verdict cannot stand and the conviction must be quashed (per Lord Hope in *Sinclair v HM Advocate* [2005] UKPC D2).

A7.6 Qualified Rights   Qualified rights are those rights that are to be balanced against the public interest and which can be restricted in times of war or other public emergency: Article 8 (right to respect for private and family life), Article 9 (right to manifest religion or belief), Article 10 (freedom of expression), Article 11 (freedom of assembly and association), Article 14 (prohibition on discrimination) and Protocol 1, Article 1 (protection of property).

These rights are in positive form, but can be restricted where it can be shown that a restriction is (a) prescribed by law; (b) legitimate; (c) necessary and proportionate; and (d) not discriminatory.

Protocol 1, Article 1 (protection of property) also probably falls into a category of its own because it is less well protected than the other qualified rights. Where property rights are interfered with, the question will be whether a 'fair balance' has been achieved between the individual's right to property and the general public interest.

The Legality of Restrictions on Convention Rights

A7.7   Any restriction on Convention rights must be lawful. In some places, such as Article 5, the word 'lawful' itself is used. In others, such as Articles 8 and 9, phrases such as 'in accordance with law' or 'prescribed by law' are used. Even where no express provision is made (e.g., in Protocol 1, Article 1), any restriction on Convention rights must nonetheless be 'lawful'.

Under the ECHR the term 'lawful' has a special meaning. A restriction on Convention rights will be 'lawful' only if: (a) there is an established legal basis in domestic law for the restriction: e.g., where it is provided for by legislation or special rules; (b) the provision in question is 'accessible': i.e. those likely to be affected by it can find out what it says; and (c) the provision in question is 'foreseeable': i.e. it is formulated with sufficient clarity to enable those likely to be affected by it to understand it and to regulate their conduct accordingly.

A7.8 Established Legal Basis   Primary and subordinate legislation is a sufficient basis in domestic law for a restriction on Convention rights; so too is the common law (*Sunday Times v UK* (1979–80) 2 EHRR 245 at [47]). Home Office guidelines and internal police guidelines are unlikely to satisfy the requirement that provisions governing restrictions on Convention rights be accessible, unless they are made publicly available (*Silver v UK* (1983) 5 EHRR 347; *Govell v UK* (1998) Appln. 27237/95, 14 January 1998 at [62]; *Khan v UK* (2001) 31 EHRR 1016). In *Christian v R* [2007] 2 AC 400, the Privy Council held that the non-promulgation of a law may be good grounds for staying a prosecution.

A7.9 Foreseeability   Absolute certainty is not required for a provision to be 'foreseeable'. In *Sunday Times v UK* (1979–80) 2 EHRR 245, the ECtHR said (at [49]):

> …whilst certainty is highly desirable, it may bring in its train excessive rigidity and the law must be able to keep pace with changing circumstances. Accordingly, many laws are inevitably couched in terms which, to a greater or lesser extent, are vague and whose interpretation and application are questions of practice.

The degree of certainty will depend on the circumstances. In some fields of application a fairly wide degree of flexibility is acceptable: e.g., general statutory provisions (*Rekvenyi v Hungary* (2000) 30 EHRR 519 at [34]; *Bronda v Italy* (2001) 33 EHRR 81 at [54]). In others, a relatively high level of certainty is required: e.g., where the deprivation of liberty is concerned (*Steel v UK* (1999) 28 EHRR 603; *Baranowski v Poland* (2000) Appln. 28358/95, 28 March 2000). In *Grigoriades v Greece* (1999) 27 EHRR 464, the ECtHR held that an offence of 'insulting' the army was sufficiently certain for Convention purposes (at [38]). But in *Hashman and Harrop v UK* (2000) 30 EHRR 241, the ECtHR held that the concept of a bind over to be of good behaviour was too vague and uncertain and thus a breach of the ECHR.

The Legitimacy of Restrictions on Convention Rights

Any restriction on Convention rights must be legitimate. For qualified rights, so long as a **A7.10** restriction genuinely pursues one of the aims set out in the article itself, it will be legitimate. The aims set out in Articles 8 to 11 include: national security, public safety, the prevention of disorder or crime and the protection of the rights and freedoms of others.

The Necessity and Proportionality of Restrictions on Convention Rights

Any restriction on Convention rights must be necessary and proportionate. For qualified rights, **A7.11** this requirement flows from the use of the phrase 'necessary in a democratic society' in Articles 8 to 11.

Necessary The word 'necessary' in the ECHR is not synonymous with 'reasonable'. In **A7.12** *Handyside v UK* (1979–80) 1 EHRR 737, the ECtHR said (at [48]):

…whilst the adjective 'necessary', within the meaning of Article 10(2), is not synonymous with 'indispensable', neither has it the flexibility of such expressions as 'admissible', 'ordinary', 'useful', 'reasonable', or 'desirable'.

Nor will a restriction be necessary just because the majority are in favour of it (*Chassagnou v France* (2000) 29 EHRR 615 at [112]).

Proportionality A restriction will be proportionate only if the objective behind the restriction **A7.13** justifies interference with a Convention right, there is a rational connection between the objective and the restriction in question and the means employed are not more than is necessary to achieve the objective.

In making this assessment, the following factors are relevant: (a) whether relevant and sufficient reasons have been advanced for the restriction; (b) whether there was a less restrictive, but equally effective, way of achieving the same objective; (c) whether sufficient regard has been paid to the rights and interests of those affected (in some cases, e.g., in family cases, those affected should be consulted); (d) whether safeguards exist to guard against error or abuse (e.g., in secret surveillance cases); and (e) whether the restriction in question destroys the very essence of the Convention right in issue.

Positive Obligations

The ECHR safeguards Convention rights by limiting the circumstances in which they can be **A7.14** restricted (if at all). Public authorities are under a duty to refrain from restricting Convention rights in any other circumstances.

The ECHR also safeguards Convention rights by imposing an obligation on public authorities to adopt positive measures to protect the Convention rights of individuals. In *Platform Ärtze für das Leben v Austria* (1991) 13 EHRR 204, the ECtHR said (at [32]):

Genuine, effective freedom of peaceful assembly cannot … be reduced to a mere duty on the part of the state not to interfere; a purely negative conception would not be compatible with the object and purpose of Article 11. Like Article 8, Article 11 sometimes requires positive measures to be taken, even in the sphere of relations between individuals, if need be.

The extent of this obligation will vary according to such factors as the nature of the Convention right in issue, the importance of the right for the individual and the nature of the activities involved in the case.

The most onerous positive obligations arise where, by very definition, a Convention right **A7.15** requires the provision of resources: e.g., the right to free legal assistance in criminal cases under

Article 6(3)(c). However, the doctrine of positive obligations under the ECHR is not restricted to the provision of resources in such circumstances. It includes a duty on the relevant authorities to put in place a legal framework which provides effective protection for Convention rights (*X and Y v Netherlands* (1986) 8 EHRR 235 at [27]). In *A v UK* (1999) 27 EHRR 611, the ECtHR held that the defence of 'reasonable chastisement' to an alleged offence of assaulting a child was so wide that the child's rights under Article 3 (the prohibition on ill-treatment) were not respected.

The ECHR can also impose a duty on the relevant authorities to take positive steps to prevent breaches of Convention rights. This duty is strictest where fundamental rights, such as the right to life or the prohibition on torture, are at stake (*Osman v UK* (2000) 29 EHRR 245 at [115]). However, such obligations must be interpreted in a way that does not impose an impossible or disproportionate burden on the authorities. Accordingly, not every claimed risk to life can entail for the authorities a Convention requirement to take operational measures to prevent that risk from materialising. It must be established that the authorities failed to do all that could reasonably be expected of them to avoid a 'real and immediate' risk to life which they knew or ought to have known about (*Osman v UK* (2000) 29 EHRR 245 at [116]). This is so even where the name of the prospective victim is unknown at the time the risk arises: it is enough that there is a risk to someone, whoever that may turn out to be (*Sarjantson v Chief Constable of Humberside Police* [2014] 1 All ER 206). In *Van Colle v Chief Constable of the Hertfordshire Police* [2009] 1 AC 225, the House of Lords held that the test in *Osman v UK* required no gloss and was to be applied whatever the circumstances of the case; no special standard applied where the risk to life arose from the State's decision to call an individual as a witness. In *MC v Bulgaria* (2005) 40 EHRR 459, the ECtHR held that States have a positive obligation under Articles 3 and 8 to enact criminal law provisions effectively punishing rape and to apply them in practice through effective investigation and prosecution; to adopt a policy of only prosecuting rape where there was evidence of resistance on the part of the alleged victim violated this duty.

Prohibition on Abuse of Rights under Article 17

A7.16   ECHR, Article 17

> Nothing in this Convention may be interpreted as implying for any State, group or person any right to engage in any activity or perform any act aimed at the destruction of any of the rights and freedoms set forth herein or at their limitation to a greater extent than is provided for in this Convention.

The purpose of Article 17 is to prevent extremists using the ECHR to destroy the rights of others (*Lawless v Ireland (No. 3)* (1979–80) 1 EHRR 15 at [7]).

Article 17 can be applied only to those rights which are capable of being exercised so as to destroy the rights of others: it cannot be used to restrict rights designed to protect the individual such as those in Articles 5 and 6 (*Lawless v Ireland (No. 3)* at [7]; *Glimmerveen and Hagenbeek v Netherlands* (1979) 18 DR 187 at p. 195). Furthermore, any measure taken under Article 17 must be strictly proportionate to the threat to the rights of others (*De Becker v Belgium* (1961) Series B, No. 4, Appln. 214/56 at [279]; *Lehideux and Isorni v France* (2000) 30 EHRR 665). Article 17 was relied on in *DPP v Collins* [2006] 4 All ER 602 when interpreting the Communications Act 2003, s. 127.

The Interpretation of Convention Rights

A7.17 A number of general principles have emerged from the case law of the ECtHR and the Commission of Human Rights about the way in which Convention rights should be interpreted.

A7.18 **Object and Purpose** Convention rights should be interpreted in light of their object and purpose: i.e. to protect individual rights, maintain the rule of law and to uphold the ideas and values of a democratic society (*Golder v UK* (1979–80) 1 EHRR 524 at [34]; *Soering v UK* (1989) 11 EHRR 439 at [87]).

Practical and Effective   Convention rights should be interpreted in such a way as to make **A7.19** them 'practical and effective'. In *Soering v UK* (1989) 11 EHRR 439, the ECtHR held (at [87]):

> In interpreting the Convention regard must be had to its special character as a treaty for the collective enforcement of human rights and fundamental freedoms…Thus, the object and purpose of the Convention as a living instrument for the protection of individual human beings require that its provisions be interpreted and applied so as to make its safeguards practical and effective.

Autonomous Meaning   Words and phrases in the ECHR are to be given an autonomous **A7.20** meaning: i.e. the meaning ascribed by the ECtHR, not (necessarily) the meaning ascribed in the domestic law of the Contracting States. This is to prevent States undermining the efficacy of the ECHR (*Chassagnou v France* (2000) 29 EHRR 615 at [100]).

Living Instrument   The ECHR is a 'living instrument' requiring a dynamic, evolving inter- **A7.21** pretation. For example, when considering what conduct might offend Article 3, the ECtHR held in the case of *Selmouni v France* (2000) 29 EHRR 365 (at [101]):

> The Court has previously examined cases in which it concluded that there had been treatment which could only be described as torture…However, having regard to the fact that the Convention is a 'living instrument' which must be interpreted in the light of present-day conditions…the Court considers that certain acts which were classified in the past as 'inhuman and degrading treatment' as opposed to 'torture' could be classified differently in future. It takes the view that the increasingly high standard being required in the area of the protection of human rights and fundamental liberties correspondingly and inevitably requires greater firmness in assessing breaches of the fundamental values of democratic societies.

Generous and Purposive Construction   A generous and purposive construction is to be given **A7.22** to Convention rights under the HRA 1998 suitable to give to individuals the full measure of the fundamental rights and freedoms to which all persons in the State are to be entitled (*DPP, ex parte Kebilene* [2000] 2 AC 326, Lord Hope at p. 998E–F; for the general principle, see *Minister of Home Affairs v Fisher* [1980] AC 319 at p. 328).

Burden and Standard of Proving a Breach of Convention Rights

It is for the complainant to show that his Convention rights have been infringed, but for the **A7.23** relevant public authority to justify any infringement established (*Jersild v Denmark* (1995) 19 EHRR 1 at [31]). Where absolute rights are at stake, the standard of proof is high: beyond reasonable doubt. However, this can be established by the coexistence of sufficiently strong, clear and concordant inferences or similar unrebutted presumptions of fact. For example, in *Aksoy v Turkey* (1997) 23 EHRR 553, the ECtHR held (at [61]):

> …where an individual is taken into police custody in good health but is found to be injured at the time of release, it is incumbent on the State to provide a plausible explanation as to the causing of the injury, failing which a clear issue arises under Article 3 of the Convention.

Failure of the relevant authority to furnish information may also lead to adverse inferences being drawn (*Timurtas v Turkey* (2000) Appln. 23531/94, 13 June 2000 at [66]).

Waiver of Convention Rights

Convention rights can be waived only in limited circumstances and waiver must be established **A7.24** in an unequivocal manner (*Zana v Turkey* (1999) 27 EHRR 671 at [70]). In *Pfeifer and Plankl v Austria* (1992) 14 EHRR 692, the ECtHR held (at [37]):

> According to the Court's case law, the waiver of a right guaranteed by the Convention — in so far as it is permissible — must be established in an unequivocal manner. Moreover…in the case of procedural rights a waiver, in order to be effective for Convention purposes, requires minimum guarantees commensurate with its importance.

Failure to raise an issue cannot be automatically equated with waiver (*McGonnell v UK* (2000) 30 EHRR 289 at [44]–[46], in the context of a fair trial).

Certain Convention rights probably cannot be waived at all: e.g., absolute rights such as the right to life and the prohibition on torture and slavery, and perhaps also fair trial rights under Article 6 (*Pfeifer and Plankl v Austria* (1992) 14 EHRR 692 at [39]). In *Jones* [2003] 1 AC 1, the House of Lords held that the appellant had waived his right to legal representation when he absconded at trial, both at common law and under the ECHR.

THE INTERPRETATION OF LEGISLATION

Primary Legislation

A7.25 **Human Rights Act 1998, s. 3**

> (1) So far as it is possible to do so, primary legislation and subordinate legislation must be read and given effect in a way which is compatible with Convention rights.

The use of the word 'possible' is intended to convey a stronger interpretative requirement than 'reasonable' (Home Secretary, *Hansard*, HC vol. 313, col. 421 (3 June 1998)).

A7.26 The scope of the approach to interpretation authorised by s. 3 has been considered in a number of cases at the highest level. The leading case is now the decision of the House of Lords in *Ghaidan v Ghodin-Mendoza* [2004] 2 AC 557, where there was broad agreement that 'excessive concentration on the linguistic features of the [statute to be interpreted]', should be substituted in favour of a 'purposive' approach concentrating on 'the importance of the fundamental right involved'. As Lord Nicholls pointed out, if it is accepted that s. 3 was intended to supersede the pre-HRA principle that legislation had to be ambiguous before it was 'possible' to interpret it compatibly with the ECHR, Parliament cannot have intended the courts to 'depend critically upon the particular form of words adopted by the parliamentary draftsman' in the legislation in question without making the application of s. 3 'something of a semantic lottery' (*Ghaidan v Ghodin-Mendoza* at [31]).

Nothing in the HRA 1998 affects the validity, continuing operation or enforcement of primary legislation which is incompatible with Convention rights (s. 3(2)(b)). But in certain circumstances a 'declaration of incompatibility' can be made.

Declarations of Incompatibility

A7.27 Under the HRA 1998, certain courts are given the power to make declarations of incompatibility if they determine that a provision in primary legislation is incompatible with Convention rights (s. 4(2)). The relevant courts for England and Wales are the Supreme Court, the Court of Appeal, the High Court and the Courts-Martial Appeal Court (s. 4(5)). A declaration of incompatibility is intended to operate as a signal to Parliament that an incompatibility has been found and to prompt remedial action. It does not affect the validity, continuing operation or enforcement of the provision in question (s. 4(6)(a)).

If a court is considering whether or not to make a declaration of incompatibility, the Crown has a right to be notified and can intervene (s. 5(1) and (2)). In criminal proceedings, if any application is to be made to the Court of Appeal for a declaration of incompatibility or any issue is to be raised which may have that effect, the procedure set out in the CrimPR, r. 65.12, must be followed. In *R (T) v Secretary of State for the Home Department* [2014] UKSC 35, the Supreme Court considered the law concerning declarations of incompatibility in the context of an appeal against a decision of the Court of Appeal to issue declarations in respect of sections of the Police Act 1997 and the Rehabilitation of Offenders Act 1974 (Exceptions) Order 1975.

Subordinate Legislation

A7.28 So far as it is possible to do so, subordinate legislation must be read and given effect in a way which is compatible with Convention rights (HRA 1998, s. 3(1)). As with primary legislation, this rule of interpretation applies whenever the subordinate legislation in question was enacted

(s. 3(2)(a)). But, unlike the position in relation to primary legislation, where subordinate legislation cannot be read and given effect in a way which is compatible with Convention rights, this *does* affect its validity, continuing operation and enforcement (s. 3(2)(b) and (c)) and it can be quashed or declared invalid by reason of incompatibility (s. 10(4)). The only exception is where primary legislation prevents the removal of any incompatibility (s. 3(1)(c)). In such circumstances, a declaration of incompatibility can be made (s. 4(4)).

Statements of Compatibility

For legislation passed after the HRA 1998 became law, s. 19 requires the minister of the Crown   **A7.29**
in charge of a Bill, before its Second Reading, to make a written, published statement that in his view the provisions of the Bill are compatible with Convention rights (a 'statement of compatibility'). If unable to do so, the minister must so state but add that the government nonetheless wishes to proceed with the Bill. A statement of compatibility does not bind a court (*A (No. 2)* [2002] 1 AC 45 per Lord Hope). The obligation to make a statement of compatibility applies only to government-sponsored Acts of Parliament.

The Relevance of Strasbourg Jurisprudence

A court or tribunal determining a question which has arisen in connection with a Convention   **A7.30**
right must take into account judgments of the ECtHR and Commission of Human Rights and decisions of the Commission and the Committee of Ministers (HRA 1998, s. 2(1)). But such judgments and decisions are not binding.

In *R (Hicks) v Commissioner of Police of the Metropolis* [2014] EWCA Civ 3 at [80], the Court of Appeal reviewed the relevant authorities and extracted the following principles:

(1) It is the duty of the national courts to enforce domestically enacted Convention rights.
(2) The ECtHR is the court that, ultimately, must interpret the meaning of the Convention.
(3) The UK courts will be bound to follow an interpretation of a provision of the Convention if given by the Grand Chamber as authoritative, unless it is apparent that it has misunderstood or overlooked some significant feature of English law or practice which, properly explained, would lead to that interpretation being reviewed by the ECtHR when its interpretation was being applied to English circumstances.
(4) The same principle and qualification applies to a 'clear and consistent' line of decisions of the ECtHR other than one of the Grand Chamber.
(5) Convention rights have to be given effect in the light of the domestic law which implements in detail the 'high level' rights set out in the ECHR.
(6) Where there are 'mixed messages' in the existing Strasbourg case law, a 'real judicial choice' will have to be made about the scope and application of the relevant provision of the Convention.

In *Horncastle* [2010] 2 AC 373, the Supreme Court decided that the judgment of the ECtHR   **A7.31**
in *Al-Khawaja and Tahery v UK* (2009) 49 EHRR 1 was not to be treated as determinative of the success of the appeals it was considering, which were concerned with the admission of hearsay evidence, because the ECtHR had not sufficiently appreciated particular aspects of domestic process in reaching its decision. Similarly, in *A-G's Ref (No. 69 of 2013)* [2014] EWCA Crim 188, the Court of Appeal declined to follow the view of the Grand Chamber in *Vinter v UK* [2013] ECHR 645 that an order for a convicted defendant to serve the remainder of his life in prison was irreducible and therefore in violation of Article 3. Lord Thomas CJ said (at [30]) that the Grand Chamber had attached too much significance to the wording of a policy document (the Lifer Manual) and thereby ignored the true scope of the powers of the Secretary of State under the C(S)A 1997, s. 30.

In *Ibrahim* [2012] 4 All ER 225 the Court of Appeal endorsed the principle (derived from *R (RJM) v Work and Pensions Secretary* [2009] 1 AC 311) that, where the Court of Appeal considers that an earlier decision of the House of Lords which would otherwise be binding on the Court of Appeal may be, or even is clearly, inconsistent with a subsequent decision of the ECtHR, the Court of Appeal must follow the decision of the House of Lords.

The UK's obligations under Article 46 do not automatically require domestic courts to quash the conviction in any case where the ECtHR finds a breach of the ECHR (*Lyons* [2003] 1 AC 976).

PUBLIC AUTHORITIES

A7.32   The HRA 1998, s. 6, makes it unlawful for a public authority to act in a way which is incompatible with Convention rights, unless required to do so to give effect to primary legislation.

Human Rights Act 1998, s. 6

(1) It is unlawful for a public authority to act in a way which is incompatible with a Convention right.

(2) Subsection (1) does not apply to an act if—

  (a) as the result of one or more provisions of primary legislation, the authority could not have acted differently; or

  (b) in the case of one or more provisions of, or made under, primary legislation which cannot be read or given effect in a way which is compatible with the Convention rights, the authority was acting so as to give effect to or enforce those provisions.

In this context, 'act' includes a failure to act; but does not include a failure to legislate or make remedial orders (s. 6(6)).

The Definition of a Public Authority

A7.33   The HRA 1998 does not fully define a 'public authority'; but s. 6(3) does include within its meaning: (a) courts and tribunals; and (b) any person certain of whose functions are functions of a public nature. The inclusion of 'any person certain of whose functions are functions of a public nature' is intended to expand, not restrict, the definition of public authority (Lord Chancellor, *Hansard*, HL vol. 583, col. 811 (24 November 1997)).

Two kinds of public authority are thus recognised under the HRA 1998: 'pure' public authorities (such as government departments, local authorities or the police) and 'functional' public authorities (those bodies that are to be treated as public authorities when they are carrying out public functions). As the Parliamentary Joint Committee on Human Rights observed in its report, *The Meaning of Public Authority under the Human Rights Act* (Seventh Report (2003–04 HL 39; 2003–04 HC 382, March 3, 2004)), the intention of Parliament in enacting this scheme was that a wide range of bodies performing public functions would fall within the obligation under s. 6 to act in a manner compatible with the 'Convention rights' established under the Act (para. 3).

A7.34   **'Pure' Public Authorities**   Identifying 'pure' public authorities is important because all of their acts are governed by s. 6(1). As the Lord Chancellor made clear when the Bill was being discussed in Parliament, 'there is no exemption for private acts' (*Hansard*, HL vol. 583, col. 811 (24 November 1997)). In *Aston Cantlow and Wilmcote with Billesley Parochial Church Council v Wallbank* [2004] 1 AC 546, Lord Hope observed that although the test as to whether a person or body is, or is not, a 'pure' public authority is not capable of being defined precisely, a distinction should be drawn between those persons who, in Convention terms, are governmental organisations on the one hand and those who are non-governmental on the other. A person who would be regarded as a non-governmental organisation within the meaning of the ECHR, Article 34, ought not to be regarded as a 'pure' public authority for the purposes of the HRA 1998, s. 6. Drawing on the case of *Holy Monasteries v Greece* (1995) 20 EHRR 1, Lord Hope observed that the test of whether a person or body is a non-governmental organisation is whether it was established with a view to public administration as part of the process of government (at [50]). Adopting that test, the Parochial Church Council was not a 'pure' public authority.

A7.35   **'Functional' Public Authorities**   Defining 'functional' public authorities has proved more difficult and controversial. In the early cases of *Poplar Housing and Regeneration Community*

A

Association Ltd v Donoghue [2002] QB 48 and *R (Heather) v Leonard Cheshire Foundation* [2002] 2 All ER 936, the Court of Appeal treated the tests for a functional public authority under the HRA 1998 and for amenability to judicial review as, for practical purposes, the same. But the House of Lords in *Aston Cantlow and Wilmcote with Billesley Parochial Church Council v Wallbank* took a wider approach. Lord Nicholls considered that there should be a generous interpretation of a public function which would ensure the fullest protection of human rights while still allowing functional bodies to rely on their Convention rights when acting privately (at [11]). He accepted that there could be no single test of universal application, but indicated that factors to be taken into account include the extent to which, in carrying out the relevant function, the body is (a) publicly funded, (b) is exercising statutory powers, (c) is taking the place of central government or local authorities, or (d) is providing a public service (at [12]). Thus the House of Lords has adopted a relatively narrow test for 'pure' public authorities, but balanced this against a correspondingly wide and flexible category of 'functional' public authority. In *YL v Birmingham City Council* [2008] 1 AC 95 the House of Lords had to determine whether a private care home fell within the meaning of 'public authority' under s. 6 when providing care. The majority of their lordships found that the care home was not exercising 'functions of a public nature' and thus upheld the narrow interpretation of the law established in the *Leonard Cheshire* case.

Remedies

A person who claims that a public authority has acted (or proposes to act) in a way that is **A7.36** incompatible with Convention rights may either bring proceedings against the authority in the appropriate court or tribunal; or rely on his Convention rights in any legal proceedings (HRA 1998, s. 7(1)). Legal proceedings in this context include proceedings brought by or at the instigation of a public authority, and any appeal against the decision of a court or tribunal (s. 7(6)).

Proceedings against a public authority can be brought only by an individual who is (or would be) a victim within the meaning of the ECHR, Article 34; likewise, only victims can rely on their Convention rights in legal proceedings (s. 6(1) and (7)).

In relation to any act (or proposed act) of a public authority which the court finds is (or would be) unlawful, it may grant such relief or remedy, or make such order, within its powers as it considers just and appropriate (s. 8(1)). But damages for breach of the HRA 1998 may be awarded only by a court which has power to award damages or to order the payment of compensation in civil proceedings (s. 8(2)). The level of damages will be assessed in accordance with the principles applied by the ECtHR (*R (Greenfield) v Secretary of State for the Home Department* [2005] 2 All ER 240).

Judicial Acts

Where individuals claim that their Convention rights have been infringed by a judicial act, they **A7.37** must bring their claim by way of an appeal or in such other forum as may be prescribed by rules (HRA 1998, s. 9(1): no rules have yet been made for England and Wales). But this does not expand the scope for judicial review of courts (s. 9(2)). The term 'judicial act' in this context includes the acts of members of tribunals, justices of the peace, clerks and other officers entitled to exercise the jurisdiction of the court (s. 9(5)). It also includes acts done on the instructions, or on behalf, of such individuals (HRA 1998, s. 9(5)).

In respect of a judicial act done in good faith, damages may not be awarded otherwise than to compensate a person to the extent required by the ECHR, Article 5(5) (s. 9(3)). An award of damages in respect of a judicial act done in good faith is to be made against the Crown, but only if the minister responsible for the court concerned, or nominated person or government department, is joined as a party (s. 9(4) and (5)).

Retrospectivity

A7.38 Proceedings against a public authority for breach of Convention rights can be brought only in relation to acts or omissions occurring after 2 October 2000 (HRA 1998, s. 22(4)). The same applies where an individual otherwise seeks to rely on his Convention rights in legal proceedings, save where proceedings are brought by or at the instigation of a public authority — in which case a breach of Convention rights can be relied upon whenever the breach took place (s. 22(4)). In *Janowiec v Russia* (2014) 58 EHRR 792, the Grand Chamber held that where agents of the state committed acts — in that case a massacre of thousands of Polish prisoners in 1940 (the triggering event) — before the State became a signatory to the ECHR — which, in Russia's case, occurred only in 1998 (the critical date) — the failure of the State to properly investigate those acts could engage Article 2 of the ECHR if there was a 'genuine connection' between the triggering event and the critical date. Such a connection could exist where (i) the lapse in time between the triggering event and the critical date was no more than ten years and (ii) a major part of the investigation into the triggering event occurred or should have occurred after the critical date because, for example, new material came to light that had not been available earlier. The Court of Appeal in *Keyu v Secretary of State for Foreign and Commonwealth Affairs* [2014] EWCA Civ 312 held (at [66]) that the Grand Chamber's decision in *Janowiec* now stands as 'the definitive exposition of the relevant principles' under the ECHR. In *Keyu*, the Secretary of State had declined to order a public inquiry into events that occurred in the former Federation of Malaya in December 1948 when British troops shot and killed 24 civilians. The appellants argued that that decision infringed Article 2 even though the UK did not ratify the ECHR until 1953. The Court concluded that, if the case was heard in Strasbourg, the appellants would succeed because the ECtHR would follow its ruling in *Janowiec*, but, nevertheless, the Court was bound by the earlier decision of the House of Lords in *Re McKerr* [2004] 1 WLR 807 to hold that, as the triggering event had occurred before 2 October 2000, there was no obligation to conduct an investigation into it.

Derogations and Reservations

A7.39 Convention rights under the HRA 1998 are subject to designated derogations (HRA 1998, s. 1(2)). Designated derogations cease to have effect after five years, unless renewed (s. 16).

Convention rights under the HRA 1998 are also subject to designated reservations (s. 1(2)). The UK has one reservation in place concerning the right to education under Protocol 1, Article 2. The terms of this derogation are set out in the HRA 1998, sch. 3, part II.

Substantive Challenges to the Criminal Law

A7.40 Subject to the ECHR, Article 7, and the procedural requirements of Articles 5 and 6, Parliament is free, in principle, to apply the criminal law to acts which are not carried out in the normal exercise of one of the rights protected under the Convention (*Engel v Netherlands* (1979–80) 1 EHRR 647 and *Salabiaku v France* (1991) 13 EHRR 379 at [27]).

In *G* [2009] 1 AC 92 the House of Lords reiterated that Article 6 was concerned with the procedural fairness of the system for the administration of justice in the Contracting States, not with the substantive content of domestic law. Lord Hope stated that when Article 6(2) used the words 'innocent' and 'guilty' it was dealing with the burden of proof regarding the elements of the offence and any defence to it; it was not dealing with what those elements were or what defences ought to be available.

Different considerations may apply where criminal offences overlap with Convention rights; particularly those contained in Articles 8 to 11. In such cases, the Strasbourg institutions will require any interference with a Convention right to be 'necessary in a democratic society' in pursuit of a legitimate aim. The tensions between sexual activity classified as criminal in Convention States and the Convention protected right of privacy provides a classic example.

In *G v UK* (2011) 53 EHRR 237, the ECtHR confirmed that the strict liability aspect of the SOA 2003, s. 5, with which G's case was concerned, was an acceptable such interference.

In *Norris v Ireland* (1991) 13 EHRR 186 the ECtHR held that maintaining in force legislation prohibiting homosexual acts committed in private between consenting adult men constituted an interference with the applicant's right to respect for his private life under Article 8, following its judgment in *Dudgeon v UK* (1982) 4 EHRR 149. A similar result followed in *Sutherland v UK* (2001) Appln. 25186/94, 27 March 2001, where the applicant complained that fixing the minimum age for lawful homosexual activities at 18, rather than 16 (the minimum age for heterosexual activities), violated his right to respect for his private life under Article 8 and was discriminatory under Article 14.

A7.41

Articles 9 and 10 have also been invoked to challenge substantive criminal law provisions. For example, in *Larissis v Greece* (1999) 27 EHRR 329, the ECtHR found that the applicants' convictions for proselytising breached Article 9 insofar as they were directed towards civilians; in *Grigoriades v Greece* (1999) 27 EHRR 464, the ECtHR held that the applicant's conviction for insulting the army when he wrote an intemperate letter to his commanding officer breached Article 10; in *Hertel v Switzerland* (1999) 28 EHRR 534, Article 10 was breached when the applicant was convicted for publishing his views on the hazardous effects of microwave ovens; and in *Gunduz v Turkey* (2005) 41 EHRR 59, the ECtHR found a breach of Article 10 when the applicant was convicted for inciting religious hatred because his speech was not an appeal to violence nor was it based on religious intolerance.

For examples going the other way, see *Laskey v UK* (1997) 24 EHRR 39, where the applicants' prosecution and conviction for assault and wounding in the course of consensual, sado-masochistic activities between adults was found not to breach Article 8; *ADT v UK* (2001) 31 EHRR 803, where the ECtHR found no breach of Article 8 in the applicants' conviction for gross indecency in respect of consensual sexual acts involving violence; and *Zana v Turkey* (1999) 27 EHRR 2667, where the ECtHR held that prosecuting a member of a terrorist organisation for comments made to a journalist did not breach Article 10. In *Shayler* [2003] 1 AC 247, the House of Lords held that the provisions of the Official Secrets Act 1989 which created criminal offences of disclosure of certain material were not incompatible with Article 10.

In *F* [2007] QB 960 the Court of Appeal held that nothing in the ECHR required terrorism under the Terrorism Act 2000 to be interpreted as including only acts directed at representative or democratic governments (see also **B10.2**).

THE INVESTIGATION OF CRIME

Duty to Investigate Crime Effectively

In certain circumstances, the ECHR obliges law enforcement bodies, such as the police, to carry out effective investigations where serious human rights issues arise, particularly where absolute rights such as the right to life or the prohibition on torture and inhuman or degrading treatment are concerned (see, e.g., *Aydin v Turkey* (1998) 25 EHRR 251 at [103] and *Labita v Italy* (2008) 46 EHRR 1228 at [131]).

A7.42

Examples where the ECtHR has found that there has been a failure to conduct a thorough and effective investigation include: (a) failing to ascertain the identity of possible eye-witnesses; (b) failing to question suspects at an early stage; (c) failing to search for corroborating evidence; (d) the adoption of an over-deferential attitude to those in authority; (e) failing to follow up proper complaints; (f) ignoring obvious evidence; (g) failing to carry out a proper autopsy; and (h) failing to test gunpowder traces (see, e.g., *Aksoy v Turkey* (1997) 23 EHRR 553; *Aydin v Turkey* (1998) 25 EHRR 251; *Kurt v Turkey* (1999) 27 EHRR 373; *Labita v Italy* (2008) 46 EHRR 1228). For a comprehensive review of many of these authorities, see *DSD and NBV v*

Commissioner of Police for the Metropolis [2014] EWHC 436 (QB), a case where the claimants were the later victims of the 'black cab rapist', John Worboys. They sought a declaration and damages under the HRA 1998, ss. 7 and 8, on account of the police's failure to arrest Worboys sooner.

Surveillance

A7.43   Secret surveillance amounts to a serious interference with an individual's private life under Article 8 (*Kopp v Switzerland* (1999) 27 EHRR 91). Therefore it must be 'prescribed by law': i.e. the applicable legal rules must be accessible and formulated with sufficient precision to enable citizens to foresee — if need be with appropriate advice — the consequences of their actions (see, e.g., *Amann v Switzerland* (2000) 30 EHRR 843). Since intercepting telephone calls constitutes a serious interference with private life, particular precision in the law is required, including the rules applicable in prisons (*Doerga v Netherlands* (2004) 41 EHRR 45).

Surveillance must also be necessary and proportionate: police surveillance should be restricted to that which is strictly necessary to achieve the required objective. What is legitimate for the prevention and detection of serious crime may not be legitimate for less serious crime. Secret surveillance is tolerable under the Convention only insofar as it is strictly necessary for the protection of national security or the prevention of disorder or crime (*Klass v Germany* (1979–80) 2 EHRR 214).

A7.44   Article 8 can be engaged where telephone calls (or other communications) are intercepted at work, even where they take place on private or internal telecommunications systems. In *Halford v UK* (1997) 24 EHRR 523, the ECtHR held (at [46]):

> …telephone calls made from business premises as well as from the home may be covered by the notions of 'private life' and 'correspondence' within the meaning of Article 8(1).

The law on secret surveillance must be particularly precise and provide effective safeguards against abuse. Although there is no requirement that individuals be given prior notice of surveillance (because in most cases that would defeat its purpose), the law governing powers of secret surveillance must be clear enough to give citizens an adequate indication of the circumstances in which, and the conditions upon which, public authorities are entitled to resort to the use of such powers (*Halford v UK* (1997) 24 EHRR 523; *Malone v UK* (1985) 7 EHRR 14; *Khan v UK* (2001) 31 EHRR 1016; *Elahi v UK* (2007) 44 EHRR 645).

The RIPA 2000 was designed to ensure that surveillance carried out within the framework it provides is compatible with Article 8. In *Kennedy v UK* (2011) 52 EHRR 207, the ECtHR found that the domestic law, together with the clarifications brought by the Code published under the Act, indicated with sufficient clarity the procedures for authorisation and processing of interception warrants as well as processing, communication and destruction of intercept material; there was no evidence of any significant shortcomings in the application and operation of the UK surveillance regime.

Informers and Undercover Police Officers

A7.45   So long as informers and undercover officers do not actively instigate criminal offences, the fact that they carry out private surveillance does not *in itself* breach the ECHR, Article 8, because those who engage in serious crime cannot have any reasonable expectation that their activities will not be observed. As the ECtHR observed in *Ludi v Switzerland* (1993) 15 EHRR 173 (at [40]):

> …the use of an undercover agent did not, either alone or in combination with the telephone interception, affect private life within the meaning of Article 8…[the applicant] must…have been aware…that he was engaged in a criminal act…and that consequently he was running the risk of encountering an undercover police officer whose task would in fact be to expose him.

However, the law governing the use of undercover agents must be clear and precise; it must also provide safeguards against abuse (*Teixeira de Castro v Portugal* (1999) 28 EHRR 101). Where informers/undercover officers go beyond observation and actively incite the commission of an offence, issues of fairness under Article 6 will arise.

Entrapment

It is unfair under the ECHR, Article 6, to prosecute an individual for a criminal offence incited   **A7.46**
by undercover agents, which, but for the incitement, would probably not have been committed. Even the public interest in the detection of serious crime cannot justify the instigation of criminal offences by undercover agents (*Teixeira de Castro v Portugal* (1999) 28 EHRR 101 at [39]). However, so long as informers and/or undercover officers keep within the reasonable limits of passive surveillance, no issue arises under Article 6 (fair trial); nor does any privacy issue arise under Article 8 (*Ludi v Switzerland* (1993) 15 EHRR 173). In *Looseley* [2001] 4 All ER 897 (see F2.36), the House of Lords held that the approach of the domestic courts to entrapment was no different to the approach taken in *Teixeira de Castro v Portugal*.

Searching Individuals

Whereas in *R (Gillan) v Commissioner of Police for the Metropolis* [2006] 2 AC 307 the House of   **A7.47**
Lords held that superficial search of the individual and the opening of bags, etc., using powers available under the Terrorism Act 2000, ss. 44 and 45 (since repealed in that form), would probably not engage Article 8, in *Gillan v UK* (2010) 50 EHRR 1105 the ECtHR held that the use of the coercive powers conferred by the Terrorism Act 2000 to require an individual to submit to a detailed search of his person, his clothing and his personal belongings amounted to a clear interference with the right to respect for private life. Such an interference could be justified under Article 8(2) only if it was, among other things, in accordance with the law. The law had to indicate with sufficient clarity the scope of any such discretion conferred on the competent authorities and the manner of its exercise. The power in question in the instant case had a basis in domestic law, namely ss. 44 to 47 of the 2000 Act, but the safeguards provided by domestic law had not been demonstrated to constitute a real curb on the wide powers afforded to the executive so as to offer the individual adequate protection against arbitrary interference. Of particular concern was the breadth of the discretion conferred on the individual police officer. The officer's decision to stop and search would be based exclusively on his professional intuition. Not only was it unnecessary for him to demonstrate the existence of any reasonable suspicion, he was not required even subjectively to suspect anything about the person stopped and searched. There was a clear risk of arbitrariness in the grant of such a broad discretion to the police officer. The powers were not therefore in accordance with the law and it followed that there had been a violation of Article 8. In the context of powers under para. 2(1) of sch. 7 to the 2000 Act to question and recover items from a person in order to determine whether he appears to be a terrorist, the Divisional Court in *Miranda v Secretary of State for the Home Department* [2014] EWHC 255 (Admin) held, *inter alia*, that those powers were prescribed by law, for the purposes of Article 10(2), and so their exercise to seize items in the hands of a partner of a journalist who was in transit from one country to another did not infringe his right to freedom of expression.

Searching Premises and Vehicles

Search and seizure interfere with the right to private and family life, home and correspondence   **A7.48**
protected by the ECHR, Article 8. Therefore such measures must be justified in accordance with Article 8(2) of the Convention. Judicial authorisation is a highly relevant factor, but not determinative of the lawfulness of search and seizure under the ECHR.

Where there has been no judicial authorisation for a search, courts should be particularly vigilant to ensure that other safeguards exist to protect individuals from unnecessary intrusion into their privacy. At the very least, a proper legal framework with very strict limits on search powers will be required (*Camenzind v Switzerland* (1999) 28 EHRR 458 at [45]). Furthermore, where the police retain a discretion whether to enter premises, that discretion must be properly exercised (*McLeod v UK* (1999) 27 EHRR 493 at [54]–[57]).

Any warrant authorising search and seizure must be clear, specific and contain safeguards against abuse. If a warrant is drawn in very broad terms or gives too much discretion to those executing it, it is likely to breach Article 8 (*Funke v France* (1993) 16 EHRR 297 at [56] and [57]). For example, the ECtHR has held that a warrant which authorised a search for 'documents' without any limitation is too broad for compliance with Article 8 (*Niemietz v Germany* (1993) 16 EHRR 97).

The notion of an individual's private life under Article 8 can be extended to his business and commercial premises (*Niemietz v Germany* (1993) 16 EHRR 97; *Sallinen v Finland* (2005) 44 EHRR 358). Therefore warrants to search business premises should comply with Article 8. Although lawyers' premises are not immune from search, professional confidentiality must be respected. In *Niemietz v Germany*, the ECtHR found a breach of Article 8 where a lawyer's offices were searched by the police acting on a court warrant in order to obtain information about the identity and whereabouts of a third party who was the subject of a criminal investigation.

Fingerprints and Other Samples

A7.49   Measures such as taking personal details, photographs and samples all engage the ECHR, Article 8, and must be justified (*Murray v UK* (1995) 19 EHRR 193). The prevention of crime can justify such measures, but only where they are prescribed by law, necessary and proportionate. In some cases, the collection of personal data from those who are not under suspicion can be justified, but only in very limited circumstances: e.g., where individuals are stopped crossing a national border and the purpose of the measures in question is the prevention of terrorism (*McVeigh, O'Neill and Evans v UK* (1983) 5 EHRR 71). In *R (R) v A Chief Constable* [2014] 1 Cr App R 222 (16), a claimant with previous criminal convictions unsuccessfully argued that the decision of the police to require him to attend a police station in order that a non-intimate sample could be taken from him, pursuant to the PACE 1984, s. 63(3B)(a) and (3BA)(a), infringed his rights under Article 8. Pitchford LJ held that the interference with the claimant's Article 8 rights was justified as a proportionate response to the need to detect crime.

The retention of personal data is different from its collection and must be separately justified (*X v Germany* 9 Coll Dec 53; Appln. 1307/61). The prevention of terrorism (or other serious offences) can justify the retention of personal data, but only for so long as it serves that purpose (*McVeigh, O'Neill and Evans v UK*).

In *S and Marper v UK* (2009) 48 EHRR 1169 the ECtHR held that the 'blanket and indiscriminate' power to retain biometric data indefinitely, provided for by the PACE 1984, was not proportionate under Article 8(2). The Supreme Court confirmed in *R (GC) v Commissioner of Police for the Metropolis* [2011] 3 All ER 859 that, in light of the decision in *S and Marper*, the retention of the DNA samples of two acquitted defendants by the Commissioner pursuant to ACPO guidelines was an unjustified interference with their Article 8(1) rights. The Protection of Freedoms Act 2012, ss. 1 to 25, provide a new scheme for the regulation of biometric data and take account of the ECtHR judgment in *R (GC)*.

International Co-operation in the Investigation of Crime

A7.50   The ECHR is relevant to questions of international co-operation in the investigation of crime. Law enforcement officers from the UK who carry out their functions in other countries remain subject to the ECHR. It will therefore be possible for a suspect arrested and detained abroad by UK law enforcement officers to claim a breach of Convention rights (*Reinette v France* (1989) 63 DR 189). The leading case on the extra-territorial application of the ECHR and the HRA 1998 is now *R (Al-Skeini) v Secretary of State for Defence* [2008] 1 AC 153.

In addition, it would breach the ECHR if international co-operation in the investigation of crime exposed an individual to the risk of torture or ill-treatment contrary to Article 3, or interfered with his right to life under Article 2 (e.g., through extradition or deportation). However, although there is no absolute rule that Contracting States to the ECHR should not co-operate with non-Contracting States merely because they do not comply with the standards set out in Article 6 (fair trial), unless there has been, or is likely to be, a flagrant denial of justice, co-operation should be refused (*Drozd and Janousek v France and Spain* (1992) 14 EHRR 745 at [110]).

In *R (Al-Skeini) v Secretary of State for Defence* the House of Lords held that s. 6 of the HRA 1998 was capable of applying to acts of UK public authorities which took place outside the territory of the UK. Whether or not any such act was unlawful would then depend on whether it was within the 'jurisdiction' of the UK within the meaning of Article 1. On that basis, s. 6 applied to the acts of UK soldiers who held an individual in their custody in Iraq. See also *Smith v Oxfordshire Assistant Deputy Coroner* [2011] 1 AC 1.

ARREST AND PRE-TRIAL DETENTION

Reasonable Suspicion

Article 5(1)(c) of the ECHR authorises arrest on 'reasonable suspicion' that an individual has   A7.51
committed an offence. Such suspicion requires objective justification. The honesty and good faith of a suspicion constitute indispensable elements of its reasonableness, but honest belief alone is not enough. There must be an objective basis justifying arrest and/or detention (*Fox, Campbell and Hartley v UK* (1991) 13 EHRR 157 at [32]). A reasonable suspicion can be based on information obtained from anonymous informers; but if challenged the authorities must furnish at least some evidence capable of satisfying a court under Article 5(3) (*O'Hara v UK* (2002) 34 EHRR 812). An arrest for failing to supply a name and address must be proportionate. In *Vasileva v Denmark* (2003) 40 EHRR 681, a breach of Article 5 was found where a 67-year-old woman was detained for 13 hours because she refused to give her name and address.

In *Ostendorf v Germany* [2013] ECHR 197, the ECtHR held that there had been no infringement of Article 5 in circumstances where the accused had been arrested and detained at a police station for four hours before being released because the police suspected that he might otherwise have engaged in acts of crowd violence at a football match. Article 5(1)(c) did not provide a justification for his detention but Article 5(1)(b) did because there was a specific and imminent risk that in the absence of detention the accused would commit a criminal offence. In *R (Hicks) v Commissioner of Police of the Metropolis* [2014] EWCA Civ 3, a case concerned with the arrest and detention of protestors during the Royal Wedding on 29 April 2011, the Court of Appeal doubted the ECtHR's interpretation of Article 5(1)(c) in *Ostendorf* and in the event declined to follow it because it did not represent a 'clear and consistent' line of authority from the Strasbourg Court. In the Court of Appeal's view, the arrest and detention of the protestors was justified under Article 5(1)(c) and may also have been justified under Article 5(1)(b).

Article 5(1) must be interpreted in a manner which takes into account the specific context in which police techniques are deployed as well as the responsibilities of the police to fulfil their duties of maintaining order and protecting the public (*Austin v UK* (2012) 55 EHRR 359); the practice of 'kettling' in the particular circumstances of the case did not involve a deprivation of liberty and Article 5(1) was not engaged.

Reasons

Article 5(2) of the ECHR requires that anyone arrested 'be informed promptly, in a language   A7.52
which he understands, of the reasons for his arrest and of any charge against him'. The promptness of reasons is to be assessed in light of all the circumstances of the case. Giving reasons

within a few hours might suffice where terrorist offences are suspected (*Fox, Campbell and Hartley v UK* (1991) 13 EHRR 157; *Murray v UK* (1995) 19 EHRR 193 at [40]).

The purpose of giving reasons for an arrest is to enable anyone arrested to challenge the lawfulness of his detention (*Fox, Campbell and Hartley v UK*; *Murray v UK*). But reasons need not be in writing (*X v Netherlands* (1966) 9 Yearbook 474; *X v Germany* (1974) 14 Yearbook 250). Merely informing an individual that he has been detained under emergency legislation is insufficient (*Ireland v UK* (1979–80) 2 EHRR 25).

Handcuffs and Restraints

A7.53 The use of handcuffs and restraints is not prohibited by the ECHR, but unless justified on the facts of each case may raise issues under Articles 3 and 8. In *Raninen v Finland* (1998) 26 EHRR 563, the ECtHR held (at [56]):

> ...handcuffing does not normally give rise to an issue under Article 3...where the measure has been imposed with lawful arrest and detention and does not entail use of force, or public exposure, exceeding what is reasonably considered necessary in the circumstances. In this regard, it is of importance for instance whether there is reason to believe that the person concerned would resist arrest or abscond, cause injury or damage or suppress evidence.

In *Henaf v France* (2005) 40 EHRR 990, the ECtHR found a breach of Article 3 where the applicant was, for no good reason, handcuffed to a hospital bed while waiting for an operation.

Access to a Lawyer

A7.54 The right to a fair trial under the ECHR, Article 6, normally requires that a suspect have access to a lawyer at the initial stages of a police investigation, particularly where steps may be taken which will impact on the defence (*Imbroscia v Switzerland* (1994) 17 EHRR 441 at [36]; *Murray (John) v UK* (1996) 22 EHRR 29 at [63], [65] and [66]). However, the actual requirements of Article 6 at the pre-trial stage will vary according to the circumstances. In *Imbroscia v Switzerland* (1994) 17 EHRR 4411, the ECtHR held (at [36]):

> ...the manner in which Article 6(1) and 3(c) is to be applied during the preliminary investigation depends on the special features of the proceedings involved and the circumstances of the case; in order to determine whether the aim of Article 6 — a fair trial — has been achieved, regard must be had to the entirety of the proceedings conducted in the case.

To deny access to a lawyer for a long period in a situation where the rights of the defence were irretrievably prejudiced is, whatever the justification, likely to be incompatible with Article 6 (*Magee v UK* (2001) 31 EHRR 822; *Averill v UK* (2001) 31 EHRR 839). But see *Brennan v UK* (2002) 34 EHRR 507, where no breach was found where denial of access to a lawyer was in good faith and on reasonable grounds.

Communications between a suspect and his lawyer should be confidential. In *Ocalan v Turkey* (2005) 41 EHRR 985 the ECtHR stated (at [146]) that 'an accused's right to communicate with his legal representative out of hearing of a third person is part of the basic requirements of fair trial in a democratic society and follows from Article 6(3)(c)'. The Court went on to acknowledge that the right of confidential communication was not an absolute right and may be subject to restrictions. However, the mere fact that a number of lawyers are co-ordinating their defence strategy cannot justify interference with lawyer/client confidentiality (*S v Switzerland* (1992) 14 EHRR 670). In *Ocalan v Turkey* (2014) Appln. 24069/03, 18 March 2014, the ECtHR held, *inter alia*, that during the course of the accused's detention following his conviction, there had been no violation of Article 3 where the accused's conversations with his lawyers had been recorded and conducted in the presence of an observer. Turkey had been entitled to impose 'legitimate restrictions' on prisoners convicted of terrorist activities insofar as they were strictly necessary to protect society against violence.

Access to Others

Suspects in custody should normally be allowed access to their families. In *McVeigh, O'Neill and*   **A7.55**
Evans v UK (1983) 5 EHRR 71, the European Commission held (at [239]):

> Unless there is a danger of accomplices being warned, a failure to allow persons so detained to make contact with their families cannot be justified under Article 8(2) as being necessary for the prevention of crime etc.

See also *Ocalan v Turkey* (2014) Appln. 24069/03, 18 March 2014 at **A7.54**.

Right to Silence

The ECHR recognises a right to remain silent during police questioning. In *Murray (John) v UK*   **A7.56**
(1996) 22 EHRR 29, the ECtHR held (at [20]):

> ...although not specifically mentioned in Article 6 of the Convention, there can be no doubt that the right to remain silent under police questioning and the privilege against self-incrimination are generally recognised international standards which lie at the heart of the notion of a fair procedure under Article 6.

That does not mean that adverse inference cannot be drawn from silence. The fairness of drawing such inferences is a matter to be determined at trial in light of all the evidence (see F19). But it does mean that the introduction into evidence in a criminal trial for the purpose of incriminating the accused of transcripts of statements made under compulsion (e.g., to non-prosecutorial inspectors) will breach Article 6 (*Saunders v UK* (1997) 23 EHRR 313; see also *Shannon v UK* (2005) Appln. 6563/03, 4 October 2005). The same applies where the authorities seek to compel a suspect to hand over incriminating documentation (*Funke v France* (1993) 16 EHRR 297). Incriminating answers obtained by the questioning of a suspect during incommunicado detention require very close scrutiny (*G v UK* (1984) 34 DR 75).

Right to be Brought Promptly before a Court

Everyone arrested for a criminal offence has the right to be brought promptly before a judge or   **A7.57**
other officer authorised by law to exercise judicial power.

ECHR, Article 5

(3) Everyone arrested or detained in accordance with the provisions of paragraph 1(c) of this Article shall be brought promptly before a judge or other officer authorised by law to exercise judicial power and shall be entitled to trial within a reasonable time or to release pending trial. Release may be conditioned by guarantees to appear for trial.

Article 5(3) does not depend on the detainee making an application for his case to be heard; it requires automatic consideration of the case by the court. It also requires provisional release once detention ceases to be reasonable (*TW v Malta; Aquilina v Malta* (2000) 29 EHRR 185). Although authorised by law to review detention, a commanding officer is not sufficiently independent and impartial to satisfy the requirements of Article 5(4) in court-martial cases (*Hood v UK* (2000) 29 EHRR 365; *Jordan v UK* (2001) 31 EHRR 201).

When determining whether an arrested person has been brought promptly before a judge or judicial officer, the scope for flexibility in interpreting and applying the notion of 'promptness' is very limited. In *Brogan v UK* (1989) 11 EHRR 117, the ECtHR held (at [62]) that a delay of four days and six hours was too long, even when an arrest is made under prevention of terrorism legislation.

Bail

Despite its wording, the ECHR, Article 5(3), does not provide for trial within a reasonable   **A7.58**
period *or* release pending trial *as alternatives*: an accused person is entitled to trial within a

reasonable period *and* release pending trial unless the prosecuting authorities advance relevant and sufficient reasons for refusing bail (*Wemhoff v Germany* (1979–80) 1 EHRR 55).

Grounds for refusing bail which have been approved by the ECtHR include: (a) fear of absconding (*Stogmuller v Austria* (1979–80) 1 EHRR 155; *Neumeister v Austria* (1979–80) 1 EHRR 91); (b) interference with the course of justice (*Wemhoff v Germany*; *Letellier v France* (1992) 14 EHRR 83); (c) prevention of further offences (*Matznetter v Austria* (1979–80) 1 EHRR 198; (d) the preservation of public order (*Letellier v France*); and (e) the protection of the defendant (*IA v France* (1998) Appln. 28213/95, 23 September 1998). The mere fact that there are reasonable grounds for suspecting that a person has committed an offence is not enough (*Letellier v France*).

A7.59   Conditional bail is permitted under the ECHR and should be granted as an alternative to pre-trial detention where objections to bail can be met with conditions (*Wemhoff v Germany*). Permissible conditions of bail include a requirement to surrender travel documents (*Stogmuller v Austria*), the imposition of a residence requirement (*Schmid v Austria* (1985) 44 DR 195) and the provision of a surety — which must be assessed by reference to the means of the accused (*Wemhoff v Germany*; *Neumeister v Austria*; *Schertenleib v Switzerland* (1980) 23 DR 137). The task of assessing appropriate bail conditions is as exacting as the task of deciding whether to grant bail at all (*Iwanczuk v Poland* (2004) 38 EHRR 148). Bail proceedings must be fair and there must be equality of arms between the prosecution and the defence. In the domestic context, in *R (KS) v Northampton Crown Court* [2010] 2 Cr App R 175 the Administrative Court held that a special advocate should have been appointed where a judge refused bail having already had sight of material relating to jury tampering when deciding that the defendant should be tried by judge alone.

Legislation depriving courts of their ability to grant bail will breach Article 5 (*Caballero v UK* (2000) 30 EHRR 643).

FAIR TRIAL IN CRIMINAL PROCEEDINGS

Meaning of 'criminal proceedings' under Article 6

A7.60   The fair trial requirements of the ECHR, Article 6, distinguish between criminal and civil proceedings. Whether proceedings are criminal or civil is to be determined according to three criteria: (a) the classification in domestic law — if classified as criminal, this is determinative; if classified as civil, this is a starting point, but not determinative; (b) the nature of the conduct in question — sanctions which apply to the population as a whole, rather than to an identifiable sub-class, point toward a criminal classification; (c) the severity of any possible penalty — severe penalties (including those with imprisonment in default) and penalties intended to deter are pointers towards a criminal classification of proceedings (*Engel v Netherlands (No. 1)* (1979–80) 1 EHRR 647; *Benham v UK* (1996) 22 EHRR 293). The second and third criteria are alternative, not cumulative (*Lauko v Slovakia* (2001) 33 EHRR 994 at [57]).

A7.61   In *Steel v UK* (1999) 28 EHRR 603, the ECtHR held that although 'breach of the peace' is not classified as a criminal offence under English law, it is nonetheless to be considered an 'offence' within the meaning of Article 6(1) (at [54]–[55]). On the other hand, in *Escoubet v Belgium* (2001) 31 EHRR 1034, the ECtHR found that a procedure whereby a driving licence could be withdrawn for 15 days on the direction of a Crown prosecutor where a driver was drunk did not amount to the determination of a criminal charge under Article 6. Similarly in *Benjafield* [2003] 1 AC 1099, the House of Lords held that confiscation proceedings were part of the sentencing process and did not involve a fresh criminal charge; accordingly Article 6(2) was not applicable to such proceedings. A similar approach had been taken by the ECtHR in *Phillips v UK* (2001)

Appln. 41087/98, 5 July 2001 (but where such proceedings follow an acquittal, see *Geerings v Netherlands* (2008) 46 EHRR 1212). In *Briggs-Price* [2009] 1 AC 1026 the House of Lords held that, where the prosecution sought to rely on criminal offending other than a conviction to prove the existence of benefit and the usual statutory assumptions had not been applied, Article 6(1) required that a statutory provision which required proof to the civil standard should be read as requiring proof to the criminal standard.

In *R (McCann) v Manchester Crown Court* [2003] 1 AC 787, the House of Lords held that the imposition of an ASBO under the CDA 1998 did not amount to the determination of a criminal charge. Such orders are preventative in character and thus no penalty is imposed. In *R v UK* (2007) Appln. 33506/05, 4 January 2007, the ECtHR held that Article 6 did not apply to the giving of a police warning to a schoolboy for indecent assault on girls at his school. The ECtHR noted that a warning is not a criminal conviction; its purpose was, largely, preventative and not retributive or deterrent and no fine or restriction of liberty was imposed.

Right to be Informed of Charge

> **ECHR, Article 6** A7.62
>
> (3) Everyone charged with a criminal offence has the following minimum rights:
>   (a) to be informed promptly, in a language which he understands and in detail, of the nature and cause of the accusation against him;
>   …

The purpose of this provision is to enable the individual to begin preparing a defence (*GSM v Austria* (1983) 34 DR 119).

Where the offence is fairly specific, it may be enough to provide a brief description of the offence, the date, place and alleged victim (*Brozicek v Italy* (1990) 12 EHRR 371). Otherwise, the information provided should be detailed (*Pelisser and Sassi v France* (2000) 30 EHRR 715).

Right to Adequate Time and Facilities to Prepare a Defence

> **ECHR, Article 6** A7.63
>
> (3) Everyone charged with a criminal offence has the following minimum rights:
>   …
>   (b) to have adequate time and facilities for the preparation of his defence.

The adequate time requirement inevitably depends on the nature and complexity of the case; it cannot be determined in the abstract but only by reference to the circumstances of each case (*X and Y v Austria* (1979) 15 DR 160). Where there is a late change of lawyer, an adjournment may be necessary. Where it is obvious that a lawyer has not had adequate time to prepare the defence properly, the court should consider adjourning the case on its own motion (*Goddi v Italy* (1984) 6 EHRR 457).

Disclosure

Under the ECHR, a disclosure requirement is based on: (a) the requirement that there be A7.64 equality of arms between prosecution and defence (*Jespers v Belgium* (1981) 27 DR 61); (b) the accused's right to adequate time and facilities to prepare a defence under ECHR, Article 6(3)(b) (*Edwards v UK* (1993) 15 EHRR 417); and (c) the requirement in Article 6(3)(d) that there be parity of conditions for the examination of witnesses (*Edwards v UK* (1993) 15 EHRR 417, Commission Report). In *Rowe and Davis v UK* (2000) 30 EHRR 1 (see **D9.61**), the ECtHR held (at [60]):

> It is a fundamental aspect of the right to a fair trial that criminal proceedings, including the elements of such proceedings which relate to procedure, should be adversarial and that there should be equality of arms between the prosecution and defence. The right to an adversarial trial means, in a criminal case, that both prosecution and defence must be given an opportunity to have knowledge

of and comment on the observations filed and the evidence adduced by the other party...In addition Article 6(1) requires...that the prosecution authorities should disclose to the defence all material evidence in their possession for or against the accused...

The requirement in Article 6(3)(d) that there be parity of conditions for the examination of witnesses requires disclosure of any material relevant to the testimony of the witnesses, including their credibility (*Edwards v UK* (1993) 15 EHRR 417, Commission Report).

A7.65   The privacy rights of complainants may require notice to be given to them, along with an opportunity to make representations, when, for example, a witness summons is directed to a hospital to produce its medical records (*R (B) v Stafford Crown Court* [2007] 1 All ER 102).

In *HM Advocate v Murtagh* [2010] 3 WLR 814, a case arising on the duty of disclosure in Scotland, it was held that the ECHR, Article 6, does not require disclosure of *all* of the previous convictions of the prosecution witnesses. A balance had to be struck between the accused's Article 6 right and the witness's Article 8 right. It would be wrong for the Crown to exclude all aspects of a witness's criminal history to which objection could possibly be taken for not being relevant. A generous approach was therefore to be taken to what might be relevant, but there were limits to that approach, bearing in mind the witness's Article 8 right. A rule that the entire criminal history of a witness must be disclosed went too far. See also **D9.15**.

Public Interest Immunity

A7.66   There may be circumstances under the ECHR in which material need not be disclosed to the defence on grounds of public interest immunity; but they must be subject to strict control by the courts. In *Rowe and Davis v UK* (2000) 30 EHRR 1, the ECtHR held (at [61]):

...the entitlement to disclosure of relevant evidence is not an absolute right. In any criminal proceedings there may be competing interests, such as national security or the need to protect witnesses at risk of reprisals or keep secret police methods of investigation of crime, which must be weighed against the rights of the accused...In some cases it may be necessary to withhold certain evidence from the defence so as to preserve the fundamental rights of another individual or to safeguard an important public interest. However, only such measures restricting the rights of the defence which are strictly necessary are permissible under Article 6(1)...Moreover, in order to ensure that the accused receives a fair trial, any difficulties caused to the defence by a limitation on its rights must be sufficiently counterbalanced by the procedures followed by the judicial authorities.

Public interest immunity hearings on an *ex parte* basis do not necessarily breach Article 6 (*Jasper v UK* (2000) 30 EHRR 97; *Fitt v UK* (2000) 30 EHRR 223; *Botmeh and Alami v UK* (2008) 46 EHRR 659). However, where material should have been disclosed to the trial judge but was not, an *ex parte* hearing at the appeal stage is unlikely to be sufficient under Article 6 (see, e.g., *Atlan v UK* (2002) 34 EHRR 833).

There is an important distinction between material that is, and material that is not, actually deployed against the accused. In *Edwards and Lewis v UK* (2005) 40 EHRR 893, the ECtHR found a breach of Article 6 where the material relevant to an issue to be decided by the judge rather than the jury (entrapment) was not disclosed on grounds of public interest immunity. In *McKeown v UK* (2011) 54 EHRR 165 the ECtHR noted this problem does not arise under the system of Diplock courts in Northern Ireland where a separate disclosure judge is appointed.

A7.67   In *Twomey* [2011] 1 Cr App R 29 the Court of Appeal held that trial by jury was not a right which was protected by the Convention nor did its removal for certain cases (by the CJA 2003, s. 44) involve interference with the rights to liberty or property or fair process protected by the Convention. It was not a pre-condition to the fairness of the trial that the procedural steps which resulted in that trial should proceed on the basis of material which was disclosed to the accused. The approach to disclosure to be adopted by domestic courts was spelt out by the House of Lords in *H* [2004] 2 AC 134, where the earlier case of *Smith* [2001] 1 WLR 1031 was overruled as being incompatible with the ECHR.

Right to an Independent and Impartial Tribunal

The ECHR, Article 6(1), provides that: 'In the determination of . . . any criminal charge against him, everyone is entitled to a fair and public hearing by an independent and impartial tribunal established by law'. Independence must be institutional and functional; but does not require trial by jury (*X and Y v Ireland* (1981) 22 DR 51).   **A7.68**

Relevant to the question of independence will be: (a) the manner of appointment and duration of office (*Le Compte, van Leuven and De Meyere v Belgium* (1982) 4 EHRR 1), but the mere fact that the executive appoint judges is not automatically a breach of Article 6 (*Campbell and Fell v UK* (1985) 7 EHRR 165); (b) protection from external influences (*Piersack v Belgium* (1983) 5 EHRR 169); (c) an appearance of independence (*Delcourt v Belgium* (1979–80) 1 EHRR 355 at [31]; *Campbell and Fell v UK* at [78]). For a case on the use of clerks in the Scottish district courts, see *Clark (Procurator Fiscal) v Kelly* [2004] 1 AC 681.

On the question of impartiality, the ECtHR has adopted a dual test: (a) first assessing whether there is any evidence of actual bias; here impartiality is presumed unless there is proof to the contrary; (b) then assessing the circumstances alleged to give rise to a risk of bias; here the question is whether there are 'ascertainable facts which may raise doubts' about the court's impartiality (*Piersack v Belgium* (1983) 5 EHRR 169; *Hauschildt v Denmark* (1990) 12 EHRR 266). The behaviour of a judge towards counsel can raise issues of impartiality (e.g., where the judge frequently interrupts counsel) and there may be a breach of Article 6 where the behaviour in question prevents counsel from pursuing a line of argument or otherwise renders the trial unfair (*CG v UK* (2002) 34 EHRR 789). Judges are free to criticise developments in the law, but they should refrain from criticism (or praise) which by its nature and language gives rise to legitimate concerns about their impartiality (*Hoekstra v HM Advocate* (2000) HRLR 410, where the judge in question had criticised the ECHR in very strong terms).

Where a judge has taken key decisions before trial, issues of impartiality may arise. But the mere fact that a judge has previously decided a bail decision based on suspicion that the accused has committed an offence will not automatically preclude that judge's participation in the trial. In *Hauschildt v Denmark* (1990) 12 EHRR 266, the ECtHR held (at [50]):   **A7.69**

> . . . the questions which the judge has to answer when taking . . . pre-trial decisions are not the same as those which are decisive for his final judgment . . . Suspicion and a formal finding of guilt are not to be treated as being the same . . . therefore, the mere fact that a trial judge or an appeal judge . . . has also made pre-trial decisions in the case, including those concerning detention on remand, cannot be held as in itself justifying fears as to his impartiality.

Nor will the fact that a judge has dealt with the accused on a previous occasion; the key issue will be the nature and character of the previous decision (*Hauschildt v Denmark*, breach where trial judge previously refused bail on a high threshold test; cf. *Brown v UK* (1986) 8 EHRR 272, no breach where appeal court judge refusing leave had previously been involved in restraint proceedings, and *Depiets v France* (2006) 43 EHRR 1206, where one member of the court had conducted ancillary pre-trial hearings).

Allegations of impartiality must be properly investigated, unless they are manifestly devoid of merit (*Remli v France* (1996) 22 EHRR 253 at [48]; *Gregory v UK* (1998) 25 EHRR 577 at [44]). In some circumstances, the nature of the alleged bias or impartiality will require decisive action; directions to the jury to try the case on the evidence may not suffice (*Sander v UK* (2001) 31 EHRR 1003, where a juror had made racist jokes and comments and the judge declined to discharge the jury, but instead directed the jury to come to a verdict without prejudice). The limits of any inquiry about the deliberations of the jury were considered by the House of Lords in *Mirza* [2004] 1 AC 1118 (see **D19.31**). In *Abdroikov* [2007] 1 All ER 315, the House of Lords observed that there is no difference between the common law and Article 6 in the requirements of an independent and impartial court and as to the importance of justice not only   **A7.70** being done, but that it should 'manifestly and undoubtedly be seen to be done'. Applying those principles, appeals were allowed in two cases where a police officer on the jury shared the same service background with a key police officer witness, and a CPS lawyer sat on the jury in a case being brought by the CPS. In the third case the mere fact that a police officer sat on the jury did not offend either the common law or Article 6 (see also *Pintori* [2007] EWCA Crim 1700). In *Hanif v UK* (2012) 55 EHRR 424, on the other hand, the ECtHR found a violation of Article 6(1) where there was a conflict regarding police evidence and a member of the jury was both a police officer and acquaintance of one of the officers who had given evidence; jury directions and judicial warnings were insufficient to guard against the risk that the juror may favour the evidence of the police.

Right to a Public Hearing

A7.71   ECHR, Article 6

(1) In the determination of...any criminal charge against him, everyone is entitled to a fair and public hearing by an independent and impartial tribunal established by law. Judgment shall be pronounced publicly but the press and public may be excluded from all or part of the trial in the interest of morals, public order or national security in a democratic society, where the interests of juveniles or the protection of the private life of the parties so require, or to the extent strictly necessary in the opinion of the court in special circumstances where publicity would prejudice the interests of justice.

There is a presumption that ordinary criminal proceedings should be public, even where they involve dangerous individuals (*Campbell and Fell v UK* (1985) 7 EHRR 165 at [87]; see also *Hummatov v Azerbaijan* (2009) 49 EHRR 960, where the importance of providing information to the public and press about hearings was emphasised). A less strict approach has, on occasion, be taken to the requirement that 'judgment shall be pronounced publicly' (*Pretto v Italy* (1984) 6 EHRR 182).

Legal Aid and Legal Representation

A7.72   ECHR, Article 6

(3) Everyone charged with a criminal offence has the following minimum rights:
...
(c) to defend himself in person or through legal assistance of his own choosing or, if he has not sufficient means to pay for legal assistance, to be given it free when the interests of justice so require.

Relevant to the 'interests of justice' test are: (a) the complexity of the case; (b) the ability of the accused to understand and present the relevant arguments without assistance; (c) the severity of the possible penalty (*Benham v UK* (1996) 22 EHRR 293; *Granger v UK* (1990) 12 EHRR 469; *Quaranta v Switzerland* (1991) Appln. 12744/87, 24 May 1991). Where deprivation of liberty is at stake, the interests of justice, in principle, call for legal aid and any refusal of legal aid should be kept under review (*Benham v UK; Granger v UK; Perks v UK* (2000) 30 EHRR 33). Rules that do not permit legal aid whatever the circumstances will invariably breach Article 6 (*Beet v UK* (2005) 41 EHRR 441; *Lloyd v UK* (2005) Appln. 29798/96, 1 March 2005).

A7.73   Merely allocating a lawyer to the accused is not enough under Article 6(3)(c) if that lawyer is manifestly unable to provide effective representation. In *Artico v Italy* (1981) 3 EHRR 1, where the applicant's nominated legal aid lawyer refused to represent him in an appeal against a fraud conviction and he was unable to secure the services of another lawyer, the ECtHR held (at [33] and [36]):

Article 6(3) speaks of 'assistance' and not of 'nomination'...[M]ere nomination does not ensure effective assistance, since the lawyer appointed for legal aid purposes may die, fall seriously ill, be prevented for a protracted period from acting or shirk his duties. If they are notified of the situation, the authorities must either replace him or cause him to fulfil his obligations...Admittedly, a State cannot be held responsible for every shortcoming on the part of a lawyer appointed for legal aid purposes, but, in the particular circumstances, it was for the ... authorities to take steps to ensure that the applicant enjoyed effectively the right to which they had recognised he was entitled.

In *Daud v Portugal* (2000) 30 EHRR 400, the ECtHR held that there had been a breach of Article 6 where defence counsel had not had sufficient time to prepare the case. Even though defence counsel made no application to adjourn the case, the court should have done so itself.

The right to be legally represented does not give an accused an absolute right to determine how **A7.74** his defence will be conducted: an accused cannot require counsel to disregard basic principles of his professional duty in the presentation of the accused's defence (*X v UK* (1980) 21 DR 126 at [6]).

In legal aid cases, an accused does not have an unqualified right to counsel of his choosing. In *Croissant v Germany* (1993) 16 EHRR 135, the ECtHR held (at [29]):

> [Article 6(3)(c)] is necessarily subject to certain limitations where free legal aid is concerned and ... it is for the courts to decide whether the interests of justice require that the accused be defended by counsel appointed by them. When appointing defence counsel the national courts must certainly have regard to the defendant's wishes ... However, they can override those wishes when there are relevant and sufficient grounds for holding that this is necessary in the interests of justice.

See also *Mayzit v Russia* (2006) 43 EHRR 805.

Rules requiring an accused to be represented by a lawyer where sexual offences are alleged will not necessarily breach Article 6(3)(c) (*Baegen v Netherlands* (Series A/327-B) (1995) at [77]).

Where a sanction such as the deprivation of liberty is at stake, the interests of justice require not only that a lawyer be appointed, but also that that lawyer be given an opportunity to make representations; see *Hooper v UK* (2005) 41 EHRR 1, where the applicant was bound over for 28 days for causing a disturbance in court without his lawyer having been heard on the matter (see also *Aerts v Belgium* (2000) 29 EHRR 50).

Right to be Present at Trial

As a general rule, the accused has a right to be present at trial (*Ekbetani v Sweden* (1991) 13 **A7.75** EHRR 504 at [25]) and adducing important evidence in the absence of the accused will usually be unfair (*Barbera, Messegue and Jabardo v Spain* (1989) 11 EHRR 360 at [89]). Consequently the authorities are under a duty to notify all accused about the proceedings against them (*Goddi v Italy* (1984) 6 EHRR 457). However, the right to be present at trial is not an absolute right. For example, an accused can be excluded where he causes disruption to the proceedings, refuses to come to court, or makes himself too ill to attend, provided that his interests are protected, e.g., because his lawyer is present (*Ensslin v Germany* (1978) 14 DR 64 at [21] and [22], where the applicants were unable to attend trial because of ill-health induced by hunger strike). But special care is needed where the accused is ill (*Romanov v Russia* (2007) 44 EHRR 479).

An accused may waive his right to be present either expressly or impliedly by failing to attend the hearing having been given effective notice (*C v Italy* (1988) 56 DR 40). But waiver must be clear and unequivocal (*Colozza v Italy* (1985) 7 EHRR 516; *Brozicek v Italy* (1990) 12 EHRR 371; *Poitrimol v France* (1994) 18 EHRR 130; *Lala v Netherlands* (1994) 18 EHRR 856; *Pelladoah v Netherlands* (1995) 19 EHRR 81). There may be circumstances where an absent defendant is entitled to a rehearing when he subsequently emerges (*Colozza v Italy*). Moreover, where an accused chooses to be absent, counsel must nonetheless be permitted to attend the trial (*Poitrimol v France* (1994) 18 EHRR 130; *Geyseghem v Belgium* (2001) 32 EHRR 554). For consideration of the issue by the House of Lords, see *Jones* [2003] 1 AC 1 (see **D15.89**), where a trial in the absence of the accused was held not to have violated his Article 6 rights.

Right to Participate in the Trial

A7.76 All accused have a right to participate effectively in the proceedings. In *Stanford v UK* (1994) Series A, No. 282 (at [26]) and in *V v UK* (2000) 30 EHRR 121 (at [85]), the ECtHR held:

> ...Article 6, read as a whole, guarantees the right of an accused to participate effectively in a criminal trial. In general this includes, inter alia, not only his right to be present, but also to hear and follow the proceedings.

Particular account must be taken of factors such as the accused's age and his ability to comprehend the proceedings. In respect of a young child charged with a grave offence attracting high levels of media and public interest, it is necessary to conduct the hearing in such a way as to reduce as far as possible his or her feelings of intimidation and inhibition (*V v UK* at [86] and [87]; *Practice Direction (Crown Court: Young Defendants)* [2000] 1 WLR 659 was made as a result). In *SC v UK* (2005) 40 EHRR 226, the ECtHR found a breach of Article 6(1) of the ECHR where the applicant, aged 11 and with limited intellectual ability, was unable to understand the criminal proceedings brought against him for robbery in the Crown Court. The ECtHR held that it was essential in such circumstances that the applicant be tried in a specialist tribunal.

The right to participate in the trial does not mean that the accused can dictate the terms on which he participates. In *R v D (R)* [2013] Eq LR 1034, HH Judge Peter Murphy ruled at Blackfriars Crown Court that the accused could give evidence at her trial only if she removed her niqaab while in the witness box, and also ruled that such an order would not infringe her rights to freedom of religion under Article 9.

Right to an Interpreter and Translation

A7.77 <center>ECHR, Article 6</center>

> (3) Everyone charged with a criminal offence has the following minimum rights:
>
> ...
>
> (e) to have the free assistance of an interpreter if he cannot understand or speak the language used in court.

This right is not subject to qualification, even if the accused is subsequently convicted; hence a convicted person cannot be ordered to pay the costs of an interpreter (*Luedicke, Delkasam and Koc v Germany* (1979–80) 2 EHRR 149 at [42] and [46]; *Ozturk v Germany* (1984) 6 EHRR 409).

The right to interpretation extends to all documentary material disclosed before trial; but this does not necessarily mean that all translations must be in written form; in limited circumstances, some oral translation is acceptable (*Luedicke, Delkasam and Koc v Germany*; *Kamasinski v Austria* (1991) 13 EHRR 36). The court has an obligation to ensure the quality of interpretation (*Kamasinski v Austria* at [74]). Responsibility for ensuring that a defendant who needs an interpreter gets appropriate assistance rests with the judge, not counsel. In *Cuscani v UK* (2003) 36 EHRR 11, the ECtHR found a breach of Article 6 where the judge acceded to counsel's suggestion that the brother of the accused could translate for him at the sentencing phase.

Article 6(3)(e) applies only where the accused does not understand or speak the language used in court; it does not provide a right to conduct proceedings in the language of the accused's choice (*K v France* (1984) 35 DR 203 at [8] — applicant who understood French wanted to conduct his defence in the Breton language). For a detailed analysis of the issues that can arise on appeal where the accused argues that he received inadequate translation services during the trial, see the decision of the Canadian Supreme Court in *Tran* 2010 SCC 58.

Pre-trial Publicity

Since pre-trial publicity can prejudice an accused's prospects of a fair trial, it can be restricted **A7.78** without necessarily breaching the ECHR, Article 10. In *Hodgson, Woolf Productions and the NUJ v UK* (1988) 10 EHRR 503, the European Commission held (at p. 509):

> ...the need to ensure a fair trial and to protect members of the jury from exposure to prejudicial influences corresponds to a pressing social need...where there is a real risk of prejudice the appropriate response...is one which must lie, in principle, with the person responsible for ensuring the fairness of the trial, namely, the trial judge.

This was reinforced by the ECtHR in *Verlags GmbH & Co KG v Austria* (2003) 36 EHRR 1059, which held (at [56]) that 'the limits of permissible comment on pending criminal proceedings may not extend to statements which are likely to prejudice, whether intentionally or not, the chances of a person receiving a fair trial or to undermine the confidence of the public in the role of the courts in the administration of justice'.

Prejudice will be harder to establish in a case tried by a judge than in a case tried by a jury **A7.79** (*Crociani v Italy* (1980) 22 DR 147 at [20]; see also *Ensslin v Germany* (1978) 14 DR 64 at [15]) and a proper balance between fair trial and press freedom must be maintained. In *Worm v Austria* (1998) 25 EHRR 454, the ECtHR held (at [50]):

> There is a general recognition of the fact that the courts cannot operate in a vacuum. Whilst the courts are the forum for the determination of a person's guilt or innocence on a criminal charge, this does not mean that there can be no prior or contemporaneous discussion of the subject-matter of criminal trials elsewhere, be it in specialised journals, in the general press or amongst the public at large...Provided that it does not overstep the bounds imposed in the interests of the proper administration of justice, reporting, including comment, on courts proceedings contributes to their publicity and is thus perfectly consonant with the requirement under Article 6(1) of the Convention that hearings be public. Not only do the media have the task of imparting such information and ideas; the public has a right to hear them.

Equality of Arms

The principle that there should be equality of arms between the parties before the court is **A7.80** fundamental to the notion of a fair trial under the ECHR, Article 6. In particular, each party must know the case being made against him, have an effective opportunity to challenge it and an effective opportunity to advance his own case. See also *Roberts v Parole Board* [2005] 2 AC 736 and see further **A7.63**.

Right to an Adversarial Hearing

All evidence and submissions should be made in the presence of the accused and in circum- **A7.81** stances in which he has an opportunity to comment upon them. The right to an adversarial trial means the opportunity for the parties to have knowledge of and comment on the observations filed or evidence adduced by the other party (*Ruiz Mateos v Spain* (1993) 16 EHRR 505 at [63]; see also *Krcmar v Czech Republic* (2001) 31 EHRR 953 at [40]). This applies even where submissions are made by an independent party — such as an *amicus* lawyer — and are wholly objective (*Van Orshoven v Belgium* (1998) 26 EHRR 55 at [39]–[42]).

Reasons

Article 6(1) of the ECHR obliges courts to give reasons for their judgments. In *Hiro Balani v* **A7.82** *Spain* (1995) 19 EHRR 566, the ECtHR held (at [27]):

> The Court reiterates that Article 6(1) obliges the courts to give reasons for their judgments, but cannot be understood as requiring a detailed answer to every argument. The extent to which this duty to give reasons applies may vary according to the nature of the decision. It is moreover necessary to take account, *inter alia*, of the diversity of the submissions that a litigant may bring before

the courts and the differences existing in the Contracting States with regard to statutory provisions, customary rules, legal opinion and the presentation and drafting of judgments.

In *Inner London Crown Court, ex parte London Borough of Lambeth* [2000] Crim LR 303, the Divisional Court held that the Crown Court is as much under a duty to give reasons for its decision when it allows an appeal against conviction as when it dismisses one.

In the context of jury trial, in *Taxquet v Belgium* (2012) 54 EHRR 933 the Grand Chamber held:

> ...the Convention does not require jurors to give reasons for their decision and...Article 6 does not preclude a defendant from being tried by a lay jury even where reasons are not given for the verdict. Nevertheless, for the requirements of a fair trial to be satisfied, the accused, and indeed the public, must be able to understand the verdict that has been given; this is a vital safeguard against arbitrariness.

Article 6 required sufficient safeguards to avoid any risk of arbitrariness. In the case of jury trial, these might include procedural safeguards such as directions or guidance provided by the judge to the jurors on legal issues arising or the evidence adduced, precise, unequivocal questions put to the jury by the judge, forming a framework on which the verdict is based, and any avenues of appeal open to the accused.

Trial within a Reasonable Period

A7.83   The right to trial within a reasonable period is guaranteed under the ECHR, Article 5(3), for those in pre-trial detention (see **A7.57**) and more generally for anyone facing criminal proceedings under Article 6(1). Since it is primarily concerned with those in pre-trial detention, the standards under Article 5(3) are more exacting than those under Article 6(1) (*Abdoella v Netherlands* (1995) 20 EHRR 585).

Time begins to run under both Article 5(3) and Article 6(1) when an individual is 'charged'. This may stretch back to arrest, rather than formal charge (*Eckle v Germany* (1983) 5 EHRR 1 at [73]; *Ewing v UK* (1988) 10 EHRR 141 at p. 143). In *A-G's Ref (No. 2 of 2001)* [2004] 2 AC 72, the House of Lords held that in England and Wales time will usually run from the time that an individual is formally charged or served with a summons. In *Burns v HM Advocate* [2009] 1 AC 720, where the appellant had been arrested, interviewed and bailed in England but a warrant to appear before a sheriff was not issued until nearly two years later in Scotland, the Privy Council held that the reasonable time requirement was to be interpreted generously so as to provide practical and effective safeguards. The term 'charge' was to be understood, having regard to the substance of the procedure in question rather than its appearance, as connoting the official notification given by the competent authority to an individual of an allegation that he had committed a criminal offence, and the relevant period began when he was first officially alerted to the likelihood of criminal proceedings against him.

Time ends for Article 5(3) purposes with the finding of guilt or innocence (*B v Austria* (1991) 13 EHRR 20); time ends for Article 6(1) purposes when the proceedings are over, including any appeal. In *Minshall v UK* (2012) 55 EHRR 36 the ECtHR found that there had been a breach of the requirement where four years and seven months had elapsed between the grant of leave to appeal against a confiscation order and the determination of the appeal.

Neither the court nor the prosecution is responsible for delays attributable to the applicant or his lawyers (*Konig v Germany* (1979–80) 2 EHRR 170). However, an accused is perfectly entitled to take legitimate points, if necessary, by way of appeal (*Ledonne (No. 1) v Italy* [1999] ECHR 25 at [25], where the applicant twice sought adjournment and twice challenged the validity of summons issued against him, but the prosecuting authorities could not provide good reason for two periods of delay totalling two years and ten months and on that basis breach of Article 6(1) was found).

Periods spent at large are discounted (*Girolami v Italy* (1991) A/196-E). The workload of the　**A7.84** court is not a good reason for delay — and, in any event, should be supported with evidence of steps taken to alleviate the position (*Majaric v Slovenia* (2000) Appln. 28400/95, 8 February 2000 at [39]) — nor is a shortage of resources. Article 6(1) imposes on Contracting States the duty to organise their judicial system in such a way that their courts can meet their requirement to hear a case within a reasonable time (*Ledonne (No. 2) v Italy* [1999] ECHR 26 at [23]).

The remedy in domestic law for a breach of the requirement that there be trial within a reasonable period has been considered at the highest level on several occasions. In *Mills v HM Advocate* [2004] 1 AC 441, the Privy Council held that quashing a conviction was a possible, but exceptional, remedy. In the subsequent case of *A-G's Ref (No. 2 of 2001)*, a nine-judge House of Lords held that, where criminal proceedings are not dealt with in a reasonable period, there is necessarily a breach of Article 6(1), but the remedy to be afforded will depend on all the circumstances of the case. See also *Crawley* [2014] EWCA Crim 1028.

Retroactive Offences

ECHR, Article 7　　　　　　　　　　　　　　　　　　　　**A7.85**

(1) No one shall be held guilty of any criminal offence on account of any act or omission which did not constitute a criminal offence under national or international law at the time when it was committed. Nor shall a heavier penalty be imposed than the one that was applicable at the time the criminal offence was committed.

(2) This Article shall not prejudice the trial and punishment of any person for any act or omission which, at the time it was committed, was criminal according to the general principles of law recognised by civilised nations.

Article 7 prohibits not only the creation of retroactive offences by legislation, but also the retroactive application of existing criminal offences through the development of the common law (*Custers v Denmark* (2008) 47 EHRR 665; *X Ltd and Y v UK* (1982) 28 DR 77; *SW and CR v UK* (1996) 21 EHRR 363). But it does not apply to the enforcement of penalties (*Grava v Italy* (2003) Appln. 43522/98, 10 July 2003).

Double Jeopardy

Double jeopardy is dealt with in Protocol 7 to the ECHR. The UK has not ratified this yet. Limited　**A7.86** protection from double jeopardy may also be provided for under Article 6 (*X v Austria* (1970) 35 EHRR CD 151; *S v Germany* (1983) 39 DR 43). For double jeopardy generally, see **D12.20** *et seq*.

Costs

There is no right to costs for an accused under the ECHR (*Lutz v Germany* (1988) 10 EHRR　**A7.87** 182 at [59], where a court refused to reimburse costs after proceedings against the applicant for road traffic offences were discontinued). However, where the court has a discretion to order costs, it must respect the presumption of innocence (*Minelli v Switzerland* (1983) 5 EHRR 554 at [37]). The presumption of innocence will not necessarily be infringed where costs are not awarded in a case where, by not disclosing his defence, the accused prolonged the proceedings against him (*Byrne v UK* [1998] EHRLR 626).

EVIDENCE

The Burden of Proof and the Presumption of Innocence

As a general rule the presumption of innocence imposes the burden of proving guilt on the pros-　**A7.88** ecution. In *Barbera, Messegue and Jabardo* (1989) 11 EHRR 360, the ECtHR held (at [77]):

> [Article 6(2)] embodies the principle of the presumption of innocence. It requires, *inter alia*, that when carrying out their duties, the members of a court should not start with the preconceived

idea that the accused has committed the offence charged; the burden of proof is on the prosecution...

(see also *Austria v Italy* (1963) 6 Yearbook 740, at p. 782).

However, where the prosecution has proved an offence, the burden of avoiding criminal liability can, within reasonable limits, pass to the defendant (*Lingens v Austria* (1981) 26 DR 171, at [4], which was a criminal prosecution of journalists for writing a defamatory article about a senior politician in which there was a burden on the accused to prove the truth of the statement which was the subject of the complaint as part of the defence).

Similarly, not all presumptions of law and/or fact will offend the presumption of innocence: the question is whether such presumptions remain within reasonable limits. In *Salabiaku v France* (1991) 13 EHRR 379, the ECtHR held (at [28]):

> Presumptions of fact or of law operate in every legal system. Clearly, the Convention does not prohibit such presumptions in principle. It does, however, require... States to remain within certain limits... Article 6(2) does not... regard presumptions of fact or of law provided for in the criminal law with indifference. It requires States to confine them within reasonable limits which take into account the importance of what is at stake and maintain the rights of the defence.

The relevant factors to be taken into account when assessing whether presumptions of fact or law are confined within reasonable limits were considered by the House of Lords in *Lambert* [2002] 2 AC 545 and *Johnstone* [2003] 3 All ER 884 (see also *Sheldrake v DPP* [2005] 1 AC 264). The relevant principles are fully discussed at **F3.18** *et seq.*

Standard of Proof

A7.89 Any doubt in criminal cases must be resolved in favour of the accused (*Austria v Italy* (1963) 6 Yearbook 740 at p. 784; *Barbera, Messegue and Jabardo* (1989) 11 EHRR 360.

Right to Call and Examine Witnesses

A7.90   **ECHR, Article 6**

(3) Everyone charged with a criminal offence has the following minimum rights:

    ...

(d) to examine or have examined witnesses against him and to obtain the attendance and examination of witnesses on his behalf under the same conditions as witnesses against him.

This rule has not been applied inflexibly and there are certain circumstances in which hearsay evidence is permitted under the ECHR (see **A7.91**). Nonetheless, Article 6(3)(d) does embody the principle that there should be equality of arms between the parties before the court and this includes the right to advance and to challenge evidence in court. In *Krcmar v Czech Republic* (2001) 31 EHRR 953, the ECtHR held (at [40]):

> ...the concept of a fair hearing also implies the right to adversarial proceedings, according to which the parties must have the opportunity not only to make known any evidence needed for their claims to succeed, but also to have knowledge of, and comment on, all evidence adduced or observations filed, with a view to influencing the courts' decision...

In addition Article 6 can require positive steps to be taken to ensure that the accused can confront and call witnesses (*Barbera, Messegue and Jabardo* (1989) 11 EHRR 360 at [78]).

Steps legitimately taken to protect witnesses will not breach Article 6, for example, where special measures are taken to protect child witnesses (*R (D) v Camberwell Green Youth Court* [2005] 1 All ER 999).

Hearsay Evidence

A7.91 As a general rule, under the ECHR, all the evidence should be produced in the presence of the accused at a public hearing and the accused has a right to examine and have examined the witnesses against him. Reliance on 'hearsay' evidence does not necessarily breach the ECHR: e.g., where there is some opportunity to challenge the evidence at an earlier committal hearing (*Kostovski v Netherlands* (1990) 12 EHRR 434 at [41]; *Trivedi v UK* (1997) EHRLR 521). But hearsay evidence must be kept within strict limits, 'having regard to the place that the right to a fair administration of justice holds in a democratic society, any measures restricting the rights of the defence should be strictly necessary. If a less restrictive measure can suffice then that measure should be applied' (*Van Mechelen v Netherlands* (1998) 25 EHRR 647 at [59]). The question in each case is whether there has been overall fairness (*Unterpertinger v Austria* (1991) 13 EHRR 175; *Kostovski v Netherlands*).

In *Horncastle* [2010] 2 AC 373 (see **A7.31**) the Supreme Court found that the common law had, **A7.92** by the hearsay rule, addressed the aspect of a fair trial that Article 6(3)(d) was designed to ensure, long before the Convention came into force. Parliament had enacted exceptions to the hearsay rule that were required in the interests of justice. The exceptions were not subject to a 'sole or decisive' rule, since the regime enacted by Parliament contained safeguards which rendered that rule unnecessary. In particular, the CJA 2003 contained a code intended to ensure that hearsay evidence was admitted only when it was fair that it should be. Hearsay was not made generally admissible by the code, but it made provision for a limited number of categories of admissible hearsay, and established special stipulations to which hearsay evidence was subject. Article 6(3)(d) did not deal with the appropriate procedure where compliance was impossible.

In *Al-Khawaja and Tahery v UK* (2011) 54 EHRR 807 a Grand Chamber of the ECtHR held that convictions based solely or decisively on statements from absent witnesses which were read out at trial will not automatically result in a breach of Article 6(1) in conjunction with Article 6(3)(d). As long as there are sufficient counterbalancing factors to compensate for the difficulties of admitting hearsay evidence, including strong procedural safeguards to ensure a fair trial, there will be no breach.

Where a hearsay statement is the sole or decisive evidence against an accused, its admission as evidence will not automatically result in a breach of Article 6(1). At the same time, where a conviction is based solely or decisively on the evidence of absent witnesses, a court must subject the proceedings to the most searching scrutiny. Because of the dangers of the admission of such evidence, it will constitute a very important factor to balance in the scales, and one which will require sufficient counterbalancing factors, including the existence of strong procedural safeguards. The question in each case is whether there are sufficient counterbalancing factors, including measures that permit a fair and proper assessment of the reliability of that evidence to take place. This will permit a conviction to be based on such evidence only if it is sufficiently reliable given its importance in the case. The safeguards contained in the CJA 1988 and the CJA 2003 regulating the admission of hearsay, supported by those contained in the PACE 1984, s. 78, and the common law, are, in principle, strong safeguards designed to ensure fairness. The ECtHR concluded that there was no breach of Article 6(1) in Al Khawaja's case because of the presence of adequate safeguards, but that there was a violation of Article 6(1) in Tahery's case.

In *Ibrahim* [2012] 4 All ER 225 the Court of Appeal further criticised the attempt of the Grand Chamber to clarify the sole and decisive test, and suggested an alternative test as to the admission of hearsay evidence. In *Riat* [2013] 1 All ER 349 the approach suggested in *Ibrahim* was further refined; the CJA 2003 did not require that a hearsay statement had to be wholly verified from an independent source before it could be admissible in evidence or left to the jury. The task of the judge was to ensure that the hearsay evidence could safely be held to be reliable; that involved looking at its strengths and weaknesses, at the tools available to the jury for testing it, and at its importance to the case as a whole. See also **F16.19** and **F16.33**.

Absconding Witnesses Hearsay evidence from witnesses who simply fail to appear at trial **A7.93** should rarely be relied upon (*Delta v France* (1993) 16 EHRR 574). However, the ECHR will not necessarily be breached where the relevant authorities can show that they have made extensive efforts to locate the witness and that his evidence is corroborated (*Doorson v Netherlands* (1996) 22 EHRR 330).

A7.94   **Fear of Reprisals**   Hearsay evidence of witnesses who genuinely fear reprisals if they attend court to give evidence can be relied upon, so long as there are counterbalancing factors to protect the defendant (*Saidi v France* (1994) 17 EHRR 251).

Anonymous Witnesses

A7.95   Evidence from anonymous witnesses should be treated with caution under the ECHR, Article 6. In *Kostovski v Netherlands* (1990) 12 EHRR 434, the ECtHR held (at [42] and [44]):

> If the defence is unaware of the identity of the person it seeks to question, it may be deprived of the very particulars enabling it to demonstrate that he or she is prejudiced, hostile or unreliable. Testimony or other declarations inculpating an accused may well be designedly untruthful or simply erroneous and the defence will scarcely be able to bring this to light if it lacks the information permitting it to test the author's reliability or cast doubt on his credibility...Although the growth in organised crime doubtless demands the introduction of appropriate measures, the Government's submissions appear...to lay insufficient weight on...'the interest of everybody in a civilised society in a controllable and fair judicial procedure.' The right to a fair administration of justice holds so prominent a place in a democratic society that it cannot be sacrificed to expediency. The Convention does not preclude reliance at the investigation stage of criminal proceedings, on sources such as anonymous informants. However, the subsequent use of anonymous statements as sufficient evidence to found a conviction...is a different matter.

But evidence from anonymous witnesses can be relied upon, where justified, so long as there are counterbalancing factors to protect the defendant (*Doorson v Netherlands* (1996) 22 EHRR 330). Cogent and specific evidence will be needed before anonymous evidence from law enforcement officers can be relied upon (*Van Mechelen v Netherlands* (1998) 25 EHRR 647 at [61]). In *Davis* [2008] 1 AC 1128, the House of Lords reviewed the use of anonymous witnesses in domestic law, quashing the appellant's conviction; that judgment led to the passing of the witness anonymity provisions now in the CAJA 2009 (see **D14.49**).

Accomplice Evidence

A7.96   Reliance on the evidence of an accomplice is not prohibited under the ECHR (*X v Austria* (1962) Appln. 1599/62) but it may put in doubt the fairness of the proceedings if there are insufficient safeguards to protect the accused. Close scrutiny and control is called for. In *Baragiola v Switzerland* (1993) 75 DR 76; *X v UK* (1976) 7 DR 115, the European Commission held (at p. 118):

> ...the sentences imposed on the co-defendants who had given evidence for the prosecution were considerably reduced and alleviated...As they ran the risk of losing the advantages they had been given if they went back on their previous statements or retracted their confessions, their statements were open to question. It was therefore necessary for the...courts to adopt a critical approach in assessing the statements.

Effective cross-examination is a minimum requirement: see *MH v UK* [1997] EHRLR 279 at pp. 279–80, the accused in that case had been unable to cross-examine a former accomplice witness on his guilty plea which had been admitted in evidence against him.

Evidence of Informers and Undercover Officers

A7.97   Reliance on the evidence of informers and undercover officers is not prohibited under the ECHR, but safeguards are necessary to protect the rights of the defence (*Ludi v Switzerland* (1993) 15 EHRR 173, see also *X v Germany* (1989) 11 EHRR 84, where evidence was obtained by a ruse when an undercover officer posed as a remand prisoner). The defence must have the opportunity to challenge the evidence (*Ludi v Switzerland* at [49]). Moreover, the proceedings as a whole will be unfair if the informer or undercover officer incited the commission of an offence which would not otherwise have been committed (see **A7.46** and **F2.36**).

Unlawfully Obtained Evidence

Evidence obtained in breach of absolute rights (such as rights under the ECHR, Article 3) should **A7.98** always be excluded from trial (*Ludi v Switzerland* (1993) 15 EHRR 173) (on the approach to be taken by domestic courts to evidence that may have been obtained by oppression, see the House of Lords' decision in *Mushtaq* [2005] 3 All ER 1013). Evidence obtained by torture is inadmissible in any legal proceedings (*A v Secretary of State (No. 2)* [2006] 2 AC 221); for the approach of the ECtHR to such evidence, see *Jalloh v Germany* (2007) 44 EHRR 667 and *Harutyunyan v Austria* (2009) 49 EHRR 202. Otherwise, the mere fact that evidence has been obtained in breach of qualified rights under the ECHR does not automatically lead to its exclusion. In *Khan v UK* (2001) 31 EHRR 1016, the ECtHR adopted the following approach (at [34]):

> The question which must be answered is whether the proceedings as a whole, including the way in which the evidence was obtained, were fair. This involves an examination of the 'unlawfulness' in question and, where violation of another Convention right is concerned, the nature of the violation found.

The central question under Article 6 is therefore overall fairness. Relevant to that assessment will be whether the breach of Convention rights was in good faith or not — and whether there was any element of entrapment or inducement. Whether the unlawfully obtained evidence is the only evidence against the accused will also be relevant, but not determinative (*Khan v UK* (2001) 31 EHRR 1016 at [36]).

The Protection against Self-incrimination

The right to a fair trial includes 'the right of anyone charged with a criminal offence . . . to remain **A7.99** silent and not to contribute to incriminating himself' (*Funke v France* (1993) 16 EHRR 297). In *Saunders v UK* (1997) 23 EHRR 313, the ECtHR explained (at [68]) that:

> . . .although not specifically mentioned in Article 6 of the Convention, the right to silence and the right not to incriminate oneself, are generally recognised international standards which lie at the heart of the notion of a fair procedure under Article 6. Their rationale lies, *inter alia*, in the protection of the accused against improper compulsion by the authorities thereby contributing to the avoidance of miscarriages of justice and to the fulfilment of the aims of Article 6. The right not to incriminate oneself, in particular, presupposes that the prosecution in a criminal case seek to prove their case against the accused without resort to evidence obtained through methods of coercion or oppression in defiance of the will of the accused. In this sense the right is closely linked to the presumption of innocence contained in Article 6(2).

The protection against self-incrimination applies to criminal proceedings in respect of all types of criminal cases without distinction from the most simple to the most complex (*Saunders v UK* at [74]). It is not confined to statements of admission of wrongdoing or to remarks which are directly incriminating (*Saunders v UK*; see also *Heaney and McGuiness v Ireland* (2001) 33 EHRR 264, where failure by the applicants to account for their movements attracted adverse inferences). However, it does not protect individuals from taking the oath, which is designed to ensure that statements made are truthful (*Serves v France* (1999) 28 EHRR 267). The mere fact that the police place a police informant in a cell with an accused prisoner in the hope that he may say something to incriminate himself will not necessarily breach Article 6. But if that individual induces the accused person to incriminate himself by persistent questioning at the insistence of the police, Article 6 will be breached (*Allan v UK* (2003) 36 EHRR 143).

However, the protection from self-incrimination is not absolute (see the comments of the **A7.100** ECtHR in *Saunders v UK* at [74]). A presumption that the owner of a car is responsible for speeding and parking offences does not necessarily breach the protection against self-incrimination (*Tora Tolmos v Spain* (1995) Appln. 23816/94, 17 May 1995; *DN v Netherlands* (1975) Appln.

6170/73; *JP, KR and GG v Austria* (1989) Appln. 15135/89, 5 September 1989). In *Brown v Stott* [2003] 1 AC 681, the Privy Council found no violation of Article 6 where the statement made by an appellant under the RTA 1988, s. 172, was used by the prosecution against her (see F9.44). That decision was considered by the Grand Chamber of the ECtHR in *O'Halloran and Francis v UK* (2008) 46 EHRR 397 and found to be compatible with Article 6. The ECtHR held that, in order to determine whether the essence of those rights was infringed, it was necessary to focus on the nature and degree of compulsion used to obtain the evidence, the existence of any relevant safeguards in the procedure, and the use to which any material so obtained was put.

It is not the compulsory questioning as such that infringes the ECHR: it is the use in criminal proceedings of answers elicited as a result of criminal proceedings to incriminate a defendant (*Saunders v UK* at [67]; *Abas v Netherlands* (1997) Appln. 27943/95, 26 February 1997). Permitting the court to draw adverse inferences from silence does not equate with compulsory questioning and is permitted within limits (*Murray (John) v UK* (1996) 22 EHRR 29 at [46]–[52]; *Condron v UK* (2001) 31 EHRR 1). But where inferences can be drawn from an accused's silence during police interview, it is essential that he should have access to a lawyer before interview (*Murray (John) v UK* at [66]). Furthermore, where inferences can be drawn from an accused's silence during police interview, it is essential that the trial judge give due weight to the explanation advanced for that silence (see *Beckles v UK* (2003) 36 EHRR 162, where the trial judge failed to direct the jury properly when the accused remained silent on his solicitor's advice).

Intimate Samples

A7.101 The protection against self-incrimination does not prevent the use in criminal proceedings of intimate body samples obtained by compulsion. In *Saunders v UK* (1997) 23 EHRR 313, the ECtHR held (at [69]):

> …[the right not to incriminate oneself] does not extend to the use in criminal proceedings of material which may be obtained from the accused through the use of compulsory powers but which has an existence independent of the will of the suspect such as, inter alia, documents acquired pursuant to a warrant, breath, blood and urine samples and bodily tissues for the purpose of DNA testing.

Expert Evidence

A7.102 The principle that there must be equality between prosecution and defence applies in relation to expert witnesses (*Bonisch v Austria* (1987) 9 EHRR 191). But the mere fact that a court-appointed expert works at the same institute as the expert relied upon by the prosecution does not automatically breach the ECHR, Article 6 (*Brandstetter v Austria* (1993) 15 EHRR 378).

SENTENCE

Fair Trial Guarantees in Sentencing

A7.103 The fair trial requirements of the ECHR, Article 6, do not cease to apply at the sentencing stage, but the requirements do not apply in the same way. The presumption of innocence ceases to apply (*Engel v Netherlands* (1979–80) 1 EHRR 647 at [90]). For a similar approach under the Canadian Charter of Rights, see *R v Gardiner* (1982) 2 SCR 368.

Retroactive Penalties

A7.104 Article 7 of the ECHR, which protects individuals from being convicted of criminal offences which did not exist at the time the act was committed, also prohibits the imposition of a more severe penalty for an offence than that which applied at the time the offence was committed. The concept of a 'penalty' is autonomous: to render the protection offered by Article 7 effective, courts must be free to go behind appearances and assess for themselves whether a particular measure amounts in substance to a penalty (*Welch v UK* (1995) 20 EHRR 247).

A

Part A Criminal Law

A requirement to register under the Sexual Offences Act 2003 is not a penalty within the meaning of Article 7 (*Ibbotson v UK* [1999] Crim LR 153: see **E23.1**). But where the definition of 'recidivist' is changed to include those convicted up to ten years before a second offence (and triggering extended sentence provisions), Article 7 may be breached (*Achour v France* (2005) 41 EHRR 751).

Proportionality in Sentencing

Where an individual is sentenced for conduct protected as a qualified right under the ECHR, **A7.105**
any punishment must be proportionate (*Arrowsmith v UK* (1978) 19 DR 5). In *Price v UK* (2002) 34 EHRR 1285, the ECtHR held that to detain a severely disabled person in conditions where she was dangerously cold, ill and unable to use the toilet constituted degrading treatment under Article 3. See also *Mouisel v France* (2004) 38 EHRR 735, where the ECtHR found a breach of Article 3 where the relevant authorities failed to take sufficient care of the conditions in which the applicant, a prisoner suffering from leukaemia, was transferred to and from hospital. The Court of Appeal in *A-G's Ref (No. 69 of 2013)* [2014] EWCA Crim 188 held that whole life orders imposed on conviction for murder did not violate Article 3 because there existed a mechanism whereby such sentences could be commuted by the Secretary of State.

Confiscation Orders: Protocol 1, Article 1

In *Waya* [2013] 1 AC 294 the Supreme Court held that, although the POCA 2002 removed **A7.106**
all discretion from the Crown Court, Protocol 1, Article 1 required that the deprivation of property as a penalty had to be proportionate to the legitimate aim, which was to remove from criminals the pecuniary proceeds of their crime, the deterrent effect being secondary. A judge should refuse to make a disproportionate confiscation order, although this was not a reincarnation of a general judicial discretion. See also **E19.7** and **E19.45**.

Preventative Sentences

ECHR, Article 5   **A7.107**

(4) Everyone who is deprived of his liberty by arrest or detention shall be entitled to take proceedings by which the lawfulness of his detention shall be decided speedily by a court and his release ordered if the detention is not lawful.

Where individuals are sentenced solely for the purposes of retribution, deterrence or protection of the public, Article 5(4) will be engaged as soon as the punitive part of the sentence is served and the preventative component begins. The key question at that stage is whether the prisoner's dangerousness continues to justify his detention.

In *James v UK* (2013) 56 EHRR 399 the ECtHR found that, in circumstances where a government sought to rely solely on the risk posed by offenders to the public in order to justify continued detention, regard must be had to the need to encourage the rehabilitation of offenders. In the applicants' cases this meant that they were required to be provided with reasonable opportunities to undertake courses aimed at helping them to address their offending behaviour and the risks they posed. There was, however, no violation of Article 5(4) as the applicants had failed to establish that the combination of Parole Board and judicial review proceedings could not have resulted in an order for their release.

APPEALS

Fair Trial Guarantees at the Appeal Stage

There is no requirement under the ECHR to set up an appeal procedure. Limitations can there- **A7.108**
fore be placed on the right to appeal, including time-limits, so long as they are reasonable and proportionate (*Bricmont v Belgium* (1986) 48 DR 106, at p. 151). If time-limits for appealing

are imposed, the relevant authorities are under a duty to inform the defendant of these limits (*Vacher v France* (1997) 24 EHRR 482 at [28]).

Although there is no requirement under the ECHR to set up an appeal procedure, where such an appeal procedure is set up, it must conform to Article 6 principles (*Delcourt v Belgium* (1979–80) 1 EHRR 335 at [25]). Inevitably, the way in which these principles are applied will not be the same as at trial and will depend upon the special features of appeal proceedings. In *Monnell and Morris v UK* (1988) 10 EHRR 205, the ECtHR held (at [56]):

> The manner in which paragraph 1, as well as paragraph 3(c), of Article 6 is to be applied in rela-tion to appellate or cassation courts depends upon the special features of the proceedings involved. Account must be taken of the entirety of the proceedings conducted in the domestic legal order and of the role of the appellate or cassation court therein.

Where a court, including a court of appeal, has power to substitute a conviction for an offence other than that with which an individual is actually charged, the defence must be afforded an opportunity to deal with the alternative charge (*Pelissier v France* (2000) 30 EHRR 715, substi-tution of aiding and abetting for principal offence by the court of appeal). This is particularly so where it is conceivable that the defence would have been different.

Leave to Appeal

A7.109   Article 6 of the ECHR applies to leave proceedings since these constitute part of the determina-tion of the criminal charge (*Monnell and Morris v UK* (1988) 10 EHRR 205, at [54]). However, the limited nature of proceedings for leave to appeal may not require a full public hearing (*Monnell and Morris v UK* at [57] and [58]). Similarly, full reasons may not be needed at the leave stage (*Webb v UK* (1997) 24 EHRR CD 73 at p. 74).

Legal Aid and Legal Representation

A7.110   The interests of justice require that an appellant be granted legal aid where the case is a complex one and/or there are serious consequences at stake. The ability of the accused to understand the proceedings and effectively participate will be relevant in determining whether he requires legal assistance (*Granger v UK* (1990) 12 EHRR 469 at [46] and [47] — refusal of legal aid in appeal against conviction for perjury).

The more severe the potential penalty if the appeal is unsuccessful, the greater the need for rep-resentation (*Maxwell v UK* (1995) 19 EHRR 97 at [38]–[40]). But the prospects of success are important (*Monnell and Morris v UK* (1988) 10 EHRR 205 at [67]). Decisions about legal aid should be kept under review (*Granger v UK* at [46]).

Right to a Hearing

A7.111   The right to a public hearing does not automatically extend to every stage of the proceedings provided the process viewed as a whole has been fair. The nature of the appellate stage will deter-mine whether a hearing is required. Where the appeal court is merely required to assess points of law which do not require oral argument, the need for a rehearing can be dispensed with (*Axen v Germany* (1984) 6 EHRR 195 at [28]). In contrast, where the court is having to determine the appellant's guilt or innocence based upon examination of law and the facts, there is a greater need for a full hearing (*Ekbatani v Sweden* (1991) 13 EHRR 504 at [32]).

Right to be Present

A7.112   There is no absolute rule that an appellant must be present during appellate proceedings: it depends what issues are being considered. Where on appeal the court is simply reviewing the findings of fact below, no new facts are adduced and there is no prospect of the sentence being increased, there is no duty on the authorities to ensure that the accused is present, particularly where he is represented (*Prinz v Austria* (2001) 31 EHRR 357 at [34]; see also *Belziuk v Poland* (2000) 30 EHRR 614). But where an assessment of the facts, or more particularly the appellant's mental state, are in issue, he should be present (*Cooke v Austria* (2001) 31 EHRR 338 at [42]; since the applicant's sentence could have been increased and the determination of this issue involved a fresh assessment of his mental state at the time of the killing, the presence of the applicant was essential; see also *Kamasinski v Austria* (1991) 13 EHRR 36 at [106]–[107]). Even where the sentence cannot be increased, the attendance of the accused may be required if the appeal court is likely to consider the motive for the offence and/or the accused's personality and character (*Pobornikoff v Austria* (2003) 36 EHRR 418).

Penalties for Appealing

Loss of time as a penalty for appealing will not necessarily breach the ECHR (*Monnell and Morris v UK* (1988) 10 EHRR 205 at [46]). Nor will an increase in sentence which reflects an appeal court's re-assessment of the facts of the offence and any aggravating features necessarily breach the ECHR (*De Salvador Torres v Spain* (1997) 23 EHRR 601). **A7.113**

Extent to which Appeal Court may Remedy Trial Defects

As a general rule, the whole of the proceedings, including any appeal, are relevant to an assessment of fairness under the ECHR, Article 6 (*Edwards v UK* (1993) 15 EHRR 417, non-disclosure at first instance). However, in some respects, an appeal court will not be able to rectify fairness problems that arose at trial: e.g., where a trial judge misdirects the jury on the question of adverse inferences (*Condron v UK* (2001) 31 EHRR 1 at [63]). Nor can an appeal court provide the required scrutiny in cases where material is not disclosed on grounds of public interest immunity (*Rowe and Davis v UK* (2000) 30 EHRR 1 at [65]). **A7.114**

Reasons in Appeal Cases

As a general rule, reasons should be given in an appeal hearing. However, full reasons need not necessarily be given at the leave stage (*Webb v UK* (1997) 24 EHRR CD 73; *X v Germany* (1981) 25 DR 240). **A7.115**

New Evidence

Once a person has been convicted and is therefore no longer 'charged with a criminal offence', establishing a duty on the relevant authorities to review the case in the light of new evidence is difficult (*X v Austria* (1962) 9 EHRR CD 17, at p. 21). However, where a procedure already exists for an appeal court to examine new evidence and determine whether it warrants a re-trial, the ECHR, Article 6, will apply (*Callaghan v UK* (1989) 60 DR 296). Failure to order a new trial will constitute a breach of the right to fair trial only if the appeal court declines to assess the new evidence (*Callaghan v UK* at pp. 300–2). **A7.116**

A

Part A Criminal Law

Section A8   Territorial and Extra-territorial Jurisdiction

INTRODUCTION

A8.1   A distinction must be drawn between the ambit of English criminal law, on the one hand, and 'venue', or the jurisdiction of particular courts, on the other. Things done beyond the ambit of English law cannot amount to offences under that law. Whether English law applies in a given case is therefore a question of substantive law, rather than one of procedure; but where English law does apply there are no longer any territorial restrictions on the jurisdiction of particular courts to try the alleged offence.

By the Senior Courts Act 1981, s. 46(1), the Crown Court has jurisdiction in proceedings on indictment for offences wherever committed, and in particular proceedings on indictment for offences within the jurisdiction of the Admiralty of England.

By the MCA 1980, s. 2(1), magistrates' courts are similarly free of territorial limitations on their criminal jurisdiction. Jurisdiction over summary offences was previously limited (with some exceptions) to offences committed within a court's own commission area, or within 500 yards of the boundary between that and another commission area, but this limitation was removed by the Courts Act 2003, s. 44.

Conduct that amounts to an offence under English law may also amount to an offence under the laws of one or more other States, especially where it involves acts or consequences in more than one jurisdiction. Within the EU, Council Framework Decision 2009/948/JHA seeks to ensure that Member States co-operate and exchange information etc. in such a way as to avoid the instigation of 'parallel proceedings' in two or more jurisdictions; note, however, that the UK Government has indicated that it does not intend to implement that Framework Decision on the basis that the practices it embodies are already well established in the UK (see **A9.24**). But if a person charged in England and Wales has already been the subject of criminal prosecution for that same offence or its equivalent abroad, he may be able to enter a plea of autrefois acquit or autrefois convict on the same basis as if he had been convicted or acquitted under English law (see *Aughet* (1919) 13 Cr App R 101 and **D12.25**).

TERRITORIAL JURISDICTION

The General Rule

A8.2   English criminal law applies throughout the realm of England and Wales and over all persons who come within the realm. Even though some such persons (e.g., foreign diplomats) may enjoy immunity from prosecution, they are nevertheless required to obey the law, and diplomatic immunity may in some cases be waived (see **A8.25**).

In contrast, English criminal law does not ordinarily extend to things done outside the realm, even when done by British citizens (*Harden* [1963] 1 QB 8). Specific statutory provision is required before any part of English criminal law can apply to conduct abroad or indeed to things done in other parts of the UK, which have their own jurisdiction over crime. The common law had no extra-territorial ambit, and in the absence of such provision, a statutory offence is presumed subject to similar constraints. As Viscount Simonds said in *Cox v Army Council* [1963] AC 48, at p. 67:

> Apart from those exceptional cases in which specific provision is made in respect of acts committed abroad, the whole body of the criminal law of England deals only with acts committed in England.

Parliament may give an offence whatever extra-territorial application it thinks fit, but must do so expressly. Lord Morris of Borth-y-Gest explained the position in *Treacy v DPP* [1971] AC 537 (at pp. 552–3):

> In general,… acts committed out of England, even though they are committed by British subjects, are not punishable under the criminal law of this country. But, as Parliament is supreme, it is open to Parliament to pass an enactment in relation to such acts. It is, however, a general rule of construction that unless there is something which points to a contrary intention a statute will be taken to apply only to the UK. It would be open to Parliament to enact that if a British subject committed anywhere an act designated as blackmail he would commit an offence punishable in England. Such an enactment would, however, have to be in clear and express terms: specific provision would have to be made with regard to acts committed abroad…

The territorial or extra-territorial ambit of an offence must be distinguished from the 'territorial extent' of the legislation creating it. The Outer Space Act 1986, for example, 'extends to England and Wales, Scotland and Northern Ireland' (so is law in all three parts of the UK), but by s. 1 of that Act it *applies* to specified activities 'whether carried on in the United Kingdom or elsewhere…[including] any activity in outer space'. **A8.3**

Even where a statute extends to Scotland or Northern Ireland, as well as to England and Wales, the commission of an offence in one part of the UK is not ordinarily punishable in another. An exception is created by the Counter-Terrorism Act 2008, s. 28 (see **B10.1**).

Where the laws of British overseas territories, or of the Channel Islands, incorporate elements of English criminal law, this does not make misconduct there punishable in England. An offence committed in Jersey, for example, is ordinarily punishable only in Jersey.

The Territorial Limits

The realm (which marks the limit of criminal jurisdiction at common law) comprises the land territory of England and Wales and the airspace above it. It now includes the English section of the Channel Tunnel system (Channel Tunnel Act 1987, s. 10). The seaward boundary of the realm is in most cases the water's edge, but the realm includes such internal waters (bays, harbours, etc.) as lie within county boundaries. **A8.4**

By the Territorial Waters Jurisdiction Act 1878, ss. 2 and 7, English criminal law also applies (in respect of offences triable on indictment) to things done on the open sea within territorial limits. This ordinarily means within 12 nautical miles of the low water mark around the coast, or of a line drawn across the mouth of a designated bay or estuary (Territorial Sea (Baselines) Order 2014 (SI 2014 No. 1353); Territorial Sea Act 1987). The limits of the territorial sea derived from these baselines are now shown on Admiralty Charts published by the UK Hydrographic Office and obtainable from Admiralty Chart agents. A person who is not a British subject (as to which see **A8.20**) may not ordinarily be prosecuted under that Act for a crime committed aboard a foreign ship, unless a Principal Secretary of State certifies that the institution of such proceedings is expedient (see s. 3 of the 1878 Act), but note that this does not apply to prosecutions for drug trafficking offences under the Criminal Justice (International Co-operation) Act 1990, s. 19. Waters adjacent to Scotland are part of Scotland (Scotland Act 1998, s. 126) and thus outwith English jurisdiction.

By the Criminal Jurisdiction (Offshore Activities) Order 1987 (SI 1987 No. 2198) and the Petroleum Act 1998, s. 10, English criminal law also extends to things done on (or within 500 metres of) platforms in designated areas of the continental shelf within which the UK claims rights to the seabed and natural resources. As to restrictions on prosecutions for certain offences, see the Petroleum Act 1998, s. 12.

CROSS-FRONTIER OFFENCES

The General Rule

A8.5   An offence may be committed within England and Wales even where some elements or consequences occur abroad, at least in cases where the last essential constituent element of the offence
takes place (i.e. the offence is completed) within England and Wales (*Harden* [1963] 1 QB 8;
Treacy v DPP [1971] AC 537). In the case of a conduct crime, such as blackmail, the offence is
complete upon the commission of the conduct in question, which in the case of blackmail is
the making of the unwarranted demand. If this occurs within the jurisdiction, it matters not
whether the intended consequences occur abroad, or indeed whether they occur at all (*Treacy*).
In the case of a result crime, jurisdiction is established upon the occurrence of any specified
result within England and Wales (*Secretary of State for Trade v Markus* [1976] AC 35). If the
victim of an act of violence abroad subsequently dies in an English hospital, it seems odd to
regard this as a case of murder or manslaughter 'committed in England', but the principle is
firmly established in English law.

The position is less clear where some essential elements take place within the jurisdiction, but
completion of the offence occurs elsewhere. The traditional approach in English law was that
in the absence of specific statutory provision (such as may be found in the CJA 1993, part 1: see
A8.10), a crime was deemed to be committed *only* where it was completed. This was sometimes
known as the 'terminatory' approach to jurisdiction. See, e.g., *Harden* [1963] 1 QB 8, *DPP v
Stonehouse* [1978] AC 55, *Nanayakkara* [1987] 1 All ER 650 and *Manning* [1998] 2 Cr App R
461. In *Smith (Wallace Duncan) (No. 4)* [2004] QB 1418, however, the Court of Appeal held
that a crime may sometimes be regarded as committed within the jurisdiction if 'a substantial
part of the offence' was committed in England and Wales, even if the last constituent element
took place abroad. This view may perhaps be open to challenge, given the weight of authority
against it, but it was supported (*obiter*) by Lord Hope in *R (Purdy) v DPP* [2010] 1 AC 345 and
was subsequently applied by the Court of Appeal in *Sheppard* [2010] 2 All ER 850.

A8.6   The terminatory approach is capable of leading to the conviction under English law of a foreigner in respect of conduct abroad that has only indirectly produced a proscribed result within
the jurisdiction. In *Perrin* [2002] EWCA Crim 747, for example, a French citizen was convicted
in England of an offence under the Obscene Publications Act 1959, s. 2(1), merely because the
contents of his foreign-based web site were downloaded (and thus 'published') by a police officer
in England. No evidence was adduced as to whether this material was illegal in the country from
which it was uploaded. Such an outcome would be less likely under the more flexible approach
adopted in *Smith,* but jurisdiction might still be asserted over foreigners in respect of acts abroad
where what happened in England was a direct consequence of their actions and forms a 'substantial part' of the offence. There is no requirement of 'double-criminality' in such cases.

Inchoate and Secondary Liability

A8.7   As to the rules governing inchoate offences of a cross-frontier kind, see **A5.33** (assistance or
encouragement under the SCA 2007, part 2); **B1.131** (solicitation of murder); **B10.76** (incitement of terrorism abroad); **A5.58** (statutory conspiracy); **A5.67** (conspiracy to defraud) and
A5.79 (criminal attempts).

In respect of secondary offenders, the general rule is that if (but only if) D commits an offence in
England, E may be liable as a secondary party to that offence, even if he has himself done nothing within the jurisdiction. In *Robert Millar (Contractors) Ltd* [1970] 2 QB 54, a fatal road accident occurred on a motorway in England when a visibly worn and defective front tyre on a lorry
blew out at speed. The driver admitted causing death by dangerous driving, and the appellants,
a Scottish haulage company and its managing director, were convicted as secondary parties, on

the basis that they knew of the defect when they despatched the lorry from its Glasgow depot. The Court of Appeal rejected an argument that the appellants had done nothing in England. Fenton Atkinson LJ said:

> The offence of causing death by dangerous driving was committed in England . . . but the appellants are guilty of participating in that crime and not of some self-subsisting crime on their own account and, therefore, they are in the same position as the principal offender and they are liable to be tried in this country.

In *R (Purdy) v DPP* [2010] 1 AC 345 the House of Lords considered (but ultimately declined **A8.8** to resolve) the argument that in the converse kind of case, where D in England aids, counsels or procures an act by E that is committed abroad, no offence is committed in England. The case concerned the Suicide Act 1961, s. 2 (see **B1.136**), which (prior to its amendment by the CAJA 2009) created a substantive offence of secondary participation in the suicide or attempted suicide of another person, but the principles applicable appear to be similar in most respects to those governing cases of secondary participation in the crime of another.

Lord Hope was minded to reject the argument, preferring the more inclusive approach to jurisdiction advanced in *Smith (Wallace Duncan) (No. 4)* [2004] QB 1418 (see **A8.5**). The majority view, however, was that the principal issue in the case (as to which, see **B1.137**) could and should be decided without deciding the jurisdiction issue, which had initially been overlooked and on which no oral argument had been heard.

Statutory Provisions

A number of statutory provisions create special jurisdictional rules for specific offences or classes **A8.9** of offence. These include the OAPA 1861, s. 10 (see **B1.10**), which makes special provision for offences of murder or manslaughter in which an unlawful wound etc. in England leads to death abroad (or vice versa) and the Perjury Act 1911, s. 1(4) and (5) (see **B14.1** *et seq.*), which deal with statements made abroad for the purpose of proceedings within the jurisdiction (and vice versa).

More recent provisions include the CJA 1993, part 1, which makes special provision for specified offences of cross-frontier fraud, blackmail or dishonesty, and the Computer Misuse Act 1990, ss. 4 to 7 (see **B17.15 to B17.17**), which make special provision for offences involving unauthorised access to or modification of computer material.

Criminal Justice Act 1993

Faced with modern forms of international fraud and dishonesty, the traditional 'terminatory' **A8.10** approach to identifying the *locus* of a crime (see **A8.5**) was manifestly inadequate. As Buxton LJ pointed out in *Manning* [1998] 2 Cr App R 461, strict application of that principle would all too often mean that 'plainly dishonest conduct with a strong connection with this country [could not] be tried here'. The CJA 1993, part 1, which did not come into force until 1 June 1999, addresses this problem by introducing special rules in respect of designated offences, which are then divided into substantive 'Group A offences' and inchoate 'Group B offences'.

The Group A offences listed in s. 1 now comprise:

- offences under the Theft Act 1968, ss. 1 (theft), 17 (false accounting), 19 (false statements by company directors, etc.), 21 (blackmail), 22 (handling stolen goods) and 24A (retaining credits from dishonest sources, etc.);
- offences under the Fraud Act 2006, ss. 1 (fraud), 6 (possession etc. of articles for use in frauds), 7 (making or supplying articles for use in frauds), 9 (participating in fraudulent business carried on by sole trader, etc.) and 11 (obtaining services dishonestly);
- offences under the Forgery and Counterfeiting Act 1981, ss. 1 (forgery), 2 (copying a false instrument), 3 (using a false instrument), 4 (using a copy of a false instrument), 5 (offences

relating to money orders, share certificates, passports, etc.), 14 (counterfeiting notes and coins), 15 (passing etc. counterfeit notes and coins), 16 (custody or control of counterfeit notes and coins), 17 (making or custody or control of counterfeiting materials, etc.), 20 (importation of counterfeit notes and coins) and 21 (exportation of counterfeit notes and coins);

- offences under the Identity Documents Act 2010, ss. 4 to 6; and
- cheating the public revenue.

The Group B offences are: conspiracy to commit a Group A offence (see **A5.58**); conspiracy to defraud (see **A5.67**); attempting to commit a Group A offence (see **A5.79**); and relevant offences under the SCA 2007, part 2 (SCA 2007, s. 63 and sch. 6).

A8.11   Prior to 15 January 2007, the Group A list included offences of deception under the Theft Act 1968, ss. 15, 15A, 16, 17 and 20(2), and under the Theft Act 1978, ss. 1 and 2. These offences were all repealed on that date by the Fraud Act 2006 but, under transitional provisions in that Act (see sch. 2, para. 3), this repeal 'does not affect any liability, investigation, legal proceeding or penalty for or in respect of any [deception] offence partly committed before commencement'.

No transitional arrangements have been made in respect of the jurisdiction provisions in the CJA 1993, however. This should not hinder prosecutions for alleged cases of cross-frontier deception dating entirely from before 15 January 2007, but may cause difficulty should the Crown seek to prosecute a defendant for a cross-frontier deception offence allegedly committed only partly before that date (e.g., where a deception before that date in England results after that date in the obtaining of property abroad). See **B5.2**.

This is unsatisfactory but, if *Smith (Wallace Duncan) (No. 4)* [2004] QB 418 is correctly decided (see **A8.5**), jurisdiction may be established over some such cases even without recourse to the Act.

Relevant Events under the Criminal Justice Act 1993

A8.12   The key to establishing jurisdiction under the CJA 1993 is the occurrence of a 'relevant event' within England and Wales. Where such an event occurs, it is irrelevant whether the accused was a British citizen or whether he was at any material time in England and Wales (s. 3(1)). A relevant event is defined for most purposes as any event that is an essential element of the offence in question. That must mean an *actus reus* element (because *mens rea* is not an event). It is not sufficient that some preparatory event occurred in England if that event is not itself a definitional element of the offence charged. Nor in a case such as *Atakpu* [1994] QB 69 (see **B4.34**), is there any relevant act of theft in England where D steals a car abroad and (having already completed that theft) brings the stolen car into England.

A8.13   Special provision is made in s. 2(1A) for the new offence of fraud. Fraud is a conduct crime in which the actual making of a gain or the causing of a loss to another forms no part of the offence at all. But for s. 2(1A), a fraud successfully practised from abroad on a victim in England would not necessarily fall within English jurisdiction. See further **B5.11**.

Criminal Justice Act 1993, s. 2

(1)   For the purposes of this Part, 'relevant event', in relation to any Group A offence, means (subject to subsection (1A)) any act or omission or other event (including any result of one or more acts or omissions) proof of which is required for conviction of the offence.

(1A)   In relation to an offence under section 1 of the Fraud Act 2006 (fraud), 'relevant event' includes—
    (a) if the fraud involved an intention to make a gain and the gain occurred, that occurrence;
    (b) if the fraud involved an intention to cause a loss or to expose another to a risk of loss and the loss occurred, that occurrence.

(2)   For the purpose of determining whether or not a particular event is a relevant event in relation to a Group A offence, any question as to where it occurred is to be disregarded.

(3)   A person may be guilty of a Group A offence if any of the events which are relevant events in relation to the offence occurred in England and Wales.

The CJA 1993, s. 4, attempts to provide guidance as to what may constitute the occurrence of **A8.14** an event in England and Wales.

Criminal Justice Act 1993, s. 4

In relation to a Group A or Group B offence—
(a) there is an obtaining of property in England and Wales if the property is either despatched from or received at a place in England and Wales; and
(b) there is a communication in England and Wales of any information, instruction, request, demand or other matter if it is sent by any means:
    (i) from a place in England and Wales to a place elsewhere; or
    (ii) from a place elsewhere to a place in England and Wales.

The wording of this section is unfortunate, because in contrast to s. 2(1A) it does not provide that such events are necessarily 'relevant events'. 'Obtaining' was of course a 'relevant event' in respect of several deception offences under the Theft Acts, but these are now repealed. The 'communication' of a blackmail demand is not a 'relevant event' for the purposes of the offence of blackmail, because a blackmail demand can be 'made' under the Theft Act 1968, s. 21, without ever being communicated (see *Treacy v DPP* [1971] AC 537 and **B5.47**).

OFFENCES ABOARD SHIPS OR AIRCRAFT

Offences aboard British or UK Ships

British ships (as defined in the Merchant Shipping Act 1995, s. 1) are not properly described as **A8.15** 'floating territory', but do sail under Admiralty jurisdiction when on the high seas (a term which in this context includes berths in foreign or Commonwealth ports (*Anderson* (1868) XI Cox CC 198; *Liverpool Justices, ex parte Molyneux* [1972] 2 QB 384). Admiralty jurisdiction over indictable offences is now exercised by the ordinary criminal courts (see **A8.1**).

A British ship registered in the UK is a 'United Kingdom ship'. By the Merchant Shipping Act 1995, s. 281, English courts have jurisdiction over any person charged with committing an offence aboard a UK ship on the high seas, 'as if it had been committed on board a UK ship within the limits of its ordinary jurisdiction'. This includes jurisdiction over summary offences. Although s. 281 confusingly refers only to 'offences under this Act', the MCA 1980, s. 3A, and the Senior Courts Act 1981, s. 46A, ensure that it is in fact of general application.

Ships include some small craft, but jet skis or other 'personal water craft' that are designed and used only for recreational purposes, rather than for navigation, are not currently considered to be ships at all, even if they have been registered as such in the UK (*Goodwin* [2005] EWCA Crim 3184).

Her Majesty's Ships and Vessels are not 'British ships' within the meaning of the Merchant Shipping Act 1995, but are subject to Admiralty jurisdiction (*Devon Justices, ex parte DPP* [1924] 1 KB 503). As to the position of civilians aboard Her Majesty's ships (or any other ships used for the purposes of any of Her Majesty's forces) see the Armed Forces Act 2006, sch. 15, para. 2.

As to the status of offshore oil and gas platforms, see **A8.4**. As to offences committed by a master or seaman from a UK ship (including offences committed after the loss of such a ship), see **A8.22**.

Offences aboard Foreign Ships, etc.

English criminal law does not ordinarily apply to things done on foreign ships outside English **A8.16** territorial limits but, by the Merchant Shipping Act 1995, s. 281 (see **A8.15**), a British citizen may be prosecuted under English law for an offence committed in a foreign port or harbour or aboard a foreign ship to which he does not belong, 'as if it had been committed on board a UK ship within the limits of its ordinary jurisdiction to try the offence…'.

In *Kelly* [1982] AC 665, the House of Lords held that the Merchant Shipping Act 1894, s. 686(1) (from which the current s. 281 is derived), was not merely a 'venue' provision, dealing with the jurisdiction of particular courts (see **A8.1**), but instead made the ordinary rules of English criminal law applicable to things done by British passengers on foreign ships. See also *Cumberworth* (1989) 89 Cr App R 187, in which what is now s. 282 was held to apply even where the foreign ship in question was docked (with its loading ramp lowered) in a foreign port.

A 'foreign ship' is defined by the Merchant Shipping Act 1995, s. 313, as one that is neither a UK ship nor a small unregistered British ship; but the term, 'foreign port or harbour' is narrower in that it excludes ports or harbours in the Republic of Ireland or in any Commonwealth country (*Liverpool Justices, ex parte Molyneux* [1972] 2 QB 384).

As to offences committed aboard ships of 'Convention countries' within the meaning of the Suppression of Terrorism Act 1978 (see **A8.23**), see s. 4(7) of that Act.

As to piracy *iure gentium* and offences under the Aviation and Maritime Security Act 1990, see **B10.198**, **B10.232** *et seq*. and **B10.202**.

Offences Committed in UK Airspace or on board Aircraft in Flight Elsewhere

A8.17   At common law, land includes the airspace above it, and accordingly it is assumed that English criminal law automatically applies to things done in English airspace; but it does not apply to conduct in the skies over Scotland or Northern Ireland, even if it takes place aboard a British controlled aircraft. Jurisdiction over things done in flight elsewhere is governed by the Civil Aviation Act 1982, s. 92.

Civil Aviation Act 1982, s. 92

(1) Any act or omission taking place on board a British-controlled aircraft or (subject to subsection (1A) below) a foreign aircraft while in flight elsewhere than in or over the UK which, if taking place in, or in a part of, the United Kingdom, would constitute an offence under the law in force in, or in that part of, the United Kingdom shall constitute that offence; but this subsection shall not apply to any act or omission which is expressly or impliedly authorised by or under that law when taking place outside the United Kingdom.

(1A) Subsection (1) above shall only apply to an act or omission which takes place on board a foreign aircraft where—

   (a) the next landing of the aircraft is in the United Kingdom, and

   (b) in the case of an aircraft registered in a country other than the United Kingdom, the act or omission would, if taking place there, also constitute an offence under the law in force in that country.

(1B) Any act or omission punishable under the law in force in any country is an offence under that law for the purposes of subsection (1A) above, however it is described in that law.

'British-controlled aircraft' are defined in s. 92(5). The consent of the DPP is required in respect of any prosecutions brought in England under s. 92 (see s. 92(2)(a)).

A8.18   No express provision has been made by legislation for criminal jurisdiction to extend to things done in the airspace above English territorial waters. Waters adjacent to England and Wales are not strictly part of England and Wales (in contrast to Scottish waters, which are now part of Scotland). By the Civil Aviation Act 1982, s. 106, references to the UK are deemed to include airspace above such waters; but this merely serves to *prevent* any possible reliance on s. 92 of the 1982 Act where aircraft are in flight above English waters. The only solution would be for the Territorial Waters Jurisdiction Act 1878 to be construed as extending by implication to such airspace.

As to offences committed in flight aboard aircraft of 'Convention countries' within the meaning of the Suppression of Terrorism Act 1978 (see **A8.23**), see s. 4(7) of that Act.

As to terrorist offences and offences under the Aviation Security Act 1982, see **B10** and in particular **B10.214** *et seq*.

EXTRA-TERRITORIAL JURISDICTION

Extra-territorial jurisdiction in English criminal law invariably has a statutory basis. Some statu- **A8.19**
tory provisions extend the ambit of English criminal law generally (or substantial parts thereof)
to specified classes of person. Persons subject to extra-territorial English criminal jurisdiction of
this type include: Crown servants acting or purporting to act in the course of their employment
(CJA 1948, s. 31(1)); masters or seamen from UK ships (Merchant Shipping Act 1995, s. 282);
and members of the British armed forces or anyone else who is for the time being subject to
service law. Such persons may be held liable under English law for extra-territorially committed
crimes such as theft, assault or even dangerous driving (as in *Cox v Army Council* [1963] AC 48)
which would otherwise have no extra-territorial ambit at all.

Legislation may alternatively provide an extra-territorial ambit to specific offences, as for example it has done in respect of murder or manslaughter on land outside the UK (see **B1.9**), sexual
offences committed against children under the age of 18 (see **B3.301**), bribery (see **B15.43** and
B15.24) and a wide range of offences involving terrorism, hijacking or piracy (see generally **B10**).

Extra-territorial jurisdiction is ordinarily limited to things done or omitted by persons who hold **A8.20**
some form of British nationality or domicile. There is little consistency in the exact form of
British nationality required. Modern statutes typically restrict any extra-territorial application to
British citizens (as does the Merchant Shipping Act 1995) or to UK nationals or residents (as does
the International Criminal Court Act 2001). Some refer instead to 'United Kingdom persons',
a term which includes Scottish partnerships and bodies incorporated in the UK. References in
older statutes imposing criminal jurisdiction over 'British subjects', 'subjects of her Majesty' or
'citizens of the United Kingdom and colonies' for things done in foreign or Commonwealth
countries or in Ireland must now be construed as references to British citizens, British overseas territories citizens, British overseas citizens, and British nationals (overseas): see the British
Nationality Act 1948, s. 3(1), read in conjunction with the British Nationality Act 1981, s. 51.

There is a strong presumption that a provision creating extra-territorial criminal liability will
not apply to things done or omitted by foreigners abroad (*Jameson* [1896] 2 QB 425; *Air India
v Wiggins* [1980] 2 All ER 593).

In exceptional cases, however, a wider basis of jurisdiction may be specified in accordance with
customary international law or specific treaty obligations. This may involve 'universal jurisdiction' over crimes (e.g., piracy, hijacking of aircraft and other offences against aviation security)
that are recognised internationally as meriting or demanding such treatment, or it may involve
(on a reciprocal convention basis) the assertion of jurisdiction over things done by persons in
specified countries or things done elsewhere by nationals of specified countries. See, e.g., the
Suppression of Terrorism Act 1978, s. 4 (at **A8.23**).

Persons Subject to Armed Service Discipline

Where a British serviceman (or a civilian subject to service discipline) is guilty of conduct any- **A8.21**
where that would in England and Wales have amounted to an offence under English law, he
may be charged with an offence under the Armed Forces Act 2006, s. 42. This provision (read
in conjunction with ss. 43 to 48) supplants three earlier provisions, namely the Army Act 1955,
s. 70, the Air Force Act 1955, s. 70, and the Naval Discipline Act 1957, s. 42.

The relationship between an offence under s. 42 of the 2006 Act and a corresponding offence
under the civilian law of England is essentially the same as that under the 1955 legislation and was
explained in that context by Lord Rodger of Earlsferry in *Spear* [2002] 3 All ER 1074 (at p. 1088):

> Where anyone who is subject to military law is guilty of an act or omission in England that would
> be punishable by the law of England, he is also guilty of an offence under [the Army Act 1955]
> s. 70. Similarly, anyone who is guilty of an act or omission that would be punishable by the law

of England if committed in England is guilty of an offence under s. 70 wherever he commits it, whether in some other part of the UK or elsewhere in the world: *Cox v Army Council*. So, for instance, a soldier or airman who possesses cocaine in England is guilty not only of an offence under s. 5(1) of the Misuse of Drugs Act 1971, but also of an offence against s. 70 of the Army Act or the Air Force Act, as the case may be, although he can, of course, be prosecuted for only one of them. If he possesses cocaine while on duty in Afghanistan, on the other hand, he does not commit an offence under s. 5(1) of the 1971 Act since the legislation does not apply there, but he is guilty of an offence under s. 70 of the relevant 1955 Act, because he would have been guilty of a contravention of s. 5(1) if he had been in possession of the drug in England. Offences of this kind, which mirror offences under English criminal law, are referred to as 'civil' offences (s. 70(2)). As s. 70(3) makes clear, these civil offences are triable by court-martial.

By the Armed Forces Act 2006, s. 51, certain offences committed abroad by civilians subject to service discipline (including some offences under s. 42 of the 2006 Act) may be tried by 'service civilian courts', but this does not extend to offences that would be triable only on indictment if committed within England and Wales.

Masters or Seamen from UK Ships

A8.22   Merchant Shipping Act 1995, s. 282

(1) Any act in relation to property or person done in or at any place (ashore or afloat) outside the United Kingdom by any master or seaman who at the time is employed in a United Kingdom ship, which, if done in any part of the United Kingdom, would be an offence under the law of any part of the United Kingdom, shall—
   (a) be an offence under that law, and
   (b) be treated for the purposes of jurisdiction and trial as if it had been done within the jurisdiction of the Admiralty of England.
(2) Subsection (1) above also applies in relation to a person who had been so employed within the period of three months expiring with the time when the act was done.
(3) Subsections (1) and (2) above apply to omissions as they apply to acts.

This provision is not expressly limited to British citizens or UK nationals, but such a limitation must arguably be inferred (see **A8.20**). Nor is it expressly limited to offences triable on indictment, but such a limitation is impliedly imposed by the fact that such offences are triable, 'as if committed within the jurisdiction of the Admiralty of England', because Admiralty jurisdiction does not extend over summary offences.

Section 282 is derived from the Merchant Shipping Act 1854, s. 267, which was the basis upon which jurisdiction was asserted over the shipwrecked cannibals in *Dudley and Stephens* (1884) 24 QBD 273. Note however that it has no application to things done by persons from British ships that are not registered in the UK, or to things done by passengers etc. from any ship. If a passenger from a sunken British vessel kills another in the sea in order to seize his lifejacket or raft, he will commit no offence under English law unless he is within territorial waters at the time.

Offences Committed in 'Convention Countries' or by Nationals of Convention Countries

A8.23   The Suppression of Terrorism Act 1978, s. 4(1), creates no new offences of its own (*Venclovas* [2013] EWCA Crim 2182) but extends the ambit of a number of existing offences under English criminal law so that they can apply to things done in 'Convention countries' by persons of any nationality. Section 4(1) meanwhile provides an even wider ambit for murder, manslaughter and certain offences under the Explosive Substances Act 1883.

Suppression of Terrorism Act 1978, s. 4

(1) If a person, whether a citizen of the United Kingdom and Colonies or not, does in a Convention country any act which, if he had done it in a part of the United Kingdom, would have made him guilty in that part of the United Kingdom of—
   (a) an offence mentioned in paragraph 1, 2, 4, 5, 10, 11, 11B, 12, 13, 14 or 15 of Schedule 1 to this Act; or

(b) an offence of attempting to commit any offence so mentioned,

he shall, in that part of the United Kingdom, be guilty of the offence or offences aforesaid of which the act would have made him guilty if he had done it there.

. . .

(3) If a person who is a national of a Convention country but not a citizen of the United Kingdom and Colonies does outside the United Kingdom and that Convention country any act which makes him in that Convention country guilty of an offence and which, if he had been a citizen of the United Kingdom and Colonies, would have made him in any part of the United Kingdom guilty of an offence mentioned in paragraph 1, 2 or 13 of Schedule 1 to this Act, he shall, in any part of the United Kingdom, be guilty of the offence or offences aforesaid of which the act would have made him guilty if he had been such a citizen.

As to offences committed aboard ships or aircraft of Convention countries, see s. 4(7).

Countries and Offences to which s. 4 Applies   'Convention countries' are those designated **A8.24** by the Secretary of State as Parties to the 1977 European Convention on the Suppression of Terrorism, namely: Albania, Austria, Belgium, Bulgaria, Croatia, Cyprus, Czech Republic, Denmark, Estonia, Finland, France, Georgia, Germany, Greece, Hungary, Iceland, Italy, Latvia, Liechtenstein, Lithuania, Luxembourg, Malta, Moldova, the Netherlands, Norway, Poland, Portugal, Republic of Ireland, Romania, Russian Federation, San Marino, Serbia and Montenegro, Slovakia, Slovenia, Spain, Sweden, Switzerland, Turkey and Ukraine. The UK, although a Party to the Convention, has not designated itself as a Convention country, which means that s. 4 gives English law no jurisdiction over things done in Scotland or Northern Ireland (or vice versa). An 'application of provisions order' made under s. 5 (see SI 1993 No. 2533) treats India for most purposes as if it were a Convention country; but an application of provisions order relating to the USA deals only with extradition, and excludes any jurisdiction under s. 4.

The offences to which s. 4(1) applies (excluding offences under Scots law or Northern Irish law) are murder, manslaughter, kidnapping and false imprisonment, together with offences under the Child Abduction Act 1984, s. 2, the OAPA 1861, ss. 28, 29 and 30, the Explosive Substances Act 1883, ss. 2 and 3, and the Firearms Act 1968, ss. 16 and 17(1).

The only offences in English law to which s. 4(3) of the 1978 Act applies are murder, manslaughter and offences under the Explosive Substances Act 1883, ss. 2 and 3.

Prosecutions brought by virtue of s. 4(1) or (3) need not have anything to do with terrorism. By s. 4(4), such prosecutions require the consent of the A-G. This provides 'a possible check on the inappropriately wide use of the provision', as the Court of Appeal noted in *Venclovas* [2013] EWCA Crim 2182 , but such consent was readily given in that case even though it had no terrorist connection whatever. The victim in *Venclovas* was D's estranged wife, V. He had abducted her in England and her body was later found in Poland. It was not clear whether V had been murdered in England or in Poland or indeed in one of the Convention countries through which D had driven en route to Poland, but the offence in each case was the same, namely murder at common law, so there was no need to prove where exactly it had been committed. Note, however, that the position would have been quite different if V's body had been found in Scotland or Northern Ireland. Neither s. 4, nor the OAPA 1861, s. 9, could be of any help in such a case.

JURISDICTIONAL IMMUNITIES

Diplomatic Immunity

Diplomatic immunity under English law is governed in the case of members of permanent dip- **A8.25** lomatic missions by the Diplomatic Privileges Act 1964, which incorporates certain provisions of the Vienna Convention on Diplomatic Relations 1961. These include Article 29, by which, 'the person of a diplomatic agent shall...not be liable to any form of arrest or detention', and Article 31(1), by which, 'a diplomatic agent shall enjoy immunity from the criminal jurisdiction of the receiving State'. By Article 37, the same privileges and immunities extend to 'the members of the family of a diplomatic agent forming part of his household..., if they are not nationals of the receiving State' and to 'members of the administrative and technical staff of the mission, together with members of their families forming part of their respective households..., if they are not nationals of or permanently resident in the receiving State'; but members of the service staff enjoy such immunity only in respect of acts performed in the course of their duties, and the private servants of members of the mission have no immunities from the criminal law other than those (if any) admitted by the receiving State.

By Article 39(2), the immunities of a diplomat 'shall normally cease when he leaves the country, or on expiry of a reasonable period in which to do so, but...with respect to acts performed...in the exercise of his functions as a member of the mission, immunity shall continue to subsist'. As to the rationale behind this rule, see *Bow Street Metropolitan Stipendiary Magistrate, ex parte Pinochet Ugarte (No. 3)* [2000] 1 AC 147, per Lord Browne-Wilkinson at p. 202.

Immunity from prosecution does not involve immunity from the duty to comply with the law. See, e.g., the Vienna Convention on Diplomatic Relations 1961, Article 41: 'It is the duty of all persons enjoying such privileges and immunities to respect the laws and regulations of the receiving state'. A foreign diplomat in England has no right or licence to ignore the rules of English law. If he commits an offence under English law he may be prosecuted for it, but only if his government waives diplomatic immunity. Even if immunity is not waived, other persons implicated as secondary parties to his offence may still face prosecution. The Vienna Convention (and thus the 1964 Act) has no application to members of ad hoc or 'special' diplomatic missions, but similar immunity arises at common law (through the incorporation of customary international law) provided that the diplomatic status of that mission (and of the individual in question) is recognised by the Foreign and Commonwealth Office on behalf of HM Government. A certificate to (or against) that effect issued by the FCO must be treated as conclusive on that issue (*Governor of Pentonville Prison, ex parte Teja* [1971] 2 QB 274; *Bat v Investigating Judge of the Federal Court, Germany* [2013] QB 349).

Consular Immunity

A8.26   Consular immunity is more limited than diplomatic immunity, and for most purposes excludes immunity from criminal prosecution, save in respect of acts performed in the course of consular duties. See generally the Consular Relations Act 1968.

Persons Connected with International Organisations

A8.27   In respect of an international organisation of which the UK is a member, the International Organisations Act 1968, s. 1, enables certain immunities to be granted to its officers or representatives. The exact terms of such immunities vary from one case to another. See, e.g., the United Nations and International Court of Justice (Immunities and Privileges) Order 1974 (SI 1974 No. 1261), the European Court of Human Rights (Immunities and Privileges) Order 2000 (SI 2000 No. 1817) and the International Maritime Organisation (Immunities and Privileges) Order 2002 (SI 2002 No. 1826). As with diplomatic immunities, these immunities may be waived by the organisation in question.

The Commonwealth Secretariat Act 1966 makes provision for immunities of officers of the Secretariat.

Foreign Heads of State and Government Ministers

A8.28   By the State Immunity Act 1978, s. 20, the Diplomatic Privileges Act 1964 applies (with appropriate modifications) to a foreign sovereign or head of State, his household and private servants, as it applies to the head of a diplomatic mission, to members of his family forming part of his household and to his private servants.

Certain other high ranking officials, such as foreign ministers, may also be able to claim State immunity from criminal liability or process, but the right to claim immunity in criminal or extradition cases is far more limited than it is in civil cases (*Bat v Investigating Judge of the Federal Court, Germany* [2013] QB 349).

A former head of State, like a former diplomat, is entitled to immunity from prosecution only in respect of acts done by him (or on his orders) in connection with his former office; and there are certain offences (such as torture committed by agents of a State that is party to the 1984 Convention against Torture and other Cruel, Inhuman or Degrading Treatment or Punishment) to which even this immunity cannot attach (*Bow Street Metropolitan Stipendiary Magistrate, ex parte Pinochet Ugarte (No. 3)* [2000] 1 AC 147).

Visiting Forces

When foreign or Commonwealth armed forces are stationed on British soil, criminal juris-   **A8.29**
diction over their personnel and families etc. is ceded in some circumstances to their own authorities. See the Visiting Forces Act 1952, s. 3. Foreign naval vessels are immune from local jurisdiction, even in respect of offences committed within English ports or harbours.

Offences Committed on or within Diplomatic Premises

The premises of diplomatic missions in England and Wales are not in any sense foreign terri-   **A8.30**
tory, although such premises may not be entered by the police or by any other agents of the UK government except with the consent of the ambassador or head of the mission (Diplomatic Privileges Act 1964, s. 2(1) and sch. 3).

Subject to any individual claims to diplomatic immunity etc., offences committed on or within such premises are accordingly triable in England and Wales under the ordinary territorial principles of English law: see *Nejad* (1981 unreported) in which acts committed by terrorists who seized the Iranian embassy in London were held to be justiciable under English law; and see also *Radwan v Radwan* [1972] 3 All ER 967.

Section A9   European Union Law

INTRODUCTION: THE RELEVANCE OF EU LAW FOR DOMESTIC CRIMINAL LAW

A9.1   EU criminal law is perhaps the fastest growing area of EU law. A number of EU criminal law measures have been adopted under the 'old' third pillar of the EU Treaties. The entry into force of the Treaty of Lisbon in December 2009 created a fresh momentum towards the adoption of new EU measures in the field. The adoption of criminal law at the level of the EU has significant consequences for domestic criminal justice systems. The principal impact of EU criminal law on domestic criminal law can be viewed at three levels:

(a) at the level of implementation of EU law: EU Member States (including the UK) are under a duty to implement in their national law EU legislation in criminal matters — the Extradition Act 2003, part of which implemented the EU Framework Decision on the European Arrest Warrant (EAW), is a prime example in this context;

(b) at the level of the development of criminal law principles: in the absence of detailed EU legislation in the field, the Court of Justice of the European Union (CJEU) has developed principles in the field of criminal justice — the interpretation of the principle of *ne bis in idem* (double jeopardy) is a prime example in this context;

(c) at the level of interpreting domestic criminal law: courts in EU Member States are called to interpret domestic law in the light of any EU criminal law measures it is designed to implement and in the light of general principles of EU law; in this context, ensuring the effective enforcement of EU law in the domestic legal order is of paramount importance after the entry into force of the Lisbon Treaty.

This section examines the impact of EU criminal law on the domestic legal system by focusing on three aspects of relevance:

(a) an overview of the institutional framework for the adoption of EU criminal law, explaining the differences between the 'old' third pillar and the Lisbon Treaty in order to clarify the differences in the nature and legal effects of EU criminal law legal instruments post-Lisbon;

(b) an overview of the applicability of general principles of EU law in the field, and their impact on the conduct of domestic criminal proceedings; and

(c) an overview of the principal EU criminal law measures and principles, focusing on measures related to judicial co-operation in criminal matters and measures with a cross-border dimension.

INSTITUTIONAL BACKGROUND AND LEGAL INSTRUMENTS

A9.2   There are two main stages in the development of the institutional framework of EU criminal law: (i) the 'third pillar' stage and (ii) the Lisbon Treaty stage.

The third pillar has been abolished by the Lisbon Treaty. However, it is important to consider it because:

(a) under the Protocol on transitional provisions agreed under the Lisbon Treaty, measures adopted under the third pillar will continue to have the same 'old' third pillar effects (unless they are amended or repealed) until 30 November 2014;

(b) the majority of EU criminal law measures (including legislation on the EAW) have taken the form of third pillar instruments (namely Framework Decisions) so, to the extent that these instruments have not been amended, they continue to have the 'old' third pillar effects.

The so-called third pillar was introduced in EU law by the Treaty of Maastricht, and was amended by the Treaty of Amsterdam to include provisions on EU action on police and judicial co-operation in criminal matters. It was one of the two more 'intergovernmental' pillars of the EU Treaty, to be contrasted with the more 'supranational' first pillar, which consisted of provisions of traditional Community (EC) law. Placing EU action in criminal matters under the third pillar (and not under the first, Community, pillar) meant that Member States would retain their sovereignty in the field by limiting the application of Community law principles in criminal law. Under the third pillar, the control of EU institutions (such as the European Commission, the European Parliament and the CJEU) over EU criminal law was limited; the general principles of EC law did not apply to EU criminal law fully; and the effects of third pillar legal instruments were less far-reaching than those of traditional EC law. Under the 'old' third pillar (Article 34(2) of the Treaty on the European Union (TEU)) binding EU criminal law mainly took the form of Framework Decisions, Conventions and Decisions. The majority of EU criminal law instruments in the third pillar have taken the form of Framework Decisions which, similarly to first pillar Directives, are binding upon the Member States as to the result to be achieved but leave to the national authorities the choice of form and methods. However, unlike Directives, Framework Decisions do not entail direct effect.

The Lisbon Treaty abolished the old third pillar and subsumed EU action in criminal matters under the full control of the EU institutions. A key change involves the form of EU legislative action in criminal matters. Following the Lisbon Treaty, Framework Decisions are no longer made. The normalisation of EU criminal law under Lisbon means that legislation in the field now takes the form of Regulations, Directives and Decisions. As regards the two main instruments, Article 288 of the Treaty on the Functioning of the European Union (TFEU) reiterates that:

- a Regulation has general application and is binding in its entirety and directly applicable in all Member States: this means that Regulations are applicable from the date of their publication in the Official Journal of the European Union to all Member States, without the need of further domestic implementation; and

- a Directive is binding as to the result to be achieved upon each Member State to which it is addressed, but leaves to the national authorities the choice of form and methods: this means that Member States will have to transpose the text of a Directive into their domestic legal system, normally by the adoption of implementing legislation.

General principles of EU law, such as direct effect, apply to EU criminal law adopted post-Lisbon and EU institutions now assume their full powers of control. In this context, it is important to note that the CJEU extends its full jurisdiction to criminal matters; in particular, it is granted jurisdiction to give preliminary rulings (Article 267 TFEU) and to rule on infringement proceedings brought against Member States by the European Commission for failing to fulfil their obligations under EU law (Articles 258 and 260 TFEU). Infringement proceedings may thus be instituted in cases where Member States are deemed not to have implemented EU criminal law fully. However, it must be emphasised that for EU law adopted under the old third pillar the Lisbon effects do not come into effect automatically. To the extent that

A9.3

'old' third pillar law has not been amended, it will assume the full effects of Union law from 1 December 2014.

EU LAW PRINCIPLES IN DOMESTIC COURTS

Fundamental Rights

A9.4   Respect for fundamental rights has been a long-standing general principle of EU law (Case C-11/70 *Internationale Handelsgesellschaft* [1970] ECR 1125). The Lisbon Treaty confirms that fundamental rights, as guaranteed by the ECHR and as they result from the constitutional traditions common to the Member States 'constitute general principles of Union law' (Article 6(3) TEU). It also recognises the provisions of the Charter of Fundamental Rights which, according to Article 6(1) TEU, has the same legal value as the EU Treaties. The opening provision of the Treaty chapter on the Area of Freedom, Security and Justice (Title V) also stresses respect for fundamental rights (Article 67(1) TFEU). EU criminal law measures and their implementation at the domestic level must be interpreted in accordance with fundamental rights. The obligation to respect fundamental rights in the context of executing a EAW (see **A9.12**) was expressly highlighted by the CJEU (see Case C-303/05 *Advocaten voor de Wereld* [2007] ECR I-3633 at **A9.13**). Key Charter provisions are the provisions in Chapter VI of the Charter, on the right to an effective remedy and fair trial, the presumption of innocence and rights of defence, the principle of legality and proportionality in criminal offences and penalties, and the principle of *ne bis in idem* (Articles 47 to 50 respectively). The CJEU has confirmed that the principle that criminal penalties must have a proper legal basis, which is enshrined in Article 49(1) of the Charter, would prohibit the imposition of criminal penalties even if the national rule were contrary to EU law (Case C-7/11 *Fabio Caronna* [2012] All ER (D) 49 (Sep)).

Direct Effect

A9.5   The principle of direct effect lies at the heart of the decentralised enforcement of EU law. It allows an individual to invoke and rely upon EU law provisions directly in *national* courts (Case 26/62 *Van Gend en Loos* [1963] ECR 13) if EU law has not been implemented or properly implemented in Member States. The principle is not absolute — EU law must be clear, unconditional and sufficiently precise to be invoked in national courts. However, the principle is of immense importance to ensure the full effectiveness of EU law and particularly relevant in measures which confer rights on individuals. Direct effect can be used in domestic courts to claim that an individual derives rights directly from EU law in cases where it is thought that EU law has not been implemented fully or properly in the UK. Framework Decisions do not currently entail direct effect. EU criminal law Directives adopted post-Lisbon can have direct effect if the relevant conditions (i.e. that the EU provision is clear, unconditional and sufficiently precise) are met.

Interpretative Obligation — Indirect Effect

A9.6   Under the principle of indirect effect, national courts are under a duty to interpret domestic law as far as possible in conformity with EU law. The principle has been developed by the CJEU in order to ensure the effective enforcement of EU law in particular in cases where EU measures were deemed not to entail direct effect. As with direct effect, indirect effect is a principle relying on national courts to give effect to EU law.

The principle of indirect effect was applicable in EU criminal law before the entry into force of the Lisbon Treaty. The CJEU in Case C-105/03 *Pupino* [2005] ECR I-5285 extended the application of the principle to the third pillar. The interpretative obligation of national courts is, however, limited by general principles of law, such as legal certainty and non-retroactivity: those principles prevent that obligation from leading to the criminal liability of persons who contravene the provisions of a Framework Decision from being judged or punished on the basis of a Framework Decision alone, independently of an implementing law (Case C-403/02 *Berlusconi* [2005] ECR I-3565). Indirect effect cannot serve as the basis for an interpretation of domestic law *contra legem* (i.e. which is inconsistent with the precise wording of a statutory provision or other rule of law), but the national court must consider the whole of domestic law in order to assess how far it can be applied in such a way as not to produce a result contrary to that envisaged by the Framework Decision. The obligation to interpret domestic law in conformity with EU law under *Pupino* has been cited repeatedly by the House of Lords in its case law on the implementation of the EAW Framework Decision (*Dabas v High Court of Justice, Madrid* [2007] 1 AC 31, *Pilecki v Circuit Court of Legnica, Poland* [2008] 4 All ER 445 and *Caldarelli v Court of Naples* [2009] 1 All ER 1). In *Assange v Swedish Prosecution Authority* [2012] 4 All ER 1249, the Supreme Court found that although the Supreme Court is not bound to apply *Pupino* to the Extradition Act 2003, it should nonetheless do so.

Primacy

The CJEU proclaimed the primacy of EU law over domestic law in the 1960s (Case 6/64 *Costa v Enel* [1964] ECR 585). The principle has been accepted by the UK courts (*Factortame Ltd v Secretary of State for Transport (No. 2)* [1991] 1 AC 603, *Equal Opportunities Commission v Secretary of State for Employment* [1994] 2 All ER 121 and *Thoburn v Sunderland City Council* [2003] QB 151). The Treaty on the European Union and the CJEU were silent as to the applicability of primacy to third pillar law. The entry into force of the Lisbon Treaty means that EU criminal law adopted post-Lisbon (and old third pillar law from December 2014) has primacy over domestic law. This finding has been confirmed by the CJEU (Case C-399/11 *Melloni v Ministerio Fiscal* [2013] QB 1067 at [55]–[59]).   **A9.7**

State Liability for Damages

A key move towards the effective enforcement of EU law has been the development by the CJEU of the principle of State liability for damages (Cases C-6, 9/90 *Francovich* [1991] ECR I-5357), which obliges States to award compensation for harm caused to individuals by breaches of EU law for which they can be held responsible. The principle of State liability for damages is central to the enforcement and implementation of EU law. It applies not only to the executive, but also to courts. Under certain conditions, failure by national courts to refer to the CJEU questions related to the interpretation of EU law may trigger State liability for damages.   **A9.8**

In particular, in Case C-224/01 *Köbler* [2003] ECR I-10239 the CJEU held that State liability is applicable where the alleged infringement of EU law stems from a decision of a court adjudicating at last instance where the rule of EU law infringed is intended to confer rights on individuals, the breach is sufficiently serious and there is a direct causal link between that breach and the loss or damage suffered by the injured parties. Determining factors include non-compliance by the court in question with its obligation to make a reference for a preliminary ruling (*Köbler* at [55]).

References for Preliminary Rulings

The extension of State liability in Case C-224/01 *Köbler* [2003] ECR I-10239 is of particular relevance in the light of the fact that national courts against whose decisions there is no judicial remedy under domestic law are under the duty to send questions on the validity or interpretation of post-Lisbon EU criminal law raised before them to the CJEU (Article 267(3) TFEU). The Lisbon Treaty extends the option of sending questions for preliminary rulings regarding EU criminal law adopted post-Lisbon to lower courts where the court considers that a decision on the question is necessary to enable it to give judgment (Article 267(2) TFEU). The government has not granted UK courts the power to send questions for preliminary rulings on third   **A9.9** pillar law. This limitation will cease on 1 December 2014, assuming that the UK accepts the full powers of the EU institutions with regard to third pillar law (see **A9.11**).

Sending references for preliminary rulings to the CJEU is a key tool for clarifying issues where the interpretation of domestic law in the light of EU criminal law or in the light of general principles of EU law is unclear. A request for a preliminary ruling may be necessary when the domestic court is called upon to rule on a provision implementing EU criminal law (e.g., the EAW Framework Decision) or on EU criminal law principles (e.g., the cross-border double jeopardy principle enshrined in Article 54 of the Schengen Implementing Convention).

Requests for preliminary rulings are of particular relevance in view of the development by the CJEU of autonomous concepts in the field of EU criminal justice. The CJEU has assigned an autonomous EU meaning to a number of terms included in the EAW Framework Decision (Case C-66/08 *Kozlowski* [2008] ECR I-6041 on residence and stay; Case C-60/12 *Balaz* [2014] RTR 61 on the concept of judicial authority — see **A9.21**). In particular, a reference to the CJEU is necessary where there is no EU law precedent on the point. The preliminary rulings mechanism provides a first class avenue of co-operation between the CJEU and national courts. In order to benefit fully from this mechanism, awareness of EU law, and of the fact that domestic legislation is actually intended to implement EU law, is key.

A9.10　Detailed guidance on how to send references for preliminary rulings is included in an Information Note produced by the CJEU ([2011] OJ C160/1):

(1) A court or tribunal against whose ruling there is no judicial remedy under domestic law must, as a rule, refer questions on the interpretation of EU law to the CJEU unless that court has ruled already on the point or unless the correct interpretation of the rule of law in question is obvious (Information Note, para. 12).

(2) A court or tribunal against whose decision there is a judicial remedy may refer a question on interpretation if it considers that it is necessary to do so in order to resolve a dispute brought before it. A reference for preliminary ruling may prove particularly useful when there is a new question of interpretation of general interest for the uniform application of EU law in all the Member States, or where the existing case law does not appear to be applicable to a new set of facts (paras. 11 and 13).

(3) A national court or tribunal may refer a question to the CJEU for a preliminary ruling as soon as it finds that a ruling on the point of validity or interpretation is necessary to enable it to give judgment. It is desirable that a decision to seek a preliminary ruling should be taken when the national proceedings have reached a stage at which the national court is able to define the factual and legal context of the question, so that the CJEU has available to it all the information necessary to check that EU law applies to the main proceedings (paras. 18 and 19).

(4) A reference for a preliminary ruling calls for the national proceedings to be stayed until the CJEU has given its ruling (para. 26).

According to Article 267(4) TFEU, if a question is raised in a case pending before a court or tribunal of a Member State with regard to a person in custody, the CJEU must act with the minimum of delay. Moreover, an urgent preliminary reference procedure has been established by the Rules of Procedure of the Court of Justice ([2012] OJ L265/1) and by the Protocol on the Statute of the Court of Justice annexed to the Lisbon Treaty (Article 23a). According to the Rules of Procedure, a national court or tribunal may request that a reference for a preliminary ruling which raises questions in the areas covered by Title V of the TFEU (on the Area of Freedom, Security and Justice, including EU criminal law) is dealt with under an urgent procedure. Detailed rules are set out in the Rules of Procedure (Articles 107 to 114) and in the Information Note on references for a preliminary ruling (paras. 38 to 41).

See **D30.6** for the text of Article 267 and domestic case law; see also the CrimPR, part 75 (see Supplement, **R-573** *et seq.*) for the procedure to be adopted in an application for a reference.

UK PARTICIPATION IN EU CRIMINAL LAW

Protocol 21 to the Lisbon Treaty extended the right of the UK not to participate in EU law to **A9.11** the whole of Title V TFEU, including criminal law measures. The right not to participate also extends to legislation amending existing measures which are binding upon the UK. The government decides on its participation in post-Lisbon measures on a case-by-case basis. As regards old third pillar law, the Protocol on Transitional Provisions grants the UK, upon the expiry of the five-year transitional period from the entry into force of the Lisbon Treaty on 30 November 2014, the right not to accept the full powers of the EU institutions in third pillar law. Where the UK has decided not to accept these powers, such legislation ceases to apply to the UK. The UK has notified the Presidency of the EU that, pursuant to Article 10(4) of Protocol 36, it does not accept the powers of the EU institutions; accordingly, those acts will cease to apply in the UK from 1 December 2014 (Council doc. 12750/13). However, the UK has indicated that it will seek to opt back into 35 of these measures including the EAW Framework Decision.

MUTUAL RECOGNITION

Under the principle of mutual recognition, judicial authorities in one Member State are under **A9.12** the duty to recognise and execute judgments and orders issued by judicial authorities in other Member States on the basis of mutual trust and with a minimum of formality. Scrutiny of the judicial decision by the issuing authority is subject to limited scrutiny. In the majority of EU mutual recognition instruments, verification of dual criminality for an extensive list of categories of serious offences has been abolished; dual criminality means that the conduct for which a EAW (or another judicial decision falling under the mutual recognition principle) has been issued constitutes an offence under both the national law of the authority issuing the EAW and the national law of the authority in the executing Member State. Moreover, the grounds available to the judicial authority in the executing State to refuse the recognition and execution of the decision by the issuing State are limited and mostly procedural (for detailed analysis see V. Mitsilegas, *EU Criminal Law* (2009), ch. 3).

The mutual recognition principle applies to a wide range of elements of the criminal justice process, from the pre-trial to the post-trial stage. Mutual recognition is applicable to judgments in the following fields.

Arrest and Surrender

The Framework Decision on the European Arrest Warrant [2002] OJ L190/1 was implemented **A9.13** by the Extradition Act 2003 (see **D31.2**). The CJEU has been called upon to interpret a number of aspects of the EAW Framework Decision. Its rulings are of relevance as regards the interpretation of these legal issues in domestic proceedings concerning EAWs. In Case C-303/05 *Advocaten voor de Wereld* [2007] ECR I-3633 the CJEU held (at [53]) that the abolition of dual criminality in the Framework Decision is not a breach of the legality principle as:

> ...the definition of those offences and of the penalties applicable continue to be matters determined by the law of the issuing Member State which, as is, moreover, stated in Article 1(3) of the Framework Decision, must respect fundamental rights and fundamental legal principles as enshrined in Article 6 EU and, consequently, the principle of the legality of criminal offences and penalties.

In Case C-306/09 *IB* [2011] 1 WLR 2227 the CJEU found that the execution of a EAW issued for the purposes of execution of a sentence imposed *in absentia* within the meaning of Article 5(1) may be subject to the condition that the person concerned should be returned to the executing State in order to serve there the sentence passed against him, following a new trial organised in his presence in the issuing State. In Case C-388/08 *Leymann and Pustovarov* [2008] ECR I-8993 the CJEU found that, to establish specialty under Article 27(2) of the Framework Decision, it must be ascertained whether the constituent elements of the offence are those in respect of which the person was surrendered and whether there is a sufficient correspondence between the information given in the arrest warrant and that contained in the later procedural document.

Two recent cases address the issue of the compatibility of the EAW with fundamental rights in cases involving judgments *in absentia*. In Case C-396/11 *Criminal proceedings against Radu* [2013] QB 1031 the CJEU found that the EAW Framework Decision, as amended by Framework Decision 2009/299/JHA on judgments *in absentia*, must be interpreted as meaning that the executing judicial authorities cannot refuse to execute a EAW issued for the purposes of conducting a criminal prosecution on the ground that the requested person was not heard in the issuing Member State before that arrest warrant was issued. In Case C-399/11 *Melloni v Ministerio Fiscal* [2013] QB 1067 the CJEU found that Article 4a(1) of the Framework Decision, as amended by the 2009 Framework Decision, precludes the executing authorities from making the execution of the warrant issued for the purposes of executing a sentence conditional upon the conviction rendered *in absentia* being open to review in the issuing Member State. The Court found that Article 4a(1) is compatible with the requirements under Articles 47 and 48(2) of the Charter of Fundamental Rights.

Evidence

A9.14   The Framework Decision on the mutual recognition of orders freezing property or evidence [2003] OJ L196/45 and the Framework Decision on the European Evidence Warrant [2008] OJ L350/72 have replaced some elements of the current system of Mutual Legal Assistance co-operation. The freezing orders Framework Decision was implemented partly by the Crime (International Co-operation) Act 2003, ss. 7 to 28. However, the European Evidence Warrant Framework Decision has not been implemented by a great number of Member States in view of the fact that a new, post-Lisbon Directive on mutual recognition of evidence is currently being negotiated in Brussels. The Directive on the European Investigation Order, which was adopted by the Council in March 2014 (Council doc. 7559/14) will replace the mutual legal assistance instruments as regards the relations between EU Member States. The European Investigation Order will establish a system for the mutual recognition of requests for evidence across the EU. The UK has opted into the European Investigation Order Directive.

Probation

A9.15   The Framework Decision on the mutual recognition of probation decisions [2008] OJ L337/102 applies.

Financial Penalties

A9.16   The Framework Decision on the mutual recognition of judgments imposing financial penalties [2005] OJ L76/16, implemented by the CJIA 2008, ss. 80 to 92 and schs. 18 and 19, applies.

Confiscation

A9.17   The Framework Decision on the mutual recognition of confiscation orders [2006] OJ L328/59 applies (see E19.77).

Supervision Measures

A9.18   The Framework Decision on the mutual recognition of decisions on supervision measures as alternatives to provisional detention [2009] OJ L294/20 and the Framework Decision on the application of the principle of mutual recognition to judgments and probation decisions with a view to the supervision of probation measures and alternative sanctions [2008] OJ L337/102 apply.

Transfer of Sentenced Persons

A9.19   The Framework Decision on the transfer of custodial sentences (sentenced persons) [2008] OJ L327/27 applies.

Examination of Effect of Recognising and Executing Judicial Decision

Important guidance on the issue of the extent to which executing authorities should examine **A9.20**
the substance of the legal system of the issuing State when deciding whether to recognise and
execute a judicial decision has been given in Case C-411/10 *R (NS) v Secretary of State for the
Home Department* [2013] QB 102. While the case involved the application of EU asylum law
(the Dublin Regulation), its key finding that there is no conclusive presumption that fundamental rights are respected in Member States does apply to the operation of mutual recognition
in criminal matters as well. *NS* precludes the automaticity in the execution of mutual recognition requests and obliges national judicial authorities to examine the impact of execution on the
fundamental rights of the affected individuals on a case-by-case basis. The Court confirmed in
NS that the Charter of Fundamental Rights (with the exception of its Chapter IV) is applicable
to the UK (at [116]–[122]).

Similar questions have arisen in domestic courts. In *Assange v Swedish Prosecution Authority*
[2011] EWHC 2849 (Admin), the Divisional Court interpreted the Extradition Act 2003
to a great extent in accordance with the EAW Framework Decision which it was designed to
implement as far as surrender to EU Member States was concerned. The need to interpret the
Extradition Act 2003 in conformity with the EAW Framework Decision was highlighted from
the outset, referring to leading judgments in both the CJEU (Case C-105/03 *Pupino* [2005]
ECR I-5285) and the House of Lords (*Dabas v High Court of Justice, Madrid* [2007] 1 AC 31).
Assange confirms that 'it is now well established that Part I of the 2003 Act must be read in
the context of the Framework Decision and that the national courts of the Member States
should construe national laws so far as possible to attain the results sought to be achieved by
the Framework Decision' (at [9]). The need to take into account the aims of the Framework
Decision under the principle of mutual recognition does not however negate any scrutiny of
EAWs by domestic courts (at [17]): the intensity of such scrutiny increases in cases where a
EAW is issued by a judicial authority who is not a judge (at [19]). However, the Divisional
Court did examine the substance of the defendant's claims.

Judicial Authority as an Autonomous Concept of EU Law

The CJEU has granted an autonomous EU meaning to the term 'court having jurisdiction in **A9.21**
particular in criminal matters'. The term must be interpreted as covering any court or tribunal
which applies a procedure that satisfies the essential characteristics of criminal procedure (Case
C-60/12 *Balaz* [2014] RTR 61). In the domestic context, in *Assange v Swedish Prosecution
Authority* [2012] 4 All ER 1249, the Supreme Court found that the meaning of the term
'judicial authority' is identical in the EAW Framework Decision and in the Extradition Act
2003 and that the term encompasses prosecutors. In *Ministry of Justice, Republic of Lithuania v
Bucnys* [2014] 2 All ER 235 the Supreme Court confirmed (at [43]–[45]) that the term 'judicial authority' for the purposes of the operation of the EAW Framework Decision is an autonomous European concept which must be interpreted in a teleological and contextual manner.
See also **D31.12**.

DOUBLE JEOPARDY

Domestic courts are obliged to respect the principle of double jeopardy or *ne bis in idem*, which **A9.22**
was introduced into EU law via the incorporation of the Schengen *acquis* in the EU legal
order. It forms part of the *acquis* which is binding on the UK. Article 54 of the Schengen
Implementing Convention (CISA) sets out the principle as follows:

> A person whose trial has been finally disposed of in one Contracting Party may not be prosecuted
> in another Contracting Party for the same acts provided that, if a penalty has been imposed, it has
> been enforced, is actually in the process of being enforced or can no longer be enforced under the
> laws of the sentencing Contracting Party.

Article 54 CISA has thus established a cross-border double jeopardy principle. The principle applies to cross-border cases involving the UK and another EU Member State and is of relevance in cases where it is thought that a defendant in domestic criminal proceedings has already been subject to criminal proceedings which have been finally disposed of in another EU Member State. The scope of the principle in EU law is broad (it applies to the same acts, and not to the same offences) and it has been extended further by the CJEU to protect the defendant. See **D12.20** *et seq.* for more detailed discussion of double jeopardy and its application in practice.

Ne bis in idem is also recognised as a fundamental right in Article 50 of the Charter of Fundamental Rights. The question has thus arisen whether Article 50 is applicable beyond cross-border cases as envisaged by Article 54 CISA, in purely domestic cases involving the implementation of EU law. The CJEU found in Case C-617/10 *Åklagaren v Åkerberg Fransson* (CJEU, 26 February 2013) that the Charter is applicable even in cases where national law has not been adopted to transpose an EU Directive, as long as a direct link is established between domestic law and the obligation of Member States to ensure the effectiveness of Union law (at [16]–[31]). The *ne bis in idem* principle applies in a domestic law context involving the imposition of criminal law and administrative law penalties only if the administrative penalties are criminal in nature. The criteria for the purposes of addressing whether administrative penalties (tax penalties in *Fransson*) are criminal are the legal classification of the offence under national law, the nature of the offence and the nature and degree of the severity of the penalty (at [34] and [35]).

TAKING ACCOUNT OF PREVIOUS CONVICTIONS

A9.23 A system of taking account of previous convictions was established by Framework Decision 2008/675/JHA [2008] OJ L220/2. It places Member States under a duty to ensure that in the course of criminal proceedings against a person, previous convictions handed down against the same person for different facts in other Member States are taken into account to the extent that previous domestic convictions are taken into account, and that equivalent legal effects are attached to them as to previous domestic convictions, in accordance with domestic law (Article 3(1)). Where, in the course of criminal proceedings in a Member State, information is available on a previous conviction in another Member State, as far as possible the person concerned should not be treated less favourably than if the previous conviction had been a domestic conviction (Preamble, recital 8). Domestic implementation has taken place via the CAJA 2009, s. 144 and sch. 17 (see **F11.1** *et seq.*, **F12.4** and **F12.36**).

CONFLICTS OF JURISDICTION

A9.24 An attempt to establish a system to prevent and settle conflicts of jurisdiction has been made by Framework Decision 2009/948/JHA [2009] OJ L328/42. The Framework Decision aims at encouraging direct contact between competent national authorities for this purpose. In October 2013, it was indicated in Parliament that the UK Government 'do not currently intend to take any steps to implement this Framework Decision' on the basis that the practices it embodies are already well established in the UK.

The Framework Decision establishes an obligation to contact when there are reasonable grounds to believe that parallel proceedings are being conducted in another Member State (Article 5) and a corresponding obligation to reply (Article 6). It also imposes a duty to enter into direct consultations when it is established that parallel proceedings exist, with the aim of reaching consensus on 'any effective solution aimed at avoiding the adverse consequences arising from such parallel proceedings, which may, where appropriate, lead to the concentration of the criminal proceedings in one Member State' (Article 10(1)). The Framework

Decision thus does not in itself impose an obligation on a Member State to prosecute or to refrain from prosecution in cases of conflicts of jurisdiction. It also does not set out a series of binding criteria which must be taken into account when deciding on conflicts of jurisdiction. The Preamble refers to relevant criteria developed by Eurojust as possible criteria to be taken into account (recital 9). However, these criteria are not binding and not hierarchical. See **A8** for jurisdiction generally.

DEFENCE RIGHTS

The Lisbon Treaty has granted the EU competence to adopt minimum standards on defence rights to the extent necessary to facilitate mutual recognition (Article 82(2) TFEU). Secondary EU law on defence rights will flesh out protection established in general human rights instruments such as that under the ECHR, Article 6. Moreover, the EU Charter of Fundamental Rights (binding upon Member States after the entry into force of the Lisbon Treaty) includes a general provision on the right to a fair trial (Article 47) and a specific provision guaranteeing respect for the rights of the defence of anyone who has been charged (Article 48(2)). Any secondary EU law in the field must be interpreted in the light of these provisions.

A9.25

The first EU measure on defence rights to be adopted was Directive 2010/64 on the right to interpretation and translation in criminal proceedings [2010] OJ L280/1. It applies to both criminal proceedings and proceedings for the execution of a EAW (Article 1(1)). It grants a right to interpretation 'without delay' (Article 2(1)) and a right to translation within a reasonable period of time of all documents which are essential to ensure that the defendant is able to exercise his right of defence and to safeguard the fairness of the proceedings (Article 3(1)). Essential documents include any decision depriving a person of his liberty, any charge or indictment, and any judgment (Article 3(2)). In proceedings for the execution of a EAW, the competent authorities must provide a written translation of it (Article 3(6)). The Directive contains a non-regression clause with regard to the ECHR, the EU Charter of Fundamental Rights, international law and domestic law which provides a higher level of protection (Article 8). The UK has opted into the Directive and the most recent changes to PACE Code C implement the Directive (see **D1.91**).

Further proposals for EU measures on defence rights are to follow. A Directive on the right to information, to which the UK has opted in was published in the Official Journal in June 2012 (Directive 2012/13/EU, [2012] OJ L142/1). The Directive grants suspects and accused persons a right to be informed about their rights (Articles 3, 4 and 5), a right to information about the accusation (Article 6) and a right of access to the materials of the case (Article 7). The deadline for implementation is 2 June 2014. A Directive on the right of access to a lawyer in criminal proceedings was published in the Official Journal in November 2013 (Directive 2013/48/EU, [2013] OJ L294/1). The UK has not opted into this Directive. These measures will be key in safeguarding fundamental rights in EU criminal law. Since they were adopted post-Lisbon and confer rights on individuals, provisions on defence rights are highly likely to have direct effect, and thus can be invoked in domestic courts in cases of perceived inadequate implementation.

VICTIMS' RIGHTS

The EU has legislated on the rights of victims in criminal proceedings by using both mutual recognition and harmonisation of criminal procedural law. Under mutual recognition, Directive 2011/99/EU on the European Protection Order ([2011] OJ L338/2) sets out rules allowing a judicial or equivalent authority in a Member State, in which a protection measure has been

A9.26

adopted with a view to protecting a person against a criminal act by another person which may endanger his life, physical or psychological integrity, dignity, personal liberty or sexual integrity, to issue a European protection order enabling a competent authority in another Member State to continue the protection of the person in the territory of that other Member State, following criminal conduct, or alleged criminal conduct, in accordance with the national law of the issuing State. Directive 2012/29, adopted under Article 82(2) TFEU, establishes minimum standards on the rights, support and protection of victims of crime ([2012] OJ L315/57). It replaces Framework Decision 2001/220/JHA and introduces a number of rights relating to the following:

(a) the provision of information and support (right to understand and be understood, right to receive information from the first contact with a competent authority, rights when making a complaint, right to receive information about a case, right to interpretation and translation, right to access victim support services: Articles 3 to 8);

(b) the victim's participation in criminal proceedings (right to be heard, rights in the event of a decision not to prosecute, right to safeguards in the context of restorative justice services, right to reimbursement of expenses, right to the return of property, right to decision on compensation from the offender in the course of criminal proceedings, rights of victims resident in another Member State: Articles 10 to 17); and

(c) the protection of victims and recognition of victims with specific protection needs, including children (Articles 18 to 24).

Section B1   Homicide and Related Offences

MURDER

Definition

> Murder is when a [person]…unlawfully killeth…any reasonable creature *in rerum natura* under   **B1.1**
> the Queen's peace, with malice aforethought…(Derived from *Coke's Institutes*, 3 Co Inst 47)

Procedure

Murder is triable only on indictment. It is a class 1A offence.   **B1.2**

Indictment

Statement of Offence   **B1.3**

Murder

Particulars of Offence

A on or about the…day of…murdered V

Alternative Verdicts

Criminal Law Act 1967, s. 6   **B1.4**

(2) On an indictment for murder a person found not guilty of murder may be found guilty—
   (a) of manslaughter, or of causing grievous bodily harm with intent to do so; or
   (b) of any offence of which he may be found guilty under an enactment specifically so provid-
       ing, or under section 4(2) of this Act [assisting offenders]; or
   (c) of an attempt to commit murder, or of an attempt to commit any other offence of which
       he might be found guilty;
but may not be found guilty of any offence not included above.

The major enactments specifically providing for an alternative verdict within s. 6(2)(b) are as
follows:

(a) Suicide Act 1961, s. 2(2) (encouraging or assisting suicide: see **B1.136**);
(b) Infant Life (Preservation) Act 1929, s. 2(2) (child destruction: see **B1.98** to **B1.106**);
(c) Infanticide Act 1938, s. 2(2) (infanticide: see **B1.88** to **B1.97**).

To these alternative verdicts must be added:

(d) manslaughter;
(e) wounding with intent (under the CLA 1967, s. 6(2)(a));

185

(f) assisting (contrary to the CLA 1967, s. 4(1)) anyone guilty of any of the above offences; and

(g) attempting to commit any of the above offences.

Murder is specifically excluded from the general rule on alternative verdicts laid down in the Criminal Law Act 1967, s. 6(3) (see **D19.50**).

Although s. 6(2)(a) refers to a person being 'found not guilty of murder', a person can still, under the common law, irrespective of s. 2, be found guilty of manslaughter as an alternative verdict where the jury are unable to agree and are discharged by the judge from returning a verdict on the charge of murder (*Saunders* [1988] AC 148). As to when it is necessary for a judge to leave an alternative verdict of manslaughter to a jury, see *Coutts* [2006] 4 All ER 353, discussed at **D19.63**. See also *JB* [2013] EWCA Crim 256 on the effect of the decision to discharge the jury from returning a verdict on the murder charge and to take the alternative verdict of manslaughter, i.e. that there can be no subsequent retrial for murder.

It is now permissible to include other counts in an indictment for murder (see *Connelly v DPP* [1964] AC 1254; as to joinder of counts generally, see **D11.63** *et seq.*).

Sentence

B1.5 The penalty for murder is as follows:

> Murder: Life imprisonment (mandatory sentence) (Murder (Abolition of Death Penalty) Act 1965, s. 1(1)).

> Murder by a person aged 18 but under 21: Custody for life (mandatory sentence) (PCC(S)A 2000, s. 93).

> Murder by person aged under 18 at the time of the offence: Detention at Her Majesty's pleasure (mandatory sentence) (PCC(S)A 2000, s. 90).

See further **E3**.

For sentencing for attempted murder, see the definitive sentencing guideline, *Attempted Murder* (see Supplement, **SG-464**). In *Terry* [2013] 1 Cr App R (S) 285 (51), where the offender struck the victim in the face many times with a claw hammer causing multiple skull fractures, an extended sentence with a custodial term of 18 years and an extension period of five years imposed after a trial was upheld on appeal. The Court of Appeal reviewed the sentencing guidelines in detail in *Barnaby* [2013] 1 Cr App R (S) 302 (53) and found that a sentence of imprisonment for public protection with a minimum term of 11 years after a trial was appropriate where the offender stabbed the victim twice causing life-threatening injuries. *Hardy* [2013] 2 Cr App R (S) 164 (24), where a husband attempted to murder his wife by hitting her on the head with a lump hammer, causing physical and psychological injury, was considered to be a level 2 offence with a starting point of 15 years, reduced to ten years to reflect a plea of guilty. An exceptional case is *Wade* [2013] 2 Cr App R (S) 52 (12), where the offender briefly tried to suffocate his partner who was ill and whose behaviour had become very difficult to cope with; the Court of Appeal reduced the sentence to 16 months' imprisonment.

Elements

B1.6 The definition set out at **B1.1** is often condensed to the form 'unlawful killing with malice aforethought', to be contrasted with those forms of manslaughter which consist of unlawful killing without malice aforethought. This contrast emphasises the point that the principal distinguishing feature of murder is malice aforethought, the *mens rea*, which can now be confidently stated to be an intention to kill or to cause grievous bodily harm. Since the *actus reus* of murder also governs both manslaughter and infanticide and affects certain other offences too, it is especially important to clarify the longer definition given by Coke.

B1.7 **Unlawful Killing** The word 'unlawfully' can be taken to exclude killings for which the accused has a complete and valid justification, such as killing (reasonably) in self-defence (see **A3.54** to

A3.70). See also *Airedale NHS Trust v Bland* [1993] AC 789 for the distinction between (lawful) withdrawal of treatment supporting life and (unlawful) active termination of a patient's life. This distinction was reiterated in *Inglis* [2011] 1 WLR 1110 by Lord Judge CJ in upholding the conviction for murder of a mother who had deliberately killed her son in his hospital bed with a carefully planned injection of heroin. She regarded it as an act of mercy but mercy killing remains unlawful and constitutes murder in the absence of e.g., diminished responsibility or some other partial defence. Similarly it was confirmed in *R (Nicklinson) v Ministry of Justice* [2012] EWHC 2381 (Admin) that voluntary euthanasia cannot provide a defence to murder by way of necessity and that the ECHR, Article 8, does not require the recognition of any such defence; that view was affirmed by the Court of Appeal (see [2014] 2 All ER 32), whose decision on this point was clearly accepted as correct by the Supreme Court ([2014] UKSC 38: see for example Lord Neuberger at [130]).

'Killeth' or 'kills' means 'causes the death of', and reference should be made to the discussion of causation in **A1.25** to **A1.40** (most of the cases there discussed being homicide cases). It should also be noted that murder is a result crime for the purposes of the rule laid down by the House of Lords in *Miller* [1983] 2 AC 161 in relation to the duty to act in the face of a danger one has created oneself (see **A1.20**).

Any Reasonable Creature *in Rerum Natura* This can be safely shortened to 'any human being' **B1.8** which includes a conjoined twin totally dependent on its twin for oxygenated blood (*Re A (Children) (Conjoined twins: surgical separation)* [2001] 4 All ER 961), provided that expression is understood as being limited to one who is born alive, i.e. when it is fully expelled from its mother's body (*Poulton* (1832) 5 C & P 329) with an existence independent of its mother. Although there are difficulties about identifying the precise time at which this occurs (Criminal Law Revision Committee, 14th Report, paras. 33–37), if death is caused before the child has an existence independent of its mother, the jury can convict of the offence of child destruction (see **B1.98** to **B1.106**). The accused's act may take place before the birth of the victim if it causes the victim to die after having been born alive but liability for murder or manslaughter will depend on the precise intention with which the act is done. The House of Lords decided in *A-G's Ref (No. 3 of 1994)* [1998] AC 245 that the child *in utero* is not simply a part of its mother as the Court of Appeal ([1996] QB 581) had held but that they are distinct organisms between which, however, the doctrine of transferred *mens rea* does not fully apply (see **A2.31**). An intention to inflict grievous bodily harm on the mother cannot ground liability for murder in respect of the subsequent live-birth-then-death of the child (although this can be manslaughter). It may however still be the case that there could be liability for the murder of the child if the intention was to kill the mother and certainly if it was intended to cause the child to die after having been born alive.

Under the Queen's Peace The original significance of this expression is somewhat unclear **B1.9** (*Page* [1954] 1 QB 170), but the only killings it would now seem to exclude are those in the actual heat and exercise of war or in putting down a rebellion. Otherwise, the killing of aliens, whether within the jurisdiction or outside it, can amount to murder (or manslaughter) and is triable in England. Any doubts about the precise position in Coke's time in relation to killings taking place outside the jurisdiction (*Page* [1954] 1 QB 170) are now resolved by the OAPA 1861, s. 9 (murder or manslaughter abroad), which provides as follows:

Offences against the Person Act 1861, s. 9

Where any murder or manslaughter shall be committed on land out of the United Kingdom, whether within the Queen's dominions or without, and whether the person killed were a subject of Her Majesty or not, every offence committed by any subject of Her Majesty in respect of any such case, whether the same shall amount to the offence of murder or manslaughter,...may be dealt with, inquired of, tried, determined, and punished...in England or Ireland.

It deals with the case where the whole of the *actus reus* takes place abroad, i.e. both the act causing death and the death itself. Section 10 is a similar provision which caters for cases where one of these two elements takes place inside, and the other outside, the jurisdiction:

B1.10　　　Offences against the Person Act 1861, s. 10

> Where any person being criminally stricken, poisoned, or otherwise hurt upon the sea, or at any place out of England or Ireland, shall die of such stroke, poisoning, or hurt in England or Ireland, or, being criminally stricken, poisoned or otherwise hurt in any place in England or Ireland, shall die of such stroke, poisoning, or hurt upon the sea, or at any place out of England or Ireland, every offence committed in respect of any such case, whether the same shall amount to the offence of murder or of manslaughter,...may be dealt with, inquired of, tried, determined, and punished...in England or Ireland.

It will be noticed that under s. 10, as contrasted with s. 9, there is no express limitation on the offence requiring it to be committed 'by any subject of Her Majesty', since at least part of the *actus reus* has taken place within the jurisdiction. Nevertheless, in *Lewis* (1857) Dears & B 182, it was held that the predecessor of s. 10 (9 Geo. IV c. 34 s. 8) did not apply to a blow struck out of the jurisdiction by a foreigner which resulted in death within the jurisdiction. But it does not necessarily follow that in the case of a blow inflicted by a foreigner within the jurisdiction, but resulting in death outside it, there would not be an offence of murder triable here. Two of the points mentioned by the court in *Lewis* were that:

(a) it is impossible to say that the blow by a foreigner out of the jurisdiction was done 'feloniously' (now 'criminally' as a result of the Criminal Law Act 1967) as required by the section; and

(b) the killing should be triable here only if it could have been triable here had the death occurred at the place where the blow was given.

In our converse case of a blow inflicted within the jurisdiction causing death outside it, these objections are not applicable, since:

(a) the blow would be inflicted 'feloniously' or 'criminally' (even without an ensuing death it would constitute an assault or an unlawful wounding) since it was given within the jurisdiction; and

(b) if the death occurred here, the killing would clearly be triable here.

Thus it is submitted that, even accepting the authority of *Lewis*, s. 10 can apply to a foreigner inflicting injury in this country which results in death abroad.

The effect of all the above is that the killing of *anyone* by a British subject anywhere in the world (except, it would seem, in Scotland or Northern Ireland — see M. Hirst at [1995] CLJ 488 and the words 'on land out of the United Kingdom' in s. 9) is triable here, and the killing of anyone by an alien is also triable here, if at least the accused's act, even if not the actual death, took place within the jurisdiction. By way of exception to all this, under the War Crimes Act 1991, certain killings in Germany or German Occupied Territory during the Second World War can be prosecuted in the UK irrespective of the nationality of the accused at the time of the alleged offence (see *Sawoniuk* [2000] 2 Cr App R 220, discussed at **F12.35**). (For offences committed on a British ship or aircraft, terrorist offences and jurisdictional questions generally, see **A8**.)

B1.11　**Abolition of Death within a Year and a Day Rule**　The former limitation that death had to occur within a year and a day of the infliction of injury was abolished, in relation to acts or omissions on or after 17 June 1996, by s. 1 of the Law Reform (Year and a Day Rule) Act 1996. The abolition is 'for all purposes' and thus affects not only murder and manslaughter but also infanticide, encouraging and assisting suicide, a coroner's verdict of suicide and any statutory offences of causing death such as causing death by dangerous driving.

However, by s. 2 of the 1996 Act, the A-G's consent is required before proceedings can be instituted for a 'fatal offence' where either:

(a) the injury alleged to have caused the death was sustained more than three years before the death occurred, or

(b) the person has previously been convicted of an offence committed in circumstances alleged to be connected with the death.

It may be noted that the three-year period is expressed to run from the date that the injury is sustained rather than the date of the accused's act or omission, which may in some cases be earlier.

Malice Aforethought   Malice aforethought, the *mens rea* for murder, is now considerably **B1.12** clearer and rather narrower than it has been in the past, the major remaining uncertainty relating to precisely how or when a jury should infer intention from foresight (see **A2.4**), a problem which is not confined to the offence of murder. Contrary to what may be suggested by the ancient term itself, neither ill will nor premeditation is *required*, and malice aforethought is satisfied by either:

(a) an intention to kill; or
(b) an intention to cause grievous bodily harm.

Care has to be taken when referring to any cases prior to 1957, since before s. 1 of the Homicide Act of that year, an intention to further any felony was also sufficient (the so-called felony-murder or constructive malice rule). Although it was clear that constructive malice was abolished by that Act, it has taken six House of Lords decisions, and further statutory intervention, to establish the following propositions:

(a) Murder requires intention, and nothing less (e.g., wicked recklessness as in Scotland) will suffice, i.e. it is a crime requiring specific intent, and, while foresight of virtual certainty may be evidence of intention, it is not to be equated with it (*Moloney* [1985] AC 905, explaining *Hyam v DPP* [1975] AC 55; see further **A2.4**).
(b) Grievous bodily harm should be given its ordinary and natural meaning, i.e. really serious bodily harm (*DPP v Smith* [1961] AC 290), and is not restricted to harm likely to endanger life (*Cunningham* [1982] AC 566). As Lord Edmund-Davies commented in that case (at pp. 582–3), 'I find it passing strange that a person can be convicted of murder if death results from, say, his intentional breaking of another's arm, an action, which, while calling for severe punishment, would in most cases be unlikely to kill'. His lordship went on to recognise, however, that any change in the law on this matter was a task for Parliament.
(c) Murder, like any other crime requiring proof of intention, involves proof of a subjective state of mind on the part of the accused.

Criminal Justice Act 1967, s. 8

A court or jury, in determining whether a person has committed an offence,—
(a) shall not be bound in law to infer that he intended or foresaw a result of his actions by reason only of its being a natural and probable consequence of those actions; but
(b) shall decide whether he did intend or foresee that result by reference to all the evidence, drawing such inferences from the evidence as appear proper in the circumstances.

(This reversed the effect of *DPP v Smith* [1961] AC 290, which had appeared to lay down an irrebuttable presumption that a man intends the natural and probable consequences of his actions, but had subsequently been said by the Privy Council in *Frankland v The Queen* [1987] AC 576 never to have accurately represented the common law of England.)

Thus, where an accused, as in *DPP v Smith* itself, does something of which the natural and prob- **B1.13** able result is death or grievous bodily harm (e.g., as in that case, driving at high speed in an erratic manner with a police officer clinging to the car), the logical processes available to the jury would appear to be as follows:

(a) They may, but do not have to, infer that death or grievous bodily harm was *intended* (CJA 1967, s. 8).
(b) They may, but do not have to, infer that death or grievous bodily harm was *foreseen* (CJA 1967, s. 8) *from which* they may, but do not have to, infer that death or grievous bodily

harm was *intended* (*Moloney* [1985] AC 905, *Nedrick* [1986] 3 All ER 1 and *Woollin* [1999] AC 82, and see **A2.4**).

(c) They may, in the light of all the evidence, decide not to draw the inferences in (a) or (b) above, and conclude that the accused lacked the *mens rea* for murder.

The difference between (a) and (b) is that in (a) the inference of intention is made directly, whereas in (b) it is made indirectly via foresight (of a virtual certainty, see *Nedrick* and *Woollin* at **B1.14**). Process (a) seems to be where the jury conclude from all the evidence that the accused intended death etc., in the sense that it was his purpose to cause it, and process (b) appears to be where a jury conclude that the accused intended death etc., even though it was not necessarily his purpose to cause it.

B1.14 **Direction on Foresight Rarely Needed**   Both the Court of Appeal and the House of Lords have clearly indicated that, normally, there will be no necessity to refer expressly to the accused's foresight (see *Fallon* [1994] Crim LR 519 for an example of a direction being needlessly complicated). In the words of Lord Lane CJ in *Nedrick* [1986] 3 All ER 1 at pp. 1027–8:

> [The jury] simply has to decide whether the defendant intended to kill or do serious bodily harm. In order to reach that decision the jury must pay regard to all the relevant circumstances, including what the defendant himself said and did.

> In the great majority of cases a direction to that effect will be enough, particularly where the defendant's actions amounted to a direct attack upon his victim, because in such cases the evidence relating to the defendant's desire or motive will be clear and his intent will have been the same as his desire or motive. But in some cases, of which this is one, the defendant does an act which is manifestly dangerous and as a result someone dies. The primary desire or motive of the defendant may not have been to harm that person, or indeed anyone. In that situation what further directions should a jury be given?…

> Where the charge is murder and in the rare cases where the simple direction is not enough, the jury should be directed that they are not entitled to infer the necessary intention, unless they feel sure that death or serious bodily harm was a virtual certainty (barring some unforeseen intervention) as a result of the defendant's actions and that the defendant appreciated that such was the case.

Lord Lane CJ used the words 'virtual certainty', but in *Walker* (1990) 90 Cr App R 226, the Court of Appeal, while obviously preferring this phrase, held that it was not a misdirection to instruct a jury in terms of 'a very high degree of probability'. This was permissible provided that the dividing line between intention and recklessness was not blurred as the House of Lords held had occurred in *Woollin* [1999] AC 82 through reference to foresight of 'a substantial risk'. Lord Steyn emphasised that the *Nedrick* direction was a 'tried and tested formula' which trial judges should continue to use. This was subject to, apparently for the purposes of clarity, the substitution of the words 'to find' for the words 'to infer'. See *Royle* [2014] 1 Cr App R (S) 296 (49), however, for another example of where the use of the tried and tested formula of foresight of virtual certainty may not be necessary if the direction actually given is appropriate to the facts of the case, especially where, if anything, it involves a higher hurdle than foresight of virtual certainty. 'You must be sure that he did not just realise that it [really serious harm] *could* happen but acted on the basis that it *would* or that he intended that it would' (at [20], emphasis added). Rafferty LJ said (at [27]) this direction 'contemplates not virtual certainty but certainty. We find it difficult to see how it can be a misdirection since it is to the benefit of the appellant…The appellant's case was complete denial. Consequently the direction upon intent avoided unnecessary elaboration and there was no need for further assistance or amplification in the *Nedrick/Woollin* tradition.'

It is perhaps worth noting, however, that the direction given is not ideal, not least because the words at the end of the quote 'or that he intended that it would', in contrasting intent with realisation of certainty, are explicable only on the basis that they refer to direct intent.

B1.15 It is instructive to look at the facts of *Nedrick*, as these illustrate the narrowing of the scope of malice aforethought over a period of time. The appellant poured paraffin through the front door of a house and set it alight, claiming that he wished to frighten the occupant but had no desire to kill or inflict grievous bodily harm. These facts are to all intents and purposes identical with those in *Hyam v DPP* [1975] AC 55, and in each case the death or deaths of child occupants were caused. Whereas the House of Lords in *Hyam v DPP* upheld a conviction for murder based on a direction that equated foresight of a high probability with intent, the same direction was held to be a misdirection in *Nedrick*. The conviction for murder was quashed and a verdict of manslaughter substituted.

It seems in such a case that the jury, if they accept the accused's evidence that he did not want to cause death or grievous bodily harm, would only be *entitled* to convict (and even then they would not be *compelled* to do so: see *Scalley* [1995] Crim LR 504 and the final observation of Lord Steyn in *Woollin*) if they felt sure that the accused foresaw death or grievous bodily harm as a 'virtual certainty'. See now the comments of the Court of Appeal in *Re A (Children) (Conjoined twins: surgical separation)* [2001] 4 All ER 961 where two of the judges (Ward and Brooke LJJ) seemed to assume that, if a doctor operates on conjoined twins knowing that the death of one of them is virtually certain to result, that in law amounts to an intention to kill. There was no reference to any discretion of the jury to find or not find intention. However, in *Mathews* [2003] 2 Cr App R 461, the Court of Appeal confirmed that it was still a matter for the jury and that 'the law has not yet reached a definition of intent in murder in terms of appreciation of virtual certainty'. The discretion left to the jury as to the inference of intention from foresight of virtual certainty was regarded as 'a strength and not a weakness' by the Law Commission in its Report on Murder Manslaughter and Infanticide (Law Com No. 304 at para. 3.27); the Commission succinctly summarised the existing law:

(1) A person should be taken to intend a result if he or she acts in order to bring it about.
(2) In cases where the judge believes that justice may not be done unless an expanded understanding of intention is given, the jury should be directed as follows: an intention to bring about a result may be found if it is shown that the defendant thought that the result was a virtually certain consequence of his or her action.

Special Defences Generally

There are three special defences to murder — loss of control (replacing the common-law **B1.16** defence of provocation), diminished responsibility, and killing in pursuance of a suicide pact. All three are partial defences, reducing the offence from murder to manslaughter rather than leading to an outright acquittal, and the last two are still governed by the Homicide Act 1957 as amended by the CAJA 2009, ss. 52 to 56. Those amendments came into force on 4 October 2010 (SI 2010 No. 816). For offences committed from that date, the common-law defence of provocation (which was also previously partly governed by s. 3 of the 1957 Act) was abolished, s. 3 repealed and provocation replaced by the new purely statutory defence of 'loss of control' (contained in the CAJA 2009, ss. 54 and 55). Diminished responsibility remains a statutory defence contained in the Homicide Act 1957, s. 2, but the amendments under the CAJA 2009 made significant changes to its constituent elements as from 4 October 2010. Killing in pursuance of a suicide pact remains the creation of s. 4 of the 1957 Act, and was not amended by the CAJA 2009. Although for some considerable time after 4 October 2010 some homicide trials will relate to offences alleged to have been committed 'wholly or partly' (see the CAJA 2009, sch. 22, para. 7) before that date, these will be increasingly rare and, where they do arise, reference should be made to the 2013 and earlier editions of this work. The law set out in the remainder of this section is the law applicable to offences committed wholly on or after 4 October 2010, incorporating the changes made by the CAJA 2009.

The three partial defences are needed principally because the mandatory life sentence for mur- **B1.17** der does not leave any discretion to the judge in sentencing whereby he can take account of mitigating factors, as he would normally be able to do on lesser charges where the sentence is not fixed by law. There is, however, a view that, even if the mandatory penalty were to be abolished, these defences should be retained as serving 'the valuable function of removing certain specific categories of acts from the stigma attaching to a conviction for murder and of ensuring that the facts were determined after a proper hearing before a jury' (House of Lords Select Committee on Murder and Life Imprisonment 1989, para. 82).

Before turning to the three special defences in more detail, it should also be noted that the offence of infanticide (see **B1.88** to **B1.97**) also reduces the stigma and introduces discretion as to sentence in relation to what would otherwise be murder. The difference is, however, that infanticide is an independent offence, which can be charged from the outset, whereas manslaughter on the basis of a partial defence such as diminished responsibility arises only by way of defence to an initial charge of murder. Infanticide is, however, an alternative verdict to murder (as, of course, is manslaughter) (see **B1.4**).

DIMINISHED RESPONSIBILITY

Basis of Defence

B1.18   This defence is purely statutory, having been introduced for the first time into English law (it had long been known to the Scottish courts) by the Homicide Act 1957, s. 2.

Homicide Act 1957, s. 2 (as amended by the CAJA 2009, s. 52)

(1) A person ('D') who kills or is a party to the killing of another is not to be convicted of murder if D was suffering from an abnormality of mental functioning which—
    (a) arose from a recognised medical condition,
    (b) substantially impaired D's ability to do one or more of the things mentioned in subsection (1A), and
    (c) provides an explanation for D's acts and omissions in doing or being a party to the killing.

(1A) Those things are—
    (a) to understand the nature of D's conduct;
    (b) to form a rational judgment;
    (c) to exercise self-control.

(1B) For the purposes of subsection (1)(c), an abnormality of mental functioning provides an explanation for D's conduct if it causes, or is a significant contributory factor in causing, D to carry out that conduct.

(2) On a charge of murder, it shall be for the defence to prove that the person charged is by virtue of this section not liable to be convicted of murder.

(3) A person who but for this section would be liable, whether as principal or as accessory, to be convicted of murder shall be liable instead to be convicted of manslaughter.

(4) The fact that one party to a killing is by virtue of this section not liable to be convicted of murder shall not affect the question whether the killing amounted to murder in the case of any other party to it.

The substitution of s. 2(1) had effect from 4 October 2010 (see SI 2010 No. 816).

Section 2(1) is the only subsection affected by the CAJA 2009, but it contains the most important definitional provisions. Section 2(2) is unaffected and has always put the burden of proof on the defence, although this burden is only required to be on the balance of probabilities rather than beyond reasonable doubt (*Dunbar* [1958] 1 QB 1, and see generally **F3.9** and **F3.54**). The placing of the burden on the defence does not breach the ECHR, Article 6, and is therefore unaffected by the HRA 1998 (*Lambert* [2001] 1 All ER 1014), more recently confirmed in *Foye* [2013] EWCA Crim 475 where the issue was thoroughly rehearsed and the legal burden was emphatically confirmed as justified and necessary. The prosecution are themselves allowed to allege diminished responsibility where the accused puts forward a defence of insanity (Criminal Procedure (Insanity) Act 1964, s. 6), and in such a case (which it is difficult to imagine arising very often, but see *Nott* (1958) 43 Cr App R 8) the prosecution must satisfy the normal burden of proof beyond a reasonable doubt.

The defence of diminished responsibility has largely replaced the insanity defence in murder cases. However, it is not available on a charge of attempted murder (*Campbell* [1997] Crim LR 495) nor under the Criminal Procedure (Insanity) Act 1964, s. 4A(2), following a finding of unfitness to plead (*Antoine* [2001] 1 AC 340). The courts have interpreted and applied the defence in a fairly flexible manner to enable it to reduce a wide range of killings, where there are compelling mitigating circumstances, from murder to manslaughter, provided that there was some supporting medical evidence to enable the court to be satisfied of the required ingredients.

Abnormality of Mental Functioning The phrase 'abnormality of mental functioning' **B1.19** replaces the original concept of 'abnormality of mind' (a concept defined in the leading case of *Byrne* [1960] 2 QB 396 as much wider than 'defect of reason' within the M'Naghten Rules (see **A3.28**) and as 'wide enough to cover the mind's activities in all its aspects' (Lord Parker CJ at p. 403)).

The change to 'abnormality of mental functioning' is not intended to have major effects in practice but is part of the attempt to use language and concepts which more accurately or appropriately focus directly on how medical conditions can affect an individual's control and understanding of his behaviour and thus to be more susceptible to relevant and coherent medical evidence consistent with up-to-date medical knowledge. Focusing on mental functioning avoids impenetrable philosophical questions about the nature of 'mind' and addresses directly the issue of how normally or abnormally did the mental processes of the accused function.

The abnormality of mental functioning must have arisen 'from a recognised medical condition'. This is a more substantial change and replaces the rather vague list of permissible causes of the abnormality in the original s. 2(1) with a concept that seems at first sight rather more precise. However, the Court of Appeal in *Dowds* [2012] 3 All ER 154 has ruled that the presence of a recognised medical condition is 'a necessary, but not always sufficient, condition to raise the issue of diminished responsibility'. In particular, the inclusion of 'acute intoxication' and 'alcohol intoxication' as disorders in the international classification systems, ICD-10 and DSM-IV respectively, does not alter the previous rule that voluntary intoxication (unclouded by alcoholism or dependence) does not give rise to the defence. Hughes LJ also pointed out (at [31]) other listed conditions which the courts are likely to be reluctant to recognise as giving rise to an abnormality of mental functioning within the section including 'unhappiness', 'irritability and anger' and 'paedophilia'. In discussing the broader question of temporary or transient conditions, Hughes LJ (at [39]) perhaps gave a clue as to the type of conditions which will qualify:

> ...there may be *genuine mental conditions, in no sense the fault of the defendant and well recognised by doctors*, which although temporary may indeed be within the ambit of the Act. Whether concussion, for example, is such a condition is a question which does not arise for decision in this case. (emphasis added)

Since it is a necessary even if not a sufficient condition, medical evidence will clearly be essential to show that the abnormality arose from a recognised medical condition. The 'practical necessity' that there should be medical evidence adduced by the accused was emphasised in *Bunch* [2013] EWCA Crim 2498, where it was also stressed that this evidence must be capable of discharging the burden on the accused to show on the balance of probabilities that each ingredient of the defence is made out. Thus, the very limited indirect evidence given of alcohol dependency, even if it could establish that medical condition, provided 'no evidence on which the jury could find that the applicant was suffering from an abnormality of mental functioning which arose from that medical condition and which substantially impaired one of the three capacities mentioned in the Act' (at [10]).

Although the Law Commission recommendations from which the new definition was devised included, in addition to abnormality of mental functioning, 'developmental immaturity' as a permissible alternative or supplementary explanation for the killing (Law Com No. 304, para. 5.125), this was rejected by the government as going too far and is not included in the

Act. The view was taken that there was sufficient protection for appropriate cases which would qualify under the heading of a 'recognised medical condition', learning disabilities and autistic spectrum disorders being given as examples that could qualify in this way (Ministry of Justice Response to Consultation CP(R) 19/08, paras. 97 to 103).

B1.20 Substantial Impairment   Notwithstanding the retention of the word 'responsibility' in the title of the defence, the thing to be substantially impaired is no longer explicitly (and somewhat obscurely) stated as D's 'mental responsibility' but instead it is his 'ability' to do one or more of the things listed in s. 2(1A) (which to a large extent echo Lord Parker's explication of abnormality of mind under the old law in *Parker* [1960] 2 QB 396), i.e. the ability to understand the nature of D's conduct, to form a rational judgement, to exercise self-control.

Medical evidence will again be highly relevant (a 'practical necessity' — see *Bunch* [2013] EWCA Crim 2498 at **B1.19**) as to whether D's ability to do these things was or could have been impaired by his abnormality of mental functioning and medical witnesses will no doubt feel more comfortable testifying directly about such matters rather than relating their evidence to the non-medical concept of responsibility. However, whilst the question of whether such abilities actually were impaired, and to what extent, may be a medical question on which the medical evidence may in most cases be effectively determinative, the evaluation of whether a particular degree of impairment should be characterised as sufficiently 'substantial' to enable the defence to succeed is still ultimately a question of fact and degree for the jury. In *Golds* [2014] EWCA Crim 748, a number of earlier cases on the meaning of the word substantial were reviewed. The view taken in some cases, that substantial meant simply 'more than trivial or minimal' was rejected. The question of whether an impairment was substantial was a matter for the jury who normally would be best left to apply the word for themselves. If further elucidation did become necessary, the (more restrictive) approach first adopted in *Simcox* (1964) *The Times*, 25 February 1964 should be followed, i.e. that there might be some impairment yet it still might not necessarily be substantial in the sense that it may not be 'something that made any really great difference'.

B1.21 Providing an Explanation for Acts and Omissions   Under the old law, the issue of 'substantial impairment' provided the main focus for the evaluative question which ultimately the jury had to decide. The new definition appears to add, in s. 2(1)(c), another evaluative component, whether the abnormality 'provides an explanation for D's acts and omissions in doing or being a party to the killing'. This phrase originates with the Law Commission which referred to an 'appropriate connection' between the abnormality and the killing (Law Com No. 304, para. 5.124) in terms of 'mitigation' rather than committing itself to a potentially problematic requirement of strict causation. However, the government was insistent that there must be an explicit causal requirement and thus s. 2(1B) was added to spell out that an abnormality of mental functioning provides an explanation within s. 2(1)(c) 'if it causes, or is a significant contributory factor in causing, D to carry out' the offence. Whether s. 2(1B) achieves its desired effect may be questioned since it could be interpreted as simply giving a common, or the most common, illustration of where the abnormality will provide an explanation but does not exclude other cases where the abnormality should be regarded as fulfilling an explanatory and mitigatory role even though it may not be possible to prove even a contributory causal effect. After all, s. 2(1B) does not say 'if, but only if' and, if it was to be read in that way, why have the primary concept of providing 'an explanation' in s. 2(1)(c) in the first place if it is to be exhaustively defined in s. 2(1B) as requiring causation? If that was the intention, it would have been perfectly possible, and simpler and clearer, to insert the causal requirement directly into s. 2(1)(c) without using the misleading mediating concept of 'provides an explanation'.

B1.22   Whether s. 2(1B) is treated as a partial or exhaustive definition of providing 'an explanation', it is clear that it does not require the abnormality to be the sole cause of the killing; it can be a contributory cause, although this must be a significant rather than trivial contribution. How one measures and proves the degree of causation of human behaviour may well throw up some difficulties but no doubt these will be matters for the jury to evaluate. It is in this context that the difficulties the courts experienced under the old law, relating to the influence of alcohol and drugs (*Dietschmann* [2003] 1 AC 1209) and how to deal with conditions such as alcohol dependency syndrome (*Tandy* [1989] 1 All ER 267; *Wood* [2008] 3 All ER 898; *Stewart* [2010] 1 All ER 260), are likely to resurface. Whatever the correct analysis of the old law might be, the position under the new law would appear to rest on the following questions:

(1) What abnormality of mental functioning arose from the recognised medical condition (i.e. not from other causes such as voluntary intoxication)?
(2) Did *that* abnormality of mental functioning substantially impair D's ability to do the things mentioned in s. 2(1A)?
(3) Did *that* abnormality of mental functioning provide an explanation for D's acts and omissions in doing or being a party to the killing as required by s. 2(1)(c)?

In relation to question (3), the fact that D may not have killed had he not been drunk should not automatically deprive him of the defence if the abnormality could also have influenced his decision to do the acts or omissions constituting the offence. On the other hand, if he would still have killed anyway, even without the abnormality of mental functioning, the exhaustive interpretation of s. 2(1B) would say that (there being no significant contributory cause, according to the Ministry of Justice Response to Consultation) there would be no defence. The partial definition interpretation of s. 2(1B), on the other hand, would say that there is still a question to be asked as to whether the abnormality provides a satisfactory (mitigatory) explanation other than a causal one (which is perhaps most likely to be relevant where the ability substantially impaired under s. 2(1A) was D's ability to form a rational judgement rather than to exercise self-control).

Accepting Plea of Diminished Responsibility

It has already been noted that one cannot initially charge manslaughter on the basis of diminished responsibility, and so the accused has to be indicted for murder no matter how clearly he appears to come within the terms of the Homicide Act 1957, s. 2(1). In some cases the prosecution may be able to accept a plea of manslaughter to an indictment for murder. In *Cox* [1968] 1 All ER 386, Winn LJ said (at p. 310):

B1.23

> ...that there are cases where, on an indictment for murder, it is perfectly proper, where the medical evidence is plainly to this effect, to treat the case as one of substantially diminished responsibility and accept, if it be tendered, a plea to manslaughter on that ground, and avoid a trial for murder.

However, the Court of Appeal in *Vinagre* (1979) 69 Cr App R 104 warned (in the context of the acceptance of a plea based on the 'Othello syndrome') that:

> ...it was never intended that pleas should be accepted on flimsy grounds [but only] when there is clear evidence of mental imbalance. We do not consider that in this case there was clear evidence of mental imbalance. There was clear evidence of killing by a jealous husband which, until modern times, no one would have thought was anything else but murder. (per Lawton LJ, at pp. 106–7)

Thus, in a novel or borderline sort of case, the plea ought not to be accepted but the evidence presented to a jury for their determination. The public interest may demand this in a notorious case such as that of the 'Yorkshire Ripper' (*The Times*, 23 May 1981). This was a striking case, in the sense that the prosecution were prepared to accept the plea in the light of unanimous psychiatric reports that the accused, Sutcliffe, was a paranoid schizophrenic, but the judge insisted that there should be a trial before a jury who convicted of murder. The nub of the problem is that, however unanimous the medical witnesses may be about there being an abnormality of mental functioning, the question of whether that abnormality 'substantially impaired D's ability' within the meaning of s. 2(1)(b) is ultimately not a medical question but one for the jury. Thus, as a general rule, the prosecution should accept a plea (and the judge should only approve that acceptance) only where there is clear and persuasive evidence of each of the required elements of diminished responsibility. There may be exceptional cases where it is desirable to accept a plea on the basis of less convincing evidence because a trial is undesirable for other reasons, e.g., the accused is himself seriously and terminally ill.

LOSS OF CONTROL

B1.24   The statutory defence of loss of control, created by the CAJA 2009, ss. 54 and 55, came into force on 4 October 2010 (SI 2010 No. 816). Section 56 abolished the common-law defence of provocation in relation to killings from that date.

Coroners and Justice Act 2009, ss. 54 and 55

54.—(1) Where a person ('D') kills or is a party to the killing of another ('V'), D is not to be convicted of murder if—

    (a) D's acts and omissions in doing or being a party to the killing resulted from D's loss of self-control,

    (b) the loss of self-control had a qualifying trigger, and

    (c) a person of D's sex and age, with a normal degree of tolerance and self-restraint and in the circumstances of D, might have reacted in the same or in a similar way to D.

(2) For the purposes of subsection (1)(a), it does not matter whether or not the loss of control was sudden.

(3) In subsection (1)(c) the reference to 'the circumstances of D' is a reference to all of D's circumstances other than those whose only relevance to D's conduct is that they bear on D's general capacity for tolerance or self-restraint.

(4) Subsection (1) does not apply if, in doing or being a party to the killing, D acted in a considered desire for revenge.

(5) On a charge of murder, if sufficient evidence is adduced to raise an issue with respect to the defence under subsection (1), the jury must assume that the defence is satisfied unless the prosecution proves beyond reasonable doubt that it is not.

(6) For the purposes of subsection (5), sufficient evidence is adduced to raise an issue with respect to the defence if evidence is adduced on which, in the opinion of the trial judge, a jury, properly directed, could reasonably conclude that the defence might apply.

(7) A person who, but for this section, would be liable to be convicted of murder is liable instead to be convicted of manslaughter.

(8) The fact that one party to a killing is by virtue of this section not liable to be convicted of murder does not affect the question whether the killing amounted to murder in the case of any other party to it.

55.—(1) This section applies for the purposes of section 54.

(2) A loss of self-control had a qualifying trigger if subsection (3), (4) or (5) applies.

(3) This subsection applies if D's loss of self-control was attributable to D's fear of serious violence from V against D or another identified person.

(4) This subsection applies if D's loss of self-control was attributable to a thing or things done or said (or both) which—

    (a)   constituted circumstances of an extremely grave character, and

    (b)   caused D to have a justifiable sense of being seriously wronged.

(5) This subsection applies if D's loss of self-control was attributable to a combination of the matters mentioned in subsections (3) and (4).

(6) In determining whether a loss of self-control had a qualifying trigger—

    (a)   D's fear of serious violence is to be disregarded to the extent that it was caused by a thing which D incited to be done or said for the purpose of providing an excuse to use violence;

    (b)   a sense of being seriously wronged by a thing done or said is not justifiable if D incited the thing to be done or said for the purpose of providing an excuse to use violence;

    (c)   the fact that a thing done or said constituted sexual infidelity is to be disregarded.

(7) In this section references to 'D' and 'V' are to be construed in accordance with section 54.

The Elements of the Defence

B1.25   **Qualifying Triggers**   The new statutory defence differs from the previous common law in that the broad concept of 'provocation' (which was thought too readily to indulge predominantly male 'anger') is abandoned in favour of more specifically limited 'qualifying triggers' for loss of control. The trigger which most closely relates to the former defence of provocation (in the CAJA 2009, s. 55(4), 'attributable to a thing or things done or said') is designed to be *much* more limited in also requiring both 'circumstances of an extremely grave character' and the causing of 'a justifiable sense of being seriously wronged'. See *Dawes* [2013] 3 All ER 308 for examples (in the cases of appellants Hatter and Bowyer) of situations which clearly do not satisfy the new more stringent trigger. These essentially objective limitations indicate a shift in philosophy from what might primarily have been seen as one of 'partial excuse' underpinning the defence of provocation to the new defence being primarily based on 'partial justification'. Similarly with the other qualifying trigger (s. 55(3)), 'fear of serious violence from V', which is clearly related to the justificatory defence of self-defence but is only a partial justification because D has not acted proportionately and has lost control and has, implicitly, used excessive force. This qualifying trigger, in contrast to the 'things done or said' trigger, does of course broaden the scope of the available partial defences to murder. It is in particular designed to accommodate more readily the dilemma faced by those, most typically women afraid of a violent partner (often as the result of violent and abusive conduct over an extended period of time), for whom the sudden and temporary requirement of the common law of provocation had frequently been a stumbling block. Furthermore, s. 55(5) makes it clear that D can rely on a combination of the two triggers as causing his or her loss of self-control.

The partially justificatory aspect of the qualifying triggers is also evident in s. 55(6)c) providing **B1.26** that the fact that 'a thing said or done constituted sexual infidelity' is to be disregarded when determining whether a loss of self-control has a qualifying trigger. The inclusion of this sub-paragraph was insisted upon by the government, despite attempts in Parliament to remove it, as being necessary to ensure that violent men could no longer hope to rely on sexual infidelity as a ground for a partial defence to murder. It was acknowledged that the thing 'said or done' may still be relevant to whether there is a qualifying trigger for reasons other than its character as sexual infidelity. Thus, for example, finding one's partner having incestuous sex or having sex with a minor might still be capable of being a qualifying trigger not because it constitutes sexual infidelity but because of the nature of the sexual activity involved. The 'formidable' difficulties of interpretation of s. 55(6)(c) have been extensively discussed by Lord Judge CJ in *Clinton* [2012] 2 All ER 947, where the prohibition on having regard to sexual infidelity has been held to apply only where sexual infidelity is the sole potential qualifying trigger. Where, however, as will often be the case, there are other matters which may potentially give rise to a qualifying trigger (e.g., as was the case in *Clinton*, the taunting of D as to his lack of courage to commit the suicide which he had contemplated) and sexual infidelity is integral to and forms an essential part of the context in which to make a just evaluation of whether those other matters are grave or serious enough to constitute a qualifying trigger, the sexual infidelity is not excluded. As to the precise meaning of sexual infidelity in terms of 'things done', it was acknowledged that there will be difficult cases at the margins in terms of what counts as infidelity (how long or strong does a relationship have to be before one can be unfaithful in it) and in terms of what sort of conduct is sufficiently 'sexual'. However, it was clarified (at [26]) that things 'said' constituting sexual infidelity include 'admissions of sexual infidelity (even if untrue) as well as reports (by others) of sexual infidelity'.

Section 55(6)(a) and (b) further limit the scope of the triggers and together have the effect of excluding from the ambit of either trigger, things 'incited...for the purpose of providing an excuse to use violence'. The new statutory limitation applies only where D acts for the 'purpose' of providing an excuse as opposed to situations where his blameworthy conduct has in fact prompted the provocation even though that was not his purpose.

See *Dawes* [2013] 3 All ER 308, where the Court of Appeal found that there was not sufficient evidence of such 'purpose'; the judge was therefore wrong to withdraw the defence from the jury on this ground (s. 55(6)(a) or (b)).

Killing Resulting from Loss of Self-control Even if the loss of self-control has a qualifying tri- **B1.27** gger, there is still a requirement that the killing resulted from the loss of self-control (CAJA 2009,

s. 54(1)(a)). This requirement can be thought of as analogous to the subjective condition in the old law of provocation but of course there are differences. In particular, s. 54(2) provides that the loss of self-control need not be sudden, a limitation which the common law of provocation had not quite managed formally to shed even though, certainly since *Ahluwalia* [1992] 4 All ER 889, it had been effectively recognised that 'sudden' did not necessarily connote 'immediately' and that a delayed but sudden reaction could come within the defence. Nevertheless, the formal removal of the suddenness requirement should be a further step in opening up the defence to the victims of domestic violence and abuse in relation to whose delayed reactions the requirement of suddenness under the old law could seem a problematic or inhibitory factor. The legitimate concern that underlay the requirement of suddenness was that partial defences should not apply to killings motivated by revenge and s. 54(4) goes directly to this point by excluding from the defence cases where D 'acted in a considered desire for revenge'. In *Clinton* [2012] 2 All ER 947 Lord Judge CJ (at [128]) approved a direction which included the statement that 'a considered act of revenge, whether performed calmly or in anger, is not a loss of self control'. There is a danger that the effect of this may be to downplay the impact of the removal of 'suddenness' insofar as a delayed but angry reaction is treated as considered revenge and not loss of control. See also *Jewell* [2014] EWCA Crim 414, where the trial judge was found to be correct not to have left the defence to the jury in a case described by the Court of Appeal as a 'planned execution'.

B1.28   **Normal Degree of Tolerance and Self-restraint**   Section 54(1)(c) of the CAJA 2009 addresses the question previously characterised in the common law as the objective question of how the reasonable man would have reacted, although it is in truth a mixture of subjective and objective considerations. It is similarly subjective to the former test laid down in the cases of *DPP v Camplin* [1978] AC 705 and *A-G for Jersey v Holley* [2005] AC 580 in that it concerns how a person of the age and sex of the accused would react and is similarly objective insofar as it assumes the 'normal degree of tolerance and self-restraint' of a person of that age and sex. Like the *Camplin/Holley* test it also recognises a further limited subjective aspect but it is formulated quite differently. Instead of asking whether the accused's characteristics would affect the gravity of the trigger for the loss of self-control (formerly the gravity of the provocation question), the statute now directs attention specifically to how a person (of normal tolerance and self restraint) '*in the circumstances of D*' might have reacted. This may open up a broader range of subjective considerations than under the *Camplin/Holley* test, notwithstanding that, rather like the old law, s. 54(3) effectively excludes circumstances 'whose only relevance to D's conduct is that they bear on D's general capacity for tolerance or self-restraint'. The difference is however that, whilst roughly the same sorts of things are *excluded*, there is now no positive requirement that, to be *included*, D's individual circumstances have to affect the gravity of the triggering conduct. Instead, all D's circumstances are included, provided only that they do not bear on his capacity for tolerance or self-restraint and they can be considered directly in terms of how he might have reacted rather than in relation to what was effectively the subsidiary question of whether they affected the gravity of the provocation/triggering conduct. Although this may be thought to be a somewhat subtle change, it is a sensible and desirable one in that juries were often baffled by the gravity of the provocation/ powers of self-control dichotomy, and it makes it more straightforward to take into account D's circumstances (such as having been the victim of a long-term abusive relationship) even though it was in principle possible to bring this in as a factor affecting the gravity of the provocation. It is no longer necessary to make this connection and all the circumstances of D may be considered provided that they do not bear 'only' on D's 'general capacity for tolerance or self-restraint'.

B1.29   **Significance of the Concept of Tolerance**   The presence of the word 'or' after 'tolerance' is important in the CAJA 2009, s. 54(3). It shows that tolerance is a distinct concept from self-restraint (contrast the word 'and' in s. 54(1)(c) which confirms nevertheless that both qualities are required). Self-restraint is very similar to the old concept of self-control in the abolished provocation defence but 'tolerance' is now added as a separate, additional component of the objective criterion. Tolerance is also apt to exclude those who are bigoted or prejudiced against individuals from minority, vulnerable or protected groups in society or who are unacceptably intolerant in other ways, e.g., because of unacceptable attitudes such as those underpinning so-called 'honour killings' or because of excessive jealousy or sexual possessiveness. The term 'tolerance' can thus be seen to be relevant to Lord Hoffmann's concern (under the old law) in *Smith (Morgan)* [2001] 1 AC 146 at p. 169 that 'male possessiveness and jealousy should not today be an acceptable reason for loss of self-control leading to homicide'. In *Clinton* [2012] 2 All ER 947, the Court of Appeal has ruled that the restriction on the relevance of sexual infidelity in s. 55(6) in relation to it being a qualifying trigger does not restrict the meaning of 'the circumstances of D' in s. 54(3) and that sexual infidelity can be taken into account in deciding whether a person with an ordinary degree of tolerance and self-restraint might have reacted in a similar way. The effect would seem to be that the jury will have to weigh the impact of the sexual infidelity (and other triggering conduct) against the ordinary degree of tolerance (and the ordinary degree of self-restraint) which they would expect to be shown and make a judgement. This seems a more nuanced and appropriate way of dealing with sexual infidelity, insisting on an ordinary degree of 'tolerance' from the accused in the face of it, rather than artificially insisting that it should be ignored altogether. It also has to be remembered that the question of what a person with an ordinary degree of tolerance and self restraint would have done, in the case of the things 'done or said' trigger, does not really arise unless there is evidence that those things done or said satisfied the test of being 'extremely grave' and caused a 'justifiable sense of being seriously wronged'. In other words, and this applies whether or not sexual infidelity is involved, there is quite a high objective test to be surmounted in the test for the qualifying trigger in s. 55(4) before one gets on to the objective aspects of the test of tolerance and self-restraint under s. 54(1)(c).

Intoxication   Although the Act does not specifically mention intoxication, it was always **B1.30** likely, given the general approach to intoxication in defences, as exemplified most recently in *Dowds* [2012] 3 All ER 154 in relation to diminished responsibility, that the effects of voluntary intoxication would not be found to be relevant to the question of whether the person of normal tolerance and self-restraint might have reacted in a similar way to D. In *Asmelash* [2014] QB 103 the Court of Appeal not unexpectedly, confirmed that, in considering the question under s. 54(1)(c) of whether 'a person of D's sex and age, with a normal degree of tolerance and self-restraint and in the circumstances of D, might have reacted in the same or similar way to D', the fact that the accused had voluntarily consumed alcohol was not to be included in D's circumstances. Lord Judge CJ upheld the following direction from the trial judge: 'Are you sure that a person of [D's] sex and age with a normal degree of tolerance and self-restraint and in the same circumstances, *but unaffected by alcohol*, would not have reacted in the same or similar way?' (emphasis added). His lordship went on to point out (at [25]) that this:

> ...does not mean that the defendant who has been drinking is deprived of any possible loss of control defence...If a sober individual in the defendant's circumstances, with normal levels of tolerance and self-restraint might have behaved in the same way as the defendant confronted by the relevant qualifying trigger, he would not be deprived of the loss of control defence just because he was not sober.

It was also acknowledged that different considerations would apply to the quite different situation of a person mercilessly taunted about a severe alcohol or drug problem which would then form part of the circumstances. The decision about the irrelevance of the voluntary intoxication has also to be read in the light of the fact that it was not suggested in this case that D's intoxication:

> ...caused him to be mistaken about anything that was going on at the relevant time, or about what he was doing. Accordingly, the only relevance of the drunkenness was that it affected the appellant's self-restraint and caused him to act in a way in which he would not have acted if sober (at [19]).

The fact that *Asmelash* was not a case of intoxicated mistake and was purely about intoxication **B1.31** affecting self-restraint may be important. Insofar as intoxication simply diminishes D's tolerance or self-restraint, it is clearly excluded anyway by s. 54(3). However, s. 54(3) appears only to exclude a circumstance if that is its 'only' relevance; so if D can point to some other relevance of his intoxication to his conduct (e.g., that it caused a relevant mistake), he might be able to bring it into consideration, although it is difficult to envisage how this would add much to the defences already available such as lack of specific intent. If the mistake was one whereby he exaggerated the nature of the triggering conduct, the issue might then be whether there is in fact a qualifying trigger in the first place and the extent to which a mistaken belief, drunken or otherwise, in the existence of a trigger can give rise to a defence under the statute. In relation to the 'things done or said' trigger, the requirement of a justifiable sense of being seriously wronged might be used to counter any such argument but, in relation to the other trigger, D's fear of serious violence seems to be a subjective matter which would in principle have to take account of D's mistaken view of the facts, just as with self-defence. However, this analogy might also suggest that no account will be taken of such mistakes due to intoxication notwithstanding that murder is a crime of specific intent (*Hatton* [2006] 1 Cr App R 247, discussed at **A3.60**).

Burden of Proof and Role of Jury

B1.32 As under the previous defence of provocation, once there is evidence capable of supporting the defence, the burden of disproving it rests with the prosecution to the usual standard of beyond reasonable doubt. The CAJA 2009, s. 54(5), refers to 'sufficient evidence. . .to raise an issue with respect to the defence'. This is then explained in s. 54(6) as being sufficient evidence 'on which, in the opinion of the trial judge, a jury, properly directed, could reasonably conclude that the defence might apply'. This presumably means that there must be sufficient evidence to raise an issue as to each of the three elements of the defence as defined in s. 54(1). With the repeal of the Homicide Act 1957, s. 3, there is no longer any equivalent to the previous duty on the judge in relation to provocation to leave the defence with the jury just because there is evidence that one element of the defence, the 'subjective condition' (roughly equating to the new s. 54(1)), was satisfied irrespective of the nature of the evidence about the 'objective condition'. On the other hand, it will no doubt continue to be incumbent on the trial judge to leave the new defence to the jury where the evidence given in the case is capable of satisfying the test in s. 54(6) even if the defence have not for tactical or other reasons themselves sought to rely on loss of control as a defence. That this approach continues to be the correct one was confirmed by Lord Judge CJ in *Dawes* [2013] 3 All ER 308 at [53] in the course of a wide-ranging judgment commenting on a number of aspects of the new defence. For an example of a case where the defence did seek to rely on the defence but which might not actually have needed to be left to the jury under the more demanding tests laid down in the new law, see the comments of Lord Judge CJ in *Clinton* [2012] 2 All ER 947 at [75] and [105] in considering the facts affecting the appellant Parker. See also the comments of Lord Judge in *Dawes* at [66] (concerning the accused Bowyer, a self-confessed burglar claiming to have a justifiable sense of being seriously wronged by the entirely reasonable response of the householder).

KILLING IN PURSUANCE OF SUICIDE PACT

B1.33   **Homicide Act 1957, s. 4**

> (1) It shall be manslaughter, and shall not be murder, for a person acting in pursuance of a suicide pact between him and another to kill the other or be a party to the other being killed by a third person.

The burden of proof that he was acting in pursuance of a suicide pact is placed on the accused by s. 4(2). This is a reverse legal burden on the balance of probabilities and is compatible with the ECHR, Article 6(2) (*A-G's Ref (No. 1 of 2004)* [2004] 4 All ER 457 (at [130]–[132])).

'Suicide pact' is defined in s. 4(3) as:

> . . .a common agreement between two or more persons having for its object the death of all of them, whether or not each is to take his own life, but nothing done by a person who enters into a suicide

pact shall be treated as done by him in pursuance of the pact unless it is done while he has the settled intention of dying in pursuance of the pact.

Thus the burden of proof on the accused involves not only proof that there was in fact a suicide pact, but also that at the time of the killing the accused still had the intention of dying himself.

Killing in pursuance of a suicide pact is closely related to the offence of complicity in suicide under the Suicide Act 1961, s. 2(1) (see **B1.136**). Section 2(2) provides that, if on an indictment for murder or manslaughter it is proved that the accused committed an offence under s. 2(1) (complicity in suicide), the jury may find him guilty of that offence. If the accused assisted or encouraged a killing by a third person, that is still potentially murder, but will be reduced to manslaughter under the Homicide Act 1957, s. 4, if it was done in pursuance of a suicide pact.

MANSLAUGHTER GENERALLY

Voluntary and Involuntary Manslaughter

Manslaughter can be classified as either voluntary or involuntary. Voluntary manslaughter has in effect already been considered, since it consists of those killings which would be murder (because the accused has the relevant *mens rea* — hence the label *voluntary* manslaughter) but which are reduced to manslaughter because of one of the three special defences, discussed at **B1.16** to **B1.33**. Voluntary manslaughter is not an offence one can be indicted for, but rather is a verdict which can result from an initial indictment for murder. The actual verdict, however, will be simply 'manslaughter' without the label of 'voluntary'.   **B1.34**

Involuntary manslaughter, on the other hand, refers to those types of manslaughter which can be charged in their own right and where the accused lacks the *mens rea* for murder, although equally they can result from an indictment for murder where the prosecution fail to prove the *mens rea*.   **B1.35**

The fact that a verdict of manslaughter can reflect a number of different views of the facts taken by the jury (or by different members of the same jury) can lead to difficulties in sentencing and in relation to the normal rule requiring unanimity of verdicts (cf. **D18.44**). It was said by the Court of Criminal Appeal in *Larkin* [1943] KB 174 that it was 'most undesirable' that the jury should be asked to explain the basis of their verdict. However, in *Matheson* [1958] 2 All ER 87 the Court of Criminal Appeal said (at p. 480) that if diminished responsibility and some other ground such as provocation are left to the jury, the judge may, and generally should, ask the jury whether the verdict was based on diminished responsibility, or on the other ground or on both. This matter was further considered in *Jones* (1999) *The Times*, 17 February 1999 (where neither of the above cases was referred to). The Court of Appeal made it clear that there is no obligation on the judge to ask any such question (of which advance warning should in any event be given), it being 'a matter entirely for him or her in the exercise of his or her discretion'. Neither is there any obligation on the jury to give an answer if asked, any such answer being merely additional information to help with sentence:

> ...provided that the jury are agreed that the defendant is guilty of manslaughter, in the sense that they are sure that he perpetrated an unlawful act which caused the death of the accused, it is unnecessary that there be any unanimity by the jury as to the route by which that verdict is achieved.

This seems right on the facts of the case and for those cases (the majority) where the offence is at least manslaughter and may be murder if malice aforethought can be established and if loss of control and diminished responsibility (if in issue) can be negatived. The prosecution has to prove causation and the unlawful act (such as an intentional assault), and negative complete defences such as self-defence if in issue, but the different possible reasons for an offence being manslaughter rather than murder are negative ones (reasonable doubt by the jury as to whether malice aforethought has been proved or whether diminished responsibility or loss of control has been negatived). It is not a question of the prosecution having to prove any of these things for manslaughter; manslaughter is merely the residual verdict for any one of these reasons. It is submitted however that it would be different if manslaughter is alleged on two fundamentally separate grounds: unlawful act and gross negligence. It should not be sufficient that six jurors thought that the accused's act causing death was unlawful but not grossly negligent and the other six thought it was grossly negligent but not unlawful. Here the prosecution have not proved either of the two forms of manslaughter beyond reasonable doubt; it is quite different from a case where what would otherwise be murder has been proved and the jurors merely differ as to the reason for *reducing* the offence to manslaughter (see Taylor, 'Jury Unanimity in Homicide' [2001] Crim LR 283 and HH Judge Clarke, 'Jury Unanimity — A Practitioner's Problem' [2001] Crim LR 301).

Definition of Involuntary Manslaughter

B1.36   Superficially, this is the same as the definition for murder (see **B1.1**) without the requirement of malice aforethought. This is only helpful in that it emphasises that requirements such as that the victim be a fully born human being are equally part of the offence of manslaughter. It is more common to refer to manslaughter as 'unlawful killing without malice aforethought', but this is not particularly helpful, because it does not indicate which killings will be regarded as unlawful in the absence of malice aforethought. In fact there now appear to be at least two main categories of killing without malice aforethought which are regarded as unlawful and hence amount to manslaughter:

(a) killing by an unlawful act likely to cause bodily harm — often called 'unlawful act manslaughter' or 'constructive manslaughter'; and
(b) killing grossly negligently.

There is also some authority (*Lidar* (11 November 1999 unreported)) for a third category of involuntary manslaughter, killing by subjective recklessness as to serious injury or death. It is arguable that such a category is not appropriate or necessary given the existence of unlawful act manslaughter, since any killing done with such recklessness would almost inevitably involve a sufficient unlawful act under the OAPA 1861 and, even if exceptionally for some reason it did not (e.g., because it was an omission rather than an act), it would be likely to come under gross negligence manslaughter. Although the latter has recently come to be limited to circumstances where there is a risk of death as opposed to serious injury, it is arguable that the same limitation should also now apply to any residual category of killing by subjective recklessness but this is as yet a matter awaiting judicial determination.

Procedure

B1.37   Manslaughter is triable only on indictment. It is a class 1A offence. It is a distinct offence from murder and attracts its own custody time-limit (*R (Wardle) v Crown Court at Leeds* [2002] 1 AC 754).

Indictment

B1.38

Statement of Offence

Manslaughter

Particulars of Offence

A on or about the...day of..., unlawfully killed V

Alternative Verdicts

These include:

B1.39

(a) child destruction (Infant Life (Preservation) Act 1929, s. 2(2)), see **B1.98** to **B1.106**;
(b) abortion (Infant Life (Preservation) Act 1929, s. 2(3)), see **B1.107** to **B1.117**;
(c) complicity in suicide (Suicide Act 1961, s. 2(2)), see **B1.136** to **B1.142**;
(d) assisting an offender (Criminal Law Act 1967, s. 4(2), see **B14.57**).

By way of exception to the general rule, there appears to be no such verdict as attempted manslaughter (*Bruzas* [1972] Crim LR 367; *Campbell* [1997] Crim LR 495).

Sentencing Guidelines: Diminished Responsibility

The maximum penalty is life imprisonment (OAPA 1861, s. 5).

B1.40

> In diminished responsibility cases there are various courses open to a judge. His choice of the right course will depend on the state of the evidence and the material before him. If the psychiatric reports recommend and justify it, and there are no contrary indications, he will make a hospital order. Where a hospital order is not recommended, or is not appropriate, and the defendant constitutes a danger to the public for an unpredictable period of time, the right sentence will, in all probabilities, be one of life imprisonment.
>
> In cases where the evidence indicates that the accused's responsibility for his acts was so grossly impaired that his degree of responsibility for them was minimal, then a lenient course will be open to the judge. Provided there is no danger of repetition of violence, it will usually be possible to make such an order as will give the accused his freedom, possibly with some supervision.
>
> There will however be cases in which there is no proper basis for a hospital order; but in which the accused's degree of responsibility is not minimal. In such cases the judge should pass a determinate sentence of imprisonment, the length of which will depend on two factors: his assessment of the degree of the accused's responsibility and his view as to the period of time, if any, for which the accused will continue to be a danger to the public. (*Chambers* (1983) 5 Cr App R (S) 190, per Leonard J at pp. 193–4)

The general approach set out in *Chambers* was endorsed by a five-member Court of Appeal in **B1.41**
Wood [2010] 1 Cr App R (S) 6. Although a life sentence would be rare in cases of diminished responsibility, in *Wood*, where the offender's culpability was very far from extinguished, and the attack on the victim had been horrific, sustained, and with a clear intent to kill, a life sentence with a minimum term of 13 years was appropriate. Subject to the specific element of reduced culpability in diminished responsibility cases, which in some cases could be small and in others very significant indeed, there plainly was a link to the principles set out in the CJA 2003, sch. 21, relating to sentencing for murder. The changes made by the 2003 Act meant that cases on sentencing diminished responsibility manslaughter decided before that Act came into effect should now be treated with the utmost caution. See also *Dighton* [2012] 1 Cr App R (S) 178, where a sentence of imprisonment for public protection with a minimum term of 12 years was imposed on a 35-year-old man who had stabbed both his parents to death. A life sentence was preferred to a hospital order in *Welsh* [2011] 2 Cr App R (S) 399 to reflect the offender's 'substantial responsibility' for the offence and a finding that the offender would remain dangerous even if his schizophrenia was brought under control by medication. The general approach set out in *Wood* should be read in light of the subsequent abolition of the sentence of imprisonment for public protection.

An example of the type of case where the court found the culpability of the offender to **B1.42**
be substantially reduced is *Derekis* [2005] 2 Cr App R (S) 1. After a long-running dispute between neighbours over levels of noise from the victim's home, the offender, a woman of 54, uttered threats after loud music came from the victim's home after 11 p.m. The female victim went to the offender's home to remonstrate with her. The offender opened the door

and stabbed the victim with a single blow to the heart, killing her. She pleaded guilty to manslaughter by reason of diminished responsibility. The Court of Appeal reduced the sentence of six years' imprisonment to three and a half years, on the basis that the offender was at the time of the offence suffering from a moderately severe depressive illness with associated anxiety and insomnia, she had no previous convictions, and the violence was completely out of character. See also *Gilliat* [2007] 1 Cr App R (S) 481. A suspended sentence was imposed in the wholly exceptional 'mercy killing' case of *Webb* [2011] 2 Cr App R (S) 353.

Sentencing Guidelines: Provocation and Loss of Control

B1.43 The definitive sentencing guideline, *Manslaughter by Reason of Provocation* (see Supplement, SG-28 *et seq.*), applies. The Court of Appeal in *O'Reilly* [2008] 2 Cr App R (S) 380 dealt with manslaughter by an 18-year-old offender who had stabbed his sister's partner following a violent attack on his sister. There was a 'substantial degree' of provocation, and a sentence of nine years' detention in a young offender institution was reduced on appeal to six years. Seven years' detention under the PCC(S)A 2000, s. 91, was reduced to four and a half years in *Calvert* [2010] 1 Cr App R (S) 321 where the 15-year-old offender stabbed his friend to death; the sentence was reduced to reflect the offender's youth and the 'high degree' of provocation from the victim prior to the killing. In *Banaszek* [2010] EWCA Crim 1076 the Court of Appeal dismissed an argument that an offender convicted of manslaughter on the ground of provocation could not qualify as a dangerous offender and receive a sentence of imprisonment for public protection. The Court did, however, reduce the minimum term from six years to four and a half years because the provocation should have been assessed by the trial judge as 'substantial', rather than 'low'. By contrast, in *Brook* [2012] 2 Cr App R (S) 433, the Court of Appeal held that a finding of dangerousness could not be based simply upon the facts of the offence together with information in the pre-sentence report, which was inconsistent with the verdict of the jury.

No specific sentencing guidelines exist as regards the loss of control defence to murder under the CAJA 2009, ss. 54 and 55. In *Thornley* [2011] 2 Cr App R (S) 361, although a case decided under the 1957 Act, the Court of Appeal said that the definitive sentencing guideline on manslaughter by reason of provocation must now be read in light of the re-casting of the offence and the indirect impact of the CJA 2003, sch. 21 (mandatory life sentences: see E3), in relation to murder, especially the increase in the minimum term for those who have committed murder having taken a knife to the scene (see E3.2). Lord Judge CJ said that the applicable starting point in the instant case was 12 years within a range of ten years to life, and that this provided 'an ample bracket', such that 'any sentence within that range would be consistent with the proper application of the Guideline'. The Court of Appeal in *Ward* [2013] 2 Cr App R (S) 233 (35) upheld a sentence of nine years' imprisonment following a plea of guilty where the offender had battered the victim to death following a low degree of provocation over a short period of time. The qualifying trigger was actual and anticipated violence. Sharp J said that the provocation guideline continued to provide useful assistance. Courts must now take into account both the higher threshold for loss of control manslaughter than for provocation manslaughter (given the need for a 'qualifying trigger' to be proved) and the increase in sentences imposed in manslaughter cases generally, but there was scope within the 'ample brackets' in the guideline to do so.

Sentencing Guidelines: Killing in Pursuance of Suicide Pact

B1.44 The maximum penalty is life imprisonment (OAPA 1861, s. 5).

The offender in *Sweeney* (1986) 8 Cr App R (S) 419 pleaded guilty to the manslaughter of his wife. He was prone to depression and had married the deceased when she was suffering from advanced muscular dystrophy. They decided to commit suicide together by taking tablets and then setting fire to their car when they were inside it. Once the fire started both tried to escape, but the wife was killed. The offender suffered serious burns. The Court of Appeal reduced a four-year prison term to one of two years, that being 'sufficient, in our judgment, to mark the seriousness of this matter'. See also *England* (1990) 12 Cr App R (S) 98.

Sentencing Guidelines: Constructive Manslaughter

The maximum penalty is life imprisonment (OAPA 1861, s. 5). **B1.45**

Fights In manslaughter arising from fights, 'the authorities demonstrate how widely the **B1.46** background facts vary in different cases' (per Bracewell J in *Cannon* [2001] 1 Cr App R (S) 286). In the leading case of *A-G's Ref (No. 60 of 2009) (Appleby)* [2010] 2 Cr App R (S) 311 a five-member Court of Appeal reviewed a large number of cases where the victim had been killed as a result of violence in which no weapon had been used and in which, but for the death of the victim, the offence would have been an assault under the OAPA 1861, s. 47 or s. 20. Lord Judge CJ referred to the well-known authority of *Coleman* (1992) 13 Cr App R (S) 508, a case in which death resulted from a single blow followed by a fall which 'almost accidentally' resulted in the deceased sustaining a fractured skull. It had been said in that case that the starting point on a plea of guilty was 12 months' imprisonment. That decision, however, should be 'strictly confined' to those facts, but it had been cited in many later cases subsumed by the generic description of 'one-punch manslaughter'. This description was apt to mislead unless so limited. Regard must now be had to the legislative changes made since that case, especially by the CJA 2003, and to the problem of gratuitous violence in streets and city centres which was a significant aggravating feature in many manslaughter cases. What is now required, without diminishing the importance of the offender's culpability, is for attention also to be given to the consequences of those actions. For the future his lordship said, 'we doubt the value of reference to any sentencing decisions prior to *Furby* [2006] 2 Cr App R (S) 64, which was also a case of manslaughter at its lowest level'. The Court then proceeded to deal with the individual appeals. Of illustrative value is *Cowles*, where sentences of seven years and seven years, six months were upheld in a case where the victim had tried to intervene in a violent attack by the two offenders on another man. The victim had been punched, seized around the neck in a headlock and punched repeatedly to the face. He never regained consciousness. Lord Judge CJ said that such a case had 'nothing whatsoever to do with one-punch manslaughter'. It is also clear from the authorities that cases where there was an accidental fall resulting in a fractured skull are to be distinguished from more serious cases where a victim on the ground has been kicked about the head or where a weapon has been used. According to Hutchinson LJ in *Harrison* [1996] 2 Cr App R (S) 250, 'cases of this sort which are superficially similar are often found on closer examination to differ in important details'. In *A-G's Ref (No. 16 of 2014) (Gill)* [2014] EWCA Crim 956 the Court of Appeal upheld a sentence of four years' imprisonment following a guilty plea where the 21-year-old offender had struck the 41-year-old victim a single blow to the face, causing him to fall and strike his head on the road. The victim died later in hospital. The Court, applying *Appleby*, said that culpability still remained an important factor in these cases, and suggested that the Sentencing Council might consider issuing a guideline to assist sentencers. Where death was occasioned by no more than a push, causing the intoxicated victim to fall down some stairs, culpability was 'very low' and, even in the light of the general increase in sentence signalled in *Appleby*, the sentence was reduced from three and a half years to two years in *Bebbington* [2012] 1 Cr App R (S) 99.

In *A-G's Ref (No. 113 of 2006)* [2007] 2 Cr App R (S) 162, the 15-year-old offender pleaded **B1.47** guilty to manslaughter after 'showing off' by striking a man with a single blow to the face. The victim suffered a fractured skull and died the following day. The Court of Appeal said that, in the light of earlier authorities (helpfully reviewed in *A-G's Ref (No. 9 of 2005)* [2005] 2 Cr App R (S) 664), the sentence in the current case could fall anywhere in a bracket between two-and-a-half and five years. Here the age of the offender was an important factor, and an extended sentence of detention with a custodial term of three years and an extension period of three years was not, in all the circumstances, an unduly lenient sentence: 'A blow sufficient to fracture an egg-shell skull is very much less culpable than one which fractures a normal skull. An unlucky punch in the course of a spontaneous fight is very different from a wholly unprovoked blow to an innocent bystander.' A classic 'eggshell skull' case is *Harvey* [2011] 1 Cr App R (S) 286 where, during a 'domestic tiff' the offender threw a television remote control at his wife, which hit her behind the ear. Unknown to anyone, she had an unusual weakness of the vertebral artery, which ruptured and caused her death. Save for the death, the offence charged would have been common assault. The Court of Appeal said that this was 'a genuinely singular set of circumstances' and reduced a sentence of three years' imprisonment to one of 21 months.

B1.48 **Weapons**   Where a knife has been taken to the scene, and has been used to kill, whether in circumstances of some provocation or excessive force being used in self-defence, or in circumstances of lack of intent to cause really serious injury, a range of ten to 12 years' imprisonment after a trial is appropriate (*Carter* [2003] 2 Cr App R (S) 524). Twelve years following a trial was upheld in *Bishop* [2012] 1 Cr App R (S) 60 where the offender had sought out a man who had been harassing his girlfriend and stabbed him seven times.

In cases of manslaughter involving firearms, much depends on the circumstances, particularly the degree of planning in the use of the firearm. In *Klair* (1995) 16 Cr App R (S) 660, following a dispute with his brother, the offender went to his brother's flat armed with a shotgun. The offender claimed that he intended only to frighten his brother, but the gun was fired and the brother was killed. On a conviction for manslaughter, the Court of Appeal upheld a sentence of seven years' imprisonment, Lord Lane CJ commenting that the case involved 'the greatest recklessness'. See also *Wesson* (1989) 11 Cr App R (S) 161, where a sentence of seven years was reduced to two years in a case where the offender had been cleaning his shotgun, waving it about but saying that it was unloaded, and it had discharged, killing his wife.

B1.49 **Course of Commission of Another Offence**   Again, a great deal depends on the precise circumstances of the killing. In *A-G's Ref (Nos. 38, 39 and 40)* [2008] 1 Cr App R (S) 319, the Court of Appeal considered sentence in a case of manslaughter committed in the course of a robbery in the victim's home. The 67-year-old victim was threatened with an iron bar and punched once. He died a week later, a scan showing that blood had collected in his skull and compressed the brain. All three offenders pleaded guilty to robbery and the second offender pleaded guilty to manslaughter. The Court of Appeal had regard to the definitive sentencing guideline on robbery (see Supplement, **SG-34**), and inferred that, following a trial, the appropriate range for a person without previous convictions who was convicted of manslaughter in such circumstances was eight to nine years' imprisonment. The sentence of three years and six months was increased to five years, having regard to the guilty plea, the element of double jeopardy, and other matters. A number of earlier similar appeals were reviewed in this case. *A-G's Ref (No. 113 of 2006)* [2007] 2 Cr App R (S) 594 was a case of manslaughter committed in the course of arson, where an 18-year-old offender of previous good character had assisted an older man in deliberately starting a fire in a family's home late in the evening. Nine people escaped but a six-year-old daughter of the family received extensive burns from which she later died. The offender was acquitted at trial of murder and attempted murder but convicted of manslaughter and arson with intent to endanger life. It was submitted that the appropriate bracket for manslaughter in such circumstances is 12 to 15 years after a trial, and the Court of Appeal accepted that such a bracket was appropriate for an adult main perpetrator. In this case the sentence was increased from eight years' detention to 11 years. A similar case is *Mahmood* [2012] 2 Cr App R (S) 373, although this time three deaths resulted from the fire. A sentence of 17 years' imprisonment after a trial was upheld on an 18-year-old offender, who had assisted his brother in the offence. The brother was convicted of murder. In *Jumah* [2011] 2 Cr App R (S) 200, applying *A-G's Ref (No. 60 of 2009) (Appleby)* [2010] 2 Cr App R (S) 311, an offender who planned and organised a robbery and was present at the scene when another offender stabbed and killed the store manager had his sentence increased from 14 years to 18 years' imprisonment.

Manslaughter of Child   Sentencing for manslaughter of a young child involving the appli-   **B1.50**
cation of violence including shaking was reviewed by the Court of Appeal in *Burridge* [2011]
2 Cr App R (S) 148. The offender, a man of previous good character, was initially convicted of
the murder of his baby son, aged eight weeks. In the light of fresh medical evidence a conviction for manslaughter was substituted. In this case culpability was high, with intent falling
just short of that necessary for murder. The fatal injury had been inflicted when the offender
had been in a temper. He had caused previous injury to the child, and had been advised and
warned about his temper by others. He was dishonest in what he told the hospital and the
police. A sentence of ten years' imprisonment was imposed. In *A-G's Ref (No. 125 of 2010)*
[2011] 2 Cr App R (S) 534 the offender, a man of previous good character, pleaded guilty to
the manslaughter of his four-month-old baby son. The offender was in a bad mood and, in a
loss of temper, forcefully shook and/or threw the baby (the exact details were unclear), causing
serious brain damage. The child died three weeks later. A sentence of three and a half years'
imprisonment was increased by the Court of Appeal to five years. The Court stressed that the
higher sentencing levels now applicable to other forms of manslaughter such as diminished
responsibility in *Wood* [2010] 1 Cr App R (S) 6 (see **B1.41**) and in manslaughter arising from
public disorder and fights in *A-G's Ref (No. 60 of 2009) (Appleby)* [2010] 2 Cr App R (S) 311
(see **B1.46**) also applied in the present context. In *Hussain* [2012] 2 Cr App R (S) 427, a child
ran out in front of the offender's car and was struck by it. The offender at first stopped, but
then drove off again, with the child trapped under the car. Fatal injuries were caused. A sentence of eight years' imprisonment after a trial was reduced to six years on appeal. For cases of
manslaughter of a child by neglect, see **B1.51**.

Gross Negligence Manslaughter   Sentences for gross negligence manslaughter vary widely,   **B1.51**
reflecting the wide variety of situations in which the offence can be committed. A case towards
the top of the scale is *H* [2009] 2 Cr App R (S) 601, where a sentence of 12 years was upheld
on a mother for neglect of her child aged three, who had been left unattended for very long
periods and allowed to starve to death. In *Abuhamza* [2011] 2 Cr App R (S) 509 one offender
received a minimum term of seven and a half years and the other a determinate sentence of
15 years for appalling cruelty involving starvation and violence to their five children resulting
in the death of one child. In *Rodgers* [2005] 2 Cr App R (S) 105, a sentence of five years was
upheld in the case of a landlord who installed a gas fire in a flat without adequate provision for
ventilation, so that two tenants died from carbon monoxide poisoning. In *Connolly* [2007] 2
Cr App R (S) 509, a sentence of seven years was appropriate in a case where the offender, who
was the owner and operator of a company which provided trailers for work on railway lines, had
disabled brake safety equipment on a trailer with the result that the trailer gathered speed on an
incline and hit a party of rail workers, four of whom were killed and others were seriously
injured; the motive for disabling the trailer had been profit and the offender had tried to cover
up what had happened, to deceive investigators. In common with other areas of manslaughter,
the Court of Appeal in *Barrass* [2012] 1 Cr App R (S) 450 has said that, following the decision
in *A-G's Ref (No. 60 of 2009) (Appleby)* [2010] 2 Cr App R (S) 311 (see **B1.46**), greater importance should now be focused on the consequences of the offence. In *Barrass* itself a sentence of
two years and eight months was upheld in a case where a socially inadequate offender failed to call
for medical assistance for his sister for two and a half weeks after she had suffered a fall at home.
The sister had suffered from various medical conditions and was unable to care for herself, but the
offender's own culpability was reduced such that he was unable to comprehend the abnormal state
of his own home. In *Holtom* [2011] 1 Cr App R (S) 128 three years was upheld in a case where a
subcontractor carrying out landscaping work failed to supervise the demolition of a wall by two
casual labourers, aged 18 and 15; the wall collapsed, causing the death of the 15-year-old who,
because of his age, should not have been employed at all. In *Brown* [2011] 2 Cr App R (S) 59, four
years was upheld where the offender admitted refusing to summon medical attention for a man
who had been stabbed by the offender's sister, with the result that the man bled to death. In *Garg*
[2013] 2 Cr App R (S) 203 (30) the offender was a 44-year-old medical practitioner employed as

a hospital consultant urologist. He was found to have been negligent in the care of a patient, and he also made changes to hospital records in the hope of evading responsibility. A sentence of two years' imprisonment was upheld by the Court of Appeal. See also *Kovvali* [2014] 1 Cr App R (S) 199 (33), where 30 months' imprisonment following a guilty plea was upheld on a 65-year-old locum doctor who failed to diagnose diabetic ketoacidosis. The patient, who displayed classic symptoms, died the next morning. In *Reeves* [2013] 2 Cr App R (S) 129 (21) a sentence of three years and nine months' imprisonment following a guilty plea was upheld where a young woman had left her baby unattended in the bath for 45 minutes and he had drowned.

CONSTRUCTIVE MANSLAUGHTER (KILLING BY AN UNLAWFUL ACT LIKELY TO CAUSE BODILY HARM)

The Unlawful Act

B1.52 The accused's act must be unlawful, in that it constitutes a criminal offence in its own right (independently of the fact that it has caused death). See *Franklin* (1883) 15 Cox CC 163, where the fact that the accused had committed a tort did not make his act an unlawful one for the purposes of manslaughter, although it should be noted that the accused was nonetheless convicted on the ground of gross negligence. Typically the unlawful act will be an assault (see, e.g., *Larkin* [1943] KB 174) or some other offence against the person such as administering a noxious thing under the OAPA 1861, s. 23.

It now seems clear that the offence need not be directed against the person; an offence of arson or criminal damage can supply the required element of unlawfulness (*Goodfellow* (1986) 83 Cr App R 23). However, being a participant in the public order offence of affray will not suffice except insofar as the accused individually commits or is party to an assault perpetrated on the victim as part of the affray (*Carey* [2006] EWCA Crim 17).

B1.53 The unlawful act must be an act which is unlawful in itself rather than one which is unlawful because of the negligent manner of its performance. Thus, driving without due care and attention does not count as an unlawful act for these purposes (*Andrews v DPP* [1937] AC 576, per Lord Atkin at p. 585), otherwise unlawful act manslaughter would swallow up both the statutory offence of causing death by dangerous driving and also killing by gross negligence in the context of road traffic deaths. Perhaps a better way of excluding driving without due care and attention would be to say that the unlawful act must be an offence which requires the proof of full *mens rea* in the sense of intention or recklessness or some equally culpable state of mind. This would have the merit of also clearly excluding offences of strict liability (e.g., under health and safety legislation) which happen to result in death. Such situations should only be capable of amounting to manslaughter (and are only so treated) if they come within the gross negligence head discussed at B1.64 to B1.71. Unfortunately, in *Andrews* [2003] Crim LR 477, the Court of Appeal treated the strict liability offence under the Medicines Act 1968 of administering a prescription only medicine (in this case insulin, in order to give someone a 'rush') as a sufficient unlawful act. The main point at issue was whether consent could be a defence by rendering the act lawful, which it clearly could not. However, the charge of administering a noxious thing contrary to the OAPA 1861, s. 23, (which had been left to lie on the file), would have been a much more appropriate offence on which to base the unlawful act.

B1.54 The type of offence sufficient for an unlawful act may also be thought to have been somewhat stretched in *Meeking* [2012] 1 WLR 3349, where the Court of Appeal upheld a conviction for constructive manslaughter based on an unlawful act contrary to the RTA 1988, s. 22A(1)(b). The specific unlawful act involved the accused pulling on the handbrake while her husband was driving their car at 60 mph, resulting in an accident which caused his death. The Court confirmed that such conduct amounts to an offence under s. 22A in that she 'interferes with a motor vehicle…in such circumstances that it would be obvious to a reasonable person that to do so would be dangerous'. The main argument raised in the Court of Appeal was whether the statutory offence should be limited to acts of interference with a vehicle prior to it being driven (see C3.58) but it was also argued that, even though the statutory offence was committed, it was not an appropriate unlawful act for the purposes of constructive manslaughter given that the offence is essentially one based on negligence and that, therefore, in line with *Andrews v DPP* [1937] AC 576, it should not count as an unlawful act for these purposes. Toulson LJ adverted to this issue (at [14]) and noted that the case might more naturally have been put forward on the basis of gross negligence and that, if it had been, it was impossible to conclude that the jury would not have convicted on that ground. One might add that it is arguable that cases such as this should *only* be prosecuted under gross negligence and that the category of unlawful acts should not be stretched to include offences which do not require full *mens rea* and which are defined in terms of negligence as to a significant element. The issue would of course be most critical if a case arose, such as the type about which Toulson LJ himself would have some concerns, 'which was essentially one of negligence, but arguably negligence falling short of gross negligence'.

The phrase 'unlawful act' connotes an act as opposed to an omission, so that the fact that the accused has committed the offence of wilful neglect of a child under the CYPA 1933, s. 1, does not supply the unlawful act required (*Lowe* [1973] QB 702). The facts may, however, justify a verdict of manslaughter on some other ground such as gross negligence.

The *Mens Rea* of the Unlawful Act

Although a person accused of manslaughter by definition lacks the *mens rea* for murder, the prosecution must normally prove that he has the *mens rea* appropriate to the unlawful act which caused the victim's death, a point well illustrated by the case of *Lamb* [1967] 2 QB 981, where the accused 'in jest' pointed a loaded revolver at his friend and pulled the trigger, believing that it was safe to do so because neither of the two bullets in the gun was in a chamber opposite the barrel. What neither the appellant nor his friend (who was similarly treating the incident as a joke) appreciated was that pulling the trigger rotated the cylinder so as to place one of the bullets opposite the barrel, and hence in the firing position. On appeal, the conviction for manslaughter was quashed on the ground that 'the element of intent without which there can be no assault' was not proved. It would have been different had Lamb intended to frighten his friend (for then he would have had the *mens rea* of an unlawful act) — see *Ball* [1989] Crim LR 730. Since the decision in *Lamb* [1967] 2 QB 981, it has been confirmed that recklessness is sufficient *mens rea* for assault (*Venna* [1976] QB 421). However, it is subjective recklessness which applies (*Spratt* [1990] 1 WLR 1073) so Lamb would still lack the necessary *mens rea*. See also *Slingsby* [1995] Crim LR 570, where vigorous consensual sexual activity did not amount to a battery or other unlawful act since there was no intention to cause, or foresight of, harm.

The accused cannot, however, rely on his lack of *mens rea* induced by voluntary intoxication, as manslaughter is a crime of basic intent (*Lipman* [1970] 1 QB 152). This was an extreme case in many ways, in which the accused killed his girlfriend whilst suffering LSD-induced hallucinations that he was at the centre of the earth being attacked by snakes. If the unlawful act alleged were to be a crime of specific intent, then the accused's intoxication *should* be relevant, but such situations are likely to be rare (see, however, *Watson* [1989] 2 All ER 865, burglary with intent to steal).

Likely to Cause Bodily Harm

The Objective Nature of the Test   The classic formulation of this requirement, sometimes referred to as the requirement that the unlawful act be 'dangerous', is that of Edmund Davies J in *Church* [1966] 1 QB 59, where he said (at p. 70):

> …the unlawful act must be such as all sober and reasonable people would inevitably recognise must subject the other person to, at least, the risk of some harm resulting therefrom, albeit not serious harm.

B1.55

B1.56

This formulation has the merit that it emphasises that the test is an objective one, which depends not on the accused's appreciation of likely harm but on what the sober and reasonable person would appreciate. The objective nature of the test was confirmed by the House of Lords in *DPP v Newbury* [1977] AC 500, where two youths pushed a paving stone off the parapet of a bridge into the path of an approaching train, thereby killing the guard. The House of Lords upheld the convictions for manslaughter and answered yes to the certified question, 'Can a defendant be properly convicted of manslaughter, when his mind is not affected by drink or drugs, if he did not foresee harm to another?'

On the other hand, the accused's foresight of harm may be relevant to the separate question of whether he has the *mens rea* of the unlawful act if the unlawful act is an offence against the person. The House of Lords in *DPP v Newbury* [1977] AC 500 did not make it clear what the unlawful act was, and indeed appeared to be rather dismissive of the requirement of *mens rea* for the unlawful act. However, it now seems clear in the light of *Goodfellow* (1986) 83 Cr App R 23 (see **B1.52**) that criminal damage would be the obvious and sufficient unlawful act in *Newbury*, and that the two accused were probably reckless as to criminal damage, so that they did have the *mens rea* for an unlawful act even if they did not foresee harm to another. Even where the unlawful act is an assault, the *mens rea* need not relate to harm; an intention to put in fear is sufficient. Thus the following dictum of Lord Denning MR in *Gray v Barr* [1971] 2 QB 554, at p. 568, on which doubt was cast by Lord Salmon in *Newbury*, is perfectly sound in the context of a case where the unlawful act is an assault: 'the accused must do a dangerous act with the *intention* of frightening or harming someone, or with the *realisation* that it is likely to frighten or harm someone'. Lord Denning was not casting doubt on the requirement that the act be *objectively* likely to cause bodily harm (he refers to a 'dangerous' act), but was making the important and separate point that the accused must be shown to have the *mens rea* for whatever is alleged to be the unlawful act. See also *Jennings* [1990] Crim LR 588 and *Scarlett* [1993] 4 All ER 629.

B1.57 **Physical Harm Not Mere Emotional Disturbance**   The harm *likely* to result from the act must be physical harm. Emotional disturbance will not suffice, even though physical harm (and death) does in fact result from the foreseeable emotional disturbance: see *Dawson* (1985) 81 Cr App R 150, where the fact that a robbery of a petrol station was likely to cause emotional disturbance to the 60-year-old attendant was held not to be sufficient, even though the attendant, who had a weak heart, suffered a heart attack and died. The heart attack did constitute physical harm but the reasonable man would not have *foreseen* physical harm as likely to result. The reasonable person is to be regarded as having the knowledge of facts that the accused has, and the accused in this case did not know that the attendant had a weak heart. A similar approach was taken in *Carey* [2006] EWCA Crim 17, where the Court of Appeal regarded it as an even clearer case than *Watson* in that the sober and reasonable bystander would not have recognised a risk of shock leading to a heart attack in the case of an apparently healthy 15-year-old girl. In *Johnston* [2007] EWCA Crim 3133, insults and spittle directed at an apparently healthy and active 67-year-old were similarly not 'dangerous acts' nor likely to give rise to a foreseeable injury. Since, however, they could not be ruled out in the light of the medical evidence as in fact the sole cause of a fatal heart attack, the later throwing of stones which struck the victim's head, whilst clearly a dangerous act, could not be proved to be a significant cause of death on which a manslaughter verdict could be sustained. However, as is shown by *M (J)* [2013] 1 WLR 1083, provided that there is a risk of physical harm that any sober and reasonable person would recognise, the actual death does not need to result from that sort of harm, if the accused's unlawful act did indeed cause the death. Thus an affray which was likely to cause bodily harm (e.g., through the direct effects of physical violence) could potentially give rise to unlawful act manslaughter even though the actual cause of death might be the effects of shock caused by the affray leading to the rupture of an aneurysm which would not have been foreseen by anyone in an apparently healthy 40-year-old.

In *Watson* [1989] 2 All ER 865, the unlawful act was burglary under the Theft Act 1968, s. 9(1)(a), which allegedly caused the elderly occupier (again with a weak heart) to suffer a heart attack and die. The Court of Appeal held (at p. 867) that, although the appellant did not know the age or physical condition of the occupier at the point of entry:

> ...the jury were entitled to ascribe to the bystander the knowledge which the appellant gained during the whole of his stay in the house...The unlawful act in the present circumstances comprised the whole of the burglarious intrusion and did not come to an end on the appellant's foot crossing the threshold...

The statement about the duration of the unlawful act seems, with respect, to stretch the definition of the offence under s. 9(1)(a) and can be regarded as *obiter*, since the conviction was quashed on another ground. However, the case is a useful illustration of the proposition that if the accused knows of the victim's susceptibility to physical harm, then that knowledge can be ascribed to the reasonable man and the accused's act can be regarded as 'likely to cause bodily harm'. See *Bristow* [2013] EWCA Crim 1540 for another example where the known features of the particular burglary were such that it was objectively likely to cause some harm.

On the other hand, the reasonable man does not share the accused's mistaken beliefs. In *Ball* [1989] Crim LR 730, the accused mistakenly believed he had loaded his gun with blank cartridges but the reasonable bystander, not sharing that belief, would have considered the act of firing the gun dangerous.

The Nature of the Causal Link   A further limitation on the type of harm required was suggested in *Dalby* [1982] 1 All ER 916, where the Court of Appeal quashed a conviction for manslaughter based on the accused unlawfully supplying his friend with drugs, which his friend subsequently injected into himself with fatal consequences. Waller LJ said that the act had to be 'directed at the victim and likely to cause *immediate* injury, however slight' (emphasis added). The harm (or injury) in this case was caused by the deceased's own act of injecting the drugs. The mere supply of the drug was not dangerous in the sense that it was likely to cause *immediate* injury. The qualification suggested in *Dalby* is capable of restricting the scope of constructive manslaughter in a number of ways but it has been distinguished in subsequent cases. **B1.58**

In *Mitchell* [1983] QB 741 the accused assaulted X, causing him to fall on top of an elderly woman who died as a result. The Court of Appeal quite rightly had no difficulty in dismissing the argument that the accused's act was directed at X rather than at the deceased, saying that in *Dalby* [1982] 1 All ER 916 the court had been concerned with 'the quality of the act rather than the identity of the victim'. This is no real restriction on *Dalby* and is similar to the familiar transferred *mens rea* rule (see **A2.31**). In *Pagett* (1983) 76 Cr App R 279, the accused, at the end of a police siege, held the victim (a girl pregnant by him) in front of him as a shield while he fired at the police. The police fired back, in what the jury found to be a lawful manner, but unfortunately killed the girl. Pagett was convicted of manslaughter. The Court of Appeal was principally concerned with the question of whether the acts of the police in firing back constituted a *novus actus interveniens* (see **A1.31** to **A1.40**), which it held it was not because the police had been acting lawfully. However, the Court briefly referred to the elements of unlawful act manslaughter and said (at p. 291): **B1.59**

> ...[the accused] committed not one but two unlawful acts, both of which were dangerous — the act of firing at the police, and the act of holding Gail Kinchen as a shield in front of him when the police might well fire shots in his direction in self-defence.

No mention was made of the *Dalby* requirement of 'directed at the victim' or 'likely to cause immediate injury'. However, the facts can be accommodated within the *Dalby* test, although with more difficulty than in *Mitchell* [1988] QB 741. Firing at the police certainly was directed at *a* victim and likely to cause immediate injury (at least to the police). Holding the girl as a shield was an act directed at her and in the circumstances likely to cause immediate harm to her, given that bullets were likely to be fired in the accused's direction as a result of the accused's own act.

B1.60   The decision in *Goodfellow* (1986) 83 Cr App R 23 moves more clearly away from the limitation suggested in *Dalby*. The accused, wishing to be rehoused, set fire to his council house. The fire spread more rapidly than he had anticipated, and his wife and child, and another woman were killed in the blaze. The Court of Appeal upheld the conviction for manslaughter, even though the accused's acts were not directed at a victim but rather against property. Lord Lane CJ said (at p. 27) that all that had been intended to be said in *Dalby* was that 'there must be no fresh intervening cause between the act and the death'. His lordship went on:

> The questions which the jury have to decide on the charge of manslaughter of this nature are: (1) Was the act intentional? (2) Was it unlawful? (3) Was it an act which any reasonable person would realise was bound to subject some other human being to the risk of physical harm, albeit not necessarily serious harm? (4) Was that act the cause of death?

The *Dalby* limitation of 'likely to cause immediate injury' seems then to have been abandoned, regrettably perhaps, inasmuch as on facts such as *Goodfellow*, as Lord Lane CJ himself recognised, gross negligence manslaughter would appear to be available. Having said that, *Willoughby* [2005] 1 WLR 1880 shows that putting this sort of case on the basis of unlawful act manslaughter is preferable; it avoids the complications inherent in establishing the duty of care required for gross negligence manslaughter. It should also be noted that, in a case such as *Lamb* [1967] 2 QB 981 (see **B1.55**), Lord Lane's second question for the jury would need to be amplified in order to stress that an act is only unlawful if the accused has the *mens rea* for the particular unlawful act alleged. To ask, 'Was the act intentional?' is not sufficient, since that can be interpreted merely as referring to voluntariness, e.g., on the facts of *Lamb*, as asking 'Did the accused intend to pull the trigger?' rather than 'Did he intend to assault his friend?' On the facts of *Goodfellow* (1986) 83 Cr App R 23, the problem does not really arise, because the accused clearly had the *mens rea* for criminal damage.

B1.61   **Drug-related Deaths, Causation and 'jointly administering'**   The essential requirement from *Dalby* [1982] 1 All ER 916 that 'there must be no intervening cause' between the accused's act and the victim's death has come into focus as a result of a number of decisions starting with *Kennedy* [1999] Crim LR 65, which was subsequently referred to the Court of Appeal by the CCRC, only for the conviction to be upheld a second time in the Court of Appeal in *Kennedy (No. 2)* [2005] 4 All ER 1083 before finally being quashed in the House of Lords in *Kennedy (No. 2)* [2008] 1 AC 269. The facts of *Kennedy* involved the accused supplying a prepared syringe of heroin with which the deceased voluntarily injected himself; that injection caused the victim's death for which Kennedy was (initially) held responsible. Precisely how the accused could be responsible for the consequences of a free and voluntary act done by the victim was never very clear. Basing his liability on the act of supply was contrary to *Dalby* since the supply, as opposed to the injection, was clearly not the cause of death. The subsequent case of *Dias* [2002] 2 Cr App R 96 demonstrated that it could not be based on aiding and abetting the act of the victim since the act of self-injection by the victim was not unlawful, there being no offence of self-manslaughter.

A third approach found favour for a time based on *Rogers* [2003] 1 WLR 1374 where the deceased injected himself with heroin whilst the appellant held his belt round the deceased's arm as a tourniquet. The appellant's conviction for manslaughter was upheld because the application of the tourniquet was regarded as part and parcel of the act of injection causing death. The appellant was regarded as playing a part in the mechanics of the injection and thus committing an unlawful act as a principal under the OAPA 1861, s. 23 (administering a noxious thing rather than simply supply of a drug). The idea of doing an act jointly with the deceased was then adopted in *Kennedy (No. 2)* in the Court of Appeal following its referral by the CCRC. Even though there was nothing done in *Kennedy* equivalent to the holding of the tourniquet in

Rogers, the conviction was again upheld on the basis that the accused and the victim were said to be acting 'in concert' and were somehow 'jointly engaged in administering the heroin' despite the fact that the act of injection was clearly done by the deceased alone.

Most of these machinations have now been swept away by the House of Lords decision in **B1.62** *Kennedy (No. 2)* which emphatically reasserts the principle that 'D is not to be treated as causing V to act in a certain way if V makes a voluntary and informed decision to act in that way rather than another' (Lord Bingham at [14]). Such a decision by V to do an act means that he is the cause of the consequences of that act and not some other person. On the facts it was clear that, whilst the syringe was prepared by D, it was V's choice to inject it and the act of injection was his alone. Kennedy had therefore not caused the injection or the death and his conviction had to be quashed and other analogous cases (such as *Finlay* [2003] EWCA Crim 3868) were disapproved of.

Even a case such as *Rogers*, where D had held the tourniquet, did not escape. Lord Bingham recognised (at [20]) that there is:

> ...a difficult borderline between contributory acts which may properly be regarded as administering a noxious thing and acts which may not...the crucial question is not whether the defendant facilitated or contributed to administration of the noxious thing but whether he went further and administered it. What matters, in a case such as *R v Rogers* and the present, is whether the injection itself was the result of a voluntary and informed decision by the person injecting himself. In *R v Rogers*, as in the present case, it was. That case was, therefore, wrongly decided.

It should not be thought however that we have heard the last of 'joint administration'. Although **B1.63** *Rogers* is not to be treated as an instance, Lord Bingham accepted (at [24]) that it is 'possible to imagine factual scenarios in which two people could properly be regarded as acting together to administer an injection' and this possibility was further discussed in *Burgess* [2008] EWCA Crim 516, where Sir Igor Judge considered (at [12]) that the accused:

> ...is not automatically entitled to be acquitted if the deceased rather than the defendant physically operated the plunger on the syringe and caused the drug to enter his body. In the present case there was evidence which might reasonably have led a jury to conclude that this appellant had indeed jointly participated in the administration of the fatal dose of heroin. From the interviews as they developed, it emerged that he supplied the deceased with the heroin, which he, the appellant, drew into the syringe...He did not hand the syringe to the deceased but he took it and the needle to the deceased's arm, where he found an appropriate vein. He laid the tip of the needle against the skin of the deceased above that vein. It is not clear from the interview that he ever in fact let go of the syringe, but on his account the deceased depressed the plunger. Having done so, the appellant assisted in the physical withdrawal of the plunger from the deceased's arm.

His lordship considered that it would have been open to the jury to convict on the basis of a joint administration on these facts but a retrial was not in fact ordered for other reasons (the accused having originally pleaded guilty on a different and false basis prior to the House of Lords decision in *Kennedy (No. 2)* and now having already served his sentence).

For an illustration of how drug-related deaths can give rise to convictions for gross negligence manslaughter based on a duty of care, see *Evans* [2009] 1 All ER 13 at **B1.70**.

MANSLAUGHTER BY GROSS NEGLIGENCE

Basis of Liability

Manslaughter has traditionally been the one offence at common law in which negligence is **B1.64** expressly recognised as a sufficient basis of liability, but even here the negligence has to be 'gross'. Defining the precise degree of negligence required has always been problematical, and ultimately the question, being one of degree, has been one for the jury. This is evident from the following test laid down by Lord Hewart CJ in *Bateman* (1925) 19 Cr App R 8, at pp. 11 to 12:

> ...the facts must be such that, in the opinion of the jury, the negligence of the accused went beyond a mere matter of compensation between subjects and showed such disregard for the life and safety of others as to amount to a crime against the State and conduct deserving punishment.

In *Andrews v DPP* [1937] AC 576, at p. 583, Lord Atkin said that whilst this was:

> ...not...a precise definition of the crime...the substance of the judgment is most valuable, and in my opinion is correct. In practice it has generally been adopted by judges in charging juries in all cases of manslaughter by negligence.

Lord Atkin went on to say that in summarising the very high degree of negligence required:

> Probably of all the epithets that can be applied 'reckless' most nearly covers the case...but it is probably not all-embracing, for 'reckless' suggests an indifference to risk, whereas the accused may have appreciated the risk and intended to avoid it and yet shown such a high degree of negligence in the means adopted to avoid as would justify a conviction. (ibid. at p. 583)

Nevertheless, judges have often used the word 'reckless' to sum up to the jury the degree of fault required without making it clear how, if at all, this differs from the concept of gross negligence. This lack of clarity was perhaps inevitable while the meaning of 'reckless' in the criminal law generally was unclear. But after the apparently authoritative House of Lords decisions on the meaning of recklessness in *Metropolitan Police Commissioner v Caldwell* [1982] AC 341 and *Lawrence* [1982] AC 510, the issue became very difficult to ignore. In *Adomako* [1995] 1 AC 171 the House of Lords restored gross negligence rather than recklessness as the essential basis of liability, but to understand the current state of the law it is necessary to outline the somewhat chequered history of this variety of manslaughter over the decade prior to *Adomako*.

B1.65 Despite the complex history, to be recounted at **B1.66** *et seq.*, the Court of Appeal, in *Misra* [2005] 1 Cr App R 328, has rejected the argument that gross negligence manslaughter offends against the principle of legal certainty inherent in the ECHR, Article 7. In the Court of Appeal's view (Judge LJ at [48]):

> The decision of the House of Lords in *Adomako* clearly identified the ingredients of manslaughter by gross negligence. In very brief summary, confirming *Andrews v DPP* [1937] AC 576, the offence requires first, death resulting from a negligent breach of the duty of care owed by the defendant to the deceased, second, that in negligent breach of that duty, the victim was exposed by the defendant to the risk of death, and third, that the circumstances were so reprehensible as to amount to gross negligence.

His lordship reiterated later in his judgment (at [64]) that:

> ...the law is clear. The ingredients of the offence have been clearly defined, and the principles decided in the House of Lords in *Adomako*. They involve no uncertainty. The hypothetical citizen, seeking to know his position, would be advised that, assuming he owed a duty of care to the deceased which he had negligently broken, and that death resulted, he would be liable to conviction for manslaughter if, on the available evidence, the jury was satisfied that his negligence was gross. A doctor would be told that grossly negligent treatment of a patient which exposed him or her to the risk of death, and caused it, would constitute manslaughter.

The common-law offence of manslaughter by gross negligence is abolished by the Corporate Manslaughter and Corporate Homicide Act 2007, s. 20, as it concerns corporations or other organisations to which s. 1 of that Act applies (see **B1.148**).

Gross Negligence as Opposed to Objective Recklessness

B1.66 **The Incursion of a Test of Recklessness** In *Seymour* [1983] 2 AC 493, the accused, having recently quarrelled with the woman with whom he lived, was involved in a minor collision between his 11-ton lorry and her car. The woman got out of the car, but was crushed between the lorry and her own car as the accused tried, allegedly, to shunt her car out of the way (moving it 10 to 20 feet and forcing a tyre off in the process). Rather than charge the statutory offence of causing death by reckless driving, the prosecution took the view (rightly in the view of the House of Lords) that this was such a bad case that the offence of common-law manslaughter was appropriate. Nevertheless, in referring to the fault element required, the judge directed the jury in terms of recklessness as then defined by the House of Lords in *Lawrence* [1982] AC 510 in relation to the statutory offence (see **A2.10**), save only that he omitted any reference to a risk of damage to property and limited the risk to 'an obvious and serious risk of causing physical harm'. Seymour appealed on the grounds that the *Lawrence* meaning of 'recklessness' was not applicable to common-law manslaughter, and that a more subjective meaning should be applied. The House of Lords dismissed the appeal and said that the *Lawrence* direction was appropriate (though without the reference to damage to property), the legal ingredients of the statutory offence and of common-law manslaughter being the same.

The decision raised many difficult issues including the question whether the *Lawrence* test of recklessness could be said to have completely supplanted the test of gross negligence in manslaughter. Clarification of this question appeared to come in the Privy Council decision in *Kong Cheuk Kwan v The Queen* (1985) 82 Cr App R 18. This case arose out of a collision in perfect weather between two hydrofoils in Hong Kong harbour, which resulted in the deaths of two passengers. Lord Roskill, in allowing the appeal, thought that here, too, a proper direction should have been based on *Lawrence*-type recklessness and appeared to confirm that the test is recklessness rather than gross negligence. Indeed Lord Roskill approved the comments of Watkins LJ in the Court of Appeal in *Seymour* (1983) 76 Cr App R 211, where he said (at p. 216): 'it is no longer necessary or helpful to make reference to compensation and negligence'.

The Restoration of the Gross Negligence Test   The start of the return to the gross negligence test can be seen in *Prentice* [1994] QB 302, where the Court of Appeal made it clear that gross negligence had by no means been totally supplanted by recklessness. Indeed it was of the view that, 'leaving motor manslaughter aside, the proper test in manslaughter based on breach of duty was the gross negligence test and that the *Lawrence/Caldwell* recklessness test was...inappropriate in the present class of case'. One of the appellants (Adomako) appealed to the House of Lords which also considered these issues.   **B1.67**

In *Adomako* [1995] 1 AC 171, the House was able to go further than the Court of Appeal and hold that the *Bateman/Andrews* gross negligence test was of general application and that there should be no separate test for motor manslaughter.

> ...the law as stated in *Seymour*...should no longer apply since the underlying statutory provisions on which it rested have not been repealed by the Road Traffic Act 1991. It may be that cases of involuntary motor manslaughter will as a result become rare but I consider it unsatisfactory that there should be any exception to the generality of the statement which I have made...(per Lord Mackay LC at p. 187)

It is not immediately apparent why the reversion from *Lawrence* recklessness to gross negligence should make convictions for involuntary motor manslaughter any more rare (they had not exactly been common in the past). Part of the explanation may lie in the fact that in the Court of Appeal the convictions of Prentice and Sulman for manslaughter (not of the motorised variety) had been quashed because the direction in terms of *Lawrence* recklessness had failed to leave it open to the jury to take account of the excuses or mitigating circumstances that might have been relevant to the issue of gross negligence. Lord Mackay and the Court of Appeal may have regarded gross negligence as a narrower basis of liability than *Lawrence* recklessness; this is surprising in the light of Lord Atkin's comments in *Andrews v DPP* [1937] AC 576 (at p. 583) that 'reckless suggests an indifference to risk whereas the accused may have appreciated the risk and intended to avoid it and yet shown such a high degree of negligence in the means adopted to avoid the risk as would justify the conviction'. This seems more consistent with the view that gross negligence is *wider* than recklessness, particularly in the sense that negligently 'ruling out the risk' may negative recklessness but not necessarily gross negligence.

B1.68   Whatever the explanation, Lord Mackay went on to answer the certified question before the House of Lords in *Adomako* (at p. 188):

> In cases of criminal negligence involving a breach of duty it is a sufficient direction to the jury to adopt the gross negligence test...it is not necessary to refer to the definition of recklessness in *Lawrence* [1982] AC 510, although it is perfectly open to the trial judge to use the word 'reckless' in its ordinary meaning as part of his exposition of the law if he deems it appropriate in the circumstances of the particular case.

His lordship emphasised that whilst a judge *may* feel it to be appropriate to use the word reckless as indicating the extent to which a defendant's conduct must deviate from a proper standard of care, it would not be right 'to *require* that this should be done and certainly not right that it should incorporate the full detail required in *Lawrence*'. Furthermore, in *A-G's Ref (No. 2 of 1999)* [2000] QB 796, the Court of Appeal held that proof of gross negligence does not require proof of any particular state of mind and does not require evidence of the accused's state of mind. Although one can agree that a specific state of mind such as recklessness is not required, it is difficult to see how one can avoid looking into what facts the individual either knew (and failed to take adequate precautions for) or did not know about (but should have done). Either way, this surely requires evidence of the accused's state of mind. In *R (Rowley) v DPP* [2003] EWHC 693 (Admin), the absence of evidence of subjective recklessness was held to be an appropriate factor to take into account in a decision not to prosecute. However, it was confirmed in *Misra* [2005] 1 Cr App R 328 that the fault element that the prosecution have to prove remains gross negligence and, despite the rehabilitation of subjective recklessness in *G* [2004] 1 AC 1034 in relation to criminal damage, there is no warrant for replacing gross negligence in manslaughter with a requirement to prove subjective recklessness. Judge LJ noted (at [55]) of *Misra* that in his speech in *G*, Lord Bingham emphasised that 'he was not addressing the meaning of "reckless" in any other statutory or common law context than section 1(1) and (2) of the Criminal Damage Act 1971'. In *Mark* [2004] EWCA Crim 2490, Scott Baker LJ made the same point in coming to the same conclusion that it is gross negligence and not subjective recklessness that has to be proved. Thus the trial judge was correct in telling the jury in relation to the facts of that case that 'actual foresight or perception of the risk is not a prerequisite of the crime of gross negligence' and that an accused could be guilty of gross negligence simply on the basis of a complete failure to advert to what is an obvious and important matter, i.e. an obvious and serious risk of death.

Nature of Gross Negligence

B1.69   Running throughout Lord Mackay's judgment in *Adomako* [1995] 1 AC 171 is a concern that directions should be 'comprehensible to an ordinary member of the public who is called to sit on a jury' and he was therefore reluctant 'to state the law more elaborately' as had perhaps been attempted by the Court of Appeal. Nevertheless it is necessary to investigate a little more closely the essentials of gross negligence manslaughter. *Bateman* (1925) 19 Cr App R 8 and *Andrews v DPP* [1937] AC 576 are not necessarily all that helpful since they say little more than that the negligence must go beyond that required for civil liability, which is a question of degree for the jury; if matters had been entirely clear from those two cases, there would not have since been the many conflicting appellate pronouncements on the issue. Having expressed his approval of those two cases, Lord Mackay set out what he regarded as the essentials of gross negligence (at p. 187):

…in my opinion the ordinary principles of the law of negligence apply to ascertain whether or not the defendant has been in breach of a duty of care towards the victim who has died. If such a breach of duty is established the next question is whether that breach of duty caused the death of the victim. If so, the jury must go on to consider whether that breach of duty should be characterised as gross negligence and therefore as a crime. This will depend on the seriousness of the breach of duty committed by the defendant in all the circumstances in which the defendant was placed when it occurred…

…The essence of the matter which is supremely a jury question is whether, having regard to the risk of death involved, the conduct of the defendant was so bad in all the circumstances as to amount in their judgment to a criminal act or omission.

The reintroduction of the ordinary principles of negligence to decide whether there is a breach of a duty of care is not necessarily a simple matter especially if the factual situation is one where policy factors might impinge (see, e.g., *Ancell v McDermott* [1993] 4 All ER 355). Is it envisaged that the types of arguments raised by that sort of case could be relevant to whether a person is guilty of manslaughter and might need to be rehearsed in a criminal prosecution? (See **B1.151** for the way in which these issues are dealt with in relation to the new statutory offence of corporate manslaughter.) Certainly the maxim '*ex turpi causa*' has no applicability in this context, as is illustrated by *Wacker* [2003] QB 1203 where the Court of Appeal confirmed that a duty of care could be owed by a lorry driver to illegal immigrants whom he had concealed in the back of his lorry. The policy factors here were clearly in favour of responsibility although in other situations they might point in the opposite direction. Nevertheless, in *Winter* [2011] 1 Cr App R (S) 476, a duty of care was still found to be owed to a civilian filming fire fighters who were responding to a massive fireworks fire and explosion caused by the negligence of the defendants, even though the civilian may have disobeyed instructions in being so close.

The issue of who decides whether there was a duty of care has now been clarified by Lord Judge CJ in *Evans* [2009] 1 All ER 13, a case involving a breach of duty to take reasonable steps to summon obviously needed medical help for a heroin overdose victim for whom the appellant had procured the drug. In accordance with normal principles, the question of whether there is a duty of care (given certain facts) is a matter of law for the trial judge although it is for the jury to decide whether any contingent facts (which the trial judge has identified the duty to depend upon) are established. As to what type of risk must be foreseeable on which the duty of care is based, various formulations have been used in the past including a risk to health and welfare, a risk of serious injury and a risk of death. *Singh* [1999] Crim LR 582 explicitly confined it to a risk of death whereby 'the circumstances must be such that a reasonably prudent person would have foreseen a serious and obvious risk not merely of injury, even serious injury, but of death' and in *Misra* [2005] 1 Cr App R 328, the Court of Appeal confirmed this approach as being in line with *Adomako* (and Lord Mackay's reference to 'having regard to the risk of death involved'). The Court was emphatic, in the face of a challenge to the compatibility of gross negligence manslaughter with the principle of legal certainty inherent in the ECHR, Article 7, that it was now quite clear that a (foreseeable) risk of death was required and the point was also made that this was consistent with the offence being one designed to protect the right to life: 'In short, the offence requires gross negligence in circumstances where what is at risk is the life of an individual to whom the defendant owes a duty of care. As such it serves to protect his or her right to life' (Judge LJ at [52]). References to risks to 'safety', or indeed to any other consequence except death, are now superfluous and should be avoided (*Yaqoob* [2005] EWCA Crim 2169).

B1.70

Sentencing Guidelines

See **B1.51**.

B1.71

MOTOR MANSLAUGHTER AND ROAD TRAFFIC ACT OFFENCES

B1.72   Until the coming into force of the Road Traffic Act 1991, s. 1, there appeared to be a complete overlap between (reckless) motor manslaughter and the statutory offence of causing death by reckless driving (*Seymour* [1983] 2 AC 493). The 1991 Act replaced the offence of causing death by reckless driving in the Road Traffic Act 1988, s. 1, by the offence of causing death by dangerous driving and s. 2A of the 1988 Act defines the meaning of dangerous driving in a way which has echoes of the *Lawrence* definition of recklessness but is not identical with it; indeed it is somewhat wider in its scope. There thus ceased to be a complete overlap with motor manslaughter but it seems that manslaughter should still be reserved for the very worst cases. If a charge of manslaughter is being considered rather than the statutory offence, it should be borne in mind that causing death by dangerous driving is an alternative verdict to manslaughter in connection with the driving of a mechanically propelled motor vehicle (RTOA 1988, s. 24(A1), inserted by the Road Safety Act 2006, s. 33). (See further **C3.3**.)

CAUSING OR ALLOWING THE DEATH OF A CHILD OR VULNERABLE ADULT

Definition

B1.73   Domestic Violence, Crime and Victims Act 2004, s. 5

(1) A person ('D') is guilty of an offence if—
    (a) a child or vulnerable adult ('V') dies or suffers serious physical harm as a result of the unlawful act of a person who—
        (i) was a member of the same household as V, and
        (ii) had frequent contact with him,
    (b) D was such a person at the time of that act,
    (c) at that time there was a significant risk of serious physical harm being caused to V by the unlawful act of such a person, and
    (d) either D was the person whose act caused the death or serious physical harm or—
        (i) D was, or ought to have been, aware of the risk mentioned in paragraph (c),
        (ii) D failed to take such steps as he could reasonably have been expected to take to protect V from the risk, and
        (iii) the act occurred in circumstances of the kind that D foresaw or ought to have foreseen.
(2) The prosecution does not have to prove whether it is the first alternative in subsection (1)(d) or the second (sub-paragraphs (i) to (iii)) that applies.

The Domestic Violence, Crime and Victims (Amendment) Act 2012, in force from 2 July 2012 (SI 2012 No. 1432), amended s. 5 and related provisions so as to extend their application to cases involving a child or vulnerable adult suffering serious physical harm. For the offence and sentence for the offence related to such harm, see **B2.157**. Notwithstanding the new non-fatal version of the offence, the procedural provisions still clearly envisage that the fatal version of the offence remains a distinct offence with its own rules.

Procedure

B1.74   The offence is triable only on indictment and is a class 1A offence if a fatality has resulted and a class 2A offence in any other case (CPD XIII, para. B: see Supplement, **PD-97**).

The DVCVA 2004, s. 6(5), expressly provides for an offence of causing or allowing a person's death under s. 5 to be treated as an offence of homicide for the purposes of:

(a) the MCA 1980, ss. 24 and 25, relating to mode of trial of a child or young person;
(b) the CDA 1998, s. 51A, relating to sending cases to the Crown Court in relation to children and young persons;

(c) the PCC(S)A 2000, s. 8, relating to the remittal of young offenders to youth courts for sentence.

The offence of causing or allowing a person's death is a 'fatal offence' for the purposes of the Law Reform (Year and a Day Rule) Act 1996, s. 2, thereby requiring the A-G's consent to a prosecution in certain circumstances, including where the death occurs more than three years after the injury alleged to have caused it (DVCVA 2004, sch. 10, para. 33).

More controversially, under s. 6(1), 'where a person is charged in the same proceedings with an **B1.75** offence of murder or manslaughter and with an offence under section 5 in respect of the same death', s. 6(2), (3) and (4) affect the evidence and procedure applicable to the offence of murder or manslaughter in three different but related ways:

(a) under s. 6(2), where by virtue of the CJPO 1994, s. 35(3), inferences may be drawn in relation to the s. 5 offence from the accused's failure to give evidence or refusal to answer a question, the court or jury may also draw such inferences in determining whether he is guilty of murder or manslaughter (or any alternative verdict offence on those charges) even if there would otherwise be no case for him to answer in relation to murder or manslaughter (or the alternative verdict offence);
(b) under s. 6(3), unless the s. 5 offence is itself dismissed, the charge of murder or manslaughter is not to be dismissed on an application to the Crown Court under the CDA 1998, sch. 3, para. 2;
(c) under s. 6(4), the question of whether there is a case for the accused to answer on the charge of murder or manslaughter is not to be considered before the close of all the evidence (unless he has already ceased to be charged with the s. 5 offence).

Domestic Violence, Crime and Victims Act 2004, s. 6 **B1.76**

(1) Subsections (2) to (4) apply where a person ('the defendant') is charged in the same proceedings with an offence of murder or manslaughter and with an offence under section 5 in respect of the same death ('the section 5 offence').
(2) Where by virtue of section 35(3) of the Criminal Justice and Public Order Act 1994 a court or jury is permitted, in relation to the section 5 offence, to draw such inferences as appear proper from the defendant's failure to give evidence or refusal to answer a question, the court or jury may also draw such inferences in determining whether he is guilty—
    (a) of murder or manslaughter, or
    (b) of any other offence of which he could lawfully be convicted on the charge of murder or manslaughter,
    even if there would otherwise be no case for him to answer in relation to that offence.
(3) The charge of murder or manslaughter is not to be dismissed under paragraph 2 of Schedule 3 to the Crime and Disorder Act 1998 (unless the section 5 offence is dismissed).
(4) At the defendant's trial the question whether there is a case for the defendant to answer on the charge of murder or manslaughter is not to be considered before the close of all the evidence (or, if at some earlier time he ceases to be charged with the section 5 offence, before that earlier time).

These provisions clearly contemplate proceedings for murder or manslaughter being brought **B1.77** where a child or vulnerable adult dies in A's (and often B's) household and there is evidence that A (and/or B) may have been guilty of an offence under s. 5 but there is not yet a prima facie case for murder or manslaughter against A or B (the problem in *Lane* (1986) 82 Cr App R 5). Proceedings for murder or manslaughter against A (and/or B), if instituted, cannot now be dismissed in advance by means of an application to dismiss in the Crown Court nor can the charges be dismissed at trial by a submission of no case to answer (the *Lane* problem) before the close of *all* the evidence, by when it will be known if and to what extent A has given evidence (and by when there may be other evidence incriminating him given by B in his or her own defence). In addition, A can actually be convicted of murder or manslaughter on the basis of inferences drawn from his failure to testify or his refusal to answer questions at his trial, even though without those inferences there would not be a case for him to answer in relation to murder or manslaughter. The fact that there would 'otherwise be no case for him to answer' does not necessarily mean that A is at risk of being convicted 'solely' on the basis of an inference from silence, since one would expect there to be other evidence, albeit not sufficient on its own to amount to a prima facie case, but there is a clear risk that it might amount to a conviction based 'mainly' on an inference from silence and, as such, it is highly likely to be subject to challenge under the ECHR, Article 6 (see **F19.49** and *Murray v UK* (1996) 22 EHRR 29). The government was of the view that the provision was compatible with the Convention (cf. Law Com No. 282, September 2003, paras 6.78 to 6.96 seeking to justify a similar but differently worded provision in their own draft Bill) because the trial judge would have the right and duty to prevent the case going to the jury at the conclusion of the evidence (rather than as normally at the half-way point) if the homicide conviction was likely to be based 'mainly' on the adverse inference from silence. This interpretation would, however, mean that there would be likely to be relatively few cases in which the judge could or would ultimately let the murder or manslaughter charge go to the jury on the basis of an adverse inference (where 'there would otherwise be no case for him to answer') and, if this is right, the phrase is of limited effect. It should be stressed that these provisions modify the evidential and procedural rules only in relation to offences of murder and manslaughter charged in the same proceedings as a s. 5 offence and do not affect the s. 5 offence itself, which is subject to the normal rules on no case to answer and adverse inferences and the like.

Indictment

B1.78
Statement of Offence

Causing or allowing the death of a child [or vulnerable adult] contrary to section 5 of the Domestic Violence, Crime and Victims Act 2004.

Particulars of Offence

A, on or about the...day of..., being a member of the same household as a child [or vulnerable adult] V and having frequent contact with him, fell into one or other of the following alternatives, it being immaterial, and unnecessary to prove, which one it was, that is to say that

either he caused the death of V as a result of his (A's) own unlawful act which carried a significant risk of serious physical harm being caused to V,

or, alternatively, he failed to take such steps as he could reasonably have been expected to take to protect V from the significant risk of serious physical harm from the unlawful act which caused V's death, the unlawful act having been committed in this alternative not by A but by another person who was a member of the same household as V and who had frequent contact with V, the significant risk in this alternative being one which A was aware of or ought to have been aware of and the other's unlawful act occurring in circumstances of the kind which A foresaw or ought to have foreseen.

Alternative Verdicts

B1.79   There are no alternative verdicts specifically provided for and the offence is not itself an alternative verdict to murder or manslaughter, but note the procedural and evidential links to murder and manslaughter (see **B1.74** *et seq.*). The offence is in a sense, within itself, one self-contained alternative verdict in that the accused is guilty provided that it can be proved that he must have satisfied one or other of the two alternatives even though it cannot be proved which particular one. Given the problems of proof underlying the creation of the offence, it is inappropriate for a special verdict, as to whether a particular defendant actually caused as opposed to allowed the death, to be sought (*Hopkinson* [2014] 1 Cr App R 22 (3)).

Sentence

B1.80   The maximum penalty for an offence under the DVCVA 2004, s. 5, where death is involved is 14 years' imprisonment (s. 5(7)). Nine years' imprisonment was upheld in respect of each of two adults convicted of this offence in *Ikram* [2008] 2 Cr App R (S) 648, where the death of the child was caused by grave violence deliberately inflicted resulting in numerous injuries to the child, but where the prosecution were unable to prove which of the offenders had inflicted the violence. The Court of Appeal said that the general approach to sentencing in cases of manslaughter of a child (see **B1.50**) provided useful assistance when sentencing for this offence. In *Vestuto* [2010] 2 Cr App R (S) 682 six years' imprisonment was upheld where the offender had administered anti-depressant drugs, which had been prescribed for her, to her two children aged three years and 18 months, causing the death of the younger child. See also *Owen* [2009] EWCA Crim 2259.

Elements

The offence is a response to the problems exemplified in *Lane* (1986) Cr App R 5 and discussed **B1.81** in Law Com No. 282, *Children: Their Non-Accidental Death or Serious Injury (Criminal Trials)*. It goes beyond the Law Commission proposals by including vulnerable adults (defined in the DVCVA 2004, s. 5(6) as 'a person aged 16 or over whose ability to protect himself from violence, abuse or neglect is significantly impaired through physical or mental disability or illness, through old age or otherwise' — see *Khan* [2009] 4 All ER 544 for a discussion of how and in what circumstances an adult's ability may become 'otherwise' impaired). As can be seen from the draft indictment (see **B1.78**) there are two ways of committing the offence (it being unnecessary to prove which one it is). The first can be compared with unlawful act manslaughter and the second with gross negligence manslaughter, but there are significant differences in each case. Unlawful act manslaughter requires only that the unlawful act carry a risk of 'some harm resulting therefrom, albeit not serious harm' whereas under s. 5(1)(c) there has to be a 'significant risk of *serious* physical harm', which is defined in s. 5(6) as 'harm that amounts to grievous bodily harm for the purposes of the Offences Against the Person Act 1861'. The risk must also be a 'significant' one; 'significant' is an ordinary English word which should not be further defined for the jury and it is incorrect to tell the jury that it means 'more than minimal' (*Stephens* [2007] 2 Cr App R 330). Comparing the second limb of the offence with gross negligence manslaughter reveals that there is no requirement under s. 5(1)(d)(ii) that the failure 'to take such steps as he reasonably could have been expected to take' has to be gross, but, on the other hand, it should be noted that as a result of s. 5(1)(a), the death must occur as a result of the unlawful act of *someone* (in the same household etc.), even if it is not the unlawful act of the accused. This introduces an element of unlawfulness that is not required for gross negligence manslaughter.

Unlawful Act   An unlawful act is defined in s. 5(5) as one that: **B1.82**

(a) constitutes an offence, or
(b) would constitute an offence but for being the act of—
   (i)   a person under the age of ten, or
   (ii) a person entitled to rely on a defence of insanity.
Paragraph (b) does not apply to an act of D.

As with unlawful act manslaughter, it might frequently be an assault or some other offence against the person that is constituted by the unlawful act but it will only constitute an offence if the person who committed it had the *mens rea* required for that offence. This requirement is also implicit in subsection (5)(b) which specifically provides that an act is still unlawful for these purposes even if the person who committed it is under the age of ten or can rely on the defence of insanity. There is no provision for the act to be unlawful even if the person who committed it lacks *mens rea*. Proving this when one is not sure whether it is the accused's act or the act of another person that caused death may cause problems, although it is enough to show that whoever committed the unlawful act must have done so with the relevant *mens rea* of that unlawful act. As far as the first limb of the offence is concerned, i.e. where it is the accused's unlawful act that has caused death, as opposed to it being the unlawful act of some other person, s. 5(5) is stated not to apply for the obvious reason that infancy or insanity would be defences available to the accused in any event.

B1.83 **Relationship of Offence with Child Cruelty**   Where it is a child who has died, the unlawful act might constitute an offence of child cruelty under the CYPA 1933 (see **B2.137**). An aggravated offence of child cruelty where death occurs was part of the Law Commission's proposed mechanisms for dealing with the problems in this area (see Law Com No. 282, para. 6.2). Child cruelty can itself be committed in a large number of different ways (see **B2.138** and **B2.144**) and note that an 'act' for the purposes of the DVCVA 2004, s. 5, 'includes a course of conduct and also includes omission' (s. 5(6)). Provided the other requirements of s. 5 are satisfied, one can envisage a successful prosecution based on s. 5 where it can be proved that a child must have died as a result of child cruelty by one or the other of the two (or more) members of the child's household. Although the offence of child cruelty requires the accused to have 'responsibility' for the child, this is not required under s. 5, whereby it is enough that the accused was a member of the same household and had frequent contact with him.

B1.84 **Member of Same Household**   Section 5(4) explains further the concepts of 'member' and 'the same household as V'.

Domestic Violence, Crime and Victims Act 2004, s. 5

(4) For the purposes of this section—
   (a) a person is to be regarded as a 'member' of a particular household, even if he does not live in that household, if he visits it so often and for such periods of time that it is reasonable to regard him as a member of it;
   (b) where V lived in different households at different times, 'the same household as V' refers to the household in which V was living at the time of the act that caused the death or serious physical harm.

Section 5(4)(a) focuses on the *accused's* membership of a household and makes it clear that he does not have to live in it to be a member whereas s. 5(4)(b) focuses on V (the child or vulnerable adult) and makes it clear that it is the household that he 'lives in' at the time of the act in question that is important. In focusing on the household V 'lives in' (as opposed to which households V is a member of), s. 5(4)(b) seems to ignore the possibility that V might be a member of different households during the period in which a course of conduct (see the definition of 'act' in s. 5(6)) took place.

It should be noted that in addition to being a member of the same household as V, D is also required to have had frequent contact with him at the time of the act (s. 5(1)(a)(ii)), an issue which in *Khan* [2009] 4 All ER 544 was said to be free-standing and independent of the question of whether D ought to have been aware of the risk to V.

B1.85 **Liability of Persons Aged under 16**   Although in principle a sibling, or other person, who is himself under 16 could be guilty of an offence under s. 5 (as unlike child cruelty, the accused does not have to have responsibility for the child or vulnerable adult), s. 5(3) effectively excludes this possibility:

...if D was not the mother or father of V—
   (a) D may not be charged with an offence under this section if he was under the age of 16 at the time of the act that caused the death or serious physical harm...

So a child sibling cannot be charged, but an under-age parent can be. Section 5(3)(b) goes on to provide that, other than for parents of V, a person cannot be held responsible for failures to take reasonable steps under s. 5(1)(d)(ii) prior to reaching the age of 16.

B1.86 **Failure to Take Steps**   In relation to the second alternative manner of commission of the offence, failing 'to take such steps as he could reasonably have been expected to take to protect V from the risk', whilst this is clearly an objective test, it is one that focuses on the steps that D could have been expected to take, not the steps that some paradigmatic reasonable person might have taken. This may be very important given that the potential accused may himself have been at risk of abuse from other members of the household and focusing on the steps that the particular accused could have been reasonably expected to take was used in the Parliamentary debates to ward off suggestions that victims of domestic violence should be specifically exempted from the scope of the offence. Account can be taken of their situation through consideration of what steps they, in their situation, could reasonably be expected to take, an approach which was also endorsed by Lord Judge CJ in *Khan* [2009] 4 All ER 544, although on the facts it was not necessary for the judge to speculate on such matters.

Directions on Offence   The offence is designed to combat difficulties of proof, but **B1.87** it will be a challenging task to explain to juries precisely what it is that they must be satisfied of (see **B1.78**). Essentially, the jury must be satisfied that the accused (being a member of the same household etc.) *either* caused the victim's death by his own unlawful act (carrying a significant risk of serious physical harm) *or, if not*, that the accused failed to take steps that *he* could reasonably have been expected to take to protect V from the risk of such harm from an unlawful act by another member of the same household and D ought to have both been aware of the significant risk and ought to have foreseen the circumstances in which the unlawful act occurred. The circumstances need only be of the same kind as, and need not be identical to, those which should have been foreseen (*Khan* [2009] 4 All ER 544, where it was also said (at [36]) that 'generally speaking a direction framed in accordance with the statute pre-empts any criticism'). See also *Ikram* [2008] 4 All ER 253 at [62] for an example of 'a helpful way of directing a jury about the ingredients of the offence'.

INFANTICIDE

Definition

Infanticide Act 1938, s. 1   **B1.88**

(1) Where a woman by any wilful act or omission causes the death of her child being a child under the age of 12 months, but at the time of the act or omission the balance of her mind was disturbed by reason of her not having fully recovered from the effect of giving birth to the child or by reason of the effect of lactation consequent upon the birth of the child, then, if the circumstances were such that but for this Act the offence would have amounted to murder or manslaughter, she shall be guilty of [an offence], to wit of infanticide, and may for such offence be dealt with and punished as if she had been guilty of the offence of manslaughter of the child.

The CAJA 2009, s. 57, in force from 4 October 2010 (SI 2010 No. 816), substituted the word 'if' for the words 'notwithstanding that' and after 'murder' inserted 'or manslaughter' (see the discussion of *Gore* [2007] EWCA 2789 at **B1.94**).

Procedure

Infanticide is triable only on indictment. It is a class 1A offence.   **B1.89**

Indictment

Statement of Offence   **B1.90**

Infanticide contrary to section 1(1) of the Infanticide Act 1938

Particulars of Offence

A on or about the...day of...did cause the death of her child V aged under 12 months by a wilful act [or omission], namely, smothering him with a pillow [failing to...], but at a time when the balance of her mind was disturbed by reason of the fact that she had not fully recovered from the effect of giving birth to V [and/or from the effect of lactation consequent on giving birth to V]

Alternative Verdicts

B1.91   Child destruction (Infant Life (Preservation) Act 1929, s. 2(2)), see **B1.98**.

Sentencing Guidelines

B1.92   The maximum sentence is life imprisonment (Infanticide Act 1938, s. 1).

The proper approach for sentencing in cases of infanticide was considered by the Court of Appeal in *Sainsbury* (1989) 11 Cr App R (S) 533. The offender had become pregnant at the age of 15. She did not tell anyone about this, and gave birth to the baby without medical assistance in the bathroom of her boyfriend's flat. The baby was then wrapped in a blanket, taken some distance away and drowned in a river. The sentencer accepted that the balance of the offender's mind was disturbed by the effect of giving birth and that she was very immature, but did not accept that her responsibility was removed altogether. He imposed a sentence of 12 months' detention in a young offender institution. The Court of Appeal, however, having regard to statistics which indicated that in 59 cases of infanticide dealt with between 1979 and 1988 there had been no custodial sentences, all offenders having been dealt with by way of probation, supervision or hospital orders, decided that although the offence was serious the mitigating factors were overwhelming, and varied the sentence to probation. See also *Lewis* (1989) 11 Cr App R (S) 457.

Elements Generally

B1.93   The offence predates the introduction of the defence of diminished responsibility, and is designed to serve a similar role in relation to killings of very young children by their mothers in circumstances where the mothers are not fully responsible for their actions. It differs from diminished responsibility (and thus has survived the introduction of that defence) in that it can be charged from the outset and can be used to avoid charging a woman with the offence of murder (or now manslaughter) in relation to her own child. Under s. 1(2) of the Infanticide Act 1938, it can also be returned as an alternative verdict to murder (or, it would now appear, as an alternative verdict to manslaughter with effect from 4 October 2010 as a result of the CAJA 2009, s. 57 (see **B1.88**)), although s. 1(3) makes it clear that that is without prejudice to the jury's power on an indictment for murder to return a verdict of manslaughter or not guilty by reason of insanity. The offence covers a narrower range of circumstances than diminished responsibility, as the disturbance of the mother's mind must be due either to 'her not having fully recovered from the effect of giving birth' or to 'the effect of lactation consequent upon the birth of the child', criteria now regarded as outdated and unduly narrow. However, a legal burden of proof is placed on the defence in a case of diminished responsibility whereas, if the prosecution are alleging the offence amounts to murder, the burden of proving that it is not a case of infanticide remains on the prosecution. Nevertheless the narrowness of the criteria for infanticide moved the Court of Appeal to conclude in *Kai-Whitewind* [2005] 2 Cr App R 457, a case where a murder conviction was upheld and where there was no evidence to support infanticide as defined under the present law, that 'the law relating to infanticide is unsatisfactory and outdated. The appeal in this sad case demonstrates the need for a thorough re-examination.' See further Law Com No. 304 (November 2006), paras. 8.44 to 8.59 for a discussion of possible procedural reforms (distinct from the change actually effected by the CAJA 2009, s. 57).

Mens Rea

B1.94   The *mens rea* for infanticide was reviewed in the case of *Gore* [2007] EWCA Crim 2789. The case was a tragic one where the accused had herself died since her conviction following a guilty plea. The case had been referred by the CCRC to the Court of Appeal on the basis that she may not have had the *mens rea* for murder, which it was said was a prerequisite to a charge of infanticide (as seemed to have been assumed in *Smith* [1983] Crim LR 789). The Court of Appeal was of the opinion that proof of an intention to cause death or grievous bodily harm was not an integral part of the crime. The words in s. 1(1), 'notwithstanding that the circumstances were such that but for this Act the offence would have amounted to murder', simply had their natural meaning of 'even if' and should not be artificially read as 'provided that'. The *mens rea* was to be found in the opening words of s. 1(1), 'by any wilful act or omission', and this had the beneficial effect in the court's view that:

> ...the offence of infanticide covers a wider range of cases...A distressed young mother in a similar position to this appellant is not forced to confront what may be the stark truth that, for whatever reason, however disturbed she may have been at the time, she killed her child intending to kill or cause really serious bodily harm...a mother in this position, often a woman in severe distress, is not required to acknowledge that she has murdered her child before she can benefit from a charge of infanticide. (Hallet LJ at [35]).

The Court did not explain in detail what precisely is required for a 'wilful' act or omission and simply said 'the prosecution must prove that the defendant acted or omitted to act wilfully' but references in the judgment to *Sheppard* [1981] AC 394 and wilful neglect under the CYPA 1933, s. 1 (see **A2.13** and **B2.147**) suggest that the Court may have had a similar interpretation in mind. Despite this involving a subjective test, it is very considerably wider than the *mens rea* for murder or even manslaughter; not only does it encompass recklessness rather than intention but the recklessness can relate simply to the child's health being at risk rather than to death or serious injury. The resultant breadth of the offence is seen by the court as a good thing insofar as it avoids detailed examination or rehearsal of the often tragic circumstances where a distressed mother kills her young child. The amendments to s. 1 of the Infanticide Act 1938 effected by the CAJA 2009, s. 57 (in force from 4 October 2010: see **B1.88**), have the effect of confirming *Gore* insofar as the killing would not be required to have otherwise amounted to murder but would narrow it in that the offence would otherwise have had to amount to at least manslaughter.

Act or Omission which Causes Death

See **A1.14** to **A1.24** for liability for omissions. See **A1.17** for the duty of parents to preserve the   **B1.95**
life of their children; essentially, parents have a duty to take any reasonable steps lying within their power to prevent harm to their child. See **A1.25** *et seq*. for the principles of causation.

'Of Her Child under the Age of 12 Months'

If the mother kills the child of another, even if it is in the course of killing her own child, then the   **B1.96**
killing of that other cannot amount to infanticide. If the mother intended to kill or cause griev- ous bodily harm, it would prima facie be murder but might be brought within the defence of diminished responsibility. Strictly speaking, the same principles apply if the mother kills, say, her own 11-month-old child as a result of giving birth to another child later in the same year, since the disturbance of her mind has to be due to the effects of the birth of the child which is killed.

The offence cannot apply once the child has reached the age of 12 months, but again, dimin- ished responsibility would be the appropriate defence to consider. If, at the other end of the scale, the child has not been fully born before the mother kills it, the offence is not infanticide but child destruction (see **B1.98** to **B1.106**) and, by virtue of the Infant Life (Preservation) Act 1929, s. 2(2), child destruction is an alternative verdict to infanticide.

Complicity and Attempt

Where a mother aids and abets the killing of her child by another (e.g., the father) but cannot   **B1.97**
be said to cause its death, it would appear that infanticide is inapplicable, and again, diminished responsibility would have to be relied on. If a third person (including, e.g., the father) aids and

to commit what is (for her) only infanticide, it would seem likely that, by analogy with the Homicide Act 1957, s. 2(4) (see **B1.18**), that third person should still be guilty of murder if he has the appropriate *mens rea*.

Some doubts have been expressed whether attempted infanticide is an offence known to the law, but such an indictment was approved in *Smith* [1983] Crim LR 789.

CHILD DESTRUCTION

Definition

B1.98

Infant Life (Preservation) Act 1929, s. 1

(1) Subject as hereinafter in this subsection provided, any person who, with intent to destroy the life of a child capable of being born alive, by any wilful act causes a child to die before it has an existence independent of its mother, shall be guilty of [an offence], to wit, of child destruction, and shall be liable on conviction thereof on indictment to life imprisonment:
Provided that no person shall be found guilty of an offence under this section unless it is proved that the act which caused the death of the child was not done in good faith for the purpose only of preserving the life of the mother.

Procedure

B1.99 Child destruction is triable only on indictment. It is a class 1A offence.

Indictment

B1.100

Statement of Offence

Child destruction contrary to section 1(1) of the Infant Life (Preservation) Act 1929

Particulars of Offence

A on or about the...day of..., with intent to destroy the life of a child capable of being born alive, did cause the death of the child of V, before it had an existence independent of the said V, by means of a wilful act, namely...

Alternative Verdict

B1.101 Abortion contrary to the OAPA 1861, s. 58 (Infant Life (Preservation) Act 1929, s. 2(3)).

Sentencing

B1.102 The maximum sentence is life imprisonment (Infant Life (Preservation) Act 1929, s. 1).

Relationship with Other Offences

B1.103 This offence was created to fill the gap between murder (which, as noted at **B1.1** and **B1.8**, requires a live birth) and abortion (which requires an attempt to procure a miscarriage, see **B1.107** to **B1.117**). A child killed in the process of being born would not be murdered, because there would be no live birth, and it would not be abortion since there was no miscarriage. The offence, however, overlaps with abortion, as it is not restricted to acts done while the child is in the process of being born and also covers the causing of miscarriage of a child 'capable of being born alive'. Abortion is an alternative verdict to child destruction (Infant Life (Preservation) Act 1929, s. 2(3)).

Meaning of 'Capable of Being Born Alive'

B1.104

Infant Life (Preservation) Act 1929, s. 1

(2) For the purposes of this Act, evidence that a woman had at any material time been pregnant for a period of 28 weeks or more shall be prima facie proof that she was at that time pregnant of a child capable of being born alive.

226

In addition to this statutory presumption, it is open to the prosecution to try to prove that a particular child was capable of being born alive even though it has not reached the relevant number of weeks' gestation. In a civil case, *C v S* [1988] QB 135, the Court of Appeal held that a child between 18 and 21 weeks was not capable of being born alive, as it could not breathe. On the other hand, in *Rance v Mid-Downs Health Authority* [1991] 1 QB 587, Brooke J held that a child of 26 or 27 weeks' gestation, who could have breathed unaided for two to three hours at least, was capable of being born alive.

Meaning of 'Wilful Act'

In contrast to the offence of infanticide discussed at **B1.88** to **B1.97**, the definition requires a **B1.105** positive act and an omission will not suffice. 'Wilful' seems here to mean merely 'voluntary', as the *mens rea* of an 'intent to destroy the life of a child capable of being born alive' is separately stated. For the meaning of wilfulness generally, see **A2.13**. Recklessness is clearly insufficient in this context.

Special Defences

Under the proviso to the Infant Life (Preservation) Act 1929, s. 1(1), 'no person shall be found **B1.106** guilty...unless it is proved that the act which caused the death of the child was not done in good faith for the purpose only of preserving the life of the mother'.

Thus, the burden is on the prosecution to negate this defence, whether or not, it would seem, the accused adduces any evidence to raise the issue. The only cases relating to the scope of this defence are first instance rulings of trial judges, and even these were prosecutions for abortion under the OAPA 1861, s. 58, where the court implied a similar defence by analogy with the proviso currently under discussion. A fairly flexible view of the meaning of 'preserving the life of the mother' was taken in these cases. In *Bourne* [1939] 1 KB 687, at p. 694, Macnaghten J took the view that the jury could properly conclude that the accused was acting in good faith to preserve the life of the mother if he believed 'that the probable consequence of the continuance of the pregnancy will be to make the woman a physical or mental wreck'. In *Newton* [1958] Crim LR 469, Ashworth J referred to 'preserving the life or health of the woman...not only her physical health but also her mental health'.

The Abortion Act 1967, s. 5(1), provides a defence to a charge of child destruction as follows:

> No offence under the Infant Life (Preservation) Act 1929 shall be committed by a registered medical practitioner who terminates a pregnancy in accordance with the provisions of this Act.

The offence of child destruction and the presumption that a child is capable of being born alive at 28 weeks' gestation no longer therefore represent one of the limits on the lawfulness of abortions under the 1967 Act. If the provisions of the 1967 Act (see **B1.115**) are complied with, an act is neither abortion nor child destruction.

ABORTION

Definition

Offences against the Person Act 1861, s. 58   **B1.107**

> Every woman, being with child, who, with intent to procure her own miscarriage, shall unlawfully administer to herself any poison or other noxious thing, or shall unlawfully use any instrument or other means whatsoever with the like intent, and whosoever, with intent to procure the miscarriage of any woman, whether she be or be not with child, shall unlawfully administer to her or cause to be taken by her any poison or other noxious thing, or shall unlawfully use any instrument or other means whatsoever with the like intent, shall be guilty of [an offence], and being convicted thereof shall be liable to [imprisonment] for life.

Procedure

B1.108　Abortion is triable only on indictment. It is a class 1A offence.

Indictment

B1.109

Statement of Offence (1)

Administering poison with intent to procure miscarriage contrary to section 58 of the Offences against the Person Act 1861

Particulars of Offence

A on or about the…day of…did unlawfully administer [or cause to be administered] to V a poison or other noxious thing, namely…, with intent to procure her miscarriage

Statement of Offence (2)

Using an instrument or other means with intent to procure miscarriage contrary to section 58 of the Offences against the Person Act 1861

Particulars of Offence

A on or about the…day of…did unlawfully use the following means, namely…, with intent to procure the miscarriage of V

Sentencing Guidelines

B1.110　The maximum penalty is life imprisonment (OAPA 1861, s. 58).

Sentences of three years' imprisonment were upheld on offenders in *Scrimaglia* (1971) 55 Cr App R 280 who pleaded guilty to using an instrument to procure a miscarriage. Lord Parker CJ endorsed the trial judge's comment that 'Now that abortions can be performed legally either under the National Health Service or at the patient's own expense, operations such as yours, carried out at a cut price and in disgraceful, insanitary and even dangerous conditions, are totally unnecessary apart from being against the law'. The offender in *Catt* [2014] 1 Cr App R (S) 210 (35) was a 36-year-old woman, married with two young children. She induced her own miscarriage when 40 weeks' pregnant by taking a drug which she had obtained over the internet. A sentence of eight years' imprisonment was reduced to three and a half years on appeal.

Elements Generally

B1.111　Given the large number of abortions now carried out legally under the provisions of the Abortion Act 1967 (see **B1.115**), the offence is comparatively rarely prosecuted. There are two peculiar features to note about the definition of the offence. First, it is in the nature of a statutory attempt. The *actus reus* does not require the actual procuring of a miscarriage, but rather an act done with the intention of procuring that result. Secondly, the requirements of the offence differ according to whether it is the (pregnant) woman herself or another person who is charged. In the case of the woman herself she must indeed be pregnant, whereas in the case of others, it is sufficient if she is believed to be pregnant and there is thus an intention to procure her miscarriage. This latter distinction is now almost redundant, because:

(a) if a non-pregnant woman is helped by another, she can be convicted either of encouraging and assisting (*Sockett* (1908) 1 Cr App R 101) or conspiring with (*Whitchurch* (1890) 24 QBD 42) that other; and

(b) even if she is acting alone, she would appear to be guilty of an attempt to commit the offence under s. 58 as a result of the Criminal Attempts Act 1981, s. 1(2) (see **A5.69** *et seq.*).

In practice, the woman herself is rarely prosecuted today, and the offence is aimed principally at third parties operating outside the terms of what is permitted under the Abortion Act 1967 and exploiting the woman's predicament for financial gain.

Intention to Procure Miscarriage

For the meaning of 'intention', see A2.4. What stage of a pregnancy has to be reached before it **B1.112**
is possible to 'miscarry' is a matter of some controversy. Is it as soon as the ovum is fertilised,
or only when the fertilised ovum is implanted in the womb some ten days later? If it were the
former, then some types of so-called contraceptives, such as 'the morning-after' pill, would be
technically illegal under the OAPA 1861, s. 58. However, in *R (Smeaton) v Secretary of State for
Health* [2002] Crim LR 664, Munby J ruled that 'miscarriage' means the termination of an
established pregnancy and that there is no established pregnancy prior to implantation. Hence
the prescription of the morning-after pill is not a criminal offence.

'Poison or other Noxious Thing...Instrument or Other Means'

If the indictment alleges the administration of a poison or noxious thing, it must either be a 'recog- **B1.113**
nised poison' or, to be a noxious thing, some substance which is either harmful in itself or administered in such a quantity as to be harmful (*Cramp* (1880) 5 QBD 307) though not necessarily
abortifacient (*Marlow* (1964) 49 Cr App R 49). However, it may be that a practical way out of the
difficulty, if there is any doubt about whether the substance administered constitutes a poison or
noxious thing, would be to utilise that form of the offence that can be committed by 'any means
whatsoever', and to frame the indictment accordingly as in Statement of Offence (2) at **B1.109**.

Special Defences

It was held in *Bourne* [1939] 1 KB 687 that, by analogy to the proviso to the Infant Life **B1.114**
(Preservation) Act 1929, s. 1(1), an act was not unlawful within s. 58 of the 1861 Act if it was
done in good faith for the purpose only of preserving the life of the mother. This defence now
seems to be entirely supplanted by the provision in the Abortion Act 1967, s. 5, that anything
done with intent to procure a woman's miscarriage is unlawfully done unless authorised by s. 1
of the 1967 Act (see **B1.115**).

Abortion Act 1967, ss. 1 and 5

Abortion Act 1967, ss. 1 and 5 **B1.115**

1.—(1) Subject to the provisions of this section, a person shall not be guilty of an offence under
the law relating to abortion when a pregnancy is terminated by a registered medical practitioner if two registered medical practitioners are of the opinion, formed in good faith—
   (a) that the pregnancy has not exceeded its twenty-fourth week and that the continuance of the pregnancy would involve risk, greater than if the pregnancy were terminated, of injury to the physical or mental health of the pregnant woman or any
   existing children of her family; or
   (b) that the termination is necessary to prevent grave permanent injury to the physical
   or mental health of the pregnant woman; or
   (c) that the continuance of the pregnancy would involve risk to the life of the pregnant
   woman, greater than if the pregnancy were terminated; or
   (d) that there is a substantial risk that if the child were born it would suffer from such
   physical or mental abnormalities as to be seriously handicapped.
(2) In determining whether the continuance of a pregnancy would involve such risk of injury
to health as is mentioned in paragraph (a) or (b) of subsection (1) of this section, account
may be taken of the pregnant woman's actual or reasonably foreseeable environment.
(3) Except as provided by subsection (4) of this section, any treatment for the termination
of pregnancy must be carried out in a hospital vested in the Secretary of State for the
purposes of his functions under the National Health Service Act 2006 or the National
Health Service (Scotland) Act 1978 or in a hospital vested in a National Health
Service trust established under section 18 of the National Health Service (Wales) Act
2006 or the National Health Service (Scotland) Act 1978 or an NHS foundation trust
or in a place approved for the purposes of this section by the Secretary of State.
(3A) The power under subsection (3) of this section to approve a place includes power, in relation to treatment consisting primarily in the use of such medicines as may be specified

    in the approval and carried out in such manner as may be so specified, to approve a class of places.

(4)   Subsection (3) of this section, and so much of subsection (1) as relates to the opinion of two registered medical practitioners, shall not apply to the termination of a pregnancy by a registered medical practitioner in a case where he is of the opinion, formed in good faith, that the termination is immediately necessary to save the life or to prevent grave permanent injury to the physical or mental health of the pregnant woman.

5. —(1)   No offence under the Infant Life (Preservation) Act 1929 shall be committed by a registered medical practitioner who terminates a pregnancy in accordance with the provisions of this Act.

(2)   For the purposes of the law relating to abortion, anything done with intent to procure a woman's miscarriage (or, in the case of a woman carrying more than one foetus, her miscarriage of any foetus) is unlawfully done unless authorised by section 1 of this Act and, in the case of a woman carrying more than one foetus, anything done with intent to procure her miscarriage of any foetus is authorised by that section if—

(a)   the ground for termination of the pregnancy specified in subsection (1)(d) of that section applies in relation to any foetus and the thing is done for the purpose of procuring the miscarriage of the foetus, or

(b)   any of the other grounds for termination of the pregnancy specified in that section applies.

Since under s. 5(1) of the 1967 Act, as amended by the Human Fertilisation and Embryology Act 1990, s. 37, compliance with the provisions of the 1967 Act is also a defence to a charge of child destruction under the Infant Life (Preservation) Act 1929 (see **B1.104**), the upper time-limits for legal abortions now are 24 weeks (believed) gestation for abortions under s. 1(1)(a) of the 1967 Act, and right up to the point of live birth under s. 1(1)(b), (c) or (d). Section 1(3A) is intended to cater for drugs such as RU 486 (mifepristone) being used in places other than National Health Service hospitals or approved nursing homes. Section 5(2) makes it clear that selective reduction (procuring the miscarriage of one or more, but not all, of the foetuses in a multiple pregnancy) may in appropriate cases be authorised by s. 1.

B1.116   Section 1 was considered by the House of Lords in *Royal College of Nursing of the UK v Department of Health and Social Security* [1981] AC 800, in which Lord Diplock said (at p. 828):

> Subsection 1 although it is expressed to apply only 'when a pregnancy is terminated by a registered medical practitioner'...also appears to contemplate treatment that is in the nature of a team effort and to extend its protection to all those who play a part in it.

Thus, methods of abortion, such as induction of premature delivery by means of prostaglandin drip, which involve nurses (or others) playing a substantial role, are covered, and all the participants are exempted provided that a registered medical practitioner accepts (loc. cit.):

> ...responsibility for all stages of the treatment for the termination of the pregnancy. The particular method to be used should be decided by the doctor in charge of the treatment for termination of the pregnancy; he should carry out any physical acts, forming part of the treatment, that in accordance with accepted medical practice are done only by qualified medical practitioners, and should give specific instructions as to the carrying out of such parts of the treatment as in accordance with accepted medical practice are carried out by nurses or other members of the hospital staff without medical qualifications. To each of them, the doctor, or his substitute, should be available to be consulted or called on for assistance from beginning to end of the treatment.

Although s. 1 refers to when 'a pregnancy *is* terminated', its protection also extends to cases where the attempt to terminate is unsuccessful (*Royal College of Nursing v DHSS* [1981] AC 800, per Lord Diplock at p. 828), a not insignificant point, since the offence under the Offences against the Person Act 1861, s. 58, is committed irrespective of whether a miscarriage is actually procured.

Medical Practitioners' Opinion   The precise scope of the grounds for abortion enumerated   **B1.117**
in s. 1 are likely to continue to escape detailed interpretation by the courts, since the question
is not whether these grounds actually exist but whether 'two registered medical practitioners
are of the opinion, formed in good faith' that they exist. It was said in *Smith* [1973] 1 All ER
376 that a conviction of a doctor without evidence as to professional practice and the medical
probabilities was likely to be unsafe, but it was stressed that the question of good faith is a matter for the jury to be determined by reference to all the evidence (and the appeal in that case
was dismissed).

Although under the Abortion Act 1967, s. 1(3), the termination must normally be carried out
in a National Health Service hospital or an approved clinic, under s. 1(4) this requirement does
not apply if just one registered medical practitioner 'is of the opinion, formed in good faith, that
the termination is immediately necessary to save the life or to prevent grave permanent injury to
the physical or mental health of the pregnant woman'. Although, as noted at **B1.114**, s. 5 makes
compliance with the Act the sole test of unlawfulness for the purposes of the law of abortion, it is
possible that this does not exclude a general defence such as duress of circumstances (see **A3.50**
and also the Canadian case of *Morgentaler v The Queen* (1975) 53 DLR (3d) 161), e.g., where
a competent medical student finds himself, rather than a registered medical practitioner, in the
sort of emergency situation outlined in s. 1(4).

Regulations have been made under s. 2(1) of the 1967 Act relating to the form of certificates of
opinions, requiring notifications etc. of terminations and prohibiting disclosure of information
in such notifications etc. Under s. 2(3) of the Act, contravention of the regulations is a summary
offence, but would not appear to render an abortion illegal if the provisions of s. 1 of the Act are
complied with. However, absence of the proper certificates may make it more difficult to show
that the relevant opinion(s) had indeed been formed in good faith.

SUPPLYING OR PROCURING THE PHYSICAL MEANS FOR ABORTION

Definition

Offences against the Person Act 1861, s. 59   B1.118

Whoever shall unlawfully supply or procure any poison or other noxious thing, or any instrument
or thing whatsoever, knowing that the same is intended to be unlawfully used or employed with
intent to procure the miscarriage of any woman, whether she be or be not with child, shall be guilty
of [an offence], and being convicted thereof shall be liable...to imprisonment...for any term not
exceeding five years.

Procedure

Supplying or procuring the physical means for abortion is triable only on indictment. It is nor-   **B1.119**
mally a class 3 offence, but see CPD XIII, para. B (see Supplement, **PD-97**) for the additional
factors that the court considers on allocation.

Indictment

Statement of Offence   B1.120

Supplying [or procuring] the physical means to procure a miscarriage contrary to section 59 of the
Offences against the Person Act 1861

Particulars of Offence

A on or about the...day of...unlawfully supplied [or procured] a poison or other noxious thing,
namely..., knowing that it was intended to be unlawfully used with intent to procure the miscarriage of V

Sentence

B1.121 The maximum sentence is five years (OAPA 1861, s. 59).

Elements

B1.122 'Supply' obviously means supply to another, and conversely 'procure' (any poison etc.) means procure *from* another, i.e. 'get possession of something of which you do not have possession already' (*Mills* [1963] 1 QB 522). Thus, the offence is not committed merely by producing the instrument or noxious thing etc. from one's cupboard (although the offence clearly is committed if it is then supplied, with the necessary knowledge, to another). In *Ahmed* [2011] QB 512, where the appellant had tried to trick his wife into undergoing an abortion procedure at a clinic, the Court of Appeal ruled that he did not fall within the section as the means or 'thing' supplied or procured must be 'some sort of article or object rather than something such as a medical procedure which has no physical existence'. The words 'or thing whatsoever' in the OAPA 1861, s. 59, were contrasted with the phrase 'any means whatsoever' in s. 58. The latter might be apt to refer to a procedure as well as to a physical thing but 'thing' in s. 59 had a narrower meaning and was in effect interpreted *sui generis* with 'poison', 'noxious thing' and 'instrument' — all of which are physical objects.

Although s. 59 refers to the accused's *knowledge* of the intentions of others, such old authorities as there are interpret this in effect as *belief* that the others intend unlawfully to use the poison etc. with intent to procure a miscarriage (*Hillman* (1863) Le & Ca 343; *Titley* (1880) 14 Cox CC 502) — i.e. the accused can be convicted even if in actual fact the other or others do not intend so to use it unlawfully. The effect of the Criminal Attempts Act 1981, s. 1(3) (see **A5.69** *et seq.*), is probably that, quite apart from these decisions, the accused could now be convicted of attempt in these circumstances.

Special Defences

B1.123 The exemption from liability provided by the Abortion Act 1967, s. 1, is equally applicable to this offence, as s. 6 of the Act defines 'the law relating to abortion' as meaning, 'sections 58 and 59 of the OAPA 1861 and any rule of law relating to the procurement of abortion'.

CONCEALMENT OF BIRTH

Definition

B1.124
> Offences against the Person Act 1861, s. 60
>
> If any woman shall be delivered of a child, every person who shall, by any secret disposition of the dead body of the said child, whether such child died before, at, or after its birth, endeavour to conceal the birth thereof, shall be guilty of [an offence], and being convicted thereof shall be liable, at the discretion of the court, to be imprisoned for any term not exceeding two years.

Procedure

B1.125 Concealing the birth of a child is triable either way. When tried on indictment it is normally a class 3 offence, but see CPD XIII, para. B (see Supplement, **PD-97**) for the additional factors that the court considers on allocation.

Indictment

B1.126
> *Statement of Offence*
>
> Endeavouring to conceal birth contrary to section 60 of the Offences against the Person Act 1861
>
> *Particulars of Offence*
>
> A on or about the…day of…endeavoured to conceal the birth of a child of which V had been delivered by a secret disposition of the dead body of that child

Alternative Verdicts

There are no alternative verdicts. It should also be noted that as a result of the Criminal Law Act 1967, sch. 2, it is no longer possible to convict of this offence on an indictment for murder, infanticide or child destruction. Other offences which should be borne in mind include the common-law misdemeanours of disposing of or destroying a dead body with intent to prevent an inquest being held (*Stephenson* (1884) 13 QBD 331) and preventing the burial of a body (*Hunter* [1974] QB 95). See also **B14.52**.

B1.127

Sentence

The maximum penalty is two years (OAPA 1861, s. 60).

B1.128

Meaning of 'Child'

In *Berriman* (1854) 6 Cox CC 388, Erle J said (at p. 390) that the child must have:

B1.129

> ...arrived at that stage of maturity at the time of birth, that it might have been a living child.... No specific limit can be assigned to the period when the chance of life begins, but it may, perhaps, be safely assumed that under seven months the great probability is that the child would not be born alive.

However, in *Colmer* (1864) 9 Cox CC 506, a child of just four or five months' gestational age, about the length of a man's finger, was said by Martin B at first instance to be within the definition. The decision has been doubted, and indeed the jury acquitted. The meaning given to 'child' in *Berriman* is probably preferable and would make the offence consistent with that of child destruction. The qualifying words 'capable of being born alive' in the Infant Life (Preservation) Act 1929 (see **B1.98**), although in one sense somewhat otiose if 'child' itself is given the more limited *Berriman* meaning, could be regarded as clarifying the ambiguity already demonstrated in these cases.

Secret Disposition

This is satisfied by putting the dead body in a place where it is unlikely to be found, even though the body is not concealed in the sense that it is completely hidden from view (*Brown* (1870) LR 1 CCR 244). Conversely, hiding the body from view is not sufficient if it is in such a manner that the body is nevertheless likely to be found (*George* (1868) 11 Cox CC 41). The accused's act must be done in relation to a dead body, so that the offence is not committed where the accused conceals a living child which later dies (*May* (1867) 10 Cox CC 448). However, there is almost certain to be liability for murder or manslaughter in this situation (or at least for attempt to commit an offence under the OAPA 1861, s. 60, where the accused believes the child is already dead). In *Hughes* (1850) 4 Cox CC 447, the accused concealed a living child, returned and found it dead, and replaced the covers which were concealing it. This was held to be an offence within a predecessor of s. 60 (9 Geo. 4 c. 31, s. 14), and to be a disposition of the dead body. An alternative and more appropriate charge would appear to be some form of homicide in relation to the initial act of concealing the living child which led to its death.

B1.130

SOLICITATION OF MURDER

Definition

| Offences against the Person Act 1861, s. 4 | **B1.131** |

Whosoever shall solicit, encourage, persuade or endeavour to persuade, or shall propose to any person, to murder any other person, whether he be a subject of Her Majesty or not, and whether he be within the Queen's dominions or not, shall be guilty of [an offence], and being convicted thereof shall be liable to imprisonment for life.

Procedure

B1.132   Solicitation of murder is triable only on indictment. It is a class 1A offence.

Indictment

B1.133

Statement of Offence

Soliciting to commit murder contrary to section 4 of the Offences against the Person Act 1861

Particulars of Offence

A on or about the…day of…, solicited [or encouraged etc.] X to murder V

Sentencing Guidelines

B1.134   The maximum penalty is life imprisonment (OAPA 1861, s. 4).

An extended sentence for soliciting murder, with a custodial term of 12 years' imprisonment and an extension period of five years, was upheld in *Ahmad* [2014] 1 Cr App R (S) 89 (17), where the offender published material on a website encouraging the murder of Members of Parliament and providing their personal details. In *Kayani* [1997] 2 Cr App R (S) 313 a sentence of 12 years' imprisonment was upheld on an offender convicted for soliciting the murder of his niece and her husband. He was arrested by an undercover police officer posing as a contract killer, to whom payment of £20,000 was tendered partly in cash and partly in heroin. The offender received concurrent sentences for supplying heroin. In *Adamthwaite* (1994) 15 Cr App R (S) 241, where the offender had met with an undercover police officer and agreed to pay £5,000 for the murder of the offender's wife, the sentence of six years on a guilty plea was said to be 'on the high side' and was reduced to four years by the Court of Appeal. See also *A-G's Ref (No. 43 of 1996)* [1997] 1 Cr App R (S) 378.

Elements

B1.135   Although the soliciting must be done from within the jurisdiction, the phrase 'whether he be a subject of Her Majesty or not, and whether he be within the Queen's dominions or not' has now in effect been interpreted so that it applies not only to the person to be murdered but also to the person being solicited. Thus in *Abu Hamza* [2007] QB 659 it was no defence that the persons being solicited were of various nationalities and the murders were to take place abroad and that it was not proved that any of those solicited to murder were British nationals. The encouragement does not in any event have to be directed to a particular individual — see *Most* (1881) 7 QBD 244, where the offence was committed by means of a newspaper article. See also *El-Faisal* [2004] EWCA Crim 456, a case involving solicitation to indiscriminate killing which was recorded on tape, the defence of limitation to self-defence on the battlefield not being made out.

The offence is not complete until someone is in receipt of the solicitation, although the act of sending it can constitute an attempt (*Krause* (1902) 66 JP 121). It does not matter that the recipient is not in fact influenced, although in this case it might be prudent to allege an 'endeavour to persuade' in the particulars. Encouraging a pregnant woman to kill her child in the future, after it shall have been born alive, is an offence within the section (*Shephard* [1919] 2 KB 125). See *Tait* [1990] 1 QB 290 and **B1.147**. The wording of the offence is wide enough to include soliciting someone to participate in murder as a secondary party, as in *Winter* [2007] EWCA Crim 3493 (e.g., by encouraging him to provide access to the intended venue of the killing).

ENCOURAGING OR ASSISTING SUICIDE

Definition

The Suicide Act 1961, s. 2, was substantially amended, and a new s. 2A was inserted, by the **B1.136** CAJA 2009, s. 59, which came into force on 1 February 2010 (see SI 2010 No. 145). For transitional provisions, see the CAJA 2009, sch. 22, para. 10.

Suicide Act 1961, ss. 2 and 2A

2.—(1) A person ('D') commits an offence if—
  (a) D does an act capable of encouraging or assisting the suicide or attempted suicide of another person, and
  (b) D's act was intended to encourage or assist suicide or an attempt at suicide.
(1A) The person referred to in subsection (1)(a) need not be a specific person (or class of persons) known to, or identified by, D.
(1B) D may commit an offence under this section whether or not a suicide, or an attempt at suicide, occurs.
(1C) An offence under this section is triable on indictment and a person convicted of such an offence is liable to imprisonment for a term not exceeding 14 years.
(2) If on the trial of an indictment for murder or manslaughter of a person it is proved that the deceased person committed suicide, and the accused committed an offence under subsection (1) in relation to that suicide, the jury may find the accused guilty of the offence under subsection (1)
2A.—(1) If D arranges for a person ('D2') to do an act that is capable of encouraging or assisting the suicide or attempted suicide of another person and D2 does that act, D is also to be treated for the purposes of this Act as having done it.
(2) Where the facts are such that an act is not capable of encouraging or assisting suicide or attempted suicide, for the purposes of this Act it is to be treated as so capable if the act would have been so capable had the facts been as D believed them to be at the time of the act or had subsequent events happened in the manner D believed they would happen (or both).
(3) A reference in this Act to a person ('P') doing an act that is capable of encouraging the suicide or attempted suicide of another person includes a reference to P doing so by threatening another person or otherwise putting pressure on another person to commit or attempt suicide.

Procedure

Encouraging or assisting suicide is triable only on indictment. It is a class 1A offence. The consent **B1.137** of the DPP is required to initiate proceedings for this offence (Suicide Act 1961, s. 2(4)). The House of Lords has held that the DPP cannot be required, nor does he have the power, to give an undertaking to withhold his consent to prosecution in advance of a contemplated assisted suicide (*R (Pretty) v DPP* [2002] 1 AC 800), notwithstanding the compassionate factors of the particular case where the contemplated assistance would involve assistance in travelling to a country where assisted suicide is lawful. However, as regards the separate question of whether the offence in such circumstances interferes with the right to respect for private life under the ECHR, Article 8(1), the House of Lords in *R (Purdy) v DPP* [2010] 1 AC 345 revised its own approach in *Pretty* (which was to the effect that Article 8 was not engaged) and followed the approach of the ECtHR in *Pretty v UK* (2002) 35 EHRR 1 in holding that Article 8 is indeed engaged in that choices about the closing moments of life are part of the act of living. Furthermore, for the interference to be 'in accordance with the law' within Article 8(2), the House of Lords in *Purdy* concluded that there was a legal requirement for the DPP 'to promulgate an offence-specific policy identifying the facts and circumstances which he will take into account in deciding, in a case such as that which Ms Purdy's case exemplifies, whether or not to consent to a prosecution under section 2(1) of the 1961 Act'. The DPP policy on prosecuting cases of assisted suicide can be found at www.cps.gov.uk/publications/prosecution/assisted_suicide_policy.pdf and 'applies when the act that constitutes the encouragement or assistance is committed in England and Wales; any suicide or attempted suicide as a result of that encouragement or assistance may take place anywhere in the world, including in England

and Wales'. In *R (Nicklinson) v Ministry of Justice* [2014] 2 All ER 32, the Court of Appeal held (with Lord Judge CJ dissenting) that the DPP had not done all that was required of him in *R (Purdy) v DPP* [2010] 1 AC 345 in publishing his policy as to the facts and circumstances he will take into account in deciding whether to consent to a prosecution. However, in the Supreme Court ([2014] UKSC 38), the DPP's appeal was unanimously allowed on this point, the content of the policy being constitutionally a matter for the DPP. In the course of the proceedings, counsel for the DPP indicated that under the 2010 Policy a stranger who is not profiteering from his or her action, but assisting to provide services which, if provided by a close relative, would not attract a prosecution, was most unlikely to be prosecuted. The Supreme Court left it as a matter for the DPP as to whether this indication should stand and whether the policy should be amended to reflect this. The Supreme Court also confirmed that the general prohibition created by s. 2 engages Article 8 of the ECHR and that the Court has jurisdiction to decide whether it is justified under Article 8(2) or incompatible under the Human Rights Act 1998. However, the majority considered that the matter was either in principle or, for the moment at least, one more appropriate for Parliament to resolve.

Indictment

B1.138
Statement of Offence

Doing an act capable of encouraging or assisting suicide contrary to section 2(1) of the Suicide Act 1961

Particulars of Offence

A on or about the…day…did an act, namely…, capable of encouraging or assisting the commission of suicide or attempted suicide, intending thereby to encourage or assist suicide or attempted suicide

Alternative Verdicts

B1.139 There are no alternative verdicts specifically provided for. The offence is itself an alternative verdict to murder or manslaughter (Suicide Act 1961, s. 2(2)).

Sentencing Guidelines

B1.140 The maximum penalty is 14 years' imprisonment (Suicide Act 1961, s. 2).

The Court of Appeal reviewed the relevant sentencing considerations for offences of encouraging or assisting suicide or attempted suicide in *Howe* [2014] EWCA Crim 114. Treacy LJ referred to cases involving 'face to face' encouragement, rather than 'remote' encouragement over the internet. On degrees of harm involved, the most serious cases were those where death resulted, then those where serious harm resulted. Harm may be psychological as well as physical, and the effects on others as well as the victim should be taken into account. At the lower end of the harm range will be cases where, despite the encouragement of the offender, the victim does not go on to attempt suicide, or where a substance is provided but it turns out to be harmless. Turning to culpability, the court will have to consider issues of premeditation, persistence, and extent of the encouragement. Motivation may be important, with compassion at one end of the range and malice or prospect of gain at the other. There may also be breach of a duty of care or trust. The court should also consider whether the victim had a settled, voluntary and informed intention to commit suicide or not, whether the victim sought assistance from the offender, the victim's capacity to choose and the offender's knowledge of the extent of the vulnerability of the victim. Evidence of threats, pressure or persuasion applied to the victim will also be relevant. In those cases where the custodial threshold is crossed, the likely sentencing range is three years' imprisonment to twelve years or more after a trial. If the victim has not attempted suicide, there may be cases where custody is not required, but the range of general aggravating and mitigating factors will apply and the particular facts in each case must be examined with care. The Court found no reason to disapprove sentences imposed in the few earlier reported cases, such as *McGranaghan* [1987] 9 Cr App R (S) 447 and *Workman* [2007] 1 Cr App R (S) 104. On the facts of *Howe* itself, the 19-year-old offender, immature but with no previous convictions, was a close friend of the victim who suffered from mental health problems and had threatened in the past to take his own life. After spending much of the day drinking together, the offender drove to a petrol station to buy petrol and a cigarette lighter and returned to the victim's home. The victim then poured petrol on himself and set himself on fire, causing 95 per cent burns. Death did not result but the victim was grievously injured. The Court reduced a sentence of 12 years' detention in a young offender institution, imposed after Howe was sentenced, after a trial, to 10 years' imprisonment. The Court noted that the Sentencing Council guideline on offences under the OAPA 1861, s. 18, was not of assistance when sentencing an offence of assisting suicide.

Elements

This special statutory offence was created because the substantive offence of suicide was abolished   **B1.141** by the Suicide Act 1961, s. 1, and it originally used the traditional language of complicity expressed in terms of aiding, abetting counselling or procuring suicide. The changes to s. 2 made by the CAJA 2009, s. 59, having effect from 1 February 2010, are designed to state the existing law more clearly and unambiguously rather than to make any particular changes and are designed to bring the offence into line with, and to make use of the terminology in, part 2 of the SCA 2007 relating to the inchoate offence of (intentionally) encouraging and assisting crime (see **A5.3** *et seq.*). Since there is in law no offence of suicide which can be encouraged or assisted, s. 2 makes the conduct which is capable of encouraging or assisting suicide an offence in its own right, just as under the previous formulation the aider and abettor of suicide was the principal offender as there was in law no principal offence of suicide to aid and abet. An inchoate basis of liability is in this sense somewhat more appropriate than one based on aiding and abetting which normally presupposes the commission of the principal offence which has been aided and abetted. The explicitly inchoate nature of the new formulation of the offence (spelled out in the new s. 2(1B)) also removes the former need to rely on a prosecution under the Criminal Attempts Act 1981 for attempt to assist suicide where no one as a result of the encouragement actually commits or attempts to commit suicide. The full inchoate offence under s. 2(1) is now committed by doing an act capable of encouraging or assisting suicide whether or not any suicide is committed or attempted and the law of attempt does not come into it (indeed the CAJA 2009, sch. 21, para. 58, excludes the operation of the Criminal Attempts Act 1981 in relation to offences under s. 2 of the Suicide Act 1961). Section 2(1A) now also makes it explicit that one can be liable for doing acts capable of encouraging or assisting persons unknown to commit suicide. One example of this would be by means of material on a web site.

The accused must, of course, intend that someone commit or attempt to commit suicide (see   **B1.142** *A-G v Able* [1984] 1 QB 795 under the old law and see now s. 2(1)(b)) but it is unnecessary for the accused to know or believe that the person encouraged had been intending or contemplating suicide (*S* (2005) 149 SJ 390). Despite the confusion over whether there can generally be a conspiracy to aid and abet (see **A5.49**), there could be liability for conspiracy to aid and abet under s. 2(1) (*Reed* [1982] Crim LR 819) and there is no reason why the position should be any different under the new version of the offence.

Section 2A also makes it clear (a) that the offence can be committed through an intermediary, (b) that there is no defence of impossibility, and (c) that encouragement by threats or other forms of pressure is covered. Section 2B clarifies that D's liability need not be based on an individual act but may be based on a course of conduct over a period of time. Again, none of this is intended significantly to change the substance as opposed to the form of the previous law.

THREATS TO KILL

Definition

Offences against the Person Act 1861, s. 16	**B1.143**

A person who without lawful excuse makes to another a threat, intending that that other would fear it would be carried out, to kill that other or a third person shall be guilty of an offence and liable on conviction on indictment to imprisonment for a term not exceeding 10 years.

Procedure

B1.144 Threatening to kill is triable either way. When tried on indictment this is normally a class 3 offence, but see CPD XIII, para. B (see Supplement, **PD-97**) for the additional factors that the court considers on allocation.

Indictment

B1.145

Statement of Offence

Making a threat to kill contrary to section 16 of the Offences against the Person Act 1861

Particulars of Offence

A on or about the…day of…, without lawful excuse, threatened V that he would kill him [or that he would kill X] intending that V would fear that the said threat would be carried out

Sentencing Guidelines

B1.146 The maximum penalty is ten years' imprisonment (Criminal Law Act 1977, sch. 12, replacing OAPA 1861, s. 16).

Sentences approved by the Court of Appeal for this offence range downwards from the five years' imprisonment imposed in *Bowden* (1986) 8 Cr App R (S) 155, where the offender, under treatment for alcoholism, went to the home of a woman with whom he had formerly lived, and threatened her with a sword. The woman barricaded herself in the bedroom and the police had to force their way into the house to arrest the offender. In *Martin* (1993) 14 Cr App R (S) 645, four years' imprisonment was reduced to three years in a case where the offender sent two anonymous notes, stained with blood. In *Gaskin* (1996) *The Times*, 15 August 1996, Judge Allen in the Court of Appeal noted that cases of making threats to kill posed difficult sentencing problems, since they ranged from threats made in the heat of the moment to cases where the victim continued to fear for the future as well as having suffered short-term terror. In recognising that the instant appeal was a case of the latter type, the Court of Appeal upheld a prison sentence of four years. Four years was reduced to 20 months in *Patel* [2013] 1 Cr App R (S) 617 (119), where the offender pleaded guilty to threatening his former partner to kill their young son, and then sending her a text message saying that he had done so. In *Choudhury* [1997] 2 Cr App R (S) 300 the offender, after being released on bail for a public order offence, made repeated threats to kill the police officer who had arrested him and also threatened the officer's family. The Court of Appeal reduced the prison sentence from three years to two years.

Elements

B1.147 The words 'without lawful excuse' in the OAPA 1861, s. 16, would exempt, for example, a threat made reasonably in self-defence to deter an apprehended attack or to prevent crime (*Cousins* [1982] QB 526). An implied threat will suffice (see the facts of *Solanke* [1970] 3 All ER 1383), as will a threat that is only to be carried out at some time in the future, although it would seem that it has to be one that will be carried out by the accused, or at least under his instructions. The victim must fear that the threat will be carried out against himself or another so it is the person to whom the threat is made, rather than the person to be killed (if different), who must fear that the threat will be carried out. A threat to a pregnant woman in respect of her unborn child is not sufficient if the threat is to kill it before its birth but if it is a threat to kill the child after its birth, then that would appear to be within s. 16 (*Tait* [1990] 1 QB 290). Alleging more than one threat in a single count may make it duplicitous but this will not necessarily result in any injustice so as to justify quashing a conviction (*Marchese* [2009] 1 WLR 992).

CORPORATE MANSLAUGHTER

B1.148 The Corporate Manslaughter and Corporate Homicide Act 2007 (CMCHA) came into force on 6 April 2008, except for s. 2(1)(d) dealing with certain aspects of deaths in custody (in force from

1 September 2011 — see SI 2011 No. 1867) and s. 10 relating to publicity orders (in force from 15 February 2010 — see SI 2010 No. 276). The Act abolishes the common-law offence of manslaughter by gross negligence in its application to corporations (s. 20) and in doing so replaces the 'identification principle' (see **A6.2**) with a new offence based on a qualified aggregation principle whereby the fault of a number of individuals may be relevant to a management or organisational failure causing death, and the organisation can be liable provided that the contribution of 'senior management' is a 'substantial element' in the breach of duty. Only corporations and certain other organisations (including partnerships that are employers, public bodies and government departments) can commit the new offence. Individual directors and managers cannot be guilty under the Act although their own potential liability at common law for their own acts and omissions still in principle remains. The Act does not operate as a principle of attribution of criminal responsibility for an existing offence to corporations, rather it creates a criminal offence which can be committed only by corporations and similar bodies. The offence is called corporate manslaughter in England, Wales and Northern Ireland (corporate homicide in Scotland) — s. 1(5).

Definition

Corporate Manslaughter and Corporate Homicide Act 2007, s. 1 B1.149

(1) An organisation to which this section applies is guilty of an offence if the way in which its activities are managed or organised—
   (a) causes a person's death, and
   (b) amounts to a gross breach of a relevant duty of care owed by the organisation to the deceased.
(2) The organisations to which this section applies are—
   (a) a corporation;
   (b) a department or other body listed in Schedule 1;
   (c) a police force;
   (d) a partnership, or a trade union or employers' association, that is an employer.
(3) An organisation is guilty of an offence under this section only if the way in which its activities are managed or organised by its senior management is a substantial element in the breach referred to in subsection (1).

Procedure and Sentence

The offence of corporate manslaughter is triable only on indictment. Proceedings may not be B1.150 instituted without the consent of the DPP (CMCHA 2007, s. 17).

The penalty available on conviction is a fine (s. 1(6)). The court may also, on the application of the prosecution, make a 'remedial order' under s. 9 requiring the organisation to take specified steps and, under s. 10, the court is now empowered to make a 'publicity order', i.e. an order for the conviction and specified particulars to be publicised. The definitive sentencing guideline, *Corporate Manslaughter and Health and Safety Offences Causing Death* (see Supplement, **SG-528**), is applicable to organisations sentenced on or after 15 February 2010. The first case successfully prosecuted under the Act, *Cotswold Geotechnical Holdings* [2012] 1 Cr App R (S) 153, resulted in a fine of £385,000 imposed on a small company which, it was accepted, would inevitably force the company into administration. The fine imposed for corporate manslaughter in *Lion Steel Equipment Ltd* (Manchester Crown Court, 20 July 2012) was, after allowing for a 20 per cent discount for an eventual guilty plea, £480,000; that sum was to be paid in four instalments over a three-year period reflecting a concern that an immediate fine of the whole amount might put the continuation of an unextravagant business in peril and unnecessarily jeopardise the livelihoods of 140 former colleagues in a close-knit workforce.

Relevant Duty of Care

Corporate Manslaughter and Corporate Homicide Act 2007, s. 2 B1.151

(1) A 'relevant duty of care', in relation to an organisation, means any of the following duties owed by it under the law of negligence—
   (a) a duty owed to its employees or to other persons working for the organisation or performing services for it;

(aa) he is detained in service custody premises
(b) a duty owed as occupier of premises;
(c) a duty owed in connection with—
  (i) the supply by the organisation of goods or services (whether for consideration or not),
  (ii) the carrying on by the organisation of any construction or maintenance operations,
  (iii) the carrying on by the organisation of any other activity on a commercial basis, or
  (iv) the use or keeping by the organisation of any plant, vehicle or other thing;
(d) a duty owed to a person who, by reason of being a person within subsection (2), is someone for whose safety the organisation is responsible.
(2) A person is within this subsection if—
  (a) he is detained at a custodial institution or in a custody area at a court or police station;
  (b) he is detained at a removal centre or short-term holding facility;
  (c) he is being transported in a vehicle, or being held in any premises, in pursuance of prison escort arrangements or immigration escort arrangements;
  (d) he is living in secure accommodation in which he has been placed;
  (e) he is a detained patient;
(3) Subsection (1) is subject to sections 3 to 7.
(4) A reference in subsection (1) to a duty owed under the law of negligence includes a reference to a duty that would be owed under the law of negligence but for any statutory provision under which liability is imposed in place of liability under that law.
(5) For the purposes of this Act, whether a particular organisation owes a duty of care to a particular individual is a question of law.
  The judge must make any findings of fact necessary to decide that question.
(6) For the purposes of this Act there is to be disregarded—
  (a) any rule of the common law that has the effect of preventing a duty of care from being owed by one person to another by reason of the fact that they are jointly engaged in unlawful conduct;
  (b) any such rule that has the effect of preventing a duty of care from being owed to a person by reason of his acceptance of a risk of harm.

B1.152 There are some very significant limitations to the above, fairly broad, meaning of 'relevant duty of care'. These are to be found in ss. 3 to 7. Sections 4, 5, 6 and 7 exclude or limit the relevant duty of care in certain specific areas of activity (i.e. military activities (s. 4), policing and law enforcement (s. 5), responses to emergency situations (s. 6) and child protection and probation functions (s. 7)). Two distinct methods of exclusion or limitation are utilised. First, duties in relation to certain activities are simply excluded as in the case of certain types of military activities or operations within s. 4. Secondly, duties as to certain other activities are not a relevant duty of care unless the duty falls within para. (a) or (b) of s. 2(1) (i.e. unless they are duties owed to employees etc. or as an occupier). This technique is used in s. 6 in relation to responses to emergency situations so that, for example, a fire and rescue authority will not be liable (e.g., to those being rescued or to bystanders) for the way it responds to an emergency but it can be liable to its own employees for breach of its duty towards them or to visitors for breach of its duty as an occupier of premises. The same applies to an NHS body responding to an emergency, although s. 6(3) and (4) further qualify this by saying that such a body can nevertheless be liable for the way in which medical treatment is carried out or is decided to be carried out but not for decisions as to the order in which persons are to be given such treatment.

Both of the techniques of exclusion referred to above are used in s. 5 whereby some police operations are simply excluded (essentially where they deal with terrorism, civil unrest or serious disorder and officers come under attack or threat of attack or violent resistance) whereas any other activities can give rise to a relevant duty of care but only under s. 2(1)(a) or (b) (as employer or occupier).

Whilst ss. 4 to 7 limit the meaning of 'relevant duty of care' in relation to certain specific types of activity, s. 3 is of potentially more general application. The broadest exclusion comes in s. 3(1), which excludes 'any duty of care owed by a public authority in respect of a decision as to matters of public policy (including in particular the allocation of public resources or the weighing of competing public interests)'. Arguments that a person's death is due to a government decision not to allocate appropriate resources to a particular service carried out by a public authority are thus not to be countenanced.

A second exclusion comes in s. 3(2) in relation to things done 'in the exercise of an exclusively **B1.153** public function', although in this instance the duty of care as employer or occupier under s. 2(1)(a) or (b) still survives. The phrase 'exclusively public function' is defined in s. 3(4) as referring to a function falling under the Crown prerogative or by nature exercisable only with authority conferred by the exercise of the prerogative or by or under a statutory provision. This exclusion is not limited to public authorities but could for example include a private sector organisation given statutory powers (e.g., licensing powers or power to detain in custody as in the case of privatised prisons). More naturally it will apply to public authorities, including the Prison Service, but it should be remembered that the duty as employer or occupier still survives.

Overall the provisions of ss. 3 to 7 significantly limit the effect of the expansion in s. 1(1) of the scope of the offence beyond corporations to government departments and other public bodies. To a large extent they also reflect some of the policy issues that at common law would come into play in deciding against a duty of care in tort and answer the question fairly directly as to how and to what extent the duty of care for the purposes of the criminal law should be limited by analogous considerations even though their precise scope and interpretation remain to be determined.

Gross Breach

Corporate Manslaughter and Corporate Homicide Act 2007, s. 8   **B1.154**

(1) This section applies where—
    (a) it is established that an organisation owed a relevant duty of care to a person, and
    (b) it falls to the jury to decide whether there was a gross breach of that duty.
(2) The jury must consider whether the evidence shows that the organisation failed to comply with any health and safety legislation that relates to the alleged breach, and if so—
    (a) how serious that failure was;
    (b) how much of a risk of death it posed.
(3) The jury may also—
    (a) consider the extent to which the evidence shows that there were attitudes, policies, systems or accepted practices within the organisation that were likely to have encouraged any such failure as is mentioned in subsection (2), or to have produced tolerance of it;
    (b) have regard to any health and safety guidance that relates to the alleged breach.
(4) This section does not prevent the jury from having regard to any other matters they consider relevant.

For a discussion in the first decided case under the Act of the potential impact of the reverse burden of proof under health and safety legislation on the burden of proof for corporate manslaughter as a result of s. 8 and the mention therein of failure to comply with health and safety legislation, see *Cotswold Geotechnical Holdings Ltd* [2012] 1 Cr App R (S) 153 and commentary by Dobson at [2012] Crim LR 200.

Related Offences

The offence cannot be committed by an individual nor can an individual be guilty of aid- **B1.155** ing, abetting, counselling or procuring the commission of an offence of corporate manslaughter (CMCHA 2007, s. 18(1)). The same principle applies in respect of assisting and encouraging crime in part 2 of the SCA 2007, s. 62 of which inserts a new s. 18(1A) into the CMCHA 2007.

Section 19 makes provision as to the relationship between corporate manslaughter and health and safety offences.

Corporate Manslaughter and Corporate Homicide Act 2007, s. 19

(1) Where in the same proceedings there is—

    (a) a charge of corporate manslaughter or corporate homicide arising out of a particular set of circumstances, and

    (b) a charge against the same defendant of a health and safety offence arising out of some or all of those circumstances, the jury may, if the interests of justice so require, be invited to return a verdict on each charge.

(2) An organisation that has been convicted of corporate manslaughter or corporate homicide arising out of a particular set of circumstances may, if the interests of justice so require, be charged with a health and safety offence arising out of some or all of those circumstances.

Section B2 Non-fatal Offences Against the Person

ASSAULT AND BATTERY

Definition

Assault and battery (or assault by beating) are separate and distinct summary offences. An assault is committed when D intentionally or recklessly causes another to apprehend immediate and unlawful violence. A battery is committed when D intentionally or recklessly inflicts unlawful force. A battery may, but does not inevitably, follow an assault. Despite this technical difference, the term 'assault', or 'common assault', has been generally used, both in cases (*Fagan v Metropolitan Police Commissioner* [1969] 1 QB 439) and in statutes (OAPA 1861, ss. 38, 42, 47), to cover either an assault or a battery.

It is now necessary to be more specific when laying an information. The Divisional Court in *DPP v Taylor* [1992] QB 645 has held that all common assaults and batteries are now offences contrary to the CJA 1988, s. 39, and that the information must include a reference to that section. An information would be bad for duplicity if the phrase 'assault and battery' were used; the court suggested that 'assault by beating' was the appropriate wording to use in cases of battery. As to the relationship between the two offences and the importance of charging them correctly, see *R (Kracher) v Leicester Magistrates' Court* [2013] EWHC 4627 (Admin).

The CDA 1998, s. 29(1)(c), creates a racially or religiously aggravated form of common assault or battery which carries a higher maximum penalty. For the meaning of 'racially or religiously aggravated', see **B11.149**.

B2.1

Procedure

Common assault is generally triable only summarily (CJA 1988, s. 39), although the racially or religiously aggravated form created by the CDA 1998, s. 29(1)(c), is triable either way. A count for the basic summary offence may be included in an indictment in the circumstances prescribed by the CJA 1988, s. 40 (see *Walton* [2011] EWCA Crim 2832 and **D11.20**), but this does not make it an indictable offence (e.g., for the purposes of the CAA 1981, s. 1). See the Interpretation Act 1978, sch. 1, which was overlooked in *Nelson* [2013] 1 WLR 2861.

B2.2

Common assault under s. 40 has the ordinary everyday meaning of that word, including battery (*Lynsey* [1995] 3 All ER 654). Furthermore, a jury may convict D of common assault on an indictment for an offence such as assault occasioning actual bodily harm (CLA 1967, s. 6(3A)). In *Nelson* it was held that s. 6(3A) does not enable a jury to convict of common assault on a count alleging assault by beating, because a battery can be committed on someone who never saw the blow coming, but with respect this overlooks *Metropolitan Police Commissioner v Wilson* [1984] AC 242 and the numerous cases that have followed it (see **D19.48**), none of which were cited to or by the court in *Nelson*.

Sentence (Basic Offence)

B2.3   The maximum penalties for common assault or battery other than in the racially or religiously aggravated form (see **B2.4**) are six months' imprisonment, a fine not exceeding level 5 on the standard scale, or both (CJA 1988, s. 39). Note the definitive sentencing guideline, *Assault* (see Supplement, **SG-211**), and the guideline and notes derived therefrom in the *Magistrates' Court Sentencing Guidelines* (see Supplement, **SG-248**).

In *Fenton* (1994) 15 Cr App R (S) 682 the offender pleaded guilty to common assault (charges of assault occasioning actual bodily harm and dangerous driving were not proceeded with). In the course of an altercation between two motorists, the offender pushed the victim in the chest. The Court of Appeal said that almost all cases of violence between motorists would be so serious that only custody could be justified. The appropriate sentence was seven days' imprisonment. See also *Ross* (1994) 15 Cr App R (S) 384.

Racial or religious aggravation cannot be taken into account by the sentencer when sentencing for the basic offence of common assault. To do so would infringe the principle that the offender must not be sentenced for an offence for which he has not been charged and convicted (*McGillivray* [2005] 2 Cr App R (S) 366; *Kentsch* [2006] 1 Cr App R (S) 737). Where there is evidence that racial or religious aggravation was present, the aggravated form of the offence should be charged.

Sentence (Racially or Religiously Aggravated Form of Offence)

B2.4   The maximum penalty for the aggravated form of common assault is two years, a fine or both on indictment; six months, a fine not exceeding the statutory maximum or both summarily (CDA 1998, s. 29(3)). Note the definitive sentencing guideline, *Assault* (see Supplement, **SG-211**), and the guideline and notes derived therefrom in the *Magistrates' Court Sentencing Guidelines* (see Supplement, **SG-248**).

The definitive sentencing guideline states that 'the court should determine the appropriate sentence for the offence without taking account of the element of aggravation and then make an addition to the sentence, considering the level of aggravation involved. It may be appropriate to move outside the identified category range, taking into account the increased statutory maximum'. In *Isitt* [2013] EWCA Crim 265 the Court of Appeal approved a sentence of 14 months' imprisonment after a guilty plea where the offender repeatedly swore at the complainant and threatened him, using highly offensive racist language. The offence took place in a doctor's surgery when the complainant's young daughter was present. The offender had many previous convictions for assault and public order matters including two racially aggravated offences. The sentence included a concurrent term for breach of a suspended sentence. In *Johnson* [2011] 2 Cr App R (S) 164, however, the Court of Appeal quashed a sentence of 18 months on a guilty plea in a case where the offender had acted aggressively towards a pregnant woman and called her a 'stupid white bitch'. The sentence was reduced because the judge had expressly taken 15 months as the starting point for the basic offence, whereas the maximum is only six months, and was varied to nine months, half of that for the basic offence and half for the racial aggravation. In *Niewulis* [2013] 2 Cr App R (S) 534 (83), a sentence of six months after a trial, comprising three months for the basic offence and three months uplift for the racial element, was appropriate for an unpleasant but relatively minor offence committed by an offender with a record of racially motivated offending.

Actus Reus of Assault

Actions and Words   An assault requires conduct which causes the victim to apprehend the **B2.5**
imminent application of unlawful force upon him (*Ireland* [1998] AC 147, per Lord Steyn at
p. 161). A fear or apprehension of *possible* violence may suffice (*Ireland*) and it may also suffice
where V is unsure as to when exactly the threatened attack may occur; but as the Court of
Appeal pointed out in *Constanza* [1997] 2 Cr App R 492, the conduct in question must at least
provoke some apprehension of violence 'at some time not excluding the immediate future'. A
threat of violence only in the more distant future cannot suffice. As to what may amount to
unlawful force, see **B2.9** and **B2.13** to **B2.21**. An omission to act arguably cannot amount to an
assault, or indeed a battery, but see **B2.10**.

The relevant conduct in cases of assault may take the form of threatening acts or gestures, as for
example where D brandishes a weapon at V or fires a shot in his direction; but it may also take
the form of threatening words, or it may involve acts and words together. It may even involve a
series of acts (*Cox* [1998] Crim LR 810). It was at one time thought that words alone, whether
written or spoken, could never amount to an assault (*Meade and Belt* (1823) 1 Lew CC 184;
Russell on Crime, 4th edn, 1865) but this view has now been rejected, both by the Court of
Appeal in *Constanza* (a case involving the sending of threatening letters) and by the House of
Lords in *Ireland* (a case involving telephone calls). Giving the judgment of the House of Lords
in *Ireland*, Lord Steyn said:

> The proposition that a gesture may amount to an assault, but that words can never suffice, is
> unrealistic and indefensible. A thing said is also a thing done. There is no reason why something
> said should be incapable of causing an apprehension of immediate personal violence…I would,
> therefore, reject the proposition that an assault can never be committed by words.

In *Ireland* D made 'silent' telephone calls to a number of women, and it was held that such **B2.6**
conduct could amount to the *actus reus* of assault if it caused victims to fear that physical
violence might be used against them in the immediate future. It may suffice for this purpose
if it causes V to fear the mere *possibility* of imminent violence, but it cannot suffice if V fears
only the prospect of receiving further calls (*Ireland*, per Lord Hope at p. 166), nor can it
suffice if it is clear to V that D or his friends can do nothing to harm her in the immediate
future.

The concept of immediacy has nevertheless been interpreted with some flexibility, and there
have been a number of recent cases in which 'stalkers' have been prosecuted for assault on that
basis. In *Smith v Chief Superintendent, Woking Police Station* (1983) 76 Cr App R 234, the
Divisional Court held that a threat of violence could be considered immediate, even though D
was still outside V's home, looking in at her through a window, and would have needed to force
an entry before he could attack her. In *Ireland*, the House of Lords adopted an even more flexible
approach, stating (at p. 162) that 'there is no reason why a telephone caller who says to a woman
in a menacing way, "I will be at your door in a minute or two" may not be guilty of an assault'.
Such conduct may alternatively, and perhaps more appropriately, be prosecuted under the
Protection from Harassment Act 1997 (see **B2.165**).

Negated and Conditional Threats   Words used by the accused may indicate that no attack **B2.7**
is threatened, even where the circumstances might otherwise suggest that one is. Thus, in
Tuberville v Savage (1669) 1 Mod 3, T, in the course of a quarrel with S, placed his hand on
the hilt of his sword (an act which might ordinarily have been construed as an assault) and
exclaimed, 'If it were not assize time, I would not take such language from you'. This was held
to be no assault, 'for the declaration of [T] was that he would not assault [S], the judges being
in town'.

A 'conditional' threat of unlawful violence may amount to an assault, even though V is told that
he may avoid such violence by complying with D's conditions. Thus, in the civil case of *Read v*

Coker (1853) 13 CB 850, the plaintiff successfully sued for assault on the basis that D and his men had surrounded him and threatened to 'break his neck' if he refused to leave D's premises. See also *Ansell v Thomas* [1974] Crim LR 31.

B2.8 **Result Crime**   Although an assault may take the form of a 'failed battery', as where D's blow fails to connect with V, assault is always a result crime (see **A1.2**). No assault can be committed unless the threats are actually perceived by V. There is no assault if a stone thrown by D sails past V's head without him noticing (although D may have attempted to commit an offence under the OAPA 1861, s. 47). If, however, D threatens V with an imitation firearm, this will indeed amount to an assault, unless V knows that the weapon cannot fire (*Logdon v DPP* [1976] Crim LR 121). If V does apprehend the threat of imminent violence, it does not matter whether he is frightened by it. He may relish the opportunity to teach D a lesson, and yet still be regarded as the victim of D's assault.

Actus Reus of Battery

B2.9 A battery requires the unlawful application of force upon the victim. It cannot include the circumstances of a telephone caller who thereby causes his victim's psychiatric injury (*Ireland* [1998] AC 147 at p. 161); but as to assault, see **B2.5**; as to liability under the Protection from Harassment Act 1997, see **B2.165**.

Battery need not necessarily be preceded by any assault. A blow may, for example, be struck from behind, without warning. Nor need a battery involve any serious violence. Any unlawful touching of another may be classed as a battery. As Goff LJ stated in *Collins v Wilcock* [1984] 3 All ER 374 (at p. 378), 'everybody is protected, not only against physical injury, but against any form of physical molestation'.

B2.10 **Direct and Indirect Application of Force**   There is authority that a battery must take the form of a positive act, rather than a mere omission, and must involve a *direct* application of force. V might, for example, suffer pain or injury if he slips on a patch of oil which D has previously spilled and omitted to clear up, but arguably that is no assault or battery, even if the spillage of the oil was deliberate. The need for a positive act was emphasised in *Fagan v Metropolitan Police Commissioner* [1969] 1 QB 439 (as to which, see **A1.8**). If *Fagan* is correct, there is no room in assault or battery cases for application of the *Miller* principle (see *Miller* [1983] 2 AC 161 explained at **A1.20**) because one cannot batter another person through mere inaction.

The question whether a battery must involve a direct application of unlawful force to V is however unclear. In *Metropolitan Police Commissioner v Wilson* [1984] AC 242, the House of Lords held (albeit by implication) that *indirect* violence, such as the setting of a trap into which P falls, may not amount to a battery, although it may involve the unlawful 'infliction' of harm, for the purpose of liability under the OAPA 1861, s. 20, and that view has been reiterated by the House of Lords, both in *Savage* [1992] 1 AC 699 and in *Ireland* [1998] AC 147 at p. 160. *Martin* (1881) 8 QBD 54 is often said to be authority to the contrary, but it merely decided that M's conduct in barring the doors to a theatre and putting out the lights could lead to the 'infliction' of grievous bodily harm on persons who were crushed in the ensuing panic. *Martin* is thus consistent with *Wilson* but has no bearing on the law of assault or battery.

Two cases do support the concept of indirect battery. In *DPP v K* [1990] 1 All ER 331, the Divisional Court held that K, a schoolboy, was guilty of an offence under the OAPA 1861, s. 47, when he poured acid into a warm-air drier in his school cloakroom, causing injury to the next pupil who used it. This appears to have been a decision *per incuriam*, however, because no account was taken of *Fagan* or *Wilson*. See Hirst, 'Assault, Battery and Indirect Violence' [1999] Crim LR 557. The point was expressly left undecided in *Haystead v Chief Constable of Derbyshire* [2000] 3 All ER 890, but *DPP v K* was followed in *DPP v Santa-Bermudez* (2004) 168 JP 373 in which D was held to have committed a battery against a police officer when he falsely assured her that he had no 'sharps' in his possession, and thus caused her to stab herself on a hypodermic needle as she searched him. However, none of the conflicting authorities or dicta was cited in that case.

The administering of a poison or noxious substance can amount to a battery (e.g., where it is sprayed directly into V's face, as in *Gillard* (1988) 87 Cr App R 189: see **B2.81**) and setting a dog on another person clearly involves a direct use of force, because the dog is used as a weapon. The same is true where D strikes P, causing her to drop and injure her child, Q. In *Haystead v Chief Constable of Derbyshire*, this was held to be a battery against both P and Q. There must also be a battery where D attacks P by pushing over a ladder on which P is standing, or by striking P's horse, so that it rears and throws him.

B2.11

Setting a spring gun or trap with intent to cause serious injury to any person may more appropriately be prosecuted under the OAPA 1861, s. 31, which may apply even if no injury is caused: see *Cockburn* [2008] 2 All ER 1153; but contrast *Munks* [1963] 3 All ER 757, where a device designed to inflict an electric shock was held not to be 'a mantrap or other engine' within the meaning of s. 31.

Mens Rea of Assault or Battery

An assault or battery must be committed intentionally or recklessly. Recklessness, in this context, means subjective or *Cunningham* recklessness: *Savage* [1992] 1 AC 699. This is true both of common assault and of aggravated assaults under the OAPA 1861, s. 47, or the Police Act 1996, s. 89. Evidence of voluntary intoxication can never assist the defence in respect of such offences because they do not require 'specific intent' (see **A3.17**).

B2.12

Lawful and Unlawful Force

Assault or battery must involve the use or threat of unlawful force. The use or threat of force is not always unlawful. In particular, it may be justified on the basis of actual or implied consent; on the basis of self-defence, crime prevention or crowd control; or on the basis that it involved the lawful correction of a child.

B2.13

A mere technical battery is unlikely to be prosecuted; but difficulties have sometimes arisen where persons are touched by police officers against their will, because even a trivial technical assault or battery by a police officer takes that officer outside the scope of his duty, and prevents him from qualifying as the victim of any offence under the Police Act 1996, s. 89 (see **B2.39**).

Self-defence and related justifications for the use or threat of force are considered in **A3** and in particular at **A3.54**. Consent and lawful correction are considered at **B2.14** and **B2.20**.

Consent   Where consent is in issue, the burden of disproving it is on the prosecution (*Donovan* [1934] 2 KB 498). The two principal questions that may arise in this context are: (1) Did the complainant in fact consent (expressly or by implication) to what was done; and (2) if so, do public policy considerations invalidate that consent?

B2.14

Whether consent was given is usually a simple question of fact, but we are all 'deemed' to consent to various harmless or unavoidable everyday contacts with our fellow citizens, which for that reason cannot be unlawful (*Wilson v Pringle* [1986] 2 All ER 440). Participants in contact sports such as football are meanwhile deemed to consent to the risk of clumsy or mistimed tackles or challenges; but this does not include tackles that are deliberately late or intended to cause harm. As Lord Woolf CJ pointed out in *Barnes* [2005] 2 All ER 113, a jury should be told the importance of the distinction between D going for the ball, albeit late, and his 'going for' an opponent. Some jobs notoriously involve the risk of being subjected to violence, but that has nothing to do with consent and no proper analogy can be drawn with implied consent in contact sports (*H v CPS* [2010] 4 All ER 264).

A person must understand what he is consenting to, if his consent is to be effective (*Burrell v Harmer* [1967] Crim LR 169; *D* [1984] AC 778). This may require more than mere agreement

B2.15

to the physical act. In *Tabassum* [2000] 2 Cr App R 328, several women allowed T to examine their breasts on the basis of his false representation that he was medically qualified and conducting a survey into breast cancer. Upholding his conviction for indecent assault, Rose LJ said, 'There was consent to the nature of the act, but not its quality'. In *Richardson* [1999] QB 444, however, R, a dentist, was not guilty of assaulting her patients through failing to tell them she had been struck off the register. R's failure to disclose her disqualification did not alter the essential quality of the treatment she carried out; but clearly she would have been guilty had she drilled healthy teeth for fraudulent financial reasons.

The concept of 'informed consent' is crucial where it is alleged that D recklessly infected a partner with a sexually transmitted disease. *Clarence* (1888) 22 QBD 23 is no longer good law. *Dica* [2004] QB 1257 and *Konzani* [2005] 2 Cr App R 198 now establish that D commits no offence if there is informed consent by his sexual partner to the risk that he might infect her, but he may be guilty if he knows he has a serious infection (or symptoms thereof), and keeps his partner in the dark. As Judge LJ observed in *Konzani*:

> There is a critical distinction between taking a risk of the various, potentially adverse and possibly problematic consequences of sexual intercourse, and giving an informed consent to the risk of infection with a fatal disease.

See also the CPS statement on policy for prosecuting cases involving the intentional or reckless sexual transmission of infection at www.cps.gov.uk/publications/prosecution/sti.html. The CPS statement was considered by the Court of Appeal in the context of a prosecution under the OAPA 1861, s. 20, in *Golding* [2014] EWCA Crim 889.

B2.16 **Invalid Consent**   Where actual bodily harm (or worse) is deliberately inflicted, consent to it will ordinarily be deemed invalid on grounds of public policy, even if V knows exactly what he is consenting to. In *Brown* [1994] 1 AC 212, the House of Lords upheld convictions for offences under the OAPA 1861, ss. 20 and 47, in respect of a group of homosexual sado-masochists, who had engaged in acts of consensual torture with each other for the purpose of sexual gratification. Lord Templeman said (at pp. 231, 234 and 236):

> In some circumstances violence is not punishable under the criminal law. When no actual bodily harm is caused, the consent of the person affected precludes him from complaining. There can be no conviction for the summary offence of common assault if the victim has consented...Even when violence is intentionally inflicted and results in...wounding or serious bodily harm the accused is entitled to be acquitted if the injury was a foreseeable incident of a lawful activity in which the person injured was participating. Surgery...is a lawful activity...ritual [male] circumcision, tattooing, ear piercing and violent sports including boxing are lawful activities.
>
> ...The question whether the defence of consent should be extended to the consequences of sadomasochistic encounters can only be decided by consideration of policy and public interest.
>
> ...The violence of sado-masochistic encounters involves the indulgence of cruelty by sadists and the degradation of victims. Such violence is injurious to the participants and unpredictably dangerous. I am not prepared to invent a defence of consent for sado-masochistic encounters which breed and glorify cruelty and result in offences under sections 47 and 20 of the Act of 1861.

The appellants in *Brown* sought redress from the ECtHR (*Laskey v UK* (1997) 24 EHRR 39), but the court ruled that state interference in this aspect of their private lives could be justified on the basis of 'protection of health'.

The approach adopted in *Brown* is consistent with earlier decisions and dicta of the Court of Appeal and Court of Criminal Appeal. Thus, in *Donovan* [1934] 2 KB 498, it was stated that a 17-year-old girl could not give valid consent to a sado-masochistic caning; and in *A-G's Ref (No. 6 of 1980)* [1981] QB 715 Lord Lane CJ held that it would not be in the public interest to allow a defence of consent in the context of a fist-fight where actual bodily harm was intended and/or caused for no good reason ('minor struggles' being excepted). As to the infliction of gratuitous pain and violence for the purpose of broadcast 'entertainment', see Cooper and James, 'The Painful Process of Rethinking Consent' [2012] Crim LR 188.

A limitation on the *Brown* principle was subsequently asserted in *Wilson* [1996] 2 Cr App R **B2.17** 241, in which the Court of Appeal held that nothing said in *Brown* prevented a wife from permitting her husband to brand his initials on her buttocks using a hot knife. The branding was considered analogous to tattooing rather than to the acts of sado-masochism condemned in *Brown*. Furthermore, 'consensual activity between husband and wife in the privacy of the matrimonial home was not. . .normally a proper matter for criminal investigation, let alone criminal prosecution'.

Wilson must now be followed by trial courts, even if it appears to modify the law as stated in *Brown*, but it is not entirely clear how far its effects extend, especially since the view of the court was that the law should be left to develop on a case-by-case basis. Some clarification has been provided by *Emmett* (1999) *The Times*, 15 October 1999, in which the Court of Appeal held that dangerous and damaging sado-masochistic games (involving suffocation and burning) were not exempted by the *Wilson* principle, even where carried out consensually in what was effectively a husband and wife relationship.

Consensual Risk-taking   One must distinguish between consent to the deliberate inflic- **B2.18** tion of injury and consent to a lawful (if dangerous) activity in which injury is accidentally caused (*Slingsby* [1995] Crim LR 571). It is clear that persons may ordinarily consent to sexual or other activities that involve a significant risk of injury, even where they could not validly consent to the deliberate infliction of such injury. In *Dica* Judge LJ explained (at [51]) why this is so:

> The problems of criminalising the consensual taking of risks. . .include the sheer impracticability of enforcement and the haphazard nature of its impact. The process would undermine the general understanding of the community that sexual relationships are pre-eminently private and essentially personal to the individuals involved in them. And if adults were to be liable to prosecution for the consequences of taking known risks with their health, it would seem odd that this should be confined to risks taken in the context of sexual intercourse, while they are nevertheless permitted to take the risks inherent in so many other aspects of everyday life. . .

See also *Meachen* [2006] EWCA Crim 2414. Another example of consensual risk-taking concerns 'rough and undisciplined horseplay'. In *Jones* (1986) 83 Cr App R 375, D and others tossed other youths into the air and let them fall to the ground. One of the victims suffered a ruptured spleen and another suffered a broken arm. The trial judge refused to allow the issue of consent to be raised, owing to the serious nature of the injuries, but the Court of Appeal held that the defence should (for what it was worth) have been left to the jury. This ruling was approved in *Brown* and followed in *Aitken* [1992] 4 All ER 541, but its proper limits must be understood. Individuals may lawfully engage in rough horseplay only where there is at least a genuine belief that the 'victim' is consenting, and then only where no injury is intended. It is not a 'bully's charter'.

In *A-G's Ref (No. 6 of 1980)* [1981] QB 715, Lord Lane CJ also identified an exception covering 'dangerous exhibitions', although the extent of that exception has never been explored.

Medical Treatment   The law concerning the limits and effectiveness of consent to medical **B2.19** treatment is a highly specialised subject which cannot be covered in detail here; but the basic issues are examined at **A1.21**.

Lawful Correction or Chastisement   At common law, a parent or any other person acting *in* **B2.20** *loco parentis* may administer reasonable corporal punishment to control the behaviour of children in his care. Concepts of reasonableness have narrowed in recent years, as the Court of Appeal recognised in *H (Assault of child: Reasonable chastisement)* [2001] 2 FLR 431, and are strongly influenced by human rights issues. Caning, for example, was condemned by Strasbourg as 'inhuman and degrading treatment' (*A v UK* (1999) 27 EHRR 611) and must now be considered unlawful.

This is now reflected in the Children Act 2004, s. 58, which clarifies the scope of reasonable correction or chastisement.

Children Act 2004, s. 58

(1) In relation to any offence specified in subsection (2), battery of a child cannot be justified on the ground that it constituted reasonable punishment.

(2) The offences referred to in subsection (1) are—

(a) an offence under section 18 or 20 of the Offences against the Person Act 1861 (wounding and causing grievous bodily harm);

(b) an offence under section 47 of that Act (assault occasioning actual bodily harm);

(c) an offence under section 1 of the Children and Young Persons Act 1933 (cruelty to persons under 16).

B2.21   Smacking, spanking or any other physical punishment is thus an offence if it causes even minor harm or injury such as significant bruising (see **B2.34**) or if it can be characterised as cruelty under the CYPA 1933, s. 1 (see **B2.137**).

It does not follow that parental chastisement, which is neither cruel within the meaning of the CYPA 1933, s. 1, nor injurious within the meaning of the OAPA 1861, must necessarily be lawful. Smacking a small child for failing to understand something he cannot be expected to understand might well be considered 'unreasonable' at common law, even if it causes no injury.

Under the Education Act 1996, s. 548, teachers (even at private schools) no longer have any right to administer corporal punishment 'by virtue of their position' but retain the right to avert an immediate danger of personal injury or damage to property (s. 548(5)). It is also unlawful for a teacher to throw an object (such as a blackboard duster) at a pupil who is misbehaving (*Taylor* (1983) *The Times*, 28 December 1983), but staff may use reasonable force to prevent a pupil from committing any offence, causing personal injury to, or damage to the property of, any person (including the pupil himself), or prejudicing the maintenance of good order and discipline at the school or among any pupils receiving education at the school, whether during a teaching session or otherwise (Education and Inspections Act 2006, s. 93).

ASSAULT WITH INTENT TO RESIST OR PREVENT ARREST

Definition

B2.22   **Offences against the Person Act 1861, s. 38**

Whosoever. . .shall assault any person with intent to resist or prevent the lawful apprehension or detainer of himself or of any other person for any offence, shall be guilty of [an offence], and being convicted thereof shall be liable, at the discretion of the court, to be imprisoned for any term not exceeding two years. . .

Procedure

B2.23   Assault with intent to resist or prevent arrest is triable either way. When tried on indictment this is normally a class 3 offence, but see CPD XIII, para. B (see Supplement, **PD-97**) for the additional factors that the court considers on allocation.

Indictment

B2.24   *Statement of Offence*

Assault with intent to resist arrest, contrary to section 38 of the Offences against the Person Act 1861

Particulars of Offence

A on or about the. . .day of. . .assaulted X with intent to resist or prevent the lawful apprehension of A [or another] for the commission of an offence

Sentence

The maximum penalty is two years (OAPA 1861, s. 38). Note the definitive sentencing guideline, *Assault* (see Supplement, **SG-209**), and the guideline and notes derived therefrom in the *Magistrates' Court Sentencing Guidelines* (see Supplement, **SG-242**).

B2.25

Elements

On a literal reading of s. 38, the only *actus reus* required is that of common assault (see **B2.5**), whereas the *mens rea* is that of common assault, coupled with an intent to resist or prevent one's own, or another person's, lawful arrest or detention, etc. Nevertheless, it is firmly established that the arrest or detention in question must in fact be lawful (*Self* [1992] 3 All ER 476; *Lee* [2001] 1 Cr App R 293) and this must accordingly be treated as a further essential *actus reus* element. The victim need not be a police officer. He may be a private citizen assisting such an officer, or a private citizen or store detective making a 'citizen's arrest'. In *Lee*, Rose LJ appears to have assumed that the victim must be the person seeking to make the lawful arrest; but this was *obiter* and (with respect) mistaken. There is no good reason why s. 38 should not extend to assaults on hapless citizens who unwittingly obstruct D's attempt to escape from pursuing officers. As to the contrast between the powers of arrest given to police officers and the more restricted powers given to private citizens, see *Self* and **D1.29**.

B2.26

The *mens rea* requirement in s. 38 may be negatived by D's mistaken view of the facts, e.g., where he mistakes CID officers for rival gangsters, and believes he is being abducted, rather than arrested. In such a case D would have no intent to resist lawful arrest. Indeed, he would not even have the *mens rea* of assault (*Kenlin v Gardiner* [1967] 2 QB 510; *Williams* [1987] 3 All ER 411; *Brightling* [1991] Crim LR 364). The mistake would not have to be a reasonable one (*Williams*; *Lee*; *Blackburn v Bowering* [1994] 3 All ER 380). In contrast, D has no defence if his mistake is merely one of law, e.g., where he does not appreciate that a citizen has a power of arrest, or where he assumes that an arrest is unlawful merely because he is (or believes himself to be) innocent of the offence in question. As Rose LJ said in *Lee*:

> Whether or not an offence has actually been committed or is believed by the defendant not to have been committed is irrelevant. We reach this conclusion without regret. Neither public order nor the clarity of the criminal law would be improved if juries were required to consider in relation to s. 38 offences the impact of a defendant's belief as to the lawfulness of his arrest in cases where a lawful arrest is being properly attempted on reasonable grounds.

ASSAULT OCCASIONING ACTUAL BODILY HARM

Definition

Offences against the Person Act 1861, s. 47

Whosoever shall be convicted upon an indictment of any assault occasioning actual bodily harm shall be liable...to [imprisonment for five years].

B2.27

The CDA 1998, s. 29(1)(b), creates a racially or religiously aggravated form of this offence which carries a higher maximum penalty. For the meaning of 'racially or religiously aggravated', see **B11.149**.

Procedure

Assault occasioning actual bodily harm (whether in its aggravated form or not) is triable either way. When tried on indictment this is normally a class 3 offence, but see CPD XIII, para. B (see Supplement, **PD-97**) for the additional factors that the court considers on allocation. See the *Magistrates' Court Sentencing Guidelines* (see Supplement, **SG-241**) for indications as to when a case should be sent to the Crown Court.

B2.28

Indictments

B2.29   Basic Offence

Statement of Offence

Assault occasioning actual bodily harm, contrary to section 47 of the Offences against the Person Act 1861

Particulars of Offence

A on or about the...day of...assaulted V thereby causing him actual bodily harm

B2.30   Aggravated Offence

Statement of Offence

Racially aggravated assault occasioning actual bodily harm, contrary to section 29(1)(b) of the Crime and Disorder Act 1998

Particulars of Offence

A on or about the...day of...assaulted V thereby causing him actual bodily harm and at the time or shortly after demonstrated to V hostility based on his membership of a racial group, by calling him a 'bloody paki'

Sentence (Basic Offence)

B2.31   The maximum penalty for the offence other than in the racially or religiously aggravated form (see **B2.33**) is five years (OAPA 1861, s. 47) on indictment; six months, or a fine not exceeding level 5, or both, summarily. Note the definitive sentencing guideline, *Assault* (see Supplement, **SG-208**), and the guideline and notes derived therefrom in the *Magistrates' Court Sentencing Guidelines* (see Supplement, **SG-241**).

Where the offence occurs in a domestic setting the definitive sentencing guideline, *Overarching Principles: Domestic Violence,* is applicable (see Supplement, **SG-51**). The terms of the guideline received a ringing endorsement from the Court of Appeal in *A-G's Ref (No. 80 of 2009)* [2010] EWCA Crim 470, in which practitioners were urged to 'read and re-read' it. See also *Caceres* [2014] 1 Cr App R (S) 128 (23).

In *Audit* (1994) 15 Cr App R (S) 36 the offender, after drinking heavily, assaulted another man by punching him in the face, causing a cut to the eyebrow which needed stitches and bruising to the face and jaw. The Court of Appeal said that a custodial sentence of three months was appropriate. In *Graham* [1993] Crim LR 628, the female offender, after an argument in a restaurant, assaulted a woman who had called her names, by hitting her in the face. She suffered black eyes and a swollen nose. Six months' imprisonment was reduced to 28 days. Four months' imprisonment was the appropriate sentence in *Marples* [1998] 1 Cr App R (S) 335 where, in the course of an altercation in a taxi queue, D struck V in the face, breaking his nose.

B2.32   Heavier sentences will be imposed where the assault was committed against a police officer or involved a vulnerable victim. Nine months' imprisonment was upheld on a guilty plea in *Broyd* [2002] 1 Cr App R (S) 197, where the offender head-butted an officer who was trying to arrest him causing a split lip and a chipped tooth. See also *Casey* [2000] 1 Cr App R (S) 221. If it is not proved that the offender knew that the victim was a police officer, then the heavier sentence will not be appropriate (*Stosiek* (1982) 4 Cr App R (S) 205). In *Glover* (1993) 14 Cr App R (S) 261 a sentence of four months' detention in a young offender institution was varied to a probation order where a 20-year-old woman, described as immature and of limited intelligence, had slapped her three-year-old son in the face, causing a swollen and bruised cheek and a bruise inside the mouth, but in *Barnes* (1993) 14 Cr App R (S) 547 a custodial sentence was upheld, though reduced from six months to 28 days, where a man left in charge of the ten-month-old daughter of the woman with whom he was living, slapped the child in the face causing bruising.

Longer sentences will also be proper, *inter alia*, where a weapon is used by the offender, or the assault is committed upon a public servant. Six months' imprisonment was appropriate in *McNally* [2000] 1 Cr App R (S) 535, where a relative of a hospital patient became abusive with medical staff and struck a doctor in the face. The victim suffered bruising and bleeding in the ear which caused a hearing loss. In *McDermott* [2007] 1 Cr App R (S) 145, a sentence of 15 months' imprisonment was upheld on a man who, while under the influence of drink, had punched an ambulance attendant to the head. Although the offender pleaded guilty he had relevant previous convictions and the offence fell into a pattern of alcohol-related violence. In *Byrne* [2000] 1 Cr App R (S) 282, where a schoolteacher was assaulted by a parent who forced his way into the staff room, 15 months' imprisonment was reduced to nine months. There is no reason to treat an assault committed by one motorist upon another after a road accident or dispute as any less serious than an assault committed in other circumstances (*Arnold* [1996] 1 Cr App R (S) 115, where six months' imprisonment was upheld for head-butting the victim, causing a broken nose). *Arnold* was followed and applied in *Maben* [1997] 2 Cr App R (S) 341 and *Sharpe* [2000] 1 Cr App R (S) 1. An offender convicted of assault committed by 'stalking' the victim over a four-year period received a sentence of 21 months' imprisonment in *Smith* [1998] 1 Cr App R (S) 138.

Racial or religious aggravation cannot be taken into account by the sentencer when sentencing for the basic offence of assault occasioning actual bodily harm (see **B2.3**).

Sentence Guidelines (Racially or Religiously Aggravated Form of Offence)

The maximum penalty for the aggravated form of the offence is seven years, a fine or both on **B2.33** indictment; six months, a fine not exceeding the statutory maximum or both summarily (CDA 1998, s. 29(2)). Note the definitive sentencing guideline, *Assault* (see Supplement, **SG-208**), and the guideline and notes derived therefrom in the *Magistrates' Court Sentencing Guidelines* (see Supplement, **SG-241**).

The relevance of racial aggravation as a factor in sentencing has been the subject of guidance from the Court of Appeal in *Saunders* [2000] 1 Cr App R 458 and in *Kelly* [2001] 2 Cr App R (S) 341, both cases of assault occasioning actual bodily harm. The court established that the sentencer should indicate what the appropriate sentence would have been for the offence in the absence of racial aggravation and then add a further term to reflect the racial element, so that the total sentence would reflect the overall criminality. Even if the basic offence would not have crossed the custody threshold, the aggravation may mean that it did so. This guidance is reflected in the current definitive sentencing guideline. In *Pells* (2004) *The Times*, 21 April 2004, the Court of Appeal stated that, when determining the degree of sentencing uplift appropriate to a racially aggravated offence, the differential maximum penalties under the CDA 1998 scheme carried no special significance. In *Saunders*, Rose LJ referred to a number of relevant features of such cases, such as the nature of the racial hostility, its duration and locality. In *Kelly*, matters said to aggravate the racial element were: where the racist element was a planned part of the offence; the offence was part of a pattern of racist offending; the offender was part of a group promoting racist activities; and the deliberate setting up of the victim to humiliate or offend. The impact on the victim was also important, such as where the offence took place in or near the victim's home; where the victim was particularly vulnerable, or was providing a service to the public; where the timing or location of the offence was such as to maximise the harm or distress it caused; if expressions of racial hostility were repeated or prolonged; if fear and distress throughout a particular community resulted from the offence; or if particular distress was caused to the victim or the victim's family.

Actus Reus

An offence under the OAPA 1861, s. 47, must involve an assault or battery (as to which see **B2.5**) **B2.34** and it must be established that this assault or battery occasioned (i.e. caused) the victim actual bodily harm. The intentional infliction of such injury cannot ordinarily be consented to (see

B2.14). As to the position where bodily harm results from the cumulative effect of a series of separate incidents, see *Cox* [1998] Crim LR 810. As long as there was a direct assault or battery, it does not matter if the bodily harm was suffered indirectly. In *Roberts* (1971) 56 Cr App R 95, R assaulted a young woman in his car, and frightened her to the extent that she leaped from it to escape whilst it was still in motion; she suffered injuries as a result. R was convicted of a s. 47 offence. Stephenson LJ said:

> The test is: was [her injury] the natural result of what [R] said and did, in the sense that it was something that could reasonably have been foreseen as the consequence of what he was saying or doing.

'Actual bodily harm' has been defined as any injury which is 'calculated to interfere with the health or comfort of the [victim]' (*Miller* [1954] 2 QB 282, per Lynskey J at p. 292). Minor cuts and bruises may satisfy this test; in *R (T) v DPP* [2003] Crim LR 622, it was held that a momentary loss of consciousness by V, following a kick to the head, could properly be regarded as actual bodily harm even where there was no other discernible evidence of injury. The CPS Charging Standards do not, however, encourage the bringing of s. 47 charges in the absence of more serious injuries, such as broken teeth, extensive bruising or cuts etc., which require medical treatment.

B2.35   It was held in *DPP v Smith* [2006] 2 All ER 16 that the cutting of a substantial part of V's hair in the course of an assault may involve actual bodily harm, even though no pain or other injury may be involved, as may putting paint on it or some unpleasant substance which marks or damages it. Sir Igor Judge P said (at [18]):

> Even if, medically and scientifically speaking, the hair above the surface of the scalp is no more than dead tissue, it remains part of the body and is attached to it. While it is so attached...it falls within the meaning of 'bodily' in the phrase 'actual bodily harm'. It is concerned with the body of the individual victim.

If this is correct, a haircut represents one more exception to the general rule that actual bodily harm cannot validly be consented to.

A recognisable psychiatric illness may amount to actual or grievous bodily harm (*Chan-Fook* [1994] 2 All ER 552; *Ireland* [1998] AC 147). Where such illness or injury is alleged, it must be proved by expert psychiatric evidence (*Chan-Fook*) and there must also be expert evidence to prove that D's conduct was the cause of that injury. For the purposes of s. 47, this conduct must involve an assault or battery. In the absence of expert evidence, there may be no case to leave to the jury (*Morris* [1998] 1 Cr App R 386). Distress, grief, anxiety or other psychological harm, not amounting to any recognisable psychiatric illness, is not bodily harm for the purposes of the 1861 Act (*Dhaliwal* [2006] 2 Cr App R 348).

Mens Rea

B2.36   The *mens rea* of a s. 47 offence is no different from that required in respect of a common assault or battery (see **B2.12**). Although the causing of actual bodily harm is an additional *actus reus* element, no *mens rea* as to it is required. If injury is caused, it need not even be proved that the injury was foreseeable, because this element of the offence is one of strict liability. This is now clear from the decision of the House of Lords in *Savage* [1992] 1 AC 699, in which S aimed to throw the contents of a beer glass over B, but inadvertently allowed the glass to slip from her hand and break, with the result that B was injured by it. It was held that a conviction for malicious wounding could not be sustained in the absence of proof that S had at least foreseen the possibility of injury to B, but a conviction for an offence under s. 47 could be substituted, because throwing beer over B was an intentional assault (indeed a battery) and that same assault had resulted in B's injury. Similarly, in a case such as *Ireland* [1998] AC 147, where threats are made by letter or by telephone etc., *mens rea* for a s. 47 offence can be established if D intends or foresees that he may cause V to apprehend immediate violence. He need not intend or foresee (nor even have any reason to foresee) that V will suffer psychiatric injury.

ASSAULT ON CONSTABLE IN EXECUTION OF DUTY

Definition

Police Act 1996, s. 89

B2.37

(1) Any person who assaults a constable in the execution of his duty, or a person assisting a constable in the execution of his duty, shall be guilty of an offence and liable on summary conviction to imprisonment for a term not exceeding six months or to a fine not exceeding level 5 on the standard scale, or to both.

Procedure and Sentencing

This offence is triable only summarily.

B2.38

The maximum penalties are six months' imprisonment, a fine not exceeding level 5, or both (Police Act 1996, s. 89(1)). Note the definitive sentencing guideline, *Assault* (see Supplement, **SG-210**), and the guideline and notes derived therefrom in the *Magistrates' Court Sentencing Guidelines* (see Supplement, **SG-243**).

See also the sentencing considerations for assault occasioning actual bodily harm, at **B2.31**.

Actus Reus

An offence under s. 89(1) must involve an assault or battery (as defined in **B2.5**) and it must be **B2.39** proved that V was a police or prison officer (of any rank) acting in the execution of his duty, or a person assisting such an officer.

Police and community support officers (CSOs) are not protected by s. 89 unless assisting a constable at the time, but as to assaults etc. on CSOs or other 'designated or accredited persons' see the Police Reform Act 2002, s. 46. As to assaults on members of international joint investigation teams, see the Police Act 1996, s. 89(4), and the SOCPA 2005, s. 57. As to assaults on persons carrying out surveillance in England and Wales under the RIPA 2000, s. 76A, see the Crime (International Co-operation) Act 2003, s. 84. As to assaults on traffic officers, see the Traffic Management Act 2004, s. 10(1); as to assaults on revenue and customs officers, see the Commissioners for Revenue and Customs Act 2005, s. 32; as to assaults on NCA officers designated as having the powers of constables, see the CCA 2013, s. 10 and sch. 5, para. 22; as to assaults on immigration officers, see the UK Borders Act 2007, ss. 22 and 23; as to assaults on accredited financial investigators exercising powers under the POCA 2002, see s. 453A of that Act.

An off-duty police officer may act in the course of duty if a breach of the peace or other incident occurs which justifies immediate action on his part (*Albert v Lavin* [1982] AC 546) but it is essential in all cases that the officer is shown to have been acting lawfully, because even a minor, technical and inadvertent act of unlawfulness on his part will mean that he cannot have been acting in the execution of his duty (*Riley v DPP* (1989) 91 Cr App R 14; *Kerr v DPP* [1995] Crim LR 394). A violent assault in response to a trivial act of unlawfulness on the part of a police officer may be punishable on some other basis (e.g., as a common assault or battery, or as assault occasioning actual bodily harm), but although common assault is necessarily included within any s. 89 assault, courts of summary jurisdiction have no power to convict of included offences, and it may therefore be desirable to draft alternative charges in cases where the legality of the officer's conduct is in doubt (*Kerr v DPP; Bentley v Brudzinski* (1982) 75 Cr App R 217; *Syed v DPP* [2010] 1 Cr App R 480 and **D1.170** *et seq.*).

The precise limits of a constable's duty remain undefined. It is clear, however, that a police **B2.40** officer may be acting in the execution of his duty, even where he is doing more than the minimum which the law requires of him (*Waterfield* [1964] 1 QB 164; *Coffin v Smith* (1980) 71 Cr App R 221). It is also clear that any action amounting to assault, battery, unlawful arrest or trespass to property takes the officer outside the course of his duty (*Davis v Lisle* [1936] 2 KB 434) but even where an officer has no legal right to remain on private property when required to leave, offensive remarks telling him to 'go away' will not necessarily suffice to withdraw any implied permission he may have had to enter or remain, and the officer must in any event be given a reasonable opportunity to leave once such permission has effectively been withdrawn (*R (Fullard) v Woking Magistrates' Court* [2005] EWHC 2922 (Admin)). Some of the most difficult cases in this area concern the power of a police officer to touch or take hold of an individual (without arresting him) in order to speak with or restrain him. In *Donnelly v Jackman* [1970] 1 All ER 987, it was held that it is not every interference with a citizen's liberty which will amount to a course of conduct sufficient to take the officer out of the execution of his duty; but how far an officer may go in attracting or retaining the citizen's attention appears to be largely a question of fact. In *Mepstead v DPP* (1996) 160 JP 475, it was held to be lawful for a police officer to take hold of a person's arm in order to attract his attention and calm him down; but in *Collins v Wilcock* [1984] 3 All ER 374, a police officer was held to have committed a battery when, without purporting to exercise any lawful power of arrest, she held a woman by the arm in order to question her. See also *Kenlin v Gardiner* [1967] 2 QB 510, *Wood v DPP* [2008] EWHC 1056 (Admin), *B v DPP* [2008] EWHC 1655 (Admin) and *Elkington v DPP* [2012] EWHC 3398 (Admin). As to the powers of CSOs, see the Police Reform Act 2002, sch. 4, and *D v DPP* [2011] 1 WLR 882. Police powers are more fully examined in **D1**.

Mens Rea

B2.41 The *mens rea* required in respect of this offence is no different from that required in respect of common assault or battery. D need not know, or even have reason to suspect, that his victim is a police officer or that the officer is acting in the execution of his duty (*Forbes* (1865) 10 Cox CC 362; *Blackburn v Bowering* [1994] 3 All ER 380). In this respect, the offence is one of strict liability. In *Albert v Lavin* [1982] AC 546, D unlawfully assaulted a man who attempted to prevent him from causing a breach of the peace. He claimed not to know that this man was a police officer, but the House of Lords held that his alleged mistake was irrelevant. He would have been guilty of an assault or battery even if the man had not been a police officer, because the officer had been doing only what any citizen would have had the right to do in the circumstances. In contrast, if D honestly believes that he is being attacked or kidnapped by criminals, and uses force to resist them, he will not be guilty of a s. 89 offence, even though the 'criminals' prove to be police officers who were acting lawfully at the time. D's honest belief in his need to act in self-defence would negative any *mens rea* for assault (*Kenlin v Gardiner* [1967] 2 QB 510; *Blackburn v Bowering*; and see generally **A3.59**).

RESISTING OR WILFULLY OBSTRUCTING A CONSTABLE, ETC.

Definition

B2.42

Police Act 1996, s. 89

(2) Any person who resists or wilfully obstructs a constable in the execution of his duty, or a person assisting a constable in the execution of his duty, shall be guilty of an offence and liable on summary conviction to imprisonment for a term not exceeding one month or to a fine not exceeding level 3 on the standard scale, or to both.

Procedure

B2.43 This offence is triable only summarily (Police Act 1996, s. 89(2)). As to powers of arrest, see **D1.14**.

Sentence

The maximum penalty is one month's imprisonment, a fine not exceeding level 3, or both **B2.44** (Police Act 1996, s. 89(2)). The *Magistrates' Court Sentencing Guidelines* (see Supplement, SG-299) provide guidance for this offence.

Elements

A person obstructs a police constable if he makes it more difficult for him to carry out his duty **B2.45** (*Hinchcliffe v Sheldon* [1955] 3 All ER 406, *obiter*). While 'resisting' implies some physical action, no physical act is necessary to constitute obstruction. Simple refusal to answer questions does not constitute an obstruction (*Rice v Connolly* [1966] 2 QB 414), neither does advising another person not to answer (*Green v DPP* (1991) 155 JP 816). Answering questions incorrectly may, however, amount to obstruction, although the distinction is not always clear (*Ledger v DPP* [1991] Crim LR 439).

A person may obstruct by omission, provided that such a person is under an initial duty to act (*Lunt v DPP* [1993] Crim LR 534). There is also a common-law offence of refusing to aid a constable who is attempting to prevent or to quell a breach of the peace and who calls for assistance (*Waugh* (1986) *The Times*, 1 October 1986).

In *Green v Moore* [1982] QB 1044 the court held that a tip-off to persons who were preparing **B2.46** to commit an offence, and who as a result of the tip-off decided not to commit such an offence, could amount to an obstruction. Police could still be said to be acting in execution of their duty even if only making general inquiries before an offence was committed. The court admitted that this was a difficult situation, since the result of the tip-off was in fact the prevention of crime. Liability would turn, however, on the *mens rea* and the question of whether D's intent was to assist the potential criminal or to assist the police. If D's intention is simply to stop or prevent the commission of the crime, no offence is committed where he warns off the potential offender by pointing out the danger of detection and arrest. If, however, D's intention is to enable the potential offender to commit his crime (or a similar crime) at a more opportune moment, he may be guilty of obstruction.

In *R (DPP) v Glendinning* (2005) 169 JP 649, the Administrative Court held (following *Bastable v Little* [1907] 1 KB 59) that no offence of wilful obstruction is committed where D warns motorists of a police speed trap ahead, unless it is established that those warned were either already speeding or were likely to do so at the location of the speed trap.

As in the offence of assaulting a constable (see **B2.39**), no offence under s. 89(2) can be committed if the officer is acting unlawfully (*Edwards v DPP* (1993) 97 Cr App R 301; *B v DPP* [2008] EWHC 1655 (Admin)). Police powers are examined in **D1**.

If obstruction (rather than resistance) is alleged, it must be proved to have been wilful. D does **B2.47** not commit wilful obstruction if he tries to help the police, even if he actually makes their job more difficult (*Wilmott v Atack* [1977] QB 498) nor can he be guilty if he is unaware that he is obstructing police officers at all (*Ostler v Elliott* [1980] Crim LR 584), but if D deliberately obstructs the police, it will be no defence to argue that he was merely trying to prevent the arrest of a person he believed to be innocent (*Lewis v Cox* [1985] QB 509). As to the obstruction of international joint investigation teams, see the Police Act 1996, s. 89(4), and the SOCPA 2005, s. 57. As to the obstruction of traffic officers, see the Traffic Management Act 2004, s. 10(2); as to the obstruction of revenue and customs officers, see the Commissioners for Revenue and Customs Act 2005, s. 31; as to resisting or wilfully obstructing NCA officers designated as having the powers of constables, see the CCA 2013, s. 10 and sch. 5, para. 21; as to the obstruction or hindrance of emergency workers or persons assisting such workers, see the Emergency Workers (Obstruction) Act 2006, ss. 1 to 4; as to resisting or wilfully obstructing an accredited financial investigator exercising powers under the POCA 2002, see s. 453A of that Act.

WOUNDING OR INFLICTING GRIEVOUS BODILY HARM

Definition

B2.48

Offences against the Person Act 1861, s. 20

Whosoever shall unlawfully and maliciously wound or inflict any grievous bodily harm upon any other person, either with or without any weapon or instrument, shall be guilty of [an offence], and being convicted thereof shall be liable to [imprisonment for not more than five years].

The CDA 1998, s. 29(1)(a), creates a racially or religiously aggravated form of this offence which carries a higher maximum penalty. For the meaning of 'racially or religiously aggravated', see **B11.149**.

Procedure

B2.49   Both forms of the offence are triable either way. When tried on indictment this is normally a class 3 offence, but see CPD XIII, para. B (see Supplement, **PD-97**) for the additional factors that the court considers on allocation. See the *Magistrates' Court Sentencing Guidelines* (see Supplement, **SG-296**) for indications as to when a case should be sent to the Crown Court.

Indictments

B2.50   **Basic Offence: Inflicting Grievous Bodily Harm**

Statement of Offence

Unlawfully inflicting grievous bodily harm, contrary to section 20 of the Offences against the Person Act 1861

Particulars of Offence

A on or about the . . . day of . . . unlawfully and maliciously inflicted grievous bodily harm on V

B2.51   **Aggravated Offence: Wounding**

Statement of Offence

Racially aggravated wounding, contrary to section 29 (1)(a) of the Crime and Disorder Act 1998

Particulars of Offence

A on or about the . . . day of . . . maliciously wounded V and was wholly or partly motivated to do so by hostility to V's racial group, namely Arabs

Alternative Verdicts

B2.52   A verdict of assault occasioning actual bodily harm under the OAPA 1861, s. 47, can be returned (see the Criminal Law Act 1967, s. 6(3)).

Sentence (Basic Offence)

B2.53   The maximum penalty for the offence other than in the racially or religiously aggravated form (see **B2.59**) is five years (OAPA 1861, s. 20) on indictment; six months, a fine not exceeding level 5, or both, summarily (MCA 1980, s. 32(1)). Note the definitive sentencing guideline, *Assault* (see Supplement, **SG-207**), and the guideline and notes derived therefrom in the *Magistrates' Court Sentencing Guidelines* (see Supplement, **SG-296**).

Where the offence occurs in a domestic setting the definitive sentencing guideline, *Overarching Principles: Domestic Violence*, is applicable (see Supplement, **SG-51**). The terms of the guideline received a ringing endorsement from the Court of Appeal in *A-G's Ref (No. 80 of 2009)* [2010] EWCA Crim 470, in which practitioners were urged to 'read and re-read' it. See also *Caceres* [2014] 1 Cr App R (S) 128 (23).

Sentences of up to three years for this offence have been upheld by the Court of Appeal where aggravating factors have been present, or where the offence has been close to the borderline with the offence of wounding with intent; such sentences will be imposed where the assault was committed against a police officer or other public servant or against a child.

In *Dodds* [2013] 2 Cr App R (S) 358 (54) a sentence of three years following a guilty plea was **B2.54** upheld where the offender had struck the victim a single blow to the face causing him to fall and strike his head on a wall. The victim incurred very serious head injuries leaving him with long-term disability and disfigurement. The Court of Appeal said that the judge had been entitled to take a starting point of four and a half years before reduction for plea even though the top of the offence range is four years. Apart from the very serious harm incurred, the offender had a record of an escalating pattern of violence and the offence involved violence in the street at night. In *Lawrence* [2012] 2 Cr App R (S) 243 the offender punched the victim in the face during a brawl in a Sunday League soccer match. The victim received facial fractures and a metal plate had to be inserted. The offender was sentenced to nine months' imprisonment following a trial. The Court of Appeal agreed with the judge that the case fell within category 2 rather than category 3, since the harm was serious in the context of the offence. Upholding the sentence, Pitchford LJ said that assessment of seriousness of injury in context was a matter of judicial knowledge and experience.

Use of Weapon   The use of a weapon is an important aggravating feature. In *Morrison* [2012] **B2.55** 2 Cr App R (S) 594 (101) the offender struck the victim on the head with a bottle. The bottle broke, and the victim received several fractures to the skull and eye socket which required an operation. The offender pleaded guilty on the day of the trial. The judge found this to be a category 1 case, and took a starting point of four and a half years. The Court of Appeal said that there was clearly greater harm, but in terms of culpability the use of the weapon had to be set against lack of premeditation. Whether one took the case as falling within category 1 or on the cusp between categories 1 and 2, the combination of aggravating and mitigating factors took the case to a starting point of three and a half years. The final sentence, allowing for the late plea, was three years' imprisonment. In *Marsh* [2012] 2 Cr App R (S) 178 (31) the female offenders became involved in a fight with a 16-year-old girl. One held the girl's arms behind her back while the second cut the girl's face with a key, causing a 4 cm laceration which would leave a permanent scar. The Court of Appeal agreed with the judge that this was a category 1 case, given that this was a cold-blooded attack which caused physical and psychological damage. Coulson J said that it was important that all the various factors in the guideline were looked at in the round. Sentences of two years' imprisonment and 20 months' detention in a young offender institution were upheld.

Glassing   Pre-guideline cases involving 'glassing' include *Robertson* [1998] 1 Cr App R (S) 21, **B2.56** where the Court of Appeal noted that, in the light of earlier authorities, any sentence of more than two years' imprisonment for unlawful wounding required careful scrutiny to see if it was justified on the facts. In that case the offender had been drinking in a public house and had thrust a beer glass into another man's face, causing wounds to his face. A sentence of 30 months was reduced to two years. In *Marsden* (1993) 15 Cr App R (S) 177, the offender became involved in an argument in a public house and, after having been asked to leave, threw a glass across the room. It hit the victim and caused a cut to the head which required hospital treatment. A sentence of 12 months' imprisonment was upheld. These two decisions were considered in *McGhee* [2008] 2 Cr App R (S) 330, where the victim was struck twice with a glass and then kicked on the ground. A sentence of 27 months' imprisonment was appropriate on a plea of guilty. See also **B2.72**.

Racial or Religious Aggravation in Basic Offence   Racial or religious aggravation cannot be **B2.57** taken into account by the sentencer when sentencing for the basic offence of wounding or inflicting grievous bodily harm (see **B2.3**).

Malicious Transmission of Sexually Transmitted Disease   In *P (SJ)* [2006] EWCA Crim **B2.58** 2599, the offender had unprotected sexual relations with a man, without informing him that she had been diagnosed as HIV positive. When he became infected, she led him to believe, to his great distress, that he had infected her. She eventually pleaded guilty to the malicious infliction of grievous bodily harm, and a sentence of 32 months' imprisonment was upheld on appeal. The Court of Appeal received representations from the Terrence Higgins Trust to the effect that deterrent sentences in cases such as this had adverse effects on the willingness of suspected HIV sufferers to seek treatment or to undergo testing, but concluded that the courts had a duty to deter those who knew that they were HIV positive from recklessly transmitting the virus.

Sentence (Racially or Religiously Aggravated Form of Offence)

B2.59   The maximum penalty for the aggravated form of wounding or inflicting grievous bodily harm is seven years, a fine or both on indictment; six months, a fine not exceeding the statutory maximum or both summarily (CDA 1998, s. 29(2)). Note the definitive sentencing guideline, *Assault* (see Supplement, **SG-207**), and the guideline and notes derived therefrom in the *Magistrates' Court Sentencing Guidelines* (see Supplement, **SG-296**).

The definitive guideline states that 'the court should determine the appropriate sentence for the offence without taking account of the element of aggravation and then make an addition to the sentence, considering the level of aggravation involved. It may be appropriate to move outside the identified category range, taking into account the increased statutory maximum' thus reflecting the Court of Appeal judgment in *Saunders* [2000] 1 Cr App R 458, as elaborated in *Kelly* [2001] 2 Cr App R (S) 341. See further **B2.33**. What was described as a 'disgraceful and unprovoked incident of racial violence' attracted a sentence of 18 months' detention in a young offender institution in *Bray* (1992) 13 Cr App R (S) 5, notwithstanding the offender's previous good character, and 30 months' detention in a young offender institution was appropriate in *Sweet* [2012] 1 Cr App R (S) 35 for an unprovoked attack by an 18-year-old on a 61-year-old man where the attack was accompanied by words of racial abuse.

Elements

B2.60   The *actus reus* of an offence under the OAPA 1861, s. 20, may involve either unlawful wounding or the infliction of grievous bodily harm. Wounding requires the breaking of the continuity of the whole of the skin (dermis and epidermis) or the breaking of the inner skin within the cheek, lip or urethra (*Smith* (1837) 8 C & P 173; *Waltham* (1849) 3 Cox 442). It does not include the rupturing of internal blood vessels (*JJC (A Minor) v Eisenhower* [1983] 3 All ER 230). In theory, even trivial wounds may qualify, but the Charging Standards agreed between the police and the CPS urge that minor wounds should not in practice be charged under s. 20. Where, however, there is evidence of a serious wound, this ought generally to be charged as wounding, rather than as inflicting grievous bodily harm (*McReady* [1978] 3 All ER 967).

Grievous bodily harm means no more and no less than really serious harm (*DPP v Smith* [1961] AC 290; *Cunningham* [1982] AC 566). It may be physical or psychiatric (*Ireland* [1998] AC 147) but not merely psychological (*Dhaliwal* [2006] 2 Cr App R 348). It may also result from infection, but need not be permanent or dangerous (*Ashman* (1858) 1 F & F 88) and in determining its seriousness account must be taken of its effect on the individual victim (*Golding* [2014] EWCA Crim 889); injury to a finger could thus be grievous bodily harm where the victim is a professional musician. A number of individually minor injuries may collectively be considered grievous (*Birmingham* [2002] EWCA Crim 2608). Expert evidence may be required, and will certainly be required (as to both cause and effect) in cases of alleged psychiatric injury, as in cases brought under s. 47 (see **B2.35**).

The CPS Charging Standards lists examples of injuries which may be considered sufficiently serious to warrant a charge, but whether an injury is 'really serious' is ultimately a question for the court or jury, subject to the judge's duty to withdraw the issue in the absence of evidence sufficient to support a conviction (*Golding*).

Infliction Section 20 refers to the 'infliction' of grievous bodily harm. The meaning of this **B2.61** term was once a matter of some uncertainty and debate, but appears to have been largely resolved by the decision of the House of Lords in *Ireland* [1998] AC 147, where Lord Steyn, in giving the majority judgment, held (at p. 160) that harm could be inflicted without the need for an assault, and that in the context of the 1861 Act, there was no radical divergence between the meanings of the words 'cause' and 'inflict' (see also *Salisbury* [1976] VR 452; *Metropolitan Police Commissioner v Wilson* [1984] AC 242). Grievous bodily harm within the meaning of s. 20 could thus be inflicted by means of menacing telephone calls which gave rise to serious psychiatric injury, whether or not the injury was caused by fear of imminent physical attack.

On the other hand, Lord Steyn later denied that the words 'cause' and 'inflict' were exactly synonymous, and this point was developed by Lord Hope, who said that, although there was no real practical difference between the two words, the word 'inflict' invariably implies detriment to the victim of some kind. Lord Steyn and Lord Hope both appear to have stopped just short of overruling the authority of *Clarence* (1888) 22 QBD 23, in which it was held that grievous bodily harm was caused, *but not inflicted*, where C enjoyed consensual sexual intercourse with his wife, without warning her that he was infected with a venereal disease, which she then contracted. The authority and rationale of *Clarence* was nevertheless gravely damaged by what was said and decided in *Ireland* and in *Dica* [2004] QB 1257 (see **B2.15**) the Court of Appeal concluded that it should no longer be followed. Judge LJ said:

> The effect of this judgment in relation to s. 20 is to remove some of the outdated restrictions against the successful prosecution of those who, knowing that they are suffering HIV or some other serious sexual disease, recklessly transmit it through consensual sexual intercourse, and inflict grievous bodily harm on a person from whom the risk is concealed and who is not consenting to it. In this context, *Clarence* has no continuing relevance. Moreover, to the extent that *Clarence* suggested that consensual sexual intercourse of itself was to be regarded as consent to the risk of consequent disease, again, it is no longer authoritative. If however, the victim consents to the risk, this continues to provide a defence under s 20...

See also *Golding* [2014] EWCA Crim 889. The injury in question must be inflicted (directly **B2.62** or indirectly) by some deliberate, non-accidental conduct on D's part. This may be deliberate or recklessly dangerous and/or drunken driving (*Kaeppner* [2012] 2 Cr App R (S) 276 (47); *Horwood* [2012] EWCA Crim 253) although the use of s. 20 in dangerous driving cases will no doubt decline now that the new offence of causing serious injury by dangerous driving (see **C3.33**) is in force. In *Brady* [2006] EWCA Crim 2413, D had consumed a significant quantity of alcohol at a nightclub. As he sat down on a low railing on the first-floor gallery above the dance floor, he lost his balance and fell, landing on V and crippling her. The Court of Appeal opined (*obiter*) that although the fall may have been accidental, the act of perching drunkenly on the rail was not. Hallett LJ said (at [25]):

> This deliberate act, on any view, led almost immediately and directly to the fall over the railing and to the infliction of grievous bodily harm. It was a substantial cause of the infliction of those injuries. We would not be inclined to accept, therefore, [counsel's] submission that, because it was the unintentional fall rather than the deliberate act which, in fact, caused [the victim's] injuries, this broke the chain of causation. The one led inevitably to the other.

D's apparent lack of *mens rea* could then be addressed under the *Majewski* rule (as to which see A3.17). His appeal against his conviction was however allowed on other grounds.

Maliciously A s. 20 offence must be committed 'maliciously'. Maliciousness requires *either* **B2.63** an intent to do some kind of bodily harm to another person *or* recklessness (in the subjective or *Cunningham* sense) as to whether any such harm might be caused. The harm intended or foreseen by D need not amount to a wound or grievous bodily harm: an intent to cause minor injury, which inadvertently results in the infliction of a wound or serious injury, is sufficient to found liability under s. 20 (*Mowatt* [1968] 1 QB 421; *Sullivan* [1981] Crim LR 46; *DPP v W* [2006] EWHC 92 (Admin)). On the other hand, there cannot ordinarily be liability under

s. 20 if D was unaware that his conduct might cause any injury at all (*Savage* [1992] 1 AC 699; *Meachen* [2006] EWCA Crim 2414). The only qualification to this rule concerns cases of voluntary intoxication: such intoxication cannot be relied upon by a defendant in order to negative *mens rea* under s. 20, because it is not a crime of 'specific intent' (*Brady* [2006] EWCA Crim 2413 at **B2.62** and see also **A3.17**).

In *Barnes* [2005] 2 All ER 113, Lord Woolf CJ suggested that recklessness in this context, 'means no more than the defendant foresaw the risk that some bodily harm (however slight) might result from what he was going to do and yet, ignoring that risk, he went on to commit the offending act'. If that were indeed so, most tackles committed in contact sports such as football would (as Lord Woolf concedes) be deemed 'malicious'. With respect, however, such conduct is not reckless at all unless the risk taking in question can be described as unreasonable or unjustified in the circumstances.

The Court of Appeal held in *Beeson* [1994] Crim LR 190 that it was unnecessary to direct the jury on the meaning of the word 'maliciously'; but whilst such an omission may have been unimportant on the facts of that particular case (where the only real issue was self-defence), there will be many cases in which careful guidance on its meaning must be vital. The concept of maliciousness is further explained at **A2.12**.

WOUNDING OR CAUSING GRIEVOUS BODILY HARM WITH INTENT

Definition

B2.64

Offences against the Person Act 1861, s. 18

Whosoever shall unlawfully and maliciously by any means whatsoever wound or cause any grievous bodily harm to any person with intent to do some grievous bodily harm to any person, or with intent to resist or prevent the lawful apprehension or detainer of any person, shall be guilty of [an offence], and being convicted thereof shall be liable to [imprisonment] for life.

Procedure

B2.65   Wounding or causing grievous bodily harm with intent is triable on indictment only. It is normally a class 3 offence, but see CPD XIII, para. B (see Supplement, **PD-97**) for the additional factors that the court considers on allocation.

Indictment

B2.66

Statement of Offence

Wounding [or causing grievous bodily harm] with intent, contrary to section 18 of the Offences against the Person Act 1861

Particulars of Offence

A on or about the…day of…unlawfully and maliciously wounded [or caused grievous bodily harm to] V with intent to do him grievous bodily harm [or to prevent the lawful apprehension of X]

As to the proper form of indictment in a 'transferred malice' case, where it is alleged that D wounded V whilst intending to do grievous bodily harm to another, see *Monger* [1973] Crim LR 301, *Slimmings* [1999] Crim LR 69. An indictment for a s. 18 offence does not become invalid merely because it refers to the 'infliction' (rather than the 'causing') of grievous bodily harm, or because it omits any reference to the specific intent required (*Hodgson* [2008] 2 Cr App R 521).

Alternative Verdicts

B2.67   This subject is complex, and is dealt with in detail at **D19.41** and **D19.58**. Where wounding is alleged in a count under the OAPA 1861, s. 18, then wounding under s. 20 and s. 47 assault are possible alternative verdicts. *Lahaye* [2006] 1 Cr App R 205, confirms that on a charge of wounding with intent to do grievous bodily harm, a conviction for malicious wounding (under the OAPA 1861, s. 20) is available even if not expressly charged on the indictment, and even if the prosecution have presented the case as one of deliberate and premeditated stabbing. The Court of Appeal nevertheless recommended that it would be preferable, in such cases, for the lesser offence to be included on the face of the indictment. If, however, the s. 18 count alleges the causing of grievous bodily harm only, the situation is more complex. Problems have arisen where an alternative count of inflicting grievous bodily harm under s. 20 has not been specified, and the alternative verdict of *causing* grievous bodily harm under s. 20 has been accepted. Strictly speaking, this is an offence unknown to law, given the use of the term 'inflicting' in the offence created by s. 20.

The House of Lords in *Mandair* [1995] 1 AC 208 held that a judge is entitled under the **B2.68** Criminal Law Act 1967, s. 6(3), to leave to a jury a conviction under s. 20 as an alternative to s. 18 because the term 'causing' is wide enough to include 'inflicting' (*Metropolitan Police Commissioner v Wilson* [1984] AC 242). Even though in *Mandair* the word 'inflicting' was not used, the meaning is clear given the context of the direction in the case and the wording of the verdict. A verdict of 'causing grievous bodily harm contrary to s. 20' can only mean causing grievous bodily harm by inflicting it, as that is the particular method referred to in s. 20. Therefore the jury had not returned a verdict unknown to law. The case was remitted to the Court of Appeal for a decision on a further point it had not considered. *Mandair* was applied in *White* [1995] Crim LR 393.

Although it is now clear that an alternative verdict can be considered following an oral direction, the House of Lords in *Mandair* re-affirmed the point that it is preferable to add an alternative specific count using the correct wording of the statute. Normally, if D is acquitted under s. 18 without an alternative indictment under s. 20, a later prosecution under s. 20 cannot be brought, but in circumstances where D was for some reason not in jeopardy of a s. 20 conviction in the first trial, a later prosecution can arguably be brought. See *Old Street Magistrates' Court, ex parte Davies* [1995] Crim LR 629, and *Brookes* [1995] Crim LR 630, where the initial charge was under s. 20, and the subsequent charge was under s. 18.

Sentence

The maximum penalties for this offence and related offences are: **B2.69**

Wounding or causing grievous bodily harm with intent to do grievous bodily harm: life imprisonment (OAPA 1861, s. 18);

Wounding or causing grievous bodily harm with intent to resist arrest: life imprisonment (OAPA 1861, s. 18);

Attempting to choke, suffocate or strangle with intent: life imprisonment (OAPA 1861, s. 21);

Throwing corrosive fluid: life imprisonment (OAPA 1861, s. 29).

Note the definitive sentencing guideline, *Assault* (see Supplement, **SG-206**) in relation to offences under s. 18. A custodial sentence will almost always be required for this offence (*A-G's Ref (No. 33 of 1997)* [1998] 1 Cr App R (S) 352).

Where the offence occurs in a domestic setting the definitive sentencing guideline, *Overarching Principles: Domestic Violence* (see Supplement, **SG-51**), is applicable. The terms of the guideline received a ringing endorsement from the Court of Appeal in *A-G's Ref (No. 80 of 2009)* [2010] EWCA Crim 470, in which practitioners were urged to 'read and re-read' it; in that case sentence was increased from two and a half years to five years on an offender who deliberately burned his wife's face with an iron. See also *A-G's Ref (No. 65 of 2010) (Dawson)* [2011] 2 Cr App R (S) 209.

Knives The Court of Appeal has considered the application of the Sentencing Council **B2.70** guidelines in a number of recent decisions. In *Collis* [2012] EWCA Crim 1335, the

40-year-old offender used a kitchen knife to stab the victim in the neck after the victim, who lived in a neighbouring flat, forced his way into the offender's flat and attacked the offender's wife in a dispute over drugs. The offender, who had many previous convictions, pleaded guilty on the basis that he had not armed himself in advance. The Court said this was a case of greater harm having regard to the life-threatening nature of the injury, but was at the borderline of higher and lower culpability and was therefore at the borderline of categories 1 and 2, requiring a starting point of nine years' imprisonment. After taking account of mitigation and the early plea of guilty, the final sentence was six years. In *Fadeiro* [2013] 1 Cr App R (S) 366 (66), the 19-year-old offender stabbed a 17-year-old youth in the face with a knife, causing a deep penetrating injury close to his eye. By great good fortune, no permanent or serious damage was done. The judge selected a starting point at the lower end of category 1 (greater harm and higher culpability), imposing a sentence of 11 years' detention in a young offender institution. The Court of Appeal agreed with the sentence, but preferred to say that it was a category 2 case given that greater harm (in the context of the offence) had not been caused. Culpability was high and there were a number of important aggravating features, not least the fact that the offender had a previous conviction for robbery in which a knife had been produced. In *Richardson* [2012] 2 Cr App R (S) 606, the victim, a convicted criminal, was attacked in a restaurant by three armed and hooded men in what appeared to have been a revenge attack. Various injuries were inflicted including a slicing wound to the thigh which was large enough for a hand to be placed inside it. The judge found this to be a category 1 case. The Court of Appeal agreed, but said that, even if it was a category 2 case of lesser harm and higher culpability, the aggravating features meant that the case was right at the top end of category 2. The correct starting point was 12 years' imprisonment, reduced to eight years to reflect full discount for a guilty plea. In *Karakas* [2013] 1 Cr App R (S) 261 (46), the offender, a man of previous good character, stabbed the victim four times following a series of disputes. The femoral artery was severed, there were injuries to bladder and bowel, and the victim lost five pints of blood and was in hospital for two months. Following a guilty plea, the judge passed a sentence of ten years' imprisonment based on a starting point of 15 years. The Court of Appeal agreed that this was a category 1 case but, in light of personal mitigation, the sentence was reduced to eight years.

B2.71   **Other Weapons**   The use of other weapons will attract comparable sentences, depending upon the extent of the injuries, taken together with relevant mitigating and aggravating factors. In *Makula* [2013] 2 Cr App R (S) 43 (9) the offender and others attacked the victim with baseball bats, and the offender also kicked the victim repeatedly when he was on the ground, causing 'catastrophic injuries' including brain damage and the amputation of both legs. A sentence of 15 years' imprisonment following a plea of guilty was upheld on appeal; the Court of Appeal stated that the case was exceptionally bad and that the judge had been right to take a starting point above the guideline offence range. In *Harrison* [2012] 2 Cr App R (S) 449 (78) the 22-year-old offender, who had many previous convictions including violence, had struck the victim on the head with a large tin concealed in a sock, causing a depressed fracture of the skull. The victim was in hospital for three days but made a full recovery. The judge found this to be a category 1 case, and passed a sentence of ten years' imprisonment following a trial. The Court of Appeal said that it was a matter of fine judgment but that on balance this was lesser harm, and so the case was category 2 rather than category 1. The appropriate sentence was at the top of that range, and should have been nine years. Eight years' imprisonment following a guilty plea was upheld in *Talbot* [2013] 2 Cr App R (S) 29 (6), where the offender caused grievous bodily harm to a police officer with intent to resist arrest. He ran his car into the victim, knocking him down, and then drove over him, fracturing the officer's leg.

B2.72   **Glassing**   The Court of Appeal has considered many cases where a broken bottle or glass has been used as a weapon. A sentence of ten years' imprisonment after a trial was upheld in *Simpson* [2012] 1 Cr App R (S) 38 (9) where, on application of the former sentencing guidelines, the attack by the offender was found to have been premeditated and involved the ramming of a broken glass into the victim's face several times, occasioning grave physical and psychological injury. On application of the current guidelines, nine years' imprisonment following a trial was upheld in *Burtenshaw* [2013] 2 Cr App R (S) 277 (41), where the offender smashed a glass and struck a man twice in the face with it, causing serious cuts which required 30 stitches and produced long-term psychological effects and permanent scarring. The Court of Appeal said that the case was on the borderline between categories 1 and 2. Six years' imprisonment was upheld in *Anani* [2013] 2 Cr App R (S) 370 (57) where the offender pleaded guilty to two s. 18 offences. After a drunken argument, he struck the first victim with a broken bottle, causing serious injury to his face, and then used the bottle to stab a second man in the arm. The Court of Appeal said the case was either a category 1 case or on the borderline with category 2, and was aggravated by its commission under the influence of alcohol in a public place.

Kicking or Stamping   It is clear that where an offender causes grievous bodily harm by kicking or stamping on the victim's head while the latter is on the ground, he should receive a substantial custodial term. The Court of Appeal said that five years' imprisonment was appropriate in *Clarke* [2006] 1 Cr App R (S) 80, where the offender, a man with no previous convictions, had, in the course of a road rage incident, pulled the victim from his car and kicked him in the head when he was on the ground. The offender was wearing steel toe-capped boots, and the Court said that the boots should be treated as equivalent to a weapon. A case decided after the Sentencing Council guideline came into effect is *Cripps* [2013] 1 Cr App R (S) 43 (7). A sentence of nine years' imprisonment was upheld where the offender had attacked a man, punched him unconscious, and then kicked his head while he lay on the floor. The victim sustained extensive fractures to the jaw, cheekbones, eye sockets and nose. His face and eye socket were reconstructed surgically. The judge regarded this as a category 1 case. The Court of Appeal said that it lay on the cusp between category 1 and category 2. Greater harm was clearly present, but in respect of culpability the lack of premeditation had to be set against the use of the shod foot as a weapon. In any event, the sentence was in no way excessive. See also *Makula* [2013] 2 Cr App R (S) 43 (9) at **B2.71**. **B2.73**

Corrosive Fluid   In cases where corrosive fluid is thrown, lengthy terms will be appropriate. The offender in *Carrington* [1999] 2 Cr App R (S) 206 threw some liquid containing sulphuric acid into the face of his former girlfriend. The victim received prompt first aid treatment, and fortunately suffered no long-term damage. In light of the fact that the attack was premeditated and that the offender had contested the case and had shown no remorse, a sentence of six years' imprisonment was upheld. In *Makeid* [2007] 2 Cr App R (S) 623 a sentence of six and a half years was appropriate where a man threw sulphuric acid at another man during the course of an argument, causing extensive injuries. There was limited credit for the offender's guilty plea because a *Newton* hearing had been substantially resolved against him. **B2.74**

Elements

An offence under the OAPA 1861, s. 18, may take one of four different forms, namely: **B2.75**

(a) wounding with intent to do grievous bodily harm;
(b) causing grievous bodily harm with intent to do so;
(c) maliciously wounding with intent to resist or prevent the lawful apprehension etc. of any person; or
(d) maliciously causing grievous bodily harm with intent to resist or prevent lawful apprehension etc. of any person.

As to the meaning of the terms 'wound' and 'grievous bodily harm', see **B2.60**. Following the decision of the House of Lords in *Ireland* [1998] AC 147, it now seems unlikely that anything of significance turns on the supposed difference between 'causing' injury in cases under s. 18 and 'inflicting' injury in cases under s. 20. This means that the *actus reus* elements of the two offences are for most purposes the same. The difference lies in the specific intent required under s. 18. Where it is alleged that D acted with intent to cause grievous bodily harm, the jury should be directed along the following or similar lines: 'You must feel sure that [D] intended to cause serious bodily harm to [V]. You can only decide what his intention was by considering all the relevant circumstances and in particular what he did and what he said about it' (*Purcell* (1986) 83 Cr App R 45).

If D is alleged to have acted with intent to do grievous bodily harm, the concept of maliciousness is rendered otiose and need not be examined (*Mowatt* [1968] 1 QB 421). Where, in contrast, it is alleged that D merely intended to resist arrest etc., maliciousness becomes an important further element to be proved. If, for example, D tries to pull free from the officer arresting him and quite unforeseeably injures the officer in the process, he could not be considered to have acted maliciously and could not therefore be convicted of an offence under s. 18. If, however, he intended or foresaw that he would cause some minor injury, he could indeed be adjudged malicious.

Where it is alleged that D acted with intent to avoid or resist the lawful apprehension of any person, it may be his own arrest or that of another that he resisted, but the lawfulness of that arrest or detention must in either event be proved by the prosecution (*Howarth* (1828) 1 Mood 207). It does not follow that D must be proved to have known that the arrest etc. was lawful, but in a case such as *Kenlin v Gardiner* [1967] 2 QB 510, where D mistook arresting officers for kidnappers, mistaken self-defence may be raised by the defence in accordance with the principles established in *Williams* [1987] 3 All ER 411 and now embodied in the CJIA 2008, s. 76 (see **A3.63**). See generally **A3.54**.

ADMINISTERING POISON ETC. SO AS TO ENDANGER LIFE ETC.

Definition

B2.76   Offences against the Person Act 1861, s. 23

Whosoever shall unlawfully and maliciously administer to or cause to be administered to or taken by any other person any poison or other destructive or noxious thing, so as thereby to endanger the life of such person, or so as thereby to inflict upon such person any grievous bodily harm, shall be guilty of [an offence], and being convicted thereof shall be liable...to [imprisonment] for any term not exceeding 10 years.

Note also the Anti-terrorism, Crime and Security Act 2001, s. 113 (see **B10.163**).

Procedure

B2.77   An offence under the OAPA 1861, s. 23, is triable only on indictment. It is normally a class 3 offence, but see CPD XIII, para. B (see Supplement, **PD-97**) for the additional factors that the court considers on allocation.

Indictment

B2.78   *Statement of Offence*

Administering poison so as to endanger life [or so as to cause grievous bodily harm], contrary to section 23 of the Offences against the Person Act 1861

Particulars of Offence

A on or about the...day of...unlawfully and maliciously administered to V a poison, namely..., so as thereby to endanger the life of the said V [or so as to inflict on the said V grievous bodily harm]

Alternative Verdicts

B2.79   Under the OAPA 1861, s. 25, if a jury are not satisfied that a person charged under s. 23 is guilty of that offence but they are satisfied that he is guilty of an offence under s. 24 (see **B2.85** to **B2.90**), then they can acquit under s. 23 and return a verdict of guilty under s. 24, and D will be sentenced as if he had been tried on indictment under s. 24.

Sentence

The maximum penalty is ten years' imprisonment (OAPA 1861, s. 23). In *MK* [2008] 2 Cr **B2.80**
App R (S) 437 the 23-year-old offender pleaded guilty to the offence under s. 23 in circumstances where he had given a three-year-old child in his care a teaspoonful of methadone. The offender planned to obtain a urine sample from the child, which would be free from Class A drugs but positive for methadone. The child suffered a life-threatening illness as a result. The offender did not admit to the doctors treating the child what he had done, so the child's suffering was prolonged. A sentence of four and a half years' imprisonment was upheld on appeal.

Actus Reus

In *Kennedy (No. 2)* [2008] 1 AC 269, the House of Lords held that s. 23 creates three distinct **B2.81**
offences. The first is committed where D administers the noxious thing directly to V, as by injecting V with the noxious thing, holding a glass containing the noxious thing to V's lips, or (as in *Gillard* (1988) 87 Cr App R 189) spraying a noxious thing (e.g., CS gas or ammonia) in V's face. See also *A-G's Ref (No. 69 of 2005)* [2005] EWCA Crim 3050 (dousing victims in petrol and threatening to light it).

The second is typically committed where D does not directly administer the noxious thing to V but causes an innocent third party (T) to administer it to V. If D, knowing a syringe to be filled with poison, instructs T to inject V, when T believes the syringe to contain a legitimate therapeutic substance, D would commit this offence.

The third covers the situation where the noxious thing is not administered to V but is taken by him, provided D causes the noxious thing to be taken by V and V does not make a voluntary and informed decision to take it. If D puts a noxious thing in food which V is about to eat and V, ignorant of the presence of the noxious thing, eats it, D commits the offence (see also *Harley* (1830) 4 C & P 369).

In each case, the administration must endanger life or inflict grievous bodily harm. If the poison etc. is not consumed by V and does not come into contact with his body in a way that may harm him, there can, at most, be an attempt to administer it (*Dale* (1852) 6 Cox CC 14).

The administering must be unlawful. Consent will normally negate unlawfulness, but not where it is procured by deception or where considerations of public policy invalidate that consent. A person cannot, for example, validly consent to being injected with a dangerous drug, such as heroin, unless this is done for bona fide medical reasons (*Cato* [1976] 1 All ER 260).

In some cases D might be said to have administered the drug to V, even though V helped him **B2.82**
to do it. Joint administration would suffice to make D guilty of an offence under s. 23 (and of manslaughter if death results). See *Burgess* [2008] EWCA Crim 516 at [12]. In *Rogers* [2003] 1 WLR 1374, D applied a tourniquet to V's arm as V self-injected. The Court of Appeal held that this made D guilty of (jointly) administering it; but in *Kennedy* (at [20]) the House of Lords disagreed:

> There is, clearly, a difficult borderline between contributory acts which may properly be regarded as administering a noxious thing and acts which may not. But the crucial question is not whether the defendant facilitated or contributed to administration of the noxious thing, but whether he went further and administered it. What matters…is whether the injection itself was the result of a voluntary and informed decision by the person injecting himself. In *R v Rogers*, as in the present case, it was. That case was, therefore, wrongly decided…

If D had injected V while V applied the tourniquet to his own arm, the House of Lords would presumably have approved the decision. The House of Lords also reversed *Kennedy (No. 2)* [2005] 4 All ER 1083, in which it had been held that D may be guilty of administering a noxious drug to V on the basis of a joint venture or agreement, even though V alone performs the physical act of injection.

B2.83   Whether a substance is a poison, etc. is largely a question of fact, but the meaning of the term 'noxious' was examined in *Marcus* [1981] 2 All ER 833, where M put sleeping pills into her neighbour's milk. Were sleeping pills a noxious substance? The question was held to be one of both quantity and quality. Something which is harmless in small doses may be noxious in larger doses or when taken at the wrong time. Its effect on V is what is important. The Court of Appeal referred to the dictionary definition of 'noxious' as 'injurious, hurtful, harmful, unwholesome' and held that it could also apply to objectionable or obnoxious substances, although the potential of such a wide definition is greater in s. 24, where no dangerous or harmful consequence is required. See also *Hill* (1986) 83 Cr App R 386 and *Gantz* [2005] 1 Cr App R(S) 587 (see **B2.90**).

Mens Rea

B2.84   The *mens rea* required under s. 23 is maliciousness, which has the same meaning as it does under s. 20 (see **B2.63**). This means that D must act either with intent or with subjective recklessness; but this *mens rea* requirement applies only to the act of administering or causing the administration of the noxious substance. It does not extend to the consequences of that administration, which are governed by strict or constructive liability. D may therefore be guilty even if he did not intend or foresee that his action would cause grievous bodily harm or endanger life. See *Cato* [1976] 1 All ER 260.

ADMINISTERING POISON ETC. WITH INTENT

Definition

B2.85   Offences against the Person Act 1861, s. 24

Whosoever shall unlawfully and maliciously administer to or cause to be administered to or taken by any other person any poison or other destructive or noxious thing, with intent to injure, aggrieve, or annoy such person, shall be guilty of [an offence] and being…convicted thereof shall be liable to [imprisonment for a term not exceeding five years].

Procedure

B2.86   Administering poison etc. with intent is triable only on indictment. It is normally a class 3 offence, but see CPD XIII, para. B (see Supplement, **PD-97**) for the additional factors that the court considers on allocation.

Indictment

B2.87   *Statement of Offence*

Administering poison with intent, contrary to section 24 of the Offences against the Person Act 1861

Particulars of Offence

D on or about the…day of…unlawfully and maliciously administered to V a poison, namely…with intent to injure, aggrieve or annoy the said V

Alternative Verdicts

B2.88   See **B2.79**.

Sentence

The maximum penalty is five years' imprisonment (OAPA 1861, s. 24). In *Jones* (1990) 12 Cr **B2.89**
App R (S) 233, Glidewell LJ accepted that the appropriate sentencing bracket for this offence
was equivalent to that for an offence of wounding or inflicting grievous bodily harm under the
OAPA 1861, s. 20 (see **B2.53**), or a serious example of an offence of assault occasioning actual
bodily harm under the OAPA 1861, s. 47 (see **B2.31**), on the basis that the maximum penalty
available for each of the three offences is five years. Nine months' imprisonment was said to be
the correct sentence in *Hogan* (1994) 15 Cr App R (S) 834, where the offender gave to a woman
a drink which contained a large quantity of a Class C drug. It caused her to fall into a deep
sleep for a day. Two years was appropriate in *Liles* [2000] 1 Cr App R (S) 31, where the offender
allowed two young boys to inhale isobutyle nitrate so that they became dizzy and unwell. Thirty
months after a trial was upheld in *Bryan* [2011] 2 Cr App R (S) 407, where the offender threw
liquid containing a mixture of chilli, black pepper and turmeric into the face of the victim, causing non-permanent damage to her eyes.

Elements

The *actus reus* of the OAPA 1861, s. 24, is similar to that of s. 23, save that no consequential **B2.90**
harm or endangerment is required. It is a conduct crime.

As with s. 23, D must act maliciously in administering the noxious thing, but there is a
further or ulterior intent, namely to injure, aggrieve or annoy, which must additionally
be proved. This means that s. 24 — the lesser offence — is one of specific intent for the
purposes of the *Majewski* rule (see **A3.17**), whereas the more serious s. 23 offence is one of
basic intent.

Section 24 has been used successfully to prosecute defendants who 'spike' their victims' drinks
with drugs such as ecstasy (*Gantz* [2005] 1 Cr App R (S) 587) or who ply children with such
drugs for improper purposes. The 'overstimulation' of a victim's metabolism that such action is
intended to cause can be viewed as a type of injury. In *Hill* (1986) 83 Cr App R 386, H administered slimming pills to young boys in order to keep them awake. The House of Lords held that
he had been properly convicted under s. 24. Lord Griffiths said:

> The defence conceded that the tablets were a noxious thing and that the respondent had unlawfully
> administered them to the boys. In these circumstances the only issue that the jury had to determine
> was whether he did so with the intent to injure them...Here was a man who admitted being sexu-
> ally attracted to young boys plying them with a drug which he knew would overstimulate and excite
> them and doing so with a reckless disregard for what might be the safe dosage and, in fact, giving
> them a gross overdose. The only reasonable inference to draw from such conduct was an intention
> that the drug should injure the boys in the sense of causing harm to the metabolism of their bodies
> by overstimulation with the motive of either ingratiating himself with them or, more probably,
> rendering them susceptible to homosexual advances.

FALSE IMPRISONMENT

Definition

False imprisonment is a common-law offence but is more common as a civil action in tort. **B2.91**
The overlap with kidnapping (see **B2.97**) and child abduction (see **B2.104**) means that those
offences may often represent more suitable charges than simple false imprisonment.

The case of *Rahman* (1985) 81 Cr App R 349 provides the following definition (at p. 353):
'False imprisonment consists in the unlawful and intentional or reckless restraint of a victim's
freedom of movement from a particular place.'

Procedure

B2.92 False imprisonment is triable only on indictment. It may be classified in class 2A, 2B or 3; see CPD XIII, para. B (see Supplement, **PD-97**) for the additional factors that the court considers on allocation.

Indictment

B2.93

Statement of Offence

False imprisonment

Particulars of Offence

D on divers days between the...day of...and the...day of...falsely imprisoned V and detained the said V against his will

Sentence

B2.94 The maximum penalty is at large (common-law offence). For indications of appropriate sentencing, see those applicable to kidnapping at **B2.100**.

Actus Reus

B2.95 This consists of preventing V's freedom of movement. V may be restrained physically or by deliberate intimidation (*James* (1997) *The Times*, 2 October 1997). V might be detained in a building or vehicle, or simply prevented from going on his way. In *Bird v Jones* (1845) 7 QB 742, a civil case, V was prevented from going in one particular direction in which he wished to go, but there was an alternative route available to him; this did not constitute a false imprisonment.

The *actus reus* is the imprisoning without lawful excuse, and there seems no logical reason for requiring that V realise this is the case. No such realisation is necessary in the tort of false imprisonment (*Meering v Grahame White Aviation Co. Ltd* (1919) 122 LT 44).

The imprisonment must be unlawful. Two main situations arise where this can be problematic. One is in respect of a parent restraining a child. In *Rahman* (1985) 81 Cr App R 349 the question arose of the limits of a parent's right to lawfully restrain a child. D had taken his 15-year-old daughter from her foster parents against her will. He was convicted and appealed. The court held that it was a question of fact in each case whether a parent had overstepped the limits of lawful correction and restraint. Whether the child's lack of consent was relevant must also be a question of fact depending on the circumstances of a particular case. In this case the appellant's appeal was dismissed. He had overstepped his right as a parent to exercise normal parental control. (See also kidnapping at **B2.97** and child abduction at **B2.104**.)

The other main situation in the context of which false imprisonment can arise is where an arrest is carried out by either a constable or a private citizen, which turns out to be unlawful. The lawfulness of an arrest is to be decided by reference to the general law, including the PACE 1984, s. 24. See, as to lawful and unlawful arrests, **D1.14**. If the arrest is unlawful, the *actus reus* of the offence will have been committed.

Mens Rea

B2.96 *Rahman* (1985) 81 Cr App R 349 states that the *mens rea* for false imprisonment is intention or recklessness. Recklessness here means subjective or *Cunningham* recklessness (*James* (1997) *The Times*, 2 October 1997).

The offence is one of basic intent, and therefore evidence of D's voluntary intoxication is irrelevant. This was confirmed in *Hutchins* [1988] Crim LR 379, which case also emphasised the overlap and analogy with kidnapping.

In that case D, having taken drugs at a party, took a neighbour hostage. He was charged with both kidnapping and false imprisonment. It was confirmed that his intoxication was irrelevant, and the court took the opportunity to define both 'false imprisonment' and 'kidnapping'. It emphasised that in kidnapping the taking must be by force or fraud, and that the definition was in terms of 'taking or carrying away' rather than a mere detaining, which would suffice for false imprisonment.

KIDNAPPING

Definition

Kidnapping is a common-law offence. It overlaps partly with false imprisonment (see **B2.91**) and partly with child abduction (see **B2.104**). **B2.97**

The offence consists of the taking or carrying away of one person by another by force or fraud, without the consent of that person and without lawful excuse.

Procedure

Kidnapping is triable only on indictment. It may be classified in class 2A, 2B or 3; see CPD XIII, para. B (see Supplement, **PD-97**) for the additional factors that the court considers on allocation. **B2.98**

Indictment

Statement of Offence **B2.99**

Kidnapping

Particulars of Offence

A on or about the...day of...unlawfully took and carried away V against his will

Despite the acknowledged overlap between the offences of kidnapping and statutory abduction, an indictment should not contain counts for both offences (*C* (1990) *The Times*, 9 November 1990).

Sentence

The maximum penalty is at large (common-law offence). **B2.100**

Some general observations on sentencing for this offence were provided in *Spence* (1983) 5 Cr App R (S) 413, where Lord Lane CJ said (at p. 416):

> ...there is a wide possible variation in seriousness between one instance of the crime and another. At the top of the scale of course, come the carefully planned abductions where the victim is used as a hostage or where ransom money is demanded. Such offences will seldom be met with less than eight years' imprisonment or thereabouts. Where violence or firearms are used, or there are other exacerbating features such as detention of the victim over a long period of time, then the proper sentence will be very much longer than that. At the other end of the scale are those offences which can perhaps scarcely be classed as kidnapping at all. They very often arise as a sequel to family tiffs or lovers' disputes, and they seldom require anything more than 18 months' imprisonment, and sometimes a great deal less.

In *Yu Hang* [2012] 1 Cr App R (S) 550 a sentence of 12 years' imprisonment following a guilty plea was appropriate where the offenders pleaded guilty to kidnap and blackmail, having abducted and detained a foreign student for six days while a ransom demand was made to his parents. Nine and a half years was upheld in *Vaz* [2012] 2 Cr App R (S) 456, where the offender took part in falsely imprisoning members of a family to facilitate the commission of a robbery. Eight years was upheld in *Razzaq* [2009] 2 Cr App R (S) 553, where the offender admitted being concerned in kidnapping and falsely imprisoning a man for ten days in the course of a large-scale fraud. The victim was tied up, assaulted, transported in the boot of a car and then held in a metal box. Five years was reduced to four years in *Parkins* [2011] 1 Cr App R (S) 686, where three women aged 19 and 20 went to the home of a 17-year-old girl, tied her up and assaulted her. The victim was then moved to a second location and assaulted again. In *Ashworth* [2010] 1 Cr App R (S) 84, a sentence of two years was appropriate for a brief period of false imprisonment of a father by his 24-year-old son after a domestic argument, and 12 months was upheld for false imprisonment in *Saker* [2012] 1 Cr App R (S) 87 where a mother was involved in tying up and imprisoning her daughter for a short time in the hope of preventing drug use by the daughter.

Actus Reus

B2.101   The *actus reus* of kidnapping (as defined at **B2.97**) is similar to that of false imprisonment (see **B2.91**) insofar as it involves the unlawful deprivation of V's liberty; but it differs from false imprisonment in that it also requires V to be taken or carried away, either by force (including the threat of force: *Archer* [2011] EWCA Crim 2252) or by fraud. He need not be carried far: in *Wellard* [1978] 3 All ER 161, D impersonated a constable and thereby tricked or coerced V into walking a few yards to his car in order to submit to a 'drugs search'. This was held to be a sufficient 'taking'.

In *D* [1984] AC 778, the House of Lords held that a parent who took custody of his own child in contravention of a court order could be guilty of kidnapping, and a majority held that the rule was more general, and that parents could be acting without lawful excuse in some circumstances by taking their children even where there was no court order. It will be a question of fact whether or not a parent has a lawful excuse to exercise such physical control over the whereabouts of the child.

Kidnapping must be committed without the valid consent of the victim. Consent or compliance procured by force or fear is not true consent (*Greenhalgh* [2001] EWCA Crim 1367). Very young children may be incapable of giving such consent (*D* [1984] AC 778); but it may sometimes prove difficult to show force or fraud if a child is simply picked up and taken. In such circumstances, a charge under the Child Abduction Act 1984 may be easier to prove, although in the most serious cases the higher maximum penalty that may be imposed for kidnapping may warrant consideration (*Kayani* [2012] 2 All ER 641). If a person initially consents to being taken away, the offence will be committed if that consent is later withdrawn and force is used to maintain a kidnapping (*Lewis* (22 March 1993 unreported)).

B2.102   As to the need for a deprivation of liberty, this appears to have been overlooked in *Cort* [2004] QB 388, in which D tricked his 'victims' into riding in his car by deceiving them into thinking that their bus had broken down. This was held to be sufficient for an offence of kidnapping, even though there was no evidence to suggest that D made any attempt to detain them against their will. But *Cort* is inconsistent with *Wellard* and was doubted in *Hendy-Freegard* [2008] QB 57, where Lord Phillips CJ said (at [55]):

> We cannot see that there was justification for extending the offence of kidnapping to cover the situation in which the driver of the car has no intention of detaining his passenger against her will nor of doing other than taking her to the destination to which she wishes to go, simply because in some such circumstances the driver may have an objectionable ulterior motive. The consequence of the decision in *Cort* would seem to be that the mini-cab driver, who obtains a fare by falsely pretending to be an authorised taxi, will be guilty of kidnapping.

In *Hendy-Freegard*, D tricked his victims into making certain journeys they would not otherwise have made; but these journeys were made independently, and D did not even accompany them. The Court of Appeal held that this could not amount to kidnapping, for otherwise, as Lord Phillips CJ pointed out at [57]:

> ...the bigamist who induces a woman to travel to the church for a wedding ceremony might be guilty not merely of bigamy but also of kidnapping. Such a submission transforms the offence of kidnapping in a manner that cannot be justified, even on the basis of the decision in *Cort*.

Mens Rea

The *mens rea* is not specifically discussed in *D* [1984] AC 778, but the Court of Appeal in **B2.103**
Hutchins [1988] Crim LR 379 pointed out the close analogy between false imprisonment and
kidnapping, the differences being in the *actus reus*. This indicates that the *mens rea* is likely to be
the same as that for false imprisonment (see **B2.96**).

CHILD ABDUCTION

Abduction by Person Connected with Child

Definition   **B2.104**

Child Abduction Act 1984, s. 1

(1) Subject to subsections (5) and (8) below, a person connected with a child under the age of
16 commits an offence if he takes or sends the child out of the United Kingdom without the
appropriate consent.

(2) A person is connected with a child for the purposes of this section if—
  (a) he is a parent of the child; or
  (b) in the case of a child whose parents were not married to each other at the time of his birth,
there are reasonable grounds for believing that he is the father of the child; or
  (c) he is a guardian of the child; or
  (ca) he is a special guardian of the child; or
  (d) he is a person in whose favour a residence order is in force with respect to the child; or
  (e) he has custody of the child.

(3) In this section 'the appropriate consent', in relation to a child, means—
  (a) the consent of each of the following—
    (i) the child's mother;
    (ii) the child's father, if he has parental responsibility for him;
    (iii) any guardian of the child;
    (iiia) any special guardian of the child;
    (iv) any person in whose favour a residence order is in force with respect to the child;
    (v) any person who has custody of the child; or
  (b) the leave of the court granted under or by virtue of any provision of part II of the Children
Act 1989; or
  (c) if any person has custody of the child, the leave of the court which awarded custody to him.

(4) A person does not commit an offence under this section by taking or sending a child out of the
United Kingdom without obtaining the appropriate consent if—
  (a) he is a person in whose favour there is a residence order in force with respect to the child, and
he takes or sends him out of the United Kingdom for a period of less than one month; or
  (b) he is a special guardian of the child and he takes or sends the child out of the United
Kingdom for a period of less than three months.

(4A) Subsection (4) above does not apply if the person taking or sending the child out of the
United Kingdom does so in breach of an order under part II of the Children Act 1989.

(5) A person does not commit an offence under this section by doing anything without the consent of another person whose consent is required under the foregoing provisions if—
  (a) he does it in the belief that the other person—
    (i) has consented; or
    (ii) would consent if he was aware of all the relevant circumstances; or
  (b) he has taken all reasonable steps to communicate with the other person but has been
unable to communicate with him; or
  (c) the other person has unreasonably refused to consent.

(5A) Subsection (5)(c) above does not apply if—
  (a) the person who refused to consent is a person—
    (i) in whose favour there is a residence order in force with respect to the child;
    (ia) who is a special guardian of the child; or
    (ii) who has custody of the child; or

(b) the person taking or sending the child out of the United Kingdom is, by so acting, in breach of an order made by a court in the United Kingdom.

(6) Where, in proceedings for an offence under this section, there is sufficient evidence to raise an issue as to the application of subsection (5) above, it shall be for the prosecution to prove that that subsection does not apply.

(7) For the purposes of this section—

(a) 'guardian of a child', 'special guardian' 'residence order' and 'parental responsibility' have the same meaning as in the Children Act 1989; and

(b) a person shall be treated as having custody of a child if there is in force an order of a court in the United Kingdom awarding him (whether solely or jointly with another person) custody, legal custody or care and control of the child.

(8) This section shall have effect subject to the provisions of the schedule to this Act in relation to a child who is in the care of a local authority, detained in a place of safety, remanded to local authority accommodation or the subject of proceedings or an order relating to adoption.

The Children and Families Act 2014, sch. 2, para. 47, amends s. 1 so as to take account of the creation of child arrangements orders.

B2.105 **Procedure** The consent of the DPP is required before a prosecution under s. 1 of the Act can be brought (Child Abduction Act 1984, s. 4(2)). The offence is triable either way (s. 4(1)). When tried on indictment this is normally a class 3 offence, but see CPD XIII, para. B (see Supplement, **PD-97**) for the additional factors that the court considers on allocation.

B2.106 **Indictment**

Statement of Offence

Child abduction by person connected with child contrary to section 1 of the Child Abduction Act 1984

Particulars of Offence

A on or about the...day of..., being a parent of V, a child under the age of 16 years, unlawfully took the said V out of the United Kingdom, to wit to Dallas, Texas, in the United States of America, without the consent of...

B2.107 **Sentence** The maximum penalty is seven years' imprisonment (Child Abduction Act 1984, s. 4(1)) on indictment; six months, a fine not exceeding level 5 or both, summarily. In *Kayani* [2012] 2 All ER 641, a sentence of five years' imprisonment following a guilty plea was upheld in a very bad case, where children had been taken abroad by their father in breach of a court order and had remained out of the jurisdiction for many years such that links with the mother had been irretrievably broken. The Court of Appeal recommended that to take account of such cases the maximum penalty for the offence should be increased. In *Brennan* [2007] 2 Cr App R (S) 313, a 'manipulative and controlling' father had prevented his partner's contact with their son, and had eventually taken the son abroad in breach of a residence order imposed by the court. A sentence of four years was held to be appropriate, although the Court of Appeal said that sentences of that length would normally be reserved for cases involving abduction by strangers. In *Downes* (1994) 15 Cr App R (S) 435 three years was upheld on a father who abducted his two-year-old daughter in defiance of a court order denying him access to the child, and took her abroad. In *SB* [2012] 2 Cr App R (S) 408, 16 months was upheld in a case where the offender, a man of positive good character, abducted his five-year-old son who was living with his mother following the parents' divorce. The child was snatched from his mother as she was taking him home from school. The registration number of the offender's car was noted, and he was arrested and the child was returned to his mother within a few hours.

B2.108 *Actus Reus* The offence can only be committed by a person 'connected with' the child, and this is defined in the Child Abduction Act 1984, s. 1(2) (see **B2.104**).

Such a person must either take, or be responsible for sending, the child out of the UK himself. This offence is not committed by holding the child within the jurisdiction, or by failing to return a child who has previously been taken abroad (*R (Nicolaou) v Redbridge Magistrates' Court* [2012] 2 Cr App R 290). The meanings of 'taking' and of 'sending' are set out in s. 3 of the Act, and include causing a child to be taken, inducing a child to accompany D or any other person, and causing a child to be sent.

Lack of appropriate consent is a necessary circumstance which must be established. Consent of each of the persons mentioned in s. 1(3)(a) is required, or if there is a custody order in force the court's permission must be sought. Alternatively, the leave of the court under part II of the Children Act 1989 will suffice. In contrast to kidnapping, however, the offence may be committed notwithstanding the consent of the child in question (see *Kayani* [2012] 2 All ER 641 and **B2.101**)

Mens Rea   No *mens rea* is specified in the definition of the offence, but it can be deduced from the 'defences' available under the Child Abduction Act 1984, s. 1(5), at least in respect of the circumstance of lack of appropriate consent (see **B2.110**).   **B2.109**

Defences   Under the Child Abduction Act 1984, s. 1(5), an accused will not be liable if he acts   **B2.110**
in the belief that the appropriate person has consented, or would have done so if he had known the relevant circumstances. There is no requirement that such belief be reasonable, and the test is therefore subjective.

There is an additional objectively based defence if either D has taken all reasonable steps to communicate with the appropriate person, or if the consent has been unreasonably withheld. The issue of reasonableness is one of fact. If the consent needed is that of the court, then, under s. 1(5A), the provision concerning unreasonably withheld consent does not apply.

Once D provides prima facie evidence of any such defence, then the burden is on the prosecution to disprove it. The scheme of the legislation leaves no scope for any wider defence of necessity (*S* [2012] 2 All ER 793).

Abduction of Child by Other Persons

Definition   The Child Abduction Act 1984, s. 2(1), creates two further offences covering   **B2.111**
cases in which someone other than a parent or other person connected to the child takes or detains a child under the age of 16. They may apply to the child's father where he was not married to the mother at the time of the child's birth, but note the defence provided by s. 2(3), discussed at **B2.116**.

Child Abduction Act 1984, s. 2

(1) Subject to subsection (3) below, a person, other than one mentioned in subsection (2) below, commits an offence if, without lawful authority or reasonable excuse, he takes or detains a child under the age of 16—
   (a) so as to remove him from the lawful control of any person having lawful control of the child; or
   (b) so as to keep him out of the lawful control of any person entitled to lawful control of the child.
(2) The persons are—
   (a) where the father and mother of the child in question were married to each other at the time of his birth, the child's father and mother;
   (b) where the father and mother of the child in question were not married to each other at the time of his birth, the child's mother; and
   (c) any other person mentioned in section 1(2)(c) to (e) above.
(3) In proceedings against any person for an offence under this section, it shall be a defence for that person to prove—
   (a) where the father and mother of the child in question were not married to each other at the time of his birth—
      (i) that he is the child's father; or
      (ii) that, at the time of the alleged offence, he believed, on reasonable grounds, that he was the child's father; or
   (b) that, at the time of the alleged offence, he believed that the child had attained the age of sixteen.

B2.112 **Procedure**   Offences under s. 2(1) are triable either way. When tried on indictment they are normally class 3 offences, but see CPD XIII, para. B (see Supplement, **PD-97**) for the additional factors that the court considers on allocation. In contrast to alleged s. 1 offences committed by persons connected with the child, prosecutions under the Child Abduction Act 1984, s. 2, do not require the consent of the DPP.

B2.113 **Indictment**

Statement of Offence

Child abduction contrary to section 2(1)(b) of the Child Abduction Act 1984

Particulars of Offence

A on or about the…day of…without lawful authority or reasonable excuse detained V, a child under the age of 16 years, so as to keep him out of the lawful control of X, a person entitled to lawful control of V

B2.114 **Sentence**   The maximum penalty is seven years' imprisonment (Child Abduction Act 1984, s. 4(1)) on indictment; six months, a fine not exceeding level 5 or both, summarily. In *Cooper* (1994) 15 Cr App R (S) 470 a sentence of 18 months' imprisonment was upheld where the offender had taken a baby from a pram outside a shop and kept it for four hours. In *Whitlock* (1994) 15 Cr App R (S) 146 the offender had induced a 13-year-old boy to get off the school bus and spend the morning with him. Three years' imprisonment was reduced to two years. Four years was upheld in *Parsons* [1996] 1 Cr App R (S) 36, where a man with a record of sexual offences attempted to abduct a 13-year-old child by offering her a lift in his car. In *Serrant* [2007] 2 Cr App R (S) 500 a sentence of four years was upheld in respect of the abduction of an 11-year-old child and detaining him for three and a half hours in order to enforce payment of a debt arising from a drug transaction. The offenders had made telephone calls to the boy's family saying that he would not be returned until the debt was paid. The boy was very distressed but physically unharmed. The Court of Appeal said that it was an extremely serious offence of its kind. See also **B2.107**.

B2.115 **Elements**   Section 2(1) of the Child Abduction Act 1984 requires an intentional or reckless taking or detention of a child under the age of 16, the effect or objective consequence of which is to remove or to keep that child within the meaning of s. 2(1)(a) or (b) — each of which creates a separate and distinct offence (*Foster v DPP* [2005] 1 WLR 1400). 'Detaining' is defined in s. 3 so as to include causing the child to be detained or inducing the child to remain with D or another person. 'Taking' is defined in s. 3 so as to include causing or inducing the child to accompany D or any other person or causing the child to be taken. A child can be removed from lawful control without necessarily being taken to another place. It may suffice if the child is deflected into some unauthorised activity induced by D (see *Leather* (1993) 98 Cr App R 179, where children were persuaded by D to go with him to look for a 'missing bicycle'). Nor need D's conduct be the sole cause of the abduction, as long as it was more than merely peripheral. It is no defence that another cause may be the child's own decision or state of mind (*A* [2000] 2 All ER 177).

The words, 'so as to' do not import any further *mens rea*; an offence may therefore be committed whether or not D intends to interfere with another person's lawful control or entitlement (*Foster v DPP*). Insofar as *Re Owens* [2000] 1 Cr App R 195 suggests otherwise, it is inconsistent with *Leather* and was not followed in *Foster v DPP*. The consent of that other person would amount to 'lawful authority', but the consent of the child is irrelevant. This distinguishes the offence from that of kidnapping, as does the absence of any requirement of force or fraud (see **B2.97**).

B2.116 **Defences**   Section 2(3)(a) of the Child Abduction Act 1984 provides a defence only if the parents of the child were not married at the time the child was born and D is, or reasonably believes himself to be, the father of that particular child. It does not apply where D mistakenly takes the wrong child from a nursery, thinking it to be his daughter, although it is just possible that D may in such circumstances be able to advance a defence of reasonable excuse under s. 2(1) (*Berry* [1996] 2 Cr App R 226). The burden of proving that such a taking or detention was committed without lawful authority or reasonable excuse rests with the Crown (*Berry*).

TAKING OF HOSTAGES

Definition

Taking of Hostages Act 1982, s. 1   B2.117

(1) A person, whatever his nationality, who, in the United Kingdom or elsewhere—
   (a) detains any other person ('the hostage'), and
   (b) in order to compel a State, international governmental organisation, or person to do or abstain from doing any act, threatens to kill, injure or continue to detain the hostage, commits an offence.

Procedure

The consent of the A-G is required before a prosecution can be brought under the Taking of   B2.118
Hostages Act 1982, s. 1. Taking hostages is triable only on indictment. It is a class 1B offence.

Indictment

Statement of Offence   B2.119

Hostage taking contrary to section 1 of the Taking of Hostages Act 1982

Particulars of Offence

A on divers days between the...day of...and the...day of..., detained V, and in order to compel the Government of the United Kingdom to release from prison certain convicted offenders, threatened to kill the said V

Sentence

The maximum penalty is life imprisonment (Taking of Hostages Act 1982, s. 1(2)).   B2.120

Elements

The *actus reus* consists of detaining any person, and making threats to kill, injure or continue to   B2.121
detain that person.

The *mens rea* defined is in terms of the purpose for which the act and threat take place, and in that respect D's motive is relevant. The offence could therefore be seen as one of further or ulterior intent to cause the doing or abstaining from any act, and such intent or purpose must be proved, although it does not have to be achieved.

BIGAMY

Definition

Offences against the Person Act 1861, s. 57   B2.122

Whosoever, being married, shall marry any other person during the life of the former husband or wife, whether the second marriage shall have taken place in England or Ireland or elsewhere, shall be guilty of [an offence], and being convicted thereof shall be liable to [imprisonment] for any term not exceeding seven years...: Provided, that nothing in this section contained shall extend to any second marriage contracted elsewhere than in England and Ireland by any other than a subject of Her Majesty, or to any person marrying a second time whose husband or wife shall have been continually absent from such person for the space of seven years then last past, and shall not have been known by such person to be living within that time, or shall extend to any person who, at the time of such second marriage, shall have been divorced from the bond of the first marriage, or to any person whose former marriage shall have been declared void by the sentence of any court of competent jurisdiction.

Procedure

B2.123 Bigamy is triable either way (MCA 1980, s. 17 and sch. 1). When tried on indictment this is normally a class 3 offence, but see CPD XIII, para. B (see Supplement, **PD-97**) for the additional factors that the court considers on allocation.

Indictment

B2.124

Statement of Offence

Bigamy contrary to section 57 of the Offences against the Person Act 1861

Particulars of Offence

A on or about the…day of…married V during the life of his wife, W

Sentence

B2.125 The maximum penalty is seven years, a fine, or both, on indictment (OAPA 1861, s. 57); six months, a fine not exceeding the statutory maximum, or both, summarily.

There are very few Court of Appeal decisions on the proper approach to sentencing for this offence. According to Waller LJ in *Crowhurst* (1978) CSP B9–43A01:

> It appears to this court that the sentence for bigamy must vary very much with the particular circumstances of the case. In many cases of bigamy it is possible to deal with the case by some sentence which does not involve deprivation of liberty. In other cases there may be a clear deception which has resulted in some injury to the woman concerned; in which an immediate custodial sentence must be passed, and the length of that sentence must depend greatly on the seriousness of the injury that has been done.

On the facts of the particular case, where the marriage was not consummated and lasted only a week, but where the woman's evidence was that she would not have married the offender had she known that he was still married, a short custodial sentence was held to be proper. The Court of Appeal reduced an 18-month sentence, which was 'wholly out of proportion to the gravity of this offence', to one of four months. *Crowhurst* was followed and applied in *Smith* (1994) 15 Cr App R (S) 407. Three months' imprisonment was appropriate in *Ballard* [2007] 2 Cr App R (S) 608, where the offender was convicted of bigamy after a trial.

This offence has also arisen in the context of bogus marriages designed to avoid immigration controls. In *Khan* [2005] 2 Cr App R (S) 273, the offender, who was lawfully married and of previous good character, went through two further marriage ceremonies with Bangladeshi nationals with intent to assist them in avoiding immigration controls. The Court of Appeal upheld sentences totalling 27 months on the offender, who pleaded guilty, and 18 months on her co-defendant, for aiding and abetting one of the offences. See also *Cairns* [1997] 1 Cr App R (S) 118.

Actus Reus

B2.126 The *actus reus* of bigamy is committed where D 'marries' another person whilst still lawfully married to a surviving spouse. No offence is committed, however, where D's original spouse has been missing for seven years or more (see **B2.131**); nor is any offence committed under English law where a foreigner commits bigamy abroad, even if his original marriage was registered in England. If, however, D is a British (or British overseas, etc.) citizen, it is irrelevant where the bigamous marriage takes place, because bigamy is punishable in England and Wales (or in Northern Ireland) if committed by such a person anywhere in the world (*Earl Russell* [1901] AC

446). This includes bigamy committed in Scotland, even though s. 57 is not applicable under Scots law (*Topping* (1856) Dears 647).

The Act of 'Marrying'   Although the OAPA 1861, s. 57, uses the term 'marry', a bigamous   **B2.127**
marriage must inevitably be void under English law. Section 57 is accordingly construed as criminalising the act of bigamously *purporting* to marry (*Allen* (1872) LR 1 CCR 367).

The existence of other reasons for invalidity of the second 'marriage', such as the second spouse's lack of age or capacity, is no defence on a charge of bigamy (*Allen*). D must, however, go through a ceremony of marriage that purports to be legally binding. D does not commit bigamy where, for example, he contracts an unregistered Islamic marriage in England without disclosing the existence of a subsisting marriage (*Al-Mudaris v Al-Mudaris* [2001] All ER (D) 288 (Feb)).

'Being Married'   The burden is on the prosecution to prove both that D was validly married   **B2.128**
on an earlier occasion *and* that this marriage was still subsisting at the time of the second ceremony. The validity of the original marriage cannot be presumed, as it might be presumed in civil cases, but may be proved by adducing a certified copy of the relevant entry in the Register of Marriages (see **F8.24** and **F16.53**) together with evidence of the identity of the parties to the marriage. See *Tolson* (1864) 4 F & F 103; *Birtles* (1911) 6 Cr App R 177. In the case of a marriage celebrated abroad, expert evidence of local marriage law may be required (*Sussex Peerage Case* (1844) 11 Cl & F 85; and see **F10.27**).

If D alleges that his earlier marriage is invalid for a particular reason, he need do no more than raise the issue, and the burden will then be on the prosecution to establish its validity (*Kay*(1887) 16 Cox CC 292). An admission by D as to the validity of his earlier marriage may suffice, but not where the marriage was celebrated abroad (*Naguib* [1917] 1 KB 359; *Flaherty* (1847) 2 Car & Kir 782).

Polygamous Marriages   A British citizen who practises polygamy abroad in accordance with   **B2.129**
local law commits no offence under s. 57. This is not because his conduct is lawful where it takes place. It is because, as far as the English law of bigamy is concerned, polygamous or even potentially polygamous marriages have never been considered to be marriages at all, even though they may be recognised as valid by the civil courts in accordance with the rules of private international law.

Nevertheless, a marriage registered in the UK is necessarily monogamous, and precludes any subsequent polygamy by either party to it; and if D is domiciled in England and Wales (or in any other country that prohibits polygamy), he cannot lawfully practise polygamy abroad. An overseas marriage contracted by someone with English domicile must accordingly be considered monogamous.

A potentially polygamous foreign marriage may become monogamous in certain circumstances, notably where the party who might otherwise have been entitled to take a second spouse subsequently acquires a domicile of choice in a country that does not permit polygamy. This may happen, for example, where D settles permanently in England and Wales, thereby acquiring an English domicile. If D were then to contract a further marriage in England and Wales, he would thereby commit bigamy (*Sagoo* [1975] QB 885). If D also acquires British citizenship, s. 57 would equally apply to any second marriage he might later enter into abroad.

Mens Rea

There is no specific mention of the requisite *mens rea* for the offence in the OAPA 1861, s. 57.   **B2.130**
This is unlikely to cause any problems in respect of the intent to go through a ceremony of marriage, but what if D mistakenly believes his first spouse to be dead or mistakenly believes himself to be lawfully divorced? In other sections of the 1861 Act strict liability was once applied

to certain circumstances of an offence (*Prince* (1875) LR 2 CCR 154), and the absence of the word 'malicious' from s. 57, in contrast to its presence in other sections, was at one time taken to suggest that strict liability applied under s. 57.

The leading case on the *mens rea* for bigamy has for many years been *Tolson* (1889) 23 QBD 168. D had remarried, reasonably, but mistakenly, believing that her first husband was dead. It was held that a mistake of this kind was a good defence to the charge, as long as it was a reasonable one. The same argument would also apply where D believed that she was divorced, or that her first marriage was void, etc. The situation has always been different as regards the proviso in s. 57, relating to seven years' absence of the first spouse, because this may provide a defence, even where D suspects that his spouse is still alive (see **B2.131**).

Tolson was followed by the Court of Appeal in *Gould* [1968] 2 QB 65, and confirmed, *obiter*, by the House of Lords in *DPP v Morgan* [1976] AC 182, but its authority has been undermined by the House of Lords in *B (a minor) v DPP* [2000] 2 AC 428 in which it was held that, where *mens rea* may be ousted by an honest but mistaken belief, it is as well ousted by an unreasonable belief as by a reasonable one. It is accordingly submitted that the same principles must apply to mistake in bigamy cases as to mistake in other crimes. The reasonableness or otherwise of any alleged mistake should now be considered irrelevant, except when assessing its credibility.

Continual Absence of First Spouse for Seven Years

B2.131 Under the proviso to the OAPA 1861, s. 57, D has a defence to a charge of bigamy if his husband or wife 'shall have been continually absent...for the space of seven years then last past, and shall not have been known [by D] to have been living within that time'. The scope and limitations of this proviso must be noted. First, it does nothing to relieve the prosecution from its duty to prove that the first spouse was indeed alive at the time of the second ceremony. Even if D remarried just a few months after his first spouse's disappearance, a prosecution for bigamy would still fail in the absence of such proof. Secondly, if D honestly believed his spouse to be dead after a shorter period than seven years (see **B2.130**) the proviso defence is not necessary. On the other hand, if the conditions of the proviso are satisfied, it does not matter whether D really believed his first spouse to be dead at all. The spouse's continuous absence (combined with the absence of any news of his being alive) is a sufficient defence in itself.

To establish the defence, D must adduce evidence of continual absence for the requisite seven- year period. The prosecution must then prove either that there was no such continual absence, or that D knew the spouse to be alive at some time during that period (*Curgerwen* (1865) LR 1 CCR 1). Actual knowledge would have to be proved. D need not even have attempted to contact his spouse or ascertain whether his spouse was alive (*Jones* (1842) C & Mar 614; *Briggs* (1856) Dears & B 98). If s. 57 had been intended to impose any such duty on D, it would surely have stipulated this expressly.

FORCED MARRIAGE

New Offences Relating to Non-consensual Marriage

B2.132 The ABCPA 2014 creates three new offences in connection with forced or non-consensual marriage, which have effect from 16 June 2014 (SI 2014 No. 949). The first relates to breach of a forced marriage protection order made under the Family Law Act 1996. Previously, such a breach was punishable only as a contempt of court, but the ABCPA 2014, s. 120, adds a new s. 63CA to that Act, under which a person who without reasonable excuse does anything that he is prohibited from doing by such an order commits an offence triable either way and is punishable following conviction on indictment by up to five years' imprisonment, or a fine, or both. Such conduct may be still be punishable as contempt, but not both as an offence and as contempt (s. 63CA(3) and (4)).

The second new offence (created by s. 121(1)) involves the use of violence, threats or other coercion for the purpose of forcing another person into a marriage. This extends (by s. 121(2)) to any other conduct intended to cause a person to marry when lacking the capacity to give valid consent to such a marriage.

The third new offence (created by s. 121(3)) involves the practice of deception with intent to lure the victim into a forced marriage abroad.

Coercion or Deception for the Purpose of Marriage

Anti-social Behaviour, Crime and Policing Act 2014, s. 121 B2.133

(1) A person commits an offence under the law of England and Wales if he or she—
  (a) uses violence, threats or any other form of coercion for the purpose of causing another person to enter into a marriage, and
  (b) believes, or ought reasonably to believe, that the conduct may cause the other person to enter into the marriage without free and full consent.
(2) In relation to a victim who lacks capacity to consent to marriage, the offence under subsection (1) is capable of being committed by any conduct carried out for the purpose of causing the victim to enter into a marriage (whether or not the conduct amounts to violence, threats or any other form coercion).
(3) A person commits an offence under the law of England and Wales if he or she—
  (a) practises any form of deception with the intention of causing another person to leave the United Kingdom, and
  (b) intends the other person to be subjected to conduct outside the United Kingdom that is an offence under subsection (1) or would be an offence under that subsection if the victim were in England or Wales.
(4) 'Marriage' means any religious or civil ceremony of marriage (whether or not legally binding).
(5) 'Lacks capacity' means lacks capacity within the meaning of the Mental Capacity Act 2005.
(6) It is irrelevant whether the conduct mentioned in paragraph (a) of subsection (1) is directed at the victim of the offence under that subsection or another person.

Procedure Offences under the ABCPA 2014, s. 121(1) or (3), are triable either way. B2.134
When tried on indictment they are normally class 3 offences, but see CPD XIII, para. B (see Supplement, PD-97) for the additional factors that the court considers on allocation.

Sentence The maximum penalty following conviction on indictment is seven years' impris- B2.135
onment or a fine or both (ABCPA 2014, s. 121(9)(a)). The maximum penalty on summary conviction is imprisonment for a term not exceeding six months or a fine, or both (s. 121(9)(b) and (10)).

Elements The offence created by the ABCPA 2014, s. 121(1), may be committed either by B2.136
the use of coercion or (in cases involving a victim who lacks the capacity to give valid consent) by any other conduct, which might include deceptive conduct; but in either case the offence is a 'conduct crime'. The purpose specified in s. 121(1) and (2) is clearly a form of ulterior intent and the substantive offence may be committed even where no marriage takes place or when the threats etc. prove wholly ineffectual.

In most cases the offending conduct will involve the coercion or attempted coercion of the very person who is to be forcibly married, but this is not essential. The coercion etc. may instead be directed towards a third party, such as a parent or sibling.

The *mens rea* requirement in s. 121(1)(b) is unlikely to be problematic in cases falling within s. 121(1)(a), but may be harder to establish in some cases falling within s. 121(2), where D may argue that he was unaware of any lack of capacity and therefore unaware of any lack of consent.

The offence under s. 121(3) requires the practising of a deception but does not in terms require that any person be actually deceived, and it would be consistent with the scheme of

s. 121 to read this as a conduct crime, as in s. 121(1). The deceptive conduct must be directed not to the proposed marriage itself, but to causing the person who is to be forcibly married (the 'victim') to leave the UK. The person D seeks to deceive may or may not be the victim, but in any event it is not enough that D lies about the real purpose of a proposed travel; he must do so 'intending' that there will be a forced marriage abroad, or at least that the victim will be subject to coercion etc. abroad for that purpose. 'Intent' here must be a wider concept than 'purpose', as used in s. 121(1), so D may be found to intend that the victim will be coerced abroad if he knows or believes it will happen in the normal course of events, even if he would prefer that it did not happen at all.

CHILD CRUELTY

Definition

B2.137   Children and Young Persons Act 1933, s. 1

(1) If any person who has attained the age of sixteen years and has responsibility for any child or young person under that age, wilfully assaults, ill-treats, neglects, abandons, or exposes him, or causes or procures him to be assaulted, ill-treated, neglected, abandoned, or exposed, in a manner likely to cause him unnecessary suffering or injury to health (including injury to or loss of sight, or hearing, or limb, or organ of the body, and any mental derangement), that person shall be guilty of [an offence], and shall be liable—

   (a) on conviction on indictment, to a fine or alternatively, or in addition thereto, to imprisonment for any term not exceeding ten years;

   (b) on summary conviction, to a fine not exceeding the prescribed sum, or alternatively or in addition thereto, to imprisonment for any term not exceeding six months.

(2) For the purposes of this section—

   (a) a parent or other person legally liable to maintain a child or young person or the legal guardian of a child or young person shall be deemed to have neglected him in a manner likely to cause injury to his health if he has failed to provide adequate food, clothing, medical aid or lodging for him, or if, having been unable otherwise to provide such food, clothing, medical aid or lodging, he has failed to take steps to procure it to be provided under the enactments applicable in that behalf;

   (b) where it is proved that the death of an infant under three years of age was caused by suffocation (not being suffocation caused by disease or the presence of any foreign body in the throat or air passages of the infant) while the infant was in bed with some other person who has attained the age of sixteen years, that other person shall, if he was, when he went to bed, under the influence of drink, be deemed to have neglected the infant in a manner likely to cause injury to its health.

(3) A person may be convicted of an offence under this section—

   (a) notwithstanding that actual suffering or injury to health, or the likelihood of actual suffering or injury to health, was obviated by the action of another person;

   (b) notwithstanding the death of the child or young person in question.

Indictment

B2.138   *Statement of Offence*

Cruelty to a person under the age of 16, contrary to s. 1(1) of the Children and Young Persons Act 1933

Particulars of Offence

A, between the...day of...and the...day of..., being a person who had attained the age of 16 and having responsibility for V, a child under that age, wilfully neglected the said V in a manner likely to cause her unnecessary suffering or injury to her health by failing to provide medical aid for her

The drafting of indictments for offences under this section may be complicated by the fact that the offence can be committed in several different ways. As to the importance of identifying the appropriate form of allegation in a given case, see *Hayles* [1969] 1 QB 364 and *Beard* (1987) 85 Cr App R 395.

Procedure

An offence under this provision is triable either way. When tried on indictment, this is normally a class 2A offence, but see CPD XIII, para. B (see Supplement, **PD-97**) for the additional factors that the court considers on allocation. Where an alleged offence is tried summarily, the CYPA 1933, s. 14, has effect. See the *Magistrates' Court Sentencing Guidelines* (see Supplement, **SG-252**) for indications as to when a case should be sent to the Crown Court.

B2.139

Children and Young Persons Act 1933, s. 14

(1) Where a person is charged with committing any of the offences mentioned in the first Schedule to this Act in respect of two or more children or young persons, the same information or summons may charge the offence in respect of all or any of them, but the person charged shall not, if he is summarily convicted, be liable to a separate penalty in respect of each child or young person except upon separate informations.

(2) The same information or summons may charge him with the offence of assault, ill-treatment, neglect, abandonment, or exposure, together or separately, and may charge him with committing all or any of those offences in a manner likely to cause unnecessary suffering or injury to health, alternatively or together, but when those offences are charged together, the person charged shall not, if he is summarily convicted, be liable to a separate penalty for each.

Sentence

The maximum penalty on conviction on indictment is ten years' imprisonment. The maximum penalty on summary conviction is six months' imprisonment, or a fine not exceeding the prescribed sum, or both. See the definitive sentencing guideline, *Assaults on Children and Cruelty to a Child* (see Supplement, **SG-213**). The following principles and illustrative cases should be read in the light of that guideline. See also the *Magistrates' Court Sentencing Guidelines* (see Supplement, **SG-252**).

B2.140

A distinction is drawn in the cases between instances of violent assault where the victim is a child, and cases of cruelty or neglect.

Infliction of Injury In the former cases, a more usual charge is assault occasioning actual bodily harm or, where appropriate, a more serious offence against the person, but sometimes a prosecution under the CYPA 1933, s. 1, will be brought instead. In *J and M* [2005] 1 Cr App R (S) 284 the Court of Appeal emphasised the importance of establishing the basis on which an offender is being sentenced, and noted that this was particularly important where two defendants blamed each other. In such a case the sentencer must either resolve the conflict by hearing evidence, or accept the mitigation, sentencing each defendant on the basis of his or her plea. A second distinction which is generally drawn is between those cases where there has been deliberate infliction of injury, of a serious nature, perhaps on more than one occasion, where a lengthy custodial sentence will be upheld, and one-off cases of less serious injury which have taken place in a context of very considerable economic or domestic pressure, where a rather lower custodial sentence is the norm.

B2.141

B [2011] EWCA Crim 2566 is a post-guideline case in which the offender maltreated four fostered children in his care, all of whom had special needs in various different forms. A total sentence of 18 months' imprisonment was upheld on a guilty plea. The case was said to fall on the borderline between the second and third levels in the guideline. Relevant aggravating factors were the number of children harmed, the duration of the ill-treatment (ten months), and the particular breach of trust involved in the harming of such vulnerable children by a person entrusted by the State with their care. There was some mitigation in the offender's inability to cope with such challenging children, but the Court of Appeal said that help was available to the offender and he had failed to access it. A community rehabilitation order with a programme in parenting skills was held not to be unduly lenient in *A-G's Ref (No. 105 of 2004)* [2005] 2 Cr App R (S) 250, a case where the 41-year-old offender pleaded guilty to using excessive chastisement on three of his children, aged eight, ten and 13. The Court of Appeal said the offences arose from a distorted view of what was appropriate, rather than from cruelty for its own sake.

In *S (Will)* [2009] 1 Cr App R (S) 220 the offender subjected his five-year-old stepdaughter to a harsh regime of discipline, by sending her to her room for long periods of time, but did not inflict any significant violence. A sentence of 30 months' imprisonment was varied to a community order on appeal. The Court of Appeal found the sentencing guideline unhelpful in this case, and said that on its facts this case should have been regarded as falling within the first rather than the second category of seriousness. Nor were the guidelines really applicable in *MB* [2014] 1 Cr App R (S) 173 (29), where the Court reduced a sentence of ten months' imprisonment (following a trial) to four months where the offender was a Nigerian woman who was in the country illegally because she had overstayed her right to remain. She failed to seek medical treatment for her baby son after she had arranged for an unqualified person to carry out circumcision. While there had been 'real neglect', there was significant personal mitigation.

B2.142 **Cruelty or Neglect**   Most of the reported cases on cruelty or neglect (as opposed to infliction of an injury) arise from the offender's culpable failure to summon medical assistance for a child. In *Taggart* [1999] 2 Cr App R (S) 68 the offender's child aged three and a half suffered severe scalding while in the bath. It was accepted that the scalding had been accidental, but the offender pleaded guilty to cruelty on the basis of his failure to summon medical attention until more than 24 hours later. The appropriate sentence was 30 months' imprisonment.

A case of more general neglect is *Harvey* (1987) 9 Cr App R (S) 524. A mother was convicted of four counts of cruelty to her four children aged between four and eight years. The mother was frequently drunk, the living accommodation was dirty, pornographic material was left lying about and the children were not kept clean and were denied affection; there was one instance of a failure to arrange medical attention when it was needed. A sentence of nine months' imprisonment was upheld. See also *Crank* [1996] 2 Cr App R (S) 363 and *Weaver* [1998] 2 Cr App R (S) 56.

Another category of neglect is where injury has been inflicted upon the offender's child by another person with the offender's knowledge. Sentences totalling five years' imprisonment were upheld in *Creed* [2000] 1 Cr App R (S) 304, where a woman had failed to protect her child from sustained violence over a period of seven months from the man with whom she was living. See also *Rawlinson* (1992) 14 Cr App R (S) 30.

Actus Reus

B2.143 **Age and Responsibility**   To be guilty of an offence under the CYPA 1933, s. 1, D must have been over the age of 16 at the time of the offence, and must have 'had responsibility' for the child or young person in question. If proof of D's or the victim's ages is an issue, reference may be made to the CYPA 1933, s. 99, which provides (s. 99(2)) that, where in such a case the person by or in respect of whom the offence was allegedly committed 'appears to the court to have been at the date of the alleged offence a child or young person or to have been under or to have attained a particular age, as the case may be, he shall...be presumed to have been under or to have attained that age, as the case may be, unless the contrary is proved'. Where this presumption applies, the defence may have the burden of proving that the young person in question was in fact over the age of 16 (s. 99(4)).

'Responsibility' in this context may be shared by more than one person, and it may involve questions both of fact and law (*Liverpool Society for the Prevention of Cruelty to Children v Jones* [1914] 3 KB 813). Any person who has parental responsibility or who has any other legal liability to maintain a child or young person will be 'presumed' to have responsibility for him under the Act and 'shall not be taken to have ceased to be responsible for him by reason of the fact that he does not have care of him' (CYPA 1933, s. 17(1)(a) and (2)); but other persons, such as baby-sitters or teachers, may also have responsibility whilst a child or young person is in their care (s. 17(1)(b)).

Conduct Although the CYPA 1933, s. 1, creates just one offence, it may take a number of **B2.144** different forms (*Hayles* [1969] 1 QB 364; *Harding* [1997] Crim LR 815). It may take the form of positive abuse (assault, ill-treatment, abandonment or exposure) or of mere neglect, or it may take the form of causing or procuring abuse or neglect. The abuse or neglect in question must be committed 'in a manner likely to cause unnecessary suffering or injury to health' (as to which see s. 1(1)); but the offence is essentially a conduct crime rather than a result crime. It need not therefore be shown that any such injury was caused, and indeed it is no defence to show that any suffering of or danger to V was obviated by the action of another person (s. 1(3)(a)).

'Assault' in this context will usually mean assault by beating, or battery as to which see **B2.9** *et seq.* Ill-treatment is self-explanatory in the context of the requirement that it must be likely to cause unnecessary suffering or injury (see **B2.146**). In *Boulden* (1957) 41 Cr App R 105, the Court of Appeal considered a case of abandonment in which a father of five children had left them and travelled to Scotland. Although the evidence was somewhat contradictory, the court found sufficient evidence to show that he had 'washed his hands' of his children, and had 'left them to their fate'; this was sufficient proof of abandonment.

The offence of exposing a child in a manner likely to cause unnecessary suffering or injury has had little consideration in case law. Exposure to bad weather in itself would not be enough, given the second limb of the *actus reus* (*Williams* (1910) 4 Cr App R 89, a case concerning the Children Act 1908).

Neglect Cases of neglect have received frequent attention in the courts. The requisite neglect **B2.145** will be deemed to have occurred, and therefore need not be proved, in the circumstances set out in s. 1(2)(a) and (b), although the Court of Appeal in *Wills* [1990] Crim LR 714 stressed that even where neglect is deemed the *mens rea* element of the offence must be proved (see **B2.147**). Where s. 1(2)(a) applies, it may be the basis for proving neglect; in any event, it gives a general indication of what constitutes neglect. For example, a relative who was not the legal guardian of, or legally liable to maintain, a child, but who was looking after him for several weeks, might be under a duty to act (see **A1.17**). Such a person would then be expected to provide care of the kind mentioned in s. 2(1)(a).

The Court of Appeal in *S and M* [1995] Crim LR 486 explained 'neglecting' in the context **B2.146** of failing to obtain medical help. Either S the parent or M the boyfriend assaulted the child, who had bruising to the spine and buttocks. There was then further neglect in the failure to get medical help. The argument that there was no neglect because there was nothing a doctor could have done, was rejected. The Court of Appeal held that S or M had neglected the child within the meaning of the statute by refraining from seeking medical help, being reckless as to whether the child might need such help. There are difficulties not addressed in this case concerning the burden of proof, given that it was clear that one party had committed the assault but it was not clear which. However, there is clearly an argument that both were liable for neglect, both being under a duty to act.

The Court of Appeal in *Wills* was concerned with the meaning of the phrase 'in a manner likely to cause unnecessary suffering or injury to health' and more particularly the exact meaning of the word 'likely'. The trial judge had relied on remarks of Lord Diplock in *Sheppard* [1981] AC 394, that 'likely' was simply meant to exclude what was highly unlikely. Although the Court of Appeal agreed that these remarks were *obiter dicta*, it found that Lord Diplock had properly construed the word in the context of this statute, given the difficulties for parents in deciding how serious an injury is, and the possible grave consequences of lack of treatment. The court went on to point out however that, because of the 'deeming' provision under s. 1(2)(a) of the Act, it was unnecessary for the court to come to a decision about the meaning of the word, and these remarks too were *obiter*. In the context of interpreting s. 1(2)(a), it was held that medical aid included medical supervision or medical care in the sense of observation to discover the gravity of any particular injury. The deeming provision was also relevant in *Sheppard* and was explained by Lord Diplock as follows:

> Did the parents fail to provide…in the period before [the child's] death medical aid that was in fact adequate in view of his actual state of health at the relevant time? This, as it seems to me, is a pure question of objective fact to be determined in the light of what has become known by *the date of the trial* to have been the child's actual state of health at the relevant time. It does not depend upon whether a reasonably careful parent, with knowledge of those facts only which such a parent might reasonably be expected to observe for himself, would have thought it prudent to have recourse to medical aid.

The requisite *mens rea* must still be proved, even when the deeming provisions apply.

Mens Rea

B2.147   The *mens rea* of this offence is defined as 'wilfully' carrying out any of the various modes of the *actus reus*. *Sheppard* [1981] AC 394 is the leading case on the interpretation of the word in this context, and although it was decided in the context of cruelty by neglect, it is now clear that it bears the same meaning wherever it is used in the CYPA 1933, s. 1 (*D* [2008] EWCA Crim 2360).

In *Sheppard*, a child aged 16 months died of hypothermia following severe gastroenteritis. The parents were poor and of low intelligence, and had not appreciated the seriousness of his condition. They were convicted under s. 1 on the basis of an objective test. The House of Lords in *Sheppard* allowed their appeals, and Lord Diplock explained the *mens rea* requirement as follows:

> The proper direction to be given to a jury on a charge of wilful neglect of a child under section 1 of the Children and Young Persons Act 1933 by failing to provide adequate medical aid, is that the jury must be satisfied (1) that the child did in fact need medical aid at the time at which the parent is charged with failing to provide it (the actus reus) and (2) either that the parent was aware at the time that the child's health might be at risk if it were not provided with medical aid, or that the parent's unawareness of this fact was due to his not caring whether the child's health was at risk or not (the *mens rea*).

This passage was formerly interpreted by some commentators as conveying *Caldwell* recklessness; but this was always difficult to reconcile with the concept of 'not caring', or with Lord Diplock's observation in *Sheppard* that the concept of what the reasonable parent would observe and understand has no part to play in the *mens rea* of this offence. In *W (Emma)* [2006] EWCA Crim 2723 it was held that a parent may be guilty of wilful neglect where he knows that his child needs medical care, but deliberately refrains from obtaining it, or fails to obtain it because he does not care whether it is needed or not. But if a parent, whether through personal inadequacy or stupidity or both, genuinely fails to appreciate that his child needs medical care, then the parent does not act wilfully and is not guilty of the offence.

General

B2.148   D can be charged under the CYPA 1933, s. 1, even if death occurs (s. 1(3)(b)) and in such circumstances the charge is often coupled with a charge of murder or manslaughter brought against that defendant and/or a co-defendant. Note also the DVCVA 2004, s. 5 (see **B1.73** and **B2.157**).

The Children Act 2004, s. 58(5), repeals the CYPA 1933, s. 1(7), which formerly provided that nothing in that section affected a parent or teacher's right to administer punishment (see **B2.20**).

ILL-TREATMENT OF MENTAL PATIENTS OR PERSONS WHO LACK CAPACITY

Ill-treatment or Neglect of Mental Patients

Mental Health Act 1983, s. 127   **B2.149**

(1) It shall be an offence for any person who is an officer on the staff of or otherwise employed in, or who is one of the managers of, a hospital, independent hospital or care home—
  (a) to ill-treat or wilfully to neglect a patient for the time being receiving treatment for mental disorder as an in-patient in that hospital or home; or
  (b) to ill-treat or wilfully to neglect, on the premises of which the hospital or home forms part, a patient for the time being receiving such treatment there as an out-patient.
(2) It shall be an offence for any individual to ill-treat or wilfully to neglect a mentally disordered patient who is for the time being subject to his guardianship under this Act or otherwise in his custody or care (whether by virtue of any legal or moral obligation or otherwise).

Procedure Offences under s. 127 are triable either way. When tried on indictment they are normally class 3 offences, but see CPD XIII, para. B (see Supplement, **PD-97**) for the additional factors that the court considers on allocation. No proceedings may be instituted except by or with the consent of the DPP (s. 127(4)).   **B2.150**

Sentence The maximum penalty following conviction on indictment on or after 1 October 2007 is five years' imprisonment and/or a fine (s. 127(3)(b)) (see SI 2007 No. 2798, art. 2). For offences committed before that date, the maximum penalty is two years' imprisonment and a fine. The maximum penalty on summary conviction is imprisonment for a term not exceeding six months or a fine not exceeding the statutory maximum, or both.   **B2.151**

Elements Ill-treatment and wilful neglect, which are separate offences (*Newington* (1990) 91 Cr App R 247), have the same meanings as under the CYPA 1933, s. 1 (see **B2.144** and *Sheppard* [1981] AC 394). It follows that neglect arising from a genuine mistake is not enough (*Morrell* [2002] EWCA Crim 2547).   **B2.152**

'Mental disorder' is defined in the Mental Health Act 1983, s. 1, as 'any disorder of disability of the mind', which includes in this context any learning disability, but not dependence on alcohol or drugs (Mental Health Act 1983, s. 1(2A) to (3)).

Ill-treatment or Neglect of Persons who Lack Capacity

Mental Capacity Act 2005, s. 44   **B2.153**

(1) Subsection (2) applies if a person ('D')—
  (a) has the care of a person ('P') who lacks, or whom D reasonably believes to lack, capacity,
  (b) is the donee of a lasting power of attorney, or an enduring power of attorney (within the meaning of Schedule 4), created by P, or
  (c) is a deputy appointed by the court for P.
(2) D is guilty of an offence if he ill-treats or wilfully neglects P.

Procedure Offences under s. 44 are triable either way. When tried on indictment they are normally class 3 offences, but see CPD XIII, para. B (see Supplement, **PD-97**) for the additional factors that the court considers on allocation.   **B2.154**

Sentence The maximum penalty following conviction on indictment is imprisonment for five years or a fine or both. The maximum penalty on summary conviction is imprisonment for six months or a fine not exceeding the statutory maximum, or both (s. 44(3)).   **B2.155**

Elements Ill-treatment and wilful neglect have the same meanings as under the CYPA 1933, s. 1 (see **B2.144** and *Sheppard* [1981] AC 394). Mere carelessness or negligence cannot therefore be equated with wilful neglect (*Turbill* [2014] 1 Cr App R 62 (7)). But, in contrast to the CYPA 1933, s. 1, the offence under the Mental Capacity Act 2005, s. 44, does not include the qualifying   **B2.156**

words 'in a manner likely to cause unnecessary suffering or injury to health'. In *Patel* [2013] EWCA Crim 965 the Court of Appeal therefore held that it could be no defence to show that a patient who was wrongly denied CPR when she stopped breathing would have died even if that treatment had been provided. 'Lack of capacity' is defined for purposes of the Mental Capacity Act 2005 in s. 2: 'a person lacks capacity in relation to a matter if at the material time he is unable to make a decision for himself in relation to the matter because of an impairment of, or a disturbance in the functioning of, the mind or brain'. This may be proved on a mere balance of probabilities and it 'does not matter whether the impairment or disturbance is permanent or temporary'. This definition is supplemented by s. 3, which provides an elaborate diagnostic test for identifying the circumstances in which an individual is to be found to be unable to make decisions for himself. But in the context of a prosecution for ill-treatment or wilful neglect it may not always be necessary or appropriate for a jury to be directed in terms of this diagnostic test. See *Dunn* [2010] EWCA Crim 2935. In *Nursing* [2013] 1 All ER 1139 the Court of Appeal considered the extent to which a person of limited mental capacity might nevertheless have, or be believed to have, the capacity to decide what care or treatment he should receive, and noted that, in areas where an individual has such capacity, his autonomy should be respected. Lord Judge CJ said (at [18]):

> [S]ection 44 did not create an absolute offence. Therefore, actions or omissions, or a combination of both, which reflect or are believed to reflect the protected autonomy of the individual needing care do not constitute wilful neglect.

CAUSING OR ALLOWING A CHILD OR VULNERABLE ADULT TO SUFFER SERIOUS PHYSICAL HARM

B2.157   The Domestic Violence, Crime and Victims (Amendment) Act 2012, in force from 2 July 2012 (SI 2012 No. 1432), amends the DVCVA 2004, s. 5 (causing or allowing the death of a child or vulnerable adult: see **B1.73**), and related provisions so as to extend their application to cases involving a child or vulnerable adult suffering serious physical harm. The amendment has no retrospective effect, so applies only to conduct on or after 2 July 2012.

Procedure and Evidence

B2.158   The offence is triable only on indictment and is normally a class 1A or 2A offence (see CPD XIII, para. B (see Supplement, **PD-97**) for the additional factors that the court considers on allocation).

Where D is charged in the same proceedings with an offence under the OAPA 1861, s. 18 or 20, or with attempted murder as well as with an offence under the DVCVA 2004, s. 5 (as amended), in respect of the same harm, s. 6A(3) to (5) affect the evidence and procedure applicable in three different but related ways:

(a)   under s. 6A(3), where by virtue of the CJPO 1994, s. 35(3), inferences may be drawn in relation to the s. 5 offence from the accused's failure to give evidence or refusal to answer a question, the court or jury may also draw such inferences in determining whether he is guilty of the offence under the OAPA 1861 or attempted murder, even if there would otherwise be no case for him to answer in relation to those offences;

(b)   under s. 6A(4), unless the s. 5 offence is itself dismissed, the charge of the offence under the OAPA 1861 or attempted murder is not to be dismissed on an application to the Crown Court under the CDA 1998, sch. 3, para. 2;

(c)   under s. 6A(5), the question of whether there is a case for the accused to answer on the charge of the offence under the OAPA 1861 or attempted murder is not to be considered before the close of all the evidence (unless he has already ceased to be charged with the s. 5 offence).

B2.159   Domestic Violence, Crime and Victims Act 2004, s. 6A

(1)   Subsections (3) to (5) apply where a person ('the defendant') is charged in the same proceedings with a relevant offence and with an offence under section 5 in respect of the same harm ('the section 5 offence').

(2) In this section 'relevant offence' means—

    (a) an offence under section 18 or 20 of the Offences against the Person Act 1861 (grievous bodily harm etc);

    (b) an offence under section 1 of the Criminal Attempts Act 1981 of attempting to commit murder.

(3) Where by virtue of section 35(3) of the Criminal Justice and Public Order Act 1994 a court or jury is permitted, in relation to the section 5 offence, to draw such inferences as appear proper from the defendant's failure to give evidence or refusal to answer a question, the court or jury may also draw such inferences in determining whether the defendant is guilty of a relevant offence, even if there would otherwise be no case for the defendant to answer in relation to that offence.

(4) The charge of the relevant offence is not to be dismissed under paragraph 2 of Schedule 3 to the Crime and Disorder Act 1998 (unless the section 5 offence is dismissed).

(5) At the defendant's trial the question whether there is a case for the defendant to answer on the charge of the relevant offence is not to be considered before the close of all the evidence (or, if at some earlier time the defendant ceases to be charged with the section 5 offence, before that earlier time).

Alternative Verdicts

B2.160 There are no alternative verdicts specifically provided for and the offence is not itself an alternative verdict to an offence under the OAPA 1861, s. 18 or 20, or to an offence of attempted murder. It does however allow for a guilty verdict in cases where the exact nature of the accused's misconduct is unclear.

Sentence

B2.161 The maximum penalty for an offence under the DVCVA 2004, s. 5, where serious physical harm is involved, is ten years' imprisonment (s. 5(8)).

Elements

B2.162 The s. 5 offence was enacted in response to the problems exemplified in *Lane* (1986) 82 Cr App R 5 and discussed in Law Com No. 282, *Children: Their Non-Accidental Death or Serious Injury (Criminal Trials)*. The 2012 amendment extends its reach to non-fatal injury cases, in accordance with the Commission's original proposals. Extension to cases involving vulnerable adults was a feature of the original offence.

As to the meaning of 'unlawful act', 'member of the same household', liability of persons aged under 16 and 'failure to take steps', see **B1.83** *et seq*.

Where it is a child who has suffered serious physical harm, the unlawful act might constitute an offence of child cruelty under the CYPA 1933 (see **B2.137**). Where a vulnerable adult is the victim, there may in some cases be an offence of ill-treatment of mental patients or persons who lack capacity (see **B2.149** *et seq*.).

FEMALE GENITAL MUTILATION

Definition

Female Genital Mutilation Act 2003, ss. 1 to 4

B2.163

1.—(1) A person is guilty of an offence if he excises, infibulates or otherwise mutilates the whole or any part of a girl's labia majora, labia minora or clitoris.

    (2) But no offence is committed by an approved person who performs—

        (a) a surgical operation on a girl which is necessary for her physical or mental health, or

        (b) a surgical operation on a girl who is in any stage of labour, or has just given birth, for purposes connected with the labour or birth.

    (3) The following are approved persons—

        (a) in relation to an operation falling within subsection (2)(a), a registered medical practitioner,

    (b) in relation to an operation falling within subsection (2)(b), a registered medical practitioner, a registered midwife or a person undergoing a course of training with a view to becoming such a practitioner or midwife.

(4) There is also no offence committed by a person who—

    (a) performs a surgical operation falling within subsection (2)(a) or (b) outside the United Kingdom, and

    (b) in relation to such an operation exercises functions corresponding to those of an approved person.

(5) For the purpose of determining whether an operation is necessary for the mental health of a girl it is immaterial whether she or any other person believes that the operation is required as a matter of custom or ritual.

2. A person is guilty of an offence if he aids, abets, counsels or procures a girl to excise, infibulate or otherwise mutilate the whole or any part of her own labia majora, labia minora or clitoris.

3.—(1) A person is guilty of an offence if he aids, abets, counsels or procures a person who is not a United Kingdom national or permanent United Kingdom resident to do a relevant act of female genital mutilation outside the United Kingdom.

(2) An act is a relevant act of female genital mutilation if—

    (a) it is done in relation to a United Kingdom national or permanent United Kingdom resident, and

    (b) it would, if done by such a person, constitute an offence under section 1.

(3) But no offence is committed if the relevant act of female genital mutilation—

    (a) is a surgical operation falling within section 1(2)(a) or (b), and

    (b) is performed by a person who, in relation to such an operation, is an approved person or exercises functions corresponding to those of an approved person.

4.—(1) Sections 1 to 3 extend to any act done outside the United Kingdom by a United Kingdom national or permanent United Kingdom resident.

(2) If an offence under this Act is committed outside the United Kingdom—

    (a) proceedings may be taken, and

    (b) the offence may for incidental purposes be treated as having been committed,

in any place in England and Wales or Northern Ireland.

This Act supplants the little-used Prohibition of Female Circumcision Act 1985. The most obvious difference is that the principal provisions of the 2003 Act extend to acts done outside the UK by UK nationals or permanent UK residents (s. 4); and this includes (by s. 3) aiding, abetting, counselling or procuring a person who is not a UK national or permanent UK resident to do a relevant act of female genital mutilation outside the UK; and (by s. 2) aiding, abetting, counselling or procuring a girl or woman to mutilate herself.

Procedure and Sentence

B2.164 Offences under the Act are triable either way. By s. 5, the maximum penalty following conviction on indictment is imprisonment for 14 years or a fine (or both); and on summary conviction imprisonment for up to six months or a fine not exceeding the statutory maximum (or both).

OFFENCES OF HARASSMENT

B2.165

Protection from Harassment Act 1997, ss. 1 and 2

1.—(1) A person must not pursue a course of conduct—

    (a) which amounts to harassment of another, and

    (b) which he knows or ought to know amounts to harassment of the other.

(1A) A person must not pursue a course of conduct—

    (a) which involves harassment of two or more persons, and

    (b) which he knows or ought to know involves harassment of those persons, and

    (c) by which he intends to persuade any person (whether or not one of those mentioned above)—

        (i) not to do something that he is entitled or required to do, or

        (ii) to do something that he is not under any obligation to do.

2.—(1) A person who pursues a course of conduct in breach of section 1(1) or (1A) is guilty of an offence.

The CDA 1998, s. 32, creates a racially or religiously aggravated form of this offence. For the meaning of 'racially or religiously aggravated', see **B11.149**.

Procedure and Alternative Verdicts

The basic offence is triable summarily (Protection from Harassment Act 1997, s. 2(2)). The **B2.166** aggravated form of the offence is triable either way. A judge who rules that there is no case to answer on an indictment alleging an offence under s. 4 of the Act (see **B2.181**) may allow the jury to consider an alternative verdict of harassment, contrary to s. 2 (*Livesey* [2006] EWCA Crim 3344, applying *Carson* (1990) 92 Cr App R 236).

Where there is a continuing offence, it is possible to take into account events occurring outside the six-month limitation period imposed by the MCA 1980, s. 127, provided that at least one of the incidents occurred within that time period (*DPP v Baker* (2005) 169 JP 140).

Sentence (Basic Offence)

The maximum penalty is imprisonment for six months, a fine not exceeding the statutory **B2.167** maximum, or both (Protection from Harassment Act 1997, s. 2(2)). As to the imposition of restraining orders, see **E21.28**.

The *Magistrates' Court Sentencing Guidelines* provide guidelines for this offence (see Supplement, **SG-293**).

Racial or religious aggravation cannot be taken into account by the sentencer when sentencing for the basic offence of harassment (see **B2.3**). See **E1.17** for increase in sentence, under the CJA 2003, s. 146, for aggravation relating to disability, sexual orientation or transgender identity.

Sentence (Racially or Religiously Aggravated Form of Offence)

The maximum penalty is two years, a fine or both on indictment; six months, a fine not exceed- **B2.168** ing the statutory maximum, or both, summarily (CDA 1998, s. 32(3)). As to the imposition of restraining orders, see **E21.28**.

The *Magistrates' Court Sentencing Guidelines* provide the same guidelines for this offence as for the basic offence (see Supplement, **SG-293**) but indicate that the sentence should be increased to reflect the racially or religiously aggravated element.

The Court of Appeal stated in *Saunders* [2000] 1 Cr App R 458 and in *Kelly* [2001] 2 Cr App R (S) 341, that when sentencing for the racially aggravated form of an offence the sentencer should indicate the appropriate sentence for the offence in the absence of racial aggravation and then add a further term for the racial element. See further **B2.33**.

Elements

Course of Conduct   **B2.169**

Protection from Harassment Act 1997, s. 7

(3) A 'course of conduct' must involve—
   (a) in the case of conduct in relation to a single person (see section 1(1)), conduct on at least two occasions in relation to that person, or
   (b) in the case of conduct in relation to two or more persons (see section 1(1A)), conduct on at least one occasion in relation to each of those persons.
(3A) A person's conduct on any occasion shall be taken, if aided, abetted, counselled or procured by another—
   (a) to be conduct on that occasion of the other (as well as conduct of the person whose conduct it is); and
   (b) to be conduct in relation to which the other's knowledge and purpose, and what he ought to have known, are the same as they were in relation to what was contemplated or reasonably foreseeable at the time of the aiding, abetting, counselling or procuring.
(4) 'Conduct' includes speech.

Establishing a course of conduct, rather than a series of unrelated acts, is crucial to the success of any prosecution for harassment, and 'it is the course of conduct which has to have the quality of amounting to harassment, rather than individual instances of conduct' (*Iqbal v Dean Manson (Solicitors)* [2011] EWCA Civ 123 per Rix LJ at [45]). The matters said to constitute the course of conduct amounting to harassment must be properly particularised in the information laid or the indictment (*C v CPS* [2008] EWHC 148 (Admin)) and must be so connected in type and in context as to justify the conclusion that they amount to a course of conduct (*Patel* [2005] 1 Cr App R 440; *Pratt v DPP* (2001) 165 JP 800; *C v CPS*). The fewer and further apart the incidents, the less likely it is that they will be so regarded, but circumstances can be conceived 'where incidents, as far apart as a year, could constitute a course of conduct' (*Lau v DPP* [2000] Crim LR 580). See also *Hills* [2001] 1 FLR 580 and *Sahin* [2009] EWCA Crim 2616. In *Baron v CPS* (13 June 2000 unreported), two letters sent some four and a half months apart were capable of constituting a course of conduct amounting to harassment. At the other end of the scale, it was held in *Kelly v DPP* (2002) 166 JP 621 that three telephone calls made over a space of five minutes could amount to a 'course of conduct', taking into account the separate and distinct nature of the calls.

A course of conduct that may initially take the form of a legitimate inquiry or complaint may descend into harassment if unreasonably prolonged or persisted in, as in *DPP v Hardy* (2009) 173 JP 10, where D made 95 telephone calls over a 90 minute period and threatened to keep calling all night. See also *James v CPS* [2009] EWHC 2925 (Admin). In *R (Taffurelli) v DPP* [2004] EWHC 2791 (Admin), it was accepted that deliberate failure to control dogs following a number of complaints could constitute 'conduct'.

B2.170 Two or More Persons Harassed   The problems previously caused where D's course of conduct harassed two or more persons separately (*DPP v Dunn* [2001] 1 Cr App R 352; *Caurti v DPP* [2002] Crim LR 131; *DPP v Dziurzynski* (2002) 166 JP 545) are resolved by the introduction of a specific statutory solution in the Protection from Harassment Act 1997, s. 1(1A). But s. 2 remains the offence-creating provision.

B2.171 Indirect Awareness of Victim   A person may become aware of a course of conduct, or parts of it, indirectly. So, the offence was complete when V knew of the relevant telephone calls made by D, even though that knowledge came from being informed by a third party, provided there was evidence on the basis of which the court can properly conclude that D was pursuing a course of conduct with the necessary *mens rea* (*Kellett v DPP* [2001] EWHC 107 (Admin)).

Definition of Harassment

B2.172   Protection from Harassment Act 1997, s. 7

(2) References to harassing a person include alarming the person or causing the person distress.
...
(5) References to a person, in the context of the harassment of a person, are references to a person who is an individual.

The definition provided by s. 7 is clearly inclusive and not exhaustive (*DPP v Ramsdale* [2001] EWHC Admin 106). 'Harassment' is generally understood to involve improper oppressive and unreasonable conduct that is targeted at an individual and calculated to produce the consequences described in s. 7. By s. 1(3) of the Act (see **B2.175**), reasonable and/or lawful courses of conduct may be excluded. The practice of stalking is arguably the prime example of harassment (*Curtis* [2010] 1 Cr App R (S) 193) but a wide range of other actions could, if persisted in, be so categorised. A course of conduct which is unattractive and unreasonable does not of itself necessarily constitute harassment; it must be unacceptable and oppressive conduct such that it should sustain criminal liability. See *Majrowski v Guy's & St Thomas's NHS Trust* [2007] 1 AC 224, per Lord Nicholls at [30]. Harassment includes negative emotion by repeated molestation, annoyance or worry. The words 'alarm and distress' are to be taken disjunctively and not conjunctively, but there is a minimum level of alarm or distress which must be suffered in order to constitute harassment.

The courts, in view of the individual's right to protest and demonstrate about issues of public interest, will resist attempts to interpret the statute widely (*Huntingdon Life Sciences Ltd v Curtin* (1997) *The Times*, 11 December 1997). However, 'whatever may have been the purpose behind [the Act], its words are clear, and it can cover harassment of any sort' (*DPP v Selvanayagam* (1999) *The Times*, 23 June 1999, per Collins J). In *Iqbal v Dean Manson (Solicitors)* [2011] EWCA Civ 123 it was held (in the context of a civil action) that a series of letters written by one litigant to another (and copied to the court), attacking the personal and professional integrity of the second litigant's solicitor, could potentially be seen as harassment of that solicitor under s. 1. Similarly, in *Plavelil v DPP* [2014] EWHC 736 (Admin), it was held that the repeated making of false and malicious assertions against a doctor in connection with an investigation by the General Medical Council could amount to harassment; they could be oppressive even if they could easily be rebutted.

Publication by Press as Harassment   It was held in *Thomas v News Group Newspapers Ltd* **B2.173** (2001) *The Times*, 25 July 2001, that the publication of press articles is, in law, capable of amounting to harassment, although only in very rare circumstances. Whether conduct is reasonable depends upon the circumstances of the particular case. It was common ground between the parties that, before press publications are capable of constituting harassment, they must be attended by some exceptional circumstances which justify sanctions and the restriction on the freedom of expression (under the ECHR, Article 10) that they involve. An example of such conduct amounting to harassment which was agreed by the parties to that case was the publication of press articles calculated to incite racial hatred of an individual.

Mens Rea

The *mens rea* for this offence, as defined in s. 1(1)(b), is that D knows or ought to know that the **B2.174** course of conduct amounts to harassment of the other. Assistance in determining when D ought to know this is provided by s. 1(2).

Protection from Harassment Act 1997, s. 1

(2) For the purposes of this section or section 2A(2)(c), the person whose course of conduct is in question ought to know that it amounts to or involves harassment of another if a reasonable person in possession of the same information would think the course of conduct amounted to or involved harassment of the other.

This is an objective test, and no allowance can be made for conditions such as paranoid schizophrenia that may affect D's perception (*Colohan* [2001] EWCA Crim 1251). Furthermore, nothing that involves cultural or racial differences should be taken into account, unless it is relevant and supported by proper evidence (*C v CPS* [2008] EWHC 148 (Admin)). But where D actually intends to cause alarm or distress and actually does so, that is likely to meet the requirements of s. 1(1)(b) (*Baron v CPS* (13 June 2000 unreported)).

Lawful Courses of Conduct

Protection from Harassment Act 1997, s. 1   **B2.175**

(3) Subsection (1) or (1A) does not apply to a course of conduct if the person who pursued it shows—

(a) that it was pursued for the purpose of preventing or detecting crime;

(b) that it was pursued under any enactment or rule of law or to comply with any condition or requirement imposed by any person under any enactment, or

(c) that in the particular circumstances the pursuit of the course of conduct was reasonable.

In *Hayes v Willoughby* [2013] 2 All ER 405, the Supreme Court held that s. 1(3)(a) may be relied upon by both law enforcement agencies and private individuals, whether or not D can prove that his behaviour was objectively reasonable. Their lordships rejected (*obiter*) the Court of Appeal's view that such a purpose must be D's sole purpose. But as Lord Sumption explained (at [15]):

> Before an alleged harasser can be said to have had the purpose of preventing or detecting crime, he must have sufficiently applied his mind to the matter. He must have thought rationally about the material suggesting the possibility of criminality and formed the view that the conduct said to constitute harassment was appropriate for the purpose of preventing or detecting it...If, on the other hand, he has not engaged in these minimum mental processes necessary to acquire the relevant state of mind...two consequences will follow. The first is that the law will not regard him as having had the relevant purpose at all. He has simply not taken the necessary steps to form one. The second is that the causal connection which section 1(3)(a) posits between the purpose of the alleged harasser and the conduct constituting the harassment, will not exist.

Section 1(3)(b) protects, *inter alia*, the right to free speech. The requirement in s. 1(3)(c) poses an objective test, namely whether D's conduct is, in the judgement of the jury or magistrates, reasonable; there is no warrant for attaching to the word 'reasonable' or via the words 'particular circumstances' the standards or characteristics of D himself (*Colohan* [2001] EWCA Crim 1251; *C v CPS* [2008] EWHC 148 (Admin)). The imposition of a legal burden upon D may be open to challenge in the light of the human rights cases on the 'reverse burden' (see **F3.7**).

B2.176   In *DPP v Selvanayagam* (1999) *The Times*, 23 June 1999, the Divisional Court considered the relevance of an injunction to the question of whether the course of conduct being pursued by M and S was reasonable. The injunction was in force against S (and others), but not against M. The terms of the injunction were crucial. It endeavoured to prevent harassment (defined as in the 1997 Act) of H and his family. Thus it was difficult to see how the course of conduct in contravention of the injunction and being harassment could be reasonable. There might be circumstances in which it was necessary for those covered by the injunction to go on to the other's land, but to make this of relevance they would have to explain away a course of conduct and not merely one emergency entry on to that land. In the case of M, it was not sufficient to be aware of the existence of the injunction. M would have to be aware of its specific terms. M was not sufficiently aware, and so the defence of reasonableness of the course of conduct was open for consideration. In the balancing exercise to determine reasonableness, the existence, in general terms, of the injunction would be relevant, though it would have little impact. On a more general level, when engaging in the balancing of different interests (such as the right of peaceful protest and the right to quiet enjoyment of property) the courts may have to get involved in the same sort of exercise as occurs when considering the exercise of the police powers to prevent a breach of the peace. It does not follow that it is always the first party's rights that are protected (e.g., to process). They may, in effect, be held responsible for the reaction of the other party. Priority will, however, always be given, where possible, to lawful activity that is not (deliberately) provocative. For consideration of this problem, see *Redmond-Bate v DPP* (1999) 163 JP 789.

For the special defence relating to national security etc., see s. 12 at **B2.188**.

Related Offence

B2.177   Where the High Court or the county court has granted an injunction under the Protection from Harassment Act 1997, s. 3(3)(a), to restrain a person from conduct which amounts to harassment, it is by s. 3(6) an offence for that person, without reasonable excuse, to do anything which he is thereby prohibited from doing. Such conduct is not punishable as a contempt of court (s. 3(7)) nor can a person be convicted of this offence for any conduct which has been punished as a contempt of court (s. 3(8)). A person guilty of this offence is liable, on conviction on indictment, to imprisonment for a term not exceeding five years or a fine or both; and, on summary conviction, to imprisonment for a term not exceeding six months or a fine not exceeding the statutory maximum or both (s. 3(9)).

OFFENCE OF STALKING

Protection from Harassment Act 1997, s. 2A

(1) A person is guilty of an offence if—
  (a) the person pursues a course of conduct in breach of section 1(1), and
  (b) the course of conduct amounts to stalking.
(2) For the purposes of subsection (1)(b) (and section 4A(1)(a)) a person's course of conduct amounts to stalking of another person if—
  (a) it amounts to harassment of that person,
  (b) the acts or omissions involved are ones associated with stalking, and
  (c) the person whose course of conduct it is knows or ought to know that the course of conduct amounts to harassment of the other person.
(3) The following are examples of acts or omissions which, in particular circumstances, are ones associated with stalking—
  (a) following a person,
  (b) contacting, or attempting to contact, a person by any means,
  (c) publishing any statement or other material—
    (i) relating or purporting to relate to a person, or
    (ii) purporting to originate from a person,
  (d) monitoring the use by a person of the internet, email or any other form of electronic communication,
  (e) loitering in any place (whether public or private),
  (f) interfering with any property in the possession of a person,
  (g) watching or spying on a person....
(6) This section is without prejudice to the generality of section 2.

Section 2A was inserted by the Protection of Freedoms Act 2012, s. 111, which was brought into force on 25 November 2012.

The CDA 1998, s. 32, has been amended to create a racially or religiously aggravated form of this offence. For the meaning of 'racially or religiously aggravated', see **B11.149**.

Procedure and Sentence

The offence is triable summarily only. The maximum penalty is imprisonment for six months, a fine not exceeding level 5 on the standard scale or both (Protection from Harassment Act 1997, s. 2A(4) and (5)).

Elements

Behaviour prior to the commencement of the Protection of Freedoms Act 2012, s. 111, cannot found an offence under the Protection from Harassment Act 1997, s. 2A, but may still constitute harassment under s.2 since the new stalking offence is nothing more than the existing offence of harassment within the meaning of s.1(1) with the added requirement that the harassment in question takes the form of stalking. The penalties are the same. To put it another way, anything that would amount to an offence of stalking on or after commencement could equally be charged as harassment either before or after commencement. But the various forms of stalking listed in s. 2A(3) are at least identified as potential forms of harassment.

For the meaning of 'course of conduct' for the purposes of s. 2A(1), see s. 7(3) and (4) at **B2.169**. For the definition of harassment, see s. 7(2) and (5) of the 1997 Act at **B2.172**. As to the specific *mens rea* required by virtue of s. 2A(2), note that s. 1(2) also applies in respect of s. 2A (see **B2.174**).

The acts or omissions mentioned in s. 2A(3) are referred to as examples and thus do not exclude, *inter alia*, newly developing forms of behaviour such as electronic tracking of an individual.

PUTTING PEOPLE IN FEAR OF VIOLENCE

B2.181   Protection from Harassment Act 1997, s. 4

> (1) A person whose course of conduct causes another to fear, on at least two occasions, that violence will be used against him is guilty of an offence if he knows or ought to know that his course of conduct will cause the other so to fear on each of those occasions.

The CDA 1998, s. 32, creates a racially or religiously aggravated form of this offence. For the meaning of 'racially or religiously aggravated', see **B11.149**.

Procedure and Alternative Verdicts

B2.182   The basic and aggravated offences are each triable either way (Protection from Harassment Act, s. 4(4); CDA 1998, s. 32(4)). When tried on indictment, they are normally class 3 offences, but see CPD XIII, para. B (see Supplement, **PD-97**) for the additional factors that the court considers on allocation. If a jury acquit D of racially aggravated harassment, they may convict him of the basic offence (s. 32(6)).

The Protection from Harassment Act 1997, s. 4(5), provides that if D is tried on indictment for the s. 4 offence the jury may instead convict him of the offence under s. 2 or (once in force) s. 2A (see **B2.165** and **B2.178**). If they do so, the Crown Court has the same powers and duties as a magistrates' court would have on convicting D of an offence under s. 2 or 2A (s. 4(6)). Similarly, a judge who rules that there is no case to answer on an indictment alleging an offence under s. 4 may allow the jury to consider an alternative verdict of harassment contrary to s. 2 (*Livesey* [2006] EWCA Crim 3344, applying *Carson* (1990) 92 Cr App R 236) or the offence of stalking under s. 2A (once in force).

The *Magistrates' Court Sentencing Guidelines* indicate that, where the nature of the activity involves sexual threats or the targeting of a vulnerable person, Crown Court trial is appropriate.

Sentence (Basic Offence)

B2.183   The maximum penalty is five years, a fine or both on indictment; six months, a fine not exceeding the statutory maximum, or both, summarily (Protection from Harassment Act 1997, s. 4(4)). As to the imposition of restraining orders, see **E21.28**.

The *Magistrates' Court Sentencing Guidelines* provide guidelines for this offence (see Supplement, **SG-236**). In *Scott* [2011] 2 Cr App R (S) 227 a sentence of three years' imprisonment together with a restraining order was upheld where the offender made a series of telephone calls to the victim threatening her that she would be put in a crate and shipped abroad. Twelve months was upheld in *Nagy* [2010] 1 Cr App R (S) 491, where the offender threatened and abused his former partner in her home.

Racial or religious aggravation cannot be taken into account by the sentencer when sentencing for the basic offence of harassment (see **B2.3**). See **E1.17** for increase in sentence, under the CJA 2003, s. 146, for aggravation relating to disability, sexual orientation or transgender identity.

Sentence (Racially or Religiously Aggravated Form of Offence)

B2.184   The maximum penalty is seven years, a fine or both on indictment; six months, a fine not exceeding the statutory maximum, or both, summarily (CDA 1998, s. 32(4)). As to the imposition of restraining orders, see **E21.28**.

The *Magistrates' Court Sentencing Guidelines* provide the same guidelines for this offence as for the basic offence (see Supplement, **SG-292**) but indicate that the sentence should be increased to reflect the racially or religiously aggravated element.

The Court of Appeal stated in *Saunders* [2000] 1 Cr App R 458 and in *Kelly* [2001] 2 Cr App R (S) 341 that when sentencing for the racially aggravated form of an offence the sentencer should indicate the appropriate sentence for the offence in the absence of racial aggravation and then add a further term for the racial element. See further **B2.33**.

Course of Conduct Causing Fear on at least Two Occasions

As to the meaning of 'course of conduct' see **B2.169**. In *R (A) v DPP* [2004] EWHC 2454 (Admin), it was confirmed that there must be at least two occasions involving threats or other conduct giving rise to the fear of violence. **B2.185**

Other Elements of the Offence

'Violence' is not defined in the Act. As to the similar, though not identical, concept defined for the purposes of the POA 1986, see **B11.23** and **B11.44**. **B2.186**

D's conduct must cause the complainant to fear that violence will be used against him; it is not sufficient for it to frighten the complainant as to what *might* happen (*Henley* [2000] Crim LR 582; *Caurti v DPP* [2002] Crim LR 131). It is always a question of fact (*Caurti* and *R (Simon Howard) v DPP* [2001] EWHC Admin 17) and, whilst it can sometimes be inferred from the evidence, there should, if possible, be direct evidence from the complainant (*R v DPP* [2001] Crim LR 396; *Caurti*).

The s. 4 offence does not in terms require proof of harassment, but it has been interpreted as if it did (*Curtis* [2010] 3 All ER 849; *Widdows* (2011)175 JP 345; *Haque* [2012] 1 Cr App R 48). The prosecution must prove that the conduct in question was targeted at an individual, that it was calculated to produce the consequences described in s. 7 of the Act (alarming the person or causing the person distress) and that it was both oppressive and unreasonable (see *Haque* at [70]–[73]). A prosecution under s. 4 is not normally appropriate for use as a means of criminalising conduct, not charged as violence, during incidents in a long and predominantly affectionate relationship in which both parties persisted and wanted to continue (see *Widdows* at [29]).

Mens Rea

Protection from Harassment Act 1997, s. 4 **B2.187**

(2) For the purposes of this section, the person whose course of conduct is in question ought to know that it will cause another to fear that violence will be used against him on any occasion if a reasonable person in possession of the same information would think the course of conduct would cause the other so to fear on that occasion.

A direction under s. 4(2) should be routinely given (*Henley* [2000] Crim LR 582). The effect of s. 4(2) is that fear must have been caused on each occasion within the course of conduct (*Kelly v DPP* (2002) 166 JP 621).

Defences

Protection from Harassment Act 1997, ss. 4 and 12 **B2.188**

4.— (3) It is a defence for a person charged with an offence under this section to show that—
    (a) his course of conduct was pursued for the purpose of preventing or detecting crime,
    (b) his course of conduct was pursued under any enactment or rule of law or to comply with any condition or requirement imposed by any person under any enactment, or
    (c) the pursuit of his course of conduct was reasonable for the protection of himself or another or for the protection of his or another's property.
12.—(1) If the Secretary of State certifies that in his opinion anything done by a specified person on a specified occasion related to—
    (a) national security,

(b) the economic well-being of the United Kingdom, or

(c) the prevention or detection of serious crime,

and was done on behalf of the Crown, the certificate is conclusive evidence that this Act does not apply to any conduct of that person on that occasion.

In s. 12, 'specified' means specified in the certificate in question (s. 12(2)). A document purporting to be such a certificate is to be received in evidence and, unless the contrary is proved, treated as being such a certificate (s. 12(3)). For consideration of when the course of conduct may be reasonable, see *Kellett v DPP* [2001] EWHC Admin 107 and **B2.175**. The imposition of a legal burden upon D may be open to challenge in the light of the human rights cases on the 'reverse burden' (see **F3.7**).

OFFENCE OF STALKING INVOLVING FEAR OF VIOLENCE OR SERIOUS ALARM OR DISTRESS

B2.189   Protection from Harassment Act 1997, s. 4A

(1) A person ('A') whose course of conduct—

(a) amounts to stalking, and

(b) either—

(i) causes another ('B') to fear, on at least two occasions, that violence will be used against B, or

(ii) causes B serious alarm or distress which has a substantial adverse effect on B's usual day-to-day activities is guilty of an offence if A knows or ought to know that A's course of conduct will cause B so to fear on each of those occasions or (as the case may be) will cause such alarm or distress.

(2) For the purposes of this section A ought to know that A's course of conduct will cause B to fear that violence will be used against B on any occasion if a reasonable person in possession of the same information would think the course of conduct would cause B so to fear on that occasion.

(3) For the purposes of this section A ought to know that A's course of conduct will cause B serious alarm or distress which has a substantial adverse effect on B's usual day-to-day activities if a reasonable person in possession of the same information would think the course of conduct would cause B such alarm or distress.

Section 4A was inserted by the Protection of Freedoms Act 2012, s.111, which was brought into force on 25 November 2012. The CDA 1998, s. 32, has been amended to create a racially or religiously aggravated form of this offence. For the meaning of 'racially or religiously aggravated', see **B11.149**.

Procedure and Alternative Verdicts

B2.190   The basic offence is triable either way (Protection from Harassment Act 1997, s. 4A(5)). The aggravated form of the offence is triable either way.

By virtue of s. 4A(7), on trial on indictment, if the jury find the accused not guilty of the offence under s. 4A, they may find him guilty of an offence under s. 2 or 2A (see **B2.165** and **B2.178**).

Sentence (Basic Offence)

B2.191   The maximum penalty is five years, a fine or both on indictment; six months, a fine not exceeding level 5 on the standard scale, or both, summarily (Protection from Harassment Act 1997, s. 4A(5) and (6)). As to the imposition of restraining orders, see **E21.28**.

Racial or religious aggravation cannot be taken into account by the sentencer when sentencing for the basic offence of harassment (see **B2.3**). See **E1.17** for increase in sentence, under the CJA 2003, s. 146, for aggravation relating to disability, sexual orientation or transgender identity.

Sentence (Racially or Religiously Aggravated Form of Offence)

B2.192 The maximum penalty is seven years, a fine or both on indictment; six months, a fine not exceeding the statutory maximum, or both, summarily (CDA 1998, s. 32(4)). As to the imposition of restraining orders, see **E21.28**.

The Court of Appeal stated in *Saunders* [2000] 1 Cr App R 458 and in *Kelly* [2001] 2 Cr App R (S) 341 that when sentencing for the racially aggravated form of an offence the sentencer should indicate the appropriate sentence for the offence in the absence of racial aggravation and then add a further term for the racial element. See further **B2.33**.

Elements

B2.193 Behaviour prior to the commencement of the Protection of Freedoms Act 2012, s. 111, cannot found an offence under the Protection from Harassment Act 1997, s. 4A.

For the meaning of 'course of conduct' for the purposes of s. 4A(1), see s. 7(3) and (4) at **B2.169**. As to fear of violence, see **B2.186**.

Some of the criticism that may be levelled against the new offence under s.2A (see **B2.180**) applies equally to the s.4A offence. In large part, it is merely the existing s.4 offence with the added requirement of stalking. But s.4A(1)(b)(ii) is both new and significant, and may sometimes enable the new offence to be proved where the s.4 offence could not be.

Defence

B2.194
Protection from Harassment Act 1997, s. 4A

(3) It is a defence for A to show that—
    (a) A's course of conduct was pursued for the purpose of preventing or detecting crime,
    (b) A's course of conduct was pursued under any enactment or rule of law or to comply with any condition or requirement imposed by any person under any enactment, or
    (c) the pursuit of A's course of conduct was reasonable for the protection of A or another or for the protection of A's or another's property.

HARASSMENT OF A PERSON IN HIS HOME

Definition

B2.195
Criminal Justice and Police Act 2001, s. 42A

(1) A person commits an offence if—
    (a) that person is present outside or in the vicinity of any premises that are used by any individual ('the resident') as his dwelling;
    (b) that person is present there for the purpose (by his presence or otherwise) of representing to the resident or another individual (whether or not one who uses the premises as his dwelling), or of persuading the resident or such another individual—
        (i) that he should not do something that he is entitled or required to do; or
        (ii) that he should do something that he is not under any obligation to do;
    (c) that person—
        (i) intends his presence to amount to the harassment of, or to cause alarm or distress to, the resident; or
        (ii) knows or ought to know that his presence is likely to result in the harassment of, or to cause alarm or distress to, the resident; and
    (d) the presence of that person—
        (i) amounts to the harassment of, or causes alarm or distress to, any person falling within subsection (2); or
        (ii) is likely to result in the harassment of, or to cause alarm or distress to, any such person.

(2) A person falls within this subsection if he is—
(a) the resident,
(b) a person in the resident's dwelling, or
(c) a person in another dwelling in the vicinity of the resident's dwelling.
(3) The references in subsection (1)(c) and (d) to a person's presence are references to his presence either alone or together with that of any other persons who are also present.

'Dwelling' has the same meaning as in the POA 1986, part 1 (s. 42A(7)). D ought to know that his presence is likely to result in the harassment of, or to cause alarm or distress to, a resident if a reasonable person in possession of the same information would think that D's presence was likely to have that effect (s. 42A(4)).

Procedure and Sentence

B2.196 Offences under s. 42A are triable summarily (CJPA 2001, s. 42A(4)). The maximum penalty is imprisonment for six months, or a fine not exceeding level 4 on the standard scale, or both.

SLAVERY, SERVITUDE AND FORCED OR COMPULSORY LABOUR

B2.197 The CAJA 2009, s. 71, which came into force on 6 April 2010, was enacted in order to ensure compliance with the ECHR, Article 4, by which (1) 'No one shall be held in slavery or servitude' and (2) 'No one shall be required to perform forced or compulsory labour'. It also seeks to ensure compliance with the UK's obligations under the International Labour Organisation Conventions on Forced Labour, which require the illegal exaction of forced or compulsory labour to be punishable as a criminal offence.

Definition

B2.198   Coroners and Justice Act 2009, s. 71

(1) A person (D) commits an offence if—
(a) D holds another person in slavery or servitude and the circumstances are such that D knows or ought to know that the person is so held, or
(b) D requires another person to perform forced or compulsory labour and the circumstances are such that D knows or ought to know that the person is being required to perform such labour.
(2) In subsection (1) the references to holding a person in slavery or servitude or requiring a person to perform forced or compulsory labour are to be construed in accordance with Article 4 of the Human Rights Convention (which prohibits a person from being held in slavery or servitude or being required to perform forced or compulsory labour).

Procedure and Sentence

B2.199 Offences under s. 71 are triable either way. The maximum penalty on conviction on indictment is 14 years' imprisonment, or six months on summary conviction. Subsections (1)(a) and (b) appear to create separate offences, and offences under the former seem likely to be considered more serious than offences under the latter. The Court of Appeal provided guidance for sentencing this offence in *A-G's Ref (Nos. 2, 3, 4 and 5 of 2013) (Connors)* [2013] 2 Cr App R (S) 451 (71). Lord Judge CJ said that, where the circumstances of the offences were broadly similar, the sentence for slavery was the gravest offence, followed by servitude and then by enforced or compulsory labour, but it was wrong to suggest that a sentence for enforced or compulsory labour would always be lower than for servitude etc. Relevant considerations were the nature and degree of the deception or coercion involved in persuading the worker to join the organisation, the nature and degree of subsequent exploitation after arrival, conditions of work, level and methods of control over the workers, level and extent of vulnerability of and harm (including psychological and financial) to the victim, and the nature and extent of the organisation and the role of the individual offender within it. These offences involved deliberate degrading of human beings. It was difficult for victims to report their plight to the authorities. When offenders were brought to justice substantial sentences were required. Offenders in this case were sentenced on conviction after a trial to terms ranging from six and a half years down to four years and three years. The Court regarded the sentences as lenient but not so lenient as to require adjustment. A degree of assistance in sentencing could also be derived from *A-G's Ref (Nos. 37, 38 and 65 of 2010)* [2011] 2 Cr App R (S) 186 (see **B22.38**).

Interpretation

In interpreting s. 71, the courts must have regard to any case law on the ECHR, Article 4. It was **B2.200** held in *Siliadin v France* (2006) 43 EHRR 16, that the terms used in Article 4 are themselves to be construed in accordance with their use in other treaties, such as the 1927 Slavery Convention, by which 'slavery is the status or condition of a person over whom any or all of the powers attaching to the right of ownership are exercised'. Slaves are, in other words, treated as chattels that can be bought and sold. In many ways, servitude is similar to slavery, because a person kept in servitude is similarly denied his liberty and compelled to provide his services under coercion, whereas one who is merely required to perform forced or compulsory labour may not necessarily be imprisoned or detained at all. 'In descending order of gravity…"slavery" stands at the top of the hierarchy, "servitude" in the middle, and "forced or compulsory labour" at the bottom.' (*K* [2012] 1 All ER 1090 at [24]). But the concept of forced labour implies an element of coercion, oppression or deception of the victim. If D is not actually aware of this, the circumstances must be such that he ought to be aware of it.

By Article 4(3), the term 'forced or compulsory labour' excludes:

(a) any work required to be done in the ordinary course of detention imposed according to the provisions of Article 5 of this Convention or during conditional release from such detention;

(b) any service of a military character or, in case of conscientious objectors in countries where they are recognised, service exacted instead of compulsory military service;

(c) any service exacted in case of an emergency or calamity threatening the life or well-being of the community; and

(d) any work or service which forms part of normal civic obligations.

Persons accused of keeping others (usually vulnerable women, children or immigrants) in servi- **B2.201** tude as 'domestic slaves' have hitherto faced prosecution for offences such as false imprisonment or assault (*Pearson-Gaballonie* [2007] EWCA Crim 3504). Prosecutions may also be brought, in appropriate cases, under the Asylum and Immigration (Treatment of Claimants etc.) Act 2004, s. 4, which makes it unlawful to traffic human beings (see *K* and **B22.36**), or under surviving provisions of the Slave Trade Acts of 1824, 1843 and 1873; but in *Siliadin v France*, the ECtHR held that it was not enough for there to be laws that *might* be used to punish cases of servitude and forced labour. Member States are required to make specific provision for the punishment of such crimes, and this is what s. 71 attempts to do. See also *CN v UK* (2013) 56 EHRR 869.

Section B3   Sexual Offences

INTRODUCTION

B3.1   The SOA 2003 represented the most important overhaul of the law governing sexual offences since at least Victorian times. Some offences have been swept away, others been redefined and many new ones have been created. Part 1 of the Act created over 50 offences. Some carry different sentences depending upon the precise factual ingredients proved, which in accordance with the decision in *Courtie* [1984] AC 463 means they actually create even more offences. The Sexual Offences Act 2003 (Commencement Order) 2004 (SI 2004 No. 874) brought the Act fully into force on 1 May 2004.

Section 141 empowered the Secretary of State to make transitional provisions, but no such provisions have been enacted. It followed that, where there was doubt as to whether an offence of rape occurred before or after the coming into force of the SOA 2003, the prosecution failed because it could not be proved whether a statutory offence was committed under the old or the new law (*A (Prosecutor's Appeal)* [2006] 1 Cr App R 433; *Newbon* [2005] Crim LR 738; *F* [2008] EWCA Crim 994). The lacuna was addressed in the VCRA 2006, s. 55. This deeming provision covers the situation where an accused is charged in respect of the same conduct both with an offence under the SOA 2003 and an offence under the old law, and the only thing preventing him being found guilty of the 2003 Act offence or the offence under the old law is the fact that it has not been proved beyond a reasonable doubt that the time when the conduct took place was either after the coming into force of the SOA 2003 or before the repeal of the old law. In such circumstances, for the purpose of determining guilt, it will be conclusively presumed that the time when the conduct took place was when the old law applied if the offence attracted a lesser maximum penalty; otherwise it will be presumed the conduct took place after the implementation of the new law. Where the evidence is likely to be unclear as to whether the offence should be charged under the old or new law, in order to rely upon s. 55 each offence should be charged in the alternative under the new regime and the old (*Chaney* [2009] 1 Cr App R 512; *F* [2008] EWCA Crim 994). Adopting a procedural device with the particulars of an offence under both the old and new law in the same count is not an appropriate solution. Such a count would be duplicitous and would impede the proper working of s. 55; directions to the jury would be difficult, if not impossible (*Marshall* (2 December 2009 unreported, Woolwich Crown Court)).

In *Stocker* [2014] 1 Cr App R 247 (18) the accused was convicted under the wrong statute in that the statement of offence of rape referred to the SOA 1956, s. 1(1), when the offence was committed in 2008 and the SOA 2003 applied. The Court of Appeal treated this mistake as a purely technical defect. From the beginning to the end of the process the charge was, in substance, one of rape under the SOA 2003.

The key objectives of the Act were to modernise the law governing sexual offences and to protect **B3.2** children and other vulnerable individuals from sexual abuse. The principles underpinning the new legislation include non-discrimination between men and women and non-discrimination between those of different sexual orientation. All offences are gender neutral in that they can be committed by either sex, apart from rape as a principal. The Act also aimed to refocus the law on critical issues such as consent and protection of sexual autonomy.

For the old law, which continues to apply to offences committed before 1 May 2004, reference may be made to the 2004 edition of this work.

Sentencing under the Sexual Offences Act 2003 and Historic Cases: General

The Sentencing Council has issued a new guideline in respect of the sentencing of offenders **B3.3** aged 18 and older convicted of sexual offences who are sentenced on or after 1 April 2014 (see Supplement, **SG-57**). In *Nicholson* [2014] EWCA Crim 834, the Court of Appeal emphasised that a judge was obliged to use the guideline in force at the time of sentencing even if a more lenient outcome might have resulted under a previous or future guideline.

Starting points apply to all offences within the corresponding category. At Step One, the court should determine which categories of harm and culpability the offence falls into by reference only to the matters specified in the tables. Once the starting point is established by assessing harm (categories 1, 2 or 3) and culpability (categories A or B), at Step Two the court should consider the table, which sets out a non-exhaustive list of further aggravating and mitigating factors and previous convictions so as to adjust the sentence within the category range. Starting points and ranges apply to all offenders, whether they have pleaded guilty or been convicted after trial.

The new guideline focuses on the extent of the harm to the victim rather than on the nature of the particular physical activity. It uses a number of models for addressing harm and culpability, each different from the model used in the previous guideline. The model used for the majority of offences, including rape and sexual assault, has a lowest level (a baseline) where inherent harm and culpability are assumed.

In contrast to the previous guideline, separate guidance applies in respect of rape and other non-consensual offences involving children under 13.

As to sentences of imprisonment, discretionary life sentences, sentences of detention for life, automatic life sentences and extended sentences, see **E4** and **E5**.

Sentencing in Historic Cases Annex B of the new *Sexual Offences Definitive Guideline* sets out **B3.4** the appropriate approach to sentencing historic sexual offences. This was clarified by the Court of Appeal in *H* [2012] 2 All ER 340.

Having reviewed a large body of earlier judicial decisions, some of which were impossible to reconcile, Lord Judge CJ summarised the following principles (at [47]). He suggested (at [46]) that reference to earlier decisions is unlikely to be helpful, and is to be discouraged, and that the following considerations should be treated as guidance.

(a) Sentence will be imposed at the date of the sentencing hearing, on the basis of the legislative provisions then current, and by measured reference to any definitive sentencing guidelines relevant to the situation revealed by the established facts.

(b) Although sentence must be limited to the maximum sentence at the date when the offence was committed, it is wholly unrealistic to attempt an assessment of sentence by seeking to identify [at the time of sentencing] what the sentence for the individual offence was likely to have been if the offence had come to light at or shortly after the date when it was committed.

(c) As always, the particular circumstances in which the offence was committed and its serious-ness must be the main focus. Due allowance for passage of time may be appropriate. The date may have a considerable bearing on the offender's culpability. If, for example, the offender was very young and immature at the time when the case was committed, that remains a continuing feature of the sentencing decision. Similarly if the allegations had come to light many years earlier, and when confronted with them, the defendant had admitted them, but for whatever reason, the complaint had not been drawn to the attention of, or investigated by, the police, or had been investigated and not then pursued to trial, these too would be relevant features.

(d) In some cases it may be safe to assume that the fact that, notwithstanding the passage of years, the victim has chosen spontaneously to report what happened to him or her in his childhood or younger years would be an indication of continuing inner turmoil. However the circum-stances in which the facts come to light varies, and careful judgment of the harm done to the victim is always a critical feature of the sentencing decision. Simultaneously, equal care needs to be taken to assess the true extent of the defendant's criminality by reference to what he actually did and the circumstances in which he did it.

(e) The passing of years may demonstrate aggravating features if, for example, the defendant has continued to commit sexual crime or he represents a continuing risk to the public. On the other hand, mitigation may be found in an unblemished life over the years since the offences were committed, particularly if accompanied by evidence of positive good character.

(f) Early admissions and a guilty plea are of particular importance in historic cases. Just because they relate to facts which are long passed, the defendant will inevitably be tempted to lie his way out of the allegations. It is greatly to his credit if he makes early admissions. Even more powerful mitigation is available to the offender who out of a sense of guilt and remorse reports himself to the authorities. Considerations like these provide the victim with vindication, often a feature of great importance to them.

For examples of the application of *H*, see *Clarke* [2012] EWCA Crim 9, *Wheller* [2012] EWCA Crim 84, and *D* [2013] 1 Cr App R (S) 674 (127), where the Court of Appeal upheld a life sentence in respect of an historic case where the offender had broken into his grandmother's home and raped her in 1983. The Court concluded that the pre-conditions for a discretionary life sentence in a pre-CJA 2003 case which were laid down in *Hodgson* (1968) 52 Cr App R 113 were satisfied. The offence was grave enough to require a very long sentence, and it appeared from the nature of the offence and from the offender's history that he was a person of unstable character likely to commit such offences in the future; if such offences were committed, the consequences to others might be especially injurious. The Court re-emphasised how seriously offences of rape committed on a lone woman in her home at night after a forced entry into the house by an offender are now regarded. The case is of significance in that the offender would have been unlikely to have received a life sentence if he had been sentenced at the time of the offence. For a recent example of a pre-CJA 2003 case where a discretionary life sentence was upheld for a brutal rape of an elderly woman after forced entry into her own home, see *Wendell Baker* [2014] EWCA Crim 242.

Presumptions and Alternative Verdicts

B3.5 In relation to rape (SOA 2003, s. 1), assault by penetration (s. 2), sexual assault (s. 3) and caus-ing a person to engage in sexual activity without consent (s. 4), presumptions as to consent and/ or reasonable belief as to consent may apply. They do not apply to inchoate offences. However, the evidential presumptions about consent (s. 75) arise very rarely in practice as in most cases it is likely that sufficient evidence will be adduced, from whatever source, to raise an issue as to consent and reasonable belief as to consent. A s. 75 presumption must not be elevated into a conclusive presumption (*Shanjil Zhang* [2007] EWCA Crim 2018; *White* [2010] EWCA Crim 1929). In contrast, s.76 creates conclusive presumptions. However, essentially the s. 76 presumptions replicate the previous common law (with some limited extension) as to deception as to the nature or purpose of the act, and impersonation, and so will rarely be triggered (see *Jheeta* [2007] 2 Cr App R 477, *Bingham* [2013] 2 Cr App R 307 (29) and *Devonald* [2008] EWCA Crim 527 at **B3.33** *et seq.*). These presumptions are dealt with fully in relation to rape and cross-referenced in respect of the other offences to which they apply. Beyond the limited type of case where s. 76 arises, and assuming that s. 75 has no application, the issue of consent has to be addressed in the context of s. 74 (see **B3.19**).

The issue of alternative offences and included offences is covered at **B3.335** and referred to throughout the text. If the jury are not sure that there was penile penetration, they may nevertheless return a verdict of guilty of attempted rape if the accused's conduct amounted to more than mere preparation and he had the requisite intent (*A-G's Ref (No. 1 of 1992)* [1993] 2 All ER 190). Nor is it necessary that the accused should have done an act of an unequivocally sexual nature (*Patnaik* [2000] 3 Arch News 2, CA). See also *Beaney* [2010] EWCA Crim 2551, where the Court of Appeal substituted a conviction for attempted sexual assault, and *Ferriter* [2012] EWCA Crim 2211, where the Court of Appeal substituted a conviction for sexual assault which had been an alternative on the indictment.

RAPE

Rape is a statutory offence which can be committed by a man upon a woman or another man. It consists of non-consensual vaginal, anal or oral intercourse.   **B3.6**

Sexual Offences Act 2003, s. 1

(1) A person (A) commits an offence if—
    (a) he intentionally penetrates the vagina, anus or mouth of another person (B) with his penis,
    (b) B does not consent to the penetration, and
    (c) A does not reasonably believe that B consents.
(2) Whether a belief is reasonable is to be determined having regard to all the circumstances, including any steps A has taken to ascertain whether B consents.
(3) Sections 75 and 76 apply to an offence under this section.

Sections 75 and 76 deal with presumptions as to consent.

Procedure

Rape is triable only on indictment. As to the classification of the offence for the purpose of listing,   **B3.7** see CPD XIII, para. B (see Supplement, **PD-97**). The presumption that a boy under the age of 14 was incapable of sexual intercourse was abolished by the SOA 1993, s. 1, and does not apply where penetration occurred after 20 September 1993. It continues to apply to rape cases where the offence is alleged to have occurred before that date (*O* [2012] EWCA Crim 2458). Where the victim of the offence was under 18 at the time of the offence, the extended jurisdiction provisions of s. 72 apply (see **B3.301**).

On 17 October 2013 the DPP published guidelines which are designed to set out the approach that prosecutors should take when dealing with child sexual abuse cases. See http://www.cps.gov.uk/legal/a_to_c/child_sexual_abuse/. For the special protections relating to complainants in sexual cases, see **F7.22**.

See **B3.335** for alternative verdicts.

Indictment

Statement of Offence   **B3.8**
    Rape, contrary to section 1 of the Sexual Offences Act 2003.

Particulars of Offence

A, on or about the…day of…penetrated the [vagina] [anus] [mouth] of V with his penis without her consent and not reasonably believing that V did consent.

Sentencing Guidelines

B3.9   The maximum penalty for rape, and attempted rape, is life imprisonment (SOA 2003, s. 1(4)). The definitive sentencing guideline, *Sexual Offences* (see Supplement, **SG-59**), applies to all offenders aged 18 and older, who are sentenced on or after 1 April 2014. In certain circumstances, the fact that there was no actual penetration will provide little or no mitigation; a recent example is *Collier* [2013] EWCA Crim 1038, where the overall circumstances included attempted oral and attempted vaginal rape so no allowance was appropriate for the fact that the offences were attempts. However, save where it can exceptionally be said that the attempt is virtually indistinguishable from the full offence or where the nature of the circumstances mean that as much harm was caused as would usually be the case for the full offence, some reduction is normally appropriate to reflect the fact the offence was an attempt, as the level of sentence is dependent upon harm done; see *Cooper* [2014] EWCA Crim 946, where the Court of Appeal observed that typically less harm is done by the attempt than the full offence.

The starting point for the least serious category of rape, reflecting the baseline of assumed harm and culpability with none of the stipulated harm and culpability factors present, is five years with a category range of four to seven years (see Harm category 3, culpability category B). At the other end of the scale, where the extreme nature or impact of one or more category 2 harm factors has elevated the case into category 1, and this is combined with the presence of one or more culpability A factors, the starting point is 15 years with a category range of 13 to 19 years.

Aggravating and mitigating factors are set out in the guideline, but these are additional to those set out in the definitive sentencing guideline, *Overarching Principles: Seriousness*, paras. 1.20 to 1.24 (see Supplement, **SG-25**). For the new automatic life sentence, discretionary life sentences and the new extended sentences, see **E4** and **E5**. In every case the court should consider a disqualification from working with children (see **E21.17** and **E21.21**) and a sexual offences prevention order (see **E21.24**). There is a notification requirement under the SOA 2003, s. 80 and sch. 3 (see **E23**).

B3.10   **Form of Penetration and Sex of the Victim**   Guidance on sentencing in respect of the offences of rape, following the change of definition of that offence in the SOA 2003, was provided by the Court of Appeal in *A-G's Ref (No. 104 of 2004) (Garvey)* [2005] 1 Cr App R (S) 666. The Court stated that the starting point for an adult for rape should be the same, whether the penetration was of the vagina, anus or mouth, and whether the victim was male or female. In *Ismail* [2005] 2 Cr App R (S) 542, a case of forcible oral sex, the Court of Appeal stressed that for the purposes of sentencing offences of rape under the new Act no distinction is to be drawn between oral rape and other forms of the offence.

B3.11   **Young Offenders**   The guideline applies only to offenders aged 18 and older. The general principles to be considered in the sentencing of youths are in the Sentencing Council's definitive guideline, *Overarching Principles – Sentencing Youths* (see Supplement, **SG-515**). The youth and immaturity of the offender must also be taken into account in every case; in many cases the maturity of the offender will be at least as important as his chronological age (*N* [2010] 2 Cr App R 97). See also *W (Daniel)* [2009] EWCA Crim 153 where the Court of Appeal held that, in the light of the evidence of the 20-year-old appellant's learning difficulties and serious immaturity, it was inappropriate to take into account an abuse of trust as an aggravating feature when sentencing him for three counts of rape of a child under 13. For young offenders, the sentence for rape should normally be significantly shorter than that for an adult. However, this approach admits of exceptions. Where the facts of the case are particularly serious, the youth of the offender will not necessarily mitigate the appropriate sentence (*Asi-Akram* [2006] 1 Cr App R (S) 260; *Patrick M* [2005] 1 Cr App R (S) 218). See *A-G's Ref (Nos. 7, 8 and 9 of 2009)* [2010] 1 Cr App R (S) 446, where the Court of Appeal stated that the trial judge had been correctly concerned at the gang mentality which infused offenders aged 14 and 15. *B* [2006] EWCA Crim 330 is an example of the Court of Appeal upholding an indeterminate sentence detaining a 15-year-old offender for life where exceptional violence had been used; the Court stated that the offender's young age had to be balanced against the seriousness of the offence.

Relationship between the Victim and the Offender   *Millberry* [2003] 2 All ER 939 estab-   **B3.12**
lished the fundamental principle that the same starting point applies for 'relationship rape' or 'acquaintance rape' as for 'stranger rape'. Any rape is a traumatic and humiliating experience and, although the particular circumstances in which the rape takes place may affect the sentence imposed, the starting point for sentencing should be the same. This principle applies to all non-consensual offences. In *MA* [2012] EWCA Crim 1646 the Court of Appeal, presided over by Lord Judge CJ, roundly rejected a submission that a man who raped his wife should be treated less severely if he came from a culture which instilled in him a belief that he had a right to do so.

Previous Consensual Activity   Previous sexual activity between the offender and the vic-   **B3.13**
tim is not included as a mitigating factor in the non-exhaustive list set out at Step Two. Cases under the old guideline suggest that it may amount to mitigation, but only if there was some level of consensual activity on the same occasion or immediately before the rape. However, the seriousness of the non-consensual act may overwhelm any other consideration. It is important to focus upon the circumstances in which the rape was committed. In *A-G's Ref (No. 77 of 2012)* [2013] EWCA Crim 202 leave to refer a sentence of two years' imprisonment for the rape of the offender's wife was refused. The Court of Appeal described the offence as one occasion of unwanted sexual intercourse during a period of consensual sexual relations. After the offence, and when the offence was known, continuing consensual relations continued over a not inconsiderable period. This case should be treated with care; the Court noted the exceptional circumstances in that there was no evidence of psychological harm nor anger. In *O'Brien* [2007] 1 Cr App R (S) 189 a sentence of six years' imprisonment for anal rape following consensual vaginal sex was reduced to four-and-a-half years on the basis that it was a case of consensual sex which went too far. See also *A-G's Ref (No. 96 of 2006) (Miles)* [2007] 2 Cr App R (S) 170 for a case where intercourse was consensual at the outset.

Highest Suggested Starting Points and Cases More Serious than Envisaged in the   **B3.14**
Guidelines   Although the top of the category range for a category 1, culpability A single offence of rape is 19 years, the new guideline acknowledges that offences may be of such severity, for example involving a campaign of rape, that sentences of 20 years and above may be appropriate. Sentences higher than envisaged in the old guideline have been held by the Court of Appeal to have been appropriate in a number of very grave cases. For example, in *C* [2009] EWCA Crim 536, the Court of Appeal upheld a sentence of 17 years for 'an appalling history of progressive sexual abuse, accompanied by cruelty, violence, perversion and corruption' of a stepdaughter 'which started at the age of 3 and progressed to vaginal assaults when the victim was 8, to oral sex and attempted rape when she was 10, and to rape when she was 11'. In *A-G's Refs (Nos. 14 and 15 of 2006) (French and Webster)* [2007] 1 All ER 718, the Court of Appeal upheld the sentence of life imprisonment on the principal offender, Webster, and observed that it was questionable whether he would ever be released. The extraordinary and abhorrent features of this case went beyond those envisaged in the guideline cases, combining aggravating features of repeated rape of a victim over a period of time, breach of trust, and the most vulnerable victim possible — a baby. The Court of

Appeal increased the appropriate minimum term from six years (based on a notional determinate sentence of 18 years and reduced by one third to reflect the plea of guilty) to one of eight years (based on a notional determinate sentence of 24 years adjusted in the same way). French received an extended sentence of ten years with a custodial term of five years and an extension period of five years, and that sentence was upheld on appeal.

B3.15 **Life Imprisonment: Automatic and Discretionary Life Sentences**   Following the implementation of LASPO 2012, discretionary life sentences and sentences of detention for life remain available for an offender convicted of a serious offence, where the court is of the opinion the offender is dangerous, the offence carries life imprisonment as a possible sentence, and the court considers that the seriousness of the offence, or the offence and one or more offences associated with it, is such as to justify the imposition of a sentence of imprisonment (or detention) for life. See *Saunders* [2014] 1 Cr App R (S) 258 (45) for an explanation from Lord Judge CJ of the impact of the removal of IPP as a sentencing option and *A-G's Ref (No. 27 of 2013) (Burinskas)* [2014] EWCA Crim 334 in which Lord Thomas CJ expressly agreed with Lord Judge's view. For a full consideration of these sentences and cases, see E4.

In *Wilkinson* [2010] 1 Cr App R (S) 628, one of the matters considered by the Court of Appeal involved Bennet, whose sentence for public protection was held to be unduly lenient; life imprisonment was substituted. Bennet's case involved a dangerous predatory paedophile who abducted a young boy, raped him, and then subjected him to potentially lethal violence. In *Wilkinson* Lord Judge CJ explained:

> ...as a matter of principle the discretionary life sentence under section 225 should continue to be reserved for offences of the utmost gravity. Without being prescriptive, we suggest that the sentence should come into contemplation when the judgement of the court is that the seriousness is such that the life sentence would have...a 'denunciatory' value, reflective of public abhorrence of the offence, and where, because of its seriousness, the notional determinate sentence would be very long measured in very many years.

Cases where life imprisonment has been upheld for offences of rape before the abolition of IPP include *Henry* [2006] EWCA Crim 2394 and *Frost* [2006] EWCA Crim 830. In *L (D)* [2009] 2 Cr App R (S) 19, the Court of Appeal took the view that the gross nature of the offending over a two-hour period, when the 18-year-old victim was detained and subjected to a succession of rapes, justified the imposition of a sentence of life imprisonment. In *Saunders* the Court of Appeal held that a life sentence was correctly imposed even though the option of IPP or an extended sentence had been available to the judge. The offender, a photography student aged 23, was sentenced to life imprisonment with a minimum term of eight years for a rape of a child under 13, contrary to the SOA 2003, s. 5. He was given concurrent sentences for various other sexual offences. He had committed truly grave offences against two girls aged eight and six respectively when 'baby sitting' and was plainly dangerous in that he had an entrenched pattern of offending against children.

B3.16 Normally a minimum term should be specified (*Burke* [2008] EWCA Crim 1077). Whole life sentences (no minimum term) are reserved for rare and exceptional cases, and the sentence must be justified by the extreme seriousness of the offence as opposed to the dangerousness of the offender (*Hogg* [2008] 1 Cr App R (S) 99). That category is most unlikely to include sexual cases, however serious they may be unless they are combined with homicide. This was confirmed in *Oakes* [2013] 2 All ER 30. Researches had revealed that, among the cases where a whole life order had been imposed, none could be found in the context of sexual crime where one or more of the victims had not been murdered. This is well illustrated by the conjoined appeal of *Roberts* [2013] 2 All ER 30 where (at [102]) a whole life order was quashed and life with a minimum of 25 years was substituted. *Roberts* was a case of the utmost depravity where women, living alone and no longer young, had been attacked and raped in their own homes. As a result an entire community in South London had been terrified and the last years of the victims' lives had been blighted. It was accepted that this was an extremely serious series of offences in which the interests of public safety amply justified the imposition of a life sentence, but it was successfully argued that the whole life order was inappropriate and wrong in principle.

Automatic Life Sentences   Under the LASPO 2012, s. 122, inserting a new s. 224A into the   **B3.17**
CJA 2003, a new automatic life sentence applies to an adult offender convicted of an offence listed in the CJA 2003, sch. 15B, part 1, where the offence was committed after the section came into force (3 December 2012), and where the sentence condition and the previous offence conditions are met. The offences listed in sch. 15B include many sexual offences. See E5 for further details.

Actus Reus

Rape, as a principal, can be committed only by a man. A woman who encourages or assists a   **B3.18**
man to penetrate another person, not reasonably believing the other person is consenting, may be convicted of aiding and abetting rape (*Cogan* [1976] QB 217).

Section 1 of the SOA 2003 makes clear that the vital ingredients of the *actus reus* consist of penetration by the penis of the vagina, anus or mouth of the complainant, together with the absence of consent of the complainant. 'Vagina' is to be taken as including the vulva (s. 79(9)). The slightest penetration is sufficient. In respect of penetration of the vagina, it is not necessary to show the hymen was ruptured. Whether the defendant ejaculates or not is irrelevant.

A count alleging that a defendant committed rape by penetrating the complainant vaginally or anally is not duplicitous. A jury needs to be sure that one of the proscribed orifices has been penetrated. They do not need to be satisfied as to which (*K* [2009] 1 Cr App R 331).

References to the parts of the body specified above include references to a part surgically constructed (in particular through gender reassignment surgery) (s. 79(3)). The offence thus protects transsexuals. It also, however, means that a person who has a surgically constructed penis can commit the offence of rape.

Under the SOA 2003, penile penetration of the mouth without consent constitutes rape, whereas formerly it amounted only to indecent assault.

Penetration is a continuing act from entry to withdrawal (s. 79(2)). It follows that if there is no longer consent to penetration, the man must withdraw (*Kaitamaki v The Queen* [1985] AC 147; *Tarmohammed* [1997] Crim LR 458). If the man is aware that a person has ceased to consent to penetration, he cannot claim that there was a consent to its continuation (*Cooper* [1994] Crim LR 531). In the event of a claim of a mistaken belief that consent persisted, an accused will be guilty of rape if he did not reasonably believe, having regard to all the circumstances, that the person continued to consent (s. 1(2)).

Absence of Consent

Section 74 of the 2003 Act defines consent to the extent that it provides: 'For the purposes of   **B3.19**
this part, a person consents if he or she agrees by choice and has the freedom and capacity to make that choice'. The definition, with its emphasis on free agreement, is designed to focus upon the complainant's autonomy. It highlights the fact that a complainant who simply freezes with no protest or resistance may nevertheless not be consenting. Violence or the threat of violence is not a necessary ingredient. To have the freedom to make a choice a person must be free from physical pressure, but it remains a matter of fact for a jury as to what degree of coercion has to be exercised upon a person's mind before he or she is not agreeing by choice with the freedom to make that choice. Context is all-important. *C* [2012] EWCA Crim 2034 provides a good illustration. It was alleged that the accused had sexually abused the complainant for many years during her childhood. It was also alleged that he raped her in later years, including when she

was at university. The complainant's actions in respect of the later counts were consistent with apparent consent. Lord Judge CJ observed that the reality of the case could not be understood without reference to the long years of the complainant's childhood when she was the victim of repeated abuse by the appellant. Evidence of prolonged grooming and potential corruption of the complainant when she was a child provided the context in which the evidence of apparent consent should be examined and assessed. It reflected upon the accused's apparent dominance and control over the complainant. The Court of Appeal approved the judge's direction that the jury could take into account the history of sexual abuse in relation to the later counts if they were sure of the history of sexual abuse. Another instructive case is *Kirk* [2008] EWCA Crim 434 where a vulnerable and destitute 14-year-old girl submitted to sexual intercourse with the appellant accused for money so as to buy food. The accused had abused her in the past. A rape conviction (under the 1956 Act) was upheld by the Court of Appeal even though there was no evidence of pressure, threats or deception at the time of the rape. Clearly the result would have been the same under the SOA 2003. Similarly, and also under the old law, in *Robinson* [2011] EWCA Crim 916 the Court of Appeal held that a jury was entitled to find that a 12-year-old's immaturity, coupled with the evidence of her acquiescence rather than enthusiastic consent (particularly in the context of what could be perceived as grooming), meant that there was no proper consent.

B3.20   Consent covers a range of behaviour from whole-hearted enthusiastic agreement to reluctant acquiescence. There are circumstances where a jury will require assistance with the distinction between reluctant but free exercise of choice, especially in the context of a long-term loving relationship, and unwilling submission due to fear of worse circumstances. A direction along the lines of the direction of Pill J approved in *Mohammed Zafar* (18 June 1993, unreported, CA: see the *Crown Court Bench Book*, p. 376) may well be appropriate in those circumstances. However, where the prosecution and defence cases are diametrically opposed, e.g., where the prosecution allege a violent rape and the defence case is free agreement without any coercion, such a direction will not be necessary provided the distinction between the respective cases is made clear. In these cases, there is no half-way position. In *Doyle* [2010] EWCA Crim 119, the Court of Appeal upheld a conviction for a violent rape of an ex-girlfriend where the defence case was free agreement and no coercion after the parties had made up. The relationship had been volatile with periods of violence by the accused followed by periods of making up. In his summing up, the judge had distinguished between consent as defined in s. 74 and 'mere submission to something she did not want'. It was argued on appeal that 'submission' was only appropriate in pre-2003 cases and the judge should have given more assistance in the context of a consensual sexual relationship, and he had failed to give any further explanation as to the distinction between 'submission' and consent freely given by choice. The Court rejected these submissions, holding that the judge's directions had made a clear distinction between the prosecution and defence cases. The directions were appropriate in the context of the case and there was no possibility that he might have given the jury the wrong impression or that the jury had convicted the accused on the basis of a misunderstanding between consent and submission.

B3.21   'Capacity' is an integral part of the definition of consent. A valid consent can be given only by a person who has the capacity to give it. The SOA 2003 does not define capacity. Common-law principles that developed under the old law suggest that a complainant will not have had capacity to agree by choice where her understanding and knowledge were so limited that she was not in a position to decide whether or not to agree (*Howard* (1965) 50 Cr App R 56). This may arise in a variety of different circumstances; for instance, when a complainant is suffering from some forms of mental disorder, very young or intoxicated by alcohol or drugs. These principles still apply under the SOA 2003. There is a clear overlap between offences under ss. 30 to 33 (see **B3.166**) and offences under ss. 1 to 4. A person who is 'unable to refuse because of or for a reason related to mental disorder' is likely not to have the capacity to agree by choice, enabling prosecutors to charge a non-consensual offence and rely on s. 74. The narrow interpretation of ss. 30 to 33 by the Court of Appeal in *C* [2009] 1 Cr App R 211 left prosecutors in a position where they might have preferred the option of proceeding under ss. 1 to 4 but the decision in *Cooper* [2009] 4 All ER 33 has given a wider interpretation to ss. 30 to 33 (see **B3.167**) and, in any event, the accused's mental element will be easier to prove (see Baroness Hale at [32]). However, there will be cases where a person with a mental disorder either did not have the capacity to agree or may have had the capacity to agree, but, nevertheless, did not freely agree within the meaning of s. 74. In such a case, the prosecution may prefer the option of charging under ss. 1 to 4 (at the very least in the alternative to s. 30). The House of Lords decision in *Cooper* has not clarified the appropriate direction on capacity in respect of a person with mental disorder charged under s. 1 as the case concerned s. 30. Before *Cooper* it had been thought that where the issue is whether a person with a mental disorder had the capacity to agree by choice, the jury need to consider whether the complainant did not have sufficient knowledge or understanding to comprehend that what was proposed to be done was the physical fact of the penetration of her body by the male organ or, if that is not proved, the sexual nature of the act. See the decision of the Supreme Court of Victoria in *Morgan* [1970] VR 337 as approved by Munby J in *X City Council v MB, NB, and MAB* [2006] EWHC 168 (Fam) and the Court of Appeal in *Cooper*. In her judgment in the House of Lords in *Cooper*, Baroness Hale did not accept Munby J's line of reasoning (at [24]). Clearly with the definition of capacity in the Mental Capacity Act 2005, ss. 2(1) and 3(1), in mind, she stressed that in order to be able to make a decision (a) a person must be able to understand the information relevant to making it and (b) must be able to weigh that information in the balance to arrive at a choice. A mentally disordered person might appreciate the sexual nature of the act but not be able to weigh the information in the balance so as to be able to arrive at a choice. In *IM v LM* [2014] EWCA Civ 37 the Court of Appeal (Civil Division) explained the apparent different approaches, stating that Munby J was not saying that consideration of the ability to 'weigh' up relevant information had no place in determining capacity to consent to sexual relations. Sir Brian Leveson P also explained the distinction between the general *capacity* to give or withhold consent to sexual relations, which is the necessary forward looking focus of the Court of Protection, and the person-specific, time and place-specific occasion when that capacity is actually deployed and consent is either given or withheld, which is the focus of criminal law. In *Avanzi* [2014] EWCA Crim 299 the Court of Appeal expressed the view that civil and criminal jurisdictions should adopt the same test for capacity to consent to sexual relations. The approach should be informed by the definition and guidance contained in the Mental Capacity Act 2005, ss. 2 and 3. That is not to say that a jury will need to be directed in strict accordance with the language used by and steps to be adopted in accordance with proceedings brought pursuant to the Mental Capacity Act 2005.

When summing-up the judge should give the jury some assistance with the meaning of 'capacity' in circumstances where a complainant was significantly affected by voluntarily induced intoxication through drink or drugs. He should also assist the jury on the issue of whether, and to what extent, they could take that voluntary intoxication into account in deciding whether the complainant had consented. See *Bree* [2008] QB 131 and *Coates* [2008] 1 Cr App R 52 at [44] per Sir Igor Judge P. The following points may need to be addressed in the summing-up.   **B3.22**

(a) Consumption of alcohol or drugs may cause someone to become disinhibited and behave differently. If she is aware of what is happening, but the consumption of alcohol or drugs has caused her to consent to activity which she would ordinarily refuse, then she has consented no matter how much she may regret it later. A drunken consent is still a consent if a person has the capacity to make the decision whether to agree by choice.

(b) However, if a complainant becomes so intoxicated that she no longer has the capacity to agree, there will be no consent. Clearly she will not have the capacity to agree by choice where she was so intoxicated through drink or drugs, and her understanding and knowledge are so limited that she was not in a position to decide whether or not to agree. (This relates to understanding and knowledge of what is going on, as opposed to the quality of the decision-making.)

(c) A person may reach such a state without losing consciousness. For instance, she may be in a state where she knows that she does not want to take part in any sexual activity with someone, but she is incapable of saying so. Alternatively, she may have been affected to such a degree, that, whilst having some limited awareness of what is happening, she is incapable of making any decision at all.

(d) If a person is asleep or has lost consciousness through drink or drugs, she cannot consent, and that is so even though her body responds to the accused's advances.

It remains unnecessary to give a direction on 'capacity' where the complainant's and accused's respective accounts are completely at odds and the issue does not arise from the evidence. In *Wright* [2007] EWCA Crim 3473 the trial judge was held to have correctly summed up the case on the basis that the jury had a stark choice namely, that either (i) the complainant had been unconscious at the time of sexual intercourse, in which case she has not consented and, if the accused had known of her unconscious state, he would be guilty; or (ii) the complainant had been affected by her own voluntarily induced intoxication, but that she had nevertheless remained capable of choosing whether or not to have intercourse and, in drink, had agreed to do so, in which case the accused would not be guilty.

B3.23   *Hysa* [2007] EWCA Crim 2056, a prosecution appeal from a terminating ruling, is a highly instructive example of the principles in operation. A 16-year-old complainant got into a car with three strangers after heavy drinking, and alleged that she was then raped. In the car, the accused asked her for sex. She could not remember her replies, but recalled her jeans being removed and the accused having sex with her. She thought she tried or might have tried to tell him to get off. She did not want to have sex with the accused, did not think she did so willingly and did not think she would have consented to having intercourse in such circumstances. She could not remember what she said to the accused, as she was drunk. When he had finished, one of the other men asked if it was his turn and she said 'No'. In *Hysa* the trial judge acceded to a defence submission of no case to answer, stating that the evidence of the complainant's drunkenness was insufficient to allow a jury to conclude that she lacked the capacity to consent. There was evidence that she had demonstrated capacity to agree or disagree by choice in relation to advances from other men. The evidence of her friends was that, although she was very drunk, she was capable of expressing herself clearly and insisting on doing what she wanted. As to whether she had in fact consented, the complainant's evidence at its highest was that she did not think that she would have done. The prosecution had accepted that she could not say that she had not said 'Yes'. When allowing the appeal and remitting the case back to the Crown Court for the trial to continue, Hallett LJ said (at [34]):

> Issues of consent and capacity to consent to intercourse in cases of alleged rape should normally be left to the jury to determine. It would be a rare case indeed where it would be appropriate for a judge to stop a case in which, on one view, a 16-year-old girl, alone at night and vulnerable through drink, is picked up by a stranger who has sex with her within minutes of meeting her and she says repeatedly she would not have consented in these circumstances.

In an important comment, Hallett LJ stated (at [31]) that simply because the complainant did not say 'No' at the moment of initial penetration was not fatal to the prosecution case. There is no requirement that absence of consent has to be demonstrated or communicated to the accused (*Malone* [1998] 2 Cr App R 447). Furthermore, the fact that a complainant cannot remember whether she has consented or not need not be fatal to the prosecution. For a recent example, see *T* [2014] EWCA Crim 954, where the complainant had no recollection whatsoever of having sexual intercourse.

There is also no requirement that the complainant should be incapable of putting up some physical resistance or actually did put up some resistance. A jury is entitled to bear in mind any lies by an accused as to whether or not he had sex with the complainant.

Capacity should not be left to the jury when it is not a live issue in the case. For an example of a conviction still being held to be safe even though the judge summed-up in relation to capacity when it was not in issue, see *S* [2011] EWCA Crim 2427. When directing a jury as to capacity, there is no obligation to use the words 'a drunken consent is still a consent', provided the critical points have been addressed (*Chedwyn Evans* [2012] EWCA Crim 2559; *Kamki* [2013] EWCA Crim 2335).

The anachronism that a woman could not in law refuse sexual intercourse with her husband was   **B3.24**
ended by the House of Lords in *R* [1992] 1 AC 599. The Court of Appeal have since held that a man may properly be convicted of raping his wife even though the offence was committed over 20 years before the final demise of the marital exemption (*Barry C* [2004] EWCA Crim 292).

Mens Rea

First, the prosecution must prove that the accused intended to penetrate the vagina, anus or   **B3.25**
mouth of another. Following the reasoning in *Heard* [2008] QB 43 in respect of sexual assault, this would seem to be no more than a requirement that the penetration be deliberate (meaning simply voluntarily willed movement), and self-induced intoxication does not provide a defence. In any event, in the vast majority of cases, if penetration is proved there will be no issue as to whether it was intentional. If a defendant is unconscious through sleep, penetration would not be deliberate; however, a jury is likely to have difficulty in accepting that an accused may have been an unconscious participant when penetration has occurred (see *F* [2014] EWCA Crim 878, a case under s. 9). Secondly, by virtue of the SOA 2003, s. 1(1)(c), the prosecution must also prove that the accused did not reasonably believe that the complainant was consenting at the time of penetration. Whilst this section reverses the decision in *DPP v Morgan* [1976] AC 182 and abolishes the wholly subjective test for the mental element, the Act does not adopt a test based on what a reasonable man would have believed. The provision focuses upon the belief of the particular accused. Since s. 1(2) provides that regard is to be had to 'all the circumstances, including any steps A has taken to ascertain whether B consents' in determining whether an accused had a reasonable belief, it is clear that a jury may take into account relevant characteristics of the accused, such as extreme youth and a learning disability.

In *Braham* [2013] EWCA Crim 3 the Court of Appeal has, to some extent, clarified whether a   **B3.26**
mental disorder that might affect a person's capacity to understand the true nature of a situation may be a relevant characteristic. Delusional thinking, psychotic or otherwise, can never be considered to be reasonable. Such a permissive construction would fly in the face of the legislative intention to reverse the decision of *DPP v Morgan*. The Court of Appeal concluded that, unless and until the state of mind of an accused amounts to insanity in law, beliefs in consent arising from conditions such as delusional psychotic illness or personality disorders must be judged by objective standards of reasonableness and by not taking into account a mental disorder which induced a belief which could not reasonably arise without it. Once a belief could be judged reasonable only by a process which labelled a plainly irrational belief as reasonable, it cannot be open to a jury to conclude that it was reasonable without straying outside the SOA 2003.

The Court did, however, acknowledge that there may be cases in which the personality and abilities of the accused may be relevant to whether his positive belief in consent was reasonable. Cases could arise in which the reasonableness of such belief depends on the reading by the accused of subtle social signals, and in which his impaired ability to do so is relevant to the reasonableness of his belief. The Court did not attempt exhaustively to foresee the circumstances which might arise in which a belief might be held which is not in any sense irrational even though most people would not have had it.

The Court illustrated the difficulty in identifying the dividing line in such cases. It gave the example of an accused of less than the ordinary intelligence or with a demonstrated inability to recognise behavioural cues as possibly such a case. The Court felt that it is possible that beliefs generated by such factors may not properly be described as irrational and might be judged by a jury not to be unreasonable on the particular facts. This has left open the relevance of conditions such as autism spectrum and Asperger's Syndrome, which might lead to an impaired or distorted perception of a complainant's behaviour. For example, in *Sultan* [2008] EWCA Crim 6, a rape case under the

B

Part B Offences

old law when the test was wholly subjective, it was accepted by the Court of Appeal that expert evidence would have been admissible to show that the accused was suffering from a psychological condition such as Asperger's Syndrome, which may have affected his ability to determine another's intentions, beliefs or desires in ambiguous situations. Following the steer given in *Braham*, there is a strong argument that such a characteristic would be admissible under the new law.

B3.27   Section 1(2) does not positively require an accused to have taken steps to ascertain whether the complainant consents. However, this is something the jury will consider when considering the reasonableness of his belief. More steps are likely to be expected where there is no established relationship.

Under the old law, rape was held to be a crime of basic intent and self-induced intoxication could not be used as the basis of a denial of *mens rea*. In *Woods* (1982) 74 Cr App R 312, the Court of Appeal held that 'reasonable grounds' under the Sexual Offences (Amendment) Act 1976, s. 1(2), were grounds that would have been reasonable had the accused been sober. See also *Fotheringham* (1989) 88 Cr App R 206. Whilst s. 1(2) does stipulate that whether a person's belief is reasonable is to be determined having regard to all the circumstances, given that the new test has become more objective it is clear that the Court of Appeal's reasoning under the old law continues to apply. Whilst self-induced intoxication may be relevant as to whether an accused may have had a genuine belief that the complainant was consenting, and a drunk person may make a reasonable mistake, it is not a relevant factor when considering whether such a belief may have been reasonable. This approach was confirmed by the Court of Appeal in *Grewal* [2010] EWCA Crim 2448.

B3.28   In *A-G's Ref (No. 79 of 2006)* [2007] 1 Cr App R (S) 752, the Court of Appeal, when dealing with an application to make a reference, expressed the view that it had doubts about the ruling of the trial judge that it is not a defence to a charge under ss. 1 or 2 of the SOA 2003 if the accused has made a mistake, however reasonable, as to the identity of the person to whom the sexual activity is directed. The judge had felt that he must adopt the narrow view in that the offences related to a named complainant (B), and the requirement in s. 1(2) cannot widen the scope of such consideration so as to allow for the accused's state of mind in relation to any third party. The Court observed that a possible alternative way of dealing with such a very rare set of circumstances would be to hold that the offence is committed if a reasonable (therefore sober) person would have realised that the person being penetrated or sexually touched was not the person whom the accused thought he was consensually penetrating.

A direction upon absence of reasonable belief falls to be given by the judge when, but only when, there is material on which a jury might come to the conclusion that (a) the complainant did not in fact consent, but (b) the accused thought she was consenting. Such a direction is not necessary where prosecution and defence cases on consent are diametrically opposed and there is simply no scope, in the case of either party, for any misunderstanding by the accused as to presence of consent (*Taran* [2006] EWCA Crim 1498).

Evidential Presumptions about Consent

B3.29   The SOA 2003 creates evidential presumptions and conclusive presumptions as to consent and reasonable belief in consent.

B3.30   **Evidential Presumptions**   Section 75 of the SOA 2003 lists circumstances in which the complainant is taken not to have consented to the relevant act *unless* sufficient evidence is adduced to raise an issue as to whether the complainant consented. Also the accused is to be taken not to have reasonably believed that the complainant consented *unless* sufficient evidence is adduced to raise an issue as to whether he reasonably believed it (s. 75(1)).

There must be some foundation in the evidence, and it must not be merely speculative or fanciful for there to be sufficient evidence. However, it is vital to understand that if the trial judge decides (presumably at the close of the evidence) that there is sufficient evidence to raise an issue as to whether the complainant consented and/or the accused reasonably believed the complainant was consenting, then the judge will put the issues to the jury in accordance with the key sections (i.e. ss. 74 and 1(2)), and the s. 75 route is barred. In the relatively rare cases where the judge decides that there is not sufficient evidence on one or both of the issues, a s. 75 direction must be given on that issue. The above summary was expressly endorsed by Goldring LJ in *White* [2010] EWCA Crim 1929 at [10].

Section 75 must not be elevated into an irrebuttable presumption (*Kapezi* [2013] EWCA Crim 560). To find absence of consent and/or absence of reasonable belief, the jury have to be sure of three matters: (i) that the accused did the relevant act (in the case of rape, it is the intentional penile penetration of the complainant's vagina, anus or mouth: s. 77) (s. 75(1)(a)); (ii) any of the s. 75(2) circumstances existed; and (iii) the accused knew those circumstances existed (s. 75(1) (c)). It should be noted that where a s. 75 evidential presumption arises there is no question of the issue being removed from the jury. In *Mba* [2012] EWCA Crim 2773 the Court of Appeal upheld a conviction where the trial judge had given both a s. 74 and a s. 75 direction. The Court was not approving a hybrid direction; rather it was considering the safety of the conviction on its own special facts. It follows that trial judges should continue to follow the approach set out in this paragraph as endorsed in *White*.

See *Ciccarelli* [2012] 1 Cr App R 190 for a classic example of a s. 75 presumption arising where there was insufficient evidence that the accused's belief that the complainant was consenting was reasonable. There must be evidence that a belief is reasonable. It follows that an accused's asserted belief may not be sufficient to raise an issue.

The circumstances in which evidential presumptions about consent apply are set out in s. 75(2) (a) to (f). **B3.31**

Sexual Offences Act 2003, s. 75

(2) The circumstances are that—

    (a) any person was, at the time of the relevant act or immediately before it began, using violence against the complainant or causing the complainant to fear that immediate violence would be used against him;

    (b) any person was, at the time of the relevant act or immediately before it began, causing the complainant to fear that violence was being used, or that immediate violence would be used, against another person;

    (c) the complainant was, and the defendant was not, unlawfully detained at the time of the relevant act;

    (d) the complainant was asleep or otherwise unconscious at the time of the relevant act;

    (e) because of the complainant's physical disability, the complainant would not have been able at the time of the relevant act to communicate to the defendant whether the complainant consented;

    (f) any person had administered to or caused to be taken by the complainant, without the complainant's consent, a substance which, having regard to when it was administered or taken, was capable of causing or enabling the complainant to be stupefied or overpowered at the time of the relevant act.

The circumstances set out in s. 75(2) are not exhaustive of the cases where consent will be absent. The categories of threats and behaviour capable of negating consent are wider than the categories to which the presumptions apply. For example, the evidential presumptions under (a) and (b) do not deal with the situation where a complainant fears future as opposed to 'immediate violence' although in such circumstances the complainant may well not be consenting within the definition in s. 74.

Section 75(3) provides that in s. 75(2)(a) and (b) the reference to the time immediately before the relevant act began is, in the case of an act which is one of a continuous series of sexual activities, a reference to the time immediately before the first sexual activity began.

B3.32 **Conclusive Presumptions about Consent**   In contrast to the rebuttable presumptions of s. 75 of the SOA 2003, s. 76 creates conclusive presumptions.

Sexual Offences Act 2003, s. 76

> (1) If in proceedings for an offence to which this section applies it is proved that the defendant did the relevant act and that any of the circumstances specified in subsection (2) existed, it is to be conclusively presumed—
>   (a) that the complainant did not consent to the relevant act, and
>   (b) that the defendant did not believe that the complainant consented to the relevant act.
> (2) The circumstances are that—
>   (a) the defendant intentionally deceived the complainant as to the nature or purpose of the relevant act;
>   (b) the defendant intentionally induced the complainant to consent to the relevant act by impersonating a person known personally to the complainant.

Section 76 essentially replicates the common law, although both limbs of s. 76(2) in some respects go further. Where the prosecution is able to prove that the accused did the relevant act (in the case of rape, the intentional penile penetration of the complainant's vagina, anus or mouth: s. 77), and either of the circumstances set out in s. 76(2) existed, it is conclusively presumed that the complainant did not consent to the relevant act and that the accused did not believe that the complainant consented to the relevant act. The jury should be directed to convict if they find either of these matters proved. For the presumption to arise, the deception or impersonation must be shown to have operated upon the mind of the complainant so as to induce consent (see Temkin and Ashworth, [2004] Crim LR 328 at p. 335).

B3.33 Section 76(2)(a) follows the common law, which established that in the comparatively rare cases where the complainant has been induced to consent on the basis of fraudulent misrepresentations as to the nature of the act there was no consent (*Williams* [1923] 1 KB 340 and *Flattery* [1877] 2 QB 410). Arguably the inclusion of the word 'purpose' extends the pre-existing law which had evolved to the extent that deceptions as to the purpose of the physical act were sufficient to vitiate consent (*Tabassum* [2000] 2 Cr App R 328 and *Green* [2002] EWCA Crim 1501). However, as was stressed by the Court of Appeal in *Jheeta* [2007] 2 Cr App R 477, s. 76(2)(a) does not address the 'quality' of the act, but confines itself to its 'purpose'. It follows that deception by representing a false medical purpose may be sufficient to trigger s. 76, but not if consent is induced by a bogus ceremony of marriage or false promise of payment (see facts of *Linekar* [1995] 2 Cr App R 49 as considered in *Jheeta* at [25]). In the Australian case of *Papadimitropoulos* (1957) 98 CLR 249 the High Court refused to find that a deception arising from a bogus ceremony of marriage invalidated a woman's consent. However, s. 76(2)(a) might apply on such facts as arguably there is a deception as to the purpose of the act, the consummation of marriage.

B3.34 In *Jheeta* the Court of Appeal held that no conclusive presumptions arose merely because the complainant had been deceived in some way by disingenuous blandishments from or the lies of the accused. The creation of a bizarre fantasy which had pressurised the complainant into having sexual intercourse with the accused more frequently than she otherwise would have done was not a deception as to the nature or purpose of sexual intercourse. Such conduct might be deceptive or persuasive, but would rarely go to the nature or purpose of intercourse. In many cases, notwithstanding deceptive conduct, the accused's motivation will be sexual gratification and so there will have been no relevant deception as to purpose operating upon the complainant's mind. In *Bingham* [2013] 2 Cr App R 307 (29) (seven counts of causing his girlfriend to engage in sexual activity without consent under s. 4), B, using pseudonyms, established an online Facebook relationship with his girlfriend so as to persuade and then blackmail her into providing him with photographs of her engaging in sexual activity. The Court of Appeal held that reliance at trial upon s. 76 was misplaced. The motive behind the conduct was sexual gratification, and there was no deception as to that. The prosecution would have had a forceful argument under s. 74 on the basis that she only complied because she was blackmailed. In the light of s. 76(2), it would appear that deception as to the identity of the recipient would not be sufficient as it was the impersonation of a person unknown to the complainant. Contrast *Devonald* [2008] EWCA Crim 527 for a case under s. 4 where the court held that s. 76 applied: it was open to the jury to conclude that the complainant was deceived into believing he was masturbating for the gratification of a 20-year-old girl via a webcam when in fact he was doing it for the father of a former girlfriend who was teaching him a lesson. Here 'purpose' has been given a wide meaning in that the deception was not as to sexual purpose, rather it was as to the purpose of the act of masturbation.

B3.35 Section 76(2)(b) extends the law by widening the categories of impersonation sufficient to vitiate consent beyond the complainant's husband or regular sexual partner to 'a person known personally to the complainant'.

B3.36 **Consent in Absence of Presumption**   In most cases neither the evidential nor conclusive presumptions will arise, and the jury must determine whether the prosecution have established absence of consent and/or absence of reasonable belief in accordance with the key definitions in ss. 74 and 1(2). Section 76 replicates and extends the common law. It simply identifies the relatively rare situations in which conclusive presumptions arise. It was designed to buttress s. 74, not to limit it. The conclusive presumptions are concerned with proof of absence of consent rather than its definition. Whilst deceptions by the accused as to purely peripheral circumstances will not vitiate consent, it does not follow from the existence of s. 76 that lesser deceptions which do not trigger the conclusive presumptions cannot ever do so.

In *Assange v Swedish Prosecution Authority* [2011] EWHC 2489 (Admin), the Divisional Court suggested that s. 76 should be given a stringent construction because it provides for a conclusive presumption. The question of consent, and the issue of the materiality of the use of a condom, fell to be determined by reference to s. 74. It would be open to a jury to hold that, if the complainant had made clear that she would consent to sexual intercourse only if the appellant used a condom, then there would be no consent if, without her consent, he did not use a condom, or removed or tore the condom without her consent.

If conduct is not within s. 76, that does not preclude reliance upon s. 74. Section 76 deals simply with a conclusive presumption in the very limited circumstances to which it applies. The court rejected the argument that if the deception was not a deception within s. 76 (a deception as to the nature and quality of the act or a case of impersonation) then the deception could not be taken into account for the purposes of s. 74. Sir John Thomas P stated (at [88]): 'It would, in our view, have been extraordinary if Parliament had legislated in terms that, if conduct that was not deceptive could be taken into account for the purposes of s. 74, conduct that was deceptive could not be.'

Following the reasoning in *Assange* the Divisional Court in *R (F) v DPP* [2014] 2 WLR 190 allowed judicial review of a decision by the DPP not to prosecute a man for rape. Ejaculation without consent could transform an incident of consensual intercourse into rape where there was evidence that the man had deliberately ignored the crucial feature upon which the claimant's original consent to penetration was based as a manifestation of his control over her. The Court of Appeal confirmed the position in the extraordinary factual context of *McNally* [2014] 2 WLR 200. When the complainant was aged 12 and the accused M was aged 13, they struck up a relationship playing a social networking game. Though M was a girl, the complainant believed that she was communicating with a boy called 'Scott Hill' from Glasgow. The internet relationship developed over the following three and a half years and the complainant began to refer to M as her boyfriend. The complainant also saw 'Scott' on a web cam. They became interested in each other sexually and, shortly after the complainant's 16th birthday, M visited the complainant in London on a total of four occasions, always dressed as a boy. On each occasion there was sexual activity and over the course of the visits it included digital penetration and oral sex. On the fourth and final visit in November 2011, M was confronted by the complainant's mother about really being a girl. M pleaded guilty to six counts of assault by penetration contrary to the SOA 2003, s. 2. It was suggested on appeal that those pleas were entered in error following incorrect legal advice and the elements of the offence were not made out. It was argued that deception as to gender cannot vitiate consent; in the same way that deception as to age, marital status, wealth or, following *B* [2007] 1 WLR 1567 (see **B3.40**), HIV status, being deceptions as to qualities or attributes, cannot vitiate consent. Thus, it was submitted that *Assange* and *R (F)* could be distinguished as the deceptions in those cases were not deceptions as to qualities or attributes. They were deceptions as to the features of the act itself.

The Court of Appeal rejected that analysis. The Court pointed out that *B* was not authority for the proposition that HIV status could not vitiate consent. *B* left the issue open and HIV status could vitiate consent if, for example, the complainant had been positively assured that the accused was not HIV positive. The argument that the deceptions in *Assange* and *R (F)* were as to the features of the act was not sustainable; the wearing of a condom and ejaculation are irrelevant to the definition of rape and are not 'features' of the offence. In those cases, it was alleged that the victim had consented on the basis of a premise that, at the time of the consent, was false. Giving the judgment of the Court, Leveson LJ said (at [25]):

> while, in a physical sense, the acts of assault by penetration of the vagina are the same whether perpetrated by a male or a female, the sexual nature of the acts is, on any common sense view, different where the complainant is deliberately deceived by a defendant into believing that the latter is a male. Assuming the facts to be proved as alleged, M chose to have sexual encounters with a boy and her preference (her freedom to choose whether or not to have a sexual encounter with a girl) was removed by the appellant's deception.

B3.37 The approach recommended in *Olugboja* [1982] QB 320 had left juries with very little guidance as to the parameters of consent apart from the standard direction that submission is not necessarily consent. Whilst the new law represents a significant improvement, it leaves juries to grapple with such concepts as freedom, choice and capacity. It remains for the jury to resolve such questions as whether the degree of coercion and/or abuse of power or authority exercised upon a complainant's mind was such that she did not agree by choice with the freedom to make that choice. It may well be, for example, that a threat to expose a woman's previous sexual conduct to her family will negate consent, particularly if the woman comes from a milieu in which such a revelation might pose the danger of physical harm or even death to her (*Sharif* [2004] EWCA Crim 3386). Such questions are left for juries to resolve.

B3.38 In *Doody* [2008] EWCA Crim 2394 the Court of Appeal considered the extent of permissible judicial comment as to the mental state of rape complainants. The court held that a judge is entitled to make comments as to the way evidence is to be approached, particularly in areas where there is a danger of a jury coming to an unjustified conclusion without an appropriate warning, but any comment should be uncontroversial. The fact that the trauma of rape can cause feelings of shame and guilt which might inhibit a woman from making a complaint is sufficiently well known to justify a comment to that effect. The Court approved an example in general terms of an appropriate direction in such circumstances which covers the following points: (i) experience shows that people react differently to the trauma of a serious sexual assault, that there is no one classic response; (ii) some may complain immediately whilst others feel shame and shock and not complain for some time; and (iii) a late complaint does not necessarily mean it is a false complaint. A judge is entitled to add mention of the particular feelings of shame and embarrassment which may arise when the allegation is of sexual assault by a partner. This general approach was attacked unsuccessfully in *Miller* [2010] EWCA Crim 1578, where it was argued that the judge's directions in a child rape case were not properly based on evidence that was adduced before the jury and that they offended the common-law principle that judicial notice can be taken only of facts of particular notoriety or common knowledge. The Court of Appeal gave short shrift to these submissions, pointing out that that was precisely what dealing with these generalisations was intended to do. For examples of further directions to juries to guard against false assumptions, see the *Crown Court Bench Book*, ch. 17. As with all directions to the jury, such directions should be couched firmly against the factual matrix of the case in hand (*Smith* [2012] EWCA Crim 404). See *CE* [2012] EWCA Crim 1324 for an example of a judicial comment which the Court of Appeal found inappropriate yet did not undermine the safety of the conviction.

Given the development of permissible neutral judicial warnings to guard against false assumptions, there is limited scope for generic expert evidence as to the possible impact of sexual offences upon victims. In *ER* [2010] EWCA Crim 2522 the Court of Appeal, when holding that the evidence of a psychotherapist should not have been admitted, took a highly restrictive approach as to the circumstances in which expert evidence may be given in this area. Hughes LJ stated that such evidence should not be given unless it is directed to something which is quite outside the experience of the jury and the ability of a judge to explain common understanding and common patterns of behaviour.

Non-disclosure of STDs and Consent   At common law a man who had consensual inter-   **B3.40**
course with another person, knowing but not disclosing that he suffers from a sexually transmitted illness, could not be convicted of rape. In *Mohammed Dica* [2004] QB 1257, the Court
of Appeal, referring to the old law, stated that consent to sexual intercourse defeated liability
for rape. Clearly, deceptions by the accused as to purely marginal matters which do not relate
to the nature and purpose of the act did not vitiate consent at common law. Nor would they
do so under the SOA 2003. However, consent in the SOA 2003, s. 74, requires agreement
by choice and a person must have the freedom and capacity to make that choice. Sections 75
and 76 are illustrations of this principle but are not exhaustive of it. As yet the parameters of
consent under s. 74 are not entirely clear. What if the deception is something of fundamental
importance to the complainant? On any view, a failure to disclose any sexually transmitted
disease (STD) is not a deception as to the nature or purpose of the act, and accordingly the
conclusive presumption under s. 76(2)(a) does not arise. In *B* [2007] 1 WLR 1567, it was held
that an accused's failure to disclose his HIV status did not affect the issue of consent in rape
where there had been no allegations that the accused had deceived the complainant. Latham
LJ stated (at [17]):

> Where one party to sexual activity has a sexually transmissible disease which is not disclosed to the other
> party any consent that may have been given to that activity by the other party is not thereby vitiated. The
> act remains a consensual act. However, the party suffering from the sexual transmissible disease will not
> have any defence to any charge which may result from harm created by that sexual activity, merely by
> virtue of that consent, because such consent did not include consent to infection by the disease.

Ignorance defeats consent under the OAPA 1861, s. 20, where the illness is life-threatening   **B3.41**
(*Konzani* [2005] 2 Cr App R 198: see **B2.15**). The position may well be different as to positive
misrepresentations as to HIV status. Even following *B*, there is an argument that a jury would be
entitled to decide that a person who agrees to unprotected sex, having been deceived by his or her
partner in respect of the fact that he was, say, HIV-positive, does not have the freedom to make
that choice as defined in s. 74 which was intended to mark a change in the previous law. At the
very least, a lie about HIV status would be relevant to a complainant's state of mind, unless he
or she was willing to run the risk of contracting the disease. Relevance to choice is not limited
to an appreciation of the barest physical nature of the act and the willingness to perform it.
For strident criticism of the decision in *B*, see Leigh 'Two cases on consent in rape' (2007) 5
Arch News 7.

In *Assange v Swedish Prosecution Authority* [2011] EWHC 2489 (Admin), Sir John Thomas P
observed that *B* went no further than deciding that failure to disclose HIV infection is not of
itself relevant to consent under s. 74; it did not permit the appellant to contend that, if he
deceived the complainant as to whether he was using a condom or one that he had not damaged, that was irrelevant to the issue of consent to sexual intercourse or his belief in consent.
In *McNally* [2014] 2 WLR 200 (see **B3.36**), the Court of Appeal also observed that *B* was not
authority for the proposition that concealment of, or deception about, HIV status could not
vitiate consent. *B* left the issue open and concealment or deception could vitiate consent if, for
example, the complainant had been positively assured that the accused was not HIV positive.

See also the CPS guidance 'Policy for prosecuting cases involving the intentional or reckless
sexual transmission of infection' (January 2008).

Attempted Rape and Conspiracy to Rape

B3.42 Attempted rape is governed by the principles of the law of attempts generally (see **A5.69**). Attempted rape may be charged as such, or may be an alternative verdict on a charge of rape where the evidence does not disclose that the accused achieved sexual intercourse with the victim.

Following the approach adopted by the Court of Appeal in *Pace* [2014] 1 Cr App R 501 (34), a case involving an allegation of an impossible attempt under the POCA 2002, s. 327 (see **A5.81**), it may be argued that the prosecution must prove that the accused intended each and every aspect of the *actus reus*, i.e. an intention to penetrate and an intention that the penetration be without consent. However, in the context of attempted rape, it is likely that the courts will continue to follow the reasoning under the old law in *Khan* [1990] 2 All ER 783 and rely upon the distinction between consequences and circumstances, taking the view that the mental element in attempted rape is the same as that required for the full offence, namely an intention to penetrate (the conduct/consequences) and the absence of reasonable belief (the circumstances). See *The Mens Rea of a Criminal Attempt*, Stark, [2014] 3 Archbold Review 7–9. Furthermore, to require the prosecution to prove the defendant intended to penetrate without consent would have serious policy implications. See *Scrapping Khan?* Dyson, [2014] Crim LR 45–50.

It is not necessary to prove that the accused had gone so far as to attempt physical penetration of the vagina, anus or mouth. It suffices if acts be proved which the jury could regard as more than merely preparatory (*A-G's Ref (No. 1 of 1992)* [1993] 2 All ER 190).

To establish a conspiracy to rape, the prosecution must prove not only an agreement to rape but also an actual intention to carry out that agreement (*Hedgecock* [2007] EWCA Crim 3486; *G and F* [2012] EWCA Crim 1756); see also **A5.51**.

ASSAULT BY PENETRATION

B3.43 This offence was created in response to the recommendation by the Sexual Offences Review, which recognised that non-consensual penetration by objects or parts of the body other than the penis can be as serious in their impact on the victim as rape. It also recommended that the offence should be defined in a way that would enable it to be used where there was doubt as to the nature of the penetration (e.g., where a child knows it was penetrated but cannot say whether it was by a penis, finger or another object).

Sexual Offences Act 2003, s. 2

(1) A person (A) commits an offence if—
   (a) he intentionally penetrates the vagina or anus of another person with a part of his body or anything else,
   (b) the penetration is sexual,
   (c) B does not consent to the penetration, and
   (d) A does not reasonably believe that B consents.
(2) Whether a belief is reasonable is to be determined having regard to all the circumstances, including any steps A has taken to ascertain whether B consents.
(3) Sections 75 and 76 apply to an offence under this section.

Procedure

B3.44 Assault by penetration is triable only on indictment. As to the classification of the offence for the purpose of listing, see CPD XIII, para. B (see Supplement, **PD-97**). The extended jurisdiction provisions of s. 72 (see **B3.301**) apply where the victim was under 18 at the time of the offence.

See **B3.335** for alternative verdicts.

Sentencing

B3.45 The maximum penalty for assault by penetration is life imprisonment (SOA 2003, s. 2(4)). The Sentencing Council has issued a new definitive guideline applicable to sex offenders aged 18 or over who are sentenced on or after 1 April 2014 (see **B3.3**). The guideline (see Supplement, **SG-63**) reflects the fact that the types of penetration that may be involved in assault by penetration are wider than in relation to rape, and range from acts as severe as the highest category rape (for example, a violent sexual attack involving penetration of the victim with an object likely or intended to cause significant injury to the victim) to an activity that, whilst involving severe violation of the victim, is more akin to a serious sex assault (e.g., momentary penetration with fingers). Under the previous guideline, a lower sentence would be given for penetration with a body part, such as a finger or a tongue, where no physical harm was sustained; a higher sentence would be given for penetration with an object (the larger or more dangerous the object, the higher the sentence would be) or penetration combined with abduction, detention, abuse of trust or more than one offender acting together.

The Council agreed with the conclusions of public research that, generally, where penetration of the genitals has occurred, the public felt that this was akin to rape regardless of what had been used to penetrate due to the inherent level of violation. The Council therefore adopted the approach that such assaults should generally be treated in very similar terms to rape in terms of harm caused with only two differences in the harm factors specified in the guidelines in relation to the two offences. The factor relating to pregnancy or an STI occurring as a consequence of the offence is not included in the guideline for assault by penetration but 'penetration using large or dangerous object(s)' is included as a harm factor in relation to assault by penetration because, whilst it is acknowledged that psychological harm results whatever the means of penetration, the Council was of the view that where a large or dangerous object is used, this increases the physical consequences of the attack and also the psychological harm, and so should increase the starting point for sentence.

The new guideline adopts a similar model as in rape in that it recognises that all examples of this offence are extremely harmful to the victim by assuming there is *always* a baseline of harm. This is reflected in offence category 3, which covers offences in which harm factors identified in category 2 are not present. The extreme nature of one or more category 2 factors or the extreme impact caused by a combination of category 2 factors may elevate the case to category 1. Having identified the offence category, the court should then determine whether any culpability A factors are present in order to ascertain the starting point. There is an assumed baseline of culpability reflected in category B.

The starting points and sentence ranges are the same as for rape, representing an increase from the levels recommended in the previous guideline. In respect of categories 2 and 3, sentencing levels are lower than for rape, but there is a discernible upwards shift. In a case involving the lowest level of harm (category 3) and lower culpability (category A), where there is sufficient prospect of rehabilitation, a community order with a sex offender treatment programme requirement can be a proper alternative to a short or moderate length custodial sentence.

The offence is a qualifying offence for an automatic life sentence under the CJA 2003, sch. 15B (see **B3.15** and **E4**).

In every case the court should consider a disqualification from working with children (see **E21.17** and **E21.21**) and a sexual offences prevention order (see **E21.24**). There is a notification requirement under the SOA 2003, s. 80 and sch. 3 (see **E23**).

Indictment

Statement of Offence   **B3.46**

Assault by penetration contrary to section 2(1) of the Sexual Offences Act 2003.

Particulars of Offence

A, on or about the...day of...penetrated the [vagina] [anus] of V with [ ] without [her][his] consent and did not reasonably believe that V was consenting.

Actus Reus

The essence of the offence is penetration of the vagina or anus of another person. The penetration may be penetration with a part of the offender's body, for example, a finger or a fist, or with   **B3.47** anything else, for example, a dildo or a sharp object. The term 'anything else' will include an animal or other living organism. As with rape, references to a vagina include a surgically constructed vagina (SOA 2003, s. 79(3)). The penetration is a continuing act from entry to withdrawal (s. 79(2)).

Penetration must be 'sexual' in character. The requirement that conduct (penetration, touching etc.) is 'sexual' recurs in a number of offences. Section 78 seeks to explain the approach to be adopted when considering whether particular conduct is 'sexual' for the purposes of the Act.

Sexual Offences Act 2003, s. 78

For the purposes of this Part (except section 71) penetration, touching or any other activity is sexual if a reasonable person would consider that—

(a) whatever its circumstances or any person's purpose in relation to it, it is because of its nature sexual, or

(b) because of its nature it may be sexual and because of its circumstances or the purpose of any person in relation to it (or both) it is sexual.

Section 78(a) covers conduct where the nature of the activity is unambiguously sexual. To determine whether the conduct is 'sexual' it should be considered without reference to its circumstances or the purpose of the accused. For example, in respect of penile penetration or oral sex, the activity is sexual whatever the accused's purpose. It follows that it will not be a defence to a charge under s. 2 to claim that penetration was performed not for sexual gratification but as an assertion of dominance.

B3.48   The correct approach to the application of s. 78(b) where the nature of the activity is ambiguous and 'may' be sexual, was set out by the Court of Appeal in *H* [2005] 2 All ER 859. The Court said that the provision contains two distinct questions for the jury: first, whether they, as 12 reasonable people, considered that, because of its nature, the touching *might* be sexual: and, if so, secondly, whether, in view of the circumstances and/or the purpose of any person in relation to it, the touching *was* in fact sexual. These are two distinct questions which must be considered separately. The nature of the touching refers to the actual touching that took place and, therefore, in considering whether the touching, because of its nature, might be sexual, the jury is not concerned with the circumstances before or after the touching or the purpose of the accused in relation to it. In *H*, there was evidence that before pulling the complainant's tracksuit bottoms, the accused had said to her 'Do you fancy a shag?' At trial, it was submitted on behalf of the accused that the touching that had occurred could not be regarded by a reasonable person as 'sexual' within the meaning of the Act. The trial judge took the view that there were clearly circumstances, including the words allegedly spoken beforehand, which could make what had occurred sexual. The Court of Appeal said that the judge had not adopted the required two-stage approach to s. 78(b) but had looked at the matter as a whole. The problem with that was that, in a borderline case, a person's intention could make a touching sexual, even though the nature of the touching could not be sexual. That, said the Court, is not an appropriate approach, even though in the great majority of cases the result will be the same.

The Court in *H* disapproved the decision in *George* [1956] Crim LR 52, an allegation of indecent assault in which it was held that a shoe fetishist's act in removing a woman's shoe was not capable of being indecent. *George* was expressly approved in *Court* [1989] AC 28, where the House of Lords set out the meaning of 'indecency' in the offence of indecent assault and the reasoning in *Court* is essentially reproduced in the definition of 'sexual' in s. 78. The potentially wide scope of the application of s. 78(b) is highlighted by the court's discussion of *George* in *H*. A wide variety of conduct is capable of being regarded by a reasonable person as possibly being 'sexual', albeit the vast majority of people would regard it as objectively innocuous.

B3.49   Section 78(b) will have the effect of making an intimate medical examination involving digital examination of the vagina or anus 'sexual' where the examination is not a bona fide examination and the doctor's purpose is sexual gratification. Arguably, even where a doctor conducts a properly required intimate medical examination, if it was conducted in an inappropriate manner, it may be concluded that the activity was 'sexual' if it can be established that the doctor had an ulterior purpose of sexual gratification. See the facts of *Bolduc and Bird* (1967) 63 DLR (2d) 82, where a doctor carried out a necessary examination but allowed a friend to be present for his sexual gratification.

It is instructive to consider examples of activities which are not unambiguously 'sexual' but may be 'sexual' following the approach outlined in s. 78(b) as interpreted in *H*. For example, a slap on an athlete's buttocks by her coach is capable of being considered 'sexual' but may not be so where the occasion, filing off a field after a game, is not obviously sexual and where no words or gestures connote a sexual purpose (*Gauthier* Can Cr L. Digest 42887 and see also *J (BJ)* (1996) 193 AR 151 (Alta SC)). Stroking the legs of another is certainly capable of being sexual (*Price (David)* [2004] 1 Cr App R 145). The accused's admission in that case that he had done it because he was a shoe fetishist would be admissible under the second question in s. 78(b).

As with all the non-consensual sexual offences, it is a fundamental requirement of the offence **B3.50** that the prosecution can establish the complainant's absence of consent. (see **B3.29** *et seq.*)

For consent and public policy, and, in particular, where an accused deliberately inflicts injury upon a complainant, see *Meachen* [2006] EWCA Crim 2414 and see **B2.14** *et seq.*

In appropriate circumstances the presumptions in ss. 75 and 76 will apply. See **B3.29** *et seq.*

Mens Rea

The accused must intend to penetrate the vagina or anus of another person. On a natural read- **B3.51** ing of the section, the prosecution need not prove that the accused intended the penetration should be 'sexual'.

As with rape, the prosecution must prove that the accused did not reasonably believe that the complainant was consenting (see **B3.30**). In appropriate circumstances, the presumptions in ss. 75 and 76 as to consent and/or reasonable belief as to consent will apply. The 'relevant act' under s. 77 is 'the defendant intentionally penetrating, with a part of his body or anything else, the vagina or anus of another person, where the penetration is sexual'.

SEXUAL ASSAULT

Sexual Offences Act 2003, s. 3 **B3.52**

(1) A person (A) commits an offence if—
    (a) he intentionally touches another person (B),
    (b) the touching is sexual,
    (c) B does not consent to the touching, and
    (d) A does not reasonably believe that B consents.
(2) Whether a belief is reasonable is to be determined having regard to all the circumstances, including any steps A has taken to ascertain whether B consents.
(3) Sections 75 and 76 apply to an offence under this section.

Sections 75 and 76 relate to the presumptions as to consent (see **B3.29** *et seq.*).

Procedure

Sexual assault is triable either way. As to the classification of the offence for the purpose of list- **B3.53** ing, see CPD XIII, para. B (see Supplement, **PD-97**). The extended jurisdiction provisions of s. 72 (see **B3.301**) apply to this offence where the victim was under 18 at the time of the offence.

See **B3.335** for alternative verdicts.

Indictment

Statement of Offence **B3.54**

Sexual assault contrary to section 3(1) of the Sexual Offences Act 2003.

Particulars of Offence

A on or about the...day of...sexually touched V without [his] [her] consent not reasonably believing that V was consenting.

Sentencing

B3.55   The maximum sentence for an offence under the SOA 2003, s. 3, on conviction on indictment is ten years' imprisonment. On summary conviction, the maximum sentence is imprisonment for a term not exceeding six months or the statutory maximum fine, or both (s. 3(4)).

The Sentencing Council has issued a new guideline applicable to all sex offenders aged 18 or over who are sentenced on or after 1 April 2014 (see **B3.3**). The previous guideline categorised the offence of sexual assault purely by reference to the type of touching involved. The new guideline is intended to reflect fully the psychological and physical harm caused by the offence (see Supplement, **SG-67**).

Four of the factors in category 2 in respect of rape and assault by penetration are placed in category 1 in respect of sexual assault: severe psychological harm, abduction, violence or threats of violence, and forced/uninvited entry into victim's home. This is because the Sentencing Council considered that category 1 sexual assaults will never be as severe as category 1 rapes or assaults by penetration, as reflected in the lower statutory maximum (ten years' imprisonment rather than life.)

As with rape and assault by penetration, category 3 does not list any factors in order to reflect the fact that there is an inherent degree of harm caused by any sexual assault.

In the draft guideline the first factor in category 2 did not distinguish between clothed and naked genitalia on the basis that the type of activity does not necessarily reflect the type of harm caused. In the face of mixed responses to the consultation document on this issue, the Council amended the factor to 'touching of naked genitalia or naked breasts'. As a result, touching of clothed genitalia or breasts, without more, will fall within category 3. However, often the context of the offence will involve other factors in the harm categories.

A case of particular gravity, reflected by multiple features of culpability or harm, could merit upward adjustment from the starting point before further adjustment for aggravating or mitigating features. In respect of the most serious category (category 1, culpability A), the recommended starting point is four years' custody with a range of three to seven years. In respect of appropriate category 2 or 3 offences where there is a sufficient prospect of rehabilitation, a community order with a sex offender treatment programme requirement can be a proper alternative to a short or moderate length custodial sentence. The court should also consider whether the custodial threshold has been passed, and, if so, whether if a custodial sentence is unavoidable, it should be suspended.

In every case the court should consider a disqualification from working with children (see **E21.17** and **E21.21**) and a sexual offences prevention order (see **E21.24**). There is a notification requirement under the SOA 2003, s. 80 and sch. 3, subject to the age of the offender and the sentence imposed (see **E23**). The *Magistrates' Court Sentencing Guidelines* (see Supplement, **SG-310**) apply when sentencing in a magistrates' court.

B3.56   **Range of Sexual Assaults**   The offence of sexual assault covers many activities formerly within the offence of indecent assault, although the most serious offences within that former category will now be prosecuted as rape, assault by penetration or a child sex offence. Sexual assault covers all forms of non-consensual sexual touching, but mainly applies to the lesser forms of assault.

B3.57   **Young Offenders**   The new guideline applies only to offenders aged 18 and older. General principles to be considered in sentencing of youths are in the Sentencing Guidance Council's definitive guideline. *Overarching principles—Sentencing Youths* (see Supplement, **SG-515**). See *Sharp* [2008] EWCA Crim 1059 for an example of the Court of Appeal dealing with a young offender. The court substituted a supervision order with elements of treatment and participation in a sexual offender programme for a sentence of four years' detention in respect of a sexual assault upon a 75-year-old woman by a boy aged nearly 13.

Elements

The *actus reus* may simply be defined as touching where the touching is 'sexual' in character. There is no requirement of force or violence: the lightest touching will suffice. Nor is any element of 'hostility' required as was held to be the case in one line of indecent assault authorities. Section 79(8) provides that touching includes touching with any part of the body, with anything else, and through anything. In particular, it includes touching amounting to penetration. Touching a person through that person's clothing clearly amounts to a touching for the purposes of this offence, so too does touching the victim's clothing even though the person of the victim is not touched through clothing (*H* [2005] 2 All ER 859 at [26]). The victim need not be aware of being touched. See *Bounekhla* [2006] EWCA Crim 1217 where the accused surreptitiously took his penis out of his trousers and ejaculated onto a woman's clothing when pressed up against her dancing at a nightclub. In one area, sexual assault is narrower than indecent assault which could be committed if the accused caused the complainant to apprehend that she was about to be touched indecently (cf. *Rolfe* (1952) 36 Cr App R 4). If touching does not occur, the offence is not completed, although the circumstances may amount to an attempt. Nevertheless, it remains arguable that ejaculation onto a victim without contact with any part of an accused's body still constitutes a touching.

     B3.58

Section 78, which provides when a touching or other activity is 'sexual', is considered at **B3.47**. If the act itself is objectively equivocal, the purpose of the accused may be a relevant consideration as provided by s. 78(b), and that must be a reference to his own (subjective) purpose.

The prosecution must establish that the complainant did not consent to the touching (see **B3.19**).

The mental element consists of an intentional touching coupled with an absence of reasonable belief that the complainant was consenting. In *Heard* [2008] QB 43, the Court of Appeal confirmed that the prosecution must prove that the touching was deliberate, and a reckless touching is not sufficient. Voluntary intoxication cannot be relied upon as defeating intentional touching. However, if the touching is an unintended accident, such as a consequence of impairment of control of the limbs, no offence under s. 3 is committed. A drunken accident is still an accident. See **B3.22**.

     B3.59

In appropriate circumstances, the evidential and conclusive presumptions about consent in ss. 75 and 76 (see **B3.29** *et seq.*) may apply to this offence (s. 77).

CAUSING A PERSON TO ENGAGE IN SEXUAL ACTIVITY WITHOUT CONSENT

Sexual Offences Act 2003, s. 4

     B3.60

(1) A person (A) commits an offence if—
  (a) he intentionally causes another person (B) to engage in an activity,
  (b) the activity is sexual,
  (c) B does not consent to engaging in the activity, and
  (d) A does not reasonably believe that B consents.
(2) Whether a belief is reasonable is to be determined having regard to all the circumstances, including any steps A has taken to ascertain whether B consents.
(3) Sections 75 and 76 apply to an offence under this section.

Procedure

Causing a person to engage in sexual activity is triable either way unless penetration is involved. As to the classification of the offence for the purpose of listing, see CPD XIII, para. B (see Supplement, **PD-97**). The extended jurisdiction provisions of the SOA 2003, s. 72 (see **B3.301**), apply to this offence where the victim was under 18.

     B3.61

See **B3.335** for alternative verdicts.

Indictment

B3.62

Statement of Offence

Causing a person to engage in sexual activity without consent contrary to section 4(1) of the Sexual Offences Act 2003.

Particulars of Offence

A, on or about the…day of…caused V to engage in a sexual activity without her [his] consent [namely, to allow her vagina [anus] [mouth] to be penetrated by [the penis of] another [or — to penetrate the anus or vagina of another by [V's body][an object] or — to penetrate the mouth of another by V's penis] not reasonably believing that V was consenting.

Sentencing

B3.63   The maximum punishment varies according to the activity concerned and is set out in the SOA 2003, s. 4(4) and (5).

Sexual Offences Act 2003, s. 4

(4) A person guilty of an offence under this section, if the activity caused involved—
  (a) penetration of B's anus or vagina,
  (b) penetration of B's mouth with a person's penis,
  (c) penetration of a person's anus or vagina with a part of B's body or by B with anything else, or
  (d) penetration of a person's mouth with B's penis,
is liable, on conviction on indictment, to imprisonment for life.
(5) Unless subsection (4) applies, a person guilty of an offence under this section is liable—
  (a) on summary conviction, to imprisonment for a term not exceeding six months or to a fine not exceeding the statutory maximum or both;
  (b) on conviction on indictment, for a term not exceeding 10 years.

The Sentencing Council has issued a new guideline applicable to sex offenders aged 18 or over who are sentenced on or after 1 April 2014 (see **B3.3**). In respect of s. 4 offences, the new guideline adopts the same approach and sentencing levels as those specified for (i) the offence of assault by penetration (where the offence involved penetration) and (ii) the offence of sexual assault (where the offence did not involve penetration). See Supplement, **SG-71** for the full text.

There is a baseline of assumed harm where no category 2 harm factors are present (category 1). The extreme nature or impact of one or more category 2 factors may elevate the case into category 1. Similarly, there is a baseline of assumed culpability (category B). One or more category A culpability factors will take the case into culpability category A. The categorisation of harm and culpability enables the court to identify the starting point and category range. Then the court should consider whether the presence of aggravating or mitigating factors should result in upward or downward adjustment from the starting point or an imposition of a sentence outside the category range. The guideline provides a non-exhaustive list of such factors. In particular, relevant convictions are likely to result in an upward adjustment. When sentencing appropriate category 2 or 3 offences, the court should also consider whether the custody threshold has been passed; if so, whether a custodial sentence is unavoidable; and if it is, whether that sentence can be suspended.

The previous guideline expressly stated that the same degree of seriousness and the same starting points apply whether an offender causes an act to take place, incites an act that actually takes place, or incites an act that does not take place only because it is prevented by factors beyond the control of the offender, though some reduction will generally be appropriate when the incited activity does not, in fact, take place. It is likely that the same principles will be followed in respect of the new guideline.

In every case the court should consider a disqualification from working with children (see **E21.17** and **E21.21**) and a sexual offences prevention order (see **E21.24**). There is a notification requirement under the SOA 2003, s. 80 and sch. 3 (see **E23**). The offence is a qualifying offence for an automatic life sentence under the CJA 2003, sch. 15B, if the offender is liable on conviction on indictment to imprisonment for life (see **B3.15**).

An offender causing his victim to masturbate him with her hand does not fall in the higher category which includes acts involving contact between naked genitalia or causing a victim to masturbate himself or herself (*Ayeva* [2010] 2 Cr App R (S) 143). **B3.64**

For an example of a case where there were serious aggravating features, see *H* [2008] EWCA Crim 1202. The visibly mentally disabled victim was forced (i) to take a dog's penis in his mouth and (ii) to be penetrated in the anus by the dog. The two accused filmed the incident on their mobile phones and the footage was extensively circulated and placed on the internet. A sentence of seven years' detention was upheld in respect of a 17-year-old. The Court of Appeal noted that s. 4(4)(b) does not apply to penetration by a dog's penis and so the PCC(S) A 2000, s. 91, could not apply. Section 4(4)(c) does, however, cover penetration of the anus by a dog's penis.

Elements

Actus Reus The offence covers the situation where A causes B to engage in sexual activity without B's consent, whether or not A also engages in it and whether or not A is present. The term 'activity' is not defined, and is capable of being given a wide interpretation, although it must have actually taken place. The activity which B is caused to engage in may involve B alone such as where A forces B to masturbate himself or herself, or it may be with A, or with a third person (whether or not the third person consents) or even an animal. It would include causing a person to act as a prostitute. The activity must be 'sexual' in accordance with s. 78 (see **B3.47**). It can include engaging A in a conversation of a sexual nature (*Grout* [2011] 1 Cr App R 472). The word 'causes' is not defined and so any causative conduct may suffice, including threats of violence, inducements or persuasion. The prosecution must establish that B did not consent to engaging in the activity (see **B3.19**). **B3.65**

This complicated offence overlaps partly with rape which is also cast in terms of vaginal, anal or oral penetration. The offence is wider than rape, in that rape can be committed only by a man, as a principal and does not involve penetration with an object. This offence can be committed by and against persons of either sex and includes cases of 'female rape', i.e. where A causes B to penetrate her vagina with his penis. Furthermore, the offence makes A criminally liable for causing B to engage in sexual activity where B cannot himself be convicted of any offence because he has a defence such as duress or is under the age of criminal responsibility (see the discussion at [2004] Crim LR 328 at p. 330).

The aggravated form of the offence covers all the activities mentioned in s. 4(4). All involve some form of penetration, either penetration of the anus or vagina with a penis or with anything else *or* the penetration of the mouth with a penis. This attracts a maximum penalty of life imprisonment. There is a residual category of sexual activities, which do not involve any of the above penetrations, which attract the lower penalty. This category is wider than sexual assault, not least because it covers the case where A forces B to take an active role in touching a third party such as coercing the victim to masturbate another or coercing B to masturbate himself. Following the principle in *Courtie* [1984] AC 463, since different factual ingredients attract different punishments, separate offences are created and this must be reflected in the indictment. See *Grout*.

Mens Rea The accused must *intend* to cause another person to enter into the activity in the sense that it must have been deliberate. However, following the reasoning in *Heard* [2008] QB 43, an accused's state of voluntary intoxication at the time of the causing is not a relevant factor when deciding whether he had this intent. Furthermore, the prosecution does not have to prove that the accused intended the activity to be 'sexual'. **B3.66**

As with all non-consensual offences, the prosecution must prove that the accused did not reasonably believe the complainant (B) was consenting (see **B3.19**). This would appear to apply to the time when the complainant engaged in the activity.

B3.67 **Presumptions**   In appropriate circumstances, the SOA 2003, ss. 75 and 76 (evidential presumptions and conclusive presumptions about consent), will apply to this offence (see **B3.29** *et seq.*, especially *Bingham* [2013] 2 Cr App R 307 (29) and the discussion of *Devonald* [2008] EWCA Crim 527, a case where the Court of Appeal held that the conclusive presumption under s. 76 applied). Under s. 77, the 'relevant act' is 'the defendant intentionally penetrating, with a part of his body or anything else, the vagina or anus of another person, where the penetration is sexual'.

RAPE AND OTHER OFFENCES AGAINST CHILDREN AGED UNDER 13

B3.68 Sections 5 to 8 of the SOA 2003 mirror the non-consensual offences in ss. 1 to 4 of the Act but apply specifically to cases where the child is under 13. In respect of each section, any apparent consent is irrelevant for the purposes of proving the offence as is any mistake as to the child's age. The offences are gender neutral.

Exceptions to Aiding, Abetting and Counselling

B3.69   Sexual Offences Act 2003, s. 73

(1) A person is not guilty of aiding, abetting or counselling the commission against a child of an offence to which this section applies if he acts for the purpose of—
  (a) protecting the child from sexually transmitted infection,
  (b) protecting the physical safety of the child,
  (c) preventing the child from becoming pregnant, or
  (d) promoting the child's emotional well-being by the giving of advice,
  and not for the purpose of obtaining sexual gratification or for the purpose of causing or encouraging the activity constituting the offence or the child's participation in it.
(2) This section applies to—
  (a) an offence under any of sections 5 to 7 (offences against children under 13);
  (b) an offence under section 9 (sexual activity with a child);
  (c) an offence under section 13 which would be an offence under section 9 if the offender were aged 18;
  (d) an offence under any of sections 16, 25, 30, 34 and 38 (sexual activity) against a person under 16.
(3) This section does not affect any other enactment or any rule of law restricting the circumstances in which a person is guilty of aiding, abetting or counselling an offence under this part.

Section 73 exempts a person from liability for aiding, abetting, or counselling the commission of an offence against a child in circumstances where the person acts for the purposes specified in the section and not for sexual gratification. Section 73 applies to a number of offences dealt with in the remainder of this section. Section 73 would not apply if an offender was charged with encouraging or assisting any such offence under the SCA 2007, s. 44 (see **A5.3**).

Rape of a Child under 13

B3.70   Sexual Offences Act 2003, s. 5

(1) A person commits an offence if—
  (a) he intentionally penetrates the vagina, anus or mouth of another person with his penis, and
  (b) the other person is under 13.

B3.71 **Procedure**   An allegation of an offence contrary to s. 5 is triable only on indictment . As to the classification of the offence for the purpose of listing, see CPD XIII, para. B (see Supplement, **PD-97**). It is also an offence to which the extra-territorial jurisdiction provisions of s. 72 apply (see **B3.301**).

See **B3.335** for alternative verdicts.

Indictment

Statement of Offence

B3.72

Rape of a child under 13 contrary to section 5 of the Sexual Offences Act 2003.

Particulars of Offence

A, on or about the...day of...penetrated the [vagina][anus][mouth] of V a child then under the age of 13 years with his penis.

Sentencing   The maximum sentence is imprisonment for life (s. 5(2)).   **B3.73**

The Sentencing Council has issued a new guideline applicable to sex offenders aged 18 or over who are sentenced on or after 1 April 2014 (see **B3.3**). The Council has issued separate guidelines for the under-13 offences (see Supplement, Supplement, **SG-75**). That approach reflects the belief that there are issues and sensitivities unique to offences against children under 13 that require a separate guideline to ensure clarity for sentencers as to the factors to be taken into account and to provide a transparent process for others concerned with these cases.

Cases where a child under 13 has been groomed into acquiescence are to be treated equally for sentencing purposes with cases of forced non-consensual activity. That is so because of the evidence that younger children are increasingly at risk of sexual exploitation. In the exceptional case of a non-exploitative relationship, the Council considered that such cases should be sentenced outside the guideline. The Council stated that:

> When dealing with the statutory offence of rape of a child under 13, the court may be faced with a wide range of offending behaviour. Sentencers should have particular regard to the fact that these offences are not only committed through force or fear of force but may include exploitative behaviour towards a child which should be considered to indicate high culpability.

> Offences may be of such severity, for example involving a campaign of rape, that sentences of 20 years and above may be appropriate.

> This guideline is designed to deal with the majority of offending behaviour which deserves a significant custodial sentence; the starting points and ranges reflect the fact that such offending merits such an approach. There may also be exceptional cases, where a lengthy community order with a requirement to participate in a sex offender treatment programme may be the best way of changing the offender's behaviour and of protecting the public by preventing any repetition of the offence. This guideline may not be appropriate where the sentencer is satisfied that on the available evidence, and in the absence of exploitation, a young or particularly immature defendant genuinely believed, on reasonable grounds, that the victim was aged 16 or over and that they were engaging in lawful sexual activity.

> Sentencers are reminded that if sentencing outside the guideline they must be satisfied that it would be contrary to the interests of justice to follow the guideline.

There is a notification requirement under the SOA 2003, s. 80 and sch. 3 (see **E23**). The offence is a qualifying offence for an automatic life sentence under the CJA 2003, sch. 15B (see **B3.15**).

In *A-G's Ref (Nos. 11 and 12 of 2012)* [2013] 1 Cr App R (S) 237 (43), the Court of Appeal   **B3.74** observed that careful analysis of the circumstances of an offence under s. 5 is always required and a *Newton* hearing may be necessary when the claim is made that the victim was consenting in fact and/or that the offender believed the victim to be significantly older than her actual age. The prosecutor bears a burden of responsibility to ensure that factual concessions to a basis of plea or mitigation of the offence are made only when justified and that, if made, the precise import of the concession is understood by the offender and the court.

Elements   Save for the issue of consent, the elements of the offence are the same as those for   **B3.75** rape and reference should therefore be made to **B3.18** to **B3.42**.

In contrast to rape of an adult, consent is no defence and so there is no requirement on the prosecution to prove that the accused did not reasonably believe that the victim was consenting. The position in respect of a child close to her 13th birthday where the accused maintains that the sex was consensual has caused some difficulties in practice. Strictly speaking, so far as it is relevant, the issue of consent is for the trial judge in a *Newton* hearing and CPS policy is simply to charge an accused with the s. 5 offence. But some judges have resisted depriving a jury of the opportunity of deciding such an important issue and encouraged the prosecution to charge rape under s. 1 with the s. 5 offence as an alternative. Plainly, this does not appear to have been the Parliamentary intention.

B3.76   In respect of ss. 5 to 8, it is necessary to prove that the complainant was under the age of 13, but ss. 5 to 8 do not require the prosecution to prove that the accused knew or suspected that the child was under that age. In *G* [2009] 1 AC 92, a 15-year-old boy had pleaded guilty to an offence under s. 5 committed in respect of a 12-year-old girl. The plea was entered on an accepted basis that the complainant consented and that the accused thought she was aged 15. The Court of Appeal (*G* [2006] 1 WLR 2052) rejected his appeal based on submissions that s. 5 was incompatible with the ECHR, Articles 6 and 8. The House of Lords also dismissed his subsequent appeal. Their lordships were unanimous in holding that s. 5 was not incompatible with Article 6; in essence, it was held that it is a matter for contracting states to define the essential elements of the offence with which a person has been charged. By a majority of three to two, the House also rejected the argument based on the incompatibility of s. 5 with Article 8. The majority (Lord Hoffmann, Baroness Hale and Lord Mance) held that the prosecution of G under s. 5 did not engage his Article 8 rights but, even if it did, the prosecution was 'both rational and proportionate in pursuit of the legitimate aims of the protection of health and morals and of the rights and freedoms of others' (Baroness Hale at [55]). The minority (Lords Hope and Carswell) expressed the view that the sanctions that can be imposed under s. 13 for mutual sexual activity by a person under 18 with a child aged under 13 provide all that is needed by way of punishment that is proportionate to the offence. Section 5 is designed for a much more serious situation, with a maximum sentence of life imprisonment and the description of the offence as rape (with all the consequences that go with that description), and a prosecution is entirely appropriate where the offence has been committed by a person over the age of 18 against a child under the age of 13. It may also be appropriate where the offender is younger than 18 but the younger the offender, the less appropriate it is (Lord Hope at [39]). As the offence committed by G fell within the ambit of s. 13, to continue to prosecute him under s. 5 was disproportionate and incompatible with his Article 8 right. Despite being in the minority, Lord Hope suggested (at [40]) that there was a lesson to be learnt from the instant case which he hoped would be taken into account in future cases of this kind. In *G v UK* [2011] ECHR 1308 the majority view of the House of Lords was supported by the ECtHR. In *Brown* [2013] UKSC 43, the Supreme Court held that the Northern Irish offence of having unlawful carnal knowledge with a girl under the age of 14 did not require proof that the accused did not honestly believe that the girl was over the age of 14.

Tolhurst v DPP [2008] EWHC 2976 (Admin) was an unsuccessful application for judicial review of a decision by the CPS to prosecute an accused under s. 5 rather than s. 9 (see **B3.93**) or s. 13 (see **B3.114**).

The provisions of s. 73 apply to this offence (see **B3.69**).

Assault of a Child under 13 by Penetration

B3.77   Sexual Offences Act 2003, s. 6

(1) A person commits an offence if—
    (a) he intentionally penetrates the vagina or anus of another person with a part of his body or anything else,
    (b) the penetration is sexual, and
    (c) the other person is under 13.

Procedure   An allegation of an offence contrary to s. 6 is triable only on indictment. As to the   **B3.78** classification of the offence for the purpose of listing, see CPD XIII, para. B (see Supplement, **PD-97**). It is an offence to which the extra-territorial jurisdiction provisions of s. 72 apply (see **B3.301**).

See **B3.335** for alternative verdicts.

Indictment   **B3.79**

Statement of Offence

Assault of a child under 13 by penetration contrary to section 6 of the Sexual Offences Act 2003.

Particulars of Offence

A, on or about the...day of...penetrated the vagina [anus] of V a child then under the age of 13 years.

Sentencing   The maximum sentence is imprisonment for life (s. 6(2)).   **B3.80**

The Sentencing Council has issued a new guideline applicable to sex offenders aged 18 or over who are sentenced on or after 1 April 2014 (see **B3.3**). The Council has issued separate guidelines for the under-13 offences (see Supplement, **SG-79**).

There is a notification requirement under the SOA 2003, s. 80 and sch. 3 (see **E23**).

The offence is a qualifying offence for an automatic life sentence under the CJA 2003, sch. 15B (see **B3.15**).

Elements   The basic elements of the offence are the same as those governing such an assault   **B3.81** on an adult and reference should therefore be made to **B3.43** to **B3.51**. However, consent is no defence and so there is no requirement on the prosecution to prove that the accused did not reasonably believe that the victim was consenting. It is necessary to prove that the victim was under the age of 13 at the time of the offence, but as with s. 5, it is not necessary to show that the accused knew or suspected that to be the case (see **B3.75**).

Section 73 applies to this offence (see **B3.69**).

Sexual Assault of a Child under 13

Sexual Offences Act 2003, s. 7   **B3.82**

(1) A person commits an offence if—
    (a) he intentionally touches another person,
    (b) the touching is sexual, and
    (c) the other person is under 13.

Procedure   An allegation of an offence contrary to s. 7 is triable either. As to the classification   **B3.83** of the offence for the purpose of listing, see CPD XIII, para. B (see Supplement, **PD-97**). The extra-territorial jurisdiction provisions of s. 72 apply (see **B3.301**).

See **B3.335** for alternative verdicts.

Indictment   **B3.84**

Statement of Offence

Sexual assault of a child under 13 contrary to section 7 of the Sexual Offences Act 2003

Particulars of Offence

A, on or about the...day of...sexually touched V, then a child under the age of 13 years.

Sentencing   The maximum sentence for an offence under the SOA 2003, s. 7, on conviction   **B3.85** on indictment is 14 years' imprisonment. On summary conviction, the maximum sentence is imprisonment for a term not exceeding six months or the statutory maximum fine, or both.

The Sentencing Council has issued a new guideline applicable to sex offenders aged 18 or over who are sentenced on or after 1 April 2014 (see **B3.3**). The Council has issued separate guidelines for the under-13 offences (see Supplement, **SG-83**).

There is a notification requirement under the SOA 2003, s. 80 and sch. 3, if the offender was aged 18 or over or was sentenced to at least 12 months' imprisonment (see **E23**). The *Magistrates' Court Sentencing Guidelines* (see Supplement, **SG-310**) apply when sentencing in a magistrates' court.

For examples of the application of the old guidelines in operation, see *Dobson* [2007] EWCA Crim 2570, *A-G's Ref (No. 29 of 2008)* [2009] 1 Cr App R (S) 515 and *Spalding* [2008] EWCA Crim 3198. The Court of Appeal emphasised the importance of the effect of the conduct on the victim in *D* [2009] EWCA Crim 1926.

The offence is a qualifying offence for an automatic life sentence under the CJA 2003, sch. 15B (see **B3.15**).

B3.86   **Elements**   The elements of this offence are the same as for the adult offence (see **B3.58**) save that consent is not a defence. It is submitted that there is a necessary implication that this offence is one of strict liability as to age: see by analogy *K* [2002] 1 AC 642.

In respect of aiding, abetting and counselling, the SOA 2003, s. 73, applies to this offence (see **B3.69**).

Causing or Inciting a Child under 13 to Engage in Sexual Activity

B3.87   Sexual Offences Act 2003, s. 8

    (1) A person commits an offence if—
        (a) he intentionally causes or incites another person (B) to engage in an activity,
        (b) the activity is sexual, and
        (c) B is under 13.

B3.88   **Procedure**   An allegation of an offence contrary to s. 8 is triable either way, except where the activity involved is penetrative when the allegation is triable on indictment only. As to the classification of the offence for the purpose of listing, see CPD XIII, para. B (see Supplement, **PD-97**). The extra-territorial jurisdiction provisions of s. 72 apply (see **B3.301**).

See **B3.335** for alternative verdicts.

B3.89   **Indictment**

Statement of Offence

Causing or inciting a child under 13 to engage in sexual activity contrary to section 8 of the Sexual Offences Act 2003.

Particulars of Offence

A, on or about the...day of...caused V, then a child under the age of 13 years, to engage in sexual activity consisting of the penetration of V's [anus] [vagina] [mouth] with a part of V's body [an object].

B3.90   **Sentencing**   The maximum sentence for an offence under the SOA 2003, s. 8, varies according to the type of activity involved.

Sexual Offences Act 2003, s. 8

    (2) A person guilty of an offence under this section, if the activity caused or incited involved—
        (a) penetration of B's anus or vagina,
        (b) penetration of B's mouth with a person's penis,
        (c) penetration of a person's anus or vagina with a part of B's body or by B with anything else, or
        (d) penetration of a person's mouth with B's penis is liable, on conviction on indictment, to imprisonment for life.
    (3) Unless subsection (2) applies, a person guilty of an offence under this section is liable—

(a) on summary conviction, to imprisonment for a term not exceeding 6 months or to a fine not exceeding the statutory maximum or both;

(b) on conviction on indictment, to imprisonment for a term not exceeding 14 years.

The Sentencing Council has issued a new guideline applicable to sex offenders aged 18 or over who are sentenced on or after 1 April 2014 (see **B3.3**). For the guideline in respect of an offence under s. 8, see Supplement, **SG-87**. There is a notification requirement under the SOA 2003, s. 80 and sch. 3 (see **E23**). For an example of the application of the old guideline in operation, see *Palmer* [2009] EWCA Crim 2671.

The offence is a qualifying offence for an automatic life sentence under the CJA 2003, sch. 15B (see **B3.15**).

Elements   The basic elements of the offence of causing a child to engage in sexual activity are   **B3.91** the same as those relating to the corresponding offence in relation to an adult and reference should therefore be made to **B3.60** to **B3.67**. In contrast to a similar offence against an adult, consent is no defence and so there is no requirement on the prosecution to prove that the accused did not reasonably believe that the victim was consenting. It is necessary to prove that the victim was under the age of 13 at the time of the offence.

In *Walker* [2006] EWCA Crim 1907, the Court of Appeal held that the essence of the offence of incitement was the encouragement of a person under the age of 13 to engage in the activity. It is that encouragement that has to be intentional or deliberate. It is not necessary to prove that the accused intended that the encouraged sexual activity should actually happen. On the face of it, that is at odds with the general position in relation to common-law incitement that a person had to intend that the activity incited actually take place. In *Jones* [2008] QB 460, the Court of Appeal held that the gravamen of the offence is the incitement of children under the age of 13 to engage in sexual activity; it is not concerned with the effect on a particular child. The criminality at which the offence is aimed is the incitement and it matters not if this is directed at a particular child or a very large group of children, or whether the child or children can be identified.

In *Grout* [2011] 1 Cr App R (S) 472 the Court of Appeal emphasised (as pointed out by the authors of *Rook and Ward on Sexual Offences: Law and Practice* (4th edn, 2010) at para. 3.92) that because there are higher maximum punishments for offences committed under s. 8(2) of the SOA 2003, the effect of the House of Lords decision in *Courtie* [1984] AC 463 is that, in practice, it creates four different offences. Each of those offences must be carried out intentionally. The first offence is causing penetrative sexual activity, the second is inciting such activity, the third is causing non-penetrative sexual activity and the fourth is inciting such activity. It is therefore important that the charge or indictment specifies which of these offences is being alleged.

For the meaning of 'sexual', see **B3.47**.

SEX OFFENCES AGAINST CHILDREN AGED 13 TO 15

The child sex offences under the SOA 2003 which protect children under the age of 16 are   **B3.92** contained in ss. 9 to 15 of the Act. In contrast to ss. 5 to 8, a reasonable mistaken belief as to the child's age will be capable of founding a defence but only if the child is 13 years of age or older. The offences are all gender neutral.

The Court Service is under an obligation to give priority to cases involving vulnerable witnesses, including child witnesses, and the prosecution should remind the court of the need for priority listing. This point is specifically addressed in the *Witness Charter: Standards of care for witnesses in the Criminal Justice System* (March 2010). The need for fast-tracking in respect of children was emphasised by the Court of Appeal in *Powell* [2006] 1 Cr App R 468 and *Malicki* [2009] EWCA Crim 365.

Sexual Activity with a Child

B3.93   Sexual Offences Act 2003, s. 9

(1) A person aged 18 or over (A) commits an offence if—
  (a) he intentionally touches another person (B),
  (b) the touching is sexual, and
  (c) either—
    (i) B is under 16 and A does not reasonably believe that B is 16 or over, or
    (ii) B is under 13.

B3.94 **Procedure**   An allegation of an offence contrary to s. 9 is triable either way unless the sexual activity involves penetration, in which case it is triable only on indictment. As to the classification of the offence for the purpose of listing, see CPD XIII, para. B (see Supplement, **PD-97**). The extra-territorial jurisdiction provisions of s. 72 apply (see **B3.301**).

See **B3.335** for alternative verdicts.

An issue may arise as to whether D is 18 or over at the time of the offence. Under s. 9, unless the jury was sure that D was over 18, he would be not guilty of the charge. In respect of an alternative count under s. 13 (see **B3.114**), the same jury may not be sure that D was under 18 at the relevant time. Should D be acquitted of both charges? Whilst there is a degree of ambiguity in the relationship between ss. 9 and 13, it is submitted that D should not be acquitted of both counts. The essence of the offence alleged in both sections is sexual touching. The age of the offender is not determinative of whether an offence has taken place. Rather, the age of the offender is only decisive of the maximum penalty which may be imposed upon conviction (14 years' imprisonment for an offender aged 18 or over, five years' imprisonment for an offender under the age of 18). It would be absurd and unjust if a jury were to find that D had committed an offence against V but D had to be acquitted because they could not decide if he was under or over 18 at the time of the offence. In such circumstances, it is submitted that the benefit of any doubt should manifest itself in the maximum sentence which might be imposed. Thus, it is submitted that the court should seek to establish at an early stage of the proceedings whether any such issue exists. If such an issue does exist, or even if the issue emerges during the course of evidence, an alternative count alleging an offence under s. 13 should be added to the indictment. Upon retirement, the jury should be asked to consider, first, whether sexual touching occurred. If the answer to that is in the affirmative, they should next ask whether they were sure that the accused was aged 18 or over at the time of the offence. If they were sure of that there would be no need for them to consider the s. 13 count and they should then go on to consider the remaining relevant considerations under s. 9. If they were not sure that D was 18 or over at the relevant time, the appropriate verdict should be not guilty of s. 9. The jury should then go on to consider the remaining elements of the s. 13 count.

B3.95 **Indictment**

Statement of Offence

Sexual activity with a child contrary to section 9(1) of the Sexual Offences Act 2003.

Particulars of Offence

A, on or about the…day of…, being then a person aged 18 or over, intentionally sexually touched V, then a child under the age of [16] [13] years or A, on or about the…day of…, being then a person aged 18 or over, intentionally sexually touched V, then a child under the age of [16] [13] years, by penetrating V's [anus] [vagina] with a part of A's body, namely…[an object].

B3.96 **Sentencing**   The maximum sentence for an offence under the SOA 2003, s. 9, varies according to the activity involved.

                          Sexual Offences Act 2003, s. 9

(2) A person guilty of an offence under this section, if the touching involved—
  (a) penetration of B's anus or vagina with a part of A's body or anything else,

     (b) penetration of B's mouth with A's penis,
     (c) penetration of A's anus or vagina with a part of B's body, or
     (d) penetration of A's mouth with B's penis,
     is liable, on conviction on indictment, to imprisonment for a term not exceeding 14 years.
  (3) Unless subsection (2) applies, a person guilty of an offence under this section is liable—
     (a) on summary conviction, to imprisonment for a term not exceeding 6 months or to a fine
        not exceeding the statutory maximum or both;
     (b) on conviction on indictment, to imprisonment for a term not exceeding 14 years.

The maximum penalty also varies with the age of the offender; if the offender is aged under 18, the maximum penalty is five years (see **B3.116**).

The Sentencing Council has issued a new guideline applicable to sex offenders aged 18 or over who are sentenced on or after 1 April 2014 (see **B3.3**). For the guideline in respect of an offence under s. 9, see Supplement, **SG-91**. There is a notification requirement under the SOA 2003, s. 80 and sch. 3 (see **E23**).

The offence is a qualifying offence for an automatic life sentence under the CJA 2003, sch. 15B (see **B3.15**).

B3.97   A suspended sentence of 12 months' imprisonment for a 40-year-old woman who had had regular sexual intercourse with a boy of 14 was varied so as to be immediate in *A-G's Ref (No. 67 of 2008) (SE)* [2009] 2 Cr App R (S) 428. Giving the judgment of the Court of Appeal, Lord Judge CJ emphasised that the then guideline provided that there should be no distinction in sentence on the grounds of the gender of the offender, save in specified circumstances where a distinction is justified on the basis of the nature of the offence. For examples of the application of the old guideline when the complainant is close to her 16th birthday, see *Cartlidge* [2008] EWCA Crim 2877 and *Kloss* [2008] EWCA Crim 2873. For further examples of the application of the old guideline, see *Shenton* [2009] EWCA Crim 590, *A-G's Ref (No. 72 of 2009)* [2010] 2 Cr App R (S) 58 and *A-G's Ref (No. 26 of 2010)* [2010] EWCA Crim 1084. For an example of the use of the guideline when sentencing for offences of sexual assault of a child pre-dating the 2003 Act, see *Millar* [2009] EWCA Crim 74.

B3.98   **Elements**   The basic elements of the offence are the same as those in respect of such an assault on an adult and reference should therefore be made to **B3.52** to **B3.59**.

As to 'sexual', see **B3.47**. For 'touching', see **B3.58**.

It is a defence if, even though the complainant was under 16, the accused reasonably believed the complainant to be 16 years old or older. The defence is not available if the child is under 13.

The provisions of s. 73 apply to this offence (see **B3.69**).

Causing or Inciting a Child to Engage in Sexual Activity

B3.99   **Sexual Offences Act 2003, s. 10**

  (1) A person aged 18 or over (A) commits an offence if—
     (a) he intentionally causes or incites another person (B) to engage in an activity,
     (b) the activity is sexual, and
     (c) either—
        (i) B is under 16 and A does not reasonably believe that B is 16 or over, or
        (ii) B is under 13.

B3.100   **Procedure**   An allegation of an offence contrary to s. 10 is ordinarily triable either way but, where the activity involves penetration, it is indictable only. As to the classification of the offence for the purpose of listing, see CPD XIII, para. B (see Supplement, **PD-97**). The extra-territorial jurisdiction provisions of s. 72 apply (see **B3.301**).

See **B3.335** for alternative verdicts.

B3.101   Indictment

Statement of Offence

Intentionally causing or inciting a child to engage in a sexual activity contrary to section 10(1) of the Sexual Offences Act 2003.

Particulars of Offence

A, on or about the...day of...[being then a person aged 18 or over] intentionally caused or incited V, then a child under [16] [13] years of age, to engage in a sexual activity, namely... or

A, on or about the...day of...[being then a person aged 18 years or over] intentionally caused or incited V, then a child under the age of [16] [13] years, to engage in sexual activity, namely the penetration of V's [anus] [vagina] by another.

B3.102   **Sentencing**   The maximum sentence for an offence under the SOA 2003, s. 10, varies according to the activity concerned. Section 10(2) and (3) indicate the maximum sentence which applies and in terms almost identical to s. 9(2) and (3) (see **B3.96**). The maximum penalty also varies with the age of the offender; if the offender is aged under 18, the maximum penalty is five years (see **B3.116**).

The Sentencing Council has issued a new guideline applicable to sex offenders aged 18 or over who are sentenced on or after 1 April 2014 (see **B3.3**). For the guideline in respect of an offence under s. 10, see Supplement, **SG-91**. There is a notification requirement under the SOA 2003, s. 80 and sch. 3 (see **E23**).

For examples of the application of the old guideline, see *Price* [2008] EWCA Crim 1974 and *Dennis* [2008] EWCA Crim 2954.

The offence is a qualifying offence for an automatic life sentence under the CJA 2003, sch. 15B (see **B3.15**).

B3.103   **Elements**   The offender must be at least 18 years of age. Plainly, when the victim is under the age of 13, then the offence will be covered by s. 8. A reasonable belief that the victim was at least 16 years of age affords a defence unless the victim was under 13.

For the meaning of 'sexual', see **B3.47**.

Engaging in Sexual Activity in the Presence of a Child

B3.104   Sexual Offences Act 2003, s. 11

(1) A person aged 18 or over (A) commits an offence if—
    (a) he intentionally engages in an activity,
    (b) the activity is sexual,
    (c) for the purpose of obtaining sexual gratification, he engages in it—
        (i) when another person (B) is present or is in a place from which A can be observed, and
        (ii) knowing or believing that B is aware, or intending that B should be aware, that he is engaging in it, and
    (d) either—
        (i) B is under 16 and A does not reasonably believe that B is 16 or over, or
        (ii) B is under 13.

B3.105   **Procedure**   An allegation of an offence contrary to s. 11 is triable either way. As to the classification of the offence for the purpose of listing, see CPD XIII, para. B (see Supplement, **PD-97**). The extra-territorial jurisdiction provisions of s. 72 apply (see **B3.301**).

See **B3.335** for alternative verdicts.

B3.106   Indictment

Statement of Offence

Intentionally engaging in sexual activity in the presence of a child contrary to section 11(1) of the Sexual Offences Act 2003.

Particulars of Offence

A, on or about the…day of…[being then a person aged 18 years or over] intentionally engaged in a sexual activity for the purpose of obtaining sexual gratification from knowing that V, then a child under the age of [16][13] years was present or was in a place from which he could observe A and knew [believed] that V was aware that he was engaging in it [intending that V should be aware that he was engaging in it].

Sentencing   The maximum sentence for an offence under the SOA 2003, s. 11, on indictment is **B3.107** ten years' imprisonment. The maximum penalty varies with the age of the offender; if the offender is aged under 18, the maximum penalty is five years (see **B3.116**). On summary conviction, the maximum sentence is six months or a fine not exceeding the statutory maximum, or both (s. 11(2)).

The Sentencing Council has issued a new guideline applicable to sex offenders aged 18 or over who are sentenced on or after 1 April 2014 (see **B3.3**). For the guideline in respect of an offence under s. 11, see Supplement, **SG-99**. There is a notification requirement under the SOA 2003, s. 80 and sch. 3 (see **E23**).

The offence is a qualifying offence for an automatic life sentence under the CJA 2003, sch. 15B (see **B3.15**).

Elements   The offender must be aged 18 or over and must intentionally engage in sexual activ- **B3.108** ity with a person other than the victim.

It is a defence that the alleged offender reasonably believed the victim to be aged at least 16 unless the victim is under 13.

For 'sexual gratification', see **B3.113**. For the meaning of 'sexual', see **B3.47**.

Causing a Child to Watch a Sex Act

Sexual Offences Act 2003, s. 12   **B3.109**

(1) A person aged 18 or over (A) commits an offence if—
     (a) for the purpose of obtaining sexual gratification, he intentionally causes another person (B) to watch a third person engaging in an activity, or to look at an image of any person engaging in an activity,
     (b) the activity is sexual, and
     (c) either—
         (i)   B is under 16 and A does not reasonably believe that B is 16 or over, or
         (ii)   B is under 13.

Procedure   An allegation of an offence contrary to s. 12 is triable either way. As to the classifi- **B3.110** cation of the offence for the purpose of listing, see CPD XIII, para. B (see Supplement, **PD-97**). The extra-territorial jurisdiction provisions of s. 72 apply (see **B3.301**).

See **B3.335** for alternative verdicts.

Indictment   **B3.111**

Statement of Offence

Causing a child to watch a sexual act contrary to section 12(1) of the Sexual Offences Act 2003.

Particulars of Offence

A, on or about the…day of…[being then a person aged 18 years or over] for the purpose of obtaining sexual gratification for himself intentionally caused V a child under the age of [16][13] years to watch a third person engaging in [or][look at an image of another person engaging in], a sexual activity, the said A not reasonably believing that V was aged 16 or over.

Sentencing   The maximum sentence for an offence under the SOA 2003, s. 12 on conviction **B3.112** on indictment is ten years' imprisonment. On summary conviction the maximum sentence is six months or a fine not exceeding the statutory maximum, or both (s. 12(2)). The maximum penalty also varies with the age of the offender; if the offender is aged under 18, the maximum penalty is five years (see **B3.116**).

The Sentencing Council has issued a new guideline applicable to sex offenders aged 18 or over who are sentenced on or after 1 April 2014 (see **B3.3**). For the guideline in respect of an offence under s. 12, see Supplement, **SG-99**. There is a notification requirement under the SOA 2003, s. 80 and sch. 3 (see **E23**).

The offence is a qualifying offence for an automatic life sentence under the CJA 2003, sch. 15B (see **B3.15**).

B3.113 **Elements** The offender must be aged 18 or over and must intentionally engage in sexual activity with a person other than the victim.

It is a defence that the alleged offender reasonably believed the victim to be aged at least 16 unless the victim was under 13.

For the meaning of 'sexual', see **B3.47**.

In *Abdullahi* [2007] 1 WLR 225, the Court of Appeal considered whether it was necessary for the purposes of s. 12 for the sexual gratification to be simultaneous or contemporaneous or synchronised with the watching of the sexual activity or image. The court ruled that there was nothing in the language of s. 12 to suggest that that was the case and consequently the gratification could be deferred until much later. (For commentary on this case by Professor David Ormerod, see [2007] Crim LR 184.)

The offence has a 'bolted on intent' in that the intentional act must be 'for the purpose of obtaining sexual gratification'. It is therefore an offence of specific intent and, consequently, voluntary intoxication may negate the intent required for the offence (*Heard* [2008] QB 43).

For consideration of the acts necessary to constitute an attempt to commit an offence contrary to s. 12 see *K* [2009] EWCA Crim 1931.

Child Sex Offences Committed by Children or Young Persons

B3.114   Sexual Offences Act 2003, s. 13

(1) A person under 18 commits an offence if he does anything which would be an offence under any of sections 9 to 12 if he were aged 18.
(2) A person guilty of an offence under this section is liable—
    (a) on summary conviction, to imprisonment for a term not exceeding 6 months or a fine not exceeding the statutory maximum or both;
    (b) on conviction on indictment, to imprisonment for a term not exceeding 5 years.

B3.115 **Procedure** An allegation of an offence contrary to s. 13 is triable either way. As to the classification of the offence for the purpose of listing, see CPD XIII, para. B (see Supplement, **PD-97**). The extra-territorial jurisdiction provisions of s. 72 apply (see **B3.301**).

See **B3.335** for alternative verdicts.

For discussion as to the appropriate course to take when there is an issue as to whether D was aged 18 or over at the time of the offence, see **B3.94**.

B3.116 **Sentencing** The maximum sentence for an offence under the SOA 2003, s. 13, on conviction on indictment is five years' imprisonment. On summary conviction, the maximum is six months or a fine not exceeding the statutory maximum, or both (s. 13(2)).

Since the new guideline on sentencing for sexual offences applies only to offenders aged 18 and older, the general principles to be considered in sentencing of youths are in the Sentencing Guidance Council's definitive guideline, *Overarching Principles—Sentencing Youths* (see Supplement, **SG-515**). There is a notification requirement under the SOA 2003, s. 80 and sch. 3, if the offender was sentenced to at least 12 months' imprisonment (see **E23**).

Elements   For the elements of the offences contrary to ss. 9 to 12, see **B3.98**, **B3.103**, **B3.108**   **B3.117**
and **B3.113**.

If the offence charged under s. 13 would amount to an offence under s. 9 if the offender was
aged 18, then the provisions of s. 73 apply (see **B3.69**).

Arranging or Facilitating Commission of a Child Sex Offence

Sexual Offences Act 2003, s. 14   **B3.118**

(1) A person commits an offence if—
   (a) he intentionally arranges or facilitates something that he intends to do, intends another
      person to do, or believes that another person will do, in any part of the world, and
   (b) doing it will involve the commission of an offence under any of sections 9 to 13.
(2) A person does not commit an offence under this section if—
   (a) he arranges or facilitates something that he believes another person will do, but that he
      does not intend to do or intend another person to do, and
   (b) any offence within subsection (1)(b) would be an offence against a child for whose protec-
      tion he acts.
(3) For the purposes of subsection (2), a person acts for the protection of a child if he acts for the
    purpose of—
   (a) protecting the child from sexually transmitted infection,
   (b) protecting the physical safety of the child,
   (c) preventing the child from becoming pregnant, or
   (d) promoting the child's emotional well-being by the giving of advice,
    and not for the purpose of obtaining sexual gratification or for the purpose of causing or
    encouraging the activity constituting the offence within subsection (1)(b) or the child's par-
    ticipation in it.

Procedure   An allegation of an offence contrary to s. 14 is triable either way. As to the classifi-   **B3.119**
cation of the offence for the purpose of listing, see CPD XIII, para. B (see Supplement, **PD-97**).
The extra-territorial jurisdiction provisions of s. 72 apply (see **B3.301**).

See **B3.335** for alternative verdicts.

Indictment   **B3.120**

Statement of Offence

Arranging or facilitating commission of a child sex offence contrary to section 14(1) of the Sexual
Offences Act 2003.

Particulars of Offence

A, on [or about] the…day of…intentionally arranged the doing or facilitating of an act [intend-
ing that it be done] [by himself] [by another] [believing that it would be done by another] [in any
part of the world] and knowing that the doing of it will involve [sexual activity with a child under
16 years of age] [causing or inciting a child under the age of 16 to engage in sexual activity][causing
or inciting a child under 16 years of age to engage in sexual activity][engaging in sexual activity
in the presence of a child under 16 years of age][causing a child under 16 years of age to watch a
sexual act].

Sentencing   The maximum sentence for an offence under the SOA 2003, s. 14, on conviction   **B3.121**
on indictment is 14 years' imprisonment. On summary conviction, the maximum sentence is
six months or a fine not exceeding the statutory maximum, or both (s. 14(4)).

The Sentencing Council has issued a new guideline applicable to sex offenders aged 18 or over
who are sentenced on or after 1 April 2014 (see **B3.3**). For the guideline in respect of an offence
under s. 14, see Supplement, **SG-103**. There is a notification requirement under the SOA 2003,
s. 80 and sch. 3, if the offender was aged 18 or over or was sentenced to at least 12 months'
imprisonment (see **E23**).

The offence is a qualifying offence for an automatic life sentence under the CJA 2003, sch. 15B (see **B3.15**).

B3.122   **Elements**   The elements of offences under the SOA 2003, ss. 9 to 13, are set out in **B3.98**, **B3.103**, **B3.108**, **B3.113** and **B3.117**.

The defence set out in s. 14(2) would cover such acts for the physical and emotional well-being of a child as the provision of contraceptives and the giving of advice as an 'agony aunt'.

R [2009] 1 WLR 713 concerned an appeal against a terminating ruling in respect of an allegation of an offence contrary to s. 14. The accused was a regular client of the principal prosecution witness, a prostitute, and asked her repeatedly whether she knew of any young girls aged 12 or 13 who were working as prostitutes. The witness did not make any inquiries and reported the matter to the police when she received two text messages reading 'Heard owt of 12 lass, let me know' and, on the following day, 'you got the 12 year old sorted yet?' The Crown Court judge ruled that the facts as alleged could not amount to an offence under s. 14, nor an attempt to commit such an offence. The Court of Appeal, in an extempore ruling from Moses LJ, varied that ruling in concluding that the request could amount to an attempt to commit an offence under s. 14, as the acts of preparation criminalised by s. 14 comprise a substantive offence and not an attempt. The purpose of the imposition of criminal liability in that way (as with other sections of the 2003 Act) was to prevent the risk of children being subjected to sexual abuse. The jury was entitled to take the view that what the accused did in making the request was an attempt and not the mere preparation to make the arrangement. The request was the final thing he needed to do to make the arrangement and if the request had been accepted the full offence would have been committed. The Court of Appeal confined itself to whether the facts could establish an attempt to commit such an offence and specifically stated that it did not need to decide whether in merely making the request the accused could properly be said to have committed the full offence. Indeed, Moses LJ said that nothing the court had said was designed to indicate that what was alleged might not indeed constitute the full offence under s. 14.

When the case returned to the Crown Court, *R* was convicted of an attempt to commit an offence contrary to s.14 and sentenced to three years' imprisonment. His conviction was later quashed because of a separate judicial misdirection (*JR* [2008] EWCA Crim 2912).

Meeting a Child following Sexual Grooming

B3.123   Sexual Offences Act 2003, s. 15

(1) A person aged 18 or over (A) commits an offence if—
  (a) A has met or communicated with another person (B) on at least two occasions and subsequently—
    (i) A intentionally meets B,
    (ii) A travels with the intention of meeting B in any part of the world or arranges to meet B in any part of the world, or
    (iii) B travels with the intention of meeting A in any part of the world,
  (b) A intends to do anything to or in respect of B, during or after the meeting mentioned in paragraph (a)(i) to (iii) and in any part of the world, which if done will involve the commission by A of a relevant offence,
  (c) B is under 16, and
  (d) A does not reasonably believe that B is 16 or over.
(2) In subsection (1)—
  (a) the reference to A having met or communicated with B is a reference to A having met B in any part of the world or having communicated with B by any means from, to or in any part of the world;
  (b) 'relevant offence' means—
    (i) an offence under this part,
    (ii) an offence within any of paragraphs 61 to 92 of Schedule 3, or

(iii) anything done outside England and Wales and Northern Ireland which is not an offence within sub-paragraph (i) or (ii) but would be an offence within sub-paragraph (i) if done in England and Wales.

Procedure   An allegation of an offence contrary to s. 15 is triable either way. As to the classification of the offence for the purpose of listing, see CPD XIII, para. B (see Supplement, **PD-97**). The extra-territorial jurisdiction provisions of s. 72 apply (see **B3.301**).   **B3.124**

See **B3.335** for alternative verdicts.

Indictment   **B3.125**

> *Statement of Offence*
>
> Meeting a child following sexual grooming contrary to section 15(1) of the Sexual Offences Act 2003.
>
> *Particulars of Offence*
>
> A, on or about the…day of…having met or communicated with V a child under the age of 16 years on two earlier occasions intentionally met V [travelled with the intention of meeting V] and with intent to [specify facts constituting relevant offence].

Sentencing   The maximum sentence for an offence under the SOA 2003, s. 15, on conviction on indictment is ten years' imprisonment. On summary conviction, the maximum is six months or a fine not exceeding the statutory maximum, or both (s. 15(4)).   **B3.126**

The Sentencing Council has issued a new guideline applicable to sex offenders aged 18 or over who are sentenced on or after 1 April 2014 (see **B3.3**). For the guideline in respect of an offence under s. 15, see Supplement, **SG-104**. There is a notification requirement under the SOA 2003, s. 80 and sch. 3 (see **E23**).

The offence is a qualifying offence for an automatic life sentence under the CJA 2003, sch. 15B (see **B3.15**).

Elements   The offender must be aged 18 or over and a reasonable belief that the victim was 16 or over constitutes a defence.   **B3.127**

A relevant offence is defined under s. 15(2) as being any offence under part 1 or paras. 61 to 92 of sch. 3 to the SOA 2003. Part 1 is comprised of ss. 1 to 79; the sch. 3 paragraphs referred to identify sexual offences under the law of Northern Ireland.

In *G* [2010] EWCA Crim 1693 the Court of Appeal explained that there is absolutely no requirement that any communication which forms part of the grooming be sexual in nature. The only requirement prior to the intentional meeting during which A (over 18) intends to do anything to B (under 16) which, if carried out, would involve the commission by A of a relevant offence is that they have met or communicated 'on at least two occasions'

ABUSE OF A POSITION OF TRUST

Offences involving abuse of a position of trust are contained in ss. 16 to 19 of the SOA 2003. The conditions giving rise to a position of trust between A and B are set out in s. 21.   **B3.128**

The offences set out in ss. 16 to 19 essentially correspond to the offences under ss. 9 to 12 but with the added element of the breach of trust and some other minor differences.

Section 22 provides further definitions relevant to the operation of ss. 16 to 19.

Sections 23 and 24 make specific provision for defences to charges under ss. 16 to 19. Section 23 provides a defence to such a charge if B is aged 16 or over and A and B are either lawfully married or civil partners of each other. Section 24 provides a defence if a lawful sexual relationship existed between A and B before the formation of a relationship between them of the type referred to in s. 21.

The defences provided for by ss. 23 and 24 must be proved by the accused. It is submitted that the burden is evidential.

B3.129   Sexual Offences Act 2003, ss. 21 to 24

21.—(1) For the purposes of sections 16 to 19, a person (A) is in a position of trust in relation to another person (B) if—
(a) any of the following subsections applies, or
(b) any condition specified in an order made by the Secretary of State is met.
(2) This subsection applies if A looks after persons under 18 who are detained in an institution by virtue of a court order or under an enactment, and B is so detained in that institution.
(3) This subsection applies if A looks after persons under 18 who are resident in a home or other place in which—
(a) accommodation and maintenance are provided by an authority in accordance with section 22C(6) of the Children Act 1989, or
(b) accommodation is provided by a voluntary organisation under section 59(1) of that Act and B is resident, and is so provided with accommodation and maintenance or accommodation, in that place.
(4) This subsection applies if A looks after persons under 18 who are accommodated and cared for in one of the following institutions—
(a) a hospital,
(b) in Wales, an independent clinic,
(c) a care home, residential care home or private hospital,
(d) a community home, voluntary home or children's home, or
(e) a home provided under section 82(5) of the Children Act 1989
(f) [repealed]
and B is accommodated and cared for in that institution.
(5) This subsection applies if A looks after persons under 18 who are receiving education at an educational institution and B is receiving, and A is not receiving, education at that institution.
(6) [repealed]
(7) This subsection applies if A is engaged in the provision of services under, or pursuant to anything done under—
(a) sections 8 to 10 of the Employment and Training Act 1973, or
(b) section 68, 70(1)(b) or 74 of the Education and Skills Act 2008,
and, in that capacity, looks after B on an individual basis.
(8) This subsection applies if A regularly has unsupervised contact with B (whether face to face or by any other means)—
(a) in the exercise of functions of a local authority under section 20 or 21 of the Children Act 1989,
(b) [repealed]
(9) This subsection applies if A, as a person who is to report to the court under section 7 of the Children Act 1989 or article 4 of the Children (Northern Ireland) Order 1995 on matters relating to the welfare of B, regularly has unsupervised contact with B (whether face to face or by any other means).
(10) This subsection applies if A is a personal adviser appointed for B under—
(a) section 23B(2) of, or paragraph 19C of Schedule 2 to, the Children Act 1989,
(b) [repealed]
and, in that capacity, looks after B on an individual basis.
(11) This subsection applies if—
(a) B is subject to a care order, a supervision order or an education supervision order, and
(b) in the exercise of functions conferred by virtue of the order on an authorised person or the authority designated by the order, A looks after B on an individual basis.
(12) This subsection applies if A—
(a) is an officer of the Service or Welsh family proceedings officer (within the meaning given by section 35 of the Children Act 2004) appointed for B under section 41(1) of the Children Act 1989,

(b) is appointed a children's guardian of B under rule 6 or rule 18 of the Adoption Rules 1984 (SI 1984/265), or

(c) is appointed to be the guardian ad litem of B under rule 9.5 of the Family Proceedings Rules 1991 (SI 1991/1247)

and, in that capacity, regularly has unsupervised contact with B (whether face to face or by any other means).

(13) This subsection applies if—

    (a) B is subject to requirements imposed by or under an enactment on his release from detention for a criminal offence, or is subject to requirements imposed by a court order made in criminal proceedings, and

    (b) A looks after B on an individual basis in pursuance of the requirements.

22.—(1) The following provisions apply for the purposes of section 21.

(2) Subject to subsection (3), a person looks after persons under 18 if he is regularly involved in caring for, training, supervising or being in sole charge of such persons.

(3) A person (A) looks after another person (B) on an individual basis if—

    (a) A is regularly involved in caring for, training or supervising B, and

    (b) in the course of his involvement, A regularly has unsupervised contact with B (whether face to face or by any other means).

(4) A person receives education at an educational institution if—

    (a) he is registered or otherwise enrolled as a pupil or student at the institution, or

    (b) he receives education at the institution under arrangements with another educational institution at which he is so registered or otherwise enrolled.

(5) [Contains various definitions.]

(6) [Lists services referred to in the definition of hospital in subsection (5).]

23.—(1) Conduct by a person (A) which would otherwise be an offence under any of sections 16 to 19 against another person (B) is not an offence under that section if at the time—

    (a) B is 16 or over, and

    (b) A and B are lawfully married or civil partners of each other.

(2) In proceedings for such an offence it is for the defendant to prove that A and B were at the time lawfully married or civil partners of each other.

24.—(1) Conduct by a person (A) which would otherwise be an offence under any of sections 16 to 19 against another person (B) is not an offence under that section if, immediately before the position of trust arose, a sexual relationship existed between A and B.

(2) Subsection (1) does not apply if at that time sexual intercourse between A and B would have been unlawful.

(3) In proceedings for an offence under any of sections 16 to 19 it is for the defendant to prove that such a relationship existed at that time.

Section 22(5) provides that 'authority' in relation to England and Wales means a local authority and contains definitions of a wide range of other terms used in s. 21.

Abuse of Position of Trust: Sexual Activity with a Child

Sexual Offences Act 2003, s. 16

B3.130

(1) A person aged 18 or over (A) commits an offence if—

    (a) he intentionally touches another person (B),

    (b) the touching is sexual,

    (c) A is in a position of trust in relation to B,

    (d) where subsection (2) applies, A knows or could reasonably be expected to know of the circumstances by virtue of which he is in a position of trust in relation to B, and

    (e) either—

        (i) B is under 18 and A does not reasonably believe that B is 18 or over, or

        (ii) B is under 13.

(2) This subsection applies where A—

    (a) is in a position of trust in relation to B by virtue of circumstances within section 21(2), (3), (4) or (5), and

    (b) is not in such a position of trust by virtue of other circumstances.

(3) Where in proceedings for an offence under this section it is proved that the other person was under 18, the defendant is to be taken not to have reasonably believed that that person was

18 or over unless sufficient evidence is adduced to raise an issue as to whether he reasonably believed it.

(4) Where in proceedings for an offence under this section—

    (a) it is proved that the defendant was in a position of trust in relation to the other person by virtue of circumstances within section 21(2), (3), (4) or (5), and

    (b) it is not proved that he was in such a position of trust by virtue of other circumstances,

it is to be taken that the defendant knew or could reasonably have been expected to know of the circumstances by virtue of which he was in such a position of trust unless sufficient evidence is adduced to raise an issue as to whether he knew or could reasonably have been expected to know of those circumstances.

B3.131   **Procedure**   An allegation of an offence contrary to s. 16 is triable either way. As to the classification of the offence for the purpose of listing, see CPD XIII, para. B (see Supplement, **PD-97**). The extra-territorial jurisdiction provisions of s. 72 apply (see **B3.301**).

See **B3.335** for alternative verdicts.

B3.132   **Indictment**

Statement of Offence

Sexual activity with a child by a person in a position of trust contrary to section 16(1) of the Sexual Offences Act 2003.

Particulars of Offence

A, on or about the…day of…being then a person in a position of trust towards V a child under the age of [18][13] sexually touched V.

B3.133   **Sentencing**   The maximum sentence for an offence under the SOA 2003, s. 16, on conviction on indictment is five years' imprisonment. On summary conviction, the maximum sentence is six months or a fine not exceeding the statutory maximum, or both (s. 16(5)).

The Sentencing Council has issued a new guideline applicable to sex offenders aged 18 or over who are sentenced on or after 1 April 2014 (see **B3.3**). For the guideline in respect of an offence under s. 16, see Supplement, **SG-108**. There is a notification requirement under the SOA 2003, s. 80 and sch. 3, if the offender is imprisoned, detained in a hospital or receives a community sentence of at least 12 months (see **E23**).

B3.134   **Elements**   The basic elements of the offence are the same as required in s. 9 (see **B3.98**). In addition, the offender must be in a position of trust and the victim may be as old as 17.

It is a defence if the accused reasonably believes that the victim is 18 or over when in fact she is not, unless the child is under 13 in which case that defence is not available.

There are two rebuttable presumptions under the SOA 2003, s. 16, which impose an evidential burden on the accused. Under s. 16(3), if it is proved that the victim was under the age of 18, the accused is taken to have not reasonably believed the victim to be over 18 unless sufficient evidence is adduced to raise an issue as to whether the accused did in fact have that reasonable belief. It is then for the prosecution to prove to the criminal standard that he did not have that reasonable belief.

Under s. 16(4), if it is proved that the accused is in a position of trust in relation to the alleged victim by virtue of circumstances within s. 21(2), (3), (4) or (5) and it is not proved that the position of trust arose because of other circumstances, then it is taken that the accused either knew or could reasonably have been expected to know of the circumstances placing him in a position of trust unless sufficient evidence is adduced to raise an issue as to whether he did in fact know or could have reasonably been expected to know of the circumstances founding the position of trust. Once sufficient evidence has been adduced then, as with s. 16(3), it is for the prosecution to prove the contrary to the criminal standard.

The provisions of s. 73 apply to this offence (see **B3.69**).

Abuse of Position of Trust: Causing or Inciting a Child to Engage in Sexual Activity

Sexual Offences Act 2003, s. 17

B3.135

(1) A person aged 18 or over (A) commits an offence if—
   (a) he intentionally causes or incites another person (B) to engage in an activity,
   (b) the activity is sexual,
   (c) A is in a position of trust in relation to B,
   (d) where subsection (2) applies, A knows or could reasonably be expected to know of the circumstances by virtue of which he is in a position of trust in relation to B, and
   (e) either—
      (i) B is under 18 and A does not reasonably believe that B is 18 or over, or
      (ii) B is under 13.

Procedure   An allegation of an offence contrary to s. 17 is triable either way. As to the classification of the offence for the purpose of listing, see CPD XIII, para. B (see Supplement, PD-97). The extra-territorial provisions of s. 72 apply (see **B3.301**).

B3.136

See **B3.335** for alternative verdicts.

Indictment

B3.137

Statement of Offence

Causing or inciting a child by a person in a position of trust to engage in sexual activity contrary to section 17(1) of the Sexual Offences Act 2003.

Particulars of Offence

A, on or about the...day of...being then in a position of trust towards V a child under the age of [18][13] caused or incited V to engage in a sexual activity.

Sentencing   The maximum sentence for an offence under the SOA 2003, s. 17, is the same as that for a s. 16 offence (see **B3.133**).

B3.138

The Sentencing Council has issued a new guideline applicable to sex offenders aged 18 or over who are sentenced on or after 1 April 2014 (see **B3.3**). For the guideline in respect of an offence under s. 17, see Supplement, **SG-108**. There is a notification requirement under the SOA 2003, s. 80 and sch. 3, if the offender is imprisoned, detained in a hospital or receives a community sentence of at least 12 months (see **E23**). For examples of the application of the old guideline, see *Howell* [2007] EWCA Crim 1863 and *Wilson* [2008] 1 Cr App R (S) 542.

Elements   The basic elements of an offence contrary to s. 17 are the same as those under s. 10 (see **B3.103**) but there are some differences: the offender must be in a position of trust and the victim may be as old as 17. The same assumptions apply as under s. 16 (see **B3.134**).

B3.139

Abuse of Position of Trust: Sexual Activity in Presence of Child

Sexual Offences Act 2003, s. 18

B3.140

(1) A person aged 18 or over (A) commits an offence if—
   (a) he intentionally engages in an activity,
   (b) the activity is sexual,
   (c) for the purpose of obtaining sexual gratification, he engages in it—
      (i) when another person (B) is present or is in a place from which A can be observed, and
      (ii) knowing or believing that B is aware, or intending that B should be aware, that he is engaging in it,
   (d) A is in a position of trust in relation to B,
   (e) where subsection (2) applies, A knows or could reasonably be expected to know of the circumstances by virtue of which he is in a position of trust in relation to B, and
   (f) either—
      (i) B is under 18 and A does not reasonably believe that B is 18 or over, or
      (ii) B is under 13.

B3.141 **Procedure** An allegation of an offence contrary to s. 18 is triable either way. As to the classification of the offence for the purpose of listing, see CPD XIII, para. B (see Supplement, **PD-97**). The extra-territorial jurisdiction provisions of s. 72 apply (see **B3.301**).

See **B3.335** for alternative verdicts.

B3.142 **Sentencing** The maximum sentence for an offence under the SOA 2003, s. 18, is the same as that for a s. 16 offence (see **B3.133**). The Sentencing Council has issued a new guideline applicable to sex offenders aged 18 or over who are sentenced on or after 1 April 2014 (see **B3.3**). For the guideline in respect of an offence under s. 18, see Supplement, **SG-112**.

There is a notification requirement under the SOA 2003, s. 80 and sch. 3, if the offender is imprisoned, detained in a hospital or receives a community sentence of at least 12 months (see **E23**).

B3.143 **Elements** The basic elements of an offence contrary to s. 18 are the same as those under s. 11 (see **B3.108**) but there are some differences. The differences are that the offender must be in a position of trust and the victim may be as old as 17. The same assumptions apply as under s. 16 (see **B3.134**).

For 'gratification', see **B3.113**.

Abuse of Position of Trust: Causing a Child to Watch a Sexual Act

B3.144

Sexual Offences Act 2003, s. 19

(1) A person aged 18 or over (A) commits an offence if—
    (a) for the purpose of obtaining sexual gratification, he intentionally causes another person (B) to watch a third person engaging in an activity, or to look at an image of any person engaging in an activity,
    (b) the activity is sexual,
    (c) A is in a position of trust in relation to B,
    (d) where subsection (2) applies, A knows or could reasonably be expected to know of the circumstances by virtue of which he is in a position of trust in relation to B, and
    (e) either—
        (i) B is under 18 and A does not reasonably believe that B is 18 or over, or
        (ii) B is under 13.

B3.145 **Procedure** An allegation of an offence contrary to s. 19 is triable either way. As to the classification of the offence for the purpose of listing, see CPD XIII, para. B (see Supplement, **PD-97**). The extra-territorial jurisdiction provisions of s. 72 apply (see **B3.301**).

See **B3.335** for alternative verdicts.

B3.146 **Sentencing** The maximum sentence for an offence under the SOA 2003, s. 19, is the same as that for an offence under s. 16 (see **B3.133**).

The Sentencing Council has issued a new guideline applicable to sex offenders aged 18 or over who are sentenced on or after 1 April 2014 (see **B3.3**). For the guideline in respect of an offence under s. 19, see Supplement, **SG-112**. There is a notification requirement under the SOA 2003, s. 80 and sch. 3, if the offender is imprisoned, detained in a hospital or receives a community sentence of at least 12 months (see **E23**).

B3.147 **Elements** The basic elements of an offence contrary to s. 19 are the same as those under s. 12 (see **B3.113**) but there are some differences. The differences are that the offender must be in a position of trust and the victim may be as old as 17. The same assumptions apply as under s. 16 (see **B3.134**).

For 'gratification', see **B3.113**.

FAMILIAL CHILD SEX OFFENCES

In ss. 25 and 26, the SOA 2003 creates two gender-neutral offences which are designed to counter the sexual abuse and exploitation of children within the 'family unit'. Section 25 creates an offence of sexual activity with a child family member and s. 26 creates an offence of inciting a child family member to engage in sexual activity. There are common features of each offence governed by ss. 27, 28 and 29. Section 27 defines which relationships between A and B are relevant for the purposes of those sections. Section 28 provides a defence to a charge under s. 25 or s. 26 if B is aged 16 or over and A and B are either lawfully married or civil partners of each other. Section 29 provides a defence if a lawful sexual relationship existed between A and B before the formation of a relationship between them of the type referred to in s. 27(3), (4) or (5). If the relationship is one referred to in s. 27(2) (see below), or would fall within that subsection if B had not been adopted by another, then the defence is not available.

B3.148

The defences provided for by ss. 28 and 29 must be proved by the accused. It is submitted that the burden is evidential.

Sexual Offences Act 2003, ss. 27 to 29

B3.149

27.—(1) The relation of one person (A) to another (B) is within this section if—
  (a) it is within any of subsections (2) to (4), or
  (b) it would be within one of those subsections but for section 39 of the Adoption Act 1976 or section 67 of the Adoption and Children Act 2002 (status conferred by adoption).
(2) The relation of A to B is within this subsection if—
  (a) one of them is the other's parent, grandparent, brother, sister, half-brother, half-sister, aunt or uncle, or
  (b) A is or has been B's foster parent.
(3) The relation of A to B is within this subsection if A and B live or have lived in the same household, or A is or has been regularly involved in caring for, training, supervising or being in sole charge of B, and—
  (a) one of them is or has been the other's step-parent,
  (b) A and B are cousins,
  (c) one of them is or has been the other's stepbrother or stepsister, or
  (d) the parent or present or former foster parent of one of them is or has been the other's foster parent.
(4) The relation of A to B is within this subsection if—
  (a) A and B live in the same household, and
  (b) A is regularly involved in caring for, training, supervising or being in sole charge of B.
(5) For the purposes of this section—
  (a) 'aunt' means the sister or half-sister of a person's parent, and 'uncle' has a corresponding meaning;
  (b) 'cousin' means the child of an aunt or uncle;
  (c) a person is a child's foster parent if—
    (i) he is a person with whom the child has been placed under section 23(2)(a) or 59(1)(a) of the Children Act 1989 in a placement falling within subsection (6)(a) or (b) of that section (placement with local authority foster parent),
    (ia) he is a person with whom the child has been placed under section 59(1)(a) of that Act (placement by voluntary organisation), or
    (ii) he fosters the child privately, within the meaning given by section 66(1)(b) of that Act;
  (d) a person is another's partner (whether they are of different sexes or the same sex) if they live together as partners in an enduring family relationship;
  (e) 'step-parent' includes a parent's partner and 'stepbrother' and 'stepsister' include the child of a parent's partner.
28.—(1) Conduct by a person (A) which would otherwise be an offence under section 25 or 26 against another person (B) is not an offence under that section if at the time—
  (a) B is 16 or over, and
  (b) A and B are lawfully married or civil partners of each other.

(2) In proceedings for such an offence it is for the defendant to prove that A and B were at the time lawfully married or civil partners of each other.

29.—(1) Conduct by a person (A) which would otherwise be an offence under section 25 or 26 against another person (B) is not an offence under that section if—

(a) the relation of A to B is not within subsection (2) of section 27,

(b) it would not be within that subsection if section 39 of the Adoption Act 1976 or section 67 of the Adoption and Children Act 2002 did not apply, and

(c) immediately before the relation of A to B first became such as to fall within section 27, a sexual relationship existed between A and B.

(2) Subsection (1) does not apply if at the time referred to in subsection (1)(c) sexual intercourse between A and B would have been unlawful.

(3) In proceedings for an offence under section 25 or 26 it is for the defendant to prove the matters mentioned in subsection (1)(a) to (c).

Sexual Activity with a Child Family Member

B3.150   Sexual Offences Act 2003, s. 25

(1) A person (A) commits an offence if—

(a) he intentionally touches another person (B),

(b) the touching is sexual,

(c) the relation of A to B is within section 27,

(d) A knows or could reasonably be expected to know that his relation to B is of a description falling within that section, and

(e) either—

(i) B is under 18 and A does not reasonably believe that B is 18 or over, or

(ii) B is under 13.

(2) Where in proceedings for an offence under this section it is proved that the other person was under 18, the defendant is to be taken not to have reasonably believed that that person was 18 or over unless sufficient evidence is adduced to raise an issue as to whether he reasonably believed it.

(3) Where in proceedings for an offence under this section it is proved that the relation of the defendant to the other person was of a description falling within section 27, it is to be taken that the defendant knew or could reasonably have been expected to know that his relation to the other person was of that description unless sufficient evidence is adduced to raise an issue as to whether he knew or could reasonably have been expected to know that it was.

B3.151 **Procedure**   An allegation of an offence contrary to s. 25 is triable either way unless the alleged offender is 18 or over at the time of the offence and penetration is involved, in which case the allegation is triable on indictment only. As to the classification of the offence for the purpose of listing, see CPD XIII, para. B (see Supplement, **PD-97**). The extra-territoriality provisions of s. 72 apply (see **B3.301**).

See **B3.335** for alternative verdicts.

B3.152 Indictment

Statement of Offence

Sexual activity with a child family member contrary to section 25(1) of the Sexual Offences Act 2003.

Particulars of Offence

A on or about the…day of…being then in a family relationship to V, a child then under the age of [18][13] years sexually touched V

or

A, on or about the…day of…being then in a family relationship to V, a child then under the age of [18] [13] years, sexually touched V by penetrating V's [anus] [vagina] with a part of his body [an object] or [by penetrating V's mouth with his penis]

or

A, on or about the…day of…being then in a family relationship to V, a child then under the age of [18] [13] years, sexually touched V by allowing V to penetrate A's [anus] [vagina] with a part of V's body [an object] or [by allowing V to penetrate A's mouth with his penis].

Sentencing Where the accused is over 18 and the activity involved penetration, the maximum penalty for an offence under the SOA 2003, s. 25, is 14 years' imprisonment. In the case of any other activity and where the offender is aged 18 or over, the maximum penalty on conviction on indictment remains at 14 years but, on summary conviction, it is six months or a fine not exceeding the statutory maximum, or both. The maximum penalty where the offender is aged under 18 is five years on conviction on indictment and, on summary conviction, it is six months or a fine not exceeding the statutory maximum, or both (s. 25(4) to (6)). **B3.153**

The Sentencing Council has issued a new guideline applicable to sex offenders aged 18 or over who are sentenced on or after 1 April 2014 (see **B3.3**). For the guideline in respect of an offence under s. 25, see Supplement, **SG-95**. There is a notification requirement under the SOA 2003, s. 80 and sch. 3, if the offender is imprisoned, detained in a hospital or receives a community sentence of at least 12 months (see **E23**).

For examples of the application of the old guideline, see *SM* [2008] EWCA Crim 1459 and *Degraag* [2008] EWCA Crim 3175. For an example of exceptional circumstances justifying the imposition of a non-custodial sentence, see *SG* [2010] EWCA Crim 1250.

The offence is a qualifying offence for an automatic life sentence under the CJA 2003, sch. 15B, if the offender is aged 18 or over at the time of the offence (see **B3.15**).

Elements The basic elements of the offence are the same as those in s. 9 (see **B3.98**) but with the additional necessity of the existence of a relationship between the parties of the kind encompassed by s. 27. **B3.154**

For 'sexual', see **B3.47**. As to 'touching', see **B3.58**.

The provisions of s. 73 apply (see **B3.69**) where the alleged victim is less than 16 years old.

Inciting a Child Family Member to Engage in Sexual Activity

Sexual Offences Act 2003, s. 26 **B3.155**

(1) A person (A) commits an offence if—
    (a) he intentionally incites another person (B) to touch, or allow himself to be touched by, A,
    (b) the touching is sexual,
    (c) the relation of A to B is within section 27,
    (d) A knows or could reasonably be expected to know that his relation to B is of a description falling within that section, and
    (e) either—
        (i) B is under 18 and A does not reasonably believe that B is 18 or over, or
        (ii) B is under 13.

Procedure An allegation of an offence contrary to s. 26 is triable either way unless the accused is aged 18 or over at the time of the offence and penetration is involved, in which case the allegation is triable on indictment only. As to the classification of the offence for the purpose of listing, see CPD XIII, para. B (see Supplement, **PD-97**). The extra-territorial jurisdiction provisions of s. 72 apply (see **B3.301**). **B3.156**

See **B3.335** for alternative verdicts.

Indictment **B3.157**

Statement of Offence

Inciting a child family member to engage in sexual activity contrary to section 26 of the Sexual Offences Act 2003.

Particulars of Offence

A, on or about the…day of…being then in a family relationship to V, a child under the age of [18] [13] years incited V [to touch A sexually] [to allow himself to be touched by A sexually].

B3.158   **Sentencing**   The provisions as to penalties for an offence under the SOA 2003, s. 26, are contained in s. 26(4) to (6) and are in identical terms to s. 25(4) to (6) (see **B3.153**).

The Sentencing Council has issued a new guideline applicable to sex offenders aged 18 or over who are sentenced on or after 1 April 2014 (see **B3.3**). For the guideline in respect of an offence under s. 26, see Supplement, **SG-95**. There is a notification requirement under the SOA 2003, s. 80 and sch. 3, if the offender was aged 18 or over or was sentenced to at least 12 months' imprisonment (see **E23**).

The offence is a qualifying offence for an automatic life sentence under the CJA 2003, sch. 15B, if the offender is aged 18 or over at the time of the offence (see **B3.15**).

B3.159   **Elements**   The elements of this offence are similar to those in respect of a s. 10 offence (see **B3.103**) but the offence is much more limited in scope, being restricted to incitement and applying only to sexual touching.

For 'incitement', see **B3.91**. For 'sexual', see **B3.47**. For 'touching', see **B3.58**.

OFFENCES AGAINST PERSONS WITH A MENTAL DISORDER IMPEDING CHOICE

B3.160   Sections 30 to 41 of the SOA 2003 cover a wide range of offences designed to protect persons of either gender who suffer from a mental disorder. The legislation is wider than any previous enactments to protect people vulnerable as a result of their mental state. By virtue of s. 79(6), 'mental disorder' is as defined in s. 1 of the Mental Health Act 1983, and so a person with a learning difficulty finds protection in the Act. In addition, activities prohibited by the Act extend beyond sexual intercourse and indecent assault to sexual touching of a mentally disordered person, the causing or inciting of sexual activity by a mentally disordered person, engaging in sexual activity in the presence of a mentally disordered person and causing a mentally disordered person to watch sexual activity.

Sections 30 to 33 govern offences arising out of sexual activity with persons with a mental disorder which impedes their capacity for choice.

Sexual Activity with a Person with a Mental Disorder Impeding Choice

B3.161   Sexual Offences Act 2003, s. 30

(1) A person (A) commits an offence if—
   (a) he intentionally touches another person (B),
   (b) the touching is sexual,
   (c) B is unable to refuse because of or for a reason related to a mental disorder, and
   (d) A knows or could reasonably be expected to know that B has a mental disorder and that because of it or for a reason related to it B is likely to be unable to refuse.
(2) B is unable to refuse if—
   (a) he lacks the capacity to choose whether to agree to the touching (whether because he lacks sufficient understanding of the nature or reasonably foreseeable consequences of what is being done, or for any other reason), or
   (b) he is unable to communicate such a choice to A.

B3.162   **Procedure**   An allegation of an offence contrary to s. 30 is triable either way unless the conduct involves penetration, in which case it is triable only on indictment. As to the classification of the offence for the purpose of listing, see CPD XIII, para. B (see Supplement, **PD-97**). The extra-territorial jurisdiction provisions of s. 72 apply when the victim was under 18 at the time of the offence (see **B3.301**).

See **B3.335** for alternative verdicts.

Indictment   **B3.163**

Statement of Offence

Sexual touching of a person who was then unable to refuse because of a reason relating to a mental disorder contrary to section 30(1) of the Sexual Offences Act 2003.

Particulars of Offence

A, on or about the...day of...intentionally sexually touched V a person who he knew [ought reasonably to have known] was unable to refuse to be touched by reason of a mental disorder

or

A, on or about the...day of...sexually touched V, a person who he knew [ought reasonably to have known] was unable to refuse to be touched by reason of a mental disorder by penetrating V's [anus] [vagina] with a part of his, A's, body [an object]

or

A, on or about the...day of...sexually touched V, a person who he knew [ought reasonably to have known] was unable to refuse to be touched by reason of a mental disorder by allowing V to penetrate A's [anus] [vagina] with a part of his, V's, body [to penetrate A's mouth with his, V's, penis].

Sentencing   The maximum penalty applicable is determined by the nature of the activity.   **B3.164**

Sexual Offences Act 2003, s. 30

(3) A person guilty of an offence under this section, if the touching involved—
    (a) penetration of B's anus or vagina with a part of A's body or anything else,
    (b) penetration of B's mouth with A's penis,
    (c) penetration of A's anus or vagina with a part of B's body, or
    (d) penetration of A's mouth with B's penis, is liable, on conviction on indictment, to imprisonment for life.
(4) Unless subsection (3) applies, a person guilty of an offence under this section is liable—
    (a) on summary conviction, to imprisonment for a term not exceeding 6 months or to a fine not exceeding the statutory maximum or both;
    (b) on conviction on indictment, to imprisonment for a term not exceeding 14 years.

It is a curiosity of the section that in the case of penetration by touching, the maximum penalty is enhanced where A commits the offence by penetration by a part of the body or by an object, but where the essence of the offence is allowing B to penetrate A's anus or vagina, penetration by an object is not comprehended. Penetration enhances the maximum penalty where it is with a part of B's body.

The Sentencing Council has issued a new guideline applicable to sex offenders aged 18 or over who are sentenced on or after 1 April 2014 (see **B3.3**). For the guideline in respect of an offence under s. 30, see Supplement, **SG-140**. There is a notification requirement under the SOA 2003, s. 80 and sch. 3 (see **E23**).

The offence is a qualifying offence for an automatic life sentence under the CJA 2003, sch. 15B, if the offender is liable on conviction to imprisonment for life (see **B3.15**).

See *A-G's Ref (No. 75 of 2007)* [2007] EWCA Crim 2266 and *Clements* [2009] 2 Cr App R (S)   **B3.165**
644 for examples of sentencing decisions under the previous guideline which may be of assistance when considering the likely sentence under the new guideline.

Elements   The elements of the offence are essentially the same as those required for an offence   **B3.166**
under s. 9 (see **B3.98**) but with the additional elements concerning the victim's mental disorder (see s. 30(1)(c)) and the *mens rea* of the accused (see s. 30(1)(d)).

In *Hulme v DPP* (2006) 170 JP 598, a woman with cerebral palsy and a mental age well below her actual age of 27 could not communicate her feelings as to sexual acts in a way that a person of her age without her disabilities would be able to. The evidence was that when H touched her private parts she did not know what to do or say but it made her sad, hurt and upset. She was therefore unable to communicate her choice within the meaning of s. 30 because of or for a reason related to a mental disorder and thus 'unable to refuse'.

B3.167 The House of Lords considered the ambit of the phrases 'capacity to choose' and 'unable to communicate' in ss. 30 to 33 of the Act in *Cooper* [2009] 4 All ER 33. Their lordships held that the Court of Appeal had been wrong in holding that a lack of capacity to choose cannot be person or situation specific and had been wrong in holding that an irrational fear that prevents the exercise of choice cannot be equated with a lack of capacity to choose. Moreover, s. 30(2)(b) did not require that a complainant was physically unable to communicate by reason of her mental disorder. In a speech with which the other Law Lords agreed, Baroness Hale observed that it was not necessary to decide whether the reasoning of Munby J contained in family law cases which had underpinned the judgment of the Court of Appeal was correct (see **B3.21**); the SOA 2003 made the position clear. Under s. 30(2)(a), a person is unable to refuse if he lacks the capacity to choose whether to agree to the touching, whether because he lacks sufficient understanding of the nature or reasonably foreseeable consequences of what is being done 'or for any other reason'. Provided that the inability to refuse is, under s. 30(2)(c) 'because of or for a reason related to a mental disorder', and the other ingredients of the offence are proved, the perpetrator is guilty. Baroness Hale said that the words 'for any other reason' are plainly capable of encompassing a wide range of circumstances in which a person's mental disorder may rob them of the ability to make an autonomous choice, even though they may have sufficient understanding of the information relevant to making it. These could include the kind of compulsion which drives a person with anorexia to refuse food or the phobia (or irrational fear) which drives a person to refuse a life-saving injection. Moreover, the capacity to choose can be situation or person specific. The SOA 2003 refers to 'the' touching and is therefore concerned with the specific act of touching with which the accused is charged. Once it is accepted that choice is an exercise of free will and that the mental disorder may rob the person of such free will then a mentally disordered person may be quite capable of refusing touching in one situation rather than another. Whilst the complainant was unable to refuse in the vulnerable and terrifying circumstances in which the accused had placed her, she might well have been able to refuse a person who had not placed her in a situation of that nature: 'One does not consent to sex in general. One consents to this act of sex with this person at this time and in this place' (at [27]). Such an approach is in keeping with the concept of autonomy in matters of private life guaranteed by the ECHR, Article 8. There is no justification for limiting the requisite inability to communicate to physical inability. Baroness Hale observed that an offence under s. 1 or s. 34 could have been proceeded with in these circumstances (see **B3.21**).

The provisions of s. 73 apply to this offence (see **B3.69**) when the alleged victim is less than 16 years old.

Causing or Inciting a Person with a Mental Disorder Impeding Choice to Engage in Sexual Activity

B3.168
Sexual Offences Act 2003, s. 31

(1) A person (A) commits an offence if—
   (a) he intentionally causes or incites another person (B) to engage in an activity,
   (b) the activity is sexual,
   (c) B is unable to refuse because of or for a reason related to a mental disorder, and
   (d) A knows or could reasonably be expected to know that B has a mental disorder and that because of it or for a reason related to it B is likely to be unable to refuse.
(2) B is unable to refuse if—
   (a) he lacks the capacity to choose whether to agree to engaging in the activity caused or incited (whether because he lacks sufficient understanding of the nature or reasonably foreseeable consequences of the activity, or for any other reason), or
   (b) he is unable to communicate such a choice to A.

Procedure   An allegation of an offence contrary to s. 31 is triable either way unless the con-   **B3.169**
duct involves penetration, in which case it is triable only on indictment. As to the classification of the offence for the purpose of listing, see CPD XIII, para. B (see Supplement, **PD-97**).
The extra-territorial jurisdiction provisions of s. 72 apply (see **B3.301**).

See **B3.335** for alternative verdicts.

Indictment   **B3.170**

Statement of Offence

Causing or inciting a person who was then unable to refuse because of a mental disorder impeding choice to engage in sexual activity contrary to section 31(1) of the Sexual Offences Act
2003.

Particulars of Offence

A, on or about the…day of…intentionally caused or incited V a person who he knew [ought
reasonably to have known] was unable to refuse consent to the said activity by reason of mental
disorder to engage in a sexual activity

or

A, on or about the…day of…intentionally caused or incited V, a person who he knew [ought
reasonably to have known] was unable to refuse consent to the said activity by reason of mental
disorder, to engage in a sexual activity, namely, causing or inciting the penetration of V's [anus]
[vagina] or [V's mouth with the penis of another]

Sentencing   The provisions as to the maximum sentence for an offence under s. 31 are the   **B3.171**
same as those which apply in respect of an offence under s. 30 (see **B3.164**).

The Sentencing Council has issued a new guideline applicable to sex offenders aged 18 or over
who are sentenced on or after 1 April 2014 (see **B3.3**). For the guideline in respect of an offence
under s. 31, see Supplement, **SG-140**. There is a notification requirement under the SOA 2003,
s. 80 and sch. 3 (see **E23**).

The offence is a qualifying offence for an automatic life sentence under the CJA 2003, sch. 15B,
if the offender is liable on conviction to imprisonment for life (see **B3.15**).

Elements   The elements of the offence are essentially the same as those required for an offence   **B3.172**
under s. 10 (see **B3.103**), but with the additional elements concerning the victim's mental disorder (see s. 31(1)(c)) and the accused's *mens rea* (see s. 31(1)(d)).

Engaging in Sexual Activity in the Presence of a Person with a Mental Disorder

Sexual Offences Act 2003, s. 32   **B3.173**

(1) A person (A) commits an offence if—
    (a) he intentionally engages in an activity,
    (b) the activity is sexual,
    (c) for the purpose of obtaining sexual gratification, he engages in it—
       (i) when another person (B) is present or is in a place from which A can be observed,
         and
      (ii) knowing or believing that B is aware, or intending that B should be aware, that he is
         engaging in it,
    (d) B is unable to refuse because of or for a reason related to a mental disorder, and
    (e) A knows or could reasonably be expected to know that B has a mental disorder and that
      because of it or for a reason related to it B is likely to be unable to refuse.
(2) B is unable to refuse if—
    (a) he lacks the capacity to choose whether to agree to being present (whether because
      he lacks sufficient understanding of the nature of the activity, or for any other rea-
      son), or
    (b) he is unable to communicate such a choice to A.

B3.174 **Procedure**   An allegation of an offence contrary to s. 32 is triable either way. As to the classification of the offence for the purpose of listing, see CPD XIII, para. B (see Supplement, **PD-97**). The extra-territorial jurisdiction provisions of s. 72 apply where the victim was aged under 18 at the time of the offence (see **B3.301**).

See **B3.335** for alternative verdicts.

B3.175 **Sentencing**   The maximum sentence for an offence under the SOA 2003, s. 32, on conviction on indictment is ten years' imprisonment. On summary conviction, the maximum sentence is six months or a fine not exceeding the statutory maximum, or both (s. 32(3)).

The Sentencing Council has issued a new guideline applicable to sex offenders aged 18 or over who are sentenced on or after 1 April 2014 (see **B3.3**). For the guideline in respect of an offence under s. 32, see Supplement, **SG-144**. There is a notification requirement under the SOA 2003, s. 80 and sch. 3 (see **E23**).

B3.176 **Elements**   The elements of the offence are essentially the same as those required for an offence under s. 11 (see **B3.108**) but with the additional elements concerning the victim's mental disorder (see s. 3(1)(c)) and the accused's *mens rea* (see s. 32(1)(d)).

For 'gratification', see **B3.113**.

Causing a Person with a Mental Disorder Impeding Choice to Watch a Sexual Act

B3.177   Sexual Offences Act 2003, s. 33

(1) A person (A) commits an offence if—
  (a) for the purpose of obtaining sexual gratification, he intentionally causes another person (B) to watch a third person engaging in an activity, or to look at an image of any person engaging in an activity,
  (b) the activity is sexual,
  (c) B is unable to refuse because of or for a reason related to a mental disorder, and
  (d) A knows or could reasonably be expected to know that B has a mental disorder and that because of it or for a reason related to it B is likely to be unable to refuse.
(2) B is unable to refuse if—
  (a) he lacks the capacity to choose whether to agree to watching or looking (whether because he lacks sufficient understanding of the nature of the activity, or for any other reason), or
  (b) he is unable to communicate such a choice to A.

B3.178 **Procedure**   An allegation of an offence contrary to s. 33 is triable either way. As to the classification of the offence for the purpose of listing, see CPD XIII, para. B (see Supplement, **PD-97**). The extra-territorial jurisdiction provisions of s. 72 apply where the victim was aged under 18 at the time of the offence (see **B3.301**).

See **B3.335** for alternative verdicts.

B3.179 **Sentencing**   The maximum sentence for an offence under the SOA 2003, s. 33, on conviction on indictment is ten years' imprisonment. On summary conviction, the maximum is six months or a fine not exceeding the statutory maximum, or both (s. 33(3)).

The Sentencing Council has issued a new guideline applicable to sex offenders aged 18 or over who are sentenced on or after 1 April 2014 (see **B3.3**). For the guideline in respect of an offence under s. 33, see Supplement, **SG-144**. There is a notification requirement under the SOA 2003, s. 80 and sch. 3 (see **E23**).

B3.180 **Elements**   The elements of the offence are essentially the same as those required for an offence under s. 12 (see **B3.113**) but with the additional elements concerning the victim's mental disorder (see s. 33(1)(c)) and the accused's *mens rea* (see s. 33(1)(d)).

For 'gratification', see **B3.113**.

INDUCEMENTS TO PERSONS WITH A MENTAL DISORDER

Sections 34 to 37 cover sexual activity in relation to a mentally disordered victim where agreement is obtained by inducement, threat or deception.   **B3.181**

Inducement, Threat or Deception to Procure Sexual Activity with a Person

Sexual Offences Act 2003, s. 34   **B3.182**

(1) A person (A) commits an offence if—
   (a) with the agreement of another person (B) he intentionally touches that person,
   (b) the touching is sexual,
   (c) A obtains B's agreement by means of an inducement offered or given, a threat made or a deception practised by A for that purpose,
   (d) B has a mental disorder, and
   (e) A knows or could reasonably be expected to know that B has a mental disorder.

Procedure   An allegation of an offence contrary to s. 34 is triable either way unless the conduct   **B3.183** involves penetration, in which case it is triable only on indictment. As to the classification of the offence for the purpose of listing, see CPD XIII, para. B (see Supplement, **PD-97**). The extra-territorial jurisdiction provisions of s. 72 apply where the victim was aged under 18 at the time of the offence (see **B3.301**).

See **B3.335** for alternative verdicts.

Indictment   **B3.184**

Statement of Offence

Intentionally sexually touching a person suffering from mental disorder by agreement procured by inducement, threat or deception contrary to section 34(1) of the Sexual Offences Act 2003.

Particulars of Offence

A, on or about the…day of…sexually touched V *[by penetration…by procuring penetration]* a person who he then knew or ought reasonably to have known suffered from a mental disorder by agreement procured by an inducement offered or given, a threat made or a deception practised on V.

Sentencing   The maximum sentence varies according to the nature of the activity involved.   **B3.185**

Sexual Offences Act 2003, s. 34

(2) A person guilty of an offence under this section, if the touching involved—
   (a) penetration of B's anus or vagina with a part of A's body or anything else,
   (b) penetration of B's mouth with A's penis,
   (c) penetration of A's anus or vagina with a part of B's body, or
   (d) penetration of A's mouth with B's penis,
is liable, on conviction on indictment, to imprisonment for life.
(3) Unless subsection (2) applies, a person guilty of an offence under this section is liable—
   (a) on summary conviction, to imprisonment for a term not exceeding 6 months or a fine not exceeding the statutory maximum or both;
   (b) on conviction on indictment, to imprisonment for a term not exceeding 14 years.

Note that where B penetrates A, the penalty is only enhanced where penetration is by part of B's body.

The Sentencing Council has issued a new guideline applicable to sex offenders aged 18 or over who are sentenced on or after 1 April 2014 (see **B3.3**). For the guideline in respect of an offence under s. 34, see Supplement, **SG-148**. There is a notification requirement under the SOA 2003, s. 80 and sch. 3 (see **E23**).

The offence is a qualifying offence for an automatic life sentence under the CJA 2003, sch. 15B, if the offender is liable on conviction to imprisonment for life (see **B3.15**).

B3.186 **Elements**   The elements of the offence are essentially the same as those under s. 9 (see **B3.98**) but also include additional features relating to the agreement obtained by means of an inducement, threat or deception, the mental disorder of the victim and the *mens rea* of the accused. The Home Office Explanatory Notes to the 2003 Act give examples of what might be sufficient to constitute an inducement, threat or deception. An inducement might be the promise of anything from sweets to a holiday; a threat might be a statement by the offender that he would hurt a member of the victim's family; and a deception might be a statement by the offender that the victim will get into trouble if he does not engage in sexual activity.

The provisions of s. 73 apply (see **B3.69**) when the alleged victim is under 16 years of age.

Causing a Person with a Mental Disorder to Engage in or Agree to Engage in Sexual Activity by Inducement, Threat or Deception

B3.187   Sexual Offences Act 2003, s. 35

   (1) A person (A) commits an offence if—
      (a) by means of an inducement offered or given, a threat made or a deception practised by him for this purpose, he intentionally causes another person (B) to engage in, or to agree to engage in, an activity,
      (b) the activity is sexual,
      (c) B has a mental disorder, and
      (d) A knows or could reasonably be expected to know that B has a mental disorder.

B3.188 **Procedure**   An allegation of an offence contrary to s. 35 is triable either way unless the conduct involves penetration, in which case it is triable only on indictment. As to the classification of the offence for the purpose of listing, see CPD XIII, para. B (see Supplement, **PD-97**). The extra-territorial jurisdiction provisions of s. 72 apply where the victim was aged under 18 at the time of the offence (see **B3.301**).

See **B3.335** for alternative verdicts.

B3.189 **Sentencing**   Where the activity concerned consists of anal, vaginal or oral penetration, the maximum penalty is life imprisonment. Otherwise, on indictment, it is 14 years' imprisonment or, on summary conviction, six months or a fine not exceeding the statutory maximum, or both (s. 35(2) and (3)).

The Sentencing Council has issued a new guideline applicable to sex offenders aged 18 or over who are sentenced on or after 1 April 2014 (see **B3.3**). For the guideline in respect of an offence under s. 35, see Supplement, **SG-148**. There is a notification requirement under the SOA 2003, s. 80 and sch. 3 (see **E23**).

The offence is a qualifying offence for an automatic life sentence under the CJA 2003, sch. 15B, if the offender is liable on conviction to imprisonment for life (see **B3.15**).

B3.190 **Elements**   The elements of the offence are essentially the same as those under s. 10 (see **B3.103**) but also include the additional features relating to the agreement obtained by means of an inducement, threat or deception, the mental disorder of the victim and the *mens rea* of the accused. It should also be noted that the scope of s. 35 is limited to causing sexual activity and unlike s. 10 does not include inciting. For examples of inducement, threat and deception, see **B3.186**.

Engaging in Sexual Activity in the Presence, Procured by Inducement, Threat or Deception, of a Person with a Mental Disorder

B3.191   Sexual Offences Act 2003, s. 36

   (1) A person (A) commits an offence if—
      (a) he intentionally engages in an activity,
      (b) the activity is sexual,
      (c) for the purpose of obtaining sexual gratification, he engages in it—
         (i) when another person (B) is present or is in a place from which A can be observed, and

      (ii) knowing or believing that B is aware, or intending that B should be aware, that he is engaging in it,

  (d) B agrees to be present or in the place referred to in paragraph (c)(i) because of an inducement offered or given, a threat made or a deception practised by A for the purpose of obtaining that agreement,

  (e) B has a mental disorder, and

  (f) A knows or could reasonably be expected to know that B has a mental disorder.

Procedure   An allegation of an offence contrary to s. 36 is triable either way. As to the classification of the offence for the purpose of listing, see CPD XIII, para. B (see Supplement, **PD-97**). The extra-territorial jurisdiction provisions of s. 72 apply where the victim was aged under 18 at the time of the offence (see **B3.301**).   **B3.192**

See **B3.335** for alternative verdicts.

Sentencing   The maximum sentence for an offence under the SOA 2003, s. 36, on conviction on indictment is ten years' imprisonment. On summary conviction, the maximum penalty is six months or a fine not exceeding the statutory maximum, or both (s. 36(2)).   **B3.193**

The Sentencing Council has issued a new guideline applicable to sex offenders aged 18 or over who are sentenced on or after 1 April 2014 (see **B3.3**). For the guideline in respect of an offence under s. 36, see Supplement, **SG-152**. There is a notification requirement under the SOA 2003, s. 80 and sch. 3 (see **E23**).

Elements   The elements of the offence are essentially the same as those under s. 11 (see **B3.108**) but also include the additional features relating to the agreement obtained by means of an inducement, threat or deception, the mental disorder of the victim and the *mens rea* of the accused. For examples of inducement, threat and deception, see **B3.186**.   **B3.194**

For 'gratification', see **B3.113**.

Causing a Person with a Mental Disorder to Watch a Sexual Act by Inducement, Threat or Deception

Sexual Offences Act 2003, s. 37   **B3.195**

(1) A person (A) commits an offence if—

  (a) for the purpose of obtaining sexual gratification, he intentionally causes another person (B) to watch a third person engaging in an activity, or to look at an image of any person engaging in an activity,

  (b) the activity is sexual,

  (c) B agrees to watch or look because of an inducement offered or given, a threat made or a deception practised by A for the purpose of obtaining that agreement,

  (d) B has a mental disorder, and

  (e) A knows or could reasonably be expected to know that B has a mental disorder.

Procedure   An allegation of an offence contrary to s. 37 is triable either way. As to the classification of the offence for the purpose of listing, see CPD XIII, para. B (see Supplement, **PD-97**). The extra-territorial jurisdiction provisions of s. 72 apply where the victim was aged under 18 at the time of the offence (see **B3.301**).   **B3.196**

See **B3.335** for alternative verdicts.

Sentencing   The maximum sentence for an offence under the SOA 2003, s. 37, on conviction on indictment is ten years' imprisonment. On summary conviction, the maximum penalty is six months or a fine not exceeding the statutory maximum, or both (s. 37(2)).   **B3.197**

The Sentencing Council has issued a new guideline applicable to sex offenders aged 18 or over who are sentenced on or after 1 April 2014 (see **B3.3**). For the guideline in respect of an offence under s. 37, see Supplement, **SG-152**. There is a notification requirement under the SOA 2003, s. 80 and sch. 3 (see **E23**).

B3.198 **Elements**   The elements of the offence are essentially the same as those under s. 12 (see **B3.113**) but also include the additional features relating to the agreement obtained by means of an inducement, threat or deception, the mental disorder of the victim and the *mens rea* of the accused. For examples of inducement, threat and deception, see **B3.186**.

For 'gratification', see **B3.113**.

CARE WORKERS FOR PERSONS WITH A MENTAL DISORDER

B3.199 Sections 38 to 41 govern offences committed by care workers against people with a mental disorder in their care. Section 42 defines a care worker for the purposes of these sections. Sections 43 and 44 provide for defences analogous to those set out in ss. 23 and 24 (see **B3.129**).

Sexual Offences Act 2003, ss. 42 to 44

42.—(1) For the purposes of sections 38 to 41, a person (A) is involved in the care of another person (B) in a way that falls within this section if any of subsections (2) to (4) applies.

(2) This subsection applies if—
  (a) B is accommodated and cared for in a care home, community home, voluntary home or children's home, and
  (b) A has functions to perform in the home in the course of employment which have brought him or are likely to bring him into regular face to face contact with B.

(3) This subsection applies if B is a patient for whom services are provided—
  (a) by a National Health Service body or an independent medical agency; or
  (b) in an independent hospital;
  (c) in Wales, in an independent clinic,
  and A has functions to perform for the body or agency or in the hospital or clinic in the course of employment which have brought A or are likely to bring A into regular face to face contact with B.

(4) This subsection applies if A—
  (a) is, whether or not in the course of employment, a provider of care, assistance or services to B in connection with B's mental disorder, and
  (b) as such, has had or is likely to have regular face to face contact with B.

(5) [Definition of terms used in the section.]
(6) [Definition of terms used in the section.]

43.—(1) Conduct by a person (A) which would otherwise be an offence under any of sections 38 to 41 against another person (B) is not an offence under that section if at the time—
  (a) B is 16 or over, and
  (b) A and B are lawfully married or civil partners of each other.

(2) In proceedings for such an offence it is for the defendant to prove that A and B were at the time lawfully married or civil partners of each other.

44.—(1) Conduct by a person (A) which would otherwise be an offence under any of sections 38 to 41 against another person (B) is not an offence under that section if, immediately before A became involved in B's care in a way that falls within section 42, a sexual relationship existed between A and B.

(2) Subsection (1) does not apply if at that time sexual intercourse between A and B would have been unlawful.

(3) In proceedings for an offence under any of sections 38 to 41 it is for the defendant to prove that such a relationship existed at that time.

Care Workers: Sexual Activity with a Person with a Mental Disorder

B3.200   Sexual Offences Act 2003, s. 38

(1) A person (A) commits an offence if—
  (a) he intentionally touches another person (B),
  (b) the touching is sexual,
  (c) B has a mental disorder,

(d) A knows or could reasonably be expected to know that B has a mental disorder, and

(e) A is involved in B's care in a way that falls within section 42.

(2) Where in proceedings for an offence under this section it is proved that the other person had a mental disorder, it is to be taken that the defendant knew or could reasonably have been expected to know that that person had a mental disorder unless sufficient evidence is adduced to raise an issue as to whether he knew or could reasonably have been expected to know it.

Procedure An allegation of an offence contrary to s. 38 is triable either way unless the conduct involves penetration, in which case it is triable only on indictment. As to the classification of the offence for the purpose of listing, see CPD XIII, para. B (see Supplement, **PD-97**). The extra-territorial jurisdiction provisions of s. 72 apply where the victim was aged under 18 at the time of the offence (see **B3.301**).   **B3.201**

See **B3.335** for alternative verdicts.

Indictment   **B3.202**

Statement of Offence

Sexual touching of a mentally disordered person by a person involved in the care of that person contrary to section 38(1) of the Sexual Offences Act 2003.

Particulars of Offence

A, on or about the…day of…being then involved in V's care, knowing that V had a mental disorder or in circumstances where he could reasonably be expected to know that V had a mental disorder, intentionally sexually touched V *[namely, by penetration…]*.

Sentencing The maximum sentence for an offence under the SOA 2003, s. 38, varies depending on the sexual activity concerned. Where the touching amounts to penetration the maximum penalty on indictment is 14 years. For these purposes penetration of B's anus or vagina may be with a part of A's body or anything else. Where B penetrates A, the higher penalty applies to bodily penetration of A's anus or vagina or mouth with B's penis. It does not extend to penetration of A's sexual organs or mouth with anything else. Where touching does not amount to penetration, the maximum penalty on indictment is ten years, and on summary conviction is six months or a fine not exceeding the statutory maximum, or both (s. 38(3) and (4)).   **B3.203**

The Sentencing Council has issued a new guideline applicable to sex offenders aged 18 or over who are sentenced on or after 1 April 2014 (see **B3.3**). For the guideline in respect of an offence under s. 38, see Supplement, **SG-156**. There is a notification requirement under the SOA 2003, s. 80 and sch. 3, subject to the age of the offender and the sentence imposed (see **E23**). See *Williams* [2009] 2 Cr App R (S) 76 and *Watts* [2010] EWCA Crim 1824 for examples of sentencing under the old guideline.

Elements The elements of the offence are essentially the same as those under s. 9 (see **B3.98**) but also include the additional features relating to the position of the accused as a care worker, the mental disorder of the victim and the *mens rea* of the accused. As a good illustration of the way in which the SOA 2003 has widened protection for persons who are vulnerable because of their mental state, proceedings have been brought successfully under s. 38 where a social worker had sexual intercourse with the complainant when she was suffering from post-natal depression (*Bradford* [2006] EWCA Crim 2629).   **B3.204**

The provisions of s. 73 apply (see **B3.69**) when the alleged victim is less than 16 years old.

Care Workers: Causing or Inciting Sexual Activity

Sexual Offences Act 2003, s. 39   **B3.205**

(1) A person (A) commits an offence if—

   (a) he intentionally causes or incites another person (B) to engage in an activity,

   (b) the activity is sexual,

   (c) B has a mental disorder,

    (d) A knows or could reasonably be expected to know that B has a mental disorder, and

    (e) A is involved in B's care in a way that falls within section 42.

  (2) Where in proceedings for an offence under this section it is proved that the other person had a mental disorder, it is to be taken that the defendant knew or could reasonably have been expected to know that that person had a mental disorder unless sufficient evidence is adduced to raise an issue as to whether he knew or could reasonably have been expected to know it.

B3.206   **Procedure**   An allegation of an offence contrary to s. 39 is triable either way unless the conduct involves penetration, in which case it is triable only on indictment. As to the classification of the offence for the purpose of listing, see CPD XIII, para. B (see Supplement, **PD-97**). The extra-territorial jurisdiction provisions of s. 72 apply where the victim was aged under 18 at the time of the offence (see **B3.301**).

See **B3.335** for alternative verdicts.

B3.207   **Indictment**

Statement of Offence

Causing or inciting a mentally disordered person to engage in a sexual activity by a care worker for whose care he was responsible contrary to section 39(1) of the Sexual Offences Act 2003.

Particulars of Offence

A, on or about the...day of...being then involved in V's care knowing that V had a mental disorder or in circumstances where he could reasonably be expected to have known that V had a mental disorder intentionally caused or incited V, to engage in a sexual activity *[namely, by penetration...]*.

B3.208   **Sentencing**   Where penetration is concerned, the maximum penalty on indictment is 14 years' imprisonment. Otherwise it is ten years on conviction on indictment or, on summary conviction, six months or a fine not exceeding the statutory maximum, or both (s. 39(3) and (4)). Note that for these purposes penetration attracting the higher penalty may be of B's anus or vagina seemingly by any part of A's body or an object, or B's mouth with a person's penis. Where, however, it is B who penetrates another's anus or vagina such penetration may be by any part of B's body or anything else or by penetration of another's mouth by B's penis.

The Sentencing Council has issued a new guideline applicable to sex offenders aged 18 or over who are sentenced on or after 1 April 2014 (see **B3.3**). For the guideline in respect of an offence under s. 39, see Supplement, **SG-156**. There is a notification requirement under the SOA 2003, s. 80 and sch. 3, subject to the age of the offender and the sentence imposed (see **E23**).

B3.209   **Elements**   The elements of the offence are essentially the same as those under s. 10 (see **B3.103**) but also include the additional features relating to the position of the accused as a care worker, the mental disorder of the victim and the *mens rea* of the accused.

Care Workers: Sexual Activity in the Presence of a Person with a Mental Disorder

B3.210   **Sexual Offences Act 2003, s. 40**

  (1) A person (A) commits an offence if—

    (a) he intentionally engages in an activity,

    (b) the activity is sexual,

    (c) for the purpose of obtaining sexual gratification, he engages in it—

      (i) when another person (B) is present or is in a place from which A can be observed, and

      (ii) knowing or believing that B is aware, or intending that B should be aware, that he is engaging in it,

    (d) B has a mental disorder,

    (e) A knows or could reasonably be expected to know that B has a mental disorder, and

    (f) A is involved in B's care in a way that falls within section 42.

  (2) Where in proceedings for an offence under this section it is proved that the other person had a mental disorder, it is to be taken that the defendant knew or could reasonably have been expected to know that that person had a mental disorder unless sufficient evidence is adduced to raise an issue as to whether he knew or could reasonably have been expected to know it.

Procedure An allegation of an offence contrary to s. 40 is triable either way. As to the classification of the offence for the purpose of listing, see CPD XIII, para. B (see Supplement, **PD-97**). The extra-territorial jurisdiction provisions of s. 72 apply where the victim was aged under 18 at the time of the offence (see **B3.301**). **B3.211**

See **B3.335** for alternative verdicts.

Sentencing The maximum sentence for an offence under the SOA 2003, s. 40, on conviction on indictment is seven years' imprisonment. On summary conviction, the maximum is six months or a fine not exceeding the statutory maximum, or both. **B3.212**

The Sentencing Council has issued a new guideline applicable to sex offenders aged 18 or over who are sentenced on or after 1 April 2014 (see **B3.3**). For the guideline in respect of an offence under s. 40, see Supplement, **SG-160**. There is a notification requirement under the SOA 2003, s. 80 and sch. 3, subject to the age of the offender and the sentence imposed (see **E23**).

Elements The elements of the offence are essentially the same as those under s. 11 (see **B3.108**) but also include the additional features relating to the position of the accused as a care worker, the mental disorder of the victim and the *mens rea* of the accused. **B3.213**

For 'gratification', see **B3.113**.

Care Workers: Causing a Person with a Mental Disorder to Watch a Sexual Act

Sexual Offences Act 2003, s. 41 **B3.214**

(1) A person (A) commits an offence if—
  (a) for the purpose of obtaining sexual gratification, he intentionally causes another person (B) to watch a third person engaging in an activity, or to look at an image of any person engaging in an activity,
  (b) the activity is sexual,
  (c) B has a mental disorder,
  (d) A knows or could reasonably be expected to know that B has a mental disorder, and
  (e) A is involved in B's care in a way that falls within section 42.
(2) Where in proceedings for an offence under this section it is proved that the other person had a mental disorder, it is to be taken that the defendant knew or could reasonably have been expected to know that that person had a mental disorder unless sufficient evidence is adduced to raise an issue as to whether he knew or could reasonably have been expected to know it.

Procedure An allegation of an offence contrary to s. 41 is triable either way. As to the classification of the offence for the purpose of listing, see CPD XIII, para. B (see Supplement, **PD-97**). The extra-territorial jurisdiction provisions of s. 72 apply (see **B3.301**). **B3.215**

See **B3.335** for alternative verdicts.

Sentencing The maximum penalties for an offence under the SOA 2003, s. 41, are the same as for an offence under s. 40 (see **B3.212**). **B3.216**

The Sentencing Council has issued a new guideline applicable to sex offenders aged 18 or over who are sentenced on or after 1 April 2014 (see **B3.3**). For the guideline in respect of an offence under s. 41, see Supplement, **SG-160**. There is a notification requirement under the SOA 2003, s. 80 and sch. 3, subject to the age of the offender and the sentence imposed (see **E23**).

Elements The elements of the offence are essentially the same as those under s. 12 (see **B3.113**) but also include the additional features relating to the position of the accused as a care worker, the mental disorder of the victim and the *mens rea* of the accused. The offence under s. 41 is also limited to 'causing' whilst s. 12 prohibits both causing and inciting. **B3.217**

For 'gratification', see **B3.113**.

ABUSE OF CHILDREN THROUGH PROSTITUTION AND PORNOGRAPHY

B3.218   Sections 47 to 50 govern offences against children that are committed in relation to prostitution or pornography. Section 51 is a definitional section of common application to each of ss. 47 to 50.

Sexual Offences Act 2003, s. 51

(1) For the purposes of sections 48 to 50, a person is involved in pornography if an indecent image of that person is recorded; and similar expressions, and 'pornography', are to be interpreted accordingly.

(2) In those sections 'prostitute' means a person (A) who, on at least one occasion and whether or not compelled to do so, offers or provides sexual services to another person in return for payment or a promise of payment to A or a third person; and 'prostitution' is to be interpreted accordingly.

(3) In subsection (2), 'payment' means any financial advantage, including the discharge of an obligation to pay or the provision of goods or services (including sexual services) gratuitously or at a discount.

Paying for Sexual Services of a Child

B3.219   ### Sexual Offences Act 2003, s. 47

(1) A person (A) commits an offence if—
   (a) he intentionally obtains for himself the sexual services of another person (B),
   (b) before obtaining those services, he has made or promised payment for those services to B or a third person, or knows that another person has made or promised such a payment, and
   (c) either—
      (i) B is under 18, and A does not reasonably believe that B is 18 or over, or
      (ii) B is under 13.

(2) In this section, 'payment' means any financial advantage, including the discharge of an obligation to pay or the provision of goods or services (including sexual services) gratuitously or at a discount.

B3.220   **Procedure**   An allegation of an offence contrary to s. 47 is triable either way unless the conduct involves penetration, in which case it is triable only on indictment. As to the classification of the offence for the purpose of listing, see CPD XIII, para. B (see Supplement, **PD-97**). The extra-territorial jurisdiction provisions of s. 72 apply (see **B3.301**).

See **B3.335** for alternative verdicts.

B3.221   **Indictment**

Statement of Offence

Intentionally obtaining the sexual services of a person under the age of 18 years by prior payment or promise of payment to that person or another person contrary to section 47(1) of the Sexual Offences Act 2003.

Particulars of Offence

A, on or about the...day of...intentionally obtained the sexual services of V then a child under the age of 18 [13] years then knowing that V was under the age of 18 years or not believing on reasonable grounds that V was over the age of 18 years by making or promising payment for such services to V or to another person before obtaining those services.

B3.222   **Sentencing**   The maximum penalty for an offence under the SOA 2003, s. 47, varies according to the age of the child and whether or not the offence involved penetration.

Sexual Offences Act 2003, s. 47

(3) A person guilty of an offence under this section against a person under 13, where subsection (6) applies, is liable on conviction on indictment to imprisonment for life.

(4) Unless subsection (3) applies, a person guilty of an offence under this section against a person under 16 is liable—

    (a) where subsection (6) applies, on conviction on indictment, to imprisonment for a term not exceeding 14 years;

    (b) in any other case—

        (i) on summary conviction, to imprisonment for a term not exceeding 6 months or a fine not exceeding the statutory maximum or both;

        (ii) on conviction on indictment, to imprisonment for a term not exceeding 14 years.

(5) Unless subsection (3) or (4) applies, a person guilty of an offence under this section is liable—

    (a) on summary conviction, to imprisonment for a term not exceeding 6 months or a fine not exceeding the statutory maximum or both;

    (b) on conviction on indictment, to imprisonment for a term not exceeding 7 years.

(6) This subsection applies where the offence involved—

    (a) penetration of B's anus or vagina with a part of A's body or anything else,

    (b) penetration of B's mouth with A's penis,

    (c) penetration of A's anus or vagina with a part of B's body or by B with anything else, or

    (d) penetration of A's mouth with B's penis.

The Sentencing Council has issued a new guideline applicable to sex offenders aged 18 or over who are sentenced on or after 1 April 2014 (see **B3.3**). For the guideline in respect of an offence under s. 47, see Supplement, **SG-132**. There is a notification requirement under the SOA 2003, s.80 and sch. 3, where the victim was under 16 and the offender was aged 18 or over or was sentenced to at least 12 months' imprisonment (see **E23**).

The offence is a qualifying offence for an automatic life sentence under the CJA 2003, sch. 15B (see **B3.15**).

Elements   The offender (A) must intentionally obtain the sexual services of a person under the age of 18 (B). Before he does so he must have either made or promised payment to the child or a third party or must be aware that such a payment has been made or promised.   **B3.223**

Section 47(2) contains a very broad definition of payment.

It is a defence for A that he reasonably believed that B was aged 18 or over, but the defence does not apply if B was aged under 13 at the material time.

Causing or Inciting Child Prostitution or Pornography

Sexual Offences Act 2003, s. 48   **B3.224**

(1) A person (A) commits an offence if—

    (a) he intentionally causes or incites another person (B) to become a prostitute, or to be involved in pornography, in any part of the world, and

    (b) either—

        (i) B is under 18, and A does not reasonably believe that B is 18 or over, or

        (ii) B is under 13.

Procedure   An allegation of an offence contrary to s. 48 is triable either way. As to the classification of the offence for the purpose of listing, see CPD XIII, para. B (see Supplement, **PD-97**). The extra-territorial jurisdiction provisions of s. 72 apply (see **B3.301**).   **B3.225**

See **B3.335** for alternative verdicts.

Indictment   **B3.226**

Statement of Offence

Intentionally causing or inciting a child under the age of 18 years to become a prostitute in any part of the world contrary so section 48(1) of the Sexual Offences Act 2003

or

Intentionally causing or inciting a child under the age of 18 years to be involved in pornography in any part of the world contrary to section 48(1) of the Sexual Offences Act 2003.

Particulars of Offence

A, on or about the…day of…intentionally caused [incited] V then a child under the age of 18 years to engage in prostitution in any part of the world [to engage in pornography in any part of the world].

B3.227   **Sentencing**   The maximum sentence for an offence under the SOA 2003, s. 48, on conviction on indictment is 14 years' imprisonment. On summary conviction, the maximum sentence is six months or a fine of the statutory maximum, or both (s. 48(2)).

The Sentencing Council has issued a new guideline applicable to sex offenders aged 18 or over who are sentenced on or after 1 April 2014 (see **B3.3**). For the guideline in respect of an offence under s. 48, see Supplement, **SG-128**.

The offence is a qualifying offence for an automatic life sentence under the CJA 2003, sch. 15B (see **B3.15**).

B3.228   **Elements**   The offender (A) must intentionally cause or incite a person under the age of 18 (B) to become a prostitute or become involved in pornography. Plainly, for an accused to be guilty of the incitement offence it is not necessary that B actually becomes a prostitute or involves himself in pornography.

It is a defence for A that he reasonably believed that B was not under 18 years of age even though B was actually under 18. However, if B was under 13 at the material time then no such defence is available.

Controlling a Child Prostitute or a Child Involved in Pornography

B3.229   Sexual Offences Act 2003, s. 49

(1) A person (A) commits an offence if—
   (a) he intentionally controls any of the activities of another person (B) relating to B's prostitution or involvement in pornography in any part of the world, and
   (b) either—
      (i) B is under 18, and A does not reasonably believe that B is 18 or over, or
      (ii) B is under 13.

B3.230   **Procedure**   An allegation of an offence contrary to s. 49 is triable either way. As to the classification of the offence for the purpose of listing, see CPD XIII, para. B (see Supplement, **PD-97**). The extra-territorial jurisdiction provisions of s. 72 apply (see **B3.301**).

See **B3.335** for alternative verdicts.

B3.231   **Indictment**

Statement of Offence

Intentionally controlling the activities of another person under the age of 18 years relating to that person's prostitution or involvement in prostitution or pornography in any part of the world contrary to section 49 of the Sexual Offences Act 2003.

Particulars of Offence

A, on or about the…day of…intentionally controlled activities of V, then a child under the age of 18 years or over relating to V's involvement in any part of the world in prostitution [pornography].

B3.232   **Sentencing**   The maximum sentence for an offence under the SOA 2003, s. 49, on conviction on indictment is 14 years' imprisonment. On summary conviction, the maximum sentence is six months or a fine of the statutory maximum, or both (s. 49(2)).

The Sentencing Council has issued a new guideline applicable to sex offenders aged 18 or over who are sentenced on or after 1 April 2014 (see **B3.3**). For the guideline in respect of an offence under s. 49, see Supplement, **SG-128**.

The offence is a qualifying offence for an automatic life sentence under the CJA 2003, sch. 15B (see **B3.15**).

Elements   The essence of the offence is that A must intentionally control the prostitution or   **B3.233**
pornography-related activities of B. For 'control' see **B3.247**.

It is a defence for A that he reasonably believed that B was aged 18 or over, but the defence does
not apply if B was aged under 13 at the material time.

Arranging or Facilitating Child Prostitution or Pornography

Sexual Offences Act 2003, s. 50   **B3.234**

(1) A person (A) commits an offence if—
  (a) he intentionally arranges or facilitates the prostitution or involvement in pornography in
      any part of the world of another person (B), and
  (b) either—
      (i) B is under 18, and A does not reasonably believe that B is 18 or over, or
      (ii) B is under 13.

Procedure   An allegation of an offence contrary to s. 50 is triable either way. As to the classifi-   **B3.235**
cation of the offence for the purpose of listing, see CPD XIII, para. B (see Supplement, **PD-97**).
The extra-territorial jurisdiction provisions of s. 72 apply (see **B3.301**).

See **B3.335** for alternative verdicts.

Sentencing   The maximum sentence for an offence under the SOA 2003, s. 50, on conviction   **B3.236**
on indictment is 14 years' imprisonment. On summary conviction, the maximum sentence is
six months or a fine of the statutory maximum, or both (s. 50(2)).

The Sentencing Council has issued a new guideline applicable to sex offenders aged 18 or over
who are sentenced on or after 1 April 2014 (see **B3.3**). For the guideline in respect of an offence
under s. 50, see Supplement, **SG-128**. The offence is a qualifying offence for an automatic life
sentence under the CJA 2003, sch. 15B (see **B3.15**).

Elements   The offender (A) must intentionally arrange or facilitate the involvement in prosti-   **B3.237**
tution or pornography of a person under the age of 18 (B).

It is a defence for A that he reasonably believed that B was aged 18 or over, but the defence does
not apply if B was aged under 13 at the material time.

EXPLOITATION OF PROSTITUTION

Offences concerning Exploitation of Prostitution

Sections 52 and 53 of the SOA 2003 concern the exploitation of prostitution. Common inter-   **B3.238**
pretation provisions in s. 54 apply to them.

Sexual Offences Act 2003, s. 54

(1) In sections 52 and 53, 'gain' means—
  (a) any financial advantage, including the discharge of an obligation to pay or the provision
      of goods or services (including sexual services) gratuitously or at a discount; or
  (b) the goodwill of any person which is or appears likely, in time, to bring financial advantage.
(2) In those sections 'prostitute' and 'prostitution' have the meaning given by section 51(2).

Gain is expressed in terms of either financial advantage or good will which appears likely to
bring financial advantage in the future. Financial advantage is widely defined by s. 54(1).

The extra-territorial jurisdiction provisions of s. 72 do not apply to these offences and
therefore the accused's acts constituting the offence must be committed in England and
Wales.

Causing or Inciting Prostitution for Gain

B3.239

Sexual Offences Act 2003, s. 52

(1) A person commits an offence if—
   (a) he intentionally causes or incites another person to become a prostitute in any part of the world, and
   (b) he does so for or in the expectation of gain for himself or a third person.

B3.240 **Procedure** An allegation of an offence contrary to s. 52 is triable either way. As to the classification of the offence for the purpose of listing, see CPD XIII, para. B (see Supplement, **PD-97**).

See **B3.335** for alternative verdicts.

B3.241 **Indictment**

Statement of Offence

Intentionally causing or inciting a person to become a prostitute in any part of the world in the expectation of gain contrary to section 52(1) of the Sexual Offences Act 2003.

Particulars of Offence

A, on or about the...day of...intentionally and in the expectation of gain to himself or another caused [incited] V to become a prostitute in any part of the world.

B3.242 **Sentencing** The maximum penalty for an offence under the SOA 2003, s. 52, on conviction on indictment is seven years' imprisonment. On summary conviction, the maximum is six months or a fine not exceeding the statutory maximum, or both (s. 52(2)).

The Sentencing Council has issued a new guideline applicable to sex offenders aged 18 or over who are sentenced on or after 1 April 2014 (see **B3.3**). For the guideline in respect of an offence under s. 52, see Supplement, **SG-120**.

B3.243 **Elements** The essence of the offence is that the accused must intentionally cause or incite another person to become a prostitute in any part of the world. The person's acts must, however, have been done in England and Wales as the extra-territorial jurisdiction provisions of s. 72 do not apply. Plainly, the person incited need not in fact have engaged in an act of prostitution. The accused must act in the expectation of gain for himself or a third person.

The wide definition of 'prostitute' contained in s. 51(2) applies to this offence by virtue of s. 54(2) (see **B3.218**).

Controlling Prostitution for Gain

B3.244

Sexual Offences Act 2003, s. 53

(1) A person commits an offence if—
   (a) he intentionally controls any of the activities of another person relating to that person's prostitution in any part of the world, and
   (b) he does so for or in the expectation of gain for himself or a third person.

B3.245 **Procedure** An allegation of an offence contrary to s. 53 is triable either way. As to the classification of the offence for the purpose of listing, see CPD XIII, para. B (see Supplement, **PD-97**).

See **B3.335** for alternative verdicts.

B3.246 **Sentencing** The maximum penalty for an offence under the SOA 2003, s. 53, on conviction on indictment is seven years' imprisonment. On summary conviction, the maximum is six months or a fine not exceeding the statutory maximum, or both (s. 53(2)).

The Sentencing Council has issued a new guideline applicable to sex offenders aged 18 or over who are sentenced on or after 1 April 2014 (see **B3.3**). For the guideline in respect of an offence under s. 53, see Supplement, **SG-120**.

Elements   The essence of the offence is that the accused must intentionally control any of the   **B3.247**
activities of another person relating to that person's prostitution in any part of the world. Such
control may be direct or through an intermediary.

The meaning of 'control' in s. 53 was considered in *Massey* [2008] 1 WLR 937. In dismissing
M's appeal against conviction, the Court of Appeal said 'control' includes but is not limited to
one who forces another to carry out an activity. The Court saw no need to lay down a comprehensive definition of an ordinary English word, it is enough that a person instructs or directs
another to carry out a particular activity or do it in a particular way. There is a wide variety of
possible reasons why a person may do as instructed. It may be, for example, because of the use
or threat of physical violence, or it may be because of emotional blackmail, or the lure of gain.
There is no necessity for the victim to have acted without free will.

In *LM* [2011] 1 Cr App R 135, the Court of Appeal considered the applicability of the   **B3.248**
European Convention on Action on Trafficking in Human Beings 2005 to proceedings concerned with controlling prostitution for gain contrary to s. 53. Article 26 of the Convention
provides for the possibility of not imposing penalties on victims for their involvement in
unlawful activities to the extent that they had been compelled to be involved. Under Article
10, a number of agencies were established and charged with the identification of persons
who had reasonable grounds for being treated as a victim of trafficking. Moreover, guidelines
issued by the CPS required prosecutors to consider whether the public interest was best
served in continuing a relevant prosecution. The accused were prosecuted for offences contrary to s. 53. The Crown's case against them had been that they had initially been victims of
trafficking, but they had subsequently become controllers of prostitution by others. At a late
stage, the Crown accepted pleas of guilty entered on the basis that the accused had been trafficked, beaten and coerced into prostitution themselves and that anything that had amounted
to controlling prostitution had been done under pressure which fell short of duress. The
Court of Appeal quashed the convictions on the basis that the Article 26 duty was ignored at
the point when the factual basis changed. If the duty had been discharged, the Crown should
have offered no evidence or an application to stay should have been successful on the basis
that any decision to continue to prosecute was one which no reasonable prosecutor could
make. The Court also observed that, whilst any breach of Article 10 is deplorable, such a
breach is not sufficient simply of itself to render a prosecution unlawful or amenable to stay.
In any case where trafficking was an obvious possibility, the police should inquire into it. In
this case they did so by raising it with the accused in interview and formed the view that the
accused probably had been trafficked. The accused ought then to have been referred to the
referral agencies, because other possible measures apart from decisions about prosecution
might have followed. If an accused was legally represented then, unless there was something
unusual about the case, it was not desirable for the police to be required to refer people to
the agencies against their wishes and following legal advice. The police fulfilled their duties
by reminding the solicitors of the availability of the relevant agencies. So far as an unrepresented offender was concerned, the situation might well be different. It had initially been the
Crown's case on a fair assessment of the evidence available that, although previously victims
of trafficking, the accused had become voluntary abusers of others. That assessment justified
a decision to prosecute. The Crown's case might or might not have been made out, but it was
not unreasonable to decide to pursue it.

Because the extra-territorial jurisdiction provisions of s. 72 do not apply, the accused's acts must
be done in or from England and Wales. Here too 'prostitution' bears the wide protective meaning in s. 51(2) (see **B3.218**). Thus, controlling an activity relating to a single act of prostitution
is sufficient to bring an offender within the section.

The accused must act with an expectation of gain for himself or a third party. 'Gain' is defined
in terms of financial advantage (see s. 54(1) at **B3.238**).

PAYING FOR SEXUAL SERVICES OF A PROSTITUTE SUBJECTED TO EXPLOITATIVE CONDUCT

B3.249 Sexual Offences Act 2003, s. 53A

(1) A person (A) commits an offence if—

    (a) A makes or promises payment for the sexual services of a prostitute (B),

    (b) a third person (C) has engaged in exploitative conduct of a kind likely to induce or encourage B to provide the sexual services for which A has made or promised payment, and

    (c) C engaged in that conduct for or in the expectation of gain for C or another person (apart from A or B).

(2) The following are irrelevant—

    (a) where in the world the sexual services are to be provided and whether those services are provided,

    (b) whether A is, or ought to be, aware that C has engaged in exploitative conduct.

(3) C engages in exploitative conduct if—

    (a) C uses force, threats (whether or not relating to violence) or any other form of coercion, or

    (b) C practises any form of deception.

B3.250 **Procedure** The offence is summary only.

B3.251 **Sentencing** The offence is punishable by a fine not exceeding level 3 on the standard scale (SOA 2003, s. 53A(4)). The new definitive sentencing guideline (see **B3.3**) does not refer to this offence.

B3.252 **Elements** It is of note that, by virtue of s. 53A(2), it is deemed to be irrelevant whether the accused was, or ought to have been, aware that B had been exploited. Moreover, by virtue of s. 53A(3)(b), it appears that A may be guilty even if B is not aware that she has been exploited because she has been deceived.

TRAFFICKING

B3.253 The Protection of Freedoms Act 2012, s. 109, which came into force on 6 April 2013, repealed the SOA 2003, ss. 57 to 59, substantially amended s. 60 and inserted a new s. 59A (see **B3.254**). The Protection of Freedoms Act 2012 (Commencement No. 5 and Saving and Transitional Provision) Order 2013 (SI 2013 No. 470) provides that the amendments and repeals made by s. 109 do not have effect in relation to offences committed wholly or partly before 6 April 2013 (art. 3) but also provides that, where D is charged under both the SOA 2003, s. 59A, and any of ss. 57 to 59, and it cannot be proved whether the conduct in question came before or after 6 April 2013, it shall be conclusively presumed that the offence was committed before that date.

For the now repealed ss. 57 to 59, see the 2014 edition of this work.

Trafficking People for Sexual Exploitation

B3.254 Sexual Offences Act 2003, s. 59A

(1) A person ('A') commits an offence if A intentionally arranges or facilitates—

    (a) the arrival in, or entry into, the United Kingdom or another country of another person ('B'),

    (b) the travel of B within the United Kingdom or another country, or

    (c) the departure of B from the United Kingdom or another country, with a view to the sexual exploitation of B.

(2) For the purposes of subsection (1)(a) and (c) A's arranging or facilitating is with a view to the sexual exploitation of B if, and only if—

    (a) A intends to do anything to or in respect of B, after B's arrival, entry or (as the case may be) departure but in any part of the world, which if done will involve the commission of a relevant offence, or

    (b) A believes that another person is likely to do something to or in respect of B, after B's arrival, entry or (as the case may be) departure but in any part of the world, which if done will involve the commission of a relevant offence.

(3) For the purposes of subsection (1)(b) A's arranging or facilitating is with a view to the sexual exploitation of B if, and only if—

    (a) A intends to do anything to or in respect of B, during or after the journey and in any part of the world, which if done will involve the commission of a relevant offence, or

    (b) A believes that another person is likely to do something to or in respect of B, during or after the journey and in any part of the world, which if done will involve the commission of a relevant offence.

(4) A person who is a UK national commits an offence under this section regardless of—

    (a) where the arranging or facilitating takes place, or

    (b) which country is the country of arrival, entry, travel or (as the case may be) departure.

(5) A person who is not a UK national commits an offence under this section if—

    (a) any part of the arranging or facilitating takes place in the United Kingdom, or

    (b) the United Kingdom is the country of arrival, entry, travel or (as the case may be) departure.

Procedure and Sentence   An allegation of an offence contrary to s. 59A is triable either way. **B3.255** As to the classification of the offence for the purpose of listing, see CPD XIII, para. B (see Supplement, **PD-97**). The maximum penalty on conviction on indictment is 14 years' imprisonment. On summary conviction, the maximum penalty is six months or a fine not exceeding the statutory maximum or both (s. 59A(6)).

The Sentencing Council has issued a new guideline applicable to sex offenders aged 18 or over who are sentenced on or after 1 April 2014 (see **B3.3**). For the guideline in respect of an offence under s. 59A, see Supplement, **SG-136**. For powers of forfeiture relating to land, vehicles, ships and aircraft used in commission of an offence under the SOA 2003, s. 59A, see s. 60A.

Elements   A relevant offence is defined by s. 60(1), as substituted by the Protection of **B3.256** Freedoms Act 2012, s. 109(3), to mean (a) any offence under the law of England and Wales which is an offence under the SOA 2003, part 1 or under the Protection of Children Act 1978, s. 1(1)(a), or (b) anything done outside England and Wales which is not an offence within (a) but would be if done in England and Wales.

PREPARATORY OFFENCES

Administering a Substance with Intent

Sexual Offences Act 2003, s. 61

                                                                B3.257

(1) A person commits an offence if he intentionally administers a substance to, or causes a substance to be taken by, another person (B)—

    (a) knowing that B does not consent, and

    (b) with the intention of stupefying or overpowering B, so as to enable any person to engage in a sexual activity that involves B.

Procedure   An allegation of an offence contrary to s. 61 is triable either way. As to the classifi- **B3.258** cation of the offence for the purpose of listing, see CPD XIII, para. B (see Supplement, **PD-97**). The extra-territorial jurisdiction provisions of s. 72 apply (see **B3.301**) if the victim was under the age of 18 at the time of the alleged offence.

See **B3.335** for alternative verdicts.

Indictment   **B3.259**

Statement of Offence

Intentionally administering a substance to or causing a substance to be taken by another with the intention of stupefying or overpowering that other in order to enable another person to engage in sexual activity with that person contrary to section 61(1) of the Sexual Offences Act 2003.

Particulars of Offence

A, on or about the...day of...intentionally administered a substance to [caused a substance to be taken by] V knowing that V did not consent and with the intention of stupefying or overpowering V so as to enable himself or another to engage in a sexual activity involving V.

B3.260   **Sentencing**   The maximum penalty for an offence under the SOA 2003, s. 61, on conviction on indictment is ten years' imprisonment. On summary conviction, the maximum is six months or a fine not exceeding the statutory maximum, or both.

The Sentencing Council has issued a new guideline applicable to sex offenders aged 18 or over who are sentenced on or after 1 April 2014 (see **B3.3**). For the guideline in respect of an offence under s. 61, see Supplement, **SG-176**.

There is a notification requirement under the SOA 2003, s. 80 and sch. 3 (see **E23**).

B3.261   **Elements**   The Home Office Explanatory Notes to the 2003 Act suggest that the substance may be administered to the victim in any way, e.g., in a drink, by injection or by covering the victim's face with a cloth impregnated with the substance. The offence is made out both where A administers the substance to the victim, B, or he persuades a third party, C, to administer the substance because C knows B and so is more easily able to do so. The intended sexual activity need not involve A but instead it may be planned that a third party have sex with B.

For the meaning of consent, see **B3.19**.

For 'sexual', see **B3.47**.

Committing an Offence with Intent to Commit a Sexual Offence

B3.262   Sexual Offences Act 2003, s. 62

(1) A person commits an offence under this section if he commits any offence with the intention of committing a relevant sexual offence.
(2) In this section, 'relevant sexual offence' means any offence under this Part (including an offence of aiding, abetting, counselling or procuring such an offence).

B3.263   **Procedure**   An allegation of an offence contrary to s. 62 is triable either way unless the offence alleged is one of either kidnapping or false imprisonment. In such a case, the alleged offence is triable on indictment only. As to the classification of the offence for the purpose of listing, see CPD XIII, para. B (see Supplement, **PD-97**). If the victim was under 18 years of age at the time of the offence, the extra-territorial jurisdiction provisions of s. 72 apply (see **B3.301**).

See **B3.335** for alternative verdicts.

B3.264   **Indictment**

Statement of Offence

Committing an offence with intent to commit a sexual offence contrary to section 62(1) of the Sexual Offences Act 2003.

Particulars of Offence

A, on or about the...day of...[e.g., unlawfully had in his possession a controlled drug of class B with intent to administer the same] with the intention of committing a relevant sexual offence, namely [specify relevant sexual offence e.g., under s. 61(1) of the Sexual Offences Act 2003].

B3.265   **Sentencing**   The maximum penalty on conviction on indictment is ten years' imprisonment. However, where the offence is committed by kidnapping or false imprisonment, the maximum penalty is imprisonment for life. On summary conviction, the maximum penalty is six months or a fine not exceeding the statutory maximum, or both (s. 62(3) and (4)).

The Sentencing Council has issued a new guideline applicable to sex offenders aged 18 or over who are sentenced on or after 1 April 2014 (see **B3.3**). For the guideline in respect of an offence under s. 62, see Supplement, **SG-180**. Essentially, it states that the starting point for any sentence should be commensurate with that for the preparatory offence actually committed but enhanced to reflect the nature and severity of the intended sexual offence. Two years' imprisonment is suggested to be a suitable enhancement where the intent was to commit rape or assault by penetration.

There is a notification requirement under the SOA 2003, s. 80 and sch. 3, subject to the age of the offender and the sentence passed and subject to the age of the victim (see **E23**).

The offence is a qualifying offence for an automatic life sentence under the CJA 2003, sch. 15B, if the offender is liable on conviction to imprisonment for life (see **B3.15**).

Elements   An offence 'under this part' means any within the SOA 2003, ss. 1 to 79.   **B3.266**

It is submitted that it is not necessary for the prosecution to prove that a specific sexual offence was intended by the offender. Instead it will be sufficient that jurors are sure that an offence under part 1 was intended even though they may disagree as to the nature of the offence that the accused intended.

Trespass with Intent to Commit a Sexual Offence

Sexual Offences Act 2003, s. 63   **B3.267**

(1) A person commits an offence if—
   (a) he is a trespasser on any premises,
   (b) he intends to commit a relevant sexual offence on the premises, and
   (c) he knows that, or is reckless as to whether, he is a trespasser.
(2) In this section—
   'premises' includes a structure or part of a structure;
   'relevant sexual offence' has the same meaning as in section 62;
   'structure' includes a tent, vehicle or vessel or other temporary or movable structure.

Procedure   An allegation of an offence contrary to s. 63 is triable either way. As to the clas- **B3.268** sification of the offence for the purpose of listing, see CPD XIII, para. B (see Supplement, PD-97). The extra-territorial jurisdiction provisions of s. 72 apply (see **B3.301**) if the victim was under the age of 18 at the time of the alleged offence.

See **B3.335** for alternative verdicts.

Indictment   **B3.269**

Statement of Offence

Trespass with intent to commit a sexual offence contrary to section 63(1) of the Sexual Offences Act 2003.

Particulars of Offence

A, on or about the…day of…being a trespasser on premises and knowing that, or being reckless as to whether he was, a trespasser, intended to commit a relevant sexual offence on the premises, namely [here specify the relevant offence].

Sentencing   The maximum penalty for an offence under the SOA 2003, s. 63, on conviction **B3.270** on indictment is ten years' imprisonment. On summary conviction, the maximum is six months or a fine not exceeding the statutory maximum, or both.

The Sentencing Council has issued a new guideline applicable to sex offenders aged 18 or over who are sentenced on or after 1 April 2014 (see **B3.3**). For the guideline in respect of an offence under s. 63, see Supplement, **SG-181**. There is a notification requirement under the SOA 2003, s. 80 and sch. 3, subject to the age of the offender and the sentence passed and subject to the age of the victim (see **E23**).

Elements   The offender must be at least reckless as to whether he is trespassing. As to **B3.271** the necessity for the prosecution to prove the nature of the relevant offence intended, see **B3.266**.

SEX WITH AN ADULT RELATIVE

Sex with an Adult Relative: Penetration

B3.272   Sexual Offences Act 2003, s. 64

(1) A person aged 16 or over (A) (subject to subsection (3A)) commits an offence if—

    (a) he intentionally penetrates another person's vagina or anus with a part of his body or anything else, or penetrates another person's mouth with his penis,

    (b) the penetration is sexual,

    (c) the other person (B) is aged 18 or over,

    (d) A is related to B in a way mentioned in subsection (2), and

    (e) A knows or could reasonably be expected to know that he is related to B in that way.

(2) The ways that A may be related to B are as parent, grandparent, child, grandchild, brother, sister, half-brother, half-sister, uncle, aunt, nephew or niece.

(3) In subsection (2)—

    (za) 'parent' includes an adoptive parent;

    (zb) 'child' includes an adopted person within the meaning of chapter 4 of part 1 of the Adoption and Children Act 2002;

    (a) 'uncle' means the brother of a person's parent, and 'aunt' has a corresponding meaning;

    (b) 'nephew' means the child of a person's brother or sister, and 'niece' has a corresponding meaning.

(3A) Where subsection (1) applies in a case where A is related to B as B's child by virtue of subsection (3)(zb), A does not commit an offence under this section unless A is 18 or over.

(4) Where in proceedings for an offence under this section it is proved that the defendant was related to the other person in any of those ways, it is to be taken that the defendant knew or could reasonably have been expected to know that he was related in that way unless sufficient evidence is adduced to raise an issue as to whether he knew or could reasonably have been expected to know that he was.

Any reference to an adoptive relationship is to be read as including a reference to the corresponding relationship arising by virtue of a parental order under the Human Fertilisation and Embryology Act 2008 (Human Fertilisation and Embryology (Parental Orders) Regulations 2010 (SI 2010 No. 985), sch. 4).

B3.273 **Procedure**   An allegation of an offence contrary to s. 64 is triable either way. As to the classification of the offence for the purpose of listing, see CPD XIII, para. B (see Supplement, **PD-97**).

See **B3.335** for alternative verdicts.

B3.274 **Sentencing**   The maximum penalty for an offence under the SOA 2003, s. 64, on conviction on indictment is two years' imprisonment. On summary conviction, the maximum is six months or a fine not exceeding the statutory maximum, or both (s. 64(5)).

The Sentencing Council has issued a new guideline applicable to sex offenders aged 18 or over who are sentenced on or after 1 April 2014 (see **B3.3**). For the guideline in respect of an offence under s. 64, see Supplement, **SG-172**. There is a notification requirement under the SOA 2003, s. 80 and sch. 3, subject to the age of the offender and the sentence imposed (see **E23**).

B3.275 **Elements**   Section 64 of the SOA 2003 contains a rebuttable presumption as to the accused's *mens rea* in respect of the relationship between him and the person he penetrates. If the prosecution prove that the relationship is a relevant one for the purposes of s. 64 then the accused is taken to have either known of that relationship, or could reasonably have been expected to know of it, unless he adduces sufficient evidence so as to raise an issue as to whether he knew or could reasonably have known of that relationship. The burden is evidential and once sufficient evidence is raised then the prosecution has the usual burden of proving the contrary to the criminal standard.

Sex with an Adult Relative: Consenting to Penetration

Sexual Offences Act 2003, s. 65   B3.276

(1) A person aged 16 or over (A) (subject to subsection (3A)) commits an offence if—
  (a) another person (B) penetrates A's vagina or anus with a part of B's body or anything else, or penetrates A's mouth with B's penis,
  (b) A consents to the penetration,
  (c) the penetration is sexual,
  (d) B is aged 18 or over,
  (e) A is related to B in a way mentioned in subsection (2), and
  (f) A knows or could reasonably be expected to know that he is related to B in that way.

Section 65(2) to (4) and (6) are in identical terms to s. 64(2) to (4) and (6) (see **B3.272**).

Any reference to an adoptive relationship is to be read as including a reference to the corresponding relationship arising by virtue of a parental order under the Human Fertilisation and Embryology Act 2008 (Human Fertilisation and Embryology (Parental Orders) Regulations 2010 (SI 2010 No. 985), sch. 4).

Procedure An allegation of an offence contrary to s. 65 is triable either way. As to the classification of the offence for the purpose of listing, see CPD XIII, para. B (see Supplement, **PD-97**).   **B3.277**

See **B3.335** for alternative verdicts.

Indictment   B3.278

Statement of Offence

Consenting to the penetration of his body by a related person contrary to section 65(1) of the Sexual Offences Act 2003.

Particulars of Offence

A on or about the...day of...being then a person aged 16 years or over permitted V a person related to her and over the age of 18 years sexually to penetrate [her vagina or anus] [his anus] [with his penis, fingers,] [with a part of her body, namely her fingers].

Sentencing The maximum sentence for an offence under the SOA 2003, s. 65, on conviction on indictment is two years. On summary conviction, the maximum is six months or a fine not exceeding the statutory maximum, or both (s. 65(5)).   **B3.279**

The Sentencing Council has issued a new guideline applicable to sex offenders aged 18 or over who are sentenced on or after 1 April 2014 (see **B3.3**). For the guideline in respect of an offence under s. 65, see Supplement, **SG-172**. There is a notification requirement under the SOA 2003, s. 80 and sch. 3, subject to the age of the offender and the sentence imposed (see **E23**).

Elements Section 65 contains a rebuttable presumption as to the accused's *mens rea* in respect of the relationship between him and the person he penetrates. The provision is identical to that contained within s. 64 and reference should therefore be had to **B3.275** for its nature and effect.   **B3.280**

OTHER OFFENCES

Exposure

Sexual Offences Act 2003, s. 66   B3.281

(1) A person commits an offence if—
  (a) he intentionally exposes his genitals, and
  (b) he intends that someone will see them and be caused alarm or distress.

B3.282 **Procedure** An allegation of an offence contrary to s. 66 is triable either way. As to the classification of the offence for the purpose of listing, see CPD XIII, para. B (see Supplement, **PD-97**).

See **B3.335** for alternative verdicts.

B3.283 **Sentencing** The maximum penalty for an offence under the SOA 2003, s. 66, on conviction on indictment is two years' imprisonment. On summary conviction, the maximum is six months or a fine not exceeding the statutory maximum, or both.

The Sentencing Council has issued a new guideline applicable to sex offenders aged 18 or over who are sentenced on or after 1 April 2014 (see **B3.3**). For the guideline in respect of an offence under s. 66, see Supplement, **SG-164**. For examples of the application of the previous guideline, see *Bell* [2008] 2 Cr App R (S) 232 and *McMahon* [2008] EWCA Crim 3104.

There is a notification requirement under the SOA 2003, s. 80 and sch. 3, subject to the age of the offender, the age of the victim, and the sentence imposed (see **E23**).

B3.284 **Elements** The essence of the offence is that the accused intentionally exposes his genitals and intends that another person see them and is thereby caused alarm or distress. The offence thus has a 'bolted on intent' and is therefore one of specific intent. Consequently, voluntary intoxication may negate the intent required for the offence (*Heard* [2008] QB 43).

Voyeurism

B3.285   Sexual Offences Act 2003, ss. 67 and 68

67.—(1) A person commits an offence if—
   (a) for the purpose of obtaining sexual gratification, he observes another person doing a private act, and
   (b) he knows that the other person does not consent to being observed for his sexual gratification.
(2) A person commits an offence if—
   (a) he operates equipment with the intention of enabling another person to observe, for the purpose of obtaining sexual gratification, a third person (B) doing a private act, and
   (b) he knows that B does not consent to his operating equipment with that intention.
(3) A person commits an offence if—
   (a) he records another person (B) doing a private act,
   (b) he does so with the intention that he or a third person will, for the purpose of obtaining sexual gratification, look at an image of B doing the act, and
   (c) he knows that B does not consent to his recording the act with that intention.
(4) A person commits an offence if he instals equipment, or constructs or adapts a structure or part of a structure, with the intention of enabling himself or another person to commit an offence under subsection (1).

68.—(1) for the purposes of section 67, a person is doing a private act if the person is in a place which, in the circumstances, would reasonably be expected to provide privacy, and—
   (a) the person's genitals, buttocks or breasts are exposed or covered only with underwear,
   (b) the person is using a lavatory, or
   (c) the person is doing a sexual act that is not of a kind ordinarily done in public.
(2) In section 67, 'structure' includes a tent, vehicle or vessel or other temporary or movable structure.

B3.286 **Procedure** An allegation of an offence contrary to s. 67 is triable either way. As to the classification of the offence for the purpose of listing, see CPD XIII, para. B (see Supplement, **PD-97**).

See **B3.335** for alternative verdicts.

Indictment   **B3.287**

Statement of Offence

Operating equipment with the intention of enabling another person to observe a private act for the purposes of sexual gratification contrary to section 67(2) of the Sexual Offences Act 2003.

Particulars of Offence

A, on or about the. . .day of. . .knowing that V did not consent thereto operated equipment with the intention of enabling another person to observe V doing a private act.

Sentencing   The maximum penalty for an offence under the SOA 2003, s. 67, on conviction **B3.288** on indictment is two years' imprisonment. On summary conviction, the maximum is six months or a fine not exceeding the statutory maximum, or both (s. 67(5)).

The Sentencing Council has issued a new guideline applicable to sex offenders aged 18 or over who are sentenced on or after 1 April 2014 (see **B3.3**). For the guideline in respect of an offence under s. 67, see Supplement, **SG-168**. For examples of the application of the old guideline, see *Hodgson* [2009] 1 Cr App R (S) 145 and *Al-Sayed* [2010] 1 Cr App R (S) 568.

There is a notification requirement under the SOA 2003, s. 80 and sch. 3, subject to the age of the offender and the sentence imposed (see **E23**).

Elements   As to 'gratification', see **B3.113**. For 'consent', see **B3.19**. 'Private act' is defined in **B3.289** s. 68 (see **B3.285**).

In *Bassett* [2009] 1 WLR 1032, the appellant had been convicted of voyeurism after using a concealed camera to film a man wearing swimming trunks in the showers of a public swimming pool. The Court of Appeal quashed the conviction on the basis that s. 68(1)(a) related only to the breasts of women and not men. The issue also arose as to whether the complainant was doing a private act at the time of the offence. The fact that the showers were open plan was not inevitably fatal to the conviction as a person may have a reasonable expectation of privacy from the type of observation which occurred whilst they were in the shower area. That issue of reasonable expectation of privacy is one for the jury. For commentary on *Bassett*, see [2008] Crim LR 998.

Intercourse with an Animal

Sexual Offences Act 2003, s. 69   **B3.290**

(1) A person commits an offence if—
    (a) he intentionally performs an act of penetration with his penis,
    (b) what is penetrated is the vagina or anus of a living animal, and
    (c) he knows that, or is reckless as to whether, that is what is penetrated.
(2) A person (A) commits an offence if—
    (a) A intentionally causes, or allows, A's vagina or anus to be penetrated,
    (b) the penetration is by the penis of a living animal, and
    (c) A knows that, or is reckless as to whether, that is what A is being penetrated by.

Procedure   An allegation of an offence contrary to s. 69 is triable either way. As to the classifi- **B3.291** cation of the offence for the purpose of listing, see CPD XIII, para. B (see Supplement, **PD-97**).

See **B3.335** for alternative verdicts.

Sentencing   The maximum penalty for an offence under the SOA 2003, s. 69, on conviction **B3.292** on indictment is two years' imprisonment. On summary conviction, the maximum is six months or a fine not exceeding the statutory maximum, or both (s. 69(3)).

The new definitive sentencing guideline (see **B3.3**) does not include this offence. There is a notification requirement under the SOA 2003, s. 80 and sch. 3, subject to the age of the offender and the sentence imposed (see **E23**).

B3.293   **Elements**   The essence of the offence under the SOA 2003, s. 69(1), is an intentional act of penetration by the penis and so it can be committed only by a male person. Penetration must be of the vagina or anus of a living animal. 'Vagina' or 'anus' is defined in s. 79(10) to include references to any similar part. The accused must know or be reckless as to whether that is what is penetrated.

By contrast, the offence under s. 69(2) can be committed by a male or female person as the essence of it is that the offender intentionally allows his or her anus or her vagina to be penetrated by the penis of a living animal. The accused must know or be reckless that it is the anus or vagina that is being penetrated.

See **B3.324** for explanation of the circumstances in which possession of an image of intercourse or oral sex with an animal is capable of constituting an offence.

Sexual Penetration of a Corpse

B3.294   Sexual Offences Act 2003, s. 70

(1) A person commits an offence if—
   (a) he intentionally performs an act of penetration with a part of his body or anything else,
   (b) what is penetrated is a part of the body of a dead person,
   (c) he knows that, or is reckless as to whether, that is what is penetrated, and
   (d) the penetration is sexual.

B3.295   **Procedure**   An allegation of an offence contrary to s. 67 is triable either way. As to the classification of the offence for the purpose of listing, see CPD XIII, para. B (see Supplement, **PD-97**).

See **B3.335** for alternative verdicts.

B3.296   **Sentencing**   The maximum penalty for an offence under the SOA 2003, s. 70, on conviction on indictment is two years' imprisonment. On summary conviction, the maximum is six months or a fine not exceeding the statutory maximum, or both (s. 70(2)).

The new definitive sentencing guideline (see **B3.3**) does not include this offence.

B3.297   **Elements**   The essence of the offence is the intentional penetration of the body of a dead person. That penetration can be by means of either a part of the body or an object. The accused must know that or be reckless as to whether he is penetrating a part of the body of a dead person and the penetration must be sexual. For 'sexual', see **B3.47**.

Sexual Activity in a Public Lavatory

B3.298   Sexual Offences Act 2003, s. 71

(1) A person commits an offence if—
   (a) he is in a lavatory to which the public or a section of the public has or is permitted to have access, whether on payment or otherwise,
   (b) he intentionally engages in an activity, and,
   (c) the activity is sexual.
(2) For the purposes of this section, an activity is sexual if a reasonable person would, in all the circumstances but regardless of any person's purpose, consider it to be sexual.

B3.299   **Procedure and Sentencing**   An allegation of an offence contrary to s. 71 is triable summarily only.

The maximum penalty upon conviction is six months' imprisonment or a fine not exceeding level 5, or both (s. 71(3)).

The new definitive sentencing guideline (see **B3.3**) does not refer to this offence. The *Magistrates' Court Sentencing Guidelines* (see Supplement, **SG-309**) apply.

B3.300   **Elements**   An offender must intentionally engage in sexual activity in a lavatory to which the public, or a section of the public, is permitted access either by payment or otherwise. The definition of 'sexual' is objective for the purposes of s. 71.

TERRITORIAL AND EXTRA-TERRITORIAL JURISDICTION

Extra-territorial jurisdiction is provided for in respect of many offences under the SOA 2003 **B3.301** by s. 72.

Sexual Offences Act 2003, s. 72

(1) If—
  (a) a United Kingdom national does an act in a country outside the United Kingdom, and
  (b) the act, if done in England and Wales, would constitute a sexual offence to which this section applies,
  the United Kingdom national is guilty in England and Wales of that sexual offence.

(2) If—
  (a) a United Kingdom resident does an act in a country outside the United Kingdom,
  (b) the act constitutes an offence under the law in force in that country, and
  (c) the act, if done in England and Wales, would constitute a sexual offence to which this section applies,
  the United Kingdom resident is guilty in England and Wales of that sexual offence.

(3) If—
  (a) a person does an act in a country outside the United Kingdom at a time when the person was not a United Kingdom national or a United Kingdom resident,
  (b) the act constituted an offence under the law in force in that country,
  (c) the act, if done in England and Wales, would have constituted a sexual offence to which this section applies, and
  (d) the person meets the residence or nationality condition at the relevant time,
  proceedings may be brought against the person in England and Wales for that sexual offence as if the person had done the act there.

(4) The person meets the residence or nationality condition at the relevant time if the person is a United Kingdom national or a United Kingdom resident at the time when the proceedings are brought.

(5) An act punishable under the law in force in any country constitutes an offence under that law for the purposes of subsections (2) and (3) however it is described in that law.

(6) The condition in subsection (2)(b) or (3)(b) is to be taken to be met unless, not later than rules of court may provide, the defendant serves on the prosecution a notice—
  (a) stating that, on the facts as alleged with respect to the act in question, the condition is not in the defendant's opinion met,
  (b) showing the grounds for that opinion, and
  (c) requiring the prosecution to prove that it is met.

(7) But the court, if it thinks fit, may permit the defendant to require the prosecution to prove that the condition is met without service of a notice under subsection (6).

(8) In the Crown Court the question whether the condition is met is to be decided by the judge alone.

(9) In this section—
  'country' includes territory;
  'United Kingdom national' means an individual who is—
  (a) a British citizen, a British overseas territories citizen, a British National (Overseas) or a British Overseas citizen;
  (b) a person who under the British Nationality Act 1981 is a British subject; or
  (c) a British protected person within the meaning of that Act;
  'United Kingdom resident' means an individual who is resident in the United Kingdom.

(10) Schedule 2 lists the sexual offences to which this section applies.

Schedule 2, para. 1 applies to England and Wales.

Sexual Offences Act 2003, sch. 2, para. 1

In relation to England and Wales, the following are sexual offences to which section 72 applies—

(a) an offence under any of sections 5 to 19, 25 and 26 and 47 to 50;
(b) an offence under any of sections 1 to 4, 30 to 41 and 61 where the victim of the offence was under 18 at the time of the offence;

(c) an offence under section 62 or 63 where the intended offence was an offence against a person under 18;

(d) an offence under—

(i) section 1 of the Protection of Children Act 1978 (indecent photographs of children), or

(ii) section 160 of the Criminal Justice Act 1988 (possession of indecent photograph of child).

Section 72 was substituted by the CJIA 2008, s. 72, with effect from 14 July 2008. It is no longer confined to offences against children under the age of 16. In respect of non-consensual offences such as rape, or offences involving child prostitution or breach of trust, the new limit is now set at 18. More controversially, by virtue of s. 72(1) (and in contrast to UK residents and others coming under ss. 72(2) and (3)), UK nationals are deprived of any defence based on lack of dual criminality. Thus a UK national who engages in consensual sexual activity with a child aged 15 in a country outside the UK may incur criminal liability even if he is not resident in the UK and the activity is perfectly lawful in the country in which it takes place.

SOLICITING

B3.302

Street Offences Act 1959, s. 1

(1) It shall be an offence for a person (whether male or female) persistently to loiter or solicit in a street or public place for the purpose of prostitution.

(2) A person guilty of an offence under this section shall be liable on summary conviction to a fine of an amount not exceeding level 2 on the standard scale or, for an offence committed after a previous conviction, to a fine of an amount not exceeding level 3 on that scale.

(3) [Repealed by SOCPA 2005, schs. 7 and 17.]

(4) For the purposes of this section—

(a) conduct is persistent if it takes place on two or more occasions in any period of three months;

(b) any reference to a person loitering or soliciting for the purposes of prostitution is a reference to a person loitering or soliciting for the purposes of offering services as a prostitute;

(c) 'street' includes any bridge, road, lane, footway, subway, square, court, alley or passage, whether a thoroughfare, or not, which is for the time being open to the public; and the doorways and entrances of premises abutting on a street (as hereinbefore defined), and any ground adjoining and open to a street, shall be treated as forming part of the street.

Sexual Offences Act 2003, s. 51A

(1) It is an offence for a person in a street or public place to solicit another (B) for the purpose of obtaining B's sexual services as a prostitute.

(2) The reference to a person in a street or public place includes a person in a vehicle in a street or public place.

Procedure

B3.303 An allegation of an offence contrary to s. 1 of the Street Offences Act 1959 or s. 51A of the SOA 2003 is triable summarily only.

Sentencing

B3.304 The maximum penalty for the offence of loitering for the purposes of prostitution under the Street Offences Act 1959 is a fine not exceeding level 2 on the standard scale; for an offence committed after a previous conviction, the maximum penalty is a fine not exceeding level 3 (Street Offences Act 1959, s. 1(2)). Soliciting contrary to the SOA 2003, s. 51A, carries a maximum penalty of a fine not exceeding level 3.

The PACA 2009, s. 17, amended the Street Offences Act 1959, s. 1, so as to provide new sentencing powers relating to offences under s. 1, namely orders requiring attendance at meetings to assist the offender to address the causes of the conduct constituting the offence.

Elements

Soliciting can be carried out by either a male or female, the essence of the offence being the **B3.305** solicitation of another to engage in prostitution (*DPP v Bull* [1995] QB 88). The person solicit-ing need not be in a public place provided the solicitation extends into a public place (*Behrendt v Burridge* [1977] 3 All ER 285). 'Loitering' is simply lingering with no intent to move on either on foot or in a vehicle (*Bridge v Campbell* (1947) 177 LT 444). There is no definition of public place and any issue will be resolved as a matter of fact and degree (*Glynn v Simmonds* [1952] 2 All ER 57; *Elkins v Cartlidge* [1947] 1 All ER 829).

A person is in a street or public place for the purposes of s. 51A if they are in a vehicle in that street or public place. The term 'street' has the same meaning under s. 51A as under the Street Offences Act 1959, s. 1 (SOA 2003, s. 51A(4)).

INDECENT PHOTOGRAPHS OF CHILDREN, ETC.

The Protection of Children Act 1978 and the CJA 1988 govern the making, possession, publi- **B3.306** cation and distribution of indecent images of children with offenders being punished with up to ten years' imprisonment. These provisions are dealt with in detail below.

Protection of Children Act 1978, ss. 1 and 1A

1.—(1) Subject to section 1A and 1B, it is an offence for a person—
   (a) to take, or permit to be taken or to make, any indecent photograph or pseudo-photograph of a child; or
   (b) to distribute or show such indecent photographs or pseudo-photographs; or
   (c) to have in his possession such indecent photographs or pseudo-photographs, with a view to their being distributed or shown by himself or others; or
   (d) to publish or cause to be published any advertisement likely to be understood as conveying that the advertiser distributes or shows such indecent photographs or pseudo-photographs, or intends to do so.

1A.—(1) This section applies where, in proceedings for an offence under section 1(1)(a) of taking or making an indecent photograph or pseudo-photograph of a child, or for an offence under section 1(1)(b) or (c) relating to an indecent photograph or pseudo-photograph of a child, the defendant proves that the photograph or pseudo-photograph was of the child aged 16 or over, and that at the time of the offence charged the child and he—
   (a) were married, or
   (b) lived together as partners in an enduring family relationship.
   (2) Subsections (5) and (6) also apply where, in proceedings for an offence under section 1(1)(b) or (c) relating to an indecent photograph or pseudo-photograph of a child, the defendant proves that the photograph or pseudo-photograph was of the child aged 16 or over, and that at the time when he obtained it the child and he—
   (a) were married, or
   (b) lived together as partners in an enduring family relationship.
   (3) This section applies whether the photograph or pseudo-photograph showed the child alone or with the defendant, but not if it showed any other person.
   (4) In the case of an offence under section 1(1)(a), if sufficient evidence is adduced to raise an issue as to whether the child consented to the photograph or pseudo-photograph being taken or made, or as to whether the defendant reasonably believed that the child so con-sented, the defendant is not guilty of the offence unless it is proved that the child did not so consent and that the defendant did not reasonably believe that the child so consented.
   (5) In the case of an offence under section 1(1)(b), the defendant is not guilty of the offence unless it is proved that the showing or distributing was to a person other than the child.
   (6) In the case of an offence under section 1(1)(c), if sufficient evidence is adduced to raise an issue both—
   (a) as to whether the child consented to the photograph or pseudo-photograph being in the defendant's possession, or as to whether the defendant reasonably believed that the child so consented, and

(b) as to whether the defendant had the photograph or pseudo-photograph in his possession with a view to its being distributed or shown to anyone other than the child,

the defendant is not guilty of the offence unless it is proved either that the child did not so consent and that the defendant did not reasonably believe that the child so consented, or that the defendant had the photograph or pseudo-photograph in his possession with a view to its being distributed or shown to a person other than the child.

B3.307

Criminal Justice Act 1988, ss. 160 and 160A

160.—(1) Subject to section 160A, it is an offence for a person to have any indecent photograph or pseudo-photograph of a child in his possession.

(2) Where a person is charged with an offence under subsection (1) above, it shall be a defence for him to prove—

(a) that he had a legitimate reason for having the photograph or pseudo-photograph in his possession; or

(b) that he had not himself seen the photograph or pseudo-photograph and did not know, nor had any cause to suspect, it to be indecent; or

(c) that the photograph or pseudo-photograph was sent to him without any prior request made by him or on his behalf and that he did not keep it for an unreasonable time.

160A.—(1) This section applies where, in proceedings for an offence under section 160 relating to an indecent photograph or pseudo-photograph of a child, the defendant proves that the photograph or pseudo-photograph was of the child aged 16 or over, and that at the time of the offence charged the child and he—

(a) were married or civil partners of each other, or

(b) lived together as partners in an enduring family relationship.

(2) This section also applies where, in proceedings for an offence under section 160 relating to an indecent photograph or pseudo-photograph of a child, the defendant proves that the photograph or pseudo-photograph was of the child aged 16 or over, and that at the time when he obtained it the child and he—

(a) were married or civil partners of each other, or

(b) lived together as partners in an enduring family relationship.

(3) This section applies whether the photograph or pseudo-photograph showed the child alone or with the defendant, but not if it showed any other person.

(4) If sufficient evidence is adduced to raise an issue as to whether the child consented to the photograph or pseudo-photograph being in the defendant's possession, or as to whether the defendant reasonably believed that the child so consented, the defendant is not guilty of the offence unless it is proved that the child did not so consent and that the defendant did not reasonably believe that the child so consented.

Procedure

B3.308 An allegation of an offence contrary to s. 1 of the Protection of Children Act 1978 is triable either way. An allegation of an offence contrary to s. 160(1) of the CJA 1988 is similarly triable either way. As to the classification of the offences for the purpose of listing, see CPD XIII, para. B (see Supplement, **PD-97**). Proceedings in relation to either offence may not be instituted without the consent of the DPP. The extra-territorial jurisdiction provisions of the SOA 2003, s. 72 (see **B3.301**) apply.

Indictment

B3.309 In *Thompson* [2004] 2 Cr App R 262, the Court of Appeal gave guidance as to the drafting of an indictment where a case involves possession of a large number of photographs under the CJA 1988, s. 160. It is submitted that the same guidance will apply to prosecutions under the 1978 Act. The following principles were set out in *Thompson*:

(1) In addition to the specific counts, a comprehensive count should be included to cover the remainder.

(2) The photographs used in the specific counts should, if practicable, be selected so as to be broadly representative of the images in the comprehensive count. If agreement can be reached

as to the number of photographs to be included at each level (*Oliver* [2003] 1 Cr App R 463), the need for the judge to view the entirety of the offending material may be avoided. It is submitted that this principle will apply in the same way to the new levels of images set out in the 2014 Sentencing Council definitive guideline (see **B3.310**).

(3) Where it is impracticable to present the court with specific counts that are agreed to be representative of the comprehensive count, there must be available to the court an approximate breakdown of the number of images at each of the five levels (*Oliver*). It is submitted that the counts settled should now be representative of the three levels identified in the 2014 Sentencing Council definitive guideline (see **B3.310**). That may best be achieved by the prosecution providing the defence with a schedule setting out the information and ensuring that the defence has an opportunity, well in advance of the sentencing hearing, of viewing the images and checking the accuracy of the schedule.

(4) The specific counts should make it clear whether the image in question is a real image or a pseudo-image: the same count should not charge both. There might be a significant difference between the two and, where there was a dispute, there should be alternative counts.

(5) Each image charged in a specific count should be identified by its 'jpg' or other reference so that it is clear with which image the specific count is dealing.

(6) The estimated age range of the child shown in each of the images should, where possible, be provided to the court.

In practice judges will usually view a selection of the material in order to establish the seriousness of the contents.

Sentencing

The maximum penalty for an offence under the Protection of Children Act 1978, s. 1, is ten years on indictment and six months and/or a fine to the statutory maximum on summary conviction (Protection of Children Act 1978, s. 8; MCA 1980, s. 32; CJCSA 2000, s. 41). The maximum penalty for an offence under the CJA 1988, s. 160, is five years on indictment and six months and/or a fine not exceeding the statutory maximum on summary conviction (CJCSA 2000, s. 41).

B3.310

The Sentencing Council has issued a new guideline applicable to sex offenders aged 18 or over who are sentenced on or after 1 April 2014 (see **B3.3**). For the guideline in respect of an offence under s. 1 of the 1978 Act or the CJA 1988, s. 160, see Supplement, **SG-116**. The new guideline has radically altered the approach to be taken by courts. The approach to sentencing in respect of the relevant offences is also different to that taken in respect of other offences covered by the new guideline. That different approach is necessary because the 'harm and culpability' model employed in relation to other offences is not so readily applicable to these offences. The Council focuses on the role of the offender as the starting point for the assessment of culpability. The three roles are:

Possession An offender falls within this category if he possesses images but there is no evidence of distributing, possession with a view to distributing, or involvement in the production of the image.

B3.311

Distribution This category includes both actual distribution and possession of images with a view to distributing them, showing them or sharing them with others.

B3.312

Production/taking This category includes involvement in the actual taking or making of an image at source, i.e. involvement in its production, and is the highest category for sentencing purposes.

B3.313

The role of the offender then has to be viewed in the context of the type of images upon which the offending is centred. The Council identified three levels (in contrast to the previous *Oliver* scale). The three levels are:

Category A: 'Images involving penetrative sexual activity' and 'images involving sexual activity with an animal or sadism'.
Category B: 'Images involving non-penetrative sexual activity'.
Category C: 'Other indecent images not falling within categories A or B'.

The collections of many offenders contain images at a mix of levels. In respect of 'mixed collections' the Council has decided that the appropriate starting point and range should initially be determined by the highest category of image level present in the collection. But if those images are unrepresentative of the offender's conduct, a lower category may be appropriate. Nevertheless, a lower category will not be appropriate if the offender has produced or taken images of a higher category. It should be noted that the quantity of material possessed is no longer used to determine the offence category.

Elements of the 1978 Act Offence

B3.314 A person's intention in making photographs of children may be relevant to his *mens rea* but it is not relevant to the question of whether they are indecent for the purposes of s. 1(1)(a) (*Smethurst* [2002] 1 Cr App R 50). 'Making' can be comprised of simply copying an indecent photograph (*Atkins v DPP* [2000] 2 All ER 425). If a person intentionally opens an attachment to an e-mail and he knows that it contains an indecent photograph of a child or is likely to contain such a photograph, then he is guilty of making a photograph for the purposes of the Act (*Smith* [2003] 1 Cr App R 212). In *Harrison* [2008] 1 Cr App R 387, it was held that a person who accesses an adult pornographic web site knowing that indecent images of children will automatically be generated as 'pop-ups' on the screen is guilty of 'making' an image each time that it appears. He is equally guilty of making an image if he knows that it will be automatically saved to the hard drive of his computer and possesses the image as long as it remains there. In *Dodd* [2013] EWCA Crim 660, where the errors in the trial were such as to undermine the safety of the conviction, the Court of Appeal did not need to decide what it described as the interesting question of whether images which are on their face innocuous can be rendered indecent by their context; in *Dodd* that context was text which surrounded the images.

In *Fox* [2009] EWCA Crim 653 the accused had been convicted of, *inter alia*, two counts of taking indecent photographs of a child contrary to s. 1(1)(a). Two photographs had been specified in the particulars of the indictment as sample counts. In relation to each count, the jury was provided with a bundle of photographs relating to that count. The trial judge directed the jury that they could convict provided they were sure that at least one in each bundle was indecent. The Court of Appeal quashed the convictions. The jury should have been directed that in order to convict on either count they had to be sure that either of the photographs specified in the indictment were indecent. The way the trial judge had directed the jury allowed for the possibility that different jurors might have different views on which photograph they considered indecent and it may have been that the jury did not consider the photograph specified in the indictment to be indecent.

B3.315 The Court of Appeal rejected an argument that s. 1A(4) should be interpreted so as to apply to a 'one night stand' in *DM* [2011] EWCA Crim 2752. It was submitted that s. 1A should be interpreted so as to apply to a casual encounter of the type which occurred. Such an interpretation was said to be compatible with the ECHR, Articles 8 and 10. Unmarried and non-cohabiting 16 or 17-year-olds are able to consent to sexual intercourse but not the taking of an indecent photograph whilst their married or cohabiting counterparts are able to consent to both. The legislation therefore failed to make allowance for sexually active 16 or 17-year-olds living with their parents and violated their rights under Articles 8 and 10. The Court held that the 1978 Act was drafted and interpreted so as to provide effective protection of children whilst balancing rights under Article 8. A defence which included a 'brief sexual relationship' would diminish the protection provided. The Act strikes the balance between keeping interference by the State in the private lives of individuals to the minimum and maintaining under the law maximum protection for children from sexual abuse and exploitation.

Section 2(3) provides that a person is to be taken as having been a child at any material time if it appears, from the evidence as a whole, that he was then under the age of 18.

For the purposes of the Protection of Children Act 1978, a child is a person under the age of 18 (s. 7(6)).

The offence is not incompatible with the ECHR, Article 10 (*Graham-Kerr* (1989) 88 Cr App R 302).

The offence of showing an indecent photograph of a child is not made out where the accused proposes to show it only to himself. This is also true of the offence of possession with intent to show (*ET* (1999) 163 JP 349). Similarly, the phrase 'with a view to' distribution of indecent photographs or pseudo-photographs in the Protection of Children Act 1978, s. 1(1)(c), requires that the distribution or showing must be at least one of the accused's purposes, but not necessarily his primary purpose. Thus in *Dooley* [2006] 1 WLR 775, the accused did not intend to show or distribute indecent images when he downloaded pornography with a view to placing it in a secure file but did not have time to remove it from a shared file before others could look at it. If an offender provides another person with a password to access a computer in order to view relevant images, that is sufficient to amount to 'showing' (*Fellows and Arnold* [1997] 1 Cr App R 244). In *Price* [2006] EWCA Crim 3363, the Court of Appeal held that the offence under s. 1(1)(b) is one of strict liability, subject only to the defence in s. 1(4).

Under s. 1(4), it is a defence to a charge of distribution or possession if the accused proves that he had a legitimate reason for either possessing, showing or distributing such photographs or he had not seen the photographs and did not know or have reason to suspect that they were indecent.

If the photograph or pseudo-photograph is made pursuant to an appropriate authorisation given by a relevant authority for the purposes of the prevention, detection or investigation of crime or criminal proceedings, then the making is exempt from criminal proceedings under s. 1B.

Photograph and pseudo-photograph are defined in detail in s. 7   B3.316

Protection of Children Act 1978, s. 7

(1) The following subsections apply for the interpretation of this Act.
(2) References to an indecent photograph include an indecent film, a copy of an indecent photograph or film, and an indecent photograph comprised in a film.
(3) Photographs (including those comprised in a film) shall, if they show children and are indecent, be treated for all purposes of this Act as indecent photographs of children and so as respects pseudo-photographs.
(4) References to a photograph include—
    (a) the negative as well as the positive version; and
    (b) data stored on a computer disc or by other electronic means which is capable of conversion into a photograph.
(4A) References to a photograph also include—
    (a) a tracing or other image, whether made by electronic or other means (of whatever nature)—
        (i) which is not itself a photograph or pseudo-photograph, but
        (ii) which is derived from the whole or part of a photograph or pseudo-photograph (or a combination of either or both); and
    (b) data stored on a computer disc or by other electronic means which is capable of conversion into an image within paragraph (a);

and subsection (8) applies in relation to such an image as it applies in relation to a pseudo-photograph.

(5) 'Film' includes any form of video-recording.

(6) 'Child', subject to subsection (8), means a person under the age of 18.

(7) 'Pseudo-photograph' means an image, whether made by computer-graphics or otherwise howsoever, which appears to be a photograph.

(8) If the impression conveyed by a pseudo-photograph is that the person shown is a child, the pseudo-photograph shall be treated for all purposes of this Act as showing a child and so shall a pseudo-photograph where the predominant impression conveyed is that the person shown is a child notwithstanding that some of the physical characteristics shown are those of an adult.

(9) References to an indecent pseudo-photograph include—

(a) a copy of an indecent pseudo-photograph; and

(b) data stored on a computer disc or by other electronic means which is capable of conversion into an indecent pseudo-photograph.

Elements of the 1988 Act Offence

B3.317 Under the CJA 1988, s. 160, simple possession of a relevant photograph or pseudo-photograph may constitute an offence.

In *Porter* [2006] 2 All ER 625, it was held that the offence of possession required that the accused had possession or control of the images. If the images had been deleted from his computer then it would be a question of fact as to whether he had control of them. That question could be answered by reference to whether he had the expertise and equipment to retrieve the images. *Porter* was applied in *Rowe* (2008) 172 JP 585 and in *Leonard* [2012] 2 Cr App R 138.

The defence set out in s. 160(2) is available if the accused did not have cause to suspect that the photograph was an indecent photograph of a child (*Collier* [2005] 1 WLR 843), albeit he suspected that the image was of an indecent nature.

Photograph and pseudo-photograph have the same meaning as in s. 7 of the Protection of Children Act 1978 (s. 160(4)).

POSSESSION OF PROHIBITED IMAGES OF CHILDREN

B3.318 The CAJA 2009, ss. 62 to 68, governs offences of possession of prohibited images of children, associated defences and ancillary provisions.

Coroners and Justice Act 2009, s. 62

(1) It is an offence for a person to be in possession of a prohibited image of a child.

(2) A prohibited image is an image which—

(a) is pornographic,

(b) falls within subsection (6), and

(c) is grossly offensive, disgusting or otherwise of an obscene character.

(3) An image is 'pornographic' if it is of such a nature that it must reasonably be assumed to have been produced solely or principally for the purpose of sexual arousal.

(4) Where (as found in the person's possession) an image forms part of a series of images, the question whether the image is of such a nature as is mentioned in subsection (3) is to be determined by reference to—

(a) the image itself, and

(b) (if the series of images is such as to be capable of providing a context for the image) the context in which it occurs in the series of images.

(5) So, for example, where—

(a) an image forms an integral part of a narrative constituted by a series of images, and

(b) having regard to those images as a whole, they are not of such a nature that they must reasonably be assumed to have been produced solely or principally for the purpose of sexual arousal,
the image may, by virtue of being part of that narrative, be found not to be pornographic, even
though it might have been found to be pornographic if taken by itself.
(6) An image falls within this subsection if it—
  (a) is an image which focuses solely or principally on a child's genitals or anal region, or
  (b) portrays any of the acts mentioned in subsection (7).
(7) Those acts are—
  (a) the performance by a person of an act of intercourse or oral sex with or in the presence of
      a child;
  (b) an act of masturbation by, of, involving or in the presence of a child;
  (c) an act which involves penetration of the vagina or anus of a child with a part of a person's
      body or with anything else;
  (d) an act of penetration, in the presence of a child, of the vagina or anus of a person with a
      part of a person's body or with anything else;
  (e) the performance by a child of an act of intercourse or oral sex with an animal (whether
      dead or alive or imaginary);
  (f) the performance by a person of an act of intercourse or oral sex with an animal (whether
      dead or alive or imaginary) in the presence of a child.
(8) For the purposes of subsection (7), penetration is a continuing act from entry to withdrawal.

Indictment

Statement of Offence   **B3.319**

Possession of a prohibited image contrary to section 62 of the Coroners and Justice Act 2009

Particulars of Offence

A, on or about the...day of...possessed a prohibited image of a child which focused principally on
the child's genitals

Procedure

The offence is triable either way. Proceedings under the CAJA 2009, s. 62, may not be instituted   **B3.320**
without the consent of the DPP.

Sentencing

The maximum penalty on conviction on indictment is three years' imprisonment or a fine or   **B3.321**
both. On summary conviction, the maximum penalty is six months' imprisonment or a fine not
exceeding the statutory maximum or both (CAJA 2009, s. 66 and sch. 22, para. 12).

Elements

An image is 'pornographic' for the purposes of the CAJA 2009 if it must reasonably be assumed   **B3.322**
to have been produced solely or principally for the purpose of sexual arousal (CAJA 2009,
s. 62(3)). Its potential pornographic nature is to be considered in the context of the whole
where it forms part of a series of images found in D's possession (s. 62(4)). 'Image' is defined to
include a moving or still image produced by any means; or data stored by any means which is
capable of conversion into a moving or still image but does not include an indecent photograph
or indecent pseudo-photograph of a child (s. 65(2) and (3)).

'Child' means a person under the age of 18 (s. 65(5)).

An image is to be treated as an image of a child if the impression created is that the person shown
is a child, or the predominant impression conveyed is that the person shown is a child despite the
fact that some of the physical characteristics shown are not those of a child (s. 65(6)).

Section 63 defines 'excluded images' to which s. 62 does not apply. Broadly speaking, excluded
images are those contained within a classified work. Classified work is work which has been

given a classification certificate by a designation certificate (whenever issued). All images contained within a classified work are, however, not necessarily exempt from s. 62. Section 63(3) states that an image or images extracted from a classified work solely or principally for the purposes of sexual arousal will not be excluded.

Defences

B3.323   Under the CAJA 2009, s. 64(1), it is a defence for a person charged under s. 62(1) to prove any of the following matters.

(a) that the person had a legitimate reason for being in possession of the image concerned;
(b) that the person had not seen the image concerned and did not know, nor had any cause to suspect, it to be a prohibited image;
(c) that the person—
   (i) was sent the image concerned without any prior request having been made by or on behalf of the person, and
   (ii) did not keep it for an unreasonable time.

It is submitted that the burden on the accused is evidential.

Section 68 and sch. 13 make special provision for persons providing information society services.

EXTREME PORNOGRAPHIC IMAGES

B3.324   In contrast to the relevant provisions of the Protection of Children Act 1978 and the CJA 1988 (see **B3.306** and **B3.307**), the images prohibited by the CJIA 2008, s. 63, are not only those of children but may also include adults and animals.

Criminal Justice and Immigration Act 2008, s. 63

(1) It is an offence for a person to be in possession of an extreme pornographic image.
(2) An 'extreme pornographic image' is an image which is both—
   (a) pornographic, and
   (b) an extreme image.
(3) An image is 'pornographic' if it is of such a nature that it must reasonably be assumed to have been produced solely or principally for the purpose of sexual arousal.
(4) Where (as found in the person's possession) an image forms part of a series of images, the question whether the image is of such a nature as is mentioned in subsection (3) is to be determined by reference to—
   (a) the image itself, and
   (b) (if the series of images is such as to be capable of providing a context for the image) the context in which it occurs in the series of images.
(5) So, for example, where—
   (a) an image forms an integral part of a narrative constituted by a series of images, and
   (b) having regard to those images as a whole, they are not of such a nature that they must reasonably be assumed to have been produced solely or principally for the purpose of sexual arousal,
   the image may, by virtue of being part of that narrative, be found not to be pornographic, even though it might have been found to be pornographic if taken by itself.
(6) An 'extreme image' is an image which—
   (a) falls within subsection (7), and
   (b) is grossly offensive, disgusting or otherwise of an obscene character.
(7) An image falls within this subsection if it portrays, in an explicit and realistic way, any of the following—
   (a) an act which threatens a person's life,
   (b) an act which results, or is likely to result, in serious injury to a person's anus, breasts or genitals,
   (c) an act which involves sexual interference with a human corpse, or
   (d) a person performing an act of intercourse or oral sex with an animal (whether dead or alive),
   and a reasonable person looking at the image would think that any such person or animal was real.

(8) In this section 'image' means—
   (a) a moving or still image (produced by any means); or
   (b) data (stored by any means) which is capable of conversion into an image within para-
       graph (a).
(9) In this section references to a part of the body include references to a part surgically constructed
   (in particular through gender reassignment surgery).

Indictment

B3.325

Statement of Offence

Possession of an extreme pornographic image contrary to section 63 of the Criminal Justice and
Immigration Act 2008

Particulars of Offence

A, on or about the…day of…possessed an extreme pornographic image.

Procedure

An allegation of an offence of possession of extreme pornographic images is triable either way. **B3.326**
As to the classification of the offence for the purpose of listing, see CPD XIII, para. B (see
Supplement, **PD-97**). Proceedings for an offence under the CJIA 2008, s. 63, may not be insti-
tuted except by or with the consent of the DPP (s. 63(10)).

Sentencing

By virtue of the CJIA 2008, s. 67, if the offending image portrays any act within s. 63(7)(a) or **B3.327**
(b), the maximum sentence on summary conviction is one of 12 months' imprisonment, a fine of
the statutory maximum or both. On conviction on indictment, the maximum sentence is three
years, a fine or both. If the image does not portray an act within s. 63(7)(a) or (b), the maximum
sentence on summary conviction is 12 months' imprisonment, a fine of the statutory maximum,
or both; on conviction on indictment, the maximum sentence is two years, a fine or both. The
new sentencing guideline (see **B3.3**) does not cover this offence.

In *Oliver* [2011] EWCA Crim 3114, the Court expressed the view that the public would be
surprised if the seriousness of possession of adult images under s. 63(1) should be equated with
those involving images of children. The need to protect children enables the courts to pass deterrent sentences when images of children are involved and on principle no narrow comparison is
to be made between images of children and adults. In that case O had downloaded extreme pornographic images before their possession became illegal under s. 63(1). An aggravating feature
of his offending was that he subsequently downloaded a software program called 'Team Viewer'
which enabled others to access the images by taking remote control of his computer, but he was
a 54-year-old man of previous positive good character with substantial personal mitigation. The
Court reduced a sentence of six months' imprisonment to one of two months.

In *Lewis* [2013] 1 Cr App R (S) 121 (23), the Court of Appeal upheld a sentence of 12 months'
imprisonment following guilty pleas to two offences under s. 63(1). The Court observed that
the offence under s. 63 is not a victimless crime and women photographed in such extreme
pornographic images are often trafficked or forced into their involvement.

In *Livesey* [2013] All ER (D) 179 (Aug) the Court of Appeal reduced the sentence for an offender
who had pleaded guilty to three offences of possessing extreme pornographic images from a
total of 14 months' imprisonment to four months. The offender had a large number of still and
moving images on his laptop of horses and dogs penetrating women. He admitted the offences
immediately upon police officers arriving at his home. The Court decided that, even though the
number of extreme images involved was large and the offender had deliberately sought them
out, since he had no previous convictions, was of good character and had demonstrated remorse
for his actions and there were no other aggravating features in his case and the personal mitigation was extremely strong, an element of leniency was justified.

Elements

B3.328 An image is 'pornographic' for the purposes of the CJIA 2008 if it must reasonably be assumed to have been produced solely or principally for the purpose of sexual arousal (s. 63(3)). Its potential pornographic nature is to be considered in the context of the whole where it forms part of a series of images found in D's possession (s. 63(4)). 'Image' is defined to include a moving or still image produced by any means; or data stored by any means which is capable of conversion into a moving or still image (s. 63(8)).

Section 64 defines 'excluded images' to which s. 63 does not apply. Broadly speaking, excluded images are those contained within a classified work. Classified work is work which has been given a classification certificate by a designation certificate (whenever issued). All images contained within a classified work are, however, not necessarily exempt from s. 63. Section 64 states that an image or images extracted from a classified work solely or principally for the purposes of sexual arousal will not be excluded.

For possession, see *Pin Chen Cheung* [2009] EWCA Crim 2963 (discussed at **B3.329**) and the various cases relating to drugs at **B19.23** *et seq.*, especially **B19.30**.

Defences

B3.329 Under the CJIA 2008, s. 65(1), it is a defence for a person charged under s. 63 to prove any of the matters set out in s. 65(2).

Criminal Justice and Immigration Act 2008, s. 65

    (2) The matters are—
        (a) that the person had a legitimate reason for being in possession of the image concerned;
        (b) that the person had not seen the image concerned and did not know, nor had any cause to suspect, it to be an extreme pornographic image;
        (c) that the person—
            (i) was sent the image concerned without any prior request having been made by or on behalf of the person, and
            (ii) did not keep it for an unreasonable time.

The nature of possession for the purposes of s. 63 and the nature of the burden on the accused in establishing a defence under s. 65(2) was considered in *Pin Chen Cheung* [2009] EWCA Crim 2963. The Court of Appeal made clear that the burden on the accused in establishing a defence under s. 65(2) is not simply evidential. Drawing on cases dealing with possession of drugs under the Misuse of Drugs Act 1971, the Court of Appeal ruled that, in order for the Crown to prove possession under s. 63, it was not enough that D simply had custody or control of them. Before the defence under s. 65(2) became relevant, the prosecution had to show that D had knowledge of the 'things' that gave rise to liability. But the prosecution did not need to go so far as to prove that D knew that the 'things' he knowingly had in his custody or control contained extreme pornographic images. If that were the case, the defence under s. 65(2)(b) would be otiose. If D may have believed that the items he possessed were of a wholly different nature to the subject matter of the allegations, such as floor-tiles, then he would not be guilty. The question of what amounted to items of a wholly different nature was one of fact and degree for a jury. Once possession had been established, the onus shifted to the accused to establish his defence under s. 65(2) on the balance of probabilities.

There are further defences available to a person charged with possessing images which come within s. 63(7)(a) to (c). In respect of s. 63(7)(a) and (b), by virtue of s. 66(2), it is a defence that the accused participated in any of the acts portrayed and that the act or acts did not involve the infliction of any non-consensual harm on any person. In respect of images within s. 67(3)(c), it is a defence that the defendant participated in any of the acts portrayed, that the act or acts did not involve the infliction of any non-consensual harm on any person and that what is portrayed is not in fact a corpse. For the purposes of s. 66, harm is 'non-consensual' if the harm is of such a nature that the person cannot in law consent to it being inflicted or him or herself; or, where the person can in law consent to it being so inflicted, he or she does not in fact consent (s. 66(3)).

OUTRAGING PUBLIC DECENCY

At common law it is an offence to outrage public decency, to expose the person or to engage in or simulate a sexual act in public. As to the offence of outraging public decency by way of obscene publication, see **B18.1**. **B3.330**

Procedure

The offence is triable either way; see **B3.335** for alternative verdicts. **B3.331**

Indictment

Statement of Offence **B3.332**

Outraging public decency.

Particulars of Offence

A on or about the…day of…outraged public decency, namely by publicly, to wit in the street at…, having sexual intercourse with X, within the sight and to the outrage of other persons then present.

Sentencing

The maximum penalty for the common-law offence on conviction on indictment is impris- **B3.333**
onment and/or a fine at large. On summary conviction, the maximum is six months or a fine not exceeding scale 5 on the standard scale, or both. See further **B3.283**. The new sentencing guideline (see **B3.3**) does not cover this offence.

In *Ferguson* [2009] 2 Cr App R (S) 39, the offender had pleaded guilty to offences of outraging public decency, exposure and harassment. A further 19 offences of exposure were taken into consideration. He was 43 years of age with a number of previous convictions including 13 for indecency in the USA. He was sentenced to concurrent terms of 21 months' imprisonment for the offences of outraging public decency and exposure and a further six months concurrent for the offence of harassment. It was argued that the sentence was manifestly excessive because the maxima for the offences of exposure and harassment were 24 and six months respectively. The Court of Appeal rejected the argument, observing that the sentence for outraging public decency is at large. The judge could therefore have passed shorter consecutive sentences for the three offences to which the offender had pleaded guilty or could have imposed shorter concurrent sentences to the one of 21 months for outraging public decency. See also *Cosco* [2005] 2 Cr App R (S) 405 and *Vaiculevicius* [2013] 2 Cr App R (S) 362 (55) in which both *Ferguson* and *Cosco* are cited.

An extended sentence may not be imposed for such an offence (*Chevron* [2005] All ER (D) 91 (Feb)).

Elements

The act must be lewd, obscene or disgusting and must be of such a nature as to outrage minimum **B3.334**
standards of public decency as judged by a jury in contemporary society (*Knuller (Publishing, Printing and Promotions) Ltd v DPP* [1973] AC 435) but it is not necessary that any particular member of the public is outraged (*Mayling* [1963] 3 QB 717 and *Choi* [1999] EWCA Crim 1279).

The public element to the offence is satisfied if at least two persons are present and could see the act even if they do not. In *Hamilton* [2008] QB 224, H had used a camera concealed in a rucksack to film up the skirts of women who were shopping. Nobody had ever noticed what he was doing but when his home was searched films produced from the activity were found. It was accepted at trial that there was a clear line of sight shown in the films, so it was contended by the prosecution (and disputed by the defence) that the camera lens must have been visible. The trial judge directed the jury that it was sufficient for the offence to be made out that there was a real possibility that when H was filming at least two people would have been able to see the act. In dismissing the appeal after a comprehensive review of the authorities, the Court of Appeal held that for the public element to be satisfied it was not necessary that two people actually see or hear the act. It is sufficient if at least two people are present and the accused's acts are capable of being seen. Whether the actions were capable of being seen was a question of fact for the jury. See also *Rose v DPP* [2006] 1 WLR 2626 and *F* (2010) 174 JP 582.

The act need not take place in a public place, it is sufficient that members of the public are able to see the act (*Wellard* (1884–85) LR 14 QBD 63).

ALTERNATIVE VERDICTS

B3.335 Plainly, there is a degree of overlap between many of the offences contained within the SOA 2003 and thus an offender may sometimes be found guilty of a lesser charge than that upon which he is indicted (see **D19.41** *et seq*. for the applicable general principles). In the case of an allegation of rape, it is possible that the accused could be alternatively found guilty of attempted rape, assault by penetration, sexual assault, sexual activity with a child, sexual activity with a child family member, sexual activity with a person having a mental disorder impeding choice, sexual activity by a care worker or sex with an adult relative. In respect of rape of a child, an accused may alternatively be found guilty of attempted rape, assault by penetration, sexual assault of a child contrary to s. 7 or sexual assault of a child contrary to s. 9.

BROTHELS AND DISORDERLY HOUSES

Keeping a Brothel

B3.336
Sexual Offences Act 1956, ss. 33 and 33A

33. It is an offence for a person to keep a brothel, or to manage, or act or assist in the management of, a brothel.

33A.—(1) It is an offence for a person to keep, or to manage, or act or assist in the management of a brothel to which people resort for practices involving prostitution (whether or not also for other practices).

(2) In this section 'prostitution' has the meaning given by section 51(2) of the Sexual Offences Act 2003.

Sexual Offences Act 1967, s. 6

Premises shall be treated for purposes of sections 33 to 35 of the Act of 1956 as a brothel if people resort to it for the purpose of lewd homosexual practices in circumstances in which resort thereto for lewd heterosexual practices would have led to its being treated as a brothel for the purposes of those sections.

B3.337 **Procedure** The offence contrary to s. 33 of the SOA 1956 is triable summarily. The offence contrary to s. 33A is triable either way.

B3.338 **Sentence** Under s. 33 of the SOA 1956, for an offence committed after a previous conviction for the same or a related offence, the maximum penalty is six months or a fine not exceeding level 4 on the standard scale, or both; otherwise three months or a fine not exceeding level 3 on the standard scale, or both (SOA 1956, s. 37 and sch. 2). For an offence under s. 33A, the maximum penalty is seven years' imprisonment; on summary conviction, it is six months or the statutory maximum fine, or both.

The Sentencing Council has issued a new guideline applicable to sex offenders aged 18 or over who are sentenced on or after 1 April 2014 (see **B3.3**). For the guideline in respect of an offence under s. 33A, see Supplement, **SG-124**.

Elements   A brothel is essentially a place where people are allowed to engage in unlawful **B3.339** sexual intercourse. For specific elaborations upon that general definition, regard should be had to *Kelly v Purvis* [1983] AC 663, *Stevens v Christy* (1987) 85 Cr App R 249, *Donovan v Gavin* [1965] 2 QB 648, and *Korie* [1966] 1 All ER 50. By virtue of s. 6 of the SOA 1967, homosexual activity is as capable as heterosexual activity of founding the existence of a brothel.

The nature and extent of the activities which comprise management or assisting in the management of a brothel have been considered in a number of cases, including *Stevens v Christy* (1987) 85 Cr App R 249, *DPP v Curley* [1991] COD 186, *Abbott v Smith* [1965] 2 QB 662 and *Jones v DPP* (1992) 96 Cr App R 130.

A person does not keep a brothel unless he is aware that the premises are to be used by more than one prostitute for the purposes of prostitution.

Landlord Letting Premises as a Brothel

Sexual Offences Act 1956, s. 34   **B3.340**

It is an offence for the lessor or landlord of any premises or his agent to let the whole or part of the premises with the knowledge that it is to be used, in whole or in part, as a brothel, or, where the whole or part of the premises is used as a brothel, to be wilfully a party to that use continuing.

Procedure   The offence contrary to s. 34 of the SOA 1956 is triable summarily.   **B3.341**

Sentence   Under s. 34 of the SOA 1956, for an offence committed after a previous conviction **B3.342** for the same or a related offence, the maximum penalty is six months or a fine not exceeding level 4 on the standard scale, or both; otherwise three months or a fine not exceeding level 3 on the standard scale, or both (SOA 1956, s. 37 and sch. 2). The new sentencing guideline (see **B3.3**) does not cover this offence.

Elements   The offence under the SOA 1956, s. 34, requires the landlord to know that the **B3.343** premises are to be used as a brothel or are being used as a brothel.

Tenant Permitting Premises to be Used as a Brothel or for Prostitution

Sexual Offences Act 1956, ss. 35 and 36   **B3.344**

35.—(1) It is an offence for the tenant or occupier, or person in charge, of any premises knowingly to permit the whole or part of the premises to be used as a brothel.

(2) Where the tenant or occupier of any premises is convicted of knowingly permitting the whole or part of the premises to be used as a brothel, the first Schedule to this Act shall apply to enlarge the rights of the lessor or landlord with respect to the assignment or determination of the lease or other contract under which the premises are held by the person convicted.

(3) Where the tenant or occupier of any premises is so convicted...and either—

(a) the lessor or landlord, after having the conviction brought to his notice, fails or failed to exercise his statutory rights in relation to the lease or contract under which the premises are or were held by the person convicted; or

(b) the lessor or landlord, after exercising his statutory rights so as to determine that lease or contract, grants or granted a new lease or enters or entered into a new contract of tenancy of the premises to, with or for the benefit of the same person, without having all reasonable provisions to prevent the recurrence of the offence inserted in the new lease or contract;

then, if subsequently an offence under this section is committed in respect of the premises during the subsistence of the lease or contract referred to in paragraph (a) of this subsection or (where paragraph (b) applies) during the subsistence of the new lease or contract, the lessor or landlord shall be deemed to be a party to that offence unless he shows that he took all reasonable steps to prevent the recurrence of the offence.

References in this subsection to the statutory rights of a lessor or landlord refer to his rights under the First Schedule to this Act.

36. It is an offence for the tenant or occupier of any premises knowingly to permit the whole or part of the premises to be used for the purposes of habitual prostitution (whether any prostitute involved is male or female).

B3.345   **Procedure**   An offence contrary to s. 34 or 35 of the SOA 1956 is triable summarily.

B3.346   **Sentence**   Under ss. 35 and 36 of the SOA 1956, for an offence committed after a previous conviction for the same or a related offence, the maximum penalty is six months or a fine not exceeding level 4 on the standard scale, or both; otherwise three months or a fine not exceeding level 3 on the standard scale, or both (SOA 1956, s. 37 and sch. 2).

The new sentencing guideline (see **B3.3**) does not cover this offence.

B3.347   **Elements**   The offence under s. 35 of the SOA 1956 applies to tenants who sublet their premises or simply allow the premises to be used as a brothel. If a tenant or occupier is convicted of allowing premises to be used as a brothel then the landlord of those premises has increased powers of eviction in relation to that tenancy under s. 35(2). If the landlord fails to exercise those powers or grants a new lease or licence to the offender, and the tenant or occupier repeats the offence, then the landlord will be liable as a party to the offence unless he shows that he took all reasonable steps to prevent the recurrence of the offence (s.35(3)).

In contrast to those sections of the SOA 1956 dealing with brothels, the offence under s. 36 can be committed if only one prostitute engages in prostitution in the premises.

Keeping a Disorderly House

B3.348   It is an offence at common law for a person to keep a disorderly house.

B3.349   **Procedure**   This common-law offence is triable either way.

B3.350   **Sentencing**   As a common-law offence, punishment is at large by imprisonment or fine, or both. The new sentencing guideline (see **B3.3**) does not cover this offence.

B3.351   **Elements**   The elements of the common-law offence of keeping a disorderly house were set out in *Tan* [1983] QB 1053:

(a) there must be some element of keeping open house;
(b) the house must not be regulated by the restraints of morality, or must be unchaste or of bad repute;
(c) it must be so conducted as to violate law and good order.

In *Moores v DPP* [1992] QB 125, it was held that the accused must also be aware that the house was used in that way. The requisite disorderliness of the house is not confined to sexual behaviour (*Berg* (1927) 20 Cr App R 38).

In *Court* [2012] 1 WLR 2260, following a review of the authorities, the Court of Appeal (presided over by Lord Judge CJ) quashed convictions for the offence. The evidence relied on at trial by the prosecution was very limited. Two unremarkable advertisements had been placed in the personal section of a local newspaper. No addresses were given but when the mobile numbers advertised were contacted by the officers they were offered sexual services. Those services went no further than normal sexual intercourse. Officers visited the premises. At one address, a woman wearing not much clothing was seen; at the other, no one was found. At both addresses, a large number of condoms were found and at one of the addresses a vibrator was recovered. There had been no complaints about the house from any of the neighbouring houses. The Court of Appeal observed that the judgment in *Tan* had proceeded on the basis that the provision of straightforward sexual intercourse could not be sufficient to constitute the offence. Therefore, taken at their highest, the circumstances of the case were not capable of falling within the common-law offence.

Section B4 Theft, Handling Stolen Goods and Related Offences

THEFT

Definition

B4.1

Theft Act 1968, s. 1

(1) A person is guilty of theft if he dishonestly appropriates property belonging to another with the intention of permanently depriving the other of it; and 'thief' and 'steal' shall be construed accordingly.

Procedure

B4.2 Save where it amounts to low value shoplifting as defined by the MCA 1980, s. 22A(3) (see **D6.29**), theft is triable either way (MCA 1980, s. 17 and sch. 1, para. 28). When tried on indictment it is normally a class 3 offence, but see CPD XIII, para. B (see Supplement, **PD-97**) for the additional factors that the court considers on allocation. It is a Group A offence for jurisdiction purposes under the CJA 1993, part I (see **A8.10**). See the *Magistrates' Court Sentencing Guidelines* (see Supplement, **SG-313**) for indications as to when a case should be sent to the Crown Court.

Where the property in question belonged to D's spouse or civil partner, a prosecution for theft (or criminal damage, or inchoate versions of those offences) may be instituted against D only by or with the consent of the DPP (Theft Act 1968, s. 30(4)). See *Withers* [1975] Crim LR 647. This restriction must also apply to charges of robbery or of burglary by stealing, etc., but does not apply to other persons charged with committing the offence jointly with D; nor does it apply where the parties are separated by judicial decree or order or under no obligation to cohabit (s. 30(4)(a)).

Indictment

B4.3

Statement of Offence

Theft contrary to section 1(1) of the Theft Act 1968.

Particulars of Offence

A on or about the. . .day of. . .stole a pearl necklace belonging to V.

It is proper to allege in a single count the theft of an aggregate sum of money or items of property where the evidence does not disclose the precise dates and amounts of each individual transaction, provided that D's conduct amounted to a continuous offence over a period of time. Such an allegation is usually referred to as theft of a 'general deficiency'. Thus it would be proper to indict for theft of the total sum missing on a day on which D was bound to account for it, even though he clearly took it in instalments (*Balls* (1871) LR 1 CCR 328) or theft of all items stolen from a department store on one day, even though the various articles emanated from different departments of the store (*Wilson* (1979) 69 Cr App R 83; *Heaton v Costello* (1984) 148 JP 688). A count drafted in this way is not bad for duplicity. This principle also applies where 'money' was in different forms and it could not be said whether what was stolen was a debt, cash drawn from a bank account or cash disposed of otherwise and representing funds provided by clients of financial advisers (*Hallam* [1995] Crim LR 323). The elements of the offence must exist throughout; otherwise there would be a lack of coincidence (see **B4.25**). As to indictments for continuous offences generally, see *DPP v Merriman* [1973] AC 584 and **D11.33** *et seq.*

Not all the items mentioned in an information or count do have to be proved to have been stolen (*Machent v Quinn* [1970] 2 All ER 255), provided it is proved that D stole at least one of them. However, there will be cases where the prosecution should not include in a single count more than one allegation of theft, for example where several items are alleged to have been stolen from an employer on different days (*Jackson* (1991) *The Guardian*, 20 November 1991). Some property must be specified in the indictment or information.

As to the relevance of conditional intention in drafting an indictment, see **B4.64**. As to the relationship between theft and handling, see **B4.178**.

Alternative Verdicts

In addition to the general power under the CLA 1967, s. 6(3), the Theft Act 1968, s. 12(4), **B4.4** provides that, as an alternative to a conviction of theft, the jury may on a trial on indictment for theft find D guilty of an offence under s. 12(1) (taking a motor vehicle or other conveyance without authority etc.; see **B4.117** to **B4.127**). He is liable then as he would have been liable under s. 12(2) on summary conviction (s. 12(4): see **B4.119**).

Sentence

The maximum penalty is seven years (Theft Act 1968, s. 1(7)) on indictment; six months **B4.5** or a fine not exceeding the statutory maximum, or both, summarily. Under the Penalties for Disorderly Behaviour (Amount of Penalty) Order 2002 (SI 2002 No. 1837), as amended, this offence is a penalty offence and the amount payable by persons aged 18 and over is £90.

Offences of Theft Generally The definitive sentencing guideline, *Theft* (see Supplement, **B4.6** SG-447), applies to adult offenders. The guideline covers four specific forms of theft: theft in breach of trust, theft in a dwelling, theft from the person, and theft from a shop, but the SGC considers that some of the principles are of general application in cases of theft. In *Moss* [2011] 1 Cr App R (S) 199 the offenders pleaded guilty to theft of 142 metres of copper wire cabling from a telephone installation. As a result of the theft 500 households lost their telephone and internet services. The value of the copper was £10,000 and the cost of repair and replacement was a further £15,000. The Court of Appeal said that there were no specific guidelines applicable, but regard was given to the SGC guideline on *Seriousness* as well as to that on *Theft*. The starting point in a case such as this was two to three years' imprisonment for a first offender after a trial. Sentences in this case were varied from three years to two years for one offender and 20 months' detention for the other. See also *Mitchell* [2012] 1 Cr App R (S) 387, *Birch* [2013] 1 Cr App R (S) 84 (16) and *Coffey* [2013] 2 Cr App R (S) 60 (14). A sentence of two years following a guilty plea was upheld in *Boyd-Hiscock* [2013] 2 Cr App R (S) 511 (78), where the 21-year-old offender removed 123 commemorative plaques from a crematorium and sold them as scrap metal. In *Jacques* [2011] 2 Cr App R (S) 237 a sentence of three and a half years was upheld on an offender for theft of rare books valued at about £27,000 from a specialist library, where the offender had a previous conviction for a similar offence. The Court of Appeal distinguished the superficially similar case of *Hakimzadeh* [2010] 1 Cr App R (S) 49 where sentence was reduced on appeal to 12 months, because there had been significant mitigating features in that case which were not present in the instant case.

Shoplifting The definitive sentencing guideline, *Theft* (see Supplement, SG-447), applies to **B4.7** adult offenders. Theft from a shop is one of four categories of theft dealt with and it supersedes the guideline case of *Page* [2005] 2 Cr App R (S) 22.

B4.8 **Theft from the Person**   The definitive sentencing guideline, *Theft* (see Supplement, **SG-447**), applies to adult offenders. Theft from the person is one of four categories of theft dealt with.

In *de Weever* [2010] 1 Cr App R (S) 16 a sentence of ten months' imprisonment was appropriate for a 46-year-old offender with numerous previous convictions for stealing a woman's purse from her shoulder bag as she waited at an underground station. The Court of Appeal said that the victim could not properly be described as 'vulnerable', but other aggravating features of the case, including the degree of planning and the offender's poor record, took it from the lowest into the middle bracket in the guidelines. A case falling well outside the guidelines because of the value of the property involved is *Maughan* [2012] EWCA Crim 692, where the 30-year-old offender with a record of dishonesty pleaded guilty to theft of a Stradivarius violin worth £1.2 million. The property was not recovered. Sentence was reduced from four and a half years' imprisonment to three and a half years on appeal.

B4.9 **Theft in Breach of Trust**   The definitive sentencing guideline, *Theft* (see Supplement, SG-447), applies to adult offenders. Theft in breach of trust is one of four categories of theft dealt with. In *Hunt* [2013] 2 Cr App R (S) 6 (2) the offender, who had been in practice as a solicitor, transferred sums from the client account to the office account to pay staff wages when the firm got into financial difficulty. This created a deficit in the client account of over £1 million. He pleaded guilty to fraud by abuse of position, but the Court of Appeal applied the guideline for theft in breach of trust. Four years' imprisonment was reduced to three years. In *Lawson* [2010] 2 Cr App R (S) 468 sentences totalling three years' imprisonment were reduced to 27 months in a case where the offender, an employee in a care home, stole cheques and bank cards from vulnerable elderly people, obtaining over £2,000.

The Five Elements of Theft

B4.10 By the Theft Act 1968, s. 1(1), theft consists of five elements: (i) dishonest (ii) appropriation (iii) of property (iv) belonging to another (v) with the intention of permanently depriving the other of it. Those five elements are amplified (but not fully defined) in ss. 2 to 6. It is usually said that the first and last elements constitute the *mens rea* of the offence, whereas the second, third and fourth constitute the *actus reus*; but this is an oversimplification, because appropriation necessarily involves a mental element and the concept of dishonesty (as explained in *Ghosh* [1982] QB 1053) is not exclusively concerned with D's state of mind.

Section 1(1) does not expressly require that the appropriation in question must be the means whereby D intends to deprive V of his property. It does not, in other words, say that D must appropriate the property 'with the intention *thereby* of permanently depriving V'. One might suppose that on a purposive reading of s. 1(1) such a requirement would be implied, but the House of Lords in *Morris* [1984] AC 320 held otherwise. If D does something to V's property that amounts to a dishonest appropriation, but intends to deprive V only by some later act (which the first appropriation may perhaps be intended to facilitate) then D has already stolen V's property (even though V may still have it); and because D cannot ordinarily re-steal property he has already stolen, the later act which actually deprives V may not then amount to theft at all. See further **B4.34** *et seq*.

'Property'

B4.11   Theft Act 1968, s. 4

(1) 'Property' includes money and all other property, real or personal, including things in action and other intangible property.
(2) A person cannot steal land, or things forming part of land and severed from it by him or by his directions, except in the following cases, that is to say—
    (a) when he is a trustee or personal representative, or is authorised by power of attorney, or as liquidator of a company, or otherwise, to sell or dispose of land belonging to another, and

he appropriates the land or anything forming part of it by dealing with it in breach of the confidence reposed in him; or

(b) when he is not in possession of the land and appropriates anything forming part of the land by severing it or causing it to be severed, or after it has been severed; or

(c) when, being in possession of the land under a tenancy, he appropriates the whole or part of any fixture or structure let to be used with the land.

For purposes of this subsection 'land' does not include incorporeal hereditaments; 'tenancy' means a tenancy for years or any less period and includes an agreement for such a tenancy, but a person who after the end of a tenancy remains in possession as statutory tenant or otherwise is to be treated as having possession under the tenancy, and 'let' shall be construed accordingly.

(3) A person who picks mushrooms growing wild on any land, or who picks flowers, fruit or foliage from a plant growing wild on any land, does not (although not in possession of the land) steal what he picks, unless he does it for reward or for sale or other commercial purpose.

For purposes of this subsection 'mushroom' includes any fungus, and 'plant' includes any shrub or tree.

(4) Wild creatures, tamed or untamed, shall be regarded as property; but a person cannot steal a wild creature not tamed nor ordinarily kept in captivity, or the carcase of any such creature, unless either it has been reduced into possession by or on behalf of another person and possession of it has not since been lost or abandoned, or another person is in course of reducing it into possession.

Money Coins and banknotes are property (*Davis* (1988) 88 Cr App R 347). 'Money' does **B4.12** not include cheques or credit balances held in banks and building societies, but see **B4.15** and **B4.16**.

Real Property and Wild Plants etc. Special rules apply to land, buildings, fixtures, and other **B4.13** things that form part of the land (including crops, plants, etc.). These can be the subject of a theft charge only in limited circumstances specified by s. 4(2). Trustees and other persons falling within the scope of s. 4(2)(a) may commit theft by appropriating any such property in breach of their fiduciary duties, assuming all other elements of theft (notably dishonesty) can be established. However, a breach of fiduciary duty may not necessarily be dishonest for the purposes of the law of theft.

Under s. 4(2)(b), persons who are not in possession of land may commit theft in a variety of ways, notably by severing fixtures, plants, topsoil, etc., from the land or by appropriating such property after it has been severed. This would not however, for example, include a person who dishonestly moves a boundary fence so as to appropriate some part of a neighbouring property.

Nor does s. 4(2)(b) apply to tenants or to persons in possession of land under a licence or tenancy. The appropriation of fixtures by tenants (as defined at the end of s. 4(2)) is governed by s. 4(2)(c), but by what appears to be an oversight this does not extend to mere licensees. So, whereas a tenant who dishonestly sells a valuable fireplace or greenhouse forming part of the property falls squarely within s. 4(2)(c) (even if he has not yet severed or removed it), a licensee doing exactly the same thing would not be caught, and since he is also excluded from s. 4(2)(b), he may not be guilty of theft at all.

Whether a particular object forms part of the land may be a difficult question. Under the law **B4.14** of real property, an article that was a chattel may become annexed to the land if it is attached to the land (or building etc.) in order to improve or facilitate the use of the land or building, but not where it is attached only to facilitate its own use as a chattel (*Elitestone Ltd v Morris* [1997] 2 All ER 513).

The restrictions imposed by s. 4(2) do not apply to incorporeal hereditaments (or intangible real property) such as easements, profits à prendre and rentcharges.

Where charges of theft are problematic because of the nature of the property involved, the dishonest obtaining of land or fixtures may in some cases be more easily prosecuted as an offence of fraud or (where it occurred before 15 January 2007) under the Theft Act 1968, s. 15 (see **B5.1**).

Section 4(3) is clumsily expressed, but is designed to ensure that persons who pick wild mushrooms, flowers or berries for non-commercial purposes cannot be guilty of theft, even if they trespass on private land when so doing. Commercial pickers may be guilty of theft in such circumstances, but only if all other elements of theft are established. The picking, destruction or uprooting of wild plants protected under the Wildlife and Countryside Act 1981, sch. 8, or the uprooting of any wild plant, may be an offence under s. 13 of that Act.

B4.15   **Personal Property**   Personal property includes tangible personal property, which might also be described as 'things (or choses) in possession', 'chattels' or 'goods'. A cheque, bill of exchange or other valuable security (or even an uncompleted cheque form or cheque book) is personal property capable of being appropriated (*Arnold* [1997] 4 All ER 1; *Clark* [2002] 1 Cr App R 141) but see *Preddy* [1996] AC 815. Personal property also includes things (or choses) in action and other intangible property.

A debt for a liquidated, or known, sum is a common form of thing in action, as are shares in a company. In *Marshall* [1998] 2 Cr App R 282, the Court of Appeal, stated, *obiter*, that, because the issuing of an underground train ticket resulted in the creation of a contract between the customer and the train operator, the contractual rights arising were enforceable by action:

> Therefore it is arguable, we suppose, that by the transaction each party has acquired a chose in action. On the side of the purchaser it is represented by a right to use the ticket to the extent which it allows travel on the underground system. On the side of [the operator] it encompasses the right to insist that the ticket is used by no one other than the purchaser. It is that right which is disregarded when the ticket is acquired by the appellant and sold on.

'Other intangible property' includes patents (Patents Act 1977, s. 30), copyright (Copyright, Designs and Patents Act 1988, s. 1) and design rights (Copyright, Designs and Patents Act 1988, s. 213), although a mere breach of copyright is not theft. See also *A-G of Hong Kong v Nai-Keung* [1987] 1 WLR 1339 (export quotas held to be intangible property). However, confidential information is not a form of property. Thus in *Oxford v Moss* (1978) 68 Cr App R 183, D, an undergraduate, committed no theft by dishonestly copying questions from an examination paper he was due to sit. It would seem to follow that no theft can be committed in cases of 'industrial espionage' where D dishonestly acquires trade secrets from V, unless D also appropriates documents etc., on which such information is recorded, and does so with the requisite *mens rea*.

B4.16   **Bank Accounts**   A credit balance in a bank or a building society account provides the holder with a thing in action. The relationship of debtor and creditor exists between the bank and the customer. This debt cannot be physically possessed, but may be enforced by legal action and is capable of being stolen (*Kohn* (1979) 69 Cr App R 395 at p. 404; see also *Chan Man-sin v The Queen* [1988] 1 All ER 1; *Wille* (1987) 86 Cr App R 296; *Preddy* [1996] AC 815 at p. 825).

Where an account is overdrawn the bank remains obliged to honour cheques as long as the account remains within agreed overdraft limits. This again is a thing in action and capable of being stolen (see *Kohn* at p. 407; *Chan Man-sin* at p. 198E); but the position is different when the account is overdrawn and not within the limit of an overdraft facility. The bank may decline to honour any cheque drawn on an account in that state. If it does honour such a cheque, it does so only as a matter of honour and not as the consequence of an obligation. Thus where the account is overdrawn without authority, there is nothing in the account that is capable of being stolen (*Kohn* at p. 408). Where however D attempts to use a forged cheque or other instrument to withdraw funds from P's account, he may instead be guilty of stealing or attempting to steal from the bank itself (cf. *Hendricks* [2003] EWCA Crim 1040) and he may be guilty of fraud or of offences under the Forgery and Counterfeiting Act 1981, regardless of the state of the account in question.

Wild Creatures   Section 4(4) restricts the circumstances in which wild creatures are covered by the law of theft. Wild creatures that are neither tamed nor kept in captivity cannot be stolen unless they have already been reduced into possession by another or are in the process of being so reduced (cf. *Cresswell v DPP* (2007) 171 JP 233) although an escaped creature can be stolen if ordinarily kept in captivity. The poaching of wild animals, birds or fish may be punishable under a number of statutes, including the Night Poaching Act 1828 and the Game Act 1831 (see **B13.91**). The intentional killing or taking of such creatures may also be punishable under the Wildlife and Countryside Act 1981, part 1.   **B4.17**

Other Forms of Property   Electricity cannot be stolen (*Low v Blease* [1975] Crim LR 513) but it is an offence to abstract electricity contrary to the Theft Act 1968, s. 13 (see **B4.141** *et seq.*).   **B4.18**

Human bodies are not ordinarily anyone's property, but bodies or body parts are capable of being stolen 'if they have acquired different attributes by virtue of the application of skill, such as dissection or preservation techniques, for exhibition or teaching purposes' (*Kelly* [1999] QB 621 at p. 632, following *Doodeward v Spence* (1907) 6 CLR 406 and *Dobson v North Tyneside Health Authority* [1997] 4 All ER 474). An Egyptian mummy, for example, may be the property of a museum. In *Kelly* the court said, at p. 632:

> It may be that if...the question arises, the courts will hold that human body parts are capable of being property for the purposes of the [Theft Act 1968, s. 4], even without the acquisition of different attributes, if they have a use or significance beyond their mere existence. This may be so if, for example, they are intended for use in an organ transplant operation, for the extraction of DNA or, for that matter, as an exhibit in a trial.

As to theft of forensic human tissue samples, see *Welsh* [1974] RTR 478. As to sperm stored by fertility clinics for future use on behalf of the donor, see *Yearworth v North Bristol NHS Trust* [2009] 2 All ER 986. The Human Tissue Act 2004, s. 5, creates specific offences in relation to the improper and unauthorised use, storage or removal of human bodies, organs and other tissue. As to embryos etc., see also the Human Fertilisation and Embryology Act 1990, s. 41.

As to unlawfully possessed drugs or other contraband, see *Smith* [2011] 1 Cr App R 379 and **B4.20**.

'Belonging to Another'

Theft Act 1968, s. 5   **B4.19**

(1) Property shall be regarded as belonging to any person having possession or control of it, or having in it any proprietary right or interest (not being an equitable interest arising only from an agreement to transfer or grant an interest).

(2) Where property is subject to a trust, the persons to whom it belongs shall be regarded as including any person having a right to enforce the trust, and an intention to defeat the trust shall be regarded accordingly as an intention to deprive of the property any person having that right.

(3) Where a person receives property from or on account of another, and is under an obligation to the other to retain and deal with that property or its proceeds in a particular way, the property or proceeds shall be regarded (as against him) as belonging to the other.

(4) Where a person gets property by another's mistake, and is under an obligation to make restoration (in whole or in part) of the property or its proceeds or of the value thereof, then to the extent of that obligation the property or proceeds shall be regarded (as against him) as belonging to the person entitled to restoration, and an intention not to make restoration shall be regarded accordingly as an intention to deprive that person of the property or proceeds.

(5) Property of a corporation sole shall be regarded as belonging to the corporation notwithstanding a vacancy in the corporation.

The identity of the owner is generally irrelevant, provided that someone other than D has a property right or interest in the property in question. In *Sullivan* [2002] Crim LR 758, a trial judge decided that money found on a dead drug dealer did not belong to anyone and could not be stolen. With respect, however, it must have belonged to someone. It may have belonged to the deceased's estate or to the Crown as bona vacantia.

B4.20   **Ownership, Possession or Control**   Theft is usually perpetrated against the owner of the property, who may or may not also be in possession of it (*Hancock* [1990] 2 QB 242) but can equally be perpetrated against persons with lesser interests, as s. 5(1) makes clear. A person may be in control of property, even though unaware of its presence, since the general principle is that control of a site by excluding others from it gives prima facie control of articles on the site (*Woodman* [1974] QB 754 at p. 758; *Waverley BC v Fletcher* [1996] QB 334). The 'owner' may even be in possession of the property unlawfully. Property may thus be stolen by one thief from another, and a drug dealer may be the victim of robbery if his stock is taken from him by force; the criminal law is concerned with keeping the Queen's peace, not with protecting private property rights (*Smith* [2011] 1 Cr App R 379).

B4.21   If the interest of a person satisfies s. 5(1), the property belongs to that person for the purposes of the Act. In *Turner (No. 2)* [1971] 2 All ER 441, the Court of Appeal held that an owner of property can steal that property from someone else with a sufficient interest, including mere possession through a bailment. On that basis, the court upheld D's conviction for stealing his own car from V who had been undertaking repairs on it. D had dishonestly removed the car from V's premises during the night, apparently with the intention of evading his duty to pay for the repairs. The trial judge had directed the jury to decide the case without reference to any repairer's lien that V might have had over the car, and the court therefore had to decide whether the conviction could be upheld even if there had been no such lien. With respect, however, it is hard to see how D's removal of the car could ever have been categorised as dishonest had he not been aware of that lien. But for V's lien, D would have had a legal right to reclaim his car (see s. 2(1)(a)). Contrast *Meredith* [1973] Crim LR 253.

The person to whom the property belongs need not be an individual. A corporation may own property which can be stolen from it, even by persons who are in total control of it by reason of shareholding and directorships (*A-G's Ref (No. 2 of 1982)* [1984] QB 624; *Philippou* (1989) 89 Cr App R 290: see **B4.45**).

Under the Treasure Act 1996, s. 4(1), when treasure is found, it vests, subject to prior interests and rights, in the franchisee (if there is one) and otherwise (and more usually) in the Crown. 'Treasure' is defined in s. 1 of that Act; 'prior interests or rights' is defined in s. 2; and 'franchisee' is defined in s. 5. Property (other than treasure) found buried on land will ordinarily belong to the owner of the land in priority to the finder, even if the public were permitted access to that land (*Waverley BC v Fletcher* [1996] QB 334).

B4.22   **Proprietary Rights or Interests**   For the purposes of the Theft Act 1968, property 'belongs' to any person who has any proprietary right or interest in it other than an equitable interest arising only from an agreement to transfer or grant an interest (s. 5(1)). A partner, who has a proprietary interest in partnership property, may steal it, as his co-partners also have such an interest (*Bonner* [1970] 2 All ER 97). In *Marshall* [1998] 2 Cr App R 282, D acquired London Underground tickets and travel cards that had not been fully used up and sold them to other travellers. The Court of Appeal held that the tickets 'belonged to London Underground'. Although the tickets had previously been issued to travellers, London Underground retained a sufficient proprietary right or interest in the tickets for the purposes of s. 5(1).

B4.23   Trust property 'belongs' to the trustee who has legal title to it, but also to 'any person having a right to enforce the trust' (s. 5(2)); that is, any beneficiary or, in the case of a charitable trust, the A-G (Charities Act 1993, s. 33). A trustee who appropriates trust property with the intention of defeating the trust is to be regarded as intending to deprive the person who has the right to enforce the trust of property (s. 5(2)).

However, secret profits which become subject to a constructive trust do not thereby 'belong', for the purposes of the Act, to the person for whose benefit the trust was imposed. In *A-G's Ref (No. 1 of 1985)* [1986] QB 491, D, a publican, sold his own beer in a tied house, keeping the profit for himself. A constructive trust arose in respect of the profits; but the Court of Appeal took the view that s. 5(2) does not result in this profit 'belonging' to the brewery for the purposes of the law of theft. Behaviour which had previously not been considered to be criminal would otherwise have been criminalised and clearer words were needed to make such a major change. There was in any event no identifiable trust property which could form the subject-matter of a theft charge. D's only obligation was to account for the profit being made, until, if ever, that profit was identified as a separate piece of property, which then could provide the basis for a theft charge. See also *Governor of Pentonville Prison, ex parte Tarling* (1978) 70 Cr App R 77. Similarly, a bribe received by an employee does not 'belong' to the employer and the employee does not commit theft when he keeps it (*Powell v MacRae* [1977] Crim LR 571).

A-G's Ref (No. 1 of 1985) was distinguished in *Re Holmes* [2005] 1 All ER 490 in which it was held that where property is fraudulently obtained from V, the proceeds of that fraud (e.g., funds credited to a bank account) may become subject to a constructive trust in V's favour and will then 'belong' to V for the purposes of s. 5(2).

Equitable Proprietary Interests   Where A transfers legal ownership of property to B, but **B4.24** retains an equitable proprietary interest in that property, it may still be said to 'belong' to him for the purposes of s. 5(1) and (2). If B dishonestly appropriates the property (e.g., by disposing of it in a way that prejudices A's interest) he may then be guilty of stealing it from A. See *Clowes (No. 2)* [1994] 2 All ER 316 and *Wain* [1995] 2 Cr App R 660). It is not strictly necessary to invoke s. 5(3) or (4) in such cases. The latter provisions (which are examined at **B4.27** and **B4.31**) *may* still be used, but are unlikely to offer any real advantages to prosecutors. In *Hallam* [1995] Crim LR 323, the Court of Appeal held that the clients of financial advisers, having paid cheques in the expectation that investments would be made on their behalf, retained an equitable interest in the cheques, their proceeds and any balance in accounts operated by D or the company through which they operated to which the payment could be traced. It was immaterial whether the property belonged to the clients within the meaning of s. 5(1) or whether it was merely deemed to belong to them under s. 5(3). See also *Governor of Brixton Prison, ex parte Levin* [1997] AC 741.

An equitable proprietary interest may also be retained by A where property is got by B on the basis of A's mistake (*Chase Manhattan Bank NA v Israel-British Bank (London) Ltd* [1981] Ch 105). Where this is the case, reliance on s 5(4) will not strictly be necessary. In *Shadrokh-Cigari* [1988] Crim LR 465, a child's bank account in England was mistakenly credited by an American bank with £286,000 instead of £286. Realising the error, D, her guardian, dishonestly appropriated all but £21,000 of this for his own use. It was held (applying *Chase Manhattan*) that the bank retained an equitable interest in the transferred funds, although the Court of Appeal accepted that an argument based on s. 5(4) would also succeed. *Chase Manhattan* has been criticised in subsequent civil cases (*Re Goldcorp Exchange Ltd* [1995] 1 AC 74; *Westdeutsche Landesbank Girozentrale v Islington London Borough Council* [1996] AC 669), but *Shadrokh-Cigari* was followed in *Webster* [2006] EWCA Crim 2894. In *Webster* D, a soldier, was charged with stealing a medal 'belonging to the Secretary of State' by selling it on the internet. His captain (C) had been issued with two of the medals by mistake, and had passed the duplicate to D. The Court of Appeal held that the Secretary of State 'clearly' retained a proprietary interest in it for the purposes of s. 5(1), and it was not open to C to permit its sale (as D alleged he had done).

Property Must Belong to Another when Appropriated   Property cannot be stolen unless it **B4.25** belonged to another at the moment of appropriation. There can be no theft where D decides not to pay for a meal only after he has eaten it (*Corcoran v Whent* [1977] Crim LR 52) or for petrol only after he has refuelled his car (*Edwards v Ddin* [1976] 1 WLR 942).

This principle can easily give rise to difficulty where intangible property is involved, as *Preddy* [1996] AC 815 demonstrated in the context of dishonestly obtained mortgage loans although many of the difficulties of the kind that arose in *Preddy* can be avoided where the facts permit a charge of fraud instead (see **B5.4** *et seq.*).

Questions of ownership in relation to property (and the passing of property) are essentially questions of civil law. In *Morris* [1984] AC 320 Lord Roskill opined that difficult questions of whether contracts were void or voidable on the ground of mistake or fraud or whether any mistake is sufficiently fundamental to vitiate a contract should, so far as possible, be confined to those fields of law to which they are immediately relevant and should not be dragged into the law of theft. This view was quoted with approval by Parker LJ in *Dobson v General Accident Fire and Life Assurance Corporation plc* [1990] 1 QB 274 and later approved by Lord Keith in *Gomez* [1993] AC 442. The intricacies of the civil law cannot, however, be ignored where they determine proprietary rights. In *Walker* [1984] Crim LR 112, D sold a video recorder to C who then returned it as faulty. D resold it to E and was charged with stealing it from C. D's defence was that under the law on sale of goods, the customer had rejected the recorder (so that ownership of it had reverted to him). Dunn LJ, giving the judgment of the Court of Appeal, rightly observed that 'a careful direction as to the law relating to the passing of property and rejection of goods under the provisions of the Sale of Goods Act was plainly required' and that on this issue 'there is no distinction between the civil law and the criminal law'. See also *Wheeler* (1991) 92 Cr App R 279; *Davies v Leighton* (1978) 68 Cr App R 4.

An example of the difficulties which may be created by failure to pay due regard to the civil law is presented by *Hinks* [2001] 2 AC 241 (see **B4.39**) in which the House of Lords contrived to hold that a person who acquires an indefeasible title to property under the civil law may still, if considered dishonest, be convicted of thereby stealing that property. On the facts of *Hinks*, D's title to the property might perhaps have been challenged on the basis of undue influence, but that was not the basis for the ruling.

B4.26 **Abandoned Goods** Where property has been abandoned by A, it cannot be stolen from him: see *Small* (1988) 86 Cr App R 170; *White* (1912) 7 Cr App R 266; *Ellerman's Wilson Line Ltd v Webster* [1952] 1 Lloyd's Rep 179. But A does not abandon property by leaving it outside a charity shop, or in a collection bag outside his front door, with a view in either case to it being collected on behalf of the charity (*R (Ricketts) v Basildon Magistrates' Court* [2011] 1 Cr App R 202; *Toleikis* [2013] EWCA Crim 600) or by setting it aside for disposal or destruction by B. Abandonment suggests that A has no further interest in what may become of it or who may then appropriate it. If, for example, A puts some unwanted property in a bag labelled 'confidential waste for incineration' and some in a box labelled, 'help yourselves', he may have abandoned the latter, but not the former; and if B has been tasked with disposal or destruction, B may now have rights over the former property (cf. *Williams v Phillips* (1957) 41 Cr App R 5). D's mistaken belief that A has abandoned the property, or his failure to appreciate that B has already acquired rights to property that A has abandoned, may mean that D lacks the requisite *mens rea* for theft (*Small* (1988) 86 Cr App R 170; *White* (1912) 7 Cr App R 266; *Ellerman's Wilson Line Ltd v Webster* [1952] 1 Lloyd's Rep 179).

Property is not abandoned merely because it has been lost (*Hibbert v McKiernan* [1948] 2 KB 142) or because the owner is not currently able to recover it. Thus, golf balls lying at the bottom of a lake within a golf club may still belong to the club, even if it has no immediate plans to dredge the lake for them (*Rostron* [2003] EWCA Crim 2206).

B4.27 **Obligation to Retain and Deal with Property or Proceeds** Section 5(3) (see **B4.19**) provides that property received by D from or on account of V shall be 'regarded' (as against D) as belonging to V if D has an obligation to deal with it or its proceeds in a particular way. What this means, in practice, is that D may be found to have stolen such property if he has (for example) disposed of it (or its proceeds) in such a way as to deprive V of his entitlement, and this may be the case whether or not V actually has any legal or equitable interest in that property such as would make him an owner of it for the purposes of s. 5(1) or (2). It is thus a 'deeming' provision so that, where D is under the specified obligation, the property may for the purposes of the law of theft be treated as if it belonged at least partly to V. In *Adams* [2003] EWCA Crim 3620, for example, s. 5(3) was applied to ensure that cheques made payable to D and belonging only to him nevertheless could be regarded as property belonging to V because their creation was a part of a process whereby D managed an investment account on V's behalf.

The obligation in s. 5(3) must be a legal one. A moral or social obligation is not sufficient (*Hall* [1973] QB 126; *Wakeman v Farrar* [1974] Crim LR 136). But D need not have been under any obligation to retain or hand over the particular monies or property received: it may suffice that he is obliged to set aside and hand over an equivalent sum (*Wain* [1995] 2 Cr App R 660).

In *Hall*, a travel agent received money from customers as deposits and payments for flights which were never provided. The business became insolvent and none of the money was refunded. But in the absence of special contractual arrangements to the contrary (of which there was no evidence) the agent's only obligation was as a debtor to the customers; he was not obliged to retain and deal with the deposits in any particular way, but was entitled to pay the proceeds into his general trading account. By failing to provide the tickets he was in breach of contract, but nothing more.

Whether an agent is obliged to keep his principal's money or property separate from his own or whether the relationship is merely that of creditor and debtor will depend upon their intentions and on the type of transaction involved. Had the travel agent in *Hall* been a solicitor who received deposits from purchasers in connection with property transactions, the position would clearly have been different.

It is necessary to identify the person to whom the obligation is owed. If the only such person is **B4.28** V, an indictment charging D with theft from X will be defective (*Dyke* [2002] 1 Cr App R 404). An obligation under s. 5(3) will normally arise where a person receives money for onward transmission to a charity (e.g., from donors or sponsors), either because the charity imposes such an obligation as a condition of involvement or because the sponsors impose such an obligation, at least implicitly, in handing over their money (*Wain* [1995] 2 Cr App R 660). In *Dyke* it was held that the 'collector of money from the public receives that money subject to the charitable trust and shall treat the money as belonging to the beneficiaries of that charity'; there is in other words an obligation within the meaning of s. 5(3), but it is owed to the charity and its beneficiaries and not to the donors who contributed the money in question. On the other hand, it would be no defence to a charge brought under s. 5(3) in such a case that liability would in any event arise under s. 5(1) or (2).

In *Klineberg* [1999] 1 Cr App R 427 the allegation was that money was stolen from intending purchasers of timeshares rather than from the company established to sell the timeshares. This meant that the necessary obligation had to be established with regard to each of the intending purchasers. This could be established on the facts (taking particular account of the element of the scheme whereby investors' money would be safeguarded by a trusteeship pending completion of the purchase) and, since it was established that the money had not been used properly, theft convictions were upheld.

It is not sufficient that a duty to account arises (*Powell v MacRae* [1977] Crim LR 571). Section **B4.29** 5(3) does not therefore apply to the secret profit scenario illustrated by *A-G's Ref (No. 1 of 1985)* [1986] QB 491 (see **B4.23**). As Lord Lane CJ explained in that case:

> [D] received the money on his own account as a result of his private venture. No doubt...he is under an obligation to account to the employers at least for the profit he has made out of his venture, but that is a different matter. The fact that A may have to account to B for money he has received from X does not mean necessarily that he received the money on account of B.

Since D's obligation must be a legal one, one might suppose that it must also be legally enforceable. Two cases cause problems with regard to this requirement and must each be regarded as questionable on that basis. In *Cullen* (1974 unreported) V gave D, his mistress, £20 to buy food and pay certain domestic debts, but she spent it on herself. Parties to domestic housekeeping arrangements do not ordinarily intend to create legally enforceable obligations (*Balfour v*

Balfour [1919] 2 KB 571) and yet the court ruled that D's obligation to deal with the money as V directed did not cease to be a legal obligation simply because she was his mistress. She was guilty of theft by virtue of s. 5(3). The other problem case is *Meech* [1974] QB 549, where V fraudulently obtained a cheque from a finance company and D undertook to cash it for him. Having discovered V's fraud, D then arranged for some accomplices to stage a fake robbery in which the proceeds of the cheque (withdrawn by D from his own account) were supposedly taken. Because of his own fraud, V could not have enforced D's undertaking to pay him the proceeds, but D was nevertheless convicted on the basis of s. 5(3).

B4.30   The courts have made clear that whether an obligation sufficient to satisfy s. 5(3) arises depends upon the particular facts of the case (*Hall* [1973] QB 126; *McHugh* (1993) 97 Cr App R 335). The functions of judge and jury were described in *Mainwaring* (1981) 74 Cr App R 99 at p. 107 in a passage later approved in *Dubar* [1994] 1 All ER 781 and *Breaks* [1998] Crim LR 349):

> Whether or not an obligation arises is a matter of law, because an obligation must be a legal obligation. But a legal obligation arises only in certain circumstances, and in many cases the circumstances cannot be known until the facts have been established. It is for the jury, not the judge, to establish the facts, if they are in dispute.

> What, in our judgment, a judge ought to do is this: if the facts relied upon by the prosecution are in dispute he should direct the jury to make their findings on the facts, and then say to them: 'If you find the facts to be such-and-such, then I direct you as a matter of law that a legal obligation arose to which section 5(3) applies'.

If the facts are not in dispute, it may be appropriate for the judge to direct the jury that an obligation had been undertaken by the person receiving the property.

According to *McHugh*, the obligation must be understood by both parties. However, it is submitted that the crucial factor is only that D be aware of it. There might be circumstances where D knows that an obligation is imposed upon him, but the other person concerned is ignorant of this obligation. This should be sufficient for liability. D must know of the obligation (*Wills* (1991) 92 Cr App R 297), but for such knowledge it is not necessary that he understand that an obligation existed, rather he must appreciate the necessary facts which, as a matter of law, amount to an obligation (*Dubar*).

B4.31   **Obligation to Make Restoration of Property**   Section 5(4) deals with the case where ownership in property is passed by mistake to another who is under an obligation to return the property or its proceeds. The property is regarded, as against the recipient, as belonging to the person entitled to restoration.

As the Court of Appeal recognised in *Gilks* [1972] 3 All ER 280, s. 5(4) was enacted to deal with the mischief of the decision in *Moynes v Cooper* [1956] 1 QB 439, in which D was overpaid in his weekly wages, having received an advance payment which was not then deducted from his pay packet at the end of the week. D committed no offence under the Larceny Act 1916 by keeping this money because, *inter alia*, he was held to be the only person with a legal interest in it. Section 5(4) would now apply to such a case: D clearly 'got' property in the form of coins and notes, and this would be deemed (as against him) to belong to his employer.

In *A-G's Ref (No. 1 of 1983)* [1985] QB 182, s. 5(4) was applied to intangible property. A policewoman was mistakenly credited with wages and overtime for a day which she had not worked. Her bank account was credited by credit transfer with £74.74. The Court of Appeal was satisfied that she had got property, since she had acquired a thing in action against her bank. This is clearly a form of property (see **B4.16**). See also *Stalham* [1993] Crim LR 310.

Not only does 'property' have a wide meaning, but so also does the word 'got'. It is about as wide a word as could possibly have been adopted (*A-G's Ref (No. 1 of 1983)*). Consequently, it would not only cover the handing over of coins and notes as in *Moynes v Cooper*, but also the crediting of a bank account by credit transfer.

Section 5(4) applies only where some error has been made by the giver of the property which **B4.32** amounts to a mistake. In *Moynes v Cooper* the mistake was the error of the wages clerk in believing that M was entitled to his full wages, whereas he should have deducted the money received in advance. In *A-G's Ref (No. 1 of 1983)* the mistake was the belief that the policewoman had worked on a particular day and was entitled to wages and overtime, when in fact she had not so worked.

Section 5(4) does not apply unless the obligation to make restoration is a legal obligation (*Gilks* [1972] 3 All ER 280). In *Gilks* D placed a bet on a horse called Flying Scot. The race was won by Flying Taff. The relief manager paid out to D as if he had backed the winning horse and so D was overpaid by £106.63. D knew that a mistake had been made, but decided to keep the money. The Court of Appeal held that D did not owe a legal obligation to return the money because the bookmaker could not have sued on a gaming transaction (*Morgan v Ashcroft* [1938] 1 KB 490). The court held further that s. 5(4) did not apply to D's moral or social obligation to return the money.

In *A-G's Ref (No. 1 of 1983)* [1985] QB 182 the Court of Appeal decided that 'restoration' has **B4.33** the same meaning as 'restitution'. Consequently, it has to be established that the recipient of the property is under an obligation within the general principles of restitution. The Court of Appeal went on to say that a recipient of property is obliged to pay for a benefit received when it has been given under a mistake on the part of the giver about a material fact. The mistake has to be about a fundamental or essential fact and the payment must have been induced by the mistaken fact (*Norwich Union Fire Insurance Society Ltd v Wm H. Price Ltd* [1934] AC 455). Consequently, not everyone who receives property under a mistake sufficient to satisfy the first element of s. 5(4) will, as a result of that mistake, be under an obligation to make restoration.

In *Davis* (1988) 88 Cr App R 347 the Court of Appeal indicated that the 'language of quasi-contract and of other parts of the civil law' are 'unwelcome visitors to a statute which is supposed to furnish lay juries with tests which they can readily grasp and apply'. It is submitted that the solution must be not a refusal to make use of the law of quasi-contract or restitution, but rather that care should be taken in directions given to juries such that the jury are clear that if they find certain facts then an obligation to restore has been established. This approach is consistent with that to be used when directing juries with regard to s. 5(3) as laid down in *Mainwaring* (1981) 74 Cr App R 99 (see **B4.30**).

'Appropriation'

Theft Act 1968, s. 3   **B4.34**

(1) Any assumption by a person of the rights of an owner amounts to an appropriation, and this includes, where he has come by the property (innocently or not) without stealing it, any later assumption of a right to it by keeping or dealing with it as owner.
(2) Where property or a right or interest in property is or purports to be transferred for value to a person acting in good faith, no later assumption by him of rights which he believed himself to be acquiring shall, by reason of any defect in the transferor's title, amount to theft of the property.

The meaning of 'appropriation' has been considered in four House of Lords cases: *Lawrence v Metropolitan Police Commissioner* [1972] AC 626; *Morris* [1984] AC 320; *Gomez* [1993] AC 442 and *Hinks* [2001] 2 AC 24 as well as by numerous decisions of the Court of Appeal. Most commentators are highly critical of these House of Lords cases, which have distorted the concept of appropriation by giving it a much wider meaning than that which was intended by Parliament. But we are obliged to live with these decisions. We must accordingly accept that an appropriation of property belonging to another (which if committed with dishonest intent, etc., will amount to theft) may be committed:

• whether or not the act is unlawful as a matter of civil law (there need be no misappropriation);
• with or without the consent or authority of the owner;

- by the assumption of any one right of ownership or of all;
- with or without any physical taking or obtaining; and even
- by receipt of a valid gift from the lawful owner.

In many everyday instances, the only difference between lawful appropriation and theft will be the presence or absence of dishonesty.

Section 3(1) itself provides that D may appropriate (and steal) property belonging to another even where he has already 'come by' that property without stealing it, but the courts have decided that D cannot be guilty of repeated thefts of property that he himself has already stolen, even if the original stealing was committed abroad and beyond the reach of English criminal law (see *Atakpu* [1994] QB 69 at **B4.42**). But D may be guilty of theft from V by dishonestly receiving or dealing with property originally stolen by E. The fact that D may more obviously be guilty of handling stolen goods does not mean he cannot also be guilty of theft (see **B4.42**).

B4.35 **The Mental Element in Appropriation** In *Gomez,* Lord Browne-Wilkinson said (at p. 495), that appropriation is an 'objective description of the act done irrespective of the mental state of either the owner or the accused'; but (with respect) an appropriation must involve some kind of mental element, sometimes referred to as *'animus appropriendi'*. If D picks up his shopping bag, he does not thereby appropriate property that E has placed in the bag without his knowledge. He cannot be said to assume rights of ownership over property of which he knows nothing.

If it can be proved that D acted dishonestly and with intent permanently to deprive V, proof of his intention to appropriate is unlikely to be an issue. But as explained at **B4.36**, it is possible for D to be charged with appropriating V's property by one act, with the intention of depriving V by some subsequent act, which may or may not have taken place as intended. The prosecution might conceivably find itself able to prove D's ulterior intent, but not that he performed any act with the requisite *'animus appropriendi'* and in such a case there can be no conviction for theft.

It is also possible for D to appropriate property already in his possession or control by 'keeping or dealing with it as owner', and there can surely be no question of an 'appropriation by keeping' in this context unless the keeping is accompanied by intent.

B4.36 **Assumption of Just One of the Rights of an Owner** In *Gomez* [1993] AC 442 the House of Lords held, approving *Morris* [1984] AC 320 on this point, that it is sufficient for the prosecution to prove the assumption by D of any one of the rights of the owner. It followed that 'the removal of an article from the shelf [of a supermarket] and the changing of the price label on it constituted an assumption of one of the rights of the owner and hence an appropriation'. Lord Keith stated in *Gomez* that 'the switching of price labels on the article is in itself an assumption of one of the rights of the owner, whether or not it is accompanied by some other act such as removing the article from the shelf and placing it in a basket or trolley' because 'no one but the owner has the right to remove a price label from an article or to place a price label upon it'.

With respect, s. 3(1) expressly refers to an assumption of the owner's rights (plural), and it is hard to see how interference with just one of the owner's rights can be equated with an assumption of ownership generally. In the label switching scenario, D replaces one of V's labels with another and then offers to buy the item from V at the lower price. This may be dishonest, but is hardly consistent with an assumption of ownership, and is not even the means by which he intends to deprive V of the item in question (but see **B4.10**).

B4.37 **Consent or Authority of Owner** The House of Lords in *Gomez* [1993] AC 442 (following *Lawrence v Metropolitan Police Commissioner* [1972] AC 626 rather than *Morris* [1984] AC 320 on this point) held that an appropriation of property (even one amounting to theft) can be committed by an act that has the consent of the owner. In *Lawrence* the House rejected an argument that s. 1(1) must be construed as though it contained the words, 'without the consent of the owner'. Viscount Dilhorne said (at pp. 631–2):

> I see no ground for concluding that the omission of the words 'without the consent of the owner' was inadvertent and not deliberate, and to read the subsection as if they were included is, in my opinion, wholly unwarranted. Parliament by the omission of these words has relieved the prosecution of the burden of establishing that the taking was without the owner's consent. That is no longer an ingredient of the offence.

In *Lawrence* D was a taxi-driver who picked up V, who spoke little English, at an airport. The proper fare for the journey was less than £1. V offered D £1, but D said it was not enough. V then offered his wallet, and D took from it another £6. As the House of Lords acknowledged, it was far from clear on these facts that V's lack of resistance amounted to consent, but consent was not in doubt in *Gomez*, where D, an assistant manager of an electrical shop, obtained the consent or authorisation of the manager for goods to be delivered to D's accomplices against two building society cheques which D knew to be worthless. D's conviction for theft was upheld. The obvious charge on those facts was one of obtaining (or enabling others to obtain) property by deception, contrary to the Theft Act 1968, s. 15. In respect of things done on or after 15 January 2007, the obvious charge would now be one of fraud (see B5.1). But in *Gomez* only Lord Lowry (dissenting) was prepared to consider the Eighth Report of the Criminal Law Revision Committee (1966) Cmnd. 2977, which clearly showed that a fraud of that kind was not meant to be included within the concept of theft.

B4.38 The majority in *Gomez* held (at p. 460) that no 'sensible distinction can be made in this context between consent and authorisation' and they approved both *Lawrence* and *Dobson v General Accident Fire and Life Assurance Corporation plc* [1990] 1 QB 274. Contrary dicta in *Morris* were rejected as erroneous and decisions of the Court of Appeal in *Skipp* [1975] Crim LR 114 and *Fritschy* [1985] Crim LR 745 were overruled. In *Fritschy* D had been contracted to collect gold coins in London and deliver them to a bank in Switzerland. He collected them as instructed, but appears to have acted with the dishonest intention of disposing of them elsewhere. The question was whether he appropriated (and stole) the coins (a) as soon as he collected them, or (b) only when he acted on his plan and took them to Italy instead of Switzerland. The Court of Appeal's answer was (b), according to which D committed no offence in England (see A8.2), but in *Gomez* the correct answer was said to be (a). D accordingly stole the coins as soon as he collected them — even though he had not at that stage done anything other than what he had been hired to do. The problem with this approach is that it can reduce theft to little more than a thought crime. An objectively innocent act may become theft because of a dishonest intent that D has not yet put into operation. In *Fritschy* D would on that basis have stolen the coins on collection even if he later changed his mind and delivered them as contracted to the Swiss bank.

Several other cases require reconsideration following *Gomez*. These include *Meech* [1974] QB 549, *Hircock* (1978) 67 Cr App R 278, *Eddy v Niman* (1981) 73 Cr App R 237, and *McPherson* [1973] Crim LR 191.

B4.39 **Appropriation and the Civil Law** *Hinks* [2001] 2 AC 241 is the hardest to defend of the House of Lords theft cases. It was held that D may be guilty of theft even when he is the recipient of a valid and indefeasible gift of property from V, provided that he acted dishonestly in receiving it. The House rejected an argument, deriving from *Mazo* [1997] 2 Cr App R 518, that a distinction should be drawn between cases (such as *Gomez* [1993] AC 442) in which V's consent was obtained by fraud or deception and cases in which his consent was untainted by such factors. Consent obtained by deception may be voidable and it would not necessarily create a conflict with the civil law if D were to be held guilty of theft in such a case. The same might be said of cases in which V's gift is procured by the exercise of undue influence, but although there was some evidence of that in *Hinks* (where V, a naïve and vulnerable man, was persuaded by D, his carer, to give her £60,000 from his savings account), the basis of the decision was that D could be convicted if the jury considered her to have acted dishonestly in accepting the gift — regardless of its legal validity.

Despite *Hinks*, it seems that the recipient of a legally valid and binding gift can rarely be categorised as guilty of theft because he will seldom be dishonest within the meaning of the Theft Act 1968, s. 2(1) (see **B4.51**), even where he might properly be described as greedy or unscrupulous. Even if dishonesty can be proved, it remains necessary to prove that the property in question was appropriated when it still 'belonged to another'. That other person would not necessarily have to be the donor and it might belong to him only in one of the extended senses provided for by s. 5 (see **B4.20**) but D cannot commit theft by appropriating property that has already become entirely his own. See *Briggs* [2004] 1 Cr App R 451.

Hinks is not concerned only with gifts. The question posed for consideration by the House of Lords in that case (and answered in the affirmative) was 'whether the acquisition of an indefeasible title to property is capable of amounting to an appropriation of property belonging to another for the purposes of s. 1(1)'. It may now be possible, following *Hinks*, for an allegation of theft to be made where D acts unscrupulously in receiving payment or other consideration under a valid contractual agreement. D may perhaps be able to escape conviction on such facts by claiming that his conduct is not dishonest under s. 2(1)(a), but he cannot simply rely on the fact that he acquired a valid legal title to the object in question. To that extent, *Hinks* again puts the criminal law potentially at odds with the civil.

B4.40 **Appropriation of Property Previously Acquired, but Not Stolen**   D may appropriate or otherwise 'come by' property belonging to another without initially stealing it. He may do so by means of an unlawful appropriation (e.g., by taking it without the owner's consent) or lawfully (e.g., by borrowing it *with* the owner's consent) but in either case any later assumption of a right to it by keeping it or dealing with it as owner will amount to an appropriation (s. 3(1)); and if committed with the requisite *mens rea*, such appropriation may constitute theft.

For this rule to operate, D must originally have 'come by the property…without stealing it'. The rule does not address the problem of successive appropriations of property that has already been stolen; but see on this **B4.42**.

In order to have appropriated property of which he already has possession, an alleged thief must 'keep or deal with it as owner'. There may be little difficulty in determining that D has 'dealt with' borrowed property as owner if he attempts to sell it as his own. However, it may not be so easy to establish that D has merely kept property as owner (see e.g., *Broom v Crowther* (1984) 148 JP 592).

B4.41 **Appropriation by Purchaser in Good Faith of Stolen Goods**   Ordinarily a person who has previously gained possession of property appropriates (and potentially steals) that property if he then keeps or deals with it as owner (s. 3(1); see **B4.40**). However, s. 3(2) (see **B4.34**) provides an exception in cases where D acquired the property in good faith and for value.

A typical example would be where D innocently purchases a used car only to discover later that it is a stolen vehicle. He would commit no theft in this scenario merely by retaining the car after discovering the truth. But s. 3(2) does not prevent the stolen property from being reclaimed, nor does it mean that D would act lawfully in attempting to sell it on to E. Such an act could not amount to theft of the property, and nor would it amount to an offence of handling stolen goods (see *Bloxham* [1983] 1 AC 109, and **B4.177**) but it would almost inevitably involve fraud, unless E has been warned of D's defective title.

As regards the words 'rights which he believed himself to be acquiring', the relevant time at which D's belief must be held is the moment when he purchased for value (*Adams* [1993] Crim LR 72).

B4.42 **Property Stolen Abroad and Brought into England**   The Theft Acts apply to England and Wales but ordinarily have no application to things done abroad (or even in other parts of the

UK). For exceptions to this rule see generally **A8**. Unless some such exception applies, an act abroad that amounts to theft or stealing under local law is not therefore an offence of theft under English law.

If property stolen abroad is then brought into England, it ordinarily remains the property of the original owner, but it was held in *Atakpu* [1994] QB 69 that it cannot be stolen again by the original thief or thieves. Anyone else who dishonestly receives or otherwise handles that property may however be guilty of handling (see **B4.160**) or indeed of theft, because a dishonest receiver of stolen goods will ordinarily appropriate them with the requisite *mens rea* for theft (see *Stapylton v O'Callaghan* [1973] 2 All ER 782 and **B4.179**). The original thief cannot be guilty of theft or handling, but may now be guilty of offences under the POCA 2002, part 7 (see **B21**).

There may sometimes be room for argument as to whether D stole V's property in England or abroad. In *Ascroft* [2004] 1 Cr App R (S) 326, D, who ran a road haulage firm, challenged a confiscation order imposed following his conviction for conspiracy to steal goods from shipping containers carried on his lorries. The prosecution proved that sealed containers were regularly opened by his accomplices, without breaking the seals, and that parts of each consignment (typically cases of spirits) were then removed before the containers were closed up again. This appears to have occurred in each case at or near the company's depot in England. Counsel for D nevertheless argued that in 17 of the 25 acts of theft to which this count of conspiracy related the goods in question had already been stolen even before the containers were opened—when the sealed containers were first loaded onto D's lorries in Scotland.

The Court of Appeal acknowledged that a charge of conspiracy to steal under English law cannot be based on an agreement to steal goods in Scotland. The question, therefore, was whether the contents of the containers in question were dishonestly appropriated (i.e. stolen) when first collected in Scotland, or whether the appropriation occurred in England, when the containers were improperly opened and the selected goods removed. The Court of Appeal preferred the latter view. Scott Baker LJ said (at [43]–[45]): **B4.43**

> We do not believe that *Gomez* was ever intended to apply to the sort of situation that obtains in this case. The reality seems to us to be that there was a conspiracy to steal goods being conveyed in the appellant's company's lorries as and when appropriate opportunities occurred, with the actual operation to achieve their removal from the lorries (which, we would add, requires some effort and subtlety) taking place at or near the appellant's premises. If the appellant's argument is correct, the theft involves not only those goods that the conspirators subsequently stole but also those that they left in the lorry.
>
> …In our judgment there never was in any ordinary sense of the word an appropriation of the stolen goods until the conspirators removed them from the containers.

The Court of Appeal's view of appropriation in *Ascroft* is a sensible and realistic one, but with respect it is not entirely easy to reconcile with the overruling of *Fritschy* [1985] Crim LR 745 in *Gomez* [1993] AC 442. The only significant difference is that the thieves in *Ascroft* needed to separate the goods they were taking from the rest of the consignment.

Appropriation as a Continuing or Ongoing Act In *Atakpu* [1994] QB 69, the Court of **B4.44** Appeal recognised (*obiter*) that appropriation might sometimes take the form of a continuous or ongoing course of action. It would thus be open to a jury to find, in a given case, that the appropriation (or act of theft) was ongoing for as long as the thief (or robber, burglar etc.) could properly be regarded as 'on the job'. This possibility is more directly supported by *Hale* (1978) 68 Cr App R 415, *Gregory* (1981) 77 Cr App R 41 and *Lockley* [1995] Crim LR 656 and is particularly relevant in cases of alleged robbery where force is used only after the initial act of appropriation.

In *Hale*, the Court of Appeal held that 'it is a matter for the jury to decide whether or not the act of appropriation has finished'. It was open to the jury in that case to decide that D's theft of a jewellery box did not finish with the initial seizure, even though the offence was complete by that point. The jury was entitled to find that the offence was ongoing as D attempted to make his getaway from the house. Force used or threatened by D in order to facilitate that getaway could then turn the theft into robbery.

B4.45   **Appropriation of Company Property by Directors**   A corporation, such as a registered company, has legal personality and may own property in its own right. Directors, managers and other officers may exercise control over the company and its property, and consent on its behalf to things being done to it, but if they dishonestly appropriate its property they may thereby commit theft. This remains possible even where the directors concerned are also the sole mangers of the company's affairs and/or the sole owners of its shares. As Lord Browne-Wilkinson explained in *Gomez* [1993] AC 442 (at p. 496), the presence of absence of consent in such a case is not decisive, and is irrelevant to the question whether there has been an appropriation:

> Whether or not those controlling the company consented or purported to consent to the abstraction of the company's property by the accused, he will have appropriated the property of the company. The question will be whether the other necessary elements are present, viz. was such appropriation dishonest and was it done with the intention of permanently depriving the company of such property?

Lord Browne-Wilkinson approved *A-G's Ref (No. 2 of 1982)* [1984] QB 624 and *Philippou* (1989) 89 Cr App R 290. See also *R (A) v Snaresbrook Crown Court* [2001] EWHC Admin 456.

B4.46   **Appropriation without Real Loss to V**   Since an appropriation may occur even though not all the rights of an owner are assumed, it follows that the owner need not necessarily lose his property, even for a moment. In *Chan Man-sin v The Queen* [1988] 1 All ER 1, D, an accountant, forged company cheques to his own benefit. The company lost nothing, since it was always entitled to have the initial debit to its account reversed, but it was held that D had appropriated the company's credit balance. An intention permanently to deprive is ordinarily required before an appropriation can amount to theft, but since D intended to dispose of the credit balance regardless of the company's rights (see **B4.58**) this requirement was deemed to be satisfied and D's conviction for theft was upheld. See also *Wille* (1989) 86 Cr App R 296, where Woolf LJ said (at p. 302):

> When what the appellant did in this case is considered, it is hard to see what more he could do to assume the rights of the owner in respect of the account at Barclays Bank to the extent of the amount for which the cheques were drawn, than to draw a cheque, issue the cheque, and then take steps which were designed to achieve that the account of the company at the bank was debited with the amount of the cheque...The fact that the company may still have rights against the bank for the amounts of those cheques is...irrelevant to the issues with which the jury were concerned.

In both *Wille* and *Chan Man-sin v The Queen*, the cheques were honoured by the banks, but D might in each case have been guilty even if the cheques had not been honoured (*Wheatley v Commissioner of Police of the British Virgin Islands* [2006] 1 WLR 1683).

A complete offence of theft may be committed by an act that D himself would regard as a failed attempt. In *Corcoran v Anderton* (1980) 71 Cr App R 104, for example, D tugged at V's handbag, causing her to drop it, but never obtained control over the bag and escaped empty-handed. This was a sufficient appropriation to make D guilty of robbery. He would indeed have committed that offence, even if V never released her hold on the bag.

B4.47   **Appropriation by Destruction**   V's property can be appropriated by D even though D never attempts to make use of or profit from that property. Dishonestly causing the destruction of such property can itself be theft (*Kohn* (1979) 69 Cr App R 395). This was confirmed in *Graham* [1997] 1 Cr App R 302, where Lord Bingham CJ said:

> We wish to make it clear that nothing we said was intended to cast doubt upon the principle that theft of a chose in action may be committed when a chose in action belonging to another is destroyed by the defendant's act of appropriation as defined by section 3(1) of the Act.

This does not make theft an appropriate charge where D merely smashes V's car window by throwing a brick though it. Criminal damage would be the only appropriate charge on such facts. But a charge of theft might be a reasonable option where D takes and ignites V's fireworks, thereby destroying them. Theft might indeed be seen as a more appropriate charge on those facts than one of arson.

Cheques, Credit Balances and Money Transfers   Where an alleged theft involves a thing in **B4.48** action such as the credit balance in V's bank account, or the right to payment on a cheque, it can sometimes be particularly difficult to identify the crucial act of appropriation, even where it seems clear that D has dishonestly enriched himself at V's expense.

In most such cases, the prosecution would be well advised to use charges other than theft. Alternative charges to consider might (depending on the facts) include fraud, forgery or using a false instrument. But if for some reason a charge of theft is brought, the following principles may require consideration.

Where V is deceived into drawing a cheque in favour of D, as payee, D thereby acquires a thing in action (the payee's right to enforce the cheque) but this thing in action is created for him and has never belonged to anyone else, so D cannot steal it (*Preddy* [1996] AC 815; *Graham* [1997] 1 Cr App R 302). Nor can he steal funds that are credited to his account under a bank transfer, because here again the thing in action is property that has only ever belonged to him.

A solution of sorts was adopted in *Williams* [2001] 1 Cr App R 362. D dishonestly tricked **B4.49** elderly customers into overpaying him by cheque for building services supposedly rendered. He was convicted of theft: not theft of the cheques themselves, nor theft of the moneys which were credited to his account, but theft of the credit balances in the bank accounts of his victims. By causing the cheques to be paid and credited to his own account he was held to have 'appropriated' their property by reducing the sizes of their bank balances. It made no difference that this appropriation took place with their consent, as long as his conduct could be described as dishonest. Once he 'banked' the cheques they would be collected and paid more or less automatically and any human involvement in that process would be the acts of innocent agents. As to the precise moment at which theft would be committed in such a case, see *Governor of Pentonville Prison, ex parte Osman* [1990] 3 All ER 701 and *Ngan* [1998] 1 Cr App R 331 (discussed in *Smith's Law of Theft* (9th edn) at paras. 2.80 *et seq.*).

In *Naviede* [1997] Crim LR 662, however, the court rejected the argument that D could appropriate property in V's account by deceiving V or V's agent into consciously making a transfer or withdrawal from that account:

> We are not satisfied that a misrepresentation which persuades the account holder to direct payment out of his account is an assumption of the rights of the account holder as owner such as to amount to an appropriation of his rights within section 3(1) of the 1968 Act.

A similar approach was adopted in *Briggs* [2004] 1 Cr App R 451, where D deceived elderly rela- **B4.50** tives into authorising a transfer of £49,500 from the proceeds of their house sale into a bank account controlled by her. It was held, as in *Naviede*, that the transfer was not an act of appropriation by D, even though her dishonest intent was not in doubt. Silber J said (at [13]):

> We are fortified in coming to that view by three further factors. First, no case has been cited to us where it has been held that an appropriation occurs where the relevant act is committed by the victim albeit as a result of deception. Second,…there would [otherwise] be little need for many deception offences as many acts of deceptive conduct would be covered by theft, but it is noteworthy that the Theft Act 1968 (as amended) contains deception offences to deal with the case where a defendant by deception induces a person to take a step which leads to the wrongdoing of gaining property by deception (section 15) or obtaining a money transfer by deception (section 15A) or obtaining a pecuniary advantage (section 16). Third, we have already referred to the explanation of the word 'appropriation' in section 3(1) of the Theft Act 1968 and it is a word which connotes a physical act rather than a more remote action triggering the payment which gives rise to the charge.

The Oxford English Dictionary defines 'appropriation' as 'to take possession for one's own, to take to oneself'. It is not easy to see why an act of deceiving an owner to do something would fall within the meaning of 'appropriation'.

The subsequent repeal of the deception offences and their replacement by new offences in the Fraud Act 2006 has not invalidated that argument.

Where D draws a cheque on V's account for an improper purpose, or forges V's cheque or purports to issue instructions to V's bank, an appropriation may be relatively easy to identify, because such acts involve misuse by D of the 'key' to V's account. See e.g., *Hilton* [1997] 2 Cr App R 445, in which D, the chairman of a charity, abused his position by instructing the bank (in two cases by fax and in another by cheque) to make payments from the charity's account which were used to settle his personal debts. D's conviction for theft was upheld.

'Dishonesty'

B4.51

Theft Act 1968, s. 2

(1) A person's appropriation of property belonging to another is not to be regarded as dishonest—
    (a) if he appropriates the property in the belief that he has in law the right to deprive the other of it, on behalf of himself or a third person; or
    (b) if he appropriates the property in the belief that he would have the other's consent if the other knew of the appropriation and the circumstances of it; or
    (c) (except where the property came to him as trustee or personal representative) if he appropriates the property in the belief that the person to whom the property belongs cannot be discovered by taking reasonable steps.
(2) A person's appropriation of property belonging to another may be dishonest notwithstanding that he is willing to pay for the property.

Section 2 provides only a partial definition of 'dishonesty'. Where D acted with any of the three states of mind listed in s. 2(1) his actions cannot be considered dishonest, but the converse is not true. In other words, it does not follow that D's conduct *must* be considered dishonest just because it falls outwith any of the s. 2(1) categories. The Court of Appeal in *Ghosh* [1982] QB 1053 has provided a supplementary test that must be applied in any case where there is an issue of dishonesty to which s. 2(1) provides no answer. This is examined at **B4.54**.

There is no requirement in s. 2(1) that D's belief must be based on reasonable grounds, but the reasonableness or otherwise of D's supposed belief may be relevant to its credibility (*Holden* [1991] Crim LR 478).

Section 2(1)(a) requires only that D genuinely believed he was entitled to take the property in question. He need not necessarily have believed he was entitled to take it in the way he did (*Robinson* [1977] Crim LR 173) although the use of improper methods (trespass to property, threats, violence, etc.) may give rise to other forms of civil or criminal liability.

The importance of drawing the jury's attention to the provisions of s. 2(1)(a) was emphasised by the Court of Appeal in *Falconer-Atlee* (1973) 58 Cr App R 348. The Court of Appeal held in *Wootton* [1990] Crim LR 201 that a jury must be directed on s. 2(1)(a) whenever a claim of right is raised. Directing the jury only in accordance with the *Ghosh* test does not suffice in such a case. See also *Forrester* [1992] Crim LR 793.

B4.52 The Court of Appeal considered s. 2(1)(a) and (b) in *A-G's Ref (No. 2 of 1982)* [1984] QB 624. It was held that where the directors of a company appropriate assets belonging to the company they cannot rely on s. 2(1)(b) to negate dishonesty if the only consent they believe they would have is their own consent, given on behalf of the company. Whether they could succeed under s. 2(1)(a) would depend on whether they honestly believed they were entitled to do what they did. The court rejected arguments that, when all the members and directors of a company agree to such action, they cannot be held to have acted dishonestly. The appropriation of company assets may prejudice the wider interests of the company and its creditors, even if its own members are not prejudiced.

As to s. 2(1)(c), this appears to cover not only cases in which D believes the owner cannot reasonably be identified but also cases in which he believes that the owner (although known to D) cannot reasonably be traced or located. An example given in *Smith's Law of Theft* (9th edn) at para. 2.285 is that D may have agreed to store V's furniture. V moves away and fails to keep in touch. Needing the space and being genuinely convinced that he cannot find V, D eventually disposes of V's furniture. This would not be theft.

Dishonesty Notwithstanding Willingness to Pay   Although under s. 2(2) D's appropriation **B4.53** of V's property may sometimes be considered dishonest even though he is willing to pay for it (notably where he knows that V is not willing to sell it to him), his willingness to pay a fair price may in other circumstances be indicative of his honesty. See *Boggeln v Williams* [1978] 2 All ER 1061. To put it another way, it is often D's evident intent to *avoid* paying that most clearly demonstrates his dishonesty.

Meaning of 'Dishonesty' according to *Ghosh*   The Court of Appeal in *Ghosh* [1982] QB **B4.54** 1053 established a dishonesty test that applies both to theft and to other offences of dishonesty. It is subordinate to s. 2(1), so where in a theft case D's conduct is deemed *not* to be dishonest under that provision the *Ghosh* test need not even be considered; but where s. 2(1) is not applicable or does not provide the answer (and it never positively defines dishonesty), the *Ghosh* test becomes paramount.

According to *Ghosh* (at p. 1064D–E) a two-part test must be applied. A jury must first be directed to decide:

> …whether according to the ordinary standards of reasonable and honest people what was done was dishonest. If it was not dishonest by those standards, that is the end of the matter and the prosecution fails.

If (but only if) D's conduct was dishonest by those standards, the jury must consider the second question, namely:

> …whether the defendant himself must have realised that what he was doing was [by the standards of reasonable and honest people] dishonest.

The *Ghosh* test has often been criticised for leaving too much to the whims of a jury, but it remains good law: see *Cornelius* [2012] EWCA Crim 500.

The first part of the test concerns the 'acceptability' of D's conduct according to the standards **B4.55** of reasonable honest people and not D's own state of mind. Strictly speaking, therefore, it is an *actus reus* issue rather than a *mens rea* one, but the second limb of the test is certainly focused on D's *mens rea*. Where a *Ghosh* direction is necessary, the exact words in *Ghosh* should be used (*Hyam* [1997] Crim LR 439). The questions must be asked in the indicated order; to reverse them is confusing (*Green* [1992] Crim LR 292). The Court of Appeal in *Ghosh* gave further explanation of the second question when it said (at p. 1064E–G):

> In most cases, where the actions are obviously dishonest by ordinary standards, there will be no doubt about it. It will be obvious that the defendant himself knew that he was acting dishonestly. It is dishonest for a defendant to act in a way which he knows ordinary people consider to be dishonest, even if he asserts or genuinely believes that he is morally justified in acting as he did. For example, Robin Hood or those ardent anti-vivisectionists who remove animals from vivisection laboratories are acting dishonestly, even though they may consider themselves to be morally justified in doing what they do, because they know that ordinary people would consider these actions to be dishonest.

With respect, the question of what an anti-vivisectionist believes may well be a question of fact that has to be left to the jury. In many other cases, however, dishonesty will not be in issue. Bank robbery, for example, is so obviously dishonest that a *Ghosh* direction will not be required in any such case. In *Roberts* (1985) 84 Cr App R 117, a decision concerned with handling stolen goods, the Court of Appeal indicated that a full *Ghosh* direction would not be necessary unless D raised the issue by, for example, suggesting that he did not know that anybody would regard his actions

B

Part B Offences

as dishonest. Further, in *Price* (1989) 90 Cr App R 409, a decision concerned with the Theft Act 1978, ss. 1 and 2, the Court of Appeal, following *Roberts*, said (at p. 411):

> ...it is by no means in every case involving dishonesty that a *Ghosh* direction is necessary. Indeed in the majority of such cases, of which this was one, it is unnecessary and potentially misleading to give such a direction. It need only be given in cases where the defendant might have believed that what he is alleged to have done was in accordance with the ordinary person's idea of honesty.

In consequence D's convictions were upheld when the judge had not given a *Ghosh* direction, since the only question relevant to dishonesty was whether D honestly believed that he was the beneficiary of a trust fund or not (see also *Buzalek* [1991] Crim LR 130 (a fraudulent trading case), *Brennen* [1990] Crim LR 118 (a handling case) and *Green* [1992] Crim LR 292 (a s. 20 case)). But in other cases failure to direct on *Ghosh* could be fatal to a conviction (*Clarke* [1996] Crim LR 824).

B4.56   In *Rostron* [2003] EWCA Crim 2206, the Court of Appeal upheld D's conviction for the theft of golf balls from a lake on a private golf course, even though no *Ghosh* direction had been provided. The court appears to have concluded that there could be no doubting D's dishonesty if he knew he had no right to go onto the golf course (at night) in order to take the balls. With respect, his knowledge that he had no 'right' (and no permission) to act in this way meant only that he had no defence under s. 2(1)(a) or (b). But D had argued that he saw no harm in fishing for the balls, given that nobody else seemed interested in recovering them, and this surely entitled him to a *Ghosh* direction. D's case elicited considerable public sympathy at the time and it seems quite possible that a jury would have given serious consideration to his argument that he was 'doing no harm to anyone'.

Rostron may be contrasted with *Clowes (No. 2)* [1994] 2 All ER 316 and *Lightfoot* (1992) 97 Cr App R 24 in which it was held that, for the purposes of the *Ghosh* test D's knowledge of the civil or criminal law is irrelevant. With respect, however, it is surely more likely that D will be considered dishonest if he realises that his actions are unlawful.

The *Ghosh* test also applies to handling stolen goods (*Roberts* (1985) 84 Cr App R 117), false accounting (*Gohill* [2007] EWHC 239 (Admin)), conspiracy to defraud and offences under the Fraud Act 2006.

Intention Permanently to Deprive

B4.57   On a charge of theft, the prosecution must prove that D had an intention permanently to deprive the owner of the property in question when he appropriated it. If this can be proved, it is no defence that D subsequently changed his mind and returned the property (*McHugh* (1993) 97 Cr App R 335). If however no such intent is proved, there can be no conviction either for theft or for any other offence (such as robbery) that involves theft or requires an intention to steal (*Warner* (1970) 55 Cr App R 93; *Cocks* (1976) 63 Cr App R 79). Even a violent carjacking cannot amount to robbery of the car if D intends only to use that car for his getaway before abandoning it (*Mitchell* [2008] EWCA Crim 850). The Theft Act 1968, s. 6, (see **B4.58**), may sometimes assist in establishing whether the requisite intention can be established, but it does not purport to define the concept and should be referred to 'in exceptional cases only' (*Lloyd* [1985] QB 829; *Coffey* [1987] Crim LR 498).

What actually amounts to 'permanent deprivation' is largely a question of fact, but may also involve questions of law. See for example the discussion of *Duru* [1974] 3 All ER 715 and *Preddy* [1996] AC 815.

Intention to Treat Property as One's Own to Dispose of

B4.58   Section 6 does not fully define what is meant by an intention to permanently deprive, but stretches the meaning of that phrase by providing that in some cases an intent to cause something less than outright or permanent deprivation will suffice.

Theft Act 1968, s. 6

(1) A person appropriating property belonging to another without meaning the other permanently to lose the thing itself is nevertheless to be regarded as having the intention of permanently depriving the other of it if his intention is to treat the thing as his own to dispose of regardless of the other's rights; and a borrowing or lending of it may amount to so treating it if, but only if, the borrowing or lending is for a period and in circumstances making it equivalent to an outright taking or disposal.

(2) Without prejudice to the generality of subsection (1) above, where a person, having possession or control (lawfully or not) of property belonging to another, parts with the property under a condition as to its return which he may not be able to perform, this (if done for purposes of his own and without the other's authority) amounts to treating the property as his own to dispose of regardless of the other's rights.

Section 6 is essentially a 'deeming' provision. It enables a court to find in appropriate cases that **B4.59** D intended permanently to deprive V of certain property, even though he may have intended that V would eventually regain that property. For s. 6 to apply, D must intend to 'dispose' of the property regardless of V's rights. Section 6(2) identifies one way in which such a disposal may be made. The 'second limb' of s. 6(1) identifies another. But what else may amount to a relevant 'disposal'?

An example suggested by the Court of Appeal in *Lloyd* [1985] QB 829 at p. 836 was:

> ...the sort of case where [D] takes things and then offers them back to the owner for the owner to buy if he wishes. If [D] intends to return them to the owner only upon such payment, then, on the wording of section 6(1), that is deemed to amount to the necessary intention permanently to deprive.

See, e.g., *Raphael* [2008] EWCA Crim 1014 (where the charge was one of conspiracy to steal). Other kinds of behaviour might also suffice, notably where it involves the 'disposal' of V's property. There is much to be said for Sir John Smith's argument that a disposal of property must involve getting rid of it or expending it (e.g., by selling it). This was accepted by the Court of Appeal in *Cahill* [1993] Crim LR 141 but *Cahill* was overlooked in *DPP v Lavender* [1994] Crim LR 297, where D had without authority taken doors from one council house and installed them in another house owned by the very same council. The Divisional Court held on these facts that s. 6(1) clearly applied, so that D was guilty of theft; but with respect, this decision must be open to question. D had no right to relocate the doors, but he never intended to dispose of them in such a way as to deprive the council of them.

The Court of Appeal in *Lloyd* interpreted s. 6 restrictively, 'in such a way as to ensure that nothing is construed as an intention permanently to deprive which would not prior to the 1968 Act have been so construed'. See also *Warner* (1970) 55 Cr App R 93. In contrast, the court in *Downes* (1983) 77 Cr App R 260 preferred to give the words of s. 6 their normal meaning, without reference to the technicalities of the law prior to 1968, and this now appears to be the preferred approach. See *Duru* [1974] 3 All ER 715, *Bagshaw* [1988] Crim LR 321, *Governor of Pentonville Prison, ex parte Osman* [1990] 3 All ER 701, *Fernandes* [1996] 1 Cr App R 175 and *Raphael*. In *Vinall* [2012] 1 Cr App R 400, Pitchford LJ said (at [16]):

> What section 6(1) requires is a state of mind in the defendant which Parliament regards as the equivalent of an intention permanently to deprive... [It] does not require that the thing has been disposed of, nor does it require that the defendant intends to dispose of the thing in any particular way. No doubt evidence of a particular disposal or a particular intention to dispose of the thing will constitute evidence of the defendant's state of mind but it is, in our view, for the jury to decide upon the circumstances proved whether the defendant harboured the statutory intention.

In *Chan Man-sin v The Queen* [1988] 1 All ER 1, D forged cheques from two companies for **B4.60** which he worked and paid them into his own account. The companies' credit balances at their banks were reduced each time, and H was charged with stealing those balances. He may perhaps have known that once the fraud was discovered the companies' accounts would have to be reimbursed and that the companies would ultimately lose nothing, but the Privy Council referred to the Hong Kong equivalent of s. 6(1) and ruled that, even if D expected this to happen, he was still on these facts 'purporting to deal with the companies' property without regard to their rights' and could be deemed to have the requisite intention.

Another example is provided by *Marshall* [1998] 2 Cr App R 282 in which D acquired unexpired London Underground tickets from travellers who no longer needed them and then dishonestly resold these tickets to other travellers. It was assumed (perhaps wrongly) that on expiry the tickets would eventually be returned to or retained by London Underground, but the court held that D would nevertheless remain guilty of theft by virtue of s. 6(1). By acquiring and reselling the tickets, said the court, D 'had the intention to treat them as his own to dispose of regardless of London Underground's rights'. But if this approach is correct it should also be possible to apply s. 6(1) in a case such as *Preddy* [1996] AC 815—a possibility that does not appear to have been properly examined in that case.

B4.61 **Borrowing or Lending as Equivalent to Outright Taking**   In *Lloyd* [1985] QB 829, D, a cinema projectionist, clandestinely removed feature films due to be shown in the cinema where he worked. His co-defendants copied them onto video tape and they sold many such 'pirate' copies; but the original films were returned in perfect working order and continued to attract audiences to the cinema. On such facts there was clearly no theft. Copyright offences had been committed, and there was a criminal conspiracy, but there was no intent to deprive the owners of any films even under the second limb of s. 6(1). For it to apply to a 'borrowing' case, said the court, D's intention must be to return the thing in question 'in such a changed state that it can truly be said that all its goodness or virtue has gone'. This might include taking a season ticket until the end of the season, or using V's (non-rechargeable) torch battery until it is discharged and 'flat'. See also *Coffey* [1987] Crim LR 498; *Bagshaw* [1988] Crim LR 321.

Despite what was said in *Lloyd,* it may perhaps be argued that D commits theft if he dishonestly 'borrows' V's season ticket with the intention of returning it halfway through the season. This would be equivalent to the outright taking of half of a complete series of individual tickets, which is what a season ticket represents. If this is correct, borrowing the season ticket for just one afternoon must then suffice to trigger s. 6(1). That afternoon's events will never be repeated and to that extent V's deprivation is not just temporary.

In *Velumyl* [1989] Crim LR 299, the Court of Appeal rejected an argument that if D 'borrows' money from his employer expecting to return an equivalent sum he has no intention permanently to deprive his employer of that money. That would be true only if D intended to return the very same notes or coins that he took, and in practice that is most improbable. Section 6 accordingly has no application on such facts.

B4.62 **Parting with Property on a Condition which D May Not be Able to Perform**   Section 6(2) covers such instances as D pawning V's property, hoping that he will be able to redeem the property at the appropriate time, but not knowing whether he will be able to do so.

B4.63 **Intention to Deprive under s. 5**   In relation to trust property, s. 5(2) (see **B4.19**) provides that 'an intention to defeat the trust shall be regarded as an intention to deprive of the property any person having that right'. The right referred to is the right to enforce the trust and 'that person' is the person to whom the trust property belongs (see **B4.24**). Section 5(2) states only that an intention to defeat the trust is an intention to deprive. An intention to deprive permanently must still be established.

In respect of property got by another's mistake (see **B4.31**), s. 5(4) provides that 'an intention not to make restoration shall be regarded accordingly as an intention to deprive that person of the property or proceeds'. 'That person' is the person who is entitled to restoration. Section 5(4) states only that the intention not to make restoration is an intention to deprive. It must still be established whether there was an intention to deprive permanently.

Conditional Intention   Problems have arisen in relation to cases of theft or attempted theft   **B4.64**
where D has been caught interfering with V's property but claims that he had not at that stage
decided to steal anything but was simply ascertaining whether there was something worth stealing. In *Easom* [1971] 2 QB 315 the Court of Appeal said that 'a conditional appropriation will
not do'. So rummaging through a handbag with that intention was not sufficient. In *Husseyn*
(1977) 67 Cr App R 131, the Court of Appeal followed *Easom* and so held that D was not guilty
of attempted theft of some sub-aqua equipment from a holdall, because he had not yet looked
into the bag and decided whether there was anything worth stealing. A solution to this problem
can usually be found in careful drafting of the charge or indictment. In a case such as *Easom* or
Husseyn, D may be charged with attempting to steal some or all of the contents of the handbag
or the holdall. There is then no need to prove that D intended to steal any of the specific items
found within the bag or holdall, but simply that he intended to steal anything worth stealing
(*A-G's Ref (Nos. 1 and 2 of 1979)* [1980] QB 180).

Where D takes a specific item with a view to ascertaining whether it is valuable, or can profitably
be disposed of, it is no defence for him to argue that he was going to return it if it proved useless
to him. He is thereby treating that item as his own to dispose of, regardless of the owner's rights.
See **B4.58**.

Theft of Mails within the British Postal Area

For most purposes, the Theft Acts apply only to things done within England and Wales or   **B4.65**
(notably where the CJA 1993, part I, applies) to things done partly in England and partly
abroad (see generally **A8**); but the Theft Act 1968, s. 14, creates a special rule in respect of mail
in transit within any part of the British Postal Area.

Theft Act 1968, s. 14

(1) Where a person—
   (a)   steals or attempts to steal any mailbag or postal packet in the course of transmission as such
       between places in different jurisdictions in the British postal area, or any of the contents of
       such a mailbag or postal packet, or
   (b)   in stealing or with intent to steal any such mailbag or postal packet or any of its contents,
       commits any robbery, attempted robbery or assault with intent to rob;
    then, notwithstanding that he does so outside England and Wales, he shall be guilty of com-
    mitting or attempting to commit the offence against this Act as if he had done so in England or
    Wales, and he shall accordingly be liable to be prosecuted, tried and punished in England and
    Wales without proof that the offence was committed there.
(2) In subsection (1) above the reference to different jurisdictions in the British postal area is to
    be construed as referring to the several jurisdictions of England and Wales, of Scotland, of
    Northern Ireland, of the Isle of Man and of the Channel Islands.

There are specific offences concerned with mail thefts: it is an offence, contrary to the Postal
Services Act 2000, s. 83, for a postal operator to interfere with the mail; and it is an offence,
contrary to s. 84, for any person to interfere with the mail. For other offences, see ss. 85 to 88.
Section 125 of that Act defines 'mail bag' and 'postal packet'.

ROBBERY AND ASSAULT WITH INTENT TO ROB

Definition

Theft Act 1968, s. 8   **B4.66**

(1) A person is guilty of robbery if he steals, and immediately before or at the time of doing so, and
    in order to do so, he uses force on any person or puts or seeks to put any person in fear of being
    then and there subjected to force.
(2) A person guilty of robbery, or of an assault with intent to rob, shall on conviction on indict-
    ment be liable to imprisonment for life.

Procedure

B4.67 Robbery and assault with intent to rob are triable only on indictment; they are normally class 3 offences, but see CPD XIII, para. B (see Supplement, **PD-97**) for the additional factors that the court considers on allocation.

Indictment

B4.68

Statement of Offence

Robbery contrary to section 8(1) of the Theft Act 1968.

Particulars of Offence

A on the … day of…robbed V of a gold watch.

As to the practice of including a count for an offence contrary to the Firearms Act 1968, see *French* (1982) 75 Cr App R 1 per Lord Lane CJ.

Alternative Verdicts

B4.69 Theft is the obvious alternative verdict by the application of the CLA 1967, s. 6(3). The House of Lords in *Maxwell* [1990] 1 All ER 801 has held that the trial judge is only obliged to leave such a lesser alternative verdict to the jury if necessary in the interests of justice, for example, if the question of force was in doubt but there was substantial evidence of theft.

The decision in *Tennant* [1976] Crim LR 133, that it is not possible under the CLA 1967, s. 6(3), to convict a person of an assault on a charge of robbery, needs to be reconsidered in the light of *Metropolitan Police Commissioner v Wilson* [1984] AC 242. An allegation of robbery may in many cases impliedly include an allegation of an assault, because most uses of force will involve an assault, even though it is not possible exactly to assimilate 'force' as required for robbery with 'assault'.

Sentence

B4.70 The maximum penalty for robbery or assault with intent to rob is life imprisonment (s. 8(2)). The combination of violence and theft makes robbery the most serious of the common offences of dishonesty. The great majority of offenders convicted of robbery receive custodial sentences.

The definitive sentencing guideline, *Robbery* (see Supplement, **SG-34**), applies to three important categories of this offence: (i) street robbery or 'mugging', (ii) robberies of small businesses, and (iii) the less sophisticated commercial robberies. Separate sentencing ranges and starting points are indicated for adults and for young offenders. In *Peloe* [2011] 1 Cr App R (S) 96 the offender accosted a woman in the street, and grabbed her bag with sufficient force to cause her to fall over. He struck her three times in the face and took her bag. He was arrested two hours later. He had 20 previous convictions for 50 offences, including robbery. The judge treated this as a level 2 offence and passed a sentence of six years' imprisonment following a trial. The Court of Appeal agreed. Significant force was used and there was an element of persistence in the violence although the offence was opportunistic. The criminal record was a significant aggravating feature. The sentence was high but not wrong in principle. By comparison, in *Hume* [2011] 2 Cr App R (S) 268 the offender approached a 76-year-old woman who had just collected her pension. When she got into her car, he pulled the door open, reached across her and grabbed her bag from her grasp. The victim suffered minor injury to her fingers. A sentence of four years following a plea of guilty was reduced to 32 months. The judge had been entitled to conclude that the victim had been targeted, and the offender had a poor record.

B4.71 The guidelines do *not* cover two other categories of robbery: (iv) professionally planned commercial robberies and (v) violent personal robberies in the home. In the former category guidance can now be found in *McCartney* [2003] EWCA Crim 1372 (where a sentence of 22 years' imprisonment was passed on a career criminal being dealt with for some 20 robberies) and *Atkinson* [2005] 2 Cr App R (S) 206 (where 22 years was appropriate for an organiser of a series of armed robberies of sub-post offices). Moses LJ in *Jenkins* [2009] 1 Cr App R (S) 109 said that the maximum sentence for a number of armed robberies, where violence is actually used, appears to be in the region of 25 years after a trial. On the particular facts, and taking guilty pleas into account, the appropriate sentences were 15, ten and eight years. In *Lawrence* [2011] EWCA Crim 2609, a case involving violent smash and grab raids of jewellers' premises in the middle of the day, in which shop-owners and customers had been put in real fear, the proper sentences were 11 or 12 years after a trial but seven and eight years in light of guilty pleas and relevant mitigation. In the latter category of violent robbery in the home the case of *O'Driscoll* (1986) 8 Cr App R (S) 121 indicates that the appropriate sentencing range is 13 to 16 years for a first-time offender pleading not guilty. Longer terms may be appropriate where extreme violence is used. This category overlaps with some cases of aggravated burglary where comparable sentences are passed (see **B4.101**). Some cases a little lower down the scale were identified in *A-G's Ref (Nos. 38, 39 & 40 of 2007) (Crummack)* [2008] 1 Cr App R (S) 319. In *Purcell* [2009] 1 Cr App R (S) 113, the Court of Appeal said that violent robberies in the home were a distinct category of robbery, but that the overall seriousness of the case should be assessed irrespective of whether charges were laid as robbery, burglary, or offences against the person. See also *Roe* [2010] 2 Cr App R (S) 561. In *Poynter* [2013] 1 Cr App R (S) 33 (5), sentences of 15 years were reduced to 12 years after a trial in a case where three men armed with weapons forced their way into the victim's home and tied him and his daughter up while the house was ransacked.

It is also clear that the robbery guidelines do not cover cases of 'ram-raiding' (*Lawlor* [2013] 1 Cr App R (S) 532 (102)). In *Lawlor* a sentence of 12 years' imprisonment after a trial was upheld for a violent and carefully planned ram-raid on a bank at a time when staff had been present and put in fear. According to the Court of Appeal, ram-raiding cases might be charged as theft, burglary or robbery, varied considerably on their facts and did not fall neatly within any particular guidelines.

Actus Reus

Robbery requires theft. In *Robinson* [1977] Crim LR 173 it was held that where D uses or **B4.72** threatens force in order to appropriate property to which he believes he is entitled, he cannot then be guilty of either theft or robbery, even if he knows the force to be unlawful. If theft is intended but not committed (e.g., because V escapes or has nothing for D to steal), a charge of assault with intent to rob under the Theft Act 1968, s. 8(2), or a charge of attempted robbery under the Criminal Attempts Act 1981, s. 1 (see **A5.69**), may still be possible. If D has at least committed an assault, a charge under s. 8(2) may be preferable in that it avoids the uncertainties that can beset a prosecution for attempt.

To be guilty of robbery, D must either use force or put another person in fear of being then and there subjected to force, and he must do this in order to steal. In *Shendley* [1970] Crim LR 49 the trial judge clearly erred by directing the jury that: '...if the violence was unconnected with the stealing but you are satisfied there was a stealing it...would be open to you to find [D] guilty of robbery...without violence'. The Court of Appeal quashed D's conviction for robbery and substituted a conviction for theft. It would not matter, however, if D also had some additional motive for using or threatening force.

In *Dawson* (1976) 64 Cr App R 170 the Court of Appeal held that 'force' is a word in ordinary **B4.73** use, which juries understand. The jury in that case were entitled to find that force was used where the defendants stood around the victim, one of them nudged him and his wallet was stolen. In such cases, an implicit threat of force may suffice, as where a gang surround the victim in order to steal from him. It does not then matter whether the victim is actually put in fear or not: it is the intention of the perpetrator that matters (*B v DPP* (2007) 171 JP 404).

Whether force has been used on a person is a question for the jury to consider, and it appears that they may conclude that force has been used when it is used indirectly. In *Clouden* [1987] Crim LR 56 the court dismissed an appeal against a conviction for robbery when D had wrenched the victim's shopping basket from her hand and run off with it. Indeed, it should not matter in such a case that V's grip on her bag is too strong for D to break: by grabbing the bag with intent, D has appropriated it and the theft (and robbery) is complete. See also *Corcoran v Anderton* (1980) 71 Cr App R 104, but contrast *P v DPP* [2013] 1 WLR 2337, where snatching a cigarette away from V's hand, without making any contact with V, was akin to picking V's pocket and could not therefore be robbery.

Force must be used or threatened immediately before or at the time of stealing. Consequently, it is important to know whether D had already finished committing the theft when the force or threat was used (see **B4.44**, *Vinall* [2012] 1 Cr App R 400 and *James* [1997] Crim LR 598).

Mens Rea

B4.74   Robbery and assault with intent to rob each require the *mens rea* elements of theft, namely dishonesty (see **B4.51** to **B4.56**) and intention permanently to deprive (see **B4.57** to **B4.64**) as well as the intention to appropriate the property in question (*Zerei* [2012] EWCA Crim 1114). There must also be intention or at least recklessness as to the use of force. The accidental use of force during the course of an ordinary theft would not suffice since D must use the force in order to steal. Similarly, D does not commit robbery merely because he is interrupted by V in the course of a theft or burglary and V momentarily fears that D will attack her.

BURGLARY

Definition

B4.75   Theft Act 1968, s. 9

(1) A person is guilty of burglary if—
  (a) he enters any building or part of a building as a trespasser and with intent to commit any such offence as is mentioned in subsection (2) below; or
  (b) having entered any building or part of a building as a trespasser he steals or attempts to steal anything in the building or that part of it or inflicts or attempts to inflict on any person therein any grievous bodily harm.
(2) The offences referred to in subsection (1)(a) above are offences of stealing anything in the building or part of a building in question, of inflicting on any person therein any grievous bodily harm, and of doing unlawful damage to the building or anything therein.

Section 9 creates two groups of offences: one of entering a building (or part of a building) as a trespasser with the requisite intent, contrary to s. 9(1)(a); the other of having entered a building (or part of a building) as a trespasser and committing a specified offence, contrary to s. 9(1)(b). In each case there are now (by s. 9(4) as amended) two offences dependent upon whether the building is or is not a dwelling. The different sentence provisions applicable (see **B4.80**) mean that, under *Courtie* [1984] AC 463, burglary of a dwelling is now a distinct offence from burglary of any other type of building.

Procedure

B4.76   By virtue of the MCA 1980, s. 17 and sch. 1, para. 28, most forms of burglary are triable either way. When tried on indictment, it is normally a class 3 offence, but see CPD XIII, para. B (see Supplement, **PD-97**) for the additional factors that the court considers on allocation. However:

(a) if the burglary comprises the commission of, or an intention to commit, an offence which is triable only on indictment, then the burglary is also triable only on indictment (sch. 1, para. 28(b));
(b) if the burglary is in a dwelling-house and any person in the dwelling was subjected to violence or the threat of violence, the offence is triable only on indictment (sch. 1, para. 28(c)) (the violence need not have been used as part of effecting the burglary: *McGrath* [2004] 1 Cr App R 173);
(c) if the burglary is a domestic burglary and the accused, who is now aged 18 or over, has two previous separate convictions for domestic burglary in respect of offences committed after 30 November 1999, the offence is triable only on indictment (PCC(S)A 2000, s. 111(4)).

See the *Magistrates' Court Sentencing Guidelines* (see Supplement, SG-246 and SG-247 for **B4.77** indications as to when a case should be sent to the Crown Court.

Indictment

Statement of Offence   **B4.78**

Burglary with intent contrary to section 9(1)(a) of the Theft Act 1968.

Particulars of Offence

A, on or about the...day of...entered a dwelling [or part of a dwelling, or a building or part of a building], namely..., as a trespasser with intent to steal therein [or inflict grievous bodily harm upon a person therein, or to do unlawful damage to the building or anything therein].

Statement of Offence

Burglary contrary to section 9(1)(b) of the Theft Act 1968.

Particulars of Offence

A on or about the...day of..., having entered a dwelling [or part of a dwelling, or a building or part of a building], namely..., as a trespasser, stole therein [or attempted to steal therein, or inflicted grievous bodily harm upon...therein].

In *Machent v Quinn* [1970] 2 All ER 255 the Divisional Court decided that it is unnecessary for the prosecution to prove that all the articles mentioned in an information or an indictment have been stolen. Proof that D stole any one of those articles is sufficient.

Alternative Verdicts

By virtue of the CLA 1967, s. 6(3), on an indictment for burglary contrary to the Theft Act **B4.79** 1968, s. 9(1)(b), D may alternatively be convicted of the underlying offence that he is alleged to have committed after entering the building (*Lillis* [1972] 2 QB 236). In *Metropolitan Police Commissioner v Wilson* [1984] AC 242, the House of Lords ruled that by virtue of s. 6(3) a conviction under the OAPA 1861, s. 47, may also be available as an alternative verdict on a charge of burglary by inflicting grievous bodily harm under s. 9(1)(b), just as it may be on an indictment alleging the commission of an offence under the OAPA 1861, s. 20. See **D19.47**.

The approach in *Wilson* has been applied in *Whiting* (1987) 85 Cr App R 78. The Court of Appeal decided that it is possible that a person may be found guilty of burglary under s. 9(1)(a) on a charge of burglary under s. 9(1)(b), because s. 9(1)(b) impliedly includes an allegation of an offence contrary to s. 9(1)(a). Such an alternative verdict can be arrived at in some, but not all cases, since these two offences are essentially different in certain respects (see **B4.83**, **B4.89** and **B4.95**).

Sentence

The maximum penalty which may be imposed for burglary, and the penalty likely to be imposed **B4.80** in a particular case, varies according to whether the burglary is in respect of a dwelling or in respect of premises other than a dwelling. The question whether the burgled building was a dwelling or not cannot be resolved by a *Newton* hearing at sentencing. It should be settled by a jury after the insertion of alternative counts in the indictment, or by an appropriate guilty plea (*Flack* [2013] 2 Cr App R (S) 366 (56)).

The maximum penalty for burglary of a building or part of a building which is a dwelling is 14 years' imprisonment on indictment, six months or a fine not exceeding the statutory maximum, or both, summarily (s. 9(3)).

A minimum custodial sentence of three years must be imposed by the court where an offender aged 18 or over is convicted of a third 'domestic burglary', where all three of the offences were committed after 30 November 1999, and where there are no particular circumstances relating to any of the offences, or the offender, such that the imposition of a custodial sentence of at least three years would be unjust in all the circumstances (PCC(S)A 2000, s. 111, and see **E5.4**).

The definitive sentencing guideline, *Burglary Offences*, applies to all offenders aged 18 and over sentenced on or after 16 January 2012 irrespective of the date of the offence. The guideline covers domestic burglary and non-domestic burglary (see Supplement, **SG-539** *et seq.*).

B4.81   **Burglary from Dwellings**   In respect of burglaries from dwellings, the definitive sentencing guideline supersedes Court of Appeal guidance provided by the case of *Saw* [2009] 2 All ER 1138. For a domestic burglary falling within category 1 (greater harm and higher culpability) the starting point is three years within a range of two to six years; for category 2 (greater harm and lower culpability or lesser harm and higher culpability) the starting point is one year within a range of high level community order to two years, and for category 3 (lesser harm and lower culpability) the starting point is a high level community order within a range of low level community order to 26 weeks. The guideline stresses that relevant recent convictions are likely to result in an upward movement. Appropriate reduction should be made for a guilty plea.

According to Lord Judge CJ in *Saw*, burglary of a home was a serious criminal offence, being an offence against the person as well as an offence against property. In sentencing, particular focus was required on the impact of the offence on those living in the burgled house. In *Mikolajczak* [2012] 1 Cr App R (S) 265, the offender pleaded guilty at a late stage to a night-time burglary when the householder was asleep upstairs. She was woken by the sound of the offender driving off in her car. She became very anxious as a result of the offence, and eventually moved house because she did not feel safe. The 19-year-old offender had 30 previous court appearances for 42 offences including burglary. He had been made subject to a community order the day before committing the burglary. The Court of Appeal upheld the sentence of 27 months' detention. The offence was within category 2 of the guidelines but there were aggravating features. Although the offender was young he was an experienced criminal. Elias LJ said that, where there were especially serious consequences of a burglary, the sentencer was entitled to 'push the case above the guidelines'. In *Brinkley* [2013] EWCA Crim 760 a persistent house burglar, whose latest offence fell within category 3 of the guideline, did not merit a sentence of 40 months after a guilty plea to reflect his very poor record. The Court of Appeal substituted a sentence of two years and five months (based on the PCC(S)A 2000, s. 111, less the limited statutory discount for plea).

Distraction burglary of the elderly or otherwise vulnerable is still a particular category of burglary which has always attracted lengthy custodial sentences. The Court of Appeal in *Dance* [2014] 1 Cr App R (S) 304 (51) said that in such cases a sentence above the offence range in the guidelines may be appropriate, particularly if there is a pattern of repeat offending. In *Brooker* [2012] 1 Cr App R (S) 298 the Court of Appeal upheld sentences totalling six years for a series of distraction burglaries committed at the homes of elderly people, by a man with a long record of drug-related property offences. In *Cash* [2012] 2 Cr App R (S) 381, a sentence of five years on a plea of guilty in respect of three distraction burglaries at the homes of people aged over 80 was 'severe' but not excessive according to the Court of Appeal. In *Roberts* [2013] 2 Cr App R (S) 84 (19) a sentence of six years was appropriate after a guilty plea for an offender who went to the home of an elderly woman, pretended to be from the council, and stole her handbag and bank books. The offender had a very long record of dishonesty, including burglary of the elderly. The Court of Appeal said that this was a category 1 case and it was right to take a starting point above the offence range. See also *Dean* [2014] EWCA Crim 609.

B4.82   **Burglary from Non-dwelling**   Burglary committed in relation to premises other than a dwelling is regarded as somewhat less serious than the previous category. The maximum penalty for burglary other than from a dwelling is ten years' imprisonment on indictment, six months or a fine not exceeding the statutory maximum, or both, summarily (Theft Act 1968, s. 9(3)). In respect of burglary from a non-dwelling, the definitive sentencing guideline, *Burglary Offences* applies. For a non-domestic burglary falling within category 1 (greater harm and higher culpability) the starting point is two years within a range of one to five years; for category 2 (greater harm and lower culpability or lesser harm and higher culpability) the starting point is 18 weeks within a range of low level community order to 51 weeks; and for category 3 (lesser harm and lower culpability) the starting point is a medium level community order within a range of Band B fine order to 18 weeks. The guideline stresses that relevant recent convictions are likely to result in an upward movement. Appropriate reduction should be made for a guilty plea. In *Rye* [2013] 2 Cr App R (S) 50 (11) the offenders had committed night-time attacks on electricity sub-stations connected with the rail network to steal copper. About £8,000 worth of damage was done. The Court of Appeal said that the case fell into category 1 of the guideline, and sentences of three and a half years would have been appropriate following a trial.

Cases of so-called 'ram-raiding' seem to fall outside these guidelines. In *Delaney* [2011] 1 Cr App R (S) 117 the Court of Appeal said that sentences of ten years were appropriate after a trial for two 'professionally executed' offences in which the offender (an 'accomplished and ruthless criminal') had used a JCB digger to remove a cash dispenser from buildings. A total of £98,000 was stolen and damage was done to the fabric of the buildings. See also *Lawlor* [2013] 1 Cr App R (S) 532 (102), considered at **B4.71**.

Elements Common to Both s. 9(1)(a) and (b)

Although the Theft Act 1968, s. 9(1)(a) and (b) create separate offences, some elements are **B4.83** common to both. A 'building or part of a building' must be or have been 'entered' as 'a trespasser' in order for burglary to have been committed. The trespassory entry requirement demands a consideration not only of whether the entry was trespassory, but also whether D knew that it was trespassory, or was reckless as to that. The difference lies in s. 9(1)(a) with the need for an intention to commit certain offences and in s. 9(1)(b) with the need to do certain things in the building (see, e.g., *O'Leary* (1986) 82 Cr App R 341 at p. 343).

Meaning of 'Building' and 'Dwelling'   The Theft Act 1968 does not define a 'building', other **B4.84** than by providing that inhabited vehicles or vessels are deemed to be buildings. Whether a given thing can be called a building is not always straightforward and may be context-dependent. The best known judicial definition is that provided by Byles J in *Stevens v Gourley* (1859) CBNS 99 at p. 112: 'a structure of considerable size and intended to be permanent or at least to endure for a considerable period'. Such structures need not be inhabited, nor need they have doors, windows or foundations. A garden shed, a multi-storey car park and a portakabin office might each be regarded as a building, although the status of a tent is doubtful. In *B v Leathley* [1979] Crim LR 314, it was held that a freezer container in a farmyard was a building. The freezer was 25 feet long with 7 feet square cross-section, weighing about three tons and had been in place for two or three years. In *Norfolk Constabulary v Seekings* [1986] Crim LR 167, however, a disconnected freezer trailer was held not to be a building. In *Manning* (1871) LR 1 CCR 338 it was decided that a building does not have to be complete. In that case the building was a house which was very nearly complete, but the court was satisfied that less complete structures could also be 'buildings'.

Section 9(4) provides:

> References in subsections (1) and (2) above to a building, and the reference in subsection (3) above to a dwelling, shall apply also to an inhabited vehicle or vessel, and shall apply to any such vehicle or vessel at times when the person having a habitation in it is not there as well as at times when he is.

'Inhabited vehicles' include caravans and motor homes (or even derelict vehicles) that are used for habitation at the relevant time. It is submitted that a caravan is not 'inhabited' when laid up unoccupied for the winter, even if it is fully stocked and furnished. Some HGVs now provide a sleeping area in the cab for long-distance drivers to rest in; but it seems unlikely that a sleeping HGV driver could properly be said to 'inhabit' his lorry, unless he has nowhere else to live at the time.

Inhabited vessels include occupied houseboats and ships on which at least some members of the crew can be said to 'live', rather than merely work. A cruise ship is also 'inhabited' by its passengers during the cruise. A person who, in order to steal, etc., boards such a ship or enters a cabin or compartment on a ship knowing he is not permitted to do so will accordingly commit burglary, provided that he is at the time subject to English law (as to which see **A8.15** *et seq.*).

B4.85   Since a person need enter only a part of a building as a trespasser to be a burglar, it is possible for a person lawfully on premises to become a burglar by entering another part of the building to which he is not entitled to enter. In *Walkington* [1979] 2 All ER 716, the Court of Appeal decided that it is for the jury to decide whether an area physically marked out is sufficiently segregated to amount to a 'part of a building'. In this case, D had gone behind the sales counter in a large store. The counter was moveable, but occupied a clearly identified area. In the circumstances, the court took the view that there was evidence on which the jury could conclude that there was a separate part of the building identified by the counter area, since there was a physical partition and the management impliedly prohibited customers from entering the area.

For the reasons given at **B4.80**, it may be important to determine whether the building in question is a 'dwelling', but there is surprisingly little authority on that question. See *Lees* [2007] EWCA Crim 94. In many cases, the facts will be plain. A building (or caravan etc.) in which someone has a home must be a dwelling, whereas a shop or factory will not be. Difficulties may however arise in the case of an hotel or time-shared holiday home. Most hotel guests do not use the hotel as their dwelling, but some may do so, as may some of the hotel staff; and difficulties may also arise in respect of a building (or part of a building) that has been constructed or adapted to serve as a dwelling but has not been (is not currently) used as such. In the absence of authority, it is submitted that the reasons for distinguishing between dwellings and other premises must be considered. If (as in *Lees*) the new house that is burgled is still unoccupied and is still owned by the building contractors, no resident occupier will be distressed, violated or endangered by that burglary, which is in effect no different from a burglary of commercial premises. The position is less clear where a house has been purchased and furnished as a home, but is burgled shortly before the new owners move in. Arguably, this should be treated as burglary of a dwelling; but cf. the Public Order Act 1986, s. 8 (see **B11.57**) and the Terrorism Act 2000, s. 121, each of which define a dwelling as a building, etc. that is currently occupied or used as a dwelling.

B4.86   **Meaning of 'Entry'**   In *Collins* [1973] QB 100, the Court of Appeal decided (at p. 106) that D has to make 'an effective and substantial entry into' a building or part of a building. This phrase was considered by the Court of Appeal in *Brown* [1985] Crim LR 212 and it took the view that the important point was whether the entry was 'effective'. A person could, therefore, enter a building when only part of the body is actually within it, so B had entered where the top half of his body was leaning into a shop window. The prosecution does not have to prove that the person was capable of stealing when only partially in a building. The issue is whether the partial entry was capable of constituting entry, as it was where D was stuck in an open window; the matter is then for the tribunal of fact to decide (*Ryan* (1996) 160 JP 610).

It was said in *Collins* that entry must be 'deliberate'. Consequently, it cannot be shown that this element of the crime has been satisfied if the entry is accidental, which it might be, for example, if boundaries of private land are unclear or obstructed by snow.

It is not clear whether a person who boards an inhabited vessel, but fails to get inside, can be said to have 'entered' the vessel. Arguably he has not, and is in the same position as someone who climbs onto the roof of a building. There may be an attempted burglary on such facts, but nothing more.

B4.87   **Meaning of 'as a Trespasser'**   It is important that at the time D entered the building, his entry was as a trespasser (*Laing* [1995] Crim LR 395). A trespasser is someone who does not have permission, express or implied, to be on the premises. Since this is an aspect of the criminal law, it must be shown that there was a trespassory entry, and also that the person entered with *mens rea* (i.e. he knew that he was entering as a trespasser or was reckless as to whether this was so).

Adequate permission can be given by someone other than the householder. In *Collins* [1973] QB 100, D climbed up a ladder to look into a girl's bedroom. As he reached the window, she woke up and, thinking D was her boyfriend, invited him in. There was some doubt as to whether he had already entered at that point. They had sexual intercourse before she realised her mistake. D was initially convicted of burglary with intent to rape (a variant now replaced by a new offence under the Sexual Offences Act 2003, s. 63). His appeal against that conviction succeeded because the jury had not been asked to consider whether he had entered the building as a trespasser and whether he knew or was reckless as to whether he was entering as a trespasser. It was held that the girl's invitation would have sufficed to make the entry non-trespassory but only if D was still outside the building at that time.

As to *mens rea* the court said (at p. 105E):   **B4.88**

> …there cannot be a conviction for entering premises 'as a trespasser' within the meaning of section 9 …unless the person entering does so knowing that he is a trespasser and nevertheless deliberately enters, or, at the very least, is reckless as to whether or not he is entering the premises of another without the other party's consent.

The matter will not always be a simple one of deciding whether at the time D entered, permission had been granted. Permission, specific or general, may be exceeded. It is then to be determined whether that makes the entry trespassory. In *Jones* [1976] 3 All ER 54 D and E dishonestly entered a house belonging to D's father and there stole two television sets. The question for the court was whether they had entered as trespassers for the purposes of s. 9. The court said:

> …a person is a trespasser for the purpose of section 9(1)(b)…if he enters premises of another knowing that he is entering in excess of the permission that has been given to him, or being reckless as to whether he is entering in excess of the permission that has been given to him to enter. Provided the facts are known to the accused which enable him to realise that he is acting in excess of the permission given or that he is acting recklessly as to whether he exceeds that permission, then that is sufficient for the jury to decide that he is in fact a trespasser.

Since the jury were satisfied that D and E acted outside the scope of any permission they might otherwise have had, their convictions were upheld.

It is essential, therefore, for the person entering to know that entry is prohibited, or at least be advertently reckless as to the prohibition. In *Walkington* [1979] 2 All ER 716 (see **B4.85**) the Court of Appeal emphasised that it was necessary in order for a conviction to be sustained that D knew he was not supposed to enter the counter area.

The common-law doctrine of trespass *ab initio* has no application to burglary (*Collins* [1973] QB 100 at p. 107). If D enters a building, etc. otherwise than as a trespasser, he does not become a burglar merely by committing a theft inside that building.

Burglary with Intent (s. 9(1)(a)): Proof of Intent

On a charge of burglary with intent contrary to s. 9(1)(a), it must be shown that, at the time of the entry (not before and not after), D intended to commit the offences listed in s. 9(2). As to intention generally, see **A2.4**.   **B4.89**

Intent to Commit an Offence of Stealing 'Stealing' is defined in the Theft Act 1968, s. 1; see **B4.1**. It is not burglary to enter a building with intent to abstract electricity because abstracting electricity is not stealing (*Low v Blease* [1975] Crim LR 513). In *Gregory* (1981) 77 Cr App R 41, the Court of Appeal said (at p. 46):   **B4.90**

> In a case of burglary of a dwelling-house and before any property is removed from it, it may consist of a continuing process and involve either a single appropriation by one or more persons or a number of appropriations of the property in the house by several persons at different times during the same incident…Thus a person who may have more the appearance of a handler than the thief can nevertheless still be convicted of theft, and thus of burglary, if the jury are satisfied that with the requisite dishonest intent he appropriated, or took part in the appropriation, of another person's goods.

As to the question whether, in theft and therefore burglary, an appropriation is instantaneous or continuing, see **B4.44**.

B4.91 **Intent to Commit an Offence of Inflicting Grievous Bodily Harm**   In order to prove an intention to commit grievous bodily harm on a charge of burglary with intent it is unnecessary to prove an assault (*Metropolitan Police Commissioner v Wilson* [1984] AC 242). As to the meaning of 'grievous bodily harm', see generally **B2.60**.

In *O'Neill* (1986) *The Times*, 17 October 1986 the Court of Appeal appears to have decided, presumably on the facts of the particular case in question, that charges of burglary by entering a building with intent to inflict grievous bodily harm should not have been left to the jury because there was no specific express evidence of such intent. No weapons had been carried and no grievous bodily harm had been committed, even though two persons on the premises had been assaulted. The offence is committed by intending, at the time of entering premises as a trespasser, to inflict grievous bodily harm, and the fact that no grievous bodily harm is actually inflicted does not affect liability, though it may make it very difficult to prove the intent.

B4.92 **Intent to Commit an Offence of Doing Unlawful Damage**   It is to be presumed that this phrase refers to what is now criminal damage, see **B8.1** to **B8.30**.

B4.93 **Intent to Commit an Offence of Rape**   The SOA 2003, s. 140 and sch. 7, removed the form of burglary, under the Theft Act 1968, s. 9(1)(a), where the person entered as a trespasser with intent of raping any person therein. A new offence of trespass with intent to commit a sexual offence has been created by the SOA 2003, s. 63 (see **B3.267**).

B4.94 **Conditional Intent**   At one stage it was thought that a 'burglar's charter' had been created by the case of *Husseyn* (1977) 67 Cr App R 131. The argument was that if a person only intended to steal that which he found worth stealing then there was no intention to steal, since it was conditional on his finding something worth stealing, which might not be the case. The solution to this problem was found by the Court of Appeal in *Walkington* [1979] 2 All ER 716 and adopted by the Court of Appeal in *A-G's Refs (Nos. 1 and 2 of 1979)* [1980] QB 180. If D is charged with burglary, contrary to s. 9(1)(a), by entering a building as a trespasser with intent to steal therein, and there is no reference to the stealing of specific items, he is guilty if he has an intention to steal anything in the building and the fact that there was nothing in the building worth his stealing is immaterial. The problem is identical to that which may arise on a charge of theft: see **B4.64**.

Burglary (s. 9(1)(b)): Proof of Stealing or Grievous Bodily Harm

B4.95 On a charge of burglary contrary to s. 9(1)(b), the prosecution must establish that D either stole or attempted to steal in the building or part of a building, or inflicted or attempted to inflict on any person in the building or part of a building any grievous bodily harm. For the meaning of 'steal' and 'inflict grievous bodily harm', see **B4.1** and **B2.60**. For the law of attempts, see **A5.69** *et seq.* It is not burglary under s. 9(1)(b) to cause unlawful damage, though intent to cause such damage is relevant to burglary with intent contrary to s. 9(1)(a).

Related Offence

B4.96 An offence that might be considered as an alternative to burglary is that contrary to the Vagrancy Act 1824, s. 4(1), by which (i) every person wandering abroad and lodging in any barn or outhouse, or in any deserted or unoccupied building, or in the open air, or under a tent, or in any cart or wagon, and not giving a good account of himself or herself; (ii) every person being found in or upon any dwelling house, warehouse, coach-house, stable, or outhouse, or in any enclosed yard, garden, or area, for any unlawful purpose; commits an offence. The maximum penalty is three months' imprisonment. Once the CJA 2003, sch. 32, para. 146, is brought into force, the maximum penalty for an offence in category (i) will be a fine on level 1 of the standard scale and for an offence in category (ii) it will be a level 3 fine. As to the restricted meaning of 'enclosed yard...or area', see *Akhurst v DPP* (2009) 173 JP 499, in which it was held that this does not include a university campus or buildings. The phrase 'for an unlawful purpose' means for the purpose of committing an offence, such as burglary. Hiding from the police is not such a purpose (*L v CPS* [2008] 1 Cr App R 131).

AGGRAVATED BURGLARY

Definition

Theft Act 1968, s. 10

    B4.97

(1) A person is guilty of aggravated burglary if he commits any burglary and at the time has with him any firearm or imitation firearm, any weapon of offence, or any explosive.

Procedure

Aggravated burglary is triable only on indictment. It is normally a class 3 offence, but see CPD   B4.98
XIII, para. B (see Supplement, **PD-97**) for the additional factors that the court considers on allocation.

Indictment

Statement of Offence

    B4.99

Aggravated burglary contrary to section 10(1) of the Theft Act 1968.

Particulars of Offence

A on or about the...day of...having entered a dwelling [or part of a dwelling, or a building or part of a building], namely..., as a trespasser stole therein [or attempted to steal therein, or inflicted grievous bodily harm upon...therein] and at the time had with him a firearm [or an imitation firearm, or a weapon of offence or an explosive], namely...

See also **B4.78**.

Alternative Verdicts

Burglary contrary to either s. 9(1)(a) or s. 9(1)(b) of the Theft Act 1968 (by virtue of the CLA   B4.100
1967, s. 6(3)). See also **B4.79**.

Sentence

The maximum penalty is: life imprisonment (Theft Act 1968, s. 10(2)). In respect of aggravated   B4.101
burglary the definitive sentencing guideline, *Burglary Offences*, provides that for an offence falling within category 1 (greater harm and higher culpability) the starting point is ten years within
a range of nine to 13 years; for category 2 (greater harm and lower culpability or lesser harm and
higher culpability), the starting point is six years within a range of four to nine years, and for
category 3 (lesser harm and lower culpability), the starting point is two years within a range of
one to four years. The guideline stresses that relevant recent convictions are likely to result in an
upward movement. Appropriate reduction should be made for a guilty plea.

Of the more important pre-guideline cases, towards the top of the scale of seriousness is
O'Driscoll (1986) 8 Cr App R (S) 121, where the offender gained access to the home of an
elderly man and struck him a number of blows with a hammer. The victim was also threatened
with a lighted gas poker, tied up with wire and gagged. A sentence of 15 years was upheld.
Subsequent decisions which treat *O'Driscoll* as a guideline case include *A-G's Refs (Nos. 32 and
33 of 1995)* [1996] 2 Cr App R (S) 345 and *Eastap* [1997] 2 Cr App R (S) 55. Seven years'
imprisonment was upheld in *Brady* [2000] 1 Cr App R (S) 410 where the offender, a man with
numerous previous convictions including three for robbery, entered a bungalow occupied by a
woman aged 70, threatened her with a chisel and demanded money. He left taking £50 and a
radio. In *A-G's Ref (No. 10 of 1996)* [1997] 1 Cr App R (S) 76 the offender, a man with a long
criminal record, together with three friends all armed with baseball bats, staged a revenge attack
at the home of a man the offender believed to have stolen property from him. The offender beat
the victim with a bat, causing a depressed fracture of the skull and other injuries. A sentence of
15 months' imprisonment was increased to four years on appeal, with an unspecified allowance

for the element of double jeopardy. In *A-G's Ref (No. 16 of 1994)* (1995) 16 Cr App R (S) 629, the offender, who had a record of violent offences and was armed with a baseball bat, went to the flat of a man he knew. He used the bat to smash property in the flat, thereby frightening the female occupant. A sentence of 18 months' imprisonment was increased to three years.

Meaning of 'Firearm', 'Imitation Firearm', 'Weapon of Offence', 'Explosive'

B4.102   **Theft Act 1968, s. 10**

(1) ...and for this purpose—
   (a) 'firearm' includes an airgun or air pistol, and 'imitation firearm' means anything which has the appearance of being a firearm, whether capable of being discharged or not, and
   (b) 'weapon of offence' means any article made or adapted for use for causing injury to or incapacitating a person, or intended by the person having it with him for such use; and
   (c) 'explosive' means any article manufactured for the purpose of producing a practical effect by explosion, or intended by the person having it with him for that purpose.

B4.103 **Paragraph (a)**   Whilst a definition of 'imitation firearm' is provided, there is no definition of 'firearm', except to make clear that it includes airguns and air pistols. It may be that the general definition of 'firearm' in the Firearms Act 1968 is appropriate (see **B12.7**).

B4.104 **Paragraph (b)**   In *Stones* [1989] 1 WLR 156, approved in *Kelly* (1992) 97 Cr App R 245, the Court of Appeal said (at p. 160):

> It is not necessary to prove the intention to use the [weapon] to cause injury etc. during the course of the burglary.

> ...The mischief at which the section is clearly aimed is that if a burglar has a weapon which he intends to use to injure some person unconnected with the premises burgled [as in the instant case], he may nevertheless be tempted to use it if challenged during the course of the burglary and put under sufficient pressure.

The court also drew attention to the similarity between this paragraph and the provisions of the Prevention of Crime Act 1953, s. 1, concerned with the possession of offensive weapons. Whilst the two provisions are not identical since the phrase 'incapacitating a person' does not appear in s. 1 of the 1953 Act, some assistance may be obtained from the cases concerned with possession of offensive weapons. The defence of lawful authority or reasonable excuse for the possession of an offensive weapon (see **B12.156** to **B12.158**) does not appear to apply to aggravated burglary.

B4.105 **Paragraph (c)**   The definition of 'explosive' for the purposes of aggravated burglary is narrower than that to be found in the Explosive Substances Act 1883, but that Act may be of assistance in determining the meaning of s. 10(1)(c).

Relevant Time

B4.106 The gravamen of the aggravated offence of burglary with intent is entry into a building with a weapon. Therefore, at least one of the entrants to the building must have a weapon with him at that time (*Klass* [1998] 1 Cr App R 453). If, however, D is charged, as in *O'Leary* (1986) 82 Cr App R 341, with aggravated burglary by stealing *after* entry, under s. 10 and s. 9(1)(b), it follows that, according to the Court of Appeal in that case (at p. 343):

> ...the time at which [D] must be proved to have had with him a weapon of offence to make him guilty of aggravated burglary was the time at which he actually stole...

In *O'Leary* D entered a building as a trespasser, armed himself with a knife from the kitchen, and confronted the occupiers to demand their cash and jewellery. This was an act of theft, and since D at that point had the kitchen knife in his hand it became aggravated burglary, even though he may have entered the building unarmed. See also *Kelly* (1992) 97 Cr App R 245.

No such offence was proved in *Chevannes* [2009] EWCA Crim 2725. D's accomplice carried a weapon when he and D assaulted V at the door of his caravan and when they chased him from it, but there was no evidence that D carried any weapon when he went on to burgle the caravan.

Meaning of 'Has with Him'

There is a requirement for a degree of immediate control of the weapon of offence or other **B4.107** article (*Kelt* [1977] 3 All ER 1099; *Pawlicki* [1992] 3 All ER 902). Indeed, 'the word will normally mean "carrying"' (*Kelt* and *Klass* [1998] 1 Cr App R 453). The cases decided on the Prevention of Crime Act 1953, s. 1 (possession of offensive weapons) are of no assistance because of the different purposes of the two offence-creating sections (*Kelly* (1992) 97 Cr App R 245). Since a dictum in *Stones* [1989] 1 WLR 156 at p. 160, it has been unclear whether the prosecution must prove that D knew he had a weapon of offence with him or knew he had something with him which was, in fact, a weapon of offence. It is submitted that the latter is to be preferred. It is more consistent with the general approach to this type of offence. For the comparable offence contrary to the Firearms Act 1968, s. 19, see **B12.105**. For the related offence contrary to the Firearms Act 1968, s. 1, see **B12.34**. For the decision on the drugs legislation that lies at the heart of many of these decisions, see **B19.23**. This issue has also recently arisen for decision under the Prevention of Crime Act 1953, s. 1 where the matter is controversial (see **B12.150**). The offence contrary to the Firearms Act 1968, s. 18, explicitly requires knowledge (see **B12.102**).

REMOVAL OF ARTICLES FROM PLACES OPEN TO THE PUBLIC

Definition

Theft Act 1968, s. 11   **B4.108**

(1) Subject to subsections (2) and (3) below, where the public have access to a building in order to view the building or part of it, or a collection or part of a collection housed in it, any person who without lawful authority removes from the building or its grounds the whole or part of any article displayed or kept for display to the public in the building or that part of it or in its grounds shall be guilty of an offence.

Procedure

Removal of an article from a place open to the public is triable either way (MCA 1980, s. 17 and **B4.109** sch. 1, para. 28). When tried on indictment it is normally a class 3 offence, but see CPD XIII, para. B (see Supplement, **PD-97**) for the additional factors that the court considers on allocation.

Indictment

Statement of Offence   **B4.110**

Removing an article from a place open to the public contrary to section 11 of the Theft Act 1968.

Particulars of Offence

A on or about the...day of...without lawful authority removed from the V art gallery, being a place to which the public then had access in order to view an art collection therein, a painting, namely *Portrait of the Madonna* by von Klomp.

Sentence

The maximum penalty is five years on indictment (s. 11(4)); six months and/or a fine not **B4.111** exceeding the statutory maximum summarily. No sentencing guidelines are reported for this offence.

Purpose for which the Public Have Access

An offence under s. 11(1), can be committed only in relation to a building to which the public **B4.112** have access for the purpose of viewing the building (or a part of it) or a collection (or part of a collection). It is the purpose of the inviter in granting access that matters (*Barr* [1978] Crim LR 244).

Meaning of 'Collection'

B4.113

Theft Act 1968, s. 11

(1) For this purpose, 'collection' includes a collection got together for a temporary purpose, but references in this section to a collection do not apply to a collection made or exhibited for the purpose of effecting sales or other commercial dealings.

Time of Public Access

B4.114

Theft Act 1968, s. 11

(2) It is immaterial for purposes of subsection (1) above, that the public's access to a building is limited to a particular period or particular occasion; but where anything removed from a building or its grounds is there otherwise than as forming part of, or being on loan for exhibition with, a collection intended for permanent exhibition to the public, the person removing it does not thereby commit an offence under this section unless he removes it on a day when the public have access to the building as mentioned in subsection (1) above.

If an art gallery, for example, is usually open it is possible for an offence under s. 11(1) to be committed on a day when the gallery is closed by removing an item which is part of a collection intended for permanent exhibition, whether it is actually on display or kept in store and exhibited on a rota basis (*Durkin* [1973] QB 786).

Meaning of 'Displayed or Kept for Display'

B4.115 Whether an article is displayed, or kept for display, depends upon the intention of the person setting out the articles. For example, in *Barr* [1978] Crim LR 244 it was found that a cross and ewer in a church were not on display but were intended to be aids to worship and devotion.

Belief in Lawful Authority

B4.116

Theft Act 1968, s. 11

(3) A person does not commit an offence under this section if he believes that he has lawful authority for the removal of the thing in question or that he would have it if the person entitled to give it knew of the removal and the circumstances of it.

It is submitted that, if an accused raises the issue of his belief, it is then for the prosecution to prove beyond reasonable doubt that he had no such belief (compare the position under s. 12 of the Act, see **B4.125**). As to the defence of mistake generally, see **A3.2** to **A3.11**.

TAKING CONVEYANCE WITHOUT AUTHORITY

Definition

B4.117

Theft Act 1968, s. 12

(1) Subject to subsections (5) and (6) below, a person shall be guilty of an offence if, without having the consent of the owner or other lawful authority, he takes any conveyance for his own or another's use or, knowing that any conveyance has been taken without such authority, drives it or allows himself to be carried in or on it.

Procedure

B4.118 An offence under s. 12(1), is triable only summarily. However, a count for such an offence may be included in an indictment for another offence in the circumstances set out in the CJA 1988, s. 40 (see **D11.18**). On the trial of an indictment for theft, the jury may find the accused guilty of an offence under s. 12(1) as an alternative verdict (s. 12(4)).

Proceedings for the offence (unless they fall within s. 12(4)) in relation to a mechanically propelled vehicle (a) shall not be commenced after the end of the period of three years beginning with the day on which the offence was committed, but (b) subject to that, may be commenced at any time within the period of six months beginning with the relevant day (s. 12(4A)). 'The relevant day' means (a) in the case of a prosecution for an offence under s. 12(1) by a public prosecutor, the day on which sufficient evidence to justify the proceedings came to the knowledge of any person responsible for deciding whether to commence any such proceedings; (b) in the case of a prosecution for an offence under s. 12(1), which is commenced by a person other than a public prosecutor after the discontinuance of a prosecution falling within s. 12(4B)(a) and relates to the same facts, the day on which sufficient evidence to justify the proceedings came to the knowledge of the person who has decided to commence the prosecution or (if later) the discontinuance of the other prosecution; (c) in the case of any other prosecution for an offence under s. 12(1), the day on which sufficient evidence to justify the proceedings came to the knowledge of the person who has decided to commence the prosecution (s. 12(4B)). For the purposes of s. 12(4A)(b), a certificate of a person responsible for deciding whether to commence a prosecution of a kind mentioned in s. 12(4B)(a) as to the date on which such evidence as is mentioned in the certificate came to the knowledge of any person responsible for deciding whether to commence any such prosecution shall be conclusive evidence of that fact (s. 12(4C)).

Sentencing Guidelines

The maximum penalty for taking a conveyance without authority is six months and/or a fine **B4.119** not exceeding level 5 (s. 12(2)). Additionally, for the offence or an attempt to commit it in respect of a motor vehicle, there is discretionary disqualification (RTOA 1988, sch. 2). The same maximum penalty and liability for disqualification applies in relation to the offence of driving or allowing oneself to be carried in or on a conveyance taken without authority.

The *Magistrates' Court Sentencing Guidelines* provide guidelines for this offence (see Supplement, SG-324).

In *Bushell* (1987) 9 Cr App R (S) 537 the offender, aged 17 and with no previous convictions, took a friend's car without permission and crashed it, damaging it beyond repair. A sentence of 180 hours' community service, together with a disqualification for one year, was upheld by the Court of Appeal. Where the offence is combined with other offences arising out of the same circumstances, an immediate custodial sentence may be appropriate. Thus in *Jeary* (1986) 8 Cr App R (S) 491 the offender, aged 18, and with one previous finding of guilt for assault occasioning actual bodily harm, pleaded guilty to two counts of taking a conveyance, two counts of theft, and asked for two other offences to be taken into consideration. He was involved with others in taking several cars in the course of an evening and driving them at high speed in a city centre 'just as a bit of fun'. Three cars were damaged, one beyond repair. The offender also admitted taking property from the cars, though most of that was recovered. The Court of Appeal agreed with the sentencer's view that the offences were so serious that a non-custodial sentence could not be justified because, in addition to the unlawful taking, the cars had been deliberately damaged. Four months' detention was upheld.

Meaning of 'Conveyance'

Whilst the marginal note to s. 12, uses the phrase 'motor vehicle or other conveyance', the sec- **B4.120** tion itself refers only to a 'conveyance'. A definition of 'conveyance' is to be found in s. 12(7)(a):

> 'conveyance' means any conveyance constructed or adapted for the carriage of a person or persons whether by land, water or air, except that it does not include a conveyance constructed or adapted for use only under the control of a person not carried in or on it, and 'drive' shall be construed accordingly.

This definition would ordinarily include a pedal cycle, but for s. 12(5), which creates a separate offence (see **B4.136**), and makes clear that the offence under s. 12(1) does not apply in relation to pedal cycles. An electrically assisted (or pedelec) cycle arguably falls within s. 12(1). In *Neal v Gribble* (1978) 68 Cr App R 9, the Divisional Court had to consider whether a horse was a conveyance within the meaning of s. 12. The court was of the view that it was not such a conveyance, since the definition in s. 12(7)(a) 'seems to be directed towards artefacts rather than towards animals'.

Taking for his Own or Another's Use

B4.121 It is essential that a conveyance be moved in order for it to be taken, however small that movement may be. Merely trying to start the engine of a motor vehicle without moving the vehicle does not amount to taking it (*Bogacki* [1973] QB 832). Attempt is not available as an alternative offence (Criminal Attempts Act 1981, s. 1(1) and (4)). On a charge of taking it is not necessary that D used the conveyance to convey himself, merely that he 'took' it. In *Pearce* [1973] Crim LR 321 an appeal against conviction was dismissed where D had placed the conveyance, an inflatable rubber dinghy, on a trailer and drove away with it.

On a charge of taking, the prosecution must prove that D took the conveyance 'for his own or another's use'. In *Bow* (1976) 64 Cr App R 54, it was argued that D had not taken the conveyance 'for his own use' when he got into a Land Rover which was obstructing his way and released its handbrake and let it coast for about 200 yards. The Court of Appeal said (at p. 58):

> The short answer. . .is that where as here, a conveyance is taken and moved in a way which necessarily involves its use as a conveyance, the taker cannot be heard to say that the taking was not for that use. If he has in fact taken the conveyance and used it as such, his motive in so doing is. . .quite immaterial.

B4.122 In *Stokes* [1983] RTR 59, D pushed a car round a corner as a practical joke. The conviction could not be upheld because the judge failed specifically to emphasise the importance of establishing that someone was being conveyed inside the car or riding on it, i.e. failed clearly to require a finding that the car was being taken for use as a conveyance, rather than merely that it was 'taken'.

Pearce, Bow and *Stokes* were further explained by the Court of Appeal in *Marchant* (1984) 80 Cr App R 361. Robert Goff LJ, giving the judgment of the court, stated that 'to be guilty of the offence, D must have both taken the vehicle, i.e. have taken control of it and caused it to be moved, and he must have done so for his own or another's use'. That phrase requires that it be taken *for use as* a conveyance, which is satisfied provided that is why the conveyance was taken, rather than that it must have been taken *as* a conveyance. For example, if a person takes a car by pushing it around a corner and leaving it, he satisfies the first element of this requirement. If, at the time he moves it, he intends to get it going after he has returned to it, his purpose is plain: it was for use as a conveyance and the offence has been committed. In *Pearce* the dinghy was clearly taken and D's purpose was to use it as a dinghy, that is, as a conveyance. In *Bow* D actually used the Land Rover as a conveyance whilst taking it. In *Stokes* D did take the conveyance, but his purpose was not to use it as a conveyance and so the offence was not committed.

Once a vehicle has been taken, it cannot be taken again by the same accused, but, where a first taker abandons a vehicle, that same vehicle may be taken by another (*DPP v Spriggs* [1994] RTR 1).

Without the Consent of the Owner or Other Lawful Authority

B4.123 On a charge of taking a conveyance without authority, the prosecution must prove that the taking was actually without the owner's consent or other lawful authority (*Ambler* [1979] RTR 217 and *Sturrock v DPP* [1996] RTR 216). 'Owner' is defined by s. 12(7)(b) of the Theft Act 1968, in relation to a conveyance which is the subject of a hiring agreement or hire-purchase agreement, as meaning the person in possession of the conveyance under that agreement.

In *Whittaker v Campbell* [1984] QB 318 the two defendants, neither of whom had a driving licence, had come by Dunn's licence. They hired a van, using that acquired licence by pretending that one of them was Dunn. They paid the appropriate hire charge and drove the van away. The Divisional Court was asked to consider the effect of the false representation on the consent that was obtained as a consequence. It stated that there is no general principle of law that fraud vitiates consent. The court took the view that where force is used, it is possible to distinguish between consent and mere submission, but that when the factor being exercised was fraud and not force, no such sensible distinction can be drawn. In common-sense terms, the owner has consented and, despite the fraud, that means that no offence is committed.

In *Peart* [1970] 2 QB 672, the Court of Appeal quashed a conviction where D had falsely represented to the owner of a car that he needed it to drive from Bedlington to Alnwick to sign a contract. The owner let him have the vehicle, provided he returned it that day. As D always intended, he drove the car instead to Burnley in the evening. The court reserved the question whether a fundamental misrepresentation can vitiate consent (according to *Whittaker v Campbell* it would appear that it does not), but decided that the sort of false pretence in the particular case did not vitiate the consent, and the activity involved was not the type of activity with which s. 12 was concerned.   **B4.124**

In *Phipps* (1970) 54 Cr App R 300 the Court of Appeal approved a direction by the trial judge that if, after a lawful purpose had been fulfilled, D then did not return the car but drove it off on his own business, the offence was committed. It is not clear whether a deception was practised upon the owner, and the decision of the Court of Appeal does not raise the issue of such a deception. It may, therefore, be that this case can be regarded as consistent with *Peart* and *Whittaker v Campbell* since in *Phipps* there may well have been no question of consent obtained by fraud or a false representation. Rather it seems that it was a case of D going beyond the limits of the consent that had been given by the owner of the car (see also *McKnight v Davies* [1974] RTR 4).

Mens Rea of Offence of Taking

There are two aspects to the mental element of the offence.   **B4.125**

First, the taking must be intentional. In *Blayney v Knight* (1974) 60 Cr App R 269, Lord Widgery CJ, giving the judgment of the court, stated, 'I do not see how anybody could be charged with taking a motor car because of the fact that the car accidentally moves forward'.

Secondly, the Theft Act 1968, s. 12(6), provides:

> A person does not commit an offence under this section by anything done in the belief that he has lawful authority to do it or that he would have the owner's consent if the owner knew of his doing it and the circumstances of it.

It is essential that this belief exist at the time of the taking. It is not enough if the owner says, later, that he would have consented had he known (*Ambler* [1979] RTR 217). This question is one for the magistrates to decide and they may well take into account a factor such as the likelihood of a person genuinely believing that an owner would authorise another to drive a car when uninsured. Clearly an owner could provide such an authorisation (*Clotworthy* [1981] RTR 477). An example of what might amount to 'unlawful authority' is given by *Briggs* [1987] Crim LR 708, where D claimed that he was repairing the motor cycle for a friend. Since the judge had not focused the attention of the jury on this matter, the conviction was quashed by the Court of Appeal.

The onus of proof of this matter lies on the prosecution (*MacPherson* [1973] RTR 157; *Gannon* (1987) 87 Cr App R 254) but before that stage is reached, it is for D to raise the issue. He must call evidence or point to some evidence which tends to show that he held the necessary belief (*Gannon*).

The offence is one of basic intent for the purposes of any defence involving voluntary intoxication (*Gannon, MacPherson*). As to basic and specific intent generally, see **A3.15** to **A3.22**.

Driving or Allowing himself to be Carried

B4.126   Section 12(7)(a) of the Theft Act 1968 indicates that 'drive' is to be construed in accordance with the meaning of 'conveyance' (see **B4.120**) and therefore includes 'driving' not only motor vehicles, but any land, water or air conveyance. The meaning of 'drives' is considered generally at **C1.2**.

On a charge of allowing himself to be carried in or on a conveyance taken without authority, it is not enough for the prosecution to prove that D was in or on the conveyance, there must have been some movement of the conveyance (*Miller* [1976] Crim LR 417; *Diggin* (1980) 72 Cr App R 204). If a taker of a motor vehicle offers a person a lift and he gets into the seat next to the driver, the person is not allowing himself to be driven before the driver turns on the ignition switch (*Diggin*).

Mens Rea of Offence of Driving or Allowing Himself to be Carried

B4.127   On a charge of driving or allowing himself to be carried in or on a conveyance taken without authority, it must be proved that D knew that the conveyance had been taken without lawful authority (*Diggin* (1980) 72 Cr App R 204; *Boldizsar v Knight* [1980] Crim LR 653). As to the meaning of these terms, see **B4.120** to **B4.125**. It seems that D need not be aware that the taker took the conveyance for his own or another's use, though no doubt ordinarily he will know this. As to knowledge generally, see **A2.14**.

Section 12(6) of the Theft Act 1968 applies to the offence of driving or allowing oneself to be carried in or on a conveyance taken without consent (see **B4.126**).

AGGRAVATED VEHICLE-TAKING

B4.128   The Theft Act 1968, s. 12A (inserted by the Aggravated Vehicle-Taking Act 1992), creates aggravated forms of the basic s. 12 offence.

Theft Act 1968, s. 12A

(1) Subject to subsection (3) below, a person is guilty of aggravated taking of a vehicle if—
    (a) he commits an offence under section 12(1) above (in this section referred to as a 'basic offence') in relation to a mechanically propelled vehicle; and
    (b) it is proved that, at any time after the vehicle was unlawfully taken (whether by him or another) and before it was recovered, the vehicle was driven, or injury or damage was caused, in one or more of the circumstances set out in paragraphs (a) to (d) of subsection (2) below.
(2) The circumstances referred to in subsection (1)(b) above are—
    (a) that the vehicle was driven dangerously on a road or other public place;
    (b) that, owing to the driving of the vehicle, an accident occurred by which injury was caused to any person;
    (c) that, owing to the driving of the vehicle, an accident occurred by which damage was caused to any property, other than the vehicle;
    (d) that damage was caused to the vehicle.

Since the maximum penalty is greater where death is caused (see **B4.131**), s. 12A creates two offences (see *Sherwood* [1995] RTR 60, following *Courtie* [1984] AC 403). Where however there is clear evidence of causing death by dangerous driving (see **C3.7**) following the unauthorised taking of a motor vehicle, that offence should ordinarily be charged in preference to a charge under s. 12A (*Roberts* [2013] RTR 436 (32)).

Procedure

B4.129   The offences are triable either way. When tried on indictment they are normally class 3 offences, but see CPD XIII, para. B (see Supplement, **PD-97**) for the additional factors that the court considers on allocation.

D has no right to elect trial on indictment where the only allegation is of damage to the vehicle or other property or both and the total value of the damage alleged to have been caused is less than the 'relevant sum' (i.e. £5,000) (MCA 1980, ss. 22 and 33 and sch. 2: see **D6.28**).

See the *Magistrates' Court Sentencing Guidelines* (see Supplement, **SG-325** for indications as to when a case should be sent to the Crown Court.

Alternative Verdict

Under the Theft Act 1968, s. 12A(5), where D is charged with either of these offences but found not guilty, he may be convicted of the basic offence, contrary to s. 12(1) (see **B4.117** *et seq.* and **D19.55**). If convicted of the basic offence at the Crown Court, that court has the same powers and duties as a magistrates' court would have had on convicting him of such an offence (s. 12A(6)) (see **B4.119**).

B4.130

Sentence

The maximum penalty is, on indictment, two years or a fine or both. The maximum penalty, on indictment, is increased to 14 years where it is proved that, in circumstances falling within the Theft Act 1968, s. 12A(2)(b), the accident caused the death of the person concerned (s. 12A(4)).

B4.131

The maximum penalty on summary conviction is a term of imprisonment not exceeding six months or a fine not exceeding the statutory maximum or both. The limit on penalties imposed by the MCA 1980, s. 33(1), with regard to an offence tried summarily in pursuance of the MCA 1980, s. 22, does not apply where the offence is aggravated vehicle-taking (MCA 1980, s. 33(3)).

By virtue of the RTOA 1988, ss. 28, 96 and 97 and sch. 2, part II, where a person is convicted of aggravated vehicle-taking, disqualification from driving is obligatory, endorsement of licence is obligatory and the penalty points which may be imposed for the offence are 3 to 11. As to disqualification, endorsement of licence and penalty points, see **C7**. The fact that D did not drive the vehicle at any particular time or at all is not a special reason to avoid obligatory disqualification (RTOA 1988, s. 34).

The *Magistrates' Court Sentencing Guidelines* provide guidelines for this offence when dealt with summarily (see Supplement, **SG-325**).

In *Bird* (1993) 14 Cr App R (S) 343, the Court of Appeal said that, when sentencing for this offence, relevant aggravating features would be related to the overall culpability of the driver: how bad the driving was and for how long it had lasted and, to a lesser extent, how much injury or damage had been caused. Drink would affect the assessment of culpability, but where drink was a major factor in the case it would be the subject of a separate charge. Mitigation might be found in a guilty plea showing contrition, but the youth of the offender would be of less significance in this type of case than in others, since the offence was aimed primarily at young offenders. See also *Evans* (1994) 15 Cr App R (S) 137, *Sealey* (1994) 15 Cr App R (S) 189, *Robinson* (1994) 15 Cr App R (S) 452 and *Frostick* [1998] 1 Cr App R (S) 257. In *Clifford* [2008] 1 Cr App R (S) 593 the offender pleaded guilty to aggravated vehicle-taking resulting in death. The offender had taken his partner's car for a drive but was not authorised to do so since he had only a provisional licence. A seven-year-old boy was killed when he stepped into the path of the car. It was accepted by the prosecution that the offender, who had no prior driving convictions, had not been speeding nor had he consumed alcohol, and that the offender could not have seen the boy and avoided the accident. The offender initially left the scene but shortly afterwards went to the police station. A sentence of two years' imprisonment was reduced to six months.

B4.132

Actus Reus

An offence of aggravated vehicle-taking can be committed only if an offence under the Theft Act 1968, s. 12(1), is committed in respect of a mechanically propelled vehicle (s. 12A(1)(a)). In the RTA 1988, s. 185, the following are defined and are all mechanically propelled vehicles: heavy

B4.133

locomotive, heavy motor car, invalid carriage, light locomotive, motor car, motor cycle, motor tractor, and motor vehicle. This excludes electrically assisted (pedelec) cycles, aircraft or boats. Secondly, the prosecution must prove that, at any time after the vehicle was taken and before it was recovered, one or more of the circumstances in s. 12A(2)(a) to (d) occurred (s. 12A(1) (b)). All that the prosecution has to prove is that the circumstances occurred, it does not have to prove that D was the cause of them (*Dawes v DPP* [1995] 1 Cr App R 65); it is for D to prove one of the specific defences if he is to avoid conviction (see **B4.135**).

The circumstances of aggravation in s. 12A(2) are listed at **B4.128**. The phrase 'driven dangerously', which occurs in s. 12A(2)(a), is defined in s. 12A(7) in identical terms to the definition which applies to the offence of dangerous driving (see **C3.10**). Whilst the vehicle must be driven dangerously for s. 12A(2)(a) to apply, there is no such requirement in s. 12A(2)(b) or (c), so the simple fact that the vehicle is being driven, without fault, is sufficient (*Marsh* [1997] 1 Cr App R 67, in which M was guilty under s. 12A(2)(b) when he drove a vehicle without permission and knocked a pedestrian down despite driving apparently carefully). The question is whether the driving was the cause of the accident. It is unnecessary for D to be the driver or even for him to be in or near the vehicle when the incident occurs. None of the other phrases used in s. 12A(2) are specifically defined. For 'damage', see **B8.6**; for 'driving', see **C1.2**; for 'accident', see **C1.1** and *Branchflower* [2005] 1 Cr App R 140, where it was decided that 'accident' in this offence is perfectly capable of applying to an untoward occurrence that has adverse physical results, notwithstanding that one event in the chain of events which led to the untoward occurrence was a deliberate act on the part of some mischievous person.

An offence under s. 12A may be committed only in the period after the vehicle is taken and before it is recovered. A vehicle is recovered when it is restored to its owner or other lawful possession or custody (s. 12A(8)); a similar concept is used in the offence of handling stolen goods, see **B4.172**. 'Owner' has the same meaning as in s. 12 (s. 12A(8)) (see **B4.124**).

Mens Rea

B4.134   *Mens rea* has to be established with regard to the first element of an offence of aggravated vehicle-taking, that is the *mens rea* of the basic offence (see **B4.125** and **B4.127**). No *mens rea* need be shown with regard to the second element, the circumstances of aggravation: the offences are offences of strict liability in that regard.

Specific Defence

B4.135   Theft Act 1968, s. 12A

> (3) A person is not guilty of an offence under this section if he proves that, as regards any such proven driving, injury or damage as is referred to in subsection (1)(b) above, either—
>> (a) the driving, accident or damage referred to in subsection (2) above occurred before he committed the basic offence; or
>> (b) he was neither in nor in the immediate vicinity of the vehicle when that driving, accident or damage occurred.

TAKING OR RIDING A PEDAL CYCLE
WITHOUT AUTHORITY

B4.136   It is an offence, contrary to the Theft Act 1968, s. 12(5), and subject to s. 12(6) (see **B4.125**), for a person, without having the consent of the owner or other lawful authority, to take a pedal cycle for his own or another's use, or ride a pedal cycle knowing it to have been taken without such authority. In *Sturrock v DPP* [1996] RTR 216, it was held that it is not necessary to have a formal statement of ownership from the owner of a cycle where the primary facts permit the inference that the cycle had not been abandoned and had an owner. The offence is punishable on summary conviction with a fine not exceeding level 3 on the standard scale.

INTERFERENCE WITH VEHICLES

Definition

Criminal Attempts Act 1981, s. 9   B4.137

(1) A person is guilty of the offence of vehicle interference if he interferes with a motor vehicle or trailer or with anything carried in or on a motor vehicle or trailer with the intention that an offence specified in subsection (2) below shall be committed by himself or some other person.
(2) The offences mentioned in subsection (1) above are—
   (a) theft of the motor vehicle or trailer or part of it;
   (b) theft of anything carried in or on the motor vehicle or trailer; and
   (c) an offence under section 12(1) of the Theft Act 1968 (taking and driving away without consent);
   and, if it is shown that a person accused of an offence under this section intended that one of those offences should be committed, it is immaterial that it cannot be shown which it was.

Procedure

The offence is triable summarily only (Criminal Attempts Act 1981, s. 9(3)).   B4.138

Sentence

The maximum penalty is imprisonment for a term not exceeding three months or a fine not   B4.139
exceeding level 4 on the standard scale or both (Criminal Attempts Act 1981, s. 9(3)).

The *Magistrates' Court Sentencing Guidelines* provide guidelines for this offence (see Supplement, SG-322).

Elements

As to theft, see **B4.1** *et seq.* As to offences under the Theft Act 1968, s. 12(1), see **B4.117** *et seq.*   B4.140

There is no definition of 'interference'. Clearly there has to be interference as well as intention. Merely looking into cars is probably not an act of interference whereas opening doors and putting pressure on the door handles is an act of interference. However, whether placing a hand on a door handle is an act of interference is not clear, nor was it clarified in the Crown Court case of *Reynolds and Warren v Metropolitan Police* [1982] Crim LR 831.

'Motor vehicle' and 'trailer', by virtue of s. 9(5), have the same meaning as in the RTA 1988, s. 185(1):

> 'motor vehicle' means, subject to section 20 of the Chronically Sick and Disabled Persons Act 1970 (which makes special provision about invalid carriages, within the meaning of that Act), a mechanically propelled vehicle intended or adapted for use on roads, and 'trailer' means a vehicle drawn by a motor vehicle.

ABSTRACTING ELECTRICITY

Definition

Theft Act 1968, s. 13   B4.141

A person who dishonestly uses without due authority, or dishonestly causes to be wasted or diverted, any electricity shall on conviction on indictment be liable to imprisonment for a term not exceeding five years.

Procedure

Abstracting electricity is triable either way (MCA 1980, s. 17 and sch. 1, para. 28). When tried on   B4.142
indictment it is normally a class 3 offence, but see CPD XIII, para. B (see Supplement, **PD-97**) for the additional factors that the court considers on allocation.

Indictment

B4.143

Statement of Offence

Abstracting electricity contrary to section 13 of the Theft Act 1968.

Particulars of Offence

A on or about the...day of...dishonestly and without due authority used [or dishonestly caused to be wasted or diverted] a quantity of electricity.

Sentencing Guidelines

B4.144   The maximum penalty on indictment is five years; six months or a fine not exceeding the statutory maximum, or both, summarily.

The *Magistrates' Court Sentencing Guidelines* provide guidelines for this offence when tried summarily (see Supplement, **SG-282**).

In *Hodkinson* (1980) 2 Cr App R (S) 331, the offender pleaded guilty to abstracting electricity, in that he had fitted a device to the electricity meter at his home, which caused the meter to give a false reading. A sentence of imprisonment for one month, together with a fine of £750, was approved.

See also *Western* (1987) 9 Cr App R (S) 6.

Actus Reus

B4.145   Electricity cannot be property and so when electricity is 'obtained' the only available offence is the present one (*Low v Blease* [1975] Crim LR 513). Any use, waste or diversion of electricity will suffice (*Low v Blease*), so a meter does not have to be tampered with (*McCreadie* (1992) 96 Cr App R 143). Electricity is abstracted where the electricity supply to a house is reconnected without the consent of the electricity supplier (*Boggeln v Williams* [1978] 2 All ER 1061). It is also abstracted where the electricity supply to a house is caused not to be registered by the meter (*Collins v DPP* (1987) *The Times*, 20 October 1987). It may well be an abstraction of electricity to make a call from a telephone belonging to another person (*Low v Blease*).

Mens Rea

B4.146   Abstracting electricity is an offence of dishonesty to which the definition provided by the Court of Appeal in *Ghosh* [1982] QB 1053 applies (see **B4.54**). This is so even though the Court of Appeal in *Boggeln v Williams* [1978] 2 All ER 1061 took the view that 'dishonesty' was to be approached as a subjective concept in s. 13.

DISHONEST USE OF TELECOMMUNICATION SYSTEMS AND DISHONEST RECEIPT OF PROGRAMMES

Electronic Communications Service

B4.147   It is an offence, contrary to the Communications Act 2003, s. 125(1), for a person dishonestly to obtain an electronic communications service where he does so with intent to avoid payment of a charge applicable to the provision of that service. Section 125(2) makes it clear that it is not an offence under s. 125 to obtain a service mentioned in the Copyright, Designs and Patents Act 1988, s. 297(1) (see **B4.148**). The offence is triable either way, and the maximum penalty is, on conviction on indictment, imprisonment for a term not exceeding five years or a fine or both and, on summary conviction, imprisonment for a term not exceeding six months or a fine not exceeding the statutory maximum or both (s. 125(3)). It is also an offence, contrary to s. 126(1) for a person to have in his possession or under his control anything which may be used for obtaining an electronic communications service, provided he has the requisite intention (which is defined in s. 126(3)). It is also an offence, contrary to s. 126(2), for a person to supply or offer to supply anything which may be so used, where he knows or believes that the intentions of the person supplied or offered fall within s. 126(3). Both offences under s. 126 are triable either way and the maximum penalty, on conviction on indictment, is a term of imprisonment not exceeding five years, a fine or both and, on summary conviction, a term of imprisonment not exceeding six months, a fine not exceeding the statutory maximum or both (s. 126(5)). For neither of these offences will an intention fall within s. 126(3) if it relates exclusively to the obtaining of a service mentioned in the Copyright, Designs and Patents Act 1988, s. 297(1) (s. 126(4)). For the definition of relevant terms, see s. 126(6) and s. 151.

Broadcast or Cable Service

It is a summary offence, contrary to the Copyright, Designs and Patents Act 1988, s. 297(1), **B4.148** dishonestly to receive a programme included in a broadcasting or cable programme service provided from a place in the UK with intent to avoid payment of any charge applicable to the reception of the programme. Section 297A of the 1988 Act (inserted by the Conditional Access (Unauthorised Decoders) Regulations 2000 (SI 2000 No. 1175) creates an offence triable either way concerned with certain commercial activities in relation to unauthorised decoders (that is apparatus to enable receipt of encrypted transmissions).

Mobile Telephone Reprogramming

The Mobile Telephones (Re-programming) Act 2002 creates four offences concerned with the **B4.149** re-programming of mobile telephones: changing a unique device identifier (s. 1(1)(a)); interfering with a unique device identifier's operation (s. 1(1)(b)); offering or agreeing to change, or interfere with the operation of, a unique device identifier (s. 1(1)(c)); and offering or agreeing to arrange for another person to do so (s. 1(1)(d)).

A unique device identifier is an electronic equipment identifier which is unique to a mobile wireless communications device (s. 1(2) and s. 2(4)); a SIM card is an obvious example. A person does not commit an offence if he is the device manufacturer or he does the act with the written consent of the manufacturer (s. 1(2)). The maximum penalty is, on indictment, five years' imprisonment or a fine or both, and summarily, six months' imprisonment or a fine not exceeding the statutory maximum or both (s. 1(4)). The Act also creates three offences concerned with the possession or supply of things for such programming. A person commits an offence by: (1) having in his custody or under his control anything which may be used for the purpose of changing or interfering with a unique device identifier's operation where he has the intention to use the thing unlawfully for that purpose or to allow it to be used unlawfully for that purpose (s. 2(1)); (2) supplying anything which may be used for the purpose of changing or interfering with a unique device identifier's operation where he knows or believes that the person to whom it is supplied intends to use it unlawfully for that purpose or to allow it to be used unlawfully for that purpose (s. 2(2)); (3) offering to supply anything which may be used for the purpose of changing or interfering with a unique device identifier's operation where he knows or believes that the person to whom it is offered intends, if it is supplied to him, to use it unlawfully for that purpose or to allow it to be used unlawfully for that purpose (s. 2(3)). The maximum penalty, on indictment, is five years' imprisonment or a fine or both and, summarily, is six months' imprisonment or a fine not exceeding the statutory maximum or both (s. 2(6)).

Sentence

In *Nadig* (1993) 14 Cr App R (S) 49 the offender was convicted of fraudulent use of a telecom- **B4.150** munications system. He used a tone-dialling device to make calls from a telephone box without paying. A suspended sentence was held to be wrong in principle for an isolated offence. Auld J, in the Court of Appeal, said that the preferred sentence was a fine, and that comparison between sentencing for this offence and sentencing for abstracting electricity (see **B4.144**) would be helpful only where the fraudulent use of the telephone had taken place over a period of time. See also *Adewale* (1994) 15 Cr App R (S) 790 and *Aslam* [1996] 2 Cr App R 377.

GOING EQUIPPED

Definition

B4.151

Theft Act 1968, s. 25

(1) A person shall be guilty of an offence if, when not at his place of abode, he has with him any article for use in the course of or in connection with any burglary or theft.

(2) A person guilty of an offence under this section shall on conviction on indictment be liable to imprisonment for a term not exceeding three years.

(3) Where a person is charged with an offence under this section, proof that he had with him any article made or adapted for use in committing a burglary or theft shall be evidence that he had it with him for such use.

(4) [Repealed.]

(5) For purposes of this section an offence under section 12(1) of this Act of taking a conveyance shall be treated as theft.

As of 15 January 2007, this provision no longer contains any reference to going equipped for a 'cheat', but the Fraud Act 2006, ss. 6 and 7, create (as of that date) new offences of possessing, making or supplying articles for use in frauds (see **B5.21** and **B5.23**).

Procedure

B4.152   Going equipped for stealing is triable either way (MCA 1980, s. 17 and sch. 1, para. 28). When tried on indictment it is normally a class 3 offence, but see CPD XIII, para. B (see Supplement, **PD-97**) for the additional factors that the court considers on allocation.

Indictment

B4.153

Statement of Offence

Going equipped for burglary contrary to section 25 of the Theft Act 1968.

Particulars of Offence

A on or about the…day of…, not being at his place of abode, had with him articles, namely a jemmy and a kitchen knife, for use in the course of or in connection with burglary.

Sentence

B4.154   The maximum penalty is three years (s. 25(2)) on indictment; six months or a fine not exceeding the statutory maximum, or both, summarily. If committed with reference to the theft or taking of motor vehicles, disqualification is discretionary (RTOA 1988, sch. 2). There are no reported sentencing guidelines for this offence, but in *Ferry* [1997] 2 Cr App R (S) 42 a sentence of 12 months' imprisonment was upheld where the offenders, found in possession of a cordless drill, screwdrivers, surgical gloves and a map, were targeting a series of telephone boxes in a rural area. A sentence of 24 weeks' imprisonment was appropriate on a guilty plea in *Flack* [2011] EWCA Crim 1112, where a man with a long record of dishonesty was found in possession of a carrier bag lined with foil (a device used to avoid shop theft detection).

The *Magistrates' Court Sentencing Guidelines* provide guidelines for this offence when tried summarily (see Supplement, **SG-289**). In *Flack* the Court of Appeal said that where the offender had elected trial in the Crown Court and then pleaded guilty, the available maximum sentence was higher than that available to the magistrates and the *Magistrates' Court Sentencing Guidelines* were of limited relevance.

Relation to Other Offences

It is not an offence under the Theft Act 1968, s. 25, to keep or possess articles intended for use in theft, burglary etc. as long as those articles are kept at home. An individual who has been found to possess a jemmy or similar implement at his place of abode may, however, be charged under the Criminal Damage Act 1971, s. 3, if it appears that the thing in question might be used to damage windows, locks etc. in the course of forcing an entry for the purpose of theft or burglary. Firearms or imitation firearms kept for the purpose of a robbery or aggravated burglary come within the scope of s. 25, but more obviously come within the provisions of the Firearms Act 1968.

B4.155

When Not at his Place of Abode

'Place of abode' is not defined in the Theft Act 1968. It could include a caravan or motor vehicle, but in *Bundy* [1977] 2 All ER 382, the Court of Appeal held that a vehicle is not to be regarded as a place of abode unless parked at a site where D abides or intends to abide. If a traveller keeps housebreaking tools in his vehicle, he will therefore commit an offence under s. 25, whenever he drives his vehicle away from that site.

B4.156

Meaning of 'Has with Him'

This phrase must bear the same meaning in s. 25 as in s. 10 of the Act (see **B4.107**) and implies a degree of immediate control (*Kelt* [1977] 3 All ER 1099). It would suffice if D had the article in his car or bag, at his place of work, or on his person. In *Re McAngus* [1994] Crim LR 602 the Divisional Court held, in relation to extradition proceedings, that a s. 25 offence could be made out where the applicant showed undercover agents counterfeit shirts stored in a bonded warehouse.

B4.157

Any Article for Use in the Course of or in Connection with any Burglary or Theft

The connection between the articles and the proposed theft etc. must not be too remote. In *Mansfield* [1975] Crim LR 101, D was charged under the Theft Act 1968, s. 25, with possessing another person's driving licence, with intent to use this to obtain employment, in the course of which he would have an opportunity to steal. Not surprisingly, the Court of Appeal quashed his conviction.

B4.158

As to the offences which may be intended, see s. 25(5). Although the taking of pedal cycles contrary to s. 12(5) of the Act is not one of those offences, the possession of bolt-cutters etc. for cutting cycle locks could readily be interpreted as intended for use in theft. Burglary includes burglary with intent to inflict grievous bodily harm etc. under s. 9(1)(a) and theft includes theft with force which would amount to robbery.

The most ordinary of articles, including footwear and clothing, could be used in the course of such crimes, but in practice s. 25 is used only in connection with articles which seem intended to play a prominent or obvious role: something which D would not have with him if he was not intending to commit such a crime. Coshes, masks, jemmies, glass-cutters and skeleton keys are obvious examples; less obvious perhaps are credit cards stolen or illicitly borrowed from their real owners (see also *Re McAngus* [1994] Crim LR 602: counterfeit clothing). This does not mean that apparently innocuous articles cannot be within the scope of the section. Bottles of wine were found to constitute such articles in *Doukas* [1978] 1 All ER 1071, where D had apparently brought the wine to the hotel where he worked as a waiter in order dishonestly to sell it to his employer's customers, who would be deceived (contrary to s. 15 of the Act) into thinking that they were buying wine from the employer. A charge under the Fraud Act 2006, s. 6, would now be more appropriate on such facts.

The article need not be intended for use that day, nor for use by D himself, but it must be intended for *future* use. The possession of articles that *have been used* in theft etc. with a view to

B4.159

disposing of them is not an offence under s. 25, although a charge under the CLA 1967, s. 4, may be appropriate (*Ellames* [1974] 3 All ER 130).

In the absence of a confession or other self-incriminating behaviour by D, it may sometimes be difficult to prove that the article was indeed intended for use in the course of or in connection with burglary or theft, and proof of intent is needed: it is not sufficient to show that D merely contemplated possible use (*Hargreaves* [1985] Crim LR 243). Section 25(3) is of very limited use in this respect, since it only states the obvious. If D was found to be carrying a jemmy or a bunch of skeleton keys, a court or jury would in any case consider this to be evidence (and possibly sufficient proof) of intent to commit burglary. Possession of a torch or screwdriver would be less likely to be considered evidence of such intent, and here s. 25(3) is of no help at all (*Harrison* [1970] Crim LR 415).

HANDLING STOLEN GOODS

Definition

B4.160   **Theft Act 1968, s. 22**

(1) A person handles stolen goods if (otherwise than in the course of the stealing) knowing or believing them to be stolen goods he dishonestly receives the goods, or dishonestly undertakes or assists in their retention, removal, disposal or realisation by or for the benefit of another person, or if he arranges to do so.

(2) A person guilty of handling stolen goods shall on conviction on indictment be liable to imprisonment for a term not exceeding 14 years.

Procedure

B4.161   Handling stolen goods is triable either way (MCA 1980, s. 17 and sch. 1, para. 28). When tried on indictment it is normally a class 3 offence, but see CPD XIII, para. B (see Supplement, **PD-97**) for the additional factors that the court considers on allocation. It is a Group A offence for jurisdiction purposes under the CJA 1993, part I (see **A8.10**).

See the *Magistrates' Court Sentencing Guidelines* (see Supplement, **SG-291**) for indications as to when a case should be sent to the Crown Court.

Indictment

B4.162   **First Count**

Statement of Offence

Handling stolen goods contrary to section 22(1) of the Theft Act 1968.

Particulars of Offence

A on or about the...day of...dishonestly received stolen goods, namely a pearl necklace belonging to V, knowing or believing the same to be stolen goods.

Second Count

Statement of Offence

Handling stolen goods contrary to section 22(1) of the Theft Act 1968.

Particulars of Offence

A on or about the...day of...dishonestly undertook or assisted in the retention, removal, disposal or realisation of stolen goods, namely a pearl necklace belonging to V, by or for the benefit of B, or dishonestly arranged to do so, knowing or believing the same to be stolen goods.

It may be prudent to include both counts unless there is clear evidence of one particular form of handling and the prosecution intend to present the case exclusively in those terms. See further *Deakin* [1972] 3 All ER 803.

The general deficiency principle applies to counts for handling stolen goods (for the application **B4.163** of this principle to theft, see **B4.3**, and for the drafting of counts for continuous offences generally, see **D11.33**). It is, therefore, proper to indict for the handling of a total amount of money if the evidence does not precisely disclose the date or amount of each dishonest transaction but the transactions are so closely linked as to be, in effect, a continuous transaction (*Cain* [1983] Crim LR 802). However, if D is charged with handling items of property which are clearly the proceeds of different thefts, burglaries or robberies, and which are received or dealt with on separate occasions, there should be a separate count of handling for each occasion (*Smythe* (1980) 72 Cr App R 8).

Theft Act 1968, s. 27

(1) Any number of persons may be charged in one indictment, with reference to the same theft, with having at different times or at the same time handled all or any of the stolen goods, and the persons so charged may be tried together.
(2) On the trial of two or more persons indicted for jointly handling any stolen goods the jury may find any of the accused guilty if the jury are satisfied that he handled all or any of the stolen goods, whether or not he did so jointly with the other accused or any of them.

Section 27(2), arguably goes further than the general rule, established in *DPP v Merriman* [1973] AC 584, that a person jointly indicted for an offence may be convicted of committing it independently of the others. It also covers cases in which two co-accused handle goods on separate occasions (*French* [1973] Crim LR 632).

Sentence

The maximum penalty is 14 years (Theft Act 1968, s. 22(2)) on indictment; six months or a fine **B4.164** not exceeding the statutory maximum, or both, summarily.

The *Magistrates' Court Sentencing Guidelines* provide guidelines for this offence when tried summarily (see Supplement, **SG-291**).

In *Webbe* [2002] 1 Cr App R (S) 82, the Court of Appeal issued sentencing guidelines for this offence. According to Rose LJ in that case, the relative seriousness of a particular case of handling depends upon the interplay of a number of different factors. One important issue is whether the handler has had advance knowledge of the original offence (or has directly or indirectly made known his willingness to receive the proceeds of the original offence), as compared with a handler who has had no connection with the original offence but who has dishonestly accepted the stolen goods at an undervalue. Where the handler has had knowledge of the original offence, the seriousness of the handling is inevitably linked to the seriousness of the original offence. The replacement value of the goods is often a helpful indication of the seriousness of the offence, but monetary value in itself should not be regarded as the determining factor. Features to be taken as aggravating the offence of handling are (i) the physical or temporal closeness of the handler to the primary offence; (ii) particular seriousness in the primary offence; (iii) high value of the goods to the loser, including sentimental value; (iv) the fact that the goods were the proceeds of a domestic burglary; (v) sophistication in relation to the handling; (vi) a high level of profit made or expected by the handler; (vii) the provision by the handler of a regular outlet for stolen goods; (viii) threats of violence or abuse of power by the handler over others (for example an adult commissioning criminal activity by children or a drug dealer pressurising addicts to steal in order to pay for their habit); and (ix) the commission of the offence while on bail. Relevant mitigating factors include (i) low monetary value of the goods; (ii) the fact that the offence was a one-off offence, committed by an otherwise honest offender; (iii) the fact that there is little or no benefit to the offender; and (iv) voluntary restitution to the victim.

Low-value Cases   Where the property handled is of low monetary value (less than £1,000) **B4.165** and was acquired for the receiver's own use, the starting point should generally be a moderate fine or, in some cases (particularly if a fine cannot be paid by a particular defendant), a discharge. Such an outcome would be appropriate in relation to someone of previous good character handling low value domestic goods for his own use. Irrespective of value, the presence of any one of the aggravating features referred to above is likely to result in a community sentence. A community sentence may be appropriate where property worth less than £1,000 is acquired for resale or where more valuable goods are acquired for the handler's own use. Such a sentence may well be appropriate in relation to a young offender with little criminal experience, playing a peripheral role. But adult offenders with a record of dishonesty are likely to attract a custodial sentence. An offender with either a record of offences for dishonesty or who engages in sophisticated law-breaking will attract a custodial sentence. When fixing the length of that sentence, the aggravating and mitigating features referred to above will come into play, as will the personal mitigation of the offender.

B4.166   **More Serious Cases**   In more serious cases of handling, factors to be taken into consideration will include whether an offence is committed in the context of a business, whether the offender is acting as an organiser or distributor of the proceeds of crime and whether the offender has made himself available to other criminals as willing to handle the proceeds of thefts or burglaries. According to these and other circumstances, sentences in the range of 12 months' to four years' imprisonment are likely to be appropriate if the value of the goods involved is up to around £100,000. Where the value of the goods is in excess of that figure, or where the offence is highly organised and bears the hallmarks of a professional commercial operation, a sentence of four years and upwards is likely to be appropriate, and it will be higher where the source of the handled property is known by the handler to be a serious violent offence such as armed robbery. An example is *Poulton* [2012] 1 Cr App R (S) 580, where sentences of eight years were appropriate following a guilty plea for an organised and professional conspiracy to handle high value motor vehicles, stolen in the course of night-time house burglaries over a wide area of the country. The aggregate value of the property was £500,000. A sentence of four years after a trial was upheld in *Noorulah* [2012] 2 Cr App R (S) 574 where pharmaceutical products worth in excess of £1 million were handled following their theft from a lorry. Goods worth £17,000 were handled by the offenders in *Daniels and Smith* [2012] 2 Cr App R (S) 532; sentences of 16 months and 12 months were appropriate, applying *Webbe*.

Meaning of 'Goods', 'Stolen Goods', 'Theft' etc.

B4.167   Sections 22 to 24 of the Theft Act 1968 deal with what are referred to therein as 'stolen goods' but the combined effect of ss. 24 and 34(2)(b) ensures that the provisions apply to a wider range of property than the ordinary meaning of that term might suggest.

Theft Act 1968, s. 34(2)(b)

'goods', except insofar as the context otherwise requires, includes money and every other description of property except land, and includes things severed from the land by stealing.

A credit balance in a bank account might be regarded as stolen goods if it directly or indirectly represents the proceeds of theft etc. (s. 24(2); *Forsyth* [1997] 2 Cr App R 299: but see **B4.190**). As to things severed from land, see **B4.13**.

The concept of stolen goods has an extended meaning by statute.

Theft Act 1968, ss. 24 and 24A

24.—(1) The provisions of this Act relating to goods which have been stolen shall apply whether the stealing occurred in England or Wales or elsewhere, and whether it occurred before or after the commencement of this Act, provided that the stealing (if not an offence under this Act) amounted to an offence where and at the time when the goods were stolen; and references to stolen goods shall be construed accordingly.

(2) For purposes of those provisions references to stolen goods shall include, in addition to the goods originally stolen and parts of them (whether in their original state or not),—

(a) any other goods which directly or indirectly represent or have at any time represented the stolen goods in the hands of the thief as being the proceeds of any disposal or realisation of the whole or part of the goods stolen or of goods so representing the stolen goods; and

(b)   any other goods which directly or indirectly represent or have at any time represented the stolen goods in the hands of a handler of the stolen goods or any part of them as being the proceeds of any disposal or realisation of the whole or part of the stolen goods handled by him or of goods so representing them.

(3)   But no goods shall be regarded as having continued to be stolen goods after they have been restored to the person from whom they were stolen or to other lawful possession or custody, or after that person and any other person claiming through him have otherwise ceased as regards those goods to have any right to restitution in respect of the theft.

(4)   For purposes of the provisions of this Act relating to goods which have been stolen (including subsections (1) to (3) above) goods obtained in England or Wales or elsewhere either by blackmail or, subject to subsection (5) below, by fraud (within the meaning of the Fraud Act 2006) shall be regarded as stolen; and 'steal', 'theft' and 'thief' shall be construed accordingly.

(5)   Subsection (1) above applies in relation to goods obtained by fraud as if—

(a)   the reference to the commencement of this Act were a reference to the commencement of the Fraud Act 2006, and

(b)   the reference to an offence under this Act were a reference to an offence under section 1 of that Act.

24A.—(8)   References to stolen goods include money which is dishonestly withdrawn from an account to which a wrongful credit has been made, but only to the extent that the money derives from the credit.

If the property in question appears to represent the proceeds of an offence that falls outside the scope of s. 24 or s. 24A(8) it may be possible to consider charges under the 'money laundering' provisions (as to which, see **B21**). These provisions overlap significantly with the offence of handling, and, even where the goods concerned are stolen, the prosecution may in some cases find it easier to charge one or more of the offences they create in preference to handling. As to the handling of dishonestly obtained money transfers, see s. 24A, discussed at **B4.187** *et seq.*

Goods Obtained by Blackmail or Fraud   Section 24(4) governs s. 24(1) to (3) and extends the   **B4.168** meaning of 'stolen goods' to cover the fruits or proceeds of fraud offences and offences under s. 21 (blackmail). No mention of burglary or robbery is needed, because any property obtained by such means must necessarily have been obtained by theft.

Goods Stolen outside England and Wales   Theft Act 1968 offences (other than theft of mails   **B4.169** under s. 14 and offences on British ships etc.) do not ordinarily apply to conduct taking place outside England or Wales (see generally **B4.65** and **A8**) but s. 24(1), read in conjunction with s. 24(4), ensures that property obtained outside the jurisdiction, by what would in England have been regarded as theft, blackmail or fraud, will be regarded as stolen property within the jurisdiction if either:

(a)   the stealing etc. was (exceptionally) punishable as an extra-territorial offence under English law (e.g., where the thief was a British citizen aboard a foreign ship to which he did not belong: Merchant Shipping Act 1995, s. 281); or

(b)   the stealing was punishable under the law then in force where it took place.

Thus, if a thief stole property in Spain, and D received it (or its proceeds) in England, knowing of the circumstances, D may be guilty of handling under s. 22, but it must be proved that the conduct of the thief was, at the time of the theft, punishable under Spanish law. It is not possible to rely on any presumption that foreign law will be similar to English law, nor can judicial notice be taken of foreign law for such a purpose (*Ofori* (1994) 99 Cr App R 223). See also **F10.27** for the general rules on evidence of foreign law.

Fruits and Proceeds of Stolen Goods   Although wide-ranging, s. 24(2), is significantly nar-   **B4.170** rower than the corresponding provision in the Larceny Act 1916, which it replaced. The old law failed to distinguish between the proceeds of stolen goods in the hands of a thief or receiver of stolen goods, and such proceeds in the hands of an innocent person. Thus, anything purchased with, or exchanged for, stolen goods or the proceeds thereof would itself become categorised as stolen goods, even if it had never itself been possessed by either the thief or a receiver. In theory, the potential spread of the contagion was almost limitless.

The present position is that property is categorised as stolen only if it is the original property stolen, or something that has at some time represented the proceeds thereof in the hands of the original thief or of a dishonest handler. For example, if a person innocently acquires a stolen bicycle and then (still innocently) part-exchanges it for a new one, the new cycle cannot be categorised as stolen goods; but it would be otherwise if he knew the original one was stolen.

B4.171   It may be difficult to determine whether property subsequently acquired by the thief or by an alleged handler represents the proceeds of a disposal of the original stolen goods. Classification may be particularly problematic where bank accounts are involved. A thief (A) may for example pay into his account both legitimately obtained moneys (such as his salary) and the proceeds of his thefts. He may then buy goods with funds drawn from that account, or arrange for funds to be transferred to other accounts. In *A-G's Ref (No. 4 of 1979)* [1981] 1 All ER 1193, the Court of Appeal held in such a case that any credit balance in A's account constitutes, in part, stolen goods and that funds withdrawn from that account by A may also constitute stolen goods, to the extent that they derive from the original theft, etc. If the withdrawal involves a sum greater than the amount covered by 'legitimate' funds in the account, it must necessarily represent (at least in part) the proceeds of theft; but in other cases, it must be proved that A intended the withdrawal to represent such proceeds, as where his intention is to settle up with an accomplice to whom he 'owes' part of the proceeds. Note that it is A's intention which matters. The recipient's belief that this is what the withdrawal represents cannot suffice (*A-G's Ref (No. 4 of 1979)*).

If A withdraws money (i.e. cash) from his account, and hands this to B as B's share of the proceeds of theft, B undoubtedly receives stolen goods (s. 24A(8): see **B4.167**). If, however, A arranges for funds to be transferred from his account to an account operated by B, then, for reasons which are explained in **B4.190**, B cannot be guilty of handling the chose in action thereby created in his favour. The proper charge would be one of dishonestly retaining a wrongful credit, contrary to s. 24A (see **B4.187** *et seq.*) or one of knowingly acquiring or possessing the proceeds of criminal conduct, contrary to the POCA 2002, s. 329 (see **B4.192** and **B21.20**).

B4.172   **Goods Restored to Owner etc.**   As to what amounts to restoration to lawful possession, see *Haughton v Smith* [1975] AC 476 and *A-G's Ref (No. 1 of 1974)* [1974] QB 744. In the latter case, a police officer immobilised a parked car he suspected to contain stolen goods, and apprehended D when he attempted to start it. The question arose whether D could be guilty of handling at the time of his arrest, or whether the goods had already been taken into lawful police custody. It was held by the Court of Appeal that, if the police officer had already resolved to prevent the removal of the goods under any circumstances, they would indeed have ceased to be stolen; but if he had remained in doubt, and had resolved only to seek a satisfactory explanation before deciding whether or not to take charge of them, then they would remain stolen.

On somewhat different facts, it was held in *Metropolitan Police Commissioner v Streeter* (1980) 71 Cr App R 113 that stolen goods were not taken into lawful custody merely because they had been marked for later identification and followed in the thief's possession to a rendezvous with the handler.

If there is any doubt about the status of such property when received, it may sometimes be desirable to charge theft (since receiving will usually amount to appropriation of property belonging to another), or it may be easier to prove that D arranged to receive the goods before they ceased to be stolen. Other possibilities are attempt (now that *Haughton v Smith* is no longer good law) and conspiracy.

'Loss of right to restitution' is a matter determined by the civil law. Briefly, this right will be lost **B4.173** where a stolen cheque or other negotiable instrument is acquired by a person who can establish title to it as a holder in due course (see Bills of Exchange Act 1882, s. 29). See also the Factors Act 1889, s. 2 (theft by mercantile agent and sale to bona fide purchaser) and the Hire Purchase Act 1964, s. 27.

Goods which are 'stolen' in the sense of being the proceeds of fraud or deception, rather than theft, may have become in law the property of the fraudster, albeit subject to the victim's right to rescind for fraud. In such a case, any bona fide purchaser may acquire good title to them (Sale of Goods Act 1979, s. 23). Property obtained by blackmail will sometimes give the blackmailer voidable title (as with fraud or deception); but since some kinds of blackmail are analogous to robbery, there will be cases in which no title passes, because the victim never 'consented' to parting with it. Loss to right to restitution of the original property need not usually prevent any proceeds from continuing to be classed as stolen goods.

Actus Reus: Goods must be Stolen

However dishonest D may be, there can be no offence of handling stolen goods unless the goods **B4.174** in question were in fact stolen goods at the time of the alleged handling. See **B4.179**. However, a person who has done an act which would be a sufficient act of handling, intended to handle, was dishonest and believed the goods to be stolen will be liable for an attempt to handle if the goods were not stolen (Criminal Attempts Act 1981, s. 1(2) and (3); *Shivpuri* [1987] AC 1; see generally **A5.81**). The cases of *Haughton v Smith* [1975] AC 476 and *Anderton v Ryan* [1985] AC 560, which were formerly authority for the contrary proposition, are no longer good law.

Proof that handled goods were stolen may be facilitated by the Theft Act 1968, s. 27(4), which provides for the use, in theft or handling cases, of statutory declarations by witnesses to loss of goods in transit where D is notified and does not require personal attendance of the witnesses.

Theft Act 1968, s. 27

(4) In any proceedings for the theft of anything in the course of transmission (whether by post or otherwise), or for handling stolen goods from such a theft, a statutory declaration made by any person that he dispatched or received or failed to receive any goods or postal packet, or that any goods or postal packet when dispatched or received by him were in a particular state or condition, shall be admissible as evidence of the facts stated in the declaration, subject to the following conditions:—

   (a) a statutory declaration shall only be admissible where and to the extent to which oral evidence to the like effect would have been admissible in the proceedings; and

   (b) a statutory declaration shall only be admissible if at least seven days before the hearing or trial a copy of it has been given to the person charged, and he has not, at least three days before the hearing or trial or within such further time as the court may in special circumstances allow, given the prosecutor written notice requiring the attendance at the hearing or trial of the person making the declaration.

(4A) Where the proceedings mentioned in subsection (4) above are proceedings before a magistrates' court inquiring into an offence as examining justices that subsection shall have effect with the omission of the words from 'subject to the following conditions' to the end of the subsection.

(5) This section is to be construed in accordance with section 24 of this Act; and in subsection (3) (b) above the reference to handling stolen goods shall include any corresponding offence committed before the commencement of this Act.

Actus Reus: The Forms of Handling

The Theft Act 1968, s. 22, must be read in conjunction with s. 24 (see **B4.167**). The term 'han- **B4.175** dling' is a form of shorthand embracing the several forms of dealing in the property specified in s. 22(1). In *Bloxham* [1983] 1 AC 109, Lord Bridge of Harwich stated, *obiter*, that s. 22 creates two distinct offences: receiving (or arranging to receive) being one and the various other forms being different variants of the other; but as most commentators have been quick to point out, this is, strictly speaking, incorrect. There is only one offence (*Griffiths v Freeman* [1970] 1 All ER 1117), and an indictment alleging 'handling' without specifying the form is not therefore bad for duplicity (*Nicklin* [1977] 2 All ER 444). On the other hand, Lord Bridge's dictum has been accepted as a good indication of proper practice. An indictment should indicate which of the two main forms of handling is alleged, and if both are alleged there should be separate counts. A person cannot be accused of one and convicted on the basis of the other (*Nicklin*).

Except in cases of receiving or arranging to receive, it must be both alleged and proved that D assisted, or acted for the benefit of, another person: this is the main difference between receiving etc. and the other variants of the offence.

Receiving and Arranging to Receive

B4.176   The Theft Act 1968 does not define 'receiving', but cases on receiving decided under the Larceny Act 1916, s. 33, defined it as involving the taking of possession or control of property, either jointly, or exclusively (*Frost* (1964) 48 Cr App R 284). Possession does not necessarily require physical handling, nor indeed would such handling suffice in the absence of any intent to possess or control the goods (*Hobson v Impett* (1957) 41 Cr App R 138). It is sufficient that the goods were handled by D's agents on his behalf (*Miller* (1854) 6 Cox CC 353). Things in action, which are not capable of physical handling, can certainly be received, as where the proceeds of a stolen cheque are credited to a bank account.

Arranging to receive is a substantive offence which may consist of the kind of preparatory arrangements that would fall short of constituting an attempt to receive, or of arrangements with an innocent party, so that there would be no conspiracy. It is not enough, however, for arrangements to be made for receipt of goods that have yet to be stolen. This might be conspiracy to steal and to handle stolen goods, but cannot be a full s. 22 offence (*Park* (1987) 87 Cr App R 164).

Undertaking or Assisting in Retention, Removal, Disposal or Realisation by or for the Benefit of Another Person

B4.177   In *Bloxham* [1983] 1 AC 109, D innocently purchased a car which he later came to realise must have been stolen. He sold it to an unidentified person at a knockdown price, and it was alleged that this amounted to realisation for the benefit of that unidentified purchaser. The House of Lords disagreed, on the basis that the sale (realisation) was for the benefit of D himself, and Lord Bridge of Harwich added (at pp. 113–14):

> The offence can be committed in relation to any one of [four named] activities in one or other of two ways. First, the offender may himself undertake the activity *for the benefit of* another person. Secondly, the activity may be undertaken *by* another person and the offender may assist him...the category of other persons contemplated by the subsection is subject to the same limitations in whichever way the offence is committed. Accordingly, a purchaser, as such, of stolen goods, cannot...be 'another person' within the subsection, since his act of purchase could not sensibly be described as a disposal or realisation of the stolen goods *by* him...therefore, even if the sale to him could be described as a disposal or realisation for his benefit, the transaction is not...within the ambit of the subsection.

See also *Gingell* (1999) 163 JP 648, *Tokeley-Parry* [1999] Crim LR 578 and *Toleikis* [2013] EWCA Crim 600 (although there is nothing in the judgment in that case to explain why it could be assumed that D acted for the benefit of anyone other than himself).

Assisting in the retention of stolen goods requires active assistance to be given to the other person. Accommodating or banking the stolen property would suffice (*Pitchley* (1972) 57 Cr App R 30); but mere failure to co-operate with the police during a search for stolen goods would not (*Brown* [1970] 1 QB 105). It is not necessary that the assistance should be successful; an attempt to deceive the police during such a search will amount to the complete offence under the Theft Act 1968, s. 22 (*Kanwar* [1982] 2 All ER 528).

Disposing of or assisting in the disposal or realisation of stolen goods typically means moving the property from one place to another or converting it from one form into another (*Forsyth* [1997] 2 Cr App R 299 at p. 317). This may be a continuing offence and may be committed in England even where much of the relevant conduct occurs abroad (*Forsyth*). Because handling is a group A offence for the purposes of the CJA 1993, part I, it would now suffice for any 'relevant event' to occur within the jurisdiction. Cases of 'money laundering', in which arrangements are made for the transfer, concealment or investment, etc., of criminal property (including stolen goods) may also involve offences under the POCA 2002, ss. 327 to 329. Such offences will in many cases be easier to prove than handling, and carry the same maximum penalties: see **B21.24**.

Relationship between Handling and other Offences

The Theft Act 1968, s. 22, stipulates that the offence of handling may only be committed **B4.178** 'otherwise than in the course of the stealing'. The stealing referred to is the crime whereby the goods become 'stolen' in the first place. (This may, under s. 24(4), take the form of blackmail or fraud: see **B4.168**). The stipulation prevents thieves or blackmailers etc. becoming handlers whilst still participating in the original offence, which may take the form of a continuous or on-going series of acts (see **B4.44**). Where, for example, burglar A passes the items he steals to his accomplice, burglar B, who carries them to the get-away car, B might otherwise become a handler through 'receiving' stolen goods. It may therefore be necessary for the prosecution to prove, in appropriate cases, that the stealing had been completed prior to the alleged act of handling and was not still in progress at the time. This was the issue in *Pitham* (1976) 65 Cr App R 45, where the appellants were invited by one M to pay him for furniture belonging to another man, who was in prison at the time. They agreed a price with M and removed the furniture, and were indicted on those facts with alternative counts of burglary and handling. (As to the joinder of 'mutually destructive' counts within a single indictment, see *Bellman* [1989] AC 836 and **D11.68**.) They were convicted of handling and their convictions were upheld on appeal; Lawton LJ took the view that the jury were fully justified in finding that the appellants had dealt with the furniture only after M had stolen it by assuming the right to dispose of it. They had either helped M to steal the goods or M had stolen them and got rid of them by sale to the appellants; but the jury had, by their verdict, rejected the former possibility.

The prosecution need not affirmatively prove every alleged handler to be innocent of the origi- **B4.179** nal theft, blackmail or deception. The courts have refused to place such a burden on the prosecution where there is no evidence to suggest that D was anything other than a handler (*Cash* [1985] QB 801). Problems may however arise where the evidence is ambiguous, as where property that has been stolen in a burglary is discovered a day later, hidden in D's attic. Under the doctrine of recent possession (see **F3.63**), the court or jury may legitimately infer, in the absence of any alternative explanation, that D must either have been the burglar or have dishonestly received the property knowing it to be stolen; but unless there is some further evidence to indicate which of the two offences D committed, it would appear to be impossible for them to draw one inference rather than the other.

The problem in such cases would not be solved merely by treating the words 'otherwise than in the course of the stealing' as a proviso or qualification to the general words of s. 22, and thus as a matter to be raised and proved by the defence under the rule as to the burden of proof which was affirmed by the House of Lords in *Hunt* [1987] AC 352 (see **F3.16**). The prosecution would still have to prove that D 'received the goods, knowing or believing them to be stolen', D would not have done so if he had appropriated them as the original burglar. Nor is it permissible for the court or jury to convict D of whichever offence appears, on balance, to be the more likely possibility. They must be sure that D is guilty of the specific offence of which they convict him (*A-G of Hong Kong v Yip Kai-foon* [1988] AC 642; cf. *Bellman* [1989] AC 836, per Lord Griffiths at p. 838).

It does not follow that D must be acquitted in such circumstances. The courts have recognised two possible solutions to the problem, each of which enables a conviction to be recorded. The first, and preferable, solution is for the prosecution to compromise by seeking a conviction for theft. Although a thief or burglar cannot become guilty of handling in the course of the original stealing, the offences of theft and handling are not mutually exclusive. Receiving property stolen or obtained in an earlier, completed theft must invariably involve a further appropriation of it, and it follows that a dishonest receiver of such goods must be a thief as well (*Stapylton v O'Callaghan* [1973] 2 All ER 782). It is accordingly open to the prosecution to include within the indictment a count for theft, drawn sufficiently widely to cover an appropriation of the property on any date between that of the original theft or burglary etc. and the date on which the property was found in D's possession (*More* [1987] 3 All ER 825). This count may be additional to more specific counts, such as for handling or burglary, or it may stand alone; but the prosecution should in either case be able to prove that D stole the property at some point, and it need not matter if they cannot prove whether it was theft by burglary or theft by receiving (*Shelton* (1986) 83 Cr App R 379).

B4.180   In *Shelton* the Court of Appeal offered the following advice (at pp. 384–5).

> As we have been asked by counsel to do so, for the guidance of judges and counsel we make the following comments. First that the long established practice of charging theft and handling as alternatives should continue whenever there is a real possibility, not a fanciful one, that at trial the evidence might support one rather than the other. Secondly, that there is a danger that juries may be confused by reference to second or later appropriations since the issue in every case is whether the defendant has in fact appropriated property belonging to another. If he has done so, it is irrelevant how he came to make the appropriation provided it was in the course of theft. Thirdly, that a jury should be told that a handler can be a thief, but he cannot be convicted of being both a thief and a handler. Fourthly, that handling is the more serious offence, carrying a heavier penalty because those who knowingly have dealings with thieves encourage stealing. Fifthly, in the unlikely event of the jury not agreeing amongst themselves whether theft or handling has been proved, they should be discharged. Finally, and perhaps most importantly, both judges and counsel when directing and addressing juries should avoid intellectual subtleties which some jurors may have difficulty in grasping; the golden rule should be 'Keep it short and simple'.

The second possible solution to the problem has the support of the Privy Council in *A-G of Hong Kong v Yip Kai-foon* [1988] AC 642 and that of the Court of Appeal in *Foreman* [1991] Crim LR 702, but is, with respect, based on doubtful logic. In *Yip Kai-foon*, the Privy Council took the view that, where the evidence was equally consistent with robbery or handling, and the jury was accordingly unable to convict D of robbery, it would then be open to them to rely upon his 'innocence' of that offence as proof that he must have committed handling. This is objectionable, in that it can lead to a conviction for handling being recorded when the jury think it more likely that D committed robbery, burglary or simple theft (see Sir John Smith's commentary on *Ryan v DPP* [1994] Crim LR 457). It is accordingly submitted that a widely drawn count for theft offers a more logical solution to cases in which it is unclear how D acquired the stolen property.

A third possible solution would be for charges to be laid instead under part 7 of the POCA 2002. Section 327 of that Act (see **B21.10**) creates offences of concealing, disguising, converting or transferring abroad 'criminal property' (as defined in s. 340). Section 329 (see **B21.20**) creates offences of acquiring, using or possessing such property. This includes property that directly or indirectly represents any person's benefit from criminal conduct (including D's own conduct). Dishonesty need not be proved, and mere suspicion as to the provenance of the property may suffice. If misused, charges of this kind could enable lazy prosecutors to sidestep the basic *mens rea* requirements of the Theft Act 1968, and it is submitted that the courts should discourage any such practice. As to the overlap between these offences and handling stolen goods, see *Wilkinson v DPP* [2006] EWHC 3012 (Admin) and **B21.24**.

See also the offences under the Scrap Metal Dealers Act 1964, as amended by the LASPO 2012, s. 146 (which inserts the offence of buying scrap metal for cash).

Mens Rea

Dishonesty　This must bear the same meaning here as it does in fraud or deception cases and (save for the fact that the Theft Act 1968, s. 2, is not directly applicable) in theft. In other words, it is dishonesty in the *Ghosh* sense (*Ghosh* [1982] QB 1053, see **B4.54**). As to the possible relationship between knowledge and dishonesty, see **B4.182**. **B4.181**

Knowledge or Belief that the Goods are Stolen　On a charge of handling stolen goods, it must **B4.182** be proved that D actually knew that the goods were stolen, or correctly believed that they were. This knowledge or belief must correspond in time with the *actus reus* (*Williams* [1994] Crim LR 934). In cases of handling by receiving, this means the moment of receipt or acquisition. If D only later becomes aware that the goods are stolen, this will not suffice, even if his retention of them is clearly dishonest (*Brook* [1993] Crim LR 455). On the other hand, dishonest retention in such circumstances may sometimes amount to theft (subject to the Theft Act 1968, s. 3(2), which precludes such liability in cases where the property was acquired bona fide and for value); or it may amount to an offence under the POCA 2002, s. 329 (see **B21.20**).

Knowledge of the circumstances which make the goods stolen will generally suffice for liability in cases of alleged handling whether or not D appreciated the legal consequences of those circumstances. An accused's belief that the proceeds of blackmail are something different from stolen goods will accordingly be no defence; nor should it be any defence that an accused believed the goods to be the proceeds of theft when they are in fact the proceeds of blackmail, fraud or deception. In either event, the goods are stolen, and his belief is not incorrect in any material sense.

Another immaterial error would be one about the precise identity of the goods. It would be no defence that an accused thought a container held stolen whisky when in fact it contained stolen cigars (*McCullum* (1973) 57 Cr App R 645).

An accused's ignorance of the law may prevent him from being considered dishonest. For example, a person may know that certain property indirectly represents the proceeds of the sale, by a thief or handler, of the original stolen goods, but may not realise that these proceeds are accordingly 'stolen goods' within the meaning of the Theft Act 1968, s. 24. Not realising the legal position, he is perhaps unlikely to realise that his handling of them would be considered dishonest according to the standards of reasonable and honest people.

Belief that goods are stolen is an alternative *mens rea* to knowledge of that fact. It is not of course **B4.183** an alternative to the goods actually *being* stolen (*Haughton v Smith* [1975] AC 485 at p. 503). If the goods are not in fact stolen, there may be an attempt to handle stolen goods (see **B4.174** or he may actually steal them himself, but he cannot be guilty of handling.

The distinction between knowledge and belief is not crucial in this context, since either state of mind may suffice for liability. In *Hall* (1985) 81 Cr App R 260, the Court of Appeal nevertheless attempted to distinguish between the two concepts. The Court suggested that a person 'knows' that goods are stolen if someone with first-hand knowledge (such as the thief) has told him so; whereas he 'believes' that fact if he does not know it for certain, but realises that there is no other reasonable conclusion to be drawn in the light of all the circumstances. With respect, however, a person cannot properly be said to 'know' a fact merely because someone else has told him about it. He can only know a fact (or indeed testify as to such a fact at a criminal trial) if he himself has first-hand knowledge of it, as for example where he personally witnesses the theft taking place or where he positively identifies property which he knows to have been stolen (cf. *Overington* [1978] Crim LR 692; *Hulbert* (1979) 69 Cr App R 243). Failing this, he can at most 'believe' the goods to be stolen.

The critical distinction in handling cases is that between knowledge or belief, on the one hand, and suspicion, on the other, because it has been held on many occasions that suspicion, even grave suspicion accompanied by dishonesty and a wilful failure to make reasonable inquiries, cannot suffice for liability (*Griffiths* (1974) 60 Cr App R 14; *Pethick* [1980] Crim LR 242; *Moys* (1984) 79 Cr App R 72; *Forsyth* [1997] 2 Cr App R 299). The Court of Appeal in *Hall* suggested that a person may believe goods to be stolen where he 'refuses to believe what his brain tells him is obvious', but this suggestion has rightly been rejected as potentially confusing (*Forsyth*). A person cannot sensibly be said to believe what he refuses to believe, and the test must be a subjective one, rather than an objective test based on what D ought to have realised. In *Forsyth*, the Court of Appeal defined belief as 'the mental acceptance of a fact as true or existing', and suggested that juries might be directed in the following terms, as previously suggested by Lord Lane CJ in *Moys*:

> ...it must be proved that the defendant was aware of the theft or that he believed the goods to be stolen. Suspicion that they were stolen, even coupled with the fact that he shut his eyes to the circumstances, is not enough, although these matters may be taken into account...in deciding whether or not the necessary knowledge or belief existed.

This is certainly preferable to the definition attempted in *Hall*, but the definition of belief remains imprecise. Does belief on balance of probabilities suffice, or must D have felt sure of it, beyond reasonable doubt? In *Forsyth*, the Court of Appeal merely observed, rather unhelpfully, that 'between suspicion and belief there may be a range of awareness' and it would therefore be safer to assume that the stricter concept of belief applies. In other words, a person believes that goods are stolen only if he harbours no serious or substantial doubt as to that fact.

B4.184   A person who deals with goods that he merely suspects *may possibly* have been stolen but 'asks no questions' might perhaps be considered dishonest, but cannot on that basis be guilty of handling, although he may be guilty of an offence under part 7 of the POCA 2002 (see **B21**). On the other hand, a person who has concluded that the goods he is being offered *must* almost certainly be stolen (e.g., because he notices that the serial number has been removed from an item he is being offered for a knock-down price) cannot then set up his failure to ask questions as a defence. Turning a blind eye to the facts, 'can be capable, depending on the circumstances, of providing evidence going to prove knowledge or belief' (*Pace* [2014] 1 Cr App R 501 (34), per Davis LJ at [81]). See also *Griffiths* (1974) 60 Cr App R 14 and **F3.63**.

As to the position where D wrongly concludes that the property in question is stolen (e.g., because he is caught in a police 'sting' operation where undercover officers pretend to be thieves), see **A5.81**.

B4.185   **Previous Convictions as Evidence**   On a charge of handling, the Theft Act 1968, s. 27(3) (which remains in force despite the enactment of the 'bad character' provisions of the CJA 2003), makes evidence of D's previous convictions for theft or handling, or of D's previous dealings in stolen goods, admissible in certain circumstances for the limited purpose of proving his knowledge or belief that the goods were stolen on the present occasion. Section 27(3), and its relationship to the regime laid down by the CJA 2003, is examined at **F12.99** *et seq*.

Effect of Conviction or Acquittal of the Alleged Thief

B4.186   A conviction for handling stolen goods does not depend on the conviction of the alleged thief (or blackmailer etc.), nor is it even necessary to identify him in every case. It follows that there is nothing necessarily inconsistent in the acquittal of the alleged thief and the conviction at the same trial of the alleged handler. It may be, for example, that the handler is convicted on the basis of a confession that is not admissible against his co-accused. On the other hand, acquittal of the alleged thief could sometimes be inconsistent with conviction of the handler at the same trial. A court must be satisfied that the goods are stolen, and this would not, for example, be consistent with acquittal of a child who is alleged to have been the thief, but who is found to be under the age of criminal responsibility (cf. *Walters v Lunt* [1951] 2 All ER 645).

At the trial of a person for handling stolen goods, conviction by a court in, or by a Service court outside, the UK of another person for stealing those goods is admissible evidence that that person did commit the theft. If the alleged handler wishes to argue that the goods were not stolen, he will have to prove it on balance of probabilities (PACE 1984, s. 74; see *Barnes* [1991] Crim LR 132 and F11.6). Conviction of the alleged thief by a foreign court is not, however, admissible as evidence that he committed the theft. This may hamper the use of the Theft Act 1968, s. 24(1) (see B4.167), although it does not preclude expert evidence that an act would have been an offence under foreign law.

DISHONESTLY RETAINING A WRONGFUL CREDIT

Definition

Theft Act 1968, s. 24A

B4.187

(1) A person is guilty of an offence if—
    (a) a wrongful credit has been made to an account kept by him or in respect of which he has any right or interest;
    (b) he knows or believes that the credit is wrongful; and
    (c) he dishonestly fails to take such steps as are reasonable in the circumstances to secure that the credit is cancelled.
(2) References to a credit are to a credit of an amount of money.
(2A) A credit to an account is wrongful to the extent that it derives from—
    (a) theft;
    (b) blackmail; or
    (c) fraud (contrary to the Fraud Act 2006); or
    (d) stolen goods.
(3) [Repealed—see below and B4.190.]
(4) [Repealed—see below and B4.190.]
(5) In determining whether a credit to an account is wrongful, it is immaterial (in particular) whether the account is overdrawn before or after the credit is made.
(6) A person guilty of an offence under this section shall be liable on conviction on indictment to imprisonment for a term not exceeding ten years.
(7) Subsection (8) below applies for purposes of provisions of this Act relating to stolen goods (including subsection (2A) above).
(8) References to stolen goods include money which is dishonestly withdrawn from an account to which a wrongful credit has been made, but only to the extent that the money derives from the credit.
(9) 'Account' means an account kept with—
    (a) a bank;
    (b) a person carrying on a business which falls within subsection (10) below; or
    (c) a person falling within any of paragraphs (a) to (j) of the definition of 'electronic money issuer' in regulation 2(1) of the Electronic Money Regulations 2011.
(10) A business falls within this subsection if—
    (a) in the course of the business money received by way of deposit is lent to others; or
    (b) any other activity of the business is financed, wholly or to any material extent, out of the capital of or the interest on money received by way of deposit.
(11) References in subsection (10) above to a deposit must be read with—
    (a) section 22 of the Financial Services and Markets Act 2000;
    (b) any relevant order under that section; and
    (c) Schedule 2 to that Act;
    but any restriction on the meaning of deposit which arises from the identity of the person making it is to be disregarded.
(12) For the purposes of subsection (10) above—
    (a) all the activities which a person carries on by way of business shall be regarded as a single business carried on by him; and
    (b) 'money' includes money expressed in a currency other than sterling.

Section 24A is shown as amended by the Fraud Act 2006, sch. 1, para. 7; but these amendments do not affect its operation in relation to credits falling within s. 24A(3) or (4) and made before 15 January 2007 (see the Fraud Act 2006, sch. 2, para. 5). This means that s. 24A will continue to apply where a credit represents or is derived from a money transfer obtained before that date, contrary to the Theft Act 1968, s. 15A. See **B4.190.**

Procedure and Sentence

B4.188   An offence under s. 24A is triable either way (MCA 1980, s. 17 and sch. 1, para. 28). When tried on indictment, it is normally a class 3 offence, but see CPD XIII, para. B (see Supplement, **PD-97**) for the additional factors that the court considers on allocation. It is a Group A offence for jurisdiction purposes under the CJA 1993, part I (see **A8.10**).

The maximum penalty is ten years (Theft Act 1968, s. 24A(6)) on indictment; six months and/ or a fine not exceeding the statutory maximum on summary conviction. There are no reported sentencing guidelines for this offence.

Indictment

B4.189
Statement of Offence

Dishonestly retaining a wrongful credit, contrary to section 24A(1) of the Theft Act 1968.

Particulars of Offence

A between the ... day of ... and the ... day of ... knowing or believing that a wrongful credit, namely a transfer of £20,000 obtained by B from Nationwide Building Society, contrary to section 1 of the Fraud Act 2006, had been made to a current account (no. ....) kept jointly by A and B at Barclays Bank plc, dishonestly failed to take such steps as were reasonable in the circumstances to secure that the credit was cancelled.

Wrongful Credits and Stolen Goods

B4.190   One (at least arguable) side-effect of the decision of the House of Lords in *Preddy* [1996] AC 815) was that, where D dishonestly obtained a money transfer from V, the sum thereby credited to D's account could no longer be categorised as stolen goods. This indeed was the view of the Law Commission when reviewing the impact of *Preddy*. To some extent, this is now addressed by the enactment of the Fraud Act 2006 and the consequential amendment of the Theft Act 1968, s. 24, so as to classify the proceeds of fraud as stolen goods; but this assists only in respect of frauds committed on or after 15 January 2007. Furthermore, even where A pays stolen bank notes directly into his account, the proceeds of a subsequent transfer from that account to an account held by B cannot be classed as stolen goods, because any credit balance thereby created in B's account is an entirely different chose in action from the credit balance which previously represented the stolen money in A's account. B's credit balance admittedly represents the proceeds of A's original crime, but it has never done so in the hands of the original thief, and any argument that it does so in the hands of a handler of the stolen property (i.e. B) is circular, because that presupposes the very point it seeks to establish, namely that the funds in B's account are stolen goods. In *A-G's Ref (No. 4 of 1979)* [1981] 1 All ER 1193, it was held that B may be guilty of handling in such circumstances; but this cannot stand with *Preddy* on that particular issue.

Section 24A addresses the problem by ensuring (originally through subsections (3) and (4) and now through subsection (2A)) that D commits an offence where he dishonestly retains a credit which he knows or correctly believes represents or is derived from theft, blackmail, s. 15A deception (prior to 15 January 2007), fraud (contrary to the Fraud Act 2006, s. 1) or stolen goods. If, for example, A pays stolen money into his account and transfers the funds from that account to an account owned by B, a wrongful credit has been made to B's account, and B may commit a s. 24A offence if he dishonestly retains it, knowing or believing it to be derived from one or other of those offences. Section 24A(8), meanwhile, provides that any *money* dishonestly withdrawn from an account to which a wrongful credit has been made can be classed as stolen goods, subject to the principles explained in **B4.170** in respect of withdrawals from accounts into which both 'clean' and 'dirty' money has been paid. It may seem strange that the proceeds of A's original theft can be classed as stolen goods when paid into A's own bank account, cease to be so classified when effectively 'transferred' to B's account, and yet revert to being stolen goods when dishonestly withdrawn as cash by B; but such is now the law.

Dishonesty, Omissions and Bona Fide Purchasers

The offence created by s. 24A(1) is one of dishonest omission. Dishonesty must bear the same **B4.191** meaning as in offences of handling or deception (i.e. the test set out in *Ghosh* [1982] QB 1053: see **B4.55**, **B4.181** and **B4.182**), but knowledge cannot always be equated with dishonesty. A may discover that B has caused the payment of a wrongful credit into their joint account. It may be difficult for her to insist on the cancellation of this credit, unless she is prepared to inform on B, but would a court or jury necessarily categorise her inactivity as dishonest? Similarly, although the bona fide purchaser of a credit is not exempted from liability under s. 24A where he retains the credit after belatedly discovering it to have been a wrongful one (contrast the Theft Act 1968, s. 3(2)) it may be very difficult to persuade a jury that such a person acted dishonestly.

The word 'cancelled' as used in s. 24A(1)(c) means cancelling the original credit so as to achieve the same effect as if it had not been made in the first place. In many cases that will be achieved by a corresponding debit reversing the original entry in the account (*Lee* [2006] EWCA Crim 156, per Moore-Bick LJ at [24]).

Wrongful Credits and the Proceeds of Criminal Conduct

The POCA 2002, s. 327 (see **B21.10**), creates offences of concealing, disguising, converting or **B4.192** transferring abroad 'criminal property' (as defined in s. 340 of the Act). Section 329 (see **B21.20**) creates offences of acquiring, using or possessing such property. This includes property that directly or indirectly represents any person's benefit from criminal conduct. Dishonesty need not be proved, and mere suspicion as to the provenance of the property may suffice. These offences nevertheless carry higher maximum penalties than offences under the Theft Act 1968, s. 24A.

Where a money transfer is made, for example, from a thief's account to an account held by D, what is credited to D's account represents the benefit to the thief of his original crime, and (in contrast to the position under the Theft Act 1968, s. 22) it does not matter for this purpose that it was never held by the thief himself. *Preddy* [1996] AC 815 does not apply to or affect the operation of money laundering offences. Section 24A applies only to wrongful credits made on or after 18 December 1996 (Theft (Amendment) Act 1996, s. 2(2)), whereas criminal property may, for the purposes of the 2002 Act, derive from more ancient crimes.

ADVERTISING REWARDS FOR RETURN OF GOODS STOLEN OR LOST

Definition

Theft Act 1968, s. 23　　B4.193

> Where any public advertisement of a reward for the return of any goods which have been stolen or lost uses any words to the effect that no questions will be asked, or that the person producing the goods will be safe from apprehension or inquiry, or that any money paid for the purchase of the goods or advanced by way of loan on them will be repaid, the person advertising the reward and any person who prints or publishes the advertisement shall on summary conviction be liable to a fine not exceeding level 3 on the standard scale.

Elements

B4.194   Section 23 does not necessarily forbid the offering of rewards for the return of stolen goods, nor does it necessarily prohibit advertisements promising that 'no questions will be asked'. What it prohibits are public advertisements which *combine* an offer of a reward with a promise that no questions will be asked or that immunity will be granted. It does not matter if the advertiser is uncertain whether the goods were lost or stolen; he may even be confident that they were only lost.

The printing or publishing of an offending advertisement is an offence of strict liability (*Denham v Scott* (1984) 77 Cr App R 210).

For the meaning of 'goods', 'stolen goods', 'theft' etc., see **B4.170** *et seq*.

UNLAWFUL DEALING IN CULTURAL OBJECTS

B4.195   The Dealing in Cultural Objects (Offences) Act 2003, s. 1, creates an offence of acquiring, disposing of, importing or exporting tainted cultural objects, or agreeing or arranging to do so.

By ss. 1 and 2 of the Act, a 'tainted cultural object' is one that has been criminally removed from a building or structure of historical, architectural or archaeological interest where the object has at any time formed part of the building or structure, or from a monument of such interest. This removal may have been criminal under UK law or 'under the law of any other country or territory', but the offence of dealing itself (extensively defined in s. 3) has not been given any extra-territorial ambit.

By s. 4, proceedings for an offence relating to the dealing in a tainted cultural object may be instituted by the Director of Revenue and Customs Prosecutions or by order of the Commissioners of HM Revenue and Customs if it appears to them that the offence has involved the importation or exportation of such an object.

Section B5   Fraud and Blackmail

DECEPTION AND FRAUD: THE OLD AND NEW LAW

The Theft Acts 1968 and 1978 created several deception offences covering situations in which **B5.1** something was dishonestly obtained, secured or procured, or in which liability was evaded, by the deception of another person.

The offences in the Theft Act 1968 were those created by s. 15 (obtaining property), s. 15A (obtaining a money transfer), s. 16 (obtaining a pecuniary advantage) and s. 20(2) (procuring the execution of a valuable security). The Theft Act 1978 added offences of obtaining services (s. 1), securing remission of an existing liability (s. 2(1)(a)), inducing a creditor to wait for or forgo payment (s. 2(1)(b)) and obtaining exemption from, or abatement of, liability to make a payment (s. 2(1)(c)).

These offences were repealed by the Fraud Act 2006, s. 14 and sch. 1, on 15 January 2007 (Fraud Act 2006 (Commencement) Order 2006 (SI 2006 No. 3200)); they were replaced on that date:

(1) by a general offence of fraud (Fraud Act 2006, s. 1) that may be committed:
   (a) by dishonestly making a false (i.e. untrue or misleading) representation with a view to gain or with intent to cause loss or to expose to a risk of loss (s. 2);
   (b) by dishonestly (and with a view to gain or with intent to cause loss etc.) failing to disclose information when under a legal duty to disclose it (s. 3); or
   (c) by dishonest abuse of a position, with a view to gain or with intent to cause loss etc. (s. 4); and
(2) by an offence of obtaining services dishonestly (s. 11).

The Fraud Act (largely based on proposals made by the Law Commission in 2002 (Cm 5560)) also creates offences of possessing or making articles for use in frauds (e.g., false identity documents, counterfeit goods or stolen credit cards) (see **B5.21** *et seq.*) but does not, as was originally proposed, abrogate the common-law offence of conspiracy to defraud (see **A5.61**).

Because the Fraud Act has no retrospective effect, it remains necessary to rely upon the old law when prosecuting frauds that predate the commencement of that Act. See *Goldsmith* [2009] EWCA Crim 1840. Some cases that involve both pre- and post-commencement elements may also fall to be prosecuted under the old law: see **B5.2**. For coverage of the old law, see the 2013 edition of this work at **B5.54** *et seq.*

Transitional Provisions and Pre-commencement Offences

The repeal of the deception offences by the Fraud Act 2006, sch. 1, para. 1, 'does not affect any **B5.2** liability, investigation, legal proceeding or penalty for or in respect of any offence partly committed before' commencement (i.e. 15 January 2007) (sch. 2, para. 3(1)). An offence will be deemed to have been partly committed before that date if a 'relevant event' (i.e. any act, omission or other event, including any result of one or more acts or omissions, proof of which is required for conviction of the offence) occurs before it, and another event occurs on or after it (sch. 2, para. 3(2) and (3)).

Where frauds are committed over a long period of time, but involve false representations etc. committed *only* prior to 15 January 2007, the old law must continue to be relied upon, even if any gain or obtaining takes place well after commencement. Whereas the old law is given transitional application under sch. 2, para. 3 (above), the new offence of fraud has no retrospective effect, and creates a conduct crime rather than a result crime. The obtaining of property in 2008 as a result of a fraudulent representation made in 2005 would not therefore satisfy the *actus reus* of the new fraud offence. If, however, fraudulent acts or omissions can be identified both before and after 15 January 2007 (and that might include a single but ongoing or repeated representation), a prosecutor might be in a position to choose between proceeding under the old law and proceeding under the new. Similarly, the new offence of obtaining services dishonestly (s. 11), which is a result crime, may perhaps result from a pre-commencement deception although no deception is strictly necessary under that section. Here again, the old and new offences may overlap so that the prosecutor can choose under which to proceed.

B5.3 Two transitional scenarios remain problematic.

(a) If it is unclear whether a 'relevant event' occurred before or after commencement, the Crown may seek to put alternative counts on the indictment (i.e. one under the 2006 Act and one under the repealed legislation). This is permissible under the principles established in *Bellman* [1989] AC 836 (see **D11.68**), but will not help unless the correct date and charge become clear during the course of the trial. Unless one of the transitional provisions applies, evidence that D must have committed either a deception offence or a Fraud Act offence will not enable him to be convicted of either.

(b) No transitional provisions have been made in respect of the jurisdiction provisions in the CJA 1993, part I (see **A8.11**). As of 15 January 2007, the deception offences ceased to be Group A offences under that Act, and are replaced in that role by Fraud Act offences (Fraud Act 2006, sch. 1, para. 24). No express provision is made in that context for deception offences partly committed before commencement. None of the transitional provisions in sch. 2 purport to qualify sch. 1, para. 24. Parliament may have assumed that this problem was covered by sch. 2, para. 3, but that provision deals only with the repeal of the deception offences by sch. 1, para. 3, whereas the jurisdiction problem referred to here arises from amendments made to the CJA 1993.

As pointed out at **A8.11**, *Smith (Wallace Duncan) (No. 4)* [2004] QB 418 arguably provides a solution to the latter problem, but only at the expense of rendering the provisions of the CJA 1993, part I, largely otiose. Alternatively, a court or prosecutor might possibly seek to draw an analogy with *C* [2008] 1 WLR 966, in which the court adopted a flexible approach to a broadly similar (but not identical) transitional difficulty in connection with changes to the laws governing sexual offences (see **F7.22**).

THE OFFENCE OF FRAUD

B5.4   Fraud Act 2006, s. 1

(1) A person is guilty of fraud if he is in breach of any of the sections listed in subsection (2) (which provide for three different ways of committing the offence).

(2) The sections are—

(a) section 2 (fraud by false representation),

(b) section 3 (fraud by failing to disclose information), and

(c) section 4 (fraud by abuse of position).

These are reproduced and examined at **B5.12** *et seq.*

In all three variants of the offence, the focus is on proscribed conduct and ulterior intent, whereas the consequences of that conduct are not legally significant. Fraud is, in other words, a conduct crime, in which causation issues cannot arise in respect of the *actus reus* and in which unsuccessful 'attempts' to defraud (or even communicate with) the victim may in law amount to a complete or substantive offence. Indeed, it is difficult (as with blackmail) to envisage conduct that could give rise to liability for an attempt to commit it, save where D tries to make a false representation, but stammers helplessly, or mistakenly tells the truth (*Deller* (1952) 36 Cr App R 184; *Cornelius* [2012] EWCA Crim 500 at [36]), or intends to withhold information, but unwittingly discloses it.

Procedure and Jurisdiction

Fraud is triable either way. When tried on indictment, it is normally a class 3 offence, but see **B5.5** CPD XIII, para. B (see Supplement, **PD-97**) for the additional factors that the court considers on allocation. It is a Group A offence for jurisdiction purposes under the CJA 1993, part I (see A8.10). Company officers may be proceeded against and punished for any such offence committed by the company with their consent or connivance (Fraud Act 2006, s. 12(2)). As to the position where a body corporate is managed by its members, see s. 12(3).

See the *Magistrates' Court Sentencing Guidelines* (see Supplement, **SG-472**) for indications as to when a case should be sent to the Crown Court.

Indictment

Statement of Offence   **B5.6**

Fraud, contrary to the Fraud Act 2006, section 1.

Particulars of Offence

A on or about the…day of…2007, dishonestly made a false representation to B, namely,…knowing this to be [might be] untrue [misleading] and intending thereby to make a gain for himself [expose B to a risk of loss].

Sentencing for Fraud Offences Generally

The maximum sentence for fraud, whether committed in breach of the Fraud Act 2006, s. 2, **B5.7** 3, or 4, is (i) on summary conviction, six months' imprisonment or a fine not exceeding the statutory maximum, or both, (ii) on conviction on indictment, ten years' imprisonment or a fine, or both (s. 1(3)).

The definitive sentencing guideline, *Fraud, Bribery and Money Laundering Offences* (see Supplement, **SG-472**) is applicable. The guideline applies to all individual offenders aged 18 and over and to organisations sentenced on or after 1 October 2014 regardless of the date of the offence. It replaces the SGC Guideline *Fraud – Statutory Offences* on that date. The new guideline is more comprehensive in its coverage of fraud offences than the old guideline. The part of the guideline on fraud is applicable to fraud by false representation (see **B5.12**), fraud by failing to disclose information (see **B5.19**), fraud by abuse of position (see **B5.20**), conspiracy to defraud, and false accounting. A separate part of the guideline applies to possessing, making or supplying articles for use in fraud, a third applies to revenue fraud, and a fourth to benefit fraud. There is a separate part of the guideline which applies in relation to fraud committed by corporate offenders.

The following cases were decided under the former guideline on fraud. In *Hartridge* [2011] 2 Cr App R (S) 543 the offender had contacted women through a dating site and gained access to their bank accounts. The offences were treated as confidence frauds (six counts) as well as three counts of theft. The total sum obtained was no more than £53,000, the guidelines for loss between £20,000 and £100,000 indicating either a starting point of three years' imprisonment (range two to five years) or a starting point of four years (range three to six years). The Court of Appeal said that it was open to debate which was the correct bracket but that the judge's sentence of four years' imprisonment on a guilty plea was too high and it was reduced to 30 months. See also *Chaytor* [2011] 2 Cr App R (S) 653 at **B6.6**. Four years was the correct sentence for a 65-year-old confidence trickster in *Clugston* [2012] EWCA Crim 98, who pleaded guilty to numerous offences of fraud. He offered to supply cheap champagne, received payment, but provided no goods. The total loss was £19,500. The Court of Appeal upheld a sentence of 54 months following a late guilty plea in *Kalian* [2012] 2 Cr App R (S) 513 where the offender had been selling useless alarm systems to elderly people. In *Yates* [2011] 1 Cr App R (S) 112 the Court of Appeal upheld a sentence of 30 months' imprisonment, on a guilty plea, for a mortgage fraud. The Court of Appeal had regard to the guideline (although this came into effect shortly after sentence was passed). Davis J said that in cases where a loan has been obtained by fraud the relevant sentencing considerations are (i) whether one or more transactions are involved, (ii) whether the fraud is committed by a professional person or otherwise in breach of trust, (iii) the nature of the fraud and the means used to commit it, (iv) whether it was isolated, or involved ongoing deception, (v) the amount of money sought or obtained, (vi) the amount of loss, (vii) whether the offender was involved with others, and (viii) whether at the time there was an intention to repay or not. Thirty months' imprisonment was upheld for an identity fraud in *McGrath* [2013] 1 Cr App R (S) 560 (108), where the offender pleaded guilty to obtaining credit cards in the name of another and using them for purchases totalling nearly £22,000. Two months was upheld following a guilty plea in *Dittman* [2013] 1 Cr App R (S) 113 (21) for a fraud by representation where one offender impersonated the other in taking the practical part of the driving test. For an offence of possession of an article for use in fraud, a sentence of eight months was appropriate after a trial in *Graduiara* [2013] 1 Cr App R (S) 282 (50); the offender was in possession of a 'Lebanese loop', a device used to retain a person's bank card within an automatic cash machine. See also *Ciomaga* [2013] 1 Cr App R (S) 553 (106) and *Munteanu* [2013] 1 Cr App R (S) 555 (107).

B5.8   **Benefit Fraud etc.**   Most cases involving the dishonest obtaining of social security benefits or payments are dealt with summarily under the Social Security Administration Act 1992, s.111A (see **B16.53**). More serious cases will be prosecuted under the Fraud Act 2006. The relevant definitive sentencing guideline is *Fraud, Bribery and Money Laundering* (see Supplement, SG-472), which is applicable to all individual offenders aged 18 or over and to organisations sentenced on or after 1 October 2014. The former guideline was considered in *Turner* [2011] 2 Cr App R (S) 102, where 14 months' imprisonment was upheld. The offender obtained £33,952 in various benefits by failing to disclose her income and assets. The Court of Appeal noted that this was a case of greed, involving a woman with a sound financial base, and was not a fraud perpetrated against a background of hardship. The fraud was prolonged and repeated. The aggravating features of the case made selection of a sentencing starting point above the normal range appropriate.

Dishonesty in Fraud Cases

B5.9   The concept of dishonesty in fraud cases is broadly similar to that which applies to offences of dishonesty under the Theft Act 1968 (see **B4.51** *et seq.*), subject to the caveat that the Theft Act 1968, s. 2, is not directly applicable to any offence that does not involve either theft or an intent to steal. The test for dishonesty in fraud cases is thus based (as it was in deception cases) on *Ghosh* [1982] QB 1053 (see *Cornelius* [2012] EWCA Crim 500 and **B4.54**).

This arguably means that D might in theory be found guilty of fraud, even where he acts with a view to securing possession of property to which he genuinely believes he has a claim of right, and in respect of which he would have had an unqualified defence under the Theft Act 1968, s. 2(1)(a), had he been charged instead with theft. This is because a jury might label D's *methods* dishonest, because they involve lies or abuse of a position of trust, even though they could not have labelled him dishonest had he openly helped himself to the property in question.

In deception cases, few such problems seem to have been caused by dependency on the *Ghosh* test, because in most respects this test is more generous to defendants than anything in s. 2(1). Belief in a moral claim of right might for example suffice to negate dishonesty under *Ghosh*, as might D's belief that his conduct, although irregular or unlawful, would nevertheless be tolerated by ordinary right thinking people (*Lightfoot* (1993) 97 Cr App R 24). In *Woolven* (1983) 77 Cr App R 231, where D was charged with attempting to obtain property by deception, the court held that a direction based on s. 2(1)(a) would have added nothing to the *Ghosh* direction actually given in that case, because the latter direction, 'seems likely to us to cover all occasions when a s. 2(1)(a) direction might otherwise have been desirable'; and yet according to *Wootton* [1990] Crim LR 201 a trial judge in a theft case must always direct the jury on s. 2(1)(a) if a claim of right is raised.

The wording of the Fraud Act 2006 arguably encourages a court or jury to focus on the honesty or dishonesty of D's methods, rather than on the honesty or dishonesty of his ulterior purpose. Section 2 of the Act, for example, deals with fraud by *dishonestly making a false representation* with a view to making a gain etc., rather than making a false representation with a view to *dishonestly making a gain*, etc. In *Clarke* [1996] Crim LR 824, however, it was held that D's lies concerning his experience and background did not *ipso facto* make him guilty of obtaining a pecuniary advantage (employment) by deception, because the jury ought to have been directed also to consider D's argument that he could do the job properly and intended to do so. It is submitted that a similar approach should be adopted in cases of fraud.

Intent to Gain or Cause Loss

Another *mens rea* element common to all variants of the fraud offence is that D must act *either* with intent to gain for himself or another *or* with intent to cause loss to another or expose another to a risk of loss. The intent in each case is ulterior. It does not matter whether any gain, loss or exposure actually occurs.

B5.10

Fraud Act 2006, s. 5

(1) The references to gain and loss in sections 2 to 4 are to be read in accordance with this section.
(2) 'Gain' and 'loss'—
　(a) extend only to gain or loss in money or other property;
　(b) include any such gain or loss whether temporary or permanent;
　and 'property' means any property whether real or personal (including things in action and other intangible property).
(3) 'Gain' includes a gain by keeping what one has, as well as a gain by getting what one does not have.
(4) 'Loss' includes a loss by not getting what one might get, as well as a loss by parting with what one has.

It has been held, in cases decided under the Theft Act 1968, s. 34(2)(a), that D may act with 'intent to gain' even where he merely seeks to acquire property that is owing to him (*A-G's Ref (No. 1 of 2001)* [2002] 3 All ER 849), although in the context of a fraud charge D would doubtless argue that he could not have acted dishonestly in such circumstances (see **B5.9**). In *Eden* (1971) 55 Cr App R 193, a false-accounting case, it was emphasised that an intent to gain or lose on a temporary basis may suffice under s. 34(2)(a); but in *Golechha* [1989] 3 All ER 908, it was held that the falsification of bills of exchange with intent to postpone the enforcement of a debt owing to a bank was not made with a view to gain, because it was designed simply to postpone the enforcement of an obligation. *Golechha* is widely considered to be wrongly decided, because clearly one purpose of the falsification in that case was to enable D to keep (if only temporarily) property that would otherwise have had to be expended in meeting his obligations. See also *Lee Cheung Wing v The Queen* (1992) 94 Cr App R 355 (**B6.13**). In *Gilbert* [2012] EWCA Crim 2392, the issue was whether an offence of fraud by false representation could be committed on the basis of lies told when opening a bank account. Such an account is not of itself 'money or other property', but it was argued that there was a possibility of gains arising from future legitimate property developments, using the account. In the Court of Appeal's view, however, the link between the false representation and any such prospective gain was simply too vague and tenuous to base a conviction upon it.

B5.11 **Jurisdictional Issues**   One consequence of fraud offences being 'conduct crimes' (see **B5.4**) is that where D is guilty of fraudulent conduct abroad, with intent to deceive a victim within England and Wales, or with intent to gain or cause loss etc. within England and Wales, no constituent element of fraud is necessarily committed in England and Wales. The offence may be completed (and thus committed) entirely abroad. The CJA 1993, part I, applies English criminal law to transnational offences of fraud or dishonesty if, but only if, a 'relevant event' takes place within the jurisdiction — and the fraudulent obtaining of property etc. following a false representation or abuse of position etc. is not itself a 'relevant event' (see **A8.5** and **A8.12** *et seq.*).

The Fraud Act 2006, sch. 1, para. 25, addresses this point (if only in part) by inserting a new s. 2(1A) into the CJA 1993. This provides that, in relation to an offence of fraud, a 'relevant event' includes:

(a) if the fraud involved an intention to make a gain *and the gain occurred*, that occurrence; and
(b) if the fraud involved an intention to cause a loss or to expose another to a risk of loss *and the loss occurred*, that occurrence. [emphasis added]

Clearly, however, this will not assist the prosecution in cases where D intended by his conduct abroad to make a gain or cause a loss within England and Wales, but failed to do so; nor does it assist even where D actually succeeds in exposing V to a risk of loss in England. This deliberate omission is curious, because it conflicts with a strong trend towards the assumption of jurisdiction over acts such as conspiracies abroad that are intended to cause, but fail to cause, harm within the jurisdiction. See *Liangsiriprasert v USA* [1991] 1 AC 225 and **A5.59**.

FRAUD BY FALSE REPRESENTATION

B5.12 Fraud Act 2006, s. 2

(1) A person is in breach of this section if he—
    (a) dishonestly makes a false representation, and
    (b) intends, by making the representation—
        (i) to make a gain for himself or another, or
        (ii) to cause loss to another or to expose another to a risk of loss.
(2) A representation is false if—
    (a) it is untrue or misleading, and
    (b) the person making it knows that it is, or might be, untrue or misleading.
(3) 'Representation' means any representation as to fact or law, including a representation as to the state of mind of—
    (a) the person making the representation, or
    (b) any other person.
(4) A representation may be express or implied.
(5) For the purposes of this section a representation may be regarded as made if it (or anything implying it) is submitted in any form to any system or device designed to receive, convey or respond to communications (with or without human intervention).

Elements

This provision must be read in conjunction with s. 1 of the Act (**B5.4**) because it creates a variant of the basic fraud offence, not an offence in its own right. Intent to gain and intent to cause loss are examined in **B5.10**. Dishonesty is examined at **B5.9**.   **B5.13**

The *actus reus* of a fraud of this kind consists solely of making a false representation, either to another person or (by subsection (5)) to a 'system or device'. No deception need result from such a representation, and no gain or loss need result. Because it is a conduct crime, the offence may be complete even if the representation is rejected out of hand, or treated with derision by those to whom it is addressed. Indeed, as with a blackmail demand, a false representation is presumably 'made' as soon as it is uttered. If that is so, there is no need for it even to be communicated to the intended recipients. An offence under s. 1 may then be complete even if (for example) the letter containing the offending representation is lost or intercepted in the post, or the person to whom it is directed fails to hear or understand it: *Treacy v DPP* [1971] AC 537 (see **B5.48**); and see also *DPP v Collins* [2006] 4 All ER 602.

Section 2 defines the elements that make up a false representation. By s. 2(2) a statement that is literally true may be treated as false if it is misleading, although this is complicated by the introduction in s. 2(2)(b) of what is in effect a *mens rea* requirement masquerading as part of the *actus reus*. An honest mistake may give rise to an untrue or misleading representation, but not to a 'false' one.

By s. 2(3), a representation may concern matters of fact or of law, and these must no doubt be matters of existing fact or law. A promise does not become a false representation merely because it is later broken; but (as was the case under the law governing deception) a representation may be considered false if it misrepresents the current intentions or state of mind of the person making it or anyone else, so a promise involves a false representation if D never intended to keep that promise in the first place.

Where D dishonestly tenders a stolen or forged credit or debit card to pay for goods or services, or shows another person's season ticket or bus pass in order to use facilities or services to which he is not entitled, it is clear that he makes a false representation. Even if he says nothing, he impliedly represents that the card or season ticket is genuine, that he is the authorised user, and that he is still entitled to use it. The same may be true (under subsection (5)) where D enters a security code, password and/or PIN so as to represent to a 'system or device' that he is authorised to access an account or use a facility that he is not in fact authorised to access or use.   **B5.14**

Another classic example of an implied representation is that made by a customer who dines in a restaurant or stays in a hotel. He does not need to state that he will pay for the food and service at the end, because an inference to that effect will in any case arise from his behaviour. Cf. *DPP v Ray* [1974] AC 370.

The making of a false representation may itself be proved by inference. Where an elderly or other vulnerable person has paid D vastly more for a job or product (such as gardening work) than it was worth, it may be open to a court or jury to infer that D must dishonestly have misrepresented the value of that job or product, even if there is no direct evidence of any such misrepresentation (*Greig* [2010] EWCA Crim 1183).

Where an unidentified imposter presented himself to take a driving test in D's name it could be inferred that D was complicit in any false representations made by that person with a view to gaining a pass certificate in his name (*Idrees v DPP* [2011] EWHC 624 (Admin)).

False Representations in Cheques   Tendering a forged or stolen cheque (or one drawn on a defunct account) will inevitably involve the making of a false representation; but where D tenders a genuine cheque in payment for goods or services, the position would appear to be much the same as it was under the law relating to deception. It is tempting to suggest that, by   **B5.15**

tendering the cheque, D represents that it will be paid by his bank in due course; but this cannot suffice as a false representation, under either the old law or the new, because it is a representation or promise concerning future events.

As the Court of Appeal pointed out in *Gilmartin* [1983] QB 953, one must identify a false representation as to an existing fact. Clearly D represents that the account is still active and that he is not barred from using it. But one cannot argue that merely by drawing the cheque D makes any representation as to whether his account currently contains adequate funds to meet it. If D tenders a cheque towards the end of the month he may know that his account is badly over-drawn; but he may also expect it to be refreshed the next day by his monthly salary. Indeed, the issue of a post-dated cheque might be seen to imply that the account is currently insufficient to meet it. The solution adopted in *Gilmartin* was that:

> ...by the simple giving of a cheque, whether postdated or not, the drawer impliedly represents that the state of facts existing at the date of delivery of the cheque is such that in the ordinary course the cheque will on presentation for payment on or after the date specified in the cheque, be met.

Arguably this differs only in phrasing from a promise that the cheque will be honoured on pre-sentation, but such is the law. What is clear is that account may be taken of existing expecta-tions, such as salaries due to be credited, standing orders due to be debited, and perhaps D's credit rating with his bank.

The representations usually associated with issuing a cheque may sometimes be overridden by express words. D may, for example, indicate that he is unsure about the state of his current account, but assure V that he will indemnify him in the event of any dishonour. Each case must thus be judged on its own facts. Thus, in *United Arab Emirates v Allen* [2012] 1 WLR 3419, the Administrative Court refused to infer that a mortgagor who issued a cheque for the full amount of the loan by way of additional security for that loan thereby represented that it would 'in the ordinary course' be honoured on presentation; if she had funds of that kind at her disposal, she would not have needed the loan in the first place.

B5.16   There will not ordinarily be any fraud if D genuinely expects sufficient funds to be credited to the account in time to meet the cheque on presentation; but in *Greenstein* [1975] 1 All ER 1 the appellants drew cheques for sums vastly exceeding their credit limits in order to subscribe for the largest possible number of shares in oversubscribed company flotations. They relied on being allocated only a small percentage of the shares applied for, and on the issuing houses' refund cheques arriving in time to ensure their own cheques would be honoured. They had been warned that such tactics were considered improper, and in some cases had given an express undertaking that their cheques would be honoured on first presentation (something of which they could not in fact be sure and which did not always happen). In those circumstances they were held to have committed offences under the Theft Act 1968, s. 15. Arguably, they would now be considered guilty of fraud by false representation.

B5.17   **Representations made to Systems or Devices**   An important difference between the old and new law concerns untrue or misleading representations that are intended to operate on ATMs, 'chip and pin' card readers, computer systems or other devices. Section 2(5) of the Fraud Act 2006 enables the offence of fraud to apply in such cases. The old law on deception was generally thought to be inapplicable in such cases on the basis that 'a machine cannot be deceived'. The Fraud Act does not of course state that a machine *can* be deceived, but only that it may be an offence dishonestly to supply a system or device with false information.

Section 2(5) also provides that the submission of a representation to an appropriate system or device, etc., may be treated as a 'making' of that representation. In the case of an 'online' fraud, this arguably should not include a case in which D merely types and saves his representation onto his own computer disk, but only one in which he has actually clicked on the 'send' button. In the lat-ter case, however, it may not matter that the system to which it is sent fails to process or receive it.

FRAUD BY FAILING TO DISCLOSE INFORMATION

Fraud Act 2006, s. 3　　　　　　　　　　　　　　　　　**B5.18**

A person is in breach of this section if he—

(a) dishonestly fails to disclose to another person information which he is under a legal duty to disclose, and

(b) intends, by failing to disclose the information—
   (i) to make a gain for himself or another, or
   (ii) to cause loss to another or to expose another to a risk of loss.

This is not an offence in its own right, but another variant of the offence of fraud under s. 1 (see **B5.4** *et seq.*). Intent to gain and intent to cause loss are examined in **B5.10**. Dishonesty is examined at **B5.9**.

Under the Theft Acts, liability for deception offences could be incurred in some cases through dishonest omissions to provide correct information (*Firth* (1989) 91 Cr App R 217). The Fraud Act 2006, s. 3, introduces a potentially broader concept of fraud through non-disclosure, but only in cases where there is a legal duty to disclose. 'Legal duty' is not defined in the Act, but the Law Commission provided this explanation in its Report (Cm. 5560, 2002) at paras. 7.28 and 7.29:

> Such a duty may derive from statute (such as the provisions governing company prospectuses), from the fact that the transaction in question is one of the utmost good faith (such as a contract of insurance), from the express or implied terms of a contract, from the custom of a particular trade or market, or from the existence of a fiduciary relationship between the parties (such as that of agent and principal).
>
> For this purpose there is a legal duty to disclose information not only if the defendant's failure to disclose it gives the victim a cause of action for damages, but also if the law gives the victim a right to set aside any change in his or her legal position to which he or she may consent as a result of the non-disclosure. For example, a person in a fiduciary position has a duty to disclose material information when entering into a contract with his or her beneficiary, in the sense that a failure to make such disclosure will entitle the beneficiary to rescind the contract and to reclaim any property transferred under it.

Whether such a duty arises on any given set of facts (assuming the jury are satisfied as to those facts) must be for the judge to decide as a question of law. Section 3 does not state whether D must be aware of his legal duty. Ignorance of the law is ordinarily no defence to any criminal charge, but may have a bearing (as in theft cases) on any question of dishonesty. If D knows he has a legal duty to make disclosure, it is that much harder for him to deny that his failure to do so was dishonest.

Non-disclosure and Misrepresentation

If D took advantage of V's misunderstanding, but was under no legal duty to disclose informa-　**B5.19**
tion to correct him, it may still be possible to argue that D is guilty of fraud by false (implied) representation (see **B5.14**). In *Rai* [2000] 1 Cr App R 233, D failed to inform his local authority that his disabled mother had died, lest he should lose the benefit of a home improvement grant that he had recently obtained on the basis of her needs. By saying nothing he impliedly represented that her needs were unchanged. But where a recipient of benefits dishonestly fails to disclose income, etc. that he is legally required to disclose, as in *El Mashta* [2010] EWCA Crim 2595, fraud by failure to disclose may be a more appropriate charge.

FRAUD BY ABUSE OF POSITION

Fraud Act 2006, s. 4　　　　　　　　　　　　　　　　　**B5.20**

(1) A person is in breach of this section if he—
   (a) occupies a position in which he is expected to safeguard, or not to act against, the financial interests of another person,

465

(b) dishonestly abuses that position, and
(c) intends, by means of the abuse of that position—
  (i)   to make a gain for himself or another, or
  (ii) to cause loss to another or to expose another to a risk of loss.
(2) A person may be regarded as having abused his position even though his conduct consisted of an omission rather than an act.

This is a variant of the offence of fraud under s. 1; not an offence in its own right. Intent to gain and intent to cause loss are examined in **B5.10**. Dishonesty is examined at **B5.9**.

Section 4 is in theory broader than the Law Commission's proposed offence of fraud by 'dishonest *and secret* abuse of position', but in practice nothing is likely to turn on this, because such abuse is most unlikely to take place openly.

The clear intention of the provision is to cover the dishonest abuse of a position of financial trust or responsibility, including that of a trustee, company director or executor, but it is not confined to such fiduciary relationships and would extend to frauds committed by employees, including acts that could not be prosecuted as theft; e.g., where a cinema projectionist copies newly released films for private profit (cf. *Scott v Metropolitan Police Commissioner* [1975] AC 819), where an officer or employee of a company or business clones software or leaks confidential client information to a rival business, or where hotel or catering staff supply (and retain the profits from) their own food or drink, thereby depriving their employer of profits that would otherwise have been made from such sales (cf. *Cooke* [1986] AC 909; *Doukas* [1978] 1 All ER 1071).

Liability for an omission might arise where, for example, a company director or employee dishonestly fails to secure or negotiate for a contract, lease or other business opportunity for the company, with the object of later securing it for himself. Whether given behaviour amounts to an abuse of D's position must largely be a question of fact for a jury, but it would be proper in many cases for a judge to make rulings or give directions as to the existence of fiduciary duties or other relationships. The abuse of information etc. legitimately acquired in connection with a *former* position of trust appears not to be covered by s. 4.

Where D has abused his position by dishonestly appropriating V's property for himself, a charge of theft may sometimes be easier to establish than a charge of fraud. In *Hinks* [2001] 2 AC 241, for example, D's liability for theft did not depend on whether her position as V's carer was one in which she was 'expected to safeguard or not to act against' V's financial interests; and indeed it seems doubtful whether it was such a position.

POSSESSION OR CONTROL OF ARTICLES FOR USE IN FRAUD

B5.21   Fraud Act 2006, s. 6

(1) A person is guilty of an offence if he has in his possession or under his control any article for use in the course of or in connection with any fraud.

Possession and control are not defined in the Act but in *Tarley* [2012] EWCA Crim 464 the Court of Appeal observed that case law on possession of drugs or firearms may assist, and that liability may arise on the basis of participation in a fraudulent joint enterprise involving the article in question, even where D lacks physical possession or control of it. An 'article' includes for this purpose (or for the purposes of the PACE 1984, s. 1(7)(b)) any program or data held in electronic form (Fraud Act 2006, s. 8(1)). This addresses the importance of computer technology in the perpetration of frauds. This offence complements the offence of having custody or control of a false instrument with intent (Forgery and Counterfeiting Act 1981, s. 5; see **B6.51**) and to some extent supplants the offence of 'going equipped' under the Theft Act 1968, s. 25 (see **B4.151**). The latter provision is amended by the Fraud Act so that it no longer applies to the possession of articles intended for use in a 'cheat'. In its application to offences of fraud, the new offence has a much wider ambit than s. 25, which did not (and in its application to burglary or theft still does not) apply to articles possessed by D at his place of abode. Moreover, the only kind of 'cheat' to which it related was an offence under the Theft Act 1968, s. 15, whereas the new offence may apply to the possession, anywhere, of articles of any description that are intended for use in respect of any fraud offence. On the other hand, the possession of articles that have *previously* been used for such purposes does not fall within the scope of this offence (*Sakalauskas* [2014] 1 All ER 1231; see also *Ellames* [1974] 3 All ER 130 and **B4.159**).

Procedure, Sentence and Jurisdiction

Fraud Act 2006, s. 6   **B5.22**

(2) A person guilty of an offence under this section is liable—
   (a) on summary conviction, to imprisonment for a term not exceeding [six] months or to a fine not exceeding the statutory maximum (or to both);
   (b) on conviction on indictment, to imprisonment for a term not exceeding 5 years or to a fine (or to both).

When tried on indictment, this is normally a class 3 offence, but see CPD XIII, para. B (see Supplement, **PD-97**) for the additional factors that the court considers on allocation. It is a Group A offence for jurisdiction purposes under the CJA 1993, part I (see **A8.10**). Company officers may be proceeded against and punished for any such offence committed by the company with their consent or connivance (Fraud Act 2006, s. 12(2)). As to the position where a body corporate is managed by its members, see s. 12(3).

The relevant definitive sentencing guideline is *Fraud, Bribery and Money Laundering* (see Supplement, **SG-472**), which is applicable to all offenders aged 18 or over sentenced on or after 1 October 2014. There is a separate part of the guideline for corporate offenders.

MAKING OR SUPPLYING ARTICLES FOR USE IN FRAUD

Fraud Act 2006, s. 7   **B5.23**

(1) A person is guilty of an offence if he makes, adapts, supplies or offers to supply any article—
   (a) knowing that it is designed or adapted for use in the course of or in connection with fraud, or
   (b) intending it to be used to commit, or assist in the commission of, fraud.

As to the meaning of the term, 'article', see the Fraud Act 2006, s. 8(1) and **B5.21**. The offence created by s. 7(1) overlaps substantially with offences such as forgery or copying a false instrument (see **B6.36** and **B6.41**) but could also be used to prosecute persons who make, adapt, advertise or supply devices such as 'black boxes' for the purpose of falsifying readings on electricity meters.

Procedure, Sentence and Jurisdiction

Fraud Act 2006, s. 7   **B5.24**

(2) A person guilty of an offence under this section is liable—
   (a) on summary conviction, to imprisonment for a term not exceeding [six] months or to a fine not exceeding the statutory maximum (or to both);
   (b) on conviction on indictment, to imprisonment for a term not exceeding 10 years or to a fine (or to both).

When tried on indictment, this is normally a class 3 offence, but see CPD XIII, para. B (see Supplement, **PD-97**) for the additional factors that the court considers on allocation. It is a Group A offence for jurisdiction purposes under the CJA 1993, part I (see **A8.10**). Company officers may be proceeded against and punished for any such offence committed by the company with their consent or connivance (Fraud Act 2006, s. 12(2)). As to the position where a body corporate is managed by its members, see s. 12(3).

The relevant definitive sentencing guideline is *Fraud, Bribery and Money Laundering* (see Supplement, **SG-472**), which is applicable to all offenders aged 18 or over sentenced on or after 1 October 2014. There is a separate part of the guideline for corporate offenders.

PARTICIPATING IN FRAUDULENT BUSINESS
CARRIED ON BY SOLE TRADER ETC.

B5.25   Fraud Act 2006, s. 9

(1) A person is guilty of an offence if he is knowingly a party to the carrying on of a business to which this section applies.

(2) This section applies to a business which is carried on—
   (a) by a person who is outside the reach of section 993 of the Companies Act 2006 (offence of fraudulent trading), and
   (b) with intent to defraud creditors of any person or for any other fraudulent purpose.

(3) The following are within the reach of that section —
   (a) a company (as defined in section 1(1) of the Companies Act 2006);
   (b) a person to whom that section applies (with or without adaptations or modifications) as if the person were a company;
   (c) a person exempted from the application of that section.

(4) [Applies only to Northern Ireland.]

(5) 'Fraudulent purpose' has the same meaning as in that section.

Procedure, Sentence and Jurisdiction

B5.26   Fraud Act 2006, s. 9

(6) A person guilty of an offence under this section is liable—
   (a) on summary conviction, to imprisonment for a term not exceeding [six] months or to a fine not exceeding the statutory maximum (or to both);
   (b) on conviction on indictment, to imprisonment for a term not exceeding 10 years or to a fine (or to both).

When tried on indictment, this is normally a class 3 offence, but see CPD XIII, para. B (see Supplement, **PD-97**) for the additional factors that the court considers on allocation. It is a Group A offence for jurisdiction purposes under the CJA 1993, part I (see **A8.10**), whereas fraudulent trading under the Companies Act 2006 is not. The maximum penalty of ten years' imprisonment is higher than that formerly applicable to fraudulent trading by companies, but the Fraud Act 2006, s. 10, increases the penalty for that offence, so the two offences now carry identical penalties.

Elements

B5.27 The offence of fraudulent trading by registered companies or by other legal persons to which the Companies Act 2006, s. 993 applies (including limited liability partnerships) is dealt with at **B7.7** *et seq*.

The Fraud Act 2006, s. 9, gives effect to a recommendation of the Law Commission in its Report on Multiple Offending (Cm 5609, 2002) by adopting the Companies Act offence and applying it to fraudulent trading committed by unincorporated businesses such as those operated by sole traders or partnership firms, or by persons (such as employees) connected with such businesses.

As to the carrying on of a business, see **B7.11**. As to intent to defraud creditors and other fraudulent purposes, see **B7.13**.

OBTAINING SERVICES DISHONESTLY

B5.28   Fraud Act 2006, s. 11

(1) A person is guilty of an offence under this section if he obtains services for himself or another—
   (a) by a dishonest act, and
   (b) in breach of subsection (2).

(2) A person obtains services in breach of this subsection if—
   (a) they are made available on the basis that payment has been, is being or will be made for or in respect of them,

    (b) he obtains them without any payment having been made for or in respect of them or without payment having been made in full, and

    (c) when he obtains them, he knows—

        (i) that they are being made available on the basis described in paragraph (a), or

        (ii) that they might be, but intends that payment will not be made, or will not be made in full.

Indictment

Statement of Offence   **B5.29**

Obtaining services dishonestly, contrary to the Fraud Act 2006, section 11(1).

Particulars of Offence

A on or about the…day of…2007, dishonestly entered the…Cinema in…without paying the required entrance fee, and viewed [a part of] the film then being screened, knowing that payment was required and intending that such payment would not be made.

Procedure, Sentence and Jurisdiction

Fraud Act 2006, s. 11   **B5.30**

(3) A person guilty of an offence under this section is liable—

    (a) on summary conviction, to imprisonment for a term not exceeding [six] months or to a fine not exceeding the statutory maximum (or to both);

    (b) on conviction on indictment, to imprisonment for a term not exceeding 5 years or to a fine (or to both).

When tried on indictment, this is normally a class 3 offence, but see CPD XIII, para. B (see Supplement, **PD-97**) for the additional factors that the court considers on allocation. It is a Group A offence for jurisdiction purposes under the CJA 1993, part I (see **A8.10**). Company officers may be proceeded against and punished for any such offence committed by the company with their consent or connivance (Fraud Act 2006, s. 12(2)). As to the position where a body corporate is managed by its members, see s. 12(3).

This may be committed in circumstances that otherwise could be charged as an offence contrary to s. 1 or may be more akin to making off without payment. If the former, the court should apply the appropriate fraud guideline (see **B5.7**); if the latter, the guideline for that offence in the *Magistrates' Court Sentencing Guidelines* should be used (see Supplement, **SG-298**).

Elements

This offence differs in several respects from fraud itself, and is in part derived from the offence **B5.31** of obtaining services by deception contrary to the Theft Act 1978, s. 1, which it replaces. It resembles the old offence in that it requires the dishonest obtaining of services, and is therefore a 'result crime', in contrast to fraud itself, which is a conduct crime. It also resembles the old offence in that it has no application to the obtaining of services other than those that are provided in return for payment.

In most other respects, however, the new offence is broader than the old. It does not require any deception, nor indeed does it require any fraudulent representation. If, for example, D sneaks into a cinema to watch a film without paying, he may commit the offence, assuming he is dishonest and succeeds in viewing at least part of the film.

Obtaining Services The terms 'services' and 'obtaining' are not defined in the Fraud Act **B5.32** 2006, but must bear a similar meaning to that given in the Theft Act 1978, s. 1(2), in which an obtaining of services was defined as the conferring of a benefit by doing an act or permitting an act to be done. As under the old law, the provision of gratuitous services is excluded, even if the whole basis of the fraud is that D is entitled to receive them free of charge, when he is not.

Also excluded is the taking by D of a benefit that V has no intention of providing to anyone. If, for example, D sneaks aboard a lorry or freight train, and obtains a free ride, he commits no offence under s. 11, because the haulage company or freight train operator does not provide such rides, even for payment. What is not excluded is the provision of a service in return for a payment that could not be enforced in a court of law. It may not be rape dishonestly to secure the services of a prostitute without intending to pay her, and D cannot then be guilty of making off without payment if he 'does a runner' (see B5.38), but under the Fraud Act 2006, s. 11, offences could be committed in such circumstances.

B5.33 Where D resorts to false representations in order to obtain (or attempt to obtain) a service, it might sometimes be more appropriate to consider a charge of fraud. According to the explanatory notes accompanying the Act, the offence under s. 11 may be committed where D uses false credit card details or other false personal information in order to obtain access to a subscription service on the internet. With respect, reliance on such a charge might cause difficulty because the prosecution would have to prove full payment was not made and that D 'intended that payment would not be made, or would not be made in full'. D might argue that his plan was for the service to be paid for — not by him, but by the lawful holder of the credit card or by the bank which issued it. Indeed, payment may already have been made in that way by the time the service was provided to him. It might accordingly be safer in such a case to charge D with fraud on the basis of a false representation (namely the implied representation that he was entitled to use the credit card). Proving an intent to gain or cause loss should not be difficult in such a case, because D certainly intends to keep his own money and he must realise that someone else will suffer a corresponding loss, even if he does not know (or care) who that loser will be.

In *Halai* [1983] Crim LR 624, the Court of Appeal held that a building society had not provided services merely by allowing D to open a savings account because building societies do not charge any fees for such accounts. The position would be different if D dishonestly opens a current or credit card account with a bank which applies charges to such accounts (*Shortland* [1995] Crim LR 893; *Sofroniou* [2004] QB 1218). It was also held in *Halai* that a mortgage advance falls outside the definition of 'services', but this ruling was abrogated (in respect of matters occurring on or after 18 December 1996) by the Theft (Amendment) Act 1996, s. 4. Even in respect of matters occurring before that date, it was held on several occasions that *Halai* should no longer be followed (see, e.g., *Graham* [1997] 1 Cr App R 302, and *Smith (Wallace Duncan) (No. 4)* [2004] QB 1418).

In one respect, the new offence is actually narrower than the old. Under the Theft Act 1978, s. 1, the deception practised by D did not have to concern the issue of payment. If D dishonestly obtained a service that he was not qualified to obtain (e.g., by attending a 'members only' event) he could be guilty of the offence, even if he paid the full entry fee. Under the new law, however, D can be guilty *only* if he intends that payment will not be made, or will not be made in full.

MAKING OFF WITHOUT PAYMENT

Definition
B5.34 Theft Act 1978, s. 3

(1) Subject to subsection (3) below, a person who, knowing that payment on the spot for any goods supplied or service done is required or expected from him, dishonestly makes off without having paid as required or expected and with intent to avoid payment of the amount due shall be guilty of an offence.
(2) For purposes of this section 'payment on the spot' includes payment at the time of collecting goods on which work has been done or in respect of which service has been provided.
(3) Subsection (1) above shall not apply where the supply of the goods or the doing of the service is contrary to law, or where the service done is such that payment is not legally enforceable.

Procedure
B5.35 Making off without payment is triable either way (s. 4(1)). When tried on indictment it is normally a class 3 offence, but see CPD XIII, para. B (see Supplement, **PD-97**) for the additional factors that the court considers on allocation.

Indictment

Statement of Offence

Making off without payment contrary to section 3(1) of the Theft Act 1978.

Particulars of Offence

A on or about the. . .day of. . ., knowing that payment on the spot of £. . .was required of him for petrol supplied to him by V, dishonestly made off without having paid the amount due as so required and with intent to avoid payment thereof.

Sentence

The maximum penalty is two years (Theft Act 1978, s. 4(2)(b)) on indictment; six months, a fine not exceeding the statutory maximum, or both, summarily. There is no guideline judgment reported for an offence under the Theft Act 1978, s. 3, when tried on indictment. For sentencing guidelines for offences of deception generally, see B5.7. For sentencing guidelines for theft offences, see B4.5 to B4.9.

The *Magistrates' Court Sentencing Guidelines* provide guidelines for this offence when tried summarily (see Supplement, SG-298).

Overlap with Other Offences

Because of the relative ease with which the offence of making off without payment can be proved, it may be charged in circumstances where a more serious charge such as theft might otherwise have been pressed. If, for example, it is clear that D dishonestly made off without paying for his meal, or for the petrol which he put into his car, the Theft Act 1978, s. 3, provides the obvious charge. It may be that D never intended to pay, and therefore committed theft or fraud, but this will be far harder to prove in the absence of a confession or other evidence of D's state of mind at the time of the original obtaining.

There may also be some overlap between the offence of making off without payment under s. 3 and that of obtaining services dishonestly (B5.28), e.g., where D tricks a taxi driver and then makes off. If, however, D deceives V into accepting a worthless cheque in payment, or into allowing him to 'put a cheque in the post' the following day, one of the other charges must be preferred, because D now leaves with V's consent and V no longer expects payment on the spot when D 'makes off' (*Hammond* [1982] Crim LR 611; *Vincent* [2001] 1 WLR 1172). In *Morris* [2014] 1 WLR 16, Leveson LJ said:

> If a passenger were to explain (honestly) to the taxi driver that he had to enter his house in order to obtain the fare, the moment for payment would be deferred for him to do so. A decision not to return to the taxi would mean that, from that moment, the passenger is making off without payment.

With respect, failing to return cannot properly be called 'making off' unless it involves continued movement away from the place where payment is expected. Hiding behind a wall is not 'making off'. But the offence may indeed be committed if, having been allowed to leave the cab to fetch payment, D changes his mind and runs off down the road. Payment at the cab is still expected in such a case, even if the driver agreed to defer it for a few minutes (see *Vincent* at [12]).

Payment on the Spot for Goods Supplied or Service Done

The phrase 'payment on the spot' used in the Theft Act 1978, s. 3(1), is partially explained in s. 3(2). The 'spot' in question is the place where payment is required, and this will usually be the premises where the transaction takes place, but it may sometimes mean something narrower (see B5.40).

Under the Theft Act 1978, s. 5(2), 'goods' in s. 3(1) is to be interpreted in accordance with the Theft Act 1968, s. 34(2)(b), and it can be assumed that 'service' bears the same meaning as in s. 1 of the 1978 Act.

The required payment must be one which is legally enforceable (Theft Act 1978, s. 3(3)). It may be possible to commit an offence of dishonestly obtaining services by tricking another person into entering into a legally unenforceable transaction; but the evasion of an unenforceable obligation, whether by deception or by making off, cannot be an offence.

Meaning of 'Making Off'

B5.40 In *Brooks* (1982) 76 Cr App R 66, it was held that the words 'dishonestly makes off' are easily understandable by a jury, and ordinarily require no elaboration in a summing-up; but such elaboration may be needed in some cases. If D practises a deception, as a result of which V allows him to leave without paying, this cannot be an offence under s. 3, and a jury must be directed accordingly. As Pill LJ explained in *Vincent* [2001] 1 WLR 1172: 'If the expectation [of payment on the spot] is defeated by an agreement, it cannot be said to exist. The fact that the agreement is obtained dishonestly does not re-instate the expectation.' A charge of fraud may be more appropriate here (cf. *Hammond* [1982] Crim LR 611).

'Making off' ordinarily means leaving the premises concerned, and if D is stopped at the exit he will usually have committed only an attempt (*McDavitt* [1981] Crim LR 843), but this must be a question of fact. If, for example, D slips away from the top-floor restaurant in a department store, without paying for his meal at the counter, and is caught on the ground floor before leaving the building, there can be little doubt that he has made off within the meaning of s. 3 (cf. *Brooks* (1982) 76 Cr App R 66). If D hires a taxi but then makes off without paying, the relevant 'spot' is in the place where the taxi is standing. See *Aziz* [1993] Crim LR 708. In *Morris* [2014] 1 WLR 16, Leveson LJ suggested that this may not always be the case (see **B5.38**). If D travels on a public transport system without a ticket and dishonestly makes off when required to produce one, it will be no defence to argue that payment should have been made before the journey began (*Moberley v Alsop* (1991) 156 JP 514). An honest passenger inadvertently travelling without a ticket would of course be expected to pay during or after the journey.

Mens Rea: Dishonesty and Intent to Avoid Payment

B5.41 On a charge of making off without payment the prosecution must prove that D intended to make permanent default (*Allen* [1985] AC 1029). If D made off, but intended to pay later, or knew he would have to do so (because the person to whom payment was due knew his address), he will not be guilty.

As to the meaning of 'dishonesty', see *Ghosh* [1982] QB 1053 and **B4.54**. The issue of dishonesty may arise where D claims that he walked out of a restaurant in protest at poor service or poor food. If he considered himself to be acting reasonably, and thought that ordinary honest people would agree with his actions, then clearly he cannot be considered dishonest.

BLACKMAIL

Definition

B5.42   Theft Act 1968, s. 21

(1) A person is guilty of blackmail if, with a view to gain for himself or another or with intent to cause loss to another, he makes any unwarranted demand with menaces; and for this purpose a demand with menaces is unwarranted unless the person making it does so in the belief—
    (a) that he has reasonable grounds for making the demand; and
    (b) that the use of the menaces is a proper means of reinforcing the demand.
(2) The nature of the act or omission demanded is immaterial, and it is also immaterial whether the menaces relate to action to be taken by the person making the demand.
(3) A person guilty of blackmail shall on conviction on indictment be liable to imprisonment for a term not exceeding 14 years.

Procedure and Jurisdiction

B5.43 Blackmail is triable only on indictment (MCA 1980, s. 17 and sch. 1, para. 28). It is normally a class 3 offence, but see CPD XIII, para. B (see Supplement, **PD-97**) for the additional factors that the court considers on allocation. It is a Group A offence for jurisdiction purposes under the CJA 1993, part I (see **A8.10**).

Indictment

Statement of Offence

Blackmail contrary to section 21(1) of the Theft Act 1968.

Particulars of Offence

A on or about the…day of…, with a view to gain for himself, made an unwarranted demand for £1,000 from V with menaces.

Sentencing Guidelines

The maximum penalty is 14 years (s. 21(3)).

In *Witchelo* (1992) 13 Cr App R (S) 371 the offender received a sentence of 13 years after conviction of six offences of blackmail. He had written to food producers and threatened to contaminate their products. Some food was contaminated, and the offender obtained £32,000. He received a further four years for related offences. See also *Telford* (1992) 13 Cr App R (S) 676, where eight years was appropriate and *Riolfo* [1997] 1 Cr App R (S) 57, where a sentence of six years was substituted. In *Ablewhite* [2007] 2 Cr App R (S) 604, 12 years' imprisonment for conspiracy to commit blackmail was upheld, where the offenders had been involved in a six-year campaign against a company engaged in breeding guinea pigs for medical research. The campaign was calculated to cause maximum fear and disruption.

Sentences of six years and five years were reduced to four years and three years in *Cox* (1979) 1 Cr App R (S) 190, where the offenders removed discs and tapes from their employer and demanded £275,000 as the price for returning them. Three years was said to be appropriate in *Stone* (1989) 11 Cr App R (S) 176, where the offender took part in homosexual activities with the victim and then demanded sums of money under the threat of disclosing the victim's behaviour to the police. The offenders in *Taberer* [2011] 2 Cr App R (S) 603 made phone calls to a wealthy businessman demanding payment of £1 million under the threat of kidnapping members of the victim's family. The Court of Appeal said that four years was the proper sentence following a guilty plea. In *Havell* [2006] 2 Cr App R (S) 633, sentences of three years' and two years' imprisonment were appropriate for offenders convicted of seven counts of blackmail. They ran an illicit wheel-clamping business. Motorists who stopped their cars on land for a short period found that they were clamped and prevented from driving away until they had paid a sum of money between £45 and £95. The offenders behaved in a hostile manner.

In *A-G's Ref (No. 67 of 2007) (W)* [2008] 1 Cr App R (S) 549, D, aged 45 and of previous good character, blackmailed his elderly uncle, V, by threatening to reveal that he had previously sexually abused D. V committed suicide as a result of the threat. The Court of Appeal substituted a sentence of four years' imprisonment for the 12-month suspended sentence originally imposed.

View to Gain or Intent to Cause Loss

Demands reinforced by improper threats do not necessarily constitute blackmail, which can only be committed 'with a view to gain…or intent to cause loss' (s. 21(1)). The concepts of gain and loss are defined for this purpose in s. 34(2)(a) of the Act:

Theft Act 1968, s. 34

(2) …

    (a) 'gain' and 'loss' are to be construed as extending only to gain or loss in money or other property, but as extending to any such gain or loss whether temporary or permanent; and—

        (i) 'gain' includes a gain by keeping what one has, as well as a gain by getting what one has not; and

(ii) 'loss' includes a loss by not getting what one might get, as well as a loss by parting with
what one has.

It is possible to commit blackmail by using improper menaces in the course of demanding
money or other property to which one is legally entitled (*Lawrence* (1971) 57 Cr App R 64); but
merely seeking sexual favours or political advantage is not blackmail, though procuring sexual
intercourse by threats etc. may amount to rape if the woman concerned is found to have submitted without genuinely consenting (see **B3.29** *et seq.*).

A blackmailer need not be seeking any kind of material profit. In *Bevans* (1987) 87 Cr App R
64, D used menaces in order to obtain a pain-killing injection from a doctor; this was held to be
blackmail as the drug involved was a form of property.

Meaning of 'Making a Demand'

B5.47   The definition of the offence of blackmail in the Theft Act 1968, s. 21, is deliberately drafted in
such a way as to penalise the making of the demand, rather than the obtaining of property or the
intimidation of the victim. In other words, it is a 'conduct crime', in which the effectiveness of
D's behaviour is irrelevant (whether for jurisdictional or any other purpose), and in which the
results thereof form no constituent part of the offence.

'Demands' are not defined in the Act. A demand need not be expressed openly. As was pointed
out in *Studer* (1915) 85 LJ KB 1017, 'it may be in language only a request'; and indeed it need
not even be that, if the context makes the blackmailer's meaning clear. A demand may even be
made by one who poses as the victim (*Lambert* [2010] 1 Cr App R 299).

The kidnapper who writes to the child's parents, asking them whether they regard the child as
being worth £10,000, would clearly be regarded as having 'demanded' that sum. Similarly, there
would be a demand where a man offers to sell a victim his 'protection' whilst his friends demonstrate their willingness to wreck the victim's premises in the event of the offer being declined
(*Colister* (1955) 39 Cr App R 100).

B5.48   The earlier authorities did not provide any definite answer to the question whether a demand could
be 'made' without successful communication to the intended recipient; but the question came
before the House of Lords in *Treacy v DPP* [1971] AC 537, where D had posted his blackmail
demand from England to a victim in Germany. If receipt of the demand was regarded as an essential
part of its 'making' then the blackmail would have been completed (and thus committed, for jurisdictional purposes) in Germany, beyond the territorial ambit of the Theft Act 1968; but it was held
that the demand was made earlier, and within the jurisdiction, when the letter was posted.

Following *Treacy*, the successful communication of the demand cannot properly be described as
an element of the offence of blackmail, and it was accordingly doubtful whether the receipt of a
demand by a victim in England could render a 'cross-frontier' blackmailer liable for any offence
under English law. The point was left open in *Treacy*, although it was suggested (*obiter*) that the concept of a 'continuing demand' might constitute a basis for jurisdiction. The CJA 1993, part I (see
A8.10). was intended to clarify the position. By s. 4(b) of that Act, there is now deemed to be a 'communication' of a demand within the jurisdiction if it is sent from England and Wales to a place elsewhere, or sent from elsewhere to a place in England and Wales. The wording is unfortunate, because
communication is not a 'relevant event' for the purposes of that Act. What s. 4(b) ought to have
said is that there is a '*making*' of a demand in England and Wales in either of those circumstances,
but it seems likely that a court would construe s. 4(b) so as to give effect to its intended meaning.

Attempted Blackmail

B5.49   It follows from the way blackmail is defined that offences of attempted blackmail must be
unlikely occurrences. One could perhaps have such an offence where a telephone call is cut off
just as the caller is starting to present his demand, or where a letter containing demands is seized
just as the demander is about to post it; but in other circumstances it would seem that either the

full offence is committed or only preparatory acts, which would not suffice for liability under the Criminal Attempts Act 1981.

Meaning of 'Menaces'

In drafting the proposals which later became incorporated into the Theft Act 1968, s. 21, the Criminal Law Revision Committee adopted the term 'menaces' in preference to 'threats', on the basis that the latter term might possibly be too wide. As the Court of Appeal later said in *Clear* [1968] 1 QB 670:

> Words or conduct which would not intimidate or influence anyone to respond to the demand would not be menaces..., but threats and conduct of such a nature and extent that the mind of an ordinary person of normal stability and courage might be influenced or made apprehensive so as to accede unwillingly to the demand would be sufficient for a jury's consideration.

Menaces are therefore serious or significant threats; but since blackmail cases rarely involve any dispute about whether the alleged threats, if proved, were serious, there is generally no need for a trial judge to define the term for the jury. (See *Lawrence* (1971) 57 Cr App R 64; and *Garwood* [1987] 1 All ER 1032, in which it was said, somewhat questionably, that the term 'menaces' is an ordinary English word which any jury can be expected to understand.)

Nevertheless, there are at least two situations in which it is recognised that the jury may need guidance:

(a) A threat which one person would find trivial may be one which another would find terrifying. Some people are more timid than others, and fear is not always rational, even in people who may otherwise be very brave. If a demander knows that his victim suffers from arachnophobia, his threat to drop a large spider down the victim's back would obviously be calculated to have at least the same impact as a threat of serious violence. In *Garwood* [1987] 1 All ER 1032, it was recognised that the victim's 'unusual timidity' could be taken into account, provided D knew of it; and it is submitted that it should suffice if D merely hoped to discover such weakness (e.g., where he mistakenly believed the victim suffers from such a phobia).
(b) In the converse situation, where an apparently serious threat failed to intimidate the victim at all (perhaps because he knew something the blackmailer did not), the jury should be told that liability may still be incurred (*Clear* [1968] 1 QB 670).

Meaning of 'Unwarranted Demands'

A demand with menaces will be unwarranted unless the demander genuinely believes both that he has reasonable grounds for making the demand, and that it is proper to reinforce it with those particular menaces. Note that he need not have reasonable grounds for his belief: it is a subjective test of what he thinks is reasonable and proper. Once the issue is raised, the prosecution will have the burden of proving that D had no such belief.

A menace may be considered improper without necessarily being a threat to do anything improper. Publicising a person's scandalous behaviour may in itself be perfectly legitimate: threatening him with such publicity in order to extract money from him would clearly be a classic case of blackmail.

In *Harvey* (1980) 72 Cr App R 139, the Court of Appeal stated that one cannot believe a threat to be proper if one knows it would be unlawful (i.e. criminal) to carry it out. This seemingly conflicts with the later pronouncement of the Court of Appeal in *Cousins* [1982] QB 526 that a threat to kill might sometimes be lawful where the killing threatened would not be; but the dicta in *Harvey* clearly indicate a link between legality and propriety. A fanatic might believe that he would be *justified* in killing or threatening to kill for the sake of his cause, but it seems that he cannot argue that he believes such threats to be *proper* when he knows that what he threatens would be criminal (*Harvey* (1980) 72 Cr App R 139 at p. 142).

B5.50

B5.51

B

Part B Offences

In this respect, blackmail can be contrasted with robbery. A person who takes back property borrowed from him by another, believing that he is entitled to recover the property, cannot be guilty of stealing it, and thus cannot be guilty of robbery if he threatens violence in order to recover it; but since he can hardly believe his threats of violence are proper, he will almost certainly be guilty of blackmail (*Lawrence* (1971) 57 Cr App R 64; *Harvey* (1980) 72 Cr App R 139).

HARASSMENT OF DEBTORS

B5.52   Administration of Justice Act 1970, s. 40

(1) A person commits an offence if, with the object of coercing another person to pay money claimed from the other as a debt due under a contract, he—

   (a) harasses the other with demands for payment which, in respect of their frequency or the manner or occasion of making any such demand, or of any threat or publicity by which any demand is accompanied, are calculated to subject him or members of his family or household to alarm, distress or humiliation;

   (b) falsely represents, in relation to the money claimed, that criminal proceedings lie for failure to pay it;

   (c) falsely represents himself to be authorised in some official capacity to claim or enforce payment; or

   (d) utters a document falsely represented by him to have some official character or purporting to have some official character which he knows it has not.

(2) A person may be guilty of an offence by virtue of subsection (1)(a) above if he concerts with others in the taking of such action as is described in that paragraph, notwithstanding that his own course of conduct does not by itself amount to harassment.

(3) Subsection (1)(a) above does not apply to anything done by a person which is reasonable (and otherwise permissible in law) for the purpose—

   (a) of securing the discharge of an obligation due, or believed by him to be due, to himself or to persons for whom he acts, or protecting himself or them from future loss; or

   (b) of the enforcement of any liability by legal process.

(3A) Subsection (1) above does not apply to anything done by a person to another in circumstances where what is done is a commercial practice within the meaning of the Consumer Protection from Unfair Trading Regulations 2008 and the other is a consumer in relation to that practice.

(4) A person guilty of an offence under this section shall be liable on summary conviction to a fine of not more than level 5 on the standard scale.

The overlap between this summary offence and blackmail is clearly significant. If a person acts for the purpose of coercing another person into paying money, he necessarily acts 'with a view to gain', and some at least of the tactics proscribed by paras. (a)–(d) of the Administration of Justice Act 1970, s. 40(1), could well amount to the use of menaces.

OTHER OFFENCES INVOLVING THREATS
OR DEMANDS

B5.53 Threats to kill, whether or not amounting to blackmail, may be punishable under the OAPA 1861, s. 16 (see **B1.143** to **B1.147**). Threats of immediate violence may be punished as assault (see **B2.5**) or under the POA 1986 (see **B11**); and if done for the purposes of theft may amount to robbery or assault with intent to rob (see **B4.66** *et seq.*). Threats to damage property may be covered by the Criminal Damage Act 1971, s. 2 (see **B8.31** to **B8.35**). Threats of violence for the purpose of securing entry to premises may be covered by the Criminal Law Act 1977, s. 6(1) (see **B13.24**). The Criminal Law Act 1977, s. 51, deals with bomb hoaxes (see **B11.96**), which may or may not be made with a view to gain etc. Contamination of goods (often connected with blackmail of the manufacturers or suppliers) is punishable under the POA 1986, s. 38 (see **B11.102**).

The demanding of payment for unsolicited goods may be an offence under the Unsolicited Goods and Services Act 1971, s. 2, or under the Consumer Protection (Distance Selling) Regulations 2000 (SI 2000 No. 2334).

Threatening letters are covered by the Malicious Communications Act 1988, s. 1 (see **B18.30**). As to the offences under the Protection from Harassment Act 1997, see **B2.165** *et seq.*

Section B6   Falsification, Forgery and Counterfeiting

COMPARISON WITH FRAUD AND DECEPTION OFFENCES

B6.1   There is a significant overlap between the offences covered in this section and the offences of fraud and deception covered in **B5**. Offences of falsification, false accounting or forgery committed on or after 15 January 2007 will often involve conduct amounting equally to fraud within the meaning of the Fraud Act 2006, s. 1 (see **B5.4** *et seq.*), although dishonesty, which is an essential element of any fraud or false accounting offence, need not be proved in cases charged under the Forgery and Counterfeiting Act 1981, the Trade Marks Act 1994 or the offences arising under the new regulations governing unfair commercial practice or misleading advertising.

Conduct pre-dating 15 January 2007 may alternatively give rise to liability for deception offences under the Theft Acts 1968 or 1978, but the differences between those offences and the offences considered in this section are more pronounced. Not only do the deception offences require proof of dishonesty, but in addition they are 'result crimes' that are committed only if D succeeds in deceiving another person and in securing some profit, gain or advantage for himself or another. If all that can be proved is that D forged an instrument or made a false statement, a deception offence cannot be established.

FALSIFICATION

Falsification, False Statements and False Instruments

B6.2   The concept of falsity, as applied to documents or instruments, is not always the same as that of falsity in statements. A lie is a false statement, but documents containing lies or false statements are not always regarded as false instruments.

As far as offences under the Forgery and Counterfeiting Act 1981 are concerned, an instrument is only false if it purports to be something it is not, or if it 'tells a lie' about its own authorship, origins or history. Conversely, such an instrument might be false in one or more of those respects, despite being a true and accurate statement of the matters with which it deals (as where an exact copy of a genuine document purports to be the original). See further, s. 9 of the Act (see **B6.28** to **B6.31**), which provides an exhaustive definition of falsity for those purposes.

For most purposes a document is not regarded as 'falsified' unless it has been fraudulently altered or interfered with. Such a document will usually be rendered 'false' for the purposes of the Forgery and Counterfeiting Act 1981, even if falsified by the same person who made it in the first place (see s. 9(1)(g) of the Act); but the concept of falsification would not necessarily extend to the inclusion of false statements in an original document or record. For example, the offence of falsification by a bankrupt of his papers (Insolvency Act 1986, s. 355(2)(b)) would not be committed where the bankrupt merely enters incorrect details when drawing up his accounts; the correct charge would be one of making false entries, contrary to s. 355(2)(c) (see **B7.61**).

There are few decided cases on the meaning of 'falsification', but the issue arose in *Edwards v Toombs* [1983] Crim LR 43, where it was held that an act which interferes with a mechanical (or presumably electronic) recording device (in that case a turnstile meter at a soccer stadium) can amount to falsification of the record, for the purpose of liability under the Theft Act 1968, s. 17(1)(a).

Falsification is 'deemed' to bear a further meaning in s. 17, by virtue of s. 17(2), but this has no wider application, and is therefore dealt with in the analysis of that provision at **B6.10** and **B6.11**.

FALSE ACCOUNTING

Theft Act 1968, s. 17   B6.3

(1) Where a person dishonestly, with a view to gain for himself or another or with intent to cause loss to another,—
  (a) destroys, defaces, conceals or falsifies any account or any record or document made or required for any accounting purpose; or
  (b) in furnishing information for any purpose produces or makes use of any account, or any such record or document as aforesaid, which to his knowledge is or may be misleading, false or deceptive in a material particular; he shall, on conviction on indictment, be liable to imprisonment for a term not exceeding seven years.
(2) For purposes of this section a person who makes or concurs in making in an account or other document an entry which is or may be misleading, false or deceptive in a material particular, or who omits or concurs in omitting a material particular from an account or other document, is to be treated as falsifying the account or document.

Procedure and Jurisdiction

False accounting is triable either way (MCA 1980, s. 17 and sch. 1, para. 28). When tried on **B6.4** indictment it is normally a class 3 offence, but see CPD XIII, para. B (see Supplement, **PD-97**) for the additional factors that the court considers on allocation. It is a Group A offence for jurisdiction purposes under the CJA 1993, part I (see **A8.10**). The *Magistrates' Court Sentencing Guidelines* relating to fraud (see Supplement, **SG-472**) offer indications as to when a case should be sent to the Crown Court.

For the liability of officers of a company for an offence committed by the company, see the Theft Act 1968, s. 18, **B6.14** and **A6.23**.

Indictment

Statement of Offence   **B6.5**

False accounting contrary to section 17(1)(a) of the Theft Act 1968.

Particulars of Offence

A on or about the . . . day of . . . dishonestly and with a view to gain for himself [or for X] [or with intent to cause loss to Y] falsified a document required for an accounting purpose, namely a ledger, by making therein an entry which was misleading, false or deceptive in a material particular in that it falsely purported to show that A had received the sum of £10,000 from Z in payment for services rendered.

Sentence

B6.6 The maximum penalty is seven years (s. 17(1)) on indictment; six months, a fine not exceeding the statutory maximum, or both, summarily. The definitive sentencing guideline *Fraud, Bribery and Money Laundering* (see Supplement, **SG-472**), is applicable to all individual offenders aged 18 or over and organisations sentenced on or after 1 October 2014 regardless of the date of the offence. It replaces the SGC Guideline *Fraud – Statutory Offences* on that date. There is a separate part of the guideline for corporate offenders. The offence of false accounting may be the relevant offence in relation to the guideline on fraud, revenue fraud or benefit fraud.

In *Chaytor* [2011] 2 Cr App R (S) 653, where a serving MP admitted three counts of false accounting relating to Parliamentary expenses, the Court of Appeal upheld a sentence of 18 months' imprisonment. The offence involved 'serious dishonesty' and had damaged the reputation of Parliament. Lord Judge CJ doubted para. 21 of the previous fraud guideline, which suggested that the sentence should reflect the amount of money involved less the sum which could legitimately have been claimed. No such adjustment was necessary in *Chaytor*, according to his lordship, since the expenses claims were 'bogus in their entirety'.

Scope of Offence

B6.7 Section 17 creates two distinct offences: destruction, concealment or falsification etc. (s. 17(1)(a)) and using false or misleading documents etc. in furnishing information (s. 17(1)(b)). The user of falsified accounts may well be the person who falsified them, but this is not necessarily so. A person does not, however, commit an offence under s. 17(1)(b) unless he knows of the misleading, false or deceptive nature of the documents in question. Section 17(2) seems incapable of applying to s. 17(1)(b) because it deals only with falsification — the subject-matter of s. 17(1)(a).

Relationship to Other Offences

B6.8 There are potential overlaps between the offence under s. 17(1)(a) and forgery; and between the s. 17(1)(b) offence and using a false instrument (see **B6.26** *et seq.*). Nevertheless it would be wrong to assume that any case of false accounting must necessarily involve forgery (*Dodge* [1972] 1 QB 416). As explained in **B6.2**, the concept of falsity in the 1981 Act is a narrow one, and does not generally extend to the making of false or misleading entries when compiling a document, or to the destruction (as opposed to the falsification) of documents or records.

A further area of significant overlap involves documents relating to the affairs of companies or bankrupts. See the Companies Act 1985, s. 450 and the Insolvency Act 1986, ss. 209 and 355(2) (see **B7.15**, **B7.50** and **B7.61**).

Cases of false accounting are often closely associated with various other offences of dishonesty. The falsification or concealment may be a cover for past, contemporaneous or future offences of theft or fraud and it is not unusual for an indictment to include counts for both false accounting and theft. In *Eden* (1971) 55 Cr App R 193, the Court of Appeal expressed the view that the inclusion of parallel counts of this kind should be discouraged if they would both stand or fall by the same evidence; but the inclusion of both counts was at the same time recognised as prudent in a situation where (as in *Eden* itself) theft might be harder to prove.

False accounting and theft are not always clearly distinguishable from each other. The courts appear prone at times to confuse the appropriation of money or things in action (such as debts) with the falsification or misuse of documents or records relating to them. *Monaghan* [1979] Crim LR 673 is an example of this. D's dishonest failure to record a payment of £3.99 on the supermarket till she was operating, with a view to taking an equivalent sum from the till later in the day, was held to amount to theft, even though the cash was properly placed in the till, where it belonged, and even though D would no doubt have taken different notes and coins anyway. Even after *Gomez* [1993] AC 442 (see **B4.34** *et seq.*), the better view must be that she had done nothing more than falsify the till roll; but if *Monaghan* is indeed correct, the overlap between s. 17(2) and theft must be very substantial.

Accounts, Records and Documents

The word 'account' must be given the meaning it bears in normal English usage (*Scot-Simmonds* [1994] Crim LR 933). A record or account need not necessarily be a document. In *Edwards v Toombs* [1983] Crim LR 43 it was held that a turnstile meter at a soccer stadium was a record, and thus within the scope of the section. See also *Solomons* [1909] 2 KB 980 (taxi meter). Conversely, a document or record need not be an account, as long as it is made or required for an accounting purpose, either by D or by another person. This purpose need not be anything more than a secondary or incidental one; thus in *A-G's Ref (No. 1 of 1980)* [1981] 1 All ER 366 it was held that loan proposal forms, which would eventually be used by the loan company for an accounting purpose, could be the subject of an offence under s. 17 (see also *Cummings-John* [1997] Crim LR 660). Whether a document is one required for an accounting purpose is a question of fact and may need to be proved by the prosecution. See *Okanta* [1997] Crim LR 451, *Osinuga v DPP* [1998] Crim LR 216, *Sundhers* [1998] Crim LR 497 and *Manning* [1998] 2 Cr App R 461, but in some cases this may be self-evident. As Hooper LJ explained in *O* [2010] EWCA Crim 2233 at [49]:   **B6.9**

> Without any further direct evidence of the accounting practices of the lender, a jury is entitled to come to the conclusion that an application for a mortgage or a loan made to a commercial institution is a document required for an accounting purpose.

Extended Meaning of Falsification under Theft Act 1968, s. 17(2)

Section 17(2) gives 'falsification' a specially extended meaning for the purposes of s. 17(1)(a). It clearly embraces the preparation of false accounts as well as the falsification of existing ones (*Scot-Simmonds* [1994] Crim LR 933). It does not, however, purport to provide an exhaustive definition of the concept, and it was held in *Edwards v Toombs* [1983] Crim LR 43 that anything amounting to falsification within the ordinary meaning of the term (see **B6.2**) would equally amount to falsification for s. 17 purposes.   **B6.10**

Falsification by Omission

Section 17(2) expressly provides that the omission of material information from a document etc. can have the effect of falsifying it. In *Shama* [1990] 2 All ER 602 the Court of Appeal upheld the conviction of a telephone operator who had failed even to start filling out standard forms provided by his employer for the recording of international calls. He was held to have falsified the forms by leaving them unmarked. See also *Neil* [2008] EWCA Crim 478. A statement or record with material omissions may be misleading for purposes of s. 17(1)(b) even if it contains no outright lies; there is authority to the effect that such statements may also be regarded as being 'false in a material particular' (*Lord Kylsant* [1932] 1 KB 442) but it would not be necessary to rely thereon.   **B6.11**

Meaning of 'Material'

Falsity etc. is not a basis of liability under the Theft Act 1968, s. 17, unless it is falsity 'in a material particular'. The meaning of this concept was examined in *Mallett* [1978] 3 All ER 10, where the Court of Appeal rejected the argument that the falsity etc. must be material in the sense of being directly connected with the accuracy etc. of an accounting process. D had furnished false   **B6.12** information to a finance company concerning the status of a potential customer. The falsity was material to the company's decision to finance the transaction, and the form containing the false information was required for accounting purposes. It was held that D had been rightly convicted even though no accounts had been rendered inaccurate by his supply of false information.

An omission is 'material' only if it makes the document misleading in a way that is significant (or in some way that 'matters'); the omission of information required by an application form does not necessarily amount to the omission of a material particular (*Lancaster* [2010] 3 All ER 402).

Mens Rea

B6.13   In false accounting there need be no proof of any intent to permanently deprive another person of his property. What is needed is dishonesty (in the *Ghosh* [1982] QB 1053 sense, see **B4.54**) coupled with a 'view to gain' or 'intent to cause loss'; and in *Eden* (1971) 55 Cr App R 193 it was said that this might involve nothing more than an intent to gain or avoid loss on a temporary basis, perhaps in order to play for time, whilst losses caused by honest incompetence are made good. In *Lee Cheung Wing v The Queen* (1992) 94 Cr App R 355, falsified documents were used by securities dealers to mask withdrawals of unauthorised profits from accounts they had kept secret from their employers. The Privy Council held that the falsification of these documents had been made with a view to gain and constituted an offence under equivalent legislation in Hong Kong.

As to the meaning of 'gain' and 'loss' in this context, see the Theft Act 1968, s. 34(2)(a), *Golechha* [1989] 3 All ER 908 and *A-G's Ref (No. 1 of 2001)* [2002] 3 All ER 840 (see **B5.10** and **B5.46**).

LIABILITY OF COMPANY OFFICERS FOR OFFENCES COMMITTED BY THE COMPANY

B6.14   Theft Act 1968, s. 18

(1) Where an offence committed by a body corporate under section 17 of this Act is proved to have been committed with the consent or connivance of any director, manager, secretary or other similar officer of the body corporate, or any person who was purporting to act in any such capacity, he as well as the body corporate shall be guilty of that offence, and shall be liable to be proceeded against and punished accordingly.

(2) Where the affairs of a body corporate are managed by its members, this section shall apply in relation to the acts and defaults of a member in connection with his functions of management as if he were a director of the body corporate.

In respect of things done wholly or partly prior to 15 January 2007, s. 18 also applies to offences under ss. 15 and 16 and to offences under the Theft Act 1978, ss. 1 and 2 (Theft Act 1978, s. 5(1); Fraud Act 2006, sch. 2, para. 3).

As to the limitations on the scope of s. 18, see the discussion of *Boal* [1992] 1 QB 591 at **A6.24**. Offences to which it applies can be committed by corporations only if the persons who control them possess the requisite *mens rea*, which can then be imputed to the corporation. Such persons will necessarily be guilty as joint perpetrators or as accessories under the general law governing complicity in offences, without any need for reference to s. 18. A junior manager or officer who knowingly assists in the commission of such an offence by his company will similarly incur secondary liability.

This leaves s. 18 with one significant function. It may apply to senior officers or directors who knowingly consent to the commission of relevant offences, without themselves doing any acts that could result in liability as accessories under the general law (see further **A6.24**).

FALSE STATEMENTS BY OFFICERS OF COMPANY OR ASSOCIATION

Theft Act 1968, s. 19   **B6.15**

(1) Where an officer of a body corporate or unincorporated association (or person purporting to act as such), with intent to deceive members or creditors of the body corporate or association about its affairs, publishes or concurs in publishing a written statement or account which to his knowledge is or may be misleading, false or deceptive in a material particular, he shall on conviction on indictment be liable to imprisonment for a term not exceeding seven years.

(2) For purposes of this section a person who has entered into a security for the benefit of a body corporate or association is to be treated as a creditor of it.

(3) Where the affairs of a body corporate or association are managed by its members, this section shall apply to any statement which a member publishes or concurs in publishing in connection with his functions of management as if he were an officer of the body corporate or association.

Procedure and Jurisdiction

An offence under s. 19 is triable either way (MCA 1980, s. 17 and sch. 1, para. 28). When tried on **B6.16** indictment it is normally a class 3 offence, but see CPD XIII, para. B (see Supplement, **PD-97**) for the additional factors that the court considers on allocation. It is a Group A offence for jurisdiction purposes under the CJA 1993, part I (see **A8.10**).

Indictment

Statement of Offence   **B6.17**

Publishing a false statement contrary to section 19(1) of the Theft Act 1968.

Particulars of Offence

A on or about the…day of…, being a director of a body corporate, namely X plc, with intent to deceive the members or creditors or the said X plc, published a written statement about the affairs of the said X plc which to his knowledge was misleading, false or deceptive in a material particular in that it falsely stated that X plc then had no contingent liabilities.

Sentence

The maximum penalty is seven years (s. 19(1)) on indictment; six months, a fine not exceeding **B6.18** the statutory maximum, or both, summarily. There is no guideline judgment reported for an offence under s. 19(1). For sentencing guidelines for offences of fraud generally, see **B5.7**. For sentencing guidelines for theft offences, see **B4.5** to **B4.9**.

Relationship to Other Offences

The commission of an offence under the Theft Act 1968, s. 19(1), by a company director may **B6.19** be in circumstances in which the company itself commits an offence under s. 17 or possibly ss. 15 or 16 for which the director may be liable under s. 18. There is clearly some overlap between such liability and possible liability under s. 19(1), subject to the consideration that under s. 19(1) there need be no successful deception, no proof of dishonesty and no need for the statement to be made or required for any accounting purpose, but, insofar as the s. 19 offence can be committed by officers of an unincorporated association, its scope is nevertheless wider than that of s. 18.

Meaning of 'Officer of a Body Corporate or Unincorporated Association'

In relation to a body corporate, the term 'officer' includes a director, manager or secretary **B6.20** (Companies Act 1985, s. 744; Companies Act 2006, s. 1121), and an auditor may also be considered to be an officer (*Shacter* [1960] 2 QB 252). As to the meaning of manager, see **A6.24**.

In relation to unincorporated associations, treasurers, secretaries and chairmen would be considered to be officers; as would any partner publishing or concurring in the publication of an offending statement in connection with his firm's affairs. Where the affairs of a company or association are managed by its members, a member may commit this offence (s. 19(3)).

Intent to Deceive Members or Creditors

B6.21   A statement published with intent to deceive only prospective members or creditors would not appear to come within the ambit of this offence, but would be likely to fall within the Financial Services Act 2012, ss. 89 or 90 (see **B7.25**) or amount to an offence under the Insolvency Act 1986 (see **B7.40** *et seq.*). The Theft Act 1968, s. 19(2), provides that for the purposes of s. 19, a person who has entered into a security for the benefit of a body corporate or association is to be treated as a creditor of it. This seems to refer to a guarantor, though the precise scope of the subsection is unclear.

SUPPRESSION OF DOCUMENTS

Definition

B6.22   Theft Act 1968, s. 20(1)

> A person who dishonestly, with a view to gain for himself or another or with intent to cause loss to another, destroys, defaces or conceals any valuable security, any will or other testamentary document or any original document of or belonging to, or filed or deposited in, any court of justice or any government department shall on conviction on indictment be liable to imprisonment for a term not exceeding seven years.

Procedure

B6.23   This offence is triable either way (MCA 1980, s. 17 and sch. 1). When tried on indictment it is normally a class 3 offence, but see CPD XIII, para. B (see Supplement, **PD-97**) for the additional factors that the court considers on allocation.

Sentence

B6.24   The maximum penalty is seven years (s. 20(1)) on indictment; six months, a fine not exceeding the statutory maximum, or both, summarily. There is no guideline judgment reported for an offence under s. 20(1). For sentencing guidelines for theft offences, see **B4.5** to **B4.9**.

Elements

B6.25   Section 20(1) is little used, perhaps because offences involving the destruction or concealment of wills etc. are difficult to detect. The defacing of such instruments may sometimes amount to forgery if intended to deceive, and destruction etc. might in many cases be charged as theft or criminal damage.

Most of the terms used in this provision have been discussed elsewhere. The meaning of 'dishonesty' is discussed in **B4.51** *et seq.* and **B5.9**. The definition of 'view to gain' etc. in s. 34(2)(a) is discussed at **B5.46**. 'Valuable security' is defined in s. 20(3).

FORGERY AND KINDRED OFFENCES: GENERAL CONSIDERATIONS

Offences and Penalties under Part I of the Forgery and Counterfeiting Act 1981

B6.26   The Forgery and Counterfeiting Act 1981, s. 30, together with the schedule to that Act, repealed a number of older statutory offences of forgery, and s. 13 abolished the offence of forgery at common law. In their place, part I (ss. 1 to 13) of the Act created the following offences:

(a) making a false instrument (s. 1);
(b) copying a false instrument (s. 2);
(c) using a false instrument (s. 3);
(d) using a copy of a false instrument (s. 4);
(e) having custody or control of specified kinds of false instrument (s. 5(1)); and
(f) making or having custody etc. of machines, paper etc. for making false instruments of that kind (s. 5(3)).

These offences all require proof of an 'intention to induce somebody to accept the instrument as genuine' (or as a copy of a genuine instrument) and 'by reason of so accepting it to do or not to do some act to his own or any other person's prejudice'. They are punishable following conviction on indictment with up to 10 years' imprisonment under s. 6(2) and (3) of the Act.

In addition, subsections (2) and (4) of s. 5 create two further, less serious, offences, which do not require proof of this ulterior intent, but which are otherwise comparable to the offences created by s. 5(1) and (3) respectively. These are punishable with up to two years' imprisonment under s. 6(4).

On summary conviction, all eight offences attract up to six months' imprisonment and/or a fine not exceeding the statutory maximum (s. 6(1)).

The above offences all use certain key terms, the meanings of which are defined in ss. 8 to 10 of the Act.

Meaning of 'Instrument'

Forgery and Counterfeiting Act 1981, s. 8   **B6.27**

(1) Subject to subsection (2) below, in this Part of this Act 'instrument' means—
    (a) any document, whether of a formal or informal character;
    (b) any stamp issued or sold by a postal operator;
    (c) any Inland Revenue stamp; and
    (d) any disc, tape, soundtrack or other device on or in which information is recorded or stored by mechanical, electronic or other means.
(2) A currency note within the meaning of Part II of this Act is not an instrument for the purposes of this Part of this Act.
(3) A mark denoting payment of postage which a postal operator authorises to be used instead of an adhesive stamp is to be treated for the purposes of this Part of this Act as if it were a stamp issued by the postal operator concerned.

It had been recognised that one of the many difficulties surrounding the old Forgery Act 1913 was uncertainty about what kinds of article fell within the scope of the offences it created. The fact that it referred to 'documents', without providing any definition of that term, meant, *inter alia*, that doubts surrounded things such as wrappers on goods or the signatures on paintings or other works of art (*Closs* (1857) Dears & B 460; *Smith* (1858) Dears & B 566; *Douce* [1972] Crim LR 105). In proposing the new legislation, the Law Commission advocated the adoption of the term 'instrument' instead, on the basis that forgery and its kindred offences should apply only to those documents, such as cheques, which create rights and duties, or which give directions that are to be accepted and acted upon. This proposal was seemingly rejected; the term 'instrument' has indeed been adopted in the Act, but it has been defined in such a way that it includes any document (still without defining that term!) and several things that might not otherwise have been thought of as documents at all. The only documents excluded are currency notes, which are covered by the counterfeiting offences in part II of the Act.

Electronic impulses representing passwords for accessing computers are too ephemeral to be instruments (*Gold* [1988] AC 1063) though the misuse of such a password may be an offence under the Computer Misuse Act 1990 (see **B17**).

Meaning of 'False' and 'Making'

B6.28   Forgery and Counterfeiting Act 1981, s. 9

(1) An instrument is false for the purposes of this Part of this Act—

   (a) if it purports to have been made in the form in which it is made by a person who did not in fact make it in that form; or

   (b) if it purports to have been made in the form in which it is made on the authority of a person who did not in fact authorise its making in that form; or

   (c) if it purports to have been made in the terms in which it is made by a person who did not in fact make it in those terms; or

   (d) if it purports to have been made in the terms in which it is made on the authority of a person who did not in fact authorise its making in those terms; or

   (e) if it purports to have been altered in any respect by a person who did not in fact alter it in that respect; or

   (f) if it purports to have been altered in any respect on the authority of a person who did not in fact authorise the alteration in that respect; or

   (g) if it purports to have been made or altered on a date on which, or at a place at which, or otherwise in circumstances in which, it was not in fact made or altered; or

   (h) if it purports to have been made or altered by an existing person but he did not in fact exist.

(2) A person is to be treated for the purposes of this Part of this Act as making a false instrument if he alters an instrument so as to make it false in any respect (whether or not it is false in some other respect apart from that alteration).

As was the position at common law and under the earlier legislation, a false statement in a document or instrument does not ordinarily make that instrument a forgery; a false instrument is one which purports to be something which it is not (*Re Windsor* (1865) 10 Cox CC 118; *Warneford* [1994] Crim LR 753).

Section 9(1) lists the ways in which an instrument may be false. It is an exhaustive list: an instrument cannot be regarded as false on any alternative basis. On the other hand, an indictment does not need to specify the exact ground on which an instrument is alleged to be false.

B6.29   **Falsity as to Authorship or Authority (s. 9(1)(a), (c), (d) or (h))**   An instrument will be false if the supposed maker did not make it at all, or if it has been altered since he made it. The obvious example of such falsity would be where one person forges another's signature on a cheque (*Lack* (1986) 84 Cr App R 342).

The concept might appear to be a simple one, but is not always so. In *Macer* [1979] Crim LR 659, decided under earlier, but essentially similar, provisions, it was held *not* to be forgery for a person to sign his own name on a cheque, but with a different signature from his normal one, with a view to later denying its authenticity. It was said that the cheque did not 'purport' to have been signed by any other person.

Another difficulty concerns the use of assumed names. There is generally no law against the use of assumed names. An instrument signed in a false name is not necessarily a forgery, even if the false name has been used for dishonest purposes (*More* [1987] 3 All ER 825). However, assuming the name of another person in the pretence of being that other person may constitute forgery. In *More*, D stole a cheque and paid it into a building society account opened in the same name as the payee. He later withdrew the proceeds, using withdrawal forms signed in that same name, and was charged, *inter alia*, with forgery of those forms. The House of Lords held that the forms were not forgeries: they purported to have been signed by the person who had opened the account, as indeed they had been, and (crucially) did not refer back to the original cheque.

More was distinguished in *Atunwa* [2006] EWCA Crim 673, in which D was found in possession of cheques purporting to have been signed on behalf of registered companies, but bearing the signatures of unknown individuals who (if they existed at all) had no connection with those companies. His convictions for possessing false instruments with intent (see **B6.51**) were upheld. Dyson LJ said (at [8]):

> If A signs a cheque on behalf of X Limited in the name of B, and B is authorised to sign cheques on behalf of X Limited, A commits the offence; he purports to make an instrument 'in the terms in which it is made on the authority of a person who did not in fact authorise its making in those terms'...But the offence may also be committed if A purports to sign a cheque on behalf of X Limited in his own name where he is not an authorised signatory. In this situation too, A purports to make an instrument in the terms in which it is made on the authority of a person who did not in fact authorise its making in those terms. In both cases the cheque tells a lie about itself, namely that it is a cheque duly signed by a person authorised to sign the cheque on behalf of the company.

Falsification by Alteration (s. 9(1)(e))   Alteration of an instrument so as to change its value or **B6.30** terms would come within s. 9(1)(c) if the alteration is intended to pass undetected. Section 9(1)(e) covers alterations which purport to be those of someone other than the person who made, or authorised the making of, the instrument, even an alteration which purports to be unauthorised (done, for example, for the purpose of falsely accusing someone else of forgery). If the person purportedly responsible for the alteration did not really exist then the instrument would be false by virtue of s. 9(1)(h).

Falsity as to Date, Place or Circumstances (s. 9(1)(g))   An instrument which is dated other- **B6.31** wise than with the date on which it is made is not necessarily false, because in some cases it is recognised that the date indicates, not the date of making, but the date at which the instrument becomes enforceable (as with a postdated cheque).

The final part of s. 9(1)(g) is a 'sweeping-up' provision, which is potentially very wide ranging. In some circumstances, the concept of falsity can be hard to distinguish from that of mere false statements which fall outside the scope of the Act (see **B6.2**).

In *Donnelly* [1984] 1 WLR 1017, the Court of Appeal held that a jeweller's certificate purport-ing to value jewellery that did not really exist was a forgery. Had the certificate merely lied about the value of real items inspected, it could not have been a forgery, and *Donnelly* has been criticised on the basis that there is no difference between a certificate which lies about real items and one which lies about fictional items. Some commentators argue that *Donnelly* cannot stand with *More* [1987] 3 All ER 825 (see **B6.29**) but, with respect, the certificate did not merely tell lies; it was not merely an inflated valuation; it purported to be something it was not: a valuation based on an inspection of real jewellery.

Donnelly was followed in *Jeraj* [1994] Crim LR 595 but disapproved in *Warneford* [1994] Crim LR 753. The issue now appears to have been settled by *A-G's Ref (No. 1 of 2000)* [2001] 1 WLR 331, in which Lord Woolf CJ followed *Donnelly* and clearly identified the principle to be applied in cases brought under s. 9(1)(g): namely that a document which tells lies about the cir-cumstances under which it is made becomes a forgery if, but only if, those circumstances need to exist before the document can properly be made. One cannot, for example, produce a valuation of jewellery (even an inaccurate one) unless the jewellery in question exists; nor can one issue a genuine receipt for a security that has not in fact been received (see *Jeraj*).

Meaning of 'Prejudice' and 'Induce'

Forgery and Counterfeiting Act 1981, s. 10   **B6.32**

(1) Subject to subsections (2) and (4) below, for the purposes of this Part of this Act an act or omission intended to be induced is to a person's prejudice if, and only if, it is one which if it occurs—

    (a) will result—

        (i)   in his temporary or permanent loss of property; or

        (ii) in his being deprived of an opportunity to earn remuneration or greater remunera-tion; or

        (iii) in his being deprived of an opportunity to gain a financial advantage otherwise than by way of remuneration; or

    (b) will result in somebody being given an opportunity—

        (i) to earn remuneration or greater remuneration from him; or

        (ii) to gain a financial advantage from him otherwise than by way of remuneration; or

    (c) will be the result of his having accepted a false instrument as genuine, or a copy of a false instrument as a copy of a genuine one, in connection with his performance of any duty.

(2) An act which a person has an enforceable duty to do and an omission to do an act which a person is not entitled to do shall be disregarded for the purposes of this Part of this Act.

(3) In this Part of this Act references to inducing somebody to accept a false instrument as genuine, or a copy of a false instrument as a copy of a genuine one, include references to inducing a machine to respond to the instrument or copy as if it were a genuine instrument or, as the case may be, a copy of a genuine one.

(4) Where subsection (3) above applies, the act or omission intended to be induced by the machine responding to the instrument or copy shall be treated as an act or omission to a person's prejudice.

(5) In this section 'loss' includes not getting what one might get as well as parting with what one has.

Section 10 provides an exhaustive definition of the concept of 'prejudice' for the purposes of the six offences which require an intent to induce another person to act or omit to act to his own or another's prejudice (see **B6.26**). 'Inducing' is only defined to the extent that it applies to machines.

To be guilty of one of these offences, an accused need not have induced any reaction at all: it is a matter of ulterior intent, rather than of *actus reus* (*Ondhia* [1998] 2 Cr App R 150). It would not however suffice that D was merely aware that prejudice might result (*Garcia* [1988] Crim LR 115).

B6.33   Section 10(1)(a) covers situations in which acceptance of a false instrument would result in loss, or loss of potential profit; s. 10(1)(b) covers situations where actual loss might be difficult to identify, but where someone might be able to obtain a pecuniary advantage from the person induced; and the broad scope of s. 10(1)(c) is illustrated by *Campbell* (1984) 80 Cr App R 47, in which it was held that a bank would be prejudiced if it was induced to pay or collect payment on a forged cheque, whether or not it suffered financially by so doing, and whether or not anyone profited thereby. Another illustration is provided by *Utting* [1987] 1 WLR 1375, where, but for a defective indictment, D might have been convicted of forging an instrument in order to induce the police to act to their prejudice by not prosecuting him. See also *A-G's Ref (No. 1 of 2001)* [2002] 3 All ER 840.

B6.34   The effect of s. 10(2) is that it cannot be an offence under the Act to make or use a false instrument in order to secure or protect one's lawful rights against anyone it is intended to deceive; but in the case of cheques and other instruments covered by s. 5, s. 10(2) and (4) might still apply.

B6.35   Section 10(3) and (4) ensure, *inter alia*, that the use of a forged card in an automatic service till could be an offence under s. 3, and making such a forged card could be an offence under s. 1. Similar provision is made by the Fraud Act 2006 (see **B5.17**). In contrast, the obtaining of cash using such a device was not regarded as a deception offence under the Theft Acts, which lacked any provisions akin to these. The correct charge in such a case was theft. Section 10(3) and (4) would also apply where forged identification cards are used in computers etc., but not where hackers merely transmit or key in false user identification numbers, these being too ephemeral to constitute 'instruments' under s. 8 (*Gold* [1988] AC 1063). Similar considerations would apply to the misuse of another person's card and personal identification number in a bank automatic service till. Misuse of a user identification may, however, be an offence under the Computer Misuse Act 1990 (see **B17**).

FORGERY

Forgery and Counterfeiting Act 1981, s. 1   **B6.36**
A person is guilty of forgery if he makes a false instrument, with the intention that he or another
shall use it to induce somebody to accept it as genuine, and by reason of so accepting it to do or not
to do some act to his own or any other person's prejudice.

Procedure and Jurisdiction

Forgery is triable either way (Forgery and Counterfeiting Act 1981, s. 6). When tried on indict-   **B6.37**
ment it is normally a class 3 offence, but see CPD XIII, para. B (see Supplement, **PD-97**) for the
additional factors that the court considers on allocation. It is a Group A offence for jurisdiction
purposes under the CJA 1993, part I (see **A8.10**).

Indictment

Statement of Offence   **B6.38**

Forgery contrary to section 1 of the Forgery and Counterfeiting Act 1981.

Particulars of Offence

A on or about the...day of...made a false instrument, namely a document purporting to be the
will of X, with the intention of using it to induce Y to accept it as genuine and by reason of so
accepting to give A a Ming vase forming part of the estate of X to the prejudice of the beneficiaries
under the true will of X.

Sentence

The maximum sentence is ten years on indictment; six months or a fine not exceeding the statu-   **B6.39**
tory maximum or both summarily (Forgery and Counterfeiting Act 1981, s. 6). There is no
guideline judgment reported for this offence but in *Mussa* [2012] 2 Cr App R (S) 585 the Court
of Appeal dealt with a case in which the offenders admitted conspiracy to produce large numbers of false French identity documents. The forged documents were of high quality, and would
have enabled false bank accounts to be set up, driving penalties to be avoided, and facilitated
illegal entry and residence in the UK. Cranston J said that the key considerations in sentencing
such a case were the role of the offender in the operation, its scale and sophistication, the type
of documents being produced, the damage caused and the income generated. The scale in this
case was 'vast', and sentences of six and half years' imprisonment on a guilty plea were upheld.
See also *Velev* [2009] 1 Cr App R (S) 554 and *Toska* [2011] 1 Cr App R (S) 601. Much lower
down the scale, in *Lincoln* (1994) 15 Cr App R 333, where the offender forged the signature of
his estranged wife on a contract for sale of a house and a Land Registry transfer, it was held that
the proper sentence was six months' imprisonment.

Elements

Most of the key terms used in s. 1 are considered in **B6.27** to **B6.32**. By virtue of s. 9(2), 'mak-   **B6.40**
ing' a false instrument includes falsifying an existing one; but however it is made, it must be
proved that it was made with the specified 'double intention': it must be proved that D intended
both that the instrument would be accepted as genuine and that someone would therefore act
to his own or another's prejudice. It is a specific intent; recklessness or foresight will not suffice
(*Garcia* [1988] Crim LR 115). In *Ondhia* [1998] 2 Cr App R 150, O created a false 'copy
bill of lading', not for the purpose of using it directly to deceive any other person, but for the
purpose of feeding it into his fax machine, so that the recipient of his call would receive the
facsimile copy thereby created. This was held to amount to an offence of forgery under s. 1. No
doubt O would also have been guilty of copying a false instrument, contrary to s. 2 of the Act,
but overlapping offences are common in English law, and there is nothing artificial or unnatural
in the argument that a person who faxes a forged document to another 'uses' that document for
the purpose of inducing that other (or indeed a third party) to accept it as genuine. A person

who relies upon a facsimile of a bill of lading will recognise it to be a facsimile; and if he is deceived by the facsimile, he is deceived by the original from which it was made.

On the other hand, dishonesty is not an essential ingredient in this or any other offences under the Act (*Campbell* (1984) 80 Cr App R 47; *Winston* [1999] 1 Cr App R 337), and the intent is ulterior, so that actual inducement or prejudice need not be proved, and need not even be intended to take place within the jurisdiction (cf. *Treacy v DPP* [1971] AC 537; *Berry* [1985] AC 246).

COPYING A FALSE INSTRUMENT

Definition

B6.41
Forgery and Counterfeiting Act 1981, s. 2

It is an offence for a person to make a copy of an instrument which is, and which he knows or believes to be, a false instrument, with the intention that he or another shall use it to induce somebody to accept it as a copy of a genuine instrument, and by reason of so accepting it to do or not to do some act to his own or any other person's prejudice.

Procedure and Jurisdiction

B6.42 The offence is triable either way (s. 6). When tried on indictment it is normally a class 3 offence, but see CPD XIII, para. B (see Supplement, **PD-97**) for the additional factors that the court considers on allocation. It is a Group A offence for jurisdiction purposes under the CJA 1993, part I (see **A8.10**).

Indictment

B6.43
Statement of Offence

Copying a false instrument contrary to section 2 of the Forgery and Counterfeiting Act 1981.

Particulars of Offence

A on or about the…day of…made a copy of an instrument, namely a document purporting to be the will of X, which was and which he knew to be a false instrument, with the intention of using it to induce Y to accept it as genuine and by reason of so accepting to give A a Ming vase forming part of the estate of X to the prejudice of the beneficiaries under the true will of X.

Sentence

B6.44 The maximum sentence is ten years on indictment; six months or a fine not exceeding the statutory maximum or both summarily (s. 6).

Elements

B6.45 Section 2 does not deal with copies which are intended to be passed off as originals, even if they are themselves copies of copies, nor does it deal with instruments which purport to be copies of originals which do not in fact exist. (The correct charge for making such copies is one of forgery under s. 1.) This provision aims instead at copies (particularly photocopies) which purport to be true copies of original instruments, but which are not, either because the original has been falsified prior to photocopying etc., or because the original was a complete forgery from the start.

It might be argued that there is really no need for such a provision, since a document which purports to be a photocopy of a genuine instrument, but which is in fact a copy of a forgery, would *ipso facto* be false under s. 9(1)(g) (and see *Utting* [1987] 1 WLR 1375). This might be true where the original is a total forgery; but difficulties could arise in other circumstances. If, for example, an individual is required to send to some person a copy of his birth certificate, and takes a photocopy for that purpose, knowing that the original was falsified in some way by his father ten years before, it could be argued that the photocopy is a true copy of the certificate, and thus not false within s. 9 at all. Section 2, however, would clearly apply in such circumstances.

USING A FALSE INSTRUMENT: USING COPY OF FALSE INSTRUMENT

Forgery and Counterfeiting Act 1981, ss. 3 and 4   **B6.46**

3. It is an offence for a person to use an instrument which is, and which he knows or believes to be, false, with the intention of inducing somebody to accept it as genuine, and by reason of so accepting it to do or not to do some act to his own or any other person's prejudice.

4. It is an offence for a person to use a copy of an instrument which is, and which he knows or believes to be, a false instrument, with the intention of inducing somebody to accept it as a copy of a genuine instrument, and by reason of so accepting it to do or not to do some act to his own or any other person's prejudice.

Procedure and Jurisdiction

Both offences are triable either way (s. 6). When tried on indictment they are normally class 3 **B6.47** offences, but see CPD XIII, para. B (see Supplement, **PD-97**) for the additional factors that the court considers on allocation. It is a Group A offence for jurisdiction purposes under the CJA 1993, part I (see **A8.10**).

Indictment

Statement of Offence   **B6.48**

Using a false instrument contrary to section 3 of the Forgery and Counterfeiting Act 1981.

Particulars of Offence

A on or about the...day of...used an instrument, namely a document purporting to be the will of X, which was and which he knew to be false, with the intention of inducing Y to accept it as genuine and by reason of so accepting to give A a Ming vase forming part of the estate of X to the prejudice of the beneficiaries under the true will of X.

This form may easily be adapted for a charge under s. 4.

Sentence

The maximum sentence is ten years on indictment; six months or a fine not exceeding the statutory **B6.49** maximum or both summarily (s. 6). There are no guideline judgments reported for these offences.

In *Singh* [1999] 1 Cr App R (S) 490, the Court of Appeal upheld a sentence of eight months' imprisonment on an offender who had pleaded guilty to an offence under s. 3, in that he had attempted to use a false British passport at Gatwick Airport in order to travel to Canada. After reviewing a number of authorities involving the misuse of passports, Rose LJ explained that a deterrent custodial sentence within the range of six to nine months would usually be merited. A guilty plea would always attract an appropriate discount, but previous good character and personal mitigation were of very limited value. *Singh* was, however, revisited by the Court of Appeal in *Kolawole* [2005] 2 Cr App R (S) 71, where Rose LJ said that in light of international events in recent years and the increase in public concern that they had generated, sentences at a higher level were now appropriate, and that in such a case as *Singh* the appropriate sentence, even on a guilty plea by a person of good character, should usually be in the range of 12 to 18 months.

Elements

Whereas s. 1 penalises the making of a false instrument, even if it is never used for its intended pur- **B6.50** pose or intended for use outside the jurisdiction, s. 3 strikes at the use of such an instrument, even if it was not originally made to be used in a way prohibited by s. 3, or made outside the jurisdiction. The same 'double intention' is required as in s. 1: see **B6.40** and *Tobierre* [1986] 1 All ER 346.

Section 4 relates to s. 2 as s. 3 relates to s. 1. Like s. 2 it does not apply to copies which purport to be originals; and like s. 3 it does not matter who made the copy, or for what purpose it was made.

'Using' is not defined in the Act. Previous legislation used the term 'uttering', and using was the principal form of uttering (*Harris* [1966] 1 QB 184). 'Use' must presumably bear its ordinary meaning: 'to put into action or service: avail oneself of:…to carry out a purpose or action by means of' (*Webster's Ninth New Collegiate Dictionary*). However, the use need not be successful: the full offence may be committed even if the instrument is at once recognised as a forgery.

OFFENCES RELATING TO STAMPS, SHARE CERTIFICATES ETC.

B6.51   Forgery and Counterfeiting Act 1981, s. 5

(1) It is an offence for a person to have in his custody or under his control an instrument to which this section applies which is, and which he knows or believes to be, false, with the intention that he or another shall use it to induce somebody to accept it as genuine, and by reason of so accepting it to do or not to do some act to his own or any other person's prejudice.

(2) It is an offence for a person to have in his custody or under his control, without lawful authority or excuse, an instrument to which this section applies which is, and which he knows or believes to be, false.

(3) It is an offence for a person to make or to have in his custody or under his control a machine or implement, or paper or any other material, which to his knowledge is or has been specially designed or adapted for the making of an instrument to which this section applies, with the intention that he or another shall make an instrument to which this section applies which is false and that he or another shall use the instrument to induce somebody to accept it as genuine, and by reason of so accepting it to do or not to do some act to his own or any other person's prejudice.

(4) It is an offence for a person to make or to have in his custody or under his control any such machine, implement, paper or material, without lawful authority or excuse.

(5) The instruments to which this section applies are—
   (a)   money orders;
   (b)   postal orders;
   (c)   United Kingdom postage stamps;
   (d)   Inland Revenue stamps;
   (e)   share certificates;
   (f)   [repealed];
   (fa)   [repealed];
   (g)   cheques and other bills of exchange;
   (h)   travellers' cheques;
   (ha)   bankers' drafts;
   (hb)   promissory notes;
   (j)   cheque cards;
   (ja)   debit cards;
   (k)   credit cards;
   (l)   certified copies relating to an entry in a register of births, adoptions, marriages, civil partnerships or deaths and issued by the Registrar-General, the Registrar-General for Northern Ireland, a registration officer or a person lawfully authorised to issue certified copies relating to such entries; and
   (m)   certificates relating to entries in such registers.

(6) In subsection (5)(e) above 'share certificate' means an instrument entitling or evidencing the title of a person to a share or interest—
   (a) in any public stock, annuity, fund or debt of any government or State, including a State which forms part of another State; or
   (b) in any stock, fund or debt of a body (whether corporate or unincorporated) established in the United Kingdom or elsewhere.

(7) An instrument is also an instrument to which this section applies if it is a monetary instrument specified for the purposes of this section by an order made by the Secretary of State.

(8) The power under subsection (7) above is exercisable by statutory instrument subject to annulment in pursuance of a resolution of either House of Parliament.

B6.52   The Forgery and Counterfeiting Act 1981, s. 5(5)(f) (knowingly having custody or control of false passports etc.) and (fa) (knowingly having custody or control of false immigration documents), were repealed as of 7 June 2006 by the Identity Cards Act 2006 and replaced by offences under s. 25 of that Act, which applied to any conduct that would previously have been punishable under the old law. See *R (CPS) v Bow Street Magistrates' Court* [2007] 4 All ER 1342, *Soule Ali* [2007] 1 WLR 1599 and the 2011 edition of this work. But as to the repeal and re-enactment of the s. 25 offences, see **B6.59**.

Procedure and Jurisdiction

Offences under the Forgery and Counterfeiting Act 1981, s. 5(1) and (3) are triable either way (Forgery and Counterfeiting Act 1981, s. 6). When tried on indictment they are normally class 3 offences, but see CPD XIII, para. B (see Supplement, **PD-97**) for the additional factors that the court considers on allocation. They are Group A offences for jurisdiction purposes under the CJA 1993, part I (see **A8.10**).   **B6.53**

Alternative Verdicts

Based on the usual principles of law governing alternative verdicts (Criminal Law Act 1967, s. 6(3): see **D19.41** *et seq*.), it is submitted that on an indictment for an offence under the Forgery and Counterfeiting Act 1981, s. 5(1), the jury may return a verdict of guilty of an offence under s. 5(2); and that on an indictment for an offence under s. 5(3) the jury may return a verdict of guilty under s. 5(4). It may, nevertheless, be prudent to add alternative counts.   **B6.54**

Sentence

The maximum sentence for an offence under s. 5(1) or 5(3) is ten years on indictment; six months or a fine not exceeding the statutory maximum or both summarily (Forgery and Counterfeiting Act 1981, s. 6).   **B6.55**

The maximum sentence for an offence under s. 5(2) or 5(4) of the Forgery and Counterfeiting Act 1981 is two years on indictment; six months or a fine not exceeding the statutory maximum or both summarily (Forgery and Counterfeiting Act 1981, s. 6).

Elements

It is not generally an offence merely to have custody or control of false instruments, or materials etc. for making them, even if the instruments or materials are intended for some unlawful purpose. The instruments listed in the Forgery and Counterfeiting Act 1981, s. 5(5), have been singled out for protection, as have those to which the Mental Health Act 1983, s. 126, applies (specified documents relating to mental health).   **B6.56**

Most of the terms used in the Forgery and Counterfeiting Act 1981, s. 5, are considered in **B6.27** to **B6.32**, but the concepts of 'custody or control' and 'lawful authority or excuse' require some comment.

Custody or Control   The offences in the Forgery and Counterfeiting Act 1981, s. 5, are not limited to having the offending items on one's person, or even 'with' one in the sense required for liability under comparable legislation dealing with offensive weapons or theft etc. (e.g., Theft Act 1968, ss. 10 and 25; see **B4.107** and **B4.157**). It will suffice if they are kept in one's home, garage, car or workplace. Problems of liability based on 'innocent possession', such as sometimes arise in other offences (e.g., possession of drugs or firearms) should not be a problem, because the prosecution must prove D's knowledge of the falsity and, in cases under s. 5(1) or 5(3), his ulterior intent. One might perhaps know of the falsity etc. without knowing one had custody or control (cf. *Wings Ltd v Ellis* [1985] AC 272), but such a case would be most unusual, and it is doubtful whether strict liability would be imposed even then.   **B6.57**

Lawful Authority or Excuse   In the absence of any definition in the Forgery and Counterfeiting Act 1981 itself, the concept of lawful excuse must presumably extend to any recognised general defences, and would also cover possession with intent to hand the relevant items to the police or   **B6.58**

493

other authorities at the first reasonable opportunity (*Wuyts* [1969] 2 QB 474; *Sunman* [1995] Crim LR 569). While the cases on reasonable excuse in the context of weapons are generally of little assistance, the approach on forgetfulness may be relevant (see, e.g., *Glidewell* [1999] EWCA Crim 1221 at **B12.156**) as may be the approach in *Densu* [1998] 1 Cr App R 400 on ignorance of the nature of the object in question (see **B12.153**). It would seem that the burden of proving lawful authority or excuse must only be evidential: contrast s. 17(4) of the Act (making or having implements etc. for counterfeiting protected coins), where the legal burden of proof is expressly placed on the defence. If this is correct, then once D raises the issue of lawful authority or excuse, the prosecution must disprove it beyond reasonable doubt. (As to the legal and evidential burdens of proof generally, see **F3.1** *et seq*. and **F3.54**.)

OFFENCES RELATING TO IDENTITY DOCUMENTS

B6.59 The Identity Cards Act 2006 was repealed on 21 January 2011 by the Identity Documents Act 2010, s. 1(1). But the offences created by s. 25 of the 2006 Act were re-enacted with consequential amendments in ss. 4, 5 and 6 of the 2010 Act. Definitions provided by s. 26 of the 2006 Act were likewise re-enacted in ss. 7 to 9 of the 2010 Act; and by s. 13(1) of that Act, '[t]he repeal and re-enactment of provisions by this Act does not affect the continuity of the law'. Thus, by s. 13(3), '[a]ny reference (express or implied) in any enactment, instrument or document to a provision of this Act is to be read as including, in relation to times, circumstances or purposes in relation to which any corresponding provision repealed by this Act had effect, a reference to that corresponding provision' — so far as the context permits.

Identity Documents Act 2010, ss. 4 to 9

4.—(1) It is an offence for a person ('P') with an improper intention to have in P's possession or under P's control—

    (a) an identity document that is false and that P knows or believes to be false,

    (b) an identity document that was improperly obtained and that P knows or believes to have been improperly obtained, or

    (c) an identity document that relates to someone else.

  (2) Each of the following is an improper intention—

    (a) the intention of using the document for establishing personal information about P;

    (b) the intention of allowing or inducing another to use it for establishing, ascertaining or verifying personal information about P or anyone else.

  (3) In subsection (2)(b) the reference to P or anyone else does not include, in the case of a document within subsection (1)(c), the individual to whom it relates.

. . .

5.—(1) It is an offence for a person ('P') with the prohibited intention to make or to have in P's possession or under P's control—

    (a) any apparatus which, to P's knowledge, is or has been specially designed or adapted for the making of false identity documents, or

    (b) any article or material which, to P's knowledge, is or has been specially designed or adapted to be used in the making of such documents.

  (2) The prohibited intention is the intention—

    (a) that P or another will make a false identity document, and

    (b) that the document will be used by somebody for establishing, ascertaining or verifying personal information about a person.

. . .

6.—(1) It is an offence for a person ('P'), without reasonable excuse, to have in P's possession or under P's control—

    (a) an identity document that is false,

    (b) an identity document that was improperly obtained,

    (c) an identity document that relates to someone else,

    (d) any apparatus which, to P's knowledge, is or has been specially designed or adapted for the making of false identity documents, or

  (e) any article or material which, to P's knowledge, is or has been specially designed or adapted to be used in the making of such documents.

...

7.—(1) For the purposes of sections 4 to 6 'identity document' means any document that is or purports to be—
  (a) an immigration document,
  (b) a United Kingdom passport (within the meaning of the Immigration Act 1971),
  (c) a passport issued by or on behalf of the authorities of a country or territory outside the United Kingdom or by or on behalf of an international organisation,
  (d) a document that can be used (in some or all circumstances) instead of a passport,
  (e) a licence to drive a motor vehicle granted under Part 3 of the Road Traffic 1988 or under Part 2 of the Road Traffic (Northern Ireland) Order 1981, or
  (f) a driving licence issued by or on behalf of the authorities of a country or territory outside the United Kingdom.
(2) In subsection (1)(a) 'immigration document' means—
  (a) a document used for confirming the right of a person under the EU Treaties in respect of entry or residence in the United Kingdom,
  (b) a document that is given in exercise of immigration functions and records information about leave granted to a person to enter or to remain in the United Kingdom, or
  (c) a registration card (within the meaning of section 26A of the Immigration Act 1971).

...

8.—(1) For the purposes of sections 4 and 5 'personal information', in relation to an individual ('A'), means—
  (a) A's full name,
  (b) other names by which A is or has previously been known,
  (c) A's gender,
  (d) A's date and place of birth,
  (e) external characteristics of A that are capable of being used for identifying A,
  (f) the address of A's principal place of residence in the United Kingdom,
  (g) the address of every other place in the United Kingdom or elsewhere where A has a place of residence,
  (h) where in the United Kingdom and elsewhere A has previously been resident,
  (i) the times at which A was resident at different places in the United Kingdom or elsewhere,
  (j) A's current residential status,
  (k) residential statuses previously held by A, and
  (l) information about numbers allocated to A for identification purposes and about the documents (including stamps or labels) to which they relate.
(2) In subsection (1) 'residential status' means—
  (a) A's nationality,
  (b) A's entitlement to remain in the United Kingdom, and
  (c) if that entitlement derives from a grant of leave to enter or remain in the United Kingdom, the terms and conditions of that leave.
9.—(1) 'Apparatus' includes any equipment, machinery or device and any wire or cable, together with any software used with it.
(2) In relation to England and Wales and Northern Ireland, an identity document is 'false' only if it is false within the meaning of Part 1 of the Forgery and Counterfeiting Act 1981 (see section 9(1)).
(3) An identity document was 'improperly obtained' if—
  (a) false information was provided in, or in connection with, the application for its issue to the person who issued it, or
  (b) false information was provided in, or in connection with, an application for its modification to a person entitled to modify it.
(4) In subsection (3)—
  (a) 'false' information includes information containing any inaccuracy or omission that results in a tendency to mislead,
  (b) 'information' includes documents (including stamps and labels) and records, and
  (c) the 'issue' of a document includes its renewal, replacement or re-issue (with or without modifications).

(5) References to the making of a false identity document include the modification of an identity document so that it becomes false.

(6) This section applies for the purposes of sections 4 to 6.

Procedure and Jurisdiction

B6.60   Offences under the Identity Documents Act 2010, ss. 4 and 5 are triable only on indictment (ss. 4(4) and 5(3)) and are normally class 3 offences, but see CPD XIII, para. B (see Supplement, **PD-97**) for the additional factors that the court considers on allocation. Offences under s. 6 are triable either way (s. 6(2)). All are Group A offences for jurisdiction purposes under the CJA 1993, part I (see **A8.10**).

Alternative Verdicts

B6.61   Based on the usual principles of law governing alternative verdicts (Criminal Law Act 1967, s. 6(3): see **D19.41** *et seq.*), it is submitted that on an indictment for an offence under the Identity Documents Act 2010, s. 4 or 5, the jury may return a verdict of guilty of an offence under s. 6. It may, nevertheless, be prudent to add alternative counts.

Sentence

B6.62   The maximum sentence for an offence under the Identity Documents Act 2010, s. 4 or 5, is ten years or a fine (or both) (ss. 4(4) and 5(3)). The maximum sentence for an offence under s. 6 when tried on indictment is two years; on summary conviction, it is six months or a fine not exceeding the statutory maximum or both.

In *Cheema* [2002] Cr App R (S) 356, the offender was convicted under the Forgery and Counterfeiting Act 1981 of having custody or control of 12 false passports, intending that they would be used as genuine passports, contrary to s. 5(1) of the 1981 Act which then applied to passports. A sentence of four years' imprisonment was reduced to three years. The Court of Appeal in *Kolawole* [2005] 2 Cr App R (S) 71 approved the sentence in *Cheema*, but disapproved *Siliavski* [2000] 1 Cr App R (S) 23 and *Balasubramaniam* [2002] Cr App R (S) 17. Five years' imprisonment for possessing 250 counterfeit passports with intent was upheld in *Kuosmanen* [2005] 1 Cr App R (S) 354. See also **B6.49**.

Elements

B6.63   Although the Identity Documents Act 2010 replaces two lengthy sections in the 2006 Act with six shorter ones, no obvious change is made to the form or structure of the three offences involved. Section 4 effectively restates the offence previously found in s. 25(1) and (2); s. 5 similarly restates the offence previously found in s. 25(3) and (4), and s. 6 is identical in every respect to the old s. 25(5). The s. 25(5) offence was considered by the Court of Appeal in *Unah* [2012] 1 All ER 122, in which it was held that whether D's ignorance of a document's falsity would amount to a 'reasonable excuse' for possessing it must be question of fact. The same must accordingly be true of the offence under the new s. 6.

One possible caveat arises from the definition of 'improper intention' in s. 4(2). In contrast to the concept of 'requisite intent' it replaces, and in contrast to that of 'prohibited intent' in s. 5(2), it might be possible to construe that definition as non-exhaustive. In other words, there may perhaps be some (as yet unidentified) forms of 'improper intention' beyond those listed in s. 5(2)(a) and (b). The fact that in this respect the wording of the new provision differs from the one it replaced might suggest this. On the other hand, such an intention could easily have been made more obvious by use of the word 'includes'.

The s. 6 offence corresponds to that in the Forgery and Counterfeiting Act 1981, s. 5(4) (see **B6.51** *et seq.*). 'Possession or control' in the former provision broadly corresponds to 'custody or control' in the latter (see **B6.57**) and the concept of 'lawful excuse' must have the same meaning in each case. As to this, see **B6.58**.

FORGERY, FALSIFICATION ETC. OF REGISTERS, CERTIFICATES OR CERTIFIED COPIES

Forgery Act 1861

Under the Forgery Act 1861, ss. 36 and 37, it is an offence, punishable with a maximum penalty **B6.64** of life imprisonment, unlawfully to destroy, deface, injure etc. any register of births, baptisms, marriages, deaths or burials; to cause or permit such damage; or knowingly to make, sign or permit the making of false entries or insertions in such registers or in copies thereof, or knowingly to issue false certificates or copies. These provisions overlap with those of the Forgery and Counterfeiting Act 1981, but deal with acts of damage and destruction as well as with falsification.

Other Provisions Relating to Registers and Certificates

As to the falsification of birth or death certificates, see the Births and Deaths Registration Act **B6.65** 1953, s. 37. As to the making of false statements and the use of false certificates in connection with births and deaths, see the Perjury Act 1911, s. 4 (see **B14.23**). Various non-parochial registers deposited with the Registrar-General are protected under the Non-parochial Registers Act 1840, s. 8.

As to dishonestly inducing another to alter entries under the Land Registration Act 2002, see s. 124 of that Act. See also s. 123 of that Act (suppression of information).

The falsification of any pedigree upon which title to land (or some interest therein) depends, with intent to defraud a purchaser who might thereby be induced to accept the title offered, is punishable with up to two years' imprisonment and/or a fine under the Law of Property Act 1925, s. 183. The A-G must give leave before any prosecution is commenced.

As to falsification of entries in the register of trade marks, see the Trade Marks Act 1994, s. 94. As to forgery of a county court summons or other process of the county court, see the County Courts Act 1984, s. 135.

COUNTERFEITING MONEY AND KINDRED OFFENCES

Introduction

The counterfeiting of currency notes and 'protected coins' is dealt with in part II (ss. 14 to 28) **B6.66** of the Forgery and Counterfeiting Act 1981; the counterfeiting of hallmarks and dies etc. is protected under the Hallmarking Act 1973, s. 6; as to 'counterfeit goods' to which false trade marks are applied, so as to imitate the products of leading manufacturers, see the Trade Marks Act 1994, ss. 92 and 97 (see **B6.102** to **B6.108**).

Scope of Offences under Part II of the Forgery and Counterfeiting Act 1981

Part II of the Forgery and Counterfeiting Act 1981 applies only in respect of currency notes and **B6.67** protected coins, as defined in s. 27.

Forgery and Counterfeiting Act 1981, s. 27

> (1) In this Part of this Act—
> 'currency note' means—
> (a) any note which—
> > (i) has been lawfully issued in England and Wales, Scotland, Northern Ireland, any of the Channel Islands, the Isle of Man or the Republic of Ireland: and
> > (ii) is or has been customarily used as money in the country where it was issued: and
> > (iii) is payable on demand: or

B

      (b) any note which—
          (i) has been lawfully issued in some country other than those mentioned in paragraph (a)(i) above: and
         (ii) is customarily used as money in that country: and
     'protected coin' means any coin which—
      (a) is customarily used as money in any country: or
      (b) is specified in an order made by the Treasury for the purposes of this Part of this Act.
  (2) The power to make an order conferred on the Treasury by subsection (1) above shall be exercisable by statutory instrument.
  (3) A statutory instrument containing such an order shall be laid before Parliament after being made.

B6.68 British or Irish notes come within the Act even if no longer customarily used as money (s. 27(1)(a)); but foreign or Commonwealth notes must be in current use (s. 27(1)(b)). Neither kind need ever have been legal tender: Scottish notes, for example, are not legal tender even in Scotland (and see also s. 28(3)).

Coins must either be in current use or be specified by the Treasury for the purpose of this Act. The following coins have been so specified: sovereigns, half-sovereigns, krugerrands, coins which are denominated in fractions of krugerrands, Maria-Theresia thalers dated 1780 and euro-coins (Forgery and Counterfeiting (Protected Coins) Orders 1981 and 1999 (SI 1981 No. 1505 and 1999 No. 2095)). The counterfeiting of ancient coins *not* specified for these purposes cannot be an offence under this Act, however dishonest the motives.

Meaning of 'Counterfeit'

B6.69   **Forgery and Counterfeiting Act 1981, s. 28**

  (1) For the purposes of this Part of this Act a thing is a counterfeit of a currency note or of a protected coin—
      (a) if it is not a currency note or a protected coin but resembles a currency note or protected coin (whether on one side only or on both) to such an extent that it is reasonably capable of passing for a currency note or protected coin of that description: or
      (b) if it is a currency note or protected coin which has been so altered that it is reasonably capable of passing for a currency note or protected coin of some other description.
  (2) For the purposes of this Part of this Act—
      (a) a thing consisting of one side only of a currency note, with or without the addition of other material, is a counterfeit of such a note:
      (b) a thing consisting—
          (i) of parts of two or more currency notes: or
         (ii) of parts of a currency note, or of parts of two or more currency notes, with the addition of other material,
     is capable of being a counterfeit of a currency note.
  (3) References in this Part of this Act to passing or tendering a counterfeit of a currency note or a protected coin are not to be construed as confined to passing or tendering it as legal tender.

It is not possible to argue that a one-sided note or coin is *ipso facto* incapable of passing for a genuine one, but in other respects the question of what kind of imitation can amount to a counterfeit is one of fact. An incompetent counterfeiter whose notes would fool nobody can be guilty of an attempt to counterfeit or of an offence under s. 17 of the Act (making or having custody of materials etc. for counterfeiting; see **B6.94** to **B6.99**).

Section 19 of the Act (imitation coins produced for promotional purposes) appears to assume that a coin may imitate a British coin in size, shape and substance, without necessarily being a counterfeit. Since any such coins could, in some circumstances, be confused with the real thing (e.g., when mixed in a handful of change in poor light), it would seem that a counterfeit must be 'reasonably capable' of bearing some direct scrutiny, if not perhaps close or careful scrutiny.

Sentencing Guidelines

The maximum penalties for the various offences are set out in the sections dealing with them **B6.70** below. There is no definitive sentencing guideline for these offences.

In *Crick* (1981) 3 Cr App R (S) 275, Mustill J made the following general remarks about the offences of counterfeiting notes or coinage:

> Coining is a serious offence. It was rightly treated as such by the learned judge, who correctly took the view that it called for an immediate custodial sentence. It must, however, be recognised that not all such offences are of the same gravity. At one extreme is the professional forger, with carefully prepared plates, and elaborate machinery, who manufactures large quantities of banknotes and puts them into circulation. A long sentence of imprisonment is appropriate in such a case. Here the offence is at the other end of the scale. The tools used to make the blanks were primitive, and were not acquired specially for the purpose; the techniques used were amateurish, and there was little real attempt to make the blanks a facsimile of a 50 pence piece. The coins were not, and could not have been, put into general circulation.

A three-year sentence was reduced to one of nine months.

Banknote Production   Longer sentences will be upheld for *production* of banknotes, but much **B6.71** depends on the sophistication of the enterprise and the success of the offenders. Sentences of ten years and eight months were appropriate in *Hartley* [2012] 1 Cr App R (S) 429, for two offences involving the production of counterfeit currency, with a total value in excess of £790,000. In *Allen* [2011] 1 Cr App R (S) 92 six years' imprisonment was upheld for an offender who pleaded guilty to conspiracy to produce counterfeit currency. He had purchased specialist equipment for the production of counterfeit notes, and forged currency with a face value of about £15,000 was seized from his home. He admitted to producing currency with a face value of up to £250,000. See also *Allyson* (1989) 11 Cr App R (S) 60, *Britton* (1994) 15 Cr App R (S) 482, and *Dossiter* [1999] 2 Cr App R (S) 248.

Passing of Banknotes   In *Howard* (1985) 82 Cr App R 262, the Court of Appeal provided guid- **B6.72** ance for sentencing in cases involving the *passing* of counterfeit notes. It was said that a custodial sentence would be required in nearly all cases, and that possession of large quantities of notes, indicating proximity to the counterfeiters, would be a most important consideration in determining the severity of the sentence. *Miller* [2010] 2 Cr App R (S) 413 is a case towards the lower end of the scale, where the offender, who had a long history of offending, tendered two £20 notes for drinks at a bar and it was noticed that the notes had the same serial number. Three more such notes were found at the offender's home. The Court of Appeal said that a sentence of 15 months' imprisonment was appropriate on a guilty plea. In *Everett* (1983) 5 Cr App R (S) 207 the offender had bought two counterfeit £20 notes for £4 each and changed them at a club. Whilst the offence was a 'one-off', the offender had previous convictions for dishonesty, and a sentence of 12 months was upheld. In *Shah* (1987) 9 Cr App R (S) 167 the offender, while on bail in relation to unrelated charges, attempted to purchase a record using a counterfeit £50 note. The offender had previous convictions, but of a nature different to the current offence. There was no evidence of dealing in counterfeit currency, and the offender contested the case on the ground that he had not realised the note to be counterfeit. Steyn J said that while this case was at the lower end of the spectrum of seriousness, 'in the absence of exceptional circumstances an immediate custodial sentence is necessary in all cases involving the tendering or passing of forged banknotes'. A 12-month prison sentence, suspended for two years, together with a supervision order, was upheld.

COUNTERFEITING NOTES OR COINS

Forgery and Counterfeiting Act 1981, s. 14   **B6.73**

(1) It is an offence for a person to make a counterfeit of a currency note or of a protected coin, intending that he or another shall pass or tender it as genuine.

(2) It is an offence for a person to make a counterfeit of a currency note or of a protected coin without lawful authority or excuse.

Procedure

B6.74   Offences under s. 14(1) are by s. 22 of the Act, triable either way. When tried on indictment they are normally a class 3 offence, but see CPD XIII, para. B (see Supplement, **PD-97**) for the additional factors that the court considers on allocation. They are Group A offences for jurisdiction purposes under the CJA 1993, part I (see **A8.10**).

Indictment

B6.75

Statement of Offence

Counterfeiting contrary to section 14(1) of the Forgery and Counterfeiting Act 1981.

Particulars of Offence

A on or about the … day of … made a counterfeit of a currency note, namely a Bank of England £5 note, intending to pass or tender the same as genuine.

Alternative Verdicts

B6.76   It is submitted that, on an indictment for an offence under s. 14(1) it is open to the jury to return a verdict of guilty of the offence under s. 14(2) (see generally the Criminal Law Act 1967, s. 6(3), and **D19.41** *et seq*.). It may, however, be prudent to add an alternative count.

Sentence

B6.77   The Forgery and Counterfeiting Act 1981, s. 22, prescribes the maximum penalties: for an offence under s. 14(1), the maximum penalty is ten years and/or a fine on indictment; six months and/or a fine not exceeding the statutory maximum summarily; for an offence under s. 14(2), it is two years and/or a fine on indictment; six months and/or a fine not exceeding the statutory maximum summarily. For sentencing guidelines, see **B6.70**.

Elements

B6.78   In s. 14, a distinction is drawn (as in s. 5 of the Act: see **B6.51** to **B6.58**) between cases in which there is proof of an intent that the fake item shall be passed as genuine (s. 14(1)) and cases in which there is not (s. 14(2)). In the latter kind of case counterfeiting is still an offence (albeit a less serious one), unless the maker has lawful authority or excuse. The reason for this is that even the honest manufacture of realistic fakes carries risks of confusion or subsequent misuse. See *Heron* [1982] 1 All ER 993, decided under the Coinage Offences Act 1936, in which the making of counterfeit coins was held to be an offence without proof of any intent to deceive; see also *Selby v DPP* [1972] AC 515.

The intent specified in s. 14(1) is ulterior. The actual passing of the counterfeit need never happen, and it would suffice even if it was intended to happen outside the jurisdiction, as long as the counterfeiting itself was committed within it. In contrast to ss. 1 to 4 and s. 5(1) of the Act, there is no need to prove an intent to induce someone to act to his own or another's prejudice.

PASSING, TENDERING OR DELIVERING COUNTERFEIT NOTES OR COINS

B6.79

Forgery and Counterfeiting Act 1981, s. 15

(1) It is an offence for a person—
   (a) to pass or tender as genuine any thing which is, and which he knows or believes to be, a counterfeit of a currency note or of a protected coin; or
   (b) to deliver to another any thing which is, and which he knows or believes to be, such a counterfeit, intending that the person to whom it is delivered or another shall pass or tender it as genuine.

(2) It is an offence for a person to deliver to another, without lawful authority or excuse, any thing which is, and which he knows or believes to be, a counterfeit of a currency note or of a protected coin.

Procedure

Offences under s. 15 are, by s. 22 of the Act, triable either way. When tried on indictment they are normally class 3 offences, but see CPD XIII, para. B (see Supplement, **PD-97**) for the additional factors that the court considers on allocation. They are Group A offences for jurisdiction purposes under the CJA 1993, part I (see **A8.10**).   **B6.80**

Alternative Verdicts

It is submitted that, on an indictment for an offence under s. 15(1)(b), it is open to the jury to return a verdict of guilty of the offence under s. 15(2) (see generally the Criminal Law Act 1967, s. 6(3), and **D19.41** *et seq.*). It may, however, be prudent to add an alternative count.   **B6.81**

Sentence

Section 22 of the Act, prescribes the maximum penalties: for an offence under s. 15(1)(a) or (b), the maximum penalty is ten years and/or a fine on indictment; six months and/or a fine not exceeding the statutory maximum summarily; for an offence under s. 15(2), it is two years and/or a fine on indictment; six months and/or a fine not exceeding the statutory maximum summarily. For sentencing guidelines, see **B6.70**.   **B6.82**

Scope of Offence

Section 15 follows the same pattern as s. 14 (see **B6.73** to **B6.78**), in that it distinguishes between cases in which a counterfeit is passed as genuine or delivered to another with intent that he should so pass it, and cases in which it is merely 'delivered', perhaps expressly described as a reproduction (*Selby v DPP* [1972] AC 515). The latter kind of case attracts less serious penalties, but is still regarded as dangerous and undesirable.   **B6.83**

Meaning of 'Passing' and 'Tendering'

'Passing' suggests acceptance by the person to whom the thing is given, but a counterfeit may be *tendered* as genuine, even if it is at once rejected, and an offence may be committed even where the item in question is not passed or tendered as legal tender (s. 28(3)). Many forms of notes etc. used as money are not legal tender (e.g., Scottish notes), and many protected coins have a collectors' value exceeding any nominal value as currency.   **B6.84**

Knowledge and Belief

It would not be an offence under s. 15 to pass or tender a note etc. which one suspects *may* be a counterfeit, even if the suspicion is a strong one. The section requires knowledge or belief, as in handling stolen goods under the Theft Act 1968, s. 22 (see **B4.160**), and those terms must presumably bear the same meanings as under that provision.   **B6.85**

Meaning of 'Delivering'

'Delivering', in s. 15(1)(b) and (2) of the 1981 Act need not involve any intent to deceive as to the nature of the thing delivered, but the more serious offence under s. 15(1)(b) may be committed if it is intended that the counterfeits should eventually be tendered as genuine, by the recipient or some other person.   **B6.86**

Lawful Authority or Excuse

An obvious example of lawful delivery, which would not be an offence under s. 15(2), would be where the counterfeits are handed over to the police; but lawful excuse could extend to general defences, such as mistake or duress. In view of the contrast with s. 17(4) (see **B6.99**), in which   **B6.87** the legal burden of proof is expressly placed on the defence, it seems clear that the defence have only an evidential burden to discharge under s. 15(2). If the issue is raised by evidence, the prosecution must disprove the existence of lawful authority or excuse (see generally **F3.1** *et seq.* and **F3.18** *et seq.*), but if there is no evidence capable of supporting such a defence, the judge need not leave it to the jury (*Sunman* [1995] Crim LR 569).

CUSTODY OR CONTROL OF COUNTERFEIT NOTES OR COINS

B6.88

Forgery and Counterfeiting Act 1981, s. 16

(1) It is an offence for a person to have in his custody or under his control any thing which is, and which he knows or believes to be, a counterfeit of a currency note or of a protected coin, intending either to pass or tender it as genuine or to deliver it to another with the intention that he or another shall pass or tender it as genuine.

(2) It is an offence for a person to have in his custody or under his control, without lawful authority or excuse, any thing which is, and which he knows or believes to be, a counterfeit of a currency note or of a protected coin.

(3) It is immaterial for the purposes of subsections (1) and (2) above that a coin or note is not in a fit state to be passed or tendered or that the making or counterfeiting of a coin or note has not been finished or perfected.

Procedure

B6.89 Offences under s. 16(1) are, by s. 22 of the Act, triable either way. When tried on indictment they are normally class 3 offences, but see CPD XIII, para. B (see Supplement, **PD-97**) for the additional factors that the court considers on allocation. They are Group A offences for jurisdiction purposes under the CJA 1993, part I (see **A8.10**).

Indictment

B6.90

Statement of Offence

Having custody or control of a counterfeit note contrary to section 16(1) of the Forgery and Counterfeiting Act 1981.

Particulars of Offence

A on or about the…day of…had in his custody or under his control a counterfeit of a currency note, namely a Bank of England £5 note, knowing or believing the same to be counterfeit and intending to pass or tender it as genuine [or to deliver it to X with the intention that X should pass or tender it as genuine].

Alternative Verdicts

B6.91 It is submitted that on an indictment for an offence under s. 16(1), it is open to the jury to return a verdict of guilty of the offence under s. 16(2) (see generally the Criminal Law Act 1967, s. 6(3), and **D19.41** *et seq.*). It may, however, be prudent to add an alternative count.

Sentence

B6.92 Section 22 of the Act prescribes the maximum penalties: for an offence under s. 16(1), the maximum penalty is ten years and/or a fine on indictment; six months and/or a fine not exceeding the statutory maximum summarily; for an offence under s. 16(2), it is two years and/or a fine on indictment; six months and/or a fine not exceeding the statutory maximum summarily. For sentencing guidelines, see **B6.70**.

Elements

B6.93 Section 16 follows the same format as ss. 14 and 15 (see **B6.73** to **B6.87**). Section 16 serves the same kind of function as that served by s. 5(1) and (2) in relation to forgery offences (see **B6.51** to **B6.58**). As to the meaning of 'custody and control' in this context, see the discussion of s. 5 at **B6.57**.

OFFENCES RELATING TO MATERIALS AND IMPLEMENTS FOR COUNTERFEITING

Definitions

Forgery and Counterfeiting Act 1981, s. 17   **B6.94**

(1) It is an offence for a person to make, or to have in his custody or under his control, any thing which he intends to use, or permit any other person to use, for the purpose of making a counterfeit of a currency note or of a protected coin with the intention that it be passed or tendered as genuine.

(2) It is an offence for a person without lawful authority or excuse—
    (a) to make; or
    (b) to have in his custody or under his control,
    any thing which, to his knowledge, is or has been specially designed or adapted for the making of a counterfeit of a currency note.

(3) Subject to subsection (4) below, it is an offence for a person to make, or to have in his custody or under his control, any implement which, to his knowledge, is capable of imparting to any thing a resemblance—
    (a) to the whole or part of either side of a protected coin: or
    (b) to the whole or part of the reverse of the image on either side of a protected coin.

(4) It shall be a defence for a person charged with an offence under subsection (3) above to show—
    (a) that he made the implement or, as the case may be, had it in his custody or under his control, with the written consent of the Treasury; or
    (b) that he had lawful authority otherwise than by virtue of paragraph (a) above, or a lawful excuse, for making it or having it in his custody or under his control.

Procedure

Both offences under s. 17 are, by s. 22 of the Act, triable either way. When tried on indictment   **B6.95** they are normally class 3 offences, but see CPD XIII, para. B (see Supplement, **PD-97**) for the additional factors that the court considers on allocation. They are Group A offences for jurisdiction purposes under the CJA 1993, part I (see **A8.10**).

Indictment

Statement of Offence   **B6.96**

Having custody or control of thing intended for use in making a counterfeit, with intent, contrary to section 17(1) of the Forgery and Counterfeiting Act 1981.

Particulars of Offence

A on or about the...day of...had in his custody or under his control a press and a quantity of inks intending to use the same to make a counterfeit of a currency note, namely a Bank of England £5 note, with the intention that such note be passed or tendered as genuine.

Sentence

Section 22 prescribes the maximum penalties: for an offence under s. 17(1), the maximum   **B6.97** penalty is ten years and/or a fine on indictment; six months and/or a fine not exceeding the statutory maximum summarily; for an offence under s. 17(2) or (3), it is two years and/or a fine on indictment; six months and/or a fine not exceeding the statutory maximum summarily. For sentencing guidelines, see **B6.70**.

Scope of Offence

Section 17 serves the same kind of function as that served by s. 5(3) and (4) of the Act in relation   **B6.98** to forgery offences (see **B6.51** to **B6.58**), and it follows s. 5 in distinguishing between cases where there is proof of an intent to pass false items as genuine and cases where there is not. Subsection (1) of s. 17 deals with the more serious kind of case; subsections (2) and (3) deal with the less serious kind. Either subsection may apply, not only to essential counterfeiting materials such as inks, but also to optional 'quality-control' devices such as chromolins (*Maltman* [1995] 1 Cr App R 239).

Lawful Authority or Excuse

B6.99   Section 17(3) is subject to subsection (4), which expressly places the burden of proving lawful authority or excuse on the defence. However, subsection (2) is not subject to subsection (4). This indicates that the legal burden lies on the prosecution to disprove beyond reasonable doubt defences of lawful excuse etc. under s. 17(2), and indeed under all other provisions in the Act except s. 17(3). See generally **F3.1** *et seq.* and **F3.18** *et seq.*

IMPORTATION AND EXPORTATION OF COUNTERFEIT NOTES OR COINS

B6.100

Forgery and Counterfeiting Act 1981, ss. 20 and 21

20. The importation, landing or unloading of a counterfeit of a currency note or of a protected coin without the consent of the Treasury is hereby prohibited.
21.—(1) The exportation of a counterfeit of a currency note or of a protected coin without the consent of the Treasury is hereby prohibited.
   (2) A counterfeit of a currency note or of a protected coin which is removed to the Isle of Man from the United Kingdom shall be deemed to be exported from the United Kingdom—
      (a) for the purposes of this section: and
      (b) for the purposes of the customs and excise Acts, in their application to the prohibition imposed by this section.

Sections 20 and 21 impose prohibitions, but are not themselves offence-creating provisions. The relevant offences are those created under the Customs and Excise Management Act 1979, ss. 50 and 68 (see **B16.28** and **B16.35**). Any such offences involving breaches of ss. 20 or 21 are Group A offences for jurisdiction purposes under the CJA 1993, part I (see **A8.10**).

POWERS OF SEARCH, SEIZURE AND FORFEITURE

B6.101   Powers of search and seizure in relation to false instruments and the means of their production are contained in the Forgery and Counterfeiting Act 1981, s. 7(1). Broadly similar powers in relation to counterfeiting are contained in s. 24(1) of that Act.

An order for the forfeiture, destruction or disposal of such objects may be obtained from a magistrates' court, if it is satisfied that the order is conducive to the public interest; but anyone claiming a proprietary right or other interest in the objects concerned must be given the opportunity to 'show cause why the order should not be made' (ss. 7(4) and 24(4)). Where convictions are imposed under the Act, the court concerned may order the destruction or forfeiture of any object which has been shown to relate to the offence, or it may order it to be dealt with in such other manner as it thinks fit (ss. 7(3) and 24(3)). Any applicant claiming an interest in the object concerned must be given the opportunity to oppose the order under s. 7(4) or 24(4).

FALSE APPLICATION OR USE OF TRADE MARKS

B6.102

Trade Marks Act 1994, s. 92

(1) A person commits an offence who with a view to gain for himself or another, or with intent to cause loss to another, and without the consent of the proprietor—
   (a) applies to goods or their packaging a sign identical to, or likely to be mistaken for, a registered trade mark, or
   (b) sells or lets for hire, offers or exposes for sale or hire or distributes goods which bear, or the packaging of which bears, such a sign, or

(c) has in his possession, custody or control in the course of a business any such goods with a view to the doing of anything, by himself or another, which would be an offence under paragraph (b).

(2) A person commits an offence who with a view to gain for himself or another, or with intent to cause loss to another, and without the consent of the proprietor—

(a) applies a sign identical to, or likely to be mistaken for, a registered trade mark to material intended to be used—
 (i) for labelling or packaging goods,
 (ii) as a business paper in relation to goods, or
 (iii) for advertising goods, or

(b) uses in the course of a business material bearing such a sign for labelling or packaging goods, as a business paper in relation to goods, or for advertising goods, or

(c) has in his possession, custody or control in the course of a business any such material with a view to the doing of anything, by himself or another, which would be an offence under paragraph (b).

(3) A person commits an offence who with a view to gain for himself or another, or with intent to cause loss to another, and without the consent of the proprietor—

(a) makes an article specifically designed or adapted for making copies of a sign identical to, or likely to be mistaken for, a registered trade mark, or

(b) has such an article in his possession, custody or control in the course of a business, knowing or having reason to believe that it has been, or is to be, used to produce goods, or material for labelling or packaging goods, as a business paper in relation to goods, or for advertising goods.

Sentence and Procedure

Offences under s. 92 are punishable on indictment with a fine and/or a maximum of ten years' **B6.103**
imprisonment; on summary conviction with imprisonment for six months and/or a fine not exceeding the statutory maximum (s. 92(6)). When tried on indictment they are normally class 3 offences, but see CPD XIII, para. B (see Supplement, **PD-97**) for the additional factors that the court considers on allocation. Relevant sentencing decisions are *Ansari* [2000] 1 Cr App R (S) 94, *Burns* [2001] 1 Cr App R (S) 220, *Gleeson* [2002] 1 Cr App R (S) 485, *Woolridge* [2006] 1 Cr App R (S) 72, *Hatton* [2008] 1 Cr App R (S) 429 and *Kirkwood* [2006] 2 Cr App R (S) 263. In *Manders* [2013] 1 Cr App R (S) 73 (13) the Court of Appeal considered the earlier cases before upholding a sentence of two years' imprisonment on an offender who pleaded guilty on the day of trial to manufacturing counterfeit DVDs on a commercial scale. The first level of his house was given over to the production of these, and 32,000 counterfeit discs were found together with computer hard drives, DVD writing machines, printers and scanners. The offender was well aware of the illegality of his operation, and had even downloaded sentencing decisions in comparable cases from the internet. Proceedings for offences committed by partnerships must be brought against the partnership in the name of the firm, and not that of the partners (s. 101(1)). As to the liability of individual partners, see **B6.107**.

Local weights and measures authorities are responsible for the enforcement of s. 92, and for this purpose are vested with the same powers to make test purchases, enter premises, seize goods and documents, etc., as under the Trade Descriptions Act 1968 or the new regulations that have largely replaced that Act (see **B6.109** *et seq.*) (Trade Marks Act 1994, s. 93).

Requirement for Specific Offence

Although commercial activities involving trade in counterfeit goods will often involve the com- **B6.104**
mission of offences under the Consumer Protection from Unfair Trading Regulations 2008 (see **B6.109** *et seq.*), and in some cases offences under the Theft Act 1968, it was felt that a set of specific offences should exist to combat this trade. Such offences were originally introduced by s. 58A of the Trade Marks Act 1938, inserted by s. 300 of the Copyright, Designs and Patents Act 1988. The Trade Marks Act 1994, s. 92, repeals and replaces these offences with broadly similar, but not identical, provisions.

Scope of Offences under Trade Marks Act 1994, s. 92

B6.105 The offences created by s. 92(1) to (3) deal only with the infringement, etc., of registered trade marks in respect of goods. A trade mark is defined in s. 1 of the 1994 Act as any sign capable of being represented graphically which is capable of distinguishing goods or services of one undertaking from those of other undertakings. It may consist of words, names, designs, letters, numerals or the shape of goods or their packaging. Registration gives the owner a property right in it, which is protected under the 1994 Act (s. 2). Section 92 does not, however, apply to infringement of trade marks in respect of services. Furthermore, s. 92(4) provides that no offence can be committed under s. 92 unless the goods involved are goods in respect of which the trade mark has been registered, or the use of the counterfeit mark, etc., would take unfair advantage of, or be detrimental to the distinctive character or reputation of, a trade mark that has a reputation in the UK.

An offence under s. 92(1), (2) or (3), can be committed only when the offending sign is used as an indication or badge of trade origin. This involves a question of fact in each case, namely whether the sign would be so perceived by the average customer of the type of goods in question. See *Johnstone* [2003] 3 All ER 884 and *Thompson* [2006] EWCA Crim 3058. But it is no defence to argue that the quality of counterfeiting is so poor that a buyer is unlikely to be deceived (*Boulter* [2008] EWCA Crim 2375).

A 'bootleg' compact disc of music by artists such as the Rolling Stones, if it does not purport to be anything *other* than a bootleg recording, does not offend under s. 92, even though the name 'Rolling Stones' is a registered trade mark. It would be otherwise if the disc purported to be (or would be perceived by customers as) a work released *by* the Rolling Stones, because the use of the trade mark under those circumstances would indeed purport to indicate the trade origin of the disc itself, and not merely serve to identify the artists. It is not however a defence for a maker or supplier to inform his immediate client that the goods are counterfeit: the focus must be on the appearance of the goods themselves, and how they might later be perceived by consumers (*Morgan* [2006] EWCA Crim 1742).

As to the scope of s. 92(1)(c), see *Kousar* [2009] 2 Cr App R 88, in which it was held that a market trader's wife did not have possession, custody or control of his stock merely because he kept it at their home and that, even if she did possess it, she could commit no offence under s. 92(1)(c) unless she was involved in the business as a participant.

Mens Rea and Defences

B6.106 D must in all cases be shown to have acted with a view to gain or with an intent to cause loss to another. This is the same ulterior intent that is required under the Theft Act 1968, ss. 17 and 21, and it must have the same meaning as it bears there (see **B5.46**). This may not necessarily mean, however, that D acted dishonestly, knowingly or fraudulently.

Under s. 92(5), it is a defence for D to prove that he believed on reasonable grounds that the use or proposed use of the offending sign concerned was not an infringement of the registered trade mark. This applies both to cases in which D reasonably believes there is no such registered trade mark and to cases in which he is aware of the trade mark but unaware that it is being infringed (*Johnstone* [2003] 3 All ER 884). The burdens imposed here are persuasive and not merely evidential (*Johnstone*).

It does not follow that someone who is simply ignorant of the existence of a registered trade mark, or who has not paid any attention to it, still less someone who has been reckless of its existence, has a defence under s. 92(5) (*McCrudden* [2005] EWCA Crim 466).

By s. 101(4), 'Where a partnership is guilty of an offence under this Act, every partner, other than a partner who is proved to have been ignorant of or to have attempted to prevent the commission of the offence, is also guilty of the offence and liable to be proceeded against and punished accordingly'. This does not require the prior conviction of the firm. It merely requires the court to be satisfied that the firm (which may no longer exist) is or was guilty of such an offence (*Wakefield* (2004) 168 JP 505).

Offences Committed by Bodies Corporate

Directors, managers or other officers of a body corporate who connive at or consent to the commission of an offence by that body will be guilty of the same offence (s. 101(5)). As to the meaning of the term 'manager', see **A6.24**. **B6.107**

Forfeiture Provisions

The Trade Marks Act 1994, s. 97, provides for the making of forfeiture orders in relation to counterfeit goods or packaging (or articles used in their production, etc.) seized in connection with the investigation or prosecution of an offence under s. 92, an offence under the Trade Descriptions Act 1968, or an offence of dishonesty or deception. Such orders may be sought either from the court before which relevant criminal proceedings have been brought or, where no such application has been made, by way of complaint to a magistrates' court (s. 97(2)). **B6.108**

If satisfied that a relevant offence has been committed in relation to the goods, etc. (or other goods which are representative of them), the court may order that they be destroyed in accordance with its directions, or that they be released to a specified person, on condition (a) that he causes offending signs to be removed or obliterated and (b) that any order against him to pay costs in those proceedings is complied with (s. 97(7)).

UNFAIR COMMERCIAL PRACTICES, MISLEADING ADVERTISEMENTS ETC.

The Consumer Protection from Unfair Trading Regulations 2008 (SI 2008 No. 1277) came into force on 26 May 2008 and supplanted provisions previously found in the Trade Descriptions Act 1968 (false or misleading descriptions in respect of goods, services, accommodation or facilities) and the Consumer Protection Act 1987, part III (misleading price indications to consumers). The Regulations implement Directive 2005/29/EC of the European Parliament and of the Council concerning unfair business-to-consumer commercial practices together with article 6.2 of Directive 1999/44/EC of the European Parliament and of the Council on certain aspects of the sale of consumer goods and associated guarantees. **B6.109**

They are supplemented by the Business Protection from Misleading Marketing Regulations 2008 (SI 2008 No. 1276) which implement Directive 2006/114/EC of the European Parliament and of the Council concerning misleading and comparative advertising.

Other repeals effected by SI 2008/1277 include the Fraudulent Mediums Act 1951, the Mock Auctions Act 1961, the Weights and Measures Act 1985, s. 29 (false representations as to quantity), the Consumer Credit Act 1974, s. 46 (false or misleading credit or hire advertisements) and the Control of Misleading Advertising Regulations 1988 (SI 1988 No. 915).

Unfair Commercial Practices

The Consumer Protection from Unfair Trading Regulations, reg. 3(1), prohibits (but does not itself criminalise) a range of 'unfair commercial practices'. Such practices are not confined to those that involve misleading acts or omissions. A commercial practice is defined in reg. 2 as an act, omission, course of conduct, representation or commercial communication (including advertising and marketing) by a trader, which is directly connected with the promotion, sale or supply of a product to or from consumers, whether occurring before, during or after a commercial transaction (if any) in relation to a product. This definition was considered by the Court of Appeal in *X Ltd* [2013] 3 All ER 995, where it was held that an unfair commercial **B6.110** practice could take the form of an isolated act and was not confined to courses of repeated malpractice. 'A commercial practice' said Leveson LJ, 'can be derived from a single incident. It will depend on the circumstances'. Moreover, there need be no actual sale or transaction, as the words 'if any' make clear. If there has been such a transaction the unfair practice may come later, as where a trader misleads a customer as to his rights or duties under that transaction.

By reg. 3(3), a commercial practice is deemed unfair if (a) it contravenes the requirements of 'professional diligence' (skill and care commensurate with honest market practice or good faith); and (b) it materially distorts or is likely to materially distort the economic behaviour of the 'average consumer' with regard to the product. These concepts are further defined in reg. 2.

By reg. 3(4), a commercial practice is also deemed unfair if (a) it is a misleading action under the provisions of reg. 5; (b) it is a misleading omission under the provisions of reg. 6; (c) it is aggressive under the provisions of reg. 7; or (d) it is listed in sch. 1.

B6.111   Regulations 5 and 6 define misleading actions and omissions. By reg. 7(1) (which should be read in conjunction with reg. 7(2) and (3)), a commercial practice is 'aggressive' if in its factual context, taking account of all of its features and circumstances:

(a) it significantly impairs or is likely significantly to impair the average consumer's freedom of choice or conduct in relation to the product concerned through the use of harassment, coercion or undue influence; and

(b) it thereby causes or is likely to cause him to take a transactional decision he would not have taken otherwise.

Schedule 1 lists over 30 commercial practices that are deemed inherently (and 'in all circumstances') unfair. Many of the practices involve false or misleading statements, and most but not all give rise to criminal liability under reg. 12 (see **B6.112**).

Offences Relating to Unfair Commercial Practices

B6.112   By regs. 8 to 12, a trader (defined in reg. 2 as any person who in relation to a commercial practice is acting for purposes relating to his business, and anyone acting in the name of or on behalf of a trader) may incur criminal liability for engaging in specified unfair commercial practices.

Consumer Protection from Unfair Trading Regulations 2008, regs. 8 to 12

8.—(1) A trader is guilty of an offence if—
(a) he knowingly or recklessly engages in a commercial practice which contravenes the requirements of professional diligence under regulation 3(3)(a); and
(b) the practice materially distorts or is likely to materially distort the economic behaviour of the average consumer with regard to the product under regulation 3(3)(b).
(2) For the purposes of paragraph (1)(a) a trader who engages in a commercial practice without regard to whether the practice contravenes the requirements of professional diligence shall be deemed recklessly to engage in the practice, whether or not the trader has reason for believing that the practice might contravene those requirements.
9. A trader is guilty of an offence if he engages in a commercial practice which is a misleading action under regulation 5 otherwise than by reason of the commercial practice satisfying the condition in regulation 5(3)(b).
10. A trader is guilty of an offence if he engages in a commercial practice which is a misleading omission under regulation 6.
11. A trader is guilty of an offence if he engages in a commercial practice which is aggressive under regulation 7.
12. A trader is guilty of an offence if he engages in a commercial practice set out in any of paragraphs 1 to 10, 12 to 27 and 29 to 31 of schedule 1.

B6.113   Strict liability is applicable to offences under regs. 9 to 12, subject to defences of due diligence (reg. 17) or innocent publication of an offending advertisement (reg. 18) but the reg. 8 offence requires proof of knowledge or recklessness, which is given an extended and objective meaning under reg. 8(2).

Persons other than traders may incur liability under reg. 16 where their acts or defaults cause traders to commit offences under regs. 9 to 12, or acts, etc., that would have involved offences but for the availability of defences under regs. 17 or 18. As to offences by corporations or Scottish partnerships, see reg. 15.

Enforcement of the regulations depends in England and Wales on the OFT, and on local weights and measures authorities. Their duties and powers of investigation and enforcement are governed by part 4 of the Regulations. By reg. 13, all offences under regs. 8 to 12 are triable either way and punishable on indictment by a fine and/or imprisonment for a term not exceeding two years. Following summary conviction, the maximum penalty is a fine not exceeding the statutory maximum. There is also a summary offence of obstructing authorised officers (reg. 23) punishable by a fine not exceeding the statutory maximum. As to the power of local authorities to prosecute for conspiracy to defraud, see **A5.63**.

By reg. 14(1), no proceedings for an offence under the regulations may be commenced after the **B6.114** end of the period of three years beginning with the date of the commission of the offence, or the end of the period of one year beginning with the date of discovery of the offence by the prosecutor, whichever is earlier. A certificate signed by or on behalf of the prosecutor and stating the date on which the offence was discovered by him shall be conclusive evidence of that fact and a certificate stating that matter and purporting to be so signed shall be treated as so signed unless the contrary is proved (reg. 14(2)).

Notwithstanding anything in the MCA 1980, s. 127(1), an information relating to an offence under the Regulations which is triable by a magistrates' court in England and Wales may be so tried if it is laid at any time before the end of the period of 12 months beginning with the date of the commission of the offence (reg. 14(3)).

Misleading Business to Business Advertising

The Business Protection from Misleading Marketing Regulations 2008 prohibit misleading **B6.115** business-to-business advertising and set out the conditions under which comparative advertisements (which is any advertisement which identifies a competitor or a competitor's product) are permitted.

The Business Protection Regulations broadly follow the pattern of the Consumer Protection from Unfair Trading Regulations. A 'misleading' advertisement (defined as one which deceives or is likely to deceive the traders to whom it is addressed or whom it reaches; and by reason of its deceptive nature is likely to affect their economic behaviour; or which for those reasons, injures or is likely to injure a competitor, is prohibited under reg. 3. By reg. 6, a trader who engages in such advertising commits a criminal offence, subject to any 'due diligence' or 'innocent publications' defences under regs. 11 and 12. In contrast, breaches of the rules relating to comparative advertising (reg. 4) are criminalised only if the advertisement thereby becomes misleading under regs. 3 and 6.

Persons other than traders may incur liability under reg. 9 where their acts or defaults cause traders to commit offences under reg. 6, or acts that would have been offences but for defences under regs. 11 or 12. As to offences by corporations or Scottish partnerships, see reg. 8.

Civil or criminal enforcement of the Regulations is entrusted in England and Wales to the OFT, and to local weights and measures authorities. Their powers of investigation and enforcement are governed by part 3 of the Regulations. By reg. 7, an offence under reg. 6 is triable either way and punishable on indictment by a fine and/or imprisonment for a term not exceeding two years. Following summary conviction, the maximum penalty is a fine not exceeding the statutory maximum. There is also a summary offence of obstructing authorised officers (reg. 25) punishable by a fine not exceeding the statutory maximum. As to the power of local authorities to prosecute for conspiracy to defraud, see **A5.63**.

Regulation 10 deals with time limits on prosecutions. These are similar to those that apply under the Consumer Protection from Unfair Trading Regulations 2008, reg. 14 (see **B6.114**).

Property Misdescriptions and Holiday Accommodation Contracts

B6.116 Misleading statements or representations concerning residential or commercial property sales or lettings fall within the ambit of the Consumer Protection from Unfair Trading Regulations or the Business Protection from Misleading Marketing Regulations but, prior to 1 October 2013, were more specifically dealt with under the Property Misdescriptions Act 1991, s. 1. The existence of largely duplicated offences in this area was however considered to be 'burdensome and confusing', and the 1991 Act was accordingly repealed on 1 October 2013 by the Property Misdescriptions Act 1991 (Repeal) Order 2013 (SI 2013 No. 1575).

Offences under the Consumer Protection from Unfair Trading Regulations committed in connection with timeshares and other regulated holiday accommodation contracts may alternatively be prosecuted under the Timeshare, Holiday Products, Resale and Exchange Contracts Regulations 2010 (SI 2010 No. 2960), part 7. As to the power of local authorities to prosecute for conspiracy to defraud, see **A5.63**.

Providing False Information as to Health Services or Adult Social Care

B6.117 When brought into force, the Care Act 2014, s. 92(1), enacted in response to issues identified by the Francis report into the Mid-Staffordshire NHS foundation trust scandal, will create an offence in cases where a 'Care Provider' as defined in s. 92(3) supplies, publishes or otherwise makes available information of a specified description that is required under an enactment or other legal obligation, but which is false or misleading in a material respect.

Regulations made under the Act will specify the information to which s. 92 will apply and the full range of care providers who will be subject to it, but s. 92 applies to any public body which provides health services or adult social care in England and to those who provide such care pursuant to arrangements made with such a public body, thus including NHS trusts and local authorities.

Liability is strict, subject to a due diligence defence provided by s. 91(2). The maximum penalty is a fine on summary conviction, or imprisonment for up to two years and a fine (or both) following conviction on indictment (s. 93(1)).

Remedial orders (requiring the provider to take specified steps to remedy any matter or deficiency) and/or publicity orders (requiring the provider to publicise in a specified manner details of the offence and conviction etc.) may be made instead of or in addition to such penalties in accordance with s. 93(3) to (7). Failure to comply with such an order is an offence (s. 93(8)).

Section B7   Company, Commercial and Insolvency Offences

OFFENCES UNDER THE COMPANIES ACTS: GENERAL

Scope of the Companies Acts

The bulk of the legislation affecting companies is contained in the Companies Act 2006. A small **B7.1** number of the provisions of the Companies Act 1985 (principally under part XIV relating to company investigations) remain in force. This chapter adopts the definition of 'the Companies Acts' in s. 2 of the Companies Act 2006 as meaning parts 1 to 39 (ss. 1 to 1181) of that Act, the provisions of the Companies Act 1985 which remain in force, and part 2 of the Companies (Audit, Investigations and Community Enterprise) Act 2004.

The Companies Acts contain over 150 offence-creating provisions, many of which must be read in conjunction with other provisions which do not themselves create offences. Some provisions create summary offences relating to comparatively minor defaults, typically involving failure to notify the Registrar of Companies of matters affecting the company and its constitution or to provide information to shareholders. But other provisions create serious crimes, many of which involve fraud. The distinction is not, however, clear-cut. Minor defaults and irregularities will often be associated with more serious crime, for example where improperly maintained accounts or records are used to conceal fraudulent trading or unlawful dealings with directors. In such cases, an indictment may include counts alleging fraud offences and counts alleging lesser defaults and irregularities, some of which are triable either way.

A general work on criminal law cannot attempt to cover all offences under the Companies Acts or to discuss the relationship between the offence-creating provisions and the rest of this massive Act. Readers requiring fuller coverage must therefore refer to specialist works on company law.

Offences Punishable with Imprisonment under the Companies Acts

The more serious offences under the Companies Acts, punishable with imprisonment, are listed **B7.2** below. Each of the listed offences is triable either way. The maximum penalty on indictment for each of these offences is a term of imprisonment not exceeding two years and/or a fine, except for (i) fraudulent trading (see **B7.7**), for which the maximum sentence is ten years' imprisonment and/or a fine, and (ii) the aggravated offences under ss. 1006 to 1007 of the Companies Act 2006 and the offences under ss. 450 to 451 of the Companies Act 1985, for which the maximum sentence is seven years and/or a fine. On summary conviction each of the offences listed is punishable with imprisonment not exceeding six months (see s. 1131) and/or a fine not exceeding the statutory maximum. The offence under s. 980 of the Companies Act 2006 also carries a daily default fine of up to one-fiftieth of the statutory maximum.

Section of Act creating offence	General nature of offence
Companies Act 2006	
119, 747 & 814	Making a misleading, false or deceptive statement in a request to inspect the register of members' names, register of debenture holders or register of interests disclosed or disclosing such information for an improper purpose.
350	Making a misleading, false or deceptive statement to an independent assessor.
387 & 389	Failing to keep and preserve accounting records.
418	Making a false statement as to audit information in a directors' report.
458	Wrongful use or disclosure of tax information.
460	Wrongful disclosure of information obtained under compulsory powers.
501	Making false, misleading or deceptive statement to an auditor.
572	Inclusion of misleading false or deceptive matter in a directors' statement under section 571(6).
643	Making a solvency statement without having reasonable grounds for the opinion expressed in it.
658	Company acquiring its own shares.
680	Financial assistance by a public company for the acquisition of its own shares or shares in its private holding company.
715	Directors' statement under section 714 without reasonable grounds for the opinion expressed in the statement.
795	Failing to comply with a notice requiring information about interests in shares in a public company or making a false statement in compliance with such a notice.
949	Wrongful disclosure of information provided to the Takeover Panel.
980	Failure to send a copy of a notice or statutory declaration under s. 979 to the company or making a false declaration.
993	Being a party to carrying on company's business with intent to defraud creditors, or for any fraudulent purpose.
1006 & 1007	Failure to send a copy of an application for voluntary striking off with intent to conceal the making of the application (aggravated offence).
1112	Making a misleading, false or deceptive statement to the Registrar of Companies.
1153	Making a misleading, false or deceptive statement to a person carrying out a valuation or making a report.
1250	Furnishing misleading, false or deceptive information in connection with an application under part 42 or in purported compliance with a requirement under part 42.
Companies Act 1985	
444(3)	Failure to give Secretary of State, when required to do so, information about interests in shares, etc.; giving false information.
449(6)	Wrongful disclosure of information to which s. 449 applies.
450	Destroying or mutilating company documents; falsifying such documents or making false entries; parting with such documents or altering them or making omissions.
451	Providing false information in purported compliance with s. 447.

Ambit of the Companies Acts

B7.3   The Companies Acts are primarily concerned with registered companies as defined in ss. 1 and 1171 of the Companies Act 2006 (i.e. those registered under this and former Companies Acts). Some of the provisions have a wider ambit. Unregistered companies are relatively uncommon, but the Secretary of State is given power by s. 1043 to make regulations applying provisions of the Companies Acts to them. More importantly, many provisions of part XIV of the Companies

Act 1985 (ss. 431 to 457: company investigations) apply also to companies incorporated outside Great Britain which are or have been carrying on business in Great Britain (s. 453). The 2006 Act extends to the whole of the UK. The Overseas Companies Regulations 2009 (SI 2009 No. 1801), made under part 34 of the 2006 Act, impose a duty on companies incorporated outside the UK which open an establishment in the UK to deliver a return and documents to the Registrar of Companies. By s. 1054 of the 2006 Act and reg. 11, failure to comply with any of the regulations is an offence punishable by a fine not exceeding level 3 on the standard scale and a daily default fine not exceeding one tenth of level 3.

Liability of Officers in Default

Companies Act 2006, s. 1121   **B7.4**

(1) This section has effect for the purposes of any provision of the Companies Acts to the effect that, in the event of a contravention of an enactment in relation to a company, an offence is committed by every officer of the company who is in default.
(2) For this purpose 'officer' includes—
  (a) any director, manager or secretary, and
  (b) any person who is to be treated as an officer of the company for the purposes of the provision in question.
(3) An officer is 'in default' for the purposes of the provision if he authorises or permits, participates in, or fails to take all reasonable steps to prevent, the contravention.

By virtue of the Companies Act 2006, s. 250, 'director' includes 'any person occupying the position of director, by whatever name called'. So long as at least one person is a natural person, a company can be a director of another company (s. 155(1)). In *Revenue and Customs Commissioners v Holland* [2010] 1 All ER 430 the Supreme Court held that a human director of a corporate director of another company was not to be treated as a director of that other company, so as to render him responsible for misuse of the other company's assets.

Companies Act 2006, s. 1122

(1) Where a company is an officer of another company, it does not commit an offence as an officer in default unless one of its officers is in default.
(2) Where any such offence is committed by a company the officer in question also commits the offence and is liable to be proceeded against and punished accordingly.
(3) In this section 'officer' and 'in default' have the meanings given by section 1121.

Section 1123 contains provisions applying s. 1121 to bodies other than companies.

Consents for Prosecutions

By s. 1126(2) of the Companies Act 2006, no proceedings are to be brought under ss. 458, 460, 949 or 953 of the 2006 Act or under ss. 448 to 451 or 453A of the 1985 Act except by or with the consent of the Secretary of State or the DPP. Proceedings under s. 798 of the 2006 Act or s. 455 of the 1985 Act require the consent of the Secretary of State.   **B7.5**

Summary Offences: General Provisions

Companies Act 2006, ss. 1125, 1127 and 1128   **B7.6**

1125.—(1) This section defines what is meant in the Companies Acts where it is provided that a person guilty of an offence is liable on summary conviction to a fine not exceeding a specified amount 'and, for continued contravention, a daily default fine' not exceeding a specified amount.
(2) This means that the person is liable on a second or subsequent summary conviction of the offence to a fine not exceeding the latter amount for each day on which the contravention is continued (instead of being liable to a fine not exceeding the former amount
...
1127.—(1) Summary proceedings for any offence under the Companies Acts may be taken—
  (a) against a body corporate, at any place at which the body has a place of business, and

513

    (b) against any other person, at any place at which he is for the time being.
  (2) This is without prejudice to any jurisdiction exercisable apart from this section.
  1128.—(1) An information relating to an offence under the Companies Acts that is triable by a magistrates' court in England and Wales may be so tried if it is laid—
    (a) at any time within three years after the commission of the offence, and
    (b) within twelve months after the date on which evidence sufficient in the opinion of the Director of Public Prosecutions or the Secretary of State (as the case may be) to justify the proceedings comes to his knowledge.
  (2) and (3) [Apply only to Scotland and Northern Ireland.]
  (4) For purposes of this section a certificate of the Director of Public Prosecutions...or the Secretary of State (as the case may be) as to the date on which such evidence as is referred to above came to his knowledge is conclusive evidence.

Section 1128(1) has no effect in relation to the summary trial of offences triable either way (*Thames Metropolitan Stipendiary Magistrate, ex parte Horgan* [1998] QB 719).

FRAUDULENT TRADING

B7.7   Companies Act 2006, s. 993

  (1) If any business of a company is carried on with intent to defraud creditors of the company or creditors of any other person, or for any fraudulent purpose, every person who is knowingly a party to the carrying on of the business in that manner commits an offence.
  (2) This applies whether or not the company has been, or is in the course of being, wound up.

The Fraud Act 2006, s. 9, makes fraudulent trading by sole traders and other non-corporate entities a criminal offence (see **B5.25**).

Procedure and Sentence

B7.8   For procedural provisions see **B7.5** and **B7.6**. For disqualification orders, see **E21.8**.

On conviction on indictment, the maximum sentence is ten years' imprisonment or a fine or both; on summary conviction, the maximum sentence is six months' imprisonment or a fine not exceeding the statutory maximum or both (ss. 993(3) and 1131). The maximum penalty for fraudulent trading was increased from seven years to ten years by the Fraud Act 2006, s. 10, with effect from 15 January 2007.

The definitive sentencing guideline, *Fraud, Bribery and Money Laundering Offences* (see Supplement, **SG-472**), does not apply to an offence under s. 993 but it was held under the previous guideline that a judge is entitled to pay regard to such a guideline where the fraudulent trading bears similarities to an offence to which the guideline does apply (*McCrae* [2013] 1 Cr App R (S) 1 (1) at [16]). See also *Mackey* [2013] 1 Cr App R (S) 522 (100).

Before the increase in the maximum penalty to ten years, in *Smith* [1997] 2 Cr App R (S) 167 the offenders had admitted using misleading accounts and false invoices to maintain the credit of a marketing company which had eventually failed, with losses of £520,000. Sentences of three years' imprisonment were reduced to 18 months. The Court of Appeal regarded the case as lying towards the lower end of a wide spectrum of offences covered by the offence of fraudulent trading. The Court also observed that, broadly speaking, a charge of fraudulent trading resulting in loss to creditors is somewhat less seriously regarded than a charge of theft or fraud of the same amount. See also *Thobani* [1998] 1 Cr App R (S) 227, *Ward* [2001] 2 Cr App R (S) 30 and *Furr* [2007] EWCA Crim 191.

An example of a case at the other extreme is *Leaf* [2008] 1 Cr App R (S) 14, in which the offender had been convicted in 2005 of 13 counts of fraudulent trading in company purchase schemes resulting in a loss of £22 million in tax. The Court of Appeal reduced consecutive sentences totalling 12 and a half years to ten years, consisting of five-year sentences on the two most serious counts, to be served consecutively with the remaining sentences to be served concurrently. In *Freeman* [2012] Cr App R (S) 629 the offender carried out an investment fraud involving losses of £14 million to 335 victims. He pleaded guilty to fraudulent trading. The Court of Appeal reduced the sentence for fraudulent trading to six years' imprisonment with a further 12 months consecutive for bankruptcy offences.

Liability of Parties

The Insolvency Act 1986, s. 213, provides that persons who were knowingly parties to such conduct may be required to contribute to the assets of the company concerned in the course of its winding-up. In those circumstances, disqualification orders can also be made against them under the Company Directors Disqualification Act 1996, s. 10 (see **B7.71**). Unlike the criminal provision, s. 213 has no application unless the company goes into liquidation. In *Bilta (UK) Ltd v Nazir (No. 2)* [2014] Ch 52 (at [84]–[93]) the Court of Appeal decided that s. 213 has extra-territorial effect and extends to persons outside the jurisdiction.

B7.9

Indictment

B7.10

Statement of Offence

Fraudulent trading contrary to section 993 of the Companies Act 2006

Particulars of Offence

A between the…day of…and the…day of…was knowingly a party to the carrying on of certain business of a company called…with intent to defraud creditors of the said company [or with intent to defraud creditors of…] [or for a fraudulent purpose, namely…]

Carrying on the Business of the Company

The meaning of the words 'any business of the company has been carried on with intent to defraud creditors' has been considered in cases under the Insolvency Act 1986, s. 213. In *Morphitis v Bernasconi* [2003] Ch 552 (at [42]–[49]) the Court of Appeal considered that the legislation is aimed at the carrying on of a business and not the execution of individual transactions in the course of carrying on that business. Thus not every fraud perpetrated on a customer amounts to fraudulent trading. But circumstances can arise, as in *Re Gerald Cooper Chemicals Ltd* [1978] Ch 262, in which a single transaction in which only one creditor is defrauded will suffice (see also *Lockwood* [1986] Crim LR 244). In *Philippou* (1989) 89 Cr App R 290, it was held that the fraudulent obtaining of an air travel organiser's licence from the Civil Aviation Authority involved carrying on a business for a fraudulent purpose, as the licence was essential to that business.

B7.11

Intent to Defraud and Knowledge

Although the concept of intent to defraud was defined in *Welham v DPP* [1961] AC 103 in a way which appeared to include no specific requirement of dishonesty, it is clear that dishonesty is an essential element both in fraudulent trading and in other fraud offences involving similar terminology. See *Cox* (1982) 75 Cr App R 291. The extent to which a jury need be directed on the meaning of dishonesty varies from case to case. A full *Ghosh* direction (see **B4.54**) would not be appropriate in a case where the accused denies any knowledge of the allegedly fraudulent activities, whereas such a direction might be essential where he admits the facts and claims that he regarded them as normal business practice. See *Miles* [1992] Crim LR 657 and *Goldman* [1997] Crim LR 894.

B7.12

Welham v DPP establishes that there need not be any intent to cause financial loss to another person. Deliberately and dishonestly putting another person's property or financial interests in

515

jeopardy may suffice (*Allsop* (1977) 64 Cr App R 29; *Wai Yu-Tsang v The Queen* [1992] 1 AC 269), whether or not there is any deception (*Scott v Metropolitan Police Commissioner* [1975] AC 819), and it may be fraud to deceive public officers into failing to perform their duty (*Welham v DPP*; cf. *Philippou* (1989) 89 Cr App R 290 at **B7.11**).

In *Bank of India v Morris* [2005] BCC 739 at [14] the Court of Appeal held (albeit on a concession) that knowledge includes 'blind-eye' knowledge, namely a firmly grounded suspicion of specific facts and a deliberate decision to avoid confirming that they exist.

Frauds on Creditors and Other Fraudulent Purposes

B7.13 A typical example of fraudulent trading involves a company which has lapsed into insolvency, but which continues to obtain credit in circumstances where its directors know that there can be little if any chance of the creditors being paid. It would probably not be considered dishonest for debts to be incurred in the expectation that they could be repaid shortly after they fall due because many debts are paid a few days or weeks late, but a jury may well consider it dishonest for debts to be incurred when they could at best be repaid months late (*Grantham* [1984] QB 675).

The argument that the words 'any fraudulent purpose' should be construed *eiusdem generis* with defrauding creditors, and that defrauding customers etc. should not be regarded as falling within the scope of this provision, was rejected in *Kemp* [1988] QB 645 where the Court of Appeal held that the mischief aimed at is fraudulent trading generally, and not just insofar as it affects creditors. In *Philippou* (1989) 89 Cr App R 290, the fraudulent obtaining of an air travel organiser's licence was held to have involved fraudulent trading. This perhaps stretches the meaning of 'purpose', because the licence was obtained as a means to an end, rather than as an end in itself; but it signals a clear rejection of any attempt to restrict the offence to frauds on creditors or potential creditors. As to the meaning of 'creditors', see *Smith* [1996] 2 Cr App R 1.

It is not necessarily fraudulent trading for a holding company to issue letters of comfort in respect of a subsidiary which it later allows to go into insolvent liquidation, though it would largely depend on whether the holding company was sincere at the time the letters were issued (*Re Augustus Barnett & Son Ltd* [1986] BCLC 170). Preference of one creditor over another may be open to attack in the civil courts under the Insolvency Act 1986, but is unlikely to be deemed fraudulent trading (*Re Sarflax Ltd* [1979] Ch 592).

Persons who May be Liable for Fraudulent Trading

B7.14 The Court of Appeal held in *Miles* [1992] Crim LR 657 that the offence of fraudulent trading can be committed only by persons who exercise some kind of controlling or managerial function within the company. But employees who exercise no such function (including junior managers and managers of local branches) might, despite this narrow interpretation, incur liability as secondary parties to offences committed by the company's directors or senior managers. And persons holding no formal position within the company, such as shadow directors, could meanwhile incur liability for fraudulent trading if they exercise de facto managerial powers.

In *Maidstone Buildings Provisions Ltd* [1971] 3 All ER 363, it was said that some positive action on the part of a company secretary, rather than inertia, was required to make him liable. Passivity on the part of an executive director might be different, but *mens rea* would be needed in any event.

See also **A6** on corporate liability generally.

DESTRUCTION, MUTILATION OR FALSIFICATION
OF COMPANY DOCUMENTS

Companies Act 1985, s. 450   **B7.15**

(1)   An officer of a company, who—
  (a) destroys, mutilates or falsifies, or is privy to the destruction, mutilation or falsification of a document affecting or relating to the company's property or affairs, or
  (b) makes, or is privy to the making of, a false entry in such a document,
  is guilty of an offence, unless he proves that he had no intention to conceal the state of affairs of the company or to defeat the law.
(1A) Subsection (1) applies to an officer of an authorised insurance company which is not a body corporate as it applies to an officer of a company.
(2)   Such a person as above mentioned who fraudulently either parts with, alters or makes an omission in any such document or is privy to fraudulent parting with, fraudulent altering or fraudulent making of an omission in, any such document, is guilty of an offence.

By s. 450(5), 'document' includes information recorded in any form.

Procedure and Sentence   No proceedings for an offence under s. 450 are to be brought except   **B7.16**
by or with the consent of the Secretary of State or the DPP (Companies Act 2006, s. 1126(2): see
B7.5). For procedural provisions, see **B7.6**.

On conviction on indictment, the maximum sentence is seven years' imprisonment or a fine or
both; on summary conviction, the maximum sentence is six months' imprisonment or a fine
not exceeding the statutory maximum or both (ss. 450(3) and 1131).

This is therefore one of the most serious offences under the Companies Acts. Such conduct is
often designed to remove evidence of serious fraud. It may also be designed to frustrate or hinder
an investigation into the company's affairs under part XIV (ss. 431 to 453) of the Companies Act
1985; but the offence may be committed whether or not any such investigation is in prospect.

Burden of Proof   The wording of the offence is similar to the Insolvency Act 1986, s. 206(1)(c)   **B7.17**
and (d) and (4)(b) (see **B7.45**). It follows from *A-G's Ref (No. 1 of 2004)* [2004] 4 All ER 457 (at
[80]–[84]) and other cases on the incidence of burden of proof (see **F3.18** *et seq.*, particularly
F3.26) that the imposition of the full persuasive burden on the accused is compatible with the
ECHR, Article 6.

FINANCIAL ASSISTANCE PROVIDED BY COMPANIES
IN CONNECTION WITH THE ACQUISITION OF
THEIR OWN SHARES

The provision by a company of financial assistance in connection with the acquisition of its own   **B7.18**
shares may in some circumstances be unobjectionable, but in other instances company funds
may be improperly depleted by loans for the purchase of its own shares and the loans never
repaid. Following particularly scandalous instances of asset-stripping of companies with cash or
other liquid assets (described in *Re VGM Holdings Ltd* [1942] Ch 235 at p. 239), widely drawn
legislation was enacted in 1929; but this rendered criminal many harmless transactions, while
providing wholly inadequate penalties for serious fraud. The legislation was recast in a more
complex form in 1981. The mischief to which it is directed is that the resources of the company
and its subsidiaries should not be used directly or indirectly to assist the purchaser financially
to make the acquisition, because this may prejudice the interests of creditors of the company
or group and the interests of shareholders other than those whose shares are bought (*Chaston v
SWP Group plc* [2002] EWCA Civ 1999 at [31]).

The current legislation is contained in ss. 677 to 683 of the Companies Act 2006. Unlike ss. 151 to 158 of the Companies Act 1985, which these sections replaced, ss. 677 to 683 apply only to public companies.

B7.19   **Companies Act 2006, s. 680**

> (1) If a company contravenes section 678(1) or (3) or section 679(1) or (3) (prohibited financial assistance) an offence is committed by—
>   (a) the company, and
>   (b) every officer of the company who is in default.

On conviction on indictment, the maximum sentence is two years' imprisonment or a fine or both; on summary conviction, the maximum sentence is six months' imprisonment or a fine not exceeding the statutory maximum or both (ss. 680(2) and 1131).

B7.20   For procedural provisions, see **B7.5** and **B7.6**. Although the only penalty expressly provided for breach of s. 678 (and its predecessors) is criminal, the civil courts held, after initial hesitation, that breaches of the prohibition also give rise to civil remedies. Readers are referred to specialist works on company law for discussions of the substantial body of case law in civil litigation on the interpretation of these provisions.

FINANCIAL SERVICES OFFENCES

Introduction

B7.21   The Financial Services and Markets Act 2000, as amended by the Financial Services Act 2012, makes provision for the regulation of financial services and markets. Section 19 contains a 'general prohibition' against carrying on a regulated activity in the UK, unless authorised or exempt. Regulated activities are specified in the Financial Services and Markets Act (Regulated Activities) Order 2001 (SI 2001 No. 544), which is regularly amended.

Under the FSMA 2000, ss. 1B to 1H, the Financial Conduct Authority (FCA) has the strategic objective of ensuring that financial markets, markets for regulated financial services and markets for services carrying on regulated activities function well. The FCA also has three operational objectives, namely, consumer protection, integrity and competition (s. 1B(3)). The Prudential Regulation Authority (PRA), part of the Bank of England, regulates deposit-takers, insurers and designated investment firms (ss. 2A to 2P).

The FSMA 2000 creates a relatively small number of criminal offences. Breaches of the Act and rules are mainly enforced by remedies in civil courts or disciplinary procedures. Where the Act creates offences, proceedings can be instituted only by the appropriate regulator, the Secretary of State or the DPP, or with the consent of the DPP (s. 401). For the role of the FCA in prosecuting, see *R (Uberoi) v City of Westminster Magistrates' Court* [2009] 1 WLR 1905, and for the power to prosecute offences beyond the Act, see s. 402 and *Rollins* [2010] 4 All ER 880.

Summary proceedings may be taken against a company or unincorporated association at any place where it has a place of business and against an individual at any place where he is for the time being (s. 403(5)). Where an offence committed by a body corporate is proved to have been committed with the consent or connivance of a director or other officer, or is attributable to his neglect, he may also be prosecuted for that offence (s. 400(1)).

Contravention of the General Prohibition

B7.22   By the FSMA 2000, s. 23(1), contravention of the general prohibition is punishable, on indictment, with a maximum penalty of two years' imprisonment or a fine, or both; on summary conviction, the maximum penalty is six months' imprisonment or a fine of the statutory maximum, or both. By s. 23(3), it is a defence for the accused to show that he took all reasonable precautions and exercised all due diligence to avoid committing the offence. In relation to aiding the commission of an offence under s. 23(1), see *O'Neil v Gale* [2013] EWCA Civ 1554 (at [10]–[22]).

In *Epton* [2009] 2 Cr App R (S) 639 a sentence of 15 months' imprisonment for contravening the general prohibition, plus nine months consecutive for transferring criminal property, was upheld.

By s. 23(1A)–(1G), an authorised person who carries on a credit-regulated activity otherwise than in accordance with permission commits an offence, punishable in the same way as an offence under s. 23(1).

False Claims to be Authorised or Exempt

Section 24 of the FSMA 2000 creates a summary offence of making false claims to be authorised   **B7.23**
or exempt, punishable by a maximum of six months' imprisonment or a fine not exceeding level 5 on the standard scale, or both. Where the offence involves or includes the public display of any material, the maximum fine is multiplied by the number of days of any public display. Again it is a defence for the accused to show that he took all reasonable precautions and exercised all due diligence to avoid committing the offence.

Section 333 of the FSMA 2000 creates a similar offence of making a false claim to be a person to whom the general prohibition does not apply.

Breach of Restrictions on Financial Promotion

Section 25 of the FSMA 2000 and the Financial Services and Markets Act 2000 (Financial   **B7.24**
Promotion) Order 2005 (SI 2005 No. 1529) impose restrictions on financial promotion (communication of an invitation or inducement to engage in investment activity) in the course of business. By s. 25, breach of the restrictions on financial promotion is an offence. It is punishable on indictment with a maximum penalty of two years' imprisonment or a fine, or both; on summary conviction, the maximum penalty is six months' imprisonment or a fine of the statutory maximum, or both (s. 25(1)). It is a defence for the accused to show that he believed on reasonable grounds that the content of the communication was prepared, or approved for the purposes of s. 21, by an authorised person or that he took all reasonable precautions and exercised all due diligence to avoid committing the offence (s. 25(2)).

In *Powell* [2009] 1 Cr App R (S) 158 sentences of 15 months' imprisonment were upheld for offences under s. 25 where the offenders had participated in an investment scam.

Misleading Statements and Impressions

Financial Services Act 2012, ss. 89 to 91 and 93   **B7.25**

89.—(1) Subsection (2) applies to a person ('P') who—
    (a) makes a statement which P knows to be false or misleading in a material respect,
    (b) makes a statement which is false or misleading in a material respect, being reckless as to whether it is, or
    (c) dishonestly conceals any material facts whether in connection with a statement made by P or otherwise.
  (2) P commits an offence if P makes the statement or conceals the facts with the intention of inducing, or is reckless as to whether making it or concealing them may induce, another person (whether or not the person to whom the statement is made)—
    (a) to enter into or offer to enter into, or to refrain from entering or offering to enter into, a relevant agreement, or
    (b) to exercise, or refrain from exercising, any rights conferred by a relevant investment.
  (3) In proceedings for an offence under subsection (2) brought against a person to whom that subsection applies as a result of paragraph (a) of subsection (1), it is a defence for the person charged ('D') to show that the statement was made in conformity with—
    (a) price stabilising rules,
    (b) control of information rules, or

(c) the relevant provisions of Commission Regulation (EC) No 2273/2003 of 22 December 2003 implementing Directive 2003/6/EC of the European Parliament and of the Council as regards exemptions for buy-back programmes and stabilisation of financial instruments.

(4) Subsections (1) and (2) do not apply unless—

(a) the statement is made in or from, or the facts are concealed in or from, the United Kingdom or arrangements are made in or from the United Kingdom for the statement to be made or the facts to be concealed,

(b) the person on whom the inducement is intended to or may have effect is in the United Kingdom, or

(c) the agreement is or would be entered into or the rights are or would be exercised in the United Kingdom.

90.—(1) A person ('P') who does any act or engages in any course of conduct which creates a false or misleading impression as to the market in or the price or value of any relevant investments commits an offence if—

(a) P intends to create the impression, and

(b) the case falls within subsection (2) or (3) (or both).

(2) The case falls within this subsection if P intends, by creating the impression, to induce another person to acquire, dispose of, subscribe for or underwrite the investments or to refrain from doing so or to exercise or refrain from exercising any rights conferred by the investments.

(3) The case falls within this subsection if—

(a) P knows that the impression is false or misleading or is reckless as to whether it is, and

(b) P intends by creating the impression to produce any of the results in subsection (4) or is aware that creating the impression is likely to produce any of the results in that subsection.

(4) Those results are—

(a) the making of a gain for P or another, or

(b) the causing of loss to another person or the exposing of another person to the risk of loss.

(5) References in subsection (4) to gain or loss are to be read in accordance with subsections (6) to (8).

(6) 'Gain' and 'loss'—

(a) extend only to gain or loss in money or other property of any kind;

(b) include such gain or loss whether temporary or permanent.

(7) 'Gain' includes a gain by keeping what one has, as well as a gain by getting what one does not have.

(8) 'Loss' includes a loss by not getting what one might get, as well as a loss by parting with what one has.

(9) In proceedings brought against any person ('D') for an offence under subsection (1) it is a defence for D to show—

(a) to the extent that the offence results from subsection (2), that D reasonably believed that D's conduct would not create an impression that was false or misleading as to the matters mentioned in subsection (1),

(b) that D acted or engaged in the conduct—

(i) for the purpose of stabilising the price of investments, and

(ii) in conformity with price stabilising rules,

(c) that D acted or engaged in the conduct in conformity with control of information rules, or

(d) that D acted or engaged in the conduct in conformity with the relevant provisions of Commission Regulation (EC) No 2273/2003 of 22 December 2003 implementing Directive 2003/6/EC of the European Parliament and of the Council as regards exemptions for buy-back programmes and stabilisation of financial instruments.

(10) This section does not apply unless—

(a) the act is done, or the course of conduct is engaged in, in the United Kingdom, or

(b) the false or misleading impression is created there.

91.—(1) A person ('A') who makes to another person ('B') a false or misleading statement commits an offence if—

(a) A makes the statement in the course of arrangements for the setting of a relevant benchmark,

(b) A intends that the statement should be used by B for the purpose of the setting of a relevant benchmark, and

(c) A knows that the statement is false or misleading or is reckless as to whether it is.

(2) A person ('C') who does any act or engages in any course of conduct which creates a false or misleading impression as to the price or value of any investment or as to the interest rate appropriate to any transaction commits an offence if—

(a) C intends to create the impression,

  (b) the impression may affect the setting of a relevant benchmark,
  (c) C knows that the impression is false or misleading or is reckless as to whether it is, and
  (d) C knows that the impression may affect the setting of a relevant benchmark.
(3) In proceedings for an offence under subsection (1), it is a defence for the person charged ('D') to show that the statement was made in conformity with—
  (a) price stabilising rules,
  (b) control of information rules, or
  (c) the relevant provisions of Commission Regulation (EC) No 2273/2003 of 22 December 2003 implementing Directive 2003/6/EC of the European Parliament and of the Council as regards exemptions for buy-back programmes and stabilisation of financial instruments.
(4) In proceedings brought against any person ('D') for an offence under subsection (2) it is a defence for D to show—
  (a) that D acted or engaged in the conduct—
    (i)   for the purpose of stabilising the price of investments, and
    (ii) in conformity with price stabilising rules,
  (b) that D acted or engaged in the conduct in conformity with control of information rules, or
  (c) that D acted or engaged in the conduct in conformity with the relevant provisions of Commission Regulation (EC) No 2273/2003 of 22 December 2003 implementing Directive 2003/6/EC of the European Parliament and of the Council as regards exemptions for buy-back programmes and stabilisation of financial instruments.
(5) Subsection (1) does not apply unless the statement is made in or from the United Kingdom or to a person in the United Kingdom.
(6) Subsection (2) does not apply unless—
  (a) the act is done, or the course of conduct is engaged in, in the United Kingdom, or
  (b) the false or misleading impression is created there.
...

93.—(1) This section has effect for the interpretation of [part XI].
(2) 'Investment' includes any asset, right or interest.
(3) "Relevant agreement' means an agreement—
  (a) the entering into or performance of which by either party constitutes an activity of a kind specified in an order made by the Treasury, and
  (b) which relates to a relevant investment.
(4) 'Relevant benchmark' means a benchmark of a kind specified in an order made by the Treasury.
(5) 'Relevant investment' means an investment of a kind specified in an order made by the Treasury.
(6) Schedule 2 to FSMA 2000 (except paragraphs 25 and 26) applies for the purposes of subsections (3) and (5) with references to section 22 of that Act being read as references to each of those subsections.
(7) Nothing in Schedule 2 to FSMA 2000, as applied by subsection (6), limits the power conferred by subsection (3) or (5).
(8) 'Price stabilising rules' and 'control of information rules' have the same meaning as in FSMA 2000.
(9) In this section 'benchmark' has the meaning given in section 22(6) of FSMA 2000.

These sections replaced the FSMA 2000, s. 397, with effect from 1 April 2013. Schedule 2 to the FSMA 2000 identifies activities which may be regulated under s. 22 of the Act.

Sentencing

Offences under the Financial Services Act 2012, ss. 89 to 91, are punishable on indictment by a maximum of seven years' imprisonment and/or a fine; on summary conviction by up to six months' imprisonment and/or a fine not exceeding the statutory maximum (s. 92). This is the same maximum as under the FSMA 2000, s. 397, and the same sentencing considerations are therefore likely to apply to the new offences.   **B7.26**

In *A-G's Ref (Nos. 14, 15 and 16 of 1995)* (1997) *The Times*, 10 April 1997, the Court of Appeal stated that offenders who took part in conspiracy to defraud involving the creation of false share markets to influence the fate of takeovers would ordinarily receive custodial sentences.

Deterrent sentences were appropriate since creating false share markets could lead both to a fraud on shareholders and to considerable damage to the City. In *Feld* [1999] 1 Cr App R (S) 1, sentences totalling six years were approved after a trial for raising in excess of £20 million by false statements relating to the financial position of a company. Factors relevant to sentence were stated to include the amount of the fraud, the manner in which it was carried out, the period over which it took place, the persistence with which it was carried out, the position of the offender in the company, abuse of trust, the consequences of the fraud, the effect on public confidence in the City and the integrity of commercial life, the loss to small investors, the personal benefit to the offender, and the plea, age and character of the offender. See also *Chauhan* [2000] 2 Cr App R (S) 230.

In *Bailey* [2006] 2 Cr App R (S) 250, offenders were convicted, after a trial, of recklessly (rather than knowingly) making the relevant statement. In light of personal mitigation, sentences were reduced to nine months and 18 months' imprisonment. Confiscation and compensation orders were also made. Similarly 18 months' imprisonment was upheld in *O'Hanlon* [2008] 2 Cr App R (S) 96, where the misrepresentations had been 'comparatively spontaneous'. See also *Hipwell* [2006] 2 Cr App R (S) 636 (six months' imprisonment upheld on a financial journalist who had tipped companies in which he had bought shares).

Elements

B7.27 A false or misleading promise must be one which is false or misleading when made (e.g., because the speaker never has any intention or expectation that it will be kept). Under previous legislation it was held that material facts include the accused's present intention (*R (Young) v Central Criminal Court* [2002] 2 Cr App R 178). It is not enough to prove that a promise was broken (cf. *Re Augustus Barnett & Son Ltd* [1986] BCLC 170, discussed at **B7.13**).

Likewise it was held that where several false or misleading statements are alleged, they may be included in a single count (*Linnell* [1969] 3 All ER 849), but the judge must warn the jury that they cannot convict merely because some jurors are satisfied as to the falsity of one statement and the others are satisfied as to the falsity of another (*Brown* (1983) 79 Cr App R 115: see **D18.44**).

Other Financial Services Offences

B7.28 Other offences created by the FSMA 2000 are listed in the table below.

Section	General nature of offence	Mode of prosecution	Punishment
55P(10)	Releasing or dealing with trust assets subject to an assets requirement without the consent of a regulator	Summary	Fine not exceeding level 5
56(4)	Breach of a prohibition order	Summary	Fine not exceeding level 5
85(3)	Dealing in transferable securities without an approved prospectus	1. On indictment 2. Summary	2 years or a fine; or both 3 months or the statutory maximum; or both
131L(3)	Breach of short selling regulation	1. On indictment 2. Summary	2 years or a fine; or both 3 months or the statutory maximum; or both
133B(2)(a)	Refusal to attend tribunal or to give evidence	Summary	Fine not exceeding level 5
133B(2)(b)	Alter, suppress, conceal, destroy or refuse to produce a document for tribunal proceedings	1. On indictment 2. Summary	2 years or a fine; or both 3 months or the statutory maximum; or both

Section	General nature of offence	Mode of prosecution	Punishment
177(3)	Falsify, conceal, destroy or dispose of a document relevant to an investigation under part XI	1. On indictment 2. Summary	2 years or a fine; or both 6 months or the statutory maximum; or both
177(4)	Provide false or misleading information in connection with an investigation	1. On indictment 2. Summary	2 years or a fine; or both 6 months or the statutory maximum; or both
177(6)	Obstruction of entry and search warrant in connection with an investigation	Summary	3 months or a fine not exceeding level 5
191F(1)	Failure to comply with an obligation to notify a regulator of change in control of a UK authorised person	1. On indictment 2. Summary	A fine The statutory maximum
191F(2)	Acquisition before the expiry of an assessment period	1. On indictment 2. Summary	A fine The statutory maximum
191F(3)	Contravention of a condition in a warning or decision notice	1. On indictment 2. Summary	A fine The statutory maximum
191F(4)	Acquisition in contravention of a notice	1. On indictment 2. Summary	2 years or a fine; or both 3 months or the statutory maximum; or both
191F(5)	Acquisition after approval ceased to be effective	1. On indictment 2. Summary	A fine The statutory maximum
191F(6)	Providing false information to a regulator	1. On indictment 2. Summary	A fine The statutory maximum
191F(7)	Breach of a direction in a restriction notice	1. On indictment 2. Summary	A fine The statutory maximum
203(9)	Contravention of a consumer credit prohibition	1. On indictment 2. Summary	A fine The statutory maximum
204(4)	Contravention of a consumer credit restriction	1. On indictment 2. Summary	A fine The statutory maximum
301L(1)	Failure to comply with an obligation to notify the FCA of acquisition or increased control over a recognised investment exchange	1. On indictment 2. Summary	A fine The statutory maximum
301L(2)	Acquisition before the expiry of an assessment period	1. On indictment 2. Summary	A fine The statutory maximum
301L(3)	Acquisition in contravention of a notice	1. On indictment 2. Summary	2 years or a fine; or both 3 months or the statutory maximum; or both
301L(4)	Acquisition after approval ceased to be effective	1. On indictment 2. Summary	A fine The statutory maximum
301L(5)	Providing false information to a regulator	1. On indictment 2. Summary	A fine The statutory maximum
301L(6)	Breach of a direction in a restriction notice	1. On indictment 2. Summary	A fine The statutory maximum
346(1)	Provision of false or misleading information to an auditor or actuary	1. On indictment 2. Summary	2 years or a fine; or both 6 months or the statutory maximum; or both
352(1)	Disclosure of confidential information	1. On indictment 2. Summary	2 years or a fine; or both 3 months or the statutory maximum; or both
352(3) & (4)	Use of confidential information in contravention of regulations or s. 350(4)	Summary	3 months or a fine not exceeding level 5

Section	General nature of offence	Mode of prosecution	Punishment
366(2)	Failure to notify the PRA of resolution to wind up voluntarily insurer of long term contracts of insurance	Summary	Fine not exceeding level 5
398(1)	Misleading the FCA or PRA	1. On indictment 2. Summary	A fine The statutory maximum
399	Misleading the OFT	1. On indictment 2. Summary	A fine The statutory maximum

INSIDER DEALING

B7.29   Part V of the Criminal Justice Act 1993 contains the offence of insider dealing. The offence is set out in s. 52 and is subject to defences set out in s. 53, which refers to further special defences set out in sch. 1. Section 62 contains territorial limits to the scope of the offence, linking it to the UK.

B7.30   Criminal Justice Act 1993, ss. 52 and 53

52.—(1) An individual who has information as an insider is guilty of insider dealing if, in the circumstances mentioned in subsection (3), he deals in securities that are price-affected securities in relation to the information.

(2) An individual who has information as an insider is also guilty of insider dealing if—

(a) he encourages another person to deal in securities that are (whether or not that other knows it) price-affected securities in relation to the information, knowing or having reasonable cause to believe that the dealing would take place in the circumstances mentioned in subsection (3); or

(b) he discloses the information, otherwise than in the proper performance of the functions of his employment, office or profession, to another person.

(3) The circumstances referred to above are that the acquisition or disposal in question occurs on a regulated market, or that the person dealing relies on a professional intermediary or is himself acting as a professional intermediary.

(4) This section has effect subject to section 53.

53.—(1) An individual is not guilty of insider dealing by virtue of dealing in securities if he shows—

(a) that he did not at the time expect the dealing to result in a profit attributable to the fact that the information in question was price-sensitive information in relation to the securities, or

(b) that at the time he believed on reasonable grounds that the information had been disclosed widely enough to ensure that none of those taking part in the dealing would be prejudiced by not having the information, or

(c) that he would have done what he did even if he had not had the information.

(2) An individual is not guilty of insider dealing by virtue of encouraging another person to deal in securities if he shows—

(a) that he did not at the time expect the dealing to result in a profit attributable to the fact that the information in question was price-sensitive information in relation to the securities, or

(b) that at the time he believed on reasonable grounds that the information had been or would be disclosed widely enough to ensure that none of those taking part in the dealing would be prejudiced by not having the information, or

(c) that he would have done what he did even if he had not had the information.

(3) An individual is not guilty of insider dealing by virtue of a disclosure of information if he shows—

(a) that he did not at the time expect any person, because of the disclosure, to deal in securities in the circumstances mentioned in subsection (3) of section 52; or

(b) that, although he had such an expectation at the time, he did not expect the dealing to result in a profit attributable to the fact that the information was price-sensitive information in relation to the securities.

...

(6) In this section references to a profit include references to the avoidance of a loss.

Section 52 does not apply to anything done by an individual acting on behalf of a public sector body in pursuit of monetary policies or policies with respect to exchange rates or the management of public debt or foreign exchange reserves (s. 63(1)).

Procedure

The offence is triable either way (CJA 1993, s. 61(1)). Proceedings cannot be instituted except by or with the consent of the Secretary of State or the DPP (s. 61(2)). The FCA has power to prosecute an offence under s. 52 (s. 402(1) of the FSMA 2000 and see *Rollins* [2010] 4 All ER 880).   **B7.31**

Summary proceedings may be brought against an individual at any place at which the individual is for the time being (s. 61A(1)). If tried summarily, the information must be laid within three years after the commission of the offence and within 12 months after the date on which evidence sufficient in the opinion of the DPP or the Secretary of State (as the case may be) to justify the proceedings comes to that person's knowledge (s. 61A(2)).

Sentencing

When tried on indictment the maximum penalty is seven years' imprisonment or a fine or both. When tried summarily, the maximum penalty is six months or a fine not exceeding the statutory maximum or both (CJA 1993, s. 61(1)).   **B7.32**

In *McQuoid* [2010] 1 Cr App R(S) 269 at [14] the Court of Appeal stated that the sentencing considerations for insider dealing are (1) the nature of the offender's employment or retainer, or involvement in the arrangements which enabled him to participate in the insider dealing of which he is guilty; (2) the circumstances in which he came into possession of confidential information and the use he made of it; (3) whether he behaved recklessly or acted deliberately, and almost inevitably therefore, dishonestly; (4) the level of planning and sophistication involved in his activity, as well as the period of trading and the number of individual trades; (5) whether he acted alone or with others and, if so, his relative culpability; (6) the amount of anticipated or intended financial benefit or loss avoided, as well as the actual benefit or loss avoided; (7) although the absence of any identified victim is not normally a matter going to mitigation, the impact, if any, on any individual victim; (8) the impact of the offence on overall confidence in the integrity of the market; because of its impact on public confidence, an offence committed jointly by more than one person trusted with confidential information will be more damaging to public confidence than an offence committed in isolation by one person acting on his own; (9) age and a guilty plea; (10) good character, but it is often the case that a person is trusted with confidential information because he is of good character and by misusing the information that trust has been breached. The Court added that valuable assistance was also to be found in the Sentencing Council's Guideline on *Theft in Breach of Trust* under chapter E (see Supplement, **SG-453**). In *Butt* [2006] 2 Cr App R (S) 44 the offender was the compliance officer at an investment bank who originated, and (with others) ran over a three-year period, a scheme based on inside information which produced a profit of £287,000. The Court of Appeal reduced his sentence for conspiracy to commit insider dealing from five years' imprisonment to four years.

Elements

Sections 54 to 60 of the CJA 1993 contain definitions of the terms used in ss. 52 and 53.   **B7.33** 'Securities' to which the provisions apply are defined in sch. 2. In summary, they consist of shares, debt securities, warrants, depositary receipts, options, futures and contracts for differences. 'Dealing' is defined in s. 55 and, again in summary, involves acquisition or disposal. Sections 56 and 57 define 'inside information' and 'insiders'.

B7.34   Criminal Justice Act 1993, ss. 56 and 57

56.—(1) For the purposes of this section and section 57, 'inside information' means information which—

(a) relates to particular securities or to a particular issuer of securities or to particular issuers of securities and not to securities generally or to issuers of securities generally;

(b) is specific or precise;

(c) has not been made public; and

(d) if it were made public would be likely to have a significant effect on the price of any securities.

(2) For the purposes of this Part, securities are 'price-affected securities' in relation to inside information, and inside information is 'price-sensitive information' in relation to securities, if and only if the information would, if made public, be likely to have a significant effect on the price of the securities.

(3) For the purposes of this section 'price' includes value.

57.—(1) For the purposes of this Part, a person has information as an insider if and only if—

(a) it is, and he knows that it is, inside information, and

(b) he has it, and knows that he has it, from an inside source.

(2) For the purposes of subsection (1), a person has information from an inside source if and only if—

(a) he has it through—

   (i) being a director, employee or shareholder of an issuer of securities; or

   (ii) having access to the information by virtue of his employment, office or profession; or

(b) the direct or indirect source of his information is a person within paragraph (a).

Section 58 contains a non-exhaustive definition of 'made public' and s. 59 defines 'professional intermediary'.

Defences

B7.35 In addition to the defences provided by the CJA 1993, s. 53(1) to (3) (see **B7.30**), sch. 1 to the Act provides special defences relating to market makers (para. 1), market information (paras. 2 to 4) and price stabilisation (para. 5).

THE CARTEL OFFENCE

B7.36 Sections 188 to 189 of the Enterprise Act 2002, as amended by the Enterprise and Regulatory Reform Act 2013, s. 47 (with effect from 1 April 2014: see SI 2014 No. 416), create a cartel offence, aimed at agreements to make or implement arrangements between undertakings which affect the price, supply or production of products or services in the UK. As with revenue and customs offences (see **B16.2**), this criminal sanction co-exists with civil remedies; those under the Competition Act 1998 are particularly relevant here.

B7.37   Enterprise Act 2002, ss. 188 to 189

188.—(1) An individual is guilty of an offence if he agrees with one or more other persons to make or implement, or to cause to be made or implemented, arrangements of the following kind relating to at least two undertakings (A and B).

(2) The arrangements must be ones which, if operating as the parties to the agreement intend, would—

(a) directly or indirectly fix a price for the supply by A in the United Kingdom (otherwise than to B) of a product or service,

(b) limit or prevent supply by A in the United Kingdom of a product or service,

(c) limit or prevent production by A in the United Kingdom of a product,

(d) divide between A and B the supply in the United Kingdom of a product or service to a customer or customers,

(e) divide between A and B customers for the supply in the United Kingdom of a product or service, or

(f) be bid-rigging arrangements.

(3) Unless subsection (2)(d), (e) or (f) applies, the arrangements must also be ones which, if operating as the parties to the agreement intend, would—
   (a) directly or indirectly fix a price for the supply by B in the United Kingdom (otherwise than to A) of a product or service,
   (b) limit or prevent supply by B in the United Kingdom of a product or service, or
   (c) limit or prevent production by B in the United Kingdom of a product.

(4) In subsections (2)(a) to (d) and (3), references to supply or production are to supply or production in the appropriate circumstances (for which see section 189).

(5) 'Bid-rigging arrangements' are arrangements under which, in response to a request for bids for the supply of a product or service in the United Kingdom, or for the production of a product in the United Kingdom—
   (a) A but not B may make a bid, or
   (b) A and B may each make a bid but, in one case or both, only a bid arrived at in accordance with the arrangements.

(6) [Repealed.]

(7) 'Undertaking' has the same meaning as in Part 1 of the [Competition Act 1998].

(8) This section is subject to section 188A.

188A.—(1) An individual does not commit an offence under section 188(1) if, under the arrangements—
   (a) in a case where the arrangements would (operating as the parties intend) affect the supply in the United Kingdom of a product or service, customers would be given relevant information about the arrangements before they enter into agreements for the supply to them of the product or service so affected,
   (b) in the case of bid-rigging arrangements, the person requesting bids would be given relevant information about them at or before the time when a bid is made, or
   (c) in any case, relevant information about the arrangements would be published, before the arrangements are implemented, in the manner specified at the time of the making of the agreement in an order made by the Secretary of State.

(2) In subsection (1), 'relevant information' means—
   (a) the names of the undertakings to which the arrangements relate,
   (b) a description of the nature of the arrangements which is sufficient to show why they are or might be arrangements of the kind to which section 188(1) applies,
   (c) the products or services to which they relate, and
   (d) such other information as may be specified in an order made by the Secretary of State.

(3) An individual does not commit an offence under section 188(1) if the agreement is made in order to comply with a legal requirement.

(4) In subsection (3), 'legal requirement' has the same meaning as in paragraph 5 of Schedule 3 to the Competition Act 1998.

(5) and (6) [Order-making powers and procedure.]

188B.—(1) In a case where the arrangements would (operating as the parties intend) affect the supply in the United Kingdom of a product or service, it is a defence for an individual charged with an offence under section 188(1) to show that, at the time of the making of the agreement, he or she did not intend that the nature of the arrangements would be concealed from customers at all times before they enter into agreements for the supply to them of the product or service.

(2) It is a defence for an individual charged with an offence under section 188(1) to show that, at the time of the making of the agreement, he or she did not intend that the nature of the arrangements would be concealed from the [Competition and Markets Authority].

(3) It is a defence for an individual charged with an offence under section 188(1) to show that, before the making of the agreement, he or she took reasonable steps to ensure that the nature of the arrangements would be disclosed to professional legal advisers for the purposes of obtaining advice about them before their making or (as the case may be) their implementation.

189.—(1) For section 188(2)(a), the appropriate circumstances are that A's supply of the product or service would be at a level in the supply chain at which the product or service would at the same time be supplied by B in the United Kingdom.

(2) For section 188(2)(b), the appropriate circumstances are that A's supply of the product or service would be at a level in the supply chain—
   (a) at which the product or service would at the same time be supplied by B in the United Kingdom, or

    (b) at which supply by B in the United Kingdom of the product or service would be limited or prevented by the arrangements.

    (3) For section 188(2)(c), the appropriate circumstances are that A's production of the product would be at a level in the production chain—

      (a) at which the product would at the same time be produced by B in the United Kingdom, or

      (b) at which production by B in the United Kingdom of the product would be limited or prevented by the arrangements.

    (4) For section 188(2)(d), the appropriate circumstances are that A's supply of the product or service would be at the same level in the supply chain as B's.

    (5) For section 188(3)(a), the appropriate circumstances are that B's supply of the product or service would be at a level in the supply chain at which the product or service would at the same time be supplied by A in the United Kingdom.

    (6) For section 188(3)(b), the appropriate circumstances are that B's supply of the product or service would be at a level in the supply chain—

      (a) at which the product or service would at the same time be supplied by A in the United Kingdom, or

      (b) at which supply by A in the United Kingdom of the product or service would be limited or prevented by the arrangements.

    (7) For section 188(3)(c), the appropriate circumstances are that B's production of the product would be at a level in the production chain—

      (a) at which the product would at the same time be produced by A in the United Kingdom, or

      (b) at which production by A in the United Kingdom of the product would be limited or prevented by the arrangements.

Procedure

B7.38 The offence is triable either way (Enterprise Act 2002, s. 190(1)). Proceedings may be instituted only by the Director of the SFO or by or with the consent of the OFT (s. 190(2)). No proceedings can be brought in respect of an agreement outside the UK, unless it has been implemented in whole or in part in the UK (s. 190(3)). In order to encourage co-operation and admissions, s. 190(4) enables the OFT to give a written notice that no proceedings will be taken for an offence under s. 188.

Sentencing

B7.39 When tried on indictment the maximum penalty is five years' imprisonment or a fine or both. When tried summarily the maximum penalty is six months or a fine not exceeding the statutory maximum or both (Enterprise Act 2002, s. 190(1)(a)).

INSOLVENCY OFFENCES: GENERAL

B7.40 The law relating to personal and corporate insolvency was consolidated in the Insolvency Act 1986. The principal offences under the Act are contained in part IV, chapter X (in relation to company insolvency), and part IX, chapter VI (in respect of bankruptcy of individuals). Some offences are created by the Insolvency Rules 1986 (SI 1986 No. 1925).

The scale, complexity and specialised subject-matter of this legislation again precludes comprehensive coverage of its offences within a general work on criminal law. This section accordingly covers only the principal offences.

Penalties

B7.41 Penalties for offences under the Insolvency Act 1986, together with brief descriptions of the offences and details of modes of trial, are set out in sch. 10. This is reproduced in abridged form at **B7.73**.

OFFENCES CONCERNING COMPANY INSOLVENCY AND LIQUIDATION

Procedure in Summary Proceedings

Insolvency Act 1986, s. 431

B7.42

(1) Summary proceedings for any offence under any of parts I to VII of this Act may (without prejudice to any jurisdiction exercisable apart from this subsection) be taken against a body corporate at any place at which the body has a place of business, and against any other person at any place at which he is for the time being.

(2) Notwithstanding anything in section 127(1) of the Magistrates' Courts Act 1980, an information relating to such an offence which is triable by a magistrates' court in England and Wales may be so tried if it is laid at any time within 3 years after the commission of the offence and within 12 months after the date on which evidence sufficient in the opinion of the Director of Public Prosecutions or the Secretary of State (as the case may be) to justify the proceedings comes to his knowledge.

(3) [Applies only to Scotland.]

(4) For purposes of this section, a certificate of the Director of Public Prosecutions, the Lord Advocate or the Secretary of State (as the case may be) as to the date on which such evidence as is referred to above came to his knowledge is conclusive evidence.

Insolvency and Winding Up

A company can be wound up by an order of the High Court or (if its paid up share capital does **B7.43** not exceed £120,000) by an order of the county court with winding-up jurisdiction for the district in which the company's registered office is situated (Insolvency Act 1986, s. 117). This is called a compulsory winding up. A company can also be wound up voluntarily if the company passes a resolution for voluntary winding up under s. 84. A company that is being wound up is referred to as being in liquidation. Companies in liquidation are not always insolvent, and the offences contained within the Insolvency Act 1986 are often capable of applying to the winding up of solvent companies. In practice, however, prosecutions under the Act usually concern the winding up of insolvent companies.

The date at which winding up commences can be crucial to the application of the relevant law. A voluntary winding up commences when the resolution for winding up is passed by the company (s. 86) and, under s. 129, this remains the relevant date even when a winding-up order is later made in respect of that company. In compulsory winding up, the relevant date is the date on which the winding-up petition was presented (s. 129(2)).

As to the application of the Insolvency Act 1986 to limited liability partnerships, see the Limited Liability Partnerships Regulations 2001 (SI 2001 No. 1090), reg. 5.

False Declarations of Solvency in Voluntary Liquidations

Insolvency Act 1986, s. 89

B7.44

(1) Where it is proposed to wind up a company voluntarily, the directors (or, in the case of a company having more than two directors, the majority of them) may at a directors' meeting make a statutory declaration to the effect that they have made a full inquiry into the company's affairs and that, having done so, they have formed the opinion that the company will be able to pay its debts in full, together with interest at the official rate (as defined in section 251), within such period, not exceeding 12 months from the commencement of the winding up, as may be specified in the declaration

...

(4) A director making a declaration under this section without having reasonable grounds for the opinion that the company will be able to pay its debts in full, together with interest at the official rate, within the period specified is liable to imprisonment or a fine, or both.

529

(5) If the company is wound up in pursuance of a resolution passed within 5 weeks after the making of the declaration, and its debts (together with interest at the official rate) are not paid or provided for in full within the period specified, it is to be presumed (unless the contrary is shown) that the director did not have reasonable grounds for his opinion.

This section also applies, subject to modifications, to friendly societies (Friendly Societies Act 1992, s. 23 and sch. 10).

For procedural provisions, see **B7.42**; for sentencing provisions, see **B7.73** and **B7.74**.

The importance of the declaration is that it determines whether the winding up will be a members' or a creditors' winding up (s. 90). In the latter, the company has to call a creditors' meeting (s. 98) and the creditors' nomination of the liquidator takes precedence over the members' nomination (s. 100). In a creditors' winding up it is an offence under s. 166 for any liquidator nominated by the members to dispose of company property (except perishables and other goods likely to diminish in value) unless and until his status is confirmed by a creditors' meeting. This prohibits the once prevalent practice of selling assets of insolvent companies to directors or others associated with the company at knock-down prices without the creditors being warned or consulted (*Re Centrebind Ltd* [1967] 3 All ER 889).

Fraud etc. in Anticipation of Winding Up

B7.45   **Insolvency Act 1986, s. 206**

(1) When a company is ordered to be wound up by the court, or passes a resolution for voluntary winding up, any person, being a past or present officer of the company, is deemed to have committed an offence if, within the 12 months immediately preceding the commencement of the winding up, he has—
   (a) concealed any part of the company's property to the value of £500 or more, or concealed any debt due to or from the company, or
   (b) fraudulently removed any part of the company's property to the value of £500 or more, or
   (c) concealed, destroyed, mutilated or falsified any book or paper affecting or relating to the company's property or affairs, or
   (d) made any false entry in any book or paper affecting or relating to the company's property or affairs, or
   (e) fraudulently parted with, altered or made any omission in any document affecting or relating to the company's property or affairs, or
   (f) pawned, pledged or disposed of any property of the company which has been obtained on credit and has not been paid for (unless the pawning, pledging or disposal was in the ordinary way of the company's business).
(2) Such a person is deemed to have committed an offence if within the period above mentioned he has been privy to the doing by others of any of the things mentioned in paragraphs (c), (d) and (e) of subsection (1); and he commits an offence if, at any time after the commencement of the winding up, he does any of the things mentioned in paragraph (a) to (f) of that subsection, or is privy to the doing by others of any of the things mentioned in paragraphs (c) to (e) of it.
(3) For purposes of this section, 'officer' includes a shadow director.
(4) It is a defence—
   (a) for a person charged under paragraph (a) or (f) of subsection (1) (or under subsection (2) in respect of the things mentioned in either of those two paragraphs) to prove that he had no intent to defraud, and
   (b) for a person charged under paragraph (c) or (d) of subsection (1) (or under subsection (2) in respect of the things mentioned in either of those two paragraphs) to prove that he had no intent to conceal the state of affairs of the company or to defeat the law.
(5) Where a person pawns, pledges or disposes of any property in circumstances which amount to an offence under subsection (1)(f), every person who takes in pawn or pledge, or otherwise receives, the property knowing it to be pawned, pledged or disposed of in such circumstances, is guilty of an offence.

For procedural provisions, see **B7.42**; for sentencing provisions, see **B7.73** and **B7.74**.

Fraud is a definitional element in the offences under s. 206(1)(b) and (e), and must therefore be proved by the prosecution. In the case of other offences under s. 206(1), liability is strict, unless an accused is able to rely on the defence provided by s. 206(4). The burden placed on the accused under this provision is the full persuasive burden. This does not infringe the ECHR, Article 6 (see *A-G's Ref (No. 1 of 2004)* [2004] 4 All ER 457 and *Sheldrake v DPP* [2005] 1 AC 624, holding that *Carass* [2002] 1 WLR 1714 was wrongly decided: see **F3.26**).

The words 'book or paper' in s. 206(1)(d) include records kept on computer (*Taylor* [2011] 1 WLR 1809). By s. 251, 'books or papers' include writing and, by s. 436B, a thing in writing includes that thing in electronic form.

The combined effect of s. 206(1) and (2) is that offences can be committed before or after commencement of winding up. Offences under s. 206(1)(c) to (e) can be committed by officers who are 'privy' to the acts of others; these others need not themselves be officers nor need they be guilty of any offence.

Subsections (1) and (2) create separate offences; a charge cannot be brought under s. 206(1) in respect of things done after the commencement of the winding up.

Fraudulent Conduct and Intent to Defraud   References to fraudulent conduct in the   **B7.46**
Insolvency Act 1986, s. 206(1), and to 'intent to defraud' in s. 206(4)(a), must be concerned with the same concept (for further discussion of this in the context of fraudulent trading, see **B7.12**). It must, in other words, involve dishonesty, but need not involve deceit.

Receipt of Property Disposed of Contrary to s. 206(1)(f) etc.   The wording of the   **B7.47**
Insolvency Act 1986, s. 206(5), seems open to two possible interpretations. One possibility is that the recipient need know only of the circumstances specified in s. 206(1)(f), and that knowledge of whether the person disposing of the property could establish a defence under s. 206(4) is irrelevant; fraud is not, after all, a definitional element in an offence under s. 206(1)(f). The other possibility is that the prosecution must prove the recipient's knowledge of the disposer's guilt, and that that guilt arises only where the disposer is unable to prove a defence under s. 206(4); the recipient would therefore need to know that no such defence could be established (in other words, he must be shown to know that the disposer is acting fraudulently). It is submitted that the latter interpretation is the correct one; the former could lead to cases in which the recipient is convicted despite the acquittal of the disposer and would be in marked contrast to the position under the corresponding bankruptcy provision (Insolvency Act 1986, s. 359 — see **B7.65**). In contrast, there is nothing illogical in a rule under which conviction of the disposer is made easier than conviction of the recipient.

For the approach to disposal otherwise than in the ordinary course of business, see *Countrywide Banking Corporation Ltd v Dean* [1998] AC 338 and the older cases of *Bolus* (1870) 23 LT 339 and *Thomas* (1870) 22 LT 138.

Transactions in Fraud of Creditors

Insolvency Act 1986, s. 207   **B7.48**

(1) When a company is ordered to be wound up by the court or passes a resolution for voluntary winding up, a person is deemed to have committed an offence if he, being at the time an officer of the company—
   (a) has made or caused to be made any gift or transfer of, or charge on, or has caused or connived at the levying of any execution against, the company's property, or
   (b) has concealed or removed any part of the company's property since, or within 2 months before, the date of any unsatisfied judgment or order for the payment of money obtained against the company.
(2) A person is not guilty of an offence under this section—
   (a) by reason of conduct constituting an offence under subsection (1)(a) which occurred more than 5 years before the commencement of the winding up, or

(b) if he proves that, at the time of the conduct constituting the offence, he had no intent to defraud the company's creditors.

For procedural provisions, see **B7.42**; for sentencing provisions, see **B7.73** and **B7.74**.

Although s. 207(1)(a) is widely expressed, its effect is heavily curtailed by s. 207(2). The burden placed on the accused under s. 207(2)(b) would appear to be the full persuasive burden (see *A-G's Ref (No. 1 of 2004)* [2004] 4 All ER 457, *Sheldrake v DPP* [2005] 1 AC 624 and **F3.18** *et seq.*).

Old authority to the effect that any intent to defraud creditors must refer to creditors at the time of the action concerned (*Hopkins* [1896] 1 QB 652) seems doubtful on principle. It would produce very unsatisfactory results where the company has a long-term debt problem, but a series of short-term creditors (*Seillon* [1982] Crim LR 676).

A person 'causes' a thing to be done when he orders or directs it to be done (*Houston v Buchanan* [1940] 2 All ER 179).

Misconduct in the Course of Winding Up

B7.49   Insolvency Act 1986, s. 208

(1) When a company is being wound up, whether by the court or voluntarily, any person, being a past or present officer of the company, commits an offence if he—
   (a) does not to the best of his knowledge and belief fully and truly discover to the liquidator all the company's property, and how and to whom and for what consideration and when the company disposed of any part of that property (except such part as has been disposed of in the ordinary way of the company's business), or
   (b) does not deliver up to the liquidator (or as he directs) all such part of the company's property as is in his custody or under his control, and which he is required by law to deliver up, or
   (c) does not deliver up to the liquidator (or as he directs) all books and papers in his custody or under his control belonging to the company and which he is required by law to deliver up, or
   (d) knowing or believing that a false debt has been proved by any person in the winding up, fails to inform the liquidator as soon as practicable, or
   (e) after the commencement of the winding up, prevents the production of any book or paper affecting or relating to the company's property or affairs.
(2) Such a person commits an offence if after the commencement of the winding up he attempts to account for any part of the company's property by fictitious losses or expenses; and he is deemed to have committed that offence if he has so attempted at any meeting of the company's creditors within the 12 months immediately preceding the commencement of the winding up.
(3) For the purposes of this section, 'officer' includes a shadow director.
(4) It is a defence—
   (a) for a person charged under paragraph (a), (b) or (c) of subsection (1) to prove that he had no intent to defraud, and
   (b) for a person charged under paragraph (e) of that subsection to prove that he had no intent to conceal the state of affairs of the company or to defeat the law.

For procedural provisions, see **B7.42**; for sentencing provisions, see **B7.73** and **B7.74**.

This is an important section, because the reason for appointing the liquidator is to ensure that the winding up is conducted by an independent person. That purpose would be defeated if the liquidator was unable to obtain access to, and control of, the company's property and records. The burden imposed on the defence by s. 208(4) is the full persuasive burden of proof (*R (Griffin) v Richmond Magistrates' Court* [2008] 3 All ER 274 and **F3.18** *et seq.*).

It is not necessary for the liquidator to have demanded the specific property in question. There is accordingly a continuing duty to disclose and deliver any valuable items of which the liquidator may be unaware (*McCredie* [2000] BCC 617). In *McCredie* the words 'books and papers' in s. 208(1)(c) were treated as including records on floppy disks. This was considered to be correct in *Taylor* [2011] 1 WLR 1809 at [24] (see also **B7.45**).

No special defences are available to the offences in s. 208(1)(d) and (2). Under s. 208(2), full and frank disclosure to the liquidator does not excuse previous lies told to creditors, and under s. 208(1)(d) mere hesitation in disclosing a false claim may be sufficient.

Falsification of Company Books

Insolvency Act 1986, s. 209   **B7.50**

(1) When a company is being wound up, an officer or contributory of the company commits an offence if he destroys, mutilates, alters or falsifies any books, papers or securities, or makes or is privy to the making of any false or fraudulent entry in any register, book of account or document belonging to the company with intent to defraud or deceive any person.

For procedural provisions, see **B7.42**; for sentencing provisions, see **B7.73** and **B7.74**.

Section 209(1) is not clearly worded. It is not clear whether the words 'belonging to the company' govern only the immediately preceding words 'register, book of account or document' or whether they also govern the words 'any books, papers or securities' earlier in the subsection. But the phrase 'with intent to defraud or deceive any person' appears to apply to each of the ways in which the offence can be committed.

The term 'documents' is defined in s. 436 as including computer records and other non-documentary records. This means, for example, that the fraudulent insertion of false entries on a company computer record would be an offence under s. 209(1) if the insertion is made with intent to defraud or deceive.

Material Omissions from Statements Relating to the Company's Affairs

Insolvency Act 1986, s. 210   **B7.51**

(1) When a company is being wound up, whether by the court or voluntarily, any person, being a past or present officer of the company, commits an offence if he makes any material omission in any statement relating to the company's affairs.
(2) When a company has been ordered to be wound up by the court, or has passed a resolution for voluntary winding up, any such person is deemed to have committed that offence if, prior to the winding up, he has made any material omission in any such statement.
(3) For the purposes of this section, 'officer' includes a shadow director.
(4) It is a defence for a person charged under this section to prove that he had no intent to defraud.

For procedural provisions, see **B7.42**; for sentencing provisions, see **B7.73** and **B7.74**.

The width of this provision is limited by the defence in s. 210(4). Unlike the equivalent provision in respect of bankruptcy (s. 356(1); see **B7.62**), it is not necessary that the material omission be made in a statement under any provision of the Act, such as the statutory statement of affairs under s. 131 in compulsory winding up; any statement, oral or written, would seem to be within its scope, whether made during winding up or prior to it. If a material omission was understandable in the circumstances (as where the statement was informal and unrehearsed), it would be difficult to conclude that there was any intent to defraud.

False Representations to Creditors

Insolvency Act 1986, s. 211   **B7.52**

(1) When a company is being wound up, whether by the court or voluntarily, any person, being a past or present officer of the company—
(a) commits an offence if he makes any false representation or commits any other fraud for the purpose of obtaining the consent of the company's creditors or any of them to an agreement with reference to the company's affairs or to the winding up, and

    (b) is deemed to have committed that offence if, prior to the winding up, he has made any false representation, or committed any other fraud, for that purpose.

  (2) For purposes of this section, 'officer' includes a shadow director.

For procedural provisions, see **B7.42**; for sentencing provisions, see **B7.73** and **B7.74**.

In view of the fact that s. 211 makes no provision for an accused to prove that he acted without fraudulent intent, and in view of the references to false representations 'or any other fraud', it is submitted that the offence of making false representations should be construed as requiring the prosecution to prove fraud. This interpretation gains some support from *Cherry* (1871) 12 Cox 32, in which it was said (in relation to bankruptcy provisions) that, in this context, 'false' means 'fraudulent'.

Re-use of Company Names

B7.53   Insolvency Act 1986, s. 216

  (1) This section applies to a person where a company ('the liquidating company') has gone into insolvent liquidation on or after the appointed day and he was a director or shadow director of the company at any time in the period of 12 months ending with the day before it went into liquidation.

  (2) For the purposes of this section, a name is a prohibited name in relation to such a person if—

    (a) it is a name by which the liquidating company was known at any time in that period of 12 months, or

    (b) it is a name which is so similar to a name falling within paragraph (a) as to suggest an association with that company.

  (3) Except with leave of the court or in such circumstances as may be prescribed, a person to whom this section applies shall not at any time in the period of 5 years beginning with the day on which the liquidating company went into liquidation—

    (a) be a director of any other company that is known by a prohibited name, or

    (b) in any way, whether directly or indirectly, be concerned or take part in the promotion, formation or management of any such company, or

    (c) in any way, whether directly or indirectly, be concerned or take part in the carrying on of a business carried on (otherwise than by a company) under a prohibited name.

For procedural provisions, see **B7.42**; for sentencing provisions, see **B7.73** and **B7.74**.

Section 216 deals with one aspect of 'Phoenix companies', where companies in insolvent liquidation would re-appear, with almost identical names, businesses and directors, a few months later. The re-born companies would in law be new enterprises, unfettered by the unpaid debts of the previous ones, but would, to outside appearances, be the same as before, and often acquired assets cheaply from the liquidator of the previous company. However, s. 216 is not limited to such cases (*Ricketts v Ad Valorem Factors Ltd* [2003] EWCA Civ 1706; *First Independent Factors and Finance Ltd v Mountford* [2008] EWHC 835 (Ch)).

Circumstances prescribed as exceptions from the prohibition in s. 216 are set out in rr. 4.228 to 4.230 of the Insolvency Rules 1986 (*Churchill v First Independent Factors and Finance Ltd* [2006] EWCA Civ 1623). The court which may give leave under s. 216(3) is the court having jurisdiction to wind up companies, and a company is regarded as going into insolvent liquidation if its assets are insufficient to meet its liabilities and the expenses of the winding up (s. 216(5) and (7)). References, in relation to a time, to a name by which a company is known, are to the name of the company at that time or to any name under which the company carries on business at that time (s. 216(6)).

Contravention of s. 216 may involve civil liability under s. 217 as well as the criminal penalties prescribed in sch. 10. The offence created by s. 216 is one of strict liability (*Cole* [1998] BCC 87 and *Doring* [2003] 1 Cr App R 143).

In *Weintroub* [2011] EWCA Crim 2167 the Court of Appeal decided that where directors had traded under a prohibited company name, the amount of benefit they had received for the purposes of the POCA 2002 was the full amount that they had received as directors and not just the proportion of that sum attributable to the prohibited name.

False Claim of Status as Creditor

Insolvency Rules 1986, r. 12.18   **B7.54**

(1) Where the rules provide for creditors, members of a company or contributories in a company's winding up a right to inspect any documents, whether on the court's file or in the hands of an office holder or other person, it is an offence for a person, with the intention of obtaining a sight of documents which he has not under the rules any right to inspect, falsely to claim a status which would entitle him to inspect them.

This offence is triable either way. On conviction on indictment for an offence contrary to r. 12.18, the maximum penalty is two years' imprisonment and/or a fine; on summary conviction, it is six months' imprisonment and/or a fine of the statutory maximum.

BANKRUPTCY OFFENCES

The provisions of the Insolvency Act 1986, part IX, chapter VI, deal with the principal bank-   **B7.55**
ruptcy offences and are in many respects similar, but not identical, to the provisions dealing with company insolvency and liquidation offences. In individual insolvency the trustee in bankruptcy performs a role similar to that of a liquidator in company liquidation.

The Tribunals, Courts and Enforcement Act 2007, sch. 17, inserted part 7A (ss. 251A to 251X) into the Insolvency Act 1986. These provisions enable an individual who is unable to pay his debts to apply for a debt relief order. For an explanation of debt relief orders, see *R (Cooper) v Secretary of State for Work and Pensions* [2012] 2 AC 1 at [7]–[11]. Sections 251O to 251S create offences in connection with debt relief orders. By s. 251T(1) proceedings for these offences can only be instituted by the Secretary of State or by or with the consent of the DPP.

Scheme of Chapter VI

Insolvency Act 1986, s. 350   **B7.56**

(1) Subject to section 360(3) below, this chapter applies where the court has made a bankruptcy order on a bankruptcy petition.
(2) This chapter applies whether or not the bankruptcy order is annulled, but proceedings for an offence under this chapter shall not be instituted after the annulment.
(3) Without prejudice to his liability in respect of a subsequent bankruptcy, the bankrupt is not guilty of an offence under this chapter in respect of anything done after his discharge; but nothing in this group of parts prevents the institution of proceedings against a discharged bankrupt for an offence committed before his discharge.
(3A) Subsection (3) is without prejudice to any provision of this chapter which applies to a person in respect of whom a bankruptcy restrictions order is in force.
(4) It is not a defence in proceedings for an offence under this chapter that anything relied on, in whole or in part, as constituting that offence was done outside England and Wales.
(5) Proceedings for an offence under this chapter or under the rules shall not be instituted except by the Secretary of State or by or with the consent of the Director of Public Prosecutions.
(6) A person guilty of any offence under this chapter is liable to imprisonment or a fine, or both.

Penalties for offences under chapter VI (ss. 353 to 362) are prescribed by sch. 10, the relevant parts of which are printed at **B7.73**.

Definitions

Insolvency Act 1986, ss. 351 and 381   **B7.57**

351. In the following provisions of this chapter—
(a) references to property comprised in the bankrupt's estate or to property possession of which is required to be delivered up to the official receiver or the trustee of the bankrupt's estate include any property which would be such property if a notice in respect of it were given under section 307 (after-acquired property), section 308 (personal property and effects of bankrupt having more than replacement value) or section 308A (vesting in trustee of certain tenancies);

(b) 'the initial period' means the period between the presentation of the bankruptcy petition and the commencement of the bankruptcy; and

(c) a reference to a number of months or years before petition is to that period ending with the presentation of the bankruptcy petition.

381.—(1) 'Bankrupt' means an individual who has been adjudged bankrupt, and, in relation to a bankruptcy order, it means the individual adjudged bankrupt by that order.

(2) 'Bankruptcy order' means an order adjudging an individual bankrupt.

(3) 'Bankruptcy petition' means a petition to the court for a bankruptcy order.

Under s. 306 the bankrupt's estate vests in his trustee in bankruptcy. Under s. 307, the bankrupt's trustee may by notice in writing claim for his estate property acquired or devolved upon the bankrupt since commencement of his bankruptcy; and under s. 308 he may similarly claim tools of trade, household effects etc., which would not ordinarily be claimed, but which appear to have a realisable value exceeding the cost of reasonable replacements.

Further definitions (not printed in this work) are to be found in ss. 382 to 385. In cases of absconding, removal of goods and concealment or destruction of goods or documents, the bankruptcy court can make an order under s. 364 for the arrest of an undischarged bankrupt or a debtor against whom a bankruptcy petition has been issued and the seizure of documents or goods in his possession. For the procedure to be followed, see *Hickling v Baker* [2007] 4 All ER 390.

Defence of Innocent Intention

B7.58
                    Insolvency Act 1986, s. 352

Where in the case of an offence under any provision of this chapter it is stated that this section applies, a person is not guilty of the offence if he proves that, at the time of the conduct constituting the offence, he had no intent to defraud or to conceal the state of his affairs.

In *A-G's Ref (No. 1 of 2004)* [2004] 4 All ER 457, Lord Woolf CJ said (at [92]):

In the light of *Lambert* [[2002] 2 AC 740], we accept that in appropriate cases [s. 352] may be read down as imposing no more than an evidential burden of proof. Its effect within chapter VI depends on the context of its application. In section 357(1), it has to be so read.

Offences of Non-disclosure

B7.59
                    Insolvency Act 1986, s. 353

(1) The bankrupt is guilty of an offence if—

(a) he does not to the best of his knowledge and belief disclose all the property comprised in his estate to the official receiver or the trustee, or

(b) he does not inform the official receiver or the trustee of any disposal of any property which but for the disposal would be so comprised, stating how, when, to whom and for what consideration the property was disposed of.

(2) Subsection (1)(b) does not apply to any disposal in the ordinary course of a business carried on by the bankrupt or to any payment of the ordinary expenses of the bankrupt or his family.

(3) Section 352 applies to this offence.

For procedural provisions, see **B7.56**; for sentencing provisions, see **B7.73** and **B7.74**. As to the meaning of 'property' see **B7.57**. Section 353(1)(b) is primarily concerned with property which the bankrupt has had at some time and which the trustee might be able to trace and reclaim through exercise of his powers under the Act.

As to what might or might not amount to disposal 'in the ordinary course of business', see **B7.47** and *Countrywide Banking Corporation Ltd v Dean* [1998] AC 338.

Concealment of Property and Failure to Account for Losses

B7.60
                    Insolvency Act 1986, s. 354

(1) The bankrupt is guilty of an offence, if—

(a) he does not deliver up possession to the official receiver or trustee, or as the official receiver or trustee may direct, of such part of the property comprised in his estate as is in his possession or under his control, and possession of which he is required by law so to deliver up,

(b) he conceals any debt due to or from him or conceals any property the value of which is not less than the prescribed amount and possession of which he is required to deliver up to the official receiver or trustee, or

(c) in the 12 months before petition, or in the initial period, he did anything which would have been an offence under paragraph (b) above if the bankruptcy order had been made immediately before he did it.

Section 352 applies to this offence.

(2) The bankrupt is guilty of an offence if he removes, or in the initial period removed, any property the value of which was not less than the prescribed amount and possession of which he has or would have been required to deliver up to the official receiver or the trustee.

Section 352 applies to this offence.

(3) The bankrupt is guilty of an offence if he without reasonable excuse fails, on being required to do so by the official receiver, the trustee or the court—

(a) to account for the loss of any substantial part of his property incurred in the 12 months before petition or in the initial period, or

(b) to give a satisfactory explanation of the manner in which such a loss was incurred.

For procedural provisions, see B7.56; for sentencing provisions, see B7.73 and B7.74. For the defence under s. 352 (defence of innocent intention), see B7.58. The 'prescribed amount' for the purposes of s. 354 is fixed by the Insolvency Proceedings (Monetary Limits) Order 1986 (SI 1986 No. 1996, as amended by SI 2004 No. 547) at £1,000.

The offence contained within s. 354(3) differs from those contained within the preceding subsections in that it is absolute, and does not allow for any possible defence under s. 352. For the jury direction in relation to a similarly worded offence under the Bankruptcy Act 1914 see *Salter* [1968] 2 QB 793 at p. 798. An explanation, if clear and true, need not also be 'satisfactory' in the sense of clearing the bankrupt of blame. If, for example, the explanation reveals heavy gambling losses, this may still be satisfactory for the purposes of s. 354.

The offence under s. 354(3)(a) is compatible with the accused's right to silence and not to incriminate himself (*Kearns* [2002] 1 WLR 2815).

Concealment or Falsification of Books and Papers

Insolvency Act 1986, s. 355   B7.61

(1) The bankrupt is guilty of an offence if he does not deliver up possession to the official receiver or the trustee, or as the official receiver or trustee may direct, of all books, papers and other records of which he has possession or control and which relate to his estate or his affairs.

Section 352 applies to this offence.

(2) The bankrupt is guilty of an offence if—

(a) he prevents, or in the initial period prevented, the production of any books, papers or records relating to his estate or affairs;

(b) he conceals, destroys, mutilates or falsifies, or causes or permits the concealment, destruction, mutilation or falsification of, any books, papers or other records relating to his estate or affairs;

(c) he makes or causes or permits the making of, any false entries in any book, document or record relating to his estate or affairs; or

(d) in the 12 months before petition, or in the initial period, he did anything which would have been an offence, under paragraph (b) or (c) above if the bankruptcy order had been made before he did it.

Section 352 applies to this offence.

(3) The bankrupt is guilty of an offence if—

(a) he disposes of, or alters or makes any omission in, or causes or permits the disposal, altering or making of any omission in, any book, document or record relating to his estate or affairs, or

(b) in the 12 months before petition, or in the initial period, he did anything which would have been an offence under paragraph (a) if the bankruptcy order had been made before he did it.

(4) In their application to a trading record subsections (2)(d) and (3)(b) shall have effect as if the reference to 12 months were a reference to two years.

(5) In subsection (4) 'trading record' means a book, document or record which shows or explains the transactions or financial position of a person's business, including—

    (a) a periodic record of cash paid and received,

    (b) a statement of periodic stock-taking, and

    (c) except in the case of goods sold by way of retail trade, a record of goods sold and purchased which identifies the buyer and seller or enables them to be identified.

Section 352 applies to this offence.

For procedural provisions, see **B7.56**; for sentencing provisions, see **B7.73** and **B7.74**. For the meaning of 'the initial period', see **B7.57**. For the defence under s. 352 (lack of fraudulent intent), see **B7.58**. Section 251P creates similar offences by a person in respect of whom a debt relief order is made.

'Causing' an act means ordering or directing it, and 'permitting' it means allowing it to happen (*Houston v Buchanan* [1940] 2 All ER 179). It is not always clear whether an accused must be proved to know the circumstances which make the act criminal, although, in this context, it is unlikely that such proof would be required. Where an accused has, for example, permitted an assistant to clear out old files in his office, and it transpires that these included papers relating to his estate or affairs, it is submitted that his only possible defence to a charge under s. 355(2)(b) would be that provided by s. 352.

The point which was argued unsuccessfully in *Taylor* [2011] 1 WLR 1809 (see **B7.45**) about company records kept on computer could not have arisen in relation to individual bankruptcy as s. 355 expressly extends to records other than books or papers.

The offences under s. 355(2) and (3) overlap with the Theft Act 1968, s. 17 (see **B6.3**), and the Forgery and Counterfeiting Act 1981, s. 1 (see **B6.36**).

False Statements

B7.62

Insolvency Act 1986, s. 356

(1) The bankrupt is guilty of an offence if he makes or has made any material omission in any statement made under any provision in this group of parts and relating to his affairs.

Section 352 applies to this offence.

(2) The bankrupt is guilty of an offence if—

    (a) knowing or believing that a false debt has been proved by any person under the bankruptcy, he fails to inform the trustee as soon as practicable; or

    (b) he attempts to account for any part of his property by fictitious losses or expenses; or

    (c) at any meeting of his creditors in the 12 months before petition or (whether or not at such a meeting) at any time in the initial period, he did anything which would have been an offence under paragraph (b) if the bankruptcy order had been made before he did it; or

    (d) he is, or at any time has been, guilty of any false representation or other fraud for the purpose of obtaining the consent of his creditors, or any of them, to an agreement with reference to his affairs or to his bankruptcy.

For procedural provisions, see **B7.56**; for sentencing provisions, see **B7.73** and **B7.74**. For the defence under s. 352 (lack of fraudulent intent), see **B7.58**. Section 251O(2) and (4) creates similar offences in respect of debt relief orders.

A charge under s. 356 remains appropriate even where the bankrupt's false statement was made prior to bankruptcy (*Edwards* [2010] EWCA Crim 1682). Section 356(1) differs from the equivalent company liquidation offence (s. 210) in that the statement concerned must be one made under relevant provisions of the Act. This might be a 'statement of affairs' under s. 288 or a statement made in purported compliance with s. 333 or any other relevant provision.

The defence under s. 352 applies only to s. 356(1); the offences under s. 356(2) require proof of knowledge or belief. Thus, proof of the inaccuracy of a bankrupt's account would not suffice to prove an offence under s. 366(2)(b): it must also be proved to be fictitious (i.e. that the inaccuracy is deliberate). In respect of s. 356(2)(d), fraud must be proved (see the discussion of the equivalent provision in s. 211 at B7.52). In respect of the other offences under s. 356(2), the requisite *mens rea* need not necessarily involve fraud, which thus becomes wholly irrelevant to the issue of guilt: the prosecution need not prove it, and it will not avail the defence to prove its absence.

Fraudulent Disposal or Concealment of Property

Insolvency Act 1986, s. 357

B7.63

(1) The bankrupt is guilty of an offence if he makes or causes to be made, or has in the period of 5 years ending with the commencement of the bankruptcy made or caused to be made, any gift or transfer of, or any charge on, his property.
Section 352 applies to this offence.
(2) The reference to making a transfer of or charge on any property includes causing or conniving at the levying of any execution against the property.
(3) The bankrupt is guilty of an offence if he conceals or removes, or has at any time before the commencement of the bankruptcy concealed or removed, any part of his property after, or within 2 months before, the date on which a judgment or order for the payment of money has been obtained against him, being a judgment or order which was not satisfied before the commencement of the bankruptcy.
Section 352 applies to this offence.

For procedural provisions, see B7.56; for sentencing provisions, see B7.73 and B7.74; for definitions, see B7.57. Section 357(1) is similar to the companies offence contained within s. 207 (see B7.48) and, like s. 207, would be of very wide application but for the defence provided under s. 352 (see B7.58). Section 251Q creates a similar offence to that under s. 357(1) in relation to the fraudulent disposal of property by a person in respect of whom a debt relief order is made, but in that case the period starts two years before the application for the debt relief order is made.

A bankrupt who commits an offence under s. 357 can expect to receive a custodial sentence, even if of previous good character (*Mungroo* [1998] BPIR 784; see also *Ferguson* [2013] EWCA Crim 1089).

The Debtors Act 1869, s. 13(3), creates an offence similar in form to the Insolvency Act 1986, s. 357(3), but it does not require there to be a bankruptcy, and places the burden of proving fraud on the prosecution. The Debtors Act 1869, s. 13(2), creates an offence of making gifts etc. with intent to defraud creditors; again this is not dependent on bankruptcy.

Absconding with Property

Insolvency Act 1986, s. 358

B7.64

The bankrupt is guilty of an offence if—
(a) he leaves, or attempts or makes preparations to leave, England and Wales with any property the value of which is not less than the prescribed amount and possession of which he is required to deliver up to the official receiver or the trustee, or
(b) in the 6 months before the petition, or in the initial period, he did anything which would have been an offence under paragraph (a) if the bankruptcy order had been made immediately before he did it.
Section 352 applies to this offence.

For procedural provisions, see B7.56; for sentencing provisions, see B7.73 and B7.74; for definitions, see B7.57. The 'prescribed amount' is fixed by the Insolvency Proceedings (Monetary Limits) Order 1986 (SI 1986 No. 1996, as amended by SI 2004 No. 547) at £1,000.

If the bankrupt has done nothing worse than travel abroad with property (e.g., his car) with which he has later returned, it may well be easy for him to show that he had no intent to defraud and thus take advantage of the defence under s. 352 (see **B7.58**).

Fraudulent Dealing with Property Obtained on Credit

B7.65   *Insolvency Act 1986, s. 359*

(1) The bankrupt is guilty of an offence if, in the 12 months before petition, or in the initial period, he disposed of any property which he had obtained on credit and, at the time he disposed of it, had not paid for.
Section 352 applies to this offence.

(2) A person is guilty of an offence if, in the 12 months before petition or in the initial period, he acquired or received property from the bankrupt knowing or believing—
   (a) that the bankrupt owed money in respect of the property, and
   (b) that the bankrupt did not intend, or was unlikely to be able, to pay the money he so owed.

(3) A person is not guilty of an offence under subsection (1) or (2) if the disposal, acquisition or receipt of the property was in the ordinary course of a business carried on by the bankrupt at the time of the disposal, acquisition or receipt.

(4) In determining for the purposes of this section whether any property is disposed of, acquired or received in the ordinary course of a business carried on by the bankrupt, regard may be had, in particular, to the price paid for the property.

(5) In this section references to disposing of property include pawning or pledging it; and references to acquiring or receiving property shall be read accordingly.

For procedural provisions, see **B7.56**; for sentencing provisions, see **B7.73** and **B7.74**. For definitions, see **B7.57**. For the defence of no intent under s. 352, see **B7.58**. Section 251R(1) and (2) creates similar offences in relation to the disposal of property by a person in respect of whom a debt relief order has been made where the property was obtained on credit and has not been paid for.

The mischief against which s. 359 strikes is that of obtaining goods on credit, and then selling or otherwise disposing of them, often on disadvantageous terms or for inadequate consideration, as a method of raising cash which may be unobtainable by more conventional means. Such methods are generally resorted to only by persons who are already in serious financial difficulties, and prejudice the interests of the unpaid suppliers.

As to what may amount to disposal 'otherwise than in the ordinary course of business', see **B7.47**.

Obtaining Credit: Engaging in Business

B7.66   *Insolvency Act 1986, s. 360*

(1) The bankrupt is guilty of an offence if—
   (a) either alone or jointly with any other person, he obtains credit to the extent of the prescribed amount or more without giving the person from whom he obtains it the relevant information about his status; or
   (b) he engages (whether directly or indirectly) in any business under a name other than that in which he was adjudged bankrupt without disclosing to all persons with whom he enters into any business transaction the name in which he was so adjudged.

(2) The reference to the bankrupt obtaining credit includes the following cases—
   (a) where goods are bailed to him under a hire-purchase agreement, or agreed to be sold to him under a conditional sale agreement, and
   (b) where he is paid in advance (whether in money or otherwise) for the supply of goods or services.

(3) A person whose estate has been sequestrated in Scotland, or who has been adjudged bankrupt in Northern Ireland, is guilty of an offence if, before his discharge, he does anything in England and Wales which would be an offence under subsection (1) if he were an undischarged bankrupt and the sequestration of his estate or the adjudication in Northern Ireland were an adjudication under this part.

(4) For the purposes of subsection (1)(a), the relevant information about the status of the person in question is the information that he is an undischarged bankrupt or, as the case may be, that his estate has been sequestrated in Scotland and that he has not been discharged.

(5) This section applies to the bankrupt after discharge while a bankruptcy restrictions order is in force in respect of him.

(6) For the purposes of subsection (1)(a) as it applies by virtue of subsection (5), the relevant information about the status of the person in question is the information that a bankruptcy restrictions order is in force in respect of him.

For procedural provisions, see **B7.56**; for sentencing provisions, see **B7.73** and **B7.74**. Section 251S creates similar offences by a person in respect of whom a debt relief order is made.

Section 360 is not subject to the defence of innocent intention under s. 352. The offences re-enacted in s. 360 have always been regarded as absolute. Thus, in *Duke of Leinster* [1924] 1 KB 311, it was held that D committed the offence even though his agent had been instructed to inform the creditor of D's status and had failed to do so. See also *Dyson* [1894] 2 QB 176.

Credit to the Extent of the Prescribed Amount   The amount prescribed by the Insolvency   **B7.67** Proceedings (Monetary Limits) Order 1986 (SI 1986 No. 1996, as amended by SI 2004 No. 547 and SI 2009 No. 465, which extends the principal Order to cover debt relief orders) is £500. This limit governs the aggregate of the credit obtained, and it cannot be circumvented merely by ensuring that no one transaction exceeds the limit (*Juby* (1886) 16 Cox 160; *Hartley* [1972] 2 QB 1). It seems to have been assumed in *Hartley* that the prescribed amount nevertheless refers to the aggregate obtained from any one creditor. If this is correct, it would be no offence for a bankrupt to obtain £499 worth of credit from each of four different persons without admitting to being a bankrupt. This proposition is of doubtful validity, for, although the section refers to 'the person' from whom credit is obtained, the general principle is that the singular includes the plural (Interpretation Act 1978, s. 6(c)) and the risk of loss to each creditor is increased by the increase in the aggregate of the bankrupt's debt.

Obtaining   Any obtaining must be of credit given to the bankrupt himself. The agree-   **B7.68** ment to provide credit does not have to be enforceable (*Roder Ltd v West* [2012] QB 752 at [17]). Credit given to the bankrupt jointly with another is expressly included, but cases where credit is obtained by the bankrupt as agent for another person to whom the creditor looks for payment would not be covered (*Godwin* (1980) 71 Cr App R 97). 'Obtaining' has a narrower meaning for the purposes of s. 360 than it has, for example, in respect of insider dealing; it must involve 'some conduct, either by words or otherwise…which amounts to an obtaining' (*Hayat* (1976) 63 Cr App R 181). There may not necessarily have been any 'obtaining' in this sense where the bankrupt's bank account becomes overdrawn as a result of the dishonouring of certain incoming cheques and the honouring of certain cheques drawn by him on that account; it will be a question of fact for the jury (*Hayat*). There is no obtaining of credit where the bankrupt defaults on an existing hire-purchase obligation and thereby becomes liable to pay the arrears (*Miller* [1977] 3 All ER 986) nor where funds are received from a business partner in the course of a joint venture. It makes no difference if the bankrupt intends to default on his side of the bargain: 'It is the nature of the agreement which determines whether or not credit has been obtained, not the intention of the defendant' (*Ramzan* [1998] 2 Cr App R 328 at p. 334).

Credit is 'obtained' where any goods or monies concerned are received (*Ellis* [1899] 1 QB 230), but the Insolvency Act 1986, s. 350(4) (see **B7.56**), ensures that the provisions of chapter VI have extra-territorial effect, and so it will be no defence to argue that credit was obtained abroad.

Engaging in Business   A bankrupt may engage in business without necessarily disclosing   **B7.69** his status, although he cannot become a company director, manager or promoter without

leave of the court (see the Company Directors Disqualification Act 1986, ss. 11 and 13, at
B7.71). He must not hide his bankruptcy by using a different name. The reference in the
Insolvency Act 1986, s. 360(1)(b), to indirectly engaging in business is designed to deal
with bankrupts who procure some other persons to 'front' businesses effectively controlled
by themselves.

FRAUD IN RESPECT OF VOLUNTARY ARRANGEMENTS

B7.70   Parts I and VIII of the Insolvency Act 1986 make provision for voluntary arrangements by
agreement with creditors for the satisfaction of debts or a scheme of arrangement.

Insolvency Act 1986, s. 6A

(1) If, for the purpose of obtaining the approval of the members or creditors of a company to a
proposal for a voluntary arrangement, a person who is an officer of the company—
(a) makes any false representation, or
(b) fraudulently does, or omits to do, anything,
he commits an offence.
(2) Subsection (1) applies even if the proposal is not approved.
(3) For purposes of this section 'officer' includes a shadow director.

Section 262A makes similar provision for fraud etc. by individual debtors. For sentencing provisions, see **B7.73** and **B7.74**.

OFFENCES RELATING TO DISQUALIFICATION

Disqualification from Company Management etc.

B7.71   Company Directors Disqualification Act 1986, ss. 11 and 13

11.—(1) It is an offence for a person to act as director of a company or directly or indirectly to take
part in or be concerned in the promotion, formation or management of a company, without
the leave of the court, at a time when—
(a) he is an undischarged bankrupt
(aa) a moratorium period under a debt relief order applies in relation to him, or
(b) a bankruptcy restrictions order is in force in respect of him.
(2) For this purpose the court is—.
(a) in the case of a person adjudged bankrupt or, in Scotland, whose estate was sequestrated, the
court by which the person was adjudged bankrupt or sequestration of his estates was awarded,
(b) in the case of a person in respect of whom a court made a debt relief restrictions order
(under Schedule 4ZB of the Insolvency Act 1986), the court by which the order was
made, and
(c) in the case of any other person, the court to which the person would make an application
under section 251M(1) of the Insolvency Act 1986 (if the person were dissatisfied as mentioned there).
(3) In England and Wales, the leave of the court shall not be given unless notice of intention to
apply for it has been served on the official receiver; and it is the latter's duty, if he is of opinion
that it is contrary to the public interest that the application should be granted, to attend on the
hearing of the application and oppose it.
(4) In this section 'company' includes a company incorporated outside Great Britain that has an
established place of business in Great Britain.
13.—If a person acts in contravention of a disqualification order or disqualification undertaking
or in contravention of section 12(2), 12A or 12B, or is guilty of an offence under section 11,
he is liable—
(a) on conviction on indictment, to imprisonment for not more than 2 years or a fine, or
both; and
(b) on summary conviction, to imprisonment for not more than 6 months or a fine not
exceeding the statutory maximum, or both.

Liability under s.11 is strict; it is no defence that the accused honestly believed that his bankruptcy had been discharged at the relevant time (*Brockley* [1994] Crim LR 671). The scope of the prohibition is illustrated by *Campbell* (1983) 78 Cr App R 95, where it was held that a disqualified person could commit the offence by advising on financial matters and on company restructuring as a 'management consultant'.

For disqualification orders by criminal courts, see E21.8. Under ss. 3, 4 and 6, a disqualification order may also be made against a person by a court with jurisdiction to wind up companies (see B7.43) (i) for persistent breaches of companies legislation; (ii) if, in the course of winding up a company, it appears that the person has been guilty of fraudulent trading (see B7.7) or any fraud or breach of duty as an officer, liquidator or receiver of the company; or (iii) his conduct as a director makes him unfit to be concerned in the management of a company. A person against whom an application is made may give a disqualification undertaking under s. 1A. By s. 10, a disqualification order can be made against a person liable to contribute to the company's assets following fraudulent or wrongful trading.

Disqualification is to be taken seriously and is enforced strictly. For sentencing decisions, see B7.74. For confiscation orders following convictions under the Company Directors Disqualification Act 1986, see *Seager* [2010] 1 WLR 815 (see E19.21).

Disqualification under the Insolvency Act 1986

It is an offence under the Insolvency Act 1986, s. 31, for a bankrupt who is undischarged or subject to a bankruptcy restrictions order to act as a receiver or manager on behalf of debenture holders, unless appointed by the court, and since such a person is also disqualified from acting as an insolvency practitioner (Insolvency Act 1986, s. 390(4) and (5)), it follows that he commits an offence under s. 389 if he acts as a liquidator, administrator, or trustee in bankruptcy. **B7.72**

SCHEDULE OF OFFENCES UNDER THE INSOLVENCY ACT 1986

Insolvency Act 1986, sch. 10, Abridged

B7.73

Section	General nature of offence	Mode of prosecution	Punishment
6A(1)	False representation or fraud for purpose of obtaining members' or creditors' approval of proposed voluntary arrangement.	1. On indictment. 2. Summary.	7 years or a fine; or both. 6 months or the statutory maximum; or both.
31	Bankrupt acting as receiver or manager.	1. On indictment. 2. Summary.	2 years or a fine; or both. 6 months or the statutory maximum; or both.
89(4)	Director making statutory declaration of company's solvency without reasonable grounds for his opinion.	1. On indictment. 2. Summary.	2 years or a fine; or both. 6 months or the statutory maximum; or both.
206(1)	Fraud, etc. in anticipation of winding up.	1. On indictment. 2. Summary.	7 years or a fine; or both. 6 months or the statutory maximum; or both.
206(2)	Privity to fraud in anticipation of winding up; fraud, or privity to fraud, after commencement of winding up.	1. On indictment. 2. Summary.	7 years or a fine; or both. 6 months or the statutory maximum; or both.
206(5)	Knowingly taking in pawn or pledge, or otherwise receiving, company property.	1. On indictment. 2. Summary.	7 years or a fine; or both. 6 months or the statutory maximum; or both.

Section	General nature of offence	Mode of prosecution	Punishment
207	Officer of company entering into transaction in fraud of company's creditors.	1. On indictment. 2. Summary.	2 years or a fine; or both. 6 months or the statutory maximum; or both.
208	Officer of company misconducting himself in course of winding up.	1. On indictment. 2. Summary.	7 years or a fine; or both. 6 months or the statutory maximum; or both.
209	Officer or contributory destroying, falsifying, etc. company's books.	1. On indictment. 2. Summary.	7 years or a fine; or both. 6 months or the statutory maximum; or both.
210	Officer of company making material omission from statement relating to company's affairs.	1. On indictment. 2. Summary.	7 years or a fine; or both. 6 months or the statutory maximum; or both.
211	False representation or fraud for purposes of obtaining creditors' consent to an agreement in connection with winding up.	1. On indictment. 2. Summary.	7 years or a fine; or both. 6 months or the statutory maximum; or both.
216(4)	Contravening restrictions on re-use of name of company in insolvent liquidation.	1. On indictment. 2. Summary.	2 years or a fine; or both. 6 months or the statutory maximum; or both.
251O(1)	False representations or omissions in making an application for a debt relief order.	1. On indictment. 2. Summary.	7 years or a fine; or both. 12 months or the statutory maximum; or both.
251O(2)(a)	Failing to comply with duty in connection with an application for a debt relief order.	1. On indictment. 2. Summary.	2 years or a fine; or both. 12 months or the statutory maximum; or both.
251O(2)(b)	False representations or omissions in connection with duty in relation to an application for a debt relief order.	1. On indictment. 2. Summary.	7 years or a fine; or both. 12 months or the statutory maximum; or both.
251O(4)(a)	Failing to comply with duty in connection with a debt relief order.	1. On indictment. 2. Summary.	2 years or a fine; or both. 12 months or the statutory maximum; or both.
251O(4)(b)	False representations or omissions in connection with a duty in relation to a debt relief order.	1. On indictment. 2. Summary.	7 years or a fine; or both. 12 months or the statutory maximum; or both.
251P(1)	Failing to deliver books, records and papers to official receiver, concealing or destroying them or making false entries in them by person in respect of whom a debt relief order is made.	1. On indictment. 2. Summary.	7 years or a fine; or both. 12 months or the statutory maximum; or both.
251P(2)	Person in respect of whom debt relief order is made doing anything falling within paragraphs (c) to (e) of section 251P(1) during the period of 12 months ending with the application date or doing anything falling within paragraphs (b) to (e) of section 251P(1) after that date but before the effective date.	1. On indictment. 2. Summary.	7 years or a fine; or both. 12 months or the statutory maximum; or both.
251Q(1)	Fraudulent disposal of property by person in respect of whom a debt relief order is made.	1. On indictment. 2. Summary.	2 years or a fine; or both. 12 months or the statutory maximum; or both.
251R(1)	Disposal of property that is not paid for by person in respect of whom a debt relief order is made.	1. On indictment. 2. Summary.	7 years or a fine; or both. 12 months or the statutory maximum; or both.

Section	General nature of offence	Mode of prosecution	Punishment
251R(2)	Obtaining property in respect of which money is owed by a person in respect of whom a debt relief order is made.	1. On indictment. 2. Summary.	7 years or a fine; or both. 12 months or the statutory maximum; or both.
251S(1)	Person in respect of whom a debt relief order is made obtaining credit or engaging in business without disclosing his status or name.	1. On indictment. 2. Summary.	2 years or a fine; or both. 12 months or the statutory maximum; or both.
262A(1)	False representation or fraud for purposes of obtaining creditors' approval of proposed voluntary arrangement.	1. On indictment. 2. Summary.	7 years or a fine; or both. 6 months or the statutory maximum; or both.
353(1)	Bankrupt failing to disclose property or disposals to official receiver or trustee.	1. On indictment. 2. Summary.	7 years or a fine; or both. 6 months or the statutory maximum; or both.
354(1)	Bankrupt failing to deliver property to, or concealing property from, official receiver or trustee.	1. On indictment. 2. Summary.	7 years or a fine; or both. 6 months or the statutory maximum; or both.
354(2)	Bankrupt removing property which he is required to deliver to official receiver or trustee.	1. On indictment. 2. Summary.	7 years or a fine; or both. 6 months or the statutory maximum; or both.
354(3)	Bankrupt failing to account for loss of substantial part of property.	1. On indictment. 2. Summary.	2 years or a fine; or both. 6 months or the statutory maximum; or both.
355(1)	Bankrupt failing to deliver books, papers and records to official receiver or trustee.	1. On indictment. 2. Summary.	7 years or a fine; or both. 6 months or the statutory maximum; or both.
355(2)	Bankrupt concealing, destroying etc. books, papers or records, or making false entries in them.	1. On indictment. 2. Summary.	7 years or a fine; or both. 6 months or the statutory maximum; or both.
355(3)	Bankrupt disposing of, or altering, books, papers or records relating to his estate or affairs.	1. On indictment. 2. Summary.	7 years or a fine; or both. 6 months or the statutory maximum; or both.
356(1)	Bankrupt making material omission in statement relating to his affairs.	1. On indictment. 2. Summary.	7 years or a fine; or both. 6 months or the statutory maximum; or both.
356(2)	Bankrupt making false statement, or failing to inform trustee, where false debt proved.	1. On indictment. 2. Summary.	7 years or a fine; or both. 6 months or the statutory maximum; or both.
357	Bankrupt fraudulently disposing of property.	1. On indictment. 2. Summary.	2 years or a fine; or both. 6 months or the statutory maximum; or both.
358	Bankrupt absconding with property he is required to deliver to official receiver or trustee.	1. On indictment. 2. Summary.	2 years or a fine; or both. 6 months or the statutory maximum; or both.
359(1)	Bankrupt disposing of property obtained on credit and not paid for.	1. On indictment. 2. Summary.	7 years or a fine; or both. 6 months or the statutory maximum; or both.
359(2)	Obtaining property in respect of which money is owed by a bankrupt	1. On indictment. 2. Summary.	7 years or a fine; or both. 6 months or the statutory maximum; or both.
360(1)	Bankrupt obtaining credit or engaging in business without disclosing his status or name in which he was made bankrupt	1. On indictment. 2. Summary.	2 years or a fine; or both. 6 months or the statutory maximum; or both.

Section	General nature of offence	Mode of prosecution	Punishment
360(3)	Person made bankrupt in Scotland or Northern Ireland obtaining credit, etc. in England and Wales.	1. On indictment. 2. Summary.	2 years or a fine; or both. 6 months or the statutory maximum; or both.
389	Acting as insolvency practitioner when not qualified.	1. On indictment. 2. Summary.	2 years or a fine; or both. 6 months or the statutory maximum; or both.
429(5)	Contravening s. 429 in respect of disabilities imposed by county court on revocation of administration.	1. On indictment. 2. Summary.	2 years or a fine; or both. 6 months or the statutory maximum; or both.

SENTENCING: INSOLVENCY AND BANKRUPTCY OFFENCES

B7.74 In *Vanderwell* [1998] 1 Cr App R (S) 439, the offender pleaded guilty to two counts of being concerned in the management of a company while an undischarged bankrupt, one count of obtaining credit as a bankrupt, one of obtaining by deception, one of failing to keep proper business accounts and one of concealment of debts. He had been made bankrupt in 1978 and in 1986, sentenced to imprisonment in 1990 and disqualified from acting as a company director. On his release he again started trading and accumulated debts of £25,000. The Court of Appeal regarded him as thoroughly dishonest, and upheld a total prison sentence of four years and three months, together with a company director disqualification for 15 years.

In contrast, many who commit insolvency and bankruptcy offences have no previous convictions. In *Mungroo* [1998] BPIR 784, the Court of Appeal stated that a bankrupt offender, against whom a judgment debt had been entered, who concealed assets and used them to pay personal debts, could expect to receive a custodial sentence, even if of previous exemplary character. In *Bevis* [2001] 1 Cr App R (S) 257, the offender was 53 years old and of previous good character. The Court of Appeal reduced a sentence for failing to disclose company property and details of its disposal contrary to the Insolvency Act 1986, s. 208(1)(a) from 18 months' imprisonment to nine months. In *Taylor* [2011] 1 WLR 1809 the offender, again of good character, pleaded guilty to acting as a director of a company while an undischarged bankrupt and was convicted of falsifying books or papers relating to the company's affairs and making a material omission in a statement relating to the company's affairs. He had effectively stolen £23,000 from the company's creditors and used three of the company's vehicles for himself. The Court of Appeal upheld a total sentence of 16 months' imprisonment. See also *Hussain* [2013] EWCA Crim 2243 (six months' imprisonment imposed on a bankrupt for making a false statement and fraudulent concealment of property), *Thompson* (1992) 14 Cr App R (S) 89, *Teece* (1993) 15 Cr App R (S) 302, *Ashby* [1998] 2 Cr App R (S) 37 and *Brownlees* [2005] EWCA Crim 532.

In *Theivendran* (1992) 13 Cr App R (S) 601, a bankrupt continued for several years to act as a director of a group of companies which he had set up and which were later wound up. The Court of Appeal found that there had been a plain flouting of the bankruptcy order, but no dishonesty. The sentence was reduced from nine months' imprisonment to six months and suspended for two years; the disqualification period was halved from ten years to five years. See also *Dawes* [1997] 1 Cr App R (S) 149.

Confiscation orders under the POCA 2002 may also be made (see *Lowe* [2009] 2 Cr App R (S) 544 and *Weintroub* [2011] EWCA Crim 2167 at **B7.53**).

Section B8   Damage to Property

SIMPLE CRIMINAL DAMAGE

Criminal Damage Act 1971, s. 1   B8.1

(1) A person who without lawful excuse destroys or damages any property belonging to another
intending to destroy or damage any such property or being reckless as to whether any such
property would be destroyed or damaged shall be guilty of an offence.

The CDA 1998, s. 30, creates a racially or religiously aggravated form of this offence which
carries a higher maximum penalty (see **B8.43**). For the meaning of racially or religiously aggravated, see **B11.149** *et seq.*

Procedure

Criminal damage is generally triable either way (MCA 1980, s. 17 and sch. 1, para. 29). When   B8.2
tried on indictment it is normally a class 3 offence, but see CPD XIII, para. B (see Supplement,
PD-97) for the additional factors that the court considers on allocation. However, where the value
of the property alleged to have been destroyed or the value of the alleged damage is not more than
£5,000 (unless the destruction or damage was by fire and thus constitutes arson, see **B8.25** to
B8.30), criminal damage (unless charged in the racially aggravated form) is treated as if it were triable only summarily (MCA 1980, s. 22 and sch. 2). This does not convert it into a summary offence
for all purposes and thus there can still be an attempt to commit low value criminal damage even
though only an attempt to commit an indictable offence is caught by the Criminal Attempts Act
1981, s. 1(4) (*Bristol Justices, ex parte E* [1999] 3 All ER 798). For consideration of the mode of
trial for criminal damage, including the method of determining the value involved, see **D6**. Even
if the value involved is not more than £5,000, a count for criminal damage may be included in
an indictment for another offence in the circumstances set out in the CJA 1988, s. 40 (see **D11**).

See the *Magistrates' Court Sentencing Guidelines* which indicate that, where the value of the dam-   B8.3
age exceeds £10,000, Crown Court trial may be appropriate.

The aggravated form of the offence is triable either way, irrespective of the value of the damage.
Even if the value is not more than £5,000, simple criminal damage is available on indictment as
an alternative verdict if the aggravated element is not made out (*Fennell* [2000] 1 WLR 2011).

Indictment

Statement of Offence   B8.4

Criminal damage contrary to section 1(1) of the Criminal Damage Act 1971.

Particulars of Offence

A on or about the. . .day of. . .did without lawful excuse damage [or destroy] a glass window, having
a value of £120, belonging to V intending to damage [or destroy] such property or being reckless as
to whether such property would be damaged [or destroyed].

Sentence

For the maximum penalty and for sentencing guidelines, see **B8.41** to **B8.46**.   B8.5

Meaning of 'Damage'

B8.6 'Damage' is left undefined in the Criminal Damage Act 1971. The courts have construed the term liberally. Criminal damage is not limited to permanent damage, so smearing mud on the walls of a police cell may be criminal damage. See *Roe v Kingerlee* [1986] Crim LR 735, where it was also said that: 'What constitutes criminal damage is a matter of fact and degree and it is for the justices, applying their common sense, to decide whether what occurred was damage or not.' In *Fiak* [2005] EWCA Crim 2381, where a blanket was soaked (but not soiled) with water from a toilet in a police cell and three cell floors were flooded, a conclusion that the blanket and floor were not damaged (even though the damage was remediable) 'would have been incomprehensible'.

Older (persuasive) authorities under pre-1971 enactments further illustrate the breadth of the notion of damage: see, e.g., *Roper v Knott* [1898] 1 QB 868 (milk damaged by adulteration with water) and *Tacey* (1821) Russ & Ry 452 (machine damaged by removal of essential part, although if the constituent part or parts are not themselves damaged it is important to charge damage to the machine, i.e. to the whole rather than to the parts — see *Woolcock* [1977] Crim LR 104 and 161). *Hardman v Chief Constable of Avon and Somerset* [1986] Crim LR 330 is a more modern illustration of the scope of the meaning of 'damage', in which water-soluble pavement paintings were held to constitute damage to the pavement.

The damage need not be tangible or visible if it affects the value or performance of the property: see *Cox v Riley* (1986) 83 Cr App R 54, where a plastic circuit card for controlling a computerised saw was held to have been damaged by the erasure of the programs electronically written on it. Nor did it matter that the damage was not permanent in that it could be remedied, as restoring the programs necessitated 'time, labour and expense'. See now *Whiteley* (1991) 93 Cr App R 25, where a computer disk was held to be damaged by the addition and deletion of files. The interference with the disk amounted to an 'impairment of the value or usefulness of the disk to the owner'. These two decisions remain significant for the general meaning of damage but are overtaken as regards their own particular facts by the Computer Misuse Act 1990, s. 3 (see further **B17.11**).

Meaning of 'Property'

B8.7 Criminal Damage Act 1971, s. 10

    (1) In this Act 'property' means property of a tangible nature, whether real or personal, including money and—

        (a) including wild creatures which have been tamed or are ordinarily kept in captivity...; but

        (b) not including mushrooms growing wild on any land or flowers, fruit or foliage or a plant growing wild on any land.

This definition of property is wider than that in the Theft Act 1968, s. 4 (see **B4.11** to **B4.18**), in that it lacks the restrictions on stealing land in that section, but, on the other hand, is narrower in that it does not include 'things in action and other intangible property'. Thus, land can be damaged by, e.g., dumping on it, even though it cannot be stolen (see discussion in *Cox v Riley* (1986) 83 Cr App 54 and **B8.6**). However, a copyright cannot be damaged by infringing it (contrast the offences under the Copyright, Designs and Patents Act 1988, s. 107), even though it can in theory be stolen. In *Cox v Riley*, even though the erased program might be said to be 'intangible property', the property alleged to be damaged was the circuit card and not the erased program itself. See also *Whiteley* (1991) 93 Cr App R 25, discussed in **B8.6**. (Note that both *Whiteley* and *Cox v Riley* have now to be read in the light of the Computer Misuse Act 1990, s. 3; see **B17.11**.)

Meaning of 'Belonging to Another'

Criminal Damage Act 1971, s. 10

(2) Property shall be treated for the purposes of this Act as belonging to any person—
  (a) having the custody or control of it;
  (b) having in it any proprietary right or interest (not being an equitable interest arising only from an agreement to transfer or grant an interest); or
  (c) having a charge on it.

The effect of this provision (as with theft, see **B4.19** to **B4.27**) is that an owner can be guilty of criminal damage to his own property if at the same time it belongs to someone else within the extended meaning of s. 10. This also means that D will be guilty even if he has a mistaken belief that property is his provided that he also believes another has a proprietary interest in it (*Seray-Wurie v DPP* [2012] EWHC 208 (Admin)). A genuine belief in that person's consent might then be a defence under s. 5(2)(a) (see **B8.12**) but such a belief does not appear to have been argued on the facts in *Seray-Wurie*.

Mens Rea

This is satisfied by either intention or recklessness, and it is the latter, wider concept which has proved crucial. It seemed clear for 20 years following *Metropolitan Police Commissioner v Caldwell* [1982] AC 341 that recklessness in this context did not require subjective appreciation of the risk of causing damage, but was also satisfied by a failure to consider an obvious risk. In *Caldwell* Lord Diplock gave the following model direction (at p. 354):

> . . .a person charged with an offence under section 1(1) of the Criminal Damage Act 1971 is 'reckless as to whether any such property would be destroyed or damaged' if (1) he does an act which in fact creates an obvious risk that property will be destroyed or damaged and (2) when he does the act he either has not given any thought to the possibility of there being any such risk or has recognised that there was some risk involved and has nonetheless gone on to do it.

The risk needed only be obvious in the sense that it would have been obvious to the reasonable man, not to the accused if he or she had stopped to think (*Elliot v C* [1983] 2 All ER 1005), nor to a person of the age of the accused or sharing the accused's characteristics (*R (Stephen Malcolm)* (1984) 79 Cr App R 334; *Miller* [1983] 2 AC 161). However in *G* [2004] 1 AC 1034, the House of Lords overruled its own previous decision in *Caldwell* and restored a subjective test to the meaning of recklessness for the purposes of the Criminal Damage Act 1971 as it ruled that this had always been Parliament's intention.

Lord Bingham adopted the meaning of recklessness given in the Law Commission's Draft Criminal Code (Law Com. No. 177) to the effect that:

> A person acts recklessly. . . . with respect to—
> (i) a circumstance when he is aware of a risk that it exists or will exist;
> (ii) a result when he is aware of a risk that it will occur;
> (iii) and it is, in the circumstances known to him, unreasonable to take the risk.

For a more detailed analysis of the implications of this return to a subjective test of recklessness, see **A2.7** to **A2.11**. Suffice to say here that in many cases the change may not make all that much practical difference; the jury will normally conclude in relation to most if not all obvious risks that the accused was actually aware of the risk and thus liable even under a subjective test. The notion of closing one's mind to an obvious risk is also likely to be pressed into service where, as in the case of *Parker* [1977] 2 All ER 37, referred to seemingly approvingly by Lord Bingham as a case of conscious awareness of risk, the accused claims not to have been aware of a risk because of his anger or other unsympathetic emotion. The concept of closing one's mind was referred to in the quite remarkable case of *Booth v CPS* (2006) 170 JP 305, which concerned the damage caused by a pedestrian to the bonnet of a vehicle into the path of which he suddenly stepped out. The Divisional Court upheld the findings of magistrates that the accused pedestrian was aware:

... of the risks associated with running into the road, namely the risk of a collision and the damage to property. Aware of those risks, he then deliberately put them out of his mind and, for reasons of his own, ran out into the path of a car.

One might have thought that the more obvious risk in such a case, as argued by the defence, is one of risk of injury to the pedestrian but the court was not sympathetic to arguments which they regarded as, in effect, inviting them to characterise the particular findings of the magistrates as perverse.

Where the accused lacks the ability to appreciate an obvious risk (e.g., as in *G* itself, because of youth, or as in *Stephenson* [1979] QB 695, because of mental illness), the subjective test will clearly make a major difference and the courts will no longer be compelled to convict because of what the accused ought to have been aware of had he had the degree of awareness of the standard reasonable man (see *Elliot v C* and *R (Stephen Malcolm)*, both of which can now be regarded as overruled along with *Caldwell*).

B8.11 It will be noted that the test of recklessness refers to both circumstances and consequences. In criminal damage cases it will normally be the awareness of risk of a consequence — damage to property — which will be relevant. In this connection it appears from *G* that it is the awareness of the risk of damage to the property named in the charge that is relevant, in that case damage to the building rather than simply to the wheelie bins (given that Lord Bingham said (at [33]) that 'they would have had little defence' to a charge of recklessly damaging the wheelie bins). On the other hand it would not be necessary to foresee the extent of the damage (i.e. in *G*, £1 million worth of damage to the building). Nor is it necessary (whether for the purposes of recklessness or intention) that the accused realises that what he is doing to the property legally constitutes damage (e.g., where he writes on a notice with a black marker pen: see *Seray-Wurie v DPP* [2012] EWHC 208 (Admin)).

Awareness of risk of circumstances can also be relevant however, the circumstance being that the property was 'belonging to another'. If A decides to destroy all his papers in his filing cabinet but is aware of the risk that some of his flat-mate's valuable papers may also be in the cabinet and may also be destroyed, he is aware of the risk of a circumstance, that some of the property belongs to another. However, if he is not aware of any such risk and believes he is simply destroying his own property, he is not guilty under a subjective test (*Smith* [1974] QB 354 for an analogous example where the mistake was one of law).

Meaning of 'Without Lawful Excuse'

B8.12 The meaning of 'lawful excuse' is specially provided for in relation to this offence in the Criminal Damage Act 1971, s. 5 (which, however, is not applicable to the aggravated offence of criminal damage under s. 1(2) — see **B8.16** to **B8.24**).

Criminal Damage Act 1971, s. 5

(2) A person charged with an offence to which this section applies shall, whether or not he would be treated for the purposes of this Act as having a lawful excuse apart from this subsection, be treated for those purposes as having a lawful excuse—

   (a) if at the time of the act or acts alleged to constitute the offence he believed that the person or persons whom he believed to be entitled to consent to the destruction of or damage to the property in question had so consented, or would have so consented to it if he or they had known of the destruction or damage and its circumstances; or

   (b) if he destroyed or damaged or threatened to destroy or damage the property in question or, in the case of a charge of an offence under section 3 above, intended to use or cause or permit the use of something to destroy or damage it, in order to protect property belonging to himself or another or a right or interest in property which was or which he believed to be vested in himself or another, and at the time of the act or acts alleged to constitute the offence he believed—

       (i) that the property, right or interest was in immediate need of protection; and

(ii) that the means of protection adopted or proposed to be adopted were or would be reasonable having regard to all the circumstances.

(3) For the purposes of this section it is immaterial whether a belief is justified or not if it is honestly held.

(4) For the purposes of subsection (2) above a right or interest in property includes any right or privilege in or over land, whether created by grant, licence or otherwise.

(5) This section shall not be construed as casting doubt on any defence recognised by law as a defence to criminal charges.

The words in s. 5(2) 'whether or not he would be treated for the purposes of this Act as having **B8.13** a lawful excuse apart from this subsection' together with s. 5(5), indicate that the section is not intended to be an exhaustive account of the circumstances of lawful excuse. Thus, general defences such as duress or prevention of crime are not excluded (cf. *Baker* [1997] Crim LR 497) but they do require the accused to be acting reasonably, and damaging perimeter fencing in order to challenge the lawful storage of nuclear weapons was held not be reasonable by the Divisional Court in *Hutchinson v DPP* (2000) *Independent*, 20 November 2000). A motorist who damages a wheel clamp to free his car, having parked on another's property knowing of the risk of being clamped, does not have a lawful excuse (*Lloyd v DPP* [1992] 1 All ER 982: contrast the entirely different approach to wheel clamping in the Scottish case *Black v Carmichael* (1992) *The Times*, 25 June 1992, and see now the Protection of Freedoms Act 2012, s. 54).

Section 5 specifically covers two alternative types of belief which are outlined in more detail in s. 5(2):

(a) belief in consent; or

(b) belief in the immediate necessity to protect property.

Subjective Nature of Belief   Section 5(3) emphasises that the question is the purely subjective **B8.14** one of whether the belief is honestly held, not whether it is justified or reasonable. In *Jaggard v Dickinson* [1981] QB 527, the accused, due to intoxication, mistakenly believed she would have had the owner's consent to breaking a window in order to gain access to a house (unfortunately she tried to break into the wrong house). The Divisional Court quashed her conviction, saying (per Mustill J, at pp. 531–2): '…the court is required by section 5(3) to focus on the existence of the belief, not its intellectual soundness; and a belief can be just as much honestly held if it is induced by intoxication, as if it stems from stupidity, forgetfulness or inattention'.

Although the test under s. 5(2)(b)(ii) is clearly *subjective* and the question is not whether the accused's action is *in fact* reasonable (contrast *Hutchinson v DPP* (2000) *Independent*, 20 November 2000 at **B8.13**) but whether the accused *believed* it to be reasonable, whether an accused is acting 'in order to protect property' under s. 5(2)(b) does seem to have an objective aspect. In *Hunt* (1977) 66 Cr App R 105, the accused set fire to bedding to draw attention to a defective fire alarm in old people's accommodation which the court ruled was not 'in order to protect property', despite the accused's belief that it would ultimately have that effect. See further *Hill* (1988) 89 Cr App R 74, where the accused's beliefs about the ultimate effects of damaging perimeter fencing at a US naval base were held not to amount to a purpose of protecting property, or to a belief that property was in *imminent* need of protection under s. 5(2)(b)(i). See however *Chamberlain v Lindon* [1998] 2 All ER 538 for a case where these two requirements were satisfied. There is no requirement that the threat to property believed to be in need of protection is a threat of *unlawful* damage (*Jones* [2005] QB 259).

If the accused does hold a belief provided for in s. 5, it is immaterial as far as his liability for **B8.15** criminal damage is concerned that he has some ulterior fraudulent or criminal purpose. Thus, in *Denton* [1981] 1 All ER 65, the accused set fire to the cotton mill where he worked, because he believed he had been asked to do so by his employer with a view to gaining the insurance money on the property. The Court of Appeal quashed his conviction for criminal damage, pointing out that if the owner himself had caused the damage he would have committed no offence (under

s. 1(1), though other charges might be possible), since he was not damaging property 'belonging to another', and hence the accused, who believed he was acting on behalf of the owner and with his consent, should be in no worse position. In fact, the 'employer' (an individual) in this case was not strictly the owner of the property, which legally belonged to the company, a separate legal entity. This did not particularly matter on the facts, since it was conceded that the accused honestly believed that his 'employer' was the person 'entitled to consent' within s. 5(2)(a). Contrast *Appleyard* (1985) 81 Cr App R 319, where a managing director was convicted of destroying the company's store, and was not allowed to claim that he himself was the person entitled to consent to the damage. It would seem, therefore, that the belief under s. 5(2)(a) must relate to some other person having the right to consent and not to the accused himself. If a person mistakenly believes he is the actual owner (as opposed to being merely the person entitled to consent), then he has a defence, not under s. 5(2) but because he lacks *mens rea* (*Smith* [1974] QB 354).

AGGRAVATED CRIMINAL DAMAGE

B8.16

Criminal Damage Act 1971, s. 1

(2) A person who without lawful excuse destroys or damages any property, whether belonging to himself or another—

   (a) intending to destroy or damage any property or being reckless as to whether any property would be destroyed or damaged; and

   (b) intending by the destruction or damage to endanger the life of another or being reckless as to whether the life of another would be thereby endangered;

shall be guilty of an offence.

Procedure

B8.17 Aggravated criminal damage is triable only on indictment. It is normally a class 3 offence, but see CPD XIII, para. B (see Supplement, **PD-97**) for the additional factors that the court considers on allocation.

Indictment

B8.18

Statement of Offence

Destroying [or damaging] property with intent to endanger life [or being reckless as to whether life would be endangered] contrary to section 1(2) of the Criminal Damage Act 1971.

Particulars of Offence

A on or about the...day of...did without lawful excuse damage [or destroy] a motor vehicle belonging to V, intending to damage [or destroy] such vehicle or being reckless as to whether such vehicle would be damaged [or destroyed] and intending by such damage [or destruction] to endanger the life of V or being reckless as to whether the life of V would be thereby endangered.

Alternative Verdicts

B8.19 It is submitted that in some cases, on an indictment for aggravated criminal damage, it may be possible for the jury to return an alternative verdict of simple criminal damage, pursuant to the Criminal Law Act 1967, s. 6(3) (see **D19.41** *et seq.*). However, this is problematic in that it will be possible only where:

   (a) it is specifically alleged that the property in question belonged not to the accused but to another (which is not an essential averment under the Criminal Damage Act 1971, s. 1(2), but is under s. 1(1)); and

   (b) there is no issue as to lawful excuse (the meaning of which differs as between the two offences, inasmuch as the provisions of the Criminal Damage Act 1971, s. 5, do not apply to offences under s. 1(2)).

It is therefore always appropriate to add an alternative count (which may be done even where the value of the property is less than £5,000 — see the CJA 1988, s. 40, and **D11.18**). In the absence of such an alternative count, trial judges may be reluctant to leave the alternative to the jury (see generally **D19.58** *et seq.*).

Sentence

For the maximum penalty and for sentencing guidelines, see **B8.41** to **B8.44**.   **B8.20**

Relationship to Simple Criminal Damage

Aggravated criminal damage is identical with the offence under the Criminal Damage Act   **B8.21**
1971, s. 1(1), as far as it relates to the meaning of damage and property (see **B8.6** and **B8.7**), but differs in three main respects:

(a) The presence of the aggravating ulterior *mens rea* of intention to endanger life or recklessness as to whether life would be endangered.
(b) The fact that the offence can be committed irrespective of whether the property 'belongs to another'.
(c) The inapplicability of s. 5 of the Act to the meaning of 'lawful excuse'.

Mens Rea The overruling of *Metropolitan Police Commissioner v Caldwell* [1982] AC 341   **B8.22**
(see **B8.9**) applies equally to this offence and therefore it must be shown in accordance with *G*
[2004] 1 AC 1034 that the accused must be subjectively aware of the risk of endangering the
life of another. Again, the more obvious the risk of endangering life, the more likely that the jury
will conclude that the accused was aware of the risk unless he gives some plausible explanation
of why he would not have appreciated the obvious. According to the Court of Appeal in *Heard*
[2008] QB 43 (see **A3.17**), recklessness as to endangering life is not a basic intent but is a specific
(ulterior) intent and it would thus seem that voluntary intoxication can be admitted in order to
show that the accused did not appreciate the risk of endangering life (but see also *Coley* [2013]
EWCA Crim 223 at **A3.18**).

In the case of attempt to commit an offence under the Criminal Damage Act 1971, s. 1(2),
recklessness as to life being endangered will suffice even though a specific intent to cause damage
is also required (*A-G's Ref (No. 3 of 1992)* [1994] 2 All ER 121).

Requirement that Danger to Life Result from Damage Intended   The accused must be at   **B8.23**
least reckless as to causing damage, as to endangering life and also as to whether life would be
endangered *as a result of the damage*. The offence was thus not made out in *Steer* [1988] AC 111,
where the accused shot through a window behind which two people were standing. Although the
accused was reckless as to whether life would be endangered, the danger to life was not due to the
damage to the window but due to the bullet itself. Compare *Webster* [1995] 2 All ER 168, where
damaging the windscreen of a moving car or ramming the car was held to be capable of endangering
life as a result of the damage. Furthermore, it is the damage which the accused intended,
or as to which he was reckless, which is relevant, rather than the actual damage which happens
to be caused. See *Dudley* [1989] Crim LR 57, where only trivial damage, not likely to endanger
life, was *actually* caused, but the appellant's conviction was upheld since he created a *risk* of much
more serious damage which was capable of endangering life. *Steer* was considered in *Wenton*
[2010] EWCA Crim 2361 where the case was even plainer in that the offence as charged was not
made out since the act charged as causing the damage (breaking a window by throwing a brick)
was a quite separate act from the act creating the risk to life (throwing through the window a petrol
canister which in the event did not ignite). Although the appeals against conviction based on
the first act of throwing the brick clearly had to be allowed, it seems that the facts could have been
successfully dealt with by charging the *second* act of throwing the canister as an attempt to cause
damage by fire, being reckless as to whether that *intended* damage by fire would endanger life.

Meaning of 'Without Lawful Excuse'   The partial definition of 'lawful excuse' in the   **B8.24**
Criminal Damage Act 1971, s. 5, is not applicable, because belief in the owner's consent

or of the immediate need to protect *property* cannot justify the endangering of human life. However, 'without lawful excuse' in any other sense remains part of the definition of the offence so that, e.g., damaging property in lawful self-defence would not be criminal even if it endangers the aggressor's (or possibly even a third party's) life, provided that it was reasonable to do so.

ARSON

B8.25
Criminal Damage Act 1971, s. 1

> (3) An offence committed under this section by destroying or damaging property by fire shall be charged as arson.

Procedure

B8.26 Simple arson contrary to the Criminal Damage Act 1971, s. 1(1) and (3), is triable either way (MCA 1980, s. 17 and sch. 1, para. 29). When tried on indictment it is normally a class 3 offence, but see CPD XIII, para. B (see Supplement, **PD-97**) for the additional factors that the court considers on allocation. See the *Magistrates' Court Sentencing Guidelines* (see Supplement, **SG-240**), which indicate that where the activity forming the basis of the charge is 'significant damage by fire' then Crown Court trial is appropriate but clearly imply that summary trial may be appropriate in other cases. The value involved in simple arson does not cause the MCA 1980, s. 22, to restrict the mode of trial because arson is, by sch. 2 to the MCA 1980, not an offence to which s. 22 applies.

Aggravated arson contrary to the Criminal Damage Act 1971, s. 1(2) and (3), is triable only on indictment. It is a class 2A offence.

Indictment

B8.27 The wording of the Criminal Damage Act 1971, s. 1(3) (see **B8.25**), has been held to be mandatory in the Crown Court and a charge of criminal damage 'contrary to s. 1(1) plus (3) of the Act' was held to be a nullity in *Booth* [1999] Crim LR 144. However, *Booth* was distinguished in *Drayton* (2005) 169 JP 593 in the context of a charge in a magistrates' court. The charge of damage by fire under s. 1(1), (3) and (4) was held to be a valid one to which the accused could lawfully plead guilty and on which he could be lawfully committed for sentence. The important issue was that the allegation was at least identified as 'damage *by fire*' rather than by the use of the specific word 'arson' with which it was synonymous, although it would be preferable to use the word 'arson'. Hedley J said (at [11]) that:

> ...the essence of section 1(3), the mischief which it is designed to address, is that the defendant shall know that he is facing an allegation of damage by fire, because by section 1(4) the penalties in relation to damage by fire are different and significantly potentially more severe than those of simple criminal damage by other means.

In *Booth*, the charge in the Crown Court was conspiracy to incite a variety of forms of criminal damage including damage by fire but it appears that the indictment whilst mentioning s. 1(3) did not specifically mention either 'arson' or 'damage *by fire*'. The focus in *Drayton* was on damage by fire and nothing else and, in describing the offence alleged in ordinary language avoiding technical terms like arson and giving reasonable information as to the nature of the charge, it complied with the requirements of the rules (now the CrimPR, r. 7.2). Hedley J left open the position in the Crown Court saying (at [10]):

> Clearly on indictment where the rules require both a statement of offence and particulars of offence it is desirable that the word arson should continue to be used in the statement of offence. Whether the absence of that word arson from a count that plainly alleges damage by fire and nothing else invalidates the count must await decision as and when that point arises.

Statement of Offence

Arson contrary to section 1(1) and (3) of the Criminal Damage Act 1971.

Particulars of Offence

A on or about the…day of…did without lawful excuse damage by fire a motor vehicle, having a value of £3,500, belonging to V intending to damage such vehicle by fire or being reckless as to whether such vehicle would be damaged by fire.

An offence under s. 1(2) by fire must also be charged as arson. In such a case there should be separate counts of arson with intent to endanger life and arson being reckless as to whether life would be endangered (*Hoof* (1980) 72 Cr App 126; *sed quaere*, the two forms of *mens rea* do not mean that the section creates two offences, and, of course, the maximum penalty is the same).

First Count

Statement of Offence

Arson contrary to section 1(2) and (3) of the Criminal Damage Act 1971.

Particulars of Offence

A on or about the…day of…did without lawful excuse damage by fire a motor vehicle, having a value of £3,500, belonging to V intending to damage such vehicle by fire and intending by such damage to endanger the life of V.

Second Count

As above, but alleging instead of the intent to endanger life: '…and being reckless as to whether the life of V would thereby be endangered'.

Alternative Verdicts

See **B8.19**. On indictment for arson under the Criminal Damage Act 1971, s. 1(1) and (3) or **B8.28** s. 1(2) and (3), it is submitted that the jury should not be invited to return an alternative verdict of guilty of criminal damage other than by fire, even under the corresponding subsection of s. 1, because of the different nature of the *actus reus*. In the unlikely event of doubt as to the method of causing the damage, an alternative count should be added.

Sentence

For the maximum penalty and for sentencing guidelines, see **B8.41** to **B8.46**.　　**B8.29**

Elements

Arson differs from simple or aggravated criminal damage only in that the destruction or dam-　**B8.30** age to the property must be 'by fire'. *Quaere* whether this might extend to damage caused, for example, by water in saving the property from imminent destruction by the fire, or by a fall resulting from the collapse due to fire of a structure on which the property had stood.

THREATS TO DESTROY OR DAMAGE PROPERTY

Criminal Damage Act 1971, s. 2　　**B8.31**

A person who without lawful excuse makes to another a threat, intending that that other would fear it would be carried out,—
(a) to destroy or damage any property belonging to that other or a third person; or
(b) to destroy or damage his own property in a way which he knows is likely to endanger the life of that other or a third person;
shall be guilty of an offence.

Procedure

A threat to destroy or damage property is triable either way (MCA 1980, s. 17 and sch. 1, para. 29).　**B8.32** When tried on indictment it is normally a class 3 offence, but see CPD XIII, para. B (see Supplement, PD-97) for the additional factors that the court considers on allocation.

B

Part B Offences

Indictment

B8.33

Statement of Offence

Threatening to destroy property contrary to section 2(a) of the Criminal Damage Act 1971.

Particulars of Offence

A on or about the...day of...did without lawful excuse make a threat to V to destroy a motor vehicle belonging to V [or X] intending that V would fear that the threat would be carried out.

Sentence

B8.34   For the maximum penalty see **B8.41**.

Elements

B8.35   For the meaning of 'without lawful excuse', see **B8.12**, but note that by virtue of the Criminal Damage Act 1971, s. 5(1), the partial definition of 'lawful excuse' does not apply where the accused knows that the threatened damage is likely to endanger life. This is no doubt for the same sorts of reasons that s. 5 does not apply to aggravated criminal damage under s. 1(2).

There is no requirement that the threat be carried out or be capable of being carried out immediately, or that the accused intended to carry it out or that the person threatened *actually* fears that it will be carried out, provided that the accused *intends* that there should be such fear.

A threat to set oneself on fire may come within s. 2(a) if, objectively considered, it constitutes a threat that another's property may be destroyed or damaged as a consequence (*Cakmak* [2002] 2 Cr App R 158).

POSSESSION WITH INTENT TO DESTROY OR DAMAGE PROPERTY

B8.36   **Criminal Damage Act 1971, s. 3**

A person who has anything in his custody or under his control intending without lawful excuse to use it or cause or permit another to use it—
(a) to destroy or damage any property belonging to some other person; or
(b) to destroy or damage his own or the user's property in a way which he knows is likely to endanger the life of some other person;
shall be guilty of an offence.

Procedure

B8.37   Possession of an article with intent to destroy or damage property is triable either way (MCA 1980, s. 17 and sch. 1, para. 29). When tried on indictment it is normally a class 3 offence, but see CPD XIII, para. B (see Supplement, **PD-97**) for the additional factors that the court considers on allocation.

Indictment

B8.38

Statement of Offence

Possession of an article with intent to destroy [or damage] property contrary to section 3 of the Criminal Damage Act 1971.

Particulars of Offence

A on or about the...day of...did have in his custody [or under his control] a can of spray paint intending without lawful excuse to use it [or cause or permit X to use it] to damage a motor vehicle belonging to V.

Sentence

For the maximum penalty, see **B8.41**.   **B8.39**

Elements

The essence of the offence is the intention to use *any article*, or to cause or permit it to be used,   **B8.40**
to cause damage. A conditional intention to so use it if given circumstances arise will suffice
(*Buckingham* (1976) 63 Cr App R 159).

The partial definition of 'lawful excuse' in the Criminal Damage Act 1971, s. 5, is applicable
only to the form of the offence in s. 3(a) and not to that in s. 3(b), although it is still open to the
accused to put forward a lawful excuse independently of s. 5.

The Criminal Damage Act 1971, s. 6, enables the police to search for articles used, or intended
to be used, to cause criminal damage.

Criminal Damage Act 1971, s. 6

(1) If it is made to appear by information on oath before a justice of the peace that there is reason-
    able cause to believe that any person has in his custody or under his control or on his premises
    anything which there is reasonable cause to believe has been used or is intended for use without
    lawful excuse—
    (a) to destroy or damage property belonging to another; or
    (b) to destroy or damage any property in a way likely to endanger the life of another,
    the justice may grant a warrant authorising any constable to search for and seize that thing.
(2) A constable who is authorised under this section to search premises for anything, may enter (if
    need be by force) and search the premises accordingly and may seize anything which he believes
    to have been used or to be intended to be used as aforesaid.
(3) The Police (Property) Act 1897 (disposal of property in the possession of the police) shall apply to
    property which has come into the possession of the police under this section as it applies to prop-
    erty which has come into the possession of the police in the circumstances mentioned in that Act.

SENTENCING: OFFENCES INVOLVING DAMAGE TO PROPERTY

Maximum Penalties

Criminal damage, with intent to endanger life or recklessness whether life is endangered: life   **B8.41**
imprisonment (Criminal Damage Act 1971, s. 4(1)).

Criminal damage: ten years (Criminal Damage Act 1971, s. 4(2)) on indictment; six months or
a fine not exceeding the statutory maximum, or both, summarily. If, however, damage is quantified at less than £5,000, so that the offence is treated as triable summarily only: three months, a
fine not exceeding level 4 on the standard scale, or both.

Racially or religiously aggravated criminal damage: 14 years on indictment (CDA 1998,
s. 30(2)); six months or a fine not exceeding the statutory maximum, or both, summarily.

Arson (where either of the above offences is committed by fire): life imprisonment (Criminal
Damage Act 1971, s. 4(1)) on indictment; where criminal damage by fire, but not criminal
damage with intent or recklessness whether life is endangered, six months or a fine not exceeding the statutory maximum, or both, summarily.

Threat to destroy or damage property: ten years (Criminal Damage Act 1971, s. 4(2)) on indictment; six months or a fine not exceeding the statutory maximum, or both, summarily.

Possessing article with intent to destroy or damage property: ten years (Criminal Damage Act
1971, s. 4(2)) on indictment; six months or a fine not exceeding the statutory maximum, or
both, summarily.

Sentencing Guidelines (Basic Offence)

B8.42 Where tried summarily, the *Magistrates' Court Sentencing Guidelines* apply (see Supplement, SG-193). The guideline sentence varies according to the degree of damage: minor damage, moderate damage, significant damage up to £5,000, damage between £5,000 and £10,000 and damage over £10,000. Revenge attacks and the targeting of a vulnerable victim are identified as factors indicating higher culpability.

By virtue of the Penalties for Disorderly Behaviour (Amount of Penalty) Order 2002 (SI 2002 No. 1837), as amended, the offence under the Criminal Damage Act 1971, s. 1(1), is a fixed penalty offence and attracts a fixed penalty of £90 for persons aged 18 or over.

There are few Court of Appeal decisions relating to simple criminal damage. In *Toomey* (1993) 14 Cr App R (S) 42, the offender smashed the windows and door of a restaurant after an argument with the owner. Customers were in the restaurant at the time and over £2,000 worth of damage was done. Eighteen months' imprisonment was reduced to 12 months on appeal. In *Austin* [2009] 2 Cr App R (S) 510 a sentence of 20 months' imprisonment was appropriate for offenders who admitted involvement in a conspiracy to commit criminal damage by painting graffiti on railway carriages, which cost £60,000 to remove. In *Brzezinski* [2012] 2 Cr App R (S) 364, 18 months' imprisonment together with an ASBO was upheld on a 23-year-old man who admitted eight counts of criminal damage, all involving the writing of graffiti in railway carriages. This case may be contrasted with *Moore* [2012] 1 Cr App R (S) 19, where graffiti was painted on railway property, and two years' imprisonment was reduced to 18 months but an ASBO was quashed because the graffiti was 'unsightly' but not threatening or abusive in nature.

Racial or religious aggravation cannot be taken into account by the sentencer when sentencing for the basic offence of criminal damage. To do so would infringe the principle that the offender must not be sentenced for an offence for which he has not been charged and convicted (*McGillivray* [2005] Crim LR 484). Where there is evidence that racial or religious aggravation was present, the aggravated form of the offence should be charged.

Sentencing Guidelines (Racially or Religiously Aggravated Form of Offence)

B8.43 The Court of Appeal indicated in *Saunders* [2000] 1 Cr App R 458 that, when sentencing for the racially aggravated form of an offence, the sentencer may usefully consider the appropriate sentence for the offence in the absence of racial aggravation and then add a further term for the racial element. See further **B2.33**. The *Magistrates' Court Sentencing Guidelines* (see Supplement, SG-251) follow this approach, indicating that sentence should be increased to reflect this element.

In *Johnston* [2006] 1 Cr App R (S) 665, a sentence of six years' detention in a young offender institution was upheld for racially aggravated criminal damage in the form of damaging headstones in a Jewish cemetery, combined with other racially aggravated offences. Sixty-two headstones had been smashed or pushed over, with damage estimated at £100,000. The judge indicated that the sentence for the basic offence would have been three years, with a further three years to reflect the racial element. The Court of Appeal noted that the case contained a number of high-level aggravating features, and had clearly been calculated to cause maximum distress to the families of those whose graves had been targeted.

Sentencing Guidelines: Criminal Damage with Intent to Endanger Life etc.

B8.44 In *Dodd* [1997] 1 Cr App R (S) 127, the offender pleaded guilty to damaging property being reckless whether life was endangered, and to driving while disqualified. He had driven his car, at between 35 and 40 mph through the glass-fronted doors of Plymouth Magistrates' Court and through inner doors, the car coming to rest against the rear wall of the building, causing £34,000 worth of damage. Nobody was injured. A sentence of four years' imprisonment for the criminal damage offence was upheld by the Court of Appeal. In *Kavanagh* [1998] 1 Cr App R (S) 241 the offender, after an argument with his partner, released gas from a gas fire and threatened to blow up their flat. The police were called and the threat was not carried out. A sentence of four years' imprisonment was reduced to three years on appeal. See also *McCann* [2000] 1 Cr App R (S) 495. In *T* [2010] 1 Cr App R (S) 377, terms of detention of four years, three years and two years were upheld on young persons aged 16, 15 and 13 who threw stones and bricks at vehicles travelling on a busy road. Eleven vehicles were damaged. An accident then occurred in which two of the cars collided and the driver of one was killed.

Sentencing Guidelines: Arson

The Court of Appeal cases taken together indicate that there should be a psychiatric report avail- **B8.45**
able on the offender in cases of arson, and that where there is appropriate psychiatric evidence, a medical disposal, such as a community order with a mental health treatment requirement or a hospital order, may be passed. Minor cases can be dealt with by non-custodial sentences. Otherwise, in the absence of mitigation, a custodial sentence will generally be appropriate. Longer custodial sentences are appropriate where substantial damage has been caused, or where death or serious injury has been risked by the offender.

In *A-G's Ref (No. 66 of 1997)* [2000] 1 Cr App R (S) 149, a case of arson with intent to endanger life, the Court of Appeal said that a sentence within the range of eight to ten years following a trial would have been appropriate in a case where the offender set fires in a bungalow in which several members of his family were asleep. The fire was extinguished before much damage had been done. Rose LJ said that the offence showed clear evidence of intention and planning. See also *A-G's Ref (No. 68 of 2008)* [2009] 2 Cr App R (S) 338, where the offender used petrol to start fires in the vicinity of an occupied house and the same range of sentencing for that offence was confirmed. Nine years was reduced to eight years on a guilty plea in *Ajmal* [2010] 2 Cr App R (S) 587, a case of attempt; the offender had thrown a home-made petrol bomb into an occupied house but the petrol had failed to ignite and, shortly afterwards, he had tried to set fire to a parked van by means of a similar bomb.

Five years was upheld for an offence of arson being reckless whether life was endangered in **B8.46**
Black [2010] 2 Cr App R (S) 583. The offender, in a 'moment of madness', had set fire to a semi-detached house in which he lived. His wife, from whom he had recently separated, alerted the emergency services. The offender was rescued, but extensive damage was done to the property. Four years and six months was upheld in *Maitland-Thomas* [2014] 1 Cr App R (S) 125 (22), where the offender, a woman of previous good character, admitted starting a fire in her flat, causing £13,000 worth of damage. The offence was not an isolated incident and arose as a result of depression made worse by alcoholism. The Court of Appeal said that the distinction between intention to endanger life and being reckless whether life is endangered can be a very fine one. Had the offence been motivated by malice, the starting point might have been eight or nine years. Two years' detention in a young offender institution was upheld in *Letham* [2000] 1 Cr App R (S) 185, where the 16-year-old offender pleaded guilty to arson. He had started a fire at a school where he had formerly been a pupil, causing damage to the extent of £400,000. Sullivan J in the Court of Appeal said that if the offender had not been young and of good character a significantly longer sentence would have been justified.

Section B9   Offences Affecting Security

ACTS PREJUDICIAL TO SAFETY OR INTERESTS OF STATE ('SPYING')

B9.1   Official Secrets Act 1911, s. 1

(1) If any person for any purpose prejudicial to the safety or interests of the State—
   (a) approaches, inspects, passes over or is in the neighbourhood of, or enters any prohibited place within the meaning of this Act, or
   (b) makes any sketch, plan, model, or note which is calculated to be or might be or is intended to be directly or indirectly useful to an enemy; or
   (c) obtains, collects, records, or publishes, or communicates to any other person any secret official code word or pass word, or any sketch, plan, model, article, or note, or other document or information which is calculated to be or might be or is intended to be directly or indirectly useful to an enemy;
   he shall be guilty of [an offence].

Procedure

B9.2   This offence is triable only on indictment. It is a class 1B offence.

Official Secrets Act 1911, s. 8

A prosecution for an offence under this Act shall not be instituted except by or with the consent of the Attorney-General.

By virtue of the Official Secrets Act 1911, s. 10(1) and (2), and the Official Secrets Act 1920, s. 8(3), a competent British court in the place where the offence was committed has jurisdiction to try a person, and a court in England has jurisdiction to try a person alleged to have committed the instant offence, even though the offence was committed elsewhere. As to territorial jurisdiction generally, see **A8**.

In addition to general powers (see **D3.122** *et seq*.), the Official Secrets Act 1920, s. 8(4), permits the court, on the application of the prosecution, on grounds of national safety to exclude all or some of the public from a trial, except during any sentencing hearing. This power applies to all offences under the 1911, 1920 and 1989 Acts, except those created by s. 8 of the 1989 Act. The ambit of s. 8(4) was considered in *A-G v Leveller Magazine Ltd* [1979] AC 440, in relation to the granting of anonymity to a prosecution witness. The judge's wide discretion in this area was upheld. Likewise, the restrictive trial arrangements in *Shayler* [2003] EWCA Crim 2218 (which included screens and anonymity for security services witnesses and a requirement of prior notice by the accused in relation to any questions or evidence relating to security or intelligence on penalty of contempt) were upheld, albeit in circumstances where the accused refused to give any assurance that he would not attempt to raise a 'public interest' defence (which the House of Lords had already ruled was unavailable to him). The procedure for applications under s. 8 is set out in the CrimPR, r. 16.6 (see **D3.125**).

Indictment

Statement of Offence

B9.3

Entering a prohibited place contrary to section 1(1)(a) of the Official Secrets Act 1911.

Particulars of Offence

A on or about the…day of…, for a purpose prejudicial to the safety or interests of the State, namely…, entered a prohibited place, namely…

Sentence

A person guilty of an offence under the Official Secrets Act 1911, s. 1, is liable to imprisonment **B9.4** for a term not exceeding 14 years (Official Secrets Act 1920, s. 8(1)).

Offences committed under the Official Secrets Act 1911, s. 1, will inevitably attract a lengthy custodial sentence. In *Prime* (1983) 5 Cr App R (S) 127, the offender pleaded guilty to seven offences against the Official Secrets Acts. Having been employed for nine years in the Government Communications Service, with access to highly sensitive intelligence information of importance to national security, he had passed on such information to the Soviet Union. He received consecutive terms of 14, 14, and seven years' imprisonment, which were upheld on appeal. In *Schulze* (1986) 8 Cr App R (S) 463, the offenders' home was found to contain a variety of spying equipment and documents and related equipment. They were convicted of doing acts preparatory to the commission of an offence under s. 1 of the Act. Sentences of ten years were upheld in each case. In *James* [2010] 1 Cr App R (S) 362 the Court of Appeal reviewed the relevant sentencing authorities and upheld a deterrent sentence of ten years' imprisonment following a conviction under s. 1 of the Act imposed on an interpreter for NATO forces in Afghanistan for spying on behalf of Iran. Lord Judge CJ emphasised that a deterrent element would necessarily govern every sentencing decision in cases of treachery. Although allied military relationships were not jeopardised by the offender's actions, it was an aggravating feature that they might have been. The fact that the spying occurred in a war zone and that material was passed to a hostile state also increased the gravity of the offence. In *Devenney* (12 December 2012 unreported, Central Criminal Court), the offender received a total of eight years' imprisonment (concurrent) having pleaded guilty to one offence under s. 1 and one offence of misconduct in public office. He was a Royal Navy petty officer who, over a period of four months, covertly passed details of a secret code to MI5 officers whom he believed to be Russian agents. His motive was retribution; he considered the Royal Navy had treated him badly, and he was depressed at the time. Saunders J considered that a deterrent sentence was required even though the offender had actually achieved nothing by his actions.

Offence Not Limited to 'Spying'

The Official Secrets Act 1911, s. 1, is stated in the marginal note as being concerned with 'penal- **B9.5** ties for spying', but it is not limited to 'spying' and extends to sabotage and temporary sabotage (*Chandler v DPP* [1964] AC 763).

Mens Rea: Purpose Prejudicial to the Safety or Interests of the State

An offence under the Official Secrets Act 1911, s. 1(1), may be committed in a number of ways, **B9.6** which must be considered separately. However, the *mens rea* requirement that a person act with a 'purpose prejudicial to the safety or interests of the State' is common to each paragraph of s. 1(1). The House of Lords in *Chandler v DPP* [1964] AC 763, held that it is not necessary to establish an overt act on the part of the accused evidencing the requisite purpose — circumstantial

B

Part B Offences

evidence will suffice. It is to be presumed that a sketch, plan, model etc. made etc. by a person not acting under lawful authority is made etc. for a purpose prejudicial to the interests of the State until the contrary is proved. Furthermore, 'prejudicial to the safety or interests of the State' does not refer to the government or the executive, or UK residents. 'The country' or 'the realm' are good synonyms as is 'the organised community' or 'the organs of government of a national community'. Whether a person's purpose is prejudicial to the safety or interests of the State is a matter for the jury to decide on the basis that it is for the Crown to decide what is for the safety or interests of the State and that decision of the Crown is not challengeable. Thus, the opinion of the accused as to what is in the safety or interests of the State is irrelevant (*Bettaney* [1985] Crim LR 104). Similarly, in a prosecution under related regulations in *M* (1916) 11 Cr App R 207, it was held that the information provided to the enemy need not be correct provided that the accused intended to inform the enemy. See further **B9.67**.

Approaching, etc. Prohibited Place

B9.7 'Prohibited place' is defined by the Official Secrets Act 1911, s. 3.

Official Secrets Act 1911, ss. 3 and 12

3. For the purposes of this Act, the expression 'prohibited place' means—
   (a) any work of a defence, arsenal, naval or air force establishment or station, factory, dockyard, mine, minefield, camp, ship, or aircraft belonging to or occupied by or on behalf of His Majesty, or any telegraph, telephone, wireless or signal station, or office so belonging or occupied, and any place belonging to or occupied by or on behalf of His Majesty and used for the purpose of building, repairing, making, or storing any munitions of war, or any sketches, plans, models, or documents relating thereto, or for the purpose of getting any metals, oil, or minerals of use in time of war;
   (b) any place not belonging to His Majesty where any munitions of war, or any sketches, models, plans or documents relating thereto, are being made, repaired, gotten or stored under contract with, or with any person on behalf of, His Majesty, or otherwise on behalf of His Majesty; and
   (c) any place belonging to or used for the purposes of His Majesty which is for the time being declared by order of a Secretary of State to be a prohibited place for the purposes of this section on the ground that information with respect thereto, or damage thereto, would be useful to an enemy; and
   (d) any railway, road, way, or channel, or other means of communication by land or water (including any works or structures being part thereof or connected therewith), or any place used for gas, water, or electricity works or other works for purposes of a public character, or any place where any munitions of war, or any sketches, models, plans or documents relating thereto, are being made, repaired, or stored otherwise than on behalf of His Majesty, which is for the time being declared by order of a Secretary of State to be a prohibited place for the purposes of this section, on the ground that information with respect thereto, or the destruction or obstruction thereof, or interference therewith, would be useful to an enemy.

12. In this Act, unless the context otherwise requires,—
   Any reference to a place belonging to His Majesty includes a place belonging to any department of the Government...whether the place is or is not actually vested in His Majesty;...
   The expression 'document' includes part of a document;
   The expression 'model' includes design, pattern and specimen;
   The expression 'sketch' includes any photograph or other mode of representing any place or thing;
   The expression 'munitions of war' includes the whole or any part of any ship, submarine, aircraft, tank or similar engine, arms and ammunition, torpedo, or mine, intended or adapted for use in war, and any other article, material, or device, whether actual or proposed, intended for such use;

The Official Secrets (Prohibited Places) Order 1994 (SI 1994 No. 968), made under s. 3(c), provide that the works and offices of the UKAEA at Dounreay, the BNF sites at Sellafield and Capenhurst, the Urenco site at Capenhurst and the UKAEA sites at Harwell and Windscale are prohibited places. Further, any place used by the Civil Aviation Authority is a place belonging to Her Majesty under s. 3(c) (Civil Aviation Act 1982, s. 18(2) to (4)); and any electronic communications station or office belonging to, or occupied by, the provider of a public electronic communications service is a prohibited place (Communications Act 2003, sch. 17, para. 2).

Making Sketches etc. Useful to Enemy

For the definitions of 'sketch' and 'model' in the Official Secrets Act 1911, s. 12, see B9.7.   **B9.8**

As to the meaning of the word 'enemy', the Court of Appeal in *Parrott* (1913) 8 Cr App R 186, held that 'it does not mean necessarily someone with whom this country is at war, but a potential enemy with whom we might some day be at war'.

Obtaining or Communicating Sketches etc. Useful to Enemy

A partial definition of the words 'obtains' and 'communicates' is provided by the Official Secrets   **B9.9**
Act 1911, s. 12:

Official Secrets Act 1911, s. 12

Expressions referring to communicating include any communicating, whether in whole or in part, and whether the sketch, plan, model, article, note, document, or information itself or the substance, effect, or description thereof only be communicated; expressions referring to obtaining or retaining any sketch, plan, model, article, note, or document, include the copying or causing to be copied the whole or any part of any sketch, plan, model, article, note, or document, and expressions referring to the communication of any sketch, plan, model, article, note or document include the transfer or transmissions of the sketch, plan, model, article, note or document.

For the definitions of 'sketch', 'model' and 'enemy', see **B9.7** and **B9.8**.

The Official Secrets Act 1920, s. 2(1), provides that communication with a foreign agent is to be evidence that the accused has obtained or communicated information useful to an enemy with a purpose prejudicial to the safety or interests of the State. Section 2(2)(a) lays down the circumstances in which a person is deemed to have been in communication with a foreign agent, unless he proves the contrary. They are:

(a) he has, either within or without the UK, visited the address of a foreign agent or consorted or associated with a foreign agent; or
(b) either within or without the UK, the name or address of, or any other information regarding a foreign agent has been found in his possession, or has been supplied by him to any other person, or has been obtained by him from any other person.

'Foreign agent' is defined by s. 2(2)(b) as including any person who is, or has been, or is reasonably suspected of being or having been employed by a foreign power either directly or indirectly for the purpose of committing an act, either within or without the UK, prejudicial to the safety or interests of the State, or who has, or is reasonably suspected of having, either within or without the UK, committed, or attempted to commit, such an act in the interests of a foreign power.

Finally, s. 2(2)(c) provides that an address, whether or not in the UK, is deemed to be the address of a foreign agent, and communications to that address deemed to be communications with a foreign agent, if the address is reasonably suspected of being an address for the receipt of communications or where he resides, or resorts for giving or receiving communications or carries on a business. The relevance of the activities of a foreign agent in proving the above requirements was considered in *Kent* (1943) 28 Cr App R 23.

Related Offences

(a) A duty to give information about the commission of an offence under the Official Secrets   **B9.10**
Act 1911, s. 1(1), may be imposed by a chief officer of police acting under the Official Secrets Act 1920, s. 6. It is an offence to fail to provide such information. A person guilty of

this offence is liable, on conviction on indictment, to imprisonment for a term not exceeding two years or a fine, or both or, on summary conviction, to a term of imprisonment not exceeding three months or a fine not exceeding the prescribed sum or both (Official Secrets Act 1920, s. 8(2)).

(b)   The Official Secrets Act 1920, s. 7, makes it an offence to attempt, solicit or endeavour to persuade, or to aid and abet or do an act preparatory to, an offence under the Official Secrets Act 1911, s. 1(1) or the Official Secrets Act 1920, s. 6. The penalty for this offence is the same as for the substantive offence.

(c)   It is an offence, contrary to the Official Secrets Act 1989, s. 5(6), for a person to disclose any information, document or other article which he knows, or has reasonable cause to believe, to have come into his possession as a result of a contravention of the Official Secrets Act 1911, s. 1.

(d)   The European Communities Act 1972, s. 11(2), protects Euratom secrets. It creates an offence which is to be regarded as an offence under the 1911 Act, and thus the provision in relation to restriction on prosecution (see **B9.2**) applies.

B9.11   European Communities Act 1972, s. 11

(2)   Where a person (whether a British subject or not) owing either—
  (a)   to his duties as a member of any Euratom institution or committee, or as an officer or servant of Euratom; or
  (b)   to his dealings in any capacity (official or unofficial) with any Euratom institution or installation or with any Euratom joint enterprise;
  has occasion to acquire, or obtain cognisance of, any classified information, he shall be guilty of [an offence] if, knowing or having reason to believe that it is classified information, he communicates it to any unauthorised person or makes any public disclosure of it, whether in the United Kingdom or elsewhere and whether before or after the termination of those duties or dealings…

Sections 10 and 11 of the 1911 Act, dealing with the extent of the Act and the place of trial of the offence, and saving for laws of British possessions, do not apply to this offence.

This offence is triable either way; it may be dealt with summarily only with the consent of the A-G. A person guilty of the offence is liable on conviction on indictment to imprisonment for a term not exceeding two years or a fine or both, or, on summary conviction, to a term of imprisonment not exceeding three months or a fine not exceeding the prescribed sum or both.

'Classified information' means any facts, information, knowledge, documents or objects that are subject to the security rules of a Member State or any Euratom institution (European Communities Act 1972, s. 11(2)).

HARBOURING 'SPIES'

B9.12   Official Secrets Act 1911, s. 7

If any person knowingly harbours any person whom he knows, or has reasonable grounds for supposing, to be a person who is about to commit or who has committed an offence under this Act, or knowingly permits to meet or assemble in any premises in his occupation or under his control any such persons, or if any person having harboured any such person, or permitted to meet or assemble in any premises in his occupation or under his control any such persons, wilfully omits or refuses to disclose to a superintendent of police any information which it is in his power to give in relation to any such person he shall be guilty of [an offence].

Procedure

B9.13   As to prosecutions requiring the consent of the A-G, see **B9.2**.

The offence is triable either way, subject to the proviso to the Official Secrets Act 1920, s. 8(2), which provides that the offence may be dealt with summarily only with the consent of the A-G. When tried on indictment it is a class 1B offence.

As to the special provisions relating to place of trial, territorial jurisdiction, excluding the public from the trial and offences tried outside the UK, see **B9.2**.

Indictment

Statement of Offence   **B9.14**

Harbouring an offender contrary to section 7 of the Official Secrets Act 1911.

Particulars of Offence

A on or about the...day of...harboured O whom he knew or had reasonable grounds for supposing was about to commit [or had committed] an offence under the Official Secrets Act 1911, namely [state the offence].

Sentence

The maximum penalty is: on conviction on indictment, imprisonment for a term not exceed-   **B9.15** ing two years or a fine or both; on summary conviction, a term of imprisonment not exceeding three months or a fine not exceeding the prescribed sum or both (Official Secrets Act 1920, s. 8(2)).

Offence Not Limited to Harbouring 'Spies'

The offence is not limited to harbouring 'spies', since the person being harboured must simply   **B9.16** have committed an 'offence under this Act', which means any act, omission, or other thing which is punishable under the 1911 Act (Official Secrets Act 1911, s. 12).

Meaning of 'Superintendent of Police'

Official Secrets Act 1911, s. 12   **B9.17**

In this Act, unless the context otherwise requires,—

...

The expression 'superintendent of police' includes any police officer of a like or superior rank and any person upon whom the powers of a superintendent of police are for the purposes of this Act conferred by a Secretary of State.

Related Offences

The Official Secrets Act 1920, s. 7, makes it an offence to attempt, solicit or endeavour to per-   **B9.18** suade, or to aid and abet or do an act preparatory to, an offence under the Official Secrets Act 1911, s. 7.

GAINING ACCESS TO PROHIBITED PLACES

Official Secrets Act 1920, s. 1   **B9.19**

(1) If any person for the purpose of gaining admission, or of assisting, any other person to gain admission, to a prohibited place, within the meaning of the Official Secrets Act 1911..., or for any other purpose prejudicial to the safety or interests of the State within the meaning of the said Act—

  (a) uses or wears, without lawful authority, any naval, military, air-force, police, or other offi-cial uniform, or any uniform so nearly resembling the same as to be calculated to deceive, or falsely represents himself to be a person who is or has been entitled to use or wear any such uniform; or

  (b) orally, or in writing in any declaration or application, or in any document signed by him or on his behalf, knowingly makes or connives at the making of any false statement or any omission; or

  (c) tampers with any passport or naval, military, air-force, police, or other official pass, permit, certificate, licence, or other document of a similar character (hereinafter in this section referred to as an official document), or has in his possession any forged, altered, or irregular official document; or

(d) personates, or falsely represents himself to be a person holding, or in the employment of a person holding office under His Majesty, or to be or not to be a person to whom an official document or secret official code word or pass word has been duly issued or communicated, or with intent to obtain an official document, secret official code word or pass word, whether for himself or any other person, knowingly makes any false statement; or

(e) uses, or has in his possession or under his control, without the authority of the Government Department or the authority concerned, any die, seal, or stamp of or belonging to, or used, made or provided by any Government Department, or by any diplomatic, naval, military, or air force authority appointed by or acting under the authority of His Majesty, or any die, seal or stamp so nearly resembling any such die, seal or stamp as to be calculated to deceive, or counterfeits any such die, seal or stamp, or uses, or has in his possession, or under his control, any such counterfeited die, seal or stamp;

he shall be guilty of [an offence].

Procedure

B9.20 As to prosecutions requiring the consent of the A-G, see **B9.2**.

The offence is triable either way, subject to the proviso to the Official Secrets Act 1920, s. 8(2), which provides that the offence may be dealt with summarily only with the consent of the A-G. When tried on indictment it is a class 1B offence.

As to the special provisions relating to place of trial, territorial jurisdiction, excluding the public from the trial and offences tried outside the UK, see **B9.2**.

Indictment

B9.21
Statement of Offence

Unlawfully wearing a uniform for the purpose of gaining access to a prohibited place contrary to section 1(1) of the Official Secrets Act 1920.

Particulars of Offence

A on or about the...day of..., for the purpose of gaining admission to a prohibited place, namely..., wore a naval [or military etc.] uniform without lawful authority.

Sentence

B9.22 The maximum penalty is: on conviction on indictment, imprisonment for a term not exceeding two years or a fine or both; on summary conviction, a term of imprisonment not exceeding three months or a fine not exceeding the prescribed sum or both (Official Secrets Act 1920, s. 8(2)).

Elements

B9.23 For the meaning of 'prohibited place', see **B9.7**. For the meaning of 'purpose prejudicial to the safety or interests of the State', see **B9.6**.

By virtue of the Official Secrets Act 1911, s. 12, 'office under His Majesty' includes any office or employment in or under any department of the government of the UK or of any British possession. A police officer is in employment under Her Majesty (*Lewis v Cattle* [1938] 2 KB 454).

Related Offences

B9.24 The Official Secrets Act 1920, s. 7, makes it an offence to attempt, solicit or endeavour to persuade, or to aid and abet or do an act preparatory to, an offence under the Official Secrets Act 1920, s. 1(1). The mental element for the s. 7 offence was considered in *Bingham* [1973] QB 870.

RETENTION AND POSSESSION OF OFFICIAL DOCUMENTS ETC.

Official Secrets Act 1920, s. 1   **B9.25**

(2) If any person—

(a) retains for any purpose prejudicial to the safety or interests of the State any official document, whether or not completed or issued for use, when he has no right to retain it, or when it is contrary to his duty to retain it, or fails to comply with any directions issued by any government department or any person authorised by such department with regard to the return or disposal thereof, or

(b) allows any other person to have possession of any official document issued for his use alone, or communicates any secret official code word or pass word so issued, or, without lawful authority or excuse, has in his possession any official document or secret official code word or pass word issued for the use of some person other than himself, or on obtaining possession of any official document by finding or otherwise, neglects or fails to restore it to the person or authority by whom or for whose use it was issued, or to a police constable; or

(c) without lawful authority or excuse, manufactures or sells, or has in his possession for sale any such die, seal or stamp as aforesaid;

he shall be guilty of [an offence].

Procedure

As to prosecutions requiring the consent of the A-G, see **B9.2**.   **B9.26**

The offence is triable either way, subject to the proviso to the Official Secrets Act 1920, s. 8(2), which provides that the offence may be dealt with summarily only with the consent of the A-G. When tried on indictment it is a class 1B offence.

As to the special provisions relating to place of trial, territorial jurisdiction, excluding the public from the trial and offences tried outside the UK, see **B9.2**.

Indictment

Statement of Offence   **B9.27**

Retaining an official document contrary to section 1(2) of the Official Secrets Act 1920.

Particulars of Offence

A on or about the...day of..., for a purpose prejudicial to the safety or interests of the State, namely..., retained an official document, namely..., when he had no right to retain it [or when it was contrary to his duty to retain it].

Sentence

The maximum penalty is: on conviction on indictment, imprisonment for a term not exceeding   **B9.28**
two years or a fine or both; on summary conviction, a term of imprisonment not exceeding three months or a fine not exceeding the prescribed sum or both (Official Secrets Act 1920, s. 8(2)).

Elements

For the meaning of 'official document', see the Official Secrets Act 1920, s. 1(1)(c) at **B9.19**. For   **B9.29**
the meaning of 'die, seal or stamp', see s. 1(1)(e) of that Act. For the meaning of 'communicate', see **B9.9**.

For the meaning of 'purpose prejudicial to the safety or interests of the State', see **B9.6**.

Related Offences

The Official Secrets Act 1920, s. 7, makes it an offence to attempt, solicit or endeavour to persuade, or to aid and abet or do an act preparatory to, an offence under the Official Secrets Act   **B9.30**
1920, s. 1(2).

INTERFERING WITH OFFICERS OF POLICE OR MEMBERS OF ARMED FORCES IN VICINITY OF PROHIBITED PLACE

B9.31   Official Secrets Act 1920, s. 3

No person in the vicinity of any prohibited place shall obstruct, knowingly mislead or otherwise interfere with or impede, the chief officer or a superintendent or other officer of police, or any member of His Majesty's forces engaged on guard, sentry, patrol, or other similar duty in relation to the prohibited place, and, if any person acts in contravention of, or fails to comply with, this provision, he shall be guilty of [an offence].

Procedure

B9.32   As to the restriction on prosecutions requiring the consent of the A-G, see **B9.2**.

This offence is triable either way, subject to the proviso to the Official Secrets Act 1920, s. 8(2), which provides that the offence may be dealt with summarily only with the consent of the A-G. When tried on indictment it is a class 1B offence.

As to the special provisions relating to territorial jurisdiction, excluding the public from the trial and offences tried outside the UK, see **B9.2**.

Sentence

B9.33   The maximum penalty is: on conviction on indictment, imprisonment for a term not exceeding two years or a fine or both; on summary conviction, a term of imprisonment not exceeding three months or a fine not exceeding the prescribed sum or both (Official Secrets Act 1920, s. 8(2)).

Elements

B9.34   For the meaning of 'prohibited place', see **B9.7**.

In *Adler v George* [1964] 2 QB 7, it was held that the phrase 'in the vicinity of' in the Official Secrets Act 1920, s. 3, is to be interpreted as 'in or in the vicinity of' so that obstruction of someone at an airbase could constitute an offence under the section.

The word 'obstruct' presumably has the same meaning as in the offence of obstruction of a police officer in the execution of his duty (see **B2.42** to **B2.47**). The meaning of 'superintendent' is considered at **B9.17**. For the meaning of 'chief officer of police', see the Police Act 1996, s. 101.

Related Offences

B9.35   The Official Secrets Act 1920, s. 7, makes it an offence to attempt, solicit or endeavour to persuade, or to aid and abet or do an act preparatory to, an offence under the Official Secrets Act 1920, s. 3. As to the offences of assaulting and obstructing a police officer in the execution of his duty, see **B2.37** to **B2.47**.

DISCLOSURE OF SECURITY AND INTELLIGENCE INFORMATION

B9.36   Official Secrets Act 1989, s. 1

(1) A person who is or has been—
   (a) a member of the security and intelligence services; or
   (b) a person notified that he is subject to the provisions of this subsection,
   shall be guilty of an offence if without lawful authority he discloses any information, document or other article relating to security or intelligence which is or has been in his possession

by virtue of his position as a member of any of those services or in the course of his work while the notification is or was in force.

Procedure and Extra-territoriality

Official Secrets Act 1989, ss. 9, 11, and 15

B9.37

9.—(1) Subject to subsection (2) below, no prosecution for an offence under this Act shall be instituted in England and Wales or in Northern Ireland except by or with the consent of the Attorney-General or, as the case may be, the Attorney-General for Northern Ireland.

(2) Subsection (1) above does not apply to an offence in respect of any such information, document or article as is mentioned in section 4(2) above but no prosecution for such an offence shall be instituted in England and Wales or in Northern Ireland except by or with the consent of the Director of Public Prosecutions or, as the case may be, the Director of Public Prosecutions for Northern Ireland.

11.—(5) Proceedings for an offence under this Act may be taken in any place in the United Kingdom.

15.—(1) Any act—
  (a) done by a British citizen or Crown servant; or
  (b) done by any person in any of the Channel Islands or the Isle of Man or any colony,
shall, if it would be an offence by that person under any provision of this Act other than section 8(1), (4) or (5) when done by him in the United Kingdom, be an offence under that provision.

This offence is triable either way (Official Secrets Act 1989, s. 10(1)). When tried on indictment it is a class 1B offence.

The power to exclude the public under the Official Secrets Act 1920, s. 8(4), applies to the instant offence by virtue of the Official Secrets Act 1989, s. 11(4) (see **B9.2**).

Indictment

Statement of Offence

B9.38

Unlawful disclosure of information contrary to section 1(1) of the Official Secrets Act 1989.

Particulars of Offence

A on or about the...day of..., being a person notified that he was subject to the provisions of section 1 of the Official Secrets Act 1989, without lawful authority disclosed to P a document, namely..., which related to security or intelligence and which the said A had in his possession in the course of his work while the said notification was in force.

Sentence

B9.39

The maximum penalty is: on conviction on indictment, imprisonment for a term not exceeding two years or a fine or both; on summary conviction, imprisonment for a term not exceeding six months or a fine not exceeding the statutory maximum or both (Official Secrets Act 1989, s. 10(1)). In *Shayler* [2003] 1 AC 247, a former member of the security service, received a total of six months' imprisonment for offences under s. 1, following a contested trial. In 2010 Daniel Houghton, a former MI6 agent, pleaded guilty to attempting to sell classified material to Dutch Intelligence and received a total of 12 months for two offences under s. 1.

Persons who Can Commit Offence

B9.40

An offence under the Official Secrets Act 1989, s. 1(1), can be committed by either a person who is or has been a member of the security and intelligence services, or someone who is or has been a notified person (i.e. notified that he is subject to s. 1 of the Act).

Official Secrets Act 1989, s. 1

(6) Notification that a person is subject to subsection (1) above shall be effected by a notice in writing served on him by a Minister of the Crown; and such a notice may be served if, in the

Minister's opinion, the work undertaken by the person in question is or includes work connected with the security and intelligence services and its nature is such that the interests of national security require that he should be subject to the provisions of that subsection.

(7) Subject to subsection (8) below, a notification for the purposes of subsection (1) above shall be in force for the period of five years beginning with the day on which it is served but may be renewed by further notices under subsection (6) above for periods of five years at a time.

(8) A notification for the purposes of subsection (1) above may at any time be revoked by a further notice in writing served by the Minister on the person concerned; and the Minister shall serve such a further notice as soon as, in his opinion, the work undertaken by that person ceases to be such as is mentioned in subsection (6) above.

Meaning of 'Security' and 'Intelligence'

B9.41

Official Secrets Act 1989, s. 1

(9) In this section 'security or intelligence' means the work of, or in support of, the security and intelligence services or any part of them, and references to information relating to security or intelligence include references to information held or transmitted by those services or by persons in support of, or of any part of, them.

The security service has now been placed on a statutory basis (see the Security Service Act 1989), as has the Secret Intelligence Service (Intelligence Services Act 1994).

Disclosure of Information

B9.42

Official Secrets Act 1989, ss. 1 and 13

1.—(2) The reference in subsection (1) above to disclosing information relating to security or intelligence includes a reference to making any statement which purports to be a disclosure of such information or is intended to be taken by those to whom it is addressed as being such a disclosure.

13.—(1) In this Act—
'disclose' and 'disclosure', in relation to a document or other article, include parting with possession of it.

'Disclose' is not defined merely as 'make public', for example. This is capable of causing difficulties in relation to the absolute right of an accused to provide his legal advisers with instructions relating to his defence. It is possible to do so only if the provision of his instructions would not involve the commission of a further offence by such disclosure to his lawyers. In cases where, for example, the alleged disclosure was not widely publicised, the accused's lawyers may need to seek authorisation under s. 7 before they can even view the subject-matter of the indictment. Undoubtedly there is likely to be an application for such trials to be held in camera. Although Lord Bingham in *Shayler* [2003] 1 AC 247, suggested a special advocate solution (at [34]), this related only to a judicial review of a refusal to authorise disclosure, not criminal proceedings in which the accused seeks to provide his lawyers with instructions/material relevant to his defence.

The issue of prior publication is relevant to whether the disclosure in question is damaging but not decisive of it: see the White Paper *Reform of Section 2 of the Official Secrets Act 1911* (1988) Cm. 408 at paras. 62 to 63. The White Paper recommendations 'bear directly on the interpretation of the Act' (*Shayler* [2003] 1 AC 247 at [11]).

Meaning of 'Without Lawful Authority'

B9.43 The Official Secrets Act 1989, s. 1(1), applies only to unauthorised disclosures. Section 7 provides for the only circumstances in which a disclosure may be made 'with lawful authority'. Only s. 7(1) applies to s. 1(1), since the offence applies only to the limited range of Crown servants who work for the security and intelligence services, or who are notified as being covered by the provisions of s. 1(1).

Official Secrets Act 1989, s. 7

(1) For the purposes of this Act a disclosure by—
   (a) a Crown servant; or
   (b) a person, not being a Crown servant or government contractor, in whose case a notification for the purposes of section 1(1) above is in force,
   is made with lawful authority if, and only if, it is made in accordance with his official duty.

As to the broader provisions relating, generally, to authorised disclosures, see **B9.54**; as to defences, see **B9.44**.

Defences

Official Secrets Act 1989, ss. 1 and 7   **B9.44**

1.—(5) It is a defence for a person charged with an offence under this section to prove that at the time of the alleged offence he did not know, and had no reasonable cause to believe, that the information, document or article in question related to security or intelligence.

7.—(4) It is a defence for a person charged with an offence under any of the foregoing provisions of this Act to prove that at the time of the alleged offence he believed that he had lawful authority to make the disclosure in question and had no reasonable cause to believe otherwise.

Although the legal burden appears to lie upon the accused, it is likely that only an evidential burden would be compatible with the ECHR, Article 6 (see *Keogh* [2007] 3 All ER 789 and **F3.18** *et seq*.). The rationale given in the White Paper *Reform of Section 2 of the Official Secrets Act 1911* (1988) Cm. 408 for the reversal of the burden of proof (that a Crown servant or government contractor can be expected to appreciate the consequences of disclosure and that it is reasonable to expect him to demonstrate that this was not the case) was insufficient justification for the imposition of a legal burden.

According to the House of Lords in *Shayler* [2003] 1 AC 247, there is no additional defence of   **B9.45** a disclosure being in the national or public interest, the offence contrary to the Official Secrets Act 1989, s. 1(1), or the offence contrary to s. 4(1). The House held that the blanket ban on disclosures by members of the security services nevertheless satisfied the requirements of the ECHR, Article 10(2). The intention to counter terrorism, criminal activity, hostile activity and subversion was a sufficient purpose to satisfy Article 10(2), and the restrictions were clear, and so prescribed by law. The restrictions were also necessary in a democratic society because of the defences that existed (which vary from offence to offence): the two means of gaining authorisation for a disclosure under s. 7 and the possibility of challenging an adverse decision under judicial review (with a suitably rigorous and intensive form of review for the alleged breach of a Convention right). Moreover, no prosecution would take place without the consent of the A-G.

'Public interest', however, remains relevant to whether any particular disclosure is damaging (i.e. for *all* offences except those under s. 1(1) and s. 4 of the Act): see White Paper *Reform of Section 2 of the Official Secrets Act 1911*, para. 61. For offences requiring damaging disclosure, it is necessary for the prosecution to prove not only that the disclosure is damaging but also that the person making the disclosure knows or has reasonable grounds to believe that it would be damaging (in the sense that it is likely to have that effect). It is insufficient for the prosecution to prove that there were reasonable grounds to believe that the disclosure might be damaging, or that this was merely a possibility.

Although the House held that Shayler himself was not 'within measurable distance' of the defence of necessity (as to which, see further **A3.47**), necessity remains available as a defence to *all* offences under the 1989 Act. The potential width of the defence is illustrated by one of the prosecution's stated reasons for not proceeding with the case against Katharine Gun, namely that it could not rebut her defence of necessity. She was a GCHQ employee who, in 2004, was charged with s. 1 disclosure of the US request for the UK to spy on the UN in the run-up to the Iraq war. Her publicly stated defence was a desire to prevent a war without a lawfully obtained second UN resolution.

Related Offences

B9.46   It is an offence, contrary to the Official Secrets Act 1989, s. 1(3), for a Crown servant or government contractor to make a damaging disclosure of security or intelligence information (see B9.47 to B9.56).

DAMAGING DISCLOSURE OF SECURITY AND INTELLIGENCE INFORMATION

B9.47   Official Secrets Act 1989, s. 1

> (3) A person who is or has been a Crown servant or government contractor shall be guilty of an offence if without lawful authority he makes a damaging disclosure of any information, document or other article relating to security or intelligence which is or has been in his possession by virtue of his position as such but otherwise than as mentioned in subsection (1) above.

Procedure

B9.48   As to the requirement of consent of the A-G, see the Official Secrets Act 1989, s. 9(1), and **B9.37**.

The offence is triable either way (s. 10(1)). When tried on indictment it is a class 1B offence.

As to provisions relating to place of trial, territorial jurisdiction and excluding the public from the trial, see **B9.37**.

Indictment

B9.49   *Statement of Offence*

Unlawfully making a damaging disclosure of information relating to security [or intelligence] contrary to section 1(3) of the Official Secrets Act 1989.

Particulars of Offence

A on or about the...day of..., being then [or having been] a Crown servant [or government contractor], without lawful authority disclosed to P information relating to security [or intelligence], namely..., which was in his possession by virtue of his position as a Crown servant [or government contractor], which disclosure caused [or disclosure of which would have been likely to cause] damage to the work of the security and intelligence services [or the work of..., being part of the security and intelligence services].

Sentence

B9.50   The maximum penalty is: on conviction on indictment, imprisonment for a term not exceeding two years or a fine or both; on summary conviction, imprisonment for a term not exceeding six months or a fine not exceeding the statutory maximum or both (Official Secrets Act 1989, s. 10(1)).

Meaning of 'Security', 'Intelligence', 'Disclosure', 'Damaging Disclosure'

B9.51   For the meaning of 'security' and 'intelligence', see **B9.41**. For the meaning of 'disclosure', see **B9.42**. The words 'damaging disclosure' are defined by the Official Secrets Act 1989, s. 1(4).

Official Secrets Act 1989, s. 1

> (4) For the purposes of subsection (3) above a disclosure is damaging if—
>   (a) it causes damage to the work of, or of any part of, the security and intelligence services; or
>   (b) it is of information or a document or other article which is such that its unauthorised disclosure would be likely to cause such damage or which falls within a class or description of information, documents or articles the unauthorised disclosure of which would be likely to have that effect.

This offence is committed whether or not the information disclosed was secret or confidential, and whether or not the disclosure was damaging to national interests (*A-G v Blake* [1997] Ch

84 (per Sir Richard Scott (*obiter*)). 'Public interest' is relevant to whether the disclosure is damaging, see **B9.44**.

Meaning of 'Crown Servant'

Official Secrets Act 1989, s. 12   **B9.52**

(1) In this Act 'Crown servant' means—
    (a)   a Minister of the Crown;
    (aa) a member of the Scottish Executive or a junior Scottish minister;
    (ab) the First Minister of Wales, a Welsh Minister appointed under section 48 of the Government of Wales Act 2006, the Counsel General to the Welsh Assembly Government or a Deputy Welsh Minister;
    (b)   [repealed]
    (c)   any person employed in the civil service of the Crown, including Her Majesty's Diplomatic Service, Her Majesty's Overseas Civil Service, the civil service of Northern Ireland and the Northern Ireland Court Service;
    (d)   any member of the naval, military or air forces of the Crown, including any person employed by an association established for the purposes of Part XI of the Reserve Forces Act 1996;
    (e)   any constable and any other person employed or appointed in or for the purposes of any police force (including the Police Service of Northern Ireland and the Police Service of Northern Ireland Reserve) or an NCA special (within the meaning of Part 1 of the Crime and Courts Act 2013);
    (f)   any person who is a member or employee of a prescribed body or a body of a prescribed class and either is prescribed for the purposes of this paragraph or belongs to a prescribed class of members or employees of any such body;
    (g)   any person who is the holder of a prescribed office or who is an employee of such a holder and either is prescribed for the purposes of this paragraph or belongs to a prescribed class of such employees.

The Official Secrets Act 1989 (Prescription) Order 1990 (SI 1990 No. 200), art. 2 and sch. 1 (as amended by SI 2013 No. 602), prescribe classes of members or employees of certain bodies (and classes of bodies) as 'Crown servants' for the purpose of s. 12(1)(f); art. 3 and sch. 2 prescribe classes of members or employees as 'Crown servants' for the purposes of s. 12(1)(g).

The 1989 Act applies to the First Minister and deputy First Minister in Northern Ireland and Northern Ireland Ministers and junior Ministers in the same way as it applies to Crown servants (Official Secrets Act 1989, s. 12(5)).

Meaning of 'Government Contractor'

Official Secrets Act 1989, ss. 12 and 13   **B9.53**

12.—(2) In this Act 'government contractor' means, subject to subsection (3) below, any person who is not a Crown servant but who provides, or is employed in the provision of, goods or services—
    (a) for the purposes of any Minister of the Crown or person mentioned in paragraph (a), (ab) or (b) of subsection (1) above, of any of the services, forces or bodies mentioned in that subsection or of the holder of any office prescribed under that subsection; or
    (b) under an agreement or arrangement certified by the Secretary of State as being one to which the government of a State other than the United Kingdom or an international organisation is a party or which is subordinate to, or made for the purposes of implementing, any such agreement or arrangement.
(3) Where an employee or class of employees of any body, or of any holder of an office, is prescribed by an order made for the purposes of subsection (1) above—
    (a) any employee of that body, or the holder of that office who is not prescribed or is not within the prescribed class; and
    (b) any person who does not provide, or is not employed in the provision of, goods or services for the purposes of the performance of those functions of the body or the holder of the office in connection with which the employee or prescribed class of employees is engaged,
shall not be a government contractor for the purposes of this Act.

13.—(1) In this Act—

...

'international organisation' means, subject to subsections (2) and (3) below, an organisation of which only States are members and includes a reference to any organ of such an organisation;

...

'State' includes the government of a State and any organ of its government and references to a State other than the United Kingdom include references to any territory outside the United Kingdom.

(2) In section 12(2)(b) above the reference to an international organisation includes a reference to any such organisation whether or not one of which only States are members and includes a commercial organisation.

(3) In determining for the purposes of subsection (1) above whether only States are members of an organisation, any member which is itself an organisation of which only States are members, or which is an organ of such an organisation, shall be treated as a State.

'Without Lawful Authority'

B9.54   An offence under the Official Secrets Act 1989, s. 1(3), is committed only if the disclosure is 'without lawful authority'. The only circumstances in which a disclosure is made with lawful authority are to be found in s. 7.

Official Secrets Act 1989, s. 7

(1) For the purposes of this Act a disclosure by—
   (a) a Crown servant; or
   (b) a person, not being a Crown servant or government contractor, in whose case a notification for the purposes of section 1(1) above is in force,
   is made with lawful authority if, and only if, it is made in accordance with his official duty.

(2) For the purposes of this Act a disclosure by a government contractor is made with lawful authority if, and only if, it is made—
   (a) in accordance with an official authorisation; or
   (b) for the purposes of the functions by virtue of which he is a government contractor and without contravening an official restriction.

(3) For the purposes of this Act a disclosure made by any other person is made with lawful authority if, and only if, it is made—
   (a) to a Crown servant for the purposes of his functions as such; or
   (b) in accordance with an official authorisation.

...

(5) In this section 'official authorisation' and 'official restriction' mean, subject to subsection (6) below, an authorisation or restriction duly given or imposed by a Crown servant or government contractor or by or on behalf of a prescribed body or a body of a prescribed class.

The Civil Aviation Authority and the Investigatory Powers Tribunal have been prescribed by the Official Secrets Act 1989 (Prescription) Order 1990 (SI 1990 No. 200), art. 4 and sch. 3, for the purpose of s. 7(5) so as to enable them to give official authorisations or restrictions.

Specific Defences

B9.55   The defence of having no knowledge or reasonable cause to believe that information related to security or intelligence, created by the Official Secrets Act 1989, s. 1(5), and the defence that the accused believed that he had lawful authority for disclosure, apply to this offence. There is no defence of disclosure in the public or national interest for an offence under s. 1(1) (*Shayler* [2003] 1 AC 247), but 'public interest' is relevant to whether the disclosure is damaging. The defences are considered at **B9.44**.

Related Offences

B9.56   It is an offence, contrary to the Official Secrets Act 1989, s. 1(1), for a present or past member of the security and intelligence services or a notified person to make a disclosure of security or intelligence information (see **B9.36** to **B9.46**).

DAMAGING DISCLOSURE OF DEFENCE INFORMATION

Official Secrets Act 1989, s. 2   **B9.57**

(1) A person who is or has been a Crown servant or government contractor shall be guilty of an offence if without lawful authority he makes a damaging disclosure of any information, document or other article relating to defence which is or has been in his possession by virtue of his position as such.

Procedure

As to the requirement of consent of the A-G, see **B9.37**. The offence is triable either way **B9.58** (Official Secrets Act 1989, s. 10(1)). When tried on indictment it is a class 1B offence.

As to provisions relating to place of trial, territorial jurisdiction and excluding the public from the trial, see **B9.37**.

Indictment

Statement of Offence   **B9.59**

Unlawfully making a damaging disclosure of information relating to defence contrary to section 2(1) of the Official Secrets Act 1989.

Particulars of Offence

A on or about the...day of..., being then [or having been] a Crown servant [or government contractor], without lawful authority disclosed to P information relating to defence, namely..., which was in his possession by virtue of his position as a Crown servant [or government contractor], which disclosure prejudiced [or disclosure of which would have been likely to prejudice] the capability of the armed forces of the Crown to carry out their tasks [or other form of damage specified in s. 2(2): see **B9.61**].

Sentence

The maximum penalty is: on conviction on indictment, imprisonment for a term not exceeding **B9.60** two years or a fine or both; on summary conviction, imprisonment for a term not exceeding six months or a fine not exceeding the statutory maximum or both.

Elements

The meaning of 'disclosure' is considered at **B9.42**.   **B9.61**

Official Secrets Act 1989, s. 2

(2) For the purposes of subsection (1) above a disclosure is damaging if—
 (a) it prejudices the capability of, or any part of, the armed forces of the Crown to carry out their tasks or leads to loss of life or injury to members of those forces or serious damage to the equipment or installations of those forces; or
 (b) otherwise than in paragraph (a) above, it endangers the interests of the United Kingdom abroad, seriously obstructs the promotion or protection by the United Kingdom of those interests or endangers the safety of British citizens abroad; or
 (c) it is of information or of a document or article which is such that its unauthorised disclosure would be likely to have any of those effects.
...
(4) In this section 'defence' means—
 (a) the size, shape, organisation, logistics, order of battle, deployment, operations, state of readiness and training of the armed forces of the Crown;
 (b) the weapons, stores or other equipment of those forces and the invention, development, production and operation of such equipment and research relating to it;
 (c) defence policy and strategy and military planning and intelligence;
 (d) plans and measures for the maintenance of essential supplies and services that are or would be needed in time of war.

The meanings of 'Crown servant' and 'government contractor' are considered at **B9.52** and **B9.53**. As to the meaning of 'without lawful authority', see s. 7 of the Act, at **B9.54**. As to the only circumstances in which a disclosure is made with lawful authority, see **B9.54**.

Specific Defences

B9.62
Official Secrets Act 1989, s. 2

(3) It is a defence for a person charged with an offence under this section to prove that at the time of the alleged offence he did not know, and had no reasonable cause to believe, that the information, document or article in question related to defence or that its disclosure would be damaging within the meaning of subsection (1) above.

To ensure compliance with the ECHR, Article 6, the accused has only an evidential burden as regards proving this defence (*Keogh* [2007] 3 All ER 789: cf. the Terrorism Act 2000, s. 118 at **B10.29** and see further **F3.18** *et seq.*).

The defence that the accused believed that he had lawful authority for disclosure, created by the Official Secrets Act 1989, s. 7(4), also applies to this offence, and is considered at **B9.44** together with other defences.

DAMAGING DISCLOSURE OF INTERNATIONAL RELATIONS INFORMATION

B9.63
Official Secrets Act 1989, s. 3

(1) A person who is or has been a Crown servant or government contractor shall be guilty of an offence if without lawful authority he makes a damaging disclosure of—
(a) any information, document or other article relating to international relations; or
(b) any confidential information, document or other article which was obtained from a State other than the United Kingdom or an international organisation,
being information or a document or article which is or has been in his possession by virtue of his position as a Crown servant or government contractor.

Procedure

B9.64 As to the requirement of the A-G's consent, see **B9.37**. The offence is triable either way (Official Secrets Act 1989, s. 10(1)). When tried on indictment it is a class 1B offence.

As to provisions relating to place of trial, territorial jurisdiction and excluding the public from the trial, see **B9.37**.

Indictment

B9.65
Statement of Offence

Unlawfully making a damaging disclosure of information relating to international relations contrary to section 3(1) of the Official Secrets Act 1989.

Particulars of Offence

A on or about the…day of…, being then [or having been] a Crown servant [or government contractor], without lawful authority disclosed to P information relating to international relations, namely…, which was in his possession by virtue of his position as a Crown servant [or government contractor], which disclosure endangered [or disclosure of which would have been likely to endanger] the interests of the United Kingdom abroad [or other form of damage specified in s. 3(2): see **B9.67**].

Sentence

B9.66 The maximum penalty is: on conviction on indictment, imprisonment for a term not exceeding two years or a fine or both; on summary conviction, imprisonment for a term not exceeding six months or a fine not exceeding the statutory maximum or both (Official Secrets Act 1989, s. 10(1)).

Elements

The meaning of 'disclosure' is considered at **B9.42**. The phrases 'damaging disclosure', **B9.67**
'international relations' and 'confidential information' are defined by the Official Secrets Act
1989, s. 3.

Official Secrets Act 1989, s. 3

(2) For the purposes of subsection (1) above a disclosure is damaging if—
   (a) it endangers the interests of the United Kingdom abroad, seriously obstructs the promo-
       tion or protection by the United Kingdom of those interests or endangers the safety of
       British citizens abroad; or
   (b) it is of information or of a document or article which is such that its unauthorised disclo-
       sure would be likely to have any of those effects.
(3) In the case of information or a document or article within subsection (1) above—
   (a) the fact that it is confidential, or
   (b) its nature or contents,
   may be sufficient to establish for the purposes of subsection (2)(b) above that the information,
   document or article is such that its unauthorised disclosure would be likely to have any of the
   effects there mentioned.
   ...
(5) In this section 'international relations' means the relations between States, between international organisations or between one or more States and one or more such organisations and
   includes any matter relating to a State other than the United Kingdom or to an international
   organisation which is capable of affecting the relations of the United Kingdom with another
   State or with an international organisation.
(6) For the purposes of this section any information, document or article obtained from a State or
   organisation is confidential at any time while the terms on which it was obtained require it to
   be held in confidence or while the circumstances in which it was obtained make it reasonable
   for the State or organisation to expect that it would be so held.

Section 13 of the Act defines 'State and international organisation' (see **B9.53**). The meanings of 'Crown servant' and 'government contractor' are considered at **B9.52** and **B9.53**. The
phrase 'without lawful authority' is defined by s. 7 of the Act (see **B9.54**). The Act does not
define the 'interests of the United Kingdom abroad'. This is an inchoate concept which raises
important and difficult issues of interpretation. There is some first instance authority for the
proposition that the concept of the national interest is to be treated as synonymous with the
interests of the government of the day. On the other hand, it is axiomatic that the interests of
any particular political party, or of any individual public official, are not to be equated with the
interests of the UK as a whole. A good indication of the kind of harm contemplated by s. 3 is
set out in the White Paper *Reform of Section 2 of the Official Secrets Act 1911* (1988) Cm. 408
at para. 27.

Specific Defences

Official Secrets Act 1989, s. 3   **B9.68**

(4) It is a defence for a person charged with an offence under this section to prove that at the time of
   the alleged offence he did not know, and had no reasonable cause to believe, that the information, document or article in question was such as is mentioned in subsection (1) above or that
   its disclosure would be damaging within the meaning of that subsection.

To ensure compliance with the ECHR, Article 6, the accused has only an evidential burden as
regards proving this defence (*Keogh* [2007] 3 All ER 789: cf. the Terrorism Act 2000, s. 118 and
see further **F3.18** *et seq.*).

The defence that the accused believed that he had lawful authority for disclosure also applies to
this offence. For defences generally, see **B9.44**.

DISCLOSURE OF INFORMATION RELEVANT TO CRIMINAL INVESTIGATIONS

B9.69   Official Secrets Act 1989, s. 4

(1) A person who is or has been a Crown servant or government contractor is guilty of an offence if without lawful authority he discloses any information, document or other article to which this section applies and which is or has been in his possession by virtue of his position as such.

(As to the materials referred to, see s. 4(2) and (3) at **B9.73**.)

Procedure

B9.70 As to the requirement of the consent of the A-G, see **B9.37**. This offence is triable either way (Official Secrets Act 1989, s. 10(1)). When tried on indictment it is a class 1B offence.

As to provisions relating to the place of trial, territorial jurisdiction and excluding the public from the trial, see **B9.37**.

Indictment

B9.71   *Statement of Offence*

Unlawful disclosure of information resulting in the commission of an offence contrary to section 4(1) of the Official Secrets Act 1989.

Particulars of Offence

A on or about the…day of…, being then [or having been] a Crown servant [or government contractor], without lawful authority disclosed to P information, which was such that its unauthorised disclosure resulted in the commission of an offence, namely…

Sentence

B9.72 The maximum penalty is: on conviction on indictment, imprisonment for a term not exceeding two years or a fine or both; on summary conviction, imprisonment for a term not exceeding six months or a fine not exceeding the statutory maximum or both (Official Secrets Act 1989, s. 10(1)).

Elements

B9.73   Official Secrets Act 1989, s. 4

(2) This section applies to any information, document or other article—
(a) the disclosure of which—
  (i) results in the commission of an offence; or
  (ii) facilitates an escape from legal custody or the doing of any other act prejudicial to the safekeeping of persons in legal custody; or
  (iii) impedes the prevention or detection of offences or the apprehension or prosecution of suspected offenders; or
(b) which is such that its unauthorised disclosure would be likely to have any of those effects.
(3) This section also applies to—
(a) any information obtained by reason of the interception of any communication in obedience to a warrant issued under section 2 of the Interception of Communications Act 1985 or under the authority of an interception warrant under section 5 of the Regulation of Investigatory Powers Act 2000, any information relating to the obtaining of information by reason of any such interception and any document or other article which is or has been used or held for use in, or has been obtained by reason of, any such interception; and
(b) any information obtained by reason of action authorised by a warrant issued under section 3 of the Security Service Act 1989, any information relating to the obtaining of information by reason of any such action and any document or other article which is or has been used or held for use in, or has been obtained by reason of, any such action.

…

(6) In this section 'legal custody' includes detention in pursuance of any enactment or any instrument made under an enactment.

The meaning of 'discloses' has been considered at **B9.42**. With regard to the meaning of 'without lawful authority', see s. 7 of the Act, at **B9.54**.

Specific Defences

Official Secrets Act 1989, s. 4   **B9.74**

(4) It is a defence for a person charged with an offence under this section in respect of a disclosure falling within subsection (2)(a) above to prove that at the time of the alleged offence he did not know, and had no reasonable cause to believe, that the disclosure would have any of the effects there mentioned.
(5) It is a defence for a person charged with an offence under this section in respect of any other disclosure to prove that at the time of the alleged offence he did not know, and had no reasonable cause to believe, that the information, document or article in question was information or a document or article to which this section applies.

Although the accused appears to have the legal burden of proving these defences, it is likely that only an evidential burden would be compatible with the ECHR, Article 6 (see *Keogh* [2007] 3 All ER 789 and **F3.18** *et seq.*).

The defence that the accused believed that he had lawful authority for disclosure also applies to this offence (see **B9.44** for all defences). There is no defence of disclosure in the public or national interest (*Shayler* [2003] 1 AC 247; see **B9.44**).

OTHER OFFENCES RELATING TO UNAUTHORISED DISCLOSURE OF INFORMATION

Other offences dealing with the unauthorised disclosure of information are listed below. They   **B9.75** are subject to the same procedural rules governing consent for commencement of proceedings, mode of trial, place of trial, territorial jurisdiction and exclusion of the public from the trial as the offence under s. 1(1) of the Act (see Official Secrets Act 1989, ss. 9, 11 and 15, and **B9.37**). As to sentence, see s. 10 of the Act.

The terms 'disclose', 'Crown servant', 'government contractor', 'State', 'international organisation' and 'without lawful authority' have the same meanings as elsewhere in the Act (see **B9.42**, **B9.52**, **B9.53** and **B9.54**).

The other offences created by the Official Secrets Act 1989 are:

(a) Disclosure of information resulting from unauthorised disclosures or entrusted in confidence (s. 5(1) and (2)). This offence provides additional protection for information 'protected against disclosure' (for the meaning of which, see s. 5(5)). Under the 1989 Act, it is not an offence merely to be the recipient of unsolicited information where the disclosure of that information involves the commission of an offence under the Act by the person who provides the information. However, the effect of s. 5 is that, where a third party comes into possession of information either directly or indirectly as a result of an unauthorised disclosure, that third party may be guilty of an offence if he further discloses it. Section 5 applies to any information, document or other article which is protected against disclosure by ss. 1 to 4.
(b) Disclosure of information possessed in contravention of the Official Secrets Act 1911, s. 1 (Official Secrets Act 1989, s. 5(6)). For s. 1 of the 1911 Act, see **B9.1** to **B9.10**.
(c) Disclosure of information entrusted in confidence to other states or an international organisation (Official Secrets Act 1989, s. 6(1) and (2)). Under this provision, a disclosure is to be regarded as 'damaging' if it would be so regarded in relation to an offence under ss. 1(3), 2(1) or 3(1) (s. 6(4)). For the meaning of 'damaging disclosure' under those provisions, see

B9.51, **B9.61** and **B9.67** and the White Paper *Reform of Section 2 of the Official Secrets Act 1911* (1988) Cm. 408 at para. 28.
(d) Disclosure of official information which can be used for gaining access to protected information (Official Secrets Act 1989, s. 8(6)). For the meaning of 'disclosure of official information', see s. 8(7).

B9.76 The CJA 1991, s. 91, creates an offence of wrongful disclosure of information by a person employed in pursuance of prison escort arrangements. The offence is triable either way. On conviction on indictment, the maximum penalty is imprisonment for a term not exceeding two years or a fine, or both; on summary conviction, the maximum penalty is imprisonment for a term not exceeding six months or a fine not exceeding the statutory maximum, or both. The CJPO 1994, s. 14, creates a similar offence in respect of the wrongful disclosure of information relating to offenders in youth detention accommodation.

Section 69 of the SCA 2007 creates an offence of wrongful further disclosure of protected information which has been disclosed to the recipient by a public authority which is a 'specified anti-fraud organisation' (as designated by the Secretary of State but subject to s. 68(8)).

Disclosure of information which is not protected by the Official Secrets Acts or other specific enactments by a person holding public office may amount to the common-law offence of misconduct in a public office (see **B15.26**).

FAILURE TO SAFEGUARD INFORMATION

B9.77 The Official Secrets Act 1989, s. 8, creates three offences concerned with failure to safeguard information:

(a) Section 8(1) makes it an offence for a Crown servant or government contractor to fail to safeguard certain information.
(b) Section 8(4) makes it an offence for a person with information as a consequence of an unauthorised disclosure or entrusted in confidence to fail to safeguard it.
(c) Section 8(5) makes it an offence for a person with information entrusted in confidence to States or international organisations to fail to comply with official directions for its return or disposal.

Official Secrets Act 1989, s. 8

(1) Where a Crown servant or government contractor, by virtue of his position as such, has in his possession or under his control any document or other article which it would be an offence under any of the foregoing provisions of this Act for him to disclose without lawful authority he shall be guilty of an offence if—
  (a) being a Crown servant, he retains the document or article contrary to his official duty; or
  (b) being a government contractor, he fails to comply with an official direction for the return or disposal of the document or article,
or if he fails to take such care to prevent the unauthorised disclosure of the document or article as a person in his position may reasonably be expected to take.
...
(4) Where a person has in his possession or under his control any document or other article which it would be an offence under section 5 above for him to disclose without lawful authority, he shall be guilty of an offence if—
  (a) he fails to comply with an official direction for its return or disposal; or
  (b) where he obtained it from a Crown servant or government contractor on terms requiring it to be held in confidence or in circumstances in which that servant or contractor could reasonably expect that it would be so held, he fails to take such care to prevent its unauthorised disclosure as a person in his position may reasonably be expected to take.
(5) Where a person has in his possession or under his control any document or other article which it would be an offence under section 6 above for him to disclose without lawful authority, he shall be guilty of an offence if he fails to comply with an official direction for its return or disposal.

Procedure

As to the requirement of consent of the A-G, see **B9.37**. These offences are triable summarily **B9.78** only (Official Secrets Act 1989, s. 10(2)). Section 11(5) (place of trial) applies to these offences (see **B9.37**).

Sentence

The maximum penalty on summary conviction is imprisonment for a term not exceeding three **B9.79** months or a fine not exceeding level 5 on the standard scale or both (Official Secrets Act 1989, s. 10(2)). In October 2008 a senior Whitehall official who pleaded guilty to leaving highly classified intelligence documents about Al-Qa'ida and the capabilities of the Iraqi security forces on a train was fined £2,500 by a magistrates' court for the offence.

Common Elements

Certain elements are common to all three offences:　　　　　　　　　　　　**B9.80**

The terms 'possession' and 'control' are not defined by the Act, but 'possession' appears as an essential requirement in a number of criminal offences, and, it is submitted, should be interpreted in the same way as in relation to, e.g., dangerous drugs (see **B19.19** *et seq.*). The meaning of the word 'disclose' is considered at **B9.42**.

As to the meaning of 'official direction', the Official Secrets Act 1989, s. 8(9), provides that 'official direction' means a direction duly given by a Crown servant or government contractor or by or on behalf of a prescribed body or a body of a prescribed class. The Official Secrets Act 1989 (Prescription) Order (SI 1990 No. 200), art. 4 and sch. 3, specify the bodies which have the power to impose official restrictions for the purpose of s. 8(9); the Civil Aviation Authority and the Investigatory Powers Tribunal have such power.

As to the only circumstances in which a disclosure is made with lawful authority, see s. 7 of the Act and **B9.54**.

Elements Specific to s. 8(1) and (4)

The meanings of 'Crown servant' and 'government contractor' are considered at **B9.52** and **B9.81** **B9.53**. However, for the purposes of this offence, the Official Secrets Act 1989, s. 8(3), provides that 'Crown servant' includes a person notified within the meaning of s. 1(1), who is not otherwise either a Crown servant or a government contractor (see **B9.40**).

Elements Specific to s. 8(5)

The information protected by this offence is that which it would be an offence to disclose under **B9.82** s. 6 of the Act (see **B9.75**). As to such information, see s. 6(1).

Specific Defences

The accused's belief that he had lawful authority for the disclosure is a defence to all three **B9.83** charges under the Official Secrets Act 1989, s. 8. As to this and other defences, see **B9.44**.

In relation to the offence under s. 8(1) only, the Official Secrets Act 1989, s. 8(2), provides that it is a defence for a Crown servant to prove that at the time of the alleged offence he believed that he was acting in accordance with his official duty and had no reasonable cause to believe otherwise. Although the legal burden of proving this defence appears to lie on the accused, it is likely that only an evidential burden would be compatible with the ECHR, Article 6 (see *Keogh* [2007] 3 All ER 789 and **F3.18** *et seq.*).

UNLAWFUL INTERCEPTION OF COMMUNICATIONS BY PUBLIC AND PRIVATE SYSTEMS

B9.84   The Regulation of Investigatory Powers Act 2000 (RIPA 2000), s. 1, creates two interception offences. One (s. 1(1)) is concerned with the interception of communications transmitted by either public postal or public telecommunications systems; the other offence (s. 1(2)) is concerned with the interception of communications transmitted by private telecommunications systems.

Definition

B9.85
Regulation of Investigatory Powers Act 2000, s. 1

(1)   It shall be an offence for a person intentionally and without lawful authority to intercept, at any place in the United Kingdom, any communication in the course of its transmission by means of—
   (a) a public postal service; or
   (b) a public telecommunication system.

(1A) The Interception of Communications Commissioner may serve a monetary penalty notice on a person if the Commissioner—
   (a) considers that the person—
      (i)   has without lawful authority intercepted, at any place in the United Kingdom, any communication in the course of its transmission by means of a public telecommunication system, and
      (ii) was not, at the time of the interception, making an attempt to act in accordance with an interception warrant which might, in the opinion of the Commissioner, explain the interception concerned, and
   (b) does not consider that the person has committed an offence under subsection (1).

(1B) Schedule A1 (which makes further provision about monetary penalty notices) has effect.

(2)   It shall be an offence for a person—
   (a) intentionally and without lawful authority, and
   (b) otherwise than in circumstances in which his conduct is excluded by subsection (6) from criminal liability under this subsection,

   to intercept, at any place in the United Kingdom, any communication in the course of its transmission by means of a private telecommunication system.

Procedure

B9.86   The offences are triable either way (RIPA 2000, s. 1(7)). When tried on indictment, this is normally a class 3 offence, but see CPD XIII, para. B (see Supplement, **PD-97**) for the additional factors that the court considers on allocation. Proceedings for an offence cannot be instituted except, in England and Wales, with the consent of the DPP (s. 1(8)(a)). Section 1(1A) and (1B), which came into force on 16 June 2011, were inserted by the Regulation of Investigatory Powers (Monetary Penalty Notices and Consents for Interceptions) Regulations 2011 (SI 2011 No. 1340) and implement Council Directives 95/46/EC (processing and free movement of personal data) and 2002/58/EC (privacy and electronic communications). They give effect to a new scheme whereby the Interception of Communications Commissioner can impose a monetary penalty notice on a person, effectively imposing a fine if that person fails to comply with a direction requiring cessation of specified interception of communications.

Sentence

B9.87   The maximum punishment is: on conviction on indictment, imprisonment for a term not exceeding two years, or a fine, or both; and, on summary conviction, a fine not exceeding the statutory maximum (RIPA 2000, s. 1(7)).

Elements of the Offence: Postal Service and Telecommunications Systems

B9.88   Section 2(1) of the RIPA 2000 defines various terms.

'Public postal service' means any postal service which is offered to or provided to, or to a substantial section of, the public in one or more parts of the UK. 'Postal service' means any service which (a) consists in the following, or in any one or more of them, namely, the collection, sorting, conveyance, distribution and delivery (whether in the UK or elsewhere) of postal items; and (b) is offered or provided as a service the main purpose of which, or one of the main purposes of which, is to make available, or to facilitate, a means of transmission from place to place of postal items containing communications.

'Public telecommunication system' means any such parts of a telecommunication system by means of which any public telecommunications service is provided as are located in the UK.

'Telecommunication system' means any system (including the apparatus comprised in it) which exists (whether wholly or partly in the UK or elsewhere) for the purpose of facilitating the transmission of communications by any means involving the use of electrical or electromagnetic energy.

'Public telecommunications service' means any telecommunications service which is offered or provided to, or to a substantial section of, the public in any one or more parts of the UK.

'Telecommunications service' means any service that consists in the provision of access to, and of facilities for making use of, any telecommunication system (whether or not one provided by the person providing the service), and this includes any case where a service consists in or includes facilitating the creation, management or storage of communications transmitted, or that may be transmitted, by means of such a system.

'Private telecommunication system' means any telecommunication system which, not being a public telecommunication system, is a system which satisfies certain conditions: (a) it is attached, directly or indirectly and whether or not for the purpose of the communication in question, to a public telecommunication system; and (b) there is apparatus comprised in the system which is both located in the UK and used (with or without other apparatus) for making the attachment to the public telecommunication system.

General terms such as 'apparatus' and 'communication' and related terms are defined in the RIPA 2000, s. 81.

Interception

Section 2(2) of the RIPA 2000 defines 'interception' for the purposes of the Act. A person intercepts a communication in the course of its transmission by means of a telecommunication system if, and only if, he (a) so modifies or interferes with the system or its operation, (b) so monitors transmissions made by means of the system, or (c) so monitors transmissions made by wireless telegraphy to or from apparatus comprised in the system, as to make some or all of the contents of the communication available, while being transmitted, to a person other than the sender or intended recipient of the communication.   **B9.89**

References to the interception of a communication do not include reference to the interception of any communication broadcast for general reception (s. 2(3)).

Modification of a telecommunication system includes references to the attachment of any apparatus to, or other modification of or interference with (a) any part of the system, or (b) any wireless telegraphy apparatus used for making transmissions to or from apparatus comprised in the system (s. 2(6)).

An interception takes place in the UK if, and only if, the modification, interference or monitoring or, in the case of a postal item, the interception is effected by conduct within the UK and the communication is either (a) intercepted in the course of its transmission by means of a public telecommunication system; or (b) intercepted in the course of its transmission by means of a private telecommunication system in a case in which the sender or intended recipient of the communication is in the UK (s. 2(4)).

The period during which a communication is being transmitted by a telecommunication system includes any time when the system by means of which the communication is being, or has been, transmitted is used for storing it in a manner that enables the intended recipient to collect it or otherwise to have access to it (s. 2(7)). Section 2(7) has the effect of extending the concept of 'in the course of transmission' so as to include a situation where a voice-mail message had been initially received by the intended recipient and was stored in the communication system where the intended recipient might have continued access to it (*Edmondson* [2013] 4 All ER 999; the Court of Appeal held that s. 2(7) went beyond the EU Directives to which the RIPA 2000 was giving effect and distinguished *R (NTL) v Ipswich Crown Court* [2003] QB 131 on the basis it had failed to consider the effect of the words 'or otherwise to have access to it' in s. 2(7); the Court declined to permit the case to proceed to the Supreme Court). The contents of a communication made available to a person while being transmitted includes any case in which any of the contents of the communication, while being transmitted, are diverted or recorded so as to be available to a person subsequently (s. 2(8)). The tape recording of a telephone call by one party to it, without the knowledge of the other party, does not amount to interception of a communication within s. 2 (*Hardy* [2003] 1 Cr App R 494). Nor does a recording of what one person said on the telephone, picked up by a surveillance device placed in his car which did not record any speech by the other party (*E* [2004] 1 WLR 3279; *Allsopp* [2005] EWCA Crim 703). The compatibility of interception (and surveillance) which has been authorised under the RIPA 2000 with the ECHR, Article 8, was confirmed in *Kennedy v UK* (2011) 52 EHRR 207.

'Postal item' means any letter, postcard or other such thing in writing as may be used by the sender for imparting information to the recipient, or any packet or parcel (s. 2(11)).

B9.90   **Traffic Data**   The exception in relation to traffic data provides that references to the interception of a communication in the course of its transmission by means of a postal service or telecommunication system do not include reference to (a) any conduct that takes place in relation only to so much of the communication as consists in any traffic data comprised in or attached to a communication (whether by the sender or otherwise) for the purposes of any postal service or telecommunication system by means of which it is being or may be transmitted; or (b) any such conduct, in connection with conduct falling within paragraph (a), as gives a person who is neither the sender nor the intended recipient only so much access to a communication as is necessary for the purpose of identifying traffic data so comprised or attached (s. 2(5)). 'Traffic data' is defined in s. 2(9).

References, in relation to traffic data comprising signals for the actuation of apparatus, to a telecommunication system by means of which a communication is being or may be transmitted include references to any telecommunication system in which that apparatus is comprised, and references to traffic data being attached to a communication include references to the data and the communication being logically associated with each other (s. 2(10)). 'Data' in relation to a postal item means anything written on the outside of the item (s. 2(10)).

Lawful Authority

B9.91   Regulation of Investigatory Powers Act 2000, ss. 1, 3 and 4

1.—(5) Conduct has lawful authority for the purposes of this section if, and only if—
   (a) it is authorised by or under section 3 or 4;
   (b) it takes place in accordance with a warrant under section 5 ('an interception warrant'); or
   (c) it is in exercise, in relation to any stored communication, of any statutory power that is exercised (apart from this section) for the purpose of obtaining information or of taking possession of any document or other property;
   and conduct (whether or not prohibited by this section) which has lawful authority for the purpose of this section by virtue of paragraph (a) or (b) shall also be taken to be lawful for all other purposes.
3.—(1) Conduct by any person consisting in the interception of a communication is authorised by this section if the communication is one which is both—
   (a) a communication sent by a person who has consented to the interception; and
   (b) a communication the intended recipient of which has so consented.

(2) Conduct by any person consisting in the interception of a communication is authorised by this section if—
  (a) the communication is one sent by, or intended for, a person who has consented to the interception; and
  (b) surveillance by means of that interception has been authorised under Part II.
(3) Conduct consisting in the interception of a communication is authorised by this section if—
  (a) it is conduct by or on behalf of a person who provides a postal service or a telecommunications service; and
  (b) it takes place for purposes connected with the provision or operation of that service or with the enforcement, in relation to that service, of any enactment relating to the use of postal services or telecommunications services.
(3A) Conduct consisting in the interception of a communication in the course of its transmission by means of a public postal service is authorised by this section if it is conduct—
  (a) under section 159 of the Customs and Excise Management Act 1979 as applied by virtue of—
    (i) section 105 of the Postal Services Act 2000 (power to open postal items etc); or
    (ii) that section 105 and another enactment; and
  (b) by an officer of Revenue and Customs.
(4) Conduct by any person consisting in the interception of a communication in the course of its transmission by means of wireless telegraphy is authorised by this section if it takes place—
  (a) with the authority of a designated person under section 48 of the Wireless Telegraphy Act 2006 (interception and disclosure of wireless telegraphy messages); and
  (b) for purposes connected with anything falling within subsection (5).
(5) Each of the following falls within this subsection—
  (a) the grant of wireless telegraphy licences under the Wireless Telegraphy Act 2006;
  (b) the prevention or detection of anything which constitutes interference with wireless telegraphy; and
  (c) the enforcement of—
    (i) any provision of Part 2 (other than chapter 2 and sections 27 to 31) or Part 3 of that Act, or
    (ii) any enactment not falling within sub-paragraph (i),
  that relates to such interference.
4.—(1) Conduct by any person ('the interceptor') consisting in the interception of a communication in the course of its transmission by means of a telecommunication system is authorised by this section if—
  (a) the interception is carried out for the purpose of obtaining information about the communications of a person who, or who the interceptor has reasonable grounds for believing, is in a country or territory outside the United Kingdom;
  (b) the interception relates to the use of a telecommunications service provided to persons in that country or territory which is either—
    (i) a public telecommunications service; or
    (ii) a telecommunications service that would be a public telecommunications service if the persons to whom it is offered or provided were members of the public in a part of the United Kingdom;
  (c) the person who provides that service (whether the interceptor or another person) is required by the law of that country or territory to carry out, secure or facilitate the interception in question;
  (d) the situation is one in relation to which such further conditions as may be prescribed by regulations made by the Secretary of State are required to be satisfied before conduct may be treated as authorised by virtue of this subsection; and
  (e) the conditions so prescribed are satisfied in relation to that situation.

The Telecommunications (Lawful Business Practice) (Interception of Communications)   **B9.92**
Regulations 2000 (SI 2000 No. 2699) have been passed under s. 4(2) of the RIPA 2000, authorising certain lawful business practices. These authorisations do not exceed those permitted by Articles 5.2 and 14.1 of Directive 97/66/EC. In particular, the Regulations specify that interceptions can only be authorised if the system controller has made all reasonable efforts to inform the users of the system that communications may be intercepted. The Information Commissioner's Office has issued guidance to businesses on employment practices which includes information on the circumstances in which interceptions may be permitted within the workplace and the precautions which must be taken by employers to protect the privacy of the workforce.

The Regulation of Investigatory Powers (Conditions for the Lawful Interception of Persons out-side the United Kingdom) Regulations 2004 (SI 2004 No. 157) prescribe the following conditions under s. 4(1)(d): (a) the interception is carried out for the purposes of a criminal investigation; and (b) the criminal investigation is being carried out in a country or territory that is party to an international agreement designated for the purposes of s. 1(4). The Regulation of Investigatory Powers (Designation of an International Agreement) Order 2004 (SI 2004 No. 158) provides that the Convention on Mutual Assistance in Criminal Matters between the Member States of the European Union is a designated international agreement for the purposes of s. 1(4).

Probably the most important means of making an interception lawful will be through action taken under an interception warrant. There are extensive statutory procedures in relation to the issuing, exercising and oversight of such warrants (RIPA 2000, ss. 5 to 11); the Protection of Freedoms Act 2012, part 2, chapter 2 (in force from 1 November 2012: SI 2012 No. 2075), creates a new requirement (and associated procedures) for local authorities to obtain judicial approval before seeking to gain access to or disclose communications data under the RIPA 2000.

The admissibility of foreign intercept evidence will often make it disclosable under the usual principles (*Koc* [2008] EWCA Crim 77).

It should be noted that providers of relevant services, including persons outside the UK (see the Data Retention and Investigatory Powers Act 2014, s. 4), have an obligation to maintain an interception capability if required by the Secretary of State under the RIPA 2000, s. 12.

B9.93 Further, there is a provision providing a general saving for lawful conduct:

Regulation of Investigatory Powers Act 2000, s. 80

Nothing in any of the provisions of this Act by virtue of which conduct of any description is or may be authorised by any warrant, authorisation or notice, or by virtue of which information may be obtained in any manner, shall be construed—

    (a) as making it unlawful to engage in any conduct of that description which is not otherwise unlawful under this Act and would not be unlawful apart from this Act;

    (b) as otherwise requiring—

        (i)   the issue, grant or giving of such a warrant, authorisation or notice, or

        (ii) the taking of any step for or towards obtaining the authority of such a warrant, authorisation or notice,

        before any such conduct of that description is engaged in; or

    (c) as prejudicing any power to obtain information by any means not involving conduct that may be authorised under this Act.

As to the continuing validity of a warrant issued under the Interception of Communications Act 1985, see the RIPA 2000, s. 82(4).

Private Telecommunications Interceptions: Defence

B9.94 A person's conduct is excluded from criminal liability for the offence contrary to the RIPA 2000, s. 1(2), if he is a person with a right to control the operation or the use of the system; or he has the express or implied consent of such a person to make the interception (s. 1(6)). In *Stanford* [2006] 1 WLR 1554, it was held that 'control' means 'authorise and forbid' and not the unre-stricted ability physically to use and operate the system. Any other approach would contravene the purposes of the legislation.

INCITEMENT TO DISAFFECTION

B9.95   Incitement to Disaffection Act 1934, ss. 1 and 2

    1. If any person maliciously and advisedly endeavours to seduce any member of His Majesty's forces from his duty or allegiance to His Majesty, he shall be guilty of an offence under this Act.

2.—(1) If any person, with intent to commit or to aid, abet, counsel, or procure the commission of an offence under section 1 of this Act, has in his possession or under his control any document of such a nature that the dissemination of copies thereof among members of His Majesty's forces would constitute such an offence, he shall be guilty of an offence under this Act.

Police Act 1996, s. 91

(1) Any person who causes, or attempts to cause, or does any act calculated to cause, disaffection amongst the members of any police force, or induces or attempts to induce, or does any act calculated to induce, any member of a police force to withhold his services, shall be guilty of an offence...

(2) This section applies in the case of—

    (a) special constables appointed for a police area,

    (b) members of the Civil Nuclear Constabulary, and

    (c) members of the British Transport Police Force,

as it applies in the case of members of a police force.

There are like offences in relation to Ministry of Defence police (see the Ministry of Defence Police Act 1987, s. 6).

Procedure

Incitement to Disaffection Act 1934, s. 3   B9.96

(2) No prosecution in England under this Act shall take place without the consent of the Director of Public Prosecutions.

(3) Where a prosecution under this Act is being carried on by the Director of Public Prosecutions, a court of summary jurisdiction shall not deal with the case summarily without the consent of the Director.

The offences under the Incitement to Disaffection Act 1934 and the Police Act 1996 are triable either way. When tried on indictment they are class 1B offences.

Sentence

The maximum penalties are: B9.97

Incitement to Disaffection Act 1934, s. 1: on indictment, two years and/or a fine; summarily, four months and/or a fine not exceeding the statutory maximum (Incitement to Disaffection Act 1934, s. 3(1)). The court also has power to order the destruction or other disposal of any documents connected with the offence after conviction of the accused and after expiration of the time during which an appeal may be lodged (Incitement to Disaffection Act 1934, s. 3(4)).

Police Act 1996, s. 91: on indictment, two years and/or a fine; summarily, six months and/or a fine not exceeding the statutory maximum.

Elements

It is not necessary to show that any particular individual was the object of the attempted seduc-   B9.98
tion; members of the armed forces, or a police force generally will suffice (*Bowman* (1912) 76 JP 271). Evidential and *mens rea* requirements were considered in *Fuller* (1797) 2 Leach 790. 'Allegiance' was considered in *Joyce v DPP* [1946] AC 347, and the correct form of the indictment was considered in *Arrowsmith* [1975] QB 678.

The method of attempted seduction, whether by written or oral communication, is irrelevant, though circumstances such as the offering of an inducement or the use of threats or blackmail will no doubt affect sentence.

Section B10   Terrorism, Piracy and Hijacking

TERRORISM: OVERVIEW

B10.1   This section deals with the investigative anti-terrorist powers, the substantive offences relating to terrorism, the sentencing guidance relevant to those offences and the financial powers which aim to obstruct terrorist funding. TPIMs and the Terrorism Prevention and Investigation Measures Act 2011 are also considered. Miscellaneous offences related to nuclear and chemical weapons and piracy and hijacking, all of which might be committed in a terrorist context, are also covered.

In terms of investigation, the TA 2000 gave permanent effect to anti-terrorist powers for the first time. Those powers have since been supplemented by the Anti-terrorism, Crime and Security Act 2001 (A-tCSA 2001), the Terrorism Act 2006 (TA 2006) and the Counter-Terrorism Act 2008 (C-TA 2008). The financial powers available to the authorities to stem the flow of funds to terrorist groups have become more extensive (see, e.g., the Terrorism Asset Freezing Act 2010).

Trials of terrorist offences are governed by the Terrorism Protocol issued by the President of the Queen's Bench Division on 30 January 2007. The Protocol provides for administrative arrangements specific to terrorist cases.

By virtue of the C-TA 2008, s. 28, specified terrorist offences may be tried in any place in the UK, irrespective of where in the UK the offence was committed. The offence is treated for jurisdictional purposes as having been committed in the place where proceedings are taken.

Definition of Terrorism

B10.2
Terrorism Act 2000, s. 1

(1)   In this Act 'terrorism' means the use or threat of action where—
   (a)   the action falls within subsection (2),
   (b)   the use or threat is designed to influence the government or an international governmental organisation or to intimidate the public or a section of the public, and
   (c)   the use or threat is made for the purpose of advancing a political, religious, ideological, or racial cause.

(2) Action falls within this subsection if it—
  (a) involves serious violence against a person,
  (b) involves serious damage to property,
  (c) endangers a person's life, other than that of the person committing the action,
  (d) creates a serious risk to the health or safety of the public or a section of the public, or
  (e) is designed seriously to interfere with or seriously to disrupt an electronic system.

The definition of terrorism is widely drawn and, in essence, involves the use or threat of violence for political, religious, ideological or racial causes. Terms used in s. 1(1) and (2) are defined in s. 1(4) and 1(5). The references to action, person, public, property and government apply equally whether the action, person, public property or government is inside or outside the UK (s. 1(4)(a)–(d) and (5)). In *F* [2007] QB 960 it was held that the meaning of the phrase 'a country other than the United Kingdom' in s. 1(4)(d) is plain and the terrorist legislation applies equally in respect of undemocratic countries as it does in relation to democratic governments. In *Gul* [2012] 1 Cr App R 504 the Court of Appeal held that there was nothing in international law that required the terms of s. 1 to be read down so as to exclude those perpetrating military attacks in a time of Non-International Armed Conflict. The Supreme Court upheld that decision in *Gul* [2014] 1 All ER 463. The certified question was whether the definition of 'terrorism' in the TA 2000, s. 1, operated so as to include any or all military attacks by a non-State armed group against any or all State or inter-governmental organisation armed forces in the context of a non-international armed conflict. The Court concluded that, although it had concerns about the breadth of the definition (referring to the reports of the Independent Reviewer and the comments on this issue from David Anderson QC in particular), there was no basis in domestic law to restrict the statutory definition in the way advanced by the appellant, namely that:

(a) some provisions of the 2000 and 2006 Acts were enacted to give effect to the UK's treaty obligations concerned with the suppression of terrorism, and that 'terrorism' should accordingly be given a meaning which accords with the international law norm, consistent with the definition in the treaty to which effect is being given, and
(b) as the 2000 and 2006 Acts criminalise certain 'terrorist' actions committed outside the UK, the meaning of 'terrorism' in those statutes should not be wider than what is accepted as an international norm.

The Court noted the absence of any accepted norm in international law as to what constitutes terrorism, citing its recent decision in *Al-Sirri v Secretary of State for the Home Department* [2013] 1 AC 745. It observed that, whilst some UN and other texts provided significant support for the argument that terrorism did not extend to the acts of insurgents or 'freedom fighters' in non-international armed conflicts, it was insufficient to demonstrate a rule of international law requiring the definition to be read down as being in conflict with the UK's ECHR or other international law obligations. It reiterated the point made in *Al-Sirri*, that 'an attack on ISAF in Afghanistan is in principle capable of being an act contrary to the purposes and principles of the United Nations' and such an attack therefore can constitute 'terrorism'. The Court pointed to UN resolutions which referred to the activities of Al-Qa'ida and the Taliban as 'terrorism', even though their actions involved insurgents attacking forces of States and inter-governmental organisations in non-international armed conflict and noted that insurgents do not benefit from combatant immunity in non-international armed conflicts.

Next, the Court considered the argument that the TA 2000, ss. 62 to 64, and some provisions of the TA 2006, gave effect to the UK's obligations under international conventions, two of which exclude insurgent attacks on military forces in non-international armed conflicts from their definitions. However, the Court declined to read down the definition of terrorism because some of the activities which became offences under the TA 2000 were included in order to fulfil international law obligations; the UK can go beyond its international law obligations in criminalising conduct. And, even if the wide definition of terrorism in s. 1 had to be read down for the purposes of ss. 62 to 64, it did not have to be read down when interpreting the rest of the Act.

INVESTIGATIVE POWERS UNDER
THE TERRORISM ACT 2000

B10.3 Sections 32 to 39 of, and schs. 5 and 6 to, the TA 2000 provide a plethora of powers to be deployed in terrorist investigations. They are dealt with below. The definition of a terrorist investigation is contained in s. 32.

Terrorism Act 2000, s. 32

(1) In this Act, 'terrorist investigation' means an investigation of—
   (a) the commission, preparation or instigation of acts of terrorism,
   (b) an act which appears to have been done for the purposes of terrorism,
   (c) the resources of a proscribed organisation,
   (d) the possibility of making an order under s. 3(3), or
   (e) the commission, preparation or instigation of an offence under this Act or under Part 1 of the Terrorism Act 2006 other than an offence under section 1 or 2 of that Act.

Cordons

B10.4 Police officers, usually of the rank of at least superintendent, are empowered under ss. 33 and 34 of the TA 2000 to designate an area as a cordoned area for the purposes of a terrorist investigation. An order may be made only when it is considered expedient for the purposes of a terrorist investigation. The cordoned area must be demarcated by tape or in any other manner that the officer considers appropriate. Sections 35 and 36 provide for the duration of a cordon and the powers of a constable in relation to that cordon respectively. A failure to comply with the requirements of a constable in relation to the cordoned area is a summary offence punishable by up to three months' imprisonment.

Securing Information and Evidence: Search and Seizure Powers

B10.5 Section 37 of the TA 2000 gives effect to sch. 5, which contains a number of provisions relating to the securing of information for the purposes of terrorist investigations. Any application in respect of sch. 5 is now governed by part 6 of the CrimPR.

Paragraph 1 of sch. 5 governs the procedure for search warrants. An application may be made to a justice of the peace for a warrant to search premises in order to seize material which a constable has reasonable grounds for believing is likely to be of substantial value to a terrorist investigation and must be seized in order to prevent it being concealed, lost, damaged or destroyed (para. 1(3)). By virtue of para. 1(2A), the premises to be searched may be specified (a 'specific premises warrant') or may concern all premises occupied or controlled by a person specified in the application (an 'all premises warrant'). A warrant cannot authorise the seizure of legally privileged material, nor may a constable executing the warrant require any person to remove any clothing in public other than headgear, footwear, an outer coat, jacket or gloves. The application may be granted if the justice of the peace is satisfied that the warrant is sought for the purposes of a terrorist investigation (para. 1(5)(a)), that the reasonable grounds for the belief held by the constable are made out and the material to be seized is not legally privileged (para. 1(5)(b)), that the warrant is likely to be necessary in the circumstances of the case (para. 1(5)(c)) and, in the case of an all premises warrant, that it is not reasonably practicable to specify all the premises owned or occupied by the person concerned (para. 1(5)(d)).

Paragraph 2 of sch. 5 concerns an application for a specified premises warrant for non-residential premises by an officer of at least the rank of superintendent. Even if the justice of the peace is not satisfied that the condition in para. 1(5)(c) is satisfied, he may grant the warrant provided that he is satisfied that para. 1(5)(a) and (b) are made out. Such a warrant must be executed within 24 hours of it being issued.

B10.6 Officers of at least the rank of superintendent (or in urgent cases, officers of lesser rank) may themselves authorise the search of specified premises by virtue of para. 3 of sch. 5. Such authorisation may be given when the premises are within an area subject to a cordon created under the TA 2000, s. 33 (see **B10.4**). Paragraph 1(3) of sch. 5 (the authorising officer must have reasonable grounds for believing that the material has value etc.) applies. No legally privileged material may be seized. Such a search may be authorised on any number of occasions during the period that the cordon is in existence. It is an offence punishable with up to three months' imprisonment and/or a fine to the level 4 maximum to obstruct such a search.

Paragraph 4 defines 'excluded material', 'items subject to legal professional privilege' and 'special procedure material' as having the meanings given to them by the PACE 1984, ss. 11, 10 and 14, respectively (see **D1.147**, **F9.62** and **D1.149**).

Applications for warrants to search for excluded material or special procedure material must be **B10.7** made to a circuit judge under sch. 5, paras. 5 and 6.

Terrorism Act 2000, sch. 5

5.—(1) A constable may apply to a circuit judge for an order under this paragraph for the purposes of a terrorist investigation.
(2) An application for an order shall relate to particular material, or material of a particular description, which consists of or includes excluded material or special procedure material.
(3) An order under this paragraph may require a specified person—
   (a) to produce to a constable within a specified period for seizure and retention any material which he has in his possession, custody or power and to which the application relates;
   (b) to give a constable access to any material of the kind mentioned in paragraph (a) within a specified period;
   (c) to state to the best of his knowledge and belief the location of material to which the application relates if it is not in, and it will not come into, his possession, custody or power within the period specified under paragraph (a) or (b).
(4) For the purposes of this paragraph—
   (a) an order may specify a person only if he appears to the circuit judge to have in his possession, custody or power any of the material to which the application relates, and
   (b) a period specified in an order shall be the period of seven days beginning with the date of the order unless it appears to the judge that a different period would be appropriate in the particular circumstances of the application.
(5) Where a circuit judge makes an order under sub-paragraph (3)(b) in relation to material on any premises, he may, on the application of a constable, order any person who appears to the judge to be entitled to grant entry to the premises to allow any constable to enter the premises to obtain access to the material.
6.—(1) A circuit judge may grant an application under paragraph 5 if satisfied—
   (a) that the material to which the application relates consists of or includes excluded material or special procedure material,
   (b) that it does not include items subject to legal privilege, and
   (c) that the conditions in sub-paragraphs (2) and (3) are satisfied in respect of that material.
(2) The first condition is that—
   (a) the order is sought for the purposes of a terrorist investigation, and
   (b) there are reasonable grounds for believing that the material is likely to be of substantial value, whether by itself or together with other material, to a terrorist investigation.
(3) The second condition is that there are reasonable grounds for believing that it is in the public interest that the material should be produced or that access to it should be given having regard—
   (a) to the benefit likely to accrue to a terrorist investigation if the material is obtained, and
   (b) to the circumstances under which the person concerned has any of the material in his possession, custody or power.

By virtue of para. 7 an order under para. 5 may be made in relation to material which is expected **B10.8** to come into existence within 28 days of the making of the order. An order under para. 5 does not confer any rights of access or production in relation to legally privileged information and has effect notwithstanding any statutory restriction on disclosure. Where a para. 5 order relates to computer material, it shall have effect as an order to produce or give access to the material in a form which is visible and legible (para. 8).

B

Part B Offences

An order under para. 5 may be made against a government department as defined by the Crown Proceedings Act 1947 (para. 9).

Paragraph 11 governs the procedure for making an application to a circuit judge by a constable for a specific premises warrant or any premises warrant, applying a similar scheme to that under para. 1. Under para. 12, a circuit judge may grant a specific premises warrant if he is satisfied that a para. 5 order relating to excluded or special procedure material at the premises has not been complied with (para. 12(1)), or (under para. 12(2)) there are reasonable grounds for believing that there is special procedure or excluded material (which is not legally privileged material) on the premises and the conditions in paras. 12(3) and (4) are met. The condition in para. 12(3) is that the warrant is for the purposes of a terrorist investigation and the material is likely to be of substantial value to a terrorist investigation. The condition in para. 12(4) is that it is not appropriate to make an order under para. 5 either because it is not practicable to communicate with any person entitled to produce or grant access to the material or grant entry to the relevant premises or because a terrorist investigation may be seriously prejudiced unless a constable can secure immediate access to the material. Under para. 12(2A), a circuit or district judge may grant an application for an all premises warrant if satisfied that an order under para. 5 has not been complied with and the person specified in the application is also specified in the order. An all premises warrant may also be granted by a circuit or district judge under para. 12(2B) if there are reasonable grounds for believing that there is excluded or special procedure material (which is not legally privileged material) in the premises in question and the conditions in para. 12(3) and (4) are met.

B10.9   Schedule 5 also provides for a system of explanation orders requiring a person to provide an explanation for any material which is seized under para. 1 or 11 or produced or made available under para. 5. Paragraph 13 provides that a constable may apply to a circuit judge for such an order. A lawyer may be required to provide the name and address of a client (para. 13(3)) but is not required to disclose information he would be entitled to refuse to disclose on the grounds of legal professional privilege in proceedings in the High Court (para. 13(2)); statements in compliance with such an order may be made orally or in writing and may only be used in evidence against the maker for prosecution for an offence under para. 14 (para. 13(4)). Paragraph 14 creates an offence; it is an offence to make a statement in purported compliance with an order under para. 13 which the maker knows is false or misleading in relation to a material particular or recklessly to make a statement which is false or misleading in a material particular. Such an offence is triable either way and punishable summarily with imprisonment up to six months and/or a fine to the statutory maximum. On indictment, the maximum sentence is one of two years' imprisonment and/or a fine up to the statutory maximum (para. 14(2)).

In circumstances where an officer of at least the rank of superintendent has reasonable grounds for believing that the case is one of great emergency and immediate action is necessary, para. 15 allows him to sign a written order giving a constable the authority to carry out a search which would be given by a warrant secured under para. 1 or para. 11 (para. 15(2)). If such a written order is signed, the particulars of the case must be notified to the Secretary of State as soon as is reasonably practicable. Any person wilfully obstructing such a search commits an offence punishable with up to three months' imprisonment and/or a fine up to level 4. Moreover, under para. 16, an officer of at least the rank of superintendent, if he has reasonable grounds for believing that the case is one of great emergency, may require by written notice a person to provide an explanation of any material seized in pursuance of an order under para. 15. A person commits an offence if he fails to comply with such a notice, punishable with up to six months' imprisonment and/or a fine up to level 5. It is a defence to the alleged offence that the person had a reasonable excuse for the failure to provide the explanation.

Financial Information

B10.10   Section 38 of the TA 2000 gives effect to sch. 6. An application for an order under sch. 6 must be made by a police officer of at least the rank of superintendent. A circuit judge should make the order only if satisfied that the order is sought for the purposes of a terrorist investigation, the tracing of terrorist property is desirable for the purposes of the investigation, and the order will enhance the effectiveness of the investigation (paras. 2, 3 and 5). Any application for an order pursuant to sch. 6 is now governed by part 6 of the CrimPR.

Where a circuit judge has made the relevant supporting order, a named constable may require a financial institution to provide customer information for the purposes of a terrorist investigation (sch. 6, para. 1(1)). That information must be supplied in such a way and within such time as the constable specifies and notwithstanding any restriction on the disclosure of information imposed by statute or otherwise (para. 1(2)). It is a summary offence for the institution to fail to comply with the requirement (para. 1(3)), but it is a defence for the institution to prove that the information required was not in the institution's possession, or that it was not reasonably practicable for the institution to comply with the requirement (para. 1(4)). The penalty for the offence is a fine not exceeding level 5 on the standard scale (para. 1(5)). If the offence was committed with the consent or connivance of an officer of the institution, or was attributable to neglect on the part of an officer of the institution, that officer, as well as the institution, is guilty of the offence (para. 8(1) and (2)). The maximum penalty is imprisonment for a term not exceeding six months, a fine not exceeding level 5 on the standard scale, or both (para. 8(3)).

Customer Information and Business Relationship 'Customer information' is defined in para. 7(1) and includes details of bank account numbers, start and end dates of accounts, past and present addresses and the identity of any person sharing the account.   **B10.11**

A 'business relationship' exists between a financial institution and a person if (and only if) (a) there is an arrangement between them designed to facilitate the carrying out of frequent or regular transactions between them, and (b) the total amount of payments to be made in the course of the arrangement is neither known nor capable of being ascertained when the arrangement is made (para. 7(2)).

If a financial institution provides 'customer information', it is not admissible in evidence in criminal proceedings against the institution or any of its officers or employees (para. 9(1)), except in relation to proceedings for an offence contrary to para. 1(3) or para. 8.

Account Monitoring Orders

Account monitoring orders can be imposed on financial institutions in relation to accounts (whether all or particular) held by any person specified in an application by virtue of s. 38A of and sch. 6A to the TA 2000. Any application for such an order is now governed by part 6 of the CrimPR. During a specified period the institution is required to provide information of a specified description to an appropriate officer (para. 2(4) and (5)). The order must be complied with irrespective of any legislative or other restriction on the disclosure of information (para. 6(2)). Ordinarily, a statement made by a financial institution in response to an account monitoring order may not be used in evidence against it in criminal proceedings. However, there are certain exceptions to that rule. The statement may be used: **B10.12**

(a) in the case of proceedings for contempt of court;
(b) in the case of proceedings under s. 23 (forfeiture) where the financial institution has been convicted of an offence under any of ss. 15 to 18 (terrorist property offences: see **B10.115** to **B10.135**); or
(c) on a prosecution for an offence where, in giving evidence, the financial institution makes a statement inconsistent with the first statement (but the statement may not be used against a financial institution unless evidence relating to it is adduced or a question relating to it is asked by or on behalf of the financial institution in the proceedings arising out of the prosecution (para. 7(1)–(3)).

Disclosure of and Interference with Information Offences

Terrorism Act 2000, s. 39   **B10.13**

(1) Subsection (2) applies where a person knows or has reasonable cause to suspect that a constable is conducting or proposes to conduct a terrorist investigation.

(2) The person commits an offence if he—
   (a) discloses to another anything which is likely to prejudice the investigation, or
   (b) interferes with material which is likely to be relevant to the investigation.
(3) Subsection (4) applies where a person knows or has reasonable cause to suspect that a disclosure has been or will be made under any of sections 19 to 21B or 38B.
(4) The person commits an offence if he—
   (a) discloses to another anything which is likely to prejudice an investigation resulting from the disclosure under that section, or
   (b) interferes with material which is likely to be relevant to an investigation resulting from the disclosure under that section.
(5) It is a defence for a person charged with an offence under subsection (2) or (4) to prove—
   (a) that he did not know and had no reasonable cause to suspect that the disclosure or interference was likely to affect a terrorist investigation, or
   (b) that he had a reasonable excuse for the disclosure or interference.
(6) Subsections (2) and (4) do not apply to a disclosure which is made by a professional legal adviser—
   (a) to his client or to his client's representative in connection with the provision of legal advice by the adviser to the client and not with a view to furthering a criminal purpose, or
   (b) to any person for the purpose of actual or contemplated legal proceedings and not with a view to furthering a criminal purpose.
(6A) Subsections (2) and (4) do not apply if—
   (a) the disclosure is of a matter within section 21D(2) or (3)(a) (terrorist property: tipping off), and
   (b) the information on which the disclosure is based came to the person in the course of a business in the regulated sector.
(7) A person guilty of an offence under this section shall be liable—
   (a) on conviction on indictment, to imprisonment for a term not exceeding five years, to a fine or to both, or
   (b) on summary conviction, to imprisonment for a term not exceeding six months, to a fine not exceeding the statutory maximum or to both.
(8) For the purposes of this section—
   (a) a reference to conducting a terrorist investigation includes a reference to taking part in the conduct of, or assisting, a terrorist investigation, and
   (b) a person interferes with material if he falsifies it, conceals it, destroys it or disposes of it, or if he causes or permits another to do any of those things.
(9) The reference in subsection (6A) to a business in the regulated sector is to be construed in accordance with Schedule 3A.

There are two offences concerned with the disclosure of or interference with information linked to a terrorist investigation created by s. 39.

The defence provided for under s. 39(5)(a) is subject to the provisions of s. 118 of the TA 2000 (see **B10.29**), but the defence under s. 39(5)(b) is not. For the significance of the reverse burden, see **F3.18** *et seq.*

COUNTER-TERRORISM POWERS UNDER THE TERRORISM ACT 2000

Arrest without Warrant

B10.14   Section 41(1) of the TA 2000 provides that a constable may arrest without warrant any person whom he reasonably suspects to be a terrorist. When a person is arrested under s. 41, he must be taken as soon as is reasonably practicable to the police station which the constable who arrests him considers the most appropriate (sch. 8, para. 1(4)). PACE Code H (see **appendix 1**) applies to such detainees. A revised Code H was brought into operation by the Police and Criminal Evidence Act 1984 (Codes of Practice) (Revisions to Codes C and H) Order 2014 (SI 2014 No. 1237) on 2 June 2014. The revisions mainly concern the right of detainees to information (including information as to their rights in criminal proceedings) in accordance with the UK's obligations under EU Directive 2012/13/EU.

The detention provisions of the TA 2000 contain no provisions about bail. The effect is that neither a custody officer nor a court has power to bail a suspect detained under the TA 2000 powers before charge, either conditionally or otherwise. Consequently, at an application for a warrant for further detention (see **B10.22**) any submission that the detained person be bailed pending further enquiries is bound to fail. Moreover, a custody officer cannot grant bail after charge; only a court can do so. If a suspect is arrested on suspicion of a terrorism offence under the PACE 1984 and dealt with in accordance with that regime, the ordinary rules about detention apply, including provisions about grant of bail before or after charge.

Detention

Where a person is arrested under the power provided by the TA 2000, s. 41, the provisions of sch. 8 **B10.15** apply to his detention, treatment, review of detention and extension of detention (s. 41(2)). A person detained under s. 41 may be detained (unless detained under any other power) for no longer than the period of 48 hours beginning (a) with the time of his arrest, or (b) if he was being detained under sch. 7 when he was arrested under s. 41, with the time when his examination under sch. 7 began (s. 41(3)). If a reviewing officer reviewing the person's detention under sch. 8, part II, does not authorise continued detention, the person must (unless detained in accordance with s. 41(5) or (6) or under any other power) be released (s. 41(4)). Where a police officer intends to make an application for a warrant of further detention under sch. 8, para. 29, the person may be detained pending the making of the application (s. 41(5)). Where an application has been made under sch. 8, para. 29 or 36, he may be detained until the proceedings in relation to the application are concluded (s. 41(6)). If an application under sch. 8, para. 29 or 36, is refused, that does not prevent his continued detention under s. 41, although he must be released at the end of the relevant period.

As to post-charge questioning under the C-TA 2008, s. 22 (see **B10.22**).

Identification

An authorised person may take any steps which are reasonably necessary for (a) photographing **B10.16** the detained person, (b) measuring him, or (c) identifying him (TA 2000, sch. 8, para. 2(1)).

Detained Person's Rights

Informing a Named Person **B10.17**

Terrorism Act 2000, sch. 8, para. 6

(1) Subject to paragraph 8, a person detained under Schedule 7 or section 41 at a place in England, Wales or Northern Ireland shall be entitled, if he so requests, to have one named person informed as soon as is reasonably practicable that he is being detained there.
(2) The person named must be—
  (a) a friend of the detained person,
  (b) a relative, or
  (c) a person who is known to the detained person or who is likely to take an interest in his welfare.
(3) Where a detained person is transferred from one place to another, he shall be entitled to exercise the right under this paragraph in respect of the place to which he is transferred.

The exercise of this right may be delayed by an officer of at least the rank of superintendent if he believes that there will be interference with the investigation, evidence or a person, or that persons will be alerted and the prevention of crime or the recovery of a criminal benefit will be made more difficult (sch. 8, para. 8(1)(a), (4) and (5)). If authorisation for delay is given orally, it must be recorded in writing as soon as reasonably practicable (para. 8(6)). The reason for the delay must be communicated to the detained person and recorded as soon as reasonably practicable (para. 8(7)) and if the reason for the delay ceases to exist the detained person must be allowed to exercise his right without further delay (para. 8(8)). The detained person must be allowed to exercise the right to inform a named person of his whereabouts before the end of his period of detention under the TA 2000 (para. 8(2)).

The ABCPA 2014, sch. 9, includes amendments to the TA 2000, sch. 8. Certain rights conferred by sch. 8, which previously applied only to persons detained at a police station or places designated as such, are extended so as to apply to persons detained at ports, airports or international rail stations under sch. 7. The rights extended include the right of a detained person to have a named person informed of the fact of his or her detention (sch. 8, para. 6) and the right to consult a solicitor in private (para. 7). A number of other provisions of the ABCPA 2014, sch. 9, amend the substance of the TA 2000, schs. 7 and 8. The Terrorism Act 2000 (Code of Practice for Examining Officers and Review Officers) Order 2014 (SI 2014 No. 1838) brings into operation a revised code of practice which takes account of these amendments.

B10.18   Informing a Solicitor

Terrorism Act 2000, sch. 8, paras. 7 and 7A

7.-(1) Subject to paragraphs 8 and 9, a person detained under Schedule 7 or section 41 in England, Wales or Northern Ireland shall be entitled, if he so requests, to consult a solicitor as soon as is reasonably practicable, privately and at any time.

(2) Where a request is made under sub-paragraph (1), the request and the time at which it was made shall be recorded.

7A.-(1) This paragraph applies where a person detained under Schedule 7 requests to consult a solicitor.

(2) The examining officer may not question the detained person under paragraph 2 or 3 of Schedule 7 until the person has consulted a solicitor (or no longer wishes to do so).

(3) Sub-paragraph (2) does not apply if the examining officer reasonably believes that postponing the questioning until then would be likely to prejudice determination of the relevant matters.

(4) The powers given by paragraph 8 of Schedule 7 (search powers where a person is questioned under paragraph 2 of Schedule 7) may be used when questioning is postponed because of sub-paragraph (2).

(5) The detained person is entitled to consult a solicitor in person.

(6) Sub-paragraph (5) does not apply if the examining officer reasonably believes that the time it would take to consult a solicitor in person would be likely to prejudice determination of the relevant matters.

(7) In that case the examining officer may require any consultation to take place in another way.

(8) In this paragraph 'the relevant matters' means the matters the examining officer seeks to determine under paragraph 2 or 3 of Schedule 7.

In *Ibrahim* [2009] 4 All ER 208, the Court of Appeal dismissed an appeal which principally concerned the admission into evidence of police 'safety' interviews of terrorist suspects conducted in the absence of a solicitor. Such interviews are often carried out to try to establish whether there are any further devices or terrorists at large which might imperil the safety of members of the public. The Court of Appeal held that the trial judge had properly exercised his discretion in allowing the interviews to go before the jury and rejected a policy-based argument that to do so would discourage terrorist suspects from providing information which might lead to lives being saved. The case concerned those arrested for the attempted bombing of the London Transport network on 21 July 2005 and so the relevant Code of Practice governing the 'safety' interviews conducted was at that time Code C. It is submitted that the same principles discussed by the Court would govern the admission of safety interviews governed by Code H. The Court of Appeal remarked that if a suspect was given an undertaking by the police to the effect that the fruits of any safety interview would not be deployed in evidence then that would provide the basis for a powerful argument to exclude any interview at trial.

Schedule 8, para. 9 provides for a direction that a consultation with a solicitor be in the sight and hearing of a police officer.

Fingerprints and Intimate and Non-intimate Samples

B10.19   Schedule 8, para. 10 to the TA 2000 regulates the taking of fingerprints and other samples from a person detained under the TA 2000.

Terrorism Act 2000, sch. 8, para. 10

(1) This paragraph applies where a person is detained in England, Wales or Northern Ireland under Schedule 7 or section 41.

(2) Fingerprints may be taken from the detained person only if they are taken by a constable—
    (a) with the appropriate consent given in writing, or
    (b) without that consent under sub-paragraph (4).

(3) A non-intimate sample may be taken from the detained person only if it is taken by a constable—
    (a) with the appropriate consent given in writing, or
    (b) without that consent under sub-paragraph (4).

(4) Fingerprints or a non-intimate sample may be taken from the detained person without the appropriate consent only if—
    (a) he is detained at a police station and a police officer of at least the rank of superintendent authorises the fingerprints or sample to be taken, or
    (b) he has been convicted of a recordable offence and, where a non-intimate sample is to be taken, he was convicted of the offence on or after 10th April 1995 (or 29th July 1996 where the non-intimate sample is to be taken in Northern Ireland).

(5) An intimate sample may be taken from a person detained under section 41, but only if—
    (a) he is detained at a police station,
    (b) the appropriate consent is given in writing,
    (c) a police officer of at least the rank of superintendent authorises the sample to be taken, and
    (d) subject to paragraph 13(2) and (3), the sample is taken by a constable.

(6) Subject to sub-paragraph (6A) an officer may give an authorisation under sub-paragraph (4)(a) or (5)(c) only if—
    (a) in the case of a person detained under section 41, the officer reasonably suspects that the person has been involved in an offence under any of the provisions mentioned in section 40(1)(a), and the officer reasonably believes that the fingerprints or sample will tend to confirm or disprove his involvement, or
    (b) in any case in which an authorisation under that sub-paragraph may be given, the officer is satisfied that the taking of the fingerprints or sample from the person is necessary in order to assist in determining whether he falls within section 40(1)(b).

(6A) An officer may also give an authorisation under sub-paragraph (4)(a) for the taking of fingerprints if—
    (a) he is satisfied that the fingerprints of the detained person will facilitate the ascertainment of that person's identity; and
    (b) that person has refused to identify himself or the officer has reasonable grounds for suspecting that that person is not who he claims to be.

(6B) In this paragraph references to ascertaining a person's identity include references to showing that he is not a particular person.

(7) If an authorisation under sub-paragraph (4)(a) or (5)(c) is given orally, the person giving it shall confirm it in writing as soon as is reasonably practicable.

If the detained person refuses to consent to the giving of a sample, a court may be entitled to draw appropriate adverse inferences against him (see **F19**).

Any fingerprints or samples or information provided may be used only for the purpose of a terrorist investigation. A check cannot be made against such samples under the PACE 1984, s. 63A(1), except for the purpose of a terrorist investigation (TA 2000, sch. 8, para. 14(3)).

Review and Extension of Detention

The Protection of Freedoms Act 2012, s. 57 reduced the maximum period of detention to 14 days. **B10.20** Section 58 provides an emergency procedure whereby the limit may be increased to 28 days.

Parts II and III of sch. 8 to the TA 2000 contain detailed provisions on review and extension of detention. As to amendments of the review and extension provisions by the ABCPA 2014, sch. 9, see **B10.21**.

Section 41 of the TA 2000 requires periodical review of the detention of a suspect. The first review must be carried out as soon as is reasonably practicable after the time of the detained person's arrest and any subsequent reviews must be carried out at intervals of not more than 12 hours (sch. 8, para. 21(1)–(3)). A review may be postponed if at the latest time when it should be carried out (a) the detained person is being questioned by a police officer and an officer is satisfied that an interruption of the questioning would prejudice the investigation, (b) no review officer is readily available, or (c) it is not practicable for any other reason to carry it out (sch. 8, para. 22(1)). If a review is postponed, a review must be carried out as soon as is reasonably practicable after the postponement (sch. 8, para. 22(2)).

B10.21   The authorisation of continued detention is governed by sch. 8, para. 23.

Terrorism Act 2000, sch. 8, para. 23

(1) A review officer may authorise a person's continued detention only if satisfied that it is necessary—
   (a) to obtain relevant evidence whether by questioning him or otherwise,
   (b) to preserve relevant evidence,
   (ba) pending the result of an examination or analysis of any relevant evidence or of anything the examination or analysis of which is to be or is being carried out with a view to obtaining relevant evidence,
   (c) pending a decision whether to apply to the Secretary of State for a deportation notice to be served on the detained person,
   (d) pending the making of an application for the Secretary of State for a deportation notice to be served on the detained person, or
   (e) pending consideration by the Secretary of State whether to serve a deportation notice on the detained person, or
   (f) pending a decision whether the detained person should be charged with an offence.

The review officer must not authorise continued detention unless the investigation or process for deportation is being conducted diligently and expeditiously (sch. 8, para. 23(2) and (3)). The detained person, or a solicitor representing him who is available at the time of the review, must be given an opportunity to make oral or written representations about the detention before the review officer decides whether to authorise detention (para. 26(1) and (2)). The review officer may refuse oral representations by the person detained if he considers that he is unfit because of his condition or behaviour (para. 26(3)). The detained person has the right to have a named person informed and to consult a solicitor (paras. 6 and 7: see **B10.17** and **B10.18**); when authorising continued detention, the review officer must inform the detained person of those rights where he has not exercised them or inform him that they have been delayed. Under para. 27(1) and (2), the review officer must also review the reasons for the delay under para. 8 (see **B10.17**).

New provisions introduced by the ABCPA 2014, sch. 9, affect the length and review of detention under the TA 2000, sch. 7. It is no longer possible to question a person for more than two hours unless they are detained. Moreover, any detained person must be released after a maximum of six hours (unless they are detained under another power). See also **B10.17**.

B10.22   A warrant of further detention may be sought by a Crown Prosecutor or a police officer of at least the rank of superintendent. The application is made to a judicial authority (a specially designated district judge) (para. 29(1) and (4)). If a warrant is granted it authorises further detention of the person under s. 41 for a specified period. Information on which the applicant for extension intends to rely may be withheld from the detained person or anyone representing him upon application to the district judge (para. 34(1)).

There may be extension or further extension of the specified period upon further application by an officer of at least the rank of superintendent (para. 36(1)). Where the application would extend the period to a time that is no more than 14 days after (in effect) arrival at the police station and no application has previously been made to a senior judge (i.e. a judge of the High Court), the application is heard by the judicial authority; in any other case, the application must be heard by a senior judge (para. 36(1A), (1B) and (7)). The decision of the High Court judge is not amenable to judicial review.

If at any time it appears to the police officer or other person in charge that any of the conditions under which the warrant of further detention was issued no longer apply, he must (a) if he has custody of the detained person, release him immediately, and (b) if he does not, immediately inform the person who does have custody that those matters no longer apply and that person must release him immediately (para. 37(1)–(3)).

Detention under s. 41 and sch. 8 was held to be compatible with the ECHR, Article 5, in *R (I) v City of Westminster Magistrates' Court and Chief Constable of Greater Manchester Police* [2008] EWHC 2146 (Admin).

Post-charge questioning is permissible under the C-TA 2008, s. 22, which came into force on 10 July 2012. Section 22 empowers a Crown Court judge to authorise questioning of a person about a terrorism offence (or an offence which appears to the judge to have a terrorist connection) after the person has been charged with it, or been officially informed that he may be prosecuted for it, or even after the person has been sent for trial for the offence. Under s. 22(3), the judge must specify the period during which questioning is authorised, and may impose such conditions as appear to be necessary in the interests of justice, including conditions as to the place where the questioning is to be carried out. The period authorised for questioning must not exceed 48 hours and runs continuously from when questioning pursuant to the authorisation begins. However, s. 22 plainly envisages that further authorisations of up to 48 hours may be allowed as s. 22(4) states that the 48-hour limit is 'without prejudice to any application for a further authorisation under this section'. If a person is in prison or detained elsewhere then, under s. 22(5), the judge may authorise his removal to another place for questioning. Section 22(6) limits the circumstances under which a Crown Court judge may allow such questioning. It stipulates that a judge must not authorise the questioning of a person under s. 22 unless satisfied that three conditions are met:

(a) that further questioning of the person is necessary in the interests of justice;
(b) that the investigation for the purposes of which the further questioning is proposed is being conducted diligently and expeditiously; and
(c) that what is authorised will not interfere unduly with the preparation of the person's defence to the charge in question or any other criminal charge.

There is no requirement in s. 22 that the questioning be based on evidence which was not available before charge, though a judge granting permission could impose that limitation. The most important safeguard is that the person may be questioned under s. 22 only about the offence for which he *has been* charged. A question may arise as to whether a person can be questioned about a more serious offence than the one charged, if it arises from the same facts.

Search of Premises for a Person

Powers of search are provided for under s. 42 of the TA 2000. Upon application by a constable, **B10.23** a magistrate may issue a warrant in relation to specified premises if he is satisfied that there are reasonable grounds for suspecting that a person whom the constable reasonably suspects to be a person falling within s. 40(1)(b) (i.e. a person who is or has been concerned in the commission, preparation or instigation of acts of terrorism) is to be found there (s. 42(1)). Any constable is thereby authorised to enter and search the specified premises for the purpose of arresting the person under s. 41 (s. 42(2)).

Search of Person and Vehicle

A constable may stop and search a person whom he reasonably suspects to be a terrorist to **B10.24** discover whether he has in his possession anything which may constitute evidence that he is a terrorist (TA 2000, s. 43(1)). In addition a constable may search a person arrested under s. 41 to discover whether he has in his possession anything which may constitute evidence that he is a terrorist (s. 43(2)). The Protection of Freedoms Act 2012, s. 60 (in force from 10 July 2012: see SI 2012 No. 1205), amends s. 43 of, and inserts a new s. 43A into, the TA 2000, so as to provide a new power to search vehicles.

Stop and Search Power

The TA 2000, ss. 44 to 47, provided for stop and search powers, exercisable where it was consi- **B10.25** dered expedient for the prevention of acts of terrorism. The powers ceased to have effect on 18 March 2011.

In *R (Gillan) v Metropolitan Police Commissioner* [2006] 2 AC 307, the House of Lords held that the powers did not infringe any of the articles of the ECHR. The ECtHR disagreed in *Gillan v UK* (2010) 50 EHRR 1105. The Court held that the requirement on a person to submit to a stop and search under the TA 2000 represented a clear interference with the right to respect for private life (see also A7.47). Under Article 8(2) its exercise thus had to be 'in accordance with the law'. An officer was not required to show the existence of any reasonable suspicion nor even subjectively to suspect anything of a person before exercising the power. The grant of such a broad power provided the potential for the arbitrary and discriminatory use of the power and there was evidence that the power had been used disproportionately against black and Asian persons.

The Terrorism Act 2000 (Remedial) Order 2011 (SI 2011 No. 631) had effect until the Protection of Freedoms Act 2012 was enacted.

The Protection of Freedoms Act 2012, s. 59 (in force from 10 July 2012), permanently repealed the TA 2000, ss. 44 to 47; by s. 61 of the 2012 Act (also in force from 10 July 2012), the temporary ss. 47A to 47C were made permanent. Section 47A and sch. 6B provide the police with replacement powers of stop and search. If a senior officer reasonably suspects that an act of terrorism will take place and considers that the stop and search powers are necessary to prevent such an act of terrorism, the senior officer may authorise the use of those powers in an area within the officer's police force area no larger than necessary and for a period no longer than necessary for that purpose (and for a maximum of 14 days). Authorisations must be confirmed by the Secretary of State within 48 hours if they are to last beyond that period and the Secretary of State has the power to restrict the scope of authorisations. Where an authorisation is in place, an officer in uniform may stop and search a person or a vehicle to search for evidence that the person is a terrorist or that the vehicle is being used for purposes of terrorism, whether or not the officer reasonably suspects that such evidence will be present. An individual or vehicle may be detained whilst a search is carried out, but only at or near the place where the person or vehicle is stopped. Written records are required to be kept and provided to a person searched, or the owner of a vehicle, if requested.

Prohibiting or Restricting Parking

B10.26 Under s. 48 of the TA 2000 authorisation may be given to prohibit or restrict the parking of vehicles on a specified road if the person authorising it considers it expedient for the prevention of acts of terrorism (s. 48(1) and (2)). The power may then be exercised by a constable placing a traffic sign on the road concerned (s. 49(1)). A constable exercising the power may suspend a parking place (s. 49(2)).

The period of authorisation must not exceed 28 days (s. 50(1) and (2)). An authorisation may be renewed in writing by the authoriser or by a person who could have authorised it; a renewed authorisation has effect as if it were a new authorisation (s. 50(3)). Section 51 penalises any person who contravenes any relevant restriction or prohibition. A person charged under s. 51 will be found not guilty if he proves that he had a reasonable excuse for the act or omission in question (s. 51(3)). Under s. 51(4), possession of a current disabled person's badge does not of itself constitute a reasonable excuse.

The offences under s. 51 are triable summarily only. For an offence contrary to s. 51(1), a person is liable to a fine not exceeding level 4 (s. 51(5)). For the offence contrary to s. 51(2), a person is liable to imprisonment for a term not exceeding three months, a fine not exceeding level 4 on the standard scale, or both (s. 51(6)).

Port and Border Controls

B10.27 A number of port and border controls are made available by s. 53(1) of, and sch. 7 to, the TA 2000. The exercise of the powers created in sch. 7 is not affected by any of the rights conferred by s. 1 of the Immigration Act 1971 (general principles regulating entry into and stay in the UK). These border controls operate in respect of Northern Ireland (TA 2000, sch. 7, para. 4). The powers created include powers of search, controls on embarkation and disembarkation and powers to compel disclosure of passenger information. It is an offence (i) wilfully to fail to comply with a duty under sch. 7, (ii) wilfully to contravene a prohibition imposed under sch. 7 or (iii) wilfully to obstruct or seek to frustrate a search or examination under sch. 7. The maximum penalty for these summary offences is imprisonment for a term not exceeding three months, a fine not exceeding level 4 on the standard scale, or both (para. 18(2)).

In *Beghal v DPP* [2014] 1 All ER 529 the Divisional Court ruled that the operation of the TA 2000, sch. 7, did not breach either Article 6 or 8 of the ECHR. The Court observed (at [151]):

> ...although the Independent Reviewer has drawn attention to the increase in litigation concerning the schedule 7 powers, he has reiterated the utility of these powers as an 'essential tool' in the fight against terrorism: see, for instance, paras. 10.35 and 10.63.

The claimant now has leave to appeal to the Supreme Court.

In *Miranda v Secretary of State for the Home Department* [2014] EWHC 255 (Admin) the Court of Appeal (Civil Division) ruled that sch. 7 is not incompatible with Article 10.

The ABCPA 2014, sch. 9, includes amendments to the TA 2000, sch. 7. See **B10.17**.

SUBSTANTIVE TERRORISM OFFENCES UNDER THE TERRORISM ACT 2000

The TA 2000 created numerous offences designed to fill perceived gaps in the legislative scheme aimed at countering acts of terrorism and developed the system of proscribing organisations, first introduced in response to Irish terrorism in 1974.   **B10.28**

Special Evidence Provisions

Terrorism Act 2000, s. 118   **B10.29**

(1) Subsection (2) applies where in accordance with a provision mentioned in subsection (5) it is a defence for a person charged with an offence to prove a particular matter.
(2) If the person adduces evidence which is sufficient to raise an issue with respect to the matter the court or jury shall assume that the defence is satisfied unless the prosecution proves beyond reasonable doubt that it is not.
(3) Subsection (4) applies where in accordance with a provision mentioned in subsection (5) a court—
  (a) may make an assumption in relation to a person charged with an offence unless a particular matter is proved, or
  (b) may accept a fact as sufficient evidence unless a particular matter is proved.
(4) If evidence is adduced which is sufficient to raise an issue with respect to the matter mentioned in subsection (3)(a) or (b) the court shall treat it as proved unless the prosecution disproves it beyond reasonable doubt.
(5) The provisions in respect of which subsections (2) and (4) apply are—
  (a) sections 12(4), 39(5)(a), 54, 57, 58, 58A, 77 and 103 of this Act, and
  (b) sections 13, 32 and 33 of the Northern Ireland (Emergency Provisions) Act 1996 (possession and information offences) as they have effect by virtue of Schedule 1 to this Act.

These special evidence provisions are concerned with many of the offences which impose a reverse burden on the accused and are designed to ensure that the legislation is not incompatible with the ECHR. (For analysis of the effect of reverse burdens, see **F3.18** *et seq.*)

Documentary Evidence   There are special rules relating to documentary evidence set out in s. 120.   **B10.30**

Terrorism Act 2000, s. 120

(1) A document which purports to be—
  (a) a notice or direction given or order made by the Secretary of State for the purposes of a provision of this Act, and
  (b) signed by him or on his behalf, shall be received in evidence and
shall, until the contrary is proved, be deemed to have been given or made by the Secretary of State.
(2) A document bearing a certificate which—
  (a) purports to be signed by or on behalf of the Secretary of State, and

(b) states that the document is a true copy of a notice or direction given or order made by the
Secretary of State for the purposes of a provision of this Act,

shall be evidence (or, in Scotland, sufficient evidence) of the document in legal proceedings.

(3) In subsections (1) and (2) a reference to an order does not include a reference to an order made
by statutory instrument.

(4) The Documentary Evidence Act 1868 shall apply to an authorisation given in writing by the
Secretary of State for the purposes of this Act as it applies to an order made by him.

Membership of a Proscribed Organisation

B10.31   Terrorism Act 2000, s. 11

(1) A person commits an offence if he belongs or professes to belong to a proscribed organisation.

B10.32 **Procedure and Jurisdiction**   The offence of belonging to a proscribed organisation is triable
either way and when tried on indictment is normally a class 3 offence, but see CPD XIII, para. B
(see Supplement, **PD-97**) for the additional factors that the court considers on allocation.
Under the TA 2000, s. 117(2), as amended by the C-TA 2008, s. 29, the consent of the DPP is
generally required for proceedings to be instituted; if it appears to him that the offence is committed outside the UK or for a purpose wholly or partly connected with the affairs of a country
other than the UK, then the A-G's consent is required (s. 117(2A)). The A-G's consent must be
obtained before any plea before venue proceedings (*Lambert* [2010] 1 WLR 898).

The procedure set out in the Proscribed Organisations (Applications for Deproscription)
Regulations 2001 (SI 2001 No. 107) enables an application to be made for an organisation to be
removed from the list of organisations contained in sch. 2. An appeal against a refusal to remove
an organisation from the list may be made to the Proscribed Organisations Appeal Committee
under the TA 2000, s. 5(1) and (2).

Under s. 10(1), the following evidence may not be called by the prosecution in proceedings for
this offence:

(a) evidence of anything done in relation to an application under s. 4 to deproscribe the organisation;
(b) evidence of anything done in relation to proceedings before the Proscribed Organisations
Appeal Commission under the TA 2000, s. 5, or the HRA 1998, s. 7(1);
(c) evidence of anything done in relation to a further appeal on a matter of law under the TA
2000, s. 6; and
(d) any document submitted for any of the above purposes.

However, s. 10(2) allows such evidence to be called by the defence. Under the TA 2006, s. 17 (see
B10.84), if a person does anything outside the UK which would amount to an offence under
s. 11(1) if done in any part of it, he will be liable for the offence in that part of the UK; see **A8**.

B10.33 **Sentencing**   The maximum penalty is: on conviction on indictment, imprisonment for a term
not exceeding ten years, a fine, or both; on summary conviction, imprisonment for a term not
exceeding six months, a fine not exceeding the statutory maximum, or both (TA 2000, s. 11(3)).

In *Hundal* [2004] 2 Cr App R (S) 355, the offenders were convicted of offences under s. 11, of
belonging to the International Sikh Youth Federation. The offenders did not know that the organisation was proscribed in the UK. Sentences of 30 months' imprisonment were reduced to 12 months.

In *Ahmed* [2011] EWCA Crim 184 concurrent sentences of two years' and nine years'
imprisonment imposed on Habib Ahmed after trial for offences of professing membership
of Al-Qa'ida and membership of Al-Qa'ida respectively were upheld by the Court of Appeal.

B10.34 **Elements**   Proscribed organisations are listed in the TA 2000, sch. 2, as amended. It is an offence
to be a member of an organisation listed in sch. 2 or an organisation operating under the name of an
organisation listed in sch. 2. The Secretary of State may amend sch. 2 by order (s. 3) and a number of
such orders have been made; five entries were most recently added to the list by SI 2014 No. 1624.

Under s. 3(6), if the Secretary of State is of the belief that a proscribed organisation is operating under
a different name than one listed in sch. 2 or is operating under a name that does not appear in sch. 2

but is to all intents and purposes the same organisation as one listed in sch. 2, he may direct that the name not specified shall be treated as the same as one listed in sch. 2. A number of such orders have been made. Most recently, the Proscribed Organisations (Name Changes) Order 2014 (SI 2014 No. 1612) stipulated that names Need4Khilafah, the Shariah Project and Islamic Dawah Association be treated as other names for the proscribed organisations Al Ghurabaa and The Saved Sect.

In *Ahmed* [2011] EWCA Crim 184, the Court of Appeal observed that what amounts to membership of a proscribed organisation is likely to depend upon the nature of the organisation in question. Membership of a loose and unstructured organisation may not require any formal steps, whereas a more structured organisation may have an express process by which a person becomes a member. A criminal association is inherently more likely to lack formality than an innocent one. Deriving assistance from the analysis by Jack J of the organisation known as the Animal Liberation Front in *Smith Kline Beecham plc v Avery* [2009] EWHC 1488 (QB), the Court expressed the view that the core elements of membership were voluntary and knowing association with others with a view to furthering the aims of the proscribed organisation. In some cases, a trial judge directing a jury may need to make clear that unilateral sympathy with the aims of an organisation, even coupled with acts designed to promote similar objectives, will not always be sufficient. The jury may need to consider whether there is the necessary element of acceptance or reciprocity from the organisation which is involved in belonging.

If a person joins an organisation in a country where the organisation is not proscribed, he nonetheless commits the offence if he remains a member of the organisation and travels to this jurisdiction (*Hundal* [2004] 2 Cr App R 307).

Specific Defence   B10.35

> **Terrorism Act 2000, s. 11**
>
> (2) It is a defence for a person charged with an offence under subsection (1) above to prove—
>   (a) that the organisation was not proscribed on the last (or only) occasion on which he became a member or began to profess to be a member, and
>   (b) that he has not taken part in the activities of the organisation at any time while it was proscribed.

In *Sheldrake v DPP* [2005] 1 AC 264 (see **F3.33**), the House of Lords read down s. 11(2) so as to interpret it as imposing only an evidential burden on the accused. See **F3.18**.

Supporting a Proscribed Organisation

> **Terrorism Act 2000, s. 12**   B10.36
>
> (1) A person commits an offence if—
>   (a) he invites support for a proscribed organisation, and
>   (b) the support is not, or is not restricted to, the provision of money or other property (within the meaning of section 15).
> (2) A person commits an offence if he arranges, manages or assists in arranging or managing a meeting which he knows is—
>   (a) to support a proscribed organisation,
>   (b) to further the activities of a proscribed organisation, or
>   (c) to be addressed by a person who belongs or professes to belong to a proscribed organisation.
> (3) A person commits an offence if he addresses a meeting and the purpose of his address is to encourage support for a proscribed organisation or to further its activities.

Procedure   An allegation of an offence contrary to the TA 2000, s. 12, is triable either way; when   B10.37
tried on indictment it is normally a class 3 offence, but see CPD XIII, para. B (see Supplement,
PD-97) for the additional factors that the court considers on allocation. For consent to prosecution, see **B10.32**.

Sentencing   The maximum penalty is: on conviction on indictment, imprisonment for a   B10.38
term not exceeding ten years, a fine, or both; on summary conviction, imprisonment for a
term not exceeding six months, a fine not exceeding the statutory maximum, or both (TA
2000, s. 12(6)).

B10.39 **Elements** For 'proscribed organisation', see **B10.34**.

A 'meeting' consists of a gathering of three or more people (TA 2000, s. 12(5)(a)).

B10.40 **Specific Defence**

> **Terrorism Act 2000, s. 12**
>
> (4) Where a person is charged with an offence under subsection (2)(c) in respect of a private meeting it is a defence for him to prove that he had no reasonable cause to believe that the address mentioned in subsection (2)(c) would support a proscribed organisation or further its activities.

The defence under s. 12(4) is subject to the provisions of s. 118 of the 2000 Act and thus an evidential burden is imposed on the accused.

Wearing a Uniform

B10.41

> **Terrorism Act 2000, s. 13**
>
> (3) A person in a public place commits an offence if he—
>   (a) wears an item of clothing, or
>   (b) wears, carries or displays an article,
> in such a way or in such circumstances as to arouse reasonable suspicion that he is a member or supporter of a proscribed organisation.

B10.42 **Procedure** An allegation of an offence contrary to the TA 2000, s. 13, is triable summarily only. For consent to prosecution, see **B10.32**.

B10.43 **Sentencing** The maximum penalty is imprisonment for a term not exceeding six months, a fine not exceeding level 5 on the standard scale, or both (TA 2000, s. 13(3)).

B10.44 **Elements** By virtue of the TA 2000, s. 121, an 'article' includes a substance or any other thing and a 'public place' is one to which the public have access, whether for payment or not.

In *Rankin v Murray* 2004 SLT 1164, the offender had worn jewellery which bore the initials 'UVF'. Even on the assumption it was established that R had received the ring as a gift, regularly visited Northern Ireland, and was not a member or supporter of the said organisation, those facts did not negate the actual suspicion of the officers nor the objectively reasonable basis for that suspicion.

For 'proscribed organisation' and deproscription, see **B10.34**.

For the related public order offence, see **B11.8**.

Information about Acts of Terrorism

B10.45

> **Terrorism Act 2000, s. 38B**
>
> (1) This section applies where a person has information which he knows or believes might be of material assistance—
>   (a) in preventing the commission by another person of an act of terrorism, or
>   (b) in securing the apprehension, prosecution or conviction of another person,
> in the United Kingdom, for an offence involving the commission, preparation or instigation of an act of terrorism.
> (2) The person commits an offence if he does not disclose the information as soon as reasonably practicable in accordance with subsection (3).
> (3) Disclosure is in accordance with this subsection if it is made—
>   (a) in England and Wales, to a constable...

B10.46 **Procedure** An offence under s. 38B is triable either way; when tried on indictment it is normally a class 3 offence, but see CPD XIII, para. B (see Supplement, **PD-97**) for the additional factors that the court considers on allocation. For consent to prosecution, see **B10.32**.

B10.47 **Sentencing** The maximum penalty is, on conviction on indictment, imprisonment for a term not exceeding five years, a fine or both; on summary conviction, imprisonment for a term not exceeding six months, a fine not exceeding the statutory maximum or both (TA 2000, s. 38B(5)). In *Sherif* [2009] 2 Cr App R (S) 235, which concerned the failed 21/7 London Underground bombings, many of the offenders had been sentenced to the maximum of five years for offences contrary to s. 38B; some had also received consecutive sentences for failure to disclose information both before and after the attempted bombings. The totality of the sentences ranged from three to 17 years. The following issues of principle were dealt with by the Court of Appeal:

(a) So far as offences contrary to s. 38B are concerned, in many cases it will be the seriousness of the terrorist activity about which an offender has failed to give information which will determine the level of criminality, rather than the extent of the information which could be provided, which will affect the sentence. The case being dealt with was so serious as to merit the imposition of the statutory maximum.

(b) There was nothing wrong in principle with imposing consecutive sentences where both limbs of s. 38B have been charged. The failure to give information before the act (said by the Court to be arguably the more serious offence) and failure to give information afterwards are entirely separate offences even though the failure may arise out of the same state of mind (e.g., misguided loyalty).

(c) There is always a place for exceptional personal mitigation, even in cases as grave as the one the Court was dealing with. There may be cases when the court may be able to show some understanding and even mercy when someone, if vulnerable either because of age or his particular relationship with an offender, mistakenly and misguidedly puts loyalty to a family or to a friend before duties to the public or before disclosing what he knows to the police.

The principles set out in *Sherif* have since been applied in *Girma* [2010] 1 Cr App R (S) 172.

Elements   Under the TA 2000, s. 38B(6), the offence may, for the purposes of the proceedings, be taken to have occurred in any place where the accused is or has been since he first knew or believed that the information might be of material assistance in the way referred to in s. 38B(1). The proceedings may also be taken in any such place.   **B10.48**

Specific Defence   Section 38B(4) of the TA 2000 provides that it is a defence for the accused to prove that he had a reasonable excuse for failing to make the required disclosure.   **B10.49**

For the compatibility of the reverse burden with the ECHR, Article 6, see **F3.18** *et seq.*

Weapons Training

Terrorism Act 2000, s. 54	**B10.50**

(1) A person commits an offence if he provides instruction or training in the making or use of—
  (a) firearms,
  (aa) radioactive material or weapons designed or adapted for the discharge of any radioactive material,
  (b) explosives, or
  (c) chemical, biological or nuclear weapons.
(2) A person commits an offence if he receives instruction or training in the making or use of—
  (a) firearms,
  (aa) radioactive material or weapons designed or adapted for the discharge of any radioactive material,
  (b) explosives, or
  (c) chemical, biological or nuclear weapons.
(3) A person commits an offence if he invites another to receive instruction or training and the receipt—
  (a) would constitute an offence under subsection (2), or
  (b) would constitute an offence under subsection (2) but for the fact that it is to take place outside the United Kingdom.

Procedure   An allegation of an offence contrary to the TA 2000, s. 54, is triable either way and if tried on indictment is normally a class 3 offence, but see CPD XIII, para. B (see Supplement, **PD-97**) for the additional factors that the court considers on allocation. For consent to prosecution, see **B10.32**.   **B10.51**

Sentencing   The maximum penalty is: on conviction on indictment, a sentence of imprisonment not exceeding ten years, a fine or both; on summary conviction, a sentence of   **B10.52**

imprisonment not exceeding six months, a fine not exceeding the statutory maximum or both (TA 2000, s. 54(6)). The court may also make a forfeiture order in accordance with s. 23A, as inserted by the C-TA 2008, s. 35 (see **B10.112**).

B10.53   **Elements**   By virtue of the TA 2000, s. 54(4), the provision of, or invitation to, training referred to in s. 54(1) and (3) can be to specific persons or generally.

Section 55 of the Act provides definitions of most of the items referred to in s. 54(1). Thus:

'biological weapon' means a biological agent or toxin (within the meaning of the Biological Weapons Act 1974) in a form capable of use for hostile purposes or anything to which s. 1(1)(b) of that Act applies;
'chemical weapon' has the meaning given by s. 1 of the Chemical Weapons Act 1996;
'radioactive material' means radioactive material capable of endangering life or causing harm to human health;
a 'firearm' is defined in s. 121 as including an air gun or air pistol.

Under s. 17 of the TA 2006 (see **B10.84**) if a person does anything outside the UK which would amount to an offence under s. 54 if done in any part of the UK, he will be liable for the offence in that part of the UK.

B10.54   **Specific Defence**

Terrorism Act 2000, s. 54

(5) It is a defence for a person charged with an offence under this section in relation to instruction or training to prove that his action or involvement was wholly for a purpose other than assisting, preparing for or participating in terrorism.

The defence under s. 54(4) is subject to the provisions of s. 118 of the 2000 Act and thus imposes an evidential burden on the accused (see **B10.29**).

Directing a Terrorist Organisation

B10.55

Terrorism Act 2000, s. 56

(1) A person commits an offence if he directs, at any level, the activities of an organisation which is concerned in the commission of acts of terrorism.

B10.56   **Procedure**   An allegation of an offence contrary to the TA 2000, s. 56, is triable on indictment only and is normally a class 1B offence, but see CPD XIII, para. B (see Supplement, **PD-97**) for the additional factors that the court considers on allocation. For consent to prosecution, see **B10.32**.

For the extended jurisdiction provisions in relation to this offence, see **B10.81**.

B10.57   **Sentencing**   A person convicted of this offence is liable to imprisonment for life (TA 2000, s. 56(2)). Rangzieb Ahmed was convicted after trial and was sentenced to life imprisonment with a minimum term of ten years to be served for the offence; that sentence was not the subject of any appeal. For the outline facts of the offence, see *Ahmed* [2011] EWCA Crim 184. In passing sentence upon him in December 2008, Saunders J said that he had to bear in mind that, while directing a terrorist organisation is a very serious offence, Ahmed had not been proved to be directly involved in any terrorist act. Moreover, while he was satisfied that at the time of his arrest Ahmed was planning something, he did not know what it was, how imminent it was, what were the chances of it succeeding or what (if any) loss of life it was likely to cause.

B10.58   **Elements**   For 'terrorism', see **B10.2**.

Possession of an Article for Terrorist Purposes

B10.59

Terrorism Act 2000, s. 57

(1) A person commits an offence if he possesses an article in circumstances which give rise to a reasonable suspicion that his possession is for a purpose connected with the commission, preparation or instigation of an act of terrorism.

Procedure   An allegation of an offence contrary to the TA 2000, s. 57, is triable either way; if   **B10.60** tried on indictment it is normally a class 3 offence, but see CPD XIII, para. B (see Supplement, PD-97) for the additional factors that the court considers on allocation. For consent to prosecution, see **B10.32**.

For the extended jurisdiction provisions in relation to this offence, see **B10.81**.

Sentence   The maximum penalty is: on conviction on indictment, imprisonment for a term   **B10.61** not exceeding 15 years, a fine, or both; on summary conviction, imprisonment for a term not exceeding six months, a fine not exceeding the statutory maximum, or both (TA 2000, s. 57(4)). The court may also make a forfeiture order in accordance with s. 23A (see **B10.112**).

In *Rowe* [2007] QB 975 (see **B10.62**) the offender was sentenced under the old statutory maximum of ten years. He appealed against two consecutive sentences of seven and a half years' duration for offences under s. 57 of possessing a substitution code and notes for the use of a mortar respectively. The Court of Appeal rejected the submission that consecutive sentences should not have been imposed, but reduced the sentence for possession of the mortar notes to two and a half years after having regard to the principle of totality.

In *Rahman* [2008] 4 All ER 661 the offender was sentenced to six years' imprisonment following a late plea of guilty to an offence contrary to s. 57 to which the new statutory maximum applied. The Court of Appeal reduced the sentence to one of five years and six months for reasons primarily concerned with the *Goodyear* procedure adopted.

Elements   Under the TA 2000, s. 57(3), if it is proved that an article was on any premises   **B10.62** at the same time as the accused, or was on premises of which the accused was the occupier or which he habitually used otherwise than as a member of the public, the court may assume that he possessed the article unless the accused proves that he did not know of the presence of the article on the premises or had no control over it. By virtue of s. 118, the burden on the accused is evidential (see **B10.29**).

In *Rowe* [2007] QB 975, the Court of Appeal held that a document or record was capable of constituting an article for the purposes of s. 57. The Court observed that ss. 57 and 58 (see **B10.63** *et seq.*) deal with different aspects of activities relating to terrorism. Section 57 deals with possession of articles *for the purpose* of terrorist acts. Section 58 is concerned with the collecting or holding of information that *is of a kind likely to be useful* to those involved in acts of terrorism. Section 57 also includes a specific intention whilst s. 58 does not. Those differences between the two sections were said to be rational features of a statute whose aims included the prohibition of different types of support for, and involvement in, terrorism. There is thus no basis for any conclusion that Parliament intended to have a completely separate regime for documents and records from that which applies to other articles. In so holding, the Court found that the decision, on interlocutory appeal from a preparatory hearing, to the opposite effect in *M (No. 1)* [2007] EWCA Crim 218 was wrongly decided *per incuriam*. *Rowe* has since been followed in *M* [2007] 3 All ER 53, and in *G* [2010] 1 AC 43 (see **B10.70**) the House of Lords said that the decision in *Rowe* was plainly correct.

The accused in *M* were subsequently convicted of offences contrary to s. 57 at the Central Criminal Court. Examination of their computers had revealed that they were in possession of radical Islamic material and other material such as a US military manual downloaded from the internet. They successfully appealed against conviction (*Zafar* [2008] QB 810). The Court of Appeal concluded (with Lord Phillips CJ giving the judgment of the Court) that, if s. 57 was to have the certainty of meaning that the law requires, it must be interpreted in a way that requires a direct connection between the object possessed and the act of terrorism. Section 57 should therefore be interpreted as if it reads that a person commits an offence if he possesses an article in circumstances which give rise to a reasonable suspicion that he intends it to be used for the purpose of the commission, preparation or instigation of an act of terrorism. Possessing a document for the purposes of inciting a person to commit an act of terrorism falls within the ambit of s. 57, as one synonym for 'instigation' is 'incitement'. In *G* it was made clear that the Crown does not have to prove what the terrorist purpose of the accused actually is.

B10.63   **Specific Defence**

Terrorism Act 2000, s. 57

(2) It is a defence for a person charged with an offence under this section to prove that his possession of the article was not for a purpose connected with the commission, preparation or instigation of an act of terrorism.

The defence under s. 57(2) is subject to the provisions of s. 118 and thus imposes an evidential burden on the accused (see **B10.29**).

Collection of Information

B10.64

Terrorism Act 2000, s. 58

(1) A person commits an offence if—
   (a) he collects or makes a record of information of a kind likely to be useful to a person committing or preparing an act of terrorism, or
   (b) he possesses a document or record containing information of that kind.

B10.65   **Procedure**   An allegation of an offence contrary to the TA 2000, s. 58, is triable either way; if tried on indictment it is normally a class 3 offence, but see CPD XIII, para. B (see Supplement, **PD-97**) for the additional factors that the court considers on allocation. For consent to prosecution, see **B10.32**.

For the extended jurisdiction provisions in relation to this offence, see **B10.81**.

B10.66   **Sentencing**   The maximum penalty is: on conviction on indictment, a term of imprisonment not exceeding ten years, a fine, or both; on summary conviction, a term of imprisonment not exceeding six months, a fine not exceeding the statutory maximum, or both (TA 2000, s. 58(4)). The court may also make a forfeiture order in accordance with s. 23A (see **B10.112**).

In *Mansha* [2007] 1 Cr App R (S) 410, a sentence of six years' imprisonment was upheld where the offender was in possession of detailed information relating to a soldier who had been decorated for bravery in Iraq.

In the sentencing of *Yahya* (5 November 2007 unreported), Calvert-Smith J observed that the offence under s. 58 is one which can be committed in an almost infinite variety of ways and the sentence appropriate for a particular offence will need to reflect the particular facts and circumstances of the offence and the offender (this dictum was approved by Lord Phillips CJ in *Rahman* [2008] 4 All ER 661: see **B10.92**). Calvert-Smith J stated that in his judgement it would be rare for the circumstances of both offence and offender to justify a sentence which did not result in the offender serving an immediate term of imprisonment or detention. Factors relevant to the sentence will include: the youth or otherwise of the offender, the degree to which the information was likely to assist a terrorist offender or offenders, the likelihood of the information actually reaching such offenders, and the degree of remorse and any evidence of a change of heart which may be evident. Y pleaded guilty to an offence under s. 58 in connection with the attempted 21/7 bombings of the London Underground. He accepted that he had made inquiries about the purchase of hydrogen peroxide on behalf of some of his co-defendants knowing that they were considering making improvised explosive devices using hydrogen peroxide as a possible component part. A man of previous good character who had left the UK almost six weeks before the attempted bombing, he was sentenced to six years and nine months' imprisonment.

In *Muhammed* [2010] 3 All ER 759, a sentence of four years' imprisonment imposed was reduced to two years by the Court of Appeal.

In the wake of *G* [2010] 1 AC 43 (see **B10.70**), it is possible for an offender to plead guilty and be sentenced on the basis of a lack of terrorist intent.

Elements   The first comprehensive guidance on the ambit of the TA 2000, s. 58, was set out by the Court of Appeal in *K* [2008] QB 827. Giving the judgment of the Court, Lord Phillips CJ explained that a document or record will fall within s. 58 only if it is of a kind that is likely to provide practical assistance to a person committing or preparing an act of terrorism. A document which simply encourages the commission of acts of terrorism does not fall within s. 58. The natural meaning of s. 58 requires that a document or record that infringes it must contain information of a nature likely to give rise to a reasonable suspicion that it is intended to be used to assist in the commission or preparation of an act of terrorism. Thus s. 58 places a burden on the accused to provide a reasonable excuse for his possession of it (see **B10.70**). Extrinsic evidence may be adduced to explain the nature of the material but it is not legitimate to call extrinsic evidence to show that a document which is innocuous on its face is intended to be used for the preparation or commission of an act of terrorism.

B10.67

In *G* [2010] 1 AC 43, s. 58 was considered by the House of Lords. The cases were prosecution appeals against the application of the *ratio* of *K* by the Court of Appeal. Confirming the dictum in *K*, it was recognised that the aim of s. 58 was to catch information which would typically be of use to terrorists, as opposed to ordinary members of the public; the information collected or possessed must, of its very nature, be designed to provide practical assistance to a person committing or preparing an act of terrorism. It is not necessary that the information should be useful only to a person involved in an act of terrorism. For instance, information on where to obtain explosives is capable of falling within s. 58(1), even though an ordinary criminal planning a bank robbery might also find it useful. The House of Lords also confirmed the dictum in *K* that the role of extrinsic evidence is limited and provided further analysis and definition of the elements of the offence. First, the Crown must prove that the accused had control of a record which contained information that was likely to provide practical assistance to a person committing or preparing an act of terrorism. Secondly, the Crown must prove that the accused knew that he had the record. Thirdly, the Crown must prove that he knew the kind of information which it contained, although it does not have to prove that he knew everything that was in the document or record. The Crown must establish all three elements beyond reasonable doubt and, if it does so, it has proved its case.

B10.68

G was applied in *Muhammed* [2010] 3 All ER 759, where it was argued that a document containing guidance as to how to maintain secrecy in respect of mobile phone and e-mail usage, along with suggestions as how to avoid surveillance by the authorities and a suggested reading list, should not fall within s. 58. Giving the judgment of the Court of Appeal, Hooper LJ said (at [47]):

> Provided that the document containing the information is not one in every day use by ordinary members of the public (e.g. published timetables and maps) and provided that a reasonable jury could properly conclude that the document contains information of a kind likely to be useful to a person committing or preparing an act of terrorism, then it will be a matter for the jury whether they are sure that it contains such information. If so, and provided the defendant has the necessary *mens rea*, then the only issue will be whether the defendant has a reasonable excuse.

In *Brown* [2011] EWCA Crim 2751, the Court of Appeal held that s. 58 constituted a proportionate restriction on freedom of expression under the ECHR and freedom of speech at common law.

Specific Defence   **B10.69**

Terrorism Act 2000, s. 58

(3) It is a defence for a person charged with an offence under this section to prove that he had a reasonable excuse for his action or possession.

The defence under s. 58(3) is subject to the provisions of s. 118 and thus imposes an evidential burden on the accused (see **B10.29**).

In *F* [2007] QB 960 it was held by the Court of Appeal that possession of documents as part of an effort to change an illegal or undemocratic regime could not constitute a reasonable excuse under s. 58(3). In the interlocutory appeal *Y (A)* [2010] 1 WLR 2644, the accused's case was that he possessed various documents in order to, amongst other things, assist Somali Muslims in self-defence against opposing forces. The Court of Appeal dismissed the Crown's appeal against a refusal by the trial judge to rule that the defence could not give rise to a reasonable excuse under s. 58(3).

B10.70   In *K* [2008] QB 827 (see **B10.67**), the Court of Appeal held that the nature of a reasonable excuse is simply an explanation that the document or record is possessed for a purpose other than to assist in the commission or preparation of an act of terrorism. It matters not that that purpose may infringe some other provision of the criminal or civil law. In *G* [2010] 1 AC 43, the House of Lords overturned the definition of reasonable excuse set out in *K*. Lord Rodger said that the Court of Appeal went wrong in *K* when it interpreted the defence of reasonable excuse in the way that it did. Their lordships accepted the submission by the appellants that the Court of Appeal had, in effect, substituted for the defence of reasonable excuse enacted in s. 58(3) a quite different defence which was in effect a reproduction of the defence in s. 57(2) (see **B10.63**). Lord Rodger stated that the real issue under s. 58 is not whether the accused had a terrorist purpose. Whether he had such a purpose is neutral. Instead the accused has to show that he had an objectively reasonable excuse for possessing the document or record which Parliament has made it prima facie a crime to possess because of its potential utility to terrorists. Possessing such a document or record for the purposes of carrying out a bank robbery is a purpose which is not connected with terrorism, but it is not a reasonable excuse. Unless a trial judge is satisfied that no reasonable jury could regard the accused's excuse as reasonable, he must leave the matter for the jury to decide. When doing so, he may indicate to the jury various factors which may be useful to them in determining the issue, such as the accused's age, his associates, his background and how long he had the item in his possession.

Eliciting, Publishing or Communicating Information About Members of Armed Forces etc.

B10.71   Terrorism Act 2000, s. 58A

(1) A person commits an offence who—
    (a) elicits or attempts to elicit information about an individual who is or has been—
        (i)   a member of Her Majesty's forces,
        (ii) a member of any of the intelligence services, or
        (iii) a constable,
        which is of a kind likely to be useful to a person committing or preparing an act of terrorism, or
    (b) publishes or communicates any such information.

B10.72   **Procedure**   An allegation of an offence contrary to the TA 2000, s. 58A, is triable either way; if tried on indictment it is normally a class 3 offence, but see CPD XIII, para. B (see Supplement, **PD-97**) for the additional factors that the court considers on allocation. For consent to prosecution, see **B10.32**.

For the extended jurisdiction provisions in relation to this offence, see **B10.81**.

B10.73   **Sentencing**   The maximum penalty is: on conviction on indictment, a term of imprisonment not exceeding ten years, a fine, or both; on summary conviction, a term of imprisonment not exceeding six months, a fine not exceeding the statutory maximum, or both (TA 2000, s. 58A(3)). The court may also make a forfeiture order in accordance with s. 23A (see **B10.112**).

B10.74   **Elements**   The scheme of s. 58A is very similar to that of s. 58 (see **B10.64**). Under s. 58, the information collected or possessed by the accused must, of its very nature, be designed to provide practical assistance to a person committing or preparing an act of terrorism. In argument in the House of Lords in *G* [2010] 1 AC 43, the Crown asserted that Parliament could never have intended to criminalise the possession of information of a kind which is useful to people for all sorts of everyday purposes and which many members of the public regularly obtain or use, simply because that information could also be useful to someone who was preparing an act of terrorism. By contrast, under s. 58A, it is submitted that the information most likely to be of use to a terrorist is the home address of the member, or former member, of the armed services etc. That information is not of its very nature of the type designed to provide practical assistance to a terrorist. If *G* is to be applied in respect of s. 58A, it would seem to be enough for the Crown to establish, for example, simply that D elicited the address, that he knew he had elicited the address and that he knew that he had elicited the address of a member of the armed forces etc. It would then be for D to establish a reasonable excuse under s. 58A(2).

Specific Defence B10.75

Terrorism Act 2000, s. 58A

(2) It is a defence for a person charged with an offence under this section to prove that they had a reasonable excuse for their action.

The defence under s. 58A(2) is subject to the provisions of s. 118 and thus imposes an evidential burden on the accused (see **B10.29**).

Section 58A contains the defence of reasonable excuse and is in almost identical terms to that in s. 58 (see **B10.69**). It is submitted that the rationale for the definition of reasonable excuse contained within *G* [2010] 1 AC 43 is more difficult to support in the context of s. 58A. It is submitted that the type of information covered by s. 58A is much more likely to be held and used by ordinary members of the public and much less demanding of an explanation than the information covered by s. 58.

TERRORISM OVERSEAS

Inciting Terrorism Overseas

Terrorism Act 2000, s. 59 B10.76

(1) A person commits an offence if—
   (a) he incites another person to commit an act of terrorism wholly or partly outside the United Kingdom, and
   (b) the act would, if committed in England and Wales, constitute one of the offences listed in subsection (2).
(2) Those offences are—
   (a) murder,
   (b) an offence under section 18 of the Offences against the Person Act 1861 (wounding with intent),
   (c) an offence under section 23 or 24 of that Act (poison),
   (d) an offence under section 28 or 29 of that Act (explosions), and
   (e) an offence under section 1(2) of the Criminal Damage Act 1971 (endangering life by damaging property).
(3) A person guilty of an offence under this section shall be liable to any penalty to which he would be liable on conviction of the offence listed in subsection (2) which corresponds to the act which he incites.
(4) For the purposes of subsection (1) it is immaterial whether or not the person incited is in the United Kingdom at the time of the incitement.
(5) Nothing in this section imposes criminal liability on any person acting on behalf of, or holding office under, the Crown.

Procedure By virtue of the TA 2000, s. 59(3), an allegation of an offence contrary to s. 59 is **B10.77** triable in the same way that the substantive offence listed in s. 59(2) would be tried. As all of those offences are triable only on indictment, s. 59 is effectively indictable only. It is a class 1B offence. For consent to prosecution, see **B10.32**.

The Terrorism Protocol (see **B10.1**) applies to this offence.

For the extended jurisdiction provisions in relation to this offence, see **B10.81**.

B10.78 **Sentencing**   The maximum penalty is that which would be available on conviction of the substantive offence (TA 2000, s. 59(3)). The court may also make a forfeiture order in accordance with s. 23A (see **B10.112**).

In *AG's Ref (Nos. 85, 86 and 87 of 2007) (Tsouli)* [2008] 2 Cr App R (S) 247, sentences of between six and a half and ten years' imprisonment following guilty pleas during the course of the trial were increased to range between ten and 16 years having allowed for double jeopardy. The offenders had maintained web sites through which they incited murder, primarily in Iraq.

B10.79 **Elements**   For murder, see **B1.1**; for the OAPA 1861, ss. 18, 23, 24, 28 and 29, see **B2.64**, **B2.76**, **B2.85**, **B12.224** and **B12.228** respectively; for the CDA 1971, s. 1(2), see **B8.16**.

Terrorist Bombing Committed Abroad and Terrorist Financing Abroad

B10.80   Terrorism Act 2000, ss. 62 and 63

62.—(1) If—
  (a) a person does anything outside the United Kingdom as an act of terrorism or for the purposes of terrorism, and
  (b) his action would have constituted the commission of one of the offences listed in subsection (2) if it had been done in the United Kingdom,
he shall be guilty of the offence.
(2) The offences referred to in subsection (1)(b) are—
  (a) an offence under section 2, 3 or 5 of the Explosive Substances Act 1883 (causing explosions, &c),
  (b) an offence under section 1 of the Biological Weapons Act 1974 (biological weapons), and
  (c) an offence under section 2 of the Chemical Weapons Act 1996 (chemical weapons).
63.—(1) If—
  (a) a person does anything outside the United Kingdom, and
  (b) his action would have constituted the commission of an offence under any of sections 15 to 18 if it had been done in the United Kingdom,
he shall be guilty of the offence.
(2) For the purposes of subsection (1)(b), section 18(1)(b) shall be read as if for 'the jurisdiction' there were substituted 'a jurisdiction'.

The 2000 Act provides for extended jurisdiction in relation to offences of terrorist bombing and terrorism finance committed outside the UK.

Extended Jurisdiction for Offences Committed Abroad for Terrorist Purposes

B10.81   Terrorism Act 2000, ss. 63A to 63E

63A.—(1) If—
  (a) a United Kingdom national or a United Kingdom resident does anything outside the United Kingdom, and
  (b) his action, if done in any part of the United Kingdom, would have constituted an offence under any of sections 56 to 61,
he shall be guilty in that part of the United Kingdom of the offence.
(2) For the purposes of this section and sections 63B and 63C a 'United Kingdom national' means an individual who is—
  (a) a British citizen, a British overseas territories citizen, a British National (Overseas) or a British Overseas citizen,
  (b) a person who under the British Nationality Act 1981 is a British subject, or
  (c) a British protected person within the meaning of that Act.
(3) For the purposes of this section and sections 63B and 63C a 'United Kingdom resident' means an individual who is resident in the United Kingdom.
63B.—(1) If—

(a) a United Kingdom national or a United Kingdom resident does anything outside the United Kingdom as an act of terrorism or for the purposes of terrorism, and

(b) his action, if done in any part of the United Kingdom, would have constituted an offence listed in subsection (2),

he shall be guilty in that part of the United Kingdom of the offence.

(2) These are the offences—

(a) murder, manslaughter, culpable homicide, rape, assault causing injury, assault to injury, kidnapping, abduction or false imprisonment,

(b) an offence under section 4, 16, 18, 20, 21, 22, 23, 24, 28, 29, 30 or 64 of the Offences against the Person Act 1861,

(c) an offence under any of sections 1 to 5 of the Forgery and Counterfeiting Act 1981,

(d) the uttering of a forged document or an offence under section 46A of the Criminal Law (Consolidation) (Scotland) Act 1995,

(e) an offence under section 1 or 2 of the Criminal Damage Act 1971,

(f) an offence under article 3 or 4 of the Criminal Damage (Northern Ireland) Order 1977,

(g) malicious mischief,

(h) wilful fire-raising.

63C.—(1) If—

(a) a person does anything outside the United Kingdom as an act of terrorism or for the purposes of terrorism,

(b) his action is done to, or in relation to, a United Kingdom national, a United Kingdom resident or a protected person, and

(c) his action, if done in any part of the United Kingdom, would have constituted an offence listed in subsection (2),

he shall be guilty in that part of the United Kingdom of the offence.

(2) These are the offences—

(a) murder, manslaughter, culpable homicide, rape, assault causing injury, assault to injury, kidnapping, abduction or false imprisonment,

(b) an offence under section 4, 16, 18, 20, 21, 22, 23, 24, 28, 29, 30 or 64 of the Offences against the Person Act 1861,

(c) an offence under section 1, 2, 3, 4 or 5(1) or (3) of the Forgery and Counterfeiting Act 1981,

(d) the uttering of a forged document or an offence under section 46A(1) of the Criminal Law (Consolidation) (Scotland) Act 1995.

(3) [Relates to the liability of protected persons].

63D.—(1) If—

(a) a person does anything outside the United Kingdom as an act of terrorism or for the purposes of terrorism,

(b) his action is done in connection with an attack on relevant premises or on a vehicle ordinarily used by a protected person,

(c) the attack is made when a protected person is on or in the premises or vehicle, and

(d) his action, if done in any part of the United Kingdom, would have constituted an offence listed in subsection (2),

he shall be guilty in that part of the United Kingdom of the offence.

(2) These are the offences—

(a) an offence under section 1 of the Criminal Damage Act 1971,

(b) an offence under article 3 of the Criminal Damage (Northern Ireland) Order 1977,

(c) malicious mischief,

(d) wilful fire-raising.

(3) If—

(a) a person does anything outside the United Kingdom as an act of terrorism or for the purposes of terrorism,

(b) his action consists of a threat of an attack on relevant premises or on a vehicle ordinarily used by a protected person,

(c) the attack is threatened to be made when a protected person is, or is likely to be, on or in the premises or vehicle, and

(d) his action, if done in any part of the United Kingdom, would have constituted an offence listed in subsection (4),

he shall be guilty in that part of the United Kingdom of the offence.

(4) These are the offences—
  (a) an offence under section 2 of the Criminal Damage Act 1971,
  (b) an offence under article 4 of the Criminal Damage (Northern Ireland) Order 1977,
  (c) breach of the peace (in relation to Scotland only).
(5) [Definition of premises]
63E.—(1) Proceedings for an offence which (disregarding the Acts listed in subsection (2)) would not be an offence apart from section 63B, 63C or 63D are not to be started—
  (a) in England and Wales, except by or with the consent of the Attorney General,
  (b) in Northern Ireland, except by or with the consent of the Advocate General for Northern Ireland.
(2) These are the Acts—
  (a) the Internationally Protected Persons Act 1978,
  (b) the Suppression of Terrorism Act 1978,
  (c) the Nuclear Material (Offences) Act 1983,
  (d) the United Nations Personnel Act 1997.
(3) For the purposes of sections 63C and 63D it is immaterial whether a person knows that another person is a United Kingdom national, a United Kingdom resident or a protected person.

Sections 63A to 63E represent important provisions extending the jurisdiction of the courts of the UK to deal with offences committed outside it by and against persons associated with the UK.

SUBSTANTIVE OFFENCES UNDER THE TERRORISM ACT 2006

B10.82 The TA 2006 was passed in the wake of the bombings and attempted bombings of the London Underground system in July 2005. The statute creates a number of new offences designed to counter the activities of terrorists which had not been previously addressed by legislation.

Encouragement of Terrorism

B10.83   Terrorism Act 2006, s. 1

(1) This section applies to a statement that is likely to be understood by some or all of the members of the public to whom it is published as a direct or indirect encouragement or other inducement to them to the commission, preparation or instigation of acts of terrorism or Convention offences.
(2) A person commits an offence if—
  (a) he publishes a statement to which this section applies or causes another to publish such a statement; and
  (b) at the time he publishes it or causes it to be published, he—
    (i) intends members of the public to be directly or indirectly encouraged or otherwise induced by the statement to commit, prepare or instigate acts of terrorism or Convention offences; or
    (ii) is reckless as to whether members of the public will be directly or indirectly encouraged or otherwise induced by the statement to commit, prepare or instigate such acts or offences.

B10.84 **Procedure** An allegation of an offence contrary to the TA 2006, s. 1, is triable either way (s. 1(7)); when tried on indictment it is normally a class 3 offence, but see CPD XIII, para. B (see Supplement, **PD-97**) for the additional factors that the court considers on allocation. The consent of the DPP is necessary for the institution of proceedings under the TA 2006 (s. 19(1)) unless the offence is committed outside the UK or wholly or partly in connection with the affairs of a country outside the UK, in which case the consent of the A-G is required (s. 19(2) as amended by the CT-A 2008, s. 29).

By virtue of s. 17, the offence under s. 1 may be committed by any person of any nationality anywhere in the world. The courts of the UK therefore have universal jurisdiction in relation to the offence. If a person does anything outside the UK which would constitute an offence in any part of the UK, he will be guilty of the offence in that part of the UK. Proceedings in respect of the offence may be taken anywhere in the UK and the offence may be treated for incidental purposes as having been committed in any such place (s. 17(4)).

Sentence   The maximum penalty is, on conviction on indictment, imprisonment for a term not exceeding seven years or a fine, or both, and, on summary conviction, imprisonment for a term not exceeding six months or a fine not exceeding the statutory maximum, or both (TA 2006, s. 1(7) and (8)).

B10.85

Elements   By virtue of s. 1(3), the statements that are likely to be understood by members of the public as indirectly encouraging the commission or preparation of acts of terrorism or Convention offences include every statement which (a) glorifies the commission or preparation (whether in the past, in the future or generally) of such acts or offences; and (b) is a statement from which those members of the public could reasonably be expected to infer that what is being glorified is being glorified as conduct that should be emulated by them in existing circumstances.

B10.86

'Terrorism' has the same definition as applies under the TA 2000 (see **B10.2**).

'Convention offence' in s. 1(1) means an offence listed in the TA 2006, sch. 1, or an equivalent offence under the law of a country or territory outside the UK.

The questions of how a statement is likely to be understood and what members of the public could reasonably be expected to infer from it must be determined having regard both (a) to the contents of the statement as a whole, and (b) to the circumstances and manner of its publication (s. 1(4)).

'Glorification' is defined in s. 20(2) as including any form of praise or celebration, and cognate expressions are to be construed accordingly.

'Conduct that should be emulated in existing circumstances' includes conduct that is illustrative of a type of conduct that should be so emulated (s. 20(7)).

By virtue of s. 20(3), references to 'the public' (a) are references to the public of any part of the UK or of a country or territory outside the UK, or any section of the public, and (b) except in s. 9(4), also include references to a meeting or other group of persons which is open to the public (whether unconditionally or on the making of a payment or the satisfaction of other conditions).

B10.87

References to a person's publishing a statement are references to (a) his publishing it in any manner to the public, (b) his providing electronically any service by means of which the public have access to the statement, or (c) his using a service provided to him electronically by another so as to enable or to facilitate access by the public to his statement (s. 20(4)). This subsection does not apply to the references to a publication in s. 2 (see **B10.90**).

Under s. 20(5), 'providing a service' includes making a facility available.

References to 'a statement' are references to a communication of any description, including a communication without words consisting of sounds or images or both (s. 20(6)).

For the purposes of s. 1(1)–(3), it is irrelevant (a) whether anything mentioned in those subsections relates to the commission, instigation or preparation of one or more particular acts of terrorism or Convention offences, of acts of terrorism or Convention offences of a particular description, or of acts of terrorism or Convention offences generally, and (b) whether any person is in fact encouraged or induced by the statement to commit, prepare or instigate any such act or offence (s. 1(5)).

Section 18 provides that, where an offence under part 1 of the Act is committed by a body corporate and is proved to have been committed with the consent or connivance of a director, manager, secretary or other similar officer of the body corporate (or a person purporting to act in that capacity), he (as well as the body corporate) is guilty of that offence and is liable to be proceeded against and punished accordingly. For the purposes of s. 18, where a body corporate is managed by its members, a member is a director.

B10.88

For extended jurisdiction in respect of suppliers of information society services who are established in the UK where a relevant act occurs in the EEA, see the Electronic Commerce Directive (Terrorism Act 2006) Regulations 2007 (SI 2007 No. 1550). The Regulations also provide for special defences and limited liability where they apply.

B10.89   **Specific Defence**   Section 1(6) of the TA 2006 provides that, where it is not proved that the accused intended the statement directly or indirectly to encourage or otherwise induce the commission, preparation or instigation of acts of terrorism or Convention offences, it is a defence for him to show (a) that the statement neither expressed his views nor had his endorsement (whether by virtue of s. 3 or otherwise); and (b) that it was clear, in all the circumstances of the statement's publication, that it did not express his views and (apart from the possibility of his having been given and failed to comply with a notice under s. 3(3); see **B10.95**) did not have his endorsement).

Dissemination of Terrorist Publications

B10.90   Terrorism Act 2006, s. 2

(1) A person commits an offence if he engages in conduct falling within subsection (2) and, at the time he does so—
  (a) he intends an effect of his conduct to be a direct or indirect encouragement or other inducement to the commission, preparation or instigation of acts of terrorism;
  (b) he intends an effect of his conduct to be the provision of assistance in the commission or preparation of such acts; or
  (c) he is reckless as to whether his conduct has an effect mentioned in paragraph (a) or (b).
(2) For the purposes of this section a person engages in conduct falling within this subsection if he—
  (a) distributes or circulates a terrorist publication;
  (b) gives, sells or lends such a publication;
  (c) offers such a publication for sale or loan;
  (d) provides a service to others that enables them to obtain, read, listen to or look at such a publication, or to acquire it by means of a gift, sale or loan;
  (e) transmits the contents of such a publication electronically; or
  (f) has such a publication in his possession with a view to its becoming the subject of conduct falling within any of paragraphs (a) to (e).

B10.91   **Procedure**   An allegation of an offence contrary to s. 2 of the TA 2006 is triable either way (s. 2(11)); when tried on indictment it is normally a class 3 offence, but see CPD XIII, para. B (see Supplement, **PD-97**) for the additional factors that the court considers on allocation. For consent to prosecution, see **B10.84**.

The provisions of s. 17 apply to this offence (see **B10.84**). For the liability of company directors, see **B10.88**.

B10.92   **Sentence**   The maximum penalty is, on conviction on indictment, imprisonment for a term not exceeding seven years or a fine, or both, and, on summary conviction, imprisonment for a term not exceeding six months or a fine not exceeding the statutory maximum, or both (TA 2006, s. 2(11) and (12)). The court may also make a forfeiture order in accordance with s. 23A (see **B10.112**).

In appeals against sentence in *Rahman* [2008] 4 All ER 661, the Court of Appeal gave some general guidance on sentencing for offences under s. 2. Lord Phillips CJ stated that the seriousness of the offence could not be said to be largely measurable simply by reference to the quality and quantity of the material. Other matters should be given the importance they deserve. Whether the offender intended dissemination of terrorist publications to encourage the commission, preparation or instigation of acts of terrorism or was merely reckless as to such consequences is likely to be significant. The volume and content of the material disseminated will be relevant to the harm caused, intended or foreseeable. The Court specifically approved the dictum of Calvert-Smith J in sentencing *Yahya* for an offence under s. 58 (see **B10.66**) when he observed that the offence could be committed in an almost infinite variety of ways and the appropriate sentence for such an offence would need to reflect the particular facts and circumstances of the offence and offender. The Court observed that those words apply with particular force to offences under s. 2 and, if sentences are imposed which are more severe than the circumstances of the case warrant, that is likely to inflame rather than deter terrorism. The Court allowed Rahman's appeal to the extent that the six-year sentence was reduced to five years and six months for reasons primarily concerned with the *Goodyear* procedure adopted. The Court stated that, had the s. 2 offence stood alone, the sentence would have been significantly too high. A co-appellant (Mohammed) had been sentenced to three years' imprisonment after he pleaded guilty to an offence contrary to s. 2. The Court of Appeal reduced the sentence to two years.

Elements   A publication is a terrorist publication, in relation to the conduct mentioned in the TA 2006, s. 2(2), if matter contained in it is likely (a) to be understood, by some or all of the persons to whom it is or may become available as a consequence of that conduct, as a direct or indirect encouragement or other inducement to them to the commission, preparation or instigation of acts of terrorism; or (b) to be useful in the commission or preparation of such acts and to be understood, by some or all of those persons, as contained in the publication, or made available to them, wholly or mainly for the purpose of being so useful to them (s. 2(3)). **B10.93**

Matter that is likely to be understood by a person as indirectly encouraging the commission or preparation of acts of terrorism includes any matter which (a) glorifies the commission or preparation (whether in the past, in the future or generally) of such acts, and (b) is matter from which that person could reasonably be expected to infer that what is being glorified is being glorified as conduct that should be emulated by him in existing circumstances (s. 2(4)).

Whether a publication is a terrorist publication must be determined (a) as at the time of the conduct, and (b) having regard both to the contents of the publication as a whole and to the circumstances in which the conduct occurs (s. 2(5)).

References to the effect of a person's conduct in relation to a terrorist publication include references to an effect of the publication on one or more persons to whom it is or may become available as a consequence of that conduct (s. 2(6)).

Evidence of possession of a publication by known terrorists is admissible, if at all, only for the 'extremely limited purpose' of demonstrating that such persons may be among those who read it. It cannot prove that they were encouraged by it to commit or instigate terrorist offences; but there is an obvious risk that a jury may be prejudiced into condemning the publication purely by reason of its association with known terrorists, and if such evidence is properly admitted at all there must be a clear warning to the jury as to what it can and cannot be used to prove (*Faraz* [2013] 1 WLR 265).

It is irrelevant whether anything in s. 2(1)–(4) is in relation to the commission, preparation or instigation of one or more particular acts of terrorism, of acts of terrorism of a particular description or of acts of terrorism generally (s. 2(7)). It is also irrelevant whether any person is in fact encouraged or induced by the matter contained in any articles to commit, prepare or instigate acts of terrorism, or in fact makes use of it in the commission or preparation of such acts (s. 2(8)).

'Article' includes anything for storing data (s. 20(2)). 'Publication' means any article or record of any description that contains any of the following, or a combination of them: matter to be read, matter to be listened to, matter to be looked at or watched (s. 2(13)).

In *Brown* [2011] EWCA Crim 2571, the Court of Appeal held that s. 2 constituted a proportionate restriction on the right to freedom of expression under the ECHR and freedom of speech at common law.

Specific Defences   The TA 2006 provides for two special defences to an allegation under s. 2. **B10.94** The first defence concerns the defendant establishing that the views were not his nor did he endorse them.

617

Terrorism Act 2006, s. 2

(9) In proceedings for an offence under this section against a person in respect of conduct to which subsection (10) applies, it is a defence for him to show—

(a) that the matter by reference to which the publication in question was a terrorist publication neither expressed his views nor had his endorsement (whether by virtue of section 3 or otherwise); and

(b) that it was clear, in all the circumstances of the conduct, that that matter did not express his views and (apart from the possibility of his having been given and failed to comply with a notice under [s. 3(3): see **B10.95**]) did not have his endorsement.

(10) This subsection applies to the conduct of a person to the extent that—

(a) the publication to which his conduct related contained matter by reference to which it was a terrorist publication by virtue of [s. 2(3)(a)]; and

(b) that person is not proved to have engaged in that conduct with the intention specified in [s. 2(1)(a)].

The second defence relates to internet activity and repeat statements.

Terrorism Act 2006, s. 3

(5) In proceedings against a person for an offence under section 1 or 2 the requirements of subsection (2)(a) to (c) are not, in his case, to be regarded as satisfied in relation to any time by virtue of subsection (4) if he shows that he—

(a) has, before that time, taken every step he reasonably could to prevent a repeat statement from becoming available to the public and to ascertain whether it does; and

(b) was, at that time, a person to whom subsection (6) applied.

(6) This subsection applies to a person at any time when he—

(a) is not aware of the publication of the repeat statement; or

(b) having become aware of its publication, has taken every step that he reasonably could to secure that it either ceased to be available to the public or was modified as mentioned in subsection (3)(b).

B10.95   **Internet Activity**   In relation to the TA 2006, ss. 1 and 2, s. 3 applies where a statement is published or caused to be published in the course of, or in connection with, the provision or use of a service provided electronically, or conduct falling within s. 2(2) was in the course of, or in connection with, the provision or use of such a service (s. 3(1)). The statement or article or record to which the conduct relates is to be regarded as having the endorsement of a person at any time more than two working days after a constable has given him notice under s. 3(3) and the relevant person has failed, without reasonable excuse, to comply with the notice (s. 3(2)).

Section 3(7) sets out when a statement or an article or record is unlawfully terrorism-related.

Section 4 deals with the delivery of s. 3 notices.

For extended jurisdiction in respect of suppliers of information society services who are established in the UK where a relevant act occurs in the EEA, see the Electronic Commerce Directive (Terrorism Act 2006) Regulations 2007 (SI 2007 No. 1550). The Regulations also provide for special defences and limited liability where they apply.

B10.96   **Search Power**   If a magistrate is satisfied that there are reasonable grounds for suspecting that articles likely to be the subject of conduct falling within s. 2(2)(a)–(e) and to be treated as a terrorist publication are likely to be found on any premises, he may issue a warrant authorising a constable (a) to enter and search the premises, and (b) to seize anything found there which the constable has reason to believe is such an article (TA 2006, s. 28(1) and (2)). The person searching may use such force as is reasonable in the circumstances for exercising the power (s. 28(3)).

Preparation of Terrorist Acts

B10.97

Terrorism Act 2006, s. 5

(1) A person commits an offence if, with the intention of—

(a) committing acts of terrorism, or

(b) assisting another to commit such acts,

he engages in any conduct in preparation for giving effect to his intention.

Procedure   The offence is indictable only (TA 2006, s. 5(1)) and is a class 1B offence. For   **B10.98**
consent to prosecution, see **B10.84**.

The Terrorism Protocol (see **B10.1**) applies to this offence.

For the liability of company directors, see **B10.88**.

Sentence   The maximum penalty is life imprisonment (TA 2006, s. 5(3)). The court may also   **B10.99**
make a forfeiture order in accordance with s. 23A (see **B10.112**).

In *Usman Khan* [2013] EWCA Crim 468 (see **B10.109**) the Court of Appeal observed that the
offence under s. 5 is 'particularly wide, covering acts just short of an attempt to conduct that only
just crosses the line into criminality' and noted the difficulty in setting guidelines for the offence.

In *A-G's Ref (No. 7 of 2008) (Quereshi)* [2008] EWCA Crim 1054 a 30-year-old offender of previous good character was sentenced to four and a half years' imprisonment following a guilty plea
to an offence under s. 5. The offender had been apprehended when about to fly to Islamabad.
He had in his possession approximately £9,000 in cash along with a number of items including
a night-sight, medical supplies, sleeping bags, asp-type batons, a hard drive and motivational
CDs, with the intention of making himself available to support his cause in one way or another.
The Court of Appeal held that the sentence was lenient but not unduly so. In *Tabbakh* (2009)
173 JP 201, the Court of Appeal rejected a renewed application for leave to appeal against a
sentence of seven years' imprisonment imposed for an offence contrary to s. 5. The applicant
was aged 39 and of previous good character. He had post-traumatic stress disorder as a result of
torture in Syria. The sentencing judge had reduced his sentence from one of eight years because
of his mental condition. Hughes LJ observed that the sentence was not manifestly excessive or
outside the range for an offender who was doing his best to make a bomb in this country with a
view to terrorist acts (being in possession of bomb-making instructions and having gone some
way towards securing the necessary ingredients) but was unable to do so at that time because
he did not have a detonator nor the right grade of ingredients. In *Parviz Khan* [2010] 1 Cr App
R (S) 215, the Court of Appeal dismissed a renewed application for leave to appeal against a
sentence of life imprisonment with a minimum term of 14 years. K had pleaded guilty to two
offences contrary to s. 5 of the TA 2006 and two offences contrary to s. 58 of the TA 2000.
The s. 5 offences concerned, first, a plot to kidnap and behead a Muslim serving in the British
army and, second, a repeated and continuing supply of equipment to jihadists on the Pakistan/
Afghanistan border. The s. 58 offences related to possession of two documents, namely 'The
Encyclopaedia of Jihad' and 'How do I prepare myself for Jihad?'. The Court of Appeal said that
the sentencing judge was right to impose a life sentence on a man of such fanatical determination and was right to take the view that there would have been consecutive sentences when he
calculated the appropriate minimum term. The Court observed (as Henriques J had done when
sentencing) that, if the kidnap plot had come to fruition, a whole life sentence would have been
appropriate.

In *Karim* [2012] 1 Cr App R (S) 503, a total sentence of 30 years' imprisonment with an extension period of five years was upheld by the Court of Appeal in respect of offences under s. 5. The
offender had, amongst other things, joined British Airways as an employee for the purposes of
acquiring a position and/or information useful to the commission of a terrorist act and indirectly corresponded with a well-known terrorist about getting a bomb on to a plane to the USA.

Elements   By virtue of the TA 2006, s. 5(2), it is irrelevant whether the intention and prepara-   **B10.100**
tion referred to in s. 5(1) relate to one or more particular acts of terrorism, acts of terrorism of a
particular description, or acts of terrorism generally. The offence under s. 5 has been prosecuted
relatively frequently. Its breadth has meant that prosecutors have not relied on the TA 2000,
ss. 57 and 58, as often as they did prior to 2006.

In *Roddis* [2009] EWCA Crim 585, the accused was in possession of two of the three component
ingredients of the primary explosive TATP, had made attempts to secure the final ingredient and

had carried out research into bomb-making and explosives. It was submitted on appeal that the evidence did not amount to a case to answer as it did not go beyond mere possession. Allied with that was a further submission that the judge ought to have directed the jury that conduct in the context of this case meant, and meant only, acquisition and accordingly the only relevant time to look at the accused's intent was the time of acquisition of the material. The acquisition of the ingredients for TATP had been some 18 months before arrest and any subsequent intent ought to have been treated as irrelevant. So far as the first submission was concerned, the Court of Appeal observed that the Crown's case was one of successive acts of acquisition of knowledge and materials for bomb-making which amounted to a continuing process. There was ample evidence of that continuing process, a simple example of which was afforded by the attempts to buy the final ingredient for the TATP. In respect of the allied submission, the Court observed that the summing-up had made clear to the jury that the coincidence of conduct and intent was essential. The conduct in which the accused was alleged to have engaged was researching on the internet into how to make home-made explosives and purchasing two of the ingredients so that he could manufacture his explosives and use them in an improvised explosive device along with the nails he had also purchased for that purpose and the fuse that he had obtained from fireworks. It follows that the conduct left to the jury was not simply the acquisition of the ingredients, but extended to acquisition of knowledge, which was on the facts a continuing process. The real issue in the case was the intent of the accused.

Training for Terrorism

B10.101
Terrorism Act 2006, s. 6

(1) A person commits an offence if—
  (a) he provides instruction or training in any of the skills mentioned in subsection (3); and
  (b) at the time he provides the instruction or training, he knows that a person receiving it intends to use the skills on which he is being instructed or trained—
    (i) for or in connection with the commission or preparation of acts of terrorism or Convention offences; or
    (ii) for assisting the commission or preparation by others of such acts or offences.
(2) A person commits an offence if—
  (a) he receives instruction or training in any of the skills mentioned in subsection (3); and
  (b) at the time of the instruction or training, he intends to use the skills which he is being instructed or trained—
    (i) for or in connection with the commission or preparation of acts of terrorism or Convention offences; or
    (ii) for assisting the commission or preparation by others of such acts or offences.
(3) The skills are—
  (a) the making, handling or use of a noxious substance, or of substances of a description of such substances;
  (b) the use of any method or technique for doing anything else that is capable of being done for the purposes of terrorism, in connection with the commission or preparation of an act of terrorism or Convention offence or in connection with assisting the commission or preparation by another of such an act or offence; and
  (c) the design or adaptation for the purposes of terrorism, or in connection with the commission or preparation of acts of terrorism or Convention offences, of any method or technique for doing anything.

B10.102 **Procedure** An allegation of an offence contrary to s. 6 of the TA 2006 is triable either way (s. 6(5)); when tried on indictment it is normally a class 3 offence, but see CPD XIII, para. B (see Supplement, **PD-97**) for the additional factors that the court considers on allocation. For consent to prosecution, see **B10.84**.

The provisions of s. 17 apply to this offence (see **B10.84**). For the liability of company directors, see **B10.88**.

B10.103 **Sentence** The maximum penalty is, on conviction on indictment, imprisonment for a term not exceeding ten years or a fine, or both, and, on summary conviction, imprisonment for a term not exceeding six months or a fine not exceeding the statutory maximum, or both (TA 2006, s. 6(5) and (6)). The court may order the forfeiture of anything the court considers to have been in the person's possession for purposes connected with the offence (s. 7(1)). The court may also make a more wide-ranging forfeiture order in accordance with s. 23A (see **B10.112**).

When dealing with the two principal offenders in *Hamid* (7 March 2008 unreported), Pitchers J said that the starting point, following conviction after trial, where training had been provided on a number of occasions, was one of seven years' imprisonment. He observed that the offence was no less serious because the primary purpose of the training was for the commission of terrorist offences abroad.

Elements   It is irrelevant (a) whether any instruction or training that is provided is provided   **B10.104**
to one or more particular persons or generally; (b) whether the acts or offences in relation to which a person intends to use such skills consist of one or more particular acts of terrorism or Convention offences, acts of terrorism or Convention offences of a particular description, or acts of terrorism or Convention offences generally; and (c) whether assistance that a person intends to provide to others is intended to be provided to one or more particular persons or to one or more persons whose identities are not yet known (TA 2006, s. 6(4)).

'Noxious substance' means (a) a dangerous substance within the meaning of the A-tCSA 2001, part 7, or (b) any other substance which is hazardous or noxious or which may be or become hazardous or noxious only in certain circumstances. 'Substance' includes any natural or artificial substance (whatever its origin or method of production and whether in solid or liquid form or in the form of a gas or vapour) and any mixture of substances (s. 6(7)).

Attendance at a Place for Terrorist Training

Terrorism Act 2006, s. 8   **B10.105**

(1) A person commits an offence if—
  (a) he attends at any place, whether in the United Kingdom or elsewhere;
  (b) while he is at that place, instruction or training of the type mentioned in section 6(1) of this Act or section 54(1) of the Terrorism Act 2000 is provided there;
  (c) that instruction or training is provided there wholly or partly for purposes connected with the commission or preparation of acts of terrorism or Convention offences; and
  (d) the requirements of subsection (2) are satisfied in relation to that person.
(2) The requirements of this subsection are satisfied in relation to a person if—
  (a) he knows or believes that instruction or training is being provided there wholly or partly for purposes connected with the commission or preparation of acts of terrorism or Convention offences; or
  (b) a person attending at that place throughout the period of that person's attendance could not reasonably have failed to understand that instruction or training was being provided there wholly or partly for such purposes.

Procedure   An allegation of an offence contrary to s. 8 of the TA 2006 is triable either way   **B10.106**
(s. 8(4)); when tried on indictment it is normally a class 3 offence, but see CPD XIII, para. B (see Supplement, **PD-97**) for the additional factors that the court considers on allocation. For consent to prosecution, see **B10.84**.

The provisions of s. 17 apply to this offence (see **B10.84**). For the liability of company directors, see **B10.88**.

Sentence   The maximum penalty is, on conviction on indictment, imprisonment for a term   **B10.107**
not exceeding ten years or a fine, or both, and, on summary conviction, imprisonment for a term not exceeding six months or a fine not exceeding the statutory maximum, or both (TA 2006, s. 8(4) and (5)). In *Hamid* (26 February 2008 unreported), Pitchers J imposed sentences ranging between three and a half years' and four and a half years' imprisonment on offenders convicted of offences under s. 8. The judge took into account that each had come under the influence of the charismatic principal offenders.

B10.108 **Elements** It is immaterial (a) whether the person concerned receives the instruction or training himself; and (b) whether the instruction or training is provided for purposes connected with one or more particular acts of terrorism or Convention offences, acts of terrorism or Convention offences of a particular description, or acts of terrorism or Convention offences generally (TA 2006, s. 8(3)). Under s. 8, and in contrast to s. 6(2) (see **B10.101**), the prosecution plainly do not have to prove that the accused intended to use the training he received for terrorist purposes.

SENTENCING FOR OFFENCES COMMITTED IN A TERRORIST CONTEXT

B10.109 In *Barot* [2008] 1 Cr App R (S) 156, the Court of Appeal gave substantial guidance (at [33]–[62]) as to the sentencing of persons committing offences in a terrorist context. Lord Phillips CJ observed that a terrorist who is in the grip of idealistic extremism to the extent that he has been plotting to commit murder of innocent citizens over a long period is likely to pose a serious risk to the public for an indefinite period if he is not confined. Thus, if he commits an offence that permits the court to impose an indeterminate sentence, that is likely to be the appropriate course. The Court considered *Taylor and Thomas* (1995) 16 Cr App R (S) 873, *Martin* [1999] 1 Cr App R (S) 477 and *Hindawi* (1988) 10 Cr App R (S) 104 in deciding how the appropriate minimum term of that indeterminate sentence should be set. The guidelines in *Martin* required review as there had been a significant increase in the minimum terms imposed in serious murders since the implementation of the CJA 2003. Where mass murder flows from the actions of the offenders, whole life terms will be imposed. Other than in exceptional circumstances, a life sentence with a minimum of 40 years should represent the maximum sentence for a terrorist who sets out to achieve mass murder but is not successful in causing any physical harm. That sentence should be reserved for a terrorist convicted, after trial, of a serious and viable attempt to commit mass murder. If the offence charged is one of conspiracy and the plot falls short of an attempt, the sentence should be lower. Where a court is of the view that the conspiracy was likely to lead to an attempt which was likely to be successful, then it may be right to draw little distinction between the conspiracy and attempt. Where the court cannot be certain that the conspiracy would have been put into practice, or would have led to a successful attempt to murder, the sentence should be significantly lower than that imposed for an attempt. The offender's role in the plot will also be significant, with a leader being subject to a more severe sentence than a follower.

In *Usman Khan* [2013] EWCA Crim 468 the Court of Appeal set out principles for sentencing in terrorism cases which, the Court observed, come in many different forms. The Court did not provide guidelines because of 'the enormous breadth of potential offences and ... the differing potential assessment of culpability and harm depending on the precise facts'. The principles to be applied are:

(a) an assessment of culpability and harm, as required by the CJA 2003, s. 143, is necessary: the Court of Appeal noted that 'in most ... terrorist offences, the former will be extremely high';
(b) 'the purpose of sentence for the most serious terrorist offences is to punish, deter and incapacitate. Rehabilitation will play little, if any part': see *Martin*;
(c) 'the starting point for sentence for an inchoate offence is the sentence that would have been imposed if the objective had been achieved, with an attempt to commit the offence being more serious than a conspiracy': see *Barot*;
(d) sentences based on *Martin* or other cases pre-dating implementation of the CJA 2003, sch. 21 are of historical interest only and do not provide any assistance as to the approach now.

B10.110 In *Saleem* [2008] 2 Cr App R (S) 70, the Court of Appeal identified factors affecting the seriousness of an allegation of solicitation to murder in a terrorist context. The case concerned demonstrations against the publication in Denmark of cartoons depicting the Prophet Mohammed.

The Court quashed sentences of six years' imprisonment imposed after trial and substituted sentences of four years. Giving the judgment of the Court, Lord Phillips CJ said (at [38] and [45]):

> These appeals relate to sentences for inchoate offences of the kind that can lead others to commit acts of terrorism. When considering the seriousness of such offences in the context of terrorism it is material to have regard to the period of time covered by the offending, the sophistication, skill and industry devoted to it, and the likelihood that the offending would lead others to commit acts of terrorism, or may even have done so. . . .
>
> The offences with which we are concerned involved a one-off demonstration, mounted at short notice without sophisticated planning. . .Insofar as this crude chanting and the messages on the placards solicited murder, we do not think that this was likely to persuade those who witnessed the demonstration in central London, or who saw the television broadcasts of it, to resort to killing, although one cannot be sure of the effect that it might have on those already inclined to terrorist activity.

The Court observed that the seriousness of the offending was less than that in *El-Faisal* [2004] EWCA Crim 465 (seven years' imprisonment for solicitation to murder upheld on appeal) and *Abu Hamza* [2007] QB 659 (no appeal against sentence of seven years' imprisonment imposed for solicitation to murder) which involved a persistent and protracted course of conduct aimed at indoctrinating young Muslims into committing terrorist murder.

In *Rahman* [2008] 4 All ER 661, Lord Phillips CJ observed that sentences which are more severe than the circumstances of the case warrant are likely to inflame rather than deter terrorism.

In *Al Daour* [2011] EWCA Crim 2392 the Court of Appeal dealt with the question of whether a period of police detention under the TA 2000 should be taken into account, by virtue of the CJA 2003, s. 240, for the purposes of any subsequent sentence and determined that it should (see **E2.14**).

Terrorism as an Aggravating Factor

B10.111
By virtue of the C-TA 2008, s. 30 (which has effect for offences committed on or after 18 June 2009), a judge considering the seriousness of an offence listed in sch. 2 to that Act (a list of offences which may have a terrorist connection) must determine whether the offence has a terrorist connection if there is material before the court which suggests that it may have such a connection. If the court decides that there is a terrorist connection to the offence, that much must be stated in open court and must be treated as an aggravating factor for the purposes of sentencing.

Forfeiture

B10.112
Sections 34 to 39 of the C-TA 2008 extend the powers of forfeiture available to the court when sentencing for terrorist offences. A new s. 23, dealing with forfeiture for offences under ss. 15 to 18 of the TA 2000, is inserted into the TA 2000 by the C-TA 2008, s. 34; ss. 23A and 23B are inserted by the C-TA 2008, ss. 35 and 36. Sections 23A and 23B of the TA 2000 create new forfeiture powers for courts sentencing for offences specified in s. 23A or other offences found to have a terrorist connection in accordance with s. 30 of the C-TA 2008 (s. 23A (2), (3) and (4)).

Notification Requirements

B10.113
A system of notification requirements for persons convicted of terrorist offences was created by the C-TA 2008, ss. 40 to 61. The scheme is similar in nature to that applying to sexual offenders (see E23). They apply to persons convicted of an offence on or after that date but also apply retrospectively to offenders who were either in custody or on licence in relation to a custodial sentence for a terrorist offence specified in s. 41(1) on the date the provisions came into force (s. 43). The provisions apply only to terrorist offenders who are sentenced to a minimum of 12 months' imprisonment or made subject to a hospital order when charged with such an offence (s. 45). Sections 47 to 52 set out the procedure for notification and the details which the offender must provide. The duration of any notification requirements will be determined by the length of sentence imposed on the offender (s. 53). Section 54 makes it an offence to fail to comply with a notification requirement. On summary conviction, the maximum penalty is 12 months' imprisonment and/or a fine

to the statutory maximum. On conviction on indictment the maximum sentence is five years' imprisonment and/or a fine (s. 54(2)). Notification requirements can also be imposed on persons who have been convicted outside the UK in respect of a corresponding foreign offence (s. 57). Section 58 implements sch. 5 and provides for the making of foreign travel restriction orders prohibiting persons subject to notification orders from travelling outside the UK.

FINANCIAL MEASURES TO COUNTER TERRORISM: GENERAL

B10.114   Provisions designed to stem the flow of funds to terrorist groups have assumed increasing importance in the international fight against terrorism. The first substantive provisions emerged in the TA 2000, creating offences relating to the funding of terrorism, money laundering and the failure to provide information relating to terrorism finance during the course of employment. The A-tCSA 2001 supplemented those provisions, enabling the forfeiture of money connected to terrorism. In the wake of the Al-Qa'ida attacks on the World Trade Center, a number of United Nations resolutions designed to prohibit the provision of funds to named individuals and groups were incorporated into English law under the auspices of the United Nations Act 1946. The C-TA 2008 implemented a range of financial directions, found in sch. 7 to the Act. The Terrorism Asset Freezing Act 2010 added to those powers and amended sch. 7 to the C-TA 2008.

FINANCIAL MEASURES UNDER THE TERRORISM ACT 2000

Terrorist Fundraising

B10.115   **Terrorism Act 2000, s. 15**

(1) A person commits an offence if he—
  (a) invites another to provide money or other property, and
  (b) intends that it should be used, or has reasonable cause to suspect that it may be used, for the purposes of terrorism.
(2) A person commits an offence if he—
  (a) receives money or other property, and
  (b) intends that it should be used, or has reasonable cause to suspect that it may be used, for the purposes of terrorism.
(3) A person commits an offence if he—
  (a) provides money or other property, and
  (b) knows or has reasonable cause to suspect that it will or may be used for the purposes of terrorism.

B10.116   **Procedure**   An allegation of an offence contrary to the TA 2000, s. 15, is triable either way and when tried on indictment is normally a class 3 offence, but see CPD XIII, para. B (see Supplement, **PD-97**) for the additional factors that the court considers on allocation. For consent to prosecution, see **B10.32**.

See **B10.81** for extended jurisdiction provisions in relation to this offence.

B10.117   **Sentencing**   The maximum penalty is: on conviction on indictment, imprisonment for a term not exceeding 14 years, a fine, or both; on summary conviction, imprisonment for a term not exceeding six months, a fine not exceeding the statutory maximum, or both (TA 2000, s. 22). A court may also make a forfeiture order (s. 23 and sch. 4). See also **B10.112**. In *Saleem* [2009] EWCA Crim 920, custodial sentences ranging from two to two and a half years for fund-raising in relation to Iraq were reduced on appeal by the Court of Appeal.

B10.118   **Elements**   By virtue of the TA 2000, s. 121, 'property' includes property wherever situated and whether real or personal, heritable or moveable, things in action and other intangible or incorporeal property.

Specific Defences Section 21 of the TA 2000 provides a number of specific defences to an allega- **B10.119**
tion of an offence contrary to s. 15. Each of the defences involves co-operation with police officers.

(1) Under s. 21(1), no offence is committed if a person who is involved in any of the actions
covered by s. 15 is acting with the express consent of a constable.
(2) By virtue of s. 21(2), if a person is involved in a transaction or arrangement relating to
money or other property, no offence is committed if he discloses to a constable (a) his suspicion or belief that the money or other property is terrorist property, and (b) the information
on which his suspicion or belief is based. This defence applies only where a person makes
a disclosure as soon as is reasonably practicable and on his own initiative after he becomes
concerned in the relevant transaction (s. 21(3)). By virtue of s. 21(4), if a constable forbids
a person from continuing his involvement in the transaction or arrangement in relation to
which the disclosure was made but he nevertheless continues, the defence does not apply.
For 'terrorist property', see **B10.124**.
(3) For any person charged with an offence under s. 15(2) or (3), but not s. 15(1), the defence
is open to him to prove that he intended to make a disclosure of the kind mentioned
in s. 21(2) and (3), but there is a reasonable excuse for his failure to do so (s. 21(5)).

The TA 2000 makes special provision for employees where their employer has established a
procedure for making any required disclosure. Under s. 21(6), in relation to all these defences,
where a person is in employment and his employer has established a procedure for making
disclosures, the duty of disclosure on the employee is to make disclosure in accordance with the
procedure. 'Transaction or arrangement relating to money or other property' includes a reference to use or possession (s. 21(7)).

The Terrorism Act 2000 and the Proceeds of Crime Act 2002 (Amendment) Regulations **B10.120**
2007 (SI 2007 No. 3398) inserted ss. 21ZA to 21ZC into the TA 2000, providing further
specific defences to a charge under ss. 15 to 18. They relate to disclosure to authorised officers
as opposed to constables.

An 'authorised officer' is an officer of the NCA.

For the compatibility of the reverse burden with the ECHR, Article 6, see **F3.18** *et seq.*

Possession of Property

Terrorism Act 2000, s. 16 **B10.121**

(1) A person commits an offence if he uses money or other property for the purposes of terrorism.
(2) A person commits an offence if he—
  (a) possesses money or other property, and
  (b) intends that it should be used, or has reasonable cause to suspect that it may be used, for
the purposes of terrorism.

Procedure An allegation of an offence contrary to the TA 2000, s. 16, is triable either way **B10.122**
and when tried on indictment is normally a class 3 offence, but see CPD XIII, para. B (see
Supplement, **PD-97**) for the additional factors that the court considers on allocation. For consent to prosecution, see **B10.32**.

See **B10.81** for extended jurisdiction provisions in relation to this offence.

Sentencing The maximum penalty is: on conviction on indictment, imprisonment for a term **B10.123**
not exceeding 14 years, a fine, or both; on summary conviction, imprisonment for a term not
exceeding six months, a fine not exceeding the statutory maximum, or both (TA 2000, s. 22).
A court may also make a forfeiture order (s. 23 and sch. 4). See also **B10.112**.

Elements For 'terrorism', see **B10.2**. By virtue of s. 14(1) of the 2000 Act, 'terrorist prop- **B10.124**
erty' means (a) money or other property which is likely to be used for the purposes of terrorism
(including any resources of a proscribed organisation), (b) proceeds of the commission of acts of

B

Part B Offences

terrorism, and (c) proceeds of acts carried out for the purposes of terrorism. The 'proceeds' of an act include any property which, wholly or partly and directly or indirectly, represents the proceeds of the act (including payments or other rewards in connection with its commission). An organisation's resources include any money or other property which is applied or made available, or is to be applied or made available, for use by the organisation (s. 14(2)). For 'property', see **B10.118**.

The offence is one of specific intent and is concerned with knowingly providing money or other property in support of a proscribed organisation. If the organisation has been properly proscribed, the offence cannot be seen as disproportionate (*O'Driscoll v Secretary of State for the Home Department* [2003] ACD 35).

B10.125   **Specific Defences**   The defences available to a person charged with an offence contrary to the TA 2000, s. 16, are the same as those available to a person charged with an offence contrary to s. 15 (see **B10.119**).

For the compatibility of the reverse burden with the ECHR, Article 6, see **F3.18** *et seq.*

Funding Arrangements

B10.126
Terrorism Act 2000, s. 17

A person commits an offence if—
(a) he enters into or becomes concerned in an arrangement as a result of which money or other property is made available or is to be made available to another, and
(b) he knows or has reasonable cause to suspect that it will or may be used for the purposes of terrorism.

B10.127   **Procedure**   An allegation of an offence contrary to the TA 2000, s. 17, is triable either way and when tried on indictment is normally a class 3 offence, but see CPD XIII, para. B (see Supplement, **PD-97**) for the additional factors that the court considers on allocation. For consent to prosecution, see **B10.32**.

See **B10.81** for extended jurisdiction provisions in relation to this offence.

B10.128   **Sentencing**   The maximum penalty is: on conviction on indictment, imprisonment for a term not exceeding 14 years, a fine, or both; on summary conviction, imprisonment for a term not exceeding six months, a fine not exceeding the statutory maximum, or both (TA 2000, s. 22). A court may also make a forfeiture order (s. 23 and sch. 4). See also **B10.112**. In *Mohammed Ajmal Khan* (17 March 2006 unreported, but for the facts of the case see [2007] EWCA Crim 2331) the offender was sentenced to eight years' imprisonment by Fulford J following a guilty plea to conspiracy to commit an offence under s. 17. He was an influential member of Lashkar-e-Tayyaba, a Kashmiri separatist organisation, and had been involved in procuring, modifying and supplying guns for the organisation.

B10.129   **Elements**   For 'terrorism', see **B10.2**.

B10.130   **Specific Defences**   The defences available to a person charged with an offence contrary to the TA 2000, s. 17, are the same as those available to a person charged with an offence contrary to s. 15 (see **B10.119**).

For the compatibility of the reverse burden with the ECHR, Article 6, see **F3.18** *et seq.*

Money Laundering

B10.131
Terrorism Act 2000, s. 18

(1) A person commits an offence if he enters into or becomes concerned in an arrangement which facilitates the retention or control by or on behalf of another person of terrorist property—
(a) by concealment,
(b) by removal from the jurisdiction,
(c) by transfer to nominees, or
(d) in any other way.

Procedure   An allegation of an offence contrary to s. 18 is triable either way and when tried on   B10.132
indictment is normally a class 3 offence, but see CPD XIII, para. B (see Supplement, PD-97) for the
additional factors that the court considers on allocation. For consent to prosecution, see **B10.32**.

See **B10.81** for extended jurisdiction provisions in relation to this offence.

Sentencing   The maximum penalty is: on conviction on indictment, imprisonment for a term   B10.133
not exceeding 14 years, a fine, or both; on summary conviction, imprisonment for a term not
exceeding six months, a fine not exceeding the statutory maximum, or both (TA 2000, s. 22).
A court may also make a forfeiture order (s. 23 and sch. 4). See also **B10.112**.

Elements   For terrorism, see **B10.2**. For terrorist property, see **B10.124**.   B10.134

Specific Defence   B10.135

Terrorism Act 2000, s. 18

(2) It is a defence for a person charged with an offence under subsection (1) to prove that he did not
know and had no reasonable cause to suspect that the arrangement related to terrorist property.

In addition to the defence set out in s. 18(2), the same defences available to a person charged
with an offence contrary to s. 15 (see **B10.115**) are available to a person charged with an offence
contrary to s. 18.

For the compatibility of the reverse burden with the ECHR, Article 6, see **F3.18** *et seq.*

FAILURE TO COMPLY WITH A DUTY OF DISCLOSURE

General Duty of Disclosure

Terrorism Act 2000, s. 19   B10.136

(1) This section applies where a person—
  (a) believes or suspects that another person has committed an offence under any of sections
15 to 18, and
  (b) bases his belief or suspicion on information which comes to his attention—
    (i)   in the course of a trade, profession or business, or
    (ii) in the course of his employment (whether or not in the course of a trade, profession
or business).
(1A)   But this section does not apply if the information came to the person in the course of a business in the regulated sector.
(2) The person commits an offence if he does not disclose to a constable as soon as is reasonably
practicable—
  (a) his belief or suspicion, and
  (b) the information on which it is based.

Procedure   An allegation of an offence contrary to the TA 2000, s. 19, is triable either way   B10.137
and when tried on indictment is normally a class 3 offence, but see CPD XIII, para. B (see
Supplement, PD-97) for the additional factors that the court considers on allocation. For consent to prosecution, see **B10.32**.

Sentencing   The maximum penalty is: on conviction on indictment, imprisonment for a term   B10.138
not exceeding five years, a fine or both; on summary conviction, imprisonment for a term not
exceeding six months, a fine not exceeding the statutory maximum, or both (TA 2000, s. 19(8)).

Elements   For the offences under the TA 2000, ss. 15 to 18, see **B10.115** *et seq.*   B10.139

By virtue of s. 19(7), a person is treated as having committed one of the offences in ss. 15 to 18
if (a) he has taken an action or been in possession of a thing, and (b) he would have committed
an offence under one of those sections if he had been in the UK at the time when he took the
action or was in possession of the thing.

The term 'a business in the regulated sector' must be construed in accordance with sch. 3A
(s. 19(7A)).

'A constable' includes an officer of the NCA (s. 19(7B)).

B10.140   Specific Defence

Terrorism Act 2000, s. 19

(3) It is a defence for a person charged with an offence under subsection (2) to prove that he had a reasonable excuse for not making the disclosure.

(4) Where—

   (a) a person is in employment,

   (b) his employer has established a procedure for the making of disclosures of the matters specified in subsection (2), and

   (c) he is charged with an offence under that subsection,

it is a defence for him to prove that he had disclosed the matters specified in that subsection in accordance with the procedure.

(5) Subsection (2) does not require disclosure by a professional legal adviser of—

   (a) information which he obtains in privileged circumstances, or

   (b) a belief or suspicion based on information which he obtains in privileged circumstances.

For the compatibility of the reverse burden with the ECHR, Article 6, see **F3.18** *et seq.*

Failure to Disclose: Regulated Sector

B10.141

Terrorism Act 2000, s. 21A

(1) A person commits an offence if each of the following three conditions is satisfied.

(2) The first condition is that he—

   (a) knows or suspects, or

   (b) has reasonable grounds for knowing or suspecting,

that another person has committed or attempted to commit an offence under any of sections 15 to 18.

(3) The second condition is that the information or other matter—

   (a) on which his knowledge or suspicion is based, or

   (b) which gives reasonable grounds for such knowledge or suspicion,

came to him in the course of a business in the regulated sector.

(4) The third condition is that he does not disclose the information or other matter to a constable or nominated officer as soon as is practicable after it comes to him.

B10.142   Procedure   An allegation of an offence contrary to the TA 2000, s. 21A, is triable either way and when tried on indictment is normally a class 3 offence, but see CPD XIII, para. B (see Supplement, **PD-97**) for the additional factors that the court considers on allocation. For consent to prosecution, see **B10.32**.

B10.143   Sentencing   The maximum penalty is, on conviction on indictment, imprisonment for a term not exceeding five years or a fine or both; and, on summary conviction, imprisonment for a term not exceeding six months or a fine not exceeding the statutory maximum or both (TA 2000, s. 21A(12)).

B10.144   Elements   Section 21A(6) of the TA 2000 provides that, when a court is deciding whether a person has committed an offence under s. 21A, it must decide whether he followed any relevant guidance issued by a supervisory authority or any other appropriate body approved by the Treasury and published in a manner that the Treasury thought appropriate in order to bring it to the attention of persons likely to be affected by it.

For the purposes of s. 21A(4), s. 21A(7) requires that disclosure is made to a nominated officer if it is made to a person nominated by the accused's employer to receive such disclosures.

By virtue of s. 21A(11), a person is taken to have committed an offence under s. 21A(2) if he has taken action or been in possession of a thing and when he did that he would have committed an offence if he had done it in the UK.

The meanings of 'supervisory authority' and 'regulated sector' are to be found in sch. 3A to the 2000 Act (s. 21A(10)).

Specific Defences   Section 21A(5) of the TA 2000 provides that a person does not commit   **B10.145**
an offence under the section if he has a reasonable excuse for not disclosing the information
or other matter or he is a professional legal adviser or relevant professional adviser and the
information or matter came to him in legally privileged circumstances. Section 21A(5A)
provides that s. 21A(5) applies to a person if the person is employed by, or is in partnership
with, a professional legal adviser or relevant professional adviser to provide the adviser with
assistance or support, and the information or other matter comes to the person in connection
with the provision of such assistance or support, and, finally, that the information or other
matter came to the adviser in privileged circumstances. For legal professional privilege, see
F9.49 *et seq*.

Legally privileged circumstances are defined in s. 21A(8) as being when information is given to
a legal adviser or relevant professional adviser by a client (or his representative) in connection
with legal advice, by a person (or his representative) seeking legal advice or by any other person
in connection with proceedings which are in progress or contemplated. Information or other
material which is provided in furtherance of a criminal purpose is not covered by s. 21A(8)
(s. 21A(9)).

By s. 21A(15), a relevant professional adviser means an accountant, auditor or tax adviser who
is a member of a professional body which is established for accountants, auditors or tax advisers
(as the case may be) and which makes provision for testing the competence of those seeking
admission to membership of such a body as a condition for such admission and, finally, imposing and maintaining professional and ethical standards for its members, as well as imposing
sanctions for non-compliance with those standards.

Under s. 21B, a disclosure is not to be taken to breach any restriction on the disclosure of information, however imposed, if it fulfils three conditions. The first is that the information or other
matter disclosed came to the person in the course of a business in the regulated sector. The
second is that the information or other matter causes the person to know or suspect, or gives
him reasonable grounds for knowing or suspecting, that another person has committed an
offence under ss. 15 to 18 of the 2000 Act. Third, the person to whom the information or other
matter has been given must inform a constable or nominated officer as soon as practicable after
receiving it.

Tipping-off: Regulated Sector

Terrorism Act 2000, s. 21D   **B10.146**

(1) A person commits an offence if—
    (a) the person discloses any matter within subsection (2);
    (b) the disclosure is likely to prejudice any investigation that might be conducted following
        the disclosure referred to in that subsection; and
    (c) the information on which the disclosure is based came to the person in the course of a
        business in the regulated sector.
(2) The matters are that the person or another person has made a disclosure under a provision of
    this part—
    (a) to a constable,
    (b) in accordance with a procedure established by that person's employer for the making of
        disclosures under that provision,
    (c) to a nominated officer, or
    (d) to a National Crime Agency officer,
    of information that came to that person in the course of a business in the regulated sector.
(3) A person commits an offence if—
    (a) the person discloses that an investigation into allegations that an offence under this Part
        has been committed is being contemplated or is being carried out;
    (b) the disclosure is likely to prejudice that investigation; and
    (c) the information on which the disclosure is based came to the person in the course of a
        business in the regulated sector.

B10.147 **Procedure**   An allegation of an offence contrary to the TA 2000, s. 21A, is triable either way and when tried on indictment is normally a class 3 offence, but see CPD XIII, para. B (see Supplement, **PD-97**) for the additional factors that the court considers on allocation. For consent to prosecution, see **B10.32**.

B10.148 **Sentencing**   The maximum penalty is, on conviction on indictment, imprisonment for a term not exceeding five years or a fine or both; and, on summary conviction, imprisonment for a term not exceeding six months or a fine not exceeding the statutory maximum or both (TA 2000, s. 21A(12)).

B10.149 **Elements**   Section 21H defines terms used in ss. 21D to 21G. The references under ss. 21D to 21G to business in the regulated sector, and to a supervisory authority, are to be construed in accordance with sch. 3A.

B10.150 **Specific Defences**   Sections 21E to 21F of the TA 2000 provide for defences relating to s. 21D.

(a) An employee, officer or partner of an undertaking does not commit an offence under s. 21D if the disclosure is to an employee, officer or partner of the same undertaking (s. 21E(1)).

(b) A person does not commit an offence under s. 21D in respect of a disclosure by a credit institution or a financial institution if the disclosure is to a credit institution or a financial institution which is situated in an EEA State or in a country or territory imposing equivalent money laundering requirements and both the institution making the disclosure and the institution to whom it is made belong to the same group (s. 21E(2)).

(c) A professional legal adviser or a relevant professional adviser does not commit an offence under s. 21D if the disclosure is to a professional legal adviser or a relevant professional adviser, both the person making the disclosure and the person to whom it is made carry on business in an EEA State or in a country or territory imposing equivalent money laundering requirements, and those persons perform their professional activities within different undertakings that share common ownership, management or control (s. 21E(4)).

(d) Section 21F applies to a disclosure by one credit institution, financial institution, professional legal adviser or relevant professional adviser to another institution or adviser having that same status. No offence is committed where such a disclosure relates to a client or former client of the institution or adviser making the disclosure and the institution or adviser to whom it is made, a transaction involving them both, or the provision of a service involving them both, provided that the disclosure is to prevent an offence under part III, and both institutions or advisers are situated in an EEA State or in a territory imposing equivalent money laundering requirements and equivalent duties of professional confidentiality with regard to the protection of personal data.

(e) Two further defences apply under s. 21G.

B10.151
Terrorism Act 2000, s. 21G

(1) A person does not commit an offence under section 21D if the disclosure is—
   (a) to the authority that is the supervisory authority for that person by virtue of the Money Laundering Regulations 2007 [see **B21.32**]; or
   (b) for the purpose of—
      (i) the detection, investigation or prosecution of a criminal offence (whether in the United Kingdom or elsewhere),
      (ii) an investigation under the Proceeds of Crime Act 2002, or
      (iii) the enforcement of any order of a court under that Act.
(2) A professional legal adviser or a relevant professional adviser does not commit an offence under section 21D if the disclosure—
   (a) is to the adviser's client, and
   (b) is made for the purpose of dissuading the client from engaging in conduct amounting to an offence.
(3) A person does not commit an offence under section 21D(1) if the person does not know or suspect that the disclosure is likely to have the effect mentioned in section 21D(1)(b).

(4) A person does not commit an offence under section 21D(3) if the person does not know or suspect that the disclosure is likely to have the effect mentioned in section 21D(3)(b).

Section 21H defines terms used in ss. 21D to 21G. In those sections 'credit institution' has the same meaning as in sch. 3A and 'financial institution' means an undertaking that carries on a business in the regulated sector by virtue of any of para. 1(1)(b)–(i) thereof. References in ss. 21D to 21G to a disclosure by or to a credit institution or a financial institution include disclosure by or to an employee, officer or partner of the institution acting on its behalf. For the purposes of those sections, a country or territory imposes 'equivalent money laundering requirements' if it imposes requirements equivalent to those laid down in Directive 2005/60/EC on the prevention of the use of the financial system for the purpose of money laundering and terrorist financing. 'Relevant professional adviser' has the same meaning as in s. 21A (see **B10.145**).

FINANCIAL MEASURES UNDER THE ANTI-TERRORISM, CRIME AND SECURITY ACT 2001

Forfeiture of Cash

Powers to seize and forfeit cash which is intended to be used for terrorist purposes, represents the resources of a proscribed organisation or represents property obtained through terrorist activities are contained in sch. 1 to the A-tCSA 2001, as amended by the C-TA 2008, ss. 83 and 84. The powers are exercisable through civil proceedings in the magistrates' courts and, under s. 1(2), apply whether or not criminal proceedings have been instituted (A-tCSA 2001, s. 1(1)).   **B10.152**

Freezing Orders

Detailed provisions in relation to the making of freezing orders are set out in the A-tCSA 2001, ss. 4 to 8 and sch. 3. The procedure for making an order is set out in ss. 10 to 14.   **B10.153**

Under s. 4, the Treasury may make such a freezing order, prohibiting any person from making funds available to a specified person or persons, if the Treasury reasonably believes:

(a) either (i) action to the detriment of the UK's economy (or part of it) has been or is likely to be taken by a person or persons, or (ii) action constituting a threat to the life or property of one or more nationals of the UK or residents of the UK has been or is likely to be taken by a person or persons; and
(b) if one person is believed to have taken or be likely to take the action, that the person is (i) the government of a country or territory outside the UK, or (ii) a resident of a country or territory outside the UK or, where two or more persons are believed to be involved, each of them falls within category (i) or (ii).

'National' and 'resident' are defined in s. 9.

By virtue of s. 62 of the C-TA 2008, any challenge to such a freezing order must be made by way of judicial review (see **B10.155**).

Disclosure by Public Authorities

Anti-terrorism, Crime and Security Act 2001, s. 17   **B10.154**

(1) This section applies to the provisions listed in Schedule 4, so far as they authorise the disclosure of information.
(2) Each of the provisions to which this section applies shall have effect, in relation to the disclosure of information by or on behalf of a public authority, as if the purposes for which the disclosure of information is authorised by that provision included each of the following—
   (a) the purposes of any criminal investigation whatever which is being or may be carried out, whether in the United Kingdom or elsewhere;

(b) the purposes of any criminal proceedings whatever which have been or may be initiated, whether in the United Kingdom or elsewhere;

(c) the purposes of the initiation or bringing to an end of any such investigation or proceedings;

(d) the purpose of facilitating a determination of whether any such investigation or proceedings should be initiated or brought to an end.

(3) The Treasury may by order made by statutory instrument add any provision contained in any subordinate legislation to the provisions to which this section applies.

(4) The Treasury shall not make an order under subsection (3) unless a draft of it has been laid before Parliament and approved by a resolution of each House.

(5) No disclosure of information shall be made by virtue of this section unless the public authority by which the disclosure is made is satisfied that the making of the disclosure is proportionate to what is sought to be achieved by it.

(6) Nothing in this section shall be taken to prejudice any power to disclose information which exists apart from this section.

(7) The information that may be disclosed by virtue of this section includes information obtained before the commencement of this section.

The duties of disclosure of information by public bodies to investigators were significantly widened by s. 17. The provisions to which the extended disclosure duties relate are set out in sch. 4. Under s. 17(5), the public body must be satisfied that the disclosure is proportionate to the objectives of the request. Section 18 places limitations on disclosure of information for the purposes of proceedings overseas.

FINANCIAL POWERS UNDER THE COUNTER-TERRORISM ACT 2008

B10.155   There is further provision for the use of financial powers against terrorism in the C-TA 2008. Section 62 and sch. 7 (as amended by the Terrorism Asset Freezing Act 2010 — see **B10.156**) confer wide powers on the Treasury to act against terrorist financing. The powers enable the Treasury to direct financial and credit institutions to take action in respect of business with persons in certain countries where there is concern about money laundering, terrorist financing or proliferation. Schedule 7 also provides for a supervisory regime, and for the imposition of civil and criminal penalties. Upon indictment, the maximum penalty for the breach of a direction from the Treasury is two years' imprisonment. Section 63 creates a structure for the challenge of any decision made by the Treasury under sch. 7, or freezing orders under part 2 of the A-tCSA 2001. Any person affected by any such decision may apply to the High Court to set it aside. The application will be determined by the court in accordance with the principles of judicial review and the court may give such relief as may be given in judicial proceedings. For an example of an unsuccessful judicial review pursuant to the C-TA 2008, s. 63, related to a freezing order under the Al-Qa'ida and Taliban (United Nations Measures Order) 2006, see *R (K) v HM Treasury* [2009] EWHC 1643 (Admin). See also *Bank Mellat v HM Treasury* [2010] EWHC 1332 (QB).

Part 2 of the Terrorist Asset-Freezing Act 2010 amends sch. 7. It clarifies the persons to whom a direction may be given, broadens the definition of persons in relation to whom restrictions may be applied, and prohibits the circumvention of the requirements of a direction. Schedule 7 is also amended so as to remove some enforcement functions of the Department of Enterprise, Trade and Investment in Northern Ireland.

THE TERRORIST ASSET-FREEZING ACT 2010

B10.156   The Terrorist Asset-Freezing Act 2010 came into force on 17 December 2010. The purpose of the Act is to give effect in the UK to resolutions of the UN Security Council. Resolution 1373 (2001) was adopted by the Security Council on 28 September 2001 and relates to terrorism.

Resolution 1452 (2002) was adopted on 20 December 2002 and relates to humanitarian exemptions. The Act also provides for enforcement of Regulation (EC) 2580/2001 on specific measures directed at certain persons and entities with a view to combating terrorism. Orders were previously made by Parliament under s. 1 of the United Nations Act 1946 in order to give effect to obligations under Resolution 1373. Those were the Terrorism (United Nations Measures) Order 2001, the Terrorism (United Nations Measures) Order 2006 and the Terrorism (United Nations Measures) Order 2009. In *Ahmed v HM Treasury* [2010] 2 AC 534, the Supreme Court held that the 2006 Order was *ultra vires* the United Nations Act 1946 and quashed the 2006 Order. It was plain that the Orders of 2001 and 2009 were susceptible to the same challenge and liable to be quashed. Consequently, interim measures were introduced. The Terrorist Asset-Freezing (Temporary Provisions) Act 2010 provided that the previous orders were deemed to have been validly made under the UN Act and allowed for directions made to impose the freezing of assets to be effective from Royal Assent (10 February 2010) until 31 December 2010. The Act supersedes those temporary provisions.

B10.157 The Terrorist Asset-Freezing Act 2010 makes provision for imposing financial restrictions on persons believed or suspected to be involved in, or to have previously been involved in, terrorism. The Act allows for actions to be taken in respect of 'designated persons', as defined in s. 1 Under s. 2, two conditions must be fulfilled before the Treasury may make a final designation of a person. First, the Treasury must reasonably believe that the person is or has been involved in terrorist activity, that the person is owned or controlled directly or indirectly by such a person or that the person is acting on behalf of or at the direction of such a person. Secondly, the Treasury must consider it necessary that financial restrictions are placed on the person for purposes connected with protecting members of the public from terrorism. By virtue of s. 6, the Treasury may make an 'interim designation' of a person. Such a designation is permissible when the Treasury merely reasonably suspects that the conditions which justify a final designation are fulfilled. An interim designation expires after 30 days but may be replaced by a final designation during that period (s. 8). The Treasury may not make more than one interim designation against a person based on the same set of facts. A final designation has a maximum duration of one year but may be renewed. A renewed final designation expires after a further year but may be renewed again (s. 4). Under s. 26, any person who is designated may appeal against the decision to the High Court. Moreover, any decisions in relation to the making of the order are susceptible to judicial review (s. 27).

B10.158 Sections 11 to 15 of the Act prohibit particular actions in respect of designated persons. A person must not deal with the funds or economic resources of a designated person (s. 11), make funds or financial services available to a designated person (s. 12), make funds or financial services available for the benefit of a designated person (s. 13), make economic resources available to a designated person (s. 14), nor make economic resources available for the benefit of a designated person (s. 15). The relevant terms are defined in ss. 39 to 42. Any person who contravenes any of the prohibitions commits an offence. Section 16 provides for exceptions for certain institutions required to pay interest credits to frozen accounts and s. 17 allows the granting of licences by the Treasury to deal with frozen accounts. Section 18 makes it an offence intentionally to participate in activities knowing that the object of them is to circumvent any of the prohibitions in ss. 11 to 15 or to enable or facilitate the circumvention of any such prohibition. By virtue of s. 32, any person who commits an offence under ss. 11 to 15 or 18 is liable upon conviction on indictment to up to seven years' imprisonment and/or a fine; on summary conviction, the maximum penalty is six months' imprisonment and/or a fine to the statutory maximum.

Under s. 10, the Treasury may provide that certain information in connection with the making of a designation be kept confidential. Any person who breaches that confidentiality commits an offence. Section 17 makes it an offence to provide false details when applying for a licence. On conviction on indictment, the maximum penalty for either offence is two years' imprisonment and/or a fine; on summary conviction, the maximum penalty is six months' imprisonment and/or a fine to the statutory maximum (s. 32).

Under s. 19, institutions have an obligation to report to the Treasury any reasonable suspicion that they are dealing with a designated person. Section 22 creates an offence of failing to comply with a request for information from the Treasury. The offences under ss. 19 and 22 are summary only and are punishable by up to six months' imprisonment and/or a fine not exceeding level 5.

The provisions of the Act have extra-territorial effect (s. 33). By virtue of s. 37, the consent of the A-G must be secured for any prosecution under the Act.

BREACH OF TERRORISM PREVENTION AND INVESTIGATION MEASURES ('TPIMS')

B10.159   TPIMs were introduced by the Terrorism Prevention and Investigation Measures Act 2011 which came into force on 15 December 2011. They have replaced the previous and much criticised system of control orders created under the Prevention of Terrorism Act 2005. It is an offence under s. 23 of the 2011 Act to breach any measure specified in the TPIM without reasonable excuse. The offence is triable either way. Upon summary conviction, the offence is punishable with up to 12 months' imprisonment and/or a fine. On conviction on indictment, the offence is punishable with up to five years' imprisonment and/or a fine.

FURTHER OFFENCES UNDER THE TERRORISM ACT 2006

B10.160   The TA 2006 provides for offences relating to radioactive material and nuclear facilities. The offences concern 'Making and Possession of Radioactive Materials' (s. 9), 'Misuse of Radioactive Devices or Material and Misuse and Damage of Nuclear Facilities' (s. 10) and 'Terrorist Threats Relating to Radioactive Devices or Materials and Nuclear Facilities' (s. 11). Each offence is triable on indictment only and the Terrorism Protocol (see **B10.1**) will apply. The maximum penalty for each of the offences is life imprisonment and a forfeiture order may also be made in accordance with s. 23A (see **B10.112**).

FURTHER OFFENCES UNDER THE ANTI-TERRORISM, CRIME AND SECURITY ACT 2001

B10.161   The A-tCSA 2001 creates a number of offences to deal with weapons of mass destruction. Section 67 makes it an offence to fail to comply with any duty or direction in relation to the security of pathogens and toxins without reasonable excuse. In addition it is an offence for a person giving information under the Act knowingly or recklessly to make a statement which is false or misleading in any material particular. The offence is triable either way. On indictment it is punishable with up to five years' imprisonment and/or a fine; on summary conviction, the maximum penalty is six months, a fine not exceeding the statutory maximum or both.

Section 47, creates a number of offences relating to the use of nuclear weapons. The offences are triable on indictment only and are punishable with life imprisonment.

Section 79 makes it an offence to disclose information which might prejudice the safety of any nuclear facility or nuclear material if the disclosure is made either intending or being reckless as to whether such prejudice occurs. The offence is triable either way and on indictment is punishable with up to seven years' imprisonment and/or a fine; on summary conviction, the maximum penalty is six months, a fine not exceeding the statutory maximum or both.

B10.162   Offences relating to noxious substances which have been the subject of prosecutions since coming into force are contained in ss. 113 and 114 of the Act.

Use or Threat of Use of Noxious Substances or Things to Cause Harm and Intimidate

Anti-terrorism, Crime and Security Act 2001, s. 113

(1) A person who takes any action which—
  (a) involves the use of a noxious substance or other noxious thing;
  (b) has or is likely to have an effect falling within subsection (2); and
  (c) is designed to influence the government or an international governmental organisation or to intimidate the public or a section of the public,
  is guilty of an offence.
(2) Action has an effect falling within this subsection if it—
  (a) causes serious violence against a person anywhere in the world;
  (b) causes serious damages to real or personal property anywhere in the world;
  (c) endangers human life or creates a serious risk to the health or safety of the public or a section of the public; or
  (d) induces in members of the public the fear that the action is likely to endanger their lives or create a serious risk to their health or safety;
  but any effect on the person taking the action is to be disregarded.
(3) A person who—
  (a) makes a threat that he or another will take any action which constitutes an offence under subsection (1); and
  (b) intends thereby to induce in a person anywhere in the world the fear that the threat is likely to be carried out,
  is guilty of an offence.

Procedure   An allegation of an offence contrary to the A-tCSA 2001, s. 113, is triable either way (s. 113(4)); when tried on indictment it is normally a class 3 offence, but see CPD XIII, para. B (see Supplement, **PD-97**) for the additional factors that the court considers on allocation.

Conduct which occurs outside the UK will be covered by s. 113 provided two conditions are met (s. 113A). The first is that the conduct is done for the purpose of advancing a political, religious, ideological or racial cause. The second is that the conduct is (a) by a UK national or a UK resident, (b) by any person if done to, or in relation to, a UK national, a UK resident or a protected person, or (c) by any person if done in the circumstances which fall within the TA 2000, s. 63D(1)(b) and (c) or (3)(b) and (c) (s. 113A(2) and (3)). As to the TA 2000, s. 63D, see **B10.81**. 'United Kingdom national', 'United Kingdom resident', and 'protected person' have the same meaning as in the TA 2000, ss. 63C and 63D (s. 113A(4)). By virtue of s. 113A(5), it is immaterial whether a person knows that another is a UK national, UK resident or a protected person.

Section 113B(1) provides that the consent of the A-G is necessary for the institution of proceedings under s. 113, and s. 113B(2) provides for such proceedings to be taken, and the offence for incidental purposes to be treated as having been committed, in any part of the UK.

Sentence   The maximum penalty is, on indictment, 14 years' imprisonment, a fine or both; on summary conviction, six months' imprisonment, a fine not exceeding the statutory maximum or both (A-tCSA 2001, s. 113(4)).

Elements   For the meaning of 'noxious thing' in the OAPA 1861, see **B2.83**.

Under the A-tCSA 2001, s. 113(5), 'government' means the government of the UK or a part of the UK or of a country other than the UK. Under the same section, 'public' includes the public of a country other than the UK.

'Substance' includes any biological agent and any other natural or artificial substance (whatever its form, origin or method of production) (s. 115(1)).

For a person to be guilty of an offence under s. 113(3), it is not necessary for him to have any particular person in mind as the person in whom he intends to induce the belief in question (s. 115(2)).

Hoaxes Involving Noxious Substances or Things

B10.167   Anti-terrorism, Crime and Security Act 2001, s. 114

(1) A person is guilty of an offence if he—
   (a) places any substance or other thing in any place; or
   (b) sends any substance or other thing from one place to another (by post, rail or any other means whatever);
   with the intention of inducing in a person anywhere in the world a belief that it is likely to be (or contain) a noxious substance or other noxious thing and thereby endanger human life or create a serious risk to human health.

(2) A person is guilty of an offence if he communicates any information which he knows or believes to be false with the intention of inducing in a person anywhere in the world a belief that a noxious substance or other noxious thing is likely to be present (whether at the time the information is communicated or later) in any place and thereby endanger human life or create a serious risk to human health.

B10.168 Procedure   The offence is triable either way (A-tCSA 2001, s. 114(3)); when tried on indictment it is normally a class 3 offence, but see CPD XIII, para. B (see Supplement, **PD-97**) for the additional factors that the court considers on allocation.

B10.169 Sentence   The maximum penalty is, on indictment, 14 years' imprisonment, a fine or both; on summary conviction, six months' imprisonment, a fine not exceeding the statutory maximum or both (A-tCSA 2001, s. 113(4)).

B10.170 Elements   See **B10.166** for definitions of the elements of the offence.

For a person to be guilty of an offence under s. 114 it is not necessary for him to have any particular person in mind as the person in whom he intends to induce the belief in question (s. 115(2)).

OTHER OFFENCES RELATING TO CHEMICAL, BIOLOGICAL AND NUCLEAR WEAPONS

B10.171   In addition to those offences provided for under the TA 2000, the A-tCSA 2001 and the TA 2006, there are a number of miscellaneous operative legislative provisions relating to chemical, biological and nuclear weapons deriving from the Biological Weapons Act 1974, the Chemical Weapons Act 1996 and the Nuclear Material (Offences) Act 1983.

Developing, Producing etc. Biological Agents, Toxins and Weapons

B10.172   Biological Weapons Act 1974, s. 1

(1) No person shall develop, produce, stockpile, acquire or retain—
   (a) any biological agent or toxin of a type and in quantity that has no justification for prophylactic, protective or other peaceful purposes; or
   (b) any weapon, equipment or means of delivery designed to use biological agents or toxins for hostile purposes or in armed conflict.

(1A) A person shall not—
   (a) transfer any biological agent or toxin to another person or enter into an agreement to do so, or
   (b) make arrangements under which another person transfers any biological agent or toxin or enters into an agreement with a third party to do so,
   if the biological agent is likely to be kept or used (whether by the transferee or any other person) otherwise than for prophylactic, protective or other peaceful purposes and he knows or has reason to believe that that is the case.

B10.173 Procedure   An allegation of an offence contrary to the Biological Weapons Act 1974, s. 1, is triable on indictment only (s. 1(3)). As to the classification of the offence for the purpose of listing, see CPD XIII, para. B (see Supplement, **PD-97**). The Terrorism Protocol (see **B10.1**) applies to proceedings taken under s. 1.

The acts founding culpability can be committed outside the UK but only by a 'United Kingdom person' (s. 1A(1)); proceedings may be instituted, and for incidental purposes taken as having been committed, anywhere in the UK (s. 1A(2)). A 'United Kingdom person' is defined by s. 1A(4) in terms identical to those used by the A-tCSA 2001, s. 56.

If the requirements of s. 1B are met, then proceedings for the offence may be instituted by the DPP or by order of the Commissioners of Revenue and Customs.

Sentence   The maximum penalty is imprisonment for life (Biological Weapons Act 1974, s. 1(3)).   **B10.174**

Elements   Under the Biological Weapons Act 1974, s. 1(2), 'biological agent' means any   **B10.175**
microbial or other biological agent and 'toxin' means any toxin, whatever its origin or method of production.

Use etc. of Chemical Weapons

B10.176

Chemical Weapons Act 1996, s. 2

(1) No person shall—
   (a) use a chemical weapon;
   (b) develop or produce a chemical weapon;
   (c) have a chemical weapon in his possession;
   (d) participate in the transfer of a chemical weapon;
   (e) engage in military preparations, or in preparations of a military nature, intending to use a chemical weapon
. . .
(8) A person contravening this section is guilty of an offence. . . .

Procedure   An allegation of an offence contrary to the Chemical Weapons Act 1996, s. 2, is   **B10.177**
triable on indictment only (s. 2(8)). As to the classification of the offence for the purpose of listing, see CPD XIII, para. B (see Supplement, **PD-97**). The Terrorism Protocol (see **B10.1**) applies to this offence. The consent of the A-G is required for the institution of proceedings under this section (s. 31(1)).

The acts founding culpability can be committed outside the UK but only by a 'United Kingdom person' (s. 3(1)) and proceedings may be instituted, and for incidental purposes taken as having been committed, anywhere in the UK (s. 3(5)). A 'United Kingdom person' is defined by s. 3(2) in terms identical to those used by the A-tCSA 2001, s. 56.

Sentence   The maximum penalty is imprisonment for life (Chemical Weapons Act 1996,   **B10.178**
s. 2(8)). As to the power of forfeiture, see s. 30.

Elements   **B10.179**

Chemical Weapons Act 1996, ss. 1 and 10

1.—(1) Chemical weapons are—
   (a) toxic chemicals and their precursors;
   (b) munitions and other devices designed to cause death or harm through the toxic properties of toxic chemicals released by them;
   (c) equipment designed for use in connection with munitions and devices falling with in paragraph (b).
(2) Subsection (1) is subject to sections 2(2) and (3), 10(1) and 11(2) (by virtue of which an object is not a chemical weapon if the use or intended use is only for permitted purposes).
(3) Permitted purposes are—
   (a) peaceful purposes;
   (b) purposes related to protection against toxic chemicals;
   (c) legitimate military purposes;
   (d) purposes of enforcing the law.
(4) Legitimate military purposes are all military purposes except those which depend on the use of the toxic properties of chemicals as a method of warfare in circumstances where the main object is to cause death, permanent harm or temporary incapacity to humans or animals.
(5) A toxic chemical is a chemical which through its chemical action on life processes can cause death, permanent harm or temporary incapacity to humans or animals; and the origin, method of production and place of production are immaterial.

(6) A precursor is a chemical reactant which takes part at any stage in the production (by whatever method) of a toxic chemical.

(7) References to an object include references to a substance.

10.—(1) If an object is in the possession of a person who intends that it will be used only for permitted purposes, it is not a chemical weapon for the purposes of sections 4(1) and (3) and 5(1) and (2); and in deciding whether permitted purposes are intended the types and quantities of objects shall be taken into account.

It should be noted that 's. 11(2)', referred to in s. 1(2) above, does not apply to this offence.

The specific provisions are as follows:

Chemical Weapons Act 1996, s. 2

(2) For the purposes of subsection (1)(a) an object is not a chemical weapon if the person uses the object only for permitted purposes; and in deciding whether permitted purposes are intended the types and quantities of objects shall be taken into account.

(3) For the purposes of subsection (1)(b), (c), (d) or (e) an object is not a chemical weapon if the person does the act there mentioned with the intention that the object will be used only for permitted purposes; and in deciding whether permitted purposes are intended the types and quantities of objects shall be taken into account.

B10.180   **Specific Defence**   Under the Chemical Weapons Act 1996, s. 2(6), it is a defence for the accused to prove (a) that he neither knew nor suspected nor had reason to suspect that the object was a chemical weapon, or (b) that he knew or suspected it to be a chemical weapon and as soon as reasonably practicable after he first so knew or suspected he took all reasonable steps to inform the Secretary of State or a constable of his knowledge or suspicion. By virtue of s. 2(7), the s. 2(6) defence does not prejudice any other defence which it is open to a person charged with this offence to raise.

Restrictive and Enforcement Powers under the Chemical Weapons Act 1996

B10.181   **Issuing of Notices in Relation to Suspicious Objects**   By virtue of s. 4 of the Chemical Weapons Act 1996, if the Secretary of State has grounds to suspect that an object is a chemical weapon and someone appears to be in possession of it or has a sufficient interest in it, a notice may be issued to that person which will state, *inter alia*, that destruction of the object is being considered and that the object must not be relinquished before a specified date.

B10.182   **Powers of Entry, Search and Seizure**   Section 5 of the Chemical Weapons Act 1996 gives powers of entry, search and seizure in relation to suspected involvement with chemical weapons. If the Secretary of State has reasonable cause to believe that, on premises to which the public have access or where the occupier consents to access, an object is on such premises and it is a chemical weapon, he may authorise entry and search of the premises (s. 5(1)). A magistrate may issue a warrant to enter premises of whatever nature if there is reasonable cause to believe that an object, which is a chemical weapon, is on the premises (s. 5(2)). The person issued with the warrant may take such people and equipment with him as are necessary, and objects found on the relevant premises may be seized and removed or immobilised and made safe (s. 5(3)–(7)).

B10.183   **Power to Destroy Removed Objects**   Section 6 of the Chemical Weapons Act 1996 provides for the destruction of objects removed under the power provided by virtue of s. 5.

Chemical Weapons Premises

B10.184   Chemical Weapons Act 1996, s. 11

(1) No person shall—
   (a) construct premises he intends to be used to produce chemical weapons;
   (b) alter premises in circumstances where he intends that they will be used to produce chemical weapons;
   (c) instal or construct equipment he intends to be used to produce chemical weapons;
   (d) alter equipment in circumstances where he intends that it will be used to produce chemical weapons;

(e) permit the construction on land he occupies of premises he intends to be used to produce chemical weapons;

(f) permit premises on land he occupies to be altered in circumstances where he intends that they will be used to produce chemical weapons;

(g) permit the installation or construction on land he occupies of equipment he intends to be used to produce chemical weapons;

(h) permit equipment on land he occupies to be altered in circumstances where he intends that it will be used to produce chemical weapons.

(2) For the purposes of subsection (1) an object is not a chemical weapon if the person intends that the object will be used only for permitted purposes; and in deciding whether permitted purposes are intended the types and quantities of objects shall be taken into account.

Procedure   An allegation of an offence contrary to the Chemical Weapons Act 1996, s. 11, is **B10.185** triable on indictment only (s. 11(3)).

Sentence   The maximum sentence is one of imprisonment for life.   **B10.186**

Chemicals Used for Permitted Purposes

Chemical Weapons Act 1996, s. 19   **B10.187**

(1) Subject to section 20 (which relates to licences) no person shall—
(a) use a Schedule 1 toxic chemical or precursor for a permitted purpose, or
(b) produce or have in his possession a Schedule 1 toxic chemical or precursor with the intention that it will be used for a permitted purpose.

(2) A Schedule 1 toxic chemical or precursor is a toxic chemical or precursor listed in Schedule 1 to the annex on chemicals to the Convention; and for ease of reference that Schedule is set out in the Schedule to this Act.

(3) A person contravening this section is guilty of an offence....

Procedure   An allegation of an offence contrary to the Chemical Weapons Act 1996, s. 19, is tria- **B10.188** ble either way (s. 19(3)); when tried on indictment it is normally a class 3 offence, but see CPD XIII, para. B (see Supplement, **PD-97**) for the additional factors that the court considers on allocation.

The consent of the Secretary of State is necessary for the institution of proceedings under the section (s. 31(2)).

Sentence   The maximum penalty, whether on summary conviction or indictment, is a fine **B10.189** (Chemical Weapons Act 1996, s. 19(3)).

Holding or Dealing with Nuclear Material

Nuclear Material (Offences) Act 1983, ss. 1, 1B and 1C   **B10.190**

1.—(1) If a person, whatever his nationality, does outside the United Kingdom, in relation to or by means of nuclear material, any act which, had he done it in any part of the United Kingdom, would have made him guilty of—
(a) the offence of murder, manslaughter, culpable homicide, assault to injury, malicious mischief or causing injury, or endangering the life of the lieges, by reckless conduct, or
(b) an offence under section 18 or 20 of the Offences against the Person Act 1861 or section 1 of the Criminal Damage Act 1971, or Article 3 of the Criminal Damage (Northern Ireland) Order 1977, or section 52 of the Criminal Law (Consolidation) (Scotland) Act 1995, or
(c) the offence of theft, embezzlement, robbery, assault with intent to rob, burglary or aggravated burglary, or
(d) the offence of fraud or extortion or an offence under section 21 of the Theft Act 1968 or section 20 of the Theft Act (Northern Ireland) 1969,
he shall in any part of the United Kingdom be guilty of such of the offences mentioned in paragraphs (a) to (d) above as are offences of which the act would have made him guilty had he done it in that part of the United Kingdom.

(1A) If—
(a) a person, whatever his nationality, does outside the United Kingdom an act directed at a nuclear facility, or which interferes with the operation of such a facility,

(b) the act causes death, injury or damage resulting from the emission of ionising radiation or the release of radioactive material, and

(c) had he done that act in any part of the United Kingdom, it would have made him guilty of an offence mentioned in subsection (1)(a) or (b) above,

the person shall in any part of the United Kingdom be guilty of such of the offences mentioned in subsection (1)(a) and (b) as are offences of which the act would have made him guilty had he done it in that part of the United Kingdom.

1B.—(1) If a person, whatever his nationality, in the United Kingdom or elsewhere contravenes subsection (2) or (3) he is guilty of an offence.

(2) A person contravenes this subsection if without lawful authority—

(a) he receives, holds or deals with nuclear material, and

(b) he does so either—

   (i) intending to cause, or for the purpose of enabling another to cause, damage to the environment by means of that material, or

   (ii) being reckless as to whether, as a result of his so receiving, holding or dealing with that material, damage would be caused to the environment by means of that material.

(3) A person contravenes this subsection if without lawful authority—

(a) he does an act directed at a nuclear facility, or which interferes with the operation of such a facility, and

(b) he does so either—

   (i) intending to cause, or for the purpose of enabling another to cause, damage to the environment by means of the emission of ionising radiation or the release of radioactive material, or

   (ii) being reckless as to whether, as a result of his act, damage would be caused to the environment by means of such an emission or release.

1C.—(1) If a person, whatever his nationality, outside the United Kingdom contravenes subsection (2) below he shall be guilty of an offence.

(2) A person contravenes this subsection if he is knowingly concerned in—

(a) the unlawful export or shipment as stores of nuclear material from one country to another, or

(b) the unlawful import of nuclear material into one country from another.

(3) For the purposes of subsection (2)—

(a) the export or shipment as stores of nuclear material from a country, or

(b) the import of nuclear material into a country,

is unlawful if it is contrary to any prohibition or restriction on the export, shipment as stores or import (as the case may be) of nuclear material having effect under or by virtue of the law of that country.

B10.191 **Procedure**   An allegation of an offence contrary to the Nuclear Material (Offences) Act 1983, s. 1, is triable on indictment only. As to the classification of the offence for the purpose of listing, see CPD XIII, para. B (see Supplement, **PD-97**). Section 1D makes provision for the conduct of investigations relating to an offence under s. 1C. Proceedings for an offence which (disregarding the Internationally Protected Persons Act 1978, the Suppression of Terrorism Act 1978, the United Nations Personnel Act 1997 and the TA 2000) would not be an offence but for the Nuclear Materials (Offences) Act 1983 must have the consent of the A-G.

The provisions of the Terrorism Protocol (see **B10.1**) will apply if the offence is committed for terrorist purposes as defined under the TA 2000 (see **B10.2**).

B10.192 **Sentence**   By virtue of s. 1A, life imprisonment is the maximum penalty for an offence under s. 1(1)(a) or (b) when the offence is committed by means of, or in relation to nuclear material and the act was directed at a nuclear facility and caused death, injury or damage as a result of the emission of nuclear material. Similarly, an offence under s. 1(1)(c) or (d) committed by means of, or in relation to, nuclear material is punishable by life imprisonment as is an offence under s. 1B. For an offence under s. 1C, the maximum penalty is 14 years' imprisonment.

B10.193 **Elements**   By virtue of the Nuclear Material (Offences) Act 1983, s. 6(1) and (5), references to 'nuclear material' relate to 'nuclear material used for peaceful purposes' within the meaning of the Convention on the Physical Protection of Nuclear Material and Nuclear Facilities. Under

s. 6(2), any statement by the Secretary of State to the effect that the nuclear material either was or was not for peaceful purposes will be conclusive as to the issue. For the implications of such a provision reversing the burden of proof in the light of the ECHR, Article 6, see **F3.18** *et seq.* Similarly for the purposes of s. 1C any statement by a foreign government that a shipment of material was contrary to a prohibition shall be conclusive unless the contrary is proved (s. 1C(4) and (5)).

Nuclear Material: Offences Involving Preparatory Acts and Threats

Nuclear Material (Offences) Act 1983 ss. 2 and 2A   **B10.194**

2.—(1) If a person, whatever his nationality, in the United Kingdom or elsewhere contravenes subsection (2), (3), (4) or (7) he shall be guilty of an offence.

(2) A person contravenes this subsection if without lawful authority—
  (a) he receives, holds or deals with nuclear material, and
  (b) he does so either—
    (i) intending to cause, or for the purpose of enabling another to cause, relevant injury or damage by means of that material, or
    (ii) being reckless as to whether, as a result of his so receiving, holding or dealing with that material, relevant injury or damage would be caused by means of that material.

(3) A person contravenes this subsection if without lawful authority—
  (a) he does an act directed at a nuclear facility, or which interferes with the operation of such a facility, and
  (b) he does so either—
    (i) intending to cause, or for the purpose of enabling another to cause, relevant injury or damage by means of the emission of ionising radiation or the release of radioactive material, or
    (ii) being reckless as to whether, as a result of his act, relevant injury or damage would be caused by means of such an emission or release.

(4) A person contravenes this subsection if he—
  (a) makes a threat of a kind falling within subsection (5), and
  (b) intends that the person to whom the threat is made shall fear that it will be carried out.

(5) A threat falls within this subsection if it is a threat that the person making it or any other person will cause any of the consequences set out in subsection (6) either—
  (a) by means of nuclear material, or
  (b) by means of the emission of ionising radiation or the release of radioactive material resulting from an act which is directed at a nuclear facility, or which interferes with the operation of such a facility.

(6) The consequences mentioned in subsection (5) are—
  (a) relevant injury or damage, or
  (b) damage to the environment.

(7) A person contravenes this subsection if, in order to compel a State, international organisation or person to do, or abstain from doing, any act, he threatens that he or any other person will obtain nuclear material by an act which, whether by virtue of section 1(1) above or otherwise, is an offence mentioned in section 1(1)(c) above.

(8) A person guilty of an offence under this section shall be liable, on conviction on indictment, to imprisonment for life.

(9) In this section references to relevant injury or damage are references to death or to injury or damage of a type which constitutes an element of any offence mentioned in section 1(1)(a) or (b) above.

2A.—(1) If a person, whatever his nationality—
  (a) does an act outside the United Kingdom, and
  (b) his act, if done in any part of the United Kingdom, would constitute an offence falling within subsection (2),
he shall be guilty in that part of the United Kingdom of the offence.

(2) The offences are—
  (a) attempting to commit a nuclear offence;
  (b) conspiring to commit a nuclear offence;
  (c) inciting the commission of a nuclear offence;
  (d) aiding, abetting, counselling or procuring the commission of a nuclear offence.

B10.195   **Procedure**   Proceedings for an offence contrary to s. 2 of the Nuclear Material (Offences) Act 1983 are triable on indictment only. The same conditions apply for the requirement of the consent of the A-G as pertain to s. 1 (see **B10.191**).

The provisions of the Terrorism Protocol (see **B10.1**) will apply if the offence is committed for terrorist purposes as defined under the TA 2000 (see **B10.2**).

B10.196   **Sentence**   The maximum sentence for an offence under s. 2 is life imprisonment (s. 2(8)).

B10.197   **Elements**   Nuclear material has the same meaning as in s.1 (see **B10.193**). The term 'nuclear offence' is defined in s. 2A(3) and (4). In essence it is one of the offences listed in s. 1(1)(a)–(d) (see **B10.190**) or blackmail committed in a nuclear context, an offence contrary to s. 1B, 1C or 2(1)–(3), or one of a number of offences under the Customs and Excise Management Act 1979.

PIRACY

B10.198   Piracy has been recognised as a common-law offence in English law since the 16th century and is recognised internationally as being a crime of universal jurisdiction. The continued existence of the offence is confirmed by its modern statutory definition.

Merchant Shipping and Maritime Security Act 1997, s. 26

(1) For the avoidance of doubt it is hereby declared that for the purposes of any proceedings before a court in the United Kingdom in respect of piracy, the provisions of the United Nations Convention on the Law of the Sea 1982 that are set out in Schedule 5 shall be treated as constituting part of the law of nations.
(2) For the purposes of those provisions the high seas shall (in accordance with paragraph 2 of Article 58 of that Convention) be taken to include all waters beyond the territorial sea of the United Kingdom or of any other state.

Merchant Shipping and Maritime Security Act 1997, sch. 5

Article 101   Piracy consists of any of the following acts:
(a) any illegal acts of violence or detention, or any act of depredation, committed for private ends by the crew or the passengers of a private ship or a private aircraft, and directed—
  (i) on the high seas, against another ship or aircraft, or against persons or property on board such ship or aircraft;
  (ii) against a ship, aircraft, persons or property in a place outside the jurisdiction of any State;
(b) any act of voluntary participation in the operation of a ship or of an aircraft with knowledge of facts making it a pirate ship or aircraft;
(c) any act of inciting or of intentionally facilitating an act described in subparagraph (a) or (b).
Article 102   The acts of piracy, as defined in article 101, committed by a warship, government ship or government aircraft whose crew has mutinied and taken control of the ship or aircraft are assimilated to acts committed by a private ship or aircraft.
Article 103   A ship or aircraft is considered a pirate ship or aircraft if it is intended by the persons in dominant control to be used for the purpose of committing one of the acts referred to in article 101. The same applies if the ship or aircraft has been used to commit any such act, so long as it remains under the control of the persons guilty of that act.

Articles 101 to 103 are from the United Nations Convention on the Law of the Sea (UNCLOS).

While there is no UK case law defining the terms contained within Article 101 of UNCLOS, courts in the USA have had recent cause to consider the meaning of both 'private ends' (*Institute of Cetacean Research v Sea Shepherd Conservation Society*, Opinion of the Ninth Circuit Courts of Appeal, No. 12-35266) and 'the high seas' (*US v Ali*, US District Court, District of Columbia, No. 11-0106). In the *Sea Shepherd* case, which concerned tactics used by anti-whaling protesters who routinely used violence against whaling ships, the appellate court approved a previous decision saying that '[t]he law looks to [piracy] as an act of hostility…being committed by a vessel not commissioned and engaged in lawful warfare' and concluded that '"private ends" include those pursued on personal, moral or philosophical grounds, such as Sea Shepherd's professed environmental goals. That the perpetrators believe themselves to be serving the public good does not render their ends public.'

Procedure and Jurisdiction

Piracy *iure gentium* is a class 1B offence and triable only on indictment.   B10.199

The fact that the accused is a foreign national does not affect the jurisdiction of a court. However, the English courts will be slow to assume jurisdiction when the alleged offence has no real connection with England and Wales (*Republic of Bolivia v Indemnity Mutual Marine Assurance Co. Ltd* [1909] 1 KB 785). There is a potential problem about enforcement of this offence outside the territorial jurisdiction of England and Wales. The 1997 Act is silent as to powers of arrest and detention for acts of piracy, and Article 105 of UNCLOS, which provides for detention, is not incorporated into English law. There is no recent authority on the point. It is arguable that a common-law power to detain survives, and a Royal Navy officer detaining a piracy suspect may be said to do so under the Royal Prerogative, that being the basis for deployment of UK forces overseas. For a ruling of the ECtHR on the lawfulness of an extended detention at sea (in a drugs case), see *Medvedyev v France* (2010) 51 EHRR 899.

Sentence

Piracy Act 1837, s. 2   B10.200

Whosoever, with intent to commit or at the time of or immediately before or immediately after committing the crime of piracy in respect of any ship or vessel, shall assault, with intent to murder, any person being on board of or belonging to such ship or vessel, or shall stab, cut or wound any such person, or unlawfully do any act, by which the life of such person may be endangered, shall be guilty of [an offence], and being convicted thereof shall be liable to imprisonment for life.

An act of piracy *iure gentium* committed without the aggravating acts described within s. 2 is punishable by imprisonment and a fine at large at common law. Any specific offences committed during the piracy are punishable as if committed on land (Offences at Sea Act 1799).

Elements

'Depredation' means an act of attacking or plundering. The offences created by Article 101   B10.201 require that illegal acts are committed 'for private ends' so as to exclude actions taken during the course of an armed conflict or by law-enforcement officials. It arguably does not exclude offences committed for terrorist or political motives, as they are personal to those committing the acts. The offence defined by Article 101(a) requires an attack by a ship (or aircraft) on another ship (the 'two-ship rule'), so an act of violence etc. committed by the passengers or crew within a ship against others in the same ship would not be piracy.

Piracy cannot be committed in UK internal waters or territorial seas, or generally, in the internal waters or territorial seas of another State. The appropriate offence would be one contrary to domestic law, e.g., robbery.

<h2>HIJACKING OF SHIPS AND RELATED OFFENCES</h2>

Hijacking of Ships

Aviation and Maritime Security Act 1990, s. 9   B10.202

(1) A person who unlawfully, by the use of force or threats of any kind, seizes a ship or exercises control of it, commits the offence of hijacking a ship, whatever his nationality and whether the ship is in the United Kingdom or elsewhere, but subject to subsection (2) below.

Procedure and Jurisdiction   Under the Aviation and Maritime Security Act 1990, s. 9(1),   B10.203 the general rule is that a person can be found guilty of an offence contrary to s. 9 whatever his nationality and wherever the ship is at the time of the offence. There are exceptions in some circumstances for warships, naval auxiliary vessels and those in naval or customs service.

An allegation of an offence contrary to s. 9 is triable only on indictment and is normally a class 3 offence, but see CPD XIII, para. B (see Supplement, **PD-97**) for the additional factors that the court considers on allocation.

Proceedings for an offence under s. 9 can be instituted only with the consent of the A-G (s. 16(1)).

B10.204   **Sentence**   The maximum penalty is life imprisonment (Aviation and Maritime Security Act 1990, s. 9(3)).

B10.205   **Elements**   For 'United Kingdom national', see **B10.217**.

In s. 17(1) of the Aviation and Maritime Security Act 1990, 'ship' is defined as meaning any vessel (including hovercraft, submersible craft and other floating craft) other than one which permanently rests on, or is permanently attached to, the seabed, or has been withdrawn from navigation or laid up.

'Naval service' includes military and air force service (s. 17(1)).

Other Maritime Security Offences

B10.206   Further offences dealing with the safety of ships and fixed platforms are provided for under the Aviation and Maritime Security Act 1990 and the Merchant Shipping Act 1995.

Aviation and Maritime Security Act 1990, ss. 10, 11, 12, and 13

10.—(1) A person who unlawfully, by the use of force or by threats of any kind, seizes a fixed platform or exercises control of it, commits an offence, whatever his nationality and whether the fixed platform is in the United Kingdom or elsewhere.

(2) A person guilty of an offence under this section is liable on conviction on indictment to imprisonment for life.

11.—(1) Subject to subsection (5) below, a person commits an offence if he unlawfully and intentionally—

(a) destroys a ship or a fixed platform,

(b) damages a ship, its cargo or a fixed platform so as to endanger, or to be likely to endanger, the safe navigation of the ship, or as the case may be, the safety of the platform, or

(c) commits on board a ship or on a fixed platform an act of violence which is likely to endanger the safe navigation of the ship, or as the case may be, the safety of the platform.

(2) Subject to subsection (5) below, a person commits an offence if he unlawfully and intentionally places, or causes to be placed, on a ship or fixed platform any device or substance which—

(a) in the case of a ship, is likely to destroy the ship or is likely so to damage it or its cargo as to endanger its safe navigation, or

(b) in the case of a fixed platform, is likely to destroy the fixed platform or so to damage it as to endanger its safety.

(3) Nothing in subsection (2) above is to be construed as limiting the circumstances in which the commission of any act—

(a) may constitute an offence under subsection (1) above, or

(b) may constitute attempting or conspiring to commit, or aiding, abetting, counselling, procuring or inciting, or being art and part in, the commission of such an offence.

(4) Except as provided by subsection (5) below, subsections (1) and (2) above apply whether any such act as is mentioned in those subsections is committed in the United Kingdom or elsewhere and whatever the nationality of the person committing the act.

(5) Subsections (1) and (2) above do not apply in relation to any act committed in relation to a warship or any other ship used as a naval auxiliary or in customs or police service unless—

(a) the person committing the act is a United Kingdom national, or

(b) his act is committed in the United Kingdom, or

(c) the ship is used in the naval or customs service of the United Kingdom or in the service of any police force in the United Kingdom.

(6) A person guilty of an offence under this section is liable on conviction on indictment to imprisonment for life.

12.—(1) Subject to subsection (6) below, it is an offence for any person unlawfully and intentionally—
  (a) to destroy or damage any property to which this subsection applies, or
  (b) seriously to interfere with the operation of any such property,
  where the destruction, damage or interference is likely to endanger the safe navigation of any ship.

(2) Subsection (1) above applies to any property used for the provision of maritime navigation facilities, including any land, building or ship so used, and including any apparatus or equipment so used, whether it is on board a ship or elsewhere.

(3) Subject to subsection (6) below, it is also an offence for any person intentionally to communicate any information which he knows to be false in a material particular, where the communication of the information endangers the safe navigation of any ship.

(4) It is a defence for a person charged with an offence under subsection (3) above to prove that, when he communicated the information, he was lawfully employed to perform duties which consisted of or included the communication of information and that he communicated the information in good faith in performance of those duties.

(5) Except as provided by subsection (6) below, subsections (1) and (3) above apply whether any such act as is mentioned in those subsections is committed in the United Kingdom or elsewhere and whatever the nationality of the person committing the act.

(6) For the purposes of subsections (1) and (3) above any danger, or likelihood of danger, to the safe navigation of a warship or any other ship used as a naval auxiliary or in customs or police service is to be disregarded unless—
  (a) the person committing the act is a United Kingdom national, or
  (b) his act is committed in the United Kingdom, or
  (c) the ship is used in the naval or customs service of the United Kingdom or in the service of any police force in the United Kingdom.

(7) A person guilty of an offence under this section is liable on conviction on indictment to imprisonment for life.

13.—(1) A person commits an offence if—
  (a) in order to compel any other person to do or abstain from doing any act, he threatens that he or some other person will do in relation to any ship or fixed platform an act which is an offence by virtue of section 11(1) of this Act, and
  (b) the making of that threat is likely to endanger the safe navigation of the ship or, as the case may be, the safety of the fixed platform.

(2) Subject to subsection (4) below, a person commits an offence if—
  (a) in order to compel any other person to do or abstain from doing any act, he threatens that he or some other person will do an act which is an offence by virtue of section 12(1) of this Act, and
  (b) the making of that threat is likely to endanger the safe navigation of any ship.

(3) Except as provided by subsection (4) below, subsections (1) and (2) above apply whether any such act as is mentioned in those subsections is committed in the United Kingdom or elsewhere and whatever the nationality of the person committing the act.

(4) Section 12(6) of this Act applies for the purposes of subsection (2)(b) above as it applies for the purposes of section 12(1) and (3) of this Act.

Procedure   Each of the offences is triable only on indictment. Proceedings may be instituted only with the consent of the A-G.   **B10.207**

Sentence   The maximum sentence for each offence is life imprisonment.   **B10.208**

Elements   For 'act of violence', see **B10.221**. For 'unlawful', see **B10.221**. Hijacking a ship is   **B10.209**
the act of unlawfully seizing a ship or exercising control of it by the use of force or by threats. The offence can be committed in the territorial seas of the UK or any other State, or in UK internal waters, as well as on the high seas. It can be committed by individuals within a ship.

Related Offences and Powers

There are ancillary offences relevant to provisions within the Aviation and Maritime Security   **B10.210**
Act 1990 along with a power of delivery to a ship's master:

Ancillary Offences under s. 14(1): Section 14(1) and (2) of the Act provide that, where a person (of whatever nationality) does any act outside the UK which, if done in the UK, would constitute an offence of murder, attempted murder, manslaughter, culpable homicide or assault, or an offence under the OAPA 1861, ss. 18, 20, 21, 22, 23, 28 and 29, or an offence contrary to s. 2 of the Explosive Substances Act 1883, his act constitutes that offence if it is done in connection with an offence under the Aviation and Maritime Security Act 1990, ss. 9, 10, 11, or 12, committed or attempted by him. These provisions are without prejudice to the jurisdiction clauses of the Merchant Shipping Act 1995, ss. 281 and 282, or the Petroleum Act 1998, s. 10 (Aviation and Maritime Security Act 1990, s. 14(3)).

Inducing or Assisting in Commission of Offences under s. 14(4): It is an offence for any person in the UK to induce or assist the commission outside the UK of any act which would, but for the Aviation and Maritime Security Act 1990, s. 9(2), be an offence under ss. 9, 11, 12 or 13 (offences involving threats). These offences can be committed against a Naval, Customs or police vessel as well as a civilian ship. The offences are triable on indictment only and the maximum penalty is life imprisonment (s. 14(5)).

Master's Power of Delivery: Section 15 of the Act provides the master of a ship with the power to deliver a person to an appropriate officer in the UK or any other Rome Convention country where he has reasonable grounds to believe that that person has (a) committed an offence under s. 9, 11, 12 or 13, (b) attempted to commit such an offence, or (c) aided, abetted, counselled, procured or incited, been art and part in, the commission of such an offence.

B10.211   Merchant Discipline   The Merchant Shipping Act 1995, s. 58, creates offences relating to conduct on ships which causes danger, concerted disobedience and neglect of duty. These offences, which carry a maximum sentence of two years' imprisonment, provide a discipline system for those working or travelling in merchant ships. Section 58 applies not only to the master and crew of a UK ship, but to the master and crew of a foreign-registered ship when it is in a port in the UK or within UK waters while proceeding to or from any UK port. But if the foreign ship in question is travelling through UK territorial seas but not on passage to or from a UK port (e.g., passing through the English Channel from Belgium to Spain), the Act does not apply. Section 106 of the 1995 Act provides that, where a person goes to sea in a ship without the consent of the master or of any other person authorised to give it, ss. 58 and 59 apply as if he were a seaman employed in the ship (s. 106 does not apply to fishing vessels).

B10.212   Stowaways and Port and Harbour Security   There are ancillary provisions within the Merchant Shipping Act 1995 which deal with persons not lawfully on board ships, and which give powers of detention to the master of a UK ship.

Section 103 deals with stowaways. A person who goes to sea or attempts to go to sea in a UK ship, without the consent of the master or of any other person authorised to give it, is guilty of a summary-only offence with a maximum penalty of a fine not exceeding level 3 on the standard scale. Section 104 makes it an offence to go on board a UK ship or a ship registered in any other country in a port in the UK without the consent of the master or of any other persons authorised to give it; or to remain on board the ship after being requested to leave by the master, a constable, an officer authorised by the Secretary of State or an officer of customs and excise. This is a summary-only offence with a maximum penalty of a fine not exceeding level 5 on the standard scale.

Section 105 provides that the master of any UK ship may cause any person on board the ship to be put under restraint if and for so long as it appears to him necessary or expedient in the interest of safety or for the preservation of good order or discipline on board the ship.

The Aviation and Maritime Security Act 1990, s. 39, makes it an offence to go into a restricted zone in a harbour without authorisation, or to remain there after being requested to leave by a competent authority or person. The offence is summary only and punishable with a level 5 fine. A constable or any person acting on behalf of the competent authority may use such force as is reasonable in the circumstances to remove from a restricted zone a person remaining in it in contravention of the section. Notices stating that the area concerned is a restricted zone must be posted so as to be readily seen and read by persons entering the restricted zone.

HIJACKING OF AIRCRAFT AND RELATED OFFENCES

A number of offences relating to the safety of and security of aircraft are provided for by the **B10.213** Aviation Security Act 1982. Part II provides for the safety of aircraft, aerodromes and air navigation installations against acts of violence and part III for the policing of airports. The Aviation and Maritime Security Act 1990, s. 1, creates the offence of endangering safety at airports.

Hijacking of Aircraft

Aviation Security Act 1982, s. 1   B10.214

(1) A person on board an aircraft in flight who unlawfully, by the use of force or by threats of any kind, seizes the aircraft or exercises control of it commits the offence of hijacking, whatever his nationality, whatever the State in which the aircraft is registered and whether the aircraft is in the United Kingdom or elsewhere but subject to subsection (2) below.

Procedure and Jurisdiction   B10.215

Aviation Security Act 1982, s. 5

(1) Any court in the United Kingdom having jurisdiction in respect of piracy committed on the high seas shall have jurisdiction in respect of piracy committed by or against an aircraft, wherever that piracy is committed.

Under s. 1(1), the general rule is that a person can be found guilty of an offence contrary to s. 1 whatever his nationality, wherever the aircraft is registered and wherever the aircraft is at the time of the offence. But, under s. 1(2), if the aircraft is used in military, police or customs service or both the place of take-off and landing are in the territory of the State where the plane is registered; s. 1(1) will not apply unless the alleged hijacker is a UK national or his act is committed in the UK or the aircraft is registered in the UK or is used in the military or customs service of the UK or the service of any police force in the UK.

An allegation of an offence contrary to s. 1 is triable only on indictment and is normally a class 3 offence, but see CPD XIII, para. B (see Supplement, **PD-97**) for the additional factors that the court considers on allocation.

Proceedings for an offence under s. 1 can be instituted only with the consent of the A-G (s. 8(1)).

Section 37 of the Act makes similar provision for the liability of bodies corporate to that contained in s. 18 of the TA 2006 (see **B10.88**).

Sentence   The maximum penalty is life imprisonment (Aviation Security Act 1982, s. 1(3)).   **B10.216**

Elements   'In flight' is defined in s. 38(3)(a) of the Aviation Security Act 1982 as being from **B10.217** the point when all an aircraft's external doors are closed following embarkation until the point when one of those doors is opened for disembarkation. When a plane is forced to land, it is 'in flight' until the competent authorities take responsibility for the plane and its occupants and any property on board.

'Military service' is defined so as to include naval and air force service; 'United Kingdom national' is a person who is (a) a British citizen, a British Dependent Territories citizen or a British overseas citizen, (b) a British subject under the British Nationality Act 1981, or (c) a British protected person (s. 38(1)).

Destroying, Damaging or Endangering the Safety of an Aircraft

Aviation Security Act 1982, s. 2   B10.218

(1) It shall, subject to subsection (4) below, be an offence for any person unlawfully and intentionally—
  (a) to destroy an aircraft in service or so to damage such an aircraft as to render it incapable of flight or as to be likely to endanger its safety in flight; or
  (b) to commit on board an aircraft in flight any act of violence which is likely to endanger the safety of the aircraft.

(2) It shall also, subject to subsection (4) below, be an offence for any person unlawfully and intentionally to place, or cause to be placed, on an aircraft in service any device or substance which is likely to destroy the aircraft, or is likely so to damage it, as to render it incapable of flight or as to be likely to endanger its safety in flight; but nothing in this subsection shall be construed as limiting the circumstances in which the commission of any act—
(a) may constitute an offence under subsection (1) above, or
(b) may constitute attempting or conspiring to commit, or aiding, abetting, counselling or procuring, or being art and part in, the commission of such an offence.

B10.219 **Procedure and Jurisdiction** The Aviation Security Act 1982, s. 2(3) is in identical terms to s. 1(1) (see **B10.215**).

An allegation of an offence contrary to s. 2 is triable only on indictment and is normally a class 3 offence, but see CPD XIII, para. B (see Supplement, **PD-97**) for the additional factors that the court considers on allocation.

Proceedings for an offence under s. 2 can be instituted only with the consent of the A-G (s. 8(1)).

B10.220 **Sentence** The maximum penalty is life imprisonment (Aviation Security Act 1982, s. 2(5)).

B10.221 **Elements** 'Unlawful' in relation to an act in the UK means that it constitutes an offence under the law of the part of the UK in which it is committed. In relation to an act outside the UK, 'unlawful' means that it would constitute an offence if it had been committed in England, Scotland or Wales (Aviation Security Act 1982, s. 2(6)).

'Act of violence' is any act in the UK which constitutes the offence of murder, manslaughter, culpable homicide or assault, an offence under any of ss. 18, 20, 21, 22, 23, 24, 28 or 29 of the OAPA 1861, or an offence under s. 2 of the Explosive Substances Act 1883. Outside the UK, it is any act which would constitute any of the offences mentioned above if it occurred in the UK (s. 2(7)).

'In service' is defined as the period from pre-flight preparation of the aircraft to a time 24 hours after it has landed following completion of the flight (s. 38(3)(b)). For 'in flight', see **B10.217**. For 'United Kingdom national', see **B10.217**.

Other Acts Endangering or Likely to Endanger the Safety of an Aircraft

B10.222
Aviation Security Act 1982, s. 3

(1) It shall, subject to subsections (5) and (6) below, be an offence for any person unlawfully and intentionally to destroy or damage any property to which this subsection applies, or to interfere with the operation of any such property, where the destruction, damage or interference is likely to endanger the safety of the aircraft in flight.
(2) Subsection (1) above applies to any property used for the provision of air navigation facilities, including any land, building or ship so used, and including any apparatus or equipment so used, whether it is on board an aircraft or elsewhere.
(3) It shall also, subject to subsections (4) and (5) below, be an offence for any person intentionally to communicate any information which is false, misleading or deceptive in a material particular, where the communication of the information endangers the safety of an aircraft in flight or is likely to endanger the safety of aircraft in flight.

B10.223 **Procedure and Jurisdiction** Provisions concerning jurisdiction are contained in the Aviation Security Act 1982, s. 3(5) and (6).

Aviation Security Act 1982, s. 3

(5) Subsections (1) and (3) above shall not apply to the commission of any act unless either the act is committed in the United Kingdom or, where it is committed outside the United Kingdom—
(a) the person committing it is a United Kingdom national; or
(b) the commission of the act endangers or is likely to endanger the safety in flight of civil aircraft registered in the United Kingdom or chartered by demise to a lessee whose principal place of business, or (if he has no place of business) whose permanent residence, is in the United Kingdom; or

(c) the act is committed on board a civil aircraft which is so registered or so chartered; or

(d) the act is committed on board a civil aircraft which lands in the United Kingdom with the person who committed the act still on board.

(6) Subsection (1) above shall also not apply to any act committed outside the United Kingdom and so committed in relation to property which is situated outside the United Kingdom and is not used for the provision of air navigation facilities in connection with international air navigation, unless the person committing the act is a United Kingdom national.

An allegation of an offence contrary to s. 3 is triable only on indictment and is normally a class 3 offence, but see CPD XIII, para. B (see Supplement, PD-97) for the additional factors that the court considers on allocation.

Proceedings for an offence under s. 3 can be instituted only with the consent of the A-G (s. 8(1)).

Sentence   The maximum penalty is life imprisonment (Aviation Security Act 1982, s. 3(7)).   **B10.224**

In *Voice* [2009] 1 Cr App R (S) 54 the Court of Appeal quashed a sentence of four months' imprisonment imposed for recklessly endangering the safety of an aircraft and substituted a community sentence. The offender had shone a high-powered torch out of the window of his flat into the cockpit of a helicopter that was attempting to land, rendering the pilot unable to see any of the cockpit instruments. The pilot was therefore required to take evasive action. The offender had acquired the torch in order to deter groups of youths which had been congregating on the estate on which he lived. He had not directed the torch at the landing helicopter, and instead was directing it at youths, but accepted that he was reckless as to the danger his behaviour had caused. In substituting the community sentence, the Court of Appeal regarded as crucial the agreed basis of plea which included an express acceptance by the Crown that the torch was not shone directly or deliberately at the helicopter but was being shone out of the window for another reason altogether. By contrast, in *Hussain* [2009] 1 Cr App R (S) 373 the Court of Appeal held that sentences of six months' imprisonment and six months' detention in a young offender institution respectively for the two offenders were the least that could properly have been imposed following guilty pleas entered at the first opportunity. The pilot of a police helicopter was forced to take emergency action when the appellants had shone a green laser beam at the cockpit. The offenders had previous convictions but they were said by the Court to have little bearing on the decision it made. *Voice* could be distinguished on two bases. First, in *Voice* the torch was shone for a legitimate reason whereas in *Hussain* there was no legitimate reason for possession of the laser pen. Secondly, in *Voice*, the helicopter flew through and out of the beam of light and the beam was not aimed at the aircraft nor did it follow the aircraft. In this case, the beam was directed at the aircraft and followed the aircraft for several minutes.

Elements   'Property' includes any land, buildings or work, any aircraft or vehicle and any bag-   **B10.225**
gage, cargo or any other article of any description (s. 38(1)).

'Civil aircraft' constitutes any aircraft other than an aircraft used in military, customs or police service (s. 3(8)).

For 'unlawful', see **B10.221**. For 'in flight', see **B10.217**. For 'United Kingdom national', see **B10.217**.

Specific Defence   **B10.226**

Aviation Security Act 1982, s. 3

(4) It shall be a defence for a person charged with an offence under subsection (3) above to prove—

(a) that he believed, and had reasonable grounds for believing, that the information was true; or

(b) that, when he communicated the information, he was lawfully employed to perform duties which consisted of or included the communication of information and that he communicated the information in good faith in the performance of those duties.

See **F3.18** *et seq*. for the significance of the reverse burden within this defence.

Dangerous Articles

B10.227

Aviation Security Act 1982, s. 4

(1) It shall be an offence for any person without lawful authority or reasonable excuse (the proof of which shall lie on him) to have with him—

    (a) in any aircraft registered in the United Kingdom, whether at a time when the aircraft is in the United Kingdom or not, or

    (b) in any other aircraft at a time when it is in, or in flight over, the United Kingdom, or

    (c) in any part of an aerodrome in the United Kingdom, or

    (d) in any air navigation installation in the United Kingdom which does not form part of an aerodrome,

any article to which this section applies.

B10.228   **Procedure**   An allegation of an offence contrary to the Aviation and Maritime Security Act 1990, s. 4, is triable either way (s. 4(4)); when tried on indictment it is normally a class 3 offence, but see CPD XIII, para. B (see Supplement, **PD-97**) for the additional factors that the court considers on allocation.

B10.229   **Sentence**   The maximum penalty on conviction on indictment is imprisonment for a term not exceeding five years or a fine or both; on summary conviction, it is imprisonment for a term not exceeding three months, a fine not exceeding the statutory maximum or both (Aviation Security Act 1982, s. 4(4)).

B10.230   Elements

Aviation Security Act 1982, s. 4

(3) For the purposes of this section a person who is for the time being in an aircraft, or in part of an aerodrome, shall be treated as having with him in an aircraft, or in that part of the aerodrome, as the case may be, an article to which this section applies if—

    (a) where he is in an aircraft, the article, or an article in which it is contained, is in the aircraft and has been caused (whether by him or by any other person) to be brought there as being, or as forming part of, his baggage on a flight in the aircraft, or has been caused by him to be brought there as being, or as forming part of, any other property to be carried on such a flight, or

    (b) where he is in part of an aerodrome (otherwise than in an aircraft), the article, or an article in which it is contained, is in that or any other part of the aerodrome and has been caused (whether by him or by any other person) to be brought into the aerodrome as being, or as forming part of, his baggage on a flight from that aerodrome or has been caused by him to be brought there as being, or as forming part of, any other property to be carried on such a flight on which he is also to be carried,

notwithstanding that the circumstance may be such that (apart from this subsection) he would not be regarded as having the article with him in the aircraft or in a part of the aerodrome, as the case may be.

B10.231   Section 4(2) sets out the articles to which s. 4 is relevant:

(a) any firearm, or any article having the appearance of being a firearm, whether capable of being discharged or not;

(b) any explosive, any article manufactured or adapted (whether in the form of a bomb, grenade or otherwise) so as to have the appearance of being an explosive, whether it is capable of producing a practical effect by explosion or not, or any article marked or labelled so as to indicate that it is or contains an explosive; and

(c) any article (not falling within either of the preceding paragraphs) made or adapted for use for causing injury to or incapacitating a person or for destroying or damaging property, or intended by the person having it with him for such use, whether by him or by any other person.

'Explosive' means any article manufactured for the purpose of producing a practical effect by explosion, or intended for that purpose by a person having the article with him. Firearm includes an airgun or air pistol (s. 38(1)).

'Have with him' receives some explanation in s. 4(3) but s. 4(5) provides that nothing in s. 4(3) shall be taken to limit the circumstances in which a person could be regarded as having an article with him.

For 'in flight', see **B10.217**. For 'United Kingdom national', see **B10.217**. For 'unlawfully', see **B10.221**.

'Air navigation installation' means any building, works, apparatus or equipment used wholly or mainly for the purpose of assisting air traffic control or as an aid to air navigation, together with any land contiguous or adjacent to any such building, works, apparatus or equipment and used wholly or mainly for purposes connected therewith (s. 38(1)).

Endangering Safety at Aerodromes

Aviation and Maritime Security Act 1990, s. 1 **B10.232**

(1) It is an offence for any person by means of any device, substance or weapon intentionally to commit at an aerodrome serving international civil aviation any act of violence which—
   (a) causes or is likely to cause death or serious personal injury, and
   (b) endangers or is likely to endanger the safe operation of the aerodrome or the safety of persons at the aerodrome.
(2) It is also, subject to subsection (4) below, an offence for any person by means of any device, substance or weapon unlawfully and intentionally—
   (a) to destroy or seriously to damage—
      (i) property used for the provision of any facilities at an aerodrome serving international civil aviation (including any apparatus or equipment so used), or
      (ii) any aircraft which is at such aerodrome but is not in service, or
   (b) to disrupt the services of such an aerodrome,
in such a way as to endanger or be likely to endanger the safe operation of the aerodrome or the safety of persons at the aerodrome.

Procedure and Jurisdiction Under s. 1(3) of the Aviation and Maritime Security Act 1990, **B10.233** the general rule is that a person can be found guilty of an offence contrary to s. 2 whatever his nationality and wherever the aircraft is at the time of the offence. But, under s. 1(4), if the aircraft is used in military, police or customs service, s. 1(1) and (2) will not apply unless the alleged act is committed in the UK or, if the act is committed outside the UK, it is committed by a UK national.

An allegation of an offence contrary to s. 1 is triable only on indictment and is normally a class 3 offence, but see CPD XIII, para. B (see Supplement, **PD-97**) for the additional factors that the court considers on allocation.

Proceedings for an offence under s. 1 can be instituted only with the consent of the A-G (s. 1(7)).

Sentence The maximum penalty is life imprisonment (Aviation and Maritime Security Act **B10.234** 1990, s. 1(5)).

Elements 'Act of violence' is defined by the Aviation and Maritime Security Act 1990, s. 1(9), **B10.235** in terms identical to those used under the Aviation Security Act 1982, s. 2(7) (see **B10.221**).

'Aerodrome' means any area of land or water designed, equipped, set apart or commonly used for affording facilities for the landing and departure of aircraft. It includes any area or space, whether on the ground, on the roof of a building or elsewhere, which is designed, equipped or set apart for affording facilities for the landing and departure of aircraft capable of descending or climbing vertically (Civil Aviation Act 1982, s. 105(1)).

For 'unlawfully', see **B10.221**. For 'United Kingdom national', see **B10.217**. For 'in service', see **B10.221**.

Section B11   Offences Affecting Public Order

INTRODUCTION

B11.1   The POA 1986 abolished a number of common-law offences, including riot, unlawful assembly and affray, replacing them with statutory offences of riot, violent disorder, affray, threatening behaviour etc. and disorderly conduct. It extended controls over processions and created controls over open-air assemblies. It expanded the law relating to the stirring up of racial hatred and provided for the exclusion of certain offenders from sporting events, notably association football matches. It has been further expanded by the Racial and Religious Hatred Act 2006, which inserted a number of new offences relating to the stirring up of religious hatred. The CJIA 2008, s. 74 and sch. 16, expanded it yet further by covering offences relating to hatred on the grounds of sexual orientation.

This section also deals with surviving offences under the POA 1936 and the common-law offence of public nuisance.

PROHIBITION OF QUASI-MILITARY ORGANISATIONS

B11.2   Public Order Act 1936, s. 2

(1) If the members or adherents of any association of persons, whether incorporated or not, are—

(a) organised or trained or equipped for the purpose of enabling them to be employed in usurping the functions of the police or of the armed forces of the Crown; or

(b) organised and trained or organised and equipped either for the purpose of enabling them to be employed for the use or display of physical force in promoting any political object, or in such manner as to arouse reasonable apprehension that they are organised and either trained or equipped for that purpose;

then any person who takes part in the control or management of the association, or in so organising or training as aforesaid any members or adherents thereof, shall be guilty of an offence under this section.

Procedure

Offences under the POA 1936, s. 2, are triable either way (POA 1936, s. 7(1)). When tried on indictment they are normally class 3 offences, but see CPD XIII, para. B (see Supplement, PD-97) for the additional factors that the court considers on allocation. By virtue of s. 2(2), no prosecution shall be instituted without the consent of the A-G.   **B11.3**

Public Order Act 1936, s. 2

(4) In any criminal or civil proceedings under this section proof of things done or of words written, spoken or published (whether or not in the presence of any party to the proceedings) by any person taking part in the control or management of an association or in organising, training or equipping members or adherents of an association shall be admissible as evidence of the purposes for which, or the manner in which, members or adherents of the association (whether those persons or others) were organised, or trained, or equipped.

Indictment

Statement of Offence   **B11.4**

Taking part in the control or management [or organising or training members or adherents] of an association contrary to section 2(1)(a) of the Public Order Act 1936.

Particulars of Offence

A between the...day of...and the...day of...took part in the management or control [or organising or training members or adherents] of an association, namely..., whose members or adherents were organised, trained or equipped for the purpose of enabling them to be employed in usurping the functions of the police or the armed forces of the Crown.

Sentence

The maximum penalty is two years or a fine or both on indictment; six months or a fine not exceeding the prescribed sum or both summarily (POA 1936, s. 7(1)).   **B11.5**

Specific Defences

Public Order Act 1936, s. 2   **B11.6**

Provided that in any proceedings against a person charged with the offence of taking part in the control or management of such an association as aforesaid it shall be a defence to that charge to prove that he neither consented to nor connived at the organisation, training, or equipment of members or adherents of the association in contravention of the provisions of this section.

Furthermore, s. 2(6) provides that s. 2 does not prohibit the employment of a reasonable number of people as stewards to assist in the preservation of order at a public meeting held on private premises, or the making of arrangements for that purpose or the instruction of people to be so employed in their lawful duties as such stewards, or their being furnished with badges or other distinguishing signs.

When the legal burden is on the accused, the standard required is proof on a balance of probabilities (see F3.5 and F3.53). For a summary of the case law relating to 'reverse burden' challenges under the HRA 1998, see F3.18 *et seq.*

Powers of High Court in Relation to Quasi-military Organisations

B11.7   **Public Order Act 1936, s. 2**

(3) If upon application being made by the Attorney-General it appears to the High Court that any association is an association of which members or adherents are organised, trained, or equipped in contravention of the provisions of this section, the court may make such order as appears necessary to prevent any disposition without the leave of the court of property held by or for the association and in accordance with rules of court may direct an inquiry and report to be made as to any such property as aforesaid and as to the affairs of the association and make such further orders as appear to the court to be just and equitable for the application of such property in or towards the discharge of the liabilities of the association lawfully incurred before the date of the application or since that date with the approval of the court, in or towards the repayment of moneys to persons who became subscribers or contributors to the association in good faith and without knowledge of any such contravention as aforesaid, and in or towards any costs incurred in connection with any such inquiry and report as aforesaid or in winding-up or dissolving the association, and may order that any property which is not directed by the court to be so applied as aforesaid shall be forfeited to the Crown.

Under s. 2(5) a High Court judge may grant a search warrant with a view to seizing evidence of the commission of an offence under s. 2. The judge must be satisfied on information under oath that there is reasonable ground for believing that an offence under s. 2 has been committed, and that evidence of it may be found at the place specified in the information. Application must be made by a police officer of a rank not lower than inspector.

PROHIBITION OF UNIFORMS IN CONNECTION WITH POLITICAL OBJECTS

B11.8   **Public Order Act 1936, s. 1**

(1) Subject as hereinafter provided, any person who in any public place or at any public meeting wears uniform signifying his association with any political organisation or with the promotion of any political object is guilty of an offence:

Provided that, if the chief officer of police is satisfied that the wearing of any such uniform as aforesaid on any ceremonial, anniversary, or other special occasion will not be likely to involve risk of public disorder, he may, with the consent of a Secretary of State, by order permit the wearing of such uniform on that occasion either absolutely or subject to such conditions as may be specified in the order.

Procedure

B11.9   An offence under the POA 1936, s. 1(1), is triable only summarily (POA 1936, s. 7(2)). By virtue of s. 1(2), no further proceedings after charge shall be instituted without the consent of the A-G.

Sentence

B11.10   The maximum penalty is imprisonment for a term not exceeding three months or a fine not exceeding level 4 on the standard scale, or both (POA 1936, s. 7(2)).

Uniform Signifying Association with a Political Organisation etc.

B11.11   In *O'Moran v DPP* [1975] QB 864 the Divisional Court held that the accused was wearing a uniform when wearing a black beret, because that beret was worn by each member of the group to signify that he was a member of a group in association with others. The court took the view that the requirement of the POA 1936, s. 1, that the uniform should signify association with a political organisation could be satisfied either by proof that the uniform had previously been worn as a uniform of a recognised, although not necessarily specified, organisation, or by judging an accused's activities at the time he was seen wearing that uniform.

Meaning of 'Public Place' and 'Public Meeting'

The concept of 'public place' in the POA 1936 was frequently litigated. All that litigation is **B11.12** relevant to the instant offence and also to the POA 1986, and probably also all other legislation in which a similar concept plays an important part.

Public Order Act 1936, s. 9

(1) In this Act the following expressions have the meanings hereby respectively assigned to them, that is to say:—

...

'Public place' includes any highway and any other premises or place to which at the material time the public have or are permitted to have access, whether on payment or otherwise.

This is an incomplete definition. The question of whether a particular place is a 'public place' depends upon a number of factors as decided by a series of cases on the since repealed s. 5 of the POA 1936. (See also **B12.155**.)

Whether a place is a public place depends upon an assessment of the factual position at 'the mate- **B11.13** rial time'. Consequently, the Divisional Court decided in *Marsh v Arscott* (1982) 75 Cr App Rep 211 that a shop car park could not be a public place at 11.30 p.m. when the shop was shut. If at the material time, the public do have access as members of the public rather than under any other provision of law, s. 9 means that that place is a public place even if entry may be refused to certain people. Accordingly a public house was held to be a public place by the Divisional Court in *Lawrenson v Oxford* [1982] Crim LR 185. On the other hand the Court of Appeal in *Edwards* (1978) 67 Cr App R 228 held that the front garden of a house was not a public place because people have access only on an individual basis as lawful visitors. The Divisional Court in *Cawley v Frost* [1976] 3 All ER 743 held that a place is a 'public place' even if the public are denied access to parts of it. Consequently, a football ground is a public place, even though members of the public are permitted only to go to certain areas and are denied access to other private areas.

Public Order Act 1936, s. 9

(1) In this Act the following expressions have the meanings hereby respectively assigned to them, that is to say:—

...

'Meeting' means a meeting held for the purpose of the discussion of matters of public interest or for the purpose of the expression of views on such matters;...

'Public meeting' includes any meeting in a public place and any meeting which the public or any section thereof are permitted to attend, whether on payment or otherwise.

Related Offence

It is an offence, contrary to the Police Act 1996, s. 90(2), for someone who is not a police officer to **B11.14** wear any article of police uniform, which includes distinctive badges, marks and documents, where it gives that person an appearance so resembling a member of a police force that it is calculated to deceive. The offence is punishable on summary conviction with a fine not exceeding level 3.

For offences relating to the use of uniforms to gain access to prohibited places (Official Secrets Act 1920, s. 1(1)), see **B9.19** to **B9.24**.

RIOT

Public Order Act 1986, s. 1   **B11.15**

(1) Where 12 or more persons who are present together use or threaten unlawful violence for a common purpose and the conduct of them (taken together) is such as would cause a person of reasonable firmness present at the scene to fear for his personal safety, each of the persons using unlawful violence for the common purpose is guilty of riot.

(2) It is immaterial whether or not the 12 or more use or threaten unlawful violence simultaneously.

(3) The common purpose may be inferred from conduct.
(4) No person of reasonable firmness need actually be, or be likely to be, present at the scene.
(5) Riot may be committed in private as well as in public places.

Procedure

B11.16   Riot is triable only on indictment (POA 1986, s. 1(6)). It is a class 1C or 2A offence, depending on whether it is in the course of a serious civil disturbance (CPD XIII, para. B (see Supplement, **PD-97**)). By s. 7(1), a prosecution for riot or incitement to riot may be commenced only by, or with the consent of, the DPP (the common-law offence of incitement has been abolished by the SCA 2007, s. 59, so the reference to incitement in s. 7(1) has effect as a reference to (or to conduct amounting to) the offences under part 2 of that Act (see **A5**): SCA 2007, s. 63 and sch. 6, para. 13). See the CPS Legal Guidance on Public Disorder for the current charging criteria.

Indictment

B11.17   *Statement of Offence*
Riot contrary to section 1 of the Public Order Act 1986.

Particulars of Offence
A on or about the...day of..., being one of 12 or more persons present together at...and using [or threatening] unlawful violence for a common purpose, namely..., used unlawful violence for the said common purpose by assaulting members of the public, the conduct of the 12 or more persons aforesaid, taken together, being such as would cause a person of reasonable firmness present at the scene to fear for his personal safety.

This form of indictment was approved by the Court of Appeal in *Tyler* (1992) 96 Cr App R 332 and *Jefferson* [1994] 1 All ER 270.

As to the importance of alleging the presence of the required 12 persons, see by analogy *Mahroof* (1989) 88 Cr App R 317 (a case concerned with violent disorder: see **B11.31** and **B11.34**). See also *Fleming* (1989) 153 JP 517; *Worton* (1989) 154 JP 201.

The POA 1986, s. 7(2), declares that for the purposes of the rules against charging more than one offence in the same count, each of ss. 1 to 5 of the Act creates one offence.

Alternative Verdicts

B11.18   The POA 1986, s. 7(3), provides for alternative verdicts on charges under the Act without mentioning s. 1. However, the CLA 1967, s. 6(3) (see **D19.42** *et seq.*), would allow the jury on an indictment for riot to return an alternative verdict of guilty of violent disorder under the POA 1986, s. 2, or of affray under s. 3 (see also **B11.32**). It may, however, be prudent to add alternative counts.

Sentencing Guidelines

B11.19   The maximum penalty is ten years or a fine or both (POA 1986, s. 1(6)). Riot is a specified offence for the purposes of the public protection provisions in the CJA 2003 (see **E4**).

Some general guidance on the gravity of public order offences, including riot, is to be found in *Caird* (1970) 54 Cr App R 499, a case, like several others cited below, decided in respect of common-law offences of public order which have been replaced by the statutory scheme in the POA 1986. In *Caird*, Sachs LJ said (at pp. 506–8) that:

When there is wanton and vicious violence of gross degree the court is not concerned with whether it originates from gang rivalry or from political motives. It is the degree of mob violence that matters and the extent to which the public peace is being broken...

In the view of this court, it is a wholly wrong approach to take the acts of any individual participator in isolation. They were not committed in isolation and, as already indicated, it is that very fact that constitutes the gravity of the offence.

In *Muranyi* (1986) 8 Cr App R (S) 176, the offender pleaded guilty to riot. He had been concerned in planning and instigating a number of attacks on football supporters. Between 30 and 150 people attacked visiting football supporters, a number of whom suffered serious injuries, including one who was stabbed in the neck with a bottle which severed an artery, although Muranyi himself had not been seen with a weapon on these occasions. Five years' imprisonment was upheld on appeal. In *Pilgrim* (1983) 5 Cr App R (S) 140, three offenders had been involved in a riot in which 100 youths, equipped with various weapons, had attacked a public house frequented by members of an opposing group, and subsequently attacked a number of people who were unconnected with the event, one of whom was killed. The first offender was convicted of manslaughter in respect of that, and received sentences totalling eight years. The other two received sentences of five years and three years respectively. The Court of Appeal upheld the sentences.

In *Najeeb* [2003] 2 Cr App R (S) 408 the offenders had been involved in a riot involving **B11.20** clashes between hundreds of white and Asian males, following a speech made by a leader of the British National Party. Police officers were attacked with stones and petrol bombs, and two officers were stabbed. Stolen cars were set alight and many premises were severely damage estimated at £27 million was caused. Rose LJ in the Court of Appeal said that, in a case of riot on this scale, the sentence for a ringleader, after a trial, should be around the maximum of ten years. In a contested case, for an active and persistent participant who used petrol bombs a sentence of eight to nine years was appropriate. Those who were present for a significant period, throwing stones, could expect five years. Where the evidence was overwhelming, because a defendant's activity had been caught on camera, little discount was to be expected for a guilty plea. In cases of serious riot deterrent sentences were required so that good character and personal mitigation would carry comparatively little weight.

The Court of Appeal gave guidance on sentencing individuals involved in the widespread public disorder that took place around the country between 6 and 11 August 2011 in *Blackshaw* [2012] 1 WLR 1126. Although the appeals involved offences other than riot, the context of the Court of Appeal's reasoning and its justification for departure from the definitive sentencing guidelines for individual offences is riot.

Twelve or More Persons Present Using or Threatening Violence for a Common Purpose

It is immaterial whether or not the 12 or more use or threaten unlawful violence simultaneously **B11.21** (POA 1986, s. 1(2)). It is also immaterial (by s. 6(7)) whether all of the 12 or more intend to use violence or are aware that their conduct may be violent (the mental element in the offence of riot: see **B11.26**). In other words, a person may be guilty of riot even if some of the 12 or more co-rioters are not guilty of riot (or of violent disorder or affray) because of lack of *mens rea* (see **B11.34**). Common purpose may be inferred from the conduct of the rioters (POA 1986, s. 1(3)) together with such circumstances as the carrying of banners, shouting of slogans, threats and the like.

Accused Must Use Violence

There must be 12 or more persons using or threatening violence but only those who actually **B11.22** use violence will be guilty of the offence of riot (*Jefferson* [1994] 1 All ER 270). In *Mitsui Sumitomo Insurance (Europe) Ltd v Mayor's Office for Policing and Crime* [2014] 1 All ER 422 the claimants sued for damages under the Riot (Damages) Act 1886 following a fire at a warehouse that occurred during the civil disorder of August 2011. The claimants had to establish that there had been a riot within the meaning of the POA 1986, s. 1. It was not in dispute that a number of youths had been responsible for the fire but there was an issue as to whether the elements of riot were made out on the facts. Flaux J (at [69]) held that there had been a riot. He said:

> ...even if not all the gang were smashing down the door or throwing petrol bombs, the others by their presence were threatening unlawful violence, or, putting it another way, they were all engaged together in the joint enterprise of breaking into the premises and looting and destroying them, even the two twelve year olds [a witness] encountered outside.

The reasoning here is open to question and it should be noted that the case was presented as one of joint enterprise. It cannot be the case that because 12 or more persons are present together with a common purpose that *some* of their number should use or threaten violence that in the event all 12 have therefore used or threatened violence. If, on different facts, 12 persons had assembled with the common purpose that one of their number should start a fight in the street and he did so while the others stood and watched, that could not be described as a riot.

Meaning of 'Unlawful Violence'

B11.23   Public Order Act 1986, s. 8

(1) In this part—
   ...
   'violence' means any violent conduct, so that—
   (a) except in the context of affray, it includes violent conduct towards property as well as violent conduct towards persons, and
   (b) it is not restricted to conduct causing or intended to cause injury or damage but includes any other violent conduct (for example, throwing at or towards a person a missile of a kind capable of causing injury which does not hit or falls short).

As to the meaning of 'unlawful', see **B11.43**.

Consequences of the Use or Threat of Violence

B11.24 Under the POA 1986, s. 1(1), riot occurs where a person of reasonable firmness present at the scene *would* be caused, not *was* caused, to fear for his personal safety. Further, s. 1(4) provides that: 'No person of reasonable firmness need actually be, or be likely to be, present at the scene' (see **B11.45**).

Place of Commission

B11.25 Riot may occur in private as well as in public places (POA 1986, s. 1(5)).

Mens Rea

B11.26 A person is guilty of riot only if he intends to use violence or is aware that his conduct may be violent (POA 1986, s. 6(1)). A direction as to *mens* rea must normally be given (*Blackwood* [2002] EWCA Crim 3102), and care must be taken to distinguish between principal offenders and aiders and abettors in that direction (see also **A4**).

Effect of Voluntary, Self-induced Intoxication on *Mens Rea*

B11.27 The POA 1986, s. 6, deals with the problem of whether a person's intoxication should be taken into account when determining that of which an accused was aware. Consequently, the problems encountered with the defence of self-induced intoxication (see **A3.16** to **A3.22**) and the effect of intoxication on mistakes which a person makes are of no direct concern in the offence of riot.

Public Order Act 1986, s. 6

(5) For the purposes of this section a person whose awareness is impaired by intoxication shall be taken to be aware of that of which he would be aware if not intoxicated, unless he shows either that his intoxication was not self-induced or that it was caused solely by the taking or administration of a substance in the course of medical treatment.

(6) In subsection (5) 'intoxication' means any intoxication, whether caused by drink, drugs or other means, or by a combination of means.

VIOLENT DISORDER

Public Order Act 1986, s. 2

(1) Where three or more persons who are present together use or threaten unlawful violence and the conduct of them (taken together) is such as would cause a person of reasonable firmness present at the scene to fear for his personal safety, each of the persons using or threatening unlawful violence is guilty of violent disorder.

(2) It is immaterial whether or not the three or more use or threaten unlawful violence simultaneously.

(3) No person of reasonable firmness need actually be, or be likely to be, present at the scene.

(4) Violent disorder may be committed in private as well as in public places.

Procedure

Violent disorder is triable either way (POA 1986, s. 2(5)). According to the *Magistrates' Court Sentencing Guidelines* (see Supplement, **SG-301**), these offences should normally be dealt with in the Crown Court although 'there may be rare cases involving minor violence or threats of violence leading to no or minor injury, with few people involved and no weapons or missiles, in which a custodial sentence within the jurisdiction of the magistrates' court may be appropriate'. For the procedure to be followed on determining mode of trial, see **D6.6**. When tried on indictment, violent disorder is normally a class 3 offence, but see CPD XIII, para. B (see Supplement, **PD-97**) for the additional factors that the court considers on allocation. See the CPS Legal Guidance on Public Disorder for the current charging criteria

Indictment

Statement of Offence

Violent disorder contrary to section 2(1) of the Public Order Act 1986.

Particulars of Offence

A on or about the...day of..., being one of three or more persons present together at...and using [or threatening] unlawful violence used [or threatened to use] unlawful violence by assaulting members of the public, the conduct of the three or more persons aforesaid, taken together, being such as would cause a person of reasonable firmness present at the scene to fear for his personal safety.

The POA 1986, s. 7(2), declares that for the purposes of the rules against charging more than one offence in the same count, each of ss. 1 to 5 of the Act creates one offence.

Violent disorder is not committed unless there are three or more persons together. In *Mahroof* (1988) 88 Cr App R 317, the jury had acquitted two of the accused named in the indictment, but had convicted Mahroof. The Court of Appeal decided that there was a sufficient allegation in the indictment, even though no other persons were named, 'subject to two *very important* qualifications':

(a) 'that there is evidence before the jury that there were three people involved in the criminal behaviour, though not necessarily those named in the indictment' (see also *Lemon* [2002] EWCA Crim 1661), and

(b) 'that the defence are apprised of what it is they have to meet'.

The Court made clear that the best way, and generally the only way, of satisfying the second qualification is by putting it in the indictment. This could be done by adding the phrase, after naming certain individuals, 'and others', which could have been pursued in this case by the defence seeking particulars, which would have led to the provision of information about two other people who were known about. In *Mahroof*, qualification (b) was not satisfied. This decision was followed in *Fleming* (1989) 153 JP 517 and was followed and applied by the Court of Appeal in *Worton* (1989) 154 JP 201, although the Court seems to have been satisfied that the defence was sufficiently apprised of the matter. It seems unsatisfactory that qualification (b) should be satisfied by the evidence given by the prosecution at the trial, rather than information provided in advance of the trial.

If one or more of the accused may lack the *mens rea* for the offence, the determination of numbers is not affected (see **B11.34**). See also *Mechen* [2004] EWCA Crim 388, confirming that acquittal of a person on the grounds of self-defence removes him from inclusion in the minimum number required for the offence.

Alternative Verdicts

B11.32   Public Order Act 1986, s. 7

(3) If on the trial on indictment of a person charged with violent disorder…the jury find him not guilty of the offence charged, they may (without prejudice to section 6(3) of the Criminal Law Act 1967) find him guilty of an offence under section 4.
(4) The Crown Court has the same powers and duties in relation to a person who is by virtue of subsection (3) convicted before it of an offence under section 4 as a magistrates' court would have on convicting him of the offence.

As to the operation of the POA 1986, s. 7(3), see *Mahroof* (1988) 88 Cr App R 317 and *Worton* (1989) 154 JP 201. Section 7(3) applies only where the jury has found the accused not guilty, whether as a result of its own deliberations or as a result of following the judge's proper direction (*Carson* (1990) 92 Cr App R 236). The CLA 1967, s. 6(3) (see **D19.42** *et seq.*), may be resorted to where the defendant on arraignment pleads not guilty to an offence contrary to the POA 1986, s. 2 or 3, but wishes to plead guilty to an offence contrary to s. 4 (*O'Brien* (1992) 156 JP 925). The operation of the 1967 Act is unaffected by the POA 1986, so, on a charge of violent disorder, it is possible, provided the elements of the offence are established, to substitute a conviction, for example, of affray under s. 3 (*Fleming* (1989) 153 JP 517). Particular attention must be paid to matters such as the different meanings of 'violence' in the offences (*McGuigan* [1991] Crim LR 719 and see **B11.34** and **B11.45**).

The same principles apply to finding a person guilty of an offence contrary to s. 4 in the alternative. However, if a judge decides to leave s. 4 as an alternative to the jury, defence counsel should be given an opportunity to address the jury (*Perrins* [1995] Crim LR 432; *Stanley* [1993] Crim LR 618). In *Mbagwu* [2007] EWCA Crim 1068 it was said to be improper to leave s. 4 in the alternative to the jury after it had been in retirement for over a day and had already acquitted eight other defendants. See also *Va Kun Hau* [1990] Crim LR 518, where s. 4 was not available because the act took place in a dwelling-house.

Sentencing Guidelines

B11.33   The maximum penalty is five years, a fine or both, on indictment (POA 1986, s. 2(5)); six months, a fine not exceeding the statutory maximum, or both, summarily. Violent disorder is a specified offence for the purposes of the public protection provisions in the CJA 2003 (see **E4**). See **B11.29** for the *Magistrates' Court Sentencing Guidelines*.

In *Greenall* [2005] 2 Cr App R (S) 276, sentences of four years' imprisonment were upheld for the organisers of a conspiracy to cause violent disorder, and sentences of two years were upheld for those who took part, when rival football supporters arranged to fight each other at a railway station. Some of the gang were armed with bottles, fighting continued for several minutes and three participants were knocked unconscious. See also *Alderson* (1989) 11 Cr App R (S) 301, where a sentence of 30 months was upheld in respect of a racially motivated attack by the offender (who had seven previous convictions, mainly for dishonesty) and three other men, upon a group of Jordanian students, who were punched, kicked, butted and struck with a chair. Eighteen months' imprisonment was upheld on three offenders of previous good character in

Watson (1990) 12 Cr App R (S) 477. One of the offenders, who had witnessed the stabbing of a workmate, who eventually died from his wound, met co-defendants and went to the scene of the stabbing, the premises of a taxi firm, to exact revenge. They broke in and attacked a taxi driver and a 17-year-old female controller, who were unconnected with the stabbing incident. See also *Sturton* (1992) 13 Cr App R (S) 116, *Betts* (1995) 16 Cr App R (S) 436, *Green* [1997] 2 Cr App R (S) 191 and *Rees* [2006] 2 Cr App R (S) 143. Where serious violence is used then it matters not that it stems from genuinely held political belief (*Alhaddad* [2011] 1 Cr App R (S) 517).

The Court of Appeal in *Gilmour* [2011] EWCA Crim 2458 emphasised that 'the law protects the right of people in this country to demonstrate, that is to say to make known and in public their feelings on matters of public concern. Equally, to do so in large numbers in public carries clear responsibilities, principally amongst them to act without disorder or violence which puts the public at risk.' The Court upheld a sentence of 16 months' imprisonment on a plea of guilty relating to disorder in the course of the university fees protests.

Actus Reus

Three or More People Present Together Using or Threatening Violence   It is immaterial whether or not the three or more use or threaten unlawful violence simultaneously (POA 1986, s. 2(2)).   **B11.34**

As stated at **B11.31**, it is essential to establish that three or more people were present together using or threatening violence. In *NW* [2010] 1 WLR 1426, the Court of Appeal considered the meaning of the expression 'present together'. It held that it means no more than being in the same place at the same time. Moore-Bick LJ stated at [19] that:

> Three or more people using or threatening violence in the same place at the same time, whether for the same purpose or different purposes, are capable of creating a daunting prospect for those who may encounter them simply by reason of the fact that they represent a breakdown of law and order which has unpredictable consequences. We are unable to accept that the phrase requires any degree of co-operation between those who are using or threatening violence; all that is required is that they be present in the same place at the same time.

The Court of Appeal in *Church* (12 November 1999 unreported) felt that assistance can be derived from the decision of the Divisional Court in *Allen v Ireland* [1984] 1 WLR 903 where Kerr LJ stated (at p. 910) that voluntary presence at an affray 'is capable of raising a prima facie case of participation…, but that mere voluntary presence is not sufficient…unless the court is satisfied that he at least also gave some overt encouragement to the others who were directly involved in the affray or threatening behaviour'. Whether any particular defendant is involved is, then, a question of fact. In *Fleming* (1989) 153 JP 517, the Court of Appeal made it clear that a jury should be directed that 'if it cannot be sure that three or more of the defendants were using or threatening violence, then it should acquit every defendant, even if satisfied that one or more particular defendants were unlawfully fighting'. See also *McGuigan* [1991] Crim LR 719. Usually, therefore, when only three are named in the indictment, the jury must acquit all three if they acquit one. This is not the case where the jury are satisfied that others not charged were taking part in the violent disorder in which case the jury may convict (*Worton* (1989) 154 JP 201). Account can be taken of such others only if the requirements established in *Mahroof* (1988) 88 Cr App R 317 (see **B11.31**) are satisfied. Further, where one (or more) defendant is acquitted as a result of lack of *mens rea* (see **B11.36**), the determination of the number of persons is unaffected (POA 1986, s. 6(7)). Thus if one (or more) of the named defendants is found not guilty because he lacks *mens rea*, the remaining defendants may be found guilty, even if there are only two of them.

Other Elements   Unlike the offence of riot, it is not part of the definition of violent disorder that those present have a common purpose (see *NW* [2010] 1 WLR 1426 at **B11.34**).   **B11.35**

For the elements of unlawful violence, producing fear in a person of reasonable firmness, and place of commission, see the discussion of those elements in the offence of riot at **B11.23** to **B11.25**.

Mens Rea

B11.36

Public Order Act 1986, s. 6

(2) A person is guilty of violent disorder...only if he intends to use or threaten violence or is aware that his conduct may be violent or threaten violence.

The *mens rea* is subjective, see **B11.79**. For the effect of voluntary, self-induced intoxication on *mens rea*, see the discussion in relation to the offence of riot at **B11.27**.

AFFRAY

B11.37

Public Order Act 1986, s. 3

(1) A person is guilty of affray if he uses or threatens unlawful violence towards another and his conduct is such as would cause a person of reasonable firmness present at the scene to fear for his personal safety.
(2) Where two or more persons use or threaten the unlawful violence, it is the conduct of them taken together that must be considered for the purposes of subsection (1).
(3) For the purposes of this section a threat cannot be made by the use of words alone.
(4) No person of reasonable firmness need actually be, or be likely to be, present at the scene.
(5) Affray may be committed in private as well as in public places.

Procedure

B11.38 Prosecutions for affray should be instituted only where the incident gives rise to serious disturbance to public order (Law Commission Report No. 123, para. 3.38, referred to in *Davison* [1992] Crim LR 31); it is thoroughly bad practice to charge what are straightforward assaults as public order offences (*Connor* (13 March 2000 unreported)). See the CPS Legal Guidance on Public Disorder for the current charging criteria.

Affray is triable either way (POA 1986, s. 3(7)). The *Magistrates' Court Sentencing Guidelines* (see **B11.41** for a summary) give guidance on offence seriousness. For the procedure to be followed on determining mode of trial, see **D6.6**. When tried on indictment, affray is normally a class 3 offence, but see CPD XIII, para. B (see Supplement, **PD-97**) for the additional factors that the court considers on allocation.

Indictment

B11.39

Statement of Offence

Affray contrary to section 3(1) of the Public Order Act 1986.

Particulars of Offence

A on or about the...day of...used [or threatened] violence towards one V, the conduct of A being such as to cause a person of reasonable firmness present at the scene to fear for his personal safety.

The POA 1986, s. 7(2), declares that for the purpose of the rules against charging more than one offence in the same count, each of ss. 1 to 5 of the Act creates one offence.

Although affray is a continuing offence, it is better practice to charge separate offences where there are distinct incidents and not all defendants are alleged to be involved in each of them (*Flounders* [2002] EWCA Crim 1325). See also *Smith* [1997] 1 Cr App R 14 as to how to direct a jury when a continuous affray has separate parts to it.

Alternative Verdicts

B11.40

Public Order Act 1986, s. 7

(3) If on the trial on indictment of a person charged with...affray the jury find him not guilty of the offence charged, they may (without prejudice to section 6(3) of the Criminal Law Act 1967) find him guilty of an offence under section 4.

(4) The Crown Court has the same powers and duties in relation to a person who is by virtue of subsection (3) convicted before it of an offence under section 4 as a magistrates' court would have on convicting him of the offence.

It is important that the jury be properly directed as to the lesser offence, which it should consider only if it is unsure that affray has been committed (*Stanley* [1993] Crim LR 618). The differences between the offences may be crucial (see *Va Kun Hau* [1990] Crim LR 518, where s. 4 was not available because the act took place in a dwelling-house).

As to the interrelationship between s. 7(3) and the CLA 1967, s. 6(3), see **B11.32**.

Sentencing Guidelines

The maximum penalty is three years, a fine, or both, on indictment (POA 1986, s. 3(7)); six   **B11.41**
months, a fine not exceeding the statutory maximum, or both, summarily. Affray is a specified offence for the purposes of the public protection provisions in the CJA 2003 (see E4).

The *Magistrates' Court Sentencing Guidelines* (see Supplement, **SG-302**) identify three starting points (for a first time offender pleading not guilty) according to the nature of the activity, each starting point having a defined range, which is adjusted according to the non-exhaustive list of aggravating and mitigating features. Offender mitigation is considered after the court has reached a provisional sentence based on its assessment of offence seriousness.

A brief offence involving low-level violence and no substantial fear created attracts a low level community order, the range being a band C fine to a medium level community order. The next level up is a degree of fighting or violence that causes substantial fear which attracts a high level community order, the range being a medium level community order to 12 weeks' custody. Fights involving a weapon/throwing objects or conduct causing risk of serious injury will attract 18 weeks' custody, with a range of '12 weeks custody to Crown Court'. Aggravating factors are identified as follows: those indicating higher culpability are group action, threats, lengthy incident; those indicating greater degree of harm are vulnerable person(s) present, injuries caused, damage to property. Mitigating factors indicating lower culpability are as follows: did not start the trouble; provocation; stopped as soon as police arrived.

In *Holmes* [1999] 2 Cr App R (S) 100 two offenders, after an evening of heavy drinking, started   **B11.42**
a fight with another customer in a fish and chip shop, in which the victim was punched and kicked. They pleaded guilty in the magistrates' court to affray, and were committed for sentence. In light of personal mitigation, custodial sentences were reduced from 15 months to nine months by the Court of Appeal. In *Oliver* [1999] 1 Cr App R (S) 394, 12 months was appropriate for a man who admitted creating a disturbance on a transatlantic flight. He assaulted his wife, was abusive to a steward and behaved in a threatening manner. See also *McCallum* [2002] 1 Cr App R (S) 488. In *Mears* [2013] EWCA Crim 106, sentences of two and a half years', two years' and 21 months' imprisonment were not excessive after the three accused had been involved in a sustained and unprovoked attack on two innocent men in the street which caused the victims serious injuries. See also *Fox* [2006] 1 Cr App R (S) 97 as to the need to look at the whole picture, not just the role of the individual offender.

Meaning of 'Threat' and 'Unlawful Violence'

The essential elements of affray, according to the Court of Appeal, are '(a) the use or threat of   **B11.43**
violence by the defendant; (b) to another person; which (c) would cause a third person to fear for his or her own safety' (*Thind* [1999] Crim LR 842). For (a) and (b), see below. For (c), see **B11.45**. Lord Bingham CJ has described affray in *Smith* [1997] 1 Cr App R 14 at p. 16:

> It typically involves a group of people who may well be shouting, struggling, threatening, waving weapons, throwing objects, exchanging and threatening blows and so on. Again, typically, it involves a continuous course of conduct, the criminal character of which depends on the general nature and effect of the conduct as a whole and not on particular incidents and events which may

take place in the course of it. Where reliance is placed on such a continuous course of conduct, it is not necessary for the Crown to identify and prove particular incidents.

These 'typical activities' must amount to the use or threat of unlawful violence (POA 1986, s. 3(1)). The definition of 'violence' in affray is different from its definition for other purposes in the POA 1986. By s. 8, violence, for affray, does not include violent conduct towards property. It is, therefore, limited to violent conduct towards persons. Otherwise, s. 8 provides:

'violence' means any violent conduct, so that—

...

(b) it is not restricted to conduct causing or intended to cause injury or damage but includes any other violent conduct (for example, throwing at or towards a person a missile of a kind capable of causing injury which does not hit or falls short).

In *Rothwell* [1993] Crim LR 626, it was held that the word 'unlawful' is intended to ensure that defences such as self-defence apply to offences under the POA 1986 (see also *Key* (24 November 1992 unreported); *Afzal* [1993] Crim LR 791; *Pulham* [1995] Crim LR 296).

B11.44 Since a threat cannot be made by words alone (POA 1986, s. 3(3)), there must be conduct on the part of the accused; the fact that the experience was frightening does not make aggressive words sufficient (*Robinson* [1993] Crim LR 581). However, in *Dixon* [1993] Crim LR 579, ordering a dog to attack was sufficient to constitute a threat, because there was conduct, the dog being used as a weapon. See also *Dackers* [2000] All ER (D) 1958.

The words 'threatens unlawful violence' carry their ordinary and natural meaning so that the carrying of dangerous weapons, such as petrol bombs by a group of persons can, in some circumstances, constitute the threat of violence, without those weapons being waved or brandished (*I v DPP* [2001] 2 All ER 583). Lord Hutton supported this view by reference to applicable cases on the common-law offence of affray: see *Sharp* [1957] 1 QB 552 and *Taylor* [1973] AC 964 (where it was said that mere words are not sufficient, but that brandishing weapons is not always required). Whether the carrying of weapons is sufficient in any given case is a matter for the tribunal of fact to decide. Unlawful violence must be used or threatened to another. That other must be present at the scene (*I v DPP*). As the only people proved to be present in *I v DPP* were the members of the gang possessing and brandishing petrol bombs, there was no 'another' to whom violence was used or threatened and so there was no affray.

The Test for Conduct Causing Fear

B11.45 The test, as for riot and violent disorder, is whether a person of reasonable firmness present at the scene *would* be caused, not *was* caused, to fear for his personal safety. No person of reasonable firmness need actually be, or be likely to be, present at the scene (POA 1986, s. 3(4)).

In *Davison* [1992] Crim LR 31, the Court of Appeal, taking account of Law Commission Report No. 123, decided that the conduct to be considered is that of the accused. Its consequences are judged by an objective standard, i.e. whether the hypothetical bystander of reasonable firmness (not the person assaulted) would be put in fear of his personal safety if he was there. Account may be taken of the nature of the premises and scene where the incident actually took place, and of the fact that the violence was limited to those involved. Account may also be taken of the reactions of others who were present, whether those reactions showed fear on the one hand (*Freeman v DPP* [2013] EWHC 610 (Admin)) or disinterest on the other (*DPP v Cotcher* (1992) *The Times*, 29 December 1992), provided that the jury is directed that in considering their verdict only the reaction of the hypothetical bystander matters. In *Sanchez* (1996) 160 JP 321, the Divisional Court approved the commentary of Professor Sir John Smith to *Davison* as being the correct approach: 'the question in the present case was not whether a person of reasonable firmness in [the victim's] shoes would have feared for his personal safety but whether [the] hypothetical person, present in the room and seeing [the accused's] conduct towards [the victim] would have so feared ... [The offence] is designed for the protection of the bystander. It is a public order offence. There are other offences for the protection of persons at whom the violence is aimed.' In *Leeson v DPP* [2010] EWHC 994 (Admin), the Administrative Court reviewed all the authorities in this area. Applying *Cotcher*, it found that the magistrates had been wrong to convict the accused of affray after she issued a drunken threat to kill her long-term partner whilst holding a knife, in a bathroom, in an otherwise unoccupied house. The Court found that there was no possibility of a hypothetical bystander fearing for his safety as the exchanges were personal and restricted to turbulence between the couple, and so could not have given rise to a fear of unlawful violence to anyone else. See also *Rafferty* (2004) *The Times*, 21 April 2004 as to a judge's obligations when directing the jury on the question of the person of reasonable firmness.

In *Carey* [2006] EWCA Crim 17, the Court of Appeal decided that affray was to be defined without reference to the Law Commission report which preceded the POA 1986 and that the words used in the legislation were to be given their ordinary unglossed meaning. Thus, it was improper to require a person of reasonable firmness to be 'terrified' (as was required under the common-law offence of affray).

Mens Rea

Public Order Act 1986, s. 6	**B11.46**

(2) A person is guilty of...affray only if he intends to use or threaten violence or is aware that his conduct may be violent or threaten violence.

The *mens rea* is subjective, see **B11.79**. A direction about *mens rea* should normally be given (*Mann* [2002] EWCA Crim 3045). For the effect of voluntary, self-induced intoxication on *mens rea*, see the discussion in relation to the offence of riot at **B11.27**.

FEAR OR PROVOCATION OF VIOLENCE

Public Order Act 1986, s. 4	**B11.47**

(1) A person is guilty of an offence if he—
   (a) uses towards another person threatening, abusive or insulting words or behaviour, or
   (b) distributes or displays to another person any writing, sign or other visible representation which is threatening, abusive or insulting,
   with intent to cause that person to believe that immediate unlawful violence will be used against him or another by any person, or to provoke the immediate use of unlawful violence by that person or another, or whereby that person is likely to believe that such violence will be used or it is likely that such violence will be provoked.
(2) An offence under this section may be committed in a public or a private place, except that no offence is committed where the words or behaviour are used, or the writing, sign or other visible representation is distributed or displayed, by a person inside a dwelling and the other person is also inside that or another dwelling.

The CDA 1998, s. 31, created a racially or religiously aggravated form of this offence. For the meaning of racially or religiously aggravated, see **B11.149**.

Procedure

An offence under the POA 1986, s. 4(1), is, by s. 4(4) of the Act, triable summarily only. The racially aggravated form of the offence is triable either way (CDA 1998, s. 31(4)). If, on trial on indictment, the jury find the accused not guilty of the racially aggravated form of the offence, they may find him guilty of the basic offence (s. 31(6)). It is not permissible for a magistrates' court to convict a person of both an offence under s. 4(1) and the racially aggravated form of the offence, where both offences arise out of the same facts. The charges are in the alternative and it is a basic principle of English justice that a person should be convicted

B11.48

only once for one wrong (*R (Dyer) v Watford Magistrates' Court* (2013) 177 JP 265: see also **D22.68**).

The POA 1986, s. 7(2), declares that for the purposes of the rules against charging more than one offence in the same information, each of ss. 1 to 5 of the Act creates one offence. The offence under s. 4 may be committed in one of four ways (*Winn v DPP* (1992) 156 JP 881, and see **B11.53**). Care must be taken in formulating the charge so that the way of committing the offence reflects the facts of the case, otherwise there may be unjustifiable variance between the charge and the particulars alleged. More than one way of committing the offence may be included and amendment is possible if necessary (*Winn v DPP; Loade v DPP* [1990] 1 QB 1052: for amendment, see **D21.11**).

The person towards whom threatening, abusive or insulting words or behaviour are used can be held to perceive the threatening words or behaviour when he does not give evidence at the trial (*Swanston v DPP* (1997) 161 JP 203). Of course, there must be other evidence, as there was in *Swanston* in view of the small area in which the incidents took place, and the evidence of the police constable.

No prosecution should be brought unless it can be established that prosecution is necessary in order to prevent public disorder, thereby avoiding breach of the ECHR, Article 10 (*Dehal v CPS* (2005) 169 JP 581). In that case Moses J indicated that in order to justify interfering with 'one of the essential foundations of democratic society', the prosecution must show that criminal proceedings were 'brought in pursuit of a legitimate aim, namely the protection of society against violence and that a criminal prosecution is the only method necessary to achieve that aim'. See the CPS Legal Guidance on Public Disorder for the current charging criteria.

Sentencing Guidelines (Basic Offence)

B11.49   The maximum penalty is six months or a fine not exceeding level 5 or both (POA 1986, s. 4(4)).

The *Magistrates' Court Sentencing Guidelines* (see Supplement, **SG-303**) identify three starting points (for a first time offender pleading not guilty) according to the nature of the activity, each starting point having a defined range which is adjusted according to the non-exhaustive list of aggravating and mitigating features. Offender mitigation is considered after the court has reached a provisional sentence based on its assessment of offence seriousness.

Where there is fear or threat of low level immediate unlawful violence such as a push, shove or spit, the starting point is a community order, the range being a band B fine to a medium level community order. Where there is fear or threat of medium level immediate unlawful violence such as a punch, the starting point is a high level community order, the range being a low level community order to 12 weeks' custody. At the top end is fear or threat of high level immediate unlawful violence such as use of a weapon; missile throwing; gang involvement, attracting a starting point of 12 weeks' custody, the range being six to 26 weeks' custody. Aggravating factors are identified as follows: those indicating higher culpability are planning, offender deliberately isolating a victim, group action, threat directed at victim because of job, history of antagonism towards victim; those indicating greater degree of harm are offence committed at a school, hospital or other place where vulnerable persons may be present, offence committed on enclosed premises such as public transport, vulnerable victim(s), victim needs medical help/counselling. Mitigating factors indicating lower culpability are impulsive action; short duration; provocation.

B11.50   Racial or religious aggravation cannot be taken into account by the sentencer when sentencing for the basic offence of fear or provocation of violence. To do so would infringe the principle that the offender must not be sentenced for an offence for which he has not been charged and convicted (*McGillivray* [2005] 2 Cr App R (S) 366). Where there is evidence that racial aggravation was present, the aggravated form of the offence should be charged (*O'Callaghan* [2005] EWCA Crim 317). See **E1.17** for increase in sentence, under the CJA 2003, s. 146, for aggravation relating to disability, sexual orientation or transgender identity. Where the offence is committed in a domestic context, reference should be made to the definitive sentencing guideline, *Overarching Principles: Domestic Violence* (see Supplement, **SG-51**).

Sentencing Guidelines (Racially or Religiously Aggravated Form of Offence)

The maximum penalty for the aggravated form of the offence is two years, a fine or both on indictment; six months, a fine not exceeding the statutory maximum or both summarily (CDA 1998, s. 31(4)). **B11.51**

The *Magistrates' Court Sentencing Guidelines* (see Supplement, **SG-303**) lay down a detailed approach to sentencing offences which are racially or religiously aggravated, incorporating the Court of Appeal's decisions on the subject to date. The extent to which the sentence will be increased will depend on the seriousness of the aggravation. The guidelines split the aggravating factors into two categories: the offender's intention and the impact on the victim or others.

In the first category, the following is identified as indicating a high level of aggravation: the racial etc. aggravation was planned; the offence was part of a pattern of offending; the offender was a member of, or was associated with, a group promoting hostility based on race etc.; the incident was deliberately set up to be offensive or humiliating to the victim or to the group of which he is a member.

In the second category, the following factors are highly aggravating: the offence was committed in the victim's home; the victim was providing a service to the public; the timing or location of the offence was calculated to maximise the harm or distress it caused; the expression of hostility was repeated or prolonged; the offence caused fear and distress throughout a local community or more widely; the offence caused particular distress to the victim and/or his family.

At the lower end of the scale, aggravation may be less serious if it was limited in scope or duration; the offence was not motivated by hostility on the basis of race etc., and the element of hostility was minor or incidental. The Court of Appeal stated in *Saunders* [2000] 1 Cr App R 458 and in *Kelly* [2001] 2 Cr App R (S) 341, that when sentencing for the racially aggravated form of an offence the sentencer should indicate the appropriate sentence for the offence in the absence of racial aggravation and then add a further term for the racial element. See further **B2.33**. In *Miller* [1999] 2 Cr App R (S) 392, the Court of Appeal upheld a sentence of 18 months' imprisonment where the offender, who had been travelling on a train without a ticket, used verbal racial abuse towards the train conductor. **B11.52**

The Four Ways of Committing an Offence under s. 4

Common to all four ways of committing an offence under the POA 1986, s. 4, are (i) the use of threatening words or behaviour or the distribution or display of threatening, abusive or insulting writing etc. (see **B11.55** to **B11.57**) and (ii) the requirement as to *mens rea* in s. 6(3) (see **B11.58**). The four ways, as indicated in *Winn v DPP* (1992) 156 JP 881, are: **B11.53**

(a) the accused must 'intend the person against whom the conduct is directed to believe that immediate unlawful violence will be used against him or another by [any] person' — as McCowan LJ put it in *Swanston v DPP* (1997) 161 JP 203, 'It is a vital component of the offence that it does not have to be shown that the other person believed: it has to be shown that the [accused] had the intention to cause that person to believe' that immediate unlawful violence would be used against him;

(b) the accused must 'intend to provoke the immediate use of unlawful violence by that person or another';

(c) 'the person against whom [the words, behaviour, distribution or display] are directed is likely to believe that such violence will be used' (note that the person who must be caused to believe that violence will be used or threatened is the person to whom the words, behaviour, distribution or display are directed, see *Loade v DPP* [1990] 1 QB 1052);

(d) 'it is likely that such violence will be provoked'.

In paragraphs (c) and (d) above, 'such violence' means 'immediate unlawful violence' (*Horseferry Road Metropolitan Stipendiary Magistrate, ex parte Siadatan* [1991] 1 QB 260).

Uses Towards

B11.54   The Divisional Court in *Atkin v DPP* (1989) 89 Cr App R 199 held that the phrase 'uses towards' in the POA 1986, s. 4(1)(a), connotes the physical presence of the person to whom the words were used. That other person must perceive with his own senses the threatening words or behaviour (see also **B11.45**). In *Atkin* the conviction had to be quashed, since the person outside the dwelling was only aware of the threat because it was relayed to him by a Customs and Excise officer.

Threatening, Abusive or Insulting

B11.55   The phrase 'threatening, abusive or insulting words or behaviour' used in the POA 1986, s. 4(1)(a), is not defined in the Act. However, 'threatening, abusive or insulting' was used with reference to words or behaviour in the POA 1936, s. 5, and the Metropolitan Police Act 1839, s. 54(13).

The House of Lords in *Brutus v Cozens* [1973] AC 854 decided that 'insulting' is to be given its ordinary meaning and the question whether words or behaviour are insulting is a question of fact. The same approach is adopted with regard to the words 'threatening' and 'abusive' and the courts have adopted this approach in interpretation of the 1986 Act (*DPP v Clarke* (1991) 94 Cr App R 359, a decision on s. 5). In *Ambrose* (1973) 57 Cr App R 538, the Court of Appeal said that rude or offensive words were not necessarily insulting. In *Vigon v DPP* (1998) 162 JP 115, it was held that secretly filming people in a changing area where they tried on swimwear could amount to insulting behaviour. Whether such behaviour can properly be described as 'insulting' must be questioned, it would seem better to have described it as a nuisance (although such behaviour falls outside the Act; it is an offence under the SOA 2003, s. 67: see **B3.285**). Describing an Asian person as a 'fucking Islam' is almost undeniably abusive, if not insulting (*R (DPP) v Humphrey* [2005] EWHC 822 (Admin)).

Meaning of 'Writing' and 'Display'

B11.56   'Writing' includes typing, printing, lithography, photography and other modes of representing or reproducing words in a visible form (Interpretation Act 1978, s. 5 and sch. 1). As to 'display', see **B11.75**.

Place of Commission

B11.57

Public Order Act 1986, ss. 4 and 8

4.—(2) An offence under this section may be committed in a public or a private place, except that no offence is committed where the words or behaviour are used, or the writing, sign or other visible representation is distributed or displayed, by a person inside a dwelling and the other person is also inside that or another dwelling.

8. In this part—
'dwelling' means any structure or part of a structure occupied as a person's home or as other living accommodation (whether the occupation is separate or shared with others) but does not include any part not so occupied, and for this purpose 'structure' includes a tent, caravan, vehicle, vessel or other temporary or movable structure.

'The other person' referred to in s. 4(2) is the same person as is referred to as 'another person' in s. 4(1)(a). Thus the offence is not committed in a dwelling if the only person to whom the words or behaviour are used, etc. (see **B11.54**) is also in that or another dwelling (*Atkin v DPP* (1989) 89 Cr App R 199). It appears to follow that the offence can be committed by the use of telephones, fax machines, e-mail and social media.

Where common parts (a communal landing) were the means of access to living accommodation, they were not part of a dwelling, even though access was via an entry phone system, and were not part of the living area or home (*Rukwira v DPP* [1993] Crim LR 882). Similarly in

Le Vine v DPP (2010) 174 JP 337, the Administrative Court, applying *Rukwira*, found that a laundry room, commonly used by tenants in sheltered housing, did not form part of a dwelling. See also *Francis* [2007] 1 WLR 1021 in which it was held that a police cell is not living accommodation.

Mens Rea

The intention with which the defendant must act is to be found in s. 4(1) (see **B11.47**) as explained further at **B11.53**. Thus, the *mens rea* that must be proved is dependent upon which form of the offence is charged. **B11.58**

For all four forms of the offence, the following applies.

Public Order Act 1986, s. 6

(3) A person is guilty of an offence under section 4 only if he intends his words or behaviour, or the writing, sign or other visible representation, to be threatening, abusive or insulting, or is aware that it may be threatening, abusive or insulting.

Whichever *mens rea* applies, the question of whether immediate unlawful violence was intended arises. In *DPP v Ramos* [2000] Crim LR 768 it was decided that it is the victim's state of mind that 'is crucial rather than the statistical risk of violence actually occurring within a very short space of time'. Thus, there was evidence on the basis of which the magistrate could infer the requisite intention as to the belief of the victims since the letters that were sent contained a very serious threat, of a bombing campaign, and there was nothing to exclude the immediate future from the period when that violence would be used. This case demonstrates the importance of identifying whether there will be immediate violence. The Divisional Court in *Horseferry Road Metropolitan Stipendiary Magistrate, ex parte Siadatan* [1991] 1 QB 260 decided that it is not sufficient that the conduct was likely to lead to violence at some unspecified time in the future. However, it decided also that 'immediate' does not mean 'instantaneous', so a relatively short time interval may elapse between the act and the violence. The court also decided that 'immediate' connotes proximity in both time and causation, i.e. the violence must result within a relatively short period of time and without any intervening occurrence. Thus, as it was not contended that immediate unlawful violence would be provoked as a result of the publication of *The Satanic Verses*, the failure to issue a summons against Penguin Viking Books Ltd was not open to challenge. The Divisional Court held in *Valentine v DPP* [1997] COD 339 that the justices were entitled to find the accused guilty where his threats caused a woman to fear 'immediate' violence the next time she went to work, but only because she might have gone to work the same night that the threat was made. Assistance on this matter may also be found in the concept of immediacy in assault (see **B2.5**), referred to by the Divisional Court in *DPP v Ramos*. As to the definition of 'violence' in the POA 1986, s. 8, see **B11.23**. **B11.59**

Since the POA 1986, s. 6, deals with intoxication when determining that of which an accused was aware, the general problems encountered with self-induced intoxication (see **A3.16** to **A3.22**), and the effect of intoxication on mistakes, are of no direct concern in this offence.

INTENTIONALLY CAUSING HARASSMENT, ALARM OR DISTRESS

Public Order Act 1986, s. 4A **B11.60**

(1) A person is guilty of an offence if, with intent to cause a person harassment, alarm or distress, he—
 (a) uses threatening, abusive or insulting words or behaviour, or disorderly behaviour, or
 (b) displays any writing, sign or other visible representation which is threatening, abusive or insulting,
 thereby causing that or another person harassment, alarm or distress.

The CDA 1998, s. 31, created a racially or religiously aggravated form of this offence. For the meaning of racially or religiously aggravated, see **B11.149** *et seq.*

Procedure and Sentencing Guidelines (Basic Offence)

B11.61   The basic offence is triable summarily only (POA 1986, s. 4A(5)). The maximum penalty is a term of imprisonment not exceeding six months or a fine not exceeding level 5 on the standard scale or both (s. 4A(5)). For the power of arrest, see **B11.67**. For the charging criteria in cases that engage the ECHR, Article 10, see **B11.48**.

The *Magistrates' Court Sentencing Guidelines* (see Supplement, **SG-304**) identify three starting points (for a first time offender pleading not guilty) according to the nature of the activity, each starting point having a defined range which is adjusted according to the non-exhaustive list of aggravating and mitigating features. Offender mitigation is considered after the court has reached a provisional sentence based on its assessment of offence seriousness.

Threats, abuse or insults made more than once but on the same occasion against the same person (e.g., while following them down the street) attract a starting point of a band C fine, with a range of band B to low level community order. Group action or deliberately planned action against a targeted victim attracts a starting point of a medium level community order, with a range of low level community order to 12 weeks' custody. If a weapon is brandished or used or threats made against a vulnerable victim or if there is a course of conduct over a long period, the starting point will be 12 weeks' custody, with a range of high level community order to 26 weeks' custody. Aggravating factors are identified as follows: those indicating higher culpability are a high degree of planning, offender deliberately isolating a victim; those indicating greater degree of harm are an offence committed in the vicinity of the victim's home, a large number of people in the vicinity, actual or potential escalation into violence, particularly serious impact on the victim. Mitigating factors indicating lower culpability are: very short duration; provocation.

Racial or religious aggravation cannot be taken into account by the sentencer when sentencing for the basic offence. See **B11.49**.

Procedure and Sentencing Guidelines (Racially or Religiously Aggravated Form of Offence)

B11.62   The aggravated form of the offence is triable either way (CDA 1998, s. 31(4)). If, on trial on indictment, the jury find the accused not guilty of the racially aggravated form of the offence, they may find him guilty of the basic offence (s. 31(6)). The maximum penalty on indictment is a term of imprisonment for two years, a fine or both and, on summary trial, a term of imprisonment for six months, or a fine not exceeding the statutory maximum, or both (s. 31(4)).

The *Magistrates' Court Sentencing Guidelines* (see Supplement, **SG-304**) lay down a detailed approach to sentencing offences which are racially or religiously aggravated. The extent to which the sentence will be increased will depend on the seriousness of the aggravation. See **B11.51** for details of what constitutes a high level of aggravation. The Court of Appeal stated in *Saunders* [2000] 1 Cr App R 458 and in *Kelly* [2001] 2 Cr App R (S) 341, that when sentencing for the racially aggravated form of an offence the sentencer should indicate the appropriate sentence for the offence in the absence of racial aggravation and then add a further term for the racial element. See further **B2.33**. Three months' imprisonment was appropriate in *Jacobs* [2001] 2 Cr App R (S) 174, where the victim was a female police officer subjected to repeated verbal racial abuse by a female suspect who had been arrested and taken to the police station. Bennett J commented that 'police officers are entitled to be protected, just as any other members of the public, from racial abuse'. See also *Jesson* [2000] 2 Cr App R (S) 200 and *Shand* [2002] 1 Cr App R (S) 291.

Meaning of 'Harassment, Alarm or Distress' etc.

Harassment, alarm or distress have not been defined, but it is assumed that they are ordinary **B11.63**
words of the English language unless and until a definition is provided. The guidance on these
words under the POA 1986, s. 5, supports this approach, see **B11.78**. In *R (R) v DPP* (2006)
170 JP 661, a prosecution under the POA 1986, s. 4A, the High Court described them as relatively strong words befitting an offence which may carry imprisonment or a substantial fine and
held that the word 'distress' in this context requires emotional disturbance or upset.

For the meaning of the phrase 'threatening, abusive or insulting', see **B11.55**. For the meaning
of 'disorderly behaviour', see **B11.74**. For the meaning of 'writing', see **B11.56**. For the meaning of 'display' in the POA 1986, s. 5, see **B11.75**.

There must be a causal connection between what the accused does and the other person's harassment, alarm or distress, as was emphasised in *Rogers v DPP* (22 July 1999 unreported). It was
held that the causal connection was not broken where a cat breeder heard the noise of the crowd
and was concerned by it and its cumulative increase, but watched the incident on his security
close circuit television. In *Steele v DPP* [2008] 1 WLR 2847 the Divisional Court held that
the offence was made out even if the material that eventually caused the harassment, alarm or
distress was no longer in the public domain at the time it caused that reaction. On the facts of
that case, material displayed on an animal rights web site was preserved by police before it was
removed by the accused and subsequently shown to the complainant by the police.

Place of Commission of Offence

Public Order Act 1986, s. 4A   **B11.64**

(2) An offence under this section may be committed in a public or a private place, except that no
offence is committed where the words or behaviour are used, or the writing, sign or other visible representation is displayed, by a person inside a dwelling and the person who is harassed,
alarmed or distressed is also inside that or another dwelling.

As to the consideration of the similar provision in s. 5(2), see **B11.78**.

A police cell is not a place which a person occupies as living accommodation, and cannot be
classified as a dwelling or living accommodation for the purposes of s. 4A (*Francis* [2007] 1
WLR 1021).

Mens Rea

This is an offence requiring proof of an intention to cause harassment, alarm or distress (POA **B11.65**
1986, s. 4A(1)). This is the fundamental question and it may be inferred where the accused's
'activities are committed in the context of a large crowd there to express disapproval of [the
other's] activities and in the context of fence removal and penetration of the police line' even
though there is no evidence that the accused knew that the other was present at the scene or
could directly experience the disorderly behaviour (*Rogers v DPP* (22 July 1999 unreported)).
It may also be inferred from the words used, though it does not necessarily follow that the requisite intention is established by the use of words such as 'black bastard' (*DPP v Weeks* (2000)
Independent, 17 July 2000). As to the meaning of 'intention', see **A2.4**. For the effect of voluntary, self-induced intoxication on *mens rea*, see the discussion in relation to the offence of riot
at **B11.27**.

Specific Defences

Public Order Act 1986, s. 4A   **B11.66**

(3) It is a defence for the accused to prove—
   (a) that he was inside a dwelling and had no reason to believe that the words or behaviour
     used, or the writing, sign or other visible representation displayed, would be heard or seen
     by a person outside that or any other dwelling; or

(b) that his conduct was reasonable.

When the legal burden is on the accused, the standard required is proof on a balance of probabilities (see **F3.5** and **F3.53**). For a summary of the case law relating to 'reverse burden' challenges under the HRA 1998, see **F3.18** *et seq.*

A person's conduct will be reasonable if he is exercising ECHR rights in circumstances in which an interference with that exercise would not be justified under Articles 10(2) (the qualifications to the right to freedom of expression) and 9(2) (the qualifications to freedom of religion) (*Hammond v DPP* (2004) 168 JP 601, a case relating to the POA 1986, s. 5). See also *Dehal v CPS* (2005) 169 JP 581 (at **B11.48**), a case in which the accused was prosecuted under the POA 1986, s. 4A, in relation to a notice he put up in a Sikh Temple denouncing those who ran the Temple and calling the president a hypocrite and a liar. It was successfully argued that his conduct was reasonable bearing in mind his Article 10 rights.

Police Powers

B11.67 Under the CJPA 2001, s. 42(1), a constable at the scene may give a direction to any person if (a) that person is present outside or in the vicinity of any premises that are used by any individual ('the resident') as his dwelling; (b) that constable believes, on reasonable grounds, that that person is present there for the purpose (by his presence or otherwise) of representing to the resident or another individual (whether or not one who uses the premises as his dwelling), or of persuading the resident or such another individual (i) that he should not do something that he is entitled or required to do, or (ii) that he should do something that he is not under an obligation to do, and (c) that constable also believes, on reasonable grounds, that the presence of that person (either alone or together with that of any other persons who are also present) (i) amounts to, or is likely to result in, the harassment of the resident, or (ii) is likely to cause alarm or distress to the resident. Further detail on the power to issue directions is contained in s. 42(2)–(6). A person who knowingly contravenes such a direction is guilty of an offence and is liable, on summary conviction, to imprisonment for a term not exceeding three months (or six months where the contravention is of a direction under s. 42(4)(b)) or a fine not exceeding level 4 on the standard scale or both (CJPA, s. 42(7)–(7C)).

For dispersal of groups and removal of persons under 16 to their place of residence, see **B11.117**.

Alternative Offence

B11.68 It is a summary offence, contrary to the CJA 1967, s. 91, where a person in any public place is, while drunk, guilty of disorderly behaviour (see **B11.202**).

HARASSMENT, ALARM OR DISTRESS

B11.69
Public Order Act 1986, s. 5

(1) A person is guilty of an offence if he—
    (a) uses threatening or abusive words or behaviour, or disorderly behaviour, or
    (b) displays any writing, sign or other visible representation which is threatening or abusive,
    within the hearing or sight of a person likely to be caused harassment, alarm or distress thereby.
[(2) and (3) concern the place of commission of the offence and a specific defence: see **B11.78** and **B11.80**.]

The CDA 1998, s. 31, created a racially or religiously aggravated form of this offence. For the meaning of racially or religiously aggravated, see **B11.149** *et seq.*; the definition has effect as if the person likely to be caused harassment, alarm or distress were the victim of the offence (s. 31(7)).

B11.70 **ECHR, Article 10** A prosecution under the POA 1986, s. 5, does not *per se* engage the ECHR, Article 10 (the right to freedom of expression): *Percy v DPP* (2002) 166 JP 93 (but see the defence of 'reasonableness' at **B11.80**). In *Abdul v DPP* [2011] EWHC 247 (Admin) the five appellants were protestors who were convicted of offences under the POA 1986, s. 5. They attended a parade in Luton town centre the purpose of which was to celebrate the home-coming of the local Royal Anglian Regiment from its duties in Afghanistan and Iraq. They carried placards, chanted slogans such as 'British soldiers burn in hell', and called the soldiers murderers, rapists and baby-killers. One of the submissions made at the close of the prosecution case was that the prosecution itself was disproportionate bearing in mind the ECHR, Article 10. The Divisional Court found that the district judge was entitled to conclude that prosecution was a proportionate response. The principles governing the relationship between s. 5 and Article 10 could be summarised as follows: the starting point was the importance of the right to freedom of expression, but it was to be recognised that legitimate protest could be offensive, at least to some; the justification for interference had to be convincingly established and the restrictions in Article 10(2) were to be construed narrowly; the justification for invoking the criminal law was the threat to public order and was for the Crown to establish; in striking the right balance when determining whether speech was threatening, abusive or insulting, the focus on minority rights was not to result in overlooking the rights of the majority; if the line between legitimate freedom of expression and a threat to public order was crossed, freedom of speech would not be impaired by 'ruling out' threatening, abusive or insulting speech. Finally, the decision was one for the judge and was not to be overturned unless shown to be plainly wrong. The Divisional Court in *Gough v DPP* (2013) 177 JP 669 upheld a finding that being naked was a form of expression such that Article 10 was engaged but that there was a pressing social need for the restriction of the accused's right to be naked in the context (walking naked in the centre of Halifax in daytime for around 15 minutes). For a decision of the Strasbourg Court, in which a political activist's conviction for insulting the French president was found to be a violation of Article 10, see *Eon v France* [2013] ECHR 216. See also **B11.48**.

See also the CPS Legal Guidance on Public Disorder for the current charging criteria.

Procedure

The offence is, by s. 5(6) of the POA 1986, triable summarily only. The racially or religiously **B11.71** aggravated form of the offence is also triable only summarily.

The POA 1986, s. 7(2), declares that, for the purposes of the rules against charging more than one offence in the same information, each of ss. 1 to 5 of the Act creates one offence.

Sentencing Guidelines (Basic Offence)

The maximum penalty is a fine not exceeding level 3 (POA 1986, s. 5(6)). Under the Penalties **B11.72** for Disorderly Behaviour (Amount of Penalty) Order 2002 (SI 2002 No. 1837), as amended, this offence is a penalty offence and the amount payable is £90.

The *Magistrates' Court Sentencing Guidelines* (see Supplement, **SG-305**) identify two starting points (for a first time offender pleading not guilty) according to the nature of the activity, each starting point having a defined range which is adjusted according to the non-exhaustive list of aggravating and mitigating features. Offender mitigation is considered after the court has reached a provisional sentence based on its assessment of offence seriousness.

If the offence involves shouting or causing a disturbance for some minutes, the starting point is a band A fine, with the range being a conditional discharge to a band B fine. If substantial disturbance is caused, the starting point is a band B fine, with the range being band A fine to band C fine (see **E15.9**). Aggravating factors are identified as follows: those indicating higher culpability are group action and lengthy incident; those indicating greater degree of harm are vulnerable persons present; offence committed at school, hospital or other place where vulnerable persons may be present; the victim is providing a public service. Mitigating factors indicating lower culpability are: the behaviour stopped as soon as police arrived; brief/minor incident; provocation.

Racial or religious aggravation cannot be taken into account by the sentencer when sentencing for the basic offence (see **B11.49**); see **E1.17** for increase in sentence, under the CJA 2003, s. 146, for aggravation relating to disability, sexual orientation or transgender identity.

Sentencing Guidelines (Racially or Religiously Aggravated Form of Offence)

B11.73   The maximum penalty is a fine not exceeding level 4 (CDA 1998, s. 31(5)).

The *Magistrates' Court Sentencing Guidelines* (see Supplement, **SG-305**) lay down a detailed approach to sentencing offences which are racially or religiously aggravated, incorporating the Court of Appeal's decisions on the subject to date. The extent to which the sentence will be increased will depend on the seriousness of the aggravation. See **B11.51** for details of what constitutes a high level of aggravation. The Court of Appeal indicated in *Saunders* [2000] 1 Cr App R 458, that when sentencing for the racially aggravated form of an offence the sentencer may usefully consider the appropriate sentence for the offence in the absence of racial aggravation and then add a further term for the racial element. See further **B11.51** and **B2.33**.

Threatening, Abusive or Insulting Words or Behaviour; Disorderly Behaviour; Writing

B11.74   For the meaning of the phrase 'threatening, abusive or insulting', see **B11.55**. This element of the offence and that of causing harassment, alarm or distress are separate and different; the two must not be equated. The approach in *Brutus v Cozens* [1973] AC 854 (i.e. that words should be given their ordinary meaning: see **B11.55**) should be adopted in considering the meaning of disorderly behaviour. The disorderly behaviour need not be threatening, abusive or insulting nor is it necessary to prove any feeling of insecurity in an apprehensive sense (*Chambers v DPP* [1995] Crim LR 896). In *Hammond v DPP* (2004) 168 JP 601, the Divisional Court decided that, in determining whether words or behaviour are insulting (or threatening or abusive), the traditional approach under *Brutus v Cozens* is to be followed, but also that full account must be taken of the ECHR, Article 10 (freedom of expression): see **B11.70**. For the meaning of 'writing', see **B11.56**.

Display

B11.75   The Divisional Court in *Chappell v DPP* (1988) 89 Cr App R 82 held that magistrates were correct to decide that the posting of an envelope, with writing containing abusive or insulting words concealed inside it, through a letter box of someone's home could not amount to a 'display'. This approach might apply to envelopes containing threatening, abusive or insulting material even in public.

Within the Hearing or Sight of a Person Likely to be Caused Harassment, Alarm or Distress

B11.76   Harassment, alarm and distress are alternatives. In *R (R) v DPP* (2006) 170 JP 661, a prosecution under the POA 1986, s. 4A, the High Court described them as relatively strong words befitting an offence which may carry imprisonment or a substantial fine and held that the word 'distress' in this context requires emotional disturbance or upset. In *Southard v DPP* [2006] EWHC 3449 (Admin)) it was held that distress, by its very nature, involves an element of emotional disturbance or upset, but harassment does not. However, the harassment has to be real as opposed to trivial. 'Harassment' does not demand any element of apprehension about personal safety (*Chambers v DPP* [1995] Crim LR 896).

In *Taylor v DPP* (2006) 170 JP 485, it was held that there must be evidence that there was someone *able* to hear or see the accused's conduct, and that the prosecution does not have to call evidence that he or she did *actually* hear the words spoken or see the behaviour. To the extent that there was a difference of approach between Collins J and Silber J in *Holloway v DPP* [2004] EWHC 2621 (Admin), the preference was for the approach of the former. See also *Reda v DPP* [2011] EWHC 1550 (Admin). In *Mladenov v Bulgaria* [2013] EWHC 903 (Admin), the accused, when in Bulgaria, had waved a newspaper in a police officer's face, shouted at him in a threatening tone and intimated that the officer would lose his job if he carried on telling the accused what to do. As to whether this conduct would amount to an offence under the POA 1986, s. 5, if it had occurred in England, Mitting J said this (at [21]):

> I have no doubt that a robust English magistrates' court would conclude that this was the sort of thing that police officers had to put up with day in, day out, and that their reaction, if not of boredom, would have been of resignation and a willingness to continue to perform their official duties without interruption. For a court to conclude that a police officer in Investigator Grigorov's position would be likely to be subjected to 'harassment' by this conduct would, in my judgment, be an erroneous conclusion which would not afford proper respect to the stoicism and fortitude of a policeman in the position of Investigator Grigorov.

In *Lodge v DPP* (1988) *The Times*, 26 October 1988, the Divisional Court decided that whether a person was likely to be caused harassment, alarm or distress is a matter of fact to be determined by the magistrates. The Court indicated that it is sufficient if the other person in question, in that case a police officer, feels alarm (or harassment or distress) for someone else, for example a child.

B11.77 In *DPP v Orum*, the Divisional Court decided that, where the only people present were the defendant, his girlfriend with whom he was having an argument and two police officers, a police officer can be a person likely to be caused harassment, alarm or distress. However, if an officer is the only other person present and he is not likely to be caused harassment, alarm or distress, no offence is committed, because the element of causation is lacking. However, the Court of Appeal in *Ball* (1989) 90 Cr App R 378, without reference to *Orum*, was of the opinion that in such circumstances a police officer could arrest the person because he could have reasonable cause to suspect that an offence had been committed, since the conduct in s. 5 does not have to be directed towards another person. As to whether a police officer could be said to have been caused distress by a 12-year-old boy calling him a 'wanker', see *R (R) v DPP* (2006) 170 JP 661, in which the court very much doubted that he could have been. By contrast see *Southard v DPP*, in which the Divisional Court stated that the words 'fuck you' or 'fuck off' were potentially abusive, whether they were addressed to a police officer or a member of the public and on the facts of the case the police officer was harassed by the use of those words directed at him by the appellant during an incident in which he was making it impossible for the officer to detain a suspect.

Place of Commission of Offence

B11.78
Public Order Act 1986, s. 5

(2) An offence under this section may be committed in a public or a private place, except that no offence is committed where the words or behaviour are used, or the writing, sign or other visible representation is displayed, by a person inside a dwelling and the other person is also inside that or another dwelling.

The Divisional Court in *Chappell v DPP* (1988) 89 Cr App R 82 held that the delivery of a letter to a person within his or her own home, where he or she reads it and is alarmed or distressed by its contents, cannot be an offence under s. 5. Such conduct would constitute an offence contrary to the Malicious Communications Act 1988, s. 1(1). See also **B11.64**.

Mens Rea

B11.79   **Public Order Act 1986, s. 6**

> (4) A person is guilty of an offence under section 5 only if he intends his words or behaviour, or
> the writing, sign or other visible representation, to be threatening or abusive, or is aware that it
> may be threatening or abusive or (as the case may be) he intends his behaviour to be or is aware
> that it may be disorderly.

Whether the accused had the intention or awareness is to be tested subjectively in the
light of the whole evidence, the burden of proof beyond a reasonable doubt lying upon
the prosecution (*DPP v Clarke* (1991) 94 Cr App R 359). The accused must intend the
behaviour to be disorderly or be aware that it might be disorderly (*Chambers v DPP* [1995]
Crim LR 896).

For the effect of voluntary, self-induced intoxication on *mens rea*, see the discussion in relation
to the offence of riot at **B11.27**.

Specific Defences

B11.80   **Public Order Act 1986, s. 5**

> (3) It is a defence for the accused to prove—
>   (a) that he had no reason to believe that there was any person within hearing or sight who was
>   likely to be caused harassment, alarm or distress, or
>   (b) that he was inside a dwelling and had no reason to believe that the words or behaviour
>   used, or the writing, sign or other visible representation displayed, would be heard or seen
>   by a person outside that or any other dwelling, or
>   (c) that his conduct was reasonable.

When the legal burden is on the accused, the standard required is proof on a balance of probabilities (see **F3.5** and **F3.53**). For a summary of the case law relating to 'reverse burden' challenges under the HRA 1998, see **F3.18** *et seq*. As to whether incompatibility with the ECHR
arises in the context of the 'reverse burden' in the POA 1986, s. 5, see Auld LJ's comments in
Norwood v DPP [2003] Crim LR 888.

An objective test must be used to assess the conduct referred to in s. 5(3)(c) (*DPP v Clarke*
(1991) 94 Cr App R 359; *Kwasi Poku v DPP* [1993] Crim LR 705; *Morrow v DPP* [1994] Crim
LR 58; *Lewis v DPP* (1996 unreported)). A person's conduct will be reasonable if he is exercising
ECHR rights in circumstances in which an interference with that exercise would not be justified under Articles 10(2) (the qualifications to the right to freedom of expression) and 9(2) (the
qualifications to freedom of religion): *Percy v DPP* (2002) 166 JP 93; *Norwood v DPP* [2003]
Crim LR 888; *Hammond v DPP* (2004) 168 JP 601.

B11.81 In *Percy v DPP*, a protester who had for many years protested against the use of weapons of mass
destruction and against US military policy defaced the American flag at a US air base by writing
'Stop Star Wars' across the stripes, stepped in front of a vehicle and placed the flag down in front
of it and then stood on it. American service personnel and/or their families were distressed to varying degrees by her actions. On appeal to the Divisional Court, she argued that her conduct was
reasonable within the meaning of s. 5(3)(c), relying on Article 10. Her conviction was quashed
on the basis that insufficient weight had been given to the question of proportionality when considering whether her conduct was reasonable. By contrast in *Hammond v DPP*, H, an Evangelical
Christian preacher, had on more than one occasion carried a large double-sided sign with the
words 'Stop Immorality! Stop Homosexuality! Stop Lesbianism!', whilst preaching in the centre of
Bournemouth. This attracted a large crowd: some found the words on the placard insulting, others
found them distressing, one person found them disgusting and annoying. The Divisional Court
considered his actions in the context of Articles 10 and 11 and found that they were not reasonable
within the meaning of s. 5(3)(c). Similarly in *Norwood v DPP* the action of a member of the BNP

in placing a sign in window saying 'Islam out of Britain' and 'Protect the British people' was not considered reasonable.

Related Offence

It is an offence, contrary to the Air Navigation Order 2009 (SI 2009 No. 3015), art. 142, (a) to use any threatening, abusive or insulting words towards an aircraft crew member, (b) to behave in a threatening, abusive, insulting or disorderly manner towards an aircraft crew member, or (c) to interfere intentionally with the performance by an aircraft crew member of his duties. The offences mentioned in (a) and (b) are triable summarily only. On conviction the maximum penalty is a fine not exceeding level 4 on the standard scale (art. 241(7) and sch. 13, parts B and C). The offence mentioned in (c) is triable either way. The maximum penalty on conviction on indictment is a term of imprisonment not exceeding two years, a fine, or both; on summary conviction, the maximum penalty is a fine not exceeding the statutory maximum. **B11.82**

Alternative Offence

The summary offence of being drunk and disorderly (see B11.202) may be an appropriate alternative offence. **B11.83**

PUBLIC NUISANCE

Definition

In recent times, the Court of Appeal has expressed approval of the following definitions of public nuisance: **B11.84**

> Public nuisance is an offence at common law. A person is guilty of a public nuisance (also known as a common nuisance) who (a) does an act not warranted by law, or (b) omits to discharge a legal duty, if the effect of the act or omission is to endanger the life, health, property, morals, or comfort of the public, or to obstruct the public in the exercise or enjoyment of rights common to all Her Majesty's subjects. (*Goldstein* [2004] 2 All ER 589 at [3].)

> A common nuisance is an act not warranted by law or an omission to discharge a legal duty, which act or omission obstructs or causes inconvenience or damage to the public in the exercise of rights common to all of His Majesty's subjects. (*Stephen's Digest of Criminal Law*, confirmed in *A-G v PYA Quarries Ltd* [1957] 2 QB 169, per Romer LJ, *Madden* [1975] 1 WLR 1379 and *Shorrock* [1994] QB 279.)

> Nuisance, nocumentum, or annoyance, signifies anything that worketh hurt, inconvenience, or damage. And nuisances are of two kinds; public or common nuisances, which affect the public, and are an annoyance to all the King's subjects; for which reason we must refer them to the class of public wrongs, or crimes and misdemeanours; and private nuisances, which are the objects of our present consideration, and may be defined, anything done to the hurt or annoyance of the lands, tenements or hereditaments of another. (*Blackstone's Commentaries*, confirmed in *A-G v PYA Quarries Ltd* [1957] 2 QB 169 and quoted, with apparent approval, in *Shorrock* [1994] QB 279.)

The courts do not have power to abolish the offence (*Rimmington* [2006] 1 AC 459 at [31]). A single act by a male on foot of soliciting a woman for prostitution within a recognised vice area cannot amount in law to the common-law offence of public nuisance; central to the concept of public nuisance was common injury to members of the public, and it was not permissible to apply the offence to multiple, separate incidents on different members of the public and call them a common injury (*DPP v Fearon* [2010] 2 Cr App R 169, applying *Rimmington*) (see B11.91).

Procedure and Limit on Prosecution

It is a common-law offence, triable either way, for a person to cause a public nuisance. When tried on indictment, it is normally a class 3 offence, but see CPD XIII, para. B (see Supplement, PD-97) for the additional factors that the court considers on allocation. **B11.85**

The House of Lords in *Rimmington* [2006] 1 AC 459 has made clear that this offence should not ordinarily be prosecuted where there is a statutory offence covering the relevant mischief. Lord Bingham said (at [30]):

> It cannot in the ordinary way be a reason for resorting to the common law offence that the prosecutor is freed from mandatory time limits or restrictions on penalty. It must rather be assumed that Parliament imposed the restrictions which it did having considered and weighed up what the protection of the public reasonably demanded. I would not go to the length of holding that conduct may never be lawfully prosecuted as a generally expressed common law crime where it falls within the terms of a specific statutory provision, but good practice and respect for the primacy of statute do in my judgment require that conduct falling within the terms of a specific statutory provision should be prosecuted under that provision unless there is good reason for doing otherwise.

The statutory offences that may be prosecuted include the following (as identified by Lord Bingham in *Rimmington* at [29]): statutory nuisance under the Environmental Protection Act 1990, s. 79(1); dumping of waste under the Environmental Protection Act 1990, s. 33; wilfully obstructing the highway under the Highways Act 1980, s. 137; harassment under the Protection from Harassment Act 1997, ss. 1 and 4; racially or religiously aggravated offences under the CDA 1998, s. 32; dealing with raves, etc. under the CJPO 1994, s. 63; bomb hoaxes under the CLA 1977, s. 51; sending substances inducing someone to believe they are noxious under the Anti-terrorism, Crime and Security Act 2001, s. 114; sending by post matter that is obscene or indecent or is likely to injure a postal worker under the Postal Services Act 2000, s. 85; sending malicious etc. communications under the Malicious Communications Act 1988, s. 1; and improperly using a public electronic communications network under the Communications Act 2003, s. 127.

Sentence

B11.86   On conviction on indictment, the maximum sentence is at the discretion of the court. On summary conviction, the statutory maxima apply. In *Ruffell* (1992) 13 Cr App R (S) 204, the offender organised an 'acid house' party in unsuitable premises which was attended by a large number of people. A road leading to the site was blocked by traffic, local residents were disturbed by noise throughout the night, and litter and excrement were deposited in adjoining woodlands. He pleaded guilty to causing a public nuisance. A 12-month suspended prison sentence was upheld by the Court of Appeal but a fine imposed in addition was quashed because of the offender's lack of means. A sentence of four years for conspiracy to cause a public nuisance was upheld in *Ong* [2001] 1 Cr App R (S) 404, where the offenders arranged with others to cause the abandoning of a Premiership football match by switching off the floodlights. Had the scheme succeeded the offenders stood to make a substantial sum from betting on the outcome of the match.

Private and Public Nuisance

B11.87   The torts and the crime are closely connected: 'public nuisance is defined by reference to private nuisance and as differing from private nuisance only in the range of its effect' (*Shorrock* [1994] QB 279). The idea that public nuisance could be committed by isolated acts or isolated acts in a series (which originated from Denning LJ's judgment in *A-G v PYA Quarries Ltd* [1957] 2 QB 169) was firmly rejected by the House of Lords in *Rimmington* [2006] 1 AC 459 (at [37]):

> …to permit a conviction of causing a public nuisance to rest on an injury caused to separate individuals rather than on an injury suffered by the community or a significant section of it as a whole was to contradict the rationale of the offence and pervert its nature.

See further **B11.91**.

Where someone suffers particular damage as a result of a public nuisance they may sue in tort for public nuisance.

Nuisance

There must be conduct by the accused which 'renders the enjoyment of life and property **B11.88** uncomfortable' (*White* (1775) 1 Burr 333, per Lord Mansfield) or 'materially affects the reasonable comfort and convenience of a class of Her Majesty's subjects' (*A-G v PYA Quarries Ltd* [1957] 2 QB 169, approved by the Court of Appeal in *Johnson* [1996] 2 Cr App R 434). Not all obstructions of the highway amount to a public nuisance (see, e.g., *Dwyer v Mansfield* [1946] KB 437 and *DPP v Jones* [1999] 2 AC 240).

Criminal convictions have, for example, been successful in the following circumstances:

(a) the accused was responsible for a house which was ruinous and likely to fall down thus endangering people using the highway (*Watts* (1757) 1 Salkeld 357);
(b) the accused sold meat unfit for human consumption (*Stephens* (1866) LR 1 QB 702);
(c) the accused caused 30 houses and the highway to be affected by dust and noise from its quarry (*A-G v PYA Quarries Ltd* [1957] 2 QB 169);
(d) the accused sniffed glue in a school playground when staff and pupils were absent (*Sykes v Homes* [1985] Crim LR 791, holding that it was a nuisance within the Local Government (Miscellaneous Provisions) Act 1982, s. 40 — whether it would be a public nuisance would depend upon the public nature of the nuisance);
(e) the accused allowed a rave to take place in his field (*Shorrock* [1994] QB 279).

Act or Omission

It is clear that a public nuisance may be caused by either an act (see, e.g., *Vantandillo* (1815) 4 **B11.89** M & S 73 and *A-G v PYA Quarries Ltd* [1957] 2 QB 169) or an omission (see, e.g., *Watts* (1757) 1 Salkeld 357 and *Shorrock* [1994] QB 279; see also *A-G v Tod Heatley* [1897] 1 Ch 560, where it was held that it was the duty of the owner of land to prevent it from being used as a dumping ground which caused a public nuisance).

The Public Nature of the Nuisance

In order to establish that a crime has been committed, it is necessary to establish the essential public **B11.90** nature of the nuisance. It is clear that not all the public need be affected. But it must be established that the act or omission was sufficiently widespread or indiscriminate as to amount to a public rather than a private nuisance. In *A-G v PYA Quarries Ltd* [1957] 2 QB 169, Romer LJ stated:

> ...any nuisance is 'public' which materially affects the reasonable comfort and convenience of life of a class of Her Majesty's subjects. The sphere of the nuisance may be described generally as 'the neighbourhood'; but the question whether the local community within that sphere comprises sufficient number of persons to constitute a class of the public is a question of fact in every case. It is not necessary, in my judgment, to prove that every member of the class has been injuriously affected; it is sufficient to show that a representative cross-section of the class has been so affected for an injunction to issue.

In the same case, Denning LJ said, 'a public nuisance is a nuisance which is so widespread in its range or so indiscriminate in its effect that it would not be reasonable to expect one person to take proceedings on his own responsibility to put a stop to it, but that it should be taken on the responsibility of the community at large'. In that case, there was a public nuisance where 30 houses and the highway were affected by dust and noise from the workings of a quarry.

In *Rimmington* [2006] 1 AC 459, the House of Lords held (at [12]) that 'a common injury **B11.91** is a, perhaps the, distinguishing feature of this offence.' Further (at [36]) that what must be looked for is whether the act of omission contemplated by the accused 'was likely to inflict significant injury on a substantial section of the public exercising their ordinary rights as such'. In consequence, the House overruled the decision in *Johnson* [1996] 2 Cr App R 434, where the conviction had been upheld after the accused had made hundreds of telephone calls to at least 13 women in South Cumbria. The error was that this was a series of acts involving individual members of the public and could not constitute the necessary effect on the public or a significant section of the public for there to be a public nuisance. So, per Lord Nicholls at [42], a telephone hoax call might involve a public nuisance if it was a call that an explosive device had been left at a railway station as opposed to a call which would only inconvenience the recipient. So R's conviction was quashed as he had sent offensive and racist messages to a series of individuals. G's conviction was quashed because of the lack of *mens rea*, but it was stated that, if the *mens rea* had been present, sending salt through the post anticipating that, if it leaked, it could be thought to be anthrax and its effect would be sufficiently serious to affect a section of the public could have been a public nuisance. Relying on *Rimmington*, the Divisional Court in *DPP v Fearon* [2010] 2 Cr App R 22 held that the accused had not committed a public nuisance when, on a public highway, he solicited an undercover police officer for sex on one occasion. The prosecution had argued that the accused's actions should be seen in the context of similar conduct carried on by other men in that area at around the same time, and so it was their collective actions that lent a 'public' air to the accused's nuisance behaviour. Elias LJ rejected that argument in emphatic terms (at [13]).

Mens Rea

B11.92   The 'requirement as to the accused's state of mind is the same whether the proceedings brought be civil or criminal. Actual knowledge of the nuisance need not be established'. The *mens rea*, therefore, is that the defendant is 'guilty of the offence charged if either he knew or he ought to have known, in the sense that the means of knowledge were available to him, that there was a real risk that the consequences of the licence granted by [the accused] in respect of his field [on which a rave took place] would be to create the sort of nuisance that in fact occurred' (*Shorrock* [1994] QB 279, approved in *Rimmington* [2006] 1 AC 459).

Vicarious Liability

B11.93   For the ordinary rules relating to vicarious liability, see **A6.8**. However, a master may be liable for a public nuisance even if the act of the servant is contrary to the master's orders (see *Stephens* (1866) LR 1 QB 702 and *Smith and Hogan's Criminal Law* (13th edn, 2011), at p. 275). The decision in *Stephens* was doubted in *Chisholm v Doulton* (1889) 22 QBD 736. It remains to be seen whether such a rule will continue to apply and, if so, if it will apply consistently to all forms of public nuisance (a view the decision in *Shorrock* [1994] QB 279 may be interpreted as implicitly supporting).

Defences

B11.94   Statutory authorisation is a defence to public nuisance, provided that the statute covers that which is done (*Hammersmith and City Railway Co. v Brand and Louisa* (1868) LR 4 QB 171; *Managers of the Metropolitan Asylum District v Hill* (1881) LR 6 AC 193; *London, Brighton and South Coast Railway v Truman* (1885) LR 11 AC 45; *Saunders v Holborn District Board of Works* [1895] 1 QB 64).

Compliance with the European Convention on Human Rights

B11.95   The House of Lords in *Rimmington* [2006] 1 AC 459 took the view that the offence of public nuisance did not breach ECHR, Article 7 (the prohibition on retrospective criminal offences: see **A7.85**). It should be noted, first, that the House decided that it should be prosecuted rarely as it should be used only where there was no statutory nuisance that ordinarily ought to be prosecuted (see **B11.85**); secondly, the House emphasised the requirement of a sufficiently serious effect on the public or a section of it (see **B11.90**); finally, it confirmed the *mens rea* requirement (see **B11.92**). The standards that the House identified were, per Lord Bingham (at [35]) that the:

> ...offence must be clearly defined in law...and a norm cannot be regarded as a law unless it is formulated with sufficient precision to enable the citizen to foresee, if need be with appropriate advice, the consequences which a given course of conduct may entail.... It is accepted that absolute certainty is

unattainable, and might entail excessive rigidity since the law must be able to keep pace with changing circumstances, some degree of vagueness is inevitable and development of the law is a recognised feature of common law courts...But the law-making function of the courts must remain within reasonable limits...existing offences may not be extended to cover facts which did not previously constitute a criminal offence. The law may be clarified and adapted to new circumstances which can reasonably be brought under the original concept of the offence.... But any development must be consistent with the essence of the offence and be reasonably foreseeable...and the criminal law must not be extensively construed to the detriment of an accused, for instance by analogy.

Lord Bingham took the view (at [36] and [37]) that these requirements would not have been met had the recent development moving the law away from the requirement for an effect on the public or a significant section of it not been re-emphasised.

BOMB HOAXES

B

Criminal Law Act 1977, s. 51   B11.96

(1) A person who—
  (a) places any article in any place whatever; or
  (b) dispatches any article by post, rail or any other means whatever of sending things from one place to another,
  with the intention (in either case) of inducing in some other person a belief that it is likely to explode or ignite and thereby cause personal injury or damage to property is guilty of an offence. In this subsection 'article' includes substance.
(2) A person who communicates any information which he knows or believes to be false to another person with the intention of inducing in him or any other person a false belief that a bomb or other thing liable to explode or ignite is present in any place or location whatever is guilty of an offence.

Procedure

Offences under the CLA 1977, s. 51, are triable either way. When tried on indictment they are normally class 3 offences, but see CPD XIII, para. B (see Supplement, **PD-97**) for the additional factors that the court considers on allocation.   **B11.97**

Indictment

First Count   **B11.98**

Statement of Offence

Perpetrating bomb hoax contrary to section 51(1) of the Criminal Law Act 1977.

Particulars of Offence

A on or about the...day of...placed an article, namely a parcel, in [or: dispatched by post (or rail etc.) an article, namely a parcel, to] the Dead Parrot Public House at...with the intention of inducing in V, the manager of the said house, a belief that the said parcel was likely to explode or ignite and thereby cause personal injury or damage to property therein.

Second Count

Statement of Offence

Perpetrating bomb hoax contrary to section 51(2) of the Criminal Law Act 1977.

Particulars of Offence

A on or about the...day of...communicated to V the information that a parcel containing a bomb liable to explode or ignite was present on the premises of the Dead Parrot Public House at..., knowing or believing the said information to be false and with the intention of inducing in V the false belief that it was true.

Sentencing Guidelines

The maximum penalty is seven years on indictment; six months, a fine not exceeding the statutory maximum, or both, summarily (CLA 1977, s. 51(4)).   **B11.99**

In *Harrison* [1997] 2 Cr App R (S) 174, a sentence of four years' imprisonment was upheld on an offender who made a series of telephone calls to a theatre saying that a bomb had been planted. The offender had previous convictions for similar offences and was said to be suffering from a personality disorder but not mental illness. In *Dunbar* (1987) 9 Cr App R (S) 393, the offenders pleaded guilty to communicating a bomb hoax. They telephoned the police to say that incendiary devices had been placed in various stores, apparently in order to cause financial loss to the stores. Sentences of 12 months' imprisonment were upheld by the Court of Appeal, Leggatt J commenting that:

> A bomb hoax of this kind, as this court has had occasion to say in the past, is a public nuisance, and it is important not to underrate the anxiety and apprehension that this kind of behaviour engenders. The public rightly expect judges to pass severe sentences as a mark of public disapprobation of this kind of offence.

In *Harris* [2005] 2 Cr App R (S) 649, the offender manufactured two devices designed to look like bombs. He took one to a police station and one to a restaurant. The premises and surrounding area had to be evacuated. There was no evidence that the offender suffered from a treatable mental disorder. Bearing in mind that his conduct had been more than a nuisance and had caused fear and disruption, a total sentence of three years' imprisonment was appropriate on a guilty plea.

In *Walter* [2013] 2 Cr App R (S) 302 (46), the accused pleaded guilty to three offences of communicating false information with intent. On each occasion he called the emergency services to say that a bomb would detonate and kill the Queen. Concurrent sentences of three years' imprisonment were held to be manifestly excessive. Concurrent sentences of two years' imprisonment were substituted. See also *McMenemy* [2009] 2 Cr App R (S) 57 and *Ahmed* [2010] 2 Cr App R (S) 85.

Elements

B11.100   A call stating 'there is a bomb' is sufficient to comprise the offence, even though there is no reference to a place or location (*Webb* (1995) *The Times*, 19 June 1995).

By the CLA 1977, s. 51(3), for a person to be guilty of an offence under s. 51(1) or (2), it is not necessary for him to have any particular person in mind as the person in whom he intends to induce the belief mentioned in the relevant subsection.

Related Offence: False Alarm of Fire

B11.101   It is an offence, contrary to the Fire and Rescue Services Act 2004, s. 49(1), if a person knowingly gives or causes to be given a false alarm of fire to a person acting on behalf of a fire and rescue authority. A person guilty of such an offence is liable, on summary conviction, to a fine not exceeding level 4 on the standard scale, or a term of imprisonment not exceeding three months, or to both (Fire and Rescue Services Act 2004, s. 49(2) and (3)). Under the Penalties for Disorderly Behaviour (Amount of Penalty) Order 2002 (SI 2002 No. 1837), as amended, this offence is a penalty offence and the amount payable is £90.

CONTAMINATION OF OR INTERFERENCE WITH GOODS

B11.102

Public Order Act 1986, s. 38

(1) It is an offence for a person, with the intention—

    (a) of causing public alarm or anxiety, or

    (b) of causing injury to members of the public consuming or using the goods, or

    (c) of causing economic loss to any person by reason of the goods being shunned by members of the public, or

    (d) of causing economic loss to any person by reason of steps taken to avoid such alarm or anxiety, injury or loss, to contaminate or interfere with goods, or make it appear that goods have been contaminated or interfered with, or to place goods which have been contaminated or interfered with, or which appear to have been contaminated or interfered with, in a place where goods of that description are consumed, used, sold or otherwise supplied.

(2) It is also an offence for a person, with any such intention as is mentioned in paragraph (a), (c) or (d) of subsection (1), to threaten that he or another will do, or claim that he or another has done, any of the acts mentioned in that subsection.

(3) It is an offence for a person to be in possession of any of the following articles with a view to the commission of an offence under subsection (1)—

(a) materials to be used for contaminating or interfering with goods or making it appear that goods have been contaminated or interfered with, or

(b) goods which have been contaminated or interfered with, or which appear to have been contaminated or interfered with.

Procedure

B11.103 Offences under the POA 1986, s. 38, are triable either way (POA 1986, s. 38(4)). When tried on indictment they are normally class 3 offences, but see CPD XIII, para. B (see Supplement, PD-97) for the additional factors that the court considers on allocation.

Indictment (for an Offence Contrary to s. 38(1)(a))

B11.104
Statement of Offence

Contamination of goods contrary to section 38(1)(a) of the Public Order Act 1986.

Particulars of Offence

A on or about the…day of…with the intention of causing public alarm or anxiety, placed certain goods, namely 100 jars of…brand honey which had been contaminated by the insertion of fragments of broken glass therein, in a place where goods of that description are sold to the public, namely V's department store,…

Sentence

B11.105 The maximum penalty is ten years, a fine or both, on indictment (POA 1986, s. 38(4)); six months, a fine not exceeding the statutory maximum, or both, summarily. In *Cruickshank* [2001] 2 Cr App R (S) 278, the offender pleaded guilty to contaminating food in a supermarket by inserting pins, needles or nails into various items. He persisted in this behaviour for three months, and some minor injuries were incurred by customers who bought the contaminated products. There was no logical explanation for the offender's behaviour, and no financial motive, but a medical disposal was not recommended. Three years' imprisonment was upheld by the Court of Appeal. Examples of cases involving *threats* to contaminate goods are *Witchelo* (1992) 13 Cr App R (S) 371 (see **B5.45**) and *Smith* (1994) 15 Cr App R (S) 106.

Meaning of 'Goods'

B11.106 In the POA 1986, s. 38, 'goods' includes substances whether natural or manufactured and whether or not incorporated in or mixed with other goods (s. 38(5)).

Meaning of 'Claim' that Acts Have Been Committed

B11.107 The reference in the POA 1986, s. 38(2), to a person claiming that certain acts have been committed does not include a person who in good faith reports or warns that such acts have been, or appear to have been, committed (s. 38(6)).

PRISON MUTINY

B11.108 The Prison Security Act 1992 created the offence of prison mutiny. For offences relating to the escape of prisoners, see **B14.70** *et seq*.

Prison Security Act 1992, s. 1

(1) Any prisoner who takes part in a prison mutiny shall be guilty of an offence and liable, on conviction on indictment, to imprisonment for a term not exceeding ten years or to a fine or to both.

(2) For the purposes of this section there is a prison mutiny where two or more prisoners, while on the premises of any prison, engage in conduct which is intended to further a common purpose of overthrowing lawful authority in that prison.

(3) For the purposes of this section the intentions and common purpose of prisoners may be inferred from the form and circumstances of their conduct and it shall be immaterial that conduct falling within subsection (2) above takes a different form in the case of different prisoners.

(4) Where there is a prison mutiny, a prisoner who has or is given a reasonable opportunity of submitting to lawful authority and fails, without reasonable excuse, to do so shall be regarded for the purposes of this section as taking part in the mutiny.

(5) Proceedings for an offence under this section shall not be brought except by or with the consent of the Director of Public Prosecutions.

(6) In this section—
'conduct' includes acts and omissions;
'prison' means any prison, young offender institution or remand centre which is under the general superintendence of, or is provided by, the Secretary of State under the Prison Act 1952, including a contracted out prison within the meaning of Part IV of the Criminal Justice Act 1991;
'prisoner' means any person for the time being in a prison as a result of any requirement imposed by a court or otherwise that he be detained in legal custody.

Sentence

B11.109   Sentences of up to nine years' imprisonment were upheld in *Lambert* [2006] 2 Cr App R (S) 107 for the instigators of a prison mutiny at Lincoln prison. During the riot, which lasted for several hours and spread to all parts of the prison, a prison officer was attacked and knocked unconscious, there were numerous other instances of violence, and damage in excess of £2 million was caused. The offenders were convicted after a trial which lasted for 13 weeks. In *Mitchell* (1995) 16 Cr App R (S) 924, custodial sentences of five years were upheld in respect of two offenders convicted of prison mutiny. They had taken a leading part in an incident involving 120 remand prisoners which had caused extensive damage at Reading prison.

Elements

B11.110   The offence may be committed in one of two ways as found in s. 1(2) and (4). Section 1(2) is committed where there is a common purpose and that is aimed at overthrowing lawful authority in the prison. This latter requirement is a stronger word than 'subversion' and is not synonymous with 'widespread failure to follow lawful orders'; it is limited to serious disturbances and does not cover a mere defiance of, or challenge to, that lawful authority. The offence in s. 1(4) is committed on a deemed basis and is parasitic to the commission of the s. 1(2) offence. An indictment should make clear on which basis the offence is charged (*Mason* [2005] 1 Cr App R 145). Where the s. 1(4) offence is charged, the prosecution must prove that there was a prison mutiny and that the defendant participated in it at some stage (*Griffin* (17 August 1999 unreported)).

CONTROL OF PROCESSIONS, ASSEMBLIES AND MEETINGS

Advance Notice of Public Procession

B11.111   It is an offence, contrary to the POA 1986, s. 11(7), for a person organising a public procession to fail to satisfy the requirements in s. 11 concerning the giving of notice of the procession to the police. By s. 11(2), notice is not required where the procession is one commonly or customarily held in the police area (or areas) in which it is proposed to be held or is a funeral procession organised by a funeral director acting in the normal course of his business. A mass cycle ride, beginning at the same place and held at the same time each month but with no predetermined route, was, assuming s. 11 applied, a commonly or customarily held procession within the meaning of s. 11(2) and so no notice of it had to be given (*R (Kay) v Commissioner of Police of the Metropolis* [2008] 2 All ER 935). Having given notice, an organiser commits an offence if the date when the procession is held, the time when it starts or its route differ from the date, time or route specified in the notice. The offence is triable only summarily and is punishable with a fine not exceeding level 3.

It is a defence, under s. 11(8), for the accused to prove that he did not know of, and neither suspected nor had reason to suspect, the failure to satisfy the requirements or (as the case may be) the difference of date, time or route. It is also a defence, under s. 11(9), when the offence turns on a difference of date, time or route, for the accused to prove that the difference arose from circumstances beyond his control or from something done with the agreement of a police officer or by his direction.

When the ABCPA 2014, part 3, is in force, if an authorisation is in force under s. 34, a constable in uniform cannot make a dispersal direction under s. 35 if the person he wishes to disperse is one of a group of persons who are taking part in a public procession of the kind mentioned in the POA 1986, s. 11(1) (ABCPA 2014, s. 36(4)(b)).

Failure to Comply with Conditions Imposed on Public Procession

Under the POA 1986, s. 12, conditions may be imposed on public processions. Conditions may be imposed either in advance or at the time of the procession by the senior police officer acting under s. 12(1)–(3). It is an offence, triable only summarily:

B11.112

(a) for a person who organises a public procession knowingly to fail to comply with a condition (s. 12(4)) (*DPP v Baillie* [1995] Crim LR 426);
(b) for a person who takes part in such a procession knowingly to fail to comply with a condition (s. 12(5));
(c) for a person to incite another to commit an offence under s. 12(5) (s. 12(6)).

In *Jukes v DPP* (2013) 177 JP 212, an appeal by way of case stated, the question for the Divisional Court to answer was the circumstances in which conditions imposed under the POA 1986, s. 12, continue to apply to those who left the route designated by those conditions for the purposes of joining a different demonstration. The Court, upholding their convictions, found that leaving the agreed route was an offence if at that time those leaving were still participating in the public procession to which the conditions applied. In *Powlesland v DPP* (2014) 178 JP 67, the accused was a participant in a Critical Mass Cycle Ride (CMCR) through London. The ride started at a certain location but there was no fixed route, end-time or destination. Before the ride started the senior police officer imposed a condition on the participants that they should not go north of the Thames. The accused went north of the Thames in breach of the condition. He was convicted and appealed by way of case stated. He argued that, as there was no fixed route for the ride, the senior police officer could not have had regard to its 'route or proposed route' (s. 12(1)) when making the condition and thus his exercise of the power under that subsection was unlawful. Ouseley J, giving the judgment of the Divisional Court, was not persuaded by that argument. All s. 12(1) states is that the senior police officer could consider the 'reasonably possible future routes of a procession' before making any direction that the procession should not take a particular route; there was nothing in s. 12(1) to suggest that a condition could only be imposed where the route the procession would take was known in advance.

In the case of the organiser's offence and the offence committed by a person taking part, it is a defence to prove that the failure to comply with a condition arose from circumstances beyond the accused's control.

The maximum penalty for the organiser's offence and the inciter's offence is imprisonment for a term not exceeding three months or a fine not exceeding level 4 or both (s. 12(10)). A person who commits an offence by taking part in a procession is liable to a fine not exceeding level 3.

Contravening Prohibition of Public Procession

B11.113   Under the POA 1986, s. 13, a public procession may be prohibited. Where the procession is to take place outside the City of London or the metropolitan police district, it is the district council, on application from the chief officer of police and with the approval of the Secretary of State, which may make a procession prohibition order (s. 13(1)–(3)). In the City of London or the metropolitan police district, it is the relevant Commissioner, with the approval of the Secretary of State, who may make a procession prohibition order (s. 13(4)).

It is an offence, triable only summarily:

(a) for a person to organise a public procession the holding of which he knows to be prohibited (s. 13(7));
(b) for a person to take part in a public procession the holding of which he knows to be prohibited (s. 13(8));
(c) for a person to incite another to commit an offence under s. 13(8) (s. 13(9)).

The maximum penalty for the organiser's offence and the inciter's offence is imprisonment for a term not exceeding three months or a fine not exceeding level 4 or both (s. 13(13)). A person who commits an offence by taking part in a procession is liable to a fine not exceeding level 3.

Failure to Comply with Conditions Imposed on Public Assembly

B11.114   Under the POA 1986, s. 14, conditions may be imposed on public assemblies. Conditions may be imposed either in advance or at the time of the assembly by the senior police officer acting under s. 14(1)–(3). It is an offence, triable only summarily:

(a) for a person who organises a public assembly knowingly to fail to comply with a condition (s. 14(4)) (*DPP v Baillie* [1995] Crim LR 426);
(b) for a person who takes part in such an assembly knowingly to fail to comply with a condition (s. 14(5)) (*Broadwith v DPP* [2000] All ER (D) 225);
(c) for a person to incite another to commit an offence under s. 14(5) (s. 14(6)).

The term 'public assembly' means an assembly of two or more persons in a public place which is wholly or partly open to the air (s. 16).

In the case of the organiser's offence and the offence committed by a person taking part, it is a defence to prove that the failure to comply with a condition arose from circumstances beyond the defendant's control.

The maximum penalty for the organiser's offence and the inciter's offence is imprisonment for a term not exceeding three months or a fine not exceeding level 4 or both (s. 14(10)). A person who commits an offence by taking part in an assembly is liable to a fine not exceeding level 3.

Contravention of Prohibition of Trespassory Assembly

B11.115   Under the POA 1986, s. 14A, the chief officer of police has the power, if he reasonably believes that it is intended to hold a trespassory assembly which may result in serious disruption to the life of the community or significant damage to the land, building or monument which is of historical, archaeological or scientific importance, to apply to the district council for an order prohibiting for a specified period the holding of all trespassory assemblies in the district or part of it, but the order must not last for more than four days and must not apply to an area greater than that represented by a circle of five miles radius from a specified centre. The council must receive the consent of the Secretary of State for the making of such an order. The Metropolitan Police Commissioner or the Commissioner of the City of London Police may make such an order with the consent of the Secretary of State.

It is an offence, triable only summarily:

(a) for a person to organise an assembly which he knows is prohibited by an order under s. 14A (s. 14B(1));
(b) for a person to take part in an assembly which he knows is prohibited by such an order (s. 14B(2));
(c) for a person to incite another to commit an offence under s. 14B(2) (s. 14B(3)).

An assembly is not trespassory where the user of the highway is reasonable. This is determined by the civil law. Use of the highway is not restricted to the right of passage and matters incidental or ancillary to it. The public has the right to use the public highway for any reasonable and usual mode, including peaceful assembly on the highway, as is consistent with and does not obstruct the general public's primary right of passage. Further the use of the highway must not amount to a public or private nuisance (*DPP v Jones* [1999] 2 AC 240).

B11.116 The maximum penalty for the organiser's offence and the inciter's offence is imprisonment for a term not exceeding three months or a fine not exceeding level 4 on the standard scale or both (s. 14B(5) and (7)). A person who commits an offence by taking part is liable to a fine not exceeding level 3 on the standard scale (s. 14B(6)).

A constable in uniform has power, which may be exercised only within the area to which an order under s. 14A applies, to stop someone he reasonably believes to be on his way to an assembly prohibited by an order under s. 14A and to direct him not to proceed in the direction of the assembly (s. 14C(1) and (2)). A person who fails to comply with such a direction which he knows has been given commits a summary offence punishable with a fine not exceeding level 3 on the standard scale (s. 14C(3) and (5)).

Dispersal of Groups and Removal of Persons under 16 to their Place of Residence

B11.117 Where a relevant officer has reasonable grounds for believing (a) that any members of the public have been intimidated, harassed, alarmed or distressed as a result of the presence or behaviour of groups of two or more persons in public places in any locality in his police area (the 'relevant locality'), and (b) that anti-social behaviour is a significant and persistent problem in the relevant locality, that officer may give an authorisation that the powers conferred on a constable under the ASBA 2003, s. 30(3)–(6), are to be exercisable for a period specified in the authorisation which does not exceed six months (ASBA 2003, s. 30(1) and (2)). Any reference to the presence or behaviour of a group of persons is to be read as including a reference to the presence or behaviour of any one or more of the persons in the group (s. 30(7)).

A constable's powers to give directions are subject to the requirement in s. 30(3) that the constable in uniform must have reasonable grounds for believing that the presence or behaviour of a group of two or more persons in any public place in the relevant locality has resulted, or is likely to result, in any members of the public being intimidated, harassed, alarmed or distressed. If so, the constable may, under s. 30(4), give one or more of the following directions: (a) a direction requiring the persons in the group to disperse (either immediately or by such time as he may specify and in such was as he may specify), (b) a direction requiring any of those persons whose place of residence is not within the relevant locality to leave it or any part of it (either immediately or by such time as he may specify and in such way as he may specify), and (c) a direction prohibiting any of those persons whose place of residence is not within the relevant locality from returning to it or any part of it for such period (not exceeding 24 hours) from the beginning of the direction as he may specify. The direction may be given orally, to any person individually or to two or more persons together, and may be withdrawn or varied by the person who gave it: s. 32(1). Mere presence in a designated dispersal area, whilst capable of being the basis for the forming of a belief under s. 30(3), was not normally sufficient for giving a direction under s. 30(4). Unless there were exceptional circumstances, a reasonable belief under s. 30(4) had normally to depend, in part at least, on some behaviour by the group indicating that harassment, alarm, intimidation or distress had resulted or would result (*Bucknell v DPP* (2007) 171 JP 10). Such a direction may not be given in respect of a group of persons (a) who are engaged in conduct which is lawful under the Trade Union and Labour Relations (Consolidation) Act 1992, s. 220, or (b) who are taking part in a public procession within the meaning of the POA 1986, s. 11(1), in respect of which (i) written notice has been given in accordance with s. 11, or (ii) such notice is not required as provided by the POA 1986, s. 11(1) and (2) (ASBA 2003, s. 30(5)).

B11.118 If, between the hours of 9 p.m. and 6 a.m., a constable in uniform finds a person in any public place in the relevant locality who he has reasonable grounds for believing (a) is under the age of 16, and (b) is not under the effective control of a parent or a responsible person aged 18 or over, he may remove the person to their place of residence unless he has reasonable grounds for believing that the person would, if removed to that place, be likely to suffer significant harm (s. 30(6)). There are supplemental provisions with regard to the issuing of an authorisation by the relevant officer to be found in ss. 31 and 32(4). A person who knowingly contravenes a s. 30(4) direction commits an offence and, on summary conviction, is liable to imprisonment for not more than three months, a fine not exceeding level 4 on the standard scale, or both (s. 32(2)). Where a person is charged with such an offence, the authorisation of the officer to give the direction must be properly proved, both as regards the reason for having the authorisation (s. 30(1)), its form (s. 31(1)), the consent of the local authority (s. 31(2)), and the extent to which it has been publicised (s. 31(3)–(5)), in order to prove that the officer acted lawfully (*Carter v CPS* (2009) 173 JP 590).

B11.119 **Meaning of 'Removal'**   In *R (W) v Metropolitan Police Commissioner* [2006] 3 All ER 458 it was held that the word 'remove' in s. 30(6) naturally and compellingly means 'take away using reasonable force if necessary'. It was also held that s. 30(6) does not have an illegitimate curfew effect. The constable is not free to act arbitrarily, he must act for the purpose for which the power was conferred. There are two purposes: (a) to protect children under 16 within a designated dispersal area at night from the physical and social risks of anti-social behaviour by others; (b) to prevent children from themselves participating in anti-social behaviour within a designated dispersal area at night. There is no power to remove a child simply because he is in the designated dispersal area. Further, the power should be exercised only if it is reasonable to do so and in so deciding constables must have regard to circumstances such as how young the child is, how late at night it is, whether the child is vulnerable or in distress, the child's explanation for his conduct and presence in the area, and the nature of the actual or imminently anticipated anti-social behaviour.

B11.120 **Protests**   In *R (Singh) v Chief Constable of West Midlands Police* [2007] 2 All ER 297 the appellant challenged the use of a s. 30 authorisation which had been created to deal with New Year revelries when used to deal with disturbances outside a theatre which was showing a play to which many Sikhs objected. First, the Court of Appeal held that s. 30 can be applied to protests. Secondly, it held that its usage was not a breach of Article 9, 10 or 11 of the ECHR as, on the critical issue of proportionality, the evidence demonstrated that the police had considered the correct questions; these involved a recognition of the particular importance of the right to protest and the need to determine whether some alternative, less intrusive means could have been used. Thirdly, it held that there was no reason to restrict the use of the authorisation and bar its use in relation to matters that were not anticipated when it was originally made as that would be absurd and unworkable.

B11.121 **Miscellaneous**   Community support officers may also have the dispersal powers (s. 33).

For the meaning of 'anti-social behaviour', 'local authority', 'public place', 'relevant locality' and 'relevant officer', see s. 36.

On a date to be appointed, the ABCPA 2014, sch. 11, para. 41, will repeal the ASBA 2003, part 4 (ss. 30 to 36).

Controls on Activities in Parliament Square Garden and Adjoining Pavements

The PRSRA 2011, ss. 142 to 149, introduced controls on activities in Parliament Square **B11.122** Garden and adjoining pavements. The ABCPA 2014, s. 153, which has effect from 13 May 2014, amends the PRSRA 2011 by adding s. 142A, thereby expanding the controlled area to include the vicinity of the Palace of Westminster as defined in that section. The Court of Appeal has ruled that neither s. 143 nor s. 145 is incompatible with the ECHR, Articles 6, 10 or 11 (*R (Gallastegui) v Westminster City Council* [2013] 2 All ER 579).

See the CPS Legal Guidance on the charging criteria in such cases at www.cps.gov.uk/legal/p_ to_r/public_protests/.

Prohibited Activities   The prohibited activities are: operating any amplified noise equipment **B11.123** in the controlled area; erecting or keeping erected a tent or any other structure that is designed, or adapted (solely or mainly) for the purpose of facilitating sleeping or staying in a place for any period in the controlled area; using any tent or other such structure in the controlled area for the purpose of sleeping or staying in that area; placing or keeping in place in the controlled area any sleeping equipment with a view to its use (whether or not by the person placing it or keeping it in place) for the purpose of sleeping overnight in that area; and using any sleeping equipment in the controlled area of Parliament Square for the purpose of sleeping overnight in that area (PRSRA 2011, s. 143(2)).

Police Powers of Direction   By s. 143(1) of the PRSRA 2011, a constable or authorised officer **B11.124** (as defined in s. 148) who has reasonable grounds for believing that a person is doing, or is about to do, a prohibited activity may direct the person (a) to cease doing that activity, or (b) (as the case may be) not to start doing that activity. By s. 143(8), a person who fails without reasonable excuse to comply with a direction under s. 143(1) commits an offence and is liable on summary conviction to a fine not exceeding level 5 on the standard scale.

Section 144 gives the relevant officer further powers of direction (a direction requiring a person to cease doing a prohibited activity may include a direction that the person does not start doing that activity again after having ceased it). Such a direction continues in force for a specified period of no more than 90 days or for 90 days from the day the direction was given (s. 144(2) and (3)). It may be given orally, may be given to any person individually or to two or more persons together, and may be withdrawn or varied by the person who gave it (s. 142(6)).

Police Powers to Seize Property   Section 145 of the PRSRA 2011 gives the relevant officer **B11.125** power to seize and retain property, namely a prohibited item that is on any land in the controlled area of Parliament Square if it appears to that constable or officer that the item is being, or has been, used in connection with the commission of an offence under s. 143. There is also a power to seize and retain a prohibited item that is on any land outside the controlled area if it appears to the constable that the item has been used in connection with the commission of an offence under s. 143. By s. 143(4), a constable may use reasonable force, if necessary, in exercising a power of seizure.

Forfeiture   The court has wide, additional powers upon conviction. These include (a) the **B11.126** power to make an order providing for the forfeiture of any item of a kind mentioned in the PRSRA 2011, s. 143(2), that was used in the commission of the offence and (b) the power to make such other order as the court considers appropriate for the purpose of preventing the defendant from engaging in any prohibited activity in the controlled area of Parliament Square (s. 146(1), including a requirement not to enter the controlled area of Parliament Square for such period as may be specified in the order (s. 146(2))).

Endeavouring to Break up a Public Meeting

B11.127 It is an offence, contrary to the Public Meeting Act 1908, s. 1(1), for a person at a lawful public meeting to act in a disorderly manner for the purpose of preventing the transaction of the business for which the meeting was called together. The offence is triable summarily only. A person guilty of the offence is liable to imprisonment for a term not exceeding six months or to a fine not exceeding level 5 or to both.

There is no definition of either 'meeting' or 'public meeting' in the Public Meeting Act 1908 though there is in the POA 1936, s. 9. The case law that exists is concerned with whether the public meeting is lawful or not and indicates that a lawful meeting may be held on a highway, even if it might amount to an obstruction of that highway (*Burden v Rigler* [1911] 1 KB 337). Further, a public meeting does not cease to be lawful just because there is disorderly opposition from other persons (*Beatty v Gillbanks* (1882) 9 QBD 308, the authority of which does not, on this point, seem to be doubted by the Divisional Court in *Duncan v Jones* [1936] 1 KB 218). It is an offence, contrary to the Public Meeting Act 1908, s. 1(2), to incite another person to commit an offence under s. 1; the offence is subject to similar punishment.

Failure to Comply with Constable's Request with Regard to Public Meeting

B11.128 It is an offence, contrary to the Public Meeting Act 1908, s. 1(3), for a person to refuse or fail to declare his name and address when asked to do so by a constable who reasonably suspects the person of committing an offence under the Public Meeting Act 1908, s. 1(1) or (2) (see **B11.127**) if the constable has been requested to ask for them by the chairman of the meeting. It is an offence to give a false name and address in such circumstances. A person guilty of the offence is liable to a fine not exceeding level 1.

Illegal Electoral Practice with Regard to Public Meeting

B11.129 It is one of the illegal electoral practices, contrary to the Representation of the People Act 1983, s. 97(1), for a person at a lawful public meeting to act, or incite others to act, in a disorderly manner for the purpose of preventing the transaction of the business for which the meeting was called together. The offence is triable summarily only. It is punishable on summary conviction with a fine not exceeding level 5.

'Lawful public meeting' in this offence means a political meeting held in any constituency between the date of the issue of the writ for the return of a Member of Parliament for the constituency and the date at which a return to the writ is made, or a meeting held with reference to a local government election in the electoral area for that election in the period beginning with the last date on which notice of the election may be published in accordance with the local government election rules and ending with the day of the election (Representation of the People Act 1983, s. 97(2)).

OFFENCES UNDER THE FOOTBALL
(OFFENCES) ACT 1991

B11.130 The Football (Offences) Act 1991 creates three offences: throwing of missiles (s. 2), indecent or racialist chanting (s. 3) and going onto the playing area (s. 4).

Football (Offences) Act 1991, ss. 2, 3, and 4

2. It is an offence for a person at a designated football match to throw anything at or towards—

 (a) the playing area, or any area adjacent to the playing area to which spectators are not generally admitted, or

 (b) any area in which spectators or other persons are or may be present, without lawful authority or lawful excuse (which shall be for him to prove).

3.—(1) It is an offence to engage or take part in chanting of an indecent or racialist nature at a designated football match.

(2) For this purpose—

    (a) 'chanting' means the repeated uttering of any words or sounds (whether alone or in concert with one or more others); and

    (b) 'of racialist nature' means consisting of or including matter which is threatening, abusive or insulting to a person by reason of his colour, race, nationality (including citizenship) or ethnic or national origins.

4. It is an offence for a person at a designated football match to go onto the playing area, or any area adjacent to the playing area to which spectators are not generally admitted, without lawful authority of lawful excuse (which shall be for him to prove).

Sentence and Procedure

The offences are all triable summarily only.   **B11.131**

The maximum penalty is a fine not exceeding level 3 on the standard scale (s. 5(2)).

The *Magistrates' Court Sentencing Guidelines* (see Supplement, **SG-287**) deal with a number of 'football ground offences' (offences under ss. 2, 3 and 4 as well as those dealt with at **B11.133** and **B11.207**) all together. They identify starting points (for a first time offender pleading not guilty) according to the nature of the activity, each starting point having a defined range which is adjusted according to the non-exhaustive list of aggravating and mitigating features. The aggravating and mitigating factors identified are common to all the football offences referred to above.

Throwing missiles (s. 2) and indecent or 'racialist' chanting (s. 3) attract a starting point of a band C fine, the range being band B to a medium level community order. Going on to prohibited areas (s. 4) attracts a starting point of a band B fine, the range being a band A to band C fine.

Aggravating factors relevant to these offences are identified as follows: inciting others to misbehave, offensive language (where not an element of the offence); those indicating greater degree of harm are missiles likely to cause serious injury (e.g., coin, glass, bottle, stone).

In relation to both offences under s. 2 and s. 4, the court must consider imposing a banning order (see **E21.3**). If no banning order is made, the court must give reasons.

Elements

A 'designated football match' is an association football match designated, or of a description   **B11.132** designated, for the purposes of the Act by the Secretary of State. The Football (Offences) (Designation of Football Matches) Order 2004 (SI 2004 No. 2410) designates football matches for this purpose.

References to things done at a designated football match include anything done at the ground:

    (a) within the period beginning two hours before the start of the match or (if earlier) two hours before the time at which it is advertised to start and ending one hour after the end of the match,

    (b) where the match is advertised to start at a particular time on a particular day but does not take place, within the period beginning two hours before and ending one hour after the advertised starting time (s. 1(2)).

When the phrase 'you're just a town of Pakis' was used at a football match, that was a chant of a racist nature. The term 'Paki' was being used in a racially derogatory or insulting sense. It is possible that the context could make it non-racist, so each use would have to be considered on a case-by-case basis (*DPP v Stoke on Trent Magistrates' Court* [2003] 3 All ER 1096).

OFFENCES UNDER THE FOOTBALL
SPECTATORS ACT 1989

B11.133   The Football Spectators Act 1989 was designed to control the admission of spectators at designated football matches and provided for the making of restriction orders on persons convicted of offences of violence or disorder at, or in connection with, such matches. In the light of the Taylor Report on the deaths which occurred at Hillsborough, many of its provisions, particularly those relating to a national football membership scheme, have not been, and are not likely to be, brought into force. However, the majority of the provisions relating to the grant of licences to admit spectators and the whole of part II (which concerns football matches taking place outside England and Wales) are in force.

Under s. 9, it is an offence to admit spectators to watch a designated football match unless it is played at licensed premises. By virtue of s. 10(13), it is a summary offence for any responsible person to contravene any term or condition of a licence granted to admit spectators to any premises for the purpose of watching any designated football match played there. It is a defence, in accordance with s. 10(14), for an accused to prove that the contravention took place without his consent and that he took all reasonable precautions and exercised all due diligence to avoid the commission of such an offence. The relevant licences are those issued by the Football Licensing Authority under the Football Spectators (Seating) Orders that are made annually. The Football Spectators (Prescription) Order 2004 (SI 2004 No. 2409) (as amended by SI 2006 No. 761, SI 2010 No. 584 and SI 2013 No. 1709) designates matches for the purposes of the Act.

As to banning orders and other powers to exclude persons from football matches, see **E21.3**.

TICKET TOUTS

B11.134   *Criminal Justice and Public Order Act 1994, s. 166*

(1) It is an offence for an unauthorised person to—
   (a) sell a ticket for a designated football match, or
   (b) otherwise to dispose of such a ticket to another person.

Sentence and Procedure

B11.135   The offence is triable summarily (CJPO 1994, s. 166(3)).

The maximum sentence is a fine not exceeding level 5 on the standard scale (CJPO 1994, s. 166(3)).

The *Magistrates' Court Sentencing Guidelines* (see Supplement, **SG-287**) deal with a number of 'football ground offences' (offences under s. 166 as well as those dealt with at **B11.130** and **B11.207**) all together. They identify starting points (for a first time offender pleading not guilty). Unauthorised sale or attempted sale of tickets attracts a starting point of a band B fine, the range being a band A to band C fine. Aggravating factors indicating higher culpability (relevant to this offence) are identified as follows: commercial ticket operation, potential high cash value, and counterfeit tickets.

The court must consider imposing a banning order (see **E21.3**). If no banning order is made, the court must give reasons.

Elements

B11.136   A person is 'an unauthorised person' unless he is authorised in writing to sell tickets for the match by the organisers of the match; 'ticket' means anything which purports to be a ticket; and 'selling' a ticket includes offering to sell it, exposing it for sale, making it available for sale by another; advertising that it is available for purchase; and giving it to a person who pays or agrees to pay for some other goods or services or offers to do so (CJPO 1994, s. 166(2)).

For the meaning of 'designated football match', see the Ticket Touting (Designation of Football Matches) Order 2007 (SI 2007 No. 790).

Search of Person and Premises

The PACE 1984, s. 32, has effect in relation to an offence under the CJPO 1994, s. 166, as if the **B11.137** power conferred on a constable to enter and search any vehicle extended to any vehicle which the constable has reasonable grounds for believing was being used for any purpose connected with the offence (s. 166(5)).

INTIMIDATION OR ANNOYANCE BY VIOLENCE OR OTHERWISE

Trade Union and Labour Relations (Consolidation) Act 1992, s. 241   **B11.138**

(1) A person commits an offence who, with a view to compelling another person to abstain from doing or to do any act which that person has a legal right to do or abstain from doing, wrongfully and without legal authority—

    (a) uses violence to or intimidates that person or his wife or children, or injures his property,

    (b) persistently follows that person about from place to place,

    (c) hides any tools, clothes or other property owned or used by that person, or deprives him of or hinders him in the use thereof,

    (d) watches or besets the house or other place where that person resides, works, carries on business or happens to be, or the approach to any such house or place, or

    (e) follows that person with two or more other persons in a disorderly manner in or through any street or road.

(2) A person guilty of an offence under this section is liable on summary conviction to imprisonment for a term not exceeding six months or a fine not exceeding level 5 on the standard scale, or both.

Sentence and Procedure

An offence under the Trade Union and Labour Relations (Consolidation) Act 1992, s. 241, is **B11.139** triable summarily only.

The maximum penalty is six months and/or a fine not exceeding level 5 (Trade Union and Labour Relations (Consolidation) Act 1992, s. 241(2)).

Elements

It was made clear by the Divisional Court in *Todd v DPP* [1996] Crim LR 344 that the offence **B11.140** is not limited to trade disputes. It can, therefore, apply to someone engaged in an anti-roads protest (as in *Todd*) and might apply, for example, to stalking (see also Professor Sir John Smith at [1996] Crim LR 345). The general elements of the offence are, first, the *mens rea*, which is dealt with below and, secondly, the requirements that the act be done 'wrongfully' and 'without lawful authority'. No special consideration has been given to the phrase 'without lawful authority' apart from the creation of a defence for trade unions acting in contemplation or furtherance of a dispute, which is treated as a defence, below.

Meaning of 'Wrongfully'   Scott J in *Thomas v National Union of Mineworkers (South Wales* **B11.141** *Area)* [1986] Ch 20 decided that the authorities established that conduct must, in order to be an offence under what was, prior to consolidation, the Conspiracy, and Protection of Property Act 1875, s. 7, be tortious (at p. 61). This approach to the question of whether there is a wrongful act does indeed seem to be consistent with the existing case law. The Court of Appeal in *Ward, Lock & Co. Ltd v Operative Printers' Assistants' Society* (1906) 22 TLR 327 clearly took the view that s. 7 (now the Trade Union and Labour Relations (Consolidation) Act 1992, s. 241) was concerned only to provide a criminal remedy to what was already recognised as being a civil wrong. Thus in order for the criminal remedy to be available, it had to be established that what was done was a civil wrong, without reference to the provisions of the Act.

B11.142   **Intimidates**   The Court of Appeal in *Jones* (1974) 59 Cr App R 120, whilst not wishing to define 'intimidation' exhaustively, said that:

> ...'intimidate' in this section includes putting persons in fear by the exhibition of force or violence or the threat of force or violence, and there is no limitation restricting the meaning to cases of violence or threats of violence to the person.

In *Connor v Kent* [1891] 2 QB 545, the court also did not want to attempt an exhaustive definition of the word, preferring instead to make clear (at p. 559) that 'intimidate' is 'a word of common speech and everyday use; and it must receive, therefore, a reasonable and sensible interpretation according to the circumstances of the cases as they arise from time to time'. Further assistance may be gleaned from the decision of Stuart-Smith J in *News Group Newspapers Ltd v SOGAT 82 (No. 2)* [1987] ICR 181, at pp. 204–5, considering the related tort of intimidation.

B11.143   **Persistently Follows**   In *Smith v Thomasson* (1890) 62 LT 68, Hawkins J stated that: 'It is impossible to define generally what is "persistently following"'. However, it was held dogging of a workman's footsteps could amount to 'persistently following' him. See also *Elsey v Smith* 1982 SCCR 218.

B11.144   **Deprivation of Property**   The Court of Appeal in *Fowler v Kibble* [1922] 1 Ch 487 made clear the significance of the requirement that the activity must be wrongful separately from a consideration of the section creating the offence. Thus there could be no offence where a workman did not let miners who were not members of a particular union have safety lamps because such an act of deprivation was not unlawful.

B11.145   **Watches or Besets**   In general, it would seem that the words 'watch' and 'beset' are viewed as words of the ordinary English language, see, e.g., *J. Lyons & Sons v Wilkins* [1899] 1 Ch 811 and *Ward, Lock & Co. Ltd v Operative Printers' Assistants' Society* (1906) 22 TLR 327. The High Court of Justiciary in *Gatt v Philp* 1983 JC 51 took the view that the essence of the offence comprised preventing access to and egress from somewhere. Thus a sit-in satisfied this element of the offence.

The watching and besetting must be 'wrongful', that is, unlawful without reference to s. 241. Thus, for example, in *J. Lyons & Sons v Wilkins* [1899] 1 Ch 811, careful consideration was given to the question of whether the activity amounted to a nuisance and was therefore 'wrongful' and within the ambit of the section. The length of time the people were present was relevant, since that would help determine whether there was a nuisance. Consequently, lawful picketing is not 'watching and besetting' unless it amounts to a nuisance, or some other tort or other wrong such as obstruction of the highway (see, e.g., *News Group Newspapers Ltd v SOGAT 82 (No. 2)* [1987] ICR 181 and *Walters v Green* [1899] 2 Ch 696; see also *Bonsall* [1985] Crim LR 150).

In *Charnock v Court* [1899] 2 Ch 35 and *Farmer v Wilson* (1900) 69 LJ QB 496, it was made clear that the offence is committed when any place where the person happens to be is watched and beset, whether or not such persons are in the service or employment of any person. This latter point in *Farmer v Wilson* makes clear that the offence is not solely concerned with employment disputes.

B11.146   **Following in a Disorderly Manner**   Whether the following is in a disorderly manner is a question of fact in each case, and therefore will depend upon the conduct of the defendant and all the circumstances of the particular case, see *McKenzie* [1892] 2 QB 519 and *Elsey v Smith* 1982 SCCR 218.

Mens Rea: With a View to Compel Any Other Person

B11.147   This is a *mens rea* requirement importing not motive but purpose according to the Divisional Court in *DPP v Fidler* [1992] 1 WLR 91, explaining *J. Lyons & Sons v Wilkins* [1899] 1 Ch 255. The Divisional Court stated that purpose is a more objective concept not concerned with the different motives with which members of the group might have joined, for example, a demonstration. The court also decided that the accused's purpose must be one to compel and not merely to persuade (see also *Bonsall* [1985] Crim LR 150 and *McKenzie* [1892] 2 QB 519). It is not necessary to show that the compulsion was in any way effective (*Agnew v Munro* (1891) 18 R (J) 22). The phrase 'such other person' refers back to the person whom the defendant has a view to compel to abstain from doing or to do something (*J. Lyons & Sons v Wilkins* [1899] 1 Ch 811).

Application to Trade or Employment Disputes

B11.148

Trade Union and Labour Relations (Consolidation) Act 1992, s. 220

(1) It shall be lawful for a person in contemplation or furtherance of a trade dispute to attend—
 (a) at or near his own place of work, or
 (b) if he is an official of a trade union, at or near the place of work of a member of that union whom he is accompanying and whom he represents,
 for the purpose only of peacefully obtaining or communicating information, or peacefully persuading any person to work or abstain from working.
(2) If a person works or normally works—
 (a) otherwise than at any one place, or
 (b) at a place the location of which is such that attendance there for a purpose mentioned in subsection (1) above is impracticable,
 his place of work for the purposes of that subsection shall be any premises of his employer from which he works or from which his work is administered.
(3) In the case of a worker who is not in employment where—
 (a) his last employment was terminated in connection with a trade dispute, or
 (b) the termination of his employment was one of the circumstances giving rise to a trade dispute,
 in relation to that dispute his former place of work shall be treated for the purposes of subsection (1) as being his place of work.
(4) A person who is an official of a trade union by virtue only of having been elected or appointed to be a representative of some of the members of the union shall be regarded for the purposes of subsection (1) above as representing only those members; but otherwise an official of a trade union shall be regarded for those purposes as representing all its members.

RACIALLY OR RELIGIOUSLY AGGRAVATED OFFENCES

The CDA 1998 introduced a series of racially aggravated offences, i.e. existing offences which are racially aggravated according to the definition in s. 28. These provisions were extended by the Anti-terrorism, Crime and Security Act 2001, s. 39, so as to include religiously aggravated offences.

B11.149

Crime and Disorder Act 1998, s. 28

(1) An offence is racially or religiously aggravated for the purposes of sections 29 to 32 below if—
 (a) at the time of committing the offence, or immediately before or after doing so, the offender demonstrates towards the victim of the offence hostility based on the victim's membership (or presumed membership) of a racial or religious group; or
 (b) the offence is motivated (wholly or partly) by hostility towards members of a racial or religious group based on their membership of that group.
(2) In subsection (1)(a) above—
 'membership', in relation to a racial or religious group, includes association with members of that group;
 'presumed' means presumed by the offender.
(3) It is immaterial for the purposes of paragraph (a) or (b) of subsection (1) above whether or not the offender's hostility is also based, to any extent, on any other factor not mentioned in that paragraph.
(4) In this section 'racial group' means a group of persons defined by reference to race, colour, nationality (including citizenship) or ethnic or national origins.
(5) In this section 'religious group' means a group of persons defined by reference to religious belief or lack of religious belief.

The offences which may be racially or religiously aggravated are an offence contrary to the OAPA 1861, ss. 20 and 47 and common assault (CDA 1998, s. 29: see **B2.1**, **B2.27** and **B2.48**), criminal damage (CDA 1998, s. 30: see **B8.1**), offences contrary to the POA 1986, ss. 4, 4A and 5 (CDA 1998, s. 31: see **B11.47**, **B11.60** and **B11.69**) and harassment and stalking etc.

contrary to the Protection from Harassment Act 1997, ss. 2, 2A, 4 and 4A (CDA 1998, s. 32: see **B2.165** to **B2.194**). In each case, the court must first establish that the basic offence has been committed and then consider whether it was racially or religiously aggravated within the meaning of s. 28 (but see also **B11.48**). The racially or religiously aggravated form of each offence carries a higher maximum penalty than the ordinary form of the offence and this is reflected by significantly higher sentences in practice (see *Kelly* [2001] 1 Cr App R (S) 341; *Bridger* [2006] EWCA Crim 3169; *A-G's Ref (No. 52 of 2013)* [2013] EWCA Crim 1733 and **E1.16**). See also **B11.51**.

If the offence is not one of those to which s. 28 applies, it is for the sentencer to decide whether it was racially aggravated and, if it was, to treat this as an aggravating factor in sentencing (CJA 2003, s. 145). See generally *Rogers* [2007] 2 AC 62.

B11.150   **Racial or Religious Groups**   By the CDA 1998, s. 28(4), a 'racial group' means a group of persons defined by reference to race, colour, nationality (including citizenship) or ethnic or national origins. This definition is derived from that used in the Race Relations Act 1976 and is also used in the POA 1986, s. 17 (see **B11.162**). In *Mandla v Dowell Lee* [1983] 2 AC 548, it was necessary to determine whether the Sikhs are a 'racial group' for the purposes of the 1976 Act. The House of Lords was satisfied that it was necessary to determine whether Sikhs are a group defined by ethnic origins, since none of the other descriptions would distinguish them from at least some other groups of people. In holding that Sikhs are an ethnic group, Lord Fraser of Tullybelton said (at pp. 562D–563A):

> For a group to constitute an ethnic group in the sense of the Act of 1976, it must, in my opinion, regard itself, and be regarded by others, as a distinct community by virtue of certain characteristics. Some of these characteristics are essential; others are not essential but one or more of them will commonly be found and will help to distinguish the group from the surrounding community. The conditions which appear to me to be essential are these: (1) a long shared history, of which the group is conscious as distinguishing it from other groups, and the memory of which it keeps alive; (2) a cultural tradition of its own, including family and social customs and manners, often but not necessarily associated with religious observance. In addition to those two essential characteristics the following characteristics are, in my opinion, relevant; (3) either a common geographical origin, or descent from a small number of common ancestors; (4) a common language, not necessarily peculiar to the group; (5) a common literature peculiar to the group; (6) a common religion different from that of neighbouring groups or from the general community surrounding it; (7) being a minority or being an oppressed or a dominant group within a larger community, for example a conquered people (say the inhabitants shortly after the Norman conquest) and their conquerors might both be ethnic groups.

> A group defined by reference to enough of these characteristics would be capable of including converts, for example, people who marry into the group, and of excluding apostates. Provided a person who joins the group feels himself or herself to be a member of it, and is accepted by other members, then he is, for the purposes of the Act, a member. … In my opinion, it is possible for a person to fall into a particular racial group either by birth or by adherence, and it makes no difference, so far as the Act of 1976 is concerned, by which route he finds his way into the group.

Lord Templeman, taking a similar approach to that of Lord Fraser, said (at p. 569E):

> In my opinion, for the purposes of the Race Relations Act a group of persons defined by reference to ethnic origins must possess some of the characteristics of a race, namely group descent, a group of geographical origin and a group history.

Lord Fraser also approved the decision of the New Zealand Court of Appeal in *King-Ansell v Police* [1979] 2 NZLR 531 that Jews form a group with common ethnic origins within the New Zealand Race Relations Act 1971. In the course of his judgment, Richardson J said (at p. 543):

> …a group is identifiable in terms of its ethnic origins if it is a segment of the population distinguished from others by a sufficient combination of shared customs, beliefs, traditions and characteristics derived from a common or presumed common past, even if not drawn from what in biological terms is a common racial stock. It is that combination which gives them an historically

determined social identity in their own eyes and in the eyes of those outside the group. They have a distinct social identity based not simply on group cohesion and solidarity but also on their belief as to their historical antecedents.

Romany gypsies are recognised as a racial group on the basis of their ethnic origin (*Commission* **B11.151**
for Racial Equality v Dutton [1989] QB 783). In more recent times and certainly since the first instance discrimination case of *O'Leary v Punch Retail* (HHJ Goldstein, Westminster County Court, 29 August 2000), Irish Travellers have also been considered an ethnic racial group. Following the test in *Mandla v Dowell Lee*, the Court of Appeal held that Rastafarians are not members of an ethnic group separate from the rest of the Afro-Caribbean community but nevertheless share beliefs that identify them as members of a religious group (*Crown Suppliers (Property Services Agency) v Dawkins* [1993] 1 CR 517).

In *White* [2001] 1 WLR 1352, the Court of Appeal, following *Mandla* and *Ealing London Borough Council v Race Relations Board* [1972] AC 342, noted that the statutory language is to be given a broad, non-technical meaning and that words are to be construed as generally used in England and Wales. In its judgment, 'the word "African" does describe a "racial group" defined by reference to race. In ordinary speech, the word "African" denotes a limited group of people regarded as of common stock and regarded as one of the major divisions of humankind having in common distinct physical features. It denotes a personal characteristic of the blacks of Africa.' On the other hand, the Court of Appeal took the view that the expression 'South American', in England and Wales, probably does not have a racial connotation.

Thus, a broad and non-technical approach has been adopted in the context of s. 28. In *Rogers* [2007] 2 AC 62, the House of Lords was asked, 'Do those who are not of British origin constitute a racial group within s. 28(4)?' The unanimous answer was 'yes'. 'Foreigners' likewise constitute such a group; and of course it follows that those who are of British origin must enjoy the same legal protection as those who are not: each forms for these purposes a 'racial group', even though many more racial groups exist within them. See also *White (Anthony Delroy)* [2001] 1 WLR 1352, *DPP v M* [2004] 1 WLR 2758, *A-G's Ref (No. 4 of 2004)* [2005] 1 WLR 2810 and *Kendall v DPP* [2008] EWHC 1848 (Admin).

Although in other contexts 'religion' has been interpreted as involving a belief in some kind **B11.152**
of god or supernatural being (*Registrar General, ex parte Segerdal* [1970] 2 QB 697), a much broader approach is clearly required in the context of s. 28. It is clear from s. 28(5) that a 'religious group' may for these purposes include a group defined by its lack of religious beliefs. If, for example, D assaults V because V is an atheist or humanist who rejects religious beliefs, D must be guilty of a religiously aggravated offence.

Proof of Hostility   A racially or religiously aggravated offence, may, but need not have been, **B11.153**
committed for racial or religious motives. It suffices if the accused formed the view that the victim was a member of a racial or religious group and then said or did something that demonstrated hostility towards him based on membership of that group. This will usually involve racist words or gestures, but may in some cases be manifested in other ways (*Rogers* [2007] 2 AC 62 per Baroness Hale at [13]). Whether, in general, words actually demonstrated racial hostility was a question of fact for the relevant tribunal (*Johnson v DPP* [2008] EWHC 509 (Admin); *DPP v Howard* [2008] EWHC 608 (Admin)).

To be guilty of an offence that is racially or religiously aggravated, it is not necessary that the accused be of a different racial, national or ethnic (or religious) group from the victim (*White* [2001] 1 WLR 1352). Section 28(2) specifically addresses the possibility that D's attack on V may be aggravated as a result of D's hostility to V's actual or supposed association with other groups. D may also be mistaken as to V's own race or religion.

In *DPP v Pal* [2000] Crim LR 756, Simon Brown LJ stated that, for the purposes of s. 28(1) **B11.154**
(a), it will always be necessary for the prosecution to prove the demonstration of racial hostility, although the use of racially abusive insults will ordinarily be found sufficient. Following this,

the Divisional Court in *DPP v McFarlane* [2002] EWHC 485 (Admin) decided that, where the expressions 'jungle bunny', 'black bastard' and 'wog' were used, the offence was properly made out as the words were used immediately before and at the time of the commission of the offence contrary to the POA 1986, s. 4 (see **B11.47** *et seq.*), those words were of a racial nature, and they were racial, threatening and abusive towards the victim. The decision in *Pal*, where the words 'white man's arse licker' and 'brown Englishman' were used, was to be limited to its own particular facts, notably that both parties were Asian. Even so, *DPP v Pal* appears hard to reconcile with s. 28(2), as Baroness Hale noted in *Rogers* at [15].

The fact that the accused may have had some additional reason for his choice of words is immaterial (*McFarlane; DPP v Woods* [2002] EWHC 85 (Admin); *DPP v Green* (2004) *The Times*, 7 July 2004; *DPP v M*). Also irrelevant is the victim's perception of the incident and the fact that the accused's frame of mind was such that he would have abused any person standing where the complainant was by reference to an obvious physical characteristic, such as obesity or baldness (*Woods*). The accused need not act for any racial or religious motive (*DPP v Green*). It would nevertheless be wrong for charges of aggravated offences to be brought where vulgar abuse has included racial epithets that did not, when all the relevant circumstances are considered, indicate hostility to the victim on account of his race or religion (*Rogers* per Baroness Hale at [17]).

B11.155   In *G and T v DPP* (2004) 168 JP 313, the Divisional Court considered the two routes to establishing racial aggravation of an offence. Section 28(1)(a) requires the prosecution to prove facts that indicate that the defendant had demonstrated racial hostility at the time of the committing the offence or immediately before or after doing so. This is not to prove the accused's state of mind, but what he did or said so as to demonstrate racial hostility towards the victim. The demonstration will often be by way of words, shouting, holding up a banner, etc. or by adherence to a group that is demonstrating racial hostility. Section 28(1)(b) is concerned with the accused's motivation, which does concern his state of mind. Often the evidence establishing this will involve the kind of demonstration referred to in relation to s. 28(1)(a). The prosecution may base its case on both of s. 28(1)(a) and (b) and cases may arise where it is legitimate to require the prosecution to make clear the basis upon which it is proceeding. In *Taylor v DPP* (2006) 170 JP 485, it was decided that use of phrases such as 'fucking nigger' and 'fucking coon bitch', patently not used in a jesting manner, must, in the circumstance of the case, have led any judge to find that the offence (in this case, the POA 1986, s. 5(1)(a)) was motivated, at least in part, by racial hostility as described in s. 28(1)(b). It is also clear that it is better that this matter be dealt with more explicitly, in particular that the two possible approaches in s. 28 be clearly identified and separated for the benefit of the jury. In relation to s. 28(1)(b), see also *DPP v Howard* [2008] EWHC 608 (Admin) and *DPP v Dykes* [2008] EWHC 2775 (Admin); in the latter the Administrative Court said the prosecutor ought to make it absolutely clear that s. 28(1)(b) is very much in play as part of the allegation made of racial aggravation in a summary trial so that the magistrates have in mind that it is not simply the abuse directed at the victim which is being alleged, but also a motivation based on racial hostility. In *R (Jones) v Bedfordshire and Mid-Bedfordshire Magistrates' Court* [2010] EWHC 523 (Admin), the Administrative Court made plain that *Howard* was a case exclusively concerned with s. 28(1)(b) and subjective motivation of racial hostility did not have to be proved for each limb. Applying *G and T v DPP*, Ouseley J stated at [18] that:

> Even though the facts of a particular case may satisfy both limbs simultaneously, limb (a) involves no examination of subjective intent or motivation behind the demonstration of racial hostility for the victim. It merely requires the demonstration of racial hostility. It contains an objective test of whether the defendant demonstrated racial hostility to the victim. That makes particular sense where a victim is present towards whom such racial hostility is demonstrated. The offence is concerned with the objective view of whether racial hostility had been demonstrated, in part because of its effect upon the victim, rather than being concerned with a subjective motivation of the defendant. By contrast, limb (b) is examining the defendant's subjective motivation whether an individual victim is present or not. The former deals with what is demonstrated by the behaviour, the latter with the motivation behind it.

The case of *H (S)* [2011] 1 Cr App R 182 demonstrates the continued misunderstanding by the lower courts of the difference between the CDA 1998, s. 28(1)(a) and s. 28(1)(b). The trial judge insisted on effectively ending the case at the close of the prosecution case. The prosecution appealed. As the Court of Appeal pointed out it is difficult to see how it could be suggested that repeated angry references to a Nigerian as a 'black monkey' or 'monkey' did not generate a prima facie case of an outward manifestation of racial hostility (s. 28(1)(a)). The Court found that the judge was quite wrong to conclude that, because the jury could not exclude vulgar abuse as a factor, there was no case to answer.

B11.156

Timing of Demonstration of Hostility   The word 'immediately' in s. 28(1) qualifies both 'before' and 'after', and this means that the subsection deals with words uttered or acts done in the immediate context of the substantive offence, so it was not possible that the section was satisfied where the accused had quit the scene and used the relevant words when sitting in his own house (which was the next door house) some 20 minutes after the criminal damage had been caused (*Parry v DPP* [2004] EWHC 3112 (Admin)). See also *Babbs* [2007] EWCA Crim 2737.

B11.157

USING WORDS OR BEHAVIOUR OR DISPLAYING WRITTEN MATERIAL STIRRING UP RACIAL HATRED

Public Order Act 1986, s. 18

B11.158

(1) A person who uses threatening, abusive or insulting words or behaviour, or displays any written material which is threatening, abusive or insulting, is guilty of an offence if—
   (a) he intends thereby to stir up racial hatred, or
   (b) having regard to all the circumstances racial hatred is likely to be stirred up thereby.

Procedure

An offence under the POA 1986, s. 18, is triable either way. When tried on indictment it is normally a class 3 offence, but see CPD XIII, para. B (see Supplement, **PD-97**) for the additional factors that the court considers on allocation. No proceeding may be instituted except by, or with the consent of, the A-G (POA 1986, s. 27(3)).

B11.159

For the liability of corporate officers, see **B11.165**.

Indictment

B11.160

Statement of Offence

Displaying threatening, abusive or insulting material with intent to stir up racial hatred contrary to section 18 of the Public Order Act 1986.

Particulars of Offence

A on or about the...day of...at...displayed certain threatening, abusive or insulting materials, namely a quantity of pamphlets entitled...with intent thereby to stir up racial hatred.

The POA 1986, s. 27(2), declares that for the purposes of the rules against charging more than one offence in the same count, each of ss. 18 to 23 of the Act creates one offence.

Sentencing Guidelines

The maximum penalty is seven years' imprisonment, a fine, or both, on indictment (POA 1986, s. 27(3)); six months, a fine not exceeding the statutory maximum, or both, summarily.

B11.161

Relevant sentencing decisions are *Relf* (1979) 1 Cr App R (S) 111 and *Edwards* (1983) 5 Cr App R (S) 145. See, however, *Gray* [1999] 1 Cr App R (S) 50 at **B11.177** as to the relevance of older cases. A more recent example is *Saleem* [2008] 2 Cr App R (S) 70, in which the defendants had participated in a demonstration in central London in response to the publication of Danish cartoons depicting the Prophet Mohammed. It was accepted by the Court of Appeal that the offences involved a one-off demonstration (albeit attracting some 300 young men), mounted at short notice without sophisticated planning. The sentences of four years and three years imposed on Saleem and Javed for stirring up racial hatred contrary to the POA 1986, s. 18, (after a trial) were reduced to 30 months and two years respectively. In relation to the offence relating to the display of written material, the court has the following forfeiture power.

Public Order Act 1986, s. 25

(1) A court by or before which a person is convicted of—
  (a) an offence under section 18 relating to the display of written material, or
  (b) an offence under section 19, 21 or 23,
  shall order to be forfeited any written material...produced to the court and shown to its satisfaction to be written material...to which the offence relates.
(2) An order made under this section shall not take effect—
  (a) in the case of an order made in proceedings in England and Wales, until the expiry of the ordinary time within which an appeal may be instituted or, where an appeal is duly instituted, until it is finally decided or abandoned...
(3) For the purposes of subsection (2)(a)—
  (a) an application for a case stated or for leave to appeal shall be treated as the institution of an appeal, and
  (b) where a decision on appeal is subject to a further appeal, the appeal is not finally determined until the expiry of the ordinary time within which a further appeal may be instituted or, where a further appeal is duly instituted, until the further appeal is finally decided or abandoned.

Elements

B11.162 The essence of the offence under the POA 1986, s. 18, lies in the use of words or behaviour or the display of material either when the accused intends to stir up racial hatred (s. 18(1)(a)) or where racial hatred is, in the circumstances, likely to be stirred up (s. 18(1)(b)). The concept of 'racial hatred' is therefore central to the offence.

Public Order Act 1986, s. 17

In this Part [i.e. ss. 17 to 29] 'racial hatred' means hatred against a group of persons defined by reference to colour, race, nationality (including citizenship) or ethnic or national origins.

For the meaning of 'racial group', see **B11.150**.

For discussion of the phrase 'threatening, abusive or insulting', see **B11.55**.

In the POA 1986, ss. 17 to 29, 'written material' includes any sign or other visible representation (s. 29). This includes articles in electronic form, such as material disseminated via a web site (*Sheppard* [2010] 2 All ER 850). For the meaning of 'writing', see **B11.56**.

For the offence under the POA 1986, s. 18(1)(a), an intention to stir up racial hatred is required. The *mens rea* of the offence under s. 18(1)(b) is established by reference to s. 18(5):

A person who is not shown to have intended to stir up racial hatred is not guilty of an offence under this section if he did not intend his words or behaviour, or the written material, to be, and was not aware that it might be, threatening, abusive or insulting.

Place of Commission

B11.163 ### Public Order Act 1986, s. 18

(2) An offence under this section may be committed in a public or a private place, except that no offence is committed where the words or behaviour are used, or the written material is displayed, by a person inside a dwelling and are not heard or seen except by other persons in that or another dwelling.
...
(4) In proceedings for an offence under this section it is a defence for the accused to prove that he was inside a dwelling and had no reason to believe that the words or behaviour used, or the written material displayed, would be heard or seen by a person outside that or any other dwelling.

Section 29 provides that, in ss. 17 to 29:

> 'dwelling' means any structure or part of a structure occupied as a person's home or other living accommodation (whether the occupation is separate or shared with others) but does not include any part not so occupied; and for this purpose 'structure' includes a tent, caravan, vehicle, vessel or other temporary or movable structure.

Offence Does Not Apply to Broadcasts or Cable Programme Services

The POA 1986, s. 18, does not (by s. 18(6)) apply to words or behaviour used, or written mate- **B11.164**
rial displayed, solely for the purpose of being included in a programme service. Such activity is
controlled by s. 22 of the Act, see **B11.176**.

Liability of Corporate Officers

Public Order Act 1986, s. 28   **B11.165**

(1) Where a body corporate is guilty of an offence under this Part and it is shown that the offence was committed with the consent or connivance of a director, manager, secretary or other similar officer of the body, or a person purporting to act in any such capacity, he as well as the body corporate is guilty of the offence and liable to be proceeded against and punished accordingly.
(2) Where the affairs of a body corporate are managed by its members, subsection (1) applies in relation to the acts and defaults of a member in connection with his functions of management as it applies to a director.

As to corporate liability generally, and the liability of corporate officers, see **A6.23**.

Defence for Reports of Parliamentary and Judicial Proceedings

Public Order Act 1986, s. 26   **B11.166**

(1) Nothing in this Part applies to a fair and accurate report of proceedings in Parliament.
(2) Nothing in this Part applies to a fair and accurate report of proceedings publicly heard before a court or tribunal exercising judicial authority where the report is published contemporaneously with the proceedings or, if it is not reasonably practicable or would be unlawful to publish a report of them contemporaneously, as soon as publication is reasonably practicable and lawful.

This and the general defences (see **A3**) are the only defences available to an accused. The truth of material, or belief in its truth, is not a defence (*Birdwood* (11 April 1995 unreported)).

PUBLISHING OR DISTRIBUTING WRITTEN MATERIAL STIRRING UP RACIAL HATRED

Public Order Act 1986, s. 19   **B11.167**

(1) A person who publishes or distributes written material which is threatening, abusive or insulting is guilty of an offence if—
    (a) he intends thereby to stir up racial hatred, or
    (b) having regard to all the circumstances racial hatred is likely to be stirred up thereby.

Procedure

An offence under the POA 1986, s. 19, is triable either way (POA 1986, s. 27(3)). When tried **B11.168**
on indictment it is normally a class 3 offence, but see CPD XIII, para. B (see Supplement, **PD-97**) for the additional factors that the court considers on allocation. No proceeding may be instituted except by, or with the consent of, the A-G (POA 1986, s. 27(3)). Where an offender had produced racially inflammatory material and posted it on a web site hosted by a remote server in the USA, he could still be tried in England and Wales as the appropriate jurisdictional test was the 'substantial measure' test laid down in *Smith (Wallace Duncan) (No. 4)* [2004] QB 1418 (*Sheppard* [2010] 2 All ER 850: see further **A8.5**). The POA 1986, s. 27(2), declares that for the purposes of the rules against charging more than one offence in the same count or information, each of ss. 18 to 23 of the Act creates one offence.

For the liability of corporate officers, see **B11.165**.

Sentence

B11.169   The maximum penalty for an offence under the POA 1986, s. 19, is, by s. 27(3) of the Act, two years' imprisonment or a fine or both, on indictment; six months, a fine not exceeding the statutory maximum or both, summarily. The court also has a power under s. 25 to order forfeiture of written material to which the offence relates where the offender has been convicted of displaying written material (see **B11.161**).

Meaning of Terms Used in Defining the Offence

B11.170   For the meaning of 'racial hatred' see **B11.162**. For the meaning of 'threatening, abusive or insulting', see **B11.55**. The POA 1986, s. 29, states that 'written material includes any sign or other visible representation' (see **B11.162**). In *Sheppard* [2010] 2 All ER 850, the Court of Appeal held that the word 'includes' was plainly intended to widen the scope of the expression and the words were sufficiently wide to include articles in electronic form, such as material disseminated by a web site. 'Publication' does not require proof that anybody had actually read or heard the material (*Sheppard*).

References in the POA 1986, ss. 17 to 29, to the publication or distribution of written material are, by s. 19(3) of the Act, to the publication or distribution of that material to the public or a section of the public.

Defences

B11.171   In proceedings for an offence under the POA 1986, s. 19, it is, by virtue of s. 19(2), a defence for an accused who is not shown to have intended to stir up racial hatred to prove that he was not aware of the content of the material and did not suspect, and had no reason to suspect, that it was threatening, abusive or insulting. The burden of proof of this defence lies on the accused on the balance of probabilities (see generally **F3.5** and **F3.53**). For a summary of the case law relating to 'reverse burden' challenges under the HRA 1998, see **F3.18** *et seq.* The defence in the POA 1986, s. 26 (savings for reports of parliamentary and judicial proceedings: see **B11.166**), applies to s. 19.

These and the general defences (see **A3**) are the only offences available to an accused. The truth of the material, or a belief in its truth, is not a defence (*Birdwood* (11 April 1995 unreported)).

PUBLIC PERFORMANCE, BROADCASTING AND POSSESSION OF MATERIALS STIRRING UP RACIAL HATRED

General Provisions

B11.172   Sections 20 to 23 of the POA 1986 deal with the public performance, broadcasting and possession of materials intended to, or likely to, stir up racial hatred. The offences are triable either way, and the following general provisions of part III of the Act apply:

(a)   Prosecution may only be by, or with the consent of, the A-G (s. 27(1)).
(b)   Each section creates one offence (s. 27(2)).
(c)   The maximum penalty is two years and/or a fine, on indictment; six months and/or a fine not exceeding the statutory maximum, summarily (s. 27(3)).
(d)   There is a saving for fair and accurate reports of parliamentary or judicial proceedings (see **B11.166**).
(e)   For the liability of corporate officers, see **B11.165**.

For the meaning of 'racial hatred' see **B11.162**. For the meaning of 'threatening, abusive or insulting', see **B11.55**. For the meaning of 'written material', see **B11.162**.

References in the POA 1986, ss. 17 to 29, to the publication or distribution of written material are, by s. 19(3) of the Act, to the publication or distribution of that material to the public or a section of the public. References to the distribution, showing or playing of a recording are, by s. 21(2), to the distribution, showing or playing of the recording to the public or a section of the public. 'Recording' means any record from which visual images or sounds may, by any means, be reproduced (s. 21(2)).

As to the limited defences available and that the truth of material, or a belief in its truth, is not a defence, see *Birdwood* (11 April 1995 unreported).

Public Performance of Play Stirring up Racial Hatred

Public Order Act 1986, s. 20 **B11.173**

(1) If a public performance of a play is given which involves the use of threatening, abusive or insulting words or behaviour, any person who presents or directs the performance is guilty of an offence if—
    (a) he intends thereby to stir up racial hatred, or
    (b) having regard to all the circumstances (and, in particular, taking the performance as a whole) racial hatred is likely to be stirred up thereby.

Section 20(5) of the POA 1986 provides that the words 'play' and 'public performance' in s. 20 have the same meaning as in the Theatres Act 1968, s. 18(1)

The meaning of 'public place' in the POA 1936 is considered at **B11.12.** **B11.174**

Public Order Act 1986, s. 20

(2) If a person presenting or directing the performance is not shown to have intended to stir up racial hatred, it is a defence for him to prove—
    (a) that he did not know and had no reason to suspect that the performance would involve the use of the offending words or behaviour, or
    (b) that he did not know and had no reason to suspect that the offending words or behaviour were threatening, abusive or insulting, or
    (c) that he did not know and had no reason to suspect that the circumstances in which the performance would be given would be such that racial hatred would be likely to be stirred up.
(3) This section does not apply to a performance given solely or primarily for one or more of the following purposes—
    (a) rehearsal,
    (b) making a recording of the performance, or
    (c) enabling the performance to be included in a programme service,
but if it is proved that the performance was attended by persons other than those directly concerned with the giving of the performance or the doing in relation to it of the things mentioned in paragraph (b) or (c), the performance shall, unless the contrary is shown, be taken not to have been given solely for the purposes mentioned above.
(4) For the purposes of this section—
    (a) a person shall not be treated as presenting a performance of a play by reason only of his taking part in it as a performer,
    (b) a person taking part as a performer in a performance directed by another shall be treated as a person who directed the performance if without reasonable excuse he performs otherwise than in accordance with that person's direction, and
    (c) a person shall be taken to have directed a performance of a play given under his direction notwithstanding that he was not present during the performance;
and a person shall not be treated as aiding or abetting the commission of an offence under this section by reason only of his taking part in a performance as a performer.

Distributing, Showing or Playing a Recording Stirring up Racial Hatred

Public Order Act 1986, s. 21 **B11.175**

(1) A person who distributes, or shows or plays, a recording of visual images or sounds which are threatening, abusive or insulting is guilty of an offence if—
    (a) he intends thereby to stir up racial hatred, or
    (b) having regard to all the circumstances racial hatred is likely to be stirred up thereby.

(2) [See **B11.172**]

(3) In proceedings for an offence under this section it is a defence for an accused who is not shown to have intended to stir up racial hatred to prove that he was not aware of the content of the recording and did not suspect, and had no reason to suspect, that it was threatening, abusive or insulting.

(4) This section does not apply to the showing or playing of a recording solely for the purpose of enabling the recording to be included in a programme service.

Broadcasting Programme Stirring up Racial Hatred

B11.176   Public Order Act 1986, s. 22

(1) If a programme involving threatening, abusive or insulting visual images or sounds is included in a programme service, each of the persons mentioned in subsection (2) is guilty of an offence if—
  (a) he intends to stir up racial hatred, or
  (b) having regard to all the circumstances racial hatred is likely to be stirred up thereby.

(2) The persons are—
  (a) the person providing the programme service,
  (b) any person by whom the programme is produced or directed, and
  (c) any person by whom offending words or behaviour are used.

(3) If the person providing the service, or a person by whom the programme was produced or directed, is not shown to have intended to stir up racial hatred, it is a defence for him to prove that—
  (a) he did not know and had no reason to suspect that the programme would involve the offending material, and
  (b) having regard to the circumstances in which the programme was included in a programme service, it was not reasonably practicable for him to secure the removal of the material.

(4) It is a defence for a person by whom the programme was produced or directed who is not shown to have intended to stir up racial hatred to prove that he did not know and had no reason to suspect—
  (a) that the programme would be included in a programme service, or
  (b) that the circumstances in which the programme would be so included would be such that racial hatred would be likely to be stirred up.

(5) It is a defence for a person by whom offending words or behaviour were used and who is not shown to have intended to stir up racial hatred to prove that he did not know and had no reason to suspect—
  (a) that a programme involving the use of the offending material would be included in a programme service, or
  (b) that the circumstances in which a programme involving the use of the offending material would be so included, or in which a programme so included would involve the use of the offending material, would be such that racial hatred would be likely to be stirred up.

(6) A person who is not shown to have intended to stir up racial hatred is not guilty of an offence under this section if he did not know, and had no reason to suspect, that the offending material was threatening, abusive or insulting.

Possession of Written Material or Recording Stirring up Racial Hatred

B11.177   Public Order Act 1986, s. 23

(1) A person who has in his possession written material which is threatening, abusive or insulting, or a recording of visual images or sounds which are threatening, abusive or insulting, with a view to—
  (a) in the case of written material, its being displayed, published, distributed, or included in a programme service, whether by himself or another, or
  (b) in the case of a recording, its being distributed, shown, played, or included in a programme service, whether by himself or another, is guilty of an offence if he intends racial hatred to be stirred up thereby or, having regard to all the circumstances, racial hatred is likely to be stirred up thereby.

(2) For this purpose regard is to be had to such display, publication, distribution, showing, playing, or inclusion in a programme service as he has, or it may reasonably be inferred that he has, in view.

(3) In proceedings for an offence under this section it is a defence for an accused who is not shown to have intended to stir up racial hatred to prove that he was not aware of the content of the written material or recording and did not suspect, and had no reason to suspect, that it was threatening, abusive or insulting.

In *Gray* [1999] 1 Cr App R (S) 50, the offender was found in possession of a quantity of magazines containing racist material, and he was involved in their distribution. A prison sentence of 12 months following a plea of guilty to the offence under s. 23(1) was upheld on appeal. The Court of Appeal commented that reported decisions dating from the 1970s and 1980s for similar offences might no longer be an adequate guide to current sentencing practice, since 'the grave social damage done by offences and remarks of a racist nature is now perhaps better known than it was then'. See **B11.161** for the power of forfeiture.

USING WORDS OR BEHAVIOUR OR DISPLAYING WRITTEN MATERIAL STIRRING UP HATRED ON RELIGIOUS GROUNDS OR ON GROUNDS OF SEXUAL ORIENTATION

The Racial and Religious Hatred Act 2006 inserted ss. 29A to 29L into part 3A of the POA 1986. SI 2007 No. 2497 brought the Act into force on 1 October 2007. The CJIA 2008, s. 74 and sch. 16, further expand part 3A to cover hatred on the grounds of sexual orientation; the Criminal Justice and Immigration Act 2008 (Commencement No. 14) Order 2010 (SI 2010 No. 712), *inter alia*, brought s. 74 and sch. 16 into force on 23 March 2010. The Electronic Commerce Directive (Hatred against Persons on Religious Grounds or the Grounds of Sexual Orientation) Regulations 2010 (SI 2010 No. 894) include provision for the application of the 2006 Act to information society services, particularly to internet service providers and the like. The Regulations ensure that offences under part 3A of the Public Order Act 1986 apply on a country of origin basis and create exceptions from liability in respect of the offences for intermediary providers of information society services where their role is limited to that of a mere conduit or they merely provide caching or hosting services. **B11.178**

Procedure

Offences under the POA 1986, ss. 29B(1), 29C(1), 29D(1), 29E(1), 29F(1) and 29G(1), are triable either way (s. 29L(3)). When tried on indictment, they are normally class 3 offences, but see CPD XIII, para. B (see Supplement, **PD-97**) for the additional factors that the court considers on allocation. No proceedings may be instituted except by or with the consent of the A-G (s. 29L(1)). For the purposes of rules against charging more than one offence in the same count or information, this section creates one offence (s. 29L(2)). For the liability of corporate offenders, see s. 29M, which is worded in the standard format. **B11.179**

Sentence

The maximum penalty for each of these offences is, on conviction on indictment, imprisonment for a term not exceeding seven years, a fine, or both; on summary conviction, the maximum is a term of imprisonment not exceeding six months, a fine not exceeding the statutory maximum, or both (POA 1986, s. 29L(3)). **B11.180**

In relation to the offences relating to the display of written material, the court has the following forfeiture power.

Public Order Act 1986, s. 29I

(1) A court by or before which a person is convicted of—
   (a) an offence under section 29B relating to the display of written material, or
   (b) an offence under section 29C, 29E or 29G,

shall order to be forfeited any written material or recording produced to the court and shown to its satisfaction to be written material or a recording to which the offence relates.

(2) An order made under this section shall not take effect—

    (a) until the expiry of the ordinary time within which an appeal may be instituted or, where an appeal is duly instituted, until it is finally decided or abandoned.

    (b) [repealed]

(3) For the purposes of subsection (2)(a)—

    (a) an application for a case stated or for leave to appeal shall be treated as the institution of an appeal, and

    (b) where a decision on appeal is subject to a further appeal, the appeal is not finally determined until the expiry of the ordinary time within which a further appeal may be instituted or, where a further appeal is duly instituted, until the further appeal is finally decided or abandoned.

Definition of Offence

B11.181

Public Order Act 1986, s. 29B

(1) A person who uses threatening words or behaviour, or displays any written material which is threatening, is guilty of an offence if he intends thereby to stir up religious hatred or hatred on the grounds of sexual orientation.

Elements

B11.182   Key concepts are the meaning of 'religious hatred' and the meaning of hatred on the grounds of sexual orientation.

Public Order Act 1986, ss. 29A and 29AB

29A.—In this part 'religious hatred' means hatred against a group of persons defined by reference to religious belief or lack of religious belief.

29AB.—In this part 'hatred on the grounds of sexual orientation' means hatred against a group of person defined by reference to sexual orientation (whether towards persons of the same sex, the opposite sex or both).

It is possible that the meaning of 'religion' will play a part in considering the offence relating to 'religious hatred'. It is a notoriously difficult concept to define. For a consideration of this issue in the context of religiously aggravated offences, see **B11.150**. It is submitted that, utilising the jurisprudence under the ECHR, Article 9, regarding these words as ordinary words of the English language is the approach that will be adopted. The government, in the *Explanatory Memorandum*, provides a list of 'religions widely recognised in this country' and lists: Christianity, Islam, Hinduism, Judaism, Buddhism, Sikhism, Rastafarianism, Baha'ism, Zoroastrianism and Jainism. For those who lack a religious belief, the government lists groups such as atheists and humanists. These offences are, according to the government, 'based on the fact that the group do not share the particular religious beliefs of the perpetrator'.

B11.183   As for 'hatred on the grounds of sexual orientation', the Ministry of Justice Circular 2010/05, para. 7, expresses the view that the definition 'is expressly limited to orientation towards persons of the same sex, the opposite sex, or both. The term does not extend to orientation based on, for example, a preference for particular sexual acts or practices. It therefore covers only groups of people who are gay, lesbian, bisexual or heterosexual.' An offence was not motivated by, nor was there a demonstration of hostility towards, the complainant's sexual orientation, where the appellant believed that the complainant was a paedophile (*B* [2013] 2 Cr App R (S) 443 (69)).

In order to meet many of the deep concerns that this kind of legislation would prevent what has been acceptable behaviour, particularly that of those wishing to convert people to their own religion or of comedians, entertainers and social commentators, and a feeling that the existence of the ECHR, Articles 9, 10 and 11, would not provide sufficient protection, the Act provides as follows.

Public Order Act 1986, ss. 29J and 29JA

29J.—Nothing in this part shall be read or given effect in a way which prohibits or restricts discussion, criticism or expressions of antipathy, dislike, ridicule, insult or abuse of particular religions or the beliefs or practices of their adherents, or of any other belief system or the beliefs or practices of its adherents, or proselytising or urging adherents of a different religion or belief system to cease practising their religion or belief system.

29JA.—In this part, for the avoidance of doubt, the discussion or criticism of sexual conduct or practices or the urging of persons to refrain from or modify such conduct or practices shall not be taken of itself to be threatening or intended to stir up hatred.

The Marriage (Same Sex Couples) Act 2013, sch. 7, para. 28, came into force on 13 March 2014 (SI 2014 No. 93) and amended s. 29JA of the 1986 Act so as to provide that 'for the avoidance of doubt, any discussion or criticism of marriage which concerns the sex of the parties to marriage shall not be taken of itself to be threatening or intended to stir up hatred'.

Ministry of Justice Circular 2010/05, para. 12, states: 'The offences are limited to threatening conduct or material which is intended to stir up hatred. Subject to those conditions, they do not prevent the telling of jokes or the preaching of religious doctrine. Hatred is a very strong emotion. Conduct or material which only stirs up ridicule or dislike, or which simply causes offence, would not meet that threshold. The offences are not intended to cover, for example, teenagers who call each other names in the playground where this is not threatening and there is no intention of stirring up hatred against a group.'

The offence may be committed in a public or a private place, but no offence is committed **B11.184** where the words or behaviour are used or the written material is displayed by a person inside a dwelling and are not heard or seen except by other persons in that or another dwelling (s. 29B(2)). The offence does not apply to words or behaviour used or written material displayed solely for the purpose of being included in a programme service (s. 29B(5)). For the relevant offence that may be committed, see **B11.196**. 'Dwelling' means any structure or part of a structure occupied as a person's home or other living accommodation (whether the occupation is separate or shared with others) but does not include any part not so occupied, and 'structure' includes a tent, caravan, vehicle, vessel or other temporary or moveable structure (s. 29N).

For a discussion of 'threatening, abusive or insulting', see **B11.55**. 'Written material' includes any sign or other visible representation (s. 29N). This includes articles in electronic form, such as material disseminated via a web site (*Sheppard* [2010] 2 All ER 850).

The accused must have the relevant intention (s. 29B(1)).

There is a special saving for reports of parliamentary and judicial proceedings.

Public Order Act 1986, s. 29K

(1) Nothing in this part applies to a fair and accurate report of proceedings in Parliament or in the Scottish Parliament.

(2) Nothing in this part applies to a fair and accurate report of proceedings publicly heard before a court or tribunal exercising judicial authority where the report is published contemporaneously with the proceedings or, if it is not reasonably practicable or would be unlawful to publish a report of them contemporaneously, as soon as publication is reasonably practicable and lawful.

Defence

It is a defence for the accused to prove that he was inside the dwelling and had no reason to **B11.185** believe that the words or behaviour used or the written material displayed would be heard or seen by a person outside that or any other dwelling (POA 1986, s. 29B(4)).

Powers of Arrest

The citizen's power of arrest in the PACE 1984, s. 24A, does not apply to this offence (PACE **B11.186** 1984, s. 24A(5)). For arrest generally, see **D1.14** *et seq*.

PUBLISHING OR DISTRIBUTING WRITTEN MATERIAL STIRRING UP HATRED ON RELIGIOUS GROUNDS OR ON GROUNDS OF SEXUAL ORIENTATION

B11.187

Public Order Act 1986, s. 29C

(1) A person who publishes or distributes written material which is threatening is guilty of an offence if he intends thereby to stir up religious hatred or hatred on the grounds of sexual orientation.

For procedure and sentence, see **B11.179** and **B11.180**.

Elements

B11.188   As to the meaning of 'religious hatred' and the special provision on the protection of freedom of expression (POA 1986, ss. 29J and 29JA), see **B11.183**. As to the meaning of 'threatening', see **B11.55**, but note that it is only material that is threatening which forms this offence.

References to the publication or distribution of written material are to its publication or distribution to the public or a section of the public (s. 29C(2)).

The accused must have the relevant intention (s. 29C(1)).

For savings for reports of parliamentary and judicial proceedings under POA 1986, s. 29K, see **B11.184**.

PUBLIC PERFORMANCE OF PLAY STIRRING UP HATRED ON RELIGIOUS GROUNDS OR ON GROUNDS OF SEXUAL ORIENTATION

B11.189

Public Order Act 1986, s. 29D

(1) If a public performance of a play is given which involves the use of threatening words or behaviour, any person who presents or directs the performance is guilty of an offence if he intends thereby to stir up religious hatred or hatred on the grounds of sexual orientation.

For procedure and sentence, see **B11.179** and **B11.180**.

Elements

B11.190   As to the meaning of 'religious hatred' and 'hatred on the grounds of sexual orientation' and the special provision on the protection of freedom of expression, see **B11.184**. As to the meaning of 'threatening', see **B11.55**, but note that it is only material that is threatening which forms this offence.

The offence does not apply to certain performances.

Public Order Act 1986, s. 29D

(2) This section does not apply to a performance given solely or primarily for one or more of the following purposes—
   (a) rehearsal,
   (b) making a recording of the performance, or
   (c) enabling the performance to be included in a programme service;
   but if it is proved that the performance was attended by persons other than those directly connected with the giving of the performance or the doing in relation to it of the things mentioned in paragraph (b) or (c), the performance shall, unless the contrary is shown, be taken not to have been given solely or primarily for the purpose mentioned above.

As regards those who may or may not be directing a performance, the following provision applies.

Public Order Act 1986, s. 29D

(3) For the purposes of this section—
   (a) a person shall not be treated as presenting a performance of a play by reason only of his taking part in it as a performer,
   (b) a person taking part as a performer in a performance directed by another shall be treated as a person who directed the performance if without reasonable excuse he performs otherwise than in accordance with that person's direction, and
   (c) a person shall be taken to have directed a performance of a play given under his direction notwithstanding that he was not present during the performance;
   and a person shall not be treated as aiding or abetting the commission of an offence under this section by reason only of his taking part in a performance as a performer.

The accused must have the relevant intention (POA 1986, s. 29D(1)).

'Play' and 'public performance' have the same meaning as in the Theatres Act 1968 (s. 29D(4)). Further, the Theatres Act 1968, ss. 9 (script as evidence of what was performed), 10 (power to make copies of script) and 15 (powers of entry and inspection) apply to this offence (s. 29D(5)).

For savings for reports of parliamentary and judicial proceedings under s. 29K, see **B11.184**.

Power of Arrest

The citizen's power of arrest in the PACE 1984, s. 24A, does not apply to this offence (PACE 1984, s. 24A(5)).   **B11.191**

DISTRIBUTING, SHOWING OR PLAYING A RECORDING STIRRING UP HATRED ON RELIGIOUS GROUNDS OR ON GROUNDS OF SEXUAL ORIENTATION

Public Order Act 1986, s. 29E   **B11.192**

(1) A person who distributes, or shows or plays, a recording of visual images or sounds which are threatening is guilty of an offence if he intends thereby to stir up religious hatred or hatred on the grounds of sexual orientation.

For procedure and sentence, see **B11.179** and **B11.180**.

Elements

As to the meaning of 'religious hatred' and 'hatred on the grounds of sexual orientation', and the special provision on the protection of freedom of expression, see **B11.184**. As to the meaning of 'threatening', see **B11.55**, but note that it is only material that is threatening which forms this offence. Section 29E defines 'recording'.   **B11.193**

Public Order Act 1986, s. 29E

(2) In this Part 'recording' means any record from which visual images or sounds may, by any means, be reproduced; and references to the distribution, showing or playing of a recording are to its distribution, showing or playing to the public or a section of the public.

The accused must have the relevant intention (s. 29E(1)).

This offence does not apply to the showing or playing of a recording solely for the purpose of enabling it to be included in a programme service (s. 29E(3)). For the relevant offence, see **B11.196**.

For savings for reports of parliamentary and judicial proceedings under s. 29K, see **B11.184**.

Power of Arrest

The citizen's power of arrest in the PACE 1984, s. 24A, does not apply to this offence (PACE 1984, s. 24A(5)).   **B11.194**

BROADCASTING OR INCLUDING PROGRAMME IN PROGRAMME SERVICE STIRRING UP HATRED ON RELIGIOUS GROUNDS OR ON GROUNDS OF SEXUAL ORIENTATION

B11.195   **Public Order Act 1986, s. 29F**

(1) If a programme involving threatening visual images or sounds is included in a programme service, each of the persons mentioned in subsection (2) is guilty of an offence if he intends thereby to stir up religious hatred or hatred on the grounds of sexual orientation.

(2) The persons are—
  (a) the person providing the programme service,
  (b) any person by whom the programme is produced or directed, and
  (c) any person by whom offending words or behaviour are used.

For procedure and sentence, see **B11.179** and **B11.180**.

Elements

B11.196 As to the meaning of 'religious hatred' and 'hatred on the grounds of sexual orientation', and the special provision on the protection of freedom of expression, see **B11.184**. As to the meaning of 'threatening', see **B11.55**, but note that it is only material that is threatening which forms this offence.

'Programme service' has the same meaning as in the Broadcasting Act 1990 (s. 29N). 'Programme' means any item which is included in a programme service (s. 29N).

The accused must have the relevant intention (s. 29F(1)).

For savings for reports of parliamentary and judicial proceedings under s. 29K, see **B11.184**.

Power of Arrest

B11.197 The citizen's power of arrest in the PACE 1984, s. 24A, does not apply to this offence (PACE 1984, s. 24A(5)).

POSSESSION OF INFLAMMATORY MATERIAL

B11.198   **Public Order Act 1986, s. 29G**

(1) A person who has in his possession written material which is threatening, or a recording of visual images or sounds which are threatening, with a view to—
  (a) in the case of written material, its being displayed, published, distributed, or included in a programme service whether by himself or another, or
  (b) in the case of a recording, its being distributed, shown, played, or included in a programme service, whether by himself or another,
  is guilty of an offence if he intends thereby to stir up religious hatred or hatred on the grounds of sexual orientation.

For procedure and sentence, see **B11.179** and **B11.180**.

Elements

B11.199 As to the meaning of 'religious hatred' and 'hatred on the grounds of sexual orientation', and the special provision on the protection of freedom of expression, see **B11.184**. As to the meaning of 'threatening', see **B11.55**, but note that it is only material that is threatening which forms this offence.

For this offence regard is had to such display, publication, distribution, showing, playing, or inclusion in a programme service as the accused has, or it may be reasonably be inferred that he has, in view (s. 29G(2)).

The accused must have the relevant intention (s. 29G(1)).

For savings for reports of parliamentary and judicial proceedings under s. 29K, see **B11.184**.

Power of Arrest

The citizen's power of arrest in the PACE 1984, s. 24A, does not apply to this offence (PACE **B11.200** 1984, s. 24A(5)).

Entry and Search

Public Order Act 1986, s. 29H   **B11.201**

(1) If a justice of the peace is satisfied by information on oath laid by a constable that there are reasonable grounds for suspecting that a person has possession of written material or a recording in contravention of section 29G, the justice may issue a warrant under his hand authorising any constable to enter and search the premises where it is suspected the material or recording is situated.

(2) [repealed]

(3) A constable entering or searching premises in pursuance of a warrant issued under this section may use reasonable force if necessary.

(4) In this section 'premises' means any place and, in particular, includes—

    (a) any vehicle, vessel, aircraft or hovercraft,

    (b) any offshore installation as defined in section 12 of the Mineral Workings (Offshore Installations) Act 1971, and

    (c) any tent or movable structure.

DRUNK AND DISORDERLY

Offence, Procedure and Sentence

It is a summary offence, contrary to the CJA 1967, s. 91(1), where 'Any person who in any **B11.202** public place is guilty, while drunk, of disorderly behaviour...'. The maximum penalty for the offence is a fine not exceeding level 3 on the standard scale. The *Magistrates' Court Sentencing Guidelines* (see Supplement, **SG-281**) identify two starting points (for a first time offender pleading not guilty) according to the nature of the activity. Shouting/causing disturbance for some minutes attracts a starting point of a band A fine. If substantial disturbance is caused, the starting point is a band B fine.

Community rehabilitation orders and curfew orders are the only available community sentences for this offence.

Under the Penalties for Disorderly Behaviour (Amount of Penalty) Order 2002 (SI 2002 No. 1837), as amended, this offence is a penalty offence and the amount payable is £90.

Drunk

It was held by the Divisional Court in *Neale v R.M.J.E. (a minor)* (1984) 80 Cr App R 20 **B11.203** that the natural and ordinary meaning of the word 'drunk' in this statutory context is that it is limited to cases of drunkenness induced by alcohol. It is not, therefore, committed where the state of the accused is a product of glue-sniffing. This decision was followed by the Divisional Court in *Lanham v Rickwood* (1984) 148 JP 737, a decision on the meaning of the word 'drunk' in the Licensing Act 1872, s. 12, which states: 'Every person found drunk in any highway or other public place, whether building or not, or on any licensed premises, shall be liable to a penalty'.

In *Lanham v Rickwood* it was also decided that the condition in which the accused was found does not have to be solely attributable to alcohol:

> In each case, the magistrates have to ask themselves, no doubt as a matter of simple common sense, whether a person's loss of self-control is attributable to his having indulged in an excessive

consumption of intoxicating liquor. If the evidence before them is that he has indulged both in an excessive consumption of intoxicating liquor and also in some other form of activity, such as glue-sniffing, which may also have affected his self-control, they have to decide, as a matter of common sense, whether they are satisfied that, apart from the glue-sniffing, he has consumed intoxicating liquor to an extent which affects his steady self-control.

This decision is important not only on multiple causes of a condition, but also because it gives an indication of what is meant by 'drunk'. In *Neale v R.J.M.E. (a minor)* Robert Goff LJ made the same point about the meaning of drunkenness: 'the word "drunk", in ordinary common speech,...refers to someone who has taken intoxicating liquor to an extent which affects his steady self control'. Note that a person may be in a condition which can be described as 'drunk' but that need not be the same condition as that necessary to raise the defence of intoxication.

In *Carroll v DPP* [2009] 173 JP 285 the Divisional Court confirmed that this is one of the most basic offences in the calendar and that it requires proof of three elements, namely that (1) the accused was drunk; (2) he was in a public place; and (3) he was guilty of disorderly behaviour. As to the first element, approving *Neale*, it said that whether an accused was drunk is a simple question of fact in each case. If the voluntary consumption of alcohol results in the accused becoming drunk then the first element is proved.

Disorderly Behaviour

B11.204   The words are to be given their ordinary and natural meaning; what is required is proof that objectively viewed the defendant was guilty of disorderly behaviour — there is no *mens rea* requirement (*Carroll v DPP* (2009) 173 JP 285). The disorderly conduct, though, must occur before the person is arrested as the gravamen of the offence is disorderly conduct whilst being drunk (*R (H) v CPS* (2006) 170 JP 4).

Public Place

B11.205   The CJA 1967, s. 91(4), provides that, in s. 91, '"public place" includes any highway and any other premises or place to which at the material time the public have or are permitted to have access, whether on payment or otherwise'. As to this definition, see *Williams v DPP* (1992) 95 Cr App R 415 and *Cleaver* [2011] EWCA Crim 983.

Related Offence: Drunk on an Aircraft

B11.206   It is an offence, contrary to the Air Navigation Order 2009 (SI 2009 No. 3015), art. 139, for a person to enter any aircraft when drunk or to be drunk in any aircraft. It is also an offence for a person, when acting as an aircraft crew member or being carried in any aircraft for the purpose of so acting, to be under the influence of drink or drugs to such an extent as to impair his capacity to act. Both offences are triable either way. The maximum penalty is: on conviction on indictment, two years' imprisonment or a fine or both; on summary conviction, a fine not exceeding the statutory maximum (art. 241(7) and sch. 13, part C). A sentence of eight months for this offence was upheld in *Ayodeji* [2001] 1 Cr App R (S) 370 (at that time the maximum sentence was five years on indictment). In *Ator* [2011] 2 Cr App R (S) 618 the offender pleaded guilty to being drunk in an aircraft and received a sentence of six months' imprisonment. Shorter concurrent terms were imposed in relation to two offences of common assault and an offence of interfering with the performance of the duties of a crew member on an aircraft. The Court of Appeal (considering *Cooper* [2004] 2 Cr App R (S) 82 and *Matlach* [2006] 2 Cr App R (S) 1) upheld the sentence, despite the appellant being a man of previous good character with a series of 'impressive personal references from a number of sources'. The aggravating features identified were that this was a prolonged series of events whilst the aircraft was in the air, a number of passengers were upset and distressed by the appellant's behaviour, he ignored numerous requests to calm down and behave, and in the course of his conduct he assaulted a passenger by biting him and also assaulted an attendant who was doing her job.

ALCOHOL OFFENCES IN CONNECTION WITH SPORTING EVENTS

Alcohol on Coaches and Trains

Sporting Events (Control of Alcohol etc.) Act 1985, s. 1   **B11.207**

(2) A person who knowingly causes or permits alcohol to be carried on a vehicle to which this section applies is guilty of an offence—
  (a) if the vehicle is a public service vehicle and he is the operator of the vehicle or the servant or agent of the operator, or
  (b) if the vehicle is a hired vehicle and he is the person to whom it is hired or the servant or agent of that person.
(3) A person who has alcohol in his possession while on a vehicle to which this section applies is guilty of an offence.
(4) A person who is drunk on a vehicle to which this section applies is guilty of an offence.

Sentence and Procedure   Offences under the Sporting Events (Control of Alcohol etc.) Act   **B11.208**
1985, s. 1, are, by s. 8 of the Act, triable summarily only and punishable:

(a) in the case of an offence under s. 1(2), a fine not exceeding level 4 on the standard scale;
(b) in the case of an offence under s. 1(3), a fine not exceeding level 3 on the standard scale or imprisonment for a term not exceeding three months, or both;
(c) in the case of an offence under s. 1(4), a fine not exceeding level 2 on the standard scale.

Meaning of 'Vehicle'   **B11.209**

Sporting Events (Control of Alcohol etc.) Act 1985, s. 1

(1) This section applies to a vehicle which—
  (a) is a public service vehicle or railway passenger vehicle, and
  (b) is being used for the principal purpose of carrying passengers for the whole or part of a journey to or from a designated sporting event.
(2) to (4) [see **B11.207**]
(5) In this section 'public service vehicle' and 'operator' have the same meaning as in the Public Passenger Vehicles Act 1981.

Meaning of 'Designated Sporting Event'   **B11.210**

Sporting Events (Control of Alcohol etc.) Act 1985, s. 9

(3) 'Designated sporting event'—
  (a) means a sporting event or proposed sporting event for the time being designated, or of a class designated, by order made by the Secretary of State, and
  (b) includes a designated sporting event within the meaning of Part II of the Criminal Law (Consolidation) (Scotland) Act 1995;
  and an order under this subsection may apply to events or proposed events outside Great Britain as well as those in England and Wales.

See the Sports Grounds and Sporting Events (Designation Order) 1985 (SI 1985 No. 1151), as amended.

Alcohol on Other Vehicles

Sporting Events (Control of Alcohol etc.) Act 1985, s. 1A   **B11.211**

(2) A person who knowingly causes or permits alcohol to be carried on a motor vehicle to which this section applies is guilty of an offence—
  (a) if he is its driver, or
  (b) if he is not its driver but is its keeper, the servant or agent of its keeper, a person to whom it is made available (by hire, loan or otherwise) by its keeper or the keeper's servant or agent, or the servant or agent of a person to whom it is so made available.

(3) A person who has alcohol in his possession while on a motor vehicle to which this section applies is guilty of an offence.

(4) A person who is drunk on a motor vehicle to which this section applies is guilty of an offence.

B11.212 Sentence and Procedure   Offences under the Sporting Events (Control of Alcohol etc.) Act 1985, s. 1A are, by s. 8, triable summarily only and punishable.

(a) in the case of an offence under s. 1A(2), a fine not exceeding level 4 on the standard scale;

(b) in the case of an offence under s. 1A(3), a fine not exceeding level 3 on the standard scale or imprisonment for a terms not exceeding three months, or both;

(c) in the case of an offence under s. 1A(4), a fine not exceeding level 2 on the standard scale.

B11.213 Meaning of Terms

Sporting Events (Control of Alcohol etc.) Act 1985, s. 1A

(1) This section applies to a motor vehicle which—

(a) is not a public service vehicle but is adapted to carry more than 8 passengers, and

(b) is being used for the principal purpose of carrying two or more passengers for the whole or part of a journey to or from a designated sporting event.

...

(5) In this section—

'keeper', in relation to a vehicle, means the person having the duty to take out a licence for it under the Vehicle Excise and Registration Act 1994,

'motor vehicle' means a mechanically propelled vehicle intended or adapted for use on roads, and

'public service vehicle' has the same meaning as in the Public Passenger Vehicles Act 1981.

Containers etc. at Sports Grounds

B11.214   **Sporting Events (Control of Alcohol etc.) Act 1985, s. 2**

(1) A person who has alcohol or an article to which this section applies in his possession—

(a) at any time during the period of a designated sporting event when he is in any area of a designated sports ground from which the event may be directly viewed, or

(b) while entering or trying to enter a designated sports ground at any time during the period of a designated sporting event at that ground, is guilty of an offence.

(1A) Subsection (1)(a) above has effect subject to section 5A(1) of this Act.

(2) A person who is drunk in a designated sports ground at any time during the period of a designated sporting event at that ground or is drunk while entering or trying to enter such a ground at any time during the period of a designated sporting event at that ground is guilty of an offence.

Special provision is made by s. 5A(1) for private rooms from which the sporting event can be viewed; although prospectively repealed by the Licensing Act 2003, s. 198 and sch. 6, this provision remains in force.

B11.215 Sentence and Procedure   Offences under the Sporting Events (Control of Alcohol etc.) Act 1985, s. 2, are, by s. 8 of the Act, triable summarily only and punishable:

(a) in the case of an offence under s. 2(1), a fine not exceeding level 3 on the standard scale or imprisonment for a term not exceeding three months, or both;

(b) in the case of an offence under s. 2(2), a fine not exceeding level 2 on the standard scale.

The *Magistrates' Court Sentencing Guidelines* (see Supplement, SG-287) deal with a number of 'football ground offences' (offences under this section as well as those dealt with at **B11.130** and **B11.133**) all together. They identify starting points (for a first time offender pleading not guilty) according to the nature of the activity, each starting point having a defined range which is adjusted according to the non-exhaustive list of aggravating and mitigating features. The aggravating and mitigating factors identified are common to all the football offences referred to above.

Being drunk in, or whilst trying to enter the ground attracts a starting point of a band A fine, the range being a conditional discharge to a band B fine. Possession of alcohol whilst entering or trying to enter a ground attracts a band C fine, the range being a band B fine to a high level community order. Aggravating factors relevant to these offences are: inciting others to misbehave, possession of a large quantity of alcohol; offensive language.

Both for the s. 2(1) and s. 2(2) offence, the court must consider imposing a banning order (see E21.3). If no banning order is made, the court must give reasons.

Meaning of Terms   B11.216

For the meaning of 'designated sporting event', see **B11.210**.

Sporting Events (Control of Alcohol etc.) Act 1985, s. 9

(2) 'Designated sports ground' means any place—
  (a) used (wholly or partly) for sporting events where accommodation is provided for spectators, and
  (b) for the time being designated, or of a class designated, by order made by the Secretary of State; and an order under this subsection may include provision for determining for the purposes of this Act the outer limit of any designated sports ground.
  ...
(4) The period of a designated sporting event is the period beginning two hours before the start of the event or (if earlier) two hours before the time at which it is advertised to start and ending one hour after the end of the event, but—
  (a) where an event advertised to start at a particular time on a particular day is postponed to a later day, the period includes the period in the day on which it is advertised to take place beginning two hours before and ending one hour after that time, and
  (b) where an event advertised to start at a particular time on a particular day does not take place, the period is the period referred to in paragraph (a) above.

The articles to which s. 2 applies are defined in s. 2(3):

This section applies to any article capable of causing injury to a person struck by it, being—
  (a) a bottle, can or other portable container (including such an article when crushed or broken) which—
    (i)   is for holding any drink, and
    (ii) is of a kind which, when empty, is normally discarded or returned to, or left to be recovered by, the supplier, or
  (b) part of an article falling within paragraph (a) above;
but does not apply to anything that is for holding any medicinal product (within the meaning of the Medicines Act 1968).

Possession of Flares, Fireworks, etc. at Sports Grounds

Sporting Events (Control of Alcohol etc.) Act 1985, s. 2A   B11.217

(1) A person is guilty of an offence if he has an article or substance to which this section applies in his possession—
  (a) at any time during the period of a designated sporting event when he is in any area of a designated sports ground from which the event may be directly viewed, or
  (b) while entering or trying to enter a designated sports ground at any time during the period of a designated sporting event at the ground.
(2) It is a defence for the accused to prove that he had possession with lawful authority.
(3) This section applies to any article or substance whose main purpose is the emission of a flare for purposes of illuminating or signalling (as opposed to igniting or heating) or the emission of smoke or a visible gas; and in particular it applies to distress flares, fog signals, and pellets and capsules intended to be used as fumigators or for testing pipes, but not to matches, cigarette lighters or heaters.
(4) This section also applies to any article which is a firework.

For the meaning of 'designated sporting event', see **B11.210**; for the meaning of 'designated sports ground', see **B11.216**.

Sentence and Procedure   Offences under the Sporting Events (Control of Alcohol etc.) Act   B11.218
1985, s. 2A are, by s. 8, triable summarily only, and punishable:

(a) in the case of an offence under s. 1A(2), a fine not exceeding level 4 on the standard scale;

(b) in the case of an offence under s. 1A(3), a fine not exceeding level 3 on the standard scale or imprisonment for a terms not exceeding three months, or both;

(c) in the case of an offence under s. 1A(4), a fine not exceeding level 2 on the standard scale.

NUISANCE OR DISTURBANCE ON NHS PREMISES

B11.219 The CJIA 2008, s. 119, introduced the offence of causing nuisance or disturbance on NHS premises. The Criminal Justice and Immigration Act 2008 (Commencement No. 13 and Transitory Provision) Order 2009 (SI 2009 No. 3074) brought ss. 119 to 121 of the Act into force on 30 November 2009 in respect of English NHS premises.

Criminal Justice and Immigration Act 2008, s. 119

(1) A person commits an offence if—

(a) the person causes, without reasonable excuse and while on NHS premises, a nuisance or disturbance to an NHS staff member who is working there or is otherwise there in connection with work,

(b) the person refuses, without reasonable excuse, to leave the NHS premises when asked to do so by a constable or an NHS staff member, and

(c) the person is not on the NHS premises for the purpose of obtaining medical advice, treatment or care for himself or herself.

Sentence

B11.220 This is a summary only offence which attracts a maximum penalty of a fine not exceeding level 3 (CJIA 2008, s. 119(2)).

Defences

B11.221 A person will not commit the offence if he has a reasonable excuse for causing the nuisance or disturbance or refusing to leave the premises. Behaviour consequential to the receipt of upsetting news or bereavement may, for example, constitute a reasonable excuse. A reasonable excuse for not leaving the premises may, for example, include a situation where a dependant is on the premises concerned and the person causing a nuisance or disturbance has a responsibility to remain on the premises with this dependant.

Meaning of 'for the purpose of obtaining medical advice, treatment, etc'

B11.222 A person ceases to be on the premises for the purpose of obtaining medical advice, treatment or care for himself in two circumstances. First, once the person has received the advice, etc. (CJIA 2008, s. 119(3)(a)) and secondly, if the person has received the advice, etc. during the last eight hours (s. 119(3)(b)).

Powers of Removal

B11.223 The CJIA 2008, s.120, gives police officers and other authorised officers the power to use reasonable force if necessary to remove a person from NHS premises who they reasonably suspect is committing an offence under s. 119 or who has committed such an offence. However, an authorised officer cannot remove such a person if he has reason to believe that the person is in need of medical advice, etc. or that removal would endanger his mental or physical health (s. 120(4)). An 'authorised officer' is a duly authorised NHS staff member (see s. 120(5)).

Section B12   Offences Relating to Weapons

FIREARMS OFFENCES GENERALLY

The Firearms Acts 1968 to 1997 control the possession etc. of firearms by dividing such weapons **B12.1** into a number of different categories, namely (i) firearms, (ii) firearms within s. 1 of the FA 1968 (certificate needed: see **B12.33**), (iii) prohibited weapons, (iv) shot guns and (v) air weapons. Section 8 of the F(A)A 1988 takes de-activated weapons out of a category into which they would otherwise have fallen (see **B12.20**) but, there can be circumstances in which a de-activated weapon constitutes an 'imitation firearm'. Care needs to be taken in respect of any 'imitation firearm' because some offences expressly make reference to imitation firearms (see **B12.24**), while the reach of other offences extends to imitation firearms by operation of the FA 1982, ss. 1 and 2 (see **B12.28**). Many of the offences control ammunition as well as firearms. It is important to distinguish between ammunition to which s.1 of the FA 1968 applies (certificate needed) and other ammunition that is not subject to s. 1.

Several areas of the legislation are unhappily drafted (notably, but not exclusively, in relation to 'air weapons') and much legislation has evolved piecemeal due, in part, to developments in the design and use of a number of devices. For example, devices that are popularly described as 'air guns' are not confined to the break-barrel piston-action type, but include carbon-dioxide bulb systems, or gas-cartridge-pellet systems. A number of air/gas powered guns have been designed to resemble traditional firearms.

Mode of Trial and Punishment

B12.2 Section 51(1) to (3) of the FA 1968 provides that the mode of trial, maximum punishments and powers of convicting courts with respect to offences created by that Act shall be as set out in sch. 6 to that Act, which is reproduced at **B12.5**.

Time-limits: Summary Trial

B12.3

Firearms Act 1968, s. 51

(4) Notwithstanding section 127(1) of the Magistrates' Courts Act 1980…[Scotland] summary proceedings for an offence under this Act, other than an offence under section 22(3) or an offence relating specifically to air weapons, may be instituted at any time within four years after the commission of the offence:

Provided that no such proceedings shall be instituted in England after the expiration of six months after the commission of the offence unless they are instituted by, or by the direction of, the Director of Public Prosecutions.

Powers of Seizure and Forfeiture

B12.4 Sections 46 to 49 of the FA 1968 provide for powers of search, the demand by a constable for production of certificates, and police powers in relation to arms traffic.

Powers of forfeiture exercisable by a convicting court may be found in two places. Part II of sch. 6 to the FA 1968 (see **B12.6**) provides certain specific powers. Section 52 provides generally for forfeiture and disposal of firearms and for cancellation of certificates. Section 50(3) of the VCRA 2006 provides for ss. 46, 51(4), 52 and 58 of the FA 1968 to apply as if ss. 28, 29 and 35 of the 2006 Act were contained in the FA 1968. The following powers, inserted or amended by the VCRA 2006, also apply: (a) Education Act 1996, s. 550AA (power of members of staff to search school pupils for weapons); (b) Further and Higher Education Act 1992, s. 85B (power to search further education students for weapons); (c) CJA 1988, s. 139B (police power to search schools etc. for weapons).

In the absence of legitimate grounds for piercing the corporate veil, firearms or other property lawfully owned by a registered company or other corporation cannot be subject to a forfeiture order merely because an individual connected to that corporation has been convicted of an offence in relation to it (*Hyde* [2014] EWCA Crim 713).

Firearms Act 1968, s. 52

(1) Where a person—

    (a) is convicted of an offence under this Act (other than an offence under section 22(3) or an offence relating specifically to air weapons) or is convicted of a crime for which he is sentenced to imprisonment, or detention in a young offender institution…[Scotland]…or is subject to a detention and training order; or

    (b) has been ordered into a recognizance to keep the peace or to be of good behaviour, a condition of which is that he shall not possess, use or carry a firearm; or

    (c) is subject to a community order containing a requirement that he shall not possess, use or carry a firearm; or

    (d) [applies to Scotland only]

the court by or before which he is convicted, or by which the order is made, may make such order as to the forfeiture or disposal of any firearm or ammunition found in his possession as the court thinks fit and may cancel any firearm certificate or shot gun certificate held by him.

(1A) In subsection (1)(c) 'community order' means—

    (a) a community order within the meaning of part 12 of the Criminal Justice Act 2003, or a youth rehabilitation order within the meaning of part 1 of the Criminal Justice and Immigration Act 2008, made in England and Wales, or

    (b) …[Scotland].

(2) Where the court cancels a certificate under this section—

  (a) the court shall cause notice to be sent to the chief officer of police by whom the certificate was granted; and

  (b) the chief officer of police shall by notice in writing require the holder of the certificate to surrender it; and

  (c) it is an offence for the holder to fail to surrender the certificate within 21 days from the date of the notice given him by the chief officer of police.

(3) A constable may seize and detain any firearm or ammunition which may be the subject of an order for forfeiture under this section.

(4) A court of summary jurisdiction or, in Scotland, the sheriff may, on the application of the chief officer of police, order any firearm or ammunition seized and detained by a constable under this Act to be destroyed or otherwise disposed of.

(5) In this section references to ammunition include references to a primer to which section 35 of the Violent Crime Reduction Act 2006 applies and to an empty cartridge case incorporating such a primer.

Punishments under the Firearms Act 1968

Firearms Act 1968, sch. 6   B12.5

PART I TABLE OF PUNISHMENT

Section of this Act creating offence	General nature of offence	Mode of prosecution	Punishment	Additional provisions
Section 1(1)	Possessing etc. firearm or ammunition without certificate.	(a) Summary (b) On indictment	6 months or a fine of the prescribed sum; or both. (i) where the offence is committed in an aggravated form within the meaning of section 4(4) of this Act, 7 years, or a fine; or both. (ii) in any other case, 5 years or a fine; or both.	[Scotland only.]
Section 1(2)	Non-compliance with condition of firearm certificate	Summary	6 months or a fine of level 5 on the standard scale; or both.	
Section 2(1)	Possessing, etc. shot gun without shot gun certificate	(a) Summary (b) On indictment	6 months or the statutory maximum; or both. 5 years or a fine; or both.	[Scotland only.]
Section 2(2)	Non-compliance with condition of shot gun certificate.	Summary	6 months or a fine of level 5 on the standard scale; or both.	[Scotland only.]
Section 3(1)	Trading in firearms without being registered as firearms dealer.	Summary	6 months or a fine of the prescribed sum; or both.	
Section 3(2)	Selling firearm to person without a certificate.	(a) Summary (b) On indictment.	6 months or a fine of the prescribed sum; or both. 5 years or a fine; or both.	
Section 3(3)	Repairing, testing etc. firearm for person without a certificate.	(a) Summary (b) On indictment	6 months or a fine of the prescribed sum; or both. 5 years of a fine; or both.	
Section 3(5)	Falsifying certificate, etc. with view to acquisition of firearm.	(a) Summary (b) On indictment	6 months or a fine of the prescribed sum; or both. 5 years or a fine; or both.	
Section 3(6)	Pawnbroker taking firearm in pawn.	Summary	3 months or a fine of level 3 on the standard scale; or both.	

Section of this Act creating offence	General nature of offence	Mode of prosecution	Punishment	Additional provisions
Section 4(1), (3)	Shortening a shot gun; conversion of firearms.	(a) Summary (b) On indictment	6 months or a fine of the prescribed sum; or both. 7 years or a fine; or both.	
Section 5(1)(a), (ab), (aba), (ac), (ad), (ae), (af) or (c)	Possessing prohibited weapons or ammunition.	On indictment	10 years or a fine, or both.	
Section 5(1)(b)	Possessing prohibited weapons designed for discharge of noxious liquid etc.	(a) Summary (b) On indictment	6 months or a fine of the statutory maximum; or both. 10 years or a fine; or both.	
Section 5(1A)(a)	Possessing firearm disguised as other object.	On indictment	10 years or a fine; or both.	
Section 5(1A)(b), (c), (d), (e), (f), or (g)	Possessing other prohibited weapons.	(a) Summary (b) On indictment	6 months or a fine of the statutory maximum; or both. 10 years or a fine; or both.	
Section 5(2A)	Manufacturing or distributing, or possessing for distribution, prohibited weapons or ammunition	On indictment	Imprisonment for life	
Section 5(5)	Non-compliance with condition of Defence Council authority.	Summary	6 months or a fine of level 5 on the standard scale; or both.	
Section 5(6)	Non-compliance with requirement to surrender authority to possess, etc. prohibited weapon or ammunition.	Summary	A fine of level 3 on the standard scale.	
Section 6(3)	Contravention of order under s. 6 (or corresponding Northern Irish order) restricting removal of arms.	Summary	3 months or, for each firearm or parcel of ammunition in respect of which the offence is committed, a fine of level 3 on the standard scale; or both.	Para. 2 of Part II of this Schedule applies.
Section 7(2)	Making false statement in order to obtain police permit.	Summary	6 months or a fine of level 5 on the standard scale; or both.	
Section 9(3)	Making false statement in order to obtain permit for auction of firearms etc.	Summary	6 months or a fine not exceeding level 5 on the standard scale; or both.	
Section 13(2)	Making false statement in order to obtain permit for removal of signalling apparatus.	Summary	6 months or a fine of level 5 on the standard scale; or both.	
Section 16	Possession of firearm with intent to endanger life or injure property.	On indictment	Life imprisonment or a fine; or both.	

Section of this Act creating offence	General nature of offence	Mode of prosecution	Punishment	Additional provisions
Section 16A	Possession of firearm or imitation firearm with intent to cause fear of violence.	On indictment	10 years or a fine; or both.	
Section 17(1)	Use of firearm or imitation firearm to resist arrest.	On indictment	Life imprisonment or a fine; or both.	Paras. 3 to 5 of Part II of this Schedule apply.
Section 17(2)	Possessing firearm or imitation firearm while committing an offence in schedule 1 or, in Scotland, an offence specified in Schedule 2.	On indictment	Life imprisonment or a fine; or both.	Paras. 3 and 6 of Part II of this Schedule apply.
Section 18(1)	Carrying firearm or imitation firearm with intent to commit indictable offence (or, in Scotland, an offence specified in Schedule 2) or to resist arrest.	On indictment	Life imprisonment or a fine; or both.	
Section 19	Carrying firearm or imitation firearm in public place.	(a) Summary except if the firearm is a firearm specified in section 5(1) (a), (ab), (aba), (ac), (ad), (ae) or (af) or section 5(1A)(a) of this Act. (b) On indictment (but not if the firearm is an air weapon).	6 months or a fine of the prescribed sum; or both. (i) if the weapon is an imitation firearm, 12 months or a fine; or both; (ii) in any other case, 7 years or a fine; or both.	
Section 20(1)	Trespassing with firearm or imitation firearm in a building	(a) Summary except if the firearm is a firearm specified in section 5(1) (a), (ab), (aba), (ac), (ad), (ae) or (af) or section 5(1A)(a) of this Act. (b) On indictment (but not in the case of an imitation firearm or if the firearm is an air weapon).	6 months or a fine of the prescribed sum; or both. 7 years or a fine; or both.	
Section 20(2)	Trespassing with firearm or imitation firearm on land.	Summary	3 months or a fine of level 4 on the standard scale; or both.	

Section of this Act creating offence	General nature of offence	Mode of prosecution	Punishment	Additional provisions
Section 21(4)	Contravention of provisions denying firearms to ex-prisoners and the like.	(a) Summary (b) On indictment	6 months or a fine of the prescribed sum; or both. 5 years or a fine; or both.	
Section 21(5)	Supplying firearms to person denied them under section 21.	(a) Summary (b) On indictment	6 months or a fine of the prescribed sum; or both. 5 years or a fine; or both.	
Section 21A	Person making improper use of air weapon.	Summary	A fine of level 3 on the standard scale.	Paras. 7 and 8 of Part II of this Schedule apply
Section 22(1)	Person under 18 acquiring firearm.	Summary	(i) Where the offence is committed in relation to a person aged 17 and in relation to a firearm other than an air weapon or ammunition other than ammunition for an air weapon, 3 months or a fine of level 5 on the standard scale; or both; (ii) in any other case, 6 months or a fine of level 5 on the standard scale; or both.	
Section 22(1A)	Person under 18 using certified firearm for unauthorised purpose.	Summary	3 months or a fine of level 5 on the standard scale or both.	
Section 22(2)	Person under 14 having firearm in his possession without lawful authority.	Summary	6 months or a fine of level 5 on the standard scale; or both.	
Section 22(3)	Person under 15 having with him a shot gun without adult supervision.	Summary	A fine of level 3 on the standard scale.	Para. 8 of Part II of this Schedule applies.
Section 22(4)	Person under 18 having with him an air weapon or ammunition therefore.	Summary	A fine of level 3 on the standard scale.	Paras. 7 and 8 of Part II of this Schedule apply.
Section 23(1)	Person supervising a person under 18 and allowing him to make improper use of air weapon.	Summary	A fine of level 3 on the standard scale.	Paras. 7 and 8 of Part II of this Schedule apply.

Section of this Act creating offence	General nature of offence	Mode of prosecution	Punishment	Additional provisions
Section 24(1)	Selling or letting on hire a firearm to person	Summary	(i) Where the offence is committed in relation to a person aged 17 and in relation to a firearm other than an air weapon or ammunition other than ammunition for an air weapon, 3 months or a fine of level 5 on the standard scale; or both; (ii) in any other case, 6 months or a fine of level 5 on the standard scale; or both.	
Section 24(2)	Supplying firearm or ammunition (being of a kind to which section 1 of this Act applies) to person under 18.	Summary	6 months or a fine of level 5 on the standard scale; or both.	
Section 24(3)	Making gift of shot gun to person under 15.	Summary	A fine of level 3 on the standard scale.	Para. 9 of Part II of this Schedule applies.
Section 24(4)	Supplying air weapon to person under 14.	Summary	A fine of level 3 on the standard scale.	Paras. 7 and 8 of Part II of this Schedule apply.
Section 24ZA(1)	Failing to prevent minors from having air weapons	Summary	A fine of level 3 on the standard scale.	Paras. 7 and 8 of Part II of this Schedule apply.
Section 24A(1) or (2)	Acquisition by a minor of an imitation firearm and supplying him.	Summary	In England and Wales, 6 months or a fine of level 5 on the standard scale, or both. [Further provision re Scotland.]	
Section 25	Supplying firearm to person drunk or insane.	Summary	3 months or a fine of level 3 on the standard scale; or both.	
Section 26(5)	Making false statement in order to procure grant or renewal of a firearm or shot gun certificate.	Summary	6 months or a fine of level 5 on the standard scale; or both.	
Section 29(3)	Making false statement in order to procure variation of a firearm certificate.	Summary	6 months or a fine of level 5 on the standard scale; or both.	
Section 30D(3)	Failing to surrender certificate on revocation.	Summary	A fine of level 3 on the standard scale.	
Section 32B(5)	Failure to surrender expired European firearms pass.	Summary	A fine of level 3 on the standard scale.	

723

Section of this Act creating offence	General nature of offence	Mode of prosecution	Punishment	Additional provisions
Section 32C(6)	Failure to produce European firearms pass or Article 7 authority for variation or cancellation etc.; failure to notify loss or theft of firearm identified in pass or to produce pass for endorsement.	Summary	3 months or a fine of level 5 on the standard scale; or both.	
Section 38(8)	Failure to surrender certificate of registration or register of transactions on removal of firearms dealer's name from register.	Summary	A fine of level 3 on the standard scale.	
Section 39(1)	Making false statement in order to secure registration or entry in register of a place of business.	Summary	6 months or a fine of level 5 on the standard scale; or both.	
Section 39(2)	Registered firearms dealer having place of business not entered in the register.	Summary	6 months or a fine of level 5 on the standard scale; or both.	
Section 39(3)	Non-compliance with condition of registration.	Summary	6 months or a fine of level 5 on the standard scale; or both.	
Section 40(5)	Non-compliance by firearms dealer with provisions as to register of transactions; making false entry in register.	Summary	6 months or a fine of level 5 on the standard scale; or both.	
Section 42A	Failure to report transaction authorised by visitor's shot gun permit.	Summary	3 months or a fine of level 5 on the standard scale or both.	
Section 46	Obstructing constable or civilian officer in exercise of search powers.	Summary	6 months or a fine of level 5 on the standard scale; or both.	
Section 47(2)	Failure to hand over firearm or ammunition on demand by constable.	Summary	3 months, or a fine of level 4 on the standard scale; or both.	
Section 48(3)	Failure to comply with requirement of a constable that a person shall declare his name and address.	Summary	A fine of level 3 on the standard scale.	

Section of this Act creating offence	General nature of offence	Mode of prosecution	Punishment	Additional provisions
Section 48A(4)	Failure to produce firearms pass issued in another Member State.	Summary	A fine of level 3 on the standard scale.	
Section 49(3)	Failure to give constable facilities for examination of firearms in transit, or to produce papers.	Summary	3 months or, for each firearm or parcel of ammunition in respect of which the offence is committed, a fine of level 3 on the standard scale; or both.	Para. 2 of Part II of this schedule applies.
Section 52(2)(c)	Failure to surrender firearm or shot gun certificate cancelled by court on conviction.	Summary	A fine of level 3 on the standard scale.	

PART II

B12.6

1. [Applies to Scotland only.]
2. In the case of an offence against section 6(3) or 49(3) of this Act, the court before which the offender is convicted may, if the offender is the owner of the firearms or ammunition, make such order as to the forfeiture of the firearms or ammunition as the court thinks fit.
3.—(1) Where in England or Wales a person who has attained the age of seventeen is charged before a magistrates' court with an offence triable either way listed in schedule 1 to the Magistrates' Courts Act 1980 ('the listed offence') and is also charged before that court with an offence under section 17(1) or (2) of this Act, the following provisions of this paragraph shall apply.
   (2) Subject to the following subparagraph the court shall proceed as if the listed offence were triable only on indictment and sections 18 to 23 of the said Act of 1980 (procedure for determining mode of trial of offences triable either way) shall not apply in relation to that offence.
   (3) [Omitted except for rare cases where committal still applies.]
4. Where a person commits an offence under section 17(1) of this Act in respect of the lawful arrest or detention of himself for any other offence committed by him, he shall be liable to the penalty provided by part I of this schedule in addition to any penalty to which he may be sentenced for the other offence.
5. If on the trial of a person for an offence under section 17(1) of this Act the jury are not satisfied that he is guilty of that offence but are satisfied that he is guilty of an offence under section 17(2), the jury may find him guilty of the offence under section 17(2) and he shall then be punishable accordingly.
6. The punishment to which a person is liable for an offence under section 17(2) of this Act shall be in addition to any punishment to which he may be liable for the offence first referred to in section 17(2).
7. The court by which a person is convicted of an offence under section 21A, 22(4), 23(1), 24(4) or 24ZA(1) of this Act may make such order as it thinks fit as to the forfeiture or disposal of the air weapon or ammunition in respect of which the offence was committed.
8. The court by which a person is convicted of an offence under section 21A, 22(3) or (4), 23(1), 24(4) or 24ZA(1) may make such order as it thinks fit as to the forfeiture or disposal of any firearm or ammunition found in his possession.
9. The court by which a person is convicted of an offence under section 24(3) of this Act may make such order is it thinks fit as to the forfeiture or disposal of the shot gun or ammunition in respect of which the offence was committed.

Schedule 6 is shown as amended by the ABCPA 2014, s. 108(7) and (8), which came into force on 14 July 2014.

725

GENERAL DEFINITIONS

Meaning of 'Firearm'

B12.7   Firearms Act 1968, s. 57

(1) In this Act, the expression 'firearm' means a lethal barrelled weapon of any description from which any shot, bullet or other missile can be discharged, and includes—

    (a) any prohibited weapon, whether it is such a lethal weapon as aforesaid or not; and

    (b) any component part of such a lethal or prohibited weapon; and

    (c) any accessory to any such weapon designed or adapted to diminish the noise or flash caused by firing the weapon.

The meaning of 'prohibited weapon' is considered at **B12.55** *et seq.*

B12.8 **Lethal Barrelled Weapon** There is no statutory definition of a 'lethal barrelled weapon'. In *Grace v DPP* (1989) 153 JP 491 the Divisional Court held that the prosecution must prove the following in order to satisfy the definition:

(a) whether the weapon was one from which any shot, bullet or other missile could be discharged or whether it could be adapted so as to be made capable of discharging such a missile, and

(b) if so satisfied, whether it was a lethal barrelled weapon.

B12.9 **Item which Could Discharge a Missile** As to the first question, *Freeman* [1970] 2 All ER 413 and *Cafferata v Wilson* [1936] 3 All ER 149 were disapproved in *Bewley* [2013] 1 All ER 1 (in which *Kelly v MacKinnon* 1983 SLT 9 was cited and discussed). There is no warrant for including within the definition in the FA 1968, s. 57(1), an item which could discharge a missile only in combination with other tools extraneous to that item. The opening words of s. 57(1) refer to the capacity of a particular item and not its capacity in combination with other pieces of equipment. Thus, an old and damaged starting pistol with a partially drilled barrel could not be regarded as a 'prohibited weapon' (see **B12.55**), and thus a 'firearm' within s. 57, merely because it could be made to discharge a pellet with the aid of a vice or clamp, a mallet and metal punch. *Bewley* was applied in *Williamson* [2012] EWCA Crim 2114.

For a discussion of the circumstances in which an item, or its parts, constitute 'component parts' within the definition of 'firearm' in s. 57, see **B12.14**.

It is submitted that the word 'discharged' may mean more than that a missile is merely capable of *passing* down a barrel (*Rogers* [2011] EWCA Crim 1459). Thus, there may be a distinction to be drawn between a barrelled weapon from which, *as a working item,* 'any shot, bullet or other missile can be *discharged*' and an incomplete defective item (issues of conversion aside) from which no such missile can be 'discharged' (e.g., because the barrel, albeit unobstructed, is incapable of withstanding pressure from the propelling gas) (cf. *Clarke* [1986] 1 All ER 846: see **B12.67**).

B12.10 **Lethality** Lord Parker CJ said in *Moore v Gooderham* [1960] 3 All ER 575 that if the article 'is capable of causing more than trifling and trivial injury when misused, then it is a weapon capable of causing injury from which death may result'. Earlier in his judgment his lordship had said that 'one is not considering whether a firearm is designed or intended to cause injury from which death results, *but rather whether it is a weapon which, however misused, may cause injury from which death may result*' (emphasis added). In *Thorpe* (1987) 85 Cr App R 107 — a case where the jury had asked the question 'In a definition of "lethal" how remote can the chance of the lethality be on the basis that anything can be lethal?' — the Court of Appeal held that it was clear that Lord Parker CJ was saying that 'a lethal weapon was one which when misused was capable of causing injury from which death might result' (per Kenneth Jones J).

The aforementioned test can create difficulties in practice (see, for example, *Street v DPP* [2004] EWHC 86 (Admin)). Despite the breadth of the test, expert evidence is often adduced where the lethality of the item in question is in issue. The reference in *Moore v Gooderham* to 'more than trifling or trivial injury' has been interpreted by experts (not by the courts) as meaning 'with a force sufficient to puncture the skin' (Home Affairs Committee, 2nd Report, 1999–2000, para. 25; and Minutes of Evidence). According to that Report, the Home Office and the (now disbanded) Forensic Science Service considered that the lowest level of muzzle energy capable of inflicting a penetrating wound is one foot-pound (or about 1.35 joules): 'below these power levels, weapons are "incapable of penetrating even vulnerable parts of the body, such as the eye"'. The Report added that analysis by the Forensic Science Agency for Northern Ireland had indicated that a more reasonable assessment of the minimum muzzle energy required to inflict a penetrating wound lies between 2.2 and 3.0 foot-pounds (3 to 4 joules) (para. 26). By contrast, a subgroup to the Firearms Consultative Committee recommended that 'a statutory threshold of one joule muzzle energy should be embodied in primary legislation as the level at which an item becomes a "firearm" for legal purposes' (11th Report, 2002, para. 24; and see, to the same effect, the Home Office *Guide on Firearms Licensing Law* (2013), para. 2.4).

It is submitted that the complexities associated with the current definition of 'lethal barrelled' is exemplified by the position in relation to airsoft BB guns and the need to differentiate between an 'air weapon', a 'realistic imitation firearm' (or an unrealistic firearm), a 'lethal barrelled weapon', and a 'prohibited weapon'. In this regard, paras. 2.5 and 2.6 of the 2013 Home Office Guide should be noted (and, in particular, the concluding words of para. 2.6):

> ...we think it is safe to conclude that fully automatic airsoft guns operating at 1.3 joules or less and single shot (or semi automatic) airsoft guns operating at 2.5 joules or less would not engage the lethality threshold crossing over into stricter controls under the Firearms Act. This would mean that airsoft firearms that are also realistic imitation firearms operating at or below these thresholds would, nonetheless, not be required to be sold by a Registered Firearms Dealer but that the other control provisions provided by the Violent Crime Reduction Act would apply.

B12.11 Whether a device is a 'lethal barrelled weapon' is a question of fact (see *Grace v DPP* (1989) 153 JP 491; and consider *Street v DPP* [2004] EWHC 86 (Admin)). The correct approach is for a judge to determine whether the device is *capable* of amounting to a firearm and then to leave to the jury the question of whether it actually is a lethal weapon (*Singh* [1989] Crim LR 724; see also *Paul* [1998] EWCA Crim 2283). In *Singh*, an army signalling kit consisting of flares and a hand-held device was held to be capable of amounting to a 'firearm' and the flares, being explosives, were held to be capable of amounting to 'ammunition'. The judge had correctly left the jury to decide, on conflicting expert evidence, whether the device was a 'lethal barrelled weapon'. It is submitted that the word 'weapon' within the definition of a 'firearm' in s. 57, ought not to be overlooked (see **B12.12**).

The following devices were found, on the facts of the particular case, to be 'lethal barrelled' weapons: (a) a Ruger.357 revolver capable of killing at short range (*Paul* [1998] EWCA Crim 2283); (b) an airgun which was capable of causing injury from which death might result if it was misused (*Moore v Gooderham* [1960] 3 All ER 575); (c) an air pellet revolver capable of causing injury from which death could result if misused (*Thorpe* [1987] 2 All ER 108, applying *Read v Donovan* [1947] KB 326 and *Moore v Gooderham*); and (d) two air rifles suitable for shooting small vermin, and two air rifles suitable for target practice, which 'could cause injury from which death might result if fired at point blank range at a vulnerable part of the body' (*Castle v DPP* [1998] EWHC Admin 309). In *Castle v DPP*, the magistrates were entitled to draw the inference that the guns were lethal barrelled weapons, having regard to assertions made by a salesman that the guns were working and for what purpose they would be suitable.

B12.12 **Meaning of Weapon for Purposes of the FA 1968, s. 57(1)** The word 'weapon' is not defined by the FA 1968 but, unlike the Prevention of Crime Act 1953 (which controls the use of 'any article made or adapted for use for causing injury to a person, [etc.]', the items brought under the control of the Firearms Acts encompass a wide range of uses and purposes in respect of 'persons', animals and property. Accordingly, it is submitted that the word 'weapon' in s. 57 may have relevance when a court is determining whether the item in question is a 'firearm' within the meaning of that section. The point is illustrated, but not answered, by *Formosa* [1991] 2 QB 1 (which held that *Titus* [1971] Crim LR 279 was correctly decided (ammonia in a water pistol was not within the FA 1968, s. 5(1)(b)). In *Formosa*, a Fairy Liquid washing-up bottle containing 400 millilitres of hydrochloric acid was held not to be a 'prohibited weapon' within the meaning of the FA 1968, s. 5(1)(b), because the bottle was not *altered* by being filled with the acid and, therefore, it was not a weapon 'designed or adapted' for the discharge of any noxious liquid within the meaning of the section. In the words of Lloyd LJ, a contrary construction 'would mean that a householder who filled a milk bottle with acid in order to destroy a wasps' nest would be in possession of a weapon adapted for the discharge of a noxious liquid and would therefore be guilty of the offence of possessing a prohibited weapon; until, of course, he had used the acid for the purpose in question when the milk bottle would revert to its pristine innocence. That could not be right.' In his commentary to *Formosa* at [1990] Crim LR 868, Professor John Smith QC said 'The answer surely is that the articles are not "weapons"...It would be hazardous to attempt an off-the-cuff definition of "weapon" but perhaps it requires something designed or adapted for use against the person of another.' Professor Smith might have gone on to include weapons for use against animals. On that analysis, neither a signalling parachute flare nor a 'firework' that emits a potentially lethal projectile would fall within s. 57 and, if so, cases such as *Singh* [1989] Crim LR 724 (see **B12.11**) should be considered in that light. However, some provisions of the firearms legislation describe as firearms apparatuses that are clearly not weapons (e.g., 'signalling apparatus' for ships and aircraft (FA 1968, s. 13), and starting pistols (F(A)A 1997, s. 5)). In any event, it may be an oversimplification to construe 'weapon' merely in terms of whether the article in question is designed, or intended, to be used offensively or defensively (consider *Bryson v Gamage* [1907] 2 KB 630, a case under the Pistols Act 1903, in which Darling J said the fact-finder 'should carefully inform his mind as to what a weapon is, what a weapon is meant for in the way of offence or defence').

B12.13 **Prohibited Weapon as Firearm (whether Lethal Barrelled or Not)**   The effect of the FA 1968, s. 57(1)(a), is that any prohibited weapon is a 'firearm' whether it is a 'lethal barrelled weapon' or not. In *Weaver* [2007] EWCA Crim 3485 the Court of Appeal held that an electronic stun gun, resembling a torch, which is a 'prohibited weapon' within the meaning of s. 5(1)(b) (see **B12.56**), must necessarily be a firearm within the meaning of s. 57(1) of the Act, even though it may not be a 'lethal barrelled weapon' or capable of firing a missile. This wider meaning is clear from s. 57(1)(a)). All prohibited weapons are firearms but not all firearms are prohibited weapons. The court added that what D actually possessed was merely a non-lethal self-defence weapon, but if convicted on the charge of possessing a disguised firearm contrary to s. 5(1A)(a), D would be subject to the minimum sentences applicable to firearms offences.

B12.14 **Any Component Part**   The expression 'component part' is not defined in the FA 1968, but the CPS Charging Standards state that the expression may include '(i) the barrel, chamber, cylinder, (ii) frame, body or receiver, (iii) breech, block, bolt or other mechanism for containing the charge at the rear of the chamber, (iv) any other part of the firearm upon which the pressure caused by firing the weapon impinges directly. Magazines, sights and furniture are not considered component parts.' This mirrors what is said at para. 13.74 of the Home Office's *Guide on Firearms Licensing Law* (2013). However, the actual meaning of 'component part', for the purposes of the Firearms Acts, is a matter for the courts.

In *Secretary of State for the Home Department, ex parte Impower Ltd* [1999] EWHC 309 (Admin), Jowitt J said that the words in s. 57(1)(b) are 'ordinary English words'. Nonetheless, the courts have drawn a distinction between parts, without which a 'lethal barrelled weapon' or 'prohibited weapon' could not function, and (for example) general purpose screws or washers. Jowitt J said:

For myself, I would suggest as a rough working aid (stressing what I say is not a substitute for the words of the statute) that a component part of a firearm is likely to be a part used to make the firearm operate as it is designed or modified to operate. Further, a component part may be an assembly of individual parts which make up a composite assembly used to make the firearm operate, as it is designed or modified to operate. I add though, that the part which is separated from other parts and in that separate form would have other uses, would not in that separate state be likely to be a component part. There obviously is a margin of appreciation, because there may be cases in which it is not easy to say whether something is or is not a component part for a gun. It is not suggested by either side that ordinary screws, washers and the like should be regarded as component parts.

Similarly, in *Ashton* [2007] EWCA Crim 234, the Courts-Martial Appeal Court held that a Judge Advocate had directed himself 'impeccably' when he distinguished between a general screw or washer (which would not be a 'component part') and a part 'that if it were removed, a General Purpose Machine Gun could not function without it' (and thus a 'component part' within the definition of 'firearm' within s. 57).

Three situations need to be considered when determining whether a part is a 'component part'.   **B12.15**

(i) Item is neither a 'lethal barrelled weapon' nor a 'prohibited weapon'. In *Bewley* [2013] 1 All ER 1, the Court of Appeal held that, if the item in question is not a 'lethal-barrelled weapon of any description from which any shot, bullet or other missile can be discharged' (FA 1968, s. 57(1)), then neither the item nor any part of it constitutes a 'component part of such a lethal weapon' (s. 57(1)(b)). The Court remarked that any other construction 'would ignore the use of the word "such". If the starting pistol does not fall within the definition of firearm within s 57(1), no part of it could do so' (per Moses LJ at [34]). Presumably, the same reasoning applies when determining whether a part of a 'prohibited weapon' falls within s. 57(1).

(ii) A part separated from the weapon which is otherwise capable of being 'lethal barrelled' or 'prohibited'. In *Ashton* (a decision which was neither cited nor referred to in skeleton arguments in *Bewley*), the Courts-Martial Appeal Court held that a gas plug, separated from a deactivated weapon, was a 'component part' that fell within the definition of 'firearm' within s. 57(1):

> So long as a de-activated weapon remains in its complete state, there is therefore a justification in permitting it to be possessed or indeed traded on the open market. But it is clear from the exception that it is not intended to apply to any component part of such a weapon and that must be for the good public policy reason that once a weapon, de-activated or not, is disassembled then the parts which are then made available are capable of being re-assembled into a working weapon. The mischief to which section 57 in particular is directed therefore exists whether or not the origin of the component part is a working or a de-activated weapon. (per Latham LJ at [7].)

It is respectfully submitted that, whereas the analysis in *Bewley* closely follows the language of s. 57(1) (and see *Bewley* at [36]), a wider reach of s. 57(1)(b) that is founded on public policy reasons, as discussed in *Ashton*, arguably requires the attention of the legislature.

(iii) The part could not function as a 'component part' in any working firearm. In *Matthews* [2013] EWCA Crim 120, the item in question was a home-made submachine gun which the judge ruled was not a firearm because of the amount of work which needed to be done to it before the item would be capable of discharging bullets. The Court of Appeal held that the judge erred in further ruling that the item included 'component parts' of a lethal barrelled weapon within the meaning of s. 57(1)(b), the error being conceded by the prosecution. The evidence showed that the components were not merely home-made but could not function as 'component parts' in any working firearm. Notwithstanding that neither *Bewley* nor *Ashton* were cited in *Matthews*, it is submitted that the judgment of the Court is correct. Given that the item was not a 'lethal barrelled weapon', it follows (applying *Bewley*) that its parts were not 'component parts' within

the meaning of s. 57. Moreover, *Ashton* (if correctly decided) is distinguishable from *Matthews* on its facts.

B12.16   **Accessory Designed or Adapted to Diminish Noise or Flash**   Whether a sound moderator ('silencer' or 'sound suppressor') is an accessory to a firearm within the meaning of the FA 1968, s. 57(1)(c) (see **B12.7**), is a question of fact (*Buckfield* [1998] EWCA Crim 1322). The question is to be answered by considering whether the device (a) can be used with the accused's firearm, and (b) whether the accused has the device for that purpose. The Court said:

> Where the silencer has been manufactured for use on the particular firearm in the defendant's possession, no further evidence will be required to establish that the silencer is an accessory to that weapon and should be shown on a firearm certificate. Where the silencer, as here, was manufactured for a weapon other than that in the defendant's possession, then the prosecution, to obtain a conviction under section 1(1)(a) of the Act, will have to prove that the device can be used with the defendant's firearm and that the defendant has the device for that purpose. The fact that the silencer may have been designed for quite a different weapon, such as a shotgun, does not prevent it being an accessory to a firearm if it can be used as such.

Professor Sir John Smith QC criticised the reasoning in *Buckfield* ([1998] Crim LR 673) on the grounds that the material question is whether the moderator was 'made or adapted' for use with the firearm in question and not whether it 'can be used' with the weapon. Furthermore, the section says nothing about the purpose of the possessor of the firearm or accessory. Accordingly, if the *purpose* of the possessor is an issue that must be proved, then this would seem to import an element of *mens rea* in connection with offences under the Firearms Acts that would otherwise be offences of strict liability (e.g., FA 1968, ss. 1, 2 and 5). It is unlikely that the Court intended to imply the existence of such a mental element in respect of these offences. It is further submitted that a person who has possession only of a sound moderator or anti-flash device is not in possession of a firearm within s. 57, and therefore the opening words of s. 57(1)(c) should be construed as if they read '*with* any such weapon'. In those circumstances, a firearms certificate (see s. 1 and s. 1(3)) is not required for the device in question: see *Broome v Walter* [1989] Crim LR 724 where the Divisional Court held that, where something is an integral part of the firearm, then (albeit that it may increase the lethal qualities of the firearm), it does not require a separate reference in a certificate or a separate certificate. The court also held that there is a distinction between a component and an accessory. Normally 'an accessory' is something readily detachable from an article that is capable of its ordinary use with or without the accessory (see also *Hedges* [1997] EWCA Crim 958).

Meaning of 'Shot gun'

B12.17   'Shot gun' has the meaning assigned to it by the FA 1968, s. 1(3)(a) (see s. 57(4): and see **B12.34**).

Meaning of Air Weapon etc. and Gas Cartridge System

B12.18   Some barrelled air/gas weapons are capable of being firearms within the meaning of the FA 1968, s. 57(1) (see **B12.11**), and a number of offences apply to such weapons, e.g., offences under the FA 1968, ss. 16, 16A, 17(1), 17(2), 18(1) and 19.

Meaning of Imitation Firearm

B12.19   See **B12.24**.

De-activated Weapons

B12.20   Any firearm (including a prohibited weapon) which is de-activated in accordance with the FA 1968, s. 8, ceases to be a firearm. But the article can constitute an 'imitation firearm' in some circumstances, see **B12.24**.

Firearms (Amendment) Act 1988, s. 8

For the purposes of the principal Act and this Act it shall be presumed, unless the contrary is shown, that a firearm has been rendered incapable of discharging any shot, bullet or other missile, and has consequently ceased to be a firearm within the meaning of those Acts, if—

(a) it bears a mark which has been approved by the Secretary of State for denoting that fact and which has been made either by one of the two companies mentioned in section 58(1) of the principal Act or by such other person as may be approved by the Secretary of State for the purposes of this section; and

(b) that company or person has certified in writing that work has been carried out on the firearm in a manner approved by the Secretary of State for rendering it incapable of discharging any shot, bullet or other missile.

The companies mentioned in s. 58(1) are the Society of the Mystery of Gunmakers of the City of London (presumably a reference to the 'Worshipful Company of Gunmakers') and the Birmingham Proof House.

As to whether a 'component part' of a de-activated weapon falls within the definition of 'firearm' within the meaning of the FA 1968, s. 57(1), see **B12.14**.

Meaning of 'Ammunition'

The FA 1968, s. 57(2), provides a general definition of 'ammunition'.   **B12.21**

Firearms Act 1968, s. 57

(2) In this Act, the expression 'ammunition' means ammunition for any firearm and includes grenades, bombs and other like missiles, whether capable of use with a firearm or not, and also includes prohibited ammunition.

Section 58(3) provides that control over ammunition is in addition to, and not in derogation of, any enactment relating to the keeping and sale of explosives.

It is submitted that the Home Office's *Guide on Firearms Licensing Law* (2013), at para. 2.12, states correctly that:

> ...the definition of ammunition does not include ingredients and components of ammunition; it is only assembled ammunition that is controlled under the Act, not component parts. Empty cartridge cases, for example, are not 'ammunition'. There are two exceptions to this. The first is missiles for ammunition prohibited under section 5 of the 1968 Act, for example, expanding or armour-piercing bullets. Such missiles are themselves defined as 'ammunition' and are subject to control accordingly [see s. 5(1A)(g) at **B12.56**] ...The second is primers — section 35 of the Violent Crime Reduction Act 2006 introduced controls on the purchase and sale of a cap type primer designed for use in metallic ammunition.

Cap-type Primers

Section 35 of the VCRA 2006 creates summary offences in connection with cap-type prim-   **B12.22**
ers designed for use in metallic ammunition for a firearm. By s. 35(2), it is an offence for a person to sell to another either (a) a primer to which s. 35 applies, or (b) an empty cartridge case incorporating such a primer, unless that other person falls within s. 35(3). The eight categories of persons falling within s. 35(3) include (a) a registered firearms dealer; (b) a person who sells by way of any trade or business either primers or empty cartridge cases incorporating primers, or both; (c) the holder of a certificate authorising him to possess a firearm of a relevant kind; (d) the holder of a certificate authorising him to possess ammunition of a relevant kind.

Section 35(4) of the VCRA 2006 makes it an offence for a person to buy or to attempt to buy (a) a primer to which s. 35 applies, or (b) an empty cartridge case incorporating such a primer, unless he falls within s. 35(5). Although slightly different in phrasing, s. 35(5) covers the same persons as are covered by s. 35(3). Section 35 binds persons in the service of Her Majesty but such a person is expressly exempted from its restrictions if he is authorised as specified under s. 35(6). By s. 50(4) 'a person is in the service of Her Majesty if he is deemed to be in such service (or to be in the naval, military or air service of Her Majesty) for the purposes of and under section 54 of the 1968 Act (Crown application)'.

Appeals Against Conviction for a Firearms Offence

B12.23   As to the power of the Court of Appeal to substitute a firearms offence pursuant to the Criminal Appeal Act 1968, s. 3A, see *Lawrence* [2014] 1 WLR 106.

OFFENCES RELATING TO IMITATION FIREARMS

Introduction

B12.24   It is important to distinguish between (a) the general definition of an 'imitation firearm' within the meaning of the FA 1968, s. 57(4) (see **B12.25** *et seq.*), (b) those imitation firearms that have the appearance of being firearms which are subject to the FA 1968, s. 1, and which are readily convertible into such firearms (see **B12.28**) and (c) 'realistic imitation firearms' within the meaning of the VCRA 2006, s. 38 (see **B12.29**). The intensity of legislative control differs in each case.

Offences Applying to Imitation Firearms by virtue of the Wording of the Section

B12.25   Some offences, by their definition, apply to 'imitation firearms', see, e.g., the FA 1968, s. 17(1). In such cases, the expression 'imitation firearm' has the following definition, according to s. 57(4).

Firearms Act 1968, s. 57

(4)   ...'imitation firearm' means any thing which has the appearance of being a firearm (other than such a weapon as is mentioned in section 5(1)(b) of this Act) whether or not it is capable of discharging any shot, bullet or other missile.

Weapons mentioned in s. 5(1)(b) constitute one category of prohibited weapons, i.e. a weapon designed or adapted for the discharge of any noxious liquid, gas or other thing (see **B12.56**).

B12.26   **'Appearance of Being a Firearm'**   Whether an item is an 'imitation firearm' is a matter for the tribunal of fact to decide, taking an objective view (*K v DPP* [2006] EWHC 2183 (Admin)), and taking into account the views of witnesses who saw the thing (*Morris and King* (1984) 79 Cr App R 104). 'In this case, the justices, having seen the BB gun, were in our judgment quite entitled to hold that it was an imitation firearm' (*K v DPP*, per Gage LJ at [13]). In *K v DPP*, the Divisional Court appears to have accepted as being correct the submission of the respondent that once the tribunal of fact had found the thing to be an imitation firearm, its character cannot change depending on the knowledge and perception of the person against whom it is used; in that case, the victim knew that a BB gun was an imitation firearm but he also knew that it was capable of firing a pellet which could cause him injury. In *Morris and King*, the accused was in possession of two metal pipes bound together, giving the appearance of being a double-barrelled shot gun that could constitute an imitation firearm. In *Williams* [2006] EWCA Crim 1650, W told the victim that he had a gun; the issue was whether, in the judgement of the jury, a bottle in a plastic bag constituted an imitation firearm.

B12.27   **Device Must Be a 'Thing' that is Distinct from the Holder of It**   In *Bentham* [2005] 2 All ER 65, the House of Lords held that, for a person to be in possession of an imitation firearm (FA 1968, s. 17(2); see **B12.99**), the 'thing' must be separate or distinct from himself. Therefore, the conviction for possession of an imitation firearm, where the accused put his hand inside a zipped-up jacket forcing the material out so as to give the impression that he had a gun, was quashed. This case does not affect the decision in *Morris* (1984) 79 Cr App R 104, where the accused was clearly in possession of a thing. In *Williams* [2006] EWCA Crim 1650, it was held that, in the context of having an imitation firearm with intention to commit an indictable offence contrary to the FA 1968, s. 18 (see **B12.102**), the relevant question was whether the thing had the appearance of a firearm at the relevant time.

Offences Applying to Imitation Firearms by virtue of the Firearms Act 1982

The FA 1982 applies to any article which has the appearance of being a firearm to which the FA 1968, s. 1, applies (see **B12.34**) and is readily convertible into such a firearm (FA 1982, s. 1(1)). In *Bewley* [2013] 1 All ER 1, the Court of Appeal held that no conclusion can be reached as to whether an imitation firearm is or was readily convertible without proper consideration of the FA 1982, s. 1(6), and, if it was raised, the defence in s. 1(5). **B12.28**

This definition of 'imitation firearm' applies to all offences which are concerned with a firearm to which the FA 1968, s. 1, applies (FA 1982, s. 1(2)), except ss. 4(3) and (4), 16 to 20 and 47 of the FA 1968 (FA 1982, s. 2(2)(a) and (b) and (3)). Air weapons are included whether or not they are specially dangerous (FA 1968, s. 1(4)(a)). The definition does not apply to component parts and accessories (s. 1(4)(b)).

Firearms Act 1982, ss. 1 and 2

1.—(1) This Act applies to an imitation firearm if—
   (a) it has the appearance of being a firearm to which section 1 of the 1968 Act (firearms requiring a firearm certificate) applies; and
   (b) it is so constructed or adapted as to be readily convertible into a firearm to which that section applies.
(2) Subject to section 2(2) of this Act and the following provisions of this section, the 1968 Act shall apply in relation to an imitation firearm to which this Act applies as it applies in relation to a firearm to which section 1 of that Act applies.
(3) Subject to the modifications in subsection (4) below, any expression given a meaning for the purposes of the 1968 Act has the same meaning in this Act.
(4) For the purposes of this section and the 1968 Act, as it applies by virtue of this section—
   (a) the definition of air weapon in section 1(3)(b) of that Act (air weapons excepted from requirement of firearm certificate) shall have effect without the exclusion of any type declared by rules made by the Secretary of State under section 53 of that Act to be specially dangerous; and
   (b) the definition of firearm in section 57(1) of that Act shall have effect without paragraphs (b) and (c) of that subsection (component parts and accessories).
   ...
(6) For the purposes of this section an imitation firearm shall be regarded as readily convertible into a firearm to which section 1 of the 1968 Act applies if—
   (a) it can be so converted without any special skill on the part of the person converting it in the construction or adaptation of firearms of any description; and
   (b) the work involved in converting it does not require equipment or tools other than such as are in common use by persons carrying out works of construction and maintenance in their own homes.
   ...
2.—(2) The following provisions of the 1968 Act do not apply by virtue of this Act to an imitation firearm to which this Act applies, that is to say—
   (a) section 4(3) and (4)...; and
   (b) the provisions of that Act which relate to, or to the enforcement of control over, the manner in which a firearm is used or the circumstances in which it is carried;
   but without prejudice, in the case of the provisions mentioned in paragraph (b) above, to the application to such an imitation firearm of such of those provisions as apply to imitation firearms apart from this Act.
(3) The provisions referred to in subsection (2)(b) are sections 16 to 20 and section 47.

If the FA 1982 does apply, a special defence is introduced by s. 1(5):

> In any proceedings brought by virtue of this section for an offence under the 1968 Act involving an imitation firearm to which this Act applies, it shall be a defence for the accused to show that he did not know and had no reason to suspect that the imitation firearm was so constructed or adapted as to be readily convertible into a firearm to which section 1 of that Act applies.

In *Williams* [2013] 2 All ER 787, the Court of Appeal held that the accused shoulders the legal burden of proving the special defence introduced by the FA 1982, s. 1(5), which, in the judgment of the Court, was justified and proportionate, given that the defence was made available as an exception or modification to the strict liability approach adopted in respect of the FA 1968, ss. 1 and 5. See also the commentary to *Williams* at [2013] Crim LR 984 and **F3.35**.

Offences Concerning 'Realistic Imitation Firearms'

B12.29 The VCRA 2006 introduced restrictions, and created offences as well as defences (rather than exceptions) in relation to 'realistic imitation firearms' (defined by s. 38). In essence, these are imitations that are visually indistinguishable from 'real firearms' (defined by s. 38(7)), typically a 'modern firearm' (i.e. other than one the appearance of which would tend to identify it as having a design and mechanism of a sort first dating from before the year 1870: s. 38(8)). The VCRA 2006 does not define the term 'imitation firearm', but the Explanatory Notes to that Act state (para. 241) that, for the purposes of s. 38, the relevant definition is the one set out in the FA 1968, s. 57(4). Many realistic imitation firearms are air-powered BB guns (single shot, semi-automatic, and fully automatic fire), which are used in airsoft sports including 'skirmishing'. Such imitations take many forms, including rifles, pistols and submachine guns. An imitation firearm is to be regarded as *'unrealistic* for a real firearm' by virtue of its size and/or colour specified in the Violent Crime Reduction Act 2006 (Realistic Imitation Firearms) Regulations 2007 (SI 2007 No. 2606) (see **B12.31**). Nevertheless, an unrealistic imitation firearm may fall within s. 57(4) and both realistic and unrealistic imitations that discharge missiles may, depending on their specifications, be 'lethal barrelled' (see **B12.10**) or even a 'prohibited weapon' (see **B12.56**; and see the Home Office *Guide on Firearms Licensing Law* (2013), paras. 2.21 to 2.37).

A person commits a summary offence contrary to s. 36(1) of the VCRA 2006 if he (a) manufactures a realistic imitation firearm; or (b) modifies an imitation firearm so that it becomes a realistic imitation firearm; or (c) sells a realistic imitation firearm; or (d) brings a realistic imitation firearm into Great Britain or causes one to be brought into Great Britain. It is submitted that the 3D printing of a 'realistic imitation firearm' would be caught by s. 36(1)(a).

Violent Crime Reduction Act 2006, s. 38

(1) In sections 36 and 37 'realistic imitation firearm' means an imitation firearm which—
    (a) has an appearance that is so realistic as to make it indistinguishable, for all practical purposes, from a real firearm; and
    (b) is neither a de-activated firearm nor itself an antique.
(2) For the purposes of this section, an imitation firearm is not (except by virtue of subsection (3)(b)) to be regarded as distinguishable from a real firearm for any practical purpose if it could be so distinguished only—
    (a) by an expert;
    (b) on a close examination; or
    (c) as a result of an attempt to load or to fire it.
(3) In determining for the purposes of this section whether an imitation firearm is distinguishable from a real firearm—
    (a) the matters that must be taken into account include any differences between the size, shape and principal colour of the imitation firearm and the size, shape and colour in which the real firearm is manufactured; and

(b) the imitation is to be regarded as distinguishable if its size, shape or principal colour is unrealistic for a real firearm.

Specific 'defences' (rather than exemptions) to charges under s. 36 are set out in s. 37, namely, that it is for the accused to show that his conduct was for the purpose only of making the imitation firearm in question available for one or more of the purposes specified in s. 37 (notably, for the purposes of a museum or gallery, theatrical performances, the production of films; the production of television programmes; certain historical re-enactments; and functions of persons in HM services). Further purposes have been added by the Violent Crime Reduction Act 2006 (Realistic Imitation Firearms) Regulations 2007 (SI 2007 No. 2606), regs. 3 and 4 (whether as a defence to proceedings under s. 36 or under sch. 2, para. 4 to that instrument), namely, (a) the organisation and holding of 'permitted activities' (i.e. 'the acting out of military or law enforcement scenarios for the purposes of recreation': reg. 2) for which public liability insurance is held in relation to liabilities to third parties arising from or in connection with the organisation and holding of those activities; and (b) the purposes of display at a permitted event. These defences are intended to give some protection to those who hold airsoft 'skirmishing' activities, or fairs at which airsoft imitations are on display: see the Home Office *Guide on Firearms Licensing Law* (2013), paras.2.33 to 2.35. The defences available under s. 37(1) and (3) of the VCRA 2006 impose an evidential burden on the accused: see s. 37(4).   **B12.30**

Offences: Not Conforming to Specifications for Realistic Imitation Firearms

Under the VCRA 2006, s. 39(1), the Secretary of State may by regulations make provision requiring imitation firearms to conform to specifications which are (a) set out in regulations; or (b) approved by such persons and in such manner as may be so set out. Although s. 39 is silent on the point, the Explanatory Notes to the Act assert (at para. 246) that the definition of 'imitation firearm' for the purpose of s. 39 is the same as that for s. 38.   **B12.31**

The Violent Crime Reduction Act 2006 (Realistic Imitation Firearms) Regulations 2007 make provision specifying sizes and colours which are to be regarded as *unrealistic* for a real firearm. The size of an imitation firearm is to be regarded as unrealistic for a real firearm only if the imitation firearm has dimensions that are less than a height of 38 millimetres and a length of 70 millimetres (reg. 6). The colour is to be regarded as unrealistic for a real firearm only if it is bright red, bright orange, bright yellow, bright green, bright pink, bright purple or bright blue (reg. 7). The Violent Crime Reduction Act 2006 (Specification for Imitation Firearms) Regulations 2011 (SI 2011 No. 1754), in force from 11 August 2011, set out specifications for 'blank-firing imitation firearms' (regs. 3 and 4) and 'blank firing imitation revolvers' (regs. 5 and 6).

By virtue of s. 39(2), a person commits a summary offence if '(a) he manufactures an imitation firearm which does not conform to the specifications required of it by regulations under that section; (b) he modifies an imitation firearm so that it ceases to conform to the specifications so required of it; (c) he modifies a firearm to create an imitation firearm that does not conform to the specifications so required of it; or (d) he brings an imitation firearm which does not conform to the specifications so required of it into Great Britain or causes such an imitation firearm to be brought into Great Britain'. Regulation 7 of SI 2011 No. 1754 provides that the offence in s. 39(2)(d) of the 2006 Act does not apply where the purpose involved was to make the imitation firearm available for one of the purposes set out in s. 37(2) (museum or gallery, theatre, film or TV production, re-enactment or HM services).

Supplying Imitation Firearms to Persons under 18

See **B12.122**.   **B12.32**

POSSESSING ETC. FIREARM OR AMMUNITION WITHOUT FIREARM CERTIFICATE

The Offence: Possessing, Purchasing or Acquiring a s. 1 Firearm

B12.33

Firearms Act 1968, s. 1

(1) Subject to any exemption under this Act, it is an offence for a person—

   (a) to have in his possession, or to purchase or acquire, a firearm to which this section applies without holding a firearm certificate in force at the time, or otherwise than as authorised by such a certificate;

   (b) to have in his possession, or to purchase or acquire, any ammunition to which this section applies without holding a firearm certificate in force at the time, or otherwise than as authorised by such a certificate, or in quantities in excess of those so authorised.

It is also an offence for a person to fail to comply with a condition subject to which a firearm certificate is held by him.

B12.34   ### Firearms to which s. 1 Applies

Firearms Act 1968, s. 1

(3) This section applies to every firearm except—

   (a) a shot gun within the meaning of this Act, that is to say a smooth-bore gun (not being an air gun) which—

     (i) has a barrel not less than 24 inches in length and does not have any barrel with a bore exceeding 2 inches in diameter;

     (ii) either has no magazine or has a non-detachable magazine incapable of holding more than two cartridges; and

     (iii) is not a revolver gun; and

   (b) an air weapon (that is to say, an air rifle, air gun or air pistol which does not fall within section 5(1) and which is not of a type declared by rules made by the Secretary of State under section 53 of this Act to be specially dangerous).

(3A) A gun which has been adapted to have such a magazine as is mentioned in subsection (3)(a)(ii) above shall not be regarded as falling within that provision unless the magazine bears a mark approved by the Secretary of State for denoting that fact and that mark has been made, and the adaptation has been certified in writing as having been carried out in a manner approved by him, either by one of the two companies mentioned in section 58(1) of this Act or by such other person as may be approved by him for that purpose.

The 'two companies' referred to in s. 58(1) are the proof houses identified at **B12.20**.

The length of the barrel of a firearm shall be measured from the muzzle to the point at which the charge is exploded on firing (s. 57(6)(a)). 'Revolver', in relation to a smoothbore gun, means a gun containing a series of chambers, which revolve when the gun is fired (s. 57(2B)).

For exemptions relating to air weapons (i.e. s. 1(3)(b)), see **B12.36**.

Extension to Imitation Firearms Having the Appearance of s. 1 Firearms

B12.35   By s. 1 of the FA 1982, that Act applies to the FA 1968, s. 1, thus extending it to imitation firearms, as defined in the FA 1982 (see **B12.25**).

Exemptions: Shot Guns and Air Weapons that are Not Specially Dangerous

B12.36   Section 1 of the FA 1968 applies to all firearms except shot guns and certain air weapons (the meaning of which is considered at **B12.17** and **B12.34**). Sawn-off shot guns are firearms to which s. 1 applies.

Section 1(3)(b) exempts 'air weapons' (air rifle, air gun or air pistol) from the certification requirements of s. 1 except in three cases:

(a) Where the air device has been declared by the Secretary of State to be 'specially dangerous' under the Firearms (Dangerous Air Weapons) Rules 1969 (SI 1969 No. 47). Air pistols that develop kinetic energy of more than 6 ft/lb, and other air guns/rifles that develop kinetic energy of more than 12 ft/lb, are declared to be 'specially dangerous' (see r. 2(1)(a)). It is submitted that, although a 'specially dangerous' weapon is likely to be 'lethal barrelled' (within the meaning of s. 57(1)), the element of lethality must also be established. Note that an air weapon is not 'specially dangerous' if it falls only within r. 2(1)(a) but is designed for use only when submerged in water (see r. 2(2), disapplying r. 3).

(b) Where the air weapon is disguised as another object (SI 1969 No. 47, r. 2(1)(b)): and note s. 5(1A)(a) (see **B12.56**).

(c) Where the air weapon is a 'prohibited weapon' (i.e. it falls within s. 5(1): see **B12.56**). Any 'air rifle, air gun or air pistol which uses, or is designed or adapted for use with, a self-contained gas cartridge system' is a 'prohibited weapon' (s. 5(1)(af): see **B12.66**). Note that a 'prohibited weapon' is a firearm (whether lethal barrelled or not) within the meaning of s. 57(1).

The exemption in s. 1(3)(b) was strictly construed by the Court of Appeal in *Thorpe* [1987] 2 All ER 108, but the FA(A)A 1997, s. 48, provides that the words 'an air rifle, airgun or air pistol' as they appear both in s. 1(3)(b), and in the Firearms (Dangerous Air Weapons) Rules 1969, include 'a rifle, pistol or gun powered by compressed carbon dioxide'. Firearms which use gases other than carbon dioxide or air would not be exempt from s. 1.

The legislation does not define the expression 'self-contained gas cartridge system' but the measure is directed against gas cartridges that contain a projectile. Home Office Circular 01/2004 makes it clear that 'weapons that use a $CO2$ bulb system are not affected because $CO2$ bulbs do not contain a projectile and are not therefore self-contained' (see also **B12.56**).

Note that the effect of r. 2(2) is to exclude an air powered underwater harpoon (unless it comes within r. 2(1)(b)).

Given that the expression 'firearm' in s. 57(1) includes the components of, and accessories to, lethal barrelled weapons, it follows that the components of, and accessories to, shot guns (other than those with a shortened barrel) and air weapons (other than those declared to be specially dangerous) are also not included in the phrase 'firearms to which s. 1 of the FA 1968 applies'.

By virtue of the F(A)A 1988, s. 7(2), the conversion of a weapon into a shot gun or air weapon does not affect its classification as a firearm to which s. 1 applies.

Firearms (Amendment) Act 1988, s. 7

(2) Any weapon which—
    (a) has at any time since the coming into force of section 2 above been a weapon to which section 1 of the principal Act applies; or
    (b) would at any previous time have been such a weapon if those sections had then been in force,
shall if it has, or at any time has had, a rifled barrel less than 24 inches in length, be treated as a weapon to which section 1 of the principal Act applies notwithstanding anything done for the purpose of converting it into a shot gun or an air weapon.

(3) For the purposes of subsection (2) above there shall be disregarded the shortening of a barrel by a registered firearms dealer for the sole purpose of replacing part of it so as to produce a barrel not less than 24 inches in length.

Ammunition to which the Firearms Act 1968, s. 1, Applies   Section 1 applies to all ammunition except that excluded by s. 1(4).   **B12.37**

Firearms Act 1968, s. 1

(4) This section applies to any ammunition for a firearm, except the following articles, namely—
    (a) cartridges containing five or more shot, none of which exceeds 0.36 inch in diameter;
    (b) ammunition for an airgun, air rifle or air pistol; and

(c) blank cartridges not more than one inch in diameter measures immediately in front of the rim or cannelure of the base of the cartridge.

Primed cartridges (ones without gunpowder) are not excluded under s. 1(4)(c) because such a cartridge is capable of producing an explosive effect and it is therefore ammunition (*Stubbings* [1990] Crim LR 811, and see *Burfitt v A & E Kille* [1939] 2 KB 743).

B12.38   Aggravated Offence: Shortened Shot Guns or Converted Firearms   The aggravated form of the offence (shortened shot guns and converted firearms) is to be found in the FA 1968, s. 4(4):

Firearms Act 1968, s. 4

(4) A person who commits an offence under section 1 of this Act by having in his possession, or pur-chasing or acquiring, a shot gun which has been shortened contrary to subsection (1) [of section 4] or a firearm which has been converted as mentioned in subsection (3) [of section 4] (whether by a registered firearms dealer or not), without holding a firearm certificate authorising him to have it in his possession, or to purchase or acquire it, shall be treated for the purposes of provisions of this Act relating to the punishment of offences as committing that offence in an aggravated form.

For the offence, contrary to s. 4(1), of shortening the barrel of a shot gun to a length less than 24 inches, see **B12.123**.

Indictment (for Offence under the Firearms Act 1968, s. 1(1)(a))

B12.39
Statement of Offence

Possessing a firearm without holding a current firearm certificate contrary to section 1(1)(a) of the Firearms Act 1968.

Particulars of Offence

A on or about the……...day of………was in possession of [or: purchased (or acquired)] a firearm to which section 1 of the Firearms Act 1968 applies, namely a…, without holding a firearm certificate in force at that time.

As to procedure and sentence, see the FA 1968, ss. 51 and 52, at **B12.3** and **B12.4**, and sch. 6 at **B12.5**. As to those firearms and ammunition to which the FA 1968, s. 1, applies, see **B12.36** and **B12.37**.

Firearm Certificate

B12.40   A person does not commit an offence contrary to the FA 1968, s. 1, if he has a firearm certificate (as defined by s. 57(4)) granted by a chief officer of police under s. 26A of the FA 1968. A fire-arm certificate is a public document. In *Paul* [1999] Crim LR 79, the Court of Appeal rejected the possibility of allowing the jury to approach the words in a firearm certificate as those of the ordinary English language (as in *Brutus v Cozens* [1973] AC 854):

If [a firearm certificate] is to fulfil the clear statutory objective of providing a certain and effective system of control of particular firearms it is obvious and a matter of common sense that it should have a certain and consistent meaning. That can only be achieved by trial judges determining the meaning as a matter of law, leaving it to the jury in each case to determine…whether the physical attributes of the firearm in question bring it within that meaning.

In *Paul* the trial judge correctly drew on the definition of 'slaughtering instrument' in s. 57(4) when defining 'humane killer' (as those words appeared in the certificate) as meaning 'a firearm specially designed or adapted for instantaneous slaughter of animals'; it would be for the jury to decide whether they covered the revolver in question, a Ruger.357. What matters is not the intention of the possessor/transferor or transferee but the physical characteristics of the weapon.

Firearm certificates are issued in accordance with the provisions of the Firearms Acts 1968 to 1997 (but see also *Leatherdale v Surrey Police Headquarters* [1999] EWHC Admin 631). Conditions may be imposed by the grant of a certificate on the use of a firearm. Certain conditions are statutorily imposed, for example, that any rifle or muzzle-loading pistol that is not a prohibited weapon (see **B12.55** *et seq.*) may be used only for target shooting (F(A)A 1997, s. 44(1)). See the Home Office *Guide on Firearms Licensing Law* (2013).

It is an offence to fail to comply with the conditions of a certificate (s. 1(2)). For rules relating to procedure and sentence, see **B12.3** and **B12.4**. As to possession authorised in accordance with a European firearms pass or other documents for European purposes, see the FA 1968, ss. 32A to 32C.

Meaning of 'Acquire'

The FA 1968, s. 57(4), provides that 'acquire' means 'hire, accept as a gift or borrow': the word 'acquisition' is to be construed accordingly.

B12.41

Possession Generally

It is submitted that the *actus reus* of the offence under the FA 1968, s. 1(1) is that the firearm is physically in the custody or under the control of the defendant: consider *DPP v Brooks* [1974] AC 862, *Warner v Metropolitan Police Commissioner* [1969] 2 AC 256. In *Uddin* [2005] EWCA Crim 2653, the Court of Appeal held that the accused was not in possession of the firearm (contrary to the FA 1968, s. 16; see **B12.88**) because, although he appeared to have intended to purchase the firearm, he never had his hands on the bag or the firearm within it. In different circumstances, the accused might have been considered to have acquired control of the firearm had the purchase gone through, even though he did not yet physically possess it. In *Prosecution Appeal; T* [2011] EWCA Crim 1646 the Court of Appeal held that, on the agreed facts of the case, the judge had been correct to hold that the momentary handling of a firearm by the accused, followed by his immediate rejection of it, did not constitute possession of it within the meaning of the FA 1968, s. 5(1). Possession is not confined to 'physical possession' (*North* [2001] EWCA Crim 544). The ability to demand that the property in question be removed (or the ability to remove it oneself) is no more than evidence of knowledge and acquiescence: it is not to be equated with actual control (consider *Kousar* [2009] 2 Cr App R 88). Custody and control of a firearm can 'reside' in different people. In *Sullivan v Earl of Caithness* [1976] QB 966, the Divisional Court held that an owner of firearms is in possession of them even if they are kept in another's custody. In *Woodage v Moss* [1974] 1 All ER 584, the accused was held to be in possession of a firearm when he was handed it by an unknown person to deliver it to a dealer as a surrendered weapon. Similarly, a person does not have to be present in the place where the firearm is kept in order to be in possession of it (*Hall v Cotton* [1987] QB 504).

B12.42

Whether a person is in possession of a firearm is a question of fact (*Hall v Cotton*). It is important to note the distinction in the FA 1968 between being in 'possession' of a firearm and 'having a firearm with him'. This is a consistent distinction, so that where the conduct element of the offence is merely the fact of possession, that fact can be proved in the sense indicated in *Sullivan v Earl of Caithness* and it does not require the Crown to go further and to show that the accused had the firearm with him at the time of his committing or being arrested for the offence in question (*North*). The distinction is reinforced (it is submitted) by the observations of the Court of Appeal in *Veira* [2013] EWCA Crim 1823 at [15].

Possession and *Mens Rea*

The offences contrary to the FA 1968, ss. 1, 3, 5 and 19 (see **B12.33**, **B12.70** and **B12.105**), are strict liability offences (*Deyemi* [2008] 1 Cr App R 345, and *Warner v Metropolitan Police Commissioner* [1969] 2 AC 256: see **B19.24**). The offences should not be described as ones of 'absolute' liability (*Gregory* [2011] EWCA Crim 1712; see the commentary to *Deyemi* [2008] Crim LR 327, and consider *Zahid* [2010] EWCA Crim 2158, noting *Williams* [2013] 2 All ER 787).

B12.43

For the purpose of s. 1, the accused need know only that he is in possession of something which is, in fact, a firearm (or ammunition, as the case may be: see *Amos* [1999] EWCA Crim

1826). See also *Pommell* [1995] 2 Cr App R 607. The accused need not know that the thing in question was a firearm (*Hussain* [1981] 2 All ER 287, followed in *Vann* [1996] Crim LR 52). Accordingly, no *mens rea* is required except insofar as it is necessary to establish that the accused was in possession of the article (or, had it 'with him', as the case may be) (see also *Howells* [1977] QB 614). In *Deyemi* [2008] 1 Cr App R 345, the Court of Appeal applied *Bradish* [1990] 1 QB 981 (see **B12.70**) and explained *Warner* and *Vann*. The case concerned the FA 1968, s. 5(1)(b) (see **B12.56**). The Court remarked that it would appear that Parliament had intended to impose a draconian prohibition on the possession of firearms for the obvious social purpose of controlling dangerous weapons. Insofar as the decision in *Vann* seeks to suggest that an accused may have a defence if he did not know the nature of the object, that went too far (per Latham LJ, at [24]):

> It is based on the slender foundation of the *obiter* exposition of the effect of *Warner*...by Lord Lane CJ in *McNamara* [(1988) 87 Cr App R 246]...which itself was based upon one short passage in Lord Pearce's speech. As Auld J said in *Bradish*...the Court's approach to 'possession' under the 1968 Act, has been to take the more restrictive view of Lord Morris and Lord Guest, and has rejected the 'half-way house' of which the 'nature' concept clearly forms part. In any event, that concept produces real logical difficulties, as its context in Lord Pearce's speech demonstrates. Sweets seem to us to be of a different nature from heroin; but according to Lord Pearce believing that the heroin tablets were sweets would not provide a defence.

B12.44 There is no distinction between cases where the accused believes that the contents of a container (e.g., a bag) were something innocent as opposed to not knowing what the contents were (*Zahid* [2010] EWCA Crim 2158). Thus, an offence contrary to s. 1 is committed even where the accused does not know there is a firearm in the container which he possesses (*Waller*; cf. the position with regard to drugs at **B19.25**). Similarly, an accused was held to have been in possession of the contents of a rucksack (ammunition) notwithstanding that he had no idea of its contents, and was indeed mistaken as to whom it belonged, or as to its nature and quality (*Price v DPP* [1996] CLY 1469, following *Bradish, Waller, Steele* [1993] Crim LR 298, and *Harrison*). See also *Cremin* [2007] EWCA Crim 666. Similarly, in *Harrison* [1996] 1 Cr App R 138, a case concerned with s. 19, the Court of Appeal, following *Waller* [1991] Crim LR 381, held that, if a person claims that he was mistaken as to whether what he possessed was a loaded shot gun or loaded air weapon, his argument will not avail, provided he knowingly had possession of the item.

Inasmuch as s. 19 provides a defence of 'reasonable excuse', consider *Densu* [1998] 1 Cr App R 400, and see **B12.106**. Given the reasoning of the court in *Densu* (at p. 404), it is submitted that D's lack of knowledge that the thing is a firearm does not constitute a 'reasonable excuse'.

In *Amos* it was held to be no defence for a person to say that he had forgotten about his possession of an item or that he erroneously believed that it had been destroyed or disposed of, even if the original acquisition had been lawful under a firearm certificate.

EXEMPTIONS AND DEFENCES FOR THE PURPOSES OF THE FIREARMS ACT 1968, s. 1

B12.45 The FA 1968, s. 1(1), indicates that the offence is 'subject to any exemption under this Act'. Exemptions include the following.

(a) A holder of a police permit from the chief officer of police is exempted (FA 1968, s. 7(1); and see the Firearms Rules 1998 (SI 1998 No. 1941)).

(b) A registered firearms dealer (or his servant) may have in his possession, or purchase or acquire a firearm or ammunition in the ordinary course of that business without a certificate (FA 1968, s. 8(1)). The term 'firearms dealer' is defined by s. 57(4). The definition has been widened to include selling or transferring air weapons (VCRA 2006, s. 31(3)).

Registration as a firearms dealer is governed by the FA 1968, ss. 33 to 39, and the Firearms Rules 1998, r. 10 and sch. 5.

(c) An auctioneer, carrier or warehouseman, or his servant, may have a firearm or ammunition in his possession in the ordinary course of business without a certificate (FA 1968, s. 9(1)).

(d) A licensed slaughterer may have in his possession, without a certificate, a slaughtering instrument (*Paul* [1999] Crim LR 79) or ammunition in any slaughterhouse or knacker's yard in which he is employed (FA 1968, s. 10). Note the European Weapons Directive (Council Directive No. 91/477/EEC, as amended by 2008/51/EC), see **B12.75**.

(e) There are a number of exemptions related to rifle or pistol clubs, sports, athletics and other approved activities (FA 1968, s. 11, and F(A)A 1988, s. 15). Approval is granted by the Secretary of State (see s. 15). As to the European Weapons Directive (Council Directive No. 91/477/EEC), see **B12.75**.

(f) A person taking part in a theatrical performance or rehearsal or the production of a film may have a firearm in his possession without a certificate, but only during and for the purpose of the performance, rehearsal or production (FA 1968, s. 12).

(g) The Proof Houses (see **B12.20**) and persons carrying firearms to or from such places.

(h) Antique firearms that are sold, transferred, purchased, acquired or possessed as a curiosity or ornament are exempted (s. 58(2)). Whether a firearm is an antique firearm is a question of fact and degree (*Richards v Curwen* [1977] 3 All ER 426; *Bennett v Brown* (1980) 71 Cr App R 109), and is therefore a matter for a jury (*Burke* (1978) 67 Cr App R 220). It is not sufficient for the accused honestly and reasonably to believe that the firearm is an antique firearm; it must actually be so (*Howells* [1977] QB 614).

(i) A person aged over 17 may, without holding a certificate, borrow a rifle from the occupier of private premises and use it on those premises in the presence of either the occupier or a servant, provided the occupier holds a certificate and the borrower's possession and use of it comply with any conditions in the certificate (F(A)A 1988, s. 16). In addition, the borrower may purchase or acquire ammunition for the rifle, if the certificate authorises the purchase of ammunition and the borrower's possession and use of the ammunition complies with any conditions in the certificate.

(j) A person who holds a visitor's permit granted by a chief officer of police under s. 17(2)–(9) of the F(A)A 1988, may have in his possession, without a certificate, a firearm or ammunition to which the FA 1968, s. 1, and the Firearms Rules 1998 (SI 1998 No. 1941) apply. A visitor's shot gun permit does not authorise the purchase or acquisition of any shot gun with a magazine, except where s. 17(1A)(a)–(d) applies (s. 17(1A)). No visitor's permit will be issued unless the visitor produces a European firearms pass (see **B12.40**) and satisfies other criteria (s. 17(3A), as amended by SI 2011 No. 2175). For summary offences relating to visitor permits, see the FA 1968, s. 17(1).

(k) Firearms acquired for export (see **B12.127** *et seq.*) may be exempted. This exemption is primarily concerned with the acquisition of firearms for export, but must also cover their possession for that purpose.

(l) The holder of a museums firearms licence (F(A)A 1988, s. 19 and sch.).

Note the amendments made to the Firearms Rules 1998 (SI 1998 No. 1941), by SI 2010 No. 1759, SI 2013 No. 1945, SI 2013 No. 2970 and SI 2014 No. 1239; and see the Home Office *Guide on Firearms Licensing Laws* (2013).

Possession etc. of Signalling Apparatus for Ship, Aircraft or Aerodrome

A person may, under the FA 1968, s. 13(1), without holding a certificate:

(a) have in his possession a firearm, signalling apparatus or ammunition on board a ship or aircraft or at an aerodrome, provided it is equipment for same;

B12.46

(b) remove signalling apparatus or ammunition, if it is aircraft equipment, from one aircraft to another at an aerodrome or into or from storage and keep such equipment in storage at an aerodrome;

(c) if he has a permit from a constable, remove a firearm, signalling apparatus or ammunition to or from a ship or aircraft at an aerodrome to or from a place specified in the permit.

It is an offence, contrary to s. 13(2), for a person knowingly or recklessly to make a statement which is false in any material particular for the purpose of procuring, either for himself or another person, the grant of a permit under s. 13(1)(c). As to procedure and sentence, see **B12.3** and **B12.4**.

Persons in the Service of the Crown

B12.47   Section 54 of the FA 1968 sets out the circumstances in which offences under the Firearms Acts are disapplied in respect of persons in the service of the Crown. See also *Heritage v Claxon* (1941) 85 SJ 323 and *Tarttelin v Bowen* [1947] 2 All ER 837. The ABCPA 2014, s. 112, amends s. 54 with effect from 13 May 2014 (see SI 2014 No. 949); it widens the exemptions that apply in relation to members and employees of the British Transport Police.

OFFENCES RELATING TO SHOT GUNS

Possessing etc. Shot Gun without Shot Gun Certificate

B12.48   Firearms Act 1968, s. 2

(1) Subject to any exemption under this Act, it is an offence for a person to have in his possession, or to purchase or acquire, a shot gun without holding a certificate under this Act authorising him to possess shot guns.

As to procedure and sentence, see **B12.3** and **B12.4**. The meaning of 'shot gun' is considered at **B12.17**. This section does not extend to imitation firearms, see **B12.24**.

The term 'shot gun certificate' is defined by the FA 1968, s. 57(4) as 'a certificate granted by a chief officer of police…authorising a person to possess shot guns'. Such certificates are issued by chief officers of police under the FA 1968, s. 26A, the related provisions in part II, and the Firearms Rules 1998 (SI 1998 No. 1941), as amended by SI 2010 No. 1759, SI 2013 No. 1945, SI 2013 No. 2970 and SI 2014 No. 1239.

For the meaning of 'acquire', see **B12.41**. For the meaning of 'possession', see **B12.42**.

The exemptions applicable in the case of firearms from liability under the FA 1968, s. 1, also apply to this offence. In addition, holders of certificates granted in Northern Ireland are exempt (FA 1968, s. 15).

For the aggravated offence under the FA 1968, ss. 1 and 4, in respect of possessing a shortened shot gun, see **B12.38**.

Failure to Comply with Condition of Shot Gun Certificate

B12.49   Firearms Act 1968, s. 2

(2) It is an offence for a person to fail to comply with a condition subject to which a shot gun certificate is held by him.

This is a summary offence. For procedure and sentence, see **B12.3** and **B12.4**. The meaning of 'shot gun certificate' is considered at **B12.48**. For the meaning of 'shot gun', see **B12.17**.

SPECIFIC OFFENCES RELATING TO AIR WEAPONS

Prohibition on Sale or Transfer of Air Weapons except by Registered Dealers

B12.50   It is an offence if a person (other than a registered firearms dealer) 'sells or transfers an air weapon, exposes such a weapon for sale or transfer or has such a weapon in his possession for sale or transfer' (FA 1968, s. 3(1)(c), inserted by the VCRA 2006, s. 31(1)). A 'firearms dealer' includes a person who sells or transfers air weapons (FA 1968, s. 57(4), as amended by the VCRA 2006, s. 31(3)). For the meaning of 'air weapon', see **B12.18** and **B12.34**.

Sales of Air Weapons by way of Trade or Business to be Face to Face

Section 32 of the VCRA 2006 makes it an offence for a person to transfer possession of an air **B12.51** weapon, by way of trade or business, to an individual in Great Britain (who is not registered as a firearms dealer) other than when the buyer and seller are in the presence of each other.

Violent Crime Reduction Act 2006, s. 32

(1) This section applies where a person sells an air weapon by way of trade or business to an individual in Great Britain who is not registered as a firearms dealer.
(2) A person is guilty of an offence if, for the purposes of the sale, he transfers possession of the air weapon to the buyer otherwise than at a time when both—
  (a) the buyer, and
  (b) either the seller or a representative of his,
  are present in person.
(3) The reference in subsection (2) to a representative of the seller is a reference to—
  (a) a person who is employed by the seller in his business as a registered firearms dealer;
  (b) a registered firearms dealer who has been authorised by the seller to act on his behalf in relation to the sale; or
  (c) a person who is employed by a person falling within paragraph (b) in his business as a registered firearms dealer.

This is a summary offence. The maximum penalty is imprisonment for six months, a fine not exceeding level 5, or both.

Age Limits on Purchasing and Selling Air Weapons

By the FA 1968, s. 22(1), 'It is an offence for a person under the age of eighteen to purchase or **B12.52** hire any firearm or ammunition' (see the Firearms (Amendment) Regulations 2010 (SI 2010 No. 1759), reg. 2(3)). Note that an air weapon, which is 'lethal barrelled', is, by definition, a firearm within the meaning of s. 57: see **B12.7**. Section 24(1) provides that '(1) It is an offence to sell or let on hire any firearm or ammunition to a person under the age of eighteen'. See also **B12.110**.

Air Weapons Safety

A person (of any age) who fires an air weapon beyond premises commits an offence (whether **B12.53** he is supervised or not) unless he has the consent of the occupier of any premises he fired into or across (FA 1968, s. 21A).

Firearms Act 1968, s. 21A

(1) A person commits an offence if—
  (a) he has with him an air weapon on any premises; and
  (b) he uses it for firing a missile beyond those premises.
(2) In proceedings against a person for an offence under this section it shall be a defence for him to show that the only premises into or across which the missile was fired were premises the occupier of which had consented to the firing of the missile (whether specifically or by way of a general consent).

From 10 February 2011 (SI 2011 No. 144) it is an offence for a person in possession of an air weapon to fail to take reasonable precautions to prevent any person under the age of 18 from having the weapon with him (s. 24ZA, inserted by the Crime and Security Act 2010, s. 46). A statutory defence exists by virtue of s. 24ZA(3).

Meaning of 'Premises', Further Defences, Penalties

'Premises' is defined by the FA 1968, s. 57(4) to include any land. Where a person is a member **B12.54** of a rifle club or miniature rifle club (for the time being approved by the Secretary of State for the purposes of the F(A)A 1988, s. 23 or s. 15), s. 23 provides that no offence is committed where a person has with him an air weapon or ammunition at a time when he is engaged as (a) a member, (b) in connection with target shooting, or (c) he is using the weapon or ammunition at a shooting gallery, and where the only firearms used are either air weapons or miniature rifles not exceeding 0.23 inch calibre (s. 23(2)).

The offence contrary to s. 23(4) carries the same penalty as the offence under s. 22(4) as well as the same forfeiture and disposal powers (see sch. 6). The offence contrary to s. 23(1) carries the same penalty as the offence under s. 22(4) as well as the same forfeiture and disposal provisions (see sch. 6).

POSSESSING OR DISTRIBUTING PROHIBITED WEAPONS OR AMMUNITION

Meaning of 'Prohibited Weapon' and 'Prohibited Ammunition'

B12.55   Section 5(2) of the FA 1968 defines 'prohibited weapon' and 'prohibited ammunition':

The weapons and ammunition specified in subsections (1) and (1A) of this section (including, in the case of ammunition, any missiles falling within subsection (1A)(g) of this section) are referred to in this Act as 'prohibited weapons' and 'prohibited ammunition' respectively.

Offence in Respect of Prohibited Weapons and/or Ammunition

B12.56   Firearms Act 1968, s. 5

(1) A person commits an offence if, without the authority, he has in his possession, or purchases, or acquires—
   (a)   any firearm which is so designed or adapted that two or more missiles can be successively discharged without repeated pressure on the trigger;
   (ab) any self-loading or pump-action rifled gun other than one which is chambered for 0.22 rim-fire cartridges;
   (aba) any firearm which either has a barrel less than 30 centimetres in length or is less than 60 centimetres in length overall, other than an air weapon, a muzzle-loading gun or a firearm designed as signalling apparatus;
   (ac) any self-loading or pump-action smooth-bore gun which is not an air weapon or chambered for 0.22 rim-fire cartridges and either has a barrel less than 24 inches in length or is less than 40 inches in length overall;
   (ad) any smooth-bore revolver gun other than one which is chambered for 9 mm rim-fire cartridges or a muzzle-loading gun;
   (ae) any rocket launcher, or any mortar, for projecting a stabilised missile, other than a launcher or mortar designed for line-throwing or pyrotechnic purposes or as signalling apparatus;
   (af) any air rifle, air gun or air pistol which uses, or is designed or adapted for use with, a self-contained gas cartridge system;
   (b)   any weapon of whatever description designed or adapted for the discharge of any noxious liquid, gas or other thing;
   (c)   any cartridge with a bullet designed to explode on or immediately before impact, any ammunition containing or designed or adapted to contain any such noxious thing as is mentioned in paragraph (b) above and, if capable of being used with a firearm of any description, any grenade, bomb (or other like missile), or rocket or shell designed to explode as aforesaid.
(1A) Subject to section 5A of this Act [see **B12.75**], a person commits an offence if, without authority, he has in his possession, or purchases or acquires—
   (a)   any firearm which is disguised as another object;
   (b)   any rocket or ammunition not falling within paragraph (c) of subsection (1) of this section which consists in or incorporates a missile designed to explode on or immediately before impact and is for military use;
   (c)   any launcher or other projecting apparatus not falling within paragraph (ae) of that subsection which is designed to be used with any rocket or ammunition falling within paragraph (b)

above or with ammunition which would fall within that paragraph but for its being ammunition falling within paragraph (c) of that subsection;

  (d)   any ammunition for military use which consists in or incorporates a missile designed so that a substance contained in the missile will ignite on or immediately before impact;

  (e)   any ammunition for military use which consists in or incorporates a missile designed, on account of its having a jacket and hard-core, to penetrate armour plating, armour screening or body armour;

  (f)   any ammunition which incorporates a missile designed or adapted to expand on impact;

  (g)   anything which is designed to be projected as a missile from any weapon and is designed to be, or has been, incorporated in—

    (i)   any ammunition falling within any of the preceding paragraphs; or

    (ii)   any ammunition which would fall within any of those paragraphs but for its being specified in subsection (1) of this section.

(2)   [See **B12.55**].

(2A)   A person commits an offence if without authority—

  (a)   he manufactures any weapon or ammunition specified in subsection (1) of this section,

  (b)   he sells or transfers any prohibited weapon or prohibited ammunition,

  (c)   he has in his possession for sale or transfer any prohibited weapon or prohibited ammunition, or

  (d)   he purchases or acquires for sale or transfer any prohibited weapon or prohibited ammunition

(3)   In this section 'authority' means an authority given in writing by—

  (a)   the Secretary of State (in or as regards England and Wales), or

  (b)   the Scottish Ministers (in or as regards Scotland).

Section 5(1) to (3) is shown as amended by the ABCPA 2014, ss. 108 (which added subsection (2A) and substituted subsection (3)) and 109, with effect from 14 July 2014.

Expressions in the Firearms Act 1968, s. 5

Prohibited Weapon   A person is in possession of a prohibited weapon even when it is in parts (*Pannell* (1982) 76 Cr App R 53, where the accused had possession of all the parts). A weapon may be a prohibited weapon even if one essential component is missing, such as the trigger (*Clarke* [1986] 1 All ER 846, and see *Brown* (1992) *The Times*, 27 March 1992, where it was held that a stun gun which did not work because of some unknown fault, and was not proved ever to have worked, was a prohibited weapon).   **B12.57**

Firearm   A 'firearm', for the purposes of the FA 1968, s. 5(1)(a), is defined by s. 57(1) so as to include the component parts of a firearm (*Clarke*). In *Rogers* [2011] EWCA Crim 1459, the Court of Appeal held (allowing R's appeal against conviction under s. 5(1)(aba)) that it was impossible to describe the components in question as components of a firearm. It is submitted that, although the result is correct, the direct route was to hold that the article did not constitute a '*lethal* barrelled weapon' within the meaning of s. 57 (see **B12.8**).   **B12.58**

Rocket or Ammunition for Military Use   By the FA 1968, s. 5(7)(a), 'any rocket or ammunition which is designed to be capable of being used with a military weapon shall be taken to be for military use'.   **B12.59**

Meaning of Missiles Igniting on Impact   By the FA 1968, s. 5(7)(b), 'references to a missile designed so that a substance contained in the missile will ignite on or immediately before impact include references to any missile containing a substance that ignites on exposure to air'.   **B12.60**

Meaning of Expanding Missiles   Section 5(1A)(f) and (7)(c) of the FA 1968 apply to expanding ammunition that is popularly referred to as 'dum-dum bullets' (*Zahid* [2010] EWCA Crim 2158). These provisions are considered in greater detail at **B12.76**. Section 5(7)(c) provides: 'references to a missile's expanding on impact include references to its deforming in any predictable manner on or immediately after impact'.   **B12.61**

B12.62   **Measuring Barrel Length and Overall Length**   The FA 1968, s. 5(8), provides that, for the purposes of s. 5(1)(aba) and (ac), 'any detachable, folding, retractable or other movable butt-stock shall be disregarded in measuring the length of any firearm'. Section 57(6)(a) provides that 'the length of the barrel of a firearm is measured from the muzzle to the point at which the charge is exploded on firing'.

B12.63   **Meaning of Muzzle-loading Gun**   The FA 1968, s. 5(9), provides that any reference in s. 5 to a muzzle-loading gun 'is a reference to a gun which is designed to be loaded at the muzzle end of the barrel or chamber with a loose charge and a separate ball (or other missile)'.

B12.64   **Meaning of Self-loading and Pump-action**   The FA 1968, s. 57(2A), provides that 'self-loading' and 'pump-action' in relation to any weapon 'mean respectively that it is designed or adapted (otherwise than as mentioned in section 5(1)(a)) so that it is automatically reloaded or that it is so designed or adapted that it is reloaded by the manual operation of the fore-end or forestock of the weapon'.

B12.65   **Meaning of Revolver Gun**   The FA 1968, s. 57(2B), provides that a 'revolver', in relation to a smooth-bore gun, 'means a gun containing a series of chambers which revolve when the gun is fired'.

B12.66   **Air Weapons with Self-contained Gas Cartridges**   For the meaning of 'air weapons' and 'self-contained gas cartridge systems', see **B12.36**. If a person has in his possession an air rifle, air gun or air pistol of the kind described in the FA 1968, s. 5(1)(af), then (a) s. 5(1) shall not prevent the person's continued possession of the air rifle, air gun or air pistol; (b) s. 1 shall apply; and (c) a chief officer of police may not refuse to grant or renew, and may not revoke or partially revoke, a firearm certificate on the ground that the person does not have a good reason for having the air rifle, air gun or air pistol in his possession (ASBA 2003, s. 39(4)). But these provisions do not apply to possession in the circumstances described in the FA 1968, s. 8, which is concerned with authorised dealing (ASBA 2003, s. 39(5)).

Specific Issues Associated with Particular Prohibited Weapons

B12.67   **FA 1968, s. 5(1)a**   Authorisation of prohibited weapons is a matter for the Secretary of State (*Leatherdale v Surrey Police Headquarters* [1999] EWHC Admin 631).

Note that s. 5(1)(a) does not apply to ammunition (*McLean* [2010] EWCA Crim 2398 at [28]). For useful examples of the types of weapons that fall within s. 5(1) and (1A), see the Home Office *Guide on Firearms Licensing Law* (2013), para. 2.55, and chapter 3. For exemptions to the obligation to have the authority of the Secretary of State with respect to any of the activities mentioned in s. 5(1A), see **B12.75**.

A weapon satisfies s. 5(1)(a) if it is capable of burst fire, making it a weapon from which 'two or more missiles can be successively discharged'. This will be the case even if a weapon has been adapted and only experts would be able to make it operate as an automatic weapon. Section 5(1)(a) does not import either explicitly or implicitly any intention on the part of the designer or the adaptor. The vital words are 'can be successfully discharged' (*Law* [1999] EWCA Crim 210). For the meaning of 'firearm', see **B12.7**.

B12.68   **FA 1968, s. 5(1)(b)**   A 'Lightning Strike' (a hand-held device from which electricity is emitted) is a prohibited weapon within s. 5(1)(b), because electricity is a noxious thing by reason of the stunning effect that it has on its victims, and is discharged from the device (*Flack v Baldry* [1988] 1 All ER 673 and see *Weaver* [2007] EWCA Crim 3485). An empty bottle is not a weapon, and filling it with hydrochloric acid does not make it a prohibited weapon; merely to fill a bottle is not to 'adapt' it within the meaning of s. 5(1)(b) (*Formosa* [1991] 2 QB 1: see **B12.12**). The court approved *Titus* [1971] Crim LR 279, where it was held that a water pistol is not a prohibited weapon even when used to discharge a noxious liquid. On the facts of *Ray* [2011] 6 Arch Rev 4 (HHJ Bevan QC, Luton Crown Court), a smoke grenade was held not to be a prohibited weapon under s. 5(1)(b).

FA 1968, s. 5(1A)   It is submitted that s. 5(1A)(a) ought to be restrictively construed. The   **B12.69**
item must appear to be something that it is not, e.g., firearms that appear to be cameras or
umbrellas, pepper or CS gas sprays that appear to be pens, or stun guns that resemble torches
(*Weaver* [2007] EWCA Crim 3485). Note that s. 5(1A) was inserted by SI 1992 No. 2823, reg.
3(1), having regard to Council Directive No. 91/477/EEC (since amended by 2008/51/EC,
and see Annex I of the Directive for the definition of 'firearm').

Strict Liability for s. 5 Offence

The offence under the FA 1968, s. 5, is one of strict liability (*Deyemi* [2008] 1 Cr App R 345,   **B12.70**
Bradish [1990] 1 QB 981, following *Howells* [1977] QB 614 and *Hussain* [1981] 2 All ER 287
(see **B12.43**), and distinguishing *Warner v Metropolitan Police Commissioner* [1969] 2 AC 256
insofar as it dealt with the 'container' cases). It is not appropriate to describe the offence as one
of 'absolute' liability (*Gregory* [2011] EWCA Crim 1712). See also *Zahid* [2010] EWCA Crim
2158.

All that the prosecution need prove is that the accused knowingly had in his possession an article which was in fact a prohibited weapon. The fact of possession must be proved (see **B12.42**,
especially *Prosecution Appeal; T* [2011] EWCA Crim 1646). It was submitted in *Bradish* that
the weapon of which the accused was in possession was a spray canister containing CS gas and,
therefore, he was not in possession of the contents of the container if he could show that he neither knew, nor could reasonably have been expected to know, that it was a prohibited weapon.
The court rejected this submission and that the facts did not disclose a 'container' case. The item
was a prohibited weapon because of the combination of the canister itself and its contents. The
'container' was an essential part of the weapon.

In *Law* [1999] EWCA Crim 210, the Court of Appeal held that s. 5(1)(a) of the FA 1968 'does
not import either explicitly or implicitly any intention on the part of the designer or the adaptor'. The vital words are 'can be successfully discharged'. (Note that the transcript wrongly refers
to 's. 5(1A)'; the case concerns s. 5(1)(a).)

As to procedure and sentence, see ss. 51, 52 and sch. 6 at **B12.3**, **B12.4** and **B12.5** and also
B12.124.

A Prohibited Weapon Keeps that Description even if Converted

The F(A)A 1988 introduced an important change into the law as regards the conversion of   **B12.71**
weapons. Consequently, care needs to be taken in reading cases on the unamended version of
s. 5 of the FA 1968, insofar as they are concerned with the conversion of weapons.

Firearms (Amendment) Act 1988, s. 7(1)

(1) Any weapon which—
    (a) has at any time (whether before or after the passing of the Firearms (Amendment) Act
        1997) been a weapon of a kind described in section 5(1) or (1A) of the principal Act
        (including any amendments to section 5(1) made under section 1(4) of this Act;
    (b) is not a self-loading or pump-action smooth-bore gun which has at any such time been
        such a weapon by reason only of having had a barrel of less than 24 inches in length,
    shall be treated as a prohibited weapon notwithstanding anything done for the purpose of
    converting it into a weapon of a different kind.

As to the de-activation of firearms, see **B12.20**.

Imitation Firearms and the Firearms Act 1968, s. 5

It is submitted that possession (etc.) of an imitation 'prohibited weapon' would be an offence contrary   **B12.72**
to the FA 1968, s. 1 (certificate needed) if the weapon falls within the FA 1982, s. 1 (i.e. is readily
convertible into a firearm: see **B12.28**). See also the Home Office's *Guide on Firearms Licensing Law*
(2013), para. 2.21.

AUTHORITY TO HANDLE PROHIBITED WEAPONS

Authority of the Defence Council as performed by the Secretary of State

B12.73 The Secretary of State may grant an authority (which must be in writing) permitting possession of a prohibited weapon or ammunition. The authority so granted must be subject to whatever conditions he sees fit to impose to secure that the prohibited weapon or ammunition does not endanger public safety or the peace (FA 1968, s. 5(1) and (2)). It is an offence to fail to comply with a condition of an authority (s. 5(5)). An authority may be revoked at any time by notice (s. 5(6)). As to procedure and sentence, see **B12.3** and **B12.4**.

Authority of the Secretary of State for Theatrical Performances

B12.74 The Secretary of State may, under the FA 1968, s. 12(2):

(a) authorise a person in charge of a theatrical performance or rehearsal or the production of a cinematograph film to have possession of a prohibited weapon if it is required for the purpose of the performance, rehearsal or production; and

(b) authorise, under s. 5, such other person as the person in charge of the performance etc. may select to have possession of it while taking part in the performance etc.

Exemptions to the Prohibitions Imposed by s. 5(1A)

B12.75 Section 5(1A) of the FA 1968 (see **B12.56**) is subject to s. 5A, which aims to ensure compliance with the European Weapons Directive (Council Directive No. 91/477/EEC; since amended by 2008/51/EC). It creates several exemptions to the obligation to have authority with regard to activities mentioned in s. 5(1A) in connection with any of the prohibited weapons or ammunition therein specified. Section 57(4A) makes provision to permit the use of a firearm or ammunition for specified purposes (e.g., sporting purposes, the shooting of vermin, competitions and estate management). Further exemptions apply in respect of persons who keep or exhibit the item in question as part of a collection (s. 5A(1)), or in connection with the carrying on of activities by a collector of firearms or a body concerned in the cultural or historical aspects of weapons (s. 5A(3)).

Expanding Ammunition Exemptions

B12.76 Expanding ammunition ('dum-dum bullets') is 'prohibited ammunition' by virtue of the FA 1968, s. 5(1A)(f), but it is important to note that a number of exemptions apply to such ammunition for the purposes, and in the situations, specified in s. 5A(3). By s. 5A(8), references in s. 5A to expanding ammunition 'are references to any ammunition which incorporates a missile which is designed to expand on impact' and references to the missile for any such ammunition 'are references to anything which, in relation to any such ammunition, falls within section 5(1A)(g)'. The Home Office's *Guide on Firearms Licensing Law* (2013), at para. 3.21 provides useful information about this type of ammunition (emphasis added):

> [Section 5(1A)(f)] refers to ammunition incorporating a projectile that is designed or adapted to expand in a controlled manner. It is the kind of ammunition used in deerstalking and vermin control because it is more likely than non-expanding ammunition to ensure a quick and humane kill. Semi-jacketed soft point and hollow point are typical forms of expanding ammunition, but care must be taken to distinguish between match target hollow point ammunition, which has a tiny hole at the front for manufacturing purposes, and true hollow point. Match hollow point rounds which are not designed to expand upon impact . . . are not prohibited. Flat-nosed bullets, which are designed to prevent a magazine explosion caused by a pointed bullet resting on the primer of the cartridge ahead of it when the ammunition is used in a tubular magazine are also not prohibited. All bullets will distort on impact, *but only those which were designed or adapted to do so in a predictable manner fit this category.*

The italicised words are important because they reflect the thinking behind the wording of s. 5(7)(c) (see **B12.61**).

There are four categories of exemptions under s. 5A relating to expanding ammunition:

(a) persons authorised by a firearm certificate or a visitor's firearm permit to possess, purchase or acquire, or to sell or transfer, expanding ammunition, or the missile for such ammunition, in order lawfully to shoot deer, to shoot vermin or (in the course of estate management activities) other wildlife, to kill animals humanely, or to shoot in order to protect other animals or humans (s. 5A(4));

(b) persons who are entitled under the FA 1968, s. 10, to have a slaughtering instrument in their possession provided the expanding ammunition, or the missile for any such ammunition, in their possession is designed to be capable of being used with a slaughtering instrument (s. 5A(5));

(c) persons who sell or transfer expanding ammunition or the missile for such ammunition to persons who hold a certificate by virtue of the FA 1968, s. 5A(4) (s. 5A(6));

(d) persons who carry on the business of a firearms dealer, and who may deal in expanding ammunition or the missile for any such ammunition in the ordinary course of that business (s. 5A(7)).

Estate management activities (see s. 5A(4)(b)) relate to estates in Great Britain (*Lacey v Commissioner of Police for the Metropolitan Police Service* [2000] Crim LR 853).

EXEMPTIONS: HANDLING PROHIBITED SMALL FIREARMS

B12.77   Exemptions to the prohibition imposed by the FA 1968, s. 5(1)(aba) (see **B12.56**) are granted by the F(A)A 1997 and the Firearms (Amendment) (No. 2) Act 1997 in the situations set out below. Note that from 14 July 2014, the reference to s. 5(1)(aba) includes a reference to the FA 1968, s. 5(2A) (ABCPA 2014, s. 108(9), inserting the FA(A)A 1997, s. 1(7A)).

B12.78   **Slaughtering Instruments**   A person may have in his possession, purchase or acquire, or sell or transfer 'a slaughtering instrument if he is authorised by a firearm certificate to have the instrument in his possession, or to purchase or acquire it' (F(A)A 1997, s. 2(a)). A person may have in his possession 'a slaughtering instrument if he is entitled, under section 10 of the 1968 Act, to have it in his possession without a firearm certificate' (s. 2(b)).

B12.79   **Firearms Used for the Humane Killing of Animals**   A person may have in his possession, purchase or acquire, or sell or transfer 'a firearm if he is authorised by a firearm certificate to have the firearm in his possession, or to purchase or acquire it, subject to a condition that it is only for use in connection with the humane killing of animals' (F(A)A 1997, s. 3).

B12.80   **Shot Pistols Used for Shooting Vermin**   A person may have in his possession, purchase or acquire, or sell or transfer 'a shot pistol if he is authorised by a firearm certificate to have the shot pistol in his possession, or to purchase or acquire it, subject to a condition that it is only for use in connection with the shooting of vermin' (F(A)A 1997, s. 4(1)). 'Shot pistol' means a smooth-bored gun which is chambered for 410 cartridges or 9mm rim-fire cartridges (s. 4(2)).

B12.81   **Races at Athletic Meetings**   A person may 'have a firearm in his possession at an athletic meeting for the purpose of starting races at that meeting' (F(A)A 1997, s. 5(1)). A person may have in his possession, purchase or acquire, or sell or transfer 'a firearm if he is authorised by a firearm certificate to have the firearm in his possession, or to purchase or acquire it, subject to a condition that it is only for use in connection with starting races at athletic meetings' (F(A)A 1997, s. 5(2)).

B12.82   **Trophies of War**   A person may have in his possession 'a firearm which was acquired as a trophy of war before 1st January 1946 if he is authorised by a firearm certificate to have it in his possession' (F(A)A 1997, s. 6). A 'trophy of war' is not defined in the Firearms Acts but the Home Office's *Guide on Firearms Licensing Law* (2013), at para. 13.62, states that it is 'generally held to refer to firearms either carried on active service or captured from the enemy'.

B12.83   Firearms of Historic Interest   The following provisions have effect without prejudice to s. 58(2) of the 1968 Act which is concerned with antique firearms, and which is an additional exception (F(A)A 1997, s. 7(4)).

(a) A person may have in his possession, purchase or acquire, or sell or transfer, a firearm which was (i) manufactured before 1 January 1919; and (ii) is of a specified description 'if he is authorised by a firearm certificate to have the firearm in his possession, or to purchase or acquire it, subject to a condition that he does so only for the purpose of its being kept or exhibited as part of a collection' (s. 7(1)). The Secretary of State may specify descriptions of firearms for the purposes of s. 7(1) if it appears to him that firearms of that description were manufactured before 1 January 1919 and ammunition for fire-arms of that type is not readily available (s. 7(2)). The Firearms (Amendment) Act 1997 (Firearms of Historic Interest) Order 1997 (SI 1997 No. 1537) has been made in exercise of that power.

(b) A person may have in his possession, or may purchase or acquire, or sell or transfer 'a fire-arm which is of particular rarity, aesthetic quality or technical interest, or is of historical importance, if he is authorised by a firearm certificate to have the firearm in his possession subject to a condition requiring it to be kept and used only at a designated place' (s. 7(3)). Places will be designated by the Secretary of State (s. 7(3)).

B12.84   Weapons and Ammunition Used for Treating Animals   This special exception applies to offences contrary to s. 5(1)(aba), (b) and (c) (see **B12.56**). A person may have in his posses-sion, purchase or acquire, or sell or transfer 'any firearm, weapon or ammunition designed or adapted for the purpose of tranquillising or otherwise treating any animal, if he is authorised by a firearm certificate to possess, or to purchase or acquire, the firearm, weapon or ammuni-tion subject to a condition restricting its use in connection with the treatment of animals' (F(A)A 1997, s. 8). Note that from 14 July 2014, the reference to s. 5(1)(aba), (b) and (c), includes a reference to the FA 1968, s. 5(2A) (ABCPA 2014, s.108(9), inserting the FA(A)A 1997, s. 1(7B)).

POSSESSION OF FIREARM WITH INTENT TO ENDANGER LIFE

B12.85   Firearms Act 1968, s. 16

It is an offence for a person to have in his possession any firearm or ammunition with intent by means thereof to endanger life or to enable another person by means thereof to endanger life whether any injury has been caused or not.

As to procedure and sentence, see ss. 51, 52 and sch. 6; **B12.3**, **B12.4** and **B12.5**.

Indictment

B12.86   *Statement of Offence*

Having a firearm [ammunition] in possession with intent to endanger life, contrary to section 16 of the Firearms Act 1968.

Particulars of Offence

A on or about the...day of...at...had in his possession a firearm [ammunition], namely..., with intent by means thereof [with intent to enable another person by means thereof] to endanger life.

Note that the section applies to any 'firearm' (as defined by s. 57(1): see **B12.7**) or 'ammunition' (s. 57(2): see **B12.21**). Section 16 does not require the firearm or the ammunition to be prohibited (*Salih* [2008] 2 All ER 319).

The accused must be 'in possession' of the firearm or ammunition: see **B12.42**.

No Extension to Imitation Firearms

Section 16 does not extend to imitation firearms, because there is no express reference to such **B12.87** firearms, and because the FA 1982, s. 2(2) and (3), makes clear that that Act does not extend to s. 16.

Intent to Endanger Life

The FA 1968, s. 16, deals with two situations. The first is where D intends, by means of the **B12.88** firearm/ammunition, to endanger life; typically, D will have physical custody and control of the item in question. The second situation is where D intends to *enable another person* by means of a firearm/ammunition to endanger life, e.g., where D makes a firearm available to P and, by means thereof, to endanger life. The intent in each case is an intention to endanger life — not to kill.
As the Court of Appeal pointed out in *Jones* [1997] QB 798, both limbs of s. 16 are concerned with possession by D of firearms or ammunition — not with their supply. It is the state of mind of D or the possessor that has to be considered.

The accused must have intended to behave in such a way as will in fact, to the accused's knowledge, endanger life (*Brown* [1995] Crim LR 328 and *Anderson* [2006] EWCA Crim 833, disapproving the dictum in *East* [1990] Crim LR 413). A specific intent to endanger life has to be established (*Bathh* (28 May 1999 unreported)). The person whose life it is intended to endanger need not be in the UK (*El-Hakkoui* [1975] 2 All ER 146) and the intent need not be an immediate or unconditional one, although it is necessary that the accused has possession of a firearm or ammunition with a view to using it, if and when the occasion arises (*Bentham* [1973] QB 357 and *Jones* [1997] QB 798; and see *Spence* [2009] EWCA Crim 2736).

An intention to endanger life is not defined by the physical capabilities of any bullet at the time when the trigger comes to be pulled, so the intention could be present where the bullet or cartridge was a misfire. If the accused knew that the ammunition could not work, that may be relevant to intention (*Anderson*). The life that the accused intends to endanger must be someone else's and not his own (*Norton* [1977] Crim LR 478).

Where the charge relates to the second limb of s. 16, i.e. possessing a firearm or ammunition **B12.89** with intent *to enable another* to endanger life, it is submitted that the prosecution must prove more than the mere fact of supply of a firearm to another. In *Jones* [1997] QB 798, the Court of Appeal said (emphasis added):

> The key to the problem is to identify the meaning of [the words 'to enable another person'] in the context in which they appear — in particular to determine the shade of meaning that the verb 'to enable' carries. *It plainly means something more than 'to give the opportunity', because to equate it with such an intent would indeed be to make the second limb offence almost one of strict liability and would certainly encompass the example of a man who negligently determines to hand a loaded firearm to an insufficiently responsible person* — conduct which one cannot sensibly contemplate as running with the first limb in a section creating offences for which life imprisonment is provided...[It] is not necessary to prove an immediate or unconditional intent that life shall be endangered — it is sufficient if the intent is that the firearm shall be used in a manner which endangers life as and when occasion requires. However, with that qualification it seems to us that *an intention on the part of the possessor that life shall be endangered is a requirement of the second as of the first limb. Whether on the facts of the particular case that intention has been proved is a question for the jury to determine, drawing such inferences as they properly may from the evidence...[T]here may be all the difference between possessing a gun with intent to supply it to a known poacher and possessing it with*

intent to supply it to a person known to have convictions for violent robberies. Our conclusion. . .recognises the fallacy of placing all the emphasis or too much emphasis on the words 'to enable' rather than having regard to the whole phrase 'with intent to enable another to endanger life'. The essence of the offence is the intent to enable life to be endangered. *That is a specific intent and accordingly, if in the circumstances of the case the judge considers it necessary to elaborate upon a simple direction as to intent, he will need to have regard to the guidance to be derived from Nedrick, Hancock and Maloney.*

For a further illustration of the application of s. 16, see *Gander* [1997] EWCA Crim 1452 and *Thompson* [2013] EWCA Crim 57.

Virtual Certainty and Intention

B12.90   The reference in *Jones* [1997] QB 798 to the cases of *Moloney* [1985] AC 905, *Nedrick* [1986] 3 All ER 1, and *Hancock* [1986] AC 455 (and see now *Woollin* [1999] AC 82) means that the court may be required to grapple with the vexed problem of defining 'intention' in the context of consequences that are 'virtually certain' (sometimes termed 'oblique intention'). In *Smith and Hogan's Criminal Law* (13th edn, 2011), at p. 112 it is said that it 'is arguable that intention, in law, should extend to results known or believed by the actor to be conditions of the achievement of his purpose but should go no further'.

In *Woollin* the House of Lords held that in the rare cases (notably of murder) where the simple direction is not enough, the jury should be directed that they are not entitled to infer the necessary intention, unless they feel sure that death or serious bodily harm (endangerment to life in the context of the FA 1968, s. 16) was a virtual certainty (barring some unforeseen intervention) as a result of the accused's actions, and that the accused appreciated that such was the case; that the decision was one for the jury to reach upon a consideration of all the evidence, and that the use of the phrase 'virtual certainty' was not confined to cases where the evidence of intent was limited to actions of the accused and the consequences of those actions.

Notwithstanding the observations of the Court of Appeal in *Jones*, there are four reasons why (it is respectfully submitted) a direction along the lines set out in *Woollin* is best avoided if possible. First, such a direction will very rarely be needed. Secondly, the 'virtual certainty' concept is not easily understood by lawyers or by juries. Thirdly, there is a risk that elaborating on the element of intention by reference to this concept will lead to further confusion. The trial judge must make it clear to the jury that intent, for the purpose of s. 16, is not to be equated with indifference, negligence, or recklessness. Fourthly, the trial judge must not leave the jury with the impression that D's appreciation that endangerment to life was a virtual certainty is to be equated with intention. Note the words of Lord Scarman, in *Hancock* (see A2.5). It is submitted that D's awareness that the consequences of his actions were 'virtually certain' may indicate whether D had the requisite intent or not, but it is not by itself the answer to the question (consider *Harte* [2006] NICC 2 at [20]). In *Royle* [2014] 1 Cr App R (S) 296 (49), the Court of Appeal, having regard to *Nedrick* [1986] 3 All ER 1 and *Woollin* [1999] AC 82, held that the direction '[y]ou must be sure that he did not just realise that it could happen but acted on the basis that it would or that he intended that it would' was far from being a misdirection but, arguably, set a hurdle higher than that in *Woollin* and *Nedrick*. It contemplated not virtual certainty but certainty.

Intention to Endanger Life for an Unlawful Purpose

B12.91   The Court of Appeal in *Georgiades* [1989] 1 WLR 759, held that it is possible for an accused to intend to endanger life for a lawful purpose, as when raising the defence of self-defence. Cases where such a plea could be successfully raised must be very rare. In *Georgiades*, the conviction under the FA 1968, s. 16, had to be quashed because the question of whether the intention to endanger life might have been a lawful one was not left to the jury. In *Stubbs* [2007] EWCA Crim 1714, the Court of Appeal held that for the issue of self-defence to be left to the jury there had to be evidence of fear of imminent attack. In *Salih* [2008] 2 All ER 319, Hooper LJ said (at [16]–[18]):

> In our view, and in accordance with *Stubbs*..., the effectiveness of legislation designed to prevent the carrying of firearms or offensive weapons...would be 'seriously impaired' if anyone who reasonably feared that he might at some time be unlawfully attacked was allowed to carry such a weapon (see the commentary of Professor J C Smith QC in [1989] Crim LR 452). If at the moment at which the defendant is alleged to be in possession of a firearm (or offensive weapon...) he is anticipating an imminent attack and carrying the weapon for his own defence against a specific danger then that may be different...*Georgiades* establishes that if the defendant was acting in self defence at the moment when he is alleged to be in possession of a firearm, then he would not be guilty. However if the possession with intent to endanger life is alleged to have occurred at some time before that moment and at a time when he was not in immediate fear of attack, then, in accordance with *Stubbs*..., *Georgiades* will not apply.

It is submitted that it would rarely, if ever, be a defence to a charge under the FA 1968, s. 16, that D possessed the firearm to effect a citizen's arrest (consider, albeit in the context of s. 17, *List* [2011] EWCA Crim 2821).

POSSESSION OF FIREARM OR IMITATION FIREARM WITH INTENT TO CAUSE FEAR OF VIOLENCE

Firearms Act 1968, s. 16A   **B12.92**

It is an offence for a person to have in his possession any firearm or imitation firearm with intent—

(a) by means thereof to cause, or
(b) to enable another person by means thereof to cause,
any person to believe that unlawful violence will be used against him or another person.

As to procedure and sentence, see **B12.3** and **B12.4**.

Indictment

Statement of Offence   **B12.93**

Having a firearm [an imitation firearm] in possession with intent to cause a person to believe that unlawful violence will be used against him or another, contrary to section 16A of the Firearms Act 1968.

Particulars of Offence

A on or about the...day of...had in his possession a firearm [an imitation firearm], namely..., with intent by means thereof to cause V, to believe that unlawful violence would be used against him or another.

Elements

For the meaning of 'firearm', see **B12.7**; for the meaning of 'imitation firearm', see **B12.24**. **B12.94** The concept of 'possession' is considered at **B12.42**. For the meaning of 'unlawful violence', see **B11.43**.

In *K v DPP* [2006] EWHC 2183 (Admin), the Divisional Court rejected the appellant's submission that the knowledge of all those present, and in particular the complainant, that the gun was an imitation firearm was such as to make the commission of the offence impossible. K's purpose or intention was to make the complainant fear violence and it was not fatal to the conviction that the complainant was aware that it was an imitation firearm (that fact might be relevant to sentence).

It is not appropriate to attempt to draw parallels with the provisions of the Prevention of Crime Act 1953 (see **B12.138**): 'the plain language of section 16A embraces the situation where an offender forms an intention to cause fear of violence at or immediately before his actions which are designed to cause such fear' (*Goluchowski* [2006] EWCA Crim 1972 at [18]).

USE OF FIREARM TO RESIST ARREST

B12.95   Firearms Act 1968, s. 17

(1) It is an offence for a person to make or attempt to make any use whatsoever of a firearm or imitation firearm with intent to resist or prevent the lawful arrest or detention of himself or another person.

As to sentence, see ss. 51 and 52 and sch. 6; **B12.3**, **B12.4** and **B12.5**.

Indictment

B12.96   *Statement of Offence*

Using firearm [imitation firearm] with intent to resist [or: prevent] arrest, contrary to section 17(1) of the Firearms Act 1968.

Particulars of Offence

A on or about the…day of…at…used a firearm [an imitation firearm], namely…with intent to resist his lawful arrest or detention [or: to prevent the lawful arrest or detention of X].

Alternative Verdicts

B12.97   Firearms Act 1968, sch. 6, part II, para. 5

If on the trial of a person for an offence under section 17(1) of this Act the jury are not satisfied that he is guilty of that offence but are satisfied that he is guilty of an offence under section 17(2), the jury may find him guilty of the offence under section 17(2) and he shall then be punishable accordingly.

As to the offence under s. 17(2), see **B12.99** to **B12.101**.

Firearms and Imitation Firearms

B12.98 By virtue of the FA 1968, s. 17(4), a restricted definition of 'firearm', as provided by s. 57(1) applies (see **B12.7**), except that component parts of and accessories to such firearms are not part of the definition for the purposes of the s. 17 offence (i.e. the definition in s. 57(1), except for paras. (b) and (c)).

Section 17 expressly refers to 'imitation firearm', and therefore it is the definition in s. 57(4), as applied by s. 17(4), that is relevant (see **B12.25**). The FA 1982 is not relevant to this offence.

POSSESSING FIREARM WHILE COMMITTING AN OFFENCE IN THE FIREARMS ACT 1968, sch. 1

B12.99   Firearms Act 1968, s. 17

(2) If a person, at the time of his committing or being arrested for an offence specified in schedule 1 to this Act, has in his possession a firearm or imitation firearm, he shall be guilty of an offence under this subsection unless he shows that he had it in his possession for a lawful object.

As to procedure and sentence, see ss. 51, 52 and sch. 6, **B12.3**, **B12.4** and **B12.5**. See also **B12.96** and **B12.97**.

Elements

B12.100 As to the meaning of 'firearm' and 'imitation firearm' in the FA 1968, s. 17, generally, see **B12.98**.

An offence under s. 17(1) is committed where the accused has possession of the firearm or an imitation firearm. He need not 'have it with him' (see **B12.103**). There is a consistent use of the expressions 'possession' (see **B12.42**) and 'have with him' (see **B12.104**) in the FA 1968. Therefore, the same meaning of possession was applied in *North* [2001] EWCA Crim 544, as is applied to the offence contrary to the FA 1968, s. 1 (see **B12.33**). Having a firearm in order to carry out a citizen's arrest would not be lawful and therefore such a purpose would not constitute a 'lawful object' within the meaning of s. 17(2) (*List* [2011] EWCA Crim 2821).

Offences Specified in the Firearms Act 1968, sch. 1

The offences specified in sch. 1 are:

B12.101

offences under the Criminal Damage Act 1971, s. 1 (damage to property);

offences under the OAPA 1861, ss. 20 to 22 (inflicting bodily injury, garrotting, criminal use of stupefying drugs), 30 (laying explosive to building), 32 (endangering railway passengers by tampering with track), 38 (assault with intent to commit offence or resist arrest) and 47 (assault);

offences under the Child Abduction Act 1984, part I (abduction of children);

theft, robbery, burglary, blackmail and any offence under the Theft Act 1968, s. 12(1);

offences under the Police Act 1996, s. 89(1) or the Police (Scotland) Act 1967, s. 41 (assaulting constable in execution of his duty);

offences under the CJA 1991, s. 90(1) (assaulting prisoner custody officer);

offences under the CJPO 1994, s. 13(1) (assaulting secure training centre custody officer);

offences under the Immigration and Asylum Act 1999, sch. 11, para. 4 (assaulting a detainee custody officer);

offences under the SOA 2003, ss. 1 (rape), 2 (assault by penetration), 4 (causing a person to engage in sexual activity involving penetration without consent), 5 (rape of a child under 13), 6 (assault by penetration of a child under 13), 8 (causing or inciting a child under 13 to engage in sexual activity involving penetration), 30 (sexual activity involving penetration with a person with a mental disorder impeding choice) and 31 (causing or inciting a person with a mental disorder impeding choice to engage in sexual activity involving penetration);

aiding or abetting the commission of any such offence;

attempting to commit any such offence.

In *Nelson* [2001] 1 QB 55, the Court of Appeal confirmed that the statute is clear that a specified offence need not have been committed, but the accused must have been lawfully arrested for one. However, in *Rutkahskas* [2014] EWCA Crim 425, a conviction under the FA 1968, s. 17, was quashed where R, having been charged with possessing a firearm at the time of committing a robbery, was acquitted of the robbery.

OFFENCES INVOLVING CARRYING OF FIREARMS

Carrying Firearm or Imitation Firearm with Intent to Commit an Indictable Offence or to Resist Arrest

Firearms Act 1968, s. 18

B12.102

(1) It is an offence for a person to have with him a firearm or imitation firearm with intent to commit an indictable offence, or to resist arrest or prevent the arrest of another, in either case while he has a firearm or imitation firearm with him.

(2) In proceedings for an offence under this section proof that the accused had a firearm or imitation firearm with him and intended to commit an offence, or to resist or prevent arrest, is evidence that he intended to have it with him while doing so.

As to procedure and sentence, see ss. 51, 52, sch. 6, **B12.3**, **B12.4** and **B12.5**.

Elements of the Offence

B12.103   The Court of Appeal in *Stoddart* [1998] 2 Cr App R 25, has made clear that there are three elements to this offence:

   (a)   that the accused had with him a firearm or imitation firearm;

   (b)   that he intended to have it with him; and

   (c)   that at the same time he had the intention to commit an indictable offence or to resist or prevent arrest.

The Court added that (b) and (c) are distinct rather than composite elements of the offence. However, proving (b) and (c) is made easier by s. 18(2) (see **B12.102**).

The Court of Appeal in *Houghton* [1982] Crim LR 112, held that it is necessary to establish the intent only at the moment to which the charge relates, which in this case was when the imitation firearm was pulled out of a holster by the accused. The intent may be formed at the same time as the accused begins to have the gun with him. It need not be formed at any earlier stage. It is not necessary to show an intention to use the firearm in the furtherance of the indictable offence (*Stoddart*). The intent must be free from duress (*Fisher* [2004] Crim LR 938).

The general definition of 'firearm' in the FA 1968, s. 57(1), applies, see **B12.7**. Since there is an express reference to 'imitation firearm', the definition in s. 57(4) applies, and the FA 1982 has no application, see **B12.25** and **B12.28**.

B12.104   **Have with Him**   Possession itself is not enough: the law requires the evidence to establish that the accused had the weapon with him (consider *North* [2001] EWCA Crim 544). The classic case is carrying it, or a person may have it with him if it is immediately available to him, but 'if all that can be shown is possession in the sense that it is in your house or in a shed or somewhere where you have ultimate control, that is not enough' (per Scarman LJ in *Kelt* [1977] 3 All ER 1099; for the meaning of 'possession', see **B12.42**). In *Pawlicki* [1992] 3 All ER 902, the Court of Appeal explained *Kelt* on the basis that the court had attempted to highlight the importance of propinquity as a necessary ingredient distinguishing this offence from those relating to possession. Whilst rejecting the possibility of a statutory definition, the Court, adopting a purposive approach, relied upon a concept of 'ready accessibility' and decided that the defendants in an auction room had firearms with them which were in a car some 50 yards away. In *Bradish* [2004] EWCA Crim 1340, the defendants had made no arrangements that would have enabled them quickly to acquire the gun (kept in premises several miles away) in the course of a robbery if they had needed it for their purposes. On a common-sense basis, they did not have the gun with them.

Carrying Firearm in Public Place

B12.105   Firearms Act 1968, s. 19

A person commits an offence if, without lawful authority or reasonable excuse (the proof whereof lies on him), he has with him in a public place—

   (a)   a loaded shot gun,

   (b)   an air weapon (whether loaded or not),

   (c)   any other firearm (whether loaded or not) together with ammunition suitable for use in that firearm, or

   (d)   an imitation firearm.

As to procedure and sentence, see ss. 51, 52, sch. 6, **B12.3**, **B12.4** and **B12.5**. The offence is triable only summarily where the firearm is an air weapon. Note that a s. 19 offence may be committed whether the air weapon is lethal barrelled or not (*Street v DPP* [2004] EWHC 86 (Admin)).

By s. 57(4), a 'public place' includes 'any highway and any other premises or place to which at the material time the public have or are permitted to have access whether on payment or otherwise' (*Anderson v Miller* (1976) 64 Cr App R 178, where it was held that the space behind a shop counter is a public place).

For the meaning of 'imitation firearm' see **B12.25**. For the definition of 'shot gun' see **B12.17**.

The term 'loaded' has an extended meaning in the circumstances set out in s. 57(6) but note that the offence is committed for the purposes of s. 19(b) or (c) whether the weapon/firearm is loaded or not.

Firearms Act 1968, s. 57

(6) For purposes of this Act—
...
(b) a shot gun or an air weapon shall be deemed to be loaded if there is ammunition in the chamber or barrel or in any magazine or other device which is in such a position that the ammunition can be fed into the chamber or barrel by the manual or automatic operation of some part of the gun or weapon.

The offence under s.19 is one of strict liability: see **B12.43**. In *Vann* [1996] Crim LR 52, V had a loaded weapon with her because 'she had the gun with her. . . .physically in her possession, and. . .was aware that she had it, even if she was ignorant of the fact that it was a gun'. In *Jones* [1995] QB 235, the Court of Appeal held, following the Divisional Court in *Ross v Collins* [1982] Crim LR 368, that possession of a firearm or ammunition certificate was not in itself lawful authority to have a firearm and ammunition in a public place.

Reasonable Excuse   Whereas an honest, mistaken belief in facts, which if true would provide a   **B12.106**
lawful authority, is capable of being a reasonable excuse, there can be no reasonable excuse where the belief is in something which could not be lawful authority even if true, such as the accused's belief that he held a valid certificate when the certificate was, in fact, invalid (see also *Taylor v Mucklow* (1973) 117 SJ 792).

Reasonable excuse is unlikely to include a plea that the accused was unaware of the nature of the item that he had with him, or that the firearm was in a container and he did not know its contents nor had a reasonable opportunity to inspect, but the point was left undecided in *Vann*. However, in *Densu* [1998] 1 Cr App R 400 — a case that was decided in the context of the Prevention of Crime Act 1953, s. 1(1) — the Court of Appeal said that as a matter of principle:

> . . .it cannot be possible for a defendant to argue, once found to have with him an offensive weapon, that he did not know it was an offensive weapon. The [Prevention of Crime Act 1953] is an Act aimed at eradicating the carrying of dangerous weapons in public. The whole purpose of the Act is to provide strict liability in respect of objects regarded as dangerous. To allow lack of knowledge to be raised as a reasonable excuse defence would defeat the purpose of imposing strict liability in respect of the possession of such a weapon.

It is unlikely that the courts would apply a contrary principle where a 'reasonable excuse' defence is raised under the Firearms Acts.

Whether the imposition of the burden on the accused is compliant with the ECHR, Article 6, remains to be determined, see **F3.18**. Arguments against the reverse burden include the fact that the offence is triable either way and, on indictment, carries a high maximum penalty. On the other hand, the definitional elements of the offence have to be proved by the prosecution and the offence deals with a serious problem.

PROHIBITION ON POSSESSION OR ACQUISITION OF FIREARMS BY CONVICTED PERSONS

Section 21 of the FA 1968 imposes restrictions on the possession and acquisition of fire-   **B12.107**
arms by convicted persons. By s. 21(4), it is an offence for a person to contravene any

of the 'foregoing provisions' of the section. The 'foregoing provisions' are the provisions of s. 21(1)–(3A), which (in summary) provides that a person who has been sentenced to custody for life or to preventive detention, or to imprisonment, or to corrective training, youth custody or detention in a young offender institution (or Scottish equivalent) for three years or more, must not at any time have a firearm or ammunition in his possession (s. 21(1)).

A person who has been sentenced to imprisonment, youth custody, detention in a young offender institution (or Scottish equivalent), a secure training order, or a detention and training order for three months or more, but less than three years, must not at any time before the expiration of the period of five years from the date of his release have a firearm or ammunition in his possession (s. 21(2)). (For the meaning of 'date of release', see s. 21(2A).) With effect from 14 July 2014, the ABCPA 2014, s. 110(1), inserts s. 21(2C), whereby a person who has been sentenced to imprisonment for a term of three months or more whose sentence is suspended must not have a firearm or ammunition in his possession at any time during the period of five years beginning with the second day after the date on which the sentence is passed.

A person who is subject to a recognizance to keep the peace or be of good behaviour with a condition relating to the possession of firearms (or the Scottish equivalent), a community order or a youth rehabilitation order must not, at any time during which he is so subject, have a firearm or ammunition in his possession (s. 21(3)).

B12.108 As to procedure and sentence, see ss. 51, 52 and sch. 6, **B12.3**, **B12.4** and **B12.5**. If a person is prohibited in Northern Ireland from having a firearm or ammunition in his possession, he is also so prohibited in Great Britain (s. 21(3A)).

A person may apply to the Crown Court for the removal of such prohibitions (FA 1968, s. 21(6); *Gordon v Northampton Crown Court* (20 December 1999 unreported)). For the procedure, see s. 21(7) and sch. 3.

Section 21 does not extend to imitation firearms, because there is no express reference to such firearms and because the FA 1982 only extends to firearms to which s. 1 of the FA 1968 applies, whereas this section applies to firearms generally.

Firearms Act 1968, s. 21

(5) It is an offence for a person to sell or transfer a firearm or ammunition to, or to repair, test or prove a firearm or ammunition for, a person whom he knows or has reasonable ground for believing to be prohibited by this section from having a firearm or ammunition in his possession.

The offence carries the same range of sentence as the offence contrary to s. 21(4) above (see sch. 6 at **B12.5**) and is triable either way.

PROHIBITION ON POSSESSION OR ACQUISITION OF FIREARMS BY PERSONS UNDER SPECIFIED AGES

B12.109 A series of summary offences created by the FA 1968, ss. 22 to 24, deals with the acquiring, having in possession, use, sale or letting to, supply to and making a gift to a young person of a variety of firearms. The requisite age of the young person is not the same in each case. As to procedure and sentence, see ss. 51, 52 and sch. 6 at **B12.3**, **B12.4** and **B12.5**. The following relevant definitions have been given above: 'firearm' (**B12.7**); 'shot gun' (**B12.17**); 'air weapon' (**B12.18**); 'ammunition' (**B12.21**); firearm to which the FA 1968, s. 1, applies (**B12.36**); ammunition to which the FA 1968, s. 1, applies (**B12.37**).

Person under 18 Acquiring Firearm or Imitation Firearm

Section 22(1) of the FA 1968 provides: '(1) It is an offence for a person under the age of eighteen   **B12.110**
to purchase or hire any firearm or ammunition' (see the Firearms (Amendment) Regulations
2010 (SI 2010 No. 1759)). See also **B12.52** in relation to air weapons.

Persons under 18 Possessing Firearm

A person under 18 may, as the holder of a certificate, have a firearm in his possession, but it is   **B12.111**
an offence to use that firearm for a purpose not authorised by the European Weapons Directive
(Council Directive No. 91/477/EEC; since amended by 2008/51/EC) (FA 1968, s. 22(1A); see
also **B12.75**).

Person under 14 Having Firearm in his Possession without Lawful Authority

It is an offence, contrary to the FA 1968, s. 22(2), for a person under the age of 14 to have   **B12.112**
in his possession any firearm or ammunition to which s. 1 of the 1968 Act or s. 15 of the
F(A)A 1988 applies, except in circumstances where under s. 11(1), (3) or (4) of the 1968
Act, or s. 15 of the F(A)A 1988, he is entitled to have possession of it without holding a
firearm certificate. Since this offence refers to firearms to which s. 1 of the FA 1968 applies,
the FA 1982 applies and so this section extends to imitation firearms within that Act,
see **B12.28**.

Person under 15 Having with Him a Shot Gun without Adult Supervision

It is an offence, contrary to the FA 1968, s. 22(3), for a person under the age of 15 to have with   **B12.113**
him an assembled shot gun except while under the supervision of a person of or over the age of
21, or while the shot gun is so covered with a securely fastened gun cover that it cannot be fired.
This section does not extend to imitation firearms because there is no express reference to such
firearms and the FA 1982 does not apply. The offence consists in a person 'having with him'
such a weapon, see **B12.104**.

Person under 18 Having with Him an Air Weapon or Ammunition

It is an offence, contrary to the FA 1968, s. 22(4), and subject to s. 23, for a person under   **B12.114**
the age of 18 to have with him an air weapon or ammunition for an air weapon. This section
does not extend to imitation firearms, because there is no express reference to such firearms
and the FA 1982 does not apply. As with the previous offence, this offence is concerned
with a person having such a weapon with him (see **B12.104**). Section 23 provides certain
defences.

Person under 18 Having with Him an Air Weapon or Ammunition and who is Acting under Supervision

By virtue of the FA 1968, s. 23(1), no offence is committed under s. 22(4) while the person is   **B12.115**
under the supervision of a person of or over the age of 21 but, where the person has with him
an air weapon on any premises in circumstances where he would be prohibited from having it
with him but for s. 23, it is an offence for the person *supervising him* to allow him to use it for
firing any missile beyond those premises. However, 'it shall be a defence for him to show that
the only premises into or across which the missile was fired were premises the occupier of which
had consented to the firing of the missile (whether specifically or by way of a general consent)'
(s. 23(1A)).

Person aged 14 or over Having with Him an Air Weapon or Ammunition and who is Acting with the Consent of the Occupier of Private Premises

B12.116   It is not an offence under the FA 1968, s 22(4), for a person of or over the age of 14 to have with him an air weapon or ammunition on private premises with the consent of the occupier (s. 23(3), as inserted by the ASBA 2003, s. 38(3)(b)). But, in those circumstances, it is an offence for him to use the air weapon for firing any missile beyond those premises (see the FA 1968, s. 21A, at **B12.53**).

Selling or Letting on Hire to Person under 18

B12.117   Section 24(1) of the FA 1968 provides: 'It is an offence to sell or let on hire any firearm or ammunition to a person under the age of eighteen'. Section 24(1) does not extend to imitation firearms, because there is no express reference to such firearms and the FA 1982 does not apply. It is a defence, according to s. 24(5), to prove that the person charged with the offence believed the other person to be of or over the age mentioned in that provision and had reasonable grounds for that belief.

Supplying Certain Firearms or Ammunition to Person under 14

B12.118   It is an offence, contrary to the FA 1968, s. 24(2):

(a) to make a gift of or lend any firearm or ammunition to which s. 1 applies to a person under the age of 14; or

(b) to part with the possession of any such firearm or ammunition to a person under that age, except in circumstances where that person is entitled under s. 11(1), (3) or (4), or under the F(A)A 1988, s. 15, to have possession thereof without holding a firearm certificate.

Since this offence refers to firearms to which s. 1 of the FA 1968, applies, the FA 1982 applies and so this section extends to imitation firearms within that Act (see **B12.28**). As with the previous offence it is a defence to make a reasonable mistake as to age (see the defence under the FA 1968, s. 24(5)). It is also a defence if possession is permitted under s. 11(1), (3) or (4); or under the F(A)A 1988, s. 15 (sports, athletics and other approved activities; rifle and pistol clubs).

Making Gift of Shot Gun to Person under 15

B12.119   It is an offence, contrary to the FA 1968, s. 24(3), to make a gift of a shot gun or ammunition for a shot gun to a person under the age of 15. This section does not extend to imitation firearms because there is no express reference to such firearms and the FA 1982 does not apply. As with the offence contrary to the FA 1968, s. 24(1), it is a defence to make a reasonable mistake as to age (see the defence under s. 24(5)).

Supplying Air Weapon to Person under 18

B12.120   It is an offence, contrary to the FA 1968, s. 24(4):

(a) to make a gift of an air weapon or ammunition for an air weapon to a person under the age of 18; or

(b) to part with the possession of an air weapon or ammunition for an air weapon to a person under the age of 18 except where by virtue of s. 23 (see above) the person is not prohibited from having it with him.

There are the following defences to this offence:

(i) As with the offence contrary to the FA 1968, s. 24(1), it is a defence to make a reasonable mistake as to age; see the defence under s. 24(5).

(ii) A person may be entitled to have the weapon or ammunition with him under s. 23, see the offence under s. 22(4).

Failing to Prevent Minors from Having Air Weapons

For the FA 1968, s. 24ZA, see **B12.53**.   **B12.121**

Supplying Imitation Firearms to Persons under 18

Section 24A of the FA 1968, inserted by the VCRA 2006, s. 40, makes it an offence for a person   **B12.122**
under the age of 18 to purchase an imitation firearm.

It is also an offence for a person to sell an imitation firearm to a person under the age of 18
(s. 24A(2)). It is a defence to show that the person charged with the offence (a) believed the other
person to be aged 18 or over; and (b) had reasonable ground for that belief (s. 24A(3)). A person
shall be taken to have shown the matters specified in s. 24A(3) if (i) sufficient evidence of those
matters is adduced to raise an issue with respect to them; and (ii) the contrary is not proved
beyond a reasonable doubt. For the definition of 'imitation firearm', see **B12.25**.

SHORTENING AND CONVERSION OF FIREARMS

Offence

Three offences are considered here.   **B12.123**

(a) Section 4(1) of the FA 1968 makes it an offence to shorten the barrel of a shot gun to a
    length less than 24 inches. For the aggravated offence under s. 1 of possessing, purchasing
    or acquiring a shot gun which has been shortened contrary to s. 4(1) and see **B12.38**.
(b) Section 4(3) makes it an offence for a person other than a registered firearms dealer to
    convert into a firearm anything which, though having the appearance of being a firearm, is
    so constructed as to be incapable of discharging any missile through its barrel. (Note that
    this offence does not extend to imitation firearms that come within the FA 1982, ss. 1 and
    2: see **B12.28**.)
(c) Section 6(1) of the F(A)A 1988 makes it an offence to shorten to a length of less than
    24 inches the barrel of any smooth-bore gun to which the FA 1968, s. 1, applies, other than
    one which has a barrel with a bore exceeding two inches in diameter.

Procedure and Sentence

All three offences are triable either way.   **B12.124**

The range of sentence for all three offences is the same, i.e. the offender is liable, on summary
conviction, to a term of imprisonment not exceeding six months, or a fine not exceeding the
prescribed sum, or both, and, on conviction on indictment, to a term of imprisonment not
exceeding five years or a fine or both.

As to the courts' power to order forfeiture or disposal of firearms and ammunition, see the FA
1968, ss. 51, 52 and sch. 6, **B12.3**, **B12.4** and **B12.5**.

Elements and Defences

As to the meaning of: 'shot gun', see **B12.17**; 'smooth-bore gun to which section 1 of the   **B12.125**
Firearms Act 1968 applies', see **B12.34**; 'registered firearms dealer', see **B12.45**; 'firearm' see
B12.7.

The length to which the barrel may be shortened is crucial for the first two offences, and this
is to be measured, by virtue of s. 57(6)(a), from the muzzle to the point at which the charge is
exploded on firing.

By virtue of the FA 1968, s. 4(2), a registered firearms dealer does not commit the offence
contrary to s. 4(1) if the barrel is shortened for the sole purpose of replacing a defective part of

the barrel so as to produce a barrel not less than 24 inches in length. The F(A)A 1988, s. 6(2), provides the same defence to the offence under s. 6(1).

TRANSFER OF FIREARMS AND AMMUNITION TO BE IN PERSON

B12.126 The F(A)A 1997 introduced measures concerned with the transfer etc. of firearms and ammunition. In all cases it is an offence to breach the provisions provided for in ss. 32 to 35 of that Act. For transfers relating to air weapons, see **B12.50**.

The punishment and mode of trial of the offences depends upon whether the weaponry is a firearm or ammunition to which the FA 1968, s. 1, applies (F(A)A 1997, s. 36(a)) or a shotgun (s. 36(b)).

The offences to which these sentence and mode of trial provisions apply are set out in the detailed provisions of ss. 32 to 35 of the F(A)A 1997. It is an offence for a transferor, or a transferee, of weapons or ammunition which are specified in s. 32(1) to fail to comply with s. 32(2) (s. 32(3)).

A failure by a party to a transaction to which s. 33 applies (transfer of a firearm, including let or hire for more than 72 hours) to give the notice required by that section is an offence (s. 33(4)). The notice must be given within seven days of the transfer and must contain a description of the firearm in question (giving its identification number if any) and state the nature of the transaction and the name and address of the other party. Any such notice must be sent by registered post, recorded delivery or 'permitted electronic means' (s. 33(3) and (3A), as amended by the Firearms (Electronic Communications) Order 2011 (SI 2011 No. 713), art. 4).

A failure, without reasonable excuse, to give the seven-day notice required by s. 34 in connection with the de-activation, destruction or loss of firearms is an offence (s. 34(4)). A firearm is de-activated 'if it would, by virtue of section 8 of the 1988 Act be presumed to be rendered incapable of discharging any shot, bullet or other missile' (s. 34(5)). (For s. 8 of the 1988 Act, see **B12.20**.) The s. 34(4) offence extends to ammunition which has been lost (whether by theft or otherwise) (see s. 34(2)).

Section 35 creates two offences relating to the notification of events taking place outside Great Britain involving firearms which, broadly, mirror the offences under ss. 33 and 34.

BUSINESS, EXPORT AND OTHER TRANSACTIONS INVOLVING FIREARMS AND AMMUNITION

Scope of Offences

B12.127 There are 15 firearms offences concerned with business and other transactions. These can be considered in four separate groups reflecting the varying modes of trial and penalties.

Either-way offences:

(a) trading in firearms without being registered as a firearms dealer (FA 1968, s. 3(1));
(b) selling firearms to person without a certificate (s. 3(2));
(c) repairing, testing etc. firearms for person without a certificate (s. 3(3));
(d) falsifying a certificate etc. with a view to the acquisition of a firearm (s. 3(5));
(e) transactions with person not a registered firearms dealer (s. 42(2));
(f) supplying firearms to person denied them under s. 21(5) (this offence is dealt with at **B12.107**).

Summary offences with maximum penalty three months' imprisonment or level 5 fine:

(a)   failure to report transaction authorised by visitor's shot gun permit (FA 1968, s. 42A(3));

(b)   failure by person who resides in Great Britain to report purchase or acquisition of firearms in other EU Member States (FA 1968, s. 18A(6));

(c)   failure of firearms dealer to include particulars of agreement as required by the European Weapons Directive (Council Directive No. 91/477/EEC) and FA 1968, s. 18(1A) (s. 18(6)).

Summary offences with maximum penalty six months' imprisonment or level 5 fine:

(a)   failure of registered firearms dealer to notify police of export transaction (F(A)A 1988, s. 18(5));

(b)   transfer of shot guns (s. 4(5));

(c)   restriction on sale of ammunition for smooth-bore guns (s. 5(2)).

Summary offences with maximum penalty six months' imprisonment or level 3 fine:

(a)   pawnbroker taking firearm in pawn (FA 1968, s. 3(6));

(b)   supplying firearm to person drunk or insane (s. 25);

(c)   contravention of order prohibiting movement of arms and ammunition (s. 6(3)).

Either-way Offences

Firearms Act 1968, s. 3

B12.128

(1)   A person commits an offence if, by way of trade or business, he—

   (a)   manufactures, sells, transfers, repairs, tests or proves any firearm or ammunition to which section 1 of this Act applies, or a shot gun; or

   (b)   exposes for sale or transfer, or has in his possession for sale, transfer, test or proof any such firearm or ammunition, or a shot gun, or

   (c)   sells or transfers an air weapon, exposes such a weapon for sale or transfer or has such a weapon in his possession for sale or transfer,

   without being registered under this Act as a firearms dealer.

(2)   It is an offence for a person to sell or transfer to any other person in the United Kingdom, other than a registered firearms dealer, any firearm or ammunition to which section 1 of this Act applies, or a shot gun, unless that other produces a firearm certificate authorising him to purchase or acquire it, or as the case may be, his shot gun certificate, or shows that he is by virtue of this Act entitled to purchase or acquire it without holding a certificate.

(3)   It is an offence for a person to undertake the repair, test or proof of a firearm or ammunition to which section 1 of this Act applies, or of a shot gun, for any other person in the United Kingdom other than a registered firearms dealer as such, unless that other produces or causes to be produced a firearm certificate authorising him to have possession of the firearm or ammunition or, as the case may be, his shot gun certificate, or shows that he is by virtue of this Act entitled to have possession of it without holding a certificate.

...

(5)   A person commits an offence if, with a view to purchasing or acquiring, or procuring the repair, test or proof of, any firearm or ammunition to which section 1 of this Act applies, or a shot gun, he produces a false certificate or a certificate in which any false entry has been made or personates a person to whom a certificate has been granted or knowingly or recklessly makes a statement false in any material particular.

As to procedure and sentence, see ss. 51, 52 and sch. 6, **B12.3**, **B12.4** and **B12.5**.

The FA 1982, on imitation firearms, applies to these offences (see **B12.28**).

For the meaning of: 'firearm or ammunition to which the FA 1968, s. 1, applies', see **B12.34**; 'shot gun', see **B12.17**; 'firearm certificate', see **B12.40**; 'shot gun certificate', see **B12.48**; 'registered firearms dealer', see **B12.45**. 'Transfer' is defined by the FA 1968, s. 57(4), as including let on hire, give, lend and part with possession, and 'transferee' and 'transferor' are construed accordingly.

The offence in s. 3(2) is one of strict liability (*Paul* [1999] Crim LR 79). This must be true of   B12.129
the similar offences. The test is an objective one: 'whether the firearm in question corresponds

with the description relied on in a certificate produced by the transferee'. The intentions of the transferee as to use are irrelevant (*Paul*).

In the offence contrary to s. 3(5), the offence requires consideration of what is a 'false certificate', a 'false entry' or a 'false statement'. The consideration of the analogous phrases in the Forgery and Counterfeiting Act 1981 (see **B6.28** to **B6.32**) may be of assistance in ascertaining the meaning of these terms.

With respect to s. 3(1), relevant exemptions include exemption where the accused is authorised to deal with firearms, for persons in the service of the Crown, for proof houses, and where the firearm is an antique firearm sold or purchased as a curiosity or ornament, although all of the exemptions in ss. 7 to 13, 15, 54 and 58(1) and (2) of the FA 1968, and ss. 15 to 19 of the F(A) A 1988 (see **B12.45** to **B12.47**) apply.

By s. 9(2) it is not an offence for an auctioneer to sell by auction, expose for sale by auction or have in his possession for sale by auction, a firearm or ammunition when he is not a registered firearms dealer, provided he has a permit from the chief officer of police and he complies with the terms of that permit. It is a summary offence for a person knowingly or recklessly to make a statement false in any material particular for the purpose of procuring for himself or another the grant of such a permit (s. 9(3)).

The same exemptions apply to offences under the FA 1968, s. 3(2) and (3). In addition, by virtue of s. 8(2), a person does not commit an offence under s. 3(2) if he (a) parts with possession of any firearm or ammunition, otherwise than in pursuance of a contract of sale or hire by way of gift or loan, to a person who shows that he is by virtue of this Act entitled to have possession of the firearm or ammunition without holding a certificate, or (b) returns to another person a shot gun which he has lawfully undertaken to repair, test or prove for another. By virtue of s. 9(4) it is not an offence under s. 3(2) for a carrier or warehouseman, or a servant, to deliver any firearm or ammunition in the ordinary course of his business or employment as such.

Summary Offences with Maximum Penalty Six or Three Months' Imprisonment and/or Level 5 Fine

B12.130   Five offences which are only triable summarily are to be found in the F(A)A 1988.

The two offences introduced in compliance with the European Weapons Directive (Council Directive No. 91/477/EEC) (breach of s. 18(6) or s. 18A(6) of the 1988 Act) are punishable with a maximum penalty of three months' imprisonment, or a fine not exceeding level 5 on the standard scale, or both.

The penalty in respect of the remaining three offences is that a guilty person is liable to a term of imprisonment not exceeding six months, or a fine not exceeding level 5 on the standard scale, or both. The provision extending the usual time within which proceedings must be instituted applies to these offences, see **B12.3**. The first offence, contrary to s. 18(5), is designed to ensure that a registered firearms dealer, who sells a firearm or shot gun to a person entitled to purchase the same under s. 18(1) without a certificate, sends a notice of the transaction within 48 hours to the chief officer of police. The required details of such a notice are laid down by s. 18(3), as amended by the Firearms (Electronic Communications) Order 2011 (SI 2011 No. 713), art. 3. The second offence, contrary to s. 4(5), is designed to enable the police to be aware of who has possession of a shot gun when it is transferred without the intervention of a registered firearms dealer. Section 4 requires the police to be given notice of such a transfer and it is an offence to fail to comply with the provisions of s. 4. The third offence, contrary to s. 5(2), makes it an offence to sell certain ammunition to a person who is not a registered firearms dealer and is not permitted by a certificate or otherwise to have the gun for which certain ammunition is required. The ammunition covered is that to which the FA 1968, s. 1, does not apply and which can be used in a shot gun or smooth-bore gun to which that section applies.

Summary Offences with Maximum Penalty Six Months' Imprisonment and/or Level 3 Fine

It is a summary offence, contrary to the FA 1968, s. 3(6), for a pawnbroker to take in pawn any firearm or ammunition to which s. 1 applies. **B12.131**

It is a summary offence, contrary to s. 25, for a person to sell or transfer any firearm or ammunition to, or to repair, prove or test any firearm or ammunition for, another person whom he knows to be, or has reasonable cause for believing to be, drunk or of unsound mind.

It is a summary offence, contrary to s. 6(3), to contravene any order prohibiting the movement of arms and ammunition made under s. 6, any earlier corresponding legislation or any corresponding Northern Ireland legislation. This offence is supported by the power of the police, under s. 49, to search for and seize any firearms or ammunition which they have reason to believe are being removed in contravention of such an order. A person having custody or control of the firearms or ammunition must allow the police reasonable facilities to examine and inspect such articles and any documentation. Failure to comply with this power is a summary offence punishable in the same way as the offence contrary to s. 6(3).

Failure to Comply with Instructions by Police Officers

It is an offence, contrary to the FA 1968, s. 47(2), for a person having a firearm or ammunition **B12.132** with him to fail to hand it over when required to do so by a constable acting under s. 47(1). This provision enables a constable to require a person whom he has reasonable cause to suspect (i) of having a firearm with him in a public place, or (ii) to be committing, or about to commit, elsewhere than in a public place, an offence contrary to ss. 18(1), (2) and 20, to hand over the firearm or any ammunition for examination by the constable. Section 47 also provides a power of search of person and vehicle (s. 47(3) and (4)).

It is also an offence, contrary to s. 48(3), for a person to refuse to declare to a constable his name and address or to fail to give his true name and address when required to do so by a constable acting under s. 48. This enables a constable to require the production of a relevant certificate when he believes a person to be in possession of a firearm to which s. 1 applies, or a shot gun.

As to procedure and sentence, see ss. 51, 52 and sch. 6 **B12.3**, **B12.4** and **B12.5**.

Miscellaneous Offences Relating to Permits, Certificates and Authorisations

A number of offences relate to the obtaining and use of permits, certificates and authorisa- **B12.133** tions under the Firearms Acts 1968 to 1992. Reference has already been made to some of these offences under specific offences in the preceding parts of this section. In addition, the following summary offences have been created:

(a) To make a false statement in order to procure the grant or renewal of a firearm or shot gun certificate (FA 1968, s. 26(5)). It is punishable with a term of imprisonment not exceeding six months, or a fine not exceeding level 5 on the standard scale, or both.
(b) To make a false statement in order to procure the variation of a firearm certificate (s. 29(3)). It is punishable with a term of imprisonment not exceeding six months, or a fine not exceeding level 5 on the standard scale, or both.
(c) To fail to surrender a certificate on revocation (s. 30(4)). It is punishable with a fine not exceeding level 3 on the standard scale.
(d) On removal of a firearms dealer's name from the register, to fail to surrender a certificate of registration or register of transactions (s. 38(8)). It is punishable with a fine not exceeding level 3 on the standard scale.

(e) To make a false statement in order to secure firearms dealer registration or entry in the register of a place of business (s. 39(1)). It is punishable with a term of imprisonment not exceeding six months, or a fine not exceeding level 5 on the standard scale, or both.

(f) For a registered firearms dealer to have a place of business not entered on the register (s. 39(2)). It is punishable with a term of imprisonment not exceeding six months, or a fine not exceeding level 5 on the standard scale, or both.

(g) Not to comply with a condition of firearms dealer registration (s. 39(3)). It is punishable with a term of imprisonment not exceeding six months, or a fine not exceeding level 5 on the standard scale, or both.

(h) For a firearms dealer not to comply with provisions as to the register of transactions and to make a false entry in the register (s. 40(5)). These offences are punishable with a term of imprisonment not exceeding six months, or a fine not exceeding level 5 on the standard scale, or both.

(i) To fail to surrender a firearm or shot gun certificate cancelled by a court on conviction (s. 52(2)(c)). It is punishable with a fine not exceeding level 3 on the standard scale.

(j) To fail to comply with a notice from a chief officer of police who has revoked a certificate requiring the holder of the certificate to surrender forthwith the certificate and any firearms and ammunition which are in the holder's possession by virtue of the certificate (s. 12(2)). The offence is punishable with imprisonment for a term not exceeding three months, or a fine not exceeding level 4 on the standard scale, or both.

Further summary offences (under the FA 1968, ss. 32B(5), 32C(6), 42A(3) and 48A(4)) have been created to ensure compliance with the European Weapons Directive (Council Directive No. 91/477/EEC).

SENTENCING GUIDELINES FOR FIREARMS OFFENCES

B12.134 Section 51A of the FA 1968 provides for minimum custodial sentences to be imposed for certain firearms offences, unless (s. 51A(2)) the court is of the opinion that there are exceptional circumstances relating to the offence or to the offender which justify its not doing so. The relevant offences are those under s. 5(1)(a), (ab), (aba), (ac), (ad), (ae), (af) or (c), (1A) or (2A) of the FA 1968. For a detailed discussion, see **E5.9**.

Several Court of Appeal decisions provide guidance on the appropriate sentencing bracket for the most serious firearms offences.

B12.135 The Court of Appeal in *Avis* [1998] 1 Cr App R 420, reviewed sentencing levels for a number of such offences. These offences had been coming before the courts more frequently in recent years, and on some occasions sentencing levels had failed properly to reflect public concern. Lord Bingham CJ said that, given the clear public need to discourage unlawful possession and use of firearms (both real and imitation) and Parliament's intention expressed by the continuing increase in maximum penalties, the courts should treat offences under the FA 1968 as serious. Save for minor infringements which might be and were properly dealt with summarily, offences committed under ss. 1(1), 2(1), 3, 4, 5(1A), 16, 16A, 17(1) and (2), 18(1), 19 and 21(4) would generally merit custodial sentences, even on a plea of guilty and where the offender had no previous record. On breaches of ss. 4, 5, 16, 16A, 17(1) and (2), 18(1), 19 or 21, the custodial term was likely to be considerable, and where the four questions suggested by the court (set out below) yielded answers adverse to the offender, terms at or approaching the maximum might in a contested case be appropriate. An indeterminate sentence should, however, be imposed only where the established criteria for imposing such a sentence were met.

His lordship said that the appropriate level of sentence for firearms offences would, as for any other offence, depend on all the particular facts relevant to the offence and the offender, and it would be wrong for the Court of Appeal to prescribe unduly restrictive sentencing guidelines. However, it would usually be appropriate for the sentencing court to ask itself four questions:

(a) What sort of weapon was involved? Genuine weapons were more dangerous than imitation firearms, loaded firearms more dangerous than unloaded, unloaded for which ammunition was available more dangerous than where none was available. Possession of a firearm which had no lawful use, such as a sawn-off shot gun, would be viewed even more seriously than possession of a firearm capable of unlawful use.

(b) What, if any, use had been made of the firearm? The court had to take account of all the circumstances surrounding any use made of the firearm; the more prolonged and premeditated and violent, the more serious the offence was likely to be.

(c) With what intention, if any, did the defendant possess or use the firearm? Generally the more serious offences under the Act were those requiring proof of a specific criminal intent to endanger life, cause fear of violence, resist arrest, or commit an indictable offence. The more serious the act intended, the more serious the offence.

(d) What was the defendant's record? The seriousness of any firearm offence was inevitably increased if the offender had an established record of committing firearms offences or crimes of violence.

The Court of Appeal in *Wilkinson* [2010] 1 Cr App R (S) 628 endorsed the guidance given in *Avis* but noted that *Avis* did not address large-scale importation and/or manufacture, sale and distribution of guns. Lord Judge CJ said that such offences were no less criminally reprehensible than the importation of drugs or possession of drugs with intent to supply. It was difficult to anticipate many such cases where an imminent risk to life was not an inevitable consequence of the offence. If so, the availability of a life sentence should not be dependent on proof of the specific intent required by s. 16 of the Act. However, where the statutory intent involving danger to life had been established, and it was clear that the firearms had subsequently been used with homicidal intent by others, the sentence on the importer or supplier should always reflect those dreadful consequences. The fact that the importer or supplier did not pull the trigger did not resolve the issue of dangerousness. In such cases, indeterminate sentences inevitably arose for consideration. See *Cardwell* [2013] 2 Cr App R (S) 284 (43), a case of this kind, where the Court of Appeal varied a life sentence to a determinate sentence of 22 years.

B12.136 In *Gourley* [1999] 2 Cr App R (S) 148, a sentence of four years' imprisonment for possessing a sawn-off shot gun without a certificate was reduced on appeal to three years. Although the offender had pleaded guilty, the offence was aggravated because live ammunition had been found along with the gun, the barrel had been shortened, and the offender had a previous conviction for violence. In *Hudson* [1998] 1 Cr App R (S) 124, the gun was of the same type but, in addition, was loaded and ready for use. The correct sentence, according to the Court of Appeal, was four years on a guilty plea. The Court of Appeal noted in *Ashman* [1997] 1 Cr App R (S) 241, that the maximum sentence for this offence had been increased to seven years by the CJPO 1994 and that a general increase in sentencing levels was in accordance with Parliament's intentions, even where possession was by a 'caretaker or minder' of the weapon. The Court of Appeal in *Higgins* [1998] 1 Cr App R (S) 333, confirmed that a distinction should be maintained when sentencing for possession of firearms other than shortened shot guns, but that sentences should nonetheless reflect public concerns about firearms generally. Fifteen months' imprisonment was appropriate in that case, where the offender was found to have a semi-automatic pistol and 55 rounds of ammunition at his home. It was accepted that the offender, who pleaded guilty, had taken the pistol from a nephew who had threatened to harm himself, but the offender had retained the weapon for six months, even after the nephew's death.

B12.137 A sentence of ten years' imprisonment was appropriate in *Sugulle* [2013] 2 Cr App R (S) 389 (61) where the offender pleaded guilty to possession of a loaded revolver with intent to endanger life. The judge had considered the questions posed in *Avis*, and found that the gun was genuine, loaded, deadly, had no lawful purpose, and was in the possession of a man connected with gang-related activity. Another case of possession of a firearm with intent to endanger life is *Kumar* [2012] 2 Cr App R (S) 487, where the Court of Appeal said that the appropriate sentence was five years and nine months on a guilty plea where the offender had acquired a gun after hearing threats that a gang was about to attack him, and had fired a shot from his house in the direction of the gang during the attack. See also *Adigun* [2013] 2 Cr App R (S) 374 (58). Possession of a firearm with intent to cause fear of violence merited a sentence of two years' imprisonment on conviction in *Carey* [2000] 1 Cr App R (S) 179, where the offender threatened police officers with an air pistol. In *Marsh* [2013] 1 Cr App R (S) 99 (18), a sentence of nine months was appropriate following a guilty plea where the offender, a man of 36 with no relevant previous convictions, pointed an imitation firearm at some youths who had come to his home to complain about the offender's son.

For the offence under the FA 1968, s. 19 (carrying a firearm in a public place: see **B12.105**), when tried summarily, see the *Magistrates' Court Sentencing Guidelines* (see Supplement, **SG-286**).

POSSESSION OF OFFENSIVE WEAPON

B12.138
Prevention of Crime Act 1953, s. 1

(1) Any person who without lawful authority or reasonable excuse, the proof whereof shall lie on him, has with him in any public place any offensive weapon shall be guilty of an offence.

Procedure

B12.139   This offence is triable either way (Prevention of Crime Act 1953, s. 1(1)).

Indictment

B12.140
Statement of Offence

Having an offensive weapon in a public place contrary to section 1 of the Prevention of Crime Act 1953.

Particulars of Offence

A on the…day of…had with him in a public place, namely…an offensive weapon, namely…without lawful authority or reasonable excuse.

'Time' and 'place' are material elements of the instant offence which must be accurately stated in the particulars of the offence (*Allamby* [1974] 3 All ER 126).

Where the weapon may be offensive under two of the categories of offensive weapons, the indictment need not contain two counts (*Flynn* (1985) 82 Cr App R 319).

Sentencing Guidelines

B12.141   The maximum penalty is: on conviction on indictment, imprisonment for a term not exceeding four years or a fine or both; on summary conviction, a term of imprisonment not exceeding six months, or a fine not exceeding £5,000 or both (Prevention of Crime Act 1953, s. 1(1)).

The Court of Appeal issued sentencing guidelines for this offence in *Celaire* [2003] 1 Cr App R (S) 610. In determining the appropriate sentence it was necessary to consider three interlinking factors: (a) the offender's intention in committing the offence, (b) the circumstances of the offence, and (c) the nature of the weapon involved. As to intention, specific factors that would aggravate the offence are: planned use of the weapon to commit or threaten violence or to intimidate, if the offence was motivated by hostility to a minority individual or group, commission of the offence while the offender was under the influence of drink or drugs, and commission of the offence in the course of carrying out another crime. As to the circumstances of the offence, specific factors that would aggravate the offence are: its commission on school premises, or in a hospital or other place where vulnerable people are likely to be found, or at public gatherings, or on public transport (or at an airport: *Charles* [2005] 1 Cr App R (S) 253), or in licensed premises. By itself the nature of the weapon would not be a prime determinant of sentence. The nature of the weapon could, however, assist the court in drawing inferences as to the offender's intention, such as where a weapon which is offensive *per se* has been carried, or a weapon has been designed or adapted to cause serious injury. Mitigation might be found if the weapon was being carried on a temporary basis, and might also arise from personal factors, co-operation with the police, and a timely guilty plea. In relation to an adult offender of previous good character, the custody threshold would almost invariably be passed where there was a combination of dangerous circumstances and use of the weapon to threaten or cause fear. Alternatively, there would be cases (no threat had been made and the weapon was not particularly dangerous), where the custody threshold might not be passed and a community sentence towards the upper end of the range might be appropriate. Where the weapons offence was ancillary to another more serious offence, concurrent sentences would normally be appropriate; if the weapons offence was distinct and independent from the other offence, a consecutive sentence was usually called for, subject to the usual considerations of totality.

In *Povey* [2009] 1 Cr App R (S) 228, the Court of Appeal remarked that carrying a knife or an **B12.142** offensive weapon without reasonable excuse was a crime committed far too often by far too many people. Every weapon carried represented a threat to public safety and public order. Such offences had recently escalated and were reaching epidemic proportions. Sentencers dealing with this offence should focus on the need for the reduction of crime, including by deterrence, and the protection of the public. This was a serious offence and should be treated with the seriousness it deserved. The guidance given in *Celaire* should be applied with the current grave situation clearly in mind. The court recommended that any relevant guidance from the SGC to magistrates (see Supplement, **SG-245**) should normally be applied at the most severe end of the appropriate range of sentences. On 1 August 2008, the SGC published an Additional Note to reflect the remarks made in *Povey*, stating that when 'the current concerns have been overcome, courts will be notified that the approach should return to the guideline as published'. In *Monteiro* [2014] EWCA Crim 747, the Court of Appeal reviewed the guidance given in Povey. Lord Thomas CJ said that no further guidance was necessary for the Crown Court, but his lordship expressed concern about some offences involving the carrying of a knife where cautions are administered or which are dealt with in the youth courts. It was important that cautions were issued only in accordance with the ACPO guidelines on Knife Crime Offences, issued in 2009, which indicated an expectation that 16 and 17-year-olds should be charged for carrying a knife unless there were exceptional circumstances. It was also essential that magistrates applied the starting point of 12 weeks' custody (as indicated in *Povey*) for the lowest level of offence involving the use of knives.

Meaning of 'Offensive Weapon'

Prevention of Crime Act 1953, s. 1 **B12.143**

(4) In this section...'offensive weapon' means any article made or adapted for use for causing injury to the person, or intended by the person having it with him for such use by him or by some other person.

According to the Court of Appeal in *Simpson* [1983] 3 All ER 789, there are three possible categories of offensive weapon:

(a) an article made for use for causing injury to the person, commonly known as a weapon that is offensive *per se*;
(b) an article adapted for use for causing injury to the person;
(c) an article which the person carrying it intends to use for the purpose of causing injury to the person.

Frequently there is little or no distinction between the first two categories, but they must be distinguished from the third category, which requires proof that the accused intended to injure another person.

Weapons Offensive *per se*

B12.144   A flick-knife is an offensive weapon *per se* (*Lawrence* (1971) 57 Cr App R 64, *Allamby* [1974] 3 All ER 126, and *Gibson v Wales* [1983] 1 All ER 869). See also the Restriction of Offensive Weapons Act 1959, s. 1, at **B12.185**. Not all knives are offensive weapons *per se* (*Simpson*). Not all sheath knives are offensive weapons (*Simpson*). However, an object which has all the characteristics of a flick-knife does not cease to be a flick-knife because it also has the secondary characteristic of being a lighter (*Vasili* [2011] EWCA Crim 615). In *Patterson v PC 108D PK* (1984) *The Times*, 21 June 1984, it was held that a lock knife is not an offensive weapon *per se*. In a decision on the Aviation Security Act 1982, s. 4(2)(c), it was held that a butterfly knife is necessarily an article for use for causing injury to the person and judicial notice can be taken of that fact (see also *DPP v Hynde* [1998] 1 All ER 649, where the Court of Appeal referred to both the definition in the CJA 1988 and the decision in *Simpson*; and *DPP v Patterson* [2004] EWHC 2744 (Admin), which also concerned a butterfly knife). In *Houghton v Chief Constable of Greater Manchester* (1986) 84 Cr App R 319, it was held that a truncheon is an offensive weapon *per se*, in part because it does not possess *per se* any innocent quality. It is submitted that a 'shuriken' (Chinese throwing star) is offensive *per se* (*McGlennan v Clark* 1993 SLT 1069).

B12.145   It is for the tribunal of fact to determine whether a weapon is offensive *per se* (see, in particular, the decision of the Court of Appeal in *Williamson* (1978) 67 Cr App R 35, and see *Chen v DPP* [1997] EWHC Admin 221, where a Kobutan martial arts bar was not, on the facts of that case, offensive *per se*). It was held in *Butler* [1988] Crim LR 695 that a sword stick is a weapon, offensive *per se*: see also *Davis v Alexander* (1970) 54 Cr App R 398, where the court held that a sword stick was an offensive weapon *per se*, being made for the purpose of causing injury to the person. The conclusion by magistrates that a rice flail was an offensive weapon *per se* could not successfully be challenged, because it was legitimately reached in accordance with the evidence (*Copus v DPP* [1989] Crim LR 577). Following *Williamson*, it was held in *Dhindsa* [2005] EWCA Crim 1198 that it was for the jury to decide whether an item was a ring or a knuckle-duster (and thus an offensive weapon *per se*).

If an article has an innocent purpose, which may have to be the main purpose for which it is produced, it will not be an offensive weapon *per se*. Thus, in *Houghton v Chief Constable of Greater Manchester* and from *Petrie* [1961] 1 All ER 466, it was held that an ordinary razor is not an offensive weapon *per se* and, in *Humphreys* [1977] Crim LR 225, an ordinary penknife was held not to be an offensive weapon *per se*.

Where there is doubt whether an article is an offensive weapon *per se*, the tribunal of fact must have its attention drawn to the statutory definition (*Williamson* (1977) 67 Cr App R 35; *Simpson* [1983] 3 All ER 789; *Humphries* (1987) *Independent*, 13 April 1987).

It is not clear to what extent trial judges are entitled to take judicial notice of the fact that an instrument is offensive *per se*.

Where the article is an offensive weapon *per se*, the prosecution must prove that the accused had possession of the offensive weapon but need not prove a specific intent to injure (*Davis v Alexander*, *Southwell v Chadwick* (1986) 85 Cr App R 235).

Note that a list of offensive weapons appears in SI 1988 No. 2019 for the purposes of the offence contrary to the CJA 1988, s. 141 (manufacture, sale or hire of offensive weapons). See **B12.186**. In Scotland, the High Court of Justiciary has held that where it was clearly stated in a statutory instrument that an article was to be regarded as an offensive weapon, it could be regarded as an offensive weapon *per se* for the purposes of the Prevention of Crime Act 1953 (*McGlennan v Clark* 1993 SLT 1069).

Weapons Adapted to Cause Injury

B12.146   Whether an article is adapted to cause injury is a question of fact to be answered by the jury or magistrates (*Williamson* (1977) 67 Cr App R 35) and see *Warne v DPP* (3 June 1997 unreported), where the Divisional Court also made clear that the fact that the item was later used for a violent purpose was not necessarily determinative of the issue whether it had been adapted to cause injury. Thus, on the facts in *Warne*, a pick-axe handle, which had lost its head, had not been adapted for use for causing injury to the person. Articles falling within this category include a bottle which is deliberately broken so that the jagged end can be used to injure (*Simpson* [1983] 3 All ER 789) and a potato with a razor blade inserted into it (*Williamson*). In *Sills* [2006] EWHC 3383 (Admin) an unscrewed pool cue was held to be capable of being treated as 'adapted'. In *R* [2007] EWCA Crim 3312, the Court of Appeal held that it was open to a jury to infer, on the facts of that case, that a pair of sand gloves had been made for use as a weapon. *Williamson* (1977) 67 Cr App R 35 was discussed in *Ashton v HM Advocate* [2011] HCJAC 124, for the purposes of s. 47(1) of the Criminal Law (Consolidation) (Scotland) Act 1995 (which re-enacts and amends the provisions of s. 1 of the Prevention of Crime Act 1953 as it applied in that jurisdiction).

Experimentation with the article may assist the jury in determining whether it is an offensive weapon but, if permitted by the court, the experiment must take place in open court to enable counsel to make representations to the court (*Higgins* (1989) *The Times*, 16 February 1989).

Weapons Intended to be Used to Cause Injury

The prosecution must prove the element of specific intention (*Petrie* [1961] 1 All ER 466). The **B12.147** use to which the weapon is put might assist in determining what the intention of the possessor was (*Harrison v Thornton* (1966) 68 Cr App R 28; *Dayle* [1974] 3 All ER 1151; *Ohlson v Hylton* [1975] 2 All ER 490).

The charge should specify the time and place that the accused formed the intention to cause injury. It is not sufficient that he had the necessary intention at some earlier stage (*Allamby* [1974] 3 All ER 126). But an intention to use the object or article as a weapon if the occasion were to arise may be sufficient. Recklessness as to how it might be used is not sufficient (*Byrne* [2004] Crim LR 582, following *Patterson v Block* (12 September 1984 unreported)). The jury must be given carefully crafted directions regarding the meaning of 'intention' (see **A2.4**).

It is not settled whether 'injury to the person' includes self-inflicted injury but a proposition that it does do so was not challenged in the Divisional Court in *Bryan v Mott* (1975) 62 Cr App R 71. Although the accused's intention to commit suicide was not unlawful, he had no reasonable excuse for having the article in a public place for that purpose. On the other hand, a judge of the Crown Court ruled that an element in the offence was injury to a person other than the possessor of the weapon (*Fleming* [1989] Crim LR 71).

An intention to frighten or to intimidate is not an intention to cause injury unless the accused's intention was to cause injury by shock (*Rapier* (1979) 70 Cr App R 17, following *Edmonds* [1963] 2 QB 142, and explaining *Woodward v Koessler* [1958] 3 All ER 557). The trial judge must give careful directions in cases where it is appropriate to make the distinction: see also *Snooks* [1997] Crim LR 230. *Edmonds* was also followed in *Ali* [2012] EWCA Crim 934.

Distinction between 'Having it with Him' and 'Use'   The offence contrary to s. 1(1) of the **B12.148** 1953 Act is concerned with the carrying of any offensive weapon and not with its use (a distinction drawn by Professor Sir John Smith, see *Smith and Hogan Criminal Law* (13th edn, 2011), at p. 708, and by the courts (see, e.g., *Dayle* (1974) 58 Cr App R 100)). See also *C v DPP* [2002] Crim LR 322. Thus, in *Jura* [1954] 1 QB 503, a conviction for an offence under the Prevention of Crime Act 1953, s. 1, was quashed where the appellant had possession of an air rifle at a shooting gallery, which he used to fire at a woman companion. Although the use of the rifle was unlawful, his carrying of it (for which he had a reasonable excuse) was not. *Jura* was followed in *Dayle* [1974] 3 All ER 1151, where the Court of Appeal held that it was open to a jury to find that there was no possession of an offensive weapon when an inoffensive article (a car jack) lawfully carried was offensively used (see also *Bryan v Mott* (1975) 62 Cr App R 71 at p. 73).

The use of an article as a weapon can (it is submitted) be dealt with by charging appropriate offences against the person.

B12.149   In *Ohlson v Hylton* [1975] 2 All ER 490, a workman was held not to be guilty of the offence where he took a hammer from his work bag and struck a fellow traveller at an Underground station. The hammer was properly in his possession. Lord Widgery CJ said at pp. 728–9:

> ...I would hold that an offence under section 1 is not committed where a person arms himself with a weapon for *instant* attack on his victim. It seems to me that the section is concerned only with a man who, possessed of a weapon, forms the necessary intent before an occasion to use actual violence has arisen. In other words, it is not the actual use of the weapon with which the section is concerned, but the carrying of a weapon with intent to use it if occasion arises...

> I accept that it is unnecessary for the prosecution to prove that the relevant intent was formed from the moment when the defendant set out on his expedition. An innocent carrying of say, a hammer can be converted into an unlawful carrying when the defendant forms the guilty intent, provided, in my view, that the intent is formed before the actual occasion to use violence has arisen.

Ohlson v Hylton was applied in *Humphreys* [1977] Crim LR 225, where the Court of Appeal held that no offence was committed where a person had a penknife on him, and then used it in desperation: it had not been carried in a public place with the necessary intent. In *Bates v Bulman* [1979] 3 All ER 170, the Divisional Court held that the accused, who acquired an unopened clasp knife with the immediate intention of using it as an offensive weapon, did not commit the instant offence, because 'the purport of the [1953] Act...is to cover the situation where an accused person...has with him and is carrying an offensive weapon intending that it shall be used, if necessary, for offensive purposes' (per Stocker J). Stocker J also said that it:

> ...would be a rather academic and over-analytical approach [to make] a distinction between an innocent weapon subsequently used with the intention of an assault and which is being carried innocently..., and a similar article which is acquired either by borrowing from somebody else or fortuitously by being picked up in the street.

Contrast the above with *Harrison v Thornton* (1966) 68 Cr App R 28, and see also **B12.103**.

In *Veasey* [1999] Crim LR 158, the Court of Appeal confirmed that in cases where the real issue is the use of an offensive weapon, a charge of assault is 'quite adequate'.

'Has with Him' and Knowledge

B12.150   **'Has with Him' and Possession Contrasted**   It was held in *McCalla* (1988) 87 Cr App R 372, that to have something with one necessarily requires closer contact than mere possession: 'Every case of "having" is one of "possessing," but it does not necessarily follow that every case of "possessing" is one of "having" within the meaning of the relevant statutory provisions' (per May LJ at p. 378).

B12.151   **Knowledge: General Principle**   As a general principle, a person has something with him or it is in his possession if he *knows* that he has with him, or is in possession of, the object in question. A judge erred in his charge to the jury when he used words that might have made the jury think that a mere belief that a knife was somewhere in the accused's van would be sufficient (*Daubney* (2000) 164 JP 519). Similarly, in *Jolie* [2004] 1 Cr App R 44 (a case decided under the CJA 1988, s. 139), the Court of Appeal ruled that relevant to the element of possession was proof that the accused was either aware of the presence of the knife in the vehicle (when he made the journey in the course of which he was stopped) or that he was responsible for putting the knife in the place where it was later found. See also *Cugullere* [1961] 2 All ER 343.

B12.152   **Lack of Knowledge that the Thing was a Weapon**   In *Densu* [1998] 1 Cr App R 400, counsel, upon being shown by the Registrar of the Court of Appeal two unreported decisions of that Court (namely, *Vann* [1996] Crim LR 52 and *Matrix* [1997] Crim LR 901) abandoned the argument that the trial judge erred in ruling that the phrase 'has with him' was satisfied 'if the prosecution proved that the appellant merely knew that he had the baton with him but did not know that it was a weapon'. The Court of Appeal makes no comment on the abandonment of the argument but it is arguable that the point remains open. The cases referred to above are not ones concerned with the Prevention of Crime Act 1953. *Vann* [1996] Crim LR 52 is concerned with a 'have with him' offence, contrary to the FA 1968, s. 19 (and which followed *Hussain* [1981] 2 All ER 287, a possession offence under the FA 1968, s. 1: see **B12.105** and **B12.43**). *Matrix* [1997] Crim LR 901 is concerned with a possession offence contrary to the Protection of Children Act 1978. In both cases, the drugs decision of *Warner v Metropolitan Police Commissioner* [1969] 2 AC 256 (see **B19.24**), is relevant.

Forgetfulness   A person who forgets that he has the offensive weapon in his possession, nevertheless has it with him (see *McCalla* (1988) 87 Cr App R 372, where the Court of Appeal declined to follow the view expressed in *Russell* (1985) 81 Cr App R 315 that the judgment in *Cugullere* [1961] 2 All ER 343 had applied 'the general principle of criminal responsibility which makes it incumbent on the prosecution to prove full *mens rea*'). It was held in *Daubney* (2000) 164 JP 519 that, as a general principle, a person must know that he has the object with him, or that it is in his possession, leaving aside whether he must know of its precise nature. Thus, the judge's summing-up, which may have made the jury think that a mere belief that a knife was somewhere in the accused's van would be sufficient, was incorrect. In *R (Bayliss) v DPP* [2003] EWHC 245 (Admin), the Divisional Court examined *Cugullere, McCalla*, and subsequent decisions and reached the conclusion that forgetfulness does not change the fact that a person had an offensive weapon with him (consider the discussion in *Nicholson* [2006] 1 WLR 2857). Forgetfulness might be relevant to the issue of whether the accused had good reason for being in possession of the article (see **B12.158**).   **B12.153**

Joint Possession   In *Edmonds* [1963] 2 QB 142, the Court of Appeal held (at pp. 149–50) that, in the case of persons alleged to have acted together to use an article to injure another, the appropriate direction is: **B12.154**

> . . . consider the nature of each article and the case of each man individually and separately, and have regard to the circumstances as a whole and the time of day. Are you sure that each man intended to use the article he carried to injure someone? Alternatively, are you satisfied that he was party to a common purpose, with one or more of the others, of using one or more of the articles for inflicting injury upon someone? And, when you consider this alternative, you must first be sure that he knew that one or both of the others had the article which each of them was shown to be carrying.

Meaning of 'Public Place'

Prevention of Crime Act 1953, s. 1   **B12.155**

(4) In this section 'public place' includes any highway and any other premises or place to which at the material time the public have or are permitted to have access, whether on payment or otherwise. . .

Whether somewhere is a 'public place' is a question of fact; but whether it is capable of being such a place is a question of law (*Hanrahan* [2004] EWCA Crim 2943). In *Knox v Anderton* (1982) 76 Cr App R 156 the Divisional Court, in part relying on decisions on other pieces of legislation such as the Public Order Act 1936 (see **B11.12**), concluded that the upper landing of a block of flats, which could be reached without hindrance, was a 'public place', as there were no barriers or notices restricting access. In *Williams v DPP* (1992) 95 Cr App R 415, the landing of a block of flats, to which access could be gained only by way of key, security code, tenants' intercom or caretaker, was not a 'public place' for the purposes of the Criminal Law Act 1967, s. 91 (being drunk and disorderly, see **B11.202**), because only those admitted by or with the implied consent of the occupiers of the block of flats had access. People with access were not present as members of the public. The justices had misread *Knox v Anderton*, believing that the mere absence of notices restricting access had been sufficient in that case to determine that the area was a public place. See also **B11.57**.

Lawful Authority or Reasonable Excuse: the Burden of Proof

B12.156   It is important to note that '[the] Act of 1953 is meant to deal with a person who goes out with
an offensive weapon, it may be a cosh or a knife, without any reasonable excuse' (per Lord
Goddard CJ in *Jura* [1954] 1 QB 503 at p. 506).

The Prevention of Crime Act 1953, s. 1(1) (see **B12.138**), lays the burden of proving either
lawful authority or reasonable excuse upon the accused, but only when the possession of an
offensive weapon has been established (*Petrie* [1961] 1 All ER 466). If the weapon is either made
or adapted to be offensive, the prosecution has to prove no more than simple possession of the
article, whereas with the third category of offensive weapons (see **B12.143**) the prosecution has
to prove the requisite intent before the burden passes to the defendant to prove either lawful
authority or reasonable excuse.

The standard of proof required to establish a lawful authority or reasonable excuse is on a balance
of probability and not beyond a reasonable doubt (*Brown* (1971) 55 Cr App R 478). See generally **F3.9** and **F3.53**. The imposition of a legal burden upon the accused might be open to challenge in the light of the human rights cases on the 'reverse burden', but see *Lynch v DPP* [2003]
QB 137. Note also *Archbold* [2007] EWCA Crim 2137 (at [10]), where it was said that 'it is for
a defendant to raise that issue as a defence if it is appropriate in the circumstances of the case'.

Lawful Authority

B12.157   The Divisional Court said in *Bryan v Mott* (1975) 62 Cr App R 71 at p. 73:

> The reference to lawful authority in the section is a reference to those people who from time to
> time carry an offensive weapon as a matter of duty — the soldier and his rifle and the police officer
> with his truncheon.

See also *Houghton v Chief Constable of Greater Manchester* (1986) 84 Cr App R 319.

Private security guards do not have explicit lawful authority to carry, for example, a truncheon.
They have neither a statutory power, nor a duty, to do so (*Bryan v Mott* (1975) 62 Cr App R 71).
Any contractual duty would be irrelevant (*Spanner* [1973] Crim LR 704). Such a person may
have a reasonable excuse, see *Malnik v DPP* [1989] Crim LR 451 (see **B12.158**).

Reasonable Excuse

B12.158   In *Densu* [1998] 1 Cr App R 400, the Court of Appeal held that 'the cases where the defence
of reasonable excuse will be available are restricted' and that the defence arises only once it is
proved that a defendant is in possession of an offensive weapon (e.g., an offensive weapon *per se*
such as a truncheon). In *Densu* the Court of Appeal referred to an example provided by May LJ
in *McCalla* (1988) 87 Cr App R 372, that might amount to a reasonable excuse:

> ...if someone driving along a road where earlier there had been a demonstration were to see and pick
> up a police truncheon which had obviously been dropped there and were to put it into the boot of
> his car, intending to take it to the nearest police station, and then were to be stopped within a few
> minutes, he would have a reasonable excuse for having the truncheon with him in the boot of the car.

In *Southwell v Chadwick* (1986) 85 Cr App R 235, the Court of Appeal accepted that, even if a
machete knife in its scabbard and a catapult for use for killing grey squirrels were offensive *per
se* (though they were not on the facts of that case), the accused had a reasonable excuse, namely to
obtain food for his wild birds which he kept under licence. In *DPP v Patterson* [2004] EWHC
2744 (Admin), the Divisional Court held that the magistrates were entitled to come to the
conclusion that the excuse advanced by P, that he required the butterfly knife (offensive *per se*)
to cut open feed for a horse and cut open bales of straw or hay, was capable of being a reasonable
excuse on the facts of that case. The court rejected the submission on behalf of the DPP that
Densu is authority for the proposition that any factor relied on by an accused, which by its nature
does not necessarily involve the possibility of the need for self-defence, is incapable of being a

reasonable excuse for possession of a weapon offensive *per se*. There is nothing to suggest that the words 'reasonable excuse' should be fettered in that way. Furthermore, there is no authority for the proposition that reasonable excuse should be determined subjectively: 'When a defendant claims that he had a reasonable excuse for possession of an offensive weapon because he believed he was at risk of imminent attack, it is for him to prove both the belief and the reasonableness of the belief on a balance of probabilities' (*N v DPP* (2011) 175 JP 337, per Supperstone J at [32]). Note **B12.171**, and the commentary to *Clancy* at [2012] Crim LR 550. When paras. 31 and 32 of the judgment in *N v DPP* are read together, it is clear (it is submitted) that the Court meant no more than that a reasonable excuse cannot be determined solely subjectively but that regard must be had to all the circumstances of the case (see *Clancy* (2012) 176 JP 111 at [18]).

The issue of reasonable excuse should be determined only after a finding that the item is offensive *per se* or that the defendant had an intention to cause injury at the material time (*Sundas* [2011] EWCA Crim 985).

Self-defence   In *Evans and Hughes* [1972] 3 All ER 412, Lord Widgery CJ made the following   **B12.159** statement of principle: '...it may be a reasonable excuse for the carrying of an offensive weapon that the carrier is in anticipation of imminent attack and is carrying it for his own personal defence'. Accordingly, the carrying of a weapon as a general precaution is insufficient to establish a reasonable excuse (see *Evans v Hughes*, following *Evans v Wright* [1964] Crim LR 466 and *Grieve v Macleod* [1967] Crim LR 424), and this view has been confirmed by the Court of Appeal in *Densu* [1998] 1 Cr App R 400 (see also *Peacock* [1973] Crim LR 639; *Bradley v Moss* [1974] Crim LR 430; *Bryan v Mott* (1975) 62 Cr App R 71). In *N v DPP* (2011) 175 JP 337, the Divisional Court rejected the submission that *Evans v Hughes* provides explicit guidance as to what lapse in time would be permissible when assessing whether an accused was in anticipation of imminent attack. The correct approach had been stated by Keene LJ in *McAuley* [2010] 1 Cr App R 148 at [13], namely: 'The reference in *Evans v Hughes* to "imminent attack" does not write those words into the statute and it remains for a jury to determine how imminent, how soon, how likely and how serious the anticipated attack has to be to constitute a good reason for possession of the bladed article'.

Ordinarily, one cannot legitimately arm oneself with an offensive weapon with which to repel unlawful violence when one has deliberately and knowingly brought about the situation in which such violence was liable to be inflicted (*Malnik v DPP* [1989] Crim LR 451, per Bingham LJ). Bingham LJ added that the position was quite different in the case of those to whom society has entrusted the responsibility for enforcing the law, and indeed there is a difference in the case of those such as security guards who are handling valuable property in the course of their ordinary occupation and have reason to fear attack.

Theatrical Occasions and Fancy Dress   Where a weapon offensive *per se* was carried merely as   **B12.160** theatrical property as part and parcel of fancy dress worn by a person going to or from a fancy dress party, the Court of Appeal accepted that the innocent motive could amount to a reasonable excuse (*Houghton v Chief Constable of Greater Manchester* (1987) 84 Cr App R 319). The accused was dressed in a police uniform and was carrying a truncheon.

Forgetfulness as 'Reasonable Excuse'   Simple forgetfulness would not be sufficient to amount   **B12.161** to a reasonable excuse, as is made clear in *Glidewell* [1999] EWCA Crim 1221 (see also *DPP v Gregson* (1993) 96 Cr App R 240 at **B12.172** and *Hargreaves* [1999] EWCA Crim 2150, disapproved in *Jolie* [2004] 1 Cr App R 44), but factors causing forgetfulness such as an illness or the taking of medication would be relevant (*Tsap* [2008] EWCA Crim 2679). However, forgetfulness may be relevant to the issue whether a person had a reasonable excuse, depending on the circumstances. See also *Hilton v Canterbury Crown Court* [2009] EWHC 2867 (Admin).

In *Glidewell*, the fact that the accused did not introduce the weapons into his car; that the weapons had been in the car for a relatively short period of time and that the accused was very busy on the night in question, all bore on the question of forgetfulness, and were matters for the jury to consider. See also *Ivey* [2000] EWCA Crim 3458, where forgetfulness was relevant to the reasonable excuse that D had put the knife in his pocket as part of moving his possessions from one house to another (the knife having been bought as an ornament) and he had had his possessions in his car for two weeks and had forgotten about the knife. See also *Lorimer* [2003] EWCA Crim 721. In *R (Bayliss) v DPP* [2003] EWHC 245 (Admin), the Divisional Court accepted that there may be circumstances where forgetfulness is relevant to the defence of good reason, but it is not relevant to having the weapon with him (as to which see **B12.150**).

In *Nicholson* [2006] EWCA Crim 1518 (a case concerning the breach of an ASBO), the Court of Appeal suggested that the reason why the court held back from holding that forgetfulness of possession of the offending article could on its own amount to a reasonable excuse or a good reason, 'can only have been because before having to consider that defence, a court in the context of these offences must be sure that a defendant is knowingly in possession. Forgetfulness, when it supervenes, and for its duration, is absence of knowledge (ignorance) and it is an all too easy assertion for a defendant to make in an attempt to avoid conviction, particularly where his or her knowledge has to be proved as part of the prosecution case.'

THREATENING WITH WEAPON IN PUBLIC

B12.162   Prevention of Crime Act 1953, s. 1A

(1) A person is guilty of an offence if that person—
  (a) has an offensive weapon with him or her in a public place,
  (b) unlawfully and intentionally threatens another person with the weapon, and
  (c) does so in such a way that there is an immediate risk of serious physical harm to that other person.
(2) For the purposes of this section physical harm is serious if it amounts to grievous bodily harm for the purposes of the Offences against the Person Act 1861.

The offence under s. 1A was created by the LASPO 2012, s. 142 (in force from 3 December 2012).

Procedure and Sentence

B12.163 The offence under the Prevention of Crime Act 1953, s. 1A, is triable either way. On conviction on indictment, the maximum penalty is four years' imprisonment, a fine or both; on summary conviction, the maximum penalty is six months' imprisonment, a fine not exceeding the statutory maximum or both (s. 1A(4)).

Where a person aged 16 or over is convicted of an offence under s. 1A, the court must impose a minimum custodial sentence (with or without a fine) unless the court is of the opinion that there are particular circumstances which relate to the offence or to the offender and which would make it unjust to do so in all the circumstances (s. 1A(5)). The minimum sentence in the case of an offender aged 16 or 17 when convicted is a detention and training order for four months, and the minimum sentence in the case of an offender aged 18 or over when convicted is imprisonment or detention in a young offender institution for six months. See **E5.17**.

Simple possession of an offensive weapon (under s. 1 of the 1953 Act) is an alternative verdict to a charge under s. 1A (s. 1A(10)).

Elements

B12.164 Physical harm is 'serious' for the purposes of s. 1A if it amounts to grievous bodily harm for the purposes of the Offences against the Person Act 1861 (s. 1A(2)). For the meaning of grievous bodily harm, see **B2.60**. The terms 'offensive weapon' and 'public place' have the same meaning as in s. 1 (see **B12.143** *et seq.* and **B12.155**).

HAVING ARTICLE WITH BLADE OR POINT IN A PUBLIC PLACE

B12.165 It is an offence triable either way, contrary to the CJA 1988, s. 139(1), for a person to have with him in a public place an article to which the section applies.

Criminal Justice Act 1988, s. 139

(1) Subject to subsections (4) and (5) below, any person who has an article to which this section applies with him in a public place shall be guilty of an offence.

(2) Subject to subsection (3) below, this section applies to any article which has a blade or is sharply pointed except a folding pocket knife.

(3) This section applies to a folding pocket knife if the cutting edge of its blade exceeds 3 inches.

(4) It shall be a defence for a person charged with an offence under this section to prove that he had good reason or lawful authority for having the article with him in a public place.

(5) Without prejudice to the generality of subsection (4) above, it shall be a defence for a person charged with an offence under this section to prove that he had the article with him—

  (a) for use at work;

  (b) for religious reasons; or

  (c) as part of any national costume.

...

(7) In this section 'public place' includes any place to which at the material time the public have or are permitted access, whether on payment or otherwise.

Procedure and Sentence

The offence is punishable, on summary conviction, with a term of imprisonment not exceeding six months or a fine not exceeding the statutory maximum or both and, on conviction on indictment, a term of imprisonment not exceeding four years or a fine or both (CJA 1988, s. 139(6)).   **B12.166**

When dealt with summarily, the *Magistrates' Court Sentencing Guidelines* apply (see Supplement, SG-245).

In *Gordon* [2013] 1 Cr App R (S) 76 (14), the offender pleaded guilty to this offence. Described as 'a troubled young man', he was seen in a state of intoxication to be carrying a knife with a four and a half inch blade. He approached two boys and a girl aged 15 and spoke to them. They saw the knife, were frightened, and reported the matter. The offender had previous convictions, including one for threatening behaviour. The Court of Appeal said that an immediate custodial sentence was inevitable and, allowing full credit for the guilty plea, agreed with the trial judge's sentence of 12 months' imprisonment. In *Burgess* [2013] 2 Cr App R (S) 57 (13), 15 months' imprisonment on conviction after a trial was appropriate for possession of a kitchen knife with a three-inch blade. Police officers saw the offender, a man of previous good character, throw the weapon into bushes when they called on him to stop. The offence took place shortly after large-scale rioting. *Celaire* [2003] 1 Cr App R (S) 610 and *Povey* [2009] 1 Cr App R (S) 228 were applied in both these cases.

Articles and 'Has with Him'

Section 139 covers any article which has a blade or is sharply pointed except 'a folding pocket knife'. A folding pocket knife is covered if the cutting edge of its blade exceeds three inches.   **B12.167**

If a knife is secured in the open position by a locking device, it is not 'a folding pocket knife' because it is not immediately foldable at all times by virtue of the folding process (*Harris v DPP* (1992) 96 Cr App R 235, and see *Fehmi v DPP* (1992) 96 Cr App R 235). *Harris* was followed in *Deegan* [1998] 2 Cr App R 121, where a challenge to the established meaning on the basis of what ministers said in *Hansard* was rejected because their statements lacked clarity. Determining whether an article falls within the CJA 1988, s. 139, is a matter of law for the judge to decide (*Davis* [1998] Crim LR 564). There is no room for applying the decision in *Brutus v Cozens* [1973] AC 854, because the 'issue was not the simple etymological meaning of the word "blade"'. The test is not whether the article is capable of causing injury, because the offence is limited to articles which 'happen to have something that could be described as a blade'. A common-sense test is to be applied, namely, that the article must be 'within the same broad category as a knife or a sharply pointed instrument'. Thus a screwdriver does not fall within s. 139, but cf. *Manning*

[1998] Crim LR 198. The item need not be sharp but it must have a blade; therefore a blunt butter knife came within s. 139 (*Brooker v DPP* [2005] EWHC 1132 (Admin)).

For the meaning of 'has with him', see **B12.150**.

Public Place

B12.168   'Public place' includes any place to which, at the material time, the public have or are permitted access, whether on payment or otherwise (s. 139(7)). In *Roberts* [2004] 1 WLR 181, the Court of Appeal held that it did not include land adjacent to that to which the public had access. Unimpeded access to a place does not necessarily make it a public place, it must be determined whether public access was implied or tolerated (*Harriott v DPP* [2005] EWHC 965 (Admin)).

Defences

B12.169   Two defences are created by the CJA 1988, s. 139(4) and (5).

B12.170   **Good Reason or Lawful Authority (s. 139(4))**   It is a defence for the accused to prove that he had good reason or lawful authority for having the article with him in a public place. The accused must prove his good reason on a balance of probabilities so that merely providing an uncontradicted explanation is not necessarily sufficient (*Godwin v DPP* (1993) 96 Cr App R 244). Having considered the effect of *Lambert* [2002] 2 AC 545 (see **F3.9**), the Divisional Court in *L v DPP* [2003] QB 137, held that the reverse onus provision in s. 139, which is readily distinguishable from that in the Misuse of Drugs Act 1971, s. 28 (see **B19.96**), as the prosecution have to prove that the accused knows that he had the relevant article in his possession. Further, there is a strong public interest in bladed articles not being carried in public without good reason and, taking into account Parliament's decision, this requirement was not an improper infringement of rights. *L v DPP* was applied in *Matthews* [2004] QB 690.

For assistance on the meaning of 'good reason', the Court of Appeal in *Emmanuel* [1998] Crim LR 347 looked to the concept of 'reasonable excuse' under the Prevention of Crime Act 1953 (see **B12.158**). Professor Sir John Smith pointed out ([1998] Crim LR 347) that the defence in the CJA 1988 was intended to be a narrower one than that of reasonable excuse in the Prevention of Crime Act 1953 (see **B12.156**). In *Emmanuel* the Court of Appeal held that 'good reason' includes self-defence.

B12.171   There are limits, as a matter of law, on the defence of good reason (*Bown* [2004] 1 Cr App R 151). It is for the judge to determine whether the explanation is capable of amounting to a good reason and, if it is so capable, it is for the jury to determine whether it did so amount. The words in s. 139(4) are ordinary words of the English language. In *Clancy* (2012) 176 JP 111, the Court of Appeal held (with regard, in particular, to *Manning* [1998] Crim LR 198 and *Jolie* [2004] 1 Cr App R 44) that the expression 'good reason' is not one that calls for judicial explanation and thus it would be wrong for judges to hedge that expression 'with rules of law designed to limit its scope or meaning' (per Moore-Bick LJ). In some cases, a judge may be justified in ruling that certain facts are incapable of constituting a good reason, but should be slow to do so. In *Asmeron* [2013] 1 WLR 3457, the Court of Appeal went further and opined (at [22]) that *Clancy* was decided *per incuriam* in this respect because it is contrary to *Wang* [2005] 1 All ER 782. If the jury consider that the accused's view of the facts was wholly unreasonable (e.g., because he was drunk or had taken drugs or was suffering from mental illness) that, ultimately, is a matter for them. A fear of attack can constitute a 'good reason' within the meaning of s. 139(4): state of mind is not wholly irrelevant. The 'good reason' must relate to both the accused having the bladed article and having it with him in a public place (consider *Mohammed v Chief Constable of South Yorkshire Police* [2002] EWHC 406 (Admin) where the Divisional Court followed the approach in *Brutus v Cozens* [1973] AC 854 (see **B12.167**): and see *Deegan* [1998] 2 Cr App R 121). In *Giles* [2003] EWCA Crim 1287, it was held not to be sufficient that, in the case of a blade satisfying s. 139, the accused thought that he might use part of it, say the corkscrew. Self-harm appears not to be a 'good reason' (*Bown*). In *McAuley* [2010] 1 Cr App R 148, where it was held that it could amount to a 'good reason' under s. 139(4) if the appellant was carrying the knife for his own protection and he could show on the balance of probabilities that he was in fear of an imminent attack. The Court of Appeal added (at [15]) that it remains for a jury to determine 'how imminent, how soon, how likely and how serious' the anticipated attack has to be to constitute a good reason for possession of the bladed article. It advised that 'it would normally be wise in such cases for a judge not to rule before hearing the evidence, because that evidence may turn out to be to some extent different from and certainly more detailed than that suggested in the documents' (such as the Defence Statement).

Forgetfulness *alone* does not amount to a good reason (*DPP v Gregson* (1992) 96 Cr App R 240, **B12.172** confirmed in *Manning* [1997] EWCA Crim 2562 and *Hargreaves* [1999] EWCA Crim 2150; see also *Jolie* [2004] 1 Cr App R 44 at **B12.161**, disapproving *DPP v Gregson* and *Hargreaves*; and see *Bird* [2004] EWCA Crim 964). However, an accused who has what might be a good reason for possession of the item (e.g., a knife used regularly at work in a restaurant) should have that left to the deciders of fact, and the fact that he has forgotten about possession of the item is a factor in deciding whether he did, indeed, have good reason for possessing it (*Bird* [2004] EWCA Crim 964). In *Chahal v DPP* [2010] 2 Cr App R 33, C's conviction for being in possession of a bladed article (a knife) in a public place was quashed because the magistrates erroneously regarded the 'casual' nature of C's work (at his uncle's factory) to be a relevant consideration. C claimed that he had forgotten about the knife after leaving the factory. See also **B12.150**.

Religious Reasons, Work, National Costume (s. 139(5)) It is a defence for the accused to **B12.173** prove that he had the article with him for use at work, or for religious reasons, or as part of any national costume. Whether an article was for use for work (and therefore the other purposes also) is a matter to be determined in accordance with the approach in *Brutus v Cozens* [1973] AC 854 (see **B12.167**), as the statute uses words of the ordinary English language. It is a matter for the jury to determine having been so directed by the judge (*Manning* [1997] EWCA Crim 2562).

In *Wang* [2005] 1 All ER 782, the House of Lords decided that there were no circumstances in which the judge could direct a conviction. W carried a bag in which he had a curved martial arts sword, in its sheath. W claimed that he was a Buddhist and that he practised Shaolin, and that the knife was of a kind in which a Shaolin follower must become expert. The House of Lords held that had the trial judge directed the jury in the ordinary way, it seemed very likely that they would have convicted. However, the nature and extent of the accused's religious motivation had been the subject of evidence and his claim that he did not want to leave the weapon at home, with no one looking after it, were pre-eminently matters for the jury.

ARTICLES AND OFFENSIVE WEAPONS ON SCHOOL PREMISES

Having Article with Blade or Point on School Premises

It is an offence triable either way, contrary to the CJA 1988, s. 139A(1), for a person to have an **B12.174** article to which s. 139 applies (see **B12.165**) with him on school premises.

Criminal Justice Act 1988, 139A

(1) Any person who has an article to which section 139 of this Act applies with him on school premises shall be guilty of an offence.

(2) Any person who has an offensive weapon within the meaning of section 1 of the Prevention of Crime Act 1953 with him on school premises shall be guilty of an offence.

(3) It shall be a defence for a person charged with an offence under subsection (1) or (2) above to prove that he had good reason or lawful authority for having the article or weapon with him on the premises in question.

(4) Without prejudice to the generality of subsection (3) above, it shall be a defence for a person charged with an offence under subsection (1) or (2) above to prove that he had the article or weapon in question with him—

(a) for use at work;

    (b) for educational purposes,

    (c) for religious reasons; or

    (d) as part of any national costume.

...

(6) In this section and section 139B, 'school premises' means land used for the purposes of a school excluding any land occupied solely as a dwelling by a person employed at the school; and 'school' has the meaning given by section 4 of the Education Act 1996.

B12.175 **Procedure and Sentence**   The offence is triable either way. It is punishable, on summary conviction, with a term of imprisonment not exceeding six months or a fine not exceeding the statutory maximum or both and, on conviction on indictment, a term of imprisonment not exceeding four years or a fine or both (CJA 1988, s. 139A(5)).

B12.176 **Elements**   'Has with him' will be understood in the same way as under the Prevention of Crime Act 1953 (see **B12.150**).

The Education Act 1996, s. 4(1) defines 'school'.

B12.177 It is a defence for a person charged with the offence to prove that he had good reason or lawful authority for having the article with him on the premises in question (s. 139A(3)); as to lawful authority, see **B12.157** and **B12.158**. It is also a defence for an accused to prove that he had the article with him for use at work, for educational purposes, for religious reasons, or as part of any national costume (s. 139A(4)). The imposition of a legal burden upon the accused is open to challenge in the light of the human rights cases on the 'reverse burden' (see **F3.18** but note **B12.169** to **B12.173**).

B12.178 **Power of Search and Seizure**   Under the CJA 1988, s. 139B, a constable has a power of entry to school premises to search the premises and any person on them for any article to which s. 139 applies or for any offensive weapon within the meaning of the Prevention of Crime Act 1953, s. 1, if he has reasonable grounds for suspecting that an offence under the CJA 1988, s. 139A or s. 139AA) is being or has been committed. If the constable finds any article which he has reasonable grounds for suspecting is such an article, he may seize and retain it. Reasonable force may be used, if necessary.

For powers of search and seizure at schools, see **B12.4**.

Having Offensive Weapon on School Premises

B12.179 It is an offence triable either way, contrary to the CJA 1988, s. 139A(2), for a person to have an offensive weapon as defined in the Prevention of Crime Act 1953 (see **B12.143** to **B12.150**) with him on school premises. 'Has with him' will be understood in the same way as under the Prevention of Crime Act 1953 (see **B12.150**). As to the meaning of 'school premises' and 'school', see **B12.174**. It is punishable, on summary conviction, with a term of imprisonment not exceeding six months or a fine not exceeding the statutory maximum or both and, on conviction on indictment, to a term of imprisonment not exceeding four years or a fine or both (CJA 1988, s. 139A(5)(b)). The same defences as for the offence contrary to s. 139A(1) apply to this offence, see **B12.174**. For the power of entry and search, see **B12.178**.

THREATENING WITH ARTICLE WITH BLADE OR POINT OR OFFENSIVE WEAPON

B12.180

Criminal Justice Act 1988, s. 139AA

(1) A person is guilty of an offence if that person—

    (a) has an article to which this section applies with him or her in a public place or on school premises,

(b) unlawfully and intentionally threatens another person with the article, and

(c) does so in such a way that there is an immediate risk of serious physical harm to that other person.

The offence under s. 139AA was created by the LASPO 2012, s. 142 (in force from 3 December 2012).

Procedure and Sentence

The offence under the CJA 1988, s. 139AA, is triable either way. On conviction on indictment, the maximum penalty is four years' imprisonment, a fine or both; on summary conviction, the maximum penalty is six months' imprisonment, a fine not exceeding the statutory maximum or both (s. 139AA(6)).   **B12.181**

Where a person aged 16 or over is convicted of an offence under s. 139AA, the court must impose a minimum custodial sentence (with or without a fine) unless the court is of the opinion that there are particular circumstances which relate to the offence or to the offender and which would make it unjust to do so in all the circumstances (s. 139AA(7)). The minimum sentence in the case of an offender aged 16 or 17 when convicted is a detention and training order for four months, and the minimum sentence in the case of an offender aged 18 or over when convicted is imprisonment or detention in a young offender institution for six months. See **E5.18**.

Possession of an article with a blade or point or of an offensive weapon (under s. 139 or 139A) is an alternative verdict to a charge under s. 139AA (s. 139AA(12)).

Elements

In relation to a 'public place', s. 139AA of the Act applies to an article to which s. 139 applies (s. 139AA(2); 'public place' has the same meaning as in s. 139: see **B12.165**). In relation to 'school premises', s. 139AA applies to (a) an article to which s. 139 applies; or (b) an 'offensive weapon' within the meaning of s. 1 of the Prevention of Crime Act 1953 (s. 139AA(3)). 'School premises' has the same meaning as in s. 139A (s. 139AA(5): see **B12.174**).   **B12.182**

Physical harm is 'serious' for the purposes of the CJA 1988, s. 139AA, if it amounts to grievous bodily harm for the purposes of the OAPA 1861 (s. 139AA(4)). For the meaning of 'grievous bodily harm', see **B2.60**. The term 'offensive weapon' has the same meaning as in the Prevention of Crime Act 1953, s. 1 (see **B12.143** *et seq.*).

POSSESSION OF CROSSBOW BY PERSON UNDER 18

It is a summary offence, contrary to the Crossbows Act 1987, s. 3, for a person under the age of 18 to have with him: (a) a crossbow which is capable of discharging a missile; or (b) parts of a crossbow which together (and without any other parts) can be assembled to form a crossbow capable of discharging a missile, unless he is under the supervision of a person who is 21 years of age or older. The offence does not apply to crossbows with a draw weight of less than 1.4 kilograms (s. 5). A person guilty of the offence is liable to a fine not exceeding level 3 on the standard scale. The court may also make such order as it thinks fit as to the forfeiture or disposal of any crossbow or part of a crossbow in respect of which the offence was committed (s. 6).   **B12.183**

For offences by trespassers on premises carrying weapons, see **B13.83** and **B13.84**.

MANUFACTURE, SALE, HIRE AND PURCHASE OF WEAPONS

There are four summary offences concerned with the manufacture etc. of various types of weapons generally: **B12.184**

(a) manufacture, sale or hire etc. of dangerous weapons, contrary to the Restriction of Offensive Weapons Act 1959, s. 1(1): **B12.185**;

781

(b) manufacture, sale and hire of offensive weapons, contrary to the CJA 1988, s. 141(1):
    B12.186;
(c) sale and letting on hire of a crossbow to a person under 18, contrary to the Crossbows Act
    1987, s. 1: **B12.191**;
(d) purchase and hiring of a crossbow by a person under 18, contrary to the Crossbows Act
    1987, s. 2: **B12.191**.

In addition to these offences, there are certain offences of a similar nature which relate only to
knives (see **B12.192** *et seq.*).

Note that the PACA 2009, s. 102, inserts new ss. 141ZB to 141ZD into the CJA 1988, which
(when in force) prohibit the importation of offensive weapons subject to specified exceptions.
Section 141(4) of the CJA 1988, which currently prohibits such importation, and related provisions will be repealed (see the PACA 2009, sch. 8, part 10). Section 102 of the 2009 Act will
come into force on a day to be appointed.

Manufacture, Sale or Hire etc. of Dangerous Weapons

B12.185   Restriction of Offensive Weapons Act 1959, s. 1

(1) Any person who manufactures, sells or hires or offers for sale or hire or exposes or has in his
    possession for the purposes of sale or hire, or lends or gives to any other person—
    (a) any knife which has a blade which opens automatically by hand pressure applied to a but-
        ton, spring or other device in or attached to the handle of the knife, sometimes known as
        a 'flick-knife' or 'flick gun'; or
    (b) any knife which has a blade which is released from the handle or sheath thereof by the force
        of gravity or the application of centrifugal force and which, when released, is locked in
        place by means of a button, spring, lever, or other device, sometimes known as a 'gravity
        knife',
    shall be guilty of an offence and shall be liable on summary conviction to imprisonment for a
    term not exceeding six months or to a fine not exceeding level 5 on the standard scale or to both
    such imprisonment and fine.

In addition, the Restriction of Offensive Weapons Act 1959, s. 1(2), prohibits the importation
of any such knife described in s. 1(1).

Manufacture, Sale and Hire of Offensive Weapons

B12.186   Criminal Justice Act 1988, s. 141

(1) Any person who manufactures, sells or hires or offers for sale or hire, exposes or has in his pos-
    session for the purpose of sale or hire, or lends or gives to any other person, a weapon to which
    this section applies shall be guilty of an offence...

Subsection (4) also prohibits the importation of a weapon to which this section applies.

By virtue of the CJA 1988, s. 141(1), a person guilty of the offence is liable to imprisonment for
a term not exceeding six months, or to a fine not exceeding level 5 on the standard scale, or both.

B12.187 The weapons to which s. 141 applies are those listed in the schedule to the Criminal Justice Act
1988 (Offensive Weapons) Order 1988 (SI 1988 No. 2019), which was made under s. 141(2).
This makes the following items offensive weapons for the purpose of the instant offence, other
than weapons which are antiques.

Criminal Justice Act 1988 (Offensive Weapons) Order 1988
(SI 1988 No. 2019), sch.

...
    (a) a knuckleduster, that is, a band of metal or other hard material worn on one or more fin-
        gers, and designed to cause injury, and any weapon incorporating a knuckleduster;
    (b) a swordstick, that is, a hollow walking-stick or cane containing a blade which may be used
        as a sword;

(c) the weapon sometimes known as a 'handclaw', being a band of metal or other hard material from which a number of sharp spikes protrude, and worn around the hand;

(d) the weapon sometimes known as a 'belt buckle knife', being a buckle which incorporates or conceals a knife;

(e) the weapon sometimes known as a 'push dagger', being a knife the handle of which fits within a clenched fist and the blade of which protrudes from between two fingers;

(f) the weapon sometimes known as a 'hollow kubotan', being a cylindrical container containing a number of sharp spikes;

(g) the weapon sometimes known as a 'footclaw', being a bar of metal or other hard material from which a number of sharp spikes protrude, and worn strapped to the foot;

(h) the weapon sometimes known as a 'shuriken', 'shaken' or 'death star', being a hard non-flexible plate having three or more sharp radiating points and designed to be thrown;

(i) the weapon sometimes known as a 'balisong' or 'butterfly knife', being a blade enclosed by its handle, which is designed to split down the middle, without the operation of a spring or other mechanical means, to reveal the blade;

(j) the weapon sometimes known as a 'telescopic truncheon', being a truncheon which extends automatically by hand pressure applied to a button, spring or other device in or attached to its handle;

(k) the weapon sometimes known as a 'blowpipe' or 'blow gun' being a hollow tube out of which hard pellets or darts are shot by the use of breath;

(l) the weapon sometimes known as a 'kusari gama', being a length of rope, cord, wire or chain fastened at one end to a sickle;

(m) the weapon sometimes known as a 'kyoketsu shoge', being a length of rope, cord, wire or chain fastened at one end to a hooked knife;

(n) the weapon sometimes known as a 'manrikigusari' or 'kusari', being a length of rope, cord, wire or chain fastened at each end to a hard weight or hand grip;

(o) a disguised knife, that is any knife which has a concealed blade or concealed sharp point and is designed to appear to be an everyday object of a kind commonly carried on the person or in a handbag, briefcase, or other hand luggage (such as a comb, brush, writing instrument, cigarette lighter, key, lipstick or telephone); [inserted by the Criminal Justice Act 1988 (Offensive Weapons) Order 2002]

(p) a stealth knife, that is a knife or spike, which has a blade, or sharp point, made from a material that is not readily detectable by apparatus used for detecting metal and which is not designed for domestic use or for use in the processing, preparation or consumption of food or as a toy;

(q) a straight, side-handled or friction-lock truncheon (sometimes known as a baton). [(p) and (q) inserted by the Criminal Justice Act 1988 (Offensive Weapons) (Amendment) Order 2004]

(r) a sword with a curved blade of 50 centimetres or over in length; and for the purposes of this sub-paragraph, the length of the blade shall be the straight line distance from the top of the handle to the tip of the blade [inserted by the Criminal Justice Act 1988 (Offensive Weapons) (Amendment) Order 2008 (SI 2008 No. 973)].

B12.188 For the purposes of the schedule, a weapon is an antique if it was manufactured more than 100 years before the date of any offence alleged to have been committed in respect of the weapon.

It is a defence for the accused to show that he is:

(a) carrying out functions on behalf of the Crown or a visiting force (see the CJA 1988, s. 141(5)–(7)); or

(b) making a weapon available to a museum or gallery (s. 141(8), (10) and (11)); or

(c) a person acting on behalf of a museum or gallery loaning or hiring a weapon for proper purposes (see s. 141(9));

(d) making the weapon available for theatre, film or television purposes (s. 141(11A)–(11C)).

Curved Blades **B12.189** SI 2008 No. 973 has added swords that have a curved blade of 50 centimetres or over in length to the list of weapons to which the CJA 1988, s. 141, applies. Defences to a charge under s. 141 (or under the Customs and Excise Management Act 1979, s. 50(2) or (3)) are added to the 1988 Order (paras. 3 to 6) by SI 2008 No. 973 as amended by the Criminal Justice Act 1988 (Offensive Weapons) (Amendment No. 2) Order 2008 (SI 2008 No. 2039). The defences apply to swords with a curved blade of 50 centimetres or over in length made anywhere in the world either before 1954 or at any other time according to traditional methods of making swords by hand or to weapons available for the purposes of religious ceremonies. Note the incidence and standard of proof mentioned in para. 6 of the 1988 Order (as amended by the 2008 Order).

B12.190   **Criminal Justice Act 1988 (Offensive Weapons) Order 1988**
                                    (SI 1988 No. 2019), paras. 3 to 6

3. It shall be a defence for a person charged—
   (a) with an offence under section 141(1) of the Criminal Justice Act 1988; or
   (b) with an offence under section 50(2) or (3) of the Customs and Excise Management Act 1979,
   in respect of any conduct of his relating to a weapon to which section 141 of the Criminal Justice Act 1988 applies by virtue of paragraph 1(r) to show that the weapon in question was made before 1954 or was made at any other time according to traditional methods of making swords by hand.

4. It shall be a defence for a person charged—
   (a) with an offence under section 141(1) of the Criminal Justice Act 1988; or
   (b) with an offence under section 50(2) or (3) of the Customs and Excise Management Act 1979,
   in respect of any conduct of his relating to a weapon to which section 141 of the Criminal Justice Act 1988 applies by virtue of paragraph 1(r) to show that his conduct was for the purpose only of making the weapon available for the purposes of the organisation and holding of a permitted activity for which public liability insurance is held in relation to liabilities to third parties arising from or in connection with the organisation and holding of such an activity.

5. For the purposes of paragraph 4—
   'historical re-enactment' means any presentation or other event held for the purpose of re-enacting an event from the past or of illustrating conduct from a particular time or period in the past;
   'insurance' means a contract of insurance or other arrangement made for the purpose of indemnifying a person or persons named in the contract or under the arrangement;
   'permitted activity' means an historical re-enactment or a sporting activity;
   'sporting activity' means the practising of a sport which requires the use of a weapon described in paragraph 1(r);
   'third parties' includes participants in, and spectators of, a permitted activity and members of the public.

5A. It shall be a defence for a person charged—
   (a) with an offence under section 141(1) of the Criminal Justice Act 1988; or
   (b) with an offence under section 50(2) or (3) of the Customs and Excise Management Act 1979,
   in respect of any conduct of his relating to a weapon to which section 141 of the Criminal Justice Act 1988 applies by virtue of paragraph 1(r) to show that his conduct was for the purpose only of making the weapon available for the purposes of use in religious ceremonies.

6. For the purposes of paragraphs 3, 4 and 5A, a person shall be taken to have shown a matter specified in those paragraphs if—
   (a) sufficient evidence of that matter is adduced to raise an issue with respect to it; and
   (b) the contrary is not proved beyond a reasonable doubt.

B12.191 **Crossbows**   It is an offence to sell or to let on hire a crossbow or a part of a crossbow to a person under the age of 18 (Crossbows Act 1987, s. 1). It is a defence that the accused believed the person to be 18 years of age or older and had reasonable ground for the belief. The maximum penalty is imprisonment for a term not exceeding six months, a fine not exceeding level 5 on the standard scale, or both.

A person under the age of 18 who buys or hires a crossbow or part of a crossbow is guilty of an offence (s. 2), and liable to a fine not exceeding level 3 on the standard scale. The crossbow or the relevant part may be forfeited or disposed of (s. 6(1) and (3)).

MANUFACTURE, MARKETING, SALE, HIRE AND PURCHASE OF KNIVES

The Offensive Weapons Act 1996, s. 6, created an offence relating to the sale of knives to persons under a specified age. The Knives Act 1997 has created two either-way offences (unlawful marketing of knives and publications in connection with the marketing of knives). All these offences are in addition to the summary offences mentioned at **B12.184**.

B12.192

Sale of Knives and Certain Articles with Blade or Point to Persons under 18

Criminal Justice Act 1988, s. 141A

B12.193

> (1) ...any person who sells to a person under the age of 18 years an article to which this section applies shall be guilty of an offence and liable on summary conviction to imprisonment for a term not exceeding six months, or a fine not exceeding level 5 on the standard scale, or both.

By the CJA 1988, s. 141A(2), the offence applies to any knife, knife blade or razor blade, any axe, and any other article which has a blade or which is sharply pointed and which is made or adapted for use for causing injury to the person.

Section 141A(1) does not apply to:

(a) a folding knife if the cutting edge of its blade does not exceed 7.62 centimetres (3 inches);
(b) razor blades permanently enclosed in a cartridge or housing where less than 2 millimetres of any blade is exposed beyond the place which intersects the highest point of the surfaces preceding and following such blades (Criminal Justice Act 1988 (Offensive Weapons) (Exemptions) Order 1996 (SI 1996 No. 3064), art. 2).

It is not an offence under s. 141A(1) to sell a knife or knife blade to a person if the person is aged 16 or over and the knife or blade is designed for domestic use (s. 141A(3A)).

A grapefruit knife is a knife within the meaning of the CJA 1988, s.141A, as amended by the Offensive Weapons Act 1996 (*R (Royal Borough of Windsor and Maidenhead) v East Berkshire Justices* [2011] 1 Cr App R 270).

As to articles made or adapted to cause injury under the Prevention of Crime Act 1953, see **B12.146** and **B12.147**. Section 141A does not apply to any article described in the Restriction of Offensive Weapons Act 1959, s. 1 (see **B12.185**), an order made under the CJA 1988, s. 141(2) (see **B12.187**), or any order made under s. 141A itself (s. 141A(3)). It is a defence for a person charged with the offence to prove that he took all reasonable precautions and exercised due diligence to avoid the commission of the offence (s. 141A(4)); the imposition of a legal burden upon the accused is open to challenge in the light of the human rights jurisprudence regarding 'reverse burdens' (see **F3.18**).

Unlawful Marketing of Knives

Knives Act 1997, s. 1

B12.194

> (1) A person is guilty of an offence if he markets a knife in a way which—
> (a) indicates, or suggests, that it is suitable for combat; or
> (b) is otherwise likely to stimulate or encourage violent behaviour involving the use of the knife as a weapon.

The offence is triable either way s. 1(5)). The maximum penalty is: on conviction on indictment, imprisonment for a term not exceeding two years or a fine, or both; on summary conviction, imprisonment for a term not exceeding six months or a fine not exceeding the statutory maximum, or both (s. 1(5)).

Elements

B12.195 'Knife' means an instrument which has a blade or is sharply pointed (s. 10). (Note that it is this definition that is relevant for the purposes of chapter 1 of part 3 of the CAJA 2009 (anonymity investigations into offences of murder or manslaughter: see **D1.197**).) A person markets a knife if he sells or hires it, he offers, or exposes, it for sale or hire or has it in his possession for the purpose of sale or hire (s. 1(4)). A knife is suitable for combat if it is suitable for use as a weapon for inflicting injury on a person or causing a person to fear injury (s. 10). 'Violent behaviour' means an unlawful act inflicting injury on a person or causing a person to fear injury (s. 10).

An indication or suggestion that a knife is suitable for combat may, in particular, be given or made by a name or description which is applied to the knife, which is on the knife or any packaging in which it is contained or which is included in any advertisement which, expressly or by implication, relates to the knife (s. 1(3)).

Defences

B12.196   Knives Act 1997, ss. 3 and 4

3.—(1) It is a defence for a person charged with an offence under section 1 to prove that—
    (a) the knife was marketed—
        (i)   for use by the armed forces of any country;
        (ii) as an antique or curio; or
        (iii) as falling within such other category (if any) as may be prescribed;
    (b) it was reasonable for the knife to be marketed in that way; and
    (c) there were no reasonable grounds for suspecting that a person into whose possession the knife might come in consequence of the way in which it was marketed would use it for an unlawful purpose.

4. (1) It is a defence for a person charged with an offence under section 1 to prove that he did not know or suspect, and had no reasonable grounds for suspecting, that the way in which the knife was marketed—
    (a) amounted to an indication or suggestion that the knife was suitable for combat; or
    (b) was likely to stimulate or encourage violent behaviour involving the use of the knife as a weapon.
(2) It is a defence for a person charged with an offence under section 2 to prove that he did not know or suspect, and had no reasonable grounds for suspecting, that the way in which the knife was marketed—
    (a) amounted to an indication or suggestion that the knife was suitable for combat; or
    (b) was likely to stimulate or encourage violent behaviour involving the use of the knife as a weapon.
(3) It is a defence for a person charged with an offence under section 1 or 2 to prove that he took all reasonable precautions and exercised all due diligence to avoid committing the offence.

The imposition of a legal burden upon the accused is open to challenge in the light of the human rights cases on the 'reverse burden' (see **F3.18**).

Publications Relating to Knives

B12.197   Knives Act 1997, s. 2

(1) A person is guilty of an offence if he publishes any written, pictorial or other material in connection with the marketing of any knife and that material—
    (a) indicates or suggests that the knife is suitable for combat; or
    (b) is otherwise likely to stimulate or encourage violent behaviour involving the use of the knife as a weapon.

The maximum penalty is: on conviction on indictment, imprisonment for a term not exceeding two years or a fine, or both; on summary conviction, imprisonment for a term not exceeding six months or a fine not exceeding the statutory maximum, or both.

For definition of the terms used in s. 2, see **B12.195**.

Specific defences are provided by s. 4(2) and (3) (see **B12.196**).

MINDING A 'DANGEROUS WEAPON'

Section 28 of the VCRA 2006 creates an offence of using a person to mind a 'dangerous weapon', **B12.198**
being a weapon intended to be made available for an unlawful purpose. By s. 28(3), 'dangerous weapon' means (a) a firearm other than an air weapon or a component part of, or accessory
to, an air weapon; or (b) a weapon to which the CJA 1988, s. 141, applies (see **B12.186**). The
penalties are set out in s. 29; the minimum sentence provisions in s. 29 are considered at **E5.14**.

Violent Crime Reduction Act 2006, ss. 28 and 29

28.—(1) A person is guilty of an offence if—
    (a) he uses another to look after, hide or transport a dangerous weapon for him; and
    (b) he does so under arrangements or in circumstances that facilitate, or are intended to facili-
        tate, the weapon's being available to him for an unlawful purpose.
(2) For the purposes of this section the cases in which a dangerous weapon is to be regarded as
    available to a person for an unlawful purpose include any case where—
    (a) the weapon is available for him to take possession of it at a time and place; and
    (b) his possession of the weapon at that time and place would constitute, or be likely to involve
        or to lead to, the commission by him of an offence.
(3) In this section 'dangerous weapon' means—
    (a) a firearm other than an air weapon or a component part of, or accessory to, an air
        weapon; or
    (b) a weapon to which section 141 or 141A of the Criminal Justice Act 1988 applies (specified
        offensive weapons, knives and bladed weapons).
(4) [Scotland.]
29.—(1) This section applies where a person ('the offender') is guilty of an offence under section 28.
(2) Where the dangerous weapon in respect of which the offence was committed is a weapon to
    which section 141 or 141A of the Criminal Justice Act 1988 (specified offensive weapons,
    knives and bladed weapons) applies, the offender shall be liable, on conviction on indictment,
    to imprisonment for a term not exceeding 4 years or to a fine, or to both.
(3) Where—
    (a) at the time of the offence, the offender was aged 16 or over, and
    (b) the dangerous weapon in respect of which the offence was committed was a firearm men-
        tioned in section 5(1)(a)–(af) or (c) or section 5(1A)(a) of the 1968 Act (firearms posses-
        sion of which attracts a minimum sentence),
    the offender shall be liable, on conviction on indictment, to imprisonment for a term not
    exceeding 10 years or to a fine, or to both.
(4) On a conviction in England and Wales, where—
    (a) subsection (3) applies, and
    (b) the offender is aged 18 or over at the time of conviction,
    the court must impose (with or without a fine) a term of imprisonment of not less than 5 years,
    unless it is of the opinion that there are exceptional circumstances relating to the offence or to
    the offender which justify its not doing so.
(5) In relation to times before the commencement of paragraph 180 of schedule 7 to the Criminal
    Justice and Court Services Act 2000, the reference in subsection (4) to a sentence of impris-
    onment, in relation to an offender aged under 21 at the time of conviction, is to be read as a
    reference to a sentence of detention in a young offender institution.
(6) On a conviction in England and Wales, where—
    (a) subsection (3) applies, and
    (b) the offender is aged under 18 at the time of conviction,
    the court must impose (with or without a fine) a term of detention under section 91 of the
    Powers of Criminal Courts (Sentencing) Act 2000 of not less than 3 years, unless it is of the
    opinion that there are exceptional circumstances relating to the offence or to the offender
    which justify its not doing so.

B

Part B: Offences

CAUSING EXPLOSION LIKELY TO ENDANGER
LIFE OR PROPERTY

B12.199   Explosive Substances Act 1883, s. 2

A person who in the United Kingdom or (being a citizen of the United Kingdom and Colonies) in the Republic of Ireland unlawfully and maliciously causes by any explosive substance an explosion of a nature likely to endanger life or to cause serious injury to property shall, whether any injury to person or property has actually been caused or not, be guilty of an offence...

Indictment

B12.200   *Statement of Offence*

Causing an explosion contrary to section 2 of the Explosive Substances Act 1883.

Particulars of Offence

A on or about the...day of...maliciously caused by an explosive substance an explosion of a nature likely to endanger life or to cause serious injury to property, namely the explosion at...Town Hall on the...day of...

Procedure

B12.201   The offence is triable on indictment only (Explosive Substances Act 1883, s. 2) and is a class 2A offence.

Proceedings for a crime under this Act shall not be instituted except by or with the consent of the A-G (s. 7(1)); remands in custody or bail are expressly excluded from the operation of s. 7(1) by the Prosecution of Offences Act 1985, s. 25(2) (see *Wale* (1991) *The Times*, 9 May 1991, in which the proceedings for the offence contrary to s. 4 were held not to be effectively instituted until the committal proceedings). Further, in *Elliott* (1984) 81 Cr App R 115 at p. 121, the Court of Appeal concluded that the Explosive Substances Act 1883, s. 7, 'should be interpreted as meaning that instituting proceedings relates to the time when a person comes to court to answer the charge' so the relevant time is 'when he attends at the magistrates' court to answer the charge'; it held that any other interpretation would 'overlook and ignore' the provisions of the Prosecution of Offences Act 1985, s. 6.

Sentence

B12.202   The maximum penalty is imprisonment for life (Explosive Substances Act 1883, s. 2). Relevant sentencing cases are *McDonald* [2002] 2 Cr App R (S) 113 and *Jones* (1995) 16 Cr App R (S) 107. Powers of forfeiture and disposal of matter are provided by the Explosives Act 1875, ss. 89 and 96; these apply to this offence (1883 Act, s. 8(1)). See also **B12.212**.

Explosive Substance and Explosion

B12.203   'Explosive substance' is 'deemed to include any materials for making any explosive substance; also any apparatus, machine, implement or materials used, or intended to be used, or adapted for causing, or aiding in causing, any explosion in or with any explosive substance; also any part of any such apparatus, machine or implement' (Explosive Substances Act 1883, s. 9(1)). Explosive substances have included a shot gun (*Downey* [1971] NI 224), a firearm (*Fegan* (1971) 78 Cr App R 189), part of a vessel filled with an explosive substance (*Charles* (1892) 17 Cox CC 499) and electronic timers (*Berry (No. 3)* [1995] 2 All ER 913; and see *G* [2010] 1 AC 43, where it was remarked (at [55]) that s. 9 would apply, for instance, to a timer), as well as the more obvious substances, such as dynamite or gunpowder (*Hallam* [1957] 1 QB 569), plaster gelatine and detonators (*Stewart* (1959) 44 Cr App R 29), and a stick of gelignite, a length of fuse and a detonator (*McCarthy* [1964] 1 All ER 95). The petrol in a petrol bomb combines with the air to create an explosive substance, so the petrol, bottle and wick are materials for making that explosive substance (*Bouch* [1983] QB 246 and *Howard* [1993] Crim LR 213).

'**Explosive**'   The Court of Appeal decided in *Wheatley* [1979] 1 All ER 954, that the definition   **B12.204**
of 'explosive' in the Explosives Act 1875, s. 3, applies to the 1883 Act.

Explosives Act 1875, s. 3

The term 'explosive' in this Act — (1) Means gunpowder, nitro-glycerine, dynamite, guncotton, blasting powders, fulminate of mercury or of other metals, coloured fires and every other substance, whether similar to those above mentioned or not, used or manufactured with a view to producing a practical effect by explosion or a pyrotechnic effect; and (2) includes fog-signals, fireworks, fuses, rockets, percussion caps, detonators, cartridges, ammunition of all description, and every adaptation or preparation of an explosive as above defined.

In *Wheatley*, fire-dampened sodium chlorate mixture, used in a pipe bomb, was an explosive substance, even if it had only a pyrotechnic effect. In *Bouch*, the Court of Appeal held that 'pyrotechnic effect' has a broad meaning and is not limited to, e.g., fireworks. A flare is a pyrotechnic device. There does not have to be an explosion. A fireball produced by a petrol bomb has a pyrotechnic effect.

'**Explosion**'   The meaning of 'explosion' was considered by the Court of Appeal in *Bouch*,   **B12.205**
where the definition used in the 1886 edition of the *Encyclopaedia Britannica* was approved:

'explosion' may for our purpose be defined as the sudden or extremely rapid conversion of a solid or liquid body of small bulk into gas or vapour, occupying very many times the volume of the original substance, and, in addition, highly expanded by the heat generated during the transformation. This sudden or very rapid expansion of volume is attained by an exhibition of force, more or less violent according to the constitution of the original substance and the circumstances of explosion. Any substance capable of undergoing such a change upon the application of heat, or other disturbing cause, is called 'explosive'.

The inevitable concomitant of a successful petrol bomb is an explosion because it produces a fireball, though it does not always have a blast effect. A petrol bomb will produce a blast effect where it does not ignite immediately upon impact but ignites after a pause. See also *Elliott* (1984) 81 Cr App R 115 adopting this approach.

Who in the United Kingdom

In *Ellis* (1991) 95 Cr App R 52, Swinton Thomas J held, on a motion to quash two counts in an   **B12.206**
indictment, that 'the words "who in the United Kingdom" do not govern the person but govern the acts'. In reaching this conclusion the judge had pointed out that 'to construe section 3…so as to limit the offence to a person who is physically present in the United Kingdom when he causes explosions runs not only wholly contrary to common sense but wholly contrary to the whole tenor of the law as it has developed over the last century and particularly over the last two decades'.

Mens Rea

The *mens rea is* that the act must be done 'maliciously' (see **B2.63** and **A2.12**). It is often said   **B12.207**
that there is no need for foresight by the defendant of (a) endangerment of life or (b) serious injury to property. The jury assesses the likelihood of either objectively. Without asserting that this proposition is incorrect, or overstated, consider *G* [2004] 1 AC 1034 and *Cunningham* [1957] 2 QB 396.

Punishment of Accessories

See **B12.222**.   **B12.208**

Power of Search etc.

Section 8(1) of the Explosive Substances Act 1883 extends certain powers in the Explosives Act   **B12.209**
1875 to this offence. The powers are: to search for explosives (s. 73); to seize and detain explosives liable to forfeiture (s. 74); and to inspect wharves, carriages, boats etc. with explosives in transit (s. 75).

ATTEMPT TO CAUSE EXPLOSION OR MAKING OR KEEPING EXPLOSIVE WITH INTENT TO ENDANGER LIFE OR PROPERTY

B12.210

Explosive Substances Act 1883, s. 3

(1) A person who in the United Kingdom or a dependency or (being a citizen of the United Kingdom and Colonies) elsewhere unlawfully and maliciously—

(a) does any act with intent to cause, or conspires to cause, by an explosive substance an explosion of a nature likely to endanger life, or cause serious injury to property, whether in the United Kingdom or elsewhere

(b) makes or has in his possession or under his control an explosive substance with intent by means thereof to endanger life, or cause serious injury to property, whether in the United Kingdom or elsewhere, or to enable any other person so to do,

shall, whether any explosion does or does not take place, and whether any injury to person or property is actually caused or not, be guilty of an offence...

Procedure

B12.211   The offence is triable on indictment only (Explosive Substances Act 1883, s. 3(1)) and is a class 2A offence. As to the need for the A-G's consent, see **B12.201**.

Sentence

B12.212   The maximum penalty is imprisonment for life (Explosive Substances Act 1883, s. 3(1)). The explosive substance is forfeited. The related provisions of the Explosives Act 1875 (ss. 89 and 96) apply (s. 8(1)).

In *Martin* [1999] 1 Cr App R (S) 477, the Court of Appeal issued guidelines for the sentencing of this offence. Lord Bingham CJ said that the appropriate sentence would depend upon a number of factors, including the nature, size and likely effect of the explosive device, the nature and extent of any death, injury or damage caused, together with the role and motivation of the individual offenders.

In cases of conspiracy to cause an explosion, key factors would be the target of that conspiracy, and the likely result of any explosion. A conspiracy whose primary object was to endanger life should attract a higher sentence than one primarily directed to damaging property. On the facts of the case before the court, the offenders were members of the IRA who had planned to cause explosions, using 37 bombs at electricity substations. They had been arrested before the plan could be implemented. The political, economic and social threat in this case had been grave, and death or personal injury, though not the primary intention, had been an obvious risk. The sentence was reduced from 35 years' imprisonment to 28 years, a term designed to correlate with the period typically served by the perpetrator of a murder with severely aggravating features. In *A-G's Ref (No. 13 of 2002)* [2003] 1 Cr App R (S) 48, the offender built a number of sophisticated explosive devices with lethal potential. A sentence of five years' imprisonment for the offence under s. 3 was increased to nine years on appeal. The Court of Appeal said that 12 years would have been appropriate without the element of double jeopardy.

Elements

B12.213   As to the significance of 'in the United Kingdom', see **B12.206**; 'dependency' means the Channel Islands, the Isle of Man and any colony, other than a colony for whose external relations a country other than the UK is responsible (Explosive Substances Act 1883, s. 3(2)). *Abedin* [2004] EWCA Crim 2232 confirms that a jury is bound to acquit if it thinks that the intention of the accused was to cause an explosion to endanger life or damage property abroad and not in the UK.

For the meaning of 'explosive substance' and 'explosive', see **B12.203** *et seq*. For the meaning of 'making explosives', see **B12.216**.

'Maliciously'

The *mens rea* is that the act, whatever it might be, must be done 'maliciously' (see **B2.63** and   **B12.214**
A2.12). It would appear not to be possible to possess a substance maliciously if it is not known what the substance is. Thus the approach in the cases decided on the Explosive Substances Act 1883, s. 4, by the Court of Criminal Appeal in *Hallam* [1957] 1 QB 569 and *Stewart* (1959) 44 Cr App R 29 (see **B12.219**), may be applicable to this offence also, rather than the rules relating to possession developed in relation to controlled drugs (see **B19.23**).

Punishment of Accessories and Powers of Search

See **B12.222** for punishment of accessories. See **B12.209** for powers of search.   **B12.215**

MAKING OR POSSESSION OF EXPLOSIVE UNDER SUSPICIOUS CIRCUMSTANCES

Explosive Substances Act 1883, s. 4   **B12.216**

(1) Any person who makes or knowingly has in his possession or under his control any explosive substance, under such circumstances as to give rise to a reasonable suspicion that he is not making it or does not have it in his possession or under his control for a lawful object, shall, unless he can show that he made it or had it in his possession or under his control for a lawful object, be guilty of [an offence]…

Procedure

The offence is triable on indictment only (Explosive Substances Act 1883, s. 4(1)) and is a class   **B12.217**
2A offence. As to the need for the A-G's consent, see **B12.201**. Note *McVitie* [1960] 2 QB 483 regarding particulars of the offence.

Sentence

On conviction on indictment, the maximum penalty is 14 years' imprisonment, and the   **B12.218**
explosive substance must be forfeited (Explosive Substances Act 1883, s. 4(1)). A sentence of 42 months was upheld in *Lloyd* [2001] 2 Cr App R (S) 493, where the offender, who had 14 previous convictions for weapons-related offences, pleaded guilty to making four explosive devices, but not intending to use them to cause harm. In *Riding* [2010] 1 Cr App R (S) 37 it was held that a sentence of imprisonment was necessary for a 21-year-old man of good character who made a pipe bomb from instructions found on the internet, and kept it at his home. The sentence was reduced from 12 months to eight months. Four years' imprisonment was upheld in *Kasprzak* [2014] 1 Cr App R (S) 115 (20), where the offender admitted eight offences of possessing an explosive substance after large quantities of chemicals and formulae for making explosives were found at his home. The sentence was ordered to run concurrently to a 20-year sentence for attempted murder, kidnapping and possession of an offensive weapon.

Possession, Control or Making and *Mens Rea*

The accused must know that he has the substance in his possession or control (*Berry (No. 3)*   **B12.219**
[1994] 2 All ER 913, at p. 918h). Note the extended meaning of 'explosive substance' in the Explosive Substances Act 1883, s. 9 (see **B12.203**). In *Hallam* [1957] 1 QB 569, the Court of Criminal Appeal decided the meaning of the section was clear and that 'the person must not only knowingly have in his possession the substance but must know that it is an explosive substance', but he does not have to have 'any particular chemical knowledge'. The Court of Criminal Appeal followed this decision in *Stewart* (1959) 44 Cr App R 29. The word 'knowingly' prefaces 'possession' and 'control' and not 'making', but, nevertheless, 'all three categories of person must be shown to have known that the substance was an explosive substance' (*Berry (No. 3)*, at p. 918g). It was said in *Berry* that 'no person who makes a substance can be unaware that he had done so' although this must be read as being subject to the general defences (see **A3**).

The Court of Appeal in *Hallam* also said that 'if evidence is given that the person had the substance in his possession, and some evidence of circumstances which give rise to a reasonable suspicion that he had not got it for a lawful purpose is given, the jury are then entitled to infer that he knew it was an explosive substance'. However, there is nothing in this approach which should be interpreted as suggesting that the burden of proof is not on the prosecution to prove *mens rea*, and that is particularly so where the substance is not so obviously an explosive substance, e.g., a timer as opposed to gunpowder or gelignite. The jury must be sure that the maker intended the timer to be used to cause explosions (*Berry (No. 3)*, at p. 919).

Reasonable Suspicion

B12.220   'Reasonable suspicion' is an objective requirement, which must be proved by the prosecution (*Fegan* (1971) 78 Cr App R 189). In *G* [2010] 1 AC 43, their lordships made the point (at [56]) that whether the circumstances in which the accused was in possession or control of the article in question give rise to a reasonable suspicion depends (in part) on the nature of the article (e.g. a timer, petrol, or fertiliser) and the purpose for which that article might legitimately be applied by him. For example, many people have good reason for having petrol, but not 'semtex'.

Lawful Object

B12.221   In *Fegan* (1971) 78 Cr App R 189, the Court of Criminal Appeal, Northern Ireland, held that 'the expression "lawful object" cannot be defined exhaustively or with precision'. The court decided that possession and purpose must not be confused, so, 'possession of a firearm for the purpose of protecting the possessor, his wife or family from acts of violence may be possession for a lawful object'. That purpose 'cannot be founded on a mere fancy, or some aggressive motive' and the 'threatened danger must be reasonably and genuinely anticipated, must appear reasonably imminent, and must be of a nature which could not reasonably be met by more pacific means' (*Fegan*). The Court of Appeal in *A-G's Ref (No. 2 of 1983)* [1984] QB 456, agreed with this approach. The House of Lords appears to have adopted the same approach in *Berry* [1985] AC 246. The court, in *Fegan*, held that a person cannot possess an item for a lawful object if he also has it for an unlawful object. The Court of Appeal in *Campbell* [2004] EWCA Crim 2309, refused to grant leave to appeal against conviction where the trial judge had ruled that the defendant never had a lawful reason for possession of the explosive substances, even if it was the case that they were made by him when he was young in order to put into hollow trees and down rabbit holes and had simply been retained as part of the detritus of childhood. It is necessary for people not to store explosive items without good reasons and this defendant was irresponsible in doing what he had done. In *Riding* [2010] 1 Cr App R (S) 37, the Court of Appeal rejected R's submission that 'lawful object' means the absence of criminal purpose rather than a positive object which is lawful. The court held that 'lawful object' means the latter and not the former and that is consistent with cases such *Fegan* and *A-G's Ref (No. 2 of 1983)*. Accordingly, mere curiosity is not a lawful object in the making of a lethal pipe bomb.

As the statute makes clear, the burden of proof of this defence lies upon the accused (see *Berry (No. 3)* [1994] 2 All ER 913 at pp. 920 *et seq.* and *Fegan*) and it must be proved on a balance of probabilities (*Fegan*). That view must be open to challenge in the light of the human rights cases on the 'reverse burden' (see F3.18).

Punishment of Accessories

B12.222   Explosive Substances Act 1883, s. 5

> Any person who within or (being a subject of Her Majesty) without Her Majesty's dominions by the supply of or solicitation for money, the providing of premises, the supply of materials, or in any manner whatsoever, procures, counsels, aids, abets, or is accessory to, the commission of any crime under this Act, shall be guilty of [an offence], and shall be liable to be tried and punished for that crime, as if he had been guilty as a principal.

Notwithstanding s. 5, the commission of an offence contrary to s. 4 may be aided and abetted (*McCarthy* [1964] 1 All ER 95). For a general consideration of participation in crime, see **A4**, and, in particular, **A4.24**.

Powers of Search

See **B12.209** for powers of search.

B12.223

CAUSING BODILY INJURY BY GUNPOWDER

Offences Against the Person Act 1861, s. 28

B12.224

Whosoever shall unlawfully and maliciously, by the explosion of gunpowder or other explosive substance, burn, maim, disfigure, disable, or do any grievous bodily harm to any person, shall be guilty of [an offence].

Procedure and Sentence

B12.225

The offence is triable on indictment (OAPA 1861, s. 28) and is a class 2A offence.

The maximum penalty is imprisonment for life (s. 28).

Elements

B12.226

In *Howard* [1993] Crim LR 213, the Court of Appeal decided that a petrol bomb is an explosive substance. The definition of 'explosive substance' under the Explosive Substances Act 1883 (see **B12.203**) was used by the trial judge and noted by the Court of Appeal. It clearly is of assistance, but may not be determinative of the concept as it appears in the OAPA 1861. It is submitted that the term should mean the same in both pieces of legislation. The Court of Appeal wondered if the trial judge should not have asked the jury to determine whether the petrol bomb was an explosive substance. This can be correct only if the jury were being asked to determine whether the facts about a petrol bomb satisfied the definition of explosive substance given to them by the judge.

It is to be assumed that the words 'burn, maim, disfigure, disable, or do any grievous bodily harm' will carry their ordinary meaning, unless a decision suggests otherwise. Indeed this was the approach of the Court of Appeal in interpreting the meaning of 'disable' in *James* (1979) 70 Cr App R 215. 'Maim' has a technical legal meaning which is injury of any part of a man's body which may make him less able to defend himself (12 *Halsbury's Statutes*, at p. 109), so there was no proof of an intent to maim or disable in *Sullivan* (1841) Car & M 209, where the blow was aimed at the head of the victim, but it would have been otherwise had it been aimed at his arm to prevent his being able to use it. 'Disfigure' means to do an external injury which may detract from the personal appearance (12 *Halsbury's Statutes*, at p. 109). 'Disable' covers both permanent and temporary disablement (*James*, a decision on s. 29, and not applying *Boyce* (1824) 1 Mood CC 29). As to 'grievous bodily harm', see **B2.48**.

Mens Rea

B12.227

The *mens rea* is 'maliciously', which, it is submitted, refers both to the consequence as well as the explosion. As to the meaning of 'maliciously', see **B2.63** and **A2.12**.

CAUSING GUNPOWDER TO EXPLODE, SENDING AN EXPLOSIVE SUBSTANCE OR THROWING CORROSIVE FLUID WITH INTENT

Offences Against the Person Act 1861, s. 29

B12.228

Whosoever shall unlawfully and maliciously cause any gunpowder or other explosive substance to explode, or send or deliver or to cause to be taken or received by any person any explosive substance or any other dangerous or noxious thing, or put or lay at any place, or cast or throw at or upon or otherwise apply to any person, any corrosive fluid or any destructive or explosive substance, with intent in any of the cases aforesaid to burn, maim, disfigure, or disable any person, or to do some grievous bodily harm to any person, shall, whether any bodily injury be effected or not, be guilty of [an offence].

Procedure and Sentence

B12.229   This offence is triable on indictment (OAPA 1861, s. 29). As to the classification of the offence for the purpose of listing, see CPD XIII, para. B (see Supplement, **PD-97**).

On conviction on indictment, the maximum penalty is life imprisonment.

Elements

B12.230   For the meaning of 'explosive substance' see **B12.203** and for 'burn, maim, disfigure, or disable', see **B12.226**. For 'grievous bodily harm', see **B2.48**.

In *Crawford* (1845) 2 Car & Kir 129, the Court for Crown Cases Reserved upheld a conviction on the basis that boiling water was 'destructive matter'. For the meaning of noxious thing, see **B2.83**.

Mens Rea

B12.231   The *mens rea* of the offence consists of 'maliciously' doing one of the prohibited acts and with intent to produce one of the prohibited consequences. As to the meaning of 'maliciously', see **B2.63** and **A2.12**. As to 'intention', see **A2.4**.

PLACING GUNPOWDER NEAR A BUILDING ETC. WITH INTENT TO DO BODILY INJURY TO ANY PERSON

B12.232   Offences Against the Person Act 1861, s. 30

Whosoever shall unlawfully and maliciously place or throw in, into, upon, against, or near any building, ship or vessel any gunpowder or other explosive substance, with intent to do any bodily injury to any person, shall, whether or not any explosion take place, and whether or not any bodily injury be effected, be guilty of [an offence].

Procedure and Sentence

B12.233   The offence is triable on indictment (OAPA 1861, s. 30) and is a class 2A offence.

The maximum penalty is 14 years' imprisonment.

Elements

B12.234   For the meaning of 'explosive substance', see **B12.203**. Although the substance need not explode, it must be capable of exploding, so to throw a bottle containing only gunpowder and an unlit fuse would not constitute the offence, because the act would merely be that of throwing a bottle (*Shephard* (1868) 19 LT 19 at p. 20).

Mens Rea

B12.235   The placing or throwing must be done 'maliciously' (as to which see **B2.63** and **A2.12**), and it must be done with intent to do bodily injury (as to 'intent', see **A2.4**). It is to be noted that the phrase is bodily injury and not grievous bodily harm. It appears to be a wider term in the sense that it need not be serious, but it may be more limited if it applies only to physical injury.

MAKING OR HAVING GUNPOWDER ETC. WITH INTENT TO COMMIT OR ENABLE ANY PERSON TO COMMIT A FELONY

Offences Against the Person Act 1861, s. 64

B12.236

Whosoever shall knowingly have in his possession, or make or manufacture, any gunpowder, explosive substance, or any dangerous or noxious thing, or any machine, engine, instrument, or thing, with intent by means thereof to commit, or for the purpose of enabling any other person to commit, any of the felonies in this Act mentioned shall be guilty of an [offence].

Procedure and Sentence

The offence is triable on indictment and is a class 2A offence.

B12.237

The maximum penalty is two years' imprisonment.

Elements

For the meaning of 'possession', see, by analogy, the drug possession cases at **B19.23**, but note that the possession in this offence must be 'knowingly', see **B12.239**.

B12.238

For the meaning of 'explosive substance', see **B12.203**. For the meaning of 'noxious thing', see **B2.83**.

Mens Rea

The *mens rea* requires that there be an act (possession, making or manufacturing) which is done 'knowingly'. As to the meaning of 'knowingly', see **A2.14**. There must also be an intent to commit a felony within the OAPA 1861. As to the meaning of 'intent', see **A2.4**. The reference to 'felonies' is to any offence within the 1861 Act for which a person (not previously convicted) may be tried on indictment otherwise than at his own instance (Criminal Law Act 1967, s. 10 and sch. 2, para. 8).

B12.239

FIREWORKS OFFENCES

There are a number of offences concerned with fireworks, including the throwing, casting, or the firing of any firework in or into any highway, street, thoroughfare or public place under the Explosives Act 1875, s. 80. On summary conviction for the s. 80 offence, the maximum penalty is a fine not exceeding level 5 on the standard scale. Under the Penalties for Disorderly Behaviour (Amount of Penalty) Order 2002 (SI 2002 No. 1837), as amended, the s. 80 offence is a penalty offence and the amount payable is £90. The Fireworks Act 2003, s. 11(1), provides that any person who contravenes a prohibition imposed by fireworks regulations is guilty of an offence: see the Fireworks Regulations 2004 (SI 2004 No. 1836). Any person guilty of such an offence is liable, on summary conviction, to imprisonment for a term not exceeding six months or a fine not exceeding level 5 on the standard scale or both (Fireworks Act 2003, s. 11(3)). The defence of due diligence, in the Consumer Protection Act 1987, s. 39, applies to this offence (Fireworks Act 2003, s. 11(7)). The offence under s. 11 is also a fixed penalty offence and attracts a penalty of £80 for persons aged 16 or over and £40 for persons under 16.

B12.240

Section B13   Offences Affecting Enjoyment of Premises

UNLAWFUL EVICTION AND HARASSMENT OF OCCUPIER

Definition

B13.1   The Protection from Eviction Act 1977, s. 1, creates three offences which may be considered together. The first offence, contrary to s. 1(2), is concerned with unlawful eviction (the statute using the words 'deprives'); the other two offences, contrary to s. 1(3) and (3A), are concerned with harassment of a residential occupier. The main differences between the two harassment offences is that the one contrary to s. 1(3) can be committed by any person and it is necessary to prove intention, whereas the offence contrary to s. 1(3A) can be committed only by the landlord or agent and no intention need be proved. Section 1(3) does not create two offences (*Schon v Camden London Borough Council* (1986) 84 LGR 830, per Glidewell LJ).

Protection from Eviction Act 1977, s. 1

(2)   If any person unlawfully deprives the residential occupier of any premises of his occupation of the premises or any part thereof, or attempts to do so, he is guilty of an offence unless he proves that he believed, and had reasonable cause to believe, that the residential occupier had ceased to reside in the premises.

(3)   If any person with intent to cause the residential occupier of any premises—

(a) to give up the occupation of the premises or any part thereof; or

(b) to refrain from exercising any right or pursuing any remedy in respect of the premises or part thereof;

does acts likely to interfere with the peace or comfort of the residential occupier or members of his household, or persistently withdraws or withholds services reasonably required for the occupation of the premises as a residence, he shall be guilty of an offence.

(3A) Subject to subsection (3B) below the landlord of a residential occupier or an agent of the landlord shall be guilty of an offence if—

(a) he does acts likely to interfere with the peace or comfort of the residential occupier or members of his household, or

(b) he persistently withdraws or withholds services reasonably required for the occupation of the premises in question as a residence,

and (in either case) he knows, or has reasonable cause to believe, that that conduct is likely to cause the residential occupier to give up the occupation of the whole or part of the premises or to refrain from exercising any right or pursuing any remedy in respect of the whole or part of the premises.

Procedure

The Protection from Eviction Act 1977, s. 6, provides that proceedings may be instituted by   **B13.2**
councils of districts and London boroughs, the Common Council of the City of London, councils of Welsh counties and county boroughs and the Council of the Scilly Isles.

The offence is triable either way. When tried on indictment it is normally a class 3 offence, but
see CPD XIII, para. B (see Supplement, **PD-97**) for the additional factors that the court considers on allocation.

Indictment

First Count   **B13.3**

Statement of Offence

Unlawful eviction contrary to section 1(2) of the Protection from Eviction Act 1977.

Particulars of Offence

A on the…day of…unlawfully deprived V, the residential occupier, of his occupation of premises,
namely…, by changing the locks of the said premises during the absence of V and the members of
his household.

Second Count

Statement of Offence

Unlawful harassment contrary to section 1(3) of the Protection from Eviction Act 1977.

Particulars of Offence

A on divers dates between…and…did acts likely to interfere with the peace and comfort of
[or: withdrew (or withheld) services reasonably required for occupation, namely…, from] V, the
residential occupier of premises at…, namely…, with intent to cause V to give up his occupation
of the said premises [or: to refrain from exercising the right to…] [or: to refrain from pursuing
a remedy of…], without reasonable cause to believe that he had ceased to reside in the premises.

Although strictly speaking in an indictment for the offence contrary to s. 1(3) there need be
no reference to a 'persistent' withdrawing or withholding of services, as a matter of practice it
is desirable that it should be included (*Abrol* [1972] Crim LR 318). It would not appear that
s. 1(3) is a possible alternative offence to s. 1(2), although Glidewell LJ, giving the judgment
of the Divisional Court in *Costelloe v Camden London Borough Council* [1986] Crim LR 249,
stated that charging the two offences in the alternative would not be objectionable.

Sentence

The maximum penalty is: on summary conviction, a fine not exceeding the prescribed sum or   **B13.4**
imprisonment for a term not exceeding six months or both; on conviction on indictment, a
fine or imprisonment for a term not exceeding two years or both (Protection from Eviction Act
1977, s. 1(4)).

In *Khan* [2001] 2 Cr App R (S) 553, a sentence of 15 months' imprisonment was upheld on
conviction after a trial where the offender and four associates kicked down the door to the victim's flat when she was out, caused wanton damage to the victim's possessions and made threats
of violence against her. See also *Pittard* (1994) 15 Cr App R (S) 108.

Persons who Can Commit Offence

The offences contrary to the Protection from Eviction Act 1977, s. 1(2) and (3), may be com-   **B13.5**
mitted by 'any person', whereas the offence contrary to s. 1(3A) may be committed only by 'the
landlord of a residential occupier or an agent of the landlord'. It may be that if the eviction is
'unlawful' within s. 1(2) only by virtue of the provisions of s. 3(1), the offence can be committed
only by a landlord or agent (see **B13.11**).

Liability of Corporate Officers

B13.6 The Protection from Eviction Act 1977, s. 1(6), makes provision for the liability of officers of a body corporate which is guilty of one of the two offences:

> **Protection from Eviction Act 1977, s. 1**
>
> (6) Where an offence under this section committed by a body corporate is proved to have been committed with the consent or connivance of, or to be attributable to any neglect on the part of, any director, manager or secretary or other similar officer of the body corporate or any person who was purporting to act in any such capacity, he as well as the body corporate shall be guilty of that offence and shall be liable to be proceeded against and punished accordingly.

Meaning of 'Residential Occupier'

B13.7
> **Protection from Eviction Act 1977, s. 1**
>
> (1) In this section 'residential occupier', in relation to any premises, means a person occupying the premises as a residence, whether under a contract or by virtue of any enactment or rule of law giving him the right to remain in occupation or restricting the right of any other person to recover possession of the premises.

Provided an occupier has a right to remain in occupation, or the right of any other person to recover possession of the premises is restricted, he is a 'residential occupier'. It has to be ascertained whether a given occupier has sufficient residential protection to qualify under this statute. In *Blankley* [1979] Crim LR 166, a Crown Court judge held, considering the earlier offence contrary to the Rent Act 1965, s. 30, that there was no case to answer since the occupier was not a tenant but merely a contractual licensee. With respect, this decision cannot be correct, since the Protection from Eviction Act 1977 is not concerned with whether the occupier is a tenant, but whether the occupation that he has, granted by whatever means, satisfies the statutory requirements. Those requirements may be satisfied under a contractual licence. Lord Widgery CJ, giving the judgment of the Divisional Court, accepted in *Thurrock Urban District Council v Shina* (1972) 70 LGR 301 that a licensee could be a residential occupier, whilst recognising that a licence may more easily be terminated than a tenancy. This case is also a decision on the Rent Act 1965, s. 30. Of course, once a licence is ended, the person is usually no longer a residential occupier and falls outside the protection provided by these offences (*Portsmouth City Council, ex parte Knight* (1983) 82 LGR 184; *Surrey Heath Borough Council, ex parte Li* (1984) 16 HLR 79).

The wider approach being advocated also follows from the decision of the Divisional Court in *Norton v Knowles* [1969] 1 QB 572 (a decision on the Rent Act 1965, s. 30) that a person living in a caravan which was not attached to the land was a residential occupier. Although the caravan was connected to the drains, water pipes and electricity supply and had a telephone, it does not appear that these factors were necessarily essential to the decision. What was essential was the relationship between the landlord and the caravan dweller.

Belief that Person Not Residential Occupier

B13.8 In relation to the harassment offence contrary to the Protection from Eviction Act 1977, s. 1(3), the Court of Appeal in *Phekoo* [1981] 3 All ER 84 held, on the basis that conviction for the offence is conviction for a truly criminal offence and attaches serious social stigma to the offender, that, where the issue is raised that the accused reasonably believed that the person who was harassed was not a residential occupier, it is for the Crown to prove that that belief was not honest. Although this decision directly applies only to the offence contrary to s. 1(3), there appears to be no good reason why it does not also apply to the offence contrary to s. 1(2) and 1(3A) (*Qureshi* [2012] 1 WLR 694). Whether it is still good law that there must be a reasonable basis for the belief, or whether the belief has only to be an honest one, is a question which is open. See the discussion of 'mistake' at **A3.2** to **A3.11**. For reasons of compliance with the ECHR, Article 6(2), it may be that the burden will be confirmed as lying on the prosecution, see *A-G's Ref (No. 1 of 2004)* [2004] 4 All ER 457 and **F3.18** *et seq.*

Meaning of 'Premises'

Lord Widgery CJ, giving the judgment of the Divisional Court in *Thurrock Urban District* **B13.9**
Council v Shina (1972) 70 LGR 301, decided that the word 'premises' in the Rent Act 1965,
s. 30, the precursor to the Protection from Eviction Act 1977, should be given its normal wide
meaning. He had no doubt that a single room, together with shared use of a bathroom and
kitchen, did fall within the meaning of 'premises'. 'Premises' may include a caravan, together
with the land upon which it stands (*Norton v Knowles* [1969] 1 QB 572).

Meaning of 'Occupying Premises as a Residence'

'Occupying premises as a residence' has the same meaning as it had in the Rent Act 1977 (*Schon* **B13.10**
v Camden London Borough Council (1986) 84 LGR 830). Thus, a person may occupy premises
as his residence although he is physically absent from them, provided that the absence is not,
and is not intended to be, permanent, and either his spouse or some other member of the family is physically in occupation or, at the very least, his furniture and belongings remain in the
premises.

Elements Specific to s. 1(2)

Unlawfully Depriving Occupier   The Protection from Eviction Act 1977, s. 3(1), makes it **B13.11**
unlawful for the owner to enforce against the occupier, otherwise than by court proceedings,
his right to recover possession of the premises where those premises have been let as a dwelling under a tenancy (which is not a statutorily protected tenancy or an excluded tenancy) and
the tenancy has come to an end but the occupier continues to reside in the premises. In *Patel v
Pirabakaran* [2006] EWCA Civ 685, a case under s. 2 of the 1977 Act on the meaning of 'let
as a dwelling', Wilson LJ said (at [34]): 'the phrase "let as a dwelling" in s. 2 of the Act of 1977
means "let wholly or partly as a dwelling" and so applies to premises which are let for mixed
residential and business purposes'.

The Court of Appeal in *Yuthiwattana* (1984) 80 Cr App R 55 was satisfied that s. 1(2) is concerned with eviction, and so an unlawful deprivation must have the character of an eviction
although it need not be of a permanent character. Kerr LJ, giving the judgment of the court,
said (at p. 63): 'cases which are more properly described as "locking out" or not admitting an
occupier on one or even more isolated occasions, so that in effect he continues to be allowed to
occupy the premises but is then unable to enter, seem to us to fall appropriately under subsection (3)(a) or (b), which deal with acts of harassment'.

Consequently the conviction under a count charging the offence contrary to s. 1(2) had to be
quashed because the occupier was excluded for only one night. This decision was followed by the
Divisional Court in *Costelloe v Camden London Borough Council* [1986] Crim LR 249, where
Glidewell LJ held that there is an offence under s. 1(2) where the landlord intends to exclude
the occupier permanently and the occupier thinks he has been excluded permanently, even if the
landlord then changes his mind and the occupier is later admitted. What matters is whether the
exclusion appears to be permanent. Woolf J put the point slightly differently saying:

> The proper test is: What was the nature of the exclusion? Was it, whether it be short or long, an
> exclusion designed to evict the tenant from the premises? If it was, then it falls within section
> 1(2). If on the other hand all that occurred was the deprivation of the occupation of the premises
> for a short period of time and that was the object of the exercise, then it would not fall within
> section 1(2).

Belief that Occupier had Ceased to Reside in Premises   No offence is committed if the **B13.12**
accused believes, on reasonable grounds, that a residential occupier has ceased to reside in the
premises. This is a matter for the jury to determine. Thus the trial judge erred in *Davidson-Acres*
[1980] Crim LR 50, when he himself decided questions as to the time and existence of the
accused's belief.

Elements Specific to s. 1(3)

B13.13 **Harassment with Intent**   It is essential under this offence to establish the necessary intent. If it is not present, it may be that an offence contrary to the Protection from Eviction Act 1977, s. 1(3A), has been committed. It has been held that the meaning of the word 'intent' must be approached in the same way as in the law of murder (*AMK (Property Management) Ltd* [1985] Crim LR 600). On the other hand, the House of Lords in *Burke* [1991] AC 135 held that 'intention' in this context means with the purpose or motive of causing the occupier to give up occupation of the premises. This would appear to be a more limited understanding of the word 'intent' than usually applies in criminal law, and might not, therefore, be followed in a case to which the usual understanding actually applied on the facts. See generally, **A2.4**. The intention must be either to cause the occupier to give up the premises (s. 1(3)(a)), or to refrain from exercising any right or pursuing any remedy in respect of the premises (s. 1(3)(b)).

B13.14 With regard to s. 1(3)(a), the Court of Appeal allowed the appeals in part in *AMK (Property Management) Ltd* [1985] Crim LR 600 because the trial judge had not made clear to the jury that the consequences of the building work designed to refurbish a block of flats were not simply to be equated with an intention to evict. An intention to evict must be established and, whilst the works could have been carried out without an intention to evict, the company's acts were reasonable and not of the kind covered by s. 1(3)(a). Ormrod LJ, giving the judgment of the Court of Appeal in *McCall v Abelesz* [1976] QB 585 (a decision on the Rent Act 1965, s. 30), held that it is not sufficient to establish that the accused was completely indifferent as to cutting off the gas supply to the occupier, nor would it be sufficient for the accused simply to allow things to happen which might have the effect of causing the occupier to leave, since these could not be equated with an intent to cause the occupier to give up the occupation of the premises. If the accused realised that there was a real likelihood that these activities would result in the occupier leaving, the general approach to the meaning of 'intent' might result in a decision that the accused did intend to cause the occupier to give up occupation of the premises. Applying the orthodox interpretation of intent, the requirement should be that the accused at least foresaw the occupier leaving as a virtually certain result of his conduct (as to the general approach to 'intent', see **A2.4**).

B13.15 With regard to s. 1(3)(b), the Divisional Court in *Schon v Camden London Borough Council* (1986) 84 LGR 830 held that 'an intention to persuade [the occupier] to leave for a limited period of time in order to enable work to be done and thereafter to allow her to return, was not an intent to cause her to give up her occupation of the premises. Notwithstanding that, it would be an intent which fell within the second intention within s. 1(3) because it would be an intention to cause her to refrain from exercising her right to live in the premises and to be physically present in the premises.' Since the charge was specifically worded to refer to s. 1(3)(b), the necessary intent was not established and the appeal against conviction was allowed.

B13.16 **Belief that Person Harassed Not Residential Occupier**   The decision of the Court of Appeal on this matter in *Phekoo* [1981] 3 All ER 84 applies to this offence, and is considered at **B13.8**.

B13.17 **Acts Likely to Interfere with Peace or Comfort**   The Protection from Eviction Act 1977, uses the phrase 'does acts', which requires that there be conduct on the part of the accused, but that phrase does not require that there be more than one act (*Polycarpou* (1978) 9 HLR 129). Consequently, removing the sole source of heat of a tenant would satisfy this requirement of the offence.

It may be that the Court of Appeal in *McCall v Abelesz* [1976] 1 QB 585 had in mind the need to establish personal conduct, as distinct from merely taking advantage of the consequences of the acts of others with the accused actually doing nothing. In *Ahmad* (1987) 84 Cr App R 64, the Court of Appeal held that the phrase 'does acts' does not impose a responsibility to rectify damage which the accused has already caused by an act done innocently. Thus, a later failure to take steps to rectify what he has caused, even if with the requisite intent, is not the doing of an act or acts for the purposes of s. 1(3). Clearly an act and not an omission is required, and the doctrine established by the House of Lords in *Miller* [1983] 2 AC 161 (see **A1.20**) does not apply. In *Yuthiwattana* (1984) 80 Cr App R 55, in addition to *the failure* to provide a front door key, which would not of itself have sufficed, there was proof of other sufficient acts which included entering the occupier's room without permission, removing his record player and records, and shouting at him.

Kerr LJ, delivering the judgment of the Court of Appeal in *Yuthiwattana* (1984) 80 Cr App R 55, and explaining the *obiter dictum* of Ormrod LJ in *McCall v Abelesz* [1976] 1 QB 585, held that it is not necessary that the acts in question should constitute a breach of the civil law, but simply that the accused's act be one calculated to interfere with the occupier's peace and comfort which was intended to cause him to give up his occupation of the premises. *Yuthiwattana* was approved by the House of Lords in *Burke* [1991] AC 135.

The relevant acts must be ones 'likely to' interfere with peace or comfort. It should be noted that until the amendment introduced by the Housing Act 1988, s. 29(1), this phrase read 'calculated to', which caused uncertainty. The phrase 'likely to' is a matter of objective analysis, not of realisation or calculation on the part of the accused.

Persistently Withdrawing or Withholding Services   The Divisional Court in *Westminster*   **B13.18**
City Council v Peart (1968) 66 LGR 561, a decision on the Rent Act 1965, s. 30, held that 'persistently' in the identically worded precursor of the present provision, refers to the withholding of as well as the withdrawing of services. Withdrawal of a service on one day was not sufficient to satisfy the element of persistency. Lord Parker CJ, giving the judgment of the court, left open the question of whether failing to pay for a gas or electricity supply, as a result of which a gas or electricity company disconnects the service, can properly be described as the landlord withholding a service. Clearly, where the accused permanently cuts off the electricity supply, there is a persistent withholding (see *Boaks* (1967) 205 EG 103, a decision on the Rent Act 1965, s. 30).

Elements Specific to s. 1(3A)

Landlord Harassing Residential Occupier   The points made in relation to the offence con-   **B13.19**
trary to s. 1(3) regarding the meaning of 'does acts likely to interfere with the peace or comfort of the residential occupier or members of his household' and 'persistently withdraws or withholds services reasonably required for the occupation of the premises in question as a residence', apply in full to the s. 1(3A) offence. However, the offence contrary to s. 1(3A) differs in that it can be committed only by a landlord (or agent) and it is not necessary to establish intention, although knowledge or belief must be established. In *Qureshi* [2012] 1 WLR 694 the issue for the Court of Appeal was whether an accused may be guilty of an offence under s. 1(3A) on the footing that he is vicariously liable for the act of another or others. The Court held that on its true construction s. 1(3A) requires the actual participation of the accused and that there is no room for vicarious liability.

Meaning of 'Landlord'

Protection from Eviction Act 1977, s. 1   **B13.20**

(3C) In subsection (3A) above 'landlord', in relation to a residential occupier of any premises, means the person who, but for—
  (a) the residential occupier's right to remain in occupation of the premises, or
  (b) a restriction on the person's right to recover possession of the premises,
  would be entitled to occupation of the premises and any superior landlord under whom that person derives title.

If it is necessary to discover the identity of the landlord, a notice may be served on his agent or other person under s. 7 of the Act, requiring the disclosure of the landlord's full name and address. If such is not forthcoming, the person on whom the notice is served is guilty of a summary offence and liable to a fine not exceeding level 4 on the standard scale.

B13.21   **Knowledge or Belief**   The landlord, though not requiring an intention, must know or have reasonable cause to believe that the residential occupier is likely to be caused to give up occupation of the premises (*R (McGowan) v Brent Justices* (2002) 166 JP 29).

Specific Defences

B13.22   The Protection from Eviction Act 1977, s. 1(2), provides that a person is not guilty of the eviction offence if 'he proves that he believed, and had reasonable cause to believe, that the residential occupier had ceased to reside in the premises'. The accused must prove the belief and its reasonable foundation on a balance of probabilities (*Desai* (1992) *The Times*, 3 February 1992).

Protection from Eviction Act 1977, s. 1

   (3B)   A person shall not be guilty of an offence under subsection (3A) above if he proves that he had reasonable grounds for doing the acts or withdrawing or withholding the services in question.

When the legal burden is on the accused, the standard required is proof on a balance of probabilities (see **F3.6** and **F3.53**). A trial judge is not obliged to leave this defence to the jury if it would be 'tenuous and specious' to do so (*Allen* [2013] EWCA Crim 676 at [14]). For a summary of the case law relating to 'reverse burden' challenges under the HRA 1998, see **F3.18** *et seq*.

Related Offences

B13.23   The offences contrary to the CLA 1977, part I (see **B13.24** to **B13.37**), may be relevant. In particular, even if a person's activity does not fall within the Protection from Eviction Act 1977 offence because, for example, the 'victim' is not a residential occupier, the offence contrary to the CLA 1977, s. 6, using or threatening violence to secure entry, may nevertheless cover the relevant activity.

USE OR THREAT OF VIOLENCE FOR PURPOSE OF SECURING ENTRY TO PREMISES

Definition

B13.24   It is a summary offence, by virtue of the CLA 1977, s. 6(1), for any person, without lawful authority, to use or threaten violence for the purpose of securing entry into any premises for himself or for any other person, provided that:

(a)   there is someone present on those premises at the time who is opposed to the entry which the violence is intended to secure; and

(b)   the person using or threatening the violence knows that that is the case.

Procedure and Sentence

B13.25   The CLA 1977, s. 12(8), provides that 'no rule of law ousting the jurisdiction of magistrates' courts to try offences where a dispute of title to property is involved shall preclude magistrates' courts from trying offences under this part of this Act'. By virtue of s. 6(5), a person found guilty of this offence is liable to imprisonment for a term not exceeding six months or to a fine not exceeding level 5 on the standard scale or to both.

Elements

B13.26   Some of the elements of this offence are further defined by the CLA 1977:

(a) *Uses or threatens violence*: according to s. 6(4)(a), it is immaterial whether the violence in question is directed against the person or against property.

(b) *Entry*: according to s. 6(4)(b), it is immaterial whether the entry which the violence is intended to secure is for the purpose of acquiring possession of the premises in question or for any other purpose. As to the meaning of entry in the analogous offence of burglary, see **B4.86**.

(c) *Premises*: according to s. 12, this means any building, any part of a building under separate occupation, any land ancillary to a building, the site comprising any building or buildings together with any land ancillary thereto. By s. 12(2) the references to a building apply to any structure other than a moveable one, and to any moveable structure, vehicle or vessel designed or adapted for residential purposes; and further that (i) part of a building is under separate occupation if anyone is in occupation or entitled to occupation of that part as distinct from the whole, and (ii) land is ancillary to a building if it is adjacent to it and used (or intended for use) in connection with the occupation of that building or any part of it.

(d) *Lawful authority* is considered in s. 6(2), which provides that the fact that a person has any interest in or right to possession or occupation of any premises shall not constitute lawful authority for the use or threat of violence by him or anyone else for the purpose of securing his entry into those premises.

Specific Defence

No offence is committed if the person is a displaced residential occupier or a protected intend- **B13.27**
ing occupier of the premises in question or is acting on behalf of such an occupier. If the accused adduces sufficient evidence that he was, or was acting on behalf of, such an occupier he is presumed to be, or to be acting on behalf of, such an occupier unless the contrary is proved by the prosecution (CLA 1977, s. 6(1A)). When the legal burden is on the accused, the standard required is proof on a balance of probabilities (see **F3.6** and **F3.53**). For a summary of the case law relating to 'reverse burden' challenges under the HRA 1998, see **F3.18** *et seq.*

Displaced Residential Occupier   Section 6(7) of the CLA 1977 makes clear that it is s. 12 **B13.28**
which determines when a person is to be regarded as a 'displaced residential occupier' of any premises or of any access to any premises, which involves also considering the meaning of 'trespasser' (the meaning of 'premises' has been considered at **B13.26**).

Section 12(3) defines 'displaced residential occupier' by providing that any person who was occupying any premises as a residence immediately before being excluded from occupation by anyone who entered those premises, or any access to those premises, as a trespasser, is a displaced residential occupier of the premises for the purposes of this part of the Act, so long as he continues to be excluded from occupation of the premises by the original trespasser or any subsequent trespasser. Such a person is also regarded, by s. 12(5), as a displaced residential occupier of any access to those premises.

Section 12(4) provides that a person, who was himself occupying the premises in question as a trespasser immediately before being excluded from occupation, is not a displaced residential occupier of the premises. Section 12(6) provides an extended meaning of 'trespasser' so that anyone who enters or is on or in occupation of any premises by virtue of (a) any title derived from a trespasser, or (b) any licence or consent given by a trespasser or by a person deriving title from a trespasser, is himself treated as a trespasser for present purposes alone, and phrases involving a reference to a trespasser will be construed accordingly. Further s. 12(7) provides that anyone who is on any premises as a trespasser does not cease to be a trespasser by virtue of being allowed time to leave the premises, nor does anyone cease to be a displaced residential occupier of any premises by virtue of any such allowance of time to a trespasser.

It is also important to consider the meaning of 'access' which is provided by s. 12. It means, in relation to any premises, any part of any site or building within which those premises are situated which constitutes an ordinary means of access to those premises (whether or not that is its sole or primary use).

B13.29   **Protected Intending Occupier**   Section 6(7) of the CLA 1977 also indicates that s. 12A has effect for determining when any person is to be regarded as a protected intending occupier of any premises (or any access to those premises: s. 12A(11)).

Criminal Law Act 1977, s. 12A

(1) For the purposes of this Part of this Act [part II] an individual is a protected intending occupier of any premises at any time if at that time he falls within subsection (2), (4) or (6) below.
(2) An individual is a protected intending occupier of any premises if—
   (a) he has in those premises a freehold interest or a leasehold interest with not less than two years still to run;
   (b) he requires the premises for his own occupation as a residence;
   (c) he is excluded from occupation of the premises by a person who entered them, or any access to them, as a trespasser; and
   (d) he or a person acting on his behalf holds a written statement—
     (i) which specifies his interest in the premises;
     (ii) which states that he requires the premises for occupation as a residence for himself; and
     (iii) with respect to which the requirements in subsection (3) below are fulfilled.
(3) The requirements referred to in subsection (2)(d)(iii) above are—
   (a) that the statement is signed by the person whose interest is specified in it in the presence of a justice of the peace or commissioner for oaths; and
   (b) that the justice of the peace or commissioner for oaths has subscribed his name as a witness to the signature.
(4) An individual is also a protected intending occupier of any premises if—
   (a) he has a tenancy of those premises (other than a tenancy falling within subsection (2)(a) above or (6)(a) below) or a licence to occupy those premises granted by a person with a freehold interest or a leasehold interest with not less than two years still to run in the premises;
   (b) he requires the premises for his own occupation as a residence;
   (c) he is excluded from occupation of the premises by a person who entered them, or any access to them, as a trespasser; and
   (d) he or a person acting on his behalf holds a written statement—
     (i) which states that he has been granted a tenancy of those premises or a licence to occupy those premises;
     (ii) which specifies the interest in the premises of the person who granted that tenancy or licence to occupy ('the landlord');
     (iii) which states that he requires the premises for occupation as a residence for himself; and
     (iv) with respect to which the requirements in subsection (5) below are fulfilled.
(5) The requirements referred to in subsection (4)(d)(iv) above are—
   (a) that the statement is signed by the landlord and by the tenant or licensee in the presence of a justice of the peace or commissioner for oaths;
   (b) that the justice of the peace or commissioner for oaths has subscribed his name as a witness to the signatures.
(6) An individual is also a protected intending occupier of any premises if—
   (a) he has a tenancy of those premises (other than a tenancy falling within subsection (2)(a) or (4)(a) above) or a licence to occupy those premises granted by an authority to which this subsection applies;
   (b) he requires the premises for his own occupation as a residence;
   (c) he is excluded from occupation of the premises by a person who entered the premises, or any access to them, as a trespasser; and
   (d) there has been issued to him by or on behalf of the authority referred to in paragraph (a) above a certificate stating that—
     (i) he has been granted a tenancy of those premises or a licence to occupy those premises as a residence by the authority; and

        (ii) the authority which granted that tenancy or licence to occupy is one to which this subsection applies, being of a description specified in the certificate.

(7) Subsection (6) above applies to the following authorities—

    (a) any body mentioned in section 14 of the Rent Act 1977 (landlord's interest belonging to local authority etc.);

    (b) the Regulator of Social Housing;

    (ba) a non-profit registered provider of social housing;

    (bb) a profit-making registered provider of social housing, but only in relation to premises which are social housing within the meaning of Part 2 of the Housing and Regeneration Act 2008;

    (c) [repealed]; and

    (d) a registered social landlord within the meaning of the Housing Act 1985 ...

(7A) Subsection (6) also applies to the Secretary of State if the tenancy or licence is granted by him under Part III of the Housing Associations Act 1985.

A freehold owner of former matrimonial premises is not a 'protected intending occupier' within the meaning of s. 12A, each of the provisions of which must be read conjunctively (*Wakolo v DPP* [2012] EWHC 611 (Admin)).

If a person makes a statement for the purposes of s. 12A(2)(d) or (4) which he knows to be **B13.30** false in a material particular (see **B6.12** for meaning), or if he recklessly makes such a statement which is false in a material particular, he commits an offence (s. 12A(8)) and is liable on summary conviction to imprisonment for a term not exceeding six months or a fine not exceeding level 5 on the standard scale or both (s. 12A(10)).

OFFENCE OF SQUATTING IN A RESIDENTIAL BUILDING

Definition

Legal Aid, Sentencing and Punishment of Offences Act 2012, s. 144   **B13.31**

(1) A person commits an offence if—

    (a) the person is in a residential building as a trespasser having entered it as a trespasser,

    (b) the person knows or ought to know that he or she is a trespasser, and

    (c) the person is living in the building or intends to live there for any period.

(2) The offence is not committed by a person holding over after the end of a lease or licence (even if the person leaves and re-enters the building).

Section 144 was brought into force on 1 September 2012 by the Legal Aid, Sentencing and Punishment of Offences (Commencement No. 1) Order 2012 (SI 2012 No. 1956).

Procedure and Sentence

The offence is triable summarily. The maximum penalty is imprisonment for a term not exceed- **B13.32** ing six months or a fine not exceeding level 5 on the standard scale or both (LASPO 2012, s. 144(5) and (6)).

Elements

By LASPO 2012, s. 144(7), it is irrelevant whether a person entered the building as a trespasser **B13.33** before or after the commencement of the section.

The term 'building' includes any structure or part of a structure (including a temporary or moveable structure) and a building is 'residential' if it is designed or adapted, before the time of entry, for use as a place to live (s. 144(3)).

The fact that a person derives title from a trespasser, or has the permission of a trespasser, does not prevent the person from being a trespasser (s. 144(4)).

ADVERSE OCCUPATION OF RESIDENTIAL PREMISES

Definition

B13.34

Criminal Law Act 1977, s. 7

(1) ...any person who is on any premises as a trespasser after having entered as such is guilty of an offence if he fails to leave those premises on being required to do so by or on behalf of—

    (a) a displaced residential occupier of the premises; or

    (b) an individual who is a protected intending occupier of the premises.

Procedure and Sentence

B13.35 The offence is triable summarily (CLA 1977, s. 7(5)). Where the offence relates to a protected intending occupier, a document purporting to be a certificate under the CLA 1977, s. 12A(6)(d) (see **B13.29**) is to be received in evidence and, unless the contrary is proved, is deemed to have been issued by or on behalf of the authority stated in the certificate (s. 12A(9)(b)).

The maximum penalty is imprisonment for a term not exceeding six months or a fine not exceeding level 5 on the standard scale or both (s. 7(5)).

Elements

B13.36 Premises includes a reference to any access to them, whether or not such access itself constitutes premises within the meaning of the CLA 1977, part II (s. 7(4)).

For the meaning of 'displaced residential occupier' and 'protected intending occupier', see **B13.28** and **B13.29**.

Specific Defences

B13.37 Section 7(3) provides that it is a defence for the accused to prove that:

(a) he believed that the person requiring him to leave the premises was not a displaced residential occupier or protected intending occupier of the premises or a person acting on behalf of a displaced residential occupier or protected intending occupier (CLA 1977, s. 7(2));

(b) the premises in question are or form part of premises used mainly for non-residential purposes, and that he was not on any part of the premises used wholly or mainly for residential purposes.

When the legal burden is on the accused, the standard required is proof on a balance of probabilities (see **F3.6** and **F3.53**). For a summary of the case law relating to 'reverse burden' challenges under the HRA 1998, see **F3.18** *et seq*. Where the accused was requested to leave the premises by a person claiming to be or to act on behalf of a protected intending occupier of the premises, it is a defence for the accused to prove that, although asked to do so by the accused at the time the accused was requested to leave, that person failed at that time to produce to the accused a s. 12A statement or certificate (s. 12A(9)(a)) (see **B13.29** and *Forest Justices, ex parte Hartman* [1991] Crim LR 641).

TRESPASSING DURING THE CURRENCY OF AN INTERIM POSSESSION ORDER

Definition

B13.38

Criminal Justice and Public Order Act 1994, s. 76

(2) ...a person who is present on premises as a trespasser at any time during the currency of the order commits an offence.

...

(4) A person who was in occupation of the premises at the time of service of the order but leaves them commits an offence if he re-enters the premises as a trespasser or attempts to do so after the expiry of the order but within the period of one year beginning with the day on which it was served.

Procedure and Sentence

The offences are triable summarily only.   **B13.39**

The maximum penalty is a term of imprisonment not exceeding six months or a fine not exceeding level 5 on the standard scale or both (CJPO 1994, s. 76(5)).

Elements

References to 'the order' are to be construed as referring to an interim possession order which   **B13.40** has been made in respect of any premises and served in accordance with rules of court (CJPO 1994, s. 76(1)); references to 'the premises' are to the premises covered by the order (s. 76(1)). For the meaning of 'premises', which has the same meaning as in the CLA 1977, part II, see **B13.26**. An interim possession order means an interim possession order (so entitled) made under rules of court for the bringing of summary proceedings for possession of premises which are occupied by trespassers (CJPO 1994, s. 75(4)).

A person who is in occupation of the premises at the time of service of the order is to be treated for the purposes of s. 76 as being present as a trespasser (s. 76(6)).

Specific Defence

Section 76(3) of the CJPO 1994 provides a specific defence to a charge under s. 76(2). No   **B13.41** offence is committed by a person if he leaves the premises within 24 hours of the time of service of the order and does not return, or a copy of the order was not fixed to the premises in accordance with rules of court. When the legal burden is on the accused, the standard required is proof on a balance of probabilities (see **F3.6** and **F3.53**). For a summary of the case law relating to 'reverse burden' challenges under the HRA 1998, see **F3.18** *et seq.*

INTERIM POSSESSION ORDERS: FALSE OR MISLEADING STATEMENTS

Definition

Criminal Justice and Public Order Act 1994, s. 75   **B13.42**

(1) A person commits an offence if, for the purpose of obtaining an interim possession order, he—
  (a) makes a statement which he knows to be false or misleading in a material particular; or
  (b) recklessly makes a statement which is false or misleading in a material particular.
(2) A person commits an offence if, for the purpose of resisting the making of an interim possession order, he—
  (a) makes a statement which he knows to be false or misleading in a material particular, or
  (b) recklessly makes a statement which is false or misleading in a material particular.

Procedure and Sentence

This offence is triable either way (CJPO 1994, s. 75(3)).   **B13.43**

The maximum penalty is, on indictment, imprisonment for a term not exceeding two years or a fine or both, and, summarily, imprisonment for a term not exceeding six months or a fine not exceeding the statutory maximum or both (s. 75(3)).

Elements

B13.44   'Statement' in relation to an interim possession order, means any statement, in writing or oral and whether as to fact or belief, made in or for the purposes of the proceedings (CJPO 1994, s. 75(4)). For the meaning of 'interim possession order', see **B13.40**; for the meaning of 'premises', see **B13.26**.

AGGRAVATED TRESPASS

Definition

B13.45   Criminal Justice and Public Order Act 1994, s. 68

(1) A person commits the offence of aggravated trespass if he trespasses on land and, in relation to any lawful activity which persons are engaging in or are about to engage in on that or adjoining land, does there anything which is intended by him to have the effect—
   (a) of intimidating those persons or any of them so as to deter them or any of them from engaging in that activity,
   (b) of obstructing that activity, or
   (c) of disrupting that activity.

Procedure and Sentence

B13.46   The offence is triable summarily (CJPO 1994, s. 68(3)). A charge is not void for duplicity where it states that the accused intended to 'deter, disrupt or obstruct' a hunt because these elements overlap. Therefore, there is no need for each element to be the subject of a separate charge (*Nelder v DPP* (1998) *The Times*, 11 June 1998).

The maximum penalty is imprisonment for a term not exceeding three months or a fine not exceeding level 4 on the standard scale or both (s. 68(3)).

Elements

B13.47   There are three elements to the offence: trespass on land; an intention to have one of three effects stated in subsections (a), (b) and (c) (despite the lack of the word 'or' after (a), Rafferty J in *Tilly v DPP* (2001) 166 JP 22 confirmed that this is the correct interpretation); and an act done towards that end (*Winder v DPP* (1996) 160 JP 713 and *Barnard v DPP* (1999) *The Times*, 9 November 1999). The act must be a 'distinct and overt act' apart from trespass, which calls for careful consideration in the context of the facts of a given case (*Peppersharp v DPP* (2012) 176 JP 257, approving *Barnard v DPP*). In *Bauer v DPP* [2013] 1 WLR 3617, the Divisional Court held that when UK Uncut protestors forced their way into a department store and, once inside, began to erect tents, beat drums and sound other loud instruments, and even play volleyball, there had been acts distinct from the initial trespass so as to justify convictions under s. 68(1). Whether the activity is lawful is defined by the CJPO 1994, s. 68(2).

                    Criminal Justice and Public Order Act 1994, s. 68

(2) Activity on any occasion on the part of a person or persons on land is 'lawful' for the purpose of this section if he or they may engage in the activity on the land on that occasion without committing an offence or trespassing on the land.

This requires that the activity or task be lawful. It does not require that the way it is to be done must be lawful. Clearing land and felling trees was the activity in question in *Hibberd v Muddle* (1996 unreported); it was held to be a lawful activity, even though the means used may have been in breach of the Health and Safety at Work etc. Act 1974.

The Supreme Court in *Richardson v DPP* [2014] 2 WLR 288 held that the intention of s. 68 is plainly to add the sanction of the criminal law to a trespass where, in addition to the accused invading the property of someone else where he is not entitled to be, he there disrupts an activity which the occupant is entitled to pursue. Section 68(2) therefore must mean that the additional criminal sanction is removed when the activity which is disrupted is, in itself, unlawful, which may be either because the occupant is himself trespassing, or because his activity is criminal. Not every incidental or collateral criminal offence can properly be said to affect the lawfulness of the activity, nor to render it criminal. It will do so only when the criminal offence is integral to the core activity carried on. It will not do so when there is some incidental or collateral offence, which is remote from the activity. If, however, a criminal offence integral to the core activity is raised, it may involve the court investigating extraneous facts or the conduct of third parties.

There is an 'activity' only where someone is present on the land who could be intimidated or not allowed to get on with what they are entitled to (*Tilly v DPP*). By the CJPO 1994, s. 68(5), 'land' does not include those highways and roads excluded for the purposes of s. 61(9) (see **B13.53**). Further, the word 'land' in the CJPO 1994, ss. 68 and 69, includes buildings. In *DPP v Chivers* [2011] 1 All ER 367, the Administrative Court held that, in its unamended form, s. 68 did not include buildings within the definition of 'land' because of the inclusion of the phrase 'in the open air' (which was removed by the ASBA 2003). The purpose and effect of the amendment was, in the Court's view, quite plainly to negative the exclusion of buildings.

B13.48   Where the charge is under s. 68(1)(c), an intention to disrupt must be proved, but actual disruption need not be established (*Winder v DPP* (1996) 160 JP 713). Further, the Divisional Court was satisfied that the decision of the magistrate that the requisite intention was present was justified, as the trespassers ran towards a hunt, that being an act that was not merely preparatory to actual disruption, although that running was not itself intended to disrupt the hunt. As to the possible application of the defence of property as an answer to the charge, see *DPP v Bayer* [2004] 1 WLR 2856.

In *Ayliffe v DPP* [2006] QB 227, the Divisional Court was concerned with whether the offence was committed where protesters trespassed on sites and interfered with activity there that was in preparation for action in the Gulf and Iraq and held that following the Court of Appeal decision in *Jones* [2005] QB 259, in the absence of express provision to the contrary, the term 'offence' in a domestic statute was ordinarily treated as referring to an offence committed in the domestic sphere against a common law or statutory rule, and, since the 1994 Act did not define the word 'offence', that term, as used in s. 68(2), was to be understood as referring to an offence under domestic criminal law and not to the crime of aggression in international law. The crime of aggression in international law had not been assimilated into domestic law. The House of Lords, considering appeals affecting the accused in *Ayliffe* among others, supported that view (*Jones* [2007] 1 AC 136).

Power to Remove Persons

B13.49   Under the CJPO 1994, s. 69(1), the senior police officer present at the scene has the power to direct a person or persons to leave land if he reasonably believes:

(a) that a person is committing, has committed or intends to commit the offence of aggravated trespass on land; or

(b) that two or more persons are trespassing on land and are present there with the common purpose of intimidating persons so as to deter them from engaging in a lawful activity or of obstructing or disrupting a lawful activity.

If a person knowing that a direction under s. 69(1) has been given which applies to him fails to leave the land as soon as practicable or, having left, again enters the land as a trespasser within the period of three months beginning with the day on which the direction was given, he commits an offence and is liable on summary conviction to imprisonment for a term not exceeding three months or a fine not exceeding level 4 on the standard scale or both (s. 69(3)). If the police officer giving the direction does not communicate it, any constable at the scene may communicate it (s. 69(2)).

It is a defence for the accused to show (i) that he was not trespassing on land, or (ii) that he has a reasonable excuse for failing to leave the land as soon as practicable or, as the case may be, for again entering the land as a trespasser (s. 69(4)). When the legal burden is on the accused, the standard required is proof on a balance of probabilities (see F3.6 and F3.53). For a summary of the case law relating to 'reverse burden' challenges under the HRA 1998, see F3.18 *et seq.*

FAILURE TO LEAVE OR RE-ENTRY TO LAND AFTER POLICE DIRECTION TO LEAVE

Definition

B13.50
Criminal Justice and Public Order Act 1994, s. 61

(4) If a person knowing that a direction under subsection (1) above has been given which applies to him—
    (a) fails to leave the land as soon as reasonably practicable, or
    (b) having left again enters the land as a trespasser within the period of three months beginning with the day on which the direction was given,
    he commits an offence . . .

Procedure and Sentence

B13.51 The offence is triable summarily.

The maximum penalty is imprisonment for a term not exceeding three months or a fine not exceeding level 4 on the standard scale or both (CJPO 1994, s. 61(4)).

Elements

B13.52
Criminal Justice and Public Order Act 1994, s. 61

(1) If the senior police officer present at the scene reasonably believes that two or more persons are trespassing on land and are present there with the common purpose of residing there for any period, that reasonable steps have been taken by or on behalf of the occupier to ask them to leave and—
    (a) that any of those persons has caused damage to the land or to property on the land or used threatening, abusive or insulting words or behaviour towards the occupier, a member of his family or an employee or agent of his, or
    (b) that those persons have between them six or more vehicles on the land, he may direct those persons, or any of them, to leave the land and to remove any vehicles or other property they have with them on the land.

In *R (Fuller) v Chief Constable of Dorset Police* [2002] 3 All ER 57, the court decided that s. 61 did not breach the ECHR, Article 6, because, although the police procedure applied without recourse to a court, it did not prevent a challenge through the courts to the power of arrest or prosecution or to the decision of the landowner (the local authority). Nor was s. 61 in breach of Article 8; whilst a measure that prevents a traveller or gypsy from residing in his vehicle on land may breach Article 8, it does not necessarily do so, following *South Buckinghamshire District Council v Porter* [2002] 1 All ER 425, as it may be justifiable under Article 8(2)) or, for similar reasons as applied to Article 8 under Article 1 of the First Protocol. Even more clearly, there was no breach of Article 3 (as to Article 8 rights and trespassers, see also *Kay v Lambeth London Borough Council* [2006] 2 AC 465).

The offence is committed only where a direction to leave has been given. The court in *Fuller* decided that it followed from construing s. 61 narrowly that, as a direction could be given to leave at some time in the future, the offence could not be committed before the time permitted in the direction had expired. Further, if the trespassers had not had an opportunity to comply with the landowner's request to leave, a direction under s. 61 was not lawful or valid.

Where the senior police officer reasonably believes that the person was not originally a trespasser on the land, a direction may still be made if the person has become a trespasser and the senior police officer reasonably believes that the conditions in s. 61(1) are satisfied after the person became a trespasser (s. 61(2)).

Definitions   Section 61(9) of the CJPO 1994 defines certain terms used in the section.   **B13.53**

(a) 'Land' does not include:
   (i) buildings other than agricultural buildings (within the meaning of the Local Government Finance Act 1988, sch. 5, paras. 3 to 8) or scheduled monuments (within the meaning of the Ancient Monuments and Archaeological Areas Act 1979);
   (ii) land forming part of a highway unless it is a footpath, bridleway or byway open to all traffic within the meaning of the Wildlife and Countryside Act 1981, part III, is a restricted byway within the meaning of the Countryside and Rights of Way Act 2000, part II or is a cycle track under the Highways Act 1980 or the Cycle Tracks Act 1984.
(b) 'Occupier' means the person entitled to possession of the land by virtue of an estate or interest held by him.
(c) Subject to the extension of its meaning with regard to common land (see below), 'trespass' means trespass as against the occupier of the land.
(d) In relation to damage to property on land, 'property' has the meaning in the Criminal Damage Act 1971, s. 10(1) (see **B8.7**), and 'damage' includes the deposit of any substance capable of polluting the land.
(e) 'Vehicle' includes:
   (i) any vehicle, whether or not it is in a fit state for use on roads, and includes any chassis or body, with or without wheels, appearing to have formed part of such a vehicle, and any load carried by, and anything attached to, such a vehicle; and
   (ii) a caravan as defined in the Caravan Sites and Control of Development Act 1960, s. 29(1).
(f) A person may be regarded as having a purpose of residing in a place notwithstanding that he has a home elsewhere.

Where the persons are on common land (i.e. land registered as common land in a register of common land kept under the Commons Act 2006, part 1, and land which is subject to rights of common as defined in that Act), the references to trespassing or trespassers are references to acts and persons doing acts which constitute either a trespass as against the occupier or an infringement of the commoners' rights; references to 'the occupier' include the commoners or any of them or, in the case of common land to which the public has access, the local authority as well as any commoner (CJPO 1994, s. 61(7)). Persons are not trespassers as against any commoner or the local authority if they are permitted to be there by the other occupier (s. 61(8)(b)). The person must know of the direction and, it would appear, that it applies to him (s. 61(4)). If the police officer giving the direction does not communicate it to the persons to be removed, any constable may do so (s. 61(3)).

Specific Defence

It is a defence for the accused to show that he was not trespassing on the land, or that he had a   **B13.54**
reasonable excuse for failing to leave the land as soon as reasonably practicable or, as the case may be, for again entering the land as a trespasser (CJPO 1994, s. 61(6)). When the legal burden is on the accused, the standard required is proof on a balance of probabilities (see **F3.6** and **F3.53**).

For a summary of the case law relating to 'reverse burden' challenges under the HRA 1998, see **F3.18** *et seq*.

Powers of Seizure

B13.55   A constable may seize and remove vehicles after a direction under the CJPO 1994, s. 61, has been given, provided the criteria in s. 62 are satisfied.

TRESPASSER'S FAILURE TO LEAVE LAND ON POLICE DIRECTION AFTER OCCUPIER'S REQUEST

Definition

B13.56
Criminal Justice and Public Order Act 1994, s. 62B

(1) A person commits an offence if he knows that a direction under section 62A(1) has been given which applies to him and—
   (a) he fails to leave the relevant land as soon as reasonably practicable, or
   (b) he enters any land in the area of the relevant local authority as a trespasser before the end of the relevant period with the intention of residing there.

The CJPO 1994, ss. 62A to 62E, create complementary offences and provide powers to remove trespassers where an alternative site is available.

Procedure and Sentence

B13.57   The offence is triable summarily.

The maximum penalty is imprisonment for a term not exceeding three months, a fine not exceeding level 4 on the standard scale, or both (CJPO 1994, s. 62B(3)).

Elements

B13.58   The power of the police to require someone to leave is provided by the CJPO 1994, s. 62A.

Criminal Justice and Public Order Act 1994, s. 62A

(1) If the senior police officer present at a scene reasonably believes that the conditions in subsection (2) are satisfied in relation to a person and land, he may direct the person—
   (a)   to leave the land:
   (b)   to remove any vehicle and other property he has with him on the land.
(2) The conditions are—
   (a)   that the person and one or more others ('the trespassers') are trespassing on the land;
   (b)   that the trespassers have between them at least one vehicle on the land;
   (c)   that the trespassers are present on the land with the common purpose of residing there for any period;
   (d)   if it appears to the officer that the person has one or more caravans in his possession or under his control on the land, that there is a suitable pitch on a relevant caravan site for that caravan or for each of those caravans;
   (e)   that the occupier of the land or a person acting on his behalf has asked the police to remove the trespassers from the land.
(3) A direction under subsection (1) may be communicated to the person to whom it applies by any constable at the scene.
(4) Subsection (5) applies if—
   (a) a police officer proposes to give a direction under subsection (1) in relation to a person and land, and
   (b) it appears to him that the person has one or more caravans in his possession or under his control on the land.

(5) The officer must consult every local authority within whose area the land is situated as to whether there is a suitable pitch for the caravan or each of the caravans on a relevant caravan site which is situated in the local authority's area.

Definitions   The following terms are defined by the CJPO 1994, s. 62A(6). 'Caravan' and   **B13.59**
'caravan site' have the same meaning as in the Caravan Sites and Control of Development
Act 1960, part 1. 'Relevant caravan site' means a caravan site which is (a) situated in the area
of a local authority within whose area the land is situated; and (b) managed by a relevant site
manager. 'Relevant site manager' means (a) a local authority within whose area the land is situated; (b) a registered social landlord (which definition may be amended by the Secretary of
State: s. 62A(7) and (8)). 'Registered social landlord' means a body registered as a social landlord
under the Housing Act 1996, chapter 1.

The 'relevant period' in s. 62B(1) is the period of three months starting with the day on which
the direction is given (s. 62B(2)).

'Land' does not include buildings other than (a) agricultural buildings within the meaning of
the Local Government Finance Act 1988, sch. 5, paras. 3 to 8, or (b) scheduled monuments
within the meaning of the Ancient Monuments and Archaeological Areas Act 1979 (s. 62E(2)).
'Local authority' means (a) in Greater London, a London borough or the Common Council of
the City of London, (b) in England outside Greater London, a county council, a district council
or the Council of the Isles of Scilly, (c) in Wales, a county council or a county borough council
(s. 62E(3)). 'Occupier', 'trespass', 'trespassing' and 'trespasser' have the meanings given by s. 61
in relation to England and Wales (see **B13.53**) (s. 62E(4)). 'The relevant land' means the land
in respect of which a direction under s. 62A(1) is given (s. 62E(5)). 'The relevant local authority' means (a) if the relevant land is situated in the area of more than one local authority (but is
not in the Isles of Scilly), the district council or county borough council within whose area the
relevant land is situated, (b) if the relevant land is situated in the Isles of Scilly, the Council of
the Isles of Scilly, (c) in any other case, the local authority within whose area the relevant land
is situated (s. 62E(6)). 'Vehicle' has the meaning given by s. 61 (see **B13.53**) (s. 62E(7)). A person may be regarded as having a purpose of residing in a place even if he has a home elsewhere
(s. 62E(8)).

Common Land Modifications   The CJPO 1994, ss. 62A to 62C, have effect in relation to   **B13.60**
common land with the modifications in s. 62D (s. 62D(1)). In that context, references to trespassing and trespassers have effect as if they were reference to acts, and persons doing acts, which
constitute (a) a trespass as against the occupier, or (b) an infringement of the commoners' rights
(s. 62D(2)). References to the occupier (a) in the case of land to which the public has access,
include the local authority and any commoner, (b) in any other case, include the commoners or
any of them (s. 62D(3)). Section 62D(1) does not (a) require action by more than one occupier,
or (b) constitute persons trespassers as against any commoner or other local authority if they are
permitted to be there by the other occupier (s. 62D(4)). 'Common land', 'commoner' and 'the
local authority' have the meanings given by s. 61 (see **B13.53**).

Defences

Criminal Justice and Public Order Act 1994, s. 62B   **B13.61**

(5) In proceedings for an offence under this section it is a defence for the accused to show—
    (a) that he was not trespassing on the land in respect of which he is alleged to have committed
        the offence, or
    (b) that he had a reasonable excuse—
        (i)   for failing to leave the relevant land as soon as reasonably practicable, or
        (ii) for entering land in the area of the relevant local authority as a trespasser with the
            intention of residing there, or
    (c) that, at the time the direction was given, he was under the age of 18 years and was residing
        with his parent or guardian.

B

Part B Offences

When the legal burden is on the accused, the standard required is proof on a balance of probabilities (see **F3.6** and **F3.53**). For a summary of the case law relating to 'reverse burden' challenges under the HRA 1998, see **F3.18** *et seq.*

Power of Seizure

B13.62   A constable may seize and remove vehicles after a direction under the CJPO 1994, s. 62A(1), has been given, provided the criteria in s. 62C are satisfied.

FAILURE TO LEAVE AN EXCLUSION ZONE AFTER BEING ORDERED TO DO SO

Definition

B13.63   Serious Organised Crime and Police Act 2005, s. 112

> (5) Any person who knowingly contravenes a direction given to him under this section is guilty of an offence...

Procedure and Sentence

B13.64   The offence is triable summarily.

The maximum penalty is imprisonment for a term not exceeding four months or a fine not exceeding level 4 on the standard scale or both (SOCPA 2005, s. 112(5)).

Elements

B13.65   Serious Organised Crime and Police Act 2005, s. 112

> (1) A constable may direct a person to leave a place if he believes, on reasonable grounds, that the person is in the place at a time when he would be prohibited from entering it by virtue of—
>   (a) an order to which subsection (2) applies, or
>   (b) a condition to which subsection (3) applies.
> (2) This subsection applies to an order which—
>   (a) was made, by virtue of any enactment, following the person's conviction of an offence, and
>   (b) prohibits the person from entering the place or from doing so during a period specified in the order.
> (3) This subsection applies to a condition which—
>   (a) was imposed, by virtue of any enactment, as a condition of the person's release from a prison in which he was serving a sentence of imprisonment following his conviction of an offence, and
>   (b) prohibits the person from entering the place or from doing so during a period specified in the condition.
> (4) A direction under this section may be given orally.

'Sentence of imprisonment' and 'prison' are to be construed in accordance with the CJCSA 2000, s. 62(5) (s. 112(8)(a)). The reference to a release from prison includes a reference to a temporary release (s. 112(8)(b)). 'Place' includes an area (s. 112(9)).

Section 112 applies whether or not the order or condition in s. 112(1) was made or imposed before or after the commencement of s. 112 (s. 112(10)).

FAILURE TO LEAVE LAND OR RE-ENTRY TO LAND: RAVES

Definition

B13.66   Criminal Justice and Public Order Act 1994, s. 63

> (6) If a person knowing that a direction has been given which applies to him—
>   (a) fails to leave the land as soon as reasonably practicable, or

(b) having left again enters the land within the period of 7 days beginning with the day on which the direction was given,

he commits an offence...

Procedure and Sentence

The offence is triable summarily.   B13.67

The maximum penalty is imprisonment for a term not exceeding three months or a fine not exceeding level 4 on the standard scale or both (CJPO 1994, s. 63(6)). Where a person has been convicted of this offence and the court is satisfied that sound equipment which has been seized from him under s. 64(4), or which was in his possession or under his control at the relevant time, has been used at the gathering, it may make an order for forfeiture in respect of that property in compliance with the provisions of s. 66 (s. 66(1)).

Elements

Section 63 of the CJPO 1994 applies only to gatherings of the kind specified in the s. 63(1);   B13.68
in the marginal note to s. 63, and in common parlance, such gatherings are called raves. The offence is committed only where a direction to leave has been given.

Criminal Justice and Public Order Act 1994, s. 63

(1) This section applies to a gathering on land in the open air of 20 or more persons (whether or not trespassers) at which amplified music is played during the night (with or without intermissions) and is such as, by reason of its loudness and duration and the time at which it is played, is likely to cause serious distress to the inhabitants of the locality; and for this purpose—
   (a) such a gathering continues during intermissions in the music and, where the gathering extends over several days, throughout the period during which the amplified music is played at night (with or without intermissions); and
   (b) 'music' includes sounds wholly or predominantly characterised by the emission of a succession of repetitive beats.
(1A) This section also applies to a gathering if—
   (a) it is a gathering of 20 or more persons who are trespassing on the land; and
   (b) it would be a gathering of a kind mentioned in subsection (1) above if it took place on land in the open air.
(2) If, as respects any land, a police officer of at least the rank of superintendent reasonably believes that—
   (a) two or more persons are making preparations for the holding there of a gathering to which this section applies,
   (b) ten or more persons are waiting for such a gathering to begin there, or
   (c) ten or more persons are attending such a gathering which is in progress, he may give a direction that those persons and any other persons who come to prepare or wait for or to attend the gathering are to leave the land and remove any vehicles or other property they have with them on the land.

The terms 'trespasser' and 'vehicle' have the same meaning as in s. 61 of the 1994 Act (see B13.53). 'Land in the open air' includes a place partly open to the air (s. 63(10)). See also *DPP v Chivers* [2011] 1 WLR 2324.

The person must know of the direction and, it would appear, that it applies to him (s. 63(6)). If the police officer giving the direction does not communicate it to the persons to be removed, any constable at the scene may do so (s. 63(3)). Persons shall be treated as having had a direction communicated to them if reasonable steps have been taken to bring it to their attention (s. 63(4)).

Exempt Persons and Gatherings

Directions do not apply to 'exempt persons' (CJPO 1994, s. 63(5)). An 'exempt person', in rela-   B13.69
tion to land (or any gathering on land), means the occupier, any member of his family and any

employee or agent of his and any person whose home is situated on the land (s. 63(10)). As to the meaning of 'occupier', see **B13.53**.

Directions do not apply, in England and Wales, to a gathering licensed by an entertainment licence (s. 63(9)(a)).

Specific Defence

B13.70 It is a defence to a charge under the CJPO 1994, s. 63(6), for the accused to show that he had a reasonable excuse for failing to leave the land as soon as reasonably practicable or, as the case may be, for again entering the land (s. 63(7)). When the legal burden is on the accused, the standard required is proof on a balance of probabilities (see **F3.6** and **F3.53**). For a summary of the case law relating to 'reverse burden' challenges under the HRA 1998, see **F3.18** *et seq*.

The offence does not apply to a gathering in relation to a licensable activity within the meaning of the Licensing Act 2003, s. 1(1)(c) (provision of certain forms of entertainment) which is carried on under and in accordance with an authorisation within the meaning of s. 136 of that Act (s. 63(9)).

Further Offence

B13.71 A person commits an offence, contrary to the CJPO 1994, s. 63(7A) if (a) he knows that a direction under s. 63(2) has been given which applies to him, and (b) he makes preparations for or attends a gathering to which s. 63 applies within the period of 24 hours starting when the direction was given. A person guilty of this offence is liable, on summary conviction, to imprisonment for a term not exceeding three months or a fine not exceeding level 4 on the standard scale, or both (s. 63(7B)).

Police Powers

B13.72 Sections 63 to 65 and 67 of the CJPO 1994 provide certain additional police powers for the purpose of controlling or prohibiting gatherings of the kind specified in s. 63(1) (see **B13.68**).

(a) A constable authorised to enter land for any purpose in accordance with s. 64(1) and (2) by a police officer of at least the rank of superintendent may enter the land without a warrant (s. 64(3)).

(b) A constable may seize and remove vehicles or sound equipment (as defined in s. 64(6)) after a s. 63 direction provided the criteria in s. 64(4) and (5) are satisfied. Any vehicles so seized and removed may be retained in accordance with regulations made by the Secretary of State (s. 67(1)). Any sound equipment so seized and removed may be retained until the conclusion of proceedings against the person from whom it was seized for an offence under s. 63 (s. 67(2)). Any authority is entitled to recover from a person from whom a vehicle has been seized such charges as may be prescribed in respect of the removal, retention, disposal and destruction of the vehicle by the authority (s. 67(4)).

(c) A constable in uniform has power, at a place within five miles of the boundary of the site of the rave, to stop a person, except an exempt person, whom the constable reasonably believes to be on his way to a rave and direct him not to proceed in the direction of the rave (s. 65(1), (2) and (3)). It is a summary offence for a person, knowing that such a direction has been given to him, to fail to comply with that direction, and such a person is liable on conviction to a fine not exceeding level 3 on the standard scale (s. 65(4)).

UNAUTHORISED CAMPERS: FAILURE TO LEAVE OR RETURNING TO THE LAND

Definition

Criminal Justice and Public Order Act 1994, s. 77

B13.73

(3) If a person knowing that a direction under subsection (1) has been given which applied to him—

    (a) fails, as soon as practicable, to leave the land or remove from the land any vehicle or other property which is the subject of the direction, or

    (b) having removed any such vehicle or property again enters the land with a vehicle within the period of three months beginning with the day on which the direction was given,

he commits an offence...

Procedure and Sentence

The offence is triable summarily only.

B13.74

The maximum penalty is a fine not exceeding level 3 on the standard scale (CJPO 1994, s. 77(3)).

Direction

Criminal Justice and Public Order Act 1994, s. 77

B13.75

(1) If it appears to a local authority that persons are for the time being residing in a vehicle or vehicles within that authority's area—

    (a) on any land forming part of a highway;

    (b) on any other unoccupied land; or

    (c) on any occupied land without the consent of the occupier,

the authority may give a direction that those persons and any others with them are to leave the land and remove the vehicle or vehicles and any other property they have with them on the land.

Notice of a direction must be served on the persons to whom the direction applies, but it is sufficient for the direction to specify the land and (except where it applies to only one person) to be addressed to all occupants of the vehicles on the land, without naming them (s. 77(2)). Where it is impracticable to serve a direction on a person named in it, it is treated as duly served on him if a copy is fixed in a prominent place to the vehicle concerned; and where the direction is directed to unnamed occupants of vehicles, it is treated as duly served on those occupants if it is fixed in a prominent place to every vehicle on the land in question at the time when service is thus effected (s. 79(2)). The local authority must take such steps as are reasonably practicable to ensure that a copy of the direction is displayed on the land in question (otherwise than by being fixed to a vehicle) in a manner designed to ensure that it is likely to be seen by any person camping on the land (s. 79(3)). Notice of a direction is to be given by the local authority to the owner of the land and to any occupier of that land unless, after reasonable inquiries, it is unable to ascertain their names and addresses (s. 79(4)).

A direction operates to require persons who re-enter the land within the period of three months with vehicles or other property to leave and remove the vehicles or other property as it operates in relation to the persons and vehicles or other property on the land when the direction was given (s. 77(4)).

Definitions

Section 77(6) of the CJPO 1994 provides definitions for certain terms used in the section. A person may be regarded as residing on any land notwithstanding that he has a home elsewhere.

B13.76

'Land' means land in the open air. 'Vehicle' and 'occupier' are defined in the same terms as in s. 61 (see **B13.53**).

Specific Defence

B13.77   It is a defence for the accused to show that his failure to leave or to remove the vehicle or other property as soon as practicable, or his re-entry with a vehicle, was due to illness, mechanical breakdown or other immediate emergency (CJPO 1994, s. 77(5)). When the legal burden is on the accused, the standard required is proof on a balance of probabilities (see **F3.6** and **F3.53**). For a summary of the case law relating to 'reverse burden' challenges under the HRA 1998, see **F3.18** *et seq*.

Magistrates' Removal Order

B13.78   On a complaint made by a local authority, a magistrates' court, if satisfied that persons and vehicles in which they are residing are present on land within that authority's area in contravention of such a direction, may make an order requiring the removal of any vehicle or other property and any person residing in it (CJPO 1994, s. 78(1)). Such an order may authorise the local authority to take such steps as are reasonably necessary to ensure that the order is complied with and, in particular, may authorise the authority, by its officers and servants, to enter upon the land specified in the order, and to take, in relation to any vehicle or property to be removed in pursuance of the order, such steps for securing entry and rendering it suitable for removal as may be specified in the order (s. 78(2)). The local authority must give to the owner and occupier at least 24 hours' notice of its intention to enter any occupied land unless after reasonable inquiries it is unable to ascertain their names and addresses (s. 78(3)). A person who wilfully obstructs any person in the exercise of any power conferred on him by an order under s. 78 commits an offence and is liable, on summary conviction, to a fine not exceeding level 3 on the standard scale (s. 78(4)). Where a complaint is made, a summons issued by the court requiring the person(s) to whom it is directed to appear before it to answer to the complaint may be directed either to the occupant of a particular vehicle on the land in question or to all occupants of vehicles on the land in question, without naming him or them (s. 78(5)). There is no power to issue a warrant for arrest upon failure to appear (s. 78(6)). The owner and occupier of the land are entitled to appear and be heard at any proceedings (s. 79(4)).

TRESPASS ON A PROTECTED SITE

Definition

B13.79   <center>Serious Organised Crime and Police Act 2005, s. 128</center>

   (1) A person commits an offence if he enters, or is on, any protected site in England and Wales or Northern Ireland as a trespasser.

Procedure and Sentence

B13.80   The offence is triable summarily only.

The maximum penalty is imprisonment for a term not exceeding six months, a fine not exceeding level 5 on the standard scale, or both (SOCPA 2005, s. 128(5)). No proceedings for the offence may be instituted against any person in England and Wales except by or with the consent of the A-G (s. 128(6)(a)).

Elements

B13.81   A 'protected site' means a nuclear site or a designated site (SOCPA 2005, s. 128(1A)). 'Nuclear site' means (a) so much of any premises in respect of which a nuclear site licence (within the meaning of the Nuclear Installations Act 1965) is for the time being in force as lies within the outer perimeter of the protection provided for those premises; and (b) so much of any other premises of which premises falling within paragraph (a) form a part as lies within that outer perimeter (s. 128(1B)). For this purpose (a) the outer perimeter of the protection provided for any premises is the line of the outermost fences, walls or other obstacles provided or relied on for protecting those premises from intruders; and (b) that line shall be determined on the assumption that every gate, door or other barrier across a way through a fence, wall or other obstacle is closed (s. 128(1C)). A 'designated site' means a site (a) specified or described (in any way) in an order made by the Secretary of State, and (b) designated for the purposes of s. 128 by the order (SOCPA 2005, s. 128(2)). The land that the Secretary of State may designate must be comprised in Crown land, or comprised in land belonging to Her Majesty in her private capacity or to the immediate heir to the Throne in his private capacity, or it must appear to the Secretary of State that it is appropriate to designate the site in the interests of national security (s. 128(3)). 'Site' means the whole or part of any building or buildings, or any land, or both (s. 128(8)(a)). 'Crown land' means land in which there is a Crown interest or a Duchy interest (s. 128(8)(b)). 'Crown interest' means an interest belonging to Her Majesty in right of the Crown and 'Duchy interest' means an interest belonging to Her Majesty in right of the Duchy of Lancaster or belonging to the Duchy of Cornwall (s. 128(9)). Sites have been designated by the Serious Organised Crime and Police Act 2005 (Designated Sites) Order 2005 (SI 2005 No. 3447) and the Serious Organised Crime and Police Act 2005 (Designated Sites under Section 128) Order 2007 (SI 2007 No. 930), as amended by SI 2012 Nos. 1769 and 2709, SI 2013 No. 1562 and SI 2014 No. 411; the former designates 13 sites of military significance and the latter designates 17 sites associated with the government, the security services and the Royal family.

A person who is on any protected site as a trespasser does not cease to be a trespasser by virtue of being allowed time to leave the site (s. 128(7)).

A person cannot claim not to be a trespasser by virtue of the rights of the public in relation to access to land under the Countryside and Rights of Way Act 2000, s. 2(1), since that provision does not apply in respect of land in respect of which a designation order is in force (s. 131(1)).

Defence

Serious Organised Crime and Police Act 2005, s. 128 B13.82

(4) It is a defence for a person charged with an offence under this section to prove that he did not know, and had no reasonable cause to suspect, that the site in relation to which the offence is alleged to have been committed was a protected site.

When the legal burden is on the accused, the standard required is proof on a balance of probabilities (see **F3.6** and **F3.53**). For a summary of the case law relating to 'reverse burden' challenges under the HRA 1998, see **F3.18** *et seq.*

OTHER OFFENCES BY TRESPASSERS

Trespassing with Firearm in a Building or on Land

Firearms Act 1968, s. 20 B13.83

(1) A person commits an offence if, while he has a firearm or imitation firearm with him, he enters or is in any building or part of a building as a trespasser and without reasonable excuse (the proof whereof lies on him).
(2) A person commits an offence if, while he has a firearm or imitation firearm with him, he enters or is on any land as a trespasser and without reasonable excuse (the proof whereof lies on him).

The mode of trial for trespassing with firearm in a building is either way, although if the weapon is an air weapon or an imitation firearm, the offence is triable summarily only. The mode of trial for trespassing with a firearm on any land is summary only. As to the extension of the usual time-limit within which summary proceedings must be instituted, see **B12.3**.

The offence of trespassing with a firearm in a building is punishable, on summary conviction, with a term of imprisonment not exceeding six months or a fine not exceeding the prescribed sum or both; and, on conviction on indictment, with a term of imprisonment not exceeding five years or a fine or both. The offence of trespassing with a firearm on any land is punishable, on summary conviction, with a term of imprisonment not exceeding three months or a fine not exceeding level 4 on the standard scale or both. As to the courts' power to order forfeiture or disposal of firearms and ammunition, see **B12.4**.

The meaning of 'firearm' is considered at **B12.7**. Imitation firearms (see **B12.25**) fall within this section. The Firearms Act 1968, s. 20(3), defines 'land' as including land covered by water.

Trespassing with Weapon of Offence

B13.84   It is a summary offence, contrary to the CLA 1977, s. 8(1), for a person who is on any premises as a trespasser, after having entered as such, without lawful authority or reasonable excuse to have with him on the premises any weapon of offence. As to disputes as to title to property on summary trial, see **B13.25**.

By virtue of s. 8(3), a person guilty of this offence is liable to imprisonment for a term not exceeding three months or to a fine not exceeding level 5 on the standard scale or to both.

The meanings of the words 'premises' and 'trespasser' have been considered at **B13.26** and **B13.28**. The phrase, 'weapon of offence' is defined by s. 8(2) as meaning any article made or adapted for causing injury to or incapacitating a person, or intended by the person having it with him for such use. The same definition of 'weapon of offence' is used in the offence of aggravated burglary contrary to the Theft Act 1968, s. 10. For further discussion of this subject, see **B4.102**.

Trespassing on Premises of Foreign Missions, etc.

B13.85   It is a summary offence, contrary to the CLA 1977, s. 9(1), for a person to enter or be on any premises to which s. 9 applies as a trespasser. As to disputes as to title to property on summary trial, see **B13.25**.

By virtue of s. 9(6), proceedings for this offence may not be instituted against any person except by or with the consent of the A-G.

By virtue of s. 9(5), a person guilty of this offence is liable to imprisonment for a term not exceeding six months or to a fine not exceeding level 5 on the standard scale or to both.

The phrase 'enters as a trespasser', is partly defined by the 1977 Act, since meanings are given for 'entry' and 'trespasser' (see **B13.26** and **B13.28** respectively). Similar terms also appear in the offence of burglary (see **B4.86** and **B4.87**).

B13.86   The premises to which s. 9 applies are listed in s. 9(2):

Criminal Law Act 1977, s. 9

(2) This section applies to any premises which are or form part of—
(a) the premises of a diplomatic mission within the meaning of the definition in Article 1(i) of the Vienna Convention on Diplomatic Relations signed in 1961 as that Article has effect in the United Kingdom by virtue of section 2 of and Schedule 1 to the Diplomatic Privileges Act 1964;
(aa) the premises of a closed diplomatic mission;
(b) consular premises within the meaning of the definition in paragraph 1(j) of Article 1 of the Vienna Convention on Consular Relations signed in 1963 as that Article has effect in the United Kingdom by virtue of section 1 of and Schedule 1 to the Consular Relations Act 1968;

(bb) the premises of a closed consular post;

(c) any other premises in respect of which any organisation or body is entitled to inviolability by or under any enactment; and

(d) any premises which are the private residence of a diplomatic agent (within the meaning of Article 1(e) of the Convention mentioned in paragraph (a) above) or of any other person who is entitled to inviolability of residence by or under any enactment.

(2A) In subsection (2) above—

'the premises of a closed diplomatic mission' means premises which fall within Article 45 of the Convention mentioned in subsection (2)(a) above (as that Article has effect in the United Kingdom by virtue of the section and Schedule mentioned in that paragraph); and

'the premises of a closed consular post' means premises which fall within Article 27 of the Convention mentioned in subsection (2)(b) above (as that Article has effect in the United Kingdom by virtue of the section and Schedule mentioned in that paragraph).

Insofar as the general meaning of 'premises' is relevant, see **B13.26**. Section 9(4) creates an important evidential provision in relation to establishing whether given premises are covered by s. 9 or not, since in any proceedings for this offence 'a certificate issued by or under the authority of the Secretary of State stating that any premises were or formed part of premises of any description mentioned in paragraphs (a) to (d) of subsection (2) above at the time of the alleged offence shall be conclusive evidence that the premises were or formed part of premises of that description at that time'.

By virtue of s. 9(3), it is a defence for the accused to prove that he believed that the premises in question were not premises to which s. 9 applies. When the legal burden is on the accused, the standard required is proof on a balance of probabilities (see **F3.6** and **F3.53**). For a summary of the case law relating to 'reverse burden' challenges under the HRA 1998, see **F3.18** *et seq.*

Obstruction of Court Officers Executing Process against Unauthorised Occupiers

It is a summary offence, contrary to the CLA 1977, s. 10(1), and without prejudice to the **B13.87** Sheriffs Act 1887, s. 8(2), if a person resists or intentionally obstructs any person who is in fact an officer of a court engaged in executing any process issued by the High Court or any county court for the purpose of enforcing any judgment or order for the recovery of any premises or for the delivery of possession of any premises. As to disputes as to title to property on summary trial, see **B13.25**.

By virtue of s. 6(5), a person guilty of this offence is liable to imprisonment for a term not exceeding six months or to a fine not exceeding level 5 on the standard scale or to both.

A similar phrase to 'resists or intentionally obstructs' appears in the offence involving the obstruction of a constable contrary to the Police Act 1996, s. 89(2) (see **B2.42**).

'Officer of a court' according to s. 10(6) means any sheriff, under sheriff, deputy sheriff, bailiff or officer of a sheriff, and officer of the county court.

The offence does not apply unless the judgment or order in question was given or made in proceedings brought under any provisions of rules of court applicable only in circumstances where the person claiming possession of any premises alleges that the premises in question are occupied solely by a person or persons (not being a tenant or tenants holding over after the termination of the tenancy) who entered into or remained in occupation of the premises without the licence or consent of the person claiming possession or any predecessor in title of his.

'Premises' in this section has a slightly wider meaning than in the other offences in part II of **B13.88** the CLA 1977. Section 12 states that 'premises' means any building, any part of a building under separate occupation, any land ancillary to a building, the site comprising any building or buildings together with any land ancillary thereto, and (for the purposes only of ss. 10 and 11) any other place. The references to a building apply also to any structure other than a moveable one, and to any moveable structure, vehicle or vessel designed or adapted for residential purposes; and:

(a) part of a building is under separate occupation if anyone is in occupation or entitled to occupation of that part as distinct from the whole; and

(b) land is ancillary to a building if it is adjacent to it and used (or intended for use) in connection with the occupation of that building or any part of it.

Note that the PACE 1984, s. 17(1)(c)(ii) (see **D1.169**) provides the police with a power of entry to premises to arrest a person for this offence.

By virtue of s. 10(3), it is a defence for the accused to prove that he believed that the person he was resisting or obstructing was not an officer of a court. When the legal burden is on the accused, the standard required is proof on a balance of probabilities (see **F3.6** and **F3.53**). For a summary of the case law relating to 'reverse burden' challenges under the HRA 1998, see **F3.18** *et seq.*

There is a related offence under s. 10(A1) of resisting or intentionally obstructing any person who is an enforcement officer, or is acting under the authority of an enforcement officer and is engaged in executing a writ issued from the High Court.

Trespassing on Licensed Aerodromes

B13.89   It is an offence, contrary to the Civil Aviation Act 1982, s. 39, for a person to trespass on any land forming part of an aerodrome licensed in pursuit of an Air Navigation Order. The maximum punishment is, on summary conviction, a fine not exceeding level 3 on the standard scale (s. 39(1)). No one may be convicted unless it is proved that, at the material time, notices warning trespassers of their liability under s. 39 were posted so as to be readily seen and read by members of the public, in such positions on or near the boundary of the aerodrome as appear to the court to be proper (s. 39(2)).

Trespassing on a Railway

B13.90   It is an offence, contrary to the British Transport Commission Act 1949, s. 55(1), to trespass on any railway lines, sidings, embankments, tunnels, cuttings or similar railway works. On summary conviction, the maximum penalty is a fine not exceeding level 3 on the standard scale. Under the Penalties for Disorderly Behaviour (Amount of Penalty) Order 2002 (SI 2002 No. 1837), as amended, this offence is a penalty offence and the amount payable is £60.

Poaching Offences

B13.91   There are five poaching offences, the primary focus of which is the protection of game rights, but which involve trespass to land, see Game Act 1831, s. 30 (poaching by day and poaching by day in company), Night Poaching Act 1828, s. 1 (night poaching by unlawfully entering land and night poaching by unlawfully being on land) and the Deer Act 1991, s. 1 (poaching of deer). Further, it is an offence to take or destroy fish from water which is private property or in which there is a private right of fishery (Theft Act 1968, sch. 1, para. 2(1)).

Section B14 Offences Against the Administration of Justice

PERJURY IN A JUDICIAL PROCEEDING

Perjury Act 1911, s. 1

B14.1

(1) If any person lawfully sworn as a witness or as an interpreter in a judicial proceeding wilfully makes a statement material in that proceeding, which he knows to be false or does not believe to be true, he shall be guilty of perjury, and shall, on conviction thereof on indictment, be liable to imprisonment for a term not exceeding seven years, or to a fine or to both imprisonment and fine.

(2) The expression 'judicial proceeding' includes a proceeding before any court, tribunal, or person having by law power to hear, receive, and examine evidence on oath.

(3) Where a statement made for the purposes of a judicial proceeding is not made before the tribunal itself, but is made on oath before a person authorised by law to administer an oath to the person who makes the statement, and to record or authenticate the statement, it shall, for the purposes of this section, be treated as having been made in a judicial proceeding.

(4) A statement made by a person lawfully sworn in England for the purposes of a judicial proceeding:
    (a) in another part of His Majesty's dominions; or
    (b) in a British tribunal lawfully constituted in any place by sea or land outside His Majesty's dominions; or
    (c) in a tribunal of any foreign state,
shall, for the purposes of this section, be treated as a statement made in a judicial proceeding in England.

(5) Where, for the purposes of a judicial proceeding in England, a person is lawfully sworn under the authority of an Act of Parliament:
    (a) in any other part of His Majesty's dominions; or
    (b) before a British tribunal or a British officer in a foreign country, or within the jurisdiction of the Admiralty of England;
a statement made by such person so sworn as aforesaid (unless the Act of Parliament under which it was made otherwise specifically provides) shall be treated for the purposes of this section as having been made in the judicial proceeding in England for the purposes whereof it was made.

(6) The question whether a statement on which perjury is assigned was material is a question of law to be determined by the court of trial.

This offence applies to intermediaries appointed under the YJCEA 1999, s. 29, as it applies to interpreters (s. 29(7)). This includes intermediaries who assist in the examination of a witness otherwise than in the course of judicial proceedings: the examination shall be taken to be part of the judicial proceeding in which that witness's evidence is given.

B14.2

Procedure

Perjury in a judicial proceeding is triable only on indictment. It is normally a class 3 offence, but see CPD XIII, para. B (see Supplement, **PD-97**) for the additional factors that the court considers on allocation.

B14.3

Perjury Act 1911, s. 8

Where an offence against this Act or any offence punishable as perjury or as subornation of perjury under any other Act of Parliament is committed in any place either on sea or land outside the United Kingdom, the offender may be proceeded against, indicted, tried, and punished...in England.

It is not altogether clear whether this provision was intended to extend the ambit of the Act in any way, or whether it was, as the marginal note ('venue') suggests, intended merely to provide for the trial of any extra-territorial offences created under the preceding sections. On balance, the latter interpretation is to be preferred. The extra-territorial scope of s. 1, for example, is precisely governed by subsections (4) and (5), and these provisions would not have been necessary if s. 8 had any wider meaning. As to territorial jurisdiction generally, see **A8**.

Indictment

B14.4

Statement of Offence

Perjury contrary to section 1(1) of the Perjury Act 1911.

Particulars of Offence

A on the...day of..., having been lawfully sworn as a witness in a judicial proceeding, namely the trial of a criminal cause at the Central Criminal Court entitled The Queen v B.C., wilfully made a statement material in that proceeding which he knew to be false, namely that the accused B.C. had been in the City of Leicester on the...day of...

Perjury Act 1911, s. 12

(1) In an indictment—
  (a) for making any false statement or false representation punishable under this Act; or
  (b) for unlawfully, wilfully, falsely, fraudulently, deceitfully, maliciously, or corruptly taking, making, signing, or subscribing any oath, affirmation, solemn declaration, statutory declaration, affidavit, deposition, notice, certificate, or other writing,
  it is sufficient to set forth the substance of the offence charged, and before which court or person (if any) the offence was committed without setting forth the proceedings or any part of the proceedings in the course of which the offence was committed, and without setting forth the authority of any court or person before whom the offence was committed.
(2) In an indictment for aiding, abetting, counselling, suborning, or procuring any other person to commit any offence hereinbefore in this section mentioned, or for conspiring with any other person, or with attempting to suborn or procure any other person, to commit any such offence, it is sufficient—
  (a) where such offence has been committed, to allege that offence, and then to allege that the defendant procured the commission of the offence; and
  (b) where such offence has not been committed, to set forth the substance of the offence charged against the defendant without setting forth any matter or thing which it is unnecessary to aver in the case of an indictment for a false statement or false representation punishable under this Act.

Sentence

B14.5 The maximum penalty for perjury is seven years (Perjury Act 1911, s. 1).

There are numerous Court of Appeal decisions dealing with sentencing for this offence. They indicate that a custodial sentence is almost always necessary since, as Roskill LJ said in *Davies* (1974) 59 Cr App R 311 at p. 313:

> It is often said there is too much perjury committed in courts, and it is regrettably true as everyone sitting in court knows. But it is one thing to suspect that perjury has been committed and another thing to prove it. Perjury is not always easy to prove. Perjurers are not easily brought to justice. When they are they must be punished.

It seems that where the original charge in relation to which the perjury was committed was one of very serious crime, the penalty for the perjury should be proportionately higher. A sentence of four years' imprisonment for perjury was upheld in *Cunningham* [2007] 2 Cr App R (S) 376, where the offender, a man with a previous conviction for an offence against justice, committed perjury in proceedings relating to a serious crime. His defence that he acted under duress was rejected by the jury. In *Archer* [2003] 1 Cr App R (S) 446, a sentence of four years was upheld in respect of an offender who was convicted of two counts of perjury and two counts of perverting the course of justice, in respect of civil proceedings for libel which he had brought against a newspaper. The Court of Appeal held that there was no inherent difference in seriousness between perjury in civil as against criminal proceedings. Other factors were more relevant, including the number of offences committed, the time scale over which they had taken place, whether the lies were planned and persisted in, whether D had implicated others, and whether the perjury had affected the outcome of the original proceedings.

In *Hall* (1982) 4 Cr App R (S) 153 Talbot J (at p. 155) said that '... it is almost inconceivable   **B14.6** that a sentence of less than three months would be given for a deliberate perjury in the face of the court', since 'such false evidence strikes at the whole basis of the administration of the law'. In that case a three-month sentence was upheld on a 62-year-old woman who had given false alibi evidence at a magistrates' court in respect of a man charged with assault occasioning actual bodily harm. A sentence of six months' imprisonment was upheld in *Healey* (1990) 12 Cr App R (S) 297, in respect of perjury committed in the course of a means inquiry in a magistrates' court. The offender appeared in court for failure to pay a fine of £200. He then gave evidence on oath that he was employed, and that the fine could be recovered by an attachment of earnings order. This evidence was untrue. In *Wittekind* [2010] EWCA Crim 646 the Court of Appeal said that a sentence of three years was too long for perjury committed in the course of an appeal in an Army disciplinary matter. No original serious offence was involved and, as a result of the custodial penalty, the offender would be discharged from the Army. The sentence was reduced to two years.

Meaning of 'Statements in Judicial Proceedings'

The effect of the Perjury Act 1911, s. 1 (2) and (3), is that perjury need not take the form of false   **B14.7** evidence in court. A false affidavit sworn in connection with a judicial proceeding may amount to perjury, as may false evidence given on oath before a tribunal.

The position is slightly different in the case of false written evidence tendered in criminal proceedings under the CJA 1967, s. 9, and of false written evidence admitted in committal proceedings under the MCA 1980, s. 5B. Wilful falsity in such cases attracts a maximum penalty of two years and/or a fine, as opposed to the seven year maximum for perjury itself, but in all other respects the principles contained within the Perjury Act 1911 are applicable. The relevant offences (under the CJA 1967, s. 89 and the MCA 1980, s. 106) are dealt with at **B14.20**.

The CJA 1988, s. 32, enables a person outside the UK to give evidence at a criminal trial in England or Wales through a live television link. As with evidence to which the Perjury Act 1911, s. 1(5), applies, any such evidence is treated for the purposes of the Perjury Act 1911, s. 1, as given in the trial concerned (CJA 1988, s. 32(3)).

By the European Communities Act 1972, s. 11(1)(a), all relevant provisions of the Perjury Act 1911 are applicable to statements made on oath before the European Court of Justice, or any court attached thereto, whether or not the person responsible is a British citizen. See also the Evidence (European Court) Order 1976 (SI 1976 No. 428).

Meaning of 'Lawfully Sworn'

Evidence Act 1851, s. 16   **B14.8**

> Every court, judge, justice, officer, commissioner, arbitrator, or other person, now or hereafter having by law or by consent of parties authority to hear, receive, and examine evidence, is hereby empowered to administer an oath to all such witnesses as are legally called before them respectively.

A conviction for perjury is impossible if D was incompetent to testify in the proceedings in which his perjury is alleged to have been committed (*Clegg* (1868) 19 LT 47).

It is possible for a witness or interpreter to make a solemn affirmation in place of the oath, whether or not the taking of an oath would be contrary to his religious beliefs, and the Perjury Act 1911, s. 15(2), provides that references therein to 'oaths' and 'swearing' embrace affirmations. The affirming witness is thus equally subject to the Perjury Act 1911.

Perjury Act 1911, s. 15

(1) For the purposes of this Act, the forms and ceremonies used in administering an oath are immaterial, if the court or person before whom the oath is taken has power to administer an oath for the purpose of verifying the statement in question, and if the oath has been administered in a form and with ceremonies which the person taking the oath has accepted without objection, or has declared to be binding on him.

As to oaths and affirmations generally, see F4.32 to F4.37.

Wilfulness

B14.9 It might seem at first sight that the requirement of wilfulness in the Perjury Act 1911, s. 1, is otiose, since the offence can be committed only by someone who does not believe his testimony to be true; but conduct is wilful only if it is deliberate or intentional (*Senior* [1899] 1 QB 283), and it must therefore be proved that any alleged perjury was not the result of a misunderstanding or a slip of the tongue, whereby D might perhaps have said something he did not mean (*Millward* [1985] QB 519). As to wilfulness generally, see A2.13.

Materiality

B14.10 'Material' means important or significant: something which matters. See *Mallett* [1978] 3 All ER 10, in which the Court of Appeal so construed the phrase 'false in a material particular', in a prosecution under the Theft Act 1968, s. 17(1) and *Lancaster* [2010] 3 All ER 402 at B6.12. Under the Perjury Act 1911, s. 1(6), the question of what is material is one of law (i.e. for the judge to decide). Although A must know of the falsity of his statement (or not believe in its truth) he need not know or believe it to be material (*Millward* [1985] QB 519).

The truth or falsity of D's statement need not be crucial to the outcome of the case. It would suffice, for example, if D's lies prevented the other side from pursuing a certain line of questioning which might have been material to the question of his credibility (*Millward* [1985] QB 519; and see also *Baker* [1895] 1 QB 797). A statement may also be material even though it ought strictly to have been excluded by the court or judge before whom it was made (*Gibbon* (1862) Le & Ca 109; cf. *Philpotts* (1851) 2 Den CC 302).

Clear examples of immaterial statements are hard to find amongst the reported cases. It was held in *Tate* (1871) 12 Cox CC 7 that it was not perjury for D to swear at X's trial for assault that he had seen X's wife commit adultery, because that would have been irrelevant to the question whether X had indeed committed the assault; but this decision has been doubted (*Hewitt* (1913) 9 Cr App R 192) and it has since been held that evidence is material if it may affect the likely penalty in criminal proceedings, even if it is immaterial to the question of liability (*Wheeler* [1917] 1 KB 283). A rare reported example of lies that were held to be immaterial is *Sweet-Escott* (1971) 55 Cr App R 316, where in committal proceedings D had denied having any previous convictions. He did have some; but these dated from over 20 years before, and it was held that they could not have made any difference to the outcome of the proceedings.

Truth or Falsity of the Statement

B14.11 On a literal interpretation of the Perjury Act 1911, s. 1, it would seem that D could be convicted of perjury as a result of a statement which he did not believe to be true, but which was in fact true after all. Prosecutions are hardly likely to be brought in respect of manifestly true statements, but if this literal interpretation is correct, it would ease the prosecution's task in cases where D's state of mind is easier to prove than the truth or falsity of his evidence. If, for example, D had testified that event X took place on 5 July, and the prosecution can prove that D had no idea whether that event took place or not, this should suffice as proof of his perjury, even if there is no evidence that it did not take place on 5 July. See *Rider* (1986) 83 Cr App R 207.

This was indeed the position at common law (*Allen v Westley* (1629) Het 97) and although the Court of Appeal appears to have assumed in *Millward* [1985] QB 519 that proof of falsity is required under the Perjury Act 1911, this was unconsidered and strictly *obiter*. Most commentators support the literal interpretation, which also found some favour with the Court of Appeal in *Rider* (1986) Cr App R 207, although the point was ultimately left open in that case.

It may at first seem rather difficult to reconcile the 'literal' interpretation of the Perjury Act 1911, s. 1, with s. 13, which effectively requires corroboration of any allegation of falsity before a conviction for perjury can be obtained, but the wording of s. 13 is not in fact inconsistent with that interpretation, as the Court of Appeal noted in *Rider* (1986) 83 Cr App R 207. As to s. 13, see **B14.16**.

False Statements of Opinion

An expression of opinion, not genuinely held by the witness making it, may amount to perjury (*Schlesinger* (1847) 10 QB 670).   **B14.12**

Perjury Based on Inconsistent Statements

Where D has on separate occasions made two or more inconsistent statements on oath, and must have been guilty of deliberate perjury on at least one of those occasions, a conviction will not be possible unless the prosecution can prove which of the statements were perjured.   **B14.13**

Prosecution for Perjury where Accused's Evidence Secured his Acquittal in Previous Trial

Problems may arise where a person has been acquitted of a criminal charge after giving evidence of his own innocence, but further evidence has come to light which tends to prove, not just that he lied in the course of his testimony, but that he must have been wrongly acquitted. If a person is tried for perjury, can the prosecution adduce evidence which is flatly inconsistent with his acquittal at the earlier trial?   **B14.14**

The House of Lords in *DPP v Humphrys* [1977] AC 1 held that issue estoppel has no place in criminal proceedings, but the related doctrine laid down in *Sambasivam v Public Prosecutor* [1950] AC 458, under which it was said that the prosecution must accept D's innocence of any alleged crimes of which he has previously been acquitted, survived until its rejection by the House in *Z* [2000] 2 AC 483. D's previous acquittal is no longer an obstacle to his prosecution for perjury.

On the other hand, it would be oppressive and unfair for D to be prosecuted for perjury after successfully defending himself on the original charge, unless significant new prosecution evidence has become available to contradict his original evidence. If the prosecution are merely hoping that a different jury might believe their original witnesses, the prosecution should be stayed as an abuse of process. This was recognised, both in *Humphrys* and in *Z*.

As to the effect of previous verdicts in criminal cases generally, see **F11**.

Proof of Previous Judicial Proceeding

If the fact of the proceeding at which the perjury is alleged to have taken place is not admitted, this may be proved by production of the record of the trial or, in the case of trials on indictment, in accordance with the Perjury Act 1911, s. 14.   **B14.15**

Perjury Act 1911, s. 14

On a prosecution—
(a) for perjury alleged to have been committed on the trial of an indictment...; or
(b) for procuring or suborning the commission of perjury on any such trial,
the fact of the former trial shall be sufficiently proved by the production of a certificate containing the substance and effect (omitting the formal parts) of the indictment and trial purporting to be signed by the clerk of the court, or other person having the custody of the records of the court where the indictment was tried, or by the deputy of that clerk or other person, without proof of the signature or official character of the clerk or person appearing to have signed the certificate.

D's allegedly perjured statements, if not admitted, may be proved by the testimony of persons who were present at the trial. One such witness would suffice, since s. 13 (see **B14.16**) applies only to evidence of falsity. Alternatively, the shorthand writer's record may be admissible under the CJA 2003, s. 117.

Requirement of Corroboration as to Falsity

B14.16   Perjury Act 1911, s. 13

A person shall not be liable to be convicted of any offence against this Act, or of any offence declared by any other Act to be perjury or subornation of perjury, or to be punishable as perjury or subornation of perjury, solely upon the evidence of one witness as to the falsity of any statement alleged to be false.

This provision does not lay down any corroboration requirement as to the fact that D made the alleged statement, or as to his knowledge or belief at the time (*O'Connor* [1980] Crim LR 43). If it is not being alleged that the statement was false (e.g., where it is alleged that neither D nor anyone else could have known whether it was true or not), then s. 13 has no application.

Where s. 13 does apply, its interpretation is troublesome. It does not expressly refer to 'corroboration' at all, and it was accordingly argued in *Hamid* (1979) 69 Cr App R 324 that, provided the prosecution case does not depend on a single witness as to falsity, the technicalities of the law relating to corroboration do not apply; but the Court of Appeal disagreed. It follows that a jury will need to be directed as to what other evidence might be capable of providing that corroboration, and the absence of any such direction will amount to a material irregularity. See also *Rider* (1986) 83 Cr App R 207, *Carroll* [1993] Crim LR 613 and *Cooper* [2010] 2 Cr App R 92.

Although a single witness to falsity must be corroborated, this corroboration may take the form of documentary evidence, and may originate from D himself, as in *Threlfall* (1914) 10 Cr App R 112, where D had written a letter, parts of which appeared to be self-incriminating.

Where D is alleged to have confessed prior to the trial, the evidence of two witnesses to the confession has been held to be sufficient for the purposes of s. 13. It is not necessary that they should have witnessed confessions on separate occasions (*Peach* [1990] 2 All ER 966).

Aiding and Abetting etc.

B14.17   Perjury Act 1911, s. 7

(1) Every person who aids, abets, counsels, procures, or suborns another person to commit an offence against this Act shall be liable to be proceeded against, indicted, tried and punished as if he were a principal offender.
(2) Every person who incites another person to commit an offence against this Act shall be guilty of an offence, and, on conviction thereof on indictment, shall be liable to imprisonment, or to a fine, or to both such imprisonment and fine.

'Suborning' is merely another term, in this context, for procuring, and s. 7(1) thus adds nothing of significance to the general law of secondary participation in crime, as governed by the Accessories and Abettors Act 1861 (see generally A4.1 *et seq.*).

The offence of incitement in s. 7(2) remains unaffected by the new law on aiding and encouraging crime because s. 7(2) is not one of the provisions listed in the SCA 2007, sch. 6, part 1 (see **A5.1**). The maximum term of imprisonment for an offence under s. 7(2) is limited by the PCC(S)A 2000, s. 77, to two years' imprisonment.

The Perjury Act 1911, s. 13 (see **B14.16**), applies to offences under this provision. All complicity offences are triable either way except complicity in an offence under the Perjury Act 1911, s. 1 (perjury in judicial proceedings).

OFFENCES AKIN TO PERJURY

False Testimony of Unsworn Child Witnesses in Criminal Proceedings

B14.18 The Perjury Act 1911, s. 16(2), provides that nothing in that Act applies to the unsworn evidence of children (see **F4.21**) but under the YJCEA 1999, s. 57, children or other persons who wilfully give false evidence in criminal proceedings when testifying unsworn (by virtue of s. 56 of that Act: see **F4.24**), and who would be guilty of perjury if testifying on oath, will be guilty of a summary offence. The penalty for children (aged under 14) is a fine not exceeding £250; others may face a fine not exceeding £1,000 and/or imprisonment for a term not exceeding six months (YJCEA 1999, s. 57(2) and (3)).

False Unsworn Evidence under the Evidence (Proceedings in Other Jurisdictions) Act 1975

B14.19

> **Perjury Act 1911, s. 1A**
>
> If any person, in giving any testimony (either orally or in writing) otherwise than on oath, where required to do so by an order under section 2 of the Evidence (Proceedings in Other Jurisdictions) Act 1975, makes a statement:
> (a) which he knows to be false in a material particular, or
> (b) which is false in a material particular and which he does not believe to be true,
> he shall be guilty of [an offence] and shall be liable on conviction on indictment to imprisonment for a term not exceeding two years or a fine or both.

This section serves a function similar to that served in respect of sworn evidence by the Perjury Act 1911, s. 1(4) (see **B14.1**). In contrast to the uncertainty concerning the need for proof of actual falsity in prosecutions under s. 1, it is clear in this case that such proof is indeed required. As to the meaning of the phrase 'false in a material particular', see the discussion at **B14.10**.

Section 13 applies (see **B14.16**); and offences under this provision are triable either way (MCA 1980, s. 17 and sch. 1, para. 14).

False Written Statements Tendered in Criminal Proceedings

B14.20

> **Criminal Justice Act 1967, s. 89**
> (1) If any person in a written statement tendered in evidence in criminal proceedings by virtue of section 9 of this Act, wilfully makes a statement material in those proceedings which he knows to be false or does not believe to be true, he shall be liable on conviction on indictment to imprisonment for a term not exceeding two years or a fine or both.
> (2) The Perjury Act 1911 shall have effect as if this section were contained in that Act.
>
> **Magistrates' Courts Act 1980, s. 106**
> (1) If any person in a written statement admitted in evidence in criminal proceedings by virtue of section 5B above wilfully makes a statement material in those proceedings which he knows to be false or does not believe to be true, he shall be liable on conviction on indictment to imprisonment for a term not exceeding two years or a fine or both.
> (2) The Perjury Act 1911 shall have effect as if this section were contained in that Act.

The only obvious distinction between these offences and perjury itself lies in the maximum penalties, which stand at two years compared with the maximum of seven under the Perjury Act 1911, s. 1. Although there is no specific provision, it would seem that these offences are triable either way, since, in each of the two sections set out above, subsection (2) assimilates them into the Perjury Act 1911 and, by virtue of the MCA 1980, s. 17 and sch. 1, para. 14, all offences under the Perjury Act 1911, except those under ss. 1, 3 and 4, are so triable. (Sections 3 and 4 of the Perjury Act 1911 expressly made offences under those sections triable either way.)

Section 13 of the Perjury Act 1911 is applicable to both offences: see **B14.16**.

False Statements Made on Oath outside Judicial Proceedings

B14.21   Perjury Act 1911, s. 2

If any person:

(1) being required or authorised by law to make any statement on oath for any purpose, and being lawfully sworn (otherwise than in a judicial proceeding) wilfully makes a statement which is material for that purpose and which he knows to be false or does not believe to be true; or

(2) wilfully uses any false affidavit for the purposes of the Bills of Sale Act 1878, as amended by any subsequent enactment,

he shall be guilty of [an offence], and, on conviction thereof on indictment, shall be liable to imprisonment for a term not exceeding seven years or to a fine or to both such imprisonment and fine.

The offence created by this section is of limited application. Affidavits sworn in connection with judicial proceedings must be dealt with under the Perjury Act 1911, s. 1(3). As to statutory declarations, see s. 5, discussed in **B14.25**.

Section 13 applies (see **B14.16**), and offences under this provision are triable either way (MCA 1980, sch. 1, para. 14).

False Statements with Reference to Marriage

B14.22   Perjury Act 1911, s. 3

(1) If any person:

(a) for the purpose of procuring a marriage, or a certificate or licence for marriage, knowingly and wilfully makes a false oath, or makes or signs a false declaration, notice or certificate required under any Act of Parliament for the time being in force relating to marriage; or

(b) knowingly and wilfully makes, or knowingly and wilfully causes to be made, for the purpose of being inserted in any register of marriage, a false statement as to any particular required by law to be known and registered relating to any marriage; or

(c) forbids the issue of any certificate or licence for marriage by falsely representing himself to be a person whose consent to the marriage is required by law knowing such representation to be false; or

(d) with respect to a declaration made under section 16(1A) or 27B(2) of the Marriage Act 1949:

(i)   enters a caveat under subsection (2) of the said section 16, or

(ii) makes a statement mentioned in subsection (4) of the said section 27B, which he knows to be false in a material particular,

he shall be guilty of [an offence,] and, on conviction thereof on indictment, shall be liable to imprisonment for a term not exceeding seven years or to a fine or to both imprisonment and fine and on summary conviction thereof shall be liable to a penalty not exceeding the prescribed sum.

(2) No prosecution for knowingly and wilfully making a false declaration for the purpose of procuring any marriage out of the district in which the parties or one of them dwell shall take place after the expiration of eighteen months from the solemnization of the marriage to which the declaration refers.

An offence under s. 3 is committed only by a person who acts for the purpose of procuring a marriage or licence etc. but whether or not he succeeds in this purpose is irrelevant. A false statement cannot, however, give rise to liability under the s. 3(1)(a) or (b), unless it concerns something which must by law be stated correctly (*Frickey* [1956] Crim LR 421).

See also the Civil Partnership Act 2004, s. 80 (false statements etc. with reference to civil partnerships).

The Perjury Act 1911, s. 13 (see **B14.16**) applies both to s. 3 and to s. 80 of the 2004 Act (by virtue of s. 80(4)).

False Statements about Births and Deaths

Perjury Act 1911, s. 4 **B14.23**

(1) If any person:
  (a) wilfully makes any false answer to any question put to him by any registrar of births or deaths relating to the particulars required to be registered concerning any birth or death, or, wilfully gives to any such registrar any false information concerning any birth or death or the cause of any death; or
  (b) wilfully makes any false certificate or declaration under or for the purposes of any Act relating to the registration of births or deaths, or, knowing any such certificate or declaration to be false, uses the same as true or gives or sends the same as true to any person; or
  (c) wilfully makes, gives or uses any false statement or declaration as to a child born alive as having been still-born, or as to the body of a deceased person or still-born child in any coffin, or falsely pretends that any child born alive was still-born; or
  (d) makes any false statement with intent to have the same inserted in any register of births or deaths:
he shall be guilty of [an offence] and shall be liable:
  (i) on conviction thereof on indictment, to imprisonment for a term not exceeding seven years, or to a fine instead of the said punishments; and
  (ii) on summary conviction thereof, to a penalty not exceeding [the prescribed sum].
(2) A prosecution on indictment for an offence against this section shall not be commenced more than three years after the commission of the offence.

As to the particulars requiring registration in relation to births or deaths, see the Births and **B14.24** Deaths Registration Act 1953, s. 39, and orders made thereunder. In contrast to the position under the Perjury Act 1911, s. 3, the wilful provision of any false information concerning a birth or death may involve liability, whether or not its provision was a strict legal requirement.

False statements as to the paternity of a child are obvious examples of the s. 4 offence, but cases of artificial insemination by donor (AID) can give rise to problems. The Family Law Reform Act 1987, s. 27, provides that, where a married couple agree to such a scheme, the child 'shall be treated as the child of the parties to the marriage', and this probably means that the husband can lawfully be registered as the father; but some doubts have been expressed as to this, especially since s. 27(3) precludes the inheritance of titles of honour by such children.

Section 13 of the Perjury Act 1911, applies: see **B14.16**.

False Statutory Declarations etc.

Perjury Act 1911, s. 5 **B14.25**

(1) If any person knowingly and wilfully makes (otherwise than on oath) a statement false in a material particular, and the statement is made:
  (a) in a statutory declaration; or
  (b) in an abstract, account, balance sheet, book, certificate, declaration, entry, estimate, inventory, notice, report, return, or other document which he is authorised or required to make, attest, or verify, by any public general Act of Parliament for the time being in force; or
  (c) in any oral declaration or oral answer which he is required to make by, under, or in pursuance of any public general Act of Parliament for the time being in force,
he shall be guilty of [an offence] and shall be liable on conviction thereof on indictment to imprisonment for any term not exceeding two years, or to a fine or to both such imprisonment and fine.

Perjury Act 1911, s. 15

(2) ...The expression 'statutory declaration' means a declaration made by virtue of the Statutory Declarations Act 1835, or of any Act, order in council, rule or regulation applying or extending the provisions thereof;

As to the meaning of the phrase 'knowingly and wilfully' in this context, see *Sood* [1998] 2 Cr App R 355. The principal limitation on the scope of s. 5 (b) and (c) is the need to prove that A was statutorily authorised or required to make the declaration etc. which is alleged to be false. It would not appear to suffice that the declaration was made in connection with, or for the purpose of procuring, some benefit which is the subject of legislative control; but false statements in such circumstances are frequently penalised under other legislation. See, e.g., the CJA 1925, s. 36, which creates an offence of making a statement which one knows to be untrue for the purpose of procuring a passport.

Section 13 applies to offences under s. 5 (see **B14.16**), and offences under s. 5 are triable either way (MCA 1980, s. 17 and sch. 1, para. 14).

False Declarations etc. to Obtain Registration for Carrying on a Vocation

B14.26

Perjury Act 1911, s. 6

(1) If any person:
  (a) procures or attempts to procure himself to be registered on any register or roll kept under or in pursuance of any public general Act of Parliament for the time being in force of persons qualified by law to practise any vocation or calling; or
  (b) procures or attempts to procure a certificate of the registration of any person on any such register or roll as aforesaid,
  by wilfully making or producing or causing to be made or produced either verbally or in writing, any declaration, certificate, or representation which he knows to be false or fraudulent, he shall be guilty of [an offence] and shall be liable on conviction thereof on indictment to imprisonment for any term not exceeding 12 months, or to a fine, or to both such imprisonment and fine.

A person should be charged with 'procuring' only where he has succeeded in his purpose under s. 6 (a) or (b). Where he fails in this, the charge should be one of attempting to procure, and this would be construed in accordance with the Criminal Attempts Act 1981, s. 3: see generally **A5.69** *et seq.*

Section 13 applies (scc **B14.16**); and offences under this section are triable either way (MCA 1980, s. 17 and sch. 1, para. 14).

Offences under the Land Registration Act 2002

B14.27

Land Registration Act 2002, ss. 123 and 124

123.—(1) A person commits an offence if in the course of proceedings relating to registration under this Act he suppresses information with the intention of—
  (a) concealing a person's right or claim, or
  (b) substantiating a false claim.
(2) A person guilty of an offence under this section is liable—
  (a) on conviction on indictment, to imprisonment for a term not exceeding two years or to a fine;
  (b) on summary conviction, to imprisonment for a term not exceeding six months or to a fine not exceeding the statutory maximum, or to both.
124.—(1) A person commits an offence if he dishonestly induces another—
  (a) to change the register of title or cautions register, or
  (b) to authorise the making of such a change.
(2) A person commits an offence if he intentionally or recklessly makes an unauthorised change in the register of title or cautions register.
(3) A person guilty of an offence under this section is liable—
  (a) on conviction on indictment, to imprisonment for a term not exceeding 2 years or to a fine;
  (b) on summary conviction, to imprisonment for a term not exceeding six months or to a fine not exceeding the statutory maximum, or to both.

(4) In this section, references to changing the register of title include changing a document referred to in it.

As to restrictions on the privilege against self-incrimination, see the Land Registration Act 2002, s. 125.

Relationship of Perjury Act 1911 to Other Enactments

Perjury Act 1911, s. 16   B14.28

(1) Where the making of a false statement is not only an offence under this Act, but also by virtue of some other Act is a corrupt practice or subjects the offender to any forfeiture or disqualification or to any penalty other than imprisonment, or fine, the liability of the offender under this Act shall be in addition to and not in substitution for his liability under such other Act.
(2) Nothing in this Act shall apply to a statement made without oath by a child under the provisions of the Prevention of Cruelty to Children Act 1904 and the Children Act 1908.
(3) Where the making of a false statement is by any other Act, whether passed before or after the commencement of this Act, made punishable on summary conviction, proceedings may be taken either under such other Act or under this Act:
Provided that where such an offence is by any Act passed before the commencement of this Act, as originally enacted, made punishable only on summary conviction, it shall remain only so punishable.

The provisions referred to in s. 16(2) have long been repealed. As to the position where a child gives false unsworn evidence in criminal proceedings, see **B14.18**.

PERVERTING THE COURSE OF JUSTICE

Definition   B14.29

It is an offence at common law to do an act tending and intended to pervert the course of public justice (including criminal investigations and proceedings before tribunals).

Procedure   B14.30

This offence is triable only on indictment. It is normally a class 3 offence, but see CPD XIII, para. B (see Supplement, **PD-97**) for the additional factors that the court considers on allocation.

Indictment

Statement of Offence   B14.31

Perverting the course of justice.

Particulars of Offence

A on or about the...day of...did an act tending to pervert the course of justice, namely falsifying a number of documents, namely..., intended to be used as evidence in the prosecution of one X on indictment number...preferred against the said X according to law in the Central Criminal Court, intending that the course of justice should thereby be perverted.

Sentence

The maximum penalty is life imprisonment and/or a fine.   B14.32

The cases reflect the wide range of circumstances in which this offence may be committed. Serious examples of witness intimidation may be prosecuted as perverting the course of justice, but there is an overlap with the statutory offence considered at **B14.46**. Other cases involve the concealing of evidence, the giving of false or misleading information to the police and false allegations of crime. In *Mitchell* [2003] 1 Cr App R (S) 508 the Court of Appeal said that the important factors in sentencing offences of this kind were the length of time during which the deception was maintained, the nature of the deception and the seriousness of the consequences.

In *Weiner* [2012] 1 Cr App R (S) 24 a sentence of ten years after a trial was appropriate for an offender who had planted indecent photographs of children on the victim's computer and then made an anonymous call to the police accusing the victim of possessing child pornography. The victim had been arrested, suffered unwelcome publicity, had been dismissed from his employment and forced to move house before the truth was uncovered. The Court of Appeal said that the degree of culpability and planning was worse than in many other false allegations of crime.

In *Matthews* [2010] 1 Cr App R (S) 373 a sentence of three years was upheld on the owner of a scrap metal company who attempted to conceal the cause of a fatal accident by arranging for the removal of evidence and telling employees to give a false account of what had happened. In *Jones* [2008] 2 Cr App R (S) 420, one of the worst cases, 12 years' imprisonment was upheld on an offender who attempted to intimidate a female witness in a murder case involving five defendants. The woman was subject to threats, and was promised a substantial sum of money if she would retract her evidence. The Court of Appeal said that the case was of 'utmost seriousness', and that the offender had set about derailing the trial for what had been a professional killing. There was no guilty plea and no mitigation.

B14.33 A sentence of three years' imprisonment was upheld in *Livesley* [2013] 1 Cr App R (S) 138 (27), where the offender had submitted false references to the court in advance of being sentenced for a benefit fraud, with the effect that his sentence was suspended. A sentence of 12 months was reduced to six months in *Burney* [2008] 1 Cr App R (S) 335, where the offender falsely claimed that he had been driving a car involved in a collision, although his son had been the driver. The offender maintained this pretence through two police interviews, but then admitted the deception. In *Snow* [2008] 2 Cr App R (S) 497 the offender pleaded guilty to two counts of perverting the course of justice where he had twice given false details when stopped by the police for motoring matters. As a result of one deception, the offender's brother was convicted in his absence by a magistrates' court. Consecutive sentences of nine months on each count were upheld on appeal. Sentences of four months were appropriate for both offenders following guilty pleas in *Henderson* [2012] 1 Cr App R (S) 95, where a lorry driver asked a friend to 'take' his penalty points for speeding so that he could avoid disqualification; the friend did so, but the deception later came to light. See also *Cerrone* [2011] EWCA Crim 2895 where custodial sentences were upheld on female offenders who gave false statements to the police, despite strong personal mitigation.

Comparable sentences would appear to be appropriate where the offence takes the form of a false allegation of crime. The Court of Appeal in *Day* [2010] 2 Cr App R (S) 73, where the offender had made a false complaint of rape, was referred to several similar cases, and found that the sentence bracket ranged from three years' imprisonment down to four months on a plea of guilty. In *Day* the man who had been accused was released from custody after ten hours. The Court said that a false accusation of rape was not just a wrong against the man concerned but was also an attack on the criminal justice system, diverting scarce and expensive police resources. Although the offender had been 'far from well' when she made the complaint, the sentence of two years after a trial in this case was entirely appropriate, and could have been longer. See also *Ngwata* [2013] 1 Cr App R (S) 576 (111), where a sentence of 29 months' imprisonment was appropriate for an offender who made false allegations of rape and violence against her husband, so that he was detained in custody for 14 hours. The Court of Appeal observed that every false allegation of rape increased the plight of women who had been victims of that crime. In *Afford* [2014] 1 Cr App R (S) 4 (2) the offender told the police that he had been attacked by four Asian men, one of whom had slashed his face and said 'no white person should walk here'. The offender later admitted that he had made up the story, and had cut his own face. The Court of Appeal reduced a sentence of 12 months to one of eight months, commenting that the case was at the lower end of the scale, but the aggravating feature had been the risk of heightened racial tension in the area.

Substantive Offences, Conspiracy and Attempt

B14.34 Indictments tended to allege attempts or conspiracies to pervert the course of justice, because it was thought that actual perversion of the course of justice would often be difficult to prove.

Indeed, this form of indictment was used even in some cases where the course of justice had been wholly frustrated (*Britton* [1973] RTR 502). It is now recognised, however, that an act which is intended to have this effect, and is capable of succeeding, may constitute the substantive offence, and should be charged accordingly. The Criminal Attempts Act 1981 does not generally have any application in such cases (unless perhaps a person has failed to perform the act he intended) and references to 'attempts' to pervert the course of justice are accordingly misleading (*Rowell* [1978] 1 All ER 665; *Machin* [1980] 3 All ER 151; *Williams* (1991) 92 Cr App R 158).

Where there appears to have been a conspiracy, there may sometimes be certain advantages in charging the statutory offence under the CLA 1977, s. 1; but see CPD II, para. 14A.3 (see Supplement, **PD-19**), on the use of conspiracy charges.

Acts which May Amount to Perverting the Course of Justice

There is no closed list of acts which may give rise to an offence of perverting the course of **B14.35** justice and neither authority nor principle supports confining such acts to those giving rise to some other independent criminal wrongdoing (*Kenny* [2013] QB 896 at [35]: see also **B14.43**). However, some acts that do amount to this offence may (depending on the circumstances) more appropriately be charged as contempt of court, offences under the CLA 1967, s. 4 or s. 5, witness intimidation, perjury, subornation of perjury or wasting police time. In *Kenny* the Court of Appeal warned that any expansion of the offence should take place only incrementally and with caution, reflecting both principles of common law reasoning and the requirements of the ECHR, Article 7.

Perverting the course of justice requires some positive act; mere failure to point out an error, as where the wrong person is prosecuted, cannot suffice (*Headley* [1995] Crim LR 737), nor is the offence committed by a motorist who fails to report an accident until any alcohol in his body has been eliminated (*Clark* [2003] 2 Cr App R 363). In *Sookoo* (2002) *The Times*, 10 April 2002, the court warned that charges of perverting the course of justice should not without good reason be added to cases in which a suspect has merely told lies when questioned. In many cases such charges 'only serve to complicate the sentencing process'. See also *Hamshaw* [2003] EWCA Crim 2435.

Deliberately Assisting a Person to Evade Arrest　*Thomas* [1979] QB 326 is an example of **B14.36** such a case. In contrast to the offence under the CLA 1967, s. 4 (see **B14.54**), it does not matter whether the offence was 'a relevant offence', and it is not strictly necessary to prove the guilt of the person assisted. Cf. *Spinks* [1982] 1 All ER 587.

Destroying, Falsifying or Concealing Potential Evidence　This form of the offence can **B14.37** occur whether or not legal proceedings have already been instigated (*Vreones* [1891] 1 QB 360; *Murray* [1982] 2 All ER 225; *Firetto* [1991] Crim LR 208; *Rafique* [1993] 4 All ER 1; *Kiffin* [1994] Crim LR 449). It was said in *Selvage* [1982] QB 372 that, if proceedings have not been instigated at that time, an investigation must have been in progress; but this would fail to deal with measures designed to prevent an offence ever being discovered, and cannot be reconciled with *Vreones* or *T* [2011] EWCA Crim 729. In *Selvage*, D attempted to falsify details on X's driving licence, so as to obscure the fact he had endorsements; but this was with a view to protecting him if he should ever commit, and be charged with, a future road traffic offence. Insofar as the dicta in that case seem to refer to evidence in actual but undiscovered crimes or potential civil disputes, it is submitted that they are *obiter* and wrong. See also *Sharpe* [1938] 1 All ER 48 and *Sinha* [1995] Crim LR 68. An offence of perverting the course of justice may be committed by falsifying or procuring false evidence, even where D's motive was to procure what he believed would be a true and fair verdict; although this is ultimately a matter for the consideration of the jury (*A-G's Ref (No. 1 of 2002)* [2003] Crim LR 410).

Interfering with Jurors or Witnesses　Successful prosecutions have been brought in cases **B14.38** involving interfering with jurors (*Mickleburgh* [1995] 1 Cr App R 297) or interfering with potential witnesses, so as to prevent or dissuade them from testifying (*Kellett* [1976] QB 372;

B

Panayiotou [1973] 3 All ER 112) or so as to persuade them to change their evidence. There must be an intent to influence the course or outcome of the case in some way (*Lalani* [1999] 1 Cr App R 481). If D knowingly sought to prevent true evidence being given, or to procure false evidence, then his guilt is clear, even if no bribe, threat, undue pressure or other unlawful means were used (*Toney* [1993] 2 All ER 409). Problems may, however, arise where D claims that his object was to prevent a witness giving false evidence. In *T* [2008] EWCA Crim 183, the court approved this dictum from *Kellett*:

> We would not consider that the offence of attempting to pervert the course of justice would necessarily be committed by a person who tried to persuade a false witness, or even a witness he believed to be false, to speak the truth or to refrain from giving false evidence... [but] we think that however proper the end, the means must not be improper. Even if the intention of the meddler with a witness is to prevent perjury and injustice, he commits the offence if he meddles by unlawful means.

What is improper is generally a question of fact, but a jury should be directed that any threats, or any use of force, amounts to perversion of the course of justice, even where the threat is to take legal action for defamation or to exercise some other legal right, as long as the prosecution can prove necessary intent to influence the witness's evidence (*Toney*). One kind of threat should however be distinguished from the rest: a mere warning to a witness that he may be prosecuted for perjury if he gives false evidence should be insufficient to constitute an offence of perverting the course of justice. The new offences of witness or jury intimidation, which are created by the CJPO 1994, s. 51, operate in addition to, rather than in derogation of, the common law: see **B14.46**.

B14.39 **Offer or Agreement by Potential Witness**   An offer or agreement by a potential witness to withhold (or, presumably, to change) his evidence in return for payment etc. may amount to perverting the course of justice (*Bassi* [1985] Crim LR 671). *Bassi* has been criticised as being inconsistent with *Murray* [1982] 2 All ER 225, where it was said that the offence would only be complete where a person has done something which might, without further action on his part, lead to potential injustice; but it could be argued that the course of justice is jeopardised as soon as any such offer or agreement is made, even if the witness could eventually decide to tell the truth after all, and if *Bassi* is inconsistent with *Murray*, it is to be preferred. See also the CLA 1967, s. 5(1), discussed in **B14.65** to **B14.69**.

B14.40 **Confession to Another's Crime**   Confessing to, or pleading guilty to, another person's crime, in order to shield him may amount to an offence (*Devito* [1975] Crim LR 175 but cf. *Headley* [1995] Crim LR 737).

B14.41 **Abuse of Police Discretion**   Knowingly acting outside the limits of one's discretion as a police officer, so as to shield or excuse another person (e.g., a friend) from criminal charges may amount to perverting the course of justice (*Coxhead* [1986] RTR 411). It is for the jury to decide whether the accused had any discretion to act as he did, and, if not, whether he might mistakenly have believed he had (*Coxhead*). See also *Ward* [1995] Crim LR 398.

B14.42 **False Allegations**   Making false allegations against another person, intending that he should be prosecuted or knowing that he might be may be an offence (*Rowell* [1978] 1 All ER 665). Where false stories merely waste police time, a charge under the CLA 1967, s. 5(2), may be more appropriate (see **B14.78**) but even where no alleged offender is named, there may be a risk that an innocent person could be arrested and/or prosecuted, and this may accordingly amount to perverting the course of justice (*Cotter* [2003] QB 951). It makes no difference if, unknown to D, the subject of these allegations has died, because the vice of the offence lies in the intent (*Brown* [2004] EWCA Crim 744). Where it can be proved that D acted with intent to pervert the course of justice (e.g., by falsely reporting a crime), it is not necessary to prove whether he intended to pervert the course of criminal or civil justice (*Iaquaniello* [2005] EWCA Crim 2029).

Breach of Restraint Orders   In *Kenny* [2013] QB 896 the Court of Appeal noted that where D   **B14.43**
deliberately defies a restraint order under the POCA 2002, condign punishment for contempt
will almost invariably be available and will ordinarily provide a sufficient punishment and deterrent, but held that, where such defiance involves determined and sophisticated criminal conduct
carefully orchestrated and designed to frustrate the intended effect of the restraint order, he cannot complain if the Crown instead pursue a charge of perverting the course of justice.

Compensation of Victims and Settlement of Disputes

No offence is committed where one person merely offers to settle his civil dispute with another   **B14.44**
by offering (or asking for) payment, or where a third party offers such a settlement on behalf of
one or other litigant (*Panayiotou* [1973] 3 All ER 112 at p. 1038).

The position becomes more complicated and uncertain where the offer is made to the victim of
a crime, who is a potential prosecution witness; but the CLA 1967, s. 5(1) (see **B14.65**), appears
to recognise that the victim would commit no offence merely by accepting an offer of 'reasonable
compensation for loss or injury' in return for not disclosing the crime, and it may be inferred
that the offeror would equally commit no offence. An agreement to accept more than such compensation (i.e. a bribe) would appear to be an offence under s. 5(1) and the offeror would be a
party to this, whether or not he is also guilty of perverting the course of justice (*Ali* [1993] Crim
LR 396). And see, with regard to advertisements offering rewards for the return of stolen goods,
the Theft Act 1968, s. 23.

OFFENCES AKIN TO PERVERSION
OF THE COURSE OF JUSTICE

Certain other kinds of conduct might be regarded as amounting to the perversion of public   **B14.45**
justice, but are more commonly charged under other heads. In addition to those dealt with
below, certain forms of advertisement offering rewards for the return of stolen goods contravene
the Theft Act 1968, s. 23 (see **B4.193** and **B4.194**). Concealing or transferring the proceeds of
criminal conduct for the purpose of avoiding prosecution may be punishable under the POCA
2002, s. 327, and 'tipping off' another person as to a proposed money laundering investigation
may be punishable under s. 333 of that Act (see **B21** for the offences).

Intimidation of, or Retaliation against, Witnesses, Jurors and Others

The intimidation of witnesses, jurors or other persons involved in legal proceedings or investi-   **B14.46**
gations may be punishable at common law, not only as tending to the perversion of the course
of justice (see **B14.38**), but also as contempt of court. Whether a judge should refer the matter
to the CPS for possible prosecution or proceed to determine the matter under his contempt
jurisdiction is a matter for the judge's discretion (*AS* [2008] EWCA Crim 138). Retaliation
against former witnesses etc. is also punishable as contempt (see **B14.98**). Indeed, any improper
interference with or approach to a witness or juror (present, past or future), whether based on
intimidation, bribery or persuasion, will almost invariably be punishable under one or other of
those heads. See, e.g., *Mickleburgh* [1995] 1 Cr App R 297 and *A-G v Judd* [1995] COD 15 at
B14.98.

Acts of intimidation or retaliation may, alternatively, be dealt with under the CJPO 1994, s. 51,   **B14.47**
or (where the victim is a witness or potential witness in a civil case) under the CJPA 2001, ss. 39
to 41 (*Sahin* [2009] EWCA Crim 2616).

Criminal Justice and Public Order Act 1994, s. 51

(1) A person commits an offence if—
    (a) he does an act which intimidates, and is intended to intimidate, another person ('the
       victim'),

   (b) he does the act knowing or believing that the victim is assisting in the investigation of an offence or is a witness or potential witness or a juror or potential juror in proceedings for an offence, and

   (c) he does it intending thereby to cause the investigation or the course of justice to be obstructed, perverted or interfered with.

(2) A person commits an offence if—

   (a) he does an act which harms, and is intended to harm, another person or, intending to cause another person to fear harm, he threatens to do an act which would harm that other person,

   (b) he does or threatens to do the act knowing or believing that the person harmed or threatened to be harmed ('the victim'), or some other person, has assisted in an investigation into an offence or has given evidence or particular evidence in proceedings for an offence, or has acted as a juror or concurred in a particular verdict in proceedings for an offence, and

   (c) he does or threatens to do it because of that knowledge or belief.

(3) For the purposes of subsections (1) and (2) it is immaterial that the act is or would be done, or that the threat is made—

   (a) otherwise than in the presence of the victim, or

   (b) to a person other than the victim.

(4) The harm that may be done or threatened may be financial as well as physical (whether to the person or a person's property) and similarly as respects an intimidatory act which consists of threats.

(5) The intention required by subsection (1)(c) and the motive required by subsection (2)(c) above need not be the only or the predominating intention or motive with which the act is done or, in the case of subsection (2), threatened.

(6) A person guilty of an offence under this section shall be liable—

   (a) on conviction on indictment, to imprisonment for a term not exceeding five years or a fine or both;

   (b) on summary conviction, to imprisonment for a term not exceeding six months or a fine not exceeding the statutory maximum or both.

(7) If, in proceedings against a person for an offence under subsection (1) above, it is proved that he did an act falling within paragraph (a) with the knowledge or belief required by paragraph (b), he shall be presumed, unless the contrary is proved, to have done the act with the intention required by paragraph (c) of that subsection.

(8) If, in proceedings against a person for an offence under subsection (2) above, it is proved that within the relevant period—

   (a) he did an act which harmed, and was intended to harm, another person, or

   (b) intending to cause another person fear of harm, he threatened to do an act which would harm that other person,

   and that he did the act, or (as the case may be) threatened to do the act with the knowledge or belief required by paragraph (b), he shall be presumed, unless the contrary is proved, to have done the act or (as the case may be) threatened to do the act with the motive required by paragraph (c) of that subsection.

(9) In this section—

   'investigation into an offence' means such an investigation by the police or other person charged with the duty of investigating offences or charging offenders;

   'offence' includes an alleged or suspected offence;

   'potential', in relation to a juror, means a person who has been summoned for jury service at the court at which proceedings for the offence are pending; and

   'the relevant period'—

   (a) in relation to a witness or juror in any proceedings for an offence, means the period beginning with the institution of the proceedings and ending with the first anniversary of the conclusion of the trial or, if there is an appeal or a reference under section 9 or 11 of the Criminal Appeal Act 1995, of the conclusion of the appeal;

   (b) in relation to a person who has or is believed by the accused to have, assisted in an investigation into an offence, but was not also a witness in proceedings for an offence, means the period of one year beginning with any act of his, or any act believed by the accused to be an act of his, assisting in the investigation; and

   (c) in relation to a person who both has or is believed by the accused to have, assisted in the investigation into an offence and was a witness in proceedings for the offence, means the period beginning with any act of his, or any act believed by the accused to be an act of his, assisting in the investigation and ending with the anniversary mentioned in paragraph (a) above.

Although, as s. 51(4) makes clear, the 'other person' in question does not have to be put in fear of physical violence, a full offence under s. 51 cannot be committed if that person refuses to be deterred or intimidated (*ZN* [2013] 4 All ER 331, not following *Patrascu* [2004] 4 All ER 1006 on that point), nor can it be committed on the basis of a mistaken belief that an investigation is in progress (*Singh* [1999] Crim LR 681). A criminal attempt may, however, be committed in either case (see **A5.57**).

Relationship with Common-law Offence   Apart from being triable either way, the offence **B14.48** created by s. 51(1) appears to offer few advantages over the common-law offence of perverting the course of justice (which is preserved under s. 51(11)). The latter would indeed be committed even if bribery or persuasion were used in place of intimidation. As to the burden of proof, the Court of Appeal in *A-G's Ref (No. 1 of 2004)* [2004] 4 All ER 457 had 'no hesitation in concluding' that for this offence the legal burden of proof imposed on a defendant by s. 51(7) is both justified and proportional under the ECHR, Article 6.

In contrast, the offence created by s. 51(2) covers conduct that would not ordinarily amount to perverting the course of justice, and carries heavier penalties than those available for contempt of court (as to which, see **B14.95**). Committal for contempt may not, in any case, be a wholly satisfactory method of dealing with conduct of this type, especially where it occurs after the original trial has ended.

Sentence   In *Smith* [2011] 2 Cr App R (S) 676 a sentence of two years and eight months was **B14.49** upheld for witness intimidation, where the offender had knocked on the door of a house occupied by a witness to an assault and threatened to kidnap her son if she did not retract her statement. The Court of Appeal reviewed several earlier cases and concluded that the factors which bore on sentencing for this offence included whether the intimidation was isolated or part of a campaign, the content of any threat, whether the intimidation was accompanied by violence, the circumstances in which any threat was uttered, whether any encounter with a witness was premeditated or by chance and the impact on the victim. Overall a key factor was the public policy of ensuring the integrity of the justice system by imposing sentences which had a general deterrent effect. In *Williams* [1997] 2 Cr App R (S) 221 the offender, after having been convicted of false imprisonment and unlawful wounding, wrote to the victim of those offences from prison, threatening her with violence. For this offence under s. 51(2), to which the offender pleaded guilty, a further sentence of two years' imprisonment, consecutive to the three-year term being served, was upheld by the Court of Appeal. Harrison J noted that the offence under s. 51(2) carried a maximum of five years, as compared with two years for contempt of court, and said that such intimidation must be viewed extremely seriously.

Witnesses in Civil Proceedings   The CJPA 2001 makes similar provision (in ss. 39 to 41) to **B14.50** protect witnesses and potential witnesses in civil cases. Section 39 corresponds to the CJPO 1994, s. 51(1); the CJPA 2001, s. 40 corresponds to s. 51(2) of the 1994 Act.

Personating a Juror

It is an offence at common law, punishable with a fine and imprisonment at large, to impersonate someone summoned for jury service, so as to sit in his place. The motive is irrelevant (*Clark* (1918) 82 JP 295). **B14.51**

Disposing of a Body with Intent to Prevent an Inquest

The concealment, disposal or destruction of a corpse is a common-law offence, punishable with **B14.52** a fine and imprisonment at large, if done to prevent the holding of a lawful inquest as to the death (*Stephenson* (1884) 13 QBD 331). There is a separate common-law offence of preventing the decent and lawful burial of a body. This may be committed by anyone who unlawfully conceals or destroys a body whether to conceal an unlawful killing (as in *Hunter* [1974] QB 95) or for other reasons. In *Skidmore* [2008] EWCA Crim 1464 the offence was committed where a funeral director forgot to put an infant's body in the coffin for burial and attempted to conceal this blunder by placing it in the coffin of another deceased, which was in due course cremated.

B14.53   **Sentence**   In *Godward* [1998] 1 Cr App R (S) 385 the offender pleaded guilty to obstructing the coroner by concealing a body. The police found the decomposed body of a man in the offender's flat. Godward had failed to disclose the whereabouts of the body, despite being twice asked by the police to assist them in tracing him. Lord Bingham CJ, in the Court of Appeal, said that the most important factor was the intention of the perpetrator. If the purpose was to obstruct the course of justice and to make it difficult to bring home a charge against the offender or another person, the offence would merit punishment towards the top of the appropriate bracket. If such intention was lacking, a lesser sentence was appropriate. On the present facts, a prison sentence of four years was reduced to three years. See also *Blakemore* [1997] 2 Cr App R (S) 255.

As to sentencing for the offence of preventing a decent and lawful burial, Ouseley J commented in *Whiteley* [2001] 2 Cr App R (S) 119 that this was a serious matter, capable of interfering with the administration of justice and causing grief for the bereaved. It deprived the deceased of a proper burial and sometimes raised anxieties in the minds of relatives as to whether the person had been dead when the attempts at concealment had been made. On the facts, where the offender had not been in any way responsible for the death but had assisted in removing the body of a man who was a drug addict from the flat where he had died to conceal it in a ditch, a sentence of 30 months was reduced to 18 months, with a further three months consecutive for failing to answer bail upheld. See also *Parry* (1986) 8 Cr App R (S) 476.

ASSISTING OFFENDERS

Definition

B14.54   Criminal Law Act 1967, s. 4

(1)   Where a person has committed a relevant offence, any other person who, knowing or believing him to be guilty of the offence or of some other relevant offence, does without lawful authority or reasonable excuse any act with intent to impede his apprehension or prosecution shall be guilty of an offence.

(1A) In this section and section 5 below, 'relevant offence' means—
  (a) an offence for which the sentence is fixed by law,
  (b) an offence for which a person of 18 years or over (not previously convicted) may be sentenced to imprisonment for a term of five years (or might be so sentenced but for the restrictions imposed by section 33 of the Magistrates' Courts Acts 1980).

At common law, a person knowingly rendering assistance to a person who had committed a felony became an accessory after the fact, and thus guilty of that felony. This provision created a specific offence to replace that principle.

Procedure

B14.55   Criminal Law Act 1967, s. 4

(4) No proceedings shall be instituted for an offence under subsection (1)...except by or with the consent of the Director of Public Prosecutions.

Indictment

B14.56   *Statement of Offence*

Assisting an offender contrary to section 4(1) of the Criminal Law Act 1967.

Particulars of Offence

A on the...day of..., X having committed a relevant offence, namely robbery, knowing or believing that X had committed the said offence or some other relevant offence, without lawful authority or reasonable excuse harboured X in his house, with intent to impede the apprehension or prosecution of X.

It must be proved that X did indeed commit the specified offence or some other offence for which he might have been convicted on an indictment alleging the specified offence (*Morgan* [1972] 1 QB 436). *Morgan* appears to have been overlooked in *Saunders* [2011] EWCA Crim 1571.

Alternative Verdicts

Criminal Law Act 1967, s. 4   **B14.57**

  (2) If on the trial of an indictment for a relevant offence the jury are satisfied that the offence charged (or some other offence of which the accused might on that charge be found guilty) was committed, but find the accused not guilty of it, they may find him guilty of any offence under subsection (1)...of which they are satisfied that he is guilty in relation to the offence charged (or that other offence).

If D is not initially charged with a s. 4 offence, but with a substantive relevant offence, and the possibility of an alternative verdict under subsection (2) manifests itself in the course of the trial, D should be given sufficient opportunity to meet such a possibility. The issue should not be raised after the court has finished hearing evidence (*Cross* [1971] 3 All ER 641; *Vincent* (1972) 56 Cr App R 281).

Sentence

Where the principal offence is subject to a sentence fixed by law the maximum penalty is ten **B14.58** years, a fine, or both, on indictment (CLA 1967, s. 4(3)(a)); and six months, a fine not exceeding the statutory maximum, or both, summarily. Where the principal offence is subject to a sentence of 14 years, the maximum penalty is seven years, a fine, or both, on indictment (s. 4(3) (b)); and six months, a fine not exceeding the statutory maximum, or both, summarily. Where the principal offence is subject to a sentence of ten years, the maximum penalty is five years, a fine, or both, on indictment (s. 4(3)(c)); and six months, a fine not exceeding the statutory maximum, or both, summarily. In other cases: the maximum penalty is three years, a fine, or both, on indictment (s. 4(3)(d)); and six months, a fine not exceeding the statutory maximum, or both, summarily.

In *A-G's Ref (No. 16 of 2009) (Yates)* [2010] 2 Cr App R (S) 64, the Court of Appeal said that, when assessing sentence for an offence of assisting an offender, the first issue is the nature and extent of the criminality of the offender for whom assistance was provided (the criminality involved the murder of a young boy). The second issue is the nature and extent of the assistance provided (in this case the offender had done all he could do, including washing down the offender in petrol to remove traces of evidence). The third issue is the extent to which the efforts to assist the offender damaged the interests of justice (here the administration of justice was slowed but ultimately not thwarted). Six years' detention in a young offender institution, imposed on a 19-year-old following conviction after a trial, was upheld in principle although reduced to five years for reasons of totality. In *Khatab* [2008] 2 Cr App R (S) 530 a sentence of four years' imprisonment for assisting an offender by disposing of a weapon used to commit a murder was reduced on appeal to three years. In *Worthington-Hale* [2011] 1 Cr App R (S) 401 the appropriate sentence was 30 months' imprisonment for an offender who harboured a man who had committed a series of violent robberies and was himself later sentenced to nine years in prison.

Offence Cannot be Committed by Omission

This offence is not capable of taking the form of an omission. Shielding another person by **B14.59** silence etc. is rarely a crime, but see the CLA 1967, s. 5, and **B14.65**.

Requirement that Relevant Offence has been Committed

An offence under the CLA 1967, s. 4, can be committed only where a relevant offence has previ- **B14.60** ously been committed by the person assisted, and proof of that person's guilt is accordingly an essential element in proof of this offence (see **B14.56**).

It is not necessary for the person allegedly assisted to be convicted of his offence before someone can be convicted of assisting (*Donald* (1986) Cr App R 49), nor is the person assisted's conviction conclusive proof of his guilt at the subsequent trial of a person accused of assisting; but the prior conviction of the person assisted will raise a presumption that he was guilty, and this will simplify the task of the prosecution at the trial. It would be for the defence to prove, on balance of probabilities, that the conviction of the person assisted was wrong. See the PACE 1984, s. 74, and **F11.7**.

An acquittal is not proof of innocence, however. If, for example, D1 is accused of assisting D2 by impeding his apprehension or prosecution, D1 may be convicted on evidence that is not admissible against D2 or he may plead guilty to assisting D2, only for D2 to be acquitted by the court or jury. In neither case need D2's acquittal undermine the safety of D1's conviction (*Zaman* [2010] 1 WLR 1304; *Saunders* [2011] EWCA Crim 1571). But if the court trying D1 has any reasonable doubts as to the guilt of D2, D1 must be acquitted. Cf. *Shannon* [1975] AC 717 (conviction of single conspirator).

Many of the problems arising from use of s. 4 can be avoided by charging an assister with perverting the course of justice: see **B14.29** to **B14.44**. In some cases there may be an overlap between s. 4 and the money laundering offences in the POCA 2002, part 7 (see **B21**).

Knowledge of or Belief in the Guilt of the Person Assisted

B14.61   By analogy with decisions concerning the offence of handling stolen goods (where knowledge or belief is similarly a *mens rea* element), it is clear that D must either know or positively believe in the guilt of the person assisted. Mere suspicion, however strong and well founded, would not suffice. On the other hand, the CLA 1967, s. 4(1), expressly provides that an accused may be guilty even if he is mistaken about what offence the person assisted has committed; and the language used is wide enough to embrace cases where D knew that the person assisted must have committed a serious offence, but had no idea what offence it may have been (*Morgan* [1972] 1 QB 436).

Intent to Impede Apprehension or Prosecution

B14.62   The intent to impede the apprehension etc. of the person assisted is an ulterior intent. It is not necessary that the person assisted should have benefited from D's actions; indeed, they may be wholly unsuccessful and lead unwittingly to his immediate arrest.

Lawful Authority or Reasonable Excuse

B14.63   The legal burden of proving absence of lawful authority etc. appears to rest on the prosecution (*Brindley* [1971] 2 QB 300). But the prosecution need not do so unless there is evidence before the court sufficient to raise the issue. See generally **F3.6** *et seq*. It is difficult to imagine what might amount to lawful authority or reasonable excuse in any normal circumstances.

No Offence of Attempting to Assist

B14.64   There can be no offence of attempting to commit an offence under the CLA 1967, s. 4 (Criminal Attempts Act 1981, s. 1(4)).

CONCEALING OFFENCES

Definition

B14.65

Criminal Law Act 1967, s. 5

(1) Where a person has committed a relevant offence, any other person who, knowing or believing that the offence or some other relevant offence has been committed, and that he has information which might be of material assistance in securing the prosecution or conviction of an

offender for it, accepts or agrees to accept for not disclosing that information any consideration other than the making good of loss or injury caused by the offence, or the making of reasonable compensation for that loss or injury, shall be liable on conviction on indictment to imprisonment for not more than two years...

(5) The compounding of an offence other than treason shall not be an offence otherwise than under this section.

The term 'relevant offence' is defined by s. 4(1A) (see **B14.54**).

Procedure

No proceedings shall be instituted for an offence under the CLA 1967, s. 5, except by or with the consent of the DPP (s. 5(3)).   **B14.66**

Concealing a relevant offence is triable either way where the underlying offence is so triable (MCA 1980, s. 17 and sch. 1, para. 26). As in the case of assisting offenders, contrary to the CLA 1967, s. 4, an anomalous position arises with respect to the purely summary offence of taking a conveyance without authority (see **B14.55**).

Indictment

Statement of Offence   **B14.67**

Concealing a relevant offence contrary to section 5(1) of the Criminal Law Act 1967.

Particulars of Offence

A on the...day of..., X having committed a relevant offence, namely robbery, knowing or believing that the said or some other relevant offence had been committed and that he had information which might be of material assistance in securing the prosecution or conviction of X for it, accepted (or agreed to accept) consideration, namely a payment of £1,000, which was neither a making good of loss or injury caused by the said offence nor the making of reasonable compensation therefor, for not disclosing the said information.

Sentence

The maximum penalty on indictment is two years (s. 5(1)). Summarily, the maximum penalty   **B14.68**
is six months and/or a fine not exceeding the statutory maximum. As to sentencing, see the cases considered in respect of assisting offenders in **B14.58**.

Elements

The common-law offences of misprision of felony and compounding a felony were both abol-   **B14.69**
ished by the CLA 1967. Misprision of treason remains an offence and there are now statutory offences of non-disclosure in relation to certain terrorist offences (see **B10.136** *et seq.*) and money laundering (see **B21.27**). With these exceptions, the non-disclosure of offences cannot ordinarily be punishable. Compounding an offence other than treason cannot now be an offence other than under the CLA 1967, s. 5(1) (s. 5(5)).

The striking of a bargain, in which a promise of silence or non-disclosure is exchanged for consideration going beyond reasonable compensation to the victim, is another matter, and is punishable under s. 5(1). It is the agreement which constitutes the gist of the offence. D will remain guilty, even if he later breaks the agreement and informs the police.

As with the CLA 1967, s. 4 (see **B14.54** to **B14.64**), the prosecution must prove that the other person did indeed commit a relevant offence (see **B14.60**); and where this might be difficult there may similarly be advantages in charging a person who has agreed to conceal a crime with perverting the course of justice. A person who demands money for his silence might also be guilty of blackmail (see **B5.42**).

As with assisting offenders there can be no offence of attempting to commit an offence under this section (Criminal Attempts Act 1981, s. 1(4)).

OTHER OFFENCES RELATING TO OFFENDERS

Escape

B14.70   It is a common-law offence, punishable on indictment by a fine and imprisonment at large, to escape from legal custody. The escape may be from police custody following arrest (*Timmis* [1976] Crim LR 129) or from custody or imprisonment etc. following remand or conviction (*Moss* (1985) 82 Cr App R 116).

In a case of alleged escape, the prosecution must prove that the D was in custody; that he knew this (or was reckless as to whether he was or not); that the custody was lawful; and that he intentionally escaped from it (*Dhillon* [2006] 1 WLR 1535; see also *Dillon v The Queen* [1982] AC 484). But it is irrelevant whether he was guilty of the crime for which he was arrested or imprisoned (*Waters* (1873) 12 Cox CC 390).

A partial definition of 'legal custody' is provided by s. 13(2) of the Prison Act 1952:

Prison Act 1952, s. 13

(2) A prisoner shall be deemed to be in legal custody while he is confined in, or is being taken to or from, any prison and while he is working, or is for any other reason, outside the prison in the custody or under the control of an officer of the prison and while he is being taken to any place to which he is required or authorised by or under this Act or the CJA 1982 to be taken, or is kept in custody in pursuance of any such requirement or authorisation.

The references to 'prison' apply equally to remand centres and young offender institutions (Prison Act 1952, s. 43(5)). The reference to 'an officer of the prison' is to be construed as a reference to a prisoner custody officer performing custodial duties at the prison (CJA 1991, s. 87(6)).

B14.71   D is not lawfully confined if he has been erroneously kept in prison after his proper release date (*O'Connor* [2010] EWCA Crim 2842). A person may be in lawful custody even though he is not physically restrained or guarded (e.g., where he is left unguarded in court). The question of whether D was in custody at the relevant time is primarily a question of fact, to be decided on a case-by-case basis (*Rumble* (2003) 167 JP 205). A juvenile who is remanded into the custody of the local authority under the CYPA 1969, s. 23, without a security requirement, and who has been told by a member of the youth offending team to remain where he is, may be guilty of escaping from lawful custody if he makes off when left unsupervised (*H v DPP* [2003] Crim LR 560). If D is granted temporary release from prison, and fails to return, he does not commit this offence (*Montgomery* [2008] 2 All ER 924) but see **B14.73**.

In *Purchase* [2008] 1 Cr App R (S) 338 the Court of Appeal suggested that 'escape' cases fell into two categories. The first category included cases where a prisoner escaped under some personal pressure to do so, where sentences would be measured in months. The instant case involved a prisoner who absconded from an open prison and was at large for a fortnight. During that time he got into further trouble. A sentence of nine months' imprisonment, consecutive to the existing sentence, was upheld. See also *Banks-Nash* [2007] 1 Cr App R (S) 87, where 12 months was reduced to nine months, and *Golding* [2007] 2 Cr App R (S) 309, where ten months was upheld, in each case consecutive to the existing sentence. The second category included cases where a criminal is aided in escape by confederates inside or outside prison, where sentences would be measured in years. An example is *Coughtrey* [1997] 2 Cr App R (S) 269, where four years' imprisonment was appropriate in the case of a man serving life imprisonment for murder who escaped from prison after burning through a perimeter fence with cutting equipment and scaling the outer wall by means of a ladder. He was at large for a week.

Breach of Prison

B14.72   This offence is similar to escape, but must involve some breaking, cutting, or forcing in the course of the escape. It need not involve escape from an actual prison (forcing open a police station window would suffice) and need not involve any deliberate damage (see *Haswell* (1821) Russ & Ry 458, where accidental dislodging of loose bricks while scaling the prison wall was held to suffice).

The case of *Coughtrey* [1997] 2 Cr App R (S) 269 provides sentencing guidelines for this offence. The offender was serving a life sentence for murder and escaped after two years by burning through the perimeter fence with cutting equipment and then scaling the outer wall. He gave himself up a week later. A sentence of seven years' imprisonment for prison breach was reduced on appeal to four years. McCowan LJ in the Court of Appeal noted that breaking prison is a very serious offence for which a substantial sentence of imprisonment is always to be expected because of the fear and apprehension it generates, the disruption to prison life, the violence and disorder that it may lead to, and the need to deter the culprit and others. Factors to be taken into account in fixing the length of the sentence will include (i) the nature and circumstances of the original offence, (ii) the offender's conduct while in prison, (iii) the methods employed in effecting escape and, in particular, whether any violence was used and whether there was extensive planning and outside assistance, (iv) whether he surrendered himself and how soon, and (v) a plea of guilty. If the original sentence is a determinate one, the sentence for prison breach should almost always be ordered to run consecutively. If the original sentence is a life sentence, the sentence for prison breach should usually be the same as if he had been serving a determinate sentence, but it will have to be served concurrently.

Remaining at Large after Temporary Release

Under the Prisoners (Return to Custody) Act 1995, s. 1(1), a person who has been temporarily **B14.73** released in pursuance of rules made under the Prison Act 1952, s. 47(5), will be guilty of a summary offence, punishable by imprisonment for a term not exceeding six months and/or a fine not exceeding level 5 on the standard scale if:

(a) without reasonable excuse he remains unlawfully at large at any time after the expiry of the period for which he was temporarily released; or

(b) knowing or believing an order recalling him to have been made, and while unlawfully at large by virtue of such an order, he fails, without reasonable excuse, to take all necessary steps for complying as soon as reasonably practicable with that order.

The offence does not apply to persons temporarily released from secure training centres (s. 1(2)).

Assisting Escape and Harbouring Escapees

Prison Act 1952, s. 39   **B14.74**

(1) A person who—
    (a) assists a prisoner in escaping or attempting to escape from a prison, or
    (b) intending to facilitate the escape of a prisoner—
        (i) brings, throws or otherwise conveys anything into a prison,
        (ii) causes another person to bring, throw or otherwise convey anything into a prison, or
        (iii) gives anything to a prisoner or leaves anything in any place (whether inside or outside a prison),
  is guilty of an offence.
(2) A person guilty of an offence under this section is liable on conviction on indictment to imprisonment for a term not exceeding ten years.

Criminal Justice Act 1961, s. 22   **B14.75**

(2) If any person knowingly harbours a person who has escaped from a prison or other institution to which…section 39 [of this Act] applies, or who, having been sentenced in any part of the United Kingdom or in any of the Channel Islands or the Isle of Man to imprisonment or detention, is otherwise unlawfully at large, or who gives to any such person any assistance with intent to prevent, hinder or interfere with his being taken into custody, he shall be liable—
    (a) on summary conviction, to imprisonment for a term not exceeding six months, or to a fine not exceeding [£5,000] or to both;

(b) on conviction on indictment, to imprisonment for a term not exceeding ten years, or to a fine, or to both.

(2A) The reference in subsection (2) to a person who has been sentenced as mentioned there includes—

(a) a person on whom a custodial sentence within the meaning of the Armed Forces Act 2006 has been passed (anywhere) in respect of a service offence within the meaning of that Act;

(b) a person in respect of whom an order under section 214 of that Act (detention for commission of offence during currency of order) has been made.

B14.76 These offences can each apply where the escape is from a prison, remand centre or young offender institution; but a s. 39 offence cannot be committed in respect of a person who escapes from custody whilst in transit to or from prison, or from court etc. (*Nicoll v Catron* (1985) 81 Cr App R 339; *Moss* (1985) 82 Cr App R 116) nor can a s. 22 offence be committed in respect of such a person unless he has already been sentenced to imprisonment or detention and is 'unlawfully at large'. It was suggested in both *Nicoll v Catron*, and *Moss* that common-law offences could be committed by assisting a remand prisoner to escape from a court, etc. No specific common law offence was identified in *Moss*, and *Nicoll v Catron* contains only a reference to perverting the course of justice; but there is also a common-law offence of forcible rescue from lawful custody (see 2 Hawk PC, ch. 21).

The most serious reported sentencing case is *Bowman* [1997] 1 Cr App R (S) 282, where a sentence of seven years' imprisonment was upheld in respect of a conspiracy to assist prisoners to escape by smuggling a pistol into Durham Prison. The pistol was found after a search by prison officers. In *Walker* (1990) 12 Cr App R (S) 65, a sentence of nine months' imprisonment was upheld on an offender who pleaded guilty to aiding a prisoner to escape from an open prison by meeting him outside the prison and giving him a lift in his car. In *Williams* (1992) 13 Cr App R (S) 236, the appropriate sentence was said to be 15 months where the offender had changed places with a prisoner in an open prison for one night to allow the prisoner to spend a night at home. Twelve months' imprisonment was reduced to nine months in *Taylor* (1994) 15 Cr App R (S) 893 where the offender pleaded guilty to harbouring an escaped prisoner, his brother.

B14.77 **Mental Health Act 1983, s. 128**

(1) Where any person induces or knowingly assists another person who is liable to be detained in a hospital within the meaning of part II of this Act or is subject to guardianship under this Act or is a community patient to absent himself without leave he shall be guilty of an offence.

(2) Where any person induces or knowingly assists another person who is in legal custody by virtue of section 137 [of this Act] to escape from such custody he shall be guilty of an offence.

(3) Where any person knowingly harbours a patient who is absent without leave or is otherwise at large and liable to be retaken under this Act or gives him any assistance with intent to prevent, hinder or interfere with his being taken into custody or returned to the hospital or other place where he ought to be he shall be guilty of an offence.

(4) Any person guilty of an offence under this section shall be liable—

(a) on summary conviction, to imprisonment for a term not exceeding six months or to a fine not exceeding the statutory maximum, or to both;

(b) on conviction on indictment, to imprisonment for a term not exceeding two years or to a fine of any amount, or to both.

Wasting Police Time

B14.78 **Criminal Law Act 1967, s. 5**

(2) Where a person causes any wasteful employment of the police by knowingly making to any person a false report tending to show that an offence has been committed, or to give rise to apprehension for the safety of any persons or property, or tending to show that he has information material to any police inquiry, he shall be liable on summary conviction to imprisonment for not more than six months or to a fine of not more than level 4 on the standard scale or to both.

No proceedings for this offence may be instituted except by or with the consent of the DPP (CLA 1967, s. 5(3)). Under the Penalties for Disorderly Behaviour (Amount of Penalty) Order 2002 (SI 2002 No. 1837), as amended, the offence under s. 5(2) is a penalty offence and the amount payable is £90.

As to the relationship between the s. 5(2) offence and the more serious offence of perverting the course of justice, see *Cotter* [2003] QB 951.

As to false (hoax) fire alarms, see the Fire and Rescue Services Act 2004, s. 49, discussed at **B11.101**.

CONTEMPT OF COURT

The next part of this section is primarily concerned with criminal contempt of court, and more   **B14.79** particularly with contempt insofar as it affects the criminal courts. Some reference is made to civil contempt by disobedience of court orders and to the jurisdiction of the civil courts in respect of criminal contempt, but those topics are not covered in detail.

Nature of Contempt

Criminal contempt of court can take a number of different forms. At common law, it has been   **B14.80** defined as behaviour 'involving an interference with the due administration of justice, either in a particular case or more generally as a continuing process' (*A-G v Leveller Magazine Ltd* [1979] AC 440, per Lord Diplock at p. 449). It is not possible to provide an exhaustive list of the ways in which such contempt can be committed, although a substantial number of typical examples are given at **B14.98** to **B14.115**. As Donaldson MR said in *A-G v Newspaper Publishing plc* [1988] Ch 333 at p. 368:

> The law of contempt is based on the broadest of principles, namely that the courts cannot and will not permit interference with the due administration of justice. Its application is universal. The fact that it is applied in novel circumstances…is not a case of widening its application. It is merely a new example of its application.

Broadly based though it is, criminal contempt can nevertheless be categorised according to whether it is committed 'in the face of the court' or committed indirectly (i.e. a 'constructive' contempt, such as the publication of a book or article prejudicing a forthcoming trial in a way which may influence potential jurors or witnesses). Only the superior courts have jurisdiction to punish for constructive contempts (*Lefroy* (1873) LR 8 QB 134), whereas any court of record (including county courts and coroners' courts) may punish contempt in the face of the court. (As to the position of magistrates' courts, see **B14.85**.) It does not follow that constructive contempt of an inferior court must go unpunished; jurisdiction to commit for such contempt may be exercised by the Divisional Court of the Queen's Bench Division (see **B14.92**).

Criminal contempt of court must be distinguished from civil contempt, which takes the form   **B14.81** of disobedience to a court order (or an undertaking in lieu of an order). Breach of a restraint order made under the POCA 2002, s. 41, is no different in this respect from breach of a civil injunction and is thus properly classified as a civil contempt (*Director of the Serious Fraud Office v O'Brien* [2014] 2 All ER 798). But either kind of contempt is subject to sanctions that include imprisonment (see **B14.95**) and the appropriate standard of proof is that of beyond reasonable doubt, even in cases of civil contempt to which civil rules of evidence apply (see, e.g., *Re Bramblevale Ltd* [1970] Ch 128). The ECHR, Article 6(2) and (3), are likewise equally applicable (*OB v Director of Serious Fraud Office* at [21]).

In cases of civil contempt it is usually left to any party aggrieved to instigate proceedings, and such party retains the right to waive the contempt. In contrast, cases of criminal contempt are generally prosecuted by the A-G or by the court acting of its own motion (*Home Office v Harman* [1983] 1 AC 280 per Lord Scarman at p. 310). This distinction is now reflected in the structure of the CrimPR, part 62, in which different procedures are prescribed for contempt in the face of the court, on the one hand and disobedience to court orders etc. on the other (see **B14.88** and Supplement, **R-453** *et seq.*). A significant point of distinction is that in cases of alleged civil contempt there is no power to remand an alleged contemnor in custody pending the hearing of his case. Furthermore, peers and Members of Parliament are generally immune from arrest for civil contempt (*Stourton v Stourton* [1963] P 302), but not for criminal contempt.

Parties

B14.82   In *Balogh v St Albans Crown Court* [1975] QB 73, Lord Denning MR held that criminal contempt of court is governed by the ordinary principles of criminal liability. If this is correct, it follows that complicity in the offence, as a secondary party, would require *mens rea*, even where liability of the principal offender is strict under the Contempt of Court Act 1981 (see **B14.118** to **B14.125**). Where a corporation publishes material amounting to contempt, the corporation itself is the obvious principal offender, but a newspaper editor (or his counterpart in television etc.) would usually be regarded as a joint principal, because of his special responsibility for the content of the publication, and, where *mens rea* is required, his *mens rea* could arguably be imputed to the company on the basis that he manages that part at least of the company's business.

The dictum of Lord Goddard CJ in *Evening Standard Co. Ltd* [1954] 1 QB 578, that the liability of the editor and company is vicarious, is contrary to principle and has generally been doubted. Employees (e.g., reporters) are not publishers, but might be liable as secondary parties if they act with *mens rea*. See *Griffiths, ex parte A-G* [1957] 2 QB 192.

Courts and Tribunals Protected by the Law of Contempt

B14.83   One must distinguish between the protection of the law of contempt, which is afforded to all courts and tribunals exercising the judicial power of the State, and the jurisdiction to punish for contempt, which is possessed at common law only by courts of record, and to differing extent according to whether the court is superior or inferior. (As to the position of magistrates' courts, which are not courts of record, but which have statutory powers to deal with some forms of contempt, see **B14.85**.)

There is no definitive list of the bodies which qualify for protection. Some do not qualify, even though they are called 'courts', e.g., local valuation courts. Others do qualify, even though they lack that title, e.g., industrial tribunals (*Peach Grey & Co. v Sommers* [1995] 2 All ER 513) and mental health review tribunals (*P v Liverpool Daily Post and Echo Newspapers plc* [1991] 2 AC 370). The ones which lack protection are those which exercise administrative, rather than judicial functions. It is not enough that they act judicially in discharging such functions (*A-G v British Broadcasting Corporation* [1981] AC 303; *General Medical Council v British Broadcasting Corporation* [1998] 3 All ER 426). Even magistrates lose the protection of the law of contempt when sitting as licensing justices, because this is an administrative function (*A-G v British Broadcasting Corporation* [1981] AC 303 at p. 348).

Mode of Trial

B14.84   Cases of alleged contempt are tried by procedures which are peculiar to that offence. Contempt may be dealt with summarily (see **B14.85** *et seq.*) or by an application for committal made to the Divisional Court of the Queen's Bench Division (see **B14.92** *et seq.*). In *DPP v Channel Four Television Co. Ltd* [1993] 2 All ER 517, it was stated that 'sensitive' contempt cases, involving such issues as the duty of a journalist to disclose the source of his information, should invariably be determined by the Divisional Court.

Jurisdiction and Procedure: Magistrates' Courts

Magistrates' courts have jurisdiction to deal with contempt only where that power is given by statute. In addition to the power to imprison fine defaulters, the MCA 1980, s. 63(3), empowers magistrates to deal with defaults in respect of other orders. This power is exercisable either of the court's own motion or by order on complaint (Contempt of Court Act 1981, s. 17). The maximum fine is £50 per day or £5,000; the maximum period of custody is two months. Some forms of contempt in the face of the court may be dealt with summarily under the MCA 1980, s. 97(4), or under the Contempt of Court Act 1981, s. 12. Under the CPIA 1996, s. 18, a court can also punish as contempt the use of disclosed prosecution material in contravention of s. 17 of that Act.

B14.85

Magistrates' Courts Act 1980, s. 97

(4) If any person attending or brought before a magistrates' court refuses without just excuse to be sworn or give evidence, or to produce any document or thing, the court may commit him to custody until the expiration of such period not exceeding one month as may be specified in the warrant or until he sooner gives evidence or produces the document or thing or impose on him a fine not exceeding £2,500 or both.

Contempt of Court Act 1981, s. 12

(1) A magistrates' court has jurisdiction under this section to deal with any person who—
  (a) wilfully insults the justice or justices, any witness before or officer of the court or any solicitor or counsel having business in the court, during his or their sitting or attendance in court or in going to or returning from the court; or
  (b) wilfully interrupts the proceedings of the court or otherwise misbehaves in court.
(2) In any such case the court may order any officer of the court, or any constable, to take the offender into custody and detain him until the rising of the court; and the court may, if it thinks fit, commit the offender to custody for a specified period not exceeding one month or impose on him a fine not exceeding £2,500, or both.
(2A) A fine imposed under subsection (2) above shall be deemed, for the purposes of any enactment, to be a sum adjudged to be paid by a conviction.
(3) [Repealed.]
(4) A magistrates' court may at any time revoke an order of committal made under subsection (2) and, if the offender is in custody, order his discharge.
(5) Section 135 of the Powers of Criminal Courts (Sentencing) Act 2000 (limit on fines in respect of young persons) and the following provisions of the Magistrates' Courts Act 1980 apply in relation to an order under this section as they apply in relation to a sentence on conviction or finding of guilty of an offence, and those provisions of the Magistrates' Courts Act 1980 are sections 75 to 91 (enforcement); section 108 (appeal to Crown Court); section 136 (overnight detention in default of payment); and section 142(1) (power to rectify mistakes).

The principles to be applied in exercising this jurisdiction are contained in the CrimPR, part 62 (see Supplement, R-453 and also **B14.88** *et seq.*).

B14.86

Section 12(1)(a) is not applicable where D has uttered threats rather than insults (*Havant Justices, ex parte Palmer* (1985) 149 JP 609, although uttering threats might involve 'misbehaviour' in court under s. 12(1)(b)). Magistrates have no jurisdiction over constructive contempts. These may, however, be dealt with by a Divisional Court under the Civil Procedure Rules 1998, part 81 (see **B14.92**).

Section 12(5) enables an appeal to be brought under the MCA 1980, s. 108, against conviction or sentence. In appropriate cases, the alleged contemnor may seek judicial review, or apply to the court to state a case for the High Court in accordance with the MCA 1980, s. 111 (*Haw v City of Westminster Magistrates' Court* [2008] QB 888).

Jurisdiction and Procedure: the Crown Court

By the Senior Courts Act 1981, s. 45(4), the Crown Court has, in relation to contempt and the enforcement of its orders, 'the like powers, rights, privileges and authority as the High Court'.

B14.87

This includes the power summarily to punish: disruptive, insulting or intimidating conduct in the courtroom or in its vicinity; disobedience to a witness summons (Criminal Procedure (Attendance of Witnesses) Act 1965, s. 3) or jury summons (Juries Act 1974, s. 20); misconduct under the Contempt of Court Act 1981, s. 8 or 9 (see **B14.107** and **B14.108**); failure to comply with its orders (such as investigation or restraint orders); and unauthorised use of disclosed prosecution material in contravention of the CPIA 1996, s. 17. As to failure to surrender to bail (which is not strictly speaking punishable as contempt), see **D7.114**.

Other forms of contempt (notably contempt involving publications prejudicial to current or forthcoming criminal trials) must be referred to a Queen's Bench Divisional Court in accordance with the Civil Procedure Rules 1998, part 81 (see **B14.92** *et seq.*).

Criminal Procedure Rules, Part 62

B14.88   The CrimPR, part 62 (see Supplement, **R-453** *et seq.*), deals with procedures to be followed in a wide range of contempt cases before magistrates' courts, the Crown Court or the Court of Appeal. Part 62 does not deal with procedures in cases brought by order of committal before the Divisional Court, which are dealt with in the Civil Procedure Rules 1998, part 81 (see **B14.93**).

Part 62 is divided into three sections. The first contains general rules (including rules governing the discharge or suspension of orders of imprisonment for contempt) and the second deals with procedures to be followed in cases involving allegations of obstruction, disruption or other forms of criminal contempt committed in the face of the court. The third section deals with procedures in cases where a party or some other person complains of disobedience to a court order, unauthorised use of disclosed prosecution material or other conduct akin to a civil contempt of court.

Where applicable, the rules supersede common-law principles and practice directions as to procedure in contempt cases, but are intended to reflect and codify previous good practice. This includes the principle that, wherever possible, a formal hearing must be held, even in cases involving contempt in the face of the court.

B14.89   **Rules Governing Proceedings for Contempt in the Face of the Court**   Case law preceding the enlargement of the CrimPR, part 62, emphasised the need to avoid unfairness to alleged contemnors. It was held that although a judge of the Crown Court has jurisdiction to deal immediately and summarily with contempt committed in the face of the court, that 'truly summary' procedure should be exercised only where 'the ends of justice really require such drastic means'. This is because 'it appears to be rough justice; it is contrary to natural justice; and it can only be justified if nothing else will do' (*Balogh v St Albans Crown Court* [1975] QB 73 per Stephenson LJ at p. 90). See also *AS* [2008] EWCA Crim 138.

An example of contempt that may call for immediate summary action is conduct which deliberately disrupts the trial, whether committed inside the courtroom or outside it. In *Morris v Crown Office* [1970] 2 QB 114, Welsh language campaigners who physically disrupted a sitting of the High Court were summarily committed to prison for three months. Less serious disruptions may also merit summary punishment, but there may be times when it would be wiser for the judge to rise, leaving those wishing to behave badly to do so in his absence (*Lewis* (1999) *The Times*, 4 November 1999).

The intimidation of witnesses or jurors during the course of a trial, or other forms of interference with them, has also been held to warrant an immediate judicial response. In *Goult* (1982) 76 Cr App R 140, the respondent was summarily committed to prison by a Crown Court judge for intimidating jurors, both in and out of court. Lord Lane CJ said (at p. 144):

> There is every reason…for the judge to take the sort of steps which the judge took here…not only for the question of the dignity of the court, but also for the reassurance of other jurors who would be awaiting their call to duty in the court.

The CrimPR, part 62, preserves (in r. 62.5(3)) the discretion to deal immediately with an apparent contempt or postpone consideration of it until later, but r. 62.5(2) requires certain steps to be taken by a court, wherever possible, before it proceeds to conduct a hearing of any kind, including providing the respondent with access to legal advice and the opportunity to reflect and (if he wishes) to explain or apologise. These steps reflect guidance previously given in cases such as *Moran* (1985) 81 Cr App R 51, *Hill* [1986] Crim LR 457 and *Wilkinson v S* [2003] 2 All ER 184.

B14.90

A court (including, where the Contempt of Court Act 1981, s. 12, applies, a magistrates' court) may order detention of the respondent in custody pending determination of the alleged contempt. By s. 12(2) and the CrimPR, r. 62.6, a magistrates' court may order such temporary detention only until the court rises, and must determine the case that same day, but the Crown Court or Court of Appeal are not so restricted and may detain him pending a review the next business day. Having reviewed the case, the court may then conduct a hearing or inquiry into the alleged contempt or postpone that inquiry and deal with it at some later date, in which case the respondent must be released pending the hearing and must be served with a written statement of the allegations and details of the hearing date etc. in accordance with r. 62.7. The hearing itself (whether postponed or not) must be conducted in accordance with r. 62.8.

Rules Governing Proceedings for Contempt by Disobedience to a Court Order The CrimPR, part 62, deals separately with cases where it is alleged that a person has disobeyed an investigation or restraint order of the Crown Court; has improperly used prosecution material disclosed under the CPIA 1996, s. 17, or is guilty of any other conduct that can be dealt with by the Crown Court or Court of Appeal as a civil contempt. Such cases are governed by rr. 62.9 to 62.17. Because proceedings for civil contempt of court are themselves civil proceedings, rr. 62.11 to 62.15 address the procedural requirements of the Civil Evidence Act 1995 in respect of hearsay evidence, any cross-examination of the maker of a hearsay statement, and any challenge to the credibility and consistency of the maker of such a statement.

B14.91

As to circumstances in which it may be appropriate to adjourn proceedings for contempt by breach of a restraint order pending the outcome of a related criminal case, see *Payton* [2006] EWCA Crim 1226 and *AA* [2010] EWCA Crim 2805.

Jurisdiction and Procedure: the Divisional Court of the Queen's Bench Division

The Divisional Court inherently possesses all the powers of a superior court and may act of its own motion in respect of contempts committed against it; but its more important jurisdiction in connection with criminal cases is in committal proceedings instituted by the A-G for alleged interference with the due administration of justice (notably in respect of publications that are alleged to create a risk of prejudice to current or forthcoming trials).

B14.92

Such proceedings are governed not by the CrimPR, part 62, but by the Civil Procedure Rules 1998, part 81, as inserted by the Civil Procedure (Amendment No. 2) Rules 2012 (SI 2012 No. 2208). Part 81, *inter alia*, supplants RSC Ord. 52, which was latterly set out in sch. 1 to the 1998 Rules, but only a few of the provisions of part 81 apply to contempt in criminal cases.

Committal proceedings to which part 81 applies are deemed to be civil proceedings for the purposes of rules of evidence and procedure, except that the criminal standard of proof applies along with the ECHR, Article 6 (*Daltel Europe Ltd v Makki* [2006] 1 WLR 2704).

Civil Procedure Rules 1998 (SI 1998 No. 3132), part 81, rr. 81.12, 81.13 and 81.14

B14.93

81.12.—(1) This section regulates committal applications in relation to interference with the due administration of justice in connection with proceedings—

...

(e) which are criminal proceedings,

except where the contempt is committed in the face of the court or consists of disobedience to an order of the court or a breach of an undertaking to the court.

. . .

(3) A committal application under this section may not be made without the permission of the court.

81.13.—(1) Where contempt of court is committed in connection with any proceedings—

. . .

(e) which are criminal proceedings, the application for permission may be made only to a Divisional Court of the Queen's Bench Division.

81.14.—(1) The application for permission to make a committal application must be made by a part 8 claim form which must include or be accompanied by—

(a) a detailed statement of the applicant's grounds for bringing the committal application; and

(b) an affidavit setting out the facts and exhibiting all documents relied upon.

(2) The claim form and the documents referred to in paragraph (1) must be served personally on the respondent unless the court otherwise directs.

(3) Within 14 days of service on the respondent of the claim form, the respondent—

(a) must file and serve an acknowledgment of service; and

(b) may file and serve evidence.

(4) The court will consider the application for permission at an oral hearing, unless it considers that such a hearing is not appropriate.

(5) If the respondent intends to appear at the permission hearing referred to in paragraph (4), the respondent must give 7 days' notice in writing of such intention to the court and any other party and at the same time provide a written summary of the submissions which the respondent proposes to make.

(6) Where permission to proceed is given, the court may give such directions as it thinks fit, and may—

(a) transfer the proceedings to another court; or

(b) direct that the application be listed for hearing before a single judge or a Divisional Court.

Jurisdiction and Procedure: The Court of Appeal and the Supreme Court

B14.94   The Court of Appeal and Supreme Court each possess the same inherent jurisdiction over contempt of court as the Crown Court and High Court. Contempt in the face of the Court of Appeal and contempt by disobedience to its orders must be dealt with according to the rules contained in the CrimPR, part 62 (see **B14.88**). Other contempts may still be dealt with by application for committal under the Civil Procedure Rules 1998, part 81 (see **B14.93**). Such an application may be made to the Court of Appeal itself. Order 52, r. 1(2), does not apply to the Court of Appeal. An alleged contempt of the House of Lords was determinable by the House alone (*Re Lonrho plc* [1990] 2 AC 154), and presumably this is true for the Supreme Court.

Penalties for Contempt

B14.95   Penalties for contempt of court are now governed by s. 14 of the Act.

Contempt of Court Act 1981, s. 14

(1) In any case where a court has power to commit a person to prison for contempt of court and (apart from this provision) no limitation applies to the period of committal, the committal shall (without prejudice to the power of the court to order his earlier discharge) be for a fixed term, and that term shall not on any occasion exceed two years in the case of committal by a superior court, or one month in the case of committal by an inferior court.

(2) In any case where an inferior court has power to fine a person for contempt of court and (apart from this provision) no limit applies to the amount of the fine, the fine shall not on any occasion exceed £2,500.

(2A) In the exercise of jurisdiction to commit for contempt of court or any kindred offence the court shall not deal with the offender by making an order under section 60 of the Powers of Criminal Courts (Sentencing) Act 2000 (an attendance centre order) if it appears to the court, after considering any available evidence, that he is under 17 years of age.

(2A) A fine imposed under subsection (2) above shall be deemed, for the purposes of any enactment, to be a sum adjudged to be paid by a conviction.

(3) [Repealed.]

(4)   Each of the superior courts shall have the like power to make a hospital order or guardianship order under section 37 of the Mental Health Act 1983 or an interim hospital order under section 38 of that Act in the case of a person suffering from mental disorder within the meaning of that Act who could otherwise be committed to prison for contempt of court as the Crown Court has under that section in the case of a person convicted of an offence.

(4A) Each of the superior courts shall have the like power to make an order under section 35 of the said Act of 1983 (remand for report on accused's mental condition) where there is reason to suspect that a person who could be committed to prison for contempt of court is suffering from mental disorder within the meaning of that Act as the Crown Court has under that section in the case of an accused person within the meaning of the section.

(4A) For the purposes of the preceding provisions of this section the county court shall be treated as a superior court and not as an inferior court.

(4B) The preceding provisions of this section do not apply to the family court, but—

(a) this is without prejudice to the operation of section 31E(1)(a) of the Matrimonial and Family Proceedings Act 1984 (family court has High Court's powers) in relation to the powers of the High Court that are limited or conferred by those provisions of this section, and

(b) section 31E(1)(b) of that Act (family court has county court's powers) does not apply in relation to the powers of the county court that are limited or conferred by those provisions of this section.

(By oversight there are now *two* subsections numbered (2A) and *two* numbered (4A).)

As to the maximum penalties which may be imposed by magistrates' courts, see **B14.85.**

Section 14(1) applies to both civil and criminal contempt of court (*OB v Director of the Serious Fraud Office* [2012] 3 All ER 1017).

There is no power to impose a custodial sentence on an offender under the age of 21 for contempt of court (PCC(S)A 2000, s. 89); *Byas* (1995) 16 Cr App R (S) 869). For offenders aged between 18 and 20 inclusive, detention may be ordered where appropriate under the PCC(S)A 2000, s. 108 (see further **E15.2**). Courts dealing with persons who are found guilty of criminal contempt have no power to make community rehabilitation orders (*Palmer* [1992] 3 All ER 289).

Contempts Amounting to Other Offences   Where the same conduct can amount both to   **B14.96** contempt of court and to a more specific statutory offence (as is the case with deliberate non-attendance by a person summoned as a witness), the courts must have some regard to the maximum penalty in respect of the statutory offence when considering a possible penalty for contempt, but they are not bound by any such maximum if there are aggravating features (*Montgomery* [1995] 2 Cr App R 23).

Imprisonment without Legal Representation   The PCC(S)A 2000, s. 83(1), which restricts   **B14.97** the imprisonment of legally unrepresented persons (see **D20.78**), does not apply in cases of committal for contempt (*Newbury Justices, ex parte Pont* (1984) 78 Cr App R 255); but where the CrimPR, r. 62.5, applies the respondent must at least be allowed an opportunity to take advice before any hearing, unless his behaviour makes this impracticable.

Forms of Contempt: Intimidation of or Interference with or Retaliation against Witnesses or Jurors

An attempt to interfere with jurors or witnesses, whether by way of intimidation, bribery or   **B14.98** persuasion, may be punished as contempt at common law. This principle extends not only to litigants and members of the public but also to court officials and jury bailiffs, who should avoid any discussion of cases with jurors (*Mickleburgh* [1995] 1 Cr App R 297). In practice, such cases will ordinarily require police investigation, and may then more appropriately be dealt with under the CJPO 1994, s. 51 (see **B14.47**) or as conduct tending to pervert the course of justice.

Intimidation or harassment of former witnesses or jurors, or retaliation against them, is an equally serious matter (*A-G v Judd* [1995] COD 15). Although the original trial may be over, it is essential that former witnesses or jurors are protected, so that they will not be afraid to do their duty (*A-G v Butterworth* [1963] 1 QB 696).

In *Connolly v Dale* [1996] QB 120, a police inspector was found to be in contempt for obstructing attempts by an accused person's inquiry agent to obtain alibi evidence on behalf of his client, and for threatening him with prosecution under what is now the Police Act 1996, s. 89(2). This was despite the fact that the officer had acted in good faith, for the purpose, as he saw it, of preventing the contamination of identification evidence.

B14.99   **Sentencing Guidelines**   In *Wedlock* [1996] 1 Cr App R (S) 391 the offender had been on trial in the Crown Court for theft. After the principal prosecution witness had finished giving her evidence in chief the case was adjourned overnight. That evening the offender drove past the witness, threw something at her, and made an abusive remark. The Court of Appeal upheld the sentence of six months' imprisonment for the contempt. Six months' imprisonment was upheld in *Bryan* [1998] 2 Cr App R (S) 109, where the offender, the brother of a man on trial for murder, mouthed threatening words from the public gallery at a witness giving evidence in the case. See also *Stredder* [1997] 1 Cr App R (S) 209, where 12 months' imprisonment was upheld in a case where the offender, who was about to stand trial for theft, approached the sole prosecution witness in the court building, referred to damage which had been done to the witness's car, and said 'that was just a warning'.

Comparable sentences have been upheld by the Court of Appeal in respect of attempts to influence jurors. In *Curtis* [2013] 1 Cr App R (S) 147 (28) the offenders had followed three jurors on to a bus and sat close to them while one of the offenders held a loud conversation on her mobile phone making comments about the course of the trial. Sentences of five months and three months were upheld. In *Sparks* (1995) 16 Cr App R (S) 480, the offenders had sat in the public gallery in the Crown Court and, for their own amusement, made threatening gestures towards a juror. The jury had to be discharged as a result. Nine months' imprisonment was reduced to six months on appeal. In *Mitchell-Crinkley* [1998] 1 Cr App R (S) 368, the offender attended the trial of a friend and recognised one of the jurors. He telephoned the juror and told him that a previous jury in the case had failed to agree. Imprisonment for 12 months was upheld. See also **B14.46** *et seq.*

Forms of Contempt: Disruption of Proceedings and Misbehaviour in Court

B14.100   A deliberate disruption of proceedings in court, whether staged by persons involved in those proceedings, or by demonstrators etc. may be punished as contempt, and in most cases will be dealt with by the court acting of its own motion. See *Morris v Crown Office* [1970] 2 QB 114. The same is true of misconduct, such as wolf-whistling at female jurors or witnesses (*Powell* (1993) 98 Cr App R 224), and of assaults on court officials whilst they are engaged in the administration of justice (*Re de Court* (1997) *The Times*, 27 November 1997). Whether noisy protests from the public gallery following conviction or sentence are so serious as to amount to contempt is a matter which the trial court or judge is usually best placed to decide, but in many cases the best way of dealing with it may be for the judge to rise, and let the disturbance subside (*Lewis* (1999) *The Times*, 4 November 1999). Outbursts in court may, however, be contempts, even in the absence of an intent to disrupt the proceedings (*Huggins* [2007] 2 Cr App R 107).

B14.101   **Sentencing Guidelines**   In *Phelps* [2010] 2 Cr App R (S) 1, during the course of the sentencing hearing the offender attacked two female dock officers, punching and spitting. An alarm button was pressed and male officers attended. The offender continued to lash out with his fists. The judge dealt with the contempt immediately, imposing the maximum sentence of two years for contempt, consecutive to the other sentences. The Court of Appeal said that it had not been wrong for the judge to deal with the contempt summarily. There was no dispute as to what had happened, and the court had to act decisively. The conventional wisdom, however, was that in most cases a cooling-off period to allow the offender to calm down and apologise was appropriate. The sentence for the contempt was reduced to 21 months. In *McDaniel* (1990) 12 Cr App R (S) 44, the offender was aged 31 and had minor previous convictions. He attended the trial of his brother at the Crown Court where he and others had been warned about noisy conversations during the proceedings. When his brother was convicted and sentenced there was a general commotion during which the offender called the judge 'a dog'. A sentence of three months' imprisonment for addressing such personal abuse to the judge was reduced on appeal to 14 days.

Forms of Contempt: Committed by Witnesses, Jurors or Defendants

A juror who fails to attend court when duly summoned commits a summary offence under the   **B14.102**
Juries Act 1974, s. 20(1), but may alternatively be punished 'as if it were criminal contempt...in the face of the court' (s. 20(2)). Jurors may likewise be punished for contempt if they refuse or fail to discharge their obligations in accordance with the jury oath (*Schot* [1997] 2 Cr App R 383) or conduct improper communications or research in defiance of the warnings given to them. As Lord Judge CJ explained in *A-G v Fraill* [2011] 2 Cr App R 271:

> If jurors make their own inquiries into aspects of the trials with which they are concerned, the jury system as we know it, so precious to the administration of criminal justice in this country, will be seriously undermined, and what is more, the public confidence on which it depends will be shaken. The jury's deliberations, and ultimately their verdict, must be based — and exclusively based — on the evidence given in court, a principle which applies as much to communication with the internet as it does to discussions by members of the jury with individuals in and around, and sometimes outside the precincts of the court.

See also *A-G v Davey* [2014] 1 Cr App R 1 (1).

A witness who refuses to be sworn, or refuses to produce documents or answer questions properly put to him, will be in contempt. In *Wicks* (31 January 1995 unreported), the Court of Appeal emphasised that witnesses who have been threatened are not thereby excused from giving evidence. As to the liability of witnesses who fail to obey witness summonses, see **D15.95**. As to the position of journalists who wish to protect their sources of information, special provision is made by the Contempt of Court Act 1981, s. 10 (see **B14.112**).

As to contempt by a convicted defendant who refuses to appear in court for sentencing, see *Santiago* [2005] 2 Cr App R 366. As to defendants who disrupt the trial or attempt to manipulate the jury, see *Baker* [2008] EWCA Crim 334.

Sentencing Guidelines   Guidance on sentencing for contempt where a witness refuses to give   **B14.103**
evidence has been provided by the Court of Appeal in *Montgomery* [1995] 2 Cr App R 23 and in *Robinson* [2006] 2 Cr App R (S) 587. In the former case a sentence of 12 months' imprisonment for failure to attend court and persistent refusal to testify or explain the refusal was reduced to three months. In the latter case, where a defence witness gave evidence in chief but refused to answer any question in cross-examination, a sentence of four months' imprisonment was upheld on appeal. It emerges from these decisions that, in the absence of wholly exceptional circumstances, an immediate custodial sentence is appropriate for a refusal to testify, but that the sentence will often be shorter than that imposed in a case of interference with a witness or juror. The principal matters affecting sentence are the gravity of the offence being tried, the extent to which the failure to testify affected the course of the trial, whether the refusal was aggravated by defiance or impertinence to the judge, and the antecedents and personal circumstances of the contemnor. The contemnor should normally be sentenced at the end of the trial, or at least at the end of the prosecution case, to allow him time to reconsider his position. See also *Cole* [1997] 1 Cr App R (S) 228.

In *A-G v Dallas* [2012] 1 WLR 991 a juror conducted online research into the accused's past, in defiance of the judge's instructions regarding misuse of the internet. She compounded this misconduct by disclosing her findings to her fellow jurors. As a result, the jury had to be discharged. In proceedings brought by the A-G, the juror was sentenced to six months' imprisonment. In *Chapman* [2013] 1 Cr App R (S) 117 (22), 56 days' imprisonment was upheld in respect of a juror who absented herself from a trial to go on holiday.

Forms of Contempt: Contempt by Advocates

B14.104   An advocate who deliberately fails to attend a hearing with intent to hinder or delay the course of justice would be guilty of contempt (*Weston v Central Criminal Court Courts Administrator* [1977] QB 32); see also *West* [2014] EWCA Crim 1480, a case concerning the behaviour of a barrister of 'breathtaking arrogance', where Sir Brian Leveson P indicated (at 50) 'that not every failure to co-operate or refusal to attend court is a contempt; that is very different, however, from saying that failure to co-operate or refusal to attend court could never be a contempt: it clearly can be'. It could also be a contempt to persist in adducing inadmissible evidence, or in a forbidden line of questioning, or generally to disobey or disregard orders of the court or to treat the court with gross disrespect. It is not, however, contempt to do whatever is ethically and professionally appropriate to provide a client with zealous representation, even if this brings the advocate into conflict with the court for such is his duty. Failure to submit a defence statement complying with the CPIA 1996, ss. 5(5) and 6A, cannot be punished as a contempt of court on the part of either the defendant or his advocate (*Rochford* [2011] 1 WLR 534).

The Legal Services Act 2007 created offences under ss. 14, 16 and 17 (carrying on a reserved activity when not entitled, employing someone to do so and pretending to be so entitled) and 181 (pretending to be a barrister). Each offence is an either-way offence punishable with imprisonment for two years on conviction on indictment and/or a fine, and with six months' imprisonment and a fine up to the statutory maximum on summary conviction.

Forms of Contempt: Conduct or Publication Scandalising the Court

B14.105   Prior to the implementation of the CCA 2013, s. 33, the publication of scurrilous criticism or abuse that tended to discredit a court or judge (or the judicial system as a whole) could potentially be punished as a criminal contempt of court (see *Gray* [1900] 2 QB 36). This law was rarely invoked in modern times, and s. 33 has now abolished it with effect from 25 June 2013.

Forms of Contempt: Publication Prejudicial to the Administration of Justice

B14.106   This is one of the most important and complex varieties of contempt. Prejudice may be caused, *inter alia*, by revealing matters which might be inadmissible in evidence, and which may influence jurors etc. (as in *Clarke, ex parte Crippen* (1910) 103 LT 636 and *Parke* [1903] 2 KB 432); by sensational and misleading coverage of a trial (see the comments of McCowan LJ in *Taylor* (1993) 98 Cr App R 361); by commenting on the merits of the case or prejudging it (*Hutchison, ex parte McMahon* [1936] 2 All ER 1514); by the vilification of a suspect under arrest (*A-G v MGN Ltd* [2012] 1 WLR 2408) or by publicly disclosing sensitive material that was subject to a court order restricting such disclosure, even where the order was addressed to another (*A-G v Newspaper Publishing plc* [1997] 3 All ER 159). The question for the court in such cases is whether the publication created a substantial risk that the course of justice would be substantially impeded or prejudiced. That court must assess that risk by looking forward from the time of publication. It is no defence that by chance no jurors saw the offending material and no prejudice was caused (*A-G v Associated Newspapers Ltd* [2011] 1 WLR 2097). Newspapers and other publishers may also commit contempt where they make payments to witnesses on terms which may encourage perjured evidence, or seek to pressurise litigants into abandoning their actions (*A-G v Hislop* [1991] 1 QB 514). Publication of material by one person, when another person has already been served with an injunction prohibiting disclosure of that material pending trial of the issue of its confidentiality, may be a criminal contempt by the publisher because it destroys the subject-matter of the dispute (*A-G v Times Newspapers Ltd* [1992] 1 AC 191; *A-G v Punch Ltd* [2003] 1 AC 1046). It is not necessary that the publisher in such a case should intend to cause the harm that the third party injunction was ultimately designed to prevent. It is not for editors or broadcasters to decide (for example) whether publication of material which a third party has been ordered not to disclose would or would not harm the national interest. An honest belief on their part that no such harm would be caused is accordingly no defence (*A-G v Punch Ltd*).

B14.107

Publication of material capable of prejudicing or impeding forthcoming legal proceedings does not necessarily amount to contempt. If the proceedings in question are not 'active' within the meaning of the Contempt of Court Act 1981 (see **B14.118**) or if there is no substantial risk of serious prejudice at the time of publication, then publication amounts to contempt only if there is proof of an intent to interfere with the course of justice in those proceedings. Recklessness or negligence will not suffice (*A-G v News Group Newspapers plc* [1989] QB 110; *A-G v Newspaper Publishing plc*). Where there is a substantial risk of serious prejudice to active proceedings, liability may be strict, but subject to certain defences (see generally **B14.118** to **B14.127**).

According to the Divisional Court in *A-G v News Group Newspapers plc*, publications which deliberately set out to prejudice possible future legal proceedings, and which do in fact create a real risk of such prejudice, may constitute contempt, even where those proceedings were not even imminent at the time of publication (e.g., where nothing had yet been done to instigate them). The case involved a highly prejudicial campaign run by the *Sun* newspaper with a view to ensuring that a doctor accused of raping a child would in due course be prosecuted. Watkins LJ acknowledged that this decision represented an extension of the law, but argued that the common law was 'a living body of law capable of adaption and expansion to meet fresh needs'. Doubts have subsequently been expressed as to the correctness of this view, which could be seen as a threat to investigative journalism. In *A-G v Sport Newspapers Ltd* [1991] 1 WLR 1194, a differently constituted Divisional Court held that material published by the *Sport* concerning a suspect in a murder inquiry did not amount to intentional interference in the course of justice, but Hodgson J went on to state (*obiter*) that *News Group Newspapers* was wrongly decided, and it seems that Bingham LJ would have been prepared to follow it only on the basis that he considered it wrong to depart from such a recent precedent.

Sentencing Guidelines In *A-G v News Group Newspapers Ltd* (1984) 6 Cr App R (S) 418 the Divisional Court dealt with a case where a newspaper had published, during the course of a trial, a picture of one of two defendants on trial for causing injury to their baby, with the headline: 'Baby was blinded by dad'. This statement was wholly misleading. The newspaper subsequently apologised and the court accepted that the contempt was not deliberate. According to Stephen Brown LJ (at p. 420):

B14.108

> We are bound to say that this newspaper headline and photograph greatly surprised us and gravely disturbed us. It is fortunate indeed that the trial was not interrupted but it has to be made plain that there is a strict duty of care placed upon those who publish news items relating to trials to see that they do not run the risk of interfering with the course of justice. There was a clear and grave risk of that in this case.
>
> Taking into account all the facts, bearing in mind the nature of the apology, and bearing in mind the fact that it was not intentional but nevertheless a serious contempt, the order of this court is that the respondents be fined the sum of £5,000.

Forms of Contempt: Disclosures Relating to Jury Deliberations

Contempt of Court Act 1981, s. 8

B14.109

(1) Subject to subsection (2) below, it is a contempt of court to obtain, disclose or solicit any particulars of statements made, opinions expressed, arguments advanced or votes cast by members of a jury in the course of their deliberations in any legal proceedings.

(2) This section does not apply to any disclosure of any particulars—

    (a) in the proceedings in question for the purpose of enabling the jury to arrive at their verdict, or in connection with the delivery of that verdict, or

    (b) in evidence in any subsequent proceedings for an offence alleged to have been committed in relation to the jury in the first mentioned proceedings,

    or to the publication of any particulars so disclosed.

(3) Proceedings for a contempt of court under this section (other than Scottish proceedings) shall not be instituted except by or with the consent of the Attorney-General or on the motion of a court having jurisdiction to deal with it.

This provision was enacted following the failure of the prosecution in *A-G v New Statesman and Nation Publishing Co. Ltd* [1981] QB 1. The contempt may be committed both by jurors and by a person who further discloses or publishes the information he has been given (see *A-G v Associated Newspapers Ltd* [1994] 2 AC 238). In *Mickleburgh* [1995] 1 Cr App R 297, Lord Taylor CJ warned that defence solicitors who take statements from former jurors, or make inquiries of former jurors, run a grave risk of being in contempt of court under s. 8, unless they first obtain leave from the Court of Appeal. Similar advice was given by Henry J in *McGlusky* (1993) 98 Cr App R 223.

If a juror genuinely believes that there had been a miscarriage of justice due to failings on the part of his fellow jurors, he would not, merely by expressing such concerns to the trial judge or the Court of Appeal, commit any contempt of court under s. 8(1) (*Mirza* [2004] 1 AC 1118). A letter detailing such concerns may even be passed to counsel, with instructions to forward it unopened to the court. But the position is different where the juror communicates with a defendant or third party who had no authority to receive disclosures on behalf of the court; this will be punishable under s. 8(1) (*A-G v Scotcher* [2005] 3 All ER 1; *A-G v Seckerson* [2009] EWHC 1023 (Admin)).

Forms of Contempt: Misuse of Tape Recorders in Court

B14.110   Contempt of Court Act 1981, s. 9

    (1) Subject to subsection (4) below, it is a contempt of court—
        (a) to use in court, or bring into court for use, any tape recorder or other instrument for recording sound, except with the leave of the court;
        (b) to publish a recording of legal proceedings made by means of any such instrument, or any recording derived directly or indirectly from it, by playing it in the hearing of the public or any section of the public, or to dispose of it or any recording so derived, with a view to such publication;
        (c) to use any such recording in contravention of any conditions of leave granted under paragraph (a).
    (2) Leave under paragraph (a) of subsection (1) may be granted or refused at the discretion of the court, and if granted may be granted subject to such conditions as the court thinks proper with respect to the use of any recording made pursuant to the leave; and where leave has been granted the court may at the like discretion withdraw or amend it either generally or in relation to any particular part of the proceedings.
    (3) Without prejudice to any other power to deal with an act of contempt under paragraph (a) of subsection (1), the court may order the instrument, or any recording made with it, or both, to be forfeited; and any object so forfeited shall (unless the court otherwise determines on application by a person appearing to be the owner) be sold or otherwise disposed of in such manner as the court may direct.
    (4) This section does not apply to the making or use of sound recordings for purposes of official transcripts of proceedings.

Section 9 does not apply to the recording and broadcasting of certain proceedings in the Court of Appeal that are made in accordance with the Court of Appeal (Recording and Broadcasting) Order 2013 (SI 2013 No. 2786). In other cases, CPD II, paras. 16A.1 to 16A.6, *Unofficial Sound Recording of Proceedings* (see Supplement, **PD-21**) provide guidance on the exercise of the discretion to grant, withhold or withdraw leave to use equipment for recording sound or to impose conditions as to the use of any recording. (As to the power to order forfeiture of unauthorised recordings, see the CrimPR, r. 16.10 (see Supplement, **R-139**).)

Forms of Contempt: Photography, Sketching, Tweeting and Mobile Telephones

B14.111   The taking of photographs in court, or the publication of such photographs, is sometimes punished as contempt (see for example, *A-G v Scarth* [2013] EWHC 194 (Admin)), but may also be punished as a summary offence (carrying a level 3 fine) under the CJA 1925, s. 41, which also deals with sketches. It is an offence under s. 41(1) to:

(a) take or attempt to take in any court any photograph, or with a view to publication make or attempt to make in any court any portrait or sketch of any person, being a judge of the court or a juror or a witness in or a party to any proceedings before the court, whether civil or criminal; or

(b) publish any photograph, portrait or sketch taken or made in contravention of the foregoing provisions of this section or any reproduction thereof.

'Judge' includes a registrar, magistrate, justice and coroner (s. 41(2)(a)). Photography includes video-tape; and the police are not exempt from the prohibition (*Loveridge* [2001] 2 Cr App R 591). Photography in the precincts of the court building is also covered (s. 41(2)(c)). The publication of sketches drawn from memory once outside the court is not prohibited; and s. 41 does not apply to the recording and broadcasting of certain proceedings in the Court of Appeal that are made in accordance with the Court of Appeal (Recording and Broadcasting) Order 2013 (SI 2013 No. 2786).

Mobile telephones must ordinarily be turned off in court, but a mobile phone (in silent mode) or small computer may be used by representatives of the media or legal commentators for the fair reporting of cases. Members of the public who wish to use such equipment must seek prior approval (see *Practice Guidance (Court Proceedings: Live Text-based Communications) (No. 2)* [2012] 1 WLR 12 at **D3.142**).

Forms of Contempt: Refusal to Disclose Sources of Published Information

A journalist or other person who refuses to disclose the source of information he has published **B14.112** may be in contempt of court, but regard must be had to the Contempt of Court Act 1981, s. 10, which provides:

> No court may require a person to disclose, nor is any person guilty of contempt of court for refusing to disclose, the source of information contained in a publication for which he is responsible, unless it be established to the satisfaction of the court that disclosure is necessary in the interests of justice or national security or for the prevention of disorder or crime.

In order to satisfy the court of the necessity of disclosure, proof is required, on balance of probabilities; it is not enough merely to assert the need (*Secretary of State for Defence v Guardian Newspapers Ltd* [1985] AC 339). Nor is convenience the same thing as necessity; but necessity is a relative concept, and may be something less than absolute indispensability (*Re an Inquiry under the Company Securities (Insider Dealing) Act 1985* [1988] AC 660). 'Prevention of crime' includes the general control of crime and not just the prevention of specific acts (*Re an Inquiry under the Company Securities (Insider Dealing) Act 1985*). See generally **F9.23**.

Forms of Contempt: Breaches of Reporting Restrictions on Cases Heard in Public

Deliberate (or perhaps reckless) breach of reporting restrictions imposed under the Contempt **B14.113** of Court Act 1981, s. 4 (see **D3.127**) would appear to be a form of statutory contempt, whether or not any real risk of prejudice is involved. See generally *Horsham Justices, ex parte Farquharson* [1982] QB 762. As to sentencing for breach, see *A-G v Harkins* [2013] EWHC 1455 (Admin) (publication of photographs on Facebook, supposedly showing the notorious child murderers Thompson and Venables as adults).

CPD II, paras. 16B.1 to 16B.7, *Restrictions on Reporting Proceedings*, provide specific guidance on the exercise of this power (see Supplement, **PD-20**).

As to reporting restrictions generally, see **D3.127** *et seq.*; for reporting restrictions when a case is sent to the Crown Court, see the CDA 1998, s. 52B at **D10.43**.

Forms of Contempt: Publication of Matter Exempted from Disclosure in Court

B14.114   Contempt of Court Act 1981, s. 11

In any case where a court (having power to do so) allows a name or other matter to be withheld from the public in proceedings before the court, the court may give such directions prohibiting the publication of that name or matter in connection with the proceedings as appear to the court to be necessary for the purpose for which it was so withheld.

CPD II, paras. 16B.1 to 16B.7, *Restrictions on Reporting Proceedings*, provide specific guidance on the exercise of this power (see Supplement, **PD-22**). Breach of an order made under s. 11 could (as with breaches of orders under the Contempt of Court Act 1981, s. 4), constitute a statutory contempt. As to the principles of 'open justice', see **D3.122** *et seq*.

The power to make such an order must not be used merely 'for the benefit of the comfort and feelings of defendants' as by safeguarding them from unwanted publicity or molestation (*Evesham Justices, ex parte McDonagh* [1988] QB 553). It is properly employed to safeguard the identity of children and young persons, complainants in rape cases, witnesses who might later be exposed to violence or blackmail, or revelation of whose identity might prejudice national security.

It may be necessary for a court to sit in camera when hearing evidence in support of an application under the Contempt of Court Act 1981, s. 11 (*Tower Bridge Magistrates' Court, ex parte Osbourne* (1989) 88 Cr App R 28).

Forms of Contempt: Publications Relating to Proceedings in Camera

B14.115   Administration of Justice Act 1960, s. 12

(1) The publication of information relating to proceedings before any court sitting in private shall not of itself be contempt of court except in the following cases, that is to say—

    (a) where the proceedings—

        (i)   relate to the exercise of the inherent jurisdiction of the High Court with respect to minors;

        (ii) are brought under the Children Act 1989 or the Adoption and Children Act 2002; or

        (iii) otherwise relate wholly or mainly to the maintenance or upbringing of a minor;

    (b) where the proceedings are brought under the Mental Capacity Act 2005, or under any provision of the Mental Health Act 1983 authorising an application or reference to be made to the First-tier Tribunal, the Mental Health Review Tribunal for Wales or to the county court;

    (c) where the court sits in private for reasons of national security during that part of the proceedings about which the information in question is published;

    (d) where the information relates to a secret process, discovery or invention which is in issue in the proceedings;

    (e) where the court (having power to do so) expressly prohibits the publication of all information relating to the proceedings or of information of the description which is published.

(2) Without prejudice to the foregoing subsection, the publication of the text or a summary of the whole or part of an order made by a court sitting in private shall not of itself be contempt of court except where the court (having power to do so) expressly prohibits the publication.

(3) In this section references to a court include references to a judge and to a tribunal and to any person exercising the functions of a court, a judge or a tribunal; and references to a court sitting in private include references to a court sitting in camera or in chambers.

(4) Nothing in this section shall be construed as implying that any publication is punishable as contempt of court which would not be so punishable apart from this section (and in particular where the publication is not so punishable by reason of being authorised by rules of court).

(5) Subsection (1) is subject to Part 2 of the Children, Schools and Families Act 2010 (family proceedings), and nothing in subsection (2) applies in relation to a contempt of court under section 11 of that Act (restriction on publication of information relating to family proceedings).

Section 12(5) was inserted by the Children, Schools and Families Act 2010, sch. 3, para. 4, and is not yet in force.

In *P v Liverpool Daily Post and Echo Newspapers plc* [1991] 2 AC 370, the House of Lords held that nothing in s. 12(1) prohibits publication of the fact that a court or tribunal is to sit etc., nor does it prohibit the naming of a person involved (but see **B14.114**).

Attempted Contempt

Criminal contempt can take the form either of conduct which is intended to interfere with the **B14.116** course of justice, or of conduct which tends to have that effect. It is not therefore essential that any real harm is done. If the intent is proved, the measures adopted may be hopelessly ineffective (*Castro, Skipworth's and the Defendant's Case* (1873) LR 9 QB 230), and if the tendency is proved, there may sometimes be an element of strict liability, although this is now largely confined to certain publications (see **B14.118**).

This leaves little scope for offences of attempted contempt, but one could have a case in which a person fails, not only to interfere with the proceedings, but to perform the act by which he intends so to do. An example of such a case is *Balogh v St Albans Crown Court* [1975] QB 73, where Balogh intended to disrupt a trial by pumping laughing-gas into the court-room, but was arrested before he could do so. Doubts were expressed by Stephenson LJ about the very existence of any crime of attempted contempt, but Balogh had not in any case got beyond the stage of mere preparation, and the doubts were left unresolved. It is submitted that there are no compelling reasons for denying the existence of that offence (see the judgment of Lord Denning MR), but the problem will seldom arise in practice.

Mens Rea

It has been recognised that *mens rea* in criminal contempt cases is something of a minefield, **B14.117** owing to the piecemeal development of the common-law offence, and the lack of codification (see the observations of Lord Donaldson MR in *A-G v Newspaper Publishing plc* [1988] Ch 333 at p. 373).

At common law, some forms of contempt carried strict liability. Thus, in *Odhams Press Ltd, ex parte A-G* [1957] 1 QB 73, Odhams Press was held to be guilty of contempt for publishing an article which tended to prejudice the course of justice in a forthcoming trial, even though it was not informed that the trial was forthcoming, and was not even proved to have been reckless as to the possibility. This rule seems to have been confined in practice to publication cases (*A-G v English* [1983] 1 AC 116 per Lord Diplock at p. 141), and insofar as interference with the course of justice in 'particular proceedings' is concerned, it is now expressly so confined by ss. 1 and 2 of the Contempt of Court Act 1981, which indeed limit its application more tightly still (see **B14.118**).

This leaves two further issues to be considered. First, whether strict liability can still apply in any areas not covered by the Contempt of Court Act 1981; and secondly, whether anything less than a specific intent may suffice where strict liability is excluded under the Act. These issues are considered at **B14.126** and **B14.127** respectively.

Strict Liability: the Contempt of Court Act 1981

Contempt of Court Act 1981, ss. 1 and 2 and sch. 1 **B14.118**

The strict liability rule
1. In this Act 'the strict liability rule' means the rule of law whereby conduct may be treated as a contempt of court as tending to interfere with the course of justice in particular legal proceedings regardless of intent to do so.

Limitation of scope of strict liability
2.—(1) The strict liability rule applies only in relation to publications, and for this purpose 'publication' includes any speech, writing, programme included in a programme service or other communication in whatever form, which is addressed to the public at large or any section of the public.
(2) The strict liability rule applies only to a publication which creates a substantial risk that the course of justice in the proceedings in question will be seriously impeded or prejudiced.

(3) The strict liability rule applies to a publication only if the proceedings in question are active within the meaning of this section at the time of the publication.

(4) Schedule 1 applies for determining the times at which proceedings are to be treated as active within the meaning of this section.

(5) In this section 'programme service' has the same meaning as in the Broadcasting Act 1990.

SCHEDULE 1

TIMES WHEN PROCEEDINGS ARE ACTIVE FOR PURPOSES OF SECTION 2

Preliminary

1. In this Schedule 'criminal proceedings' means proceedings against a person in respect of an offence, not being appellate proceedings or proceedings commenced by motion for committal or attachment in England and Wales or Northern Ireland; and 'appellate proceedings' means proceedings on appeal from or for the review of the decision of a court in any proceedings.

1ZA. [Scotland.]

1A. In paragraph 1 the reference to an offence includes a service offence within the meaning of the Armed Forces Act 2006.

2. Criminal, appellate and other proceedings are active within the meaning of section 2 at the times respectively prescribed by the following paragraphs of this Schedule; and in relation to proceedings in which more than one of the steps described in any of those paragraphs is taken, the reference in that paragraph is a reference to the first of those steps.

Criminal proceedings

3. Subject to the following provisions of this Schedule, criminal proceedings are active from the relevant initial step specified in paragraph 4 until concluded as described in paragraph 5.

4. The initial steps of criminal proceedings are:—
    (a) arrest without warrant;
    (b) the issue, or in Scotland the grant, of a warrant for arrest;
    (c) the issue of a summons to appear; [or in Scotland the grant of a warrant to cite;]
    (d) the service of an indictment or other document specifying the charge;
    (e) except in Scotland, oral charge.
    (f) [Scotland].

4A. Where as a result of an order under section 54 of the Criminal Procedure and Investigations Act 1996 (acquittal tainted by an administration of justice offence) proceedings are brought against a person for an offence of which he has previously been acquitted, the initial step of the proceedings is a certification under subsection (2) of that section; and paragraph 4 has effect subject to this.

5. Criminal proceedings are concluded—
    (a) by acquittal or, as the case may be, by sentence;
    (b) by any other verdict, finding, order or decision which puts an end to the proceedings;
    (c) by discontinuance or by operation of law.
    (d) [Scotland].

6. The reference in paragraph 5(a) to sentence includes any order or decision consequent on conviction or finding of guilt which disposes of the case, either absolutely or subject to future events, and a deferment of sentence under section 1 of the Powers of Criminal Courts (Sentencing) Act 2000, section 202 of the Criminal Procedure (Scotland) Act 1995 or Article 14 of the Treatment of Offenders (Northern Ireland) Order 1976.

7. Proceedings are discontinued within the meaning of paragraph 5(c)—
    (a) in England and Wales or Northern Ireland, if the charge or summons is withdrawn or a *nolle prosequi* entered;
    (aa) in England and Wales, if they are discontinued by virtue of section 23 of the Prosecution of Offences Act 1985;
    (ab) in England and Wales, if they are discontinued by virtue of paragraph 11 of Schedule 17 to the Crime and Courts Act 2013 (deferred prosecution agreements);
    (b) [Scotland];
    (c) in the case of proceedings in England and Wales or Northern Ireland commenced by arrest without warrant, if the person arrested is released, otherwise than on bail, without having been charged.
    (d) [Scotland].

8. [Repealed.]

9. Criminal proceedings in England and Wales or Northern Ireland cease to be active if an order is made for the charge to lie on the file, but become active again if leave is later given for the proceedings to continue.

9A. Where proceedings in England and Wales have been discontinued by virtue of section 23 of the Prosecution of Offences Act 1985, but notice is given by the accused under subsection (7) of that section to the effect that he wants the proceedings to continue, they become active again with the giving of that notice.

10. Without prejudice to paragraph 5(b) above, criminal proceedings against a person cease to be active—

    (a) if the accused is found to be under a disability such as to render him unfit to be tried or unfit to plead or, in Scotland, is found to be insane in bar of trial; or

    (b) if a hospital order is made in his case under section 51(5) of the Mental Health Act 1983 or Article 57(5) of the Mental Health (Northern Ireland) Order 1986 or, in Scotland, where an assessment order or a treatment order ceases to have effect by virtue of sections 52H or 52R respectively of the Criminal Procedure (Scotland) Act 1995,

    but become active again if they are later resumed.

11. Criminal proceedings against a person which become active on the issue or the grant of a warrant for his arrest cease to be active at the end of the period of 12 months beginning with the date of the warrant unless he has been arrested within that period, but become active again if he is subsequently arrested.

Other proceedings at first instance

12. Proceedings other than criminal proceedings and appellate proceedings are active from the time when arrangements for the hearing are made or, if no such arrangements are previously made, from the time the hearing begins, until the proceedings are disposed of or discontinued or withdrawn; and for the purposes of this paragraph any motion or application made in or for the purposes of any proceedings, and any pre-trial review in the county court, is to be treated as a distinct proceeding.

13. In England and Wales or Northern Ireland arrangements for the hearing of proceedings to which paragraph 12 applies are made within the meaning of that paragraph—

    (a) in the case of proceedings in the High Court for which provision is made by rules of court for setting down for trial, when the case is set down;

    (b) in the case of any proceedings, when a date for the trial or hearing is fixed.

14. [Scotland].

Appellate proceedings

15. Appellate proceedings are active from the time when they are commenced—

    (a) by application for leave to appeal or apply for review, or by notice of such an application;

    (b) by notice of appeal or of application for review;

    (c) by other originating process,

    until disposed of or abandoned, discontinued or withdrawn.

16. Where, in appellate proceedings relating to criminal proceedings, the court—

    (a) remits the case to the court below; or

    (b) orders a new trial or a *venire de novo*, or in Scotland grants authority to bring a new prosecution,

    any further or new proceedings which result shall be treated as active from the conclusion of the appellate proceedings.

B14.119 Prior to the enactment of these provisions, it had been held that the prejudging of court proceedings was necessarily contempt (see e.g., *A-G v Times Newspapers Ltd* [1974] AC 273), and this is still true of publications which create a real risk of prejudicing a fair trial and which are intended to influence jurors, to dissuade one of the parties from contesting the case, or otherwise to interfere with the proceedings (*A-G v Hislop* [1991] 1 QB 514); but in the absence of proof of such intent, it would have to be proved that the prejudgment or other comment created a substantial risk of serious prejudice etc. in respect of active proceedings (as defined in sch. 1). Strict liability will then apply, subject to qualifications and defences contained or preserved within the Contempt of Court Act 1981, ss. 3 to 5 (**B14.122** *et seq.*).

B14.120   **Substantial Risk of Prejudice**   The question whether a publication creates a substantial risk of serious prejudice etc. is ultimately one of fact (*Re Lonrho plc* [1990] 2 AC 154, per Lord Bridge at p. 208; *A-G v Times Newspapers Ltd* [2012] EWHC 3195 (Admin)). The creation of such a risk must accordingly be proved beyond reasonable doubt (*A-G v Unger* [1998] 1 Cr App R 308). 'Substantial' in this context does not mean 'weighty', but rather 'not insubstantial' or 'not minimal' (*A-G v News Group Newspapers Ltd* [1987] QB 1). Account may be taken of the likely effect of the publication on the parties, witnesses or court. Whilst it may sometimes be material, in assessing the risk of prejudice to any proceedings, that a defendant has already confessed or has intimated an intention to plead guilty, it would be most dangerous for publishers to rely on such considerations, because pleas may be changed and confessions retracted or excluded from evidence (*A-G v Unger*). Still less should a publisher assume that the weight of evidence against a defendant would place the outcome of any contested trial beyond doubt (*A-G v Unger*). The courts do however recognise that the proximity of the publication to any future trial may be an important consideration. The longer the interval between publication and trial, the less likely it is that any serious prejudice will be caused, especially if the publication contains nothing that could amount to inadmissible evidence (*A-G v News Group Newspapers Ltd*; *A-G v Independent Television News Ltd* [1995] 2 All ER 370; *A-G v Times Newspapers Ltd* [2012] EWHC 3195 (Admin); *A-G v Unger*). In contrast, the risk of prejudicing the court (and especially a jury) may be heightened by the vulnerability of the defendant, the high profile of the case or any inaccuracy in the reporting (*A-G v Unger*). The vilification of a suspect under arrest readily falls within the protective ambit of s. 2(2) as a potential impediment to the course of justice (*A-G v MGN Ltd* [2012] 1 WLR 2408).

B14.121   In considering the test under s. 2(2) the question is whether the publication would have given rise to a seriously arguable ground of appeal if the trial had been allowed to continue and had proceeded to conviction (*A-G v Birmingham Post and Mail* [1999] 4 All ER 49 at 371; *A-G v Associated Newspapers Ltd* [2012] EWHC 2029 (Admin) at [11]).

Where several prejudicial media accounts have been published, the conduct of each publisher must be looked at separately: the cumulative effect of the various publications cannot be lumped together. But if several newspapers etc. each publish prejudicial material, they cannot escape by contending that the damage has already been done by the others. It is sufficient that the latest publication has afforded an additional or further risk of prejudice or exacerbated and increased that risk (*A-G v Independent Television News* [1995] 2 All ER 370 at p. 381; *A-G v MGN Ltd* [1997] 1 All ER 456 at p. 460; *A-G v Associated Newspapers Ltd* [2012] EWHC 2029 (Admin) at [11]).

In *A-G v Associated Newspapers* an avalanche of material highlighting the depravity of the recently convicted serial child murderer, Levi Bellfield, appeared in the defendant's newspapers while the jury were still considering a further charge against him. This included material that had been ruled inadmissible at the trial. The jury was at once discharged and the publications were later found to have created substantial risk of prejudice within the scope of s. 2(2) even though the jury already knew many terrible things about Bellfield's character and had already convicted him of kidnapping and child murder.

Applied this way, s. 2(2) applies the right kind of balance for the purposes of the ECHR, Article 10 (*A-G v MGN Ltd* [2012] 1 WLR 2408 at [32] and *A-G v Associated Newspapers Ltd* at [11]).

Innocent Publication or Distribution

B14.122   **Contempt of Court Act 1981, s. 3**

    (1) A person is not guilty of contempt of court under the strict liability rule as the publisher of any matter to which that rule applies if at the time of publication (having taken all reasonable care) he does not know and has no reason to suspect that relevant proceedings are active.

    (2) A person is not guilty of contempt of court under the strict liability rule as the distributor of a publication containing any such matter if at the time of distribution (having taken all reasonable care) he does not know that it contains such matter and has no reason to suspect that it is likely to do so.

(3) The burden of proof of any fact tending to establish a defence a afforded by this section to any person lies upon that person.

This section falls short of providing a general 'no fault' defence. In particular it does not protect publishers who are aware of the proceedings, but blamelessly unaware of the prejudicial effect of the publication (*Evening Standard Co. Ltd* [1954] 1 QB 578).

Fair and Accurate Reports of Proceedings

A person is not guilty of contempt of court under the strict liability rule in respect of a fair and accurate report of legal proceedings held in public, published contemporaneously and in good faith (Contempt of Court Act 1981, s. 4(1)). As to the limitations on that defence and the power to order postponement of a report, see **D3.127** (where s. 4 is set out) and **B14.115**.

B14.123

Discussion of Public Affairs

B14.124

Contempt of Court Act 1981, s. 5

A publication made as or as part of a discussion in good faith of public affairs or other matters of general public interest is not to be treated as a contempt of court under the strict liability rule if the risk of impediment or prejudice to particular legal proceedings is merely incidental to the discussion.

Whereas the Contempt of Court Act 1981, s. 3, creates defences to charges of contempt, s. 5 follows ss. 2 and 4(1) in restricting the scope of the strict liability rule itself, and the burden of proof does not lie on the alleged contemnor. If the publication is part of a wider discussion, the publisher is guilty of contempt under the strict liability rule only if it is proved that there is a substantial risk of prejudice to active proceedings (s. 2) and that this is not merely incidental to the wider discussion. See generally *A-G v English* [1983] 1 AC 116.

If, in the course of a wider discussion, the publisher intends to influence the outcome of proceedings, then (even apart from the good faith issue) he may be guilty of contempt independently of the Act (see s. 6(c) at **B14.125**).

Contempt of Court Act 1981: General Provisions

B14.125

Contempt of Court Act 1981, ss. 6 and 7

6. Nothing in the foregoing provisions of this Act—
   (a) prejudices any defence available at common law to a charge of contempt of court under the strict liability rule;
   (b) implies that any publication is punishable as contempt of court under that rule which would not be so punishable apart from those provisions;
   (c) restricts liability for contempt of court in respect of conduct intended to impede or prejudice the administration of justice.
7. Proceedings for a contempt of court under the strict liability rule (other than Scottish proceedings) shall not be instituted except by or with the consent of the A-G or on the motion of a court having jurisdiction to deal with it.

Strict Liability: Where the Act Does Not Apply

It is possible (but, it is submitted, unlikely) that strict liability may apply in certain circumstances not covered by the Contempt of Court Act 1981. This is because the Act only defines the scope of the strict liability rule insofar as it applies to conduct tending to interfere with particular proceedings. In *A-G v Newspaper Publishing plc* [1988] Ch 333, Sir John Donaldson MR suggested that examples of possible strict liability outside the scope of the Contempt of Court Act 1981 could include retaliation against a person who has given evidence in previous proceedings (which could themselves no longer be affected) and marrying a ward of court without the court's consent. The better view, however, would seem to be that such contempts do not carry strict liability. A person who punishes another for giving evidence or serving on a jury

B14.126

must at the very least be reckless as to the implications of his conduct on the due administration of justice, and this recklessness is the more probable basis of his liability. As for the wardship example (or other cases of interference with a court order), there is clear authority to the effect that recklessness as to the existence of the order is the minimum *mens rea* that will suffice (*Re F (A Minor) (Publication of Information)* [1977] Fam 58).

Cases in which Intent is Required by the Contempt of Court Act 1981

B14.127 Where the Contempt of Court Act 1981 expressly rules out any question of strict liability (e.g., in respect of publications tending to prejudice proceedings which may be forthcoming but which are not active), it is clear that a specific intent must be present. In *A-G v Newspaper Publishing plc* [1988] Ch 333, Lloyd LJ said:

> In cases covered by the Act to which the strict liability rule does not apply, there is no room for a state of mind which falls short of intention. There is no middle way.

> I would therefore hold that the *mens rea* required in the present case is an intent to interfere with the course of justice. As in other branches of the criminal law, that intent may exist, even though there is no desire to interfere with the course of justice. Nor need it be the sole intent. It may be inferred, even though there is no overt proof. The more obvious the interference with the course of justice, the more readily will the requisite intent be inferred.

See also *A-G v Newspaper Publishing plc* [1997] 3 All ER 159 per Lord Bingham CJ at p. 936.

Appeals

B14.128 Appeals in contempt cases are usually governed by the Administration of Justice Act 1960, s. 13. An appeal against a finding of criminal contempt lies as of right. Leave is not required (*Hourigan* [2003] EWCA Crim 2306).

Administration of Justice Act 1960, s. 13

(1) Subject to the provisions of this section, an appeal shall lie under this section from any order or decision of a court in the exercise of jurisdiction to punish for contempt of court (including criminal contempt); and in relation to any such order or decision the provisions of this section shall have effect in substitution for any other enactment relating to appeals in civil or criminal proceedings.

(2) An appeal under this section shall lie in any case at the instance of the defendant and, in the case of an application for committal or attachment, at the instance of the applicant; and the appeal shall lie—
   (a) from an order or decision of any inferior court not referred to in the next following paragraph, to the High Court;
   (b) from an order or decision of the county court or any other inferior court from which appeals generally lie to the Court of Appeal, and from an order or decision (other than a decision on an appeal under this section) of a single judge of the High Court, or of any court having the powers of the High Court or of a judge of that court, to the Court of Appeal;
   (bb) from an order or decision of the Crown Court to the Court of Appeal;
   (c) from a decision of a single judge of the High Court on an appeal under this section, from an order or decision of a divisional court or the Court of Appeal (including a decision of either of those courts on an appeal under this section), and from an order or decision of the...Courts-Martial Appeal Court, to the Supreme Court.

(3) The court to which an appeal is brought under this section may reverse or vary the order or decision of the court below and make such other order as may be just; and without prejudice to the inherent powers of any court referred to in subsection (2) of this section, provision may be made by rules of court for authorising the release on bail of an appellant under this section.

(4) Subsections (2) to (4) of section 1 and section 2 of this Act shall apply to an appeal to the Supreme Court under this section as they apply to an appeal to the Supreme Court under the said section 1, except that so much of the said subsection (2) as restricts the grant of leave to appeal shall apply only where the decision of the court below is a decision on appeal to that court under this section.

(5) In this section 'court' includes any tribunal or person having power to punish for contempt; and references in this section to an order or decision of a court in the exercise of jurisdiction to punish for contempt of court include references—

(a) to an order or decision of the High Court, the Crown Court or the county court under any enactment enabling that court to deal with an offence as if it were contempt of court;

(b) to an order or decision of the county court, or of any court having the powers of the county court, under section 14, 92 or 118 of the County Courts Act 1984;

(c) to an order or decision of a magistrates' court under subsection (3) of section 63 of the Magistrates' Courts Act 1980,

(d) to an order or decision (except one made in Scotland or Northern Ireland) of the Court Martial, the Summary Appeal Court or the Service Civilian Court under section 309 of the Armed Forces Act 2006,

but do not include references to orders under section 5 of the Debtors Act 1869, or under any provision of the Magistrates' Courts Act 1980, or the County Courts Act 1984, except those referred to in paragraphs (b) and (c) of this subsection and except section 38 and 142 of the last mentioned Act so far as those sections confer jurisdiction in respect of contempt of court.

(6) This section does not apply to a conviction or sentence in respect of which an appeal lies under Part I of the Criminal Appeal Act 1968, or to a decision of the Criminal Division of the Court of Appeal under that Part of that Act.

Section 13(1) and (2)(bb) give the Court of Appeal jurisdiction to hear an appeal against a refusal of bail by the Crown Court pending the determination of contempt proceedings against him (*Serumaga* [2005] 2 All ER 160). **B14.129**

Section 13(2) was considered by the Court of Appeal in *A-G v Hislop* [1991] 1 QB 514. It was held that the words 'application for committal or attachment' refer to the original application, rather than to the appeal itself: in other words, it gives a right of appeal to an unsuccessful applicant for a committal or attachment order. It does not matter if the applicant is actually seeking to have the alleged contemnor fined rather than committed to prison (this in any case being a matter for the court), nor if the alleged contemnor is a corporation which could not be committed or attached.

Appeals from the Crown Court were originally heard by the Civil Division of the Court of Appeal, but are now, more appropriately, heard by the Criminal Division; see the Senior Courts Act 1981, s. 53(2)(b). Applying normal principles of statutory interpretation, the reference to the Court of Appeal in s. 13(2)(c) would be a reference to the civil division of that court (Senior Courts Act 1981, sch. 4, para. 3) but that would have the quite unintended effect of precluding any contempt appeal from the criminal division to the Supreme Court, and in *OB v Director of the Serious Fraud Office* [2012] 3 All ER 1017 the Court of Appeal held that this error should be judicially rectified in accordance with principles established in *Inco Europe v First Choice Distribution* [2000] 2 All ER 109. As to appeals from magistrates' courts, see *Haw v City of Westminster Magistrates' Court* [2008] QB 888 (see **B14.86**).

BREACH OF NON-MOLESTATION OR
RESTRAINING ORDERS

The DVCVA 2004, s. 1, inserted s. 42A into the Family Law Act 1996. This makes breach of a non-molestation order (defined in s. 42 of the 1996 Act) a criminal offence, but only if committed on or after 1 July 2007 (see the DVCVA 2004, sch. 12, para. 1) and not where a power of arrest under the Family Law Act 1996, s. 47, has been attached to a non-molestation order before that date, unless that power of arrest no longer has effect (Domestic Violence, Crime and Victims Act (Commencement No. 9 and Transitional Provisions) Order 2007 (SI 2007 No. 1845), art. 3). It remains possible for breach of a non-molestation order to be dealt with as a civil contempt of court, but s. 42A(3) and (4) prevent a defendant being punished twice for the same breach. **B14.130**

Family Law Act 1996, s. 42A

(1) A person who without reasonable excuse does anything that he is prohibited from doing by a non-molestation order is guilty of an offence.

(2) In the case of a non-molestation order made by virtue of section 45(1), a person can be guilty of an offence under this section only in respect of conduct engaged in at a time when he was aware of the existence of the order.

(3) Where a person is convicted of an offence under this section in respect of any conduct, that conduct is not punishable as a contempt of court.

(4) A person cannot be convicted of an offence under this section in respect of any conduct which has been punished as a contempt of court.

(5) A person guilty of an offence under this section is liable—

   (a) on conviction on indictment, to imprisonment for a term not exceeding five years, or a fine, or both;

   (b) on summary conviction, to imprisonment for a term not exceeding 12 months, or a fine not exceeding the statutory maximum, or both.

(6) A reference in any enactment to proceedings under this Part, or to an order under this Part, does not include a reference to proceedings for an offence under this section or to an order made in such proceedings.

'Enactment' includes an enactment contained in subordinate legislation within the meaning of the Interpretation Act 1978.

The penalties that may be imposed for an offence under s. 42A are identical to those that may be imposed under the Protection from Harassment Act 1997, s. 5(5), for breach of restraining orders made under ss. 5 or 5A of that Act, as to which see the definitive sentencing guideline, *Breach of a Protective Order*, considered at E21.29 and set out in the Supplement at SG-45.

Section B15   Corruption

THE BRIBERY ACT 2010 AND THE OLD LAW

B15.1 The Bribery Act 2010 was brought into force on 1 July 2011. Section 17 and sch. 2 abolished the common-law offences of bribery and embracery, and repealed the Public Bodies Corrupt Practices Act 1889 and the Prevention of Corruption Acts 1889 to 1916, but not the Honours (Prevention of Abuses) Act 1925 or the common-law offence of misconduct in public office. New offences were created by the Bribery Act 2010, ss. 1, 2, 6 and 7, subject to transitional provisions set out in s. 19(5) and (6).

Bribery Act 2010, s. 19

(5) This Act does not affect any liability, investigation, legal proceeding or penalty for or in respect
    of—
    (a) a common law offence mentioned in subsection (1) of section 17 which is committed
        wholly or partly before the coming into force of that subsection in relation to such an
        offence, or
    (b) an offence under the Public Bodies Corrupt Practices Act 1889 or the Prevention of
        Corruption Act 1906 committed wholly or partly before the coming into force of the
        repeal of the Act by schedule 2 to this Act.
(6) For the purposes of subsection (5) an offence is partly committed before a particular time if any
    act or omission which forms part of the offence takes place before that time.

The new offences have no retrospective effect and thus apply only to things done on or after the appointed date. But some overlap between the old and new law remains possible. If, for example, P offered a bribe to R (a public official) before the commencement date, but R agreed to receive it only on or after that date, R may then be charged with the new offence of 'being bribed' (Bribery Act 2010, s. 2, see **B15.11** *et seq.*); whereas P would have to be charged under the old law with offering that bribe, and R might also face charges under the old law if there is evidence that he 'corruptly solicited' the bribe before commencement (see the Public Bodies Corrupt Practices Act 1889, s. 1 at **B15.32**). If, however, the promised bribe was eventually given and received after commencement, there should be no difficulty in prosecuting both parties under the new law, without any need to resort to transitional provisions.

OFFENCES UNDER THE BRIBERY ACT 2010

The Structure of the Act

B15.2 The Bribery Act 2010 came into force on 1 July 2011. As to commencement, repeals and transitional provisions, see **B15.1**. The main or 'general' offences under the Act can be divided into the bribery of another person (contrary to s. 1) and being bribed (contrary to s. 2). These are

869

separate and distinct offences because one can (for example) offer or request a bribe without the prior knowledge or agreement of the person who is intended to receive or provide it. The two general offences are supplemented by s. 6, which creates a discrete offence of bribing a foreign public official, and by s. 7, under which a commercial organisation may incur criminal liability if a person who performs services for it (such as an agent or employee) commits bribery on its behalf and it cannot prove that it had adopted appropriate procedures to prevent such conduct.

The general offences apply equally to bribery in the public sector and to bribery in connection with a business, trade or profession, thus largely eliminating the problematic distinctions that are discussed at **B15.31**. The Act bases the new concept of bribery on the offer, promise or provision (or request, agreement to receive or acceptance) of a financial or other advantage for the purpose of inducing or rewarding the 'improper performance of a relevant function or activity'. It applies to individuals in the public service of the Crown as it applies to other individuals (s. 16), although there is a specific defence in s. 13 in respect of conduct that is necessary for the proper exercise of any function of one of the intelligence services, or for the proper exercise of any function of the armed forces when engaged on active service.

Meaning of Terms

B15.3 Sections 3 and 4 of the Bribery Act 2010 define 'relevant function or activity' and 'improper performance' for the purposes of ss. 1 and 2, and are themselves supplemented by s. 5, which further defines the 'expectation test' used in those provisions. Between them, these provisions adopt and apply 'threshold' and 'wrongfulness' tests developed by the Law Commission, on whose 2008 Report, *Reforming Bribery* (LC 313) the Act is closely based. They are designed to ensure that personal or family arrangements and matters of private morality are kept outside the ambit of the new law, and to distinguish improper bribery on the one hand from legitimate rewards or inducements, on the other.

B15.4   **Bribery Act 2010, ss. 3, 4 and 5**

3.—(1) For the purposes of this Act a function or activity is a relevant function or activity if—
    (a) it falls within subsection (2), and
    (b) meets one or more of conditions A to C.
(2) The following functions and activities fall within this subsection—
    (a) any function of a public nature,
    (b) any activity connected with a business,
    (c) any activity performed in the course of a person's employment,
    (d) any activity performed by or on behalf of a body of persons (whether corporate or unincorporate).
(3) Condition A is that a person performing the function or activity is expected to perform it in good faith.
(4) Condition B is that a person performing the function or activity is expected to perform it impartially.
(5) Condition C is that a person performing the function or activity is in a position of trust by virtue of performing it.
(6) A function or activity is a relevant function or activity even if it—
    (a) has no connection with the United Kingdom, and
    (b) is performed in a country or territory outside the United Kingdom.
(7) In this section 'business' includes trade or profession.
4.—(1) For the purposes of this Act a relevant function or activity—
    (a) is performed improperly if it is performed in breach of a relevant expectation, and
    (b) is to be treated as being performed improperly if there is a failure to perform the function or activity and that failure is itself a breach of a relevant expectation.
(2) In subsection (1) 'relevant expectation'—
    (a) in relation to a function or activity which meets condition A or B, means the expectation mentioned in the condition concerned, and

(b) in relation to a function or activity which meets condition C, means any expectation as to the manner in which, or the reasons for which, the function or activity will be performed that arises from the position of trust mentioned in that condition.

(3) Anything that a person does (or omits to do) arising from or in connection with that person's past performance of a relevant function or activity is to be treated for the purposes of this Act as being done (or omitted) by that person in the performance of that function or activity.

5.—(1) For the purposes of sections 3 and 4, the test of what is expected is a test of what a reasonable person in the United Kingdom would expect in relation to the performance of the type of function or activity concerned.

(2) In deciding what such a person would expect in relation to the performance of a function or activity where the performance is not subject to the law of any part of the United Kingdom, any local custom or practice is to be disregarded unless it is permitted or required by the written law applicable to the country or territory concerned.

(3) In subsection (2) 'written law' means law contained in—

(a) any written constitution, or provision made by or under legislation, applicable to the country or territory concerned, or

(b) any judicial decision which is so applicable and is evidenced in published written sources.

B15.5 The offer, request, provision or receipt of a financial or other advantage may thus fall beyond the scope of the new offences for a number of reasons. One possibility is that the offer, etc., is not intended to influence or reward the conduct of any public, business-related, employment or corporate function or activity, or any function or activity carried on by an unincorporated body of persons. But even if it is intended to influence or reward the performance of some such function or activity, the new general offences cannot be engaged unless at least one of the conditions in s. 3(3), (4) or (5) is also satisfied. There must in other words be an expectation (as defined in s. 5) that the functions in question will be carried out in good faith (condition A), or impartially (condition B), or the person performing it must be in a position of trust (condition C). In the absence of any such expectation, there can be no 'improper' performance of the relevant function or activity, as defined in s. 4. If however those tests are satisfied, it does not matter whether the function or activity in question was, or was intended to be, performed within the UK.

The Act does not attempt to define a 'financial or other advantage' (an expression also used in s. 6). If any issue arises as to whether something amounts to such an advantage for the purpose of the Act, it must be determined as a matter of common sense by the court or jury.

Commission Payments and Corporate Hospitality

B15.6 The Law Commission and the Government each took the view that the provision or acceptance of 'corporate hospitality' in the business world does not ordinarily involve anything capable of amounting to a bribe. Although such hospitality may involve the provision and acceptance of 'financial or other advantages', there will ordinarily be no breach of any relevant expectation about the way that the recipients will behave. This is also the stated view of the DPP and the Director of the Serious Fraud Office, who issued joint guidance in March 2011 on prosecutorial decision-making under the Bribery Act 2010 (see www.cps.gov.uk/legal/a_to_c/bribery_act_2010/). There may, however, be circumstances in which the sheer scale of the hospitality is such as to suggest the opposite, and in other cases the offer or acceptance of 'hospitality' (e.g., to or by a judge or some other person acting in a position of trust or impartiality) would clearly be improper.

Similarly, an agent or broker who acts for a buyer of goods or services, but seeks or receives a commission payment from the supplier, will not ordinarily be regarded as acting improperly, but the prospect of earning such commission does create a potential conflict of interest and a prosecution for bribery might be possible if it can be proved that the purpose was to induce the agent to ignore the best interests of his client in order to maximise his own earnings.

GENERAL OFFENCES: BRIBING ANOTHER PERSON

Definition

B15.7   Bribery Act 2010, s. 1

(1) A person ('P') is guilty of an offence if either of the following cases applies.
(2) Case 1 is where—
   (a) P offers, promises or gives a financial or other advantage to another person, and
   (b) P intends the advantage—
      (i) to induce a person to perform improperly a relevant function or activity, or
      (ii) to reward a person for the improper performance of such a function or activity.
(3) Case 2 is where—
   (a) P offers, promises or gives a financial or other advantage to another person, and
   (b) P knows or believes that the acceptance of the advantage would itself constitute the improper performance of a relevant function or activity.
(4) In case 1 it does not matter whether the person to whom the advantage is offered, promised or given is the same person as the person who is to perform, or has performed, the function or activity concerned.
(5) In cases 1 and 2 it does not matter whether the advantage is offered, promised or given by P directly or through a third party.

Procedure

B15.8   An offence under the Bribery Act 2010, s. 1, is triable either way. When tried on indictment it is normally a class 2C or 3 offence (depending on the complexity of the offence), but see CPD XIII, para. B (see Supplement, **PD-97**) for the additional factors that the court considers on allocation. No prosecution may be instituted in England and Wales except by or with the consent of the DPP or the Director of the Serious Fraud Office (Bribery Act 2010, s. 10(1)). The relevant Director must exercise this function in person, unless he is incapacitated or out of the country, in which case he may give written authorisation to another person to exercise (but not sub-delegate) that function (s. 10(4) and (5)). For guidance setting out the Directors' approach to prosecutorial decision-making in respect of offences under the Act, see www.cps.gov.uk/legal/a_to_c/bribery_act_2010/.

Some cases potentially falling within s. 1 may alternatively be prosecuted as offences under s. 6 (bribery of a foreign official: see **B15.15**).

Sentence

B15.9   The maximum penalty for an offence under s. 1 is ten years' imprisonment and/or a fine. On summary conviction the maximum penalty is six months' imprisonment, and/or a fine not exceeding the statutory maximum (Bribery Act 2010, s. 11). In *Patel* [2013] 1 Cr App R (S) 269 (48) the offender, a court clerk, had solicited bribes from motoring offenders due to appear before the magistrates' court. He offered to help avoid conviction in return for a payment of £500. He pleaded guilty to bribery and to misconduct in public office and was sentenced to three years' imprisonment for the former offence and six years for the latter, concurrently. The Court of Appeal reduced the overall sentence to four years.

The definitive sentencing guideline, *Fraud, Bribery and Money Laundering Offences* (see Supplement, **SG-500**) is applicable. The guideline applies to individual offenders aged 18 and over and organisations. It applies to all offenders sentenced on or after 1 October 2014 regardless of the date of the offence. There is a separate part of the guideline applicable to corporate offenders.

Elements

B15.10 The Bribery Act 2010, s. 1, appears to create a single umbrella offence that can be committed in either of two main ways (case 1 or case 2). In either case it is a conduct crime. P's offer, gift or promise need not be accepted by the person to whom it is offered and in a 'case 1' scenario it need not, even if accepted, result in the improper performance of any relevant function or activity. P must however intend such a result. If P offers a financial or other advantage to R, who undertakes no relevant function or activity, on the understanding that R will then seek to approach and influence a third party (S) who does, the criminality of P's conduct under s. 1 will depend on whether he intends that S would be induced to act improperly within the meaning of s. 4. If he does not intend to corrupt S, it is irrelevant whether P views his payment to R as a bribe or whether R accepts or receives it on that basis.

P may have a defence under s. 13 if he can prove (on a balance of probabilities) that his conduct was necessary for the proper exercise of any function of one of the intelligence services, or for the proper exercise of any function of the armed forces when engaged on active service. By s. 13(6), this defence extends to secondary participation and inchoate offences, but it is excluded in cases that also infringe s. 6 (bribery of a foreign official: see **B15.15**).

As to jurisdiction over cases with a foreign element, see s. 12(1)–(4) at **B15.24**. As to the liability of senior officers of corporations (or persons purporting to act as such) for offences committed by the corporation with their consent or connivance, see s. 14 at **B15.25**.

GENERAL OFFENCES: BEING BRIBED

Definition

Bribery Act 2010, s. 2   **B15.11**

(1) A person ('R') is guilty of an offence if any of the following cases applies.
(2) Case 3 is where R requests, agrees to receive or accepts a financial or other advantage intending that, in consequence, a relevant function or activity should be performed improperly (whether by R or another person).
(3) Case 4 is where—
    (a) R requests, agrees to receive or accepts a financial or other advantage, and
    (b) the request, agreement or acceptance itself constitutes the improper performance by R of a relevant function or activity.
(4) Case 5 is where R requests, agrees to receive or accepts a financial or other advantage as a reward for the improper performance (whether by R or another person) of a relevant function or activity.
(5) Case 6 is where, in anticipation of or in consequence of R requesting, agreeing to receive or accepting a financial or other advantage, a relevant function or activity is performed improperly—
    (a) by R, or
    (b) by another person at R's request or with R's assent or acquiescence.
(6) In cases 3 to 6 it does not matter—
    (a) whether R requests, agrees to receive or accepts (or is to request, agree to receive or accept) the advantage directly or through a third party,
    (b) whether the advantage is (or is to be) for the benefit of R or another person.
(7) In cases 4 to 6 it does not matter whether R knows or believes that the performance of the function or activity is improper.
(8) In case 6, where a person other than R is performing the function or activity, it also does not matter whether that person knows or believes that the performance of the function or activity is improper.

Procedure

An offence under the Bribery Act 2010, s. 2, is triable either way. When tried on indictment it is   **B15.12**
normally a class 2C or 3 offence (depending on the complexity of the offence), but see CPD XIII, para. B (see Supplement, **PD-97**) for the additional factors that the court considers on allocation. No prosecution may be instituted in England and Wales except by or with the consent of the DPP or the Director of the Serious Fraud Office (Bribery Act 2010, s. 10(1)). For s. 10(4) and (5) and the Directors' published guidance, see **B15.8**.

Sentence

The maximum penalty for an offence under s. 2 is ten years' imprisonment and/or a fine. On   **B15.13**
summary conviction the maximum penalty is six months' imprisonment, and/or a fine not exceeding the statutory maximum (Bribery Act 2010, s. 11).

The definitive sentencing guideline, *Fraud, Bribery and Money Laundering Offences* (see Supplement, **SG-500**) is applicable. The guideline applies to individual offenders aged 18 and over and organisations. It applies to all offenders sentenced on or after 1 October 2014 regardless of the date of the offence. There is a separate part of the guideline applicable to corporate offenders.

Elements

B15.14 Section 2 of the Bribery Act 2010 creates a single umbrella offence that can be committed in a number of different ways, the principal forms of which are labelled as cases 3, 4, 5 and 6. These will ordinarily be conduct crimes. This is true even of some offences falling within case 6, which reflects the Law Commission's view that, 'improper conduct may come before the advantage is conferred, and the other way around' (LC 313 at para. 3.197). A case 6 offence may however take the form of a result crime if what is alleged is that a relevant function or activity was performed improperly by a third person at R's request, etc., in consequence of R requesting, agreeing to receive or accepting a financial or other advantage.

In a case 4 scenario, R must himself be a person who performs (or is to perform) the relevant function or activity, as defined in s. 3, but in each of the other scenarios falling within s. 2 he need not be that person. There must however be a link between the advantage received or requested etc. by R and the improper performance (actual or intended) of a relevant function or activity by R or by some other person. In a case 3 scenario, R must intend that he or someone else will improperly perform a relevant function activity as a consequence of the advantage R has received, requested or agreed to receive; and in a case 5 scenario R must request, agree to receive or accept a reward for some such improper performance.

Mens rea is addressed in s. 2(7). D can commit an offence falling within cases 4, 5 or 6 without being aware of the wrongfulness of what is being done or proposed, but such awareness clearly *is* required in cases falling only within case 3.

P has a defence under s. 13 if he can prove (on a balance of probabilities) that his conduct was necessary for the proper exercise of any function of one of the intelligence services, or for the proper exercise of any function of the armed forces when engaged on active service. This defence also extends to secondary participation and inchoate offences (s. 13(6)).

As to jurisdiction over cases with a foreign element, see s. 12(1)–(4) at **B15.24**. As to the liability of senior officers of corporations (or persons purporting to act as such) for offences committed by the corporation with their consent or connivance, see s. 14 at **B15.25**.

BRIBERY OF FOREIGN PUBLIC OFFICIALS

Definition

B15.15   Bribery Act 2010, s. 6

(1) A person ('P') who bribes a foreign public official ('F') is guilty of an offence if P's intention is to influence F in F's capacity as a foreign public official.

(2) P must also intend to obtain or retain—
   (a) business, or
   (b) an advantage in the conduct of business.

(3) P bribes F if, and only if—
   (a) directly or through a third party, P offers, promises or gives any financial or other advantage—
      (i) to F, or
      (ii) to another person at F's request or with F's assent or acquiescence, and
   (b) F is neither permitted nor required by the written law applicable to F to be influenced in F's capacity as a foreign public official by the offer, promise or gift.

(4) References in this section to influencing F in F's capacity as a foreign public official mean influencing F in the performance of F's functions as such an official, which includes—
   (a) any omission to exercise those functions, and
   (b) any use of F's position as such an official, even if not within F's authority.

(5) 'Foreign public official' means an individual who—

   (a) holds a legislative, administrative or judicial position of any kind, whether appointed or elected, of a country or territory outside the United Kingdom (or any subdivision of such a country or territory),

   (b) exercises a public function—

      (i) for or on behalf of a country or territory outside the United Kingdom (or any subdivision of such a country or territory), or

      (ii) for any public agency or public enterprise of that country or territory (or subdivision), or

   (c) is an official or agent of a public international organisation.

(6) 'Public international organisation' means an organisation whose members are any of the following—

   (a) countries or territories,

   (b) governments of countries or territories,

   (c) other public international organisations,

   (d) a mixture of any of the above.

(7) For the purposes of subsection (3)(b), the written law applicable to F is—

   (a) where the performance of the functions of F which P intends to influence would be subject to the law of any part of the United Kingdom, the law of that part of the United Kingdom,

   (b) where paragraph (a) does not apply and F is an official or agent of a public international organisation, the applicable written rules of that organisation,

   (c) where paragraphs (a) and (b) do not apply, the law of the country or territory in relation to which F is a foreign public official so far as that law is contained in—

      (i) any written constitution, or provision made by or under legislation, applicable to the country or territory concerned, or

      (ii) any judicial decision which is so applicable and is evidenced in published written sources.

(8) For the purposes of this section, a trade or profession is a business.

Procedure

An offence under the Bribery Act 2010, s. 6, is triable either way. When tried on indictment it is normally a class 2C or 3 offence (depending on the complexity of the offence), but see CPD XIII, para. B (see Supplement, **PD-97**) for the additional factors that the court considers on allocation. No prosecution may be instituted in England and Wales except by or with the consent of the DPP or the Director of the Serious Fraud Office (s. 10(1)). For s. 10(4) and (5) and the Directors' published guidance, see **B15.8**.   **B15.16**

Sentence

The maximum penalty for an offence under s. 6 is ten years' imprisonment and/or a fine. On summary conviction the maximum penalty is six months' imprisonment, and/or a fine not exceeding the statutory maximum (Bribery Act 2010, s. 11).   **B15.17**

The definitive sentencing guideline, *Fraud, Bribery and Money Laundering Offences* (see Supplement, **SG-500**) is applicable. The guideline applies to individual offenders aged 18 and over and organisations. It applies to all offenders sentenced on or after 1 October 2014 regardless of the date of the offence. There is a separate part of the guideline applicable to corporate offenders.

Elements

The bribery of a public official (as defined in the Bribery Act 2010, s. 6(5)) may in some circumstances fall equally within the ambit of the general offence of bribery created by s. 1 (see **B15.7**) and the receipt of a bribe by such an official (which is not dealt with in s. 6) may sometimes fall within the ambit of s. 2 (see **B15.11**). The discrete offence created by s. 6, which shares the same territorial and extra-territorial ambit as the general offences, was included in order to ensure that the UK would comply with its obligations under the OECD *Convention on Combating Bribery of Foreign Public Officials in International Business Transactions*, and many of its terms are accordingly based on the terms of that Convention. The s. 6 offence can be developed and interpreted in light of those obligations and in line with international developments in the interpretation of the Convention without forcing the courts to develop or interpret the general offences in the same way.   **B15.18**

The s. 6 offence has a narrower focus than the general offence created by s. 1, but will in some circumstances be easier to prove. P must act with the intent specified in s. 6(2) and must intend to influence the conduct of the official (F) in the performance of his functions, but it need not be proved that P intended to induce or reward any 'improper performance' of those functions. No reference need be made to ss. 3, 4 or 5 of the Act. An attempt to influence F (directly or indirectly) through the offer or gift of a financial or other advantage will be lawful only where F is 'permitted or required by the written law applicable to F to be influenced in his capacity as a foreign public official by the offer, promise or gift'.

B15.19   The advice of the Law Commission (at para. 5.76) was that a person who is anxious to avoid any infringement of this provision can almost always rely on one simple rule of thumb: 'Do not intentionally give advantages to foreign public officials, to gain or retain business, without a legal justification.' In some countries, however, 'facilitation payments' are routinely expected if officials are to perform the very functions that might legitimately be expected of them. In such circumstances, a prosecution for bribery brought under s. 1 might result in acquittal on the basis that no 'improper performance' by F was being encouraged, but a prosecution brought under s. 6 might well succeed, on the basis that the payment was nevertheless intended to influence F. This indeed is the firm view of the DPP and the Director of the Serious Fraud Office, although the guidance issued by the Directors (see **B15.8**) is that in some such cases (e.g., those involving small payments or payments made under duress) the public interest may not always favour prosecution.

As to jurisdiction over bribery cases with a foreign element, see s. 12(1)–(4) at **B15.24**. As to the liability of senior officers of corporations (or persons purporting to act as such) for offences committed by the corporation with their consent or connivance, see s. 14 at **B15.25**.

FAILURE OF COMMERCIAL ORGANISATIONS TO PREVENT BRIBERY

Definition

B15.20   Bribery Act 2010, ss. 7 and 8

7.—(1) A relevant commercial organisation ('C') is guilty of an offence under this section if a person ('A') associated with C bribes another person intending—
  (a) to obtain or retain business for C, or
  (b) to obtain or retain an advantage in the conduct of business for C.
(2) But it is a defence for C to prove that C had in place adequate procedures designed to prevent persons associated with C from undertaking such conduct.
(3) For the purposes of this section, A bribes another person if, and only if, A—
  (a) is, or would be, guilty of an offence under section 1 or 6 (whether or not A has been prosecuted for such an offence), or
  (b) would be guilty of such an offence if section 12(2)(c) and (4) were omitted.
(4) See section 8 for the meaning of a person associated with C and see section 9 for a duty on the Secretary of State to publish guidance.
(5) In this section—
  'partnership' means—
  (a) a partnership within the Partnership Act 1890, or
  (b) a limited partnership registered under the Limited Partnerships Act 1907, or a firm or entity of a similar character formed under the law of a country or territory outside the United Kingdom,
  'relevant commercial organisation' means—
  (a) a body which is incorporated under the law of any part of the United Kingdom and which carries on a business (whether there or elsewhere),
  (b) any other body corporate (wherever incorporated) which carries on a business, or part of a business, in any part of the United Kingdom,
  (c) a partnership which is formed under the law of any part of the United Kingdom and which carries on a business (whether there or elsewhere), or

(d) any other partnership (wherever formed) which carries on a business, or part of a business, in any part of the United Kingdom,

and, for the purposes of this section, a trade or profession is a business.

8.—(1) For the purposes of section 7, a person ('A') is associated with C if (disregarding any bribe under consideration) A is a person who performs services for or on behalf of C.

(2) The capacity in which A performs services for or on behalf of C does not matter.

(3) Accordingly A may (for example) be C's employee, agent or subsidiary.

(4) Whether or not A is a person who performs services for or on behalf of C is to be determined by reference to all the relevant circumstances and not merely by reference to the nature of the relationship between A and C.

(5) But if A is an employee of C, it is to be presumed unless the contrary is shown that A is a person who performs services for or on behalf of C.

Procedure

An offence under the Bribery Act 2010, s. 7, is triable only on indictment (s. 11(3)). No **B15.21** prosecution may be instituted in England and Wales except by or with the consent of the DPP or the Director of the Serious Fraud Office (s. 10(1)). For s. 10(4) and (5) and the Directors' published guidance, see **B15.8**.

An offence is committed under s. 7 irrespective of whether the acts or omissions which form part of the offence take place in the UK or elsewhere. Where no such acts or omissions take place in the UK, proceedings for the offence may be taken at any place in the UK (s. 12(5) and (6)).

Special rules apply to the prosecution of a partnership (as defined in s. 7(5)). Proceedings for an offence under s. 7 must be brought in the name of the partnership (not in that of any of the partners) and for the purposes of such proceedings the CJA 1925, s. 33, the MCA 1980, sch. 3, and the CrimPR, part 4 (service of documents), apply as if the partnership were a body corporate (Bribery Act 2010, s. 15).

Sentence

A relevant commercial organisation convicted of an offence under s. 7 is liable to a fine (Bribery Act **B15.22** 2010, s. 11(3)). A fine imposed on a partnership is to be paid out of partnership assets (s. 15(3)).

The definitive sentencing guideline, *Fraud, Bribery and Money Laundering Offences* (see Supplement, **SG-504**) is applicable. It applies to all offenders sentenced on or after 1 October 2014 regardless of the date of the offence. The guidance is to be found in the part of the guideline applicable to corporate offenders.

Elements

The offence created by the Bribery Act 2010, s. 7 is not an offence of negligence, but an offence **B15.23** of strict liability, subject to a due diligence (or 'adequate procedures') defence contained in s. 7(2) that must be proved by C on a balance of probabilities. If no such defence is offered, C may be convicted without any evidence of fault on its part.

The prosecution must however prove that the associated person (A) is guilty of bribery committed on C's behalf, contrary to s. 1 or s. 6, or that he would have been so guilty but for the fact that his acts were committed abroad and he himself has no 'close connection with the United Kingdom' as defined in s. 12 (see **B15.24**).

In accordance with the Bribery Act 2010, s. 9, the Secretary of State has published guidance on procedures that relevant commercial organisations should put in place to prevent bribery by persons associated with them — the so-called 'six principles' (see www.justice.gov.uk/legislation/bribery). These are not intended to be prescriptive and lack the force of law, but evidence of compliance with the six principles will inevitably assist a company or organisation that faces, or might otherwise face, a charge under s. 7. The six principles can be summarised as:

1. top-level commitment — senior management should provide leadership and demonstrate commitment to the prevention of bribery;

2. proportionality — greater efforts to prevent bribery may be expected of larger organisations and those exposed to potentially corrupt overseas markets, and/or high-risk transactions etc.;

3. risk assessment — research may be needed to assess the risks relating to markets and clients etc. with whom business is transacted;

4. due diligence — this is linked to risk assessment and may be linked to due diligence procedures familiar in other contexts;

5. communication (including training) — relevant employees etc. should be made aware of the law and receive training proportionate to the risks involved;

6. monitoring and review — this may involve internal and/or external review mechanisms that are proportionate to the organisation and the risks to which it is exposed.

TERRITORIAL AND EXTRA-TERRITORIAL APPLICATION

B15.24

Bribery Act 2010, s. 12

(1) An offence is committed under section 1, 2 or 6 in England and Wales, Scotland or Northern Ireland if any act or omission which forms part of the offence takes place in that part of the United Kingdom.

(2) Subsection (3) applies if—

    (a) no act or omission which forms part of an offence under section 1, 2 or 6 takes place in the United Kingdom,

    (b) a person's acts or omissions done or made outside the United Kingdom would form part of such an offence if done or made in the United Kingdom, and

    (c) that person has a close connection with the United Kingdom.

(3) In such a case—

    (a) the acts or omissions form part of the offence referred to in subsection (2)(a), and

    (b) proceedings for the offence may be taken at any place in the United Kingdom.

(4) For the purposes of subsection (2)(c) a person has a close connection with the United Kingdom if, and only if, the person was one of the following at the time the acts or omissions concerned were done or made—

    (a) a British citizen,

    (b) a British overseas territories citizen,

    (c) a British National (Overseas),

    (d) a British Overseas citizen,

    (e) a person who under the British Nationality Act 1981 was a British subject,

    (f) a British protected person within the meaning of that Act,

    (g) an individual ordinarily resident in the United Kingdom,

    (h) a body incorporated under the law of any part of the United Kingdom,

    (i) a Scottish partnership.

(5) An offence is committed under section 7 irrespective of whether the acts or omissions which form part of the offence take place in the United Kingdom or elsewhere.

(6) Where no act or omission which forms part of an offence under section 7 takes place in the United Kingdom, proceedings for the offence may be taken at any place in the United Kingdom.

Although s. 12(2) ensures that ss. 1, 2 or 6 may apply to things done abroad by persons (such as British citizens) who have a close UK connection, this ceases to be the case (as far as English law is concerned) if the only relevant acts or omissions take place in other parts of the UK. English jurisdiction may however be asserted (by virtue of s. 12(1)) if relevant acts or omissions take place both in England and Wales and elsewhere.

The offence under s. 7 has been described as one of 'universal jurisdiction', but this cannot be so because it can be committed only by a 'relevant commercial organisation' with close links to the UK (see s. 7(5)). Moreover, s. 12(6) implies that if no act or omission occurs in England and Wales, English law still has no application to things done elsewhere in the UK.

LIABILITY OF SENIOR OFFICERS OF CORPORATIONS

Bribery Act 2010, s. 14   **B15.25**

(1) This section applies if an offence under section 1, 2 or 6 is committed by a body corporate or a Scottish partnership.

(2) If the offence is proved to have been committed with the consent or connivance of—
   (a) a senior officer of the body corporate or Scottish partnership, or
   (b) a person purporting to act in such a capacity,
   the senior officer or person (as well as the body corporate or partnership) is guilty of the offence and liable to be proceeded against and punished accordingly.

(3) But subsection (2) does not apply, in the case of an offence which is committed under section 1, 2 or 6 by virtue of section 12(2) to (4), to a senior officer or person purporting to act in such a capacity unless the senior officer or person has a close connection with the United Kingdom (within the meaning given by section 12(4)).

(4) In this section—
   'director', in relation to a body corporate whose affairs are managed by its members, means a member of the body corporate,
   'senior officer' means—
   (a) in relation to a body corporate, a director, manager, secretary or other similar officer of the body corporate, and
   (b) in relation to a Scottish partnership, a partner in the partnership.

MISCONDUCT IN PUBLIC OFFICE

In *Bembridge* (1783) 3 Doug 327, Lord Mansfield set out two basic principles which underpin **B15.26** the offence of misconduct in public office. The first is that 'a man accepting an office of trust concerning the public, especially if attended with profit, is answerable criminally to the King for misbehaviour in his office'. The second is that, 'where there is a breach of trust, fraud, or imposition, in a matter concerning the public, though as between individuals it would only be actionable, yet as between the King and the subject it is indictable'. The offence was subsequently examined by the Court of Appeal in *Dytham* [1979] QB 722 and *A-G's Ref (No. 3 of 2003)* [2005] 1 QB 73. The concept of 'public office' was examined in *Belton* [2011] QB 934. An extensive exploration of both English and Commonwealth authorities can also be found in the judgment of the Supreme Court of Canada in *Boulanger* [2006] 2 SCR 49.

These cases establish that the offence may take many forms, and may involve either an improper act or an omission, but the misconduct must be wilful, and the offender must (whether remunerated or not) be a public officer acting as such. Magistrates, judges, registrars, council officials, ministers, civil servants and police officers are all public officers as are prison staff (*King* [2014] 1 Cr App R (S) 462 (73)) and prison nursing officers, including those employed by private companies operating prisons. As Leveson LJ explained in *Cosford* [2014] QB 81:

> Whether the prison is run directly by the state or indirectly through a private company paid by the state to perform this function does not alter the public nature of the duties of those undertaking the work: the responsibilities to the public are identical.

Police community support officers (*Bunyan* [2014] 1 Cr App R (S) 428 (65)) and some police civilian employees may also be regarded as holding public office. In *DL* [2011] 2 Cr App R 159, a civilian employee in an Investigative Support Unit was convicted of conspiracy to commit the offence by passing confidential police information to a private investigator and to a member of the criminal fraternity. In contrast, NHS paramedics or ambulance staff cannot in this context be regarded as holding public office. As Sir Brian Leveson P observed in *Mitchell* [2014] EWCA Crim 318 (at [17]), the public may have an interest in the duty owed by the NHS trust that employs them, but 'to focus on the overarching duty of the Trust would be to mean that every... employee of the Trust is a public officer; for an education authority, it would mean that every teacher... or other employee at a school is a public officer. This is not correct.'

Wilful misconduct involves 'deliberately doing something which is wrong, knowing it to be wrong or with reckless indifference as to whether it is wrong or not' (*A-G's Ref (No. 3 of 2003)* at [28]). There must be 'an element of culpability which is not restricted to corruption or dishonesty but…must be of such a degree that the misconduct impugned is calculated to injure the public interest so as to call for condemnation and punishment' (*Dytham,* per Lord Widgery CJ at p. 394). 'The threshold is a high one requiring conduct so far below acceptable standards as to amount to an abuse of the public's trust in the office holder. A mistake, even a serious one, will not suffice' (*A-G's Ref (No. 3 of 2003)* at [56]).

When misconduct in a public office is alleged to have been committed in circumstances which involve the acquisition of property by theft or fraud, and in particular when the holder of a public office is alleged to have made improper claims for public funds in circumstances which are said to be criminal, it must be proved that the accused acted dishonestly. It is not enough that his behaviour was irregular or improper. The question whether the accused was acting dishonestly or not is pre-eminently one for the jury after a correct direction from the judge (*W (M)* [2010] QB 787).

In *Dytham* (see **A1.19**), a police officer was convicted of this offence for ignoring a serious and violent offence that was being committed in front of his eyes. In *A-G's Ref (No. 1 of 2007)* [2007] 2 Cr App R (S) 544 a police officer was convicted of it for misusing the Police National Computer in order to supply confidential information to a known criminal. In *Bowden* [1996] 4 All ER 505 a local authority manager was convicted of it for improperly arranging for his men to carry out work at his girlfriend's house. See also *Borron* (1820) 3 B & Ald 432 and *Llewellyn-Jones* [1968] 1 QB 429.

Sentence

B15.27 Misconduct in public office is triable only on indictment and is normally a class 3 offence, but see CPD XIII, para. B (see Supplement, **PD-97**) for the additional factors that the court considers on allocation. The penalty is imprisonment and/or a fine, at the discretion of the court.

Sentencing cases on the common-law offence of misconduct in public office, all involving police officers, are *Kassim* [2006] 1 Cr App R (S) 12, *O'Leary* [2007] 2 Cr App R (S) 317, *A-G's Ref (No. 1 of 2007)* [2007] 2 Cr App R (S) 544, *A-G's Ref (No. 68 of 2009) (Turner)* [2010] 1 Cr App R (S) 684 and *Lewis* [2010] 2 Cr App R (S) 666. Cases involving prison officers include *McDade* [2010] 2 Cr App R (S) 530 and *King* [2014] 1 Cr App R (S) 462 (73). In *Bunyan* [2014] 1 Cr App R (S) 428 (65), a sentence of seven years' imprisonment in total was reduced by the Court of Appeal to one of three years, in the case of an offender who used his position as a Community Support Officer to engage in consensual sexual relationships with vulnerable women, with whom he came into contact as a result of his position, and to access police records without any legitimate reason. He had sent sexualised text messages, neglected his legitimate police work in furtherance of these sexual relationships, and disclosed unauthorised information. In *Shoyeju* [2014] EWCA Crim 486, a sentence of seven years' imprisonment on a senior official working at the United Kingdom Border Agency's Asylum Screening Unit (following a late guilty plea) was not considered excessive and the limited guidance in *John-Ayo* [2009] 1 Cr App R (S) 416, where the offender received a nine-year prison sentence after trial, was approved.

ABUSES IN RESPECT OF HONOURS

B15.28 Under the Honours (Prevention of Abuses) Act 1925, s. 1, a person who accepts, obtains, gives or offers gifts or other valuable consideration, or who agrees to do so, as an inducement or reward for procuring, assisting or endeavouring to procure the grant of a dignity or title of honour to any person, is liable on conviction on indictment to imprisonment for a term not exceeding two years, and/or to a fine, or on summary conviction to three months' imprisonment and/or a fine not exceeding £5,000. This provision remains unaffected by the Bribery Act 2010.

DISCLOSURE OF INTERESTS BY THOSE IN LOCAL GOVERNMENT

B15.29 Under the Local Government Act 1972, s. 94(1) (which remains in force despite prospective repeal by the Local Government Act 2000 and is not directly affected by the Bribery Act 2010), any member of a local authority who has a direct pecuniary interest in a contract or a proposed contract involving that authority must disclose it and refrain from taking part in consideration of the matter. Pecuniary interests are defined for this purpose in s. 95. By s. 94(2), failure to comply is punishable on summary conviction by a fine not exceeding level 4 on the standard scale unless the accused proves that he did not know that the contract, proposed contract or other matter in which he had a pecuniary interest was the subject of consideration at that meeting. By s. 94(3), a prosecution for an offence under s. 94(1) may be instituted only by or on behalf of the DPP.

OLD OFFENCE OF BRIBERY AT COMMON LAW

B15.30 Prior to the implementation of the Bribery Act 2010 (see **B15.1**), it was an offence at common law to bribe the holder of a public office, or for any such office holder to accept such a bribe (*Whitaker* [1914] 3 KB 1283; *Lancaster* (1890) 16 Cox CC 737). There was considerable overlap in this respect with the offence of misconduct in public office (see **B15.26**). It was immaterial for the purposes of the common-law offence if the functions of the person who received or was offered the bribe had no connection with the UK and were performed abroad (A-tCSA 2001, s. 108(1)). Where the offer of a bribe was not accepted, the offeror could still be guilty of attempting to commit the offence.

A charge of bribery at common law (relating to conduct before 1 July 2011) remains triable only on indictment and is a class 2A or 3 offence, depending on the complexity of the offence. The penalty is imprisonment and/or a fine, at the discretion of the court.

REPEALED STATUTORY OFFENCES

B15.31 Prior to the implementation of the Bribery Act 2010 (see **B15.1**), the principal legislation dealing with corruption was to be found in the Public Bodies Corrupt Practices Act 1889 and the Prevention of Corruption Act 1906, which were supplemented by the Prevention of Corruption Act 1916 and the A-tCSA 2001, part 12. The 1889 Act dealt with corruption in local government and in other public bodies; the 1906 Act dealt with the corruption of agents, whether the agents of public bodies or not. There was a degree of overlap between the two principal Acts where the agents of public bodies were involved, but since councillors in local government are not agents, corruption of such councillors cannot be dealt with under the 1906 Act. The Crown, meanwhile, is not a public body, and the corruption of Crown servants cannot be prosecuted under the 1889 Act (*Natji* [2002] 1 WLR 2337).

OLD OFFENCE OF CORRUPTION IN PUBLIC OFFICE

Definition

B15.32
Public Bodies Corrupt Practices Act 1889, s. 1

(1) Every person who shall by himself or by or in conjunction with any other person, corruptly solicit or receive, or agree to receive, for himself, or for any other person, any gift, loan, fee, reward, or advantage whatever as an inducement to, or reward for, or otherwise on account of any member, officer, or servant of a public body as in this Act defined, doing or forbearing to do anything in respect of any matter or transaction whatsoever, actual or proposed, in which the said public body is concerned, shall be guilty of [an offence].
(2) Every person who shall by himself or by or in conjunction with any other person corruptly give, promise, or offer any gift, loan, fee, reward, or advantage whatsoever to any person, whether for

the benefit of that person or of another person, as an inducement to or reward for or otherwise on account of any member, officer, or servant of any public body as in this Act defined, doing or forbearing to do anything in respect of any matter or transaction whatsoever, actual or proposed, in which such public body as aforesaid is concerned, shall be guilty of [an offence].

As to the liability of a corporation for the corrupt acts of its officers, see *Andrews-Weatherfoil Ltd* [1972] 1 All ER 65 and **A6.2**. As to the repeal of this Act by the Bribery Act 2010 and transitional provisions, see **B15.1**.

Procedure

B15.33   No prosecution may be instituted except by or with the consent of the A-G (Public Bodies Corrupt Practices Act 1889, s. 4). The offence is triable either way (s. 2(a)). When tried on indictment it is a class 2C offence.

Penalties

B15.34   Public Bodies Corrupt Practices Act 1889, s. 2

Any person on conviction for offending as aforesaid shall, at the discretion of the court before which he is convicted,—

   (a) be liable—
      (i) on summary conviction, to imprisonment for a term not exceeding six months or to a fine not exceeding the statutory maximum, or to both; and
      (ii) on conviction on indictment, to imprisonment for a term not exceeding seven years or to a fine, or to both; and

   (b) in addition be liable to be ordered to pay to such body, and in such manner as the court directs, the amount or value of any gift, loan, fee, or reward received by him or any part thereof; and

   (c) be liable to be adjudged incapable of being elected or appointed to any public office for five years from the date of his conviction, and to forfeit any such office held by him at the time of his conviction; and

   (d) in the event of a second conviction for a like offence he shall, in addition to the foregoing penalties, be liable to be adjudged to be for ever incapable of holding any public office, and to be incapable for five years of being registered as an elector, or voting at an election either of members to serve in Parliament or of members of any public body, and the enactments for preventing the voting and registration of persons declared by reason of corrupt practices to be incapable of voting shall apply to a person adjudged in pursuance of this section to be incapable of voting; and

   (e) if such person is an officer or servant in the employ of any public body upon such conviction he shall, at the discretion of the court, be liable to forfeit his right and claim to any compensation or pension to which he would otherwise have been entitled.

For sentencing guidelines, see **B15.44**.

Definition of Relevant Terms

B15.35   Public Bodies Corrupt Practices Act 1889, s. 7

The expression 'public body' means any council of a county or council of a city or town, any council of a municipal borough, also any board, commissioners, select vestry, or other body which has power to act under and for the purposes of any Act relating to local government, or the public health, or to poor law or otherwise to administer money raised by rates in pursuance of any public general Act, and includes any body which exists in a country or territory outside the United Kingdom and is equivalent to any body described above:

The expression 'public office' means any office or employment of a person as a member, officer, or servant of such public body:

The expression 'person' includes a body of persons, corporate or unincorporate:

The expression 'advantage' includes any office or dignity, and any forbearance to demand any money or money's worth or valuable thing, and includes any aid, vote, consent, or influence, or pretended aid, vote, consent, or influence, and also includes any promise or procurement of or agreement or endeavour to procure, or the holding out of any expectation of any gift, loan, fee, reward, or advantage, as before defined.

By the Prevention of Corruption Act 1916, s. 4(2), 'local and public authorities of all descriptions' are public bodies for this purpose. See *DPP v Holly* [1978] AC 43. The Crown, however, is not a public body (*Natji* [2002] 1 WLR 2337). By the Public Bodies Corrupt Practices Act 1889, s. 3, the invalidity of any appointment or election to a public office is no defence to a charge under s. 1.

Meaning of 'Corruptly'

'Corruptly' means purposefully doing an act which the law forbids as tending to corrupt   **B15.36**
(*Wellburn* (1979) 69 Cr App R 254). Any improper and unauthorised gift, payment or other inducement offered to a councillor or other such officer is likely to be considered corrupt. D need not be proved to have acted dishonestly, as long as he knew that the gift or bribe was connected with the performance of public duties, whether by way of reward for past performance, or of inducement to secure future performance. No bargain need be struck between the parties involved (*Andrews-Weatherfoil Ltd* [1972] 1 All ER 65), and it is no defence for the recipient to prove that his acceptance of a corrupt gift failed to influence him in the performance of his duties (*Parker* (1985) 82 Cr App R 69). Nor is it necessary to prove that any person serving under the state or other public body, or holding a public office, was aware of the transaction or offer, provided that its purpose was to corrupt (*Jagdeo Singh v The State of Trinidad and Tobago* [2006] 4 All ER 781).

In *Smith* [1960] 2 QB 423, S's offer of a bribe to a mayor was held to amount to an offence under s. 1, even if S's motive was to expose the mayor as corrupt. This must be contrasted with the position where D is offered a bribe by E and purports to accept it for the purpose of exposing E or of procuring evidence against him; this 'would plainly not be corrupt' (*Mills* (1978) 68 Cr App R 154 at p. 159). On such facts, D would neither be acting corruptly himself, nor inducing another person to so act.

The Presumption of Corruption

Prevention of Corruption Act 1916, s. 2   **B15.37**

Where in any proceedings against a person for an offence under the Prevention of Corruption Act 1906, or the Public Bodies Corrupt Practices Act 1889, it is proved that any money, gift, or other consideration has been paid or given to or received by a person in the employment of His Majesty or any government department or a public body by or from a person, or agent of a person, holding or seeking to obtain a contract from His Majesty or any government department or public body, the money, gift, or consideration shall be deemed to have been paid or given and received corruptly as such inducement or reward as is mentioned in such Act unless the contrary is proved.

This presumption applies only to gifts etc. given to or received by relevant employees before 1 July 2011, and then only to cases in which a relevant contract was sought or obtained (*Dickinson* (1948) 33 Cr App R 5). It cannot apply to conspiracy charges (*A-G, ex parte Rockall* [2000] 4 All ER 312) or to cases that fall within English jurisdiction only by virtue of the A-tCSA 2001 (see s. 110 of that Act). Even where it does apply, it imposes a mere evidential burden on the defence (*Webster* [2011] 1 Cr App R 207).

OLD OFFENCE OF CORRUPTION OF AGENTS

Definition and Penalty

Prevention of Corruption Act 1906, s. 1   **B15.38**

(1) If any agent corruptly accepts or obtains, or agrees to accept or attempts to obtain, from any person, for himself or for any other person, any gift or consideration as an inducement or reward for doing or forbearing to do, or for having after the passing of this Act done or forborne to do, any act in relation to his principal's affairs or business, or for showing or forbearing to show favour or disfavour to any person in relation to his principal's affairs or business; or

If any person corruptly gives or agrees to give or offers any gift or consideration to any agent as an inducement or reward for doing or forbearing to do, or for having after the passing of this Act done or forborne to do, any act in relation to his principal's affairs or business, or for showing or forbearing to show favour or disfavour to any person in relation to his principal's affairs or business; or
If any person knowingly gives to any agent, or if any agent knowingly uses with intent to deceive his principal, any receipt, account, or other document in respect of which the principal is interested, and which contains any statement which is false or erroneous or defective in any material particular, and which to his knowledge is intended to mislead the principal;
he shall be guilty of [an offence] and shall be liable:

(a)   on summary conviction, to imprisonment for a term not exceeding 6 months or to a fine not exceeding the statutory maximum, or to both; and

(b)   on conviction on indictment, to imprisonment for a term not exceeding seven years or to a fine, or to both.

(2)   For the purposes of this Act the expression 'consideration' includes valuable consideration of any kind; the expression 'agent' includes any person employed by or acting for another; and the expression 'principal' includes an employer.

(3)   A person serving under the Crown or under any corporation or any...borough, county, or district council, or any board of guardians, is an agent within the meaning of this Act.

(4)   For the purposes of this Act it is immaterial if—

(a)   the principal's affairs or business have no connection with the United Kingdom and are conducted in a country or territory outside the United Kingdom;

(b)   the agent's functions have no connection with the United Kingdom and are carried out in a country or territory outside the United Kingdom.

For sentencing guidelines, see **B15.44**. As to the liability of a corporation for the corrupt acts of its officers, see *Andrews-Weatherfoil Ltd* [1972] 1 All ER 65 and **A6.2**. As to the repeal of this Act by the Bribery Act 2010 and transitional provisions, see **B15.1**.

Procedure

B15.39   No prosecution for this offence may be instituted except by or with the consent of the A-G and every information for an offence must be on oath (Prevention of Corruption Act 1906, s. 2; *Ghafar* [2009] EWCA Crim 2270). The offence is triable either way (Prevention of Corruption Act 1906, s. 1). When tried on indictment it is a class 2C offence.

Meaning of 'Agent'

B15.40   The definition of an agent in the Prevention of Corruption Act 1906, s. 1(2) and (3), was supplemented by the Prevention of Corruption Act 1916, s. 4(3), by which a person serving under any other public body within the meaning of that Act was an agent for the purposes of the 1906 Act. As to the term 'public body', see **B15.35**. As to the status of local authority councillors, see **B15.31**. In *Barrett* [1976] 3 All ER 895 it was held that a superintendent registrar was an agent, serving under the Crown.

Outside the public domain, the term 'agent' applies only to employees and agents in the strict sense (i.e. those who act on behalf of others). But an agent need not have acted as an agent of his principal at the relevant time, as long as the Act in question was done 'in relation to his principal's affairs' (*Morgan v DPP* [1970] 3 All ER 1053; *Majeed* [2012] 3 All ER 737).

Comparison with the Public Bodies Corrupt Practices Act 1889

B15.41   In most respects the offences created by the Prevention of Corruption Act 1906 corresponded with those in the Public Bodies Corrupt Practices Act 1889. The concept of corruption was the same (*Harvey* [1999] Crim LR 70; *J (P)* [2014] 1 WLR 1857); and although the 1906 Act used the words, 'gift or consideration' instead of the 1889 formula, 'gift, loan, fee, reward or advantage', this does not seem to be a significant difference. An issue may arise as to whether the agent's principal had consented to what was done, but whether evidence as to this is material depends on the facts of the case. In some cases a payment may be corrupt in any event (*J (P)*).

False Statements under the Prevention of Corruption Act 1906

The Prevention of Corruption Act 1906, s. 1(1), created one offence which had no equivalent in the 1889 legislation: that of knowingly giving to an agent, or knowing use by an agent, of documents etc. which were false, erroneous or defective, and which were intended to mislead the agent's principal. See *Sage v Eicholz* [1919] 2 KB 171. But such liability could arise only where the document originated from outside any business or organisation in which both principal and agent were involved. Otherwise, 'an employee who put a false entry on his timesheet would be guilty of an offence under the Act' (*Tweedie* [1984] QB 729 per Lawton LJ at p. 734).

'Knowingly' must here mean knowledge of the falsity etc. as well as of the giving, but wilful blindness could suffice. See *Westminster City Council v Croyalgrange Ltd* [1986] 2 All ER 353.

BRIBERY AND CORRUPTION ABROAD (OLD LAW)

Anti-terrorism, Crime and Security Act 2001, s. 109

(1) This section applies if—
    (a) a national of the United Kingdom or a body incorporated under the law of any part of the United Kingdom does anything in a country or territory outside the United Kingdom, and
    (b) the act would, if done in the United Kingdom, constitute a corruption offence (as defined below).
(2) In such a case—
    (a) the act constitutes the offence concerned, and
    (b) proceedings for the offence may be taken in the United Kingdom.
(3) These are corruption offences—
    (a) any common law offence of bribery;
    (b) the offences under section 1 of the Public Bodies Corrupt Practices Act 1889 (corruption in office);
    (c) the first two offences under section 1 of the Prevention of Corruption Act 1906 (bribes obtained by or given to agents).
(4) A national of the United Kingdom is an individual who is—
    (a) a British citizen, a British Overseas Territories citizen, a British National (Overseas) or a British Overseas citizen,
    (b) a person who under the British Nationality Act 1981 is a British subject, or
    (c) a British protected person within the meaning of that Act.

This provision was repealed by the Bribery Act 2010, s. 17 and sch. 2, as of 1 July 2011. The extra-territorial reach of the new law is in some respects greater: see **B15.24**.

SENTENCING GUIDELINES FOR CORRUPTION OFFENCES (OLD LAW)

In *Dougall* [2011] 1 Cr App R (S) 227, Lord Judge CJ stressed the seriousness of the offences of bribery and corruption, noting that 'corruption is an insidious plague that has a wide range of corrosive effects on society'. At the top end of the scale of seriousness is *Donald* [1997] 2 Cr App R (S) 272, where sentences totalling 11 years were upheld in respect of a detective-constable in a regional crime squad who pleaded guilty, at a late stage of his trial, to four counts of corruption. He had accepted various sums of money from a man against whom criminal proceedings were being brought to disclose confidential information about the inquiry and to destroy surveillance logs. The officer had agreed to accept about £50,000 and actually received about £18,500. The sentencing judge commented that the case was 'almost unique' in its seriousness. The Court of Appeal said the sentence was severe, but not manifestly excessive. In *Welcher* [2007] 2 Cr App R (S) 519, sentences totalling six and a half years were upheld in respect of two men convicted of conspiracy to corrupt and conspiracy to defraud. They had been involved in paying sums of money in the order of £3 million to an employee of a major company, in return for showing favour to the offenders' company by placing major orders and authorising over-payments to the company. A sentence of 30 months' imprisonment was upheld in *Ozakpinar* [2009] 1 Cr App R (S) 35 where the offender, who was chief procurement officer for the CPS, was convicted of corruption in respect of employing persons who were personal friends and receiving payments in connection with three separate contracts. The Court of Appeal did not accept an argument that guidelines for theft in breach of trust were helpful in dealing with corruption cases.

In *Wilson* (1982) 4 Cr App R (S) 337 the offender, a man of previous good character, was con-victed of conspiracy to commit corruption and three counts of corruption. He was a purchasing agent and chief buyer with a manufacturing concern, and he accepted gifts of £2,500 in return for showing favour to a company supplying parts to his employer. A sentence of three and a half years was reduced to 18 months, taking into account personal mitigation, including the break-up of his family, the loss of his home and his business. In *Dearnley* [2001] 2 Cr App R (S) 201, a council employee and a supplier of security services to the council pleaded guilty to corruption in the form of supplying a car worth £5,445 and misrepresenting a loan in order to pay off a per-sonal debt. A sentence of 18 months was reduced to 12 months by the Court of Appeal, Rafferty J noting that custody was required as a deterrent and was inevitable, but that there had been no lack of value for the security services paid for by the council, the car was a modest one, and that both defendants, previously of good character, were now 'broken men'.

B15.45   The offenders in *Garner* (1988) 10 Cr App R (S) 445 pleaded guilty to conspiracy to corrupt. They were concerned in bribing a prison officer to take various items, including luxury foods, alcohol and cigars to one of the offenders who was serving a prison sentence: sentences of 18 months, 12 months, and 12 months suspended were upheld. Offering a bribe to a police officer was the nature of the corruption in *McGovern* (1980) 2 Cr App R (S) 389. The offender was arrested in connection with a burglary, and offered a bribe of £2,000 to the police involved in the case. Fifteen months was reduced to nine months' imprisonment for the corruption offence. In *Oxdemir* (1985) 7 Cr App R (S) 382 the offender tried to bribe a police officer with £50 or a free meal at the offender's restaurant if he did not report a driving offence by the offender's son. The appropriate sentence was said by the Court of Appeal to be three months' imprisonment.

Section B16 Revenue, Customs and Social Security Offences

INTRODUCTION

Because the Inland Revenue and Customs and Excise used to be separate government depart- **B16.1**
ments, legislation creating offences against the public revenue is contained in different Acts of
Parliament. The Commissioners for Revenue and Customs Act 2005 created the department
called HM Revenue and Customs, which exercises the functions previously exercised by those
two departments.

PROSECUTIONS, PENALTIES AND MONEY SETTLEMENTS

Frauds committed against the public revenue often involve Theft Act offences, such as false **B16.2**
accounting (see **B6.3**), Fraud Act offences (see **B5.4**) or offences under the Perjury Act 1911,
s. 5(1)(b) (see **B14.25**). They may instead be prosecuted as offences under revenue and customs
legislation or as the common-law offence of cheating the public revenue. In many cases, tax
frauds are not prosecuted. HM Revenue and Customs are often content to impose financial
penalties and accept a money settlement, once full disclosure has been made. Civil remedies in
tort may also be available to the Commissioners (*Revenue and Customs Commissioners v Total
Network SL* [2008] 1 AC 1174; see **B16.8**). Taxpayers under investigation are nevertheless
warned that the Revenue gives no undertaking that it will refrain from prosecuting, even if
the taxpayer fully co-operates (*Allen* [2002] 1 AC 509). As to the need for interviews with suspected tax offenders to be conducted in accordance with PACE Code C, even in cases where the
Revenue would ordinarily seek to reach a monetary settlement and avoid any criminal prosecution, see *Gill* [2004] 4 All ER 681.

CHEATING THE PUBLIC REVENUE

The common-law offence of cheating the public revenue is triable only on indictment and punish- **B16.3**
able by a fine and/or imprisonment at large. It is a Group A offence for jurisdiction purposes under
the CJA 1993, part I (see **A8.10**).

In *Steed* [2011] EWCA Crim 75 the Court of Appeal stated (at [11]): 'Cheating consists of any
form of fraudulent conduct, whether by making positive false representations,. . .or by concealing or omitting to disclose liability or income with the result that money is diverted from the
Revenue and the Revenue is deprived of money to which it is entitled'. The offence may therefore be committed by dishonestly making false statements with intent to deceive or prejudice
HM Revenue and Customs or the Department of Social Security (*Hudson* [1956] 2 QB 252) or

by dishonestly failing to declare a tax or national insurance liability. In *Mavji* [1987] 2 All ER 758, Michael Davies J said (at p. 1392): 'This appellant...had a statutory duty to make VAT returns and pay over to the Crown the VAT due. He dishonestly failed to do either. Accordingly, he was guilty of cheating...the public revenue. No further act or omission is required.' See also *Redford* (1988) 89 Cr App R 1 and *Allen* [2002] 1 AC 509.

Prosecutions for cheating the public revenue are generally reserved for the most serious and unusual offences. In *Dosanjh* [2014] 1 WLR 1780 the Court of Appeal decided that Parliament had deliberately left this common-law offence untouched by statutory changes. It therefore remains appropriate to charge cheating the public revenue for the most serious revenue frauds for which statutory offences do not adequately reflect the criminality involved.

The definitive sentencing guideline, *Fraud, Bribery and Money Laundering Offences* (see Supplement, **SG-488**) includes guidance on sentencing for cheating the public revenue. The guideline applies to individual offenders aged 18 and over and organisations. It applies to all offenders sentenced on or after 1 October 2014 regardless of the date of the offence. There is a separate part of the guideline applicable to corporate offenders. Previous sentencing levels for the offence had been discussed in *Dosanjh*. See also *Randhawa* [2012] 2 Cr App R (S) 298, *Chaudhery* [2012] EWCA Crim 12, *Bajwa* [2013] EWCA Crim 811 and *Hackney* [2014] 1 Cr App R (S) 235 (41).

FRAUDULENT EVASION OF INCOME TAX

B16.4

Taxes Management Act 1970, s. 106A

(1) A person commits an offence if that person is knowingly concerned in the fraudulent evasion of income tax by that or any other person.
(2) A person guilty of an offence under this section is liable—
   (a) on summary conviction, to imprisonment for a term not exceeding [six]months or a fine not exceeding the statutory maximum, or both;
   (b) on conviction on indictment, to imprisonment for a term not exceeding seven years or a fine, or both.

In many respects, this offence mirrors the common-law offence of cheating, but only in respect of income tax evasion. The words 'knowingly concerned' and 'fraudulent evasion' appear in the Customs and Excise Management Act 1979, s. 170(2) (see **B16.38**), and reference should be made to the case law under that section (see **B16.43** *et seq.*). Any dishonest attempt to evade or conceal one's income tax liabilities would appear to amount to an offence under s. 144; as would conduct that is intended to facilitate fraudulent evasion by another taxpayer. Dishonest financial advisers, or clients who provide the taxpayer with false invoices etc. may also be 'knowingly concerned' in the act of evasion. Paying a taxpayer a specially reduced fee in cash might also suffice, but only if the person making this payment knows that he is thereby facilitating the dishonest non-disclosure of this payment by the taxpayer. See D Ormerod, 'Fraudulent Evasion of Income Tax' [2002] Crim LR 3.

The definitive sentencing guideline, *Fraud, Bribery and Money Laundering Offences* (see Supplement, **SG-488**) includes guidance on sentencing for fraudulent evasion of income tax. See **B16.52** for a fuller discussion of sentencing in revenue fraud cases.

FRAUD IN RELATION TO TAX CREDITS

B16.5 The Tax Credits Act 2002 and regulations made thereunder make provision for means-tested awards of tax credits, primarily for working families with dependent children.

Tax Credits Act 2002, s. 35

(1) A person commits an offence if he is knowingly concerned in any fraudulent activity undertaken with a view to obtaining payments of a tax credit by him or any other person.

(2) A person who commits an offence under subsection (1) is liable—

  (a) on summary conviction, to imprisonment for a term not exceeding six months, or a fine not exceeding the statutory maximum, or both, or

  (b) on conviction on indictment, to imprisonment for a term not exceeding seven years, or a fine, or both.

The new sentencing guideline, *Fraud, Bribery and Money Laundering Offences* (see Supplement, **SG-492**) includes a section relating to benefit fraud which provides guidance on offences under s. 35. For further discussion, see **B16.60**.

In *Gardiner* [2012] EWCA Crim 1318 the offender pleaded guilty to obtaining £14,820 tax credit over a period of more than three years after he had stopped working and to failing to notify a change of circumstances as a result of which he obtained £7,300 in housing and council tax benefit. Sentences of six months' imprisonment concurrent were reduced by the Court of Appeal to four months' imprisonment concurrent. Other cases decided by reference to the previous guideline, and relating to benefit fraud more generally, are summarised at **B16.61**.

For the words 'knowingly concerned' see **B16.43** to **B16.46**. The words 'fraudulent activity undertaken with a view to obtaining payments of a tax credit' would clearly cover the dishonest completion of an application form for tax credits. The words 'with a view to obtaining' require proof of behaviour calculated to obtain payment of a tax credit, rather than to capitalise on payment already received (*Nolan* [2012] EWCA Crim 671). But a person involved in the disposing of the proceeds might be charged with conspiracy to commit fraud (*Kolapo* [2009] EWCA Crim 545).

FALSIFICATION ETC. OF DOCUMENTS CALLED FOR INSPECTION

Falsification of documents with a view to deceiving tax inspectors may be charged as offences under various general provisions (e.g., false accounting, cheating or fraudulent evasion of income tax), but s. 20BB deals specifically with such behaviour.   **B16.6**

Taxes Management Act 1970, s. 20BB

(1) Subject to subsections (2) and (3) below, a person shall be guilty of an offence if he intentionally falsifies, conceals, destroys or otherwise disposes of, or causes or permits the falsification, concealment, destruction or disposal of, a document which he has been required by an order under section 20BA above to deliver, or to deliver or to make available for inspection.

(2) A person does not commit an offence under subsection (1) above if he acts—

  (a) with the written permission of the tribunal, or an officer of the Board, or

  (b) after the document has been delivered.

(3) A person does not commit an offence under subsection (1) above if he acts after the end of the period of two years beginning with the date on which the order is made, unless before the end of that period an officer of Revenue and Customs has notified the person in writing that the order has not been complied with to the officer's satisfaction.

(4) *[repealed]*

(5) A person guilty of an offence under subsection (1) above shall be liable—

  (a) on summary conviction, to a fine not exceeding the statutory maximum;

  (b) on conviction on indictment, to imprisonment for a term not exceeding two years or to a fine or to both.

Section 20BB is shown as amended, with effect from 1 April 2013, by the Finance Act 2012, sch. 38, para. 46.

For the similar offence under the Customs and Excise Management Act 1979, s. 168, see **B16.51**.

VAT FRAUDS

B16.7   **Value Added Tax Act 1994, s. 72**

(1) If any person is knowingly concerned in, or in the taking of steps with a view to, the fraudulent evasion of VAT by him or any other person, he shall be liable—

    (a) on summary conviction, to a penalty of the statutory maximum or of three times the amount of the VAT, whichever is the greater, or to imprisonment for a term not exceeding 6 months or to both; or

    (b) on conviction on indictment, to a penalty of any amount or to imprisonment for a term not exceeding 7 years or to both.

(2) Any reference in subsection (1) above or subsection (8) below to the evasion of VAT includes a reference to the obtaining of—

    (a) the payment of a VAT credit; or

    (b) a refund under section 35, 36 or 40 of this Act or section 22 of the [Value Added Tax Act 1983]; or

    (c) a refund under any regulations made by virtue of section 13(5); or

    (d) a repayment under section 39;

    and any reference in those subsections to the amount of the VAT shall be construed—

        (i) in relation to VAT itself or a VAT credit, as a reference to the aggregate of the amount (if any) falsely claimed by way of credit for input tax and the amount (if any) by which output was falsely understated, and

        (ii) in relation to a refund or repayment falling within paragraph (b), (c) or (d) above, as a reference to the amount falsely claimed by way of refund or repayment.

(3) If any person—

    (a) with intent to deceive produces, furnishes or sends for the purposes of this Act or otherwise makes use for those purposes of any document which is false in a material particular; or

    (b) in furnishing any information for the purposes of this Act makes any statement which he knows to be false in a material particular or recklessly makes a statement which is false in a material particular,

    he shall be liable—

        (i) on summary conviction, to a penalty of the statutory maximum or, where subsection (4) or (5) below applies, to the alternative penalty specified in that subsection if it is greater, or to imprisonment for a term not exceeding 6 months or to both; or

        (ii) on conviction on indictment, to a penalty of any amount or to imprisonment for a term not exceeding 7 years or to both.

(4) In any case where—

    (a) the document referred to in subsection (3)(a) above is a return required under this Act, or

    (b) the information referred to in subsection (3)(b) above is contained in or otherwise relevant to such a return,

    the alternative penalty referred to in subsection (3)(i) above is a penalty equal to three times the aggregate of the amount (if any) falsely claimed by way of credit for input tax and the amount (if any) by which output tax was falsely understated.

(5) In any case where—

    (a) the document referred to in subsection (3)(a) above is a claim for a refund under section 35, 36 or 40 of this Act or section 22 of the [Value Added Tax Act 1983] for a refund under any regulations made by virtue of section 13(5) or for a repayment under section 39, or

    (b) the information referred to in subsection (3)(b) above is contained in or otherwise relevant to such a claim,

    the alternative penalty referred to in subsection (3)(i) above is a penalty equal to three times the amount falsely claimed.

(6) The reference in subsection (3)(a) above to furnishing, sending or otherwise making use of a document which is false in a material particular, with intent to deceive, includes a reference to furnishing, sending or otherwise making use of such a document, with intent to secure that a machine will respond to the document as if it were a true document.

(7) Any reference in subsection (3)(a) or subsection (6) above to producing, furnishing or sending a document includes a reference to causing a document to be produced, furnished or sent.

(8) Where a person's conduct during any specified period must have involved the commission by him of one or more offences under the preceding provisions of this section, then, whether

or not the particulars of that offence or those offences are known, he shall, by virtue of this subsection, be guilty of an offence and liable—

    (a) on summary conviction, to a penalty of the statutory maximum or, if greater, three times the amount of any VAT that was or was intended to be evaded by his conduct, or to imprisonment for a term not exceeding 6 months or to both; or

    (b) on conviction on indictment to a penalty of any amount or to imprisonment for a term not exceeding 7 years or to both.

(9) [Repealed.]

(10) If any person acquires possession of or deals with any goods, or accepts the supply of any services, having reason to believe that VAT on the supply of the goods or services, on the acquisition of the goods from another member State or on the importation of the goods from a place outside the member States has been or will be evaded, he shall be liable on summary conviction to a penalty of level 5 on the standard scale or three times the amount of the VAT, whichever is the greater.

(11) If any person supplies or is supplied with goods or services in contravention of paragraph 4(2) of Schedule 11, he shall be liable on summary conviction to a penalty of level 5 on the standard scale.

(12) Subject to subsection (13) below, sections 145 to 155 of the [Customs and Excise Management Act 1979] (proceedings for offences, mitigation of penalties and certain other matters) shall apply in relation to offences under this Act (which include any act or omission in respect of which a penalty is imposed) and penalties imposed under this Act as they apply in relation to offences and penalties under the customs and excise Acts as defined in that Act; and accordingly in section 154(2) as it applies by virtue of this subsection the reference to duty shall be construed as a reference to VAT.

(13) In subsection (12) above the references to penalties do not include references to penalties under sections 60 to 70.

B16.8 For the Customs and Excise Management Act 1979, ss. 145 to 154, see **B16.18** to **B16.23**. For case law on 'knowingly concerned' and 'fraudulent evasion', see **B16.37** and **B16.43** *et seq*. The Court of Appeal held in *McCarthy* [1981] STC 298 that a dishonest omission to register for VAT may constitute an offence of taking steps to evade that tax under what is now s. 72(1).

In *Hashash* [2006] EWCA Crim 2518 the Court of Appeal, applying the decision of the European Court of Justice in *Optigen Ltd v Customs and Excise Commissioners* [2006] Ch 218, upheld convictions under s. 72 for participating in a 'carousel' fraud, whereby payment of VAT is avoided by a series of sales passing between different Member States. Liability to VAT is determined by the objective appearance of the transaction, regardless of any fraudulent intention.

HM Revenue and Customs may also recover the VAT evaded by a 'carousel' fraud as damages in the tort of conspiracy (*Revenue and Customs Commissioners v Total Network SL* [2008] 1 AC 1174; *Revenue and Customs Commissioners v Sunico A/S* [2013] EWHC 941 (Ch)). Such a judgment is enforceable in other Member States as a civil and commercial matter (*Revenue and Customs Commissioners v Sunico ApS* [2014] QB 391).

Section 72(8) enables a charge to be brought on the basis of a general deficiency. As to the circumstances in which this should be resorted to, see *Rasool* [1997] 4 All ER 439. As to the wording of indictments generally, see *Ike* [1996] Crim LR 515.

The definitive sentencing guideline, *Fraud, Bribery and Money Laundering Offences* (see Supplement, **SG-488**) includes guidance on sentencing for fraudulent evasion of VAT and the making of a false statement for VAT purposes. See **B16.52** for a fuller discussion of sentencing in revenue fraud cases. For sentencing in VAT fraud cases charged as cheating the public revenue, see **B16.3**.

TAXATION ETC. IN THE EUROPEAN UNION

B16.9 The CJA 1993, s. 71, creates an offence of involvement, within the UK, in specified EU fraud offences committed against the laws of other Member States. Despite this international dimension, the offence is not an extra-territorial one. The courts of England and Wales are not concerned with acts committed in other parts of the UK, nor does s. 71 penalise frauds in other Member States.

Definition

B16.10   Criminal Justice Act 1993, s. 71

(1) A person who, in the United Kingdom, assists in or induces any conduct outside the United Kingdom which involves the commission of a serious offence against the law of another Member State is guilty of an offence under this section if—

   (a) the offence involved is one consisting in or including the contravention of provisions of the law of that Member State which relate to any of the matters specified in subsection (2);

   (b) the offence involved is one consisting in or including the contravention of other provisions of that law so far as they have effect in relation to any of those matters; or

   (c) the conduct is such as to be calculated to have an effect in that Member State in relation to any of those matters.

(2) The matters mentioned in subsection (1) are—

   (a) the determination, discharge or enforcement of any liability for a Community duty or tax;

   (b) the operation of arrangements under which reliefs or exemptions from any such duty or tax are provided or sums in respect of any such duty or tax are repaid or refunded;

   (c) the making of payments in pursuance of Community arrangements made in connection with the regulation of the market for agricultural products and the enforcement of the conditions of any such payments;

   (d) the movement into or out of any Member State of anything in relation to the movement of which any EU instrument imposes, or requires the imposition of, any prohibition or restriction; and

   (e) such other matters in relation to which provision is made by any EU instrument as the Secretary of State may by order specify.

(3) For the purposes of this section—

   (a) an offence against the law of a Member State is a serious offence if provision is in force in that Member State authorising the sentencing, in some or all cases, of a person convicted of that offence to imprisonment for a maximum term of twelve months or more; and

   (b) the question whether any conduct involves the commission of such an offence shall be determined according to the law in force in the Member State in question at the time of the assistance or inducement.

...

(9) In this section—

'another Member State' means a Member State other than the United Kingdom;

'Community duty or tax' means any of the following, that is to say—

   (a) any EU customs duty;

   (b) an agricultural levy of the Economic Community;

   (c) value added tax under the law of another Member State;

   (d) any duty or tax on tobacco products, alcoholic liquors or hydrocarbon oils which, in another Member State, corresponds to any excise duty;

   (e) any duty, tax or other charge not falling within paragraphs (a) to (d) of this definition which is imposed by or in pursuance of any EU instrument on the movement of goods into or out of any Member State;

'conduct' includes acts, omissions and statements;

'contravention' includes a failure to comply; and

'the customs and excise Acts' has the same meaning as in the Customs and Excise Management Act 1979.

(10) References in this section, in relation to an EU instrument, to the movement of anything into or out of a Member State include references to the movement of anything between Member States and to the doing of anything which falls to be treated for the purposes of that instrument as involving the entry into, or departure from, the territory of the European Union of any goods (within the meaning of that Act of 1979).

Procedure and Sentence

An offence under the CJA 1993, s. 71, is triable either way, and is punishable following convic- **B16.11**
tion on indictment by imprisonment for up to seven years or by a fine or both; six months and/
or a fine not exceeding the statutory maximum following summary conviction (CJA 1993,
s. 71(6)). When tried on indictment, it is normally a class 3 offence, but see CPD XIII, para. B
(see Supplement, **PD-97**) for the additional factors that the court considers on allocation.

Elements

The term 'induce' in the CJA 1993, s. 71(1) is an ordinary English word meaning 'to prevail **B16.12**
upon, persuade, bring about or give rise to'. This suggests that an offence against the laws of
another Member State must actually be committed before liability can arise under s. 71. The
conduct giving rise to that offence may involve or may merely be 'calculated' (i.e. likely) to have
an effect in relation to the matters listed in s. 71(2).

Evidence of Foreign Law

Proof of the relevant law in the Member State concerned is facilitated by the CJA 1993, s. 71(5) **B16.13**
which enables English courts to ascertain whether specified conduct would, if proved, amount
to a specified offence under foreign law. Other methods of proving foreign law may also be used
(see **F10.26**, **F8.19** and *Kordasinski* [2007] 1 Cr App R 238). The obtaining of evidence may be
facilitated by procedures established under the Crime (International Co-operation) Act 2003.

Defences

Criminal Justice Act 1993, s. 71   B16.14

(4) In any proceedings against any person for an offence under this section it shall be a defence for
that person to show—
(a) that the conduct in question would not have involved the commission of an offence
against the law of the Member State in question but for circumstances of which he had no
knowledge; and
(b) that he did not suspect or anticipate the existence of those circumstances and did not have
reasonable grounds for doing so.

The burden of proving any such matter is ostensibly placed on the defence, but this burden may
need to be construed as evidential only, following the views expressed by the House of Lords in
Sheldrake v DPP [2005] 1 AC 204 (see **F3.18** *et seq.*).

CUSTOMS AND EXCISE: INTRODUCTION

The following paragraphs deal with the most important offences under the Customs and Excise **B16.15**
Management Act 1979 and the Commissioners for Revenue and Customs Act 2005. Many such
offences involve defrauding Her Majesty of duty payable on goods. It is therefore important to
check not only the terms of the section creating the offence, but also the regulations setting out
the circumstances in which a liability to duty arises. This affects not only the question whether
the offence charged has been committed (*Chambers* [2008] EWCA Crim 2467; *Khan* [2009]
EWCA Crim 588), but also the question whether the accused personally owed duty on goods
for the purposes of confiscation proceedings (*Mackle* [2014] 2 WLR 267: for further detail, see
E19.24 and **E19.29**).

Time of Importation, Exportation, etc.

Most of the important offences involve breach of import or export control. Section 5 of the **B16.16**
Customs and Excise Management Act 1979 identifies the time at which import or export takes
place.

Customs and Excise Management Act 1979, s. 5

(1) The provisions of this section shall have effect for the purposes of the customs and excise Acts.

(2) Subject to subsections (3) and (6) below, the time of importation of any goods shall be deemed to be—

   (a) where the goods are brought by sea, the time when the ship carrying them comes within the limits of a port;

   (b) where the goods are brought by air, the time when the aircraft carrying them lands in the United Kingdom or the time when the goods are unloaded in the United Kingdom, whichever is the earlier;

   (c) where the goods are brought by land, the time when the goods are brought across the boundary into Northern Ireland.

(3) In the case of goods brought by sea of which entry is not required under regulation 5 of the Customs Controls on Importation of Goods Regulations 1991, the time of importation shall be deemed to be the time when the ship carrying them came within the limits of the port at which the goods are discharged.

(4) Subject to subsections (5) and (7) below, the time of exportation of any goods from the United Kingdom shall be deemed to be—

   (a) where the goods are exported by sea or air, the time when the goods are shipped for exportation;

   (b) where the goods are exported by land, the time when they are cleared by the proper officer at the last customs and excise station on their way to the boundary.

(5) In the case of goods of a class or description with respect to the exportation of which any prohibition or restriction is for the time being in force under or by virtue of any enactment which are exported by sea or air, the time of exportation shall be deemed to be the time when the exporting ship or aircraft departs from the last port or customs and excise airport at which it is cleared before departing for a destination outside the United Kingdom.

(6) Goods imported by means of a pipe-line shall be treated as imported at the time when they are brought within the limits of a port or brought across the boundary into Northern Ireland.

(7) Goods exported by means of a pipe-line shall be treated as exported at the time when they are charged into that pipe-line for exportation.

(8) A ship shall be deemed to have arrived at or departed from a port at the time when the ship comes within or, as the case may be, leaves the limits of that port.

Procedural Provisions

B16.17 A number of specific procedural provisions apply to prosecutions for any offence under the 1979 and 2005 Acts, and it will be convenient to consider these before turning to the offences themselves.

Institution of Proceedings

B16.18 With limited exceptions, prosecutions under the Acts may be commenced by the Commissioners and in the name of an officer of the Customs and Excise Service. The functions of the Director of Revenue and Customs Prosecutions were transferred to the Director of Public Prosecutions on 27 March 2014 (Public Bodies (Merger of the Director of Public Prosecutions and the Director of Revenue and Customs Prosecutions) Order 2014 (SI 2014 No. 834)).

Customs and Excise Management Act 1979, s. 145

(1) Subject to the following provisions of this section, no proceedings for an offence under the customs and excise Acts or for condemnation under Schedule 3 to this Act shall be instituted except—

   (a) by or with the consent of the Director of Public Prosecutions, or

   (b) by order of, or with the consent of, the Commissioners for Her Majesty's Revenue and Customs.

(2) Subject to the following provisions of this section, any proceedings under the customs and excise Acts instituted by order of the Commissioners in a magistrates court. . .shall be commenced in the name of an officer of Revenue and Customs.

(3) [Applies to Scotland only.]

(4) [Repealed by the Commissioners for Revenue and Customs Act 2005, sch. 5.]

(5) Nothing in the foregoing provisions of this section, shall prevent the institution of proceedings for an offence under the customs and excise Acts by order and in any case in which he thinks it proper that proceedings should be so instituted.

(6) Notwithstanding anything in the foregoing provisions of this section, where any person has been detained for any offence for which he is liable to be detained under the customs and excise Acts, any court before which he is brought may proceed to deal with the case although the proceedings have not been instituted in accordance with this section.

This provision applies also to conspiracy to commit an offence under the Acts (*Whitehead* [1982] QB 1272).

Time-limits Section 146A provides the following time-limits for instituting proceedings, which override the general limitation provisions of the MCA 1980, s. 127. **B16.19**

Customs and Excise Management Act 1979, s. 146A

(1) Except as otherwise provided in the customs and excise Acts, and notwithstanding anything in any other enactment, the following provisions shall apply in relation to proceedings for an offence under those Acts.

(2) Proceedings for an indictable offence shall not be commenced after the end of the period of 20 years beginning with the day on which the offence was committed.

(3) Proceedings for a summary offence shall not be commenced after the end of the period of three years beginning with that day but, subject to that, may be commenced at any time within six months from that date on which sufficient evidence to warrant the proceedings came to the knowledge of the prosecuting authority.

(4) For the purposes of subsection (3) above, a certificate of the prosecuting authority as to the date on which such evidence as is there mentioned came to that authority's knowledge shall be conclusive evidence of that fact.

(5) [Applies to Scotland only.]

(6) [Applies to Northern Ireland only.]

(7) In this section 'prosecuting authority', (a) in England and Wales means the DPP…

Knowledge of the prosecuting authority (formerly the Director of Revenue and Customs Prosecutions and now the DPP) does not include knowledge of Revenue and Customs staff (*Director of Revenue and Customs Prosecutions v NE Plastics Ltd* [2009] 2 Cr App R 358).

Appeals from Decisions of Magistrates' Courts B16.20

Customs and Excise Management Act 1979, s. 147

(3) In the case of proceedings in England and Wales, without prejudice to any right to require the statement of a case for the opinion of the High Court, the prosecutor may appeal to the Crown Court against any decision of a magistrates' court in proceedings for an offence under the customs and excise acts.

Place of Trial B16.21

Customs and Excise Management Act 1979, s. 148

(1) Proceedings for an offence under the customs and excise Acts may be commenced—
  (a) in any court having jurisdiction in the place where the person charged with the offence resides or is found; or
  (b) if any thing was detained or seized in connection with the offence, in any court having jurisdiction in the place where that thing was so detained or seized or was found or condemned as forfeited; or
  (c) in any court having jurisdiction anywhere in that part of the United Kingdom, namely—
    (i) England and Wales,
    (ii) Scotland, or
    (iii) Northern Ireland,
in which the place where the offence was committed is situated.

(2) Where any such offence was committed at some place outside the area of any commission of the peace, the place of the commission of the offence shall, for the purposes of the jurisdiction of any court, be deemed to be any place in the United Kingdom where the offender is found or to which he is first brought after the commission of the offence.

(3) The jurisdiction under subsection (2) above shall be in addition to and not in derogation of any jurisdiction or power of any court under any other enactment.

Powers of Court and Commissioners in Relation to Penalties

B16.22   Customs and Excise Management Act 1979, ss. 149 to 150 and 152

149.—(1) Where, in any proceedings for an offence under the customs and excise Acts, a magistrates court in England or Wales or a court of summary jurisdiction in Scotland, in addition to ordering the person convicted to pay a penalty for the offence—

(a) orders him to be imprisoned for a term in respect of the same offence; and

(b) further (whether at the same time or subsequently) orders him to be imprisoned for a term in respect of non-payment of that penalty or default of a sufficient distress to satisfy the amount of that penalty,

the aggregate of the terms for which he is so ordered to be imprisoned shall not exceed 15 months.

(2) [Repealed.]

(3) [Applies to Northern Ireland only.]

150.—(1) Where liability for any offence under the customs and excise Acts is incurred by two or more persons jointly, those persons shall each be liable for the full amount of any pecuniary penalty and may be proceeded against jointly or severally as the Director of Public Prosecutions (in relation to proceedings instituted in England and Wales) or the Commissioners (in relation to proceedings instituted in Scotland or Northern Ireland) may see fit.

(2) In any proceedings for an offence under the customs and excise Acts instituted in England, Wales or Northern Ireland, any court by whom the matter is considered may mitigate any pecuniary penalty as they see fit.

(3) In any proceedings for an offence or for the condemnation of any thing as being forfeited under the customs and excise Acts, the fact that security has been given by bond or otherwise for the payment of any duty or for compliance with any condition in respect of the non-payment of which or non-compliance with which the proceedings are instituted shall not be a defence.

. . .

152. The Commissioners may, as they see fit—

(a) compound an offence (whether or not proceedings have been instituted in respect of it) and compound proceedings or for the condemnation of any thing as being forfeited under the customs and excise Acts; or

(b) restore, subject to such conditions (if any) as they think proper, any thing forfeited or seized under those Acts; or

(c) and (d) [repealed];

but paragraph (a) above shall not apply to proceedings on indictment in Scotland.

Evidential Provisions

B16.23 The following important provisions relate to the burden of proof as to certain documents and frequently recurring facts.

                    Customs and Excise Management Act 1979, s. 154

(1) An averment in any process in proceedings under the customs and excise Acts—

(a) that those proceedings were instituted by the order of the Commissioners; or

(b) that any person is or was a Commissioner, officer or constable, or a member of Her Majesty's armed forces or coastguard; or

(c) that any person is or was appointed or authorised by the Commissioners to discharge, or was engaged by the orders or with the concurrence of the Commissioners in the discharge of, any duty; or

(d) that the Commissioners have or have not been satisfied as to any matter as to which they are required by any provision of those Acts to be satisfied; or

(e) that any ship is a British ship; or

(f) that any goods thrown overboard, staved or destroyed were so dealt with in order to prevent or avoid the seizure of those goods,

shall, until the contrary is proved, be sufficient evidence of the matter in question.

(2) Where in any proceedings relating to customs or excise any question arises as to the place from which any goods have been brought or as to whether or not—

(a) any duty has been paid or secured in respect of any goods; or

(b) any goods or other things whatsoever are of the description or nature alleged in the information, writ or other process; or

(c) any goods have been lawfully imported or lawfully unloaded from any ship or aircraft; or

(d) any goods have been lawfully loaded into any ship or aircraft or lawfully exported or were lawfully water-borne; or

(e) any goods were lawfully brought to any place for the purpose of being loaded into any ship or aircraft or exported; or

(f) any goods are or were subject to any prohibition of or restriction on their importation or exportation,

then where those proceedings are brought by or against the Commissioners, a law officer of the Crown or an officer, or against any other person in respect of anything purporting to have been done in pursuance of any power or duty conferred or imposed on him by or under the custom and excise Acts, the burden of proof shall be upon the other party to the proceedings.

Commissioners for Revenue and Customs Act 2005, s. 24 B16.24

(1) A document that purports to have been issued or signed by or with the authority of the Commissioners—

(a) shall be treated as having been so issued or signed unless the contrary is proved, and

(b) shall be admissible in any legal proceedings.

(2) A document that purports to have been issued by the Commissioners and which certifies any of the matters specified in subsection (3) shall (in addition to the matters provided for by subsection (1)(a) and (b)) be treated as accurate unless the contrary is proved.

(3) The matters mentioned in subsection (2) are—

(a) that a specified person was appointed as a commissioner on a specified date,

(b) that a specified person was appointed as an officer of Revenue and Customs on a specified date,

(c) that at a specified time or for a specified purpose (or both) a function was delegated to a specified Commissioner,

(d) that at a specified time or for a specified purpose (or both) a function was delegated to a specified committee, and

(e) that at a specified time or for a specified purpose (or both) a function was delegated to another specified person.

(4) A photographic or other copy of a document acquired by the Commissioners shall, if certified by them to be an accurate copy, be admissible in any legal proceedings to the same extent as the document itself.

(5) Section 2 of the Documentary Evidence Act 1868 (proof of documents) shall apply to a Revenue and Customs document as it applies in relation to the documents mentioned in that section.

(6) In the application of that section to a Revenue and Customs document the Schedule to that Act shall be treated as if—

(a) the first column contained a reference to the Commissioners, and

(b) the second column contained a reference to a Commissioner or a person acting on his authority.

(7) In this section—

(a) 'Revenue and Customs document' means a document issued by or on behalf of the Commissioners, and

(b) a reference to the Commissioners includes a reference to the Commissioners of Inland Revenue and to the Commissioners of Customs and Excise.

OFFENCES IN CONNECTION WITH COMMISSIONERS AND OFFICERS

Section 33 of the Commissioners for Revenue and Customs Act 2005 confers a power of **B16.25** arrest on an authorised officer of the Revenue and Customs if the officer reasonably suspects that a person has committed, is committing or is about to commit an offence under any of ss. 30 to 32.

Unlawful Assumption of Character of Commissioner or Officer

B16.26

Commissioners for Revenue and Customs Act 2005, s. 30

(1) A person commits an offence if he pretends to be a Commissioner or an officer of Revenue and Customs with a view to obtaining—
- (a) admission to premises,
- (b) information, or
- (c) any other benefit.

This is a summary offence with a maximum penalty of six months' imprisonment and a fine at level 5 on the standard scale, or both.

Obstruction of and Assaults upon Officers etc.

B16.27

Commissioners for Revenue and Customs Act 2005, ss. 31 and 32

31.—(1) A person commits an offence if without reasonable excuse he obstructs—
- (a) an officer of Revenue and Customs,
- (b) a person acting on behalf of the Commissioners or an officer of Revenue and Customs, or
- (c) a person assisting an officer of Revenue and Customs.

32.—(1) A person commits an offence if he assaults an officer of Revenue and Customs.

Section 31 creates a summary offence with a maximum penalty of six months' imprisonment and a fine at level 3 on the standard scale, or both. The general principles concerning obstruction of a police officer (see **B2.42** to **B2.47**) apply. Thus a person who gives false information to officers of the Revenue and Customs, so making it harder for officers to perform their duty, is guilty of obstruction (*George* [1981] Crim LR 185). For the powers of Customs officers to seize and detain goods, see the Customs and Excise Management Act 1979, s. 139, the two decisions of the Court of Appeal in *R (Eastenders Cash & Carry plc) v Revenue and Customs Commissioners* [2012] 1 WLR 2067 and [2012] 1 WLR 2912, *Revenue and Customs Commissioners v First Stop Wholesale Ltd* [2013] EWCA Civ 183 and *R (Blackside Ltd) v Secretary of State for the Home Department* [2013] EWHC 2087 (Admin).

Section 32 creates a summary offence with a maximum penalty of six months' imprisonment and a fine at level 5 on the standard scale, or both.

<h1 style="text-align:center">IMPROPER IMPORTATION AND
EXPORTATION OF GOODS</h1>

Improper Importation of Goods

B16.28

Customs and Excise Management Act 1979, s. 50

(1) Subsection (2) below applies to goods of the following descriptions, that is to say—
- (a) goods chargeable with a duty which has not been paid; and
- (b) goods the importation, landing or unloading of which is for the time being prohibited or restricted by or under any enactment.

(2) If any person with intent to defraud Her Majesty of any such duty or to evade any such prohibition or restriction as is mentioned in subsection (1) above—
- (a) unships or lands in any port or unloads from any aircraft in the United Kingdom or from any vehicle in Northern Ireland any goods to which this subsection applies, or assists or is otherwise concerned in such unshipping, landing or unloading; or
- (b) removes from their place of importation or from any approved wharf, examination station, transit shed or customs and excise station any goods to which this subsection applies or assists or is otherwise concerned in such removal,

he shall be guilty of an offence under this subsection and may be arrested.

(3) If any person imports or is concerned in importing any goods contrary to any prohibition or restriction for the time being in force under or by virtue of any enactment with respect to those goods, whether or not the goods are unloaded, and does so with intent to evade

the prohibition or restriction, he shall be guilty of an offence under this subsection and may be arrested.

Procedure and Penalties   This offence is triable either way. When tried on indictment it is normally a class 3 offence, but see CPD XIII, para. B (see Supplement, **PD-97**) for the additional factors that the court considers on allocation. As to the power of arrest, see *Smith* [1973] QB 924.   **B16.29**

Penalties are provided by the Customs and Excise Management Act 1979, s. 50(4): on indictment, a penalty of any amount, or imprisonment for a term not exceeding seven years or both; on summary conviction, a penalty of the prescribed sum or of three times the value of the goods, whichever is the greater, or imprisonment for a term not exceeding six months, or both. Enhanced penalties are provided for by s. 50(5) and sch. 1 and are imposed in the following types of cases.

(i) Where the goods in respect of which the offence is committed are drugs, the importation of which is prohibited by the Misuse of Drugs Act 1971, s. 3 (see **B16.32**). If the drug is a Class A or Class B or temporary class drug (as to the meaning of which, see **B19.2**), on summary conviction, the penalty is six months and/or a penalty not exceeding the prescribed amount, or three times the value of the goods, whichever is the greater; on indictment, there is a penalty of unlimited amount and, in the case of a Class A drug, life imprisonment, or, in the case of a Class B drug, 14 years' imprisonment. If the drug is a Class C drug (see **B19.2**), the penalty is, on summary conviction, three months and/or a penalty of £500, or three times the value of the goods, whichever is the greater. On indictment there is a penalty of unlimited amount and 14 years' imprisonment.

(ii) Where the importation is of any weapon or ammunition of a kind mentioned in the Firearms Act 1968, s. 5(1)(a), (ab), (aba), (ac), (ad), (ae), (af) or (c) or (1A)(a) (see **B12.56**) or of a counterfeit of a currency note or of a protected coin without the Treasury's consent (Forgery and Counterfeiting Act 1981, s. 20: see **B6.100**), the maximum penalty on indictment is enhanced to ten years by s. 50(5A) of, and sch. 1 to, the Act.

(iii) Where the offence is in connection with nuclear material, the maximum penalty on indictment is 14 years' imprisonment.

The definitive sentencing guideline, *Fraud, Bribery and Money Laundering Offences* (see Supplement, **SG-488**) includes guidance on sentencing for improper importation of goods. See **B16.52** for a fuller discussion of sentencing in revenue fraud cases.

Elements   As to prohibition or restriction, see *Superheater Co. Ltd v Commissioners of Customs and Excise* [1969] 2 All ER 469.   **B16.30**

Goods which are unloaded at an airport and held in a customs area pending trans-shipment to a foreign destination are regarded as having been imported into the UK (*Smith* [1973] QB 924).

A person who brings in items for others, e.g., a bus driver bringing in goods for his passengers, is an importer of the goods and if they are beneficially his he can be convicted of being knowingly concerned in the fraudulent evasion of duty payable on them (*Collins* [1987] Crim LR 256).

Duplication of Offences   Section 50(7) of the Customs and Excise Management Act 1979   **B16.31** prevents duplication of offences and possible double jeopardy problems.

Customs and Excise Management Act 1979, s. 50

(7) In any case where a person would, apart from this subsection, be guilty of—
    (a) an offence under this section in connection with the importation of goods contrary to a prohibition or restriction; and
    (b) a corresponding offence under the enactment or other instrument imposing the prohibition or restriction, being an offence for which a fine or other penalty is expressly provided by that enactment or other instrument,
he shall not be guilty of the offence mentioned in paragraph (a) of this subsection.

B

Part B Offences

Prohibition on Importation and Exportation of Controlled Drugs

B16.32   Misuse of Drugs Act 1971, s. 3

(1) Subject to subsection (2) below—
   (a) the importation of a controlled drug; and
   (b) the exportation of a controlled drug,
   are hereby prohibited.
(2) Subsection (1) above does not apply—
   (a) to the importation or exportation of a controlled drug which is for the time being excepted from paragraph (a) or, as the case may be, paragraph (b) of subsection (1) above by regulations under section 7 of this Act or by provision made in a temporary class drug order by virtue of section 7A; or
   (b) to the importation or exportation of a controlled drug under and in accordance with the terms of a licence issued by the Secretary of State and in compliance with any conditions attached thereto.

Section 18(2) of the Misuse of Drugs Act 1971 makes it an offence to contravene any conditions imposed on a licence under s. 3. As to controlled drugs generally, see **B19.2**.

Section 3 of the Misuse of Drugs Act 1971 creates a prohibition, but does not expressly create an offence. Consequently, evasion of this prohibition should be charged as an offence of fraudulent evasion of duty (under the Customs and Excise Management Act 1979, s. 170; **B16.38**) or as improper importation or exportation of goods (under ss. 50 and 68; **B16.28** and **B16.35**). It is also possible, where appropriate, to charge a conspiracy to evade the prohibition imposed by the Misuse of Drugs Act 1971, s. 3.

For sentencing guidelines relating to controlled drugs, including importation, see **B19.132** *et seq*.

Misdescription of Imported Goods

B16.33   Customs and Excise Management Act 1979, s. 50

(6) If any person—
   (a) imports or causes to be imported any goods concealed in a container holding goods of a different description; or
   (b) directly or indirectly imports or causes to be imported or entered any goods found, whether before or after delivery, not to correspond with the entry made thereof,
   he shall be liable on summary conviction to a penalty of three times the value of the goods or level 3 on the standard scale, whichever is the greater.

This offence appears clearly to be a strict liability offence. It meets the criteria for strict liability and in particular it emphasises the need to take care in the furnishing of information, packaging of imports, etc. (*Gammon (Hong Kong) Ltd v A-G of Hong Kong* [1985] AC 1; and see generally **A2.20**).

Improper Unloading of Goods Loaded etc. for Exportation

B16.34   Customs and Excise Management Act 1979, s. 67

(1) If any goods which have been loaded or retained on board any ship or aircraft for exportation are not exported to and discharged at a place outside the United Kingdom but are unloaded in the United Kingdom, then, unless—
   (a) the unloading was authorised by the proper officer; and
   (b) except where the officer otherwise permits, any duty chargeable and unpaid on the goods is paid and any drawback or allowance paid in respect thereof is repaid,
   the master of the ship or the commander of the aircraft and any person concerned in the unshipping, relanding, landing, unloading or carrying of the goods from the ship or aircraft without such authority, payment or repayment shall each be guilty of an offence under this section.

(2) The Commissioners may impose such conditions as they see fit with respect to any goods loaded or retained as mentioned in subsection (1) above which are permitted to be unloaded in the United Kingdom.

(3) If any person contravenes or fails to comply with, or is concerned in any contravention of or failure to comply with, any condition imposed under subsection (2) above he shall be guilty of an offence under this section.

(4) Where any goods loaded or retained as mentioned in subsection (1) above or brought to a customs and excise station for exportation by land are—

(a) goods from a warehouse, other than goods which have been kept, without being warehoused, in a warehouse by virtue of section 92(4). . .;

(b) transit goods;

(c) other goods chargeable with a duty which has not been paid; or

(d) drawback goods,

then if any container in which the goods are held is without the authority of the proper officer opened, or any mark, letter or device on any such container or on any lot of the goods is without that authority cancelled, obliterated or altered, every person concerned in the opening, cancellation, obliteration or alteration shall be guilty of an offence under this section.

The offence is triable only summarily. The penalty is forfeiture of goods and a penalty of three times the value of the goods or level 3 on the standard scale, whichever is the greater (s. 67(5)).

Offences in Relation to Exportation of Prohibited or Restricted Goods

Customs and Excise Management Act 1979, s. 68   B16.35

(1) If any goods are—

(a) exported or shipped as stores; or

(b) brought to any place in the United Kingdom for the purpose of being exported or shipped as stores,

and the exportation or shipment is or would be contrary to any prohibition or restriction for the time being in force with respect to those goods under or by virtue of any enactment, the goods shall be liable to forfeiture and the exporter or intending exporter of the goods and any agent of his concerned in the exportation or shipment or intended exportation or shipment shall each be liable on summary conviction to a penalty of three times the value of the goods or level three on the standard scale, whichever is the greater.

(2) Any person knowingly concerned in the exportation or shipment as stores, or in the attempted exportation or shipment as stores, of any goods with intent to evade any such prohibition or restriction as is mentioned in subsection (1) above shall be guilty of an offence under this subsection and may be arrested

. . .

(5) If by virtue of any such restriction as is mentioned in subsection (1) above any goods may be exported only when consigned to a particular place or person and any goods so consigned are delivered to some other place or person, the ship, aircraft or vehicle in which they were exported shall be liable to forfeiture unless it is proved to the satisfaction of the Commissioners that both the owner of the ship, aircraft or vehicle and the master of the ship, commander of the aircraft or person in charge of the vehicle—

(a) took all reasonable steps to secure that the goods were delivered to the particular place to which or person to whom they were consigned; and

(b) did not connive at or, except under duress, consent to the delivery of the goods to that other place or person.

(6) In any case where a person would, apart from this subsection be guilty of—

(a) an offence under subsection (1) or (2) above; and

(b) a corresponding offence under the enactment or instrument imposing the prohibition or restriction in question, being an offence for which a fine or other penalty is expressly provided by that enactment or other instrument,

he shall not be guilty of the offence mentioned in paragraph (a) of this subsection.

Procedure and Penalties   The offence is triable either way. When tried on indictment it is normally a class 3 offence, but see CPD XIII, para. B (see Supplement, **PD-97**) for the additional factors that the court considers on allocation. As to the power of arrest, see *Smith* [1973] QB 924.   B16.36

The Customs and Excise Management Act 1979, s. 68(3), (4) and (4A) and sch. 1, prescribe penalties. On summary conviction there may be imposed a penalty of the prescribed sum or of three times the value of the goods whichever is the greater, or imprisonment for a term not exceeding six months or both. On conviction on indictment there may be imposed a penalty of any amount, or imprisonment for a term not exceeding seven years, or both. Enhanced penalties as under s. 50 (see **B16.29**) apply to dealing respectively with drugs, firearms and counterfeit notes and currency.

The penalties are also modified where a person is convicted of an offence contrary to s. 68 by virtue of the application of reg. 6 of the Controlled Drugs (Drug Precursors) (Community External Trade) Regulations 2008 (SI 2008 No. 296), which makes provision in relation to the breach of EU legislation enabling authorities to obtain information about operations involving substances useful for the manufacture of controlled drugs. In these cases, the maximum penalty under s. 68(1) is not to exceed level 5 on the standard scale, and, for an offence under s. 68(2), the maximum penalty on indictment is two years' imprisonment and, on summary conviction, is not to exceed the statutory maximum and three months' imprisonment.

Provision for forfeiture is made, subject to defences, by s. 68(5) above.

B16.37   **Elements**   Under other legislation relating to national defence, it was held that a person may be convicted of an offence of unlawful exportation even though he intends to bring the goods back to the UK (*Berner* (1953) 37 Cr App R 113).

A person can be concerned with the exportation of goods even if the acts which he performs take place at a time other than that which constitutes exportation. A person can be so concerned, for example, at a time prior to the departure of an aircraft (*Garrett v Arthur Churchill (Glass) Ltd* [1970] 1 QB 92).

The prosecution must show both that the export of the goods was prohibited (e.g., by the Export Control Order 2008 (SI 2008 No. 3231)), and that the accused knew that the goods fell into a prohibited category (*Daghir* [1994] Crim LR 945). The Customs and Excise Management Act 1979, s. 68(2), is cast in terms of evasion. This does not require an element of fraud or dishonesty, but is, rather, given its ordinary English meaning, i.e. 'to get around or avoid' (*Hurford-Jones* (1977) 65 Cr App R 263; see also *Bajwa* [2012] 1 All ER 348 at [90] (see **B16.43**)).

In *Garrett v Arthur Churchill (Glass) Ltd* [1970] 1 QB 92, it was held that a person who hands over goods belonging to another, knowing that the other proposes to export them unlawfully, is knowingly concerned in the unlawful importation. The duty to hand over goods to their owner yields to the public interest in preventing such exportation.

Under art. 26 of the Export Control Order 2008 (SI 2008 No. 3231), an export which would otherwise be forbidden may be licensed by the Secretary of State. Such a licence will not bar a prosecution under s. 68(2) where a shipment is in fact to a destination other than that specified in the licence. Even if it cannot be proved that a licence was obtained by misrepresentation, a prosecution may still be brought if the actor seeks to evade the prohibition by specifying a sham consignee (*Redfern and Dunlop Ltd (Aircraft Division)* [1993] Crim LR 43).

An order prohibiting exportation is no less valid where its substance falls within a matter governed by the common commercial policy of the EU, provided that the order and any EEC Regulation are not incompatible (*Searle and KCS Products* [1996] Crim LR 58).

FRAUDULENT EVASION OF DUTY ('SMUGGLING')

B16.38   **Customs and Excise Management Act 1979, s. 170**

(1) Without prejudice to any other provision of the Customs and Excise Acts 1979, if any person—
   (a) knowingly acquires possession of any of the following goods, that is to say—
      (i)   goods which have been unlawfully removed from a warehouse or Queens warehouse;
      (ii) goods which are chargeable with a duty which has not been paid;

>   (iii) goods with respect to the importation or exportation of which any prohibition or restriction is for the time being in force under or by virtue of any enactment; or
>
>   (b) is in any way knowingly concerned in carrying, removing, depositing, harbouring, keeping or concealing or in any manner dealing with any such goods,
>
> and does so with intent to defraud Her Majesty of any duty payable on the goods or to evade any such prohibition or restriction with respect to the goods he shall be guilty of an offence under this section and may be arrested.
>
> (2) Without prejudice to any other provision of the Customs and Excise Acts 1979, if any person is, in relation to any goods, in any way knowingly concerned in any fraudulent evasion or attempt at evasion—
>
>   (a) of any duty chargeable on the goods;
>
>   (b) of any prohibition or restriction for the time being in force with respect to the goods under or by virtue of any enactment; or
>
>   (c) of any provision of the Customs and Excise Acts 1979 applicable to the goods,
>
> he shall be guilty of an offence under this section and may be arrested
>
> ...
>
> (5) In any case where a person would, apart from this subsection, be guilty of—
>
>   (a) an offence under this section in connection with a prohibition or restriction; and
>
>   (b) a corresponding offence under the enactment or other instrument imposing the prohibition or restriction, being an offence for which a fine or other penalty is expressly provided by that enactment or other instrument,
>
> he shall not be guilty of the offence mentioned in paragraph (a) of this subsection.

For the offence of 'people smuggling' under the Immigration Act 1971, s. 25, see **B22.21**.

Procedure

The offence is triable either way. When tried on indictment it is normally a class 3 offence, but see CPD XIII, para. B (see Supplement, **PD-97**) for the additional factors that the court considers on allocation. The Customs and Excise Management Act 1979, s. 170(5), operates to prevent duplication of proceedings and possible double jeopardy problems. **B16.39**

Indictment (for Offences under s. 170(1)(b))

Statement of Offence **B16.40**

Being knowingly concerned in concealing goods with intent to avoid prohibition on importation contrary to section 170(1)(b) of the Customs and Excise Management Act 1979.

Particulars of Offence

A on the...day of...was knowingly concerned in concealing goods, that is to say a quantity of a controlled drug, namely...valued at £..., with intent to evade the prohibition on importation of the said goods then in force pursuant to section 3 of the Misuse of Drugs Act 1971.

As to the Misuse of Drugs Act 1971, s. 3, see **B16.32** and as to controlled drugs generally, see **B19.2**.

Sentencing

The maximum penalty on summary conviction is a penalty of the prescribed sum or of three times the value of the goods, whichever is the greater, and/or to imprisonment for a term not exceeding six months. The maximum penalty on indictment is a penalty of any amount and/or imprisonment for a term not exceeding seven years (Customs and Excise Management Act 1979, s.170(3)). **B16.41**

In cases involving drugs, firearms and counterfeiting, penalties may be enhanced (s. 170(4) and (4A) and sch. 1). The enhancement is identical to that provided for in the case of s. 50 of the Act (see **B16.29**). For sentencing guidelines in drugs cases, see **B19.132** *et seq*. In cases involving seal skins the maximum penalty is two years' imprisonment (s. 170(4B)).

The definitive sentencing guideline, *Fraud, Bribery and Money Laundering Offences* (see Supplement, **SG-488**), includes guidance on sentencing for fraudulent evasion of excise duty. See **B16.52** for a fuller discussion of sentencing in revenue fraud cases.

Scope of Offence

B16.42 These are wide prohibitions. Section 170 covers importing, exporting, those concerned in actual import and export, and even persons who cannot be proved to be implicated in an actual import or export; it is hard to think of anything in s. 170(2) which does not in fact come within s. 170(1) (*Neal* [1984] 3 All ER 156). One possibility may be, however, that a person could knowingly come into possession of unlawfully imported goods contrary to s. 170(1)(a)(iii) without himself being concerned in their importation contrary to s. 170(2)(b).

Actus Reus

B16.43 A person evades an obligation if he deliberately so organises affairs that he is able to avoid doing what he knows he has to do (*Bajwa* [2012] 1 All ER 348 at [90]–[93]). The words 'fraudulent evasion' in s. 170(2) do not require proof of acts of deceit practised on a customs officer (*A-G's Ref (No. 1 of 1981)* [1982] QB 848). When goods are smuggled into the UK by boat with the intention of avoiding the payment of duty, evasion takes place when the vessel enters the limits of the port (*Bajwa* [2012] 1 All ER 348 at [94]). Section 170(2) does not require an actual fraudulent importation; the offence can be committed by attempted evasion even if the accused's acts took place abroad (*Latif* [1996] 1 All ER 353).

The offence in s. 170(2) could relate to a single incident or a series of incidents forming an activity, any of which could be charged in a single count (*Martin* [1998] 2 Cr App R 385). Neither s. 170(1) nor (2) is restricted to those who form part of an original smuggling team (*Neal* [1984] 3 All ER 156).

A person may be liable for acts done abroad prior to the actual smuggling, as well as for participation in the act of entry itself, and for acts subsequent to entry relating, for example, to disposal of the goods (*Jakeman* (1983) 76 Cr App R 223). In *Wall* [1974] 2 All ER 254 the accused took part in Afghanistan in the loading of cannabis for the purpose of exporting it to the UK. Section 170B (see **B16.49**) creates a separate offence of being knowingly concerned in the taking of steps with a view to the fraudulent evasion of excise duty.

B16.44 In *Green* [1976] QB 985, the accused and another arranged customs clearance for a crate which, at the moment of importation, contained cannabis. Customs officials substituted a harmless substance before the crate left the warehouse. The accused, who assisted in the operation by renting a garage and unloading a crate, was held liable on the footing that the evasion of the prohibition continues until the goods cease to be prohibited goods or, possibly, are exported. Renting a garage may be an act concerned in the evasion of the prohibition. A narrower and, it is submitted, less difficult ground for decision might be that the making of such arrangements constituted being concerned in the evasion, at least if it was done before substitution of the contents, though such an approach could encounter difficulties of proof. Evasion of the relevant prohibition is a continuing process; thus a person who, even after goods have been innocently imported by a carrier, falsely declares that his possessions contain no prohibited material, commits the offence (*Coughlan* (12 May 1997 unreported); *Bell* [2011] EWCA Crim 6 at [10]).

The same principles as to when the offence begins and ends appear in cases of conspiracy to evade a prohibition, etc. There can, it is said, be no abstract limit to the time when or place at which the crime is committed, provided always that the goods, the subject-matter of the charge, are goods which are the subject of a prohibition on importation and the acquisition is done knowingly and with intent to evade that prohibition or restriction (*Ardalan* [1972] 2 All ER 257). In *Caippara* (1987) 87 Cr App R 316, in the context of importation of drugs, the Court of Appeal held that a person may be guilty if it be proved that he was willing to participate in a chain of activities which would result in drugs being imported into the UK, notwithstanding that the Customs has substituted a harmless substance for them before delivery to the recipient.

Acts done after importation can be done in furtherance of a conspiracy since the conspiracy is not to import but to evade a restriction (*Borro* [1973] Crim LR 513).

B16.45 EC Council regulations are enactments the evasion of which is an offence under s. 170(2)(b). For the purpose of prohibiting trade in endangered species, the offence is committed under English law by a person concerned in importation notwithstanding that the initial country of entry is not the UK (*Sissen* [2001] 1 WLR 962).

No defence of necessity at common law in the interests of pain relief, whether for the person importing or others, can be raised to an unauthorised importation of a prohibited drug (*Quayle* [2005] 1 All ER 988; *Altham* [2006] 1 WLR 3287).

The fact of importation, where relevant, must be proved. It is then incumbent on the accused to prove factors in justification mentioned in s. 154 of the Act (see **B16.23**), such as that the goods were made here or that duty has been paid (*Watts* (1979) 70 Cr App R 187; *Mizel v Warren* [1973] 2 All ER 1149).

Mens Rea

B16.46 Under s. 170(1), it must be shown that the accused knowingly performed certain acts with intent to defraud Her Majesty or with intent to evade a relevant prohibition or restriction. In relation to knowingly harbouring goods, it is usually enough to show that goods which were subject to duty were found in the possession of the accused. This will establish a prima facie case of knowingly harbouring subject to the accused's ability to rebut this by evidence casting doubt upon his knowledge. Once the Crown has adduced a case of knowing possession, the accused must prove that the goods were in fact customed; see s. 154 (at **B16.23**) and *Cohen* [1951] 1 KB 505. In respect of the importation of indecent material, it is enough if the person knows the material to be indecent; he need not know the precise nature of the indecency portrayed (*Forbes* [2002] 2 AC 512).

It was held in *Latif* [1996] 1 All ER 353, that the guilty mind need not subsist at the time of the importation: thus one who is recruited to pick up a package which has already arrived has a sufficient *mens rea* because he is then concerned with bringing about the importation.

A person who presents goods for an assessment of duty does not act fraudulently by not disclosing his assessment of their worth, or by failing to alert a customs officer that the officer's valuation is wrong. In the absence of a false statement or concealment, the payment of duty demanded by a customs officer discharges the person's liability (*Customs and Excise Commissioners v Tan* [1977] AC 650).

B16.47 The prosecution must under s. 170(2) prove both an intent to evade a prohibition and knowledge on the part of the accused of the relevant circumstances, for example in a case of smuggling by sea that he had in fact entered territorial waters. Mere knowledge by the accused that he was at the relevant time running the risk of entering territorial waters is not enough (*Panayi (No. 2)* [1989] 1 WLR 187).

The accused may have formed a guilty intent outside the UK. If the intent is formed abroad and acts constituting the offence are done there, liability will be complete. Subsequent repentance will not found a defence (*Jakeman* (1983) 76 Cr App R 223).

It need not be proved that the accused was aware of the exact nature of the articles to which a restriction applies. If a person believes himself to be engaged in the importation of goods which are not subject to a restriction or prohibition, he cannot be convicted (*Taaffe* [1984] AC 539). He is to be judged on the facts as he believed them to be. If he believes himself to be importing narcotics whereas the substance is snuff, he may be convicted of attempting to evade a prohibition or restriction (*Shivpuri* [1987] AC 1). If on the other hand he imports drugs believing them to be pornography, he will be liable for the offence (*Ellis* (1986) 84 Cr App R 235; *Hennessey*

905

(1978) 68 Cr App R 419). A person who knows the nature of the material imported and who believes it to be obscene will be liable for the offence even though no jury trying a case under the Obscene Publications Act 1959 has determined the article to be so: knowledge and belief suffice for guilt (*Dunne* (1998) 162 JP 399).

B16.48 Particular problems concern drugs where importation and exportation offences vary in severity according to whether the drug is a Class A, B, or C drug. Lord Bridge stated in *Shivpuri* [1987] AC 1 that the legislative history of the Misuse of Drugs Act 1971 makes clear that, while possession of class A, B, or C drugs are distinct offences, the offence of being concerned in importation requires proof only that the accused knew that he was engaged in evading restrictions on the importation of a prohibited article. Lord Bridge's dictum was followed in *Siracusa* (1989) 90 Cr App R 340. The prosecution must prove that the accused knew that the goods in question were prohibited goods, but need not prove that the accused knew (precisely) what they were.

On a charge of conspiracy to supply controlled drugs, the prosecution must prove that the accused either (i) knew that the agreement related to the particular drug mentioned in the indictment, or (ii) knew that it related to a drug of the same class, without having any knowledge or belief as to it involving any particular drug, or (iii) believed that it related to another particular drug of the same class, or of a class attracting a greater penalty, or (iv) believed that it related to a drug of a class attracting a greater maximum penalty, without having any belief as to any particular drug, or (v) did not care at all what particular drug was involved. An accused would escape liability only where he mistakenly believed that the conspiracy related to a controlled drug of a class attracting a lesser maximum penalty (*Hanif* [2012] EWCA Crim 1968 at [14], following *Ayala* [2003] EWCA Crim 2047).

Offences under other provisions, e.g., regulations relating to the importation of animal products intended for human consumption, carry strict liability (see *Matudi* [2003] EWCA Crim 697 and **A2.20**).

Taking Preparatory Steps for Evasion of Excise Duty

B16.49   Customs and Excise Management Act 1979, s. 170B

(1) If any person is knowingly concerned in the taking of any steps with a view to the fraudulent evasion, whether by himself or another, of any duty of excise on any goods, he shall be liable—
   (a) on summary conviction, to a penalty of the prescribed sum or of three times the amount of the duty, whichever is the greater, or to imprisonment for a term not exceeding six months or to both; and
   (b) on conviction on indictment, to a penalty of any amount or to imprisonment for a term not exceeding seven years or to both.
(2) Where any person is guilty of an offence under this section, the goods in respect of which the offence was committed shall be liable to forfeiture.

Untrue Declarations

B16.50   Customs and Excise Management Act 1979, s. 167

(1) If any person either knowingly or recklessly—
   (a) makes or signs, or causes to be made or signed, or delivers or causes to be delivered to the Commissioners or an officer, any declaration, notice, certificate or other document whatsoever; or
   (b) makes any statement in answer to any question put to him by an officer which he is required by or under any enactment to answer,
being a document or statement produced or made for any purpose or any assigned matter, which is untrue in any material particular, he shall be guilty of an offence under this subsection and may be arrested; and any goods in relation to which the document or statement was made shall be liable to forfeiture.

(2) Without prejudice to subsection (4) below, a person who commits an offence under subsection (1) above shall be liable—

    (a) on summary conviction, to a penalty of the prescribed sum, or to imprisonment for a term not exceeding six months, or to both; or

    (b) on conviction on indictment, to a penalty of any amount, or to imprisonment for a term not exceeding two years, or to both.

(3) If any person—

    (a) makes or signs, or causes to be made or signed, or delivers or causes to be delivered to the Commissioners or an officer, any declaration, notice, certificate or other document whatsoever; or

    (b) makes any statement in answer to any question put to him by an officer which he is required by or under any enactment to answer,

being a document or statement produced or made for any purpose of any assigned matter, which is untrue in any material particular, then, without prejudice to subsection (4) below, he shall be liable on summary conviction to a penalty of level 4 on the standard scale.

In *Cross* [1987] Crim LR 43, it was held that the construction of documents is for the judge and not the jury; see also *Pioneer Shipping Ltd v BTP Tioxide Ltd (The Nema)* [1982] AC 724 at p. 736.

As to recklessness in this context, see *G* [2004] 1 AC 1034 and **A2.8** *et seq.* generally. The offence under s. 167(3) would seem to be an offence of strict liability (*Patel v Comptroller of Customs* [1966] AC 356).

Counterfeiting Documents

Customs and Excise Management Act 1979, s. 168

B16.51

(1) If any person—

    (a) counterfeits or falsifies any document which is required by or under any enactment relating to an assigned matter or which is used in the transaction of any business relating to an assigned matter; or

    (b) knowingly accepts, receives or uses any such document so counterfeited or falsified; or

    (c) alters any such document after it is officially issued; or

    (d) counterfeits any seal, signature, initials or other mark of, or used by, any officer for the verification of such a document or for the security of goods or for any other purpose relating to an assigned matter,

he shall be guilty of an offence under this section and may be arrested.

Offences under s. 168(1) are triable either way. Under s. 168(2) the penalty, on indictment, is a penalty of any amount and/or imprisonment for a term not exceeding two years. The penalty on summary conviction, is a penalty of the prescribed sum and/or imprisonment for a term not exceeding six months. See also **B16.6** for the similar offence under the Taxes Management Act 1970, s. 20BB.

In *Patel v Comptroller of Customs* [1966] AC 356, it was held that falsification and counterfeiting require *mens rea*. It may be helpful to refer to the law on these subjects under the Forgery and Counterfeiting Act 1981. See generally **B6.26** to **B6.29** and **B6.66**.

SENTENCING GUIDELINES FOR REVENUE FRAUD

Charges in respect of revenue fraud may be brought under a range of statutory provisions. **B16.52** The principal ones are likely to be fraud (see **B5.4**), false accounting (see **B6.3**), fraudulent evasion of VAT, false statement for VAT purposes, conduct amounting to an offence under the Value Added Tax Act 1994, s. 72 (see **B16.7**), fraudulent evasion of income tax (see **B16.4**), fraudulent evasion of excise duty (see **B16.38**) and improper importation of goods (see **B16.28**).

The definitive sentencing guideline, *Fraud, Bribery and Money Laundering Offences* (see Supplement, **SG-488**), sets out guidance for sentencing for a range of revenue fraud offences. The guideline applies to individual offenders aged 18 and over and organisations. It applies to all offenders sentenced on or after 1 October 2014 regardless of the date of the offence. There is a separate part of the guideline applicable to corporate offenders which covers offences under the Value Added Tax Act 1994, s. 72, and the Customs and Excise Management Act 1979, s. 170. The court is required to determine the offender's level of culpability and the harm, in monetary terms. A table in the guideline sets out starting points and ranges of sentences.

The previous guideline was considered in *Wood* [2010] EWCA Crim 1742 (sentences of four years' and three years, eight months' imprisonment on pleas of guilty to defrauding the public revenue of £1.7 million VAT), *Tariq* [2012] EWCA Crim 1842 at [40]–[51] (five years' imprisonment upheld following conviction after trial for conspiracy to evade £600,000 duty payable on alcohol), *Lamb* [2013] EWCA Crim 1365 (sentences of six and five years' imprisonment on former police officers for conspiracy to evade duty on cigarettes), *Lachman* [2013] EWCA Crim 1528 (sentence of five and a half years' imprisonment on a drugs courier importing 1.18 kg of cocaine) and *Sedani* [2013] EWCA Crim 1763 (sentence of 20 months' imprisonment for evading duty on tobacco suspended for reasons of serious ill-health); see also *Lendrum* [2011] 2 Cr App R (S) 404 (18 months' imprisonment for being knowingly concerned in carrying peregrine falcon eggs with intent to evade the prohibition or restriction on export).

SOCIAL SECURITY OFFENCES

B16.53   The dishonest obtaining and/or retention of benefits may well involve the commission of offences under the Fraud Act 2006 (see **B5.4** *et seq.*) or false accounting (see **B6.3**), but the Social Security Administration Act 1992, s. 111A, creates further offences carrying comparable penalties while s. 112 creates a range of summary offences.

Dishonest Representations for Obtaining Benefit, etc.

B16.54   Social Security Administration Act 1992, s. 111A

(1) If a person dishonestly—
    (a) makes a false statement or representation; or
    (b) produces or furnishes, or causes or allows to be produced or furnished, any document or information which is false in a material particular,
with a view to obtaining any benefit or other payment or advantage under the relevant social security legislation (whether for himself or for some other person), he shall be guilty of an offence.

(1A) A person shall be guilty of an offence if—
    (a) there has been a change of circumstances affecting any entitlement of his to any benefit or other payment or advantage under any provision of the relevant social security legislation;
    (b) the change is not a change that is excluded by regulations from the changes that are required to be notified;
    (c) he knows that the change affects an entitlement of his to such a benefit or other payment or advantage; and
    (d) he dishonestly fails to give a prompt notification of that change in the prescribed manner to the prescribed person.

(1B) A person shall be guilty of an offence if—
    (a) there has been a change of circumstances affecting any entitlement of another person to any benefit or other payment or advantage under any provision of the relevant social security legislation;

(b) the change is not a change that is excluded by regulations from the changes that are required to be notified;

(c) he knows that the change affects an entitlement of that other person to such a benefit or other payment or advantage; and

(d) he dishonestly causes or allows that other person to fail to give a prompt notification of that change in the prescribed manner to the prescribed person.

(1C) This subsection applies where—

(a) there has been a change of circumstances affecting any entitlement of a person ('the claimant') to any benefit or other payment or advantage under any provision of the relevant social security legislation;

(b) the benefit, payment or advantage is one in respect of which there is another person ('the recipient') who for the time being has a right to receive payments to which the claimant has, or (but for the arrangements under which they are payable to the recipient) would have, an entitlement; and

(c) the change is not a change that is excluded by regulations from the changes that are required to be notified.

(1D) In a case where subsection (1C) above applies, the recipient is guilty of an offence if—

(a) he knows that the change affects an entitlement of the claimant to a benefit or other payment or advantage under a provision of the relevant social security legislation;

(b) the entitlement is one in respect of which he has a right to receive payments to which the claimant has, or (but for the arrangements under which they are payable to the recipient) would have, an entitlement; and

(c) he dishonestly fails to give a prompt notification of that change in the prescribed manner to the prescribed person.

(1E) In a case where that subsection applies, a person other than the recipient is guilty of an offence if—

(a) he knows that the change affects an entitlement of the claimant to a benefit or other payment or advantage under a provision of the relevant social security legislation;

(b) the entitlement is one in respect of which the recipient has a right to receive payments to which the claimant has, or (but for the arrangements under which they are payable to the recipient) would have, an entitlement; and

(c) he dishonestly causes or allows the recipient to fail to give a prompt notification of that change in the prescribed manner to the prescribed person.

(1F) In any case where subsection (1C) above applies but the right of the recipient is confined to a right, by reason of his being a person to whom the claimant is required to make payments in respect of a dwelling, to receive payments of housing benefit—

(a) a person shall not be guilty of an offence under subsection (1D) or (1E) above unless the change is one relating to one or both of the following—

(i)   the claimant's occupation of that dwelling;

(ii) the claimant's liability to make payments in respect of that dwelling; but

(b) subsections (1D)(a) and (1E)(a) above shall each have effect as if after 'knows' there were inserted 'or could reasonably be expected to know'.

(1G) For the purposes of subsections (1A) to (1E) above a notification of a change is prompt if, and only if, it is given as soon as reasonably practicable after the change occurs.

(2) [repealed]

Elements 'Dishonestly' in the Social Security Administration Act 1992, s. 111A, has its normal meaning in criminal offences, namely that the accused must have realised that what he was doing was, by the standards of reasonable and honest people, dishonest and that that was what it was (*Department for Work and Pensions v Courts* [2006] EWHC 1156 (Admin) at [3]). For the direction on dishonesty in cases under s. 111A, see *Marsden* [2006] EWCA Crim 2236 at [15]. The prosecution have to prove that the accused knew that the change of circumstances had to be notified (*Zorlu* [2009] EWCA Crim 589).   **B16.55**

The prosecution must prove that any 'change of circumstances' which a person failed to report would (and not merely could or might) have affected an entitlement to benefit etc. (*King v Kerrier District Council* [2006] EWHC 500 (Admin); *Coventry City Council v Vassell* [2011] EWHC 1542 (Admin) at [32]–[35]; *Webster* [2013] EWCA Crim 1714 at [41]). A change of circumstances will not affect entitlement unless, upon computation, the entitlement to benefit would be altered by the change (*Croydon London Borough Council v Shanahan* (2010) 174 JP 172 at [18]). See also *Passmore* [2008] 1 Cr App R 165, where it was held that the accused committed no offence by failing to disclose that he had formed a company from which he had received no income, and *Mote* [2007] EWCA Crim 313.

Where the prosecution rely on the word 'allows' in s. 111A(1B), they must prove that the accused failed to take some action which he could appropriately have taken that would have resulted in the other person discharging his obligation to report (*Tilley* [2010] 1 WLR 605).

The word 'prompt' in s. 111A is an ordinary word to be given its natural meaning. The question whether 'prompt notification' has been given is one of fact (*Coventry City Council v Vassell* [2011] EWHC 1542 (Admin) at [37]–[39]).

False Representations for Obtaining Benefit, etc.

B16.56   Section 112 complements s. 111A with a range of purely summary offences. These largely mirror the offences created by s. 111A and require similar knowledge of relevant matters, but do not require proof of dishonesty.

Social Security Administration Act 1992, s. 112

(1) If a person for the purpose of obtaining any benefit or other payment under the [relevant social security legislation] whether for himself or some other person, or for any other purpose connected with that legislation—
   (a) makes a statement or representation which he knows to be false; or
   (b) produces or furnishes, or knowingly causes or knowingly allows to be produced or furnished, any document or information which he knows to be false in a material particular,
   he shall be guilty of an offence.
(1A)   A person shall be guilty of an offence if—
   (a) there has been a change of circumstances affecting any entitlement of his to any benefit or other payment or advantage under any provision of the relevant social security legislation;
   (b) the change is not a change that is excluded by regulations from the changes that are required to be notified;
   (c) he knows that the change affects an entitlement of his to such a benefit or other payment or advantage; and
   (d) he fails to give a prompt notification of that change in the prescribed manner to the prescribed person.
(1B)   A person is guilty of an offence under this section if—
   (a) there has been a change of circumstances affecting any entitlement of another person to any benefit or other payment or advantage under any provision of the relevant social security legislation;
   (b) the change is not a change that is excluded by regulations from the changes that are required to be notified;
   (c) he knows that the change affects an entitlement of that other person to such a benefit or other payment or advantage; and
   (d) he causes or allows that other person to fail to give a prompt notification of that change in the prescribed manner to the prescribed person.
(1C)   In a case where subsection (1C) of section 111A above applies, the recipient is guilty of an offence if—
   (a) he knows that the change affects an entitlement of the claimant to a benefit or other payment or advantage under a provision of the relevant social security legislation;
   (b) the entitlement is one in respect of which he has a right to receive payments to which the claimant has, or (but for the arrangements under which they are payable to the recipient) would have, an entitlement; and
   (c) he fails to give a prompt notification of that change in the prescribed manner to the prescribed person.

(1D) In a case where that subsection applies, a person other than the recipient is guilty of an offence if—

    (a) he knows that the change affects an entitlement of the claimant to a benefit or other payment or advantage under a provision of the relevant social security legislation;

    (b) the entitlement is one in respect of which the recipient has a right to receive payments to which the claimant has, or (but for the arrangements under which they are payable to the recipient) would have, an entitlement; and

    (c) he causes or allows the recipient to fail to give a prompt notification of that change in the prescribed manner to the prescribed person.

(1E) Subsection (1F) of section 111A above applies in relation to subsections (1C) and (1D) above as it applies in relation to subsections (1D) and (1E) of that section.

(1F) For the purposes of subsections (1A) to (1D) above a notification of a change is prompt if, and only if, it is given as soon as reasonably practicable after the change occurs.

Elements While the offences under the Social Security Administration Act 1992, s. 112, do not require proof of dishonesty, s. 112(1A)(d) is to be read as requiring the prosecution to prove a mental element of knowingly failing to notify (*Coventry City Council v Vassell* [2011] EWHC 1542 (Admin) at [50]–[70]). Moreover, any 'change of circumstance' must be proved to have affected an entitlement (see **B16.55**). As to the meaning of 'allows' and 'prompt', see **B16.55**.   **B16.57**

Related Offences The fraudulent evasion of an obligation to make social security contributions is dealt with under the Social Security Administration Act 1992, s. 114. Any person 'knowingly concerned in the fraudulent evasion of any contributions which he or any other person is liable to pay' may be sentenced on indictment to imprisonment for up to seven years; or on summary conviction to a fine not exceeding the statutory maximum.   **B16.58**

Procedure

The DPP has published (on www.cps.gov.uk) guidelines for the prosecution of benefit fraud cases. In addition, procedural provisions relating to the prosecution of offences under the Social Security Administration Act 1992 are contained in s. 116.   **B16.59**

Social Security Administration Act 1992, s. 116

(1) Any person authorised by the Secretary of State in that behalf may conduct any proceedings under any provision of this Act other than section 114 or under any provision of the Jobseekers Act 1995 before a magistrates' court although not a barrister or solicitor.

(2) Notwithstanding anything in any Act—

    (a) proceedings for an offence under this Act (other than proceedings to which paragraph (b) applies) or for an offence under the Jobseekers Act 1995 may be begun at any time within the period of 3 months from the date on which evidence, sufficient in the opinion of the Secretary of State to justify a prosecution for the offence, comes to his knowledge or within a period of 12 months from the commission of the offence, whichever period last expires; and

    (b) proceedings brought by the appropriate authority for an offence under this Act relating to housing benefit or council tax benefit may be begun at any time within the period of 3 months from the date on which evidence, sufficient in the opinion of the appropriate authority to justify a prosecution for the offence, comes to the authority's knowledge or within a period of 12 months from the commission of the offence, whichever period last expires.

(2A) Subsection 2 above shall not be taken to impose any restriction on the time when proceedings may be begun for an offence under section 111A above.

(3) For the purposes of subsection (2) above—

    (a) a certificate purporting to be signed by or on behalf of the Secretary of State as to the date on which such evidence as is mentioned in paragraph (a) of that subsection came to his knowledge shall be conclusive evidence of that date; and

    (b) a certificate of the appropriate authority as to the date on which such evidence as is mentioned in paragraph (b) of that subsection came to the authority's knowledge shall be conclusive evidence of that date.

For the running of time within which a prosecution must be brought under s. 116(2), see *Eyeson v Milton Keynes Council* [2005] EWHC 1160 (Admin) and *Smith v North Somerset Council* (2007) 171 JP 509. A certificate under s. 116(3) is conclusive unless it is inaccurate on its face or fraudulent (*Azam v Epping Forest District Council* [2009] EWHC 3177 (Admin)). The Secretary of State may delegate the power to issue a certificate under s. 116 to a lawyer or prosecutor (*Mohammed v Department for Work and Pensions* [2012] EWHC 4220 (Admin)).

A heavy burden has to be discharged to stay prosecutions on the ground of abuse of process (*Department of Work and Pensions v Courts* [2006] EWHC 1156 (Admin)).

B16.60 **Sentencing**   The maximum sentence for an offence under the Social Security Administration Act 1992, s. 111A, is (i) on indictment, seven years' imprisonment, a fine or both and (ii) on summary conviction, six months' imprisonment, a fine not exceeding the statutory maximum or both. The maximum sentence for the offences under s. 112 is three months' imprisonment, a fine not exceeding level 5 on the standard scale or both.

The definitive sentencing guideline, *Fraud, Bribery and Money Laundering Offences* (see Supplement, **SG-492**), sets out guidance for sentencing for benefit fraud offences under s. 111A. The court is required to determine the offender's level of culpability and the harm, in monetary terms. A table in the guideline sets out starting points and ranges of sentences. Unlike the previous guideline (see *Noel* [2012] EWCA Crim 956), the new guideline also contains a table setting out starting points and ranges for sentences for offences under s. 112. The guideline applies to individual offenders aged 18 and over who are sentenced on or after 1 October 2014 regardless of the date of the offence.

B16.61 The previous guideline was considered in *Gardiner* [2012] EWCA Crim 1318 (at **B16.5**) and *Fiaz* [2012] EWCA Crim 1823, in which the offender had received over £16,000 Job Seekers allowance and council tax benefit over a period of two years. He was responsible for the care of his ailing wife. Six months' imprisonment following his plea of guilty was reduced by the Court of Appeal to three months. Contrast *Kireche* [2013] 1 Cr App R (S) 488 (91), in which 11 months' imprisonment following trial was upheld; although not dishonest from the outset, the offender had obtained £30,000 in housing and council tax benefits from a careful, long-lasting and extremely productive multiple fraud. See also *Bonner* [2013] EWCA Crim 1534 (mother of a young child) and *Taylor* [2013] EWCA Crim 1668 (whether to suspend a sentence of imprisonment), in each of which immediate custodial sentences were, on the facts, upheld.

In *Pettigrew* [2012] EWCA Crim 1998 the offender, who had a serious record for dishonesty, pleaded guilty to offences of fraud, obtaining by deception and failing to notify a change of circumstances. The Court of Appeal observed (at [13]) that it was not particularly helpful to attempt slavishly to bring the combination of offences into particular categories in the previous guideline and that a broader view, with assistance from that guideline, needed to be taken. In *Turner* [2011] 2 Cr App R (S) 18 the Court of Appeal upheld a judge's departure from that guideline in a case of repeated false declarations by an offender of substantial means. See also *Jairam* [2013] EWCA Crim 1140 (sentence of three years' imprisonment upheld on an elderly offender who had obtained at least £280,000 by fraud over 16 years).

Section B17   Offences Involving Misuse of Computers

INTRODUCTION

In many instances involving the use of a computer to commit an offence, such as theft or fraud, **B17.1** the means of commission creates no special difficulty in achieving a conviction. This section is concerned with a limited range of situations involving unauthorised access by a person to data or programs held in a computer, whether for a further criminal purpose or not, and with the improper processing of personal data. For offences involving possession or distribution of indecent pseudo-photographs of children downloaded from the internet, see **B3.306**.

UNAUTHORISED ACCESS OFFENCE ('HACKING')

Computer Misuse Act 1990, s. 1   **B17.2**

(1) A person is guilty of an offence if—
   (a) he causes a computer to perform any function with intent to secure access to any program or data held in any computer;
   (b) the access he intends to secure is unauthorised; and
   (c) he knows at the time when he causes the computer to perform the function that that is the case.
(2) The intent a person has to have to commit an offence under this section need not be directed at—
   (a) any particular program or data;
   (b) a program or data of any particular kind; or
   (c) a program or data held in any particular computer.

Procedure and Sentence

The maximum penalty on indictment is two years' imprisonment or a fine or both. On sum- **B17.3** mary conviction, the maximum sentence is imprisonment for a term not exceeding six months, or a fine not exceeding the statutory maximum, or both. For cases giving some guidance on sentencing for offences under the Computer Misuse Act 1990, see **B17.14**.

Actus Reus

The *actus reus* of the offence requires the accused to 'cause a computer to perform any func- **B17.4** tion'. This is meant to exclude mere physical contact with a computer and the scrutiny of data without any interaction with a computer (thus the reading of confidential computer output, the reading of data displayed on the screen, or 'computer eavesdropping', are not covered). On the other hand there is no requirement that the accused should succeed in obtaining access to the program or data, or be successful in subverting computer security measures in place. A remote hacker would, thus, 'cause a computer to perform any function' if he accessed it remotely and the computer responded, for example, by activating a computer security device or by offering a log-on menu. The substantive offence is thus drafted in such a way as to include conduct which might usually be thought to fall within the scope of the law of attempt. Secondary liability may arise where, for example, a person supplies a hacker with information which would assist him, such as a confidential computer password. The operator of a computer hacker 'bulletin board' might, therefore, come within the reach of the offence. The words 'any computer' in s. 1(1)(a) entail that the offence is not restricted to a case where the accused uses one computer to gain unauthorised access to the target computer. Direct access to the target computer is also covered (*A-G's Ref (No. 1 of 1991)* [1993] QB 94; *Bow Street Metropolitan Stipendiary Magistrate, ex parte Government of the United States* [2000] 1 Cr App R 61 per Lord Hobhouse at p. 72).

B17.5   The access to the program or data which the accused intends to secure must be 'unauthorised' access (s. 1(1)(b)). In *DPP v Bignell* [1998] 1 Cr App R 1, the Divisional Court held that an offence under s. 1 of the Computer Misuse Act 1990 was not committed where police officers, for private purposes, instructed a computer operator to extract details of two cars from a police computer. This was because the officers were entitled to access the computer, albeit only for legitimate police purposes. Astill J commented that the Act was designed to criminalise 'breaking into computer systems', and noted that misuse of the data once obtained was not covered by the Act but might constitute an offence under the Data Protection Act 1984, s. 5(2)(b) (which was then in force), and this clearly influenced the Divisional Court in holding that the conduct lay outside the 1990 Act. The decision in *Bignell* is open to criticism on the ground that, on an ordinary construction of language, authorising a person's access for one (legitimate) purpose ought not to be regarded as authorising his access for another (non-legitimate) purpose (see, by analogy, the burglary case of *Jones* [1976] 3 All ER 54 at **B4.88**). The authority of *Bignell* is to some extent undermined by the decision of the House of Lords in *Bow Street Metropolitan Stipendiary Magistrate, ex parte Government of the United States*. In that case one Allison, an employee of American Express, was authorised to access certain client accounts to check matters relating to credit. It was alleged that she in fact obtained access to other accounts and passed on confidential details to accomplices who were able to forge credit cards and obtain large sums of money. The issue was whether Allison could be extradited from England to the USA and the House of Lords, reversing the decision of the Divisional Court, held that she could. Lord Hobhouse had no difficulty in finding that the alleged conduct of Allison fell within the provisions of s. 1. His lordship then considered the decision in *Bignell*, and pointed out that the Divisional Court in that case had fallen into error in asking itself whether the accused had authority to access data of that general kind, a mistake also made by the same court in the instant case. The correct question (applying the wording of s. 1 and s. 17(5)(a)) was whether the officers had authority to access the *actual data* involved. Even so, Lord Hobhouse thought that the outcome in *Bignell* was 'probably right'. It was distinguishable from the instant case because the police officers in *Bignell* had instructed the (innocent) computer operator to access the data. The access had been made by that person, and he had not exceeded his authority in doing so. It seems that in the circumstances there had been no 'unauthorised access', and hence an essential element of the *actus reus* was missing.

Mens Rea

B17.6   There are two limbs to the *mens rea* of the offence. The first limb is the 'intent to secure access to any program or data held in any computer'. The word 'any' makes it clear that the intent need not relate to the computer which the accused is at that time operating. The Computer Misuse Act 1990, s. 1(2), explains that the intent of the accused need not be directed at any particular program or data, so as to include the hacker who accesses a computer without any clear idea of what he will find there. Recklessness is insufficient; still less would careless or inattentive accessing of the computer suffice for liability. The second limb is that the accused must know at the time when he causes the computer to perform the function that the access which he intends to secure is unauthorised. The prosecution must prove both limbs.

Definitions

Computer Misuse Act 1990, s. 17

(1) The following provisions of this section apply for the interpretation of this Act.

(2) A person secures access to any program or data held in a computer if by causing a computer to perform any function he—

    (a) alters or erases the program or data;

    (b) copies or moves it to any storage medium other than that in which it is held or to a different location in the storage medium in which it is held;

    (c) uses it; or

    (d) has it output from the computer in which it is held (whether by having it displayed or in any other manner);

and references to access to a program or data (and to an intent to secure such access) shall be read accordingly.

(3) For the purposes of subsection (2)(c) above a person uses a program if the function he causes the computer to perform—

    (a) causes the program to be executed; or

    (b) is itself a function of the program.

(4) For the purposes of subsection (2)(d) above—

    (a) program is output if the instructions of which it consists are output; and

    (b) the form in which any such instructions or any other data is output (and in particular whether or not it represents a form in which, in the case of instructions, they are capable of being executed or, in the case of data, it is capable of being processed by a computer) is immaterial.

(5) Access of any kind by any person to any program or data held in a computer is unauthorised if—

    (a) he is not himself entitled to control access of the kind in question to the program or data; and

    (b) he does not have consent to access by him of the kind in question to the program or data from any person who is so entitled,

but this subsection is subject to section 10.

(6) References to any program or data held in a computer include references to any program or data held in any removable storage medium which is for the time being in the computer; and a computer is to be regarded as containing any program or data held in any such medium.

(7) [Repealed]

(8) An act done in relation to a computer is unauthorised if the person doing the act (or causing it to be done)

    (a) is not himself a person who has responsibility for the computer and is entitled to determine whether the act may be done; and

    (b) does not have consent to the act from any such person.

In this subsection 'act' includes a series of acts.

The terms 'computer', 'data' and 'program' are not defined in the Computer Misuse Act 1990 and should, therefore, be given their ordinary meaning by the courts. Section 10 of the Act deals with access to computer material for law enforcement purposes.

UNAUTHORISED ACCESS OFFENCE WITH INTENT TO COMMIT FURTHER OFFENCES

Computer Misuse Act 1990, s. 2

(1) A person is guilty of an offence under this section if he commits an offence under section 1 above ('the unauthorised access offence') with intent—

    (a) to commit an offence to which this section applies; or

    (b) to facilitate the commission of such an offence (whether by himself or by any other person);

and the offence he intends to commit or facilitate is referred to below in this section as the further offence.

(2) This section applies to offences—
  (a) for which the sentence is fixed by law; or
  (b) for which a person of 21 years of age or over (not previously convicted) may be sentenced to imprisonment for a term of five years (or, in England and Wales, might be so sentenced but for the restrictions imposed by section 33 of the Magistrates' Courts Act 1980).
(3) It is immaterial for the purposes of this section whether the further offence is to be committed on the same occasion as the unauthorised access offence or on any future occasion.
(4) A person may be guilty of an offence under this section even though the facts are such that the commission of the further offence is impossible.

Procedure and Sentence

B17.9   Section 2 of the Computer Misuse Act 1990 creates an offence triable either way. The maximum penalty on conviction on indictment is five years' imprisonment, or a fine or both; on summary conviction, the maximum is six months or a fine of the statutory maximum or both (s. 2(5)). For cases giving some guidance on sentencing for offences under the Computer Misuse Act 1990, see **B17.14**.

Elements

B17.10   The offence under s. 2 of the Computer Misuse Act 1990 is committing the unauthorised access offence under s. 1 (see **B17.2**) with intent to commit or facilitate the commission of a more serious 'further' offence. It is not necessary to prove that the intended further offence has actually been committed.

A person will be guilty of an offence under s. 2 in a range of situations. Obtaining the unauthorised access may, for example, be done with the intention of committing theft, such as by diverting funds, which are in the course of an electronic funds transfer, to the accused's own bank account, or to the bank account of an accomplice. It would also cover the case where the accused gained unauthorised access to sensitive information held on computer with a view to blackmailing the person to whom that information related.

Section 2(2) explains what qualifies as a further offence for the purposes of the s. 2 offence. Section 2(3) makes clear that the accused may intend to commit the further offence on the same occasion as the unauthorised access offence (as in the theft example just given) or on a future occasion (as in the blackmail example). Section 2(4) makes it possible to convict a person who intended to commit the further offence even if, on the facts, that would be impossible (e.g., where the intended blackmail victim was, unknown to the accused, dead). This rule is analogous to that in the Criminal Attempts Act 1981, s. 1(2), as applied in *Shivpuri* [1987] AC 1. See **A5.81**.

UNAUTHORISED ACTS WITH INTENT TO IMPAIR OPERATION OF COMPUTER ETC.

B17.11

Computer Misuse Act 1990, s. 3

(1) A person is guilty of an offence if—
  (a) he does any unauthorised act in relation to a computer;
  (b) at the time when he does the act he knows that it is unauthorised; and
  (c) either subsection (2) or subsection (3) below applies.
(2) This subsection applies if the person intends by doing the act—
  (a) to impair the operation of any computer;
  (b) to prevent or hinder access to any program or data held in any computer;
  (c) to impair the operation of any such program or the reliability of any such data.
(3) This subsection applies if the person is reckless as to whether the act will do any of the things mentioned in paragraphs (a) to (c) of subsection (2) above.

(4) The intention referred to in subsection (2) above, or the recklessness referred to in sub-section (3) above, need not relate to—
   (a) any particular computer;
   (b) any particular program or data; or
   (c) a program or data of any particular kind.
(5) In this section—
   (a) a reference to doing an act includes a reference to causing an act to be done;
   (b) 'act' includes a series of acts;
   (c) a reference to impairing, preventing or hindering something includes a reference to doing so temporarily.

Section 3 is an offence triable either way, punishable, on conviction on indictment, to imprisonment for a term not exceeding ten years or to a fine or both and, on summary conviction, with six months or a fine up to the statutory maximum or both (s. 3(6)). **B17.12**

The effect of s. 3 is that a person commits an offence if he performs any unauthorised act in relation to a computer, knowing it to be unauthorised, if he intends by doing the act to do one of the things set out in s. 3(2), or if he is reckless as to whether by doing the act he will do one of the things set out in s. 3(2). The inclusion of liability for recklessness is a significant extension of liability from that which applied prior to 1 October 2008.

When read in the context of the Computer Misuse Act 1990, s. 17 (see **B17.7**), it is clear that a wide range of different forms of conduct are included by s. 3. It covers all cases involving deliberate or reckless impairment of a computer's operation, preventing or hindering access to computer material by a legitimate user or impairing the operation or reliability of computer-held material. The offender must know that the act was unauthorised. In *DPP v Lennon* (2006) 170 JP 532 the Divisional Court held that an offence under the substituted s. 3 was committed where a former employee of a company, acting on a grudge, impaired the operation of the company's computer by using a program to generate and send 5 million e-mails to the company. The court rejected a defence argument under s. 17(8)(b) that the owner of a computer set up to receive e-mails must be taken to have consented to the sending of e-mails, holding that such implied consent was not without limits and that the owner could not be taken to consent to multiple e-mails being sent for the purposes of swamping his computer system. In *Zezev and Yarimaka v Governor of HM Prison Brixton* [2002] 2 Cr App R 515, it was held that an offence was committed under the substituted s. 3 where the accused placed on the files of another person's computer a bogus e-mail which purported to come from a person who had not sent it. It does not have to be proved that the defendant had any specific target computer, program or data in mind.

MAKING, SUPPLYING OR OBTAINING ARTICLES FOR USE IN OFFENCES UNDER s. 1 OR 3

Computer Misuse Act 1990, s. 3A **B17.13**

(1) A person is guilty of an offence if he makes, adapts, supplies or offers to supply any article intending it to be used to commit, or to assist in the commission of, an offence under section 1 or 3.
(2) A person is guilty of an offence if he supplies or offers to supply any article believing that it is likely to be used to commit, or to assist in the commission of, an offence under section 1 or 3.
(3) A person is guilty of an offence if he obtains any article with a view to its being supplied for use to commit, or to assist in the commission of, an offence under section 1 or 3.
(4) In this section 'article' includes any program or data held in electronic form.

Section 3A creates three offences triable either way, each punishable, on conviction on indictment, with imprisonment for a term not exceeding two years or to a fine or both and, on summary conviction, with six months or a fine up to the statutory maximum or both (s. 3A(5)).

It is clear that the reason for the creation of this offence is the market in electronic 'hacker tools'; which can be used for breaking into, or compromising, computer systems. According to guidance notes published together with the Police and Justice Act 2006, if the accused is charged with an offence under s. 3A(2) in relation to a quantity of articles, the prosecution would need to prove its case in relation to any particular one or more of those articles, but it would not be enough to prove that the accused believed that a certain proportion of the articles was likely to be used in connection with an offence under s. 1 or 3. In the offence under s. 3A(2) the relevant *mens rea* is 'belief' — by analogy with the offence of handling stolen goods it is submitted that mere suspicion would not be enough.

SENTENCING FOR OFFENCES UNDER THE COMPUTER MISUSE ACT 1990

B17.14   There are no official guideline cases on sentencing for offences under the Computer Misuse Act 1990, although a number of earlier cases were considered in *Mangham* [2013] 1 Cr App R (S) 62 (11), where the offender pleaded guilty to offences under ss. 1 and 3. He had hacked into Facebook's computer and accessed and downloaded source code, which compromised confidential corporate information but not personal data. Facebook investigated and remedied the damage, which cost $200,000. A sentence of four months' imprisonment was appropriate. Cranston J said (at [19]) that aggravating features in computer misuse cases would be (i) whether the offence was planned or persistent, (ii) nature of the damage caused to the system and to the wider public interest, (iii) motive (including revenge) and extent of gain by the offender and (iv) whether the information had been passed on to others. Among the mitigating factors the psychological profile of the offender would be important. In *Martin* [2014] 1 Cr App R (S) 414 (63) the Court of Appeal dealt with a 21-year-old offender with a record of dishonesty offences, who pleaded guilty to five offences under s. 3 of the Act, one offence under s. 2, one offence under s. 1, and two offences contrary to s. 3A. The total sentence of two years' imprisonment was upheld, together with a deprivation order under the PCC(S)A 2000, s. 143, in relation to various IT equipment. The offender had launched denial of service attacks on two university websites, which involved flooding the sites with internet traffic from a single device. Some two weeks of man hours were expended in each case in dealing with these attacks. Three days later he launched a similar attack on a police force website. Other illegal activity which the offender admitted involved the obtaining of bank account and other personal details on a named individual, requiring that individual to cancel his bank cards and change his passwords. A list of further potential targets was found at his home address. Leveson LJ said that the offences fell into the highest level of culpability, being carefully planned and targeted. The prevalence of computer crime, its potential to cause enormous damage, both to the credibility of IT systems and the way in which our society now operates, and the apparent ease with which hackers, from the confines of their own homes, can damage important institutions and individuals, cannot be understated. His lordship said that *Mangham* should not be considered a benchmark for such cases, which, in the ordinary course, are now likely to attract sentences that are very considerably longer; for offending on the scale of *Martin*, sentences will be measured in years rather than months. A sentence of four months' imprisonment was appropriate in *Baker* [2011] EWCA Crim 928 for an offence under s. 1 committed by a disgruntled Welsh Assembly ex-employee, who retained computer equipment after his dismissal and used it to access his former employer's computers. In *Delamare* [2003] 2 Cr App R (S) 474 four months' detention was appropriate for a bank employee who committed an offence under s. 2 by selling confidential details of two bank account holders. In *Lindesay* [2002] 1 Cr App R (S) 370, nine months' imprisonment was upheld on a computer consultant who corrupted the web sites of clients of a company which had dismissed him. In *Crosskey* [2013] 1 Cr App R (S) 420 (76) eight months' detention was deemed appropriate for offences under ss. 1 and

3 which involved hacking into a celebrity's Facebook account. He pleaded guilty to three charges under the substituted s. 3 of the 1990 Act. In *Vallor* [2004] 1 Cr App R (S) 319, two years' imprisonment was upheld on an offender who pleaded guilty to three offences of releasing computer viruses on the internet, contrary to the substituted s. 3. In some serious cases involving misuse of information held on police computers, offenders have been prosecuted for misconduct in public office (see **B15.26**) rather than for an offence under the 1990 Act. See, e.g., *Kassim* [2006] 1 Cr App R (S) 12, *O'Leary* [2007] 2 Cr App R (S) 317, *A-G's Ref (No. 1 of 2007)* [2007] 2 Cr App R (S) 544, *A-G's Ref (No. 68 of 2009) (Turner)* [2010] 1 Cr App R (S) 684 and *Lewis* [2010] 2 Cr App R (S) 666.

JURISDICTIONAL PROVISIONS

Liability for offences under the Computer Misuse Act 1990, s. 1 or s. 3, requires proof of at least one 'significant link' with the 'home country concerned' which for the purposes of English law means England and Wales. By ss. 4 and 5, this link is satisfied where the accused was in England and Wales when he committed the act in question. Alternatively, it is satisfied where the targeted computer was situated in England and Wales. For territorial jurisdiction generally, see **A8.2**. **B17.15**

In contrast, s. 4(3) enables a s. 2 offence to be committed entirely abroad, provided that the 'further offence' would itself fall within English jurisdiction. If that offence is itself an extra-territorial offence, there need be no connection with England and Wales at all.

Section 4(4), read in conjunction with s. 8(1), applies s. 2 to cases in which the 'further offence' is an offence only under a foreign system of law, but would have qualified as a further offence within the meaning of s. 2(2) if committed within England and Wales. This applies only where the underlying s. 1 offence *does* have a significant link with England and Wales. It would, for example, cover a case in which D, in England, gains unauthorised access to a computer in France, with a view to committing a crime under French law that would have been punishable with imprisonment for five years or more if committed by an adult in England and Wales.

Computer Misuse Act 1990, ss. 4 and 5 **B17.16**

4.—(1) Except as provided below in this section, it is immaterial for the purposes of any offence under section 1 or 3 above—
   (a) whether any act or other event proof of which is required for conviction of the offence occurred in [England and Wales]; or
   (b) whether the accused was in [England and Wales] at the time of any such act or event.
(2) Subject to subsection (3) below, in the case of such an offence at least one significant link with domestic jurisdiction must exist in the circumstances of the case for the offence to be committed.
(3) There is no need for any such link to exist for the commission of an offence under section 1 above to be established in proof of an allegation to that effect in proceedings for an offence under section 2 above.
(4) Subject to section 8 below, where—
   (a) any such link does in fact exist in the case of an offence under section 1 above; and
   (b) commission of that offence is alleged in proceedings for an offence under section 2 above;
section 2 above shall apply as if anything the accused intended to do or facilitate in any place outside [England and Wales] which would be an offence to which section 2 applies if it took place in [England and Wales] were the offence in question.
5.—(1) The following provisions of this section apply for the interpretation of section 4 above.
(2) In relation to an offence under section 1, either of the following is a significant link with domestic jurisdiction—
   (a) that the accused was in [England and Wales] at the time when he did the act which caused the computer to perform the function; or

(b) that any computer containing any program or data to which the accused by doing that act secured or intended to secure unauthorised access, or enabled or intended to enable unauthorised access to be secured, was in [England and Wales] at that time.

(3) In relation to an offence under section 3, either of the following is a significant link with domestic jurisdiction—
  (a) that the accused was in [England and Wales] at the time when he did the unauthorised act (or caused it to be done); or
  (b) that the unauthorised act was done in relation to a computer in [England and Wales].

JURISDICTION OVER CONSPIRACY AND ATTEMPT

B17.17   Section 6 of the Computer Misuse Act 1990 makes special provision for jurisdiction over inchoate offences of computer misuse, as does the Criminal Attempts Act 1981, s. 1(1A) and (1B); but in practice, s. 1(1A) and (1B) are of no conceivable use to prosecutors, for the same reason that s. 1A of that Act is of no use: see A5.79.

Computer Misuse Act 1990, s. 6

(1) On a charge of conspiracy to commit an offence under section 1, 2 or 3 above, the following questions are immaterial to the accused's guilt—
  (a) the question where any person became a party to the conspiracy; and
  (b) the question whether any act, omission or other event occurred in the home country concerned.

(2) On a charge of attempting to commit an offence under section 3 above the following questions are immaterial to the accused's guilt—
  (a) the question where the attempt was made; and
  (b) the question whether it had an effect in the home country concerned.

EVIDENCE OF FOREIGN LAW

B17.18
Computer Misuse Act 1990, s. 8

(1) A person is guilty of an offence triable by virtue of section 4(4) above only if what he intended to do or facilitate would involve the commission of an offence under the law in force where the whole or any part of it was intended to take place.

(2) [Repealed.]

(3) A person is guilty of an offence triable by virtue of section 1(1A) of the Criminal Attempts Act 1981 only if what he had in view would involve the commission of an offence under the law in force where the whole or any part of it was intended to take place.

(4) Conduct punishable under the law in force in any place is an offence under that law for the purposes of this section, however it is described in that law.

(5) Subject to subsection (7) below, a condition specified in [subsection (1) or (3)] above shall be taken to be satisfied unless not later than rules of court may provide the defence serve on the prosecution a notice—
  (a) stating that, on the facts as alleged with respect to the relevant conduct, the condition is not in their opinion satisfied;
  (b) showing their grounds for that opinion; and
  (c) requiring the prosecution to show that it is satisfied.

(6) In subsection (5) above 'the relevant conduct' means—
  (a) where the condition in subsection (1) above is in question, what the accused intended to do or facilitate;
  (b) [Repealed.]
  (c) where the condition in subsection (3) above is in question, what the accused had in view.

(7) The court, if it thinks fit, may permit the defence to require the prosecution to show that the condition is satisfied without the prior service of a notice under subsection (5) above.

(8) [Scotland.]

(9) In the Crown Court the question whether the condition is satisfied shall be decided by the judge alone.

OFFENCES UNDER THE DATA PROTECTION ACT 1998

Proceedings for any criminal offence under the 1998 Act may be brought only by the Information **B17.19**
Commissioner, or by or with the consent of the DPP (s. 60(1)). The maximum penalties for
the offences created are, in summary proceedings, a fine not exceeding the statutory maximum
and, on indictment, an unlimited fine (s. 60(2)). Whenever a person is convicted of an offence
under the Act, the court may in addition order that data material appearing to the court to be
connected with the offence be forfeited or erased (s. 60(4)). An order under s. 60(4) must not
be made before any person (other than the offender) claiming to be the owner or otherwise
interested in the data material who has applied to the court is given an opportunity to show
cause why the order should not be made. For liability of directors, see s. 61.

Data Processing Offences

Section 17(1) requires that personal data within the meaning of the Act must not be processed **B17.20**
unless an entry in respect of the data controller is included in the register maintained by the
Commissioner under s. 19, although by s. 17(3) regulations may provide that s. 17(1) does not
apply in respect of processing of a particular description, where that processing is unlikely to
prejudice the rights and freedoms of data subjects. Contravention of s. 17(1) by a data controller
is an offence under s. 21(1). Section 20 imposes a duty on every data controller included in the
register to notify the Commissioner, as and when required by regulations, of details of the reg-
istrable particulars and of measures taken by the data controller to ensure compliance with the
seventh data protection principle (that appropriate technical and organisational measures shall
be taken against unauthorised or unlawful processing of personal data and against accidental
loss or destruction of, or damage to, personal data). Failure by a data controller to comply with
this duty is an offence (s. 21(2)). This is an offence of strict liability, although s. 21(3) provides
for a due diligence defence.

It is an offence for a person to fail to comply with an enforcement notice issued under s. 40
where the Commissioner is satisfied that a data controller has contravened or is contravening
any of the data protection principles, or an information notice issued under s. 43 or a special
information notice issued under s. 44 (s. 47(1)). This is an offence of strict liability, although
s. 47(3) provides for a due diligence defence. It is also an offence under s. 47(2), for a person to
make a statement in purported compliance with an information notice or a special information
notice which he knows to be false in a material particular, or where he recklessly makes such a
statement which is false.

Obtaining or Disclosing Personal Data etc.

Data Protection Act 1998, s. 55   **B17.21**

(1) A person must not knowingly or recklessly, without the consent of the data controller—
    (a) obtain or disclose personal data or the information contained in personal data, or
    (b) procure the disclosure to another person of the information contained in personal data.
(2) Subsection (1) does not apply to a person who shows—
    (a) that the obtaining, disclosing or procuring—
        (i)   was necessary for the purpose of preventing or detecting crime, or
        (ii) was required or authorised by or under any enactment, by any rule of law or by the
            order of a court.
    (b) that he acted in the reasonable belief that he had in law the right to obtain or disclose the
        data or information or, as the case may be, to procure the disclosure of the information to
        the other person,
    (c) that he acted in the reasonable belief that he would have had the consent of the data con-
        troller if the data controller had known of the obtaining, disclosing or procuring, and the
        circumstances of it, or
    (d) that in the particular circumstance the obtaining, disclosing or procuring was justified as
        being in the public interest.

B

Part B Offences

(3) A person who contravenes subsection (1) is guilty of an offence.
(4) A person who sells personal data is guilty of an offence if he has obtained the data in contravention of subsection (1).
(5) A person who offers to sell personal data is guilty of an offence if—
   (a) he has obtained the data in contravention of subsection (1), or
   (b) he subsequently obtains the data in contravention of that subsection.
(6) For the purposes of subsection (5) an advertisement indicating that personal data are or may be for sale is an offer to sell the data.

Further it is made an offence under s. 56 for a person, in connection with the recruitment of another person as an employee, or the continued employment of another person, or any contract for the provision of services to him by another person, to require that other person to supply or produce certain records which, by s. 56(6), includes records of that other person's previous convictions and cautions.

The CJIA 2008, s. 78 (not yet in force), inserts a new defence in s. 55(2) to cover the situation where a person acts either for the special purposes (i.e. journalistic, literary and artistic purposes) or with a view to the publication by any person of any journalistic, literary or artistic material, *and* in the reasonable belief that in the particular circumstances the obtaining, disclosing or procuring was justified as being in the public interest.

This offence is currently punishable by way of a fine. The only reported consideration of sentencing for this offence in the Crown Court is *Rooney* [2006] EWCA Crim 1841, a case involving inappropriate access of a police computer, where a fine of £700 was imposed. See also *A-G's Ref (No. 140 of 2004)* [2004] EWCA Crim 3525, where the offence under s. 55 was considered in the more serious context of a prosecution for misconduct in public office. The CJIA 2008, s. 77, empowers the Secretary of State to increase the maximum penalty by order to two years' imprisonment on indictment. No such order has yet been made.

Section B18   Offences Involving Writing, Speech or Publication

PUBLISHING, OR HAVING FOR PUBLICATION FOR GAIN, AN OBSCENE ARTICLE

Definition

Obscene Publications Act 1959, s. 2   **B18.1**

(1) Subject as hereinafter provided, any person who, whether for gain or not, publishes an obscene article or who has an obscene article for publication for gain (whether gain to himself or gain to another) shall be liable...

Procedure

Offences under the Obscene Publications Act 1959, s. 2(1), are triable either way. When tried   **B18.2** on indictment they are normally class 3 offences, but see CPD XIII, para. B (see Supplement, **PD-97**) for the additional factors that the court considers on allocation. A prosecution must not be commenced more than two years after the commission of the offence (s. 2(3)).

Where the article in question is a moving picture film of width 16 mm or more, and the publication in question is by a film exhibition as defined in the Cinemas Act 1985, then proceeding may not be instituted except by, or with the consent of, the DPP (Obscene Publications Act 1959, s. 2(3A)).

The Obscene Publications Act 1959, s. 2(4), provides that 'A person publishing an article shall   **B18.3** not be proceeded against for an offence at common law consisting of the publication of any matter contained or embodied in the article where it is of the essence of the offence that the matter is obscene'. Subsection (4A) makes similar provision in respect of a film exhibition as defined in the Cinemas Act 1985. The rationale for these provisions was to prevent evasion by the prosecution of the defences available under the 1959 Act by charging the common-law offence of publishing an obscene libel. This common-law offence (together with defamatory libel and sedition and seditious libel) was abolished by the CAJA 2009, s. 73, on 12 January 2010. Section 2(4) never did technically apply to the common-law offence of conspiracy to corrupt public morals since such a conspiracy does not consist of publication within s. 2(4) but rather the *agreement* to corrupt public morals by publishing (*Shaw v DPP* [1962] AC 220). The law officers, however, gave undertakings to Parliament in 1964 (*Parliamentary Debates (Hansard), House of Commons*, 3 June 1964, col. 1212) that conspiracy to corrupt public morals would not be used so as to circumvent the defences available under s. 4 of the 1959 Act. On the other hand, there is a separate offence at common law of outraging public decency (see **B3.330**), and conspiracy to do so, and this, it was held in *Gibson* [1990] 2 QB 619, is not barred by s. 2(4), even though in that case the offence involved the publication of an article (a human foetus earring) which was, in a loose sense, obscene. The article was not likely to deprave or corrupt and was therefore not obscene within the meaning of the 1959 Act and thus was not covered by s. 2(4). The Court of Appeal therefore upheld the convictions for outraging public decency.

For conspiracy to outrage public decency and conspiracy to corrupt public morals, see **A5.39**.

Indictment (for Offence of Having for Gain)

B18.4

Statement of Offence

Having an obscene article for publication for gain, contrary to section 2(1) of the Obscene Publications Act 1959.

Particulars of Offence

A on or about the…day of…had an obscene article, namely…for publication for gain to himself or another.

Sentence

B18.5 The maximum penalty is five years' imprisonment, a fine, or both, on indictment (Obscene Publications Act 1959, s. 2(1), as amended by the CJIA 2008, s. 71, with effect from 26 January 2009); six months' imprisonment, a fine not exceeding the statutory maximum, or both, summarily.

A number of Court of Appeal decisions deal with sentencing for offences in relation to obscene publications. In *Holloway* (1982) 4 Cr App R (S) 128, where the offender had been selling pornographic books, films and tapes on a commercial scale, Lawton LJ said:

> Experience has shown…that fining these pornographers does not discourage them. Fines merely become an expense of the trade and are passed on to purchasers of the pornographic matter, so that prices go up and sales go on.

> In the judgment of this court, the only way of stamping out this filthy trade is by imposing sentences of imprisonment on first offenders and all connected with the commercial exploitation of pornography: otherwise front men will be put up and the real villains will hide behind them. It follows, in our judgment, that the salesmen, projectionists, owners and suppliers behind the owners should on conviction lose their liberty. For first offenders sentences need only be comparatively short, but persistent offenders should get the full rigour of the law. In addition, the courts should take the profit out of this illegal filthy trade by imposing very substantial fines.

> …We wish to make it clear that the guidelines we have indicated apply to those who commercially exploit pornography. We do not suggest that sentences of imprisonment would be appropriate for a newsagent who is carrying on a legitimate trade in selling newspapers and magazines and who has the odd pornographic magazine in his possession, probably because he has been careless in not looking to see what he is selling…he can be discouraged, and usually should be, by a substantial fine from repeating his carelessness. Nor do we suggest that a young man who comes into possession of a pornographic videotape and who takes it along to his rugby or cricket club to amuse his friends by showing it should be sentenced to imprisonment. On conviction he too can be dealt with by the imposition of a fine. The matter might be very different if owners or managers of clubs were to make a weekly practice of showing 'blue' films to attract custom. Like the pornographers of Soho they would be engaging in the commercial exploitation of pornography.

B18.6 A case towards the top end of the scale is *Snowden* [2010] 1 Cr App R (S) 233, where 30 months' imprisonment following a guilty plea was upheld. The offender was found to be in possession of some 55 DVDs categorised as obscene within the terms of the 1959 Act. Several involved scenes of sexual activity with animals. The offender admitted copying and distributing the DVDs to paying customers.

Custodial sentences of six months were approved in *Doorgashurn* (1988) 10 Cr App R (S) 195 and *Knight* (1990) 12 Cr App R (S) 319 where, in both cases, shopkeepers kept obscene books and video tapes for sale as part of their general trade. A fine of £2,000 was also imposed in the latter case; in the former case the shopkeeper was bankrupt by the time of sentence. In *Knight*, Wright J regarded it as a significant aggravating factor that children's comics were for sale in the shop and that children could and sometimes did see the obscene material which was on display. In *Ibrahim*, Lord Bingham CJ referred to the comments of Maurice Kay J in *Mather* (10 June 1997 unreported) to the effect that there is now a greater awareness of the link between the supply of pornographic material and the commission of serious sexual offences, and that sentences in this area are likely to increase rather than remain at the level indicated in *Knight*. Three months' imprisonment was appropriate in *Pace* [1998] 1 Cr App R (S) 121 for an offender who worked as a 'front man' in a shop selling pornographic videos, who was convicted in respect of possession of one tape. The Court of Appeal indicated the continuing relevance of the guidelines in *Holloway*.

Meaning of 'Obscenity'

Obscene Publications Act 1959, s. 1   **B18.7**

(1) For the purposes of this Act an article shall be deemed to be obscene if its effect or (where the article comprises two or more distinct items) the effect of any one of its items is, if taken as a whole, such as to tend to deprave and corrupt persons who are likely, having regard to all relevant circumstances, to read, see or hear the matter contained or embodied in it.

Although this does not purport to be an exhaustive definition of obscenity it is the only definition which counts for the purposes of the Act and the judge must not leave the jury with the impression that it is sufficient if the article is obscene in the ordinary sense of being 'filthy', 'loathsome' or 'lewd' (*Anderson* [1972] 1 QB 304; *Anderson* [1971] 3 All ER 1152). It is the tendency to deprave and corrupt which is important. This can refer merely to the effect on the mind in terms of stimulating fantasies and it is not necessary that physical or overt sexual activity should result (*DPP v Whyte* [1972] AC 849). Indeed obscenity is not necessarily concerned with sexual depravity but has included in the past material advocating drug taking or violence (*John Calder (Publications) Ltd v Powell* [1965] 1 QB 509; *Calder and Boyars Ltd* [1969] 1 QB 151).

The persons likely to be depraved or corrupted need not be wholly innocent to begin with: the further corruption of the less innocent is also included. Nor is it necessary that all those likely to read, see or hear the article should be corrupted. It is sufficient that the article should tend to deprave or corrupt a significant proportion of them. This may be much less than 50 per cent but must not be numerically negligible (*DPP v Whyte* [1972] AC 849). However, where publication has been only to one person, the tendency to deprave and corrupt (or to further deprave and corrupt) that one person is sufficient (*GS* [2012] 1 WLR 3368).

It is the effect of the publication by the accused that counts (that is, the effect on persons likely   **B18.8**
to read, see or hear the article as a result of *that* publication) rather than the effect of publication by anyone else, 'unless it could reasonably have been expected that the publication by the other person would follow from publication by the person charged' (Obscene Publications Act 1959, s. 2(6)).

The fact that there are other materials in circulation which are as obscene as, or which are not materially different from, the articles in question is not of itself relevant nor does it render the articles in question acceptable. The jury should apply the standards of 'ordinary, decent right-minded people' to the actual articles before them (*Elliott* [1996] 1 Cr App R 432).

Admittedly shocking, disgusting and outrageous material may not be obscene if instead of tending to encourage, it would have precisely the opposite effect (per Salmon LJ in *Calder and Boyars Ltd* [1969] 1 QB 151 at p. 169) — a limitation on the meaning of obscenity approved by the Court of Appeal in *Anderson* [1972] 1 QB 304 as the 'aversion argument'.

Meaning of 'Article'

The term 'article' is defined in the Obscene Publications Act 1959, s. 1(2), as 'any description of   **B18.9**
article containing or embodying matter to be read or looked at or both, any sound record, and any film or other record of a picture or pictures'. A video cassette is within s. 1(2) (*A-G's Ref (No. 5 of 1980)* [1981] 3 All ER 816).

Articles which are not themselves to be read or looked at or listened to are still treated as within s. 1(2) if they are 'intended to be used…for the reproduction or manufacture therefrom of articles containing or embodying matter to be read, looked at or listened to' (Obscene Publications Act 1964, s. 2(1), which thus now makes it clear that, for example, a photographic negative would be an article within the Obscene Publications Act 1959, s. 1(2), even if it was not itself to be looked at but merely used for producing prints). See also *Fellows* [1997] 1 Cr App R 244 (images held on computer disk in digitised form).

An 'article' may be regarded as a single item (e.g., a novel as in *Penguin Books* [1961] Crim LR 176), in which case, in assessing whether it has a tendency to deprave and corrupt, the jury should look at the effect of the article as a whole rather than at the effect in isolation of specific passages within it. However, an article may comprise a number of items (as in the case of the magazine in *Anderson* [1972] 1 QB 304); each item must then be judged individually and it is sufficient if the effect of any one of the items, taken as a whole, is to tend to deprave and corrupt. In *Anderson* [1972] 1 QB 304, Lord Widgery CJ said (at p. 312):

> A novelist who writes a complete novel and who cannot cut out particular passages without destroying the theme of the novel is entitled to have his work judged as a whole, but a magazine publisher who has a far wider discretion as to what he will and will not insert by way of items is to be judged under the 1959 Act on what we call the item to item basis.

In *Goring* [1999] Crim LR 670, one film was treated as containing a number of distinct items, and whether a particular film is to be judged as a whole or on an item by item basis is a question of law for the judge.

Role of Expert Evidence

B18.10 Expert evidence is not admissible on the question whether an article is obscene since that is a matter for the jury. However, where the subject-matter of an article is beyond the experience of the ordinary person, such as the characteristics and effects of cocaine and the methods of ingesting it, expert evidence is admissible to inform the jury about that subject-matter. It then remains a matter entirely for the jury, armed with this information, whether an article advocating the taking of cocaine has a tendency to deprave or corrupt (*Skirving* [1985] QB 819). In contrast, where an article is concerned with sexual activity, the jury need no special information to assess that activity before proceeding to the question of whether the article itself is obscene.

Where the persons likely to be depraved or corrupted are members of a special class, such as primary schoolchildren, there may be a special rule allowing expert evidence on the likely effect of unusual material on them if a jury cannot be expected to understand the likely impact of the material without assistance (*DPP v A & BC Chewing Gum Ltd* [1968] 1 QB 159). However, it still remains, even in this 'highly exceptional' (*Anderson* [1972] 1 QB 304 at p. 313) type of case, for the jury to decide whether the factual effect should be classified as depraving or corrupting, and expert evidence would not be admissible on that issue.

As to expert evidence generally, see **F10**, especially **F10.16**.

Meaning of 'Publication'

B18.11   Obscene Publications Act 1959, s. 1

(3) For the purposes of this Act a person publishes an article who—
(a) distributes, circulates, sells, lets on hire, gives, or lends it, or who offers it for sale or for letting for hire; or
(b) in the case of an article containing or embodying matter to be looked at or a record, shows, plays or projects it, or, where the matter is data stored electronically, transmits that data.
(4) For the purposes of this Act a person also publishes an article to the extent that any matter recorded on it is included by him in a programme included in a programme service.
(5) Where the inclusion of any matter in a programme so included would, if that matter were recorded matter, constitute the publication of an obscene article for the purposes of this Act by virtue of subsection (4) above, this Act shall have effect in relation to the inclusion of that matter in that programme as if it were recorded matter.

(6) In this section 'programme' and 'programme service' have the same meaning as in the Broadcasting Act 1990.

In *Taylor* [1995] 1 Cr App R 131, the Court of Appeal held that a photographic developer, who develops a film sent to him by customers depicting obscene acts and who makes prints as requested and sends the prints back to those customers, publishes the prints by way of selling or distributing them. Even if there was only one customer to whom the print was sold, that would still be a publication as is now confirmed in *GS* [2012] 1 WLR 3368, where it was explicitly decided that there can be publication to a single recipient (in this case not of photographic prints but of data — obscene paedophile comments — via internet relay chat).

The concluding words of s. 1(3)(b) relating to the transmission of electronically stored data were added by the CJPO 1994, sch. 9, para. 3, and were applied in *Waddon* [2000] All ER (D) 502 to the transmission of obscene images to a web site in the USA and then back again to a subscriber in the UK, which constituted publication within the jurisdiction. It seems from *Perrin* [2002] EWCA Crim 747 that it is immaterial where the major steps to set up a web site are taken; it is access to the web pages within the jurisdiction which constitutes evidence of publication within s. 1(3)(b). See also *Sheppard* [2010] 2 All ER 850 and **A8.5**. In *GS* the publication was not the chat logs themselves but the logs were evidence of the 'comments that the defendant had typed and transmitted to the other party to the chat' so it seems that the act which transmits the data can be simultaneous with the act which stores the data electronically rather than the data having to be stored previously and then subsequently transmitted.

Having an Obscene Article for Publication for Gain

B18.12

This form of the offence was added by the Obscene Publications Act 1964, s. 1(1), to deal with limitations on the publication form of the offence, notably that displaying an obscene article in a shop window does not amount to offering it for sale (*Mella v Monahan* [1961] Crim LR 175) and that supplying to a supposedly non-corruptible person (e.g., a police officer) may not be a publication tending to deprave or corrupt anyone (*Clayton* [1963] 1 QB 163).

By s. 1(2) of the 1964 Act '...a person shall be deemed to have an article for publication for gain if with a view to such publication he has the article in his ownership, possession or control'. Thus a person having obscene articles for sale in sex shops (cf. *O'Sullivan* [1995] 1 Cr App R 455) 'has' them '*for* publication for gain' even though he may not yet have technically offered them for sale and actually published them in that sense. Since the provision deals with prospective publication rather than actual publication, s. 1(3)(b) of the 1964 Act provides that:

> ...the question whether the article is obscene shall be determined by reference to such publication for gain of the article as in the circumstances it may reasonably be inferred he had in contemplation and to any further publication that could reasonably be expected to follow from it, but not to any other publication.

In a case such as *O'Sullivan*, the original prospective publication which it may reasonably be inferred D had in contemplation would be the sale in a sex shop, and the further publication that may reasonably be expected to follow from it (note the absence here of any reference to reasonably inferring *D's contemplation*) might (or might not, depending on the circumstances) include such matters as further circulation, lending, selling or showing the article by the original purchaser from the sex shop. The jury then has to consider the tendency to deprave and corrupt as a result of those prospective publications. The Court of Appeal in *O'Sullivan* thought that the complexity of the direction to the jury necessitated by this provision and its relationship with the provisions of the Obscene Publications Act 1959 was such that the judge would be best advised to follow the order of the statutory provisions without attempting to improve upon them or to redefine the wording of the Acts. If a judge had any doubts about his proposed direction, he ought to commit it to writing and invite comment from counsel before they made their final speeches.

Things (such as negatives) from which obscene articles are to be made for publication but which things are not themselves to be published are deemed by s. 2(2) of the 1964 Act to be had for publication.

Defence of Having No Reasonable Cause to Suspect

B18.13   Under the Obscene Publications Act 1959, s. 2(5), it is a defence for the accused to prove that 'he had not examined the article in respect of which he is charged' and that he 'had no reasonable cause to suspect that it was such that his publication of it would make him liable to be convicted of an offence under this section'.

This defence applies where the form of the alleged offence is publishing. Where the alleged offence is having for publication for gain, the Obscene Publications Act 1964, s. 1(3)(a), provides a similar defence except that it refers to 'no reasonable cause to suspect that it was such that his having it would make him liable'.

Defence of Public Good

B18.14   Obscene Publications Act 1959, s. 4

   (1) Subject to subsection (1A) of this section a person shall not be convicted of an offence against section 2 of this Act...if it is proved that publication of the article in question is justified as being for the public good on the ground that it is in the interests of science, literature, art or learning, or of other objects of general concern.

Under s. 4(1A) the defence of public good does not apply to moving picture films or soundtracks but in relation to such articles there is instead a defence of public good 'on the ground that it is in the interests of drama, opera, ballet or any other art, or of literature or learning'. Section 4(2) declares: 'that the opinion of experts as to the literary, artistic, scientific or other merits of an article may be admitted in any proceedings under this Act either to establish or to negative the said ground'. The issue of public good arises only if the article is first shown to be obscene and the expert evidence authorised by s. 4(2) is only admissible in relation to whether the article is in the interests of science, literature, art etc. and not in relation to whether the article is obscene in the first place. This should be pointed out to the jury (*A-G's Ref (No. 3 of 1977)* [1978] 3 All ER 1166). In *DPP v Jordan* [1978] AC 699, Lord Wilberforce said (at p. 719):

   The judgment to be reached under section 4(1) and the evidence to be given under section 4(2) must be in order to show that publication should be permitted in spite of obscenity — not to negative obscenity.

B18.15   The jury need some explanation of their task under s. 4, and should not be left, as was said in *Calder and Boyars Ltd* [1969] 1 QB 151 at p. 172, 'to sink or swim in its dark waters'. The Court of Appeal went on to say that the jury should consider:

   ...on the one hand, the number of readers they believe would tend to be depraved and corrupted by the book, the strength of the tendency to deprave and corrupt and the nature of the depravity or corruption. On the other hand they should assess the strength of the literary, sociological or ethical merit which they consider the book to possess. They should then weigh up all these factors and decide whether on balance the publication is proved to be justified as being for the public good.

It is for the jury to decide the issue of public good, the evidence of the experts going merely to the literary merits etc. which the jury then have to balance against the admitted obscenity of the article (*Penguin Books* [1961] Crim LR 176).

The phrase 'other objects of general concern' in s. 4(1), refers to objects falling within the same area as those specifically mentioned there, namely science, literature, art or learning, and thus expert evidence that obscene material is psychologically beneficial to persons with certain sexual tendencies in that it would relieve their sexual tensions and might divert them from antisocial activities is inadmissible

(*DPP v Jordan* [1977] AC 699). On the other hand, the ethical merits of a book do come within 'other merits' in s. 4(2) and expert evidence on that issue is admissible (*Penguin Books*).

The word 'learning' in s. 4(1) is a noun and means the product of scholarship, rather than being a verb encompassing teaching. Expert evidence that obscene articles have merit for the purposes of sex education, or value in teaching or providing information about sexual matters, is not admissible because such matters are not in the interests of 'learning' as that word is used in s. 4(1) (*A-G's Ref (No. 3 of 1977)* [1978] 3 All ER 1166).

Search, Seizure and Forfeiture

Section 3 of the Obscene Publications Act 1959 empowers a justice of the peace to issue a war-   **B18.16**
rant for the search and seizure of obscene articles kept for publication for gain. A warrant which authorised a search for 'any other material of a sexually explicit nature' is on the face of it bad since such articles are not necessarily obscene (*Darbo v DPP* [1991] Crim LR 56).

The CJA 1967, s. 25, requires that the information must be laid by, or on behalf of, the DPP, or by a constable. The articles must then be brought before a justice of the peace who may issue a summons to the occupier of the premises from where the articles were seized to show cause why the articles should not be forfeited. See *Olympia Press Ltd v Hollis* [1973] 1 All ER 108 and R.T.H. Stone, 'Obscene Publications: the problems persist' [1986] Crim LR 139 for discussion of the procedure. The defence of public good under s. 4(1) applies to the procedure under s. 3. So also does s. 2(2) of the Obscene Publications Act 1964 deeming negatives etc. to be had or kept for publication even though not themselves to be published. By virtue of the Prosecution of Offences Act 1985, s. 3(2)(d), it is the duty of the DPP to take over the conduct of any pro-ceedings commenced by summons under the Obscene Publications Act 1959, s. 3. Section 3 (and, no doubt, the offence of having for publication for gain) applies equally to articles kept for publication abroad as it does to articles kept for publication in England and Wales (*Gold Star Publications Ltd v DPP* [1981] 2 All ER 257).

OBSCENE PERFORMANCES OF PLAYS

The obscene *performance* of a play, being unlike the written script of the play a transient thing,   **B18.17**
cannot amount to an article within the Obscene Publications Act 1959. Nor, it seems does the performance of an obscene play amount to the publication of its script. However, the Theatres Act 1968, s. 2(2), makes it an offence 'if an obscene performance of a play is given, whether in public or private'. The offence is committed by 'anyone who (whether for gain or not) presented or directed' the performance and the penalties are the same as under the Obscene Publications Act 1959 (see **B18.1**), which is also echoed in the definition of obscenity (Theatres Act 1968, s. 2(1); cf. **B18.7**), in the time-limit of two years for prosecution (s. 2(3); cf. **B18.2**), the exclu-sion of proceedings at common law in respect of the performance of a play (s. 2(4)) and the defence of public good (s. 3, cf. **B18.14**). Section 7 of the Theatres Act 1968 contains a number of exceptions to the offence under s. 2 including the performance of a play given on a domestic occasion in a private dwelling, and s. 18 contains interpretation provisions explaining, *inter alia*, what is a play and who is, and who is not, to be treated as a presenter or director.

INDECENT DISPLAYS

Definition

Indecent Displays (Control) Act 1981, s. 1   **B18.18**

(1) If any indecent matter is publicly displayed the person making the display and any person caus-ing or permitting the display to be made shall be guilty of an offence.

Procedure

B18.19   Offences under the Indecent Displays (Control) Act 1981, s. 1(1), are, by s. 4(1) of the Act, tri-able either way. When tried on indictment they are normally class 3 offences, but see CPD XIII, para. B (see Supplement, **PD-97**) for the additional factors that the court considers on allocation.

Sentence

B18.20   The maximum penalty is two years or a fine or both, on indictment; a fine not exceeding the statutory maximum, summarily (Indecent Displays (Control) Act 1981, s. 4(1)).

Meaning of 'Indecent'

B18.21   It seems clear that something can be indecent for the purposes of the Indecent Displays (Control) Act 1981 without being obscene for the purposes of the Obscene Publications Act 1959 (see *Stanley* [1965] 2 QB 327, decided under the Post Office Act 1953, s. 11 — posting obscene or indecent matter). There is no defence of public good to a charge under the Indecent Displays (Control) Act 1981, s. 1(1). Section 1(5) provides that, in determining whether any displayed matter is indecent, '(a) there shall be disregarded any part of that matter which is not exposed to view'. This underlines the fact that the offence is only concerned with that which is publicly displayed, so this is one occasion where one can judge a book (or magazine or any other article) by its cover. On the other hand, in assessing indecency, 'account may be taken of the effect of juxtaposing one thing with another' (s. 1(5)(b)).

Meaning of 'Matter'

B18.22   'Matter' includes 'anything capable of being displayed, except that it does not include an actual human body or any part thereof' (Indecent Displays (Control) Act 1981, s. 1(5)). By s. 1(2), 'Any matter which is displayed in or so as to be visible from any public place shall, for the pur-poses of this section, be deemed to be publicly displayed'.

Meaning of 'Public Place'

B18.23   Indecent Displays (Control) Act 1981, s. 1

(3) In subsection (2) above, 'public place', in relation to the display of any matter, means any place to which the public have or are permitted to have access (whether on payment or otherwise) while that matter is displayed except—
   (a) a place to which the public are permitted to have access only on payment which is or includes payment for that display; or
   (b) a shop or any part of a shop to which the public can only gain access by passing beyond an adequate warning notice;
   but the exclusions contained in paragraphs (a) and (b) above shall only apply where persons under the age of 18 years are not permitted to enter while the display in question is continuing.

Section 1(6) sets out minimum requirements with which an adequate warning notice must comply.

Exclusions

B18.24   Section 1(4) of the Indecent Displays (Control) Act 1981 contains a number of exclusions for matter:

(a) included in a television broadcasting service or other television programme service (as defined in the Broadcasting Act 1990), or
(b) displayed in an art gallery or museum and only visible from within the gallery or museum, or
(c) displayed by or with the authority of, and visible only from within a building occupied by, the Crown or a local authority, or
(d) included in a performance of a play (as defined in the Theatres Act 1968) or a film exhibi-tion (as defined in the Cinemas Act 1985).

OTHER OFFENCES

Sending Indecent etc. Articles through Post

Postal Services Act 2000, s. 85

(3) A person commits an offence if he sends by post a postal packet which encloses—
   (a) any indecent or obscene print, painting, photograph, lithograph, engraving, cinemato-graph film or other record of a picture or pictures, book, card or written communication, or
   (b) any other indecent or obscene article (whether or not of a similar kind to those mentioned in paragraph (a)).
(4) A person commits an offence if he sends by post a postal packet which has on the packet, or on the cover of the packet, any words, marks or designs which are of an indecent or obscene character.

This offence is triable either way. The maximum penalty is 12 months, on indictment; a fine not exceeding the statutory maximum, summarily.

Whether something is 'obscene' under this section does not depend on the person or persons to whom the packet is addressed, but is to be determined using an objective test, regardless of the addressees (*Kosmos Publications Ltd v DPP* [1975] Crim LR 345; see also *Stanley* [1965] 2 QB 327; *Stamford* [1972] 2 QB 391). See also *Kirk* [2006] EWCA Crim 725.

Unsolicited Publications

Unsolicited Goods and Services Act 1971, s. 4

(1) A person shall be guilty of an offence if he sends or causes to be sent to another person any book, magazine or leaflet (or advertising material for any such publication) which he knows or ought reasonably to know is unsolicited and which describes or illustrates human sexual techniques.
(2) A person found guilty of an offence under this section shall be liable on summary conviction to a fine not exceeding level 5 on the standard scale.
(3) A prosecution for an offence under this section shall not in England and Wales be instituted except by, or with the consent of, the DPP.

The sending of advertising material may be an offence even if that material does not itself describe or illustrate human sexual techniques (*DPP v Beate Uhse Ltd* [1974] QB 158).

Improper Use of Public Electronic Communications Network

Communications Act 2003, s. 127

(1) A person is guilty of an offence if he—
   (a) sends by means of a public electronic communications network a message or other matter that is grossly offensive or of an indecent, obscene or menacing character; or
   (b) causes any such message or matter to be so sent.
(2) A person is guilty of an offence if, for the purpose of causing annoyance, inconvenience or needless anxiety to another, he—
   (a) sends by means of a public electronic communications network, a message that he knows to be false,
   (b) causes such a message to be sent; or
   (c) persistently makes use of a public electronic communications network.
(3) A person guilty of an offence under this section shall be liable, on summary conviction, to imprisonment for a term not exceeding six months or to a fine not exceeding level 5 on the standard scale, or to both.
(4) Subsections (1) and (2) do not apply to anything done in the course of providing a programme service (within the meaning of the Broadcasting Act 1990).

The term 'public electronic communications network' is defined in chapter 1 of part 2 of the 2003 Act. Messages (or 'tweets') on Twitter which are communicated and are accessible via the internet are covered (*Chambers v DPP* [2013] 1 All ER 149). Programme services (excluded by

s. 127(4)) are covered by the Obscene Publications Act 1959 (see **B18.11**). As to the meaning of *grossly* offensive under s. 127(1), see *DPP v Collins* [2006] 4 All ER 602, where it was held by the House of Lords, contrary to the findings of the magistrates, that telephone messages sent to an MP about immigration and asylum issues (referring to 'Wogs', 'Pakis', 'Black bastards' and 'Niggers') were grossly offensive, irrespective of the actual reaction of the particular recipients. The offence is complete as soon as the message is sent and the test was said to be (at [10]) whether the message is 'couched in terms liable to cause gross offence to those to whom it relates' (not necessarily the recipients). Although intention or awareness of the grossly offensive nature of the message was required, Lord Bingham said (at [12]) that:

> ...a culpable state of mind will ordinarily be found where a message is couched in terms showing an intention to insult those to whom the message relates or giving rise to the inference that a risk of doing so must have been recognised by the sender.

Lord Carswell (at [22]) concluded that:

> ...the messages would be regarded as grossly offensive by reasonable persons in general, judged by the standards of an open and just multiracial society. The terms used were opprobrious and insulting, and not accidentally so. I am satisfied that reasonable citizens, not only members of the ethnic minorities referred to by the terms, would find them grossly offensive.

Lord Brown of Eaton-under-Heywood recognised (at [26]–[27]) that a conversation in these terms between two racists, neither of whom were offended, would be caught since the speakers would certainly know that the grossly offensive terms used were insulting to those to whom they applied and the section was intended to protect the integrity of the public communication system. The possible implications for certain types of telephone chat lines, given that the section also refers to messages of an obscene or indecent character, were expressly left open for another day.

In *Chambers v DPP* the meaning of 'menacing character' was considered. A 'tweet' intended to be a joke (and treated as such by all who read it), about blowing up an airport if it did not reopen by the time D was intending to travel the following week, was not of such character since it did not 'create fear or apprehension in those to whom it is communicated, or who may reasonably [be] expected to see it'. Quite apart from the absence of this *actus reus* requirement, on the facts, the mental element of this variation of the offence would further require (consistently with *DPP v Collins*) proof that D intended that the message should be of a menacing character or that he was aware of or recognised the risk at the time of sending the message 'that it may create fear or apprehension in any reasonable member of the public who reads or sees it'.

Chambers v DPP led to the DPP issuing guidelines as to the approach to be taken to the prosecution of messages on social media. A final version of the guidance was published on the CPS web site on 20 June 2013.

B18.29   Under the Penalties for Disorderly Behaviour (Amount of Penalty) Order 2002 (SI 2002 No. 1837), an offence under s. 127 is a fixed penalty offence and the amount payable is £90.

The *Magistrates' Court Sentencing Guidelines* include guidance on 'communication network offences' (see Supplement, SG-249). Four months' imprisonment was appropriate in *Harris* [2012] 1 Cr App R (S) 57, where the offender sent text messages to a 15-year-old boy inviting him to participate in sexual activity.

Indecent or Offensive or Threatening Letters etc.

B18.30   Malicious Communications Act 1988, s. 1

(1) Any person who sends to another person—
    (a) a letter, electronic communication or article of any description which conveys—
        (i) a message which is indecent or grossly offensive;
        (ii) a threat; or

(iii) information which is false and known or believed to be false by the sender; or

(b) any article or electronic communication which is, in whole or part, of an indecent or grossly offensive nature,

is guilty of an offence if his purpose, or one of his purposes, in sending it is that it should, so far as falling within paragraph (a) or (b) above, cause distress or anxiety to the recipient or to any other person to whom he intends that it or its contents or nature should be communicated.

(2) A person is not guilty of an offence by virtue of subsection (1)(a)(ii) above if he shows—

(a) that the threat was used to reinforce a demand made by him on reasonable grounds; and

(b) that he believed, and had reasonable grounds for believing, that the use of the threat was a proper means of reinforcing the demand.

(2A) In this section 'electronic communication' includes—

(a) any oral or other communication by means of an electronic communications network; and

(b) any communication (however sent) that is in electronic form.

(3) In this section references to sending include references to delivering or transmitting and to causing to be sent, delivered or transmitted or delivered and 'sender' shall be construed accordingly.

(4) A person guilty of an offence under this section shall be liable on summary conviction to imprisonment for a term not exceeding six months or to a fine not exceeding level 5 on the standard scale.

The terms of s. 1 were considered in *Connolly v DPP* [2008] 2 All ER 1012. 'Indecent or grossly offensive' were said to be ordinary English words and thus it was impossible to say that the court below was not entitled to conclude that 'shocking and disturbing' close-up photographs of aborted foetuses and of an abortion were grossly offensive. They were intended to cause distress and anxiety to those who received them and the fact that there was also a political or educational motive behind the accused's actions was of no avail. Furthermore, to the extent that the accused was exercising her rights under the ECHR, Articles 9 and 10, to freedom of speech or religion in sending the material, the restriction on those rights effected by the criminal prosecution was justified under Articles 9(2) and 10(2) as being necessary for the protection of the rights of others, namely the rights of the employees of the three pharmacies who were in receipt of the photographs.

Publications Harmful to Children and Young Persons

Children and Young Persons (Harmful Publications) Act 1955, s. 2   **B18.31**

(1) A person who prints, publishes, sells or lets on hire a work to which this Act applies, or has any such work in his possession for the purpose of selling it or letting it on hire, shall be guilty of an offence and liable, on summary conviction, to imprisonment for a term not exceeding four months or to a fine not exceeding level 3 on the standard scale or to both.

Provided that, in any proceedings taken under this subsection against a person in respect of selling or letting on hire a work or of having it in his possession for the purpose of selling it or letting it on hire, it shall be a defence for him to prove that he had not examined the contents of the work and had no reasonable cause to suspect that it was one to which this Act applies.

(2) A prosecution for an offence under this section shall not, in England and Wales, be instituted except by, or with the consent of, the Attorney-General.

By s. 1, the works to which the Act applies are:

…any book, magazine or other like work which is of a kind likely to fall into the hands of children or young persons and consists wholly or mainly of stories told in pictures (with or without the addition of written matter) being stories portraying—

(a) the commission of crimes; or

(b) acts of violence or cruelty; or

(c) incidents of a repulsive or horrible nature;

in such a way that the work as a whole would tend to corrupt a child or young person into whose hands it might fall.

Section 3 provides powers of entry, search, seizure and, on conviction, forfeiture.

Indecent Photographs of Children

B18.32   The offences under the Protection of Children Act 1978 dealing with indecent photographs of children are dealt with at **B3.306** *et seq.*

Video Recordings Act 1984 Offences

B18.33   The Video Recordings Act 1984, repealed and revived by the Video Recordings Act 2010, established a system for the classification by the British Board of Film Classification of video recordings supplied to the public through video rental and other outlets. Sections 9 to 14 of the 1984 Act create various offences, all originally summary and punishable only by fines, relating to the supply, or possession for supply, of video recordings which have not been classified or with a false indication as to their classification etc. However, the CJPO 1994, s. 88, made the two most serious offences (under ss. 9 and 10 of the 1984 Act) indictable and punishable by a maximum of two years' imprisonment or six months on summary conviction. The other offences under the 1984 Act remain summary but the offences under ss. 11, 12 and 14 of the Act have been made imprisonable with a maximum sentence of six months.

The Video Recordings Act 2010 remedied a technical defect that had been discovered in the Video Recordings Act 1984, namely failure to notify the European Commission in accordance with applicable EU law (the Technical Standards Directive, Directive 83/189/EEC). This meant that provisions relating to video classification and distribution were unenforceable within the UK, and when the defect came to light all current prosecutions were discontinued. The status of convictions already imposed has now been considered in *Budimir; Interfact Ltd v Liverpool City Council (No. 2)* [2011] 2 WLR 396. Lord Judge CJ concluded:

> . . .the convictions remain safe convictions.
>
> (1) Applying principles of national law, the convictions in these cases have not given rise to any substantial injustice and therefore there are no grounds to set aside the convictions.
> (2) There is no obligation on this court, either under EU law or under the European Convention on Human Rights, as given effect by the Human Rights Act 1998, to set aside the convictions.
>
> In view of these conclusions it is not strictly necessary to address the power of the court to re-open a final determination of an appeal to the Divisional Court or to extend time for appealing against conviction to the Court of Appeal Criminal Division.

The issues were nevertheless thought to be such as might merit consideration by the Supreme Court.

B18.34   In brief, the offences under the revived 1984 Act are as follows.

(a) supplying a video recording of an unclassified work (s. 9);
(b) possessing a video recording of an unclassified work for the purposes of supply (s. 10);
(c) supplying a video recording of a classified work to a person who has not attained the age specified in the classification certificate (s. 11);
(d) supplying a video recording with a restricted classification from a place other than a licensed sex shop (s. 12) (*Interfact Ltd v Liverpool City Council* (2005) 169 JP 353: it is the place of delivery rather than each despatch which counts, and mail order catalogues constitute 'offers' to supply illegally);
(e) supplying a video recording which does not comply with the requirements as to labelling (s. 13);
(f) supplying a video recording containing a false indication as to classification (s. 14).

Section 10 is set out below as an example of the provision made. An offence under the section is punishable, on indictment, with two years' imprisonment or a fine or both and, on summary conviction, with six months or a fine not exceeding £20,000 or both.

Video Recordings Act 1984, s. 10

(1) Where a video recording contains a video work in respect of which no classification certificate has been issued, a person who has the recording in his possession for the purpose of supplying it is guilty of an offence unless—

    (a) he has it in his possession for the purpose only of a supply which, if it took place, would be an exempted supply, or

    (b) the video work is an exempted work.

(2) It is a defence to a charge of committing an offence under this section to prove—

    (a) that the accused believed on reasonable grounds that the video work concerned or, if the video recording contained more than one work to which the charge relates, each of those works was either an exempted work or a work in respect of which a classification certificate had been issued,

    (b) that the accused had the video recording in his possession for the purpose only of a supply which he believed on reasonable grounds would, if it took place, be an exempted supply by virtue of section 3(4) or (5) of this Act, or

    (c) that the accused did not intend to supply the video recording until a classification certificate had been issued in respect of the video work concerned.

Certain video works are exempted from the provisions of the 1984 Act. The meaning of an exempted work is set out in s. 2 of the Act. Broadly, a work is exempted if it is designed to inform, educate or instruct, it is concerned with sport, religion or music or it is a video game. However, there are restrictions on these exemptions where, for example, the video work depicts, to any significant extent, human sexual activity, gross violence, human excretory functions or techniques likely to be useful in the commission of offences. For a minimalist view of what is required for such depictions, see *Kent County Council v Multi Media Marketing (Canterbury) Ltd* (1995) *The Times*, 9 May 1995. 'Human sexual activity' does not require material that would be regarded as hard pornography or as offensive. A video work is also not exempted if to any significant extent it depicts criminal activity which is likely to any significant extent to stimulate or encourage the commission of offences. Section 3 of the 1984 Act provides for the meaning of exempted supply, which includes a supply which is neither for reward nor in the course or furtherance of a business.

Possession of Extreme Pornographic Images

This offence, created under the CJIA 2008, s. 63, is dealt with at **B3.324**.   **B18.35**

Section B19   Offences Related to Drugs

CONTROLLED DRUGS

The Statutory Regime

B19.1   The UK is a party to the three main United Nations Conventions that aim to promote the global implementation of measures to restrict the use of substances that are included in the three classes of controlled drugs set out in sch. 2 to the Misuse of Drugs Act 1971 (MDA 1971) to medical, therapeutic and research purposes. The three UN Conventions are the Single Convention on Narcotic Drugs, 1961 (as amended by the 1972 Protocol), the Convention on Psychotropic Substances 1971, and the United Nations Convention Against Illicit Traffic in Narcotic Drugs and Psychotropic Substances 1988. There are a number of EU initiatives and measures that have similar objectives to those of the three main UN Conventions (e.g., Council Decision 2013/129/ EU (March 2013) on subjecting 4-methylamphetamine to control measures) and see the EU Action Plan on Drugs 2013–2020 (2013/C351/01).

The restrictions and prohibitions imposed by the MDA 1971 are subject to the exceptions and exemptions set out in secondary legislation (notably in the Misuse of Drugs Regulations 2001 (SI 2001 No. 3998)). Many products and substances are (from 14 August 2012) subject to the Human Medicines Regulations 2012 (SI 2012 No. 1916); the expression 'medicinal product' has the meaning given by reg. 2 of the 2012 Regulations (see SI 2012 No. 1916, sch. 34, para. 31).

Meaning of 'Controlled Drug' and 'Temporary Class Drugs'

B19.2   Misuse of Drugs Act 1971, s. 2

(1) In this Act —
(a) the expression 'controlled drug' means any substance or product for the time being specified —
    (i) in Part I, II or III of Schedule 2, or
    (ii) in a temporary class drug order as a drug subject to temporary control (but this is subject
        to section 2A(6));

(b) the expressions 'Class A drug', 'Class B drug' and 'Class C drug' mean any of the substances and products for the time being specified respectively in Part I, Part II and Part III of that Schedule; and

(c) the expression 'temporary class drug' means any substance or product which is for the time being a controlled drug by virtue of a temporary class drug order;

and the provisions of Part IV of that Schedule shall have effect with respect to the meanings of expressions used in that Schedule.

Temporary Class Drugs

Section 2 of the MDA 1971 was amended by the PRSRA 2011, s. 151 and sch. 17, para. 2, with the effect that substances and products that are the subject of a Temporary Class Drug Order are 'controlled drugs' (see s. 2(1)(a)(ii) at **B19.2**). The relevant penalties are those that apply to Class B drugs (s. 25(2B)). **B19.3**

Offences that Apply to Temporary Class Drugs   Subject to a statutory exception or exemption (and noting s. 28 of the MDA: see **B19.96**), it is unlawful and an offence to: **B19.4**

(a) import or to export a temporary class drug (MDA 1971, s. 3: see **B19.61**);
(b) supply, or offer to supply etc. a temporary class drug (s. 4(1) and (3): see **B19.37**);
(c) produce a temporary class drug (s. 4(2): see **B19.55**);
(d) possess a temporary class drug, intending to supply it (s. 5(3): see **B19.48**): but note, below, the saving in relation to the simple possession of a temporary class drug.

There can be circumstances in which s. 8 (see **B19.78**) and s. 19 (see **B19.95**) also apply in relation to temporary class drugs.

Section 9A(1) (see **B19.73**) is amended so that the administration of a temporary class drug is unlawful (where the other ingredients of s. 9A are proved) unless the administration is 'by any person of a temporary class drug to himself in circumstances where having the drug in his possession is to be treated as excepted possession for the purposes of this Act' (see s. 7A(2)(c)).

It is neither unlawful nor a criminal offence to be in *simple possession* of a temporary class drug (s. 5(2A): see **B19.19**). Confusingly, s. 7A(2)(c) (see **B19.6**), states that a Temporary Class Order may stipulate the circumstances 'in which a person's possession of the drug is to be treated as excepted possession for the purposes of this Act'. This provision is not intended to limit the circumstances in which the simple possession of a temporary class drug is lawful (see the Explanatory Notes to the PRSRA 2011, paras. 410 to 417).

Status of Temporary Class Drug Orders

A substance or product specified in a temporary class drug order as a drug subject to temporary control ceases to be a controlled drug by virtue of the order at the end of one year beginning with the day on which the order comes into force, or any earlier date on which the substance or product is specified as a controlled drug under sch. 2 (s. 2A(6)); but this is without prejudice to the need for Parliamentary approval of the order. **B19.5**

Making Provision to Exempt or Exclude Temporary Class Drugs from Offences

Section 7A of the MDA 1971 (inserted by the PRSRA 2011, s. 151 and sch. 17, para. 8) empowers the Secretary of State to make lawful certain activities that would otherwise be unlawful in respect of a temporary class drug, for example, exempting the drug from the application of s. 3(1)(a) or (b) or 4(1)(a) or (b) of the MDA 1971. **B19.6**

'Substances and Products' Specified as Controlled Drugs in Class A, B, or C

B19.7　Schedule 2 is frequently amended, including recently by SI 2014 Nos. 1106 and 1352. The principal purpose of having the three classes of controlled drugs is to identify the maximum statutory penalty for a given class (*Free* [2013] EWCA Crim 589).

Note that para. (e) to Part 2 of Sch. 2 was inserted by SI 2014 No. 1106, art. 4(b). That paragraph adds substances by way of a generic definition which includes 2-ethylaminobenzofurans. However, it is submitted that the legislature may have intended to control 2-aminoethylbenzofurans rather than ethylamino compounds.

Misuse of Drugs Act 1971, sch. 2

CONTROLLED DRUGS
PART I CLASS A DRUGS

1.　The following substances and products, namely:—
　　(a)　Acetorphine.
　　　　Alfentanil.
　　Allylprodine.
　　Alphacetylmethadol.
　　Alphameprodine.
　　Alphamethadol.
　　Alphaprodine.
　　Anileridine.
　　Benzethidine.
　　Benzylmorphine (3-benzylmorphine).
　　Betacetylmethadol.
　　Betameprodine.
　　Betamethadol.
　　Betaprodine.
　　Bezitramide.
　　Bufotenine.
　　Carfentanil.
　　Clonitazene.
　　Coca leaf.
　　Cocaine.
　　Desomorphine.
　　Dextromoramide.
　　Diamorphine.
　　Diampromide.
　　Diethylthiambutene.
　　Difenoxin (1-(3-cyano-3, 3-diphenylpropyl)-4-phenylpiperidine-4-carboxylic acid).
　　Dihydrocodeinone O-carboxymethyloxime.
　　Dihydroetorphine.
　　Dihydromorphine.
　　Dimenoxadole.
　　Dimepheptanol.
　　Dimethylthiambutene.
　　Dioxaphetyl butyrate.
　　Diphenoxylate.
　　Dipipanone.
　　Drotebanol (3,4-dimethoxy-17-methylmorphinan-6b, 14-diol).

Ecgonine, and any derivative of ecgonine which is convertible to ecgonine or to cocaine.
Ethylmethylthiambutene.
Eticyclidine.
Etonitazene.
Etorphine.
Etoxeridine.
Etryptamine.
Fentanyl.
Fungus (of any kind) which contains psilocin or an ester of psilocin.
Furethidine.
Hydrocodone.
Hydromorphinol.
Hydromorphone.
Hydroxypethidine.
Isomethadone.
Ketobemidone.
Levomethorphan.
Levomoramide.
Levophenacylmorphan.
Levorphanol.
Lofentanil.
Lysergamide.
Lysergide and other *N*-alkyl derivatives of lysergamide.
Mescaline.
Metazocine.
Methadone.
Methadyl acetate.
Methylamphetamine
Methyldesorphine.
Methyldihydromorphine (6-methyldihydromorphine).
Metopon.
Morpheridine.
Morphine.
Morphine methoromide, morphine *N*-oxide and other pentavalent nitrogen morphine derivatives.
Myrophine.

Nicomorphine
(3,6-dinicotinoyl- morphine).
Noracymethadol.
Norlevorphanol.
Normethadone.
Normorphine.
Norpipanone.
Opium, whether raw, prepared or
medicinal.
Oxycodone.
Oxymorphone.
Pethidine.
Phenadoxone.
Phenampromide.
Phenazocine.
Phencyclidine.
Phenomorphan.
Phenoperidine.
Piminodine.
Piritramide.
Poppy-straw and concentrate of
poppy-straw.
Proheptazine.
Properidine (1-methyl-4-phenyl-
piperidine-4-carboxylic acid
isopropyl ester).
Psilocin.
Racemethorphan.

Racemoramide.
Racemorphan.
Remifentanil.
Rolicyclidine.
Sufentanil.
Tapentadol.
Tenocylidine.
Thebacon.
Thebaine.
Tilidate.
Trimeperidine.
4-Bromo-2,5-dimethoxy-a-me
thylphenethylamine.
4-Cyano-2-dimethylamino-4,4-
diphenylbutane.
4-Cyano-1-methyl-4-phenyl-piperidine.
N,N-Diethyltryptamine.
N,N-Dimethyltryptamine.
2,5-Dimethoxy-a,
4-dimethylphenethylamine.
N-Hydroxy-tenamphetamine
1-Methyl-4-phenylpiperidine-
4-carboxylic acid.
2-Methyl-3-morpholino-1,1- diphe-
nylpropanecarboxylic acid.
4-Methyl-aminorex
4-Phenylpiperidine-4-carboxylic acid
ethyl ester.

(b) any compound (not being a compound for the time being specified in subparagraph
(a) above) structurally derived from tryptamine or from a ring-hydroxy tryptamine by
substitution at the nitrogen atom of the sidechain with one or more alkyl substituents
but no other substituent;

(ba) the following phenethylamine derivatives, namely:

Allyl(a-methyl-3,4-methylenedioxyphenethyl)amine
2-Amino-1-(2,5-dimethoxy-4-methylphenyl)ethanol
2-Amino-1-(3,4-dimethoxyphenyl)ethanol
Benzyl(a-methyl-3,4-methylenedioxyphenethyl)amine
4-Bromo-b,2,5-trimethoxyphenethylamine
N-(4-sec-Butylthio-2,5-dimethoxyphenethyl)hydroxylamine
Cyclopropylmethyl(a-methyl-3,4-methylenedioxyphenethyl)amine
2-(4,7-Dimethoxy-2,3-dihydro-1H-indan-5-yl)ethylamine
2-(4,7-Dimethoxy-2,3-dihydro-1H-indan-5-yl)-1-methylethylamine
2-(2,5-Dimethoxy-4-methylphenyl)cyclopropylamine
2-(1,4-Dimethoxy-2-naphthyl)ethylamine
2-(1,4-Dimethoxy-2-naphthyl)-1-methylethylamine
N-(2,5-Dimethoxy-4-propylthiophenethyl)hydroxylamine
2-(1,4-Dimethoxy-5, 6, 7,8-tetrahydro-2-naphthyl)ethylamine
2-(1,4-Dimethoxy-5,6,7,8-tetrahydro-2-naphthy1)-1-methylethylamine
a,a-Dimethyl-3,4-methylenedioxyphenethylamine
a,a-Dimethyl-3,4-methylenedioxyphenethyl(methyl)amine
Dimethyl(a-methyl-3,4-methylenedioxyphenethyl)amine
N-(4-Ethylthio-2,5-dimethoxyphenethyl)hydroxylamine
4-lodo-2,5-dimethoxy-a-methylphenethyl(dimethyl)amine
2-(1,4-Methano-5,8-dimethoxy-1,2,3,4-tetrahydro-6-naphthyl)ethylamine
2-(1,4-Methano-5,8-dimethoxy-1,2,3,4-tetrahydro-6-naphthyl)1-methylethylamine
2-(5-Methoxy-2,2-dimethyl-2,3-dihydrobenzo[b]furan-6-yl)-1-methylethylamine
2-Methoxyethyl(a-methyl-3,4-methylenedioxyphenethyl)amine
2-(5-Methoxy-2-methyl-2,3-dihydrobenzo[b]furan-6-yl)-1-methylethylamine

b-Methoxy-3,4-methylenedioxyphenethylamine
1-(3,4-Methylenedioxybenzyl)butyl(ethyl)amine
1-(3,4-Methylenedioxybenzyl)butyl(methyl)amine
2-(a-Methyl-3,4-methylenedioxyphenethylamino)ethanol
a-Methyl-3,4-methylenedioxyphenethyl(prop-2-ynyl)amine
N-Methyl-N-(a-methyl-3,4-methylenedioxyphenethyl)hydroxylamine
O-Methyl-N-(a-methyl-3,4methylenedioxyphenethyl)hydroxylamine
a-Methyl-4-(methylthio)phenethylamine
b,3,4,5-Tetramethoxyphenethylamine
b,2,5-Trimethoxy-4-methylphenethylamine.

(c) any compound (not being methoxyphenamine or a compound for the time being specified in subparagraph (a) above) structurally derived from phenethylamine, an *N*-alkylphenethylamine, a-methylphenethylamine, an *N*-alkyl-a-methylphenethylamine, a-ethylphenethylamine, or an *N*-alkyl-a-ethylphenethylamine by substitution in the ring to any extent with alkyl, alkoxy, alkylenedioxy or halide substituents, whether or not further substituted in the ring by one or more other univalent substituents.

(d) any compound (not being a compound for the time being specified in subparagraph (a) above) structurally derived from fentanyl by modification in any of the following ways, that is to say,

(i) by replacement of the phenyl portion of the phenethyl group by any heteromonocycle whether or not further substituted in the heterocycle;

(ii) by substitution in the phenethyl group with alkyl, alkenyl, alkoxy, hydoxy, halogeno, haloalkyl, amino or nitro groups;

(iii) by substitution in the piperidine ring with alkyl or alkenyl groups;

(iv) by substitution in the aniline ring with alkyl, alkoxy, alkylenedioxy, halogeno or haloalkyl groups;

(v) by substitution at the 4-position of the piperidine ring with any alkoxycarbonyl or alkoxyalkyl or acyloxy group;

(vi) by replacement of the *N*-propionyl group by another acyl group;

(e) any compound (not being a compound for the time being specified in subparagraph (a) above) structurally derived from pethidine by modification in any of the following ways, that is to say,

(i) by replacement of the 1-methyl group by an acyl, alkyl whether or not unsaturated, benzyl or phenethyl group, whether or not further substituted;

(ii) by substitution in the piperidine ring with alkyl or alkenyl groups or with a propano bridge, whether or not further substituted;

(iii) by substitution in the 4-phenyl ring with alkyl, alkoxy, aryloxy, halogeno or haloalkyl groups;

(iv) by replacement of the 4-ethoxycarbonyl by any other alkoxycarbonyl or any alkoxyalkyl or acyloxy group;

(v) by formation of an *N*-oxide or of a quaternary base.

(f) any compound (not being benzyl(α-methyl-3,4-methylenedioxyphenethyl)amine) structurally derived from mescaline, 4-bromo-2,5-dimethoxy-α-methylphenethylamine, 2,5-dimethoxy-α,4-dimethylphenethylamine, *N*-hydroxytenamphetamine, or a compound specified in sub-paragraph (ba) or (c) above, by substitution at the nitrogen atom of the amino group with a benzyl substituent, whether or not substituted in the phenyl ring of the benzyl group to any extent.

2. Any stereoisomeric form of a substance for the time being specified in paragraph 1 above not being dextromethorphan or dextrorphan.

3. Any ester or ether of a substance for the time being specified in paragraph 1 or 2 above not being a substance for the time being specified in Part II of this Schedule.

4. Any salt of a substance for the time being specified in any of paragraphs 1 to 3 above.

5. Any preparation or other product containing a substance or product for the time being specified in any of paragraphs 1 to 4 above.

6. Any preparation designed for administration by injection which includes a substance or product for the time being specified in any of paragraphs 1 to 3 of Part II of this Schedule.

PART II CLASS B DRUGS

1. The following substances and products, namely:—

   (a) Acetyldihydrocodeine.
   Amphetamine.
   Cannabinol.
   Cannabinol derivatives.
   Cannabis and cannabis resin.
   Codeine.
   Dihydrocodeine.
   Ethylmorphine (3-ethylmorphine).
   Glutethimide.
   Ketamine.
   Lefetamine.
   Lisdexamphetamine.
   Mecloqualone.
   Methaqualone.
   Methcathinone.
   Methylphenidate.
   a-Methylphenethylthydroxylamine
   Methylphenobarbitone.
   Nicodine.
   Nicodicodine
       (6-nicotinoyldihydrocodeine).
   Norcodeine.
   Pentazocine.
   Phenmetrazine.
   Pholcodine.
   Propiram.
   Zipeprol.
   2-((Dimethylamino)methyl)-1-
       (3-hydroxyphenyl)cyclohexanol.

   (aa) Any compound (not being bupropion, cathinone, diethylpropion, pyrovalerone or a compound for the time being specified in sub-paragraph (a) above) structurally derived from 2–amino–1–phenyl–1–propanone by modification in any of the following ways, that is to say,

   (i) by substitution in the phenyl ring to any extent with alkyl, alkoxy, alkylenedioxy, haloalkyl or halide substituents, whether or not further substituted in the phenyl ring by one or more other univalent substituents;

   (ii) by substitution at the 3–position with an alkyl substituent;

   (iii) by substitution at the nitrogen atom with alkyl or dialkyl groups, or by inclusion of the nitrogen atom in a cyclic structure.

   (ab) Any compound structurally derived from 2–aminopropan–1–one by substitution at the 1-position with any monocyclic, or fused polycyclic ring system (not being a phenyl ring or alkylenedioxyphenyl ring system), whether or not the compound is further modified in any of the following ways, that is to say,

   (i) by substitution in the ring system to any extent with alkyl, alkoxy, haloalkyl or halide substituents, whether or not further substituted in the ring system by one or more other univalent substituents;

   (ii) by substitution at the 3–position with an alkyl substituent;

   (iii) by substitution at the 2 amino nitrogen atom with alkyl or dialkyl groups, or by inclusion of the 2 amino nitrogen atom in a cyclic structure.

   (ac) Any compound (not being pipradrol) structurally derived from piperidine, pyrrolidine, azepane, morpholine or pyridine by substitution at a ring carbon atom with a diphenyl-methyl group, whether or not the compound is further modified in any of the following ways, that is to say,

   (i) by substitution in any of the phenyl rings to any extent with alkyl, alkoxy, haloalkyl or halide groups;

   (ii) by substitution at the methyl carbon atom with an alkyl, hydroxyalkyl or hydroxy group;

   (iii) by substitution at the ring nitrogen atom with an alkyl, alkenyl, haloalkyl or hydroxyalkyl group.

   (b) Any 5,5 disubstituted barbituric acid.

   (c) [2,3–Dihydro–5–methyl–3–(4–morpholinylmethyl)pyrrolo[1, 2, 3–de]–1,4–benzoxazin–6–yl]–1–naphthalenylmethanone.

   [9–Hydroxy–6–methyl–3–[5–phenylpentan–2–yl] oxy–5, 6, 6a, 7, 8, 9, 10, 10a–octahydrophenanthridin–1–yl] acetate.

   9-(Hydroxymethyl)–6, 6–dimethyl–3–(2–methyloctan–2–yl)–6a, 7, 10, 10a–tetrahydrobenzo[c]chromen–1–ol.

   Nabilone

   Any compound structurally derived from 3–(1–naphthoyl)indole, 3-(2-naphthoyl) indole, 1H–indol–3–yl–(1–naphthyl)methane or 1H-indol-3-yl-(2-naphthyl)methane

by substitution at the nitrogen atom of the indole ring by alkyl, haloalkyl, alkenyl, cyanoalkyl, hydroxyalkyl, cycloalkylmethyl, cycloalkylethyl, (N-methylpiperidin-2-yl) methyl or 2–(4–morpholinyl)ethyl, whether or not further substituted in the indole ring to any extent and whether or not substituted in the naphthyl ring to any extent.

Any compound structurally derived from 3–(1–naphthoyl)pyrrole or 3-(2-naphthoyl) pyrrole by substitution at the nitrogen atom of the pyrrole ring by alkyl, haloalkyl, alkenyl, cyanoalkyl, hydroxyalkyl, cycloalkylmethyl, cycloalkylethyl, (N-methylpiperidin-2-yl)methyl or 2–(4–morpholinyl)ethyl, whether or not further substituted in the pyrrole ring to any extent and whether or not substituted in the naphthyl ring to any extent.

Any compound structurally derived from 1–(1–naphthylmethylene)indene or 1-(2-naphthylmethylene)indene by substitution at the 3–position of the indene ring by alkyl, haloalkyl, alkenyl, cyanoalkyl, hydroxyalkyl, cycloalkylmethyl, cycloalkylethyl, (N-methylpiperidin-2-yl)methyl or 2–(4–morpholinyl)ethyl, whether or not further substituted in the indene ring to any extent and whether or not substituted in the naphthyl ring to any extent.

Any compound structurally derived from 3–phenylacetylindole by substitution at the nitrogen atom of the indole ring by alkyl, haloalkyl, alkenyl, cyanoalkyl, hydroxyalkyl, cycloalkylmethyl, cycloalkylethyl, (N-methylpiperidin-2-yl)methyl or 2–(4–morpholinyl)ethyl, whether or not further substituted in the indole ring to any extent and whether or not substituted in the phenyl ring to any extent.

Any compound structurally derived from 2–(3–hydroxycyclohexyl)phenol by substitution at the 5–position of the phenolic ring by alkyl, alkenyl, cycloalkylmethyl, cycloalkylethyl or 2–(4–morpholinyl)ethyl, whether or not further substituted in the cyclohexyl ring to any extent.

Any compound structurally derived from 3-benzoylindole by substitution at the nitrogen atom of the indole ring by alkyl, haloalkyl, alkenyl, cyanoalkyl, hydroxyalkyl, cycloalkylmethyl, cycloalkylethyl, (N-methylpiperidin-2-yl)methyl or 2–(4–morpholinyl)ethyl, whether or not further substituted in the indole ring to any extent and whether or not substituted in the phenyl ring to any extent.

Any compound structurally derived from 3-(1-adamantoyl)indole or 3-(2-adamantoyl) indole by substitution at the nitrogen atom of the indole ring by alkyl, haloalkyl, alkenyl, cyanoalkyl, hydroxyalkyl, cycloalkylmethyl, cycloalkylethyl, (N-methylpiperidin-2-yl)methyl or 2–(4–morpholinyl)ethyl, whether or not further substituted in the indole ring to any extent and whether or not substituted in the adamantyl ring to any extent.

Any compound structurally derived from 3-(2,2,3,3-tetramethylcyclopropylcarbonyl)indole by substitution at the nitrogen atom of the indole ring by alkyl, haloalkyl, alkenyl, cyanoalkyl, hydroxyalkyl, cycloalkylmethyl, cycloalkylethyl, (N-methylpiperidin-2-yl) methyl or 2–(4–morpholinyl)ethyl, whether or not further substituted in the indole ring to any extent.

(d) 1-Phenylcyclohexylamine or any compound (not being ketamine, tiletamine or a compound for the time being specified in paragraph 1(a) of Part 1 of this Schedule) structurally derived from 1-phenylcyclohexylamine or 2-amino-2-phenylcyclohexanone by modification in any of the following ways, that is to say,

(i) by substitution at the nitrogen atom to any extent by alkyl, alkenyl or hydroxyalkyl groups, or replacement of the amino group with a 1-piperidyl, 1-pyrrolidyl or 1-azepyl group, whether or not the nitrogen containing ring is further substituted by one or more alkyl groups;

(ii) by substitution in the phenyl ring to any extent by amino, alkyl, hydroxy, alkoxy or halide substituents, whether or not further substituted in the phenyl ring to any extent;

(iii) by substitution in the cyclohexyl or cyclohexanone ring by one or more alkyl substituents;

(iv) by replacement of the phenyl ring with a thienyl ring.

(e) Any compound (not being a compound for the time being specified in paragraph 1(ba) of Part 1 of this Schedule) structurally derived from 1-benzofuran, 2,3-dihydro-1-benzofuran, 1H-indole, indoline, 1H-indene, or indane by substitution in the 6-membered ring with a 2-ethylamino substituent whether or not further substituted in the ring system to any extent with alkyl, alkoxy, halide or haloalkyl substituents and whether or not substituted in the ethylamino side-chain with one or more alkyl substituents

2. Any stereoisomeric form of a substance for the time being specified in paragraph 1 of this Part of this Schedule.

2A. Any ester or ether of cannabinol or of a cannabinol derivative or of a substance for the time being specified in paragraph 1(ac), (c) or (d) of this Part of this Schedule.

3. Any salt of a substance for the time being specified in paragraph 1, 2 or 2A of this Part of this Schedule.

4. Any preparation or other product containing a substance or product for the time being specified in any of paragraphs 1 to 3 of this Part of this Schedule, not being a preparation falling within paragraph 6 of Part I of this Schedule.

Part III Class C Drugs

1. The following substances, namely:—
(a) Alprazolam.
Amineptine
Aminorex.
Benzphetamine.
Bromazepam.
7-bromo-5-(2-chlorophenyl)-1,3-dihy-dro-2H-1, 4-benzodiazepin-2-one
Brotizolam.
Buprenorphine.
Camazepam.
Cathine.
Cathinone.
Chlordiazepoxide.
Chlorphentermine.
Clobazam.
Clonazepam.
Clorazepic acid.
Clotiazepam.
Cloxazolam.
Delorazepam.
Dextropropoxyphene.
Diazepam.
Diethylpropion.
Estazolam.
Ethchlorvynol.
Ethinamate.
Ethyl loflazepate.
Fencamfamin.
Fenethylline.
Fenproporex.
Fludiazepam.
Flunitrazepam.
Flurazepam.
Gamma–butyrolactone
Halazepam.
Haloxazolam.
4-Hydroxy-n-butyric acid.
Ketazolam.
Khat
Loprazolam.
Lorazepam.
Lormetazepam.
Mazindol.
Medazepam.
Mefenorex.
Mephentermine.
Meprobamate.
Mesocarb.
Methyprylone.
Midazolam.
Nimetazepam.
Nitrazepam.
Nordazepam.
Oxazepam.
Oxazolam.
Pemoline.
Phendimetrazine.
Phentermine.
Pinazepam.
Prazepam.
Pyrovalerone.
Temazepam.
Tetrazepam.
Tramadol.
Triazolam.
N-Ethylamphetamine.
Zaleplon.
Zolpidem.
Zopiclone.
(b) 5α–Androstane–3,17–diol.
Androst-4-ene-3,17-diol.
1–Androstenediol.
1–Androstenedione
4-Androstene-3, 17-dione.
5–Androstenedione.
5-Androstene-3, 17-diol.
Atamestane.
Bolandiol.
Bolasterone.
Bolazine.
Boldenone.
Boldione.
Bolenol.
Bolmantalate.
1,4–Butanediol.
Calusterone.
4-Chloromethandienone.
Clostebol.
Danazol.
Desoxymethyltestosterone.
Drostanolone.

Enestebol.

Epitiostanol.

Ethyloestrenol.

Fluoxymesterone.

Formebolone.

Furazabol.

Gestrinone.

3–Hydroxy–5–androstan–17–one.

Mebolazine.

Mepitiostane.

Mesabolone.

Mestanolone.

Mesterolone.

Methandienone.

Methandriol.

Methenolone.

Methyltestosterone.

Metribolone.

Mibolerone.

Nandrolone.

19–Norandrostenedione.

19-Nor-4-Androstene-3, 17-dione.

19-Nor-5-Androstene-3, 17-diol.

19–Norandrosterone.

Norboletone.

Norclostebol.

Norethandrolone.

19–Noretiocholanolone.

Oripavine.

Ovandrotone.

Oxabolone.

Oxandrolone.

Oxymesterone.

Oxymetholone.

Pipradrol.

Prasterone.

Propetandrol.

Prostanozol.

Quinbolone.

Roxibolone.

Silandrone.

Stanolone.

Stanozolol.

Stenbolone.

Testosterone.

Tetrahydrogestrinone.

Thiomesterone.

Trenbolone.

(c) any compound (not being Trilostane or a compound for the time being specified in sub-paragraph (b) above) structurally derived from 17-hydroxyandrostan-3-one or from 17-hydroxyestran-3-one by modification in any of the following ways, that is to say,
  (i) by further substitution at position 17 by a methyl or ethyl group;
  (ii) by substitution to any extent at one or more of positions 1, 2, 4, 6, 7, 9, 11 or 16, but at no other position;
  (iii) by unsaturation in the carbocyclic ring system to any extent, provided that there are no more than two ethylenic bonds in any one carbocyclic ring;
  (iv) by fusion of ring A with a heterocyclic system;

(ca) 1–benzylpiperazine or any compound structurally derived from 1–benzylpiperazine or 1–phenylpiperazine by modification in any of the following ways—
  (i) by substitution at the second nitrogen atom of the piperazine ring with alkyl, benzyl, haloalkyl or phenyl groups;
  (ii) by substitution in the aromatic ring to any extent with alkyl, alkoxy, alkylenedioxy, halide or haloalkyl groups.

(d) any substance which is an ester or ether (or, where more than one hydroxyl function is available, both an ester and an ether) of a substance specified in sub-paragraph (b) or described in sub-paragraph (c) above;

(e) Chorionic Gonadotrophin (HCG).   Clenbuterol.
Non-human chorionic gonadotrophin.   Somatotropin.
Somatrem.   Somatropin.
Zeranol.   Zilpatero

2. Any stereoisomeric form of a substance for the time being specified in paragraph 1 of this Part of this Schedule not being phenylpropanolamine.

3. Any salt of a substance for the time being specified in paragraph 1 or 2 of this Part of this Schedule.

4. Any preparation or other product containing a substance for the time being specified in any of paragraphs 1 to 3 of this Part of this Schedule.

PART IV MEANING OF CERTAIN EXPRESSIONS USED IN THIS SCHEDULE

For the purposes of this Schedule the following expressions (which are not among those defined in section 37(1) of this Act) have the meanings hereby assigned to them respectively, that is to say—

'cannabinol derivatives' means the following substances, except where contained in cannabis or cannabis resin, namely tetrahydro derivatives of cannabinol and 3-alkyl homologues of cannabinol or of its tetrahydro derivatives;

'coca leaf' means the leaf of any plant of the genus *Erythroxylon* from whose leaves cocaine can be extracted either directly or by chemical transformation;

'concentrate of poppy-straw' means the material produced when poppy-straw has entered into a process for the concentration of its alkaloids;

'khat' means the leaves, stems or shoots of the plant of the species *Catha edulis*;

'medicinal opium' means raw opium which has undergone the process necessary to adapt it for medicinal use in accordance with the requirements of the British Pharmacopoeia, whether it is in the form of powder or is granulated or is in any other form, and whether it is or is not mixed with neutral substances;

'opium poppy' means the plant of the species *Papaver somniferum* L;

'poppy straw' means all parts, except the seeds, of the opium poppy after mowing;

'raw opium' includes powdered or granulated opium but does not include medicinal opium.

Unnecessary to Distinguish between Drugs in Usual Form and Stereoisomeric Forms, Salts or Esters   **B19.8** The MDA 1971, sch. 2, lists drugs in their basic and stereoisomeric forms, as well as their esters or salts. The Court of Appeal in *Greensmith* [1983] 3 All ER 444 held that the word 'cocaine' as used in para. 1 of sch. 2, part I (Class A drugs) is a generic word which includes within its ambit both the direct extracts of the coca leaf, the natural form, and whatever results from a chemical transformation listed in paras. 2 to 5. Having regard to *DPP v Goodchild* [1978] 2 All ER 161 it is submitted that it would have been preferable had coca-leaf (which is separately specified as a controlled drug in sch. 2) not been described by the court as 'cocaine'. *Greensmith* was applied in *A-G for the Cayman Islands v Roberts* [2002] 1 WLR 1842.

The Court of Appeal held in *Watts* [1984] 2 All ER 380 that 'amphetamine' in sch. 2, part II, para. 1 (Class B drugs), includes generically all of its stereoisomers, pure dexamphetamine, pure levoamphetamine, or a racemic mixture of dexamphetamine and levoamphetamine.

Material Occurring Naturally   **B19.9** Controlled drugs are defined by their chemical name (e.g., 'diamorphine' (heroin)). But 'any controlled drug described in [the MDA 1971, sch. 2] by its scientific name was not established by proof of possession of naturally occurring material of which the described drug was one of the constituents unseparated from the others...and that was so whether or not the naturally occurring material was also included as another item in the list of controlled drugs' (*DPP v Goodchild* [1978] 2 All ER 161, per Lord Diplock, at p. 583). In the case of the latter possibility, the offence would allude to the naturally occurring material, and not its constituent elements. Thus, cannabis, and fungus that contains psilocin, are described as such in sch. 2.

'Preparations' and 'Products' which Contain a Controlled Drug are Controlled   **B19.10** The word 'preparation' is not a technical word but 'a word to be addressed in its ordinary English meaning' (*Thomson* [2003] EWCA Crim 3477). The majority of appellate decisions that have considered the meaning of 'preparation' concern psilocybin mushrooms (now specifically controlled in the MDA 1971, sch. 2, part 1, para. 1(a)). In *Hodder v DPP* [1990] Crim LR 261, the Divisional Court held that to 'prepare' means 'to make ready or fit; to bring into a suitable state; to subject to a process of bringing it to a required state'. Freezing is not an act of preparation but of preservation. In order to prepare something it is not necessary to undertake a chemical or technical process (see *Stevens* [1981] Crim LR 568 and *Martin* [2006] EWCA Crim 109 in relation to naturally occurring material). A 'preparation' requires the substance to be altered by human action to put it into a condition in which it can be used for human consumption (*Stevens*; *Cunliffe* [1986] Crim LR 547). Although *obiter*, it was remarked by the Divisional Court in *Jama v Senior Public Prosecutor, Germany* [2014] 1 WLR 1843 at [38], that *Hodder v DPP* 'does not sit comfortably' with the observations of Lord Diplock in *DPP v Goodchild* [1978] 2 All ER 161. It did not seem to the Court that bundles of khat plants (as described in a European Arrest Warrant) could properly be regarded as a 'preparation or other product' containing cathinone, within the meaning of the MDA 1971, sch. 2, part III, para. 4, so as to bring the importation, exportation and supply of the plants themselves within the scope of the offences in ss. 3(1) and 4(1). The warrant did not suggest that anything had been done to the khat beyond picking it and bundling it up in parcels. In the opinion of the Court, it remained the natural plant, not a 'product' within the meaning of the statute (per Richards LJ at [38]). Note that khat is now a Class C controlled drug (see SI 2014 No. 1352).

B19.11 In *Walker* [1987] Crim LR 565, the Court of Appeal declined to express any view as to whether merely picking psilocybin mushrooms is an act of preparation. Whether or to what extent the word 'product' includes packaged substances is not clear, but in *Hodder v DPP*, the Court of Appeal held that psilocybin mushrooms as 'picked, packaged and frozen' came within the meaning of the word 'product' or within the phrase 'or other product' as used in sch. 2, para. 5. Note that in *Greensmith* [1983] 3 All ER 444, the Court of Appeal remarked that any kind of matter comes within 'substance' whereas 'product' envisages the result of some kind of process. Difficulties have arisen in connection with *echinopsis peruviana* (cacti) in which mescaline sub-sists. In at least three cases concerning this plant material, proceedings for an offence under the MDA 1971 have been stayed (*Mardle* (14 December 2004 unreported), *Francis* (20 April 2005 unreported) and *Sette* (13 March 2006 unreported)). In *Sette*, the learned recorder stayed the case on the basis that the law was uncertain, and that HMRC has levied VAT on some vendors of this species of cactus. None of these first decision rulings has been the subject of detailed analysis by a higher court (but see *H* [2012] EWCA Crim 525, which raised similar issues with the same result). In any future cases involving this species of cactus, expert assistance might be required to specify the steps that need to be taken in order to put the plant into a usable condition. In *Aziz* [2012] EWCA Crim 1063, the Court of Appeal held (at [4]):

> ...that making an infusion out of the B-Caapi and the Chacruna amounted to producing by mak-ing a preparation. It did in any ordinary language and it did in law. It is not a question of altering the chemical make up of DMT. It is a question of putting it into a form in which it can be consumed, which is in any ordinary language preparation.

See also the commentary on *Aziz* at [2012] Crim LR 801. The Court of Appeal's reasoning would appear to be that, because the MDA 1971 controls 'preparations' that contain a con-trolled drug, a person can 'produce' a preparation (contrary to s. 4): consider *Williams* [2011] EWCA Crim 232 (see **B19.59**). If this means that every 'preparation' involved an act of 'pro-duction' then *Aziz* goes significantly further (it is submitted) than decisions such as *Hodder v DPP* and *Stevens*.

Meaning of 'Cannabis' and 'Cannabis Resin'

B19.12   Misuse of Drugs Act 1971, s. 37

'cannabis' (except in the expression 'cannabis resin') means any plant of the genus Cannabis or any part of any such plant (by whatever name designated) except that it does not include cannabis resin or any of the following products after separation from the rest of the plant, namely—
(a) mature stalk of any such plant,
(b) fibre produced from mature stalk of any such plant, and
(c) seed of any such plant,
'cannabis resin' means the separated resin, whether crude or purified, obtained from any plant of the genus *Cannabis*.

In *Thomas* [1981] Crim LR 496, the Court of Appeal held that the substance was cannabis resin, even though on microscopic examination it was shown to contain elements of the natural form from which the resin had not been extracted. There was sufficient separated material, and *DPP v Goodchild* [1978] 2 All ER 161 did not lead to the conclusion that the wrong charge had been laid. In *Hill* (1993) 96 Cr App R 456, the Court of Appeal held that where the charge specifies the supply of 'cannabis resin' it is not enough to prove that the accused supplied either 'cannabis' or 'cannabis resin'. The Court distinguished *Best* (1979) 70 Cr App R 21 (see **B19.21**) where the charge particularised the drug as either cannabis or cannabis resin.

Proof of Substance as Controlled Drug

Expert evidence (such as an analyst's certificate) is not required in all cases, but the prosecution **B19.13** must establish the identity of the drug referred to in the charge with sufficient certainty (*Hill* (1993) 96 Cr App R 456). In *Chatwood* [1980] 1 All ER 467, it was held that the admissions of an accused as to his knowledge of the substance may constitute sufficient evidence to identify what it is. The Court of Appeal approved the statement of the law made by Lord Widgery CJ in *Bird v Adams* [1972] Crim LR 174:

> If a man admits possession of a substance which he says is a dangerous drug, if he admits it in circumstances like the present where he also admits that he has been peddling the drug, it is of course possible that the item in question was not a specified drug at all but the admission in those circumstances is not an admission of some fact about which the admitter knows nothing. This is the kind of case in which the appellant had certainly sufficient knowledge of the circumstances of his conduct to make his admission at least prima facie evidence of its truth and that was all that was required at the stage of the proceedings at which the submission to the justices was made.

The statements of the accused in *Chatwood* were sufficient to provide prima facie evidence of the nature of the substance in their possession. The opinion of the accused as to the nature of the substance he possessed must be such that his opinion is reliable. As to admissions by the accused generally, see **F17**. See also *Bagshaw* [1995] Crim LR 433. For a useful discussion of this problem and the aforementioned cases, see *DPP v Buckley* [2007] IEHC 150 (a decision of the High Court of Ireland).

Regulations that Permit Actions with Respect to 'Controlled Drugs'

Section 7(1) of the MDA 1971 empowers the Secretary of State to make regulations to except **B19.14** from s. 5(1) (and ss. 3(1)(a) or (b) and 4(1)(a)) specified controlled drugs (and to make such other provision as he thinks fit) to make lawful an activity which, under ss. 4(1), 5(1), and 6(1), would otherwise be unlawful (and criminal): see the Misuse of Drugs Regulations 2001 at **B19.17**. The Secretary of State is required to exercise this power to ensure that it is not unlawful under s. 5(1) for a doctor, dentist, veterinary practitioner, veterinary surgeon, pharmacist or person lawfully conducting a retail pharmacy business to have a controlled drug in his possession for the purpose of his acting in such a capacity; similar provision is made with regard to the offence in s. 4(1) (s. 7(3)). However, that power is subject to s. 7(4), whereby the production, supply and possession of a drug may be made wholly unlawful, or unlawful except for research or other special purposes, or whereby the activities of practitioners, pharmacists and persons lawfully conducting retail pharmacy businesses may be made unlawful except where they act under a licence or other authority from the Secretary of State (see the Misuse of Drugs (Designation) Order 2001 (SI 2001 No. 3997), as amended).

Although cannabis is designated in para. 1(a) of the schedule to the Misuse of Drugs (Designation) Order 2001 as a drug to which s. 7(4) applies, SI 2013 No. 624 excludes the cannabis-based medicine known as 'Sativex', from that designation.

In relation to regulations made under the MDA 1971, it is important to distinguish between 'controlled drugs' and 'temporary class drugs'. The Secretary of State is empowered by s. 7A to make specific provision in relation to temporary class drugs (see **B19.6**). Accordingly, s. 7(10) (inserted by the PRSRA 2011, s. 151 and sch. 17, para. 7), reads: 'In this section a reference to "controlled drugs" does not include a reference to temporary class drugs (see instead section 7A)'. Similarly, insofar as s. 10 of the MDA 1971 empowers the Secretary of State to make regulations for preventing misuse of 'controlled drugs', s. 10(3) (inserted by the PRSRA 2011, sch. 17, para. 10) provides that references in s. 10 to 'controlled drugs' do not include a reference to temporary class drugs (see, instead, s. 7A).

Whether an accused was acting in his capacity as a medical practitioner is a matter for the jury to decide (*Abraham* [2002] EWCA Crim 2870).

The Misuse of Drugs Regulations 2001 contain provisions which make lawful certain acts which, otherwise, would be offences under the MDA 1971. The regulations have been heavily amended. Regulations 2 to 10 and 12 and 13 have been reproduced at **B19.17**. Regulations 15 to 17 provide for exemptions in relation to prescriptions. Other regulations deal with requirements as to the marking of bottles and other containers, keeping of registers and records, furnishing of information and destruction of controlled drugs. There are eight schedules.

B19.15   **Burden of Proof Relating to Exceptions under Regulations**   The leading case is *Hunt* [1987] AC 352. A statute may place a burden of proof on the accused by implication, although it does not do so expressly (as to the significance of *Hunt* on issues of burden of proof generally, see **F3.16**). Lord Griffiths said that the MDA 1971, s. 7(1), gives the Secretary of State power to make two kinds of exceptions:

(a) exceptions under s. 7(1)(a), whereby the power is given to provide that it is not an offence to possess certain drugs;
(b) exceptions under s. 7(1)(b), where the power is given to clothe certain persons with immunity from what would otherwise be unlawful acts, which is achieved by the remainder of the regulations.

Lord Griffiths said (at pp. 376–7):

> These latter regulations provide special defences to what would otherwise be unlawful acts and would, I accept, place a burden upon defendants to bring themselves within the exceptions if it were necessary to do so. I say 'if it were necessary to do so' because of the extreme improbability that an exempted person would be charged with an offence.

This *obiter dictum* appears to mean that establishing the protection of any of regs. 5 to 13 places a burden of proof on the accused. Where, however, reg. 4 defines the essential ingredient of an offence, the prosecution must prove possession of the drug alleged beyond reasonable doubt. In *Hunt*, preparations of morphine containing not more than 0.2 per cent of morphine were exempted from the offence under s. 5(2), and the prosecution adduced no evidence of the composition of the preparation in question. It was held that the prosecution had failed to prove its case, and that the accused was entitled to an acquittal.

It follows that the incidence of proof may vary, depending upon which regulation is engaged. Where the accused shoulders a burden of proving a particular fact or matter, regard should be had to the decision of the House of Lords in *Lambert* [2002] 2 AC 545 (see **B19.100** and **F3.18**; and consider *Keogh* [2007] 3 All ER 789).

Extracts from the 2001 Regulations, as amended

B19.16   The 2001 Regulations have been heavily amended, most recently by SI 2014 Nos. 1275 and 1377.

B19.17   **Misuse of Drugs Regulations 2001 (SI 2001 No. 3998), regs. 2 to 13 and schs. 1 to 5**

Interpretation

2.—(1) In these Regulations, unless the context otherwise requires—
'the Act' means the Misuse of Drugs Act 1971;
'accountable officer' has the same meaning as in the Health Act 2006;
'authorised as a member of a group' means authorised by virtue of being a member of a class as respects which the Secretary of State has granted an authority under and for the purposes of regulation 8(3), 9(3) or 10(3) which is in force, and 'his group authority', in relation to a person who is a member of such a class, means the authority so granted to that class;
'care home' in relation to—
(a) England and Wales has the same meaning as in the Care Standards Act 2000; and
(b) Scotland means the accommodation provided by a care home service;

'care home service' has the same meaning as in the Public Service Reform (Scotland) Act 2010;

'clinical management plan' has the same meaning as in the Human Medicines Regulations 2012;

'the Common Services Agency for the health service' means the body established under section 10 of the National Health Service (Scotland) Act 1978;

'document' means anything in which information of any description is recorded (within the meaning of the Civil Evidence Act 1995);

'equivalent body' means a Local Health Board in Wales, a Health Board in Scotland or the Northern Ireland Central Services Agency for the Health and Social Services in Northern Ireland;

'exempt product' means a preparation or other product consisting of one or more component parts, any of which contains a controlled drug, where—

    (a)   the preparation or other product is not designed for administration of the controlled drug to a human being or animal;

    (b)   the controlled drug in any component part is packaged in such a form, or in combination with other active or inert substances in such a manner, that it cannot be recovered by readily applicable means or in a yield which constitutes a risk to health; and

    (c)   no one component part of the product or preparation contains more than one milligram of the controlled drug or one microgram in the case of lysergide or any other N-alkyl derivative of lysergamide;

'Health Board' means a board constituted under section 2 of the National Health Service (Scotland) Act 1978;

'health prescription' means a prescription issued by a doctor or a dentist under the National Health Service Act 1977, the National Health Service (Scotland) Act 1978, the Health and Personal Social Services (Northern Ireland) Order 1972 or the National Health Service (Isle of Man) Acts 1948 to 1979 (Acts of Tynwald) or upon a form issued by a local authority for use in connection with the health service of that authority;

'installation manager' and 'offshore installation' have the same meanings as in the Mineral Workings (Offshore Installations) Act 1971;

'Local Health Board' means a Local Health Board established in accordance with section 16BA of the National Health Service Act 1977;

'master' and 'seamen' have the same meanings as in the Merchant Shipping Act 1995;

'NHS Business Services Authority' means the special health authority established under Article 2 of the NHS Business Services Authority (Awdurdod Gwasanaethau Busnes-y-GIG) (Establishment and Constitution) Order 2005;

'the Northern Ireland Central Services Agency for the Health and Social Services' means the body established under Article 26 of the Health and Personal Social Services (Northern Ireland) Order 1972;

'nurse independent prescriber' has the same meaning as in the Human Medicines Regulations 2012, and such a person may only prescribe controlled drugs in accordance with regulation 6B;

'officer of customs and excise' means an officer within the meaning of the Customs and Excise Management Act 1979;

'operating department practitioner' means a person who is registered under the Health Professions Order 2001 as an operating department practitioner;

'patient group direction' has the same meaning as in the Human Medicines Regulations 2012;

'pharmacist' has the same meaning as in the Human Medicines Regulations 2012;

'pharmacist independent prescriber' has the same meaning as in the Human Medicines Regulations 2012, and such a person may only prescribe controlled drugs in accordance with regulation 6B;

'prescriber identification number' means the number recorded against a person's name by the relevant National Health Service agency for the purposes of that person's private prescribing;

'prescription' means a prescription issued by a doctor for the medical treatment of a single individual, by a supplementary prescriber for the medical treatment of a single individual; by a nurse independent prescriber for the medical treatment of a single individual, by a pharmacist independent prescriber for the medical treatment of a single individual, by a dentist for the dental treatment of a single individual or by a veterinary surgeon or veterinary practitioner for the purposes of animal treatment;

'private prescribing' means issuing prescriptions other than health prescriptions, or veterinary
  prescriptions;

'professional register' means the register maintained by the Nursing and Midwifery Council
  under article 5 of the Nursing and Midwifery Order 2001;

'professional registration number' means the number recorded against a person's name in the
  register of any body that licenses or regulates any profession of which that person is a
  member;

'register' means either a bound book, which does not include any form of loose leaf register or
  card index, or a computerised system which is in accordance with best practice guidance
  endorsed by the Secretary of State under section 2 of the National Health Service Act
  1977;

'registered chiropodist' has the same meaning as in the Human Medicines Regulations 2012;

'registered midwife' has the same meaning as in the Human Medicines Regulations 2012;

'registered nurse' has the same meaning as in the Human Medicines Regulations 2012;

'registered occupational therapist' has the same meaning as in the Human Medicines
  Regulations 2012;

'registered optometrist' has the same meaning as in the Human Medicines Regulations 2012;

'registered orthoptist' has the same meaning as in the Human Medicines Regulations 2012;

'registered orthotist and prosthetist' has the same meaning as in the Human Medicines
  Regulations 2012;

'registered paramedic' has the same meaning as in the Human Medicines Regulations 2012;

'registered pharmacy' has the same meaning as in the Human Medicines Regulations 2012;

'registered physiotherapist' has the same meaning as in the Human Medicines Regulations
  2012;

'registered radiographer' has the same meaning as in the Human Medicines Regulations 2012;

'relevant National Health Service agency' means, for England and Wales, the NHS Business
  Services Authority; for Scotland, the Common Services Agency for the health service; and
  for Northern Ireland, the Northern Ireland Central Services Agency for the Health and
  Social Services;

'retail dealer' means a person lawfully conducting a retail pharmacy business or a pharmacist
  engaged in supplying drugs to the public at a health centre within the meaning of the
  Medicines Act 1968;

'specialist community public health nurse' means a registered nurse or midwife who is also
  registered in the Specialist Community Public Health Nurses' Part of the professional
  register and against whose name in that Part of the register there is an annotation that she
  has a qualification in health visiting;

'supplementary prescriber' has the same meaning as in the Human Medicines Regulations
  2012;

'veterinary prescription' means a prescription issued by a veterinary surgeon or veterinary practitioner for the purposes of animal treatment;

'wholesale dealer' means a person who carries on the business of selling drugs to persons who
  buy to sell again.

(2) In these Regulations any reference to a regulation or schedule shall be construed as a reference
to a regulation contained in these Regulations or, as the case may be, to a schedule to these
Regulations, and any reference in a regulation or schedule to a paragraph shall be construed as
a reference to a paragraph of that regulation or schedule.

(3) Nothing in these Regulations shall be construed as derogating from any power or immunity of
the Crown, its servants or agents.

Specification of controlled drugs for purposes of Regulations

3.   Schedules 1 to 5 shall have effect for the purpose of specifying the controlled drugs to which
certain provisions of these Regulations apply.

Exceptions for drugs in Schedules 4 and 5 and poppy-straw

4.—(1) Section 3(1) of the Act (which prohibits the importation and exportation of controlled
drugs) shall not have effect in relation to the drugs specified in Schedule 5.

(2) The application of section 3(1) of the Act, in so far as it creates an offence, and the application of sections 50(1) to (4), 68(2) and (3) or 170 of the Customs and Excise Management
Act 1979, in so far as they apply in relation to a prohibition or restriction on importation or

exportation having effect by virtue of section 3 of the Act, are hereby excluded in the case of importation or exportation which is carried out in person for administration to that person of any drug specified in Part II of Schedule 4.

(3) Section 5(1) of the Act (which prohibits the possession of controlled drugs) shall not have effect in relation to—
(a) any drug specified in Part II of Schedule 4;
(b) the drugs specified in Schedule 5.

(4) Sections 4(1) (which prohibits the production and supply of controlled drugs) and 5(1) of the Act shall not have effect in relation to poppy-straw.

(5) Sections 3(1), 4(1) and 5(1) of the Act shall not have effect in relation to any exempt product.

Exceptions for drugs in Schedule 1

4A.—(1) Section 5(1) of the Act (which prohibits the possession of controlled drugs) shall not have effect in relation to a fungus (of any kind) which contains psilocin or an ester of psilocin where that fungus—
(a) is growing uncultivated;
(b) is picked by a person already in lawful possession of it for the purpose of delivering it as soon as is reasonably practicable into the custody of a person lawfully entitled to take custody of it and it remains in that person's possession for and in accordance with that purpose;
(c) is picked for either of the purposes specified in paragraph (2) and is held for and in accordance with the purpose specified in paragraph (2)(b), either by the person who picked it or by another person; or
(d) is picked for the purpose specified in paragraph (2)(b) and is held for and in accordance with the purpose in paragraph (2)(a), either by the person who picked it or by another person.

(2) The purposes specified for the purposes of this paragraph are—
(a) the purpose of delivering the fungus as soon as is reasonably practicable into the custody of a person lawfully entitled to take custody of it; and
(b) the purpose of destroying the fungus as soon as is reasonably practicable.

Exceptions for gamma–butyrolactone and 1,4–butanediol

4B.—(1) Gamma–butyrolactone and 1,4–butanediol are excepted from sections 3(1) (import and export), 4(1) (production and supply) and 5(1) (possession) of the Act save where a person imports, exports, produces, supplies or offers to supply either substance, or has either substance in his possession, knowing or believing that it will be used for the purpose of human ingestion whether by himself or another person other than as a flavouring in food.

(2) In this regulation references to gamma–butyrolactone include—
(a) any salt of gamma–butyrolactone; and
(b) any preparation or other product containing gamma–butyrolactone or a substance specified in sub–paragraph (a) of this paragraph.

(3) In this regulation references to 1,4-butanediol include—
(a) any substance which is an ester or ether or both an ester and ether of 1,4 butanediol;
(b) any salt of 1,4–butanediol or of a substance specified in sub-paragraph (a) of this paragraph; and
(c) any preparation or other product containing 1,4–butanediol or a substance specified in sub-paragraph (a) or (b) of this paragraph.

Licences to produce etc. controlled drugs

5. Where any person is authorised by a licence of the Secretary of State issued under this regulation and for the time being in force to produce, supply, offer to supply or have in his possession any controlled drug, it shall not by virtue of section 4(1) or 5(1) of the Act be unlawful for that person to produce, supply, offer to supply or have in his possession that drug in accordance with the terms of the licence and in compliance with any conditions attached to the licence.

General authority to supply and possess

6.—(1) Notwithstanding the provisions of section 4(1)(b) of the Act, any person who is lawfully in possession of a controlled drug may supply that drug to the person from whom he obtained it.

(2) Notwithstanding the provisions of section 4(1)(b) of the Act, any person who has in his possession a drug specified in Schedule 2, 3, 4 or 5 which has been supplied by or on the prescription of a practitioner, a registered nurse, a pharmacist independent prescriber, a supplementary prescriber or a person specified in Schedule 8 acting in accordance with a patient group direction for the treatment of that person, or of a person whom he represents, may supply that drug to any doctor, dentist or pharmacist for the purpose of destruction.

(3) Notwithstanding the provisions of section 4(1)(b) of the Act, any person who is lawfully in possession of a drug specified in Schedule 2, 3, 4 or 5 which has been supplied by or on the prescription of a veterinary practitioner or veterinary surgeon for the treatment of animals may supply that drug to any veterinary practitioner, veterinary surgeon or pharmacist for the purpose of destruction.

(4) It shall not by virtue of section 4(1)(b) or 5(1) of the Act be unlawful for any person in respect of whom a licence has been granted and is in force under section 16(1) of the Wildlife and Countryside Act 1981 to supply, offer to supply or have in his possession any drug specified in Schedule 2 or 3 for the purposes for which that licence was granted.

(5) Notwithstanding the provisions of section 4(1)(b) of the Act, any of the persons specified in paragraph (7) may supply any controlled drug to any person who may lawfully have that drug in his possession.

(6) Notwithstanding the provisions of section 5(1) of the Act, any of the persons so specified may have any controlled drug in his possession.

(7) The persons referred to in paragraphs (5) and (6) are
   (a) a constable when acting in the course of his duty as such;
   (b) a person engaged in the business of a carrier when acting in the course of that business;
   (c) a person engaged in the business of a postal operator (within the meaning of Part 3 of the Postal Services Act 2011) when acting in the course of that business;
   (d) an officer of customs and excise when acting in the course of his duty as such;
   (e) a person engaged in the work of any laboratory to which the drug has been sent for forensic examination when acting in the course of his duty as a person so engaged;
   (f) a person engaged in conveying the drug to a person who may lawfully have that drug in his possession.

Supply of articles for administering or preparing controlled drugs

6A.—(1) Notwithstanding the provisions of section 9A(1) and (3) of the Act, any of the persons specified in paragraph (2) may, when acting in their capacity as such, supply or offer to supply the following articles—
   (a) a swab;
   (b) utensils for the preparation of a controlled drug;
   (c) citric acid;
   (d) a filter;
   (e) ampoules of water for injection, only when supplied or offered for supply in accordance with the Medicines Act 1968 and of any instrument which is in force thereunder.
   (f) ascorbic acid

(2) The persons referred to in paragraph (1) are—
   (a) a practitioner;
   (b) a pharmacist;
   (c) a person employed or engaged in the lawful provision of drug treatment services;
   (d) a supplementary prescriber acting under and in accordance with the terms of a clinical management plan; and
   (e) a nurse independent prescriber.

Authority for Nurse Independent Prescribers and Pharmacist Independent Prescribers to Prescribe

6B. —(1) Subject to paragraph (2) of this regulation, a nurse independent prescriber or a pharmacist independent prescriber may prescribe any controlled drug specified in Schedule 2, 3, 4 or 5.

(2) Neither a nurse independent prescriber nor a pharmacist independent prescriber may prescribe any of the following substances to a person he considers, or has reasonable grounds to suspect, is addicted to any controlled drug listed in the Schedule to the Misuse of Drugs (Supply to Addicts) Regulations 1997 save for the purpose of treating organic disease or injury:
   (a) cocaine, any salt of cocaine, and any preparation or other product containing cocaine or any salt of cocaine;

(b) diamorphine, any salt of diamorphine, and any preparation or other product containing diamorphine or any salt of diamorphine;

(c) dipipanone, any salt of dipipanone, and any preparation or other product containing dipipanone or any salt of dipipanone.

(3) For the purposes of paragraph (2) a person is addicted to a controlled drug if, and only if, he has as a result of repeated administration become so dependent upon that controlled drug that he has an overpowering desire for the administration of it to be continued.

Administration of drugs in Schedules 2, 3, 4 and 5

7.—(1) Any person may administer to another any drug specified in Schedule 5.

(2) A doctor or dentist may administer to a patient any drug specified in Schedule 2, 3 or 4.

(3) Any person other than a doctor or dentist may administer to a patient, in accordance with the directions of a doctor or dentist, any drug specified in Schedule 2, 3 or 4, and for these purposes the circumstances in which a person is to be regarded as administering in accordance with the directions of a doctor or dentist include where that person is acting in accordance with a patient group direction.

(4) Notwithstanding the provisions of paragraph (3), a nurse independent prescriber or a pharmacist independent prescriber may administer to a patient, without the directions of a doctor or dentist, any controlled drug which such nurse independent prescriber or such pharmacist independent prescriber respectively may prescribe under regulation 6B provided it is administered for a purpose for which it may be prescribed under that regulation.

(5) Notwithstanding the provisions of paragraph (3), any person may administer to a patient in accordance with the specific directions of a nurse independent prescriber or a pharmacist independent prescriber any controlled drug which such nurse independent prescriber or such pharmacist independent prescriber may prescribe under regulation 6B provided it is administered for a purpose for which it may be prescribed under that regulation.

(6) Notwithstanding the provisions of paragraph (3), a supplementary prescriber acting under and in accordance with the terms of a clinical management plan may administer to a patient, without the directions of a doctor or dentist, any drug specified in Schedule 2, 3 or 4.

(7) Notwithstanding the provisions of paragraph (3), any person may administer to a patient, in accordance with the directions of a supplementary prescriber acting under and in accordance with the terms of a clinical management plan, any drug specified in Schedule 2, 3 or 4.

Production and supply of drugs in Schedules 2 and 5

8.—(1) Notwithstanding the provisions of section 4(1)(a) of the Act—

(a) a practitioner or pharmacist, acting in his capacity as such, may manufacture or compound any drug specified in Schedule 2 or 5;

(b) a person lawfully conducting a retail pharmacy business and acting in his capacity as such may, at the registered pharmacy at which he carries on that business, manufacture or compound any drug specified in Schedule 2 or 5;

(c) a nurse independent prescriber acting in her capacity as such, or a supplementary prescriber acting under and in accordance with the terms of a clinical management plan, may compound any drug specified in Schedule 2 or 5 for the purposes of administration in accordance with regulation 7;

(d) any person acting in accordance with the written directions of a doctor, a dentist, a nurse independent prescriber, a pharmacist independent prescriber, or a supplementary prescriber acting under and in accordance with the terms of a clinical management plan, may compound any drug specified in Schedule 2 or 5 for the purposes of administration in accordance with regulation 7.

(2) Notwithstanding the provisions of section 4(1)(b) of the Act, any of the following persons, that is to say—

(a) a practitioner;

(b) a pharmacist;

(c) a person lawfully conducting a retail pharmacy business;

(d) the person in charge or acting person in charge of a hospital or care home which is wholly or mainly maintained by a public authority out of public funds or by a charity or by voluntary subscriptions;

(e) in the case of such a drug supplied to her by a person responsible for the dispensing and supply of medicines at the hospital or care home, the senior registered nurse or acting senior registered nurse for the time being in charge of a ward, theatre or other department in such a hospital or care home as aforesaid;

(ea) in the case of such a drug supplied to him by a person responsible for the dispensing and supply of medicines at a hospital, an operating department practitioner practising in that hospital;

(f) a person who is in charge of a laboratory the recognised activities of which consist in, or include, the conduct of scientific education or research and which is attached to a university, university college or such a hospital as aforesaid or to any other institution approved for the purpose under this sub-paragraph by the Secretary of State;

(g) a public analyst appointed under section 27 of the Food Safety Act 1990;

(h) a sampling officer within the meaning of Schedule 3 to the Medicines Act 1968;

(i) a person employed or engaged in connection with a scheme for testing the quality or amount of the drugs, preparations and appliances supplied under the National Health Service Act 1977 or the National Health Service (Scotland) Act 1978 and the regulations made thereunder;

(j) a person authorised by the General Pharmaceutical Council for the purposes of section 108 or 109 of the Medicines Act 1968,

(k) a supplementary prescriber acting under and in accordance with the terms of a clinical management plan,

may, when acting in his capacity as such, supply or offer to supply any drug specified in Schedule 2 or 5 to any person who may lawfully have that drug in his possession, except that nothing in this paragraph authorises—

(i) the person in charge or acting person in charge of a hospital or care home, having a pharmacist responsible for the dispensing and supply of medicines, to supply or offer to supply any drug;

(ii) a senior registered nurse or acting senior registered nurse for the time being in charge of a ward, theatre or other department to supply any drug otherwise than for administration to a patient in that ward, theatre or department in accordance with the directions of a doctor, dentist, supplementary prescriber acting under and in accordance with the terms of a clinical management plan or, subject to paragraph (2A), a nurse independent prescriber or a pharmacist independent prescriber; or

(iii) an operating department practitioner to supply any drug otherwise than for administration to a patient in a ward, theatre or other department in accordance with the directions of a doctor, dentist, supplementary prescriber acting under and in accordance with the terms of a clinical management plan or, subject to paragraph (2A), a nurse independent prescriber or a pharmacist independent prescriber.

(2A) The directions given by a nurse independent prescriber or a pharmacist independent prescriber referred to in paragraph (2)(k)(ii) and (iii) shall relate only to a controlled drug which such nurse independent prescriber or such pharmacist independent prescriber respectively may prescribe under regulation 6B and a purpose for which it may be prescribed under that regulation.

(3) Notwithstanding the provisions of section 4(1)(b) of the Act, a person who is authorised as a member of a group may, under and in accordance with the terms of his group authority and in compliance with any conditions attached thereto, supply or offer to supply any drug specified in Schedule 2 or 5 to any person who may lawfully have that drug in his possession.

(4) Notwithstanding the provisions of section 4(1)(b) of the Act, a person who is authorised by a written authority issued by the Secretary of State under and for the purposes of this paragraph and for the time being in force may, at the premises specified in that authority and in compliance with any conditions so specified, supply or offer to supply any drug specified in Schedule 5 to any person who may lawfully have that drug in his possession.

(5) Notwithstanding the provisions of section 4(1)(b) of the Act—

(a) the owner of a ship, or the master of a ship which does not carry a doctor among the seamen employed in it; or

(b) the installation manager of an offshore installation,

may supply or offer to supply any drug specified in Schedule 2 or 5—

(i) for the purpose of compliance with any of the provisions specified in paragraph (6), to any person on that ship or installation;

(ii) to any person who may lawfully supply that drug to him;

(iii) to any constable for the purpose of the destruction of that drug.

(6) The provisions referred to in paragraph (5) are any provision of, or of any instrument which is in force under—

    (a) the Mineral Workings (Offshore Installations) Act 1971;

    (b) the Health and Safety at Work etc. Act 1974 or

    (c) the Merchant Shipping Act 1995.

(7) Notwithstanding the provisions of section 4(1)(b) of the Act, a nurse independent prescriber may, when acting in her capacity as such, supply or offer to supply any controlled drug specified in Schedule 2 or 5 to any person who may lawfully have any of those drugs in his possession provided it is supplied or offered in circumstances where she may prescribe it under regulation 6B.

(8) Notwithstanding the provisions of section 4(1)(b) of the Act—

    (a) a registered nurse or a pharmacist, when acting in her capacity as such, may supply or offer to supply, under and in accordance with the terms of a patient group direction, diamorphine or morphine where administration of such drugs is required for the immediate, necessary treatment of sick or injured persons;

    (b) a registered nurse or a person specified in Schedule 8 may, when acting in their capacity as such, supply or offer to supply, under and in accordance with the terms of a patient group direction, any drug specified in Schedule 5 to any person who may lawfully have that drug in his possession.

Production and supply of drugs in Schedules 3 and 4

9.—(1) Notwithstanding the provisions of section 4(1)(a) of the Act—

    (a) a practitioner or pharmacist, acting in his capacity as such, may manufacture or compound any drug specified in Schedule 3 or 4;

    (b) a person lawfully conducting a retail pharmacy business and acting in his capacity as such may, at the registered pharmacy at which he carries on that business, manufacture or compound any drug specified in Schedule 3 or 4;

    (c) a person who is authorised by a written authority issued by the Secretary of State under and for the purposes of this sub-paragraph and for the time being in force may, at the premises specified in that authority and in compliance with any conditions so specified, produce any drug specified in Schedule 3 or 4;

    (d) a nurse independent prescriber acting in her capacity as such, or a supplementary prescriber acting under and in accordance with the terms of a clinical management plan, may compound any drug specified in Schedule 3 or 4 for the purposes of administration in accordance with regulation 7;

    (e) any person acting in accordance with the written directions of a doctor, a dentist, a nurse independent prescriber, a pharmacist independent prescriber, or a supplementary prescriber acting under and in accordance with the terms of a clinical management plan, may compound any drug specified in Schedule 3 or 4 for the purposes of administration in accordance with regulation 7.

(2) Notwithstanding the provisions of section 4(1)(b) of the Act, any of the following persons, that is to say—

    (a) a practitioner;

    (b) a pharmacist;

    (c) a person lawfully conducting a retail pharmacy business;

    (d) a person in charge of a laboratory the recognised activities of which consist in, or include, the conduct of scientific education or research;

    (e) a public analyst appointed under section 27 of the Food Safety Act 1990;

    (f) a sampling officer within the meaning of Schedule 3 to the Medicines Act 1968;

    (g) a person employed or engaged in connection with a scheme for testing the quality or amount of the drugs, preparations and appliances supplied under the National Health Service Act 1977 or the National Health Service (Scotland) Act 1978 and the regulations made thereunder;

    (h) a person authorised by the General Pharmaceutical Council for the purposes of section 108 or 109 of the Medicines Act 1968,

    (i) a supplementary prescriber acting under and in accordance with the terms of a clinical management plan,

may, when acting in his capacity as such, supply or offer to supply any drug specified in Schedule 3 or 4 to any person who may lawfully have that drug in his possession.

(3) Notwithstanding the provisions of section 4(1)(b) of the Act—

    (a) a person who is authorised as a member of a group, under and in accordance with the terms of his group authority and in compliance with any conditions attached thereto;

    (b) the person in charge or acting person in charge of a hospital or care home;

    (c) in the case of such a drug supplied to her by a person responsible for the dispensing and supply of medicines at that hospital or care home, the senior registered nurse or acting senior registered nurse for the time being in charge of a ward, theatre or other department in a hospital or care home,

    (d) in the case of such a drug supplied to him by a person responsible for the dispensing and supply of medicines at a hospital, an operating department practitioner practising in that hospital;

may, when acting in his capacity as such, supply or offer to supply any drug specified in Schedule 3, or any drug specified in Schedule 4, to any person who may lawfully have that drug in his possession, except that nothing in this paragraph authorises—

    (i) the person in charge or acting person in charge of a hospital or care home, having a pharmacist responsible for the dispensing and supply of medicines, to supply or offer to supply any drug;

    (ii) a senior registered nurse or acting senior registered nurse for the time being in charge of a ward, theatre or other department to supply any drug otherwise than for administration to a patient in that ward, theatre or department in accordance with the directions of a doctor, dentist, supplementary prescriber acting under and in accordance with the terms of a clinical management plan or, subject to paragraph (3A), a nurse independent prescriber or a pharmacist independent prescriber; or

    (iii) an operating department practitioner to supply any drug otherwise than for administration to a patient in a ward, theatre or other department in accordance with the directions of a doctor, dentist, supplementary prescriber acting under and in accordance with the terms of a clinical management plan or, subject to paragraph (3A), a nurse independent prescriber or a pharmacist independent prescriber.

(3A) The directions given by a nurse independent prescriber or a pharmacist independent prescriber referred to in paragraph (3)(d)(ii) and (iii) shall relate only to a controlled drug which such nurse independent prescriber or such pharmacist independent prescriber respectively may prescribe under regulation 6B and a purpose for which it may be prescribed under that regulation.

(4) Notwithstanding the provisions of section 4(1)(b) of the Act—

    (a) a person who is authorised by a written authority issued by the Secretary of State under and for the purposes of this sub-paragraph and for the time being in force may, at the premises specified in that authority and in compliance with any conditions so specified, supply or offer to supply any drug specified in Schedule 3 or 4 to any person who may lawfully have that drug in his possession;

    (b) a person who is authorised under paragraph (1)(c) may supply or offer to supply any drug which he may, by virtue of being so authorised, lawfully produce to any person who may lawfully have that drug in his possession.

(5) Notwithstanding the provisions of section 4(1)(b) of the Act—

    (a) the owner of a ship, or the master of a ship which does not carry a doctor among the seamen employed in it;

    (b) the installation manager of an offshore installation,

may supply or offer to supply any drug specified in Schedule 3, or any drug specified in Schedule 4—

    (i) for the purpose of compliance with any of the provisions specified in regulation 8(6), to any person on that ship or installation; or

    (ii) to any person who may lawfully supply that drug to him.

(6) Notwithstanding the provisions of section 4(1)(b) of the Act, a person in charge of a laboratory may, when acting in his capacity as such, supply or offer to supply any drug specified in Schedule 3 which is required for use as a buffering agent in chemical analysis to any person who may lawfully have that drug in his possession.

(7) Notwithstanding the provisions of section 4(1)(b) of the Act, a nurse independent prescriber may, when acting in her capacity as such, supply or offer to supply any controlled drug specified in Schedule 3 or 4 to any person who may lawfully have any of those drugs in his possession provided it is supplied or offered in circumstances where she may prescribe it under regulation 6B.

(8) Notwithstanding the provisions of section 4(1)(b) of the Act, a registered nurse or a person specified in Schedule 8, when acting in their capacity as such, may supply or offer to supply,

under and in accordance with the terms of a patient group direction, any drug specified in Schedule 4 or Midazolam to any person who may lawfully have that drug in his possession, except that this paragraph shall not have effect in the case of—

(a) the supply or offer to supply of any of the anabolic steroid drugs specified in Part II of Schedule 4; and

(b) any drug or preparation which is designed for administration by injection and which is to be used for the purpose of treating a person who is addicted to a drug;

(c) for the purposes of paragraph (b) above, a person shall be regarded as being addicted to a drug if, and only if, he has as a result of repeated administration become so dependent upon the drug that he has an overpowering desire for the administration of it to be continued.

Possession of drugs in Schedules 2, 3 and 4

10.—(1) Notwithstanding the provisions of section 5(1) of the Act—

(a) a person specified in one of sub-paragraphs (a) to (k) of regulation 8(2) may have in his possession any drug specified in Schedule 2;

(b) a person specified in one of sub-paragraphs (a) to (i) of regulation 9(2) may have in his possession any drug specified in Schedule 3 or 4;

(c) a person specified in regulation 9(3)(b) to (d) or (6) may have in his possession any drug specified in Schedule 3;

(d) a person specified in regulation 9(3)(b) to (d) may have in his possession any drug specified in Part I of Schedule 4;

(e) a person specified in regulation 8(7), regulation 8(8)(a), regulation 9(7) or regulation 9(8) may have in her possession any drug specified in that regulation in accordance with the conditions specified in those regulations;

for the purpose of acting in his capacity as such a person, except that nothing in this paragraph authorises—

(i) a person specified in sub-paragraph (e) or (ea) of regulation 8(2);

(ii) a person specified in sub-paragraph (c) or (d) of regulation 9(3); or

(iii) a person specified in regulation 9(6),

to have in his possession any drug other than such a drug as is mentioned in the paragraph or sub-paragraph in question specifying him.

(2) Notwithstanding the provisions of section 5(1) of the Act, a person may have in his possession any drug specified in Schedule 2, 3 or Part I of Schedule 4 for administration for medical, dental or veterinary purposes in accordance with the directions of a practitioner, a supplementary prescriber acting under and in accordance with the terms of a clinical management plan a nurse independent prescriber or a pharmacist independent prescriber, except that this paragraph shall not have effect in the case of a person to whom the drug has been supplied by or on the prescription of a doctor, a supplementary prescriber, a nurse independent prescriber, a pharmacist independent prescriber or a person specified in Schedule 8 acting in accordance with a patient group direction, if—

(a) that person was then being supplied with any controlled drug by or on the prescription of another doctor, another supplementary prescriber, another nurse independent prescriber, another pharmacist independent prescriber or another person specified in Schedule 8 acting in accordance with a patient group direction and failed to disclose that fact to the first mentioned doctor, supplementary prescriber, nurse independent prescriber, pharmacist independent prescriber or person specified in Schedule 8 acting in accordance with a patient group direction before the supply by him or on his prescription; or

(b) that or any other person on his behalf made a declaration or statement, which was false in any particular, for the purpose of obtaining the supply or prescription.

(3) Notwithstanding the provisions of section 5(1) of the Act, a person who is authorised as a member of a group may, under and in accordance with the terms of his group authority and in compliance with any conditions attached thereto, have any drug specified in Schedule 2, 3 or Part I of Schedule 4 in his possession.

(4) Notwithstanding the provisions of section 5(1) of the Act—

(a) a person who is authorised by a written authority issued by the Secretary of State under and for the purposes of this sub-paragraph and for the time being in force may, at the premises specified in that authority and in compliance with any conditions so specified, have in his possession any drug specified in Schedule 3 or 4;

(b) a person who is authorised under regulation 9(1)(c) may have in his possession any drug which he may, by virtue of being so authorised, lawfully produce;

    (c) a person who is authorised under regulation 9(4)(a) may have in his possession any drug which he may, by virtue of being so authorised, lawfully supply or offer to supply.

(5) Notwithstanding the provisions of section 5(1) of the Act—

    (a) any person may have in his possession any drug specified in Schedule 2, 3 or Part I of Schedule 4 for the purpose of compliance with any of the provisions specified in regulation 8(6);

    (b) the master of a foreign ship which is in a port in Great Britain may have in his possession any drug specified in Schedule 2, 3 or Part I of Schedule 4 so far as necessary for the equipment of the ship.

(6) The foregoing provisions of this regulation are without prejudice to the provisions of regulation 4(3)(a).

11. —[*Exemption for midwives*]

Cultivation under licence of cannabis plant

12. Where any person is authorised by a licence of the Secretary of State issued under this regulation and for the time being in force to cultivate plants of the genus Cannabis, it shall not by virtue of section 6 of the Act be unlawful for that person to cultivate any such plant in accordance with the terms of the licence and in compliance with any conditions attached to the licence.

Approval of premises for cannabis smoking for research purposes

13. Section 8 of the Act (which makes it an offence for the occupier of premises to permit certain activities there) shall not have effect in relation to the smoking of cannabis or cannabis resin for the purposes of research on any premises for the time being approved for the purpose under this regulation by the Secretary of State.

[Regulations 14 to 28 have not been reproduced.]

SCHEDULE 1

CONTROLLED DRUGS SUBJECT TO THE REQUIREMENTS OF REGULATIONS 14,
15, 16, 18, 19, 20, 23, 26 AND 27

1. The following substances and products, namely:—

    (a) Bufotenine
        Cannabinol
        Cannabinol derivatives not being dronabinol or its stereoisomers
        Cannabis (not being the substance specified in paragraph 5 of Part 1 of Schedule 4) and
           cannabis resin
        Cathinone
        Coca leaf
        Concentrate of poppy-straw
        (2,3–Dihydro–5–methyl–3–(4–morpholinylmethyl)
           pyrrole(1,2,3–de)–1,4–benzoxazin–6–yl)–1–naphthalenylmethanone.
        3–Dimethylheptyl–11–hydroxyhexahydrocannabinol
        Eticyclidine
        Etryptamine
        Fungus (of any kind) which contains psilocin or an ester of psilocin
        (9–Hydroxy–6–methyl–3–(5–phenylpentan–2–yl) oxy–5, 6, 6a, 7, 8, 9, 10, 10a–
           octahydrophenanthridin–1–yl) acetate
        9-(Hydroxymethyl)–6, 6–dimethyl–3–(2–methyloctan–2–yl)–6a, 7, 10,
           10a–tetrahydrobenzo[c]chromen–1–ol.
        Khat
        Lysergamide
        Lysergide and other N-alkyl derivatives of lysergamide
        Mescaline
        Methcathinone
        Psilocin
        Raw opium
        Rolicyclidine
        Tenocyclidine

hydroxyalkyl, cycloalkylmethyl, cycloalkylethyl, (N-methylpiperidin-2-yl)methyl or 2–(4–morpholinyl)ethyl, whether or not further substituted in the indole ring to any extent.

(m) Any compound (not being bupropion, diethylpropion, pyrovalerone or a compound for the time being specified in sub–paragraph (a) above) structurally derived from 2–amino–1–phenyl–1–propanone by modification in any of the following ways, that is to say—

    (i)   by substitution in the phenyl ring to any extent with alkyl, alkoxy, alkylenedioxy, haloalkyl or halide substituents, whether or not further substituted in the phenyl ring by one or more other univalent substituents;

    (ii) by substitution at the 3–position with an alkyl substituent;

    (iii) by substitution at the nitrogen atom with alkyl or dialkyl groups, or by inclusion of the nitrogen atom in a cyclic structure.

(n) Any compound structurally derived from 2–aminopropan–1–one by substitution at the 1-position with any monocyclic, or fused-polycyclic ring system (not being a phenyl ring or alkylenedioxyphenyl ring system), whether or not the compound is further modified in any of the following ways, that is to say—

    (i)   by substitution in the ring system to any extent with alkyl, alkoxy, haloalkyl or halide substituents, whether or not further substituted in the ring system by one or more other univalent substituents;

    (ii) by substitution at the 3–position with an alkyl substituent;

    (iii) by substitution at the 2–amino nitrogen atom with alkyl or dialkyl groups, or by inclusion of the 2–amino nitrogen atom in a cyclic structure.

(o) Any compound (not being pipradrol) structurally derived from piperidine, pyrrolidine, azepane, morpholine or pyridine by substitution at a ring carbon atom with a diphenylmethyl group, whether or not the compound is further modified in any of the following ways, that is to say,

    (i)   by substitution in any of the phenyl rings to any extent with alkyl, alkoxy, haloalkyl or halide groups;

    (ii) by substitution at the methyl carbon atom with an alkyl, hydroxyalkyl or hydroxy group;

    (iii) by substitution at the ring nitrogen atom with an alkyl, alkenyl, haloalkyl or hydroxy-alkyl group.

(p) 1-Phenylcyclohexylamine or any compound (not being eticyclidine, ketamine, phencyclidine, rolicyclidine, tenocyclidine or tiletamine) structurally derived from 1-phenylcyclohexylamine or 2-amino-2-phenylcyclohexanone by modification in any of the following ways, that is to say,

    (i)   by substitution at the nitrogen atom to any extent by alkyl, alkenyl or hydroxy-alkyl groups, or replacement of the amino group with a 1-piperidyl, 1-pyrrolidyl or 1-azepyl group, whether or not the nitrogen containing ring is further substituted by one or more alkyl groups;

    (ii) by substitution in the phenyl ring to any extent by amino, alkyl, hydroxy, alkoxy or halide substituents, whether or not further substituted in the phenyl ring to any extent;

    (iii) by substitution in the cyclohexyl or cyclohexanone ring by one or more alkyl substituents;

    (iv) by replacement of the phenyl ring with a thienyl ring;

(q) Any compound (not being benzyl(a-methyl-3,4-methylenedioxyphenethyl)amine) structurally derived from mescaline, 4-bromo-2,5-dimethoxy-a-methylphenethylamine, 2,5-dimethoxy-a,4-dimethylphenethylamine, Nhydroxytenamphetamine, or a compound specified in sub-paragraph (c) or (d) above, by substitution at the nitrogen atom of the amino group with a benzyl substituent, whether or not substituted in the phenyl ring of the benzyl group to any extent;

(r) Any compound (not being a compound for the time being specified in sub-paragraph (c) above) structurally derived from 1-benzofuran, 2,3-dihydro-1-benzofuran, 1H-indole, indoline, 1H-indene, or indane by substitution in the 6-membered ring with a 2-eth-ylamino substituent whether or not further substituted in the ring system to any extent with alkyl, alkoxy, halide or haloalkyl substituents and whether or not substituted in the ethylamino side-chain with one or more alkyl substituents.

2.   Any stereoisomeric form of a substance specified in paragraph 1.

3.   Any ester or ether of a substance specified in paragraph 1 (not being 2-((dimethylamino)methyl)-1-(3-hydroxyphenyl)cyclohexanol) or paragraph 2.

4.   Any salt of a substance specified in any of paragraphs 1 to 3.

5.   Any preparation or other product containing a substance or product specified in any of paragraphs 1 to 4, not being a preparation specified in Schedule 5.

SCHEDULE 2

CONTROLLED DRUGS SUBJECT TO THE REQUIREMENTS OF REGULATIONS 14,
15, 16, 18, 19, 20, 21, 23, 26 AND 27

1.   The following substances and products,
     namely:
     Acetorphine
     Alfentanil
     Allylprodine
     Alphacetylmethadol
     Alphameprodine
     Alphamethadol
     Alphaprodine
     Amineptine
     Anileridine
     Benzethidine
     Benzylmorphine (3-benzylmorphine)
     Betacetylmethadol
     Betameprodine
     Betamethadol
     Betaprodine
     Bezitramide
     Carfentanil
     Clonitazene
     Cocaine
     Desomorphine
     Dextromoramide
     Diamorphine
     Diampromide
     Diethylthiambutene
     Difenoxin
     Dihydrocodeinone
         O-carboxymethyloxime
     Dihydroetorphine
     Dihydromorphine
     Dimenoxadole
     Dimepheptanol
     Dimethylthiambutene
     Dioxaphetyl butyrate
     Diphenoxylate
     Dipipanone
     Dronabinol
     Drotebanol
     Ecgonine, and any derivative of
         ecgonine which is convertible to
         ecgonine or to cocaine
     Ethylmethylthiambutene
     Etonitazene
     Etorphine
     Etoxeridine
     Fentanyl
     Furethidine
     Hydrocodone
     Hydromorphinol
     Hydromorphone
     Hydroxypethidine
     Isomethadone

Ketobemidone
Levomethorphan
Levomoramide
Levophenacylmorphan
Levorphanol
Lisdexamphetamine
Lofentanil
Medicinal opium
Metazocine
Methadone
Methadyl acetate
methobromide, morphine N-oxide
    and other pentavalent nitrogen
    morphine derivatives
Methyldesorphine
Methyldihydromorphine
    (6-methyldihydromorphine)
Metopon
Morpheridine
Morphine
Morphine methobromide, morphine
    N-oxide and other pentavalent
    nitrogen morphine derivatives
Myrophine
Nabilone
Nicomorphine
Noracymethadol
Norlevorphanol
Normethadone
Normorphine
Norpipanone
Oripavine
Oxycodone
Oxymorphone
Pethidine
Phenadoxone
Phenampromide
Phenazocine
Phencyclidine
Phenomorphan
Phenoperidine
Piminodine
Piritramide
Proheptazine
Properidine
Racemethorphan
Racemoramide
Racemorphan
Remifentanil
Sufentanil
Tapentadol
Thebacon
Thebaine

Tilidate
Trimeperidine
Zipeprol
4-Cyano-2-dimethylamino-4,4-
diphenylbutane
4-Cyano-1-methyl-4-
phenylpiperidine

1-Methyl-4-phenylpiperidine-4-
carboxylic acid
2-Methyl-3-morpholino-1,1-
diphenylpropane- carboxylic acid
a-Methylphenethylhydroxlamine
4-Phenylpiperidine-4-carboxylic acid
ethyl ester

2. Any stereoisomeric form of a substance specified in paragraph 1 not being dextromethorphan or dextrorphan.

3. Any ester or ether of a substance specified in paragraph 1 or 2, not being a substance specified in paragraph 6.

4. Any salt of a substance specified in any of paragraphs 1 to 3.

5. Any preparation or other product containing a substance or product specified in any of paragraphs 1 to 4, not being a preparation specified in Schedule 5.

6. The following substances and products, namely—

Acetyldihydrocodeine
Amphetamine
Codeine
Dextropropoxyphene
Dihydrocodeine
Ethylmorphine (3-ethylmorphine)
Fenethylline
Glutethimide
Lefetamine
Mecloqualone
Methaqualone

Methylamphetamine
Methylphenidate
Nicocodine
Nicodicodine
(6-nicotinoyldihydrocodeine)
Norcodeine
Phenmetrazine
Pholcodine
Propiram
Quinalbarbitone

7. Any stereoisomeric form of a substance specified in paragraph 6.

8. Any salt of a substance specified in paragraph 6 or 7.

9. Any preparation or other product containing a substance or product specified in any of paragraphs 6 to 8, not being a preparation specified in Schedule 5.

SCHEDULE 3

CONTROLLED DRUGS SUBJECT TO THE REQUIREMENTS OF REGULATIONS 14, 15 (EXCEPT TEMAZEPAM), 16, 18, 22, 23, 24, 26 AND 27

1. The following substances, namely:—
(a) Benzphetamine
Buprenorphine
7-bromo-5-(2-chlorophenyl)-1,
3-dihydro-2H-1,
4-benzodiazepin-2-one
Cathine
Chlorphentermine
Diethylpropion
Ethchlorvynol
Ethinamate
Flunitrazepam

Mazindol
Mephentermine
Meprobamate
Methylphenobarbitone
Methyprylone
Midazolam
Pentazocine
Phendimetrazine
Phenterminc
Pipradrol
Temazepam
Tramadol

(b) any 5, 5 disubstituted barbituric acid not being quinalbarbitone.

2. Any stereoisomeric form of a substance specified in paragraph 1 or 3 not being phenylpropanolamine.

3. Any ester or ether of pipradrol.

4. Any salt of a substance specified in any of paragraphs 1 to 3.

5. Any preparation or other product containing a substance specified in any of paragraphs 1 to 4, not being a preparation specified in Schedule 5.

SCHEDULE 4

PART I   CONTROLLED DRUGS SUBJECT TO THE REQUIREMENTS OF
REGULATIONS 22, 23 26 AND 27

1. The following substances and products, namely:—

Alprazolam
Aminorex
Bromazepam
Brotizolam
Camazepam
Chlordiazepoxide
1–(3–chlorophenyl)piperazine
1–(3–chlorophenyl)–4–(3–chloropropyl)piperazine
Clobazam
Clonazepam
Clorazepic acid
Clotiazepam
Cloxazolam
Delorazepam
Diazepam
Estazolam
Ethyl loflazepate
Fencamfamin
Fenproporex
Fludiazepam
Flurazepam
Halazepam
Haloxazolam
4-Hydroxy-n-butyric acid
Ketamine
Ketazolam
Loprazolam
Lorazepam
Lormetazepam
Medazepam
Mefenorex
Mesocarb
Nimetazepam
Nitrazepam
Nordazepam
Oxazepam
Oxazolam
Pemoline
Pinazepam
Prazepam
Pyrovalerone
Tetrazepam
Triazolam
N-Ethylamphetamine
Zaleplon
Zolpidem
Zopiclone

2. Any stereoisomeric form of a substance specified in paragraph 1.

3. Any salt of a substance specified in paragraph 1 or 2.

4. Any preparation or other product containing a substance or product specified in any of paragraphs 1 to 3, not being a preparation specified in Schedule 5.

5. A liquid formulation—
    (a) containing a botanical extract of cannabis—
        (i)   with a concentration of not more than 30 milligrams of cannabidiol per millilitre, and not more than 30 milligrams of delta-9-tetrahydrocannabinol per millilitre, and
        (ii) where the ratio of cannabidiol todelta-9-tetrahydrocannabinol is between 0.7 and 1.3,
    (b) which is dispensed through a metered dose pump as a mucosal mouth spray, and
    (c) which was approved for marketing by the Medicines and Healthcare Products Regulatory Agency on 16th June 2010.

PART II   CONTROLLED DRUGS EXCEPTED FROM THE PROHIBITION ON POSSESSION;
EXCLUDED FROM THE APPLICATION OF OFFENCES ARISING FROM THE PROHIBITION ON
IMPORTATION AND EXPORTATION WHEN CARRIED OUT IN PERSON FOR ADMINISTRATION TO
THAT PERSON; AND SUBJECT TO THE REQUIREMENTS OF REGULATIONS 22, 23, 26 AND 27

1. The following substances, namely—

5α–Androstane–3,17–diol
Androst-4-ene-3,17-diol
1–Androstenediol
1–Androstenedione
4-Androstene-3, 17-dione
5–Androstenedione
5-Androstene-3, 17 diol
Atamestane
Bolandiol
Bolasterone
Bolazine
Boldenone
Boldione
Bolenol
Bolmantalate
Calusterone
Clostebol
Danazol
Desoxymethyltestosterone
4-Chloromethandienone
Drostanolone

964

Enestebol	19–Norandrosterone
Epitiostanol	Norboletone
Ethyloestrenol	Norclostebol
Fluoxymesterone	Norethandrolone
Formebolone	19–Noretiocholanolone
Furazabol	Ovandrotone
Gestrinone	Oxabolone
3–Hydroxy–5α–androstan–17–one	Oxandrolone
Mebolazine	Oxymesterone
Mepitiostane	Oxymetholone
Mesabolone	Prasterone
Mestanolone	Propetandrol
Mesterolone	Prostanozol
Methandienone	Quinbolone
Methandriol	Roxibolone
Methenolone	Silandrone
Methyltestosterone	Stanolone
Metribolone	Stanozolol
Mibolerone	Stenbolone
Nandrolone	Testosterone
19–Norandrostenedione	Tetrahydrogestrinone
19-Nor-4-Androstene-3, 17-dione	Thiomesterone
19-Nor-5-Androstene-3, 17 diol	Trenbolone

2. Any compound (not being Trilostane or a compound for the time being specified in paragraph 1 of this Part of this Schedule) structurally derived from 17-hydroxyandrostan-3-one or from 17-hydroxyestran-3-one by modification in any of the following ways, that is to say—
   (a) by further substitution at position 17 by a methyl or ethyl group;
   (b) by substitution to any extent at one or more of positions 1, 2, 4, 6, 7, 9, 11 or 16, but at no other position;
   (c) by unsaturation in the carbocyclic ring system to any extent, provided that there are no more than two ethylenic bonds in any one carbocyclic ring;
   (d) by fusion of ring A with a heterocyclic system.
3. Any substance which is an ester or ether (or, where more than one hydroxyl function is available, both an ester and an ether) of a substance specified in paragraph 1 or described in paragraph 2 of this Part of this Schedule.
4. The following substances, namely—
   Chorionic Gonadotrophin (HCG)
   Clenbuterol
   Non-human chorionic gonadotrophin
   Somatotropin
   Somatrem
   Somatropin
   Zeranol
   Zilpaterol
5. Any stereoisomeric form of a substance specified or described in any of paragraphs 1 to 4 of this Part of this Schedule.
6. Any salt of a substance specified or described in any of paragraphs 1 to 5 of this Part of this Schedule.
7. Any preparation or other product containing a substance or product specified or described in any of paragraphs 1 to 6 of this Part of this Schedule, not being a preparation specified in Schedule 5.

SCHEDULE 5

CONTROLLED DRUGS EXCEPTED FROM THE PROHIBITION ON IMPORTATION, EXPORTATION AND POSSESSION AND SUBJECT TO THE REQUIREMENTS OF REGULATIONS 24 AND 26

1. (1) Any preparation of one or more of the substances to which this paragraph applies, not being a preparation designed for administration by injection, when compounded with one or more other active or inert ingredients and containing a total of not more than 100 milligrams

of the substance or substances (calculated as base) per dosage unit or with a total concentration of not more than 2.5% (calculated as base) in undivided preparations.

(2) The substances to which this paragraph applies are acetyldihydrocodeine, codeine, dihydrocodeine, ethylmorphine, nicocodine, nicodicodine (6-nicotinoyldihydrocodeine), norcodeine and pholcodine and their respective salts.

2. [Revoked.]

3. Any preparation of medicinal opium or of morphine containing (in either case) not more than 0.2% of morphine calculated as anhydrous morphine base, being a preparation compounded with one or more other active or inert ingredients in such a way that the opium or, as the case may be, the morphine cannot be recovered by readily applicable means or in a yield which would constitute a risk to health.

4. Any preparation of dextropropoxyphene, being a preparation designed for oral administration, containing not more than 135 milligrams of dextropropoxyphene (calculated as base) per dosage unit or with a total concentration of not more than 2.5% (calculated as base) in undivided preparations.

5. Any preparation of difenoxin containing, per dosage unit, not more than 0.5 milligrams of difenoxin and a quantity of atropine sulphate equivalent to at least 5% of the dose of difenoxin.

6. Any preparation of diphenoxylate containing, per dosage unit, not more than 2.5 milligrams of diphenoxylate calculated as base, and a quantity of atropine sulphate equivalent to at least 1% of the dose of diphenoxylate.

7. Any preparation of propiram containing, per dosage unit, not more than 100 milligrams of propiram calculated as base and compounded with at least the same amount (by weight) of methylcellulose.

8. Any powder of ipecacuanha and opium comprising—
    10% opium, in powder,
    10% ipecacuanha root, in powder, well mixed with
    80% of any other powdered ingredient containing no controlled drug.

9. Any mixture containing one or more of the preparations specified in paragraphs 1 to 8, being a mixture of which none of the other ingredients is a controlled drug.

B19.18 The MDA 1971, s. 30, provides that a licence or other authority issued by the Secretary of State may be general or specific, and it may be issued on such terms and subject to such conditions (including, in the case of a licence, the payment of a prescribed fee) as the Secretary of State thinks proper, and may be modified or revoked by him at any time.

In *Dunbar* [1981] 1 All ER 188, the Court of Appeal had to consider the meaning of the Misuse of Drugs Regulations 1973 (SI 1973 No. 797), reg. 10(2), in determining whether or not a doctor was unlawfully in possession of drugs. This case states a principle which is probably applicable to licences and authorisations generally. It was held that, for the purposes of reg. 10(2), it is not necessary for the doctor to have patients, since self-administration may well be appropriate. What matters is whether the doctor was acting bona fide in his capacity as a medical practitioner. This is a matter for the jury to decide. In *Dunbar*, the jury had not been given the opportunity to consider whether the doctor wanted the drugs for self-treatment or to commit suicide, and his conviction of unlawful possession was quashed. The mere fact that a person holds a licence, or authorisation, will not afford a defence where the possession of the drug is clearly outside the terms or conditions of the licence or authorisation, or is for an improper purpose. The issue must be left to the tribunal of fact to determine (*Abraham* [2002] EWCA Crim 2870).

OFFENCES UNDER THE MISUSE OF DRUGS ACT 1971

B19.19 It is submitted that, in the light of *L* [2014] 1 All ER 113 (see **B22.10**), the fact that the alleged offender was a trafficked child and that his criminal activities were integral to the circumstances in which he was a victim is relevant when deciding whether to prosecute on the basis of the public interest test (and to an 'abuse of process' argument). This consideration applies in relation to any offence under the MDA 1971.

Possession of 'Controlled Drugs'

Misuse of Drugs Act 1971, s. 5

(1) Subject to any regulations under section 7 of this Act for the time being in force, it shall not be lawful for a person to have a controlled drug in his possession.

(2) Subject to section 28 of this Act and to subsection (4) below, it is an offence for a person to have a controlled drug in his possession in contravention of subsection (1) above.

(2A) Subsections (1) and (2) do not apply in relation to a temporary class drug.

'Contravention' includes a failure to comply (s. 37(1)).

Given that the maximum sentence for the purposes of ss. 4(2) and (3)(a)–(c) and 5(2) and (3) depends upon the class of drug involved (see **B19.132**), it is arguable that the House of Lords decision in *Courtie* [1984] AC 463, establishes that these provisions create more than one offence. However, the point is not free of difficulty having regard to s. 28(3)(a) and cases such as *Leeson* [2000] 1 Cr App R 233. See also *Ellis* (1986) 84 Cr App R 235. Notwithstanding that it is unnecessary for the Crown to prove that the accused knew of the precise type and class of drug that he actually handled (see, e.g., *Bett* [1999] 1 All ER 600), it is submitted that it is best practice to charge by way of separate counts, on a single indictment, those controlled drugs that attract different maximum penalties.

Procedure

For powers of entry, search and seizure under the MDA 1971, see **B19.103**.   **B19.20**

Offences under the MDA 1971, s. 5(2), are (by s. 25 of and sch. 4 to the Act) triable either way. When tried on indictment they are normally class 3 offences, but see CPD XIII, para. B (see Supplement, **PD-97**) for the additional factors that the court considers on allocation.

Summary trial may be instituted by an information laid 12, rather than the usual six, months from the date of commission of the offence (MDA 1971, s. 25(4)).

For the liability of corporate officers, see **B19.36**.

Indictment

Statement of Offence   **B19.21**

Possession of controlled drug contrary to section 5(2) of the Misuse of Drugs Act 1971.

Particulars of Offence

A on the...day of...unlawfully had in his possession a controlled drug of Class [A, B, or C] namely...contrary to section 5(1) of the Misuse of Drugs Act 1971.

Where a count specifies more than one drug in the same class, the count does not offend the rules against duplicity (*Best* (1979) 70 Cr App R 21). But if the count specifies a particular controlled drug then the existence of that substance must be established (*Muir v Smith* [1978] Crim LR 293). Where a charge specifies a quantity of drugs, it is sufficient to prove that the accused acted in relation to part of that quantity and no question of a 'partial verdict' arises (*Peevey* (1973) 57 Cr App R 554).

It is not necessary to distinguish between a controlled drug and its stereoisomeric form, or a salt or ester in a count (see **B19.8**).

Sentencing Guidelines

See **B19.132** to **B19.152**.   **B19.22**

Meaning of 'Possession'

Lord Hope in the House of Lords in *Lambert* [2002] 2 AC 545, stated that 'there are two   **B19.23** elements to possession. There is the physical element, and there is the mental element.' The approach of Lord Hope is reflected in the other judgments delivered in that case. It confirms the approach taken by the Court of Appeal in *McNamara* (1988) 87 Cr App R 246 (see **B19.25**), and is settled law (consider also *DPP v Brooks* [1974] AC 862 at **B19.29**).

B19.24 **Custody or Control** 'The physical element involves proof that the thing is in the custody of the defendant or subject to his control', per Lord Hope in *Lambert* [2002] 2 AC 545 (see also Lord Scarman in *Boyesen* [1982] AC 768). This is enlarged by the MDA 1971, s. 37(3): 'For the purposes of this Act the things which a person has in his possession shall be taken to include any thing subject to his control which is in the custody of another'. The ability to demand that the property in question be removed (or the ability to remove it oneself) is no more than evidence of knowledge and acquiescence: it is not to be equated with control (*Kousar* [2009] 2 Cr App R 88, a case decided in the context of the Trade Marks Act 1994 but which, it is submitted, has relevance here).

The description of possession given by Lord Wilberforce in *Warner v Metropolitan Police Commissioner* [1969] 2 AC 256, at pp. 310–11, remains relevant:

> The question, to which an answer is required, and in the end a jury must answer it, is whether in the circumstances the accused should be held to have possession of the substance, rather than mere control. In order to decide between these two, the jury should, in my opinion, be invited to consider all the circumstances — to use again the words of *Pollock and Wright* — the 'Modes or events' — by which the custody commences and the legal incident in which it is held. By these I mean relating them to typical situations, that they must consider the manner and circumstances in which the substance, or something which contains it, has been received, what knowledge or means of knowledge or guilty knowledge as to the presence of the substance, or as to the nature of what has been received, he had at the time of receipt or thereafter up to the moment when he is found with it; his legal relation to the substance or package (including his right of access to it). On such matters as these (not exhaustively stated) they must make the decision whether, in addition to physical control, he has, or ought to have imputed to him the intention to possess, or knowledge that he does possess, what is in fact a prohibited substance. If he has this intention or knowledge, it is not additionally necessary that he should know the nature of the substance.

For an interesting discussion of *Warner v Metropolitan Police Commissioner*, see *Tan Kiam Peng v Public Prosecutor* [2007] SGCA 38. The aspect of knowledge as a component of possession is dealt with at **B19.25**.

If a person orders a controlled drug, directing that it be sent by post to his address, he is in possession of that drug from the time it arrives through the letter box (*Peaston* (1978) 69 Cr App R 203). A person smoking cannabis resin has that drug in his possession at the time of the smoking (*Chief Constable of Cheshire Constabulary v Hunt* (1983) 147 JP 567).

B19.25 **Knowledge of Possession** A person must know that he is in possession of something which is, in fact, a controlled drug (regardless of whether he knows it is a controlled drug or not): see *Warner v Metropolitan Police Commissioner* [1969] 2 AC 256, *Boyesen* [1982] AC 768 (at pp. 773–4), *McNamara* (1988) 87 Cr App R 246, and *Lambert* [2002] 2 AC 545, where, for example, Lord Clyde states, 'The second element involves that the defendant knows that the thing in question is under his control. He need not know what its nature is, but so long as he knows that the thing, whatever it is, is under his control, it is in his possession.' (and see *HKSAR v Hung Chan Wa* [2005] HKCA 231 at [36]–[37]). Ignorance of, or mistake as to the quality of, the substance in question does not prevent the accused being in possession of it, provided that the substance turns out to be a controlled drug. Thus, the accused was in possession of the amphetamine tablets in a bottle in her holdall, even if she was mistaken as to their quality, in *Lockyer v Gibb* [1967] 2 QB 243 (consider also *Irving* [1970] Crim LR 642). In *Searle v Randolph* [1972] Crim LR 779, the accused knew that he had cigarettes; he simply made a mistake about the quality of the tobacco, and so was in possession of a controlled drug since one of the cigarettes contained cannabis. An accused's lack of knowledge of the quality of the thing might be a defence under the MDA 1971, s. 28 (see **B19.96**). It is important to keep this often neglected provision in mind (see *Choudhury* [2008] EWCA Crim 3179 at **B19.97**).

A person does not possess something of which he is completely unaware. If a drug is put into someone's pocket without his knowledge, he is not in possession of it (*Warner v Metropolitan Police Commissioner* and *McNamara*). The accused was not in possession in *Marriott* [1971] 1 All ER 595, where the cannabis resin on the knife could only be detected by a forensic scientist and the accused had no knowledge of any substance. A person remains in possession of something even if he has forgotten about it (*Martindale* [1986] 3 All ER 25, following *Buswell* [1972] 1 All ER 75; cf. *Russell* (1984) 81 Cr App R 315).

Joint Possession   The expression 'joint possession' is liable to mislead. It is submitted that **B19.26** two situations need to be carefully contrasted. The first is where two or more persons are in possession of a controlled drug because each exercises control over the substance. A mere ability to control is not enough (see *Kousar* [2009] 2 Cr App R 88 at **B19.24**). Mere knowledge of the presence of a drug in the hands of a confederate is not enough: joint possession must be established (*Searle* [1971] Crim LR 592). Lord Widgery CJ, giving the judgment of the court, said: 'The sort of direction to which the deputy recorder should have opened the jury's mind was to ask them to consider whether these drugs formed a common pool from which all had the right to draw'. See also *Wright* (1975) 119 SJ 825, and consider *Montague* [2013] EWCA Crim 1781 (albeit in the context of firearms). In *Strong* (1989) *The Times*, 26 January 1990, the prosecution put the case on the basis that there was joint possession, that is, that each of the co-accused had control of one or more of the packages of cannabis. The Court of Appeal followed *Searle*, and said that what was being looked for was whether each person had the right to say what should be done with the cannabis. Mere presence in the same vehicle as the drugs, and knowing they were there, was not sufficient (and see *Irala-Prevost* [1965] Crim LR 606).

The second situation is where D aids and abets another to be in possession of a controlled drug. In this situation, there must be some evidence of assistance, or encouragement, or some element of control: consider *Bland* [1988] Crim LR 41, *Conway* [1994] Crim LR 826, *McNamara* [1998] Crim LR 278, *Arshad* [2002] EWCA Crim 1549, *Jacobs* [2002] EWCA Crim 610, and *Bailey* [2004] EWCA Crim 2169. It should be noted that, on the question of knowledge, the prosecution is required to prove a stricter intent in the case of an aider or an abettor, namely that the accused knew that the principal was in possession of a controlled drug. It is not necessary that the prosecution prove the type of drug in question (see *Patel* [1970] Crim LR 274, contrast with *Fernandez* [1970] Crim LR 277).

Cases Involving Small Quantities of Controlled Drug

There are two points. First, the quantity of drug might be so slight as to amount, in reality, **B19.27** to nothing. Secondly, the fact that the quantity of drug is miniscule might be evidence of an accused's lack of knowledge of the existence of the thing.

Whether a Drug is Visible or Measurable   Lord Widgery CJ, giving the majority judgment of **B19.28** the Divisional Court in *Bocking v Roberts* [1974] QB 307, said (at pp. 309–10):

> …it is quite clear that the prosecution have to prove that there was some of the drug in the possession of the defendant to justify the charge, and the distinction which has to be drawn in cases of this kind is whether the quantity of the drug was enough to justify the conclusion that he was possessed of a quantity of the drug or whether, on the other hand, the traces were so slight that they really indicated no more than that at some previous time he had been in possession of the drug. It seems to me that that is the distinction that has to be drawn, although its application to individual cases is by no means easy.

This test was approved by the House of Lords in *Boyesen* [1982] AC 768. Lord Scarman said 'if it is visible, tangible, and measurable, it is certainly something'. See also *Worsell* [1970] 2 All ER 1183, *Graham* [1970] 2 All ER 1181, *Searle v Randolph* [1972] Crim LR 779, and see the discussion in *Williams v The Queen* [1978] HCA 49 at [18]. The House of Lords rejected a 'usability' test requiring that there be an amount of a drug sufficient to be used (or misused) for there to be something present. *Carver* [1978] QB 472 was overruled.

Minute Amount as Evidence of Lack of Knowledge   Lord Scarman, in *Boyesen*, drew atten- **B19.29** tion to the statement of Lord Diplock delivering the opinion of the Privy Council in *DPP v*

B

Part B Offences

Brooks [1974] AC 862, where he said: 'In the ordinary use of the word "possession", one has in one's possession whatever is, to one's own knowledge, physically in one's custody or under one's physical control'. Lord Scarman added, 'If the quantity in custody or control is so minute, the question arises: was it so minute that it cannot be proved that the accused knew he had it?' A good illustration, said Lord Scarman, is the New Zealand case of *Police v Emirali* [1976] 1 NZLR 286. Small quantities of drug were found in a vacuum cleaner which others had used, as well as a burned deposit on a metal clip of the type used for smoking marijuana cigarettes. The amount of the drug on the clip was only just measurable. On such facts an accused might properly argue that he was not in possession of the substance at all; and see the approach taken by Stinson J in *Colyer* [1974] Crim LR 243.

Drugs in Containers

B19.30   Two leading cases are *McNamara* (1988) 87 Cr App R 270, and *Lambert* [2002] 2 AC 545 at [126]. In *Lambert*, Lord Clyde said:

> ...if the defendant is in possession of the container and knows that there is something in it, he will be taken to be in possession of the contents of the container. ... Where the drug is in a container, it is sufficient for the prosecution to prove that the defendant had control of the container, that he knew of its existence and that there was something in it, and that the something was in fact the controlled drug which the prosecution alleges it to be. The prosecution does not require to prove that the accused knew that the thing was a controlled drug.

If the accused had no right to open the container and ascertain its contents, it is arguable that the accused was not in possession of the contents (*Warner v Metropolitan Police Commissioner* [1969] 2 AC 256, per Lord Morris at pp. 287 and 296, Lord Pearce at p. 306 and Lord Wilberforce at p. 312; *McNamara*; *Wright* (1975) 62 Cr App R 169. But consider, albeit in the context of firearms, *Deyemi* [2007] 1 Cr App R 345 at **B12.43**).

Subject to s. 28 of the MDA 1971, a mistake as to the nature of the contents will not avail the accused (cf. some of the statements in the House of Lords in *Warner v Metropolitan Police Commissioner* [1969] 2 AC 256, per Lord Reid at p. 281, Lord Morris at pp. 285, 290 and 296, Lord Guest at p. 302, Lord Pearce at p. 305 and Lord Wilberforce at p. 311).

Evidence Establishing Earlier Possession

B19.31   The existence of drug traces, or a minute quantity of a controlled drug, might be evidence that the accused had been in possession of a measurable/usable quantity of the substance (*Worsell* [1970] 2 All ER 1183; *Graham* [1970] 2 All ER 1181; and consider *Hambleton v Callinan* [1968] 2 QB 427 concerning traces of a drug in a urine sample). However, it is important that care is taken in bringing charges on this basis. In *Pragliola* [1977] Crim LR 612, the Court of Appeal held that the charge of unlawful possession was oppressive and not justifiable where the accused was charged solely on the basis that a pipe, which contained a drug trace, was returned to him.

Mens Rea

B19.32   In *Lewis* (1988) 87 Cr App R 270, the Court of Appeal remarked that 'it is clear that if a defendant is proved to have knowledge of this control of prohibited articles, it is generally immaterial that he is in ignorance or under a mistake as to their extent or qualities'. This is the basic rule, but it is essential to read *Lewis* (and *Warner v Metropolitan Police Commissioner* [1969] 2 AC 256) with s. 28 of the MDA 1971 in mind (see *Lambert* [2002] 2 AC 545 at **B19.100**, and note the commentary to *Lewis* by Professor Sir John Smith QC [1988] Crim LR 517. See also *Tan Kiam Peng v Public Prosecutor* [2007] SGCA 38).

Defence under s. 5(4)

B19.33   The MDA 1971, s. 5(4), provides a defence to simple possession (s. 5(2)) but the existence of that defence does not preclude any other defences being raised.

Misuse of Drugs Act 1971, s. 5

(4) In any proceedings for an offence under subsection (2) above in which it is proved that the accused had a controlled drug in his possession, it shall be a defence for him to prove—

(a) that, knowing or suspecting it to be a controlled drug, he took possession of it for the purpose of preventing another from committing or continuing to commit an offence in connection with that drug and that as soon as possible after taking possession of it he took all such steps as were reasonably open to him to destroy the drug or to deliver it into the custody of a person lawfully entitled to take custody of it; or

(b) that, knowing or suspecting it to be a controlled drug, he took possession of it for the purpose of delivering it into the custody of a person lawfully entitled to take custody of it and that as soon as possible after taking possession of it he took all such steps as were reasonably open to him to deliver it into the custody of such a person.

...

(6) Nothing in subsection (4) above shall prejudice any defence which it is open to a person charged with an offence under this section to raise apart from that subsection.

Where the accused buried drugs (e.g., cannabis) it was not sufficient to satisfy the defence in s. 5(4)(a) that the forces of nature might or would destroy the drugs eventually: rather it was for the accused to show that he took all such steps as were reasonably open to him to destroy them and the acts of destruction must be his (*Murphy* [2003] 1 WLR 422). The Court of Appeal in *Dempsey* (1985) 82 Cr App R 291 made clear that the defence in s. 5(4)(b) is available only if the accused's purpose is to act in accordance with that subsection.

The decision in *Lambert* [2002] 2 AC 545 (see **B19.100** and **F3.18**) means that the imposition of the persuasive burden in s. 5(4) is open to challenge (and consider *Keogh* [2007] 3 All ER 789).

Unavailable Defences

Necessity *Quayle* [2005] 1 All ER 988 and *Altham* [2006] 1 WLR 3287 decide that neces- **B19.34**
sity is not a defence to any of the offences under the MDA 1971 in circumstances where someone has possession of, is cultivating or is supplying cannabis in order to relieve pain. See also *Cotton* [2008] EWCA Crim 1279. In *Quayle*, the Court of Appeal pointed out that cannabis, cannabis resin and most cannabinoids are designated as drugs which may be used only for medical or scientific research (and they are drugs to which s. 7(4) of the MDA 1971 applies). Mance LJ said (at [54]):

> The effect of that designation is that, whatever benefits might be perceived or suggested for any individual patients, if these particular drugs were available for medical prescription and use (other than research), such individual benefits were and are in the legislator's view outweighed by disbenefits of strength sufficient in the national interest to require a general prohibition.

For further consideration of necessity, see **A3.47** to **A3.49**.

ECHR, Article 8 The ECHR, Article 8, is not engaged because a right to private life does **B19.35**
not include a right to the possession of (or to cultivate) cannabis (*Morgan* [2002] EWCA Crim 721, and see (in the context of the ECHR, Article 9) *Taylor* [2002] 1 Cr App R 519 at **B19.54**).

Liability of Corporate Officers

Misuse of Drugs Act 1971, s. 21 **B19.36**

Where any offence under this Act or Part II of the Criminal Justice (International Cooperation) Act 1990 committed by a body corporate is proved to have been committed with the consent or connivance of, or to be attributable to any neglect on the part of, any director, manager, secretary or other similar officer of the body corporate, or any person purporting to act in such capacity, he as well as the body corporate shall be guilty of that offence and liable to be proceeded against accordingly.

As to corporate liability generally, see **A6**.

SUPPLYING OR OFFERING TO SUPPLY ETC.
CONTROLLED DRUG

B19.37   *Misuse of Drugs Act 1971, s. 4*

(1) Subject to any regulations under section 7 of this Act, or any provision made in a temporary class drug order by virtue of section 7A, for the time being in force, it shall not be lawful for a person—
   (a) to produce a controlled drug; or
   (b) to supply or offer to supply a controlled drug to another.

(2) ...

(3) Subject to section 28 of this Act, it is an offence for a person—
   (a) to supply or offer to supply, a controlled drug to another in contravention of subsection 1 above; or
   (b) to be concerned in the supplying of such a drug to another in contravention of that subsection; or
   (c) to be concerned in the making to another in contravention of that subsection of an offer to supply such a drug.

As to whether the effect of the decision of the House of Lords in *Courtie* [1984] AC 463 is that there is more than one offence under s. 4(3), see **B19.19**.

Note that a 'controlled drug' includes substances or products subject to a 'temporary class drug order' (see s. 2(1)(a)(ii) at **B19.2**).

A number of elements are common to each of these offences (save for offers to supply), namely, (a) that there must be a 'controlled drug'; (b) that the activity with regard to that drug must involve a 'supply' in some form; and (c) that the activity must be in contravention of s. 4(1). The question of what substances are 'controlled drugs' is dealt with at **B19.2** *et seq*. It is important to keep in mind the potential reach of the offences of 'encouraging or assisting' an offence, created under the SCA 2007, part 2 (see also *S* [2012] 2 All ER 793).

Procedure

B19.38   Offences under the MDA 1971, s. 4(3), are (by s. 25 of and sch. 4 to the Act) triable either way. When tried on indictment they are normally class 3 offences, but see CPD XIII, para. B (see Supplement, **PD-97**) for the additional factors that the court considers on allocation.

Summary trial may be instituted by an information laid 12, rather than the usual six, months from the date of commission of the offence (MDA 1971, s. 25(4)).

For the liability of corporate officers, see **B19.36**.

Sentencing

B19.39   See **B19.132** to **B19.152**. The Drugs Act 2005 inserted s. 4A into the MDA 1971, which specifies for sentencing purposes an aggravating feature of supply of a controlled drug. If the offender convicted of an offence under s. 4(3) is aged 18 or over and the offence was committed on or in the vicinity of school premises, or the offence involved commission by the offender of a courier who at the relevant time was under 18, the sentencing court must treat such fact as an aggravating feature of the offence and must state in open court that the offence is so aggravated. It is submitted that s. 4A adds little to pre-existing sentencing principles that apply in cases of drug trafficking.

A minimum custodial sentence of seven years applies for the third Class A drug trafficking offence (see **E5.1**).

An offence under s. 4(3) is a drug trafficking offence within the meaning of the POCA 2002, sch. 2 (see **E19.17**).

A forfeiture order (see **E18.7**) or a confiscation order (see **E19**) may be imposed.

Meaning of 'Supply'

The words 'supply' and 'supplying' mean the same whenever those words appear in the   **B19.40**
MDA 1971, as well as for the purposes of the regulations and orders made under the Act (see
B19.14): see *Maginnis* [1987] AC 303. By s. 37(1) of the 1971 Act, 'supplying' includes distributing (consider *Moore* [1979] Crim LR 789 in which *King* [1978] Crim LR 288 was not
followed). There is a 'supply' where the accused purchases drugs on behalf of a third party, and
then transfers the drug to that party (or where a drug is distributed within a small social group)
(*Buckley* (1979) 69 Cr App R 371; *Denslow* [1998] Crim LR 566).

In *Maginnis*, Lord Keith, in a speech with which three other members of the House of Lords
concurred, held that the word 'supply' is to be ascertained 'by reference to the ordinary natural
meaning of the word together with any assistance which may be afforded by the context' (see also
Holmes v Chief Constable Merseyside Police [1976] Crim LR 125). Lord Keith said (at p. 309):

> The word 'supply', in its ordinary natural meaning, conveys the idea of furnishing or providing to
> another something which is wanted or required in order to meet the wants or requirements of that
> other. It connotes more than the mere transfer of physical control of some chattel or object from
> one person to another. No one would ordinarily say that to hand over something to a mere cus-
> todier was to supply him with it. The additional concept is that of enabling the recipient to apply
> the thing handed over to purposes for which he desires or has a duty to apply it. In my opinion it
> is not a necessary element in the conception of supply that the provision should be made out of
> the personal resources of the person who does the supplying. Thus if an employee draws from his
> employer's store materials or equipment which he requires for purposes of his work, it involves no
> straining of language to say that the storekeeper supplies him with those materials or that equip-
> ment, notwithstanding that they do not form part of the storekeeper's own resources and that he
> is merely the custodier of them. I think the same is true if it is the owner of the business who is
> drawing from his own storekeeper tools or materials which form part of his own resources. The
> storekeeper can be said to be supplying him with what he needs. If a trafficker in controlled drugs
> sets up a store of these in the custody of a friend whom he thinks unlikely to attract the suspicions of
> the police, and later draws on the store for the purposes of his trade, or for his own use, the custodier
> is in my opinion rightly to be regarded as supplying him with drugs.

The *Maginnis* approach provides little difficulty in a typical case where a person transfers both
the custody and control of a controlled drug to another (*Mills* [1963] 1 QB 522).

Maginnis also deals with cases where D1 transfers drugs to D2 for 'safekeeping'. In *Maginnis*, the   **B19.41**
House of Lords reconciled the cases of *Dempsey* (1985) 82 Cr App R 201 and *Delgado* [1984] 1
All ER 449, by holding that 'supply' involves more than a mere transfer of physical control of the
item from one person to another but includes a further concept, namely, that of 'enabling the
recipient to apply the thing handed over to purposes for which he desires or has a duty to apply
it'. The result appears to be that if A gives drugs to B for safekeeping, A has not supplied B with
them for the purposes of s. 4. But, were B to return the drugs to A (or where he intends to do
so), B would be guilty of supplying the drugs to A (or possessing them with that intention) (see
Panton [2001] EWCA Crim 611, following *Maginnis*, where P, acting as a custodian of drugs,
intended to return them to the depositor — he had therefore committed an offence contrary to
s. 5(3)). In *Pentecost* [1998] EWCA Crim 865, the Court of Appeal held that the trial judge had
not erred when he directed the jury that 'supply does not require a physical handing over as such
by the custodian. It would be sufficient if, with the intention that the trafficker retakes the drugs,
the custodian did something to enable the trafficker to achieve that object.' *Maginnis* [1987] AC
303 was considered in *Watson* [2014] EWCA Crim 196, where the Court of Appeal agreed with
the single judge that questions of joint possession were irrelevant and that, on the facts of that
case, the key elements of unlawful possession and intent to supply were established.

It is important not to confuse purpose, or intention, with motive (which is irrelevant) (see *X*
[1994] Crim LR 827, where X was a registered police informer; his motive of causing a drugs
dealer to be caught did not affect whether there was a supply).

In *Harris* [1968] 2 All ER 49, it was held that injecting another with a drug in the recipient's possession is not 'supplying' that drug to the recipient, particularly since physical control was not transferred to the recipient. This case must be read with care (having regard to the fact that it pre-dates the MDA 1971).

Extra-territorial Effect

B19.42 In *Hussain (Shabbir)* [2011] QB 1 the Court of Appeal held (applying *Seymour* [2008] 1 AC 713) that the prohibition imposed by the MDA 1971 on supplying a controlled drug proscribes only the supply in the UK. H routinely transferred Class C drugs to a courier within the UK who would then deliver them to a customer abroad. The transfer to the courier did not amount to supply (*Maginnis* [1987] AC 303 applied). The fact that a custodian might act for profit did not turn him into a supplier under the Act. The essence of supply was that the transfer had to be for the benefit of the transferee. Furthermore, the supply had to be within the jurisdiction.

When Supply etc. is Lawful

B19.43 Conduct otherwise proscribed by the MDA 1971, s. 4(1), may be licensed or authorised by the Misuse of Drugs Regulations 2001 (see generally, **B19.14**).Various regulations provide exceptions and exemptions for medical personnel, pharmacists and midwives, and for research activities.

Section 4(1)(b) and (3)(a): Offering to Supply

B19.44 An offer may be by words or conduct. If it is by words, it must be ascertained whether an offer to supply a controlled drug was made. Whether the accused had a controlled drug in his possession or had access to controlled drugs or whether the substance in his possession was a controlled drug at all is immaterial. The position might be different where the offer is made by conduct (*Mitchell* [1992] Crim LR 723; *Haggard v Mason* [1976] 1 All ER 337). Whether the accused intends to carry the offer into effect is irrelevant; the offence is complete upon the making of an offer to supply (*Goodard* [1992] Crim LR 588, see also *Gill* (1993) 97 Cr App R 215, *Showers* [1995] Crim LR 400, and *Haslock* [2001] EWCA Crim 1321). The offence is committed whether or not the offer is genuine. Once made, an offer cannot be withdrawn (*Prior* [2004] EWCA Crim 1147). It is not helpful to refer to principles of contract law in determining whether there is an offer (*Dhillon* [2000] Crim LR 760 and see *Prior*).

Section 4(3)(b): Being Concerned in Supply to Another

B19.45 The three ingredients of this offence were set out by the Court of Appeal in *Hughes* (1985) 81 Cr App R 344, at p. 348:

(a) the supply of a drug to another, or, as the case may be, the making of an offer to supply the drug to another in contravention of s. 4(1) of the MDA 1971;

(b) participation by the accused in an enterprise involving such supply or, as the case may be, such an offer to supply; and

(c) knowledge by the accused of the nature of the enterprise, i.e. that it involved supply of a drug or, as the case may be, offering to supply a drug.

It would seem to be the law of England and Wales that proof of an actual supply is a prerequisite for an offence charged under s. 4(3)(b). Indeed, in *Akinsete* [2012] EWCA Crim 2377, the Court of Appeal held that it is 'quite clear that the court in *Hughes* accepted and followed the analysis of Eveleigh LJ in *Blake and O'Connor'* (per Aikens LJ at [21]): i.e. elements (a)–(c) above. The law is different in Scotland (*Atkinson v HM Advocate* [2010] HCJAC 77), and *Hughes* was not followed in Jersey (*A-G v Antunes* [2003] JLR 144), or in Guernsey (*Law Officers of the Crown v Bishop* (30 May 2013 unreported, Royal Court of Guernsey).

In *Dunn* [2008] EWCA Crim 2308, the Court of Appeal proceeded on the basis that, for the purposes of s. 4(1) and (2) (production), it must be shown that the accused participated in the enterprise with knowledge of the nature of the enterprise (at [24]). D had submitted that the requirements set out in *Hughes* in relation to the supply limb of s. 4(1) can be transferred to the 'production limb' in s. 4 (see also **B19.58**). Although both *Hughes* and *Dunn* must be taken to represent the law, it is to be noted that in neither case does it appear that the Court heard argument regarding the effect of s. 28 on s. 4 (consider *Choudhury* [2008] EWCA Crim 3179). The Court of Appeal has pointed out in *Baker* [2009] EWCA Crim 535 that neither the word 'enterprise' nor the word 'participate', as used by Robert Goff LJ in *Hughes*, appear in s. 4(3)(b). Accordingly, 'if a person introduces someone who wants to obtain heroin to someone who he knows is willing and able to supply it, and together they obtain heroin for which the person introduced to the vendor pays, on the basis that in due course the introducer will pay for his share, it is open to a jury to conclude that the introducer is concerned in the supplying of the heroin to the other person'.

It is the duty of the judge to assist the jury as to the meaning of the phrase 'concerned in' (*Hughes* (1985) 81 Cr App R 344). A person may be concerned by being involved at a distance in making an offer to supply a controlled drug (*Blake* (1978) 68 Cr App R 1). **B19.46**

For the purposes of ss. 4 and 5(3), the 'another' cannot be someone charged in the same count, but it can be someone charged in other counts in the same indictment (*Smith* (14 February 1983 unreported), *Ferrera* (1984 unreported), *Adepoju* [1988] Crim LR 378, *Connelly* (1991) 156 JP 406, *Reeves* [2001] EWCA Crim 91, and note *Gingell* (1999) 163 JP 648, which makes the same point in the context of a charge of handling stolen goods; see **B4.177**). For cases of conspiracy to supply to 'another' where that other is a co-conspirator, see *Drew* [2000] 1 Cr App R 91 and *Jackson* (1999) *The Times*, 13 May 1999; in neither judgment was the effect of *Adepoju* discussed. It is not clear whether the law in England and Wales mirrors that in Scotland, namely, that a single count, charged under s. 4(3)(a) or (b), may embrace more than one act of supply etc. (*HM Advocate v Grant* [2007] HCJAC 71).

Defence under s. 28

The defence under the MDA 1971, s. 28, is discussed at **B19.96**. Note that s. 28 does not apply to *an offer* to supply a controlled drug (*Mitchell* [1992] Crim LR 723). This is because the offence is rooted in the making of the offer, and not in the quality of the substance offered (which, if it existed at all, might be innocuous). **B19.47**

POSSESSION OF CONTROLLED DRUG WITH INTENT TO SUPPLY

Misuse of Drugs Act 1971, s. 5   **B19.48**

(3) Subject to section 28 of this Act, it is an offence for a person to have a controlled drug in his possession, whether lawfully or not, with intent to supply it to another in contravention of section 4(1) of this Act.

As to whether the effect of the House of Lords decision in *Courtie* [1984] AC 463 is that there is more than one offence under s. 5(3), see **B19.19**.

For the meaning of 'controlled drug', see **B19.2** *et seq.*); as to the meaning of 'possession', see **B19.23** *et seq.*

For circumstances in which possession may be lawful by virtue of the Misuse of Drugs Regulations 2001, see **B19.14**.

Procedure

Offences under the MDA 1971, s. 5(3), are (by s. 25 of and sch. 4 to the Act) triable either way. When tried on indictment they are normally class 3 offences, but see CPD XIII, para. B (see Supplement, **PD-97**) for the additional factors that the court considers on allocation. **B19.49**

Summary trial may be instituted by an information laid 12, rather than the usual six, months from the date of commission of the offence (MDA 1971, s. 25(4)).

For the liability of corporate officers, see **B19.36**.

Indictment

B19.50   The form of indictment provided at **B19.21** may be adapted by addition of the specific intent to the particulars of the offence.

Alternative Verdicts

B19.51   In *Blackford* (1989) 89 Cr App R 239, the Court of Appeal, exercising its general power under the CLA 1967, substituted a conviction of possession under the MDA 1971, s. 5(2), for that under s. 5(3) (but note *Yeardley* [2000] 2 WLR 366). In *Johnson* [2013] EWCA Crim 2001, the Court of Appeal, when quashing a conviction for an offence under the MDA 1971, s. 5(3), held that it did not suggest, any more than did the Court in *Hodson* [2009] EWCA Crim 1590, that every time that a jury is considering a count under s. 5(3) it will be necessary to leave simple possession in the alternative. It depends on the circumstances and the assessment of the trial judge as to what is fair. In the instant case, the jury should, at the least, have received assistance as to the evidence that was capable of establishing an intention to supply.

Sentencing

B19.52   See **B19.132** to **B19.152**. This is a drug trafficking offence within the meaning of the POCA 2002, sch. 2 (see **E19.17**). A minimum custodial sentence of seven years applies for the third Class A drug trafficking offence (see **E5.1**). A forfeiture order (see **E18.7**) or a confiscation order (see **E19**) may be imposed.

Intent to Supply

B19.53   The expression 'supply', used in both ss. 4(3) and 5(3) of the MDA 1971, means the same in both contexts (*Maginnis* [1987] AC 303). For the meaning of 'supply', see **B19.40**.

For the purposes of s. 5(3), the prosecution need only establish that the accused had the controlled drug in his possession with the intention of supplying it to another. A mistake as to the drug in question is (subject to the MDA 1971, s. 28) irrelevant (*Leeson* [2000] 1 Cr App R 233).

'Intent to supply' means an intent on the part of the possessor of the drugs to supply, and not an intention that the drug should be supplied by another person (*Greenfield* (1983) 78 Cr App R 179).

To come within s. 5(3), the intention to supply must be an intention to supply the thing of which the accused is in possession (*Wright* [2011] 2 Cr App R 168). It is submitted that *Wright* was decided on its special facts, namely, that there was no suggestion that the accused intended to supply the immature and unusable cannabis plants that were in his possession. *Wright* was doubted and distinguished in *McAtarsney* [2013] NICA 59.

As to proving an intent to supply, and the admissibility of evidence of large amounts of money, an extravagant lifestyle or drug equipment, see **F1.14**.

In *Downes* [1984] Crim LR 552, the Court of Appeal decided that where two people were in joint possession (for the meaning of this phrase, see **B19.26**) they were not both involved in a joint venture to supply unless both had an intention to supply. Mere knowledge on the part of one that the other intended to supply is not sufficient. It is submitted that this holds true if the case is put on the basis that each person was a principal offender. However, the s. 5(3) offence may be committed by way of secondary participation (Accessories and Abettors Act 1861, s. 8); it remains to be seen to what extent prosecutions are brought under the SCA 2007, part 2.

For the purposes of ss. 4 and 5(3), the 'another' cannot be someone charged in the same count, but it can be someone charged in other counts in the same indictment (see **B19.45**).

Defences

The defence under s. 28 is dealt with at **B19.96**.   **B19.54**

In *Taylor* [2002] 1 Cr App R 519, D, a Rastafarian, argued that, as the prosecution had conceded that his possession with intent to supply cannabis was purely for religious purposes (see also **B11.150**), convicting him would be a breach of the ECHR, Article 9. The Court of Appeal held that there was no breach of Article 9 (or Article 8). Article 9(2) was satisfied as there was a pressing social need to combat the public health and public safety dangers arising from drugs such as cannabis. This was evidenced, in part, by the Single Convention on Narcotic Drugs 1971; and see *Andrews* [2004] EWCA Crim 947 (a case under the Customs and Excise Management Act 1979, s. 170).

PRODUCTION OF CONTROLLED DRUG

Misuse of Drugs Act 1971, s. 4   **B19.55**

(2) Subject to section 28 of this Act, it is an offence for a person—
    (a) to produce a controlled drug in contravention of subsection (1) [of section 4]; or
    (b) to be concerned in the production of such a drug in contravention of that subsection by another.

For the meaning of 'controlled drug', see **B19.2** *et seq*. As to the circumstances in which production may be lawful pursuant to the Misuse of Drugs Regulations 2001 (SI 2001 No. 3998), see **B19.14**.

Each of paras. (a) and (b) creates separate offences. As to whether the effect of the House of Lords decision in *Courtie* [1984] AC 463 is that there is more than one offence under s. 4(2), see **B19.19**.

Procedure

Offences under the MDA 1971, s. 4(2), are (by s. 25 of and sch. 4 to the Act) triable either way.   **B19.56**
When tried on indictment they are normally class 3 offences, but see CPD XIII, para. B (see Supplement, **PD-97**) for the additional factors that the court considers on allocation.

Summary trial may be instituted by an information laid 12, rather than the usual six, months from the date of commission of the offence (MDA 1971, s. 25(4)).

For the liability of corporate officers, see **B19.36**.

Sentencing

See **B19.132** to **B19.152**. This is a drug trafficking offence within the meaning of the POCA   **B19.57**
2002, sch. 2 (see **E19.17**). A minimum custodial sentence of seven years applies for the third Class A drug trafficking offence (see **E5.1**). A forfeiture order (see **E18.7**) or a confiscation order (see **E19**) may be imposed for a drug trafficking offence.

Meaning of 'Produce', 'Concerned in Production'

Misuse of Drugs Act 1971, s. 37   **B19.58**

(1) …'produce', where the reference is to producing a controlled drug, means producing it by manufacture, cultivation or any other method, and 'production' has a corresponding meaning;…

The Court of Appeal in *Russell* (1991) 94 Cr App R 351 held that the conversion of one form of Class A drug into another form of the same genus may be production and thus the conversion of the salt cocaine hydrochloride to free base cocaine, i.e. from a substance described in the MDA 1971, sch. 2, para. 4, to a substance described in sch. 2, para. 5, was an act of production. This was because it was 'the production of a substance (not by manufacture or cultivation but by "other means" [referring to the definition in s. 37(1)]) with physical and chemical features different from the cocaine hydrochloride from which it springs, albeit sharing the same generic term, cocaine'.

Stripping a cannabis plant, which had been cut and harvested, is producing a controlled drug because the action, by 'other means', produces a part of the plant which is a controlled drug

(*Harris* [1996] 1 Cr App R 369). On the issue of whether a 'preparation' involves an act of 'production', see *Aziz* [2012] EWCA Crim 1063 (discussed at **B19.11**).

B19.59   Being 'concerned in the production' (s. 4(2)(b)) does not require proof that the accused played an identifiable role in the production of the drug in question (*Nguyen* [2010] EWCA Crim 2658). However, in *Dunn* [2008] EWCA Crim 2308 (see **B19.45**), the Court of Appeal proceeded on the basis that, for the purposes of s. 4(2), it must be shown that the accused participated in the enterprise and had knowledge of the nature of the enterprise. D had submitted that the words of Robert Goff LJ in *Hughes* (1985) 81 Cr App R 344 at p. 348, in relation to the supply limb of s. 4(1), could be transferred to the 'production limb'. Robert Goff LJ stated:

> It appears to us that, for an offence to be shown to have been committed by a defendant contrary to subsection (b) or subsection (c), as the case may be, the prosecution has to prove (1) the supply of a drug to another, or as the case may be the making of an offer to supply a drug to another, in contravention of section 4(1) of the Act; (2) participation by the defendant in an enterprise involving such supply or, as the case may be, such offer to supply; and (3) knowledge by the defendant of the nature of the enterprise, i.e. that it involved supply of a drug or, as the case may be, offering to supply a drug.

But, in *Baker* [2009] EWCA Crim 535, the Court of Appeal remarked that neither the word 'enterprise' nor the word 'participate' appear in s. 4. Contrast the foregoing with *Farr* [1982] Crim LR 745. Although both *Hughes* and *Dunn* must be taken to represent the law, it is to be noted that in neither case does it appear that the Court heard argument regarding the effect of s. 28 on s. 4 (consider *Choudhury* [2008] EWCA Crim 3179).

In *Williams* [2011] EWCA Crim 232, the Court of Appeal held as a correct statement of the law that the addition of adulterants or bulking agents can amount to the production of a controlled drug. Presumably, users of heroin who mix the drug with water and cannabis users who mix the drug with tobacco (and those who bake a cannabis cake?) will have to rely on the discretion of prosecutors not to charge inappropriately.

In cases where it is alleged that the accused conspired to produce a controlled drug, it was held in *Kenning* [2009] QB 221 that an agreement to aid and abet an offence cannot constitute a statutory conspiracy under the Criminal Law Act 1977, s. 1(1), but contrast *Dang* [2014] EWCA Crim 348 and see further **A5.49**. There could be no conviction for aiding, abetting and counselling or procuring an offence unless the *actus reus* of the substantive offence was shown to have occurred. Even if the aiders and abettors do all that they agree to do, their course of conduct will not 'necessarily amount' to the commission of an offence as required by s. 1(1).

Defence under s. 28

B19.60   As to the defence under the MDA 1971, s. 28, see **B19.96**.

PROHIBITION ON IMPORTATION AND EXPORTATION OF CONTROLLED DRUGS

B19.61   **Misuse of Drugs Act 1971, s. 3**

(1) Subject to subsection (2) below—
   (a) the importation of a controlled drug: and
   (b) the exportation of a controlled drug,
   are hereby prohibited.
(2) Subsection (1) above does not apply—
   (a) to the importation or exportation of a controlled drug which is for the time being excepted from paragraph (a) or, as the case may be, paragraph (b) of subsection (1) above by regulations under section 7 of this Act or by provision made in a temporary class drug order by virtue of section 7A; or
   (b) to the importation or exportation of a controlled drug under and in accordance with the terms of a licence issued by the Secretary of State and in compliance with any conditions attached thereto.

Section 3, which is of considerable importance, imposes a prohibition, but it does not create an offence. It is generally enforced by offences charged under the Customs and Excise Management Act 1979, namely, improper importation or exportation of goods, or the fraudulent evasion of a prohibition on importation or exportation of goods or, where appropriate, conspiracy to evade the prohibition contained in the section. As to these offences, see **B16.28** *et seq.* For the relationship between s. 3 offences and offences under the Customs and Excise Acts, see *Whitehead* [1982] QB 1272; and note *Marron* [2011] EWCA Crim 792.

The meaning of the term 'controlled drug' and the circumstances in which exemptions may be permitted by regulation are discussed in **B19.2** and **B19.14**.

CULTIVATING PLANT OF THE GENUS CANNABIS

Misuse of Drugs Act 1971, s. 6

B19.62

(1) Subject to any regulations under section 7 of this Act for the time being in force, it shall not be lawful for a person to cultivate any plant of the genus Cannabis.

(2) Subject to section 28 of this Act, it is an offence to cultivate any such plant in contravention of subsection (1) above.

Procedure

Offences under the MDA 1971, s. 6, are (by s. 25 of and sch. 4 to the Act) triable either way. **B19.63** When tried on indictment they are normally class 3 offences, but see CPD XIII, para. B (see Supplement, PD-97) for the additional factors that the court considers on allocation.

Summary trial may be instituted by an information laid 12, rather than the usual six, months from the date of commission of the offence (MDA 1971, s. 25(4)).

For the liability of corporate officers, see **B19.36**.

In the light of *L* [2014] 1 All ER 113 (see **B22.10**), the fact that the alleged offender was a trafficked child and that his criminal activities were integral to the circumstances in which he was a victim is relevant when deciding whether to prosecute on the basis of the public interest test (and to an 'abuse of process' argument).

Sentencing

See **B19.132** to **B19.152**.

B19.64

Meaning of 'Cannabis'

The definition of 'cannabis' provided in the MDA 1971, s. 37(1) (see **B19.12**), does not apply **B19.65** to the use of the word 'cannabis' in s. 6 of the Act, since the context of the instant offence clearly requires that the plant of the genus cannabis itself be cultivated (note the opening words to s. 37(1) 'except insofar as the context otherwise requires').

Meaning of 'Cultivate'

This term is not defined in the Act. *Quaere*, whether it would be sufficient that a person who **B19.66** did not introduce a plant of the genus *Cannabis* passively permitted it to thrive in a place over which he has control without tending it, or whether some active steps must be taken to keep the plant alive or to cause it to grow. It may be more appropriate to charge possession in the former case. Note also *Kenning* [2009] QB 221 (see **B19.59**).

Mens Rea

The prosecution is not required to prove that the accused knew that the plant he cultivated was **B19.67** in fact cannabis (*Champ* (1981) 73 Cr App R 367), but note that an accused may have a defence under the MDA 1971, s. 28 (see **B19.96**).

When Cultivation May be Lawful

B19.68 The Misuse of Drugs Regulations 2001 (**B19.17**) contain various exemptions from this prohibition. See, in particular, reg. 12, by virtue of which a person licensed by the Secretary of State may cultivate a plant of the genus *Cannabis* in accordance with the terms of the licence and in compliance with any conditions attached to it.

OFFENCES RELATING TO OPIUM

B19.69   Misuse of Drugs Act 1971, s. 9

Subject to section 28 of this Act, it is an offence for a person—
(a) to smoke or otherwise use prepared opium; or
(b) to frequent a place used for the purpose of opium smoking; or
(c) to have in his possession
  (i) any pipes or other utensils made or adapted for use in connection with the smoking of opium, being pipes or utensils which have been used by him or with his knowledge and permission in that connection or which he intends to use or permit others to use in that connection; or
  (ii) any utensils which have been used by him or with his knowledge and permission in connection with the preparation of opium for smoking.

Section 9 creates three discrete offences, rather than three methods of committing the same offence, in paras. (a), (b), and (c). Section 9(a) creates the only offence under the MDA 1971 where the actual use of a specified controlled drug is a criminal offence.

Procedure

B19.70 Offences under the MDA 1971, s. 9, are (by s. 25 of and sch. 4 to the Act) triable either way. When tried on indictment they are normally class 3 offences, but see CPD XIII, para. B (see Supplement, **PD-97**) for the additional factors that the court considers on allocation.

Summary trial may be instituted by an information laid 12, rather than the usual six, months from the date of commission of the offence (MDA 1971, s. 25(4)).

For the liability of corporate officers, see **B19.36**.

Sentencing

B19.71 See **B19.143** *et seq*.

Elements and Defence

B19.72 By the MDA 1971, s. 37(1), 'prepared opium' means opium prepared for smoking and includes dross and any other residues remaining after opium has been smoked.

For the meaning of 'possession' in relation to the offence of the unlawful possession of a controlled drug, see **B19.23**.

The defence under s. 28 of the Act also applies to these offences (see **B19.96**).

PROHIBITION ON SUPPLY ETC. OF ARTICLES FOR ADMINISTERING OR PREPARING CONTROLLED DRUGS

B19.73   Misuse of Drugs Act 1971, s. 9A

(1) A person who supplies or offers to supply any article which may be used or adapted to be used (whether by itself or in combination with another article or other articles) in the administration by any person of a controlled drug to himself or another, believing that the article (or the article as adapted) is to be so used in circumstances where the administration is unlawful, is guilty of an offence.

(2) It is not an offence under subsection (1) above to supply or offer to supply a hypodermic syringe, or any part of one.

(3) A person who supplies or offers to supply any article which may be used to prepare a controlled drug for administration by any person to himself or another believing that the article is to be so used in circumstances where the administration is unlawful is guilty of an offence.

(4) [See **B19.77**]

(5) In this section, references to administration by any person of a controlled drug to himself include a reference to his administering it to himself with the assistance of another.

Note that a 'controlled drug' includes substances or products subject to a 'temporary class drug order': see **B19.2** *et seq*.

Given that the penalty does not vary with the controlled drug in question, there are only two offences, one under s. 9A(1), and the other under s. 9A(3).

Procedure

Offences under the MDA 1971, s. 9A, are (by s. 25 of and sch. 4 to the Act) triable only summarily. Summary trial may be instituted by an information laid 12, rather than the usual six, months from the date of commission of the offence (MDA 1971, s. 25(4)).   **B19.74**

For the liability of corporate officers, see **B19.36**.

Sentencing

See **B19.132** to **B19.152**.   **B19.75**

Elements

This offence deals with articles which enable people to administer controlled drugs to themselves or others. The section was intended to outlaw 'drug kits', but the offence has rarely been invoked. It is subject to the Misuse of Drugs Regulations 2001, reg. 6A (permitting the supply of articles for administering or preparing controlled drugs by certain persons; see **B19.17**).   **B19.76**

As to the meaning of 'controlled drug', see **B19.2**.

It is not clear whether the definition given in *Maginnis* [1987] AC 303 of 'supply' applies to this offence (see **B19.40**).

Defences

To fall within the MDA 1971, s. 9A, the articles must be for the unlawful administration of a controlled drug.   **B19.77**

Misuse of Drugs Act 1971, s. 9A

(4) For the purposes of this section, any administration of a controlled drug is unlawful except —

(a) the administration by any person of a controlled drug to another in circumstances where the administration of the drug is not unlawful under section 4(1) of this Act,

(b) the administration by any person of a controlled drug, other than a temporary class drug, to himself in circumstances where having the controlled drug in his possession is not unlawful under section 5(1) of this Act, or

(c) the administration by any person of a temporary class drug to himself in circumstances where having the drug in his possession is to be treated as excepted possession for the purposes of this Act (see section 7A(2)(c)).

Notwithstanding s. 9A(1) and (3), certain persons may supply or offer to supply certain articles as laid down in the Misuse of Drugs Regulations 2001, reg. 6A (see **B19.17**).

OCCUPIERS AND THOSE CONCERNED IN MANAGEMENT OF PREMISES KNOWINGLY PERMITTING OR SUFFERING DRUG-RELATED ACTIVITIES

B19.78   Misuse of Drugs Act 1971, s. 8

A person commits an offence if, being the occupier or concerned in the management of any premises, he knowingly permits or suffers any of the following activities to take place on those premises, that is to say—

(a) producing or attempting to produce a controlled drug in contravention of section 4(1) of this Act;

(b) supplying or attempting to supply a controlled drug to another in contravention of section 4(1) of this Act, or offering to supply a controlled drug to another in contravention of section 4(1);

(c) preparing opium for smoking;

(d) smoking cannabis, cannabis resin or prepared opium.

It is submitted that, for the purpose of s. 8(a) and (b), although it would be appropriate to charge by way of discrete counts those controlled drugs that attract different maximum penalties, it is not necessary for the Crown to prove with regard to a given count that the accused knew the particular identity and class of drug that was in fact being handled (*Bett* [1999] 1 All ER 600).

As to the meaning of 'controlled drug', see **B19.2** *et seq.*; for 'producing', see **B19.58**; for 'supplying', see **B19.40**.

There is no definition of 'premises' in the MDA 1971, although it appears in other legislation where it is provided with a wide definition, e.g., under the Protection from Eviction Act 1977 (see **B13.9**).

It is a necessary ingredient of the offence under s. 8 that the requisite activity had actually taken place before a conviction can be sustained (see **B19.87**). For the purposes of s. 8(6), it is necessary for the supply actually to take place *on* the premises as s. 8 does not say 'from the premises' (*McGee* [2012] EWCA Crim 613, applying *Auguste* [2004] 4 All ER 373).

Procedure

B19.79   Offences under the MDA 1971, s. 9, are (by s. 25 of and sch. 4 to the Act) triable either way. When tried on indictment they are normally class 3 offences, but see CPD XIII, para. B (see Supplement, **PD-97**) for the additional factors that the court considers on allocation.

Summary trial may be instituted by an information laid 12, rather than the usual six, months from the date of commission of the offence (MDA 1971, s. 25(4)).

For the liability of corporate officers, see **B19.36**.

Indictment

B19.80   *Statement of Offence*

Being the occupier [or: concerned in the management] of premises knowingly permitting or suffering [production] of a controlled drug, contrary to section 8 of the Misuse of Drugs Act 1971.

Particulars of Offence

A on or about the…day of…, being the occupier [or: being concerned in the management] of certain premises situated at and known as…, knowingly permitted or suffered on the said premises the [production] of a controlled drug of Class B, namely…, such [production] being contrary to section [4(1)] of the Misuse of Drugs Act 1971.

Sentencing

B19.81   See **B19.132** to **B19.152**.

Meaning of 'Occupier'

Section 8 of the MDA 1971 is aimed at the occupiers or the managers of premises because it **B19.82**
is they who may exercise immediate supervision over the activities carried on within them.
It was held in *Tao* [1977] QB 141 that the term 'occupier' should be given a commonsense
interpretation. What should be avoided is an overly narrow or legalistic definition of that
term. For the purposes of s. 8, a person is in occupation of premises, whatever his legal status, if the prosecution can show that the accused exercised control, or had the authority of
another, to exclude persons from premises or to prohibit any of the activities referred to in
s. 8. Accordingly, a person does not have to be a tenant, or to have an estate in land, in order
to be an 'occupier' for the purposes of s. 8. The Court of Appeal disapproved the reasoning
in *Mogford* (1970) 63 Cr App R 168, where the trial judge (Neild J) had ruled that an 'occupier' was a person in 'legal possession of the premises and had control over them'. The Court
pointed out that a person can be in legal possession of premises without being a tenant or
having any estate in land (see *Errington v Errington* [1952] 1 KB 290 and contrast *Heslop v
Burns* [1974] 3 All ER 406).

In *Tao*, the Court dismissed an undergraduate's appeal against conviction for an offence
under s. 8, in circumstances where he had an exclusive contractual licence in respect of a
college room, which gave him not merely a right to use the room but also sufficient exclu-
sivity of possession to ensure that he was an occupier. Although he may not have been able
to exclude college staff from entering his room, he could exclude cannabis smokers or, for
that matter, any smoker. He was in a position to exercise control over the activities that took
place there.

Two further cases usefully illustrate the meaning of 'occupier' for the purposes of s. 8. In **B19.83**
Read v DPP [1997] 10 CL 120, the Divisional Court dismissed an appeal by way of case
stated against R's conviction of being the occupier of premises in which he knowingly permitted or suffered the smoking of cannabis to take place contrary to s. 8(d). R contended
that he was not the occupier of the premises because the tenancy of the council house was
in the name of his girlfriend with whom he had been cohabiting for some nine years. The
court held that R was clearly an occupier and his claim to the contrary was unrealistic. In
Coid [1998] Crim LR 199, C was charged under s. 8. C was the boyfriend of Miss M: he
cohabited with her at the premises although she was the tenant. When she was away, C
would look after the premises. Drugs paraphernalia were found in the premises. When interviewed, C gave the address as being his. C's defence was in part that he was not an occupier
for the purposes of the MDA 1971. The Court of Appeal held that Miss M's tenancy did not
preclude C from being an occupier, which was a question of fact for the jury, and the judge
gave a proper direction.

Meaning of 'Concerned in the Management of Premises'

To be a manager, the accused must run, organise and plan the use of the premises (*Josephs* (1977) **B19.84**
65 Cr App R 253), and so must be involved in more than menial or routine duties (*Abbott v
Smith* [1964] 2 QB 662). A person satisfies the requirement of a manager even if he has no lawful right or title to be on the premises.

'Knowingly Permits or Suffers'

The Court of Appeal in *Thomas* (1976) 63 Cr App R 65 held that 'knowingly' adds nothing to **B19.85**
the words 'permits or suffers'. The word was probably included in the MDA 1971, s. 8, to put
beyond doubt that proof of knowledge is required. This explains why the offence is not made
subject to s. 28. Note that in *Sweet v Parsley* [1970] AC 132, the House of Lords decided that
the word 'permits' in the forerunner to s. 8, imported *mens rea*. Wilful blindness as to forbidden activity taking place on premises may be sufficient, but mere suspicion is not (*Thomas*).
For the purposes of s. 8(a) and (b), even where the particular drug is specified, it is not

necessary for the Crown to prove more than knowledge of the production or supply of a controlled drug (*Bett* [1999] 1 All ER 600). The accused need not know the identity of the drug or its class.

In *Brock* [2001] 1 WLR 1159, a drop-in centre operated a policy that protected the confidentiality of clients in that no information was to be passed on without the express permission of the individual unless there was an element of danger, safety or personal harm involved. Whilst relevant, such policies are not determinative of the matter. It was for that reason that the trial judge directed the jury that 'the law does not permit you to write or operate a private policy so as to exempt you from the law's requirements'. The Court of Appeal held that: 'A belief by a defendant that he has taken reasonable steps does not afford any defence...It is not for the defendant to judge his own conduct', per Rose LJ. The Court added that: 'What the prosecution must prove to establish the offence of permitting under section 8(b) is (i) knowledge, actual or by closing eyes to the obvious, that heroin dealing is taking place; and (ii) unwillingness to prevent it, which can be inferred from failure to take reasonable steps readily available to prevent it'.

B19.86 In *Souter* [1971] 2 All ER 1151 (decided under s. 5 of the Dangerous Drugs Act 1965), Edmund Davies LJ said: 'The best indication of such unwillingness [to prevent the prohibited activity] is proof of failure to take reasonable steps readily available to prevent [it]. Conversely, all steps taken by the accused to prevent it have a direct bearing on the charge and should be brought to the attention of the jury.'

It is submitted that a further factor for the court to consider is whether the accused allowed the activity to go on 'not caring whether an offence was committed or not'. In *Souter*, Edmund Davies LJ adopted the test of 'permitting' as expressed by Lord Parker CJ in *Gray's Haulage v Arnold* [1966] 1 All ER 896:

> Actual knowledge or knowledge of circumstances so that it could be said that they had shut their eyes to the obvious, or had allowed something to go on, not caring whether an offence was committed or not.

Not caring whether a contravention of the prohibited activity takes place or not was held to be a relevant feature of 'permitting' in *James v Smee* [1955] 1 QB 89. Mere acquiescence in what is taking place on premises is unlikely to amount to permitting that activity (*Bradbury* [1996] Crim LR 808).

The Divisional Court stated in *Taylor v Chief Constable of Kent* [1981] 1 WLR 606 that an occupier who permits another to cultivate cannabis plants permits or suffers their production (i.e. there is an overlap between the offences contrary to the MDA 1971, ss. 4 and 6: see **B19.55** and **B19.62**), and so commits an offence contrary to s. 8.

B19.87 In *Auguste* [2004] 4 All ER 373 the Court of Appeal considered s. 8(d), and held that Parliament was seeking to deal with the situation where a person might discover, by reason of the smell of smoked cannabis, that this activity was taking place. Accordingly, the requisite activity had to be taking place for the offence to be committed.

ASSISTING IN OR INDUCING COMMISSION OUTSIDE UK OF OFFENCE PUNISHABLE UNDER CORRESPONDING LAW

B19.88   Misuse of Drugs Act 1971, s. 20

A person commits an offence if in the United Kingdom he assists in or induces the commission in any place outside the United Kingdom of an offence punishable under the provisions of a corresponding law in force in that place.

Procedure

The offence under the MDA 1971, s. 20, is (by s. 25 of and sch. 4 to the Act) triable either way. When tried on indictment it is normally a class 3 offence, but see CPD XIII, para. B (see Supplement, PD-97) for the additional factors that the court considers on allocation. It is a 'listed offence' for the purposes of the SCA 2007, sch. 3 (encouraging or assisting a person to commit an inchoate offence: see A5.32). **B19.89**

Summary trial may be instituted by an information laid 12, rather than the usual six, months from the date of commission of the offence (MDA 1971, s. 25(4)).

For the liability of corporate officers, see B19.36.

Sentencing

See B19.132 to B19.152. This is a drug trafficking offence within the meaning of the POCA 2002, sch. 2 (see E19.17). A minimum custodial sentence of seven years applies for the third Class A drug trafficking offence (see E5.1). A forfeiture order (see E18.7) or a confiscation order (see E19) may be imposed for a drug trafficking offence. **B19.90**

Meaning of 'Assisting'

Assisting is not to be narrowly construed but must be construed as an ordinary English word (*Vickers* [1975] 2 All ER 945; *Evans* (1977) 64 Cr App R 237; *Panayi* (1987) 86 Cr App R 261). In *Vickers* the accused was guilty when, as he had agreed, he took speaker cabinets to Italy, knowing that cannabis would then be loaded into them and shipped to the USA. In *Evans* the accused had assisted in the UK in the importation of cannabis into Canada from Brussels by the making of arrangements to provide for a human carrier and by carrying out those arrangements. **B19.91**

Commission of Offence outside UK

The offence outside the UK must have been committed (*Panayi* (1987) 86 Cr App R 261). It is only if such an offence is committed that there is something which can be assisted, so the convictions of the accused in *Panayi* were quashed when they had been arrested in British territorial waters having sailed from Spain in a yacht with a quantity of cannabis destined for Holland. If an offence is committed and the accused did an act of assistance, the offence under s. 20 of the MDA 1971 is committed even if it is not possible to identify the principal offender and the final act of importation was effected by an innocent third party (*Ahmed* [1990] Crim LR 648). **B19.92**

Meaning of 'Corresponding Law'

Misuse of Drugs Act 1971, s. 36 **B19.93**

(1) In this Act the expression 'corresponding law' means a law stated in a certificate purporting to be issued by or on behalf of the government of a country outside the United Kingdom to be a law providing for the control and regulation in that country of the production, supply, use, export and import of drugs and other substances in accordance with the provisions of the Single Convention on Narcotic Drugs signed at New York on 30 March 1961 or a law providing for the control and regulation in that country of the production, supply, use, export and import of dangerous or otherwise harmful drugs in pursuance of any treaty, convention or other agreement or arrangement to which the government of that country and Her Majesty's Government in the United Kingdom are for the time being parties.
(2) A statement in any such certificate as aforesaid to the effect that any facts constitute an offence against the law mentioned in the certificate shall be evidence, and in Scotland sufficient evidence, of the matters stated.

Mens Rea

The offence is not one of strict liability (*Vickers* [1975] 2 All ER 945). It is required that (a) the accused intended to assist, i.e. he must know what he is doing and the purpose with which it **B19.94** is done (*Vickers*, at p. 818), and (b) the accused was aware that the person he was assisting was involved in drug smuggling (*Ahmed* [1990] Crim LR 648). It is not necessary to establish that the accused intended that the goods be imported into a particular country (*Ahmed*).

INCITEMENT

B19.95

Misuse of Drugs Act 1971, s. 19

It is an offence for a person...to incite another to commit an offence under any other provision of this Act.

The offence of incitement is triable and punishable in the same way as the substantive offence incited (MDA 1971, s. 25(3) and sch. 4). For examples, see *Marlow* [1997] EWCA Crim 1833 and *Jones* [2010] 2 Cr App R 69. It is a 'listed offence' for the purposes of the SCA 2007, sch. 3 (encouraging or assisting a person to commit an inchoate offence: see **A5.32**).

DEFENCE UNDER THE MISUSE OF DRUGS ACT 1971, s. 28

B19.96

Misuse of Drugs Act 1971, s. 28

(1) This section applies to offences under any of the following provisions of this Act, that is to say section 4(2) and (3), section 5(2) and (3), section 6(2) and section 9.

(2) Subject to subsection (3) below, in any proceedings for an offence to which this section applies it shall be a defence for the accused to prove that he neither knew of nor suspected nor had reason to suspect the existence of some fact alleged by the prosecution which it is necessary for the prosecution to prove if he is to be convicted of the offence charged.

(3) Where in any proceedings for an offence to which this section applies it is necessary, if the accused is to be convicted of the offence charged, for the prosecution to prove that some substance or product involved in the alleged offence was the controlled drug which the prosecution alleges it to have been, and it is proved that the substance or product in question was that controlled drug, the accused—

(a) shall not be acquitted of the offence charged by reason only of proving that he neither knew nor suspected nor had reason to suspect that the substance or product in question was the particular controlled drug alleged; but

(b) shall be acquitted thereof—

(i) if he proves that he neither believed nor suspected nor had reason to suspect that the substance or product in question was a controlled drug; or

(ii) if he proves that he believed the substance or product in question to be a controlled drug, or a controlled drug of a description, such that, if it had in fact been that controlled drug or a controlled drug of that description, he would not at the material time have been committing any offence to which this section applies.

(4) Nothing in this section shall prejudice any defence which it is open to a person charged with an offence to which this section applies to raise apart from this section.

Note that the s. 28 defence cannot be 'read down', in reliance on the ECHR, Article 9, in order to provide for a religious exemption from the offence of possessing a Class A drug (*Aziz* [2012] EWCA Crim 1063, following *Taylor* [2002] 1 Cr App R 519).

Relationship between s. 28(2) and (3)

B19.97 If an accused asserts 'that he did not know that the bag or other container which he was carrying contained a controlled drug and believed it contained a different type of article such as a video film, this defence arises under section 28(2) and not under section 28(3)' (per Lord Hutton in *Lambert* [2002] 2 AC 545 at [181], applying *Salmon v HM Advocate* 1999 JC 67). The cases of *Lambert* and *Salmon* are essential reading as they lucidly explain the operation of s. 28 — a section which is often misunderstood: see *Barr* [2005] EWCA Crim 1764 (where *Lambert* was followed), and note *Carrera* [2002] EWCA Crim 2527, where the Court of Appeal said that 'following *Lambert* there may well be further debate as to the extent of the burden on the prosecution given the wording of s 28(2) and (3), but it is not necessary or appropriate to conduct that debate in order to resolve this appeal'. See also *Choudhury* [2008] EWCA Crim 3179.

It is possible to read s. 28(2) and (3) in a highly restrictive way by focusing on the phrase 'which it is necessary for the prosecution to prove'. The point is best demonstrated by an example. If D is charged with possessing cocaine, with intent to supply it to another, contrary to s. 5(3), the prosecution must prove that D was in possession of a controlled drug of some description which turned out to be cocaine. But, on one interpretation, it would not be necessary for the prosecution to prove that D knew, believed, or suspected that the drug was cocaine, and it would be no defence for D to say that he thought the thing was amphetamine, and therefore (so the argument might run) the defendant cannot avail himself of s. 28. However, if this construction of s. 28 is correct, it would mean that D would have no defence under s. 5(3) if he thought the substance was table salt. It is submitted that this is not a proper construction of s. 28. The offences under s. 6 (cultivating cannabis) and s. 9 (opium smoking) are 'subject to' s. 28. In each case, the controlled drug is specified in the section, but s. 28 is not confined to those two offences. The starting point is s. 28(2) which is qualified by s. 28(3). Thus, for the purposes of s. 5(3) it is necessary to prove that D was in possession of a substance that was a controlled drug of some description. As the Court of Appeal said in *Salmon*, 'subsection (3) turns out to be simply a particular example of the wider class of situations covered by subsection (2), viz. situations where the accused proves "that he neither knew nor suspected nor had reason to suspect the existence of some fact alleged by the prosecution which it is necessary for the prosecution to prove if he is to be convicted of the offence charged"'.

B19.98

However, in *Leeson* [2000] 1 Cr App R 233 — a case that was decided prior to the decision of the House of Lords in *Lambert* and, in which *Salmon* was not cited — the Court of Appeal appears to have favoured a narrow interpretation of s. 28. The accused testified that he had stolen a bag out of a motor vehicle initially anticipating that the bag contained a quantity of 'smart clothes': he later noticed that the bag contained cannabis resin, scales and substances that he thought were amphetamine but which were in fact cocaine. The Court rejected the appellant's submission that his error afforded him a defence under s. 28 on the grounds, (a) that proof that he 'neither knew of, nor suspected nor had reason to suspect' that a substance was cocaine, was not a lack of knowledge of the existence of a fact, alleged by the prosecution, which it was necessary for the prosecution to prove if he were to be convicted of the offence charged; (b) that the particulars of a count on an indictment that identified a substance as a particular controlled drug were not matters that the prosecution had to prove in order to obtain a conviction under s. 5(3); and (c) that s. 28(3)(b)(ii) did not afford the appellant a defence because this was not a case where it was necessary for the prosecution to prove that some substance or product involved in the alleged offence was the controlled drug which the prosecution alleged it to have been. The Court held that 'under [s. 28(3)(a)] the accused is not to be acquitted by reason only of proving that he neither knew nor suspected nor had reason to suspect that the substance or product in question was the particular controlled drug alleged' because the appellant admitted that he thought the substance was amphetamine and therefore he had no defence under s. 28 anyway.

It is respectfully submitted that *Leeson* is best regarded as having been superseded by the decision of the House of Lords in *Lambert* in which the reasoning of the High Court of Justiciary in *Salmon* was discussed with approval (and see the commentary to *Leeson* at [2000] Crim LR 196). In *Salmon*, the Lord Justice General said (at pp. 72 to 73):

B19.99

> The first part of subsec (3) shows that the subsection concerns the situation where it is necessary for the prosecution to prove that 'some *substance or product* involved in the alleged offence was the

controlled drug which the prosecution alleges it to have been, and it is proved that the *substance or product* in question was that controlled drug' (emphasis added).

It is significant that Parliament uses the words 'substance or product' rather than some more general word such as 'article'. In the clauses which I have quoted the words 'substance or product' can refer only to a substance or product which is actually a controlled drug — so it must be, say, the powder or tablets in question. That meaning must be carried through to the remainder of the subsection. Therefore in subsec (3)(b)(i), for instance, Parliament is saying that an accused is to be acquitted if he proves that he neither believed nor suspected nor had reason to suspect that the *powder or tablets* in question were a controlled drug. It follows that the subsection is intended to deal with the limited situation where the Crown have proved that the accused person possessed or was concerned in supplying, say, tablets ('the substance or product'), which are proved to be Ecstasy tablets, but he says that he was mistaken about the nature or quality of the tablets.

A person in that position may say one of three things about the tablets. First, he may say that he did not know that they were Ecstasy tablets and had always thought that they were heroin. Even if the jury accept his evidence on this point, it does not constitute a defence, however, since he is not to be acquitted of possessing ecstasy tablets by proving that he did not know that the substance or product in question was the particular controlled drug alleged rather than another controlled drug (sec 28(3)(a)). Secondly, the accused may prove that he thought that the tablets in the bottle were aspirin and that he neither suspected nor had reason to suspect that they were a controlled drug. In that situation he is to be acquitted (sec 28(3)(b)(i)). Thirdly, there are situations where people are authorised to possess or supply particular drugs…If a doctor were found to have Ecstasy tablets in his possession, it would be a defence for him to prove that he believed that the tablets were heroin tablets which he had in his possession for the purpose of acting in his capacity as a doctor (sec 28(3)(b)(ii)).

That being the scope of subsec (3), it is not apt to apply to the kind of case envisaged in *McNamara* where an accused says that he thought that the contents of a box on his motorcycle were pornographic or pirate videos rather than cannabis resin. In such a case the accused is not claiming that he did not know that the organic matter ('the substance or product in question') was a controlled drug. Rather, he is saying that he did not think that the cannabis resin was there at all: he thought that the box contained videos. It follows that, if the only possible basis for the motorcyclist's defence were sec 28(3), he would have no defence.

Incidence and Standard of Proof

B19.100   In *Lambert* [2002] 2 AC 545, the House of Lords decided that the placing of a legal burden on the defence was contrary to the ECHR, Article 6. It did not issue a declaration of incompatibility, but, using the HRA 1998, s. 3, their lordships interpreted the MDA 1971, s. 28, so as to avoid incompatibility. The effect of *Lambert* seems to be that s. 28 imposes only an evidential burden upon the accused (but see further **F3.18**). *Lambert* was applied in *Lang* [2002] EWCA Crim 298; note also *Choudhury* [2008] EWCA Crim 3179 and *R v CPS* (10 July 2008, unreported) and see *Carrera* [2002] EWCA Crim 2527, the judgment of the Appeal Court of the High Court of Justiciary in *Henvey v HM Advocate* [2005] ScotHC HCJAC 10, and consider *Keogh* [2007] 3 All ER 789.

In *Malinina* [2007] EWCA Crim 3228, the Court of Appeal purported to follow *Lambert* but, in doing so, it uncharacteristically fell into serious error (at [11]). The Court said that the trial judge's direction to the jury 'must explain the difference between an evidential burden and a legal burden of proof in terms that a jury can understand. It must then also explain that the evidential burden can be discharged on a balance of probabilities, but the legal burden on the Crown has to be discharged to a criminal burden of making the jury sure.' It is submitted that, following *Lambert*, a defence that is pursued under s. 28 ought to be dealt with in a manner akin to many other defences to a criminal charge such as self-defence (see, e.g., *DPP v Bailey* [1995] 1 Cr App R 257). In short, the question whether there is evidence sufficient to raise the issue under s. 28 for the jury's consideration is one for the trial judge to answer by applying common sense to the evidence in the case. Hopeless defences which have no factual basis of support do not have to be left to the jury.

It is submitted that the correct approach was that stated by the High Court of Justiciary in **B19.101**
Henvey v HM Advocate [2005] HCJAC 10:

(a) It must be emphasised that for the discharge of the burden there has to be evidence. As Lord
Slynn of Hadley observed in *Lambert* (at [17]): 'It is not enough that the defendant in seek-
ing to establish the evidential burden should merely mouth the words of the section'. Lord
Hope stated (at [90]):

> But an evidential burden is not to be thought of as a burden which is illusory. What the accused
> must do is put evidence before the court which, if believed, could be taken by a reasonable jury
> to support his defence. . .It is what the common law requires of a defendant who wishes to invoke
> one of the common law defences such as provocation or duress.

(b) The evidence would have to cover each of the elements in the relevant subsection of s. 28.
Thus, in the case of s. 28(2), the evidence would have to be to the effect that the accused
neither knew of nor suspected nor had reason to suspect the existence of the fact alleged by
the prosecution which it was necessary for the prosecution to prove if he was to be convicted
of the offence charged.

(c) As was pointed out by the Lord Justice General in *Salmon v HM Advocate* 1999 JC 67 at
p. 75, s. 28(2) does not require that the accused must necessarily have given evidence:

> Doubtless, that would often be the simplest mode of proof, but the necessary evidence might
> come, for example, from a 'mixed' statement or from witnesses speaking to what the accused
> was told was in the container or to the accused's apparent astonishment when the contents of the
> container were revealed and found to be a controlled drug.

(d) It is important to bear in mind that the question of whether the evidential burden has
been discharged is a question of whether there is sufficient evidence for the purposes of the
relevant subsection, for which it must be assumed that the evidence relied on is believed.
Hence, as we have noted, Lord Hope spoke of the need for the accused to put evidence
before the court 'which, if believed, could be taken by a reasonable jury to support his
defence'. That is a matter for the trial judge, who would direct the jury accordingly.

(e) If that is the case, the Crown must meet that defence and satisfy the jury beyond reasonable
doubt that it should be rejected. If the jury believe evidence that the accused neither knew
of nor suspected nor had reason to suspect the existence of the relevant fact, he must be
acquitted. Even if they are not prepared to go so far as to believe that evidence, but are left in
reasonable doubt about that matter, he must also be acquitted. Thus, as Lord Clyde stated
in *Lambert* (at [158]) in regard to a s. 5 case:

> If the jury are satisfied beyond reasonable doubt that the accused possessed the substance or prod-
> uct in question but are not satisfied beyond reasonable doubt that he knew that it was a controlled
> drug (or suspected or had reason to suspect that it was) then again they should acquit him. They
> can only convict if they are satisfied beyond reasonable doubt that the prosecution has proved
> possession of the controlled drug and, if the issue is raised, that the lines of defence set out in sec-
> tion 28 are without foundation.

(f) Where there is no issue as to whether the accused did not know or suspect or have reason to
suspect the relevant fact, there is no need for the jury to be given directions in regard to s. 28.
Thus, in a s. 4(3)(b) case where no such issue is raised on the evidence, the conviction of the
accused will depend on whether the tribunal of fact is satisfied that the accused knew that
he was concerned in the supplying of something, and is further satisfied that that thing was
in fact a controlled drug. If, on the other hand, there is evidence which, if believed, could
support a defence under s. 28, the jury must be directed to acquit the accused if (a) they
accept that evidence, or (b) they are left in reasonable doubt about that matter.

Self-induced intoxication is not a relevant consideration in the exercise of the statutory defence **B19.102**
under s. 28(3)(b) (*Young* [1984] 2 All ER 164).

Section 28 does not apply to conspiracies to commit an MDA offence as they are not statutory
offences created under the 1971 Act (*McGowan* [1990] Crim LR 399).

ENFORCEMENT PROVISIONS

Powers of Entry, Search and Seizure

B19.103   Misuse of Drugs Act 1971, s. 23

(1) A constable or other person authorised in that behalf by a general or special order of the Secretary of State (or in Northern Ireland either of the Secretary of State or the Ministry of Home Affairs for Northern Ireland) shall, for the purposes of the execution of this Act, have power to enter the premises of a person carrying on business as a producer or supplier of any controlled drugs and to demand the production of, and to inspect, any books or documents relating to dealings in any such drugs and to inspect any stocks of any such drugs.

(2) If a constable has reasonable grounds to suspect that any person is in possession of a controlled drug in contravention of this Act or of any regulations or orders made thereunder, the constable may—

(a) search that person, and detain him for the purpose of searching him;

(b) search any vehicle or vessel in which the constable suspects that the drug may be found, and for that purpose require the person in control of the vehicle or vessel to stop it;

(c) seize and detain, for the purposes of proceedings under this Act, anything found in the course of the search which appears to the constable to be evidence of an offence under this Act.

In this subsection 'vessel' includes a hovercraft within the meaning of the Hovercraft Act 1968; and nothing in this subsection shall prejudice any power of search or any power to seize or detain property which is exercisable by a constable apart from this subsection.

(3) If a justice of the peace (or in Scotland a justice of the peace, a magistrate or a sheriff) is satisfied by information on oath that there is reasonable ground for suspecting—

(a) that any controlled drugs are, in contravention of this Act or of any regulations or orders made thereunder, in the possession of a person on any premises; or

(b) that a document directly or indirectly relating to, or connected with, a transaction or dealing which was, or an intended transaction or dealing which would if carried out be, an offence under this Act, or in the case of a transaction or dealing carried out or intended to be carried out in a place outside the United Kingdom, an offence against the provisions of a corresponding law in force in that place, is in the possession of a person on any premises,

he may grant a warrant authorising any constable at any time or times within one month from the date of the warrant, to enter, if need be by force, the premises named in the warrant, and to search the premises and any persons found therein and, if there is reasonable ground for suspecting that an offence under this Act has been committed in relation to any controlled drugs found on the premises or in the possession of any such persons, or that a document so found is such a document as is mentioned in paragraph (b) above, to seize and detain those drugs or that document, as the case may be.

(3A) The powers conferred by subsection (1) above shall be exercisable also for the purposes of the execution of Part II of the Criminal Justice (International Co-operation) Act 1990 and subsection (3) above (excluding paragraph (a)) shall apply also to offences under section 12 or 13 of that Act of 1990, taking references in those provisions to controlled drugs as references to scheduled substances within the meaning of that Part.

B19.104 Note also s. 20 of the Health Act 2006 (power to enter and inspect 'relevant premises' for controlled drugs). As to what amounts to 'reasonable grounds to suspect', see *O'Hara v Chief Constable of the RUC* [1997] AC 286 at p. 298 and *Coalter v HM Advocate* [2013] HCJAC 115. Where there is an application for the details of the information laid in support of a warrant to be disclosed, see *Commissioner of Police for the Metropolis v Bangs* [2014] EWHC 546 (Admin).

In exercising any of the powers pursuant to s. 23, it is essential that constables comply with the PACE 1984, s. 2(2): see *Garjo* [2011] EWCA Crim 1169, citing *Bristol* (2007) 172 JP 171, and see *Michaels v Highbury Corner Magistrates' Court* [2009] EWHC 2928 (Admin). A pat-down search, as was conducted in *James v DPP* (2012) 176 JP 346, is not 'a forcible search' (contrary to PACE Code C, para. 3.2), nor is the placing of a hand on the body of the individual, except perhaps in sensitive parts, the application of force or 'a forcible search'. If a suspect is to be kept in lawful custody for any period of time after the police search has been completed, the police must exercise another power to do so (such as arrest) (*Young v Procurator Fiscal* [2012] HCJAC 104). See also **B19.105**.

Note that the powers conferred by s. 23(1) are also exercisable for the purposes of Articles 6 and 7 of Council Regulation (EC) No. 111/2005: see reg. 10 of the Controlled Drugs (Drug Precursors) (Community External Trade) Regulations 2008 (SI 2008 No. 296). Note also SI 2008 No. 295 with regard to intra-community trade.

The requirements set out in regs. 6 and 7 of the 2008 Regulations, and s. 23(3) of the MDA 1971 (but excluding para. (a)), also apply to an offence preferred under reg. 6, 7 or 8. For these purposes, references made in s. 23 to 'controlled drugs', are to be taken as references to 'scheduled substances' within the meaning of Council Regulation (EC) No. 111/2005 (see reg. 2).

Paragraph 16 of sch. 17 to the PRSRA 2011 inserted s. 23A into the MDA 1971 (temporary class drugs). It is submitted that s. 23A and s. 5(2A) (see **B19.19**) should be read with paras. 405 to 421 of the Explanatory Notes to the PRSRA 2011 in mind.

Misuse of Drugs Act 1971, s. 23A   **B19.105**

(1) Subsection (3) applies in any case where —
  (a) a constable has reasonable grounds to suspect that a person ('P') is in possession of a temporary class drug, and
  (b) it does not appear to the constable that a power under section 23(2) applies to the case.
(2) But if any provision has been made by virtue of section 7A(2)(c) (excepted possession) that applies to the temporary class drug in question, subsection (3) applies only if the constable has no reason to believe that P's possession of the drug is to be treated as excepted possession for the purposes of this Act.
(3) The constable may —
  (a) search P, and detain P for the purposes of searching P;
  (b) and for that purpose require the person in control of the vehicle or vessel to stop it;
  (c) seize and detain anything found in the course of the search which appears to the constable to be a temporary class drug or to be evidence of an offence under this Act.
In this subsection, 'vessel' has the same meaning as in section 23(2).
(4) Subsection (5) applies if a constable reasonably believes that anything detained under subsection (3)(c) is a temporary class drug but is not evidence of any offence under this Act.
(5) The constable may dispose of the drug in such manner as the constable thinks appropriate.
(6) A person who intentionally obstructs a constable in the exercise of the constable's powers under subsection (3) commits an offence.

Offences of Obstruction, Concealment etc.

The powers of enforcement are supported by offences created by the MDA 1971, s. 23(4).   **B19.106**

Misuse of Drugs Act 1971, s. 23

(4) A person commits an offence if he—
  (a) intentionally obstructs a person in the exercise of his powers under this section; or
  (b) conceals from a person acting in the exercise of his powers under subsection (1) above any such books, documents, stocks or drugs as are mentioned in that subsection; or
  (c) without reasonable excuse (proof of which shall lie on him) fails to produce any such books or documents as are so mentioned where their production is demanded by a person in the exercise of his powers under that subsection.

These offences are triable either way (MDA 1971, s. 25 and sch. 4).

As to sentence, see **B19.132** to **B19.152**.

In *Forde* (1985) 81 Cr App R 19, the Court of Appeal held that a person committed an offence under s. 23(4)(a) only if, on the facts of that case, the accused knew that he was being detained for the purposes of a search under s. 23(2)(a) and if the obstruction was intentional, that is to say the act viewed objectively, through the eyes of a bystander, did obstruct the constable's detention or search, and viewed subjectively, that is to say through the eyes of the accused himself, was intended so to obstruct. Note the case of *Bristol* (2008) 172 JP 161, which concerned a charge under s. 23(4)(a) where there was no evidence that the police constable had taken reasonable steps to bring to B's attention the constable's name and name of the police station, and, until he had done so, he could not commence the search; *Osman v DPP* (1999) 163 JP 725 was cited. *Bristol* was followed in *B v DPP* [2008] EWHC 1655 (Admin), and applied in *R (Michaels) v Highbury Corner Magistrates' Court* [2009] EWHC 2928 (Admin). These cases must be considered in conjunction with the PACE 1984, s. 2(2) and (3), which provide that a constable must not commence a search until he has taken reasonable steps to bring to the attention of the appropriate person (among other things) the constable's name and the name of the police station to which he is attached. A failure by the constable to identify his name and station renders the subsequent search unlawful: 'It means that the officers were not then acting in the execution of their duty and no offence was committed under section 23(4)' (*R (Michaels) v Highbury Corner Magistrates' Court* at [9]; and see *Garjo* [2011] EWCA Crim 1169).

For consideration of the similar phrasing in the offence of the wilful obstruction of a police officer in the execution of his duty contrary to the Police Act 1996, s. 89(2), see **B2.42** to **B2.47** and *DPP v Meaden* [2003] EWHC 3005 (Admin) in which s. 89(2) and the MDA 1971, s. 23, are discussed.

Note s. 21 of the Health Act 2006 (offences in connection with power to enter and inspect 'relevant premises' under s. 20 of that Act).

OTHER OFFENCES RELATED TO MISUSE OF DRUGS

Contravention of Directions Relating to Safe Custody of Controlled Drugs

B19.107   It is an offence, contrary to the MDA 1971, s. 11(2), to contravene any directions given under s. 11(1). The offence, under s.11(2), is punishable, on summary conviction, with imprisonment for a term not exceeding six months or a fine not exceeding the prescribed sum or both, and, on conviction on indictment, with imprisonment for a term not exceeding two years or a fine or both. Section 11(1) enables the Secretary of State, by notice in writing to be served on the occupier of any premises on which controlled drugs (including temporary class drugs) are or are proposed to be kept, to give directions as to the taking of precautions or further precautions for the safe custody of any controlled drugs of a description specified in the notice which are kept on those premises.

Contravention of Direction Prohibiting Practitioner etc. from Possessing, Supplying etc. Controlled Drugs

B19.108   It is an offence, contrary to the MDA 1971, s. 12(6), to contravene a direction given under s. 12(2). When tried on indictment, the penalties are the same regardless of the class of drug involved. For the penalties available on conviction, see sch. 4 to the 1971 Act (set out at **B19.133**).

Directions under s. 12(2) can be made by the Secretary of State with regard to people who fall within s. 12(1), that is, a practitioner or pharmacist who has been convicted of offences under:

(a)   the MDA 1971 or under the Dangerous Drugs Act 1965 or any enactment repealed by that Act; or

(b)   the Customs and Excise Act 1952, s. 45, 56 or 30, the Customs and Excise Management Act 1979, s. 50, 68 or 170, in connection with a prohibition of or restriction on importation or exportation of a controlled drug having effect by virtue of s. 3 of the MDA 1971 or which had effect by virtue of any provision contained in or repealed by the Dangerous Drugs Act 1965;

(c)   the Criminal Justice (International Co-operation) Act 1990, s. 12 or 13.

Contravention of Direction Prohibiting Practitioner etc. from Prescribing etc. Controlled Drugs

It is an offence, contrary to s. 13(3) of the MDA 1971, to contravene a direction given under **B19.109**
s. 13(1) or (2) of that Act. When an offence under s. 13(3) is tried on indictment, the penalties
are the same regardless of the class of drug involved. For the penalties available on conviction,
see sch. 4 (set out at **B19.133**). Note that s. 13 applies to a provision made in a temporary class
drug order.

Failure to Comply with Notice Requiring Information Relating to Prescribing Supply etc. of Drugs

Section 17(1) of the MDA 1971 empowers the Secretary of State to issue notices requiring **B19.110**
information from doctors, pharmacists etc. in an area where it appears to him that a social
problem caused by the extensive misuse of dangerous or otherwise harmful drugs exists. It
is an offence, contrary to s. 17(3), if a person without reasonable excuse (proof of which
shall lie on him) fails to comply with any requirement to which he is subject by virtue of
s. 17(1). The offence is punishable, on summary conviction, with a fine not exceeding level
3 on the standard scale. Where the burden of proof lies on D, it is open to challenge in the
light of *Lambert* [2002] 2 AC 545 (see **B19.100** and **F3.18**; and consider *Keogh* [2007] 3
All ER 789).

It is an offence, contrary to the MDA 1971, s. 17(4), if a person, in purported compliance with
a requirement imposed under s. 17(1), gives any information which he knows to be false in a
material particular or recklessly gives any information which is false. The offence is punishable,
on summary conviction, with a term of imprisonment not exceeding six months or a fine not
exceeding the prescribed sum or both, and, on conviction on indictment, with a term of imprisonment not exceeding two years or a fine or both.

Contravention of Regulations (other than Regulations Relating to Addicts)

It is an offence, contrary to the MDA 1971, s. 18(1), for a person to contravene any regula- **B19.111**
tions made under the 1971 Act (including temporary class drug orders: see **B19.3**) other
than regulations relating to addicts. The offence is punishable, on summary conviction, with
a term of imprisonment not exceeding six months or a fine not exceeding the prescribed
sum or both, and, on conviction on indictment, with a term of imprisonment not exceeding two years or a fine or both. The significance of this offence, in particular, is that it means
any breach of the Misuse of Drugs (Safe Custody) Regulations 1973 (SI 1973 No. 798), as
amended by SI 1986 No. 2332, SI 2007 No. 2154, and SI 2014 No. 1275, is an offence.

Contravention of Terms of Licence or other Authority (other than Licence Issued under Regulations Relating to Addicts)

It is an offence, contrary to the MDA 1971, s. 18(2), for a person to contravene a condition **B19.112**
or other term of a licence issued under s. 3 of the 1971 Act or of a licence or other authority
under regulations made under the 1971 Act, not being a licence issued under regulations
relating to addicts. The offence is punishable, on summary conviction, with a term of imprisonment not exceeding six months or a fine not exceeding the prescribed sum or both, and,
on conviction on indictment, with a term of imprisonment not exceeding two years or a fine
or both.

Giving False Information in Purported Compliance with Obligation to give Information Imposed under Regulations

It is an offence, contrary to the MDA 1971, s. 18(3), if a person, in purported compliance with **B19.113**
any obligation to give information to which he is subject under or by virtue of regulations made

under the 1971 Act, gives any information which he knows to be false in a material particular or recklessly gives any information which is so false. The offence is punishable, on summary conviction, with a term of imprisonment not exceeding six months or a fine not exceeding the prescribed sum or both, and, on conviction on indictment, with a term of imprisonment not exceeding two years or a fine or both.

Giving False Information, or Producing Document Containing False Statement etc. for Purpose of Obtaining Issue of Licence

B19.114   It is an offence, contrary to the MDA 1971, s. 18(4), if a person for the purpose of obtaining, whether for himself or another, the issue or renewal of a licence or other authority under the 1971 Act or any regulations made under it:

(a) makes any statement or gives any information which he knows to be false in a material particular or recklessly gives any information which is so false; or

(b) produces or otherwise makes use of any book, record or other document which to his knowledge contains any statement or information which he knows to be false in a material particular.

The offence is punishable, on summary conviction, with a term of imprisonment not exceeding six months or a fine not exceeding the prescribed sum or both, and, on conviction on indictment, with a term of imprisonment not exceeding two years or a fine or both.

SUPPLY OF INTOXICATING SUBSTANCE

B19.115   **Intoxicating Substances (Supply) Act 1985, s. 1**

(1) It is an offence for a person to supply or offer to supply a substance other than a controlled drug—

    (a) to a person under the age of 18 whom he knows, or has reasonable cause to believe, to be under that age; or

    (b) to a person—

        (i)   who is acting on behalf of a person under that age; and

        (ii) whom he knows, or has reasonable cause to believe, to be so acting,

if he knows or has reasonable cause to believe that the substance is, or its fumes are, likely to be inhaled by the person under the age of 18 for the purpose of causing intoxication.

Procedure and Sentencing

B19.116   The offence is triable summarily only.

The maximum penalty is imprisonment for a term not exceeding six months or a fine not exceeding level 5 or both (Intoxicating Substances (Supply) Act 1985, s. 1(3)).

Elements and Defence

B19.117   Since similar concepts apply in the MDA 1971, s. 4(3) (see **B19.37** and **B19.39**), it may be that the same meaning of 'supply or offer to supply' appertains in the 1985 Act, but the statute does not make that clear and the point remains open.

The Intoxicating Substances (Supply) Act 1985, s. 1(4), makes clear that 'controlled drug' has the same meaning as in the MDA 1971 (see **B19.2**).

Intoxicating Substances (Supply) Act 1985, s. 1

(2) In proceedings against any person for an offence under subsection (1) above it is a defence for him to show that at the time he made the supply or offer he was under the age of 18 and was acting otherwise than in the course or furtherance of a business.

As to the incidence of proof, consider *Lambert* [2002] 2 AC 545 (see **F3.18**; and consider *Keogh* [2007] 3 All ER 789).

MANUFACTURE AND SUPPLY OF
SCHEDULED SUBSTANCES

Criminal Justice (International Co-Operation) Act 1990, s. 12   **B19.118**

(1) It is an offence for a person—
   (a) to manufacture a scheduled substance; or
   (b) to supply such a substance to another person,
knowing or suspecting that the substance is to be used in or for the unlawful production of a controlled drug.

Procedure

No proceedings may be instituted in England and Wales except by or with the consent of **B19.119** the DPP or the Commissioners of Customs and Excise (Criminal Justice (International Co-operation) Act 1990, s. 21(2)(a)). The offence is triable either way (s. 12(2)). When tried on indictment it is a class 4 offence.

As to the position where the offence is committed on a British ship, see ss. 18 and 24. Section 21 of the MDA 1971 (liability of corporate officers — see **B19.36**) applies to this offence.

Sentencing

The maximum penalty on conviction on indictment is imprisonment for a term not exceed- **B19.120** ing 14 years or a fine or both; on summary conviction, the maximum penalty is imprisonment for a term not exceeding six months or a fine not exceeding the statutory maximum or both (Criminal Justice (International Co-operation) Act 1990, s. 12(2)). This is a drug trafficking offence within the meaning of the POCA 2002, sch. 2 (see **E19.17**). A minimum custodial sentence of seven years applies for the third Class A drug trafficking offence (see **E5.1**). A con-fiscation order (see **E19**) or forfeiture order (see **E18.7**) may be imposed for a drug trafficking offence. Note that this is a 'serious offence' for the purposes of the SCA 2007, part 1 (serious crime prevention orders: see **D25.72**).

Scheduled Substance

A 'scheduled substance' for the purposes of the Criminal Justice (International Co-operation) **B19.121** Act 1990 is a substance specified in sch. 2 to that Act. Schedule 2 may be amended by Her Majesty by Order in Council. The substances are (in Table I) n-acetylanthranilic acid, ephed-rine, ergometrine, ergotamine, isosafrole, lysergic acid, 3,4-methylene-dioxyphenyl-2-pr opanone, norephedrine, 1-phenyl-2-propanone, phenylacetic acid (moved from Table I to Table II, March 2010), piperonal, pseudoephedrine, safrole and, (in Table II) acetic anhydride, acetone, anthranilic acid, ethyl ether, hydrochloric acid, methyl ethyl ketone (also referred to as 2-butanone or M.E.K.), piperidine, potassium permanganate, sulphuric acid, and toluene.

Unlawful Production of a Controlled Drug

The phrase 'controlled drug' has the same meaning as in the MDA 1971 (Criminal Justice **B19.122** (International Co-operation) Act 1990, s. 12(3)). For that definition, see **B19.2**. 'Unlawful production of a controlled drug' means production of such a drug which is unlawful by virtue of the MDA 1971, s. 4(1)(a) (Criminal Justice (International Co-operation) Act 1990, s. 12(3)). See **B19.55** *et seq*.

A person does not commit this offence if 'he manufactures or, as the case may be, supplies the scheduled substance with the express consent of a constable' (s. 12(1A)).

Supply

Supply is not defined in the Criminal Justice (International Co-operation) Act 1990, but it is **B19.123** presumed that it has the same meaning as in the MDA 1971 (see **B19.40**), as is explicitly the case in the regulations made under the Criminal Justice (International Co-operation) Act 1990, s. 13 (see **B19.124**).

CONTROLLED DRUGS (SUBSTANCES USEFUL FOR MANUFACTURE) REGULATIONS 1991

Controlling the Production and Supply of Certain Scheduled Substances

B19.124 **Intra-community Trade**   The Controlled Drugs (Drugs Precursors) (Intra-Community Trade) Regulations 2008 (SI 2008 No. 295) revoked the Controlled Drugs (Substances Useful for Manufacture) (Intra-Community Trade) Regulations 1993 (SI 1993 No. 2166), and the Controlled Drugs (Substances Useful for Manufacture) (Intra-Community Trade) (Amendment) Regulations 2004 (SI 2004 No. 850).

It is an offence, under the Criminal Justice (International Co-operation) Act 1990, s. 13, for a person to fail to comply with any requirement imposed by regulations made under that Act or, in purported compliance with any such requirement, to furnish information which he knows to be false in a material particular or recklessly to furnish information which is false in a material particular. The offence is triable either way and it is punishable on indictment with a maximum term of two years' imprisonment, or a fine, or both. The maximum penalty, on summary conviction, is six months' imprisonment, or a fine not exceeding the statutory maximum, or both (s. 13(5)).

By reg. 6(1) of the 2008 Regulations, the obligations that are imposed by Regulation (EC) No. 273/2004, on 'operators' (as defined by Regulation (EC) No. 273/2004) by Article 5 (documentation), Article 7 (labelling) and Article 8 (notification of the competent authorities) shall be treated as if they are requirements imposed on them by regulations made under s. 13(1) of the 1990 Act, and as if references in those articles to 'scheduled substances' are references to scheduled substances within the meaning of part 2 of that Act. Where a person is convicted of an offence contrary to s. 13(5) of the 1990 Act, by virtue of reg. 6(1), s. 13(5)(a) of the 1990 Act shall have effect as if for the words '6 months' there are substituted the words '3 months'.

By reg. 7(1), an 'operator' who fails to comply with any of the requirements imposed by Article 3 of Regulation (EC) No. 273/2004 (requirements for placing on the market of scheduled substances) is guilty of an offence and liable (a) on summary conviction, to imprisonment for a term not exceeding three months or a fine not exceeding the statutory maximum or both; (b) on conviction on indictment, to imprisonment for a term not exceeding two years or a fine or both.

B19.125 **Community External Trade**   The Controlled Drugs (Drugs Precursors) (External Trade) Regulations 2008 (SI 2008 No. 296) revoked the Controlled Drugs (Substances Useful for Manufacture) Regulations 1991 (SI 1991 No. 1285), and the Controlled Drugs (Substances Useful for Manufacture) (Amendment) Regulations 1992 (SI 1992 No. 2914). By reg. 5(2), the obligations imposed under Articles 3 to 5, 8 and 9 of Regulation (EC) No. 111/2005 shall be treated as if they are requirements imposed by regulations made under s. 13(1) of the 1990 Act (see **B19.124**), and as if references in those articles to scheduled substances are references to scheduled substances within the meaning of part 2 of that Act. Where a person is convicted of an offence contrary to s. 13(5) of the 1990 Act as a result of the application of reg. 5(2), s. 13(5)(a) of the 1990 Act (penalty on summary conviction) shall have effect as if for the words '6 months' there is substituted '3 months'.

SHIPS USED FOR ILLICIT TRAFFIC

B19.126 For offences in relation to controlled drugs on a British ship, see the Criminal Justice (International Co-operation) Act 1990, s. 19. Proceedings must be instituted by or with the consent of the DPP or the Director of Revenue and Customs Prosecutions (s. 21(2)(a)). For jurisdiction, see s. 21(1).

Temporary Class Drugs   Section 19(4)(b) of the Criminal Justice (International Co-operation) **B19.127**
Act 1990 (ships used for illicit traffic) was amended by the PRSRA 2011, s. 151 and sch. 17, para. 22 (in force from 15 November 2011: see SI 2011 No. 2515), so that the words 'or a temporary class drug' are inserted after the words 'Class B drug'.

Sentences for the offence vary according to the class of drug involved. As to whether the effect of the House of Lords decision in *Courtie* [1984] AC 463 is that there is more than one offence, see **B19.19**. The offences are all triable either way (s. 19(4)). When tried on indictment they are class 4 offences.

Section 21 of the MDA 1971 (liability of corporate officers — see **B19.36**) applies to this offence.

Sentence

Where a class A drug is involved, the maximum penalty on indictment is imprisonment for life **B19.128** or a fine or both; on summary conviction, the maximum penalty is imprisonment for a term not exceeding six months or a fine not exceeding the statutory maximum or both (Criminal Justice (International Co-operation) Act 1990, s. 19(4)(a)). A minimum custodial sentence of seven years applies for the third Class A drug trafficking offence (see **E5.1**).

Where a Class B drug, or a temporary class drug, is involved, the maximum penalty on indictment is imprisonment for a term not exceeding 14 years or a fine or both; on summary conviction, the maximum penalty is imprisonment for a term not exceeding six [12] months or a fine not exceeding the statutory maximum or both (s. 19(4)(b)).

Where a Class C drug is involved, the maximum penalty on indictment is imprisonment for a term not exceeding 14 years or a fine or both; on summary conviction, the maximum penalty is imprisonment for a term not exceeding three months or a fine not exceeding the statutory maximum or both (s. 19(4)(c)).

It is clearly established that where drugs have been intercepted on the high seas and those drugs were destined for a country other than England or Wales, the maximum available sentence for such offences in that other country is not a relevant sentencing consideration (*Maguire* [1997] 1 Cr App R (S) 130; *Wagenaar* [1997] 1 Cr App R (S) 178).

These are drug trafficking offences within the meaning of the POCA 2002, sch. 2 (see **E19.17**), so a forfeiture order (see **E18.7**) or a confiscation order (see **E19**) may be imposed.

Elements

The Criminal Justice (International Co-operation) Act 1990, s. 19(2), applies to a British ship, **B19.129** a ship registered in a state other than the UK which is a party to the Vienna Convention (a Convention state), and a ship not registered in any country or territory (s. 19(1)). Ship includes any vessel used in navigation; British ship means a ship registered in the UK or a colony (s. 24(1)).

'Controlled drug', and the classes of controlled drugs, have the same meaning as in the MDA 1971, see **B19.2** *et seq*. (s. 19(5)).

Since the defence in the MDA 1971, s. 28, applies, the meaning of possession in that Act should apply to the present offence. See **B19.23** *et seq*.

As to the MDA 1971, s. 3(1), see **B19.61**. A certificate purporting to be issued by or on behalf of the government of any state to the effect that the importation or export of a controlled drug is prohibited by the law of that state shall be evidence of the matters stated (s. 19(3)).

It was made clear in *Dean* [1998] 2 Cr App R 171 that it is for the prosecution to prove, to the criminal standard of proof, that the ship in question is one to which s. 19 applies. The Court of

Appeal said that it is 'sensible' to decide that issue at the outset of the trial rather than at the end of the prosecution case. On the facts of that particular case, the judge found that the ship was not registered anywhere and thus s. 19 was engaged.

B19.130 Enforcement powers, conferred by the 1990 Act, appear in sch. 3 to that Act. Section 20(1) of the Act provides that: 'The powers conferred on an enforcement officer by schedule 3 to this Act shall be exercisable in relation to any ship to which section 18 or 19 above applies for the purpose of detecting and the taking of appropriate action in respect of the offences mentioned in those sections'. Paragraph 2(1) of sch. 3 provides that: 'An enforcement officer may stop the ship, board it and, if he thinks it necessary in the exercise of his functions, require it to be taken to a port in the United Kingdom and detain it there'. Paragraph 4 provides that: 'If an enforcement officer has reasonable grounds to suspect that an offence mentioned in section 18 or 19 of this Act has been committed on a ship to which that section applies, he may (a) arrest without warrant any one whom he has reasonable grounds for suspecting to be guilty of the offence; and (b) seize and detain anything found on the ship which appears to him to be evidence of the offence'. In *Hoestra v HM Advocate* [2002] Scot HC 343, the Appeal Court of the High Court of Justiciary held that before an enforcement officer could act under para. 4, he had to have pre-existing knowledge of reasonable grounds to suspect that an offence, mentioned in s. 18 or 19, had been committed. The wording of s. 19(2) meant that the aforementioned pre-existing knowledge (of reasonable grounds to suspect) extended to the issue of whether the ship concerned was one to which s. 19 applied. The court had regard to a principle applied in *Leckie v Miln* 1982 SLT 177, that law enforcement officers cannot be treated as acting under and in terms of legal powers of which they are, at the time in question, ignorant and heedless. For requests made by UK customs officials to another state, to board a vessel that is flying an ensign of that state, see *Bolden* [1998] 2 Cr App R 171.

Defence

B19.131 The defence in the MDA 1971, s. 28, applies (Criminal Justice (International Co-operation) Act 1990, s. 19(5)). See **B19.96** for full details of the s. 28 defence.

SENTENCING GUIDELINES FOR OFFENCES UNDER THE MISUSE OF DRUGS ACT 1971

Maximum and Minimum Sentences

B19.132 For sentencing purposes it is necessary to draw a distinction between three different types of drugs:

(a) Class A drugs (especially heroin, morphine, cocaine, LSD, opium and Ecstasy);
(b) Class B drugs (especially cannabis, cannabis resin, amphetamine and codeine); and
(c) Class C drugs (especially anabolic steroids, benzphetamine and pemoline).

A minimum custodial sentence of seven years must be imposed by the court where an offender aged 18 or over is convicted of a Class A drug trafficking offence committed after 1 October 1997, he has been convicted of two other Class A drug trafficking offences, and there are no particular circumstances relating to any of the offences, or the offender, such that the imposition of a custodial sentence of at least seven years would be unjust in all the circumstances (PCC(S) A 2000, s. 110; see **E5.1**).

Section 25 of the 1971 Act provides for the range of punishment for offences under the Act to be as set out in sch. 4 (see **B19.133**).

Forfeiture and Confiscation

B19.133 For the court's powers of forfeiture under the MDA 1971, s. 27, see **E18.7**. For powers of confiscation, see **E19**.

Misuse of **Drugs Act**, sch. 4

SCHEDULE 4   PROTECTION AND PUNISHMENT OF OFFENCES

SECTION 25

Section Creating Offence	General Nature of Offence	Mode of Prosecution	Punishment			
			Class A drug involved	Class B drug involved	Class C drug involved	General
Section 4(2)	Production, or being concerned in the production, of a controlled drug	(a) Summary	6 months or the prescribed sum, or both	6 months or the prescribed sum, or both	3 months or £2,500, or both	
		(b) On indictment	Life or a fine, or both	14 years or a fine, or both	14 years or a fine, or both	
Section 4(3)	Supplying or offering to supply a controlled drug or being concerned in the doing of either activity by another	(a) Summary	6 months or the prescribed sum, or both	6 months or the prescribed sum, or both	3 months or £2,500 or both	
		(b) On indictment	Life or a fine, or both	14 years or a fine, or both	14 years or a fine, or both	
Section 5(2)	Having possession of a controlled drug	(a) Summary	6 months or the prescribed sum, or both	3 months or £2,500 or both	3 months or £1,000 or both	
		(b) On indictment	7 years or a fine, or both	5 years or a fine, or both	2 years or a fine, or both	
Section 5(3)	Having possession of a controlled drug with intent to supply it to another	(a) Summary	6 months or the prescribed sum, or both	6 months or the prescribed sum, or both	3 months or £2,500 or both	
		(b) On indictment	Life or a fine, or both	14 years or a fine, or both	14 years or a fine, or both	
Section 6(2)	Cultivation of cannabis plant	(a) Summary	—	—	—	6 months or the prescribed sum, or both
		(b) On indictment	—	—	—	14 years or a fine, or both

Section Creating Offence	General Nature of Offence	Mode of Prosecution	Punishment			
			Class A drug involved	Class B drug involved	Class C drug involved	General
Section 8	Being the occupier, or concerned in the management, of premises and permitting or suffering certain activities to take place there	(a) Summary	6 months or the prescribed sum, or both	6 months or the prescribed sum, or both	3 months or £2,500 or both	
		(b) On indictment	14 years or a fine, or both	14 years or a fine, or both	14 years or a fine, or both	
Section 9	Offences relating to opium	(a) Summary	—	—	—	6 months or the prescribed sum, or both
		(b) On indictment	—	—	—	14 years or a fine, or both
Section 11(2)	Contravention of direction relating to safe custody of controlled drugs	(a) Summary	—	—	—	6 months or the prescribed sum, or both
		(b) On indictment	—	—	—	2 years or a fine, or both
Section 12(6)	Contravention of direction prohibiting practitioner etc. from possessing, supply etc. of controlled drugs	(a) Summary	6 months or the prescribed sum, or both	6 months or the prescribed sum, or both	3 months or £2,500 or both	
		(b) On indictment	14 years or a fine, or both	14 years or a fine, or both	14 years or a fine, or both	
Section 13(3)	Contravention of direction prohibiting practitioner etc. from prescribing, supplying etc. controlled drugs	(a) Summary	6 months or the prescribed sum, or both	6 months or the prescribed sum, or both	3 months or £2,500 or both	
		(b) On indictment	14 years or a fine, or both	14 years or a fine, or both	14 years or a fine, or both	
Section 17(3)	Failure to comply with notice requiring information relating to prescribing, supplying etc. of drugs	Summary	—	—	—	level 3 on the standard scale
Section 17(4)	Giving false information in purported compliance with notice requiring information relating to prescribing, supply etc. of drugs	(a) Summary	—	—	—	6 months or the prescribed sum, or both
		(b) On indictment	—	—	—	2 years or a fine, or both

Section 18(1)	Contravention of regulations (other than regulations relating to addicts)	(a) Summary	—	6 months or prescribed sum, or both
Section 18(2)	Contravention of terms of licence or other authority (other than licence issued under regulations relating to addicts)	(a) Summary	—	6 months or the prescribed sum, or both
		(b) On indictment	—	2 years or a fine, or both
Section 18(3)	Giving false information in purported compliance with obligation to give information imposed under or by virtue of regulations	(a) Summary	—	6 months or the prescribed sum, or both
		(b) On indictment	—	2 years or a fine, or both
Section 18(4)	Giving false information, or producing documents etc. containing false statement etc. for purposes of obtaining issue or renewal of a licence or other authority	(a) Summary	—	6 months or the prescribed sum, or both
		(b) On indictment	—	2 years or a fine, or both
Section 20	Assisting in or inducing commission outside United Kingdom of an offence punishable under a corresponding law	(a) Summary	—	6 months or the prescribed sum, or both
		(b) On indictment	—	14 years or a fine, or both
Section 23(4)	Obstructing exercise of powers of search etc or concealing books, drugs, etc	(a) Summary	—	6 months or the prescribed sum, or both
		(b) On indictment	—	2 years or a fine, or both

B19.134 The definitive sentencing guideline, *Drugs Offences* (see Supplement, SG-545), applies to all offenders aged 18 and over who are sentenced on or after 27 February 2012 irrespective of the date of the offence. The guideline covers (a) fraudulent evasion of a prohibition by bringing into or taking out of the UK a controlled drug, (b) supplying or offering to supply a controlled drug, (c) production of a controlled drug, (d) permitting premises to be used, and (e) possession of a controlled drug. The guideline supersedes a mass of case law issued under earlier authority. It was said by the Court of Appeal in *Dyer* [2013] EWCA Crim 2114, in the context of street-dealing in Class A drugs, that the old case-law had been superseded by the guideline and should no longer be relied upon. The press release issued by the Sentencing Council states that:

> Under the new guidelines there are likely to be increased sentence lengths for those guilty of large scale production offences, and reduced sentence lengths for drug mules. Sentences for drug mules — who are usually vulnerable and exploited by organised criminals — will have a starting point of six years imprisonment. There will be no change in sentencing for possession or drug supply offences. Where an offender profits from selling drugs, a prison sentence can be expected. Street dealers who have a significant role in selling Class A drugs, particularly those who sell drugs for profit can expect a custodial sentence with a starting point of four and a half years.

In the decisions in *Boakye* [2013] 1 Cr App R (S) 6 (2) and in *A-G's Refs (Nos. 15, 16 & 17 of 2012) (Lewis)* [2013] 1 Cr App R (S) 289 (52), the Court of Appeal confirmed that, although the guideline on *Drug Offences* adopted a modified form of reasoning, it was expected to produce sentences broadly in line with former practice save for the special sub-class of couriers known as drug mules.

Guideline Structure and Approach

B19.135 The definitive sentencing guideline, *Drugs Offences* (see Supplement, SG-545), requires the sentencer at Step One to determine the offence category by reference to the category of drug, the offender's culpability, and to the harm caused. The guideline sets out, for each of the forms of offence covered, three levels of culpability at Step One: 'leading role', 'significant role' and 'lesser role'. A non-exhaustive list of characteristics which may demonstrate the particular offender's role is provided. The guideline then sets out, for each of the forms of offence covered, a three-fold or four-fold classification of 'category of harm' based upon indicative quantity of the drug concerned (upon which the sentencing starting point in each category is based). In assessing harm, quantity is determined by the weight of the product. Purity of the drug concerned is not taken into account at Step One, but is dealt with at Step Two. Having determined the applicable category under Step One, the sentencer should use the corresponding starting point to reach a sentence within the category range indicated in the guideline. The starting point applies to all offenders, irrespective of plea or previous convictions. The court should then consider further adjustment within the category range for aggravating or mitigating features, as set out in a non-exhaustive list.

The Court of Appeal in *Healey* [2013] 1 Cr App R (S) 176 (33) provided a valuable detailed exposition on the proper approach of the courts to the guideline. Hughes LJ said that the sentencer's job was to read the guidelines for what they were, and it was not open to a judge to prefer and apply appellate guidance which pre-dated the guidelines. His lordship also said:

> The format which is adopted by the Sentencing Council in producing its guidelines is to present the broad categories of offence frequently encountered pictorially in boxes. That is perhaps convenient, especially since it is necessary to condense the presentation as much as possible and to avoid discursive narrative on so wide a range of offending. It may be that the pictorial boxes which are part of the presentation may lead a superficial reader to think that adjacent boxes are mutually exclusive, one of the other. They are not. There is an inevitable overlap between the scenarios which are described in adjacent boxes. In real life, offending is found on a sliding scale of gravity with few hard lines. The guidelines set out to describe such sliding scales and graduations. In these guidelines, as in almost all such, there is a recognition that the two principal factors which affect sentencing for crime can broadly be collected together as, first, the harm the offence does, and secondly, the culpability of the offender...Quantity, which is a broad appreciation of harm, may

well colour participation, which is a broad appreciation of culpability, and vice versa. What we have just said about sliding scales applies equally to both elements, both to culpability and to harm. In neither case do the boxes have hard edges.

These remarks were endorsed in *A-G's Refs (Nos. 15, 16 & 17 of 2012) (Lewis)* [2013] 1 Cr App R (S) 289 (52), where Hallett LJ also said that the Council's choice of words in categorising the role of an offender within a drugs hierarchy (leading, significant, lesser) was not a change in substance from earlier practice.

The guidelines apply to cases of conspiracy. This was confirmed by the Court of Appeal in *Khan* [2014] 1 Cr App R (S) 42 (10), a case of conspiracy to supply Class A drugs. Treacy LJ said that in such a case a judge was entitled to consider the aggregate quantity of the drug (or drugs) involved. The role of the offender within the conspiracy would be very important, and an individual offender's limited part in the conspiracy had to be balanced against the seriousness of the offending as a whole.

Class A Drug Offences

Importation   A minimum custodial sentence of seven years applies for the third Class A drug trafficking offence (see E5.1).   **B19.136**

The guideline indicates that for an offender playing a 'leading role' in this offence, involving a Class A drug, and depending on the category of harm, the starting points are 14 years (category 1), 11 years (category 2), or eight years, six months (category 3). For an offender playing a 'significant role', the starting points are ten years, eight years, or six years. For an offender playing a 'lesser role', the starting points are eight years, six years, or four years, six months. In *Talebi* [2013] 2 Cr App R (S) 339 (49), a case involving importation of 3.92 kg of opium, the Court of Appeal noted that the categories of harm in the guideline were based on indicative quantities of the drug concerned. While heroin and cocaine were listed there was no reference to opium. The Court concluded that for these purposes 1 kg of heroin should be regarded as equivalent to 8 kg of opium. The instant case was a category 2 importation with a starting point of 11 years. Applying 25 per cent discount for the guilty plea, the proper sentence was eight years' imprisonment. In *A-G's Refs (Nos. 15, 16 & 17 of 2012) (Lewis)* [2013] 1 Cr App R (S) 289 (52), in the case of two offenders (Wijtvliet and Lewis) convicted of 'a massive importation' of 100 kg of diamorphine and 6 kg of cocaine, the Court of Appeal increased sentences totalling 13 years to 20 years for the first offender and sentences totalling nine years to 13 years for the second, saying that Wijtvliet had played a 'leading/significant' role and Lewis a 'significant' role in the offence.

Drug Couriers   In *Attuh-Benson* [2005] 2 Cr App R (S) 52, the Court of Appeal stated that   **B19.137** it was not appropriate at that time to reconsider the policy of passing long deterrent custodial sentences on drug couriers, who were not infrequently women with dependent children who came from under-developed countries and who would suffer considerable hardship in prison. The Court did say, however, that there was sufficient flexibility to allow judges to assess the role of the offender, the extent of his culpability, his attitude to the offence and his personal circumstances. In *Robinson* [2004] 2 Cr App R (S) 392, the Court of Appeal observed that, in some cases involving importation of drugs where a defence of duress has been run without success, it may still be necessary for the sentencer to hold a *Newton* hearing to determine whether there had been a degree of coercion short of duress. See also *Quinn* [2010] 1 Cr App R (S) 209. The Sentencing Council has signalled a change of sentencing policy with respect to this particular group of drug offenders, with lower sentences now appropriate in some cases. It is significant, however, that the Council's press release which accompanies the guideline stresses that: 'A drug mule should not be confused with other types of offender sentenced for importation offences— if the court decides that he or she has a more significant role in importing drugs, then a longer sentence [sh]ould be passed'. In *Jaramillo* [2013] 1 Cr App R (S) 569 (110), a case decided after the guideline came into effect, the four offenders pleaded guilty to importation of cocaine. They travelled as two couples, the first pair carrying 42.81 kg worth £7.2 million and the second pair carrying 33.89 kg, worth £5.29 million. It was accepted that the offenders were not organisers or managers. Sentences of ten years' detention in a young offender institution and 11 years' imprisonment respectively, were reduced to seven years and eight years. The offenders were, for the purposes of the guidelines, performing a lesser role, but importations of 5 kg or more fell within the scope of category 1. This was much more than 5 kg and the operation was on the most serious and commercial scale. Even so, the offenders had limited roles as couriers, but did not properly fall within the category of 'mules'. The original sentences did not recognise sufficiently the gap in culpability between those who managed and organised and those towards the lower end of the hierarchy.

B19.138 **Supply**   A minimum custodial sentence of seven years applies for the third Class A drug trafficking offence (see E5.1).

The guideline indicates that for an offender playing a 'leading role' in the offence, involving a Class A drug and depending on the category of harm, the starting point is 14 years (category 1), 11 years (category 2), eight years, six months (category 3), or five years six months (category 4). For an offender playing a 'significant role', the starting point is ten years, eight years, four years six months, or three years six months. For an offender playing a 'lesser role', the starting point is seven years, five years, three years or 18 months.

In *Dyer* [2013] EWCA Crim 2114 the offenders were eight people arrested as part of a single police operation. They appealed against sentences imposed following their guilty pleas to various offences of street dealing in Class A drugs. All had sold drugs to test purchase police officers. They appealed on the basis that the judge had misapplied the guideline. Leveson LJ said that for cases involving street dealing of drugs the harm caused was not quantified by the quantity of drugs. The particular guideline on supply, offering to supply, and possession with intent to supply operates slightly differently from the norm. A street dealer who was funding his own habit was 'motivated by financial advantage' and therefore played a *significant role* for the purpose of assessing his culpability under the guideline. The characteristic of 'some awareness and understanding of scale of operation' that pointed in other cases to the offender playing a significant role was less relevant to street dealing. Any case of 'selling direct to users' drops straight into category 3. The fact that the sale was to a test purchase officer was not a reason to reduce the category since the identity of the person to whom the drugs were sold by the offender was a matter of chance. That leads (assuming Class A drugs) to a starting point of four years, six months and a category range of three years, six months to seven years. Drug purity becomes relevant at Step Two in the guideline, together with all relevant aggravating and mitigating factors (including but not limited to those listed). Then, of course, there should be an appropriate reduction for plea. The Court adjusted sentences in this case to terms ranging from three to five-and-a-half years. Leveson LJ also said that the pre-guideline authorities on supply of drugs had been overtaken by the guideline, so reliance on *Afonso* [2005] 1 Cr App R (S) 99 was no longer appropriate.

B19.139 **Supply to Serving Prisoner**   Numerous pre-guideline decisions of the Court of Appeal show that supply of drugs to a serving prisoner is a serious aggravating feature of this offence. In *Happe* [2011] 1 Cr App R (S) 108 a sentence of 30 months was upheld on a 71-year-old woman who supplied 36.7 grammes of heroin to her son, a serving prisoner, despite her previous good character and other personal mitigation. In *A-G's Ref (No. 34 of 2011)* [2012] 1 Cr App R (S) 288 the Court of Appeal increased sentence from 12 months' imprisonment to four years on an offender with many previous convictions who had smuggled 29 grams of heroin at 20 per cent purity, and a quantity of Class C drug, into prison. Lord Judge CJ stressed the need for deterrent sentences in such cases. In *Sanchez-Canadas* [2013] 1 Cr App R (S) 588 (114) the Court of Appeal upheld a sentence of 45 months on a man who attempted to supply heroin and cannabis into a prison by sending them concealed in a pair of trainers. The Court said that this was a category 4 case where the offender played a significant role. The guideline placed drug supply by prison officers automatically into category 3, but that did not apply here. Taken in the round a starting point of five years after a trial could not be faulted. In *Sterling* [2013] 2 Cr App R (S) 386 (60) the offenders were convicted of conspiracy to convey a List A article (namely cannabis) and a List B article (mobile phones) into prison. Sentences of five years to three years were imposed, with the Court of Appeal commenting that for these offences the guideline was not directly relevant but might provide indirect assistance.

Production A minimum custodial sentence of seven years applies for the third Class A drug **B19.140** trafficking offence (see **E5.1**).

The guideline indicates that for an offender playing a 'leading role' in the offence, involving a Class A drug and depending on the category of harm, the starting point is 14 years (category 1), 11 years (category 2), eight years six months (category 3), or five years six months (category 4). For an offender playing a 'significant role', the starting point is ten years, eight years, four years six months, or three years six months. For an offender playing a 'lesser role', the starting point is seven years, five years, three years or 18 months.

Permitting Use of Premises A minimum custodial sentence of seven years applies for the **B19.141** third Class A drug trafficking offence (see **E5.1**).

The guideline indicates that for category 1 (higher culpability and greater harm) the starting point is two years six months, for offence category 2 (lower culpability and greater harm, or higher culpability and lesser harm) the starting point is 36 weeks, and for offence category 3 (lower culpability and lesser harm) the starting point is a medium level community order.

Possession The guideline indicates that for possession of a Class A controlled drug the start- **B19.142** ing point is a Band C fine within a category range of a Band A fine to 51 weeks' custody. In the pre-guideline case of *Roberts* [1997] 2 Cr App R (S) 187, a prisoner serving a four-year sentence for possession of heroin with intent to supply was found to be in possession of a small quantity of heroin when searched by prison officers. The Court of Appeal stated that possession of drugs by a prisoner was more serious than possession of drugs outside prison, and upheld a consecutive sentence of 15 months' imprisonment. Possession of drugs in prison is an aggravating factor in the guideline.

Class B Drug Offences

Importation The guideline indicates that for an offender playing a 'leading role' in this **B19.143** offence, involving a Class B drug, and depending on the category of harm, the starting points are eight years (category 1), six years (category 2), or four years (category 3). For an offender playing a 'significant role', the starting points are five years six months, four years, or two years. For an offender playing a 'lesser role', the starting points are four years, two years, or one year.

In *A-G's Refs (Nos. 15, 16 & 17 of 2012) (Lewis)* [2013] 1 Cr App R (S) 289 (52), the offender Vriezen pleaded guilty to importation of 120 packages (240 kg) of methylethcathinone (street value around £3 million), 4 kg of cannabis resin (street value around £11,000) and 971 grams of moist (591 grams dry) amphetamine sulphate (street value around £9,000). The Court of Appeal found that this had been a highly professional commercial operation, and the offender played a very significant role in the chain of supply. There was little mitigation save for previous good character and a guilty plea. The Court said that the overall sentence should have been at least eight years before credit for plea, and the sentence of 42 months was increased to six years.

Supply The guideline indicates that for an offender playing a 'leading role' in the offence, **B19.144** and depending on the category of harm, the starting point is eight years (category 1), six years (category 2), four years (category 3) and 18 months (category 4). For an offender playing a 'significant role', the starting point is five years six months, four years, one year, and a high level community order. For an offender playing a 'lesser role', the starting point is three years, one year, a high level community order, or a low level community order.

B19.145   **Production**   The guideline indicates that for an offender playing a 'leading role' in the offence, and depending on the category of harm, the starting points are eight years (category 1), six years (category 2), four years (category 3) and one year (category 4). For an offender playing a 'significant role', the starting points are five years six months, four years, one year, and a high level community order. For an offender playing a 'lesser role', the starting points are three years, one year, a high level community order, and a Band C fine.

In *Healey* [2013] 1 Cr App R (S) 176 (33) the Court of Appeal dealt with a number of unrelated cases involving individual offenders growing relatively small numbers of cannabis plants in a loft or cellar, having invested in equipment for watering and lighting the plants which were intended for repeated cropping. Such offenders, displaying a 'determined approach to cultivation' play, according to the Court, a 'significant role', rather than a 'lesser role'. The offender Brearley, dealt with in *Healey*, was aged 45. He had a specially constructed room at the back of his garage, containing the usual equipment for the intensive cultivation of cannabis. At the time of arrest he had six plants but their potential yield was very high, as much as one and a third kilograms. He had spent £600 on the equipment. The offence was aggravated by involving other people to assist him crop the plants. In addition he had bypassed the electricity meter. He claimed that the product was all for his own use, and that was accepted by the judge. The Court said that the proper sentence based on a significant role, category 3, would have been 12 months after a trial, eight months on a plea of guilty. In *Bamford* [2013] 1 Cr App R (S) 26 (4), a rather similar case decided under the guideline but before the decision in *Healey*, six months' imprisonment was reduced on appeal to nine weeks on the basis of the offender's 'lesser role'. In *Descombre* [2013] 2 Cr App R (S) 345 (51) the offender had established a 'cannabis factory' in an out-building which had produced three crops of cannabis. There were 60 mature plants with a potential yield of about 5 kg. The Court approved the judge's finding that the offender performed a leading role in a commercial operation and upheld a sentence of 40 months' imprisonment following a plea of guilty. In *Lawson* [2012] EWCA Crim 1931 the offender pleaded guilty to producing cannabis and to possession of cannabis with intent to supply. A search warrant was executed at his home and a cannabis grinder, bags of herbal cannabis and weighing scales were found. There were four cannabis plants, ready for harvesting, with an estimated profit of over £5,000. The offender had many previous convictions, mainly for dishonesty. The Court of Appeal found that this was not a case of domestic production for personal use, and the element of intention to supply meant that this case was different from *Healey*. A sentence of 18 months after a trial would have been appropriate, which was reduced to 12 months following the plea of guilty.

B19.146   **Permitting Use of Premises**   The guideline indicates that for a Class B controlled drug the starting point for category 1 is one year within a category range of 26 weeks to 18 months, for category 2 the starting point is a high level community order within a category range of low level community order to 26 weeks and for category 3 the starting point is a Band C fine within a category range of a Band A fine to a low level community order.

B19.147   **Possession**   The guideline indicates that for possession of a Class B controlled drug the starting point is a Band B fine within a category range of a discharge to 26 weeks custody.

Class C Drug Offences

B19.148   **Importation**   The guideline indicates that for an offender playing a 'leading role' in this offence, involving a Class C drug, and depending on the category of harm, the starting points are five years (category 1), three years six months (category 2), or 18 months (category 3). For an offender playing a 'significant role', the starting points are three years, 18 months, or 26 weeks.

For an offender playing a 'lesser role', the starting points are 18 months, 26 weeks, or a high level community order.

Supply The guideline indicates that for an offender playing a 'leading role' in the offence, and depending on the category of harm, the starting point is five years (category 1), three years six months (category 2), 18 months (category 3) and 26 weeks (category 4). For an offender playing a 'significant role', the starting point is three years, 18 months, 26 weeks, and a high level community order. For an offender playing a 'lesser role', the starting point is 18 months, 26 weeks, a high level community order, or a low level community order.

B19.149

Sentences of 21 months and three years were appropriate on pleas of guilty for two offenders involved in the commercial supply of steroids in the pre-guideline case of *Higgins* [2011] 2 Cr App R (S) 3. In *Dalessandro* [2009] 1 Cr App R (S) 154 sentences totalling two years' imprisonment would have been appropriate for an offender who pleaded guilty to possession of various Class C drugs, including anabolic steroids and GHB, with intent to supply them to competitive bodybuilders. The sentences were in fact reduced to 18 months for reasons of delay in prosecuting the case. In *Dix* [2011] 1 Cr App R (S) 305 a sentence of 21 months was upheld on an offender who pleaded guilty to supplying ketamine on a regular basis to his friends for a profit. He was not a user of the drug. His involvement occurred over a substantial period of time and involved a substantial quantity of the drug, significantly more than that found in *Johnson* [2010] 2 Cr App R (S) 154, where 18 months' imprisonment was reduced to 12 months in the case of an offender convicted after a trial of possession of ketamine with intent to supply. Containers of the drug were found at his home in sufficient quantity to make 2,600 deals with a retail price of about £11,000.

Production The guideline indicates that for an offender playing a 'leading role' in the offence, and depending on the category of harm, the starting points are five years (category 1), three years six months (category 2), 18 months (category 3) and 26 weeks (category 4). For an offender playing a 'significant role', the starting points are three years, 18 months, 26 weeks, and a high level community order. For an offender playing a 'lesser role', the starting points are 18 months, 26 weeks, a high level community order and a Band C fine.

B19.150

Permitting Use of Premises The guideline indicates that for a Class C controlled drug the starting point for category 1 is 12 weeks within a category range of high level community order to 26 weeks (although when tried summarily the maximum penalty is 12 weeks), for category 2 the starting point is a low level community order within a category range of a Band C fine to a high level community order and for category 3 the starting point is a Band A fine within a category range of a discharge to a Band C fine.

B19.151

Possession The guideline indicates that for possession of a Class C controlled drug the starting point is a Band A fine within a category range of a discharge to a medium level community order.

B19.152

Section B20   Offences Relating to Dangerous Dogs and Animal Welfare

OFFENCES UNDER THE DANGEROUS DOGS ACT 1991

Control and Possession of Dogs Bred for Fighting

B20.1 The Dangerous Dogs Act 1991, s. 1, controls the possession, disposal and breeding of pit bull terriers. It also applies to the Japanese tosa, dogo Argentino and fila Braziliero. In *Knightsbridge Crown Court, ex parte Dunne* [1994] 4 All ER 491, it was held that s. 1 applies to dogs possessing a substantial number of breed characteristics, even if some other characteristics are missing. Some pit bull/Staffordshire crosses may therefore fall within s. 1. As to the burden of proof, s. 5(5) provides:

> If in any proceedings it is alleged by the prosecution that a dog is one to which section 1...applies it shall be presumed that it is such a dog unless the contrary is shown by the accused by such evidence as the court considers sufficient; and the accused shall not be permitted to adduce such evidence unless he has given the prosecution notice of his intention to do so not later than the 14th day before that on which the evidence is to be adduced.

Section 5(5) applies only to criminal proceedings and not where a destruction order is sought without a prosecution (*Walton Street Magistrates' Court, ex parte Crothers* (1996) 160 JP 427). In *Bates v UK* (1996) Appln 26280/95, 16 January, the European Human Rights Commission considered the burden imposed by s. 5(5) to be compatible with the presumption of innocence under the ECHR, Article 6(2), but this is difficult to reconcile with *Lambert* [2002] 2 AC 545. It may yet be necessary for s. 5 to be reinterpreted as imposing only an evidential burden on the defence (see **F3.18**).

B20.2 **Offences**   Under s. 1(3) of the Act, it is an offence to possess or have custody of any dog to which s. 1 applies (except under a power of seizure or a destruction order), unless a certificate of exemption has been obtained from DEFRA and its terms complied with (see s. 1(5), the Dangerous Dogs Compensation and Exemption Schemes Order 1991 (SI 1991 No. 1744) and the Dangerous Dogs (Amendment) Act 1997, s. 4(1)). Section 1(2) of the 1991 Act creates further offences:

Dangerous Dogs Act 1991, s. 1

(2) No person shall—
    (a) breed, or breed from, a dog to which this section applies;
    (b) sell or exchange such a dog or offer, advertise or expose such a dog for sale or exchange;
    (c) make or offer to make a gift of such a dog or advertise or expose such a dog as a gift;
    (d) allow such a dog of which he is the owner or of which he is for the time being in charge to be in a public place without being muzzled and kept on a lead; or
    (e) abandon such a dog of which he is the owner or, being the owner or for the time being in charge of such a dog, allow it to stray.

B20.3 **Penalties and Defences in relation to Offences under s. 1**

Dangerous Dogs Act 1991, s. 1

(7) Any person who contravenes this section is guilty of an offence and liable on summary conviction to imprisonment for a term not exceeding six months or a fine not exceeding level 5 on the

standard scale or both except that a person who publishes an advertisement in contravention of subsection 2(b) or (c)—
- (a) shall not on being convicted be liable to imprisonment if he shows that he published the advertisement to the order of someone else and did not himself devise it; and
- (b) shall not be convicted if, in addition, he shows that he did not know and had no reasonable cause to suspect that it related to a dog to which this section applies.

Voluntary intoxication is no defence to a charge under s. 1(7) (*DPP v Kellett* [1994] Crim LR 916). Indeed it seems clear from s. 1(7)(b) that the offence is one of strict liability, as are those created by s. 3 (see **B20.5**). The definitive sentencing guideline on *Dangerous Dog Offences* (see Supplement, SG-595) applies to all offenders aged 18 and over sentenced on or after 20 August 2012. The guidelines apply, *inter alia*, to the offences under s. 1(2) and (3). As to disqualification and destruction orders, see **B20.11**.

Definitions   The term 'advertisement' is defined in the Dangerous Dogs Act 1991, s. 10(2), **B20.4** as including any means of bringing a matter to the attention of the public; 'public place' is defined in s. 10(2) as meaning any street, road or other place to which the public have or are permitted access, whether for payment or otherwise (*Cummings v DPP* (1999) *The Times*, 26 March 1999), and includes the common parts of a building containing two or more separate dwellings. A pit bull terrier sitting in a car parked in a public place is itself in a public place and must be muzzled in accordance with s. 1(2)(d) (*Bates v DPP* (1993) 157 JP 1004). Muzzling remains necessary even if the dog is ill and would be distressed by muzzling; no defence of necessity applies in such circumstances (*Cichon v DPP* [1994] Crim LR 918). However, a private path or driveway is not a public place merely because visitors or postmen may use it when calling on the owner (*Fellowes v DPP* (1993) 157 JP 936) The same may be true even of a shared driveway, if this is private property (*Bogdal* (2008) 172 JP 178; and see also *C* [2007] EWCA Crim 1757).

Dangerous Dogs Act 1991, ss. 6 and 7

6. Where a dog is owned by a person who is less than sixteen years old any reference to its owner in section 1(2)(d) or (e) or 3 above shall include a reference to the head of the household, if any, of which that person is a member or, in Scotland, to the person who has his actual care and control.
7.—(1) In this Act—
- (a) references to a dog being muzzled are to its being securely fitted with a muzzle sufficient to prevent it biting any person; and
- (b) references to its being kept on a lead are to its being securely held on a lead by a person who is not less than sixteen years old.
(2) [Power of Secretary of State to prescribe the type of muzzle or lead to be used.]

Failing to Keep Dogs under Proper Control

The offences of failing to keep a dog under proper control have been significantly amended **B20.5** by the ABCPA 2014, with effect from 13 May 2014. The text below shows the relevant provision as amended. For the unamended version, see the 2014 edition of this work. The principal amendment involves the repeal of s. 3(3) and with it the need for any offence to take place in a public place or in a place where the dog is not permitted to be. Special provision is, however, made for 'householder' cases involving trespassers or supposed trespassers within a dwelling.

Dangerous Dogs Act 1991, s. 3

(1) If a dog is dangerously out of control in any place in England or Wales (whether or not a public place)—
- (a) the owner; and
- (b) if different, the person for the time being in charge of the dog,

is guilty of an offence, or, if the dog while so out of control injures any person or assistance dog, an aggravated offence, under this subsection.

(1A) A person ('D') is not guilty of an offence under subsection (1) in a case which is a householder case.

(1B) For the purposes of subsection (1A) 'a householder case' is a case where—

(a) the dog is dangerously out of control while in or partly in a building, or part of a building, that is a dwelling or is forces accommodation (or is both), and

(b) at that time—

(i) the person in relation to whom the dog is dangerously out of control ('V') is in, or is entering, the building or part as a trespasser, or

(ii) D (if present at that time) believed V to be in, or entering, the building or part as a trespasser.

Section 76(8B) to (8F) of the Criminal Justice and Immigration Act 2008 (use of force at place of residence) apply for the purposes of this subsection as they apply for the purposes of subsection (8A) of that section (and for those purposes the reference in section 76(8D) to subsection (8A)(d) is to be read as if it were a reference to paragraph (b)(ii) of this subsection).

(2) In proceedings for an offence under subsection (1) above against a person who is the owner of a dog but was not at the material time in charge of it, it shall be a defence for the accused to prove that the dog was at the material time in the charge of a person whom he reasonably believed to be a fit and proper person to be in charge of it.

B20.6   Sentence

Dangerous Dogs Act 1991, s. 3

(4) A person guilty of an offence under subsection (1) above other than an aggravated offence is liable on summary conviction to imprisonment for a term not exceeding six months or a fine not exceeding level 5 on the standard scale or both; and a person guilty of an aggravated offence under that subsection is liable—

(a) on summary conviction, to imprisonment for a term not exceeding six months or a fine not exceeding the statutory maximum or both;

(b) on conviction on indictment, to imprisonment for a term not exceeding the relevant maximum specified in subsection (4A) or a fine or both.

(4A) For the purposes of subsection (4)(b), the relevant maximum is—

(a) 14 years if a person dies as a result of being injured;

(b) 5 years in any other case where a person is injured;

(c) 3 years in any case where an assistance dog is injured (whether or not it dies).

The definitive sentencing guideline on *Dangerous Dog Offences* (see Supplement, **SG-595**) applies to all offenders aged 18 and over sentenced on or after 20 August 2012. The guidelines apply, *inter alia*, to the offences under s. 3(1), (3)(a) and (3)(b). Note that the guidelines pre-date the amendments made by the ABCPA 2014 (see **B20.5**).

A sentence of six months' imprisonment, suspended for 12 months, was upheld following a guilty plea in *Murphy* [2013] 2 Cr App R (S) 448 (70). The offender's dog, a Staffordshire bull terrier cross, which was known to be aggressive, attacked and killed another man's dog and bit the man when he tried to rescue his dog. The Court of Appeal said that there had been greater harm and, since the offender had behaved recklessly and had done nothing to restrain his dog, there was higher culpability and the judge was entitled to treat it as a category 1 offence.

In *Cox* [2004] 2 Cr App R (S) 287 the Court of Appeal reduced a term of nine months' imprisonment to one of three months in a case where a woman pleaded guilty to an aggravated offence under s. 3(1) of the 1991 Act. Dogs belonging to the offender had escaped from her property and attacked a seven-year-old boy, causing multiple wounds which required surgery. Leveson J said that the available maximum penalty in such a case was two years, and the legislation required that the courts should look to the consequences of the offence. The sentence was, however, too long given that the offender was a woman of good character who had pleaded guilty. See also *Shallow* [2012] 1 Cr App R (S) 197.

Alternative Verdict   When D is charged on indictment with an aggravated offence it is not open to a jury to convict D of a simple (non-aggravated) offence because, by s. 3(4), such an offence is summary only and is not specified for the purposes of the CLA 1967, s. 6(3) (*Williams* [2011] EWCA Crim 1716).

Actus Reus   Save where s. 3(1A) applies ('householder cases') and provided that the offence is alleged to have occurred after 1 October 2014 (see **B20.5**), it no longer matters whether a dog is out of control on the owner's property or elsewhere. An aggravated offence may now be committed where, for example, D's dog bites a visitor inside his house, a postman walking up his front path, or somebody stealing strawberries in his garden.

The question whether someone other than the owner is 'in charge' of the dog is one of fact and degree and should ordinarily be left to the jury (*Rawlings* [1994] Crim LR 433). More than one person may be in charge of a dog at any given time (*L v CPS* (2010) 174 JP 209). As to the scope of the defence under s. 3(2), see *Huddart* [1999] Crim LR 568.

The offences created by s. 3(1) may be committed by both the owner (subject to the s. 3(2) defence) *and* the person in charge of the dog. The owner is not exempt from liability just because someone else is in charge of the dog at the time.

Under s. 3, the type of dog is irrelevant; it is enough to show that it was dangerously out of control. Section 10(3) provides:

> ...a dog shall be regarded as dangerously out of control on any occasion on which there are grounds for reasonable apprehension that it will injure any person, whether or not it actually does so, but references to a dog injuring a person or there being grounds for reasonable apprehension that it will do so do not include references to any case in which the dog is being used for a lawful purpose by a constable or a person in the service of the Crown.

It is submitted that references to dogs injuring persons must, in this context, be confined to bites, etc., directly inflicted by dogs and should not include traffic injuries indirectly caused by dogs running loose on a road, but the point has yet to be decided in the courts.

A dog may be dangerously out of control even when on a lead, if its handler cannot properly control or restrain it (*Gedminintaite* [2008] EWCA Crim 814). By s. 10(3) liability can arise only where the dog behaves in such a way that there are 'reasonable grounds for apprehension that it will injure any person', but in *Rafiq v DPP* (1997) 161 JP 412 it was held that, even if a dog bites without warning, 'this is itself capable of being conduct giving grounds for reasonable apprehension of injury'. Anyone witnessing it is likely to fear it will cause further harm.

Even where it seems likely that a dog may injure someone, the words 'dangerously out of control' must be given their natural meaning. If, for example, X teases Y's dog in a cruel and stupid way, it may be apparent to any onlooker that X is likely to be bitten unless he desists, but it does not follow that the dog is out of control.

Where the dog is owned by a person under the age of 16, s. 6 (see **B20.4**) applies.

Strict Liability   It is clear that s. 3 imposes strict liability. It was enacted for reasons of public safety, and would become very much harder to enforce if some fault element, such as negligence, had to be proved against the owner or handler of a dog which becomes dangerously out of control. It therefore places the onus squarely upon dog owners, etc., to ensure their dogs are kept under control (*Bezzina* [1994] 3 All ER 964). But, although this provision creates an offence of 'situational liability' and does not specify how or why the dog may have come to be thus out of control, the Court of Appeal in *Robinson-Pierre* [2014] 1 Cr App R 305 (22) rejected an argument that Parliament intended liability to be absolute, 'in the sense that criminal liability may follow notwithstanding the absence of any act or omission of the defendant contributing to the prohibited state of affairs'. The offence instead requires 'proof of an act or omission by the defendant (with or without fault) that to some more than minimal degree caused or permitted the prohibited state of affairs to come about' (per Pitchford LJ at [42]). It follows that a defendant cannot properly be convicted if the dog in question was allowed to get out of control as a result of third-party acts or omissions that he did not cause and had no power to control or prevent.

Seizure

B20.10 The Dangerous Dogs Act 1991, s. 5(1), provides for the seizure of dogs to which s. 1 of the Act applies or dogs that appear to be dangerously out of control in a public place. Section 5(2) deals with warrants for the seizure of dogs on private premises. Guidance as to enforcement is provided by Defra (see *Dangerous dogs law: Guidance for enforcers* at https://www.gov.uk/government/publications/dangerous-dogs-law-guidance-for-enforcers).

Destruction and Disqualification

B20.11
Dangerous Dogs Act 1991, ss. 4 and 4A

4.—(1) Where a person is convicted of an offence under section 1 or 3(1) above or of an offence under an order made under section 2 above the court—
- (a) may order the destruction of any dog in respect of which the offence was committed and, subject to subsection (1A) below, shall do so in the case of an offence under section 1 or an aggravated offence under section 3(1) above; and
- (b) may order the offender to be disqualified, for such period as the court thinks fit, for having custody of a dog.

(1A) Nothing in subsection (1)(a) above shall require the court to order the destruction of a dog if the court is satisfied—
- (a) that the dog would not constitute a danger to public safety; and
- (b) where the dog was born before 30th November 1991 and is subject to the prohibition in section 1(3) above, that there is a good reason why the dog has not been exempted from that prohibition.

(1B) For the purposes of subsection (1A)(a), when deciding whether a dog would constitute a danger to public safety, the court—
- (a) must consider—
  - (i) the temperament of the dog and its past behaviour, and
  - (ii) whether the owner of the dog, or the person for the time being in charge of it, is a fit and proper person to be in charge of the dog, and
- (b) may consider any other relevant circumstances.

(2) Where a court makes an order under subsection (1)(a) above for the destruction of a dog owned by a person other than the offender, the owner may appeal to the Crown Court against the order.

(3) A dog shall not be destroyed pursuant to an order under subsection (1)(a) above—
- (a) until the end of the period for giving notice of appeal against the conviction, or against the order; and
- (b) if notice of appeal is given within that period, until the appeal is determined or withdrawn,

unless the offender and, in a case to which subsection (2) above applies, the owner of the dog give notice to the court that made the order that there is to be no appeal.

(4) Where a court makes an order under subsection (1)(a) above it may—
- (a) appoint a person to undertake the destruction of the dog and require any person having custody of it to deliver it up for that purpose; and
- (b) order the offender to pay such sum as the court may determine to be the reasonable expenses of destroying the dog and of keeping it pending its destruction.

(5) Any sum ordered to be paid under subsection (4)(b) above shall be treated for the purposes of enforcement as if it were a fine imposed on conviction.

4A.—(1) Where—
- (a) a person is convicted of an offence under section 1 above or an aggravated offence under section 3(1) above;
- (b) the court does not order the destruction of the dog under section 4(1)(a) above; and
- (c) in the case of an offence under section 1 above, the dog is subject to the prohibition in section 1(3) above,

the court shall order that, unless the dog is exempted from that prohibition within the requisite period, the dog shall be destroyed.

(2) Where an order is made under subsection (1) above in respect of a dog, and the dog is not exempted from the prohibition in section 1(3) above within the requisite period, the court may extend that period.

(3) Subject to subsection (2) above, the requisite period for the purposes of such an order is the period of two months beginning with the date of the order.

(4) Where a person is convicted of an offence under section 3(1) above, the court may order that, unless the owner of the dog keeps it under proper control, the dog shall be destroyed.

(5) An order under subsection (4) above—

 (a) may specify the measures to be taken for keeping the dog under proper control, whether by muzzling, keeping on a lead, excluding it from specified places or otherwise; and

 (b) if it appears to the court that the dog is a male and would be less dangerous if neutered, may require it to be neutered.

(6) Subsections (2) to (4) of section 4 above shall apply in relation to an order under subsection (1) or (4) above as they apply in relation to an order under subsection (1)(a) of that section.

Any person who has custody of a dog in contravention of s. 4(1)(b), or who fails to comply with a requirement imposed on him under s. 4(4)(a) commits a summary offence and is liable to a fine not exceeding level 5 on the standard scale (s. 4(8)). **B20.12**

The considerations listed in s. 4(1B) were in practice taken into account even before that provision was inserted by the ABCPA 2014. In *Flack* [2008] 2 Cr App R (S) 395 (a case involving an aggravated offence under s. 3(1)), it was held that a 'suspended destruction order' was appropriate in a case where D was a conscientious dog owner of good character, and where the dog had not previously been aggressive. D was ordered to comply with conditions relating to the muzzling of the dog, that the dog wear a special collar and be kept on a lead at all times in public. See also *Davies* (2010) 174 JP 514 (order conditional on muzzling and keeping under control on a lead), *Harry* [2010] 2 Cr App R (S) 626 (conditional on neutering); *Devon* [2011] EWCA Crim 1073 (conditional on rehousing with suitable owners) and *Singh* [2013] EWCA Crim 2416 (conditional on muzzling, neutering and keeping on a lead).

Sections 4 and 4A were further examined by Collins J in *Kelleher v DPP* (2012) 176 JP 729, **B20.13** with particular reference to the distinction between aggravated and non-aggravated offences under s. 3 and the burden of proof governing destruction orders in each case. He said (at [11], [12] and [15]):

> It is clear that section 4A(4) applies both to aggravated and non-aggravated offences. The power to make a destruction order applies in both cases…in the case of an aggravated offence the burden is on the defendant to show that the dog is not a danger to public safety, otherwise a destruction order is mandatory. It is, as it were, the other way around in the case of a non-aggravated offence: the court will not make a destruction order unless, on the material, the court takes the view that a destruction order is necessary

> The test, which, as it seems to me, should be applied in either case, essentially relates to whether the dog is a danger to the public. If it is, whichever way round, as it were, the burden lies for showing it, then the destruction order is appropriate. What the court must do in the case of a non-aggravated offence is to decide whether, on the basis that the dog is a danger to the public, a destruction order should follow. However, section 4A enables the court, instead of making an immediate destruction order, to make what is described as a 'contingent destruction order', that is to say a destruction order unless the dog is kept under proper control by whatever measures are considered to be appropriate…

> The court is only required to make a destruction order in the case of a pit bull or an aggravated offence [under s. 3]. Accordingly section 4(1A), as it seems to me, cannot have been intended to apply to non-aggravated offences and discretionary orders.

As to cases involving pit bulls etc. and offences under s. 1(3), see *Baballa* [2011] 1 Cr App R (S) 329 and *R (Sandhu) v Isleworth Crown Court* (2012) 176 JP 537. The only conditions that may be imposed when making a contingent destruction order in relation to a dog falling under s. 1 are those that may be imposed under the Dangerous Dogs Compensation and Exemption Schemes Order 1991 (see *Sandhu* and **B20.2**).

As to the making of destruction orders otherwise than on conviction (i.e. where the proceedings are not strictly criminal), see *Walton Street Magistrates' Court, ex parte Crothers* (1996) 160 JP 427 and s. 4B.

B20.14   In deciding whether to make a disqualification order and whether to order the forfeiture of any dog, a court may have regard to any voluntary undertaking offered by D as to his future conduct (*Haynes* [2004] 2 Cr App R (S) 36; see also *Singh* [2013] EWCA Crim 2416).

In *Holland* [2003] 1 Cr App R (S) 288 (a case involving an aggravated offence under s. 3(3)(a) in which the grandchild of D's neighbour was attacked by D's bull terrier in the neighbour's own garden), it was held that a disqualification order was appropriate in addition to the destruction of the dog, and that such an order could not solely limit D from keeping dangerous dogs but would necessarily ban her from keeping any dog at all. It was open to her to apply to have the disqualification lifted after one year, but the success of such an application might turn on the breed she intended to keep, the security of her property and who her neighbours were at that time.

OTHER OFFENCES RELATING TO DANGEROUS DOGS

B20.15   The Dangerous Dogs Act 1991 does not reduce the powers of courts under the Dogs Act 1871, s. 2. Orders requiring the destruction or proper control of dangerous dogs may still be made under that provision, whether or not any person has been injured, and may require a dog to be muzzled and/or castrated (Dangerous Dogs Act 1991, s. 3(5) and (6)). Under the Dangerous Dogs Act 1989, s. 1(3), it is an offence, punishable on summary conviction by a fine not exceeding level 3 on the standard scale, not to comply with a control or destruction order; and where under that Act an owner has been disqualified from having custody of a dog, contravention of that order is punishable by a fine not exceeding level 5 on the standard scale (Dangerous Dogs Act 1989, s. 1(6)).

Control of Guard Dogs

B20.16   Guard Dogs Act 1975, s. 1

(1) A person shall not use or permit the use of a guard dog at any premises unless a person ('the handler') who is capable of controlling the dog is present on the premises and the dog is under the control of the handler at all times while it is being so used except while it is secured so that it is not at liberty to go freely about the premises.
(2) The handler of a guard dog shall keep the dog under his control at all times while it is being used as a guard dog at any premises except—
    (a) while another handler has control over the dog; or
    (b) while the dog is secured so that it is not at liberty to go freely about the premises.
(3) A person shall not use or permit the use of a guard dog at any premises unless a notice containing a warning that a guard dog is present is clearly exhibited at each entrance to the premises.

Under the Guard Dogs Act 1975, s. 5, non-compliance with s. 1 is an offence punishable on summary conviction by a fine not exceeding level 5 on the standard scale.

Before any liability can be imposed under the Guard Dogs Act 1975, it must be proved or admitted that the dog was being used 'to protect — (a) premises; or (b) property kept on the premises; or (c) a person guarding the premises or such property' (s. 7). It is not enough that a large dog (even one kept on commercial premises) may have developed a 'guard dog's instinct' (*Kelly v DPP* [2008] EWHC 597 (Admin)).

OFFENCES UNDER THE ANIMAL WELFARE ACT 2006

The principal provisions of the Animal Welfare Act 2006 came into force in England on 6 **B20.17**
April 2007 and in Wales on 28 March 2007. A number of other provisions relating to animals
and animal welfare remain in force, including substantial parts of the Performing Animals
(Regulation) Act 1925, the Pet Animals Act 1951, the Animal Boarding Establishments Act
1963, the Riding Establishments Acts 1964 and 1970, the Breeding of Dogs Acts 1973 and
1991 and the Sale of Dogs (Welfare) Act 1999.

The Animal Welfare Act 2006 does not apply to any invertebrate creature (see s. 1(1) and (5)),
nor to any foetus or embryo (s. 1(2)), but regulations made under the Act may amend its scope
in either respect in accordance with s. 1(3) and (4).

The protection of the Act extends only to 'protected animals'. A protected animal is defined
in s. 2 as one of a kind commonly domesticated in the British Isles or one which is under the
control of man (whether on a permanent or temporary basis) or not living in a wild state. Feral
cats and stray dogs fall within this definition, as do pets, farm animals, animals kept in zoos or
wildlife parks, and animals which may recently have escaped from human control, but which
are not yet 'living wild'. Wild animals such as foxes or badgers are not ordinarily protected under
the Act, but any that have been captured or rescued are protected for as long as they remain in
care or captivity. As to the prohibition of certain cruel or potentially cruel methods of taking or
killing wild animals, see the Wildlife and Countryside Act 1981, s. 11. Captive wild birds may
be protected both under the 2006 Act and under s. 8 of the 1981 Act (*R (RSPCA) v Shinton*
(2003) 167 JP 512).

Some offences under the Act can be committed only by a person who is 'responsible for an **B20.18**
animal'. An animal for which some person is responsible (such as a pet rat) must necessarily
be a protected animal, even if other animals of the same species, living wild, would not be.

By s. 3, a person may be responsible for an animal either on a permanent or temporary basis.
Persons running boarding kennels or veterinary practices clearly have temporary responsibility
for animals in their care, but responsibility may also extend to a person who agrees to feed, clean
and water his neighbour's animals for a few days. A person who owns an animal shall always be
regarded as responsible for it, but references to being responsible for an animal include being
in charge of it; and by s. 3(4) a person shall be treated as responsible for any animal for which a
person under the age of 16 years of whom he has actual care and control is responsible. For an
illustration of the kind of case in which this rule may be important, see *R (RSPCA) v C* (2006)
170 JP 463 and **B20.28**.

By ss. 58 and 59, nothing in the Act applies to anything lawfully done under the Animals **B20.19**
(Scientific Procedures) Act 1986 or to anything which occurs in the normal course of fishing.
As to application to the Crown, see s. 60; as to the liability of directors, managers and officers
for offences committed by bodies corporate, see s. 57.

The only offences examined in this work are those created by ss. 4, 7, 8 and 9. Offences to which
reference must be made elsewhere include those concerned with the docking of dogs' tails and
other prohibited procedures involving protected animals (ss. 5 and 6, together with associated
regulations), the unlawful transfer of animals by way of sale or prize to children under the age of
16 (s. 11), and the unlicensed commission of specified activities for which a licence under the
Act is required (s. 13).

Prosecutions

The Animal Welfare Act 2006, s. 30, permits prosecutions to be brought by local authorities. **B20.20**
No specific provision is made for prosecutions to be brought by the RSPCA, but it retains (and
exercises) its common-law power to prosecute, and in *Lamont-Perkins v RSPCA* (2012) 176 JP

369 it was held that any prosecutor, including the RSPCA, may in appropriate cases invoke the provisions of s. 31.

Animal Welfare Act 2006, s. 31

(1) Notwithstanding anything in section 127(1) of the Magistrates' Courts Act 1980, a magistrates' court may try an information relating to an offence under this Act if the information is laid—

   (a) before the end of the period of three years beginning with the date of the commission of the offence, and

   (b) before the end of the period of six months beginning with the date on which evidence which the prosecutor thinks is sufficient to justify the proceedings comes to his knowledge.

(2) For the purposes of subsection (1)(b)—

   (a) a certificate signed by or on behalf of the prosecutor and stating the date on which such evidence came to his knowledge shall be conclusive evidence of that fact, and

   (b) a certificate stating that matter and purporting to be so signed shall be treated as so signed unless the contrary is proved.

Section 31 was considered by the Divisional Court in *RSPCA v King* [2010] EWHC 637 (Admin). The court concluded that a prosecutor can avail himself of the benefits of a s. 31 certificate only if that certificate fully complies with the statutory requirements. An unsigned file copy of a missing certificate does not so comply, even if accompanied by a signed letter stating that such a certificate was indeed signed and issued.

Subject to those requirements, such a certificate is ordinarily conclusive and may be challenged only on the basis that it constitutes a fraud or on the basis that it is plainly wrong (*Lamont-Perkins v RSPCA*), but in *RSPCA v King* Toulson LJ considered (*obiter*) whether a certificate would be valid if issued only after commencement of the proceedings:

> There is no requirement in terms of the statute that a certificate for the purposes of section 31(2) must come into existence prior to the commencement of legal proceedings. [Counsel] submitted as a matter of statutory construction that that should be read into the Act as Parliament's intention. She submitted that it would be objectionable if, for example, in a case where no such certificate had been issued and the defence had explored the question of date of knowledge in the evidence, and there was real reason to suppose that the prosecution would not be able to demonstrate that the proceedings were begun in time, for that inquiry to be cut off conclusively by the issue of a certificate. Were such a scenario to arise one can envisage issues about whether the making of such a certificate would be in good faith but in my judgment it is unnecessary to deal with any such arguments in this case. The matter would be better left to be dealt with on actual facts if such a situation were to arise.

Penalties and Orders

B20.21   Offences under the Animal Welfare Act 2006 are triable only summarily. The maximum penalty in respect of any of the offences considered below (other than an offence under s. 9 or s. 34(9)) is imprisonment for a term not exceeding 51 weeks, or a fine not exceeding £20,000, or both. The maximum penalty for an offence under s. 9 or s. 34(9) is similar, save that the fine may not exceed level 5 on the standard scale (s. 32). The *Magistrates' Court Sentencing Guidelines* on animal cruelty apply (see Supplement, **SG-238**).

On conviction, a person may be deprived of the animal in question (s. 33), and may be disqualified from owning, keeping or participating in the keeping of animals (s. 34(2)), disqualified from dealing in animals (s. 34(3)) and/or disqualified from transporting or arranging for the transport of animals (s. 34(4)), but such an order cannot prevent him from living at an address where animals are kept by other members of the same household (*Patterson v RSPCA* [2013] EWHC 4531 (Admin)). As to what may amount to 'keeping' an animal, see *R (Arthur) v RSPCA* (2005) 169 JP 676. Disqualification may be ordered in respect of animals generally or in respect of animals of one or more kinds (s. 34(5)) and may be made for such period as the court thinks fit (s. 34(1) and see *Ward* [2010] EWHC 347 (Admin)). However, disqualification must ordinarily extend to each of the relevant activities specified in the subsection under which the order is made (*R (RSPCA) v Guildford Crown Court* (2013) 177 JP 154). So a court cannot ordinarily make or vary an order under s. 34(2) by disqualifying D from keeping animals while at the same time permitting him to participate in the keeping of such animals, unless perhaps the HRA 1998, s. 3, requires such an interpretation of s. 34. Breach of a disqualification order is an offence under s. 34(9).

Section 34 does not address the problem that arose in *R (RSPCA) v Chester Crown Court* (2006) 170 JP 725, in which the court reluctantly concluded that a disqualification under the Protection of Animals Act 1911, s. 1, could not impose a limit on the number of animals that could be kept. Sedley J suggested in that case that, 'Parliament [may] want to consider whether [that] kind of order…should not be authorised by future animal protection legislation', but the new legislation makes no such provision.

As to the seizure of animals in connection with a disqualification order, see ss. 35 and 36. As to the making of orders for the destruction of animals, see ss. 37 and 38. As to the forfeiture of equipment used in connection with offences, see s. 40. As to the cancellation of licences or the disqualification of a person from holding a licence, see s. 42.

Unnecessary Suffering

Animal Welfare Act 2006, s. 4 **B20.22**

(1) A person commits an offence if—
  (a) an act of his, or a failure of his to act, causes an animal to suffer,
  (b) he knew, or ought reasonably to have known, that the act, or failure to act, would have that effect or be likely to do so,
  (c) the animal is a protected animal, and
  (d) the suffering is unnecessary.
(2) A person commits an offence if—
  (a) he is responsible for an animal,
  (b) an act, or failure to act, of another person causes the animal to suffer,
  (c) he permitted that to happen or failed to take such steps (whether by way of supervising the other person or otherwise) as were reasonable in all the circumstances to prevent that happening, and
  (d) the suffering is unnecessary.
(3) The considerations to which it is relevant to have regard when determining for the purposes of this section whether suffering is unnecessary include—
  (a) whether the suffering could reasonably have been avoided or reduced;
  (b) whether the conduct which caused the suffering was in compliance with any relevant enactment or any relevant provisions of a licence or code of practice issued under an enactment;
  (c) whether the conduct which caused the suffering was for a legitimate purpose, such as—
    (i) the purpose of benefiting the animal, or
    (ii) the purpose of protecting a person, property or another animal;
  (d) whether the suffering was proportionate to the purpose of the conduct concerned;
  (e) whether the conduct concerned was in all the circumstances that of a reasonably competent and humane person.
(4) Nothing in this section applies to the destruction of an animal in an appropriate and humane manner.

The offence created by s. 4(1) extends to omissions as well as to positive acts, and to men- **B20.23** tal suffering as well as physical (see s. 62(1)); but on general principles an omission can be seen as 'causing' suffering only in cases where the person in question was under a duty to prevent it. Thus, if D ignores the suffering of an injured dog he finds lying in the road he will ordinarily commit no offence; but if D was himself responsible for the injury (or care of the dog), he may be under a duty to mitigate the animal's suffering. See generally **A1.14** *et seq.*

The *mens rea* required for an offence under s. 4 was considered in *R (Gray) v Aylesbury Crown Court* [2013] 3 All ER 346. It must be proved that D knew, or ought reasonably to have known, both that his conduct would cause an animal to suffer and that the suffering was unnecessary. He would commit no offence if he acted in the honest and reasonable, albeit mistaken, belief that he was doing what was necessary for the animal's welfare. But ignorance of an animal's illness or condition may not necessarily be a defence, because a person having care of an animal must ensure that it is inspected sufficiently regularly for conditions that would cause suffering to be brought to veterinary attention (*Patterson v RSPCA* [2013] EWHC 4531 (Admin)).

Section 4(3) requires allowance to be made for a number of possible factors when determining whether any suffering was 'unnecessary'. Police horses used for riot control may, for example, be exposed to a risk of injury from flying stones or even petrol bombs, but their exposure to such risks may be considered necessary.

Administration of Poisons

B20.24

Animal Welfare Act 2006, s. 7

(1) A person commits an offence if, without lawful authority or reasonable excuse, he—
  (a) administers any poisonous or injurious drug or substance to a protected animal, knowing it to be poisonous or injurious, or
  (b) causes any poisonous or injurious drug or substance to be taken by a protected animal, knowing it to be poisonous or injurious.
(2) A person commits an offence if—
  (a) he is responsible for an animal,
  (b) without lawful authority or reasonable excuse, another person administers a poisonous or injurious drug or substance to the animal or causes the animal to take such a drug or substance, and
  (c) he permitted that to happen or, knowing the drug or substance to be poisonous or injurious, he failed to take such steps (whether by way of supervising the other person or otherwise) as were reasonable in all the circumstances to prevent that happening.
(3) In this section, references to a poisonous or injurious drug or substance include a drug or substance which, by virtue of the quantity or manner in which it is administered or taken, has the effect of a poisonous or injurious drug or substance.

This provision, which replaces the offence of wilful poisoning formerly contained in the Protection of Animals Act 1911, s. 1(1)(d), is not intended to cover cases of accidental poisoning. According to the accompanying notes for guidance, the term 'administer' should be understood as indicating a deliberate action.

Animal Fights and Related Activities

B20.25

Animal Welfare Act 2006, s. 8

(1) A person commits an offence if he—
  (a) causes an animal fight to take place, or attempts to do so;
  (b) knowingly receives money for admission to an animal fight;
  (c) knowingly publicises a proposed animal fight;
  (d) provides information about an animal fight to another with the intention of enabling or encouraging attendance at the fight;
  (e) makes or accepts a bet on the outcome of an animal fight or on the likelihood of anything occurring or not occurring in the course of an animal fight;
  (f) takes part in an animal fight;
  (g) has in his possession anything designed or adapted for use in connection with an animal fight with the intention of its being so used;
  (h) keeps or trains an animal for use for in connection with an animal fight;

    (i) keeps any premises for use for an animal fight.

(2) A person commits an offence if, without lawful authority or reasonable excuse, he is present at an animal fight.

(3) A person commits an offence if, without lawful authority or reasonable excuse, he—

    (a) knowingly supplies a video recording of an animal fight,

    (b) knowingly publishes a video recording of an animal fight,

    (c) knowingly shows a video recording of an animal fight to another, or

    (d) possesses a video recording of an animal fight, knowing it to be such a recording, with the intention of supplying it.

(4) Subsection (3) does not apply if the video recording is of an animal fight that took place—

    (a) outside Great Britain, or

    (b) before the commencement date.

(5) Subsection (3) does not apply—

    (a) in the case of paragraph (a), to the supply of a video recording for inclusion in a programme service;

    (b) in the case of paragraph (b) or (c), to the publication or showing of a video recording by means of its inclusion in a programme service;

    (c) in the case of paragraph (d), by virtue of intention to supply for inclusion in a programme service.

Note that s. 8(3) to (5) have not yet been brought into force.

B20.26 This provision targets a wide range of activities connected with animal fights — defined as 'an occasion on which a protected animal is placed with an animal, or with a human, for the purpose of fighting, wrestling or baiting' (s. 8(7)). A wild animal, such as a badger, which has been captured for the purpose of being baited by dogs, will itself be a protected animal whilst in captivity.

Section 8 does not proscribe the use of an animal (such as a terrier or ferret) for legitimate pest control or the video-recording of an animal being used for such a purpose. Where, however, pest control is combined with sport or betting (e.g., betting on the number of rats killed by a terrier) it would appear to fall within the scope of s. 8.

The Welfare Offence

B20.27

Animal Welfare Act 2006, s. 9

(1) A person commits an offence if he does not take such steps as are reasonable in all the circumstances to ensure that the needs of an animal for which he is responsible are met to the extent required by good practice.

(2) For the purposes of this Act, an animal's needs shall be taken to include—

    (a) its need for a suitable environment,

    (b) its need for a suitable diet,

    (c) its need to be able to exhibit normal behaviour patterns,

    (d) any need it has to be housed with, or apart from, other animals, and

    (e) its need to be protected from pain, suffering, injury and disease.

(3) The circumstances to which it is relevant to have regard when applying subsection (1) include, in particular—

    (a) any lawful purpose for which the animal is kept, and

    (b) any lawful activity undertaken in relation to the animal.

(4) Nothing in this section applies to the destruction of an animal in an appropriate and humane manner.

B20.28 The current regulations applicable to farmed animals in England (Welfare of Farmed Animals (England) Regulations 2007 (SI 2007 No. 2078)) cover the welfare of all farmed animals (as defined in reg. 3), including those kept on common land. Other codes of practice deal with the welfare of cats, dogs, donkeys, rabbits, privately kept non-human primates and game birds reared for sporting purposes. The Welsh Assembly publishes codes of practice for Wales that may differ in some respects from those applicable to England.

Section 9(1) sets a purely objective standard of care which a person responsible for an animal is required to provide (*R (Gray) v Aylesbury Crown Court* [2013] 3 All ER 346). There is some potential overlap between s. 9 and s. 4 of the Act (see **B20.22**). Where, for example, an animal that requires human care is abandoned, or deprived of essential veterinary care, an offence will ordinarily be committed under s. 9; if as is likely, this leads to suffering (cold, hunger, distress, etc.) there may be a further offence under s. 4. There should however be no conviction and certainly no penalty imposed under s. 9 where the facts relied upon for that conviction are essentially the same as those that gave rise to a conviction under s. 4; but that may not be the case where (as in *Gray*) the s. 9 conviction relates to different incidents and/or different or additional animals.

Although the test under s. 9 is an objective one, it may be necessary for a court to consider, not just whether the animal(s) in question received a reasonable standard of care, but whether the accused acted reasonably in the particular circumstances with which he was faced. In *R (RSPCA) v C* (2006) 170 JP 463, in which a girl aged 15 was charged under the Protection of Animals Act 1911, s. 1, with causing unnecessary suffering to her cat by 'unreasonably' failing to secure essential veterinary treatment for it, it was held that account must be taken of her youth and of the fact that she had been told by her father (who pleaded guilty) that no such treatment was required. Newman J said (at [15]):

> The issue which the justices had to decide was whether or not this...girl had acted reasonably or unreasonably in acceding to the opinion her father had expressed...That involved considering whether it was reasonable for her to go along with her father's view of the position, having regard to her age and position in the household, whether it was for her to take any other action, as she could have done, and whether it was reasonable or unreasonable for her to fail to take that other action.

Cases decided under the 1911 Act cannot necessarily be relied upon when construing provisions of the 2006 Act (a point strongly emphasised in *R (Gray) v Aylesbury Crown Court*), but the reasoning in *R (RSPCA) v C* appears wholly consistent with the wording of s. 9 itself so may still be considered good law.

B20.29 It remains to be seen how strictly the concept of 'good practice' will be interpreted and enforced outside the highly regulated farming context; but arguably any dog or cat owner who fails to keep his animal fully vaccinated against common diseases now risks prosecution under s. 9, because 'good practice' surely requires regular vaccination.

Section 10 of the Act enables inspectors (as defined in s. 51) to issue 'improvement notices' where they are of the opinion that s. 9 requirements are not being met. Such notices must give the responsible person time in which to rectify the problem specified in the notice; but this does not preclude the instigation of proceedings without notice for clear breaches of welfare principles.

Section B21 Offences Relating to Money Laundering and the Proceeds of Criminal Conduct

INTRODUCTION

Part 7 of the POCA 2002 creates a series of 'money laundering' offences (ss. 327 to 329) which **B21.1** (subject to the transitional arrangements explained below) have supplanted offences previously contained in the CJA 1988, ss. 93A to 93C, and the Drug Trafficking Act 1994, ss. 49 to 51. Sections 330 to 332 of the 2002 Act create offences of failure to disclose cases of suspected money laundering. The non-disclosure offences (which supplant the Drug Trafficking Act 1994, s. 52) are capable of commission only by persons in the 'regulated sector' of the financial services industry as defined in sch. 9 to the Act (as amended). The current offences differ from s. 52 of the 1994 Act in that they extend to matters concern ing the proceeds of all types of criminal conduct, and not just to those concerning the proceeds of drug trafficking. Finally, s. 333 creates an offence of 'tipping off' another person as to the fact that a report of suspected money laundering has been made, where this tip-off is likely to prejudice any subsequent investigation. This provision supplants s. 93D(2) of the 1988 Act and s. 53(2) of the 1994 Act. As to the origins, scope and purpose of part 7 generally, see parts 5 to 8 of Brooke LJ's judgment in *Bowman v Fels* [2005] 4 All ER 609.

In part 8 of the 2002 Act, s. 342 creates an offence involving conduct likely to obstruct or prejudice a money laundering, civil recovery, 'detained cash' or confiscation investigation. This goes well beyond the offences previously contained in s. 93D(1) of the 1988 Act and s. 53(1) of the 1994 Act.

Parts 7 and 8 of the Act were brought into force on 24 February 2003 (Proceeds of Crime Act **B21.2** 2002 (Commencement No. 4, Transitional Provisions and Savings) Order 2003 (SI 2003 No. 120)), but subject to article 3 of that Order. This provides that the current provisions do *not* apply where the conduct allegedly constituting an offence under those provisions began before 24 February 2003 and ended on or after that date. The old law continues to apply in such circumstances. See *Montila* [2005] 1 All ER 113, *Saik* [2007] 1 AC 18 (see **A5.55**) and *Khanani* [2009] EWCA Crim 276.

As to the power of the FCA (the successor in this respect to the FSA) to bring prosecutions for offences under the POCA 2002, see *Rollins* [2010] 4 All ER 880.

Criminal liability may also be incurred by 'relevant persons' in the financial services sector for failure to comply with requirements imposed on them by the Money Laundering Regulations 2007 (SI 2007 No. 2157). See **B21.32**.

MONEY LAUNDERING AND CRIMINAL PROPERTY

Meaning of Terms

The term 'money laundering', although widely used in the POCA 2002, is misleading. By **B21.3** s. 340(11), 'money laundering' is defined as an act which constitutes an offence under ss. 327,

1021

328 or 329, an inchoate version of such an offence, secondary participation in such an offence or an act which would constitute any of the above if it were done in the UK. The offences under ss. 327 to 329 do not, however, use the terms 'money' or 'laundering' to define their scope. They are concerned instead with 'criminal property', as defined in s. 340(2)–(10).

Proceeds of Crime Act 2002, s. 340

(2) Criminal conduct is conduct which—
  (a) constitutes an offence in any part of the United Kingdom, or
  (b) would constitute an offence in any part of the United Kingdom if it occurred there.
(3) Property is criminal property if—
  (a) it constitutes a person's benefit from criminal conduct or it represents such a benefit (in whole or part and whether directly or indirectly), and
  (b) the alleged offender knows or suspects that it constitutes or represents such a benefit.
(4) It is immaterial—
  (a) who carried out the conduct;
  (b) who benefited from it;
  (c) whether the conduct occurred before or after the passing of this Act.
(5) A person benefits from conduct if he obtains property as a result of or in connection with the conduct.
(6) If a person obtains a pecuniary advantage as a result of or in connection with conduct, he is to be taken to obtain as a result of or in connection with the conduct a sum of money equal to the value of the pecuniary advantage.
(7) References to property or a pecuniary advantage obtained in connection with conduct include references to property or a pecuniary advantage obtained in both that connection and some other.
(8) If a person benefits from conduct his benefit is the property obtained as a result of or in connection with the conduct.
(9) Property is all property wherever situated and includes—
  (a) money;
  (b) all forms of property, real or personal, heritable or moveable;
  (c) things in action and other intangible or incorporeal property.
(10) The following rules apply in relation to property—
  (a) property is obtained by a person if he obtains an interest in it;
  (b) references to an interest, in relation to land in England and Wales or Northern Ireland, are to any legal estate or equitable interest or power;
  (c) references to an interest, in relation to land in Scotland, are to any estate, interest, servitude or other heritable right in or over land, including a heritable security;
  (d) references to an interest, in relation to property other than land, include references to a right (including a right to possession).

'Criminal property' is essentially defined in s. 340(2) and (3). See also *Wilkinson v DPP* [2006] EWHC 3012 (Admin) and *Pace* [2014] 1 Cr App R 501 (34) at [26]. Property that does not fall within the terms of those provisions cannot be criminal property under part 7 of the Act. Subsections (4)–(10) expand upon and illustrate that concept, but do not purport to be exhaustive. In *Rose* [2008] EWCA Crim 239, the court left open the question whether a thief can be said to 'obtain' property stolen by him if he acquires no legal interest in it, preferring to rely on the fact that in most cases a thief does indeed acquire a limited interest of that kind (*Costello v Chief Constable of Derbyshire* [2001] 3 All ER 150). Section 340(3)(b) purports to be part of this definition of 'criminal property', but for practical purposes it also specifies the key *mens rea* element in money laundering offences.

B21.4 Criminal property must be proved to represent, in whole or in part, a person's benefit from *actual* criminal conduct. Unfounded suspicion as to its derivation cannot suffice (*Montila* [2005] 1 All ER 113 at [41]). Where D mistakenly believes that he is dealing with criminal property (e.g., in the course of a police undercover operation), he can potentially be guilty of an 'impossible' attempt to commit a money laundering offence, but only on the basis of a positive belief as to the character of the property in question. Mere suspicion suffices (if well-founded) for the commission of a substantive money laundering offence, but cannot suffice (if unfounded) for an attempt

(*Pace*). The money laundering offences require either knowledge or suspicion, and do not refer to 'belief' at all, but under the CAA 1981, s. 1(3), D's liability for an attempt may be based on the facts as he mistakenly believed them to be (see **A5.77** and **A5.81**).

Section 340 contains no reference to any need to particularise the class of crime from which the property is derived (*Craig* [2007] EWCA Crim 2913). In *K* [2007] 1 WLR 2262 the Court of Appeal held that it was open to a jury to infer that a large sum concealed in the assets of a money transfer business represented criminal property, even though 'the prosecution could not identify the provenance of the money'. This inference was possible because of the elaborate false documentation that had been created in an attempt to disguise its existence and origins. But in *Prosecution Appeal (No. 11 of 2007); NW* [2008] EWCA Crim 2, the court held that the class or type of crime involved must indeed be identified, as in civil proceedings for recovery under part 5 of the Act. A claim for civil recovery cannot be sustained solely on the basis that a respondent has no identifiable lawful income to warrant his lifestyle: the applicant must first establish a good arguable case that a certain kind of unlawful conduct occurred and then a good arguable case that property was obtained through that kind of unlawful conduct (*R (Director of the Assets Recovery Agency) v Green* [2005] EWHC 3168 (Admin); *Director of the Assets Recovery Agency v Szepietowski* [2007] EWCA Civ 766; *Director of the Assets Recovery Agency v Olupitan* [2008] EWCA Civ 104). But those cases leave open the possibility that an action could succeed where there is clear evidence (as in *K*) of money laundering (e.g., concealment of origin and fabrication of receipts, etc.) even if the real source remains unknown. Nobody needs to launder clean money, and one of the purposes of the 2002 Act was to avoid the problems that used to arise where it was clear that property had criminal origins, but unclear whether it derived from drug trafficking or other criminal activity (cf. *El Kurd* [2001] Crim LR 234). This interpretation is confirmed by *Anwoir* [2009] 4 All ER 582 and *F* [2008] EWCA Crim 1868. According to *Anwoir*, there are two ways in which the Crown can prove the property derives from crime, namely: (a) by showing that it derives from criminal conduct of a specific kind; or (b) by proving that the circumstances in which it was handled create an irresistible inference that it can only have been derived from crime. See also *DPP v Bolah* [2011] UKPC 44.

The concept of 'criminal property' may still in some circumstances include property derived from activities abroad that are lawful under local law. As originally drafted, the Act made no concessions to local law, but amendments to the principal money laundering offences came into force on 15 May 2006 (see ss. 327(2A), 328(3) and 329(2A)). These effectively exempt the proceeds of most, but not all, 'locally lawful' activities from the operation of the Act. By virtue of the Proceeds of Crime Act 2002 (Money Laundering: Exceptions to Overseas Conduct Defence) Order 2006 (SI 2006 No. 1070), they do not however exempt the proceeds of conduct which would have constituted an offence punishable by imprisonment for a maximum term in excess of 12 months in any part of the UK if it occurred there, other than the proceeds of conduct that would have amounted to: **B21.5**

(a) an offence under the Gaming Act 1968 (now repealed);
(b) an offence under the Lotteries and Amusements Act 1976 (now repealed), or
(c) an offence under ss. 23 or 25 of the Financial Services and Markets Act 2000.

In *Gabriel* [2007] 2 Cr App R 139, the Court of Appeal rejected arguments that profits made from legitimate trading would, if not declared to the Revenue (or, in the case of benefit claimants, to the Department of Work and Pensions) thereby become criminal property. Gage LJ said (at [21] and [22]):

> We recognise that the failure to declare profits for the purposes of income tax may give rise to an offence, but that does not make the legitimate trading in goods an offence of itself. . . .

> We can see how benefits obtained on the basis of a false declaration or a failure to disclose a change in circumstances may amount to obtaining a pecuniary advantage, namely the benefits: see section 340(6)...But in this case no attempt was made to prove that the appellant or anyone else in her family had made any false declaration or failed to disclose a change of circumstances.

B21.6   In *Loizou* [2005] 2 Cr App R 618, Clarke LJ said (at [30]), in the context of an alleged offence of transferring criminal property contrary to s. 327(1) of the Act:

> The property concealed, disguised, converted or transferred, as the case may be, must be criminal property at the time it is concealed, disguised, converted or transferred. . .In a case of transfer, if the property is not criminal property at the time of the transfer, the offence is not committed.

The same concept of criminal property applies in relation to alleged offences under ss. 328 and 329, so a dishonest or unlawful arrangement relating to property that becomes criminal property only once that arrangement has been carried out is not itself a money laundering arrangement (*Geary* [2011] 1 Cr App R 73); *Akhtar* [2011] 4 All ER 417). If, however, D fraudulently under-declares his profits with the result that he deprives the public revenue of tax, he thereby derives a pecuniary advantage from cheating the public revenue (see **B16.3**). In such cases the entirety of the undeclared turnover or profit becomes criminal property and not merely the tax due because the benefit is represented in part by that sum (*K* [2007] 1 WLR 2262; *William* [2013] EWCA Crim 1262).

AUTHORISED DISCLOSURE AND APPROPRIATE CONSENT

B21.7   A person is not guilty of a money laundering offence if he makes an 'authorised disclosure' and acts with the 'appropriate consent'. These terms are defined in ss. 338 and 335, respectively.

Proceeds of Crime Act 2002, s. 338

(1) For the purposes of this Part a disclosure is authorised if—
  (a) it is a disclosure to a constable, a customs officer or a nominated officer by the alleged offender that property is criminal property, and
  (b) [repealed]
  (c) the first, second or third condition set out below is satisfied.
(2) The first condition is that the disclosure is made before the alleged offender does the prohibited act.
(2A)   The second condition is that—
  (a) the disclosure is made while the alleged offender is doing the prohibited act,
  (b) he began to do the act at a time when, because he did not then know or suspect that the property constituted or represented a person's benefit from criminal conduct, the act was not a prohibited act, and
  (c) the disclosure is made on his own initiative and as soon as is practicable after he first knows or suspects that the property constitutes or represents a person's benefit from criminal conduct.
(3) The third condition is that—
  (a) the disclosure is made after the alleged offender does the prohibited act,
  (b) he has a reasonable excuse for his failure to make the disclosure before he did the act, and
  (c) the disclosure is made on his own initiative and as soon as it is practicable for him to make it.
(4) An authorised disclosure is not to be taken to breach any restriction on the disclosure of information (however imposed).
(5) A disclosure to a nominated officer is a disclosure which—
  (a) is made to a person nominated by the alleged offender's employer to receive authorised disclosures, and
  (b) is made in the course of the alleged offender's employment.
(6) References to the prohibited act are to an act mentioned in section 327(1), 328(1) or 329(1) (as the case may be).

References to a constable include a person authorised for these purposes by the NCA (s. 340(13)).

B21.8   **Proceeds of Crime Act 2002, s. 335**

(1) The appropriate consent is—
  (a) the consent of a nominated officer to do a prohibited act if an authorised disclosure is made to the nominated officer;

    (b) the consent of a constable to do a prohibited act if an authorised disclosure is made to a constable;

    (c) the consent of a customs officer to do a prohibited act if an authorised disclosure is made to a customs officer.

(2) A person must be treated as having the appropriate consent if—

    (a) he makes an authorised disclosure to a constable or a customs officer, and

    (b) the condition in subsection (3) or the condition in subsection (4) is satisfied.

(3) The condition is that before the end of the notice period he does not receive notice from a constable or customs officer that consent to the doing of the act is refused.

(4) The condition is that—

    (a) before the end of the notice period he receives notice from a constable or customs officer that consent to the doing of the act is refused, and

    (b) the moratorium period has expired.

(5) The notice period is the period of seven working days starting with the first working day after the person makes the disclosure.

(6) The moratorium period is the period of 31 days starting with the day on which the person receives notice that consent to the doing of the act is refused.

(7) A working day is a day other than a Saturday, a Sunday, Christmas Day, Good Friday or a day which is a bank holiday under the Banking and Financial Dealings Act 1971 in the part of the United Kingdom in which the person is when he makes the disclosure.

(8) References to a prohibited act are to an act mentioned in section 327(1), 328(1) or 329(1) (as the case may be).

(9) A nominated officer is a person nominated to receive disclosures under section 338.

Section 336 details conditions under which a nominated officer may give appropriate consent.

In *Bowman v Fels* [2005] 4 All ER 609 the Court of Appeal held that, 'the issue or pursuit of **B21.9** ordinary legal proceedings with a view to obtaining the court's adjudication upon the parties' rights and duties is not to be regarded as an arrangement or a prohibited act within ss. 327–9'. It follows that lawyers conducting litigation are not required to make disclosure to the NCA and obtain NCA consent merely because of a suspicion that the proceedings might in some way facilitate the acquisition, retention, use or control of criminal property by one or more of the parties.

Where disclosure is required, as Laddie J explained in *Squirrell Ltd v National Westminster Bank plc* [2006] 2 All ER 784 at [17], the constable (or NCA officer) or customs officer may simply give consent (s. 335(1)). Alternatively, consent may be assumed if the party has made an authorised disclosure and has not received, within seven working days, notice that consent is refused. If notice of refusal is indeed given then a further 31 calendar days (the moratorium) must pass before the party can safely deal with the property in question.

OFFENCES UNDER THE PROCEEDS OF CRIME ACT 2002

Offences of Concealment, etc.

Proceeds of Crime Act 2002, s. 327   **B21.10**

(1) A person commits an offence if he—

    (a) conceals criminal property;

    (b) disguises criminal property;

    (c) converts criminal property;

    (d) transfers criminal property;

    (e) removes criminal property from England and Wales or from Scotland or from Northern Ireland.

(2) But a person does not commit such an offence if—

    (a) he makes an authorised disclosure under section 338 and (if the disclosure is made before he does the act mentioned in subsection (1)) he has the appropriate consent;

(b) he intended to make such a disclosure but had a reasonable excuse for not doing so;

(c) the act he does is done in carrying out a function he has relating to the enforcement of any provision of this Act or of any other enactment relating to criminal conduct or benefit from criminal conduct.

(2A)   Nor does a person commit an offence under subsection (1) if—

(a) he knows, or believes on reasonable grounds, that the relevant criminal conduct occurred in a particular country or territory outside the United Kingdom, and

(b) the relevant criminal conduct—

(i)   was not, at the time it occurred, unlawful under the criminal law then applying in that country or territory, and

(ii) is not of a description prescribed by an order made by the Secretary of State.

(2B)   In subsection (2A) 'the relevant criminal conduct' is the criminal conduct by reference to which the property concerned is criminal property.

(2C)   A deposit-taking body that does an act mentioned in paragraph (c) or (d) of subsection (1) does not commit an offence under that subsection if—

(a) it does the act in operating an account maintained with it, and

(b) the value of the criminal property concerned is less than the threshold amount determined under section 339A for the act.

(3) Concealing or disguising criminal property includes concealing or disguising its nature, source, location, disposition, movement or ownership or any rights with respect to it.

Indictment

B21.11

Statement of Offence

Concealing criminal property, contrary to section 327(1)(e) of the Proceeds of Crime Act 2002.

Particulars of Offence

D on or about the…day of…concealed in his home criminal property, namely…knowing or suspecting it to represent in whole or in part the proceeds of drug trafficking committed by E.

The explanatory notes to the Act suggest that s. 327 'creates one of three principal money laundering offences', but the structure of the section suggests that it creates not one but five separate offences (one in each of s. 327(1)(a)–(e)) and the Act contains no clear indication to the contrary. This contrasts with other statutes, such as the Public Order Act 1986, which specifically states in s. 7(2) that ss. 1 to 5 of that Act each create only one offence. An indictment that merely alleges 'money laundering, contrary to s. 327' would thus appear to be duplicitous. See generally **D11.46** *et seq.*

B21.12   Procedure and Sentence   Offences under ss. 327 to 329 are triable either way (s. 334). When tried on indictment they are class 2C or 3 offences (CPD XIII, para. B: see Supplement, **PD-97**). The maximum penalty is 14 years' imprisonment and/or a fine following conviction on indictment; six months and/or a fine not exceeding the statutory maximum on summary conviction. Where criminal property has been laundered or disposed of in various ways over a period of time, it may be legitimate for the prosecution to allege a general deficiency as in comparable cases of handling or theft. See the CrimPR 2011, r. 14.2(2), and *Martin* [2012] EWCA Crim 902.

The definitive sentencing guideline, *Fraud, Bribery and Money Laundering Offences* (see Supplement, **SG-496**) covers offences under ss. 327 to 329. The guideline applies to all individual offenders aged 18 and over and to organisations sentenced on or after 1 October 2014 regardless of the date of the offence. A separate part of the guideline applies to corporate offenders.

Prior to the guideline, in *Griffiths* [2007] 1 Cr App R (S) 581, the Court of Appeal dealt with the offender estate agent, who had been convicted of offences under ss. 328 and 329. He had agreed to buy a house from a drug dealer at a substantial undervalue, in an attempt by the drug dealer to frustrate confiscation proceedings against him. Sentence was reduced from three years' imprisonment to 27 months.

B21.13   In *Greaves* [2011] 1 Cr App R (S) 72, the Court of Appeal identified principles relating to the relationship between the money laundering offence and 'the primary crime' and these continue to be of value following the issuing of the definitive sentencing guideline. Jack J stated (at [24]):

(a) Offences contrary to sections 327 to 329…are separate, 'free-standing', offences to the offences or offences which give rise to the criminal property with which the Proceeds of Crime Act is concerned.

(b) Where the offender responsible for the primary crime is not the offender guilty of the Proceeds of Crime Act offence, the position is more straightforward than when they are the same…

(c) Where the offenders are one and the same, if the conduct involved in the Proceeds of Crime Act offence in reality adds nothing to the culpability of the conduct involved in the primary offence, there should be no additional penalty. A person should not be punished twice for the same conduct. That can be achieved either by imposing 'no separate penalty' on the Proceeds of Crime Act offence or by a concurrent sentence where the primary sentence is imprisonment.

(d) Where conduct involved in a Proceeds of Crime Act offence does add to the culpability of the conduct involved in the primary offence an additional penalty is appropriate: see *Brown* [[2007] 1 Cr App R (S) 77] and *Linegar* [[2009] EWCA Crim 648].

(e) Where the primary offence has a maximum sentence, that is the maximum which Parliament has thought appropriate for conduct constituting the offence. In a case where the Proceeds of Crime Act offence does not add to the culpability of the conduct involved in the primary offence, there should not be a consecutive sentence on the latter on the ground that the maximum permitted on the primary offence is too low…

(f) Where the conduct involved in the Proceeds of Crime Act offence does add to the culpability of the conduct involved in the primary offence, the maximum sentence permitted on the primary offence may be relevant to the sentence on the Proceeds of Crime Act offence because the seriousness of the primary offence reflects on the seriousness of the laundering: see, for instance,…*Basra*. But it does not as a matter of principle provide a limit: see *Linegar*. If the Proceeds of Crime Act offence merits it, the sentence for it may add to that for the primary offence bringing it above the maximum for the latter, and it may if appropriate itself exceed the maximum on the latter.

In *Adekutasi* [2014] 1 Cr App R (S) 52 (11), another case preceding the issue of the guidelines, a sentence of 16 months was appropriate for an offender who pleaded guilty to a single count under s. 329. A sum of just over £20,000, being the proceeds of three separate frauds, was passed through the offender's bank account on to the principal fraudster.

Elements　The scope of the offences created is potentially very broad. Dishonesty is not **B21.14** required, nor is knowledge of the provenance of the property. On a literal reading of s. 327, a thief who conceals, disguises or sells property that he has just stolen may thereby commit offences under that section, as may someone who merely suspects that the property he converts or exports represents the benefit of another person's crime (see s. 340(3)(b)). In *Fazal* [2010] 1 WLR 694, D allowed his bank account to be used by a friend to launder money, and it was held that he was guilty of converting criminal property (contrary to s. 327(1)(c)) whenever such monies were deposited in, retained in, or withdrawn from the account. Where property is purchased for 'adequate consideration', s. 329(2) provides a defence to a charge of unlawful acquisition, use or possession under s. 329(1) (see **B21.20**) but this defence cannot apply if the charge is converting, transferring or removing the property under s. 327.

Section 327(2) creates defences to charges under s. 327(1). The accused does not bear any legal or persuasive burden in respect of those defences, but he must presumably bear an evidential burden. The prosecution therefore need not address any such issues unless these are raised by admissible evidence.

Money Laundering Arrangements

Proceeds of Crime Act 2002, s. 328　　**B21.15**

(1) A person commits an offence if he enters into or becomes concerned in an arrangement which he knows or suspects facilitates (by whatever means) the acquisition, retention, use or control of criminal property by or on behalf of another person.

(2) But a person does not commit such an offence if—
  (a) he makes an authorised disclosure under section 338 and (if the disclosure is made before he does the act mentioned in subsection (1)) he has the appropriate consent;
  (b) he intended to make such a disclosure but had a reasonable excuse for not doing so;
  (c) the act he does is done in carrying out a function he has relating to the enforcement of any provision of this Act or of any other enactment relating to criminal conduct or benefit from criminal conduct.
(3) Nor does a person commit an offence under subsection (1) if—
  (a) he knows, or believes on reasonable grounds, that the relevant criminal conduct occurred in a particular country or territory outside the United Kingdom, and
  (b) the relevant criminal conduct—
    (i) was not, at the time it occurred, unlawful under the criminal law then applying in that country or territory, and
    (ii) is not of a description prescribed by an order made by the Secretary of State.
(4) In subsection (3) 'the relevant criminal conduct' is the criminal conduct by reference to which the property concerned is criminal property.
(5) A deposit-taking body that does an act mentioned in subsection (1) does not commit an offence under that subsection if—
  (a) it does the act in operating an account maintained with it, and
  (b) the arrangement facilitates the acquisition, retention, use or control of criminal property of a value that is less than the threshold amount determined under section 339A for the act.

B21.16 Indictment, etc.

Statement of Offence

Entering into or becoming concerned in a money laundering arrangement, contrary to section 328(1) of the Proceeds of Crime Act 2002.

Particulars of Offence

D on or about the day of...entered into or became concerned in an arrangement, namely the opening by E of an account at...under a false name, knowing or suspecting that this arrangement would facilitate the retention, use or control of criminal property by E or by other persons unknown.

In contrast to ss. 327 and 329, s. 328 appears to create a single offence, which may be committed in various ways. It is analogous in this respect to the offence of handling stolen goods (see **B4.160**). As to procedure and sentence, see **B21.12**.

B21.17 Elements Section 328 requires a definite arrangement which D knows or suspects facilitates (and not just 'will or may facilitate') the acquisition of criminal property by or on behalf of another person, who must already be identified or at least identifiable. See *Dare v CPS* (2013) 177 JP 37. It potentially affects not only deliberate or dishonest offenders, but also banks, accountants and legal advisers, etc., who become suspicious as to the legality of the means by which their clients have acquired any of the funds or other property they are asked to deal with or manage. As Laddie J explained in *Squirrell Ltd v National Westminster Bank plc* [2006] 2 All ER 784 at [16]:

> The purpose of s. 328(1) is not to turn innocent third parties...into criminals. It is to put them under pressure to provide information to the relevant authorities to enable the latter to obtain information about possible criminal activity and to increase their prospects of being able to freeze the proceeds of crime...A party caught by s. 328(1) can avoid liability if he brings himself within the statutory defence created by s. 328(2)...

B21.18 The concept of 'suspicion' was considered by the Court of Appeal in *Da Silva* [2007] 4 All ER 900, in the context of an alleged offence under the CJA 1988, s. 93A. Longmore LJ said:

> It seems to us that the essential element in the word 'suspect' and its affiliates, in this context, is that the defendant must think that there is a possibility, which is more than fanciful, that the

relevant facts exist. A vague feeling of unease would not suffice. But the statute does not require the suspicion to be 'clear' or 'firmly grounded and targeted on specific facts', or based upon 'reasonable grounds'. To require the prosecution to satisfy such criteria as to the strength of the suspicion would, in our view, be putting a gloss on the section.

In *Squirrell*, Laddie J's view was that 'Even if [the client's account] does *not* contain funds which are, in fact, criminal property and no offence has been committed [by the client] s. 328(1) bites if [the bank] has a relevant suspicion'. A similar interpretation seems to have been assumed in *K Ltd v National Westminster Bank plc* [2007] 4 All ER 907. Unfounded suspicions may, if that view is correct, lead to the commission of a s. 328 offence. Such an interpretation nevertheless looks wrong in light of the decision of the House of Lords in *Montila* [2005] 1 All ER 113 (not referred to in *Squirrell* or *K Ltd*), in which it was held that a conviction for a similarly worded offence under the CJA 1988, s. 93C(2), required proof that the property in question was *in fact* (and was not merely suspected to be) the proceeds of criminal conduct. The House of Lords thought that this interpretation was strongly supported by the absence of any defence where the property in question was later proved to be 'clean'. Given that the 2002 Act similarly contains no such defence, the same argument would seem to apply. Indeed, the Appellate Committee expressly noted in *Montila* (at [41]) that, in the 2002 legislation, 'there is no room for any ambiguity. The property that is being dealt with in each case must be shown to have been criminal property.' This was accepted by Hamblen J in *Shah v HSBC* [2009] EWHC 79 (QB) (at [39]):

> If the property in question is not in fact 'criminal property' then no offence is committed. For the purpose of the present applications it should be assumed that it was not criminal property...On that basis it would not therefore have been illegal for HSBC to execute the payment instructions and the rights under the contract cannot have been suspended by illegality.

The Court of Appeal agreed with Hamblen J's interpretation. See *Shah v HSBC* [2010] 3 All ER 477 at [13]. In *Bowman v Fels* [2005] 4 All ER 609, the Court of Appeal rejected arguments that, if a lawyer acting for a client in legal proceedings discovers or suspects anything in the proceedings that may facilitate the acquisition, retention, use or control (usually by his own client or his client's opponent) of criminal property, he must immediately notify the relevant authority (now the NCA) of his belief if he is to avoid being guilty of a s. 328 offence. Brooke LJ said (at [83]):

> [Section 328] is...not intended to cover or affect the ordinary conduct of litigation by legal professionals. That includes any step taken by them in litigation from the issue of proceedings and the securing of injunctive relief or a freezing order up to its final disposal by judgment. We do not consider that either the European or the United Kingdom legislator can have envisaged that any of these ordinary activities could fall within the concept of 'becoming concerned in an arrangement which...facilitates the acquisition, retention, use or control of criminal property'.

B21.19 The wording of s. 328(2) does not suggest that the accused bears any legal or persuasive burden in respect of the defences it creates, but he must bear an evidential burden. The prosecution therefore need not address any such issues unless these have been raised by admissible evidence.

Offences of Acquisition, Use or Possession

Proceeds of Crime Act 2002, s. 329   **B21.20**

(1) A person commits an offence if he—
  (a) acquires criminal property;
  (b) uses criminal property;
  (c) has possession of criminal property.
(2) But a person does not commit such an offence if—
  (a) he makes an authorised disclosure under section 338 and (if the disclosure is made before he does the act mentioned in subsection (1)) he has the appropriate consent;

(b) he intended to make such a disclosure but had a reasonable excuse for not doing so;

(c) he acquired or used or had possession of the property for adequate consideration;

(d) the act he does is done in carrying out a function he has relating to the enforcement of any provision of this Act or of any other enactment relating to criminal conduct or benefit from criminal conduct.

(2A) Nor does a person commit an offence under subsection (1) if—

(a) he knows, or believes on reasonable grounds, that the relevant criminal conduct occurred in a particular country or territory outside the United Kingdom, and

(b) the relevant criminal conduct—

(i) was not, at the time it occurred, unlawful under the criminal law then applying in that country or territory, and

(ii) is not of a description prescribed by an order made by the Secretary of State.

(2B) In subsection (2A) 'the relevant criminal conduct' is the criminal conduct by reference to which the property concerned is criminal property.

(2C) A deposit-taking body that does an act mentioned in subsection (1) does not commit an offence under that subsection if—

(a) it does the act in operating an account maintained with it, and

(b) the arrangement facilitates the acquisition, retention, use or control of criminal property of a value that is less than the threshold amount determined under section 339A for the act.

(3) For the purposes of this section—

(a) a person acquires property for inadequate consideration if the value of the consideration is significantly less than the value of the property;

(b) a person uses or has possession of property for inadequate consideration if the value of the consideration is significantly less than the value of the use or possession;

(c) the provision by a person of goods or services which he knows or suspects may help another to carry out criminal conduct is not consideration.

B21.21 Indictment, etc.

Statement of Offence

Acquiring criminal property, contrary to section 329(1)(a) of the Proceeds of Crime Act 2002.

Particulars of Offence

D on or about the day of...acquired criminal property, namely...knowing or suspecting it to represent in whole or in part the proceeds of drug trafficking committed by E.

There may be room for argument as to whether s. 329(1)(a)–(c) each create a distinct offence, or whether they represent three different ways of committing a single offence created by s. 329(1). See the discussion of s. 327 at **B21.11**. The form of indictment shown above should be acceptable in either case. As to procedure and sentence, see **B21.12**.

B21.22 Elements Section 329 does not distinguish between criminal property that represents the benefit of some other person's crime and that which represents the benefits of a crime which the accused himself has just committed. A thief who uses or retains possession of property that he has just stolen (this being criminal property as defined in s. 340) must therefore be guilty of an offence under s. 329(1)(b) or (c), the maximum penalty for which is twice that for basic theft. It does not follow that such a charge would be appropriate. It might indeed be considered perverse. The structure of the new money laundering offences appears to rely on the assumption that they will be applied sensibly and that prosecutors will not attempt to exploit the more bizarre or extreme possibilities that they create. On the other hand, it is apparent that charges are now being laid under s. 329 in some cases where an accused might previously have faced more charges of theft or handling (see, e.g., *Hogan v DPP* [2007] 1 WLR 2944 and *Wilkinson v DPP* [2006] EWHC 3012 (Admin)).

Dishonesty is not required under s. 329, nor need the accused know or believe that the property in question is criminal property. Mere suspicion will suffice (see s. 340(3)(b)).

B21.23 Defences are provided under s. 329(2)–(2C). The accused bears no legal or persuasive burden in respect of those defences, but he does bear an evidential burden (*Hogan v DPP*). The prosecution therefore need not address any such issues unless these have been raised by the accused. Where property is purchased for 'adequate consideration', s. 329(2)(c) provides a defence to someone who is charged with unlawful acquisition, use or possession under s. 329(1), but this cannot apply if he is charged instead with an offence under s. 327.

In *Gabriel* [2007] 2 Cr App R 139, Gage LJ offered this advice to prosecutors in cases involving s. 329 (at [29]):

> There can be no doubt that the money laundering provisions of the Proceeds of Crime Act 2002 are draconian. The scope of section 329 is wide. It requires proof of no more *mens rea* than suspicion. The danger is that juries will be tempted to think that it is for the defence to prove innocence rather than the prosecution to prove guilt. In *R v Loizou* [2005] EWCA 1579, the prosecution had set out the factors upon which it relied and from which it submitted the jury could draw proper inferences. In our judgment it is a sensible practice for the prosecution, as was done in *Loizou*, either by giving particulars, or at least in opening, to set out the facts upon which it relies and the inferences which it will invite the jury to draw as proof that the property was criminal property. In doing so it may very well be that the prosecution will be able to limit the scope of the criminal conduct alleged.

A sentence of 12 months' imprisonment for the offence under s. 329 was upheld in *Valentine* [2012] 1 Cr App R (S) 246. The offender was married to a man who was eventually sentenced to life imprisonment for offences including robbery and conspiracy to murder. The man headed a criminal gang, and the profits made from criminal activity funded a lavish lifestyle for the couple, including expensive cars and jewellery and many foreign trips.

Money Laundering, Stolen Goods and Wrongful Credits

B21.24 There are overlaps between the new money laundering offences and several existing offences, including those of assisting offenders, concealing offences and perverting the course of justice. The most important overlaps, however, appear to be with handling stolen goods (Theft Act 1968, s. 22; see **B4.160** *et seq.*) and dishonestly retaining a wrongful credit (Theft Act 1968, s. 24A: see **B4.187** *et seq.*).

The term, 'stolen goods', as defined in s. 24 of the Theft Act 1968, includes money and other property which directly or indirectly represents (or has previously represented) the proceeds of theft, blackmail, a s. 15 deception offence, or fraud (within the meaning of the Fraud Act 2006) in the hands of the original thief, etc., or in the hands of a dishonest handler of stolen goods. Such property may be criminally 'handled' in a number of ways, but D must be proved to have been dishonest and to have 'known or believed' that the property in question was stolen goods. Mere suspicion is never enough (see **B4.182**). If the goods were allegedly stolen abroad, outside English jurisdiction, it will be necessary to prove the content of the relevant foreign law (*Ofori* (1994) 99 Cr App R 223). D cannot ordinarily be convicted of handling the proceeds of his own crime, unless he is proved to have done so for the benefit of another. Finally, in cases involving cheques, money transfers or the proceeds of bank accounts, care must be taken to avoid the problems identified (or created) by the House of Lords in *Preddy* [1996] AC 815 (see **B4.190**).

B21.25 A money laundering offence may be easier to establish than any Theft Act offence. By the POCA 2002, s. 340(3), the property in question may represent the proceeds of any crime under UK law, and it suffices that D merely suspects this (*Pace* [2014] 1 Cr App R 501 (34)). In *Hickey* [2007] EWCA Crim 542, D pleaded guilty to an offence under s. 327(1)(c) (see **B21.10**) on the basis that he had suspected that a vehicle he delivered to a buyer had been stolen. It is not clear whether a charge of handling could ever have been proved on the facts of that case, but it was accepted that there was no reason to suppose that he had been aware that the theft of the vehicle had been connected to a domestic burglary. See also *Hogan v DPP* [2007] 1 WLR 2944 and *Wilkinson v DPP* [2006] EWHC 3012 (Admin).

The exact crime from which the property is derived need not be established, nor need anyone have been convicted in respect of it. D may even be guilty of 'money laundering', by using, possessing or retaining the proceeds of his own (previous) criminal conduct (cf. *Rose* [2008] EWCA

Crim 239 noted at **B21.3**); but amendments made to the 2002 Act by the SOCPA 2005, s. 102, now ensure that D will not ordinarily be guilty of any of the principal money laundering offences where he knows, or believes on reasonable grounds, that the relevant 'criminal' conduct occurred (or is occurring) in a country or territory outside the UK, and is not (or was not at that time) criminal under the applicable local law. This defence will not apply if the relevant conduct is of a type described by an order made by the Secretary of State.

Where D's bank or building society account contains the proceeds of thefts or frauds, a money laundering charge may similarly be an easier charge to prove than a charge under the Theft Act 1968, s. 24A. It would again avoid the need for proof of D's dishonesty or of his knowledge as to the provenance of the funds; and D may commit a money laundering offence by retaining or using the proceeds of a crime committed at any time in the past (e.g., a robbery committed 20 years ago) whereas the s. 24A offence can apply only to wrongful credits made on or after 18 December 1996.

Jurisdiction

B21.26   None of the money laundering offences in the POCA 2002 are listed as Group A offences for jurisdictional purposes under the CJA 1993, part I (see **A8.10**) but, as long as the money laundering offence takes place in England and Wales, it does not matter if the property concerned is the product of criminal conduct committed elsewhere in the world.

Failure to Disclose Possible Money Laundering

B21.27   Sections 330, 331 and 332 create offences of failure to disclose possible money laundering activities (as defined in s. 340(11)). Actual knowledge or suspicion is not essential under ss. 330 or 331. It suffices in either case that the accused has 'reasonable grounds' for suspicion. Section 330 deals with failures by persons working in the 'regulated sector' (financial services etc.) as defined in sch. 9 to the Act.

Proceeds of Crime Act 2002, s. 330

(1) A person commits an offence if the conditions in subsections (2) to (4) are satisfied.
(2) The first condition is that he—
    (a) knows or suspects, or
    (b) has reasonable grounds for knowing or suspecting,
    that another person is engaged in money laundering.
(3) The second condition is that the information or other matter—
    (a) on which his knowledge or suspicion is based, or
    (b) which gives reasonable grounds for such knowledge or suspicion,
    came to him in the course of a business in the regulated sector.
(3A)   The third condition is—
    (a) that he can identify the other person mentioned in subsection (2) or the whereabouts of any of the laundered property, or
    (b) that he believes, or it is reasonable to expect him to believe, that the information or other matter mentioned in subsection (3) will or may assist in identifying that other person or the whereabouts of any of the laundered property.
(4) The fourth condition is that he does not make the required disclosure to—
    (a) a nominated officer, or
    (b) a person authorised for the purposes of this Part by the Director General of the National Crime Agency,
    as soon as is practicable after the information or other matter mentioned in subsection (3) comes to him.
(5) The required disclosure is a disclosure of—
    (a) the identity of the other person mentioned in subsection (2), if he knows it,
    (b) the whereabouts of the laundered property, so far as he knows it, and
    (c) the information or other matter mentioned in subsection (3).
(5A) The laundered property is the property forming the subject-matter of the money laundering that he knows or suspects, or has reasonable grounds for knowing or suspecting, that other person to be engaged in.

(6) But he does not commit an offence under this section if—
   (a) he has a reasonable excuse for not making the required disclosure,
   (b) he is a professional legal adviser or relevant professional adviser and—
      (i) if he knows either of the things mentioned in subsection (5)(a) and (b), he knows the thing because of information or other matter that came to him in privileged circumstances, or
      (ii) the information or other matter mentioned in subsection (3) came to him in privileged circumstances, or
   (c) subsection (7) or (7B) applies to him.
(7) This subsection applies to a person if—
   (a) he does not know or suspect that another person is engaged in money laundering, and
   (b) he has not been provided by his employer with such training as is specified by the Secretary of State by order for the purposes of this section.
(7A) Nor does a person commit an offence under this section if—
   (a) he knows, or believes on reasonable grounds, that the money laundering is occurring in a particular country or territory outside the United Kingdom, and
   (b) the money laundering—
      (i) is not unlawful under the criminal law applying in that country or territory, and
      (ii) is not of a description prescribed in an order made by the Secretary of State.
(7B) This subsection applies to a person if—
   (a) he is employed by, or is in partnership with, a professional legal adviser or a relevant professional adviser to provide the adviser with assistance or support,
   (b) the information or other matter mentioned in subsection (3) comes to the person in connection with the provision of such assistance or support, and
   (c) the information or other matter came to the adviser in privileged circumstances.
(8) In deciding whether a person committed an offence under this section the court must consider whether he followed any relevant guidance which was at the time concerned—
   (a) issued by a supervisory authority or any other appropriate body,
   (b) approved by the Treasury, and
   (c) published in a manner it approved as appropriate in its opinion to bring the guidance to the attention of persons likely to be affected by it.
(9) A disclosure to a nominated officer is a disclosure which—
   (a) is made to a person nominated by the alleged offender's employer to receive disclosures under this section, and
   (b) is made in the course of the alleged offender's employment.
(9A) But a disclosure which satisfies paragraphs (a) and (b) of subsection (9) is not to be taken as a disclosure to a nominated officer if the person making the disclosure—
   (a) is a professional legal adviser or relevant professional adviser,
   (b) makes it for the purpose of obtaining advice about making a disclosure under this section, and
   (c) does not intend it to be a disclosure under this section.
(10) Information or other matter comes to a professional legal adviser or relevant professional adviser in privileged circumstances if it is communicated or given to him—
   (a) by (or by a representative of) a client of his in connection with the giving by the adviser of legal advice to the client,
   (b) by (or by a representative of) a person seeking legal advice from the adviser, or
   (c) by a person in connection with legal proceedings or contemplated legal proceedings.
(11) But subsection (10) does not apply to information or other matter which is communicated or given with the intention of furthering a criminal purpose.
(12) Schedule 9 has effect for the purpose of determining what is—
   (a) a business in the regulated sector;
   (b) a supervisory authority.
(13) An appropriate body is any body which regulates or is representative of any trade, profession, business or employment carried on by the alleged offender.
(14) A relevant professional adviser is an accountant, auditor or tax adviser who is a member of a professional body which is established for accountants, auditors or tax advisers (as the case may be) and which makes provision for—
   (a) testing the competence of those seeking admission to membership of such a body as a condition for such admission; and

(b) imposing and maintaining professional and ethical standards for its members, as well as imposing sanctions for non-compliance with those standards.

B21.28   The guidance referred to in s. 330(8) includes that issued by the Joint Money Laundering Steering Group, in association with the British Bankers' Association. Subscribers to this service may assess their anti-money laundering procedures against current regulatory requirements.

Section 330 differs from the other provisions in part 7 in that it refers not to 'criminal property', but to 'the laundered property', which is defined in s. 330(5A). This is a narrower concept than 'criminal property' in that property may be criminal property whether it has been laundered or not. Read in isolation, s. 330(5A) might *perhaps* appear capable of referring to unfounded suspicions of money laundering. This seems indeed to have been the view of the High Court of Justiciary in *Ahmad v HM Advocate* [2009] HCJAC 60; but if this was the intended meaning, it is remarkable that a defendant could not then escape conviction by proving that no money laundering was in fact taking place, whereas he *could* escape conviction by proving (under s. 330(7A)) that he believed it was occurring abroad, in circumstances where it would then have been legal. See *Montila* [2005] 1 All ER 113.

Section 331 creates a broadly similar offence, applicable to nominated officers in the regulated sector, who have themselves received information as to suspected money laundering in consequence of disclosures made to them under s. 330.

Section 332 deals with failures by nominated officers to whom disclosures have been made under s. 337 (protected disclosures) or s. 338 (authorised disclosures).

B21.29   **Penalties and Procedure for Offences under ss. 330 to 332**   Offences under ss. 330 to 332 are triable either way (s. 334). When tried on indictment they are normally a class 3 offence, but see CPD XIII, para. B (see Supplement, **PD-97**) for the additional factors that the court considers on allocation. The maximum penalty is five years' imprisonment and/or a fine following conviction on indictment; six months and/or a fine not exceeding the statutory maximum on summary conviction.

In *Swan* [2012] 1 Cr App R (S) 542 a sentence of nine months' imprisonment was appropriate where the offenders, who ran a safe deposit company, failed to disclose circumstances giving rise to reasonable grounds to suspect that money laundering was taking place. The Court of Appeal noted that the maximum penalty for the offence was five years, and that sentences towards the top of the range would be reserved for those involved in regulated businesses who knew that money laundering was going on. In the instant case, if the Court had been dealing with an isolated instance a lower sentence would have been proper, but there had been guilty pleas to seven counts of assisting undercover police officers in laundering money without being reported and advising how identity might be concealed.

In *Griffiths* [2007] 1 Cr App R (S) 581, the solicitor offender, was convicted of failing to make a required disclosure under s. 330. He had carried out a conveyance on a house in circumstances where he had reasonable grounds to suspect that others were engaged in money laundering. Sentence was reduced from 15 months' imprisonment to six months. See also *Duff* [2003] 1 Cr App R (S) 466.

Tipping-off

B21.30   The POCA 2002, s. 333(1), created an offence of making a disclosure likely to prejudice a money laundering investigation which is being undertaken or may in the future be undertaken by law enforcement authorities. This supplanted the Drug Trafficking Act 1994, s. 53(2), and the CJA 1988, s. 93D(2), but was itself repealed (as of 26 December 2007) by the Terrorism Act 2000 and the Proceeds of Crime Act 2002 (Amendment) Regulations 2007 (SI 2007 No. 3398), reg. 3 and sch. 2, which replace it with five new sections (ss. 333A to 333E) in accordance with Directive 2005/60/EC on the prevention of the use of the financial system for the purpose of money laundering and terrorist financing. Section 333A provides a direct replacement for

s. 333, whereas ss. 333B to 333D give effect to certain exceptions specified in Article 28 of the Directive. Section 333E provides definitions.

Proceeds of Crime Act 2002, s. 333A

(1) A person commits an offence if—
- (a) the person discloses any matter within subsection (2);
- (b) the disclosure is likely to prejudice any investigation that might be conducted following the disclosure referred to in that subsection; and
- (c) the information on which the disclosure is based came to the person in the course of a business in the regulated sector.

(2) The matters are that the person or another person has made a disclosure under this Part—
- (a) to a constable,
- (b) to an officer of Revenue and Customs,
- (c) to a nominated officer, or
- (d) to a National Crime Agency officer authorised for the purposes of this Part by the Director General of that Agency,

of information that came to that person in the course of a business in the regulated sector.

(3) A person commits an offence if—
- (a) the person discloses that an investigation into allegations that an offence under this Part has been committed is being contemplated or is being carried out;
- (b) the disclosure is likely to prejudice that investigation; and
- (c) the information on which the disclosure is based came to the person in the course of a business in the regulated sector.

(4) A person guilty of an offence under this section is liable—
- (a) on summary conviction to imprisonment for a term not exceeding three months, or to a fine not exceeding level 5 on the standard scale, or to both;
- (b) on conviction on indictment to imprisonment for a term not exceeding two years, or to a fine, or to both.

(5) This section is subject to—
- (a) section 333B (disclosures within an undertaking or group etc),
- (b) section 333C (other permitted disclosures between institutions etc), and
- (c) section 333D (other permitted disclosures etc).

Prejudicing Investigations

Part 8 of the Act deals with criminal and civil investigations into suspected money laundering activities.   **B21.31**

Proceeds of Crime Act 2002, s. 342

(1) This section applies if a person knows or suspects that an appropriate officer...is acting (or proposing to act) in connection with a confiscation investigation, a civil recovery investigation, a detained cash investigation, an exploitation proceeds investigation or a money laundering investigation which is being or is about to be conducted.

(2) The person commits an offence if—
- (a) he makes a disclosure which is likely to prejudice the investigation, or
- (b) he falsifies, conceals, destroys or otherwise disposes of, or causes or permits the falsification, concealment, destruction or disposal of, documents which are relevant to the investigation.

(3) A person does not commit an offence under subsection (2)(a) if—
- (a) he does not know or suspect that the disclosure is likely to prejudice the investigation,
- (b) the disclosure is made in the exercise of a function under this Act or any other enactment relating to criminal conduct or benefit from criminal conduct or in compliance with a requirement imposed under or by virtue of this Act,
- (ba) the disclosure is of a matter within section 333A(2) or (3)(a) (money laundering: tipping off) and the information on which the disclosure is based came to the person in the course of a business in the regulated sector, or
- (bb) the disclosure is made in the exercise of a function under Part 7 of the Coroners and Justice Act 2009 (criminal memoirs etc) or in compliance with a requirement imposed under or by virtue of that Act, or
- (c) he is a professional legal adviser and the disclosure falls within subsection (4).

(4) A disclosure falls within this subsection if it is a disclosure—
    (a) to (or to a representative of) a client of the professional legal adviser in connection with the giving by the adviser of legal advice to the client, or
    (b) to any person in connection with legal proceedings or contemplated legal proceedings.
(5) But a disclosure does not fall within subsection (4) if it is made with the intention of furthering a criminal purpose.
(6) A person does not commit an offence under subsection (2)(b) if—
    (a) he does not know or suspect that the documents are relevant to the investigation, or
    (b) he does not intend to conceal any facts disclosed by the documents from any appropriate officer...carrying out the investigation.

This provision replaced the CJA 1988, s. 93D(1), and the Drug Trafficking Act 1994, s. 53(1). It must be read in conjunction with the POCA 2002, s. 341, which defines the various investigations listed in s. 342(1).

It is clear that s. 342(2)(a) and s. 342(2)(b) each create a separate offence. Penalties and procedure for either offence are the same as for offences under ss. 330 to 332 (see **B21.29**).

See also the SCA 2007, s. 69 (improper 'further disclosure' by D of protected information which has been directly or indirectly disclosed to him by a public authority).

OFFENCES UNDER THE MONEY LAUNDERING REGULATIONS 2007

B21.32 The Money Laundering Regulations 2007 (SI 2007 No. 2157) came into force on 15 December 2007, in compliance with the EU 3rd Money Laundering Directive 2005. The Regulations require that 'relevant persons' acting in the course of any business carried on by them in the UK take appropriate steps to detect and prevent both money laundering (i.e. the exchanging of monies or assets that have been criminally obtained for monies or assets that appear 'clean') and the financing of terrorism, although the application of the Regulations is subject to exemptions and exclusions listed in reg. 4.

Relevant persons are identified in reg. 3(1) and (1A) as: credit institutions; financial institutions; auditors, insolvency practitioners, external accountants and tax advisers; independent legal professionals; trust or company service providers; estate agents; high value dealers; and casinos; and for limited purposes also auction platforms in the UK.

Parts 2, 3 and 4 of the Regulations impose various responsibilities on such persons in the conduct of their businesses. These include in particular a duty to put in place and apply 'customer due diligence' measures, along with a duty to operate internal controls, training and monitoring systems that are appropriate to the business in question. Some such requirements are specific to certain kinds of business, such as casinos. Relevant businesses must also be monitored by an appropriate supervisory authority (e.g., the Law Society, the FCA or HMRC).

A person who fails to comply with any requirement in reg. 7(1), (2) or (3), 8(1) or (3), 9(2), 10(1), 11(1)(a), (b) or (c), 14(1), 15(1) or (2), 16(1), (2), (3) or (4), 19(1), (4), (5) or (6), 20(1), (4) or (5), 21, 26, 27(4) or 33, or a direction made under reg. 18, is guilty of an offence and liable on summary conviction to a fine not exceeding the statutory maximum or, on conviction on indictment to imprisonment for a term not exceeding two years, to a fine or to both (reg. 45(1)).

Section B22   Immigration Offences

ILLEGAL ENTRY AND DECEPTION

Immigration Act 1971, ss. 24 and 24A

B22.1

24.—(1) A person who is not a British citizen shall be guilty of an offence punishable on summary conviction with a fine of not more than level 5 on the standard scale or with imprisonment for not more than six months, or with both, in any of the following cases—

(a) if contrary to this Act he knowingly enters the United Kingdom in breach of a deportation order or without leave;

(b) if, having only a limited leave to enter or remain in the United Kingdom, he knowingly either—

   (i)   remains beyond the time limited by the leave; or

   (ii) fails to observe a condition of the leave;

(c) if, having lawfully entered the United Kingdom without leave by virtue of section 8(1) above, he remains without leave beyond the time allowed by section 8(1);

(d) if, without reasonable excuse, he fails to comply with any requirement imposed on him under Schedule 2 to this Act to report to a medical officer of health, or to attend, or submit to a test or examination, as required by such an officer;

(e) if, without reasonable excuse, he fails to observe any restriction imposed on him under Schedule 2 or 3 to this Act as to residence, as to his employment or occupation or as to reporting to the police, to an immigration officer or to the Secretary of State;

(f) if he disembarks in the United Kingdom from a ship or aircraft after being placed on board under Schedule 2 or 3 to this Act with a view to his removal from the United Kingdom;

(g) if he embarks in contravention of a restriction imposed by or under an Order in Council under section 3(7) of this Act.

24A.—(1) A person who is not a British citizen is guilty of an offence if, by means which include deception by him:—

(a) he obtains or seeks to obtain leave to enter or remain in the United Kingdom; or

(b) he secures or seeks to secure the avoidance, postponement or revocation of enforcement action against him.

(2) 'Enforcement action', in relation to a person, means—

(a) the giving of directions for his removal from the United Kingdom ('directions') under Schedule 2 to this Act or section 10 of the Immigration and Asylum Act 1999;

(b) the making of a deportation order against him under section 5 of this Act; or

(c) his removal from the United Kingdom in consequence of directions or a deportation order.

Procedure

An immigration officer may arrest without warrant any person who has committed or attempted **B22.2** to commit any offence under the Immigration Act 1971, ss. 24 (except s. 24(1)(d)) or 24A or whom he has reasonable grounds for suspecting of committing or attempting to commit such

B
Part B Offences

an offence (Immigration Act 1971, s. 28A(1) and (2)). The offence of deception can be committed in a control zone in France or Belgium, and powers of arrest are exercisable by police there (Nationality, Immigration and Asylum Act 2002 (Juxtaposed Controls) Order 2003 (SI 2003 No. 2818), arts. 11 to 13).

An offence under the Immigration Act 1971, s. 24, is a summary only offence (s. 24(1)). An extended time-limit for prosecution applies to offences under s. 24(1)(a) and (c) (ss. 24(3) and 28), but not to the offence of deception under s. 24A. The offence of overstaying under s. 24(1)(b) is committed at any time when the immigrant knows his leave has expired but remains in the UK, but can be charged only once for any period of overstay (s. 24(1A)).

The deception offence under s. 24A is triable either way (s. 24A(3)).

B22.3 Indictment

Statement of Offence

Obtaining leave to enter or remain in the United Kingdom by deception contrary to section 24A(1) and (3) of the Immigration Act 1971.

Particulars of Offence

A on the...day of.../on a day between the...day of...and the...day of...not being a British citizen, obtained/sought to obtain leave to enter or remain in the United Kingdom/the avoidance, postponement or revocation of enforcement against him by means of deception namely [*specify deception*].

Sentencing

B22.4 The maximum sentence for illegal entry and any other offence under the Immigration Act 1971, s. 24, is a fine not exceeding level 5 on the standard scale, six months' imprisonment or both (s. 24(1)). The maximum sentence for the deception offence when tried summarily is the same as that for illegal entry; trial on indictment carries the maximum of two years' imprisonment, a fine or both (s. 24A(3)).

If an offender is convicted or pleads guilty before a magistrates' court in respect of the s. 24A offence, it is likely that he will be committed to the Crown Court for sentence. For all but the most minor offences, an immediate custodial sentence can be expected.

Similarly, an immediate custodial sentence would ordinarily be imposed for possession of false documents with or without intent (contrary to the Identity Cards Act 2006, s. 25(1) and (5)) in an immigration context because such offences are inimical to proper immigration control (*Carneiro* [2008] 1 Cr App R (S) 571). In *Ovieriakhi* [2009] EWCA Crim 452 the Court of Appeal reviewed its sentencing decisions and explained their divergence by reference to a scale ranging from the use or possession of false passports for the purpose of evading controls on entry into the UK to the use of a document other than a passport by a person lawfully present in order to obtain employment or a bank account. Earlier guidance in *Kolawole* [2005] 2 Cr App R (S) 14 (12 to 18 months for a person of good character on a guilty plea) was said to apply to the former category which is to be distinguished from cases where a false passport is used to gain work or open a bank account whether the individual is lawfully present in the UK or not. Unlawful presence in the UK is not an aggravating factor for sentencing purposes (*Omowanle* [2009] EWCA Crim 2286). Six months 'has now become a standard sentence for somebody using a false document to obtain employment contrary to immigration controls, in circumstances where they plead at the first opportunity and have a good character' (*Osei* [2009] EWCA Crim 2287). Where the effect of the deception had been long-term and very advantageous to the offender, the sentence of 12 months was deemed appropriate (*Boateng* [2013] EWCA Crim 2306). For possession of false passports, see also **B6.62**.

Where the purpose of the entry is to claim asylum, different considerations apply. In *R (K) v Croydon Crown Court* [2005] 2 Cr App R (S) 578, a four-month detention and training order imposed by a youth court on a 17-year-old asylum seeker who used deception on entry was quashed as wrong in principle, and a conditional discharge substituted. The court emphasised the role and the power of the agent in that case.

In *Kishientine* [2005] 2 Cr App R (S) 156, the Court of Appeal held that a court should not take into consideration the apparent strength of an asylum claim where that claim had not yet been determined by the Secretary of State. Nor should it treat the imminent removal of the offender as justifying a lower sentence than would otherwise have been given (*A-G's Ref (Nos. 1 and 6 of 2008* [2008] 2 Cr App R (S) 557).

B22.5 A recommendation for deportation (see E20.1) is appropriate in cases which go well beyond the commission of a 'mere' immigration offence, such as entering a bogus marriage in order to remain in the UK (*Ahemed* [2006] 1 Cr App R (S) 419), or where a fraudulently obtained or forged passport is used to obtain a national insurance number (*Bennabas* [2005] EWCA Crim 2113). However, recommendations for deportation were quashed in *Ahaiwe* [2007] EWCA Crim 1018, and *Isah* [2007] EWCA Crim 1975, where false vignettes in passports were used to obtain employment, in *Olajide* [2008] EWCA Crim 1655 and *Mvumi* [2008] EWCA Crim 2144, where false passports were used to obtain employment, and in *Scafe* [2009] EWCA Crim 41, where a false driving licence had been used to open a bank account. Aggravating features of similar offences meant that recommendations were upheld in *Halili* [2009] EWCA Crim 25, where the offender had used documents in a number of different identities, and *Clarke* [2008] EWCA Crim 3023, where the false driving licence had been used to commit additional offences.

Elements

B22.6 A person who is a British citizen cannot commit the offences. The offence of illegal entry requires actual entry and will not have been committed if entry has not occurred. The deception offence can be committed by seeking to enter as well as by actually entering, and also embraces action taken to remain in the UK and to prevent or defer removal. It has been used against failed asylum seekers who have sought asylum again under a different identity (*Nagmadeen* [2003] EWCA Crim 2004). The deception must be material (but it does not have to be the sole means of obtaining entry, etc.) and must be by the immigrant personally. The burden of proof for both offences is normally on the prosecution. However, for the illegal entry offence an exception is made in cases brought within six months of the date of entry. In those cases the burden is on the accused to show on the balance of probabilities that he entered the UK legally (Immigration Act 1971, s. 24(4)(b)). It is arguable that this reversal of the legal burden of proof is contrary to the presumption of innocence contained in the ECHR, Article 6(2), particularly since leave to enter may be granted orally (Immigration (Leave to Enter and Remain) Order 2000 (SI 2000 No. 1161), art. 8(3)) and so might be difficult to prove. On the presumption of innocence and Article 6(2), see further **F3.18**.

There are also offences relating to false registration cards and immigration stamps under ss. 26A and 26B of the 1971 Act.

Defences

B22.7 **Article 31 of the Convention Relating to the Status of Refugees**   Section 31 of the Immigration and Asylum Act 1999 sets out defences, based on Article 31 of the Convention Relating to the Status of Refugees ('the Refugee Convention'), to the deception offence. The statutory defence in s. 31 was introduced following the decision of the Divisional Court in *Uxbridge Magistrates' Court, ex parte Adimi* [1999] 4 All ER 520 that the government's obligations under Article 31 of the Refugee Convention required that criminal sanctions were not imposed on refugees who entered the UK illegally provided that they made themselves known to the relevant authorities without delay. A 'refugee' is as defined in Article 1A of the Refugee Convention. Section 31 of the Immigration and Asylum Act 1999 is a defence to the deception offence and certain other offences, including offences under part I of the Forgery and Counterfeiting Act 1981 (see **B6.26**) or s. 4 or 6 of the Identity Document Act 2010 (see **B6.59**). In *Mateta* [2014] 1 All ER 152 the Court of Appeal summarised the main elements of this defence as follows (at [21]):

i) The defendant must provide sufficient evidence in support of his claim to refugee status to raise the issue and thereafter the burden falls on the prosecution to prove to the criminal standard that he is not a refugee (s. 31 of the [Immigration and Asylum Act 1999] and *Mukuwa* [[2006] 1 WLR 2755 at] [26]) unless an application by the defendant for asylum has been refused by the Secretary of State, when the legal burden rests on him to establish on a balance of probabilities that he is a refugee (s. 31(7) of the [1999 Act] and *Sadighipour* . . . [2012] 1 Cr App R 269 at [38]–[40]);

ii) If the Crown fails to disprove that the defendant was a refugee (or if the defendant proves on a balance of probabilities he is a refugee following the Secretary of State's refusal of his application for asylum), it then falls to a defendant to prove on the balance of probabilities that
a) he did not stop in any country in transit to the United Kingdom for more than a short stopover (which, on the facts, was explicable, see (iv) below) or, alternatively, that he could not reasonably have expected to be given protection under the Refugee Convention in countries outside the United Kingdom in which he stopped; and, if so:
b) he, presented himself to the authorities in the United Kingdom 'without delay', unless (again, depending on the facts) it was explicable that he did not present himself to the authorities in the United Kingdom during a short stopover in this country when travelling through to the nation where he intended to claim asylum;
c) he had good cause for his illegal entry or presence in the United Kingdom; and
d) he made a claim for asylum as soon as was reasonably practicable after his arrival in the United Kingdom, unless (once again, depending on the facts) it was explicable that he did not present himself to the authorities in the United Kingdom during a short stopover in this country when travelling through to the nation where he intended to claim asylum, (Section 31(1) of the 1999 Act; *Sadighpour* [38]–[40]; *Jaddi* [2012] EWCA Crim 2565 at [16] and [30]).

iii) The requirement that the claim for asylum must be made as soon as was reasonably practicable does not necessarily mean at the earliest possible moment (*Asfaw* [2008] 1 AC 1061 . . .; *R v M (A)* [[2011] 1 Cr App R 432 at] [9]).

iv) It follows that the fact that a refugee stopped in a third country in transit is not necessarily fatal and may be explicable: the refugee has some choice as to where he might properly claim asylum. The main touchstones by which exclusion from protection should be judged are the length of the stay in the intermediate country, the reasons for delaying there and whether or not the refugee sought or found protection de jure or de facto from the persecution from which he or she was seeking to escape [(*Asfaw* at [26]; *R v M (A)* at [9])].

v) The requirement that the refugee demonstrates 'good cause' for his illegal entry or presence in the United Kingdom will be satisfied by him showing he was reasonably travelling on false papers (*Ex p Adimi* [2001] QB 667 at 679H).

B22.8 The Court went on to consider the obligation to provide advice on the parameters of the s. 31 defence (at [24]):

i) There is an obligation on those representing defendants charged with an offence of possession of an identity document with improper intention to advise them of the existence of a possible s. 31 defence if the circumstances and instructions generate the possibility of mounting this defence, and they should explain its parameters (*R v M (A)* at [10]).

ii) The advisers should properly note the instructions and the advice given (*R v M (A)* at [56]).

iii) If an accused's representatives failed to advise him about the availability of this defence, on an appeal to the Court of Appeal . . . the court will assess whether the defence would 'quite probably' have succeeded (*R v M (A)* at [13]).

iv) It is appropriate for the Court of Appeal to assess the prospects of an asylum defence succeeding by reference to the findings of the First-tier Tribunal (Immigration and Asylum Chamber), if available (*Sadighpour* at [35]).

B22.9 The statutory defence under s. 31, does not apply to the offence of illegal entry, and did not apply to the statutory predecessor of s. 24A. A conviction for deception under s. 24A was quashed in *R (Badur) v Birmingham Crown Court and Solihull Magistrates' Court (DPP, Secretary of State for the Home Department and CPS interested parties)* [2006] EWHC 539 (Admin), on the basis that it should have been charged under the statutory predecessor of s. 24A, and the accused would have been able to avail himself of the broader defence which relied directly on the Refugee Convention, Article 31, instead of being limited to the statutory defence under s. 31 of the 1999 Act. In *Asfaw* [2008] 1 AC 1061, the House of Lords (by a majority of three to two) held, reversing the Court of Appeal, that it was an abuse of process to charge the offence of obtaining air services by deception (to which the statutory defence does not apply) where a jury had accepted the defence in acquitting of a charge under the Forgery and Counterfeiting Act 1981. Their lordships held that the defence applied equally to offences committed while leaving the UK in transit to a destination country as it did to offences committed in the course of entry. See also *Kamalanathan* [2010] EWCA Crim 1335.

The defence under s. 31 does not apply to the offence of facilitating the entry into the UK of another (*Sternaj v DPP* [2011] EWHC 1094 (Admin)).

Victims of Human Trafficking   A victim of human trafficking is defined in Article 4 of **B22.10** the Council of Europe Convention on Action against Trafficking in Human Beings, 2005 (ECAT) and Article 2 of EU Directive 2011/36/EU on preventing and combating trafficking in human beings and protecting its victims (the Trafficking Directive). The jurisdiction to stay an indictment as an abuse of process where a defendant is a victim of human trafficking has been considered by the Court of Appeal in the cases of *M (L)* (2011) 1 Cr App R 135 and *L* [2014] 1 All ER 113. The protection principles behind such an abuse of process submission are provided for in the non-punishment provisions in Article 26 (ECAT) and Article 8 (Trafficking Directive).

Hughes LJ, when ruling on the application of Article 26, held in *M (L)* (at [10]]) that prosecutors are required to conduct a three-stage exercise of judgement: (1) is there reason to believe that the person has been trafficked? If so, then (2) if there is clear evidence of a credible common law defence the case will be discontinued in the ordinary way on evidential grounds, but, importantly, (3) even where there is not, but the offence may have been committed as a result of compulsion arising from the trafficking, prosecutors should consider whether the public interest lies in proceeding to prosecute or not. In *M (L)* the Court of Appeal held that the word 'compelled' was not limited to the circumstances in which the English common-law defences of duress and necessity apply. In respect of (3), where the accused is a child (under 18 years old), the prosecutors should treat as a primary consideration whether it would be in the best interests of the child to prosecute (*L* at [20]–[21]).

Lord Judge CJ further held in *L* (at [17]):

> In the context of an abuse of process argument on behalf of an alleged victim of trafficking, the court will reach its own decision on the basis of the material advanced in support of and against the continuation of the prosecution. Where a court considers issues relevant to age, trafficking and exploitation, the prosecution will be stayed if the court disagrees with the decision to prosecute. The fears that the exercise of the jurisdiction to stay will be inadequate are groundless.

Lord Judge CJ had earlier stated (at [16]):

> In any case, where it is necessary to do so, whether issues of trafficking or other questions arise, the court reviews the decision to prosecute through the exercise of its jurisdiction to stay. The court protects the rights of a victim of trafficking by overseeing the decision of the prosecutor and refusing to countenance any prosecution which fails to acknowledge and address the victim's subservient situation, and the international obligations to which the United Kingdom is a party. The role of the court replicates its role in relation to *agent provocateurs*. It stands between the prosecution and the victim of trafficking where the crimes are committed as an aspect of the victim's exploitation (see *R v Loosely A-G's Ref (No. 3 of 2000)* [[2001] All ER 897]...).

B22.11 The Secretary of State provides for a formal identification of a victim of trafficking, known as the National Referral Mechanism. In *L* the Court held (at [28]) that, when considering the weight to be placed on such decisions:

> Whether the concluded decision of the competent authority is favourable or adverse to the individual it will have been made by an authority vested with the responsibility for investigating these issues, and although the court is not bound by the decision, unless there is evidence to contradict it, or significant evidence that was not considered, it is likely that the criminal courts will abide by it.

B22.12 Where an accused has not come forward as a victim of trafficking until after conviction and sentence, the Court of Appeal has still quashed the conviction as unsafe on the premise that had the evidence been made known to the prosecution at the material time, no prosecution would have been brought (*O* [2011] EWCA Crim 2226 and *LZ* [2012] EWCA Crim 1867)

The CPS has published detailed guidance on 'Human Trafficking, Smuggling and Slavery', which considers the prosecutorial discretion concerning accused potential victims of trafficking and provides examples of offences most frequently committed by victims of trafficking in its section on 'Indicators of trafficking'. These offences are wide reaching and include benefit fraud, drug production and identity offences.

FAILURE TO PRODUCE IMMIGRATION DOCUMENTS, ETC.

Definition

B22.13 **Asylum and Immigration (Treatment of Claimants, etc.) Act 2004, s. 2**

(1) A person commits an offence if at a leave or asylum interview he does not have with him an immigration document which—
   (a) is in force, and
   (b) satisfactorily establishes his identity and nationality or citizenship.
(2) A person commits an offence if at a leave or asylum interview he does not have with him, in respect of any dependent child with whom he claims to be travelling or living, an immigration document which—
   (a) is in force, and
   (b) satisfactorily establishes the child's identity and nationality or citizenship.
(3) But a person does not commit an offence under subsection (1) or (2) if—
   (a) the interview referred to in that subsection takes place after the person has entered the United Kingdom, and
   (b) within the period of three days beginning with the date of the interview the person provides to an immigration officer or to the Secretary of State a document of the kind referred to in that subsection.
(4) It is a defence for a person charged with an offence under subsection (1)—
   (a) to prove that he is an EEA national,
   (b) to prove that he is a member of the family of an EEA national and that he is exercising a right under the Community Treaties in respect of entry to or residence in the United Kingdom,
   (c) to prove that he has a reasonable excuse for not being in possession of a document of the kind specified in subsection (1),
   (d) to produce a false immigration document and to prove that he used that document as an immigration document for all purposes in connection with his journey to the United Kingdom, or
   (e) to prove that he travelled to the United Kingdom without, at any stage since he set out on the journey, having possession of an immigration document.
(5) It is a defence for a person charged with an offence under subsection (2) in respect of a child—
   (a) to prove that the child is an EEA national,
   (b) to prove that the child is a member of the family of an EEA national and that the child is exercising a right under the Community Treaties in respect of entry to or residence in the United Kingdom,

(c) to prove that the person has a reasonable excuse for not being in possession of a document of the kind specified in subsection (2),

(d) to produce a false immigration document and to prove that it was used as an immigration document for all purposes in connection with the child's journey to the United Kingdom, or

(e) to prove that he travelled to the United Kingdom with the child without, at any stage since he set out on the journey, having possession of an immigration document in respect of the child.

(6) Where the charge for an offence under subsection (1) or (2) relates to an interview which takes place after the defendant has entered the United Kingdom—

(a) subsections (4)(c) and (5)(c) shall not apply, but

(b) it is a defence for the defendant to prove that he has a reasonable excuse for not providing a document in accordance with subsection (3).

(7) For the purposes of subsections (4) to (6)—

(a) the fact that a document was deliberately destroyed or disposed of is not a reasonable excuse for not being in possession of it or for not providing it in accordance with subsection (3), unless it is shown that the destruction or disposal was—

  (i) for a reasonable cause, or

  (ii) beyond the control of the person charged with the offence, and

(b) in paragraph (a)(i) 'reasonable cause' does not include the purpose of—

  (i) delaying the handling or resolution of a claim or application or the taking of a decision,

  (ii) increasing the chances of success of a claim or application, or

  (iii) complying with instructions or advice given by a person who offers advice about, or facilitates, immigration into the United Kingdom, unless in the circumstances of the case it is unreasonable to expect non-compliance with the instructions or advice.

(8) A person shall be presumed for the purposes of this section not to have a document with him if he fails to produce it to an immigration officer or official of the Secretary of State on request.

Procedure

A power of arrest is granted to an immigration officer who reasonably suspects that a person has **B22.14** committed an offence under the Asylum and Immigration (Treatment of Claimants, etc.) Act 2004, s. 2 (s. 2(10)).

The offence is triable either way.

Sentencing

The maximum penalty on conviction on indictment is two years' imprisonment, a fine or **B22.15** both. On summary conviction, the maximum is six months, a fine not exceeding the statutory maximum, or both. In normal circumstances, a custodial sentence is inevitable (*Bei Bei Wang* [2005] 2 Cr App R (S) 492, in which a ten-month sentence in a young offender institute on an 18-year-old offender was reduced to two months, and a recommendation for deportation quashed). However, in *MJ* (20 July 2007 unreported), the Court of Appeal held that a custodial sentence was generally inappropriate for an unaccompanied minor committing the offence. In *Weng and Wang* [2005] EWCA Crim 2248, sentences of 36 weeks were reduced to three months, and in *Ai (Lu Zhu)* [2006] 1 Cr App R (S) 18, a sentence of nine months imposed on an adult male was reduced to five months. In *Safari and Zanganeh* [2006] 1 Cr App R (S) 1, in reducing a nine-month sentence on an Iranian husband and wife to three months, the Court of Appeal held that it was not open to a trial judge to conclude, without holding a *Newton* hearing, that the offenders gave their documents to an agent to conceal their identities and details of their movements. A recommendation for deportation was upheld as appropriate following conviction for failure to produce immigration documents by an asylum seeker in *Osman (Abdullah)* [2007] EWCA Crim 39, although the conviction was subsequently quashed on referral by the CCRC (see **B22.16**).

Elements

B22.16   The Home Office indicated in the Explanatory Notes issued with the Bill that the essence of the offence is that the accused has destroyed a document en route since carriers are required to ensure that their passengers have appropriate documentation prior to embarking on their journey: 'Someone who arrives in the UK, therefore, without a passport may in many cases be assumed to have destroyed it en route.' In addition to defences available to EEA nationals, no offence is committed where a person produces a false immigration document and proves that it was used for all purposes in connection with the journey or where he proves that he was at no stage in possession of an immigration document. Further, a defence is available where a reasonable excuse is provided for not having an immigration document. In *Thet v DPP* [2007] 2 All ER 425 Lord Phillips CJ held that the Asylum and Immigration (Treatment of Claimants, etc.) Act 2004, s. 2(3), (4)(c) and (6) referred to valid documents only. Someone who has been unable to obtain a valid passport in his home country has a reasonable excuse for not producing it, and does not have to prove additionally that he has a reasonable excuse for disposal of a false immigration document used to enter the UK. In *Mohammed and Osman* [2008] 1 WLR 1130, the Court of Appeal accepted this interpretation of s. 2(4)(c) and (6)(b), but held that the fact that a claimant never had a genuine travel document did not provide a defence under s. 2(4)(e). This judgment results in the phrase 'immigration document' having different meanings in different subsections, which is unsatisfactory. A conviction for entering the UK without a passport was quashed where a judge had wrongly withdrawn the defence of reasonable excuse under s. 2(4)(c) before the trial had begun; there was evidence to support the defence and it would not have been perverse of the jury to conclude that the defence was made out on the evidence before it (*Asmeron* [2013] 1 WLR 3457).

The Court of Appeal held in *Embaye* [2005] EWCA Crim 2865 that the imposition of a legal burden of proof on an accused seeking to rely on the statutory defence is not incompatible with the presumption of innocence contained in the ECHR, Article 6(2) (see further **F3.18** *et seq.*), even if the defence may not fully comply with Article 31 of the Refugee Convention where the defendant is a bona fide asylum claimant. For Article 31, see **B22.7**.

FAILURE TO COMPLY WITH REQUIREMENT TO PROVIDE INFORMATION REQUIRED TO OBTAIN TRAVEL DOCUMENT

B22.17   **Asylum and Immigration (Treatment of Claimants, etc.) Act 2004, s. 35**

   (3) A person commits an offence if he fails without reasonable excuse to comply with a requirement of the Secretary of State under subsection 1.

Under s. 35(1), the Secretary of State may require a person to take specified action if the Secretary of State thinks that the action will or may enable a travel document to be obtained to facilitate the person's deportation or removal.

Procedure

B22.18   A power of arrest is granted to an immigration officer who reasonably suspects that a person has committed an offence under the Asylum and Immigration (Treatment of Claimants, etc.) Act 2004, s. 35(3) (s. 35(5)).

The offence is triable either way.

Sentencing

B22.19   The maximum penalty on conviction on indictment is two years' imprisonment, a fine or both. On summary conviction, the maximum is six months, a fine not exceeding the statutory maximum or both (s. 35(4)).

Elements

Fear of persecution in the home country was held not to constitute a reasonable excuse for **B22.20**
non-compliance with a requirement to attend for interview by officials of that country's
Embassy in *Tabnak* [2007] 1 WLR 1317, where the Court of Appeal held that the criminal
court should not become a battleground to determine whether deportation was legitimate.
It was for the specialist immigration judges and tribunals to assess the merits of an asylum claim. Reasonable excuse should relate to ability, not willingness to comply. Home
Office guidance on the Asylum and Immigration (Treatment of Claimants, etc.) Act 2004,
s. 35(3), indicates that travel difficulties and health emergencies might constitute reasonable excuses.

ASSISTING UNLAWFUL IMMIGRATION AND
RELATED OFFENCES

Definitions

Immigration Act 1971, s. 25

B22.21

(1) A person commits an offence if he—
  (a) does an act which facilitates the commission of a breach of immigration law by an indi-
      vidual who is not a citizen of the European Union,
  (b) knows or has reasonable cause for believing that the act facilitates the commission of a
      breach of immigration law by the individual, and
  (c) knows or has reasonable cause for believing that the individual is not a citizen of the
      European Union.

Procedure and Jurisdiction

An immigration officer may arrest without warrant a person who has committed or is attempt- **B22.22**
ing to commit this offence, or whom he has reasonable grounds for suspecting of committing
or attempting to commit the offence (Immigration Act 1971, s. 28A(3)).

The offence is triable either way (Immigration Act 1971, s. 25(6)). The offence applies to things
done (to assist unlawful immigration to a Member State) whether inside or outside the UK
(s. 25(4) as amended by UK Borders Act 2007, s. 30(2)). The offence applies to assisting
unlawful immigration into any Member State of the European Union (s. 25(2)) or Iceland
and Norway, which are treated as Member States for this purpose by virtue of art. 2 of the
Immigration (Assisting Unlawful Immigration) (Section 25 List of Schengen Acquis States)
Order 2004 (SI 2004 No. 2877). This is a measure required to enable the UK to comply with
its obligations under Article 27 of the Schengen Convention to make it a criminal offence to
breach the immigration law of the UK or any Member State.

Indictment

B22.23

Statement of Offence

Assisting unlawful immigration to the United Kingdom contrary to section 25 of the Immigration
Act 1971.

Particulars of Offence

A on the...day of.../on a day between the...day of...and the...day of...did an act which
facilitated the commission of a breach of immigration law by [*specify name*], who is not a citizen
of the European Union, knowing or having reasonable cause to believe that the act facilitated
the commission of a breach of immigration law by him, and that he is not a citizen of the
European Union.

Sentencing Guidelines

B22.24 The maximum sentence is 14 years' imprisonment, a fine or both on indictment; six months' imprisonment, a fine not exceeding the statutory maximum or both summarily (Immigration Act 1971, s. 25(6)).

This offence is generally regarded as a serious one and would often attract a custodial sentence even where no profit motive or commercial organisation is involved. An important guideline judgment was given by the Court of Appeal in *Le and Stark* [1999] 1 Cr App R (S) 422 in relation to the previous s. 25(1)(a) offence of 'assisting illegal entry' into the UK. In that case Lord Bingham stated: 'The offence is one which calls very often for deterrent sentences and as the statistics make plain, the problem of illegal entry is on the increase'. The Court of Appeal indicated that the appropriate penalty would normally be a custodial sentence and that the offence would be aggravated where (a) it was committed for financial gain, (b) the illegal entry was facilitated for strangers as opposed to a spouse or a close family member, (c) there had been a high degree of planning, organisation and sophistication, or (d) the offence was committed in relation to a large number of illegal entrants. *Le and Stark* was considered and applied in *Oliviera* [2013] 2 Cr App R (S) 18 (4) in the context of sham marriages, the Court of Appeal noting that the statutory maximum at the time of *Le* had since increased from seven years' imprisonment to 14 years. In *Rotsias* [2013] EWCA Crim 2470, the Court of Appeal referred to the 'net effect' of *A-G's Ref (Nos. 37, 38 and 65)* [2011] 2 Cr App R (S) 31, namely that offences under s. 25 of the 1971 Act will routinely attract sentences of between three and eight years—where an individual sentence will stand in this range will depend on the features of aggravation identified by Lord Bingham in *Le and Stark*.

B22.25 In *Akrout (Lofti Ben Salem)* [2003] EWCA Crim 491, the Court of Appeal upheld a sentence of six years' imprisonment for an offence under the previous version of s. 25(1)(a) (when the maximum sentence was ten years). The sentence was said by the Court of Appeal to be severe but not manifestly excessive. In that case a large number of illegal immigrants (24) were involved and the immigrants were strangers to the accused. See also *Saini* [2005] 1 Cr App R (S) 278 (sentence of seven and a half years held not excessive for conspiracy to organise large-scale entry). Sentences totalling ten years for facilitating illegal entry, living on the earnings of prostitution, kidnapping and incitement to rape, for men involved in arranging the illegal entry of women who were then required to work as prostitutes, were increased to a total of 23 years in *A-G's Ref (No. 6 of 2004) (Plakici)* [2005] 1 Cr App R (S) 83. The Court of Appeal upheld a sentence of nine years' imprisonment for a conspiracy to facilitate a breach of immigration law. It was an operation that ran for three months but was sophisticated, planned and organised (*Wolanski* [2013] EWCA Crim 1020). At the other end of the scale, a sentence of 15 months was reduced to ten months on appeal where the offender had brought her husband to the UK using a false passport (*Nenartoniene* [2009] EWCA Crim 2659) and from 15 to nine months where the offender had brought his widowed sister-in-law to the UK using his wife's passport (*Darays* [2009] EWCA Crim 2654). See also *Olusanya* [2013] 1 Cr App R (S) 170 (32), a case of conspiracy to facilitate the commission of a breach of UK immigration laws by non-EU persons. Where a 20-year-old woman was convicted of assisting unlawful immigration after an illegal entrant was found in the boot of her car, a 12-month custodial sentence was deemed appropriate (*Seferi* [2013] 1 Cr App R (S) 350 (63)).

A person convicted of an offence under s. 25 will also be subject to the forfeiture provisions in s. 25C. An offence under s. 25 is designated a 'lifestyle offence' under the POCA 2002 (see **E19.16**).

Elements

B22.26 The offence applies only where the person (or persons) 'assisted' is not a citizen of a Member State of the European Union or a citizen of Iceland or Norway (see **B22.22**), and the term 'citizen of the European Union' is defined so as to include such citizens (s. 25(7)(b)). The offence refers to an act which 'facilitates' a breach of 'immigration law'. Thus, the first element in the offence is complicit dishonesty on the part of the person whose entry or stay is facilitated (e.g., that the visa applicant knew that the documents with which he had been provided by the accused and on which he relied in making his visa application were false); proof of dishonesty on the part of the accused is not sufficient (*Kaile* [2009] EWCA Crim 2868). 'Immigration law' is defined in s. 25(2) as a law which has effect in a Member State which regulates entitlement to (a) enter the State, (b) transit across the State, or (c) be in the State. The offence thus covers acts facilitating illegal entry or stay in other Member States. The immigration laws of Member States are to be conclusively proved by a certificate from the government concerned (s. 25(3)). It also includes acts assisting non-EU citizens who entered the UK lawfully to remain unlawfully. In *Javaherifard* [2005] EWCA Crim 3231, the Court of Appeal held, following *Singh and Meeuwsen* [1972] 1 All ER 122, that it is possible to facilitate entry by acts close to but following actual entry (e.g., by making arrangements to get illegal entrants away quickly from the port of disembarkation). In *Kapoor* [2012] 2 All ER 1205 the Court of Appeal held that for the purposes of s. 25(2) an immigration law is a law which determines whether a person is lawfully or unlawfully either entering the UK, or in transit or being in the UK. Thus if a person, with the necessary knowledge or reasonable cause to believe, facilitates the unlawful entry or unlawful presence in the UK of a person who is not a citizen of the EU, he commits the offence. The Court held that s. 2 of the Asylum and Immigration (Treatment of Claimants) Act 2004 (as to which see **B22.13**) was not an 'immigration law' for the purposes of s. 25(2).

The Court of Appeal held in *Dhall* [2013] EWCA Crim 1610 that an indictment charging an offence of assisting unlawful immigration which did not set out the particular immigration law alleged to have been breached had not rendered a conviction unsafe where there had been no request to provide further particulars and the accused had conceded that he had carried out acts that had facilitated breaches in immigration laws.

Acts done abroad before 30 January 2008 (before s. 25(4) was amended) by persons who are not British nationals cannot constitute an offence under s. 25 (*Rechack* [2006] EWCA Crim 2975).

An accused cannot rely on the protection of Article 31 of the Refugee Convention (see **B22.7**) in relation to facilitating the entry into the UK of another (*Sternaj v DPP* [2011] EWHC 1094 (Admin)).

OTHER OFFENCES RELATING TO ASSISTING ENTRY

Helping Asylum-Seeker to Enter the UK

Immigration Act 1971, s. 25A B22.27

(1) A person commits an offence if—
  (a) he knowingly and for gain facilitates the arrival in the United Kingdom of an individual, and
  (b) he knows or has reasonable cause to believe that the individual is an asylum-seeker.

Procedure and Jurisdiction An immigration officer may arrest without warrant a person who   B22.28
has committed or is attempting to commit this offence, or whom he has reasonable grounds for suspecting of committing or attempting to commit the offence (Immigration Act 1971, s. 28A(3)).

The offence is triable either way (Immigration Act 1971, ss. 25A(4) and 25(6)). The offence applies to things done inside or outside the UK (ss. 25A(4) and 25(4), as amended).

B22.29   Indictment

Statement of Offence

Helping an asylum-seeker to enter the United Kingdom contrary to section 25A of the Immigration Act 1971.

Particulars of Offence

A on the...day of.../on a day between the...day of...and the...day of...knowingly and for gain facilitated the arrival in the United Kingdom of [*specify name*], a person whom he knew or had reasonable cause for believing to be an asylum-seeker.

B22.30   Sentence   The maximum sentence is 14 years' imprisonment, a fine or both on indictment; six months' imprisonment, a fine not exceeding the statutory maximum or both summarily (Immigration Act 1971, ss. 25A(4) and 25(6)).

The forfeiture provisions discussed at **B22.25** also apply to this offence (s. 25C(1)). The offence is designated a 'lifestyle offence' for the purposes of the POCA 2002 (see **E19.16**).

B22.31   Elements   Section 25A of the Immigration Act 1971 reproduces the offence which was previously set out in Immigration Act 1971, s. 25(1)(b). Since the right to claim asylum is protected by the Universal Declaration on Human Rights, the act of assisting asylum-seekers to arrive in the UK and claim asylum cannot therefore be unlawful *per se*, and the gravamen of this offence is profiteering. Thus financial gain is an essential element of the offence. The section does not apply to anything done by persons acting on behalf of an organisation which aims to assist asylum-seekers and does not charge for its services (s. 25A(3)). The accused must know or 'have reasonable cause to believe' that the individual he is assisting is an 'asylum-seeker'. 'Asylum-seeker' is defined in s. 25A(2) as someone who 'intends' to claim that to remove him from the UK would be a breach of the UK's obligations under (a) the Refugee Convention or (b) the ECHR. This presumably means that a person could be guilty of this offence even though the immigrant did not make a claim under the Refugee Convention or the ECHR, provided it can be established that the immigrant intended to make such a claim. Section 25A applies in the case of an asylum-seeker who arrives in or enters the UK without any breach of immigration law being committed by the person gaining entry (*Sternaj v DPP* [2011] EWHC 1094 (Admin)).

A conspiracy to 'assist persons claiming asylum in the United Kingdom' is not an offence known to law (*Hadi* [2001] EWCA Crim 2534).

Assisting Entry to the UK in Breach of Deportation or Exclusion Order

B22.32   **Immigration Act 1971, s. 25B**

(1) A person commits an offence if he—
   (a) does an act which facilitates a breach of a deportation order in force against an individual who is a citizen of the European Union, and
   (b) knows or has reasonable cause for believing that the act facilitates a breach of the deportation order.
(2) Subsection (3) applies where the Secretary of State personally directs that the exclusion from the United Kingdom of an individual who is a citizen of the European Union is conducive to the public good.
(3) A person commits an offence if he—
   (a) does an act which assists the individual to arrive in, enter or remain in the United Kingdom,
   (b) knows or has reasonable cause for believing that the act assists the individual to arrive in, enter or remain in the United Kingdom, and
   (c) knows or has reasonable cause for believing that the Secretary of State has personally directed that the individual's exclusion from the United Kingdom is conducive to the public good.

B22.33   Procedure and Jurisdiction   An immigration officer may arrest without warrant a person who has committed or is attempting to commit this offence, or whom he has reasonable grounds for suspecting of committing or attempting to commit the offence (Immigration Act 1971, s. 28A(3)).

The offence is triable either way (Immigration Act 1971, ss. 25A(4) and 25(6)). The offence also applies to things done inside or outside the UK (ss. 25B(4) and 25(4), as amended).

Sentence   The maximum sentence is 14 years' imprisonment, a fine or both on indictment; **B22.34** six months' imprisonment, a fine not exceeding the statutory maximum or both summarily (Immigration Act 1971, ss. 25B(4) and 25(6)). There are no guideline judgments issued for this offence.

The forfeiture provisions discussed at **B22.25** also apply to this offence (s. 25C(1)). The offence is designated a 'lifestyle offence' for the purposes of the POCA 2002 (see **E19.16**).

Elements   An offence under the Immigration Act 1971 s. 25B, applies only where the per- **B22.35** son being assisted is a citizen of the European Union. It therefore complements the offence at s. 25, which applies only where the person assisted is not an EU citizen. It is a defence that the accused did not know or have reason to believe that the person being assisted was the subject of a deportation or exclusion order.

TRAFFICKING PEOPLE FOR EXPLOITATION

Asylum and Immigration (Treatment of Claimants, etc.) Act 2004, s. 4   **B22.36**

(1A)   A person ('A') commits an offence if A intentionally arranges or facilitates—
    (a)   the arrival in, or entry into, the United Kingdom or another country of another person ('B'),
    (b)   the travel of B within the United Kingdom or another country, or
    (c)   the departure of B from the United Kingdom or another country,
with a view to the exploitation of B.

(1B)   For the purposes of subsection (1A)(a) and (c) A's arranging or facilitating is with a view to the exploitation of B if (and only if)—
    (a)   A intends to exploit B, after B's arrival, entry or (as the case may be) departure but in any part of the world, or
    (b)   A believes that another person is likely to exploit B, after B's arrival, entry or (as the case may be) departure but in any part of the world.

(1C)   For the purposes of subsection (1A)(b) A's arranging or facilitating is with a view to the exploitation of B if (and only if)—
    (a)   A intends to exploit B, during or after the journey and in any part of the world, or
    (b)   A believes that another person is likely to exploit B, during or after the journey and in any part of the world.

(4)   For the purposes of this section a person is exploited if (and only if)—
    (a)   he is the victim of behaviour that contravenes Article 4 of the Human Rights Convention (slavery and forced labour),
    (b)   he is encouraged, required or expected to do anything—
        (i)   as a result of which he or another person would commit an offence under section 32 or 33 of the Human Tissue Act 2004 as it has effect in the law of England and Wales, or
        (ii)   which, were it done in England and Wales, would constitute an offence within sub-paragraph (i),
    (c)   he is subjected to force, threats or deception designed to induce him—
        (i)   to provide services of any kind,
        (ii)   to provide another person with benefits of any kind, or
        (iii)   to enable another person to acquire benefits of any kind, or
    (d)   a person uses or attempts to use him for any purpose within sub-paragraph (i), (ii) or (iii) of paragraph (c), having chosen him for that purpose on the grounds that—
        (i)   he is mentally or physically ill or disabled, he is young or he has a family relationship with a person, and
        (ii)   a person without the illness, disability, youth or family relationship would be likely to refuse to be used for that purpose.

    (4A)   A person who is a UK national commits an offence under this section regardless of—

        (a)   where the arranging or facilitating takes place, or

        (b)   which country is the country of arrival, entry, travel or (as the case may be) departure.

    (4B)   A person who is not a UK national commits an offence under this section if—

        (a)   any part of the arranging or facilitating takes place in the United Kingdom, or

        (b)   the United Kingdom is the country of arrival, entry, travel or (as the case may be) departure.

Procedure and Jurisdiction

B22.37   An immigration officer has a power of arrest in respect of this offence (Asylum and Immigration (Treatment of Claimants, etc.) Act 2004, s. 14(2)(p)).

Extended jurisdiction provisions apply by virtue of s. 4.

Sentencing

B22.38   The maximum penalty on conviction on indictment is 14 years' imprisonment, a fine or both. On summary conviction, the maximum is six months, a fine not exceeding the statutory maximum, or both (ss. 4(5) and 5(11)). In *A-G's Ref (Nos. 37, 38 and 65 of 2010)* [2010] EWCA Crim 2880, sentences of three years' imprisonment imposed, following a trial, on three offenders for an offence of statutory conspiracy to traffic persons for the purpose of exploitation were referred to the Court of Appeal as unduly lenient. The Court gave guidance on the relevant factors to be considered when sentencing, which it said should include the following: (a) the nature and degree of deception or coercion exercised upon the incoming worker; (b) the nature and degree of exploitation exercised upon the worker on arrival in the workplace; (c) the level and methods of control exercised; (d) the level of vulnerability of the incoming worker; (e) the degree of harm suffered by the worker; (f) the level of organisation and planning behind the scheme, the gain sought or achieved, and the offender's role within the organisation; (g) the numbers of those exploited; and (h) previous convictions for similar offences. On the particular facts, the Court found that there was a persistent campaign of exploitation, the motivation was financial and the victims were particularly vulnerable and badly affected by their experience. It considered that an element of general deterrence was appropriate when assessing the sentence and that the starting point would have been six years. Allowing for double jeopardy, the Court imposed sentences of four years' imprisonment on two of the offenders, and left the third sentence unaltered on the basis of the uncertain and fluctuating state of that offender's mental health.

The forfeiture provisions discussed at **B22.25** also apply to this offence (Asylum and Immigration (Treatment of Claimants, etc.) Act 2004, s. 5(4)). The offence is designated a 'lifestyle offence' for the purposes of the POCA 2002 (see **E19.16**). The offence is included in the schedule of offences against a child listed in the CJCSA 2000, sch. 4.

Elements

B22.39   'Exploitation' encompasses slavery or forced labour, organ removal, the use of force or threats to induce the victim to provide services or the abuse of the mentally or physically ill, young persons or relatives. The core elements of the ECHR, Article 4, namely 'slavery', 'servitude' and 'forced or compulsory labour', which are integral to the offence, must be defined with sufficient clarity to a jury (*SK* [2011] EWCA Crim 1691, approving the definitions in *Siliadin v France* (2005) 43 EHRR 16). In *Siliadin* the ECtHR held that slavery is the status of a person over whom powers attached to the right of ownership are exercised; servitude is an obligation to provide one's services that is imposed by the use of coercion and that forced or compulsory labour is work performed involuntarily and under the threat of a penalty. In *SK* the Court of Appeal said that these concepts are not necessarily mutually exclusive. In *Siliadin* the ECtHR also confirmed that Article 4 entails a specific positive obligation on Member States to penalise and prosecute effectively any act aimed at maintaining a person in a situation of slavery, servitude or forced or compulsory labour and that domestic servitude is a specific offence, distinct from trafficking and exploitation, which involves a complex set of dynamics, involving both overt and more subtle forms of coercion, to force compliance. See also *CN v UK* (2012) 56 EHRR 24 where s. 4 alone did not meet that obligation and **B2.197** *et seq.*

Trafficking into the UK for Sexual Exploitation

For this offence and related offences under the Sexual Offences Act 2003, see **B3.253** *et seq.*   **B22.40**

EMPLOYING PERSONS KNOWN TO BE NOT ENTITLED TO WORK IN THE UK

Immigration, Asylum and Nationality Act 2006, s. 21   **B22.41**

(1) A person commits an offence if he employs another ('the employee') knowing that the employee is an adult subject to immigration control and that—
   (a) he has not been granted leave to enter or remain in the United Kingdom, or
   (b) his leave to enter or remain in the United Kingdom—
      (i) is invalid,
      (ii) has ceased to have effect (whether by means of curtailment, revocation, cancellation, passage of time or otherwise), or
      (iii) is subject to a condition preventing him from accepting the employment.

The provisions of the 2006 Act apply only in respect of employment commenced on or after 29 February 2008 (Immigration, Asylum and Nationality Act 2006 (Commencement No. 8 and Transitional and Saving Provisions) Order 2008 (SI 2008 No. 310), art. 2(1)(b)).

Procedure   The offence is triable either way (Immigration, Asylum and Nationality Act 2006,   **B22.42**
s. 21(2)). A body corporate can commit the offence (s. 22).

Sentencing   The maximum penalty on conviction on indictment is two years' imprisonment,   **B22.43**
a fine or both. On summary conviction, the maximum is six months, a fine not exceeding the statutory maximum, or both.

Elements   The offence is committed only where the employer knows that the employee either   **B22.44**
has no valid leave to remain or is subject to a condition preventing him from accepting employment. Where the element of knowledge is not made out, the employer may be subject to a regulatory penalty under the Immigration, Asylum and Nationality Act 2006, s. 15.

Section C1　Definitions and Basic Principles in Road Traffic Cases

DEFINITIONS

Accident

The word 'accident' has been given a number of different meanings depending upon the con-　**C1.1**
text in which it is used. In *Chief Constable of West Midlands Police v Billingham* [1979] 2 All ER
182, the Divisional Court expressed a preference for an 'ordinary man' test, stating that the definition of the word by the Court of Appeal in *Morris* [1972] 1 All ER 384 as 'some unintended
occurrence which has an adverse physical result' should be understood in relation to the facts of
that case. Nonetheless, the court did state (per Bridge LJ) that the word 'accident' was 'capable
of applying to an untoward occurrence which has adverse physical results' even if one event in
the chain was deliberate. The main doubt was at one time whether an accident could result from
one or more intentional or deliberate acts.

In *Chief Constable of Staffordshire v Lees* [1981] RTR 506, the argument that a 'deliberate act'
does not constitute an 'accident' for the purposes of the Road Traffic Acts was rejected. In that
case the defendant deliberately drove his car at a locked gate. The Divisional Court held that an
'accident' could be said to have occurred within the meaning of the RTA 1972, s. 8(2), when
arising through a deliberate and intended act, provided that any ordinary person would say that
there had been an accident owing to the presence of a motor vehicle on a road. Bingham J stated
(at p. 510):

> It would be an insult to common sense if a collision involving a motor car arising from some careless
> and inadvertent act entitled a constable to exercise his powers under the [Road Traffic] Act but a
> similar result caused by a deliberate antisocial act did not. Previous cases have made it clear that one
> should look at the ordinary meaning of the word 'accident'.

See also *Charlton v Fisher* [2001] RTR 479. In *Morris* [1972] 1 All ER 384, Lord Widgery CJ
acknowledged the possibility of a *de minimis* argument where the physical consequences were
so trivial that an ordinary person would not regard the occurrence as an accident. In *Currie*
[2007] 2 Cr App R 246, the Court of Appeal held that the term must be given a common-sense
meaning and that an accident is not restricted to untoward or unintended consequences having
an adverse physical effect, confirming that some physical impact is not an essential element.

Stapylton [2012] EWCA Crim 728, applying *Mayor v Oxford* (1980) 2 Cr App R (S) 280, confirmed that any accident resulting from driving where the vehicle has run off the road and collided with some stationary object was clearly an accident which occurred 'owing to the presence
of a motor vehicle on a road', even though the collision happened off the road.

Driver and Driving

The definition of 'driver' is set out in the RTA 1988, s. 192 (see **C1.31**). It includes, except in　**C1.2**
cases of causing death by dangerous driving, a person who is steering, as well as any other person
engaged in driving. As respects establishing the identity of the driver of a vehicle concerned in
an offence, there is no general presumption that the owner of a vehicle is the driver of it at a
particular time, notwithstanding the various statutory provisions that establish owner liability

1053

in certain specific circumstances; the question of the driver's identity is one of fact on which the tribunal must be sure (*Clarke v DPP* (1992) 156 JP 605; *Powell v DPP* [1992] RTR 270; *Browning* (1991) 94 Cr App R 109, concerning car identification). Evidence of ownership is merely one strand in the evidential rope which may go to establish the identity of the driver. All the evidence relating to the issue, including circumstantial evidence, can properly be considered together (*McCombie v CPS* [2011] EWHC 758 (Admin)).

In *Evans v Walkden* [1956] 3 All ER 64, occupying the front passenger seat and supervising the driver, thereby being in a position to assume control if necessary, was held not to be equivalent to being in control, with the result that the supervisor was not a 'driver'. *Langman v Valentine* [1952] 2 All ER 803 was distinguished because there the degree of control exercised throughout by the supervisor was considerably greater.

The act of driving is a physical one which can only be performed by a natural person, and the words 'drive' and 'driver' should be construed accordingly. Consequently, the Divisional Court declined to make the respondent, a limited company, vicariously liable for an offence under the RTRA 1984, s. 8(1) (*Richmond London Borough Council v Pinn and Wheeler Ltd* [1989] RTR 354).

C1.3   In *MacDonagh* [1974] QB 448 (a five-judge Court of Appeal), the essence of driving was said to be the use of 'the driver's controls for the purpose of directing the movement of the vehicle'. The defendant, who was disqualified from driving, had been asked to move his car by a police officer and explained that he had pushed it with his two feet on the road and one hand on the steering wheel. The jury were directed that this could properly be described as driving. Allowing the appeal, Lord Widgery CJ stated (at p. 451):

> There are an infinite number of ways in which a person may control the movement of a motor vehicle, apart from the orthodox one of sitting in the driving seat and using the engine for propulsion. He may be coasting down a hill with the gears in neutral and the engine switched off; he may be steering a vehicle which is being towed by another. As has already been pointed out, he may be sitting in the driving seat while others push, or half sitting in the driving seat but keeping one foot on the road in order to induce the car to move. Finally, as in the present case, he may be standing in the road and himself pushing the car with or without using the steering wheel to direct it. Although the word 'drive' must be given a wide meaning, the courts must be alert to see that the net is not thrown so widely that it includes activities which cannot be said to be driving a motor vehicle in any ordinary use of that word in the English language.

Controlling the movement and direction of a motor cycle by pushing and steering with the ignition and lights on constituted 'driving', as long as the defendant was wearing motor cyclist's clothing and a crash helmet (*McKoen v Ellis* [1987] RTR 26).

In *Selby v DPP* [1994] RTR 157n, Taylor LJ stated (at p. 162) that 'riding' is carried out 'if a person is being carried on a motor cycle as it moves on its wheels, whether propelled by the engine or by his feet or by gravity', which would seem to be equally applicable as the test for 'driving' a motor cycle (*Gunnell v DPP* [1994] RTR 151). See also *Coates v CPS* (2011) 175 JP 401.

C1.4   Once the act of driving has commenced, ascertained by applying the *MacDonagh* test, it continues until it terminates, and a person may still be 'driving' although the vehicle is stationary (*Pinner v Everett* [1969] 3 All ER 257; *Skelton* [1995] Crim LR 635). In *Edkins v Knowles* [1973] QB 748, it was emphasised that the reason for stopping is relevant, as it may be part of the journey, e.g., traffic lights or a junction, or may mark a break in the journey, in which case the length of break and whether the driver leaves the vehicle become important. The issue is one of fact and degree, just as it is at the end of a journey, when various activities connected with driving must be completed before the driving is terminated, e.g., switching off the ignition and securing the vehicle. The court must consider the period of time and the circumstances to decide whether the person still in the driving seat was 'driving' (*Planton v DPP* [2002] RTR 107).

Examples of Driving *MacDonagh* [1974] QB 448 was followed in *McQuaid v Anderton* **C1.5** [1981] 3 All ER 540, in which the appellant, who was disqualified, was steering a towed vehicle which had an operational braking system. The court held that the method of propulsion was irrelevant and dismissed his appeal.

A person steering a vehicle from the passenger seat, over an appreciable period of time, was driving, as was the person sitting in the driver's seat (*Tyler v Whatmore* [1976] RTR 83), but a momentary seizure of the steering wheel causing the vehicle to leave the road, whilst borderline, could not properly be described as 'driving' (*Jones v Pratt* [1983] RTR 54). In neither case did the court consider the interpretation provisions and any possible definition of 'steersman'. *Jones v Pratt* was followed in *DPP v Hastings* [1993] RTR 205, where there was a similar momentary seizure of the wheel. Although the seizure in *Hastings* was intended to cause danger there was no finding that the driver relinquished control and the seizure was regarded as 'an act of interfering with the driving of the car rather than an act of driving in itself'.

In *Burgoyne v Phillips* [1983] RTR 49, releasing the handbrake and sitting in the car with the **C1.6** steering locked and the engine off whilst the vehicle moved by reason of gravity was held to be driving, although the defendant had left the keys to the car elsewhere. In *Leach v DPP* [1993] RTR 161, however, sitting in the driving seat of a stationary motor vehicle with hands on the steering wheel and the engine off was held not to be, *per se*, driving within the meaning of the RTA 1988, s. 163(1), so as to make it an offence to fail to stop for a constable. Where the engine is on but forward propulsion is being prevented because the handbrake remains applied so that the vehicle's wheels merely spin then, applying *MacDonagh*, this amounts to driving (*DPP v Alderton* [2004] RTR 367). However, in *Whelehan v DPP* [1995] RTR 177, quite apart from the defendant's admission to driving to the location where he was found by a constable, the Divisional Court concluded that being discovered in the driving seat of a stationary motor vehicle on a road at 1.20 a.m. with the keys in the ignition switch afforded sufficient evidence from which to infer that the defendant had driven to that location.

Kneeling on the driving seat, releasing the handbrake and attempting to re-apply the handbrake was material upon which justices might find a defendant was driving (*Rowan v Chief Constable of Merseyside* (1985) *The Times*, 10 December 1985).

Mechanical Defect

Where a driver is deprived of control of a motor vehicle as a result of a mechanical defect of **C1.7** which he has no knowledge, real or constructive, then such a defect is a defence to a charge of careless driving and a charge of contravening the regulations relating to pedestrian crossings and there seems little or no reason why its principles should not be of wider application.

This defence of mechanical or latent defect stems from *Kay v Butterworth* (1945) 61 TLR 452, *Simpson v Peat* [1952] 2 QB 24, *Hill v Baxter* [1958] 1 QB 227, and the general proposition that in cases not involving fault the law should seek to avoid the imposition of any criminal sanction.

In *Spurge* [1961] 2 QB 205, the appellant had recently purchased a car with a tendency to move to the right when the brakes were applied, and had been convicted of dangerous driving. His appeal was dismissed and Salmon J stressed that successful reliance on the defence would be rare and that it did not apply where the defect was known, or would have been discovered by the exercise of reasonable prudence. He stated (at p. 212) that: 'The essence of the defence is that the danger has been created by a sudden total loss of control in no way due to any fault on the part of the driver'. It is for the defence to raise the issue, but the onus of disproving it remains with the prosecution.

C1.8   In *Burns v Bidder* [1967] 2 QB 227, the Divisional Court allowed an appeal against a pedestrian crossing offence as the convicting magistrate failed to consider the defence of mechanical defect at all, wrongly believing the offence to be absolute. James J stated (at pp. 240–1):

> The cases of the driver suddenly stung by a swarm of bees or suffering a sudden epileptic form of disabling attack, or a vehicle being propelled forward by reason of another vehicle hitting it from behind, are illustrations of where no offence may be shown, because control over the vehicle is taken completely out of the hands of the driver, and his failure to accord precedence on that account would be no offence.

> Likewise in my view a sudden removal of control over the vehicle occasioned by a latent defect of which the driver did not know and could not reasonably be expected to know would render the resulting failure to accord precedence no offence, provided he is in no way at fault himself.

In *Beckford* [1996] 1 Cr App R 96, the Court of Appeal hoped that procedures have been put in place to ensure that vehicles are not scrapped before express permission is given by the police and that such permission will not be forthcoming if serious criminal charges which may involve the possibility of some mechanical defect in the vehicle have been brought.

Motor Vehicle and Mechanically Propelled Vehicle

C1.9   The term 'motor vehicle' is defined in the RTA 1988, s. 185 (see **C1.31**), as a mechanically propelled vehicle intended or adapted for use on roads. A mechanically propelled vehicle does not need to be intended or adapted for such use; whether a vehicle is mechanically propelled remains a question of fact.

A vehicle which has more than one source of power does not cease to be 'mechanically propelled', even though it is propelled by means other than an engine at the relevant time (*Floyd v Bush* [1953] 1 All ER 265). This extends to a vehicle which is being towed, even though that vehicle may be in such a poor condition that it could not be propelled under its own power, and even though it was at the same time a 'trailer', a 'vehicle' drawn by a 'motor vehicle' (*Cobb v Whorton* [1971] RTR 392).

A suitably adapted vehicle, even though originally constructed for use on the roads, may, as a question of fact, cease to be a 'motor vehicle' within the meaning of s. 185, as in *Lawrence v Howlett* [1952] 2 All ER 74, where the auxiliary engine had been removed from a moped making it into a 'pedal cycle'. Normally, however, only when it is clear that a vehicle will not become mobile again can it be said that it ceases to be a 'motor vehicle', and in each case that is a question of fact for the court.

C1.10   In *Burns v Currell* [1963] 2 QB 433, Lord Parker CJ, adopting a 'reasonable person' test as to the use of the vehicle, stated (at p. 440):

> . . . in the ordinary case . . . there will be little difficulty in saying whether a particular vehicle is a motor vehicle or not. But to define exactly the meaning of the words 'intended or adapted' is by no means easy. I think that the expression 'intended' . . . does not mean 'intended by the user of the vehicle either at the moment of the alleged offence or for the future'.

This case was followed in *Chief Constable of Avon and Somerset Constabulary v F (A Juvenile)* [1987] RTR 378, where Glidewell LJ said (at pp. 382–3):

> I emphasise that that test is what would be the view of the reasonable man as to the general user of this particular vehicle; not what was the particular user to which this particular defendant put it. . . if a reasonable man were to say 'Yes, this vehicle might well be used on the road', then, applying the test, the vehicle is intended or adapted for such use. If that be the case, it is nothing to the point if the individual defendant says: 'I normally use it for scrambling and I am only pushing it along the road on this occasion because I have no other means of getting it home', or something of that sort.

The test was also applied in *DPP v Saddington* [2001] RTR 227, in relation to a motorised scooter, the 'Go-ped', to conclude that, although the vehicle was incapable of being registered as such and fell foul of the construction and use regulations, it was a 'motor vehicle' for the purposes of the RTA 1988, s. 185(1). This conclusion was reached because a reasonable person would say that one of the scooter's uses would be general use on the roads. See also *DPP v King* [2008] EWHC 447 (Admin) and, in relation to a Segway, *Coates v CPS* (2011) 175 JP 401.

For a motor vehicle to change its character from that intended by the manufacturer a very sub- **C1.11**
stantial or dramatic alteration would be required for it to cease to be a motor vehicle; the addition of something that may make the vehicle unusable on a road might suffice, but the absence
of registration plates, reflectors, lights or the speedometer would be insufficient (*DPP v Ryan*
[1992] RTR 13).

In *Maddox v Storer* [1962] 1 All ER 831, the court stated that it was necessary to look to the
context in which the word 'adapted' was used, and when used alone it was held to have the
adjectival meaning of 'being fit and apt for the purpose'. If used disjunctively, as an alternative
to 'constructed', its meaning was 'being altered so as to make it fit'.

In *Millard v Turvey* [1968] 2 QB 390, a chassis without a cab, doors, roof, windscreen or seats
for the accommodation of passengers was held to be a motor vehicle, albeit under construction,
but was not a 'motor tractor'. In *Tahsin* [1970] RTR 88, it was held that a moped did not cease
to be a 'motor vehicle' merely because its engine would not work. A moped, however, does not
become a motor cycle merely because one pedal is missing (*G (A Minor) v Jarrett* [1981] RTR
186). For a vehicle to change in such a manner requires an alteration in its design or
construction.

Owner

See the RTA 1988, s. 192, at **C1.31**. **C1.12**

In relation to a vehicle which is subject to a hiring or hire-purchase agreement, 'owner' includes
the person in possession of the vehicle under that agreement. Even if the person lawfully in possession of the vehicle under a hiring agreement parts with it to a third party, who may then drive
the vehicle without documents, insurance etc., unless the agreement provides for instant termination of the hire, so that property in the vehicle immediately reverts to the person who has legal
title to the vehicle, the third party would not commit an offence under the Theft Act 1968,
s. 12, although both he and the person in possession of the vehicle under the hiring agreement
may be guilty of other offences relating to the absence of insurance, etc.

Road or Other Public Place

Road The word 'road' is defined by the RTA 1988, s. 192 (see **C1.31**). It includes any high- **C1.13**
way and any other road to which the public has access, including bridges over which a road
passes. The *Concise Oxford Dictionary* defines 'road' as 'a line of communication between places
for use of pedestrians, riders, and vehicles'. Section 34(1)(b) of the 1988 Act includes footpaths
and bridleways as being within the definition of a road.

In *Clarke v Kato* [1998] 4 All ER 417, the House of Lords confirmed that whether a place which
is not a highway is a 'road' within the meaning of the RTA 1988, s. 192, is a question of fact to
be determined after consideration of its physical character and the function it exists to serve.
Lord Clyde gave the following guidance (at p. 1652):

> One obvious feature of a road as commonly understood is that its physical limits are defined or at
> least definable. It should always be possible to ascertain the sides of a road or to have them ascer-
> tained. Its location should be identifiable as a route or way. It will often have a prepared surface and
> have been manufactured or constructed. But it may simply have developed by the repeated passage
> of traffic over the same area of land. It may be continuous, like a circular route, or it may come to a
> termination, as in the case of a cul-de-sac. A road may run on a single line without diversion or it
> may have branches.
>
> . . . it is also necessary to consider the function of the place in order to see if it qualifies as a road.
> Essentially a road serves as a means of access. It leads from one place to another and constitutes a

route whereby travellers may move conveniently between the places to which and from which it leads. It is thus a defined or at least a definable way intended to enable those who pass over it to reach a destination. Its precise extent will require to be a matter of detailed decision as matter of fact in the particular circumstances. Lines may require to be drawn to determine the point at which the road ends and the destination has been reached. Where there is a door or a gate the problem may be readily resolved. Where there is no physical point which can be readily identified, then by an exercise of reasonable judgment an imaginary line will have to be drawn to mark the point where it should be held that the road has ended. Whether or not a particular area is or is not a road eventually comes to be a matter of fact.

Accordingly, a place that can reasonably be described as a car park does not, save in exceptional circumstances, qualify as a road, and in the event of a carriageway being found to exist within its bounds which does so qualify, the remaining area will retain its integrity as a car park. Trafalgar Square is a road (*Sadiku v DPP* [2000] RTR 155). In *Barrett v DPP* [2010] RTR 8, a route between points marked on a plan which was a roadway with defined edges, road marking and signs was confirmed to be a road.

C1.14   In *Price v DPP* [1990] RTR 413, where the defendant drove across a pavement (part of which was maintained at public expense and part of which was privately owned) thereby causing a pedestrian to jump out of the way, it was held that the justices were fully entitled to conclude that the pavement as a whole constituted a road and the defendant was, therefore, properly convicted of driving without reasonable consideration for another road user.

In *Hawkins v Phillips* [1980] RTR 197, a filter lane or slip road was held to be part of the main carriageway for the purposes of the RTRA 1967. 'Highway' is defined as a 'public road, main route by land or water'. In *Lang v Hindhaugh* [1986] RTR 271, a footpath which was not designed for motor vehicles or passable by motor cars was held to be a highway.

In *Worth v Brooks* [1959] Crim LR 855, the grass verge by the side of a carriageway was held to form part of the highway which itself constituted a road. See also *Griffiths (Contractors) Ltd v Driver and Vehicle Licensing Agency* [2009] EWHC 3132 (Admin). In *Avery v CPS* [2012] RTR 87, where the physical boundary of the road was in issue, it being asserted that the wheels of the vehicle driven by the defendant remained on a private driveway, the Divisional Court held that any material encroachment on the air-space vertically above the road was sufficient to justify a conclusion that the vehicle concerned was on the road, because the legislation seeks to protect the public from the effects of drunken driving in a place where they might be expected to pass and repass in safety. In *Dunmill v DPP* (2004) *The Times*, 15 July 2004, a grass area within a camp site, which may have been a public place, was held not to be a road.

In *Holliday v Henry* [1974] RTR 101, an ingenious attempt to avoid a vehicle being 'on' a road by placing a roller skate under each wheel was rejected by the Divisional Court, which stated that it was perfectly clear that the vehicle was 'on' the road.

C1.15   The question of whether or not a particular road is one to which the public has access is one of fact and degree (*Waterfield* [1964] 1 QB 164). In any case where use by the public may not be readily apparent, *Hallett v DPP* [2011] EWHC 488 (Admin) emphasises the need for the prosecution to adduce evidence of such use.

The primary intended use of a place, irrespective of whether it is publicly or privately owned, does not appear to be of relevance (*Price v DPP*). A road which is not maintainable and manageable at public expense does not preclude it from being 'a road open to the public' as that expression refers to a road to which the public has access (*DPP v Cargo Handling Ltd* [1992] RTR 318).

C1.16   **Other Public Place**   It is a truism to state that a public place is one to which the public has access. It is not, however, definitive. Whether or not such access is sufficient for a finding that the place is a 'public place' for the purposes of the Road Traffic Acts is a question of fact and degree to be arrived at after consideration of the evidence (*Planton v DPP* [2002] RTR 107).

Justices are entitled to use their 'local knowledge' in arriving at their conclusion on this point, but it is good practice to inform the prosecution and defence so that they can comment (*Bowman v DPP* [1991] RTR 263).

In *DPP v Vivier* [1991] RTR 205, a case under the RTA 1988, s. 5(1)(a), the Divisional Court gave wide consideration to the meaning of 'public place'. The defendant had been driving a car in a caravan park which covered 80 acres and contained between three and four miles of road. The number of people present in the caravan park, whether admitted as caravanners, campers, or their guests, varied between 800 and 3,500, depending on the time of year. The Divisional Court referred to *Montgomery v Loney* [1959] NILR 171, in which the distinction was drawn between members of the general public and persons who belong to a special class of members of the public and who have 'some reason personal to them for their admittance', such as postmen, meter readers and employees going to work along a factory road, concluding that 'the decision whether a place was a place to which the public had access . . . was a matter of fact and degree but whether the material for consideration sufficed to support one view or the other was a matter of law'.

Whether a place is a public place or not can be identified by looking at the people who use it and their reasons for doing so. In *DPP v Vivier*, Simon Brown J separated such persons into two categories: those who seek entry for the purposes of the occupier, including guests, postmen or meter readers going to a private house, recognised as a special class of people distinct from members of the general public, and those who seek entry for their own purposes and yet are screened in the sense of having to satisfy certain conditions for admission. In the latter case, the court needs to ask whether 'those admitted pass through the screening process for a reason, or on account of some characteristic, personal to themselves', or whether in truth they are 'merely members of the public who are being admitted as such and processed simply so as to make them subject to payment and whatever other conditions the landowner chooses to impose'.   **C1.17**

In *DPP v Coulman* [1993] RTR 230, the Divisional Court concluded that, after disembarking at Dover Eastern Docks into the Freight Immigration Lanes, the respondent continued to be present there as a member of the public, rather than in any other special capacity, with the consequence that the Lanes constituted a public place for the purposes of the RTA 1988, s. 5. In *Havell v DPP* (1994) 158 JP 680, however, use of a car park, which was readily accessible from the road, without restricted access and not marked as being private, as a member of a bona fide club whose membership was not of such a size 'that it was indistinguishable from the public at large in the locality' did not constitute use as a member of the general public; therefore the defendant's appeal against a conviction for being 'in charge' of a motor vehicle on a road or other public place whilst unfit through drink or drugs was allowed. A company car park for the use of staff, customers and other visitors is not a public place unless there is proof of actual use of that car park by members of the public (*Spence* [1999] RTR 353). A car park adjoining a main road and used by members of the public generally is a public place (*May v DPP* [2005] EWHC 1280 (Admin)). In *Filmer v DPP* [2007] RTR 330, Fulford J indicated that 'the critical distinction is between private land to which the public have access at the time in question, on the one hand, and private land which is closed to the public at the material time or is only open to particular people, on the other'. In *Cowan v DPP* (2013) 177 JP 474, an internal roadway within Kingston Hill University campus was held not to be a public place; students, having a right to occupy their rooms and use the facilities on the campus, were doing so not as members of the public but by virtue of being students, and their visitors were accessing the site, not as ordinary members of the public but for the purposes of those occupiers of the site.

Vehicle

The word 'vehicle' does not appear to have been given any statutory meaning, and may therefore include things as diverse as a bicycle or a poultry shed on wheels (*Garner v Burr* [1951] 1   **C1.18**

KB 31). The *Concise Oxford Dictionary* defines 'vehicle' as a 'carriage or conveyance of any kind used on land'.

BASIC PRINCIPLES

Aiding, Abetting, Counselling, Procuring

C1.19 For the meaning of these terms, see generally the Accessories and Abettors Act 1861, s. 8; the MCA 1980, s. 44(1); and **A4.1** *et seq*. See also *Martin* [2011] RTR 46 for guidance on jury directions that could be used in respect of a qualified supervising driver who is charged with aiding and abetting resulting from failing to act to intervene when accompanying a learner driver.

By the MCA 1980, s. 44, a person convicted of aiding, abetting, counselling or procuring a summary offence is guilty of the like offence, and if the substantive offence carries endorsement the defendant must have his licence endorsed and may be disqualified.

Where disqualification is mandatory for the principal offence (e.g., driving with excess alcohol in the breath), a person convicted of aiding and abetting etc. is liable to discretionary disqualification by virtue of the RTOA 1988, s. 34(5) (see **C7.8**), and his licence must be endorsed with ten penalty points (RTOA 1988, s. 28(1)(b)).

Attempts

C1.20 As to attempts generally, see **A5.69** *et seq*.

By virtue of the Criminal Attempts Act 1981, s. 1(4), it is not possible to attempt the commission of an offence which is purely summary, unless such an offence is created by statute (e.g., the RTA 1988, s. 5(1)(a), attempting to drive a motor vehicle on a road after consuming so much alcohol that the proportion of it in the breath etc. exceeds the prescribed limit). In *Mason v DPP* [2010] RTR 120, the Divisional Court suggested that embarking on the full offence of driving would occur when turning on the engine, but not when merely opening the vehicle's door. The Criminal Attempts Act 1981, s. 3, enacts similar provisions in relation to statutory attempts as are contained in ss. 1(2), (3) and (4) of the Act.

Automatism and Insanity

C1.21 As to insanity generally, see **A3.23** to **A3.33**. As to automatism generally, see **A3.12**.

Questions of fitness to plead and insanity are triable under the Criminal Procedure (Insanity) Act 1964 (see **D12.2** *et seq*.). In indictable offences, where these issues are raised, the magistrates' court is obliged to commit to the Crown Court in pursuance of that statute.

In the magistrates' court questions relating to automatism usually arise in the form of defences of involuntary behaviour on the part of the driver. (See also mechanical defect at **C1.7**, and duress or necessity at **A3.35** to **A3.49**.)

C1.22 In *Hill v Baxter* [1958] 1 QB 277, Lord Goddard CJ, having quoted a famous dictum of Humphreys J in *Kay v Butterworth* (1945) 61 TLR 452, went on to say (at p. 283):

> I agree that there may be cases where the circumstances are such that the accused could not really be said to be driving at all. Suppose he had a stroke or an epileptic fit, both instances of what may properly be called acts of God; he might well be in the driver's seat even with his hands on the wheel, but in such a state of unconsciousness that he could not be said to be driving. A blow from a stone or an attack by a swarm of bees I think introduces some conception akin to *novus actus interveniens*.

In such circumstances, the defendant is not 'driving' but has been rendered incapable of physical control of the vehicle. This is not automatism of the type considered in *Bailey* [1983] 2 All ER 503 and *Hardie* [1985] 3 All ER 848, but nonetheless arises without fault and should not therefore be the subject of any criminal sanction. There must, however, be 'a total destruction of voluntary control'; impaired or reduced control is not enough (*A-G's Ref (No. 2 of 1992)* [1994] QB 91). The prosecution must establish the manner of the defendant's driving and then the defendant must adduce evidence that he was totally unable to control the car (*C* [2007] EWCA Crim 1862). The lack of control must arise from causes which do not bring the defendant within the M'Naghten rules. Thus driving with 'a reduced or imperfect awareness', which is brought on by the repetitive stimuli experienced on a long journey and which reduces a driver's capacity to avoid collisions, cannot, as a matter of law, found a defence of automatism. Similarly, in *Watmore v Jenkins* [1962] 2 QB 572, Winn J pointed out that a finding by the justices that the defendant 'continued to perform the functions of driving, after a fashion' for five miles on a road which was not straight, was inconsistent with a finding of automatism 'extending throughout the whole of the distance . . . to which it related'.

Causing

A number of offences in the Road Traffic Acts may be committed by causing or permitting the use of, as well as using, a vehicle in a prohibited manner. Each of these gives rise to a separate offence.

C1.23

'Causing' demands a positive act on the part of the defendant (*Price v Cromack* [1975] 2 All ER 113). It also requires prior knowledge. In *Milstead v Sexton* [1964] Crim LR 474, the defendant was convicted of causing a car to be used on a road where the car was being towed and he was driving the towing vehicle. In *Ross Hillman Ltd v Bond* [1974] QB 435, the defendant was a limited company which owned a number of vehicles and employed a number of drivers, all of whom had been warned against driving their vehicles while overloaded. One of the employees drove his vehicle while it was overloaded. Allowing the defendant's appeal, May J stated (at p. 446):

> Unassisted by any authority I would as a matter of ordinary English construe both the word 'causes' and the word 'permits' in section 40(5)(b) of the Act of 1972 as requiring prior knowledge of the facts constituting the unlawful user . . . if, as I think and as is supported by authority, actual user of a vehicle in contravention of the regulations is an absolute offence, and if, as I also think, a master 'uses' the vehicle which his servant is driving on that master's business, then I think that the mischief against which the regulations are directed, that of having unsafe vehicles on the roads is adequately dealt with. Having regard to the ordinary meaning of 'causes' I do not find it surprising that, whereas on given facts a master charged with using will be convicted, on the same facts a master charged with causing that use will be acquitted.

In *Mounsey v Campbell* [1983] RTR 36, the defendant caused an obstruction by parking his van immediately in front of another motor vehicle so that vehicle was unable to move. The defence had argued that it was only when the defendant refused to move the van that the vehicle became an obstruction, and therefore the proper charge should have been one of 'permitting'. This argument was described as 'nebulous' by the court, which found that the initial act of parking and subsequent refusal to move the vehicle could both constitute 'causing'.

C1.24

A company which shut its eyes to the failure of its employee to fill in tachograph records could not be said to have 'caused' that failure. Such wilful ignorance may amount to 'permitting' but falls short of the 'positive mandate or . . . other sufficient act required for the offence' (*Redhead Freight Ltd v Shulman* [1989] RTR 1).

Permitting

In *Vehicle Inspectorate v Nuttall* [1999] 3 All ER 833, the House of Lords drew a distinction between positive acts where a person 'allows' or 'authorises' the use of the vehicle by another and omissions which amount to 'failure to take reasonable steps to prevent' such use. When the second, wider meaning applies to the context of the offence charged, it is not an offence of strict liability and, therefore, requires proof of nothing less than wilfulness or recklessness. This may

C1.25

be demonstrated by adducing actual evidence or by raising a rebuttable presumption. For example, in respect of regulatory tachograph requirements, if the employer fails to take reasonable steps to prevent employee drivers from contravening the statutory provisions, it raises a rebuttable presumption that the necessary mental element has been established (per Lord Steyn at p. 637C). The evidence adduced must, however, be capable of supporting such a presumption (*Yorkshire Traction Co. Ltd v Vehicle Inspectorate* [2001] RTR 518).

For 'permission' involving a positive act, proof of prior knowledge remains necessary (*Ross Hillman Ltd v Bond* [1974] QB 435). This connotes express or implied permission or acquiescence as much as direct participation.

'Knowledge' includes actual and constructive knowledge, such as 'the state of mind of a man who shuts his eyes to the obvious or allows his servant to do something in the circumstances where a contravention is likely, not caring whether a contravention takes place or not' (*James & Son Ltd v Smee* [1955] 1 QB 78, per Parker J at p. 91). Where justices had found that an employer did not know and had no reasonable cause to suspect that one of his vehicles had a defective braking system, it was not open to them to convict of an offence of permitting the vehicle's use, notwithstanding that he would have had no answer to a charge of 'using' the vehicle in a defective condition (*Robinson v DPP* [1991] RTR 315).

C1.26   Negligence not amounting to recklessness did not justify an inference that a managing director, someone who might be said to be 'the "brains" of the company rather than its hands', was wilfully closing his eyes to the obvious, and therefore that a company was guilty of permitting the use of a vehicle on a road with defective brakes (*Hill & Sons (Botley and Denmead) Ltd v Hampshire Chief Constable* [1972] RTR 29).

That decision closely follows *Magna Plant Ltd v Mitchell* [1966] Crim LR 394, in which Lord Parker CJ said:

> A company was not criminally liable in the absence of knowledge of the facts constituting the offence for the failure of a servant to whom it had delegated a task. The servant was not in the position of the brains of the company and his knowledge could not be imputed to a director . . .

See also *Vehicle Operator Services Agency v FM Conway Ltd* [2013] RTR 242. However, an employer's failure to operate an adequate, or any, system of checking tachograph charts was regarded as sufficiently reckless 'shutting of the eyes' so as to amount to implied knowledge in *Vehicle Inspectorate v Shane Raymond Nuttall t/a Redline Coaches* (1997) 161 JP 701. The test is one of fact and degree.

C1.27   In cases of no insurance, permitting has a stricter interpretation. Where an owner allows the use of a vehicle, believing that use to be insured, such a belief is no defence to a charge of permitting the uninsured use of the vehicle (*Lyons v May* [1948] 2 All ER 1062; *Baugh v Crago* [1975] RTR 453). In exceptional circumstances a conditional permission to use a vehicle only with insurance does not constitute an offence (*Sheldon Deliveries Ltd v Willis* [1972] RTR 217; *Newbury v Davis* [1974] RTR 367), but such a defence must be regarded with extreme caution before it is capable of application (see *DPP v Fisher* [1991] RTR 93, where it was held that the permission must be given direct to the would-be driver).

Using

C1.28   'Using' has a restricted meaning when found in the same section as 'causing' and 'permitting'. In such cases it is only the driver, or his employer, when the driver is driving on his employer's business, who can be said to be 'using' the vehicle (*Mickleborough v BRS (Contracts) Ltd* [1977] RTR 389; *Jones v DPP* [1999] RTR 1; *Interlink Express Parcels Ltd v Night Truckers Ltd* [2000] RTR 324, where the vehicles were owned by another party). 'User' must involve an element of controlling, managing or operating the vehicle by the person concerned (*Hatton v Hall* [1997] RTR 212). For a non-driver of the vehicle, this element could exist as a result of a joint venture to use it for a particular purpose or where the passenger procures the making of the journey (*O'Mahoney v Joliffe* [1999] RTR 245); whether it does is a question of fact and degree.

These propositions extend to cases where the word 'use' is found, either alone, or in conjunction with another word such as 'keeps' (*James & Son Ltd v Smee* [1955] 1 QB 78; *Richardson v Baker* [1976] RTR 56). Use, however, by a person other than a servant, even a business partner, does not constitute use by the owner, albeit that the vehicle is being driven at his request and with his full knowledge (*Crawford v Haughton* [1972] 1 All ER 535; *Garrett v Hooper* [1973] RTR 1). That sort of use may, of course, amount to 'permitting' or even 'causing'. However, *Hallett Silberman v Cheshire County Council* [1993] RTR 32 shows that a vehicle which exceeds its permitted weight may be being used by the owner even if its driver is self-employed and provides the tractor unit. The decision rests heavily on the degree of control exercised by the defendants, who supplied the trailer and chose the route; as such their position was analogous to that of an employer. By contrast, in *DPP v Seawheel Ltd* (1994) 158 JP 444, mere ownership of a part of the assembly on which a load was carried and which was secured to the trailer was insufficient to establish use; the tractor and trailer unit were owned by a person who had contracted to transport the load and there was no finding that the defendants were in possession of any of the relevant parts. It was suggested *obiter*, however, that a wider meaning should be given to 'use' when applied to a trailer rather than when applied to a lorry. However, where 'use' appears in a provision in conjunction with 'drive or cause or permit to be driven', 'use' will be construed more broadly so as to cover the owner of a vehicle used for his purposes or on his behalf and being driven by someone other than an employee (*Richmond upon Thames London Borough Council v Morton* [2000] RTR 79). **C1.29**

Vehicles left unattended on a road can still be regarded as being used, as 'use' has been held to mean 'having the use of' for these purposes (*Eden v Mitchell* [1975] RTR 425). Accordingly, the mere fact of having two defective tyres did not preclude the vehicle's use and the owner's intention in respect of using the vehicle was held to be irrelevant. Similarly, in *Elliott v Grey* [1960] 1 QB 367, despite having an engine that did not work, no battery and no petrol, the vehicle in question was being 'used' without insurance, as it could be moved, albeit not driven. The distinction drawn in *Hewer v Cutler* [1974] RTR 155, that immobile vehicles whose wheels would not rotate were outside the definition of 'use', was found to be unjustified by Mitchell J in *Pumbien v Vines* [1996] RTR 37. In that case the vehicle's tyres were deflated, the handbrake was on, the rear brakes were seized and the gearbox contained no oil because there was a leak in the transmission pipe. It was held that, provided that vehicle was a 'motor vehicle' within the definition of the RTA 1988, s. 185 (see generally **C1.31**), and was on a road, the owner had the use of it on a road, whether at the material time it could move on its wheels or not. This decision has also apparently removed the requirement of an 'element of controlling, managing or operating the vehicle as a vehicle' (*Nichol v Leach* [1972] RTR 476), in the sense of the vehicle being capable of movement 'as a vehicle'. Consequently, for the purposes of the RTA 1988, ss. 47 and 143, 'use' should be accorded the same meaning and mobility of the vehicle is irrelevant. **C1.30**

INTERPRETATION PROVISIONS OF ROAD TRAFFIC ACT 1988

Road Traffic Act 1988, ss. 185, 186, 189, 192   **C1.31**

185.—(1) In this Act—
> 'heavy locomotive' means a mechanically propelled vehicle which is not constructed itself to carry a load other than any of the excepted articles and the weight of which unladen exceeds 11690 kilograms,
> 'heavy motor car' means a mechanically propelled vehicle, not being a motor car, which is constructed itself to carry a load or passengers and the weight of which unladen exceeds 2540 kilograms,
> 'invalid carriage' means a mechanically propelled vehicle the weight of which unladen does not exceed 254 kilograms and which is specially designed and constructed, and not merely

adapted, for the use of a person suffering from some physical defect or disability and is used solely by such a person,

'light locomotive' means a mechanically propelled vehicle which is not constructed itself to carry a load other than any of the excepted articles and the weight of which unladen does not exceed 11690 kilograms but does exceed 7370 kilograms,

'motor car' means a mechanically propelled vehicle, not being a motor cycle or an invalid carriage, which is constructed itself to carry a load or passengers and the weight of which unladen—

(a)   if it is constructed solely for the carriage of passengers and their effects, is adapted to carry not more than seven passengers exclusive of the driver and is fitted with tyres of such type as may be specified in regulations made by the Secretary of State, does not exceed 3050 kilograms,

(b)   if it is constructed or adapted for use for the conveyance of goods or burden of any description, does not exceed 3050 kilograms, or 3500 kilograms if the vehicle carries a container or containers for holding for the purposes of its propulsion any fuel which is wholly gaseous at 17.5 degrees Celsius under a pressure of 1.013 bar or plant and material for producing such fuel,

(c)   does not exceed 2540 kilograms in a case not falling within subparagraph (a) or (b) above,

'motor cycle' means a mechanically propelled vehicle, not being an invalid carriage, with less than four wheels and the weight of which unladen does not exceed 410 kilograms,

'motor tractor' means a mechanically propelled vehicle which is not constructed itself to carry a load, other than the excepted articles, and the weight of which unladen does not exceed 7370 kilograms,

'motor vehicle' means, subject to section 20 of the Chronically Sick and Disabled Persons Act 1970 (which makes special provision about invalid carriages, within the meaning of that Act), a mechanically propelled vehicle intended or adapted for use on roads, and

'trailer' means a vehicle drawn by a motor vehicle.

(2)   In subsection (1) above 'excepted articles' means any of the following: water, fuel, accumulators and other equipment used for the purpose of propulsion, loose tools and loose equipment.

186.—(1)   For the purposes of section 185 of this Act, a side car attached to a motor vehicle, if it complies with such conditions as may be specified in regulations made by the Secretary of State, is to be regarded as forming part of the vehicle to which it is attached and as not being a trailer.

(2)   For the purposes of section 185 of this Act, in a case where a motor vehicle is so constructed that a trailer may by partial super-imposition be attached to the vehicle in such a manner as to cause a substantial part of the weight of the trailer to be borne by the vehicle, that vehicle is to be deemed to be a vehicle itself constructed to carry a load.

(3)   For the purposes of section 185 of this Act, in the case of a motor vehicle fitted with a crane, dynamo, welding plant or other special appliance or apparatus which is a permanent or essentially permanent fixture, the appliance or apparatus is not to be deemed to constitute a load or goods or burden of any description, but is to be deemed to form part of the vehicle.

(4)–(6)   [Regulations.]

189.—(1)   For the purposes of the Road Traffic Acts—

(a)   a mechanically propelled vehicle being an implement for cutting grass which is controlled by a pedestrian and is not capable of being used or adapted for any other purpose,

(b)   any other mechanically propelled vehicle controlled by a pedestrian which may be specified by regulations made by the Secretary of State for the purposes of this section and section 140 of the Road Traffic Regulation Act 1984, and

(c)   an electrically assisted pedal cycle of such a class as may be prescribed by regulations so made,

is to be treated as not being a motor vehicle.

(2)   In subsection (1) above 'controlled by a pedestrian' means that the vehicle either—

(a)   is constructed or adapted for use only under such control, or

(b)   is constructed or adapted for use either under such control or under the control of a person carried on it, but is not for the time being in use under, or proceeding under, the control of a person carried on it.

192.—(1) In this Act—

...

'bridleway' means a way over which the public have the following, but no other, rights of way: a right of way on foot and a right of way on horseback or leading a horse, with or without a right to drive animals of any description along the way,

'carriage of goods' includes the haulage of goods,

'cycle' means a bicycle, a tricycle, or a cycle having four or more wheels, not being in any case a motor vehicle,

'driver', where a separate person acts as a steersman of a motor vehicle, includes (except for the purposes of section 1 of this Act) that person as well as any other person engaged in the driving of the vehicle, and 'drive' is to be interpreted accordingly,

'footpath', in relation to England and Wales, means a way over which the public have a right of way on foot only,

'goods' includes goods or burden of any description,

'goods vehicle' means a motor vehicle constructed or adapted for use for the carriage of goods, or a trailer so constructed or adapted,

'highway authority', in England and Wales, means—

    (a) in relation to a road for which he is the highway authority within the meaning of the Highways Act 1980, the Secretary of State, and

    (b) in relation to any other road, the council of the county, metropolitan district or London borough, or the Common Council of the City of London, as the case may be;

'international road haulage permit' means a licence, permit, authorisation or other document issued in pursuance of a Community instrument relating to the carriage of goods by road between member States or an international agreement to which the United Kingdom is a party and which relates to the international carriage of goods by road,

'owner', in relation to a vehicle which is the subject of a hiring agreement or hire-purchase agreement, means the person in possession of the vehicle under that agreement,

'prescribed' means prescribed by regulations made by the Secretary of State,

'road'—

    (a) in relation to England and Wales, means any highway and any other road to which the public has access, and includes bridges over which a road passes, and

    (b) [Applies only to Scotland.];

'the Road Traffic Acts' means the Road Traffic Offenders Act 1988, the Road Traffic (Consequential Provisions) Act 1988 (so far as it reproduces the effect of provisions repealed by that Act) and this Act,

'statutory', in relation to any prohibition, restriction, requirement or provision, means contained in, or having effect under, any enactment (including any enactment contained in this Act),

'the Traffic Acts' means the Road Traffic Acts and the Road Traffic Regulation Act 1984,

'traffic sign' has the meaning given by section 64(1) of the Road Traffic Regulation Act 1984,

'tramcar' includes any carriage used on any road by virtue of an order under the Light Railways Act 1896, and

'trolley vehicle' means a mechanically propelled vehicle adapted for use on roads without rails under power transmitted to it from some external source (whether or not there is in addition a source of power on board the vehicle).

(1A) In this Act—

    (a) any reference to a county shall be construed in relation to Wales as including a reference to a county borough; and

    (b) section 17(4) and (5) of the Local Government (Wales) Act 1994 (references to counties and districts to be construed generally in relation to Wales as references to counties and county boroughs) shall not apply.

(2) [Applies only to Scotland.]

(3) References in this Act to a class of vehicles are to be interpreted as references to a class defined or described by reference to any characteristics of the vehicles or to any other circumstances whatsoever and accordingly as authorising the use of 'category' to indicate a class of vehicles, however defined or described.

Section C2   Procedure and Evidence in Road Traffic Cases

PROCEDURE

Notice of Intended Prosecution

C2.1   Road Traffic Offenders Act 1988, ss. 1 and 2

1.—(1) Subject to section 2 of this Act, a person shall not be convicted of an offence to which this section applies unless—

(a) he was warned at the time the offence was committed that the question of prosecuting him for some one or other of the offences to which this section applies would be taken into consideration, or

(b) within 14 days of the commission of the offence a summons (or, in Scotland, a complaint) for the offence was served on him, or

(c) within 14 days of the commission of the offence a notice of the intended prosecution specifying the nature of the alleged offence and the time and place where it is alleged to have been committed, was—

(i) in the case of an offence under section 28 or 29 of the Road Traffic Act 1988 (cycling offences), served on him,

(ii) in the case of any other offence, served on him or on the person, if any, registered as the keeper of the vehicle at the time of the commission of the offence.

(1A)   A notice required by this section to be served on any person may be served on that person—

(a) by delivering it to him;

(b) by addressing it to him and leaving it at his last known address;

(c) by sending it by registered post, recorded delivery service or first class post addressed to him at his last known address.

(2) A notice shall be deemed for the purposes of subsection (1)(c) above to have been served on a person if it was sent by registered post or recorded delivery service addressed to him at his last known address, notwithstanding that the notice was returned as undelivered or was for any other reason not received by him.

(3) The requirement of subsection (1) above shall in every case be deemed to have been complied with unless and until the contrary is proved.

(4) Schedule 1 to this Act shows the offences to which this section applies.

2.—(1) The requirement of section 1(1) of this Act does not apply in relation to an offence if, at the time of the offence or immediately after it, an accident occurs owing to the presence on a road of the vehicle in respect of which the offence was committed.

(2) [Exception for fixed penalty notices.]

(3) Failure to comply with the requirement of section 1(1) of this Act is not a bar to the conviction of the accused in a case where the court is satisfied—

(a) that neither the name and address of the accused nor the name and address of the registered keeper, if any, could with reasonable diligence have been ascertained in time for a summons or, as the case may be, a complaint to be served or for a notice to be served or sent in compliance with the requirement, or

(b) that the accused by his own conduct contributed to the failure.

(4) Failure to comply with the requirement of section 1(1) of this Act in relation to an offence is not a bar to the conviction of a person of that offence by virtue of the provisions of—

(a) section 24 of this Act, or

(b) any of the enactments mentioned in section 24(6);

but a person is not to be convicted of an offence by virtue of any of those provisions if section 1 applies to the offence with which he was charged and the requirement of section 1(1) was not satisfied in relation to the offence charged.

The oral warning referred to in s. 1(1)(a) must have been understood by the defendant. The test **C2.2** was set out in *Gibson v Dalton* [1980] RTR 410, by Donaldson LJ (at pp. 413–14):

> The obligation on the prosecutor is to warn the accused, not merely to address a warning to him or to give a warning. The mischief to which this section is directed is clear. It is that motorists are entitled to have it brought to their attention at a relatively early stage that there is likely to be a prosecution in order that they may recall and, it may be, record the facts as they occurred at the time.... But a warning which does not get through to the accused person is of no value at all, and prima facie, therefore, the words might be expected to mean that the warning must get through....

> If, viewing the matter objectively, one would expect that the words addressed to the accused person would have been heard and understood by him, then prima facie he was warned within the meaning of the statute. But it is only a prima facie case. It is open to the defendant to prove, if he can, that he did not understand or hear or appreciate the warning and therefore that he was not warned.

The warning must have been given 'at the time' the offence was committed, which is a matter of fact and degree judged on what was reasonable (*Okike* [1978] RTR 489). In *Stacey* [1982] RTR 20, the Court of Appeal held that this issue was to be decided by the judge and added that whether or not the chain of circumstances was unbroken and whether or not all that took place was connected with the incident were relevant factors.

The warning must relate to one or other of the offences to which s. 1 applies as set out in sch. 1 to the Act. These include: dangerous driving (see **C3.39**); careless, and inconsiderate, driving (see **C6.1**); leaving vehicle in dangerous position (see **C6.16**); failing to comply with traffic directions (see **C6.22**) and traffic signs (see **C6.25**); and speeding (see **C6.58**). It need not specify the particular offence or offences but rather their nature. Alternative verdicts may be entered in accordance with the provisions of the Criminal Law Act 1967, s. 6(3), or the RTOA 1988, s. 24 (see **C2.8**), if the requirements of s. 1(1) have been complied with in relation to the original offence charged.

If the warning was not given at the time then a summons must be served within 14 days. The **C2.3** MCA 1980, s. 47, offers a saving provision where service by post has not been proved, enabling a second summons to be issued on the same information. In other cases a notice of intended prosecution must be served within 14 days on the driver or registered keeper of the vehicle. Service is deemed under s. 1(2) if sent by registered post or recorded delivery service, as long as it was sent so as to be delivered, in the ordinary course of post, within the 14 days (*Groome v Driscoll* [1969] 3 All ER 1638). Such deeming of service is unavailable where the notice of intended prosecution was actually delivered after the end of the 14-day period, despite having been posted in accordance with the rebuttable presumption in the CrimPR, r. 4.10, so that it would be delivered within that time-limit (*Gidden v Chief Constable of Humberside* [2010] 2 All ER 75, where the cause was a postal strike).

Section 1(3) places the burden of proving failure to comply with the section on the defence on a balance of probabilities. Unless and until the defendant has given evidence that he had not received the notice, the warning that has to be given is deemed to have been given under s. 1(3) (*Hall v CPS* [2013] EWHC 2544 (Admin)). Because the question of service is a highly technical point, where the evidence is lacking on this issue it falls within the discretion of the court to grant an adjournment to allow the parties the chance to deal with the matter properly and fully (*R (Taylor) v Southampton Magistrates' Court* (2009) 173 JP 17).

The requirement in s. 1 does not apply if there has been an accident of which the defendant was **C2.4** aware or to the occurrence of which he has shut his eyes but if the incident was so trivial that the driver was unaware of it a notice of intended prosecution is necessary (*Bentley v Dickinson* [1983] RTR 356). For these purposes, 'accident' should be given a common-sense meaning and not be restricted to untoward or unintended consequences having an adverse physical effect (*Currie* [2007] 2 Cr App R 246). The principle applied in *Bentley v Dickinson*, however, does

Part C Road Traffic Offences

not extend to cases where the driver's injuries are so severe that he has no recollection of the accident (*DPP v Pidhajeckyj* [1991] RTR 136). There must be a sufficient causal link between the offence and the accident before the warning can be dispensed with (*Myers* [2007] 2 Cr App R 258).

Section 2(3) contains a saving where the prosecution have acted with reasonable diligence or the accused has by his own conduct contributed to a failure to comply with s. 1. Where the court is satisfied that s. 2(3)(a) applies, that is the end of the requirement to serve a summons within 14 days; it does not set a second period of 14 days running once the name and address have been ascertained (*R* [2012] EWCA Crim 2887). In the Crown Court, determining this issue is a matter for the judge rather than the jury (*Currie*).

Time-limits

C2.5 The MCA 1980, s. 127, lays down a general time-limit of six months for the laying of an information for a summary offence, subject to any enactment which expressly permits a longer period.

The RTOA 1988, s. 6, provides for an extended time-limit in relation to certain offences specified in sch. 1 to the Act. These include: driving while disqualified (see **C6.40**); insurance offences (see **C6.46** and **C6.50**); false statements (see **C4.20**) and certain offences relating to driving licences. In those cases proceedings may be commenced within a period of six months from the date on which sufficient evidence came to the prosecutor's knowledge; that date is conclusively proved by a signed certificate (*Haringey Magistrates' Court, ex parte Amvrosiou* [1996] EWHC (Admin) 14, which raised the possibility that fraud or inaccuracy on the face of the certificate might have an effect on conclusiveness). No proceedings are to be brought more than three years after the offence.

A traffic examiner employed by the vehicle inspectorate to investigate traffic offences, but not authorised to decide whether to prosecute, is not a prosecutor for the purposes of the 1988 Act (*Swan v Vehicle Inspectorate* [1997] RTR 187).

Duty to Produce Licence to Court

C2.6   Road Traffic Offenders Act 1988, s. 7

(1) A person who is prosecuted for an offence involving obligatory or discretionary disqualification and who is the holder of a licence must—
   (a) cause it to be delivered to the proper officer of the court not later than the day before the date appointed for the hearing, or
   (b) post it, at such a time that in the ordinary course of post it would be delivered not later than that day, in a letter duly addressed to the clerk and either registered or sent by the recorded delivery service, or
   (c) have it with him at the hearing,
   the foregoing obligations imposed on him as respects the licence also apply as respects the counterpart.

'Licence' includes a Community licence (RTOA 1988, s. 91A(1)).

Notification as to Disabilities

C2.7   Road Traffic Offenders Act 1988, s. 22

(1) If in any proceedings for an offence committed in respect of a motor vehicle it appears to the court that the accused may be suffering from any relevant disability or prospective disability (within the meaning of Part III of the Road Traffic Act 1988) the court must notify the Secretary of State.
(2) A notice sent by a court to the Secretary of State in pursuance of this section must be sent in such manner and to such address and contain such particulars as the Secretary of State may determine.

'Relevant disability' means the disabilities set out in the Motor Vehicles (Driving Licences) Regulations 1999 (SI 1999 No. 2864), part VI. There must be some evidence of such a disability before the court may notify the Secretary of State.

Alternative Verdicts

Road Traffic Offenders Act 1988, s. 24

C2.8

(A1) Where—
  (a) a person charged with manslaughter in connection with the driving of a mechanically propelled vehicle by him is found not guilty of that offence, but
  (b) the allegations in the indictment amount to or include an allegation of any of the relevant offences,
  he may be convicted of that offence.
(A2) For the purposes of subsection (A1) above the following are the relevant offences—
  (a) an offence under section 1 of the Road Traffic Act 1988 (causing death by dangerous driving),
  (aa) an offence under section 1A of that Act (causing serious injury by dangerous driving),
  (b) an offence under section 2 of that Act (dangerous driving),
  (c) an offence under section 3A of that Act (causing death by careless driving when under the influence of drink or drugs), and
  (d) an offence under section 35 of the Offences against the Person Act 1861 (furious driving).
(1) Where—
  (a) a person charged with an offence under a provision of the Road Traffic Act 1988 specified in the first column of the table below (where the general nature of the offences is also indicated) is found not guilty of that offence, but
  (b) the allegations in the indictment or information (or in Scotland complaint) amount to or include an allegation of an offence under one or more of the provisions specified in the corresponding entry in the second column,
  he may be convicted of that offence or of one or more of those offences.

Offence charged	Alternative
Section 1 (causing death by dangerous driving)	Section 2 (dangerous driving)
	Section 2B (causing death by careless, or inconsiderate, driving)
	Section 3 (careless, and inconsiderate, driving)
Section 1A (causing serious injury by dangerous driving)	Section 2 (dangerous driving)
	Section 3 (careless and inconsiderate driving)
Section 2 (dangerous driving)	Section 3 (careless, and inconsiderate, driving)
Section 2B (causing death by careless, or inconsiderate, driving)	Section 3 (careless, and inconsiderate, driving)
Section 3A (causing death by careless driving when under influence of drink or drugs)	Section 2B (causing death by careless, or inconsiderate, driving)
	Section 3 (careless and inconsiderate driving)
	Section 4(1) (driving when unfit to drive through drink or drugs)
	Section 5(1)(a) (driving with excess alcohol in breath, blood or urine)
	Section 7(6) (failing to provide specimen)
	Section 7A(6) (failing to give permission for laboratory test)
Section 4(1) (driving or attempting to drive when unfit to drive through drink or drugs)	Section 4(2) (being in charge of a vehicle when unfit to drive through drink or drugs)
Section 5(1)(a) (driving or attempting to drive with excess alcohol in breath, blood or urine)	Section 5(1)(b) (being in charge of a vehicle with excess alcohol in breath, blood or urine)
Section 28 (dangerous cycling)	Section 29 (careless, and inconsiderate, cycling)

(2) Where the offence with which a person is charged is an offence under section 3A of the Road Traffic Act 1988, subsection (1) above shall not authorise his conviction of any offence of attempting to drive.

(3) Where a person is charged with having committed an offence under section 4(1) or 5(1)(a) of the Road Traffic Act 1988 by driving a vehicle, he may be convicted of having committed an offence under the provision in question by attempting to drive.

(4) Where by virtue of this section a person is convicted before the Crown Court of an offence triable only summarily, the court shall have the same powers and duties as a magistrates' court would have had on convicting him of that offence.

(5) [Applies only to Scotland.]

(6) This section has effect without prejudice to section 6(3) of the Criminal Law Act 1967 (alternative verdicts on trial on indictment) . . . and section 23 of this Act.

C2.9   Where the offence charged is one under the RTA 1988, s. 4(1) (driving, or attempting to drive, when unfit through drink or drugs: see **C5.61**) or s. 5(1)(a) (driving, or attempting to drive, with excess alcohol in breath, blood or urine: see **C5.35**), it is open to the magistrates to convict of the alternative offence of 'being in charge of' or, if the allegation is of driving, to convict of the alternative of attempting to drive (s. 24(3)). When the CCA 2013, sch. 22, is implemented, similar alternative convictions will be available in respect of the new s. 5A offence (see **C5.57**). However, s. 24(2) states that where the offence charged is that under the RTA 1988, s. 3A, no alternative verdict involving attempting to drive is authorised. If the conviction is in the Crown Court and the offence is one that is triable only summarily, for example, where the conviction is under s. 3 of the 1988 Act (careless driving) as an alternative to a count alleging causing death by dangerous driving under s. 1, the powers of the Crown Court will be the same as those of the magistrates (s. 24(4)).

The six-month time-limit imposed by the MCA 1980, s. 127, does not apply (*Coventry Justices, ex parte Sayers* [1979] RTR 22).

C2.10   In *Jeavons* [1990] RTR 263, a case of reckless driving, the prosecution alleged that the accused and another were racing, although this was denied in interview. The co-accused pleaded guilty and the appellant did not give evidence. The judge did not leave an alternative verdict of careless driving to the jury. His decision was upheld on the basis that it is for the judge to exclude irrelevant charges and allegations as well as to ensure that the indictment covers offences which the facts might disclose. In the instant case, if the prosecution's case of 'racing' was rejected by the jury there was, in the circumstances, no ground for an allegation of careless driving. However, where there is a live issue as to the quality of a defendant's driving, the alternative verdict of careless driving should be left to the jury (*Cambray* [2007] RTR 128). In *Griffiths* [1998] Crim LR 348, the Court of Appeal held that, in the absence of a verdict of not guilty on the count of dangerous driving, there was no power under s. 24(1) for the jury to return a verdict of guilty of careless driving. For these purposes, a finding of no case to answer is equivalent to a finding of not guilty, thus making available the alternative verdict (*DPP v Smith* [2002] Crim LR 970). Where the defendant has already been acquitted of the 'lesser' charge (by the prosecution offering no evidence or otherwise), the alternative verdict is not available on the trial of the 'greater' charge and that should be made clear to the arbiters of fact (*DPP v Khan* [1997] RTR 82). For a full discussion of alternative verdicts and the relevant procedure, see **D19.41** *et seq.*

Information as to Date of Birth and Sex

C2.11   The RTOA 1988, s. 25, imposes requirements on magistrates' courts convicting a person of an offence involving obligatory or discretionary disqualification, or any offence prescribed by regulations under the RTA 1988, s. 105, to ascertain the defendant's date of birth, if unknown, through ordering its provision in writing. A person, having provided his date of birth, may be required by written notice from the Secretary of State left at, delivered or sent to the person's latest known address, to provide verification of that date of birth or to give a statement in writing specifying his different name at the time of birth (s. 25(5)). When dealing with a written guilty plea, if the defendant's sex is unknown, the court must order it to be provided in writing.

The duty of the court officer under s. 25 is set out in the CrimPR, r. 37.15. Knowingly failing to comply with any s. 25 requirement is punishable by a fine up to level 3.

Duty to Provide Information

Road Traffic Act 1988, s. 172

C2.12

(1) This section applies—
    (a) to any offence under the preceding provisions of this Act except—
        (i) an offence under Part V, or
        (ii) an offence under section 13, 16, 51(2), 61(4), 67(9), 68(4), 96 or 120, and to an offence under section 178 of this Act,
    (b) to any offence under sections 25, 26 and 27 of the Road Traffic Offenders Act 1988,
    (c) to any offence against any other enactment relating to the use of vehicles on roads, and
    (d) to manslaughter, or in Scotland culpable homicide, by the driver of a motor vehicle.

(2) Where the driver of a vehicle is alleged to be guilty of an offence to which this section applies—
    (a) the person keeping the vehicle shall give such information as to the identity of the driver as he may be required to give by or on behalf of a chief officer of police, and
    (b) any other person shall if required as stated above give any information which it is in his power to give and may lead to identification of the driver.

(3) Subject to the following provisions, a person who fails to comply with a requirement under subsection (2) above shall be guilty of an offence.

(4) A person shall not be guilty of an offence by virtue of paragraph (a) of subsection (2) above if he shows that he did not know and could not with reasonable diligence have ascertained who the driver of the vehicle was.

(5) Where a body corporate is guilty of an offence under this section and the offence is proved to have been committed with the consent or connivance of, or to be attributable to neglect on the part of, a director, manager, secretary or other similar officer of the body corporate, or a person who was purporting to act in any such capacity, he, as well as the body corporate, is guilty of that offence and liable to be proceeded against and punished accordingly.

(6) Where the alleged offender is a body corporate, . . . or the proceedings are brought against him by virtue of subsection (5) above or subsection (11) below, subsection (4) above shall not apply unless, in addition to the matters there mentioned, the alleged offender shows that no record was kept of the persons who drove the vehicle and that the failure to keep a record was reasonable.

(7) A requirement under subsection (2) may be made by written notice served by post; and where it is so made—
    (a) it shall have effect as a requirement to give the information within the period of 28 days beginning with the day on which the notice is served, and
    (b) the person on whom the notice is served shall not be guilty of an offence under this section if he shows either that he gave the information as soon as reasonably practicable after the end of that period or that it has not been reasonably practicable for him to give it.

(8) Where the person on whom a notice under subsection (7) above is to be served is a body corporate, the notice is duly served if it is served on the secretary or clerk of that body.

(9) For the purposes of section 7 of the Interpretation Act 1978 as it applies for the purposes of this section the proper address of any person in relation to the service on him of a notice under subsection (7) above is—
    (a) in the case of the secretary or clerk of a body corporate, that of the registered or principal office of that body or (if the body corporate is the registered keeper of the vehicle concerned) the registered address, and
    (b) in any other case, his last known address at the time of service.

(10) In this section—
    'registered address', in relation to the registered keeper of a vehicle, means the address recorded in the record kept under the Vehicle Excise and Registration Act 1994 with respect to that vehicle as being that person's address, and
    'registered keeper', in relation to a vehicle, means the person in whose name the vehicle is registered under that Act;
    and references to the driver of a vehicle include references to the rider of a cycle.

C2.13 *Foster v DPP* (2014) 178 JP 15 highlights the necessity of a charge for non-compliance specifying a date for the offence as one *after* the period of 28 days following service of the notice requiring information to be given (s. 172(7)(a)) has passed.

The justices must be satisfied that the document requiring information as to the identity of the driver was sent on behalf of a chief officer of police, but there is no need for that document to be signed, provided the document's authenticity can clearly be established by the prosecution (*Arnold v DPP* [1999] RTR 99). The justices need to be aware whether it is alleged the defendant was the keeper of the vehicle or 'any other person', although, for the purpose of submissions on duplicity, s. 172 creates only one offence (*Mohindra v DPP* [2005] RTR 95). Where there are joint registered keepers with a common last known address, a single notice, attaching only one form on which to reply, constitutes making a lawful requirement for the purposes of s. 172 (*Lynes v DPP* [2013] RTR 199). Section 172 does not create a duty, as such, on a registered keeper to make sure he is available at the registered address to receive relevant communications; however, a failure to be available for this purpose is a factor making it difficult, if not impossible, for a registered keeper to discharge the burden of proving a defence under s. 172(7)(b) (*R (Purnell) v Snaresbrook Crown Court* [2011] RTR 452 and *Whiteside v DPP* (2012) 176 JP 103, where it was suggested a registered keeper may need to consider establishing some system to handle correspondence sent during extended absences). *Whiteside v DPP* also confirmed that the offence does not require proof of *mens rea*, being within the exception articulated in *Sweet v Parsley* [1970] AC 132 (see **A2.23**) by Lord Reid because the offence was 'not criminal in any real sense but was an act which in the public interest was prohibited under penalty', and that service by post in accordance with the CrimPR, r. 4.4(2)(a), is effective even if the defendant has not personally received the notice but accepts that it was delivered to his address.

The obligation to provide information is mandatory. Where a written response is required, giving the information sought orally will not suffice to fulfil the obligation because the scheme of the section is designed to produce a document that can be accepted as evidence against the driver (*DPP v Broomfield* [2003] RTR 108). However, responding in writing, albeit not on the official form, but providing all the information required and signing the letter can suffice to bring the defendant within the defence in s. 172(4) (*Jones v DPP* [2004] RTR 331). A response by the driver to an earlier request sent to a different person as the registered keeper does not provide a defence to failing to respond to a subsequent notice sent directly to the defendant in his capacity as driver (*Duff v DPP* [2009] EWHC 675 (Admin)). Because of the relationship with the RTOA 1988, s. 12, where the form is not signed then, even where it contains the information required, its return will not fulfil the s. 172 requirements (*Mawdesley v Chief Constable of Cheshire Constabulary* [2004] 1 All ER 58 and *Francis v DPP* (2004) 168 JP 492). Attempting to limit the use to which the provision of the required information can be put will not prevent it being used for the purpose envisaged by the RTOA 1988, s. 12 (see **C2.18**: *R (Hatton) v Chief Constable of Devon and Cornwall Constabulary* [2008] EWHC 209 (Admin)). If the keeper of the vehicle pleads ignorance as to who was the driver, the onus is on him to show that he did not know, and could not with reasonable diligence have ascertained, the identity of the driver. For the purposes of the defence in s. 172(4), the relevant date at which knowledge of who was driving needs to be assessed is the time at which the request is made, rather than the earlier time of when the driving occurred (*Atkinson v DPP* (2012) 176 JP 57). Where the defendant does not believe he was the driver and knew that only one other person had access to the vehicle, it is a clear inference that that other person was the driver at the time in question and the defendant is obliged to say so (*R (Flegg) v Southampton and New Forest Justices* (2006) 170 JP 373). In those circumstances, the defence in s. 172(4) is unavailable. When the justices reject a defence under s. 172(4), they must exercise care to ensure that they provide readily understandable reasons for doing so (*Weightman v DPP* [2007] RTR 565). In the case of any person other than the keeper, the onus is on the prosecution to establish that the person had information which may have led to the identification of the driver and which it was in his power to give.

C2.14 Where the defendant admits to having been the driver concerned in the alleged offence, the statement provided under s. 172 can still be used by the prosecution to prove that fact, because to do so does not violate the right to a fair trial conferred by the ECHR, Article 6, and the privilege against self-incrimination implicit in that general right because s. 172 is not a disproportionate measure (*Brown v Stott* [2003] 1 AC 681, which was applied by the Divisional Court in *DPP v Wilson* [2001] RTR 37 and *Hayes v DPP* [2004] EWHC 227 (Admin)). This domestic approach was endorsed by the ECtHR in *O'Halloran and Francis v UK* (2007) 46 EHRR 397, in which it was confirmed that people 'who choose to keep and drive motor cars can be taken to have accepted certain responsibilities and obligation as part of the regulatory regime relating to motor vehicles, and in the legal framework of the United Kingdom, these responsibilities include the obligation, in the event of suspected commission of road traffic offences, to inform the authorities of the identity of the driver on that occasion'. In doing so, the court focused on the nature and degree of compulsion used to obtain the evidence, the existence of any relevant safeguards in the procedure, and the use to which any material so obtained is put. When balancing these issues the court concluded that the essence of the right to remain silent and the privilege against self-incrimination had not been destroyed.

It is not hearsay evidence to refer to records relating to the making of the requirement and note the absence of any reply (*DPP v Leigh* [2010] EWHC 345 (Admin)); the record is not being used for the purpose of establishing any fact or opinion because what counts is what it does not say.

Contravention of s. 172 constitutes an offence for which the defendant can be disqualified **C2.15** or have his licence endorsed with six penalty points. It also attracts a fine up to level 3 on the standard scale. A fixed penalty of £200 is available in respect of this offence. The *Magistrates' Court Sentencing Guidelines* (see Supplement, **SG-344**) give fine band C as the starting point.

EVIDENCE

Admissibility of Highway Code

The RTA 1988, s. 38(8), defines 'the Highway Code' as the Code comprising directions for **C2.16** the guidance of persons using roads issued under the RTA 1930, s. 45, and subsequently revised.

Section 38(7) provides that a failure to observe a provision of the Code shall not of itself render a person liable to criminal proceedings, but any such failure may be relied upon by any party to civil or criminal proceedings as tending to establish or negative any liability in question in those proceedings. In appropriate cases, the provisions of the Code can be used as guidance when a judge sums up to the jury, e.g., on what might constitute dangerous driving (*Taylor* [2004] EWCA Crim 213). The subsection does not provide for the admissibility of evidence of due observance of the Code. But a defendant may rely on the failure of any other person to observe a relevant provision of the Code (*Baker v E. Longhurst & Sons Ltd* [1933] 2 KB 461; *Croston v Vaughan* [1938] 1 KB 540).

Evidence by Certificate as to Driver, Owner or User

The RTOA 1988, s. 11, makes provision for evidence relating to the driver, user or owner to be **C2.17** adduced through a certificate in the prescribed form signed by a constable or a traffic warden (Functions of Traffic Wardens Order 1970 (SI 1970 No. 1958)). The certificate confirms that the person specified therein stated that on a particular occasion the mechanically propelled vehicle referred to was driven or used by, or belonged to, him, or a firm in which he was a partner or a corporation of which he was a director, officer or employee at the time of the statement. The certificate is admissible as evidence as to who drove or used the vehicle, or to whom it belonged on that occasion.

Its admissibility is dependent on a copy being served in the prescribed manner not less than seven days before the hearing or trial and the absence of any counter-notice from the defendant served on the prosecution not later than three days before the hearing or trial requiring the person who signed the certificate to attend. The form of the certificate and rules for service are prescribed by the Evidence by Certificate Rules 1961 (SI 1961 No. 248).

Section 11 provides an exception to the 'hearsay' rule. The offences to which the section applies are set out in sch. 1 to the RTOA 1988. These include: causing death by dangerous driving (see **C3.7**); causing death by careless, or inconsiderate, driving (see **C3.27**); causing serious injury by dangerous driving (see **C3.33**); dangerous driving (see **C3.39**); careless, and inconsiderate, driving (see **C6.1**); causing death by driving: unlicensed, disqualified or uninsured drivers (see **C3.47**); causing death by careless driving when under the influence of drink or drugs (see **C3.20**); driving or attempting to drive, or being in charge, when unfit to drive through drink or drugs (see **C5.61**); driving or attempting to drive, or being in charge, with excess alcohol in breath, blood or urine (see **C5.35**); (when implemented) driving or attempting to drive, or being in charge, with concentration of specified controlled drug above specified limit (see **C5.57**); failing to co-operate with a preliminary test (see **C5.6**); failures relating to evidential specimens (see **C5.9**); motor racing on highways (see **C6.13**); leaving vehicle in dangerous position (see **C6.16**); carrying passenger on motor cycle contrary to the RTA 1988, s. 23 (see **C6.19**); failing to comply with traffic directions (see **C6.22**) and traffic signs (see **C6.25**); using vehicle in dangerous condition (see **C6.29**); contraventions of construction and use requirements (see **C6.32** and **C6.33**); driving otherwise than in accordance with a licence (see **C6.37**); driving while disqualified (see **C6.40**); insurance offences (see **C6.46** and **C6.50**); and failure by driver to stop, report accident or give information or documents (see **C6.51**). Section 11 also applies to other offences contrary to the RTA 1988 listed in the RTOA 1988, sch. 1, and to 'any offence against any other enactment relating to the use of vehicles on roads'.

Proof of Identity of Driver in Summary Proceedings

C2.18   Road Traffic Offenders Act 1988, s. 12

(1) Where on the summary trial in England and Wales of an information for an offence to which this subsection applies—
   (a) it is proved to the satisfaction of the court, on oath or in manner prescribed by Criminal Procedure Rules, that a requirement under section 172(2) of the Road Traffic Act 1988 to give information as to the identity of the driver of a particular vehicle on the particular occasion to which the information relates has been served on the accused by post, and
   (b) a statement in writing is produced to the court purporting to be signed by the accused that the accused was the driver of that vehicle on that occasion,
   the court may accept that statement as evidence that the accused was the driver of that vehicle on that occasion.

The relevant rule for proving service is the CrimPR, r. 4.11. The offences to which s. 12 applies are set out in sch. 1 to the RTOA 1988. These include all the offences listed in **C2.17** to which the RTOA 1988, s. 11, also applies, with the exception of the two offences triable only on indictment: causing death by dangerous driving (see **C3.7**) and causing death by careless driving when under the influence of drink or drugs (see **C3.20**). Section 12(1) also applies to other offences contrary to the RTA 1988 listed in the RTOA 1988, sch. 1, and to 'any offence against any other enactment relating to the use of vehicles on roads'.

C2.19   In cases where identity becomes an issue and there is no s. 12 statement, the justices will be permitted to assess the sufficiency of the evidence from other sources (*Creed v Scott* [1976] RTR 488), such as relevant information about the registered keeper given to the police when questioned, which, when checked, corresponds to details held on the Police National Computer (*DPP v Bayliff* [2003] EWHC 539 (Admin)). Indeed, where there has been no prior notice that identity is an issue, relying on evidence by way of a dock identification may be permissible (*Karia v DPP* (2002) 166 JP 753).

Admissibility of Records of Secretary of State

The RTOA 1988, s. 13, enables statements reflecting the content of a part of the records main- **C2.20**
tained by the Secretary of State in connection with any functions exercisable by him by virtue of
the RTA 1988, part III, or a part of any other records maintained by the Secretary of State with
respect to vehicles, to be admissible in proceedings as evidence of any fact stated therein to the same
extent as oral evidence would be admissible. The document containing the statement must be
authenticated by a person duly authorised by the Secretary of State. Upon conviction of a summary offence under the Traffic Acts or the Road Traffic (Driver Licensing and Information
Systems) Act 1989, s. 13 permits the court, in the absence of the defendant, to take account of any
previous conviction or order specified in the document as if he had appeared and admitted it
(s. 13(3A)). Similarly, in respect of other offences involving obligatory or discretionary disqualification, where the document refers to a previous conviction for such an offence or any order made
on conviction and is proved to have been served on the defendant not less than seven days before
its production in court, in the absence of the defendant, the court may take it into account on the
same basis (s. 13(4)).

The records to be maintained and which are admissible (s. 13(5)) are set out in the Vehicle and
Driving Licences Records (Evidence) Regulations 1970 (SI 1970 No. 1997). They usually take
the form of a computer printout from DVLA at Swansea, appropriately endorsed for use in
accordance with the general rules for adducing evidence at trial or producing information for
sentencing purposes set out in the CrimPR, part 37.

Admissibility of Evidence from Prescribed Devices

Road Traffic Offenders Act 1988, s. 20   **C2.21**

(1) Evidence (which in Scotland shall be sufficient evidence) of a fact relevant to proceedings for
an offence to which this section applies may be given by the production of—
(a) a record produced by a prescribed device, and
(b) (in the same or another document) a certificate as to the circumstances in which the record
was produced signed by a constable or by a person authorised by or on behalf of the chief
officer of police for the police area in which the offence is alleged to have been committed;
but subject to the following provisions of this section.
...
(6) In proceedings for an offence to which this section applies, evidence (which in Scotland shall
be sufficient evidence)—
(a) of a measurement made by a device, or of the circumstances in which it was made, or
(b) that a device was of a type approved for the purposes of this section, or that any conditions
subject to which an approval was given were satisfied,
may be given by the production of a document which is signed as mentioned in subsection (1)
above and which, as the case may be, gives particulars of the measurement or of the circumstances
in which it was made, or states that the device was of such a type or that, to the best of the knowledge and belief of the person making the statement, all such conditions were satisfied.
(7) For the purposes of this section a document purporting to be a record of the kind mentioned
in subsection (1) above, or to be a certificate or other document signed as mentioned in that
subsection or in subsection (6) above, shall be deemed to be such a record, or to be so signed,
unless the contrary is proved.
(8) Nothing in subsection (1) or (6) above makes a document admissible as evidence in proceedings
for an offence unless a copy of it has, not less than seven days before the hearing or trial, been
served on the person charged with the offence; and nothing in those subsections makes a document admissible as evidence of anything other than the matters shown on a record produced by
a prescribed device if that person, not less than three days before the hearing or trial or within such
further time as the court may in special circumstances allow, serves a notice on the prosecutor
requiring attendance at the hearing or trial of the person who signed the document.

As to the requirement for corroboration of the opinion evidence of a witness concerning speed **C2.22**
in such cases, and the use of measurements as corroboration, see the RTRA 1984, s. 89; *Nicholas
v Penny* [1950] 2 KB 466; and *Swain v Gillet* [1974] RTR 446.

Section 20(2) provides that s. 20 applies to offences under the RTRA 1984, ss. 16, 17(4), 88(7) and 89(1) (speeding offences: see **C6.58**), offences under that Act in respect of bus lanes or routes for use by buses only, and offences under the RTA 1988, s. 36(1) (failure to comply with automatic traffic light signal: see **C6.25**), offences under the Vehicle Excise and Registration Act 1994, s. 29(1) (using or keeping an unlicensed vehicle on a public road), and offences under the HGV Road User Levy Act 2013, s. 11(1) (using or keeping heavy goods vehicle if levy not paid). Section 20 is just one of the means of proving the offence; other methods of proof remain available (*R (Seroka) v Redhill Magistrates' Court* [2012] EWHC 3827 (Admin)).

In the case of any offence to which s. 20 applies, the prosecution will be able to rely on evidence produced by automatic devices of a specified and approved type, without the need for corroboration. For these purposes, a photograph is accepted as a record produced by the device, even though it is not produced directly because of the need for developing the negative before it becomes readable, after which printing is the most convenient medium for use (*Griffiths v DPP* [2007] RTR 547). The evidence must be accompanied by the appropriate certificate signed by a constable or other authorised person, and, where there is such a certificate, s. 20(7) imposes the burden on the defence of disproving that the document is a record. Where that evidence and certificate are served not less than seven days before the hearing or trial and there is no counter-notice from the defendant in accordance with s. 20(8), they may be tendered in evidence without the necessity of anyone being called to prove them (*DPP v Thornley* (2006) 170 JP 385). Any document served under s. 20(8) must be capable of being used for the purpose intended; if it is only a poor quality copy, that does not constitute 'service' and the document itself is rendered inadmissible under the subsection. However, in any case where s. 20(8) does not apply, the evidence from the prescribed device can be adduced in the conventional way.

C2.23 Prescribed devices include those facilitating radar measurement of speed (Road Traffic Offenders (Prescribed Devices) Order 1992 (SI 1992 No. 1209)); photographic imaging to calculate speed (Road Traffic Offenders (Prescribed Devices) Order 1999 (SI 1999 No. 162)); and measurement of odometer pulses between two points (Road Traffic Offenders (Prescribed Devices) Order 2008 (SI 2008 No. 1332)). In addition, there are bus lane cameras (Road Traffic Offenders (Additional Offences and Prescribed Devices) Order 1997 (SI 1997 No. 384)) and traffic light cameras (Road Traffic Offenders (Prescribed Devices) (No. 2) Order 1992 (SI 1992 No. 2843), and see *The Pict v CPS* [2009] EWHC 1176 (Admin)). *Brotherston v DPP* (2012) 176 JP 153 confirms that the RTOA 1988, s. 20, enables technological advances to be accommodated without the need for amending primary legislation. There is nothing in the provisions to suggest that Parliament intended that the description of the device in the statutory instrument needed to be more specific than the generic description in the original form of the section. In particular, the 'description' of the device does not need to identify the particular brand of the product.

Connell v DPP (2011) 175 JP 151 confirms that the RTOA 1988, s. 20, constitutes a self-contained code, offering a particular method of adducing evidence before the court. Accordingly, an officer providing oral evidence of his opinion of a vehicle's speed, supported by a reading from a prescribed but non-approved device, can lawfully found a conviction for speeding (see **C6.61**). In *Barber v DPP* [2006] EWHC 3137 (Admin), the constable's explanation about why 'Timeout' appeared on stills produced by the device in question was accepted and this did not render the stills inadmissible. A device remains an approved device even if one of the pre-operative tests is not performed (*R (Bray) v Bristol Crown Court* [2009] EWHC 3018 (Admin)). See also *Iaciofano v DPP* [2011] RTR 205, in respect of the Police Pilot Provida device. Unlike in Scotland, there is no requirement to prove that the device had been tested for accuracy before it can provide corroborating evidence (*Clarke v CPS* (2014) 178 JP 7).

Section C3 Offences Relating to Driving Triable on Indictment

MANSLAUGHTER

Manslaughter is considered here only in relation to so-called 'motor' or 'vehicular' manslaughter. As to manslaughter generally, see **B1.34** to **B1.51**.   **C3.1**

Indictment

For the form of indictment for manslaughter, see **B1.38**.   **C3.2**

Elements

In general see **B1.64** *et seq*.   **C3.3**

The RTA 1988, s. 38, is applicable; see **C2.16**.

Where the prosecution can satisfy the terms of the direction in *Adomako* [1995] 1 AC 171 (see **B1.88**), charging 'motor manslaughter' may still be appropriate, albeit rare, even if the test for dangerous driving in the RTA 1988, s. 2A (see **C3.10** *et seq*.), is also satisfied.

In 'motor manslaughter', however, the risk of death involved in an offence must be very high (*Pimm* [1994] RTR 391; *Brown (Uriah) v The Queen* [2005] 2 WLR 1558), thereby reflecting the greater degree of turpitude that Parliament must be taken to have intended by restricting the maximum penalty for the statutory offence under s. 1 to 14 years' imprisonment.

Defences

Automatism, mechanical defect, and duress. See **C1.21**, **C1.7** and **A3.35** to **A3.52**. See also **C3.4** *Renouf* [1986] 2 All ER 449 at **C3.42**.

Punishment

See generally, **B1.51**.   **C3.5**

Life imprisonment and/or a fine. See *Pimm* [1994] RTR 391.

By the RTOA 1988, s. 34 and sch. 2, part II, disqualification for at least two years and endorsement are obligatory, unless the court finds 'special reasons'. Manslaughter by the use of a motor vehicle carries between three and 11 penalty points for the purposes of the RTOA 1988, s. 35. The offence also carries mandatory retesting by way of an extended driving test (see **C7.32**). Forfeiture of a motor vehicle used in connection with the crime may be ordered (see **E18.1**).

Sentencing

The Court of Appeal has emphasised that real assistance from previous decisions is often unavailable because no two cases are the same (*Brown* [2006] 1 Cr App R (S) 727, where a sentence of ten years' detention in a young offender institution was upheld in respect of a driver who had been   **C3.6** trying to kill himself by driving into another vehicle at speed). The sentencing judge must bear in mind that the defendant did not intend to cause serious injury to, or kill, anyone else, which would constitute murder, and that the offence is more serious than causing death by dangerous driving. The risk of death is higher, so the offence will generally merit a proportionately greater sentence than for the statutory offence (*A-G's Ref (No. 14 of 2001)* [2002] 1 Cr App R (S) 106). In *Hussain* [2012] 2 Cr App R (S) 427, where a young defendant with a low IQ had driven off knowing a two-year-old child he had knocked over accidentally was trapped beneath the vehicle, the Court of Appeal indicated that some assistance could be derived from *Richardson* [2007] 2 All ER 601, but that the instant case was more serious than dangerous driving because of knowingly taking the risk of killing or seriously injuring the child. The sentence of eight years' imprisonment was reduced to six. Aggravating features include hostility or aggressive action taken towards another and the consumption of alcohol or drugs. Other relevant factors include the number of deaths, whether the gross negligence was prolonged or shortlived and whether it took place in the context of some other offence, e.g., seeking to steal the vehicle (*A-G's Ref (No. 11 of 2006)* [2007] 2 Cr App R (S) 146, which acknowledged that none of the recent cases purport to be guideline cases). See also *Bissell* [2008] 1 Cr App R (S) 452. In addition to the cases cited in *Brown*, other examples of sentencing exercises for motor manslaughter include *Pimm* [1994] RTR 391, *Ripley* [1997] 1 Cr App R (S) 19 and *A-G's Ref (No. 64 of 2001)* [2002] 1 Cr App R (S) 409.

CAUSING DEATH BY DANGEROUS DRIVING

C3.7   Road Traffic Act 1988, s. 1

A person who causes the death of another person by driving a mechanically propelled vehicle dangerously on a road or other public place is guilty of an offence.

This offence is triable only on indictment.

Indictment

C3.8   *Statement of Offence*

Causing death by dangerous driving, contrary to section 1 of the Road Traffic Act 1988.

Particulars of Offence

D, on the...day of..., drove a mechanically propelled vehicle dangerously on a road [or public place], namely..., and thereby caused the death of V.

In *Roberts* [2013] RTR 436, the Court of Appeal commented that, because in sentencing terms it is generally considered more serious, charging causing death by dangerous driving (when supported by the evidence) was preferable to opting to charge aggravated vehicle taking instead.

Elements

C3.9   The RTA 1988, s. 38, and the RTOA 1988, s. 11, are applicable; see **C2.16** and **C2.17**. For the meaning of 'public place', see **C1.16**.

For the purposes of the RTA 1988, s. 1, the definition of 'driver' does not include a separate person acting as a steersman. One of the tests for dangerous driving must be satisfied, producing a causal link to the death.

C3.10   **Tests for Dangerous Driving**   Section 2A sets out to define what constitutes dangerous driving.

Road Traffic Act 1988, s. 2A

(1) For the purposes of sections 1, 1A and 2 above a person is to be regarded as driving dangerously if (and, subject to subsection (2) below, only if)—
    (a) the way he drives falls far below what would be expected of a competent and careful driver, and
    (b) it would be obvious to a competent and careful driver that driving in that way would be dangerous.
(2) A person is also to be regarded as driving dangerously for the purposes of sections 1 and 2 above if it would be obvious to a competent and careful driver that driving the vehicle in its current state would be dangerous.

(3) In subsections (1) and (2) above 'dangerous' refers to danger either of injury to any person or of serious damage to property; and in determining for the purposes of those subsections what would be expected of, or obvious to, a competent and careful driver in a particular case, regard shall be had not only to the circumstances of which he could be expected to be aware but also to any circumstances shown to have been within the knowledge of the accused.

(4) In determining for the purposes of subsection (2) above the state of a vehicle, regard may be had to anything attached to or carried on or in it and to the manner in which it is attached or carried.

Section 2A relies on an objective test. Danger refers to the danger of injury to a person or serious **C3.11** damage to property. *Mens rea* plays no part in the offence (*Loukes* [1996] 1 Cr App R 444 at p. 450):

> Proof of guilt depends on an objective standard of driving, namely, what would have been obvious to a competent and careful driver. The accused driver's state of mind is relevant only if and to the extent that it attributes additional knowledge to the notional competent and careful driver...It should be noted too that the threshold of proof is high. It must be shown that the defect was 'obvious' to a 'competent and careful driver'. It is not enough to show in the case of such a driver that, say, if he had examined the vehicle by going underneath it, he would have seen the defect.

The standard of driving must fall 'far below' that expected of a 'competent and careful' driver and it must be obvious to a 'competent and careful' driver that the manner of driving is dangerous. The prosecution must demonstrate both elements before s. 2A(1) is satisfied (*Brooks* [2001] EWCA Crim 1944). Care needs to be taken by the prosecution not to seek to adduce inadmissible evidence about the defendant's past bad driving (*McKenzie* [2008] RTR 277). When directing a jury, the judge must avoid watering down the requirement for the driving to fall 'far below' the standard expected so that it confuses the test with that for careless driving (*Jeshani* [2005] EWCA Crim 146). The introduction of the concept of a careful driver as an objective observer places the question of what constitutes dangerous driving within the province of the tribunal of fact. Speed alone is not sufficient to found a conviction for dangerous driving (*DPP v Milton* [2006] RTR 264). When determining what was expected of the competent and careful driver in the situation in which the defendant was driving, taking into account the driving skills of the particular defendant is inconsistent with the objective test set out in the RTA 1988, s. 2A(3) (*Bannister* [2010] RTR 28). Accordingly, the special skill (or indeed lack of skill) of a driver is an irrelevant circumstance in considering whether the driving is dangerous. The provisions of the Highway Code, whilst certainly not conclusive, may still merit careful consideration as guidance as to the standards to be attributed to a careful and competent driver (*Taylor* [2004] EWCA Crim 213).

The CPS 'Policy for prosecuting cases of bad driving' gives the following examples of driving **C3.12** that may support an allegation of dangerous driving: racing or competitive driving; speed which is highly inappropriate for the prevailing road or traffic conditions; aggressive driving, such as sudden lane changes, cutting into a line of vehicles or driving much too close to the vehicle in front; disregard of traffic lights and other road signs, which, on an objective analysis, would appear to be deliberate; disregard of warnings from fellow passengers; overtaking that could not have been carried out safely; driving a vehicle with a load that presents a danger to other road users; where the driver is suffering from impaired ability such as having an arm or leg in plaster, or impaired eyesight; driving when too tired to stay awake; driving a vehicle knowing it has a dangerous defect; using a hand-held mobile phone or other hand-held electronic equipment when the driver was avoidably and dangerously distracted by that use; reading a newspaper/map; talking to and looking at a passenger where the driver was avoidably and dangerously distracted by that; selecting and lighting a cigarette, or similar, in circumstances where the driver was avoidably and dangerously distracted by that. In *A-G's Ref (No. 17 of 2009)* [2010] RTR 1, the Court of Appeal confirmed that there is never any excuse for texting or using a hand-held mobile phone while driving. In addition, by reference to the guidance in *Cooksley* [2003] 3 All ER 40, further factors might be callous behaviour at the time, e.g., throwing a victim off the vehicle or failing to stop, or causing death (and presumably serious injury) in the course of an escape or an attempt to avoid detection. These are indicative only and not conclusive as to the type of behaviour which might constitute dangerous driving.

C3.13 **Dangerous State of Driver**   The fact that a driver was adversely affected by alcohol is a circumstance relevant to the issue of dangerous driving, but it is not in itself determinative to prove the offence (*Webster* [2006] 2 Cr App R 103). In *Woodward* [1995] 3 All ER 79, the Court of Appeal distinguished the line of cases which had developed in relation to reckless driving and reaffirmed the earlier principle from *McBride* [1962] 2 QB 167 (a five-judge Court of Appeal), where Ashworth J stated (at p. 172):

> ... if a driver is adversely affected by drink, this fact is a circumstance relevant to the issue whether he was driving dangerously. Evidence to this effect is of probative value and is admissible in law. In the application of this principle two further points should be noticed. In the first place, the mere fact that the driver has had drink is not of itself relevant: in order to render evidence as to the drink taken by the driver admissible, such evidence must tend to show that the amount of drink taken was such as would adversely affect a driver or, alternatively, that the driver was in fact adversely affected. Secondly, there remains in the court an overriding discretion to exclude such evidence if in the opinion of the court its prejudicial effect outweighs its probative value.

The provisions of the RTOA 1988, s. 15 (see **C5.43**), are applicable only to the alcohol-related offences specified therein. Accordingly, where only a single specimen has been taken from which to assess the level of the defendant's alcohol consumption, such evidence is still admissible on the issue of whether the defendant drove dangerously (*Ash* [1999] RTR 347). There is no requirement to prove whether the defendant was above or below the prescribed limit, as that is not an element of the offence (*Mari* [2010] RTR 192); evidence of the amount of alcohol consumed and said to affect the defendant's ability to drive suffices.

A similar approach is likely to be to a driver adversely affected by drugs once the offence under the RTA 1988, s. 5A (see **C5.57**) is in force.

In *Marison* [1997] RTR 457, driving in a dangerously defective state owing to diabetes was considered no different to driving in a dangerously defective state owing to alcohol, constituting circumstances of which the defendant could be expected to be aware and of which he had knowledge, within the meaning of the RTA 1988, s. 2A(3). See also *C* [2007] EWCA Crim 1862.

C3.14 **Dangerous State of Vehicle**   The offence may also be committed if the state of a vehicle, including any attachment or load and the way in which it is attached or carried, would make driving it dangerous in the eyes of a 'competent and careful' driver. In relation to the dangerous state of the vehicle being 'obvious', no special definition is required when directing the jury; however it would not be a misdirection to indicate that it can arise from an inspection which is something between a fleeting glance and a long look (*Marsh* [2002] EWCA Crim 137). It could be argued that some loads and vehicles (e.g., certain tractor units and their attachments) are inherently dangerous. See also *Crossman* (1986) 82 Cr App R 333. However, where the vehicle benefits from specific authorisation from the Secretary of State for use on public roads, there must usually be evidence that the vehicle has been manoeuvred in such a way as to create a danger beyond that otherwise inherent in its use on a road, because 'current state' implies something different from the vehicle's original or manufactured state (*Marchant* [2004] 1 All ER 1187).

Where the mere act of taking an inherently dangerous vehicle on the road amounts to dangerous driving, it potentially falls within the RTA 1988, s. 2A(2) and also s. 2A(1)(a) and (b). To that extent s. 2A(2) is superfluous, but it underlines the point that driving a vehicle in a dangerous condition may well constitute an offence under s. 1, 1A or 2 (depending on the consequences of the dangerous driving) as well as under the construction and use regulations (see also *Spurge* [1961] 2 QB 205 and *Robert Millar Contractors Ltd* [1970] 2 QB 54). The danger presented by the current state of the vehicle must, however, be capable of being seen or realised at first glance, in the sense of being 'evident to' the competent and careful driver, before it can be regarded as 'obvious'; it should not be discoverable only by taking some additional steps to ascertain the vehicle's defective state (*Strong* [1995] Crim LR 428). Moreover, where the driver is an employee driving the employer's vehicle, it will be important to consider the instructions given to him about checking the vehicle's condition. Unless those instructions appear inadequate, the driver cannot be expected to do more than comply with them (*Roberts* [1997] RTR 462); such compliance satisfies the 'competent and careful driver' test.

Causal Link to Fatality   The prosecution need to establish that death resulted from the   **C3.15**
accused's dangerous driving. In *Jenkins* [2013] RTR 288, which involved parking a vehicle so as
to restrict visibility for other road users, the Court of Appeal stressed that the offence relates to
causing death *by* driving and not causing death *while* driving, clarifying that the driving is not
required to be coterminous with the impact resulting in the death. It should be noted that danger to the person is not qualified by any adjective and therefore, as long as it is not *de minimis*,
any danger to any person, even though slight, if obvious to the 'competent and careful' driver,
would suffice. In *Hennigan* [1971] 3 All ER 133, a case of causing death by reckless driving
under the RTA 1960, the recklessness consisted mainly of the speed at which the defendant was
driving; the driver of the other car, which contained the two persons who were killed, may well
have been substantially to blame for the accident. The court held that there was nothing in the
legislation which required the manner of the accused's driving to be a substantial or major cause
of the accident, as long as it was 'a cause and something more than *de minimis*'. Similarly, it was
said in *Skelton* [1995] Crim LR 635 that no particular degree of contribution to the death,
beyond a negligible one, is required. An acceptable direction to the jury is that they do not have
to be sure that the defendant's driving 'was the principal, or a substantial, cause of the death, as
long as [they] are sure that it was a cause and that there was something more than a slight or a
trifling link' (*Kimsey* [1996] Crim LR 35). In *Girdler* [2010] RTR 307, the Court of Appeal
offered guidance about the most appropriate way to direct the jury where the accused alleges
that a second collision is the immediate cause of death and so constitutes a *novus actus interveniens*, breaking the chain of causation. If the jury are sure that the accused drove dangerously
and also sure that his dangerous driving was more than a slight or trifling link to the death(s),
the jury could also be told that the accused 'will have caused the death(s) only if you are sure that
it could sensibly have been anticipated that a fatal collision might occur in the circumstances in
which the second collision did occur'. Hooper LJ added that, if necessary, the judge could make
clear to the jury that they are not concerned with what the accused foresaw.

Defences

Automatism, mechanical defect, and duress. See **C1.21**, **C1.7** and **A3.35** to **A3.52**. See also *Renouf*   **C3.16**
[1986] 2 All ER 449 at **C3.42**. No offence is committed under s. 1 where the driving was in a public
place other than a road in the course of an authorised motoring event (RTA 1988, s. 13A).

Alternative Verdicts

The RTOA 1988, s. 24, provides alternative verdicts of dangerous driving and careless, and   **C3.17**
inconsiderate, driving under the RTA 1988, ss. 2 and 3 (see **C2.8**). See also *Fairbanks* [1986] 1
WLR 1202 (discussed at **D19.60**) and *Jeavons* [1990] RTR 263. An alternative verdict of causing death by careless or inconsiderate driving under the RTA 1988, s. 2B, is also available (see
C3.27). Section 24 operates without prejudice to the Criminal Law Act 1967, s. 6(3).
Accordingly, no separate count for such an offence is required. Indeed, as careless driving has
not been specified under the CJA 1988, s. 40, a separate count for that offence would be invalid,
thereby rendering ineffective a guilty plea entered in respect of it (*Davis* (19 April 1996 unreported)). By the RTOA 1988, s. 2, a failure to warn a suspect of an intended prosecution or to
serve such a warning notice does not act as a bar to conviction of the alternative offences.

Punishment

The maximum sentence is 14 years' imprisonment and/or a fine. Obligatory disqualification for   **C3.18**
two years and endorsement, unless the court finds 'special reasons' (RTOA 1988, s. 34(4) and
sch. 2). The offence carries between three and 11 penalty points and mandatory retesting by way
of an extended driving test (see **C7.32**). Forfeiture of the motor vehicle used for the purpose of
the crime may be ordered (see **E18.1**).

Sentencing

C3.19   The sentencing guideline *Causing Death by Driving* (see Supplement, SG-437) must generally be followed where the offender is aged 18 or over. Earlier cases may no longer provide particular assistance for the sentencing exercise. The guideline creates three levels of seriousness drawn principally by reference to the standard of the offender's driving. Determinants of seriousness include the offender's awareness of the risk associated with his driving, the effect of alcohol or drug consumption, driving at an inappropriate speed, other instances of serious culpable behaviour and where the victim was a vulnerable road user. Examples are provided to enable the offending behaviour to be categorised. For the most serious level 1 offences, involving a deliberate decision to drive very badly and an apparent disregard for the great danger to others resulting, the sentencing range is from seven to 14 years' imprisonment, with a starting point of eight years. For level 2 offences, which create a substantial risk of danger, the sentencing range is four to seven years' imprisonment, with a starting point of five years. For level 3 offences, which create a significant risk of danger, the sentencing range is two to five years' imprisonment, with a starting point of three years. Because of the consequences flowing therefrom, it is important to select the correct level (*Carswell* [2009] EWCA Crim 1848) and to indicate clearly what it is when pronouncing sentence (*Farmer* [2010] EWCA Crim 2851), although some overlap exists and the levels are not 'impermeable' (*Salam* [2012] EWCA Crim 2264). The guideline is to be interpreted flexibly, in a nuanced way sensitive to the facts of the case (*Paul* [2013] EWCA Crim 2034) and it was further recognised in *Torkington* [2013] EWCA Crim 2183 that the list of circumstances set out in it is not exhaustive, meaning that not all cases will fit precisely into a given level. The guideline also lists the additional aggravating and mitigating factors to be taken into account in adjusting the sentence from the starting point applicable for each level of offence. Mobile telephone use during the period shortly preceding the offence is likely to be regarded as an aggravating factor (*Arora* [2014] EWCA Crim 104). Where the offender is of good character and has an impeccable driving record, a bigger discount than would be the case through slavishly following the guideline can be justified (*Bolam* [2009] EWCA Crim 2462). See also *A-G's Ref (No. 61 of 2009)* [2010] 2 Cr App R (S) 21 and *Oughton* [2011] 1 Cr App R (S) 390.

CAUSING DEATH BY CARELESS DRIVING WHEN UNDER THE INFLUENCE OF DRINK OR DRUGS

C3.20   Road Traffic Act 1988, s. 3A

   (1) If a person causes the death of another person by driving a mechanically propelled vehicle on a road or other public place without due care and attention, or without reasonable consideration for other persons using the road or place, and—

   (a) he is, at the time when he is driving, unfit to drive through drink or drugs, or

   (b) he has consumed so much alcohol that the proportion of it in his breath, blood or urine at that time exceeds the prescribed limit, or

   (c) he is, within 18 hours after that time, required to provide a specimen in pursuance of section 7 of this Act, but without reasonable excuse fails to provide it, or

   (d) he is required by a constable to give his permission for a laboratory test of a specimen of blood taken from him under section 7A of this Act, but without reasonable excuse fails to do so,

   he is guilty of an offence.

   (2) For the purposes of this section a person shall be taken to be unfit to drive at any time when his ability to drive properly is impaired.

   (3) Subsection (1)(b), (c) and (d) above shall not apply in relation to a person driving a mechanically propelled vehicle other than a motor vehicle.

This offence is triable only on indictment. When the CCA 2013, sch. 22, is implemented, a new s. 3A(1)(ba), referring to the new drug-driving offence in the RTA, s. 5A (see C5.57), will be inserted.

Indictment

C3.21

Statement of Offence

Causing death by careless driving when under the influence of drink or drugs, contrary to s. 3A(1) of the Road Traffic Act 1988.

Particulars of Offence

D, on the...day of..., caused the death of V by driving a motor [or mechanically propelled] vehicle on a road [or public place], namely..., without due care and attention and after having consumed so much alcohol that the proportion of it in his breath [or blood or urine] at the time exceeded the prescribed limit [or when unfit to drive through drink or drugs].

Elements

C3.22

For the meaning of 'careless' and 'without reasonable consideration', see **C6.3** and **C6.6**. For the meaning of 'public place', see **C1.16**.

The RTA 1988, s. 38, and the RTOA 1988, s. 11, are applicable; see **C2.16** and **C2.17**.

The offence can be committed in eight separate ways. The prosecution need to establish either that the accused was driving without due care and attention or without reasonable consideration for other persons using the road, that the death of another person was caused by the manner of his driving and that at the time he came within one of the four paragraphs in s. 3A(1). The prosecution would therefore have to prove careless driving, the requisite causal link and the related 'drink driving' offence in exactly the same way as if both offences had been charged (see **C6.1** *et seq*. and **C5.35**, **C5.61** and **C5.9**). The offence does not require any causal connection between the alcohol or drugs and the death (*Shepherd* [1994] 2 All ER 242).

In applying the appropriate test to determine whether a defendant has driven without due care and attention, the jury is entitled to look at all the circumstances of the case, including evidence that the defendant had been affected by alcohol or had taken such an amount of alcohol as would be likely to affect a driver (*Millington* [1996] RTR 80). Thus, the principle stated in *McBride* [1962] 2 QB 167 (see **C3.13**) in relation to causing death by dangerous driving applies equally to the offence in s. 3A(1). See also *Coe* [2010] 3 All ER 83, especially relating to the RTA 1988, s. 3A(1)(c).

Evidence of impairment would normally be provided by a doctor who examines the accused, but evidence may also be provided by non-expert witnesses. It may take the form of a description of the actions of the accused, including the manner of driving, as long as the witness does not express an opinion as to the condition of the accused. In relation to any drug not used in the UK, the jury need to consider in the round whether its presence in the accused's body makes him unfit (*Beach* [2013] EWCA Crim 1783).

If the offence relates to s. 3A(1)(c), the request to provide a specimen must be made within 18 hours, presumably from the time of driving rather than the time of death.

Section 3A(1)(b), (c) and (d) apply only where the driving is of a 'motor vehicle', but the offence under s. 3A(1)(a) may be committed whilst driving any 'mechanically propelled vehicle'.

Defences

C3.23

Duress and mechanical defect. See **A3.35** to **A3.52** and **C1.7**. Automatism may be a defence (see **C1.21**), but in practice will be very difficult to establish given the nature of this offence and the possibility of interpreting such a situation as arising from self-induced intoxication. See also **C5.54**.

Alternative Verdicts

C3.24

The RTOA 1988, s. 24 (see **C2.8**), provides alternative verdicts under the RTA 1988, ss. 3, 4(1), 5(1)(a), 7(6) and 7A(6). An alternative verdict under the RTA 1988, s. 2B, is also available (see **C3.27**). It would therefore seem that, if someone is accused of an offence based on s. 3A(1)(c), he could theoretically be convicted, for example, of driving whilst unfit even though the indictment contains an allegation that he refused to provide a specimen.

Punishment

C3.25   The maximum sentence is 14 years' imprisonment and/or a fine (CJA 2003, s. 285). In the absence of 'special reasons', obligatory disqualification for not less than two years and endorsement with between three and 11 penalty points. Retesting by way of an extended driving test is mandatory (see **C7.32**). Forfeiture of the motor vehicle used for the purpose of the crime may be ordered (see **E18.1**).

Sentencing

C3.26   The sentencing guideline *Causing Death by Driving* (see Supplement, SG-437) must generally be followed where the offender is aged 18 or over. The guideline creates three bands of seriousness depending on the amount by which the offender exceeded the prescribed limit or the manner of the failure to provide the specimen required. In respect of each of those bands, the sentencing range and starting point is then fixed by reference to whether the careless or inconsiderate driving arose from momentary inattention with no aggravating factors or was not far short of dangerousness, or whether it fell somewhere in-between (see, e.g., *Nwokedi* [2010] EWCA Crim 132). The lowest starting point is 18 months' imprisonment, where the sentencing range is from 26 weeks to four years, and the highest is eight years' imprisonment, where the sentencing range is seven to 14 years. The guideline also lists the additional aggravating and mitigating factors to be taken into account in adjusting the sentence from the starting point applicable for each category of offence. In *Williams* [2014] EWCA Crim 147, it was suggested that a compassionate act of shepherding the accused from the scene should be distinguished from the aggravating factor of fleeing after the offence. The sentencing judge should remember that the consumption of alcohol and carelessness, e.g., arising from speeding, are constituent elements of the offence and not of themselves aggravating factors (*Smith* [2011] EWCA Crim 2844). In *Thorogood* [2010] EWCA Crim 2123, the Court of Appeal confirmed the appropriateness of a sentencing court taking into account the age of the offender as personal mitigation, warranting a further reduction in the starting point before applying any discount arising from a guilty plea. See also *Cockroft* [2013] 2 Cr App R (S) 199 (29).

CAUSING DEATH BY CARELESS, OR INCONSIDERATE, DRIVING

C3.27   Road Traffic Act 1988, s. 2B

A person who causes the death of another person by driving a mechanically propelled vehicle on a road or other public place without due care and attention, or without reasonable consideration for other persons using the road or place, is guilty of an offence.

This offence is triable either way.

Indictment

C3.28   *Statement of Offence*

Causing death by careless [or inconsiderate] driving, contrary to s. 2B of the Road Traffic Act 1988.

Particulars of Offence

D, on the … day of …, drove a mechanically propelled vehicle on a road [or public place], namely …, without due care and attention [or reasonable consideration for other persons using the road [or place]], and thereby caused the death of V.

Elements

C3.29   The offence will require proof of an underlying offence under the RTA 1988, s. 3 (see **C6.1** *et seq.*), together with a causal link to a fatality (see **C3.15**).

The RTA 1988, s. 38, and the RTOA 1988, ss. 1, 11 and 12(1), are applicable; see **C2.1**, **C2.16**, **C2.17** and **C2.18**.

Although there is no rule of law which requires a magistrates' court to adjourn any trial involving a fatal road traffic accident until the inquest has been concluded, as a matter of practice it is desirable to do so (*Smith v DPP* [2000] RTR 36). However, a s. 2B offence should not be treated as 'unlawful killing' for the purposes of the conclusion of an inquest (*R (Wilkinson) v HM Coroner for the Greater Manchester District* (2012) 176 JP 665).

Alternative Verdicts

The RTOA 1988, s. 24, provides an alternative verdict under the RTA 1988, s. 3 (see **C2.8**). As   **C3.30**
for other offences, where the defendant has already been acquitted of the s. 3 charge (by the prosecution offering no evidence), the alternative verdict is no longer available and that should be made clear to the arbiters of fact (*DPP v Khan* [1997] RTR 82).

Punishment

On indictment, the maximum sentence is five years' imprisonment and/or a fine; on summary   **C3.31**
trial, it is six months' imprisonment and/or the statutory maximum. Disqualification is obligatory. The offence carries obligatory endorsement with between three and 11 penalty points.

Sentencing

The sentencing guideline *Causing Death by Driving* (see Supplement, **SG-437**) must generally be   **C3.32**
followed where the offender is aged 18 or over. For the least serious offences arising from momentary inattention with no aggravating factors, a community order is indicated. For the most serious offences where the driving falls not far short of dangerous driving, the starting point is 15 months' imprisonment, with the sentencing range being 36 weeks to three years. For all other cases of careless or inconsiderate driving, the starting point is 36 weeks' imprisonment, with the sentencing range being a community order (high) to two years' imprisonment. The guideline also lists the additional aggravating and mitigating factors to be taken into account in adjusting the sentence from the starting point applicable for each band of offence. *Landon* [2012] 1 Cr App R (S) 402, in which a sentence of 20 months' youth detention was upheld, provides an example of the difficulties encountered in cases in the highest category of culpability involving a young driver. For a significant lapse of concentration for 14 seconds, a sentence of 12 months' imprisonment was justified (*Forster* [2012] EWCA Crim 2142), whereas a single misjudgment could be regarded as momentary inattention where a custodial sentence may not even be warranted (*Campbell* [2010] RTR 295). See also *Fleury* [2013] EWCA Crim 2273, relating to a foreign driver's forgetfulness. The statutory minimum disqualification period may be all that is justified in respect of one short instance of inattention (*Hall* [2010] EWCA Crim 2135), although there is no reason in principle or fact where the offending is outside the bottom category not to consider increasing the disqualification period (*Bagshawe* [2013] 2 Cr App R (S) 393 (62)). There is highly likely to be a reduction in the offender's culpability where the fatal accident was largely the responsibility of the deceased (*Arshad* [2012] 1 Cr App R (S) 511). See also *Hassan* [2013] 2 Cr App R (S) 170 (25) and *Pattison* [2014] EWCA Crim 544.

CAUSING SERIOUS INJURY BY DANGEROUS DRIVING

Road Traffic Act 1988, s. 1A   **C3.33**

(1) A person who causes serious injury to another person by driving a mechanically propelled vehicle dangerously on a road or other public place is guilty of an offence.
(2) In this section 'serious injury' means—
    (a) in England and Wales, physical harm which amounts to grievous bodily harm for the purposes of the Offences Against the Person Act 1861 ...

This offence is triable either way.

The LASPO 2012, s. 143, inserted s. 1A into the RTA 1988. It was brought into force on 3 December 2012 (SI 2012 No. 2770) in relation to driving occurring on or after that date (LASPO 2012, s. 143(4)).

Elements

C3.34   For the meaning of 'dangerous' and 'dangerous driving', see **C3.10** *et seq*. For the meaning of 'public place', see **C1.16**. For 'grievous bodily harm', see **B2.60**.

The RTA 1988, s. 38, and the RTOA 1988, ss. 11 and 12(1), are applicable; see **C2.16**, **C2.17** and **C2.18**.

Defences

C3.35   Automatism, mechanical defect and duress. See **C1.21**, **C1.7** and **A3.35** *et seq*. No offence is committed under the RTA 1988, s. 1A, where the driving took place in a public place other than a road in the course of an authorised motoring event (s. 13A).

Alternative Verdicts

C3.36   The RTOA 1988, s. 24, provides an alternative verdict under the RTA 1988, ss. 2 (dangerous driving) and 3 (careless, and inconsiderate, driving); see **C2.8**. *DPP v Khan* [1997] RTR 82 (see **C3.30**) must also be borne in mind.

Punishment

C3.37   The maximum sentence on indictment is five years' imprisonment and/or a fine; on summary trial, it is six months' imprisonment and/or the statutory maximum. Disqualification is obligatory. The offence carries obligatory endorsement with between three and 11 penalty points. Retesting by way of an extended driving test is mandatory (see **C7.32**). Forfeiture of the vehicle used may also be ordered (see **E18.1**).

Sentencing

C3.38   Pending any Sentencing Council guidelines, reference to the principles set out in the guidelines for fatal driving offences, albeit making allowances where the standard of driving differs and recognising the less serious consequence of a s. 1A offence, may assist, as may sentences for dangerous driving where serious injury has been caused (e.g., *Stranney* [2008] 1 Cr App R (S) 611: see **C3.46**). See *Ellis* [2014] EWCA Crim 593 in relation to disqualification for the offence.

DANGEROUS DRIVING

C3.39   Road Traffic Act 1988, s. 2

> A person who drives a mechanically propelled vehicle dangerously on a road or other public place is guilty of an offence.

This offence is triable either way. In the absence of an election by the defendant, the *Allocation* sentencing guideline requires that cases should generally be tried summarily unless the magistrates' court's sentencing powers are insufficient (see Supplement, **SG-590**). The CPD, paras. 9A.1 to 9A.3 (see Supplement, **PD-17**), provide further guidance in relation to taking this decision.

Indictment

C3.40   *Statement of Offence*

Dangerous driving, contrary to section 2 of the Road Traffic Act 1988.

Particulars of Offence

D, on the…day of…, drove a mechanically propelled vehicle dangerously on a road [or public place], namely…

Elements

For the meaning of 'dangerous' and 'dangerous driving', see **C3.10** *et seq*. For the meaning of **C3.41**
'public place', see **C1.16**.

The RTA 1988, s. 38, and the RTOA 1988, ss. 1, 11 and 12(1), are applicable; see **C2.1**, **C2.16**, **C2.17** and **C2.18**.

Where the evidence permits, charging aggravated vehicle-taking as well as dangerous driving does not result in double jeopardy nor in itself does it amount to an abuse of process (*Harding* [1995] Crim LR 733). However, where the defendant has previously been convicted of another offence arising out of the same incident, e.g., an excess alcohol offence, then pursuing a separate charge of dangerous driving subsequently is wrong; the prosecution must choose its course of action from the outset or no later than before the conclusion of the first set of proceedings (*Phipps* [2005] EWCA Crim 33).

Defences

Automatism, mechanical defect and duress. See **C1.21**, **C1.7** and **A3.35** to **A3.52**. No offence **C3.42**
is committed under this section where the driving took place in a public place other than a road in the course of an authorised motoring event (RTA 1988, s. 13A).

In *Renouf* [1986] 2 All ER 449, the appellant pursued a Volvo containing persons who had thrown a barrage of objects which struck the appellant, occasioning actual bodily harm, and damaged the windscreen of his car. The appellant caught up with the Volvo and edged it off the road and on to the grass verge. The only risk caused was that of damage to the Volvo and, in response to a charge of reckless driving, the defence submitted that, in creating that risk, the appellant was using only such force as was reasonable to assist in the lawful arrest of the offenders in accordance with the CLA 1967, s. 3(1) (see **A3.54**). The trial judge directed that s. 3(1) was incapable of affording a defence to reckless driving. The Court of Appeal, however, held that the jury might, on the unusual evidence in the case, have accepted such a defence, which should therefore have been left to them. Accordingly, in appropriate circumstances, this unusual defence could excuse or provide a defence to a charge of dangerous driving, causing death by dangerous driving, causing serious injury by dangerous driving or manslaughter.

Alternative Verdicts

The RTOA 1988, s. 24, provides an alternative verdict under the RTA 1988, s. 3 (see **C2.8**). **C3.43**
DPP v Khan [1997] RTR 82 (see **C3.30**) must also be borne in mind.

Punishment

The maximum sentence on indictment is two years' imprisonment and/or a fine; on summary **C3.44**
trial, it is six months' imprisonment and/or the statutory maximum. Disqualification is obligatory. The offence carries obligatory endorsement with between three and 11 penalty points. Retesting by way of an extended driving test is mandatory (see **C7.32**). Forfeiture of the vehicle used may also be ordered (see **E18.1**).

Sentencing

When conducting a sentencing exercise, it is a point of principle that proper regard needs to be **C3.45**
taken of the maximum sentence of two years' imprisonment and the extent of the culpability of the offender (*Pettit* [2010] EWCA Crim 2107; *Raynham* [2011] EWCA Crim 1032 and *Gaskin* [2013] EWCA Crim 244). The introduction of the RTA 1988, s. 1A (see **C3.33**), is designed to meet the criticisms about the maximum sentence aired in *Skinner* [2011] EWCA Crim 239.

When selecting the appropriate starting point, sentencers must be realistic about just how bad the driving was (*Wilson* [2013] EWCA Crim 1745).

In *Shoaib* [2012] EWCA Crim 2742, which involved prolonged high-speed driving where it was lucky no damage or injury was inflicted, the sentence of 22 months' imprisonment was upheld. In *Templeton* [1996] 1 Cr App R (S) 380, the offender drove for nearly four minutes at speeds of up to 70 mph in a built up area, travelling about three miles and crossing seven red lights. Nine months' imprisonment and disqualification for two years was upheld. In *Joseph* [2002] 1 Cr App R (S) 74, dangerous driving resulting in personal injury to a traffic warden attracted a deterrent sentence of ten months' imprisonment and disqualification for two years. Even where the defendant is young and the period of driving involved is short, a short custodial sentence can still be warranted (*Barnes* [2011] EWCA Crim 2127). In *Jenkinson* [2011] EWCA Crim 2330, a sentence of 12 months' imprisonment and disqualification for five years was reduced to nine months and three years respectively in respect of momentary inattention by an HGV driver driving face-on to the sun, who had not displayed any disregard for the rules of the road and had good personal mitigation. See also *Bateman* [2012] EWCA Crim 2626. In *Kennion* [1997] RTR 421, the Court of Appeal commented that 'where otherwise perfectly respectable people of impeccable character lose control when sitting behind the wheel of a motor car because they imagine in some way that they have been provoked', i.e. road rage, they 'can expect immediate custodial sentences'. See also *Joel* [2013] EWCA Crim 634. Even in such cases, general principles about the appropriate period of disqualification apply (see **C7.36**) and should not be so long as to impair the prospects of rehabilitation (*Chivers* [2005] EWCA Crim 2252, where the disqualification was reduced from five years to 18 months). *McCafferty* [2011] EWCA Crim 509 provides an example of a case in which the minimum period of disqualification was appropriate.

C3.46 Where the judge is also sentencing for a count of inflicting grievous bodily harm arising from the dangerous driving, it is not wrong in principle for the overall sentence to rise above two years' imprisonment (*Stranney* [2008] 1 Cr App R (S) 611). In *Fitzpatrick* [2003] EWCA Crim 1399, the trial judge was criticised for wrongly taking into account that the driving had resulted in a fatality where this was not the offender's fault or even part of the prosecution case against him.

Reference can also usefully be made to the *Magistrates' Court Sentencing Guidelines* (see Supplement, **SG-332**); where the offence is being dealt with summarily, the guideline must generally be followed.

CAUSING DEATH BY DRIVING: UNLICENSED, DISQUALIFIED OR UNINSURED DRIVERS

C3.47   Road Traffic Act 1988, s. 3ZB

A person is guilty of an offence under this section if he causes the death of another person by driving a motor vehicle on a road and, at the time when he is driving, the circumstances are such that he is committing an offence under—
(a) section 87(1) of this Act (driving otherwise than in accordance with a licence),
(b) section 103(1)(b) of this Act (driving while disqualified), or
(c) section 143 of this Act (using motor vehicle while uninsured or unsecured against third party risks).

This offence is triable either way.

The introduction of this offence (by the Road Safety Act 2006, s. 21) means that where a fatality results from driving that is not even careless driving (see **C6.1** *et seq*. and also the offence under the RTA 1988, s. 2B, at **C3.27**), the fact that the driver should not even have been on the road at the time, whether because he does not hold the requisite driving licence, was disqualified from driving by a court order or did not have the necessary insurance cover to be using the vehicle, will convert that basic offence into the more serious offence under this provision.

Elements

The offence requires proof of one of the underlying offences under the RTA 1988 (see C6.37, **C3.48** C6.40 or C6.46), together with a causal link to a fatality (see generally C3.15). In *Hughes* [2013] 1 WLR 2461, the Supreme Court clarified that that the key words in s. 3ZB are 'causes… death… by driving' and, because this is a penal statute, it falls to be construed with a degree of strictness in favour of the accused. There must be something more than 'but for' causation. Section 3ZB 'requires at least some act or omission in the control of the car, which involves some element of fault, whether amounting to careless/inconsiderate driving or not, and which contributes in some more than minimal way to the death. It is not necessary that such act or omission be the principal cause of the death' (at [36]). In terms of directions to the jury, 'it is not necessary for the Crown to prove careless or inconsiderate driving, but…there must be something open to proper criticism in the driving of the defendant, beyond the mere presence of the vehicle on the road, and which contributed in some more than minimal way to the death' (at [33]). See also *Uthayakmar* [2014] EWCA Crim 123.

The RTOA 1988, ss. 11 and 12(1), are applicable; see C2.17 and C2.18.

Punishment

The maximum sentence on indictment is two years' imprisonment and/or a fine; on summary **C3.49** trial, it is six months' imprisonment and/or the statutory maximum. Disqualification is obligatory. The offence carries obligatory endorsement with between three and 11 penalty points.

Sentencing

The sentencing guideline *Causing Death by Driving* (see Supplement, SG-437) must generally **C3.50** be followed where the offender is aged 18 or over. The guideline sets out the starting points and sentencing ranges for the various ways in which the offence can be committed and lists the additional aggravating and mitigating factors to be taken into account in adjusting the sentence from the starting point applicable for each band of offence.

WANTON OR FURIOUS DRIVING

Offences Against the Person Act 1861, s. 35 **C3.51**

Whosoever, having the charge of any carriage or vehicle, shall by wanton or furious driving or racing, or other wilful misconduct, or by wilful neglect, do or cause to be done any bodily harm to any person whatsoever, shall be guilty of an offence…

This offence is triable only on indictment.

Indictment

Statement of Offence **C3.52**

Causing bodily harm, contrary to section 35 of the Offences Against the Person Act 1861.

Particulars of Offence

D, on the…day of…, having the charge of a taxi cab [or carriage etc.], by wanton [or furious] driving [or racing etc.] caused bodily harm to V.

Elements

The RTA 1988, s. 38, is applicable if the offence is committed on a 'road'. See C1.13 and **C3.53** C2.16.

The offence can be committed whether or not the conduct takes place on a road (*Cooke* [1971] Crim LR 44; *Knight* [2004] EWCA Crim 2998). It also covers any kind of vehicle or carriage, including bicycles (*Parker* (1895) 59 JP 793).

The definition of 'driving' in this context is generally thought to be the older definition, which would include bicycles and even box carts, although such 'vehicles' or 'carriages' would often be propelled manually or by means of pedals and could rarely be said to be 'driven' in the modern sense of that term. 'Wanton' has no technical meaning, and may be construed in the light of its ordinary dictionary definition of irresponsible, capricious, unrestrained or random. In *Knight*, the Court of Appeal accepted as correct the trial judge's direction on the meaning of 'wanton' as effectively recklessness, involving the defendant in 'driving in such a manner as to create an obvious and serious risk of causing physical harm to some other person who might happen to be using the road, or doing substantial damage to property' and 'that in driving in that manner [the defendant] did so without having given any thought to the possibility of there being any such risk, or having recognised that there was some risk involved, had nonetheless gone on to take it'.

Alternative Verdicts

C3.54   Assault occasioning actual bodily harm, contrary to the OAPA 1861, s. 47. Common assault, contrary to the CJA 1988, s. 39, but only if specifically included as a separate count on the indictment (*Mearns* [1991] QB 82).

Punishment

C3.55   The offence carries two years' imprisonment and/or a fine. Where the offence is committed in respect of a mechanically propelled vehicle, endorsement is obligatory, it carries between three and nine penalty points and disqualification is discretionary (Road Safety Act 2006, s. 28). The offence is not otherwise endorsable but disqualification may be ordered under the PCC(S)A 2000, s. 147 (see **E21.14**), if an assault is involved and the accused was driving a motor vehicle. Forfeiture of the vehicle used for the purposes of the crime may be ordered (see **E18.1**).

CAUSING DANGER TO ROAD-USERS

C3.56   **Road Traffic Act 1988, s. 22A**

(1) A person is guilty of an offence if he intentionally and without lawful authority or reasonable cause—
   (a) causes anything to be on or over a road, or
   (b) interferes with a motor vehicle, trailer or cycle, or
   (c) interferes (directly or indirectly) with traffic equipment,
   in such circumstances that it would be obvious to a reasonable person that to do so would be dangerous.

(2) In subsection (1) above 'dangerous' refers to danger either of injury to any person while on or near a road, or of serious damage to property on or near a road; and in determining for the purposes of that subsection what would be obvious to a reasonable person in a particular case, regard shall be had not only to the circumstances of which he could be expected to be aware but also to any circumstances shown to have been within the knowledge of the accused.

(3) In subsection (1) above 'traffic equipment' means—
   (a) anything lawfully placed on or near a road by a highway authority;
   (b) a traffic sign lawfully placed on or near a road by a person other than a highway authority;
   (c) any fence, barrier or light lawfully placed on or near a road—
      (i)   in pursuance of section 174 of the Highways Act 1980, or section 65 of the New Roads and Street Works Act 1991 (which provide for guarding, lighting and signing in streets where works are undertaken), or
      (ii) by a constable or a person acting under the instructions (whether general or specific) of a chief officer of police.

(4) For the purposes of subsection (3) above anything placed on or near a road shall unless the contrary is proved be deemed to have been lawfully placed there.

(5) In this section 'road' does not include a footpath or bridleway.

This offence is triable either way. In *Curtis* [2010] 1 Cr App R (S) 193, it was suggested that, because of the prejudice involved, an offence under s. 22A(1) should not have been dealt with at the trial of offences under the Protection from Harassment Act 1997, s. 4(1).

Indictment

Statement of Offence   C3.57

Causing danger to road users, contrary to section 22A(1) of the Road Traffic Act 1988.

Particulars of Offence

D, on the ... day of ..., intentionally and without lawful authority or reasonable cause interfered with a motor vehicle [or trailer, cycle or traffic equipment], namely ..., [or caused ... to be on [or over] a road, namely ...,] in such circumstances that to do so was dangerous.

Elements

The prosecution must establish that the accused intentionally performed the act. As to the   C3.58
burden of proof in relation to a defence of acting with lawful authority or reasonable cause, see F3.11 *et seq.*

The danger which arises must be of serious damage to property or of injury to any person while on or near a road. The test is an objective one but the danger must exist and must be obvious to a reasonable person. In other words there has to be a serious likelihood that injury or serious damage may be the result of the actions of the accused. In *DPP v D* [2006] RTR 461, where a large road sign had been placed by the defendant and another on the carriageway without authorisation, the Divisional Court held that the proper test is not what would be obvious to a reasonable and prudent driver but rather whether a reasonable bystander, whether a motorist or not and being fully aware that not all drivers do drive carefully and well, would consider the act in question to represent an obvious danger. It is not necessary for injury or damage to result and it seems that any injury, however slight and as long as it could be termed an injury, would qualify. The extent of the potential damage or injury must, of course, have relevance to any sentence.

In *Meeking* [2012] 1 WLR 3349, a case of unlawful act manslaughter in which the act involved endangering road users contrary to the RTA 1988, s. 22A(1)(b), the Court of Appeal clarified that s. 22A(1)(b) is not confined to acts done to the vehicle before it is driven, but also covers interference creating a danger while the vehicle is in the process of being driven. Further, the conduct can take place within the vehicle rather than only external to it, such as dropping objects on to it. It is, however, a misdirection for the judge to refer to interference with the driver of the vehicle as opposed to interference with the vehicle itself (*Maxwell* [2014] EWCA Crim 417).

Punishment

The maximum sentence on indictment is seven years' imprisonment and/or a fine; on summary   C3.59
trial, it is six months' imprisonment and/or the statutory maximum fine. The offence is not endorsable.

Section C4 Offences Relating to Documents Triable on Indictment

FORGERY, ALTERATION ETC. OF DOCUMENTS ETC.

C4.1

Goods Vehicles (Licensing of Operators) Act 1995, s. 38

(1) A person is guilty of an offence if, with intent to deceive, he—

  (a) forges, alters or uses a document or other thing to which this section applies;

  (b) lends to, or allows to be used by, any other person a document or other thing to which this section applies; or

  (c) makes or has in his possession any document or other thing so closely resembling a document or other thing to which this section applies as to be calculated to deceive.

(2) This section applies to the following documents and other things, namely—

  (a) any operator's licence;

  (b) any document, plate, mark or other thing by which, in pursuance of regulations, a vehicle is to be identified as being authorised to be used, or as being used, under an operator's licence;

  (c) any document evidencing the authorisation of any person for the purposes of sections 40 and 41;

  (d) any certificate of qualification under section 49; and

  (e) any certificate or diploma such as is mentioned in paragraph 13(1) of Schedule 3.

Indictment

C4.2

Statement of Offence

Forgery [or Use etc.] of a document [or licence etc.] with intent to deceive, contrary to section 38(1) of the Goods Vehicles (Licensing of Operators) Act 1995.

Particulars of Offence

D, on the . . . day of . . ., with intent to deceive, forged [or used etc.] a document [or licence etc.], namely . . .

Statement of Offence

Making [or Possessing] a document [or licence etc.] with intent to deceive, contrary to section 38(1) of the Goods Vehicles (Licensing of Operators) Act 1995.

Particulars of Offence

D, on the . . . day of . . ., with intent to deceive, made [or had in his possession] a document [or thing] so closely resembling an operator's licence [or document etc.] as to be calculated to deceive.

This offence is triable either way.

Elements

C4.3 The RTOA 1988, s. 6 (see C2.5), applies by virtue of the Goods Vehicles (Licensing of Operators) Act 1995, s. 51.

As to forgery, see s. 38(4) of the 1995 Act and, generally, **B6.36** *et seq*. The term 'operator's licence' is defined in s. 2(1) of the 1995 Act and the vehicles authorised to be used under such a licence are set out in s. 5(1). Power to seize documents or articles is contained in s. 41. See also *Vehicle Operator Services Agency v FM Conway Ltd* [2013] RTR 242.

Punishment

The offence under s. 38 is punishable on summary conviction by a fine up to the statutory   **C4.4**
maximum, or on indictment by a term of imprisonment not exceeding two years and/or a fine
(s. 38(3)).

Sentencing

See *Raven* (1988) 10 Cr App R (S) 354 and **C4.9**.   **C4.5**

FALSE RECORDS OR ENTRIES RELATING TO DRIVERS' HOURS

Transport Act 1968, s. 99   **C4.6**

(5) Any person who makes, or causes to be made, any entry in a book, register or document kept or carried for the purposes of regulations under section 98 [of this Act] which he knows to be false or, with intent to deceive, alters or causes to be altered any such record or entry shall be liable—
(a) on summary conviction, to a fine not exceeding the prescribed sum;
(b) on conviction on indictment, to imprisonment for a term not exceeding two years.

Indictment

Statement of Offence   **C4.7**

Making [or Causing] a false record [or entry] [to be made], contrary to section 99(5) of the Transport Act 1968.

Particulars of Offence

D, on the…day of…, made [or caused to be made] an entry in a book [or register etc.] kept [or carried] for the purposes of regulations under section 98 of the Transport Act 1968, namely…, which he knew to be false.

This offence is triable either way.

Elements

This offence has a narrower application following the introduction by the Passenger and   **C4.8**
Goods Vehicles (Recording Equipment) Regulations 2005 (SI 2005 No. 1904) of separate provisions resulting from Council Regulation (EC) No. 2135/98 relating to digital tachographs. Regulations made under s. 98 are the Drivers' Hours (Goods Vehicles) (Keeping of Records) Regulations 1987 (SI 1987 No. 1421) which provide for the making of entries in the driver's record book according to the instructions contained therein. These regulations apply to certain domestic journeys and impose obligations upon employers, where relevant, as well as drivers. In any proceedings under s. 99(5), it is necessary for the prosecution to establish that the record or book etc. is being 'carried for the purpose' of the relevant regulation, and as certain vehicles are exempt, a thorough examination of the various provisions is essential. In *J. F. Alford Transport Ltd* [1997] 2 Cr App R 326, the Court of Appeal held that knowledge of and passive acquiescence in a principal's offence under s. 99(5) is insufficient to amount to aiding and abetting its commission, but indicated that such knowledge and an ability to control the action of an offender coupled with a deliberate decision to refrain from doing so might suffice.

C

Part C   Road Traffic Offences

Sentencing

C4.9   In *Raven* (1988) 10 Cr App R (S) 354, the offender was involved in the running of a haulage business, a number of whose vehicles had their tachograph wiring interfered with. He had entered into an agreement with another man to operate using that man's operator's licence and discs. Two drivers said that they were instructed by the appellant, from time to time, to drive with the tachograph switched off. He had previous relevant convictions. The sentence of nine months' imprisonment following guilty pleas to six counts was upheld. In *Potter* [1999] 2 Cr App R (S) 448, the Court of Appeal substituted three months' imprisonment for the nine months imposed and concluded that where the offender is not in a managerial position and had not therefore corrupted others, a lower sentence may be justified. However, in *Saunders* [2001] 2 Cr App R (S) 301, eight months' imprisonment was upheld in spite of the offenders not occupying managerial positions because of the number of offences and the lengthy period over which they were committed. The Court of Appeal approved the judge's sentencing remarks, which stressed the importance of safety provisions, the unfairness of competition to 'fair traders', the level of sophistication shown, the public danger which must have arisen, and the fraudulent nature of the offenders' activities.

FORGERY, ALTERATION ETC. OF LICENCES, MARKS, TRADE PLATES ETC.

C4.10   Vehicle Excise and Registration Act 1994, s. 44

(1)   A person is guilty of an offence if he forges, fraudulently alters, fraudulently uses, fraudulently lends or fraudulently allows to be used by another person anything to which subsection (2) applies.

(2)   This subsection applies to—

    (a)   a vehicle licence,

    (b)   a trade licence,

    (c)   a nil licence,

    (d)   a registration mark,

    (e)   a registration document, and

    (f)   a trade plate (including a replacement trade plate).

Indictment

C4.11   *Statement of Offence*

Forgery [or Fraudulent use etc.] of a vehicle licence [or trade licence etc.], contrary to section 44(1) of the Vehicle Excise and Registration Act 1994.

Particulars of Offence

D, on the . . . day of . . ., forged [or fraudulently used etc.] a vehicle licence [or trade licence etc.], namely . . .

Procedure and Evidence

C4.12   The admissibility of records maintained by the Secretary of State is governed by the Vehicle Excise and Registration Act 1994, s. 52.

Elements

C4.13   For the purposes of the Vehicle Excise and Registration Act 1994, s. 44, 'fraudulently' means dishonestly deceiving a police officer or other person responsible for a public duty. There is no requirement to prove an intention to cause any economic loss (*Terry* [1984] AC 374). In *Johnson* [1995] RTR 15, it was held that an offence under the Vehicles (Excise) Act 1971, s. 26 (which s. 44 of the 1994 Act replaced), relating to fraudulent use of a licence could be committed only where there was evidence that the vehicle was being or had been used on a public road while displaying the offending licence.

Forgery does not necessarily connote an intention to defraud but may be taken to include an intention to deceive for the purposes of the Vehicle Excise and Registration Act 1994 (*Clifford v Bloom* [1977] RTR 351; *Clayton* (1980) 72 Cr App R 135).

In *Macrae* (1995) 159 JP 359, the offence of forging a licence was said to involve the defendant making a false licence, with the intent that he or another should use it to induce a third party to accept it as genuine and by reason of so accepting it to do or not to do some act to his own or another's prejudice as a result of such acceptance of the false licence as genuine in connection with the performance of any duty, i.e. akin to the ulterior intent found in the Forgery and Counterfeiting Act 1981, see **B6.36** *et seq*.

Section 44 applies to any application for a licence in respect of a duty exempt vehicle.

Punishment

On indictment, the maximum sentence for an offence under the Vehicle Excise and Registration **C4.14** Act 1994, s. 44, is two years' imprisonment and/or a fine; on summary conviction, a fine not exceeding the statutory maximum. See *Weston* [2011] EWCA Crim 2334 and *Galluccio* [2014] EWCA Crim 766.

FORGERY OF DOCUMENTS ETC.: ROAD TRAFFIC ACT 1988, s. 173

Road Traffic Act 1988, s. 173   **C4.15**

(1) A person who, with intent to deceive—
   (a) forges, alters or uses a document or other thing to which this section applies, or
   (b) lends to, or allows to be used by, any other person a document or other thing to which this section applies, or
   (c) makes or has in his possession any document or other thing so closely resembling a document or other thing to which this section applies as to be calculated to deceive,
   is guilty of an offence.
(2) This section applies to the following documents and other things—
   (a) any licence under any Part of this Act or, in the case of a licence to drive, any counterpart of such a licence,
   (aa) any counterpart of a Northern Ireland licence or Community licence,
   (b) any test certificate, goods vehicle test certificate, plating certificate, certificate of conformity or Minister's approval certificate (within the meaning of Part II of this Act),
   (c) any certificate required as a condition of any exception prescribed under section 14 of this Act,
   (cc) any seal required by regulations made under section 41 of this Act with respect to speed limiters,
   (d) any plate containing particulars required to be marked on a vehicle by regulations under section 41 of this Act or containing other particulars required to be marked on a goods vehicle by sections 54 to 58 of this Act or regulations under those sections,
   (dd) any document evidencing the appointment of an examiner under section 66A of this Act,
   (e) any records required to be kept by virtue of section 74 of this Act,
   (f) any document which, in pursuance of section 89(3) of this Act, is issued as evidence of the result of a test of competence to drive,
   (ff) any document evidencing the successful completion of a driver training course provided in accordance with regulations under section 99ZA of this Act,
   (g) any certificate under section 133A or any badge or certificate prescribed by regulations made by virtue of section 135 of this Act,
   (h) any certificate of insurance or certificate of security under Part VI of this Act,
   (j) any document produced as evidence of insurance in pursuance of Regulation 6 of the Motor Vehicles (Compulsory Insurance) (No. 2) Regulations 1973 (SI 1973 No. 2143),

(k) any document issued under regulations made by the Secretary of State in pursuance of his power under section 165(2)(a) of this Act to prescribe evidence which may be produced in lieu of a certificate of insurance or a certificate of security,

(l) any international road haulage permit, and

(m) a certificate of the kind referred to in section 34B(1) of the Road Traffic Offenders Act 1988.

(3) In the application of this section to England and Wales 'forges' means makes a false document or other thing in order that it may be used as genuine.

(4) In this section 'counterpart', 'Community licence' and 'Northern Ireland licence' have the same meanings as in Part III of this Act.

C4.16   When s. 37(8) of the Road Safety Act 2006 is brought into force, a new s. 173(2)(n) will be inserted so as to include 'any document produced as evidence of the passing of an appropriate driving test' (as defined in the RTOA 1988, s. 36) within s. 173. When para. 27 of sch. 6 to that Act is implemented, s. 173(2)(g) will be replaced with three paragraphs expanding the documents already mentioned to include reference to a document evidencing the passing of an examination to give driving instruction or the completion of training for such instructors.

Indictment

C4.17   The form provided in **C4.2** may be adapted for use in relation to offences under this section.

Elements

C4.18   'Use' extends to use by an employer, see **C1.28**.

Particular words must be read 'against the mischief which that particular section seeks to avoid or prevent'; the production of a driving licence unconnected with any driving on the road is not 'using' it for the purposes of the RTA 1988, s. 173 (*Howe* [1982] RTR 45).

A document which has been completed by someone other than the proper person does not cease to be a document to which the section applies for the purposes of 'using' (*Pilditch* [1981] RTR 303).

A forged document which is not specified within s. 173 but which closely resembles a document there specified is not 'used', but may fall within s. 173(1)(c) (*Holloway v Brown* [1978] RTR 537).

Where an 'intent to deceive' has been established, it is not necessary for the prosecution to prove that the defendant knew the documents were false; if that was the case, the statute would include the word 'knowingly'. Such an intent may be shown by evidence that 'they were irregular documents either by way of irregular acquisition or by the irregular disposing of them' (*Greenberg* [1942] 2 All ER 344, per Birkett J at p. 347). The court in *Greenberg* also stated that it is unnecessary to allege or prove an intent to deceive any particular person. Knowledge that the documents are false may, however, be relevant to the issue of whether the defendant had an 'intent to deceive'.

In *Cleghorn* [1938] 3 All ER 398, a certificate of insurance which had been cancelled was held to be properly described as one resembling a certificate of insurance. Similarly, in *Aworinde* [1996] RTR 66, bogus blank insurance certificates were held to be documents so closely resembling certificates as to be calculated to deceive.

'Calculated to deceive' means 'likely to deceive' (*Davison* [1972] 3 All ER 1121; *Turner v Shearer* [1972] 1 All ER 397).

Punishment

C4.19   On conviction on indictment, the maximum sentence is two years' imprisonment and/or a fine; on summary conviction, a fine not exceeding the statutory maximum.

FALSE STATEMENTS ETC.: ROAD TRAFFIC
ACT 1988, s. 174

Road Traffic Act 1988, s. 174

C4.20

(1) A person who knowingly makes a false statement for the purpose—
   (a) of obtaining the grant of a licence under any Part of this Act to himself or any other person, or
   (b) of preventing the grant of any such licence, or
   (c) of procuring the imposition of a condition or limitation in relation to any such licence, or
   (ca) of obtaining a document evidencing the successful completion of a driver training course provided in accordance with regulations under section 99ZA of this Act, or
   (d) of securing the entry or retention of the name of any person in the register of approved instructors maintained under Part V of this Act, or
   (dd) of obtaining the grant to any person of a certificate under section 133A of this Act, or
   (e) of obtaining the grant of an international road haulage permit to himself or any other person,
   is guilty of an offence.
(2) A person who, in supplying information or producing documents for the purposes either of sections 53 to 60 and 63 of this Act or of regulations made under sections 49 to 51, 61, 62 and 66(3) of this Act—
   (a) makes a statement which he knows to be false in a material particular or recklessly makes a statement which is false in a material particular, or
   (b) produces, provides, sends or otherwise makes use of a document which he knows to be false in a material particular or recklessly produces, provides, sends or otherwise makes use of a document which is false in a material particular,
   is guilty of an offence.
(3) A person who—
   (a) knowingly produces false evidence for the purposes of regulations under section 66(1) of this Act, or
   (b) knowingly makes a false statement in a declaration required to be made by the regulations,
   is guilty of an offence.
(4) A person who—
   (a) wilfully makes a false entry in any record required to be made or kept by regulations under section 74 of this Act, or
   (b) with intent to deceive, makes use of any such entry which he knows to be false,
   is guilty of an offence.
(5) A person who makes a false statement or withholds any material information for the purpose of obtaining the issue—
   (a) of a certificate of insurance or certificate of security under Part VI of this Act, or
   (b) of any document issued under regulations made by the Secretary of State in pursuance of his power under section 165(2)(a) of this Act to prescribe evidence which may be produced in lieu of a certificate of insurance or a certificate of security,
   is guilty of an offence.

When para. 28 of sch. 6 to the Road Safety Act 2006 is brought into force, a new s. 174(1)(da) will be inserted, referring to a document evidencing the passing of an examination to give driving instruction or the completion of training for such instructors.

Elements

There is no requirement that the making of the false statement results in any gain or advantage accruing to the defendant (*Jones v Meatyard* [1939] 1 All ER 140) or, presumably, to a third person. **C4.21**

The offence in s. 174(5) of making a false statement for the purpose of obtaining the issue of an insurance certificate is an absolute one. However, in *Cummerson* [1968] 2 QB 534, it was indicated that the other offence created by the provision of withholding material information for that purpose may well require proof that the act was done consciously. In *Power v Provincial Insurance plc* [1998] RTR 60, the Court of Appeal decided that a motorist correctly regarded his conviction for driving whilst unfit as being 'spent' by reference to the rehabilitation period applying to the fine imposed and not the period of effectiveness of the endorsement on the driving licence relating to a period of disqualification. This meant that he had been entitled to answer negatively the question whether he had been convicted of an offence for which an order of endorsement had been made, which in turn meant that he had not made a false statement under s. 174(5).

Punishment

C4.22   On conviction on indictment, the maximum sentence is two years' imprisonment and/or a fine; on summary conviction, six months' imprisonment and/or a fine not exceeding the statutory maximum.

Section C5   Drink-Driving Offences

PRELIMINARY TESTING

Road Traffic Act 1988, ss. 6, 6A, 6B, 6C, 6D and 6E

C5.1

6.—(1) If any of subsections (2) to (5) applies a constable may require a person to co-operate with any one or more preliminary tests administered to the person by that constable or another constable.

(2) This subsection applies if a constable reasonably suspects that the person—
  (a) is driving, is attempting to drive or is in charge of a motor vehicle on a road or other public place, and
  (b) has alcohol or a drug in his body or is under the influence of a drug.

(3) This subsection applies if a constable reasonably suspects that the person—
  (a) has been driving, attempting to drive or in charge of a motor vehicle on a road or other public place while having alcohol or a drug in his body or while unfit to drive because of a drug, and
  (b) still has alcohol or a drug in his body or is still under the influence of a drug.

(4) This subsection applies if a constable reasonably suspects that the person—
  (a) is or has been driving, attempting to drive or in charge of a motor vehicle on a road or other public place, and
  (b) has committed a traffic offence while the vehicle was in motion.

(5) This subsection applies if—
  (a) an accident occurs owing to the presence of a motor vehicle on a road or other public place, and
  (b) a constable reasonably believes that the person was driving, attempting to drive or in charge of the vehicle at the time of the accident.

(6) A person commits an offence if without reasonable excuse he fails to co-operate with a preliminary test in pursuance of a requirement imposed under this section.

(7) A constable may administer a preliminary test by virtue of any of subsections (2) to (4) only if he is in uniform.

(8) In this section—
  (a) a reference to a preliminary test is to any of the tests described in sections 6A to 6C, and
  (b) 'traffic offence' means an offence under—
    (i) a provision of part II of the Public Passenger Vehicles Act 1981,
    (ii) a provision of the Road Traffic Regulation Act 1984,
    (iii) a provision of the Road Traffic Offenders Act 1988 other than a provision of part III, or
    (iv) a provision of this Act other than a provision of part V.

6A.—(1) A preliminary breath test is a procedure whereby the person to whom the test is administered provides a specimen of breath to be used for the purpose of obtaining, by means of a device of a type approved by the Secretary of State, an indication whether the proportion of alcohol in the person's breath or blood is likely to exceed the prescribed limit.

(2) A preliminary breath test administered in reliance on section 6(2) to (4) may be administered only at or near the place where the requirement to co-operate with the test is imposed.

(3) A preliminary breath test administered in reliance on section 6(5) may be administered—
  (a) at or near the place where the requirement to co-operate with the test is imposed, or
  (b) if the constable who imposes the requirement thinks it expedient, at a police station specified by him.

6B.—(1) A preliminary impairment test is a procedure whereby the constable administering the test—

  (a) observes the person to whom the test is administered in his performance of tasks specified by the constable, and

  (b) makes such other observations of the person's physical state as the constable thinks expedient.

(2) and (3) [Secretary of State's power to issue code of practice and contents of such a code.]

(4) A preliminary impairment test may be administered—

  (a) at or near the place where the requirement to co-operate with the test is imposed, or

  (b) if the constable who imposes the requirement thinks it expedient, at a police station specified by him.

(5) A constable administering a preliminary impairment test shall have regard to the code of practice under this section.

(6) A constable may administer a preliminary impairment test only if he is approved for that purpose by the chief officer of the police force to which he belongs.

(7) A code of practice under this section may include provision about—

  (a) the giving of approval under subsection (6), and

  (b) in particular, the kind of training that a constable should have undergone, or the kind of qualification that a constable should possess, before being approved under that subsection.

6C.—(1) A preliminary drug test is a procedure by which a specimen of sweat or saliva is—

  (a) obtained, and

  (b) used for the purpose of obtaining, by means of a device of a type approved by the Secretary of State, an indication whether the person to whom the test is administered has a drug in his body.

(2) A preliminary drug test may be administered—

  (a) at or near the place where the requirement to co-operate with the test is imposed, or

  (b) if the constable who imposes the requirement thinks it expedient, at a police station specified by him.

6D.—(1) A constable may arrest a person without warrant if as a result of a preliminary breath test the constable reasonably suspects that the proportion of alcohol in the person's breath or blood exceeds the prescribed limit.

(1A) The fact that specimens of breath have been provided under section 7 of this Act by the person concerned does not prevent subsection (1) above having effect if the constable who imposed on him the requirement to provide the specimens has reasonable cause to believe that the device used to analyse the specimens has not produced a reliable indication of the proportion of alcohol in the breath of the person.

(2) A constable may arrest a person without warrant if—

  (a) the person fails to co-operate with a preliminary test in pursuance of a requirement imposed under section 6, and

  (b) the constable reasonably suspects that the person has alcohol or a drug in his body or is under the influence of a drug.

(2A)   A person arrested under this section may, instead of being taken to a police station, be detained at or near the place where the preliminary test was, or would have been, administered, with a view to imposing on him there a requirement under section 7 of this Act.

(3) A person may not be arrested under this section while at a hospital as a patient.

6E.—(1) A constable may enter any place (using reasonable force if necessary) for the purpose of—

  (a) imposing a requirement by virtue of section 6(5) following an accident in a case where the constable reasonably suspects that the accident involved injury of any person, or

  (b) arresting a person under section 6D following an accident in a case where the constable reasonably suspects that the accident involved injury of any person.

(2) This section—

  (a) does not extend to Scotland, and

  (b) is without prejudice to any rule of law or enactment about the right of a constable in Scotland to enter any place.

Constables may now decide to administer preliminary breath, impairment or drug tests as may be appropriate. Accordingly, investigations into 'unfit' offences can properly commence at the earliest opportunity. When the CCA 2013, sch. 22, is implemented, s. 6C will be amended to reflect that up to three preliminary drug tests may be administered to ascertain whether the person has a specified controlled drug in his body and, if so, whether it is likely it exceeds the specified limit and s. 6D will be amended so as to permit a constable to arrest a person reasonably suspected of exceeding such a limit.

Making the Requirement

Circumstances in which Requirement can be Imposed A preliminary test may be required C5.2
only when one of the situations specified in s. 6(2) to (5) is satisfied. Hospital patients are
accorded added protection (see the RTA 1988, s. 9, and **C5.25**). If reliance is placed on 'reasonable belief' following an accident, a higher standard than 'reasonable suspicion' can still be
expected (see, e.g., *Johnson v Whitehouse* [1984] RTR 38), although 'belief' does not equate to
'knowledge' (*Bunyard v Hayes* [1985] RTR 348).

The power of the police to stop a vehicle is contained in the RTA 1988, s. 163. There is nothing
to prevent random stopping, but the law requires one of the conditions in s. 6(2) to (5) to be
complied with before a preliminary test is administered. In *Chief Constable of Gwent v Dash*
[1986] RTR 41, police were stopping vehicles at random in order to apprehend drivers who
might be suspected of having excess alcohol in their bodies. Macpherson J, giving the judgment
of the Divisional Court, said (at p. 46, emphasis added):

> ... there is no restriction upon the stopping of motorists by a policeman *in the execution of his duty*
> and the subsequent requirement for a breath test should the policeman then and there genuinely
> suspect the ingestion of alcohol. It may be said by some to be bad luck that such a situation arises
> but it is not unlawful provided the officer is in uniform and acts without oppression, or caprice, or
> some false pretence or proved 'malpractice'.

The court did, however, distinguish cases where a person is arrested in his own house in a situation similar to that in *Morris v Beardmore* [1981] AC 446. See *DPP v Godwin* [1991] RTR 303
and **C5.49**.

The necessary suspicion may result from information supplied by others and may arise after a C5.3
motorist has ceased to drive, so long as it relates to the period when he was actually driving
(s. 6(3) and (5) and see also *Moss v Jenkins* [1975] RTR 25 and *Blake v Pope* [1986] 3 All ER
185). Evidence of what the officer has been told is admissible if it goes to his state of mind at the
time that he required the specimen of breath. Whilst the absence of a ground under which to
administer a preliminary test may invalidate an arrest under s. 6D, it should not invalidate the
subsequent procedure unless the court exercises its discretion to exclude evidence under the
PACE 1984, s. 78 (*Griffiths v Willett* [1979] RTR 195) or as a result of human rights violations.
In *DPP v Wilson* [1991] RTR 284, it was held that the power to exclude evidence could arise
from *Fox* [1986] AC 281 or *Chief Constable of Gwent v Dash*, and co-existed with a wide discretion under s. 78, but there is no duty on the police to warn a driver of a potential offence and
failure to do so may not be oppressive.

If the device used is itself specified in the schedule to the approval order, no further identification or specification is required from the prosecution (*Breckon v DPP* [2008] RTR 96). If the
device used to administer a roadside breath test is of a type that could be used to obtain an evidential specimen (see **C5.9**), the justices must exercise care to ensure that they understand
which type of test was being conducted and the consequences flowing therefrom. If the police
evidence is that the device was not operating so as to give an accurate evidential reading and that
goes unchallenged, or is preferred, the test is a s. 6 preliminary test (*DPP v Karamouzis* [2006]
EWHC 2634 (Admin)). Where the test is a preliminary one, the prosecution are not obliged to
disclose to the defence the results in figures from that roadside test (*Smith v DPP* [2007] 4 All
ER 1135; *Breckon v DPP*); the test remains indicative only as to whether the constable should
arrest the suspect with a view to securing an evidential specimen thereafter.

Where consumption of alcohol is suspected, the constable is likely to continue to require a C5.4
roadside breath test. Where, however, the suspect appears unfit, the constable may, if he has
been given approval by his chief officer in accordance with s. 6B(6), administer an impairment
test in accordance with the code of practice issued by the Secretary of State, which is designed
to ascertain whether the perceived unfitness to drive is due to drink or drugs. Alternatively, a
decision to administer a preliminary drug test by means of an approved device and to take a

specimen of sweat or saliva might be taken. As s. 6(1) refers to 'any one or more preliminary tests', it is clear that they are not mutually exclusive and the constable could require co-operation with each of the tests in turn, if only to eliminate his suspicions as to both alcohol and drugs.

As regards requiring a preliminary breath test, failing to follow the manufacturer's instructions about allowing a 20-minute gap to elapse after the consumption of alcohol before commencing the test will render the roadside procedure unlawful so that no offence under s. 6(6) will be committed, but that does not of itself affect the lawfulness of the subsequent Intoximeter procedure (*DPP v Kay* [1999] RTR 109).

C5.5   **Other Conditions for Requirement**   The constable making a requirement by virtue of any of s. 6(2) to (4) must be 'in uniform', i.e. he should be easily identifiable as a constable. The absence of a helmet (*Wallwork v Giles* [1970] RTR 117) or the wearing of a raincoat (*Taylor v Baldwin* [1976] RTR 265) did not affect the conclusion that the constable was still in uniform. Justices are also able to rely on their knowledge of how the local constabulary operates (*Cooper v Rowlands* [1971] RTR 291, in relation to a motor patrol officer; *Richards v West* [1980] RTR 215, in relation to special constables) and, in the absence of evidence to the contrary, they are entitled to infer or assume from the surrounding circumstances that a constable is in uniform (*Gage v Jones* [1983] RTR 508).

Under s. 6A(2), a preliminary breath test in a situation not involving an accident must be administered at or near the place where the requirement is made but, in relation to a person required to undertake a preliminary breath test as a result of an accident or a preliminary impairment or drug test, it may be administered either at or near the place where the requirement is made (usually the roadside) or at a police station (see, e.g., *Moore* [1994] RTR 360).

The requirement must be made using words of sufficient clarity, although there is no set formula for any particular words to be uttered. In relation to the old s. 6 offence, using 'I wish to give you a breath test' (*Clarke* [1969] 2 QB 91) or 'I intend to give you a breath test' (*O'Boyle* [1973] RTR 445) sufficed. Adapting such wording to cover the impairment or drug test, adding whatever further explanation is appropriate, should be adequate. As long as the words used are reasonably believed by the constable to be capable of, and were, being heard and understood, it is not necessary to prove they were actually both heard and understood (*Nicholls* [1972] 2 All ER 186). There is no need to produce physically a breath test device, provided that an opportunity to comply with the requirement is given (*DPP v Swan* [2004] EWHC 2432 (Admin)).

Failure to Co-operate with a Preliminary Test

C5.6   Section 6(6) creates a single offence of failing, without a reasonable excuse, to co-operate with a preliminary test when required to do so. The RTOA 1988, ss. 11 and 12(1), apply; see **C2.17** and **C2.18**. For the meaning of the terms 'accident', 'driving', 'motor vehicle', 'road or other public place', and 'attempting to drive', see **C1.1, C1.2, C1.9, C1.13, C1.19** and **C1.20**. For the meaning of 'in charge', see **C5.38**. The term 'fail' includes a refusal (RTA 1988, s. 11). Whether there is a failure is a question of fact and degree. If a person does not take advantage of the opportunity to take the test provided by the constable, there will in principle be a failure (*Ferguson* [1970] RTR 395).

C5.7   **Reasonable Excuse**   Once the defence have raised a 'reasonable excuse', it is for the prosecution to negative it (*Rowland v Thorpe* [1970] 3 All ER 195). A claim by the defendant that none of the pre-conditions for making the requirement existed does not constitute a reasonable excuse (*Downey* [1970] RTR 257). In *Chief Constable of Avon and Somerset Constabulary v Singh* [1988] RTR 107, it was held that a failure to provide a roadside breath test merely because the accused claimed that he had not been driving at the time did not constitute a reasonable excuse. His understanding of what was being required of him was held to be irrelevant, because he was putting forward a false story as to the driving of the vehicle. The court did accept that, in certain circumstances, a failure to understand the nature of the obligation might constitute a reasonable excuse, but added that before something could amount to an excuse 'it has to be causative in this sense, that it was the reason why the thing was not done'. This reasoning would seem to be equally valid in relation to the new impairment and drug preliminary tests. A medical condition, such as a chest complaint, may constitute a reasonable excuse for failing to co-operate, or where the person required to provide a specimen is 'physically or mentally unable to provide it or its provision would entail a substantial risk to health' (*Lennard* [1973] 2 All ER 831). See also **C5.28** and **C5.31**.

Punishment   The penalty is a fine up to level 3 on the standard scale. The *Magistrates' Court*   **C5.8**
Sentencing Guidelines (see Supplement, **SG-344**) give fine band B as the starting point. Disqualification is discretionary but, in the absence of 'special reasons', endorsement with four penalty points is obligatory.

EVIDENTIAL SPECIMENS

Road Traffic Act 1988, ss. 7 and 7A   C5.9

7.—(1) In the course of an investigation into whether a person has committed an offence under section 3A, 4 or 5 of this Act a constable may, subject to the following provisions of this section and section 9 of this Act, require him—
  (a) to provide two specimens of breath for analysis by means of a device of a type approved by the Secretary of State, or
  (b) to provide a specimen of blood or urine for a laboratory test.
(2) A requirement under this section to provide specimens of breath can only be made—
  (a) at a police station,
  (b) at a hospital, or
  (c) at or near a place where a relevant breath test has been administered to the person concerned or would have been so administered but for his failure to co-operate with it.
(2A) For the purposes of this section 'a relevant breath test' is a procedure involving the provision by the person concerned of a specimen of breath to be used for the purpose of obtaining an indication whether the proportion of alcohol in his breath or blood is likely to exceed the prescribed limit.
(2B) A requirement under this section to provide specimens of breath may not be made at or near a place mentioned in subsection (2)(c) above unless the constable making it—
  (a) is in uniform, or
  (b) has imposed a requirement on the person concerned to co-operate with the relevant breath test in circumstances in which section 6(5) of this Act applies.
(2C) Where a constable has imposed a requirement on the person concerned to co-operate with a relevant breath test at any place, he is entitled to remain at or near that place in order to impose on him there a requirement under this section.
(2D) If a requirement under subsection (1)(a) above has been made at a place other than at a police station, such a requirement may subsequently be made at a police station if (but only if)—
  (a) a device or a reliable device of the type mentioned in subsection (1)(a) above was not available at that place or it was for any other reason not practicable to use such a device there, or
  (b) the constable who made the previous requirement has reasonable cause to believe that the device used there has not produced a reliable indication of the proportion of alcohol in the breath of the person concerned.
(3) A requirement under this section to provide a specimen of blood or urine can only be made at a police station or at a hospital; and it cannot be made at a police station unless—
  (a) the constable making the requirement has reasonable cause to believe that for medical reasons a specimen of breath cannot be provided or should not be required, or
  (b) specimens of breath have not been provided elsewhere and at the time the requirement is made a device or a reliable device of the type mentioned in subsection (1)(a) above is not available at the police station or it is then for any other reason not practicable to use such a device there,
  (bb) a device of the type mentioned in subsection (1)(a) above has been used (at the police station or elsewhere) but the constable who required the specimens of breath has reasonable

cause to believe that the device has not produced a reliable indication of the proportion of alcohol in the breath of the person concerned,

(bc) as a result of the administration of a preliminary drug test, the constable making the requirement has reasonable cause to believe that the person required to provide a specimen of blood or urine has a drug in his body, or

(c) the suspected offence is one under section 3A or 4 of this Act and the constable making the requirement has been advised by a medical practitioner that the condition of the person required to provide the specimen might be due to some drug;

but may then be made notwithstanding that the person required to provide the specimen has already provided or been required to provide two specimens of breath.

(4) If the provision of a specimen other than a specimen of breath may be required in pursuance of this section the question whether it is to be a specimen of blood or a specimen of urine and, in the case of a specimen of blood, the question who is to be asked to take it shall be decided (subject to subsection (4A)) by the constable making the requirement.

(4A) Where a constable decides for the purposes of subsection (4) to require the provision of a specimen of blood, there shall be no requirement to provide such a specimen if—

(a) the medical practitioner who is asked to take the specimen is of the opinion that, for medical reasons, it cannot or should not be taken; or

(b) the registered health care professional who is asked to take it is of that opinion and there is no contrary opinion from a medical practitioner;

and, where by virtue of this subsection there can be no requirement to provide a specimen of blood, the constable may require a specimen of urine instead.

(5) A specimen of urine shall be provided within one hour of the requirement for its provision being made and after the provision of a previous specimen of urine.

(6) A person who, without reasonable excuse, fails to provide a specimen when required to do so in pursuance of this section is guilty of an offence.

(7) A constable must, on requiring any person to provide a specimen in pursuance of this section, warn him that a failure to provide it may render him liable to prosecution.

7A.—(1) A constable may make a request to a medical practitioner for him to take a specimen of blood from a person ('the person concerned') irrespective of whether that person consents if—

(a) that person is a person from whom the constable would (in the absence of any incapacity of that person and of any objection under section 9) be entitled under section 7 to require the provision of a specimen of blood for a laboratory test;

(b) it appears to that constable that that person has been involved in an accident that constitutes or is comprised in the matter that is under investigation or the circumstances of that matter;

(c) it appears to that constable that that person is or may be incapable (whether or not he has purported to do so) of giving a valid consent to the taking of a specimen of blood; and

(d) it appears to that constable that that person's incapacity is attributable to medical reasons.

(2) A request under this section—

(a) shall not be made to a medical practitioner who for the time being has any responsibility (apart from the request) for the clinical care of the person concerned; and

(b) shall not be made to a medical practitioner other than a police medical practitioner unless—

(i) it is not reasonably practicable for the request to be made to a police medical practitioner; or

(ii) it is not reasonably practicable for such a medical practitioner (assuming him to be willing to do so) to take the specimen.

(3) It shall be lawful for a medical practitioner to whom a request is made under this section, if he thinks fit—

(a) to take a specimen of blood from the person concerned irrespective of whether that person consents; and

(b) to provide the sample to a constable.

(4) If a specimen is taken in pursuance of a request under this section, the specimen shall not be subjected to a laboratory test unless the person from whom it was taken—

(a) has been informed that it was taken; and

(b) has been required by a constable to give his permission for a laboratory test of the specimen; and

(c) has given his permission.

(5) A constable must, on requiring a person to give his permission for the purposes of this section for a laboratory test of a specimen, warn that person that a failure to give the permission may render him liable to prosecution.

(6) A person who, without reasonable excuse, fails to give his permission for a laboratory test of a specimen of blood taken from him under this section is guilty of an offence.

(7) In this section 'police medical practitioner' means a medical practitioner who is engaged under any agreement to provide medical services for purposes connected with the activities of a police force.

When the CCA 2013, sch. 22, is implemented, s. 7(1A) will be inserted, permitting the making of a requirement for a specimen of blood or urine in the course of an investigation of the newly created drug-driving offence (RTA 1988, s. 5A; see **C5.57**).

Initial Procedural Requirements

The requirement to provide specimens must arise 'in the course of an investigation', which does **C5.10** not imply any greater formality than is normally involved in the plain and ordinary meaning of the word 'investigation' (*Graham v Albert* [1985] RTR 352). As with a preliminary test (see **C5.2**), the 'requirement' does not have to be in any formalised language, provided it amounts to a requirement and is made at a permitted location. A requirement made otherwise than by strictly following the guidance contained in a standard form covering the police station testing process is not automatically unlawful (*DPP v Coulter* [2005] EWHC 1533 (Admin)). The requirement can be made at or near the place where a roadside procedure was carried out, at a police station or, when appropriate, at a hospital (see **C5.25**). Having made the requirement at such a place, the RTA 1988, s. 7, is silent as to the actual taking of the specimen, which implies that it can be done elsewhere (*Pascoe v Nicholson* [1981] 2 All ER 769; *Russell v Devine* [2003] 1 WLR 1187), when taken by a medical practitioner. Any challenge to the qualifications of the person who took the blood sample must be raised in a timely fashion and not left as a last-minute defence ambush in closing (*Whitfield v DPP* [2006] EWHC 1414 (Admin)). When the requirement is made at a hospital, there is no obligation to explain why a breath specimen cannot be required (*Jones v DPP* [2004] RTR 331).

In *Brown v Gallacher* [2003] RTR 239, the Scottish High Court of Justiciary dismissed an argument that the answers given and specimens provided under this statutory procedure should be disregarded because they infringe the privilege against self-incrimination protected by the ECHR, Article 6.

Where there is some doubt as to who was driving the motor vehicle at the relevant time, a constable may require all the persons suspected of driving to provide a specimen (*Pearson v Metropolitan Police Commissioner* [1988] RTR 276). Indeed, the defendant need not have been driving the motor vehicle on a road or other public place provided the requirement for a specimen is made in the course of an investigation and is made in good faith (*Hawes v DPP* [1993] RTR 116).

At a police station, where there has been a positive result from administering a preliminary drug **C5.11** test, the constable will move directly to requiring a specimen of blood or urine under s. 7(3)(bc), but where consumption of alcohol is suspected, the constable will first consider whether the person should be required to provide two specimens of breath. Unless one of the situations set out in s. 7(3) arises, the constable will proceed to make that requirement, which involves giving the statutory warning necessary under s. 7(7) (see **C5.23**). If the person provides two specimens of breath as required, the lower reading will dictate whether no further action is taken, an offer is made for the person to provide a replacement specimen of blood or urine (see **C5.12**) or a charge under the RTA 1988, s. 5(1), will be pursued (see **C5.35**). If the person fails to provide the specimens as required, the constable may proceed to require an alternative specimen of blood or urine (see **C5.12**) or a charge under the RTA 1988, s. 7(6), may be pursued (see **C5.27**). In order to make himself understood, the constable may repeat any requirement as many times as he feels is appropriate.

Replacement Specimens

C5.12

Road Traffic Act 1988, s. 8

(1) Subject to subsection (2) below, of any two specimens of breath provided by any person in pursuance of section 7 of this Act that with the lower proportion of alcohol in the breath shall be used and the other shall be disregarded.

(2) If the specimen with the lower proportion of alcohol contains no more than 50 microgrammes of alcohol in 100 millilitres of breath, the person who provided it may claim that it should be replaced by such specimen as may be required under section 7(4) of this Act and, if he then provides such a specimen, neither specimen of breath shall be used.

(2A) If the person who makes a claim under subsection (2) above was required to provide specimens of breath under section 7 of this Act at or near a place mentioned in subsection (2)(c) of that section, a constable may arrest him without warrant.

(3) The Secretary of State may by regulations substitute another proportion of alcohol in the breath for that specified in subsection (2) above.

If the lower of the two specimens of breath provided is 39 microgrammes in 100 millilitres or less, proceedings under the RTA 1988, s. 5(1), are not usually instituted. For readings of 50 microgrammes or less, the person providing the specimen must be offered the option of supplying another specimen, either of blood or urine, under the RTA 1988, s. 7(4). Failure to offer this statutory option when required is fatal (*Clwyd Justices, ex parte Charles* (1990) 154 JP 486). There is however no requirement to give the warning in s. 7(7) when asking a person whether he wishes to give a replacement specimen (*Hayes v DPP* [1994] RTR 163).

There is no obligation on the prosecution to prove that the device was operating accurately prior to the defendant being offered a replacement specimen (*Branagan v DPP* [2000] RTR 235; *Wright v DPP* [2005] EWHC 1211 (Admin)) because, if the device were thought to be unreliable, s. 7(3) provides the grounds for requiring blood or urine anyway (see **C5.17**). It is not unfair or improper for the police to insist on a specimen being provided before legal advice is obtained, except possibly where the police refuse to allow a suspect access to a solicitor who is ready and immediately available; even then there would be powerful arguments why the discretion to exclude evidence under the PACE 1984, s. 78, should not be exercised (*Chalupa v CPS* (2010) 174 JP 111). When dealing with a juvenile, there is no requirement to delay the investigation so that an appropriate adult can be in attendance before proceeding to allow him to choose whether to provide a replacement specimen (*DPP v Evans* [2003] Crim LR 338).

C5.13 The option must be given fairly and properly so that the person concerned can make an informed choice about exercising it (*Baldwin v DPP* [1996] RTR 238) and the explanation must therefore be sufficiently detailed (*Turner v DPP* [1996] RTR 274n). However, in *Fraser v DPP* [1997] RTR 373, Lord Bingham CJ confirmed that, whilst there were plainly several things for the driver to be told at some stage in the procedure, it did not follow that he had to be told all of them at the very outset; it is the totality of the process that matters. An explanation that accepting the option may give a more reliable reading than the breath may be given by the police, but there is no obligation to do so (*CPS v Jolly* [2010] EWHC 1616 (Admin)). Where a defendant is offered the option of a replacement specimen and refuses but then consents, the prosecution are still entitled to rely on the breath specimen because the statutory procedure ends when the defendant rejects the option (*Smith v DPP* [1989] RTR 159). Caution is required to ensure that the process for provision of a replacement specimen is not terminated prematurely (*Persaud v DPP* [2010] RTR 322, where, by reference to standard form MG DD/B, the court emphasised the importance of the defendant clearly demonstrating that his election to provide a replacement specimen had been abandoned, even if continuing the process might result in fruitless attendance by a medical practitioner). Where justices found that an unrecorded conversation may have taken place between the police and the defendant, which may have had the effect of dissuading the defendant from exercising the right to provide a replacement specimen, the prosecutor had failed to prove beyond a reasonable doubt that the correct statutory procedure had been followed and an acquittal properly resulted (*Rush v DPP* [1994]

RTR 268). Where words said by the custody sergeant constitute an invitation to reconsider whether to provide a replacement specimen, in the absence of the defendant saying or doing something in response, the justices can still rely on the breath specimen (*McClean v DPP* [2009] EWHC 189 (Admin)). Where the defendant consents to providing a replacement blood specimen, then raises issues about how it can or cannot be taken, which are overcome by the investigating officer stating inaccurate information about the consequences of him maintaining that stance, the original consent is not vitiated by the technically improper procedure and the replacement specimen remains admissible, rather than the prosecution having to revert to the original breath analysis (*R (Rainsbury) v DPP* [2007] EWHC 1138 (Admin)).

A failure by the driver to provide a replacement specimen does not render the specimen of breath unavailable for use; a condition precedent to the exclusion of the results of the Intoximeter procedure is the provision of an actual replacement specimen (*DPP v Winstanley* [1993] RTR 222; *Hague v DPP* [1997] RTR 146). In *Winstanley* the defendant wished to provide a replacement specimen and did not object to it being of blood. The doctor was called but did not arrive. After waiting an hour, the investigating officer required two specimens of urine instead. The defendant, through no fault of his own, could not oblige. As no actual specimen had been provided to replace the breath specimens, they remained admissible. Similarly, where a defendant frustrates the efforts of the officer to explain the blood/urine option so that no replacement specimen is supplied, the prosecution are entitled to rely on the breath test results (*DPP v Poole* [1992] RTR 177) and where the defendant's consumption of alcohol results, at least partly, in an inability to comprehend the offer being made, the breath analysis is not rendered inadmissible (*DPP v Berry* (1996) 160 JP 707). **C5.14**

Use of Replaced Specimen Where a replacement specimen is supplied, the effect of the RTA 1988, s. 8(2), is mandatory in precluding the use of the breath specimen, even if the replacement specimen is inadmissible as a result of any irregularity or the prosecution do not, for any reason, rely upon it (*Archbold v Jones* [1986] RTR 178; *Wakely v Hyams* [1987] RTR 49). This principle extends to cases in which the defendant advances 'special reasons' (*Smith v Geraghty* [1986] RTR 222). **C5.15**

In *Yhnell v DPP* [1989] RTR 250, however, evidence of both the breath specimens and the blood specimen supplied as a replacement was admissible to demonstrate to the justices that reliance on the blood sample by the prosecution was correct. The defendant had falsified his part of the blood specimen by injecting into it blood unaffected by alcohol, thereby producing a disproportionately low analysis. The justices were able to have regard to the evidence of the breath readings so as to satisfy themselves that the prosecution analysis of the other part of the blood specimen could be relied upon and that the correct statutory procedure had been followed. In such circumstances, the breath specimens were not being 'used' in the manner prohibited by s. 8(2) so as to found a conviction. Similarly, where a court had regard to the breath specimen (and other matters) to help it determine if the defendant's evidence was capable of belief, the specimen was not being 'used' for the purposes of s. 8(2), which is concerned with the process of proof of the reliability of the sample in order to found a conviction (*Carter v DPP* [2007] RTR 257).

Medical Reason

The question of what constitutes a 'medical reason' by virtue of which a specimen of breath cannot be provided or should not be required for the purposes of the RTA 1988, s. 7(3)(a) (see C5.9), is a question for the constable. What is important is the state of knowledge of the constable and his reasonable state of belief, bearing in mind that he is a layman. Unlike under s. 7(4), there is no obligation for the constable to take medical advice before reaching a conclusion (*Steadman v DPP* [2003] RTR 10). As long as he has 'reasonable cause to believe' that a specimen of breath cannot be provided or should not be required for medical reasons then that is sufficient, whether or not the medical reason advanced appears, 'in the cold light of day', to **C5.16** be an unsatisfactory one for declining to provide a specimen of breath (*Davies v DPP* [1989] RTR 391, per Neill LJ).

Where the defendant does his best to provide a specimen, and in the absence of any other reason for not complying, incapacity due to being upset, shaken, intoxicated and distressed can amount to a medical reason (*Webb v DPP* [1992] RTR 299, applying *Davies v DPP*). Intoxication alone may constitute such a medical reason (*Young v DPP* [1992] RTR 328). The taking of medication is also capable of amounting to a medical reason (*Wade v DPP* [1996] RTR 177). If a medical opinion is given to the constable, it will properly inform the reasonableness of his conclusion on this issue, however wrong that opinion may be (*Andrews v DPP* [1992] RTR 1). If the conclusion is that there was no medical reason for the defendant's failure to provide, the officer may proceed to charge a s. 7(6) offence (*Longstaff v DPP* [2008] RTR 212).

In relation to tendering advice in accordance with the RTA 1988, s. 7(3)(c), that the condition of the person might be due to some drug, the doctor is not limited to the findings of his own examination at the police station, but is entitled to take into account all relevant information, including what he has been told by police officers (*Angel v Chief Constable of South Yorkshire* [2010] EWHC 883 (Admin)).

If a medical reason is advanced as to why a specimen of blood, which a constable has decided to be appropriate, cannot or should not be taken, the validity of the reason can be determined under s. 7(4A) only by a medical practitioner (*Townson v DPP* [2006] EWHC 2007 (Admin)). See also *Bodhaniya v CPS* (2014) 178 JP 1.

Reliability of Device

C5.17 Two situations may arise. The constable may already know that the device at the police station is not working properly or may discover its malfunctioning during the procedure (RTA 1988, s. 7(3)(b)) and move directly to consideration of whether to advance the investigation by requiring a blood or urine sample. In this context, the question of reliability is subjective and depends upon the officer's reasonable belief (*Thompson v Thynne* [1986] RTR 293). That reasonable belief can be formed as a result of information provided to the officer by another (*Kelsey v DPP* [2008] EWHC 127 (Admin)). Alternatively, breath specimens may have been provided as a result of which the investigating officer is presented objectively with reasonable cause to believe in the unreliability of the analysis produced (RTA 1988, s. 7(3)(bb)). This might occur where the difference between the two readings is considerable (e.g., above 20 per cent: *DPP v Smith* [2000] RTR 341; above 15 per cent: *Stewart v DPP* [2003] RTR 529) or where the reading that is produced is wholly inconsistent with the defendant's admitted alcohol consumption and perceived physical state (although this course of action was not taken in the circumstances considered in *DPP v Spurrier* [2000] RTR 60). This might also arise where the officer has attempted two cycles of specimens with the device with the second specimen each time being recorded as 'ambient failure' (*Hussain v DPP* [2008] RTR 82). See also *DPP v Taylor* [2009] EWHC 2824 (Admin). However, where the officer is told that the defendant burped during the process, that information does not render the analysis produced by the device unreliable (*McNeil v DPP* [2008] RTR 359, explaining the consequences of *Zafar v DPP* [2005] RTR 220: see **C5.36**).

Where the device is regarded as unreliable, the printout can be adduced in evidence to support the belief of the investigating officer without the need to comply with prior service in accordance with the RTOA 1988, s. 16 (see **C5.39**). Where no valid specimens for the purposes of the RTA 1988, s. 11(3), have been provided, the officer is entitled to require provision of two further specimens of breath (*Hussain*), and in other circumstances, the officer may choose first to invite (but not require) provision of further specimens of breath or proceed directly to considering the requirement for blood or urine (*Jubb v DPP* [2003] RTR 272).

C5.18 An officer may be entitled to decide that a device is not reliable if it does not produce the correct date (*Slender v Boothby* [1986] RTR 385n) or if it operates outside its range of tolerance. Even if the malfunctioning is the fault of the operator, the alternative sample provided in accordance with s. 7(4) remains admissible (*Jones v DPP* [1991] RTR 41, where the modem switch on the device was not turned on resulting in no printout being generated).

Challenges to the reliability of a device tend to occur where the defendant claims the reading relied on by the prosecution is falsely high (see **C5.47**) or where the failure to provide the specimens required is attributable to the device rather than the defendant's fault. The principles pointing towards or against reliability can be used by analogy where it is asserted that the investigating officer's decision to proceed to require a blood or urine specimen is flawed.

Choosing Blood or Urine

The choice as to which alternative or replacement specimen to require rests with the investigating officer, unless under the RTA 1988, s. 7(4) and (4A), a medical practitioner or a registered health care professional opines that blood is inappropriate so that urine must be taken. In *DPP v Warren* [1993] AC 319, the House of Lords held that, where an alternative or replacement specimen is required, the driver need not be invited to express a preference for giving blood or urine but, if a specimen of blood is required, he must have the opportunity to raise objection to giving blood on medical grounds (to be determined by a medical practitioner or registered health care professional: see **C5.16**) or for any other reason which might afford a reasonable excuse. The standard wording apparently approved in that case (at p. 327) is as follows:

> I require you to provide an alternative specimen, which will be submitted for laboratory analysis. The specimen may be of blood or urine, but it is for me to decide which. If you provide a specimen you will be offered part of it in a suitable container. If you fail to provide a specimen you may be liable to prosecution. Are there any reasons why a specimen of blood cannot or should not be taken by a doctor?

The officer is entitled to rely on a negative answer specifically given in response (*Jubb v DPP* [2003] RTR 272). In *Baldwin v DPP* [1996] RTR 238, the Divisional Court pointed out that these words were guidelines as to interpretation only rather than having statutory force themselves.

The requirements stated by Lord Bridge in *Warren* were reviewed in *DPP v Jackson* [1999] 1 AC **C5.20** 406. The House of Lords decided that, with three exceptions, those requirements were not to be treated as mandatory but as indicating the matters of which a driver should be aware so that he could know the role of the medical person in the taking of a specimen and in determining any medical objection that he might raise to the giving of such a specimen. The three mandatory exceptions, where particular matters must be mentioned, are:

(a) in a s. 7(3) case, the warning as to the risk of prosecution required by s. 7(7) (see **C5.23**);
(b) in a s. 7(3) case, the statement of the reason under that subsection why breath could not be used; and
(c) in a s. 8(2) case (see **C5.12**), the statement that the specimen of breath which the driver had given containing the lower proportion of alcohol did not exceed 50 microgrammes in 100 millilitres of breath.

As well as complying with those mandatory requirements, investigating officers, in order to seek to ensure that a driver is aware of the role of the medical person, should continue to use the formula set out in *Warren* or words to the same effect. Thus, in addition to telling the driver that a specimen of blood will be taken by an appropriate person unless he considers that there are medical reasons for not taking the blood, the officer should ask the driver if there are any medical reasons why a specimen could not or should not be taken by a medical practitioner or a registered health care professional. The driver should be told of the medical person's role at the outset before he has to make the decision to give blood. Fear of needles may constitute a medical reason in relation to providing blood (*Epping Justices, ex parte Quy* [1998] RTR 158n); thus a failure to investigate further the validity of that claim may preclude the prosecution from relying on any breath specimen already provided but, as it is a question of fact whether any statement by the driver raises a potential medical reason, the justices may be entitled to find that the officer is not obliged to investigate further.

C5.21 In general, the justices must first decide whether the matters set out in the *Warren* formula were brought to the driver's attention by the investigating officer. If the answer is 'No', the second issue is whether, in relation to the non-mandatory requirements, the officer's failure to give the full formula deprived the driver of the opportunity to express his position or caused him to express it in a way which he would not have done had everything been said. If the answer to the second issue is 'Yes', the driver should be acquitted. But if the answer to the second issue is 'No', the officer's failure to use the full formula should not be a reason for acquittal. Both issues are questions of fact, so that if the justices, having heard the defendant's evidence, are not satisfied beyond a reasonable doubt that he was not prejudiced, they should acquit. However, where any such procedural irregularity is raised where there has been an unequivocal plea of guilty, in the absence of conduct on the part of the prosecutor which is either fraudulent or analogous to fraud, the Divisional Court has doubted its jurisdiction to grant judicial review (*Burton upon Trent Justices, ex parte Woolley* [1995] RTR 139; *Dolgellau Justices, ex parte Cartledge* [1996] RTR 207), thereby significantly reducing the scope for reopening such convictions.

There is no requirement for a police officer to ask a driver if there is any non-medical reason why a specimen of blood should not be taken (*DPP v Jackson*). However, where such a reason is advanced, the officer should not completely disregard it when deciding how to exercise the discretion between requiring blood or urine, otherwise the decision may be quashed as *Wednesbury* unreasonable (*Joseph v DPP* [2004] RTR 341).

A failure to allow the defendant the right to object to the giving of blood for medical reasons will lead to any subsequent conviction being quashed (*Meade v DPP* [1993] RTR 151; *Edge v DPP* [1993] RTR 146).

C5.22 **Blood and Urine Specimens** The RTA 1988, s. 11(4) (see **C2.17**), and the RTOA 1988, s. 15(4) (see **C5.43**), provide that a blood specimen may be taken only with the consent of the person who provides it and must be taken by a medical practitioner or a registered health care professional in a police station. Otherwise it is to be disregarded.

Under the RTA 1988, s. 7A (see **C5.9**), a specimen of blood may be taken from a person who is, or may be, incapable of consenting to it being taken for medical reasons without that person actually consenting. Thereafter, before the police can have the sample analysed by a laboratory, the person from whom it was taken must be required by a constable to give permission for that analysis. Failure, without reasonable excuse, to give permission for a laboratory test of the specimen will constitute an offence comparable to the offence under s. 7(6).

An invalid but unproductive request for a specimen of blood does not render evidence of a subsequent correctly-taken specimen of urine inadmissible (*DPP v Garrett* [1995] RTR 302). The investigating officer is entitled to change his mind as to the type of specimen being required until the defendant has complied with the requirement in s. 7(1). However, where the defendant refuses to consent to the taking of blood, in the absence of any medical reason explaining that stance, the officer is not obliged to require a specimen of urine (*DPP v Gibbons* (2001) 165 JP 812).

A specimen of urine provided after the one-hour period referred to in the RTA 1988, s. 7(5), is still admissible to prove an offence under s. 5(1) (*DPP v Baldwin* [2000] RTR 314). The significance of the one-hour limit is that, once it passes, the investigating officer can charge a s. 7(6) offence or rely on the original specimen of breath but, should he so choose to exercise his discretion, he can await provision of the specimen of urine required.

In *Ryder v CPS* (2012) 176 JP 558, where the defendant had been catheterised at the time of consenting to provide a sample of urine, the Court of Appeal concluded that the 'providing' occurred when the catheter bag was emptied and not at the time the urine left the defendant. Consequently, the fact that there was evidence of a continuous flow of urine from the defendant's body into the catheter bag did not mean that there had only been a single specimen provided (unlike the conclusion on different facts in *Prosser v Dickeson* [1982] RTR 96, where the investigating officer had inappropriately interfered in the process of providing samples); the earlier emptying and discarding of the contents of the catheter bag amounting to provision of a previous specimen, as required by the RTA 1988, s. 7(5). This conclusion is consistent with the guidance offered by May LJ in *Nugent v Ridley* [1987] RTR 412 that the specimen to be analysed must be 'a fresh specimen and properly reflects the bodily condition of the person from whom it is taken'.

Warning

The warning in the RTA 1988, s. 7(7), is mandatory and must be understood by the person required to provide the specimen, although it does not need to be repeated in respect of replacement specimens (see **C5.12**). However, it is mandatory only when a requirement is actually made and is not needed if the constable *invites* a suspect to provide further samples (*Edmond v DPP* [2006] RTR 229). If the suspect does not understand the warning, it is invalid; the subsequent procedure is then ineffectual and a defence becomes available to a charge under s. 7(6) (*Simpson v Spalding* [1987] RTR 221; *Chief Constable of Avon and Somerset Constabulary v Singh* [1988] RTR 107). A court is permitted to draw the inference, if the evidence supports it, that someone being asked to do something in a police station by a police officer with the assistance of an accredited interpreter of the relevant language has been asked the correct question, understands it and also the consequences of not responding (*Bielecki v DPP* (2011) 175 JP 369). A finding that the defendant understood the request for a specimen being made and the penal warning attached thereto is not affected by the fact that the defendant was being detained under the Mental Health Act 1983, s. 136 (*Francis v DPP* [1997] RTR 113). At a hospital (see **C5.25**), the warning must still be given by a constable and cannot lawfully be given by a doctor (*Beatrice v DPP* [2004] EWHC 2416 (Admin)). However, self-induced intoxication rendering a person incapable of understanding what was being said does not provide such a defence or a reasonable excuse for failing to provide as required (*DPP v Beech* [1992] RTR 239). See also *R (DPP) v Preston* [2003] EWHC 729 (Admin). **C5.23**

A failure to give the warning in s. 7(7) or to comply with any of the appropriate statutory procedures will render evidence of the specimen inadmissible under the RTOA 1988, s. 15(2), even if there is no prejudice to the defendant (*Murray v DPP* [1993] RTR 209). There is no automatic requirement for the prosecution to retain CCTV footage of the custody suite in order to show that the warning was given (*Morris v DPP* (2009) 173 JP 41). If the defence wish to take issue about the alleged failure to warn, this should occur openly and during the course of the evidence rather than only in closing submissions (*R (Parker) v Crown Court at Bradford* [2007] RTR 369; *Malcolm v DPP* [2007] 3 All ER 578, where the late timing of the submission provided special circumstances justifying the court, even after retiring to consider its verdict, giving permission for further prosecution evidence to be adduced; *Cox v DPP* [2009] EWHC 3595 (Admin)).

Detention of Persons Affected by Alcohol or a Drug

By virtue of the RTA 1988, s. 10, following a requirement for a specimen of breath, blood or urine, a person may be detained at a police station until it appears to a constable that, if he were driving or attempting to drive, he would not be committing an offence under s. 4 or 5 of the Act. If the specimen was provided otherwise than at the police station, the constable may arrest the person and take him to a police station for detention on the same basis, unless the person is at a hospital as a patient and such action would be prejudicial to his proper care and treatment as a patient. If, however, it appears to the constable that there is no likelihood of that person driving or attempting to drive whilst his ability is impaired or he is above the prescribed limit **C5.24** then he may not be detained under s. 10. If a question arises in relation to detention as to whether or not a person's ability to drive is, or might be, impaired through drugs, the constable must consult a medical practitioner and act on his advice.

Protection for Hospital Patients

C5.25

Road Traffic Act 1988, s. 9

(1) While a person is at a hospital as a patient he shall not be required to co-operate with a preliminary test or to provide a specimen under section 7 of this Act unless the medical practitioner in immediate charge of his case has been notified of the proposal to make the requirement; and—
  (a) if the requirement is then made, it shall be for co-operation with a test administered, or for the provision of a specimen, at the hospital, but
  (b) if the medical practitioner objects on the ground specified in subsection (2) below, the requirement shall not be made.

(1A) While a person is at a hospital as a patient, no specimen of blood shall be taken from him under section 7A of this Act and he shall not be required to give his permission for a laboratory test of a specimen taken under that section unless the medical practitioner in immediate charge of his case—
  (a) has been notified of the proposal to take the specimen or to make the requirement; and
  (b) has not objected on the ground specified in subsection (2).

(2) The ground on which the medical practitioner may object is—
  (a) in a case falling within subsection (1), that the requirement or the provision of the specimen or (if one is required) the warning required by section 7(7) of this Act would be prejudicial to the proper care and treatment of the patient; and
  (b) in a case falling within subsection (1A), that the taking of the specimen, the requirement or the warning required by section 7A(5) of this Act would be so prejudicial.

For the RTA 1988, s. 7A, see **C5.9**.

C5.26 A person is at a hospital when he is within the hospital's curtilage and he is there for treatment, even as an out-patient. Once the treatment has been completed, the person is no longer a patient within the meaning of s. 9 (*A-G's Ref (No. 1 of 1976)* [1977] 3 All ER 557). The doctor who is directly responsible for the patient is the medical practitioner in immediate charge of his case. Common-sense evidential conclusions when identifying that medical practitioner are permissible (*Cherpion v DPP* [2013] EWHC 615 (Admin)). The medical practitioner must be notified of the proposal to take blood and must not raise any objection; formal consent is not mandatory (*Bryan* [2009] RTR 29).

In *Burton upon Trent Justices, ex parte Woolley* [1995] RTR 139, the Divisional Court decided that there is no obligation for the constable to inform a driver who is a patient at a hospital why a specimen of breath cannot be taken but, at some stage during the process at the hospital, the constable has to ask the driver whether there is any reason why a specimen of blood should not be taken. Thereafter, the details of the procedure laid down in *DPP v Warren* [1993] AC 319 and *DPP v Jackson* [1999] 1 AC 406 (see **C5.19** *et seq.*) should be followed. See also *Jones v DPP* [2004] EWHC 3165 (Admin). Where a constable has information supplied by, or presumably about, a person under investigation which relates to a possible medical reason for being unable to provide a specimen, he is required to relay that specific information to the doctor dealing with the patient (*Butler v DPP* [2001] RTR 430). A requirement lawfully made under s. 9 remains valid after the patient's discharge from hospital; it must therefore be complied with unless it is abundantly plain that, following discharge, the investigating officer is setting in train the s. 7 procedure (*Webber v DPP* [1998] RTR 111).

Failure to Provide an Evidential Specimen

C5.27 The RTOA 1988, ss. 11 and 12(1), apply; see **C2.17** and **C2.18**. 'Fail' includes a refusal (RTA 1988, s. 11). Whether there is a refusal is a matter of fact for the justices to decide (*Smyth v DPP* [1996] RTR 59; *Plackett v DPP* (2008) 172 JP 455). Where a motorist initially declined to provide the required specimens of breath but indicated a desire to change his mind within some five seconds, the only possible conclusion was that there had not been a refusal. Clear words of

denial, such as saying 'No, no, no', even before the investigating officer chooses between a specimen of blood or urine, will probably amount to a refusal (*Burke v DPP* [1999] RTR 387). If the
defendant's conduct shows he is not willing to provide the specimen required, or he imposes
unacceptable terms for the specimen to be provided, then a failure may well be made out (*DPP
v Swan* [2004] EWHC 2432 (Admin), where the court commented that *Mackey* [1977] RTR
146 should not be understood as imposing a threshold of outrageousness in behaviour before it
can constitute a failure to provide).

In *DPP v Darwen* [2007] EWHC 337 (Admin) and *Rweikiza v DPP* [2008] EWHC 386
(Admin), the importance of the conjunctive 'and' in s. 11(3) was stressed, making it clear that
the specimen provided must both be sufficient (e.g., in volume) and provided in such a way as
to enable the analysis of it to be satisfactorily achieved. If either of these criteria is not satisfied,
there will be a failure to provide the required specimen.

In *DPP v Butterworth* [1995] 1 AC 381, the House of Lords confirmed that the RTA 1988,
s. 7(6), creates only one offence. Accordingly, a charge stating that 'having been required to
provide a specimen of breath/blood/urine for analysis, [the defendant] failed without reasonable excuse to do so' was found not to be duplicitous (*Worsley v DPP* [1995] Crim LR 572,
where the prosecution then adduced evidence of failure to provide only one type of specimen),
even though the information looks capable of relating to three separate demands for three separate specimens. Amending the charge to substitute the correct type of specimen required for the
type mistakenly included is permissible, although this should usually occur prior to the date
fixed for trial (*Williams v DPP* [2009] EWHC 2354 (Admin)). The essence of the offence is that
the police are investigating whether the person committed any of the offences in ss. 3A, 4 and 5
of the 1988 Act and so there is no need to identify in the charge a specific offence to which the
mind of the investigating officer was directed.

Although s. 7(6) creates a single offence, two charges can be brought against the same defendant
where two separate failures are alleged (*Chichester Justices, ex parte DPP* [1994] RTR 175).
Moreover, the subsequent provision of a different specimen below the prescribed limit as a
consequence of a separate request may not cure the initial failure to provide without a reasonable excuse (*Lorimer v Russell* 1996 SLT 501).

Reasonable Excuse   It is a defence to a charge under the RTA 1988, s. 7(6), to have had a rea-   **C5.28**
sonable excuse for the failure to provide the specimen required. Although there is no statutory
requirement to advance a medical reason at the time of attempting but failing to provide the
specimen, if the defendant omits to mention a condition of which he is aware, this is unlikely to
be accepted by the justices subsequently as a reasonable excuse (*Piggott v DPP* [2008] RTR 199).
However, where there is a refusal or deliberate failure to provide the specimen required, it cannot
subsequently be justified by reference to a medical condition which was not alluded to at the time
(*DPP v Furby* [2000] RTR 181; *DPP v Lonsdale* [2001] RTR 444; *R (Martiner) v DPP* [2004]
EWHC 2484 (Admin)). There must be an attempt to provide which is unsuccessful because of a
physical or mental disability before reasonable excuse can be raised as a defence.

Once a defence of reasonable excuse is raised, it is for the prosecution to negative it. If the justices' decision suggests they have misapplied these respective burdens, the resulting conviction
will be liable to be quashed (*McKeon v DPP* [2008] RTR 165). What constitutes a 'reasonable
excuse' must always remain a matter of fact for the court. But in *Lennard* [1973] 2 All ER 831,
Lawton LJ said (at p. 487):

> In our judgment no excuse can be adjudged a reasonable one unless the person from whom the
> specimen is required is physically or mentally unable to provide it or the provision of the specimen
> would entail a substantial risk to his health.

Normally, expert medical evidence of the physical or mental incapacity to provide the specimen   **C5.29**
is required to support the defence and demonstrate the existence of the necessary causative link
between the incapacity and the failure to provide (*DPP v Crofton* [1994] RTR 279; *DPP v*

Brodzky [1997] RTR 425n; *DPP v Grundy* [2006] EWHC 1157 (Admin)). To be admissible, evidence supporting the defence must be indicated appropriately and in a timely fashion (see *Writtle v DPP* [2009] RTR 367, deploring defence ambushes). Where a substantial risk to health is advanced, alternative approaches to the provision of the specimen should be considered before assessing the reasonableness of the excuse (*DPP v Mukandiwa* [2006] RTR 304, where a potentially dangerous trance state triggered by the sight of blood could have been avoided by looking away and did not relate directly to the taking of the blood specimen required).

C5.30   Post-accident stress cannot, without evidence showing mental or physical disability, constitute a reasonable excuse for failing to provide a specimen (*DPP v Eddowes* [1991] RTR 35). See also *DPP v Ambrose* [1992] RTR 285, *DPP v Falzarano* [2001] RTR 217 and *DPP v Meller* [2002] EWHC 733 (Admin). In *De Freitas v DPP* [1993] RTR 98, a phobia of catching AIDS, established by medical evidence, amounted to a reasonable excuse. If a medical reason is claimed as a reason for not providing a specimen of blood, a medical practitioner's opinion that such a reason is not a medical one is conclusive.

Where a medical reason is advanced as a reasonable excuse, the justices should still give proper weight to the other evidence relating to the defendant's failure to provide, e.g., where the defendant, after having satisfactorily provided a roadside test and the first specimen of breath required, put the device's tube to his mouth and no breath was registered (*DPP v Radford* [1995] RTR 86). Only if the justices' decision in this respect is perverse will there be grounds to interfere on appeal.

Even without medical evidence justices are entitled, if they have the test in *Lennard* well in mind, to find that shock combined with inebriation which renders a defendant physically incapable may amount to a reasonable excuse (*DPP v Pearman* [1992] RTR 407; *DPP v Crofton* [1994] RTR 279). Justices should however be wary of using their own knowledge of a medical condition which is not supported by or is beyond the evidence before them (*DPP v Curtis* [1993] RTR 72).

C5.31   **Non-medical Reasons**   Omitting to warn the defendant that there is a time-limit for completing the breathalyser process, after which the Intoximeter stops functioning, will not amount to a reasonable excuse (*DPP v Coyle* [1996] RTR 287). Indeed *Cosgrove v DPP* [1997] RTR 153 confirmed that the investigating officer is not obliged to permit the driver the test's full three minutes in which to provide the required specimens. This was reaffirmed in *Watson v DPP* [2006] EWHC 3429 (Admin), where the defendant's insistence on being permitted to go to the lavatory between provision of the first and second breath specimens was not accepted as a reasonable excuse.

Failure to provide a specimen because the defendant was waiting for the arrival of, or telephone advice from, a solicitor did not amount to a reasonable excuse (*DPP v Skinner* [1990] RTR 231 and *DPP v Varley* (1999) 163 JP 443, following *DPP v Billington* [1988] 1 All ER 435). The decision in *Smith v Hand* [1986] RTR 265 was explained as applying only to cases where the defendant has been told positively that he can wait for his solicitor, although *Billington* clearly makes the distinction between imposing a condition and merely making a request in relation to the provision of legal advice. This principle remains unaffected after the HRA 1998 and does not violate the ECHR, Article 6(3) (*Campbell v CPS* (2002) 166 JP 742; *Kennedy v DPP* (2003) 167 JP 267; *Myles v DPP* [2004] 2 All ER 902). A very short delay before carrying out the test may be accommodated to permit a suspect to consult a solicitor, but thereafter the balance lies in favour of conducting the test promptly (*Gearing v DPP* [2008] RTR 72; *Chalupa v CPS* (2010) 174 JP 111, suggesting the solicitor must be immediately available). In *Dickinson v DPP* [1989] Crim LR 741, legal advice given to the defendant by a solicitor who accompanied him to the police station to the effect that he should refuse a specimen was held not to constitute a reasonable excuse. Where the defendant makes provision of the specimen required conditional on having sight of a law book, that does not amount to a reasonable excuse (*DPP v Noe* [2000]

RTR 351). Neither is insisting upon reading the PACE 1984 codes of practice before providing a specimen of breath a 'reasonable excuse' for failing to provide it (*DPP v Cornell* [1990] RTR 254).

In *DPP v Rous* [1992] RTR 246, it was held that the procedure as to the provision of specimens, **C5.32** whether relating to s. 7(4) or 8(2), does not constitute an interview and therefore there is no discretion under the PACE 1984, s. 78, to exclude evidence relating to the procedure. Indeed para. 11.1A of PACE Code C specifically states that procedures under s. 7 do not constitute interviewing. In *DPP v Whalley* [1991] RTR 161, a finding that the notice given to detained persons misled the accused to think he had a right to consult the codes before further procedures were undertaken was not enough to constitute a reasonable excuse for failing to provide a specimen. It was reiterated that an excuse would not be reasonable unless it followed *Lennard*, or was as a result of failing to understand the obligation to provide a specimen (*Chief Constable of Avon and Somerset Constabulary v Singh* [1988] RTR 107).

Punishment   Where the offender was driving or attempting to drive, the penalty is six months' **C5.33** imprisonment and/or a fine up to level 5 on the standard scale. Disqualification and endorsement are, in the absence of 'special reasons', obligatory. The offence carries between three and 11 penalty points.

In any other case, the penalty is three months' imprisonment and/or a fine up to level 4. Disqualification is discretionary, but endorsement with ten penalty points, in the absence of 'special reasons', is obligatory.

Forfeiture of the vehicle may be ordered under either situation (see **E18.1**).

Sentencing   In *Waltham Forest Justices, ex parte Barton* [1990] RTR 49, the Divisional Court **C5.34** indicated that, where a defendant is charged with failing to provide a specimen at the police station, the charge itself should indicate that 'the specimen was required to ascertain the ability of the defendant at the time he was driving or attempting to drive'. The decision in *DPP v Butterworth* [1995] 1 AC 381, however, makes it clear that there is no need to specify in the charge whether the allegation is that the defendant was only 'in charge' or driving or attempting to drive. Lord Slynn stated (at p. 394) that 'the question whether the person was driving or in charge of the motor vehicle is not part of the inquiry into whether there has been a refusal for the purposes of section 7(6). That question only becomes relevant after conviction and goes to the appropriate penalty.' Accordingly, the charge itself does not need to indicate whether the defendant faces a mandatory or discretionary disqualification, although the prosecution might be asked informally on what basis the case is being put.

Where the prosecution case is put on the 'in charge' basis, sentence can be passed only on the basis that the defendant was 'in charge' and not driving (*George v DPP* [1989] RTR 217). Consequently, if there is no evidence adduced that the defendant was driving, the court must sentence only on the 'in charge' basis (*Cawley v DPP* [2001] EWHC (Admin) 83).

The *Magistrates' Court Sentencing Guidelines* (see Supplement, **SG-337** and **SG-338**) must generally be followed; the Guidelines explain how to assess the offence seriousness by reference to the nature of the offending activity and provide examples of aggravating and mitigating factors.

DRIVING, OR BEING IN CHARGE, WITH ALCOHOL CONCENTRATION ABOVE PRESCRIBED LIMIT

Road Traffic Act 1988, s. 5

C5.35

(1) If a person—
    (a) drives or attempts to drive a motor vehicle on a road or other public place, or
    (b) is in charge of a motor vehicle on a road or other public place,

after consuming so much alcohol that the proportion of it in his breath, blood or urine exceeds the prescribed limit he is guilty of an offence.

(2) It is a defence for a person charged with an offence under subsection (1)(b) above to prove that at the time he is alleged to have committed the offence the circumstances were such that there was no likelihood of his driving the vehicle whilst the proportion of alcohol in his breath, blood or urine remained likely to exceed the prescribed limit.

(3) The court may, in determining whether there was such a likelihood as is mentioned in subsection (2) above, disregard any injury to him and any damage to the vehicle.

Elements

C5.36 The RTOA 1988, ss. 11 and 12(1), apply; see **C2.17** and **C2.18**. For the meaning of the terms 'driving', 'road or other public place' and 'attempting', see **C1.2** and **C1.5**, **C1.13** and **C1.16**, and **C1.20**. Where the only evidence of 'driving' is in a confession that is inadmissible as a result of non-compliance with the PACE 1984, it cannot be relied upon to found a conviction under the RTA 1988, s. 5(1)(a) (*Charles v DPP* [2010] RTR 402). An intoxicated driver who is intending to drive but who is prevented from doing so before getting into the vehicle has not committed the *actus reus* of attempting to drive (*Mason v DPP* [2010] RTR 120). The RTA 1988, s. 11, sets out the 'prescribed limit'. If the lower reading in breath is 39 microgrammes in 100 millilitres or less, proceedings are not usually instituted. In *DPP v Johnson* [1995] 4 All ER 53, the Divisional Court held that the meaning of 'consuming' was sufficiently wide to cover ingestion otherwise than by mouth and the important element of the offence was the concentration of alcohol in the driver's body at the relevant time. In *Zafar v DPP* [2005] RTR 220, it was confirmed that 'breath' in this context is not confined to deep lung air and should be given its dictionary definition ('air exhaled from any thing'). See also *Woolfe v DPP* [2007] RTR 187.

C5.37 Section 5 creates nine separate offences of driving, or attempting to drive or being in charge of a vehicle, each with an alcohol concentration above the prescribed limit in relation to breath, blood or urine (*Bolton Justices, ex parte Khan* [1999] Crim LR 912). The charge must state which specimen is to be relied upon by the prosecution. Referring to more than one type of specimen renders the charge bad for duplicity. However, a late amendment to the charge to refer to the correct specimen is likely to be permitted as it should not prejudice the defendant, who knows that driving with excess alcohol in his body is what is being alleged (*Fenwick v Valentine* 1994 SLT 485).

As regards secondary participation in an offence under s. 5, a supervising driver who was aware that the learner driver had drunk so much that the alcohol level in his body must have exceeded the prescribed limit was held to have been properly convicted of aiding and abetting the offence, even though the driver had not been required to provide a specimen (*Carter v Richardson* [1974] RTR 314, where this was a proper inference to draw from the behaviour of the defendant when the police arrived, because he had lied about who was the driver). Lacing the drinks of a person who then drives may involve procuring an offence under s. 5; the defendant must be proved to have known that the person whose drink was laced was going to drive and that the ordinary result of lacing the drinks would be to raise the driver's alcohol level above the prescribed limit (*A-G's Ref (No. 1 of 1975)* [1975] QB 773). Alternatively, as McCullough J stated in *Blakely v DPP* [1991] RTR 405 (at p. 415):

> It must, at the least, be shown that the accused contemplated that his act would or might bring about or assist the commission of the principal offence: ... The requirements match those needed to convict principals in the second degree. And they fit well with the liability of the parties to a joint enterprise.

C5.38 In Charge It was confirmed in *Drake v DPP* [1994] RTR 411 that a person can be in charge of a motor vehicle when the vehicle is immobile. In *Leach v Evans* [1952] 2 All ER 264, a motorist emerging from a public house considerably under the influence of alcohol told a police officer that he was looking for his van, walked towards it and was then arrested within three yards of it. Lord Goddard CJ posed the question: if the motorist was not in charge of the van who was?

This principle was followed in *Haines v Roberts* [1953] 1 All ER 344, where Lord Goddard CJ said (at p. 311):

> It may be that, if a man goes to a public house and leaves his car outside or in the car park and, getting drunk, asks a friend to look after the car for him or to take it home, he has put it in charge of somebody else; but if he has not put it in charge of somebody else he is in charge until he does. His car is out on the road or in the car park — it matters not which — and he is in charge.

In *DPP v Watkins* [1989] QB 821, it was held that a person was in charge of a vehicle if he acted in a manner which showed that he had assumed control or intended to assume control of the vehicle preparatory to driving it. Thereafter the burden of proving the statutory defence in the RTA 1988, s. 5(2), shifts to the defendant (see **C5.54**). Amongst factors which merited consideration were:

(a) whether and where he was in the vehicle or how far he was from it;
(b) what he was doing at the relevant time;
(c) whether he was in possession of a key that fitted the ignition;
(d) whether there was evidence of an intention to take or assert control of the car by driving or otherwise;
(e) whether any other person was in, at or near the vehicle and, if so, the like particulars in respect of that person.

Where the defendant was the owner of the car in which he was sitting with the ignition keys in his hand, in the absence of any suggestion of another person being in charge, it is an inescapable conclusion that the defendant was in charge (*CPS v Bate* [2004] EWHC 2811 (Admin)).

Evidence as to Specimens

Road Traffic Offenders Act 1988, s. 16   C5.39

(1) Evidence of the proportion of alcohol or a drug in a specimen of breath, blood or urine may, subject to subsections (3) and (4) below and to section 15(5) and (5A) of this Act, be given by the production of a document or documents purporting to be whichever of the following is appropriate, that is to say—
    (a) a statement automatically produced by the device by which the proportion of alcohol in a specimen of breath was measured and a certificate signed by a constable (which may but need not be contained in the same document as the statement) that the statement relates to a specimen provided by the accused at the date and time shown in the statement, and
    (b) a certificate signed by an authorised analyst as to the proportion of alcohol or any drug found in a specimen of blood or urine identified in the certificate.
(2) Subject to subsections (3) and (4) below, evidence that a specimen of blood was taken from the accused with his consent by a medical practitioner or a registered health care professional may be given by the production of a document purporting to certify that fact and to be signed by a medical practitioner or a registered health care professional.
(3) Subject to subsection (4) below—
    (a) a document purporting to be such a statement or such a certificate (or both such a statement and such a certificate) as is mentioned in subsection (1)(a) above is admissible in evidence on behalf of the prosecution in pursuance of this section only if a copy of it either has been handed to the accused when the document was produced or has been served on him not later than seven days before the hearing, and
    (b) any other document is so admissible only if a copy of it has been served on the accused not later than seven days before the hearing.
(4) A document purporting to be a certificate (or so much of a document as purports to be a certificate) is not so admissible if the accused, not later than three days before the hearing or within such further time as the court may in special circumstances allow, has served notice on the prosecutor requiring the attendance at the hearing of the person by whom the document purports to be signed.
(5) [Applies only to Scotland.]

(6) A copy of a certificate required by this section to be served on the accused or a notice required by this section to be served on the prosecutor may be served personally or sent by registered post or recorded delivery service.

C5.40 **Printouts** In *Garner v DPP* [1990] RTR 208 (following *Castle v Cross* [1984] 1 All ER 87), the Court of Appeal held that the admissibility of the 'statement automatically produced by the device' (commonly called 'the printout') did not just arise through the RTOA 1988, s. 16(1). The statement is in itself an admissible document and represents real evidence as long as it is properly produced. The purpose and effect of s. 16 is to enable the printout together with an appropriate certificate to be tendered at the hearing and to 'be capable of establishing the facts stated in it without the necessity of anybody being called' (per Stocker LJ at p. 184). In short, s. 16(1)(a) is permissive. It does not stipulate the only manner in which evidence of analysis can be given. It provides one method for proving the proportion of alcohol in a breath specimen (*Thom v DPP* [1994] RTR 11; *R (Leong) v DPP* [2006] EWHC 1575 (Admin); *R (CPS) v Sedgemoor Justices* [2007] EWHC 1803 (Admin)). Other routes of admissibility are available, including the hearsay provisions of the CJA 2003, s. 116 (*Brett v DPP* [2009] 1 WLR 2530: see **C5.42**).

The printout and the operator's certificate may be separate or contained in the same document. Section 16(4) relates to the operator's, medical practitioner's and analyst's certificates, and not to the printout (*Temple v Botha* [1985] Crim LR 517). On a plea of guilty, there is no need to produce the original printout from the device. If there is a genuine change of plea, reasonable adjournments must be given to the prosecution if there is a problem about production of the printout (*Tower Bridge Magistrates' Court, ex parte DPP* [1989] RTR 118).

C5.41 A failure to produce the printout in evidence in a case where the officer does not give evidence of the reading, his familiarity with the device, its working or calibration means that the prosecution have failed to establish a case against the defendant (*Hasler v DPP* [1989] RTR 148). Evidence of the breath alcohol reading, in the absence of the printout, is not, in itself, sufficient to found a conviction (*Owen v Chesters* [1985] RTR 191). The prosecution should establish that the device is working correctly by evidence relating to the calibration. An officer giving such evidence has to be trained in the use and manner of performance of the device so as to understand the calibration process and to recognise that, unless the result of the process lies within accepted limits, the device may be unreliable (*Denneny v Harding* [1986] RTR 350). Even where the operator's knowledge of the device has been shown in cross-examination to be less than perfect, provided there is nothing to show the decision was irrational, it is still open to the court to conclude that the operator has been adequately trained so as to be qualified to conduct the procedure and that the device has functioned reliably (*Haggis v DPP* [2004] 3 All ER 382). The operator is entitled to give oral evidence, without production of the printout being a pre-condition, so as to support a conviction, provided that the evidence demonstrates the actual reading on which the charge is founded and demonstrates that the device was working properly and reliably, i.e. by the operator looking at the figures on the device's display (*Thom v DPP*; *Greenaway v DPP* [1994] RTR 17). See also *Sneyd v DPP* [2007] RTR 53. There is also a discretion to permit the prosecution to remedy an oversight to adduce such evidence during their case by calling appropriate evidence later on, especially where the interests of justice outweigh any prejudice to the defendant (*Cook v DPP* [2001] Crim LR 321 and *Leeson v DPP* [2000] RTR 385). The exact procedures of various approved devices differ, so that reliance on the steps in respect of the wrong one, perhaps as a result of references in authorities, will not assist (*Mercer v DPP* (2003) 167 JP 441, which drew the distinction between the Lion Intoxilyser 6000 and the old Lion Intoximeter 3000).

A printout timed according to Greenwich Mean Time is admissible even though British Summer Time was operating at the time the defendant provided the specimen (*Parker v DPP* [1993] RTR 283). Indeed, in *DPP v McKeown* [1997] 1 All ER 737, a printout recording a wholly inaccurate time due to a malfunctioning clock was still held admissible because that malfunction did not affect the way in which the computer processed, stored or retrieved the information used to generate the statement in evidence. This reasoning has been applied to typographical errors on the face of printouts which clearly do not affect the proper functioning of the device (*Reid v DPP* [1999] RTR 357; *DPP v Barber* (1999) 163 JP 457).

Service of Certificate   The certificate under the RTOA 1988, s. 16(2), is termed an HORT/5. C5.42
Section 16(3) imposes a duty to serve the analyst's certificate, which cannot be waived if this method of admissibility is relied upon (*Tobi v Nicholas* [1988] RTR 343). However, where only the lack of a signature on the certificate is an issue, and not service itself, strict proof of service can be waived (*Louis v DPP* [1998] RTR 354). The obligation imposed is treated as being to offer a copy of the printout to the defendant, so that a refusal to accept it in order to argue that it has not been 'handed' as required will not render the contents of the printout inadmissible (*McCormack v DPP* [2002] RTR 355). If the defendant wishes to challenge the lack of service of any of the certificates, this must be done before the contents are put in evidence (*Banks* [1972] 1 All ER 1041), although the challenge does not have to be made immediately and may be permitted if made a few minutes later, so that the defendant first has time to consider the implications of the issue (*R (Wooldridge) v DPP* [2003] EWHC 1663 (Admin)), but attempting to do so only in closing is too late (*Jeffreys v DPP* [2006] EWHC 1377 (Admin)).

Section 16(6) provides for service of various notices, and s. 16(4) for the service of a counter-notice. Oral notice will not suffice and, if there is any issue as to whether a document complies with these provisions, the justices will have to determine as a matter of fact whether it constitutes a notice (*R (Stavrinou) v Horseferry Road Justices* [2006] EWHC 566 (Admin); *R (DPP) v Chorley Justices* [2006] EWHC 1795 (Admin)). This procedure provides an alternative method of service to that contained in the CJA 1967, s. 9 (*DPP v Stephens* [2006] EWHC 1860 (Admin), where it was pointed out that the methods specified in s. 16(6) are exhaustively listed). In *Brett v DPP* [2009] 1 WLR 2530, upon service of a s. 16(4) counter-notice, if the analyst is unavailable to attend in person, the CJA 2003, s. 116 (see **F16.7**), may enable the evidence to be admitted as hearsay, although, in the event of the trial being adjourned, the position on whether attendance can be achieved must be reviewed.

Where evidence is adduced from someone who is not an authorised analyst, the s. 16 mechanism is not applicable and the usual process for admitting expert evidence must be followed (*R (CPS) v Sedgemoor Justices* [2007] EWHC 1803 (Admin)).

Admissibility of Specimens

Road Traffic Offenders Act 1988, s. 15   C5.43

(1) This section and section 16 of this Act apply in respect of proceedings for an offence under section 3A, 4 or 5 of the Road Traffic Act 1988 (driving offences connected with drink or drugs); and expressions used in this section and section 16 of this Act have the same meaning as in sections 3A to 10 of that Act.
(2) Evidence of the proportion of alcohol or any drug in a specimen of breath, blood or urine provided by or taken from the accused shall, in all cases (including cases where the specimen was not provided or taken in connection with the alleged offence), be taken into account and, subject to subsection (3) below, it shall be assumed that the proportion of alcohol in the accused's breath, blood or urine at the time of the alleged offence was not less than in the specimen.
(3) That assumption shall not be made if the accused proves—
   (a) that he consumed alcohol before he provided the specimen or had it taken from him and—
      (i) in relation to an offence under section 3A, after the time of the alleged offence, and
      (ii) otherwise, after he had ceased to drive, attempt to drive or be in charge of a vehicle on a road or other public place, and
   (b) that had he not done so the proportion of alcohol in his breath, blood or urine would not have exceeded the prescribed limit and, if it is alleged that he was unfit to drive through drink, would not have been such as to impair his ability to drive properly.

(4) A specimen of blood shall be disregarded unless—
- (a) it was taken from the accused with his consent and either—
  - (i) in a police station by a medical practitioner or a registered health care professional; or
  - (ii) elsewhere by a medical practitioner; or
- (b) it was taken from the accused by a medical practitioner under section 7A of the Road Traffic Act 1988 and the accused subsequently gave his permission for a laboratory test of the specimen.

(5) Where, at the time a specimen of blood or urine was provided by the accused, he asked to be provided with such a specimen, evidence of the proportion of alcohol or any drug found in the specimen is not admissible on behalf of the prosecution unless—
- (a) the specimen in which the alcohol or drug was found is one of two parts into which the specimen provided by the accused was divided at the time it was provided, and
- (b) the other part was supplied to the accused.

(5A) Where a specimen of blood was taken from the accused under section 7A of the Road Traffic Act 1988, evidence of the proportion of alcohol or any drug found in the specimen is not admissible on behalf of the prosecution unless—
- (a) the specimen in which the alcohol or drug was found is one of two parts into which the specimen taken from the accused was divided at the time it was taken; and
- (b) any request to be supplied with the other part which was made by the accused at the time when he gave his permission for a laboratory test of the specimen was complied with.

Section 15 does not apply to offences contrary to the RTA 1988, s. 3A(1)(c) and (d) (*Coe* [2010] 3 All ER 83).

C5.44   Incomplete breath specimens, even if they purport to give a reading, are inadmissible against the defendant (*R (Willicott) v DPP* (2002) 166 JP 385). Under the RTA 1988, s. 7(1)(a), a constable may require provision of two specimens of breath. Accordingly, only the first two specimens actually provided are admissible (*Howard v Hallett* [1984] RTR 353). In this case, the first Intoximeter procedure resulted in only one specimen being provided because of the constable's error, so the full procedure was recommended resulting in the provision of three specimens in total. The Divisional Court rejected the prosecution's attempt to ignore the first procedure entirely and so rely on the lower of the second and third specimens provided. It ruled that the third specimen was the one to be disregarded as being outside the s. 7 statutory procedure and that the lower of the first two readings was the specimen on which the prosecution was obliged to found its case. On the basis that s. 7(1)(b) enables a constable to require a specimen of blood, only the first specimen of blood or urine taken ought to be admissible.

C5.45   Where blood has been taken on two occasions and then divided, the resulting analysis is inadmissible (*Dear v DPP* [1988] RTR 148). In *DPP v Elstob* [1992] RTR 45, it was held that the phrase 'divided at the time' in the RTOA 1988, s. 15(5)(a), meant that the taking and division of the specimen had to be closely linked in time and performed as part of the same event, even though it is inevitable that some time will pass between the two acts. It is important to maintain the integrity of what occurs, and therefore it is desirable (albeit not strictly necessary for compliance with the statute) for the defendant to be present. Incorrect labelling by a police doctor of the part specimen handed to the defendant, in pursuance of s. 15(5)(b), is not fatal to the admissibility of evidence relating to the proportion of alcohol or drug found in the specimen, unless it is supplied in such a way as to deter or prevent the defendant from having it analysed (*Butler v DPP* [1990] RTR 377). In order to comply with s. 15(5)(b), the defendant's part does not need to be handed physically to him but can be supplied by being made available, e.g., through provision to a friend in such a way that the defendant must have known what had become of it (*O'Connell v DPP* [2006] EWHC 1419 (Admin)). There is no obligation to give the defendant a choice as to which of the two parts of the sample to take (*R (Lidington) v DPP* [2006] EWHC 1984 (Admin)). In *Afolayan v CPS* [2012] EWHC 1322 (Admin), although Form MG DD/A had not been properly completed, the Divisional Court concluded that the justices had evidence from the police and from what the analyst said about the specimen she received entitling them to prefer that evidence to the defendant's evidence that the blood sample taken from him had not been sealed, as required, in his presence. As there is no statutory requirement to inform a driver that his breath specimen is above the prescribed limit, failing to do so does not render any replacement specimen provided inadmissible (*DPP v Ormsby* [1997] RTR 394n).

Where the laboratory analysing the sample subdivides it for the purpose of analysis, it is lawful to use the average result and not necessary to use only the lowest result (*DPP v Welsh* (1997) 161 JP 57). In *Bolton Magistrates' Court, ex parte Scally* [1991] 1 QB 537, where the reliability of the blood analysis was impugned because the sample had been taken using a cleaning swab impregnated with alcohol, the Divisional Court quashed the conviction. Similarly, in *Gregory v DPP* (2002) 166 JP 400, opinion evidence explaining possible discrepancies in the analysis in a borderline case, which resulted from contact with the fluoride preservative in the container into which the blood was transferred after being divided, should not have been disregarded at trial, with the consequence that the conviction was quashed. However, in *Carter v DPP* [2007] RTR 257, following *R (Dhaliwal) v DPP* [2006] EWHC 1149 (Admin), the court concluded that, unless there is something suggesting otherwise, justices are entitled to presume that the procedures laid down for the preparation of analysts' kits have been carried out correctly. Any failure to notify the defendant of the procedure set out in s. 15(5) will harm the prosecution's case irreparably (*Anderton v Lythgoe* [1985] 1 WLR 222); the same consequence is likely in respect of the procedure in s. 15(5A). Where a point is taken on this procedure, it must be taken before evidence of the analysis is adduced (*Hudson v Hornby* [1973] RTR 4).

Where the defendant has exercised the right to provide a replacement specimen under the RTA 1988, s. 8, and then challenges the reliability of the results of the blood analysis, the breath test results, with the benefit of expert evidence linking both, can be admitted to demonstrate compatibility (*Slasor v DPP* [1999] RTR 432). Conversely, the defendant should have the opportunity to adduce evidence of a breath test below the prescribed limit taken shortly after provision of blood analysed as being above the prescribed limit in order to support a challenge to the reliability of that blood analysis (*Parish v DPP* [2000] RTR 143).   C5.46

Challenging the Specimen Evidence   A general challenge to the admissibility of the printout   C5.47
from the Intoximeter (e.g., relating to the compensatory element where the device detects a substance believed to be acetone, reducing the alcohol reading accordingly) can be made using the PACE 1984, s. 78 (*Ashton v DPP* [1998] RTR 45). However, challenging the reliability of the device so as to render the evidence produced inadmissible is notoriously difficult. The justices should assume the device to have been in good working order until the contrary is proved (*Anderton v Waring* [1986] RTR 74). They can infer from the device being of a type approved by the Secretary of State that it contains the original and approved software (*Skinner v DPP* [2005] RTR 202).

In *Tower Bridge Magistrates' Court, ex parte DPP* [1989] RTR 118, the Divisional Court quashed a witness summons issued by the magistrates' court for a police officer to produce the service record and machine log in respect of the device used, castigating the defence for engaging on a fishing expedition. Disclosure to establish that an approved device has been altered in such a way as to take it out of type approval should be ordered only after production of some material justifying the application, not on the basis of mere assertion from the defendant that there had been an unapproved modification (*DPP v Wood* (2006) 170 JP 177). Any suggestion that the device was working unreliably must be related to the particular facts of the case before the justices rather than generally (*DPP v Brown* [2002] RTR 395). There should be evidence raising a realistic possibility that the device malfunctioned and a general assertion alleging failure to comply with the manufacturer's recommendations does not amount to such evidence (*Scheiner v DPP* [2006] EWHC 1516 (Admin)). Whether a modification made to a device which is ordinarily an approved device takes it out of type approval involves a broad common-sense consideration of whether the build and function of the device still has the character, essence and identity of the device with type approval (*R (Coxon) v Manchester City Magistrates' Court* [2010] EWHC 712 (Admin)). Tests by experts pointing to the unreliability of the device in relation to an aspect of its functions that is wholly irrelevant to the reliability of the evidence adduced in the defendant's case will not deprive the device of its type approval by the Secretary of State (*DPP v Memery* [2003] RTR 249). See also *Grant v DPP* (2003) 167 JP 159 and *Rose v DPP* [2010] RTR 269.

C5.48   There is no obligation on the prosecution to disclose to the defence the evidence of the proportion of alcohol found in a roadside breath test where it is not being put in evidence and relied upon in accordance with s. 15(2). Applications under the CPIA 1996, s. 8(2), for such disclosure, with a view to seeing if those readings provided the foundation for a challenge to the evidential specimen on which the prosecutions were based, were rejected in *Murphy v DPP* [2006] EWHC 1753 (Admin) and *Smith v DPP* [2007] 4 All ER 1135.

Evidence of the amount of alcohol allegedly taken prior to providing the specimen relied on by the prosecution may be used to challenge the reliability of the evidence relating to the specimen (*Cracknell v Willis* [1988] AC 450). However, this will often depend on the evidence of the defendant alone and, in the absence of the right to provide a sample of blood or urine, he is unlikely to prevail. For example, in *Lafferty v DPP* [1995] Crim LR 429, the defendant adduced evidence as to the amount of alcohol consumed supported by expert evidence indicating that, on such a level of consumption, the Intoximeter reading should not have been as high as it was; if the defendant's evidence to that effect was accepted, it followed that the device was unreliable. The Divisional Court decided that the justices had properly admitted evidence of the results of the roadside breath test, as this went to the veracity of the defendant when attacking the reliability of the device, which attack the prosecution was entitled to rebut by any relevant evidence. See also *Williams v DPP* [2001] EWHC 932 (Admin). It is not strictly necessary to adduce expert evidence establishing the reading which should have been produced on the basis of what the defendant claims to have consumed (*DPP v Spurrier* [2000] RTR 60) but, except in exceptional circumstances, to do so is always likely to make the defendant's evidence more credible.

In summary, for evidence of a specimen required under the RTA 1988, s. 7(1), to be admissible under the RTOA 1988, s. 15(2), all the procedural requirements of the RTA 1988, ss. 7 and 8, including the mandatory warning under s. 7(7), must be fully complied with, even where no prejudice results from a breach of those requirements (*Murray v DPP* [1993] RTR 209). A blood sample provided voluntarily by the defendant before he is suspected of an excess alcohol offence is also admissible under s. 15(2) (*DPP v Carless* [2005] EWHC 3234 (Admin)).

Excluding Improperly Obtained Specimens

C5.49   Since the decision in *Fox* [1986] AC 281, a lawful arrest is not an essential prerequisite for lawfully requiring a specimen under the RTA 1988, s. 7. Indeed, subject to general principles about the admissibility of evidence illegally or unlawfully obtained (see **F2.12** *et seq.*), it is arguable that no irregularity in the preliminary testing procedure under ss. 6 to 6E can have any effect on the subsequent procedure under s. 7 (*DPP v Wilson* [2009] RTR 375 and *R (CPS) v Wolverhampton Magistrates' Court* [2009] EWHC 3467 (Admin)). Similarly, because time is of the essence and the police are not required to delay the breath test procedure in order for the defendant to obtain legal advice (see **C5.31**), the PACE 1984, s. 58 (right of access to solicitor: see **D1.55**), will not usually be breached, enabling s. 78 of that Act to be invoked to justify exclusion of the evidence of the test (*Chalupa v CPS* (2010) 174 JP 111).

The decision in *Fox* did, however, recognise a discretion to exclude otherwise admissible evidence obtained by some trick, deception or other impropriety as envisaged in *Sang* [1980] AC 402. In *Matto v Wolverhampton Crown Court* [1987] RTR 337, officers followed the appellant on to private property, continued to administer a breath test to him and thereafter arrested him after their implied licence to remain had been terminated. The Crown Court was of the opinion that, in order to exercise the discretion under the PACE 1984, s. 78, it must find that the police officers were knowingly acting in excess of their powers, and therefore acting in bad faith, and that evidence had been obtained other than voluntarily. In allowing the appeal, Woolf LJ stated that the approach of the Crown Court was wrong (at p. 347):

> ... it was at least open to the Crown Court, if the matter had been properly left before them, for them to have come to a conclusion that what happened at the house was still affecting the fairness of what happened in the police station and, because it affected the fairness of what happened at the police station, that would in turn give rise to an argument as to the admissibility of the evidence under section 78 of the Police and Criminal Evidence Act 1984.

In *Thomas* [1991] RTR 292, Tudor-Evans J stated (at p. 294):   **C5.50**

> ... in principle and upon authority, it is open to a defendant to argue that the procedures at the police station were so tainted by the previous conduct of the police at the roadside that there was a discretion to exclude the evidence of what happened at the police station.

It is not normally permissible, however, to raise this type of issue before the Divisional Court if it was not raised initially before the justices themselves (*Braham v DPP* [1996] RTR 30).

The Statutory Assumption

The assumption in the RTA 1988, s. 15(2) (see **C5.43**), relates to the proportion of alcohol in   **C5.51** the defendant's specimen at the time of the offence. It applies only to trials and is not the sole basis, whether guilt is established by plea or otherwise, on which to sentence (*Goldsmith v DPP* [2010] RTR 219). The assumption is not rebuttable (*Beauchamp-Thompson v DPP* [1988] RTR 54; *Millard v DPP* [1990] RTR 201) and a court is not competent to receive expert evidence aimed at undermining the assumption (*Griffiths v DPP* (2002) 166 JP 629). The assumption has been found not to be incompatible with the presumption of innocence in the ECHR, Article 6(2) (*Parker v DPP* [2001] RTR 240; *Drummond* [2002] RTR 371).

The assumption provides the 'floor' in relation to the amount of alcohol in the defendant's breath, blood or urine at the relevant time. Accordingly, the prosecution are entitled to produce evidence by way of back-calculation to show that, at the time of driving, attempting to drive or being in charge, the proportion was even higher than the specimen shows and was therefore in excess of the prescribed limit. In *Gumbley v Cunningham* [1988] QB 170, the appellant driver was involved in a fatal accident at 11.15 p.m. Four hours and 20 minutes later, he provided a specimen of blood analysed at 59 milligrammes per 100 millilitres. The prosecution adduced evidence to demonstrate that a person of the height, age, weight and physical condition of the appellant would, at the time of driving, have had alcohol in his body in the range of 120 to 130 milligrammes in blood. In upholding his conviction in the Divisional Court, Mann J said (at p. 181):

> Evidence which is material to the question of what was the proportion of alcohol at the moment of driving must be admissible. The provisions of [the RTOA 1988, s. 15(2) and (3)] do not preclude evidence other than that revealed by a specimen to show a greater level of alcohol although, subject to the 'hip-flask' defence, the specimen will always provide a 'not less' or base figure. If that figure is above the prescribed limit, other evidence is unnecessary to establish the offence.

> Our conclusion means that those who drive whilst above the prescribed limits cannot necessarily escape punishment because of the lapse of time. However, our conclusion also means that in cases where a sample provided a substantial period of time after driving has ceased shows a level below the prescribed limit justices may find themselves confronted with evidence of a complicated and scientific nature. ... We think it needs to be said, therefore, that in our view the prosecution should not seek to rely on evidence of back-calculation save where that evidence is easily understood and clearly persuasive of the presence of excess alcohol at the time when a defendant was driving. Moreover, justices must be very careful especially where there is conflicting evidence not to convict unless, upon the scientific and other evidence which they find it safe to rely on, they are sure an excess of alcohol was in the defendant's body when he was actually driving as charged.

Where the analyses of two specimens of blood or urine differ in the amount of alcohol contained in them, it is for the justices to evaluate all the evidence before them. If in any reasonable doubt, they should choose that most favourable to the defendant (*Froggatt v Allcock* [1975] RTR 372n).

Defences

C5.52 **The Statutory 'Hip-flask' Defence**   Section 15(3) of the RTOA 1988 (see **C5.43**) affords a defence to a charge under the RTA 1988, s. 5, where the defendant claims that the fact that he has alcohol in his body above the prescribed limit is attributable to consumption after the event to an extent that, but for that later consumption of alcohol, evidence from the specimen would not have resulted in an offence being made out. Once the statutory assumption (see **C5.51**) has to be made, the onus shifts to the defendant to raise the 'hip-flask' defence (*Patterson v Charlton* [1986] RTR 18). The defendant must prove, on the balance of probabilities, not only that the reading was wrong but also that at the relevant time his alcohol level was below the prescribed limit (*DPP v Tooze* [2007] EWHC 2186 (Admin)). In *Drummond* [2002] RTR 371, the Court of Appeal decided not to 'read down' s. 15(3) under the HRA 1998, s. 3, so that it imposes only an evidential burden (see, e.g., *Lambert* [2002] 2 AC 545 at **F3.18**) and ruled that the persuasive burden imposed does not interfere with the presumption of innocence in the ECHR, Article 6(2), because it is no greater an interference than is necessary. This approach was confirmed as remaining correct post-*Sheldrake* (see **C5.54**) in *DPP v Ellery* [2005] EWHC 2513 (Admin).

C5.53 The defence also extends to offences under the RTA 1988, ss. 3A and 4 (see **C3.20** and **C5.61**). In the case of an offence under s. 3A, evidence of post-accident consumption of alcohol is admissible even if the defendant drove after the accident because s. 3A looks at the state of intoxication at the time the cause of death arose. In *Dawson v Lunn* [1986] RTR 234, Robert Goff LJ said (at p. 238):

> ... there are circumstances in which, as a matter of common sense, laymen can reach a perfectly sensible conclusion unaided by scientific evidence. We need only to take the simple case of somebody who satisfies the justices on the evidence that he had drunk only a small amount before driving, and that after ceasing to drive he had drunk a substantial quantity of alcohol. The justices can then conclude as laymen, reliably and confidently ... that the defendant has satisfied them, on the balance of probabilities, that he has consumed alcohol after ceasing to drive and that had he not done so the proportion of alcohol in his breath, or blood, or urine would not have exceeded the prescribed limit. But there must be cases where the justices cannot sensibly draw that conclusion themselves unaided by expert evidence.

The court then went on to adopt the passage in *Pugsley v Hunter* [1973] 2 All ER 10 (a case on 'special reasons'), where Lord Widgery CJ observed that 'unless the case really is an obvious one ... the only way in which a defendant can discharge the onus is by calling medical evidence'. The court also discouraged reliance upon extracts from scientific journals. Except perhaps in the clearest of cases, the defendant must therefore call scientific evidence (*DPP v Singh* [1988] RTR 209). Where there is no expert evidence, the justices should avoid drawing their own conclusions about the probable effect of the claimed consumption of alcohol (*Lonergan v DPP* [2003] RTR 188) and must be careful when assessing the credibility of the defendant (*DPP v Dukolli* [2009] EWHC 3097 (Admin)). Where the justices have the benefit of expert evidence, despite apparent discrepancies, they may be entitled to find that the defendant has discharged the onus on him (*DPP v Lowden* [1993] RTR 349).

If expert evidence is to be called, it should be disclosed to the prosecution to avoid unnecessary adjournments (*DPP v O'Connor* [1992] RTR 66).

C5.54 **Other Defences**   Section 5(2) of the RTA 1988 provides a defence to an allegation of 'in charge' of the vehicle, based on the likelihood of the defendant driving while still above the prescribed limit. In *Sheldrake v DPP* [2004] 1 AC 264, the House of Lords determined that there was no need to 'read down' this reverse onus of proof as an evidential burden only (as the majority of the Divisional Court had, relying on the presumption of innocence in the ECHR, Article 6(2)) and that this was a provision properly imposing a legal burden on the defendant, which was justified as pursuing a legitimate objective that was neither unreasonable or arbitrary. See **F3.18** for a full discussion of the 'reverse burden'.

It is not sufficient for the defendant to prove that he did not intend to drive. The question is whether he has shown that there is no likelihood of driving while still over the prescribed limit (*CPS v Thompson* [2008] RTR 70); 'likelihood' means real risk (*Sheldrake v DPP* [2004] QB 487). In *Drake v DPP* [1994] RTR 411, the Divisional Court held that the presence of a wheel clamp on a motor vehicle could not be disregarded when considering the likelihood of the defendant driving. Medical or other expert evidence will almost inevitably be required to establish the probable alcohol level at the time at which the defendant will next drive (*DPP v Frost* [1989] RTR 11), unless the length of time involved makes that conclusion obvious. As to duress, see **A3.35** to **A3.52**.

Insanity cannot be raised as a defence as there is no *mens rea* element to which it can relate (*DPP v H* [1997] 1 WLR 1406, but see **A3.24** for discussion of doubts expressed about this decision).

Punishment

For offences of driving or attempting to drive, the penalty is six months' imprisonment and/or a fine up to level 5 on the standard scale. Disqualification and endorsement are obligatory unless there are 'special reasons', and the offence carries between three and 11 penalty points. An order for forfeiture may be made under either offence (see **E18.1**).   **C5.55**

The offence of being 'in charge' is punishable by imprisonment for up to three months and/or a fine up to level 4. Disqualification is discretionary; endorsement with ten penalty points is obligatory.

Sentencing

The *Magistrates' Court Sentencing Guidelines* (see Supplement, **SG-334** and **SG-335**) must generally be followed; the Guidelines explain how to assess the offence seriousness by reference to the nature of the offending activity and provide examples of aggravating and mitigating factors. In particular, they indicate that, as a starting point, a custodial sentence might properly be considered for readings of 120 microgrammes in 100 millilitres of breath (equating to 276 milligrammes in 100 millilitres of blood or 367 milligrammes in 100 millilitres of urine). In *Nokes* [1978] RTR 101, it was accepted that there is no rule that a first offence should not attract a custodial sentence if the facts show it to be appropriate.   **C5.56**

DRIVING, OR BEING IN CHARGE, WITH CONTROLLED DRUG ABOVE SPECIFIED LIMIT

Road Traffic Act 1988, s. 5A   **C5.57**

(1) This section applies where a person ('D')—
   (a) drives or attempts to drive a motor vehicle on a road or other public place, or
   (b) is in charge of a motor vehicle on a road or other public place,
   and there is in D's body a specified controlled drug.
(2) D is guilty of an offence if the proportion of the drug in D's blood or urine exceeds the specified limit for that drug.
(3) It is a defence for a person ('D') charged with an offence under this section to show that—
   (a) the specified controlled drug had been prescribed or supplied to D for medical or dental purposes,
   (b) D took the drug in accordance with any directions given by the person by whom the drug was prescribed or supplied, and with any accompanying instructions (so far as consistent with any such directions) given by the manufacturer or distributor of the drug, and
   (c) D's possession of the drug immediately before taking it was not unlawful under section 5(1) of the Misuse of Drugs Act 1971 (restriction of possession of controlled drugs)

because of an exemption in regulations made under section 7 of that Act (authorisation of activities otherwise unlawful under foregoing provisions).

(4) The defence in subsection (3) is not available if D's actions were—

    (a) contrary to any advice, given by the person by whom the drug was prescribed or supplied, about the amount of time that should elapse between taking the drug and driving a motor vehicle, or

    (b) contrary to any accompanying instructions about that matter (so far as consistent with any such advice) given by the manufacturer or distributor of the drug.

(5) If evidence is adduced that is sufficient to raise an issue with respect to the defence in subsection (3), the court must assume that the defence is satisfied unless the prosecution proves beyond reasonable doubt that it is not.

(6) It is a defence for a person ('D') charged with an offence by virtue of subsection (1)(b) to prove that at the time D is alleged to have committed the offence the circumstances were such that there was no likelihood of D driving the vehicle whilst the proportion of the specified controlled drug in D's blood or urine remained likely to exceed the specified limit for that drug.

(7) The court may, in determining whether there was such a likelihood, disregard any injury to D and any damage to the vehicle.

This is a new offence expressly dealing with drug-driving that has been inserted into the RTA 1988 by the CCA 2013, s. 56, but is not yet in force. It can be regarded as a development of the 'unfit' offence in the RTA 1988, s. 4, although there is no requirement to prove impairment (see C5.64). It is broadly similar to the alcohol-related offence in the RTA 1988, s. 5.

Elements

C5.58 The RTOA 1988, ss. 11 and 12(1) apply; see C2.17 and C2.18. For the meaning of the terms 'driving', 'road or other public place' and 'attempting', see C1.2 and C1.5, C1.13 and C1.16 and C1.20.

Because of the similarities with the offences in the RTA 1988, s. 5, see also generally C5.36 to C5.38. The RTOA 1988, ss. 15 and 16, apply, see generally C5.39 to C5.50. The statutory assumption in respect of the proportion of a specified controlled drug in a person's body (see C5.51) will be dealt with by amendments made by the CCA 2013, sch. 22, para. 10.

The drugs to be 'specified' will be set out in regulations to be made by the Secretary of State, as will the limits of drug permitted, which may be set at zero (s. 5A(8) and (9)).

Defences

C5.59 Section 5A(3) and (4) provides a defence for a defendant who shows that the drug in question was prescribed or supplied for medical or dental purposes, was used in accordance with appropriate instructions or directions and was not possessed by him contrary to the MDA 1971. The defendant bears the evidential burden of raising the defence and thereafter the prosecution must disprove it beyond reasonable doubt (s. 5A(5)).

The RTA 1988, s. 5A(6), provides a defence in respect of an allegation that the defendant was 'in charge' of the vehicle similar to that contained in s. 5(2) (see C5.54). In determining the likelihood, the court is permitted to disregard any injury to the defendant or damage to the vehicle (s. 5A(7)).

Punishment

C5.60 For offences of driving or attempting to drive, the penalty is six months' imprisonment and/or a fine up to level 5 on the standard scale. Disqualification and endorsement are obligatory unless there are 'special reasons', and the offence carries between three and 11 penalty points. Forfeiture of the vehicle may be ordered (see E18.1).

The offence of being 'in charge' carries six months' imprisonment and/or a fine up to level 4. Disqualification is discretionary; endorsement with ten penalty points is obligatory.

The *Magistrates' Court Sentencing Guidelines*, which must generally be followed, are likely to be supplemented to explain how to assess the offence seriousness by reference to the different levels of controlled drug found in the defendant's body, as well as by reference to the nature of the offending activity, and provide examples of aggravating and mitigating factors.

DRIVING, OR BEING IN CHARGE, WHEN UNDER THE INFLUENCE OF DRINK OR DRUGS

Road Traffic Act 1988, s. 4   C5.61

(1) A person who, when driving or attempting to drive a mechanically propelled vehicle on a road or other public place, is unfit to drive through drink or drugs is guilty of an offence.

(2) Without prejudice to subsection (1) above, a person who, when in charge of a mechanically propelled vehicle which is on a road or other public place, is unfit to drive through drink or drugs is guilty of an offence.

(3) For the purposes of subsection (2) above, a person shall be deemed not to have been in charge of a mechanically propelled vehicle if he proves that at the material time the circumstances were such that there was no likelihood of his driving it so long as he remained unfit to drive through drink or drugs.

(4) The court may, in determining whether there was such a likelihood as is mentioned in subsection (3) above, disregard any injury to him and any damage to the vehicle.

(5) For the purposes of this section, a person shall be taken to be unfit to drive if his ability to drive properly is for the time being impaired.

Elements

The RTOA 1988, ss. 11 and 12(1), apply; see **C2.17** and **C2.18**. The RTA 1988, s. 11, defines   **C5.62** 'drugs' as including any intoxicant other than alcohol. For the meaning of the terms 'driving', 'motor vehicle', 'road or other public place' and 'attempting', see **C1.2** and **C1.5**, **C1.9**, **C1.13** and **C1.16** and **C1.20**. For 'in charge', see **C5.38**.

Section 4 creates three separate offences. The prosecution must establish that the defendant was driving or attempting to drive, or was in charge of a motor vehicle on a road or public place, and that at the time his ability to drive properly was impaired though drink or drugs. The charge may read 'drink or drugs' without either being duplicitous or bad for uncertainty.

Drugs

Medicines are drugs for the purposes of the RTA 1988, s. 4, and include, e.g., insulin and tolu-   **C5.63** ene (*Armstrong v Clark* [1957] 2 QB 391; *Bradford v Wilson* (1983) 78 Cr App R 77). In *Watmore v Jenkins* [1962] 2 QB 572, the defendant had been overtaken by a hypoglycaemic episode and coma through a fall in his cortisone level and a consequent increase in his insulin level, brought about by a combination of injected insulin and an improvement in his liver function following recovery from an attack of jaundice. In those unusual circumstances, the Divisional Court upheld an acquittal of driving whilst unfit through drugs as the justices were entitled to 'entertain a reasonable doubt whether the injected insulin was more than a predisposing or historical cause' of the defendant's state.

In *Ealing Magistrates' Court, ex parte Woodman* [1994] RTR 181, the conviction of a diabetic suffering a hypoglycaemic attack was quashed because there was no evidence entitling the stipendiary magistrate to conclude that the presence of insulin in the applicant's blood was the real effective cause of the attack. The Divisional Court decided that it would only be appropriate to rely on s. 4 in such cases where there is evidence of a clear overdose of insulin having been taken by the defendant.

Evidence of Impairment

This may be provided by the opinion evidence of an expert witness, normally a doctor, who has   **C5.64** examined the defendant, even if he has refused to be examined, and his testimony should be treated as that of any 'independent expert witness giving evidence to assist the court', whether he be a police surgeon or anyone else (*Lanfear* [1968] 2 QB 77). Opinion evidence of the defendant's state or of the amount he has drunk may be given even by a lay witness, but the opinion of such a lay witness as to whether or not the defendant was fit to drive is not admissible. Nor could a lay witness give evidence as to the amount of alcohol in the defendant's blood. As to opinion evidence by lay witnesses generally, see **F10.2**.

The prosecution are not obliged to adduce opinion evidence of an expert witness in order to establish the defendant's impairment to drive, provided that the totality of the evidence actually adduced suffices to satisfy the justices of this element (*Leetham v DPP* [1999] RTR 29). Such evidence may include the manner of the driving, the defendant's apparent physical state and any admission made relating to the consumption of drugs and, presumably, alcohol. Presumably observations of a defendant's performance in a preliminary impairment test under the RTA 1988, s. 6B, will also be capable of being adduced as relevant evidence on this point.

The prosecution may adduce evidence of the amount of alcohol or a drug in a specimen properly provided by the defendant under the RTA 1988, s. 7. Such evidence is admissible by virtue of the RTOA 1988, ss. 15 and 16 (see **C5.43** and **C5.39**).

Defences

C5.65   The RTA 1988, s. 4(3), provides a defence to an allegation that the defendant was 'in charge' of the vehicle similar to that contained in s. 5(2) (see **C5.54**). The defence imposes a permissible legal burden, rather than just an evidential burden, on the defendant (*Sheldrake v DPP* [2004] 1 AC 264: see **C5.54**).

The defence may also adduce evidence of post-incident consumption to rebut the assumption that he was unfit at the time of the alleged offence (see the RTOA 1988, s. 15(3) and **C5.52**). Evidence of post-incident drug use may provide a defence in comparable circumstances.

Punishment

C5.66   For offences of driving or attempting to drive when unfit, the penalty is a maximum of six months' imprisonment and/or a fine up to level 5 on the standard scale. Endorsement and disqualification for one year are obligatory unless there are 'special reasons'. The offence carries between three and 11 penalty points. Forfeiture of the vehicle may be ordered (see **E18.1**).

The offence of being 'in charge' carries three months' imprisonment and/or a fine up to level 4. Disqualification is discretionary but endorsement with ten penalty points is obligatory.

The *Magistrates' Court Sentencing Guidelines* (see Supplement, **SG-341** and **SG-342**) must generally be followed; the Guidelines explain how to assess the offence seriousness by reference to the nature of the offending activity and provide examples of aggravating and mitigating factors.

INTERPRETATION OF THE ROAD TRAFFIC
ACT 1988, ss. 3A to 10

C5.67   Road Traffic Act 1988, s. 11

(1) The following provisions apply for the interpretation of sections 3A to 10 of this Act.
(2) In those sections—
       'drug' includes any intoxicant other than alcohol,
       'fail' includes refuse,
       'hospital' means an institution which provides medical or surgical treatment for in-patients or
          out-patients,
       'the prescribed limit' means, as the case may require—

    (a) 35 microgrammes of alcohol in 100 millilitres of breath,

    (b) 80 milligrammes of alcohol in 100 millilitres of blood, or

    (c) 107 milligrammes of alcohol in 100 millilitres of urine,

or such other proportion as may be prescribed by regulations made by the Secretary of State, 'registered health care professional' means a person (other than a medical practitioner) who is—

    (a) a registered nurse; or

    (b) a registered member of a health care profession which is designated for the purposes of this paragraph by an order made by the Secretary of State.

(2A) A health care profession is any profession mentioned in section 60(2) of the Health Act 1999 other than the profession of practising medicine and the profession of nursing.

(2B) An order under subsection (2) shall be made by statutory instrument; and any such statutory instrument shall be subject to annulment in pursuance of a resolution of either House of Parliament.

  (3) A person does not co-operate with a preliminary test or provide a specimen of breath for analysis unless his co-operation or the specimen—

    (a) is sufficient to enable the test or the analysis to be carried out, and

    (b) is provided in such a way as to enable the objective of the test or analysis to be satisfactorily achieved.

  (4) A person provides a specimen of blood if and only if—

    (a) he consents to the taking of such a specimen from him; and

    (b) the specimen is taken from him by a medical practitioner or, if it is taken in a police station, either by a medical practitioner or by a registered health care professional.

Section C6   Summary Traffic Offences

CARELESS AND INCONSIDERATE DRIVING

C6.1

Road Traffic Act 1988, s. 3

If a person drives a mechanically propelled vehicle on a road or other public place without due care and attention, or without reasonable consideration for other persons using the road or place, he is guilty of an offence.

Elements

C6.2 The RTOA 1988, ss. 1, 11 and 12(1), apply; see **C2.1**, **C2.17** and **C2.18**.

For the meaning of the terms 'drive', 'mechanically propelled vehicle' and 'road or other public place' see **C1.2** and **C1.5**, **C1.9** and **C1.13**, and **C1.16**. Section 3 creates two separate offences, commonly called 'careless driving' and 'driving without reasonable consideration'.

The term 'other persons using the road' includes persons who are pedestrians or passengers in vehicles, including that driven by the defendant, as well as other motorists (*Pawley v Wharldall* [1966] 1 QB 373).

Careless Driving

C6.3 Under the RTA 1988, s. 3ZA(2) and (3), the single test for driving without due care and attention is 'if (and only if)' the way the person drives 'falls below what would be expected of a competent and careful driver'. In addition to this objective standard, the court can consider any particular matters known at the time to the driver because, in determining what would be expected of a careful and competent driver, 'regard shall be had not only to the circumstances of which he could have been expected to be aware but also to any circumstances shown to have been within the knowledge of the accused'.

Previous case law, e.g., *Simpson v Peat* [1952] 2 QB 24, *DPP v Cox* (1993) 157 JP 1044 and the *obiter* comments of Lord Diplock in *Lawrence* [1982] AC 510, has effectively been codified.

C6.4 Departure from the standard of driving required by the Highway Code, whilst not in itself an offence, may well establish liability under the RTA 1988, s. 3, but adherence to the Highway Code may, equally, negative such a liability. For the admissibility of the provisions of the Highway Code, see the RTA 1988, s. 38, and **C2.16**. Each case must be objectively decided on its own facts in the surrounding circumstances. Only if the court considers that the driver has or must have failed to exercise the degree of care and attention which the reasonable, prudent and competent driver would have exercised, should a conviction result. It follows that a particular manner of driving may be careless in one situation but not in another.

On occasions, e.g., where a driver veers off in the course of overtaking and collides with an oncoming vehicle, the only inference that can be drawn is that the defendant drove carelessly. To draw another inference, such as mechanical defect, without any evidence to support that inference means that the justices have misdirected themselves (*DPP v Tipton* (1992) 156 JP 172). Crossing a road's dividing line is prima facie evidence of carelessness, necessitating an explanation which is acceptable on the facts (*Mundi v Warwickshire Police* [2001] EWHC 447 (Admin)).

In *DPP v Parker* [1989] RTR 413, the respondent had been driving in a line of traffic which came to a halt, and he ran into the back of the car in front which then ran into another car in front. He was not driving fast immediately before the accident and because of the rain, road conditions were wet and slippery. The Divisional Court held that while such driving might in other circumstances be sufficient to constitute an offence, whether it was sufficient in this case had been a question of fact. There was insufficient material to justify a finding that the justices' decision on the facts was perverse, and the appeal accordingly failed.

The CPS 'Policy for prosecuting cases of bad driving' gives the following examples of driving which **C6.5** may amount to driving without due care and attention: overtaking on the inside; driving inappropriately close to another vehicle; driving through a red light; emerging from a side road into the path of another vehicle; tuning a car radio; using a hand-held mobile phone or other hand-held electronic equipment where the driver was avoidably distracted by that use; and selecting and lighting a cigarette or similar where the driver was avoidably distracted by that use. These are indicative only and not conclusive as to the type of behaviour which might constitute careless driving.

Driving without Reasonable Consideration

By virtue of the RTA 1988, s. 3ZA(4), this offence is made out *only* if other road users are inconvenienced by the driving of the defendant. Evidence of such inconvenience may be provided either by the direct testimony of another road user, or by inference to be drawn from evidence of the reactions or behaviour of other road users. **C6.6**

The CPS 'Policy for prosecuting cases of bad driving' gives the following examples of conduct appropriate for a charge of driving without reasonable consideration: flashing of lights to *force* other drivers in front to give way; misuse of any lane to avoid queuing or gain some other advantage over other drivers; unnecessarily remaining in an overtaking lane; unnecessarily slow driving or braking without good cause; driving with undipped headlights that dazzle oncoming drivers; driving through a puddle causing pedestrians to be splashed; and driving a bus in such a way as to alarm passengers.

Defences

Mechanical defect, automatism, and necessity (*Backshall* [1998] 1 WLR 1506); see **C1.7**, **C6.7** **C1.21** and **A3.47**. No offence is committed under s. 3 where the driving took place in a public place other than a road in the course of an authorised motoring event (RTA 1988, s. 13A).

Alternative Verdicts

See the RTOA 1988, s. 24, set out at **C2.8**. **C6.8**

On a trial on indictment for an offence under the RTA 1988, s. 1, 1A, 2, 2B or 3A, the jury may find the defendant guilty of an offence under s. 3 (unless he has already been acquitted of it: *DPP v Khan* [1997] RTR 82), and the Crown Court has the same sentencing powers as a magistrates' court when that occurs. Where the prosecution have not accepted a guilty plea to careless driving and the defendant has been found not guilty of dangerous driving, without an alternative verdict having been entered, the previous guilty plea is a nullity and the court cannot proceed to sentence in respect of it (*McGregor-Read* [1999] Crim LR 860). The requirement for a notice under s. 1(1) of the RTOA 1988 is waived by s. 2(4) of that Act as long as the original requirement for a warning notice, if any, has been complied with.

It is not open to the prosecution to accept a plea of guilty to a charge of careless driving which has been committed for trial under the CJA 1988, s. 41, and offer no evidence on the indictable offence of reckless (now dangerous) driving (*Foote* [1993] RTR 171). Offences committed for trial under s. 41 can be dealt with only following a conviction for an indictable offence arising out of circumstances which are the same as or connected with the summary offence. The question whether the alternative finding of careless driving can be accepted as a guilty plea was left open in *Foote*, and now seems to have been answered in the affirmative in *Davis* (19 April 1996 unreported), which decided that a separate count for careless driving on an indictment containing a fatal driving count was invalid — the inference being that a plea to the latter count is available, despite the wording of s. 24 militating against any alternative finding of guilt other than by the jury.

If a defendant is acquitted, by magistrates, of an offence under s. 2, the court may direct or allow a charge for an offence under s. 3 to be preferred (RTOA 1988, s. 24(3)). This power extends to the Crown Court on an appeal against conviction for dangerous driving (*Killington v Butcher* [1979] Crim LR 458; Senior Courts Act 1981, s. 79(3)). The requirement for a notice of intended prosecution is waived by the RTOA 1988, s. 2(6), as long as the original requirement for a warning notice, if any, has been complied with.

In *Coventry Justices, ex parte Sayers* [1979] RTR 22, the court held that the six-month time limit did not apply to a charge preferred under s. 24(3).

Powers to Stop, Seize and Remove Vehicles

C6.9   Police Reform Act 2002, s. 59

    (1) Where a constable in uniform has reasonable grounds for believing that a motor vehicle is being used on any occasion in a manner which—
        (a) contravenes section 3 or 34 of the Road Traffic Act 1988 (careless and inconsiderate driving and prohibition of off-road driving), and
        (b) is causing, or is likely to cause, alarm, distress or annoyance to members of the public,
        he shall have the powers set out in subsection (3).
    (2) A constable in uniform shall also have the powers set out in subsection (3) where he has reasonable grounds for believing that a motor vehicle has been used on any occasion in a manner falling within subsection (1).
    (3) Those powers are—
        (a) power, if the motor vehicle is moving, to order the person driving it to stop the vehicle;
        (b) power to seize and remove the motor vehicle;
        (c) power, for the purposes of exercising a power falling within paragraph (a) or (b), to enter any premises on which he has reasonable grounds for believing the motor vehicle to be;
        (d) power to use reasonable force, if necessary, in the exercise of any power conferred by any of paragraphs (a) to (c).
    (4) A constable shall not seize a motor vehicle in the exercise of the powers conferred on him by this section unless—
        (a) he has warned the person appearing to him to be the person whose use falls within subsection (1) that he will seize it, if that use continues or is repeated; and
        (b) it appears to him that the use has continued or been repeated after the warning.
    (5) Subsection (4) does not require a warning to be given by a constable on any occasion on which he would otherwise have the power to seize a motor vehicle under this section if—
        (a) the circumstances make it impracticable for him to give the warning;
        (b) the constable has already on that occasion given a warning under that subsection in respect of any use of that motor vehicle or of another motor vehicle by that person or any other person;
        (c) the constable has reasonable grounds for believing that such a warning has been given on that occasion otherwise than by him; or
        (d) the constable has reasonable grounds for believing that the person whose use of that motor vehicle on that occasion would justify the seizure is a person to whom a warning under that

subsection has been given (whether or not by that constable or in respect the same vehicle or the same or a similar use) on a previous occasion in the previous twelve months.

(6) A person who fails to comply with an order under subsection (3)(a) is guilty of an offence and shall be liable, on summary conviction, to a fine not exceeding level 3 on the standard scale.

(7) Subsection (3)(c) does not authorise entry into a private dwelling house.

(8) The powers conferred on a constable by this section shall be exercisable only at a time when regulations under section 60 are in force.

(9) In this section—

'driving' has the same meaning as in the Road Traffic Act 1988;

'motor vehicle' means any mechanically propelled vehicle, whether or not it is intended or adapted for use on roads; and

'private dwelling house' does not include any garage or other structure occupied with the dwelling house, or any land appurtenant to the dwelling house.

The Police (Retention and Disposal of Motor Vehicles) Regulations 2002 (SI 2002 No. 3049) have been made under s. 60. **C6.10**

The Secretary of State is empowered to appoint 'stopping officers' for specified purposes in relation to commercial vehicles (Road Vehicles (Powers to Stop) Regulations 2011 (SI 2011 No. 996)).

Punishment

The offence carries a fine up to level 5 on the standard scale. Disqualification is discretionary but **C6.11** endorsement, in the absence of 'special reasons', with between three and nine penalty points is obligatory. In appropriate cases, the court may disqualify the defendant until a driving test is passed under the RTOA 1988, s. 36 (see *Miller* (1994) 15 Cr App R (S) 505 at **C7.34**). Because the offence does not carry obligatory disqualification, it is not permitted to disqualify until an extended driving test is passed (*Kruger* [2013] 1 Cr App R (S) 608 (17)). A fixed penalty of £100 is available for this offence (Fixed Penalty Offences Order 2013 (SI 2013 No. 1565)).

Sentencing

The *Magistrates' Court Sentencing Guidelines* (see Supplement, **SG-329**) must generally be fol- **C6.12** lowed; the Guidelines explain how to assess the offence seriousness by reference to the nature of the offending activity and provide examples of aggravating and mitigating factors. The maximum fine of £5,000 should be reserved only for the worst instances of careless driving where the defendant also has the means to pay (*Holman* [2010] RTR 257 and *Christie* [2012] 2 Cr App R (S) 273, where the fine was reduced to £3,000 in respect of a defendant, recently returned from America, pulling out from a car park into a main road causing an approaching vehicle to take evasive action and driving the wrong way down the road for 185 metres before being involved in a head-on collision). An argument that it was wrong in principle to disqualify two police officers, who had driven separate vehicles on a motorway at speeds exceeding 90 mph when there was no operational need to do so, because it would deprive the public of the services they provided, was rejected in *Perkins* [2012] EWCA Crim 218 (although, having regard to all the circumstances of the case, the eight month discretionary disqualifications were quashed).

As to compensation orders, see **E16**, particularly **E16.1**.

MOTOR RACING ON HIGHWAYS

Road Traffic Act 1988, s. 12 **C6.13**

(1) A person who promotes or takes part in a race or trial of speed between motor vehicles on a public way is guilty of an offence.

Elements

C6.14 The RTOA 1988, ss. 11 and 12(1), apply; see **C2.17** and **C2.18**.

This offence seems intended to prohibit organised motor racing on a highway, but might equally apply where two or more drivers are engaged in an unofficial race or speed trial. Such conduct may, of course, be an offence under the RTRA 1984, s. 88(7), or the RTA 1988, s. 2 or 3, but its ambit appears to be wider as persons who 'promote' or 'take part' may be convicted, and there is thus no requirement to prove an act of driving but merely of participation.

Punishment

C6.15 The offence carries a fine of up to level 4 on the standard scale. Unless 'special reasons' are established, there is a minimum disqualification from driving for a period of 12 months. Persons who 'promote' or 'take part' must be disqualified even though they are not drivers. The offence is endorsable with between three and 11 penalty points.

LEAVING VEHICLE IN DANGEROUS POSITION

C6.16   Road Traffic Act 1988, s. 22

If a person in charge of a vehicle causes or permits the vehicle or a trailer drawn by it to remain at rest on a road in such a position or in such condition or in such circumstances as to involve a danger of injury to other persons using the road, he is guilty of an offence.

Elements

C6.17 For the meaning of the terms 'causing', 'permitting' and 'using', see **C1.23**, **C1.25** and **C1.28**. The RTOA 1988, ss. 1, 11 and 12(1), apply; see **C2.1**, **C2.17** and **C2.18**.

Section 22 applies to any vehicle, not just a motor vehicle. The offence may be established either where the vehicle itself involves a danger of injury (e.g., if it is on fire or parked on a hill without brakes and secured only by stones or bricks placed under the wheels), or where, because of its position on the road, it creates a danger. For example, parking a car or other vehicle on the corner of a busy intersection, obstructing the view of other motorists emerging from a side road, involves a danger of injury, because motorists would be forced to emerge 'blind' and, however cautiously this was done, the likelihood of a collision and consequent injury would remain.

Punishment

C6.18 A fine up to level 3 on the standard scale. If committed in respect of a motor vehicle, disqualification is discretionary and endorsement with three penalty points is obligatory. A fixed penalty of £100 is available for this offence.

RESTRICTION OF CARRIAGE OF PERSONS ON MOTOR CYCLES

C6.19   Road Traffic Act 1988, s. 23

(1) Not more than one person in addition to the driver may be carried on a motor bicycle.
(2) No person in addition to the driver may be carried on a motor bicycle otherwise than sitting astride the motor cycle and on a proper seat securely fixed to the motor cycle behind the driver's seat.
(3) If a person is carried on a motor cycle in contravention of this section, the driver of the motor cycle is guilty of an offence.

Elements

The RTOA 1988, ss. 11 and 12(1), apply; see **C2.17** and **C2.18**.   C6.20

Punishment

The offence carries a fine up to level 3. Disqualification is discretionary and endorsement with   C6.21
three penalty points obligatory. A fixed penalty of £100 is available for this offence.

NEGLECT OR REFUSAL TO COMPLY WITH TRAFFIC DIRECTIONS GIVEN BY CONSTABLE

Road Traffic Act 1988, s. 35   C6.22

(1) Where a constable or traffic officer is for the time being engaged in the regulation of traffic in
a road, a person driving or propelling a vehicle who neglects or refuses—
(a) to stop the vehicle, or
(b) to make it proceed in, or keep to, a particular line of traffic,
when directed to do so by the constable in the execution of his duty or the traffic officer (as the
case may be) is guilty of an offence.
(2) Where—
(a) a traffic survey of any description is being carried out on or in the vicinity of a
road, and
(b) a constable or traffic officer gives to a person driving or propelling a vehicle a direction—
(i) to stop the vehicle,
(ii) to make it proceed in, or keep to, a particular line of traffic, or
(iii) to proceed to a particular point on or near the road on which the vehicle is being
driven or propelled,
being a direction given for the purposes of the survey (but not a direction requiring any
person to provide any information for the purposes of a traffic survey),
the person is guilty of an offence if he neglects or refuses to comply with the direction.
(3) The power to give such a direction as is referred to in subsection (2) above for the purposes
of a traffic survey shall be so exercised as not to cause any unreasonable delay to a person
who indicates that he is unwilling to provide any information for the purposes of the
survey.

Elements

The RTOA 1988, ss. 1, 11 and 12(1), apply; see **C2.1**, **C2.17**, and **C2.18**.   C6.23

This section extends to any vehicle as long as it is being driven or propelled. The reference to a
constable includes a traffic warden if he is engaged in accordance with s. 35 in the regulation of
traffic in the road.

There are two offences created. For an offence under s. 35(2), the constable must be giving a
direction for the purposes of a traffic survey. Under s. 35(1), the constable must be acting in the
execution of his duty, which in this case means a duty to protect life and property arising from
the dangers created by unregulated traffic (*Hoffman v Thomas* [1974] 2 All ER 233; *Johnson v
Phillips* [1976] 3 All ER 682). It is arguable, therefore, that for s. 35 to operate, the constable
must have been engaged upon traffic duties and not exercising his powers either under the
PACE 1984 or the RTA 1988, s. 163.

Punishment

The offence carries a fine up to level 3. If the offence is committed in respect of a motor vehicle,   C6.24
disqualification is discretionary, but endorsement with three penalty points is obligatory. The
Magistrates' Court Sentencing Guidelines (see Supplement, SG-346) give fine band A as the starting point. A fixed penalty of £100 is available for this offence.

FAILURE TO COMPLY WITH INDICATION
GIVEN BY TRAFFIC SIGN

C6.25   Road Traffic Act 1988, s. 36

(1) Where a traffic sign, being a sign—
    (a) of the prescribed size, colour and type, or
    (b) of another character authorised by the Secretary of State under the provisions in that behalf of the Road Traffic Regulation Act 1984,
    has been lawfully placed on or near a road, a person driving or propelling a vehicle who fails to comply with the indication given by the sign is guilty of an offence.
(2) A traffic sign shall not be treated for the purposes of this section as having been lawfully placed unless either—
    (a) the indication given by the sign is an indication of a statutory prohibition, restriction or requirement, or
    (b) it is expressly provided by or under any provision of the Traffic Acts that this section shall apply to the sign or to signs of a type of which the sign is one; and, where the indication mentioned in paragraph (a) of this subsection is of the general nature only of the prohibition, restriction or requirement to which the sign relates, a person shall not be convicted of failure to comply with the indication unless he has failed to comply with the prohibition, restriction or requirement to which the sign relates.

Elements

C6.26 The RTOA 1988, ss. 1, 11, 12(1) and 20, apply; see **C2.1**, **C2.17**, **C2.18**, and **C2.21**.

Traffic signs are prescribed by regulations made under the RTRA 1984, s. 64. If a sign indicates a statutory prohibition, restriction or requirement, or if it is expressly provided under any provision of the Traffic Acts that the section applies to the sign, a failure to comply with it is an offence.

The main relevant statutory instrument is the Traffic Signs Regulations and General Directions 2002 (SI 2002 No. 3113). Failure to comply with any traffic sign may constitute an offence but only failure by a person driving a motor vehicle to comply with a sign of a kind specified in reg. 10(2) of the regulations carries endorsement and disqualification. The signs so specified are 'Stop' signs at the junction of minor and major roads; 'double white lines'; 'Drivers of Large or Slow Vehicles Must Phone' signs at automatic half-barrier level crossings or automatic open crossings; and the red signal when shown by light signals prescribed by the regulations.

Emergency traffic signs are included, and all signs are deemed to conform unless the contrary is proved.

Save for possible defences of mechanical defect or automatism (as to which, see **C1.7** and **C1.21**), the section creates an absolute offence.

For contravention of the 'Stop' sign, it is necessary to prove either that the vehicle did not stop before crossing the line or, if the line is unclear, before entering the major road, or that the vehicle when proceeding past the line or entering the major road, if that line is not clearly visible, did so in a manner likely to cause danger to the driver of another vehicle on the major road, or so as to cause that driver to change his speed or course so as to avoid an accident.

For contravention of a red light, it is necessary to prove that the vehicle proceeded beyond the stop line or, if that is not visible or there is no stop line, beyond the mounting of the primary signal.

C6.27 Regulation 36(1)(b) contains a waiver of the prohibition conveyed by the red light for vehicles being used for fire brigade, ambulance or police purposes, and substitutes instead a requirement that the vehicle will not proceed so as to cause danger to the driver of another vehicle, or to necessitate the driver of any such vehicle to change his speed or course in order to avoid an accident or so as to cause danger to non-vehicular traffic. As to when a vehicle is properly classified as a vehicle used for ambulance purposes, see *DPP v Issler* [2014] EWHC 669 (Admin), discussed at **C6.34**. In *Craggy v Chief Constable of Cleveland Police* [2009] EWCA Civ 1128, albeit in a civil context, expecting the driver of an emergency vehicle to drive in such a manner that he could stop in the event of another emergency vehicle emerging from the junction was held to impose an unreasonably high burden well beyond what can be expected of a reasonable and prudent driver.

The prohibition contained by 'double white lines' operates not only to prevent the vehicle crossing those lines, but also to forbid vehicles stopping on any length of road along which the marking has been placed. Regulation 26 does, however, contain certain exemptions for vehicles which have to cross the line for the purposes of obtaining access or to pass a stationary vehicle, to enable passengers to board and alight, and so forth. Stopping within double white lines to pick up a taxi fare is not an offence (*McKenzie v DPP* [1997] RTR 175).

Where there was a failure to place a white arrow before solid double white lines in the centre of the road the lines were not a sign 'lawfully placed' for the purposes of the regulations and directions then in force and failure to comply with the double white lines was, therefore, not an offence contrary to s. 36 of the RTA 1988 (*O'Halloran v DPP* [1990] RTR 62).

Punishment

The offence carries a fine up to level 3. If committed in respect of a motor vehicle by a failure to comply with a specified sign (see **C6.26**), disqualification is discretionary, but endorsement with three penalty points is obligatory. The *Magistrates' Court Sentencing Guidelines* (see Supplement, **SG-346**) give fine band A as the starting point. A fixed penalty of £100 is available for this offence.   **C6.28**

USING VEHICLE IN DANGEROUS CONDITION

Road Traffic Act 1988, s. 40A   **C6.29**

(1) A person is guilty of an offence if he uses, or causes or permits another to use, a motor vehicle or trailer on a road when—
  (a) the condition of the motor vehicle or trailer, or of its accessories or equipment, or
  (b) the purpose for which it is used, or
  (c) the number of passengers carried by it, or the manner in which they are carried, or
  (d) the weight, position or distribution of its load, or the manner in which it is secured, is such that the use of the motor vehicle or trailer involves a danger of injury to any person.

Elements

The RTOA 1988, ss. 11 and 12(1), apply; see **C2.17** and **C2.18**. For the meaning of the terms 'using', 'causing' and 'permitting' see **C1.28**, **C1.23**, and **C1.25**. The RTOA 1988, ss. 14 and 17, make provision about the admissibility of authenticated records as evidence of matters stated therein and of evidence relating to weights and dates of manufacture being presumed to be accurately marked on vehicles.   **C6.30**

Section 40A puts into statute the more important construction and use requirements and widens the scope of their operation. For example, if the circumstances applying in *Young and C F Abraham (Transport) Ltd v CPS* [1992] RTR 194 (see **C6.35**) were to be repeated, s. 40A(d) would apply. Where a passenger is carried in the rear of a van and there are no seats or restraints of any kind there, the speed at which the van is driven will be a material consideration in relation to whether the manner of carriage is such as to involve a danger of injury under s. 40A(c) (*Akelis v Normand* 1997 SLT 136). Section 40A(c) involves considering objectively whether there was a danger inherent in the circumstances in which the vehicle was being driven at the material time (*Gray v DPP* [1999] RTR 339). Accordingly, when assessing that danger, justices can take into account the locality of the offence and the prevailing traffic conditions but must disregard any consequences, such as a serious accident, of the driving involved (*DPP v Potts* [2000] RTR 1).

Punishment

C6.31 The offence is endorsable with three penalty points; disqualification is discretionary. In respect of a second offence committed within three years of a previous s. 40A offence, in the absence of 'special reasons', disqualification for six months is obligatory, although for other offences it will remain discretionary only (Road Safety Act 2006, s. 25(1)). However, the RTOA 1988, s. 48(1), forbids the court from disqualifying or ordering any penalty points to be ordered if the defendant proves he did not know, and had no reasonable cause to suspect, that the use of the vehicle involved a danger of injury to any person. Where the offence is committed in respect of a goods vehicle or a vehicle adapted to carry more than eight passengers, a fine of up to level 5 may be imposed; in other cases, a fine up to level 4 may be imposed. The *Magistrates' Court Sentencing Guidelines* (see Supplement, SG-345) must generally be followed; they apply to the various offences covered and explain the appropriate starting points for fine bands, differentiating between drivers, driver-owners and owner-companies. A fixed penalty of £100 is available for this offence.

CONTRAVENTION OF CONSTRUCTION AND USE REGULATIONS

C6.32 Road Traffic Act 1988, s. 41A

(1) A person who—
   (a) contravenes or fails to comply with a construction and use requirement as to brakes, steering-gear or tyres, or
   (b) uses on a road a motor vehicle or trailer which does not comply with such a requirement, or causes or permits a motor vehicle or trailer to be so used,
   is guilty of an offence.

Section 41B makes contravention of a requirement in relation to the weight of a goods vehicle or a passenger vehicle adapted to carry more than eight passengers an offence. It is a defence if the vehicle is proceeding to or from the nearest available weighbridge, which means the nearest one factually, irrespective of the driver's knowledge of its existence (*Vehicle and Operator Services Agency v F & S Gibbs Transport Services Ltd* [2007] RTR 193). In addition a 5 per cent excess may be excluded in certain circumstances. It is not essential for a certificate as to the accuracy of the weighbridge to be produced provided there is other evidence from which its accuracy can be ascertained (*Kelly Communications Ltd v DPP* (2003) 167 JP 73).

When the Road Safety Act 2006, s. 18, is brought into force, a new offence under the RTA 1988, s. 41C, will be created prohibiting vehicles being fitted with, or a person using a vehicle carrying, 'speed assessment equipment detection devices', which are devices 'the purpose, or one of the purposes, of which is to detect, or interfere with the operation of, equipment used to assess the speed of motor vehicles'.

Section 42 makes contravention of the other construction and use requirements an offence and extends this to cover 'using', 'causing' or 'permitting'.

Mobile Telephones, etc.

C6.33 The Road Safety Act 2006, s. 26, introduced an offence under the RTA 1988, s. 41D, dealing specifically with a contravention or failure to comply with a requirement about not driving a motor vehicle in a position which does not give proper control or a full view of the road or traffic ahead or not driving, or supervising the driving, of a motor vehicle while using a hand-held mobile telephone or other hand-held interactive communication device. The offence extends to 'causing' or 'permitting' (see **C1.23** and **C1.25**). The principal reason for carving out such a specific offence was to make endorsement with penalty points obligatory and disqualification discretionary, thereby raising its seriousness closer to the alternative of charging driving without due care and attention.

Elements

The RTOA 1988, ss. 11 and 12(1), apply to the RTA 1988, ss. 41A, 41B, 41D and 42 (and, in due course, will apply to the RTA 1988, s. 41C); see **C2.17** and **C2.18**. For the meaning of the terms 'using', 'causing' and 'permitting', see **C1.28**, **C1.23**, and **C1.25**. The relevant requirements are those contained in the Road Vehicles (Construction and Use) Regulations 1986 (SI 1986 No. 1078).

C6.34

In order to show that a vehicle does not fall within any of the definitions contained either in the regulations or the Act, the burden of proof is on the defendant (*Wakeman v Catlow* [1977] RTR 174). To qualify as a motor vehicle used for ambulance purposes, the vehicle used 'must at the very least be capable of conveying sick, injured or disabled persons and do so with such frequency that this core activity may fairly and properly be designated as its primary use' (*DPP v Issler* [2014] EWHC 669 (Admin)).

Regulations 13 to 18 and sch. 3 deal with brakes. Even if a trailer is not required to have brakes under reg. 18, any brakes fitted must be maintained in efficient working order (*DPP v Young* [1991] RTR 56). Regulation 27 deals with tyres.

C6.35

Regulation 100 deals with vehicles which are in a dangerous condition and loads which cause a danger. See the RTA 1988, s. 42(2), for a statutory defence to a summons alleging a failure to comply with a requirement relating to any description of weight applicable to a goods vehicle. In *Young and C F Abraham (Transport) Ltd v CPS* [1992] RTR 194, a trailer loaded with an excavator collided with a footbridge because the excavator arms and bucket had not been lowered. The driver and the company were prosecuted for using a trailer for an unsuitable purpose 'as to cause or be likely to cause danger or nuisance to any person . . . on a road'. The Divisional Court decided that the risk came from the incorrect loading rather than the use of the trailer and that, in such circumstances, the offence was not made out.

In respect of an offence under the RTA 1988, s. 41D, reg. 110 imposes a range of restrictions involving driving-related activities that cannot be undertaken whilst the person is using a hand-held mobile telephone or a prescribed hand-held device. Regulation 110(5) contains specific exceptions for calls to the emergency services, where it is a response to a genuine emergency and if it would be unsafe or impracticable to cease the driving-related activity before making the call.

An examination of a vehicle, for the purposes of a prosecution, which involves a permanent alteration to its condition does not render the evidence thereby obtained inadmissible under the PACE 1984, s. 78, merely because the defence are unable to examine the vehicle in its original condition. It would be prudent for the prosecution to inform the defence of their examination and to afford them an opportunity to be present, but justices should hear such evidence and the fact that the defence are denied an opportunity to examine the vehicle goes to weight rather than admissibility (*DPP v British Telecommunications plc* [1991] Crim LR 532).

Punishment

A breach of s. 41A is endorsable with three penalty points; disqualification is discretionary. However, the RTOA 1988, s. 48(2), forbids the court to disqualify or order any penalty points if the defendant proves he did not know, and had no reasonable cause to suspect, that the facts of the case were such that the offence would be committed. Where an offence is committed in respect of a goods vehicle or a vehicle adapted to carry more than eight passengers, a fine of up to level 5 may be imposed; in other cases, a fine up to level 4. A fixed penalty of £200 is available.

C6.36

Breaches of s. 41B or 42 are not endorsable. Section 41B carries a fine up to level 5 and graduated fixed penalties (see **C7.3**) are applicable to various offences thereunder, up to a maximum of £300. Section 42 carries a fine up to level 4 if committed in respect of a goods vehicle or a vehicle adapted to carry more than eight passengers; in other cases, a fine of up to level 3.

The s. 41D offence is endorsable with three penalty points; disqualification is discretionary. Where an offence is committed in respect of a goods vehicle or a vehicle adapted to carry more than eight passengers, a fine up to level 4 may be imposed; in other cases, a fine up to level 3. A fixed penalty of £100 is available.

Breach of s. 41C (not yet in force) will be subject to the same penalty as a speeding offence, i.e. it is endorsable with between three and six penalty points or three points when a fixed penalty is imposed. It will carry a fine up to level 4 if committed on a special road (such as a motorway); in other cases, a fine up to level 3.

The *Magistrates' Court Sentencing Guidelines* (see Supplement, **SG-345** and **SG-346**) must generally be followed; they apply to the various offences covered and explain the appropriate starting points for fine bands, differentiating between drivers, driver-owners and owner-companies.

DRIVING OTHERWISE THAN IN ACCORDANCE WITH A LICENCE

C6.37   Road Traffic Act 1988, s. 87

(1) It is an offence for a person to drive on a road a motor vehicle of any class otherwise than in accordance with a licence authorising him to drive a motor vehicle of that class.
(2) It is an offence for a person to cause or permit another person to drive on a road a motor vehicle of any class otherwise than in accordance with a licence authorising that other person to drive a motor vehicle of that class.

This offence encompasses driving without 'L' plates or (an alternative applicable only within Wales) 'D' plates, without supervision, driving under age and driving without a licence.

Elements

C6.38   The RTOA 1988, ss. 11 and 12(1), apply; see **C2.17** and **C2.18**. For the meaning of 'cause' and 'permit', see **C1.23** and **C1.25**.

Section 88 of the Act creates certain exceptions. The approach to proof is the same as for the offence of no insurance (see **C6.47**).

Foreign drivers are subject to the Motor Vehicles (International Circulation) Order 1975 (SI 1975 No. 1208). If a person resident abroad and temporarily resident in Great Britain holds a Convention driving permit, a foreign driving permit or a British Forces (BFG) driving licence, it shall be lawful for him to drive during a period of 12 months from his last entry into the UK (unless he is under the minimum age or disqualified by court order). Community licence holders normally resident in Great Britain are no longer obliged to exchange their licences for ones issued under the 1988 Act so as to obtain continuing authorisation to drive (s. 99A of the Act), the only requirement being to deliver their Community licences within the prescribed period to the Secretary of State to enable counterparts to be issued (s. 99B of the Act). When dealing with Community licence holders, it is not inconsistent with Directive 91/439/EEC for a person to hold, or to have held, more than one valid driving licence simultaneously (*Criminal proceedings concerning Schwarz (Case C-321/07)* [2009] RTR 23). However, where the right to drive in Great Britain has been withdrawn, that status prevails over any claim to be entitled to drive by virtue of a licence issued by another Member State (*Criminal proceedings concerning Weber (Case C-1/07)* [2009] RTR 57; *Schwarz*).

Punishment

C6.39   The offence carries a fine up to level 3. If the offender's driving would not have been in accordance with a licence that could have been granted, then, in the absence of 'special reasons', disqualification is discretionary and endorsement with between three and six penalty points is obligatory. A fixed penalty of £100 is available.

An offence of causing or permitting a person to drive without an appropriate licence contrary to s. 87(2) is punishable only by a fine up to level 3 on the standard scale. The *Magistrates' Court*

Sentencing Guidelines (see Supplement, **SG-344**) give fine band A as the starting point and note that if no licence has ever been held that is an aggravating factor.

DRIVING WHILE DISQUALIFIED

Road Traffic Act 1988, s. 103

C6.40

(1) A person is guilty of an offence if, while disqualified for holding or obtaining a licence, he—
 (a) obtains a licence, or
 (b) drives a motor vehicle on a road.
(2) A licence obtained by a person who is disqualified is of no effect (or, where the disqualification relates only to vehicles of a particular class, is of no effect in relation to vehicles of that class).
(3) [Repealed.]
(4) Subsection (1) above does not apply in relation to disqualification by virtue of section 101 of this Act.
(5) Subsection (1)(b) above does not apply in relation to disqualification by virtue of section 102 of this Act.
(6) In the application of subsection (1) above to a person whose disqualification is limited to the driving of motor vehicles of a particular class by virtue of—
 (a) section 102, 117 or 117A of this Act, or
 (b) subsection (9) of section 36 of the Road Traffic Offenders Act 1988 (disqualification until test is passed),
 the references to disqualification for holding or obtaining a licence and driving motor vehicles are references to disqualification for holding or obtaining a licence to drive and driving motor vehicles of that class.

Elements

In the absence of duress, the RTA 1988, s. 103(1)(b), creates an absolute offence. It is usual to produce either the register of the magistrates' court where the defendant was disqualified, or a properly certified extract. A conviction may be proved under the PACE 1984, s. 73, by the production of a certificate signed by the clerk of the court. (As to the proof of convictions generally, see **F11.1** *et seq.*) Other authorised methods of proving the conviction are equally admissible, but it is not necessary to prove that the defendant knew of the disqualification (*Taylor v Kenyon* [1952] 2 All ER 726).

C6.41

In *Derwentside Justices, ex parte Heaviside* [1996] RTR 384, the Divisional Court held that strict proof linking the defendant to the person named in the certificate of conviction is required. In doing so, it identified three methods by which this requirement could be satisfied: an admission under the CJA 1967, s. 10; comparison of fingerprints; or evidence from a person who was present in court when the disqualification was imposed. The fear that this list was exhaustive has been allayed by subsequent decisions of the Divisional Court (*Derwentside Justices, ex parte Swift* [1997] RTR 89; *DPP v Mansfield* [1997] RTR 96; *DPP v Mooney* [1997] RTR 434). Consequently, whilst strict proof is necessary (and failure by the prosecution to adduce any such evidence cannot be cured by information provided by the clerk to the court from computerised court records (*Kingsnorth v DPP* [2003] EWHC 768 (Admin)), the prosecution can rely on any admissible evidence from which it could properly be concluded that the defendant and the individual named in the certificate are one and the same person, and the issue is one for the court to determine on the basis of the evidence placed before it. For example, admissions in an interview with the police provide sufficient evidence (*Moran v CPS* (2000) 164 JP 562). Where the defendant has an unusual name, proof that it is identical to that of a person previously disqualified raises a prima facie case that the defendant is that disqualified person (*Olakunori v DPP* [1998] COD 443), especially if he has also lied about his identity. Even where the personal details of the defendant are not uncommon, a match with those recorded on the certificate of conviction establishes a prima facie case which, in the absence of any contradictory evidence, will be sufficient for the court to convict (*Pattison v DPP* [2006] 2 All ER 317).

In *Thames Magistrates' Court, ex parte Levy* (1997) *The Times*, 17 July 1997, it was confirmed that the offence of driving while disqualified can be committed during a period of disqualification

C6.42

Part C Road Traffic Offences

which is not suspended pending an appeal (see the RTOA 1988, s. 39, and **C7.40**), even where the conviction which led to the disqualification is subsequently quashed. Similarly, the offence can be committed in the period between disqualification following conviction and the swearing of a statutory declaration under the MCA 1980, s. 14, as the earlier proceedings become void from the time of the declaration and not *ab initio* (*Singh v DPP* [1999] RTR 424).

Where a person has been disqualified until he passes a test, under the RTOA 1988, s. 36, a failure to comply with the conditions of a provisional driving licence is an offence under s. 103(1)(b). This would seem to be the case whether or not the defendant has actually obtained such a licence (*Scott v Jelf* [1974] RTR 256). In order to avoid conviction, the defendant bears the burden of showing that he holds a provisional licence and that he was complying with the conditions attached to it at the time of the driving in question (*DPP v Baker* (2004) 168 JP 617). For the purposes of s. 103, such disqualifications persist regardless of whether elements of the original sentence would enable the offence in respect of which disqualification was imposed to be regarded as spent (*Re Hamill* [2001] EWHC Admin 762).

If a defendant drives on a 'road', his mistaken belief that it was not a road is incapable of amounting to a defence (*Miller* [1975] 2 All ER 974).

Aiding and abetting the offence of driving while disqualified requires knowledge of the disqualification; this may be actual or constructive, in the sense that the defendant failed to make inquiries which a reasonable person should have made, or deliberately closed his eyes to the possibility of the driver being disqualified (*Pope v Minton* [1954] Crim LR 711; *Bateman v Evans* [1964] Crim LR 601).

Defences

C6.43 Duress or necessity may provide a defence in the proper circumstances. See **A3.35** to **A3.52**.

Indictment

C6.44 The CJA 1988 made the offence summary only, but provides in s. 40 (see **D11.17**) for certain circumstances where it may be included in an indictment and that thereafter it 'shall be tried in the same manner as if it were an indictable offence'. Consequently, the offence is therefore no longer an 'indictable offence' within the meaning of the Criminal Attempts Act 1981 (see **A5.68**), and the offence of attempting to drive while disqualified has ceased to exist.

Punishment

C6.45 The maximum sentence is six months' imprisonment and/or a fine up to level 5 on the standard scale. Disqualification is discretionary but endorsement is obligatory. The offence carries six penalty points. Forfeiture of the vehicle used may also be ordered (see **E18.1**). The *Magistrates' Court Sentencing Guidelines* (see Supplement, **SG-333**) must generally be followed; the Guidelines explain how to assess the offence seriousness by reference to the nature of the offending activity and provide examples of aggravating and mitigating factors. See *Pegrum* (1986) 8 Cr App R (S) 27 for a case in which the maximum term of imprisonment (then one year) was upheld. There is nothing wrong in principle in imposing a consecutive sentence to that imposed for another offence arising out of the same incident, e.g., aggravated vehicle-taking (*Forbes* [2005] EWCA Crim 2069).

USING ETC. MOTOR VEHICLE WITHOUT INSURANCE

C6.46
Road Traffic Act 1988, s. 143

(1) Subject to the provisions of this Part of this Act—
  (a) a person must not use a motor vehicle on a road or other public place unless there is in force in relation to the use of the vehicle by that person such a policy of insurance or such a security in respect of third party risks as complies with the requirements of this Part of this Act, and

(b) a person must not cause or permit any other person to use a motor vehicle on a road or other public place unless there is in force in relation to the use of the vehicle by that other person such a policy of insurance or such a security in respect of third party risks as complies with the requirements of this Part of this Act.

(2) If a person acts in contravention of subsection (1) above he is guilty of an offence.

(3) A person charged with using a motor vehicle in contravention of this section shall not be convicted if he proves—

(a) that the vehicle did not belong to him and was not in his possession under a contract of hiring or of loan,

(b) that he was using the vehicle in the course of his employment, and

(c) that he neither knew nor had reason to believe that there was not in force in relation to the vehicle such a policy of insurance or security as is mentioned in subsection (1) above.

(4) This Part of this Act does not apply to invalid carriages.

Elements

The RTOA 1988, ss. 6, 11, and 12(1), apply; see **C2.5**, **C2.17**, and **C2.18**. For the meaning of **C6.47** the terms 'use', 'cause', and 'permit', see **C1.28**, **C1.23**, and **C1.25**.

The burden of proof rests on the defendant, i.e. he is required to produce evidence of a valid insurance policy (*DPP v Kavaz* [1999] RTR 40), whether or not there has been any requirement to produce this under the pro forma HORT/1 or otherwise (*DPP v Hay* [2006] RTR 32).

For the owner of a vehicle to be convicted of using without insurance when it was being driven by someone else, it has to be proved that the defendant owned the vehicle and that the driver at the time was employed by the owner and was, at the material time, acting in the course of his employment (*Jones v DPP* [1999] RTR 1).

The section imposes an absolute liability irrespective of knowledge, even if the charge is for 'causing' or 'permitting' (*Lyons v May* [1948] 2 All ER 1062; *Tapsell v Maslen* [1967] Crim LR 53). However, if the person who allows the use of a vehicle does so on the express condition that the user insures it, he is not 'permitting' the uninsured use of the vehicle within the meaning of s. 143 (*Newbury v Davis* [1974] RTR 367). That case, however, appears to be confined to its own facts. In *DPP v Fisher* [1992] RTR 93, the Divisional Court declined to follow *Newbury* where the driver of the vehicle was not in communication directly with the owner even though the owner only authorised the use of the vehicle by a suitably insured person. Lack of knowledge of unauthorised use of a vehicle does not constitute 'permitting'.

Section 144 of the RTA 1988 contains certain exceptions. The requirements of a policy of insurance are set out in the RTA 1988, s. 145.

By s. 161, 'policy of insurance' includes a covering note. By s. 147(1), a policy of insurance is of no effect under s. 143 until delivered to the party by whom the policy is effected. The burden is on the defendant to prove the facts necessary to establish the statutory defence for employees in s. 143(3).

A policy of insurance obtained by misrepresentation or non-disclosure of material facts is not a **C6.48** 'policy of insurance' for the purposes of the RTA 1930, s. 36(4) (*Guardian Assurance Co. Ltd v Sutherland* [1939] 2 All ER 246, per Branson J). A voidable policy does, however, satisfy the requirements of s. 143 until it is avoided (*Durrant v MacLaren* [1956] 2 Lloyd's Rep 70; *Adams v Dunne* [1978] RTR 281).

Payment of petrol money on a regular 'school run' which went beyond the bounds of mere social kindness may bring the vehicle (if it is adapted to carry more than eight passengers) within the meaning of the term 'public service vehicle' (*DPP v Sikondar* [1993] RTR 90). This may in turn vitiate a policy of insurance so as to bring the driver within the ambit of s. 143.

Punishment

C6.49 Disqualification is discretionary, but endorsement with between six and eight penalty points is obligatory. A fine up to level 5 may be imposed. A fixed penalty of £300 is available in respect of this offence (Fixed Penalty Offences Order 2003 (SI 2003 No. 1253)). The *Magistrates' Court Sentencing Guidelines* (see Supplement, **SG-339**) must generally be followed; the Guidelines indicate starting points to be considered and provide examples of aggravating and mitigating factors.

KEEPING VEHICLE NOT MEETING INSURANCE REQUIREMENTS

C6.50 The RTA 1988, s. 144A, was inserted by the Road Safety Act 2006, s. 22, with effect from 4 February 2011 (see SI 2011 No. 19) and introduces the offence of keeping a vehicle which does not meet the insurance requirements (as defined therein). The new offence is designed to ensure so far as possible that all relevant vehicles are covered by appropriate minimum levels of insurance. Various exceptions to the requirement are established under s. 144B and in the Motor Vehicles (Insurance Requirements) Regulations 2011 (SI 2011 No. 20), which also deal with disclosure of information by the Motor Insurers' Information Centre and the availability of a fixed penalty. The offence is not endorsable.

FAILING TO STOP AND FAILING TO REPORT ACCIDENT

C6.51

Road Traffic Act 1988, s. 170

(1) This section applies in a case where, owing to the presence of a mechanically propelled vehicle on a road or other public place, an accident occurs by which—
  (a) personal injury is caused to a person other than the driver of that mechanically propelled vehicle, or
  (b) damage is caused—
    (i) to a vehicle other than that mechanically propelled vehicle or a trailer drawn by that mechanically propelled vehicle, or
    (ii) to an animal other than an animal in or on that mechanically propelled vehicle or a trailer drawn by that mechanically propelled vehicle, or
    (iii) to any other property constructed on, fixed to, growing in or otherwise forming part of the land on which the road or place in question is situated or land adjacent to such land.
(2) The driver of the mechanically propelled vehicle must stop and, if required to do so by any person having reasonable grounds for so requiring, give his name and address and also the name and address of the owner and the identification marks of the vehicle.
(3) If for any reason the driver of the mechanically propelled vehicle does not give his name and address under subsection (2) above, he must report the accident.
(4) A person who fails to comply with subsection (2) or (3) above is guilty of an offence.
(5) If, in a case where this section applies by virtue of subsection (1)(a) above, the driver of a motor vehicle does not at the time of the accident produce such a certificate of insurance or security, or other evidence, as is mentioned in section 165(2)(a) of this Act—
  (a) to a constable, or
  (b) to some person who, having reasonable grounds for so doing, has required him to produce it, the driver must report the accident and produce such a certificate or other evidence.
  This subsection does not apply to the driver of an invalid carriage.
(6) To comply with a duty under this section to report an accident or to produce such a certificate of insurance or security, or other evidence, as is mentioned in section 165(2)(a) of this Act, the driver—
  (a) must do so at a police station or to a constable, and
  (b) must do so as soon as is reasonably practicable and, in any case, within 24 hours of the occurrence of the accident.

(7) A person who fails to comply with a duty under subsection (5) above is guilty of an offence, but he shall not be convicted by reason only of a failure to produce a certificate or other evidence if, within seven days after the occurrence of the accident, the certificate or other evidence is produced at a police station that was specified by him at the time when the accident was reported.

(8) In this section 'animal' means horse, cattle, ass, mule, sheep, pig, goat or dog.

Elements

For the meaning of the terms 'accident', 'driver' and 'vehicle', see **C1.1, C1.2** and **C1.18**.   C6.52

The RTOA 1988, ss. 11 and 12(1), apply; see **C2.17** and **C2.18**.

Section 170(2) creates one offence which may be committed in a number of different ways. Section 170(3) creates a separate offence, as does s. 170(7) (*DPP v Bennett* [1993] RTR 175). In *R (Parker) v Crown Court at Bradford* [2007] RTR 369, an attempt to challenge the insertion in s. 170(1) of 'or other public place' by the Motor Vehicles (Compulsory Insurance) Regulations 2000 (SI 2000 No. 726) was unsuccessful.

The object of s. 170 is to identify the parties involved for the purposes of both civil and criminal proceedings. To that end, it is a question of fact whether providing the name and address of a third party satisfies the requirements of the section (*DPP v McCarthy* [1999] RTR 323); in that case, the driver gave his name and the address of his solicitors, which was found to be sufficient. It is not necessary for the motor vehicle to be directly involved with the accident, but the prosecution must establish causation because of the presence of the defendant's motor vehicle on the road (*Quelch v Phipps* [1955] 2 QB 107). Nor is it necessary for the driver to be physically present in the vehicle at the time of the accident (provided his absence does not terminate the act of 'driving': (see **C1.2** and **C1.5**) (*Cawthorn v DPP* [2000] RTR 45). In *Harding v Price* [1948] 1 KB 695, it was established that where a driver is unaware of an accident, he cannot be aware of a duty to stop or report and is entitled to be acquitted. When it is sought to establish this, the onus of proof rests on the defendant (see also *Hampson v Powell* [1970] 1 All ER 929).

Following such an accident as is mentioned in s. 170(1), the driver is obliged to remain at the scene for a reasonable time so that he can fulfil his obligations under s. 170(2) (*Lee v Knapp* [1967] 2 QB 442; *Ward v Rawson* [1978] RTR 498). The obligation does not extend to searching out persons who might be entitled to the information required under s. 170(2) (*Mutton v Bates* [1984] RTR 256).

Whether or not the vehicle is stopped at the appropriate point is a question of fact; where a   C6.53 driver chose to drive on for 80 yards before stopping and returning to the scene of the accident, the Divisional Court was not prepared to interfere with a decision finding that this constituted a failure to stop as required, because it could not be said to be one which no court, properly directing itself upon the law, could rationally have arrived at (*McDermott v DPP* [1997] RTR 474). Under s. 170(2), a driver is required to stop immediately so that witnesses might make themselves known and any person wishing to request the driver's particulars might do so (*Hallinan v DPP* [1998] Crim LR 754). The requirement to stop imposed by the RTA 1988, s. 170, arises almost immediately the relevant event takes place and so the offence is complete as soon as the failure to do so occurs. Consequently, in *Attwater* [2011] RTR 173, it was confirmed that, once that moment has passed, the driver in question is no longer committing an offence and the use of force envisaged by the CJA 1967, s. 3 (to prevent an offence being committed), cannot be relied upon as a defence.

Partial compliance with the requirements will not suffice, but if he has stopped and has not been required to provide any or all of the details mentioned in s. 170(2), the driver will fulfil his obligation, subject, however, to a duty to report the accident in the manner prescribed by s. 170(6) if he has not given his name and address. The obligation to report an accident under s. 170(3) therefore exists whenever a driver has not provided his name and address.

In *DPP v Drury* [1989] RTR 165, it was held that a driver who is not aware of an accident but who subsequently becomes aware of it, must report the accident to a police station personally if he becomes aware within 24 hours of the accident occurring. Reporting an accident by telephone is insufficient, and the obligation appears to be one that must, in the absence of physical impossibility, be performed personally (*Wisdom v Macdonald* [1983] RTR 186). The obligations under s. 170 are not negated by police attendance at the scene of the accident and the defendant being conveyed to hospital (*DPP v Hay* [2006] RTR 32).

C6.54 In an accident involving more than one other person or vehicle, the driver may be required to provide details to a number of people, and failure to provide those details to anyone who has reasonable grounds for requiring them is an offence. If, however, the driver has furnished particulars, including his name and address, to at least one person and has satisfied all other requests made, then it is suggested he is not obliged to report the accident in the manner prescribed by s. 170(6), unless personal injury has been caused to someone other than the driver.

Where personal injury is caused to anyone other than the driver of the vehicle, the driver must produce his insurance certificate (or such other documentation as would satisfy s. 165(2)(a) of the Act) at the time of the accident either to a constable or any other person who has reasonable grounds for requesting him to produce it. If he does not produce insurance (or such other documentation as would satisfy s. 165(2)(a) of the Act), either because he was not able to or because he was not so required, he must report the accident in the manner prescribed by s. 170(6).

Punishment

C6.55 An offence under s. 170(4) is punishable with up to six months' imprisonment and/or a fine up to level 5 on the standard scale. Disqualification is discretionary but endorsement, with between five and ten penalty points, is obligatory. Forfeiture of the vehicle concerned may also be ordered (see **E18.1**). The *Magistrates' Court Sentencing Guidelines* (see Supplement, **SG-336**) must generally be followed.

PEDESTRIAN CROSSING REGULATIONS

C6.56 The RTRA 1984, s. 25, enables the Secretary of State to make regulations in respect of vehicles and pedestrians at and in the vicinity of crossings. The current regulations are the Zebra, Pelican and Puffin Pedestrian Crossings Regulations and General Directions 1997 (SI 1997 No. 2400). Contravention of the regulations is an offence punishable by a fine up to level 3 on the standard scale. Disqualification when a motor vehicle is involved is discretionary, but endorsement with three penalty points is obligatory. The regulations apply to all vehicles. The *Magistrates' Court Sentencing Guidelines* (see Supplement, **SG-346**) give fine band A as the starting point.

FAILING TO STOP AT SCHOOL CROSSING

C6.57 The RTRA 1984, s. 28, creates specific offences of failing to comply with a stop sign exhibited by a uniformed school crossing patrol and causing a vehicle to be put in motion so long as the sign continues to be exhibited. The sign is prescribed by the School Crossing Patrol Sign (England and Wales) Regulations 2006 (SI 2006 No. 2215). The driver of a motor vehicle must stop unless the sign has been removed by the time he arrives at the crossing (*Franklin v Langdown* [1971] 3 All ER 662). A fine up to level 3 on the standard scale may be imposed. Disqualification when a motor vehicle is involved is discretionary, but endorsement with three penalty points is obligatory.

SPEEDING

Road Traffic Regulation Act 1984, s. 89

(1) A person who drives a motor vehicle on a road at a speed exceeding a limit imposed by or under any enactment to which this section applies shall be guilty of an offence.

(2) A person prosecuted for such an offence shall not be liable to be convicted solely on the evidence of one witness to the effect that, in the opinion of the witness, the person prosecuted was driving the vehicle at a speed exceeding a specified limit.

(3) The enactments to which this section applies are—

    (a) any enactment contained in this Act except section 17(2);

    (b) section 2 of the Parks Regulation (Amendment) Act 1926; and

    (c) any enactment not contained in this Act, but passed after 1 September 1960, whether before or after the passing of this Act.

(4) If a person who employs other persons to drive motor vehicles on roads publishes or issues any timetable or schedule, or gives any directions, under which any journey, or any stage or part of any journey, is to be completed within some specified time, and it is not practicable in the circumstances of the case for that journey (or that stage or part of it) to be completed in the specified time without the commission of such an offence as is mentioned in subsection (1) above, the publication or issue of the timetable or schedule, or the giving of the directions, may be produced as prima facie evidence that the employer procured or (as the case may be) incited the persons employed by him to drive the vehicle to commit such an offence.

Elements

The section applies only to 'motor vehicles', see **C1.9**. The RTOA 1988, ss. 1, 11 and 12(1)   **C6.59** apply; see **C2.1**, **C2.17** and **C2.18**.

Depending on the context and circumstances, driving at grossly excessive speed might constitute dangerous driving (*DPP v Milton* [2006] RTR 264: see **C3.11**).

Section 87 of the 1984 Act exempts motor vehicles being used for fire service, ambulance or police purposes, if observance of the speed limit would be likely to hinder the purpose for which they are being used. Where a vehicle is not constructed, adapted or used for the purpose of conveying sick, injured or disabled persons, it may not be an ambulance benefiting from this exemption (*Ashton v CPS* [2005] EWHC 2729 (Admin); *Lord-Castle v DPP* [2009] EWHC 87 (Admin); *DPP v Issler* [2014] EWHC 669 (Admin) and see **C6.34**). When the Road Safety Act 2006, s. 19, is brought into force, it will substitute a new s. 87, which will enable the coverage to include additional purposes whilst limiting the exemption to drivers who have satisfactorily completed an appropriate course of training.

Incorrectly sited speed restriction signs will not invalidate the speed limit imposed by a relevant enactment (*Wawrzynczyk v Chief Constable of Staffordshire Constabulary* (2000) *The Times*, 16 March 2000), provided no doubt that they sufficiently advise drivers of that speed limit in the location of the alleged offence and do not mislead. At the geographical point where the motorist exceeds the speed limit, the requisite signs must be capable of conveying the reduced limit to the motorist in sufficient time to enable the reduction from a previously lawful speed to within the new limit, which will not be the case if the signs are obscured by overgrown hedgerows (*Coombes v DPP* [2007] RTR 383). See also *Werbiski* [2012] EWHC 2073 (Admin).

The specific defence available in respect of inadequate signage applies only where the road is not   **C6.60** a restricted one by reason of the system of street lighting (*Humber v DPP* [2008] EWHC 2932 (Admin)). The requirement for the prosecution to adduce evidence demonstrating compliance with the Traffic Signs Regulations and General Directions 2002 (SI 2002 No. 3113) was confirmed in *DPP v Butler* [2010] EWHC 669 (Admin), where a terminal speed limit sign located within 50 metres of a street lamp was not illuminated, as required, in darkness. However, in order to secure a conviction, there is no requirement that all the signage in the whole area to which a limit applies is compliant, provided that there is adequate compliant signage providing guidance as to the speed limit to be observed in the road leading up to the point of enforcement (*Peake v DPP* [2011] RTR 33). Where there is more than *de minimis* non-compliance with the statutory obligations relating to signage, the court needs to engage in a balancing exercise, weighing the public interest in setting and enforcing speed limits and the protections afforded to motorists and assessing whether adequate guidance has been given about the speed limit to be observed at the point on the road where the offence occurs (*Jones v DPP* [2012] RTR 19).

If it is alleged that the road in question is a restricted road by reason of the street lighting being no more than 200 yards apart and the defendant puts the prosecution to strict proof, such proof must be provided (*R (Martin) v Harrow Crown Court* [2007] EWHC 3193 (Admin)). A traffic authority for a road can make an order that a road that is not a restricted road by reason of the positioning of street lighting shall become a restricted road for the purpose of imposing a 30 mph speed limit (see, e.g., *DPP v Evans* [2004] EWHC 2785 (Admin)). In *DPP v Wells* [2007] EWHC 3259 (Admin), it was held that charging such an offence under s. 89 is permissible even where the offence could alternatively be charged under s. 14 (temporary prohibition or restriction).

Evidence from an approved device is admissible to prove speeding offences under s. 89 (see the RTOA 1988, s. 20 at **C2.21**).

C6.61 Section 89(2) provides a statutory requirement of corroboration. Opinion evidence as to speed is admissible but, because of the danger of inaccuracy inherent in such evidence, it was felt necessary to require corroboration. See generally *Nicholas v Penny* [1950] 2 KB 466 and *Swain v Gillet* [1974] RTR 446. The reading of a police car's speedometer is capable of supplying the necessary corroboration, even if there is no evidence of testing, though the weight of such evidence is open to question (*Swain v Gillet*). It would satisfy the statutory requirement to have the opinion evidence of two or more witnesses, provided that their observations occurred at the same time (*Brighty v Pearson* [1938] 4 All ER 127).

Factual evidence, however, does not require corroboration, and evidence of the speed recorded on the speedometer of a police car, driven at an even distance behind the appellant's car, was held to be sufficient to sustain a conviction (*Nicholas v Penny* [1950] 2 KB 466). The speedometer does not need to be tested, and in the absence of evidence to the contrary can be presumed, as can radar guns, radar speed meters and other mechanical instruments, to be in order at the material time (*Castle v Cross* [1984] 1 All ER 87; *Burton v Gilbert* [1984] RTR 162).

The expert evidence of an 'Accident Examiner' which entails the reconstruction of events from various tests, skid marks and damage, is considered to be based on more than mere opinion where he describes the facts on which his opinion is based (*Crossland v DPP* [1988] 3 All ER 712).

It is not open to the prosecution to accept a plea of guilty to a charge of speeding which had been committed for trial under the CJA 1988, s. 41, and offer no evidence on the indictable offence (*Avey* [1994] RTR 419). Offences committed for trial under s. 41 can be dealt with only following a conviction for an indictable offence arising out of circumstances which are the same as or connected with the summary offence. In such circumstances, the proper course for the Crown Court is to remit the s. 41 offence to be dealt with by the magistrates' court.

Punishment

C6.62 A fine up to level 3 may be imposed. Disqualification is discretionary. Endorsement, with three penalty points when a fixed penalty is imposed and with between three and six penalty points in any other case, is obligatory. When the Road Safety Act 2006, s. 17, is brought into force, the range of penalty points applicable will increase to between two and six points; the 2006 Act also provides for a range of penalty points when a fixed penalty is imposed (see C7.3). Special reasons may be capable of being advanced, e.g., when driving too quickly to deal with an emergency situation (see C7.58). The *Magistrates' Court Sentencing Guidelines* (see Supplement, SG-340) must generally be followed; the Guidelines indicate starting points to be considered by reference to the speed recorded relative to the limit in question and provide examples of aggravating and mitigating factors.

Section C7   Sentencing

GENERAL PRINCIPLES

Fines and Imprisonment

The RTOA 1988, s. 33, provides that the maximum punishments for offences against the **C7.1**
Traffic Acts should be those set out in sch. 2, part I, col. 4 (see **C8.1**). References therein to years
or months are references to terms of imprisonment.

Forfeiture of Motor Vehicle

Section 143 of the PCC(S)A 2000 (see **E18.1** *et seq*.) makes it possible, in some circumstances, **C7.2**
for a court to order the forfeiture of a motor vehicle where it has been used in committing or
facilitating the commission of an offence.

Fixed Penalties

Part III of the RTOA 1988 contains provisions relating to fixed penalties. The 'fixed penalty **C7.3**
offences' are listed in the RTOA 1988, sch. 3 (see **C8.3**), and include many of the less serious
offences which are most commonly committed. A 'fixed penalty notice' is 'a notice offering the
opportunity of the discharge of any liability to conviction for the offence to which the notice
relates by payment of a fixed penalty' which 'must give such particulars of the circumstances
alleged to constitute the offence to which it relates as are necessary for giving reasonable information about the alleged offence' (RTOA 1988, s. 52(1) and (2)). The amount of fixed penalty
is specified by the Fixed Penalty Order 2000 (SI 2000 No. 2792), made under the RTOA 1988,
s. 53. Section 53 was amended by the Road Safety Act 2006, s. 3, thereby enabling the making
of the Fixed Penalty (Amendment) Order 2009 (SI 2009 No. 488), which introduced into the
Fixed Penalty Order 2000 graduated fixed penalties in relation to offences in respect of drivers'
hours (and related recording equipment) for goods and passenger vehicles, certain roadworthi-
ness defects, and overloading; the amounts payable are determined by reference to the nature of
the offence, its severity, where it has taken place and whether the offender appears to have committed other prescribed offences during a prescribed period.

A fixed penalty notice may be given to a person where a constable in uniform or a vehicle
examiner has reason to believe that a fixed penalty offence is being, or has been, committed by
that person (RTOA 1988, s. 54). If the offence in question is endorsable, however, a fixed
penalty notice can be given only if the person produces his driving licence for inspection and
it shows that the person will not be liable, once the penalty points for the instant offence are
added, to disqualification under the RTOA 1988, s. 35 (see **C7.24**) and the person surrenders
that licence to be dealt with in accordance with the provisions of part III. Where no licence can
be produced at the time, the constable or examiner may give the person a notice to produce his
licence at a police station, within seven days if the notice is given by a constable or within
14 days if given by an examiner. If, upon inspection, a fixed penalty is similarly available, a fixed
penalty notice must be given at that time. A similar procedure now exists for drivers who do
not have a GB licence but whose driving records enable endorsement of a fixed penalty offence
(see **C7.50**).

C7.4 A suspended enforcement period follows the giving of a fixed penalty notice, during which no proceedings may be brought against the recipient in respect of the offence (RTOA 1988, s. 78(2)). The period must be at least 21 days and is usually 28 days. If the fixed penalty is paid before the end of the suspended enforcement period that ends matters except, in the case of an endorsable offence, the person's licence is endorsed and returned (RTOA 1988, s. 57(3)). Instead of paying the fixed penalty, the recipient may give notice that he requests a hearing in respect of the offence, in which case it will subsequently be tried summarily (RTOA 1988, s. 55(2)). If the recipient takes no action before the end of the suspended enforcement period, an amount of one and a half times the amount of the fixed penalty may be registered under the RTOA 1988, s. 71, for enforcement against that person as a fine (RTOA 1988, s. 55(3)). For an endorsable offence, upon notice of the registration as a fine, the person's surrendered licence is duly endorsed and returned.

A fixed penalty notice may be affixed to a stationary vehicle by a constable or vehicle examiner who has reason to believe that an offence which does not carry obligatory endorsement is being, or has on that occasion been, committed (RTOA 1988, s. 62). A similar suspended enforcement period follows and, if the fixed penalty is paid within that period, that ends the matter (RTOA 1988, s 78(2)) or, if the person gives notice requesting a hearing, stating therein that he was the driver at the time of the alleged offence, he will subsequently be tried summarily (RTOA 1988, s. 63(3)). If no payment is made or hearing requested, a notice may be served on the person appearing to be the owner of the vehicle concerned (RTOA 1988, s. 63(2)). If there is no response to that notice within the time permitted by it, an amount of one and a half times the amount of the fixed penalty may be registered under the RTOA 1988, s. 71, for enforcement against the person so served as a fine (RTOA 1988, s. 64(2)). Alternatively, the person served may request a hearing on his own behalf or on behalf of some other person who was the driver at the relevant time (RTOA 1988, s. 63(6)). Unless it is proved that the vehicle in question was in the possession of some other person without the consent of the person served with the s. 63 notice, the person so served is conclusively presumed to have been the driver of the vehicle at the time of the alleged offence (RTOA 1988, s. 64(5) and (6)).

Financial Penalty Deposits

C7.5 Under the RTOA 1988, part 3A, consisting of ss. 90A to 90F, in an appropriate case, where a person believed to have committed an applicable offence fails to provide 'an address in the United Kingdom at which the constable or vehicle examiner considers it is likely that it would be possible to find the person whenever necessary to do so in connection with the proceedings, fixed penalty notice or conditional offer', a requirement for a financial penalty deposit can be made (s. 90A(4)). The requirement is to make payment of 'the appropriate amount' immediately or within 'the relevant period' which varies according to the situation. The Road Safety (Financial Penalty Deposit) Order 2009 (SI 2009 No. 491) specifies that the requirement can be made in respect of the person in charge of the vehicle for any offence listed being committed, or which has been committed, on a road or other public place. The appropriate amount is set out in the Road Safety (Financial Penalty Deposit) (Appropriate Amount) Order 2009 (SI 2009 No. 492, as amended by SI 2013 No. 2025 and SI 2014 No. 267), and is generally fixed by reference to the size of the applicable fixed penalty or graduated fixed penalty but, for offences likely to be tried by a court, is set at £500. Where more than one offence is involved on a single occasion, the maximum aggregate amount that can be required is £1,500.

The amount so paid is then used to pay any uncontested fixed penalty notice. If the person chooses to contest the commission of the offence and is unsuccessful, the payment made is off-set against all, or part, of the fine imposed. If the offender is successful, or the matter does not come to court within the time permitted for a prosecution to be commenced or 12 months, whichever is shorter, the amount is refunded with interest, calculated by reference to the Bank of England base rate at the beginning of the day on which the financial penalty deposit was made (Road Safety (Financial Penalty Deposit) (Interest) Order 2009 (SI 2009 No. 498)).

Prohibition on Driving   Under the RTOA 1988, s. 90D, where a person on whom a financial **C7.6**
penalty deposit requirement is imposed does not make an immediate payment of the amount
required, the constable or vehicle examiner is entitled, but not obliged, to give notice in writing
to the person prohibiting the driving of the vehicle of which the person was in charge at the time
of the offence. In doing so, a direction in writing may also be given to the person concerned that
the vehicle in question must be removed to another specified place. The prohibition on driving
will continue until the deposit is paid, a fixed penalty arising from the offence is paid, the person
is convicted or acquitted of the offence, the person is told there will be no prosecution for the
offence, or the prosecution period expires. Detailed provisions relating to these powers, also
covering other instances where driving is prohibited in accordance with the Road Safety Act
2006, sch. 4, are contained in the Road Safety (Immobilisation, Removal and Disposal of
Vehicles) Regulations 2009 (SI 2009 No. 493).

Production of Licence

Road Traffic Offenders Act 1988, s. 27 **C7.7**

(1) Where a person who is the holder of a licence is convicted of an offence involving obligatory or
discretionary disqualification, and a court proposes to make an order disqualifying him or an
order under section 44 of this Act, the court must, unless it has already received them, require
the licence and its counterpart to be produced to it.
(2) [Repealed.]
(3) If the holder of the licence has not caused it and its counterpart to be delivered, or posted it and
its counterpart, in accordance with section 7 of this Act and does not produce it and its counterpart as required under this section or section 301 of the Criminal Justice Act 2003, section
146 or 147 of the Powers of Criminal Courts (Sentencing) Act 2000, . . . then, unless he satisfies
the court that he has applied for a new licence and has not received it—
  (a) he is guilty of an offence, and
  (b) the licence shall be suspended from the time when its production was required until it and
  its counterpart are produced to the court and shall, while suspended, be of no effect.
(4) Subsection (3) above does not apply where the holder of the licence—
  (a) has caused a current receipt for the licence and its counterpart issued under section 56 of
  this Act to be delivered to the proper officer of the court not later than the day before the
  date appointed for the hearing, or
  (b) has posted such a receipt, at such time that in the ordinary course of post it would be
  delivered not later than that day, in a letter duly addressed to the proper officer and either
  registered or sent by the recorded delivery service, or
  (c) surrenders such a receipt to the court at the hearing,
  and produces the licence and its counterpart to the court immediately on their return.

'Licence' includes a Community licence and 'new licence' includes a counterpart of a Community
licence (RTOA 1988, s. 91A(1) and (2)).

When an offender has been requested to produce his driving licence, a failure to produce it is,
unless he has applied for a new licence which he has not received or s. 27(4) applies, an offence
punishable by a fine up to level 3 on the standard scale. The licence is also suspended until it is
produced, and if the offender drives during that suspension, he is guilty of an offence under the
RTA 1988, s. 87(1) (see **C6.37**).

OBLIGATORY AND DISCRETIONARY DISQUALIFICATION

Obligatory Disqualification

Road Traffic Offenders Act 1988, s. 34 **C7.8**

(1) Where a person is convicted of an offence involving obligatory disqualification, the court must
order him to be disqualified for such period not less than 12 months as the court thinks fit
unless the court for special reasons thinks fit to order him to be disqualified for a shorter period
or not to order him to be disqualified.

(1A) Where a person is convicted of an offence under section 12A of the Theft Act 1968 (aggravated
       vehicle-taking), the fact that he did not drive the vehicle in question at any particular time or
       at all shall not be regarded as a special reason for the purposes of subsection (1) above.
  (2) Where a person is convicted of an offence involving discretionary disqualification, and
       either—
       (a) the penalty points to be taken into account on that occasion number fewer than 12, or
       (b) the offence is not one involving obligatory endorsement,
       the court may order him to be disqualified for such period as the court thinks fit.
  (3) Where a person convicted of an offence under any of the following provisions of the Road
       Traffic Act 1988, that is—
       (aa) section 3A (causing death by careless driving when under the influence of drink or drugs),
       (a) section 4(1) (driving or attempting to drive while unfit),
       (b) section 5(1)(a) (driving or attempting to drive with excess alcohol),
       (c) section 7(6) (failing to provide a specimen) where that is an offence involving obligatory
            disqualification,
       (d) section 7A(b) (failing to allow a specimen to be subjected to laboratory test) where that is
            an offence involving obligatory disqualification;
       has within the 10 years immediately preceding the commission of the offence been convicted
       of any such offence, subsection (1) above shall apply in relation to him as if the reference to
       12 months were a reference to three years.
  (4) Subject to subsection (3) above, subsection (1) above shall apply as if the reference to
       12 months were a reference to two years—
       (a) in relation to a person convicted of—
            (i)   manslaughter, ... or
            (ii) an offence under section 1 of the Road Traffic Act 1988 (causing death by dangerous
                  driving), or
            (iia) an offence under section 1A of that Act (causing serious injury by dangerous driving), or
            (iii) an offence under section 3A of that Act (causing death by careless driving while under
                  the influence of drink or drugs), and
       (b) in relation to a person on whom more than one disqualification for a fixed period of
            56 days or more has been imposed within the three years immediately preceding the com-
            mission of the offence.
(4A) For the purposes of subsection (4)(b) above there shall be disregarded any disqualification
       imposed under section 26 of this Act or section 147 of the Powers of Criminal Courts
       (Sentencing) Act 2000 or section 248 of the Criminal Procedure (Scotland) Act 1995 (offences
       committed by using vehicles) and any disqualification imposed in respect of an offence of steal-
       ing a motor vehicle, an offence under section 12 or 25 of the Theft Act 1968, an offence under
       section 178 of the Road Traffic Act 1988, or an attempt to commit such an offence.
(4B) Where a person convicted of an offence under section 40A of the Road Traffic Act 1988 (using
       vehicle in dangerous condition etc.) has within the three years immediately preceding the com-
       mission of the offence been convicted of any such offence, subsection (1) above shall apply in
       relation to him as if the reference to twelve months were a reference to six months.
  (5) The preceding provisions of this section shall apply in relation to a conviction of an offence
       committed by aiding, abetting, counselling or procuring, or inciting to the commission of, an
       offence involving obligatory disqualification as if the offence were an offence involving discre-
       tionary disqualification.
  (6) This section is subject to section 48 of this Act.

When the CCA 2013, sch. 22, is implemented, s. 34(3)(ba), referring to the new drug-driving
offence in the RTA 1988, s. 5A, will be inserted. The reference in s. 34(5) to incitement has
effect as a reference to (or to conduct amounting to) encouraging or assisting the offences under
part 2 of the SCA 2007 (see SI 2008 No. 2504).

C7.9 Where a person is convicted of an offence involving obligatory disqualification, the court must
         order him to be disqualified for a minimum period of 12 months in the absence of special rea-
         sons (see C7.53). Where the offence is one of manslaughter by the driver of a motor vehicle or
         is an offence under the RTA 1988, s. 1 or 3A, the minimum period of disqualification is two
         years; the minimum period is also two years where the offender has had two or more periods of
         disqualification of 56 days or more within the period of three years preceding the commission

of the offence. A second or subsequent conviction for an offence relating to 'drink driving' (i.e. under s. 3A, 4(1), 5(1)(a), 7(6) or 7A(6)) carries a minimum period of disqualification of three years, if it is committed within ten years of another such conviction. However, for a s. 7(6) or 7A(6) offence which does not involve driving (in respect of which disqualification is therefore discretionary: see **C5.34**), it would be surprising if the period chosen by the sentencer approached three years by reference to a previous drink-drive offence (*R (Cawley) v Warrington Crown Court* [2001] EWHC Admin 494). See also **C7.36**.

In *Learmont v DPP* [1994] RTR 286, the Divisional Court ruled that the justices, when sentencing the appellant for the instant offence of dangerous driving, had been wrong to conclude that an 18-month disqualification and a concurrent disqualification arising from the four notional penalty points imposed for that offence were two disqualifications of 56 days or more within the relevant three-year period; they were imposed for a single offence, thereby rendering the increased minimum period for disqualification inapplicable.

A person convicted of aiding and abetting etc. an offence mentioned in the RTOA 1988, s. 34(3), must be disqualified for three years if he is subsequently convicted of an offence mentioned in s. 34(3) (*Makeham v Donaldson* [1981] RTR 511).

C7.10 If the court disqualifies for any of the substantive offences under the RTOA 1988, s. 34, it does not order endorsement of the counterpart with any penalty points relating to that offence; the counterpart is merely endorsed with particulars of the offence. The points relating to that offence are disregarded for the purposes of s. 35 (*Martin v DPP* [2000] RTR 188).

The effect of s. 34(4A) is that disqualifications under the RTOA 1988, s. 26, the PCC(S)A 2000, s. 147, and any disqualification imposed in respect of an offence of stealing a motor vehicle, or an offence under s. 12 or 25 of the Theft Act 1968, are to be disregarded for the purposes of s. 34(4)(b).

Discretionary Disqualification

C7.11 Where a disqualification is discretionary, courts may not consider, except in the more serious cases, that disqualification is appropriate, particularly where it is a first offence. It 'should generally be restricted to cases involving bad driving, persistent motoring offences or the use of vehicles for the purposes of crime' (per Morland J in *Callister* [1993] RTR 70). In that case, theft of a vehicle by sale while it was subject to a credit agreement did not fall into any of those categories. Each case must be taken on its own merits, bearing in mind that certain types of offence will be viewed with greater seriousness. Offences of using a vehicle without insurance and failing to stop after an accident or to report an accident are always viewed seriously and often attract disqualification, even as a first offence. Also viewed seriously is driving while disqualified.

The penalty points to be taken into account are set out in the RTOA 1988, s. 29 (see **C7.19**), and include any attributable to the offence or offences for which the defendant is before the court and any points previously endorsed, unless the defendant has been disqualified under s. 35 since their imposition. The effect of s. 29 is that, where an offender has 12 or more points to be taken into account, the court may not disqualify for the substantive offence unless the offence is one which carries discretionary disqualification without obligatory endorsement; in such circumstances, it would seem that Parliament intended the penalty points procedure to take priority.

C7.12 In any case where a magistrates' court is considering imposing a period of disqualification and the person to be disqualified is not present in court, the court must, by virtue of the MCA 1980, s. 11(4), adjourn in order to warn the defendant that it has disqualification in mind. If the defendant fails to attend, the court may disqualify in his absence or, more usually, issue a warrant under the MCA 1980, s. 13, to compel his attendance. Before a court imposes disqualification in a case where it is discretionary, either the defendant or his representative should be warned and then given the opportunity to address the court (*Ireland* (1988) 10 Cr App R (S) 474 and *Money* (1988) 10 Cr App R (S) 237).

Meaning of 'Offence Involving Obligatory Disqualification' and 'Offence Involving Discretionary Disqualification'

C7.13   Road Traffic Offenders Act 1988, s. 97

(1) For the purposes of this Act, an offence involves obligatory disqualification if it is an offence under a provision of the Traffic Acts specified in column 1 of Part I of Schedule 2 to this Act or an offence specified in column 1 of Part II of that Schedule and either—

    (a) the word 'obligatory' (without qualification) appears in column 5 (in the case of Part I) or column 2 (in the case of Part II) against the offence, or

    (b) that word appears there qualified by conditions or circumstances relating to the offence which are satisfied or obtain.

(2) For the purposes of this Act, an offence involves discretionary disqualification if it is an offence under a provision of the Traffic Acts specified in column 1 of Part I of Schedule 2 to this Act or an offence specified in column 1 of Part II of that Schedule and either—

    (a) the word 'discretionary' (without qualification) appears in column 5 (in the case of Part I) or column 2 (in the case of Part II) against the offence, or

    (b) that word appears there qualified by conditions or circumstances relating to the offence which are satisfied or obtain.

Reduced Disqualification following Course

C7.14 Sections 34A to 34C of the RTOA 1988 set up a procedure for driver retraining for offenders convicted of drink-driving offences under the RTA 1988, s. 3A, 4, 5 or 7, where the court has disqualified for not less than 12 months under the RTOA 1988, s. 34, and provide an incentive to drivers to attend such courses by reducing the period of disqualification for those who do.

C7.15 For an order to be made, the period of disqualification must be at least 12 months and the 'reduced period' of disqualification cannot be less than three months or more than a quarter of the entire period of disqualification. An order cannot be made if the offender has completed an approved course under the RTOA 1988, s. 30A or s. 34A, for a specified offence within the previous three years (see **C7.22**) or in respect of an offender still within the probationary period for newly qualified drivers (see **C7.44**). The offender has to be aged at least 17. Before making a s. 34A order, the court must be satisfied that a place is available, that the offender agrees to the order and that it is explained to him that he must pay the fees for the course in advance and how much those fees are. This provision has certain disadvantages for the impecunious offender, particularly if that offender has relied on driving for previous employment.

Section 34B deals with certificates in relation to completion of the course. The order reducing the period of disqualification does not come into effect until the certificate has been received by the proper officer of the supervising court. If the certificate is received by the court before the end of the 'reduced period', the order reducing the period of disqualification comes into effect on the day that the certificate is received. The organiser of the retraining course may refuse to give a certificate for the reasons specified in s. 34B(4). If a certificate is not given to the offender in accordance with s. 34B, an application may be made to the supervising court which, if successful, has the effect of a certificate duly received by the court. Section 41A of the RTOA 1988 enables the court to suspend a disqualification pending determination of such an application.

Section 34BA makes provision for approval of courses and s. 34C deals with the powers of the Secretary of State or the National Assembly of Wales to give guidance to course organisers and other supplementary matters. See the Rehabilitation Courses (Relevant Drink Offences) Regulations 2012 (SI 2012 No. 2939) or, as the case may be, the Rehabilitation Courses (Relevant Drink Offences) (Wales) Regulations 2013 (SI 2013 No. 372), for further details.

PENALTY POINTS

Road Traffic Offenders Act 1988, s. 28

C7.16

(1) Where a person is convicted of an offence involving obligatory endorsement, then, subject to the following provisions of this section, the number of penalty points to be attributed to the offence is—
   (a) the number shown in relation to the offence in the last column of Part I or Part II of Schedule 2 to this Act, or
   (b) where a range of numbers is shown, a number within that range.

(2) Where a person is convicted of an offence committed by aiding, abetting, counselling or procuring, or inciting to the commission of, an offence involving obligatory disqualification, then, subject to the following provisions of this section, the number of penalty points to be attributed to the offence is 10.

(3) For the purposes of sections 57(5) and 77(5) of this Act, the number of penalty points to be attributed to an offence is—
   (a) where both a range of numbers and a number followed by the words '(fixed penalty)' is shown in the last column of part 1 of Schedule 2 to this Act in relation to the offence, that number,
   (b) where a range of numbers followed by the words 'or appropriate penalty points (fixed penalty)' is shown there in relation to the offence, the appropriate number of penalty points for the offence, and
   (c) where only a range of numbers is shown there in relation to the offence, the lowest number in the range.

(3A) For the purposes of subsection (3)(b) above the appropriate number of penalty points for an offence is such number of penalty points as the Secretary of State may by order made by statutory instrument prescribe.

(3B) An order made under subsection (3A) above in relation to an offence may make provision for the appropriate number of penalty points for the offence to be different depending on the circumstances, including (in particular)—
   (a) the nature of the contravention or failure constituting the offence,
   (b) how serious it is,
   (c) the area, or sort of place, where it takes place, and
   (d) whether the offender appears to have committed an offence or offences of a description in the order during a period so specified.

(4) Where a person is convicted (whether on the same occasion or not) of two or more offences committed on the same occasion and involving obligatory endorsement, the total number of penalty points to be attributed to them is the number or highest number that would be attributed on a conviction of one of them (so that if the convictions are on different occasions the number of penalty points to be attributed to the offences on the later occasion or occasions shall be restricted accordingly).

(5) In a case where (apart from this subsection) subsection (4) above would apply to two or more offences, the court may if it thinks fit determine that that subsection shall not apply to the offences (or, where three or more offences are concerned, to any one or more of them).

(6) Where a court makes such a determination it shall state its reasons in open court and, if it is a magistrates' court . . . shall cause them to be entered in the register . . . of its proceedings.

(7) to (9) [Powers of Secretary of State to alter penalty points and matters consequent.]

The reference in s. 28(2) to incitement has effect as a reference to (or to conduct amounting to) encouraging or assisting the offences under part 2 of the SCA 2007 (SI 2008 No. 2504).

Aiding and abetting etc. an offence involving obligatory disqualification, such as driving with excess alcohol, carries ten penalty points but does not entail mandatory disqualification. In offences not involving obligatory disqualification, secondary participation entails the same punishment as for the principal.

C7.17

If an attempted offence is summary only, then it must be statutory (e.g., attempting to drive while unfit through drink or drugs), and the penalty is set out in the RTOA 1988, sch. 2, part I, col. 7 (see **C8.1**). If it is triable either way then, by virtue of the Criminal Attempts Act 1981, s. 4(1)(b), the same liability to penalties exists as for the complete offence.

By virtue of the RTOA 1988, s. 28, the court may, following a determination under s. 28(5), order the endorsement of the counterpart to the licence with penalty points in relation to more than one offence committed on the same occasion. Points would then be aggregated for the purposes of the RTOA 1988, s. 35 (disqualification for repeated offences: see **C7.24**) and the Road Traffic (New Drivers) Act 1995 (surrender of licences: see **C7.44**).

The effect of s. 28 is to give the court a discretion to impose penalty points in respect of two or more offences committed on the same occasion and thereby aggregate the penalty points imposed in order to disqualify under the 'penalty points' system (s. 28(5)). Reasons must be given in open court and magistrates have to enter the reasons in the court register. The power can be used where none of the offences is so serious as to merit disqualification in its own right but the totality of the offending merits disqualification, possibly because of the number of offences or because the offences are of different types.

C7.18 In *Johnson v Finbow* [1983] 1 WLR 879, the appellant was charged with offences of failing to stop after an accident and failing to report the accident to the police. The Divisional Court accepted that there was an argument that the offences were not committed on the 'same occasion', but Robert Goff LJ, giving the judgment of the court, went on to say (at pp. 882–3):

> . . . looking at the matter more broadly (and, for my part, I think more sensibly), it can be said that the lapse of time, although significant, is not sufficiently great to be able to say, as a matter of common sense, that those offences were committed on different occasions. It is true that they were committed at different moments of time; indeed, they might even have been committed on different days. On the other hand, they certainly arose out of the same accident. And when one sees how closely they are connected with the accident, and how very similar, in fact, the two offences are in their nature, then I think the proper conclusion is that when arising out of the same accident these two offences are committed on the same occasion.

In *Johnston v Over* (1984) 6 Cr App R (S) 420, the defendant had parked two vehicles outside his home. He was charged with two offences of 'using' a vehicle without insurance. The Divisional Court stated that whether or not an offence was 'committed on the same or on different occasions' depended upon the facts of each case, and that in this case, as a matter of common sense, both offences were committed on the same occasion.

Offences which are committed on separate occasions have the number or highest number of penalty points awarded separately, and, if committed within three years of each other, those points are added up for the purposes of the RTOA 1988, s. 35.

Points to be Taken into Account on Conviction

C7.19 Road Traffic Offenders Act 1988, s. 29

(1) Where a person is convicted of an offence involving obligatory endorsement, the penalty points to be taken into account on that occasion are (subject to subsection (2) below)—
  (a) any that are to be attributed to the offence or offences of which he is convicted, disregarding any offence in respect of which an order under section 34 of this Act is made, and
  (b) any that were on a previous occasion ordered to be endorsed on the counterpart of any licence held by him, unless the offender has since that occasion and before the conviction been disqualified under section 35 of this Act.
(2) If any of the offences was committed more than three years before another, the penalty points in respect of that offence shall not be added to those in respect of the other.

C7.20 The effect of s. 29 is that penalty points remain on the licence; it is not 'wiped clean' by a disqualification under the RTOA 1988, s. 34. If a disqualification is imposed under s. 34, any points attributable to that offence are to be disregarded for the purposes of penalty points to be taken into account on conviction. Thus if a defendant is convicted of two offences committed on the same occasion, one of which carries mandatory disqualification, points on the other offence will be taken into account for the purposes of s. 35. Where there is a disqualification under s. 34, the licence is not endorsed with penalty points (*Campbell* (2010) 174 JP 73).

Even if the offender is disqualified for an offence before the court, the relevant number of penalty points (denoted in the RTOA 1988, sch. 2, part I, col. 7) must still be 'taken into account' for the purposes of s. 35.

A previous disqualification under the penalty points system has the effect of wiping the licence clean. Points ordered since the disqualification have to be taken into account even if they are imposed in respect of an offence committed before the disqualification, unless, of course, the offence was committed more than three years before another.

For the purposes of s. 29, the date of conviction means the date on which sentence is imposed (*Brentwood Justices, ex parte Richardson* (1992) 95 Cr App R 187).

Modification where Fixed Penalty Points also in Question

Road Traffic Offenders Act 1988, s. 30   **C7.21**

(1) Sections 28 and 29 of this Act shall have effect subject to this section in any case where—
   (a) a person is convicted of an offence involving obligatory endorsement, and
   (b) the court is satisfied that the counterpart of his licence has been or is liable to be endorsed under section 57 or 77 of this Act in respect of an offence (referred to in this section as the 'connected offence') committed on the same occasion as the offence of which he is convicted.
(2) The number of penalty points to be attributed to the offence of which he is convicted is—
   (a) the number of penalty points to be attributed to that offence under section 28 of this Act apart from this section, less
   (b) the number of penalty points required to be endorsed on the counterpart of his licence under section 57 or 77 of this Act in respect of the connected offence (except so far as they have already been deducted by virtue of this paragraph).

The offences to which the procedure applies are set out in the RTOA 1988, sch. 3 (see **C8.3**). Where the 'fixed penalty' procedure (see **C7.3**) has been, or is being, used in respect of an offence which arose on the 'same occasion' as the offence for which the defendant's licence is to be endorsed, the number of penalty points to be imposed in respect of that offence is the highest number of points attributable under the RTOA 1988, s. 28, less the number of points already endorsed under the fixed penalty procedure.

Reduced Penalty Points for Attendance on Courses   When the Road Safety Act 2006, s. 34, **C7.22**
is brought into force, it will introduce a new range of courses designed, when successfully completed, to remove from the offender's licence three penalty points (or fewer where, for the instant offence, the court endorsed fewer). This is intended to offer an element of retraining for repeat offenders and enable such offenders to benefit from the incentive of reducing the risk of being disqualified on reaching 12 or more penalty points under the RTOA 1988, s. 35 (see **C7.24**).

Sections 30A to 30D will be inserted into the RTOA 1988. The offences to be covered are (a) careless, and inconsiderate, driving; (b) failing to comply with traffic signs; and (c) speeding. The opportunity to attend a course will not be available to anyone who has completed a course under s. 30A or 34A (see **C7.14**) in the previous three years or a person who commits the offence during the probationary period for newly qualified drivers (see **C7.44**). These courses will be quite distinct from the Driver Improvement Scheme and Speed Awareness Courses operated by the police without court involvement.

Previously Endorsed Particulars

Road Traffic Offenders Act 1988, s. 31   **C7.23**

(1) Where a person is convicted of an offence involving obligatory or discretionary disqualification and his licence and its counterpart are produced to the court—
   (a) any existing endorsement on his licence is prima facie evidence of the matters endorsed, and

(b) the court may, in determining what order to make in pursuance of the conviction, take those matters into consideration.

   (2) [Applies only to Scotland.]

This is one of a number of ways by which previous convictions may be proved. In addition, an extract from the Criminal Records Office may be produced by the prosecution and is admissible if agreed by the defendant. On a number of occasions the only evidence relating to the defendant's driving record will be contained in a computer printout from the DVLA, which may be admitted under the RTOA 1988, s. 13 (see **C2.20**). In other circumstances previous convictions may be proved under the PACE 1984, ss. 73 to 75 (see generally, **F11.1** *et seq.*).

PENALTY POINTS DISQUALIFICATION

C7.24

Road Traffic Offenders Act 1988, s. 35

   (1) Where—

      (a) a person is convicted of an offence to which this subsection applies, and

      (b) the penalty points to be taken into account on that occasion number 12 or more,

the court must order him to be disqualified for not less than the minimum period unless the court is satisfied, having regard to all the circumstances, that there are grounds for mitigating the normal consequences of the conviction and thinks fit to order him to be disqualified for a shorter period or not to order him to be disqualified.

(1A) Subsection (1) above applies to—

      (a) an offence involving discretionary disqualification and obligatory endorsement, and

      (b) an offence involving obligatory disqualification in respect of which no order is made under section 34 of this Act.

   (2) The minimum period referred to in subsection (1) above is—

      (a) six months if no previous disqualification imposed on the offender is to be taken into account, and

      (b) one year if one, and two years if more than one, such disqualification is to be taken into account;

and a previous disqualification imposed on an offender is to be taken into account if it was for a fixed period of 56 days or more and was imposed within the three years immediately preceding the commission of the latest offence in respect of which penalty points are taken into account under section 29 of this Act.

   (3) Where an offender is convicted on the same occasion of more than one offence to which subsection (1) above applies—

      (a) not more than one disqualification shall be imposed on him under subsection (1) above,

      (b) in determining the period of the disqualification the court must take into account all the offences, and

      (c) for the purposes of any appeal any disqualification imposed under subsection (1) above shall be treated as an order made on the conviction of each of the offences.

   (4) No account is to be taken under subsection (1) above of any of the following circumstances—

      (a) any circumstances that are alleged to make the offence or any of the offences not a serious one,

      (b) hardship, other than exceptional hardship, or

      (c) any circumstances which, within the three years immediately preceding the conviction, have been taken into account under that subsection in ordering the offender to be disqualified for a shorter period or not ordering him to be disqualified.

   (5) References in this section to disqualification do not include a disqualification imposed under section 26 of this Act or section 147 of the Powers of Criminal Courts (Sentencing) Act 2000 … or a disqualification imposed in respect of an offence of stealing a motor vehicle, an offence under section 12 or 25 of the Theft Act 1968, an offence under section 178 of the Road Traffic Act 1988, or an attempt to commit such an offence.

(5A) The preceding provisions of this section shall apply in relation to a conviction of an offence committed by aiding, abetting, counselling, procuring, or inciting to the commission of, an offence involving obligatory disqualification as if the offence were an offence involving discretionary disqualification.

(6) [Applies only to Scotland.]

(7) This section is subject to section 48 of this Act.

The reference in s. 35(5A) to incitement has effect as a reference to (or to conduct amounting to) encouraging or assisting the offences under part 2 of the SCA 2007 (SI 2008 No. 2504).

C7.25 The purpose of the procedure is to punish repeated offences which in themselves are not sufficiently grave to warrant disqualification, but which taken together indicate repeated offences of bad driving or disregard for the law. When considering the proper sentence for an offence carrying discretionary disqualification, the court should first consider whether that is warranted. In doing so, it will have regard to the defendant's full relevant driving record. If it considers that a mandatory period of disqualification under the RTOA 1988, s. 35, would be the best disposal, the court can exercise its discretion not to disqualify under the RTOA, s. 34, and to impose an appropriate number of penalty points to bring the defendant within s. 35 (*Jones v DPP* [2001] RTR 80). As such, ss. 34 and 35 are complementary rather than mutually exclusive.

Once points have been imposed they are added to any other points imposed in respect of offences committed within three years of the latest offence or offences (points to be taken into consideration). If the total is 12 or more, the court is obliged to disqualify under the RTOA 1988, s. 35. This disqualification is mandatory unless the court finds mitigating circumstances. It is in addition to, but not consecutive to, any disqualification which the court may order for the offences before it on that day.

C7.26 Even if the court disqualifies for a substantive offence, it is obliged to take into account other offences which were committed and to take into account and attribute points in accordance with the RTOA 1988, ss. 28 and 29, with a view to disqualification under s. 35. Points are not endorsed on the counterpart under s. 44 if there is a penalty points disqualification.

The effect of a disqualification under the penalty points procedure is to wipe the licence and its counterpart clean. If the defendant is subsequently convicted of an offence, previously endorsed points are not taken into consideration, but the fact of a penalty points disqualification is relevant to any future points disqualification.

C7.27 **Period of Disqualification under the Road Traffic Offenders Act 1988, s. 35** The disqualification must be for a minimum period, unless there are grounds for mitigating the normal consequences and the court thinks fit to order a shorter period or no disqualification at all. See also **C7.36**.

If the offender has no previous disqualification of 56 days or more imposed within three years of the commission of the latest offence for which penalty points are to be taken into account, the period is six months. If there is one such disqualification in the three years, the period is a minimum of one year. If there are two or more such disqualifications imposed within three years of the commission of the latest offence, the minimum period is two years. Disqualifications under the RTOA 1988, s. 26, and the PCC(S)A 2000, s. 147, are not to be taken into account.

C7.28 **Mitigating Circumstances** Mitigating circumstances may be circumstances which relate to the offender or the offence, and may include the offender's record and good works.

The RTOA 1988, s. 35(4), specifically excludes circumstances which are alleged to make the offence not serious, hardship, other than exceptional hardship, and any 'mitigating circumstances' which have been advanced as such during the three years preceding the conviction for the latest offence. For those reasons the RTOA 1988, s. 47, requires grounds for mitigating the normal consequences of the conviction to be stated in open court, and entered in the court register if the case is heard by a magistrates' court.

It is for the offender to establish that grounds being advanced are different from any previously put before the court (*Sandbach Justices, ex parte Pescud* (1983) 5 Cr App R (S) 177). In practice, most of the mitigating circumstances advanced relate to 'exceptional hardship'. In *Owen v Jones* (1987) 9 Cr App R (S) 34, the court expressed the view that in the vast majority of cases justices would need to have evidence to satisfy themselves of the existence of exceptional hardship, but that on occasions they might rely upon their own knowledge. In that case a police officer had acquired a total of 13 points and, if disqualified, would have, by the usual practice of his Chief Constable, been forced to resign, thereby losing his job and his home. This practice was known to the bench, who did not require the defendant to provide evidence, as they found that the facts amounted to exceptional hardship.

C7.29 'Exceptional hardship' is often advanced in relation to the offender's employment. In those circumstances the court might consider whether or not a licence to drive is necessary for the offender either to go to work or because his occupation is, or entails, driving. Such matters as his hours and pattern of work, together with the distances he must travel in order to reach his work and the availability of public transport, are relevant, as are details of his age and health and any other means of transport available to him. If loss of his licence may mean loss of his job or reduced wages, the court may consider any unusual hardship that may result to the family of the defendant and any unusual hardship that may be occasioned to them if he were to lose his licence. The fact that he is a businessman, with employees dependent upon him and his ability to drive, may be considered, but the court should be careful to inquire as to other means of transport or available methods of effecting his necessary business.

The court must have regard to all the circumstances. This has been held to include, in the case of a young offender with a bad record who was disqualified for two years under the penalty points procedure, the counter-productive nature of long periods of disqualification. In *Thomas* [1983] 3 All ER 756, upon reducing the disqualification from two years to one, Lord Lane CJ said (at p. 1491):

> ...with persons like the present appellant, who seem to be incapable of leaving motor vehicles alone, to impose a period of disqualification which will extend for a substantial period after their release from prison may well, and in many cases certainly will, invite the offender to commit further offences in relation to motor vehicles. In other words a long period of disqualification may well be counter-productive and so contrary to the public interest. So well established has this sentencing policy become in recent years that it is not necessary to refer to a line of cases.

Given the breadth of the discretion under s. 35(1), it can be exercised in cases where the unreasonable length of time between the offence resulting in a penalty points disqualification and the imposition of that sentence violates the ECHR, Article 6; in such a case, an appropriate remedy may be the reduction of the usual period of disqualification, or even imposing no disqualification at all (*Miller v DPP* [2005] RTR 44, applying *A-G's Ref (No. 2 of 2001)* [2001] 1 WLR 1869).

DISQUALIFICATION GENERALLY

Interim Disqualification

C7.30 Road Traffic Offenders Act 1988, s. 26

(1) Where a magistrates' court—
  (a) commits an offender to the Crown Court under section 6 of the Powers of Criminal Courts (Sentencing) Act 2000 or any enactment mentioned in subsection (4) of that section, or
  (b) remits an offender to another magistrates' court under section 10 of that Act,
  to be dealt with for an offence involving obligatory or discretionary disqualification, it may order him to be disqualified until he has been dealt with in respect of the offence.
(2) Where a court in England and Wales—
  (a) defers passing sentence on an offender under section 1 of that Act in respect of an offence involving obligatory or discretionary disqualification, or

(b) adjourns after convicting an offender of such an offence but before dealing with him for the offence,

it may order the offender to be disqualified until he has been dealt with in respect of the offence.

(3) [Applies only to Scotland.]

(4) Subject to subsection (5) below, an order under this section shall cease to have effect at the end of the period of six months beginning with the day on which it is made, if it has not ceased to have effect before that time.

(5) [Applies only to Scotland.]

(6) Where a court orders a person to be disqualified under this section ('the first order'), no court shall make a further order under this section in respect of the same offence or any offence in respect of which an order could have been made under this section at the time the first order was made.

(7) to (9) [Production of licences and consequences of failure to produce.]

(10) to (11) [Duty to send notice of order to Secretary of State and contents of notice.]

(12) Where on any occasion a court deals with an offender—

(a) for an offence in respect of which an order was made under this section, or

(b) for two or more offences in respect of any of which such an order was made,

any period of disqualification which is on that occasion imposed under section 34 or 35 of this Act shall be treated as reduced by any period during which he was disqualified by reason only of an order made under this section in respect of any of those offences.

(13) Any reference in this or any other Act (including any Act passed after this Act) to the length of a period of disqualification shall, unless the context otherwise requires, be construed as a reference to its length before any reduction under this section.

(14) [References to counterparts to be disregarded for pre-June 1990 licences.]

Section 26 enables magistrates, when committing an offender to the Crown Court under the **C7.31** PCC(S)A 2000, s. 6 (see **D23.57**), remitting him to another court, deferring sentence or adjourning, to disqualify him from driving until he has been finally dealt with. Any period of disqualification finally imposed by the court, without regard to the period of interim disqualification, is reduced accordingly by the administrative authorities (*Edwards v Wheelan* 1999 SLT 917). Such an order is termed a 'first order' and only one such order may be made under s. 26. The order may only be made for a maximum of six months inclusive of the day on which the order is made. The defendant must produce his licence and, where appropriate, its counterpart, which the court must retain. Failure to do so is an offence unless the licence and its counterpart have been posted in accordance with s. 7 of the Act (see **C2.6**), a new licence and counterpart have been applied for but not received, or the defendant tenders a valid receipt under s. 56 of the Act and immediately produces the licence and counterpart to the court on their return.

Disqualification Pending Passing of Driving Test

Road Traffic Offenders Act 1988, s. 36   C7.32

(1) Where this subsection applies to a person the court must order him to be disqualified until he passes the appropriate driving test.

(2) Subsection (1) above applies to a person who is disqualified under section 34 of this Act on conviction of—

(a) manslaughter... by the driver of a motor vehicle, or

(b) an offence under section 1 (causing death by dangerous driving), section 1A (causing serious injury by dangerous driving) or section 2 (dangerous driving) of the Road Traffic Act 1988.

(3) Subsection (1) above also applies—

(a) to a person who is disqualified under section 34 or 35 of this Act in such circumstances or for such period as the Secretary of State may by order prescribe, or

(b) to such other persons convicted of such offences involving obligatory endorsement as may be so prescribed.

(4) Where a person to whom subsection (1) above does not apply is convicted of an offence involving obligatory endorsement, the court may order him to be disqualified until he passes the appropriate driving test (whether or not he has previously passed any test).

(5) In this section—
'appropriate driving test' means—
(a) an extended driving test, where a person is convicted of an offence involving obligatory disqualification or is disqualified under section 35 of this Act,
(b) a test of competence to drive, other than an extended driving test, in any other case,
'extended driving test' means a test of competence to drive prescribed for the purposes of this section, and
'test of competence to drive' means a test prescribed by virtue of section 89(3) of the Road Traffic Act 1988.
(6) In determining whether to make an order under subsection (4) above, the court shall have regard to the safety of road users.
(7) Where a person is disqualified until he passes the extended driving test—
(a) any earlier order under this section shall cease to have effect, and
(b) a court shall not make a further order under this section while he is so disqualified.
(8) Subject to subsection (9) below, a disqualification by virtue of an order under this section shall be deemed to have expired on production to the Secretary of State of evidence, in such form as may be prescribed by regulations under section 105 of the RTA 1988, that the person disqualified has passed the test in question since the order was made.
(9) A disqualification shall be deemed to have expired only in relation to vehicles of such classes as may be prescribed in relation to the test passed by regulations under that section.
(10) Where there is issued to a person a licence on the counterpart of which are endorsed particulars of a disqualification under this section, there shall also be endorsed the particulars of any test of competence to drive that he has passed since the order of disqualification was made.
(11) and (11A) [Extensions to tests taken in Northern Ireland, the Isle of Man, the Channel Islands, an EEA State, Gibraltar, or a designated country or territory or for the purposes of a British Forces licence, if passing such a test would give entitlement to an exchangeable licence.]

C7.33   The effect of s. 36 is to make disqualification until a test is passed mandatory for those offenders convicted of offences specified in s. 36(2). The obligation to disqualify under s. 36 also extends to such persons disqualified under ss. 34 and 35 as may be prescribed and to such other persons convicted of offences involving obligatory endorsement as may be prescribed. If the sentencer erroneously omits to impose this element of the sentence, the appeal court can remedy that mistake (*Broad* [2007] EWCA Crim 2146). Where an offender is already subject to an order to take an extended driving test, by virtue of the RTOA 1988, s. 36(7)(b), a sentencing court cannot impose a further order to take such a test (*Abdullahi* [2010] EWCA Crim 1886; *Green* [2013] EWCA Crim 2517).

The matters to be tested during an 'extended driving test' are broadly similar to those prescribed for the 'ordinary' driving test, but its minimum length is 60 minutes, considerably longer than the normal test of competence to drive (Motor Vehicles (Driving Licences) Regulations 1999 (SI 1999 No. 2864), reg. 41). Under the RTOA 1988, s. 36(5), when imposing a discretionary disqualification, e.g., for careless driving (*Owen* [2012] EWCA Crim 170), driving while disqualified (*Watson* [2013] EWCA Crim 2316) or assault occasioning actual bodily harm (*Large* [2011] EWCA Crim 2970), the sentencing court cannot disqualify until an extended driving test is passed; that option is confined to cases where the offence involves obligatory disqualification or the defendant is being disqualified for accumulating penalty points under the RTOA 1988, s. 35, but the court is permitted to order an ordinary test to be retaken. When the Road Safety Act 2006, s. 37, is brought into force, the definition of 'appropriate driving test' will be modified so that it will enable the Secretary of State to prescribe by regulations the circumstances in which the test to be passed must be an extended one. This is clearly intended to broaden the circumstances in which the more stringent post-disqualification test will be applicable before the driver fully returns to the roads.

C7.34   The power to order a person to take a driving test where he has been convicted of an offence involving obligatory endorsement which has not been prescribed under s. 36(3)(b) may be exercised only after the court has had regard to the safety of road users in accordance with s. 36(6). The insertion of s. 36(6) seems to indicate that such a regard is paramount in deciding whether to exercise the discretion to disqualify. This implies that all courts should consider using s. 36 when it is not mandatory to order a retest. Nonetheless, on the previous authorities an order was to be made only on evidence that the ability of the defendant to drive is in some way in question. It should not be used as an additional punishment but only where because of 'age or infirmity or the circumstances of the offence a person may not be a competent driver' (*Buckley* (1988) 10 Cr App R (S) 477).

In *Miller* (1994) 15 Cr App R (S) 505, the Court of Appeal upheld the sentencing judge's order that the offender be disqualified until passing a driving test on the ground that it was clear his driving was grossly incompetent. He had pleaded guilty to careless driving on an indictment alleging dangerous driving. He had never passed a driving test and had numerous previous convictions, including ten for driving while disqualified. In *Bannister* [1991] RTR 1, where the offender was imprisoned for three months and disqualified for two years and thereafter until he passed a test, the court took the view that competence to drive included proper regard for other road users as well as control of the vehicle.

If an offender is disqualified under the RTOA 1988, s. 36, he must obtain a provisional driving licence before driving and comply with its conditions of use, or else he may run the risk of being convicted under the RTA 1988, s. 103 (*Hunter v Coombs* [1962] 1 All ER 904; *DPP v Barker* (2004) 168 JP 617).

Offender Escaping Consequences of Endorsable Offence by Deception

Where a sentencing court was deceived by a defendant being dealt with for an offence involving obligatory endorsement about any circumstance that may have had a bearing on whether to disqualify him or the length of disqualification to impose, the RTOA 1988, s. 49, enables the court subsequently dealing with the defendant on conviction for an offence arising from that deception, after taking into account any order made by the original sentencing court, to exercise the same powers and duties regarding an order for disqualification as were available to the original court, i.e. to resentence for the original endorsable offence. **C7.35**

Length of Disqualification

A period of disqualification is forward-looking and designed to be preventative rather than backward-looking and punitive (*Hussain* [2009] EWCA Crim 2582; *Bell* [2013] EWCA Crim 2549). **C7.36**

When the CAJA 2009, s. 137 and sch. 16, are brought into force, ss. 35A and 35B will be inserted into the RTOA 1988. As a result, a defendant who is sentenced to a custodial sentence as well as a disqualification under the RTOA 1988, s. 34 or 35, must be disqualified for 'the appropriate extension period', as set out in s. 35A(4), in addition to the period being imposed in respect of s. 34 or 35. The overall period of disqualification will effectively be increased by the period actually spent in custody. In cases where the court proposes to impose a period of disqualification as well as imposing, for a separate offence, immediate custody (or where the defendant is already a serving prisoner), s. 35B will require the court to consider the diminished effect of disqualification as a distinct penalty.

In arriving at the length of disqualification which is appropriate, the court should not have regard to the application of the RTOA 1988, s. 42 (see C7.42), and the power of the court to remove a disqualification, but merely to the length of time that is appropriate for the offence before it (*Bannister* [1991] RTR 1). **C7.37**

In general, when considering the length of disqualification courts should attempt to avoid long periods, particularly when the disqualification is imposed at the same time as a sentence of imprisonment as it may have an adverse effect on 'the defendant's prospects of effective rehabilitation upon his release from custody' (per Ognall J in *Russell* [1993] RTR 249n). In considering the length of disqualification when combined with a term of imprisonment,

Part C Road Traffic Offences

there is no principle that the period should extend only for a short time beyond the length of the custodial sentence; each case must be decided on its own facts (*Playford* [2010] EWCA Crim 2171). In addition lengthy disqualifications tend to be counterproductive and often hamper the offender in the job market, sometimes leading to further crime, in particular, driving while disqualified. See *Lawson* [2006] 1 Cr App R (S) 323 and *Zar* [2013] EWCA Crim 1897. Care needs to be taken not to over-sentence in a case where there is no apparent appreciable risk to the public (*Dadson* [2013] EWCA Crim 1887). Against those considerations the court must also consider its duty to protect the public, and a lengthy period of disqualification to enable the defendant to mature may be justified (*Gibbons* (1987) 9 Cr App R (S) 21). See also *Cook* [2010] EWCA Crim 121, *Backhouse* [2010] EWCA Crim 1111 and *Geale* [2013] 2 Cr App R (S) 74 (17).

C7.38 Disqualification for life may be imposed (*Tunde-Olarinde* [1967] 2 All ER 491), but such a disqualification is inappropriate and wrong in principle in the absence of either psychiatric evidence or evidence of many previous convictions which indicates that the defendant would be a danger to the public for an indefinite period if he is allowed to drive (per Morland J in *King* (1992) 13 Cr App R (S) 668). In *King*, although the appellant had used his car as a weapon, he had no previous convictions which related to dangerous or careless driving. The Court of Appeal reduced the period of disqualification from life to five years on the basis that the judge had failed to give weight to the rehabilitative principle set out in *Russell* [1993] RTR 249n. Similarly, in *Rivano* (1994) 158 JP 288, the Court of Appeal decided that there were no very exceptional circumstances requiring disqualification for life or leading to the conclusion that, as a man of only 30, the appellant would be a danger to the public indefinitely. See also *Fazal* [1999] 1 Cr App R (S) 152. In *Buckley* (1994) 15 Cr App R (S) 695, however, the fact that the appellant had such an appalling driving record, including six convictions for reckless driving, demonstrated an astonishing readiness to imperil the public and clearly satisfied the second limb in *King*; in those circumstances disqualification for life was justified.

When considering the period for which to disqualify a defendant whose licence has already been revoked because of a relevant disability, it is wrong in principle for the court to disqualify indefinitely (*Harrison* [2004] EWCA Crim 1527). The period of disqualification should reflect the offence and the offender's driving record and concerns about public safety arising from that disability are more appropriately dealt with through DVLA procedures for restoring the licence once the disability is no longer a factor.

C7.39 Where the length of sentence alone is being challenged on appeal (which is preferable to instituting proceedings for judicial review), the appropriate test to apply is whether the sentence is 'truly astonishing' (*Tucker v DPP* [1992] 4 All ER 901; *Ealing Justices, ex parte Scrafield* [1994] RTR 195). In cases involving additional factors, the 'harsh and oppressive' test might be more appropriate.

Appeal against and Suspension of Disqualification

C7.40 Under the RTOA 1988, s. 38(1), a person disqualified by an order of a magistrates' court under s. 34 or 35 may appeal against the order in the same manner as against a conviction. Section 39(1) provides that any court which makes an order disqualifying a person may, if it thinks fit, suspend the disqualification pending an appeal against the order.

Effect of Order of Disqualification

C7.41 Upon being disqualified by court order, under the RTOA 1988, s. 37, the defendant's licence is generally treated as being revoked from the beginning of the disqualification. Revocation does not operate for short disqualifications of less than 56 days for endorsable offences or on interim disqualification under the RTOA 1988, s. 26 (see **C7.30**). If disqualified under the RTOA

1988, s. 36, until a retest is passed (see **C7.32**), and if not otherwise disqualified, a provisional licence can be obtained at the end of the fixed period of disqualification.

Removal of Disqualification

The RTOA 1988, s. 42, enables a person to apply to the court by which he was disqualified to **C7.42** remove that disqualification. This option is not available for a disqualification imposed under the RTOA 1988, s. 36(1) (requiring a retest: see **C7.32**). An application can be made only after a certain period of the disqualification has been served: two years if the disqualification was for less than four years; otherwise half of the period of disqualification, subject to never having to wait longer than five years. The court is able to reconsider the length of disqualification and may take into account the person's conduct since the disqualification was imposed. If an application is refused, a further application may not be made until at least three months have elapsed.

By the RTOA 1988, s. 43, any period of suspension shall be disregarded in determining the **C7.43** expiration of a period of disqualification. Thus, if a defendant is disqualified for three years and during that period the disqualification is suspended for three months, then the expiry of the disqualification is three years and three months after the date of disqualification.

An applicant under s. 42 is eligible to apply for publicly funded representation (*Liverpool Crown Court, ex parte McCann* [1995] RTR 23). The chances of such an application being successful, however, are slim.

The CrimPR, r. 55.1, sets out the requirements for an application under s. 42. There is no power to award the applicant costs but even if successful he may be ordered to pay the costs of the application. There appears to be nothing to prevent the court from fixing the hearing date at any stage as long as the application is actually heard after the expiry of the 'relevant time'.

Probationary Period for Newly Qualified Drivers

The Road Traffic (New Drivers) Act 1995, s. 1, establishes a probationary period of two years **C7.44** commencing from the day on which a person becomes a qualified driver, during which time a driver is more at risk of his driving licence being withdrawn than following its completion.

A person becomes a 'qualified driver' on the first occasion of passing a UK driving test or a driving test conducted in any EEA State, the Isle of Man, any of the Channel Islands or Gibraltar (s. 1(2)). By virtue of s. 7, the period may be terminated early if the person is disqualified until a driving test is passed under the RTOA 1988, s. 36 (see **C7.32**), or if he has already had to surrender his licence under the terms of the 1995 Act and has since been granted a full driving licence after retaking and passing a driving test.

During the probationary period, if the driver commits an offence or offences involving obligatory endorsement where the penalty points to be taken into account under the RTOA 1988, s. 29 (see **C7.19**), are six or more, the sentencing court or fixed penalty clerk must send a notice, together with the driver's licence and its counterpart, to the Secretary of State (s. 2), who must then serve a notice on the driver revoking the licence (s. 3). (Schedule 1 to the 1995 Act makes similar provisions for the surrender and revocation of test certificates and provisional driving licences, where the driver has not yet applied for his full driving licence.) There is no discretion involved although 'special reasons' (see **C7.53**) may, if appropriate, be raised against endorsement to prevent such an eventuality. In *Benson* [2012] EWCA Crim 2993, having indicated that the defendant's careless driving did not merit disqualification, but warranted a 'significant number' of points, without consideration of the effect of the 1995 Act, the sentencer imposed six penalty points. Revocation of the licence was only discovered some years later when the appellant sought to change the address on her licence. The situation was remedied by granting leave to appeal out of time and then substituting five penalty points instead.

C7.45 Where a licence is revoked the holder has to retake and pass an 'ordinary' driving test for each class of vehicle affected by the revocation before being able to drive unsupervised and being eligible to apply once again for a full driving licence (s. 4). After passing the retest, however, no probationary period attaches, otherwise persistent offenders could find themselves in a vicious circle of retesting.

By s. 5, if the driver appeals against the conviction or penalty points that led to his licence being revoked under s. 3 and the Secretary of State receives due notification, his licence will be temporarily restored to him pending determination of the appeal. If the appeal is successful, a new full licence will be granted and, if appropriate, the probationary period will continue to run. If the appeal fails to reduce the relevant penalty points below six, the temporary licence will be treated as revoked. These provisions are supplemented by the New Drivers (Appeals Procedure) Regulations 1997 (SI 1997 No. 1098).

Any penalty points which lead to the revocation of a licence remain effective for the normal three-year period from the date of commission of the offence (RTOA 1988, s. 29(2): see **C7.19**). Revocation of the driving licence does not 'wipe clean' the person's driving record for the purposes of disqualification for repeated offences under s. 35 (see **C7.24**). A short discretionary disqualification under s. 34(2), would, however, lead to there being no penalty points to be taken into account. If the sentencer declines to impose a discretionary disqualification, there should be some consideration of the effect on the defendant of awarding six or more penalty points, where the range for the offence permits a lower number (*Edmunds* [2000] 2 Cr App R (S) 62). The sentencing court should bear in mind the intention of the 1995 Act to require newly qualified drivers whose driving is poor to face retesting.

ENDORSEMENT

C7.46   Road Traffic Offenders Act 1988, ss. 44, 44A and 45

    44.—(1) Where a person is convicted of an offence involving obligatory endorsement, the court must order there to be endorsed on the counterpart of any licence held by him particulars of the conviction and also—

    (a) if the court orders him to be disqualified, particulars of the disqualification, or

    (b) if the court does not order him to be disqualified—

      (i) particulars of the offence, including the date when it was committed, and

      (ii) the penalty points to be attributed to the offence.

    (2) Where the court does not order the person convicted to be disqualified, it need not make an order under subsection (1) above if for special reasons it thinks fit not to do so.

    (3) [Applies only to Scotland.]

    (3A) Where a person who is not the holder of a licence is convicted of an offence involving obligatory disqualification, subsection (1) above applies as if the reference to the counterpart of any licence held by him were a reference to his driving record.

    (4) This section is subject to section 48 of this Act.

    44A.—(1) Where the court orders the endorsement of a person's driving record with any particulars or penalty points it must send notice of the order to the Secretary of State.

    (2) On receiving the notice, the Secretary of State must endorse those particulars or penalty points on the person's driving record.

    (3) A notice sent by the court to the Secretary of State in pursuance of this section must be sent in such manner and to such address and contain such particulars as the Secretary of State may require.

    45.—(1) An order that any particulars or penalty points are to be endorsed on the counterpart of any licence held by the person convicted shall, whether he is at the time the holder of a licence or not, operate as an order that the counterpart of any licence he may then hold or may subsequently obtain is to be so endorsed until he becomes entitled under subsection (4) below to have a licence issued to him with its counterpart free from the particulars or penalty points.

    (2) On the issue of a new licence to a person, any particulars or penalty points ordered to be endorsed on the counterpart of any licence held by him shall be entered on the counterpart of

the licence unless he has become entitled under subsection (4) below to have a licence issued to him with its counterpart free from those particulars or penalty points.

(3) [Repealed.]

(4) A person the counterpart of whose licence has been ordered to be endorsed is entitled to have issued to him with effect from the end of the period for which the endorsement remains effective a new licence with a counterpart free from the endorsement if he applies for a new licence in pursuance of section 97(1) of the Road Traffic Act 1988, surrenders any subsisting licence and its counterpart, pays the fee prescribed by regulations under Part III of that Act and satisfies the other requirements of section 97(1).

(5) An endorsement ordered on a person's conviction of an offence remains effective (subject to subsections (6) and (7) below)—

   (a) if an order is made for the disqualification of the offender, until four years have elapsed since the conviction, and

   (b) if no such order is made, until either—

      (i) four years have elapsed since the commission of the offence, or

      (ii) an order is made for the disqualification of the offender under section 35 of this Act.

(6) Where the offence was one under section 1, 1A or 2 of the Road Traffic Act 1988 (causing death by dangerous driving, causing serious injury by dangerous driving and dangerous driving), the endorsement remains in any case effective until four years have elapsed since the conviction.

(7) Where the offence was one—

   (a) under section 3A, 4(1) or 5(1)(a) of that Act (driving offences connected with drink or drugs), or

   (b) under section 7(6) of that Act (failing to provide specimen) involving obligatory disqualification, or

   (c) under section 7A(6) of that Act (failing to allow a specimen to be subjected to laboratory testing),

the endorsement remains effective until 11 years have elapsed since the conviction.

In all cases involving obligatory or discretionary disqualification, the court, in the absence of 'special reasons' (see **C7.53**) or the operation of the RTOA 1988, s. 48, or the Mental Health Act 1983, s. 37 (see **E22.1**), is obliged to order particulars of the offence to be endorsed on the counterpart of the offender's licence or any licence that might be held by the defendant in the future (or, where applicable, on the offender's driving record: see **C7.50**). Each offence is denoted by a particular code, and the DVLA is notified. Where the offender is not disqualified, penalty points must also be endorsed (RTOA 1988, s. 44). **C7.47**

The number of points applicable to an offence is set out in the RTOA 1988, sch. 2, part I, col. 7. Certain offences carry a variable number of points (see **C8.1**). In cases involving variable penalty points, the court should allow mitigation before arriving at any decision as to the number of points that should be imposed.

The points to be endorsed should reflect the seriousness of the offence. Therefore, an offence of driving without due care and attention consisting of momentary inattention might be suitably endorsed with three or four penalty points, whereas an offence consisting of prolonged, blatantly bad driving should carry a higher number of points to reflect the greater degree of culpability.

If there are a number of offences committed on the 'same occasion' then, subject to the RTOA 1988, s. 28 (see **C7.16**), the points to be endorsed are those relating to the offence which carries the highest number. Thus, if a defendant is convicted of careless driving and a construction and use offence, the highest number of penalty points relates to the careless driving. If the penalty points are the same for both offences, then it is normal practice to endorse the more serious offence with the points. Where penalty points for a fixed penalty have already been endorsed, the maximum number of points available to the court in respect of an offence committed on the same occasion must be reduced accordingly (see **C7.21**; *Green v O'Donnell* 1997 SCCR 315). If a period of disqualification is obligatory or imposed under the court's discretionary powers, no penalty points in respect of other offences committed on the 'same occasion' are endorsed **C7.48**

(*Martin v DPP* [2000] RTR 188 and *Ahmed v McLeod* [2000] RTR 201n, respectively). See also *Campbell* (2010) 174 JP 73.

It is not unusual for a defendant to face a number of charges relating to different occasions. In those circumstances the court must establish the total number of points for each occasion, and is then obliged to aggregate those points for the purposes of the penalty points procedure.

The fact that an endorsement to which s. 45(7) applies remains effective beyond the time after which the conviction to which it attaches may be spent under the Rehabilitation of Offenders Act 1974 (see **E24**) does not constitute a violation of the right to private life in the ECHR, Article 8(1) (*R (Pearson) v DVLA* [2003] RTR 292).

Meaning of 'Offence Involving Obligatory Endorsement'

C7.49   Road Traffic Offenders Act 1988, s. 96

For the purposes of this Act, an offence involves obligatory endorsement if it is an offence under a provision of the Traffic Acts specified in column 1 of Part I of Schedule 2 to this Act or an offence specified in column 1 of Part II of that Schedule and either—
(a) the word 'obligatory' (without qualification) appears in column 6 (in the case of Part I) or column 3 (in the case of Part II) against the offence, or
(b) that word appears there qualified by conditions relating to the offence which are satisfied.

For the RTOA 1988, sch. 2, see **C8.1**.

New System of Endorsement

C7.50 **Driving Record**   The Road Safety Act 2006, ss. 8 and 9 and sch. 2, were brought into force on 1 April 2009 as the first phase of the new system being introduced in accordance with s. 61(8) of the 2006 Act.

In order to remove the differences in treatment between those who do and those who do not hold GB driving licences, these provisions introduce the notion of a 'driving record' being established in relation to a person, to be maintained by the Secretary of State and 'designed to be endorsed with particulars relating to offences committed by the person under the Traffic Acts' (RTA 1988, s. 97A). Driving records will now be created and maintained in respect of unlicensed and foreign drivers. The RTOA 1988, s. 44(3A) (see **C7.46**), makes it a requirement to order endorsement on the driving record of an offender who does not hold a driving licence. Notice of that endorsement is then sent to the Secretary of State in accordance with the RTOA 1988, s. 44A (see **C7.46**). Thereafter, those driving records can be accessed in order to ascertain whether the person in question is liable to disqualification under the RTOA 1988, s. 35 (see **C7.24**).

Endorsement of a driving record is also available by virtue of amendments made to the RTOA 1988, s. 54 (see **C7.3**). The recipient is required to deliver the notice to enable an appropriate check to be made as to whether or not he is going to be liable to be disqualified for the offence; if that is not the case, a fixed penalty notice must follow. Similarly, the RTOA 1988, s. 57A, enables a fixed penalty clerk to deal with a person who does not hold a driving licence in much the same way as someone who does, save that, instead of endorsing the person's counterpart, upon payment of the fixed penalty before the end of the suspended enforcement period, the clerk sends notice to the Secretary of State of the relevant particulars to be endorsed on the person's driving record.

C7.51 **Extension to All Drivers**   The second phase of the new system will be introduced when the Road Safety Act 2006, s. 10 and sch. 3, are brought into force. When this stage is reached, driving records will be created for everyone and references to 'the counterpart' will disappear, so that it will no longer have any function. Drivers who hold GB licences will still be required to produce them in order to be given a fixed penalty notice; for all others, they will be dealt with like unlicensed and foreign drivers under the first phase. The benefit will be the centralisation of the offending records in respect of all drivers in a uniform manner.

Combination of Disqualification and Endorsement with Orders for Discharge

The RTOA 1988, s. 46, makes provision as to the combination of orders for disqualification **C7.52** and endorsement with the provisions in the PCC(S)A 2000, s. 14, which have the effect of treating a conviction in respect of which a discharge is imposed as if it were not a conviction at all (see E12.6). Section 46(1) provides that the PCC(S)A 2000, s. 14(3), does not operate to prevent the court from endorsing an offender's licence or disqualifying him from driving. Section 46(2) provides that the PCC(S)A 2000, s. 14(1), does not operate to prevent a court from taking into account previous orders of disqualification or endorsement imposed on an occasion when the offender was discharged.

SPECIAL REASONS

General   A finding of 'special reasons' allows the court a discretion as to whether or not it: **C7.53**

(a) disqualifies under the RTOA 1988, s. 34(1); or
(b) endorses under the RTOA 1988, s. 44.

A 'special reason' was defined in *Whittal v Kirby* [1947] KB 194 as being special to the facts of the offence and not the offender. In doing so the Divisional Court adopted the definition in *Crossan* [1939] NI 106 (at pp. 112–13):

> A 'special reason' within the exception is one which is special to the facts of the particular case, that is, special to the facts which constitute the offence. It is, in other words, a mitigating or extenuating circumstance, not amounting in law to a defence to the charge, yet directly connected with the commission of the offence, and one which the court ought properly to take into consideration when imposing punishment. A circumstance peculiar to the offender as distinguished from the offence is not a 'special reason' within the exception.

Although *Wickins* (1958) 42 Cr App R 236 broadly confirmed these requirements, in *Jarvis v DPP* (2001) 165 JP 15, in respect of cases where excess alcohol offending is in issue, preference was expressed for the analysis of the position contained in *Jackson and Hart* [1970] 1 QB 647. See also *Kinsella v DPP* [2002] EWHC 545 (Admin). Where a defendant's medical condition is found not to amount to a defence to a charge of failing to provide a specimen, it does not automatically mean that the same medical condition cannot constitute 'special reasons' (*Woolfe v DPP* [2007] RTR 187).

As unreasonable delay in the determination of the charge does not relate to the facts of the offence so such delay cannot constitute a special reason (*Miller v DPP* [2005] RTR 44).

The onus of establishing that there are 'special reasons' lies with the defence on a balance of   **C7.54** probabilities. Where there has been a trial resulting in a conviction and the defendant then advances special reasons, justices should readily accede to an application that a defendant be recalled when the earlier evidence has not fully dealt with the relevant facts (*DPP v Kinnersley* [1993] RTR 105). In most cases (save for obvious ones), the justices might expect to hear expert evidence, particularly where the defence seek to establish that drinks were laced, although where corroboration does not exist or is unavailable for some good reason it is still open to the court to find special reasons where the defendant's evidence is believed (*Watson v Adam* 1996 SLT 459). Notice of the defence's intention to produce evidence of such special reasons should be given to the prosecution so that unnecessary adjournments are avoided. Failure to notify the prosecution could reflect on the bona fides of the defendant (*DPP v O'Connor* [1992] RTR 66; see also *Pugsley v Hunter* [1973] 2 All ER 10). The defendant's failure to give an appropriate explanation or account at the time of arrest or commission of the offence does not, as a matter of law, exclude the possibility of a finding that special reasons exist, but it would usually form an important factor for the court in considering all the relevant circumstances of a case (*DPP v Kinnersley*).

'Special reasons' may be advanced on appeal to the Crown Court as part of an appeal against sentence, or, if an appeal against conviction includes an appeal against sentence, where the Crown Court have upheld the conviction. The appeal is by way of rehearing of the evidence relevant to the issue of whether or not there are special reasons and, if so, as to how the discretion is to be exercised. Where special reasons have not been found an appeal by way of case stated is a more convenient procedure than an application for judicial review (*DPP v O'Connor*).

C7.55 **Exercise of Power Discretionary**   In *St. Albans Crown Court, ex parte O'Donovan* [2000] 1 Cr App R (S) 344, the Divisional Court noted that, whilst it did not rule out the possibility, following a finding of 'special reasons', of imposing a period of disqualification greater than the mandatory minimum, there would have to be compelling reasons to do so. In *Ex parte Donovan*, the defendant was nearly three times above the prescribed limit but had only driven a very short distance and had not posed any appreciable risk of danger to anyone. A disqualification of 12 months was substituted for the original 20 months.

Even where 'special reasons' have been established, there is no obligation to exercise the discretion and the court may still disqualify and endorse as it considers appropriate. In cases involving obligatory disqualification, the court may find 'special reasons' and not disqualify but still endorse. In cases where disqualification is discretionary, the court may find 'special reasons' and still endorse. In *Agnew v DPP* [1991] RTR 147, a case of careless driving, the Divisional Court found that the conditions were satisfied but refused to exercise its discretion. The applicant was a police officer on a training exercise who had gone through a red light, failing to follow instructions in treating the light in the same way as a 'give way' sign. Morland J quoted Lord Widgery CJ in *Taylor v Rajan* [1974] QB 424, that 'justices should only exercise the discretion in favour of the driver in clear and compelling circumstances'. He then went on to say (at p. 150):

> There are two competing considerations: the need for realistic police driver training in actual road conditions and the safety of lawful users of the highway, motorists and pedestrians. The second must always be paramount.

C7.56 Whether or not to exercise the discretion 'is peculiarly a question for [the justices], seeing and hearing the witnesses and making their assessment of the answers which are given to them, to determine whether in the circumstances it is a case in which they, in the exercise of that discretion, feel justified in imposing penalties other than disqualification' (per Beldam J in *Donahue v DPP* [1993] RTR 156). In *DPP v Bristow* [1998] RTR 100, the Divisional Court held that the key question justices should ask themselves when assessing if special reasons exist and whether their discretion should be exercised is what a sober, reasonable and responsible friend of the defendant, who was present at the time but who was a non-driver and thus unable to help, would have advised in the circumstances: drive or not drive. Unless the justices thought it was a real possibility rather than just an off-chance that such a friend would have advised the defendant to drive, they should not find special reasons and exercise their discretion.

Endorsement under s. 44 includes endorsement with penalty points. If the court does exercise the discretion not to endorse with particulars of the conviction, there is no power to endorse penalty points separately. Nor is there any power to endorse either without penalty points or with a lesser number than the amount set out in sch. 2 to the Act.

As shown in the examples that follow, the question of what constitutes 'special reasons' depends upon the facts of any particular case within the overall test as expressed in *Whittal v Kirby* [1947] KB 194 (see **C7.53**). As long as the justices or Crown Court have properly directed themselves in accordance with that test, the appellate courts will not interfere with their finding. Many of the cases relate to drink-related offences where the defendant may be anxious to avoid a mandatory disqualification. The courts have consistently sought to limit the application of 'special reasons' to cases which are plainly meritorious.

'Laced' Drinks   'Laced' drinks as a special reason received a comprehensive review in *DPP v*   **C7.57**
O'Connor [1992] RTR 66. The Divisional Court held that the defence must show:

(a) that the defendant's drink or drinks had been laced;
(b) that the defendant did not know or suspect that his drink had been laced;
(c) that, if the defendant had not taken the laced drink, his level of alcohol would not have
     exceeded the prescribed limit.

Evidence needs to be examined with some care and expert evidence, which justices should normally expect to receive, is usually highly relevant as it goes to both credibility and whether or not
the driver's admitted, voluntary consumption of alcohol would have taken him above the prescribed limit (per Woolf LJ at p. 79). In appropriate cases, public funding should be made available to enable a defendant to adduce expert evidence to support a plea of special reasons in 'laced
drinks' cases (*Gravesham Magistrates' Court, ex parte Baker* [1998] RTR 451).

The need for a two-stage process was stressed, and Woolf LJ stated (at p. 81E):

> . . . in cases where there is erratic driving, or there is a substantial amount of alcohol in the defen-
> dant's bloodstream, justices will want to consider carefully whether, even if special reasons are
> established, this is a case where the defendant should have appreciated that he was not in a condi-
> tion in which he should have driven.

An inability to distinguish between the relative alcoholic strengths of different drinks will not
suffice (*Beauchamp-Thompson v DPP* [1988] RTR 54), otherwise it could give rise to a licence
to 'lace' one's own drinks. Assuming, without inquiry, that a drink contains no alcohol will not
constitute special reasons (*Robinson v DPP* (2004) 168 JP 522, where the court suggested *obiter*
that even after inquiry and being told that the drink did not contain alcohol, readings that are
very high should still not result in the justices exercising their discretion in favour of the defendant). See also *DPP v Sharma* [2005] RTR 361. The difficulties presented when advancing
special reasons were highlighted in *R (Knifton) v DPP* [2011] EWHC 3850 (Admin), where the
Divisional Court decided that the justices, following careful scrutiny of the evidence given, had
been entitled to conclude that the defendant had known, or at very least suspected, that her
drinks had been laced.

Handling Emergencies   In principle, driving in an emergency is recognised as being capable   **C7.58**
of amounting to special reasons. When raised, it is the justices' task to decide whether the facts
amount to, and were, special reasons and then to decide what effect, if any, this has on the sentence to be imposed (*DPP v Upchurch* [1994] RTR 366; *DPP v Knight* [1994] RTR 374). In
doing so, the court can divide the driving into separate chapters to ascertain whether there was
any interruption after which a fresh explanation would be required as to why the defendant had
chosen to drive again (*DPP v Goddard* [1998] RTR 463).

In *Aichroth v Cottee* [1954] 2 All ER 856, Lord Goddard CJ stated (at p. 1127) that the 'mere
fact that there is a sudden emergency will not be enough if it is shown that there are other reasonable methods of meeting it'. In *DPP v Cox* [1996] RTR 123, the defendant was a key-holder at
a golf club and was contacted in the night when the burglar alarm was activated. Despite the
short distance involved and having consumed a considerable amount of alcohol, he drove to the
club premises without considering alternative methods of responding to the alarm. The
Divisional Court confirmed that the issue of whether an emergency exists must be viewed
objectively and held that the justices were justified in concluding that this was an emergency
within the guidelines of *Aichroth v Cottee*. When considering if special reasons not to disqualify
exist and deciding objectively whether a reasonable or sober person would have advised the
defendant to drive in the perceived urgent situation in which he found himself, it is appropriate
to take into account the amount of alcohol consumed and the fact that the danger to road users
would have been obvious (*DPP v Heathcote* (2011) 175 JP 530). Where it was apparent to the
defendant that he was suffering the onset of a diabetic hypoglycaemic attack, special reasons
may be available on a charge of speeding if, and only if, the decision to exceed the speed limit

was a reasonable means by which to bring the vehicle to a halt at the nearest convenient moment (*Warring Davies v CPS Bradford* [2009] EWHC 1172 (Admin)).

C7.59   A private crisis, such as being blackmailed by a threat of crying rape, can justify a finding of special reasons as long as the justices guard against being taken in by hard luck stories and approach the issue in the proper objective fashion (*DPP v Enston* [1996] RTR 324). Provided justices have considered all the relevant facts, have reached a conclusion on those facts that could not be said to be perverse and have directed themselves properly on the law, the Divisional Court should be very slow to overturn the decision of the justices, even if it does not agree with the conclusions of the justices as to the facts (*Chapman v O'Hagan* [1949] 2 All ER 690). See also *Ashton v CPS* [2005] EWHC 2729 (Admin), which involved a defendant on his way to collect a liveried ambulance to answer a call-out.

In *DPP v Whittle* [1996] RTR 154, however, the Divisional Court overturned a finding of special reasons on grounds of a medical emergency, reaffirming the objective approach required, because the reasonable man would not have regarded the situation as one in which no other course of action was possible. The defendant had taken over the driving from his wife, who had complained of dizziness and blurred vision, but was driving fellow passengers home when stopped by the police. In passing, Simon Brown LJ wondered whether a genuine medical emergency might more properly fall within the complete defence of duress of circumstances (see A3.50) rather than being raised only as a special reason. In cases involving the risk of death or serious injury, such a course would certainly be advisable.

C7.60   **Relevance of Distance Driven**   In *Chatters v Burke* [1986] 3 All ER 168, following an accident the defendant drove his motor vehicle a very short distance from a field onto the side of the highway, where he stopped, got out, and waited for the arrival of the police. He was charged with driving with excess alcohol in his breath and no insurance. The finding of 'special reasons' was upheld and seven matters which ought to be taken into account in such cases were listed (at p. 1327):

> First of all they should consider how far the vehicle was in fact driven; secondly, in what manner it was driven; thirdly, what was the state of the vehicle; fourthly, whether it was the intention of the driver to drive any further; fifthly, the prevailing conditions with regard to the road and the traffic upon it; sixthly, whether there was any possibility of danger by contact with other road users; and finally, what was the reason for the vehicle being driven at all.

C7.61   In *DPP v Humphries* [2000] RTR 52, the Divisional Court recognised the importance of this guidance whilst adding that the presence or absence of any factor would not automatically produce a particular conclusion. In this case, an argument in favour of finding 'special reasons' founded on the short distance actually driven was rejected because the intention of the defendant had been to drive much further had he not been apprehended. In contrast, in *DPP v Heritage* (2002) 166 JP 772, where the vehicle had been moved to a parking place and was then involved in a collision, having regard to the very short distance driven and all the surrounding circumstances, the justices were entitled to conclude that special reasons existed on a conviction for no insurance.

In *DPP v Corcoran* [1991] RTR 329, the respondent, having parked in the street because he was late for the theatre, drove some 40 yards to a car park from which a colleague was to collect the car on the following day. The car was travelling without lights, albeit slowly, and there were pedestrians in the vicinity but no other vehicles were visible and no danger was caused to other road users. The lack of danger by contact with other road users and the distance travelled were central to the decision to uphold the justices' finding of special reasons. But other factors, such as the availability of alternative courses of action to that of driving, can lead to the opposite conclusion (*R (DPP) v Oram* [2005] EWHC 964 (Admin)).

In *Daniels v DPP* [1992] RTR 140, the appellant, in the course of attempting to start his motor cycle, travelled 35 yards and was then arrested on suspicion of theft. As the defendant claimed that his refusal to provide the required specimen was attributable to having been distracted by the charge of theft (which was not being pursued), on those particular facts the Divisional Court accepted that this could be found to amount to 'special reasons'.

No Insurance   In cases concerning no insurance, a mistaken, albeit honest, belief that there **C7.62** was insurance has been held to be insufficient to amount to 'special reasons' in the absence of reasonable grounds for the belief (*Knowles v Rennison* [1947] KB 488; *DPP v Robson* [2001] EWHC Admin 496), particularly where responsibility for withdrawal of insurance cover rested on the defendant (*R (Smith) v DPP* [2003] EWHC 1080 (Admin)); where a defendant has inquired as to whether he is insured and has been assured that he is, this may amount to reasonable grounds, and special reasons (*Marshall v McLeod* 1998 SCCR 317). The mere fact that a vehicle is parked and unlikely to be driven while uninsured will not amount to 'special reasons' (*Heywood v O'Connor* 1994 SLT 254). In *DPP v Powell* [1993] RTR 266, the defendant's view that he did not require insurance to road test a motorised children's bike, which he regarded as a toy, was held to come within the test set out in *Whittal v Kirby* [1947] KB 194 (see **C7.53**). See also *DPP v Murray* [2001] EWHC 848 (Admin), which concerned a Go-Ped.

Other Reasons   It can be 'special reasons' where the investigating officer incorrectly informs **C7.63** the defendant that failure to provide the required specimen will not necessarily lead to a period of disqualification (*Bobin v DPP* [1999] RTR 375).

Although fear of AIDS is potentially a defence to a charge of refusing to provide a specimen if it is medically established as a phobia (see *De Freitas v DPP* [1993] RTR 98 at **C5.30**), it was also held, in *DPP v Kinnersley* [1993] RTR 105, to be capable of being a 'special reason' for not disqualifying after a refusal to give a breath specimen.

Stating Grounds for Not Disqualifying or Endorsing or Shortening Period of Disqualification

Road Traffic Offenders Act 1988, s. 47 **C7.64**

(1) In any case where a court exercises its power under section 34, 35 or 44 of this Act not to order any disqualification or endorsement or to order disqualification for a shorter period than would otherwise be required, it must state the grounds for doing so in open court and, if it is a magistrates' court…, must cause them to be entered in the register…of its proceedings.

Any court must state, in open court, the grounds on which it has found 'special reasons' or 'mitigating circumstances', but despite the use of the word 'must', the Divisional Court in *Barnes v Gevaux* [1981] RTR 236 held that this requirement was discretionary in cases where the power to disqualify is discretionary.

INTERPRETATION PROVISIONS

Road Traffic Offenders Act 1988, s. 98 **C7.65**

(1) In this Act—
'disqualified' means disqualified for holding or obtaining a licence and 'disqualification' is to be construed accordingly,
'drive' has the same meaning as in the Road Traffic Act 1988,
'licence' means a licence to drive a motor vehicle granted under Part III of that Act,
'provisional licence' means a licence granted by virtue of section 97(2) of that Act,
'the provisions connected with the licensing of drivers' means sections 7, 8, 22, 25 to 29, 31, 32, 34 to 48, 91ZA to 91B, 96 and 97 of this Act,
'road'—
    (a) in relation to England and Wales, means any highway and any other road to which the public has access, and includes bridges over which a road passes, and
    (b) [Applies only to Scotland.],

'the Road Traffic Acts' means the Road Traffic Act 1988, the Road Traffic (Consequential Provisions) Act 1988 (so far as it reproduces the effect of provisions repealed by that Act) and this Act, and

'the Traffic Acts' means the Road Traffic Acts and the Road Traffic Regulation Act 1984, and 'Community licence', 'counterpart', 'EEA State' and 'Northern Ireland licence' have the same meanings as in Part III of the Road Traffic Act 1988.

(2) Sections 185 and 186 of the Road Traffic Act 1988 (meaning of 'motor vehicle' and other expressions relating to vehicles) apply for the purposes of this Act as they apply for the purposes of that Act.

(3) In the Schedules to this Act—

'RTRA' is used as an abbreviation for the Road Traffic Regulation Act 1984, and

'RTA' is used as an abbreviation for the Road Traffic Act 1988 or, if followed by '1989', the Road Traffic (Driver Licensing and Information Systems) Act 1989.

(4) Subject to any express exception, references in this Act to any Part of this Act include a reference to any Schedule to this Act so far as relating to that Part.

Road Traffic Offenders Act 1988, sch. 2   **C8.1**

SCHEDULE 2

PROSECUTION AND PUNISHMENT OF OFFENCES

PART I

OFFENCES UNDER THE TRAFFIC ACTS

(1) Provision creating offence	(2) General nature of offence	(3) Mode of prosecution	(4) Punishment	(5) Disqualification	(6) Endorsement	(7) Penalty points
Offences under the Road Traffic Regulation Act 1984						
RTRA section 5	Contravention of traffic regulation order.	Summarily.	Level 3 on the standard scale.			
RTRA section 8	Contravention of order regulating traffic in Greater London.	Summarily.	Level 3 on the standard scale.			
RTRA section 11	Contravention of experimental traffic order.	Summarily.	Level 3 on the standard scale.			
RTRA section 13	Contravention of experimental traffic scheme in Greater London.	Summarily.	Level 3 on the standard scale.			
RTRA section 16(1)	Contravention of temporary prohibition or restriction.	Summarily.	Level 3 on the standard scale.	Discretionary if committed in respect of a speed restriction.	Obligatory if committed in respect of a speed restriction.	3–6 or 3 (fixed penalty).
RTRA section 16C(1)	Contravention of prohibition or restriction relating to relevant event.	Summarily.	Level 3 on the standard scale.			
RTRA section 17(4)	Use of special road contrary to scheme or regulations.	Summarily.	Level 4 on the standard scale.	Discretionary if committed in respect of a motor vehicle otherwise than by unlawfully stopping or allowing the vehicle to remain at rest on a part of a special road on which vehicles are in certain circumstances permitted to remain at rest.	Obligatory if committed as mentioned in the entry in column 5.	3–6 or 3 (fixed penalty) if committed in respect of a speed restriction, 3 in any other case.
RTRA section 18(3)	One-way traffic on trunk road.	Summarily.	Level 3 on the standard scale.			

(1) Provision creating offence	(2) General nature of offence	(3) Mode of prosecution	(4) Punishment	(5) Disqualification	(6) Endorsement	(7) Penalty points
RTRA section 20(5)	Contravention of prohibition or restriction for roads of certain classes.	Summarily.	Level 3 on the standard scale.			
RTRA section 25(5)	Contravention of pedestrian crossing regulations.	Summarily.	Level 3 on the standard scale.	Discretionary if committed in respect of a motor vehicle.	Obligatory if committed in respect of a motor vehicle.	3
RTRA section 28(3)	Not stopping at school crossing.	Summarily.	Level 3 on the standard scale.	Discretionary if committed in respect of a motor vehicle.	Obligatory if committed in respect of a motor vehicle.	3
RTRA section 29(3)	Contravention of order relating to street playground.	Summarily.	Level 3 on the standard scale.	Discretionary if committed in respect of a motor vehicle.	Obligatory if committed in respect of a motor vehicle.	2
RTRA section 35A(1)	Contravention of order as to use of parking place.	Summarily.	(a) Level 3 on the standard scale in the case of an offence committed by a person in a street parking place reserved for disabled persons' vehicles or in an off-street parking place reserved for such vehicles, where that person would not have been guilty of that offence if the motor vehicle in respect of which it was committed had been a disabled person's vehicle. (b) Level 2 on the standard scale in any other case.			
RTRA section 35A(2)	Misuse of apparatus for collecting charges or of parking device or connected apparatus.	Summarily.	Level 3 on the standard scale.			
RTRA section 35A(5)	Plying for hire in parking place.	Summarily.	Level 2 on the standard scale.			
RTRA section 43(5)	Unauthorised disclosure of information in respect of licensed parking place.	Summarily.	Level 3 on the standard scale.			
RTRA section 43(10)	Failure to comply with term or conditions of licence to operate parking place.	Summarily.	Level 3 on the standard scale.			
RTRA section 43(12)	Operation of public offstreet parking place without licence.	Summarily.	Level 5 on the standard scale.			

1176

(1) Provision creating offence	(2) General nature of offence	(3) Mode of prosecution	(4) Punishment	(5) Disqualification	(6) Endorsement	(7) Penalty points
RTRA section 47(1)	Contraventions relating to designated parking places.	Summarily.	(a) Level 3 on the standard scale in the case of an offence committed by a person in a street parking place reserved for disabled persons' vehicles where that person would not have been guilty of the offence if the motor vehicle in respect of which it was committed had been a disabled person's vehicle. (b) Level 2 in any other case.			
RTRA section 47(3)	Tampering with parking meter.	Summarily.	Level 3 on the standard scale.			
RTRA section 52(1)	Misuse of parking device.	Summarily.	Level 2 on the standard scale.			
RTRA section 53(5)	Contravention of certain provisions of designation orders.	Summarily.	Level 3 on the standard scale.			
RTRA section 53(6)	Other contraventions of designation orders.	Summarily.	Level 2 on the standard scale.			
RTRA section 61(5)	Unauthorised use of loading area.	Summarily.	Level 3 on the standard scale.			
RTRA section 88(7)	Contravention of minimum speed limit.	Summarily.	Level 3 on the standard scale.			
RTRA section 89(1)	Exceeding speed limit.	Summarily.	Level 3 on the standard scale.	Discretionary.	Obligatory.	3–6 or 3 (fixed penalty).
RTRA section 104(5)	Interference with notice as to immobilisation device.	Summarily.	Level 2 on the standard scale.			
RTRA section 104(6)	Interference with immobilisation device.	Summarily.	Level 3 on the standard scale.			
RTRA section 105(5)	Misuse of disabled person's badge (immobilisation devices).	Summarily.	Level 3 on the standard scale.			
RTRA section 105(6A)	Misuse of recognised badge (immobilisation devices).	Summarily.	Level 3 on the standard scale.			

(1) Provision creating offence	(2) General nature of offence	(3) Mode of prosecution	(4) Punishment	(5) Disqualification	(6) Endorsement	(7) Penalty points
RTRA section 108(2) (or that subsection as modified by section 109(2) and (3))	Non-compliance with notice (excess charge).	Summarily.	Level 3 on the standard scale.			
RTRA section 108(3) (or that subsection as modified by section 109(2) and (3))	False response to notice (excess charge).	Summarily.	Level 5 on the standard scale.			
RTRA section 112(4)	Failure to give information as to identity of driver.	Summarily.	Level 3 on the standard scale.			
RTRA section 115(1)	Mishandling or faking parking documents.	(a) Summarily. (b) On indictment.	(a) The statutory maximum. (b) 2 years.			
RTRA section 115(2)	False statement for procuring authorisation.	Summarily.	Level 4 on the standard scale.			
RTRA section 116(1)	Non-delivery of suspect document or article.	Summarily.	Level 3 on the standard scale.			
RTRA section 117	Wrongful use of disabled person's badge.	Summarily.	Level 3 on the standard scale.			
RTRA section 117(1A)	Wrongful use of recognised badge.	Summarily.	Level 3 on the standard scale.			
RTRA section 129(3)	Failure to give evidence at inquiry.	Summarily.	Level 3 on the standard scale.			

Offences under the Road Traffic Act 1988

(1)	(2)	(3)	(4)	(5)	(6)	(7)
RTA section 1	Causing death by dangerous driving	On indictment.	14 years.	Obligatory.	Obligatory.	3–11
RTA section 1A	Causing serious injury by dangerous driving	(a) Summarily. (b) On indictment.	(a) [6 months] or the statutory maximum or both. (b) 5 years or a fine or both.	Obligatory	Obligatory.	3–11
RTA section 2	Dangerous driving.	(a) Summarily. (b) On indictment.	(a) 6 months or the statutory maximum or both. (b) 2 years or a fine or both.	Obligatory.	Obligatory.	3–11
RTA section 2B	Causing death by careless, or inconsiderate, driving.	(a) Summarily. (b) On indictment.	(a) [6 months] or the statutory maximum or both. (b) 5 years or a fine or both.	Obligatory.	Obligatory.	3–11

(1) Provision creating offence	(2) General nature of offence	(3) Mode of prosecution	(4) Punishment	(5) Disqualification	(6) Endorsement	(7) Penalty points
RTA section 3	Careless, and inconsiderate, driving.	Summarily.	Level 5 on the standard scale.	Discretionary.	Obligatory.	3–9
RTA section 3ZB	Causing death by driving: unlicensed, disqualified or uninsured drivers.	(a) Summarily. (b) On indictment.	(a) [6 months] or the statutory maximum or both. (b) 2 years or a fine or both.	Obligatory.	Obligatory.	3–11
RTA section 3A	Causing death by careless driving when under influence of drink or drugs.	On indictment.	14 years or a fine or both.	Obligatory.	Obligatory.	3–11
RTA section 4(1)	Driving or attempting to drive when unfit to drive through drink or drugs.	Summarily.	6 months or level 5 on the standard scale or both.	Obligatory.	Obligatory.	3–11
RTA section 4(2)	Being in charge of a mechanically propelled vehicle when unfit to drive through drink or drugs	Summarily.	3 months or level 4 on the standard scale or both.	Discretionary.	Obligatory.	10
RTA section 5(1)(a)	Driving or attempting to drive with excess alcohol in breath, blood or urine.	Summarily.	6 months or level 5 on the standard scale or both.	Obligatory.	Obligatory.	3–11
RTA section 5(1)(b)	Being in charge of a motor vehicle with excess alcohol in breath, blood or urine.	Summarily.	3 months or level 4 on the standard scale or both.	Discretionary.	Obligatory.	10
RTA section 5A(1)(a) and (2)	Driving or attempting to drive with concentration of specified controlled drug above specified limit.	Summarily.	On conviction in England and Wales: 51 weeks or level 5 on the standard scale or both. On conviction in Scotland: 6 months or level 5 on the standard scale or both.	Obligatory.	Obligatory.	3–11
RTA section 5A(1)(b) and (2)	Being in charge of a motor vehicle with concentration of specified controlled drug above specified limit.	Summarily.	On conviction in England and Wales: 51 weeks or level 4 on the standard scale or both. On conviction in Scotland: 3 months or level 4 on the standard scale or both.	Discretionary.	Obligatory.	10
RTA section 6	Failing to co-operate with a preliminary test.	Summarily.	Level 3 on the standard scale.	Discretionary.	Obligatory.	4
RTA section 7	Failing to provide specimen for analysis or laboratory test.	Summarily.	(a) Where the specimen was required to ascertain ability to drive or proportion of alcohol at the time offender was driving or attempting to drive, 6 months or level 5 on the standard scale or both. (b) In any other case, 3 months or level 4 on the standard scale or both.	(a) Obligatory in case mentioned in column 4(a). (b) Discretionary in any other case.	Obligatory.	(a) 3–11 in case mentioned in column 4(a). (b) 10 in any other case.

(1) Provision creating offence	(2) General nature of offence	(3) Mode of prosecution	(4) Punishment	(5) Disqualification	(6) Endorsement	(7) Penalty points
RTA section 7A	Failing to allow specimen to be subjected to laboratory test.	Summarily.	(a) Where the test would be for ascertaining ability to drive or proportion of alcohol at the time offender was driving or attempting to drive, 6 months or level 5 on the standard scale or both. (b) In any other case, 3 months or level 4 on the standard scale or both.	(a) Obligatory in the case mentioned in column 4(a). (b) Discretionary in any other case.	Obligatory.	(a) 3–11, in case mentioned in column 4(a). (b) 10 in any other case.
RTA section 12	Motor racing and speed trials on public ways.	Summarily.	Level 4 on the standard scale.	Obligatory.	Obligatory.	3–11
RTA section 13	Other unauthorised or irregular competitions or trials on public ways.	Summarily.	Level 3 on the standard scale.			
RTA section 14	Driving or riding in a motor vehicle in contravention of regulations requiring wearing of seat belts.	Summarily.	Level 2 on the standard scale.			
RTA section 15(2)	Driving motor vehicle with child in front not wearing seat belt.	Summarily.	Level 2 on the standard scale.			
RTA section 15(4)	Driving motor vehicle with child in rear not wearing seat belt or with child in a rear-facing child restraint in front seat with an active air bag.	Summarily.	Level 2 on the standard scale.			
RTA section 15A(3) or (4)	Selling etc. in certain circumstances equipment as conducive to the safety of children in motor vehicles.	Summarily.	Level 3 on the standard scale.			
RTA section 15B	Failure to notify bus passengers of the requirement to wear seat belt.	Summarily.	Level 4 on the standard scale.			
RTA section 16	Driving or riding motor cycles in contravention of regulations requiring wearing of protective headgear.	Summarily.	Level 2 on the standard scale.			
RTA section 17	Selling, etc., helmet not of the prescribed type as helmet for affording protection for motor cyclists.	Summarily.	Level 3 on the standard scale.			
RTA section 18(3)	Contravention of regulations with respect to use of headworn appliances on motor cycles.	Summarily.	Level 2 on the standard scale.			

(1) Provision creating offence	(2) General nature of offence	(3) Mode of prosecution	(4) Punishment	(5) Disqualification	(6) Endorsement	(7) Penalty points
RTA section 18(4)	Selling, etc., appliance not of prescribed type as approved for use on motor cycles.	Summarily.	Level 3 on the standard scale.			
RTA section 19	Prohibition of parking of heavy commercial vehicles on verges, etc.	Summarily.	Level 3 on the standard scale.			
RTA section 21	Driving or parking on cycle track.	Summarily.	Level 3 on the standard scale.			
RTA section 22	Leaving vehicles in dangerous positions.	Summarily.	Level 3 on the standard scale.	Discretionary if committed in respect of a motor vehicle.	Obligatory if committed in respect of a motor vehicle.	3
RTA section 22A	Causing danger to road users.	(a) Summarily. (b) On indictment.	(a) 6 months or the statutory maximum or both. (b) 7 years or a fine or both.			
RTA section 23	Carrying passenger on motor-cycle contrary to section 23.	Summarily.	Level 3 on the standard scale.	Discretionary.	Obligatory.	3
RTA section 24	Carrying passenger on bicycle contrary to section 24.	Summarily.	Level 1 on the standard scale.			
RTA section 25	Tampering with motor vehicles.	Summarily.	Level 3 on the standard scale.			
RTA section 26	Holding or getting on to vehicle, etc., in order to be towed or carried.	Summarily.	Level 1 on the standard scale.			
RTA section 27	Dogs on designated roads without being held on lead.	Summarily.	Level 1 on the standard scale.			
RTA section 28	Dangerous cycling.	Summarily.	Level 4 on the standard scale.			
RTA section 29	Careless, and inconsiderate, cycling.	Summarily.	Level 3 on the standard scale.			
RTA section 30	Cycling when unfit through drink or drugs.	Summarily.	Level 3 on the standard scale.			
RTA section 31	Unauthorised or irregular cycle racing or trials of speed on public ways.	Summarily.	Level 1 on the standard scale.			
RTA section 32	Contravening prohibition on persons under 14 driving electronically assisted pedal cycles.	Summarily.	Level 2 on the standard scale.			
RTA section 33	Unauthorised motor vehicle trial on footpaths or bridleways.	Summarily.	Level 3 on the standard scale.			
RTA section 34	Driving mechanically propelled vehicles elsewhere than on roads.	Summarily.	Level 3 on the standard scale.			
RTA section 35	Failing to comply with traffic directions.	Summarily.	Level 3 on the standard scale.	Discretionary, if committed in respect of a motor vehicle by failure to comply with a direction of a constable, traffic officer or traffic warden.	Obligatory if committed as described in column 5.	3

C

Part C Road Traffic Offences

(1) Provision creating offence	(2) General nature of offence	(3) Mode of prosecution	(4) Punishment	(5) Disqualification	(6) Endorsement	(7) Penalty points
RTA section 36	Failing to comply with traffic signs.	Summarily.	Level 3 on the standard scale.	Discretionary, if committed in respect of a motor vehicle by failure to comply with an indication given by a sign specified for the purposes of this paragraph in regulations under RTA section 36.	Obligatory if committed as described in column 5.	
RTA section 37	Pedestrian failing to stop when directed.	Summarily.	Level 3 on the standard scale.			
RTA section 40A	Using vehicle in dangerous condition etc.	Summarily.	(a) Level 5 on the standard scale if committed in respect of a goods vehicle or a vehicle adapted to carry more than eight passengers. (b) Level 4 on the standard scale in any other case.	(a) Obligatory if committed within three years of a previous conviction of the offender under section 40A. (b) Discretionary in any other case.	Obligatory.	3
RTA section 41A	Breach of requirement as to brakes, steering-gear or tyres.	Summarily.	(a) Level 5 on the standard scale if committed in respect of a goods vehicle or a vehicle adapted to carry more than eight passengers. (b) Level 4 on the standard scale in any other case.	Discretionary.	Obligatory.	3
RTA section 41B	Breach of requirement as to weight: goods and passenger vehicles.	Summarily.	Level 5 on the standard scale.			
RTA section 41D	Breach of requirements as to control of vehicle, mobile telephones etc.	Summarily.	(a) Level 4 on the standard scale if committed in respect of a goods vehicle or a vehicle adapted to carry more than eight passengers. (b) Level 3 on the standard scale in any other case.	Discretionary.	Obligatory.	3
RTA section 42	Breach of other construction and use requirements.	Summarily.	(a) Level 4 on the standard scale if committed in respect of a goods vehicle or a vehicle adapted to carry more than eight passengers. (b) Level 3 on the standard scale in any other case.			

(1) Provision creating offence	(2) General nature of offence	(3) Mode of prosecution	(4) Punishment	(5) Disqualification	(6) Endorsement	(7) Penalty points
RTA section 47	Using, etc., vehicle without required test certificate being in force.	Summarily.	(a) Level 4 on the standard scale in the case of a vehicle adapted to carry more than eight passengers. (b) Level 2 on the standard scale in any other case.			
Regulations under RTA section 49 made by virtue of section 51(2)	Contravention of requirement of regulations (which is declared by regulations to be an offence) that driver of goods vehicle being tested be present throughout tests or drive, etc., vehicle as and when directed.	Summarily.	Level 3 on the standard scale.			
RTA section 53(1)	Using, etc., goods vehicle without required plating certificate being in force.	Summarily.	Level 3 on the standard scale.			
RTA section 53(2)	Using, etc., goods vehicle without required goods vehicle test certificate being in force.	Summarily.	Level 4 on the standard scale.			
RTA section 53(3)	Using, etc., goods vehicle where Secretary of State is required by regulations under section 49 to be notified of an alteration to the vehicle or its equipment but has not been notified.	Summarily.	Level 3 on the standard scale.			
Regulations under RTA section 61 made by virtue of subsection (4)	Contravention of requirement of regulations (which is declared by regulations to be an offence) that driver of goods vehicle being tested after notifiable alteration be present throughout test and drive, etc., vehicle as and when directed.	Summarily.	Level 3 on the standard scale.			
RTA section 63(1)	Using, etc., goods vehicle without required certificate being in force showing that it complies with type approval requirements applicable to it.	Summarily.	Level 4 on the standard scale.			
RTA section 63(2)	Using, etc., certain goods vehicles for drawing trailer when plating certificate does not specify maximum laden weight for vehicle and trailer.	Summarily.	Level 3 on the standard scale.			
RTA section 63(3)	Using, etc., goods vehicle where Secretary of State is required to be notified under section 59 of alteration to it or its equipment but has not been notified.	Summarily.	Level 3 on the standard scale.			

C

(1) Provision creating offence	(2) General nature of offence	(3) Mode of prosecution	(4) Punishment	(5) Disqualification	(6) Endorsement	(7) Penalty points
RTA section 64	Using goods vehicle with unauthorised weights as well as authorised weights marked on it.	Summarily.	Level 3 on the standard scale.			
RTA section 64A	Failure to hold EC certificate of conformity for unregistered light passenger vehicle or motor cycle.	Summarily.	Level 3 on the standard scale.			
RTA section 65	Supplying vehicle or vehicle part without required certificate being in force showing that it complies with type approval requirements applicable to it.	Summarily.	Level 5 on the standard scale.			
RTA section 65A	Light passenger vehicles and motor cycles not to be sold without EC certificate of conformity.	Summarily.	Level 5 on the standard scale.			
RTA section 66C(1)	Impersonating a stopping officer etc. with intent to deceive	Summarily.	Level 5 on the standard scale.			
RTA section 66C(2)	Resisting or wilfully obstructing a stopping officer	Summarily.	One month or level 3 on the standard scale or both.			
RTA section 67	Obstructing testing of vehicle by examiner on road or failing to comply with requirements of RTA section 67 or Schedule 2.	Summarily.	Level 3 on the standard scale.			
RTA section 68	Obstructing inspection, etc., of vehicle by examiner or failing to comply with requirement to take vehicle for inspection.	Summarily.	Level 3 on the standard scale.			
RTA section 71	Driving, etc., vehicle in contravention of prohibition on driving it as being unfit for service, or refusing, neglecting or otherwise failing to comply with direction to remove a vehicle found overloaded.	Summarily.	Level 5 on the standard scale.			
RTA section 74	Contravention of regulations requiring goods vehicle operator to inspect, and keep records of inspection of, goods vehicles.	Summarily.	Level 3 on the standard scale.			
RTA section 75	Selling, etc., unroadworthy vehicle or trailer or altering vehicle or trailer so as to make it unroadworthy.	Summarily.	Level 5 on the standard scale.			
RTA section 76(1)	Fitting of defective or unsuitable vehicle parts.	Summarily.	Level 5 on the standard scale.			

(1) Provision creating offence	(2) General nature of offence	(3) Mode of prosecution	(4) Punishment	(5) Disqualification	(6) Endorsement	(7) Penalty points
RTA section 76(3)	Supplying defective or unsuitable vehicle parts.	Summarily.	Level 4 on the standard scale.			
RTA section 76(8)	Obstructing examiner testing vehicles to ascertain whether defective or unsuitable part has been fitted, etc.	Summarily.	Level 3 on the standard scale.			
RTA section 77	Obstructing examiner testing condition of used vehicle at sale rooms, etc.	Summarily.	Level 3 on the standard scale.			
RTA section 78	Failing to comply with requirement about weighing motor vehicle or obstructing authorised person.	Summarily.	Level 5 on the standard scale.			
RTA section 81	Selling, etc., pedal cycle in contravention of regulations as to brakes, bells, etc.	Summarily.	Level 3 on the standard scale.			
RTA section 83	Selling, etc., wrongly made tail lamps or reflectors.	Summarily.	Level 5 on the standard scale.			
RTA section 87(1)	Driving otherwise than in accordance with a licence.	Summarily.	Level 3 on the standard scale.	Discretionary in a case where the offender's driving would not have been in accordance with any licence that could have been granted to him.	Obligatory in the case mentioned in column 5.	3–6
RTA section 87(2)	Causing or permitting a person to drive otherwise than in accordance with a licence.	Summarily.	Level 3 on the standard scale.			
RTA section 92(7C)	Failure to deliver licence revoked by virtue of section 92(7A) and counterpart to Secretary of State.	Summarily.	Level 3 on the standard scale.			
RTA section 92(10)	Driving after making false declaration as to physical fitness.	Summarily.	Level 4 on the standard scale.	Discretionary.	Obligatory.	3–6
RTA section 93(3)	Failure to deliver revoked licence and counterpart to Secretary of State.	Summarily.	Level 3 on the standard scale.			
RTA section 94(3) and that subsection as applied by RTA section 99D or 109C	Failure to notify Secretary of State of onset of, or deterioration in, relevant or prospective disability.	Summarily.	Level 3 on the standard scale.			

(1) Provision creating offence	(2) General nature of offence	(3) Mode of prosecution	(4) Punishment	(5) Disqualification	(6) Endorsement	(7) Penalty points
RTA section 94(3A) and that subsection as applied by RTA section 99D(b) or 109C(c)	Driving after such a failure.	Summarily.	Level 3 on the standard scale.	Discretionary.	Obligatory.	3–6
RTA section 94A	Driving after refusal of licence under section 92(3), revocation under section 93 or service of a notice under section 99C or 109B.	Summarily.	6 months or level 5 on the standard scale or both.	Discretionary.	Obligatory.	3–6
RTA section 96	Driving with uncorrected defective eyesight, or refusing to submit to test of eyesight.	Summarily.	Level 3 on the standard scale.	Discretionary.	Obligatory.	3
RTA section 99(5)	Driving licence holder failing to surrender licence and counterpart.	Summarily.	Level 3 on the standard scale.			
RTA section 99B(11) and that subsection as applied by RTA section 109A(5)	Driving after failure to comply with a requirement under section 99B(6), (7) or (10) or a requirement under section 99B(6) or (7) as applied by section 109A(5).	Summarily.	Level 3 on the standard scale.			
RTA section 99C(4)	Failure to deliver Community licence to Secretary of State when required by notice under section 99C.	Summarily.	Level 3 on the standard scale.			
RTA section 103(1)(a)	Obtaining driving licence while disqualified.	Summarily.	Level 3 on the standard scale.			
RTA section 103(1)(b)	Driving while disqualified.	(a) Summarily, in England and Wales. (b) [Scotland] (c) [Scotland]	(a) 6 months or level 5 on the standard scale or both. (b) 6 months or the statutory maximum or both. (c) 12 months or a fine or both.	Discretionary.	Obligatory.	6
RTA section 109B(4)	Failing to deliver Northern Ireland licence to Secretary of State when required by notice under section 109B.	Summarily.	Level 3 on the standard scale.			
RTA section 114	Failing to comply with conditions of LGV, PCV licence or LGV Community licence, or causing or permitting person under 21 to drive LGV or PCV in contravention of such conditions.	Summarily.	Level 3 on the standard scale.			

(1) Provision creating offence	(2) General nature of offence	(3) Mode of prosecution	(4) Punishment	(5) Disqualification	(6) Endorsement	(7) Penalty points
RTA section 115A(4)	Failure to deliver LGV or PCV Community licence when required by notice under section 115A.	Summarily.	Level 3 on the standard scale.			
RTA section 118	Failing to surrender revoked or suspended LGV or PCV licence and counterpart.	Summarily.	Level 3 on the standard scale.			
Regulations made by virtue of RTA section 120(5)	Contravention of provision of regulations (which is declared by regulations to be an offence) about LGV or PCV drivers; licences or LGV or PCV Community licence.	Summarily.	Level 3 on the standard scale.			
RTA section 123(4)	Giving of paid driving instruction by unregistered and unlicensed person or their employers.	Summarily.	Level 4 on the standard scale.			
RTA section 123(6)	Giving of paid instruction without there being exhibited on the motor car a certificate of registration or a licence under RTA part V.	Summarily.	Level 3 on the standard scale.			
RTA section 125A(4)	Failure, on application for registration as disabled driving instructor, to notify Registrar of onset of, or deterioration in, relevant or prospective disability.	Summarily.	Level 3 on the standard scale.			
RTA section 133C(4)	Failure by registered or licensed disabled driving instructor to notify Registrar of onset of, or deterioration in, relevant or prospective disability.	Summarily.	Level 3 on the standard scale.			
RTA section 133D	Giving of paid driving instruction by disabled persons or their employers without emergency control certificate or in unauthorised motor car.	Summarily.	Level 3 on the standard scale.			
RTA section 135	Unregistered instructor using title or displaying badge, etc., prescribed for registered instructor, or employer using such title, etc., in relation to his unregistered instructor or issuing misleading advertisement, etc.	Summarily.	Level 4 on the standard scale.			
RTA section 136	Failure of instructor to surrender to Registrar certificate or licence.	Summarily.	Level 3 on the standard scale.			

(1) Provision creating offence	(2) General nature of offence	(3) Mode of prosecution	(4) Punishment	(5) Disqualification	(6) Endorsement	(7) Penalty points
RTA section 137	Failing to produce certificate of registration or licence as driving instructor.	Summarily.	Level 3 on the standard scale.			
RTA section 143	Using motor vehicle while uninsured or unsecured against third-party risks.	Summarily.	Level 5 on the standard scale.	Discretionary.	Obligatory.	6–8
RTA section 144A	Keeping vehicle which does not meet insurance requirements.	Summarily.	Level 2 on the standard scale.			
RTA section 147	Failing to surrender certificate of insurance or security to insurer on cancellation or to make statutory declaration of loss or destruction.	Summarily.	Level 3 on the standard scale.			
RTA section 154	Failing to give information, or wilfully making a false statement, as to insurance or security when claim made.	Summarily.	Level 4 on the standard scale.			
Regulations under RTA section 160 made by virtue of paragraph 2(1) of schedule 2A	Contravention of provisions of regulations (which is declared by regulations to be an offence) prohibiting removal of or interference with immobilisation notice.	Summarily.	Level 2 on the standard scale.			
Regulations under RTA section 160 made by virtue of paragraph 2(2) of schedule 2A	Contravention of provisions of regulations (which is declared by regulations to be an offence) prohibiting removal or attempted removal of immobilisation device.	Summarily.	Level 3 on the standard scale.			
Regulations under RTA section 160 made by virtue of paragraph 2(3) of schedule 2A	Contravention of provisions of regulations (which is declared by regulations to be an offence) about display of disabled person's badge.	Summarily.	Level 3 on the standard scale.			
RTA section 163	Failing to stop motor vehicle or cycle when required.	Summarily.	(a) Level 5 on the standard scale if committed by a person driving a mechanically propelled vehicle. (b) Level 3 on the standard scale if committed by a person riding a cycle.			

(1) Provision creating offence	(2) General nature of offence	(3) Mode of prosecution	(4) Punishment	(5) Disqualification	(6) Endorsement	(7) Penalty points
RTA section 164	Failing to produce driving licence and its counterpart or to state date of birth, or failing to provide the Secretary of State with evidence of date of birth, etc.	Summarily.	Level 3 on the standard scale.			
RTA section 165	Failing to give certain names and addresses or to produce certain documents.	Summarily.	Level 3 on the standard scale.			
RTA section 168	Refusing to give, or giving false, name and address in case of reckless, careless or inconsiderate driving or cycling.	Summarily.	Level 3 on the standard scale.			
RTA section 169	Pedestrian failing to give constable his name and address after failing to stop when directed by constable controlling traffic.	Summarily.	Level 1 on the standard scale.			
RTA section 170(4)	Failing to stop after accident and give particulars or report accident.	Summarily.	6 months or level 5 on the standard scale or both.	Discretionary.	Obligatory.	5–10
RTA section 170(7)	Failure by driver, in case of accident involving injury to another, to produce evidence of insurance or security or to report accident.	Summarily.	Level 3 on the standard scale.			
RTA section 171	Failure by owner of motor vehicle to give police information for verifying compliance with requirement of compulsory insurance or security.	Summarily.	Level 4 on the standard scale.			
RTA section 172	Failure of person keeping vehicle and others to give police information as to identity of driver, etc., in the case of certain offences.	Summarily.	Level 3 on the standard scale.	Discretionary if committed otherwise than by virtue of subsection (5) or (11).	Obligatory if committed otherwise than by virtue of subsection (5) or (11).	6
RTA section 173	Forgery, etc., of licences, counterparts of Community licences, certificates of insurance and other documents and things.	(a) Summarily. (b) On indictment.	(a) The statutory maximum. (b) 2 years.			
RTA section 174	Making certain false statements, etc., and withholding certain material information.	(a) Summarily. (b) On indictment.	6 months or the statutory maximum or both. 2 years or a fine or both.			
RTA section 175	Issuing false documents.	Summarily.	Level 4 on the standard scale.			

(1) Provision creating offence	(2) General nature of offence	(3) Mode of prosecution	(4) Punishment	(5) Disqualification	(6) Endorsement	(7) Penalty points
RTA section 177	Impersonation of, or of person employed by, authorised examiner.	Summarily.	Level 3 on the standard scale.			
RTA section 178	[Scotland.]					
RTA section 180	Failing to attend, give evidence or produce documents to, inquiry held by Secretary of State, etc.	Summarily.	Level 3 on the standard scale.			
RTA section 181	Obstructing inspection of vehicles after accident.	Summarily.	Level 3 on the standard scale.			
RTA schedule 1 paragraph 6	Applying warranty to equipment, protective helmet, appliance or information in defending proceedings under RTA section 15A, 17 or 18(4) where no warranty given, or applying false warranty.	Summarily.	Level 3 on the standard scale.			
Section 25 of this Act.	Failing to give information as to date of birth or sex to court or to provide Secretary of State with evidence of date of birth, etc.	Summarily.	Level 3 on the standard scale.			
Section 26 of this Act.	Failing to produce driving licence and counterpart to court making order for interim disqualification.	Summarily.	Level 3 on the standard scale.			
Section 27 of this Act.	Failing to produce licence and counterpart to court for endorsement on conviction of offence involving obligatory endorsement or on committal for sentence, etc., for offence involving obligatory or discretionary disqualification when no interim disqualification ordered.	Summarily.	Level 3 on the standard scale.			
Section 62 of this Act.	Removing fixed penalty notice fixed to vehicle.	Summarily.	Level 2 on the standard scale.			
Section 67 of this Act.	False statement in response to notice to owner.	Summarily.	Level 5 on the standard scale.			

C8.2

PART II
OTHER OFFENCES

(1) Offence	(2) Disqualification	(3) Endorsement	(4) Penalty points
Manslaughter or, in Scotland, culpable homicide by the driver of a motor vehicle.	Obligatory.	Obligatory.	3–11
An offence under section 35 of the Offences against the Persons Act 1861 (furious driving).	Discretionary.	Obligatory if committed in respect of a mechanically propelled vehicle.	3–9

(1) Offence	(2) Disqualification	(3) Endorsement	(4) Penalty points
Stealing or attempting to steal a motor vehicle.	Discretionary.		
An offence or attempt to commit an offence in respect of a motor vehicle under section 12 of the Theft Act 1968 (taking conveyance without consent of owner etc. or, knowing it has been so taken, driving it or allowing oneself to be carried in it).	Discretionary.		
An offence under section 25 of the Theft Act 1968 (going equipped for stealing, etc.) committed with reference to the theft or taking of motor vehicles.	Discretionary.		

Road Traffic Offenders Act 1988, sch. 3   C8.3

Schedule 3
Fixed Penalty Offences

(1) Provision creating offence	(2) General nature of offence
Offence under the Highways Act 1835	
Sections 72 of the Highways Act 1835	Cycling/driving on the footway.
Offences under the Transport Act 1968	
Section 96(11) of the Transport Act 1968	Contravention of any requirement of domestic drivers' hours code.
Section 96(11A) of that Act	Contravention of any requirement of applicable community rules as to periods of driving, etc.
Section 97(1) of that Act	Using vehicle in contravention of requirements relating to installation, use or repair of recording equipment in accordance with Community Recording Equipment Regulation.
Section 98(4) of that Act	Contravention of regulations made under section 98 or any requirement as to books, records or documents of applicable Community rules.
Section 99(4) of that Act	Failing to comply with requirements relating to inspection or records or obstructing an officer, but only insofar as the offences relates to:— (i) failing to comply with any requirement under section 99(1)(a); or (ii) obstructing an officer in exercise of powers under 99(2)(a) or 99(3).
Section 99ZD (1) of that Act	Failing to comply with requirements relating to inspection of recording equipment or records (whether electronic or hard copy) made by or stored on recording equipment except where that offence is committed by:— (i) failing to sign a hard copy of downloaded data when required to do so under section 99ZC (1); or (ii) obstructing an officer in exercise of powers under section 99ZF.
Section 99C of that Act	Failure to comply with prohibition or direction in relation to driving vehicle.

(1) Provision creating offence	(2) General nature of offence
Offence under the Road Traffic (Foreign Vehicles) Act 1972	
Section 3(1) of the Road Traffic (Foreign Vehicles) Act 1972.	Driving, etc., foreign goods vehicle or foreign public service vehicle in contravention of prohibition etc.
Offence under the Greater London Council (General Powers) Act 1974	
Section 15 of the Greater London Council (General Powers) Act 1974.	Parking vehicles on footways, verges, etc.
Offence under the Highways Act 1980	
Section 137 of the Highways Act 1980.	Obstructing a highway, but only where the offence is committed in respect of a vehicle.
Offences under the Public Passenger Vehicles Act 1981	
Section 12(5) of the Public Passenger Vehicles Act 1981.	Using public service vehicle on road except under PSV operators' licence.
Offences under the Road Traffic Regulation Act 1984	
RTA section 3	Driving mechanically propelled vehicle on a road or other public place without due care and attention, or without reasonable consideration.
RTRA section 5(1)	Using a vehicle in contravention of a traffic regulation order outside Greater London.
RTRA section 8(1)	Breach of traffic regulation order in Greater London.
RTRA section 11	Breach of experimental traffic order.
RTRA section 13	Breach of experimental traffic scheme regulations in Greater London.
RTRA section 16(1)	Using a vehicle in contravention of temporary prohibition or restriction of traffic in case of execution of works, etc.
RTRA section 17(4)	Wrongful use of special road.
RTRA section 18(3)	Using a vehicle in contravention of provision for oneway traffic on trunk road.
RTRA section 20(5)	Driving a vehicle in contravention of order prohibiting or restricting driving vehicles on certain classes of roads.
RTRA section 25(5)	Breach of pedestrian crossing regulations, except an offence in respect of a moving motor vehicle other than a contravention of regulations 23, 24, 25 and 26 of the Zebra, Pelican and Puffin Pedestrian Crossings Regulations and General Directions 1997.
RTRA section 29(3)	Using a vehicle in contravention of a street playground order.
RTRA section 35A(1)	Breach of an order regulating the use, etc., of a parking place provided by a local authority, but only where the offence is committed in relation to a parking place provided on a road.
RTRA section 47(1)	Breach of a provision of a parking place designation order and other offences committed in relation to a parking place designated by such an order, except any offence of failing to pay an excess charge within the meaning of section 46.

(1) Provision creating offence	(2) General nature of offence
RTRA section 53(5)	Using vehicle in contravention of any provision of a parking place designation order having effect by virtue of section 53(1)(a) (inclusion of certain traffic regulation provisions).
RTRA section 53(6)	Breach of a provision of a parking place designation order having effect by virtue of section 53(1)(b) (use of any part of a road for parking without charge).
RTRA section 88(7)	Driving a motor vehicle in contravention of an order imposing a minimum speed limit under section 88(1)(b).
RTRA section 89(1)	Speeding offences under RTRA and other Acts.

Offences under the Road Transport (International Passenger Services) Regulations 1984 (SI 1984/748)

Regulation 19(1) of the Road Transport (International Passenger Services) Regulations 1984.	Using vehicle for Community regulated carriage of passengers by road otherwise than in accordance with authorisation or certificate, etc.
Regulation 19(2) of those Regulations	Using vehicle for ASOR regulated or Community regulated carriage of passengers by road without having correctly completed passenger waybill or without carrying top copy of waybill on vehicle throughout journey.

Offences under the Road Traffic Act 1988

RTA section 14	Breach of regulations requiring wearing of seat belts.
RTA section 15(2)	Breach of restriction on carrying children in the front of vehicles.
RTA section 15(4)	Breach of restriction on carrying children in the rear of vehicles.
RTA section 16	Breach of regulations relating to protective headgear for motor cycle drivers and passengers.
RTA section 18(3)	Breach of regulations relating to head-worn appliances (eye protectors) for use on motor cycles.
RTA section 19	Parking a heavy commercial vehicle on verge or footway.
RTA section 22	Leaving vehicle in dangerous position.
RTA section 23	Unlawful carrying of passengers on motor cycles.
RTA section 24	Carrying more than one person on a pedal cycle.
RTA section 34	Driving mechanically propelled vehicle elsewhere than on a road.
RTA section 35	Failure to comply with traffic directions.
RTA section 36	Failure to comply with traffic signs.
RTA section 40A	Using vehicle in dangerous condition, etc.
RTA section 41A	Breach of requirement as to brakes, steering-gear or tyres.
RTA section 41B	Breach of requirement as to weight: goods and passenger vehicles.
RTA section 41D	Breach of requirements as to control of vehicle, mobile telephone etc.

(1) Provision creating offence	(2) General nature of offence
RTA section 42	Breach of other construction and use requirements.
RTA section 47	Using, etc., vehicle without required test certificate being in force.
RTA section 71(1)	Driving, etc., vehicle in contravention of prohibition on driving it as being unfit for service or overloaded, or failing to comply with direction to remove a vehicle found overloaded.
RTA section 87(1)	Driving vehicle otherwise than in accordance with requisite licence.
RTA section 143	Using motor vehicle while uninsured or unsecured against third party risks.
RTA section 163	Failure to stop vehicle on being so required.
RTA section 172	Failure of person keeping vehicle and others to give the police information as to identity of driver, etc., in the case of certain offences.
Offence under this Act	
Section 90D(6)	Driving, etc., vehicle in contravention of prohibition on driving, or failing to comply with direction to remove vehicle on failure to make a financial penalty deposit payment.
Offences under the Goods Vehicles (Community Authorisations) Regulations 1992 (SI 1992/3077)	
Regulation 3 of the Goods Vehicles (Community Authorisations) Regulations 1992.	Using goods vehicle without Community authorisation.
Regulation 7 of those Regulations	Using vehicle under Community authorisation in contravention of conditions governing authorisation.
Offences under the Vehicle Excise and Registration Act 1994	
Section 33 of the Vehicle Excise and Registration Act 1994.	Using or keeping a vehicle on a public road without vehicle licence, trade licence or nil licence being exhibited in manner prescribed by regulations.
Section 34 of that Act.	Using trade licence for unauthorised purposes or in unauthorised circumstances, etc.
Section 42 of that Act.	Driving or keeping a vehicle without required registration mark.
Section 43 of that Act.	Driving or keeping a vehicle with registration mark obscured, etc.
Section 43C of that Act.	Using an incorrectly registered vehicle.
Section 59 of that Act.	Failure to fix prescribed registration mark to a vehicle in accordance with regulations made under section 23(4)(a) of that Act.
Offence under the Goods Vehicles (Licensing of Operators) Act 1995	
Section 2(5) of the Goods Vehicles (Licensing of Operators) Act 1995.	Using goods vehicle on road for carriage of goods except under operator's licence.
Offences under the Public Service Vehicles (Community Licences) Regulations 1999 (SI 1999/1322)	
Regulation 3 of the Public Service Vehicles (Community Licences) Regulations 1999.	Using public service vehicle on road without Community licence.
Regulation 7 of those Regulations	Using public service vehicle under Community licence in contravention of conditions governing use of licence.

(1) Provision creating offence	(2) General nature of offence
Offences under the Road Transport (Passenger Vehicles Cabotage) Regulations 1999 (SI 1999/3413)	
Regulation 3 of the Road Transport (Passenger Vehicles Cabotage) Regulations 1999.	Using vehicle on road for UK cabotage operations without Community licence.
Regulation 4 of those Regulations	Using vehicle on road for UK cabotage operation without control document.
Regulation 7(1) of those Regulations	Driver failing to produce Community licence on request when vehicle required to have licence on board.
Regulation 7(3) of those Regulations	Driver failing to produce control document on request when vehicle required to have control document on board.
Offence under the Vehicle Drivers (Certificates of Professional Competence) Regulations 2007 (SI 2007/605)	
Regulation 11(7) of the Vehicle Drivers (Certificates of Professional Competence) Regulations 2007.	Driver of relevant vehicle failing to produce on request evidence or document required to be carried under regulation 11(1), (3) or (5).
Offence under the HGV Road User Levy Act 2013	
Section 11 of the HGV Road User Levy Act 2013.	Using or keeping heavy goods vehicle if HGV road user levy not paid.

Section D1   Powers of Investigation

POLICE POWERS IN THE INVESTIGATION OF CRIME

D1.1 Police powers of investigation, including arrest, detention, interrogation, entry and search of premises, personal search and the taking of samples and various procedures for identification are largely governed by the PACE 1984 and/or the associated PACE Codes of Practice. These powers are dealt with in this section, but see **F2** for the admission (and exclusion) of evidence obtained in breach of the PACE 1984 or the PACE Codes, **F17** for the admission of confession evidence and **F18** for the treatment of identification evidence at trial.

The PACE Codes of Practice are issued by the Secretary of State under the authority of the PACE 1984, ss. 66 and 67. There are eight Codes of Practice, A to H. Codes A to D and G are set out in **appendix 1**. Codes A, B, E and F came into force in their current form on 27 October 2013 (Police and Criminal Evidence Act 1984 (Codes of Practice) (Revisions to Codes A, B, C, E, F and H) Order 2013 (SI 2013 No. 2685). Revised versions of Codes C and H came into force on 2 June 2014 (Police and Criminal Evidence Act 1984 (Codes of Practice) (Revisions to Codes C and H) Order 2014 (SI 2014 No. 1237)). The revisions, together with those made to the two codes in October 2013, are intended, *inter alia*, to give effect to the EU Directives 2010/64 (the right to interpretation and translation) and 2012/13 (the right to information) (see **A9.24**). The current version of Code D came into force on 7 March 2011 (Police and Criminal Evidence Act 1984 (Codes of Practice) (Revisions of Codes A, B and D) Order 2011 (SI 2011 No. 412)), and the current version of Code G came into force on 12 November 2012 (Police and Criminal Evidence Act 1984 (Codes of Practice) (Revision of Codes C, G and H) Order 2012 (SI 2012 No. 1798)). Code A does not apply to stop and search powers under the TA 2000, which are governed by separate codes of practice given effect by the Terrorism Act 2000 (Codes of Practice for the Exercise of Stop and Search Powers) Order 2012 (SI 2012 No. 1794) (see **B10.25**). However, it does apply to powers under the Terrorism Prevention and Investigations Measures Act 2011 to search persons without them being arrested. Code B includes powers to enter and search premises for the purposes of serving, monitoring and enforcing TPIM notices.

A failure by a police officer or other person required to have regard to provisions of the codes does not, of itself, render him liable to criminal or civil proceedings (PACE 1984, s. 67(10)). However, to the extent that they are relevant, the codes are admissible in evidence in criminal or civil proceedings (PACE 1984, s. 67(11)). See further **F17.8** (in relation to exclusion of confession evidence under the PACE 1984, s. 76) and **F2.28** (in relation to the exclusion of any prosecution evidence under the PACE 1984, s. 78).

D

Part D Procedure

Investigations in Connection with Terrorism

D1.2   Where persons are detained for examination under the TA 2000, s. 53 and sch. 7, their treatment is governed by the TA 2000, sch. 8, part 1. They are not treated as being in police detention for the purpose of the PACE 1984, and the PACE Codes do not apply to them. The detention of persons arrested under the TA 2000, s. 41 (on suspicion of being a terrorist), and associated police powers, is governed by sch. 8 to that Act rather than by the PACE 1984. They are not treated as being arrested for an offence, but whilst they are detained at a police station they are deemed to be in police detention for the purposes of the PACE 1984 (PACE 1984, s. 118(2)). PACE Code H applies to their detention whilst they have not been charged, and if they are detained for post-charge questioning under the C-TA 2008, s. 22. Subject to the latter, Code C will apply if they are charged with an offence or if they are being questioned about any offence after charge without a s. 22 authorisation having been given. Note that there is a separate code of practice for video recording with sound of interviews of persons detained under the TA 2000, s. 42 or sch. 7, and of persons detained for post-charge questioning (see the Terrorism Act 2000 (Video Recording with Sound of Interviews and Associated Code of Practice) Order 2012 (SI 2012 No. 1792), and Counter-Terrorism Act 2008 (Code of Practice for the Video Recording with Sound of Post-Charge Questioning) Order 2012 (SI 2012 No. 1793)). PACE Code D does apply to persons arrested under the TA 2000, s. 41, except for those provisions relating to photographs, fingerprints, skin impressions, body samples and impressions of people. PACE Codes E and F also do not apply to such persons. See generally **B10.14** *et seq*.

Investigations by Non-Police Officers

D1.3   The PACE 1984 is applied (with modifications) to investigations conducted and persons detained by Revenue and Customs officers (PACE 1984, s. 114(2), and the Police and Criminal Evidence Act 1984 (Application to Revenue and Customs) Order 2007 (SI 2007 No. 3175), as amended by SI 2014 No. 788). The PACE 1984 is also applied (with modifications) to investigations conducted by immigration officers and designated customs officers under the Borders, Citizenship and Immigration Act 2009, part 1, by s. 23 of that Act and the Police and Criminal Evidence Act 1984 (Application to immigration officers and designated customs officers in England and Wales) Order 2013 (SI 2013 No. 1542). The PACE 1984 is applied to investigations conducted under the Armed Forces Act 2006 and to persons under arrest under that Act by the PACE 1984, s. 113(1), and the Police and Criminal Evidence Act 1984 (Armed Forces) Order 2009 (SI 2009 No. 1922). The National Crime Agency may designate a member of the Agency staff as having the powers and privileges of a police constable (CCA 2013, s. 10 and sch. 5). See **D1.191** *et seq*.

Persons other than police officers who are charged with the duty of investigating offences or charging offenders are required in the discharge of that duty to have regard to any relevant provision of the codes (PACE 1984, s. 67(9)). Whether a person is charged with such a duty is a question of fact in each case. It has been held to include officers of the Serious Fraud Office (*Director of the Serious Fraud Office, ex parte Saunders* [1988] Crim LR 837 and *Gill* [2004] 4 All ER 681); trading standards officers (*Dudley MBC v Debenhams* (1994) 159 JP 18 and *Tiplady* (1995) 159 JP 548); commercial investigators when interviewing an employee (*Twaites and Brown* (1990) 92 Cr App R 106); store detectives (*Bayliss* (1993) 98 Cr App R 235); and investigators employed by the Federation Against Copyright Theft (*Joy v Federation Against Copyright Theft Ltd* [1993] Crim LR 588 and *Halawa v Federation Against Copyright Theft* [1995] 1 Cr App R 21). However, it was decided in *Seelig and Spens* [1992] 4 All ER 429 that inspectors from the Department of Trade and Industry (now the Department of Business, Innovation and Skills) appointed under the Companies Acts, were not persons charged with such a duty. A similar conclusion was drawn in respect of local tax inspectors in *Doncaster* (2008) 172 JP 202, and of a line manager investigating possible fraud by an employee in *Welcher* [2007] 2 Cr App R (S) 519. In *Taylor (Martin)* [2000] EWCA Crim 2922 it was held that a prison officer was not a person charged with the duty of investigating offences, but on the facts in *Devani* [2008] 1 Cr App R 65 the contrary conclusion was drawn.

The PACE Codes apply to Revenue and Customs officers where they are conducting 'relevant investigations' (Police and Criminal Evidence Act 1984 (Application to Revenue and Customs) Order 2007 (SI 2007 No. 3175), art. 2(1) and sch. 1). However, it has been held that they do not apply where they are interviewing a person under the Value Added Tax Act 1994, s. 60 (*Khan v Revenue and Customs* [2006] EWCA Civ 89). They also do not apply to the civil investigation of tax fraud procedure (see HM Revenue and Customs Code of Practice 9 (July 2011) available at www.hmrc.gov.uk/leaflets/cop9-2011.htm). The PACE Codes do not apply to an investigation under the Armed Forces Act 2006, but dedicated codes have been issued under the PACE 1984, s. 113(2). For the detention and treatment of a person arrested on a European Arrest Warrant, see **D1.38**.

Certain police powers can be exercised by civilians designated by chief police officers as community support officers, investigating officers, detention officers or escort officers under the Police Reform Act 2002, part 4 and sch. 4. The full list of standard powers, discretionary powers and powers to issue penalty notices for disorder under the CJPA 2001, part 1, chapter 1, applicable to community support officers is set out in the annex to Home Office Circular 033/2007, *Standard Powers and Duties of Police Community Support Officers*. Normally, a designated person may use his powers only if he is in uniform (Police Reform Act 2002, s. 42(2)), although an officer of at least the rank of inspector may authorise a designated investigating officer not to wear a uniform for the purposes of a particular investigation (s. 42(2A)). A designated person must have regard to any relevant provision of the PACE Codes in the exercise or performance of his powers and duties (PACE 1984, s. 67(9A)).

REASONABLE SUSPICION

A number of police powers are premised upon the constable having reasonable grounds for **D1.4** suspicion. For example, stop and search under the PACE 1984, part I, requires a constable to have 'reasonable grounds for suspecting that he will find stolen or prohibited articles' etc. and some, but not all, powers of arrest under s. 24 depend on the officer having reasonable grounds for suspicion. This reflects the ECHR, Article 5(1)(c), which permits a person to be deprived of his liberty 'on reasonable suspicion of having committed an offence or when it is reasonably considered necessary to prevent his committing an offence or fleeing after having done so'. It should be contrasted with the expression 'reasonable grounds for believing', found in the PACE 1984, s. 24(4) (the necessity for arrest), s. 37(2) (detention without charge) and s. 38(1) (bail following charge), which implies a more stringent test. Reasonable suspicion relates to the existence of facts and not to the state of the law. An officer who reasonably but mistakenly proceeds on a particular view of the law, and thus exercises his power of arrest, does not have reasonable suspicion (*Todd v DPP* [1996] Crim LR 344). However, in the absence of a specific statutory requirement to such effect, the constable does not have to have identified the precise legal power under which he acts (*R (Rutherford) v Independent Police Complaints Commission* [2010] EWHC 2881 (Admin)).

Reasonable suspicion is not defined in the PACE 1984. It is explained in relation to stop and search powers in PACE Code A, para. 2.2 of which states that 'there must be an objective basis for that suspicion based on facts, information, and/or intelligence'. It goes on to state that it 'can never be supported on the basis of personal factors. It must rely on intelligence or information about, or some specific behaviour by, the person concerned', although this is qualified by paras. 2.3 and 2.4. In relation to arrest, Code G provides that there 'must be some reasonable, objective grounds for the suspicion, based on known facts and information' (para. 2.3A). Note for Guidance 2 states that facts and information should not be confined to those which tend to indicate guilt, but should include facts and information that tend to dispel suspicion, and Note for Guidance 2A provides examples in respect of self-defence and the use of force by school staff.

It has been held that reasonable suspicion requires both that the constable carrying out the arrest actually suspects (a subjective test) and that a reasonable person in possession of the same facts as the constable would also suspect (an objective test). In addition the arrest must be *Wednesbury* reasonable (*Castorina v Chief Constable of Surrey* (1988) 138 NLJ 180). The test for whether an officer has reasonable grounds for suspicion for the purposes of stop and search under the PACE 1984, part I, is the same in all material respects (*Howarth v Commissioner of Police of the Metropolis* [2011] EWHC 2818 (Admin)). Whether the constable had reasonable suspicion must be determined according to what he knew and perceived at the time; reasonableness is to be evaluated without reference to hindsight (*Redmond-Bate v DPP* (1999) 163 JP 789). Information required to form a reasonable suspicion is of a lower standard than that required to establish a prima facie case. Prima facie proof must be based on admissible evidence whereas reasonable suspicion may take into account matters which are not admissible in evidence or matters which, while admissible, could not form part of a prima facie case (*Hussien v Chong Fook Kam* [1970] AC 942). Whilst it is not necessary for the constable to have identified the specific offence of which he is suspicious (*Coudrat v Commissioners of Her Majesty's Revenue and Customs* [2005] EWCA Civ 616), he must reasonably suspect the existence of facts amounting to an offence of a kind that he has in mind (*Chapman v DPP* (1988) 89 Cr App R 190).

D1.5 In forming a reasonable suspicion a constable may rely on hearsay, provided that it is reasonable and that he believes it (*Clarke v Chief Constable of North Wales Police* [2000] All ER (D) 477). Thus a constable may arrest a person as a result of radio information, or even an anonymous telephone call, provided that the person arrested corresponds to the description in the message (*King v Gardner* (1979) 71 Cr App R 13; *DPP v Wilson* [1991] RTR 284); he may act on the word of an informant, although such a source should be treated with considerable reserve (*James v Chief Constable of South Wales* [1991] 6 CL 80). The constable may rely on an entry in the police national computer, unless in the light of all the circumstances some further inquiry is called for before suspicion can properly crystallise (*Hough v Chief Constable of Staffordshire Police* [2001] EWCA Civ 39); or on a briefing from another police officer (*Alford v Chief Constable of Cambridgeshire* [2009] EWCA Civ 100) or investigator such as an officer from the SFO (*R (Rawlinson) v Central Criminal Court* [2013] 1 WLR 1634). The mere fact that an arresting officer has been instructed by his superior to effect an arrest is not sufficient (*O'Hara v Chief Constable of the Royal Ulster Constabulary* [1997] AC 286; *Olden* [2007] EWCA Crim 726), but the existence of such instruction does not necessarily undermine the arresting officer's subjective belief that grounds for arrest exist (*R (Hicks) v Commissioner of Police for the Metropolis* [2012] EWHC 1947 (Admin), which was overruled on appeal, but not on this point: see [2014] 1 WLR 2152). A belief that a superior officer probably did have information justifying an arrest which he had not conveyed to the arresting officer does not suffice (*Metropolitan Police Commissioner v Raissi* [2009] QB 564).

Evidence of particular opportunity may give rise to reasonable suspicion. Where police, having taken all reasonable steps to discover the perpetrator of an offence, are left with the suspicion that one of a number of persons must have been the culprit, this may be sufficient to arrest those persons (*Cummings v Chief Constable of Northumbria Police* [2003] EWCA Civ 1844). The police may be justified in making such arrests even though there is a possibility that another or other persons may have committed the offence. The matter is one of degree (*Al Fayed v Metropolitan Police Commissioner* [2004] EWCA Civ 1579). Similar principles also apply to search of groups of people under the PACE 1984, part I (*Howarth v Commissioner of Police of the Metropolis* [2011] EWHC 2818 (Admin), followed in *Tuthill v York Magistrates' Court* [2011] EWHC 3760 (Admin)). A constable who has reasonable grounds to suspect that an offence has been committed is not obliged to discount all possible defences or seek complete proof before carrying out an arrest (*Ward v Chief Constable of Avon and Somerset Constabulary* (1986) *The Times*, 26 June 1986; *McCarrick v Oxford* [1983] RTR 117; but see Code G, Note for Guidance 2).

D1.6 Use of arrest in order to interview and/or seek further evidence from a suspect, or to arrest as a means of exercising control over a suspect with a view to securing a confession or other information where it is necessary to bring matters to a head speedily, to preserve evidence or to prevent the further commission of crime, is permissible (*Al Fayed v Metropolitan Police Commissioner*). Furthermore, an arrest carried out for an ulterior purpose, e.g., to install a listening device in the arrested person's house for the purpose of investigating another offence, is lawful provided that there are reasonable grounds for suspicion in relation to the offence for which the person was arrested (*Chalkley* [1998] QB 848). However, these cases must now be considered in the context of the requirement that an arrest must be necessary (see **D1.25**). The police must not mislead the suspect as to the true nature of the investigation, e.g., by failing to tell a suspect arrested for burglary that the victim has died (*Kirk* [1999] 4 All ER 698, and see **D1.17**).

THE USE OF FORCE

The PACE 1984, s. 117, provides that where any provision of the Act confers a power on a constable and does not provide that the power may be exercised only with the consent of a person other than a police officer, the officer may use reasonable force, if necessary, in the exercise of the power. This would include force used in connection with a stop and search under the PACE 1984, part I, entry and search of premises under s. 17, arrest under s. 24, detention of a person at a police station under the PACE 1984, part IV, search of a person under s. 54, intimate search of a detained person under s. 55, fingerprinting without consent under s. 61 and the taking of a non-intimate sample without consent under s. 63. It would not include the use of force in connection with the conduct of a visual identification procedure governed by PACE Code D, or the taking of an intimate sample under s. 62, since these require consent. A civilian designated under the Police Reform Act 2002, s. 38, may, in exercising powers in respect of which he has been designated, use reasonable force in the same circumstances as a constable (Police Reform Act 2002, s. 38(8) and Code C, para. 1.14). In addition, the CLA 1967, s. 3, empowers any person to use such force as is reasonable in the circumstances in the prevention of crime, or in effecting or assisting in the lawful arrest of an offender or suspected offender or of persons unlawfully at large (see **A3.54** *et seq.*). **D1.7**

In determining what force is reasonable, the court may take into account all the circumstances including the nature and degree of the force used, the gravity of the offence for which arrest is to be made, the harm that would flow from the use of force against the suspect, and the possibility of effecting the arrest or preventing the harm by other means. See *Roberts v Chief Constable of Kent* [2008] EWCA Civ 1588, in which it was held that reasonable force had been used despite the fact that a police dog had caused serious bite injuries, and *Minio-Paluello v Commissioner of Police of the Metropolis* [2011] EWHC 3411 (QB), in which it was held that excessive force had been used. The use of excessive force will not render the arrest unlawful (*Simpson v Chief Constable of South Yorkshire Police* (1991) *The Times*, 7 March 1991).

Use of Handcuffs Handcuffs should be used only where they are reasonably necessary to prevent an escape or to prevent a violent breach of the peace by a prisoner (*Lockley* (1864) 4 F & F 155). The same rule applies to the handcuffing of prisoners in court (*Cambridge Justices, ex parte Peacock* (1992) 156 JP 895; *Horden* [2009] 2 Cr App R 406). It would seem that, where handcuffs are unjustifiably resorted to, their use will constitute a trespass even though the arrest itself is lawful (*Taylor* (1895) 59 JP 393; *Bibby v Chief Constable of Essex* (2000) 164 JP 297). Association of Chief Police Officers guidance on the use of handcuffs is available at www.acpo.police.uk/documents/uniformed/2009/Handcuffs_Guidance_Amended_08x05x09_website.pdf. **D1.8**

POWERS TO STOP AND SEARCH

Police powers to stop and search people and vehicles are conferred by the PACE 1984, and a range of other legislation. See PACE Code A, annex A (see **appendix 1**) for a summary of the **D1.9** main stop and search powers. The PACE 1984, ss. 2 and 3, impose a number of obligations on officers conducting a stop and search irrespective of the legislative authority for it. Code A applies to all police powers of stop and search other than those conducted under the Aviation Security Act 1982, s. 27(2), and the PACE 1984, s. 6(1) (see the unnumbered introductory paragraphs to Code A), and stop and search under the TA 2000 (see **B10.25**). Community support officers designated under the Police Reform Act 2002, part 4, do not have powers of stop and search under the PACE 1984, but do have such powers under some other legislation (see Code A, annex C for a summary of such powers).

Stop and Search Powers Requiring Reasonable Suspicion

D1.10   The main stop and search power requiring reasonable suspicion is that under the PACE 1984, part I. For reasonable suspicion see **D1.4** and PACE Code A, paras. 2.2 to 2.11 (see **appendix 1**).

Police and Criminal Evidence Act 1984, s. 1

(1) A constable may exercise any power conferred by this section—

   (a) in any place to which at the time when he proposes to exercise the power the public or any section of the public has access, on payment or otherwise, as of right or by virtue of express or implied permission; or

   (b) in any other place to which people have ready access at the time when he proposes to exercise the power but which is not a dwelling.

(2) Subject to subsection (3) to (5) below, a constable—

   (a) may search—

      (i)   any person or vehicle;

      (ii) anything which is in or on a vehicle,

for stolen or prohibited articles, any article to which subsection (8A) below applies or any firework to which subsection (8B) below applies; and

   (b) may detain a person or vehicle for the purpose of such a search.

(3) This section does not give a constable power to search a person or vehicle or anything in or on a vehicle unless he has reasonable grounds for suspecting that he will find stolen or prohibited articles or, any article to which subsection (8A) below applies or any firework to which subsection (8B) below applies.

(4) If a person is in a garden or yard occupied with and used for the purposes of a dwelling or on other land so occupied and used, a constable may not search him in the exercise of the power conferred by this section unless the constable has reasonable grounds for believing—

   (a) that he does not reside in the dwelling; and

   (b) that he is not in the place in question with the express or implied permission of a person who resides in the dwelling.

(5) If a vehicle is in a garden or yard occupied with and used for the purposes of a dwelling or on other land so occupied and used, a constable may not search the vehicle or anything in or on it in the exercise of the power conferred by this section unless he has reasonable grounds for believing—

   (a) that the person in charge of the vehicle does not reside in the dwelling; and

   (b) that the vehicle is not in the place in question with the express or implied permission of a person who resides in the dwelling.

(6) If in the course of such a search a constable discovers an article which he has reasonable grounds for suspecting to be a stolen or prohibited article, an article to which subsection (8A) below applies or a firework to which subsection (8B) below applies, he may seize it.

(7) An article is prohibited for the purposes of this Part of this Act if it is—

   (a) an offensive weapon; or

   (b) an article—

      (i)   made or adapted for use in the course of or in connection with an offence to which this sub-paragraph applies; or

      (ii) intended by the person having it with him for such use by him or by some other person.

(8) The offences to which subsection (7)(b)(i) above applies are—

   (a) burglary;

   (b) theft;

(c) offences under section 12 of the Theft Act 1968 (taking motor vehicle or other conveyance without authority);

(d) fraud (contrary to section 1 of the Fraud Act 2006); and

(e) offences under section 1 of the Criminal Damage Act 1971 (destroying or damaging property).

(8A) This subsection applies to any article in relation to which a person has committed, or is committing or is going to commit an offence under section 139 or section 139AA of the Criminal Justice Act 1988.

(8B) This subsection applies to any firework which a person possesses in contravention of a prohibition imposed by fireworks regulations.

(8C) In this section—

(a) 'firework' shall be construed in accordance with the definition of 'fireworks' in section 1(1) of the Fireworks Act 2003; and

(b) 'fireworks regulations' has the same meaning as in that Act.

(9) In this Part of this Act 'offensive weapon' means any article—

(a) made or adapted for use for causing injury to persons; or

(b) intended by the person having it with him for such use by him or by some other person.

The power is available only in public places, but this is given a particular meaning by s. 1(1)(a) and (b), (4) and (5).

Stop and Search Powers Not Requiring Reasonable Suspicion

Stop and search powers that do not require reasonable suspicion include those under the **D1.11** CJPO 1994, ss. 60 and 60AA, and the CJA 1988, s. 139B, although under the latter power the constable must have reasonable grounds to believe that an offence under s. 139A (having a bladed or pointed article or offensive weapon on school premises) or s. 139AA (threatening with article with blade or point or offensive weapon) has been or is being committed. For stop and search powers under the TA 2000 that do not require reasonable suspicion, see **B10.25**.

Section 60 of the CJPO 1994 gives the police the power to stop and search where an officer of the **D1.12** rank of inspector or above has given the appropriate authorisation under s. 60(1). Authorisation may be granted if the officer reasonably believes:

(a) that incidents involving serious violence may take place in any locality in his police area, and that it is expedient to give an authorisation under this section to prevent their occurrence (s. 60(1)(a));

(b) that an incident involving serious violence has occurred in his police area, a dangerous instrument or offensive weapon used in the incident is being carried by a person in that area, and it is expedient to give an authorisation to find the instrument or weapon (s. 60(1)(aa)); or

(c) that persons are carrying dangerous instruments or offensive weapons in any locality in his police area without good reason (s. 60(1)(b)).

Authorisation may be granted for up to 24 hours, although this may be extended by an officer of the rank of superintendent or above by a further 24 hours (CJPO 1994, s. 60(1) and (3)). It must be given in writing specifying the grounds on which it is given, and the locality in which and the period during which the powers are exercisable (s. 60(9)). An authorisation given under s. 60(1)(aa) need not be in writing if that is not practicable, but must be recorded in writing as soon as is practicable (s. 60(9ZA)).

Where an authorisation is in force any constable in uniform may stop any pedestrian and search him or anything carried by him for offensive weapons or dangerous instruments, or may stop any vehicle and search the vehicle, the driver and any passenger for a like purpose (s. 60(4)). Section 60(5) provides that this power may be exercised whether or not the constable has any grounds for suspecting that the person or vehicle is carrying such weapons or instruments. However, under Code A, para. 2.14A, the selection of persons and vehicles to be stopped and, if appropriate, searched should reflect an objective assessment of the nature of the incident or

Part D Procedure

weapon in question and the individuals and vehicles thought likely to be associated with that incident or those weapons. It was held in *R (Roberts) v Commissioner of Police for the Metropolis* [2014] 2 Cr App R 80 (6) that, while engaging the ECHR, Article 8, exercise of the power of stop and search under s. 60 did not breach Article 8 rights.

A person, or driver of a vehicle, stopped or searched under s. 60 is entitled to a written statement that he was so stopped or searched if he applies within 12 months (s. 60(10) and (10A)). In addition, the information and recording requirements of the PACE 1984, ss. 2 and 3, apply (see **D1.13**).

The CJPO 1994, s. 60AA, provides for a power to require the removal of any item which a constable reasonably believes a person is wearing wholly or mainly for the purpose of concealing his identity, and power to seize an item which a person intends to wear for such a purpose. The power is exercisable where an authorisation under s. 60 is in place, but a separate authorisation may be given under s. 60AA(3) and (4).

Conduct of Stop and Search Powers

D1.13   The consent of the person concerned is not a sufficient authority for a search. PACE Code A, para. 1.5, provides that a search must not be conducted in the absence of a relevant power. The various statutory powers contain different provisions regarding the conduct of a stop and search. Most enable both persons and vehicles to be searched, although some are confined to one or the other. Some are exercisable anywhere whereas others can only be carried out in a public place or in specific premises or areas such as schools or ports. Some require the officer to be in uniform, but others do not. For a summary, see Code A, annex A (**appendix 1**). The requirement, under the PACE 1984, s. 2(b)(i), and Code A, para. 3.9, that an officer who is not in uniform provide documentary evidence that he is a constable before carrying out a search is mandatory (*B v DPP* (2008) 172 JP 449).

Code A sets out minimum requirements that must be observed when powers to stop and search to which Code A applies are exercised. Reasonable force may be used, although co-operation should be sought even if the person initially objects to the search (PACE 1984, s. 117; Code A, para. 3.2; *James v DPP* (2012) 176 JP 346; see also **D1.7**). A person may be detained for the purpose of carrying out a search although the period for which he is detained must be reasonable and be kept to a minimum (PACE 1984, s. 1(2)(b); Code A, para. 3.3). It was held in *R (Gillan) v Metropolitan Police Commissioner* [2006] 2 AC 307, that, provided it is properly conducted, a short period of detention (in that case 20 minutes) for the purposes of stop and search does not engage the ECHR, Article 5 (but see **B10.25**). The search must be conducted at or near the place where the person or vehicle was stopped (Code A, para. 3.4), although a place is 'near' if it is within a reasonable travelling distance (Code A, Note for Guidance 6). If a search requires the removal of more than outer clothing this cannot normally be done in public (PACE 1984, s. 2(9)(a); Code A, para. 3.5). Before a search of a person or an attended vehicle is conducted the officer must take reasonable steps to give the person the information set out in the PACE 1984, s. 2, and Code A, paras. 3.8 to 3.11 (*Bristol* (2008) 172 JP 161). It was held in *R (Michaels) v Highbury Corner Magistrates' Court* [2009] EWHC 2928 (Admin) that this applies even if the officer conducting the search and the person who is the subject of the search are well known to each other. Recording requirements are set out in the PACE 1984, s. 3, and Code A, sect. 4.

POWERS OF ARREST: GENERAL PROVISIONS

Powers of Arrest

D1.14   Police powers of arrest without a warrant in relation to criminal offences are principally governed by the PACE 1984, s. 24. Most other statutory powers of arrest were repealed by the SOCPA 2005, s. 111 and sch. 7, although a number of pre-PACE statutory powers are preserved by the PACE 1984, sch. 2, and there are extensive cross-border powers of arrest under the CJPO 1994 (see **D1.33** *et seq.*). Civilian powers of arrest are governed by the PACE 1984, s. 24A. The other remaining power of arrest without a warrant is the common-law power of arrest for breach of the peace (see **D1.33**). Arrest under a warrant is governed by a number of statutory provisions (see **D1.35** *et seq.*).

Legal Characteristics of Arrest

'Arrest' is not defined by the PACE 1984, or other legislation, and there is some inconsistency in **D1.15** the case law. One approach is that a person is arrested if, as a result of what is said or done, he is under compulsion and is not free to go as he pleases (*Alderson v Booth* [1969] 2 QB 216; *Inwood* (1973) 57 Cr App R 529; *Spicer v Holt* [1977] AC 987). Arrest, is an ordinary English word, and whether or not a person has been arrested depends not on the legality of the arrest but on whether he has been deprived of his liberty to go where he pleases (*Lewis v Chief Constable of the South Wales Constabulary* [1991] 1 All ER 206). A second approach is that context and purpose are relevant. In *Austin v Commissioner of Police of the Metropolis* [2009] 1 AC 564 the House of Lords distinguished between a deprivation of liberty and a restriction of movement. Whether a situation amounts to a deprivation of liberty as opposed to a restriction of movement is a matter of degree and intensity and is highly fact-sensitive. A whole range of factors has to be considered including the individual's specific situation, the context in which the restriction occurs and the purpose of the confinement or restriction (see also *Austin v UK* (2012) 55 EHRR 359 and *Shields v Chief Constable of Merseyside Police* [2010] EWCA Civ 1281). In *Iqbal* [2011] 1 WLR 1541 it was held that a person who was handcuffed by a police officer and told that he would be arrested later by other officers was not under arrest (although he was unlawfully detained). Under the *Lewis* approach these circumstances would clearly have amounted to an arrest, albeit an unlawful arrest because the appellant was not told that he was under arrest as required by the PACE 1984, s. 28(1). Taking hold of a person's arm for the purpose of simply drawing his attention to what is being said to him, without an intention to detain or arrest, is neither an arrest nor an actionable trespass to the person unless it goes beyond what is acceptable by the ordinary standards of everyday life (*Mepstead v DPP* (1996) 160 JP 475); and the same is true where an officer takes a drunk person by the arm to steady him for his own safety (*McMillan v CPS* (2008) 172 JP 485). However, if an officer takes hold of a person's arm to detain him while the officer decides whether to arrest, this does amount to a trespass (*Elkington v DPP* [2012] EWHC 3398 (Admin)); and detaining a person by confining them to a restricted space, without intending to arrest them, amounts to unlawful imprisonment (*Walker v Commissioner of Police of the Metropolis* [2014] EWCA Civ 897).

There is no necessary assumption that an arrest will be followed by a charge (*Holgate-Mohammed* **D1.16** *v Duke* [1984] AC 437). Although the power to arrest must be exercised for a proper purpose, it was affirmed in *Chalkley* [1998] QB 848 that the fact that an arrest is motivated by a desire to investigate another, more serious, offence does not render it invalid provided there are valid grounds for the arrest. An arrest for an offence will, however, be unlawful, even though made on the basis of reasonable suspicion, where the officer knows at the time of arrest that there is no possibility of a charge being made. Conversely, it is clear that, even though a complainant withdraws his complaint, a constable may still arrest a suspect where he hopes by so doing to obtain a confession (*Plange v Chief Constable of South Humberside Police* (1992) *The Times*, 23 March 1992).

Reasonable force may be used to effect an arrest (PACE 1984, s. 117; CLA 1967, s. 3; and see **D1.7**).

Communication of Fact of and Grounds for Arrest

Where a person is arrested (whether or not for an offence), otherwise than by being informed **D1.17** that he is under arrest, the arrest is unlawful unless he is informed that he is under arrest as soon as is practicable after the arrest (PACE 1984, s. 28(1)). If the arrest is by a constable, this applies even if the fact of arrest is obvious (s. 28(2)). Further, an arrest is unlawful unless the arrested person is informed of the ground for the arrest at the time of the arrest, or as soon as is

D

Part D Procedure

practicable after the arrest (s. 28(3)). If the arrest is by a constable, this applies even if the grounds for arrest are obvious (s. 28(4)). The person must also be informed why arrest was believed to be necessary (for the purposes of s. 24(4)), although failure to do so will not render the arrest unlawful (Code G, para. 2.2).

The test for whether the words used were sufficient is whether, having regard to all the circumstances of the case, the person arrested was told, in simple, non-technical language that he could understand, the essential legal and factual grounds for his arrest (*Taylor v Chief Constable of Thames Valley Police* [2004] 3 All ER 503; *Adler v CPS* (2013) 178 JP 558). According to PACE Code C, Note for Guidance 10B, and Code G, Note for Guidance 3, where a person is arrested for an offence he must be informed of the nature of the suspected offence, and when and where it was allegedly committed.

D1.18   The information need not be given by the arresting officer but may be given by a colleague (*Nicholas v Parsonage* [1987] RTR 199; *Dhesi v Chief Constable of West Midlands Police* (2000) *The Times*, 9 May 2000). Where no reasons are given at the time of arrest because it is impracticable to inform the suspect, acts done at the time of arrest do not become retrospectively invalid because of a later failure to inform him (*DPP v Hawkins* [1988] 3 All ER 673; *Lewis v Chief Constable of the South Wales Constabulary* [1991] 1 All ER 206). The words used will suffice even though they are apt to describe more than one offence, provided that they aptly describe the offence for which the arrest is made (*Abbassy v Metropolitan Police Commissioner* [1990] 1 All ER 193; *Clarke v Chief Constable of North Wales Police* [2000] All ER (D) 477). An arresting officer may not, however, properly give reasons on which he does not rely; that is, he may not lead a person to think that he is arresting him for one offence when in truth he wishes to arrest him for another (*Christie v Leachinsky* [1947] AC 573; *Abbassy v Metropolitan Police Commissioner*; *Waters v Bigmore* [1981] RTR 356).

In addition to the information required under s. 28, a person who is arrested, or who is further arrested (e.g., under the PACE 1984, s. 31), must be cautioned at the time of arrest or as soon as is practicable afterwards unless it is impracticable to do so because of his condition or behaviour at the time or he has already been cautioned immediately before arrest (e.g., where he was initially questioned regarding a suspected offence without being arrested) (Code C, para. 10.4, and Code G, para. 3.4). The terms of the caution are set out in Code C, para. 10.5 (see **appendix 1**). Failure to administer a caution does not render the arrest unlawful, although it may provide grounds for exclusion of evidence under the PACE 1984, s. 76 or 78 (*Miller* [2007] EWCA Crim 1891).

The nature and circumstances of the offence leading to the arrest, the reason(s) why the arrest was necessary, the giving of the caution, and anything said by the arrested person at the time of his arrest must be recorded by the arresting officer in his pocket book (or other method used for recording information) (Code G, para. 4.1). This record must be made at the time of the arrest unless impracticable, in which case it must be completed as soon as possible thereafter (Code G, para 4.2). If the arrested person is subsequently detained at a police station, the information given by the arresting officer as to the circumstances and reason(s) for the arrest must be recorded in, or attached to, the custody record (Code G, para. 4.3).

Resisting Arrest

D1.19   A person has an unqualified right at common law to resist an unlawful arrest (*Christie v Leachinsky* [1947] AC 573), but he must not use excessive force in doing so (*Wilson* [1955] 1 All ER 744; *Long* (1836) 7 C & P 314). Whilst excessive force in resisting arrest may amount to an offence, the person using excessive force would not be guilty of assaulting a constable in the execution of his duty (*Kenlin v Gardiner* [1967] 2 QB 510). These principles extend to a person resisting or assaulting an officer who goes to the assistance of another officer who is carrying out an unlawful arrest (*Cumberbatch v CPS* (2010) 174 JP 149).

It would seem that avoiding arrest, or even questioning short of arrest, by running away when approached by police can amount to wilful obstruction of the police in the execution of their duty, contrary to the Police Act 1996, s. 89(2) (*Sekfali v DPP* (2006) 170 JP 393). However, there is some difficulty in reconciling this with the established principle that a person does not commit wilful obstruction or any other offence (except where statute provides otherwise) if he refuses to give the police his name and address or to answer police questions (*Rice v Connolly* [1966] 2 QB 414); and with the decision in *Iqbal* [2011] 1 WLR 1541, in which it was held that a person did not commit an offence by refusing to wait to be arrested.

Action following Arrest

Where a person is arrested at any place other than a police station, or is taken into custody by a **D1.20** constable following an arrest made by a civilian, the constable is normally obliged to take him to a designated police station as soon as is practicable thereafter (PACE 1984, s. 30(1), (1A), (1B) and (2)). In exceptional circumstances the person may be taken to a non-designated station (s. 30(3)–(6)). The constable may delay taking the arrested person to a police station or releasing him on bail under s. 30A if his presence at a place other than a police station is necessary in order to carry out such investigations as it is reasonable to carry out immediately (s. 30(10) and (10A)), but the reasons must be recorded (s. 30(11)). This might include taking the suspect from one place to another to check his alibi (*Dallison v Caffery* [1965] 1 QB 348), search of the arrested person under s. 32(2)(a) (see **D1.96**), or entry and search of premises under s. 32(2)(b) or s. 18(1) and (5) (see **D1.169**). A constable who is satisfied that there are no grounds for keeping the arrested person under arrest or releasing him on bail under s. 30A must release him (s. 30(7) and (7A)), and the facts must be recorded (s. 30(8) and (9)).

Notwithstanding the above, an arrested person may, instead of being taken to a police station, **D1.21** be released on bail, to attend at a police station on a future date (s. 30A(1)–(3)). Conditions may be imposed for the purpose of securing surrender, preventing further offences, preventing interference with witnesses or obstruction of the administration of justice, or for the person's own protection (s. 30A(3B)). An application to vary conditions may be made to the police and, thereafter, to a magistrates' court (ss. 30CA and 30CB).

A person released on bail in these circumstances must be given a notice informing him of the offence for which he was arrested, of the grounds of arrest, that he is required to attend a police station and of any conditions imposed, and opportunities for seeking a variation of those conditions. The notice may also specify the police station which he is required to attend and the time when he is required to attend; if it does not do so, it must specify the police station at which a request for variation of a condition may be made. If the notice does not give the requisite information, the arrested person must subsequently be given a further written notice which contains that information. He may be required to attend a different police station from that originally notified (s. 30B(1)–(6)). There is no statutory limit on the period for which bail may be granted under these provisions.

A person released on bail under s. 30A may be rearrested without warrant if new evidence justifying his arrest has come to light since his release (s. 30C(4)). Any person released under s. 30A who fails to attend at a police station as required and any person whom a constable has reasonable grounds for suspecting has broken any conditions imposed may be arrested without warrant; but the police have no power to arrest for an anticipated breach of conditions or failure to surrender. He must then be taken to a police station (which may be the specified police station or any other police station) as soon as practicable after an arrest. Although breach of conditions, and failure to attend a police station, do not constitute offences, an arrest under these provisions counts as an arrest for an offence for the purposes of the PACE 1984, ss. 30 and 31 (s. 30D).

ARREST WITHOUT WARRANT

D1.22   Police powers of arrest without warrant are largely governed by the PACE 1984, s. 24 (but see **D1.30** *et seq.*), and civilian powers of arrest by s. 24A. Under s. 24 a police officer may arrest for any offence, but civilian powers of arrest are confined to indictable offences. In both cases the power is subject to a test of necessity. Section 24 is supplemented by PACE Code of Practice G (see **D1.1**). Other powers of arrest without warrant, cross-border powers of arrest, and arrest for breach of the peace, are also dealt with in this section.

Powers of arrest are generally discretionary; if the conditions are satisfied the officer (or civilian) may arrest, but is not required to. However, where a person has been arrested for an offence and is at a police station in consequence of that arrest, and it appears to the police that, if released, he would be liable to arrest for some other offence, the person must be arrested for that other offence (PACE 1984, s. 31).

Police Powers of Arrest

D1.23   **Police and Criminal Evidence Act 1984, s. 24**

(1) A constable may arrest without a warrant—
  (a) anyone who is about to commit an offence;
  (b) anyone who is in the act of committing an offence;
  (c) anyone whom he has reasonable grounds for suspecting to be about to commit an offence;
  (d) anyone whom he has reasonable grounds for suspecting to be committing an offence.
(2) If a constable has reasonable grounds for suspecting that an offence has been committed, he may arrest without a warrant anyone whom he has reasonable grounds to suspect of being guilty of it.
(3) If an offence has been committed, a constable may arrest without a warrant—
  (a) anyone who is guilty of the offence;
  (b) anyone whom he has reasonable grounds for suspecting to be guilty of it.
(4) But the power of summary arrest conferred by subsection (1), (2) or (3) is exercisable only if the constable has reasonable grounds for believing that for any of the reasons mentioned in subsection (5) it is necessary to arrest the person in question.
(5) The reasons are—
  (a) to enable the name of the person in question to be ascertained (in the case where the constable does not know, and cannot readily ascertain, the person's name, or has reasonable grounds for doubting whether a name given by the person as his name is his real name);
  (b) correspondingly as regards the person's address;
  (c) to prevent the person in question—
    (i) causing physical injury to himself or any other person;
    (ii) suffering physical injury;
    (iii) causing loss of or damage to property;
    (iv) committing an offence against public decency (subject to subsection (6)); or
    (v) causing an unlawful obstruction of the highway;
  (d) to protect a child or other vulnerable person from the person in question;
  (e) to allow the prompt and effective investigation of the offence or of the conduct of the person in question;
  (f) to prevent any prosecution for the offence from being hindered by the disappearance of the person in question.
(6) Subsection (5)(c)(iv) applies only where members of the public going about their normal business cannot reasonably be expected to avoid the person in question.

D1.24   **Reasonable Suspicion**   Arrest under the PACE 1984, s. 24(1)(c) and (d), (2) and (3)(b), requires the officer to have reasonable grounds for suspicion (see **D1.4**). However, the PACE 1984, s. 24(1)(a) and (b), and (3)(a), permit arrest without reasonable suspicion. Thus, provided that it can be established that the relevant condition is satisfied (e.g., that the person was in the act of committing an offence), the arrest will be lawful even if it cannot be established that the officer had reasonable grounds for suspicion. The scope for justifying an arrest by reference to the powers that do not require reasonable suspicion was emphasised in *Shields v Chief Constable of Merseyside Police* [2010] EWCA Civ 1281, although the court did not consider whether these powers comply with the reasonable suspicion requirement of the ECHR, Article 5(1)(c) (see **D1.4**).

Necessity In addition to the conditions set out in the PACE 1984, s. 24(1)–(3), the officer **D1.25** must have reasonable grounds for believing that arrest is necessary for any of the reasons set out in s. 24(5) (s. 24(4)). It was held in *Graham v West (Chief Constable of West Mercia)* [2011] EWHC 4 (QB), that the necessity test involves a similar mixed objective/subjective test to that required for reasonable grounds for suspicion (see **D1.4**). This requires the officer to have 'solid grounds' for believing that, for example, the suspect would hide or destroy evidence; a theoretical possibility that he might do so is not sufficient (*Hanningfield v Chief Constable of Essex* [2013] 1 WLR 3632). PACE Code G notes that arrest 'represents an obvious and significant interference' with the right to liberty (para. 1.2), and a person must not be arrested simply because the power is available. The decision to arrest must be fully justified and the officer must consider whether the necessary objectives can be met by other, less intrusive, means (para. 1.3). The necessity requirement, contained in identical provisions, was considered by the Northern Ireland Divisional Court in *Re Alexander* [2009] NIQB 20. It held that in order to satisfy the necessity requirement the arresting officer must make some evaluation of the feasibility of achieving the object of the arrest by some alternative means, such as by inviting the suspect to attend for interview. The officer does not have to be satisfied that there is no viable alternative to arrest; concluding that arrest is the practical and sensible option is sufficient. An officer who does not apply his mind to alternatives short of arrest is open to challenge (*Richardson v Chief Constable of West Midlands Police* [2011] 2 Cr App R 1), but 'the challenge, if it comes, is not one which requires the officer's decision to be subjected to a full-blown public law reasons challenge. It is one which requires it to be shown that on the information known to the officer he had reasonable grounds for believing arrest to be necessary, for an identified section 24(5) reason' (*Hayes v Chief Constable of Merseyside Police* [2012] 1 WLR 517, followed in *Fitzpatrick, Wilkey and Thomas, Body and White (a firm) v Commissioner of Police of the Metropolis* [2012] EWHC 12 (Admin)); and see Code G, para. 2.6, and Note for Guidance 2C (see **D1.4**).

Code G, para. 1.3, provides that it is essential that the power of arrest is exercised in a 'non- **D1.26** discriminatory and proportionate manner' and it is submitted that, in considering whether arrest is necessary, the officer must take into account the nature and seriousness of the suspected offence (and see Code G, para. 2.8). Further, in considering whether the police have sufficiently considered alternatives to arrest, it would seem to follow from *Hanningfield* that account should be taken of whether an arrest was carried out in the context of a planned operation, or was a response to immediate and urgent events.

Code G, para 2.9, provides some explanation of the various necessity conditions. In rela- **D1.27** tion to s. 24(5)(a) and (b) it states that an address is satisfactory for the purposes of serving a summons, or requisition and charge, if the person will be at the address for a sufficiently long period to facilitate service, or if some other person at the address given will accept service on his behalf. Where the suspect gives his name and/or address, the officer must have reasonable grounds for doubting the name or address given for arrest to be necessary (Code G, para. 2.9(b)). A constable cannot be said to doubt it simply because in the past other persons suspected of a like offence have not given correct particulars (*G v DPP* [1989] Crim LR 150).

In certain circumstances, loss of or damage to property, for the purposes of s. 24(5)(c)(iii), could include the offender's own property, such as where a violent husband, having assaulted his wife, is believed likely to damage the matrimonial home or objects in it. The condition under s. 24(5)(c)(iv) applies only where members of the public going about their normal business cannot reasonably be expected to avoid the person in question (s. 24(6)). In relation to s. 24(5)(c)(v) it is irrelevant that the police have previously permitted an act of obstruction to take place there (*Arrowsmith v Jenkins* [1963] 2 QB 561).

D1.28 Section 24(5)(e) permits arrest in order to allow the prompt and effective investigation of the offence or of the conduct of the person in question. It is difficult to see how an arrest could be justified by reference to a need to investigate the conduct of the person unless that involves investigation of the offence of which he is suspected. Code G, para. 2.9(e), gives examples of the circumstances in which this condition may be satisfied, including where there is a need to enter and search property, search the person, or take fingerprints, photographs, etc. However, many such investigative acts may be carried out with the consent of the person concerned so they may not, in themselves, justify an arrest of a person willing to co-operate. Where a person attends at a police station voluntarily, arrest is justified only if new information coming to light after the arrangements were made indicates that voluntary attendance is no longer a practical alternative. The possibility that a volunteer may leave during the interview is not a valid reason for arresting him before the interview commences (Code G, Note for Guidance 2G; cf. *Hayes v Chief Constable of Merseyside Police* [2012] 1 WLR 517).

In relation to s. 24(5)(f), Code G, para 2.9, states that the condition may be satisfied if there are reasonable grounds for believing that the person will fail to attend court if not arrested, or if the grant of bail under the PACE 1984, s. 30A, would not be enough to deter him from trying to evade prosecution. Given the reasonable belief requirement in s. 24(4), there should be some objective basis for the belief. Mere suspicion that the person may not turn up in court should not be sufficient.

Civilian Powers of Arrest

D1.29   Police and Criminal Evidence Act 1984, s. 24A

(1) A person other than a constable may arrest without a warrant—
  (a) anyone who is in the act of committing an indictable offence;
  (b) anyone whom he has reasonable grounds for suspecting to be committing an indictable offence.
(2) Where an indictable offence has been committed, a person other than a constable may arrest without a warrant—
  (a) anyone who is guilty of the offence;
  (b) anyone whom he has reasonable grounds for suspecting to be guilty of it.
(3) But the power of summary arrest conferred by subsection (1) or (2) is exercisable only if —
  (a) the person making the arrest has reasonable grounds for believing that for any of the reasons mentioned in subsection (4) it is necessary to arrest the person in question; and
  (b) it appears to the person making the arrest that it is not reasonably practicable for a constable to make it instead.
(4) The reasons are to prevent the person in question—
  (a) causing physical injury to himself or any other person;
  (b) suffering physical injury;
  (c) causing loss of or damage to property; or
  (d) making off before a constable can assume responsibility for him.
(5) This section does not apply in relation to an offence under Part 3 or 3A of the Public Order Act 1986.

Section 24A provides for a more restricted scheme of powers of arrest for persons other than constables. These powers apply only to indictable offences (s. 24A(1) and (2)), which includes offences triable either-way as well as indictable-only offences (see **D1.69**). Unlike a constable, a civilian cannot arrest for an anticipated offence. If a civilian arrests a person under s. 24A(2) for an offence he believes has been committed, the arrest will be unlawful if it cannot be established that an indictable offence was in fact committed (*Self* [1992] 3 All ER 476, decided under the former version of s. 24, but the same principles apply). A civilian making an arrest must have reasonable grounds for believing that, for any of the reasons mentioned in s. 24A(4), it is necessary to arrest the person and it must appear to him that it is not practicable for a constable to make the arrest instead (s. 24A(3)). The necessity conditions under s. 24A(4) are more limited than those that apply to constables under s. 24(5).

Other Powers of Arrest

The PACE 1984, s. 26 and sch. 2, preserve certain powers of arrest enacted prior to the **D1.30** PACE 1984.

Police and Criminal Evidence Act 1984, sch. 2

PRESERVED POWERS OF ARREST

1952 c. 52	Section 49 of the Prison Act 1952.
1952 c. 67	Section 13 of the Visiting Forces Act 1952.
1969 c. 54	Section 32 of the Children and Young Persons Act 1969.
1971 c. 77	Section 24(2) of the Immigration Act 1971 and paragraphs 17, 24 and 33 of Schedule 2 and paragraph 7 of Schedule 3 to that Act.
1976 c. 63	Section 7 of the Bail Act 1976.
1983 c. 20	Sections 18, 35(10), 36(8), 38(7), 136(1) and 138 of the Mental Health Act 1983.
1984 c. 47	Section 5(5) of the Repatriation of Prisoners Act 1984.

A constable has a power to arrest a person released on bail in criminal proceedings where (a) he has reasonable grounds to believe the person is not likely to surrender to custody or is likely to break any bail conditions, (b) he has reasonable grounds to suspect that the person has broken the conditions of his bail, or (c) where that person was released on bail with a surety or sureties, a surety notifies the constable in writing that the bailed person is unlikely to surrender to custody and that for that reason the surety wishes to be relieved of his obligations as a surety (Bail Act 1976, s. 7(3)). A Customs and Excise officer has a similar power to arrest a suspect who he has reasonable grounds for believing is not likely to surrender to custody where the person has been released on bail in respect of possession of controlled drugs, drug trafficking or money launder- ing (CJA 1988, s. 151). For powers of arrest in respect of a person granted bail before being taken to a police station, see **D1.21**, and in respect of a person granted bail under the PACE 1984, part IV, see **D1.186**.

Many statutory powers of arrest enacted before and after the PACE 1984 were repealed by the SOCPA 2005, s. 111 and sch. 7. However, the police still have various statutory powers of arrest other than those granted by the PACE 1984, s. 24, or preserved by sch. 2. For example, they may arrest a person for the purpose of taking fingerprints or samples (PACE 1984, s. 63A(4) and sch. 2A, para. 17), and may arrest a person who is reasonably suspected to be a terrorist (see **B10.14** *et seq.*). The police also have powers to arrest a person under the Mental Health Act 1983, s. 136(1). For powers of arrest in respect of service offences, see the Armed Forces Act 2006, part 3, chapter 1.

Cross-border Powers of Arrest

The CJPO 1994, part X (ss. 136 to 140), makes extensive provision for cross-border powers of **D1.31** arrest within the UK. Section 136 concerns the cross-border execution of warrants. A warrant issued in one part of the UK in the name of an innocent person (as in the context of personation by the true offender) remains valid until annulled. Where police arrest the person named in the warrant, they will not be liable for wrongful arrest or false imprisonment provided that they acted without malice (*McGrath v Chief Constable of the Royal Ulster Constabulary* [2001] 2 AC 731).

By s. 137, a constable from one part of the UK who has reasonable grounds for suspecting that an offence has been committed or attempted in his jurisdiction may arrest a suspected person in another part of the UK. An arrest can be carried out under this provision where the conditions which would enable the officer to arrest lawfully in his own jurisdiction are satisfied. Following arrest, the arrested person must be taken to a police station in accordance with s. 137(7).

A constable may use reasonable force in effecting an arrest in the other jurisdiction (s. 137(8)(a)). A constable from Scotland arresting or detaining a suspect in England or Wales has the same powers and duties, and the arrested person the same rights, as if the arrest had taken place in Scotland (s. 137(8)(b) and (c) and s. 138(2)). Scottish procedure is modified in certain respects to take account of the exigencies of this scheme.

D1.32 Search powers are available under these cross-border schemes in respect of arrests under warrant or without warrant. A constable from England and Wales arresting under warrant in Scotland or Northern Ireland, or a constable from Scotland or Northern Ireland arresting under warrant in England or Wales, is given extensive powers under s. 139. The same powers apply to arrests without warrant by a constable from England or Wales making an arrest in Scotland or Northern Ireland or a constable from Northern Ireland making an arrest in England or Wales (s. 139(1)). Under these powers a constable may search the person if he has reasonable grounds for believing that the person may present a danger to himself or to others (s. 139(2)). The powers are virtually the same as those which apply under the PACE 1984, s. 32, to a search of the person or premises on arrest (see **D1.96** and **D1.173**).

The scheme further provides for reciprocal powers of arrest. Where a police constable in England or Wales would have powers to arrest, a constable from Scotland or Northern Ireland who is in England or Wales has the same powers of arrest (s. 140(1)). Reciprocal powers apply in favour of a constable from England or Wales in Scotland or Northern Ireland (s. 140(3), (4) and (5)). The scheme is premised upon the arresting officer having the same powers and coming under the same obligations as he would were he a local constable operating under local law.

Arrest for Breach of the Peace

D1.33 Any person, whether constable or civilian, has a common-law power of arrest where (a) a breach of the peace is committed in his presence, (b) the person effecting the arrest reasonably believes that such a breach will be committed in the immediate future by the person arrested, or (c) a breach of the peace has been committed or the person effecting the arrest reasonably believes that a breach of the peace has occurred and that a further breach is threatened. In order to comply with the ECHR, Article 5(1)(c), an arrest must be for the purpose of bringing the person before a competent legal authority, but an intention to do so 'if that were to become necessary' is sufficient (*R (Hicks) v Commissioner of Police for the Metropolis* [2014] 1 WLR 2152. A breach of the peace occurs whenever harm is actually done or is likely to be done to a person or, in his presence, to his property, or where a person is in fear of being harmed through an assault, affray, riot, unlawful assembly or other disturbance (*Howell* [1982] QB 416). For guidance on immediacy in relation to conduct in a domestic setting, see *Wragg v DPP* [2005] EWHC 1389 (Admin) and *Demetriou v DPP* [2012] EWHC 2443 (Admin).

Reasonable belief is an objective requirement in the sense that the court must determine whether the belief was reasonable having regard to the circumstances as perceived by the person carrying out the arrest at the time (*Redmond-Bate v DPP* (1999) 163 JP 789). Where a reasonable apprehension of an imminent breach of the peace exists, the preventive action taken must be reasonable, necessary and proportionate. For action short of arrest, see *R (Laporte) v Chief Constable of Gloucestershire* [2007] 2 All ER 529, *Austin v Commissioner of Police of the Metropolis* [2009] 1 AC 564, and *R (McClure and Moos) v Commissioner of Police of the Metropolis* [2012] EWCA Civ 12. The power to arrest for an apprehended breach of the peace caused by apparently lawful conduct is exceptional (*Foulkes v Chief Constable of Merseyside Police* [1998] 3 All ER 705; *Bibby v Chief Constable of Essex Police* (2000) 164 JP 297). For powers of entry to deal with a breach of the peace, see **D1.172**.

D1.34 A person arrested for breach of the peace may be held in custody at a police station, but the officer concerned must have an honest belief, based upon objective and reasonable grounds, that detention is necessary in order to prevent a breach of the peace. If this condition is not satisfied, and no other grounds for detention exist, the person must be released (*Chief Constable of Cleveland Police v McGrogan* [2002] EWCA Civ 86). Breach of the peace is not an offence under domestic law, although it may be treated as criminal for the purposes of the ECHR (*Steel v UK* (1999) 28

EHRR 603) and, therefore, detention of a person arrested for breach of the peace is not governed by the PACE 1984, s. 37. It was held in *Williamson v Chief Constable of West Midlands Police* [2004] 1 WLR 14 (followed in *Hicks*) that PACE Code C did not apply to a person detained at a police station following arrest for breach of the peace because such a person was not arrested for an offence and therefore was not in police detention. However, whilst some powers and obligations under the PACE 1984 apply only in respect of persons in police detention (see **D1.40**), the right to consult a solicitor (see **D1.55**) and the right to notification (see **D1.52**) apply to persons 'arrested and held in custody'. Furthermore, Code C, para. 1.10, states that the code (other than the detention review provisions in s. 15) applies to people in custody at police stations 'whether or not they have been arrested', and it would be a strange result if a person arrested for breach of the peace had less protection than a person who is in custody without having been arrested.

ARREST UNDER WARRANT

Warrants Issued by Magistrates' Courts

The most important of the statutes which authorise arrest under warrant for a criminal offence is the MCA 1980. Section 1 empowers a justice to issue a warrant on the basis of a written information substantiated on oath that a person has, or is suspected of having, committed an offence. Such a warrant may or may not be endorsed for bail. If endorsed for bail, the warrant will (if relevant) specify the amounts in which any sureties are to be bound. If bail is to be granted with sureties, the police must release the offender if the sureties approved by the officer enter into recognizances in accordance with the endorsement. The person bailed is then obliged to appear before a magistrates' court at the time and place named in the recognizance (s. 117). **D1.35**

The power of a magistrates' court to issue a warrant for the arrest of any person who has attained the age of 18 years is limited by s. 1(4). The offence concerned must be indictable, or punishable with imprisonment, or the person's address must be not sufficiently established for a summons to be served on him. A warrant to arrest any person for non-appearance before a magistrates' court must not be issued unless the offence to which the warrant relates is also punishable with imprisonment or where the court, having convicted the defendant, proposes to impose a disqualification upon him. In the case of private prosecutions for certain offences, listed in s. 1(4D), a warrant must not be issued without consent of the DPP (s. 1(4A)).

Power is given under the MCA 1980, s. 13, to issue a warrant for the arrest of a person who has failed to appear to answer a summons. Power to issue a warrant for arrest in respect of a person who has been granted bail and who fails to surrender to custody or who, having surrendered to custody, then absents himself before the court is ready to deal with the case, is governed by the Bail Act 1976, s. 7.

Warrants Issued by the Crown Court

Section 80(2) of the Senior Courts Act 1981 provides that, where an indictment has been signed but the person charged has not been sent for trial, the Crown Court may issue a summons requiring that person to appear before it or may issue a warrant for his arrest. A similar power applies where a person charged with or convicted of an offence has entered into a recognizance to appear at the Crown Court and fails to do so. A warrant for arrest may be endorsed for bail, in which case the officer in charge of the police station to which the accused is taken has the same powers and duties as in the parallel case where the warrant is issued by magistrates (s. 81). **D1.36**

Procedural Requirements Governing Arrest Warrants For the procedural requirements governing arrest warrants, see the CrimPR, rr. 18.2 (terms of warrants for arrest), 18.4 (information to be included in a warrant), 18.5 (execution of a warrant) and 18.7 (warrant issued when the court office is closed). **D1.37**

Part D Procedure

Extradition Cases

D1.38 For powers of arrest in extradition cases, see **D31.4** and **D31.7**.

A person arrested under the extradition provisions may be held in custody at a police station until he is produced before the appropriate court, but is not treated as being in police detention for the purposes of the PACE 1984, s. 118(2) (see **D1.40**). His treatment whilst at a police station is governed by codes of practice issued under the Extradition Act 2003, s. 173 (see the Extradition Act 2003 (Police Powers: Codes of Practice) Order 2003 (SI 2003 No. 3336)).

Execution of Warrants

D1.39 The principal provision dealing with the execution of warrants is the MCA 1980, s. 125. This is supplemented by ss. 125A and 125B, which extend powers of execution to civilian enforcement officers and other approved persons and bodies. Section 125 provides that a warrant of arrest issued by a justice of the peace remains in force until it is executed or ceases to have effect in accordance with rules of court, and that it may be executed anywhere in England and Wales by any person to whom it is directed or by any constable acting within his police area. The effect of this, taken together with the Police Act 1996, s. 30, is to enable such a warrant to be executed by a constable anywhere in England and Wales and adjacent UK waters. Furthermore, any constable may execute the warrant in his own police area even though it is addressed to a constable in another police area. Police have a discretion as to when to execute a warrant, but the discretion must be exercised reasonably. The term 'immediately' in such a warrant refers to taking the person before the court and not to when the arrest may be made. In certain circumstances, it may be reasonable for police to investigate a criminal matter before executing a default warrant of which they are aware (*Henderson v Chief Constable of Cleveland Police* [2001] 1 WLR 1103).

A warrant to which s. 125A(1) or s. 125D applies may be executed by any person entitled to execute it even though it is not in his possession at the time (s. 125D(1) and (2)). It must be shown to the person arrested, if he demands it, as soon as practicable (s. 125D(4)). These provisions do not, however, apply to a search warrant or other warrant which must be in the constable's possession at the time (*Purdy* [1975] QB 288, and see **D1.167**).

A constable who arrests a person under warrant must inform the person of the reason for his arrest and that he is acting under warrant (PACE 1984, s. 28).

DETENTION AND TREATMENT OF SUSPECTS

Applicability of PACE and Codes of Practice

D1.40 **General**   The detention and treatments of suspects is regulated by the PACE 1984, parts IV and V, and PACE Code C. The PACE 1984 distinguishes between persons in police detention and others who may be held in custody at a police station. A person is in police detention if he has been taken to a police station after being arrested for an offence or under the TA 2000, s. 41, or has been arrested at a police station after attending voluntarily or accompanying a constable to it, and he is detained there or detained elsewhere in the charge of a constable (PACE 1984, s. 118(2)). Similarly, a person is in police detention if he is in the custody of a designated civilian detention, investigating or escort officer by virtue of the Police Reform Act 2002, sch. 4, paras. 22, 34(1) or 35(3) (PACE 1984, s. 118(2A)). A person who is at court after being charged is not in police detention (s. 118(2)); neither is a person who attends a police station to answer to live-link bail in accordance with a direction under the CDA 1998, s. 57C (PACE 1984, s. 46ZA(2)), unless an exception in s. 46ZA(3) applies (see **D2.46**).

Many of the police powers in the PACE 1984 relate only to persons in police detention. However, certain rights such as the right of intimation (under s. 56) and the right to legal advice (under s. 58), apply to persons arrested and held in custody at a police station or other premises, and apply irrespective of whether the person was arrested for an offence.

Code C applies to persons in custody at a police station whether or not they have been arrested **D1.41**
(subject to the exceptions in Code C, para. 1.12), and to persons removed to a police station as
a place of safety under the Mental Health Act 1983, ss. 135 and 136 (in respect of which, see
Home Office Circular 007/2008, *The Use of Police Stations As Places of Safety Under Section 136
of The Mental Health Act 1983*). However, sect. 15 of Code C (concerning reviews of detention)
applies only to persons in police detention. Whilst a person arrested under the TA 2000, s. 41,
and taken to a police station is in police detention, Code H rather than Code C applies unless
and until he is charged with an offence (Code H, para. 1.2, and see **D1.2**), and many aspects
of detention are governed by the TA 2000, sch. 8. For the application of Code C to a person
detained following arrest for breach of the peace, see **D1.34**.

Persons Remanded to Police Custody   Where a magistrates' court has power to remand a person **D1.42**
in custody, it may commit him to detention at a police station (MCA 1980, s. 128(7)). A person so
committed is treated as being in police detention for the purposes of the PACE 1984, s. 39 (duty of
the custody officer to ensure that detainees are treated in accordance with PACE and the Codes),
and his detention is subject to review under the PACE 1984, s. 40 (MCA 1980, s. 128(8)(c)
and (d)). The person is not to be kept in police detention unless it is necessary so to detain him for
the purpose of inquiring into other offences, and must be taken back before the magistrates' court
that committed him as soon as that need ceases (s. 128(8)(a) and (b)). A magistrates' court has a
similar power, under the CJA 1988, s. 152(1) and (1A), to commit a person brought before the
court in respect of certain drugs offences to the custody of a constable for up to 192 hours, but the
legislation is silent on the applicability of the PACE 1984. In any event Code C applies (other than
sect. 15) if, as a result, he is held in custody in a police station.

Volunteers   A person who, for the purpose of assisting with an investigation, attends voluntar- **D1.43**
ily at a police station or at any other place where a constable is present, or who accompanies a
constable to a police station or such other place without having been arrested, is entitled to leave
at will unless he is arrested. This could include victims and witnesses as well as suspects. If the
constable decides that the person is to be prevented from leaving at will, he is to inform the suspect at once that he is under arrest and (presumably only if at a police station) bring him before
the custody officer (PACE 1984, s. 29; Code C, para. 3.21). If he is not placed under arrest but
is cautioned (see **D1.83**), the officer administering the caution must immediately inform him
that he is not under arrest, and that he is free to leave if he wishes, and that he may obtain free
and independent legal advice if he wishes (Code C, para. 3.21). The officer must also inform the
person of the grounds and reasons for suspecting him of the offence(s) concerned. If the relevant location is any place or premises for which the interviewer requires the person's informed
consent to remain, reference to being free to leave means that the person may withdraw their
consent and require the officer to leave (Code C, para. 3.22).

Many of the provisions of the PACE 1984 and Code C do not apply to a volunteer even if he is at a
police station since he is neither in police detention nor held in custody. However, a volunteer is entitled to legal advice at any time, and to communicate with anyone outside a police station, and must be
treated with no less consideration than a person who is in custody (Code C, Note for Guidance 1A).

The Custody Officer

Where a person has been arrested, he must normally be taken to a police station (subject to the **D1.44**
power to release him under the PACE 1984, ss. 30(7) and 30A (s. 30(1): see **D1.20** *et seq.*).
He may be taken to any police station, unless it is anticipated that it will be necessary to detain
him for more than six hours, in which case he should be taken to a police station designated
under s. 35 (s. 30(3)–(6)). One or more custody officers must be appointed for each designated
police station (s. 36(1)). A custody officer must be of at least the rank of sergeant (s. 36(3)). If a
custody officer is not readily available, or if a person is taken to a non-designated police station,
another officer may perform the role although that officer must normally not be involved in the
investigation of an offence for which the person is in detention (s. 36(4)–(7)).

D

Part D Procedure

A person who has been arrested for an offence can only be kept in police detention in accordance with the PACE 1984, part IV (s. 34(1)). Such a person may be detained at a police station only on the authority of the custody officer (s. 37(1)), and may not be released except on his authority (s. 34(2) and (3)). Generally, it is the responsibility of the custody officer to ensure that a person in police detention is treated in accordance with the PACE 1984 and the Codes of Practice, although responsibility is temporarily transferred to any officer to whom custody of the person is transferred in accordance with the Codes of Practice (s. 39(1)–(3)).

Custody Records

D1.45   A custody record must be opened as soon as is practicable in respect of each person who is brought to a police station under arrest, or who is arrested at a police station after having attended voluntarily, or who attends a police station in accordance with bail granted under the PACE 1984, s. 30A (Code C, para. 2.1: see **D1.20**). In the past, custody officers have not opened a custody record if, on an arrested person being produced before them, they have determined that there is sufficient evidence to charge. It is doubtful whether this practice is compliant with Code C and, especially since many charge decisions are made by Crown Prosecutors and this often entails some delay, this practice should be reviewed (see further **D2.7**). A custody record does not have to be opened in respect of a volunteer who is not arrested. The custody officer is responsible for recording in the custody record all matters that are required by the PACE 1984 or the Codes of Practice to be recorded (s. 39(1)(b) and Code C, para. 2.3). If the detained person is transferred to another police station, the custody record or a copy of it must accompany him, and must show the time of and reason for the transfer (Code C, para. 2.3). It is not clear whether a new custody record should be opened where a person is further detained on surrendering to custody following a release on police bail or whether the original custody record should be continued. However, time in police detention before the release on bail will normally count for the purpose of calculating the maximum periods of detention (see **D1.67**).

D1.46   Both the PACE 1984 and the Codes of Practice provide for the many matters that must be recorded in the custody record. The former requirement to record everything that a person has with him when he is detained is now at the discretion of the custody officer (PACE 1984, s. 54, as amended by the CJA 2003, s. 8). If a record is made, it does not have to be in the custody record (s. 54(2A)), although Home Office Circular 60/2003, para. 5.5, states that the detained person should be asked to check any record that is made, and sign it as correct. For details of what must be recorded when a health care professional is called in to examine a detained person, see Code C, paras. 9.15 and 9.16.

A solicitor or appropriate adult must be permitted to inspect the custody record of a detained person as soon as practicable after his arrival at a police station, and at any time during the period of detention (Code C, para. 2.4). A detained person, his lawyer or his appropriate adult must be permitted, on giving reasonable notice, to inspect the custody record after the person has left police detention (Code C, para. 2.5), and is entitled to receive a copy of the custody record for up to 12 months after release (Code C, para 2.4A).

The Decision to Detain

D1.47   **The Initial Decision**   Where a person is arrested for an offence, whether without a warrant or under a warrant not endorsed for bail, the custody officer at the station where he is detained must determine whether he has sufficient evidence to charge the suspect with the offence for which he is arrested (PACE 1984, s. 37(1)). In making his determination the custody officer is not required to inquire into the lawfulness of the arrest (*DPP v L* [1999] Crim LR 752; *Al Fayed v Metropolitan Police Commissioner* [2004] EWCA Civ 1579). The test for determining whether there is sufficient evidence to charge is not statutorily defined. The DPP has issued statutory guidance for the purposes of s. 37(7) (see **D2.1**), but this is not binding in respect of a decision under s. 37(1) (*R (G) v Chief Constable of West Yorkshire Police* [2008] 1 WLR 550). It seems likely that the test is sufficient evidence to give a realistic prospect of conviction (see Code C, para. 16.1). However, the *Director's Guidance on Charging* creates an anomaly since, where a person had been detained following a determination that there is not sufficient evidence to charge under s. 37(1), it provides that in some circumstances the test for determining whether there is sufficient evidence to charge for the purposes of s. 37(7) is the lower threshold test (see **D2.3**).

The custody officer must make his determination as soon as is practicable after the arrested person arrives at the station or, if the arrest occurs there, as soon as possible after the arrest (s. 37(10)). He may detain the person at the police station for so long as is necessary to enable him to discharge this function (s. 37(1)). If the custody officer determines that he does not have sufficient evidence to charge, the arrested person is to be dealt with in accordance with the PACE 1984, s. 37(2) (see **D1.49**). If the custody officer determines that he does have sufficient evidence to charge, the arrested person must be dealt with in accordance with s. 37(7) (see *R (G) v Chief Constable of West Yorkshire Police* and **D2.2** and **D2.6**).

D1.48 A person who attends a police station to answer to bail granted under s. 30A, or returns to a police station to answer to bail otherwise granted by police under the PACE 1984, part IV, or is arrested under s. 30D (having failed to answer to bail granted under s. 30A) or s. 46A (having failed to answer to bail otherwise granted under part IV), is to be treated as arrested for the offence for which he was granted bail (s. 34(7)). A person arrested under the RTA 1988, s. 6D, or the Transport and Works Act 1992, s. 30(2) (arrest under the breath-test procedure), is also to be treated as having been arrested for an offence (PACE 1984, s. 34(6)).

A custody officer who becomes aware at any time that the grounds for detaining a suspect in police custody have ceased to apply and who is not aware of any other grounds which would justify his continued detention must release him immediately (s. 34(2)), such release normally being without bail (s. 34(5)). He is not, however, to release a suspect who appears to him to have been unlawfully at large when arrested (s. 34(4)). Further, if the offence for which the person was arrested is one in respect of which a sample for the purpose of drug-testing may be taken (see **D1.120**), release may be delayed for up to 24 hours from the relevant time (see **D1.68**) for the purpose of enabling a sample to be taken (s. 37(8A) and (8B)).

D1.49 **Insufficient Evidence to Charge**　If the custody officer determines that he does not have sufficient evidence to charge an arrested person, he must release him with or without bail unless he has reasonable grounds for believing that detention of the suspect without charge is necessary to secure or preserve evidence relating to an offence for which he is under arrest or to obtain evidence by questioning him (PACE 1984, s. 37(2)). If the custody officer does have such a belief, he may authorise the person to be kept in police detention (s. 37(3)), and must make a written record of the grounds for detention as soon as is practicable (s. 37(4); Code C, para. 3.4), normally in the presence of the person (s. 37(5) and (6)).

The requirement that the officer believes that detention is necessary creates, in principle, a stringent test. That was certainly the view of the then Secretary of State when he explained the provision to Parliament during passage of the original Bill, indicating that it meant more than simply desirable or convenient. It was held in *Al Fayed v Metropolitan Police Commissioner* [2004] EWCA Civ 1579, that whilst the question of reasonable belief that detention is necessary involves an objective element, it is to be determined by reference to whether the custody officer acted reasonably in deciding that detention was necessary. However, it is submitted that if, viewed objectively, detention was not necessary, the officer could not have acted reasonably in so believing.

D1.50 **The Procedural Requirements**　Where the custody officer authorises detention, the procedural requirements are largely governed by PACE Code C. The officer must inform the detained person of his right to legal advice (**D1.55**) and his right to have someone informed of his arrest (**D1.52**), and ask the person whether he wishes to exercise those rights (Code C, paras. 3.1

Part D Procedure

and 3.5). The officer must also inform the person of his right to consult the Codes of Practice, his right to interpretation and translation (if applicable), and his right to be informed about the offence (para. 3.1). In addition the custody officer must give the person a written notice containing the information set out in para. 3.2. A risk assessment must be carried out, and any necessary steps taken (paras. 3.6 to 3.10). The revision to Code C in June 2014 (see **D1.1**) introduced a new obligation on the police to make available to the suspect or his solicitor documents and materials which are essential to effectively challenging the lawfulness of the person's arrest and detention (para. 3.4(b) and Note for Guidance 3ZA).

If the detained person is a juvenile (which, for these purposes, includes those under 18 years: see Code C, paras. 1.5 and 1.5A), the custody officer, or other custody staff under his direction, must ascertain the person responsible for his welfare and inform that person of the arrest and detention (Code C, para. 3.13, and see **D1.63**). If the juvenile is known to be the subject of a court order under which a person or organisation is responsible for supervising or monitoring him, the custody officer must also inform that person or organisation (para. 3.14). Where the detained person is a juvenile or mentally disordered or otherwise mentally vulnerable, the officer must inform the appropriate adult and ask that adult to come to the police station (para. 3.15). If the detained person is deaf or there is doubt about his hearing or speaking ability, or doubt about his ability to speak or understand English, and the custody officer cannot establish effective communication, the custody officer must call in an interpreter (para. 3.12: see **D1.91**). If the person is blind or seriously visually handicapped or is unable to read, the custody officer should ensure that his solicitor, relative, the appropriate adult or some other person likely to take an interest in him is available to help him in checking any documentation. Where Code C requires written consent or signification then the person who is assisting may be asked to sign instead if the detained person so wishes (para. 3.20). In each case, a person who appears to come within the category of persons requiring special treatment must be treated as such.

D1.51   A detained person who is a foreign national must be informed of his right to communicate with his High Commission, embassy or consulate (Code C, para. 3.3 and sect. 7). If the person is a citizen of a foreign country with which a bilateral consular convention or agreement is in force, the appropriate High Commission, embassy or consulate must be informed, unless the person is a refugee or is seeking political asylum, in which case the United Kingdom Borders Agency must be informed, and the Agency will determine whether notification is to be given (paras. 7.2 and 7.4). These obligations and rights apply in addition to the right to notification of arrest under the PACE 1984, s. 56. There is no provision for delay even where delay in notification of arrest (see **D1.53**) or delay in access to legal advice (see **D1.61**) is authorised.

Notification of Arrest

D1.52   **The Right to Notification**   A person who has been arrested (whether or not for an offence) and who is being held in custody at a police station or other premises has a right, at his request, to have one friend, or relative or other person who is known to him or who is likely to take an interest in his welfare, told of his arrest and the place where he is being detained. This is to be done as soon as is practicable (PACE 1984, s. 56(1)). The custody officer must inform the suspect of this right (Code C, para. 3.1(i)), and ask him whether he wishes to exercise it (para. 3.5(a)(iii)).

The person chosen by the detainee is to be informed of the detainee's whereabouts at public expense and, if the detainee requests, on each occasion that he is taken to another police station (s. 56(8) and Code C, para. 5.3). If that person cannot be contacted, the detainee may choose up to two alternatives. If they too cannot be contacted, the custody officer or the person in charge of the investigation has discretion to allow further attempts until the information has been conveyed (para. 5.1). If the detainee does not know of anyone to contact for advice, the custody officer should bear in mind local voluntary bodies who may be able to help (Code C, Note for Guidance 5C).

D1.53   **Delaying Notification**   Where a person is detained for an indictable offence (i.e. indictable-only or either-way), an officer of the rank of inspector or above may authorise delay in giving notification of the detention for up to 36 hours from the relevant time (PACE 1984, s. 56(2) and (3)). For the meaning of 'relevant time', see **D1.68**. Authorisation may be given either orally or in writing, but if done orally the authorisation is to be confirmed in writing as soon as practicable (s. 56(4)). The officer may authorise delay only if he has reasonable grounds for believing that any of the conditions in s. 56(5) or (5A) is satisfied. These are the same conditions that apply to a decision to delay access to a lawyer under s. 58 (see **D1.61**). If delay is authorised, the detained person must be told the reason for it, and that reason must be noted on his custody record (s. 56(6)).

Other Similar Rights   A detainee may receive visits at the custody officer's discretion (Code **D1.54** C, para. 5.4), and Code C Note for Guidance 5B indicates that visits should be allowed where possible.

A detainee is entitled to writing materials and to speak on the telephone for a reasonable time to one person, although this may be delayed or denied if the person is detained in respect of an indictable offence and an officer of the rank of inspector or above considers that sending a letter or making a telephone call may result in any of the consequences set out in Code C, annex B, paras. 1 and 2 (Code C, para. 5.6). Any delay or denial of the above rights should be proportionate and should last for no longer than is necessary (para. 5.7A). The detainee must be told that what he says in any communication, other than one to his solicitor, may be read or listened to and may be given in evidence (para. 5.7).

If a friend or relative of a detainee, or a person with an interest in a detainee's welfare, asks where the detainee is then this information must be given provided that the detainee agrees and delay in notification under the PACE 1984, s. 56, has not been authorised (Code C, para. 5.5 and annex B).

Right of Access to Solicitor

The Right to Consult a Solicitor   A person who is arrested (whether or not for an offence) **D1.55** and held in custody at a police station or other premises has a right, at his request, to consult a solicitor privately at any time (PACE 1984, s. 58; Code C, para. 6.1). 'Held in custody' has been given a more restricted meaning than simply 'in custody', and describes the situation where a custody officer has made a decision that the person should be detained (*Kerawalla* [1991] Crim LR 451). However, in *Ambrose v Harris* [2011] 1 WLR 2435 the Supreme Court held that the ECHR, Article 6(1) and (3)(c), require that a person who suffers a significant curtailment of his freedom of action is entitled to legal assistance. Thus the right to legal assistance may apply prior to the decision to detain a person at a police station, and even before he has been formally arrested. The right applies to all persons held in custody including those who are juveniles, or mentally disordered or vulnerable. An appropriate adult has an independent right to legal advice even if the juvenile or vulnerable adult does not want one, although a juvenile cannot be forced to see a solicitor if he does not wish to do so (Code C, paras. 3.19 and 6.5A). While the statutory right does not apply in respect of a prisoner on remand in custody at a magistrates' court, there is a common-law right to consult a solicitor as soon as is reasonably practicable and police cannot refuse access to a prisoner in custody simply because the request falls outside customary hours (*Chief Constable of South Wales, ex parte Merrick* [1994] 2 All ER 560).

A person must be told of his right to free legal advice when he is brought to a police station under arrest, or when he is arrested having initially attended voluntarily (Code C, paras. 3.1 and 6.1); immediately before the beginning or recommencement of any interview at a police station or other authorised place of detention (para. 11.2); before a review of detention is conducted or before a decision is made whether to extend the period of detention (para. 15.4); after charge or being informed that he may be prosecuted, where a police officer wishes to bring to his attention any statement or the content of any interview, or where he is re-interviewed (paras. 16.4 and 16.5); before being asked to provide an intimate sample (Code D, para. 6.3); before an intimate drug search is conducted under the PACE 1984, s. 55(1)(b) (Code C, annex A, para. 2B), or an

D

Part D Procedure

x-ray or ultrasound scan is taken under s. 55A(1) (Code C, annex K, para. 3); before he is (exceptionally) interviewed after charge (Code C, para. 16.5); and before an identification parade or group or video identification is conducted (Code D, para. 3.17). Where appropriate, information should be provided regarding the availability of the duty solicitor (*Vernon* [1988] Crim LR 445, distinguished in *Beeres v CPS* [2014] EWHC 283 (Admin)). (See also **D1.43** as to the position of volunteers attending police stations.)

D1.56 If, on being informed or reminded of the right to legal advice, the person declines to speak to a solicitor, the officer must tell him that the right to legal advice includes the right to speak to a solicitor on the telephone, and ask him whether he wishes to do so. If the person still declines legal advice, the officer must ask him why, and record any answer. Once it is clear that the person does not wish to speak to a solicitor at all, the officer must cease to ask him for reasons for his decision (Code C, para. 6.5). No attempt should be made to dissuade a suspect from obtaining legal advice (para. 6.4). It was held in *McGowan v B* [2011] 1 WLR 3121 that for waiver of the right to legal assistance to be valid it is normally sufficient that the person is told of the right, that he understands what the right is, and that the waiver is made freely and voluntarily. The prosecution are not required to establish that a suspect understood all of the implications of his decision (*Saunders* [2012] 2 Cr App R 321). However, suspects 'who are of low intelligence or are vulnerable for other reasons or who are under the influence of drugs or alcohol may need to be given more than the standard formulae if their right to fair trial is not to be compromised' (*McGowan v B* at [47]). See also *Jude v HM Advocate* [2011] UKSC 55. Wrongful denial of access to a solicitor may lead to the exclusion of evidence (see **F2.28** and **F17.34**). A suspect cannot be refused access to a solicitor simply because the police fear that the solicitor will advise the suspect not to answer questions (Code C, annex B, para. 4; *Alladice* (1988) 87 Cr App R 380).

The word 'solicitor' is not defined in the PACE 1984, but Code C defines it for the purposes of the Code to include a solicitor holding a practising certificate, or an accredited or probationary representative included on the register maintained by the Legal Services Commission (Code C, para. 6.12, and see Code D, para. 2.6, Code E, para. 1.5, and Code F, para. 1.5; Code C, para. 6.12 refers to the Legal Services Commission, although this was replaced by the Legal Aid Agency by virtue of the LASPO 2012, s. 38). By implication, 'solicitor' does not include a representative (who is neither accredited nor probationary) of a solicitor acting privately, although arguably a solicitor acting privately can send such a representative to advise at the police station if the client consents.

D1.57 By Code C, para. 6.12A, an accredited or probationary representative may be denied access to a police station if an officer of the rank of inspector or above considers that to grant access will hinder the investigation. Hindering of the investigation does not include giving proper legal advice. Code C, para. 6.13, provides that the officer should take into account whether the credentials of an accredited or probationary representative have been satisfactorily established, whether the person is of suitable character to give advice, and any other matters in any written letter or authorisation provided by the solicitor concerned. A person with a criminal record, save for a minor offence, is unlikely to be suitable. Responsibility for assessing these matters rests with the investigating officer, who may have regard to but is not fettered by general statements of force policy. The primary question is whether allowing a particular individual access to advise the detainee may prejudice the investigation (*R (Thompson) v Chief Constable of the Northumberland Constabulary* [2001] 4 All ER 354). As the Divisional Court said in *Chief Constable of Avon and Somerset, ex parte Robinson* [1989] 2 All ER 15, where a person is ostensibly capable of giving advice, he cannot be excluded simply because the police believe that he will give poor advice.

There is no similar provision for a solicitor (as opposed to a representative) to be excluded from a police station. However, a solicitor (including a representative) may be required to leave an interview if an officer of the rank of superintendent or above considers that by his misconduct the solicitor has prevented the proper putting of questions to his client (Code C, paras. 6.9 to 6.11). A solicitor is not guilty of misconduct if he seeks to challenge an improper question or the manner in which it is put or if he advises his client not to reply to particular questions or if he wishes to give his client further legal advice. Code C, Note for Guidance 6D, suggests that misconduct could include answering questions on the client's behalf or providing written replies for the client to quote. However, this would not include the situation where a solicitor drafts a statement to be handed, or read out, to the police in interview (see, e.g., *Knight* [2004] 1 WLR 340).

Section 58(1) of the PACE 1984 grants a right to consult 'privately' with a solicitor. Code C, **D1.58** Note for Guidance 6J, describes this as 'fundamental', and states that facilities to enable private consultation with a solicitor, whether in person or on the telephone, should normally be provided. The consultation should be both unsupervised and unobserved by police officers (*R (L)* [2011] 3 All ER 969). The House of Lords determined that the power to conduct surveillance under the RIPA 2000, part II, overrides s. 58(1) (*McE v Prison Service of Northern Ireland* [2009] 1 AC 908), but that authorisation under the provisions governing directed surveillance (as opposed to intrusive surveillance) is not proportionate, and infringes the ECHR, Article 8(2). The Regulation of Investigatory Powers (Extension of Authorisation Provisions: Legal Consultation) Order 2010 (SI 2010 No. 461) provides that directed surveillance to be carried out on premises used for the purpose of legal consultations (which include police stations) must be treated as intrusive surveillance. The Regulation of Investigatory Powers (Covert Human Intelligence Sources: Matters Subject to Legal Privilege) Order 2010 (SI 2010 No. 123) makes similar provision regarding the authorisation of the use of covert human intelligence sources whose activities involve obtaining access to matters subject to legal privilege. For further limitations on the right to consult in terrorist investigations, see **B10.18**.

Action When a Request is Made Where a person makes a request to consult a solicitor he must, **D1.59** subject to the power to delay (see **D1.61**), be permitted to consult a solicitor as soon as practicable and the custody officer must act without delay to secure the provision of advice (PACE 1984, s. 58(4), and Code C, para. 6.5). It was held in *Gearing v DPP* [2009] RTR 72 that a delay of 22 minutes between the request for legal advice and action by the police to contact a solicitor amounted to a breach of s. 58(4). Code C, Note for Guidance 6B, sets out the arrangements for obtaining legal advice. The arrangements for obtaining legal advice, as set out in Code C, Note for Guidance 6B, give rise to considerable practical difficulties. In particular, given the lack of private telephone facilities in many police stations, securing advice under the CDS Direct scheme may lead to a breach of the right to consult a solicitor privately (see **D1.58**) A solicitor may advise more than one client in an investigation, and any question of a conflict of interest is for the solicitor to determine in accordance with their professional code of conduct (Code C, Note for Guidance 6G, and see *R (McDonagh) v Chief Constable of Leicestershire Constabulary* [2013] EWHC 4690 (Admin)).

Although s.58 does not expressly give a right to have a solicitor present in a police interview, **D1.60** s. 58(1) states that the person has a right to consult a solicitor 'at any time', and Code C, para. 6.8, provides that a detainee who has been permitted to consult a solicitor must, on request, be allowed to have him present while he is interviewed unless the exceptions in para. 6.6 apply.

Subject to the power to delay access to a solicitor under s. 58(8)–(11), once a person has asked to consult a solicitor he must not be interviewed or continue to be interviewed until he has been able to have that consultation unless any of the conditions in Code C, para. 6.6 (b)–(d), is satisfied. Note that if an interview is conducted in the absence of legal advice under para. 6.6(b) (but not para. 6.6(c) or (d)), inferences under the CJPO 1994, ss. 34, 36 or 37 (see **F19**), cannot be drawn and the modified caution under Code C, annex C, para. 2, must be given. Notwithstanding these provisions, in the absence of compelling reasons, interviewing a person who has requested legal advice before he has received it, or the use of evidence so obtained, is likely to amount to a breach of the right to fair trial under the ECHR, Article 6 (*Cadder v HM Advocate* [2010] 1 WLR 2601). The statutory drink/driving procedure under the RTA 1988 (or the Transport and Works Act 1992, s. 31) is not an interview and is therefore not subject to delay pending legal advice (Code C, para. 11.1A). Thus failure to permit access to a solicitor before the procedure is carried out does not afford the suspect with a reasonable excuse for failure to provide a specimen (*DPP v Billington* [1988] 1 All ER 435; and see also *Kennedy v CPS* (2003) 167 JP 267; *Cowper v DPP* [2009] EWHC 2165 (Admin); and *Chalupa v CPS* (2010) 174 JP 111).

D1.61   **Delaying Access to a Solicitor**   Delaying access to a solicitor is permitted only where the person is detained in respect of an indictable offence (i.e. indictable-only or either-way), he has not been charged, and delay is authorised by an officer of the rank of superintendent or above (PACE 1984, s. 58(6), and Code C, annex B). The officer may authorise delay only if there are reasonable grounds for believing that exercising the right:

(a) will lead to interference with or harm to evidence connected with an indictable offence or interference with or physical injury to other people (s. 58(8)(a));

(b) will lead to the alerting of other people suspected of having committed such an offence but not yet arrested for it (s. 58(8)(b));

(c) will hinder the recovery of any property obtained as a result of such an offence (s. 58(8)(c)); or

(d) where the person detained for the indictable offence has benefited from his criminal conduct (within the meaning of the POCA 2002, part 2), it will hinder the recovery of the value of the property constituting the benefit (s. 58A).

Where these conditions are satisfied, access to a solicitor may be delayed only for as long as the grounds exist, and in any case no longer than 36 hours from the relevant time (s. 58(5); Code C, annex B, para. 6). For the meaning of 'relevant time' see **D1.68**. If the police seek a warrant of further detention (see **D1.72**), the suspect must be allowed access to a solicitor in reasonable time before the hearing even if this is within the 36-hour period (Code C, annex B, para. 7).

D1.62   These provisions create a stringent test for delaying access to a solicitor and, given that the authorising officer must have 'reasonable grounds' for his 'belief' that access 'will' lead to one or more of the consequences, there should be some objective basis for that belief. In *Samuel* [1988] QB 615, the Court of Appeal held that (a) the police officer must believe that one of the statutory grounds for exclusion applies, and (b) that belief must be reasonable. He must believe that the consequence will very probably happen. It will rarely happen that a police officer will be entitled to believe that a solicitor will knowingly pass on information in breach of the statute, and any grounds put forward would have to be specific to the solicitor concerned. Solicitors are also unlikely to be unwitting dupes, and suspicion that the suspect will try to use the solicitor thus must be specific to him, e.g., where he is known or suspected to be a member of a criminal gang. This is reinforced by Code C, annex B, Note for Guidance B3. See also *Alladice* (1988) 87 Cr App R 380; *Davison* [1988] Crim LR 442 and *James* [2008] EWCA Crim 1869.

If a decision is made to delay access to a particular solicitor the suspect must be allowed to choose another solicitor (Code C, annex B, para. 3). If delay is authorised, the detained person must be told the reason for it, and the reason must be noted on his custody record (annex B, para. 13). Once the grounds for delay cease to exist the suspect must be asked, as soon as is practicable, whether he wants to exercise the right to a solicitor and the custody record must be noted accordingly (annex B, para. 6).

In the absence of compelling reasons, delaying access to a solicitor under these provisions is likely to amount to a breach of the right to fair trial under the ECHR, Article 6 (*Cadder v HM Advocate* [2010] 1 WLR 2601). Note that inferences under the CJPO 1994, ss. 34, 36 or 37 (see **F19**), are not permitted where the person was at an authorised place of detention and he had not been allowed an opportunity to consult a solicitor prior to being questioned (CJPO 1994, ss. 34(2A), 36(4A) and 37(3A), and see **D1.85**).

Juveniles and Mentally Disordered or Vulnerable Persons

For the initial action to be taken in respect of persons who have special needs, see **D1.50**. In the case **D1.63** of young people, anyone who appears to be under the age of 17 years must be treated as a juvenile for the purposes of the PACE 1984 and the Codes in the absence of clear evidence to the contrary (PACE 1984, s. 37(15); Code C, para. 1.5). Code C was amended in October 2013 to take account of the judgment in *R (HC) v Secretary of State for the Home Department* [2014] 1 WLR 1234. Code C, para. 1.5A, provides that, if anyone appears to have attained the age of 17, but appears to be under 18, that person must be treated as a 17-year-old for the purposes of Code C and the other PACE Codes. However, the definition of 'juvenile' in the PACE 1984, s. 37(15), has not been amended so that powers governed by the PACE 1984 rather than the Codes (for example, detention after charge under s. 38 (see **D2.52**), and appropriate consent for the purposes of taking biometric samples (s. 61, and see **D1.66**)) still apply to 17-year-olds as if they were adults. The Children Act 2004, s. 11, requires the police to take into account the need to safeguard and promote the welfare of children in discharging their functions, but does not impose additional obligations (*R (C) v Commissioner of Police of the Metropolis* [2012] 1 All ER 953). With regard to mental disorder or vulnerability, if a police officer has any suspicion, or is told in good faith, that a person of any age may be mentally disordered or otherwise mentally vulnerable, in the absence of clear evidence to dispel that suspicion, the person must be treated as such for the purposes of the Codes of Practice (Code C, para. 1.4). 'Mental disorder' is defined by the Mental Health Act 1983, s. 1(2), as 'any disorder or disability of the mind'. The term 'mentally vulnerable' applies to any person who, because of his mental state or capacity, may not understand the significance of what is said, of questions or of his replies. Where the custody officer has any doubt about the mental state or capacity of a detainee, the detainee must be treated as mentally vulnerable, and an appropriate adult called (Code C, Note for Guidance 1G). It is imperative that a mentally disordered or otherwise mentally vulnerable person detained under the Mental Health Act 1983, s. 136, be assessed as soon as possible (Code C, para. 3.16).

Appropriate Adult   'Appropriate adult', in the case of a juvenile suspect, is defined as a parent **D1.64** or guardian or, if the juvenile is in care or being looked after under the Children Act 1989, a representative of the care authority or a voluntary organisation, or a social worker, or (failing these) another responsible adult aged 18 years or older who is not a police officer or police employee (Code C, para. 1.7(a)). An estranged parent whom an arrested juvenile does not wish to attend and to whom the juvenile specifically objects should not act as an appropriate adult (Code C, Note for Guidance 1B; *DPP v Blake* [1989] 1 WLR 432). Similarly, an illiterate parent with a low IQ who cannot appreciate the gravity of the situation in which his child is placed should not act as an appropriate adult (*Morse* [1991] Crim LR 195). Where the juvenile is in care, the relevant social worker or his representative should be prepared to attend as soon as practicable (*DPP v Blake*).

'Appropriate adult' in the case of a person who is mentally disordered or vulnerable is defined as a relative, guardian or other person responsible for care or custody of the person, someone who has experience of dealing with such persons (but who is not a police officer or police employee) or, failing these, some other responsible adult aged 18 years or older who is not a police officer or police employee (Code C, para. 1.7(b)). Code C, Note for Guidance 1D, states that it may be more satisfactory for the appropriate adult to be someone who is experienced or trained in the care of mentally disordered or vulnerable people, although the suspect's wishes should be respected where practicable.

A solicitor attending a police station on a suspect's behalf should not act as an appropriate adult **D1.65** (Code C, Note for Guidance 1F; *Lewis* [1996] Crim LR 260). A person should not be the appropriate adult if he (a) is suspected of involvement in the suspected offence, (b) is the victim or a witness, (c) is involved in the investigation, or (d) has received admissions from the suspect before acting as the appropriate adult (Code C, Note for Guidance 1B). A social worker or a member of a youth offending team should also refrain from acting as an appropriate adult if the suspect has made admissions to him (Code C, Note for Guidance 1C).

Role of the Appropriate Adult   The Codes of Practice do not specify the general role of appro- **D1.66** priate adults, although Home Office Guidance for Appropriate Adults states that their role is

(a) to ensure that the detained person understands what is happening to him and why; (b) to support, advise and assist him; (c) to observe whether the police are acting properly and fairly and to intervene if they are not; (d) to assist with communication between the detained person and the police; and (e) to ensure that the detained person understands his rights and the appropriate adult's role in protecting those rights. Code C, para. 11.17, describes a similar role for appropriate adults during police interviews. The detainee should be advised of the duties of the appropriate adult and that he can consult with the adult privately at any time (Code C, para. 3.18). If the appropriate adult or the detainee asks for legal advice, the provisions of Code C, sect. 6, apply (para. 3.19, and see **D1.55**). The presence of an appropriate adult during a consultation between a suspect and his lawyer which would otherwise attract legal advice privilege does not destroy that privilege (*A Local Authority v B* [2009] 1 FLR 289).

Generally, a juvenile or mentally disordered or vulnerable person must not be interviewed by the police or asked to provide a written statement in the absence of an appropriate adult, unless delay would be likely to lead to interference with or harm to evidence connected with an offence, interference with or physical harm to other people or serious loss of or damage to property, to alerting other suspects not yet arrested, or to hindering the recovery of property obtained in consequence of commission of the offence. If an interview at a police station is necessary for one or more of these reasons, it must be authorised by an officer of the rank of superintendent or above (Code C, paras 11.1, 11.15 and 11.18 to 11.20). Further, the appropriate adult has specific roles in respect of legal advice (para. 3.9) and intimate and strip searches (Code C, annex A, paras 5 and 11(c)). In the case of identification and other evidential procedures that require 'appropriate consent', the PACE 1984, s. 65(1), provides that, in the case of a person who has attained the age of 14 years but is under 17 years (see **D1.63**), consent is required from the juvenile and his parent or guardian, but that, in the case of a person under 14 years, only the consent of the parent or guardian is required. Note that if the appropriate adult is not a parent or guardian, he cannot give consent.

Detention Time-limits

D1.67   The normal maximum period of detention without charge is 24 hours from the relevant time (PACE 1984, s. 41(1)). For the meaning of 'relevant time' see **D1.68**. Subject to the powers to extend detention without charge, if at the expiry of that time the person has not been charged, he must be released, either on bail or without bail (s. 41(7)). The period of detention without charge may be extended in respect of a person under arrest for an indictable offence; for up to a total of 36 hours from the relevant time by an officer of the rank of superintendent or above (see **D1.69**); and for up to a total of 96 hours from the relevant time by a magistrates' court (see **D1.72**). Where a detention time-limit has expired and the person is released without charge, he may not be rearrested without warrant for the offence for which he was previously arrested (subject to the power to arrest for failure to answer to police bail under s. 46A) unless new evidence justifying a further arrest has come to light since the original arrest (ss. 41(9), 42(11) and 43(19)). It is unclear precisely what 'new evidence justifying a further arrest' means, but it is submitted that it means evidence that was not available to the police at the time of the original arrest and detention. If a person is released at the expiry of a detention time-limit, and subsequent analysis of fingerprints or samples taken during their detention implicates him, does this amount to 'new evidence'? Arguably it does, but if that is correct it has the effect of potentially extending the maximum period of detention whenever a person is released pending forensic analysis or further investigation.

For the purpose of calculating maximum periods of detention, time normally runs continuously from the relevant time. However, where a detainee is removed to hospital for medical treatment, time spent at the hospital or travelling to or from hospital does not count, except for any time spent questioning the person for the purpose of obtaining evidence in respect of an offence (s. 41(6)). Note that a person in police detention at a hospital must not be questioned without the agreement of a responsible doctor (Code C, para. 14.2). If a person is questioned in these circumstances, he is entitled to consult a solicitor (see **D1.55**).

The Relevant Time Normally, the relevant time is the time an arrested person arrives at the first D1.68
police station that he is taken to, or 24 hours after arrest, whichever is the earlier (PACE 1984,
s. 41(2)(a)). However, this basic definition is modified in the circumstances set out in s. 41(2)(b)
to (6). Where a person released on police bail under the PACE 1984, part IV, is detained when
he attends at the police station to surrender to custody, or is arrested under s. 46A for failure to
surrender to custody, the relevant time is that which applies to the original detention; however,
any time during which the person was on bail is not included (PACE 1984, s. 47(6)).

If a person is arrested other than under s. 46A, e.g., because there is new evidence justifying a further arrest (see **D1.67**), the relevant time will be that relating to the subsequent arrest (s. 47(7)).

Note that the relevant time is not necessarily the same time as that for determining the timing
of reviews of detention, which may be some time later (see **D1.76**).

Detention for More than 24 Hours, up to 36 Hours

A person can be detained without charge beyond 24 hours only if three conditions are met D1.69
(PACE 1984, s. 42(1)). These are:

(a) that a police officer of the rank of superintendent or above who is responsible for the police
station at which the person is detained has reasonable grounds for believing that such detention is necessary to secure or preserve evidence relating to an offence for which the person is
under arrest or to obtain such evidence by questioning him;
(b) that the offence for which he is under arrest is an indictable offence;
(c) that the investigation is being conducted diligently and expeditiously.

As to (a), the requirement for reasonable grounds for belief that detention is necessary is the same as
under the PACE 1984, s. 37(2) (see **D1.49**). As to (b), an indictable offence is one that is triable only
on indictment or is triable either-way. Low-value shoplifting (as defined by the MCA 1980, s. 22A(3):
see **D6.29**) is an indictable offence for the purposes of the PACE 1984 (ABCPA 2014, s. 176(6)).

Documents and materials essential to challenging the lawfulness of a detainee's arrest and detention must be made available to him or his solicitor (Code C, paras. 3.4(b) and 15.0).

If the above conditions are met, the officer may authorise detention for up to 36 hours from the
relevant time (see **D1.68**). If he authorises detention for less than 36 hours, he may authorise
further detention up to the maximum 36 hours provided that the above conditions still apply
(PACE 1984, s. 42(2)). No authorisation under s. 42(1) may be made more than 24 hours after
the relevant time. Thus retrospective authorisation is not permitted. Further, by s. 42(4), the
decision to authorise detention beyond 24 hours cannot be made before the second review of
detention under s. 40 (see **D1.76**). Unlike reviews under s. 40, an extension of detention under
these provisions must be dealt with by the officer in person rather than by telephone or video
link (Code C, Note for Guidance 15F).

If it is proposed to transfer a person to police detention in another police area, in determining D1.70
whether to authorise detention without charge beyond 24 hours, the officer must have regard
to the distance and the time the journey would take (s. 42(3)). Presumably, if the time involved
is likely to take detention beyond the 36 hours permitted, the review officer will have either to
refuse the transfer or a warrant of further detention will have to be sought (see **D1.72**).

A person whose extended detention has been ordered under the foregoing procedure must be
released from detention either with or without bail at the expiration of 36 hours unless either
he has been charged with an offence or a warrant of further detention has been granted by a
magistrates' court (s. 42(10)). A person who has been released may not be rearrested for the same
offence unless new evidence justifying such a course has come to light (s. 42(11) and see **D1.67**).

Before deciding whether to authorise detention under s. 42(1) or (2), the officer must give the D1.71
detained person, or his solicitor if he is available at the time that the decision is to be made (and

appropriate adult, if relevant (Code C, para. 15.3)), an opportunity to make representations about the decision (s. 42(6)). If the detainee is likely to be asleep at the time the decision is made it should, if the legal obligations and time constraints permit, be brought forward, but if the detainee is asleep he need not be woken (Code C, Note for Guidance 15C). Representations may be given orally or in writing (s. 42(7)). It has been held that the requirement under s. 42(6) is mandatory, so that a purported authorisation without providing such an opportunity was invalid (*In the matter of an application for a warrant of further detention* [1988] Crim LR 296, although this is a magistrates' court decision). The officer may decline to hear oral representations from the suspect himself if he considers that the detainee's condition or behaviour is such as to render him unfit to do so (s. 42(8)).

If an officer authorises detention beyond 24 hours, and the detainee has not at that time availed himself of the right to have someone informed of his arrest or the right to consult a solicitor, the officer must (a) inform the detainee of his rights, (b) decide whether the detainee should be permitted to exercise them, (c) record his decision in the custody record, and (d) if he decides to refuse to allow the detainee to exercise either of the rights, must also record the grounds for the decision in the detainee's custody record (s. 42(9)).

Detention for More than 36 Hours

D1.72 **Warrant of Further Detention**   Detention without charge beyond 36 hours from the relevant time (see **D1.68**) is permitted only where a magistrates' court issues a warrant of further detention (PACE 1984, s. 43(1)). A magistrates' court is defined for this purpose as a court consisting of two or more justices sitting otherwise than in open court (PACE 1984, s. 45(1)).

The application must be made on oath by a constable and supported by an information (s. 43(1) and (14)). In order to issue a warrant the court must be satisfied that there are reasonable grounds for believing that further detention is justified (s. 43(1)), which must be determined in accordance with the criteria set out in s. 43(4). The hearing is *inter partes*. The detainee must be given a copy of the information and be brought before the court for the hearing (s. 43(2)). Prior to the hearing, documents and materials that are essential to challenging the lawfulness of the detainee's arrest and detention must be made available to him or his solicitor (Code C, paras. 3.4(b) and 15.0(b)). The detainee is entitled to be legally represented at the hearing. If he is not so represented but wishes to be, the court must adjourn the hearing to enable him to be represented. He may be held in detention during the adjournment (s. 41(3)). No limit is placed on the time for which an adjournment may be granted.

D1.73 An application for a warrant of further detention must, as a general rule, be made before the expiry of 36 hours from the relevant time (s. 43(4)(a): but see also **D1.68**). For this purpose, the time of the application is the time that the constable makes the application on oath and gives evidence (*Sedgefield Justices, ex parte Milne* (5 November 1987 unreported)). This period may be extended where it is not practicable for the magistrates' court to which the application will be made to sit before the expiry of the period but where it will sit within six hours following the 36-hour period (s. 43(4)(c)). If the application cannot be heard before the expiry of the 36-hour period, the custody officer is to note in the detainee's custody record the fact that he was detained for the extra period and the reason why he was so kept (s. 43(6)). If the application is made outside the 36-hour period and the magistrates' court considers that it would have been reasonable for the police to have made the application before the expiry of the period, it must dismiss the application (s. 43(7), and see *Slough Justices, ex parte Stirling* (1987) 151 JP 603).

If the court is not satisfied that there are reasonable grounds for believing that further detention is justified, it must dismiss the application or adjourn the hearing of it to a time not later than 36 hours from the relevant time (s. 43(8)). The person may be kept in police detention during any period of adjournment (s. 43(9)). If, therefore, the court sits at a time close to the 36-hour limit, it may well not be possible for the police to obtain an adjournment in order to strengthen their case. Furthermore, where an application for a warrant of further detention has been refused, no further application may be made under s. 43 unless fresh evidence has come to light since the refusal (s. 43(17)). This, of course, assumes that the hearing took place before the expiry of the 36-hour period and that it is possible for the detainee still to be in lawful custody. If the application for a warrant is refused, the police must either charge the detainee or release him, either on bail or without bail (s. 43(15)). However, if the refusal was made before the expiry of the 24-hour limit (**D1.67**) or any extension granted under s. 42 (see **D1.69**), the detainee need not be released before the expiry of that period (provided that the conditions for detention without charge continue to be satisfied) (s. 43(16)).

If the court is satisfied that there are reasonable grounds for believing that further detention is justified, it may issue a warrant of further detention for a maximum period of 36 hours (s. 43(12)). Within that limit, where it is intended to transfer a detainee to another police area, the court must have regard to the distance and time involved in a journey (s. 43(13)). The warrant must state the time at which it is issued and the period for which it is granted (s. 43(10)). At the expiry of a warrant of further detention the detainee must, unless the warrant is extended under the PACE 1984, s. 44, be charged or released, either on bail or without bail. If released on bail, he may not be rearrested without a warrant for the offence for which he was previously arrested unless new evidence justifying a further arrest has come to light since his release (s. 43(19), and see **D1.67**).

Extension of Warrant of Further Detention   A magistrates' court may, on an application on oath **D1.74** and supported by an information, extend a warrant of further detention issued under the PACE 1984, s. 43, provided it is satisfied that there are reasonable grounds for believing that the further detention is justified (s. 44(1)). Such extension may be made for any period which the court thinks fit, having regard to the evidence before it, but it may not be for longer than 36 hours, and the total period for which the person is to be held in detention may not exceed 96 hours from the relevant time (see **D1.68**). There is no formal limit to the number of occasions on which such a further extension may be granted, but the total period of 96 hours cannot be exceeded (s. 44(1)–(4)).

The court must be furnished with the same particulars as are required in the original application, and the detainee has the same rights of representation (s. 44(6)). The police are under the same obligation to provide documents and materials that are essential to challenging the lawfulness of the arrest and detention as for the original warrant application (see **D1.72**). If the extension is refused, the detainee must either be released (with or without bail) or charged save that, if the application for extension is made before the expiry of the period specified in the warrant itself, he may be held until the expiry of that period (provided that the conditions for detention without charge continue to be satisfied) (s. 44(7)–(8)).

Reviews of Detention

The PACE 1984, s. 40, requires that the detention of persons in police detention (see **D1.40**) **D1.75** be periodically reviewed in order to determine whether continued detention is justified (see also Code C, sect. 15). The review requirement applies both to persons who have not been charged and those who have been charged, but does not apply to a person who is at court after being charged since such a person is not in police detention (PACE 1984, s. 118(2)). The statutory review requirement does not apply to volunteers (see **D1.43**), to persons who have been taken to a police station as a place of safety under the Mental Health Act 1983, nor to persons who have been arrested other than for an offence (e.g., under a fine default warrant or for fingerprints to be taken under the PACE 1984, s. 63A(4) and sch. 2A, para. 17). However, the detention of persons who are held in custody but who are not in police detention as defined by the PACE 1984, s. 118(2), should still be reviewed periodically, as a matter of good practice, in order to check the power under which they are held, the conditions of their detention, and that appropriate action is being taken in respect of them (Code C, Note for Guidance 15B). The statutory review requirements do apply to persons who are deemed to be arrested for an offence (see **D1.40**) and to persons who have been remanded to a police station under the MCA 1980, s. 128(7) (see **D1.42**). They also apply to persons detained at a police station in respect of whom a warrant of further detention has been issued or extended by a magistrates' court (see **D1.72**).

In the case of persons who have been arrested and charged, reviews of detention must be conducted by the custody officer. For persons who have not been charged, they must be conducted by an officer of at least the rank of inspector who has not been directly involved in the investigation (PACE 1984, s. 40(1)). In either case the officer concerned is referred to as a 'review officer' (s. 40(2)).

D1.76 **Timing of Reviews**   The first review must be conducted no later than six hours after detention was first authorised under the PACE 1984, s. 37 (which may be later than the 'relevant time': see **D1.68**) (PACE 1984, s. 40(3)(a)). The second and subsequent reviews must be carried out no later than nine hours after the previous review (s. 40(3)(b) and (c)). A review may be postponed if it is impracticable to carry it out by the latest time specified (s. 40(4)(a)). The statute gives two examples. The first is where the review officer is satisfied that a review would interrupt questioning then in progress and would prejudice the investigation. The second is where no review officer is readily available at that time (s. 40(4)(b)). However, these are not exhaustive. If a detainee is asleep when a review is conducted he need not be woken up, but if he is likely to be asleep when a review is due to be conducted, the review officer should consider bringing the review forward (Code C, Note for Guidance 15C). A postponed review must be carried out as soon as is practicable (s. 40(5)), and the review officer is required to record the reasons for any postponement in the custody record (s. 40(7); Code C, para. 15.3). The timing of subsequent reviews is not affected, so that they must be carried out no later than nine hours after the latest time at which the review should have been conducted (s. 40(6)). However, if a review is brought forward, the next review must be conducted no later than nine hours after the time that the review was in fact conducted.

Failure to carry out a timely review of a person's detention in custody before charge renders previously lawful detention unlawful and amounts to the tort of false imprisonment (*Roberts v Chief Constable of the Cheshire Constabulary* [1999] 2 All ER 326).

D1.77 **Criteria for Reviews**   In the case of a person not yet charged at the time of the review, the review officer must determine whether there is sufficient evidence to charge and, if not, whether detention is necessary for the reasons set out in the PACE 1984, s. 37(2) (s. 40(8) and (8A) and see **D1.49**). If a person is held because he was not in a fit state to be dealt with, the review officer must determine whether or not he is now in a fit state (s. 40(9)).

If a person has already been charged at the time of review, the review officer must consider whether to order his release on bail, applying the same principles as those which the custody officer is obliged to employ under s. 38(1)–(6B) (s. 40(10) and (10A) and see **D2.50**).

If directions relating to a person in police detention given by a higher-ranking officer are at variance with an actual or proposed decision or action of the review officer, the matter must be immediately referred to an officer of the rank of superintendent or above who is in charge of the station (s. 40(11)).

D1.78 **Procedural Requirements**   Reviews of detention prior to charge (other than those involving consideration of whether detention is to continue beyond 24 hours: see **D1.69**) may be carried out by video-link facilities where regulations have been issued by the Secretary of State under the PACE 1984, s. 45A(1), and the review officer has access to the use of such facilities enabling him to communicate with persons at the police station (s. 45A(1)). In police stations in respect of which such regulations have not been made, or where they have but such facilities are not available, reviews (other than those involving consideration of whether detention is to continue beyond 24 hours) may be conducted by telephone (s. 40A(1)). It is for the officer conducting the review to determine whether to conduct the review in person or by telephone or video-link facilities (where authorised and available), and in making this decision the officer should take into account the factors set out in Code C, para. 15.3C. If a review is conducted using such facilities, there is provision for representations to be made by telephone or video-link (as appropriate) or by fax (PACE 1984, ss. 40A(3) and (4), and 45A(6) and (7)), and for the review to be entered in the custody record by another officer (ss. 40(A)(3) and 45A(5)). See Code C, paras. 15.9 to 15.11, for further explanation.

Before determining whether to authorise continued detention the review officer must decide, in consultation with the investigating officer, what documents and materials which are essential for challenging the lawfulness of the arrest and detention must be made available to the detainee (Code C, paras. 3.4(b) and 15.0(a)). He must also give either the detained person (unless he is asleep), or any solicitor representing him who is available at the time of the review, an opportunity to make representations about the detention (PACE 1984, s. 40(12)). Code C, para. 15.3, however, provides that this opportunity is to be given to the detainee 'and' to his solicitor and, where relevant, to the appropriate adult. The review officer may also, in his discretion, allow other persons having an interest in the person's welfare to make representations to him (para. 15.3A). Before conducting a review, the review officer must ensure that the detained person is reminded of his entitlement to free legal advice (para. 15.4). The detainee or his solicitor may make representations either orally or in writing, but the review officer need not hear oral representations from a detainee whom he considers unfit to make such representations by reason of his condition or behaviour (PACE 1984, s. 40(13) and (14); Code C, para. 15.3B).

D1.79 A note must be made in the custody record of the fact that the detainee was reminded of his right to legal advice, details of a review conducted by telephone and the outcome of the review (Code C, paras. 15.12, 15.14 and 15.16); if continued detention is authorised, any comment made by the detainee or his solicitor must also be recorded (para. 15.3). Any written representations made must be retained (para. 15.15).

INTERROGATION OF SUSPECTS

D1.80 The interrogation of suspects is governed partly by common law, partly by the PACE 1984, but primarily by PACE Code C (see **appendix 1**). Code C contains rules regulating the treatment of persons who are being questioned, and the questioning itself, principally in sects. 10, 11 and 12. For the application of Code C to the police and to others, see **D1.1** and **D1.3**. Recording of interviews is governed by Code E (audio-recording) and Code F (visual recording with sound). Code C, sect. 12, lays down certain rules governing the physical conditions of, and the treatment of detainees in, interviews conducted at police stations.

Interviews Generally

D1.81 **Definition of Interview** 'Interview' is widely defined by Code C, para. 11.1A, in purposive terms. An interview is the 'questioning of a person regarding their involvement or suspected involvement in a criminal offence or offences which, under para. 10.1, must be carried out under caution'. By para. 10.1, a person whom there are grounds to suspect of an offence 'must be cautioned before any questions about an offence, or further questions if the answers provide the grounds for suspicion, are put to them if either the suspect's answers or their silence, (i.e. failure or refusal to answer or answer satisfactorily) may be given in evidence to a court in a prosecution'. However, it further provides that a caution is not necessary if questions are for other purposes, such as:

(a) solely to establish identify or ownership of a vehicle;
(b) to obtain information in accordance with a statutory requirement, e.g., under the RTA 1988, s. 165 (note that the statutory drink-driving procedure is not an interview: *DPP v D (a Juvenile)* (1992) 94 Cr App R 185);
(c) in furtherance of the proper and effective conduct of a search (although if questioning goes further, e.g., to establish whether drugs found were intended to be supplied to another, a caution will be necessary: *Langiert* [1991] Crim LR 777; *Khan* [1993] Crim LR 54; *Raphaie* [1996] Crim LR 812); or
(d) to seek verification of a written record of comments made by the person outside of an interview.

It follows that questioning of a person in circumstances where a caution does not have to be administered does not amount to an interview for the purposes of Code C. Conversely, questioning of a person about an offence of which there are grounds to suspect him will amount to an interview even if he has not been arrested and no decision to arrest him has been made. The reference to 'an offence' means that a caution must be given if the person is questioned about an offence other than for which he has been arrested if there are grounds to suspect him of it. See further **D1.83** regarding cautioning.

D1.82 **Where an Interview May be Conducted** The general rules for the conduct of interviews are contained in Code C, sect. 11. Following a decision to arrest a suspect, he must normally be interviewed only at a police station or other authorised place of detention (Code C, para. 11.1). The reference to 'a decision to arrest' means that if a police officer has decided to arrest a person, he should not delay the arrest in order to question the suspect before doing so. The requirement that an interview be conducted at a police station is subject to exception where delay would be likely to:

(a) lead to interference with or harm to evidence connected with an offence, interference with or physical harm to other persons, or serious loss of, or damage to, property; or
(b) lead to the alerting of other persons suspected of having committed an offence but not yet arrested for it; or
(c) hinder the recovery of property obtained in consequence of the commission of an offence (para. 11.1).

Interviewing in any of these circumstances must cease once the relevant risk has been averted or the necessary questions have been put to avert the risk (Code C, para. 11.1).

D1.83 **Cautions and Special Warnings** It follows from Code C, para. 10.1 (see **D1.81**) that a caution must be administered at the commencement of an interview as defined in Code C, para. 11.1A, whether or not it is conducted at a police station. The suspect must also be reminded that he is under caution at the recommencement of an interview after any break, and if there is any doubt, the caution should be given again in full (para. 10.8). The caution must also be given on arrest (para. 10.4, and see **D1.18**).

The normal caution is set out in Code C, para. 10.5, as follows:

> You do not have to say anything. But it may harm your defence if you do not mention when questioned something which you later rely on in Court. Anything you do say may be given in evidence.

Minor deviation from these words is permissible provided that the sense of the caution is preserved (para. 10.7). Where an interpreter is used, the fact that the caution is not perfectly translated will not render it invalid provided that the essential features are adequately conveyed to the suspect (*Koc* [2008] EWCA Crim 77). If it appears that the suspect does not understand the caution, the person giving it should explain it in his own words (Code C, Note for Guidance 10D).

If a suspect is (exceptionally) interviewed after charge (see **D1.93**), or if he is interviewed in circumstances where he has requested a solicitor but has not been permitted to consult with one (see **D1.55** *et seq.*), the terms of the caution are those set out in Code C, annex C, para. 2 as follows: 'You do not have to say anything, but anything you do say may be given in evidence'. The reason for the different caution is that in such circumstances inferences cannot be drawn under the CJPO 1994, ss. 34, 36 or 37. Although Code C does not require a caution to be given if a statement is taken after charge, it should be given (*Pall* (1992) 156 JP 424).

D1.84 Whilst Code C, para. 10.1, requires a caution to be given to a person 'whom there are grounds to suspect' of an offence, Note for Guidance 10A explains this phrase by stating that there must be 'some reasonable, objective grounds for the suspicion, based on known facts or information...'. This accords with the decision in *James* [1996] Crim LR 650, and this qualification of the expression was not disputed in *Shillibier* [2006] EWCA Crim 793. If correct, however, it means that insofar as the caution has a protective purpose, it does not apply to the questioning of a person in respect of whom there is some suspicion not amounting to a reasonable suspicion, even though what he says may subsequently be used in evidence against him. Whether there are sufficient grounds for a caution to be administered is an objective question, and does not simply depend on how the police officer regarded the matter (*Williams* [2012] EWCA Crim 264). For examples of interpretation of the cautioning requirement by the courts, see *Senior* [2004] 3 All ER 9, in which it was held that a caution should have been given, and *Perpont* [2004] EWCA Crim 2562, *Ridehalgh v DPP* [2005] RTR 353 and *Sneyd v DPP* (2006) 170 JP 545, in which the decision went the other way. Failure to administer a caution in circumstances where it is required is a significant and substantial breach of Code C, although it will not necessarily result in exclusion of evidence of the interview (compare *Armas-Rodriguez* [2005] EWCA Crim 1981 and *Devani* [2008] 1 Cr App R 65 with *Miller* [2007] EWCA Crim 1891). Similarly, giving the wrong caution will not necessarily lead to exclusion (*Ibrahim* [2009] 4 All ER 208; but see *Charles v DPP* [2010] RTR 402).

Whenever a person is interviewed he, and his solicitor if represented, must be given, before the interview, sufficient information to make it possible to understand the nature of the suspected offence and why the person is suspected of committing it (Code C, para. 11.1A). In *Kirk* [1999] 4 All ER 698, the suspect was arrested for theft and was not told that his victim had died; believing himself to be facing a charge of theft only, he made admissions. It was held that these should have been excluded. See also *Charles v DPP*. The disclosure obligation in Code C, para. 11.1A, has been extended to reflect the requirements of EU Directive 2012/13/EU, Article 6 (see **D1.1**), but does not require the disclosure of details at a time which might prejudice the investigation. The decision on what should be disclosed rests with the investigating officer, who must make a record of what was disclosed and when it was disclosed.

In addition to the caution, where a suspect is interviewed at a police station or other authorised place of detention following arrest and: **D1.85**

(a) is asked to account for any object, mark or substance, or mark on such objects found on his person, in or on his clothing or footwear, otherwise in his possession, or in the place where he was arrested; or

(b) to account for his presence at the place where he was arrested,

a special warning must be given in the terms set out in Code C, para. 10.11. Inferences cannot be drawn if the warning is not given (CJPO 1994, ss. 36(4) and 37(3)). The requirement to give a special warning does not apply where the person who has requested a solicitor is interviewed without having been given an opportunity to consult him, since inferences from refusal or failure to account cannot be drawn as a result of the CJPO 1994, ss. 36(4A) and 37(3A) (Code C, para. 10.10).

Information about Legal Advice   Prior to the commencement or recommencement of an   **D1.86**
interview at a police station or other authorised place of detention, the interviewing officer must, unless access to a solicitor has been delayed or one of the exceptions applies, remind the suspect of his entitlement to free legal advice and that the interview can be delayed for legal advice to be obtained (Code C, para. 11.2, and see **D1.55** *et seq.*). Violations of a suspect's entitlement to legal advice may lead to the exclusion of evidence (see **F2.28** and **F17.34**).

Significant Statement or Silence   At the beginning of an interview carried out at a police sta-   **D1.87**
tion or other authorised place of detention, the interviewing officer must, after cautioning the suspect, put to him any significant statement or silence which occurred in the presence and hearing of a police officer or other police staff (and which has not been put to him in the course of a previous interview) (Code C, para. 11.4). A significant statement is one which appears to be capable of being used in evidence, and in particular a direct admission of guilt. It does not include what a suspect is alleged to have said as part of the conduct constituting the offence (*DPP v Lawrence* [2008] 1 Cr App R 147). A significant silence is a failure or refusal to answer a question, or answer satisfactorily when under caution which might, allowing for the restrictions on drawing inferences from silence, give rise to an adverse inference under the CJPO 1994 (para. 11.4A).

Conduct of the Interview   No police officer or other interviewer may try to obtain answers to   **D1.88**
questions or to elicit a statement by the use of oppression, nor shall he indicate, except in answer

to a direct question, what action the police will take if the suspect answers or refuses to answer questions or make a statement. If the suspect asks the officer directly what action will be taken in any of those events, the officer may inform the suspect of his proposed action, which could be, e.g., keeping the person in detention if further action is to be taken. The proposed action must, however, be proper and warranted (Code C, para. 11.5). Thus it was improper for the police to tell a church organist accused of theft from choirboys that the police would interview all of the choirboys if he did not confess (*Howden-Simpson* [1991] Crim LR 49). The police should not seek a confession by offering a caution (*R (U) v Metropolitan Police Commissioner* [2003] 4 All ER 419, overturned but not in this respect by *R (R) v Durham Constabulary* [2005] 2 All ER 369). Home Office Circular 16/2008, *Simple Cautioning of Adult Offenders*, para. 18, states that 'under no circumstances should suspects be pressed, or induced in any way to admit offences in order to receive a Simple Caution as an alternative to being charged'.

Apart from this, the PACE 1984 and Code C provide little, if any, guidance on the proper conduct of interviews, although the case law provides some indication of what is acceptable. It has been held to be legitimate for police officers to pursue their interrogation of a suspect with a view to eliciting admissions even where the suspect denies involvement in the offence or declines to answer specific questions (*Holgate-Mohammed v Duke* [1984] AC 437). In *Mason* [1988] 3 All ER 481, it was held that a confession should be excluded where the police falsely informed the suspect that incriminating fingerprints had been found, although the fact that his solicitor was also deceived may have been an important factor. In *Maclean* [1993] Crim LR 687, it was noted that not every trick will result in exclusion of evidence, but in *Imran and Hussain* [1997] Crim LR 754, the Court of Appeal stated that there was a positive duty on the police not to actively mislead a suspect. The asking of hypothetical questions is permissible, although it may need to be approached with care (*Stringer* [2008] EWCA Crim 1222). Police questioning which is carried on after repeated denials or refusals may become oppressive (*Paris* (1993) 97 Cr App R 99). Hectoring and bullying throughout an interview has been held to be oppressive (*Beales* [1991] Crim LR 118), whereas questioning that was rude and discourteous, with raised voices and some bad language, was not (*Emmerson* (1991) 92 Cr App R 284). See further **F2.48** and **F17.34** *et seq.* on exclusion of evidence.

D1.89   **When Interviews Should Cease**   The interview of a person who has not been charged or informed that he may be prosecuted must cease when the officer in charge of the investigation is satisfied that all the questions he considers relevant to obtaining accurate and reliable information about the offence have been put to the suspect, the officer has taken account of other available evidence, and he (or the custody officer in the case of a detained suspect) reasonably believes there is sufficient evidence to provide a realistic prospect of conviction (Code C, para. 11.6). This, of course, is subject to the limits imposed by the PACE 1984 on the maximum periods of detention without charge (see **D1.67**), and the provisions regarding breaks in interviews and rest periods in Code C, sect. 12 (for application of the provision regarding rest periods, see *Beeres v CPS* [2014] EWHC 283 (Admin)). The fact that the conditions in para. 11.6 are satisfied does not preclude officers in Revenue cases or acting under the confiscation provisions of the POCA 2002 from inviting a suspect to complete a formal question-and-answer record after the interview is completed. (Code C, para. 11.6 refers to the confiscation provisions of the CJA 1988 or the Drug Trafficking Act 1994, but presumably this is an error.)

Code C, para. 11.6, gives the police a large degree of latitude in determining when interviewing should cease since it appears to permit the police to continue questioning beyond the point when they are satisfied that there is sufficient evidence to charge if, e.g., the officer believes that further questions could or should be put to the suspect. However, there is some inconsistency within Code C and thus uncertainty about the effect of para. 11.6. It provides that in the case of a detained suspect (presumably, as opposed to a volunteer) it is for the custody officer and not the investigating officer to determine whether there is sufficient evidence to charge. On the other hand, para. 16.1 states that when the officer in charge of the investigation believes that there is sufficient evidence to provide a realistic prospect of conviction, he must take the suspect to the custody officer without delay. It may be that this is intended to reflect the fact that the custody officer has formal responsibility for making the decision as to whether there is sufficient evidence to charge. However, para. 16.1 implies that when the officer in charge of the investigation is so satisfied he must take the suspect to the custody officer even though the investigating officer still may have further questions to put to the suspect. In any event, by the PACE 1984, s. 37(7), once the custody officer determines that he has before him sufficient evidence to charge the person he must proceed under that subsection, which would normally preclude further interviewing. 'Sufficient evidence to charge' is not defined, but the *Director's Guidance on Charging* provides that the custody officer must normally apply the full code test (see **D2.3**).

Where a person is detained in respect of more than one offence, Code C, para. 16.1, provides that it is permissible to delay informing the custody officer until the conditions are satisfied in respect of each of the offences. This, however, conflicts with the mandatory provisions of s. 37(7).

Recording of Interviews

Interviews of suspects must normally be contemporaneously recorded (Code C, para. 11.7). **D1.90** Further, any comment that might be relevant to the suspected offence made by a suspect outside the context of an interview, including unsolicited comments, must be recorded and, where practicable, the suspect must be given the opportunity to verify the record (para. 11.13). Failure to comply with the recording requirements has led to exclusion of evidence of what was allegedly said (see, e.g., *Canale* [1990] 2 All ER 187; *Keenan* [1990] 2 QB 54), but this is not always so (see, e.g., *Waters* [1989] Crim LR 62; *Dures* [1997] 2 Cr App R 247).

Interviews conducted at a police station in respect of any indictable offence must normally be audio-recorded (Code E, para. 3.1). In practice, most interviews are audio-recorded irrespective of the suspected offence. For the provisions governing the audio-recording of interviews generally, see Code E. Visual recording of police interviews is not mandatory in any police force area, but where such facilities are available and a police officer chooses to use them, he must have regard to Code F.

Special Categories of Persons

A juvenile or a mentally disordered or vulnerable person (see **D1.63**) must not be interviewed **D1.91** or asked to provide or sign a written statement in the absence of the appropriate adult unless the conditions for conducting an interview away from a police station under Code C, para 11.1, are satisfied (see **D1.82**), or the interview is authorised by an officer of the rank of superintendent or above under Code C, para. 11.18 (Code C, para. 11.15, and annex E). A juvenile should be interviewed at his place of education only in exceptional circumstances and then only if the principal or his nominee agrees. Efforts should be made to notify parents and the appropriate adult. In cases of necessity, and provided that the school was not the victim of the alleged offence, the principal may act as the appropriate adult (Code C, para. 11.16). The appropriate adult is to be reminded of his functions as adviser and observer as well as that of facilitating communication with the person being interviewed (para. 11.17). As to the special rules applying where a child who is to be interviewed is a ward of court, see CPD V, paras. 28A.1 to 28A.8 (see Supplement, **PD-41**).

A person whom the custody officer has determined requires an interpreter (see Code C, paras. 3.5(c)(ii) and 3.12) must not be interviewed without an interpreter unless authorised by an officer of the rank of superintendent or above, being satisfied that delaying the interview will lead to the consequences in Code C, para. 11.1(a)–(c), and that the interview would not significantly harm the person's physical or mental state (para. 11.18). Where a suspect cannot read and an interview is recorded in writing, the record must be read over to the suspect who must be asked to verify it (Code C, para. 11.11).

Intoxicated Persons

D1.92 Code C, para. 11.18, precludes the interviewing of any person who is unable to appreciate the significance of questions and their answers, or to understand what is happening because of the effects of drink, drugs or any illness, ailment or condition, unless it is authorised by an officer of the rank of superintendent (such authorisation being subject to the same conditions as for a person who requires an interpreter).

Effect of Charge

D1.93 Generally, a person who has been charged with, or informed that he may be prosecuted for, an offence cannot be interviewed or otherwise asked questions about that offence (Code C, para. 16.5). Different provisions apply where the offence is a terrorism offence within the meaning of the C-TA 2008, s. 27 (see **B10.14** *et seq.*). In *Charles v DPP* [2010] RTR 402, interviewing a person about an offence of driving whilst under the influence of alcohol in circumstances where he had already been informed that he would be charged with the offence of being in charge of a motor vehicle whilst under the influence was held to be a breach of para. 16.5. There are two exceptions to the prohibition on interviewing after charge. First, the person may be questioned if an officer wishes to bring to his notice any written statement made by another person or the content of an interview with another person. In such a case, the officer must hand to the accused a true copy of any such statement or interview record, but he must not do or say anything to invite any reply or comment, except to caution him (Code C, para. 16.4). A police officer may read the statement or record to an illiterate person. If the person is a juvenile or is mentally disordered or mentally vulnerable, the copy or interview record must be given or shown to the appropriate adult (para. 16.4A).

The second exception is where an interview is necessary for the purpose of preventing or minimising harm or loss to some other person or to the public, to clear up an ambiguity in a previous answer or statement, or where it is in the interests of justice that the person should have put to him and should have an opportunity to comment on information concerning the offence which has come to light since he was charged or informed that he may be prosecuted (para. 16.5).

In either case, the person must first be cautioned in the terms set out in paras. 16.4(a) or 16.5(a). Inferences under the CJPO 1994 cannot be drawn in such circumstances (see Code C, annex C, para. 1(b)). The person must also be reminded of his right to legal advice.

Serious Fraud and other Serious Crime

D1.94 Different rules apply in relation to investigation of certain serious or complex frauds. While the police are obliged to follow the normal procedure when questioning suspects, including the administration of a caution, the Director of the Serious Fraud Office has power under the CJA 1987, s. 2, to require a person under investigation or any other person whom he has reason to believe has relevant information to produce documents and to provide an explanation of them. This includes the right to re-interview witnesses even following the delivery of a case statement by the defence (*Turner* (1993) *The Times*, 2 July 1993). The Director is not obliged to provide the interviewee with advance information on the subject-matter of the interview but he may do so should he deem it helpful and not likely to prejudice the investigation (*Serious Fraud Office, ex parte Maxwell* (1992) *The Independent*, 7 October 1992). The court has no power to direct liquidators of an insolvent company not to comply with a notice served by the Serious Fraud Office requesting production of transcripts of examinations under the Insolvency Act 1986, s. 236. It is for the judge at the criminal trial to determine whether to admit such a transcript at the criminal trial. A person who without reasonable excuse fails to comply with a requirement under s. 2 commits an offence punishable on summary conviction with up to six months' imprisonment and/or a fine not exceeding level 5. Note however that compulsion to attend for interview or to provide information where the person is at risk of criminal prosecution in respect of those matters is likely to amount to an interference with his rights under the ECHR, Article 6 (*Shannon v UK* (2006) 42 EHRR 660).

It would seem that the fact that a person who is required to answer questions in the course of an inquiry by the Serious Fraud Office is the spouse of a party charged with fraud is not a reasonable excuse for declining to answer questions (*Director of the Serious Fraud Office, ex parte Johnson* [1993] COD 58). This seemingly follows from the consideration that such inquiries are administrative, and must represent something of a triumph of form over function.

For restrictions on the use in evidence of information obtained by virtue of the CJA 1987, s. 2, see s. 2(8) and (8AA), and see further **F9.73** and **F19.1**.

D1.95

For powers of search under the CJA 1987, s. 2, see the review of the procedure and authorities in *R (Energy Financing Team Ltd) v Bow Street Magistrates' Court* [2006] 4 All ER 285.

Similar powers to those under CJA 1987, s. 2, are available to the DPP under the SOCPA 2005, part 2, in respect of certain offences. See further **D1.192** *et seq.*

For the obligation to answer questions or to provide information under a serious crime prevention order granted under the SCA 2007, part 1, see **D25.72**.

SEARCH OF THE PERSON

Search on Arrest

A constable who arrests a person elsewhere than at a police station may search that person if he has reason to believe that the person may present a danger to himself or others (PACE 1984, s. 32(1)), and may seize and retain anything he finds if he has reasonable grounds for believing that the person might use it to cause physical injury to himself or others (s. 32(8)). He may also search the person for anything which that person might use to escape from lawful custody or which might be evidence in relation to an offence, provided that he has reasonable cause to believe that the arrested person has such material on his person (s. 32(2) and (5)). The officer may seize and retain anything, other than an item subject to legal privilege, if he has reasonable grounds for believing that the person may use it to assist with his escape from lawful custody or that it is evidence of an offence or has been obtained in consequence of the commission of an offence (s. 32(9)). 'Reasonable grounds' implies a mixed subjective/objective test (see **D1.4**). Seizure of car keys under s. 32 from a person arrested on suspicion of burglary and who had been placed in a police car was held in *Churchill* [1989] Crim LR 226 to be unlawful since the keys were not evidence of any crime, although they could have been seized under the officer's general duty to preserve property.

D1.96

Search under s. 32(2) is authorised only to the extent that it is reasonably required for the purpose of discovering any such thing or evidence (s. 32(3)). The reference to 'an' offence means that the power is not limited to search for or seizure of an item which may be evidence relating to the offence for which the person has been arrested. Unlike the power to search premises under s. 32(2)(b), the offence for which the person has been arrested does not have to be an indictable offence. Where the search takes place in public, the constable may only require the arrested person to remove an outer coat, jacket or gloves, but he is authorised to search a person's mouth (s. 32(4)). Hats, turbans and other forms of head-wear, are not mentioned in s. 32(4) and thus it would seem that a person cannot be required to remove them in public. However, note the power of a constable in uniform, in an area where an authorisation under the CJPO 1994, s. 60, is in force (see **D1.12**), to require a person to remove any item which the constable reasonably believes is being worn wholly or mainly for the purpose of concealing identity (CJPO 1994, s. 60AA). Note also that the power to photograph an arrested person without consent under the PACE 1984, s. 64A(1), is supplemented by a power to require the person to remove any item worn on or over the whole or part of the face or head (s. 64A(2)).

Search at the Police Station

D1.97 With the exception of searches following arrest under the TA 2000, s. 41 (for which see **B10.24**), searches by a constable of persons in police detention (see **D1.40**), including intimate searches, can take place only under the authority of the PACE 1984 (s. 53(1)). A person who attends at a police station to answer to 'live link bail' (see **D2.46**) is not in police detention, but see **D1.98** regarding search and seizure powers.

The custody officer at a police station is obliged to ascertain everything which a person has with him when he is brought to the station after having been arrested (PACE 1984, s. 54(1); Code C, para. 4.1). In order to do so, the person may be searched if the custody officer considers it necessary in order to ascertain what property the person has, but only to the extent that he considers it necessary for that purpose (s. 54(6); para. 4.1). The custody officer must also ascertain what property the suspect may have acquired for an unlawful or harmful purpose while in custody, and is responsible for the safe-keeping of property taken from the detainee and kept at the police station (Code C, para. 4.1). For recording requirements, see **D1.45**.

The custody officer may seize and retain anything in the possession of the detainee, save for clothes and personal effects. These may be seized only if the custody officer believes that the person from whom they are seized may use them to cause physical injury to himself or another, to damage property, to interfere with evidence, to escape, or if the custody officer has reasonable grounds for believing that they may be evidence relating to an offence (PACE 1984, s. 54(3), (4), (6B) and (6C); Code C, para. 4.2). In respect of most of these criteria, the custody officer need only have a subjective belief that seizure is necessary, but in respect of articles of supposed evidentiary value, his belief must be based on reasonable grounds. Paragraphs 4.2 and 4.3 of Code C expressly state that a detained person may retain clothing and personal effects other than cash and other items of value, at his own risk, unless the custody officer considers that the detainee might use them in the manner noted above or they are needed as evidence.

A person from whom an article is seized is to be told the reason for the seizure unless he is either violent or likely to become so, is incapable of understanding what is said to him, or is in urgent need of medical attention (PACE 1984, s. 54(5); Code C, paras. 1.8 and 4.2).

D1.98 Under the PACE 1984, s. 54A, searches and examinations may be authorised by an officer of the rank of inspector or above for the purpose of ascertaining whether a detained person has any mark (such as a tattoo) that would tend to identify him as a person involved in the commission of an offence (s. 54A(1)(a)), or so as to facilitate the ascertainment of his identity (s. 54A(1)(b)). See also Code D, paras. 5.1 to 5.11. By s. 54A(2), authorisation may be given under s. 54A(1)(a) only if appropriate consent (see the PACE 1984, s. 65(1)) has been withheld or it is not practicable to obtain it (for examples, see Code D, Note for Guidance 5D). Authorisation may be given under s. 54A(1)(b) only if the person has refused to identify himself or the officer has reasonable grounds for suspecting that the person is not who he claims to be (s. 54A(3)). An identifying mark found on such a search or examination may be photographed (s. 54A(5)). In local justice areas where live link police bail is available (see **D2.46**), the PACE 1984, ss. 54B and 54C, permit a police constable to search a person attending a police station to answer to live link bail, and to seize and retain any thing that may jeopardise the maintenance of order, or the safety of any person, in the police station, or which may be evidence of, or relating to, an offence. An intimate search cannot be carried out under s. 54A (s. 54A(8)) or s. 54B (s. 54B(5)), and if the search or examination requires the removal of more than outer clothing it must be treated as a strip search and conducted in accordance with Code C, annex A, para. 11.

Strip Searches

D1.99 A strip search is a search that is not an intimate search, but which involves the removal of more than outer clothing (Code C, annex A, para. 9). It may be conducted only for the purposes of search or examination under the PACE 1984, s. 54A, or where the custody officer thinks it necessary in order to remove an article which the detained person would not be allowed to keep and the officer reasonably considers that the detainee may have concealed such an article (Code C, annex A, para. 10). It is likely that such articles are those referred to in s. 54 (see D1.97). It was held in the pre-PACE case of *Lindley v Rutter* [1981] QB 128, that strip searches 'involve an affront to the dignity and privacy of the individual' and that actions such as removal of a brassiere would require considerable justification. The conduct of strip searches is governed by Code C, annex A, para. 11; in particular, they may be carried out only by a constable of the same sex as the person being searched (annex A, para. 11(a)). See Code C, annex L, for the procedure to be followed in establishing gender for the purposes of searching.

Intimate Searches, X-rays and Ultrasound Scans

Intimate Searches   A person who has been arrested and is in police detention (see D1.40) **D1.100** may, under certain circumstances, be subjected to an intimate search, i.e. a search consisting of a physical examination of the bodily orifices other than the mouth (PACE 1984, ss. 54 and 65(1)). An intimate search cannot be authorised for the purpose of securing evidence relating to an offence, nor must it be conducted whilst carrying out a search or examination under s. 54A. 'Bodily orifice' is not defined but would include ears, nose, anus and vagina. Physical insertion into a bodily orifice amounts to an intimate search, as does any application of force to an orifice or its immediate surroundings, such as the removal of something within an orifice. Code C, annex A, para. 11(e), implies that touching an orifice in these circumstances would also amount to an intimate search.

An intimate search can be conducted only if an officer of the rank of inspector or above authorises it. Such officer must have reasonable grounds for believing that the detained person has concealed on him an article which he could use to cause physical injury to himself or others, and which he might so use while he is in police detention or in the custody of a court (s. 55(1)(a)). Authorisation may also be granted if the officer has reasonable grounds for believing that such a person may have concealed on him a Class A drug and is in possession of it with the appropriate criminal intent (i.e. either to supply it to another or to export it with intent to evade a prohibition or restriction: s. 55(17)) (s. 55(1)(b)). In either case the officer must have reasonable grounds for believing that the article in question cannot be found unless the detainee is intimately searched (s. 55(2)). The reasons why an intimate search is considered necessary must be explained to the person before the search takes place (Code C, annex A, para. 2A). Intimate searches are not limited to circumstances where a person has been arrested for an indictable or recordable offence, although searches conducted under s. 55(1)(b) will, by definition, relate to such offences.

Authorisation may be given either orally, subject to confirmation in writing, or in writing (PACE 1984, s. 55(3)). Consent of the person to be searched is not required for a search under s. 55(1)(a), and reasonable force can be used in order to carry it out (PACE 1984, s. 117). Appropriate consent (see s. 65(1) for definition) in writing is required for a search under s. 55(1)(b). In the latter case the person to be searched must be told of the authorisation and the reasons for it (s. 55(3B)). If consent to a search under s. 55(1)(b) (but not a search under s. 55(1)(a)) is refused without good cause, proper inferences may be drawn (s. 55(13A)), but where consent has been refused force may not be used.

The general rule is that an intimate search should be carried out by a suitably qualified person, **D1.101** i.e. a registered medical practitioner or a registered nurse (s. 55(17)). Searches under s. 55(1)(b) must always be so carried out (s. 55(4) and (5)). Searches under s. 55(1)(a) must normally be carried out by a suitably qualified person, but may be conducted by a constable where an officer of the rank of inspector or above considers that this would not be practicable (s. 55(5) and (6)); such a search may be carried out by a civilian detention officer (Police Reform Act 2002, sch. 4, para. 28). A search under s. 55(1)(a) by anyone other than a suitably qualified person should be considered only as a last resort (Code C, annex A, para. 3A) — an example might be where a suspect is believed to have concealed a poisonous drug in his anus. No intimate search of an arrested juvenile or a mentally vulnerable person may be carried out unless the appropriate adult of the same sex is present or the suspect requests the presence of a particular adult of the opposite sex who is readily available. In the case of a juvenile, the search may take place in the absence of the appropriate adult only if the juvenile approves this in the adult's presence (Code C, annex A, para. 5). A constable may not carry out an intimate search of a person of the opposite sex, but this restriction does not apply to a search carried out by a medically qualified person; a minimum of two people other than the detainee must be present (Code C, annex A, para. 6). The person to be searched, if not legally represented, must be reminded of his entitlement to free legal advice (Code C, para. 6.5, and annex A, para. 2B).

Intimate searches may be carried out only at a police station, a hospital, surgery or other medical premises, although an intimate search under s. 55(1)(b) may not be carried out at a police station (PACE 1984, s. 55(8) and (9); Code C, annex A, para. 4). 'Medical premises' is not defined but presumably could, e.g., include a workplace health centre. As soon as possible after completion of an intimate search, the parts of the body searched and the reason for the search (and in the case of a search under s. 55(1)(b), the fact of and grounds for the authorisation and the fact that appropriate consent was given) must be recorded in the custody record (s. 55(10) and (11)).

D1.102 A person from whom anything is seized is to be told the reason why, unless he is incapable of understanding or is violent or likely to become so (s. 55(13)). Articles found in an intimate search may be seized and retained by the police for the same reasons as justify seizure and retention in the case of a non-intimate search (s. 55(12), and see **D1.97**).

D1.103 **X-rays and Ultrasound Scans**   By the PACE 1984, s. 55A(1), an X-ray or ultrasound scan may be taken if authorised by an officer of at least the rank of inspector, who has reasonable grounds for believing that a person who has been arrested and is in police detention (see **D1.40**) may have swallowed a Class A drug and was in possession of it with the appropriate criminal intent (see s. 55A(1) and **D1.100**) before his arrest. The officer granting the authorisation must inform the person concerned of the authorisation and of the reasons for it (s. 55A(3)). Neither an X-ray nor an ultrasound scan may be taken without appropriate consent (see s. 65(1) for definition) (s. 55A(2)). The procedures may be carried out by the same categories of person, and at the same places, as for an intimate search under s. 55(1)(b) (s. 55A(4)), and similar recording requirements apply (s. 55A(5)). Inferences may be drawn against a person who refuses consent (s. 55A(9)), but force may not be used.

BIOMETRIC IMPRESSIONS AND SAMPLES

D1.104 The police have wide powers to take, use and retain biometric samples and impressions, and also footwear impressions, both with and without consent, although intimate samples cannot be taken without consent in any circumstances. Generally there is a distinction between powers that may be exercised in respect of a person who is in police detention (see **D1.40**) and powers where the person is not in police detention, although there are wide powers to require a person to attend a police station for the purpose of taking fingerprints or samples with a power of arrest in default (PACE 1984, s. 63A(4) and sch. 2A). The powers are also governed by Code D, sects. 4 and 6.

Fingerprints and Footwear Impressions

D1.105 **Fingerprints**   The taking of fingerprints in connection with a criminal investigation is governed by the PACE 1984, s. 61, and by PACE Code D, sect. 4(A) (see **appendix 1**).

Police and Criminal Evidence Act 1984, s. 61

(1) Except as provided by this section no person's fingerprints may be taken without the appropriate consent.
(2) Consent to the taking of a person's fingerprints must be in writing if it is given at a time when he is at a police station.

(3) The fingerprints of a person detained at a police station may be taken without the appropriate consent if—
   (a) he is detained in consequence of his arrest for a recordable offence; and
   (b) he has not had his fingerprints taken in the course of the investigation of the offence by the police.

(3A) Where a person mentioned in paragraph (a) of subsection (3) or (4) has already had his fingerprints taken in the course of the investigation of the offence by the police, that fact shall be disregarded for the purposes of that subsection if—
   (a) the fingerprints taken on the previous occasion do not constitute a complete set of his fingerprints; or
   (b) some or all of the fingerprints taken on the previous occasion are not of sufficient quality to allow satisfactory analysis, comparison or matching (whether in the case in question or generally).

(4) The fingerprints of a person detained at a police station may be taken without the appropriate consent if—
   (a) he has been charged with a recordable offence or informed that he will be reported for such an offence; and
   (b) he has not had his fingerprints taken in the course of the investigation of the offence by the police.

(4A) The fingerprints of a person who has answered to bail at a court or police station may be taken without the appropriate consent at the court or station if—
   (a) the court, or
   (b) an officer of at least the rank of inspector,
   authorises them to be taken.

(4B) A court or officer may only give an authorisation under subsection (4A) if—
   (a) the person who has answered to bail has answered to it for a person whose fingerprints were taken on a previous occasion and there are reasonable grounds for believing that he is not the same person; or
   (b) the person who has answered to bail claims to be a different person from a person whose fingerprints were taken on a previous occasion.

(5) An officer may give an authorisation under subsection (4A) above orally or in writing but, if he gives it orally, he shall confirm it in writing as soon as is practicable.

(5A) The fingerprints of a person may be taken without the appropriate consent if (before or after the coming into force of this subsection) he has been arrested for a recordable offence and released and—
   (a) in the case of a person who is on bail, he has not had his fingerprints taken in the course of the investigation of the offence by the police; or
   (b) in any case, he has had his fingerprints taken in the course of that investigation but
      (i) subsection (3A)(a) or (b) above applies, or
      (ii) subsection (5C) below applies.

(5B) The fingerprints of a person not detained at a police station may be taken without the appropriate consent if (before or after the coming into force of this subsection) he has been charged with a recordable offence or informed that he will be reported for such an offence and—
   (a) he has not had his fingerprints taken in the course of the investigation of the offence by the police; or
   (b) he has had his fingerprints taken in the course of that investigation but subsection (3A)(a) or (b) above applies.

(5C) This subsection applies where—
   (a) the investigation was discontinued but subsequently resumed, and
   (b) before the resumption of the investigation the fingerprints were destroyed pursuant to section 63D(3) below.

(6) Subject to this section, the fingerprints of a person may be taken without the appropriate consent if (before or after the coming into force of this subsection)—
   (a) he has been convicted of a recordable offence, or
   (b) he has been given a caution in respect of a recordable offence which, at the time of the caution, he has admitted, and
   either of the conditions mentioned in subsection (6ZA) below is met.

(6ZA) The conditions referred to in subsection (6) above are—
   (a) the person has not had his fingerprints taken since he was convicted or cautioned;
   (b) he has had his fingerprints taken since then but subsection (3A)(a) or (b) above applies.

(6ZB) Fingerprints may only be taken as specified in subsection (6) above with the authorisation of an officer of at least the rank of inspector.

(6ZC) An officer may only give an authorisation under subsection (6ZB) above if the officer is satisfied that taking the fingerprints is necessary to assist in the prevention or detection of crime.

(6A) A constable may take a person's fingerprints without the appropriate consent if—
   (a) the constable reasonably suspects that the person is committing or attempting to commit an offence, or has committed or attempted to commit an offence; and
   (b) either of the two conditions mentioned in subsection (6B) is met.

(6B) The conditions are that—
   (a) the name of the person is unknown to, and cannot be readily ascertained by, the constable;
   (b) the constable has reasonable grounds for doubting whether a name furnished by the person as his name is his real name.

(6C) The taking of fingerprints by virtue of subsection (6A) does not count for any of the purposes of this Act as taking them in the course of the investigation of an offence by the police.

(6D) Subject to this section, the fingerprints of a person may be taken without the appropriate consent if—
   (a) under the law in force in a country or territory outside England and Wales the person has been convicted of an offence under that law (whether before or after the coming into force of this subsection and whether or not he has been punished for it);
   (b) the act constituting the offence would constitute a qualifying offence if done in England and Wales (whether or not it constituted such an offence when the person was convicted); and
   (c) either of the conditions mentioned in subsection (6E) below is met.

(6E) The conditions referred to in subsection (6D)(c) above are—
   (a) the person has not had his fingerprints taken on a previous occasion under subsection (6D) above;
   (b) he has had his fingerprints taken on a previous occasion under that subsection but subsection (3A)(a) or (b) above applies.

(6F) Fingerprints may only be taken as specified in subsection (6D) above with the authorisation of an officer of at least the rank of inspector.

(6G) An officer may only give an authorisation under subsection (6F) above if the officer is satisfied that taking the fingerprints is necessary to assist in the prevention or detection of crime.

(7) Where a person's fingerprints are taken without the appropriate consent by virtue of any power conferred by this section—
   (a) before the fingerprints are taken, the person shall be informed of—
      (i) the reason for taking the fingerprints;
      (ii) the power by virtue of which they are taken; and
      (iii) in a case where the authorisation of the court or an officer is required for the exercise of the power, the fact that the authorisation has been given; and
   (b) those matters shall be recorded as soon as practicable after the fingerprints are taken.

(7A) If a person's fingerprints are taken at a police station, or by virtue of subsection (4A), (6A) at a place other than a police station, whether with or without the appropriate consent—
   (a) before the fingerprints are taken, an officer (or, where by virtue of subsection (4A), (6A) the fingerprints are taken at a place other than a police station, the constable taking the fingerprints) shall inform him that they may be the subject of a speculative search; and
   (b) the fact that the person has been informed of this possibility shall be recorded as soon as is practicable after the fingerprints have been taken.

(8) If he is detained at a police station when the fingerprints are taken, the matters referred to in subsection (7)(a)(i) to (iii) above and, in the case falling within subsection (7A) above, the fact referred to in paragraph (b) of that subsection shall be recorded on his custody record.

(8B) Any power under this section to take the fingerprints of a person without the appropriate consent, if not otherwise specified to be exercisable by a constable, shall be exercisable by a constable.

(9) Nothing in this section—
   (a) affects any power conferred by paragraph 18(2) of Schedule 2 to the Immigration Act 1971; or
   (b) applies to a person arrested or detained under the terrorism provisions.

(10) Nothing in this section applies to a person arrested under an extradition arrest power.

The ABCPA 2014, s. 144, in force from 13 May 2014, added a power to take fingerprints under s. 61(5A) and (5B) where an investigation was discontinued, and subsequently resumed, but before resumption fingerprints were destroyed pursuant to s. 63D(3).

'Fingerprints' means any record, produced by any method, of the skin pattern and other physical **D1.106** characteristics or features of a person's fingers or palms (s. 65(1)). 'Appropriate consent' means: (a) in relation to a person who has attained the age of 17 years, the consent of that person; (b) in relation to a person who has not attained that age but has attained the age of 14 years, the consent of that person and his parent or guardian; and (c) in relation to a person who has not attained the age of 14 years, the consent of his parent or guardian (s. 65(1)). A 17-year-old is treated as an adult for these purposes (see **D1.63**). If the person is at a police station, consent must be in writing (Code D, para. 4.2). 'Recordable offence' means an offence specified by the Secretary of State in regulations issued under the PACE 1984, s. 27(4), and includes all imprisonable offences and certain non-imprisonable offences (and see Code D, Note for Guidance 4A). The reference to a person 'detained at a police station' is assumed to be a reference to a person in 'police detention' (see **D1.40**).

The power under s. 61(6A)–(6C) to take the fingerprints of a person who has not been arrested is not confined to circumstances where the person is suspected of a recordable offence. Furthermore, since the absence of an arrest is not a precondition, the power could be used to take the fingerprints of a person who has been arrested for a non-recordable offence provided that one of the conditions in s. 61(6B) is satisfied (and see Code D, Note for Guidance 4C). Although fingerprints taken under s. 61(6A) are not regarded as being taken in the course of the investigation of an offence (s. 61(6C)), they can be used for the purpose of a speculative search (s. 63A(1ZA)).

Footwear Impressions The taking of footwear impressions in connection with a criminal **D1.107** investigation is governed by the PACE 1984, s. 61A, and Code D, sect. 4(C). 'Footwear' is not defined in the PACE 1984, nor in Code D.

Police and Criminal Evidence Act 1984, s. 61A

(1) Except as provided by this section, no impression of a person's footwear may be taken without the appropriate consent.

(2) Consent to the taking of an impression of a person's footwear must be in writing if it is given at a time when he is at a police station.

(3) Where a person is detained at a police station, an impression of his footwear may be taken without the appropriate consent if—
  (a) he is detained in consequence of his arrest for a recordable offence, or has been charged with a recordable offence, or informed that he will be reported for a recordable offence; and
  (b) he has not had an impression taken of his footwear in the course of the investigation of the offence by the police.

(4) Where a person mentioned in paragraph (a) of subsection (3) above has already had an impression taken of his footwear in the course of the investigation of the offence by the police, that fact shall be disregarded for the purposes of that subsection if the impression of his footwear taken previously is—
  (a) incomplete; or
  (b) is not of sufficient quality to allow satisfactory analysis, comparison or matching (whether in the case in question or generally).

(5) If an impression of a person's footwear is taken at a police station, whether with or without the appropriate consent—
  (a) before it is taken, an officer shall inform him that it may be the subject of a speculative search; and
  (b) the fact that the person has been informed of this possibility shall be recorded as soon as is practicable after the impression has been taken, and if he is detained at a police station, the record shall be made on his custody record.

(6) In a case where, by virtue of subsection (3) above, an impression of a person's footwear is taken without the appropriate consent—
  (a) he shall be told the reason before it is taken; and
  (b) the reason shall be recorded on his custody record as soon as is practicable after the impression is taken.

(7) The power to take an impression of the footwear of a person detained at a police station without the appropriate consent shall be exercisable by any constable.

(8) Nothing in this section applies to any person—

  (a) arrested or detained under the terrorism provisions;

  (b) arrested under an extradition arrest power.

For the meanings of 'appropriate consent', 'recordable offence' and 'detained at a police station', see **D1.106**.

Body Samples and Dental or Skin Impressions

D1.108   The taking of body samples, skin impressions (including footprints) and dental impressions in connection with a criminal investigation is governed by the PACE 1984, ss. 62 and 63, and by Code D, sect. 6 (see **appendix 1**). The powers differ as between intimate and non-intimate samples.

D1.109   **Intimate Samples**   Intimate samples are defined as blood, semen or tissue fluid; urine; pubic hair; dental impressions; and swabs taken from the genitals or pubic hair or from orifices other than the mouth (s. 65(1)). Hair samples (other than pubic hair) are non-intimate, even if plucked with roots for DNA testing, provided that no more are plucked than the person taking the sample reasonably considers to be necessary for a sufficient sample (s. 63A(2)). Section 62 does not apply to the taking of urine and blood samples for the purposes of the RTA 1988, ss. 4 to 11, or the Transport and Works Act 1992, ss. 26 to 38 (see **C5.1** *et seq.*).

D1.110   Police and Criminal Evidence Act 1984, s. 62

(1) Subject to section 63B below an intimate sample may be taken from a person in police detention only—

  (a) if a police officer of at least the rank of inspector authorises it to be taken; and

  (b) if the appropriate consent is given.

(1A) An intimate sample may be taken from a person who is not in police detention but from whom, in the course of the investigation of an offence, two or more non-intimate samples suitable for the same means of analysis have been taken which have proved insufficient—

  (a) if a police officer of at least the rank of inspector authorises it to be taken; and

  (b) if the appropriate consent is given.

(2) An officer may only give an authorisation under subsection (1) or (1A) above if he has reasonable grounds—

  (a) for suspecting the involvement of the person from whom the sample is to be taken in a recordable offence; and

  (b) for believing that the sample will tend to confirm or disprove his involvement.

(2A) An intimate sample may be taken from a person where—

  (a) two or more non-intimate samples suitable for the same means of analysis have been taken from the person under section 63(3E) below (persons convicted of offences outside England and Wales etc) but have proved insufficient;

  (b) a police officer of at least the rank of inspector authorises it to be taken; and

  (c) the appropriate consent is given.

(2B) An officer may only give an authorisation under subsection (2A) above if the officer is satisfied that taking the sample is necessary to assist in the prevention or detection of crime.

(3) An officer may give an authorisation under subsection (1) or (1A) or (2A) above orally or in writing but, if he gives it orally, he shall confirm it in writing as soon as is practicable.

(4) The appropriate consent must be given in writing.

(5) Before an intimate sample is taken from a person, an officer shall inform him of the following—

  (a) the reason for taking the sample;

  (b) the fact that authorisation has been given and the provision of this section under which it has been given; and

  (c) if the sample was taken at a police station, the fact that the sample may be the subject of a speculative search.

(6) The reason referred to in subsection (5)(a) above must include, except in a case where the sample is taken under subsection (2A) above, a statement of the nature of the offence in which it is suspected that the person has been involved.

(7) After an intimate sample has been taken from a person, the following shall be recorded as soon as practicable—

(a) the matters referred to in subsection (5)(a) and (b) above;

(b) if the sample was taken at a police station, the fact that the person has been informed as specified in subsection (5)(c) above; and

(c) the fact that the appropriate consent was given.

(8) If an intimate sample is taken from a person detained at a police station, the matters required to be recorded by subsection (7) above shall be recorded in his custody record.

(9) In the case of an intimate sample which is a dental impression, the sample may be taken from a person only by a registered dentist.

(9A) In the case of any other form of intimate sample, except in the case of a sample of urine, the sample may be taken from a person only by—

(a) a registered medical practitioner; or

(b) a registered health care professional.

(10) Where the appropriate consent to the taking of an intimate sample from a person was refused without good cause, in any proceedings against that person for an offence—

(a) the court, in determining—

(i) whether to commit that person for trial; or

(ii) whether there is a case to answer; and

(aa) a judge, in deciding whether to grant an application made by the accused under paragraph 2 of Schedule 3 to the Crime and Disorder Act 1998 (applications for dismissal); and

(b) the court or jury, in determining whether that person is guilty of the offence charged, may draw such inferences from the refusal as appear proper.

(11) Nothing in this section applies to the taking of a specimen for the purposes of any of the provisions of sections 4 to 11 of the Road Traffic Act 1988 or of sections 26 to 38 of the Transport and Works Act 1992.

(12) Nothing in this section applies to a person arrested or detained under the terrorism provisions; and subsection (1A) shall not apply where the non-intimate samples mentioned in that subsection were taken under paragraph 10 of Schedule 8 to the Terrorism Act 2000.

For the meanings of 'appropriate consent' and 'recordable offence', see **D1.106**, and for 'police detention' see **D1.40**. In addition to the information that must be given under s. 62(5), the person must also be warned of the consequences of refusal under s. 62(10) (Code D, para 6.3(b)).

Non-intimate Samples Non-intimate samples are defined as a sample of hair other than pubic hair; a sample taken from a nail or from under a nail; a swab taken from any part of a person's body other than a part from which a swab taken would be an intimate sample; saliva; or a skin impression (s. 65(1)). Unlike intimate samples, non-intimate samples may be taken without consent in a wide range of circumstances. **D1.111**

Police and Criminal Evidence Act 1984, s. 63 **D1.112**

(1) Except as provided by this section, a non-intimate sample may not be taken from a person without the appropriate consent.

(2) Consent to the taking of a non-intimate sample must be given in writing.

(2A) A non-intimate sample may be taken from a person without the appropriate consent if two conditions are satisfied.

(2B) The first is that the person is in police detention in consequence of his arrest for a recordable offence.

(2C) The second is that—

(a) he has not had a non-intimate sample of the same type and from the same part of the body taken in the course of the investigation of the offence by the police, or

(b) he has had such a sample taken but it proved insufficient.

(3) A non-intimate sample may be taken from a person without the appropriate consent if—

(a) he is being held in custody by the police on the authority of a court; and

(b) an officer of at least the rank of inspector authorises it to be taken without the appropriate consent.

(3ZA) A non-intimate sample may be taken from a person without the appropriate consent if (before or after the coming into force of this subsection) he has been arrested for a recordable offence and released and—

(a) in the case of a person who is on bail, he has not had a non-intimate sample of the same type and from the same part of the body taken from him in the course of the investigation of the offence by the police; or

    (b) in any case, he has had a non-intimate sample taken from him in the course of that investigation but—

        (i) it was not suitable for the same means of analysis, or

        (ii) it proved insufficient, or

        (iii) subsection (3AA) below applies.

(3A) A non-intimate sample may be taken from a person (whether or not he is in police detention or held in custody by the police on the authority of a court) without the appropriate consent if he has been charged with a recordable offence or informed that he will be reported for such an offence and—

    (a) he has not had a non-intimate sample taken from him in the course of the investigation of the offence by the police; or

    (b) he has had a non-intimate sample taken from him in the course of that investigation but—

        (i) it was not suitable for the same means of analysis, or

        (ii) it proved insufficient,

        (iii) subsection (3AA) below applies or

    (c) he has had a non-intimate sample taken from him in the course of that investigation and—

        (i) the sample has been destroyed pursuant to section 64ZA below or any other enactment, and

        (ii) it is disputed, in relation to any proceedings relating to the offence, whether a DNA profile relevant to the proceedings is derived from the sample.

(3AA) This subsection applies where the investigation was discontinued but subsequently resumed, and before the resumption of the investigation—

    (a) any DNA profile derived from the sample was destroyed pursuant to section 63D(3) below, and

    (b) the sample itself was destroyed pursuant to section 63R(4), (5) or (12) below.

(3B) Subject to this section, a non-intimate sample may be taken from a person without the appropriate consent if (before or after the coming into force of this subsection)—

    (a) he has been convicted of a recordable offence, or

    (b) he has been given a caution in respect of a recordable offence which, at the time of the caution, he has admitted, and

either of the conditions mentioned in subsection (3BA) below is met.

(3BA) The conditions referred to in subsection (3B) above are—

    (a) a non-intimate sample has not been taken from the person since he was convicted or cautioned;

    (b) such a sample has been taken from him since then but—

        (i) it was not suitable for the same means of analysis, or

        (ii) it proved insufficient.

(3BB) A non-intimate sample may only be taken as specified in subsection (3B) above with the authorisation of an officer of at least the rank of inspector.

(3BC) An officer may only give an authorisation under subsection (3BB) above if the officer is satisfied that taking the sample is necessary to assist in the prevention or detection of crime.

(3C) A non-intimate sample may also be taken from a person without the appropriate consent if he is a person to whom section 2 of the Criminal Evidence (Amendment) Act 1997 applies (persons detained following acquittal on grounds of insanity or finding of unfitness to plead).

(3D) [Not in force.]

(3E) Subject to this section, a non-intimate sample may be taken without the appropriate consent from a person if—

    (a) under the law in force in a country or territory outside England and Wales the person has been convicted of an offence under that law (whether before or after the coming into force of this subsection and whether or not he has been punished for it);

    (b) the act constituting the offence would constitute a qualifying offence if done in England and Wales (whether or not it constituted such an offence when the person was convicted); and

    (c) either of the conditions mentioned in subsection (3F) below is met.

(3F) The conditions referred to in subsection (3E)(c) above are—

    (a) the person has not had a non-intimate sample taken from him on a previous occasion under subsection (3E) above;

    (b) he has had such a sample taken from him on a previous occasion under that subsection but—

        (i) the sample was not suitable for the same means of analysis, or

        (ii) it proved insufficient.

(3G) A non-intimate sample may only be taken as specified in subsection (3E) above with the authorisation of an officer of at least the rank of inspector.

(3H) An officer may only give an authorisation under subsection (3G) above if the officer is satisfied that taking the sample is necessary to assist in the prevention or detection of crime.

(4) An officer may only give an authorisation under subsection (3) above if he has reasonable grounds—

    (a) for suspecting the involvement of the person from whom the sample is to be taken in a recordable offence; and

    (b) for believing that the sample will tend to confirm or disprove his involvement.

(5) An officer may give an authorisation under subsection (3) above orally or in writing but, if he gives it orally, he shall confirm it in writing as soon as is practicable.

(5A) An officer shall not give an authorisation under subsection (3) above for the taking from any person of a non-intimate sample consisting of a skin impression if—

    (a) a skin impression of the same part of the body has already been taken from that person in the course of the investigation of the offence; and

    (b) the impression previously taken is not one that has proved insufficient.

(6) Where a non-intimate sample is taken from a person without the appropriate consent by virtue of any power conferred by this section—

    (a) before the sample is taken, an officer shall inform him of—

        (i) the reason for taking the sample;

        (ii) the power by virtue of which it is taken; and

        (iii) in a case where the authorisation of an officer is required for the exercise of the power, the fact that the authorisation has been given; and

    (b) those matters shall be recorded as soon as practicable after the sample is taken.

(7) The reason referred to in subsection (6)(a)(i) above must include, except in a case where the non-intimate sample is taken under subsection (3B) or (3E) above, a statement of the nature of the offence in which it is suspected that the person has been involved.

(8B) If a non-intimate sample is taken from a person at a police station, whether with or without the appropriate consent—

    (a) before the sample is taken, an officer shall inform him that it may be the subject of a speculative search; and

    (b) the fact that the person has been informed of this possibility shall be recorded as soon as practicable after the sample has been taken.

(9) If a non-intimate sample is taken from a person detained at a police station, the matters required to be recorded by subsection (6) or (8B) above shall be recorded in his custody record.

(9ZA) The power to take a non-intimate sample from a person without the appropriate consent shall be exercisable by any constable.

(9A) Subsection (3B) above shall not apply to

    (a) any person convicted before 10th April 1995 unless he is a person to whom section 1 of the Criminal Evidence (Amendment) Act 1997 applies (persons imprisoned or detained by virtue of pre-existing conviction for sexual offence etc.); or

    (b) a person given a caution before 10th April 1995.

(10) Nothing in this section applies to a person arrested or detained under the terrorism provisions.

(11) Nothing in this section applies to a person arrested under an extradition arrest power.

The ABCPA 2014, s. 144, in force from 13 May 2014, added a power to take a non-intimate sample under s. 63(3ZA) and (3A) where an investigation is discontinued, and subsequently resumed, but before resumption any DNA profile derived from a sample was destroyed pursuant to s. 63D(3) and the sample itself was destroyed pursuant to s. 63R(4), (5) or (12).

For the meanings of 'appropriate consent' and 'recordable offence', see **D1.106**, and for 'police detention' see **D1.40**. A 'qualifying offence' for the purpose of s. 63(3E) is defined in s. 65A (as amended, *inter alia*, by the Police and Criminal Evidence Act 1984 (Amendment: Qualifying Offences) Order 2013 (2013 No. 2774)), and includes certain violent, sexual or terrorist offences, or inchoate versions thereof. For skin impressions consisting of ear-prints see *Kempster* [2008] 2 Cr App R 256, and **F18.37**.

Speculative Searches

Under the PACE 1984, s. 63A, fingerprints, impressions of footwear, samples or the information   **D1.113** derived from samples may be used for the purpose of speculative searches as prescribed in that section.

Police and Criminal Evidence Act 1984, s. 63A

(1) Where a person has been arrested on suspicion of being involved in a recordable offence or has been charged with such an offence or has been informed that he will be reported for such an

offence, fingerprints, impressions of footwear or samples or the information derived from samples taken under any power conferred by this Part of this Act from the person may be checked against—

    (a)   other fingerprints, impressions of footwear or samples to which the person seeking to check has access and which are held by or on behalf of any one or more relevant law-enforcement authorities or which are held in connection with or as a result of an investigation of an offence;

    (b)   information derived from other samples if the information is contained in records to which the person seeking to check has access and which are held as mentioned in paragraph (a) above.

(1ZA) Fingerprints taken by virtue of section 61(6A) above may be checked against other fingerprints to which the person seeking to check has access and which are held by or on behalf of any one or more relevant law-enforcement authorities or which are held in connection with or as a result of an investigation of an offence.

(1A) In subsection (1) and (1ZA) above 'relevant law-enforcement authority' means–

    (a)   a police force;

    (b)   the National Crime Agency;

    (d)   a public authority (not falling within paragraphs (a) to (c)) with functions in any part of the British Islands which consist of or include the investigation of crimes or the charging of offenders;

    (e)   any person with functions in any country or territory outside the United Kingdom which–

        (i)   correspond to those of a police force; or

        (ii)   otherwise consist of or include the investigation of conduct contrary to the law of that country or territory, or the apprehension of persons guilty of such conduct;

    (f)   any person with functions under any international agreement which consist of or include the investigation of conduct which is–

        (i)   unlawful under the law of one or more places,

        (ii)   prohibited by such an agreement, or

        (iii)   contrary to international law,

    or the apprehension of persons guilty of such conduct.

(1B) The reference in subsection (1A) above to a police force is a reference to any of the following–

...

(1C) Where–

    (a)   fingerprints, impressions of footwear or samples have been taken from any person in connection with the investigation of an offence but otherwise than in circumstances to which subsection (1) above applies, and

    (b)   that person has given his consent in writing to the use in a speculative search of the fingerprints, of the impressions of footwear or of the samples and of information derived from them,

the fingerprints or impressions of footwear or, as the case may be, those samples and that information may be checked against any of the fingerprints, impressions of footwear, samples or information mentioned in paragraph (a) or (b) of that subsection.

(1D) A consent given for the purposes of subsection (1C) above shall not be capable of being withdrawn.

(1E) Where fingerprints or samples have been taken from any person under section 61(6) or 63(3B) above (persons convicted etc), the fingerprints or samples, or information derived from the samples, may be checked against any of the fingerprints, samples or information mentioned in subsection (1)(a) or (b) above.

(1F) Where fingerprints or samples have been taken from any person under section 61(6D), 62(2A) or 63(3E) above (offences outside England and Wales etc), the fingerprints or samples, or information derived from the samples, may be checked against any of the fingerprints, samples or information mentioned in subsection (1)(a) or (b) above.

...

For the meaning of 'recordable offence', see **D1.106**.

Powers to Require Attendance at Police Station

D1.114   The PACE 1984, s. 63A(4) and sch. 2A, replacing more limited powers in the PACE 1984, s. 63A(4)–(8), contain powers to require attendance at a police station for the purpose of taking fingerprints and samples.

Police and Criminal Evidence Act 1984, sch. 2A   D1.115
PART I
FINGERPRINTING

Persons arrested and released

1.—(1) A constable may require a person to attend a police station for the purpose of taking his fingerprints under section 61(5A).

(2) The power under sub-paragraph (1) above may not be exercised in a case falling within section 61(5A)(b)(i) (fingerprints taken on previous occasion insufficient etc.) after the end of the period of six months beginning with the day on which the appropriate officer was informed that section 61(3A)(a) or (b) applied.

(3) In sub-paragraph (2) above 'appropriate officer' means the officer investigating the offence for which the person was arrested.

(4) The power under sub-paragraph (1) above may not be exercised in a case falling within section 61(5A)(b)(ii) (fingerprints destroyed where investigation interrupted) after the end of the period of six months beginning with the day on which the investigation was resumed.

Persons charged etc

2.—(1) A constable may require a person to attend a police station for the purpose of taking his fingerprints under section 61(5B).

(2) The power under sub-paragraph (1) above may not be exercised after the end of the period of six months beginning with—
 (a) in a case falling within section 61(5B)(a) (fingerprints not taken previously), the day on which the person was charged or informed that he would be reported, or
 (b) in a case falling within section 61(5B)(b)(i) (fingerprints taken on previous occasion insufficient etc.), the day on which the appropriate officer was informed that section 61(3A)(a) or (b) applied, or
 (c) in a case falling within section 61(5B)(b)(ii) (fingerprints destroyed where investigation interrupted), the day on which the investigation was resumed.

(3) In sub-paragraph (2)(b) above 'appropriate officer' means the officer investigating the offence for which the person was charged or informed that he would be reported.

Persons convicted etc. of an offence in England and Wales

3.—(1) A constable may require a person to attend a police station for the purpose of taking his fingerprints under section 61(6).

(2) Where the condition in section 61(6ZA)(a) is satisfied (fingerprints not taken previously), the power under sub-paragraph (1) above may not be exercised after the end of the period of two years beginning with—
 (a) the day on which the person was convicted or cautioned or
 (b) if later, the day on which this schedule comes into force.

(3) Where the condition in section 61(6ZA)(b) is satisfied (fingerprints taken on previous occasion insufficient etc.), the power under sub-paragraph (1) above may not be exercised after the end of the period of two years beginning with—
 (a) the day on which an appropriate officer was informed that section 61(3A)(a) or (b) applied, or
 (b) if later, the day on which this Schedule comes into force.

(4) In sub-paragraph (3)(a) above 'appropriate officer' means an officer of the police force which investigated the offence in question.

(5) Sub-paragraphs (2) and (3) above do not apply where the offence is a qualifying offence (whether or not it was such an offence at the time of the conviction or caution).

4. [Repealed.]

Persons convicted etc. of an offence outside England and Wales

5. A constable may require a person to attend a police station for the purpose of taking his fingerprints under section 61(6D).

Multiple attendance

6.—(1) Where a person's fingerprints have been taken under section 61 on two occasions in relation to any offence, he may not under this schedule be required to attend a police station to have his fingerprints taken under that section in relation to that offence on a subsequent occasion without the authorisation of an officer of at least the rank of inspector.

(2) Where an authorisation is given under sub-paragraph (1) above—
 (a) the fact of the authorisation, and
 (b) the reasons for giving it,
shall be recorded as soon as practicable after it has been given.

PART 2

INTIMATE SAMPLES

Persons suspected to be involved in an offence

7. A constable may require a person to attend a police station for the purpose of taking an intimate sample from him under section 62(1A) if, in the course of the investigation of an offence, two or more non-intimate samples suitable for the same means of analysis have been taken from him but have proved insufficient.

Persons convicted etc. of an offence outside England and Wales

8. A constable may require a person to attend a police station for the purpose of taking a sample from him under section 62(2A) if two or more non-intimate samples suitable for the same means of analysis have been taken from him under section 63(3E) but have proved insufficient.

PART 3

NON-INTIMATE SAMPLES

Persons arrested and released

9.—(1) A constable may require a person to attend a police station for the purpose of taking a non-intimate sample from him under section 63(3ZA).

(2) The power under sub-paragraph (1) above may not be exercised in a case falling within section 63(3ZA)(b)(i) or (ii) (sample taken on a previous occasion not suitable etc.) after the end of the period of six months beginning with the day on which the appropriate officer was informed of the matters specified in section 63(3ZA)(b)(i) or (ii).

(3) In sub-paragraph (2) above, 'appropriate officer' means the officer investigating the offence for which the person was arrested.

(4) The power under sub-paragraph (1) above may not be exercised in a case falling within section 63(3ZA)(b)(iii) (sample, and any DNA profile, destroyed where investigation interrupted) after the end of the period of six months beginning with the day on which the investigation was resumed.

Persons charged etc.

10.—(1) A constable may require a person to attend a police station for the purpose of taking a non-intimate sample from him under section 63(3A).

(2) The power under sub-paragraph (1) above may not be exercised in a case falling within section 63(3A)(a) (sample not taken previously) after the end of the period of six months beginning with the day on which he was charged or informed that he would be reported.

(3) The power under sub-paragraph (1) above may not be exercised in a case falling within section 63(3A)(b)(i) or (ii) (sample taken on a previous occasion not suitable etc.) after the end of the period of six months beginning with the day on which the appropriate officer was informed of the matters specified in section 63(3A)(b)(i) or (ii).

(4) In sub-paragraph (3) above 'appropriate officer' means the officer investigating the offence for which the person was charged or informed that he would be reported.

(5) The power under sub-paragraph (1) above may not be exercised in a case falling within section 63(3A)(b)(iii) (sample, and any DNA profile, destroyed where investigation interrupted) after the end of the period of six months beginning with the day on which the investigation was resumed.

Persons convicted etc. of an offence in England and Wales

11.—(1) A constable may require a person to attend a police station for the purpose of taking a non-intimate sample from him under section 63(3B).

(2) Where the condition in section 63(3BA)(a) is satisfied (sample not taken previously), the power under sub-paragraph (1) above may not be exercised after the end of the period of two years beginning with—

(a) the day on which the person was convicted or cautioned, or

(b) if later, the day on which this schedule comes into force.

(3) Where the condition in section 63(3BA)(b) is satisfied (sample taken on a previous occasion not suitable etc.), the power under sub-paragraph (1) above may not be exercised after the end of the period of two years beginning with—

(a) the day on which an appropriate officer was informed of the matters specified in section 63(3BA)(b)(i) or (ii), or

(b) if later, the day on which this schedule comes into force.

(4) In sub-paragraph (3)(a) above 'appropriate officer' means an officer of the police force which investigated the offence in question.

(5) Sub-paragraphs (2) and (3) above do not apply where—
(a) the offence is a qualifying offence (whether or not it was such an offence at the time of the conviction or caution), or
(b) he was convicted before 10th April 1995 and is a person to whom section 1 of the Criminal Evidence (Amendment) Act 1997 applies.

12. [Repealed.]

Persons convicted etc. of an offence outside England and Wales

13. A constable may require a person to attend a police station for the purpose of taking a non-intimate sample from him under section 63(3E).

Multiple exercise of power

14.—(1) Where a non-intimate sample has been taken from a person under section 63 on two occasions in relation to any offence, he may not under this schedule be required to attend a police station to have another such sample taken from him under that section in relation to that offence on a subsequent occasion without the authorisation of an officer of at least the rank of inspector.
(2) Where an authorisation is given under sub-paragraph (1) above—
(a) the fact of the authorisation, and
(b) the reasons for giving it, shall be recorded as soon as practicable after it has been given.

PART 4
GENERAL AND SUPPLEMENTARY

Requirement to have power to take fingerprints or sample

15. A power conferred by this schedule to require a person to attend a police station for the purposes of taking fingerprints or a sample under any provision of this Act may be exercised only in a case where the fingerprints or sample may be taken from the person under that provision (and, in particular, if any necessary authorisation for taking the fingerprints or sample under that provision has been obtained).

Date and time of attendance

16.—(1) A requirement under this schedule—
(a) shall give the person a period of at least seven days within which he must attend the police station; and
(b) may direct him so to attend at a specified time of day or between specified times of day.
(2) In specifying a period or time or times of day for the purposes of sub-paragraph (1) above, the constable shall consider whether the fingerprints or sample could reasonably be taken at a time when the person is for any other reason required to attend the police station.
(3) A requirement under this schedule may specify a period shorter than seven days if—
(a) there is an urgent need for the fingerprints or sample for the purposes of the investigation of an offence; and
(b) the shorter period is authorised by an officer of at least the rank of inspector.
(4) Where an authorisation is given under sub-paragraph (3)(b) above—
(a) the fact of the authorisation, and
(b) the reasons for giving it, shall be recorded as soon as practicable after it has been given.
(5) If the constable giving a requirement under this Schedule and the person to whom it is given so agree, it may be varied so as to specify any period within which, or date or time at which, the person must attend; but a variation shall not have effect unless confirmed by the constable in writing.

Enforcement

17. A constable may arrest without warrant a person who has failed to comply with a requirement under this schedule.

The ABCPA 2014, sch. 11, para. 86, in force from 13 May 2014, amended the PACE 1984, sch. 2A, enabling a police constable to require a person to attend a police station for the purpose of taking fingerprints or a non-intimate sample in circumstances governed by the amended s. 61(5A) or (5B), and s. 63 (3ZA) or (3A) (see **D1.105** and **D1.112**).

D1.116 Where a person is required under sch. 2A to attend a police station for the purpose of having fingerprints or samples taken he must be given be given at least seven days' notice unless there is an urgent need for them to be taken for the purposes of an investigation (Code D, annex G). A non-intimate sample may be taken under s. 63(3B) only if it is authorised by an officer of at least the rank of inspector, and a requirement to attend in order to provide such a sample under sch. 2A, para. 11, is unlawful if the demand was made before authorisation was given (*R (R) v A Chief Constable* [2014] 1 Cr App R 222 (16)). A person arrested under sch. 2A, para. 17, and taken to a police station is not in police detention (see **D1.40**). Paragraph 17 permits a constable to arrest a person for failing to attend a police station for the purpose of taking an intimate sample under sch. 2A, paras. 7 or 8, despite the fact that such a sample can only be taken with appropriate consent (see **D1.106**); although refusal to consent could result in inferences under s. 62(10).

Retention or Destruction of Biometric Data

D1.117 Provisions governing the retention and destruction of fingerprints, footwear impressions, and samples, and information derived from samples, are set out in the PACE 1984, ss. 63D to 63U, as inserted by the Protection of Freedoms Act 2012, part 1 and amended with effect from 13 May 2014 by the ABCPA 2014, ss. 145 and 146. For a detailed examination of these provisions see E. Cape, 'The Protection of Freedoms Act 2012: The Retention and Use of Biometric Data Provisions' [2013] Crim LR 23. For the use in evidence of biometric data, see **F18.27** *et seq.*

POWERS TO PHOTOGRAPH SUSPECTS

D1.118 Powers to take, retain and use photographs are governed by the PACE 1984, s. 64A(1), which provides that a person detained at a police station (see **D1.106**) may be photographed with the appropriate consent (see **D1.106**), or without such consent if it is withheld or it is not practicable to obtain it. Section 64A(1A) gives power to the police to photograph a person other than at a police station where that person has been: (a) arrested by a constable; (b) taken into custody by a constable after being arrested by a person other than a constable; (c) made the subject of a requirement to wait with a community support officer under the Police Reform Act 2002, sch. 4, paras. 2(3) or (3B); (d) been given a direction by a constable under the VCRA 2006, s. 27 (once the ABCPA 2014, sch. 11, para. 4, is in force, given a direction under s. 35 of the 2014 Act); or (e) been given a notice under various provisions set out in s. 64A(1B)(d)–(g) which relate to penalty notices and fixed penalty offences. Again, the power may be exercised with appropriate consent or without it if it is withheld or it is not practicable to obtain it (s. 64A(1A)). References to taking a photograph include references to using any process by means of which a visual image may be produced, and include a moving image (s. 64A(6) and (6A)). The powers to take photographs of persons detained in a police station or elsewhere are also governed by Code D, paras. 5.12 to 5.18, and powers to photograph persons at a police station but who are not detained (i.e. those who are voluntarily at a police station) are set out in paras. 5.19 to 5.24. Taking and retaining photographs of persons who have not been arrested may amount to a breach of the ECHR, Article 8 (*Mengesha v Commissioner of Police for the Metropolis* [2013] EWHC 1695 (Admin)).

D1.119 The particular relevance of the statutory power to take photographs is that the police may use force in order to take them. In addition to their general powers to use force under the PACE 1984, s. 117 (see **D1.7**), s. 64A(2) provides that for the purpose of taking a photograph the police may require the removal of any item or substance worn on or over the whole or any part of the head or face of the person, and may remove the item or substance if the requirement is not complied with. Force may not be used in connection with taking the photograph of a person who is voluntarily at a police station (Code D, para. 5.21).

A photograph taken under s. 64A may be used by, or disclosed to, any person for any purpose related to the prevention or detection of crime, the investigation of an offence, or the conduct of a prosecution, or to the enforcement of any sentence (s. 64A(4)(a)). After being so used or disclosed, the photograph may be retained but may not be used or disclosed except for a purpose so related (s. 64A(4)(b)). In *R (RMC and FJ) v Metropolitan Police Commissioner* [2012] 4 All ER 510, the Divisional Court concluded that the law and guidance currently in force (see the National Policing Improvement Agency Code of Practice and Guidance on the Management of Police Information) failed to strike a fair balance between competing public and private interests or meet the requirements of proportionality, and was objectionable for the same reasons as those that led to the judgment of the ECtHR in *S v United Kingdom* (2009) 48 EHRR 1169.

In particular, no adequate distinction was drawn between those convicted and those who were not charged or not convicted.

The search or examination of a suspect with a view to finding and, if necessary, photographing, any distinguishing marks or injuries is governed by the PACE 1984, s. 54A, and Code D, paras. 5.1 to 5.11 (see **D1.98**).

DRUG TESTING FOR CLASS A DRUGS

The power to test for Class A drugs is governed by the PACE 1984 s. 63B, supplemented by s. 63C, and by Code C, sect. 17. **D1.120**

Where a person is in police detention (see **D1.40**), a sample of urine or a non-intimate sample may be taken from him for the purpose of ascertaining whether he has any specified Class A drug in his body provided that he has been brought before a custody officer (s. 63B(5D)) and the following conditions are satisfied:

(a) either the arrest condition or the charge condition is met;
(b) both the age condition and the request condition are met; and
(c) the notification condition is met in relation to the arrest condition, the charge condition or the age condition (as relevant) (s. 63B(1)(a)–(c)).

The Arrest and Charge Conditions

The 'arrest condition' is satisfied if the suspect has been arrested for, but not charged with, a trigger offence or any offence where an inspector or above, having reasonable grounds for suspecting that the misuse by that person of any specified Class A drug caused or contributed to the offence, authorises a sample to be taken (PACE 1984, s. 63B(1A)). The 'charge condition' is satisfied if the suspect has been charged with a trigger offence or any offence where an inspector or above, having reasonable grounds for suspecting that the misuse by that person of any specified Class A drug caused or contributed to the offence, authorises a sample to be taken (s. 63B(2)). If a sample is taken on the basis that the arrest condition was satisfied, no further sample can be taken under s. 63B during the same continuous period of detention unless the suspect remains in police detention in respect of another offence in respect of which the arrest condition is satisfied (s. 63B(5B) and (5C); Code C, para. 17.9). A 'specified' Class A drug has the same meaning as in the CJCSA 2000, part III. The term 'trigger offence' is defined in the CJCSA 2000, sch. 6, and the offences are conveniently set out in Code C, Note for Guidance 17E (see **appendix 1**). **D1.121**

The Age and Request Conditions

Where the arrest condition is met, the 'age condition' is that the person has attained the age of 18; where the charge condition is met, the 'age condition' is that the person has attained the age of 14 (PACE 1984, s. 63B(3)). The 'request condition' is simply that a police officer has requested the suspect to give the sample (s. 63B(4)). Before requesting a sample the suspect must be warned that failure without good cause to provide the sample requested renders him liable to prosecution (s. 63B(5); Code C, Note for Guidance 17A). He must also be told the purpose of taking the sample, that authorisation has been given (where required), and his right to have someone informed of his arrest, to obtain legal advice and to consult the Codes of Practice (Code C, para. 17.6). Where the suspect is a juvenile, the making of the request, the warning that refusal may amount to an offence, and the taking of a sample must be in the presence of an appropriate adult (s. 63B(5A); Code C, para. 17.7). **D1.122**

The Notification Condition

The 'notification condition' is that the relevant chief officer has been notified by the Secretary of State that appropriate arrangements have been made for the police area as a whole, or for the particular police station in which the suspect is in police detention (PACE 1984, s. 63B(4A)). All police forces are permitted to introduce drug-testing, although not all forces have done so. **D1.123**

The authorisation and grounds for suspicion (where authorisation is required), the warning as to the consequences of refusal, and the time at which the sample is given, must be recorded in the custody record (s. 63C(3) and (4); Code C, para. 17.2).

Failure without good cause to provide a sample is an offence punishable, on summary conviction, with up to three months' imprisonment and/or a fine not exceeding level 4 (ss. 63B(8) and 63C(1)). If the suspect does refuse to provide a sample, the police cannot use force to obtain one (Code C, para. 17.14).

Detention for the Purposes of Drug-testing

D1.124 Where a person has been arrested for a relevant offence (see **D1.121**), he may be detained for up to 24 hours from the relevant time (see **D1.68**) in order for a sample to be taken even though the custody officer would otherwise have decided that the suspect should be released on bail under the PACE 1984, s. 37(2) (bail without charge), s. 37(7)(a)(i) (release without charge and on bail with a view to the CPS making the charge decision), or s. 37(7)(b) (release without charge and on bail but not for that purpose) (s. 37(8A) and (8B); Code C, para. 17.10). Where the arrest condition (but not the charge condition) is satisfied in respect of one offence (offence 1) and the suspect's release would be required before a sample could be taken but for his continued detention in respect of an offence that does not satisfy the arrest condition (offence 2), the suspect may have a sample taken whilst he continues to be detained provided that it is taken within 24 hours of his arrest for offence 1 (s. 63B(5C); Code C, para. 17.10). Thus, if a person is charged with an offence that did satisfy the arrest condition, and a sample could not be taken before he was charged, but he continues to be detained in respect of an offence that does not satisfy the arrest condition, a sample may be taken during that period of further detention, provided that it is taken within 24 hours of the arrest for the first offence. Where a sample may be taken from a person under s. 63B, but he is charged before a sample is taken and the custody officer would otherwise release him on bail under s. 38, the custody officer may authorise his detention for up to six hours from the time of charge in order for a sample to be taken (s. 38(1)(a)(iiia) and (2); Code C, para. 17.10).

Consequences of a Positive Drug-Test

D1.125 Where a suspect aged 18 years or older has tested positive for a specified Class A drug under the PACE 1984, s. 63B, the police may, before the suspect is released, impose a requirement that he attend an initial assessment of his drug misuse and remain for the duration of the assessment. Where the suspect is tested prior to charge, the requirement can be imposed even if the suspect is not subsequently charged with an offence. Failure to attend or to remain at the assessment is an offence carrying imprisonment up to three months and/or a fine not exceeding level 4 (Drugs Act 2005, s. 12(3) and (4); Code C, para. 17.17). When such a requirement is imposed the suspect must be told of the time and place for the assessment and be warned that failure without good cause to attend and to remain renders him liable for prosecution (Code C, para. 17.18). The suspect must also be given a written notice containing this information (Code C, para. 17.19) and the process must be entered in the custody record (Code C, para. 17.20). There are also provisions (in police stations where the chief officer has been notified by the Secretary of State that follow-up assessment arrangements are available) to require a person who is required to attend an initial assessment also to attend a follow-up assessment, and there are similar provisions regarding enforcement (Drugs Act 2005, ss. 10 to 12 and Code C, paras. 17.17 to 17.20).

D1.126 A sample taken under s. 63B may be disclosed only for the purposes set out in s. 63B(7). Although it must be retained until the person has made his first appearance at court (Code C, para. 17.16(b)), it cannot be used for the purpose of prosecuting for an offence, other than those offences mentioned in s. 63B(7). The purposes are:

(a) for the purpose of informing a decision as to bail, whether by the police or by a court (s. 63B(7)(a));

(b) for the purpose of informing a decision about the imposition of a conditional caution (s. 63B(7)(aa));
(c) for the purpose of informing any decision about the supervision of the person in police detention, in custody or on bail (s. 63B(7)(b));
(d) following conviction, for the purpose of informing any decision about sentence, and any decision about supervision or release (s. 63B(7)(c));
(e) for the purpose of a drugs assessment which the suspect is required to attend by the police by virtue of the Drugs Act 2005, s. 9(2) (initial assessment) or s. 10(2) (follow-up assessment) (s. 63B(7)(ca));
(f) for the purposes of a prosecution under the Drugs Act 2005, s. 12(3) (for failure to attend or remain at an initial assessment), or s. 24(3) (for failure to attend or remain at a follow-up assessment) (s. 63B(7)(cb));
(g) for the purpose of ensuring that appropriate advice and treatment is made available to the person concerned (s. 63B(7)(d)).

VISUAL IDENTIFICATION AND RECOGNITION PROCEDURES

D1.127 Visual identification and recognition procedures are governed by PACE Code D (see **D1.1**). In a departure from previous versions, the current version of Code D, sect. 3, distinguishes between identification of a suspect by an eye-witness (sect. 3(A)), and recognition by showing films, photographs and other images (sect. 3(B)), and sets out different procedures to be followed in accordance with that distinction. For the evidential implications of failure by the police to comply with relevant identification procedures, see **F18.4**. It has been held that Code D was not designed to apply to situations in which the police seek to connect a suspect with events that occurred many years previously, when his appearance was markedly different (*Folan* [2003] EWCA Crim 908). Code D makes no reference to identification procedures after charge, although it was implied in *Joseph* [1994] Crim LR 48 that this is permissible.

Identification or Recognition

D1.128 Code D, para 3.0, states that sect. 3(A) applies when an eye-witness has seen the offender committing the crime or in any other circumstances which tend to prove or disprove the involvement of the person he saw in the crime. Section 3(A) sets out the procedures to be used to test the ability of that eye-witness to identify a person suspected of involvement in the offence as the person he saw on the previous occasion (see **D1.130** *et seq.*). Section 3(B), on the other hand, sets out the procedure to be followed when, for the purposes of obtaining evidence of recognition, any person (including a police officer) views the image of another person in a film, photograph or other visual medium, and is asked whether he recognises that individual as someone who is known to him (Code D, para. 3.34). Note for Guidance 3AA states that the procedure in sect. 3(A) should not be used to test whether a witness can recognise a person as someone he knows and where he would be able to give evidence of recognition along the lines of 'On (describe date, time, location) I saw an image of an individual whom I recognised as AB'. In such cases, the note states, the procedures in sect. 3(B) should be used. The Note for Guidance is confusing since it does not adequately distinguish between (a) an eye-witness (in the sense described in Code D, para. 3.0) who may be able to identify the offender, (b) an eye-witness who purports to have recognised the offender and (c) a person who is not an eye-witness but who may be able to identify an offender from a visual image. It is clear that Code D, sect. 3(A) applies to a person in category (a) and that sect. 3(B) applies to a person in category (c). The Note for Guidance suggests that the procedures under sect. 3(B) also apply to a person in category (b), but this is contrary to some of the relevant case law and may result in unfairness; an identification procedure under sect. 3(A) may usefully test whether an uncertain recognition by an eye-witness is accurate, whereas applying the procedures under sect. 3(B) cannot.

D1.129   The case law on the distinction between identification and recognition (and thus on the question of whether an identification procedure should be conducted) has not always been consistent. If a witness clearly knows the person suspected of committing a crime and is able to name him, an identification procedure would not be mandatory (*H v DPP* [2003] EWHC 133 (Admin)). However, if the recognition is less certain, the courts have held that an identification procedure should be held. See, e.g., *Fergus* [1992] Crim LR 363, where the witness had only seen the suspect once before and had been told his name by a third party (see also *Byrne* [2004] EWCA Crim 979; and cf. *France* [2012] UKPC 28). Further, it has been held that an identification procedure should have been held, even though the witness named the suspect, where the latter disputed the purported recognition (*Conway* (1990) 91 Cr App R 143; *Harris* [2003] EWCA Crim 174). However, police officers who view CCTV footage to see if they might recognise a person are not in the same position as a witness asked to identify someone seen committing a crime (*Smith* [2009] 1 Cr App R 521; *Chaney* [2009] 1 Cr App R 512; *Moss* [2011] EWCA Crim 252; and see **D1.143**).

Identification of a Suspect by an Eye-witness

D1.130   In all potential identification cases, Code D, para. 3.1, requires a record to be made of the description of the 'suspect' (meaning the person allegedly seen at the scene of the crime etc.) as first given by the witness. This must, where practicable, be disclosed to the 'suspect' or his solicitor before any identification procedures are undertaken. The procedure to be followed depends upon whether or not there is a 'known' suspect. References to a suspect being 'known' mean there is sufficient information known to the police to justify the arrest of a particular person for suspected involvement in the offence under investigation (Code D, para. 3.4). In *Preddie* [2011] EWCA Crim 312 a street identification of suspects who had already been arrested on the basis that they fitted the description given by the witness was held to be a breach of Code D.

D1.131   **Procedures Where the Suspect is Not Known**   Where a suspect's identity is not known, Code D, paras. 3.2 and 3.3, allow witnesses to be taken to a particular neighbourhood or place, or to be shown photographs or other visual images, to see whether they can recognise the offender. Paragraph 3.2 governs the procedures to be followed where a witness is taken to a particular neighbourhood or place to see whether he can identify the person whom he saw on the relevant occasion. Whilst the features of the people seen by the witness cannot be controlled, para. 3.2 states that the principles applicable to the formal identification procedures should be followed as far as practicable.

The showing of photographs must be done in accordance with Code D, annex E (Code D, para. 3.3). Once one witness has made a positive identification from photographs then, unless the person identified can be eliminated from the inquiry, no further witnesses should be shown photographs; instead, a video identification or parade etc. should be arranged unless there is no dispute about the suspect's identification. Similarly, if the use of other visual images points to a known suspect who can be asked to participate in an identification procedure, the likeness must not then be shown to other witnesses (annex E, paras. 6 and 8).

Code D does not prevent the showing of films, photographs or other visual images to the public through national or local media, or to police officers for the purposes of recognition and tracing suspects. However, when such material is shown to obtain evidence of recognition, the procedures in sect. 3(B) apply (para. 3.28, and see **D1.128**). The procedures to be followed when a broadcast or publication is made are set out in para. 3.29. For guidance where a complainant identified a suspect via Facebook prior to reporting the offence to the police, see *Alexander* [2013] 1 Cr App R 334 (26).

D1.132   **Procedures Where the Suspect is Known**   Where a suspect is 'known' (see **D1.130**), the procedure to be followed depends upon whether the suspect is 'available'. A suspect is 'available' if he is immediately available or will be within a reasonably short time and is willing to take an effective part in a video identification, identification parade or group identification which it is practicable to arrange (para. 3.4). A suspect may be available even if not under arrest provided he is likely to be arrested, or will otherwise be available (e.g., by agreeing to attend a video identification voluntarily) in the near future. If a suspect who is 'known' refuses the identification procedure which is proposed by the police, he (or his solicitor or appropriate adult) may make representations as to why another procedure should be used. The identification officer (see D1.136) 'shall, if appropriate,' arrange for him to be offered a suitable and practicable alternative. The words 'if appropriate' indicate that the police need not give in to objections that appear to be merely obstructive, misguided or petulant. If for any reason the identification officer decides that it is not suitable and practicable to offer an alternative procedure, the reasons for that decision must be recorded (para. 3.15). If the consent of the suspect cannot be obtained he may, in effect, be treated as not being available.

D1.133 If a suspect is known but not available, the identification officer may make arrangements for a video identification or a group identification if this is practicable (para. 3.21). If not practicable, he may make arrangements for a confrontation by the witness (para. 3.23). Force may not be used in order to facilitate an identification procedure where the suspect attempts to hide his face (see *Jones* (1999) *The Times*, 26 March 1999, and Code D, annex D, para. 3) but, where there are reasonable grounds to suspect that, if forewarned, the suspect would take steps to avoid being identified, para. 3.20 permits the identification officer to arrange for images to be obtained for use in a video identification procedure before the usual information and notice is given to the suspect under paras. 3.17 and 3.18.

If a suspect is known and available, Code D, para. 3.4, provides that a video identification, identification parade or group identification 'may' be used (para. 3.4). However, this should be read subject to para 3.12, which sets out the circumstances in which such a procedure must be held, as follows:

(a) where an eye-witness has identified or purported to have identified a suspect; or there is a witness who expresses an ability to identify the suspect, or where there is a reasonable chance of the witness being able to do so; and
(b) the suspect disputes being the person the witness claims to have seen;
(c) an identification procedure must be held unless it is not practicable or it would serve no useful purpose in proving or disproving whether the suspect was involved in committing the offence.

An identification procedure may also be held if the officer in charge of the investigation considers that this would be useful (para. 3.13).

The term 'suspect' in para. 3.12 is, unfortunately, used to convey two different meanings: in (a) above it refers to the person that the witness says he saw committing the crime etc.; in (b) and (c) above it refers to the person who is now under arrest or is otherwise suspected of having committed the offence, and who is asked to participate in the identification procedure.

D1.134 Whether a witness expresses an ability to identify the suspect or there is a reasonable chance of him being able to do so is, of course, a matter of fact, but it is suggested that the police should err on the side of caution.

> If an eyewitness of a criminal incident makes plain to the police that he cannot identify the culprit, it will very probably be futile to invite that witness to attend an identification [procedure]. If an eyewitness may be able to identify clothing worn by a culprit, but not the culprit himself, it will probably be futile to mount an identification [procedure] rather than simply inviting the witness to identify the clothing. If a case is one of pure recognition of someone well known to the eyewitness, it may again be futile to hold an identification [procedure]. But save in cases such as these, or other exceptional circumstances, the effect of [Code D] is clear: if (a) the police have sufficient information to justify the arrest of a particular person for suspected involvement in an offence, and (b) an eyewitness has identified or may be able to identify that person, and (c) the suspect disputes his identification as a person involved in the commission of that offence, an identification [procedure] must be held.... (*Forbes* [2001] 1 AC 473 at p. 486, per Lord Bingham)

Code D was revised after the decision in *Forbes* so that an identification procedure does not have to be held if it would serve no useful purpose. However, it was held in *Callie* [2009] EWCA Crim 283 that this does not permit the police to carry out a proportionality exercise.

The relevant question is whether an identification procedure might produce relevant evidence. Thus, for example, the fact that one witness has made a positive identification does not mean that inviting other witnesses to view an identification procedure would serve no useful purpose (*Gojra* [2010] EWCA Crim 1939).

Whether the suspect disputes being the person the witness claims to have seen should normally be straightforward. It would include circumstances where the suspect admits being at the scene but denies being involved in the offence (*Hope* [1994] Crim LR 118; *K* [2003] EWHC 351 (QB)). However, it does not include circumstances where the suspect merely disagrees with his level of involvement in an alleged offence.

D1.135 Given the availability of the video identification procedure, cases where an identification procedure is not practicable should be relatively rare. A procedure may be impracticable if the suspect has distinctive features that cannot be appropriately disguised, although it is permissible for the police to modify video images, or to use other means of modifying the appearance of the suspect and/or the comparators used in the identification procedure, provided care is taken (*Martin* [2002] EWCA Crim 251; *Pecco* [2010] EWCA Crim 972; and see Code D, annex A, paras. 2A to 2C). The police must make their decision regarding practicability on reasonable grounds (*Britton* [1989] Crim LR 144).

The question of whether an identification procedure would serve a useful purpose has arisen in cases where there has previously been a positive identification, and also where the circumstances are on the cusp of recognition. In *Popat (No. 2)* [2000] Crim LR 54, decided under a former version of Code D, it was held that an identification parade was not necessary where there had been a 'full and satisfactory informal identification of the suspect by the witness' (although note that the circumstances where an 'informal' identification can be conducted are limited to where the suspect is not 'known': see **D1.130**). In *Harris* [2003] EWCA Crim 174 it was held that a formal identification procedure would have served a useful purpose where a purported recognition, based upon the accused having attended the same school as the witnesses two years previously, was disputed by the accused.

Types and Conduct of Identification Procedures

D1.136 **The Identification Officer and Investigating Officers** The arrangements for, and conduct of, identification procedures under Code D are the responsibility of the 'identification officer', an officer not below the rank of inspector who is not otherwise involved with the investigation (Code D, para. 3.11). However, Code D permits substantial delegation of this officer's duties (and those of the custody officer: see **D1.44**) to other officers or to civilian police employees (para. 2.21). Certain duties may also be performed by the custody officer, in respect of the 'notice to suspect' requirements under paras. 3.17 to 3.19, where the identification procedure is to be carried out at a later date, and an inspector is not available to act as identification officer. No officer or other person involved in the investigation may take part in the formal identification procedures, except as specifically provided by Code D, or act as the identification officer (para. 3.11). In particular, an officer involved in the investigation must not take witnesses to the identification procedure (*Gall* (1990) 90 Cr App R 64; *Ryan* [1992] Crim LR 187), although it appears that he is permitted to take the suspect to the procedure (*Jones* [1992] Crim LR 365, and see **D1.139**).

D1.137 **The Choice of Identification Procedure** Code D provides for four possible procedures by which a known suspect may be placed before witnesses in order to establish if they can identify him. Priority is given to video identification, but an identification parade may be offered if a video identification is not practicable or if a parade is both practicable and more suitable than a video identification. The identification officer and the officer in charge of the investigation must consult with each other to determine which procedure is to be offered (para. 3.14). A group identification may be offered initially only if the officer in charge of the investigation considers it is more suitable than either a video identification or an identification parade and the identification officer considers it is practicable to arrange (para. 3.16). Confrontation remains the last resort, to be used only if all other options (including covertly recorded video, etc.) are impracticable (para. 3.23). Whichever procedure is adopted, it must be carried out in accordance with the appropriate annex to Code D.

Video Identification   Code D, annex A, sets out the procedures to be followed in a video **D1.138** identification. A video identification must ordinarily be conducted with the suspect's consent, but may in certain circumstances be conducted covertly (Code D, paras. 3.21 and 3.22, and Note for Guidance 3D). Annex A, paras. 2A to 2C, set out the procedures to be followed if the suspect has unusual physical features, and paras. 7 to 9 deal with the opportunities to be given to the suspect or his solicitor to be involved in the procedure.

Identification Parades   Code D, annex B, sets out the procedures to be followed in holding an **D1.139** identification parade, and includes a requirement that a video recording normally be made of a parade (para. 23). Annex B, para. 10, sets out the procedure to be followed if the suspect has unusual physical features, and paras. 1, 3, 6, 8 and 13 deal with the opportunities to be given to the suspect or his solicitor to be involved in the procedure.

Regrettably, some deficiencies revealed in past cases have not been addressed by the revisions to Code D. Annex B lays down strict rules to prevent contact between witnesses, or between witnesses and investigating officers, during a parade or immediately before it (see paras. 14 to 16) but still says nothing about the propriety of such contact once the witnesses in question have viewed the parade. See *Willoughby* [1999] 2 Cr App R 82 and **F18.4**.

Group Identification   Code D, annex C, sets out the procedures to be followed in holding a group **D1.140** identification. It seeks to ensure that, as far as possible, such procedures follow the same principles as identification parades so that the conditions are fair to the suspect in the way they test the witness's ability to make an identification. The conditions under which group identifications take place cannot be controlled to the same degree as video identification or parades but, under para. 6, the identification officer must reasonably expect that over the period the witness observes the group he will be able to see, from time to time, a number of others (in addition to the suspect) whose appearance is broadly similar. In *Jamel* [1993] Crim LR 52, a group identification was arranged on the basis that a parade was impracticable. J was of mixed race, and the identification was held in a street where one might have expected a variety of individuals of various races to pass by. In the event, nobody of mixed race but J appeared, and he was identified by the witness. The Court of Appeal declined to find fault with this procedure, but indicated that a different view would have been taken had the identification procedure been held in an overwhelmingly white neighbourhood.

A group identification must ordinarily be conducted with the suspect's consent, but may in certain circumstances be conducted covertly (Code D, paras. 3.21 and 3.22, and Note for Guidance 3D). It may be held in either a public place or a secure environment (such as a prison or police station) and the suspect may be part of either a moving or a stationary group. Annex C makes provision for each type of case. An identification carried out in accordance with annex C remains a group identification notwithstanding that at the time of being seen by the witness the suspect was on his own rather than in a group (para. 10).

Paragraphs 3, 11, 13, and 27 deal with the opportunities to be given to the suspect or his solicitor to be involved in the procedure.

Confrontation   Confrontation of a suspect by a witness is governed by Code D, annex D. **D1.141** Force may not be used even if the suspect attempts to hide his face (see para. 3, and **D1.132**). A confrontation must normally not take place in the absence of the suspect's legal adviser etc. (para. 4). Confrontation is in some respects little better than dock identification, and the courts will almost certainly exclude such evidence if the limited safeguards required under annex D have been breached. See, e.g., *Powell v DPP* [1992] RTR 270 and *Samms* [1991] Crim LR 197. Judicial mistrust of confrontation can most clearly be seen in *Joseph* [1994] Crim LR 48, where the police had done their best to arrange for a parade, group identification or video identification, but without success. The prosecution sought to proceed on the basis of other evidence, but

D

Part D Procedure

J demanded a confrontation before the trial, in the misguided hope that the witnesses would not identify him. He was in fact identified by two witnesses, and the trial judge admitted that evidence on the basis that J had asked for the confrontation. However, the Court of Appeal considered that the weakness of this evidence required its exclusion under the PACE 1984, s. 78.

D1.142   **Qualified Identification**   In some cases, a witness may qualify his identification of the suspect by indicating that he 'cannot be quite certain', or that he is only '90 per cent sure'. An accused should not be convicted on qualified identification evidence alone (*George* [2003] Crim LR 282), but it may still have some probative value when adduced in support of other more positive evidence. Although Code D states in a number of places (e.g., annex A, para. 13) that care must be taken not to direct the witness's attention to any particular image or person, it remains largely silent on the subject of a qualified identification. It would clearly be improper for the police to encourage a witness to be more positive once the initial video identification or parade process has been concluded (e.g., by telling him that he has 'got the right one'). As Lord Bingham CJ observed in *Willoughby* [1999] 2 Cr App R 82:

> There … would be the utmost ground for concern if there were any question of the police nudging, prompting or encouraging any witness … to make a more positive identification of a suspect…. It would seem to us important that a witness should not be told whether an identification is right or wrong until after the witness has made any further statement that the witness may wish.

Evidence of Recognition by Showing Films, Photographs and Other Images

D1.143   Part B of sect. 3 of Code D applies when, for the purposes of obtaining evidence of recognition, a person (including a police officer) views the image of an individual in a film, photograph or other visual medium and is asked whether he recognises that individual as someone who is known to him. Note for Guidance 3AA states, in effect, that the procedure under part B should be used in order to test whether a witness can recognise a person as someone he knows and would be able to give evidence of recognition (but see **D1.128**). The procedure adopted should, as far as possible, follow the principles applicable to a video identification if the suspect is 'known' (see **D1.130**), or identification by photographs if the suspect is not known (para. 3.35). Paragraph 3.36 sets out the information that must be recorded, which includes what the person viewing the film etc. was told before viewing it, and whether he was alone or with others when the procedure was conducted.

D1.144   The revision of Code D to include a procedure for the showing of films etc. to obtain evidence of recognition was prompted by the Court of Appeal's decision in *Smith* [2009] 1 Cr App R 521, which concerned the viewing of CCTV footage by a police officer. In *JD* (2013) 177 JP 158, the fact that a police officer who was asked to view CCTV footage was told that the suspect was believed to be on it was described as a 'wholesale failure to comply with the requirements' of Code D, para. 3.35. Conversely, conducting a viewing of CCTV footage in the presence of another officer, the reason for which was not recorded, has been treated as a technical breach of para. 3.36(d) (*Selwyn* [2012] EWCA Crim 2968). See also on recognition by police officers, *McGrath* [2009] EWCA Crim 1758 and *Moss* [2011] EWCA Crim 252.

VOICE IDENTIFICATION

D1.145   There is no PACE code on voice identification, and it is mentioned only briefly in Code D. Paragraph 1.2 states that nothing in Code D precludes the use of aural identification procedures, and annex B, para. 18, states that a witness may ask any member of an identification parade to speak. In such a case, the witness should first be asked if he can make a purely visual identification, and must be reminded that participants will have been chosen on the basis of their appearance only. Members of the parade may then be asked to comply with the request of the witness to hear them speak. Code D makes no direct provision for cases in which the attempted identification is to be made on the basis of voice alone. This is unfortunate, because there is clear evidence that the risks of mistaken identification are very great. See *Roberts* [2000]

Crim LR 183, *Chenia* [2003] 2 Cr App R 83, and *Flynn* [2008] 2 Cr App R 266. For a detailed examination of the issues, see D. Ormerod, 'Sounds Familiar? — Voice Identification Evidence' [2001] Crim LR 595 and 'Sounding out Expert Voice Identification' [2002] Crim LR 771.

One possible approach is to adapt the usual Code D procedures, so as to hold what is in effect a 'voice identification parade'. In *Hersey* [1998] Crim LR 281, the Court of Appeal upheld a conviction based largely on evidence derived from such a parade. The victim of a masked robbery claimed that he had recognised the voice of one of the robbers as being that of H, and was then able to identify H's voice on a 'parade' in which H and 11 volunteers each read out a passage from an earlier interview with H himself. It would clearly be necessary in such cases for the 'parade' to be composed of persons with broadly similar accents to that of the suspect, but it may not be helpful or realistic to assemble an entire parade of similarly-pitched voices. It was acknowledged in *Hersey* that voice identification shares many of the dangers of visual identification, and should be subject at trial to analogous warnings derived or adapted from the *Turnbull* guidelines. See further **F18.24**.

ENTRY AND SEARCH UNDER WARRANT

Powers of entry and search of premises, both under a warrant and without a warrant, are gov-   **D1.146**
erned by a number of statutes, although the main general power of search under warrant is
governed by the PACE 1984, part II. The PACE 1984, ss. 15 (safeguards) and 16 (execution of
warrants), apply to warrants issued to a constable under any enactment. For examples of other
powers of search under warrant, see PACE Code B, Note for Guidance 2A (see **appendix 1**). The
CrimPR, rr. 6.29 to 6.33 (see Supplement, **R-83**) include provisions governing applications for
and the content of warrants. Search of premises and seizure is also governed by Code B which
applies to search of premises for the purposes and under the powers set out in Code B, para 2.3.
For the powers of designated civilian investigating officers to apply for a warrant under the PACE
1984, s. 8, and the application of other provisions governing search and seizure to such civilians,
see the Police Reform Act 2002, sch. 4, part 2. For the powers to search for and seize the proceeds
of crime, see **D8**. For disclosure by courts of information or documents from records or case
materials, see the CrimPR, r. 5.7 (see Supplement, **R-52**).

All statutory powers of search enacted before the PACE 1984 ceased to have effect in relation
to the authorisation of searches for items subject to legal professional privilege, excluded material and special procedure material consisting of documents or other records (PACE 1984,
s. 9(2)). The TA 2000 makes separate provision for the search of premises in respect of terrorism
(**B10.23**). For powers of entry and search in relation to serious fraud, see the CJA 1987, s. 2 and
the CrimPR, r. 6.31; those powers were comprehensively reviewed in *R (Energy Financing Team
Ltd) v Bow Street Magistrates' Court* [2006] 4 All ER 285. For powers of entry and search under
the SOCPA 2005, part 2, see **D1.195**.

Items Subject to Legal Privilege

The term 'items subject to legal privilege' is defined in the PACE 1984, s. 10(1). It includes   **D1.147**
lawyer-client communications made in connection with the giving of legal advice to the client,
and also: (a) communications between either of these or a representative and another person if
it was in connection with or in contemplation of and for the purpose of legal proceedings; and
(b) items enclosed with or referred to in any of these communications when such items are in
the possession of a person entitled to possession of them. If such items are in the possession of
a person not so entitled it would appear that the protection afforded by the PACE 1984 is lost.
Material in the hands of a solicitor which is not subject to legal privilege is special procedure
material (*Norwich Crown Court, ex parte Chethams* [1991] COD 271). However, in accordance
with the common-law rule governing privilege (see **F9.65**), if any items are held with the intention of furthering a criminal purpose they are not to be regarded as items subject to legal privilege
(s. 10(2): see also *R (Hallinan Blackburn Gittings & Nott (a firm)) v Crown Court at Middlesex
Guildhall* [2005] 1 WLR 766).

Excluded Material

D1.148 'Excluded material' means the following material *if it is held in confidence* (PACE 1984, s. 11(1)):

(a) personal records acquired or created in a trade, business, profession or other occupation or for the purpose of any office, paid or unpaid;

(b) human tissue or tissue fluid taken for purposes of diagnosis or medical treatment;

(c) journalistic material consisting of documents or records.

Material of types (a) and (b) is held in confidence if there is an express or implied undertaking to that effect, or a statutory requirement to restrict disclosure or maintain secrecy (s. 11(2)). Material of type (c) is held in confidence if it is held subject to such an undertaking, restriction or obligation and has been so held since it was first acquired or created for the purpose of journalism (s. 11(3)). It cannot acquire the status of excluded material at a later time in order to avoid a search and seizure.

'Personal records' means records concerning an individual (living or dead) who can be identified from them, and relating to that person's physical or mental health, spiritual counselling, or counselling for his personal welfare by a voluntary organisation, or a person with responsibility for so doing, either by virtue of his office or occupation or on authority from a court to supervise that person (e.g., probation officers, members of the clergy) (s. 12). Hospital records of patients' admissions and discharges are excluded material because they relate to the physical or mental health of persons who could be identified from them (*Cardiff Crown Court, ex parte Kellam* (1993) *The Times*, 3 May 1993).

'Journalistic material' means material acquired or created for the purposes of journalism, but only if it is in the possession of a person who acquired it or created it for that purpose. That person will be deemed to have acquired it for that purpose if it was given to him with the intention that it be used for that purpose (s. 13).

Special Procedure Material

D1.149 'Special procedure material' means (PACE 1984, s. 14(1) and (2)):

(a) material, other than items subject to legal privilege and excluded material, acquired or created in a trade, business, profession or occupation, or for the purpose of any office paid or unpaid, where it is held in confidence subject to an express or implied undertaking to that effect or a statutory requirement to restrict disclosure or maintain secrecy; and

(b) 'journalistic material' other than that already falling within the meaning of excluded material.

Material acquired by an employee in the course of his employment, or by a company from an associated company, is special procedure material only if it was so immediately before it was acquired (s. 14(3)); it cannot later be redesignated as confidential. Material created by an employee in the course of his employment, or by a company on behalf of an associated company, is special procedure material only if it would have been had the employer or associated company created it (s. 14(4) and (5)). For guidance on applications for 'special procedure' search warrants see *R (S) v Chief Constable of British Transport Police* [2014] 1 All ER 268.

Warrant Issued by a Justice of the Peace

D1.150 On application by a constable, a justice of the peace may issue a warrant to a constable to enter and search premises if the justice has reasonable grounds for believing: (a) that an indictable offence (see **D1.69**) has been committed; and (b) that there is material on the premises (defined below) which is likely to be of substantial value (whether by itself or together with other material) to the investigation of the offence (PACE 1984, s. 8(1)) and is likely to be admissible in evidence at a trial for the offence (s. 8(4)). Such material must not consist of or include items subject to legal privilege, excluded material or special procedure material (s. 8(1)(d); see *Bates v Chief Constable of Avon and Somerset Constabulary* (2009) 173 JP 313 and *Power-Hynes v Norwich Magistrates' Court* (2010) 173 JP 573). See further the CrimPR, r. 6.30.

Although warrants under s. 8 relate to premises rather than persons, an 'all premises warrant' may be issued in respect of all premises occupied or controlled by the person named in the application (see **D1.152**). 'Premises' is defined for all purposes in the PACE 1984 as including any place and, in particular, includes:

(a) any vehicle, vessel, aircraft or hovercraft;
(b) any offshore installation within the meaning of the Mineral Workings (Offshore Installations) Act 1971, s. 1;
(c) any renewable energy installation within the meaning of the Energy Act 2004, part 2, chapter 2;
(d) any tent or movable structure (PACE 1984, s. 23).

D1.151 Section 23 does not refer to premises that consist of a number of dwellings. However, s. 32(7), in respect of search on arrest, limits the power to search in respect of such premises to the dwelling in which the person was arrested or in which he was immediately before his arrest, and any parts of the premises which the occupier of any such dwelling uses in common with other occupiers of dwellings comprised in the premises. There are similar provisions in s. 17(2)(b). It is submitted that the same principles should apply to entry and search under other powers. There is no statutory test to determine whether rooms in premises that are individually occupied constitute separate dwellings. On the facts in *Thomas v DPP* [2009] EWHC 3906 (Admin) it was held that, where homeless persons were granted a licence to occupy a bedroom in a house containing three bedrooms, with use of communal parts, each bedroom comprised a separate dwelling.

D1.152 **All Premises and Specific Premises Warrants** Warrants fall into one of two categories. The first is a 'specific premises warrant' which permits search of one or more sets of premises specified in the application (PACE 1984, s. 8(1A)(a)). The second is an 'all premises warrant' which permits search of any premises occupied or controlled by a person specified in the application, including such sets of premises as are so specified (s. 8(1A)(b)). In addition to the conditions in s. 8(1) (see **D1.150**), before granting an 'all premises warrant' a justice of the peace must be satisfied that, because of the particulars of the indictable offence specified in s. 8(1)(a), there are reasonable grounds for believing that it is necessary to search premises occupied or controlled by the person in question which are not specified in the application in order to find material of substantial value to the investigation and that it is not reasonably practicable to specify in the application all the premises which he controls which might need to be searched (s. 8(1B)). Where an all premises warrant is issued, premises that are not specified in the warrant must not be entered or searched without the prior written authority of an officer of the rank of inspector who is not involved in the investigation (s. 16(3A)).

Either form of warrant may authorise multiple entries and searches of the premises if a justice of the peace is satisfied that it is necessary so to authorise in order to achieve the purpose for which the warrant is issued (s. 8(1C)). A warrant authorising multiple entries may authorise an unlimited number of entries or limit them to a maximum (s. 8(1D)), but any entry or search must be made within three months from the date of issue of the warrant (s. 16(3)). After the first entry and search under such a warrant, subsequent entries or searches may be conducted only with the prior written authority of an officer of the rank of inspector who is not involved in the investigation (s. 16(3B)).

D1.153 **Conditions for Issuing a Warrant** A warrant under s. 8(1) cannot be issued unless at least one of the conditions in s. 8(3) is satisfied:

(a) that it is not practicable to communicate with any person entitled to grant entry to the premises; or
(b) if it is, that it is not practicable to communicate with any person entitled to grant access to the evidence; or
(c) that entry to the premises will not be granted unless a warrant is produced; or
(d) that the purpose of a search may be frustrated or seriously prejudiced unless a constable arriving at the premises can secure immediate entry to them.

It is not a condition precedent to the issue of a magistrates' court warrant that other methods have been tried and failed or would be bound to fail, nor that no other statutory procedure for securing the material exists (*Billericay Justices, ex parte Frank Harris (Coaches) Ltd* [1991] Crim LR 472). Where there are grounds for seeking search warrants, the police are entitled to choose when to apply for them and when, within the time permitted by law, to execute them (*Chief Constable of Warwickshire Constabulary, ex parte Fitzpatrick*). However, the warrant is invalid if the police do not identify the s. 8(3) condition(s) that they rely upon (*Redknapp v Commissioner of the City of London Police* [2008] 1 All ER 229).

A constable may obtain access to excluded material or special procedure material for the purposes of a criminal investigation by making an application under the PACE 1984, sch. 1 (see **D1.160**). However, a magistrate is not barred from issuing a search warrant under s. 8(1) because there may be special procedure or excluded material on the premises; the issue of a warrant is barred only if the material falls into these categories and is or forms part of the subject-matter of such an application (*Ex parte Fitzpatrick* [1999] 1 All ER 65). The position is otherwise if the warrant is not sufficiently specific so that such material is likely to be included (*Power-Hynes v Norwich Magistrates' Court* (2009) 173 JP 573).

D1.154 **Powers on Executing a Warrant**   A constable may seize and retain anything for which a search has been authorised under a warrant issued under the PACE 1984, s. 8 (s. 8(2)). This does not extend to seizing a car parked in a car park where there was insufficient evidence that the car park was part of the premises within the scope of the warrant (*Wood v North Avon Magistrates' Court* (2010) 174 JP 157). See further **D1.176** *et seq.*

Unless the statute explicitly so provides, a warrant to enter and search premises does not confer a power to search persons found therein (*Hepburn v Chief Constable of Thames Valley* (2002) *The Times*, 19 December 2002; *DPP v Meaden* [2004] 4 All ER 75). However, it is permissible to take reasonable and necessary steps to detain persons found therein in the course of execution of the warrant (*Connor v Chief Constable of Merseyside* [2006] EWCA Civ 1549).

Access to Excluded or Special Procedure Material

D1.155 The PACE 1984, s. 9(1), enables access to be obtained to excluded material and special procedure material for the purposes of a criminal investigation if the procedures set out in sch. 1 to the Act are followed. Schedule 1 applies not only to police investigations but also to investigations of indictable offences by the Department for Business Innovations and Skills (BIS). A BIS investigator may apply for an order or warrant to obtain special procedure material in connection with a BIS investigation (PACE 1984, s. 114A, and Police and Criminal Evidence Act (Department of Trade and Industry Investigations) Order 2002 (SI 2002 No. 2326)). Special procedure material in the hands of a court can be made the subject of a production order, pursuant to the Crime (International Co-operation) Act 2003, s. 13, notwithstanding the absence of express provision in that section (*R (Secretary of State for the Home Department) v Southwark Crown Court* [2013] EWHC 4366 (Admin)).

D1.156 **Access Conditions**   There are two sets of access conditions in the PACE 1984, sch. 1, one of which must be satisfied. The first set of access conditions (sch. 1, para. 2) requires that:

(a) There are reasonable grounds for believing that an indictable offence (see **D1.69**) has been committed; that there is material which consists of special procedure material or includes special procedure material and does not include excluded material on premises specified in the application or on premises occupied or controlled by a person specified in the application (including all such premises on which there are reasonable grounds for believing that there is such material as it is reasonably practicable so to specify); that the material is likely to be of substantial value; and that the material is likely to be relevant evidence. Material is not relevant evidence simply because it could be used as the basis for cross-examination (*Norwich Crown Court, ex parte Chethams* [1991] COD 271).

(b) Other methods of obtaining the special procedure material have failed or have not been tried because it appeared they would be bound to fail. Thus if, e.g., a motion under the Bankers' Books Evidence Act 1879 (see F8.35) would be possible, it must be shown that such a motion was brought and failed or that the material could not have been secured by such a motion (*Crown Court at Lewes, ex parte Hill* (1991) 93 Cr App R 60). An application cannot however be impugned simply because some further and remote step to uncover evidence might possibly have been taken.

(c) It is in the public interest to produce or allow access to the material, having regard to the benefit to the investigation and the circumstances under which the person holds the material.

The second set of access conditions (sch. 1, para. 3) requires that there are reasonable grounds for believing that there is material which consists of or includes excluded or special procedure material:

(a) on such premises specified in the application; or

(b) on premises occupied or controlled by a person specified in the application (including such premises on which there are reasonable grounds for believing that there is such material as it is reasonably practicable so to specify),

in respect of which the issue of a warrant under an enactment other than sch. 1 would have been appropriate and available but for the repeal by s. 9(2) of all the provisions allowing warrants to be issued to search for this type of material.

Procedure   An application must be made to a circuit judge (extended to a district judge (magistrates' court) if and when the Courts Act 2003, sch. 4, para. 6, is brought into force). Before an order to produce or a search warrant is applied for, careful consideration must be given to what material it is hoped a search might reveal, and the application must also make it clear that the material sought relates to the crime under investigation (*Central Criminal Court, ex parte AJD Holdings* [1992] Crim LR 669). It is not sufficient for the information laid in support of the application merely to recite the statutory conditions, without any statement of the facts or matters on which the application is based (*R (S) v Chief Constable of the British Transport Police* [2014] 1 All ER 268). An order to produce special procedure material may be made even though some of the material is not of that description. This avoids making separate but necessarily sequential applications (*Preston Crown Court, ex parte McGrath* [1993] COD 103). **D1.157**

Notice of an application to make an order must be served on the person in possession of the material (sch. 1, para. 8), and all information on which the applicant intends to rely must be made available to him (*R (British Sky Broadcasting Ltd) v Central Criminal Court* [2012] QB 785). That person must not conceal, destroy, alter or dispose of the material without leave of a judge or written permission of a constable until the application is dismissed or abandoned, or he has complied with the order (para. 11). Failure to comply with an order is to be treated as a contempt of court (para. 15).

Bodies such as banks in respect of which such applications are made often let them go by default. It is thus particularly important that the judge be given adequate material to enable him to form a reliable judgement. This will include details of the charges, the dates covered by them, whether previous steps to secure the evidence have been tried and failed, and what the nature of the material is.

A suspect has no statutory right to be heard on an application for access, but the judge may in his discretion hear him where this appears likely to be helpful (*Crown Court at Lewes, ex parte Hill* (1991) 93 Cr App R 60).

The Order   If satisfied that one or other of the access conditions is fulfilled, the judge may make an order requiring the person in possession of the material to produce it to a constable for him to take away, or to give a constable access to it, within a specified period, normally seven days (PACE 1984, sch. 1, paras. 1 and 4). Once such an order has been made it cannot be rescinded; the only recourse is judicial review (*Liverpool Crown Court, ex parte Wimpey plc* [1991] Crim LR 635). **D1.158**

The approach which a judge should take towards applications is set out in *Crown Court at Lewes, ex parte Hill* (1991) 93 Cr App R 60 and *R (Bright) v Central Criminal Court* [2001] 2 All ER 244. The Divisional Court in *Ex parte Hill* stated that the Act provides a careful balance between the public interest in the effective investigation and prosecution of crime and the interests of citizens in protecting their personal and property rights. The circuit judge is entrusted with the primary duty of giving effect to that scheme (and in so doing must take full account of rights under the ECHR, Article 10: *R (Malik) v Manchester Crown Court* [2008] 4 All ER 403). He must exercise his powers with great care and caution. He must be shown such material as is necessary to enable him to be satisfied before making the order, and he should be told anything which, to the knowledge of the applicant, might weigh against his making such an order (*Leeds Crown Court, ex parte Hill* [1991] COD 197; *Acton Crown Court, ex parte Layton* [1993] Crim LR 458). He should not allow the police to engage in a fishing expedition. Any order which he makes must be specific as to the material sought. For an application of these principles, when production orders were quashed, see *R (British Sky Broadcasting Ltd) v Chelmsford Crown Court* [2012] 2 Cr App R 454. In cases involving national security the judge must at least be presented with a properly drafted, careful summary. In particularly sensitive cases he may wish to adapt the procedure which applies to applications for public interest immunity to deal with the matter (*R (Bright) v Central Criminal Court*).

Even if the access conditions are made out, the judge may, in his discretion, refuse to grant the order. Such an exercise of discretion would no doubt be rare. Discretion, however, enables the judge to weigh fundamental principles and, for example, may in a proper case lead to the conclusion that there would be disproportion between what might be gained to the investigation as against the stifling of public debate (*R (Bright) v Central Criminal Court* per Judge LJ, explaining *Northamptonshire Magistrates' Court, ex parte DPP* (1991) 93 Cr App R 396).

D1.159 There seems to be doubt whether a judge is inhibited in making an order for production by reason of the fact that the person to whom it is addressed may incriminate himself. In most cases a person against whom an order is made will not be a suspect and the matter may not arise. Where it does, it may be that a simple order to produce does not lead to self-incrimination in any event. In *R (Bright)* there was a lively debate on the issue which, it would seem, cannot be treated as concluded. A production order may be made even though the material sought might incriminate a journalist (*R (Bright) v Central Criminal Court* [2001] 2 All ER 244 per Kay and Gibbs JJ).

Where the material consists of information stored in any electronic form, the order is to produce material in a form in which it can be taken away and in which it is visible and legible or from which it can be produced in a visible and legible form. An order to give access is to be understood in the same sense (sch. 1, para. 5).

Where an order to produce requires the presentation or production of e-mails, which require the recipient of the order to modify or interfere with a telecommunications system (an offence under the RIPA 2000), the order takes precedence over the prohibition in the 2000 Act (*R (NTL Group Ltd) v Ipswich Crown Court* [2003] QB 131).

Search Warrant Issued by Judge

D1.160 A judge may issue a warrant authorising a constable to enter and search premises if one or other of two conditions is satisfied (PACE 1984, sch. 1, para. 12).

The first condition is that he is satisfied that either set of access conditions (see **D1.156**) is fulfilled and that any of the following are also fulfilled (sch. 1, para. 14):

(a) that it is not practicable to communicate with a person entitled to grant entry to the premises;

(b) if it is, that it is not practicable to communicate with a person entitled to grant access to the material;

(c) that there is a statutory restriction on disclosure or obligation of secrecy and disclosure contained in any enactment, and disclosure would be in breach of the statute unless a warrant is issued; or

(d) that service of notice of an application for an order would seriously prejudice the investigation.

The term 'practicable' bears a wider meaning than feasible or physically possible. The court may consider not only the available means of communication, but also all the circumstances, including the nature of the inquiries and the persons against whom they are directed. The usual procedure where a solicitor's office is to be searched would be by order to produce, but a search warrant may be proper where the firm is under investigation (*Leeds Crown Court, ex parte Switalski* [1991] Crim LR 559; *Maidstone Crown Court, ex parte Waitt* [1988] Crim LR 384; *Central Criminal Court, ex parte Hutchinson* [1996] COD 14). However, a search warrant was quashed in *R (Faisaltex Ltd) v Preston Crown Court* [2009] 1 Cr App R 549 where there was no evidence that proceeding by way of a production order might seriously prejudice the investigation: 'A solicitor was not to be regarded as somehow tainted and unreliable because, e.g., he acted for someone charged with or convicted of a criminal offence'.

The second condition is that the second set of access conditions (see **D1.156**) is fulfilled and that there has been a failure to comply with an order under sch. 1, para. 4 (**D1.158**).

The approach which a judge must take towards an application for a search warrant is set out in *Crown Court at Lewes, ex parte Hill* (1991) 93 Cr App R 60 (see **D1.158**). **D1.161**

The judge may not issue an 'all premises warrant' (**D1.152**) unless he is satisfied that there are reasonable grounds for believing that it is necessary to search premises occupied or controlled by the person in question which are not specified in the application, as well as those which are, in order to find the material in question, and that it is not reasonably practicable to specify all the premises that he occupies or controls which might need to be searched (sch. 1, para. 12A).

In searching premises, a constable is entitled to impose reasonable obligations on persons found therein in order to make the search effective. He may, thus, require persons found in the premises to go to or remain in a particular part of the premises while the search is carried out (*DPP v Meaden* [2004] 4 All ER 75, and see **D1.154**).

A constable may seize and retain anything for which such a search has been authorised (sch. 1, para. 13). See further **D1.176** *et seq.*

Procedural Requirements and Safeguards

Courts have consistently held that the issue of a search warrant is a very severe interference with individual liberty, is a step which should be taken only after mature consideration of the facts, and that the officer making the application is under a duty of full disclosure of relevant matters. The necessary foundation for the issue of a warrant should be on the face of the information unless there are good reasons for not including it, and both the applicant (subject to public interest immunity) and the court must be able to identify the basis for the grant of the warrant. If information additional to that in the information is provided to the court, both the applicant and the court must keep a written record of it (*R (Austen) v Chief Constable of Wiltshire* [2011] EWHC 3385 (Admin)). Whilst the PACE 1984 does not require a court to give reasons why the conditions for issue of a warrant are satisfied, in most cases, and particularly where the information is given or supplemented orally, the court should ensure that reasons for its decision are given and recorded (*R (Glenn & Co. (Essex) Ltd) v HM Commissioners for Revenue and Customs* [2012] 1 Cr App R 291). **D1.162**

All entries on and searches of premises under a warrant issued *under any enactment* are unlawful unless they comply with ss. 15 and 16 of the PACE 1984, although see *R (Glenn & Co. (Essex) Ltd) v HM Commissioners for Revenue and Customs*, in which a failure to supply a copy of a warrant to the occupier did not, on the facts, render the search unlawful. Code B, para 1.3A, provides a reminder that the Equality Act 2010 makes it unlawful for police officers to discriminate against, harass or victimise any person on the grounds of the 'protected characteristics' of age, disability, gender reassignment, race, religion or belief, sex and sexual orientation, marriage and civil partnership, pregnancy and maternity when using their powers.

D1.163   **The Application**   Procedure on an application for a warrant, and the conduct of the hearing, is governed by the PACE 1984, s. 15, and the CrimPR, r. 6.29 (see Supplement, **R-83**). A constable who applies for a warrant must state the ground on which he makes the application; the enactment under which the warrant would be issued; and, if the application is for a warrant authorising entry and search on more than one occasion, the ground on which he applies for such a warrant, and whether he seeks a warrant authorising an unlimited number of entries or (if not) the maximum number of entries desired (PACE 1984, s. 15(2)(i)–(iii)). In *R (Lees) v Solihull Magistrates' Court* [2013] EWHC 3779 (Admin) warrants were declared unlawful because they were too vague and general, and failed properly to identify the items to which they related (see also *R (Cheema) v Nottingham and Newark Magistrates' Court* [2013] EWHC 3790 (Admin)).

PACE Code B, requires, *inter alia*, that before making an application the officer must take reasonable steps to check the accuracy of his information, that it is recent, and that it has not been provided maliciously or irresponsibly (and see *R (G) v Commissioner of Police of the Metropolis* [2011] EWHC 3331 (Admin)). It also prohibits any application being made on the basis of information provided anonymously unless corroboration has been sought (Code B, para. 3.1). The officer must make reasonable inquiries to ascertain information about the premises to be searched, the likely occupier and the articles concerned (Code B, paras. 3.2 and 3.3). A failure to carry out basic steps to verify the connection between the premises and the offence under investigation may amount to a breach of the ECHR, Article 8 (*Keegan v UK* (2007) 44 EHRR 716). If there is reason to believe that a search might have an adverse effect on community relations, the local police/community liaison officer must be consulted, unless the search is needed urgently in which case he must be consulted as soon as practicable after the search (Code B, para. 3.5). Furthermore, a constable must not, when applying for a warrant, state that the purposes of the search will be frustrated or prejudiced unless immediate access is granted where he does not believe this to be so. In particular no such statement can properly be made where the subject of the search has already demonstrated that he is prepared to co-operate in producing material. Police acting in conjunction with another agency must form their own opinion whether it is necessary to apply for a warrant (*Reading Justices, ex parte South West Meat Ltd* [1992] Crim LR 672).

D1.164   No application for a search warrant or production order under the PACE 1984, sch. 1, may be made without the prior written authority of an officer of at least the rank of inspector, except in the case of urgency when an application to a justice of the peace may be authorised by the senior officer on duty (Code B, para. 3.4(a)). In the case of an application for a production order under the TA 2000, sch. 5, authorisation must be given by an officer of at least the rank of superintendent (Code B, para 3.4(b)).

D1.165   An application for a warrant covering one or more sets of premises specified in the application must specify each set of premises which it is desired to enter and search (s. 15(2A)(a)). Under s. 15(2A)(b), an application for an all premises warrant (see **D1.152**) must specify (i) as many sets of premises which it is desired to enter and search as it is reasonably practicable to specify; (ii) the person who is in occupation or control of those premises and any other premises which it is desired to enter and search; (iii) why it is necessary to search more premises than those specified in sub-para. (i); and (iv) why it is not reasonably practicable to specify all the premises which it is desired to enter and search (see also Code B, para. 3.6). A constable who wishes to search only a part of premises divided into separate dwellings and the common parts of those premises must make this clear in the information when applying for the warrant (*South Western Magistrates' Court, ex parte Cofie* [1996] 1 WLR 885). The application must be made *ex parte* and supported by an information in writing (s. 15(3)). The constable must answer on oath any questions put to him by the justice of the peace or the judge at a hearing of an application (s. 15(4)).

If an application is refused, no further application may be made unless supported by additional grounds (Code B, para 3.8).

Bare compliance with the statutory requirements regarding the information to be disclosed on an application for a warrant may not be sufficient. The test adopted in *R (Rawlinson) v Central Criminal Court* [2013] 1 WLR 1634 was whether the errors or non-disclosure in the application would in fact have made a difference to the decision to issue a warrant (and not whether they *might* have made a difference). This was followed in *R (Golfrate) v Southwark Crown Court* [2014] EWHC 840 (Admin), in which the lack of 'full and frank' disclosure resulted in the warrants being set aside, and in *Zinga* [2012] EWCA Crim 2357, in which failure to disclose the intended prosecutor did not vitiate the warrant. See also *Vuciterni v Brent Magistrates' Court* (2012) 176 JP 705, in which warrants were quashed where there was a failure to disclose doubts about whether the activities being investigated were unlawful.

Note that a court may consider a request for disclosure of information laid in support of an application for a warrant after the warrant has been executed, and for any additional information relied upon by the court when granting the warrant. However, this is subject to a power to refuse disclosure on the grounds of public interest immunity (*Commissioner of Police for the Metropolis v Bangs* (2014) 178 JP 158). See further CrimPR, r. 5.7 (see Supplement, **R-52**).

The Warrant   The requirements governing warrants are contained in the PACE 1984, s. 15(5)– (7), and the CrimPR, rr. 6.29(6) and 6.33 (see Supplement, **R-83**). A warrant can authorise entry on only one occasion unless it specifies that it authorises multiple entries (PACE 1984, s. 15(5)). If it authorises multiple entries, it must also specify whether the number of entries authorised is unlimited or limited to a specified maximum (s. 15(5A)). It must specify the name of the person applying for it (the name of the police unit is not sufficient: *R (G) v Commissioner of Police of the Metropolis* [2011] EWHC 3331 (Admin)), the date of issue, the Act under which it is issued, the premises to be searched, and, so far as is practicable, the identity of the articles or persons sought (s. 15(6), and see *R (Anand) v Revenue and Customs Commissioners* [2012] EWHC 2989, *Van der Pijl v Kingston Crown Court* [2013] 1 WLR 2706, and *R (Hoque) v City of London Magistrates' Court* [2013] EWHC 725 (Admin)). Each set of premises to be searched must be specified or, in the case of an all premises warrant, the person who is in occupation or control of the premises to be searched together with any premises under his occupation or control which can be specified and are to be searched (s. 15(6)(a)(iv)). Two copies must be made of a specific premises warrant which specifies only one set of premises and does not authorise multiple entries; and as many copies as are reasonably required may be made of any other kind of warrant (s. 15(7)). A warrant may be issued which is directed at all premises occupied or controlled by a specified person and, at the same time, one which specifies some of those premises (CrimPR, r. 6.29(6)(c); and see *Redknapp v Commissioner of the City of London Police* [2008] 1 All ER 229). As to specifying the articles sought, see *R (Hicks) v Commissioner of Police for the Metropolis* [2012] EWHC 1947 (Admin).   **D1.166**

Execution of the Warrant   Entry and search under a warrant must be at a reasonable hour unless it appears to the constable executing it that its purpose may otherwise be frustrated (PACE 1984, s. 16(5)). It must carried out within three months from the date of its issue (s. 16(3)). A warrant authorising entry and search 'on one occasion' does not require the police to complete the search in one calendar day (*R (Sher) v Chief Constable of Greater Manchester Police* [2011] 2 All ER 364). A warrant may be executed by any constable and may authorise persons to accompany him (s. 16(2)). A person so authorised has the same powers as the accompanied constable in respect of the execution of the warrant and the seizure of anything to which it relates (s. 16(2A)). Such a person may, however, exercise those powers only when in the company of and under the supervision of a constable (s. 16(2B); *Reading Justices, ex parte South West Meat Ltd* [1992] Crim LR 672). Civilians designated as investigating officers under the Police Reform Act 2002 have certain powers to execute warrants (see sch. 4 to that Act).   **D1.167**

Where the occupier of premises is present, the constable must identify himself and, if not in uniform, produce his identity (warrant) card, produce the search warrant and supply a copy to

D

Part D Procedure

the occupier, including any schedule (PACE 1984, s. 16(5); *R (Glenn & Co. (Essex) Ltd) v HM Commissioners for Revenue and Customs* [2012] 1 Cr App R 291; *R (Global Cash & Carry Ltd) v Birmingham Magistrates' Court* [2013] EWHC 528 (Admin)). If the occupier is not present, the constable must do these things in relation to the person who appears to be in charge of the premises (s. 16(6)). If there is no person present who appears to be in charge, a copy of the warrant must be left in a prominent place on the premises (s. 16(7)). The police practice of completing the address by hand as the warrant is executed amounts to a breach of s. 16(5) (*R (Bhatti) v Croydon Magistrates' Court* [2011] 3 All ER 671).

D1.168 The search may be conducted only to the extent required for the purpose for which it was issued (s. 16(8)), but provided a warrant is executed for the purpose for which it had been obtained, it is irrelevant that execution was timed to produce some collateral advantage (*R (Pearce) v Commissioner of Police of the Metropolis* [2013] EWCA Civ 866). As to what may be seized by a constable lawfully in premises, see **D1.176**. An executed warrant must be endorsed with information about whether the articles or persons sought were found, and whether any other articles were seized. Unless the warrant is a specific premises warrant specifying one set of premises only, the constable must endorse separately in respect of each set of premises entered and searched (s. 16(9)). The warrant must be returned to the appropriate officer in the magistrates' court or other court that issued it when it has been executed or, in the case of a specific premises warrant which has not been executed, an all premises warrant or any warrant authorising multiple entries, upon the expiry of three months or sooner (s. 16(10) and (10A)). Returned warrants are to be retained by those persons for 12 months (s. 16(11)). This is so that the occupier of the premises to which the warrant related may exercise his right under s. 16(12) to inspect the warrant.

ENTRY AND SEARCH WITHOUT WARRANT

D1.169 A search of premises is always permissible with the consent of a person entitled to grant entry, although consent should be obtained in writing (Code B, sect. 5). Police constables have powers of entry and search without a warrant under the PACE 1984, ss. 17, 18 and 32, and also under a variety of other statutes (see Code B, Note for Guidance 2B, for examples: see **appendix 1**). The police also have common-law powers of entry in respect of breach of the peace (**D1.33**). Designated civilian investigating officers also have certain powers of entry and search without a warrant (Police Reform Act 2002, s. 38(9) and sch. 4). Code B applies to searches under the PACE 1984, ss. 17, 18 and 32, and to most other searches by police for the purposes of investigation of an alleged offence, whether with or without consent (see Code B, para. 2.3).

Entry for the Purposes of Arrest etc.

D1.170 The PACE 1984, s. 17(1), empowers a constable to enter and search any premises (for definition, see **D1.150**):

(a) to execute a warrant of arrest issued in connection with or arising out of criminal proceedings, or a warrant of commitment issued under the MCA 1980, s. 76 (s. 17(1)(a));

(b) to arrest a person for an indictable offence (s. 17(1)(b), and see **D1.69** for the meaning of indictable offence);

(c) to arrest a person for an offence under the Public Order Act 1936, s. 1 (prohibition of uniforms in connection with political objects) or the Public Order Act 1986, s. 4 (fear or provocation of violence); the RTA 1988, s. 4 (driving etc. when under the influence of drink or drugs) or s. 163 (failure to stop when required to do so by a constable in uniform); the Transport and Works Act 1992, s. 27 (offences involving drink or drugs); for an offence to which the Animals Health Act 1981, s. 61, applies; or an offence under the Animal Welfare Act 2006, ss. 4, 5, 6(1) and (2), 7 and 8(1) and (2) (s. 17(1)(c) and (caa));

(d) provided he is in uniform, to arrest a person for an offence under any enactment contained in the CLA 1977, ss. 6 to 8 or 10 (offences relating to entering and remaining on property), or the CJPO 1994, s. 76 (failure to comply with an interim possession order) (s. 17(1)(c) and (3));

(e) to arrest a child or young person who has been remanded or committed to local authority accommodation under the CYPA 1969, s. 23(1) (s. 17(1)(ca));

(f) to recapture a person who is, or who is deemed to be, unlawfully at large while liable to be detained in a prison, remand centre, young offender institution, or secure training centre, or in pursuance of the PCC(S)A 2000, s. 92 (dealing with children and young persons guilty of grave crimes), or to recapture a person who is unlawfully at large and whom he is pursuing (s 17(1)(cb) and (d));

(g) to save life or limb or prevent serious damage to property (s. 17(1)(e)), which includes saving someone from self-harm (*Baker v CPS* (2009) 173 JP 215).

When entering premises to search for a person (except for the purpose of saving life or prevent- **D1.171** ing property damage), the constable must have reasonable grounds for believing that the person he is seeking is on the premises (s. 17(2)(a)). A constable may enter any dwelling in which he has reasonable grounds for believing the person may be, and, where the premises consist of two or more dwellings, he may enter any parts of the premises used in common by the occupiers (s. 17(2)(b)). For entry under s. 17(1)(e), the officer must apprehend that some serious or dangerous incident has occurred, or is likely to occur; it is not enough that the officer is merely concerned for the welfare of someone in the premises (*Syed v DPP* [2010] 1 Cr App R 480).

If a constable has power to arrest a person under an extradition arrest power, he may enter and search any premises for the purposes of exercising the power of arrest if he has reasonable grounds for believing that the person is on the premises (Extradition Act 2003, s. 161(2)). In this case, the relevant Code of Practice is the Extradition Act Code B (see **D1.38**).

Force may be used to enter premises where it is necessary to do so. Where the occupier of the premises is present and can be spoken to, forcible entry will not be justified unless the constable explains by what right and for what purpose he seeks to enter (*Lineham v DPP* [2000] Crim LR 861). That reason must be lawful: a wish to talk to a suspect cannot, for example, be elided into a wish to arrest a suspect. There is an exception to the duty above where the circumstances are such as to make it impossible, impracticable or unnecessary to give such an explanation to the occupier (*O'Loughlin v Chief Constable of Essex* [1998] 1 WLR 374).

Any search made must be restricted to that which is reasonably required to achieve the object of the search (s. 17(4)).

Other than the power of entry to deal with or prevent a breach of the peace, all common-law **D1.172** powers of a constable to enter premises without a warrant were abolished by the PACE 1984, s. 17(5). A constable does not have the power to enter premises to carry out an investigation as to whether a further breach of the peace would occur (*Friswell v Chief Constable of Essex Police* [2004] EWHC 3009 (QB)). The power of a constable under s. 17(1)(d) to enter and search premises to recapture a person who is unlawfully at large and whom he is pursuing extends to entry to retake a mental patient unlawfully at large provided that such a patient is liable to be retaken and returned to a hospital and provided that the pursuit of such person is almost contemporaneous with the entry to the premises, a term which is somewhat wider than 'hot pursuit'. Where the element of contemporaneity cannot be satisfied, but the situation is one of real emergency, the police could enter the premises under their common-law powers relating to breach of the peace which were specifically preserved by s. 17(6) (*D'Souza v DPP* (1993) 96 Cr App R 278).

Entry and Search on Arrest

Where a person is arrested for an indictable offence (see **D1.69**), a constable may enter and **D1.173** search any premises (for definition, see **D1.150**) where the person was at the time of or immediately before the arrest, for evidence relating to the offence for which he was arrested (PACE 1984, s. 32(2)(b)). Despite the wording of s. 32(1), the power is not confined to circumstances where a constable has reasonable grounds for believing that the arrested person may present a danger to himself or others (*Hanningfield v Chief Constable of Essex Police* [2013] 1 WLR 3632).

D

Part D Procedure

Where the premises consist of two or more dwellings, the power is confined to the dwelling where the arrest took place, or where the person arrested was immediately before arrest, and to common areas (s. 32(7)). The power extends to the search of vehicles and, in the case of ticket touting (see **B11.137**), extends to the search of any vehicle which the constable has reasonable grounds for believing was being used for any purpose connected with the offence. Unlike the power under the PACE 1984, s. 18, the power under s. 32 applies to premises irrespective of whether the person arrested owns, occupies or controls them. However, it does not extend to the search of premises belonging to the arrested person's friends and associates at which the person was not arrested even though it may be suspected that incriminating items are to be found there (*R (Hewitson) v Chief Constable of Dorset Police* (2004) *The Times*, 6 January 2004).

Entry and search is limited to premises that the person was in at the time of the arrest or 'immediately before' the arrest. In contrast to the power under s. 18, s. 32 is an immediate power and it is not permissible for the police to return to premises to search them several hours after the arrest (*Badham* [1987] Crim LR 202). In *Hewitson* it was indicated that a gap of two hours and ten minutes was too long. In such circumstances a power of search may, but will not necessarily, be available under s. 18.

The power of entry and search is available only if the constable has reasonable grounds for believing that there is evidence for which a search is permitted (s. 32(6)). Search is permitted only to the extent that is reasonably required for the purpose of discovering any such thing (s. 32(3)). Whether police entered for that purpose is a question of fact (*Beckford* (1991) 94 Cr App R 43).

Powers of seizure are governed by the PACE 1984, s. 19 (see **D1.176**).

Entry and Search after Arrest

D1.174   Where a person is arrested for an indictable offence (see **D1.69**), a constable may enter and search any premises (for definition, see **D1.150**) occupied or controlled by that person provided that the constable has reasonable grounds for suspecting that there is on the premises evidence (other than items subject to legal privilege) relating to that offence or to some other indictable offence which is connected with or similar to that offence (PACE 1984, s. 18(1)). The premises must as a fact, or perhaps as a matter of mixed fact and law, be occupied or controlled by the person under arrest; reasonable suspicion that the person occupies or controls them is not enough (*Khan v Commissioner of Police of the Metropolis* [2008] EWCA Civ 723 and see Code B, para. 4.3). It would be possible, provided the conditions are satisfied, for a search to be conducted under both s. 18 and s. 32. For example, where a person is arrested at the house of an acquaintance, that house could be searched under s. 32 and his own house searched under s. 18.

Generally, entry and search under s. 18 is permissible only if it is authorised in writing in advance by an officer of at least the rank of inspector (s. 18(4)). The officer must not give authorisation unless he is satisfied that the premises are occupied or controlled by the arrested person and that the necessary grounds exist (Code B, para. 4.3). Code B gives no guidance on what action the officer should take to satisfy himself that the premises are occupied or controlled by the arrested person, but it is submitted that the same principles as apply prior to making an application for a search warrant should apply to authorisation under s. 18 (see **D1.163**). A constable can enter and search under s. 18 without such authorisation and before the person is taken to a police station or released on bail under s. 30A (see **D1.20**) if the presence of the person at a place other than a police station is necessary for the effective investigation of the offence (s. 18(5) and (5A)). In such a case, the constable must inform an officer of at least the rank of inspector as soon as practicable (s. 18(6)). An officer who authorises or is informed under s. 18(6) of such a search must make a written record of the grounds for the search and the nature of the evidence sought (s. 18(7)). If the person in occupation or control of the premises at the time of the search is in police detention at the time the record is to be made, it must be made a part of his custody record (s. 18(8)).

While the authorisation requirements of s. 18 are mandatory, a failure to comply with them **D1.175** fully (as by not specifying precisely the grounds of the search and the property to be searched for) will not necessarily render the search unlawful. While the section is to be obeyed, the court will, in determining the consequences of any breach, have regard to whether the failure to record prejudiced the person arrested (*Krohn v DPP* [1997] COD 345). As with entry to arrest, it is submitted that a constable must first demand entry (where this is practicable) before resorting to force (see **D1.170**).

The constable may seize and retain anything for which he may search (s. 18(2)). The scope of the search must be restricted to that which is reasonably required for the purpose of discovering such evidence (s. 18(3)).

Where a constable has entered premises in order to arrest under an extradition arrest power (**D1.38**), he may seize and retain anything on the premises that he has reasonable grounds for believing has been obtained in consequence of the commission of an offence, or is evidence in relation to an offence, and that it is necessary to seize it in order to prevent it being concealed, lost, damaged, altered or destroyed (Extradition Act 2003, s. 161(4)). In this case, the relevant code of practice is the Extradition Act Code B (see **D1.38**).

SEIZURE OF, ACCESS TO AND RETENTION OF MATERIALS

Powers of Seizure

Where a constable executes a warrant under the PACE 1984, s. 8 or sch. 1, he has specific pow- **D1.176** ers to seize and retain anything for which the search has been authorised (s. 8(2) and sch. 1, paras. 4 and 13). Similarly, where a search of premises is conducted under s. 18, or a search of the person under s. 32(1) or s. 32(2)(a) (but not of premises under s. 32(2)(b)), a constable has specific powers to seize and retain materials (ss. 18(2), and 32(8) and (9)). In addition to specific powers of seizure and retention, a constable who is lawfully on any premises (see **D1.150** for definition) has power:

(a) to seize anything which is on the premises if he has reasonable grounds to believe that it has been obtained in consequence of the commission of an offence, or that it is evidence in relation to an offence, and that it is necessary to seize it in order to prevent it being concealed, lost, altered or destroyed (PACE 1984, s. 19(2) and (3));
(b) where he has similar reasonable grounds, to require that information which is stored in any electronic form and is accessible from the premises be produced in a form in which it can be taken away and which is in a visible and legible form or in a form (such as a disk) from which a visible and legible version can be produced (s. 19(4)) — this power is in addition to any power otherwise conferred (s. 19(5)), including common-law powers (*Cowan v Condon* [2000] 1 All ER 504).

The power under s. 19(2) and (3) to seize anything 'which is on the premises' includes the prem- **D1.177** ises themselves if they are readily movcable, e.g., a car or caravan (*Cowan v Condon*). However, it does not extend to seizing things that are not on the premises, such as a car parked in a car park adjacent to the premises (*Wood v North Avon Magistrates' Court* (2010) 174 JP 157). A trivial excess of power in seizing an object not authorised by a warrant will not vitiate the legality of a search (*Inland Revenue Commissioners, ex parte Rossminster* [1980] AC 952; *A-G of Jamaica v Williams* [1998] AC 351; *Chesterfield Justices, ex parte Bramley* [2000] QB 576). Property that has been unlawfully seized cannot be re-seized at a police station to which it has been taken on the basis that the officer is then lawfully on those premises (*R (Cook) v SOCA* [2011] 1 WLR 144). However, in such circumstances, if an application is made under the CJPA 2001, s. 59(5)(b), a judge may authorise retention under s. 59(6) (*R (El-Kurd) v Winchester Crown Court* [2011] EWHC 1853 (Admin)).

The power to require any information stored in electronic form and which is accessible from the premises to be produced in a form in which it can be taken away etc. is specifically extended to powers of seizure under any enactment contained in an Act passed before or after the PACE 1984, and under the PACE 1984, ss. 8 and 18 and sch. 1, para. 13 (s. 20).

The power under s. 19 is exercisable whether the constable is lawfully on premises by consent or as a result of a statutory or common-law power, and is not limited to indictable offences.

For powers to seize and retain the proceeds of crime, see **D8**.

Seizure of Legally Privileged Material

D1.178   No power of seizure conferred by any statute applies to items which the constable has reasonable grounds for believing to be subject to legal privilege (PACE 1984, s. 19(6)). However, this must be interpreted by reference to the CJPA 2001, s. 50. This enables a person who is lawfully on premises and to whom a power of seizure listed in the CJPA 2001, sch. 1, part 1 applies, to seize the whole or part of a suspect item so as to remove it from the premises for the purpose of determining whether it falls within the power. It is a condition of exercise of the power that the determination cannot be reasonably practicably determined on the premises (s. 50(1)). Where the seizable property cannot reasonably practicably be separated from something else in which it is comprised, both the article and that from which it cannot be separated may be seized (s. 50(2)). The factors to be considered in determining reasonable practicability are set out in s. 50(3) and include length of time, numbers of persons needed, damage to property from separation, the apparatus necessary and prejudice to the use of separated property. The powers of seizure referred to in the CJPA 2001, sch. 1, are remarkably comprehensive and include powers of seizure under the PACE 1984, parts II and III. They go beyond the normal range of police activities and include enforcement activities conducted by a wide range of other authorities. Note that Revenue and Customs officers have the same powers in respect of the provisions concerning legally privileged material as police officers (s. 67).

The CJPA 2001, s. 51, contains similar powers in respect of seizure from the person. The powers to which s. 51 apply are set out in the CJPA 2001, sch. 1, part 2 (s. 51(5)). For guidance on seizure, retention and return of property seized under ss. 50 and 51, see Code B, paras. 7.7 to 7.17 (see **appendix 1**).

Provision is made under s. 52 for giving notice of the exercise of the powers under ss. 50 and 51. It was held in *R (Dulai) v Chelmsford Magistrates' Court* [2013] 3 All ER 764 that non-compliance with s. 52 did not necessarily render a seizure under s. 50 unlawful. Examination and return of anything seized under ss. 50 and 51 is governed by s. 53. Essentially, the examination should be carried out as soon as possible, should be confined to the purpose of verification, and the property should be kept separate from other articles seized.

D1.179   Specific provision is made in s. 54 for the return of articles seized under ss. 50 or 51 which attract legal privilege. The meaning of 'legal privilege' depends upon the statute in which the phrase is used. The definition in the PACE 1984, s. 10 (see **D1.147**), remains unaltered (CJPA 2001, s. 65). If at any time after seizure it appears to the person having possession of the seized property that it is an item subject to legal privilege or has such an item comprised in it, that person is under a duty to return the property as soon as reasonably practicable after the seizure. This is subject to exception where the legally privileged item is comprised within property for which the person had power to search and which he is not required to return either under s. 54 or s. 55 (s. 55 concerns excluded and special procedure material). This is itself subject to the proviso that return is not required where separation is not reasonably practicable without prejudicing the use, for lawful purposes, of that part of the article (s. 54(1) and (2)). The power of retention under s. 56 does not authorise retention of anything that must be returned under s. 54 (s. 56(4)).

The CJPA 2001, s. 56, concerns property seized by any constable who is lawfully on premises or by 'relevant persons' (as to which see s. 56(4A) and (5), referring, e.g., to warrants under the

Companies Act 1985) accompanying a constable, and to property seized by a constable carrying out a lawful search of any person. Retention of such property is authorised if there are reasonable grounds for believing that it is property obtained in consequence of the commission of an offence and that its retention is necessary to prevent it being concealed, lost, damaged, altered or destroyed (s. 56(2) and see *R (Chief Constable of South Yorkshire) v Sheffield Crown Court* [2014] EWHC 81 (Admin)). The power also extends to property that is believed to be evidence in relation to any offence where its retention is required for the same purposes (s. 56(3)). This is in addition to the powers of retention under the PACE 1984, s. 22 (see **D1.181**).

Powers to obtain hard copies of information stored in electronic form are powers of seizure (s. 60). It follows that the powers of retention etc. apply to such material.

Remedies and safeguards, including applications to the court for return of articles, are contained in s. 59.

Access to and Retention of Seized Material

In respect of seizures under any enactment, on the request of either the occupier of premises on which the material was seized or the person having custody or control of it immediately before seizure, the constable or accompanying person must provide a record of what was seized within a reasonable time of the request (PACE 1984, s. 21(1) and (2)). If requested by the person who had custody or control of the item immediately before it was seized, or by someone acting on his behalf, the officer in charge of the investigation must allow that person access to the item under the supervision of a constable (s. 21(3)). Similarly he must allow access for photographing or copying, or arrange for it to be photographed or copied and supply the photograph or copy to the person requesting it within a reasonable time (s. 21(4), (6) and (7)). A constable may also photograph or copy anything he has power to seize without such a request (s. 21(5)). The requests do not need to be acceded to if there are reasonable grounds to believe that it would prejudice any investigation, or any criminal proceedings resulting therefrom, to do so (s. 21(8)).

D1.180

The common-law power of the police to preserve *exhibits* is well established (*Lushington, ex parte Otto* [1894] 1 QB 420). Anything seized or taken away by a constable or accompanying person under s. 19 or s. 20 may be retained as long as is necessary in all the circumstances (s. 22(1)). In particular, anything seized for the purposes of a criminal investigation may be retained for use as evidence at a trial, or forensic examination or further investigation, unless a photograph or copy would suffice, and where there are reasonable grounds for believing it has been obtained in consequence of the commission of an offence, anything may be retained in order to establish its lawful owner (s. 22(2) and (4)). In relation to the latter, the police may retain the material only for so long as that purpose continues (*Malone v Metropolitan Police Commissioner* [1980] QB 49; *Gough v Chief Constable of the West Midlands Police* [2004] EWCA Civ 206; *Settelen v Commissioner of Police of the Metropolis* [2004] EWHC 2171 (Ch)). However, the police have a short 'period of grace' during which they can retain the material to consider whether, for example, an application should be made to retain it under the POCA 2002 (*R (Iqbal) v Luton and South Bedfordshire Magistrates' Court* [2011] EWHC 705 (Admin)). Where the thing seized is a residential caravan, the legality of its retention must be determined by whether it strikes a fair balance between the right to private life under the ECHR, Article 8, and the public interest, including the prevention of disorder or crime (*Chief Constable of Wiltshire Constabulary v McDonagh* [2008] EWHC 654 (QB)).

D1.181

The police cannot retain items seized because they may be used to cause physical injury, or to damage property, or to interfere with evidence, or to assist in escape from lawful custody, when the person from whom they were seized is no longer in police detention or the custody of the court or has been released on bail (s. 22(3), and see *Chief Constable of Merseyside Police v Owens* (2012) 176 JP 688). However, they can retain material, even after the CPS has decided not

Part D Procedure

D

to prosecute, for use in a private prosecution (*Scopelight Ltd v Chief Constable of Northumbria Police Force* [2010] QB 438).

For retention of property under the CJPA 2001, s. 56, see **D1.179**.

It follows from these provisions that the only permitted use of seized material is for the purpose of investigating and prosecuting crime, after which they must be returned to their true owner. Documents and information may be communicated to others for the purpose of investigation and prosecution, and may perhaps be disclosed to other public authorities. They may not be made available to private individuals for private purposes (*Marcel v Metropolitan Police Commissioner* [1992] Ch 225).

D1.182 Section 22(5) declares that the provisions of s. 22 do not affect the power of a court to make an order in respect of property under the Police (Property) Act 1897, s. 1.

Code B, para. 8.1, requires that records be kept of all searches of premises and specifies the information that must be recorded, which includes anything seized. A search register, containing all search records, must be kept at each sub-divisional (or equivalent) police station (Code B, para. 9.1).

POLICE BAIL BEFORE CHARGE

Powers to Grant Bail

D1.183 The police have a variety of powers and duties to grant bail to persons arrested for an offence but not charged (but not in respect of a person arrested and detained under the TA 2000, s. 41; see *R (I) v City of Westminster Magistrates' Court* [2008] EWHC 2146 (Admin)). For the power to grant bail to an arrested person without taking them to a police station, see **D1.20**. The PACE 1984, s. 34(2), provides that, where a custody officer becomes aware, in relation to a person in police detention (see **D1.40**), that grounds for detention have ceased to apply and the officer is not aware of any other grounds to justify detention, he must order the immediate release from custody of the detained person (unless it appears to the officer that the person was unlawfully at large when arrested: s. 34(4)). Such release must be without bail unless it appears to the custody officer that there is a need for further investigation of any matter in connection with which the person was detained at any time during the period of detention or that in respect of any such matter proceedings may be taken against him (or, if a juvenile, that he may be reprimanded or warned under the CDA 1998, s. 65), in which case the release may be on bail (s. 34(5)).

Where a person arrested either without warrant or under a warrant not endorsed for bail is taken before a custody officer under s. 37(1), and the officer determines that he does not have before him sufficient evidence to charge, the person must be released either without bail or on bail unless the officer has reasonable grounds for believing that detention is necessary for one or more of the specified grounds (s. 37(2), and see **D1.49**). If the officer determines that there is sufficient evidence to charge, the detainee must be dealt with in accordance with s. 37(7) (see **D2.2**).

D1.184 If the officer conducting a review of detention under s. 40 (see **D1.75**) concludes that detention can no longer be justified by reference to the conditions in s. 37, he must release the person with or without bail (s. 40(8)). Where a detained person has not been charged at the expiry of 24 hours after the relevant time, he must be released with or without bail unless further detention is authorised under s. 42 or 43 (s. 41(7)). A similar provision applies at the expiry of the 36-hour time-limit (s. 42(10)), or where an application for a warrant or extension of a warrant of further detention is refused (unless the 36 hours or the existing warrant has not expired (s. 43(15) and (16) and s. 44(7) and (8)), or where a warrant expires (s. 43(18)). There is no similar provision where an extended warrant expires, but it is submitted that the same principles must apply.

The PACE 1984 imposes no limit on the period for which bail can be granted, and it would seem that a court would only be willing to intervene in exceptional circumstances (*R (C) v Chief Constable of A* [2006] EWHC 2352 (Admin)).

Powers to Impose Conditions

A release on bail under the PACE 1984, part IV (which includes all of the powers to grant **D1.185** bail mentioned in **D1.183** except for bail granted under s. 30A), is deemed to be a release on bail in accordance with the Bail Act 1976, ss. 3, 3A, 5 and 5A, as those sections apply to bail granted by a constable. However, conditions can be attached to bail granted prior to charge only where it is granted under s. 37 (s. 47(1A), and see *R (Torres) v Commissioner of Police of the Metropolis* [2007] EWHC 3212 (Admin)). For the power to attach conditions to bail granted under s. 30A, see **D1.20**. Such conditions (including requiring a surety or security) can be imposed as appear necessary for the purpose of ensuring that the person surrenders to custody, does not commit an offence on bail, does not interfere with witnesses or otherwise obstruct the course of justice, and/or for his own protection (or where the person is under 17 years, for his own welfare or in his own interests) (PACE 1984, s. 47(1A), and BA 1976, ss. 3(6) and 3A(5)). Any condition may be imposed other than a condition that the person reside in a bail hostel, make himself available for the purposes of a court report, or attend an interview with a lawyer (BA 1976, s. 3A(2)). A surety can be required only for the purpose of securing surrender to custody (*R (Shea) v Winchester Crown Court* [2013] EWHC 1050 (Admin)). It has been held in relation to a court's power to impose bail conditions that in considering whether and what conditions to impose, the court must perceive a real and not merely fanciful risk of the relevant outcome (*Mansfield Justices, ex parte Sharkey* [1985] QB 613), and it is submitted that the same principle must apply to a decision by a police officer.

For the right of a person to apply for variation or removal of bail conditions, see **D2.47**.

Enforcement

A person who has been released on bail under the PACE 1984, part IV, may be rearrested if **D1.186** new evidence justifying a further arrest comes to light after his release (PACE 1984, s. 47(2) and see **D1.67**). Where a person has been released on conditional bail, he may be arrested by a constable having reasonable grounds for suspecting that he has broken any of the conditions (s. 46A(1A)). Further, a person granted bail to return to a police station (whether conditional or not) is under a duty to do so, and may be arrested if he fails to attend the police station at the appointed time (s. 46A(1)). He must then be taken to the police station at which he was required to surrender as soon as practicable (s. 46A(1A)), and he is treated as having been arrested for an offence for the purposes of ss. 30 (duty to take arrested person to a police station) and 31 (arrest for further offence) (s. 46A(2) and (3)). If the person had been released under s. 37(7)(a) and the Crown Prosecutor has not made a charge decision under the PACE 1984, s. 37B, the custody officer may either charge him or release him on bail again (s. 37C(2) and (3)). The duty to attend at the police station on the appointed date is subject to the power of a custody officer to give notice in writing to the person that his attendance is not required (s. 47(4)). Unlike under the BA 1976, s. 7(3), there is no power of arrest in respect of an anticipated breach of conditions or failure to surrender. Breach of conditions is not an offence, but failure without reasonable cause to surrender to custody is an offence (BA 1976, s. 6, as applied by the PACE 1984, s. 47(1)).

Where a person returns to the police station in accordance with his bail (or fails to surrender and is arrested and taken to the police station), the custody officer may authorise his further detention only if the grounds in s. 37(2) are satisfied (as a result of s. 34(7)). However, this does not apply where the person was released on bail under s. 37(7)(a), in which case he may be kept in police detention to enable a charge decision to be made in accordance with ss. 37B or 37C (s. 37D(4)). Normally, time spent in police detention before the release on bail (but not any time whilst on bail) counts for the purpose of calculating the maximum period of detention without charge, whether the person surrendered as required, or failed to surrender and was arrested under s. 46A(1) (s. 47(6): see also **D1.67**). However, this is not the case if he has been arrested under s. 47(2) — in that case the detention clock starts again (s. 47(7)).

INTERCEPTION OF COMMUNICATIONS AND SURVEILLANCE

D1.187 Interception of communications and surveillance is principally regulated by the RIPA 2000, although there are a number of other relevant statutes including the Police Act 1997 and the Intelligence Services Act 1994. A number of RIPA Codes of Practice have been issued by the Secretary of State under the RIPA 2000, s. 71, and they must be taken into account by any court insofar as they are relevant (RIPA 2000, s. 72). Further, a large number of regulations have been issued under the Act. The provisions are complex and only a brief summary is provided here.

Interception of Communications

D1.188 Chapter 1 of part I of the RIPA 2000 regulates the interception of communications in the course of their transmission by a public postal service or by a public or private telecommunications service. A conversation between two people face-to-face which is overheard by means of a listening device does not constitute a conversation in the course of a transmission (*Allsopp* [2005] EWCA Crim 703). Interception of communications without authorisation under the Act is an offence (s. 1(1) and (2) and see **B9.84**), and may also be a tort (s. 1(3)). Certain interceptions may be lawfully carried out without a warrant (ss. 3 and 4). Note in particular that interception of a communication that is sent by, or intended for, a person who has consented to the interception is lawful provided that it is authorised as directed surveillance (s. 3(2)). Other than interceptions under ss. 3 and 4, interception requires a warrant issued by the Secretary of State (s. 5). The grounds for issuing a warrant are set out in s. 5(2) and (3).

Substantial restrictions apply to the use of intercepted material, see **F2.51** *et seq.*

Surveillance and Covert Human Intelligence Sources

D1.189 Part II of the RIPA 2000 regulates the use of intrusive and directed surveillance, and covert human intelligence sources. Use of these methods without authorisation does not amount to an offence, and there is no similar limitation on evidence to that found in s. 17 (*Kelly* [2007] EWCA Crim 1715). They are defined in s. 26, and it is an essential feature of each that the activity be 'covert' (defined in s. 26(9)). Surveillance is intrusive if it is carried out in relation to anything taking place on any residential premises or private vehicle, and involves the presence of an individual on the premises or vehicle or is carried out by means of a surveillance device (s. 26(3)). A police van is not a private vehicle (*Plunkett* [2013] 1 WLR 3121). However, there are certain exceptions to this definition in s. 26(4)–(6). Surveillance is directed if it is undertaken for the purposes of a specific investigation or operation in such a manner as is likely to result in private information being obtained, and is otherwise than by way of an immediate response to events or circumstances the nature of which is that it would not be reasonably practicable for an authorisation to have been sought (s. 26(2)). In this way, surveillance by general CCTV cameras, or by an officer who in the course of a routine patrol decides to follow a suspicious looking person in the street, does not come within the definition, and therefore does not require authorisation under the Act. There is an overlap between the provisions governing the authorisation of intrusive surveillance under the RIPA 2000 and those in the Police Act 1997, part III, and the Intelligence Services Act 1994, s. 5, governing entry on to or interference with property. A covert human intelligence source is defined in the RIPA 2000, s. 26(7) and (8), and could include both an informant and a police officer acting undercover.

D1.190 Authorisation of intrusive surveillance must be by a senior authorising officer (of the rank of chief constable or equivalent) or by the Secretary of State (s. 32(1)). The grounds for authorisation are set out in s. 32(2)–(4). Authorisation of directed surveillance or the use of a covert human intelligence source must be by designated persons (of the rank of superintendent or equivalent) (ss. 28(1) and 29(1)). Authorisations granted by designated local authority officers do not take effect unless approved by a judicial authority (s. 32A). The grounds for authorisation are set out in s. 28(2) and (3), and s. 29(2) and (3) respectively. The person giving authorisation must believe that the operation is necessary (*Brett* [2005] EWCA Crim 983). In the absence of exceptional circumstances, the lawfulness of surveillance would normally be sufficiently demonstrated by the production of the surveillance commissioner's or authorising officer's signed approval and the defence would not normally be entitled to see the authorisation or the material on which it was based (*GS* [2005] EWCA Crim 887). For surveillance carried out on premises used for the purpose of legal consultations and the use of covert human intelligence sources whose activities involve obtaining access to matters subject to legal privilege, see D1.58.

The RIPA 2000 does not apply to surveillance which is not covert or not conducted by the police (or other regulated agency). Thus, for example, it does not govern the non-covert taking of photographs of potential demonstrators (which it was held in *R (Wood) v Commissioner of Police of the Metropolis* [2010] 4 All ER 951 may breach the ECHR, Article 5). Evidence discovered by means of a camera erected by the accused's neighbours and the location of which was known to the accused could be used at the instance of the prosecution and would not be excluded under the PACE 1984, s. 78 (*Rosenberg* [2006] EWCA Crim 6).

INVESTIGATORY POWERS UNDER THE CRIME AND COURTS ACT 2013

Powers of NCA Staff

The Director General of the NCA has the power to designate a member of Agency staff as a **D1.191** person having the powers of a constable, Revenue and Customs officer and/or immigration officer (CCA 2013, s. 10 and sch. 5), in force from 7 October 2013 by virtue of SI 2013 No. 1682). Where a person is designated as having powers of a constable, he has all the powers and privileges of a constable (sch. 5, para. 11). The PACE 1984 applies to them and the exercise of their powers by virtue of the Crime and Courts Act 2013 (Application and Modification of Certain Enactments) Order 2014 (SI 2014 No. 1704), art. 3, which applies in respect of the NCA by virtue of the CCA 2013, sch. 8, part 4. For this purpose, the PACE 1984 is subject to the modifications set out in sch. 1 to the Order, the most important of which are:

(a) references to 'police officer' and 'officer' are normally to be treated as references to a 'designated person' under the CCA 2013;
(b) where authorisation is required for a search under the PACE 1984, s. 18, reference to an inspector is replaced by reference to a grade 3 officer;
(c) references to 'police station' (e.g., in relation to fingerprinting, volunteers and fingerprints and samples) are to be treated as references to a 'National Crime Agency office';
(d) 'National Crime Agency office' means a place for the time being occupied by the National Crime Agency.

INVESTIGATORY POWERS UNDER THE SERIOUS ORGANISED CRIME AND POLICE ACT 2005

Powers Relating to Disclosure and Production

Part 2 of the SOCPA 2005 confers powers on the DPP, referred to as 'the Investigating Authority', **D1.192** in relation to the giving of disclosure notices (s. 60(1) and (5)). These may be delegated to a Crown Prosecutor or to a Revenue and Customs Prosecutor (s. 60(2) and (3)). These powers apply to the offences specified in s. 61(1).

Serious Organised Crime and Police Act 2005, s. 61

(1) This Chapter applies to the following offences —

 (a) any offence listed in Schedule 2 to the Proceeds of Crime Act 2002 (lifestyle offences: England and Wales);

 (b) any offence listed in Schedule 4 to that Act (lifestyle offences: Scotland);

 (ba) any offence listed in Schedule 5 to that Act (lifestyle offences: Northern Ireland);

 (c) any offence under sections 15 to 18 of the Terrorism Act 2000 (offences relating to fundraising, money laundering etc.);

 (d) any offence under section 170 of the Customs and Excise Management Act 1979 (fraudulent evasion of duty) or section 72 of the Value Added Tax Act 1994 (offences relating to VAT) which is a qualifying offence;

 (e) any offence under section 17 of the Theft Act 1968 (false accounting), or section 17 of the Theft Act (Northern Ireland) 1969 (false accounting) or any offence at common law of cheating in relation to the public revenue, which is a qualifying offence;

 (f) any offence under section 1 of the Criminal Attempts Act 1981, or Article 3 of the Criminal Attempts and Conspiracy (Northern Ireland) Order 1983 or in Scotland at common law, of attempting to commit any offence in paragraph (c) or any offence in paragraph (d) or (e) which is a qualifying offence;

 (g) any offence under section 1 of the Criminal Law Act 1977, or Article 9 of the Criminal Attempts and Conspiracy (Northern Ireland) Order 1983 or in Scotland at common law, of conspiracy to commit any offence in paragraph (c) or any offence in paragraph (d) or (e) which is a qualifying offence;

 (h) any offence under the Bribery Act 2010.

(2) For the purposes of subsection (1) an offence in paragraph (d) or (e) of that subsection is a qualifying offence if the Investigating Authority certifies that in his opinion—

 (a) in the case of an offence in paragraph (d) or an offence of cheating the public revenue, the offence involved or would have involved a loss, or potential loss, to the public revenue of an amount not less than £5,000;

 (b) in the case of an offence under section 17 of the Theft Act 1968 or section 17 of the Theft Act (Northern Ireland) 1969, the offence involved or would have involved a loss or gain, or potential loss or gain, of an amount not less than £5,000.

D1.193 **Disclosure, Production and Retention**   The Investigating Authority may issue a disclosure notice where it appears to him: (a) that there are reasonable grounds for suspecting that an offence specified in the SOCPA 2005, s. 61, has been committed; (b) that any person has information, whether documentary or not, which relates to a matter relevant to the investigation of the offence; and (c) that there are reasonable grounds for believing that information which may be provided by that person in compliance with a disclosure notice is likely to be of substantial value (whether or not by itself) to that investigation (s. 62(1)). Note that the information sought need not be directly probative of an offence nor need it be admissible in evidence.

A disclosure notice, which must be in writing and signed or countersigned by the Investigating Authority, may require the person to answer questions, provide information or produce a document, or documents of any particular description, relevant to the offence (s. 62(3)–(5)).

An authorised person may take copies of or extracts from any documents produced and may require the person producing them to provide an explanation for any of them (s. 62(2)). Documents so produced may be retained for so long as the Investigating Authority considers it necessary to retain them (rather than copies) (s. 62(3)). He may retain such documents if he has reasonable grounds for believing that any such documents may have to be produced for the purpose of legal proceedings and that they might otherwise be unavailable for such purposes (s. 62(3)). If a person required to produce documents does not do so, an authorised person may require him to state, to the best of his knowledge and belief, where they are (s. 63(5)).

D1.194 **Privilege**   Legal professional privilege is fully protected. A person may not be required to answer any privileged question, provide any privileged information, or produce any privileged document (SOCPA 2005, s. 64(1)–(4)), nor may he be required to produce any excluded material (s. 64(5) and PACE 1984, s. 11). Furthermore, a person may not be required to disclose any information or produce any document in respect of which he owes an obligation of confidence by virtue of carrying on any banking business unless the person to whom the obligation is owed consents to disclosure or production, or the requirement is made by or in accordance with a specific authorisation given by the Investigating Authority (s. 64(8) and (9)). It is thus apparent that, while legal professional privilege cannot be overridden by the Investigating Authority, banking secrecy may be so overridden.

Power to Enter, and to Seize Documents

Where a person has been required by a disclosure notice to produce documents but has not done **D1.195** so, or it is not practicable to give a disclosure notice requiring production, or the giving of such a notice might seriously prejudice the investigation into a relevant offence, a justice of the peace may issue a warrant at the instance of the Investigating Authority. Such an application must be made by way of information on oath (SOCPA 2005, s. 66(1) and (2)). The justice must be satisfied that the documents are on the premises specified.

The warrant authorises an appropriate person named in it, accompanied by such other persons as he deems necessary, to enter and search the specified premises using such reasonable force as is necessary, to take possession of documents appearing to be of a description specified in the information or to take any other steps which appear to be necessary for preserving or preventing interference with any such documents. Similar steps may be taken in respect of computer disks which appear to contain the information sought. Copies and extracts of documents may be taken. Any person in the premises may be required to provide an explanation of any such documents or information or to state where any such documents or information may be found and may be required to give the person executing the warrant such assistance as he may reasonably require for the taking of copies or extracts (s. 66(1) and (4)).

It would seem that the obligation to provide an explanation of documents or information must, consistent with the HRA 1998, not require the person directly to incriminate himself.

Provision is made to ensure that premises entered in the absence of the occupier are left secure (s. 66(6)).

As with documents or devices produced under notice, the Investigating Authority may retain **D1.196** the document or device for so long as the Authority considers it necessary to retain it rather than a copy in aid of the investigation (s. 66(7)). Retention of the document or device is also authorised where the Investigating Authority has reasonable grounds for believing that the document or device may have to be produced for the purposes of any legal proceedings and that it might otherwise be unavailable for those purposes (s. 66(8)). Note that there is no 'reasonable cause to believe' requirement where retention is for the purposes of the investigation but that there is such a requirement where retention is in aid of the possible production of the document or device in legal proceedings.

The power to take possession of or make copies extends only to those items disclosure or production of which can be compelled under this statutory scheme (s. 66(9)).

Failure without reasonable cause to comply with any requirement imposed under ss. 62 or 63 is a summary offence punishable with imprisonment not exceeding six months and/or a fine not exceeding level 5 (ss. 67(1) and (4) and 175). Knowingly or recklessly making a false or misleading statement in a material particular is an either-way offence punishable on indictment with imprisonment for up to two years and/or an unlimited fine and punishable on summary conviction with six months and/or a fine not exceeding the statutory maximum (ss. 67(2) and (5) and 175). Wilful obstruction of any person in the exercise of any of the warrant powers conferred by s. 66 is a summary offence punishable in the same way as an offence under s. 67(1) (s. 67(3) and (4)).

ANONYMITY IN INVESTIGATIONS

D1.197   The CAJA 2009, part 3, chapter 1 (ss. 74 to 85) contains provisions for investigation anonymity orders, which are a response to the difficulties in persuading witnesses of serious gang-related crime to give evidence.

By s. 74, an 'investigation anonymity order' is an order in respect of a specified person which prohibits the disclosure of information which identifies the specified person as a person who is or was able and willing to assist a 'specified qualifying criminal investigation' or that might enable the specified person to be identified as such a person. The qualifying offences are murder and manslaughter, provided death is caused either by the victim being shot with a firearm or being injured with a knife. A criminal investigation is a qualifying criminal investigation if it is conducted wholly or in part with a view to ascertaining whether a person should be charged with a 'qualifying offence' or whether a person charged with a qualifying offence is guilty of it (s. 75).

Section 76(10) makes it an offence to disclose information in contravention of an investigation anonymity order. Section 76(3)–(9) set out circumstances in which the prohibition against disclosure would not be contravened.

D1.198   An order may be made on application by, *inter alia*, a police force, the Director General of the NCA or the DPP (s. 77). The order is made by a justice of the peace who must be satisfied that there are reasonable grounds for believing that the following conditions, set out in s. 78(3)–(8), are satisfied:

(a) a qualifying offence has been committed;

(b) the person likely to have committed the offence — the 'relevant person' — is a person aged at least 11 but under 30;

(c) that at the time the offence was committed the relevant person is likely to have been a member of a group which it is possible to identify from the criminal activities that its members appear to engage in and it appears that the majority of the persons in the group are aged at least 11 but under 30;

(d) the person who would be specified in the order has reasonable grounds for fearing intimidation or harm if identified as a person who is or was willing and able to assist the investigation;

(e) the person who would be specified in the order is able to provide information that would assist the criminal investigation and is more likely than not, as a consequence of the making of the order, to provide such information.

For witness anonymity orders, see **D14.49**.

Section D2　The Decision to Prosecute and Diversion

THE DECISION TO PROSECUTE

The decision to prosecute is governed by the PACE 1984, ss. 37, 37A and 37B, the Code for **D2.1**
Crown Prosecutors and the *Director's Guidance on Charging*. The Code for Crown Prosecutors
was most recently revised in January 2013 (see **appendix 3**). The *Director's Guidance on Charging*
was most recently revised in May 2013 (5th edn, at www.cps.gov.uk/publications/directors_
guidance/dpp_guidance_5.html). In January 2010, the Revenue and Customs Prosecutions
Office became a specialist division in the CPS, but there is separate guidance on charging for
revenue and customs cases. The general scheme governing the decision to prosecute in police
investigations is that the custody officer has responsibility for determining whether there is sufficient evidence to charge, but the decision to charge rests with either the custody officer or a
Crown Prosecutor, depending on the nature of the charge and the likely plea.

Commencement of criminal proceedings by way of charge is dealt with in this section. For commencement by way of summons, or written charge and requisition, see **D5.2** *et seq.*

Sufficient Evidence to Charge

If the custody officer determines that he has before him sufficient evidence to charge an **D2.2**
arrested person with the offence for which he was arrested, the person must be (PACE 1984,
s. 37(7)):

(a) released without charge and on bail (s. 37(7)(a)(i)), or kept in police detention (s. 37(7)
　　(a)(ii)), for the purpose of enabling the DPP (in practice, normally a Crown Prosecutor)
　　to make a decision under s. 37B (whether there is sufficient evidence to charge and, if so,
　　whether the person should be charged and what the charge should be, or whether he should
　　be given a caution);
(b) released without charge and on bail but not for that purpose (s. 37(7)(b));
(c) released without charge and without bail (s. 37(7)(c)); or
(d) charged (s. 37(7)(d)).

This is subject to s. 41(7), which provides that at the expiry of a detention time-limit a person
who has not been charged must be released either on bail or without bail (see **D1.67** *et seq.*).
The decision as to how a person is to be dealt with under s. 37(7) is that of the custody officer
(s. 37(7A)), but in making the decision the custody officer must have regard to the *Director's
Guidance on Charging* (s. 37A(3)). Once the custody officer has determined that there is sufficient evidence to charge, action under s. 37(7) is mandatory (*R (G) v Chief Constable of West
Yorkshire Police* [2008] 1 WLR 550). For the test for determining when interviewing should
cease and a person be brought before a custody officer, see **D1.89**.

The test for whether there is sufficient evidence to charge is not statutorily defined. PACE Code **D2.3**
C, paras. 11.6 and 16.1, imply that it means sufficient evidence to provide a realistic prospect
of conviction (which is the test for the evidential stage of the 'full code test' — see **D2.10**).
Under the *Director's Guidance on Charging* this is the test that must normally be applied both
in determining whether there is sufficient evidence to charge and in determining whether to
charge (para. 8). However, the *Guidance* provides that a lower, threshold test may be applied by

custody officers in determining whether to refer a case to a Crown Prosecutor for a charge decision where the conditions for making a charge decision on the basis of the threshold test are met (paras. 8 and 11, and see **D2.13**); or, exceptionally, where the custody officer makes a charge decision in a case that should normally be referred to a prosecutor for a charge decision (see **D2.8**). The *Guidance* and the Code for Crown Prosecutors provide that a Crown Prosecutor can make a charge decision on the basis of the threshold test in certain circumstances (see **D2.13**).

Where the person is dealt with under s. 37(7)(a), an officer involved in the investigation must, as soon as practicable, send to the DPP (in practice a Crown Prosecutor) such information as is specified in the *Director's Guidance on Charging* (s. 37B(1) and *Guidance*, para. 26 and annex A). If the prosecutor determines that there is sufficient evidence to charge, the person may be charged having been detained for this purpose under s. 37(7)(a)(ii), or may be charged when answering to bail granted under s. 37(7)(a)(i). Alternatively, the person may be charged by means of a written charge and requisition (s. 37B(8)). If the prosecutor determines that there is not sufficient evidence to charge, it would follow from the fact that the custody officer has already determined that there is sufficient evidence to charge that they could not continue to detain, or further detain, the person without charge unless, perhaps as a result of the prosecutor's decision, the custody officer no longer believes that there is sufficient evidence to charge.

D2.4   It would seem that the purpose of s. 37(7)(b) is, where the custody officer has determined that there is sufficient evidence to charge, to permit the person to be released without charge whilst further investigations are carried out. There is no statutory limit on the number of times that a person may be bailed under this provision, and no time-limit on the period for which bail is granted (see **D1.184**). However, for the purpose of the maximum period of detention without charge, periods of detention at a police station in relation to the same investigation are normally cumulative (see **D1.67**).

The question arises whether, on surrendering to custody following release under s. 37(7)(b), the person can then be further detained without charge. On returning to the police station, the person is to be treated as arrested for the offence in connection with which bail was granted (s. 34(7)). If the test for determining whether there is sufficient evidence to charge is the same for s. 37(1) and s. 37(7) (or was so treated in a particular case), it is difficult to see how detention under s. 37(2) would be possible since the custody officer would have determined that there was sufficient evidence to charge in order to grant bail under s. 37(7)(b). Since under the current version of the *Director's Guidance on Charging* the test for determining whether there is sufficient evidence to charge is normally the 'full code test', it would seem that the meaning is the same.

The PACE 1984, s. 37(7)(c), permits the custody officer to release the person without charge even if he determines that there is sufficient evidence to charge, but it also enables the officer to divert the person from prosecution, such as by means of a caution (**D2.23**).

D2.5   Where a person is arrested under the provisions of the CJA 2003, part 10, which allow a person to be retried after being acquitted of a serious offence which is a qualifying offence under sch. 5, and further prosecution is not precluded by s. 75(3) (see **D12.40** *et seq.*), the PACE 1984, s. 37, is modified and, in particular, an officer of at least the rank of superintendent (who has not directly been involved in the investigation) must determine whether the evidence available or known to him is sufficient for the case to be referred to a prosecutor to consider whether consent should be sought for an application in respect of that person under the CJA 2003, s. 76 (CJA 2003, s. 87).

If the police continue to detain a person without charge beyond the point at which the charge decision should have been made, that detention is likely to be unlawful. Further, it may be argued that inferences should not be drawn from any 'silence' (see **F19.42**) since the CJPO 1994, s. 34, does not permit inferences from 'silence' after charge.

Detention for More than One Offence   Code C, para. 16.1, provides that, where a person is **D2.6** detained in respect of more than one offence, it is permissible to delay bringing him before the custody officer with a view to a decision being made under s. 37(7) until the officer in charge of the investigation reasonably believes that there is sufficient evidence to provide a realistic prospect of conviction in respect of all the offences in respect of which the person is being detained. This may be *ultra vires* since s. 37(7) is in mandatory terms and does not cater for such circumstances, but the point does not appear to have been authoritatively determined.

Responsibility for Making the Charge Decision

Under the *Director's Guidance on Charging*, responsibility for making a charge decision may **D2.7** rest with either a Crown Prosecutor or a custody officer. A Crown Prosecutor must make a charge decision in respect of all indictable-only offences, and any either-way offence in respect of which, under the *Guidance*, a custody officer is not permitted to make a charge decision (see below). In cases where more than one charge may be appropriate, and at least one of them must be referred to a prosecutor for a charge decision, all matters must be referred to the prosecutor. The decision on charge may be made by a custody officer (under the PACE 1984, s. 37(7)(d)) in respect of any summary only offence (including criminal damage where the value of the loss or damage is less than £5,000) irrespective of likely plea. A custody officer may also make a charge decision in respect of an either-way offence where it is anticipated that the person charged will plead guilty and it is suitable for sentence in a magistrates' court provided it is not one of the following (*Director's Guidance on Charging*, para. 15):

- a case requiring the consent to prosecute of the DPP or a law officer (see **D2.15**);
- a case involving death;
- connected with terrorist activity or official secrets;
- classified as hate crime or domestic violence under CPS policies;
- an offence of violent disorder or affray;
- causing grievous bodily harm or wounding, or actual bodily harm;
- an offence under the SOA 2003 committed by or upon a person under 18 years; or
- an offence under the Licensing Act 2003.

The *Guidance* provides that a case may be considered suitable for sentence in a magistrates' court unless the loss or damage relating to the charge is more than £5,000 or would exceed that sum if more than one offence is charged (or taken into consideration); or the overall circumstances of the offence are so serious that the court may decide that a sentence of more than six months' imprisonment justifies sending the case to the Crown Court; or the offence has been committed whilst the suspect was subject to a Crown Court order then in force (para. 18).

A custody officer may also, provided it is authorised by an inspector, charge a person with an **D2.8** offence that under the *Guidance* should be referred to a Crown Prosecutor for a charge decision where the continued detention of the suspect after charge is justified and it is not possible to obtain a prosecutor's authority for the charge before the expiry of any relevant detention time-limit (see **D1.67** *et seq.*). In making a charge decision, the custody officer may apply the threshold test (see **D2.13**) and the case must be referred to a prosecutor as soon as possible after charge and not later than the time proposed for the first appearance in a magistrates' court (*Director's Guidance on Charging*, para. 20).

The Tests for Deciding Whether to Charge

The Full Code Test   In deciding whether to charge, a Crown Prosecutor or custody officer **D2.9** (where they are permitted to charge) must normally apply the 'full code test' set out in the Code for Crown Prosecutors (*Director's Guidance on Charging*, para. 8, and see **appendix 3**). The full code test has two stages: the evidential stage and the public interest stage.

Part D Procedure

D

D2.10   **The Evidential Stage**   The evidential stage requires the prosecutor (or custody officer, as the case may be) to be satisfied that there is sufficient evidence to provide a realistic prospect of conviction in respect of each charge. He must consider what the defence case may be and how it is likely to affect the prosecution case. The Code for Crown Prosecutors describes it as an objective test (para. 4.5), meaning that a court properly directed and acting in accordance with the law is more likely than not to convict the defendant of the alleged offence. However, it was held in *R (FB) v DPP* [2009] 1 Cr App R 580 that in deciding whether there is a realistic prospect of conviction, rather than take a statistical approach the prosecutor should imagine himself to be the fact finder and ask himself whether, on balance, the evidence was sufficient to merit a conviction taking into account what he knew about the defence case. See further the Code for Crown Prosecutors, paras. 4.4 to 4.6, at **appendix 3**.

D2.11   **The Public Interest Stage**   The public interest stage of the test must be applied only after the prosecutor (or custody officer, as the case may be) has determined that the evidential stage is satisfied. If the prosecutor (or custody officer) has determined that there is sufficient evidence to give a realistic prospect of conviction, a prosecution should normally proceed unless there are public interest factors that outweigh those in favour of prosecution, or the prosecutor (or custody officer) is satisfied that the public interest may be properly served by offering the offender the opportunity to have the matter dealt with by an out-of-court disposal (Code for Crown Prosecutors, para. 4.8). The factors to be taken into account are set out in the Code for Crown Prosecutors, para. 4.12, and now include whether prosecution is proportionate to the likely outcome (para. 4.12(f)). Although not specifically mentioned in the Code for Crown Prosecutors, in cases where the trafficking of human beings is an obvious possibility the police should make suitable inquiries and the prosecutor should take it into account in deciding, especially, whether to prosecute or to continue a prosecution (*M (L)* [2011] 1 Cr App R 135, and see *N* [2013] QB 379 and *L* [2014] 1 All ER 113); for a full discussion of the treatment of victims of trafficking, see **B22.36**. As to factors relevant to determining whether it is in the public interest to prosecute complainants in rape or domestic violence cases who have apparently been pressurised or coerced into retracting their initial complaint, see *A (RJ)* [2012] 2 Cr App R 80. Decisions to prosecute in such cases must always be referred to the DPP. CPS legal guidance on prosecution decisions in such cases, and in respect of other offences, is available via www.cps.gov.uk/legal.

D2.12   **Selecting the Charges**   Charges should be selected which reflect the seriousness and extent of the offending, give the court adequate powers to sentence and impose appropriate post-conviction orders, and enable the case to be presented in a clear and simple way (Code for Crown Prosecutors, para. 6.1). A prosecutor (or custody officer, as the case may be) should not proceed with more charges than are necessary just to encourage an accused to plead guilty to a few, nor proceed with a more serious charge just to encourage an accused to plead guilty to a less serious one (Code for Crown Prosecutors, para. 6.3). In making a charge decision, consideration should be given to alternatives to prosecution (Code for Crown Prosecutors, paras. 7.1 and 7.2, and see **D2.23**).

D2.13   **The Threshold Test**   As an exception to the normal rule, Crown Prosecutors may charge on the basis of the threshold test in the circumstances set out in the Code for Crown Prosecutors, para. 5.2. The test is in two parts. First, 'the prosecutor must be satisfied that there is at least a reasonable suspicion that the person to be charged has committed the offence' (para. 5.5), taking into account the factors set out in para. 5.6. Secondly, if so satisfied, 'the prosecutor must be satisfied that there are reasonable grounds for believing that the continuing investigation will provide further evidence, within a reasonable period of time, so that all the evidence taken together is capable of establishing a realistic prospect of conviction in accordance with the Full Code Test' (para. 5.8). In applying the second part of the test the prosecutor must take into account the factors set out in para. 5.10. A decision to charge under the threshold test must be kept under review, and the full code test must be applied as soon as is reasonably practicable and in any event before the expiry of any applicable custody time-limit or extended custody time-limit (para. 5.12). A previous version of the threshold test was disapproved of in *G v Chief Constable of West Yorkshire Police* [2006] EWHC 3485 (Admin) as a test for determining whether to charge. The revised version of the test still enables a person to be charged on the basis of a level of suspicion that is little different than that required for arrest, although there is a requirement that the prosecutor (and exceptionally a custody officer) has reasonable grounds for believing that continuing investigation will produce sufficient evidence within a reasonable period of time to establish a realistic prospect of conviction.

For the circumstances in which a custody officer may apply the threshold test, see **D2.3**.

The Process of Charging

D2.14 Responsibility for charging a person rests with the custody officer. Where the charge decision is made by a Crown Prosecutor, the decision must be notified to an officer involved in the investigation of the case (PACE 1984, s. 37B(4)). The person to be charged must, if still in police detention, be charged in accordance with the prosecutor's decision; if he has been released on bail, he must be charged when he returns to a police station to answer bail or through the written charge and requisition procedure established by the CJA 2003, s. 29 (s. 37B(6) and (8)). On being charged the person must be cautioned in the terms set out in Code C, para. 16.2, unless the restrictions on drawing inferences apply (see **D1.83**), in which case he must be cautioned in the terms set out in Code C, annex C, para. 2. The person must be given a written notice showing particulars of the offence(s) for which he is charged, including the name of the officer in the case (or warrant number in cases where Code C, para. 2.6A, or Code H, para. 2.8, apply), the police station and reference number for the case, and confirmation of the caution. As far as possible, the particulars of the charge must be stated in simple terms, but they must show the precise offence with which the person is charged (Code C, para. 16.3). By article 5(2) of the ECHR, an arrested person must be promptly informed of any charge in a language which he understands.

Cases where Consent is Required

D2.15 **Offences Requiring Consent** The institution of criminal proceedings for certain offences, or for offences in certain circumstances, requires the consent of either the A-G or the DPP or, in some cases, some other person such as a relevant government minister.

In general, the A-G's consent is required where issues of public policy, national security or relations with other countries may affect the decision whether to prosecute. An example is the Suppression of Terrorism Act 1978, s. 4(4) (see **A8.23**), by which he must sanction any proceedings in the UK for terrorist offences allegedly committed in a convention country. Other examples are offences of bribery under the Official Secrets Act 1911 (s. 8); offences of stirring up racial hatred etc. contrary to part III of the POA 1986 (s. 27); contempt of court under the strict liability rule (Contempt of Court Act 1981, s. 8); war crimes (War Crimes Act 1991, s. 1); and offences contrary to the Explosive Substances Act 1883 (s. 7).

Offences for which consent of the DPP is required include: offences of theft or criminal damage where the property in question belongs to the accused's spouse (Theft Act 1968, s. 30(4)); offences of assisting offenders and wasting police time (Criminal Law Act 1967, ss. 4(4) and 5(3)); encouraging or assisting another's suicide (Suicide Act 1961, s. 2(4)); riot (POA 1986, s. 7(1)); offences under the Bribery Act 2010; and certain terrorism offences under the TA 2000 (TA 2000, s. 117). For the DPP's policy on prosecuting in cases of encouraging or assisting suicide, see **B1.137**.

It was held in *R (Uberoi) v City of Westminster Magistrates' Court* [2009] 1 WLR 1905 that, despite the clear wording of the CJA 1993, s. 61(2), the Financial Services Authority has power to prosecute for insider dealing under part V of that Act without obtaining consent. The Financial Services and Markets Act 2000, s. 402, empowered the FSA to institute proceedings for such an offence and s. 401(2) enabled it to do so on its own authority. The principle would apply equally to the powers of the Financial Conduct Authority to institute proceedings: see **B7.21**.

CPS guidance, *Consents to Prosecute*, annex 1, contains a useful list of prosecutions requiring consent by the A-G or the DPP (available via www.cps.gov.uk/legal).

D2.16   **The Form and Timing of Consent**   The A-G's consent to a prosecution is normally signified in writing, although there would appear to be no bar to its being given orally (per Lord Widgery CJ in *Cain* [1976] QB 496 at p. 502C). The consent need not specify the precise form of charges to which approval is given. Thus, in *Cain*, the Court of Appeal held that the Crown Court had had jurisdiction to try C for possessing explosives under suspicious circumstances contrary to the Explosive Substances Act 1883, s. 4, even though the A-G's consent did not refer specifically to s. 4, but merely stated in general terms that he consented to the prosecution of C 'for an offence or offences contrary to the provisions of the [1883 Act]'. Although it is theoretically open to an accused to challenge the validity of an apparent consent on the basis that the A-G did not genuinely consider the propriety or otherwise of a prosecution, the initial presumption in the case of a written consent is that it would not have been issued unless the A-G had 'applied himself to his duty, considered the relevant facts, and reached a conclusion upon them' (*Cain* at p. 502F).

By the Prosecution of Offences Act 1985, s. 1(7), the consent of the DPP to a prosecution may be given on his behalf by a Crown Prosecutor. CPS guidance states that a prosecutor must specifically consider the case and decide whether proceedings should be instituted or continued.

Section 26 provides that a document duly signed and purporting to be a consent to prosecution shall be admissible as prima facie evidence that consent has in fact been given.

D2.17   Legislation requiring consent normally states that consent is required in order that proceedings be instituted. However, the Prosecution of Offences Act 1985, s. 25(2), provides that lack of consent does not prevent the arrest without warrant, or the issue or execution of a warrant for arrest, of a person for any offence, or the remand in custody or on bail, of any person. Taking account of the relevant case law, the CPS guidance, *Consents to Prosecute*, states that consent should be obtained or given: in the case of indictable-only offences, before service of the case or, where this is not possible, prior to the effective plea and case management hearing; in the case of either-way offences, before the plea before venue procedure; and in the case of summary-only offences, before plea is taken. Where a prosecution is commenced by summons, consent should be sought or given before the information is laid; where commencement is by written charge and requisition, consent should be sought before they are issued. Where the voluntary bill procedure is used, consent must be obtained or given before the application for the bill is made. In the case of proceedings in magistrates' courts, failure to comply renders the proceedings a nullity. In Crown Court proceedings, however, the court may use its powers under the Courts Act 2003, s. 66, to reconvene as a magistrates' court and, provided consent has by then been given, can proceed from the point at which proceedings are instituted.

Time-limits

D2.18   For time-limits relating to summary offences, see **D21.17** *et seq*. For abuse of process resulting from delay, see **D3.77** *et seq*.

Immunity from Prosecution

D2.19   For immunity by reason of age see **A3.72**. For jurisdictional immunities see **A8.25**.

Judicial Review of Prosecution Decisions

Decision to Prosecute Generally, a decision to prosecute is not susceptible to judicial review **D2.20** since it may be challenged within the trial process itself, notably by an application to stay proceedings on the grounds of abuse of process. Arguments relating to abuse of process may and should be raised in the course of the criminal trial itself save in wholly exceptional circumstances (*R (Pepushi) v CPS* (2004) *The Times*, 21 May 2004). It thus appears that in the absence of dishonesty, *mala fides* or some exceptional circumstance, a decision to prosecute cannot normally be challenged by way of judicial review (*DPP, ex parte Kebilene* [2000] 2 AC 326). In *R (E) v DPP* [2012] 1 Cr App R 68 the Divisional Court was willing to quash a decision to prosecute a young girl for sexual offences on her infant sisters, although the facts were unusual. It has been held that a decision to prosecute rather than caution is susceptible to judicial review, but there is a heavy burden on the applicant which may be insurmountable (*Chief Constable of Kent, ex parte L* (1991) 93 Cr App R 416). The courts are reluctant to intervene in such a decision unless breach of an authority's clear and settled policy is established (*Metropolitan Police Commissioner, ex parte Thompson* [1977] 1 WLR 1519; *R (Mondelly) v Metropolitan Police Commissioner* (2007) 171 JP 121). For abuse of process see **D3.70** *et seq.*

Decision Not to Prosecute A decision not to prosecute is susceptible to judicial review because **D2.21** no other remedy is available (*DPP, ex parte Manning* [2001] QB 330), but the cases show that the power to review such a decision will be exercised sparingly. Generally, the court will only intervene if the decision not to prosecute was arrived at as a result of some unlawful policy, or from a failure to act in accordance with the DPP's settled policy, or because the decision was perverse (i.e. it was a decision which no reasonable prosecutor could have made) (*DPP, ex parte C* [1995] 1 Cr App R 136, followed in *R (O'Brien) v DPP* [2013] EWHC 3741 (Admin)). In *Ex parte Manning* the court was willing to intervene in respect of a decision, made without giving reasons, not to prosecute a person who had been identified in an inquest as being responsible for an unlawful killing. Relief has also been granted where a decision not to prosecute amounted to a breach of the victim's right to private life under the ECHR, Article 8 (*R (Waxman) v CPS* (2012) 176 JP 121). See also *R (Dennis) v DPP* [2006] EWHC 3211 (Admin), *R (Da Silva) v DPP* [2006] EWHC 3204 (Admin), and *R (FB) v DPP* [2009] 1 Cr App R 580.

A policy not to prosecute for certain classes of offence or in certain situations is, in principle, susceptible to judicial review (*Metropolitan Police Commissioner, ex parte Blackburn* [1968] 2 QB 118). Conversely, a refusal by the DPP to undertake not to prosecute an offence or a class of offences may not be reviewed. The executive may not suspend or dispense with the execution of the laws without Parliamentary consent. Exercise of the discretion not to prosecute must depend upon a consideration of the public interest in the light of offences already committed (*R (Pretty) v DPP* [2002] 1 AC 800).

When considering whether to issue a summons for a private prosecution after the CPS had discontinued a prosecution in respect of the same facts, magistrates should consider whether the allegation was of an offence known to law and, if so, whether the ingredients of the offence are prima facie present; whether a summons was time barred; whether the court had jurisdiction; whether the informant had the necessary authority to prosecute; and any other relevant facts. However, a private prosecutor is not bound by the full code test in the Code for Crown Prosecutors (*R (Charlson) v Guildford Magistrates' Court* [2006] 3 All ER 163).

Decision to Caution A decision to caution rather than to prosecute is susceptible to review at **D2.22** the instance of the victim. The giving of a conditional caution as an alternative to prosecution was successfully challenged by the victim in *R (Guest) v DPP* [2009] 2 Cr App R 426 on the grounds that it was inappropriate for an offence of assault occasioning actual bodily harm and that the decision did not comply with the Conditional Cautioning Code of Practice. Further, a prosecution following the quashing of the conditional caution would not necessarily be stayed as an abuse of process.

D

Part D Procedure

The courts are reluctant to interfere with a decision to caution at the instance of the person cautioned, but a decision to caution may be challenged if it is made in breach of settled policy (e.g., the relevant Home Office circular); such as where there was no clear and reliable admission (*R (Wyman) v Chief Constable of Hampshire Constabulary* [2006] EWHC 1904 (Admin)) or where there was insufficient evidence to give a realistic prospect of conviction, and the resulting caution was in breach of the recipient's rights under the ECHR, Article 8 (*R (Mohammed) v Chief Constable of West Midlands* [2010] EWHC 1228 (Admin)). In *Caetano v Commissioner of the Police for the Metropolis* (2013) 177 JP 314 the Divisional Court was willing to quash a caution where it was not in the public interest. Reliance by the police on an out-of-date circular may, but will not necessarily, result in quashing of a caution (*R (Lee) v Chief Constable of Essex* [2012] EWHC 283 (Admin)).

A private prosecution commenced after a police decision to caution for the same offence may be stayed as an abuse (*Jones v Whalley* [2007] 1 AC 63). The court indicated that if the complainant had grounds to impugn the decision to caution he could have applied for judicial review to quash the decision and, if successful, could then have commenced a private prosecution. The case of *Jones v Whalley* may be contrasted with *Hayter v L* [1998] 1 WLR 854, where two defendants who had been cautioned were thereafter privately prosecuted, and the prosecution was held by the Divisional Court not to be an abuse of process. The point of distinction between the two cases is that in *Hayter* the forms signed by the defendants indicated, in terms, that such cautions did not preclude the bringing of proceedings by an aggrieved party. In *Jones v Whalley*, the House of Lords declined to rule on the correctness of the decision in *Hayter*. In any event, it should be borne in mind that the DPP has power under the Prosecution of Offences Act 1985 to take over and terminate a private prosecution if it is in the public interest to do so (see **D3.56**).

ALTERNATIVES TO PROSECUTION

D2.23   There are two main alternatives to prosecution. The first is the system of cautions: simple cautions and conditional cautions for adults; and youth cautions and youth conditional cautions. There is also a non-statutory cautioning scheme for possession of small amounts of cannabis, set out in *ACPO Guidance on Cannabis Possession for Personal Use*. The second alternative is fixed penalty notices. Ministry of Justice guidance on out-of-court disposals is available at www.justice.gov.uk/out-of-court-disposals. See **D2.11** for the general factors to be taken into account by prosecutors in deciding whether to offer an out-of-court disposal rather than to prosecute. For deferred prosecution agreements under the CCA 2013, see **D12.106**.

Simple Cautions (Adults)

D2.24   Simple cautions for adults, unlike youth cautions and conditional cautions, are a non-statutory disposal and are available only in respect of persons who have attained the age of 18 years. Their use is governed by Ministry of Justice guidance, *Simple Cautions for Adult Offenders*, the most recent version of which was issued in November 2013 (available via www.justice.gov.uk/out-of-court-disposals).

The Ministry of Justice guidance should be used in conjunction with the *Director's Guidance on Charging (Simple Cautions for Adult Offenders)*, para. 3; see **D2.1**). The decision-making process is set out in section two of *Simple Cautions for Adult Offenders*. Generally, the decision whether to offer a simple caution is for the police, but a Crown Prosecutor may instruct the police to offer a simple caution (para. 39), and should always take the decision in respect of indictable-only offences (para. 37).

D2.25   **Criteria for a Simple Caution**   In determining whether a simple caution is appropriate, the police or Crown Prosecutor must apply the Full Code Test, which includes both the evidential and public interest stages (see **D2.9** *et seq.*) (*Simple Cautions for Adult Offenders*, para. 41). A simple caution cannot be given to a person who does not make a clear and reliable admission (para. 60, and see *R (Wyman) v Chief Constable of Hampshire Constabulary* [2006] EWHC 1904 (Admin), in which there was not a clear and reliable admission in respect of an offence under the SOA 2003, s. 3). If the admission is made outside the context of a formal interview, the method of obtaining and recording the admission must be compliant with the provisions of the PACE 1984 (para. 62). The admission of guilt must be made before the person can be invited to accept a caution, and the admission must not be induced by the offer of a caution (para. 59 and *R (R) v Durham Constabulary* [2005] 2 All ER 369).

An overview of the factors to be taken into account in considering whether a simple caution is appropriate is set out in annex A of the guidance.

Consent of the Suspect   A simple caution cannot be imposed on a person who refuses to accept it, and the implications of accepting a caution must be explained to the person before he is invited to accept it (*Simple Cautions for Adult Offenders*, paras. 63 and 75). The person must be given the opportunity to consult a solicitor before a simple caution is administered (para. 76).   **D2.26**

Repeat Cautions   A simple caution should not be given to a person who has been cautioned for or convicted of the same or similar offences within two years of commission of the current offence unless there are exceptional circumstances (*Simple Cautions for Adult Offenders*, para. 46). However, a caution may be appropriate if there has been a sufficient lapse of time (at least two years) following a previous conviction, etc., for the same or a similar type of offence, to suggest that it had a sufficient deterrent effect; if the current offence is low level; if the current offence is not the same as or similar to any previous offence; if the offender has previously complied with another form of out-of-court disposal; or the giving of a simple caution is likely to be the best outcome for the victim and the offender (para. 49).   **D2.27**

Consequences of a Simple Caution   A simple caution should be administered by a custody officer or a suitably trained person to whom authority to administer cautions has been delegated (*Simple Cautions for Adult Offenders*, para. 77). The officer must ensure that the offender understands that he does not have to make an immediate decision on whether to accept a simple caution, and can take legal advice on whether to accept it, and ensure that he understands the implications of the caution. The offender should be asked to sign a form setting out the implications of the caution (para. 78). Although a caution is not a criminal conviction, if it is imposed for a recordable offence it is entered on the Police National Computer and forms part of the offender's criminal record. Fingerprints and other identification data can be taken and retained, and in the case of a relevant sexual offence the person is placed on the sex offenders register for two years (see **E23.1** *et seq.*). A simple caution may be taken into account by the Disclosure and Barring Service in making a decision about the suitability of persons to work with children and adults (para. 61). A caution may be cited in any subsequent court proceedings. However, simple cautions are covered by the Rehabilitation of Offenders Act 1974, so that they are immediately spent when administered (paras. 65 to 74, and see further **E24.1** *et seq.*). A caution may be quashed if the person is not informed of the consequences of accepting a caution (*R (Stratton) v Chief Constable of Thames Valley Police* [2013] EWHC 1561 (Admin)). Normally, a person cannot be prosecuted for an offence in respect of which he has been cautioned, although he may be prosecuted if new evidence comes to light suggesting that the offence committed is more serious than appeared at the time the decision to offer a caution was made. The fact that a simple caution has been administered may not preclude a private prosecution (para. 88).   **D2.28**

Youth Cautions

The CDA 1988, ss. 65 and 66, which provided for a system of reprimands and warnings for offenders aged 17 and under, was repealed by the LASPO 2012, s. 135. They were replaced by a   **D2.29** new statutory youth caution governed by the CDA 1988, ss. 66ZA and 66ZB. The new provisions do not apply to an offence committed before 8 April 2013 (LASPO 2012, s. 135(4)). A reprimand or warning imposed before the provisions came into effect is to be treated as a youth caution (s. 135(5)). The Ministry of Justice and Youth Justice Board have issued guidance on youth cautions and other out-of-court disposals: see *Youth Out-of-Court Disposals* (available at www.justice.gov.uk/downloads/youth-justice/courts-and-orders/laspo/out-court-disposal-guide.pdf).

D2.30   **Criteria for a Youth Caution**   A constable may give a child or young person a youth caution if:

   (a) the constable decides that there is sufficient evidence to charge the child or young person,
   (b) the child or young person admits to the constable that he committed the offence, and
   (c) the constable does not consider that the child or young person should be prosecuted or given a youth conditional caution in respect of the offence (s. 66ZA(1)).

In making a decision, the constable should have regard to the ACPO Youth Offender Case Disposal Gravity Factor System (available at http://cps.gov.uk/legal/assets/uploads/files/Gravity%20Matrix%20May09.pdf).

With regard to (b) above, it was held in *R (M) v Leicestershire Constabulary* [2009] EWHC 3640 (Admin) that the admission must be a clear and reliable admission to all elements of the offence. This was in respect of a decision to administer a final warning, but the same principles should apply. For the relevance of age in determining whether the *mens rea* of certain crimes is satisfied, or the availability of certain defences, see **A3.73**.

Unlike simple cautions for adults, and conditional cautions, there is no requirement that the child or young person (or his parent or guardian) give his consent before a youth caution is administered. It was held in *R (R) v Durham Constabulary* [2005] 2 All ER 369, in relation to a final warning, that since a warning was not the determination of a criminal charge, the absence of a consent requirement was not a breach of the ECHR, Article 6 (confirmed by the ECtHR in *R v UK* (2007) 44 EHRR 228).

D2.31   **Decision to Give a Youth Caution**   The CDA 1998, s. 66ZA(5), provides that the Secretary of State must publish guidance as to the circumstances in which it is appropriate to give a youth caution. There is no statutory prohibition on administering a youth caution to a child or young person who has previously been given a caution or youth conditional caution, or who has previously been convicted of an offence. It is for the police (rather than a Crown Prosecutor) to decide whether to administer a youth caution but presumably, as with a simple caution for an adult (see **D2.24**), a Crown Prosecutor may advise on, or authorise, the giving of a youth caution.

D2.32   **The Process of Administering a Youth Caution**   The Secretary of State must publish guidance as to the places where a youth caution may be given, the category of constable by whom it may be given, the form which youth cautions are to take, and the manner in which they are to be given and recorded (CDA 1998, s. 66ZA(5)). If given to a person under the age of 17, a youth caution must be given in the presence of an appropriate adult as defined in s. 66ZA(7) (s. 66ZA(2)). The constable administering a youth caution must explain to the child or young person (and to the appropriate adult if relevant) in ordinary language the effect of the caution and any relevant guidance published by the Secretary of State (s. 66ZA(3) and (4)).

D2.33   **The Consequences of a Youth Caution**   Where a youth caution has been administered, the constable must refer the child or young person to a youth offending team as soon as practicable (CDA 1998, s. 66ZB(1)). If the child or young person has not previously been so referred and has not previously been given a youth conditional caution, the youth offending team may assess him and may arrange for him to participate in a rehabilitation programme (s. 66ZB(3)). Otherwise, the youth offending team must assess him, and must arrange for him to participate in a rehabilitation programme unless they consider it inappropriate to do so (s. 66ZB(2)). The Secretary of State must publish guidance on what should be included in a rehabilitation programme, the manner in which any failure to participate in such a programme is to be recorded, and the persons to be notified of such failure (s. 66ZB(4)).

A youth caution does not count as a conviction, but the caution and any report on failure to participate in a rehabilitation programme may be cited in criminal proceedings in the same circumstances as a conviction may be cited (s. 66ZB(7)). Youth cautions are covered by the Rehabilitation of Offenders Act 1974, and are immediately spent when administered (see further E24.1 *et seq.*). If the offence is one that is covered by the SOA 2003, part 2 (see E23.1 *et seq.*), the child or young person will be placed on the sex offenders register for a period of two and a half years.

Where a person who has received two or more youth cautions is convicted of an offence committed within two years beginning with the date of the last of those cautions, or has received a youth conditional caution followed by a youth caution and is convicted of an offence committed within two years beginning with the date of the youth caution, the court must not impose a conditional discharge unless it is of the opinion that there are exceptional circumstances relating to the offence or the person that justify it doing so. If so justified, the fact that the court is of that opinion and the reasons for that opinion must be stated in open court (s. 66ZB(5) and (6)). **D2.34**

Where a child or young person is informed that he will be reported for a recordable offence, the usual rules regarding the taking of fingerprints and non-intimate samples apply. Where a child or young person is released, on bail or otherwise (e.g., for a decision to be taken about a youth caution), and a youth caution is subsequently administered for a recordable offence, fingerprints or a non-intimate sample may be taken without consent (see **D1.105** and **D1.112**).

Conditional Cautions

Conditional cautions for those who have attained the age of 18 are governed by the CJA 2003, part 3, and the *Code of Practice for Adult Conditional Cautions*, issued under the CJA 2003, s. 25 (and introduced by the Criminal Justice Act 2003 (Conditional Cautions: Code of Practice) Order 2013 (SI 2013 No. 801)). In addition, regard should be had to the *Director's Guidance on Adult Conditional Cautions*, issued by the DPP under the PACE 1984, s. 37A (available via www. cps.gov.uk/publications/directors_guidance). Youth conditional cautions for persons under the age of 18 are governed by the CDA 1998, ss. 66A to 66H, and the *Code of Practice for Youth Conditional Cautions* (introduced by the Crime and Disorder Act 1998 (Youth Conditional Cautions: Code of Practice) Order 2013 (SI 2013 No. 613)). The provisions are now fully in force in all police areas (see the Criminal Justice and Immigration Act 2008 (Commencement No. 15) Order 2013 (SI 2013 No. 616)). In addition, regard should be had to the *Director's Guidance on Youth Conditional Cautions*, issued by the DPP under the PACE 1984, s. 37A (available via www.cps.gov.uk/publications/directors_guidance). The codes of practice for adult and youth conditional cautions are available via www.justice.gov.uk/out-of-court-disposals. **D2.35**

A conditional caution may be imposed on an adult only in respect of offences listed in annex A of the *Director's Guidance on Adult Conditional Cautions*, and on youths in respect of offences listed in annex A of the *Director's Guidance on Youth Conditional Cautions*. In *R (Guest) v DPP* [2009] 2 Cr App R 426 a conditional caution was quashed where it was given for an offence not listed in annex A. A conditional caution is defined as 'a caution which is given in respect of an offence committed by the offender and which has conditions attached to it' (CJA 2003, s. 22(2); CDA 1998, s. 66A(2)). Formerly, the decision whether there was sufficient evidence to charge and that a conditional caution should be given was for a Crown Prosecutor, and not a police officer. However, as a result of amendments introduced by the LASPO 2012, ss. 133 (adults) and 138 (youths), those decisions can now be made by either. In deciding whether a conditional caution is a suitable disposal, both police officers and Crown Prosecutors must take into account the factors set out in the relevant guidance. Where a youth conditional caution is given the authorised person must refer the offender to a youth offending team as soon as practicable (CDA 1998, s. 66A(6A)). **D2.36**

D

Part D Procedure

D2.37 **Criteria for a Conditional Caution** A conditional caution may be imposed if each of five requirements is satisfied (CJA 2003, s. 23 (adults); CDA 1998, s. 66B (youths)):

(a) The *authorised person* has evidence that the offender has committed an offence.

(b) The *relevant prosecutor or authorised person* decides there is sufficient evidence to charge and that a conditional caution should be given. In making this decision, the evidential and public interest stages of the full code test must be applied (see **D2.9** to **D2.11**).

(c) The offender admits the offence to the *authorised person*. Following authority on similar provisions relating to simple cautions, and reprimands and warnings, the admission must be clear and reliable, and must not be induced by the offer of a conditional caution (see **D2.25**).

(d) The *authorised person* explains the effects of the conditional caution to the offender and warns him that failure to comply with any of the conditions renders him liable to being prosecuted for the original offence. If the offender is aged 16 or under, the explanation and warning must be given in the presence of an appropriate adult (CDA 1998, s. 66B(5)).

(e) The offender signs a document which contains details of the offence, an admission that he committed it, his consent to the conditional caution, and the conditions that are attached to the caution.

An *authorised person* is a constable, a designated civilian investigating officer or a person authorised for this purpose by the relevant prosecutor (CJA 2003, s. 22(4); CDA 1998, s. 66A(7)). A *relevant prosecutor* means the A-G, Director of the Serious Fraud Office, DPP, Secretary of State or a person specified in an order made by the Secretary of State (CJA 2003, s. 27; CDA 1998, s. 66H(e)).

D2.38 **Conditions that May be Imposed** A condition can be imposed provided it has the purpose of facilitating the rehabilitation of the offender, ensuring that the offender makes reparation for the offence or punishing the offender (CJA 2003, s. 22(3); CDA 1998, s. 66A(3)). A condition can include a requirement that the offender pay a financial penalty, (see the Police and Justice Act 2006 (Commencement No. 16) Order 2013 (SI 2013 No. 592) and the Criminal Justice Act 2003 (Conditional Cautions: Financial Penalties) Order 2013 (SI 2013 No. 615)). SI 2013 No. 615 also prescribes the maximum amounts of a financial penalty. The position is likewise for youth conditional cautions, although the maximum amounts of financial penalties are lower (see the Criminal Justice and Immigration Act 2008 (Commencement No. 15) Order 2013 (SI 2013 No. 616) and the Crime and Disorder Act 1998 (Youth Conditional Cautions: Financial Penalties) Order 2013 (SI 2013 No. 608)). Home Office guidance, *Using Conditional Cautions with Sobriety Requirements*, is available at www.gov.uk/government/publications/using-conditional-cautions-with-sobriety-requirements.

The CJA 2003, s. 22(3D)–(3G) (inserted by the LASPO 2012, s. 134), enables conditions to be attached to an adult conditional caution given to a relevant foreign offender that have the objective of bringing about the departure of the offender and/or ensuring that he does not return to the UK for a specified period of time. The term 'relevant foreign offender' is defined by s. 22(3G).

Conditions must be appropriate, proportionate and achievable (*Code of Practice for Adult Conditional Cautions*, para. 2.21; *Code of Practice for Youth Conditional Cautions*, para. 8.1). A relevant prosecutor or authorised person may, with consent of the offender, vary the conditions attached to a conditional caution by modifying or omitting any of the conditions or adding a condition (CJA 2003, s. 23B; CDA 1998, s. 66D).

D2.39 **Repeat Cautions** A previous conviction or caution does not preclude the use of a conditional caution or youth conditional caution, although a second caution should not normally be given for the same or a similar offence unless there are exceptional circumstances indicating that it may be appropriate (*Code of Practice for Adult Conditional Cautions*, paras. 2.11 and 2.13; *Code of Practice for Youth Conditional Cautions*, paras. 6.4 and 6.6).

D2.40 **Consequences of a Conditional Caution** Failure without reasonable cause to comply with any of the conditions imposed under a conditional caution renders the person liable to prosecution for the original offence (CJA 2003, s. 24(1); CDA 1998, s. 66E(1)), and the document that the person has signed (see **D2.37**) will be admissible in evidence (CJA 2003, s. 24(2); CDA 1998, s. 66E(2)). Although a conditional caution is not a criminal conviction, if it is imposed for a recordable offence it is entered on the Police National Computer and forms part of the offender's criminal record. Fingerprints and other identification data can be taken and retained and, in the case of a relevant sexual offence, the person is placed on the sex offenders register for two years (see **E23.1** *et seq.*). Conditional cautions may be cited in any subsequent court proceedings. They are covered by the Rehabilitation of Offenders Act 1974, and are spent at the end of the 'relevant period for the caution', i.e. normally three months after the date on which they were given (see further **E24.1** *et seq.*). A constable having reasonable grounds for believing that a person who is subject to a conditional caution has failed, without reasonable cause, to comply with any of its conditions, may arrest the person without warrant (CJA 2003, s. 24A(1)). Following arrest, the person may be charged with the offence for which the conditional caution was imposed, released without charge to enable a charge decision to be made, or released without charge and without bail (with or without any variation in the conditions attached to the caution) (s. 24A(2)). Where a person is so arrested, various provisions of the PACE 1984 apply with modifications (s. 24B). These provisions are applied to youth conditional cautions by the CDA 1998, s. 66E(4) and (5).

Fixed Penalty Notices

Fixed Penalty Notices under the CJPA 2001   The CJPA 2001, ss. 1 and 2, make provision for **D2.41** fixed penalty notices in respect of the list of offences set out in s. 1. They include being drunk in a highway, other public place or licensed premises (Licensing Act 1872, s. 12), disorderly behaviour while drunk in a public place (CJA 1967, s. 91), wasting police time or giving a false report (Criminal Law Act 1967, s. 5(2)), theft (Theft Act 1968, s. 1, but limited by guidance to retail thefts up to £100), destroying or damaging property (Criminal Damage Act 1971, s. 1(1), but limited by guidance to damage not exceeding £300), behaviour likely to cause harassment, alarm or distress (POA 1986, s. 5), and possession of cannabis or Khat and related offences (Misuse of Drugs Act 1971, s. 5(2)).

Penalty notices are defined in the CJPA 2001, s. 2(4), as notices that offer the opportunity, by paying a penalty, 'to discharge any liability to be convicted of the offence to which the notice relates'. Where a police officer has reason to believe that a person aged 18 or over has committed a penalty offence, he may give him a penalty notice in respect of the offence (s. 2(1)). Guidance provides that only one penalty notice should be issued to a person for retail theft, and a notice should not be issued for retail theft or criminal damage to a person who is a known substance misuser. Guidance on fixed penalty notices is provided by the Ministry of Justice (*Penalty Notices for Disorder (PNDs)*, available at www.justice.gov.uk/downloads/oocd/pnd-guidance-oocd.pdf).

Section 3 sets out the requirements to be met for the notice to be valid. It must: **D2.42**

(a) state the alleged offence;
(b) give such particulars of the circumstances alleged to constitute the offence as are necessary to provide reasonable information about it;
(c) specify the suspended enforcement period (as to which see s. 5) and explain its effect;
(d) state the amount of the penalty;
(e) state where the penalty may be paid; and
(f) inform the recipient of his right to ask to be tried for the alleged offence and explain how that right may be exercised.

The amount of the penalty is fixed by order of the Secretary of State (s. 3(1)). See the Penalties for Disorderly Behaviour (Amount of Penalty) Order 2002 (SI 2002 No. 1837), as amended, *inter alia*, by SI 2013 No. 1579, which increased the fixed penalties payable (from £80 to £90 and from £50 to £60) with effect from 1 July 2013. As a result of amendments to the CJPA 2001, by

D

Part D Procedure

the LASPO 2012, sch. 23 (in force from 8 April 2013), a person may be given a penalty notice with an education option for a relevant offence.

D2.43 Section 4 sets out the effect of a penalty notice. Where the recipient of a notice asks to be tried for the alleged offence, proceedings may be brought against him. Such a request must be made by the recipient in the manner specified in the penalty notice and before the end of the period of suspended enforcement (defined in s. 5). If, by the end of the suspended enforcement period, the penalty has not been paid but the recipient has not made a request to be tried, a sum equal to one and a half times the amount of the penalty may be registered under s. 8 for enforcement against him as a fine. These provisions are modified in the case of a penalty notice with an education option (see the CJPA 2001, ss. 4(6)–(10) and 5(2)).

Proceedings for the offence to which a penalty notice relates may not be brought until the end of the period of 21 days beginning with the date on which the notice was given. If the penalty is paid before the end of this 'suspended enforcement period', no proceedings may be brought for the offence (s. 5). Section 5 does not apply if the person to whom the penalty notice was given has made a request to be tried. Where a fixed penalty notice has been imposed, prosecution for an offence arising from the same circumstances is permissible if evidence of a more serious offence than that for which the penalty was imposed comes to light (*Gore* [2009] 1 WLR 2454). A penalty notice is not a conviction, and does not amount to an admission of guilt nor to proof that a crime has been committed (*Hamer* [2011] 1 WLR 528: see also **F13.12**).

D2.44 **Fixed Penalty Notices under the ASBA 2003** The ASBA 2003, s. 43, makes provision for penalty notices in respect of offences listed in s. 44(1).

Where an authorised officer of a local authority has reason to believe that a person has committed an offence to which these provisions apply, he may give that person a notice offering him the opportunity of discharging any liability to conviction for that offence by payment of a penalty (s. 43(1)). However, this does not apply if the authorised officer considers that the commission of the offence, in the case of damage to property, also involves the commission of an offence under the CDA 1998, s. 30 (racially or religiously aggravated criminal damage) or, in the case of any other relevant offence, was motivated (wholly or partly) by hostility towards a person based upon their membership (or presumed membership) of a racial or religious group, or towards members of a racial or religious group based on their membership of that group (s. 43(2)).

Where a person is given a penalty notice in respect of an offence, no proceedings may be instituted for that offence (or any other offence to which the provisions apply arising out of the same circumstances) until 14 days after the date of the notice (s. 43(4)). The person cannot be convicted of that offence (or any other relevant offence arising out of the same circumstances) if he pays the penalty specified in the notice within 14 days. The penalty notice must 'give such particulars of the circumstances alleged to constitute the offence as are necessary for giving reasonable information of the offence' (s. 43(5)). Where payment is made by post, it is deemed to have been made at the time at which that letter would be delivered in the ordinary course of post (s. 43(8)).

Section 43B empowers the authorised officer of the local authority to require the person to give his name and address. Failure to give name and address (or giving a false or inaccurate address) is an offence under s. 43B(2), punishable with a fine on level 3 of the standard scale.

D2.45 **Other Fixed Penalty Notice Provisions** There are a number of statutory provisions for fixed penalty notices in environmental protection legislation. These include fixed penalties for:

* leaving litter (Environmental Protection Act 1990, ss. 87 and 88);
* failure to provide specified receptacles for household or commercial waste (Environmental Protection Act 1990, s. 47ZA);
* failure to comply with a litter clearing notice served under the Environmental Protection Act 1990, s. 92A (s. 94A);

- exceeding permitted noise levels in a dwelling after service of a notice contrary to the Noise Act 1996, s. 4 (s. 8 of that Act);
- abandoning a vehicle contrary to the Refuse Disposal (Amenity) Act 1978, s. 2 (s. 2A of that Act);
- exposing two or more vehicles for sale on a road or repairing vehicles on a road for profit contrary to the Clean Neighbourhoods and Environment Act 2005, ss. 3 or 4 (s. 6 of that Act);
- failure to nominate a key-holder where an audible intruder alarm is installed on premises in an alarm notification area contrary to the Clean Neighbourhoods and Environment Act 2005, s. 71(4) (s. 73 of that Act).

For traffic offences in respect of which a fixed penalty notice can be imposed under the RTOA 1988, part 3, see **C8.3**.

BAIL FOLLOWING CHARGE

Where a person arrested for an offence otherwise than under a warrant endorsed for bail is charged with an offence the custody officer must, subject to the CJPO 1994, s. 25 (see **D2.50**), release him from detention either on bail or without bail, unless one or more of the conditions in the PACE 1984, s. 38, is satisfied (PACE 1984, s. 38(1); see **D2.50**). This is subject to the power under the PACE 1984, s. 37(8A) and (8B), to detain the person for the purpose of a Class A drug test (see **D1.124**). A person charged with murder cannot be granted bail by a custody officer (s. 38(1)(c)). Where a person is granted bail under s. 38(1), the custody officer must appoint for the court appearance a date which is no later than the first sitting of the relevant magistrates' court after the date on which the person is charged, unless notified that the appearance cannot be accommodated until a later date, in which case the officer must appoint that later date (PACE 1984, s. 47(3A)). Alternatively, the custody officer may bail a person to attend a police station pursuant to a live link direction under the CDA 1998, s. 57C (PACE 1984, s. 47(3)(b)). Live link bail is now available in all local justice areas (see the Police and Justice Act 2006 (Commencement No. 15) Order 2012 (SI 2012 No. 2373, art. 2, and the Coroners and Justice Act 2009 (Commencement No. 10) Order 2012 (SI 2012 No. 2374), art. 3). For pre-trial hearings by television link, see **D5.38**; for bail from a court, see **D7**.   **D2.46**

Power to Impose Conditions

A release on bail under s. 38(1) is deemed to be a release on bail granted in accordance with the BA 1976, ss. 3, 3A, 5 and 5A, as they apply to bail granted by a constable (PACE 1984, s. 47(1)), and the 'normal powers to impose conditions of bail' (as defined in the BA 1976, s. 3(6)) apply (PACE 1984, s. 47(1A)). Such conditions (including requiring a surety or security) can be imposed as appear necessary for the purpose of ensuring that the person surrenders to custody, does not commit an offence on bail, does not interfere with witnesses or otherwise obstruct the course of justice and/or for his own protection (or where the person is under 17 years, for his own welfare or in his own interests) (PACE 1984, s. 47(1A) and BA 1976, ss. 3(6) and 3A(5)). Any condition may be imposed other than a condition that the person reside in a bail hostel, make himself available for the purposes of a court report, or attend an interview with a lawyer (BA 1976, s. 3A(2)). A surety can be required only for the purpose of securing surrender to custody (*R (Shea) v Winchester Crown Court* [2013] EWHC 1050 (Admin)). It has been held in relation to a court's power to impose bail conditions that, in considering whether and what conditions to impose, the court must perceive a real and not merely fanciful risk of the relevant outcome (*Mansfield Justices, ex parte Sharkey* [1985] QB 613), and it is submitted that the same principle must apply to a decision by a police officer.   **D2.47**

A person who has been made subject to bail conditions may apply to the same or another custody officer serving at the same station for the conditions to be varied, and in doing so the officer may impose conditions or more onerous conditions (BA 1976, s. 3A(4)). The person may, alternatively or in addition, apply to a magistrates' court for variation, and again the court may impose conditions or more onerous conditions (PACE 1984, s. 47(1D) and (1E)). The procedure for reconsideration by a magistrates' court of a bail decision by a police officer, including a decision as to the imposition of conditions, is set out in the CrimPR, r. 19.6. The application must be made in writing and served on the other party, the court officer and any surety. It must specify any decision that the applicant wants the court to make, each offence charged (or for which the person was arrested) and the decision and the reasons given for it. In considering variation or removal of conditions, a court can take into account a police officer's opinion that the person is a flight risk even though the source of the information giving rise to the officer's opinion has not been disclosed (*R (Ajaib) v Birmingham Magistrates' Court* [2009] EWHC 2127 (Admin)). There is no appeal against the decision of a magistrates' court, but the decision is susceptible to judicial review (*R (Carson) v Ealing Magistrates' Court* [2012] EWHC 1456 (Admin)).

Enforcement of Bail

D2.48   Police bail granted under the PACE 1984, s. 38, is enforceable in the same way as bail granted by a court. Failure to surrender to custody at the appointed time without reasonable cause is an offence under the BA 1976, s. 6, and the person subject to bail may be arrested if he fails to surrender or if a police officer has reasonable grounds for believing that he is not likely to surrender to custody (BA 1976, s. 7). Breach of bail conditions is not an offence but a person released on bail subject to conditions may be arrested if a constable has reasonable grounds for believing that the person is likely to breach any of the conditions, or for suspecting that he has broken any of the conditions. Furthermore, if the person was released subject to a surety, the person on bail may be arrested if the surety notifies the police in writing that the person is unlikely to surrender to custody and that the surety wants to be relieved of the obligations as surety (BA 1976, s. 7(3)). The court at which the suspect is due to appear may extend bail by fixing a later time at which the suspect is to surrender, whether or not bail was granted subject to a surety (MCA 1980, s. 43(1)).

DETENTION FOLLOWING CHARGE

D2.49   As noted in D2.46, where a person arrested for an offence otherwise than under a warrant endorsed for bail is charged with an offence, the custody officer must, subject to the CJPO 1994, s. 25, release him from detention either on bail or without bail, unless one of more of the conditions in the PACE 1984, s. 38, is satisfied (PACE 1984, s. 38(1)). The officer must determine what, if any, documents or materials should be made available to the detained person by virtue of Code C, para. 3.4(b) (documents and materials that are essential for challenging the lawfulness of the arrest and detention) (Code C, para. 16.7A). It was held in *Hutt v Metropolitan Police Commissioner* [2003] EWCA Civ 1911 that where the arrest leading to the detention was unlawful, bail could not be denied under s. 38(1). However, it is submitted that this would not be the case if the nature of the illegality was such that it could be, and was, 'cured' (e.g., where a failure to comply with the requirement under the PACE 1984, s. 28, to inform the arrested person of the grounds for arrest is 'cured' by the arrested person subsequently being given this information). It is an abuse of process for the investigating officer to oppose bail following charge where he had promised that, if the person voluntarily returned to the UK and surrendered to the police, bail would be granted (*R (Hauschildt) v Highbury Corner Magistrates' Court* [2007] EWHC 3494 (Admin)).

Where a person charged with an offence is kept in police detention or, in the case of a juvenile, is detained by a local authority in accordance with the PACE 1984, s. 38(6) (see D2.52), the police must bring him before a magistrates' court (PACE 1984, s. 46(1)). A person may be treated as having been so brought if he attends through a live link (see D5.38). If he is to be brought before a magistrates' court in the local justice area in which the police station is situated, that must be done as soon as is practicable, and in any event no later than the first sitting after he is charged with the offence (s. 46(2)). This will result in the accused person being brought before the court on the day on which he is charged or on the next day, unless the next day is a Sunday, Christmas Day or Good Friday (s. 46(8)). If no magistrates' court for the area is due to sit in either period, the custody officer must inform the relevant court office that there is a charged and detained person who must be brought before the court (s. 46(3)). Arrangements must then be made for a magistrates' court to sit not later than the day after the day following the date of charge (s. 46(6)(a) and (7)(a)).

Grounds for Withholding Bail

The restrictions on bail under the CJPO 1994, s. 25, mean that where a person is charged **D2.50** with certain specified offences, and they already have a conviction (including a finding of not guilty by reason of insanity, a finding under the Criminal Procedure (Insanity) Act 1964, s. 4A(3) (unfitness to plead) that a person did the act or made the omission charged against him, or conviction for an offence for which the person was absolutely or conditionally discharged) for any of certain specified offences in any part of the UK (or a conviction for culpable homicide), bail may only be granted if the custody officer is satisfied that there are exceptional circumstances which justify the grant of bail. The offences concerned are set out in s. 25(2) (see **D7.10**).

Where the previous conviction was for manslaughter or culpable homicide, the restriction only applies if the person received a custodial sentence (CJPO 1994, s. 25(3)). No guidance is given in the Act as to the meaning of 'exceptional circumstances' nor as to the relationship between s. 25 and the PACE 1984, s. 38. It would seem that the custody officer would still have to be satisfied that one or more of the s. 38 conditions applies before withholding bail, but in practice, it is highly unlikely that a custody officer would grant bail in the circumstances covered by s. 25. It was held in *R (O) v Crown Court at Harrow* [2003] 1 WLR 2756, that s. 25 does not violate the ECHR, Article 5 (right to liberty and security), provided that it is not construed too narrowly.

The grounds for withholding bail under the PACE 1984, s. 38(1), are as follows. **D2.51**

(a) The person's name or address cannot be ascertained, or the custody officer has reasonable grounds for doubting whether the name or address given by the suspect is real (s. 38(1)(a)(i)).
(b) The custody officer has reasonable grounds for believing that the person arrested will fail to appear in court to answer bail (s. 38(1)(a)(ii)).
(c) Where the person was arrested for an imprisonable offence, the custody officer has reasonable grounds for believing that the detention of the person is necessary to prevent him from committing an offence (s. 38(1)(a)(iii)). Note that it refers to a person *arrested* for as opposed to *charged* with an imprisonable offence. It is suggested that the wording follows from the general structure of the section, and that the ground should be relied upon to deny bail only where a person is charged with such an offence.
(d) In a case where a sample may be taken under the PACE 1984, s. 63B (testing for Class A drugs), the custody officer has reasonable grounds for believing that the detention of the person is necessary to enable the sample to be taken (s. 38(1)(a)(iiia)). In this case the person cannot be kept in police detention after the end of the period of six hours beginning when he was charged with the offence (s. 38(2)).
(e) Where the person was arrested for a non-imprisonable offence, the custody officer has reasonable grounds for believing that detention is necessary to prevent him from causing physical injury to any other person or from causing loss of or damage to property (s. 38(1)(a)(iv)).
(f) The custody officer has reasonable grounds for believing that detention is necessary to prevent the person from interfering with the administration of justice or with the investigation of offences or of a particular offence (s. 38(1)(a)(v)).
(g) The custody officer has reasonable grounds for believing that detention is necessary for the person's own protection (s. 38(1)(a)(vi)).
(h) The person is charged with murder (s. 38(1)(c)).

By s. 38(7A), 'imprisonable offence' has the same meaning as in the Bail Act 1976, sch. 1 (see **D7.136**). In considering the above grounds, other than (a) and (g), the custody officer must have regard to the nature and seriousness of the offence, and the probable penalty; the character, antecedents, associations and community ties of the detained person; his record in respect of previous grant of bail; the strength of the evidence; and any other relevant consideration (PACE 1984, s. 38(2A)).

Detention of Juveniles after Charge

D2.52   The grounds for withholding bail under the PACE 1984, s. 38(1), apply to juveniles in the same way as they apply to adults except that ground (d) applies only if the juvenile has attained the minimum age (see **D1.122**), and that bail may also be withheld if the custody officer has reasonable grounds for believing that the juvenile ought to be detained in his own interests (s. 38(1)(b)). Note that a 17-year-old is not a juvenile for the purposes of s. 38 (see **D1.63**).

Where a juvenile is kept in police detention after charge under s. 38(1) (but not where he is detained under some other power), he must be dealt with in accordance with s. 38(6)–(7). Section 38(6) provides that the custody officer must arrange for the juvenile to be transferred to local authority accommodation unless the officer certifies:

(a) that, by reason of such circumstances as are specified in the certificate, it is impracticable for him to do so; or

(b) in the case of an arrested juvenile who has attained the age of 12 years, that no secure accommodation is available and that keeping the juvenile in other local authority accommodation would not be adequate to protect the public from serious harm from him.

D2.53   With regard to practicability, Code C, Note for Guidance 16D, provides that neither the juvenile's behaviour nor the nature of the offence with which he is charged provides grounds for the custody officer to retain him in police custody rather than to arrange a transfer to local authority accommodation. It also states that lack of secure local authority accommodation does not make it impracticable for the custody officer to transfer the juvenile, noting that the availability of secure accommodation is only a factor in relation to a juvenile aged 12 or over when the local authority accommodation would not be adequate to protect the public from serious harm from the juvenile. Home Office Circular 78/1992, *Criminal Justice Act 1991: Detention, etc, of Juveniles* states that 'impractical' means circumstances where transfer would be physically impossible by reason of, e.g., floods, blizzards, or the impossibility, despite repeated efforts, of contacting the local authority.

Furthermore, Note for Guidance 16D provides that the obligation to transfer a juvenile to local authority accommodation applies as much to a juvenile charged during the daytime as to a juvenile who is to be held overnight, subject to the requirement under s. 46(1) and (2) to bring a person charged and kept in police detention or detained in local authority accommodation under these provisions before a court as soon as is practicable. In *R (M) v Gateshead MBC* [2006] QB 650, the court held that local authorities should have a reasonable system in place to enable them to respond to such requests under s. 38(6), but that they were not under an absolute duty to provide secure accommodation. Where the request was made at 00.20 a.m., with a view to the juvenile being produced in court at 10 a.m. the same day, it was wholly impracticable for the local authority to provide accommodation. If this case is followed, it will in practice significantly reduce the effectiveness of s. 38(6) in ensuring that juveniles are not detained at police stations after charge.

D2.54   The PACE 1984, s. 38(6)(b), provides that, in the case of juveniles between the ages of 12 and 16, the custody officer can take into account the lack of secure accommodation where keeping the suspect in other local authority accommodation would not be adequate to protect the public from the risk of serious harm from him. It is understood that this subsection was intended to apply only to juveniles of that age who were charged with violent or sexual offences. However, somewhat strangely, s. 38(6A) provides that 'any reference, in relation to an arrested juvenile charged with a violent or sexual offence, to protecting the public from serious harm from him shall be construed as a reference to protecting members of the public from death or serious personal injury, whether physical or psychological, occasioned by further such offences committed by him'. Therefore, the possibility of keeping a juvenile in police custody after charge under s. 38(6) is not confined to those charged with a violent or sexual offence. Furthermore, the justification of 'protecting the public from serious harm' is defined only in respect of those charged with a violent or sexual offence. It is suggested, however, that this definition gives an indication of the gravity of the threat of harm to the public that would be required in order to keep a juvenile charged with any other offence in police custody.

Note that although s. 38(6)(b) refers to the non-availability of secure accommodation, the police cannot insist that the local authority place the juvenile in secure accommodation even if it is available. 'Secure accommodation' has a technical meaning, and a local authority cannot restrict the liberty of a juvenile in its care otherwise than in approved secure accommodation. A child aged 12 or over but under the age of 17, who is detained following charge under the PACE 1984, s. 38(6), may not be placed in secure accommodation unless it appears that any accommodation other than that provided for the purpose of restricting liberty is inappropriate because the child is likely to abscond from other accommodation, or is likely to injure himself or other people if kept in other accommodation. A child aged 10 or 11 who is detained under s. 38(6) may not be placed in secure accommodation unless it appears that he has a history of absconding and is likely to abscond from any other description of accommodation, and is likely, if he absconds, to suffer significant harm, or it appears that if he is kept in any other description of accommodation he is likely to injure himself or other persons (Children (Secure Accommodation) Regulations 1991 (SI 1991 No.1505), as amended by the Children (Secure Accommodation) (Amendment) (England) Regulations 2012 (SI 2012 No. 3134), reg. 2).

If a juvenile is kept in police custody under s. 38(6)(a) or (b), the custody officer must certify **D2.55** the reasons, and this certificate must be produced to the court before which the juvenile first appears (s. 38(7)).

Section D3   Courts, Parties and Abuse of Process

INTRODUCTION

D3.1   The criminal trial of an adult takes place either in the Crown Court or in a magistrates' court. The criminal trial of a juvenile usually takes place in a special form of magistrates' court, known as the youth court, but sometimes takes place in either the Crown Court or an ordinary magistrates' court. The first part of this section describes the status, structure, judges and main heads of jurisdiction of the Crown Court and ordinary magistrates' courts. Youth courts are described in **D24**.

THE CROWN COURT

Creation and Status

D3.2   The Crown Court was created by the Courts Act 1971, and replaced the former courts of assize and quarter sessions and a number of other criminal courts. The Crown Court derives its jurisdiction from the Senior Courts Act 1981. Its practice and procedure are prescribed, *inter alia*, by the CrimPR (see Supplement, **R-1** *et seq.*).

The Crown Court is regarded as a *single* court. It follows that, although the Crown Court sits in many different locations and a case will normally be tried at a location near where the offence allegedly occurred, the trial may take place at any location of the Crown Court. The choice of location will depend on the nature of the offence charged (offences are divided into three classes, determining the level of judge who should preside), the convenience of the parties, the desirability of expediting the trial and any directions given by the presiding judge of the relevant circuit as to the locations to which the magistrates' courts in the area of the circuit should normally send cases for trial. See CPD XIII for detailed guidance on listing, especially para. E on allocation of business within the Crown Court (see Supplement, **PD-96**).

In status, the Crown Court occupies a somewhat ambiguous position. Like the High Court, it is a Senior Court and a superior court of record (Senior Courts Act 1981, s. 45(1)), with the same powers in relation to, e.g., contempt and enforcement of its orders as are possessed by the High Court (s. 45(4)). Furthermore, when it exercises its jurisdiction in relation to trials on indictment, appeals from its decisions lie only to the Court of Appeal (Criminal Division), just as appeals from the High Court go to the Court of Appeal (Civil Division). On the other hand, decisions of the Crown Court which do not relate to trial on indictment (e.g., a decision taken in respect of an appeal from a magistrates' court) may be challenged in the High Court either by an appeal by way of case stated or by application for judicial review (see ss. 28(2) and 29(3) of the 1981 Act). Thus, for some purposes the Crown Court is treated as on a par with the High Court, while for other purposes it is subject to the same supervisory jurisdiction that the High Court exercises in relation to magistrates' courts.

Structure

The many different locations in which the Crown Court sits are classified according to (a) geographical position and (b) status. As to (a), every location belongs to one of six 'circuits': (i) Midlands, (ii) North-Eastern, (iii) Northern, (iv) Wales and Chester, (v) Western, and (vi) South-Eastern. Each circuit is presided over by a High Court judge called the 'presiding judge' who has responsibility for taking certain decisions about the administration and distribution of work on the circuit. If considered desirable, a circuit may have both a senior presiding judge and one or more other presiding judges to assist him. As to (b), locations are either first, second or third tier. At first-tier locations, High Court judges regularly sit; at third-tier locations, High Court judges do not normally sit. Each circuit contains locations of each of the three tiers. The most serious cases will normally be committed to either a first or second-tier location, so that there will be at least the possibility of the trial being conducted by a High Court judge. The presiding judge for the circuit has overall responsibility for listing at all courts on his circuit (see CPD XIII, which deals with listing in detail (see Supplement, **PD-96**)). At each location of the Crown Court, there is a senior judge (known as the 'resident judge') who is responsible, *inter alia*, for the distribution of work amongst the judges allocated to that court.

Judges

Senior Courts Act 1981, s. 8

(1) The jurisdiction of the Crown Court shall be exercisable by—
    (a) any judge of the High Court; or
    (b) any circuit judge, recorder, qualifying judge advocate or District Judge (Magistrates' Courts); or
    (c) subject to and in accordance with the provisions of sections 74 and 75(2), a judge of the High Court, circuit judge, recorder or qualifying judge advocate sitting with not more than four justices of the peace,
and any such persons when exercising the jurisdiction of the Crown Court shall be judges of the Crown Court.

For ss. 74 and 75(2) (justices sitting in Crown Court), see **D3.9**. Section 8(1) must be read in conjunction with s. 24 (deputy circuit judges) — see **D3.8**.

There are thus three principal categories of Crown Court judge, namely High Court judges, circuit judges and recorders. All proceedings in the Crown Court must be heard before a single professional judge of the court except where there is provision for justices to sit with such a judge (s. 73(1)).

The Armed Forces Act 2011 amended s. 8(1)(b) to add any 'qualifying judge advocate' to the list of judges who can exercise the jurisdiction of the Crown Court; however, such judges will not have jurisdiction in relation to an appeal from a youth court (s. 8(1A)).

High Court Judges By virtue of the Senior Courts Act 1981, s. 10(2)(c), a person cannot be appointed as a judge of the High Court unless he satisfies the judicial-appointment eligibility condition on a seven-year basis or has been a circuit judge for at least two years. The process for appointing High Court judges is governed by the Constitutional Reform Act 2005, ss. 85 to 93. The Senior Courts Act 1981, s. 9(4), also enables the appointment of deputy High Court judges to facilitate the disposal of business in the High Court or the Crown Court (those appointed must be eligible for appointment as High Court judges).

CPD XII, para. E requires that certain categories of case must normally be tried by a High Court judge (see Supplement, **PD-94**).

Circuit Judges The office of circuit judge was created by the Courts Act 1971. Circuit judges are appointed 'to serve in the Crown Court and county courts and to carry out such other judicial functions as may be conferred on them under this or any other enactment' (Courts Act 1971, s. 16(1)). To be appointed as a circuit judge, the applicant must satisfy the judicial-appointment eligibility condition on a seven-year basis, or else be a recorder, or a person who has held (as a full-time appointment for at least three years) one of the offices listed in the Courts Act 1971, sch. 2, part 1A (s. 16(3)). Retirement is normally at the age of 70, though the Lord Chancellor has a discretion to allow the judge to continue in office until his 75th birthday (s. 17(1)). Conversely, the Lord Chancellor (with the agreement of the Lord Chief Justice) may remove a circuit judge from office before retirement age on the ground of 'incapacity or misbehaviour' (s. 17(4)).

At each Crown Court, there is a 'Resident Judge', who leads the team of judges who sit there and provides a link between the judiciary and the court administration. City and borough councils are able to appoint a judge as 'Honorary Recorder' (a title which is not to be confused with the part-time judges discussed at D3.7); Honorary Recorders have no additional judicial functions but are expected to engage in local civic affairs and events. If an Honorary Recorder is appointed, it is usually the Resident Judge.

D3.7   **Recorders**   Recorders are appointed 'to act as part-time judges of the Crown Court and to carry out such other judicial functions as may be conferred on them under this or any other enactment' (Courts Act 1971, s. 21(1)). By s. 21(2), to be appointed as a recorder, the applicant must satisfy the judicial-appointment eligibility condition on a seven-year basis. The appointment must specify the term for which the recorder is appointed and the frequency and duration of the occasions during that term on which he must be available to undertake his duties (s. 21(3)). The original term of appointment must be extended by the Lord Chancellor (with the agreement of the recorder) unless the Lord Chief Justice agrees that the Lord Chancellor should decline to extend the appointment because of the incapacity or misbehaviour of the recorder (s. 21(4A)–(4C)). When not sitting, the recorder may (and normally does) revert to private practice. Neither the initial term of appointment, nor any extension thereof, may be such as to last beyond the date on which the recorder attains the age of 70 (subject to the power to extend the term of office until the recorder reaches the age of 75) (s. 21(5)). A recorder's appointment may be terminated by the Lord Chancellor on grounds of incapacity, misbehaviour or failure to comply with the terms of his appointment (s. 21(6)). Thus, the major difference between a circuit judge and a recorder is that the former is a full-time and the latter a part-time appointment.

D3.8   **Deputy Circuit Judges**   The Courts Act 1971, s. 24, enables the Lord Chief Justice (with the concurrence of the Lord Chancellor) to appoint deputy circuit judges where it is expedient to do so as a temporary measure in order to facilitate the disposal of business in (*inter alia*) the Crown Court. A person may be appointed as a deputy circuit judge if he has previously held office as a judge of the Court of Appeal or of the High Court or as a circuit judge.

D3.9   **Justices**   For the hearing of appeals from a magistrates' court, the Crown Court *must* normally include not less than two and not more than four justices, none of whom took part in the decision under appeal (Senior Courts Act 1981, s. 74(1); CrimPR, r. 63.10(a)). The exceptions are that the Crown Court may include only one justice of the peace if the presiding judge decides that the start of the appeal hearing would otherwise be delayed unreasonably, or else one or more of the justices who started hearing the appeal is absent (r. 63.10(c)).

Rule 63.10(b) provides that, where the appeal is from a youth court, each justice of the peace must be qualified to sit as a member of a youth court, and the Crown Court must include a man and a woman (unless either of the exceptions set out in r. 63.10(c) applies).

Role of the Justices in the Crown Court

D3.10   When the Crown Court comprises a judge sitting with a justice or justices, the decision of the court may be by a majority (Senior Courts Act 1981, s. 73(3)). It follows that the justices may out-vote the professional judge, although if an even-numbered court is equally divided the professional judge has a casting vote (s. 73(3)). The principle that the justices participate equally with the judge in the decisions of the court applies not only to the determination of the appeal, but also to interlocutory decisions (e.g., about the admissibility of evidence). Thus, in *Orpin* [1975] QB 283, Lord Widgery CJ said (at p. 287) that the justices should be given an opportunity of taking part in the decision as to whether disputed evidence was admissible or not. It is up to the judge whether he chooses to retire for the purpose, or whether he consults with the justices briefly and informally on the bench. However, his lordship went on to say that, in matters of law, 'the lay justices must take a ruling from the presiding judge in precisely the same way as the jury is required to take his ruling when the jury considers its verdict'.

The role of the justices was further considered in *Newby* (1984) 6 Cr App R (S) 148. Criticising the judge for announcing sentence immediately after defence counsel's plea in mitigation, and without any apparent consultation with the justices (although there had been consultation before coming into court and the passing of notes during counsel's speech), Caulfield J said (at p. 150):

> One would hardly need *Orpin* to recognise that where a ... judge is sitting with justices, the court consists of the presiding judge and the justices who sit with the judge, and of course on matters of fact the majority decision decides. So obviously there has to be consultation between the presiding judge and the justices who sit with him. [In the present case there had, in fact, been consultation but there had been no appearance of consultation.] ...

> This court would like to emphasise that where a learned judge is sitting with magistrates, not only should he consult his fellow magistrates by law but he should make sure that the court appreciates that he has consulted. It is not necessary for the court to retire after each particular case. There is nothing wrong in notes being passed between members of the court. But when it comes to the point of sentence having to be given, it is far wiser for the court to show the public that the court is a composite court and that each member has a view which is expressed eventually through the president or chairman of the court.

It is submitted that his lordship's remarks are applicable not only to the passing of sentence but to all decisions (whether interlocutory or final) taken by a court which includes justices.

Modes of Address

According to CPD XII, paras. B.1 and B.2 (see Supplement, **PD-91**), circuit judges, recorders and deputy circuit judges should all be addressed when sitting in court as 'Your Honour', save that any circuit judge sitting at the Central Criminal Court (and any senior circuit judge who is the honorary recorder of the city in which he or she sits) should be addressed as 'My Lord' or 'My Lady'. **D3.11**

High Court judges sitting in the Crown Court should be addressed as 'My Lord' or 'My Lady', as they would in the High Court. In cause lists, forms and orders, the following descriptions are appropriate:

Circuit judges	His (or Her) Honour Judge A
Recorders	Mr (or Mrs) Recorder B
Deputy circuit judges	His (or Her) Honour CD, sitting as a deputy circuit judge.

Jurisdiction

Under the Senior Courts Act 1981, s. 45(2): **D3.12**

> there shall be exercisable by the Crown Court—
> (a) all such appellate and other jurisdiction as is conferred on it by or under this or any other Act; and
> (b) all such other jurisdiction as was exercisable by it immediately before the commencement of this Act.

Immediately before the commencement of the 1981 Act, the Crown Court exercised the jurisdiction which had been given to it by the Courts Act 1971, which jurisdiction included the appellate and other jurisdiction conferred on any court of quarter sessions. The Crown Court has thus inherited the jurisdiction of the older quarter sessions. Furthermore, s. 79(1) of the 1981 Act provides that: 'All enactments and rules of law relating to proceedings in connection with indictable offences shall continue to have effect in relation to proceedings in the Crown Court'. It follows that, although the great bulk of the Crown Court's jurisdiction is statute-based, there may still be occasions when — before, during or after a trial on indictment — it is able to exercise a power derived from a rule of common law.

Trial on Indictment

D3.13   The Crown Court has exclusive jurisdiction over trials on indictment (Senior Courts Act 1981, s. 46(1), which provides that 'all proceedings on indictment shall be brought before the Crown Court'). This jurisdiction is not geographically restricted: 'The jurisdiction of the Crown Court...shall include jurisdiction in proceedings on indictment for offences *wherever committed*, and in particular proceedings on indictment for offences within the jurisdiction of the Admiralty of England' (s. 46(2), emphasis added). This should not, however, be construed to mean that the Crown Court will in general accept jurisdiction over offences committed abroad. The basic rule is that the English criminal courts only inquire into offences allegedly committed in England or Wales or on British ships on the high seas or on British or foreign ships in British territorial waters (see **A8** both for the general rule and the exceptions to it). Thus, the effect of s. 46(2) is that, assuming the alleged offence is indictable and is an offence in respect of which the English criminal courts accept jurisdiction, the Crown Court will have jurisdiction to try the accused for it.

Appeals

D3.14   A person convicted by a magistrates' court may, if he pleaded not guilty, appeal to the Crown Court against conviction and/or sentence; if he pleaded guilty, he may appeal only against sentence (MCA 1980, s. 108, and see **D29.2** *et seq.*).

Committal for Sentence

D3.15   Various statutory provisions enable magistrates' courts to commit an offender to the Crown Court to be sentenced. These are described fully elsewhere in this work (see **D23.30** *et seq.*).

Summary Offences

D3.16   In certain circumstances the Crown Court may have jurisdiction to deal with certain summary offences, pursuant to the CJA 1988, s. 40 (see **D11.17**). Moreover, by virtue of the Courts Act 2003, s. 66, a Crown Court judge (whether a High Court judge, circuit judge, or recorder) may exercise the powers of a District Judge (Magistrates' Court). So, for example, it would be possible for a Crown Court judge in the Crown Court to deal with a summary offence that is linked with an indictable offence without the case having to go back to a magistrates' court: under s. 66, the judge would be able to deal with the summary offence as if he were a magistrate (following the procedure that would be adopted in the magistrates' court).

Bail

D3.17   As well as being able to grant bail during the course of a trial on indictment or other proceedings before it, the Crown Court has jurisdiction, *inter alia*, to grant bail to a person: (a) who has been sent to it in custody for trial or sentence; (b) who is appealing to it from a magistrates' court following the imposition of a custodial sentence by the justices; (c) who is appealing from it to the Court of Appeal and has been granted a certificate that the case is fit for appeal; or (d) who has been remanded in custody by a magistrates' court following an argued bail application (see Senior Courts Act 1981, s. 81). Bail is covered in detail in **D7**.

Contempt etc.

The Senior Courts Act 1981, s. 45(4), provides that 'the Crown Court shall, in relation to the **D3.18** attendance and examination of witnesses, any contempt of court, the enforcement of its orders and all other matters incidental to its jurisdiction, have the like powers, rights, privileges and authority as the High Court'. In particular, the Crown Court is able to deal summarily (i.e. without the empanelling of a jury) with any contempt committed in the face of the court (see generally **B14.79** *et seq.*). The generality of s. 45(4) is subject to the proviso that, for purposes of securing the attendance of witnesses, the Crown Court must use the powers given to it by the Criminal Procedure (Attendance of Witnesses) Act 1965, s. 8, and not proceed by way of subpoena.

In *Ex parte HTV Cymru (Wales) Ltd* [2002] EMLR 11, Aikens J (sitting in the Crown Court at Cardiff) ruled (at [40]) that s. 45(4) gives the Crown Court jurisdiction to grant an injunction to restrain an anticipated or threatened contempt of court. In order to grant such an injunction, the court must be satisfied to the criminal standard (i.e. so that it is sure) that the threatened actions will take place unless restrained and that those actions, if complete, would amount to a contempt (in other words, they amount to a risk, which is more than minimal, that the course of justice in the present trial would be seriously impeded or prejudiced). However, his lordship added that a court must not do anything that is contrary to the rights of freedom of expression under the ECHR, Article 10; it follows that a court will not grant an injunction to restrain a threatened contempt unless it is 'necessary' and 'proportionate' to do so, and it must only grant an injunction to the minimum extent necessary to safeguard the course of justice.

Judicial Discipline

The Judicial Discipline (Prescribed Procedures) Regulations 2006 (SI 2006 No. 676) set out the **D3.19** procedures to be followed in the investigation and determination of allegations of misconduct by judicial office holders.

MAGISTRATES' COURTS

Magistrates' courts consist of justices of the peace. The great majority of justices are unpaid lay **D3.20** men or women; a minority are salaried District Judges (Magistrates' Courts) who are legally qualified. The bulk of the criminal jurisdiction of magistrates' courts has to be exercised by a court consisting of at least two lay justices sitting in open court. However, District Judges almost invariably sit alone. The law on justices and magistrates' courts is contained principally in: (a) the Courts Act 2003 (appointment, removal etc. of justices and organisation of magistrates' courts); (b) the MCA 1980 (jurisdiction and powers of the courts); and (c) the CrimPR (detailed practice and procedure).

The MCA 1980, s. 148(1), provides that 'the expression "magistrates' court" means any justice or justices of the peace acting under any enactment or by virtue of his or their commission or under the common law'. Thus, whenever a justice or justices sit for the purpose of exercising their jurisdiction as justices they constitute a magistrates' court. Where proceedings fall into a number of distinct stages (as when a magistrates' court, after convicting an offender and imposing a fine, subsequently takes steps to enforce payment of the fine), the court for the later stage need not be constituted by the same justices as constituted the court on the first occasion, so long as both magistrates' courts are acting in the same local justice area (s. 148(2)).

Justices of the Peace (Magistrates)

The titles 'justice' or 'justice of the peace' and 'magistrate' are interchangeable. Justices are **D3.21** appointed by the Lord Chancellor 'on behalf and in the name of Her Majesty' (Courts Act 2003, s. 10). The Lord Chancellor normally acts on the recommendation of local advisory committees.

D

Save in the special case of District Judges (Magistrates' Courts) (see **D3.22**), justices are not required to possess any particular qualifications, whether legal or otherwise. There is, however, an obligation on new justices to complete, within a year of appointment, a course of basic instruction in the duties which they will be carrying out. Also, a minority of justices are academic lawyers, and there is no objection to the holders or past holders of high judicial office serving as justices. For the special restrictions on the practice of solicitors who are justices, see the Solicitors Act 1974, s. 38.

A justice may be removed from office by the Lord Chancellor, with the concurrence of the Lord Chief Justice (Courts Act 2003, s. 11(2)) for incapacity or misbehaviour, persistent failure to meet prescribed standards of competence, or for declining or neglecting to take a proper part in the exercise of his functions as a magistrate. Assuming that does not occur, he retains his status as a justice for life. However, upon his attaining the age of 70, a justice's name is put on the 'supplemental list' (s. 13(1)), which means that he may no longer act as a magistrate (s. 12(2)).

Justices, other than District Judges (Magistrates' Courts), are not paid a salary for their work. They are, however, entitled to a travelling and/or subsistence allowance, and to compensation for loss of earnings etc. (Courts Act 2003, s. 15).

District Judges (Magistrates' Courts)

D3.22 Although the great majority of justices are lay, a minority are both paid and legally qualified. The latter (formerly known as stipendiary magistrates) are now properly described as District Judges (Magistrates' Courts). Provisions regarding their appointment, removal, remuneration etc. are contained in the Courts Act 2003, ss. 22 to 26.

To be appointed as a District Judge, the applicant must satisfy the judicial-appointment eligibility condition on a five-year basis (s. 22(1)); the same applies to Deputy District Judges (s. 24(1)). A District Judge has jurisdiction to sit as a magistrate anywhere in England and Wales (s. 25(1)). District Judges (and Deputy District Judges) sit alone in the magistrates' court.

According to CPD XIII, Annex 1 (see Supplement, **PD-103**), District Judges should generally be deployed to hear cases involving complex points of law, evidence, or procedure, as well as longer cases, but are also expected to take a share of the more routine work and, occasionally, to sit with lay justices.

Under the Courts Act 2003, s. 65, a District Judge (Magistrates' Courts) is empowered to exercise some of the powers of a Crown Court judge: sch. 4 sets out a number of interlocutory matters falling within the jurisdiction of District Judges before a case is ready to go before a Crown Court judge.

Structure of the Magistrates' Courts System

D3.23 Magistrates' courts are organised on the basis of local justice areas (Courts Act 2003, s. 8), which are listed in the Local Justice Areas Order 2005 (SI 2005 No. 554), sch. 1, as amended. Section 10 of the 2003 Act makes provision for the appointment of lay justices (i.e. justices of the peace who are not District Judges). They are appointed for the whole of England and Wales but are assigned to one or more local justice areas by the Lord Chief Justice. Under s. 10(3), every lay justice is capable of acting in any local justice area. However, lay justices are deployed to sit in the areas where they live or work, thus continuing the ethos that magistrates' court justice should essentially be local justice.

Jurisdiction

D3.24 Under the MCA 1980, s. 2(1), a magistrates' court has jurisdiction to try any summary offence and (subject to the mode of trial procedure) any offence which is triable either-way, irrespective of where the offence was committed. If the accused is convicted of a summary offence, the court may sentence him to anything up to the maximum penalty provided for by the statute creating the offence. A magistrates' court may try an either-way offence allegedly committed by an adult if (a) the offence is not so serious that the court's powers of punishment in the event of conviction would be inadequate, and (b) the accused agrees (ss. 18 to 21); in the event of conviction, the court may impose a penalty of anything up to six months' imprisonment and/or a fine of £5,000 (s. 32(1)). When implemented, the CJA 2003, s. 282(1), will increase the custodial sentencing powers of a magistrates' court to 12 months for a single offence; a maximum of 65 weeks will apply for two or more offences once the amendment of the MCA 1980, s. 133, by the CJA 2003, s. 155(2), is brought into force. Where a magistrates' court has convicted an adult of an either-way offence, it may commit him to the Crown Court for sentence if the court considers its powers of punishment to be inadequate (PCC(S)A 2000, s. 3).

A magistrates' court may send someone accused of an indictable offence (whether triable only on indictment or triable either way) for trial in the Crown Court no matter where the offence was allegedly committed.

A youth court has jurisdiction to try juveniles (i.e. persons who have not attained the age of 18) for any offence (other than homicide and certain firearms offences), whether indictable or summary, although in certain circumstances the court may choose instead to send the juvenile to the Crown Court for trial (MCA 1980, s. 24).

A magistrates' court may adjourn proceedings and remand the accused either on bail (except **D3.25** where the charge is murder) or in custody (ss. 10(1) and 128). There is also power to grant bail to: (a) an offender whose case has been adjourned for inquiries to be made about him prior to the passing of sentence (s. 10(3)); (b) a person, other than one charged with murder, who is being committed to the Crown Court for sentence (PCC(S)A 2000, s. 3); and (c) a person who is appealing to the Crown Court or the High Court against conviction or sentence by the magistrates (MCA 1980, s. 113).

Magistrates' courts are responsible for enforcing the payment of fines, both those fines imposed by a magistrates' court and those imposed by the Crown Court (Courts Act 2003, s. 97 and schs. 5 and 6; PCC(S)A 2000, s. 140; MCA 1980, ss. 75 to 91). Magistrates' courts act as supervising courts for community orders and, if an offender is brought before the court for allegedly failing to comply with the requirements of the order, the court may impose a penalty for the breach of the community order, or (if the community order was imposed by a magistrates' court) resentence the offender for the original offence, or (if the original order was made by the Crown Court) commit the offender to the Crown Court to be dealt with (CJA 2003, sch. 8, part 2). A magistrates' court may deal with a person for misbehaviour etc. in court by imposing imprisonment for up to a month and a fine of £2,500 (Contempt of Court Act 1981, s. 12(2)).

Constitution and Place of Sitting

Unless an enactment specifically provides to the contrary, a magistrates' court may not try a **D3.26** charge summarily unless it is composed of at least two justices (MCA 1980, s. 121(1)). This applies whether the offence charged is summary or indictable. Similarly, a court holding a means inquiry under s. 82 of the 1980 Act in respect of a fine defaulter must comprise at least two justices (s. 121(2)). The maximum number of justices who may sit in a criminal case is three (Justices of the Peace (Size and Chairmanship of Bench) Rules 2005 (SI 2005 No. 553), r. 3). In practice, the court almost always consists of two or three justices. If they include the chairman or one of the deputy chairmen elected by the justices for the local justice area at their annual meeting, then he presides unless he asks one of the others to do so (Courts Act 2003, s. 18). A justice may preside before he has been included on a list of approved court chairmen only if he is under the supervision of a justice who is on the list of approved court chairmen and has completed the prescribed chairman training course (reg. 4). In the absence of a justice entitled to preside, the justices present may appoint one of their number to preside in court to deal with any case if the justices present are satisfied as to the suitability of the magistrate proposed and (unless by reason of illness, circumstances unforeseen when the justices to sit were chosen, or

D

Part D Procedure

other emergency no such justice is present) that magistrate has completed (or is undergoing) a chairman training course (reg. 15).

The justices composing the court before which any proceedings take place must remain present throughout the proceedings, save that (a) if one or more absent themselves but the court nonetheless is still validly constituted having regard to the nature of the proceedings and the provisions of the MCA 1980, s. 121, then the proceedings may continue before the remaining justices (s. 121(6)), and (b) where the court has convicted an accused and adjourned before sentencing him, the court which passes sentence need not be composed of the same justices who formed the 'convicting' court (s. 121(7)).

D3.27   Any decision of the bench may be arrived at by a majority. In the event of an even-numbered court being equally divided, the court must adjourn for rehearing before a differently constituted bench.

District Judges (Magistrates' Courts) may, and normally do, sit alone in criminal proceedings (Courts Act 2003, s. 26).

For the special rules governing the constitution of youth courts, see **D24.11** *et seq.*

Under the MCA 1980, s. 121(4), a magistrates' court must sit in open court if it is conducting a summary trial, imposing imprisonment, or holding an inquiry into the means of an offender under s. 82 of that Act. Moreover, a magistrates' court composed of a single justice may not impose imprisonment for a period exceeding 14 days, and may not order a person to pay more than £1, whether by way of fine, costs, compensation or otherwise (s. 121(5)).

Under the Courts Act 2003, s. 30(3), the Lord Chancellor may, with the concurrence of the Lord Chief Justice, give directions as to the distribution and transfer of the general business of magistrates' courts between the places where magistrates' courts sit. Such directions may, under s. 30(5), require a defendant to appear at a place in the local justice area in which the offence is alleged to have been committed, or in which the person charged with the offence resides, or in which the witnesses (or the majority of the witnesses) reside; or a place (not necessarily in the same local justice area) where other cases raising similar issues are being dealt with. Section 30(7) empowers the Lord Chancellor to give directions as to the days on which, and times at which, magistrates' courts may sit; subject to these directions, the business of magistrates' courts may be conducted on any day and at any time (s. 30(8)).

Powers of a Single Lay Justice

D3.28   The CDA 1998, s. 49(1), provides that a number of powers of a magistrates' court may be exercised by a single justice of the peace. The list includes extending bail, or imposing or varying conditions of bail; dismissing a charge where no evidence is offered by the prosecution; making an order for the payment of defence costs out of central funds; requesting a presentence report following a plea of guilty and, for that purpose, giving an indication of the seriousness of the offence; requesting a medical report and, for that purpose, remanding the accused in custody or on bail; remitting an offender to another court for sentence; extending, with the consent of the accused, a custody time-limit or an overall time-limit; giving, varying or revoking directions for the conduct of a trial (including directions as to the timetable for the proceedings, the attendance of the parties, the service of documents (including summaries of any legal arguments relied on by the parties), and the manner in which evidence is to be given); and giving, varying or revoking orders for separate or joint trials in the case of two or more accused or two or more charges.

Justices' Clerks/Justices' Legal Advisers

D3.29   Justices' clerks are appointed by the Lord Chancellor (Courts Act 2003, s. 27(1)). A justices' clerk must have a five-year magistrates' court qualification (i.e. must have had a right of audience in the magistrates' court for at least five years), or be a barrister or solicitor who has served for not less than five years as an assistant to a justices' clerk, or be a person who has previously been a justices' clerk (s. 27(2)). Section 27(6) empowers the Lord Chancellor to appoint assistant justices' clerks; a person may be so designated if he has a five-year magistrates' court qualification, or has such qualifications as may be prescribed by the Lord Chancellor.

Under the Justices' Clerks Rules 2005 (SI 2005 No. 545), r. 2, the acts specified in sch. 1 to the rules may be done by a justices' clerk or (under r. 3) assistant clerk. The list includes: issuing any summons (including a witness summons); issuing a warrant of arrest (whether or not endorsed for bail) for failure to surrender to the court, where there is no objection on behalf of the accused; dismissing a charge where no evidence is offered by the prosecution; making an order for the payment of defence costs out of central funds; extending bail on the same conditions as those (if any) previously imposed or, with the consent of the prosecutor and the accused, imposing or varying conditions of bail; further adjourning criminal proceedings with the consent of the prosecutor and the accused, provided that the accused either is not remanded or else is remanded on bail on the same terms as previously (or, with the consent of both the prosecutor and the accused, on different terms); further adjourning criminal proceedings, where there has been no objection by the prosecutor and where the accused is remanded on bail in his absence on the same terms as before; asking an accused whether he pleads guilty or not guilty to a charge; fixing or setting aside a date, time and place for the trial of a charge; giving, varying or revoking directions for the conduct of a criminal trial (including directions as to the timetable for proceedings, the attendance of the parties, the service of documents (including summaries of any legal arguments relied on by the parties), and the manner in which evidence is to be given); with the consent of the parties, giving, varying or revoking orders for separate or joint trials in the case of two or more accused or two or more charges; extending, with the consent of the accused, an overall time-limit under the Prosecution of Offences Act 1985, s. 22; requesting a pre-sentence report following a plea of guilty; requesting a medical report and, for that purpose, remanding the accused on bail on the same conditions as those (if any) previously imposed (or, with the consent of the prosecutor and the accused, on other conditions); remitting an offender to another court for sentence; giving consent for another magistrates' court to deal with an offender for breach of a conditional discharge; allowing further time for payment of a sum enforceable by a magistrates' court; varying the number of instalments payable, the amount of any instalment payable and the date on which any instalment becomes payable where a magistrates' court has ordered that a sum adjudged to be paid is to be paid by instalments; requiring an offender to furnish details of his means.

The role of the justices' legal adviser in granting adjournments was considered in *R (DPP) v Lancaster Magistrates' Court* (2010) 174 JP 320. Foskett J noted (at [30]) that it is clear from the Justices' Clerks Rules 2005 (referring to what is now sch. 1, para. 7) that a justices' legal adviser or a duly authorised assistant may sanction the adjournment of a case where both parties agree. However, this does not mean that he has the power to refuse an adjournment simply because one party objects: 'questions of adjournment essentially involve the exercise of a judicial discretion, ... where there is no agreement about adjourning a case, the application for the adjournment should be listed before the magistrates for consideration'. **D3.30**

For the purposes of the CrimPR, the phrase 'justices' legal adviser' means a justices' clerk or an assistant to a justices' clerk (r. 2.2(1)). Rule 37.14 provides that a justices' legal adviser must be in attendance when the court is sitting unless that court includes a District Judge who directs that the court may sit without a legal adviser.

Assistant Clerks

The Assistants to Justices' Clerks Regulations 2006 (SI 2006 No. 3405) provide that an assistant clerk may be employed as a clerk in court if he is a barrister or solicitor, or has passed the necessary examinations for either of those professions, or has been granted an exemption in relation to any such examination by the appropriate examining body, or whose employment as an assistant is registered by the Law Society as a training contract (reg. 3). However, under reg. 4, the Lord Chancellor may designate a person to be employed as a clerk in court for a period **D3.31** of up to six months if he is satisfied that the person is a suitable person to be employed as a clerk in court and that no other arrangements can reasonably be made for the hearing of proceedings before the court. Moreover, under reg. 5, the Lord Chancellor may permit a person who is not qualified under reg. 3 to carry out some of the functions set out in sch. 1 to the Justices' Clerks Rules 2005, to the extent that these functions are performed out of court and provided that that person has been specifically authorised by the justices' clerk for that purpose.

DISQUALIFICATION OF JUDGES AND MAGISTRATES FROM HEARING PARTICULAR CASES

D3.32 A magistrate may be disqualified from adjudicating in certain proceedings either by reason of the rule of natural justice that a member of a tribunal must not be biased, or by reason of a specific statutory provision. Where a justice sits when he ought not to have done, the decision of the court is liable to be quashed through the High Court issuing a quashing order upon an application for judicial review. However, the issue of such an order is discretionary, and so, if a party knew of an objection to a justice before the commencement of the proceedings but failed to ask him to withdraw, the order may be refused.

Judicial review is not available to challenge matters relating to trial on indictment (Senior Courts Act 1981, s. 29(3)), though any issue regarding bias on the part of the trial judge could be raised in any appeal to the Court of Appeal (Criminal Division) to show that the conviction was unsafe.

Actual or Apparent Bias

D3.33 If a magistrate or judge has a direct interest in the outcome of the case, he will obviously be disqualified from hearing that case. In other cases where the question of possible bias is raised, the question is whether the fair-minded and informed observer, having considered the facts, would conclude that there was a real possibility that the tribunal was biased (*Porter v Magill* [2002] 2 AC 357). In that case, Lord Hope of Craighead noted (at [88]) that there is a close relationship between the concepts of independence and impartiality. He quoted from the case of *Findlay v UK* (1997) 24 EHRR 221 at [73], where the ECtHR said:

> ... in order to establish whether a tribunal can be considered as 'independent', regard must be had *inter alia* to the manner of appointment of its members and their term of office, the existence of guarantees against outside pressures and the question whether the body presents an appearance of independence. As to the question of 'impartiality', there are two aspects to this requirement. First, the tribunal must be subjectively free from personal prejudice or bias. Secondly, it must also be impartial from an objective viewpoint, that is, it must offer sufficient guarantees to exclude any legitimate doubt in this respect. The concepts of independence and objective impartiality are closely linked ...

Lord Hope commented that, in both cases, the concept requires not only that the tribunal must be truly independent and free from actual bias (proof of which is likely to be very difficult), but also that it must not appear, in the objective sense, to lack these essential qualities.

D3.34 **The *Gough* Test** The test for apparent bias was set out by Lord Goff of Chieveley in *Gough* [1993] AC 646 at 670, in these terms:

> I think it unnecessary, in formulating the appropriate test, to require that the court should look at the matter through the eyes of a reasonable man, because the court in cases such as these personifies the reasonable man; and in any event the court has first to ascertain the relevant circumstances from the available evidence, knowledge of which would not necessarily be available to an observer in court at the relevant time ... I prefer to state the test in terms of real danger rather than real likelihood, to ensure that the court is thinking of possibility rather than probability of bias. Accordingly, having ascertained the relevant circumstances, the court should ask itself whether, having regard to those circumstances, there was a real danger of bias on the part of the relevant member of the tribunal in question, in the sense that he might unfairly regard (or have unfairly regarded) with favour, or disfavour, the case of a party to the issue under consideration by him ...

In *Porter v Magill*, Lord Hope noted (at [100]) that the 'reasonable likelihood' and 'real danger' tests propounded by Lord Goff in *Gough* had been criticised on the ground that they tend to emphasise the court's view of the facts and to place inadequate emphasis on the public perception of the irregular incident. The Scottish courts (see, e.g., *Bradford v McLeod* (1986) SLT 244) had adopted a test which looked at the question whether there was suspicion of bias through the eyes of the reasonable man who was aware of the circumstances. Lord Hope observed that this approach (sometimes described as 'the reasonable apprehension of bias' test) is in line with that adopted in most common-law jurisdictions and by the ECtHR (which looks at the question whether there was a risk of bias objectively in the light of the circumstances which the court has identified: see, e.g., *Pullar v UK* (1996) 22 EHRR 391 at [30] and *Hauschildt v Denmark* (1990) 12 EHRR 266 at [48]).

***Porter v Magill*: the *Gough* Test Revisited**   In *Bow Street Metropolitan Stipendiary Magistrate,*   **D3.35**
ex parte Pinochet Ugarte (No. 2) [2000] 1 AC 119, the House of Lords declined to review the *Gough* test. In that case, Lord Hope had expressed the view that the English and Scottish tests were described differently but that their application was likely, in practice, to lead to results that were so similar as to be indistinguishable (p. 142). Moreover, the Court of Appeal, having examined the question whether the 'real danger' test might lead to a different result from that which the informed observer would reach on the same facts, concluded in *Locabail (UK) Ltd v Bayfield Properties Ltd* [2000] QB 451 at p. 477 that, in the overwhelming majority of cases, the application of the two tests would lead to the same outcome. However, in *Re Medicaments and Related Classes of Goods (No. 2)* [2001] 1 WLR 700, the Court of Appeal reconsidered the question of bias. Lord Phillips of Worth Matravers MR, giving the judgment of the court, concluded as follows (at [85]):

> When the Strasbourg jurisprudence is taken into account, we believe that a modest adjustment of the test in *R v Gough* is called for, which makes it plain that it is, in effect, no different from the test applied in most of the Commonwealth and in Scotland. The court must first ascertain all the circumstances which have a bearing on the suggestion that the judge was biased. It must then ask whether those circumstances would lead a fair-minded and informed observer to conclude that there was a real possibility, or a real danger, the two being the same, that the tribunal was biased.

In *Porter v Magill*, Lord Hope (with whom the other Law Lords agreed) approved this 'modest adjustment' of the test in *Gough* subject to one modification. Lord Hope (at [103]) said the test formulated by Lord Phillips:

> ... expresses in clear and simple language a test which is in harmony with the objective test which the Strasbourg court applies when it is considering whether the circumstances give rise to a reasonable apprehension of bias. It removes any possible conflict with the test which is now applied in most Commonwealth countries and in Scotland. I would however delete from it the reference to 'a real danger'. Those words no longer serve a useful purpose here, and they are not used in the jurisprudence of the Strasbourg court. The question is whether the fair-minded and informed observer, having considered the facts, would conclude that there was a real possibility that the tribunal was biased.

In *Helow v Secretary of State for the Home Department* [2008] 2 All ER 1031, Lord Hope of   **D3.36**
Craighead (at [2]) observed that the fair-minded and informed observer 'is the sort of person who always reserves judgment on every point until she has seen and fully understood both sides of the argument. She is not unduly sensitive or suspicious... But she is not complacent either. She knows that fairness requires that a judge must be, and must be seen to be, unbiased.' Lord Mance (at [39]) said that the question of whether a tribunal is biased is one of law, to be answered in the light of the relevant facts, which may include a statement from the judge as to what he knew at the time. The court is not necessarily bound to accept any such statement at face value, but there can be no question of cross-examining the judge on it, and no attention will be paid to any statement by the judge as to the impact of any knowledge on his mind. In *Oldfield* [2012] 1 Cr App R 211, Jackson LJ said (at [34]) that (in light of authorities such as *Gillies v Secretary of State for Work and Pensions* [2006] 1 All ER 731 and *Belize Bank Ltd v A-G*

of Belize [2011] UKPC 36), it was clear that the fair-minded and informed observer is 'neither complacent nor unduly sensitive or suspicious. He or she has access to all facts known by the general public. He or she knows how things are usually done. He or she is aware that judges have years of relevant training and experience. He or she is aware of the terms of the judicial oath.'

The importance of avoiding the appearance of bias was emphasised in *R v S (K)* [2010] 1 All ER 1084. The Court of Appeal had to consider a case where a judge had discharged the jury because jury-tampering had come to light and ruled (pursuant to the CJA 2003, s. 46) that a judge-only trial was appropriate. The defence argued that the judge could not continue to try the case because of bias. Lord Judge CJ (at [41]) said that the court could not 'countenance, let alone permit the verdicts in a criminal trial to be returned by a jury which is actually or apparently biased. An identical principle must apply whenever the verdict is to be returned by a judge sitting on his own.' His lordship went on to say that: 'It is clear that the absence of judicial bias does not answer the separate question whether an informed objective bystander might legitimately conclude that such bias is a realistic possibility'. So far as the CJA 2003, s. 46, is concerned, his lordship said (at [42]) that 'it is inconceivable that the consequence of discharging a jury on the ground that it has been contaminated could result in a trial by judge alone which was inconsistent with the well-established principles relating to the necessary absence of bias or apparent bias in the tribunal'.

D3.37 The test for bias was also considered, in the context of a magistrates' court, in *R (B) v Wolverhampton Youth Court* (2010) 174 JP 90, where the Divisional Court held that there was no automatic bar to a magistrate hearing a case on the basis that she taught at a school where the accused had formerly been a pupil; nor would it normally be a bar if a justice had previously dealt with someone from the same family (per Pill LJ at [11]).

Bench's Knowledge of Accused's Record or Pending Matters

D3.38 There is no blanket rule that the justices must be unaware that there are other charges outstanding against the accused in the same court or that there are offences for which he is awaiting sentence. Where a submission is made that such knowledge disqualifies the justices from acting, they have a discretion to order that the case be tried by a differently constituted bench, but if, having applied the correct test, they conclude that it is proper for them to continue with the case, the Divisional Court will not interfere with their decision (*Weston-super-Mare Justices, ex parte Shaw* [1987] QB 640).

Similar considerations apply where a justice knows from previous dealings with the accused that he is of bad character. The question is whether, having regard to the circumstances of the particular case, there is a real danger of bias on the part of the justice were he to sit. In *Downham Market Magistrates' Court, ex parte Nudd* [1989] RTR 169, at p. 175, Watkins LJ approved earlier authority to the effect that 'mere knowledge of the defendant's previous convictions does not necessarily preclude the court from trying the case. It would only be wrong for the magistrates to proceed where the previous convictions are disclosed to the court in a way which might lead to bias or a suggestion of bias in the minds of the public.' Indeed, in *R (Robinson) v Sutton Coldfield Magistrates' Court* [2006] 4 All ER 1029, the Divisional Court considered the position of the justices where an application is made to adduce bad character evidence pursuant to the CJA 2003, s. 101. Hallett LJ said (at [21]):

> Where an application is made to adduce bad character evidence before a magistrates' court, the justices will, of necessity, hear details of the conviction in order to rule on the application. If the application fails they will put the convictions out of mind when they hear the case. The fact that they know the details of the previous convictions does not disqualify them from discharging their role as fact finders in the trial.

D3.39 In *Johnson v Leicestershire Constabulary* (1998) *The Times*, 7 October 1998, it was held by the Divisional Court that, where magistrates wrongly become aware that an accused has previous convictions, or has previously been before the court, the test to be applied is whether there is any real danger of bias arising from the magistrates finding out something they should not have discovered. The court said that it has to be borne in mind that lay justices are capable of putting out of their minds matters which are irrelevant. Similarly, in *R (S) v Camberwell Green Youth Court* [2004] EWHC 1043 (QB), it was held that a magistrate is not disqualified from hearing the trial of an accused where he has sat in an earlier hearing to issue a bench warrant. The court went on to say that the mere fact that a justice is aware of a previous conviction is not sufficient to disqualify that justice from trying the case of an accused of whose previous conviction the justice is aware (per Moses J at [40]). This case involved a district judge (rather than lay justices), but it is submitted that the outcome would have been the same had the court comprised lay justices.

The fact that previous convictions may be admissible in the range of circumstances set out in the CJA 2003, ss. 101 to 106, makes it even less likely that knowledge of previous convictions will be sufficient to disqualify a magistrate from hearing a case. The MCA 1980, s. 42, formerly prevented a magistrate from being a member of the court which tried the accused if he had become aware that the accused has any previous conviction during a bail application in those proceedings. However, s. 42 was repealed by the CJA 2003, sch. 3, para. 14 with effect from 18 June 2012 (see SI 2012 No. 1320).

Other Interlocutory Rulings by Justices

Unless there are special circumstances, the making of an interlocutory ruling on the admissibil-   **D3.40**
ity of evidence does not deprive justices of the ability to continue the hearing of the trial. Justices should, therefore, not normally disqualify themselves from hearing a trial merely because they have ruled in favour of an *ex parte* application by the prosecution for non-disclosure of material on the ground of public interest immunity (*R (DPP) v Acton Youth Court* [2001] 1 WLR 1828, following *Stipendiary Magistrate for Norfolk, ex parte Taylor* (1997) 161 JP 773 and expressly approved by the House of Lords in *H* [2004] 2 AC 134).

Specific Statutory Provision Disqualifying Justices from Hearing Particular Cases

A justice who is a member of a local authority as defined by the Courts Act 2003, s. 41(6) (e.g.,   **D3.41**
a county council, district council, London borough council, parish or community council or police authority) may not be a member of the Crown Court or of a magistrates' court in any proceedings brought by or against (or by way of appeal from the decision of) the authority or any committee or officer of the authority (Courts Act 2003, s. 41). However, s. 41(5) states that 'no act is invalidated merely because of the disqualification under this section of the person by whom it is done'.

Disqualification of Judges of the Crown Court from Hearing Particular Cases

The rule that nobody may be a judge in his own cause applies to all courts. The position as   **D3.42**
far as Crown Court judges are concerned was considered in *Mulvihill* [1990] 1 All ER 436. The accused was charged with conspiracy to rob a number of banks and building societies, including the National Westminster Bank. The trial judge owned a number of shares in National Westminster Bank plc. Brooke J, giving the judgment of the Court of Appeal, said (at p. 444):

> The function of a Crown Court judge conducting a criminal trial on indictment with a jury is very different from that of a lay justice who is one of the primary decision makers in summary proceedings in a magistrates' court; and although [the trial judge] had to make direct decisions on the admissibility of evidence, ... we do not consider that the hypothetical reasonable bystander would reasonably suspect that it was not possible for him to reach a fair decision because of the existence of his shareholding in one of the institutions whose branch office was robbed ... a judge in a criminal trial is not, save possibly in some very exceptional circumstances, called upon to declare that he has some remote interest in premises which have become the scene of a crime.

So far as lay justices sitting in the Crown Court are concerned, the CrimPR, r 63.10(a)(ii), provides that a lay justice may sit in the Crown Court only if he did not take part in the decision under appeal. It follows that a justice is disqualified from sitting only if he sat on the bench which convicted the accused or passed sentence on him. If a justice was involved in a hearing other than the trial (or sentencing hearing), such as a bail application or mode of trial hearing, the usual principles governing bias would apply.

PARTIES TO CRIMINAL PROCEEDINGS

D3.43 The usual parties to criminal proceedings are the prosecutor and the accused. In *Re Pinochet Ugarte* (2000) *The Times*, 16 February 2000, it was indicated that, while there were many bodies representing the interests of victims and other persons who might wish to take part in such proceedings, there would need to be overwhelming reasons why they should be allowed to intervene in cases other than those being heard by the Supreme Court, which concern pure points of law, and which might well merit different consideration.

Prosecutor

D3.44 The great majority of prosecutions are commenced either by the police and the CPS or by the officers of governmental or quasi-governmental organisations such as local authorities, the Environment Agency and the Department for Work and Pensions.

So far as 'private' prosecutions are concerned (in other words, those not brought by the police or by another public authority), these have to be brought by the laying of an information (following which the court issues a summons). In *R (Gladstone) v Manchester City Magistrates' Court* [2005] 2 All ER 56, the Divisional Court held that, unless an information is required by statute to be laid by any particular person, any person may lay it where the offence is not an individual grievance, provided that the prosecution can establish a public interest and benefit as opposed to a purely private interest in criminal proceedings. However, in *Ewing v Davis* [2007] 1 WLR 3223, Mitting J pointed out that, historically, there has never been a requirement that a private prosecutor has to show a public interest where the prosecution is brought under a public general Act. This power has not been fettered by modern statute. His lordship went on to hold that public interest in a private prosecution is established by the nature of the offence as defined in the statute that creates it, not by the circumstances leading up to it. His lordship concluded that *R (Gladstone plc) v Manchester City Magistrates' Court* should not be taken as an invitation to magistrates to examine the circumstances of alleged offences and their relation to the private prosecutor. The fact that a prosecution may be brought by a public authority does not prevent a private prosecution taking place. For example, a prosecution for causing unnecessary suffering to an animal, contrary to the Animal Welfare Act 2006, s.4, could be brought by a local authority (pursuant to its powers under the Local Government Act 1972, s. 222) but this does not prevent a private prosecution being brought by, for example, the RSPCA (*Lamont-Perkins v RSPCA* (2012) 176 JP 369).

Who Should Commence a Prosecution?

D3.45 The CrimPR, r. 7.2, refers to a prosecution being started by 'a prosecutor'. In *Rubin v DPP* [1990] 2 QB 80, Watkins LJ expressed the view that a prosecution should be brought in the name of an individual. This proposition was, however, doubted by Woolf LJ in *Ealing Justices, ex parte Dixon* [1990] 2 QB 91; even so, his lordship thought it preferable for an individual to start the prosecution, albeit that he was acting on behalf of a body corporate.

Commencement of Proceedings against Suspects Arrested by the Police

D3.46 The procedure for charging a suspect at a police station is described at D2. It is a procedure which, by its very nature, must take place at a police station. In a minority of cases, under the PACE 1984, s. 37(1), the responsibility for deciding whether or not a person should be charged rests with the custody officer on duty at the station where the suspect is being detained at the relevant time (see s. 37(7) especially). However, in most cases the custody officer must first consult with a Crown Prosecutor before charging the suspect, or release the suspect on bail under s. 37(7)(a), to enable a charging decision to be taken by the CPS. The DPP (in practice, this means a Crown Prosecutor) will decide whether there is sufficient evidence to charge the person with an offence. Moreover, under the Prosecution of Offences Act 1985, s. 3(2), it is the duty of the DPP to take over the conduct of all criminal proceedings instituted on behalf of a police force. Proceedings are instituted on behalf of a police force only where the police force has investigated and arrested the suspect and brought him before the custody officer (*R (Hunt) v Criminal Cases Review Commission* [2001] QB 1108, where the Divisional Court rejected the argument that an Inland Revenue prosecution should have been conducted by the CPS because the suspect had been charged by a custody officer at a police station). Similarly, in *Stafford Justices, ex parte Commissioners of Customs and Excise* [1991] 2 QB 339, where the defendant was arrested by customs officers for alleged drug trafficking offences but was taken to a police station and formally charged by the custody officer, it was held by the Divisional Court that where a person such as a customs officer has investigated an offence and arrested a suspect, he does not, by taking that suspect to a police station to be charged by a custody officer, thereby surrender prosecution of the proceedings to the DPP. This reasoning was followed in *Croydon Justices, ex parte Holmberg* (1993) 157 JP 277, where it was held that the seeking of police assistance (in this case by a trading standards officer) does not of itself turn proceedings into police proceedings.

In both cases, the Divisional Court declined to follow *Ealing Justices, ex parte Dixon* [1990] 2 QB 91, where the defendants were charged at a police station with alleged offences under copyright legislation following an investigation by the Federation Against Copyright Theft (FACT) and it was held that a solicitor representing FACT had no right to conduct the prosecution. In light of the later decisions of the Divisional Court, it is submitted that *Dixon* was wrongly decided. Indeed, in *R (Hunt) v Criminal Cases Review Commission* [2001] QB 1108, Lord Woolf accepted that the approach he had taken in *Dixon* was wrong.

The Director of Public Prosecutions

Insofar as the State plays a direct role in the prosecution system, it does so through the DPP and the law officers of the Crown (the A-G and Solicitor-General).   **D3.47**

The office of DPP is governed by the Prosecution of Offences Act 1985. He is a barrister or solicitor of at least ten years' standing, appointed by the A-G (Prosecution of Offences Act 1985, s. 2). He discharges his functions under the superintendence of the A-G (s. 3(1)). The DPP's duties are listed in s. 3(2) and include (amongst other duties) the following:

(a) To take over the conduct of all criminal proceedings instituted by or on behalf of a police force, other than 'specified proceedings', namely those listed in the schedule to the Prosecution of Offences Act 1985 (Specified Proceedings) Order 1999 (SI 1999 No. 904), as amended. The list of specified offences includes various road traffic offences, offences under the POA 1986, s. 5, criminal damage where the value involved does not exceed £5,000 and theft where the offence constitutes low-value shoplifting (see **D6.29**). An offence ceases to be a specified offence if a summons or requisition has been issued in respect of it, unless (if the offence is a summary one) the accused is also served with the paperwork necessary to enable him to plead guilty by post under the MCA 1980, s. 12, or (if the offence is triable either way) the accused is served with the statement of facts, or prosecution witness statements, which will be placed before the court if he pleads guilty. Moreover, proceedings for an offence cease to be specified once a magistrates' court has begun to hear evidence in those proceedings. Proceedings which would otherwise be 'specified' for the purposes of s. 3 are not so specified if they were instituted by way of charge under the PACE 1984, s. 37(7)(d), if the accused was aged under 16 when proceedings were started, or if at any time a magistrates' court indicates that it is considering imposing a custodial sentence for the offence in question.

(b) To institute and conduct criminal proceedings in any case where it appears to him appropriate to do so either on account of the importance or difficulty of the case or for any other reason.

(c) To take over the conduct of all binding-over proceedings instituted on behalf of a police force.

(d) To take over the conduct of any criminal proceedings instituted by the NCA;

(e) To have the conduct of extradition proceedings (see **D31**).

(f) To advise police forces, to the extent he considers appropriate, on all matters relating to criminal offences.

(g) To appear for the prosecution when directed by the court to do so on:
   (i) appeals from the High Court to the Supreme Court in criminal cases;
   (ii) appeals from the Crown Court to the Court of Appeal (Criminal Division) and from thence to the Supreme Court; and
   (iii) appeals to the Crown Court against the exercise by a magistrates' court of its powers under s. 12 of the Contempt of Court Act 1981 to deal with offences of contempt of the court.

(h) To have the conduct of applications for orders under the CDA 1998, s. 1C (anti-social behaviour orders following conviction), and to apply for discharge or variation of such orders.

(i) To discharge the duties conferred under the POCA 2002, parts 5 and 8 (civil recovery of the proceeds of unlawful conduct, civil recovery investigations and disclosure orders in relation to confiscation investigations).

(j) To discharge such other functions as may from time to time be assigned to him by the A-G.

Section 3(2) will be amended by the ABCPA 2014, sch. 11, para. 5, when that provision is brought into force. The effect is that the reference in (h) above to the CDA 1998, s. 1C, will be replaced by a reference to the ABCPA 2014, s. 22 (criminal behaviour orders made on conviction: see **D25.5**).

D3.48 Where the DPP has the conduct of proceedings in consequence of the duties imposed upon him under s. 3 of the 1985 Act, he may discontinue the proceedings or take any other step in relation to them, including the bringing of an appeal and the making of representations in respect of applications for bail (s. 15(3)).

Further duties imposed on the DPP by the 1985 Act include issuing a Code for the guidance of Crown Prosecutors in the performance of various aspects of their duties (s. 10). Another duty resting on the DPP is to give or refuse his consent to a prosecution in those cases where statute provides that the prosecutor may not proceed without it (see **D2.15** for prosecutions requiring the DPP's consent).

The Crown Prosecution Service

D3.49 Section 3(2)(a) of the Prosecution of Offences Act 1985 requires the DPP to 'take over the conduct of all criminal proceedings . . . instituted on behalf of a police force'. To enable him to perform this task, the Act also provided for the creation of the CPS, of which the DPP is the head (s. 1(1)(a)).

The CPS is not instructed by the police — acting on behalf of the DPP it *takes over* prosecutions begun by the police, and therefore exercises an independent judgment in deciding any legal questions which arise.

D3.50 **CPS Involvement in the Charging Process** The CPS are involved in deciding what charges (if any) should be preferred in all but the most minor cases. For discussion of the CPS involvement in the charging process, see **D2.1** *et seq.*

D3.51 **Crown Prosecutors** For CPS administrative purposes, the country is divided into areas, with a Chief Crown Prosecutor for each area (Prosecution of Offences Act 1985, s. 1(4)). The DPP may designate any member of the CPS who is a barrister or solicitor to be a Crown Prosecutor (s. 1(3)). Crown Prosecutors have the same rights of audience as practising solicitors, which means essentially that they may appear for the Service in magistrates' courts but, unless they have been granted rights of audience in the higher courts, not in the Crown Court (see **D3.117** for rights of audience in general). Furthermore, without prejudice to any other functions assigned to him as a member of the CPS, a Crown Prosecutor has 'all the powers of the Director as to the institution and conduct of proceedings but shall exercise those powers under the direction of the Director' (s. 1(6)). Where an enactment prevents any step being taken without the DPP's consent, or requires any step to be taken by or in relation to him, the consent or step may be taken by or in relation to a Crown Prosecutor (s. 1(7)). Thus, the DPP may delegate to Crown Prosecutors his power to sanction a prosecution in cases where proceedings require his consent. In deciding whether to prosecute a suspect and, if so, with what charges, a Crown Prosecutor has to follow the guidance contained in the Code for Crown Prosecutors (see **D2.9** and, for the full text of the Code, see **appendix 3**).

In *Liverpool Crown Court, ex parte Bray* [1987] Crim LR 51, it was held that the DPP's powers   **D3.52** may be exercised by Crown Prosecutors acting within the general authority delegated to them and without express instructions from the DPP. Thus, the DPP's powers to take over the conduct of privately commenced prosecutions and to serve a notice discontinuing a prosecution are, in practice, exercised by Crown Prosecutors rather than the DPP himself. The risk of individual Crown Prosecutors coming to widely divergent decisions in similar factual situations is reduced to some extent by s. 10 of the Prosecution of Offences Act 1985, which requires the DPP to issue a Code for Crown Prosecutors giving guidance on the general principles to be applied by them in: (a) determining whether proceedings for an offence should be instituted or (if already instituted) continued; (b) determining what charge(s) should be preferred; and (c) considering what representations should be made to a magistrates' court about mode of trial. The Code is reproduced in **appendix 3**.

The Prosecution of Offences Act 1985 also empowers the DPP to appoint persons who are not   **D3.53** members of the Service to institute or take over the conduct of such criminal proceedings as he may assign to them (s. 5(1)). The appointed person must have a general qualification (within the meaning of the Courts and Legal Services Act 1990, s. 71). A person appointed under s. 5(1) has, in conducting the proceedings assigned to him, all the powers of a Crown Prosecutor, but has to exercise those powers subject to any instructions given to him by a Crown Prosecutor (s. 5(2)). Section 5 places no fetter on the circumstances in which the DPP may exercise the power to assign cases to non-CPS personnel. In practice, the volume of CPS work in the magistrates' courts is such that some has to be delegated to agents under s. 5. An agent is, however, expected to obtain authority from a CPS lawyer before taking steps in relation to a case such as offering no evidence on a charge or accepting a bind-over (contrast the independence that prosecuting counsel in the Crown Court enjoys: see **D16.4**).

Section 7A of the Prosecution of Offences Act 1985 gives the DPP power to appoint staff who are not legally qualified. These staff are now known as 'associate prosecutors' (they used to be called 'designated caseworkers'). They may represent the CPS on bail applications and on other pre-trial applications, such as requests for adjournments. The conduct of trials was excluded from their remit in the original version of s. 7A, but the CJIA 2008, s. 55(2)(a), removes this restriction by amending s. 7A(2)(a)(ii) of the 1985 Act, so that trials are excluded from the remit of associate prosecutors only if they relate to either-way offences or offences which are punishable with imprisonment. The effect of this provision is that associate prosecutors may conduct trials only where the offence in question is a non-imprisonable summary offence. Section 7A of the 1985 Act also empowers associate prosecutors to represent the CPS in proceedings relating to 'preventative civil orders' (including ASBOs).

The DPP was also the Director of Revenue and Customs Prosecutions (DRCP) for the purposes   **D3.54** of the Commissioners for Revenue and Customs Act 2005, s. 35, which empowered the DRCP to institute and conduct criminal proceedings in England and Wales relating to criminal investigations by HM Revenue and Customs (who prosecute offences such as tax evasion, VAT fraud and illegal

D

importation of drugs and other contraband). However, as a result of the Public Bodies (Merger of the Director of Public Prosecutions and the Director of Revenue and Customs Prosecutions) Order 2014 (SI 2014 No. 834), that office has now ceased to exist and its functions are fully subsumed into the role of the DPP.

Prosecutions by Other Persons

D3.55   Section 6(1) of the Prosecution of Offences Act 1985 provides that: 'Nothing in this Part [of the Act] shall preclude any person from instituting any criminal proceedings to which the Director's duty to take over the conduct of proceedings does not apply'. Since the DPP is only required to take over prosecutions begun by the police, it follows that, save in those limited categories of cases where a statute other than the 1985 Act requires a prosecution to have the prior consent of either the DPP or the A-G, there is no restriction on the right of any individual to bring criminal proceedings. This applies whether the individual acts in a purely personal capacity or in the course of his duties for a local authority, government department, business enterprise or other organisation.

It should be borne in mind that a private prosecution is initiated by the laying of an information (with a summons then being issued by a magistrates' court). The laying of the information amounts to the commencement of proceedings and is therefore the 'conduct of litigation' under the Legal Services Act 2007, sch. 2, and a 'reserved legal activity' within the meaning of s. 12 of that Act. If proceedings are commenced on behalf of a private prosecutor by someone who is acting as an agent for the prosecutor, those proceedings will be void if the agent is not authorised to conduct litigation under the 2007 Act (*Media Protection Services Ltd v Crawford* [2013] 1 WLR 1068).

In *Zinga* [2014] 3 All ER 90, it was held that a private prosecutor is entitled to initiate confiscation proceedings under the POCA 2002, s. 6.

D3.56   **CPS Taking over Private Prosecutions**   The POA 1985, s. 6(2), gives the DPP discretion to take over the conduct of proceedings begun by somebody other than himself. Since the DPP also has power to discontinue proceedings of which he has the conduct, it follows that he can, in effect, bar the continuance of a privately commenced prosecution by taking over its conduct and then serving notice of discontinuance. Alternatively, he can take over a prosecution to ensure its more efficient conduct in the public interest. Where a non-CPS prosecution is withdrawn or not proceeded with within a reasonable time, and there is some ground for suspecting that there is no satisfactory reason for the withdrawal or failure to proceed, the magistrates' court is under a duty to send copies of the documents in the case to the DPP (s. 7(4)); the DPP may then consider whether it is appropriate for him to take over the proceedings.

D3.57   The DPP has a published policy setting out the circumstances in which the CPS will take over a private prosecution. The section of the policy dealing with taking over private prosecutions in order to discontinue them states that:

> A private prosecution should be taken over and stopped if, upon review of the case papers, either the evidential sufficiency stage or the public interest stage of the Full Code Test is not met.

> However, even if the Full Code Test is met, it may be necessary to take over and stop the prosecution on behalf of the public where there is a particular need to do so, such as where the prosecution is likely to damage the interests of justice.

The lawfulness of this policy was considered by the Supreme Court in *R (Gujra) v CPS* [2013] 1 All ER 612. It was held (by a 3:2 majority) that this policy did not frustrate the right, under the POA 1985, s. 6(1), to bring a private prosecution. It was therefore lawful for the DPP to apply to private prosecutions the same tests (namely, evidential sufficiency and public interest) which apply to cases brought by the CPS.

In *Bow Street Metropolitan Stipendiary Magistrate, ex parte South Coast Shipping Co.* [1993] **D3.58**
QB 645, the Divisional Court held that the fact that the public prosecuting authorities
had instituted proceedings for a minor offence arising out of an incident did not preclude a
private prosecution for a more serious offence, where there was evidence suggesting culpability. The case arose from the sinking of the Thames pleasure cruiser, the *Marchioness*, by the
Bowbelle, a disaster in which 51 people died. The master of the *Bowbelle* had been charged
under merchant shipping legislation, and was tried twice, the jury failing to reach a verdict on
each occasion. A private prosecution for manslaughter was then instituted against the owners
of the *Bowbelle* and others. The magistrate's decision to send them for trial was upheld by the
Divisional Court.

In *Barry v Birmingham Magistrates' Court* [2010] 1 Cr App R 160, Cranston J said (at [13]) that
'there is no requirement for a person seeking to have a summons issued to approach the police
first'. He observed that, 'in a particular case it may be a relevant circumstance whether or not
the person seeking a summons has approached the police. The failure of the police to proceed
in a particular case may demonstrate that it is hopeless.'

A private prosecutor may wish to see evidence, such as witness statements, in the possession of **D3.59**
the police or the CPS. In *Scopelight Ltd v Chief Constable of Northumbria* [2010] QB 438, it was
held that the PACE 1984, s. 22, does not preclude the police from retaining seized property
where that property was required for the purpose of investigating or prosecuting an offence,
even where the CPS had notified the parties of its decision not to prosecute those from whom
the property had been seized. The police then have power to determine whether it is necessary
in all the circumstances that the property seized should be retained for further examination or
for use as evidence at a trial for an offence. Leveson LJ, at [53], said:

> If a prosecution is not to be pursued by the CPS but some other public or private body wishes to
> pursue a private prosecution, the relevant circumstances include (but are not limited to): the iden-
> tity and motive of the potential prosecutor; the gravity of the allegation along with the reasoning
> behind the negative decision of the CPS and thus the extent to which, in this case, the public have a
> legitimate interest in the criminal prosecution of this conduct; the police view of the significance of
> what has been retained; and any material fact concerning the proposed defendant. All this falls to be
> considered so that a balanced decision can be reached upon whether retention is necessary 'in all the
> circumstances'. Such a decision would be capable of challenge on traditional public law grounds.

However, the bringing of a private prosecution does not confer a right of access to statements,
photographs or reports in the hands of the police or the CPS, even if the request is a legitimate
one and even if they are essential to the success of the prosecution (*DPP, ex parte Hallas* (1987)
87 Cr App R 340). Nonetheless, once the matter has been sent for Crown Court trial, the
prosecution is deemed to be on behalf of the Crown, and so disclosure may be ordered (*Pawsey*
[1989] Crim LR 152).

On restraint of vexatious prosecutions, see **D3.69**.

The Attorney-General

The main functions of the A-G in respect of criminal proceedings are as follows: **D3.60**

(a) He appoints the DPP, who discharges his functions 'under the superintendence of the
    Attorney-General' (Prosecution of Offences Act 1985, ss. 2 and 3(1)).
(b) Through his office, he may institute and conduct the prosecution of offences of exceptional
    gravity or complexity, especially those which impinge upon the security of the State and/or
    this country's relationships with other countries. He may bring prosecutions for contempt
    of court. He may also take over the conduct of a privately commenced prosecution (or direct
    the DPP to do so). Very occasionally, the A-G appears in court to represent the prosecution.
(c) Certain offences may only be prosecuted by or with the consent of the A-G (see **D2.15**).

(d) From time to time he issues guidelines on aspects of prosecution practice (e.g., in relation to the decision to institute proceedings or the prosecution material which should be made available to the defence).

(e) At any stage after the indictment against an accused has been signed and before the verdict, the A-G may enter a *nolle prosequi*, which terminates the prosecution.

(f) He may invite the Court of Appeal to clarify a point of law where an accused has been acquitted (CJA 1972, s. 36; see **D28.5**).

(g) He may refer a sentence to the Court of Appeal on the ground that it is unduly lenient (CJA 1988, s. 36; see **D28.7**).

By virtue of the Law Officers Act 1997, s. 1, the functions of the A-G may be discharged by the Solicitor-General.

D3.61 *Nolle Prosequi*   Either the prosecution or defence may apply informally to the A-G for entry of a *nolle prosequi*. The commonest reason for the power being exercised is that the accused is physically or mentally unfit to be produced in court and his incapacity is likely to be permanent, but there may be other exceptional situations in which a *nolle prosequi* is the best means of halting proceedings which the prosecution agree ought not to be continued.

The power of the A-G to enter a *nolle prosequi* is not shared by the DPP, but it may be viewed as complementing the latter's powers under the Prosecution of Offences Act 1985, ss. 23 and 23A.

The Serious Fraud Office

D3.62 The Serious Fraud Office was set up by the CJA 1987. It is headed by a Director, who is appointed and superintended by the A-G (s. 1(2)). Its functions are to 'investigate any suspected offence which appears to [the Director] on reasonable grounds to involve serious or complex fraud', and to initiate and conduct (or take over and then conduct) any criminal proceedings relating to such fraud (s. 1(3) and (5)). Functions are also conferred under the POCA 2002, parts 5 and 8 (civil recovery of the proceeds of unlawful conduct, civil recovery investigations and disclosure orders in relation to confiscation investigations). The Director may designate any barrister or solicitor who is a member of the Office to have the same powers as the Director in relation to the institution and conduct of proceedings (s. 1(7) and (8)). The DPP's duties in relation to the initiation and/or conduct of proceedings where a case appears to be of difficulty or importance do not extend to serious frauds under investigation by the Serious Fraud Office (Prosecution of Offences Act 1985, s. 3(2)).

National Crime Agency

D3.63 Section 1 of the CCA 2013 created the National Crime Agency (NCA) to replace the Serious Organised Crime Agency (SOCA). By virtue of s. 1(4) and (5), the NCA has a 'crime-reduction function' (securing that efficient and effective activities to combat organised crime and serious crime are carried out, whether by the NCA or by other law enforcement agencies) and a 'criminal intelligence function' (gathering, storing, processing, analysing, and disseminating information that is relevant to activities to combat crime, including organised or serious crime). The NCA discharges the crime-reduction function through (for example) investigating offences relating to organised or serious crime, and carrying out activities to combat organised and serious crime, including by instituting criminal proceedings (s. 1(7)), as well as by working with other enforcement agencies (s. 1(8)). The crime-reduction function does not include the function of the NCA itself prosecuting offences (s. 1(10)), and so any prosecutions instituted by the NCA are carried on by the CPS.

Government Departments and Statutory Bodies

D3.64 Several government departments regularly initiate and conduct criminal prosecutions, e.g., the Department for Business, Innovation and Skills for violations of the Companies Acts and the Department for Work and Pensions for fraudulent benefit claims.

Some non-governmental statutory bodies also have the power to institute criminal proceedings. For example, the Financial Conduct Authority has power to bring prosecutions for offences under the FSMA 2000 (see s. 401 of that Act and **B7.21**) and for certain other offences, such as offences under the CJA 1993, part V (insider dealing) (see the FSMA 2000, s. 402). In *Rollins* [2010] 4 All ER 880, the issue was whether the Financial Services Authority had power to prosecute offences of money laundering contrary to the POCA 2002, ss. 327 and 328, or whether the FSA's powers to prosecute criminal offences were limited to the offences referred to in the FSMA 2000, ss. 401 and 402 (which do not include offences under the POCA 2002). The Supreme Court rejected the contention that ss. 401 and 402 create a complete regime of offences that the FSA has the power to prosecute, holding that the FSA was entitled to prosecute other offences (e.g., offences under the POCA 2002). In reaching this conclusion, which is presumably equally applicable to the FCA, Sir John Dyson SCJ noted (at [15]) that the purpose of s. 401 is not to *confer* the power to prosecute, but to *limit* the persons who may prosecute for offences under that Act. His lordship also referred (at [10]) to the judgment of Lord Woolf CJ in *R (Hunt) v Criminal Cases Review Commission* [2001] QB 1108, where his lordship had said (at [20]) that, if an ordinary member of the public can bring proceedings for breaches of the criminal law, it would be surprising if the Inland Revenue (as HMRC was then known) were not in a similar position.

DISCONTINUANCE OF AND JUDICIAL RESTRAINT ON CRIMINAL PROSECUTION

Discontinuance of Prosecutions Conducted by the DPP

D3.65 Where the DPP is conducting a prosecution (this includes CPS prosecutions), he (or a Crown Prosecutor) may, at any time during the 'preliminary stages' of the proceedings, give notice to the court that he does not want the proceedings to continue (Prosecution of Offences Act 1985, s. 23(3)). 'Preliminary stage' does *not* include: (a) any stage of the proceedings after the court has begun to hear evidence for the prosecution at a summary trial of the offence; or (b) any stage of the proceedings after the accused has been sent for trial for the offence. However, the exclusion (by s. 23(2)) of cases that have been sent for trial to the Crown Court is negated to a large extent by s. 23A. This specifically provides for a notice of discontinuance to be served where a case has been sent to the Crown Court for trial under the CDA 1998, s. 51. The notice may be served on the Crown Court 'at any time before the indictment is preferred' (s. 23A(2)).

The effect of the DPP giving notice of discontinuance under s. 23 is that the proceedings are discontinued from the giving of notice. However, they may be revived by the accused himself giving notice that he wishes them to continue (s. 23(3) and (7)). The apparent purpose of allowing the accused to insist on the case continuing is, first, that a full hearing may establish innocence and vindicate him in a way which the mere withdrawal of proceedings could not, and, secondly, if there is an acquittal following trial he may rely on the plea of autrefois acquit if further proceedings are commenced. This is significant because notice of discontinuance does not guarantee that the proceedings will not be revived should additional evidence later be discovered (see s. 23(9), which provides that discontinuance shall not prevent the subsequent institution of fresh proceedings in respect of the same offence).

D3.66 When giving notice to the court under s. 23(3) the DPP must give his reasons for not wanting the proceedings to continue (s. 23(5)). He must also inform the accused that notice has been given and that he (the accused) has the right to require the proceedings to be continued, but he is not obliged to indicate to the accused his reasons for desiring discontinuance (s. 23(6)). If the accused has been charged at the police station and the DPP wishes to discontinue before there has even been a court appearance, it is merely necessary to serve notice to that effect on the accused himself, and he does not then have the right to require the proceedings to continue (s. 23(4)).

Where proceedings are discontinued under s. 23A, the discontinuance takes effect from the giving of that notice (s. 23A(2)). The notice must give reasons for the decision to discontinue the proceedings (s. 23A(3)) but the DPP (or Crown Prosecutor) is not obliged to give the accused any indication of his reasons for not wanting the proceedings to continue (s. 23A(4)). Under s. 23A(5), the discontinuance of proceedings under s. 23A does not prevent the institution of fresh proceedings in respect of the same offence. However, unlike discontinuance under s. 23, there is no provision for the accused to insist that the proceedings continue.

The procedure to be followed under s. 23 or s. 23A is set out in part 8 of the CrimPR (see Supplement, R-95).

The decision to discontinue a prosecution may be challenged by way of judicial review if that decision is based on an irrational (and therefore) unlawful application of the provisions of the Code for Crown Prosecutors which govern the decision to prosecute (*R (FB) v DPP* [2009] 1 Cr App R 580).

Offering No Evidence

D3.67 Instead of discontinuing proceedings under the Prosecution of Offences Act 1985, s. 23 or 23A (see **D3.65**), the prosecution may simply offer no evidence at the trial. *Cooke v DPP* (1992) 95 Cr App R 233 makes it clear that the statutory power to discontinue a prosecution is additional to the common-law power to offer no evidence.

The court has no power to prevent the offering of no evidence (see Lord Lane CJ in *Canterbury and St Augustine Justices, ex parte Klisiak* [1982] QB 398 at p. 411C–D and *Horseferry Road Magistrates' Court, ex parte O'Regan* (1986) 150 JP 535).

In *Raymond v A-G* [1982] QB 839 the Court of Appeal considered whether it was legitimate for the Director to take over a prosecution with the sole purpose of offering no evidence. It was held that the DPP's decision was not open to attack unless it was so manifestly wrong that it could not have been honestly and reasonably arrived at. Giving the judgment of the court, Sir Sebag Shaw said (at pp. 846H–847D):

> ...when the Director intervenes in a prosecution which has been privately instituted he may do so not exclusively for the purpose of pursuing it by carrying it on, but also with the object of aborting it; that is to say, he may 'conduct' the proceedings in whatever manner may appear expedient in the public interest. The Director will thus intervene in a private prosecution where the issues in the public interest are so grave that the expertise and the resources of the Director's office should be brought to bear in order to ensure that the proceedings are properly conducted from the point of view of the prosecution.
>
> On the other hand, there may be what appear to the Director substantial reasons in the public interest for not pursuing a prosecution privately commenced. What may emerge from those proceedings might have an adverse effect upon a pending prosecution involving far more serious issues. The Director, in such a case, is called upon to make a value judgment. Unless his decision is manifestly such that it could not be honestly and reasonably arrived at it cannot, in our opinion, be impugned.

D3.68 　　　　　　　　　Prosecution of Offences Act 1985, ss. 23 and 23A

23.—(1) Where the Director of Public Prosecutions has the conduct of proceedings for an offence, this section applies in relation to the preliminary stages of those proceedings.
(2) In this section, 'preliminary stage' in relation to proceedings for an offence does not include—
　(a) any stage of the proceedings after the court has begun to hear evidence for the prosecution at a summary trial of the offence; or
　(b) any stage of the proceedings after the accused has been sent for trial for the offence.

(3) Where, at any time during the preliminary stages of the proceedings, the Director gives notice under this section to the designated officer for the court that he does not want the proceedings to continue, they shall be discontinued with effect from the giving of that notice but may be revived by notice given by the accused under subsection (7) below.

(4) Where, in the case of a person charged with an offence after being taken into custody without a warrant, the Director gives him notice, at a time when no magistrates' court has been informed of the charge, that the proceedings against him are discontinued, they shall be discontinued with effect from the giving of that notice.

(5) The Director shall, in any notice given under subsection (3) above, give reasons for not wanting the proceedings to continue.

(6) On giving any notice under subsection (3) above the Director shall inform the accused of the notice and of the accused's right to require the proceedings to be continued; but the Director shall not be obliged to give the accused any indication of his reasons for not wanting the proceedings to continue.

(7) Where the Director has given notice under subsection (3) above, the accused shall, if he wants the proceedings to continue, give notice to that effect to the designated officer for the court within the prescribed period; and where notice is so given the proceedings shall continue as if no notice had been given by the Director under subsection (3) above.

(8) Where the designated officer for the court has been so notified by the accused he shall inform the Director.

(9) The discontinuance of any proceedings by virtue of this section shall not prevent the institution of fresh proceedings in respect of the same offence.

[(10) Meaning of 'prescribed'.]

23A.—(1) This section applies where—

  (a) the Director of Public Prosecutions, or a public authority (within the meaning of section 17 of this Act), has the conduct of proceedings for an offence; and

  (b) the accused has been sent for trial for the offence.

(2) Where, at any time before the indictment is preferred, the Director or authority gives notice under this section to the Crown Court sitting at the place specified in the notice under section 51D(1) of the Crime and Disorder Act 1998 that he or it does not want the proceedings to continue, they shall be discontinued with effect from the giving of that notice.

(3) The Director or authority shall, in any notice given under subsection (2) above, give reasons for not wanting the proceedings to continue.

(4) On giving any notice under subsection (2) above the Director or authority shall inform the accused of the notice; but the Director or authority shall not be obliged to give the accused any indication of his reasons for not wanting the proceedings to continue.

(5) The discontinuance of any proceedings by virtue of this section shall not prevent the institution of fresh proceedings in respect of the same offence.

Court Order Restricting the Commencement of a Prosecution

By s. 42(1)(c) of the Senior Courts Act 1981, the A-G may apply to the High Court for a **D3.69**
'criminal proceedings order'. Such an order prevents the person against whom it is made laying an information or applying for a voluntary bill of indictment without leave of the High Court (s. 42(1A)). Before making the order, the High Court must, after giving the proposed subject the opportunity of making representations, be satisfied that he has 'habitually and persistently and without any reasonable ground . . . instituted vexatious prosecutions (whether against the same person or different persons)'. Where an order has been made, leave to lay an information or apply for a voluntary bill may not be given unless the High Court is satisfied that (a) the institution of the prosecution would not be an abuse of the criminal process; and (b) the applicant has reasonable grounds for instituting it (s. 42(3A)). There is no appeal against refusal of leave (s. 42(4)).

An application for permission to apply for judicial review falls within the definition of 'civil proceedings' even if the decision under challenge relates to a criminal cause or matter, and so a person who has been declared a vexatious litigant and who is subject to a 'civil proceedings order' under s. 42(1A) of the 1981 Act, requires leave (under s. 42) to make the application (*Ewing v DPP* [2010] EWCA Civ 70, following *Re Ewing (No. 2)* [1994] 1 WLR 1553).

ABUSE OF PROCESS: THE POWER TO STAY PROCEEDINGS

D3.70   According to *County of London Quarter Sessions, ex parte Downes* [1954] 1 QB 1 at p. 6, once an indictment has been preferred, the accused must be tried unless:

(a) the indictment is defective (e.g., it contains counts that are improperly joined and so does not comply with the CrimPR, r. 14.2(3));

(b) a 'plea in bar' applies (such as autrefois acquit);

(c) a '*nolle prosequi*' is entered by the A-G to stop the proceedings; or

(d) the indictment discloses no offence that the court has jurisdiction to try (e.g., the offence is based on a statutory provision that was not in force at the date the accused allegedly did the act complained of).

To this list must be added cases where it would amount to an abuse of process to continue with the prosecution. Where proceedings would amount to an abuse of process, the court may order that those proceedings be stayed. The effect of a stay is that the case against the accused is stopped permanently. Given the nature of the grounds upon which a case may properly be regarded as an abuse of process, it is unlikely that there would be any basis for lifting a stay that has been imposed.

D3.71   In *Beckford* [1996] 1 Cr App R 94, Neill LJ said (at p. 100) that the 'constitutional principle which underlies the jurisdiction to stay proceedings is that the courts have the power and the duty to protect the law by protecting its own purposes and functions'. His lordship quoted the words of Lord Devlin in *Connelly v DPP* [1964] AC 1254 at p. 1354, that the courts have 'an inescapable duty to secure fair treatment for those who come or are brought before them'. In *Maxwell* [2011] 4 All ER 941 (at [13]), cited in *Warren v Attorney General for Jersey* [2012] 1 AC 22 (at [22]), Lord Dyson summarised the two categories of case in which the court has the power to stay proceedings for abuse of process:

> It is well established that the court has the power to stay proceedings in two categories of case, namely (i) where it will be impossible to give the accused a fair trial, and (ii) where it offends the court's sense of justice and propriety to be asked to try the accused in the particular circumstances of the case. In the first category of case, if the court concludes that an accused cannot receive a fair trial, it will stay the proceedings without more. No question of the balancing of competing interests arises. In the second category of case, the court is concerned to protect the integrity of the criminal justice system. Here a stay will be granted where the court concludes that in all the circumstances a trial will offend the court's sense of justice and propriety (per Lord Lowry in *R v Horseferry Road Magistrates' Court, ex p Bennett* [1994] 1 AC 42 (at 74G)), or will undermine public confidence in the criminal justice system and bring it into disrepute (per Lord Steyn in *Latif* [1996] 1 WLR 104 (at 112F)).

More recently, in *Crawley* [2014] EWCA Crim 1028, Sir Brian Leveson P summarised the scope of abuse of process thus (at [17]):

> [T]here are two categories of case in which the court has the power to stay proceedings for abuse of process. These are, first, where the court concludes that the accused can no longer receive a fair hearing; and, second, where it would otherwise be unfair to try the accused or, put another way, where a stay is necessary to protect the integrity of the criminal justice system. The first limb focuses on the trial process and where the court concludes that the accused would not receive a fair hearing it will stay the proceedings; no balancing exercise is required. The second limb concerns the integrity of the criminal justice system and applies where the Court considers that the accused should not be standing trial at all, irrespective of the potential fairness of the trial itself.

He added (at [18]):

> [T]here is a strong public interest in the prosecution of crime and in ensuring that those charged with serious criminal offences are tried. Ordering a stay of proceedings, which in criminal law is effectively a permanent remedy, is thus a remedy of last resort.

His lordship observed (at [21]) that 'cases in which it may be unfair to try the accused (the second category of case) will include, but are not confined to, those cases where there has been bad faith, unlawfulness or executive misconduct'. In such case, 'the court is concerned not to create the perception that it is condoning malpractice by law enforcement agencies or to convey the impression that it will adopt the approach that the end justifies the means: the touchstone is the integrity of the criminal justice system' (at [23]). In *Horseferry Road Magistrates' Court, ex parte Bennett* [1994] 1 AC 42, Lord Griffiths (at p. 61H) said that if the courts have a power to interfere with the prosecution in such cases:

> it must be because the judiciary accept a responsibility for the maintenance of the rule of law that embraces a willingness to oversee executive action and to refuse to countenance behaviour that threatens either basic human rights or the rule of law ... I have no doubt that the judiciary should accept this responsibility in the field of criminal law.

There are thus two main categories of abuse of process: **D3.72**

(a) cases where the court concludes that the accused cannot receive a fair trial;
(b) cases where the court concludes that it would be unfair for the accused to be tried.

The former focuses on the trial process; the latter is applicable where the accused should not be standing trial at all (irrespective of the fairness of the actual trial).

In *DPP v Humphrys* [1977] AC 1, Lord Salmon (at p. 46) commented that a judge does not have 'any power to refuse to allow a prosecution to proceed merely because he considers that, as a matter of policy, it ought not to have been brought. It is only if the prosecution amounts to an abuse of the process of the court and is oppressive and vexatious that the judge has the power to intervene.'

In very rare cases, the court may intervene to prevent an abuse of process before a suspect has   **D3.73**
been formally charged. However, the court will order that a police investigation be discontinued, on the basis that there is no prospect of an eventual prosecution, only in the most exceptional cases. Where there were unquestionably reasonable grounds initially to suspect a person under investigation, the court should be very slow to second-guess the police in deciding at what point he can be dismissed from the inquiry. To hold otherwise would involve an unwelcome blurring of the separate roles of court and prosecutor/investigator (*R (C) v Chief Constable of A* [2006] EWHC 2352 (Admin), per Underhill J at [32]).

Important Issues

Two key questions run through many of the authorities: (1) To what extent is the accused preju-   **D3.74**
diced? (2) To what degree are the rule of law and the administration of justice undermined by the behaviour of the investigators or the prosecution?

There is no definitive list of complaints which are capable of amounting to abuse of process, but it is possible to derive some categories of abuse from the case law. For example: lengthy delay which causes prejudice to the accused; failure to honour an undertaking given to the accused; failing to secure evidence or destroying evidence; tactical manipulation or misuse of procedures in order to deprive the accused of some protection provided by the law, or taking unfair advantage of a technicality; entrapment; abuse of executive power.

One consequence of the fact that the test for abuse of process is much higher than the judge simply taking the view that the case should not have been brought is that it is not an abuse of process to prosecute someone where the evidence against him is weak. It follows that a judge has no power to prevent the prosecution from presenting their evidence merely on the basis that he considers a conviction unlikely (*A-G's Ref (No. 2 of 2000)* [2001] 1 Cr App R 36), but the judge may, if he sees fit, stop the case at the close of the prosecution evidence .

As well as invoking the right to a fair trial under the ECHR, Article 6, those seeking to establish abuse of process will also rely on the overriding objective set out in the CrimPR, part 1, which requires everyone involved in any way in a criminal case to prepare and conduct the case in accordance with the overriding objective to deal with the case 'justly' (which term includes the requirement to deal with the defence fairly and to deal with the case efficiently and expeditiously: see **D4**).

Magistrates' Courts

D3.75   Much of the case law on abuse of process comes from cases tried in the Crown Court. However, abuse of process can also be raised in a magistrates' court. In *Horseferry Road Magistrates' Court, ex parte Bennett* [1994] 1 AC 42, the House of Lords ruled that the jurisdiction exercised by magistrates to protect the court's process from abuse is confined strictly to matters directly affecting the fairness of the trial of the particular accused with whom they were dealing (such as delay or unfair manipulation of court procedures). It does not extend to a wider supervisory jurisdiction to uphold the rule of law. The rationale is that supervision of the use of executive power is a responsibility that is vested in the High Court. Where such an issue arises, the magistrates should adjourn the matter so that an application can be made to the Divisional Court, which is the proper forum for deciding the matter (per Lord Griffiths at p. 64).

In *R (Salubi) v Bow Street Magistrates' Court* [2002] 1 WLR 3073, it was held that the fact that magistrates are required, under the transfer procedure in the CDA 1998, s. 51(1), to send cases to Crown Court 'forthwith' does not necessarily preclude them from exercising their jurisdiction to stay the proceedings as an abuse of process in an appropriate case. However, it would be appropriate to do so only in rare cases where the defence establish bad faith or serious misconduct. The Divisional Court reiterated that a magistrates' court's power to stay criminal proceedings for abuse of process is strictly confined to matters directly affecting the fairness of a trial before it and that this power should be exercised sparingly. The Court said that where the point is complex or novel it should normally be left for resolution in the Crown Court or the High Court. It should be borne in mind that an abuse of process application may be made immediately after the case arrives at the Crown Court (per Auld LJ at [20]–[21]).

Where it is contended that a summary trial should not take place because it would be unfair to try the defendant (as opposed to the question being whether he can have a fair trial), the issue of abuse of process has to be dealt with by the High Court, not in the magistrates' court (*Nembhard v DPP* [2009] EWHC 194 (Admin); *R (Smith) v CPS* [2010] EWHC 3593 (Admin)). In *DPP v Gowing* (2014) 178 JP 181, Beatson LJ (at [29]) emphasised that it is important that magistrates who are considering staying proceedings recognise 'the exceptional nature of the jurisdiction to stay proceedings'. This means that there must be 'a firm factual basis for staying' (namely bad faith or an inability to have a fair trial). His lordship added (at [31]) that, where there are failures on the part of prosecutors, the power to stay proceedings 'should not be used to punish prosecutors where a fair trial remains possible'.

Burden and Standard of Proof

D3.76   The normal rule is that he who asserts the abuse of process must prove it; it follows that the defence bear the burden of establishing abuse on the balance of probabilities (*Telford Justices, ex parte Badhan* [1991] 2 QB 78).

It should be noted that in *S (SP)* [2006] 2 Cr App R 341, the Court of Appeal observed that the discretionary decision whether or not to grant a stay by reason of delay is an exercise in judicial assessment dependent on judgement, rather than on any conclusion as to fact based on evidence. It is, therefore, potentially misleading to use the language of burden and standard of proof, which is more apt to an evidence-based fact-finding process (per Rose LJ at [20]). It may well be that this comment should be taken as applying to abuse of process applications generally (i.e. it is not limited to those where delay is an issue), since the balancing of competing interests is at the heart of all abuse claims. It is doubtful, however, that the Court of Appeal intended to signal a new approach to abuse cases: it is likely to remain the case that there is, effectively, a presumption that the trial should go ahead unless there is a compelling reason for stopping the trial from taking place. In the case of delay, for example, the Court of Appeal confirmed in *E* [2012] EWCA Crim 791 that, where delay is said to amount to abuse of process, 'the burden of proof or persuasion lies on the defendant' to show that a fair trial is no longer possible (per Rix LJ at [22]).

In *R (Barons Pub Co. Ltd) v Staines Magistrates' Court* [2013] EWHC 898 (Admin), Sir John Thomas P made it clear (at [36]) that a magistrates' court has 'no power of review of a prosecutorial decision other than through an abuse of process application'. His lordship added that such an application 'in itself is an exceptional remedy'; moreover, it is only where an abuse of process application cannot be made that an application can be made to the High Court by way of judicial review of the decision to prosecute.

Delay

There is no general time-limit within which proceedings have to be commenced where the alleged offence is indictable. However, in the case of summary offences, there is a six-month time-limit by virtue of the MCA 1980, s. 127 (see **D21.17**).   **D3.77**

Where delay is deliberate, it is likely to be held to amount to an abuse of process. For example, in *Brentford Justices, ex parte Wong* [1981] QB 445, proceedings (for careless driving) were commenced (just) within the six-month period permitted for summary offences by the MCA 1980, s. 127, but the summons was not served until three months later. The prosecutor accepted that the delay was because he had not then reached a firm decision on whether to take proceedings, and he was trying to keep his options open. The Divisional Court held that the case could properly be regarded as one where the proceedings should be stayed, since this was a deliberate attempt by the prosecutor to gain further time in which to reach a decision, thereby defeating the time-limit set by s. 127.

Inadvertent Delay   Where deliberate delay in bringing the case to court cannot be shown, the defence may nonetheless apply for the proceedings to be stayed on the ground of abuse of process if (a) there has been inordinate or unconscionable delay due to the prosecution's inefficiency, and (b) prejudice to the defence from the delay is either proved or to be inferred (per Lloyd LJ in *Gateshead Justices, ex parte Smith* (1985) 149 JP 681). This followed the approach taken by the court in *Grays Justices, ex parte Graham* [1982] QB 1239, where it was held that, although delay alone could be sufficient to justify a stay of proceedings, if sufficiently prolonged, some other impropriety is generally required. The test to be applied is whether the delay in bringing the proceedings is of such magnitude as to render them vexatious and an abuse of the court's process. At p. 1247, May LJ said, 'we do not think that this court should create any form of artificial limitation period for criminal proceedings where it cannot truly be said that the due process of the criminal courts is being used improperly to harass a defendant'.   **D3.78**

In *Derby Crown Court, ex parte Brooks* (1985) 80 Cr App R 164, Sir Roger Ormrod propounded a general test for abuse of process (quoted at **D3.72**) but also made specific reference to delay. To amount to abuse of process, the delay must cause prejudice to the accused, and the delay must be unjustified. In *Bow Street Stipendiary Magistrate, ex parte DPP* (1989) 91 Cr App R 283, the Divisional Court made it clear that, to amount to an abuse of process, delay has to produce 'genuine prejudice and unfairness' (per Watkins LJ at p. 296). In some cases, however, prejudice will be inferred from substantial delay, and the prosecution will then have to rebut that inference of prejudice (p. 297). Such an inference 'is more easily drawn when dealing with a single brief but confused event which must depend on the recollections of those involved' (p. 300). Similarly, in *Telford Justices, ex parte Badhan* [1991] 2 QB 78, the Divisional Court said (at p. 91) that, where the period of delay is long, it is legitimate for the court to infer prejudice without proof of specific prejudice,. The period in question in that case was some 15 or 16 years, and so the court was entitled to infer prejudice and conclude that a fair trial was impossible.

Effect of Delay on Fairness of Trial   In *Bell v DPP of Jamaica* [1985] AC 937, the Privy Council laid down guidelines for determining whether delay would deprive the accused of a fair trial. The relevant factors were said to be: **D3.79**

(a) the length of delay;
(b) the reasons given by the prosecution to justify the delay;
(c) the responsibility of the accused for asserting his rights; and

(d) the prejudice to the accused.

In *A-G's Ref (No. 1 of 1990)* [1992] QB 630 (at pp. 643–4), Lord Lane CJ said that:

> Stays imposed on the grounds of delay or for any other reason should only be employed in exceptional circumstances...In principle, therefore, even where the delay can be said to be unjustifiable, the imposition of a permanent stay should be the exception rather than the rule. Still more rare should be cases where a stay can properly be imposed in the absence of any fault on the part of the complainant or prosecution. Delay due merely to the complexity of the case or contributed to by the actions of the defendant himself should never be the foundation for a stay... [N]o stay should be imposed unless the defendant shows on the balance of probabilities that owing to the delay he will suffer serious prejudice to the extent that no fair trial can be held: in other words, that the continuance of the prosecution amounts to a misuse of the process of the court. In assessing whether there is likely to be prejudice and if so whether it can properly be described as serious, the following matters should be borne in mind: first, the power of the judge at common law and under the PACE 1984 to regulate the admissibility of evidence; secondly, the trial process itself, which should ensure that all relevant factual issues arising from delay will be placed before the jury as part of the evidence for their consideration, together with the powers of the judge to give appropriate directions to the jury before they consider their verdict.

The same approach was adopted by the House of Lords in *A-G's Ref (No. 2 of 2001)* [2004] 2 AC 72. Two questions had been certified by the Court of Appeal: (1) whether criminal proceedings may be stayed on the ground that there had been a breach of the reasonable time requirement in the ECHR, Article 6(1), in circumstances where the accused cannot demonstrate any prejudice arising from the delay; and (2) when the relevant time period commences in the determination of whether, for the purposes of Article 6(1), a criminal charge has been heard within a reasonable time. The House of Lords ruled that criminal proceedings may be stayed on the ground that there had been a violation of the reasonable time requirement in the Article 6(1), only if '(a) there can no longer be a fair hearing, or (b) it would otherwise be unfair to try the defendant' (per Lord Bingham at [24]). It was said that it would be anomalous if breach of the reasonable time requirement were to have an effect that is more far-reaching than breach of the accused's other Article 6(1) rights. Lord Bingham said that the remedy for such a breach must be 'effective, just and proportionate'. It follows that a stay of the proceedings would not be an appropriate remedy 'if any lesser remedy will be just and proportionate in all the circumstances'. His lordship added that, if breach of the reasonable time requirement is established retrospectively (in other words, used as a ground for appeal against conviction), it would not be appropriate to quash any conviction unless the hearing was unfair or it was unfair to try the accused at all (at [24]).

D3.80 So far as the second question is concerned, it was held that, for the purposes of the requirement under Article 6(1) that a criminal charge must be heard within a reasonable time, the relevant period commences at the earliest time at which a person was officially alerted to the likelihood of criminal proceedings against him (per Lord Bingham at [27]). This will normally be when he is charged or served with a summons or written charge. In *Burns v HM Advocate* [2009] 1 AC 720, it was held that the reasonable time requirement must be interpreted and applied in a way that will tend to achieve its purpose, which is to avoid undue uncertainty on the part of a person charged, and so the matter ought to be examined from the perspective of the individual concerned (per Lady Cosgrove at [53]).

In *Dyer v Watson* [2004] 1 AC 379, Lord Bingham, giving the opinion of the Privy Council, said (at [52]) that the threshold of proving that a trial has not taken place within a reasonable time 'is a high one, not easily crossed'. However, his lordship went on to say that, if the period which has elapsed is one which, on its face, 'gives ground for real concern', it is necessary to look into the detailed facts and circumstances of the particular case and it must be possible to explain and justify any lapse of time which appears to be excessive. His lordship said (at [53]) that regard must be had to the complexity of the case, the conduct of the accused (he cannot properly complain of delay of which he is the author) and the manner in which the case has been dealt with by the prosecution and the courts. As regards the latter, Lord Bingham said that there is no general obligation on a prosecutor to act with all due expedition and diligence, but a marked lack of expedition, if unjustified, would point towards a breach of the reasonable time requirement (at [55]).

So far as the ECtHR is concerned, 'the reasonableness of the length of proceedings must be **D3.81** assessed in the light of the circumstances of the case and with reference to the following criteria: the complexity of the case, the conduct of the applicants and the relevant authorities and what was at stake for the applicants' (*Bullen and Soneji v UK* [2009] ECHR 28).

In *S (SP)* [2006] 2 Cr App R 341, the Court of Appeal summarised the position as follows: (a) even where delay is unjustifiable, a permanent stay should be the exception rather than the rule; (b) where there is no fault on the part of the complainant or prosecution, it will be very rare for a stay to be granted; (c) no stay should be granted in the absence of serious prejudice to the accused, so that no fair trial can be held; (d) when assessing possible serious prejudice, the judge should bear in mind his power to regulate the admissibility of evidence, and that the trial process itself should ensure that all the relevant factual issues arising from delay will be placed before the jury for their consideration; (e) if the judge's assessment is that a fair trial is possible, a stay should not be granted (per Rose LJ at [21]).

The Privy Council revisited the question of delay in *Spiers v Ruddy* [2008] 1 AC 873, emphasising that a stay of proceedings is a last resort. Lord Bingham of Cornhill CJ said (at [16]) that where there has (or may have been) such delay in the conduct of proceedings as to breach a party's right to trial within a reasonable time, but where the fairness of the trial has not been or will not be compromised, 'such delay does not give rise to a continuing breach which cannot be cured save by a discontinuation of proceedings. It gives rise to a breach which can be cured, even where it cannot be prevented, by expedition, reduction of sentence or compensation, provided always that the breach, where it occurs, is publicly acknowledged and addressed.'

The need for the accused to demonstrate that the delay has caused prejudice was emphasised in *Brants v DPP* (2011) 175 JP 246. Jackson LJ said (at [47]) that delay alone by the prosecution cannot warrant the staying of proceedings as an abuse of process: 'There is a public interest in prosecuting offences which transcends any consideration of punishing the prosecution for delay. If delay by the prosecution does not cause prejudice to the defence, then normally it would not be appropriate to stay proceedings for abuse of process.'

Where the issue of delay is raised at the stage when the magistrates are contemplating the transfer **D3.82** of the case to the Crown Court, it is submitted that the magistrates should refuse to transfer the case on the basis of delay only in cases where it is patent that a fair trial could not take place; in other cases, the magistrates should send the case to the Crown Court and allow a Crown Court judge to consider whether steps can be taken to enable the accused to have a fair trial (e.g., specific directions to the jury about the effect of the delay on the ability of the accused to conduct his defence).

So far as appeals are concerned, *Khalid Ali v CPS, West Midlands* [2007] EWCA Crim 691 emphasises that the question for the Court of Appeal is not whether the judge was correct to refuse to stay the proceedings, but rather whether the effect of the delay is such as to lead the court to the conclusion that the verdict was unsafe.

Mitigating the Effects of Delay Where the defence argue that the proceedings amount to an **D3.83** abuse of process because of delay in bringing the prosecution, an important consideration is whether a direction to the jury about the effect of the delay is a sufficient remedy for the accused. The *Crown Court Bench Book* (at p. 33) recommends that the judge 'should refer to the fact that the passage of time is bound to affect memory'. The guidance also points out that the inability of a witness to recall detail applies equally to prosecution and defence witnesses, but it is the prosecution which bears the burden of proof. If, as a result of delay, specific lines of inquiry have been closed to the defence, the disadvantage this presents should be identified and explained to the jury 'by reference to the burden of proof'. Any direction about delay 'must make clear that the jury should give careful consideration to the exigencies of delay'. In *H* [1998] 2 Cr App R 161 at p. 168, the Court of Appeal said that a direction on delay 'is not to be regarded as invariably required except in cases where some significant difficulty or aspect of prejudice is aired or otherwise becomes apparent to the judge in the course of the trial'. However, 'such a direction should be given in any case where it is necessary for the purposes of being even-handed as between complainant and defendant'. In *M* [2000] 1 Cr App R 49, it was said that trial judges should tailor their directions to the circumstances of the particular case. The Court of Appeal added that, where the evidence was cogent, such a warning might not be necessary and its absence would not necessarily render a conviction unsafe, particularly when counsel's submissions at trial had not highlighted any specific risk of prejudice.

An example of a case where there was held to be a lack of prejudice (and hence no abuse of process) was *Central Criminal Court, ex parte Randle* [1991] 1 All ER 370. The applicants were charged with offences arising out of the escape from custody of George Blake while he was serving a lengthy prison sentence for spying. They appeared in court some 23 years after the alleged offences, and applied for the proceedings to be stayed on the grounds of unreasonable delay. The Divisional Court noted that they had published a book in 1989, which had provided much of the material upon which the prosecution relied. In the light of its contents, the plea of failing memory could not be advanced, and so there was no prejudice to them. Similarly, in *Buzalek* [1991] Crim LR 115, the fact that the case turned largely on documentary evidence, and that it was possible for witnesses to refresh their memories from the documents, meant that delay did not cause prejudice to the accused.

D3.84 **Sexual Offences and Delay**   Cases involving sexual offences, such as child abuse cases, may be regarded as an exceptional category in their own right. It is often the case that such allegations emerge a long time after the alleged abuse took place. The view generally taken by the courts is that the unfairness can be minimised by a direction to the jury to take proper account of the fact that the accused was handicapped in defending the case because of the length of time which has elapsed since the alleged offence was committed. Any residual prejudice is regarded as outweighed by the importance of prosecuting such serious offences. In *E* [2004] 2 Cr App R 621, the Court of Appeal said that juries should be trusted to make allowances not only for the lapse of time but also for the difficulties faced by an accused who could only deny the offence (per Keith J at [17]).

It is important to note that there will be cases where the effect of the delay cannot be assessed until after the evidence has been heard. In *Smolinski* [2004] 2 Cr App R 40, the Court of Appeal said that applications to stay proceedings based on abuse of process where there has been delay should be discouraged. In cases of alleged sexual offences, it is sometimes very difficult for young children to speak about such matters and therefore it is only many years later that the offences come to light. Lord Woolf CJ said (at [8]) that, when a long time has elapsed, careful consideration must be given by the prosecution as to whether it is right to bring the prosecution at all. If, having considered the evidence to be called, and the witnesses having been interviewed on behalf of the prosecution, a decision is reached that the case should proceed, then it is normally better not to make an application based on abuse of process. Unless the case is exceptional, the application would be unsuccessful.

D3.85 In *Joynson* [2008] EWCA Crim 3049, Toulson LJ (at [13]) said that where the evidence of one complainant, if believed, could support that of another, it is necessary, when considering prejudice, to consider the prejudicial effect of delay not only in relation to any particular complainant, but also its secondary effect in relation to others whose evidence may be bolstered by the evidence of another complainant. Thus, it is necessary to consider the prejudice alleged in relation to the specific complainants and then to stand back and look at the matter in the round.

In *E* [2008] EWCA Crim 604 (where the offences were alleged to have occurred some 30 years earlier), the Court of Appeal, upholding the convictions, said that there is no quantifiable cut-off point in terms of the number of years in cases of delay, since each case turns on its own facts. The key issue is whether a fair trial is possible.

D3.86 In *MacKreth* [2009] EWCA Crim 1849, Rix LJ noted (at [39]) that, despite the matter being considered in a number of subsequent cases, the relevant principles regarding delay, including delay in cases involving alleged sexual offences, are still to be found in *A-G's Ref (No. 1 of 1990)* [1992] QB 630 (see **D3.79**). It follows that this case should be the first point of reference regarding delay. Nonetheless, in *F (T B)* [2011] 2 Cr App R 145 (a case concerning a 62-year-old man who had been convicted of committing sexual offences against his step-daughter and daughter between 30 and 40 years earlier) Jackson LJ, having reviewed the relevant authorities, set out the following five propositions in relation to criminal prosecutions brought after a long delay (at [37]):

i) The court should stay proceedings on some or all counts of the indictment for abuse of process if, and only if, it is satisfied on balance of probabilities that by reason of delay a fair trial is not possible on those counts.

ii) It is now recognised that usually the proper time for the defence to make such an application and for the judge to rule upon it is at trial, after all the evidence has been called.

iii) In assessing what prejudice has been caused to the defendant on any particular count by reason of delay, the court should consider what evidence directly relevant to the defence case has been lost through the passage of time. Vague speculation that lost documents or deceased witnesses might have assisted the defendant is not helpful. The court should also consider what evidence has survived the passage of time. The court should then examine critically how important the missing evidence is in the context of the case as a whole.

iv) Having identified the prejudice caused to the defence by reason of the delay, it is then necessary to consider to what extent the judge can compensate for that prejudice by emphasising guidance given in standard directions or formulating special directions to the jury. Where important independent evidence has been lost over time, it may not be known which party that evidence would have supported. There may be cases in which no direction to the jury can dispel the resultant prejudice which one or other of the parties must suffer, but this depends on the facts of the case.

v) If the complainant's delay in coming forward is unjustified, that is relevant to the question whether it is fair to try the defendant so long after the events in issue. In determining whether the complainant's delay is unjustified, it must be firmly borne in mind that victims of sexual abuse are often unwilling to reveal or talk about their experiences for some time and for good reason.

In *F (S)* [2012] QB 703, a five-judge court presided over by Lord Judge CJ repeated that, where **D3.87** a judge is considering an application to stay proceedings on the ground of prejudice resulting from delay in the institution of proceedings, the appropriate test is to be found in *A-G's Ref (No. 1 of 1990)*. Lord Judge emphasised (at [39]) that the decision whether the trial should be stayed because it would constitute an abuse of process is not to be elided with the separate and distinct question which may arise at the end of the prosecution case, namely whether (applying the principles in *Galbraith* [1981] 2 All ER 1060) there is a case to answer. A judge should not decide the question of whether there should be a stay by assessing whether a conviction would be unsafe. In most cases involving allegations of sexual offences which occurred a long time ago, the reasons for the delay in making the complaint, and whether and how the delay is explained or justified, will bear directly on the credibility of the complainant and so will be an essential part of the factual matrix on which the jury must make its decision. An abuse of process argument cannot succeed unless prejudice has been caused to the accused, and so the explanation for delay is relevant to an application to stay only if it bears on how readily the fact of prejudice to the accused may be shown. Unjustified delay is not, by itself, a sufficient reason for a stay (at [40]). Most importantly, Lord Judge CJ said (at [45]) that it is only in the exceptional cases where a fair trial is not possible that abuse of process applications are justified on the grounds of delay. His lordship said that the best safeguard against unfairness to either side in such cases is the trial process itself, and an evaluation by the jury of the evidence.

An important question is when an abuse application should be made, if one is to be made. In *Smolinski*, Lord Woolf CJ said (at [9]) that, if an abuse of process application is to be made, the best time for doing so is after any evidence has been called: the judge, having had an opportunity of seeing the witnesses, can then come to a conclusion as to whether the trial should proceed or whether the evidence is such that it would not be safe for a jury to convict. A similar point was made by Hooper LJ in *Burke* [2005] EWCA Crim 29 (at [32]), where his lordship reasoned that, prior to the start of the case, it will often be difficult, if not impossible, to determine whether an accused can have a fair trial because of the delay. This is because issues 'which might seem very important before the trial may become unimportant or of less importance as a result of developments during the trial, including the evidence of the complainant and of other witnesses including the defendant should he choose to give evidence'. However, in *F*, the Court of Appeal signalled a different approach. Lord Judge CJ said (at [45]):

> Where there are genuine grounds for an application to stay on the basis that a fair trial will be impossible because of incurable prejudice to the defendant caused by delay, that application is, by its nature, preliminary to rather than part of the trial process. The contention is that the trial should not take place at all. If it is to be made, notice should be given before the trial begins. In the end of course the time when it should be dealt with by argument and ruling is a matter for the trial judge. Although we can envisage cases in which, for example, the application is based on prejudice resulting from the absence of long-lost evidence . . . and where the evaluation of the significance of the absence of such evidence may best be undertaken at the close of the Crown's case, in general the question whether the trial should proceed at all should take place before evidence is called.

His lordship reasoned that, if the ruling is deferred, there is a significant danger that the submissions to the judge would conflate the principles applicable to a submission of no case to answer with those applicable to abuse of process. There is also the point that, if the issue is not dealt with before the evidence is heard, the complainant will have been through the ordeal of giving evidence, which is unfair if the proceedings are then held to be an abuse of process. His lordship went on to say, though the court did not propose to be prescriptive, 'unless there is a specific reason for deferment, an application to stay on abuse of process grounds is preliminary to the trial, and ought normally to be dealt with at the outset'.

Failing to Obtain, Losing or Destroying Evidence

D3.88   In *Medway* [2000] Crim LR 415, the accused was convicted of robbery. It was alleged that he robbed an elderly lady of her handbag. A closed-circuit television camera was operating in the area, but the police, having looked at the film, decided that it contained nothing of value. The tape was destroyed. The judge refused to stay the trial as an abuse of process in the absence of the tape. The Court of Appeal dismissed the appeal, saying that there was no evidence of malice, and nothing to show that the absence of the tape made the conviction unsafe. The Court observed that where evidence had been tampered with, lost or destroyed, it may well be that an accused will be disadvantaged, but it does not necessarily follow that he cannot receive a fair trial. The clear implication is that an accused is disadvantaged only if the absence of the evidence might have made a difference to the outcome of the trial.

D3.89   In *Dobson* [2001] EWCA Crim 1606, the Court of Appeal considered the position where police had failed to obtain CCTV footage relating to the accused's defence of alibi. Potter LJ said (at [34]) that, in determining whether there was an abuse of process, it was appropriate to consider:

(a) What was the duty of the police?
(b) Did the police fail in their duty by not obtaining or retaining the appropriate video footage?
(c) If so, was there serious prejudice which rendered a fair trial impossible in the light of such failure?
(d) Alternatively, did the police failure result from such bad behaviour, in the sense of bad faith or serious fault, as to render it unfair that the accused should be tried at all?

In the instant case, the police should have looked at the CCTV footage, and had failed in their duty to do so. However, the prejudice was not 'serious' because it was uncertain that the footage would have assisted the defence; moreover, the accused was in a position to understand the relevance of the footage and could have requested it and/or sought other evidence to support his alibi. There was no question of malice or intentional omission, as opposed to oversight, on behalf of the police. The judge was therefore right to conclude that a fair trial was possible and the conviction was upheld.

D3.90

In reaching that conclusion, the court in *Dobson* adopted the approach which was taken in what is now to be regarded as the leading authority on such cases, *R (Ebrahim) v Feltham Magistrates' Court* [2001] 1 All ER 831. Brooke LJ said (at [74]) that the starting point must be whether there was a duty on the investigator to obtain or retain the material in question. That question will be answered mainly through the provisions of the Code of Practice issued under part II of the CPIA 1996 (see **D9**). If there was no duty to obtain or retain the evidence in question, there can be no grounds to stay the proceedings for failure to do so. If there was a duty, and that duty has been breached, there has to be either an element of bad faith, or at the very least some serious fault, on the part of the police or the prosecution authorities, for this ground of challenge to succeed (at [23]). It follows that a stay will, unless there has been bad faith on the part of the prosecution, only be granted where the accused could not have a fair trial. At [25] Brooke LJ said:

> Two well-known principles are frequently invoked in this context when a court is invited to stay proceedings for abuse of process:
> (i) The ultimate objective of this discretionary power is to ensure that there should be a fair trial according to law, which involves fairness both to the defendant and the prosecution, because the fairness of a trial is not all one sided; it requires that those who are undoubtedly guilty should be convicted as well as that those about whose guilt there is any reasonable doubt should be acquitted.
> (ii) The trial process itself is equipped to deal with the bulk of the complaints on which applications for a stay are founded.

At [27], his lordship went on:

> It must be remembered that it is a commonplace in criminal trials for a defendant to rely on 'holes' in the prosecution case, for example, a failure to take fingerprints or a failure to submit evidential material to forensic examination. If, in such a case, there is sufficient credible evidence, apart from the missing evidence, which, if believed, would justify a safe conviction, then a trial should proceed, leaving the defendant to seek to persuade the jury or justices not to convict because evidence which might otherwise have been available was not before the court through no fault of his. Often the absence of a video film or fingerprints or DNA material is likely to hamper the prosecution as much as the defence.

The relevance of fault on the part of the prosecution is open to question. In *Clay* [2014] EWHC 321 (Admin), the accused had been driving a lorry which collided with the rear of a car. The police had released the car and allowed the insurer to dispose of it. The accused argued that, because he had been deprived of the ability to examine the state of the car (in particular, whether the brake lights were working), the failure by the police to retain the vehicle resulted in the proceedings amounting to an abuse of process. Pitchford LJ (at [46]–[48]) considered the decision in *Ebrahim*, and concluded:

> With great respect to the court in *Ebrahim*, it seems to me that the question of whether the defendant can have a fair trial does not logically depend upon whether anyone was 'at fault' in causing the exigency that created the unfairness. If vital evidence has as a matter of fact been lost to the defendant whether occasioned by the fault of the police or not, the issue is whether that disadvantage can be accommodated at his trial so as to ensure that his trial is fair. There is in this respect no difference between an unfair trial occasioned by delay and an unfair trial occasioned by the loss of vital evidence.

Burton J added (at [75]) that the justices in the present case were entitled to conclude that 'injustice to the defendant could be avoided by judicious regulation of the trial'.

D3.91

In *Khalid Ali v CPS, West Midlands* [2007] EWCA Crim 691, the Court of Appeal emphasised that, in such cases, the mere fact that missing material might have assisted the defence will not necessarily lead to a stay. In considering whether or not to order a stay, the court will have regard to whether there is sufficiently credible evidence, apart from the missing evidence, leaving the defence to exploit the gaps left by the missing evidence. Moses LJ said (at [30]) that the 'rationale for refusing a stay is the existence of credible evidence, itself untainted by what has gone missing'. A similar approach was taken in *DPP v Cooper* [2008] EWHC 507 (Admin), where the prosecution case was that bank notes in the accused's possession had tested positive for the

D

Part D Procedure

presence of heroin. The forensic test had been video-taped. However, the video had been lost. Moreover, the defence were unable to carry out their own independent tests on the bank notes because they had been tested using a spray that would make subsequent testing impossible. The defence therefore submitted that they had been denied access to material which was clearly relevant to the issues in the case, and that a fair trial could not take place as they had been denied the ability to rebut the expert evidence of the prosecution as a result of a failure on the part of the police to preserve evidence until the conclusion of the proceedings. The Divisional Court held that the proceedings did not constitute an abuse of process. Silber J pointed out (at [9]) that the accused still had adequate means to challenge the prosecution case, since the forensic scientist who conducted the tests on the bank notes could have been questioned about the way she conducted those tests and how she had reached her results; moreover, the magistrates would have been able to make adequate allowance for the fact that the defence had not been able to see a video of the tests being carried out or carry out their own tests.

The principles relevant to cases involving lost evidence were helpfully summarised by Gross LJ in *DPP v Fell* [2013] EWHC 562 (Admin) (at [15]), emphasising that a stay is to be granted only in exceptional cases:

> …the burden of proof is on the party seeking a stay; the standard of proof is a balance of probabilities, the civil standard. The party seeking a stay must make good to the civil standard that, owing to the missing evidence, he will suffer serious prejudice to the extent that no fair trial can be held and that, accordingly, the continuance of the prosecution would amount to a misuse of the process of the court.

His lordship added that the grant of the stay in a case where it is not suggested that there has been serious culpability or bad faith on the part of the prosecutor or investigator 'is, effectively, a measure of last resort. It caters for and only for those cases which cannot be accommodated with all their imperfections within the trial process'. It would, however, be 'a very different situation' if evidence had gone missing through serious culpability or bad faith.

Going Back on a Promise, Legitimate Expectation and Double Jeopardy

D3.92   In *Croydon Justices, ex parte Dean* [1993] QB 769, Staughton LJ said (at p. 778) that 'the prosecution of a person who has received a promise, undertaking or representation from the police that he will not be prosecuted is *capable* of being an abuse of process' (emphasis added). In such circumstances, it is not necessary for the accused to show that there was bad faith on the part of the police.

An example of a prosecution change of mind amounting to an abuse of process is *Bloomfield* [1997] 1 Cr App R 135. B was charged with possession of a Class A controlled drug. At a preliminary hearing, prosecuting counsel indicated to the defence that the Crown wished to offer no evidence because it was accepted that B had been the victim of a set-up. Owing to the presence in court of certain people it would have been embarrassing to the police and prosecution if no evidence had been offered that day, so counsel spoke to the judge in his room. An order was then made in open court to adjourn the case and relist it 'for mention'. The CPS subsequently arranged a conference with new prosecuting counsel and informed the defence that there had been a change of plan and that the Crown intended to continue the prosecution against B. It was held by the Court of Appeal that allowing the prosecution to go ahead amounted to an abuse of process since, whether or not there was prejudice to the accused, it would bring the administration of justice into disrepute if the Crown were permitted to revoke its original decision, particularly as it had been made in the presence of the judge (per Staughton LJ at p. 143). The court also held that it was irrelevant whether prosecuting counsel had the authority to drop the case, since neither the court nor the accused could be expected to inquire whether prosecuting counsel had authority to conduct a case in court in any particular way and so were entitled to assume that counsel did have such authority (p.139).

D3.93   **Cautions**   The administration of a caution may lead to a subsequent prosecution being held to be an abuse of process. In *Jones v Whalley* [2007] 1 AC 63 (see **D2.22**), a private prosecution was held to be an abuse of process because the accused had previously been cautioned by the police for the offence in question, and the terms of the caution had said, expressly, that he would not have to go before a criminal court in connection with the matter. The House of Lords observed that allowing private prosecutions to proceed, despite an assurance that the offender would not have to go to court, would tend to undermine not only the non-statutory system of cautions, but also the schemes for cautioning young offenders and adult offenders that Parliament had endorsed in the CDA 1998 (since replaced by the caution provisions of the LASPO 2012) and the CJA 2003 (per Lord Rodger of Earlsferry at [25]). Their lordships also noted that the abuse complained of was not abuse impairing the fairness of the trial (since evidence of the accused's admission to the offence, and of the caution administered by the police, could be excluded), but went to the fairness of trying the accused at all (per Lord Bingham at [13]). The same principles apply to young offenders. *R (H) v Guildford Youth Court* [2008] EWHC 506 (Admin) concerned a juvenile accused of assault. Before he was interviewed by the police, it was intimated to his solicitor that it was possible that the case would be dealt with by way of a final warning as a way of resolving the matter. The juvenile admitted the offence and was bailed to an 'intervention clinic', when it was indicated that the matter would be dealt with by way of a final warning. The CPS subsequently decided that a prosecution would be appropriate, and the juvenile was charged. Silber J at [16] ruled that 'the fact that a promise was made by an officer of the State, namely the police officer who was in charge at that stage deciding whether or not to prosecute, is something that there is a clear public interest in upholding'. The proceedings should therefore have been stayed as an abuse of process.

In *DPP v Alexander* [2011] 1 WLR 653, the Divisional Court again had to consider the effect of   **D3.94**
a caution. Stanley Burnton LJ said (at [6]) that the doctrine of autrefois (see **D12.20** *et seq.*) has no application where what has occurred is a caution:

> A caution is not a conviction for the purposes of those defences, notwithstanding that a caution will only be administered if the accused person admits his guilt. The principles of autrefois convict and autrefois acquit are applicable only where there has been a finding by a court of guilt or innocence. They have no application to an extra-judicial procedure, such as the administration of a simple caution

However, his lordship went on to say (at [9]) that, where criminal conduct has been the subject of an agreed caution, 'in the absence of good reason for it to be the subject of a subsequent prosecution, such a prosecution will generally constitute an abuse of the process of the court'. He added that examples of cases where a prosecution might be justified despite the earlier administration of caution include instances where information or evidence is obtained subsequent to the caution (e.g., details of injury to a victim significantly exceeding what had previously been known).

Prosecution Changes of Mind   Giving an indication that the case will be dropped does not   **D3.95**
necessarily mean that it will be an abuse of process for the prosecution to have a change of mind. In *Mulla* [2004] 1 Cr App R 6, the accused was charged with causing death by dangerous driving. On the morning of the first day of the trial, the prosecution indicated that they would be willing to accept a plea of guilty to careless driving. The judge was dissatisfied with the decision and asked the prosecutor to reconsider. In the afternoon, after having reconsidered the matter, the prosecution indicated that they had decided to proceed with the original charge of causing death by dangerous driving. The Court of Appeal held that this did not amount to an abuse of process. This was not a case in which the accused's hopes were raised, later to be dashed, since he knew from the beginning of the proceedings in court that the judge did not approve of the course which the prosecution were proposing to take. The Court said that factors to be considered include what view is expressed by the judge when the prosecution gives its indication, the period of time over which the prosecution reconsiders the matter before they change their mind, whether or not the accused's hopes have been inappropriately raised, and whether there has been, by reason of the change of course by the prosecution, any prejudice to the defence (per Rose LJ at [22]).

In *Abu Hamza* [2007] QB 659, the Court of Appeal said that, where a person has been   **D3.96**
told he will not be prosecuted for an offence, 'it is not likely to constitute an abuse of process to proceed with a prosecution unless (i) there has been an unequivocal representation

by those with the conduct of the investigation or prosecution of a case that the defendant will not be prosecuted and (ii) the defendant has acted on that representation to his detriment. Even then, if facts come to light which were not known when the representation was made, these may justify proceeding with the prosecution despite the representation' (per Lord Phillips CJ at [54]). His lordship added (at [51]) that 'it is usually in the public interest that those who are reasonably suspected of criminal conduct should be brought to trial. Only in rare circumstances will it be offensive to justice to give effect to this public interest'. In *Killick* [2012] 1 Cr App R 121, it was argued that proceedings should be stayed because of two representations from the CPS that the accused would not be prosecuted. The decision not to prosecute had been changed following a review which took place at the request of the complainant. Thomas LJ noted (at [43]) that 'if a clear unequivocal representation has been made and upon which the defendant relies to his detriment, it will be open to a court to find that to proceed against him will be an abuse of process. [However,] there can be circumstances where, even in that situation, it would not be an abuse of process to proceed'. On the facts, the Court of Appeal found that what had been said did not amount to representations of the nature that would justify a stay of proceedings. Thomas LJ went on to say (at [56]) that even if a representation had been made, 'there was good reason why the prosecution had to review the matter; the delay arising out of the review caused no prejudice'. It followed that there was no abuse of process.

In *R (Guest) v DPP* [2009] 2 Cr App R 426, judicial review was sought of a decision to administer a conditional caution (rather than prosecute) in a case involving a serious assault. The court noted that it could not be said that, where a conditional caution in respect of an alleged offence is quashed, any subsequent prosecution in respect of that alleged offence would inevitably amount to an abuse of process. However, in *Gore* [2009] 1 WLR 2454, the two accused had each received a fixed penalty notice for public disorder. The following day, the police reviewed the CCTV evidence of the incident and decided that the fixed penalty notices were inappropriate, arrested the two accused and charged them with inflicting grievous bodily harm. The Court of Appeal ruled that there had been no improper escalation of charge, nor any departure from any reasonable expectation that the accused would not be prosecuted, where more serious consequences of their conduct and evidence justifying prosecution for an offence of violence came to light after the issue of the notice (per Lord Judge CJ at [16]).

In *R (Gavigan) v Enfield Magistrates' Court* (2013) 177 JP 609, the accused received fixed penalty notices but, rather than paying the fixed penalty, they indicated that they wished the matter to be dealt with by a court. The decision was then taken to prosecute them for the offence (rather than dealing with the matter as a contested fixed penalty notice). This had the consequence that, if convicted, the accused were liable to a custodial sentence. However, Mitting J said (at [15]) that there is 'simply no principle or policy reason that requires that a person, who has rejected the opportunity to pay a fixed penalty … should not thereafter be prosecuted for any offence arising out of the same set of facts for those in respect of which the notice was issued'.

D3.97   A key question is whether the accused has been treated unjustly. In *DPP v B* [2008] EWHC 201 (Admin), the accused was originally charged with a single charge of sexual assault. However, when he appeared before the Crown Court, the judge considered that the single count failed to reflect the criminality which was alleged against the accused, the complainant having alleged that she had been sexually abused by the accused over a period of years. The prosecution subsequently sought to bring 17 charges of sexual assault against the accused, to reflect the years over which the sexual abuse had occurred. The Divisional Court held that this did not amount to an abuse of process. Latham LJ pointed out (at [10]) that proceedings should be stayed for abuse of process only 'in very exceptional circumstances, where it can properly be said that the consequence would be injustice, or where the circumstances giving rise to the proceedings in respect of which the application is made offend one's sense of justice overall'. His lordship accepted (at [12]) that the accused was clearly at risk of a substantially greater sentence than he would have been under the original charge, but said that this was not unjust since the accused was not going to be exposed to any sentence other than the proper sentence that should be imposed for the offences which were established (whether through guilty pleas or following trial) against him. *CPS v Mattu* [2009] EWCA Crim 1483 concerned a detailed 'basis of plea' which had been agreed upon and approved by the court. It was held that it would be an abuse of process to prosecute related matters where the case advanced by the prosecution was wholly inconsistent with that basis of plea. In the instant case, the basis of plea was comprehensive and carefully drafted, with the prosecution involved in agreeing its terms for submission to the court; the judge considered it to be a suitable basis for sentence and proceeded to sentence. The basis of plea had therefore achieved a status which precluded the prosecution from attempting to go behind it (per Pill LJ at [19]). However, his lordship observed (at [20]) that 'there will be cases, where, for example, fresh evidence emerges and circumstances change, in which it may be possible for the prosecution to circumvent a basis of plea they have agreed'.

In *Gripton* [2010] EWCA Crim 2260, the accused had been a prosecution witness in a rape **D3.98** trial. She had changed her evidence during the course of the proceedings. At the trial, a juror had asked whether the prosecution witness would be charged with perjury if the accused in those proceedings was acquitted. The prosecution advocate told the judge that there would be no prosecution, and the judge told the jury that, whatever their decision, nobody in the case would face other proceedings in another court on another day. The accused was subsequently prosecuted for perjury. She sought a stay. The Court of Appeal ruled (at [32]) that it would not be 'an affront to justice' to permit the proceedings to continue. Lloyd Jones J, at [29], noted that it was not suggested that the appellant had relied to her detriment on the representation made by prosecuting counsel at the trial. His lordship went on to say that the question for a court was whether, in the absence of any detrimental reliance by the appellant, the prosecution was nevertheless an abuse of process. The Court of Appeal (at [30]) considered it:

> …highly significant that the appellant was not aware of the representation until after she had been arrested for this offence. The representation was made in court in proceedings in which she had been a witness. She was not present when it was made, nor was it made in the presence of anyone representing her. Her understanding remained, no doubt, that she could be prosecuted for perjury. That remained her understanding until she was arrested.

Moreover, a stay was inappropriate despite the fact that it is 'clearly undesirable, and a matter of concern, that the Crown, having informed the court of its position, should change its stance on a matter of such importance in the absence of a good reason' (at [31]).

In *Dowty* [2011] EWCA Crim 3138 and *Killick* [2012] 1 Cr App R 121, the Court of Appeal referred to what is now para. 10 of the Code for Crown Prosecutors (see **appendix 3**), which says that occasionally there may be reasons why the CPS will overturn a decision not to prosecute or when it will re-start a prosecution, particularly if the case is serious. The examples given include cases where a review of the original decision shows that it was wrong and, in order to maintain confidence in the criminal justice system, a prosecution should be brought despite the earlier decision, and cases which are stopped because of a lack of evidence but where more significant evidence is discovered later. It is submitted that a decision taken in accordance with the Code is unlikely to be overturned by the courts.

Legitimate Expectation An important aspect of abuse of process is whether the decision to **D3.99** prosecute is inconsistent with a legitimate expectation held by the accused. In *LM* [2011] 1 Cr App R 135, Hughes LJ said (at [15]) that:

> Criminal courts in England and Wales do not decide whether a person ought to be prosecuted or not. They decide whether an offence has been committed. They may, however, also have to decide whether a legal process to which a person is entitled, or to which he has a legitimate expectation, has been neglected to his disadvantage.

D

Part D Procedure

His lordship went on to cite *Uxbridge Magistrates' Court, ex parte Adimi* [2001] QB 667, where the Divisional Court had to consider the position where a treaty provision (Article 31(1) of the Convention relating to the Status of Refugees) bound the UK not to impose a penalty, but defendants had nevertheless been prosecuted (see also **B3.248** and **B22.10**). The Court had held that the obligation, accepted by the State by ratification of the Convention, created a legitimate expectation that the immunity given by the Convention would be applied to a defendant if he fell within the Article (per Simon Brown LJ at [57] and Newman J at [80]). Hughes LJ went on (at [17]) to refer to the decision of the House of Lords in *Asfaw* [2008] 1 AC 1061, where the same Convention provision was considered and where 'the existence of the abuse of process jurisdiction was recognised to a limited extent and in effect for the purpose of ensuring that the UK's international obligation under the convention was not infringed'. The appeal in *LM* concerned Article 26 of the Council of Europe Convention on Action against Trafficking in Human Beings 2005, which creates an obligation to put in place a means by which active consideration is given to whether it is in the public interest to prosecute. Hughes LJ said (at [18]) that the court accepted that 'the power to stay for "abuse" exists as a safety net to ensure that this obligation is not wrongly neglected in an individual case to the disadvantage of the defendant' but went on to say (at [19]) that:

> …the jurisdiction to stay does not mean that the court is entitled to substitute its own view for that of the prosecutor upon the assessment of the public policy question whether a prosecution is justified or not. The power to stay is a power to ensure that the convention obligation under Article 26 is met…[T]he convention obligation is that a prosecuting authority must apply its mind conscientiously to the question of public policy and reach an informed decision…If…this exercise of judgment has not properly been carried out and would or might well have resulted in a decision not to prosecute, then there will be a breach of the convention and hence grounds for a stay. Likewise, if a decision has been reached at which no reasonable prosecutor could arrive, there will be grounds for a stay. Thus in effect the role of the court is one of review. The test is akin to that upon judicial review.

A decision to prosecute has to be taken in accordance with the Code for Crown Prosecutors and other guidance issued by the DPP. It should be noted, however, that a 'prosecution which did not constitute an abuse of process at the date of conviction cannot acquire that characteristic, on the basis of new or amended prosecutorial guidance or policy subsequently issued' (*A (RJ)* [2012] 2 Cr App R 80, per Lord Judge CJ at [86]).

Immunity from Prosecution

D3.100 The SOCPA 2005, s. 71, makes provision for immunity from prosecution. It provides that, if a specified prosecutor (i.e. the DPP, the Director of the Serious Fraud Office, the FSA and the Secretary of State for Business, Innovation and Skills, or a prosecutor acting on their behalf) thinks that, for the purposes of the investigation or prosecution of any offence, it is appropriate to offer any person immunity from prosecution, he may give the person a written 'immunity notice' (s. 71(1)). A person who has been given such a notice cannot be prosecuted for an offence of a description specified in the notice unless he fails to comply with any of the conditions specified in the notice, in which case the notice ceases to have effect (s. 71(2) and (3)). Given the clear statutory wording, a court would have little option but to regard a prosecution brought in breach of s. 71 as an abuse of process. The issue of immunity notices is restricted to indictable and either-way offences (s. 71(1)).

Manipulation of Procedure

D3.101 An example of something that may amount to manipulation of procedure is where a charge alleging a summary offence is replaced with one alleging an indictable offence, or vice versa. Paragraph 6.4 of the Code for Crown Prosecutors (see **appendix 3**) makes it clear that the charge should not be changed simply because of the decision made as to trial venue. In *Canterbury and St Augustine Justices, ex parte Klisiak* [1982] QB 398, it was said that the court should interfere with the prosecution's decision as to what offences to proceed upon only 'in the most obvious circumstances which disclose blatant injustice' (per Lord Lane CJ at p. 411). It has to be clear that the change in the charge is not a bona fide result of a reassessment of the appropriateness of the original charge. It is only appropriate to interfere where the court concludes that the prosecution were acting in bad faith, in the sense of deliberately manipulating the system to deprive an accused of his rights (*Sheffield Justices, ex parte DPP* [1993] Crim LR 136).

Another situation where allegations of manipulation can be made is where the accused is charged with a different offence at the time when the custody time-limit for the original offence is about to expire (or has expired), so that a new custody time-limit starts to run. In *R (Wardle) v Leeds Crown Court* [2002] 1 AC 754, a murder charge was replaced with a manslaughter charge when the custody time-limit was about to expire. Their lordships held that the bringing of a new charge would be an abuse of process if the bringing of that charge cannot be justified on the facts of the case by the prosecutor and the court is satisfied that it has been brought solely with a view to obtaining the substitution of a fresh custody time-limit (per Lord Hope of Craighead at [99]).

Abuse of process can also be used in cases which fall just outside the scope of the autrefois doctrine but where it would nonetheless be unfair to allow a further prosecution to take place. For example, in *Beedie* [1998] QB 356, the accused was charged with offences under health and safety legislation and, following his conviction, he was charged with manslaughter arising out of the same facts. The Court of Appeal ruled that it was an abuse of process to have sequential trials for offences on an ascending scale of gravity. **D3.102**

As to prosecution for a more serious offence after the issue of a fixed penalty, see *Gore* [2009] 1 WLR 2454 at **D3.96**.

Entrapment

In *Looseley* [2001] 4 All ER 897, the House of Lords said that, although entrapment is not a substantive defence in English law, where an accused can show entrapment, the court may stay the proceedings as an abuse of the court's process or it may exclude evidence pursuant to the PACE 1984, s. 78. Of these two remedies, the grant of stay (rather than the exclusion of evidence at the trial) should normally be regarded as the appropriate response, since a prosecution founded on entrapment would be an abuse of the court's process. Police conduct which brings about state-created crime is unacceptable and improper, and to prosecute in such circumstances would be an affront to the public conscience. However, if the accused already had the intent to commit a crime of the same or a similar kind, and the police did no more than give him the opportunity to fulfil his existing intent, that is unobjectionable (per Lord Nicholls of Birkenhead at [19] and [21]). A useful guide is to consider whether the police did no more than present the accused with an unexceptional opportunity to commit a crime. The yardstick for the purposes of this test is, in general, whether the police conduct preceding the commission of the offence was no more than might have been expected from others in the circumstances ([23]). As Lord Hutton put it (at [101]), particular emphasis is placed on the need: **D3.103**

> ... to consider whether a person has been persuaded or pressurised by a law enforcement officer into committing a crime which he would not otherwise have committed, or whether the officer did not go beyond giving the person an opportunity to break the law, when he would have behaved in the same way if some other person had offered him the opportunity to commit a similar crime, and when he freely took advantage of the opportunity presented to him by the officer.

Ultimately, however, the overall consideration is always whether the conduct of the police or other law enforcement agency was so seriously improper as to bring the administration of justice into disrepute (Lord Nicholls at [25]). In applying this test, the court has regard to all the circumstances of the case, including those listed by Lord Nicholls at [26]–[28]: (a) the nature of the offence (the use of proactive techniques is more appropriate in some circumstances than others, depending on secrecy and difficulty of detection, and the manner in which the particular criminal activity is carried on); (b) the reason for the particular police operation (having reasonable grounds for suspicion is one way good faith may be established, but having grounds for suspicion of a particular individual was not always essential); (c) the nature and extent of police participation in the crime (the greater the inducement held out by the police, and the more forceful or persistent the police overtures, the more readily might a court conclude that the police overstepped the boundary). It is also clear from this case that there is no appreciable difference between the requirements of Article 6 (or the Strasbourg jurisprudence on Article 6, such as *Teixeira de Castro v Portugal* (1999) 28 EHRR 101: see **A7.46**) and English law.

D3.104   In *M* (2011) 175 JP 273, Stanley Burnton LJ said (at [15]) that there 'may be a difficult line to draw between legitimate police conduct and improper entrapment. In general, however, conduct that is open to a finding of such entrapment as to render a prosecution improper involves some pressure or persuasion on the defendant to commit the crime. Providing the opportunity for the commission of the crime will not of itself lead to a finding of entrapment.' His lordship concluded (at [18]) that it is:

> . . . an inherent aspect of any undercover police operation that the undercover police officer insinuates himself into the confidence of those involved in the criminal conduct at which the operation is directed. For an officer who has so insinuated himself to offer an opportunity to a defendant to commit a criminal offence, in the absence of persuasion or pressure or the offer of a significant inducement, will not generally result in its being an abuse of the process to prosecute the person who takes that opportunity to commit an offence.

The principles to be applied where entrapment is alleged were set out *Moore* [2013] EWCA Crim 85. Rix LJ referred (at [52]) to Professor D. Ormerod's article, 'Recent Developments in Entrapment' [2006] Covert Policing Review 65, and noted that Professor Ormerod identifies five factors as of particular relevance: (i) reasonable suspicion of criminal activity as a legitimate trigger for the police operation (a control mechanism for testing the police's good faith); (ii) authorisation and supervision of the operation as a legitimate control mechanism (to ensure proper control of the operation); (iii) necessity and proportionality of the means employed to police particular types of offence; (iv) the concepts of 'unexceptional opportunity' and causation; and (v) authentication of the evidence (i.e. of the conversations and contacts).

Abuse of Executive Power

D3.105   In *Horseferry Road Magistrates' Court, ex parte Bennett* [1994] 1 AC 42, the accused had been brought back forcibly to the UK in disregard of extradition procedures that were available. This was held to amount to an abuse of process even though a fair trial was possible. The point was that the accused should not have been before the court in the first place.

In *Mullen* [2000] QB 520, the security services and police had procured M's unlawful deportation from Zimbabwe. The Court of Appeal ruled that, even if no complaint can be made as to the fairness of the trial itself, unconscionable conduct on the part of the authorities in bringing the accused before the court *may* amount to an abuse of process. However, it is not invariably an abuse of process, since every case should be approached on its own facts. There may be cases where the 'seriousness of the crime is so great relative to the nature of the abuse of process that it would be a proper exercise of judicial discretion to permit a prosecution to proceed or to allow a conviction to stand notwithstanding an abuse of process in relation to the defendant's presence within the jurisdiction' (per Rose LJ at pp. 536–7).

This was the approach adopted by the House of Lords in *Latif* [1996] 1 All ER 353. L was convicted of being knowingly concerned in the importation into the UK of heroin which had been brought into the country by an undercover customs officer. The House of Lords held that whether the proceedings should have been stayed on the ground of abuse was a matter of discretion for the judge, who had to decide whether the matters said to constitute abuse of process amounted to what Lord Steyn described (at p. 112) as an 'affront to the public conscience'. His lordship added that this requires the judge to balance the public interest in ensuring that those who are charged with serious crimes should be tried against the competing public interest in not conveying the impression that the court will adopt the approach that the end justifies any means (p. 113). In the instant case, the judge had been entitled to conclude the proceedings should not be stayed; for similar reasons, the judge had not erred in not exercising his discretion to exclude the core of the prosecution case.

In cases such as these, a stay will be granted where the court concludes that, in all the circumstances, a trial will 'offend the court's sense of justice and propriety' (per Lord Lowry in *Ex parte Bennett*, at p. 74G) or will 'undermine public confidence in the criminal justice system and bring it into disrepute' (per Lord Steyn in *Latif*, at p. 112F).

In *Ahmed* [2011] EWCA Crim 184 (a case where the accused had allegedly been subject to torture outside the UK), Hughes LJ said (at [24]) that the jurisdiction to stay for abuse of process may be exercised 'where, by reason of gross executive misconduct manipulating the process of the court, the defendant has been deprived of the protection of the rule of law and it would as a result be unfair to put him on trial at all'. His lordship added that 'the jurisdiction does not exist to discipline the police or other executive arms of the State (although of course it will incidentally do so), but rather to protect the integrity of the processes of justice'. The Court of Appeal upheld the refusal of a stay on the basis that the judge had been right to hold that what is required is a connection between the alleged wrongdoing and the trial. In *Ahmed*, no evidence which was the product of torture or other ill-treatment was adduced at the trial, and the investigation did not amount, directly or indirectly, to employing the product of torture to make a case against the accused (at [39]). **D3.106**

Bringing Justice into Disrepute

Closely related to abuse of executive power are cases where the investigators have behaved in a way that is wholly improper. In *Grant* [2006] QB 60, for example, the police unlawfully recorded privileged conversations between the suspect and his legal adviser. No useful evidence was gathered in this way, and so there was nothing to exclude under the PACE 1984, s. 78. The Court of Appeal said that such unlawful acts, amounting as they did to a deliberate violation of a suspect's right to legal professional privilege, were 'so great an affront to the integrity of the justice system, and therefore the rule of law, that the associated prosecution was thereby rendered abusive and ought not to be countenanced by the court' (per Laws LJ at [54]), despite the absence of any actual prejudice to the accused. (As to covert surveillance and the RIPA 2000, see *McE v Prison Service of Northern Ireland* [2009] 1 AC 908 at **D1.58**.) **D3.107**

However, in *Warren v A-G for Jersey* [2012] 1 AC 22, the Privy Council said that the decision in *Grant* was wrong (per Lord Dyson, at [36]). This was because it was 'difficult to avoid the conclusion that in *Grant* the proceedings were stayed in order to express the court's disapproval of the police misconduct and to discipline the police', which is an impermissible use of the power to stay proceedings. Lord Dyson referred to an earlier decision of the Supreme Court, *Maxwell* [2011] 4 All ER 941 (a case involving serious misconduct by the police), where he had said (at [13]) that: **D3.108**

> It is well established that the court has the power to stay proceedings in two categories of case, namely (i) where it will be impossible to give the accused a fair trial, and (ii) where it offends the court's sense of justice and propriety to be asked to try the accused in the particular circumstances of the case. In the first category of case, if the court concludes that an accused cannot receive a fair trial, it will stay the proceedings without more. No question of the balancing of competing interests

arises. In the second category of case, the court is concerned to protect the integrity of the criminal justice system...

Warren involved illegal cross-border audio surveillance and so fell within the second category of case. The arguments for and against a stay were set out by Lord Dyson at [46]–[50]. The case for a stay was 'of considerable weight': the misconduct was very serious (it involved misleading the Jersey Attorney-General and the Chief of Police, and the authorities of three foreign States) and, without the product of the unlawfulness, there would have been no trial. However, there were also factors which, taken cumulatively, 'weighed heavily against a stay': the offence was very serious; the ringleader 'was a professional drug dealer of the first order'; the 'unwise' advice of the Crown Advocate mitigated, to some extent, the gravity of the misconduct of the police; there had been no attempt to mislead the Jersey court; and there was 'real urgency' in the case and it was 'in these circumstances that the police cut corners and acted unlawfully'. Lord Kerr (at [83]) went on to summarise some of the principles which have emerged from recent case law on abuse of process:

  (i) [a stay in the second category of case] should be granted where necessary to protect the integrity of the criminal justice system.
  (ii) A balancing of interests should be conducted in deciding whether a stay is required to fulfil this primary purpose... [W]here a stay is being considered in order to protect the integrity of the criminal justice system, 'the public interest in ensuring that those that are charged with grave crimes should be tried' will always weigh in the balance [per Lord Steyn in *Latif* [1996] 1 All ER 353 at p. 113A-B, who] mentioned that a possible counter-vailing factor was that the impression should not be created that the court is giving its sanction to an approach that the end justifies any means. With the emphasis that is given in this and other cases to statements that prosecutorial or police misbehaviour will never be condoned, this may not be as significant a consideration as heretofore...
  (iii) The 'but for' factor (i.e. where it can be shown that the defendant would not have stood trial but for executive abuse of power) is merely one of various matters that will influence the outcome of the inquiry as to whether a stay should be granted. It is not necessarily determinative of that issue.
  (iv) A stay should not be ordered for the purpose of punishing or disciplining prosecutorial or police misconduct. The focus should always be on whether the stay is required in order to safeguard the integrity of the criminal justice system.

D3.109 **Private Prosecutions** In *R (Dacre) v City of Westminster Magistrates' Court* [2009] 1 All ER 639, the Divisional Court considered abuse in the context of private prosecutions. Latham LJ (at [26]) said that in deciding whether 'it would offend the court's sense of justice for the prosecution to proceed... both motive and conduct can clearly be relevant. As far as motive is concerned, proceedings tainted by *mala fides* or spite or some other oblique motive may fall into this category.' However, he went on to note (at [27]) that it had been held in *Bow Street Metropolitan Stipendiary Magistrate, ex parte South Coast Shipping Co. Ltd* [1993] QB 645, that the mere presence of an indirect or improper motive in launching a prosecution did not necessarily vitiate it, and the court would be slow to halt such a prosecution in the case of mixed motives unless the conduct was truly oppressive. Drawing an analogy with the principles relating to entrapment in relation to public prosecutions (set out in *Looseley* [2001] 4 All ER 897: see **D3.103**), his lordship went on to hold (at [31]) that there is 'no reason in principle why... a private prosecution should not be considered an abuse of process if the crime which is the subject of the prosecution is one that has been encouraged by the private prosecutor or when in some other way the private prosecutor has essentially created the same mischief as that about which he or she complains'.

D3.110 **Actions of Third Parties** In *Momodou* [2005] 2 All ER 571, Judge LJ (at [54]) observed that 'notwithstanding that the prosecution or prosecuting authority may be blameless... [t]he activities of third parties may constitute an abuse of process', although in most cases 'difficulties, even great difficulties, created for the defence are almost always capable of being addressed by the trial process itself', making it unnecessary to halt a prosecution as an abuse (see **D15.104** for further discussion of this case). Whether or not a fair trial is possible is, of course, a fact-specific question (see, e.g., *Athwal* [2009] 1 WLR 2430, where the Court of Appeal rejected an argument that refusal by the Legal Services Commission to fund particular inquiries had rendered the trial unfair).

Procedure for Making Abuse of Process Applications

Crown Court The CrimPR, r. 3.20 (see Supplement, **R-27**), applies where the accused wants **D3.111**
the Crown Court to stay the case on the grounds that the proceedings are an abuse of the court, or otherwise unfair. The accused must give written notice of the application to the prosecutor (and to any co-accused) and to the court, as soon as practicable after becoming aware of the grounds for applying. The application should be dealt with at a pre-trial hearing, unless the grounds for the application do not arise until trial. The application must explain the grounds on which it is made; include or identify all supporting material; specify 'relevant events, dates and propositions of law'; and identify any witness the accused wants to call to give evidence in person. A party who wishes to make representations in opposition to the application must serve written representations on the court and the other parties within 14 days of the service of the application. According to CPD I, para 3C.3 and 3C.4 (see Supplement, **PD-5**), the advocate appearing for the applicant must serve a skeleton argument on the court and on the other parties at least five clear working days before the application is due to be heard, and the prosecution advocate must serve a responsive skeleton argument at least two clear working days before the hearing. The skeleton arguments must set out any propositions of law to be advanced, together with any authorities (identifying specific passages) that are relied on.

Magistrates' Courts As to the procedure that the magistrates ought to adopt where abuse **D3.112**
of process is raised, it is essential that they hear from both the prosecution and the defence. In *Clerkenwell Stipendiary Magistrate, ex parte Bell* (1991) 159 JP 669, the magistrate heard evidence from a police officer explaining the reason for the delay but declined to hear evidence from the accused. The Divisional Court held that this was a breach of natural justice and quashed the decision to send the accused to the Crown Court for trial. Similarly, in *Crawley Justices, ex parte DPP* (1991) 155 JP 841, the Divisional Court quashed the decision of the justices to dismiss the case because of delay, since the bench had not heard the full facts before coming to their decision.

LEGAL REPRESENTATION AND RIGHTS OF AUDIENCE

Rights of Audience

Under the Legal Services Act 2007, s. 12(1)(a), the exercise of a right of audience is a 'reserved **D3.113**
legal activity'. By virtue of s. 13, a person is permitted to carry out a reserved legal activity only if he is an 'authorised person' in relation to that activity, and under s. 18 an 'authorised person' is someone who is 'authorised to carry on the relevant activity by a relevant approved regulator' (such as the Bar Standards Board or the Solicitors Regulation Authority).

Section 19 makes provision exempting certain persons from the requirement to be authorised to conduct particular reserved legal activities. One example is that, under sch. 3, para. 1(2), a person is exempt if he is not an authorised person but has a right of audience granted by the court 'in relation to those proceedings'. In *Southwark Crown Court, ex parte Tawfick* [1995] Crim LR 658, Glidewell LJ, construing a similar provision in earlier legislation (the Courts and Legal Services Act 1990), accepted the argument that the statute gave 'any court the power in its discretion to grant to any person a right of audience related to particular proceedings'.

The Prosecution in the Crown Court

At common law, the prosecution at a trial on indictment had to be legally represented. In *George* **D3.114**
Maxwell (Developments) Ltd [1980] 2 All ER 99, the trial judge ruled that the case would fail for want of prosecution unless the complainant (who had brought a private prosecution) instructed

solicitors and counsel (since, once the indictment was signed, the proceedings continued in the name of the Crown). However, in *Southwark Crown Court, ex parte Tawfick* [1995] Crim LR 658, it was said that the discretion which was then conferred on the court by the Courts and Legal Services Act 1990 (and which is now to be found in the Legal Services Act 2007, sch. 3) could be used to allow an unrepresented prosecutor to conduct a prosecution in the Crown Court. However, Glidewell LJ added that the discretion would be exercised only 'occasionally', and that it would be in 'exceptional circumstances' that a Crown Court judge would allow the complainant to conduct the prosecution case.

The Accused in the Crown Court

D3.115   The accused is entitled to decline legal representation and present his case in person. If he is represented during the initial stages of a trial on indictment and then wishes to dispense with the services of counsel, application to that effect must be made to the trial judge, who has a discretion to refuse to release counsel. It is, however, rare for the accused's application to be refused. In *Lyons* (1979) 68 Cr App R 104, Waller LJ said (at p. 108) that 'it may well be that in the vast majority of cases a judge, faced with an application to dispense with counsel ... would allow the application ... But at the end of the day it is a matter for the discretion of the learned judge.'

The court has a common-law power to prevent an unrepresented accused from cross-examining in an oppressive manner (*Brown* [1998] 2 Cr App R 364). Moreover, the YJCEA 1999, ss. 34 to 39, prohibits unrepresented defendants from cross-examining complainants and child witnesses in trials for certain specified offences, and the court has the power to prohibit cross-examination of witnesses by unrepresented defendants in any other case if satisfied that the quality of evidence given by the witness on cross-examination is likely to be diminished if the cross-examination is conducted or continued by the accused in person, and that a prohibition would not be contrary to the interests of justice. There are provisions for the appointment of representatives to conduct cross-examination on behalf of unrepresented defendants. The procedural aspects of the restriction on cross-examination by an accused acting in person are set out in the CrimPR, part 31 (which applies both to the Crown Court and to the magistrates' courts).

D3.116   In *Ulcay* [2008] 1 All ER 547, the accused changed his instructions at the close of the prosecution case, and his legal representatives withdrew on the grounds of professional embarrassment. The judge refused an application from the new representatives for a two-week adjournment and the new representatives also withdrew. The accused remained unrepresented during the trial. The Court of Appeal had to decide whether his subsequent conviction was safe. Sir Igor Judge P gave guidance (at [28]) on what should be done by defence counsel where the accused changes his instructions during the trial:

> It is for counsel to decide whether, consistent with his obligations to his client, and the court, and the rules of his profession, he is so professionally embarrassed that he cannot continue with the case. If so, again consistent with his duty to the court, but without contravening the legal privilege which underpins his professional relationship with his client, he should inform the court of his situation, providing such explanation as he can, to enable the judge to decide how to proceed. It is difficult to imagine cases in which it would be appropriate for the trial judge to direct counsel that he must continue with a case, or refuse him permission to withdraw on the grounds of professional embarrassment if, having heard counsel explain his position, counsel remains unpersuaded that he may properly continue to act, not least because counsel will almost certainly be better informed than the judge, in particular because there are likely to be considerations which he may be unable to reveal.

His lordship held (at [36]) that the judge was entitled to exercise his discretion to refuse the lengthy adjournment sought by counsel, since a lengthy adjournment would have necessitated the discharge of the jury, thereby causing prejudice to the co-accused and public inconvenience and cost (or else trying the accused separately from his co-accused, with the cost and inconvenience that would involve). His lordship went on (at [41]) to hold that the cab-rank rule (r. 602 of the Bar Code of Conduct) 'applies whenever, and however late, the barrister is instructed. The absence of what he would regard as sufficient time for the purpose of preparation does not constitute an exception.' Moreover, r. 701(b)(ii), which says that a barrister should not undertake any task for which 'he does not have adequate time and opportunity to prepare for or perform' does not constitute an exception to the cab-rank rule. It follows that newly instructed counsel should 'soldier on and do the best he can notwithstanding the judge's decision that the period of adjournment should be significantly shorter than the time sought by counsel' (at [42]). Finally, his lordship said that r 2.01(b) of the Law Society rules, which requires the solicitor without sufficient resources or lacking the necessary competence to cease to act, does not prevent a solicitor from acting (nor does it require him to cease to act) where an order of the court creates difficulties and makes it harder for him to discharge his professional obligations to his client (at [44]).

Rights of Audience in the Crown Court

By virtue of the regulatory regime established by the Legal Services Act 2007 (see D3.113), **D3.117** rights of audience in the Crown Court are conferred upon barristers, and upon solicitors with rights of audience in the higher courts.

Magistrates' Courts

In the magistrates' court, neither the prosecutor nor the accused need be legally represented. **D3.118** A private prosecutor, for example, may appear in person, as when the victim of an alleged assault takes out a summons against his assailant and then both argues the case himself and gives the principal evidence for the prosecution. In the case of police prosecutions, however, the Prosecution of Offences Act 1985, s. 3(2)(a), requires that the DPP, through the CPS, must take over the conduct of the prosecution.

Representation in a magistrates' court may be either by counsel or by solicitor, since both have rights of audience. Legal Executives (regulated by the Institute of Legal Executives) also have a right of audience in magistrates' courts.

Arranging for Legal Representation for the Prosecution

It is the responsibility of the CPS to arrange for the prosecution to be legally represented in **D3.119** cases where the DPP has the conduct of the proceedings. Crown Prosecutors commonly represent the CPS at proceedings in magistrates' courts. For trials on indictment (and, in practice, for appeals to the Crown Court and committals for sentence), the CPS are obliged to brief an advocate with the right of audience in the Crown Court unless the case is conducted by a Crown Prosecutor with a right of audience in the higher courts. There is nothing to stop the CPS briefing an advocate for a specific case in a magistrates' court, although the usual practice is to employ a solicitor or barrister as agent (under the Prosecution of Offences Act 1985, s. 5) to handle the entire CPS list for a court session.

Major prosecuting authorities other than the CPS (such as the Department of Work and Pensions and local authorities) have legally qualified staff to prepare and present cases. Otherwise, a private prosecutor who wishes to be legally represented must instruct solicitors (who may, of course, brief counsel). Various enactments also permit certain types of prosecution in the magistrates' courts to be presented by officials who are not practising solicitors and may not even be lawyers (e.g., Local Government Act 1972, s. 223, and Social Security Administration Act 1992, s. 116).

Arranging for Legal Representation for the Accused

An accused secures legal representation by instructing solicitors. It is open to him to apply for **D3.120** public funding (through the Criminal Defence Service) to cover the costs. To be eligible for legal aid (whether in the Crown Court or in a magistrates' court), the accused must satisfy both a merits test (that public funding is in the 'interests of justice') and a means test (see **D32.1** *et seq.* for details). Some publicly funded representation is provided through a system of salaried public defenders, but the majority is provided through solicitors in private practice who carry out what is still generally referred to as 'legal aid' work.

Use of a McKenzie Friend

D3.121   Any person may attend the court as a 'McKenzie friend' of either party (*McKenzie v McKenzie* [1971] P 33), taking notes, quietly making suggestions, and giving advice, although this is subject to the discretion of the court and may therefore not properly be described as a right (*R v Leicester City Justices, ex parte Barrow* [1991] 3 All ER 935, per Watkins LJ at p. 275). A McKenzie friend has no right to address the court on behalf of the party he is supporting.

OPEN JUSTICE

The General Rule that Proceedings Should be in Open Court

D3.122   It has long been established that criminal trials should take place in open court and be freely reported. The following principles may be derived from Lord Diplock's speech in *A-G v Leveller Magazine Ltd* [1979] AC 440 at p. 450:

(a) The normal rule is that criminal proceedings should be conducted publicly.

(b) Nonetheless, courts do have power to order that the public be excluded.

(c) The exercise of the power, in common with any other derogation from the principles of open justice, should be strictly confined to cases where the public's presence would 'frustrate or render impracticable the administration of justice'.

In *Re Times Newspapers Ltd* [2009] 1 WLR 1015, the Court of Appeal reiterated that 'justice requires proceedings in court to be held in public, with all the consequences that that entails. It is only where the proper administration of justice would be affected that any derogation from this principle can be permitted' (Latham LJ at [4]).

The importance of open justice is emphasised in the CrimPR, r. 38.2, which provides that, in the case of Crown Court trials, the general rule is that the trial must be in public. However, this is subject to the court's power to impose a restriction on reporting what takes place at a public hearing, or public access to what otherwise would be a public hearing, or to withhold information from the public during a public hearing, or to order that a trial is to take place in private. There is corresponding provision for magistrates' court trials in r. 37.2 (which provides that the general rule is that the hearing must be in public, but the court may exercise its power to impose reporting restrictions, withhold information from the public or order a hearing in private).

It should also be noted that rr. 38.12 (Crown Court) and 37.5 (magistrates' courts) stipulate that, where the written statement of a witness (including an expert witness) is admitted into evidence, each relevant part of the statement must be read or summarised aloud, or else the court (and the jury, if there is one) must read the statement and its gist must be summarised aloud.

D3.123   In *R (Guardian News and Media Ltd) v City of Westminster Magistrates' Court* [2012] 3 All ER 551, the Court of Appeal (Civil Division) had to consider whether a District Judge had power to allow a newspaper to inspect and take copies of affidavits, witness statements and correspondence, which had been supplied to the judge for the purposes of extradition hearings but which had not been read out in open court (though they were referred to during the course of the hearings). Toulson LJ, with whose judgment the Master of the Rolls agreed, said (at [69]) that the courts have an inherent jurisdiction to determine how the principle of open justice should be applied. His lordship observed (at [76]) that the newspaper had 'a serious journalistic purpose in seeking access to the documents', and said that, unless 'some strong contrary argument can be made out, the courts should assist rather than impede such an exercise' (at [77]). He observed (at [79]) that 'the purpose of the open justice principle...is to enable the public to understand and scrutinise the justice system of which the courts are the administrators'. His lordship added (at [83]) that 'the practice of receiving evidence without it being read in open court potentially has the side effect of making the proceedings less intelligible to the press and the public', and went on to say that the time has now come for the courts to acknowledge that in some cases public access to documents referred to in open court might be necessary. He went on to say (at [85]):

> In a case where documents have been placed before a judge and referred to in the course of proceedings, in my judgment the default position should be that access should be permitted on the open justice principle; and where access is sought for a proper journalistic purpose, the case for allowing it will be particularly strong. However, there may be countervailing reasons...The court has to carry out a proportionality exercise which will be fact-specific. Central to the court's evaluation will be the purpose of the open justice principle, the potential value of the material in advancing that purpose and, conversely, any risk of harm which access to the documents may cause to the legitimate interests of others.

His lordship concluded (at [87]) that, since the newspaper had put forward good reasons for having access to the documents sought, and that there was no suggestion that this would give rise to any risk of harm to any other party, or that it would place any great burden on the court, the application should be allowed.

This case was cited in *Marine A* [2014] 1 Cr App R 353 (26), where Lord Judge CJ (at [52]), applying CPD I, para. 5B.9 (see Supplement, **PD-14**), said that the court is bound to 'have regard to the rights of victims, parties, witnesses and any third parties whose rights may be engaged by the release to the public of material presented in court'. His lordship went on to consider the position of journalists, saying (at [56]) that:

> ...it is clear that those who inform public debate on matters of public interest as journalists (whether in the print, broadcasting or internet media) are accorded a special position, given the role of journalism in enabling proper and effective participation in a democratic society.

Lord Judge went on to consider the test to be applied where restrictions on publication of the identity of the accused are sought. His lordship said (at [84]) that 'a defendant in a criminal trial must be named save in rare circumstances'. However, 'the Court has a power to withhold the name and address of a defendant in cases where circumstances justify that', although 'such cases would be rare. Any derogation from open justice, and any interference with the right to report a criminal trial, must be both necessary and proportionate' (at [85]). His lordship added that an order that an accused should not be identified 'will not be necessary, if some other measure is available to protect those rights of the individuals, and that other measure would be proportionate' (at [88]).

Sitting 'In Camera' A decision to sit in camera (i.e. in private) is not justified merely on the ground that, having regard to the nature of the witness's proposed evidence, he would find it embarrassing to testify publicly (*Malvern Justices, ex parte Evans* [1988] QB 540, in which the Divisional Court held that the justices had erred when they agreed to sit in camera in a case involving special reasons for not disqualifying, for the sole purpose of sparing the accused the ordeal of giving evidence of 'embarrassing and intimate details' of her personal life). Even when it is claimed that the safety of a witness or party will be endangered by an open hearing, the court should consider carefully whether he can be adequately protected by means less drastic than totally excluding the public. In *Reigate Justices, ex parte Argus Newspapers* (1983) 5 Cr App R (S) 181, the Divisional Court emphasised that it is only in exceptional circumstances that a court may depart from the rule that justice has to be administered in public. Hearing a matter in camera is a course of last resort and the justices should have applied their minds to how else they might have dealt with the matter (in the instant case, an order could have been made at the beginning of the proceedings under the Contempt of Court Act 1981, s. 11, protecting the identity of the accused).

D3.124

It should also be borne in mind that a witness's fears may be overcome by the use of special measures (e.g., under the YJCEA 1999: see **D14**), and in other cases it may be more appropriate to deal with a reluctant witness by the threat of contempt proceedings than by depriving the public of access to the courts.

In *Yam* [2008] EWCA Crim 269, Lord Phillips CJ said (at [6]) that the court has 'an inherent power to exclude the press and the public where the interests of justice required it' but 'the interests of justice could never justify excluding the press and the public if the consequence would be that the trial would not be fair'.

D3.125   The CrimPR empower Crown Court judges to sit in chambers when exercising certain functions, e.g., hearing bail applications (and appeals under the Bail (Amendment) Act 1993); hearing applications relating to procedural matters that are preliminary or incidental to the Crown Court proceedings. Although bail applications in the Crown Court are generally listed to be heard in chambers, any application to sit in public must be approached on the footing that it must be acceded to unless there is a sound reason for excluding the public. When considering such applications, the court must start from the 'fundamental presumption in favour of open justice' (*R (Malik) v Central Criminal Court* [2007] 4 All ER 1141, per Gray J at [40]).

In *Guardian News and Media Ltd v AB and CD* [2014] EWCA Crim (B1), there was an application for a trial to be held in camera. Gross LJ said (at [2]):

> One aspect of the Rule of Law – both a hallmark and a safeguard – is open justice, which includes criminal trials being held in public and the publication of the names of defendants. Open justice is both a fundamental principle of the common law and a means of ensuring public confidence in our legal system; exceptions are rare and must be justified on the facts. Any such exceptions must be necessary and proportionate. No more than the minimum departure from open justice will be countenanced.

His lordship added (at [5]) that considerations of national security 'will not by themselves justify a departure from the principle of open justice' and that:

> Open justice must, however, give way to the yet more fundamental principle that the paramount object of the court is to do justice; accordingly, where there is a serious possibility that an insistence on open justice in the national security context would frustrate the administration of justice, for example, by deterring the Crown from prosecuting a case where it otherwise should do so, a departure from open justice may be justified.

His lordship added (at [21]) that the Court of Appeal found it difficult to conceive of a situation where it would appropriate both to hold a criminal trial in camera and to anonymise the accused.

The CrimPR, rr. 16.6 and 16.7, set out the procedure for an application for an order that all or part of a trial be held in private. Such applications are normally relevant to trial involving offences affecting national security (see the Official Secrets Act 1920, s. 8(4)), where the court receives evidence from a person under the age of 18 (see the CYPA 1933, s. 37) or where the court reviews a sentence passed on a person who assisted an investigation (see the SOCPA 2005, s. 75). The court retains an inherent power to hear a trial in private. The application must be made not less than five business days before the trial is due to begin and the application must be served on the Crown Court and each other party. The appropriate officer of the Crown Court must then ensure that a copy of the notice is prominently displayed in the vicinity of the courtroom. The application must be determined at a hearing, which must be in private unless the court otherwise directs, after the accused has been arraigned but before the jury is sworn. A court must not hear a trial in private until the business day after it orders such a trial or the disposal of any appeal or review of the order, if later.

D3.126   Under the Administration of Justice Act 1960, s. 12 (see **B14.115**), there is no automatic rule that the reporting of proceedings held in private amounts to contempt — just as when public proceedings were reported, it has to be shown that the reporting involved a substantial risk of prejudice to the administration of justice (per Lord Scarman in *A-G v Leveller Magazine Ltd* [1979] AC 440 at p. 472F–G).

Special rules govern public access to youth courts (see **D24.13**).

Freedom of the Media to Report Court Proceedings

Section 4 of the Contempt of Court Act 1981 governs liability for the reporting of court **D3.127** proceedings.

Contempt of Court Act 1981, s. 4

(1) Subject to this section a person is not guilty of contempt of court under the strict liability rule in respect of a fair and accurate report of legal proceedings held in public, published contemporaneously and in good faith.

(2) In any such proceedings the court may, where it appears to be necessary for avoiding a substantial risk of prejudice to the administration of justice in those proceedings, or in any other proceedings pending or imminent, order that the publication of any report of the proceedings, or any part of the proceedings, be postponed for such period as the court thinks necessary for that purpose.

(2A) Where in proceedings for any offence which is an administration of justice offence for the purposes of section 54 of the Criminal Procedure and Investigations Act 1996 (acquittal tainted by an administration of justice offence) it appears to the court that there is a possibility that (by virtue of that section) proceedings may be taken against a person for an offence of which he has been acquitted, subsection (2) of this section shall apply as if those proceedings were pending or imminent.

(3) For the purposes of subsection (1) of this section ... a report of proceedings shall be treated as published contemporaneously—

  (a) in the case of a report of which publication is postponed pursuant to an order under subsection (2) of this section, if published as soon as practicable after that order expires;

  (b) in the case of a report of allocation or sending proceedings of which publication is permitted by virtue only of subsection (6) of section 52A of the Crime and Disorder Act 1998 ('the 1998 Act'), if published as soon as practicable after publication is so permitted;

  (c) in the case of a report of an application of which publication is permitted by virtue only of sub-paragraph (5) or (7) of paragraph 3 of Schedule 3 to the 1998 Act, if published as soon as practicable after publication is so permitted.

Scope of Order   CPD II, para. 16B.3 (see Supplement, **PD-22**), makes it clear that, before **D3.128** exercising its discretion to impose reporting restrictions, the court must 'follow precisely the statutory provisions under which the order is to be made, paying particular regard to what has to be established, by whom and to what standard'. Paragraph 16B.4 sets out a number of general principles, for example: that the court must 'keep in mind the fact that every order is a departure from the general principle that proceedings shall be open and freely reported'; that the court 'must be satisfied that the purpose of the proposed order cannot be achieved by some lesser measure'; that the terms of the order must be 'proportionate' (so as to comply with the ECHR, Article 10); that the parties (and any interested party, including representatives of the media) must be given a chance to make representations; that the order must be in precise terms (if practicable, agreed with the advocates in the case), stating the power under which it is made, its precise scope and purpose, and when it will cease to have effect. Paragraph 16B.1 makes reference to a document entitled 'Reporting Restrictions in the Criminal Courts' (the most recent edition of which was published by the Judicial College in June 2014), a practical guide for judges and the media on the statutory and common-law principles which should be applied.

Examples of situations in which the power given to the courts by the Contempt of Court Act 1981, s. 4(2), may be of value include: (a) when an accused is to be tried successively on

D

separate indictments (or several accused are to be tried separately for connected offences) and reports of the evidence given at the trial held first are likely to prejudice jurors for the later trials; and (b) when evidence and/or argument is put before the judge at a trial on indictment in the absence of the jury, the purpose of sending the jury out being to prevent their being prejudiced by, for example, evidence which the judge ultimately rules to be inadmissible.

D3.129   In *Ex parte The Telegraph plc* [1993] 2 All ER 971, it was held that, in forming a view whether the making of an order under s. 4(2) is necessary for avoiding a substantial risk of prejudice in the administration of justice, the court should have regard to the 'competing public considerations of ensuring a fair trial and of open justice' (per Lord Taylor of Gosforth CJ at p. 984). The Court of Appeal went on to observe that the two main requirements of s. 4(2) are distinct and so the judge must first identify the risk of substantial prejudice, and then go on to consider whether, in the light of the competing public interests, an order is necessary in order to avoid the risk, whether in his discretion he should make it and, if so, with all or only some of the restrictions sought. It is submitted that the consequence of this is that the court ought not to make an order under s. 4(2) if there is another way of avoiding a substantial risk of prejudice; if an alternative is available, it should be used rather than an order under s. 4(2).

In *Ex parte MGN Ltd* [2011] 1 Cr App R 387, Lord Judge CJ (at [14]) referred to *Sherwood, ex parte Telegraph Group plc* [2001] 1 WLR 1983, and said that:

> The first question is whether the reporting would give rise to a not insubstantial risk of prejudice to the administration of justice. The second question is whether an order under s. 4(2) would eliminate that risk. If not, there would be no necessity to impose such a ban. Again, that would be the end of the matter. If, on the other hand, an order would achieve the objective, the court still has to consider whether the risk could satisfactorily be overcome by less restrictive measures. Third, even if there is no other way of eliminating the perceived risk of prejudice, it still does not follow necessarily that an order has to be made. This requires a value judgment. The . . . court's approach should be that, unless it is necessary to impose an order, it is necessary not to impose one; and if it is necessary to impose an order at all, it must go no further than necessary. In summary, an order under s 4(2) of the 1981 Act should be regarded as a last resort.

The order in that case had been made to protect witnesses in a murder trial. His lordship went on (at [22]) to say that the use of s. 4(2) 'for the purposes of alleviating the difficulties of giving evidence, even if evidence has to be given in more than one trial, is rarely appropriate'. If the conditions for an order under s. 4(2) are established in the case of a particular witness, so that the order is 'justified in accordance with principle, then the order should be made'. However, the protection of witnesses is 'more appropriately secured by statutory measures designed for the purpose', such as the reporting restrictions under the CYPA 1933, s. 39, or special measures under the YJCEA 1999, ss. 23 to 30, 'designed to enable witnesses to give of their best'.

D3.130   In *R (Press Association) v Cambridge Crown Court* [2013] 1 All ER 1361, Lord Judge CJ (at [13]) emphasised that orders under s. 4(2) are intended to avoid 'a substantial risk of prejudice' to the proceedings in respect of which they are made, or to linked or related proceedings (such as a subsequent trial involving the same defendants or witnesses). Examples of the use of the power in s. 4(2) include prohibiting the publication of evidence or argument heard by the judge in the absence of the jury, and where a new trial is ordered after a successful appeal against conviction (to avoid prejudice to any retrial). His lordship added that an order under s. 4(2) should be made only 'when it is necessary to do so and as a last resort'. Moreover, his lordship pointed out that s. 4(2) 'is aimed at the postponement of publication rather than a permanent ban'. It follows that an order prohibiting publication for an indefinite period, which amounts in effect to the imposition of a permanent ban, should not be made under s. 4(2).

The powers of the court to postpone publication under s. 4(2) are exhaustive, and so the court has no inherent power in addition to the terms of that provision (*Newtownabbey Magistrates'*

Court, ex parte Belfast Telegraph Newspapers Ltd (1997) *The Times*, 27 August 1997, where it was held that the court had no power to prohibit the publication of the name and address of the accused, and the nature of the sexual assault charge against him, on the ground that publication might be prejudicial to the accused's own welfare).

In *A-G v Guardian Newspapers Ltd* [1992] 3 All ER 38, one of the issues considered by the **D3.131** Divisional Court was whether the making of an order under s. 4(2), and its terms, could themselves be reported. Mann LJ (at p. 882) thought it 'very doubtful' whether such a report fell within the ambit of s. 4(1). However, his lordship observed that any reporting of the order could cause the very mischief which the order was intended to prevent. It might therefore be appropriate in some cases for the judge to make plain whether, and to what extent, the making of the order and its terms could be published. Brooke J added (at p. 887) that, if the judge needed help in determining whether to make an order under s. 4(2), he could adjourn consideration of the matter until the press was represented, or he had the help of an *amicus curiae*. In *Clerkenwell Stipendiary Magistrate, ex parte The Telegraph plc* [1993] QB 462, the Divisional Court confirmed that the court has a discretion to hear representations from the press regarding the making of a s. 4(2) order. Although the power is discretionary, it would generally be right to exercise it by hearing from the press, who are best qualified to represent that public interest in publicity which the court has to take into account in performing the necessary balancing exercise (per Mann LJ at p. 471).

In *Times Newspapers Ltd* [2008] 1 All ER 343, the Court of Appeal held that s. 4(2) is designed to enable the court to prevent the publication of a report of proceedings where such publication will prejudice the conduct of those proceedings, or specific pending proceedings. It permits only postponement, and the need for postponement cannot subsist beyond the end of the proceedings in question. The court added that posing and answering a question in open court does not mean that the evidence is in the public domain, and so the court may prevent publication of the answer.

Effect of the ECHR: the Balancing Exercise In *Re S (a Child) (Identification: restriction on pub-* **D3.132** *lication)* [2005] 1 AC 593, the House of Lords reiterated the substance of the decision about the interplay between the ECHR, Articles 8 (respect for private and family life) and 10 (freedom of expression), in *Campbell v MGN Ltd* [2004] 2 AC 457: (a) neither article has precedence over the other; (b) where the values under the two articles are in conflict, an intense focus on the comparative importance of the specific rights being claimed in the individual case is necessary; (c) the justifications for interfering with or restricting each right must be taken into account; (d) the proportionality test must be applied to each (per Lord Steyn at [17]). His lordship went on to say (at [30]):

> A criminal trial is a public event. The principle of open justice puts, as has often been said, the judge and all who participate in the trial under intense scrutiny. The glare of contemporaneous publicity ensures that trials are properly conducted. It is a valuable check on the criminal process. Moreover, the public interest may be as much involved in the circumstances of a remarkable acquittal as in a surprising conviction. Informed public debate is necessary about all such matters. Full contemporaneous reporting of criminal trials in progress promotes public confidence in the administration of justice. It promotes the values of the rule of law.

On this basis, it was held that the press should not be restrained from publishing the identity of the accused in a murder trial in order to protect the privacy of the accused's child, who was not involved in the criminal proceedings.

Lord Steyn's speech was analysed carefully in the case of *A Local Authority v W, L, W, T and R* **D3.133** [2006] 1 FLR 1, where the court considered again the relationship between Articles 8 and 10 of the ECHR. Sir Mark Potter (at [53]) said that each propounds a fundamental right which there is a pressing social need to protect; equally, each qualifies the right it propounds so far as it may be lawful, necessary and proportionate to do so in order to accommodate the other. He went on to say that the exercise to be performed is one of parallel analysis in which the starting point is 'presumptive parity', in that neither article has precedence over or 'trumps' the other.

Part D Procedure

This exercise of parallel analysis requires the court to examine the justification for interfering with each right, and the issue of proportionality is to be considered in respect of each. It is not a mechanical exercise to be decided upon the basis of rival generalities. An intense focus on the comparative importance of the specific rights being claimed in the individual case is necessary before the ultimate balancing test in terms of proportionality is carried out. The interest in open justice is a factor to be accorded great weight in both the parallel analysis and the ultimate balancing test. However, the weight to be accorded to the right freely to report criminal proceedings is not invariably determinative of the outcome; indeed, although it is the ordinary rule that the press, as public watchdog, may report everything that takes place in a criminal court, that rule might nonetheless be displaced in 'unusual or exceptional circumstances'.

D3.134   In *Re Trinity Mirror plc* [2008] QB 770, a five-judge Court of Appeal (including the Presidents of the QBD and the Family Division) said that it is 'impossible to over-emphasise the importance to be attached to the ability of the media to report criminal trials...this represents the embodiment of the principle of open justice in a free country. An important aspect of the public interest in the administration of criminal justice is that the identity of those convicted and sentenced for criminal offices should not be concealed' (Sir Igor Judge P at [32]). On this basis, the court set aside an order protecting the identity of the children of the accused, saying (at [33]) that:

> Everyone appreciates the risk that innocent children may suffer prejudice and damage when a parent is convicted of a serious offence...However...if the court were to uphold this ruling so as to protect the rights of the defendant's children under Article 8, it would be countenancing a substantial erosion of the principle of open justice, to the overwhelming disadvantage of public confidence in the criminal justice system, the free reporting of criminal trials and the proper identification of those convicted and sentenced in them. Such an order cannot begin to be contemplated unless the circumstances are indeed properly to be described as exceptional.

In *C v CPS* (2008) 172 JP 273, Lloyd LJ said (at [3]–[5]) that great care must be taken when making orders restricting the reporting of criminal proceedings. Such orders should not be made as a matter of routine. They require a careful balance of matters relating to the public interest. Before making such an order, the court should generally ask members of the press whether they wish to make any submissions.

D3.135   In *Re Guardian News and Media Ltd* [2010] 2 AC 697, the Supreme Court reaffirmed the general rule that the press and law reporters should ordinarily be permitted to name litigants or parties to proceedings before the courts. Some exceptions have been created by statute, but in other cases where the granting of an anonymity order might be thought necessary in order to protect the litigant's rights to privacy under the ECHR, Article 8, consideration must also be given to the right of free expression that is protected by Article 10. Judges must perform a balancing exercise between these two potentially conflicting rights and in the instances considered by the Supreme Court in the main proceedings (*Ahmed v HM Treasury* [2010] 2 AC 534), the balance came down firmly in favour of setting aside the anonymity orders that had originally been imposed.

Imposition of a Permanent Ban on Reporting Certain Matters

D3.136   In addition to their power to postpone publication of court reports by virtue of an order under the Contempt of Court Act 1981, s. 4(2), the courts are empowered to impose a *permanent* ban on the reporting of certain matters.

Contempt of Court Act 1981, s. 11

In any case where a court (having power to do so) allows a name or other matter to be withheld from the public in proceedings before the court, the court may give such directions prohibiting the publication of that name or matter in connection with the proceedings as appear to the court to be necessary for the purpose for which it was so withheld.

Section 11 complements the common-law power of a court, sitting in public, to receive certain evidence (such as the name and address of a witness) in a form which is not communicated to the public. The terms of s. 11 show that an order under it may be without limitation of time but may only be made where the court has legitimately exercised its common law power to receive evidence or other information without allowing it to be disclosed to the public (*Arundel Justices, ex parte Westminster Press Ltd* [1985] 2 All ER 390; *Re Trinity Mirror plc* [2008] QB 770). It is therefore a pre-condition to the making of an order on the basis of s. 11 that the court, having the power to do so, has withheld the name or other matter from the public in the proceedings before it (*R (Press Association) v Cambridge Crown Court* [2013] 1 All ER 1361, per Lord Judge CJ, at [14]). CPD II, paras. 16B.1 to 16B.7 (see Supplement, **PD-22**) apply to orders under s. 11 as well as to orders under s. 4(2).

In *Re Times Newspapers Ltd* [2009] 1 WLR 1015, Latham LJ (at [12]) noted that an important aspect of open justice is that defendants' names should be made public. However, 'there is no doubt that a court may, in appropriate circumstances, order that the identity of a defendant can be protected from publicity by withholding his or her name'. The power to do so comes, not from the Contempt of Court Act 1981, s. 11, but from the common law, which enables an order for anonymity to be made if the court is satisfied that the administration of justice would otherwise be seriously affected (at [17]). Nonetheless, as Lord Hope of Craighead said in *A-G's Ref (No. 3 of 1999): BBC's application to set aside or vary a reporting restriction order* [2010] 1 AC 145 (at [28]), even 'significant' interference with the rights of the accused under the ECHR, Article 8 may be 'proportionate when account is taken of the weight that must be given to the competing right to freedom of expression' under Article 10. **D3.137**

In *R (Harper and Johncox) v Aldershot Magistrates' Court* (2010) 174 JP 410, an application was made for reporting restrictions under the Contempt of Court Act 1981, s. 11, namely the withholding of the addresses of the accused. They were high-ranking police officers and it was argued on their behalf that there was a danger that publication of their addresses would put them, and their families, at risk. The Divisional Court upheld the justices' refusal to make the order sought. Pill LJ (at [24]) said that there is 'a burden on the claimants to establish not only that the derogation they seek is in the circumstances a very limited one but also that there is a justification in the particular case for interfering at all with the principle of open justice'. The accused in the present case had failed to discharge that burden. His lordship said that:

> ... if there is a risk, it would not in the circumstances be enhanced by publication of addresses ... any approach to them is likely to be a targeted one which would not be deterred by the need to discover a home address. While the charges against the claimants are serious, they are unlikely to provoke that response by vigilantes which occasionally occurs in some categories of offence, for example, charges involving abuse of young children. Moreover, it is inconceivable that these or other police officers would be deterred from performing their duties if it is known that their addresses would be disclosed in circumstances such as the present.

Juveniles So far as juveniles appearing in an adult court are concerned, under the CYPA 1933, s. 39, the onus is on the Crown Court or magistrates' court to make an order protecting the juvenile's anonymity (see **D24.78**). The opposite applies in the youth court, where reporting restrictions to protect the juvenile's identity apply automatically (see CYPA 1933, s. 49, and **D24.14**). In *Jolleys* [2014] 1 Cr App R 215 (15), Leveson LJ said (at [19]) that orders made under the CYPA 1933, s. 39, 'should be restricted to the language of the legislation'. It is submitted that this dictum applies to orders made under any legislation which restricts the freedom of the press to report court proceedings. **D3.138**

Sexual Offences Under the Sexual Offences (Amendment) Act 1992, the alleged victim in a case involving one of the sexual offences listed in s. 2 of the Act (including rape) is entitled to anonymity. Once an allegation of one of the offences in question has been made, nothing may be published which is likely to lead members of the public to identify the alleged victim (s. 1(1)). **D3.139**

In reporting the proceedings at and prior to a trial for rape or one of the offences covered by the 1992 Act, the media are obliged to omit anything likely to disclose the complainant's identity, even if that information was given in open court. Under s. 1(1), the restriction continues for the lifetime of the complainant. Under s. 3, the prohibition on publicity may be lifted by order of the court if either: (a) publicity is required by the accused so that witnesses will come forward and the conduct of the defence is likely to be seriously prejudiced if the direction is not given (s. 3(1)); or (b) the trial judge is satisfied that imposition of the prohibition imposes a substantial and unreasonable restriction on the reporting of the proceedings and it is in the public interest to relax the restriction (s. 3(2)).

D3.140 'Reporting and Access Restrictions'   The YJCEA 1999, s. 46, provides for a party to make an application for the court to give reporting directions in relation to a witness other than the accused. The court may make such a direction in respect of an eligible witness if it determines that the direction is likely to improve the quality of the evidence of the witness or his co-operation in the case preparation of any party to the proceedings (s. 46(2)). Eligibility for a direction arises where the quality of evidence or co-operation is likely to be diminished by reason of fear or distress on the part of the witness in connection with being identified by members of the public as a witness in the proceedings (s. 46(3)). Generally, the direction has effect for the lifetime of the witness (s. 46(6)).

In *ITN News v R* [2014] 1 WLR 199, the Court of Appeal noted (at [31]) that a still or moving picture of a witness may be prohibited if the 'eligibility' test is satisfied, even if the name and identity of that witness is otherwise known. The Court added that, even when a reporting restriction is appropriate, 'it should be no wider than necessary to avoid any diminution in the quality of the evidence to be given by the witness'.

Under the CrimPR, r. 16.2, where a court is (i) imposing a restriction on the reporting of what takes place at a public hearing or on public access to what otherwise would be a public hearing, (ii) is allowing the withholding of information from the public during a public hearing or (iii) is ordering that a trial should take place in private, the court must have regard to the importance of dealing with criminal cases in public and of allowing a public hearing to be reported to the public. Rule 16.4 sets out the procedure to be followed where such restrictions are sought, including any application for a 'reporting direction' (under the YJCEA 1999, s. 46). Under r. 16.6, a party who is seeking an order that some or all of a trial should be heard in private must make a written application not less than five business days before the trial is due to begin, explaining the reasons for the application and, in particular, why no measures other than a private trial order would suffice.

Access to Information Held by the Court

D3.141 The CrimPR, r. 5.8, applies where a member of the public, including a reporter, wants information about a case from the court. Certain information (such as the charge(s), the identity of the parties and the outcome of the case) has to be supplied, but the court can permit the disclosure of other information. CPD I, para. 5B.9 (see Supplement, **PD-14**), sets out a number of factors that the court should take into account, including: whether the request is for the purpose of contemporaneous reporting; the nature of the information or documents being sought; the purpose for which they are required; the value of the documents in advancing the open justice principle, including enabling the media to discharge its role as a 'public watchdog'; and any risk of harm which access to them may cause to the legitimate interests of others. If a document has been read aloud to the court in its entirety, it should usually be provided on request (para. 5B.10). Where only part of a document has been read aloud, open justice requires only access to the part of the document that has been read aloud (para. 5B.14).

Text-based Communications from Court

D3.142 *Practice Guidance (Court Proceedings: Live Text-based Communications) (No. 2)* [2012] 1 WLR 12 'clarifies the use which may be made of live text-based communications, such as mobile email, social media (including Twitter) and internet enabled laptops in and from courts throughout England and Wales'. A member of the public who is in court and who wishes to use live text-based communications during court proceedings, must first apply for permission to activate and use a mobile phone, small laptop or similar piece of equipment which can, if permission is granted, be used solely to make live, text-based communications of the proceedings (at [9]). The 'paramount question' for the judge, when deciding whether to give permission, is whether it may 'interfere with the proper administration of justice' (at [11]). In the context of a criminal trial, the danger to the administration of justice is likely to be most acute where, for example, 'witnesses who are out of court may be informed of what has already happened in court and so coached or briefed before they then give evidence', or where information posted (e.g., on Twitter) 'about inadmissible evidence may influence members of a jury' (at [13]). However, to enable the media to produce fair and accurate reports of the proceedings, a representative of the media or a legal commentator who wishes to use live, text-based communications from court may do so without making an application to the court (at [10]). It may be necessary for the judge to limit live, text-based communications to representatives of the media for journalistic purposes, and to disallow their use by the wider public in court, if (for example) it is necessary to limit the number of mobile electronic devices in use at any given time (at [14]). Permission to use live, text-based communications from court may be withdrawn by the court at any time (at [16]).

The Principle of Open Justice and Magistrates' Courts

The MCA 1980, s. 121(4), requires a magistrates' court to sit in open court when trying an accused or imposing imprisonment; moreover, the CrimPR, r. 37.2(1)(a), states that, subject to the powers to impose reporting restrictions, to withhold information from the public, or to order a hearing in private, the 'general rule is that the hearing must be in public'. **D3.143**

In *Malvern Justices, ex parte Evans* [1988] QB 540, it was held that justices have an inherent power to exclude the public and thus conduct the proceedings in camera, although that power should be exercised only in the exceptional circumstances where it was necessary for the proper administration of justice. Watkins LJ, at p. 552, said that it is undesirable that any part of proceedings in a magistrates' court should be heard in camera unless there are compelling reasons, and that this exceptional step should be avoided if there is any other way of serving the interests of justice. Thus, in determining whether to exclude the public, magistrates' courts are in the same position as other courts.

Disclosure of the Names of Judges and Magistrates A further aspect of the principle of open justice is that the names of those administering it shall not be concealed. It has never been suggested that the name of a Crown Court judge should, or could, be kept secret. So far as justices are concerned, there is no statutory rule entitling them to anonymity. Since the principle of open justice requires that nothing should be done to discourage the fair and accurate reporting of proceedings in court, a bona fide inquirer is entitled to know the name of a justice who is sitting or who has sat on a case heard recently. However, a clerk may be justified in refusing (during or after a hearing) to give the name of one of the justices to a person whom the clerk reasonably believes to be seeking that information solely for a 'mischievous purpose' (*Felixstowe Justices, ex parte Leigh* [1987] QB 582, per Watkins LJ, at p. 595). **D3.144**

Appeals against Derogations from Open Justice

Criminal Justice Act 1988, s. 159 **D3.145**

(1) A person aggrieved may appeal to the Court of Appeal, if that court grants leave, against—
 (a) an order under section 4 or 11 of the Contempt of Court Act 1981 made in relation to a trial on indictment;
 (aa) an order made by the Crown Court under section 58(7) or (8) of the Criminal Procedure and Investigations Act 1996 in a case where the court has convicted a person on a trial on indictment;

(b) any order restricting the access of the public to the whole or any part of a trial on indictment or to any proceedings ancillary to such a trial; and

(c) any order restricting the publication of any report of the whole or any part of a trial on indictment or any such ancillary proceedings;

and the decision of the Court of Appeal shall be final.

...

(5) On the hearing of an appeal under this section the Court of Appeal shall have power—

(a) to stay any proceedings in any other court until after the appeal is disposed of;

(b) to confirm, reverse or vary the order complained of; and

(c) to make such order as to costs as it thinks fit.

D3.146   Section 159 creates a specific right to appeal against orders of the Crown Court derogating from the principle of open justice. The procedure to be followed is set out in the CrimPR, part 69 (see Supplement, **R-532** *et seq.*). In *Re A* [2006] 2 All ER 1, the Court of Appeal confirmed that media representatives and the accused both fall within the description of persons who may be 'aggrieved' within s. 159(1).

Section 159(5), contemplates the trial on indictment being stayed while the appeal is determined. The power to stay the trial is necessary because quashing an order derogating from open justice after the relevant proceedings have been completed will often serve no practical purpose, since by that time any harm resulting from the order has already been done.

The CrimPR, r. 65.6(3) (see Supplement, **R-490**), stipulates that, where the appellant wants to appeal against an order restricting public access to a trial, the court may decide both the application for permission to appeal and the appeal itself without a hearing but must, in any event, announce its decision on such an appeal at a hearing in public. The Court of Appeal therefore has a discretion to hold a hearing.

D3.147   **Magistrates' Court Cases**   Section 159 of the CJA 1988 does not extend to decisions of magistrates' courts or to decisions made by the Crown Court otherwise than in connection with trials on indictment (e.g., on an appeal from magistrates). In respect of such decisions, the remedy of an aggrieved person is to apply to the Divisional Court for judicial review. This has the disadvantage that, even if the remedy sought is granted, it may come too late to be of practical value. Also, an application to quash an order of the lower court or have it declared unlawful is liable to be refused on the basis that, although the order was misguided, it was within the court's jurisdiction (see, e.g., *Malvern Justices, ex parte Evans* [1988] QB 540).

Section D4   Criminal Procedure Rules and Case Management

THE EVOLUTION OF THE RULES

The Criminal Procedure Rules 2014 (SI 2014 No. 1610), which have effect from 6 October **D4.1**
2014, (CrimPR) represent a concise and simply expressed statement of the statutory and
common-law procedural rules that apply to criminal cases. Similar rules have applied since 4
April 2005 (when the Criminal Procedure Rules 2005 came into effect) to all cases in the magistrates' court, the Crown Court and the Criminal Division of the Court of Appeal. Revisions
and expansions of the rules were consolidated as the Criminal Procedure Rules 2010 (SI 2010
No. 60), the Criminal Procedure Rules 2011 (SI 2011 No. 1709), the Criminal Procedure
Rules 2012 (SI 2012 No. 1726) and the Criminal Procedure Rules 2013 (SI 2013 No. 1554).
They now work in conjunction with the Criminal Practice Directions ('CPD') as an integrated
procedural framework for criminal cases.

The inspiration for the rules came, in large part, from the *Review of the Criminal Courts of
England and Wales* carried out by Auld LJ (the 'Auld report'). It recommended:

> . . . an exercise of both systematic restatement and reform, with the aim of producing a single cor-
> pus of rules for a unified criminal court. That instrument should begin with a clear statement of
> purpose and general rules of application and interpretation, as successfully pioneered in the Civil
> Justice Rules flowing from Lord Woolf's reforms of the civil law. It should combine the various
> sources into a concise summary of rules, reducing them so far as possible into a discipline common
> to all levels of jurisdiction, using the same language and prescribing the same forms. It should make
> separate provision only in so far as necessary to allow for procedural differences at each level flowing
> from the court's composition and nature and volume of its work.

The CrimPR are divided into subject divisions, which essentially follow the chronological progress of a criminal case. They are set out in full in the Supplement together with the comparable
parts of the CPD, and individual rules are dealt with in the relevant sections of this work.

Two parts of the CrimPR particularly give effect to the intention of the Rules Committee to
enhance the efficiency of the criminal justice system. Those parts are:

(a) part 1: the Overriding Objective (see **D4.2**); and
(b) part 3: Case Management (see **D4.6**).

THE OVERRIDING OBJECTIVE

Criminal Procedure Rules 2013, rr. 1.1 to 1.3   **D4.2**

1.1—(1) The overriding objective of this new code is that criminal cases be dealt with justly.
(2) Dealing with a criminal case justly includes—
(a) acquitting the innocent and convicting the guilty;
(b) dealing with the prosecution and the defence fairly;
(c) recognising the rights of a defendant, particularly those under Article 6 of the European
Convention on Human Rights;
(d) respecting the interests of witnesses, victims and jurors and keeping them informed of the
progress of the case;
(e) dealing with the case efficiently and expeditiously;
(f) ensuring that appropriate information is available to the court when bail and sentence are
considered; and

(g) dealing with the case in ways that take into account—
    (i)   the gravity of the offence alleged,
    (ii)   the complexity of what is in issue,
    (iii) the severity of the consequences for the defendant and others affected, and
    (iv)   the needs of other cases.
1.2—(1) Each participant, in the conduct of each case, must—
    (a) prepare and conduct the case in accordance with the overriding objective;
    (b) comply with these Rules, practice directions and directions made by the court; and
    (c) at once inform the court and all parties of any significant failure (whether or not that participant is responsible for that failure) to take any procedural step required by these Rules, any practice direction or any direction of the court. A failure is significant if it might hinder the court in furthering the overriding objective.
(2) Anyone involved in any way with a criminal case is a participant in its conduct for the purposes of this rule.
1.3—(1) The court must further the overriding objective in particular when—
    (a) exercising any power given to it by legislation (including these Rules);
    (b) applying any practice direction; or
    (c) interpreting any rule or practice direction.

The Balance of Rights and Duties

D4.3 Whilst the overriding objective 'that cases be dealt with justly' (r. 1.1(1)) may appear simply to be an explicit statement of the existing objective of the criminal courts, r. 1.1(2) specifies a number of elements that are included within its ambit. These import recognition that all of those who participate in proceedings have rights to be considered as well as obligations to undertake so as to ensure the efficient expedition of justice.

This approach was elaborated by the Court of Appeal in *Jisl* [2004] EWCA Crim 696 (at [114]–[118]):

> The starting point is simple. Justice must be done. The defendant is entitled to a fair trial: and, which is sometimes overlooked, the prosecution is equally entitled to a reasonable opportunity to present the evidence against the defendant. It is not however a concomitant of the entitlement to a fair trial that either or both sides are further entitled to take as much time as they like, or for that matter, as long as counsel and solicitors or the defendants themselves think appropriate. Resources are limited. The funding for courts and judges, for prosecuting and the vast majority of defence lawyers is dependent on public money, for which there are many competing demands. Time itself is a resource. Every day unnecessarily used, while the trial meanders sluggishly to its eventual conclusion, represents another day's stressful waiting for the remaining witnesses and the jurors in that particular trial, and no less important, continuing and increasing tension and worry for another defendant or defendants, some of whom are remanded in custody, and the witnesses in trials which are waiting their turn to be listed. It follows that the sensible use of time requires judicial management and control . . .

This has been echoed, more recently, in *R (Robinson) v Sutton Coldfield Magistrates' Court* [2006] 4 All ER 1029, where it was made clear that 'the objective of the Criminal Procedure Rules "to deal with all cases efficiently and expeditiously" depends upon adherence to the timetable set out in the rules' (the requirement that parties abide by the timetable set out in the rules in the context of applications to adduce evidence relating to bad character and hearsay, pursuant to the CJA 2003, which was the subject of that Administrative Court decision, is considered below).

The Balance of the Criteria

D4.4 In *Holmes v SGB Services* [2001] EWCA Civ 354, addressing the corresponding provisions of the Civil Procedure Rules, Buxton LJ said that the court had to balance all the criteria identified in r.1.1 without giving any one of them undue weight. However, this should not be interpreted as undermining the traditional status of the presumption of innocence. This was made clear by the Lord Chief Justice when he introduced the CrimPR, stating:

The presumption of innocence and a robust adversarial process are essential features of English legal tradition and of the defendant's right to a fair trial. The overriding objective acknowledges those rights. It must not be read as detracting from a defendant's right to silence or from the confidentiality properly attaching to what passes between a lawyer and his client.

Similarly, the requirement in r. 1.1(2)(b) of 'dealing with the prosecution and the defence fairly' should be read in the context of jurisprudence of the ECtHR, which emphasises the principle of equality of arms (see, e.g., *Kaufman v Belgium* (1986) 50 DR 98 at p. 115). In the same way, there is a notable contrast between the formulae in r. 1.1(2)(c) and (d), which properly reflects the presumption of innocence. Whereas the rights of the defendant (particularly those under the ECHR, Article 6) have to be recognised (r. 1.1(2)(c)), there is a different formula, namely 'respecting the interests', in r. 1.1(2)(d), in relation to other parties in the case. It is therefore clear that proposition (c) takes precedence over proposition (d) where they come into conflict.

Rules 1.1(2)(e) and (f) aim at efficient management of cases. Rule 1(2)(e) is closely related to the provisions on case management, which are dealt with in **D4.6**. Rule 1.1(2)(f) applies to agencies responsible for records of antecedents, and pre-sentence and medical reports, and underlines their duty to assist the court by ensuring that the relevant information is available at the crucial time when decisions as to bail and sentence are considered.

Rule 1.1(2)(g) imports the civil concept of proportionality into the overall objective, in accordance with the concern for resources identified by the Court of Appeal in *Jisl* [2004] EWCA Crim 696. It would be unrealistic to expect equivalent resources to be devoted to a case that ought to be tried in the magistrates' court and one that was indictable only. Again, the factors to be taken into account under this element of 'dealing justly' must be fleshed out by the approach of the courts to case management (see **D4.6**).

Duties Imposed on Participants

After the concept of 'dealing justly' has been elaborated in r. 1.1(2), the remaining rules in part 1 deal with the duty of the participants in the case to prepare and conduct the case in accordance with the overriding objective, and to comply with the rules and directions that the court makes. That this applies equally to the legal representatives of the parties was demonstrated in the context of the Civil Procedure Rules by the judgment of Arden LJ in *Geveran Trading v Skjeveslan* [2003] 1 All ER 1 (at [37]):

D4.5

> It is well established that as an officer of the court an advocate has a duty to the court which overrides his duty to his client — see *Rondell v Worsley*. Accordingly an advocate may not deceive or knowingly mislead the court. The advocate must bring to the attention of the court all relevant decisions and legislative provisions of which he is aware — *Copeland v Smith*. The advocate must bring to the attention of the court any procedural irregularity during the course of the trial — *R v Langford*. The advocate must conduct the proceedings economically ... under the Civil Procedure Rules, it is the express duty of the parties and hence their legal advisers, including advocates, to help the court to further the overriding objective in Rule 1.3. These are merely some examples of the practical application of the advocate's duty to the court.

This obligation was stressed by the Court of Appeal in *Phillips* [2007] EWCA Crim 1042, when Clarke J said (at [37]) 'not only must judges be robust in their case management decisions ... but the parties who are ordered to take steps must take them'. See also *Penner* [2010] EWCA Crim 1155.

The obligation on 'participants' does not just relate to their own compliance with the Rules. They are also expected to notify the court and all parties 'at once ... of any significant failure' of compliance. These so-called 'grassing' provisions require one party to report the failures of another. The court itself is fixed with a duty to implement the overriding objective by r. 1.3, through its case management functions.

D

Part D Procedure

CASE MANAGEMENT

D4.6   Rules 3.1 to 3.12 of the CrimPR (see Supplement, **R-8** *et seq.*) apply to the management of all cases in the magistrates' courts and the Crown Court, including the Crown Court acting in its appellate capacity with respect to a magistrates' court; rr. 3.13 to 3.26 apply, broadly, to Crown Court trials (r. 3.1). Part 3 operates together with CPD I (see Supplement, **PD-2**).

The Rationale

D4.7   Rule 3.2(1) lays down that the court must further the overriding objective (see **D4.2**) by 'actively managing the case'. This aim underpinned the recommendations of the Auld report (especially at chapter 10, paras. 229 to 231), and was explicitly the aim of the CrimPR, as is demonstrated by the words of Lord Woolf CJ in March 2005:

> Most importantly, they promote a culture change in criminal case management. They introduce new rules, written in plain English, that give courts explicit powers and responsibilities to manage cases effectively, and to reduce the numbers of ineffective hearings that cause distress to witnesses and inconvenience and expense to everyone.

The need for active case management is a theme that the Court of Appeal has emphasised in a series of decisions. For example, in *Jisl* [2004] EWCA Crim 696, Judge LJ stated (at [116]–[118]):

> Active, hands on, case management, both pre-trial and throughout the trial itself, is now regarded as an essential part of the judge's duty. The profession must understand that this has become and will remain part of the normal trial process, and that cases must be prepared and conducted accordingly . . . .

> Once the issue has been identified, in a case of any substance at all, (and this particular case was undoubtedly a case of substance and difficulty) the judge should consider whether to direct a time-table to cover pre-trial steps, and eventually the conduct of the trial itself, not rigid, nor immutable, and fully recognising that during the trial at any rate the unexpected must be treated as normal, and making due allowance for it in the interests of justice. To enable the trial judge to manage the case in a way which is fair to every participant, pre-trial, the potential problems, as well as the possible areas for time saving, should be canvassed. In short, a sensible informed discussion about the future management of the case and the most convenient way to present the evidence, whether disputed or not, and where appropriate, with admissions by one or other or both sides, should enable the judge to make a fully informed analysis of the future timetable, and the proper conduct of the trial. The objective is not haste and rush, but greater efficiency and better use of limited resources by closer identification of and focus on critical rather than peripheral issues. When trial judges act in accordance with these principles, the directions they give, and where appropriate, the timetables they prescribe in the exercise of their case management responsibilities, will be supported in this Court. Criticism is more likely to be addressed to those who ignore them.

The Court's Role

D4.8   Rule 3.2(2) sets out a list of elements of active case management, based upon early identification of the issues and the setting of a procedural timetable.

As far as the conduct of the trial itself is concerned, the duty of the court is set out in r. 3.2(2)(e), which reflects the overriding objective of dealing with each case 'efficiently and expeditiously' (r. 1.1(2)(e)). It states that the court must further the overriding objective by 'ensuring that evidence, whether disputed or not, is presented in the shortest and clearest way'. In addition, r. 3.2(2)(f) charges the court with the duty of 'discouraging delay'. The court's obligations have now been supplemented by r. 3.9(3)(a), which requires the court to take steps to encourage and facilitate the attendance of witnesses. Rules 3.13 to 3.26 have been added and these encourage case management at pre-trial hearings, and especially preparatory hearings.

Judicial action to apply this objective has received the support of the Court of Appeal on a number of occasions. For example:

(a) In *Bryant* [2005] EWCA Crim 2079, the Court of Appeal stated that it will support efforts by the trial judge to move a case forward at a reasonable speed, provided that the accused receives a fair trial.

(b) In *B* [2005] EWCA Crim 805, the case management powers of the judge were exercised to place limits on cross-examination conducted by defence counsel. The Court of Appeal stated that judges were entitled, and indeed obliged, to impose reasonable time-limits where necessary. The entitlement to a fair trial was not inconsistent with proper judicial control over the use of court time. Similarly, the Court of Appeal in *Heppenstall* [2007] EWCA Crim 2485 observed that case management involved cases being presented in a focused manner, and that a judge was entitled to seek an estimate for the length of cross-examination from counsel, and ensure that they kept to it. This aspect of the court's role is now covered in r. 3.11(d).

(c) In *K* [2006] 2 All ER 552, the Court of Appeal made it clear that the case management powers in the CrimPR enabled a judge to deal with issues preliminary to trial by way of written submissions, and to limit the length of those submissions (see **D9.26**). Rule 3.5(2)(h) now empowers the court to require the issues in the case similarly to be reduced to writing to allow their resolution to be timetabled.

(d) Similarly, in *Lashley* [2005] EWCA Crim 2016, the Court of Appeal gave guidance on the question of the judge's response to counsel who pressed a judge to reconsider a ruling with which he disagreed. Judge LJ stated:

> Right or wrong, the judge's ruling is or should be the end of an argument, or an application...Counsel is not entitled to keep pressing the judge about a ruling with which he disagrees on the basis of his duty to his client. The remedy for an incorrect ruling is provided in this Court. It does not take the form of trying to re-embark on the argument in an endeavour to persuade the judge to a judicial rethink of a ruling that he has already given, at any rate unless and until the circumstances have changed.

However, case management must be tempered by the imperatives of justice. This was emphasised by the Administrative Court in *S v DPP* (2007) 170 JP 707, and illustrated by the approach in *R (Drinkwater) v Solihull Magistrates' Court* (2012) 176 JP 401, where it was stressed that the decision to proceed with a trial in the absence of the accused was not to be made solely for reasons of expedition. Moreover, the court's power does not extend to the quashing of properly preferred indictments or otherwise using the overriding objective to challenge established legal principles (*B (F)* [2011] 1 WLR 844, and see also *H (S)* [2011] 1 Cr App R 182).

Protocols Relating to Complex Cases Further guidance as to the way in which case man- **D4.9** agement ought to be conducted is provided in the Protocol for 'Control and Management of Heavy Fraud and Other Complex Criminal Cases'. Whilst the Protocol is primarily directed at the control of complex cases, certain parts of the guidance have equal relevance to shorter and simpler cases. For example, in para. 3(vii) of the Protocol, there is some stress laid upon the need for caution by judges in the use of their case management powers:

> The Criminal Procedure Rules require the court to take a more active part in case management. These are salutary provisions which should bring to an end interminable criminal trials of the kind which the Court of Appeal criticised in *Jisl*. ... Nevertheless these salutary provisions do not have to be used on every occasion. Where the advocates have done their job properly, by narrowing the issues, pruning the evidence and so forth, it may be quite inappropriate for the judge to 'weigh in' and start cutting out more evidence or more charges of his own volition. It behoves the judge to make a careful assessment of the degree of judicial intervention which is warranted in each case.

The Protocol goes on to indicate that this note of caution is supported by the experience gained of the Civil Procedure Rules, which has shown that parties to litigation have been aggrieved on isolated occasions at 'what was perceived to be unnecessary intermeddling by the court'.

There is a similar Protocol relating to the management of terrorism cases (see **B10.1**).

The Role of the Parties

D4.10 Rule 3.2, which lays down the duty of the court, is supplemented by r. 3.3, which fixes the parties with a corresponding duty. To a large extent, the duty on the defence to help identify the 'real issues' is already to be found in the statutory provisions relating to disclosure (see **D9.29**, where detail of the duties in question is to be found). In this regard see *R (DPP) v Chorley Justices* [2006] EWHC 1795 (Admin), where Thomas LJ made clear the importance of co-operation from those defending in narrowing the issues:

> If a defendant refuses to identify what the issues are, one thing is clear: he can derive no advantage from that or seek, as appears to have happened in this case, to attempt an ambush at trial. The days of ambushing and taking last-minute technical points are gone. They are not consistent with the overriding objective of deciding cases justly, acquitting the innocent and convicting the guilty.

See also *R (Lawson) v Stafford Magistrates' Court* [2007] EWHC 2490 (Admin), *Writtle v DPP* [2009] RTR 369 and *Penner* [2010] EWCA Crim 1155. However, the limits to the scope of a case management order which required disclosure of details of defence witnesses, and the implications for litigation privilege and legal professional privilege, were demonstrated in *R (Kelly) v Warley Magistrates' Court* [2008] 1 WLR 2001.

Rules 3.5 and 3.9 give the court detailed case management powers and duties, including the power and duty to give directions, which can be varied in accordance with rr. 3.6 and 3.8. Rule 3.10 deals with readiness for trial (or appeal), while r. 3.11 allows the court to require a party to take various steps to help it manage the trial (or appeal). Again, the powers involved in this latter set of provisions (e.g., to identify 'any point of law that could affect the conduct of the trial or appeal': see r. 3.11(c)(viii)) in essence reflect the statutory provisions introduced by the CJA 2003 in relation to disclosure (see the CPIA 1996, s. 6A, and **D9.29**).

Case Progression Officers

D4.11 Rule 3.4 requires each of the parties, and the court, to appoint a case progression officer at the commencement of proceedings, and to inform the other participants of how to contact that person. The case progression officer is thereafter responsible for progressing the case. It is his responsibility to ensure that party's compliance with court directions, and to alert other parties to anything which may interfere with the smooth progress of the case. In reality, therefore, it will be the case progression officers who will enforce the 'grassing provisions' described at **D4.5**. The Criminal Case Management Framework describes in detail the obligations imposed on such officers, which makes it clear that it is not a role suitable for court-based professionals, such as barristers or solicitor advocates.

Practical Case Management

D4.12 Rules 3.1 to 3.12 of the CrimPR are supplemented by CPD I, paras. 3A.1 to 3A.15 (see Supplement **PD-2**), and the forms to be used for case management purposes, set out in the CPD, annex D.

The CPD stresses the necessity of active case management at pre-trial hearings in order to reduce the number of ineffective and cracked trials, and the delays that occur within trials. To that end, it addresses early guilty plea hearings (para. 3A.6), preliminary hearings in other cases (para. 3A.9) and plea and case management hearings (para. 3A.10). In the context of the latter, para. 3A.13 flags the need for preparation by all concerned and emphasises the desirability of the presence of the trial advocate at the plea and case management hearing, or at least of an advocate able to make decisions and assist the court to the maximum extent. In order to achieve this objective, listing policy should ensure that list officers as far as possible fix cases to enable the trial advocate to conduct the plea and case management hearing as well as the trial. Paragraph 3A.15 stresses the importance of avoiding other pre-trial hearings thereafter. Plea and case management hearings are addressed at **D15.47**.

Issues of case management that are addressed in more detail elsewhere in the book include the following:

(a) the automatic case management directions made by the magistrates' court at the time that cases are sent or transferred to the Crown Court, including the notice periods for applications for special measures for witnesses and in relation to hearsay, bad character and expert evidence (see **D15.41**);

(b) the provisions relating to issues of disclosure (see **D9**);

(c) the provisions relating to preparatory hearings (see **D15.49**).

Failure to Abide by Time-limits

An important aspect of the exercise of the court's case management powers is the consequences **D4.13** of any failure of the parties to comply with time-limits imposed by the CrimPR. The proper approach to be adopted appears to be that identified in *Musone* [2007] 1 WLR 2467, where the Court of Appeal was concerned with whether the trial judge had correctly rejected the attempt by one accused to adduce evidence of the previous bad character of the other at a late stage — so late as to be in breach of the time-limit for service of a notice of an application to adduce such evidence (see also **F12.68**).

The Court observed that the trial judge was entitled to exclude such evidence where he concluded that the applicant was deliberately manipulating the process so as to prevent the co-accused from dealing with the evidence properly. Their lordships went on to make clear that it would be rare for a judge to exclude evidence of substantial probative value just because the time-limits had not been complied with, but it would be proper to do so where such exclusion was the only means to ensure fairness.

The same approach was also adopted in cases such as *R (Robinson) v Sutton Coldfield Magistrates' Court* [2006] 4 All ER 1029 and *Delay* (2006) 170 JP 581, namely that the court should consider whether the other parties have been prejudiced by the late notice of the application, and the reasons for the delay, before deciding whether evidence should be excluded as a consequence of the breach of the rules.

Although these cases all relate to notice of a bad character application, the same approach has been taken in relation to the consequences of failures to comply with the rules in other areas (*R (Robinson) v Abergavenny Magistrates' Court* (2007) 171 JP 683). See also *Ensor* [2010] 1 Cr App R 255, where the failure of the defence to comply with the notice requirements for expert evidence resulted in the exclusion of that evidence.

It should, however, be noted that r. 3.8(1)(a) allows the court to extend a time-limit set by the CrimPR even after it has expired.

Section D5   Preliminary Proceedings in Magistrates' Courts

INTRODUCTION

D5.1 This section describes the preliminary proceedings in the magistrates' court which precede either the summary trial of an accused or his being sent for trial.

PROCEDURE FOR SECURING PRESENCE OF ACCUSED

Introduction

D5.2 The first appearance of an accused before a magistrates' court may be secured in a number of different ways:

(a) The accused may be arrested and, after the police have sought advice from the CPS, charged by the police (the details of the offence(s) will appear on a charge sheet).

(b) The accused may be arrested and then granted police bail while the CPS decide whether there is sufficient evidence to justify a charge; the CPS may then start a prosecution against the accused by using the 'written charge and requisition' procedure established by the CJA 2003, s. 29 (where available).

(c) The accused may be arrested and then be granted police bail, subject to a requirement that he must return to the police station on a specified date; during the intervening period the CPS decide whether there is sufficient evidence to justify a charge and, if so, when the accused returns to the police station, he will be charged (by the police) with the offence(s) specified by the CPS.

(d) The accused may be served with a written charge and requisition (under the CJA 2003, s. 29) without first having been arrested.

(e) An information may be served on a magistrates' court (this process is referred to as 'laying an information') and the court will then issue a summons (or an arrest warrant) requiring the accused to attend before it. By virtue of the CJA 2003, s. 29, laying an information (followed by issue of a summons by the court) is available only in the case of private prosecutions.

Much of the relevant legislation (such as the MCA 1980) refers to trial of an 'information' by a magistrates' court. The CJA 2003, s. 30(5), provides that references to an 'information' are to be construed as including a 'written charge', and references to a 'summons' are to be construed as including a 'requisition'.

D5.3 The powers and procedures for arresting an accused without warrant, questioning him at a police station and then charging him are dealt with in detail in **D1**, which also deals with the circumstances in which the police may refuse to bail a person once he has been charged and the period within which they must bring such a person before the magistrates' court. This section considers the other means of securing the presence of the accused before the court.

The Written Charge and Requisition Procedure

The CJA 2003, s. 29, created (in the case of public prosecutions) a new method of commencing **D5.4** criminal proceedings.

Section 29(1) provides that a public prosecutor may institute criminal proceedings against a person by issuing a 'written charge', which charges the person with an offence. Under s. 29(2), where a public prosecutor issues a written charge, a 'requisition' must be issued at the same time; this requires the accused to appear before a magistrates' court to answer the written charge. The written charge and requisition must be served on the accused and a copy of both must be served on the court named in the requisition (s. 29(3)). A public prosecutor who issues a written charge must notify the relevant magistrates' court immediately (CrimPR, r. 7.2(3)).

This method of commencing criminal proceedings is available only in the case of 'public' prosecutions. These are defined in s. 29(5) as meaning prosecutions brought by the following (or by someone authorised by that person or body to institute criminal proceedings on their behalf):

(a) a police force;
(b) the Director of the Serious Fraud Office;
(c) the DPP (SI 2012 No. 825);
(d) the Director General of the National Crime Agency;
(e) the A-G (not yet in force);
(f) a person specified by the Secretary of State in an order under the CJA 2003, s. 29(5)(h);
(g) the Secretary of State for Work and Pensions and the Secretary of State for Health in England and Wales;
(h) the Secretary of State for Business, Innovation and Skills;
(i) the Driver and Vehicle Standards Agency;
(j) Transport for London (added by the Criminal Justice Act 2003 (New Method of Instituting Proceedings) (Public Prosecutor Specification) Order 2011 (SI 2011 No. 2224)).

Section 29(4) provides that public prosecutors do not have the power to commence proceedings **D5.5** by means of the laying of an information for the purpose of obtaining the issue of a summons under the MCA 1980, s. 1 (see **D5.8**).

Notification of the requirement to attend court is communicated to the accused by the prosecutor (not by the magistrates' court, as is the case where a summons is issued).

Section 30(4) makes it clear that the written charge and requisition procedure does not affect the ability of a public prosecutor to lay an information for the purpose of obtaining an arrest warrant under the MCA 1980, s. 1 (see **D5.8**). It follows that an information still has to be laid in order to secure the grant of an arrest warrant.

As the magistrates' court is not involved in the issuing of the written charge and requisition, there will be no possibility of the magistrates preventing a prosecution from being brought in this way. However, it is submitted that the decision to issue a written charge and requisition would be amenable to judicial review, and an application for the case to be dismissed as an abuse of process would be available in appropriate cases.

Laying an Information and Issuing a Summons

The Information   The written charge and requisition procedure is not available in the case **D5.6** of private prosecutions (i.e. prosecutions where the prosecutor is not a 'public prosecutor', as defined by the CJA 2003, s. 29(5)); these have to be commenced by serving an 'information' on

D

the court (see the CJA 2003, s. 30(4)(b), which provides that nothing in s. 29 affects the power of a person who is not a public prosecutor to serve an information for the purpose of obtaining the issue of a summons, or a warrant, under the MCA 1980, s. 1). The process of serving an information is traditionally referred to as 'laying' an information, though this phrase does not appear in the CrimPR, part 7. In those areas where the CJA 2003, s. 29 has not yet been implemented, public prosecutors will continue to commence prosecutions by laying an information where proceedings are not started following the arrest of the suspect.

Under the CrimPR, r. 7.2(1), a prosecutor who wants the court to issue a summons must either serve an information in writing on the court, or present an information orally to the court (but with a written record of the allegation that it contains). In *Kennet Justices, ex parte Humphrey* [1993] Crim LR 787, the Divisional Court held that an information could be served by the prosecutor sending a letter to the justices' clerk (which would, it is submitted, count as valid service under the CrimPR, r. 4.4(1)).

D5.7   The Crim PR, r 7.2, refers to 'a prosecutor' serving an information. It is questionable whether an information may be served on behalf of an unincorporated association. It seems to follow from *Rubin v DPP* [1990] 2 QB 80 that an information should be served by a named, actual person and must disclose the identity of that person. However, in *Ealing Justices, ex parte Dixon* [1990] 2 QB 91, Woolf LJ said that he had reservations as to the reasoning which had underpinned the conclusion reached in *Rubin*, that a prosecution has to be by an individual rather than a corporate person. Nonetheless, his lordship said (at p. 101) that he would 'regard it as preferable' for an individual to be named, albeit that he is acting on behalf of a body corporate.

In *Norwich Justices, ex parte Texas Homecare* [1991] Crim LR 555, the informations had been signed by the senior environmental health officer, who had no authority to do so under the relevant legislation. The informations were later amended to substitute the signature of the person who did have the necessary authority, but the amendment took place after the six-month deadline for commencing the prosecution had elapsed. The Divisional Court quashed the convictions, holding that where the person serving an information has no authority to do so, the information is rendered a nullity. Since the informations as served were invalid, they could not found any jurisdiction, and this was not curable by amendment.

D5.8   The Summons   The MCA 1980, s. 1(1), provides that:

(1) On an information being laid before a justice of the peace that a person has, or is suspected of having, committed an offence, the justice may issue—
   (a) a summons directed to that person requiring him to appear before a magistrates' court to answer the information, or
   (b) a warrant to arrest that person and bring him before a magistrates' court.

A justices' clerk (or an assistant clerk who has been specifically authorised by the justices' clerk for that purpose) may issue a summons but not a warrant (see the Justices' Clerks Rules 2005 (SI 2005 No. 545), sch. 1, paras. 1 and 2).

D5.9   The Decision to Issue a Summons   The decision to issue a summons is judicial, not merely administrative (*Gateshead Justices, ex parte Tesco Stores Ltd* [1981] QB 470). Therefore, a justice or clerk must actually apply his mind to the information on the basis of which a summons is sought: 'no summons can be issued... without a prior judicial consideration by [the justice or clerk] of the information upon which the summons is based' (*Ex parte Tesco Stores Ltd* at p. 478A, per Donaldson LJ). The decision whether or not to issue a summons 'is a judicial function which must, therefore, be performed judicially' (per Lord Roskill in *Manchester Stipendiary Magistrate, ex parte Hill* [1983] 1 AC 328 at pp. 342F–343D). The magistrate or clerk issuing the summons should be satisfied that:

(a) the information alleges an offence known to the law;
(b) it was served on the court within any time-limit applicable to commencing a prosecution for the offence in question;

(c) that the court has jurisdiction; and

(d) that the informant has any necessary authority to prosecute (per Donaldson LJ in *Ex parte Tesco Stores Ltd* at p. 478).

There is, however, a residual discretion to refuse to issue a summons. That discretion is not, however, unfettered; the magistrate ought to issue a summons unless there are compelling reasons not to do so, e.g., if an abuse of process or other impropriety is involved (*R (Mayor and Burgesses of Newham LBC) v Stratford Magistrates' Court* (2004) 168 JP 658). It was held in *Clerk to the Bradford Justices, ex parte Sykes* (1999) 163 JP 224 that the magistrate or clerk is not obliged to make inquiries before issuing a summons. If there is material which persuades him that it would be wrong to issue a summons, he is entitled to act on that information, and should not shut his eyes to it. If, for example, he was aware that the individual informant was one who had plagued the court with vexatious informations, he could and probably should act upon that knowledge. Collins J pointed out that, even if a summons is issued, the individual summoned may apply to the magistrates' court to dismiss it, or stay it on the grounds of abuse of process (see **D3.70** *et seq.*). It is therefore unnecessary to provide that there should be, at an earlier stage, an obligation to investigate before the summons was issued.

In *R (Charlson) v Guildford Magistrates' Court* [2006] 3 All ER 163, the court considered the **D5.10** approach to be adopted by magistrates if they are considering whether to issue a summons for a private prosecution where the CPS had already brought and discontinued a prosecution arising out of the same events. Silber J, giving the judgment of the court, said (at [19]) that the magistrates should not require special circumstances before agreeing to the issue of the summons. However, his lordship added that, in the different situation where justices are considering whether to accede to an application to issue a summons for a private prosecution where CPS has already brought a prosecution which is still proceeding, the justices should, in the absence of special circumstances, be slow to issue a summons at the behest of a private prosecutor.

It is not the practice for the justice or clerk to consider the evidence before issuing a summons. Neither is it the practice for the person named in the information to attend and oppose the issue of a summons, although the justice or clerk has a discretion to allow him to do so in exceptional circumstances (*West London Stipendiary Magistrate, ex parte Klahn* [1979] 2 All ER 221).

Delay in Issue of Summons   The MCA 1980, s. 1, does not require that the issue of a sum- **D5.11** mons must follow immediately upon the consideration of the information by the justice or clerk (*Fairford Justices, ex parte Brewster* [1976] QB 600). It is open to the prosecutor to serve the information on the court and then suggest that a summons should not be issued immediately (e.g., because the accused is out of the country and service could not be effected for a considerable time). However, if the delay between the laying of the information and issue of the summons is so great as to be unreasonable and to cause prejudice, then the High Court has a discretion to intervene and quash the summons (*Ex parte Brewster* at p. 604F–H). Moreover, an information should be served on the court with the intention of having the consequent summons served as soon as reasonably possible. Therefore, if the prosecutor has not in fact made his mind up whether to proceed at the time of serving the information but is concerned merely that any possible prosecution should not be out of time, then his conduct amounts to an abuse of the process of the court and the magistrates should stay the proceedings if ultimately he does decide to proceed (*Brentford Justices, ex parte Wong* [1981] QB 445).

Content of the Written Charge or Information

The CrimPR, r. 7.3(1) (see Supplement, **R-93**), provides that an information or written charge **D5.12** must contain:

(a) a statement of the offence which describes the offence 'in ordinary language' and (if the offence is created by statute) identifies the legislation that creates it; and

(b) sufficient particulars of the conduct constituting the commission of the offence to make clear what the prosecutor alleges against the defendant.

Where a number of incidents, taken together, amount to a course of conduct (having regard to the time, place or purpose of commission), those incidents may be included in the allegation (r. 7.3(2)). Moreover, a single document may contain more than one charge (r 7.2(4)).

Under r. 7.4(3) (see Supplement, R-94), a requisition or summons must contain a notice setting out when and where the accused must attend the court, and must specify each offence in respect of which it has been issued. Additionally, a summons must identify the issuing court, and a requisition must identify the person under whose authority it is issued.

Beyond the general statement in r. 7.3 that an information or written charge should be in ordinary language and give sufficient particulars of the conduct alleged, there is little guidance on how they should be drafted. However, reference to a particular statutory provision may cure an apparent defect by making plain what might otherwise be ambiguous (*Karpinski v City of Westminster* [1993] Crim LR 606, followed in *DPP v Short* (2002) 166 JP 474).

D5.13   **Insufficient Particulars**   If the information or written charge, as originally drafted, gives insufficient particulars, application for further particulars may be made at any time after the charge has been preferred (*Aylesbury Justices, ex parte Wisbey* [1965] 1 All ER 602 at p. 345). In *Nash v Birmingham Crown Court* (2005) 169 JP 157, it was held that if the information (or written charge) fails to give sufficient information to the accused as to the nature of the charge he faces, that does not of itself render the proceedings a nullity or any resulting conviction unsafe, provided that the requisite information is given to the accused in good time for him to be able fairly to meet the case against him. The accused is entitled to that information and its provision is capable of curing the defect in the information or written charge (per Stanley Burnton J at [26]). In such a case it may well be appropriate for the prosecution to apply to amend the information or charge (under the MCA 1980, s. 123), with the defence being granted an adjournment if they may have been misled by the original error.

Service of the Summons or Requisition

D5.14   A summons or requisition may be served on an individual by handing it to him (r. 4.3(1)(a)) or by leaving it at, or sending it by first class post to, an address where it is reasonably believed that he will receive it (r. 4.4(1) and (2)(a)).

Service of a summons or requisition on a corporation may be effected by handing it to a person holding a senior position in that corporation (r. 4.3(1)(b)) or by leaving it at, or sending it by first class post to, its principal office in England and Wales or, if there is no readily identifiable principal office, any place in England and Wales where it carries on its activities or business (r. 4.4(1) and (2)(b)).

Issue of Warrant for Arrest

D5.15   The MCA 1980, s. 1(1)(b), provides that, whenever a justice before whom an information is laid has power to issue a summons, he may alternatively issue a warrant for the arrest of the person named in the information, provided that:

(a) the information is in writing (s. 1(3); CrimPR, r. 7.2(2)); and
(b) where the person in respect of whom the warrant is to be issued has attained the age of 18, the offence to which the warrant relates is an indictable offence or is punishable with imprisonment or else the person's address is not sufficiently established for a summons, or a written charge and requisition, to be served on him (s. 1(4)).

It is submitted that a magistrate should not issue a warrant if a summons or requisition, as the case may be, would appear to be an effective means of securing the accused's attendance before the court. Moreover, given that a police officer may arrest (without warrant) a person for any offence provided that the officer has reasonable grounds for believing that the arrest is necessary (for example) to allow the prompt and effective investigation of the offence or to prevent any prosecution for the offence from being hindered by the disappearance of the suspect (see the PACE 1984, s. 24, and **D1.14**), an application for an arrest warrant will generally be unnecessary, as the suspect can be arrested without one. It follows that the use of a warrant for arrest issued under s. 1 of the 1980 Act is the least common means of commencing proceedings.

Whenever magistrates issue a warrant for arrest they have a discretion to 'back it for bail', i.e. they may direct that, having been arrested, the person arrested shall thereafter be bailed by the police to attend court on a named day (see s. 117 of the 1980 Act). The backing for bail may be unconditional or conditional on the accused providing sureties.

Under the MCA 1980, s. 1(4A), inserted by the PRSRA 2011, s. 153, where a person who is not a public prosecutor (defined in the same way as under the CJA 2003, s. 29) lays an information in respect of a qualifying offence (i.e. an offence listed in s. 1(4C)) committed outside the UK, an arrest warrant can be issued only with the consent of the DPP.

The MCA 1980, s. 1(6), specifically provides that, if the offence alleged is indictable (this term **D5.16** includes either-way offences), a warrant for arrest may be issued under s. 1 notwithstanding that a summons (or written charge and requisition) has already been issued on the basis of the information. If the offence is summary and process initially takes the form of a summons or a requisition, it would seem that there is no power to issue a warrant under s. 1, although circumstances may subsequently arise which justify a warrant under other provisions of the Act. Under s. 1(6A), inserted by the CJA 2003, sch. 36, para. 8 (not yet in force), where the offence charged is an indictable offence and a written charge and requisition have previously been issued, a warrant may be issued by a justice upon a copy of the written charge being laid before him by a public prosecutor; this would be appropriate where, for example, the accused has absconded and so the requisition has not been served on him.

Effect of Defect in Process on Jurisdiction of Court

The jurisdiction of a magistrates' court to determine mode of trial for an either-way offence, **D5.17** to try such an offence summarily or to send such offence to the Crown Court to be tried on indictment is dependent, *inter alia*, on the accused appearing or being brought before the court (see the MCA 1980, ss. 2(3)–(4) and 18). However, there is no express requirement in those provisions that the accused's presence shall have been obtained by lawful means. Therefore, if he in fact appears before the court (e.g., in answer to a summons or requisition) or is brought before the court following arrest, the magistrates will have jurisdiction to deal with his case even if the process by which his attendance was secured was faulty, provided, of course, that any other preconditions of jurisdiction are satisfied (*Hughes* (1879) 4 QBD 614, approved by the House of Lords in *Manchester Stipendiary Magistrate, ex parte Hill* [1983] 1 AC 328 at pp. 344–5).

DISCLOSURE OF INITIAL DETAILS OF PROSECUTION CASE

The CrimPR, part 21, applies to any offence which may be tried in a magistrates' court, and **D5.18** so encompasses both summary and either-way offences (r. 10.1(1)). Rule 10.2(1)(a) requires the prosecutor, as soon as practicable (and, in any event, no later than the beginning of the day of the first hearing), to provide to the court 'initial details' of the prosecution case. These initial details of the prosecution case do not have to be supplied automatically to the accused; rather, r. 10.2(2) provides that, if the accused requests the initial details, the prosecutor has to serve them as soon as practicable (and, in any event, no later than the beginning of the day of the first hearing); if the accused does not request those details, the prosecutor must make them available to the accused at, or before, the beginning of the day of the first hearing (r. 10.2(3)).

Under r. 10.3, the initial details served by the prosecutor must include a summary of the evidence on which the prosecution case will be based, or any statement(s) or document(s) setting out facts or other matters on which that case will be based, or a combination of summary and statements or documents. The prosecution also have to provide details of the accused's previous convictions (if any). The effect of r. 10.3 is that the prosecution have the choice of providing a summary of their case or statements of prosecution witnesses (plus any supporting documents) or a combination of the two. Thus, the accused is not entitled to receive prosecution witness statements under these provisions.

The word 'document' in this context is to be construed widely. It could, for example, include a video recording (as in *Calderdale Magistrates' Court, ex parte Donahue* [2001] Crim LR 141, although this decision was founded on a concession that the video was a 'document' for these purposes, and so the case might not be regarded as formally deciding that point).

The reference to a magistrates' court in part 10 should be taken to include youth courts, and so these provisions apply equally to cases in the youth court where the accused is under the age of 18.

Failure to Comply

D5.19   Case law decided under the predecessor rules to the original version of the CrimPR, part 21, made it clear that, if the prosecution failed to comply with the initial duty of disclosure, the magistrates could do nothing more than adjourn the proceedings. According to *Dunmow Justices, ex parte Nash* (1993) 157 JP 1153, this was the only power available to the court where the defence has not had proper disclosure from the prosecution, since the justices had no power to order the prosecution to make disclosure. However, this decision pre-dates the general case management powers conferred by the CrimPR. It is submitted that, taking account of the overriding objective set out in the CrimPR, part 1, and the case management powers conferred by part 3, the court may now be able to order the provision of disclosure of initial details of the prosecution case despite the absence of a specific power to do so under part 21. Moreover, r. 3.5(6)(a) provides that, if a party fails to comply with a rule or direction, the court may (for example) adjourn the hearing. Failure on the part of the prosecution to comply with part 10 is likely to result in an adjournment (and possibly a costs sanction under r. 3.5(6)(b)).

However, it would seem to remain the case that the court cannot dismiss the charge(s) brought by the prosecution because of non-compliance with a request for initial details of the prosecution case (*King v Kucharz* (1989) 153 JP 336). In *R (AP, MD and JS)* (2001) 165 JP 684, the Divisional Court held that, even taking into account the coming into force of the HRA 1998, the court does not have jurisdiction to dismiss proceedings for abuse of process simply on the basis of the failure to supply the information now required by part 10.

CJS Efficiency Programme

D5.20   Since April 2012, the CPS has been producing digital case files. A digital file is used in all cases in which a defence practitioner has been identified. The files are to be made available to the defence through the *CJSM Secure eMail service* and/or via a link to the *Document Repository Service* (DRS).

ADJOURNMENTS AND REMANDS

Power to Adjourn

D5.21   At any stage before the case is sent to the Crown Court for trial or before (or during) a summary trial, a magistrates' court may adjourn the proceedings. Whether to grant an adjournment is always a matter for the court's discretion but that discretion must be exercised judicially. For example, an accused is entitled to a reasonable opportunity to prepare his case (*Thames Magistrates' Court, ex parte Polemis* [1974] 2 All ER 1219). Depending on the nature and complexity of the charge, this will almost certainly necessitate allowing him to take legal advice if he wishes. Similarly, a prosecution application for an adjournment must not be refused unreasonably (*Neath and Port Talbot Justices, ex parte DPP* [2000] 1 WLR 1376). In *S v DPP* (2006) 170 JP 707, it was said that, if it is necessary to adjourn the case to enable justice to be done following a failure by the prosecution properly to disclose matters which ought to be disclosed, then the adjournment must be granted, unless the court is satisfied that no prejudice would be caused to the accused by proceeding (per Openshaw J at [16]).

It is possible to challenge the grant or refusal of an adjournment by way of judicial review. However, the Divisional Court will be 'particularly slow' to interfere with a decision to refuse an adjournment, given the discretionary nature of that decision (Clarke J in *R(CPS) v Uxbridge Magistrates* (2007) 171 JP 279, at [5]). Nonetheless, in *Balogun v DPP* [2010] 1 WLR 1915, the accused's conviction was quashed because the magistrates' court had agreed to a request for an adjournment from the prosecution without submitting the application to the 'rigorous scrutiny' required by Lord Bingham in *Rowlands* (see **D5.24**). Leveson LJ (at [32]) said that 'challenges to such a decision will be difficult to mount and should only be commenced if the circumstances are exceptional'. His lordship added that such applications, if brought, 'must be pursued as a matter of extreme urgency — within days rather than weeks', so that the case can continue if permission to proceed with the claim for judicial review is refused.

On the role of the clerk where the parties cannot agree on an adjournment, see *R (DPP) v Lancaster Magistrates' Court* (2010) 174 JP 320, discussed at **D3.30**.

Relevant Factors   In *Neath and Port Talbot Justices, ex parte DPP*, Simon Brown LJ (at p. 1381)   **D5.22** identified the factors relevant to the decision whether or not to interfere with the decision of the lower court not to grant an adjournment. Those factors, which are also highly relevant to the original decision whether or not to adjourn, included:

(a) the seriousness of the criminal charges, (b) the nature of the evidence in the case and in particular the extent to which its quality may be affected by the delay, (c) the extent, if any, to which the defendant has brought about or contributed to the justice's error, (d) the extent, if any, to which the defendant has brought about or contributed to the delay in the hearing of the challenge, and (e) how far the complainant would feel justifiably aggrieved by the proceedings being halted and the defendant would feel justifiably aggrieved by their being continued.

In *Kingston-upon-Thames Justices, ex parte Martin* [1994] Imm AR 172, it was said that the following factors should be taken into account in deciding whether or not to grant an adjournment:

(a) the importance of the proceedings and the likely adverse consequences to the party seeking the adjournment,
(b) the risk of the party being prejudiced in the conduct of the proceedings if the application is refused,
(c) the risk of prejudice or other disadvantage to the other party if the adjournment is granted,
(d) the convenience of the court,
(e) the interests of justice generally in the efficient despatch of court business,
(f) the desirability of not delaying future litigants by adjourning early and thus leaving the court empty,
(g) the extent to which the party applying for the adjournment had been responsible for creating the difficulty which had led to the application.

Ex parte Martin was cited with approval in *R (Costello) v North East Essex Magistrates* (2007) 171 JP 153, where it was held that if, through no fault of the accused, witnesses do not attend who should have attended, or the accused does not attend because he is unfit to attend, the magistrates ought generally to grant an adjournment (Collins J at [11]). The same principle applies where a prosecution witness fails to attend, since an adjournment should not be refused to punish the inefficiency of the CPS or the supposed default of one of their witnesses (*R (DPP) v North and East Hertfordshire Justices* (2008) 172 JP 193, per Cooke J at [27]).

D5.23   In *CPS v Picton* (2006) 170 JP 567, the Divisional Court once again considered the discretion of the justices to grant an adjournment. Jack J, giving the judgment of the court, said (at [9]) that the following points emerge from a review of the authorities (including *Essen v DPP* [2005] EWHC 1077 (Admin) and the judgments of Lord Bingham in *Aberdare Justices, ex parte DPP* (1990) 155 JP 324 and *Hereford Magistrates' Court, ex parte Rowlands* [1998] QB 110):

(a) A decision whether to adjourn is a decision within the discretion of the trial court. An appellate court will interfere only if very clear grounds for doing so are shown.

(b) Magistrates should pay great attention to the need for expedition in the prosecution of criminal proceedings; delays are scandalous; they bring the law into disrepute; summary justice should be speedy justice; an application for an adjournment should be rigorously scrutinised.

(c) Where an adjournment is sought by the prosecution, magistrates must consider both the interest of the defendant in getting the matter dealt with, and the interest of the public that criminal charges should be adjudicated upon, and the guilty convicted as well as the innocent acquitted. With a more serious charge the public interest that there be a trial will carry greater weight.

(d) Where an adjournment is sought by the accused, the magistrates must consider whether, if it is not granted, he will be able fully to present his defence and, if he will not be able to do so, the degree to which his ability to do so is compromised.

(e) In considering the competing interests of the parties the magistrates should examine the likely consequences of the proposed adjournment, in particular its likely length, and the need to decide the facts while recollections are fresh.

(f) The reason that the adjournment is required should be examined and, if it arises through the fault of the party asking for the adjournment, that is a factor against granting the adjournment, carrying weight in accordance with the gravity of the fault. If that party was not at fault, that may favour an adjournment. Likewise if the party opposing the adjournment has been at fault, that will favour an adjournment.

(g) The magistrates should take appropriate account of the history of the case, and whether there have been earlier adjournments and at whose request and why.

(h) Lastly, of course the factors to be considered cannot be comprehensively stated but depend upon the particular circumstances of each case, and they will often overlap. The court's duty is to do justice between the parties in the circumstances as they have arisen.

Although not specifically mentioned by Jack J in this summary, it is clear that the court had the overriding objective in the CrimPR, r. 1, much in mind when formulating this list of considerations.

D5.24   In *Hereford Magistrates' Court, ex parte Rowlands*, Lord Bingham (at pp. 127–8) said:

> It is not possible or desirable to identify hard and fast rules as to when adjournments should or should not be granted. The guiding principle must be that justices should fully examine the circumstances leading to applications for delay, the reasons for those applications and the consequences both to the prosecution and the defence. Ultimately, they must decide what is fair in the light of all those circumstances. This court will only interfere with the exercise of the justices' discretion whether to grant an adjournment in cases where it is plain that a refusal will cause substantial unfairness to one of the parties. Such unfairness may arise when a defendant is denied a full opportunity to present his case. But neither defendants nor their legal advisers should be permitted to frustrate the objective of a speedy trial without substantial grounds. Applications for adjournments must be subjected to rigorous scrutiny. Any defendant who is guilty of deliberately seeking to postpone a trial without good reason has no cause for complaint if his application for an adjournment is refused . . . In deciding whether to grant an adjournment justices will bear in mind that they have a responsibility for ensuring, so far as possible, that summary justice is speedy justice.

Reasons for granting, or refusing, an adjournment should be given, but they do not have to be elaborate, so long as the basis for the decision is clear (*Essen v DPP*).

Approach Where Accused Claims to be Unfit to Attend Where an application for an adjourn- **D5.25**
ment is made on behalf of the defence on the ground that the accused cannot attend court by
reason of illness, and there is a medical certificate or doctor's letter to support this claim, but
the magistrates think that the excuse is spurious, they should nevertheless give the accused the
chance to answer their doubts and not simply proceed with the trial. Guidance on the approach
to be taken in such cases was given in *Bolton Magistrates' Court, ex parte Merna* (1991) 155 JP
612 and *R (Killick) v West London Magistrates' Court* [2012] EWHC 3864 (Admin) (see **D22.17**
and **D22.18**). CPD III, para. 19B.2 (see Supplement, **PD-30**), requires that an accused who is
on bail and who will be unable for medical reasons to attend court should obtain a certificate
from his GP (or hospital doctor, as the case may be) in advance of the hearing.

Repeated Applications Where an adjournment has been refused, the court can change its **D5.26**
mind only if there is a good reason. In *R (Watson) v Dartford Magistrates' Court* [2005] EWHC
905 (Admin), the prosecution (before the date fixed for trial) sought an adjournment due to the
non-availability of two witnesses. The magistrates refused the application. The parties returned
to court on the trial date and the prosecution made a further application for an adjournment.
This time, the application was successful. The Divisional Court held that the magistrates were
wrong to allow the adjournment, since there had not been a change in circumstances since the
first request to adjourn the trial.

It follows that, where an adjournment has been refused, a further application should be made
only if there has been a material change of circumstances. In *R (F) v Knowsley Youth Court*
[2006] EWHC 695 (Admin), for example, the case was listed for trial. Shortly before the trial,
the prosecution indicated that they would be applying to vacate the trial date because they had
not received the full file from the police. The application for an adjournment was heard by a
bench of lay justices on the morning of the day of the trial. The application was refused. In the
afternoon, at the beginning of the trial (before a district judge), the prosecution made another
application for an adjournment. The district judge, who was made aware that a similar application had been made to a different bench that morning, allowed the application. The defendants sought judicial review of the district judge's decision. The prosecution conceded that the
afternoon application was essentially the same application as the morning one, and that there
had been no material change in circumstances between the making of the two applications. It
was held that the district judge should have refused the application. In the absence of a change
of circumstances, he was not entitled to revisit the decision to refuse an adjournment.

Case Management and Adjournments In December 2009, Leveson LJ (then Senior Presiding **D5.27**
Judge for England and Wales) issued guidance to magistrates' courts in a document entitled
Essential Case Management: Applying the Criminal Procedure Rules. This document emphasises
that 'unnecessary hearings should be avoided by dealing with as many aspects of the case as possible at the same time'. The plea should therefore be taken at the first hearing; if this does not
happen (or if the offence is triable only on indictment), the court must find out what the plea is
likely to be. If a plea is not taken, the obligation to take it applies to the next hearing (the point
being that a plea should be taken as soon as possible). The guidance points out that the obligation to take a plea, if one has not already been entered, 'does not depend on the extent of advance
information, service of evidence, disclosure of unused material, or the grant of legal aid'. This
guidance is clearly aimed at discouraging applications for adjournments by the defence, though
it is submitted that defence advocates may have to take a robust approach in resisting demands
for a plea to be entered where, for example, the defence have insufficient information about
the nature of the prosecution case. Applications for adjournments by the prosecution are also
discouraged. In *Visvaratnam v Brent Magistrates' Court* (2010) 174 JP 61, Openshaw J said (at
[18]) that the 'prosecution must not think that they are always allowed at least one application
to adjourn the case'. He added (at [19]) that 'there is a high public interest in trials taking place
on the date set for trial, and that trials should not be adjourned unless there is a good and compelling reason to do so...An improvement in timeliness and the achievement of a more effective

and efficient system of criminal justice in the magistrates' court will bring about great benefits to victims and to witnesses and huge savings in time and money.'

D5.28 **Offering No Evidence where Adjournment Refused**   If the prosecution seek an adjournment but the magistrates refuse to adjourn and the prosecutor offers no evidence, with the effect that the charge is dismissed, the magistrates cannot subsequently hear the case. In *R (O) v Stratford Youth Court* (2004) 168 JP 469, key prosecution witnesses failed to attend. The justices refused an adjournment; the prosecution thereupon offered no evidence and the justices dismissed the charge. The prosecutor then discovered that the complainant had by then arrived at court and made a request that the court be reconvened. The magistrates agreed to do so; they overturned their refusal to adjourn and rescinded their dismissal of the charge. It was held by the Divisional Court that, where the prosecution have offered no evidence and the court has dismissed the charge, it is not open to the justices to reopen the case. In such a case, the justices are *functus officio*, and any further hearing against the accused in relation to that matter will inevitably give rise to a successful plea of autrefois acquit on his behalf (per Rose LJ at [8]).

D5.29 **Statutory Provisions on Power to Adjourn**   The power to adjourn is contained in the MCA 1980, ss. 10(1) and 18(4).

Magistrates' Courts Act 1980, ss. 10 and 18

10.—(1) A magistrates' court may at any time, whether before or after beginning to try an information, adjourn the trial, and may do so, notwithstanding anything in this Act, when composed of a single justice.

(2) The court may when adjourning either fix the time and place at which the trial is to be resumed, or, unless it remands the accused, leave the time and place to be determined later by the court . . . .

(4) On adjourning the trial of an information the court may remand the accused and, where the accused has attained the age of 18 years, shall do so if the offence is triable either way and—

(a) on the occasion on which the accused first appeared, or was brought, before the court to answer to the information he was in custody or, having been released on bail, surrendered to the custody of the court; or

(b) the accused has been remanded at any time in the course of proceedings on the information; and, where the court remands the accused, the time fixed for the resumption of the trial shall be that at which he is required to appear or be brought before the court in pursuance of the remand or would be required to be brought before the court but for section 128(3A) below.

18.—(1) Sections 19 to 23 below shall have effect where a person who has attained the age of 18 years appears or is brought before a magistrates' court on an information charging him with an offence triable either way and—

(a) he indicates under section 17A above that (if the offence were to proceed to trial) he would plead not guilty, or

(b) his representative indicates under section 17B above that (if the offence were to proceed to trial) he would plead not guilty.

. . .

(4) A magistrates' court proceeding under sections 19 to 23 below may adjourn the proceedings at any time, and on doing so on any occasion when the accused is present may remand the accused, and shall remand him if—

(a) on the occasion on which he first appeared, or was brought, before the court to answer to the information he was in custody or, having been released on bail, surrendered to the custody of the court; or

(b) he has been remanded at any time in the course of proceedings on the information; and where the court remands the accused, the time fixed for the resumption of the proceedings shall be that at which he is required to appear or be brought before the court in pursuance of the remand or would be required to be brought before the court but for section 128(3A) below.

D5.30 **Remanding the Accused on Adjournments**   References in the MCA 1980, ss. 10 and 18, to 'remanding' an accused mean either remanding him in custody (i.e. committing him to custody to be brought before the court at the end of the period of remand or at such earlier time as the court may require), or remanding him on bail in accordance with the provisions of the BA 1976 (i.e. directing him to appear before the court at the end of the period of the remand or, if bail is made continuous, directing him to appear at every time to which the proceedings may be adjourned) (see the MCA 1980, s. 128(1) and (4)).

Section 18 governs adjournments until mode of trial has been determined. Section 10 applies (a) to appearances for summary offences up until conviction, and (b) to appearances for either-way offences from after mode of trial has been determined in favour of summary trial to conviction. Sections 10(4) and 18(4) provide (in almost identical terms) that, on adjourning proceedings for an either-way offence, the court must remand the accused unless: (a) he first appeared in answer to a summons or requisition (as opposed to being brought before the court in custody or appearing in answer to police bail); and (b) he has not been remanded at an earlier hearing.

It follows that the magistrates may, at their discretion, adjourn without remanding the accused: (a) at all appearances for summary offences up to conviction; and (b) at appearances for either-way offences up to either a determination for trial on indictment or summary conviction, provided the accused initially appeared in answer to a summons or requisition and has not subsequently been remanded. Where a case is simply adjourned, there is no need to fix the date for the next hearing at the time of adjourning, whereas if there is a remand the adjournment date must be fixed forthwith and is the date to which the accused is remanded. An accused who is not remanded and who then fails to appear on the date to which his case is adjourned commits no offence, but it may be possible either for a warrant to be issued for his arrest or for the proceedings to be conducted in his absence. An accused who has been remanded on bail commits an offence under the BA 1976, s. 6, if he fails without reasonable cause to answer to his bail. The MCA 1980, s. 128(1), provides that, whenever a magistrates' court has power to remand a person, it may either remand him in custody or remand him on bail, in accordance with the BA 1976.

Period of Remand in Custody

The maximum period for which a magistrates' court may remand an accused in custody is 'eight clear days' (MCA 1980, s. 128(6)). This is subject to the following exceptions: **D5.31**

(a) following summary conviction, there may be a remand in custody of up to three weeks (four weeks if the remand is not in custody) for inquiries, such as a pre-sentence report, to be made into the most suitable method of dealing with the accused (MCA 1980, s. 10(3));
(b) following the court being satisfied that the accused 'did the act or made the omission charged', there may be a remand in custody of up to three weeks (four weeks if on bail) for a medical examination and reports if the court considers that an inquiry should be made into his physical or mental condition before deciding how to deal with him (PCC(S)A 2000, s. 11(1) and (2));
(c) where mode of trial is determined in favour of summary trial but the court is not constituted so as to proceed immediately to trial (e.g., because it consists of a single lay justice), there may be a remand in custody to a date on which the court will be properly constituted even if the remand is for a period exceeding eight clear days (MCA 1980, s. 128(6)(c));
(d) where s. 128A of the MCA 1980 applies, a second or subsequent remand in custody may be for up to 28 clear days; and
(e) if the accused is already being detained under a custodial sentence he may be remanded in custody for up to 28 clear days or his anticipated release date whichever is the shorter (MCA 1980, s. 131).

Further Remands   Where a person is brought before the court after an earlier remand, the court may remand him again (MCA 1980, s. 128(3)). Thus, there may be several remand hearings before the case is sent to the Crown Court or the commencement of summary trial. The only limitation on the number of remands is the general discretion of magistrates to refuse an adjournment if it would be against the interests of justice (e.g., because they consider that the **D5.32**

party requesting the adjournment should have been ready to proceed on the present occasion). By s. 130, a court remanding an accused in custody may order that, for subsequent remands, he be brought up before a different magistrates' court nearer to the prison where he is to be confined while on remand. That alternate court then enjoys the same powers in relation to remand that the original court would otherwise have.

The MCA 1980, s. 128, is without prejudice to the provisions of s. 129. Under s. 129(1), the magistrates may remand the accused in his absence to a convenient date, and any restrictions on the period of the remand which would otherwise be imposed by s. 128(6) do not apply. Section 129(1) applies whether the remand is in custody or on bail, but is restricted to cases where non-attendance on the day originally fixed is due to 'illness or accident'. In *Hillman v Governor of Bronzefield Prison* (24 May 2013 unreported), it was held that the failure to produce an accused in court because of an error in the administrative process is capable of amounting to an 'accident' within the meaning of s. 129(1), thus enabling the magistrates to remand the accused in custody in his absence. Moreover, by virtue of s. 129(3), where an accused has been remanded on bail, the court may grant him bail in his absence by appointing a later time for him to appear. Section 129(3) applies only to remands on bail but places no restrictions on the reasons for which the court may choose to exercise its powers under the subsection. Thus, bail may be granted under s. 129(3) where it becomes apparent during the remand period that the court will not have time to deal with the case on the day originally fixed, or where the accused fails to attend but some acceptable reason is advanced for his non-appearance (not necessarily sickness or accident). Where bail is granted in such a case, the court may also 'enlarge' the recognizances of any sureties (i.e. they will be under an obligation to secure the accused's attendance on the new hearing date).

Remands in Custody in the Absence of Accused

D5.33   To avoid the necessity for an accused to be brought before the court in custody when it is apparent that no effective progress in his case will be possible at the hearing to which he is brought, he may be remanded in custody in his absence under the MCA 1980, s. 128(3A)–(3E). The conditions that must be satisfied for there to be a custodial remand in absence are that:

(a) the accused has consented (at an earlier hearing) to not being present at future remands (s. 128(3A)(a));

(b) he has a legal representative acting for him in the case, although the representative need not be present in court (s. 128(3B));

(c) he has not been remanded in absence on more than two consecutive occasions prior to the present application for remand in absence (s. 128(3A)(b)); and

(d) he has not withdrawn his original consent (s. 128(3A)(d)).

D5.34   To facilitate the giving of consent to remands in absence, it is provided in s. 128(1A)–(1C) that, where magistrates are proposing to remand in custody an accused who is present in court (s. 128(1A)(b)), they shall, assuming he is legally represented in court (s. 128(1A)(d)), explain to him the possibility of further remands being in his absence and ask him whether he consents to that procedure being adopted. It is a precondition of the accused being asked in court for his consent to remands *in absentia* that his legal representative is present in court (s. 128(1B)), whereas (assuming consent has been given) the remands *in absentia* themselves can, and normally do, take place without the attendance of a lawyer, provided the accused still has a lawyer acting for him in the case. The restriction on the number of consecutive remands *in absentia* to a maximum of three means that the accused cannot be remanded for more than approximately a month without being brought before the court. He could, on attending after three remands in his absence, again agree to the next three remands being in his absence. If a case is listed for a formal remand *in absentia*, but it appears to the magistrates that the conditions for such a remand are not in fact satisfied (e.g., because the accused has withdrawn his consent or no longer has legal representatives acting for him), they must remand the accused for the shortest period possible that will enable him to be brought before them (s. 128(3C)–(3D)). It should be noted that, although remands *in absentia* are pure formalities, the rule that remands in custody shall not exceed eight clear days must still be complied with in the sense that the accused's case must be listed within each eight-day period so that the magistrates can formally remand him to the next appropriate date.

Remands *in absentia* are limited to cases where the court is adjourning under s. 5, 10(1) or 18(4) of the 1980 Act (i.e. adjournments prior to or during summary trial or sending the case for Crown Court trial). If the adjournment is under s. 10(3) or the PCC(S)A 2000, s. 11 (see D5.31), the period of a custodial remand may extend to three weeks but there is no power to remand *in absentia*.

Remands in Custody for up to 28 Days

Under s. 128A of the MCA 1980, a magistrates' court may remand an accused in custody for a **D5.35** period exceeding eight clear days if (by virtue of s. 128A(2)):

(a) he has previously been remanded in custody for the same offence;
(b) he is now before the court; and
(c) the court (after allowing the parties to make representations) has fixed a date on which it expects that it will be possible for the next stage in the proceedings, other than a hearing relating to a further remand in custody or on bail, to take place.

This final requirement is that the next hearing should be an effective hearing. In the case of either-way offences, the next effective hearing after the accused becomes eligible for an extended remand will be the hearing to determine plea and mode of trial. The maximum period of a remand under s. 128A is 28 clear days or to the date of the next effective hearing whichever is the shorter (s. 128A(2)(i) and (ii)). Section 128A does not apply on the occasion of a first remand in custody (s. 128A(2)(a)), although the accused may at that stage be invited to consent to the next three remands being in his absence (see D5.33). The making of a remand under s. 128A does not affect the right of the accused to apply for bail during the period of that remand (s. 128A(3)). The preservation of the right to make a bail application even though there has been a 28-day remand in custody entitles the defence to put before the magistrates forthwith any relevant change in circumstances that arises during the period of the remand.

Remand on Bail

Under the MCA 1980, s. 128(6)(a), the accused may be remanded for a period greater than **D5.36** eight clear days if he is remanded on bail and both he and the prosecution agree to a longer period of remand.

Statutory Provisions on Duration of Remands

Magistrates' Courts Act 1980, ss. 128 to 131   **D5.37**

128.—(1) Where a magistrates' court has power to remand any person, then, subject to section 4 of the Bail Act 1976 and to any other enactment modifying that power, the court may—
(a) remand him in custody, that is to say, commit him to custody to be brought before the court, subject to subsection (3A) below, at the end of the period of remand or at such earlier time as the court may require; or
(b) where it is trying an offence alleged to have been committed by that person or has convicted him of an offence, remand him on bail in accordance with the Bail Act 1976, that is to say, by directing him to appear as provided in subsection (4) below; or
[(c) relates to bail in non-criminal proceedings.]
(1A) Where—
(a) on adjourning a case under section 10(1), 17C, 18(4) or 24C above the court proposes to remand or further remand a person in custody; and
(b) he is before the court; and
(c) [repealed]; and
(d) he is legally represented in that court,

it shall be the duty of the court—
- (i) to explain the effect of subsections (3A) and (3B) below to him in ordinary language; and
- (ii) to inform him in ordinary language that, notwithstanding the procedure for a remand without his being brought before a court, he would be brought before a court for the hearing and determination of at least every fourth application for his remand, and of every application for his remand heard at a time when it appeared to the court that he had no solicitor acting for him in the case.

(1B)   For the purposes of subsection (1A) above a person is to be treated as legally represented in a court if, but only if, he has the assistance of counsel or a solicitor to represent him in the proceedings in that court.

(1C)   After explaining to an accused as provided by subsection (1A) above the court shall ask him whether he consents to hearing and determination of such applications in his absence.

(2)   Where the court fixes the amount of a recognizance under subsection (1) above or section 8(3) of the Bail Act 1976 with a view to its being taken subsequently the court shall in the meantime commit the person so remanded to custody in accordance with paragraph (a) of the said subsection (1).

(3)   Where a person is brought before the court after remand, the court may further remand him.

(3A)   Subject to subsection (3B) below, where a person has been remanded in custody and the remand was not a remand under section 128A below for a period exceeding eight clear days, the court may further remand him (otherwise than in the exercise of the power conferred by that section) on an adjournment under section 10(1), 17C, 18(4) or 24C above without his being brought before it if it is satisfied—
- (a) that he gave his consent, either in response to a question under subsection (1C) above or otherwise, to the hearing and determination in his absence of any application for his remand on an adjournment of the case under any of those provisions; and
- (b) that he has not by virtue of this subsection been remanded without being brought before the court on more than two such applications immediately preceding the application which the court is hearing; and
- (c) [repealed]; and
- (d) that he has not withdrawn his consent...

(3B)   The court may not exercise the power conferred by subsection (3A) above if it appears to the court, on an application for a further remand being made to it, that the person to whom the application relates has no solicitor acting for him in the case (whether present in court or not).

(3C)   Where—
- (a) a person has been remanded in custody on an adjournment of a case under section 10(1), 17C, 18(4) or 24C above; and
- (b) an application is subsequently made for his further remand on such an adjournment; and
- (c) he is not brought before the court which hears and determines the application; and
- (d) that court is not satisfied as mentioned in subsection (3A) above, the court shall adjourn the case and remand him in custody for the period for which it stands adjourned.

(3D)   An adjournment under subsection (3C) above shall be for the shortest period that appears to the court to make it possible for the accused to be brought before it.

(3E)   Where—
- (a) on an adjournment of a case under section 10(1), 17C, 18(4) or 24C above a person has been remanded in custody without being brought before the court; and
- (b) it subsequently appears—
  - (i) to the court which remanded him in custody; or
  - (ii) to an alternate magistrates' court to which he is remanded under section 130 below, that he ought not to have been remanded in custody in his absence, the court shall require him to be brought before it at the earliest time that appears to the court to be possible..

(4)   Where a person is remanded on bail under subsection (1) above the court may...direct him to appear...—
- (a) before that court at the end of the period of remand; or
- (b) at every time and place to which during the course of the proceedings the hearing may be from time to time adjourned;

and, where it remands him on bail conditionally on his providing a surety when it is proceeding with a view to transfer for trial, may direct that the recognisance of the surety be conditioned to secure that the person so bailed appears—

(c) at every time and place to which during the course of the proceedings the hearing may be from time to time adjourned and also before the Crown Court in the event of the person so bailed being committed for trial there.

(5) Where a person is directed to appear or a recognisance is conditioned for a person's appearance in accordance with paragraph (b) or (c) of subsection (4) above, the fixing at any time of the time for him next to appear shall be deemed to be a remand; but nothing in this subsection or subsection (4) above shall deprive the court of power at any subsequent hearing to remand him afresh.

(6) Subject to the provisions of sections 128A and 129 below, a magistrates' court shall not remand a person for a period exceeding eight clear days, except that—

(a) if the court remands him on bail, it may remand him for a longer period if he and the other party consent;

(b) where the court adjourns a trial under section 10(3) or section 11 of the Powers of Criminal Courts (Sentencing) Act 2000, the court may remand him for the period of the adjournment;

(c) where a person is charged with an offence triable either way, then, if it falls to the court to try the case summarily but the court is not at the time so constituted, and sitting in such a place, as will enable it to proceed with the trial, the court may remand him until the next occasion on which it will be practicable for the court to be so constituted, and to sit in such a place, as aforesaid, notwithstanding that the remand is for a period exceeding eight clear days.

[(7) and (8) concern committing an accused to police detention for a period not exceeding three clear days where there is a need to question him about other offences — see **D1.42**.]

128A.—(1) [Power of Secretary of State to implement this section in specified areas or for specified proceedings.]

(2) A magistrates' court may remand the accused in custody for a period exceeding eight clear days if—

(a) it has previously remanded him in custody for the same offence; and

(b) he is before the court,

but only if, after affording the parties an opportunity to make representations, it has set a date on which it expects that it will be possible for the next stage in the proceedings, other than a hearing relating to a further remand in custody or on bail, to take place, and only—

(i) for a period ending not later than that date; or

(ii) for a period of 28 clear days,

whichever is the less.

(3) Nothing in this section affects the right of the accused to apply for bail during the period of remand.

[(4) Making of statutory instruments under the section.]

129.—(1) If a magistrates' court is satisfied that any person who has been remanded is unable by reason of illness or accident to appear or be brought before the court at the expiration of the period for which he was remanded, the court may, in his absence, remand him for a further time; and section 128(6) above shall not apply.

(2) Notwithstanding anything in section 128(1) above, the power of a court under subsection (1) above to remand a person on bail for a further time—

(a) where he was granted bail in criminal proceedings, includes power to enlarge the recognisance of any surety for him to a later time;

[(b) concerns bail in non-criminal proceedings.]

(3) Where a person remanded on bail is bound to appear before a magistrates' court at any time and the court has no power to remand him under subsection (1) above, the court may in his absence—

(a) where he was granted bail in criminal proceedings, appoint a later time as the time at which he is to appear and enlarge the recognisances of any sureties for him to that time;

[(b) concerns bail in non-criminal proceedings];

and the appointment of the time . . . shall be deemed to be a further remand.

[(4) concerns enlargement of a surety's recognisance upon sending for trial.]

130.—(1) A magistrates' court adjourning a case under section 10(1), 17C, 18(4) or 24C above, and remanding the accused in custody, may, if he has attained the age of 17, order that he be brought up for any subsequent remands before an alternate magistrates' court nearer to the prison where he is to be confined while on remand.

[(2)–(5) and sch. 5 contain detailed provisions governing remands to alternate magistrates' courts.]

131.—(1) When a magistrates' court remands an accused person in custody and he is already detained under a custodial sentence, the period for which he is remanded may be up to 28 clear days.

(2) But the court shall inquire as to the expected date of his release from that detention; and if it appears that it will be before 28 clear days have expired, he shall not be remanded in custody for more than eight clear days or (if longer) a period ending with that date.

PRE-TRIAL HEARINGS BY TELEVISION LINK

D5.38   The CDA 1998, ss. 57A, 57B, 57D and 57E, enable the court to direct that an accused in custody may appear at preliminary hearings, and at sentencing hearings, via a 'live link' from prison or from a police station. Under s. 57A(2), the accused is to be treated as present in court when he attends via a live link (defined, by s. 57A(3), so as to require that that the accused be able to see and hear, and to be seen and heard by, the court during the hearing).

Preliminary Hearings where Accused in Custody

D5.39   Under s. 57B, the Crown Court or a magistrates' court (for these purposes, this includes a single justice: s. 57B(7)) may direct that an accused who is likely to be held in custody during a preliminary hearing is to attend that hearing by way of live link (a 'live link direction'). Under s. 57B(4), if there is a hearing in relation to the making (or rescinding) of such a direction, the court may require or permit attendance via a live link. It follows that the accused does not have to be physically present in court for a live link direction to be given (and so the court may give such a direction in writing or immediately before the start of a hearing with the accused present via a live link). Under s. 57B(5), the court is required to give the parties the opportunity to make representations before giving (or rescinding) a live link direction. If a magistrates' court decides not to give a live link direction where it has power to do so, it must state its reasons in open court and record the reasons in the court register (s. 57B(6)).

Preliminary Hearings where Accused at Police Station

D5.40   Section 57C empowers a magistrates' court (but not the Crown Court) to direct the accused to attend a preliminary hearing via a live link from a police station. By virtue of s. 57C(3) and (4), this provision applies both to an accused who is detained at the police station in connection with the offence in question, and to an accused who has been bailed to return to the police station for a live link appearance in connection with the offence, known as 'live link bail' (PACE 1984, s. 47(3), allows the police to grant bail subject to a duty to appear at a police station for the purpose of a live link hearing). Section 57C(10) makes it clear that an accused answering to 'live link bail' is to be treated as having surrendered to the custody of the court as from the time when it makes a live link direction in respect of him. Under s. 57C(6A), a live link direction may be given only if the court is satisfied that it is not contrary to the interests of justice to do so. However, the consent of the accused is not required. These provisions are now in force in all local justice areas from 8 October 2012, pursuant to the Police and Justice Act 2006 (Commencement No. 15) Order 2012 (SI 2012 No. 2373) and the Coroners and Justice Act 2009 (Commencement No. 10) Order 2012 (SI 2012 No. 2374).

Proceeding to Sentence

D5.41   Under s. 57D, where an accused attends a preliminary hearing over a live link (pursuant to s. 57B or 57C) and pleads guilty to the offence (or, if it is an either-way offence, indicates a guilty plea and so is deemed to have pleaded guilty under the 'plea before venue' procedure), and the court proposes to proceed immediately to sentencing, the accused may continue to attend through the live link provided that the court is satisfied that it is not contrary to the interests of justice for him to do so (s. 57D(2)). Section 57D(3) provides that, where a preliminary hearing over a live link continues as a sentencing hearing, the offender can give oral evidence over the live link only if the court is satisfied that it is not contrary to the interests of justice for him to do so.

OPTIONS WHEN THE ACCUSED FAILS TO APPEAR

If an accused who has been bailed to appear at a magistrates' court fails to do so, the court may: **D5.42**

(a) issue a warrant for his arrest under the BA 1976, s. 7; or
(b) extend his bail in accordance with the MCA 1980, s. 129(3); or
(c) proceed in his absence under the MCA 1980, s. 11(1) (see **D5.43**).

Trial in Absence of the Accused

If the accused fails to appear for the trial in the magistrates' court, the case may (if the accused is   **D5.43** under 18) or must (if the accused has attained the age of 18 and it does not appear to the court to be contrary to the interests of justice to do so) proceed in his absence. However, where the prosecution commenced by issue of a summons or requisition, it must be proved to the satisfaction of the court that either the summons (or requisition, as the case may be) was served a reasonable time before the hearing or the accused appeared on a previous occasion to answer the charge (MCA 1980, s. 11(1) and (2)). Summary trial in the absence of the accused is considered in more detail in **D22.13**.

Bench Warrants

Should the court decide to adjourn the trial rather than proceeding in the absence of the accused,   **D5.44** it may issue a warrant for his arrest under the MCA 1980, s. 13(1), provided that the offence to which the warrant relates is punishable with imprisonment, or the court, having convicted the accused, is proposing to impose a disqualification on him (s. 13(3) and (3A)). Where proceedings were begun by the issue of a summons (or requisition), it must be proved to the satisfaction of the court that the summons (or requisition) was served on the accused a reasonable time before the trial (or adjourned trial, as the case may be), unless the current adjournment is a second or subsequent adjournment and the accused was present in court on the occasion of the last adjournment and was informed of the time for the adjourned hearing on that occasion (s. 13(2), (2A) and (2B)).

Although warrants under s. 13 are not expressly limited to prosecutions commenced by way of summons or requisition, reliance on that section in cases where the accused has been bailed to appear is unnecessary because non-attendance in answer to bail may be dealt with by issue of a warrant under the BA 1976, s. 7. If a prosecution for an indictable offence is commenced by way of summons (or by written charge and requisition) and the accused does not appear, a warrant cannot be issued under s. 13 of the 1980 Act unless and until it is determined to try the information summarily, but the prosecutor is entitled to apply for the issue of a warrant for arrest under the MCA 1980, s. 1 (see s. 1(6) which provides that, where the offence charged is indictable, a warrant may be issued under s. 1 notwithstanding the previous issue of a summons or written charge and requisition).

If a warrant for arrest is issued the court may, at its discretion, 'back it for bail' (MCA 1980,   **D5.45** s. 117); the court directs that, once arrested, the person may thereafter be bailed by the police to attend court on a specified date. This is appropriate where, for example, there is some suggestion that the accused has a good reason for non-attendance but there is no (or insufficient) evidence to support this suggestion (making it inappropriate simply to extend his bail under the MCA 1980, s. 129(3)). The execution of such warrants is sometimes seen as a waste of police resources, and so magistrates' courts have been encouraged to use warning letters instead (see **D7.99**).

Full discussion of the options open to the court where an accused who is on bail fails to attend court may be found in **D7**.

D

Part D Procedure

Section D6 Classification of Offences and Determining Mode of Trial

INTRODUCTION

D6.1 Criminal trials in England and Wales are either trials on indictment or summary trials. The former take place in the Crown Court, before a judge and jury; the latter take place in a magistrates' court, before at least two lay justices or a single district judge. This section deals with (a) the classification of offences according to whether they: (i) must be tried on indictment, or (ii) may be tried either on indictment or summarily, or (iii) must be tried summarily; and (b) the procedure for determining the appropriate mode of trial in those cases where there is a choice.

CLASSIFICATION OF OFFENCES

Definition of the Classes of Offences

D6.2 There are, as regards mode of trial, three classes of offence — namely, (a) those triable only on indictment, (b) those triable only summarily, and (c) those triable either way: see the MCA 1980, ss. 17 to 25. These sections must be read in conjunction with sch. 1 to the Interpretation Act 1978.

> **Interpretation Act 1978, sch. 1**
> (a) 'indictable offence' means an offence which, if committed by an adult, is triable on indictment, whether it is exclusively so triable or triable either way;
> (b) 'summary offence' means an offence which, if committed by an adult, is triable only summarily;
> (c) 'offence triable either way' means an offence, other than an offence triable on indictment only by virtue of [s. 40] of the Criminal Justice Act 1988 which, if committed by an adult, is triable either on indictment or summarily;
> and the terms 'indictable', 'summary' and 'triable either way', in their application to offences, are to be construed accordingly.

The Interpretation Act 1978 qualifies the above definitions with the rider that: 'references [in the definitions] to the way or ways in which an offence is triable are to be construed without regard to the effect, if any, of section 22 of the Magistrates' Courts Act 1980 on the mode of trial in a particular case'. The broad effect of s. 22 of the MCA 1980 is that offences under s. 1 of the Criminal Damage Act 1971 involving damage worth less than the relevant sum (currently £5,000) must be dealt with as if they were triable only summarily (see **D6.22**).

D6.3 Where an Act contains the phrase 'indictable offence' without any further qualification, it must be understood to mean both those offences which, in the case of an adult, *must* be tried on indictment and those which (again in the case of an adult) carry the right to trial on indictment although they can be tried summarily with the agreement of the accused and of the magistrates.

Summary offences, on the other hand, are entirely distinct from indictable offences and must always be tried summarily, unless s. 40 of the CJA 1988 applies. The reason for the Interpretation Act 1978 definitions referring each time to the possible mode of trial in the case of an adult is that special rules apply to the trial of juveniles, greatly restricting the use of trial on indictment (see s. 24 of the MCA 1980 and **D24**).

The CJA 1988, s. 40, enables certain specified summary offences to appear on an indictment if they are linked to an indictable offence for which the accused has been sent to the Crown Court for trial (see **D11.17**). Those offences include common assault, taking a motor vehicle without consent, driving whilst disqualified, and criminal damage to which the provisions of the MCA 1980, s. 22, apply. Moreover, under the CLA 1967, s. 6(3A), a jury can (by way of alternative verdict under s. 6(3)) convict an accused of a summary offence to which the CJA 1988, s. 40, applies, even if a count charging the offence is not included in the indictment (see **D19.42**).

Determining Which Class an Offence Is In

An offence is triable either way if either (a) it is listed in the MCA 1980, sch. 1 (the MCA 1980, **D6.4** s. 17, provides that, without prejudice to any other enactment by virtue of which an offence is triable either way, the offences listed in sch. 1 shall be so triable), or (b) the enactment creating the offence (where the offence is a statutory one) specifies one penalty on summary conviction and a different (invariably greater) penalty on conviction on indictment. If the statute provides for a maximum penalty imposable on summary conviction but does not provide for a penalty on conviction on indictment, the offence is summary. If the statute provides only for a penalty on conviction on indictment, the offence is triable only on indictment (unless the offence is listed in the MCA 1980, sch. 1). Common-law offences (i.e. offences not created by statute) are all indictable offences and are triable only on indictment unless listed in the MCA 1980, sch. 1.

It will be apparent from the above that some statutory offences are triable either way, even though there is no indication in the statute itself that that is so. Similarly, some common law offences are triable either way even though common law offences are prima facie triable only on indictment. As regards determining the mode of trial, it makes no difference whether an offence is listed in sch. 1 or is made triable either way because the statute creating the offence specifically provides for differing penalties on summary conviction and on conviction on indictment. The significance of the distinction is that, on summary conviction for a sch. 1 offence, the maximum penalty that a magistrates' court may impose is six months' imprisonment and/or a fine not exceeding the 'prescribed sum', presently £5,000, whereas, on summary conviction for an offence made triable either way by the statute creating it, the maximum is whatever is prescribed in the statute, save that the maximum prison term imposable may not exceed six months (s. 32). The limit on the maximum fine that may be imposed by a magistrates' court will be removed when the LASPO 2012, s. 85, is brought fully into force.

Attempts are covered by the Criminal Attempts Act 1981, s. 4(1)(c), the rule being — as it is for allegations of aiding and abetting — that the offence is triable either way only if the substantive offence is so triable.

The Criminal Attempts Act 1981, s. 1(4), provides that s. 1 (which creates the offence of attempting to commit an offence) applies to any offence which, if it were completed, would be triable in England and Wales as an indictable offence. Section 4(1)(c) provides that a person guilty under s. 1 of attempting to commit an either-way offence is liable, on summary conviction, to any penalty to which he would have been liable on summary conviction of that offence. As regards *Nelson* [2013] 1 WLR 2861, see **A5.69**.

Magistrates' Courts Act 1980, s. 17 and sch. 1   D6.5

17.—(1) The offences listed in Schedule 1 to this Act shall be triable either way.

(2) Subsection (1) above is without prejudice to any other enactment by virtue of which any offence is triable either way.

SCHEDULE 1

OFFENCES TRIABLE EITHER WAY BY VIRTUE OF SECTION 17

1. Offences at common law of public nuisance.

1A. An offence at common law of outraging public decency.

3. Offences consisting in contravention of section 13 of the Statutory Declarations Act 1835 (administration by a person of an oath etc. touching matters in which he has no jurisdiction).

4. Offences under section 36 of the Malicious Damage Act 1861 (obstructing engines or carriages on railways).

5. Offences under the following provisions of the Offences against the Person Act 1861—
    (a) section 16 (threats to kill);
    (b) section 20 (inflicting bodily injury, with or without a weapon);
    (c) section 26 (not providing apprentices or servants with food etc.);
    (d) section 27 (abandoning or exposing a child);
    (e) section 34 (doing or omitting to do anything so as to endanger railway passengers);
    (f) section 36 (assaulting a clergyman at a place of worship etc.);
    (g) section 38 (assault with intent to resist apprehension);
    (h) section 47 (assault occasioning bodily harm);
    (i) section 57 (bigamy);
    (j) section 60 (concealing the birth of a child).

6. Offences under section 20 of the Telegraph Act 1868 (disclosing or intercepting messages).

7. Offences under section 13 of the Debtors Act 1869 (transactions intended to defraud creditors).

8. Offences under section 5 of the Public Stores Act 1875 (obliteration of marks with intent to conceal).

9. Offences under section 12 of the Corn Returns Act 1882 (false returns).

11. Offences under section 3 of the Submarine Telegraph Act 1885 (damaging submarine cables).

12. Offences under section 13 of the Stamp Duties Management Act 1891 (offences in relation to dies and stamps).

13. Offences under section 8(2) of the Cremation Act 1902 (making false representations etc. with a view to procuring the burning of any human remains).

14. All offences under the Perjury Act 1911 except offences under—
    (a) section 1 (perjury in judicial proceedings);
    (b) section 3 (false statements etc. with reference to marriage).
    (c) section 4 (false statements etc. as to births or deaths).

16. Offences under section 17 of the Deeds of Arrangement Act 1914 (trustee making preferential payments).

18. Offences under section 8(2) of the Census Act 1920 (disclosing census information).

19. Offences under section 36 of the Criminal Justice Act 1925 (forgery of passports etc.).

20. Offences under section 11 of the Agricultural Credits Act 1928 (frauds by farmers).

26. The following offences under the Criminal Law Act 1967—
    (a) offences under section 4(1) (assisting offenders); and
    (b) offences under section 5(1) (concealing arrestable offences and giving false information), where the offence to which they relate is triable either way.

28. All indictable offences under the Theft Act 1968 except—
    (a) robbery, aggravated burglary, blackmail and assault with intent to rob;
    (b) burglary comprising the commission of, or an intention to commit, an offence which is triable only on indictment;
    (c) burglary in a dwelling if any person in the dwelling was subjected to violence or the threat of violence.

29. Offences under the following provisions of the Criminal Damage Act 1971—
    section 1(1) (destroying or damaging property);
    section 1(1) and (3) (arson);
    section 2 (threats to destroy or damage property);
    section 3 (possessing anything with intent to destroy or damage property).

30. Offences in relation to stamps issued for the purpose of national insurance under the provisions of any enactments as applied to those stamps.

33. Aiding, abetting, counselling or procuring the commission of any offence listed in the preceding paragraphs of this Schedule except paragraph 26.

DETERMINATION OF MODE OF TRIAL

Introduction

Sections 17A to 21 of the MCA 1980 set out the method of determining the mode of trial when **D6.6** an adult is charged with an either-way offence. Section 22 provides for a special procedure where the charge is one of criminal damage, and s. 23 allows for proceedings under ss. 19 to 22 to be carried out in the absence of the accused provided certain conditions are satisfied. Section 25 relates to changing the decision about mode of trial originally taken.

Plea Before Venue

The initial procedure set out in the MCA 1980, s. 17A, applies whenever a person who has **D6.7** attained the age of 18 appears before a magistrates' court charged with an either-way offence (MCA 1980, s. 17A(1)). This procedure must be complied with before any evidence is called for purposes of a summary trial or the case is sent for Crown Court trial, and (subject to certain exceptions, considered below) should take place in the presence of the accused (s. 17A(2)). The steps in the standard procedure are as follows:

(a) The charge is written down (if that has not already been done) and read to the accused (s. 17A(3)).
(b) The court explains to the accused that he may indicate whether he would plead guilty or not guilty if the offence were to proceed to trial. The court should explain that, if the accused indicates a plea of guilty, the proceedings will be treated as a summary trial at which a guilty plea has been tendered. It must also explain that he may be committed for sentence under the PCC(S)A 2000, s. 3, if it is of the opinion that its powers of punishment are inadequate, or under s. 3A, if it appears to the court that the criteria for the imposition of a sentence under the CJA 2003, s. 226A (the 'dangerous offender' provisions), apply (s. 17A(4)).
(c) The court asks the accused whether (if the offence were to proceed to trial) he would plead guilty or not guilty (s. 17A(5)).
(d) If the accused indicates a guilty plea, the court proceeds as if he had pleaded guilty at summary trial (s. 17A(6)). Thus, the court proceeds to the sentencing stage.
(e) If the accused indicates a not guilty plea, a 'mode of trial' hearing has to take place, pursuant to s. 18 (s. 17A(7)). Similarly, if the accused fails to give an indication of intended plea, the court will regard him as having indicated an intention to plead not guilty and so will go on to determine mode of trial under s. 18 (s. 17A(8)).

Mode of Trial

Where the accused has indicated an intention to plead not guilty to an either-way offence (or **D6.8** has failed to give an indication as to plea), the court must proceed to determine mode of trial (s. 18(1)). The steps in this stage of the procedure are as follows:

(a) The court affords the prosecution and defence the opportunity to make representations about whether the offence is more suitable for summary trial or trial on indictment (s. 19(2)(b)). At that stage, the prosecution must also be given the opportunity of informing the magistrates of any previous convictions recorded against the accused (s. 19(2)(a)), since the existence of relevant previous convictions would affect the appropriate sentence.
(b) The court then has to decide whether the offence appears to be more suitable for summary trial or for trial on indictment (s. 19(1)). Section 19(3) provides that the court, when deciding which mode of trial is more suitable, has to consider:
(i) whether the sentence which a magistrates' court would have power to impose for the offence would be adequate;

(ii)   any representations made by the prosecution or the accused; and

(iii) allocation guidelines issued by the Sentencing Council under the CAJA 2009, s.120. Where the accused is charged with two or more offences which could be joined in the same indictment (under the CrimPR, r. 14.2(3)) or that the offences arise out of the same or connected circumstances (and so could be tried together in a magistrates' court), the court must have regard to the maximum aggregate sentence which a magistrates' court would have power to impose for all the offences taken together (s. 19(4)).

(c) If it appears to the court that summary trial is more appropriate, the court (almost invariably through the clerk) explains to the accused:

(i)   that such is the court's view, and that he can either consent to be tried summarily or, if he wishes, elect to be tried on indictment in the Crown Court; and

(ii) if he is tried summarily and convicted, he may be committed for sentence to the Crown Court if the magistrates are of the opinion that greater punishment should be inflicted than they have power to inflict (PCC(S)A 2000, s. 3) or if it appears to the court that the criteria for the imposition of a sentence under the CJA 2003, s. 226A (dangerous offenders), would be met (s. 20(1) and (2)).

(d) At that point, the accused may request an indication from the magistrates of whether, if he were to be tried summarily and were to plead guilty at that stage, the sentence would be custodial or non-custodial (s. 20(3)). The magistrates are not obliged to give such an indication (s. 20(4)). If the court does give an indication of sentence, it must ask the accused whether he wishes, on the basis of the indication, to reconsider the indication of plea which was given (s. 20(5)). If he does wish to do so, the court has to ask for a fresh indication of intended plea, and so the 'plea before venue' stage is repeated (s. 20(6)).

(e) If the accused indicates an intention to plead guilty following an indication of sentence, he will be regarded as having entered a guilty plea (s. 20(7)), and the magistrates' court will proceed to sentence, if necessary adjourning for a pre-sentence report; in such a case, a custodial sentence will be available only if such a sentence was indicated by the court (s. 20A(1)). Where an indication of sentence is given and the accused does not choose to plead guilty on the basis of it, the sentence indication is not binding on the magistrates who later try the case summarily, or on the Crown Court if the accused elects trial on indictment (s. 20A(3)).

(f) If the court does not give an indication of sentence (either because the accused does not seek one or the court declines to give one), or if the accused seeks and receives an indication of sentence but does not then wish to reconsider his indication of plea, or if he goes through the plea before venue stage a second time but does not indicate an intention to plead guilty, then he is asked whether he consents to summary trial (s. 20(8) and (9)).

(g) Depending on his choice, the court either proceeds to summary trial or sends the case to the Crown Court for trial under the CDA 1998, s. 51 (s. 20(9)).

(h) If, on the other hand, it appears to the court that trial on indictment is more appropriate, it tells the accused that this is so and proceeds to send the case to the Crown Court under the CDA 1998, s. 51 (s. 21).

It follows that summary trial of an either-way offence is possible only if the magistrates' court and the accused both agree to summary trial. If the magistrates decline jurisdiction, the case will be sent to the Crown Court for trial; likewise, if the magistrates accept jurisdiction but the accused elects trial on indictment, the case will be sent to the Crown Court.

Presence of the Accused

D6.9 The accused must be present at the 'plea before venue' hearing (MCA 1980, s. 17A(2)) and while mode of trial is determined (s. 18(2)), unless any of the exceptions apply.

For the 'plea before venue' hearing the exception is set out in s. 17B. This applies where:

(a) the accused is represented by a legal representative;

(b) the court considers that, by reason of the accused's disorderly conduct before the court, it is not practicable for proceedings under s. 17A to be conducted in his presence; and
(c) the court considers that it should proceed in the absence of the accused.

In such a case, the representative is asked to indicate whether the accused intends to plead guilty or not guilty (s. 17B(2)(b)); if the representative indicates a guilty plea, the court proceeds as if the accused had pleaded guilty (s. 17B(2)(c)). Otherwise, the court proceeds to determine mode of trial under s. 18 (s. 17B(2)(d) and (3)).

Mode of trial can be determined in the absence of the accused under s. 18(3) or s. 23.

(a) Under s. 18(3), the court may determine mode of trial in the absence of the accused if it considers that, by reason of his disorderly conduct before the court, it is not practicable for the proceedings to be conducted in his presence. Where there is a legal representative present in court, he speaks on behalf of the accused (s. 18(3)).
(b) Under s. 23, the court may determine mode of trial in the absence of the accused if he is represented by a legal representative who signifies to the court that the accused consents to the mode of trial proceedings being conducted in his absence, and the court is satisfied that there is good reason for the proceedings being so conducted (s. 23(1)). The phrase 'good reason' is not defined; sickness is an obvious example, but it is submitted that 'good reason' extends beyond that. Assuming the court does proceed in the accused's absence and considers that the offence is more suitable for summary trial, his consent to such a trial may be signified by his legal representative, in which event 'the court shall proceed to . . . summary trial' (s. 23(4) (a)). Clearly, this does not require the magistrates to commence the trial forthwith, as they are entitled to adjourn under the general power given them by s. 10(1) if an immediate hearing is impracticable or undesirable (e.g., because of the accused's absence). If the court considers that trial on indictment is more appropriate, or if the legal representative does not signify that the accused consents to summary trial, then the court must proceed to send the case to the Crown Court for trial under the CDA 1998, s. 51 (s. 23(4)(b) and (5)).

It should be noted that the court may use a live television link in a case where the accused is held in custody and facilities are available at the institution where he is held (CDA 1998, s. 57B: see D5.38).

JURISDICTION TO CONDUCT PLEA BEFORE VENUE AND MODE OF TRIAL HEARINGS

General

The 'plea before venue' hearing and the subsequent hearing to determine mode of trial may **D6.10** take place before a single justice (ss. 17E(1) and 18(5) respectively), but in practice it is almost invariably the case that a lay bench will consist of at least two justices.

The determination of mode of trial need not necessarily take place on the first occasion when an accused charged with an either-way offence appears before magistrates. Section 17C empowers the court to adjourn proceedings under s. 17A or s. 17B (the 'plea before venue' hearing) and s. 18(4) allows the court to adjourn proceedings under ss. 19 to 23 (the mode of trial hearing). In either case, if the court does adjourn, it must remand the accused (either in custody or on bail) to the date fixed for the resumption of the proceedings, unless he first appeared in answer to a summons, or written charge and requisition, and has not subsequently been remanded, in which case the court has a discretion simply to adjourn.

It is submitted that magistrates are to be regarded as proceeding under ss. 17A to 23 from when an accused first appears charged with an either-way offence to when mode of trial is finally determined. Therefore, any adjournment during that period will be by virtue of s. 17C or s. 18(4).

Effect of Guilty Plea Indication at Plea Before Venue Hearing

D6.11   In *Rafferty* [1999] 1 Cr App R 235, the Court of Appeal held that where a plea of guilty is entered at the 'plea before venue' hearing, this will not usually alter the position regarding bail or custody. When a person who has been on bail enters a guilty plea at the 'plea before venue' hearing, the usual practice should be to continue his bail, even if it is anticipated that a custodial sentence will be imposed by the Crown Court, unless there is good reason for remanding him in custody (per Thomas LJ at p. 237).

By virtue of the definitive sentencing guideline, *Reduction in Sentence for a Guilty Plea* (see **E1.8**), 'the greatest reduction will be given where the plea was indicated at the "first reasonable opportunity"' (para. 4.1; see Supplement, SG-4). Paragraph 3(c) of the annex to the Guideline says that, where an either-way offence is sent to the Crown Court for trial and the accused pleads guilty at the first hearing in the Crown Court, the reduction will be less than if there had been an indication of a guilty plea given to the magistrates' court (a recommended reduction of one third). It follows that, unless the case is one where the court considers that it would have been reasonable to expect an indication of willingness to plead guilty even earlier, perhaps whilst under interview (para. 3(b)), the one-third discount in sentence in respect of either-way offences is reserved for an accused who indicates a guilty plea at the 'plea before venue' hearing. In *Cundell* [2008] EWCA Crim 1420, Burnett J said (at [16]) that the earliest reasonable opportunity to accept guilt may be at the first hearing before the magistrates' court, but in some cases that opportunity may come rather sooner (e.g., when interviewed by the police). The accused had pleaded guilty at the plea and case management hearing in the Crown Court but had not indicated a guilty plea at the 'plea before venue' hearing in the magistrates' court. The court held that a discount of about 25 per cent would have been reasonable in the circumstances.

Legitimate Expectations

D6.12   Where the court does not pass sentence immediately, the magistrates must be careful not to create an expectation that the accused will ultimately be sentenced in that court if they wish the option of committal for sentence to the Crown Court to remain open. In *Horseferry Road Magistrates' Court, ex parte Rugless* (2000) 164 JP 311, the accused indicated a guilty plea at the 'plea before venue' hearing; the court ordered a pre-sentence report, stating that all sentencing options were to remain open with the exception of committal to the Crown Court for sentence. At the next hearing, the accused was committed to the Crown Court for sentence (under what is now the PCC(S)A 2000, s. 3). The Divisional Court held that the accused had a 'legitimate expectation' that he would be sentenced in the magistrates' court. The subsequent decision to commit him for sentence was in breach of this legitimate expectation; accordingly it was appropriate to quash the decision to commit for sentence.

However, the expectation has to be a legitimate one. In *R (White) v Barking Magistrates' Court* [2004] EWHC 417 (Admin), the accused was charged with production of cannabis contrary to the MDA 1971, s. 4(2). The charges related to a large-scale production operation. When he appeared before the justices, they adjourned the matter for a pre-sentence report to be prepared. At the next hearing they committed him to the Crown Court for sentence. He applied for judicial review of the decision to commit, contending that, at the first hearing, the justices had created a legitimate expectation that they would deal with sentence themselves. It was held that, although an expectation had been created by the justices at the earlier hearing that they would not commit the accused to the Crown Court, that expectation would not be fulfilled, since it would have been an unreasonable decision by the justices. Given the gravity of the offending, it would have been unreasonable, and therefore unlawful, for the justices not to have committed the accused for sentencing in the Crown Court.

D6.13   In *Nicholas v Chester Magistrates' Court* (2009) 173 JP 542, Wilkie J (at [10]) referred to *R (White) v Barking Magistrates' Court* and *R (Sumner) v Wirral Borough Magistrates' Court* [2005] EWHC 3166 (Admin) and summarised their effect as deciding that 'no judicial review would lie on the basis of legitimate expectation if the legitimate expectation was founded on a decision of a bench which was so unreasonable as to be perverse or such that no reasonable bench properly directing itself could have reached'.

Binding Effect of Indication of Sentence

Where the court gives an indication of sentence under the MCA 1980, s. 20(4), and the accused **D6.14** then indicates a guilty plea (under s. 20(7)), s. 20A(1) stipulates that 'no court (whether a magistrates' court or not) may impose a custodial sentence for the offence unless such a sentence was indicated in the indication of sentence' given under s. 20(4). However, this is subject to the proviso contained in s. 20A(2), which refers to the PCC(S)A 2000, ss. 3A(4), 4(8) and 5(3).

The PCC(S)A 2000, s. 3A(2), requires a magistrates' court to commit an offender to the Crown Court for sentence where it appears to the magistrates' court that the criteria for the imposition of a sentence under the CJA 2003, s. 226A (extended sentences for dangerous offenders) would be met; it follows that an indication of a non-custodial sentence does not oust the power of the court to commit for sentence under s. 3A (see s. 3A(4)), or the power of the Crown Court to impose an extended sentence under s. 226A (see s. 5(3)).

Section 4(8) applies where the magistrates' court commits an offender to the Crown Court for sentence under s. 4(2) on the basis that the accused has indicated an intention to plead guilty to an either-way offence (and therefore is deemed to have pleaded guilty to it) and is also being sent to the Crown Court for trial in respect of one or more related offences. This power to commit for sentence is not ousted by an indication of sentence under the MCA 1980, s. 20(4). However, the ambit of this provision is limited by the PCC(S)A 2000, s. 5(3), which makes it clear that the powers of the Crown Court are freed from the restriction imposed by s. 20A(1) only where the offence committed for sentence under the PCC(S)A 2000, s. 4(2), is a specified offence (i.e. specified under the CJA 2003, s. 224) in respect of which the magistrates' court has stated (under s. 4(4)) that, in its opinion, it also had power to commit the offender for sentence under s. 3A(2).

The Magistrates' Decision Whether to Accept Jurisdiction

Section 19(3) of the MCA 1980 sets out the matters to which the magistrates must have regard **D6.15** in considering whether summary trial or trial on indictment is more appropriate. The most important consideration for the magistrates (and for the parties, when making their representations) is whether the sentencing powers of the magistrates would be adequate to deal with the offence(s) in the event of the accused being convicted. Where the accused is charged with more than one offence, the magistrates are required to look at the totality of the allegations, and not at each offence in isolation. Thus the magistrates can, and should, decline jurisdiction if they take the view that their sentencing powers are insufficient to deal with the totality of the offending, even if each offence taken by itself would not merit a harsher sentence than the magistrates could impose for that individual offence. The maximum penalty which magistrates can currently impose on summary conviction for an either-way offence is usually six months' imprisonment and/or a fine of up to £5,000 (an aggregate of one year and/or £5,000 per offence on conviction for two or more such offences). The £5,000 maximum will become an unlimited maximum when the LASPO 2012, s. 85, comes fully into effect. It is plainly wrong for magistrates to agree to summary trial if the offences charged are so serious that the court's powers would be insufficient to deal properly with the accused should he be convicted (see, e.g., *Coe* [1968] 1 All ER 65). In *Flax Bourton Magistrates' Court, ex parte Commissioners of Customs and Excise* (1996) 160 JP 481, the Divisional Court emphasised that the justices are bound by the statutory obligation set out in s. 19(3) to apply their minds to the question whether or not their powers of punishment would be adequate if they dealt with the case summarily; if in doubt as to what the level of sentence should be, they should seek advice from their clerk.

Although the maximum sentence available in the magistrates' court is the most important factor when considering whether or not a case is suitable for summary trial, it is submitted that it is

D

Part D Procedure

open to the magistrates to consider other factors. In *Horseferry Road Magistrates' Court, ex parte K* [1997] QB 23, for example, the Divisional Court accepted that a possible defence of insanity might make the case more suitable for trial on indictment.

D6.16   **Allocation Guideline**   The Allocation Guideline issued by the Sentencing Council (see Supplement, SG-590) indicates that either-way offences should generally be tried summarily unless it is likely that the court's sentencing powers will be insufficient. The guideline states that the court should assess the likely sentence in the light of the facts alleged by the prosecution case, but also taking into account aspects of the case advanced by the defence.

Given that it is open to the magistrates to commit an either-way offence to the Crown Court for sentence after a finding that a case is suitable for summary trial and then convicting the accused, the guideline makes the point that, where the court decides that the case is suitable to be dealt with in the magistrates' court, it should remind the accused that all sentencing options remain open (including committal to the Crown Court for sentence) at the time it informs the accused of this decision.

CPD II, para. 9A.2 (see Supplement, **PD-17**), states that, where cases involve complex questions of fact or difficult questions of law (including difficult issues of disclosure of sensitive material), the court should consider sending for trial. Paragraph 9A.3 states that the fact that the defendant will be asking for other offences to be taken into consideration, if convicted, is not a relevant consideration; this is, with respect, rather surprising, given that the presence of 'TICs' is likely to result in an increase in the sentence for the offence(s) to which the accused pleads guilty.

D6.17   **Mode of Trial where there are Co-accused**   The CrimPR, r. 9.2(6)(a), provides that, where the court is dealing on the same occasion with two or more accused who are charged jointly with an offence that can be tried in the Crown Court, the court must explain that, if one of them is sent to the Crown Court for trial, the other(s) must also be sent for trial in the Crown Court for the offence that is jointly charged and for any other offence which the court decides is related to that offence. This is so even if the court by then has decided that the case against the other accused is suitable for summary trial. To prevent having to repeat the procedure where the case has been found suitable for summary trial in respect of one accused but a co-accused then elects Crown Court trial, r. 9.2(6)(b) states that the court may ask the accused questions to help it decide in what order to deal with them (this would include questions about intention to elect Crown Court trial). In any event, by virtue of r. 9.2(7), if the court is dealing on the same occasion with two or more accused who are jointly charged and it accepts jurisdiction in respect of one of them but another is then sent for Crown Court trial (this would be as a result of that accused electing Crown Court trial), the court must deal again with the accused in respect of whom it has accepted jurisdiction (sending him instead to the Crown Court for trial). This has the effect of reversing the decision of the House of Lords in *Brentwood Justices, ex parte Nicholls* [1992] 1 AC 1, where it had been held that a case remained suitable for summary trial even if a co-accused had elected Crown Court trial.

The Prosecution Influence on the Decision

D6.18   The overall effect of the mode of trial provisions in the MCA 1980 is that summary trial may be vetoed either by the court or by the accused, but not by the prosecution. The most the prosecution can do is to make representations that trial on indictment would be more appropriate having regard to the gravity of the offence. However, where either (a) the case involves fraud of such seriousness or complexity that it is appropriate that the management of the case should without delay be taken over by the Crown Court, or (b) the accused is charged with an offence which involves an assault on, or injury or a threat of injury to, a person or is charged with certain other specified offences and a child will be called as a witness at the trial and, for the purpose of avoiding any prejudice to the welfare of the child, the case should be taken over and proceeded with without delay by the Crown Court, then the prosecutor can serve a notice, under the CDA 1998, s. 51B or s. 51C respectively, the effect of which is that the magistrates' court is required, by s. 51(2)(c), to send the case forthwith to the Crown Court for trial instead of conducting a plea before venue hearing under s. 17A (s. 17A(10)).

The Accused's Decision Whether to Consent to Summary Trial

It is sometimes asserted that one advantage of summary trial is that there is a limit on the sentence which the magistrates' court can pass (six months' imprisonment for one 'either-way' offence, 12 months for two or more). This advantage is largely nullified by the power of the magistrates to commit the accused to be sentenced in the Crown Court under the PCC(S)A 2000, s. 3. An advantage of trial on indictment is said to be that submissions on the admissibility of evidence can be made in the absence of the jury, with the obvious benefit that the jury do not find out about any matters that are ruled inadmissible. However, under the Courts Act 2003, sch. 3, a bench of magistrates may give a pre-trial ruling on the admissibility of evidence and that ruling binds the bench that tries the case (see **D21.35**).

Another supposed advantage of trial on indictment is that the defence are entitled to receive copies of the written statements of the witnesses to be called by the prosecution. However, para. 57 of the A-G's Guidelines on Disclosure (see **appendix** 4) provides that, in the case of summary trial, the prosecutor should provide to the defence all evidence upon which the Crown proposes to rely in a summary trial. Thus, an accused who is to be tried in the magistrates' court should be in the same position as one being tried in the Crown Court as regards obtaining copies of the prosecution witness statements.

Statutory Provisions on Mode of Trial

Magistrates' Courts Act 1980, ss. 17A to 17C, 18 to 21 and 23

17A.—(1) This section shall have effect where a person who has attained the age of 18 years appears or is brought before a magistrates' court on an information charging him with an offence triable either way.

(2) Everything that the court is required to do under the following provisions of this section must be done with the accused present in court.

(3) The court shall cause the charge to be written down, if this has not already been done, and to be read to the accused.

(4) The court shall then explain to the accused in ordinary language that he may indicate whether (if the offence were to proceed to trial) he would plead guilty or not guilty, and that if he indicates that he would plead guilty—

    (a) the court must proceed as mentioned in subsection (6) below; and

    (b) he may be committed for sentence to the Crown Court under section 3 of the Powers of Criminal Courts (Sentencing) Act 2000 if the court is of such opinion as is mentioned in subsection (2) of that section.

(5) The court shall then ask the accused whether (if the offence were to proceed to trial) he would plead guilty or not guilty.

(6) If the accused indicates that he would plead guilty the court shall proceed as if—

    (a) the proceedings constituted from the beginning the summary trial of the information; and

    (b) section 9(1) above was complied with and he pleaded guilty under it.

(7) If the accused indicates that he would plead not guilty section 18(1) below shall apply.

(8) If the accused in fact fails to indicate how he would plead, for the purposes of this section and section 18(1) below he shall be taken to indicate that he would plead not guilty.

(9) Subject to subsection (6) above, the following shall not for any purpose be taken to constitute the taking of a plea—

    (a) asking the accused under this section whether (if the offence were to proceed to trial) he would plead guilty or not guilty;

    (b) an indication by the accused under this section of how he would plead.

17B.—(1) This section shall have effect where—

    (a) a person who has attained the age of 18 years appears or is brought before a magistrates' court on an information charging him with an offence triable either way,

    (b) the accused is represented by a legal representative,

    (c) the court considers that by reason of the accused's disorderly conduct before the court it is not practicable for proceedings under section 17A above to be conducted in his presence, and

    (d) the court considers that it should proceed in the absence of the accused.

(2) In such a case—
- (a) the court shall cause the charge to be written down, if this has not already been done, and to be read to the representative;
- (b) the court shall ask the representative whether (if the offence were to proceed to trial) the accused would plead guilty or not guilty;
- (c) if the representative indicates that the accused would plead guilty the court shall proceed as if the proceedings constituted from the beginning the summary trial of the information, and as if section 9(1) above was complied with and the accused pleaded guilty under it;
- (d) if the representative indicates that the accused would plead not guilty section 18(1) below shall apply.

(3) If the representative in fact fails to indicate how the accused would plead, for the purposes of this section and section 18(1) below he shall be taken to indicate that the accused would plead not guilty.

(4) Subject to subsection (2)(c) above, the following shall not for any purpose be taken to constitute the taking of a plea—
- (a) asking the representative under this section whether (if the offence were to proceed to trial) the accused would plead guilty or not guilty;
- (b) an indication by the representative under this section of how the accused would plead.

17C. A magistrates' court proceeding under section 17A or 17B above may adjourn the proceedings at any time, and on doing so on any occasion when the accused is present may remand the accused, and shall remand him if—
- (a) on the occasion on which he first appeared, or was brought, before the court to answer to the information he was in custody or, having been released on bail, surrendered to the custody of the court; or
- (b) he has been remanded at any time in the course of proceedings on the information;

and where the court remands the accused, the time fixed for the resumption of proceedings shall be that at which he is required to appear or be brought before the court in pursuance of the remand or would be required to be brought before the court but for section 128(3A) below.

18.—(1) Sections 19 to 23 below shall have effect where a person who has attained the age of 18 years appears or is brought before a magistrates' court on an information charging him with an offence triable either way and—
- (a) he indicates under section 17A above that (if the offence were to proceed to trial) he would plead not guilty, or
- (b) his representative indicates under section 17B above that (if the offence were to proceed to trial) he would plead not guilty.

(2) Without prejudice to section 11(1) above [proceeding to summary trial of an information in the absence of the accused if he does not appear], everything that the court is required to do under sections 19 to 22 below must be done before any evidence is called and, subject to subsection (3) below and section 23 below, with the accused present in court.

(3) The court may proceed in the absence of the accused in accordance with such of the provisions of sections 19 to 22 below as are applicable in the circumstances if the court considers that by reason of his disorderly conduct before the court it is not practicable for the proceedings to be conducted in his presence; and subsections (3) to (5) of section 23 below, so far as applicable, shall have effect in relation to proceedings conducted in the absence of the accused by virtue of this subsection (references in those subsections to the person representing the accused being for this purpose read as references to the person, if any, representing him).

(4) A magistrates' court proceeding under sections 19 to 23 below may adjourn the proceedings at any time, and on doing so on any occasion when the accused is present may remand the accused, and shall remand him if—
- (a) on the occasion on which he first appeared, or was brought, before the court to answer to the information he was in custody or, having been released on bail, surrendered to the custody of the court; or
- (b) if he has been remanded at any time in the course of proceedings on the information;

and where the court remands the accused, the time fixed for the resumption of the proceedings shall be that at which he is required to appear or be brought before the court in pursuance of the remand or would be required to be brought before the court but for section 128(3A) below [accused being remanded in custody agreeing to future remands in custody taking place in his absence].

(5) The functions of a magistrates' court under sections 19 to 23 below may be discharged by a single justice, but the foregoing provision shall not be taken to authorise the summary trial of an information by a magistrates' court composed of less than two justices.

19.—(1) The court shall decide whether the offence appears to it more suitable for summary trial or for trial on indictment.

(2) Before making a decision under this section, the court—

(a) shall give the prosecution an opportunity to inform the court of the accused's previous convictions (if any); and

(b) shall give the prosecution and the accused an opportunity to make representations as to whether summary trial or trial on indictment would be more suitable.

(3) In making a decision under this section, the court shall consider—

(a) whether the sentence which a magistrates' court would have power to impose for the offence would be adequate; and

(b) any representations made by the prosecution or the accused under subsection (2)(b) above,

and shall have regard to any allocation guidelines (or revised allocation guidelines) issued as definitive guidelines under section 170 of the Criminal Justice Act 2003.

(4) Where—

(a) the accused is charged with two or more offences; and

(b) it appears to the court that the charges for the offences could be joined in the same indictment or that the offences arise out of the same or connected circumstances,

subsection (3)(a) above shall have effect as if references to the sentence which a magistrates' court would have power to impose for the offence were a reference to the maximum aggregate sentence which a magistrates' court would have power to impose for all of the offences taken together.

(5) In this section any reference to a previous conviction is a reference to—

(a) a previous conviction by a court in the United Kingdom;

(aa) a previous conviction by a court in another member State of a relevant offence under the law of that State; or

(b) a previous conviction of a service offence within the meaning of the Armed Forces Act 2006.

(5A) For the purposes of subsection (5)(aa) an offence is 'relevant' if the offence would constitute an offence under the law of any part of the United Kingdom if it were done in that part at the time when the allocation decision is made.

(6) If, in respect of the offence, the court receives a notice under section 51B or 51C of the Crime and Disorder Act 1998 (which relate to serious or complex fraud cases and to certain cases involving children respectively), the preceding provisions of this section and sections 20, 20A and 21 below shall not apply, and the court shall proceed in relation to the offence in accordance with section 51(1) of that Act.

20.—(1) If the court decides under section 19 above that the offence appears to it more suitable for summary trial, the following provisions of this section shall apply (unless they are excluded by section 23 below).

(2) The court shall explain to the accused in ordinary language—

(a) that it appears to the court more suitable for him to be tried summarily for the offence;

(b) that he can either consent to be so tried or, if he wishes, be tried on indictment;

(c) that if he is tried summarily and is convicted by the court, he may be committed for sentence to the Crown Court under section 3 or (if applicable) section 3A of the Powers of Criminal Courts (Sentencing) Act 2000 if the court is of such opinion as is mentioned in subsection (2) of the applicable section.

(3) The accused may then request an indication ('an indication of sentence') of whether a custodial sentence or non-custodial sentence would be more likely to be imposed if he were to be tried summarily for the offence and to plead guilty.

(4) If the accused requests an indication of sentence, the court may, but need not, give such an indication.

(5) If the accused requests and the court gives an indication of sentence, the court shall ask the accused whether he wishes, on the basis of the indication, to reconsider the indication of plea which was given, or is taken to have been given, under section 17A or 17B above.

(6) If the accused indicates that he wishes to reconsider the indication under section 17A or 17B above, the court shall ask the accused whether (if the offence were to proceed to trial) he would plead guilty or not guilty.

(7) If the accused indicates that he would plead guilty the court shall proceed as if—

(a) the proceedings constituted from that time the summary trial of the information; and

(b) section 9(1) above were complied with and he pleaded guilty under it.

(8) Subsection (9) below applies where—

(a) the court does not give an indication of sentence (whether because the accused does not request one or because the court does not agree to give one);

(b) the accused either—

  (i)   does not indicate, in accordance with subsection (5) above, that he wishes; or

  (ii) indicates, in accordance with subsection (5) above, that he does not wish, to reconsider the indication of plea under section 17A or 17B above; or

(c) the accused does not indicate, in accordance with subsection (6) above, that he would plead guilty.

(9) The court shall ask the accused whether he consents to be tried summarily or wishes to be tried on indictment and—

(a) if he consents to be tried summarily, shall proceed to the summary trial of the information; and

(b) if he does not so consent, shall proceed in relation to the offence in accordance with section 51(1) of the Crime and Disorder Act 1998.

20A.—(1) Where the case is dealt with in accordance with section 20(7) above, no court (whether a magistrates' court or not) may impose a custodial sentence for the offence unless such a sentence was indicated in the indication of sentence referred to in section 20 above.

(2) Subsection (1) above is subject to sections 3A(4), 4(8) and 5(3) of the Powers of Criminal Courts (Sentencing) Act 2000.

(3) Except as provided in subsection (1) above—

(a) an indication of sentence shall not be binding on any court (whether a magistrates' court or not); and

(b) no sentence may be challenged or be the subject of appeal in any court on the ground that it is not consistent with an indication of sentence.

21. If the court decides under section 19 above that the offence appears to it more suitable for trial on indictment, the court shall tell the accused that the court has decided that it is more suitable for him to be tried on indictment, and shall proceed in relation to the offence in accordance with section 51(1) of the Crime and Disorder Act 1998.

23.—(1) Where—

(a) the accused is represented by counsel or a solicitor who in his absence signifies to the court the accused's consent to the proceedings for determining how he is to be tried for the offence being conducted in his absence; and

(b) the court is satisfied that there is good reason for proceeding in the absence of the accused,

the following provisions of this section shall apply.

(2) Subject to the following provisions of this section, the court may proceed in the absence of the accused in accordance with such of the provisions of sections 19 to 22 above as are applicable in the circumstances.

(3) If, in a case where subsection (1) of section 22 above applies, it appears to the court as mentioned in subsection (4) of that section, subsections (5) and (6) of that section shall not apply and the court—

(a) if the accused's consent to be tried summarily has been or is signified by the person representing him, shall proceed in accordance with subsection (2) of that section as if that subsection applied; or

(b) if that consent has not been and is not so signified, shall proceed in accordance with subsection (3) of that section as if that subsection applied.

(4) If the court decides under section 19 above that the offence appears to it more suitable for summary trial then—

(a) if the accused's consent to be tried summarily has been or is signified by the person representing him, section 20 above shall not apply, and the court shall proceed to the summary trial of the information; or

(b) if that consent has not been and is not so signified, section 20 above shall not apply and the court shall proceed in relation to the offence in accordance with section 51(1) of the Crime and Disorder Act 1998.

(5) If the court decides under section 19 above that the offence appears to it more suitable for trial on indictment, section 21 above shall not apply and the court shall proceed in relation to the offence in accordance with section 51(1) of the Crime and Disorder Act 1998.

[**26.** Powers ancillary to s. 23 to issue a summons or warrant for arrest in respect of the accused if either the court considers that he should be present while the mode of trial is determined or, having proceeded in his absence and adjourned without remanding him prior to committal or transfer proceedings, he does not appear for the resumption of the hearing.]

Form of Words on Election as to Mode of Trial

Annex to Home Office Circular 45/1997 (excerpt)

PLEA BEFORE VENUE PROCEDURE: INDICATION OF PLEA

Suggested form of wording for the use of the magistrates' court when inviting the defendant to indicate his plea.

This offence(s) may be tried either by this court or by the Crown Court before a judge and jury.

Whether or not this court can deal with your case today will depend upon your answers to the questions which I am going to put to you. Do you understand?

You will shortly be asked to tell the court whether you intend to plead guilty or not guilty to (certain of) the offence(s) with which you are charged. Do you understand?

If you tell us that you intend to plead guilty, you will be convicted of the offence. We may then be able to deal with (part of) your case at this hearing. The prosecutor will tell us about the facts of the case, you (your representative) will have the opportunity to respond (on your behalf), and we shall then go on to consider how to sentence you. Do you understand?

We may be able to sentence you today, or we may need to adjourn the proceedings until a later date for the preparation of a pre-sentence report by the Probation Service. If we believe that you deserve a greater sentence than we have the power to give you in this court, we may decide to send you to the Crown Court, either on bail or in custody, and you will be sentenced by that court which has greater sentencing powers. Do you understand?

[In cases where s. 4 of the PCC(S)A 2000 applies:

If you indicate a guilty plea for this/these offence(s), even if we believe that our own sentencing powers are great enough to deal with you here, we may still send you to the Crown Court to be sentenced there for this/these offence(s) because you have also been charged with a related offence(s) [for which you have already been committed for trial in that court.] [for which you will be committed for trial in that court.] Do you understand?]

If, on the other hand, you tell us that you intend to plead not guilty, or if you do not tell us what you intend to do, we shall go on to consider whether you should be tried by this court or by the Crown Court on some future date. If we decide that it would be appropriate to deal with your case in this court, we shall ask whether you are content for us to do so or whether you wish your case to be tried in the Crown Court.

Before I ask you how you intend to plead, do you understand everything I have said or is there any part of what I have said which you would like me to repeat or explain?

THE SPECIAL PROCEDURE FOR CRIMINAL DAMAGE CHARGES

Procedure on Criminal Damage Charges

Whenever the accused is charged with a 'scheduled offence', the mode of trial procedure must be preceded by consideration of the value involved in the offence (s. 22(1)). Depending on what that value is, the accused may be deprived of his right to elect trial on indictment, notwithstanding that the offence is otherwise triable either way.

Scheduled offences comprise: (a) offences of damaging or destroying property contrary to s. 1 of the Criminal Damage Act 1971, excluding those committed by fire; and (b) aiding, abetting, counselling or procuring such offences, or attempting or encouraging them (MCA 1980, sch. 2). Some offences under the Criminal Damage Act 1971 are *not* scheduled offences, including:

(a) those committed by damaging or destroying property by fire (these are expressly excluded from scheduled offences by the terms of the MCA 1980, sch. 2); and
(b) those committed with intent to endanger life or being reckless as to the endangering of life contrary to the Criminal Damage Act 1971, s. 1(2): although not expressly dealt with in

sch. 2, these cannot be scheduled offences because they are not in the list of offences under the 1971 Act that are triable either way (see the MCA 1980, sch. 1, para. 29), and so they are triable only on indictment.

It should also be noted that conspiracy to commit criminal damage is not a scheduled offence (*Ward* [1997] 1 Cr App R (S) 442).

D6.23   **Value Involved**   If the accused is charged with an offence of criminal damage to which the provisions of the MCA 1980, s. 22, apply, then the court must give the accused the opportunity to indicate his plea (pursuant to s. 17A). It must then consider, having regard to any representations made by the prosecution and defence, whether the 'value involved' in the offence exceeds the 'relevant sum', currently £5,000 (MCA 1980, s. 22(1)). If the property was allegedly destroyed or damaged beyond repair, the value involved is what it would probably have cost to purchase a replacement in the open market at the time of the offence; if the property was repairable, the value involved is the probable market cost of repairs or the probable market replacement cost, whichever is the less (sch. 2). In *Colchester Magistrates' Court, ex parte Abbott* (2001) 165 JP 386, the Divisional Court made it clear that the value on which the magistrates must focus is the value of the damage to the property itself; they should not concern themselves with any consequential losses which might have been sustained as a result of the damage.

If it appears to the magistrates that the value involved clearly does *not* exceed the relevant sum, they must proceed as if the offence charged were triable only summarily (s. 22(2)). Consequently, the mode of trial provisions of the 1980 Act do not apply and the accused has no right to elect trial on indictment.

If it appears to the court clear that the value involved exceeds the relevant sum, it is obliged to determine the mode of trial in accordance with the usual mode of trial procedure, just as it would for any other either-way offence (s. 22(3)).

Where, for any reason, it is not clear to the court whether the value involved does or does not exceed the relevant sum, it must explain to the accused that he can, if he wishes, consent to summary trial and that, if he does, he will be so tried and his liability to imprisonment or a fine will be limited in accordance with the provisions of s. 33 of the 1980 Act (see **D6.28**). The accused is then asked if he consents. Depending on his response, the court either proceeds to summary trial or embarks on the ordinary procedure for determining mode of trial, which will presumably result in the accused electing trial on indictment (s. 22(5) and (6)).

D6.24   The MCA 1980, s. 17D(1), provides that where the accused, at the plea before venue hearing, indicated a guilty plea to an offence to which s. 22 applies (and so is deemed to have pleaded guilty to it), the court must consider whether, having regard to any representations made by the accused or by the prosecutor, the value involved exceeds £5,000. If it appears clear to the court that the value involved does not exceed £5,000, or it is unclear whether the value involved exceeds £5,000, the court's sentencing powers are subject to the limits set out in the MCA 1980, s. 33, and there is no power to commit for sentence under the PCC(S)A 2000, s. 3 or s. 4. Section 33 provides that where the accused is convicted of an offence to which s. 22 applies (this includes conviction following a guilty plea under s. 17A(6) and conviction following summary trial of a criminal damage offence where either the court decided that the value involved clearly did not exceed £5,000 or, by virtue of s. 22(5), the accused consented to summary trial in a case where the court was in doubt as to the value involved), then the maximum penalty that may be imposed in the event of conviction is three months' imprisonment or a fine of £2,500, and the court has no power to commit for sentence under the PCC(S)A 2000, s. 3. If the accused is tried summarily in a case where the value involved clearly exceeded the relevant sum but he was nevertheless offered and accepted summary trial, the penalties available are as for any either-way offence (currently six months' imprisonment and/or a fine of £5,000); moreover, there may be a committal for sentence under the PCC(S)A 2000, s. 3.

When the CJA 2003, sch. 3, para. 27, comes into force, the maximum sentence of imprisonment under the MCA 1980, s. 33, will be increased to 51 weeks (effectively negating a significant advantage conferred by s. 33).

Procedure for Determining the Value Involved   The court is required by the MCA 1980,   **D6.25**
s. 22(1), to have regard to the 'representations' of the parties when considering the value involved in a criminal damage offence. This does not entail an obligation to hear evidence. In *Canterbury & St Augustine Justices, ex parte Klisiak* [1982] QB 398 at p. 413D–E, Lord Lane CJ said that 'the word "representations" implies something less than evidence. It comprises submissions, coupled with assertions of fact and sometimes production of documents…The nearest analogy is, perhaps, the speech in mitigation after a finding or plea of guilty in a criminal trial.' However, the court has a discretion to hear evidence on the question of the value involved if it wishes to do so (*Ex parte Klisiak* at p. 413D–E).

In a case where there is real difficulty in arriving at an appropriate basis for calculating the value involved, the prosecution are entitled to say that they will not seek to prove that the accused caused any more damage than can be established with clarity. Acting on that assurance, the court may conclude that the value was clearly less than the relevant sum even though, in the absence of such an assurance and adopting an alternative method of calculation, the question would have remained doubtful and the accused could therefore have elected trial on indictment (*Salisbury Magistrates' Court, ex parte Mastin* (1986) 84 Cr App R 248).

Two or More Criminal Damage Charges

If the accused is 'charged on the same occasion with two or more scheduled offences and it   **D6.26**
appears to the court that they constitute or form part of a series of two or more offences of the same or a similar character', then the relevant consideration is the *aggregate* value involved in the offences (MCA 1980, s. 22(11)). In other words, the accused will retain his right to trial on indictment if the value of the offences added together exceeds the relevant sum (£5,000), even if the value of each offence taken individually was under the relevant sum.

The reference in s. 22(11) to a 'series of two or more offences of the same or similar character' connotes that the aggregate value is the relevant value where the offences could be joined together in the same indictment without infringing the CrimPR, r. 14.2(3), which governs joinder of counts in an indictment (see **D11.63** *et seq.*). Thus, s. 22(11) applies where the offences are founded on the same facts (effectively, amounting to a single incident) or constitute a series of offences that are linked by both a legal and a factual nexus (e.g., the offences of criminal damage are linked by closeness in time and geographical location).

Section 22(11) applies where the accused is 'charged on one occasion' with two or more   **D6.27**
scheduled offences. The phrase could be construed to mean either being charged at the police station or appearing before a magistrates' court to answer charges. It is submitted that the latter interpretation is to be preferred, since there can be no reason of policy why mode of trial should depend on the method of commencing proceedings. A further question arises of whether s. 22(11) extends to cases where the accused originally appears charged with only one offence but further charges are added prior to the determination of mode of trial; again, it is submitted that s. 22(11) ought to apply (otherwise, for example, the prosecution might artificially deprive an accused of the right to trial on indictment by initially bringing him before the court on only one charge even though they already have the evidence to found further charges).

Statutory Provisions on Criminal Damage Mode of Trial

        Magistrates' Courts Act 1980, ss. 17D, 22 and 33 and sch. 2   **D6.28**

17D.—(1) If—
   (a) the offence is a scheduled offence (as defined in section 22(1) below);

(b) the court proceeds in relation to the offence in accordance with section 17A(6) or 17B(2) (c) above; and

(c) the court convicts the accused of the offence,

the court shall consider whether, having regard to any representations made by him or by the prosecutor, the value involved (as defined in section 22(10) below) appears to the court to exceed the relevant sum (as specified for the purposes of section 22 below).

(2) If it appears to the court clear that the value involved does not exceed the relevant sum, or it appears to the court for any reason not clear whether the value involved does or does not exceed the relevant sum—

(a) subject to subsection (4) below, the court shall not have power to impose on the accused in respect of the offence a sentence in excess of the limits mentioned in section 33(1)(a) below; and

(b) sections 3 and 4 of the Powers of Criminal Courts (Sentencing) Act 2000 shall not apply as regards that offence.

(3) Subsections (9) to (12) of section 22 below shall apply for the purposes of this section as they apply for the purposes of that section (reading the reference to subsection (1) in section 22(9) as a reference to subsection (1) of this section).

(4) Subsection (2)(a) above does not apply to an offence under section 12A of the Theft Act 1968 (aggravated vehicle-taking).

22.—(1) If the offence charged by the information is one of those mentioned in the first column of Schedule 2 to this Act (in this section referred to as 'scheduled offences') then the court shall, before proceeding in accordance with section 19 above, consider whether, having regard to any representations made by the prosecutor or the accused, the value involved (as defined in subsection (10) below) appears to exceed the relevant sum. For the purposes of this section the relevant sum is £5,000.

(2) If, where subsection (1) above applies, it appears to the court clear that, for the offence charged, the value involved does not exceed the relevant sum, the court shall proceed as if the offence were triable only summarily, and sections 19 to 21 above shall not apply.

(3) If, where subsection (1) above applies, it appears to the court clear that, for the offence charged, the value involved exceeds that relevant sum, the court shall thereupon proceed in accordance with section 19 above in the ordinary way without further regard to the provisions of this section.

(4) If, where subsection (1) above applies, it appears to the court for any reason not clear whether, for the offence charged, the value involved does or does not exceed the relevant sum, the provisions of subsections (5) and (6) below shall apply.

(5) The court shall cause the charge to be written down, if this has not already been done, and read to the accused, and shall explain to him in ordinary language—

(a) that he can, if he wishes, consent to be tried summarily for the offence and that if he consents to be so tried, he will definitely be tried in that way; and

(b) that if he is tried summarily and is convicted by the court, his liability to imprisonment or a fine will be limited as provided in section 33 below.

(6) After explaining to the accused as provided by subsection (5) above, the court shall ask him whether he consents to be tried summarily and—

(a) if he so consents, shall proceed in accordance with subsection (2) above as if that subsection applied;

(b) if he does not so consent, shall proceed in accordance with subsection (3) above as if that subsection applied.

[(7) Repealed.]

[(8) No appeal to the Crown Court against conviction for a scheduled offence on the ground that the decision as to the value involved was mistaken.]

[(9) Where a juvenile and an adult are jointly charged with a scheduled offence, the juvenile as well as the adult may make representations as to the value involved.]

[(10) 'The value involved' to be given the meaning set out in sch. 2, and 'material time', when used in sch. 2, means the time of the alleged offence.]

(11) Where—

(a) the accused is charged on the same occasion with two or more scheduled offences and it appears to the court that they constitute or form part of a series of two or more offences of the same or a similar character; or

(b) the offence charged consists in [intentionally encouraging or assisting a person] to commit two or more scheduled offences,

this section shall have effect as if any reference in it to the value involved were a reference to the aggregate of the values involved.

(12) Subsection (8) of section 12A of the Theft Act 1968 (which determines when a vehicle is recovered) shall apply for the purposes of paragraph 3 of Schedule 2 to this Act as it applies for the purposes of that section.

33.—(1) Where in pursuance of subsection (2) of section 22 above a magistrates' court proceeds to the summary trial of an information, then, if the accused is summarily convicted of the offence—

(a) subject to subsection (3) below the court shall not have power to impose on him in respect of that offence imprisonment for more than 3 months or a fine greater than level 4 on the standard scale; and

(b) Section 3 of the Powers of Criminal Courts (Sentencing) Act 2000 [committal for sentence if the magistrates' powers of punishment inadequate] shall not apply as regards that offence.

(2) In subsection (1) above 'fine' includes a pecuniary penalty but does not include a pecuniary forfeiture or pecuniary compensation.

(3) Paragraph (a) of subsection (1) above does not apply to an offence under section 12A of the Theft Act 1968 (aggravated vehicle-taking).

SCHEDULE 2

OFFENCES FOR WHICH THE VALUE INVOLVED IS RELEVANT TO THE MODE OF TRIAL

[Column 1 shows the offences subject to the special procedure; column 2 defines the value involved, and column 3 indicates how the value involved is calculated.]

Offence	Value involved	How measured

1. Offences under section 1 of the Criminal Damage Act 1971 (destroying or damaging property), excluding any offence committed by destroying or damaging property by fire.	As regards property alleged to have been destroyed, its value.
	
	As regards property alleged to have been damaged, the value of the alleged damage.
		What the property would probably have cost to buy in the open market at the material time.
		(a) If immediately after the material time the damage was capable of repair—
		  (i) what would probably then have been the market price for the repair of the damage, or
		  (ii) what the property alleged to have been damaged would probably have cost to buy in the open market at the material time, whichever is the less; or
		(b) if immediately after the material time the damage was beyond repair, what the said property would probably have cost to buy in the open market at the material time.

2. The following offences, namely (a) aiding, abetting, counselling or procuring the commission of any offence mentioned in paragraph 1 above; (b) attempting to commit any offence so mentioned; and (c) inciting another to commit any offence so mentioned.	The value indicated in paragraph 1 above for the offence alleged to have been aided, abetted, counselled or procured, or attempted or incited.	As for the corresponding entry in paragraph 1 above.

| 3. Offences under section 12A of the Theft Act 1968 (aggravated vehicle-taking) where no allegation is made under subsection (1)(b) other than of damage, whether to the vehicle or other property or both. | The total value of the damage alleged to have been caused. | (1) In the case of damage to any property other than the vehicle involved in the offence, as for the corresponding entry in paragraph 1 above, substituting a reference to the time of the accident concerned for any reference to the material time.
(2) In the case of damage to the vehicle involved in the offence—
  (a) if immediately after the vehicle was recovered the damage was capable of repair—
    (i) what would probably then have been the market price for the repair of the damage, or
    (ii) what the vehicle would probably have cost to buy in the open market immediately before it was unlawfully taken, whichever is the less; or
  (b) if immediately after the vehicle was recovered the damage was beyond repair, what the vehicle would probably have cost to buy in the open market immediately before it was unlawfully taken. |

SPECIAL PROVISION FOR LOW-VALUE SHOPLIFTING

D6.29   The MCA 1980, s 22A, which was inserted by the ABCPA 2014, s. 176, in force from 13 May 2014, provides that 'low-value' shoplifting (defined as shoplifting where the value of the stolen goods does not exceed £200) is triable only summarily. However, s. 22A(2) goes on to provide that, where an accused who has attained the age of 18 is charged with low-value shoplifting, the court must, before the summary trial of the offence begins, give the accused the opportunity of electing Crown Court trial for the offence; if he elects to be so tried, the magistrates' court must send him to the Crown Court for trial. Unlike the special procedure for criminal damage (under the MCA 1980, s. 22), in the case of low-value shoplifting the accused retains the right to elect Crown Court trial. The CrimPR, r. 9.7(4)(c), makes it clear that, where the offence is low-value shoplifting, the magistrates' court must offer the accused the opportunity to require trial in the Crown Court.

D6.30   Magistrates' Courts Act 1980, s. 22A

(1) Low-value shoplifting is triable only summarily.
(2) But where a person accused of low-value shoplifting is aged 18 or over, and appears or is brought before the court before the summary trial of the offence begins, the court must give the person the opportunity of electing to be tried by the Crown Court for the offence and, if the person elects to be so tried—
  (a) subsection (1) does not apply, and
  (b) the court must send the person to the Crown Court for trial for the offence.
(3) 'Low-value shoplifting' means an offence under section 1 of the Theft Act 1968 in circumstances where—
  (a) the value of the stolen goods does not exceed £200,
  (b) the goods were being offered for sale in a shop or any other premises, stall, vehicle or place from which there is carried on a trade or business, and
  (c) at the time of the offence, the person accused of low-value shoplifting was, or was purporting to be, a customer or potential customer of the person offering the goods for sale.
(4) For the purposes of subsection (3)(a)—
  (a) the value of the stolen goods is the price at which they were being offered for sale at the time of the offence, and

(b) where the accused is charged on the same occasion with two or more offences of low-value shoplifting, the reference to the value involved has effect as if it were a reference to the aggregate of the values involved.

(5) A person guilty of low-value shoplifting is liable on summary conviction to—

    (a) imprisonment for a period not exceeding 51 weeks (or 6 months, if the offence was committed before the commencement of section 281(4) and (5) of the Criminal Justice Act 2003),

    (b) a fine, or

    (c) both.

(6) A person convicted of low-value shoplifting by a magistrates' court may not appeal to the Crown Court against the conviction on the ground that the convicting court was mistaken as to whether the offence was one of low-value shoplifting.

(7) For the purposes of this section, any reference to low-value shoplifting includes aiding, abetting, counselling or procuring the commission of low-value shoplifting.

FAILURE TO COMPLY WITH THE MODE OF TRIAL PROCEDURE

In *Kent Justices, ex parte Machin* [1952] 2 QB 355, it was held that, because the jurisdiction of **D6.31** magistrates' courts to try either-way offences derives solely from statute, any failure to comply with the statutory procedure laid down for determining mode of trial renders any summary trial which follows that defective procedure *ultra vires* and therefore a nullity. In *Ashton* [2007] 1 WLR 181, it was held that, in the absence of a clear indication that Parliament intended jurisdiction automatically to be removed following a procedural failure, the decision of the court should be based on an assessment of the interests of justice, with particular focus on whether there was a real possibility that the prosecution or the defence may suffer prejudice. If that risk is present, the court should then decide whether it is just to permit the proceedings to continue. This meant that a number of authorities, including *Machin*, would have to be reconsidered (at [67]–[69]). However, in *R (Rahmdezfouli) v Wood Green Crown Court* [2014] 1 All ER 567, Mackay J said (at [16]):

> [T]he legislature in enacting s. 17A must have intended . . . that where a magistrates' court declined or failed to follow the requirements of the section it was acting without jurisdiction every bit as much as if, for instance, it had purported to try a defendant on a charge of homicide.

The effect of this decision is that failure to comply with the mode of trial process as it is set out in the MCA 1980 is to be regarded as nullifying any proceedings which follow that defective procedure.

VARIATION OF ORIGINAL DECISION AS TO MODE OF TRIAL

Introduction

Variation of the mode of trial decision is governed by the MCA 1980, s. 25, which enables the **D6.32** prosecution to make an application to the magistrates (before the start of the summary trial) to reconsider their acceptance of summary jurisdiction.

By virtue of s. 25(2), where the accused has consented to summary trial (the magistrates having first accepted jurisdiction), the prosecution may apply to the court for the offence to be tried on indictment instead (s. 25(2)). This application must be made before the summary trial begins and must be dealt with by the court before any other application or issue in relation to the summary trial is dealt with (s. 25(2A)). Under s. 25(2B), the court may accede to the application 'only if it is satisfied that the sentence which a magistrates' court would have power to impose for the offence (or offences, where they constitute or form part of a series of two or more offences of the same or a similar character) would be inadequate'. If the court agrees to the prosecution application, the case is sent to the Crown Court for trial under the CDA 1998, s. 51.

D6.33   Magistrates' Courts Act 1980, s. 25

(1) Subsections (2) to (2D) below shall have effect where a person who has attained the age of 18 appears or is brought before a magistrates' court on an information charging him with an offence triable either way.

(2) Where the court is required under section 20(9) above to proceed to the summary trial of the information, the prosecution may apply to the court for the offence to be tried on indictment instead.

(2A) An application under subsection (2) above—
    (a) must be made before the summary trial begins; and
    (b) must be dealt with by the court before any other application or issue in relation to the summary trial is dealt with.

(2B) The court may grant an application under subsection (2) above but only if it is satisfied that the sentence which a magistrates' court would have power to impose for the offence would be inadequate.

(2C) Where—
    (a) the accused is charged on the same occasion with two or more offences; and
    (b) it appears to the court that they constitute or form part of a series of two or more offences of the same or a similar character,
subsection (2B) above shall have effect as if references to the sentence which a magistrates' court would have power to impose for the offence were a reference to the maximum aggregate sentence which a magistrates' court would have power to impose for all of the offences taken together.

(2D) Where the court grants an application under subsection (2) above, it shall proceed in relation to the offence in accordance with section 51(1) of the Crime and Disorder Act 1998.

WITHDRAWAL BY ACCUSED OF ORIGINAL CONSENT

General

D6.34 The approach a magistrates' court should adopt when an accused who has already chosen between summary trial and trial on indictment asks to withdraw his original consent to summary trial was considered by McCullough J in *Birmingham Justices, ex parte Hodgson* [1985] QB 1131. The following propositions emerge from his judgment:

(a) The magistrates have a discretion to permit the accused to withdraw consent to summary trial, notwithstanding that the provisions now contained in the MCA 1980, s. 20(9)(a), state that, if an accused consents to be tried summarily, the court *shall* proceed to summary trial. The existence of this discretion was affirmed by *Craske, ex parte Metropolitan Police Commissioner* [1957] 2 QB 591, where Devlin J said (at pp. 599–600):

> I do not think that [the use of the word 'shall'] means that once the procedure is set in motion, the court has ineluctably to allow the wheels to revolve without any power to stop them if the accused wants to change his mind…. I can find nothing… which would deprive a magistrate… of the ordinary right which they must have in the interests of justice of allowing an accused who has given his consent ill-advisedly to abandoning his right to trial by jury, to be given the opportunity of reconsidering it.

It would seem that the accused can in theory be allowed to re-elect even after his trial on a not guilty plea has begun. However, it is submitted that, once a significant portion of the prosecution evidence has been given, a change of election should be allowed only in very exceptional circumstances, since otherwise the defence might be tempted to ask to re-elect as a tactical ploy simply because the trial seems to be going badly.

(b) In exercising their discretion whether or not to accede to an application to withdraw consent, magistrates must have regard to the 'broad justice' of the situation (per Lord Widgery CJ in *Southampton Justices, ex parte Briggs* [1972] 1 All ER 573 at p. 280). They are entitled to take into account: (i) that the defendant had his rights as to mode of trial fully explained to him; (ii) that he understood those rights; (iii) that he voluntarily consented to be tried summarily; and (iv) that there were no unusual, difficult or grave features in the case (*Lambeth Metropolitan Stipendiary Magistrate, ex parte Wright* [1974] Crim LR 444, as explained by McCullough J in *Ex parte Hodgson* [1985] QB 1131 at p. 1140A–C).

(c) Since one of the most important factors in the mind of an accused deciding which court he would like to deal with his case is whether or not he believes he has any defence, a consent to summary trial made when unrepresented and intending to plead guilty through a misunderstanding of the law is invalid because, even if the accused understands the nature of the choice put to him in the sense of knowing the difference between trial on indictment and summary trial, he does not truly appreciate the *significance* of the choice for him (*Ex parte Hodgson*, see especially p. 1146D–H).

(d) It is implicit in the judgment of McCullough J that the fact that the accused was unrepresented when he consented to summary trial is not sufficient by itself to compel the court to allow a withdrawal of consent, even if he is subsequently advised that trial on indictment would be preferable. Conversely, although having had legal advice before consenting would obviously be a very powerful argument against an application to withdraw consent, there is no reason to suppose that it must inevitably be decisive. In *Highbury Corner Metropolitan Stipendiary Magistrate, ex parte Weekes* [1985] QB 1147, McCullough J (at pp. 1152F–1153A) held that there is no rule of law that a magistrates' court *must* adjourn before asking an unrepresented accused to decide if he consents so as to allow him to apply for legal aid.

(e) Most important, where the material before the magistrates shows that the accused, when he consented to summary trial, did not properly understand the 'nature and significance' of the choice put to him, the broad justice of the situation demands that he be allowed to withdraw consent (*Ex parte Hodgson* [1985] QB 1131 at pp. 1144–5).

(f) Where it is said that the accused did not understand the nature and significance of his choice, the court's view that the case is, in fact, more suitable for summary trial is *not* a factor which should tell against an application to withdraw consent (per McCullough J in *Ex parte Hodgson* [1985] QB 1131 at p. 1145A–B and *Ex parte Weekes* [1985] QB 1147 at p. 1152C–E).

Where the accused is arguing that he did not understand the consequences of his original consent to summary trial, it is for him to establish that fact, whether by his own evidence or other means. Moreover, if the justices hearing the application are different from those who originally sat, they must receive evidence as to what occurred at the earlier hearing (*Forest Magistrates' Court, ex parte Spicer* (1989) 153 JP 81). His consent to summary trial is likely, in practice, to be closely connected to whether he is pleading guilty or not. If, therefore, having consented to summary trial, he pleads guilty but is then allowed to change his plea, he should be allowed to withdraw his consent to summary trial and be put to his election again (*Bow Street Magistrates' Court, ex parte Welcombe* (1992) 156 JP 609). **D6.35**

Challenging Refusal of Magistrates to Allow Withdrawal of Consent

If an application by the accused to withdraw his consent to summary trial is refused, the refusal may be challenged by means of an application for judicial review. It will, however, be necessary to show either that the magistrates took into account irrelevant factors or ignored relevant ones when deciding to hold the accused to his original decision, or that they acted so unreasonably that no bench properly directing itself could have reached their decision. In *Highbury Corner Metropolitan Stipendiary Magistrate, ex parte Weekes* [1985] QB 1147, for example, the accused, who was aged 17, had not had the opportunity to consult a lawyer and did not properly understand what a Crown Court was. In those circumstances, it was plainly unreasonable for the magistrate to have rejected the defence application that the consent to summary trial be withdrawn. **D6.36**

ADJUSTMENT OF CHARGES TO DICTATE MODE OF TRIAL

It is possible for the prosecution to replace an existing charge with a new charge. Where the prosecution choose to replace an offence which is triable either way with an offence which is triable only summarily, the accused is thereby deprived of the possibility of trial by jury. In *Canterbury & St Augustine Justices, ex parte Klisiak* [1982] QB 398, it was held that the court **D6.37**

Part D Procedure

D

can prevent the prosecution from doing this only 'in the most obvious circumstances which disclose blatant injustice' (per Lord Lane CJ at p. 411F). In *Sheffield Justices, ex parte DPP* [1993] Crim LR 136, the Divisional Court said that it would be appropriate to interfere with the prosecutor's decision to replace an either-way charge with a summary-only charge only if there was evidence that the prosecutor had done so in order to manipulate the system (in other words, acting in bad faith). However, in *DPP v Hammerton* [2010] QB 79, where the accused was charged with attempted theft (triable either way) but the prosecution subsequently sought to replace the charge with one of interfering with a motor vehicle (a summary offence), Davis J pointed out that the courts now have to take into account the CrimPR, and in particular the overriding objective and said (at [24] and [30]) that:

> ... the language of 'proper and appropriate' better conveys the correct approach in cases of this kind ... I doubt if it now needs be shown that bad faith as such needs be shown in all cases before an application to substitute a new charge can be disallowed ...

> ... in the vast majority of cases everyone concerned will be entirely content for a lesser charge to be substituted. But where a lesser charge is to be substituted, first, it must be proper and appropriate to the facts of the case; secondly, the application should be made promptly and not left until the last minute, at all events without any proper explanation; and, thirdly, an eye should also be kept on considerations of the good administration of justice and the wider picture.

For example, the impact on any co-accused might be relevant.

D6.38   It is also possible for a charge which is triable either way to be replaced with a charge that is triable only on indictment. However, in *Brooks* [1985] Crim LR 385, the Court of Appeal warned that it would be unjust and wrong for the prosecution to do this if the magistrates have already accepted jurisdiction in respect of the either-way offence, since the prosecution would be frustrating the decision reached by the justices. The principles were summarised by Neill LJ in *Redbridge Justices, ex parte Whitehouse* [1992] 94 Cr App R 332 (at p. 338):

> (3) ... If the prosecution ... seek to prefer new charges or to substitute charges or to offer no evidence on certain charges the justices should consider the matter on its merits. The fact that the prosecution wish to add or substitute new charges either to ensure that the case is tried summarily or to ensure that it is tried in the Crown Court is not a ground for refusing the issue of a summons or other process provided that on the facts disclosed the justices are satisfied that the course proposed by the prosecution is proper and appropriate in the light of the facts put before them. Thus clearly the justices should not agree to the addition of a charge which is triable only on indictment if the facts are incapable of supporting such a charge and the fresh charge can be seen to be a device designed to deprive the justices of their jurisdiction to try the case themselves. (4) If the justices have already decided to try a matter summarily and the case is then adjourned, any later application by the prosecution to add an additional charge which would have the effect of making summary trial no longer possible should be scrutinised with particular care. The prosecution cannot be allowed improperly to frustrate the earlier decision of the justices. However, I do not understand the decision in *Brooks* ... as meaning that once the justices have decided on summary trial there are no circumstances in which the prosecutor can properly seek to add a further charge which is triable only on indictment ... (5) If the justices acting within their jurisdiction exercise their discretion bona fide and bring their minds to bear on the question whether they ought to grant a further summons or not, this Court is very unlikely to interfere except in an exceptional case where the decision satisfies the strict test of being unreasonable in a *Wednesbury* sense.

It must also be borne in mind that the Code for Crown Prosecutors, para. 6.4 (see **appendix 3**), states that: 'Prosecutors should not change the charge simply because of the decision made by the court or the defendant about where the case will be heard'.

CHALLENGING A DECISION BY A MAGISTRATES' COURT TO ACCEPT JURISDICTION

D6.39   It is difficult for the prosecution to mount a challenge against a decision in favour of summary trial, since it is essentially a matter within the magistrates' discretion. An application to quash a decision to accept jurisdiction will succeed only if the magistrates' decision was so obviously wrong that no reasonable magistrate could have arrived at it (*McLean, ex parte Metropolitan Police Commissioner* [1975] Crim LR 289). Nevertheless, in an appropriately clear-cut case, the Divisional Court will grant judicial review. In *Northampton Magistrates' Court, ex parte Commissioners of Customs and Excise* [1994] Crim LR 598, for example, the accused was charged with a VAT fraud which, on the prosecution case, had caused a loss of £193,000. The magistrates decided to try him summarily and the prosecution sought judicial review. The Divisional Court said that the correct approach was to ask whether the acceptance of jurisdiction was 'truly astonishing'. Here they must have concluded that it was, as they allowed the application and remitted the matter with a direction to the magistrates to reject jurisdiction.

MODE OF TRIAL FOR SUMMARY OFFENCES

D6.40 It follows from the basic definition of a summary offence as one which is triable *only* summarily that the question of mode of trial for such an offence does not normally arise. However, the CJA 1988, s. 40, provides that where certain specified summary offences (including common assault, driving while disqualified, taking a motor vehicle without the owner's consent, and criminal damage where the value involved is less than £5,000) are disclosed by the evidence on the basis of which an accused has been sent for trial in respect of an indictable offence, and the summary offence is either founded on the same facts as the indictable offence or forms with it a series of offences of the same or similar character, then the prosecution may include a count for the summary offence on the indictment and, if the accused pleads not guilty, the charge will be tried by a jury (see D11.17).

The CDA 1998, s. 51(6), provides that, where the court sends an accused for trial in respect of an indictable-only or either-way offence, it must also send him to the Crown Court for trial for any summary offence which appears to the court to be related to the offence(s) for which he is sent for trial, provided that the summary offence is punishable with imprisonment or involves disqualification from driving. Under sch. 3, para. 6, if the accused is convicted on the indictment, the Crown Court must, assuming it agrees that the summary offence is related to the offence(s) sent for trial under s. 51, ask the accused to enter a plea to the summary offence. If he pleads guilty, the Crown Court may deal with him in respect of that offence in any way in which a magistrates' court could have dealt with him; if he pleads not guilty, the powers of the Crown Court cease in respect of the summary offence (save that the court may dismiss the charge if the prosecution inform the court that they would not desire to submit evidence in respect of it). It is submitted that (even though para. 6 is silent as to the possibility) it would also be open to a Crown Court judge to try the summary offence, sitting as a District Judge (Magistrates' Courts) under the Courts Act 2003, s. 66 (see D3.16).

Section D7 Bail

INTRODUCTION

D7.1 Bail in criminal proceedings is governed by the Bail Act 1976 (BA 1976) (see s. 1(6) of the Act). 'Bail in criminal proceedings' is defined in s. 1(1) of the Act as: '(a) bail grantable in or in connection with proceedings for an offence to a person who is accused or convicted of the offence, or (b) bail grantable in connection with an offence to a person who is under arrest for the offence or for whose arrest for the offence a warrant (endorsed for bail) is being issued'. The procedural rules relating to bail are set out in the CrimPR, part 19 (see Supplement, **R-144**). This section is chiefly concerned with bail from magistrates' courts and the Crown Court. For bail in appeals to the Court of Appeal, see **D7.5** and **D27.14**.

The BA 1976 is set out at **D7.136**.

COURTS' POWER TO GRANT BAIL

Bail by Magistrates' Courts

D7.2 A magistrates' court, when adjourning a case where the proceedings were commenced by the accused being charged at the police station (rather than by the issue of a summons or a written charge and requisition), has to remand the accused. The remand may be in custody or on bail (see the MCA 1980, ss. 5(1), 10(1) and 18(4), at **D5.29**, for the jurisdiction to adjourn and remand at the preliminary stages of a case). Under the MCA 1980, s. 128(1), whenever a magistrates' court has power to remand a person, it may either remand him in custody or remand him on bail, in accordance with the BA 1976. For the time restrictions on remands in custody and the possibility of remanding an accused in his absence, see **D5.33**. Magistrates also have power to grant bail for the period of any remand for reports etc. after summary conviction (see the MCA 1980, s. 10(3), and also the PCC(S)A 2000, s. 11, for remands on bail for medical examination). Where a magistrates' court sends an accused to the Crown Court for trial, he may be kept in custody or released on bail (see **D10**). Similarly, committals for sentence may be in custody or on bail. Where a magistrates' court has summarily convicted an accused and passed a custodial sentence, it may grant him bail pending the determination of an appeal to the Crown Court or to the Divisional Court by way of case stated (MCA 1980, s. 113). The CAJA 2009, s. 115, provides that a person charged with murder may not be granted bail except by order of a Crown Court judge (see **D7.3**).

Bail by the Crown Court

The persons to whom the Crown Court may grant bail are listed in the Senior Courts Act 1981, **D7.3**
s. 81(1)(a)–(g). They are as follows:

(a) any person who has been sent in custody for trial in the Crown Court;
(b) any person who has been given a custodial sentence following conviction in the magistrates'
     court (whether he pleaded guilty or was found guilty) and who is appealing to the Crown
     Court against conviction and/or sentence;
(c) any person who is in the custody of the Crown Court pending disposal of his case (so when-
     ever the Crown Court adjourns a trial or adjourns between conviction and sentence, it has
     a discretion to grant the accused bail for the period of the adjournment);
(d) and (e) any person whose case has been decided by the Crown Court but who has applied
     to the court to state a case for the Divisional Court's opinion or is seeking judicial review of
     the decision;
(f) any person to whom the Crown Court has granted a certificate that his case is fit for appeal
     to the Court of Appeal, whether against conviction or against sentence; and
(g) any person who has been remanded in custody by a magistrates' court on adjourning a case
     under the PCC(S)A 2000, s. 11, the CDA 1998, s. 52(5), or the MCA 1980, ss. 5, 10, 17C,
     18 or 24C, provided the magistrates' court has granted a certificate that, before refusing
     bail, it heard full argument.

All the above powers are subject to the CJPO 1994, s. 25 (see **D7.8**).

Murder Cases   The CAJA 2009, s. 115(1), provides that a person charged with murder   **D7.4**
may not be granted bail except by order of a Crown Court judge. Where a person appears
before a magistrates' court charged with murder, the magistrates' court must commit him
(in custody) to the Crown Court (s. 115(4)). A Crown Court judge must then make a decision about bail as soon as reasonably practicable and, in any event, within the period of 48
hours (excluding weekends and public holidays) beginning with the day after the day on
which the person appears before the magistrates' court (s. 115(3)). These provisions apply
whether or not the accused is charged with one or more other offences as well as the murder
charge (s. 115(6)).

Bail by Court of Appeal (Criminal Division)

The Court of Appeal has jurisdiction to grant bail to a person who has served notice of appeal   **D7.5**
or notice of application for leave to appeal against his conviction and/or sentence in the Crown
Court (Criminal Appeal Act 1968, s. 19). The Court of Appeal also has power to bail a person
who is appealing from it to the Supreme Court (s. 36). These powers are again subject to the
CJPO 1994, s. 25 (see **D7.8**).

In *X* [2004] All ER (D) 400 (Feb), it was held that where a fresh indictment has been
preferred in the Crown Court following the quashing of a conviction and the ordering of
a retrial, the Court of Appeal no longer has jurisdiction in relation to bail. It follows that,
once a fresh indictment has been preferred, jurisdiction in relation to bail belongs with the
Crown Court.

PRINCIPLES GOVERNING BAIL

Presumption in Favour of Bail

Section 4(1) of the BA 1976, together with sch. 1, creates a rebuttable presumption in favour   **D7.6**
of bail (sometimes referred to, somewhat inaccurately, as a 'right to bail'). It provides that: 'A
person to whom this section applies shall be granted bail except as provided in Schedule 1 to

this Act'. Subsections (2)–(4) of s. 4 then define the persons who benefit from the presumption in favour of bail. They are:

(a) any person who appears before the Crown Court or a magistrates' court in the course of or in connection with proceedings for an offence, or applies to a court for bail (or for a variation of the conditions of bail) in connection with those proceedings (s. 4(2));

(b) any person who has been convicted of an offence and whose case is adjourned for reports before sentencing (s. 4(4)); and

(c) any person brought before the court under the CJA 2003, sch. 8, for alleged breach of a requirement of a community order (s. 4(3)).

Apart from cases where the accused has been convicted and the hearing has been adjourned for pre-sentence reports, s. 4(1) does *not* apply once a person has been convicted of an offence (as is made clear in the proviso to s. 4(2)). Therefore, an appellant seeking bail pending determination of his appeal has no presumption of bail operating in his favour. Neither does an offender who is committed to the Crown Court for sentence following conviction in a magistrates' court. In both those situations, there is power to grant bail, but its grant or refusal is entirely at the discretion of the court. It should also be noted that s. 4(1) does not apply to bail from the police station, although, once a detainee has been charged, the PACE 1984, s. 38(1), imposes on the custody officer a duty to grant him bail unless its refusal can be justified on grounds similar to those which would justify refusing bail to a person prima facie entitled to bail under s. 4(1). Despite the fact that there is no presumption in favour of bail in these situations, if bail is granted, it is 'bail in criminal proceedings' within the definition in the BA 1976, s. 1(1), and so the general provisions of the Act concerning bail apply (e.g., if the person fails without reasonable cause to surrender, he commits an offence under s. 6).

D7.7   **Bail following Indication of Guilty Plea at 'Plea before Venue' Hearing**   In *Rafferty* [1991] 1 Cr App R 235, the Court of Appeal dealt with the position where an accused gives an indication, as part of the 'plea before venue' procedure (see **D6.11** *et seq.*), that he will plead guilty, and is then committed for sentence to the Crown Court. Their lordships stated that, in most such cases, it would not be usual to alter the position as regards bail or custody. When a person who had been on bail pleads guilty at the plea before venue, the usual practice should be to continue bail, even if it is anticipated that a custodial sentence will be imposed by the Crown Court, unless there are good reasons for remanding the accused in custody. If the accused is in custody, then it would be unusual, if the reasons for remanding him in custody remained unchanged, to alter the position.

No Bail for Homicide or Rape if Previous Conviction

D7.8   Under the CJPO 1994, s. 25, the court may not grant bail to an accused who is charged with (or has been convicted of) murder, attempted murder, manslaughter, rape or attempted rape, or certain other offences under the SOA 2003, if he has been convicted of any of these offences (or culpable homicide) in the past unless it is of the opinion that there are exceptional circumstances which justify it. In a case where the previous conviction was for manslaughter, the restriction applies only if the accused received a custodial sentence for that offence. 'Conviction' is widely defined to include a finding that the defendant was not guilty by reason of insanity, or was found to have done the act or made the omission charged in a case where he was unfit to plead. Previous convictions in other EU Member States are treated as being relevant previous convictions if the corresponding offences in the UK would be so treated.

It was suggested by the Law Commission in its paper *Bail and the Human Rights Act 1998* (Law Com No. 269) that the CJPO 1994, s. 25, is liable to be misunderstood and applied in a way which is incompatible with ECHR, Article 5. The problem with s. 25 is that it appears to create a statutory presumption against the grant of bail in cases to which it applies. If so, it conflicts with the Convention's starting point of the presumption of liberty, and substitutes a presumption of custodial remand. The Commission suggested that the court should go through the usual process of balancing factors for and against the granting of bail. Because of the provisions of s. 25, however, it should give special weight to those counting against the grant of bail. Thus the court would take all relevant circumstances into account, but might nonetheless deny bail because the case fell within s. 25, where it might not otherwise have done so.

Section 25 was considered by the House of Lords in *R (O) v Harrow Crown Court* [2007] 1 **D7.9** AC 249. The House had to consider, in particular, the effect of s. 25 upon the right to bail of a defendant during the currency of the custody time-limit provided by the Prosecution of Offences Act 1985, s. 22, and upon the expiry of such a custody time-limit (see **D15.7** *et seq.* for detailed discussion of custody time-limits). The claimant submitted that, once the court had refused to extend a custody time-limit because of the prosecution's failure to act 'with all due diligence and expedition' within the meaning of s. 22(3)(b) of the 1985 Act, the court could not refuse bail without thereby violating the ECHR, Article 5(3). The House of Lords held that, where an application for bail is made during the currency of the custody time-limit, s. 25 should be read as placing an evidential burden on the defendant to 'point to or produce material which supports the existence of exceptional circumstances' (per Lord Carswell at [12]); if he fails to do so, bail should be denied. Lord Brown of Eaton-under-Heywood (at [35]) said that in the vast majority of cases, the court will be able to reach a clear view one way or the other whether the conditions for withholding bail, specified by the BA 1976, sch. 1, are satisfied. However, the court may occasionally be left unsure as to whether the defendant should be released on bail. This is the only situation in which the burden of proof assumes any relevance, and in such a case bail would have to be granted. That must be, said his lordship, the 'default position', and s. 25 should be read down to make that plain. Dealing with the relationship between s. 25 and the custody time-limit provisions, it was held that s. 25 operates to disapply the ordinary requirement under the Prosecution of Offences (Custody Time Limits) Regulations 1987, reg. 6(6), that bail should be granted automatically to anyone whose custody time-limit has expired. Their lordships held that, thus applied, s. 25 is compatible with Article 5(3). They reasoned that the jurisprudence of the Strasbourg court demonstrates that, even where a lack of due diligence is causative of delay, it will not necessarily find a violation of Article 5(3), although in such circumstances the English courts would be likely to refuse an extension of the custody time-limit. Their lordships would not expect there to be many cases where bail is refused notwithstanding the court's refusal to extend the custody time-limit, but there is no necessary inconsistency between the two, and Article 5(3) is not necessarily thereby breached.

In *O'Dowd v UK* (2012) 54 EHRR 187, the accused complained, under the ECHR, Article 5(3) (taken together with Article 14), that the CJPO 1994, s. 25, unfairly discriminates against those with previous convictions for certain offences. The ECtHR noted (at [81]) that the accused's previous convictions arose from an incident which was factually very similar to the alleged offences with which he was subsequently charged and so were 'comparable both in nature and degree of seriousness'. In those circumstances, the accused could not 'claim to be in an analogous position to a defendant charged with the same offence who does not have a previous similar offence' (at [82]). It followed that his complaint was 'manifestly ill-founded'. Presumably, the answer would be different if the offences lacked that degree of similarity.

Criminal Justice and Public Order Act 1994, s. 25　　　　**D7.10**

(1) A person who in any proceedings has been charged with or convicted of an offence to which this section applies in circumstances to which it applies shall be granted bail in those proceedings only if the court or, as the case may be, the constable considering the grant of bail is of the opinion that there are exceptional circumstances which justify it.

(2) This section applies, subject to subsection (3) below, to the following offences, that is to say—
  (a) murder;
  (b) attempted murder;
  (c) manslaughter;
  (d) rape under the law of Scotland;

    (e)   an offence under section 1 of the Sexual Offences Act 1956 (rape);

    (f)   an offence under section 1 of the Sexual Offences Act 2003 (rape);

    (g)   an offence under section 2 of that Act (assault by penetration);

    (h)   an offence under section 4 of that Act (causing a person to engage in sexual activity without consent), where the activity caused involved penetration within subsection (4)(a) to (d) of that section;

    (i)   an offence under section 5 of that Act (rape of a child under 13);

    (j)   an offence under section 6 of that Act (assault of a child under 13 by penetration);

    (k)   an offence under section 8 of that Act (causing or inciting a child under 13 to engage in sexual activity), where an activity involving penetration within subsection (2)(a) to (d) of that section was caused;

    (l)   an offence under section 30 of that Act (sexual activity with a person with a mental disorder impeding choice), where the touching involved penetration within subsection (3)(a) to (d) of that section;

    (m)   an offence under section 31 of that Act (causing or inciting a person, with a mental disorder impeding choice, to engage in sexual activity), where an activity involving penetration within subsection (3)(a) to (d) of that section was caused;

    (ma)–(mh)   [equivalent offences under the law of Northern Ireland]

    (n)   an attempt to commit an offence within any of paragraphs (d) to (mh).

(3) This section applies in the circumstances described in subsection (3A) or (3B) only.

(3A) This section applies where—

    (a)   the person has been previously convicted by or before a court in any part of the United Kingdom of any offence within subsection (2) or of culpable homicide, and

    (b)   if that previous conviction is one of manslaughter or culpable homicide—

       (i)   the person was then a child or young person, and was sentenced to long-term detention under any of the relevant enactments, or

       (ii)   the person was not then a child or young person, and was sentenced to imprisonment or detention.

(3B) This section applies where—

    (a)   the person has been previously convicted by or before a court in another member State of any relevant foreign offence corresponding to an offence within subsection (2) or to culpable homicide, and

    (b)   if the previous conviction is of a relevant foreign offence corresponding to the offence of manslaughter or culpable homicide—

       (i)   the person was then a child or young person, and was sentenced to detention for a period in excess of 2 years, or

       (ii)   the person was not then a child or young person, and was sentenced to detention.

(4) This section applies whether or not an appeal is pending against conviction or sentence.

(5) In this section—

'conviction' includes—

    (a)   a finding that a person is not guilty by reason of insanity;

    (b)   a finding under section 4A(3) of the Criminal Procedure (Insanity) Act 1964 (cases of unfitness to plead) that a person did the act or made the omission charged against him; and

    (c)   a conviction of an offence for which an order is made discharging the offender absolutely or conditionally;

and 'convicted' shall be construed accordingly;

'the relevant enactments' means—

    (a)   as respects England and Wales, section 91 of the Powers of Criminal Courts (Sentencing) Act 2000;

    (b)   as respects Scotland, sections 205(1) to (3) and 208 of the Criminal Procedure (Scotland) Act 1995;

    (c)   as respects Northern Ireland, section 73(2) of the Children and Young Persons Act (Northern Ireland) 1968;

'relevant foreign offence', in relation to a member State other than the United Kingdom, means an offence under the law in force in that member State.

(5A) For the purposes of subsection (3B), a relevant foreign offence corresponds to another offence if the relevant foreign offence would have constituted that other offence if it had been done in any part of the United Kingdom at the time when the relevant foreign offence was committed.

REFUSING BAIL TO AN ACCUSED CHARGED WITH AN IMPRISONABLE OFFENCE

Part I of sch. 1 to the 1976 Act sets out the circumstances in which an accused may be refused   **D7.11**
bail if at least one offence with which he is charged (or for which he awaits sentence) is triable on indictment and punishable with imprisonment (part IA applies where the offences(s)
are imprisonable summary offences, and part II applies when none of the offences are
imprisonable).

An unconvicted accused charged with an offence which is imprisonable and triable on indictment need not be granted bail if one or more of the grounds for a remand in custody (listed in
the BA 1976, sch. 1, part I, paras. 2 to 6A) is applicable. The first — and most commonly relied
on — ground (para. 2) subdivides into three. As regards offenders convicted but remanded for
reports, there is a further ground (para. 7) on which reliance may also be placed. The statutory
grounds for refusing bail are as follows.

Risk of Absconding, Further Offences or Interference with Witnesses

Bail Act 1976, sch. 1, para. 2   **D7.12**

(1) The defendant need not be granted bail if the court is satisfied that there are substantial
    grounds for believing that the defendant, if released on bail (whether subject to conditions or
    not) would—
    (a) fail to surrender to custody, or
    (b) commit an offence while on bail, or
    (c) interfere with witnesses or otherwise obstruct the course of justice, whether in relation to
        himself or any other person.

Standard of Proof   The opening words of para. 2(1) do *not* require the court to be satisfied that   **D7.13**
the consequences specified in subparagraphs (a)–(c) will in fact occur in the event of bail being
granted, or even to be satisfied that they are more likely than not to occur. The court merely has
to be satisfied that there are 'substantial grounds for believing' that they would occur. Although
the question posed by para. 2 is whether substantial grounds exist for believing that a future
event will occur and to that extent is a question of fact, it is not a question which can be answered
according to the usual rules of evidence. Thus in *Re Moles* [1981] Crim LR 170 it was held that
a police officer explaining the objections to bail was entitled to recount what he had been told
by a potential witness about the threats the latter had received, with a view to showing that the
granting of bail would lead to further interference with witnesses. In *Mansfield Justices, ex parte
Sharkey* [1985] QB 613, Lord Lane CJ referred to *Re Moles* and said (at p. 626A): '...there is
no requirement for formal evidence to be given [at an application for bail]...It was for example
sufficient for the facts to be related to the justices at second hand by a police officer.' Current
practice when presenting objections to bail in a magistrates' court is not even to have a police
officer present, but for the CPS representative to argue that bail is inappropriate on the basis of
information supplied by the police and included in the file.

In *R (F) v Southampton Crown Court* [2009] EWHC 2206 (Admin), the judge had refused to   **D7.14**
grant bail because he was 'not sure' the accused would 'turn up or stay out of trouble'. On appeal,
Collins J (at [3]) noted that the correct test under the BA 1976 'requires the judge to have substantial grounds for believing that the defendant before him would fail to surrender, commit
offences on bail, or transgress one of the other provisions in schedule 1'. The judge had therefore
applied the wrong test. As Collins J said (at [8]): 'It is not a question of him not being sure that
the defendant would turn up or stay out of trouble'; rather, 'he was only entitled to refuse bail
if there were substantial grounds for believing that he would breach [his bail], he would fail to
turn up or would commit further offences'. The case was therefore remitted to the Crown Court
for reconsideration applying the correct test.

The importance of applying the correct test was emphasised again in *R (Shehzad) v Newcastle Crown Court* [2012] EWHC 1453 (Admin). In that case, the Crown Court judge had said that the accused had 'every reason to fail to surrender, there is the possibility of further offences and there is a risk of interference with witnesses, principally of course the principal witness for the prosecution. In those circumstances I refuse his application for bail'. An application for judicial review was made on the basis that the judge's phraseology suggested that he had applied a lower threshold of satisfaction in relation to the various matters that can operate as a basis for refusing bail than the 'substantial grounds for believing' test. Foskett J (at [10] and [11]) said that the Crown Court judge was extremely experienced, applied the statutory test on an almost daily basis and was therefore 'very unlikely to have misapplied the usual approach to decisions of this nature'. However, it was right for the accused to have his case 'assessed by the correct statutory formulation' so the refusal of bail was quashed and the matter remitted to the Crown Court to be dealt with by another judge. A similar approach was taken in *Charles* [2012] EWHC 2581 (Admin), where the court accepted (at [24]) the accused's submission that, when the bail ruling was read as a whole, it appeared that 'the learned judge failed to ask himself the right questions'.

D7.15　**No Real Prospect of a Custodial Sentence**　Paragraph 1A of sch. 1 provides that para. 2 does not apply where the accused has attained the age of 18, and has not been convicted of an offence in those proceedings, and it appears to the court that there is no real prospect that the accused will be sentenced to a custodial sentence in the proceedings. In such a case, bail cannot be withheld on any of the grounds set out in para. 2. Moreover, para. 2(2) of sch. 1 provides that, where the accused falls within para. 6B (drugs offences), para. 2 does not apply unless the court is of the opinion that there is no significant risk of the accused committing an offence while on bail (para. 6A: see **D7.30**).

D7.16　**Relevant Factors**　Certain factors to which the court should have regard when taking a decision under para. 2 are listed in para. 9. These factors are:

(a) the nature and seriousness of the offence and the probable method of dealing with the offender for it;
(b) the character, antecedents, associations and community ties of the accused;
(c) his 'record' for having answered bail in the past;
(d) the strength of the evidence against him; and
(e) if the court is satisfied that there are substantial grounds for believing that the accused would commit an offence while on bail, the risk that the accused may engage in conduct likely to cause physical or mental injury to anyone else.

D7.17　*Nature and seriousness of offence (para. 9(a)).* The relevance of the offence alleged being serious is that the accused will know that, if convicted, he is likely to receive a severe sentence and will therefore be tempted to abscond rather than run the risk of such a sentence. The gravity of the charge is not an automatic reason for refusing bail (although, by virtue of the CJPO 1994, s. 25, an accused must normally be refused bail where the charge is, e.g., homicide or rape and he has previously been convicted of such an offence (see **D7.8**)). Indeed, in *Hurnam v State of Mauritius* [2006] 1 WLR 857, the Privy Council said that the seriousness of an offence cannot be treated as a conclusive reason for refusing bail to an unconvicted suspect: the right to personal liberty is an important constitutional right and a suspect should remain at large unless it is necessary to refuse bail in order to serve one of the ends for which detention before trial is permissible. Lord Bingham said (at [15]):

> The seriousness of the offence and the severity of the penalty likely to be imposed on conviction may well…provide grounds for refusing bail, but they do not do so of themselves, without more: they are factors relevant to the judgment whether, in all the circumstances, it is necessary to deprive the applicant of his liberty. Whether or not that is the conclusion reached, clear and explicit reasons should be given.

The statutory presumption in favour of bail continues to apply after conviction where there is an adjournment before sentence is passed. In *R (R) v Snaresbrook Crown Court* [2011] EWHC

3569 (Admin), the Divisional Court considered the refusal of bail because of the likelihood of a custodial sentence. Holman J said (at [24]) that, of itself, 'the mere fact that a person has been convicted and a custodial sentence is inevitable, is not sufficient to trigger the exception to bail. It still is necessary that the court is satisfied that there are substantial grounds for believing that one of the statutory exceptions [to the presumption in favour of bail] applies.' This point is reiterated at [31], where his lordship said that, 'even the inevitability of a custodial sentence is not itself an exception to the right to bail, unless it justifies a court being satisfied that there are substantial grounds for believing that the defendant would fail to surrender to custody'.

Character and antecedents (para. 9(b)). This refers primarily to previous convictions. These may **D7.18** make a custodial sentence more likely (especially if the accused, if convicted of the present offence, will be in breach of a suspended sentence of imprisonment). Moreover, a person of previous good character is more likely to be trusted by the courts than one with a criminal record. Previous convictions under the BA 1976, s. 6, for failing to surrender to custody in answer to bail are especially relevant (see subparagraph (c)).

Associations and community ties (para. 9(b)). The word 'associations' is generally taken to refer **D7.19** to undesirable friends with criminal records. Examining the 'community ties' of the accused involves looking at how easy it would be for the accused to abscond and how much he has to lose by absconding. How long has he lived at his present address? Is he single or married? Does he have dependent children? Is he in employment? How long has he had his present job? Does he have a mortgage or a protected tenancy? An accused of 'no fixed abode' or living in short-term accommodation is not automatically debarred from bail, but the ease with which he could disappear to another address is a factor to be considered.

Bail record (para. 9(c)). Considering the bail record of the accused requires the court to consider **D7.20** whether he has absconded in the past. Absconding in earlier proceedings is regarded as evidence of a risk that he may do so again.

Strength of the prosecution evidence (para. 9(d)). This is relevant to whether an accused would **D7.21** answer bail, in the sense that one who knows there is a good chance of being acquitted is less likely to abscond than one who anticipates almost certain conviction. It can be argued that there is no point in the accused absconding if he is likely to be acquitted anyway. Conversely, if the prosecution case is strong, so that conviction is likely, he may abscond rather than 'face the music' (especially if a custodial sentence is likely). It is also relevant that a remand in custody followed by acquittal creates a manifest, if sometimes unavoidable, injustice. In borderline cases, where the arguments against bail are strong but not overwhelming, the court may prefer to run the risk of the accused absconding etc. rather than run the risk of his being acquitted after a long period in custody on remand.

Risk of injury to someone else (para. 9(e)). Where the court is satisfied that there are substantial **D7.22** grounds for believing that the accused would commit an offence while on bail, the court considers whether that offence is likely to cause physical or mental injury to any other person.

Paragraph 9 concludes with the words 'as well as to any others [i.e. considerations] which appear to be relevant', thus making it clear that the considerations mentioned in para. 9(a)–(e) are *not* exhaustive. Those 'others' might include the fact that the accused has previously committed offences while on bail, or the suggestion that potential prosecution witnesses have already received threats and/or are known to the accused and could easily be contacted by him if he were at liberty. Also, it should be noted that the BA 1976, s. 4(9), stipulates that 'in taking any decisions required by Part I or II of Schedule 1 to this Act, the considerations to which the court is to have regard include, so far as relevant, any misuse of controlled drugs by the defendant'.

Other Grounds for Withholding Bail

Part I of sch. 1 to the BA 1976 sets out a number of other grounds for withholding bail: risk of **D7.23** injury to an 'associated person' (para. 2ZA); where the accused is charged with an indictable offence and is already on bail (para. 2A); for the accused's own protection (para. 3); where the accused is already serving a custodial sentence for another offence (para. 4); where the court has insufficient information (para. 5); where the accused has absconded in the present proceedings (para. 6). Additionally, where the accused is charged with murder, para. 6ZA restricts the circumstances in which bail can be granted.

D7.24   **Risk to an 'associated person'**   By virtue of para. 2ZA, the accused need not be granted bail if the court is satisfied that there are substantial grounds for believing that he would, if released on bail, commit an offence while on bail by engaging in conduct that would, or would be likely to, cause physical or mental injury to an associated person, or else cause such a person to fear such injury. For this purpose, an 'associated person' is a person who is associated with the accused within the meaning of the Family Law Act 1996, s. 62.

D7.25   **Accused Already on Bail**   Under para. 2A, if the offence is an indictable one (this includes either-way offences), the accused need not be granted bail if it appears to the court that the accused was on bail in criminal proceedings on the date of the offence. However, by virtue of para. 1A, para. 2A does not apply where the accused has attained the age of 18, and has not been convicted of an offence in the current proceedings, and it appears to the court that there is no real prospect that he will be sentenced to a custodial sentence in the proceedings.

D7.26   **Own Protection**   Under para. 3, the accused need not be granted bail if the court is satisfied that he should be kept in custody for his own protection. This will cover cases where the offence alleged has caused anger in the area where it was committed and there is a risk of members of the public exacting instant revenge on the person believed to be responsible. Where the accused is a juvenile, bail may be refused under para. 3 if he should be kept in custody 'for his own welfare'.

D7.27   **Already in Custody**   Under para. 4, the accused need not be granted bail if he is already serving a custodial sentence (whether imposed by a civilian court or by a court-martial). Paragraph 4 applies only if the accused is in custody pursuant to a sentence, not when he is in custody as a result of a remand in other proceedings currently outstanding against him. Where an accused is certain to be in custody for the foreseeable future, the court may find it more convenient to grant what may be regarded as technical bail; this avoids the restrictions on the periods for which remands in custody may be ordered and the consequent need to bring the accused back to court for further remand hearings. A frequently occurring practical problem where an accused is in custody to another court or is a serving prisoner is that the onus is on the CPS to obtain a Home Office production order (HOPO) obliging the prison service to arrange for the accused's attendance. This problem is mitigated to some extent by the availability of live links under the CDA 1998, s. 57B (see **D5.38**).

D7.28   **Insufficient Time**   Under para. 5, the accused need not be granted bail if the court is satisfied that, owing to lack of time since the commencement of the proceedings, it has not been practicable to obtain sufficient information for the purposes of taking the decision on bail. In such cases, the court might remand in custody (possibly for a shorter than usual period) to enable the necessary information to be discovered. Paragraph 5 might apply, for example, where the police are not satisfied that the accused has given them his correct particulars and think he may have previous convictions under another name, or if time is needed to check an address given by the accused, or if inquiries are still in hand which may reveal the offence to be more serious than originally supposed and/or that the accused has committed additional offences. It is submitted that para. 5 should be relied on sparingly, and should not be used to justify dilatoriness on the part of the police or the prosecution in marshalling the objections to bail.

A remand in custody under para. 5 does not amount to a decision not to grant bail for the purposes of para. 2 of part IIA, and so does not restrict further applications for bail (see **D7.70**).

D7.29   **Absconded in the Present Proceedings**   Under para. 6, the accused need not be granted bail if, having previously been released on bail in connection with the current proceedings, he has been arrested under the BA 1976, s. 7 (see D7.136). However, by virtue of para. 1A, para. 6 does not apply where the accused has attained the age of 18, and has not been convicted of an offence in the current proceedings, and it appears to the court that there is no real prospect that he will be sentenced to a custodial sentence in the proceedings.

Bail in Cases involving Abuse of Drugs   Paragraphs 6A to 6C of the BA 1976, sch. 1, part I,   **D7.30** provide that an accused aged 18 or over may not be granted bail, unless the court is of the opinion that there is no significant risk of his committing an offence while on bail, where the three conditions set out in para. 6B apply, namely:

(1) there is drug test evidence (by way of a lawful test obtained under the PACE 1984, s. 63B, or the CJA 2003, s. 161) that the person has a specified Class A drug in his body;
(2) either he is charged with an offence under the Misuse of Drugs Act 1971, s. 5(2) or (3), and the offence relates to a specified Class A drug, or the court is satisfied that there are substantial grounds for believing that the misuse of a specified Class A drug caused or contributed to the offence with which he is charged or that offence was motivated wholly or partly by his intended misuse of a specified Class A drug; and
(3) the person does not agree to undergo an assessment (carried out by a suitably qualified person) of whether he is dependent upon or has a propensity to misuse any specified Class A drugs, or he has undergone such an assessment but does not agree to participate in any relevant follow-up which has been offered.

If an assessment or follow-up is proposed and agreed to, it will be a condition of bail that it is undertaken (BA 1976, s. 3(6D)).

The phrase 'may not' is a prohibitive one and makes it plain that the court should not grant bail unless satisfied that there was no significant risk of the accused committing offences while on bail. In essence, the presumption created by the BA 1976, s. 4, is reversed and it becomes necessary for the court to be persuaded that there is no significant risk of the accused committing an offence if released on bail (cf. *R (Wiggins) v Harrow Crown Court* [2005] EWHC 882 (Admin), per Collins J, at [24]).

Murder   Under para. 6ZA, an accused who is charged with murder may not be granted bail   **D7.31** unless the court is of the opinion that there is no significant risk that he will, if released on bail, commit an offence that would, or would be likely to, cause physical or mental injury to any other person. Again, the presumption in favour of bail is effectively reversed.

Convicted Offenders: Adjourning for Reports

Under the BA 1976, sch. 1, part I, para. 7, if the case of a convicted offender is adjourned for   **D7.32** inquiries or reports, he need not be granted bail if it appears to the court that it would be impracticable to complete the inquiries or make the report without keeping him in custody (e.g., because he would not voluntarily attend for purposes such as seeing a probation officer or being medically examined). It is submitted that, where a court needs a pre-sentence report before it will be in a position to decide the appropriate sentence, the normal practice should be to grant bail unless there are exceptional reasons for keeping the offender in custody. It should be borne in mind that a remand in custody might appear to be prejudging the question of whether the ultimate sentence should be custodial.

Juveniles

The BA 1976, sch. 1, contains some additional provisions that are specific to cases where the acc-   **D7.33** used is under the age of 18. Paragraph 9AA provides that, if the accused is under the age of 18 and it appears to the court that he was on bail (in respect of other proceedings) at the date of the current alleged offence, the court must (when deciding whether it is satisfied that there are substantial grounds for believing that he will, if released on bail, commit an offence) give 'particular weight' to the fact that he was on bail in respect of another alleged offence on the date of the current alleged offence.

Paragraph 9AB(3) applies where the accused is under the age of 18 and it appears to the court that, having been released on bail in connection with the proceedings for the present offence, he has failed to surrender to custody. In such a case, the court must (when deciding whether it is satisfied that there are substantial grounds for believing that the accused will, if released on bail, fail to surrender to custody) give 'particular weight' to certain matters: where the accused did not have reasonable cause for his failure to surrender to custody, the fact that he failed to surrender to custody; and where he did have reasonable cause for his failure to surrender to custody, the fact that he failed to surrender to custody as soon as reasonably practicable after the time when he should have done so.

D7.34   The BA 1976, s. 9A, provides that, where an accused under the age of 18 is charged with an offence to which the MCA 1980, s. 22, applies (criminal damage where the value involved is £5,000 or less), and the trial of that offence has not begun, a magistrates' court (this includes a youth court) considering whether to withhold or grant bail must consider, having regard to any representations from the prosecution and the accused person, whether the value exceeds £5,000. If the value involved is less than £5,000, the BA 1976, sch. 1, part IA (see **D7.136**) will apply.

REFUSING BAIL TO AN ACCUSED CHARGED WITH SUMMARY AND NON-IMPRISONABLE OFFENCES

Imprisonable Summary Offences

D7.35   Under the BA 1976, sch. 1, part I, para. 1(2), where the imprisonable offence is a summary offence, or an offence to which the MCA 1980, s. 22, applies (criminal damage where the value involved is £5,000 or less), part I of sch. 1 does not apply. In such cases, the BA 1976, sch. 1, part IA, applies instead. Under part 1A, the exceptions to the presumption in favour of bail are as follows:

(a) where the accused has previously been granted bail and has failed to surrender to custody in those proceedings, and the court believes, in view of that failure, that he would, if released on bail, fail to surrender to custody (para. 2);

(b) where the accused was on bail on the date of the current alleged offence and the court is satisfied that there are substantial grounds for believing that, if released on bail, he would commit an offence while on bail (para. 3);

(c) where the court is satisfied that there are substantial grounds for believing that, if released on bail, the accused would commit an offence while on bail by engaging in conduct that would, or would be likely to, cause physical or mental injury to an associated person (as defined by the Family Law Act 1996, s. 62), or cause such a person to fear physical or mental injury (para. 4);

(d) where the court is satisfied that the accused should be kept in custody for his own protection (or welfare, if a juvenile) (para. 5);

(e) where the accused is already serving a custodial sentence (para. 6);

(f) where the accused has been arrested under the BA 1976, s. 7, and the court is satisfied that there are substantial grounds for believing that, if released on bail, he would fail to surrender to custody, commit an offence while on bail or interfere with witnesses or otherwise obstruct the course of justice (whether in relation to himself or any other person) (para. 7);

(g) where the court is satisfied that it has not been practicable to obtain sufficient information for the purpose of taking the decision on whether or not to grant bail for want of time since the institution of the proceedings against him (para. 8); and

(h) where part 1, paras. 6A to 6C, would otherwise be applicable were the current offence an indictable one (para. 9).

The BA 1976, sch. 1, part IA, para. 1A, provides that para. 2 (failure to surrender to custody), para. 3 (committing offences while on bail) and para. 7 (accused arrested under s. 7) do not apply where the accused has attained the age of 18, and has not been convicted of an offence in the proceedings, and it appears to the court that there is 'no real prospect that the defendant will be sentenced to a custodial sentence in the proceedings'.

Non-imprisonable Offences

Part II of sch. 1 to the BA 1976 sets out the reasons which permit the refusal of bail to an accused charged solely with one or more non-imprisonable offences. The grounds for withholding bail in such cases are as follows: **D7.36**

(a) where the accused is under the age of 18 or has been convicted of an offence in those pro-
    ceedings and (in either case) having been previously granted bail in criminal proceedings,
    he has failed to surrender to custody and the court believes, in view of that failure, that he
    would fail to surrender to custody (para. 2);
(b) where the court is satisfied that the accused should be kept in custody for his own protection
    (or welfare, if a juvenile) (para. 3);
(c) where the accused is already serving a custodial sentence (para. 4);
(d) where the accused is under the age of 18 or has been convicted of an offence in those pro-
    ceedings, and (in either case) he has been arrested under the BA 1976, s. 7, and the court
    is satisfied that there are substantial grounds to believe that he would fail to surrender to
    custody, commit an offence on bail, or interfere with witnesses or otherwise obstruct the
    course of justice (para. 5);
(e) where the accused has been arrested under s. 7 and the court is satisfied that there are sub-
    stantial grounds for believing that, if released on bail, he would commit an offence while
    on bail by engaging in conduct that would, or would be likely to, cause physical or mental
    injury to an associated person (as defined by the Family Law Act 1996, s. 62), or to cause
    such a person to fear such injury (para. 6).

It should be noted that the grounds of 'risk of absconding etc.' and 'insufficient time' for refusing bail to someone charged with imprisonable offences do *not* apply where the offences are
non-imprisonable.

BAIL AND THE EUROPEAN CONVENTION ON HUMAN RIGHTS

Article 5 of the ECHR (see **A7.58**), which provides that 'everyone has the right to liberty and security of the person', has clear relevance to bail. It lays down that no one shall be deprived of his liberty save in the six sets of circumstances specified in Article 5(1)(a)–(f). The list of excep-tions is exhaustive, and has been described in Strasbourg as ensuring that no one is deprived of liberty in an 'arbitrary fashion' (*Engel v Netherlands* (1979–80) 1 EHRR 647).   **D7.37**

The Law Commission (Law Com No. 269) considered the impact of the HRA 1998 on the law governing decisions taken by the police and the courts to grant or refuse bail in criminal pro-ceedings. The Commission noted that Article 5 of the ECHR states that, although reasonable suspicion that the detained person has committed an offence can be sufficient to justify pre-trial detention for a short time, the national authorities must thereafter show additional grounds for detention. They summarised the five additional grounds recognised under the ECHR as follows, namely where the purpose of detention is to avoid a real risk that, were the accused to be released:

(1) he would fail to attend trial;
(2) he would interfere with evidence or witnesses, or otherwise obstruct the course of justice;
(3) he would commit an offence while on bail;
(4) he would be at risk of harm against which he would be inadequately protected; or
(5) a disturbance to public order would result.

The Law Commission concluded that there are no provisions in the BA 1976 which are incompatible with Convention rights. However, the Commission did produce a guide to assist decision-makers to apply the Act in a way that is compatible with the ECHR. This emphasises that an accused should be refused bail only where detention is necessary for a purpose which Strasbourg jurisprudence has recognised as legitimate, in the sense that detention may be compatible with the accused's right to release under Article 5(3). Thus, a domestic court exercising its powers in a way which is compatible with the Convention rights should refuse bail only where it can be justified both under the ECHR, as interpreted in Strasbourg jurisprudence, and domestic legislation. The guidance also points out that detention will be necessary only if the risk relied upon as the ground for withholding bail could not be adequately addressed by the imposition of appropriate bail conditions. Thus, the Commission concluded that conditional bail should be used in preference to detention where a bail condition could adequately address the risk that would otherwise justify detention. Furthermore, the court refusing bail should give reasons for finding that detention is necessary. Those reasons should be closely related to the individual circumstances pertaining to the accused, and be capable of supporting the conclusion of the court.

D7.38 In *R (Fergus) v Southampton Crown Court* [2008] EWHC 3273 (Admin), Silber J (at [19]) referred to *R (Thompson) v Central Criminal Court* [2005] EWHC 2345 (Admin), in which Collins J (at [10]) had said:

> The approach under the Bail Act is entirely consistent with the approach which the European Court has regarded as proper under Article 5, namely there must be a grant of bail unless there are good reasons to refuse. The approach therefore really is not should there be bail granted but should custody be opposed, that is, is it necessary for the defendant to be in custody. That is the approach that the court should take. Only if persuaded that it is necessary should a remand in custody take place. It would be necessary if the court decides that whatever conditions can be reasonably imposed in relation to bail there are nevertheless substantial grounds for believing that the defendant will either fail to surrender to custody, commit an offence, interfere with witnesses or otherwise obstruct justice.

Silber J concluded (at [21]) that certain consequences flowed from this:

> First, it is not reasonable for a court to withdraw bail unless it is necessary to do so especially as any decision to withdraw bail engages rights under Article 5. Second, any such reason justifying the decision to withdraw bail must be stated by the decision maker explaining why bail should be withdrawn and that reason must relate to the facts. Such a reason must be more than merely reciting that one of the statutory grounds has been made out. The underlying facts have to be put forward.

Strasbourg Case Law

D7.39 Under Article 5, a person charged with an offence must be released pending trial unless there are 'relevant and sufficient' reasons to justify continued detention (*Wemhoff v Germany* (1979–80) 1 EHRR 55, at [12]). The case law of the European Court shows that this is interpreted in a way that is very similar to the UK's BA 1976. The grounds accepted by the ECtHR for withholding bail include:

(1) *the risk that the accused will fail to appear at the trial*. This has been defined as requiring 'a whole set of circumstances. . .which give reason to suppose that the consequences and hazards of flight will seem to him to be a lesser evil than continued imprisonment' (*Stogmuller v Austria* (1979–80) 1 EHRR 155, at [15]). The court can take account of 'the character of the person involved, his morals, his home, his occupation, his assets, his family ties, and all kinds of links with the country in which he is being prosecuted' (*Neumeister v Austria* (1979–80) 1 EHRR 91, at [10]). The likely sentence is relevant but cannot of itself justify the refusal of bail (*Letellier v France* (1992) 14 EHRR 83, at [43]);

(2) *the risk that the accused will interfere with the course of justice* (e.g., interfering with witnesses, warning other suspects, destroying relevant evidence). There must be an identifiable risk and there must be plausible evidence in support (cf. *Clooth v Belgium* (1992) 14 EHRR 717);

(3) *preventing the commission of further offences*. There must be good reason to believe that the accused will commit offences while on bail (cf. *Toth v Austria* (1992) 14 EHRR 551);

(4) *the preservation of public order*. Bail may be withheld where the nature of the alleged crime and the likely public reaction to it are such that the release of the accused may give rise to public disorder (*Letellier v France*, at [51]).

Article 5 of the Convention also allows the imposition of conditions on the grant of bail.

In *O'Dowd v UK* (2012) 54 EHRR 187, the ECtHR observed (at [68]) that: **D7.40**

> Whether it is reasonable for an accused to remain in detention must be assessed in each case according to its special features. Continued detention can be justified in a given case only if there are specific indications of a genuine requirement of public interest which, notwithstanding the presumption of innocence, outweighs the rule of respect for individual liberty laid down in Article 5 of the Convention...

It follows, said the Court (at [69]), that it falls to the 'national judicial authorities to ensure that, in a given case, the pre-trial detention of an accused person does not exceed a reasonable time'. The Court went on to say (at [70]) that the 'persistence of reasonable suspicion that the person arrested has committed an offence is a condition *sine qua non* for the lawfulness of the continued detention, but after a certain lapse of time it no longer suffices'. At that point, there must not only be 'sufficient' grounds to justify the deprivation of liberty, but the 'national authorities' (i.e. the prosecution) must display 'special diligence' in the conduct of the proceedings. In assessing whether the 'special diligence' requirement has been met, regard must be had 'to periods of unjustified delay, to the overall complexity of the proceedings and to any steps taken by the authorities to speed up proceedings to ensure that the overall length of detention remains "reasonable"'.

The Court ruled (at [73]) that the 'due diligence' required by the Prosecution of Offences Act 1985, s. 22(3) (extension of custody time-limits: see **D7.42**), cannot be equated to the 'special diligence' required by Article 5(3). The Court went on to explain that:

> ...unlike the approach of the domestic courts to compliance with the 1985 Act, in assessing compliance with Article 5(3), this Court will examine the proceedings as a whole and assess any particular periods of inactivity or delay by the authorities within the context of the overall period of pre-trial detention, with particular regard to any recognition by the authorities of the length of time already spent in detention and the need to take additional steps to bring about a more speedy trial.

The Court found no breach of Article 5(3) on the facts in *O'Dowd*. This was largely because the accused had contributed substantially to the overall length of his pre-trial detention (e.g., by dismissing his legal advisers shortly before hearings, which resulted in the hearings being postponed).

'Equality of Arms'

It should be noted that the 'equality of arms' principle applies to bail applications (*Woukam Moudefo v France* (1991) 13 EHRR 549). This includes: **D7.41**

(a) the right to disclosure of prosecution evidence for purposes of making a bail application: *Lamy v Belgium* (1989) 11 EHRR 529, at [29] (the decision of the Divisional Court, *DPP, ex parte Lee* [1999] 2 Cr App R 304, largely accords with this);

(b) the requirement that the court should give reasons for the refusal of bail (*Tomasi v France* (1993) 15 EHRR 1, at [84]) and should permit renewed applications for bail at reasonable intervals (*Bezicheri v Italy* (1990) 12 EHRR 210, at [21]).

BAIL AND CUSTODY TIME-LIMITS

Grafted on to the general system of a presumption in favour of bail which is lost if one or more of the exceptions described above applies are special rules applying where the prosecution fail to **D7.42** comply with the custody time-limits contained in the Prosecution of Offences (Custody Time Limits) Regulations 1987 (SI 1987 No. 299). For either-way offences, the maximum period of custody between the accused's first appearance and the start of summary trial, or the time when the court decides to send the accused to the Crown Court for trial, is 70 days (reg. 4(2)). However, if, before the expiry of 56 days following the day of the accused's first appearance, the court decides to proceed to summary trial, the maximum period of custody between the accused's first appearance and the start of the summary trial is 56 days (reg. 4(3)). For indictable-only offences, the maximum period of custody between the accused's first appearance and the time when the court decides to send the accused to the Crown Court for trial is 70 days (reg. 4(4)). For summary offences, the maximum period of custody beginning with the date of the accused's first appearance and ending with the date of the start of the summary trial is 56 days (reg. 4(4A)). Where a case is sent for trial in the Crown Court, the maximum period of custody between the time when the accused is sent for trial and the start of the trial is 182 days (reg. 5(6B)).

Under reg. 6(6), where the Crown Court is notified that the custody time-limit applicable to an accused in custody pending his trial on indictment is about to expire, it must grant him bail as from the expiry of the time-limit. By reg. 6(1)–(5), the prosecution are obliged to notify the Crown Court at least five days before the limit's expiry of whether they intend to ask the Crown Court to impose conditions on the grant of bail. They must also arrange for the accused to be brought before the court within the two days preceding expiry. This is without prejudice to the prosecution's right to apply for an extension of the time-limit under the Prosecution of Offences Act 1985, s. 22(3).

The 1987 Regulations make no express provision as to the procedure to be adopted in a magistrates' court when a custody time-limit is about to expire. The fact that an accused who has not been granted bail has to appear before the magistrates at regular intervals (because of the restrictions on the period for which he may be remanded in custody) perhaps makes it unnecessary to provide expressly for bringing him before the court in anticipation of the expiry of a custody time-limit.

D7.43 Regulation 8 modifies the BA 1976 in that, where a custody time-limit has expired, the words 'except as provided in Schedule 1 to this Act' are treated as omitted from s. 4(1) of the Act. The effect is to give the accused an absolute right to bail. Moreover, s. 3 of the 1976 Act (which deals with the conditions which may be imposed when granting bail) is also modified so as to prevent a court, when bailing an accused entitled to bail by reason of the expiry of a custody time-limit, from imposing requirements of a surety or deposit of security or any other condition which has to be complied with *before* release on bail (although it can impose conditions such as residence, curfew or reporting to a police station which have to be complied with *after* release). Moreover, following the grant of bail, the accused may not be arrested without warrant (under s. 7 of the BA 1976) on the ground that a police officer believes he is unlikely to surrender to custody or that he has, or is likely, to break a condition of bail.

If the accused is granted bail because the custody time-limit has expired, his right to bail continues only until he enters a plea. Thereafter, the court can withhold bail if any of the reasons for doing so under the BA 1976 apply (*Croydon Crown Court, ex parte Lewis* (1994) 158 JP 886).

These provisions apply to proceedings in the youth court even though the usual distinction between summary and indictable offences does not apply there (*Stratford Youth Court, ex parte S* [1998] 1 WLR 1758).

For a full discussion of custody time-limits, see **D15.7** *et seq.*

CONDITIONS OF BAIL

D7.44 The BA 1976, s. 3, governs the duties resting on a person granted bail in criminal proceedings and the various requirements which may be attached to a grant of bail. Where the court grants 'unconditional' bail, the accused has simply to surrender to custody (i.e. attend court) at the date and time specified (s. 3(1)). However, the court may impose a wide range of additional requirements by granting bail subject to specific conditions, known as 'conditional bail' (s. 3(6)).

Duty to Surrender to Custody

A person granted bail in criminal proceedings is under a duty to surrender to custody (BA **D7.45** 1976, s. 3(1)). 'Surrender to custody' is defined in s. 2(2) as surrendering into the custody of the court the accused has been bailed to attend. For discussion of what precisely is meant by surrendering to the custody of a court, see **D7.101**. The date and place at which the accused should surrender is fixed when bail is granted, save that when he is sent to the Crown Court for trial or sentence the obligation is to surrender on the day his case comes up for hearing if it is not possible to notify him of the hearing date at the time the case is sent to the Crown Court. The date originally fixed for surrender to custody may be varied to a later date (see the MCA 1980, ss. 43 and 129, for a magistrates' court's powers in this respect). Failure without reasonable cause to surrender to custody is an offence under the BA 1976, s. 6 (see **D7.111**).

By s. 3(2) of the 1976 Act, an accused granted bail in criminal proceedings may not be bailed on his own recognizance. The accused may, however, be required to provide other people to stand surety for him, under s. 3(4) (see **D7.55**), or he may be required to give security for his surrender to custody, under s. 3(5) (see **D7.60**).

Conditions that May be Imposed by the Court

By virtue of the BA 1976, s. 3(6), a person who is granted bail may be required by the court to **D7.46** comply with such requirements as appear to the court necessary to secure that he:

(a) surrenders to custody;
(b) does not commit an offence on bail;
(c) does not interfere with witnesses or otherwise obstruct the course of justice;
(d) makes himself available for the making of inquiries or a report to assist in sentencing (this condition may be imposed only it appears to be necessary to do so for the purpose of enabling inquiries or a report to be made: sch. 1, part I, para. 8(1A)); and
(e) attends an interview with a legal representative (this will nearly always be a solicitor).

Conditions may also be imposed for the protection of the accused (or, if he is a juvenile, for his own welfare or in his own interests).

The BA 1976, sch. 1, part I, para. 8(1), provides that no conditions may be imposed unless **D7.47** it appears to the court that it is necessary to do so either (a) for the purpose of preventing the occurrence of any of the events mentioned in sch. 1, para. 2(1), or for the accused's own protection or, if he is a child or young person, for his own welfare or in his own interests. The events mentioned in sch. 1, part I, para. 2, are precisely the same as those mentioned in paras. (a)–(c) of s. 3(6): failure to surrender to custody, further offences and interference with witnesses. There is thus an almost complete overlap between s. 3(6) and sch. 1, part I, para. 8. This was attributed by Lord Lane CJ in *Mansfield Justices, ex parte Sharkey* [1985] QB 613 to 'indifferent drafting' (at p. 625C). Counsel for the applicants argued that para. 8 impliedly restricted the imposition of requirements to cases where the court was satisfied that there were substantial grounds for believing that one of the adverse consequences would occur unless bail was made conditional. However, this argument was rejected by the Divisional Court. Having quoted s. 3(6) and para. 8, Lord Lane explained their effect in the context of a condition imposed to prevent further offences. His lordship said (at p. 625E):

> In the present circumstances the question the justices should ask themselves is a simple one: 'Is this condition *necessary* for the prevention of the commission of an offence when on bail?' They are not obliged to have substantial grounds. It is enough if they perceive a *real and not a fanciful risk* of the

offence being committed. Thus, section 3(6) and paragraph 8 give the court a wide discretion to inquire whether the condition is necessary [emphasis added].

It followed that the justices were *not* obliged to have substantial grounds for believing that a repetition of the accused's conduct would occur. It was enough that they perceived a real risk of that happening. Although given the context of determining the legality of conditions imposed to prevent offences while on bail, the Lord Chief Justice's judgment is obviously applicable, *mutatis mutandis*, to conditions designed to prevent the accused absconding or interfering with witnesses.

A similar approach was adopted in *R (CPS) v Chorley Justices* (2002) 166 JP 764, where the Divisional Court noted that the only prerequisite for imposing conditions on bail is that, in the circumstances of the particular case, imposition of the condition is necessary to achieve the aims specified in that section (e.g., preventing the accused from absconding, or committing offences while on bail, or interfering with witnesses or otherwise obstructing the course of justice).

D7.48   The BA 1976 refers to some specific conditions (such as sureties and security) but it does not contain a definitive list of conditions that may be imposed. The court may impose any condition so long as it is necessary to prevent the accused from absconding, committing offences etc. Under the CrimPR, r. 19.5(4), a prosecutor who wants the court to impose a condition must specify the condition and explain what purpose it would serve.

Commonly imposed conditions include:

(a)   a condition of residence, often expressed as a condition that the accused is to live and sleep at a specified address;

(b)   a condition that the accused is to notify any changes of address to the police;

(c)   a condition of reporting (whether daily, weekly or at other intervals) to a local police station;

(d)   a curfew (i.e. the accused must be at a specified address between certain hours);

(e)   a condition that the accused is not to enter a certain area or building or go within a specified distance of a certain address;

(f)   a condition that he is not to contact (whether directly or indirectly) the victim of the alleged offence and/or any other probable prosecution witness; and

(g)   a condition that he is to surrender his passport to the police (sometimes with an additional restriction to prevent the accused from applying for travel documents).

Conditions (a), (b), (c) and (g) are particularly relevant to reducing the risk of absconding. A special form of residential condition is that the accused is to reside at a bail hostel or probation hostel. When imposing such a condition the court may, and normally will, impose an additional requirement that the accused is to comply with the rules of the hostel (s. 3(6ZA)). In the case of a convicted offender being remanded for reports, a requirement of residence at a hostel may be imposed not simply to reduce the risk of absconding but, additionally or alternatively, to assess his suitability for being dealt with by a means which would involve residence at a probation hostel. Conditions (d) and (e) are designed to prevent the commission of offences when on bail. A curfew may be appropriate where the offence with which the accused is charged was allegedly committed at night; a geographical restriction is useful if the offence was one of violence committed at a certain address (in effect, the accused is ordered to stay away from the address). Conditions (e) and (f) may be imposed to minimise the risk of interference with witnesses.

D7.49   Under the CrimPR, r. 19.11, the accused must notify the prosecutor of the address at which he will live and sleep if released on bail with a condition of residence as soon as practicable. The prosecutor must help the court to assess the suitability of an address proposed as a condition of residence.

In *McDonald v Procurator Fiscal, Elgin* (2003) *The Times*, 17 April 2003 (a case which came before the High Court of Justiciary in Scotland), the accused had been granted bail subject to a condition that he remain in his dwelling at all times except between 10.00 a.m. and noon. It was held that this (rather onerous) requirement did not amount to detention or deprivation of his liberty and did not constitute an infringement of his right to liberty under the ECHR, Article 5.

Similarly, in *R (CPS) v Chorley Justices*, the question at issue was whether justices are empowered to attach a condition to the grant of bail that the accused present himself at the door of his residence when required to do so by a police officer during the hours of curfew. It was held that there is power under s. 3(6) to impose such 'door-step' conditions, but it is a question of fact in each case whether such a condition is necessary.

Electronic Monitoring

Electronic monitoring ('tagging') is available as a condition of bail. The system does not enable the accused to be tracked, as it does not provide continuous information on the whereabouts of the accused. Rather, an alert is generated at a monitoring centre if the accused leaves the specified address, or attempts to remove or tamper with the tag. Tagging is generally used as an alternative to a remand in custody, and is often combined with a curfew condition. The BA 1976, s. 3(6ZAA), enables electronic tagging of both juveniles and adults. **D7.50**

Juveniles   Section 3AA applies where the accused is under the age of 18. It stipulates that an **D7.51** electronic monitoring requirement cannot be imposed unless the accused is at least 12 years old. Moreover, the juvenile must have been charged with, or convicted of, either (a) a violent or sexual offence, or an offence punishable in the case of an adult with at least 14 years' imprisonment, or (b) one or more imprisonable offences which amount (or would amount if he is convicted of the present charge) to a recent history of repeatedly committing imprisonable offences while remanded on bail or subject to a custodial remand (s. 3AA(3)). Moreover, a youth offending team must have confirmed the suitability of the requirement for the accused (s. 3AA(5)).

Adults   Section 3AB of the 1976 Act governs the imposition of electronic monitoring require- **D7.52** ments where the accused has attained the age of 18. Such a requirement may be imposed only if the court is satisfied that, without the electronic monitoring requirement, the accused would not be granted bail (s. 3AB(2)).

Guidance on Bail Conditions

On 5 May 2006, Thomas LJ, then Senior Presiding Judge for England and Wales, issued a letter **D7.53** of guidance to judges and magistrates on the subject of bail. To enable the court to contact the accused, the guidance notes that, 'where a defendant is reluctant to provide a telephone number and the court considers that conditions are necessary to secure his attendance, the court can consider making as a condition of bail the provision of a telephone number (and notifying the court of any change or of the fact that he/she cannot be contacted on that number)'. The guidance also notes that, if a court decides to use a curfew backed by electronic monitoring, it is 'important to consider including in the conditions of bail a condition that it is the responsibility of the defendant to gain the approval of the court for the designated bail address to be changed'.

Non-imprisonable Offences

In *Bournemouth Magistrates' Court, ex parte Cross* (1989) 89 Cr App R 90, the point at issue was **D7.54** whether conditions could be imposed on bail for non-imprisonable offences. The accused, who was a hunt protester, was charged with a non-imprisonable offence under public order legislation. He was bailed on condition he did not attend another hunt meeting before his next court appearance. He was arrested for alleged breach of this condition and remanded in custody. On application for judicial review, the Divisional Court held that the condition had been validly imposed under the BA 1976, s. 3(6).

Sureties

A person granted bail in criminal proceedings may be required, before release on bail, to provide **D7.55** one or more sureties to secure his surrender to custody (BA 1976, s. 3(4)). Section 3(4) does not place any fetter on the discretion to demand a surety (cf. s. 3(6)). However, sch. 1, part I, para. 8, provides that no conditions shall be imposed under any of subsections (4)–(6B) or (7) of s. 3 (apart from s. 3(6)(d) or (e)) unless they appear to the court necessary to prevent the occurrence of any of the events mentioned in sch. 1, part I, para. 2(1) (i.e. failure to surrender to custody, the commission of one or more offences while on bail, or interference with witnesses or obstruction of the course of justice). Moreover, it is sometimes argued that, where the prosecution object to bail on the basis that the accused is likely to commit further offences, it is possible to require both a surety under the BA 1976 to secure the accused's attendance at court and also a surety to secure his good behaviour under the general powers given to magistrates by the Justices of the Peace Act 1968, s. 1(7) (see E13 for the power to bind persons over to keep the peace and be of good behaviour). It is submitted, however, that use of s. 1(7) in this way would contravene the BA 1976, s. 3(3)(c), which provides that: 'Except as provided *by this section*...no other requirement shall be imposed [on the accused] as a condition of bail' (emphasis added).

In *R (Shea) v Winchester Crown Court* [2013] EWHC 1050 (Admin), the Divisional Court confirmed that there is no power (under the BA 1976 or otherwise) to grant conditional bail with a surety to ensure no further offending: a surety can be sought only for the purpose of securing surrender to custody, and not for any other purpose. It follows that one or more sureties should be required only in cases where there appears to be a risk of absconding.

D7.56   **Who Can be a Surety?**   The BA 1976, s. 8, contains detailed provisions about the taking of sureties. In considering whether a proposed surety is suitable, regard may be had, *inter alia*, to the factors set out in s. 8(2).

(a) The financial resources of the proposed surety: could the surety pay the sum which he is promising to pay? In *Birmingham Crown Court, ex parte Rashid Ali* (1999) 163 JP 145, Kennedy LJ (at p. 147) said that 'it is irresponsible (and possibly a matter for consideration by a professional disciplinary body) for a qualified lawyer or legal executive to tender anyone as a surety unless he or she has reasonable grounds for believing that the surety will, if necessary, be able to meet his or her financial undertaking'.

(b) The character of the proposed surety and whether he has any previous convictions: is the surety a trustworthy person?

(c) The proximity (whether kinship, place of residence or otherwise) of the proposed surety to the person for whom he is to be surety: is the proposed surety a friend, relative or employer? How far away does he live from the accused? The most important consideration under this heading is the relationship of the proposed surety to the accused: will the surety have the ability to control the accused so as to ensure that he attends court when he should? Put another way, would the fact that the surety stands to lose money if the accused absconds operate on the mind of the accused so as to deter him from absconding?

D7.57   **Taking the Surety**   The normal consequence for a surety if an accused fails to answer to his bail is that the surety is ordered to forfeit the entire sum in which he stood surety. As the surety is promising to pay money rather than handing over any money at the outset, it is important for the court to be assured that the surety has sufficient funds with which to honour the undertaking to the court. When a surety is taken in court, he is asked how he would pay the sum in which he is to stand surety were the accused to abscond. It is also standard practice for the police to check whether the surety has previous convictions; if he has, and depending on their age and nature, objection may be made to him acting as a surety. If no satisfactory surety is forthcoming at court, but the court is willing to grant bail subject to the provision of a satisfactory surety, the court simply fixes the amount in which the surety is to be bound and the accused remains in custody until the court's requirement can be fulfilled (BA 1976, s. 8(3)). To facilitate early release where the sureties are not at court, they may enter into their recognizances outside court (s. 8(4)). Paragraphs (a)–(d) of s. 8(4), in conjunction with the CrimPR, r. 19.14(3)(b), list the persons who may accept a surety's recognizance. They are: a justice of the peace; a justices' clerk; a police officer who is either of the rank of inspector or above or who is in charge of a police station; or the 'defendant's custodian' (i.e. the governor of the prison or remand centre where he is being held); or, if bail has been granted by the Crown Court, an officer of that court. The court granting bail may, however, specify the person (or class of person) before whom the surety is to be taken or require that the surety be taken in court (see the opening words of s. 8(4)). If a person asked to accept a surety outside court refuses to do so because he is not satisfied about the surety's suitability, the surety may apply either to the court which fixed the amount of the recognizance in which the surety was to be bound, or to any magistrates' court, for that court to take his recognizance; that court must, if satisfied of his suitability, take his recognizance (s. 8(5)).

It is quite common to have two or more sureties. If the court will grant bail only subject to a recognizance of a certain amount and that amount is beyond the means of one the proposed sureties, then one or more additional sureties will have to be found.

For discussion of the consequences for the surety if the accused absconds, see **D7.122**.

Making Sureties Continuous   Where an accused is granted bail at a remand hearing and it **D7.58** is anticipated that there may be several further appearances in the magistrates' court before his case is finally disposed of or sent to the Crown Court for trial, the court may, instead of simply directing him to appear at the end of the period of the remand, direct that he appear 'at every time and place to which during the course of the proceedings the hearing may be from time to time adjourned' (MCA 1980, s. 128(4)). Similarly, where bail is granted subject to a requirement for sureties, the surety's recognizance may be conditioned to secure that the accused 'appears at every time and place to which during the course of the proceedings the hearing may be from time to time adjourned' and also before the Crown Court in the event of the accused being sent there for trial (MCA 1980, s. 128(4)). Making the sureties continuous in this way is a useful device to avoid their having to come to court for each remand hearing. If they have not been made continuous and are not at court, the accused, even if granted bail on precisely the same terms as previously, cannot be released until the undertakings have been renewed (e.g., by going to a local police station). Section 128(4)(c) even empowers magistrates to make the sureties' recognizances extend beyond the date when the case is sent to the Crown Court for trial (i.e. at a remand hearing they undertake to secure the accused's attendance before the Crown Court if he is sent there for trial). Where the accused's bail is conditional both on sureties and other conditions, there is no obligation to inform the sureties should the other conditions be relaxed or varied, but it might be good practice to warn sureties of this possibility at the time they enter into their recognizances (*Wells Street Magistrates' Court, ex parte Albanese* [1982] QB 333).

In *Evans* [2012] 1 WLR 1192, Hughes LJ (at [33]) said that, where a magistrates' court has sent the accused to Crown Court, bail and any recognizance will lapse on the first appearance in the Crown Court and cannot carry through to subsequent adjournments in the Crown Court. However, if the Crown Court renews bail, it does have the power to make the recognizance continuous for all future appearances. This, said his lordship:

> ...underlines the importance of attention being paid to the terms of a defendant's bail, particularly at the conclusion of the first hearing in the Crown Court. At that point conditions of bail should always be considered. Of course it is sufficient to do so briefly by simply reimposing conditions previously placed there by the magistrates, if that is appropriate and especially if there is no objection. But in both surety cases and non-surety cases an assessment of bail is required at the end of the first hearing in each Crown Court.

Parent Standing Surety for a Juvenile   The general rule is that the obligations of a surety **D7.59** extend only to securing the accused's attendance at court, and so a surety is *not* responsible for preventing any other possible defaults of the accused while on bail (e.g., intimidation of witnesses or breach of a condition of bail). However, the BA 1976, s. 3(7), provides that, where the accused is under the age of 17, and his parent or guardian stands surety for him, the court may require the parent or guardian to secure that the accused complies with any condition of bail imposed by virtue of s. 3(6), (6ZAA), or (6A). A requirement under s. 3(7) can be imposed only with the consent of the parent or guardian, and the sum in which he is to be bound may not exceed £50.

Deposit of Security

D7.60 Under the BA 1976, s. 3(2), a person cannot stand as surety for himself. However, a person granted bail may be required to give security for his surrender to custody, i.e. deposit with the court money or some other valuable item which will be liable to forfeiture in the event of non-attendance in answer to bail (BA 1976, s. 3(5)). As with sureties, security may be required as a condition of bail only if it is considered necessary to prevent absconding. Where security has been given in pursuance of s. 3(5) and the person bailed absconds, the court may, unless there appears to have been reasonable cause for the failure to surrender to custody, order forfeiture of the security (see s. 5(7)–(9)).

In *R (Stevens) v Truro Magistrates' Court* [2002] 1 WLR 144, it was held that it is permissible for a third party to make available an asset to an accused in order to enable him to give it as security for his release on bail and that the court can accept such an asset. However, as it is the accused himself who gives the security, the arrangements the accused might make with those who helped him put up the requisite security are not a matter for the court. There is no obligation for the third party to be notified before the security is forfeited on the accused's non-attendance.

Other Statutory Bail Conditions

D7.61 There are a number of other conditions which may be imposed on the grant of bail pursuant to various provisions of the BA 1976.

D7.62 **Drug Assessments**   Section 3(6C)–(6E) of the BA 1976 provide that where:

(a) the conditions set out in para. 6B of part I of sch. 1 are satisfied (namely, the accused is aged 18 or over, there is drug test evidence that he has a specified Class A drug in his body, and either the offence is a drugs offence associated with a specified Class A drug or the court is satisfied that there are substantial grounds for believing that the misuse of a specified Class A drug caused or contributed to that offence or provided its motivation), and

(b) the accused has been offered an assessment of whether he is dependent upon or has a propensity to misuse any specified Class A drugs (or such an assessment has been carried out and he has been offered follow-up), and

(c) he has agreed to undergo that assessment or participate in any follow-up,

then the court, if it grants bail, shall impose as a condition of bail that the accused both undergo the relevant assessment and participate in any relevant follow-up proposed to him or, if a relevant assessment has been carried out, that he participate in the relevant follow-up (s. 3(6D)).

D7.63 **Co-operation in the Making of Reports**   One of the purposes for which the court may impose a requirement under the BA 1976, s. 3(6), is to ensure that the accused will make himself 'available for the purpose of enabling inquiries or a report to be made to assist the court in dealing with him for the offence' (see s. 3(6)(d)). For obvious reasons, such a requirement will not generally be considered until the stage of an adjournment between conviction and sentence. However, there are two situations in which the court is obliged — not merely empowered — to make a requirement under s. 3(6)(d), and both can arise even before conviction. Those situations are:

(a) Where a magistrates' court is dealing with an imprisonable offence, it may adjourn the case under the PCC(S)A 2000, s. 11(1), for a medical examination of the accused, provided that the court is satisfied that the accused did the act or made the omission charged, and is of the opinion that an inquiry ought to be made into his physical or mental condition before the method of dealing with him is determined. Although such an adjournment is conditional on the court being satisfied that the accused committed the *actus reus* of the offence, there is no need for a conviction to have been recorded. The purpose of ordering the examination is usually to discover whether the accused's mental condition is such that he might be dealt with by means such as a hospital order (whether with or without a prior conviction for the offence charged) or a community order with a condition for medical treatment. Under s. 11(3), where there is an adjournment under s. 11(1) and the magistrates remand the accused on bail, the court *shall* impose conditions under the BA 1976, s. 3(6). Those conditions must include requirements that he: (i) submits to examination by a duly qualified medical practitioner (or, if the inquiry is into his mental condition and the court so directs, by two practitioners); and (ii) for the purpose of the examination, attends at such place as the court directs and complies with any directions given to him for the purpose.

(b) Where a court grants bail to an accused charged with murder, it must, unless satisfied that satisfactory reports on his mental condition have already been obtained, impose as conditions of bail requirements that he undergo examination by two medical practitioners (including a psychiatrist approved under the Mental Health Act 1983) and attend such place as directed for the purpose of the examination (BA 1976, s. 3(6A) and (6B)). The importance in such cases of obtaining full medical and, in particular, psychiatric reports on the accused while he is still on remand prior to trial is that the reports may lay the foundation for a defence of diminished responsibility or, alternatively, assist the prosecution in rebutting such a defence. In *Central Criminal Court, ex parte Porter* [1992] Crim LR 121, the Divisional Court said that if no such condition was imposed, then the decision to grant bail would be a nullity.

Taking Legal Advice   The court also has power to require an accused, as a condition of bail, to attend an interview with a legal adviser before his next appearance in court (BA 1976, s. 3(6)(e)). The aim is to save the time of the court by ensuring that he receives legal advice, in advance of the hearing, to decide on how to respond to the charge. Clearly, if the accused indicates that he does not wish to be legally represented, such a condition should not be imposed. If the condition is attached, then the accused should be told of the consequences of failing to comply. Guidance issued to judges and magistrates has made it clear that, if the accused fails to attend an interview, his solicitor should not be expected to report the breach of the condition (see Home Office Circular 34/1998, para. 11).   **D7.64**

Applications to Vary the Conditions of Bail

Where bail has been granted subject to conditions, the accused may apply for the conditions to be varied (BA 1976, s. 3(8)(a)). The application should be made to the court which granted bail (or, where the accused has been sent to the Crown Court for trial, or committed to the Crown Court for sentence, to the Crown Court). Furthermore, the prosecution may make a similar application either for existing conditions to be varied or, in a case where the court originally granted unconditional bail, for conditions to be imposed (s. 3(8)(b)). Where a party intends to apply for a variation of bail conditions, he must give advance notice to the court and to the other party, explaining what is sought and why. The CrimPR, r. 19.7 applies to such applications (see D7.67). Under r. 19.7(2)(c), the application must be served not less than two business days before any hearing in the case at which the applicant wants the court to consider it, if such a hearing is already due. The court may determine an application to vary a condition without a hearing if the variation has been agreed by the parties (r. 19.7(7)(c)); if there is to be a hearing, it should take place no later than the fifth business day after the application was served (r. 19.7(6)(b)).   **D7.65**

Breach of Bail Conditions

Breach of any condition which has been imposed may result in the accused being arrested without warrant under the BA 1976, s. 7(3) and his bail being withdrawn. See D7.102.   **D7.66**

PROCEDURE FOR BAIL APPLICATIONS IN MAGISTRATES' COURTS

Application Procedure

D7.67 Guidance on the procedure to be followed for bail applications is contained in the CrimPR, part 19 (see Supplement, **R-178**). Rule 19.2(1)(a) states that a decision on bail cannot be made unless each party (and any surety directly affected by the decision) is present or has had an opportunity to make representations. However, where the accused is in custody, bail may be considered in his absence if either he has waived the right to attend or he was present when bail was refused on a previous occasion and he has been in custody continuously since then (r. 19.2(1)(b)). Rule 19.2(2) states that a bail hearing may take place in public or in private.

Assuming the presumption in favour of bail applies by virtue of the BA 1976, s. 4(1), the onus is on the court to justify any refusal of bail in accordance with sch. 1 to the Act. This applies both when the accused first appears and at all subsequent appearances while he remains within the scope of s. 4(1) (see sch. 1, part IIA, para. 1).

The question of bail is always a matter for the court. However, when adjourning the case of an unconvicted accused to whom s. 4(1) applies and who is entitled to make an argued bail application under sch. 1, part IIA (see **D7.70**), normal practice is to ask the prosecution if they have any objections to bail. The prosecution representative then summarises the objections (or, as the case may be, states that there are no objections). The CPS file will contain information, supplied by the police, which sets out the objections to bail, if any, and the basis of those objections. The prosecution advocate usually has little alternative but to base his remarks on this information as no police officer connected with the case will be present in court. The justices will normally be told of the accused's previous convictions (including any convictions for failure to surrender to custody) when the prosecution give their objections to bail. Following the prosecution objections, the defence representative (or the accused in person if unrepresented) may present the arguments for bail (whether conditional or unconditional). Even where the defence choose not to make a bail application, it is submitted that the prosecution should present at least cursory objections to bail so that the court will be able to base a refusal on one or more of the reasons contained in sch. 1.

D7.68 The question of bail is normally dealt with on the basis of submissions from the prosecution and defence. Rule 19.5(2) requires the prosecutor to provide the court with all information in the prosecutor's possession that is relevant to the question of bail. Where the prosecution oppose bail, the prosecutor is required to specify each statutory exception to the presumption in favour of bail on which the prosecution rely, and each consideration the prosecution argue to be relevant (r. 19.5(3)).

There is no requirement for formal evidence to be given (*Re Moles* [1981] Crim LR 170 and *Mansfield JJ, ex parte Sharkey* [1985] QB 613 at p. 626, per Lord Lane CJ). Either party may, however, adduce evidence in support of their respective arguments, e.g., a police officer to substantiate the objections to bail, or proposed sureties to further the application for bail. Such witnesses give their evidence on the *voir dire* form of oath, to answer truthfully all such questions as the court may ask.

The prosecution will not normally reply to the application for bail by the defence. However, the prosecutor does have a right to reply to the defence submissions if this is necessary to correct alleged misstatements of fact in what the defence have said (*Isleworth Crown Court, ex parte Commissioner of Customs and Excise* [1990] Crim LR 859).

Where a case is adjourned for reports following conviction, the prosecution are *not* usually asked if they object to bail. At this stage the question is conventionally regarded as one for the court, subject to representations from the defence. This may reflect the general rule that, in matters of sentencing, the prosecution remain neutral rather than trying to influence the court one way or the other.

Having heard the prosecution objections to bail, and the answer of the defence to those objections, the court announces its decision on the grant or withholding of bail.

Effect on Procedure of the Human Rights Act 1998   The compatibility of the procedure adopted   **D7.69**
in the case of contested bail hearings with the safeguards in the ECHR, Articles 5 and 6, was examined (in the context of a hearing involving an accused arrested for breach of a bail condition) in *R (DPP) v Havering Magistrates' Court* [2001] 3 All ER 997 (see **D7.107**). In that case the need for formal evidence and procedures was rejected in favour of proper account being taken of the quality of the material upon which the court is asked to adjudicate, with the accused being given a full and fair opportunity to comment on, and answer, that material (per Latham LJ, at [41]).

Right to Make Repeated Argued Bail Applications

Where the accused is remanded in custody, he may make a fully argued application at the next   **D7.70**
hearing, regardless of whether he is repeating arguments already placed before the previous bench
(BA 1976, sch. 1, part IIA, para. 2). Unless he consents to being remanded in his absence, the next hearing will take place within eight clear days (MCA 1980, s. 128(6)). (Section 128A of the MCA 1980, which permits remands in custody of up to 28 days, applies only if the accused has already been remanded in custody for the offence on at least one previous occasion.) Therefore, the wait between being refused bail on a first appearance and being able to argue again for bail on a second appearance is relatively short. However, should that second argued application fail, the BA 1976, sch. 1, part IIA, para. 3, is applicable. This provides that, at subsequent hearings, the court 'need not hear arguments as to fact or law which it has heard previously'. This is so even though at each hearing the court should nominally consider whether he ought to remain in custody (sch. 1, part IIA, para. 1). Paragraph 3 effectively entitles the magistrates to treat the finding of the previous bench (that there were grounds for refusing bail) as a form of *res iudicata*. They may therefore refuse to hear argument in favour of bail, and need consider the question only to the limited extent of satisfying themselves that the accused has exhausted the argued bail applications to which he is entitled as of right and that there has been no material change of circumstances since the last argued application to entitle him to reopen the matter.

The Law Commission Paper, *Bail and the Human Rights Act 1998* (Law Com No. 269), contains guidance aiming to ensure that the provisions relating to a change in circumstances are applied in a way that is compatible with the ECHR. This guidance states (at paras. 12.23 and 13.33) that courts should be willing, at regular intervals of 28 days, to consider arguments that the passage of time constitutes, in the particular case before the court, a change in circumstances so as to require full argument. If the court finds that the passage of time does amount to a relevant changed circumstance, or that there are other circumstances which may be relevant to the need to detain the accused that have changed or come to notice since the last fully argued bail hearing, then a full bail application should follow in which all the arguments, old and new, could be put forward and taken into account.

Part IIA of sch. 1 to the BA 1976 was intended to give statutory effect to the decision of the   **D7.71**
Divisional Court in *Nottingham Justices, ex parte Davies* [1981] QB 38. That decision may therefore be regarded as a useful aid to the interpretation of part IIA. In *Ex parte Davies*, the court was asked to rule on the lawfulness of a local policy that the defence would be allowed to make a full bail application at the first and second hearings, but that at all subsequent hearings, the bench would refuse to consider matters previously before the court. In other words, from the third remand hearing onwards, they would not entertain an argued bail application unless there had been a change in circumstances since the last such application. The court upheld the policy. Donaldson LJ said (at pp. 43–4, emphasis added):

> …I accept that the fact that a bench of the same or a different constitution has decided on a previous occasion or occasions that one or more of the schedule 1 exceptions applies and has accordingly remanded the accused in custody, does not absolve the bench on each subsequent occasion from considering whether the accused is entitled to bail, whether or not an application is made.

However, this does not mean that the justices should ignore their own previous decision or a previous decision of their colleagues. Far from it. On those previous occasions, the court will have been under an obligation to grant bail unless it was satisfied that a schedule 1 exception was made out. If it was so satisfied, it will have recorded the exceptions which in its judgment were applicable. This...is a finding by the court that schedule 1 circumstances then existed and it is to be treated like every other finding of the court. It is *res iudicata* or analogous thereto. It stands as a finding unless and until it is overturned on appeal..... It follows that on the next occasion when bail is considered [by the magistrates] the court should treat, as an essential fact, that at the time when the matter of bail was last considered, schedule 1 circumstances did indeed exist. Strictly speaking, they can and should only investigate whether that situation has changed since then....

I would inject only one qualification to the general rule that justices can and should only investigate whether the situation has changed since the last remand in custody. The finding on that occasion that schedule 1 circumstances existed will have been based upon matters known to the court at that time. The court considering afresh the question of bail is both entitled and bound to take account not only of a change in circumstances which has occurred since that last occasion, but also of circumstances which, although they then existed, were not brought to the attention of the court.... The question is a little wider than 'Has there been a change?' It is 'Are there any new considerations which were not before the court when the accused was last remanded in custody?'

Applying these principles, Donaldson LJ held that the practice of allowing two (rather than one) argued applications was justified because, although the finding that there were sch. 1 circumstances for refusing bail on the occasion of the first remand in custody was in theory as much a finding of the court as the similar finding on the second occasion and so ought to have precluded the making of the second application, in practice the experience of the justices showed that first bail applications were almost invariably under-prepared, so that there would in fact be new considerations before the second bench which were not before the first. For a recent application of the approach of Donaldson LJ, see *R (B) v Brent Youth Court* [2010] EWHC 1893 (Admin).

D7.72   Interpretation of Part IIA   The BA 1976, part IIA, paras. 2 and 3, oblige the court to consider any relevant arguments, whether of fact or of law, which were not before the court when bail was refused. This is so whether the argument arises out of a change in circumstances since the last unsuccessful application, or is an argument that could have been put on the previous occasion but, for whatever reason, was not. In *R (B) v Brent Youth Court* [2010] EWHC 1893 (Admin), there had been two bail applications to the magistrates' court and one at the Crown Court; the defence sought to make a further application to the magistrates on the basis, *inter alia*, of a new set of possible conditions. The magistrates ruled that the possibility of new conditions did not amount to a change of circumstances and that the revised conditions could have been put before the court on a previous occasion; accordingly, they refused to hear the application. This refusal was quashed by the Divisional Court. Wilkie J referred to part IIA and said (at [9]) that the:

...effect of this is that the court is obliged to entertain two bail applications regardless of whether the arguments put forward in the second are arguments which have been advanced previously. But if those arguments are sought to be put forward a third time the court is not obliged to entertain them, though it may do so. But this only applies to the extent that arguments put forward as to fact or law are arguments which the court has heard previously.

He went on to say that this is almost invariably referred to as the 'change of circumstance' condition but that this phrase 'does not accurately reflect the statutory provisions'. Thus, the key question is whether the argument (of fact or law) was one which was put before the court on an earlier occasion, not whether it could have been put to the court previously.

Paragraph 2 does not state, as it might have done, that the accused is entitled to two fully argued bail applications. It merely provides that, *at the first hearing* after he was refused bail, he may support his application with any argument of fact or law, regardless of whether it was previously advanced. Thus, on a literal interpretation of para. 2, if an accused chooses not to make a bail application on the occasion of his first appearance and is accordingly remanded in custody, he may make an argued application at his next appearance but, if that application fails, he is debarred from a further argued application unless he can rely on matters which were not earlier placed before the court. It follows that an accused seeking bail who wants two opportunities to do so in the magistrates' court should make applications on both the first and second remand appearances — otherwise a court interpreting part IIA strictly would be justified in saying that he had neglected to avail himself of one opportunity by not making a fully argued application on his first appearance.

In *Calder Justices, ex parte Kennedy* (1992) 156 JP 716, the Divisional Court held that a decision under sch. 1, part 1, para. 5 (that it has not been practicable to obtain sufficient information whether to grant bail) is not a decision not to grant bail, since the justices are merely saying that they are not in a position to decide the question of bail. It does not therefore count for the purposes of para. 2 of part IIA of sch. 1.

In *Dover and East Kent Justices, ex parte Dean* (1992) 156 JP 357, the accused made no bail application on his first appearance and consented to be remanded in his absence for three weeks under the MCA 1980, s. 128 (see **D5.37**). He appeared before the justices at the end of that period and wished to make a bail application. The Divisional Court held that the occasions when he had been remanded in his absence were not 'hearings' for the purpose of para. 2, and so he had a right to make a bail application when he came before the justices at the end of the period of remand by consent.

Where the accused has exhausted his automatic entitlement of fully argued applications but claims that a new consideration has arisen which was not placed before the court on the earlier occasions, para. 3 could be construed merely as obliging the court to hear the argument of fact or law not previously advanced, rather than obliging it to reopen the entire question of bail. It is submitted, however, that to consider only the new consideration in isolation from the other arguments for bail would be an artificial exercise, and that the identifying of a new consideration relevant to bail should entitle the accused to make a further full bail application in which both the fresh and the old arguments may be relied on.

It must also be borne in mind that para. 3 merely states that, at the third and subsequent remand hearings, the court 'need not' hear arguments which it has heard previously. Prima facie the paragraph does not debar the court from entertaining yet another fully argued application, but merely gives it a discretion in the matter. On the other hand, Donaldson LJ in *Nottingham Justices, ex parte Davies* [1981] QB 38 based his approval of the practice of the Nottingham Justices on the principle of *res iudicata*. It is unclear from the wording of para. 3 whether it is meant to override *Ex parte Davies* (in which case magistrates always have a discretion to hear as many fully argued applications for bail as they wish), or is merely giving statutory force to the main thrust of the decision (in which case a scrupulous bench might say that, much as they would like to reopen the question of bail, they are bound by their colleagues' earlier decisions and can do nothing in the absence of fresh arguments or considerations). Given the wording of para. 3 ('need not'), it is submitted that the justices retain a discretion to hear a further bail application even in the absence of fresh information. This interpretation is consistent with the dictum of Wilkie J in *R (B) v Brent Youth Court*, quoted above.

Care has to be taken by the court in expressing the reason for the refusal of bail where para. 3 is applicable. Since in theory the court is obliged to consider bail each time an accused who is entitled to the benefit of the BA 1976, s. 4(1), appears before it in custody, it is unwise for the magistrates simply to say that they were not prepared to consider the matter of bail. It is more appropriate to say: 'As there is no new material before us relevant to the question of bail, bail will be refused'. This avoids giving the impression that they have simply refused to consider the question (per Ormrod LJ in *Slough Justices, ex parte Duncan* (1982) 75 Cr App R 384 at p. 389).

D

Part D Procedure

Extending Bail in the Absence of the Accused

D7.73   The MCA 1980, s. 129(1), applies if the court is satisfied that, on the day to which the accused was remanded, he is unable to attend 'by reason of illness or accident'. It may then remand him again in his absence. Notwithstanding s. 128(6), a remand in custody under s. 129(1) may exceed eight clear days. Section 129(1) applies regardless of whether the remand is in custody or on bail. Thus, if an accused remanded in custody on an earlier occasion is ill in prison and will not be well enough to attend court for several weeks, the magistrates may extend the period of the remand until such time as he is likely to have recovered.

By contrast with s. 129(1), s. 129(3) applies only if the accused has been remanded on bail. The subsection permits the court to appoint, in his absence, a later time as the time at which he is to appear. The appointment of the new time is deemed to be a further remand (s. 129(3)). This power is useful when unforeseen developments mean that the case will not be able to proceed on the date to which it was originally adjourned. By agreement between the court and the parties, a new date can be fixed without the necessity for the accused appearing. The power is also useful when the accused fails to appear on the date to which he was bailed but an acceptable explanation for his non-appearance is put before the court. Instead of issuing a warrant for his arrest, the magistrates may simply adjourn and enlarge bail in his absence.

Whenever bail is extended under either s. 129(1) or s. 129(3), the recognizances of the sureties may be correspondingly 'enlarged' to secure the accused's appearance on the new date (s. 129(2)(a) and (3)(a)).

The powers conferred by the MCA 1980, s 129, should be distinguished from the power under s. 128(3A) to remand an accused in custody on up to three consecutive occasions without his being brought before the court if he has consented not to be produced (see **D5.33**).

STATING AND RECORDING DECISIONS ABOUT BAIL

D7.74   Section 5 of the BA 1976 imposes a number of requirements about the giving and recording of decisions about bail and the reasons for those decisions.

Duty to Make a Record of the Decision

D7.75   Where a court grants bail, or withholds bail from someone to whom the BA 1976, s. 4, applies, or appoints a different time or place for a person granted bail to surrender to custody, or varies any conditions of bail or imposes conditions in respect of bail, it must make a record of the decision. The accused is entitled to a copy of the record on request (BA 1976, s. 5(1)). By virtue of the CrimPR, r. 19.4(1), the court officer must arrange for a record to be made of the court's reasons for any decision made in respect of bail.

Reasons for Decisions relating to Bail

D7.76   Where a magistrates' court or the Crown Court: (a) withholds bail from an accused prima facie entitled to bail under the BA 1976, s. 4, or (b) imposes conditions on the grant of bail to such a person (or varies conditions already imposed upon him), it must give reasons for withholding bail or, as the case may be, imposing or varying conditions of bail (BA 1976, s. 5(3)). The purpose of the giving of reasons is to enable the accused to consider making an application for bail (or for the variation or removal of conditions of bail) to another court. A note of the reasons must be included in the record of the court's decision (s. 5(4)). Also, the accused must be given a copy of the note (s. 5(4)), unless the decision was taken by the Crown Court and the accused is legally represented, in which case a copy need be provided only if his legal representative so requests (s. 5(5)). It should be noted that the obligation to give reasons under s. 5(4) arises only if the accused has the benefit of s. 4. If, for example, bail pending appeal is refused to a person summarily convicted and given a custodial sentence, the court is not required by the BA 1976 to explain the refusal, since the case falls outside s. 4.

In *R (R) v Snaresbrook Crown Court* [2011] EWHC 3569 (Admin), the Divisional Court considered the duty under s. 5(3) to give reasons for withholding bail. Holman J said (at [21]) that such reasons had to 'extend to a minimum reasonable level of adequacy, and had to identify the ground or grounds upon which the court was satisfied that bail should now be refused, and with a minimum level of adequacy identify the case specific reasons for being so satisfied'. His lordship added that, although the BA 1976 does not say so in terms, before any court makes a decision as to bail (and especially a decision withdrawing bail which had previously been granted), it must give to that person or his advocate 'a fair opportunity to make submissions'.

Reasons for Granting Bail

Where a magistrates' court or the Crown Court grants bail to a person to whom the BA 1976, s. 4, applies after hearing representations from the prosecutor in favour of withholding bail, it must give reasons for its decision (s. 5(2A)), and those reasons must be included in the record of the court's decision, a copy of which must be given to the prosecutor if he so requests (s. 5(2B)).   **D7.77**

Certificates of Full Argument

Section 5(6A)–(6C) of the BA 1976 deal with certificates of full argument. Section 5(6A) applies where a magistrates' court adjourns a case under the PCC(S)A 2000, s. 11, or the CDA 1998, s. 52(5), or the MCA 1980, s. 10, 17C, 18 or 24C, and remands the accused in custody after hearing a fully argued bail application (s. 5(6A)(a)). In such a case, the court must issue a certificate confirming that full argument was heard if either the court has not previously heard full argument on a bail application made by the accused in the proceedings in question, or it has previously heard such argument but is satisfied that there has been a change in circumstances or that new considerations have been placed before it (s. 5(6A)(b)). In a case where the court heard a second or subsequent fully argued application on the basis of a change in circumstances or new considerations, the certificate must state what the change was (s. 5(6B)). The accused must be given a copy of the certificate (s. 5(6C)). The significance of the issue of a certificate of full argument is that the right to apply to the Crown Court for bail is dependent on it (Senior Courts Act 1981, s. 81(1)(g) and (1J)).   **D7.78**

It should be noted that an adjournment during a summary trial (under the MCA 1980, s. 10) includes an adjournment for reports after conviction, so the obligation to issue a certificate may arise if the accused is remanded in custody at that stage. Moreover, the obligation to issue a certificate also applies where bail is refused on an adjournment under the PCC(S)A 2000, s. 11, for medical reports.

Informing Unrepresented Accused of his Right to Apply to Other Courts

Where a magistrates' court withholds bail from an unrepresented accused and sends him for trial to the Crown Court or issues a certificate under s. 5(6A), he must be informed that he may apply to the Crown Court for bail (BA 1976, s. 5(6)).   **D7.79**

OPTIONS OPEN TO AN ACCUSED REMANDED IN CUSTODY OR ON CONDITIONAL BAIL BY MAGISTRATES

Where the accused is refused bail by the magistrates' court, he may apply for bail to the Crown Court. An appeal can also be made against a decision of the magistrates' court to impose conditions on bail.   **D7.80**

Appeal to the Crown Court

D7.81   The restrictions on the right of an accused to make repeated bail applications to the magistrates' court are offset to some extent by the possibility of applying to the Crown Court for bail. The right to apply is contained in the Senior Courts Act 1981, s. 81(1) (see **D27.17**). Section 81(1)(g) provides that the Crown Court may grant bail to any person who has been remanded in custody by a magistrates' court on adjourning a case under the PCC(S)A 2000, s. 11, or the CDA 1998, s. 52(5), or the MCA 1980, s. 10, 17C, 18 or 24C. Section 81(1J) provides that the Crown Court may grant bail under s. 81(1)(g) only if the magistrates' court which remanded the accused in custody has certified (under the BA 1976, s. 5(6A)) that it 'heard full argument on his application for bail before it refused the application'. As we have seen, the BA 1976, s. 5(6A), imposes a duty on a magistrates' court which refuses bail following full argument to issue a certificate to that effect if either it was the first occasion of such argument or there has been a change in circumstances or new considerations since the previous argued application. The combined effect of the SCA 1981, s. 81(1)(g) and (1J), and the BA 1976, s. 5(6A), is that, where a fully argued bail application is refused by magistrates, the defence should obtain a certificate of full argument from the court which they may then use to found a further application to the Crown Court. The right to apply to the Crown Court is thus dependent on a fully argued application having been made before the magistrates.

If the Crown Court confirms the refusal of bail, it may be possible (in exceptional cases) for the accused to seek judicial review of that decision (see **D7.89**).

Once the accused has been sent for trial under the CDA 1998, s. 51 or 51A, he may apply to the Crown Court for bail by virtue of s. 81(1)(a) of the 1981 Act, which empowers the Crown Court to grant bail to any person who has been sent in custody to appear before it. At this stage, there is no need to rely on a certificate of full argument.

Appeal against Imposition of Conditions

D7.82   The CJA 2003, s. 16(1), enables an accused to appeal to the Crown Court against the imposition of certain bail conditions, namely those set out in s. 16(3), that the person concerned:

(a) resides away from a particular place or area,
(b) resides at a particular place other than a bail hostel,
(c) has to provide a surety or sureties, or security,
(d) remains indoors between certain hours,
(e) is to be subject to an electronic monitoring requirement under the BA 1976, s. 3(6ZAA), or
(f) makes no contact with another person.

The right of appeal under s. 16 can be exercised only if the accused has previously made an application to the magistrates (under the BA 1976, s. 3(8)(a): see **D7.136**) for the conditions to be varied or if the conditions were imposed following an application by the prosecution under the BA 1976, s. 3(8)(b) or 5B(1) (s. 16(4), (5) and (6)). Once the Crown Court has disposed of the appeal, no further appeal can be brought under s. 16 unless an application or further application under the BA 1976, s. 3(8)(a), is made to the magistrates' court after the appeal (s. 16(8)).

PROCEDURE FOR BAIL APPLICATIONS IN THE CROWN COURT

Notice of Appeal

D7.83   The procedure for bail applications in the Crown Court is governed by the CrimPR, r. 19.8. The rule applies when the accused wants to apply to the Crown Court for bail after bail has been withheld by a magistrates' court or to appeal to the Crown Court after a magistrates' court has refused an application by the accused (under the BA 1976, s. 3(8)(a)) to vary a condition of bail (r. 19.8(1)).

Written notice of the intention to make the application must be given to the magistrates' court, the Crown Court and the prosecutor (and any surety affected or proposed) as soon as reasonably practicable after the decision of the magistrates' court (r. 19.8(2)). The notice must explain why bail should not be withheld, or why the condition of bail under appeal should be varied (as the case may be), should identify any further information or legal argument that has become available since the decision of the magistrates' court and, where it is an application for bail, should attach a copy of the certificate that the magistrates heard full argument as to bail (r. 19.8(3)).

If the prosecutor opposes the application, he must notify the Crown Court and the accused at once, and must serve notice of the reasons for opposing the application (r. 19.8(5)).

Unless the Crown Court directs otherwise, the application or appeal should be heard no later than the business day after notice of the application or appeal was served (r. 19.8(6)).

The Hearing

The application may be heard in public or in private (CrimPR, r. 19.2(2)); such applications are often heard in chambers. The application will be heard by a circuit judge or recorder. The hearing follows the pattern of a bail application in the magistrates' court, with counsel for the prosecution summarising the objections to bail and counsel for the applicant responding to those objections.   **D7.84**

If bail is granted to an accused who was refused it by magistrates at a remand hearing, the Crown Court may direct him to appear 'at a time and place which the magistrates' court could have directed' and the recognizance of any surety shall be conditioned accordingly (Senior Courts Act 1981, s. 81(1H)). Any sureties required by the Crown Court may enter into their recognizances before, *inter alia*, an officer of the Crown Court, a police officer who is either in charge of a police station or of the rank of inspector or above, or the governor of the prison where the accused is presently detained (BA 1976, s. 8(4); CrimPR, r. 19.14(3)(b)).

When considering whether a bail application should be heard in public, the Crown Court should apply the principles laid down in *R (Malik) v Central Criminal Court* [2007] 4 All ER 1141. The court must start from the 'fundamental presumption in favour of open justice' (per Gray J at [40]). The court therefore has to consider whether it is necessary, in the interests of justice, to depart from the ordinary rule of open justice. The judgment makes it clear that this is not an exercise of discretion (which implies a judicial choice between two or more equally proper courses), but of judgement as to whether a departure from the norm is justified (at [30]). It may, for example, be appropriate for the court to sit in chambers if the delay involved in arranging a public hearing would defeat the purpose of the application (at [31]). It may be in the interests of the accused for the bail application to be heard in private, e.g., (a) where the prosecution need to rehearse a damaging case against the accused; (b) where the prosecution intend to give detailed reasons for fearing that the accused will not surrender if given bail; (c) where the accused's previous convictions will be referred to; (d) where it will or may be necessary to reveal personal and confidential information about the accused or about prosecution witnesses or others; and (e) where the court may need to be told about information which has been provided to the prosecuting authorities by the accused or by someone else connected with the case (at [33]). Gray J added that it does not follow that bail applications have to be listed and called on in open court and then adjourned to chambers only if a case is made for doing so. He said that there is nothing objectionable in listing bail applications on the provisional assumption that the interests of justice call for a closed hearing, so long as any application to sit in public is approached on the footing that it must be acceded to unless there is a sound reason for excluding the public. Such an application will ordinarily come from one or both of the parties, but it may also legitimately come from the media or some other third party (at [35]). Another point which emerges from *Malik* is that, where the accused has legal representation, he has no right to be produced from prison for the purposes of a bail application. Gray J pointed out that the increasing use of video links between the court and the prison where the accused is detained   **D7.85**

D

effectively removes any disadvantage to the accused by reason of his not being physically present when the application for bail is heard (at [38]). It is submitted that it follows from this that where no video link is available a request for an accused to be produced should be looked on more favourably by the court.

Repeated Bail Applications in the Crown Court

D7.86   Part IIA of sch. 1 to the BA 1976 applies to bail applications in the Crown Court just as it applies to applications before the magistrates. Therefore, if one application for bail has already been made to the Crown Court, a further argued application may not be presented unless there are fresh arguments or considerations to put before the court (see **D7.70**).

Application for Bail during the Crown Court Proceedings

D7.87   CPD III, para. 19G.2 (see Supplement, **PD-35**), makes the point that, once the trial has begun, the grant of bail during adjournments (such as lunch-time or overnight) is a matter for the discretion of the trial judge (or magistrates, as the case may be). Paragraph 19G.3 states that, where the accused was on bail before the trial, he should not be refused bail during the trial (for example, lunch-time or overnight adjournments) unless, in the opinion of the court, there are 'positive reasons' to justify such refusal. Two examples are given: (a) a point has been reached where there is a real danger that the accused will abscond, either because the case is going badly for him, or for any other reason, or (b) there is a real danger that he may interfere with witnesses, jurors or a co-accused. Paragraph 19G.4 states that, where the accused has been found guilty, the question of bail should be decided in the light of the gravity of the offence, any friction between co-accused, and the likely sentence.

BAIL BY THE HIGH COURT

Statutory Bail Jurisdiction of the High Court

D7.88   The CJA 2003, s. 17, abolished the free-standing jurisdiction of the High Court to grant bail where it had been refused by a magistrates' court. There remain, however, a number of instances where the High Court has a statutory jurisdiction to grant bail:

(1) Under the CJA 1967, s. 22(1), the High Court may entertain an application for bail (or to vary bail conditions) if the accused is appealing by way of case stated against conviction (or sentence, although such appeals are rarely appropriate) and the magistrates have withheld bail or granted only conditional bail (see **D29.23**).

(2) Under the CJA 1948, s. 37, the High Court may also grant bail to a person in three circumstances:

(a) where he is appealing to the High Court by way of case stated from a decision of the Crown Court (s. 37(1)(b)(i)) — in practice, this will be where an accused appeals from the magistrates' court to the Crown Court and then seeks to appeal to the High Court from the decision of the Crown Court (see **D29.37**);

(b) where he is appealing from the Crown Court to the High Court by way of judicial review, seeking an order quashing the decision of the Crown Court (s. 37(1)(b)(ii)) — again this will be the case where the accused is challenging a decision of the Crown Court in its appellate capacity (see **D29.25**); and

(c) where he has been convicted or sentenced by a magistrates' court and is appealing to the High Court by way of judicial review, seeking an order quashing the decision of the magistrates (s. 37(1)(d)).

Challenging Refusal of Bail by Way of Judicial Review

D7.89   There is also the possibility of challenging a refusal of bail by way of judicial review. Although Stanley Burnton J in *R (Lipinski) v Wolverhampton Crown Court* [2005] EWHC 1950

(Admin) (at [17]–[20]), expressed doubts about the availability of judicial review to challenge the refusal of bail by a Crown Court judge because of the effect of the Senior Courts Act 1981, s. 29(3) (which excludes judicial review of the Crown Court 'in matters relating to trial on indictment'), the weight of authority clearly establishes that s. 29 is not to be regarded as a bar to judicial review of bail decisions. In *R (M) v Isleworth Crown Court* [2005] EWHC 363 (Admin), Maurice Kay LJ considered the effect of s. 29(3), and said that 'a decision as to *bail at an early stage of criminal proceedings* [emphasis added] does not relate to trial on indictment as that expression has been interpreted in cases such as *R v Manchester Crown Court, ex parte DPP* (1994) 98 Cr App R 461', in that such a decision does not arise in the issue between the Crown and the accused formulated by the indictment (the test propounded in that case by Lord Browne-Wilkinson). His lordship referred to the case of *Cox* [1997] 1 Cr App R 20, where it had been held that a refusal of bail was not susceptible to judicial review, saying that the rationale of that decision was the availability of an alternative remedy, namely the possibility that then existed of an application to a High Court judge. However, that right has been abolished by the CJA 2003, s. 17. His lordship went on to point out that s. 17(6)(b) of the 2003 Act provides that: 'Nothing in this section affects…any right of a person to apply for a writ of habeas corpus or any other prerogative remedy'. He said that he had no doubt that 'prerogative remedies' in that context embraced those set out in the Senior Courts Act 1981, s. 29(1), namely mandatory orders, prohibiting orders and quashing orders. That meant, he said, that the Divisional Court now has jurisdiction to review a bail decision by the Crown Court. Having ruled that judicial review was available in such cases, Maurice Kay LJ went on to say (at [11]–[12]):

> Although we have jurisdiction by reason of s. 17(6)(b), I am in no doubt that it is a jurisdiction which we should exercise very sparingly indeed. It would be ironic and retrograde if, having abolished a relatively short and simple remedy on the basis that it amounted to wasteful duplication, Parliament has, by a side wind, created a more protracted and expensive remedy of common application…The test must be on *Wednesbury* principles, but robustly applied and with this court always keeping in mind that Parliament has understandably vested the decision in judges in the Crown Court who have everyday experience of, and feel for, bail applications. Of course if bail were to be refused on a basis such as 'I always refuse in this type of case', or some other unjudicial basis, then this court would and should interfere.

This decision was followed in *R (Shergill) v Harrow Crown Court* [2005] EWHC 648 (Admin), **D7.90** confirming that s. 29(3) of the 1981 Act does not preclude the Divisional Court from considering applications for judicial review of a decision to refuse bail, but that it was only in exceptional cases that the court would consider it right to review the decision of a Crown Court judge in whom the relevant powers had been vested. The court went on to make two observations. First, a claim for judicial review of the decision of a Crown Court judge to refuse bail should be put before a judge of the Administrative Court or, in the vacation, the vacation judge. The judge may indicate that there is absolutely no chance that the decision would be overturned and reject it out of hand. Otherwise, the matter should then be heard orally as soon as possible, normally within 48 hours (with notice being given to the Crown Court and the prosecution). Secondly, it is essential that reasons given by a Crown Court judge for refusing bail are recorded so that, if any application for judicial review is made, the Administrative Court has a record of the reasons for refusal. In *R (Galliano) v Crown Court at Manchester* [2005] EWHC 1125 (Admin), the court made it clear that an accused who has been refused bail by a Crown Court judge can succeed on a claim for judicial review only if he persuades the High Court judge that the decision made by the Crown Court judge was one which fell outside the bounds of what could be regarded as reasonable: nothing short of irrationality will entitle the High Court to interfere. Parliament has decided that the right to go to the High Court to seek bail should be abolished, and so the normal court of last resort in questions of bail is the Crown Court. It follows that the High Court will be reluctant to entertain claims for judicial review of a failure to grant bail and will only do so if satisfied that the decision of the Crown Court judge was an irrational one (per Collins J at [11]).

It should be noted that s. 29(3) of the 1981 Act prevents a challenge by way of judicial review to a decision by a trial judge during a Crown Court trial to revoke the bail of the accused (*R (Uddin) v Leeds Crown Court* [2014] 1 WLR 1742).

D7.91   Further guidance on procedure was given in *R (Allwin) v Snaresbrook Crown Court* [2005] EWHC 742 (Admin), where it was said that it will not generally be appropriate to grant bail on an interim application on the papers. The Administrative Court judge should direct an oral hearing within a day or two to determine the issue. If, at that hearing, the court is minded to review the Crown Court's decision, permission will be granted, all procedural requirements will be abridged, and the matter will be remitted to the Crown Court to formally grant bail. Such hearings will normally be dealt with by a single judge.

Where the High Court does quash a refusal of bail, it will normally remit the matter to the court below for the question of bail to be reconsidered. It will be rare for the High Court to substitute its own decision. In *R (R) v Snaresbrook Crown Court* [2011] EWHC 3569 (Admin), Holman J said (at [29]) that the High Court:

> ...must be very especially sparing before, in the course of a trial itself, it substitutes its own decision as to bail for that of the judge conducting the trial. If this court considers...that there has been significant procedural error, it should remit the substantive issue of bail for reconsideration by the judge, who is currently conducting this case in the Crown Court, unless this court can properly conclude that no reasonable judge, properly directing himself, could have withdrawn or could now withdraw bail (subject to any appropriate conditions or varied conditions). If I am satisfied that not only this judge, but no judge acting reasonably and lawfully, could fail to grant bail (subject to any appropriate conditions), then it is no more than a waste of time and expense to remit the matter to the Crown Court. If, however, there is still room for a discretionary decision to withdraw bail, then that is a decision which should be made by the Crown Court judge, but after hearing submissions on behalf of the claimant and possibly the prosecution.

PROSECUTION APPLICATIONS RELATING TO BAIL

Prosecution Right of Appeal against Decision to Grant Bail

D7.92   The Bail (Amendment) Act 1993 (see **D7.137**) confers upon the prosecution the right to appeal to the Crown Court against a decision by a magistrates' court to grant bail (s. 1(1)), and also to appeal to the High Court when the Crown Court grants bail other than in the context of an appeal against the grant of bail by a magistrates' court under s. 1(1) (s. 1(1B) and (1C)).

Under s. 1(1)–(3), this right is limited to cases where:

(a) the accused is charged with, or convicted of, an offence which is (or would be in the case of an adult) punishable by imprisonment; and

(b) the prosecution is conducted by or on behalf of the DPP (this includes prosecutions conducted by the CPS), or by a prosecutor specified in the schedule to the Bail (Amendment) Act 1993 (Prescription of Prosecuting Authorities) Order 1994 (SI 1994 No. 1438), which includes the Revenue and Customs Prosecutions Office, the Serious Fraud Office, the Department of Business, Innovation and Skills, the Department of Work and Pensions and a universal service provider within the meaning of the Postal Services Act 2011); and

(c) before bail was granted, the prosecution made representations that bail should not be granted.

Procedure

D7.93   The Bail (Amendment) Act 1993 (see **D7.137**) and the CrimPR, r. 19.9 (see Supplement, **R-186**), lay down the procedural requirements with which the prosecution must comply in order to exercise its right. It must give oral notice of appeal at the conclusion of the proceedings in which bail was granted, and before the accused is released from custody (s. 1(4) of the 1993 Act). In *Isleworth Crown Court, ex parte Clarke* [1998] 1 Cr App R 257, this requirement was held to be satisfied where notice was given to the justices' clerk about five minutes after the court rose and before the accused had been released from custody. The Divisional Court held that a delay of five minutes or so, especially where an accused had not yet been released from custody, did not bring the case into a category in which it could be said that oral notice was not given at the conclusion of the proceedings. Moreover, since notice can properly be given to the justices' clerk, it is not necessary that the justices should themselves be in court.

Following the oral notice of appeal, the magistrates must remand the accused in custody (s. 1(6)). The oral notice given under s. 1(4) must be confirmed in writing and served on the accused within two hours after the conclusion of the proceedings (s. 1(5)); otherwise the appeal is deemed to be disposed of (s. 1(7)) and the accused will be released on bail on the terms granted by the magistrates' court.

In *R (Jeffrey) v Warwick Crown Court* [2002] EWHC 2469 (Admin), the prosecutor served the written notice of appeal on the accused three minutes late. The Divisional Court held that Parliament did not intend that the time-limit for serving notice of appeal should defeat an appeal if the prosecution had given itself ample time to serve the notice on the accused within the two-hour period, had used due diligence to serve the notice within that period, and the failure to do so was not the fault of the prosecution but was due to circumstances outside its control (per Hooper J at [11]). Furthermore, the court said that the delay of three minutes had not caused the accused any prejudice, since he knew at the conclusion of the proceedings before the magistrates that the prosecution was exercising its right of appeal and he knew that he was being detained in custody as a result of the oral application for him to be remanded in custody until the appeal was disposed of (at [9]).

The Crown Court must hear the appeal within 48 hours, excluding weekends and public holidays (s. 1(8)). In *Middlesex Guildhall Crown Court, ex parte Okoli* [2001] 1 Cr App R 1, the Divisional Court construed this as meaning that the appeal hearing must commence within two working days of the date of the decision of the magistrates' court. The court rejected the contention that the appeal had to commence literally within 48 hours of the moment upon which oral notice had been given.

D7.94 The appeal takes the form of a rehearing. The judge may remand the accused in custody or grant bail with or without conditions (s. 1(9)). The hearing may be in held in public or in private (CrimPR, r. 19.2(2)). Under r. 19.2(1)(c), the accused is entitled to be present at the hearing of the appeal unless the court is satisfied that he has waived his right to attend or that it would be just to proceed in his absence. It is submitted that it will rarely be 'just' to proceed in the absence of the accused if he wishes to be present. In *Allen v UK* (2010) 51 EHRR 555 it was held that a refusal to allow the applicant to attend the hearing of the prosecution's appeal against bail being granted amounted to a breach of Article 5(4), mainly because the prosecution appeal against bail is regarded as a re-hearing of the application for bail; it followed that 'the applicant should have been afforded the same guarantees at the prosecution's appeal as at first instance'. It should be noted, however, that a person is to be treated as present in court when, by virtue of a live link direction, he attends the hearing through a live link (see the CDA 1998, ss. 57A and 57B at **D5.38**).

Although the MCA 1980, ss. 128, 128A and 129 (see **D5.31** *et seq.*), do not directly bind the Crown Court, where the accused has not yet been sent to the Crown Court for trial, and the judge decides to remand him in custody, the judge must stipulate a date which is in accordance with the powers of the justices under those sections (*Re Szakal* [2000] 1 Cr App R 248, followed in *Remice v HMP Belmarsh* [2007] EWHC 936 (Admin)).

D7.95 **Guidance on the Use of the Power of Prosecution Appeal** Guidance issued by the CPS in their Legal Guidance Manual (www.cps.gov.uk/legal/a_to_c/bail/) states that the right of appeal against a grant of bail must be used 'judiciously and responsibly'. It should be used only 'in cases of grave concern'. The 'overarching test' is 'whether there is a serious risk of harm to any member of the public or any other significant risk of harm to any member of the public or any other significant public interest ground'.

Prosecution Application for Reconsideration of Bail

D7.96 Under the BA 1976, s. 5B, the prosecution can, in certain circumstances, apply for the grant of bail by a magistrates' court (or by a police officer) to be reconsidered (s. 5B(A1)). The power to make such an application is limited to indictable offences, including those that are triable either way (s. 5B(2)). Any application must be based on information which was not available to the court (or police officer) granting bail when the decision was taken (s. 5B(3)).

The CrimPR, r. 19.7 (see Supplement, **R-184**), applies (*inter alia*) to an application by the prosecution to withdraw bail granted by a court, or to impose or vary a bail condition. The application must be in writing and must explain the reason for the application and identify the material information that has come to light since the most recent bail decision was made (r. 19.7(2)(a) and (3)(c)). The notice must be served on the accused and the court (and on any surety affected) not less than two business days before the hearing of the application (r. 19.7(2)(b) and (c)). Unless the court directs otherwise, an application to withdraw bail should be heard no later than the second business day after service of the notice, and an application to impose or vary a bail condition should be heard no later than the fifth business day after service of the notice (r. 19.7(6)). Where the application is for reconsideration of the grant of police bail, the CrimPR, r. 19.6, which is in similar terms to r. 19.7, applies.

When an application is made by the prosecutor under the BA 1976, s. 5B, the court may vary the bail conditions, or impose conditions if the original grant of bail was unconditional, or with-hold bail altogether (s. 5B(1)). In deciding what order to make, the court must act in accordance with the presumption in favour of bail contained in s. 4 and sch. 1 (s. 5B(4)). If the decision is to withhold bail and the accused is before the court, he will be remanded in custody. If not before the court, he must be ordered to surrender to custody (s. 5B(5)(b)) and is liable to arrest without warrant if he fails without reasonable cause to surrender to custody in accordance with the order (s. 5B(7)). Where the accused is arrested pursuant to s. 5B(7), he must be taken before a magistrate within 24 hours (excluding Sundays), and the magistrate must remand him in custody (s. 5B(8)).

Section 5B(8A) stipulates that, where the court refuses to withhold bail from the accused after hearing representations from the prosecutor in favour of withholding bail, the court must give reasons for refusing to withhold bail. Those reasons must be set out in the record of the court's decision, a copy of which must be given to the prosecutor if he so requests (s. 5B(8C)).

FAILURE TO COMPLY WITH BAIL

D7.97 Where an accused who has been granted bail in criminal proceedings fails to comply with the obligations imposed upon him, two main questions arise. The first is how the court should ensure that he will attend court for the remaining stages of the proceedings; the second is how he (and any sureties) will be dealt with in consequence of his breach of bail.

Powers of the Court when a Bailed Accused Fails to Appear

D7.98 When a person who is on bail fails to surrender to custody in answer to his bail, the court has a number of options.

(1) The court may issue a warrant (often called a 'bench warrant') for his arrest, under the BA 1976, s. 7(1). This applies whatever court he was bailed to attend and regardless of whether bail was granted by the custody officer at the police station or by the court itself at an earlier hearing. The usual form of warrant simply orders the arrest of the accused and that he be brought to court. However, at the court's discretion, the warrant may be 'backed for bail' (see **D7.99**), either with

or without a requirement for sureties. Where the accused fails to appear, a bench warrant will normally be issued. It should be noted that the Justices' Clerks Rules 2005 (SI 2005 No. 545), sch. 1, para. 3, empowers a clerk to issue a warrant of arrest, whether or not endorsed for bail, for failure to surrender to court, where there is no objection on behalf of the accused.

(2) Instead of issuing a warrant, a magistrates' court may adjourn and extend the accused's bail under the MCA 1980, s. 129 (see D7.73). Similarly, the Crown Court, in appropriate cases, may simply order that the case be stood out of the list and take no further action in respect of the accused (who will remain under an obligation to attend whenever the case is next listed). Such a course of action is appropriate only where the court is satisfied that there is a good reason for the accused's non-attendance (e.g., a doctor's certificate has been sent to the court indicating that he is unfit to attend).

(3) It may be possible to proceed in the absence of the accused (though it should be borne in mind that if the offence is triable either way, a magistrates' court may try the case only with the consent of the accused, and that consent has to be given at a hearing at which the accused is present unless the court is satisfied that there is a good reason for the absence of the accused and he is represented by a lawyer who consents to summary trial on his behalf: see D6.9).

Warrants Backed for Bail Where the court decides to issue an arrest warrant, the warrant **D7.99** may be endorsed with a direction that the person named in it, having been arrested, shall then be released on bail (see the MCA 1980, s. 117, and the SCA 1981, s. 81(4), respectively, for the power of magistrates and the Crown Court). This is generally known as 'backing the warrant for bail'. The accused has to be taken to a police station before being bailed only if his bail is subject to one or more sureties. Such warrants are, however, sometimes viewed as consuming a disproportionate amount of police time and effort in return for little or no advantage. Guidance issued by Thomas LJ (the Senior Presiding Judge for England and Wales) in May 2006 (see www.judiciary.gov.uk/wp-content/uploads/JCO/Documents/Protocols/bail_trials_absence.pdf) encouraged the use of warning letters instead of warrants backed for bail: where the accused does not attend, and the court decides not to proceed in his absence and is considering the issue of a warrant backed for bail (described in the guidance as 'likely to be uncommon cases'), the court should consider whether it is better to send a letter to the accused:

...directing him to attend and warning him of the consequences of non-attendance, instead of issuing a warrant backed for bail.

The guidance carries on:

...if the defendant does not attend the rearranged hearing without good reason, the court should then consider proceeding in absence or issuing a warrant not backed for bail. Unless there were unusual circumstances, any other course of action would undermine the process. The letter to the defendant should make it clear that, if the defendant did not attend the rearranged hearing, a court might well proceed in absence or issue a warrant not backed for bail.

Proof of Inability to Attend Court The guidance issued by Thomas LJ also deals with the **D7.100** question of evidence of inability to attend court through sickness, and makes the point that:

Proper evidence must be supplied if a defendant claims he is unwell and unable to attend court; the standard 'off-work' or 'unfit to work' sick note will generally not establish that a person is too ill to attend court. There should normally be a letter from a doctor expressly stating that the defendant is too ill to attend court; this should be provided to the court before the date the defendant is due to appear. A letter can be followed up by a phone call from the clerk or legal adviser to the surgery if the court has doubts about its validity. Unless there is such evidence, the court should consider proceeding in the defendant's absence.

CPD III, para. 19B.2 (see Supplement, **PD-30**), states that an accused who will be unable to attend court for medical reasons must supply the court with a certificate from his GP (or another appropriate medical practitioner, such as a hospital doctor) in advance of the hearing. Without a medical certificate, or if an unsatisfactory certificate is provided, the court is likely to consider that the accused has failed to surrender and deal with him accordingly (para. 19B.3).

Surrender to Custody

D7.101 The power to issue a warrant under the BA 1976, s. 7(1), arises only if the accused fails to surrender to custody at the time appointed. In this context, 'surrendering to custody' merely connotes complying with whatever procedure is prescribed by the court for those answering to their bail: 'if a court provides a procedure which, by some form of direction, by notice or orally, instructs a person surrendering to bail to report to a particular office or to a particular official, when he complies with that direction he surrenders to his bail' (*DPP v Richards* [1988] QB 701, per Glidewell LJ at p. 711). Thus, if a court operates a system whereby persons on bail are required to report to an usher and are then allowed to wait in the court precincts until their case is called, a person who so reports has surrendered to custody, even though he is under no physical restraint and is not in the cell area. It follows that, if he subsequently goes away before the court is ready to deal with his case, he has not absconded within the meaning of s. 6, and a warrant may *not* be issued under s. 7(1). However, that situation is covered by s. 7(2), which provides that, where a person who has been released on bail in criminal proceedings absents himself from the court (without permission from the court) at any time after he has surrendered to custody but before the court is ready to begin or resume the hearing of the proceedings, the court may issue a warrant for his arrest.

In *Central Criminal Court, ex parte Guney* [1996] AC 616, the House of Lords held that, where an accused is formally arraigned, the arraignment amounts to surrender to the custody of the court. The accused's further detention is therefore within the discretion and power of the judge and, unless the judge grants him bail, he will remain in custody pending and during his trial. It also followed that the obligations of any surety are also extinguished at that point. In *Kent Crown Court, ex parte Jodka* (1997) 161 JP 638, the Divisional Court held that bail granted by magistrates ceases when the defendant surrenders to the custody of the Crown Court, whether or not the defendant is arraigned (i.e. enters a plea) at that hearing. It follows that the jurisdiction of the magistrates to grant bail does not extend beyond the first occasion on which a defendant surrenders to the Crown Court (*Choudhry v Birmingham Crown Court* (2008) 172 JP 33, per Gibbs J at [33]).

In *Evans* [2012] 1 WLR 1192, the Court of Appeal had to consider what amounts to surrender to custody in the Crown Court. Hughes LJ noted (at [15]) that 'what constitutes surrender has necessarily to vary to some extent according to the arrangements which are made for accepting surrender at any particular court'. His lordship (at [20]) summarised the practical effect of the decision of the House of Lords in *Guney* thus: 'once arraignment has taken place, however informal its particular circumstances may be, the court must review the question of bail and if a surety is involved direct a fresh taking of a recognizance...[W]henever else it may happen surrender is deemed to have taken place on arraignment'. His lordship went on to say (at [27]) that surrender is normally accomplished by way of entry into the dock. However, in the Crown Court, 'surrender may also be accomplished by the commencement of any hearing before the judge where the defendant is formally identified and whether he enters the dock or not'. Consequently, the Court rejected (at [28]) the suggestion that reporting to the usher amounts to surrender. The Court reasoned (at [29], [32] and [36]):

> ...in the absence of either stepping into the dock in a Crown Court or in such a court being formally identified for the purposes of hearing, the defendant has not put himself into anything which can properly be called 'custody'. Nor...has he overtly subjected himself to the directions of the court.

> ...once a defendant arrives at the Crown Court building he is in one sense not entirely at liberty to come and go as he wishes. That, however, does not...mean that he has thereby surrendered...[M]ere arrival at the Crown Court building does not constitute surrender and could not do so. The correct analysis seems to us to be not that he has surrendered but that he knows that he may be required at any moment to do so and in consequence he would be very unwise to wander away.

> ...in the absence of special arrangements either particular to the court or particular to the individual case, surrender to the Crown Court is accomplished when the defendant presents himself to the custody officers by entering the dock or where a hearing before the judge commences at which he is formally identified as present...[I]f there has been no previous surrender, as ordinarily there will have been, it is also accomplished by arraignment...[T]he position in the Magistrates' Court may be the same, but may easily differ as explained in *DPP v Richards*.

Breach of Bail Conditions

Under s. 7(3) of the BA 1976, where a person has been bailed to attend a court, a police officer **D7.102**
may arrest him without warrant prior to the surrender date if:

(a) the officer has reasonable grounds for believing that he is not likely to surrender to custody; or
(b) the officer has reasonable grounds for believing that he has broken, or is likely to break, any
condition of his bail; or
(c) a surety has given written notice to the police that the person bailed is unlikely to surrender
to custody and for that reason the surety wishes to be relieved of his obligations.

Following arrest under s. 7(3), s. 7(4) stipulates that the person arrested must be brought before
a magistrate as soon as practicable and, in any event, within 24 hours (excluding Sundays
(s. 7(7)), and so a person arrested on a Saturday under s. 7(3) need not be brought before a
magistrate until the following Monday). The wording of s. 7(4) makes it clear that the person
arrested must be brought before a single justice (s. 7(4)(a)); the justice need not be sitting in a
courtroom. Where, however, the accused is arrested under s. 7(3) within 24 hours of the time
appointed for him to surrender to custody, he must be brought before the court at which he was
to have surrendered to custody (s. 7(4)(b)).

In *Governor of Glen Parva Young Offender Institution, ex parte G* [1998] QB 877, the accused was
arrested for breach of bail conditions. He was taken to the cells of a magistrates' court within 24
hours of arrest but was not brought before a magistrate until two hours after the expiry of the
24-hour time-limit. The Divisional Court held that the detention after 24 hours was unlawful as
s. 7(4) requires the defendant to be brought before a justice of the peace (not merely brought within
the court precincts or to the court cells) within 24 hours of arrest. The importance of dealing with
the accused within 24 hours was again emphasised in *R (Culley) v Crown Court sitting at Dorchester*
(2007) 171 JP 373, where it was held that the time-limit under s. 7 is a strict one. It follows that
the justice is required to complete his investigation and decision-making in relation to this matter
within the 24-hour period. If the justice fails to do so, the continued custody of the accused becomes
unlawful from the moment the 24-hour period has expired. If the justice purports to remand the
accused in custody after that time, the order is *ultra vires* and unlawful (per Forbes J at [20]).

Arrest following Grant of Conditional Bail by the Crown Court   In *R (Ellison) v Teesside* **D7.103**
Magistrates' Court (2001) 165 JP 355, the Divisional Court held that, where an accused has
been sent for trial to the Crown Court, and is subsequently arrested for breach of a bail condition, the jurisdiction to deal with the accused under s. 7 of the BA 1976 must be exercised by a
magistrate. Thus, the magistrate must deal with the matter; there is no power simply to commit
the accused to the Crown Court to be dealt with. Lord Woolf CJ (at [9]) said that:

> The idea of remanding in custody to the Crown Court a defendant who breaches a condition of his
> bail so that the Crown Court can then deal with bail thereafter is misconceived. The appropriate
> course for the magistrates to take is to remand or commit the defendant to the Crown Court until
> his trial or further order. If the superior court wishes to grant bail, that can be done. Any order made
> by the superior court would then override the decision of the magistrates. But the making of an
> order to a fixed date (as was done in this case) was inappropriate.

It follows from this that, even after the accused has been sent to the Crown Court for trial,
an alleged breach of a bail condition has to be dealt with by a magistrate (since that is what is
required under the BA 1976, s. 7(4)). It is therefore inappropriate for the magistrate to commit
the accused to the Crown Court so that the Crown Court can then deal with the breach of bail.
If the magistrate finds that there has been no breach of a bail condition, the accused will remain
on bail as before. If the magistrate finds that there has been a breach of bail, he may allow bail to
continue as before, or he may impose more stringent conditions. If the magistrate finds that
the accused has indeed breached a bail condition, and decides that the withholding of bail (as
opposed to granting bail but on more onerous conditions) would be appropriate, he should

revoke bail and remand the accused in custody until the date fixed for his trial or further order of the Crown Court. It is then open to the Crown Court to grant bail should the accused then apply for bail to the Crown Court.

D7.104 **Procedure where the Accused is Brought before the Court under s. 7** The question for a magistrate before whom a person is brought under the BA 1976, s. 7, is whether that person is likely to fail to surrender to custody, or else has broken or is likely to break any condition of his bail (as the case may be). If of the opinion that any of those matters is established, the magistrate may remand him in custody (s. 7(5)). Alternatively, he may grant him bail subject to different conditions (or even grant him bail on the same conditions as before if he considers that new conditions would not assist but it is nevertheless not a case where a remand in custody would be justified). Where the magistrate is *not* of the opinion that the accused is likely to fail to surrender to custody or has broken, or is likely to break, a condition of his bail, he *must* grant him bail on the same conditions (if any) as were originally imposed.

These powers are subject to the proviso contained in s. 7(5A). This applies where an accused who has attained the age of 18 was released on bail, and has not yet been convicted in the current proceedings. In such a case, a magistrate cannot withhold bail under s. 7 if it appears to him that there is 'no real prospect that the person will be sentenced to a custodial sentence in the proceedings'.

D7.105 The guidance to judges and magistrates on the subject of bail from Thomas LJ issued in May 2006 (see **D7.53**) also deals with the action to be taken where the accused is arrested for breaching his bail. The guidance says that:

> ...when the offender is to be re-bailed, the court must always consider whether the conditions need strengthening and give reasons for its decision as to continuing the existing terms or strengthening the terms, such as by adding a tagging condition or requiring a surety or security. If a defendant has failed to surrender to bail, it will usually only be in the unusual case that a defendant will be re-bailed on the same terms.

D7.106 **Nature of a s. 7 Inquiry** In *R (Hussain) v Derby Magistrates' Court* [2001] 1 WLR 2454, the court confirmed that investigation into alleged breach of a bail condition is not concerned with the trial of a criminal charge; there is nothing in the language of s. 7(5) which demands that the court should adopt the procedural rigidities appropriate for a more formal hearing such as a summary trial. It follows that there is no need for the court to hear evidence; instead it can base its decision on representations from the prosecution and the defence.

In *R (Vickers) v West London Magistrates' Court* (2003) 167 JP 473, the accused was arrested and brought before the justices for failing to comply with the bail conditions. He sought to raise a defence of reasonable excuse; however, the justices ruled that no such defence exists under the BA 1976, s. 7. Gage J (at [16]–[18]) held that s. 7(5) requires a two-stage approach. First, the justice has to determine whether there has been a breach of a bail condition (if there has been no breach of a condition, then the accused is entitled to be granted bail on precisely the same conditions as before); secondly, if there has been a breach, the justice is obliged to consider whether or not the bailed person should be granted bail again. In carrying out the first stage of that process, the justice must act fairly and give the accused a chance to answer the accusations against him. That does not, however, include an inquiry as to whether the arrested person had any reasonable excuse for breaching bail (since s. 7 makes no mention of such a defence and, indeed, s. 7 does not create a criminal offence). The second stage (assuming that the justice is satisfied that there has been a breach) is the point at which the reasons for the breach of bail become relevant. At that stage, the justice has to consider all the issues relating to 'reasonable excuse' when deciding whether or not to grant bail. The breach of bail will be a factor, but only one factor as to whether or not the bailed person is granted bail again.

In *R (Thomas) v Greenwich Magistrates' Court* (2009) 173 JP 345, Hickinbottom J ruled that, in considering whether the accused has broken any condition of bail, a justice is entitled to rely upon hearsay material, so long as the material is properly evaluated.

Human Rights Issues and the Summary Procedure under s. 7   In its Paper, *Bail and the*   **D7.107**
Human Rights Act 1998 (Law Com No. 269), the Law Commission expressed the view that
the BA 1976, s. 7, is compatible with the ECHR, Article 5 (the right to liberty). See further
D7.37.

In *R (DPP) v Havering Magistrates' Court* [2001] 3 All ER 997, the Divisional Court considered
s. 7 in the context of the ECHR, Articles 5 and 6. It held that Article 6 (the right to a fair trial)
has no direct relevance where a magistrate is exercising his judgement whether or not to remand
a person in custody following breach of bail conditions, since s. 7 does not create any criminal
offence. However, the Court went on to hold that Article 5 is directly relevant. Latham LJ
summarised (at [35]) the effect of Article 5 and the relevant Strasbourg case law thus: 'where a
decision is taken to deprive somebody of his liberty, that should only be done after he has been
given a fair opportunity to answer the basis upon which such an order is sought'. His lordship
went on to hold that the procedure adopted under s. 7 is entirely compatible with the requirements of Article 5. These proceedings are, by their nature, emergency proceedings to determine
whether or not a person, who had not been considered to present risks which would have
justified a remand in custody in the first instance, did subsequently present such risks. When
exercising the power to detain, the magistrate is not entitled to order detention by reason simply
of the finding of a breach. The fact of a breach is evidence of a relevant risk arising, but it is no
more than one of the factors which the magistrate has to consider in exercising his discretion.
The magistrate is required to come to an honest and rational opinion on the material put before
him, that material not being restricted to admissible evidence in the strict sense. In doing so, he
has to bear in mind the consequences for the person arrested, namely the fact that he is at risk
of losing his liberty, in the context of the presumption of innocence. The procedural task of the
magistrate is to ensure that the person arrested has a full and fair opportunity to comment on,
and answer, the material before the court; if that material includes evidence from a witness who
gives oral testimony, there must be an opportunity to cross-examine. Likewise, if the person
arrested wishes to give oral evidence, he is entitled to do so (*R (DPP) v Havering Magistrates'
Court* at [38]–[41]).

No Power to Adjourn Proceedings under s. 7   In *R (DPP) v Havering Magistrates' Court*   **D7.108**
[2001] 3 All ER 997, the Divisional Court confirmed that there is no power for a magistrate
to adjourn the hearing once a person has been brought before him under s. 7 of the BA 1976.
Parliament has to be taken to have determined that there should be a swift and relatively informal resolution of the issues raised, and so the court has to do its best to come to a fair conclusion
on the relevant day; if it cannot do so, it will not be of the opinion that the relevant matters have
been made out which could justify detention (per Latham LJ at [44]). In *R (Hussain) v Derby
Magistrates' Court* [2001] 1 WLR 2454, the accused was arrested for breach of bail conditions.
The magistrates made a preliminary ruling and adjourned the case to the afternoon of the same
day. The Divisional Court held that, under s. 7(4) and (5), justices have power to stand an application out of their list after being seized of it and making a preliminary ruling, with the effect
that a different bench embark on the hearing afresh and determine it on the same day. What has
to be ensured is that the question of continuing detention is placed before a justice within the
24-hour period. The Court added that, where such proceedings are heard by a different court
following adjournment, the relevant allegation should be put to the accused formally at the start
of that hearing.

No Separate Offence under s. 7   It should be emphasised that the BA 1976, s. 7, merely   **D7.109**
confers a power of arrest. It does not create a separate offence (per Hobhouse J in *Rowland*
(14 February 1991 unreported, CA), cited by Dyson LJ in *Gangar* [2008] EWCA Crim 2987
at [12]).

Breach of Bail Conditions as Contempt of Court   Failure to comply with conditions of bail   **D7.110**
can also amount to contempt of court, but that fact is of limited practical relevance. In *Ashley*
[2004] 1 WLR 2057, the accused was convicted of contempt of court, arising out of breaches

of bail conditions. He had been released on bail subject to conditions that required him to surrender his passport and not to leave the country. He broke both conditions but returned to face trial on the appointed day. The Divisional Court held that the purpose of placing restrictions on an individual's movement under the BA 1976 is to ensure that he attends the trial. If the conduct breaching bail is known about at the time, that bail could be revoked. Furthermore, even though s. 7 does not itself create any offence, there may be cases where breach of a bail condition gives rise to a further offence (e.g., where witnesses are intimidated). In the present case, although the defendant had breached bail conditions by leaving the country, he did return for his trial. It followed that the judge did not have power to deal with him by way of contempt of court.

The Offence of Absconding

D7.111   The BA 1976, s. 6, creates the offence of absconding. Under s. 6(1), if a person who has been released on bail fails, without reasonable cause, to surrender to custody, he is guilty of an offence. The burden of showing reasonable cause is on the accused (s. 6(3)). Moreover, a person who had reasonable cause for failing to surrender on the appointed day nevertheless commits an offence if he fails to surrender as soon after the appointed time as is reasonably practicable (s. 6(2)). It follows that where an accused has a reasonable excuse for failing to attend court, he must surrender to custody as soon as reasonably practicable after that excuse ceases to apply (and he commits an offence under s. 6 if he does not). The meaning of 'surrendering to custody' in s. 6(1) and (2) is considered at **D7.101**.

D7.112   An offence under s. 6(1) or (2) is 'punishable either on summary conviction or as if it were a criminal contempt of court' (s. 6(5)). An offender summarily convicted of an offence under s. 6 is liable to imprisonment for up to three months and/or a fine of up to £5,000 (s. 6(7)). A magistrates' court which has convicted the offender of a s. 6 offence may commit him to the Crown Court for sentence if either it considers that the offence merits greater punishment than it has power to inflict, or it is sending the offender for trial to the Crown Court for another offence and it considers that the Crown Court should deal with him for the absconding as well (s. 6(6)). An offender who is committed to the Crown Court for sentence, or who is dealt with in the Crown Court as if he had been guilty of a criminal contempt, is liable to imprisonment for up to 12 months and/or an unlimited fine (s. 6(7)).

D7.113   The accused in *Scott* (2008) 172 JP 149 arrived at court over half an hour late, because he had overslept. The defence argued that this was *de minimis*, and that no Bail Act offence should have been put to him. The Court of Appeal rejected this argument, holding that 'the mere fact that a defendant is only slightly late cannot afford him a defence' (per Toulson LJ at [14]). His lordship added (at [15]) that, even accepting, for the sake of argument, the possibility that there could be circumstances where an accused's late arrival at court was so truly marginal that it would be 'Wednesbury unreasonable' to pursue it, that would be a rare case. His lordship explained this approach (at [16]–[17]):

> Even if a delay is small it can still cause inconvenience and waste of time. If a culture of lateness is tolerated the results can be cumulative and bad for the administration of justice. If the message given to this appellant had been that being half-an-hour late did not really matter, it would have been the wrong message to him and to other people...It was submitted that it was disproportionate and draconian that it should now be on his record that he failed to surrender at the appointed time. Why so? It is a matter of fact he did fail to attend at the appointed time. It was submitted that this could have an unduly harsh effect in the future because another court might refuse him bail. If the message received by defendants is that a failure to answer to their bail on time may have an adverse effect on obtaining bail in future, we cannot see this as a cause for complaint.

D7.114   **Procedure for Prosecuting Offences under the Bail Act 1976, s. 6**   The BA 1976, s. 6(5), provides that an offence under s. 6(1) or (2) is punishable either on summary conviction or as if it were a criminal contempt of court.

However, in *Lubega* (1999) 163 JP 221, the Court of Appeal confirmed that s. 6(5) did not have the effect of converting an offence under the Act to a contempt of court. It followed that the judge was not entitled to deal with the matter in the same way as an ordinary contempt of court.

The procedure to be followed under the BA 1976, s. 6, is set out in CPD III, paras. 19C.1 to 19C.8 (see Supplement, **PD-31**). Where the accused has absconded after being granted bail by a court, he should normally be brought, as soon as appropriate after arrest, before the court at which the proceedings in respect of which bail was granted are to be heard (para. 19C.3). There is no requirement to lay an information or to issue a written charge and requisition. It is regarded as more appropriate that the court itself should initiate the proceedings by its own motion, although the prosecutor may invite the court to take proceedings (para. 19C.4). Where the court initiates proceedings (with or without an invitation from the prosecutor), the prosecutor is expected to assist the court, for example by cross-examining the accused (para. 19C.7). In practice, many magistrates' courts informally ask the absconder or his legal representative what the reason for his non-appearance was. If the explanation seems prima facie satisfactory, the bench indicates that no further action is necessary; otherwise the clerk is instructed to put the charge to the accused. Where a bench, on the occasion of an absconder's first appearance after his absconding, indicates, albeit informally, that no charge need be preferred, that decision is binding on subsequent benches (*France v Dewsbury Magistrates' Court* (1988) 152 JP 301).

D7.115 Where bail was granted by a magistrates' court on sending the accused to the Crown Court for trial or sentence, the trial for the Bail Act offence should take place in the Crown Court. The Crown Court judge will sit alone, without a jury (*Schiavo v Anderton* [1987] QB 20, at p. 34A).

CPD III, para. 19C.5, states that the court should not, without good reason, adjourn proceedings under s. 6 until the conclusion of the proceedings in respect of which bail was granted; rather, the court should deal with the bail matter 'as soon as is practicable' (taking into account when the proceedings in respect of which bail was granted are expected to conclude, the seriousness of the offence for which the defendant is already being prosecuted, the type of penalty that might be imposed for the Bail Act offence and the original offence, and any other relevant circumstances).

A certified copy of the record made under the BA 1976, s. 5(1), of the granting of bail is evidence of the time and place at which the accused should have surrendered. The court file will show whether he did in fact surrender. Thus, although it is in theory possible for the prosecution to call the evidence of absconding, the basic facts will usually be established from court documents. The prosecution's role is therefore essentially one of testing in cross-examination any reason put forward by the accused to explain his non-appearance.

D7.116 **Failure to Answer Police Bail** When the accused has absconded after being granted police bail, the decision whether to initiate proceedings under the BA 1976, s. 6, will be taken by the police and/or the CPS (CPD III, para. 19C.1: see Supplement, **PD-31**); the offence should be dealt with on the first appearance after arrest, unless an adjournment is necessary (para. 19C.2). The prosecutor will conduct the proceedings and, if the accused denies absconding, will call the evidence to prove the case (para. 19C.7). Failure to answer police bail is dealt with by commencement of proceedings in the usual way, using the written charge and requisition procedure, under s. 6(11). Section 6(10) disapplies the MCA 1980, s. 127 (which prevents summary proceedings from being instituted more than six months after the commission of an offence), in respect of offences under the BA 1976, s. 6: instead s. 6(12)–(14) provide that such an offence may not be tried unless proceedings are commenced either within six months of the commission of the offence, or within three months of the date when the defendant surrenders to custody, or is arrested in connection with the offence for which bail was granted, or appears in court in respect of that offence. This ensures that a defendant cannot escape prosecution under s. 6 merely by absconding for more than six months.

D7.117   **Reasonable Excuse**   The offence under the BA 1976, s. 6, is made out only if the court finds that the accused did not have a 'reasonable cause' for failing to surrender to custody. It follows that it is imperative that the accused be given the opportunity to put forward any explanation he may have for his non-attendance. In *Davis* (1986) 8 Cr App R (S) 64, it was said that the court should give the accused an opportunity to explain himself, and invite submissions from counsel; if the accused was unrepresented he should be given the chance to apply for legal representation or, at the very least, be given the fullest possible opportunity of offering some excuse (if he has any) for absenting himself. In *Boyle* [1993] Crim LR 40, Steyn LJ said that it is necessary to invite counsel to call evidence on the s. 6 charge if he wants to do so and, if he does not wish to do so, counsel should be invited to address the judge on the question of guilt or otherwise. The judge should then announce his finding and, if it be a finding of guilt, the judge should give his reasons at that stage. If there is a finding of guilt, the judge should then invite counsel to address him in relation to the question of mitigation and only then impose a sentence. A similar approach was taken in *How* [1993] Crim LR 201, where the accused had not been asked to explain his failure to answer bail or been given an opportunity to put forward any mitigation, and *Hourigan* [2003] EWCA Crim 2306, where the Court of Appeal criticised both the judge and counsel, who had apparently overlooked the fact that, for an offence to be committed under s. 6(1), the failure to surrender has to have been without reasonable cause.

Being mistaken about the day on which one should have appeared was held in *Laidlaw v Atkinson* (1986) *The Times*, 2 August 1986 not to amount to a reasonable cause.

A medical certificate will usually provide the accused with sufficient evidence to defend a charge of failure to surrender, but it should be noted that the court is not absolutely bound by a medical certificate and may require the medical practitioner who issued it to give evidence or the court may exercise its discretion to disregard a certificate it finds to be unsatisfactory (CPD I, para. 5C.3: see Supplement, **PD-15**).

D7.118   **Sentencing Guidelines**   Definitive guidelines for failure to surrender to bail, under the BA 1976, s. 6 (see Supplement, **SG-202**), identify aggravating factors, including: lengthy absence (causing lengthy delay to the administration of justice), serious attempts to evade justice, determined attempt seriously to avoid the jurisdiction of the court and thereby undermine the course of justice, previous relevant convictions and/or repeated breach of court orders or police bail. They also identify mitigating factors, including: prompt voluntary surrender and (when not amounting to a defence) misunderstanding, failure to comprehend bail significance or requirements, and caring responsibilities (as to which para. 22 (see Supplement, **SG-198**) makes the point that an offender's position as the sole or primary carer of dependent relatives may be personal mitigation when it is the reason why he has failed to surrender to custody).

So far as previous convictions are concerned, annex E, para. 6 (see Supplement, **SG-201**), indicates that a previous conviction is likely to be 'relevant' for the purposes of this offence if it demonstrates failure to comply with an order of a court.

D7.119   Annex E, para. 8, makes the important point that 'the fact that an offender has a disorganised or chaotic lifestyle should not normally be treated as mitigation of the offence, but may be regarded as personal mitigation depending on the particular facts of a case'.

Annex E, para. 10, says that the sentence for the Bail Act offence should normally be in addition to any sentence for the original offence, and that, where custodial sentences are being imposed for a Bail Act offence and the original offence, the sentences should normally be consecutive. The same point is made in CPD III, para. 19C.10 (see Supplement, **PD-31**). *Leigh* [2012] EWCA Crim 621 confirms that the starting point for failure to surrender is a consecutive custodial sentence.

Paragraph 13 of the sentencing guidelines (see Supplement, **SG-198**) makes it clear that failure to surrender is a completely separate offence to the one in respect of which bail was granted. It follows that the seriousness of the Bail Act offence is not reduced by subsequent acquittal of the original offence. The rationale for this is that both the culpability and the likely harm (delay, distress and inconvenience to witnesses, and additional costs) are the same whether or not the accused was guilty of the original offence. Annex E, para. 7 (see Supplement, **SG-201**), reiterates that 'acquittal of the original offence does not automatically mitigate this offence'.

Moreover, the Court of Appeal in *White* held that there is no principle of law that the sentence for failing to surrender to custody should be proportionate to the sentence for the substantive offence of which the accused stands convicted. Indeed, it pointed out that in *Neve* (1986) 8 Cr App R (S) 270, a sentence of six months' imprisonment for failing to surrender to custody was upheld, even though the accused had been acquitted of the substantive offence.

Taking a similar approach to *Scott* (2008) 172 JP 149 (see **D7.113**), the sentencing guidelines note, in para. 15, that the period of time for which an accused absconds is likely to influence the court when considering sentence. Being absent for a long period of time will aggravate an offence. However, the fact that an accused arrives at court only a few days (or even only a few hours) late, is not a factor that will necessarily mitigate sentence. This is because, in many cases, the harm will already have been done (e.g., the trial may have been put back, witnesses may have been inconvenienced and there may be an increased likelihood that witnesses will fail to attend at a future hearing). **D7.120**

In *Hourigan* [2003] EWCA Crim 2306, the Court of Appeal made the point that it is inappropriate for a judge in the Crown Court to impose a sentence of less than five days' imprisonment for an offence under s. 6, having regard to the fact that the MCA 1980, s. 132, prohibits magistrates from imposing sentences of less than five days' imprisonment.

Relationship between the BA 1976, ss. 6 and 7

In *Evans* [2012] 1 WLR 1192, the accused's advocate in the Crown Court went into the courtroom where the case was likely to be heard and told the usher that the accused was in the building. The accused later walked out of the building and did not return. When his case was called on, he was not there, and a bench warrant for his arrest was issued. He was subsequently dealt with for the offence of failing to surrender to bail, contrary to the BA 1976, s. 6(1). Hughes LJ (at [9]–[11]) noted that the Act distinguishes between two situations: first, where an accused is on bail but fails without reasonable excuse to surrender to custody (defined in s. 2(2) as 'surrendering himself into the custody of the court…at the time and place for the time being appointed for him to do so'); secondly, where an accused has surrendered to bail but then absents himself from the court before the hearing either begins or resumes, as the case may be. The first situation constitutes an offence under s. 6(1); the second situation, however, does not, but the court may issue a warrant for the accused's arrest under s. 7(2). His lordship observed that the second situation would fall within the common-law offence of escape (*Rumble* (2003) 167 JP 205); the purpose of s. 7(2) is simply to enable the absconder to be apprehended as soon as possible so that the proceedings can begin or continue, as the case may be. His lordship went on (at [15]) to confirm that 'what constitutes surrender has necessarily to vary to some extent according to the arrangements which are made for accepting surrender at any particular court'. **D7.121**

Consequences for Sureties when Accused Absconds

If an accused who is granted bail subject to the provision of one or more sureties fails to surrender at the appointed time, there is a presumption that the court will order forfeiture of the recognizance(s) (i.e. order the sureties to pay the amounts which they had promised to pay). The court does, however, have a discretion, in exceptional circumstances, to order that the surety pay less than the full sum or even to order that none of the sum promised should in fact be forfeited. **D7.122**

The power to forfeit recognizances which relate to the accused appearing in a magistrates' court is contained in the MCA 1980, s. 120(1) and (1A). Section 120(1A)(a) provides that if the

D

Part D Procedure

accused fails to appear in court, the court 'shall…declare the recognizance to be forfeited'. The word 'shall' connotes a duty rather than mere power. However, having declared the automatic forfeiture of any recognizance entered into by a surety, the court is required to issue a summons to the surety to appear before it (unless, of course, he is present) to explain why he should not pay the sum (s. 120(1A)(b)). If the surety fails to answer the summons, the court has the discretion to proceed in his absence, provided that it is satisfied that the summons has been correctly served (s. 120(1A)). The MCA 1980, s. 120(3), provides that the court may, instead of adjudging the surety to pay the whole sum in which he is bound, adjudge him to pay part only of that sum or remit the sum altogether.

There is no express provision for forfeiture of recognizances which relate to the accused appearing in the Crown Court. It is clear from case law, however, that the Crown Court is to be regarded as having the power to order the forfeiture of a recognizance.

Forfeiture of a recognizance given by a surety, whether in respect of appearance by the accused in a magistrates' court or the Crown Court, is dealt with by r. 19.15, which requires the court to serve notice on the surety (and on the accused and the prosecution) of the hearing at which the court will consider forfeiture of the recognizance, and stipulates that forfeiture must not be ordered within five business days of the service of the notice.

Principles Governing Forfeiture of Surety

D7.123 The principles governing forfeiture of a surety's recognizance have been set out in a number of cases, including *Southampton Justices, ex parte Green* [1976] QB 11, *Horseferry Road Stipendiary Magistrate, ex parte Pearson* [1976] 2 All ER 264 and *Crown Court at Wood Green, ex parte Howe* [1992] 1 WLR 702. Before making an order, the court should consider both the surety's means and the extent of his responsibility for the accused's non-appearance, including any steps he took to ensure that he would surrender. However, there is a strong presumption that the surety should forfeit the full recognizance. As it was put in *Ex parte Pearson* at p. 514C:

> …the surety has seriously entered into a serious obligation and ought to pay the amount which he or she has promised unless there are circumstances in the case, either relating to…means or…culpability, which make it fair and just to pay a smaller sum.

The authorities were reviewed extensively by McCullough J in *Uxbridge Justices, ex parte Heward-Mills* [1983] 1 All ER 530. His lordship then summarised their effect thus (at p. 62A–B):

> …the more important principles to be derived from the authorities [are] as follows. (1) When a defendant for whose attendance a person has stood surety fails to appear, the full recognisance should be forfeited, unless it appears fair and just that a lesser sum should be forfeited or none at all. (2) The burden of satisfying the court that the full sum should not be forfeited rests on the surety and is a heavy one. It is for him to lay before the court the evidence of want of culpability and of means on which he relies. (3) Where a surety is unrepresented the court should assist him by explaining these principles in ordinary language, and giving him the opportunity to call evidence and advance argument in relation to them.

D7.124 **Want of Means**   In both *Southampton Justices, ex parte Green* [1976] QB 11 and *Uxbridge Justices, ex parte Heward-Mills* [1983] 1 All ER 530, the orders for forfeiture were quashed because the magistrates had failed properly to take into account the surety's want of means. Nevertheless, the cases emphasise that the burden is on the surety to show impecuniosity. If he wishes to put forward evidence on the matter, the court is under a duty to consider it, even if he had earlier claimed when being accepted as surety that he was worth the sum which he now states he cannot pay (*Ex parte Heward-Mills*, at p. 63). However, there is no obligation on the court to initiate the inquiry (*Ex parte Heward-Mills*, at p. 63). Moreover, it is submitted that, if a proper inquiry was conducted into the surety's means at the time he stood, he should be relieved from his obligations on financial grounds only if something unforeseen has arisen between then and the consideration of forfeiture which prevents him meeting his obligation. Otherwise he benefits from having misled the court which accepted him as surety.

In *Leicestershire Stipendiary Magistrate, ex parte Kaur* (2000) 164 JP 127, the appellant had stood surety in the sum of £150,000. To pay that sum she would have had to sell the matrimonial home. Rose LJ, having reviewed the authorities, summarised the guiding principles thus:

1. Justices have a wide discretion under s. 120 whether to remit in whole or in part;
2. In exercising that discretion, they must plainly have regard only to the surety's assets. The assets of other persons are not assets which can properly be called upon to satisfy a surety's liability;
3. Want of culpability by a surety in the accused's failure to appear is not in itself a reason for not forfeiting or for remitting a recognisance. But there may be circumstances...where the amount forfeited may be reduced because a culpable surety has made very considerable efforts to carry out his or her undertaking;
4. Regard may properly be had to a surety's share in the equity of a matrimonial home when a recognisance is being entered into;
5. When enforcement of a recognisance is being considered under s. 120, the means of the surety at that time is one of the factors to be considered and, at that stage, the impact on both the surety and on others, if the matrimonial home has to be sold to satisfy the recognisance, is a relevant factor when deciding whether to remit a recognisance in whole or in part.

Culpability   According to *Warwick Crown Court, ex parte Smalley* [1987] 1 WLR 237, there is **D7.125** no requirement of proof that any blame attached to the surety for the accused's failure to surrender. The court rejected the suggestion that there had to be some fault on the part of the surety for the recognizance to be forfeited. The authorities on this point were reviewed in *Reading Crown Court, ex parte Bello* [1992] 3 All ER 353. Parker LJ (at p. 363C–D) summarised the position as follows:

> The failure of the accused to surrender when required triggers the power to forfeit but the court, before deciding what should be done, must enquire into the question of fault. If it is satisfied that the surety was blameless throughout it would then be proper to remit the whole of the amount of the recognisance and in exceptional circumstances this would...be the only proper course.

One issue in *Ex parte Bello* was the failure of the court to notify the surety of the date on which the accused had to surrender. Parker LJ said (at p. 364G–J) that justice should require that the surety was notified by the court of the date. However, it was impossible to say that ignorance of the date must always be an answer to proceedings for forfeiture: each case will depend on its facts.

In *Maidstone Crown Court, ex parte Lever* [1995] 2 All ER 35, the Court of Appeal signalled a **D7.126** robust approach to the question of culpability. One of two sureties discovered that the accused had not been home for two nights. That surety telephoned the other surety and the police. Attempts by the police to apprehend the accused were unsuccessful. The judge ordered the first surety to forfeit £35,000 (out of a recognizance of £40,000) and the other £16,000 (out of a recognizance of £19,000). The Court of Appeal upheld this decision. Butler-Sloss LJ said (at p. 930) that 'the presence or absence of culpability is a factor but the absence of culpability...is not in itself a reason to reduce or set aside the obligations entered into by the surety to pay in the event of a failure to bring the defendant to court'. The reason for the adoption of a fairly strict approach to the forfeiture of recognizances was set out by Butler-Sloss LJ at p. 931, where her ladyship quotes from Lord Widgery CJ in *Southampton Justices, ex parte Corker* (1976) 120 SJ 214:

> The real pull of bail, the real effective force that it exerts, is that it may cause the offender to attend his trial rather than subject his nearest and dearest who has gone surety for him to undue pain and discomfort.

Nonetheless, it is clear that there may be circumstances where the amount forfeited might be reduced because the surety has made considerable efforts to carry out his undertakings.

In *Choudhry v Birmingham Crown Court* (2008) 172 JP 33, Gibbs J helpfully summarised (at **D7.127** [15]) the principles to be derived from *Ex parte Lever*:

(a) The purpose of a recognizance is to bring the defendant to court for trial.
(b) The forfeiture of recognizance is not a penalty imposed on the surety for misconduct.
(c) It is for the surety to establish to the satisfaction of the court that there are grounds upon which the court may remit from forfeiture part or, wholly exceptionally, the whole recognizance.

D

(d) The absence of culpability on the part of the surety is not of itself a reason to set aside or reduce the obligation entered into.

(e) Absence of culpability is a factor to be considered. The court may, in the exercise of a wide discretion, decide it would be fair and just to estreat some or all of the recognizance.

His lordship added (on the basis of *Uxbridge Justices, ex parte Heward-Mills* [1983] 1 All ER 530) that 'the burden of satisfying the court that the full sum should not be forfeited rests upon the surety and is a heavy one'.

In *Harrow Crown Court, ex parte Lingard* [1998] EWHC 233 (Admin), Dyson J (at [20]), with whom Lord Bingham CJ agreed, said that it was clear that in an exceptional case, where the surety is entirely blameless and the failure of the defendant to surrender to bail is wholly outside the control of the surety and not foreseeable by him, the court may in the exercise of its discretion remit the whole or a substantial part of the amount of the recognizance. In *Choudhry v Birmingham Crown Court*, however, Gibbs J (at [43]) emphasised that, although the court may so remit, there is no principle of law which requires it to do so. It is thus a matter entirely within the discretion of the court.

The position regarding forfeiture of recognizances is summarised in CPD III, para. 19F.5 (see Supplement, **PD-34**), which states that, even if a surety does his best to ensure the attendance of the accused at court, the surety remains liable for the full amount, except at the discretion of the court. However, the court should take into account the presence or absence of culpability on the part of the surety (though this 'is not in itself a reason to reduce or set aside the obligations entered into by the surety'), and the means of a surety (particularly if those means have changed since the obligation was taken on). Moreover, the court should order forfeiture of 'no more than is necessary, in public policy, to maintain the integrity and confidence of the system of taking sureties'.

D7.128   In *Wells Street Magistrates' Court, ex parte Albanese* [1982] QB 333, the court considered the position where the conditions of bail have been varied. Ralph Gibson J, giving the judgment of the court, declined to hold that a court, if it varies the conditions of bail in a case in which there is a surety, is under a duty to give notice of the change to the surety. However, an unnotified variation in bail conditions may be relevant to the question of forfeiture of the recognizance. In *Choudhry v Birmingham Crown Court*, Gibbs J (at [35]), ruled that it is both possible and lawful for a recognizance in Crown Court proceedings to be expressed as continuous until the conclusion of proceedings in the Crown Court. If an order is subsequently made varying the conditions of bail, unconnected with the sureties, this does not give rise to the need for sureties to be taken afresh. His lordship went on to say (at [36]) that if, at the commencement of the trial (when bail falls to be reconsidered), the accused is allowed to continue on bail (whether on the same or varied terms), that amounts to a fresh grant of bail. However, that does not necessarily mean that sureties have to be taken again. Provided that the recognizances were in terms which made it clear that they continued to bind the surety until the end of the trial, they would remain in force so long as bail was granted in terms which required that they did so (at [37]).

Forfeiture of Security

D7.129   Where the accused (or somebody on his behalf) has given security for his surrender to custody in pursuance of a requirement imposed under the BA 1976, s. 3(5), and the court is satisfied that the accused has absconded, then the court may, unless satisfied that he had reasonable cause for his failure, order forfeiture of part or all of the security (s. 5(7) and (8)). Section 5(8A)–(8C) set out a procedure by which the accused may apply to have an order under s. 5(7) remitted on the grounds that he did in fact have reasonable cause for not surrendering to custody. The principles to be applied in deciding whether or not to order forfeiture of a security are no doubt analogous to those which apply when forfeiture of a surety's recognizance is under consideration.

DETENTION WHEN BAIL IS REFUSED

Detention of Adults

Where a court refuses bail to an accused aged 21 or over he is detained in a prison until the next **D7.130** hearing (MCA 1980, ss. 128(1) and 150(1)). As regards an accused aged 18 to 20 inclusive who is remanded in custody, the court — if it has been notified that a remand centre is available for the reception from that court of persons of the accused's class or description — must commit him to a remand centre (CJA 1948, s. 27(1)). Otherwise it commits him to a prison. When the sentence of detention in a young offender institution is abolished for this age group, committal will be to a prison in any event.

Remands to Police Custody

A magistrates' court may, instead of remanding the accused in custody, commit him to deten- **D7.131** tion at a police station for a period not exceeding three clear days (MCA 1980, s. 128(7)). This may be done only if it is necessary for the purposes of inquiries into offences other than the one(s) for which he is appearing before the court (s. 128(8)(a)). He must be brought back before the magistrates' court as soon as that need ceases (s. 128(8)(b)). While detained at the police station, he is entitled to the same protection as regards conditions of detention, and periodic review of the continuing need for detention, as would have been the case had he simply been arrested without warrant on suspicion of having committed an offence (s. 128(8)(c) and (d)).

Juveniles Refused Bail

As regards a court's decision whether or not to grant bail to a child or young person (defined in the **D7.132** BA 1976, s. 2(2), as someone under the age of 18), the only special rules applying are that (a) bail can be refused if that is necessary for his own welfare (sch. 1, para. 3), and (b) his parent or guardian may be asked to stand surety for his compliance with such conditions of bail as may have been imposed, as well as standing surety for his appearance at court (s. 3(7)). However, where bail is *refused* in the case of a person aged under 18, the consequences are significantly different.

The LASPO 2012, ss. 91 to 107, set out the options open to the court where a juvenile is refused bail. Section 91 applies where a person under 18 is charged with, or convicted of, one or more offences: it provides that, if the juvenile is not released on bail, the court must remand him to local authority accommodation, in accordance with s. 92, or to youth detention accommodation, in accordance with s. 102.

Remands to Local Authority Accommodation

Under the LASPO 2012, s. 92, a remand to local authority accommodation is defined as a remand **D7.133** to accommodation provided by or on behalf of the local authority designated by the court; that authority must provide or arrange for the provision of accommodation for the juvenile. Section 93 enables the court to impose conditions when remanding to local authority accommodation: s. 93(1) provides that the juvenile can be required to comply with any conditions that could be imposed under the BA 1976, s. 3(6). Also, under s. 93(2), compliance with those conditions may be secured through the imposition of electronic monitoring, provided that the requirements set out in s. 94 are met. Those requirements are as follows: (i) the juvenile must have attained the age of 12; (ii) one or more of the offences must be imprisonable; (iii) one or more of the offences must be a violent or sexual offence (as specified in the CJA 2003, sch. 15) or an offence punishable (in the case of an adult) with at least 14 years' imprisonment, or else the offence(s) must amount, or (assuming the juvenile is convicted) would amount, to a recent history of committing imprisonable offences while on bail or subject to a custodial remand; (iv) the court must be satisfied that electronic monitoring is available; and (v) a youth offending team must have informed the court that the imposition of an electronic monitoring condition would be suitable for that juvenile.

Under s. 93(3), a court remanding a juvenile to local authority accommodation may also impose requirements on the designated authority to secure compliance with the conditions imposed on the juvenile; the court can also stipulate that the juvenile must not be placed with a named person. The court must first consult with the designated authority (s. 93(4)). Under s. 93(5), where a juvenile has been remanded to local authority accommodation, the court may, on the application of the designated authority, impose any conditions that could be imposed when a court is remanding a juvenile to local authority, Under s. 93(6), the local authority or the juvenile can apply for the variation or revocation of any of the conditions which have been imposed.

Section 97 enables a juvenile to be arrested for breaking conditions of the remand to local authority accommodation. A police officer may arrest a juvenile without warrant if the juvenile has been remanded to local authority accommodation, conditions were imposed on the juvenile under s. 93, and the officer has reasonable grounds for suspecting that the juvenile has broken any of those conditions (s. 97(1)). A juvenile arrested under s. 97(1) must be brought before a magistrate within 24 hours of arrest (excluding Sundays). Under s. 97(5), if the magistrate is of the opinion that the juvenile has broken any condition imposed under s. 93, he must remand the juvenile under s. 91 (i.e. either to local authority accommodation or to youth detention accommodation). If the magistrate is not of that opinion, he must remand the juvenile to the place to which he had been remanded at the time of the arrest, subject to the same conditions as before.

Remands to Youth Detention Accommodation

D7.134   Remand to 'youth detention accommodation' means remand to a secure children's home, a secure training centre, a young offender institution, or detention accommodation for detention and training orders (s. 102). Remand to youth detention accommodation is possible only where either of two sets of conditions (set out in ss. 98 and 99) is satisfied (s. 91(4)).

The conditions in s. 98 are as follows: (i) the juvenile must have attained the age of 12; (ii) one or more of the offences must be a violent or sexual offence (as specified in the CJA 2003, sch. 15), or an offence punishable (in the case of an adult) with at least 14 years' imprisonment; (iii) the court must be of the opinion, after considering all the options for the remand of the juvenile, that only a remand to youth detention accommodation would be adequate to protect the public from death or serious personal injury (whether physical or psychological) occasioned by further offences committed by the juvenile, or to prevent the juvenile committing imprisonable offences; (iv) either the juvenile is legally represented at court, or else one of the following applies: representation was provided but has been withdrawn because of the juvenile's conduct or because it appeared that the juvenile's financial resources were such that he was not eligible for such representation, or representation was refused because it appeared that the juvenile's financial resources rendered him ineligible for such representation, or the juvenile has refused or failed to apply for representation.

The conditions in s. 99 are (i) the juvenile must have attained the age of 12; (ii) there must be a real prospect that the juvenile will be sentenced to a custodial sentence; (iii) one or more of the offences is imprisonable; (iv) either the juvenile has a recent history of absconding while subject to a custodial remand and one or more of the present offences is alleged (or found) to have been committed while he was remanded to local authority accommodation or youth detention accommodation, or the offence(s) amount, or (assuming the juvenile is convicted) would amount, to a recent history of committing imprisonable offences while on bail or subject to a custodial remand. Additional conditions (the necessity condition and the legal representation conditions) apply — they are the same as those set out at (iii) and (iv) under s. 98.

D7.135   The Legal Aid, Sentencing and Punishment of Offenders Act 2012 (Children Act 1989) (Children Remanded to Youth Detention Accommodation) Regulations 2012 (SI 2012 No. 2813) provide that certain duties which are placed on local authorities under the Children Act 1989, in respect of children in care, do not apply in relation to children who are remanded to youth detention accommodation. The duties which are excluded include those in s. 22C (ways in which looked after children are to be accommodated and maintained), s. 22D (review of a child's case before making alternative arrangements for accommodation), and sch. 2, para. 21 (liability to contribute towards maintenance of looked after children). Additionally, a reg. 5A is added to the Children (Secure Accommodation) Regulations 1991 (SI 1991 No. 1505), to provide that s. 25 of the 1989 Act, which limits the circumstances in which a looked after child may be placed and kept in secure accommodation by a local authority, does not apply in relation to children remanded to youth detention accommodation.

TEXT OF THE BAIL ACT 1976

Bail Act 1976   D7.136

Preliminary

Meaning of 'bail in criminal proceedings'

1.—(1) In this Act 'bail in criminal proceedings' means—
  (a) bail grantable in or in connection with proceedings for an offence to a person who is accused or convicted of the offence, or
  (b) bail grantable in connection with an offence to a person who is under arrest for the offence or for whose arrest for the offence a warrant (endorsed for bail) is being issued, or
  (c) bail grantable in connection with extradition proceedings in respect of an offence.
(2) In this Act 'bail' means bail grantable under the law (including common law) for the time being in force.
(3) Except as provided by section 13(3) of this Act, this section does not apply to bail in or in connection with proceedings outside England and Wales.
. . .
(5) This section applies—
  (a) whether the offence was committed in England or Wales or elsewhere, and
  (b) whether it is an offence under the law of England and Wales, or of any other country or territory.
(6) Bail in criminal proceedings shall be granted (and in particular shall be granted unconditionally or conditionally), in accordance with this Act.

Other definitions

2.—(1) In this Act, unless the context otherwise requires, 'conviction' includes—
  (a) a finding of guilt,
  (b) a finding that a person is not guilty by reason of insanity,
  (c) a finding under section 11(1) of the Powers of Criminal Courts (Sentencing) Act 2000 (remand for medical examination) that the person in question did the act or made the omission charged, and
  (d) a conviction of an offence for which an order is made discharging the offender absolutely or conditionally, and 'convicted' shall be construed accordingly.
(2) In this Act, unless the context otherwise requires—
  'bail hostel' means premises for the accommodation of persons remanded on bail,
  'bail in non-extradition proceedings' means bail in criminal proceedings of the kind mentioned in section 1(1)(a),
  'child' means a person under the age of fourteen,
  'court' includes a judge of a court or a justice of the peace and, in the case of a specified court, includes a judge or (as the case may be) justice having powers to act in connection with proceedings before that court,
  'Courts Martial Appeal rules' means rules made under section 49 of the Courts Martial Appeals Act 1968,
  'custodial sentence' means a sentence or order mentioned in section 76(1) of the Powers of Criminal Courts (Sentencing) Act 2000 or any corresponding sentence or order imposed or made under any earlier enactment,
  'extradition proceedings' means proceedings under the Extradition Act 2003,
  'imprisonable offence' means an offence punishable in the case of an adult with imprisonment,
  'offence' includes an alleged offence,

'probation hostel' means premises for the accommodation of persons who may be required to reside there by a community order under section 177 of the Criminal Justice Act 2003,

'prosecutor', in relation to extradition proceedings, means the person acting on behalf of the territory to which extradition is sought,

'sexual offence' means an offence specified in Part 2 of Schedule 15 to the Criminal Justice Act 2003,

'surrender to custody' means, in relation to a person released on bail, surrendering himself into the custody of the court or of the constable (according to the requirements of the grant of bail) at the time and place for the time being appointed for him to do so,

'vary', in relation to bail, means imposing further conditions after bail is granted, or varying or rescinding conditions,

'violent offence' means murder or an offence specified in Part 1 of Schedule 15 to the Criminal Justice Act 2003,

'young person' means a person who has attained the age of 14 and is under the age of 18.

(3) Where an enactment (whenever passed) which relates to bail in criminal proceedings refers to the person bailed appearing before a court it is to be construed unless the context otherwise requires as referring to his surrendering himself into the custody of the court.

(4) Any reference in this Act to any other enactment is a reference thereto as amended, and includes a reference thereto as extended or applied, by or under any other enactment, including this Act.

Incidents of bail in criminal proceedings

General provisions

3.—(1) A person granted bail in criminal proceedings shall be under a duty to surrender to custody, and that duty is enforceable in accordance with section 6 of this Act.

(2) No recognizance for his surrender to custody shall be taken from him.

(3) Except as provided by this section—
   (a) no security for his surrender to custody shall be taken from him,
   (b) he shall not be required to provide a surety or sureties for his surrender to custody, and
   (c) no other requirement shall be imposed on him as a condition of bail.

(4) He may be required, before release on bail, to provide a surety or sureties to secure his surrender to custody.

(5) He may be required, before release on bail, to give security for his surrender to custody. The security may be given by him or on his behalf.

(6) He may be required to comply, before release on bail or later, with such requirements as appear to the court to be necessary—
   (a) to secure that he surrenders to custody,
   (b) to secure that he does not commit an offence while on bail,
   (c) to secure that he does not interfere with witnesses or otherwise obstruct the course of justice whether in relation to himself or any other person,
   (ca) for his own protection or, if he is a child or young person, for his own welfare or in his own interests,
   (d) to secure that he makes himself available for the purpose of enabling inquiries or a report to be made to assist the court in dealing with him for the offence,
   (e) to secure that before the time appointed for him to surrender to custody, he attends an interview with an authorised advocate or authorised litigator, as defined by section 119(1) of the Courts and Legal Services Act 1990;

and, in any Act, 'the normal powers to impose conditions of bail' means the powers to impose conditions under paragraph (a), (b), (c) or (ca) above.

(6ZAA) The requirements which may be imposed under subsection (6) include electronic monitoring requirements.

The imposition of electronic monitoring requirements is subject to section 3AA (in the case of a child or young person granted bail in criminal proceedings of the kind mentioned in section 1(1) (a) or (b)), section 3AAA (in the case of a child or young person granted bail in connection with extradition proceedings), section 3AB (in the case of other persons) and section 3AC (in all cases).

(6ZAB) In this section and sections 3AA to 3AC 'electronic monitoring requirements' means requirements imposed for the purpose of securing the electronic monitoring of a person's compliance with any other requirement imposed on him as a condition of bail.

(6ZA) Where he is required under subsection (6) above to reside in a bail hostel or probation hostel, he may also be required to comply with the rules of the hostel.

(6A) In the case of a person accused of murder the court granting bail shall, unless it considers that satis-factory reports on his mental condition have already been obtained, impose as conditions of bail—

    (a) a requirement that the accused shall undergo examination by two medical practitioners for the purpose of enabling such reports to be prepared; and

    (b) a requirement that he shall for that purpose attend such an institution or place as the court directs and comply with any other directions which may be given to him for that purpose by either of those practitioners.

(6B) Of the medical practitioners referred to in subsection (6A) above at least one shall be a prac-titioner approved for the purposes of section 12 of the Mental Health Act 1983.

(6C) Subsection (6D) below applies where—

    (a) the court has been notified by the Secretary of State that arrangements for conducting a relevant assessment or, as the case may be, providing relevant follow-up have been made for the local justice area in which it appears to the court that the person referred to in sub-section (6D) would reside if granted bail; and

    (b) the notice has not been withdrawn.

(6D) In the case of a person ('P')—

    (a) in relation to whom paragraphs (a) to (c) of paragraph 6B(1) of part 1 of schedule 1 to this Act apply (including where P is a person to whom the provisions of part 1A of schedule 1 apply);

    (b) who, after analysis of the sample referred to in paragraph (b) of that paragraph, has been offered a relevant assessment or, if a relevant assessment has been carried out, has had relevant follow-up proposed to him; and

    (c) who has agreed to undergo the relevant assessment or, as the case may be, to participate in the relevant follow-up,

the court, if it grants bail, shall impose as a condition of bail that P both undergo the relevant assessment and participate in any relevant follow-up proposed to him or, if a relevant assess-ment has been carried out, that P participate in the relevant follow-up.

(6E) In subsections (6C) and (6D) above—

    (a) 'relevant assessment' means an assessment conducted by a suitably qualified person of whether P is dependent upon or has a propensity to misuse any specified Class A drugs;

    (b) 'relevant follow-up' means, in a case where the person who conducted the relevant assessment believes P to have such a dependency or propensity, such further assessment, and such assis-tance or treatment (or both) in connection with the dependency or propensity, as the person who conducted the relevant assessment (or conducts any later assessment) considers to be appropriate in P's case, and in paragraph (a) above 'Class A drug' and 'misuse' have the same meaning as in the Misuse of Drugs Act 1971, and 'specified' (in relation to a Class A drug) has the same meaning as in Part 3 of the Criminal Justice and Court Services Act 2000.

(6F) In subsection (6E)(a) above, 'suitably qualified person' means a person who has such quali-fications or experience as are from time to time specified by the Secretary of State for the purposes of this subsection.

(7) If a parent or guardian of a person under the age of seventeen consents to be surety for the person for the purposes of this subsection, the parent or guardian may be required to secure that the person complies with any requirement imposed on him by virtue of subsection (6), (6ZAA) or (6A) above but—

    (a) no requirement shall be imposed on the parent or the guardian by virtue of this subsection where it appears that the person will attain the age of 17 before the time to be appointed for him to surrender to custody; and

    (b) the parent or guardian shall not be required to secure compliance with any requirement to which his consent does not extend and shall not, in respect of those requirements to which his consent does extend, be bound in a sum greater than £50.

(8) Where a court has granted bail in criminal proceedings that court or, where that court has sent a person on bail to the Crown Court for trial or committed him on bail to the Crown Court to be sentenced or otherwise dealt with, that court or the Crown Court may on application—

    (a) by or on behalf of the person to whom bail was granted, or

    (b) by the prosecutor or a constable,

vary the conditions of bail or impose conditions in respect of bail which has been granted unconditionally.

(9) This section is subject to subsection (3) of section 11 of the Powers of Criminal Courts (Sentencing) Act 2000 (conditions of bail on remand for medical examination).

(10) This section is subject, in its application to bail granted by a constable, to section 3A of this Act.

3AA.—(1) A court may not impose electronic monitoring requirements on a child or young person released on bail in criminal proceedings of the kind mentioned in section 1(1)(a) or (b) unless each of the following conditions is met.

(2) The first condition is that the child or young person has attained the age of twelve years.

(3) The second condition is that—

(a) the child or young person is charged with or has been convicted of a violent or sexual offence, or an offence punishable in the case of an adult with imprisonment for a term of fourteen years or more; or

(b) he is charged with or has been convicted of one or more imprisonable offences which, together with any other imprisonable offences of which he has been convicted in any proceedings—
   (i) amount, or
   (ii) would, if he were convicted of the offences with which he is charged, amount, to a recent history of repeatedly committing imprisonable offences while remanded on bail or subject to a custodial remand.

(4) The third condition is that the court is satisfied that the necessary provision for dealing with the person concerned can be made under arrangements for the electronic monitoring of persons released on bail that are currently available in each local justice area which is a relevant area.

(5) The fourth condition is that a youth offending team has informed the court that in its opinion the imposition of electronic monitoring requirements will be suitable in the case of the child or young person.

(6) to (10) [Repealed.]

(11) The references in subsection (3)(b) to an imprisonable offence include a reference to an offence—

(a) of which the child or young person has been convicted outside England and Wales, and

(b) which is equivalent to an offence that is punishable with imprisonment in England and Wales.

(12) The reference in subsection (3)(b) to a child or young person being subject to a custodial remand is to the child or young person being—

(a) remanded to local authority accommodation or youth detention accommodation under section 91 of the Legal Aid, Sentencing and Punishment of Offenders Act 2012,

(b) remanded to local authority accommodation under section 23 of the Children and Young Persons Act 1969 or to prison under that section as modified by section 98 of the Crime and Disorder Act 1998 or under section 27 of the Criminal Justice Act 1948, or

(c) subject to a form of custodial detention in a country or territory outside England and Wales while awaiting trial or sentence in that country or territory or during a trial in that country or territory.

3AAA.—(1) A court may not impose electronic monitoring requirements on a child or young person released on bail in connection with extradition proceedings unless each of the following conditions is met.

(2) The first condition is that the child or young person has attained the age of twelve years.

(3) The second condition is that—

(a) the conduct constituting the offence to which the extradition proceedings relate, or one or more of those offences, would, if committed in England and Wales, constitute a violent or sexual offence or an offence punishable in the case of an adult with imprisonment for a term of fourteen years or more, or

(b) the offence or offences to which the extradition proceedings relate, together with any other imprisonable offences of which the child or young person has been convicted in any proceedings—
   (i) amount, or
   (ii) would, if the child or young person were convicted of that offence or those offences, amount,
   to a recent history of committing imprisonable offences while on bail or subject to a custodial remand.

(4) The third condition is that the court is satisfied that the necessary provision for dealing with the child or young person concerned can be made under arrangements for the electronic monitoring of persons released on bail that are currently available in each local justice area which is a relevant area.

(5) The fourth condition is that a youth offending team has informed the court that in its opinion the imposition of electronic monitoring requirements will be suitable in the case of the child or young person.

(6) The references in subsection (3)(b) to an imprisonable offence include a reference to an offence—
  (a) of which the child or young person has been accused or convicted outside England and Wales, and
  (b) which is equivalent to an offence that is punishable with imprisonment in England and Wales.
(7) The reference in subsection (3)(b) to a child or young person being subject to a custodial remand is to the child or young person being—
  (a) remanded to local authority accommodation or youth detention accommodation under section 91 of the Legal Aid, Sentencing and Punishment of Offenders Act 2012,
  (b) remanded to local authority accommodation under section 23 of the Children and Young Persons Act 1969 or to prison under that section as modified by section 98 of the Crime and Disorder Act 1998 or under section 27 of the Criminal Justice Act 1948, or
  (c) subject to a form of custodial detention in a country or territory outside England and Wales while awaiting trial or sentence in that country or territory or during a trial in that country or territory.
3AB.—(1) A court may not impose electronic monitoring requirements on a person who has attained the age of eighteen unless each of the following conditions is met.
(2) The first condition is that the court is satisfied that without the electronic monitoring requirements the person would not be granted bail.
(3) The second condition is that the court is satisfied that the necessary provision for dealing with the person concerned can be made under arrangements for the electronic monitoring of persons released on bail that are currently available in each local justice area which is a relevant area.
3AC.—(1) Where a court imposes electronic monitoring requirements as a condition of bail, the requirements must include provision for making a person responsible for the monitoring.
(2) A person may not be made responsible for the electronic monitoring of a person on bail unless he is of a description specified in an order made by the Secretary of State.
(3) to (6) [Rule-making powers.]
(7) For the purposes of section 3AA, 3AAA or 3AB a local justice area is a relevant area in relation to a proposed electronic monitoring requirement if the court considers that it will not be practicable to secure the electronic monitoring in question unless electronic monitoring arrangements are available in that area.
(8) Nothing in sections 3, 3AA, 3AAA or 3AB is to be taken to require the Secretary of State to ensure that arrangements are made for the electronic monitoring of persons released on bail.

Conditions of bail in case of police bail

3A.—(1) Section 3 of this Act applies, in relation to bail granted by a custody officer under Part IV of the Police and Criminal Evidence Act 1984 in cases where the normal powers to impose conditions of bail are available to him, subject to the following modifications.
(2) Subsection (6) does not authorise the imposition of a requirement to reside in a bail hostel or any requirement under paragraph (d) or (e).
(3) Subsections (6ZAA), (6ZA), (6A) to (6F) shall be omitted.
(4) For subsection (8), substitute the following—
'(8) Where a custody officer has granted bail in criminal proceedings he or another custody officer serving at the same police station may, at the request of the person to whom it was granted, vary the conditions of bail; and in doing so he may impose conditions or more onerous conditions.'
(5) Where a constable grants bail to a person no conditions shall be imposed under subsections (4), (5), (6) or (7) of section 3 of this Act unless it appears to the constable that it is necessary to do so—
  (a) for the purpose of preventing that person from failing to surrender to custody, or
  (b) for the purpose of preventing that person from committing an offence while on bail, or
  (c) for the purpose of preventing that person from interfering with witnesses or other-wise obstructing the course of justice, whether in relation to himself or any other person, or
  (d) for that person's own protection or, if he is a child or young person, for his own welfare or in his own interests.
(6) Subsection (5) above also applies on any request to a custody officer under subsection (8) of section 3 of this Act to vary the conditions of bail.

Bail for accused persons and others

General right to bail of accused persons and others

4.—(1) A person to whom this section applies shall be granted bail except as provided in Schedule 1 to this Act.

(2) This section applies to a person who is accused of an offence when—
   (a) he appears or is brought before a magistrates' court or the Crown Court in the course of or in connection with proceedings for the offence, or
   (b) he applies to a court for bail or for a variation of the conditions of bail in connection with the proceedings.
   This subsection does not apply as respects proceedings on or after a person's conviction of the offence.

(2A) This section also applies to a person whose extradition is sought in respect of an offence, when—
   (a) he appears or is brought before a court in the course of or in connection with extradition proceedings in respect of the offence, or
   (b) he applies to a court for bail or for a variation of the conditions of bail in connection with the proceedings.

(2B) But subsection (2A) above does not apply if the person is alleged to have been convicted of the offence.

(3) This section also applies to a person who, having been convicted of an offence, appears or is brought before a magistrates' court or the Crown Court to be dealt with under—
   (za) Schedule 1 to the Powers of Criminal Courts (Sentencing) Act 2000 (referral orders: referral back to appropriate court),
   (zb) Schedule 8 to that Act (breach of reparation order),
   (a)   Schedule 2 to the Criminal Justice and Immigration Act 2008 (breach, revocation or amendment of youth rehabilitation orders),
   (b)   Part 2 of Schedule 8 to the Criminal Justice Act 2003 (breach of requirement of community order), or
   (c)   the Schedule to the Street Offences Act 1959 (breach of orders under section 1(2A) of that Act).

(4) This section also applies to a person who has been convicted of an offence and whose case is adjourned by the court for the purpose of enabling inquiries or a report to be made to assist the court in dealing with him for the offence.

(5) Schedule 1 to this Act also has effect as respects conditions of bail for a person to whom this section applies.

(6) In Schedule 1 to this Act 'the defendant' means a person to whom this section applies and any reference to a defendant whose case is adjourned for inquiries or a report is a reference to a person to whom this section applies by virtue of subsection (4) above.

(7) This section is subject to section 41 of the Magistrates' Courts Act 1980 (restriction of bail by magistrates' court in cases of treason).

(8) This section is subject to section 25 of the Criminal Justice and Public Order Act 1994 (exclusion of bail in cases of homicide and rape).

(9) In taking any decisions required by Part I or II of Schedule 1 to this Act, the considerations to which the court is to have regard include, so far as relevant, any misuse of controlled drugs by the defendant ('controlled drugs' and 'misuse' having the same meanings as in the Misuse of Drugs Act 1971).

Supplementary

Supplementary provisions about decisions on bail

5.—(1) Subject to subsection (2) below, where—
   (a) a court or constable grants bail in criminal proceedings, or
   (b) a court withholds bail in criminal proceedings from a person to whom section 4 of this Act applies, or
   (c) a court, or officer of a court or constable appoints a different time or place for a person granted bail in criminal proceedings to surrender to custody, or
   (d) a court or constable varies any conditions of bail or imposes conditions in respect of bail in criminal proceedings,
   that court, officer or constable shall make a record of the decision in the prescribed manner and containing the prescribed particulars and, if requested to do so by the person in relation to whom the decision was taken, shall cause him to be given a copy of the record of the decision as soon as practicable after the record is made.

(2) Where bail in criminal proceedings is granted by endorsing a warrant of arrest for bail the constable who releases on bail the person arrested shall make the record required by subsection (1) above instead of the judge or justice who issued the warrant.

(2A) Where a magistrates' court or the Crown Court grants bail in criminal proceedings to a person to whom section 4 of this Act applies after hearing representations from the prosecutor in favour of withholding bail, then the court shall give reasons for granting bail.

(2B) A court which is by virtue of subsection (2A) above required to give reasons for its decision shall include a note of those reasons in the record of its decision and, if requested to do so by the prosecutor, shall cause the prosecutor to be given a copy of the record of the decision as soon as practicable after the record is made.

(3) Where a magistrates' court or the Crown Court—

    (a) withholds bail in criminal proceedings, or

    (b) imposes conditions in granting bail in criminal proceedings, or

    (c) varies any conditions of bail or imposes conditions in respect of bail in criminal proceedings,

and does so in relation to a person to whom section 4 of this Act applies, then the court shall, with a view to enabling him to consider making an application in the matter to another court, give reasons for withholding bail or for imposing or varying the conditions.

(4) A court which is by virtue of subsection (3) above required to give reasons for its decision shall include a note of those reasons in the record of its decision and shall (except in a case where, by virtue of subsection (5) below, this need not be done) give a copy of that note to the person in relation to whom the decision was taken.

(5) The Crown Court need not give a copy of the note of the reasons for its decision to the person in relation to whom the decision was taken where that person is represented by counsel or a solicitor unless his counsel or solicitor requests the court to do so.

(6) Where a magistrates' court withholds bail in criminal proceedings from a person who is not represented by counsel or a solicitor, the court shall—

    (a) if it is sending him for trial to the Crown Court, or if it issues a certificate under subsection (6A) below inform him that he may apply to the High Court or to the Crown Court to be granted bail;

    (b) [Repealed].

(6A) Where in criminal proceedings—

    (a) a magistrates' court remands a person in custody under section 52(5) of the Crime and Disorder Act 1998, section 11 of the Powers of Criminal Courts (Sentencing) Act 2000 or any of the following provisions of the Magistrates' Courts Act 1980—

        (i) [Repealed.]

        (ii) section 10 (adjournment of trial);

        (iia) section 17C (intention as to plea: adjournment);

        (iii) section 18 (initial procedure on information against adult for offence triable either way),

        (iv) section 24C (intention as to plea by child or young person: adjournment),

    after hearing full argument on an application for bail from him; and

    (b) either—

        (i) it has not previously heard such argument on an application for bail from him in those proceedings; or

        (ii) it has previously heard full argument from him on such an application but it is satisfied that there has been a change in his circumstances or that new considerations have been placed before it,

it shall be the duty of the court to issue a certificate in the prescribed form that they heard full argument on his application for bail before they refused the application.

(6B) Where the court issues a certificate under subsection (6A) above in a case to which paragraph (b)(ii) of that subsection applies, it shall state in the certificate the nature of the change of circumstances or the new considerations which caused it to hear a further fully argued bail application.

(6C) Where a court issues a certificate under subsection (6A) above it shall cause the person to whom it refuses bail to be given a copy of the certificate.

(7) Where a person has given security in pursuance of section 3(5) above, and a court is satisfied that he failed to surrender to custody then, unless it appears that he had reasonable cause for his failure, the court may order the forfeiture of the security.

(8) If a court orders the forfeiture of a security under subsection (7) above, the court may declare that the forfeiture extends to such amount less than the full value of the security as it thinks fit to order.

[Subsections (8A) to (9A) detail procedure for taking and forfeiting a security.]

(10) [Meaning of 'prescribed'.]

(11) This section is subject, in its application to bail granted by a constable, to section 5A of this Act.

Supplementary provisions in cases of police bail

5A.—(1) Section 5 of this Act applies, in relation to bail granted by a custody officer under Part IV of the Police and Criminal Evidence Act 1984 in cases where the normal powers to impose conditions of bail are available to him, subject to the following modifications.

(1A)   Subsections (2A) and (2B) shall be omitted.

(2) For subsection (3) substitute the following—

'(3) Where a custody officer, in relation to any person,—

(a) imposes conditions in granting bail in criminal proceedings, or

(b) varies any conditions of bail or imposes conditions in respect of bail, in criminal proceedings,

the custody officer shall, with a view to enabling that person to consider requesting him or another custody officer, or making an application to a magistrates' court, to vary the conditions, give reasons for imposing or varying the conditions.'

(3) For subsection (4) substitute the following—

'(4) A custody officer who is by virtue of subsection (3) above required to give reasons for his decision shall include a note of those reasons in the custody record and shall give a copy of that note to the person in relation to whom the decision was taken.'

(4) Subsections (5) and (6) shall be omitted.

Reconsideration of decisions granting bail

5B.—(A1) This section applies in any of these cases—

(a) a magistrates' court has granted bail in criminal proceedings in connection with an offence to which this section applies or proceedings for such an offence;

(b) a constable has granted bail in criminal proceedings in connection with proceedings for such an offence;

(c) a magistrates' court or a constable has granted bail in connection with extradition proceedings.

(1) The court or the appropriate court in relation to the constable may, on application by the prosecutor for the decision to be reconsidered,—

(a) vary the conditions of bail,

(b) impose conditions in respect of bail which has been granted unconditionally, or

(c) withhold bail.

(2) The offences to which this section applies are offences triable on indictment and offences triable either way.

(3) No application for the reconsideration of a decision under this section shall be made unless it is based on information which was not available to the court or constable when the decision was taken.

(4) Whether or not the person to whom the application relates appears before it, the magistrates' court shall take the decision in accordance with section 4(1) (and Schedule 1) of this Act.

(5) Where the decision of the court on a reconsideration under this section is to withhold bail from the person to whom it was originally granted the court shall—

(a) if that person is before the court, remand him in custody, and

(b) if that person is not before the court, order him to surrender himself forthwith into the custody of the court.

(6) Where a person surrenders himself into the custody of the court in compliance with an order under subsection (5) above, the court shall remand him in custody.

(7) A person who has been ordered to surrender to custody under subsection (5) above may be arrested without warrant by a constable if he fails without reasonable cause to surrender to custody in accordance with the order.

(8) A person arrested in pursuance of subsection (7) above shall be brought as soon as practicable, and in any event within 24 hours after his arrest, before a justice of the peace for the local justice area in which he was arrested and the justice shall remand him in custody.

In reckoning for the purposes of this subsection any period of 24 hours, no account shall be taken of Christmas Day, Good Friday or any Sunday.

(8A) Where the court, on a reconsideration under this section, refuses to withhold bail from a relevant person after hearing representations from the prosecutor in favour of withholding bail, then the court shall give reasons for refusing to withhold bail.

(8B) In subsection (8A) above, 'relevant person' means a person to whom section 4(1) (and Schedule 1) of this Act is applicable in accordance with subsection (4) above.

(8C) A court which is by virtue of subsection (8A) above required to give reasons for its decision shall include a note of those reasons in any record of its decision and, if requested to do so by the prosecutor, shall cause the prosecutor to be given a copy of any such record as soon as practicable after the record is made.

(9) [Indicates what may be covered by the CrimPR.]

Offence of absconding by person released on bail

6.—(1) If a person who has been released on bail in criminal proceedings fails without reasonable cause to surrender to custody he shall be guilty of an offence.

(2) If a person who—
(a) has been released on bail in criminal proceedings, and
(b) having reasonable cause therefor, has failed to surrender to custody,
fails to surrender to custody at the appointed place as soon after the appointed time as is reasonably practicable he shall be guilty of an offence.

(3) It shall be for the accused to prove that he had reasonable cause for his failure to surrender to custody.

(4) A failure to give to a person granted bail in criminal proceedings a copy of the record of the decision shall not constitute a reasonable cause for that person's failure to surrender to custody.

(5) An offence under subsection (1) or (2) above shall be punishable either on summary conviction or as if it were a criminal contempt of court.

(6) Where a magistrates' court convicts a person of an offence under subsection (1) or (2) above the court may, if it thinks—
(a) that the circumstances of the offence are such that greater punishment should be inflicted for that offence than the court has power to inflict, or
(b) in a case where it sends that person for trial to the Crown Court for another offence, that it would be appropriate for him to be dealt with for the offence under subsection (1) or (2) above by the court before which he is tried for the other offence, commit him in custody or on bail to the Crown Court for sentence.

(7) A person who is convicted summarily of an offence under subsection (1) or (2) above and is not committed to the Crown Court for sentence shall be liable to imprisonment for a term not exceeding three months or to a fine not exceeding level 5 on the standard scale or to both and a person who is so committed for sentence or is dealt with as for such a contempt shall be liable to imprisonment for a term not exceeding 12 months or to a fine or to both.

(8) In any proceedings for an offence under subsection (1) or (2) above a document purporting to be a copy of the part of the prescribed record which relates to the time and place appointed for the person specified in the record to surrender to custody and to be duly certified to be a true copy of that part of the record shall be evidence of the time and place appointed for that person to surrender to custody.

(9) For the purposes of subsection (8) above—
(a) 'the prescribed record' means the record of the decision of the court, officer or constable made in pursuance of section 5(1) of this Act;
(b) the copy of the prescribed record is duly certified if it is certified by the appropriate officer of the court or, as the case may be, by the constable who took the decision or a constable designated for the purpose by the officer in charge of the police station from which the person to whom the record relates was released;
(c) 'the appropriate officer' of the court is—
(i) in the case of a magistrates' court, the designated officer for the court;
(ii) in the case of the Crown Court, such officer as may be designated for the purpose in accordance with arrangements made by the Lord Chancellor;
(iii) in the case of the High Court, such officer as may be designated for the purpose in accordance with arrangements made by the Lord Chancellor;
(iv) in the case of the Court of Appeal, the registrar of criminal appeals or such other officer as may be authorised by him to act for the purpose;

(v) in the case of the Courts Martial Appeal Court, the registrar or such other officer as may be authorised by him to act for the purpose.

(10) Section 127 of the Magistrates' Courts Act 1980 shall not apply in relation to an offence under subsection (1) or (2) above.

(11) Where a person has been released on bail in criminal proceedings and that bail was granted by a constable, a magistrates' court shall not try that person for an offence under subsection (1) or (2) above in relation to that bail (the 'relevant offence') unless either or both of subsections (12) and (13) below applies.

(12) This subsection applies if an information is laid for the relevant offence within 6 months from the time of the commission of the relevant offence.

(13) This subsection applies if an information is laid for the relevant offence no later than 3 months from the time of the occurrence of the first of the events mentioned in subsection (14) below to occur after the commission of the relevant offence.

(14) Those events are—

(a) the person surrenders to custody at the appointed place;

(b) the person is arrested, or attends at a police station, in connection with the relevant offence or the offence for which he was granted bail;

(c) the person appears or is brought before a court in connection with the relevant offence or the offence for which he was granted bail.

Liability to arrest for absconding or breaking conditions of bail

7.—(1) If a person who has been released on bail in criminal proceedings and is under a duty to surrender into the custody of a court fails to surrender to custody at the time appointed for him to do so the court may issue a warrant for his arrest.

(1A) Subsection (1B) applies if—

(a) a person has been released on bail in connection with extradition proceedings,

(b) the person is under a duty to surrender into the custody of a constable, and

(c) the person fails to surrender to custody at the time appointed for him to do so.

(1B) A magistrates' court may issue a warrant for the person's arrest.

(2) If a person who has been released on bail in criminal proceedings absents himself from the court at any time after he has surrendered into the custody of the court and before the court is ready to begin or to resume the hearing of the proceedings, the court may issue a warrant for his arrest; but no warrant shall be issued under this subsection where that person is absent in accordance with leave given to him by or on behalf of the court.

(3) A person who has been released on bail in criminal proceedings and is under a duty to surrender into the custody of a court may be arrested without warrant by a constable—

(a) if the constable has reasonable grounds for believing that that person is not likely to surrender to custody;

(b) if the constable has reasonable grounds for believing that that person is likely to break any of the conditions of his bail or has reasonable grounds for suspecting that that person has broken any of those conditions; or

(c) in a case where that person was released on bail with one or more surety or sureties, if a surety notifies a constable in writing that that person is unlikely to surrender to custody and that for that reason the surety wishes to be relieved of his obligations as a surety.

(4) A person arrested in pursuance of subsection (3) above—

(a) shall, except where he was arrested within 24 hours of the time appointed for him to surrender to custody, be brought as soon as practicable and in any event within 24 hours after his arrest before a justice of the peace; and

(b) in the said excepted case shall be brought before the court at which he was to have surrendered to custody.

(4A) A person who has been released on bail in connection with extradition proceedings and is under a duty to surrender into the custody of a constable may be arrested without warrant by a constable on any of the grounds set out in paragraphs (a) to (c) of subsection (3).

(4B) A person arrested in pursuance of subsection (4A) above shall be brought as soon as practicable and in any event within 24 hours after his arrest before a justice of the peace for the petty sessions area in which he was arrested.

(5) A justice of the peace before whom a person is brought under subsection (4) above may, subject to subsections (5A) and (6) below, if of the opinion that that person—

(a) is not likely to surrender to custody, or

(b) has broken or is likely to break any condition of his bail,

remand him in custody or commit him to custody, as the case may require, or alternatively, grant him bail subject to the same or to different conditions, but if not of that opinion shall grant him bail subject to the same conditions (if any) as were originally imposed.

(5A) A justice of the peace may not remand a person in, or commit a person to, custody under subsection (5) if—

(a) the person has attained the age of eighteen,

(b) the person was released on bail in non-extradition proceedings,

(c) the person has not been convicted of an offence in those proceedings, and

(d) it appears to the justice of the peace that there is no real prospect that the person will be sentenced to a custodial sentence in the proceedings.

(6) Where a person brought before a justice under subsection (4) or (4B) is a child or young person and the justice does not grant him bail, subsection (5) above shall have effect subject to the provisions of section 23 of the Children and Young Persons Act 1969 (remands to the care of local authorities).

(7) In reckoning for the purposes of this subsection any period of 24 hours, no account shall be taken of Christmas Day, Good Friday or any Sunday.

(8) In the case of a person charged with murder or with murder and one or more other offences—

(a) subsections (4) and (5) have effect as if for 'justice of the peace' there were substituted 'judge of the Crown Court',

(b) subsection (6) has effect as if for 'justice' (in both places) there were substituted 'judge', and

(c) subsection (7) has effect, for the purposes of subsection (4), as if at the end there were added 'Saturday or bank holiday'.

Bail with sureties

8.—(1) This section applies where a person is granted bail in criminal proceedings on condition that he provides one or more surety or sureties for the purpose of securing that he surrenders to custody.

(2) In considering the suitability for that purpose of a proposed surety, regard may be had (amongst other things) to—

(a) the surety's financial resources;

(b) his character and any previous convictions of his; and

(c) his proximity (whether in point of kinship, place of residence or otherwise) to the person for whom he is to be surety.

(3) Where a court grants a person bail in criminal proceedings on such a condition but is unable to release him because no surety or no suitable surety is available, the court shall fix the amount in which the surety is to be found and subsections (4) and (5) below, or in a case where the proposed surety resides in Scotland subsection (6) below, shall apply for the purpose of enabling the recognizance of the surety to be entered into subsequently.

(4) Where this subsection applies the recognizance of the surety may be entered into before such of the following persons or descriptions of persons as the court may by order specify or, if it makes no such order, before any of the following persons, that is to say—

(a) where the decision is taken by a magistrates' court, before a justice of the peace, a justices' clerk or a police officer who either is of the rank of inspector or above or is in charge of a police station or, if Criminal Procedure Rules so provide, by a person of such other description as is specified in the rules;

(b) where the decision is taken by the Crown Court, before any of the persons specified in paragraph (a) above or, if Criminal Procedure Rules so provide, by a person of such other description as is specified in the rules;

(c) where the decision is taken by the High Court or the Court of Appeal, before any of the persons specified in paragraph (a) above or, if Criminal Procedure Rules so provide, by a person of such other description as is specified in the rules;

(d) where the decision is taken by the Court Martial Appeal Court, before any of the persons specified in paragraph (a) above or, if Court Martial Appeal Rules so provide, by a person of such other description as is specified in the rules;

and Civil Procedure Rules, Criminal Procedure Rules or Court Martial Appeal Rules may also prescribe the manner in which a recognizance which is to be entered into before such a person is to be entered into and the persons by whom and the manner in which the recognizance may be enforced.

(5) Where a surety seeks to enter into his recognizance before any person in accordance with sub-section (4) above but that person declines to take his recognizance because he is not satisfied of the surety's suitability, the surety may apply to—
   (a) the court which fixed the amount of the recognizance in which the surety was to be bound, or
   (b) a magistrates' court.

(6) Where this subsection applies, the court, if satisfied of the suitability of the proposed surety, may direct that arrangements be made for the recognizance of the surety to be entered into in Scotland before any constable, within the meaning of the Police (Scotland) Act 1967, having charge at any police office or station in like manner as the recognizance would be entered into in England or Wales.

(7) Where, in pursuance of subsection (4) or (6) above, a recognizance is entered into otherwise than before the court that fixed the amount of the recognizance, the same consequences shall follow as if it had been entered into before that court.

Miscellaneous

Offence of agreeing to indemnify sureties in criminal proceedings

9.—(1) If a person agrees with another to indemnify that other against any liability which that other may incur as a surety to secure the surrender to custody of a person accused or convicted of or under arrest for an offence, he and that other person shall be guilty of an offence.

(2) An offence under subsection (1) above is committed whether the agreement is made before or after the person to be indemnified becomes a surety and whether or not he becomes a surety and whether the agreement contemplates compensation in money or in money's worth.

(3) Where a magistrates' court convicts a person of an offence under subsection (1) above the court may, if it thinks—
   (a) that the circumstances of the offence are such that greater punishment should be inflicted for that offence than the court has power to inflict, or
   (b) in a case where it sends that person for trial to the Crown Court for another offence, that it would be appropriate for him to be dealt with for the offence under subsection (1) above by the court before which he is tried for the other offence,
   commit him in custody or on bail to the Crown Court for sentence.

(4) A person guilty of an offence under subsection (1) above shall be liable—
   (a) on summary conviction, to imprisonment for a term not exceeding 3 months or to a fine not exceeding the prescribed sum or to both; or
   (b) on conviction on indictment or if sentenced by the Crown Court on committal for sentence under subsection (3) above, to imprisonment for a term not exceeding 12 months or to a fine or to both.

(5) No proceedings for an offence under subsection (1) above shall be instituted except by or with the consent of the Director of Public Prosecutions.

Bail decisions relating to persons aged under 18 who are accused of offences mentioned in schedule 2 to the Magistrates' Courts Act 1980

9A.—(1) This section applies whenever—
   (a) a magistrates' court is considering whether to withhold or grant bail in relation to a child or young person who is accused of a scheduled offence; and
   (b) the trial of that offence has not begun.

(2) The court shall, before deciding whether to withhold or grant bail, consider whether, having regard to any representations made by the prosecutor or the accused child or young person, the value involved does not exceed the relevant sum for the purposes of section 22.

(3) The duty in subsection (2) does not apply in relation to an offence if—
   (a) a determination under subsection (4) has already been made in relation to that offence; or
   (b) the accused child or young person is, in relation to any other offence of which he is accused which is not a scheduled offence, a person to whom part 1 of schedule 1 to this Act applies.

(4) If where the duty in subsection (2) applies it appears to the court clear that, for the offence in question, the amount involved does not exceed the relevant sum, the court shall make a determination to that effect.

(5) In this section—
 (a) 'relevant sum' has the same meaning as in section 22(1) of the Magistrates' Courts Act 1980 (certain either way offences to be tried summarily if value involved is less than the relevant sum);
 (b) 'scheduled offence' means an offence mentioned in schedule 2 to that Act (offences for which the value involved is relevant to the mode of trial); and
 (c) 'the value involved' is to be construed in accordance with section 22(10) to (12) of that Act.
[**10.** and **11.** Repealed.]
[**12.** Amendments, repeals and transitional provisions.]
[**13.** Short title, commencement, application and extent.]

SCHEDULE 1

PERSONS ENTITLED TO BAIL: SUPPLEMENTARY PROVISIONS

PART I

DEFENDANTS ACCUSED OR CONVICTED OF IMPRISONABLE OFFENCES

Defendants to whom Part I applies

1.—(1) Subject to sub-paragraph (2) and paragraph 1A, the following provisions of this Part of this Schedule apply to the defendant if—
 (a) the offence or one of the offences of which he is accused or convicted in the proceedings is punishable with imprisonment, or
 (b) his extradition is sought in respect of an offence.
(2) But those provisions do not apply by virtue of sub-paragraph (1)(a) if the offence, or each of the offences punishable with imprisonment, is—
 (a) a summary offence; or
 (b) an offence mentioned in schedule 2 to the Magistrates' Courts Act 1980 (offences for which the value involved is relevant to the mode of trial) in relation to which—
  (i) a determination has been made under section 22(2) of that Act (certain either way offences to be tried summarily if value involved is less than the relevant sum) that it is clear that the value does not exceed the relevant sum for the purposes of that section; or
  (ii) a determination has been made under section 9A(4) of this Act to the same effect.

1A.—(1) The paragraphs of this Part of this Schedule mentioned in sub-paragraph (2) do not apply in relation to bail in non-extradition proceedings where—
 (a) the defendant has attained the age of 18,
 (b) the defendant has not been convicted of an offence in those proceedings, and
 (c) it appears to the court that there is no real prospect that the defendant will be sentenced to a custodial sentence in the proceedings.
(2) The paragraphs are—
 (a) paragraph 2 (refusal of bail where defendant may fail to surrender to custody, commit offences on bail or interfere with witnesses),
 (b) paragraph 2A (refusal of bail where defendant appears to have committed indictable or either way offence while on bail), and
 (c) paragraph 6 (refusal of bail where defendant has been arrested under section 7).

Exceptions to right to bail

2.—(1) The defendant need not be granted bail if the court is satisfied that there are substantial grounds for believing that the defendant, if released on bail (whether subject to conditions or not) would—
 (a) fail to surrender to custody, or
 (b) commit an offence while on bail, or
 (c) interfere with witnesses or otherwise obstruct the course of justice, whether in relation to himself or any other person.
(2) Where the defendant falls within paragraph 6B, this paragraph does not apply unless—
 (a) the court is of the opinion mentioned in paragraph 6A, or
 (b) paragraph 6A does not apply by virtue of paragraph 6C.
2ZA.—(1) The defendant need not be granted bail if the court is satisfied that there are substantial grounds for believing that the defendant, if released on bail (whether subject to conditions or

not), would commit an offence while on bail by engaging in conduct that would, or would be likely to, cause—

  (a) physical or mental injury to an associated person; or
  (b) an associated person to fear physical or mental injury.

(2) In sub-paragraph (1) 'associated person' means a person who is associated with the defendant within the meaning of section 62 of the Family Law Act 1996.

2A. The defendant need not be granted bail if—
  (a) the offence is an indictable offence or an offence triable either way, and
  (b) it appears to the court that the defendant was on bail in criminal proceedings on the date of the offence.

2B. The defendant need not be granted bail in connection with extradition proceedings if—
  (a) the conduct constituting the offence would, if carried out by the defendant in England and Wales, constitute an indictable offence or an offence triable either way; and
  (b) it appears to the court that the defendant was on bail on the date of the offence.

3. The defendant need not be granted bail if the court is satisfied that the defendant should be kept in custody for his own protection or, if he is a child or young person, for his own welfare.

4. The defendant need not be granted bail if he is in custody in pursuance of a sentence of a court or a sentence imposed by an officer under the Armed Forces Act 2006.

5. The defendant need not be granted bail where the court is satisfied that it has not been practicable to obtain sufficient information for the purpose of taking the decisions required by this Part of this Schedule for want of time since the institution of the proceedings against him.

6.—(1) The defendant need not be granted bail if, having previously been released on bail in, or in connection with, the proceedings, the defendant has been arrested in pursuance of section 7.

6ZA. If the defendant is charged with murder, the defendant may not be granted bail unless the court is of the opinion that there is no significant risk of the defendant committing, while on bail, an offence that would, or would be likely to, cause physical or mental injury to any person other than the defendant.

Exception applicable to drug users in certain areas

6A. Subject to paragraph 6C below, a defendant who falls within paragraph 6B below may not be granted bail unless the court is of the opinion that there is no significant risk of his committing an offence while on bail (whether subject to conditions or not).

6B.—(1) A defendant falls within this paragraph if—
  (a) he is aged 18 or over,
  (b) a sample taken—
    (i) under section 63B of the Police and Criminal Evidence Act 1984 (testing for presence of Class A drugs) in connection with the offence; or
    (ii) under section 161 of the Criminal Justice Act 2003 (drug testing after conviction of an offence but before sentence),
  has revealed the presence in his body of a specified Class A drug;
  (c) either the offence is one under section 5(2) or (3) of the Misuse of Drugs Act 1971 and relates to a specified Class A drug, or the court is satisfied that there are substantial grounds for believing—
    (i) that misuse by him of any specified Class A drug caused or contributed to the offence; or
    (ii) (even if it did not) that the offence was motivated wholly or partly by his intended misuse of such a drug; and
  (d) the condition set out in sub-paragraph (2) below is satisfied or (if the court is considering on a second or subsequent occasion whether or not to grant bail) has been, and continues to be, satisfied.

(2) The condition referred to is that after the taking and analysis of the sample—
  (a) a relevant assessment has been offered to the defendant but he does not agree to undergo it; or
  (b) he has undergone a relevant assessment, and relevant follow-up has been proposed to him, but he does not agree to participate in it.

(3) In this paragraph and paragraph 6C below—
  (a) 'Class A drug' and 'misuse' have the same meaning as in the Misuse of Drugs Act 1971;
  (b) 'relevant assessment' and 'relevant follow-up' have the meaning given by section 3(6E) of this Act;

    (c) 'specified' (in relation to a Class A drug) has the same meaning as in Part 3 of the Criminal Justice and Court Services Act 2000.

6C. Paragraph 6A above does not apply unless—

    (a) the court has been notified by the Secretary of State that arrangements for conducting a relevant assessment or, as the case may be, providing relevant follow-up have been made for the local justice area in which it appears to the court that the defendant would reside if granted bail; and

    (b) the notice has not been withdrawn.

Exception applicable only to defendant whose case is adjourned for inquiries or a report

7. Where his case is adjourned for inquiries or a report, the defendant need not be granted bail if it appears to the court that it would be impracticable to complete the inquiries or make the report without keeping the defendant in custody.

Restriction of conditions of bail

8.—(1) Subject to subparagraph (3) below, where the defendant is granted bail, no conditions shall be imposed under subsections (4) to (6B) or (7) (except subsection (6)(d) or (e)) of section 3 of this Act unless it appears to the court that it is necessary to do so—

    (a) for the purpose of preventing the occurrence of any of the events mentioned in paragraph 2(1) of this Part of this Schedule, or

    (b) for the defendant's own protection or, if he is a child or young person, for his own welfare or in his own interests.

(1A) No condition shall be imposed under section 3(6)(d) of this Act unless it appears to be necessary to do so for the purpose of enabling inquiries or a report to be made.

(2) Subparagraphs (1) and (1A) above also apply on any application to the court to vary the conditions of bail or to impose conditions in respect of bail which has been granted unconditionally.

(3) The restriction imposed by subparagraph (1A) above shall not apply to the conditions required to be imposed under section 3(6A) of this Act or operate to override the direction in section 11(3) of the Powers of Criminal Courts (Sentencing) Act 2000 to a magistrates' court to impose conditions of bail under section 3(6)(d) of this Act of the description specified in the said section 11(3) in the circumstances so specified.

Decisions under paragraph 2

9. In taking the decisions required by paragraph 2(1), or in deciding whether it is satisfied as mentioned in paragraph 2ZA(1), or of the opinion mentioned in paragraph 6ZA or 6A of this Part of this Schedule, the court shall have regard to such of the following considerations as appear to it to be relevant, that is to say—

    (a) the nature and seriousness of the offence or default (and the probable method of dealing with the defendant for it),

    (b) the character, antecedents, associations and community ties of the defendant,

    (c) the defendant's record as respects the fulfilment of his obligations under previous grants of bail in criminal proceedings,

    (d) except in the case of a defendant whose case is adjourned for inquiries or a report, the strength of the evidence of his having committed the offence or having defaulted,

    (e) if the court is satisfied that there are substantial grounds for believing that the defendant, if released on bail (whether subject to conditions or not), would commit an offence while on bail, the risk that the defendant may do so by engaging in conduct that would, or would be likely to, cause physical or mental injury to any person other than the defendant,

as well as to any others which appear to be relevant.

9AA.—(1) This paragraph applies if—

    (a) the defendant is a child or young person, and

    (b) it appears to the court that he was on bail in criminal proceedings on the date of the offence.

(2) In deciding for the purposes of paragraph 2(1) of this Part of this Schedule whether it is satisfied that there are substantial grounds for believing that the defendant, if released on bail (whether subject to conditions or not), would commit an offence while on bail, the court shall give particular weight to the fact that the defendant was on bail in criminal proceedings on the date of the offence.

9AB.—(1) Subject to sub-paragraph (2) below, this paragraph applies if—

    (a) the defendant is a child or young person, and

D

Part D Procedure

1469

(b) it appears to the court that, having been released on bail in or in connection with the proceedings for the offence, he failed to surrender to custody.

(2) Where it appears to the court that the defendant had reasonable cause for his failure to surrender to custody, this paragraph does not apply unless it also appears to the court that he failed to surrender to custody at the appointed place as soon as reasonably practicable after the appointed time.

(3) In deciding for the purposes of paragraph 2(1) of this Part of this Schedule whether it is satisfied that there are substantial grounds for believing that the defendant, if released on bail (whether subject to conditions or not), would fail to surrender to custody, the court shall give particular weight to—

(a) where the defendant did not have reasonable cause for his failure to surrender to custody, the fact that he failed to surrender to custody, or

(b) where he did have reasonable cause for his failure to surrender to custody, the fact that he failed to surrender to custody at the appointed place as soon as reasonably practicable after the appointed time.

(4) For the purposes of this paragraph, a failure to give to the defendant a copy of the record of the decision to grant him bail shall not constitute a reasonable cause for his failure to surrender to custody.

[Note: Paragraphs 9AA and 9AB are in force only in respect of offences which attract a life sentence: see SI 2006 No. 3217.]

Cases under section 128A of Magistrates' Courts Act 1980

9B. Where the court is considering exercising the power conferred by section 128A of the Magistrates' Courts Act 1980 (power to remand in custody for more than 8 clear days), it shall have regard to the total length of time which the accused would spend in custody if it were to exercise the power.

PART IA

DEFENDANTS ACCUSED OR CONVICTED OF IMPRISONABLE OFFENCES TO WHICH PART I DOES NOT APPLY

Defendants to whom Part IA applies

1. Subject to paragraph 1A, the following provisions of this Part apply to the defendant if—

(a) the offence or one of the offences of which he is accused or convicted is punishable with imprisonment, but

(b) Part 1 does not apply to him by virtue of paragraph 1(2) of that part.

1A.—(1) The paragraphs of this Part of this Schedule mentioned in sub-paragraph (2) do not apply in relation to bail in, or in connection with, proceedings where—

(a) the defendant has attained the age of 18,

(b) the defendant has not been convicted of an offence in those proceedings, and

(c) it appears to the court that there is no real prospect that the defendant will be sentenced to a custodial sentence in the proceedings.

(2) The paragraphs are—

(a) paragraph 2 (refusal of bail for failure to surrender to custody),

(b) paragraph 3 (refusal of bail where defendant would commit further offences on bail), and

(c) paragraph 7 (refusal of bail in certain circumstances when arrested under section 7).

Exceptions to right to bail

2. The defendant need not be granted bail if—

(a) it appears to the court that, having been previously granted bail in criminal proceedings, he has failed to surrender to custody in accordance with his obligations under the grant of bail; and

(b) the court believes, in view of that failure, that the defendant, if released on bail (whether subject to conditions or not) would fail to surrender to custody.

3. The defendant need not be granted bail if—

(a) it appears to the court that the defendant was on bail in criminal proceedings on the date of the offence; and

(b) the court is satisfied that there are substantial grounds for believing that the defendant, if released on bail (whether subject to conditions or not) would commit an offence while on bail.

4.—(1) The defendant need not be granted bail if the court is satisfied that there are substantial grounds for believing that the defendant, if released on bail (whether subject to conditions or not), would commit an offence while on bail by engaging in conduct that would, or would be likely to, cause—

(a) physical or mental injury to an associated person; or

(b) an associated person to fear physical or mental injury.

(2) In sub-paragraph (1) 'associated person' means a person who is associated with the defendant within the meaning of section 62 of the Family Law Act 1996.

5. The defendant need not be granted bail if the court is satisfied that the defendant should be kept in custody for his own protection or, if he is a child or young person, for his own welfare.

6. The defendant need not be granted bail if he is in custody in pursuance of a sentence of a court or a sentence imposed by an officer under the Armed Forces Act 2006

7. The defendant need not be granted bail if—

(a) having been released on bail in or in connection with the proceedings for the offence, he has been arrested in pursuance of section 7 of this Act; and

(b) the court is satisfied that there are substantial grounds for believing that the defendant, if released on bail (whether subject to conditions or not) would fail to surrender to custody, commit an offence while on bail or interfere with witnesses or otherwise obstruct the course of justice (whether in relation to himself or any other person).

8. The defendant need not be granted bail where the court is satisfied that it has not been practicable to obtain sufficient information for the purpose of taking the decisions required by this Part of this Schedule for want of time since the institution of the proceedings against him.

Application of paragraphs 6A to 6C of Part 1

9. Paragraphs 6A to 6C of Part 1 (exception applicable to drug users in certain areas and related provisions) apply to a defendant to whom this Part applies as they apply to a defendant to whom that Part applies.

PART II

DEFENDANTS ACCUSED OR CONVICTED OF NON-IMPRISONABLE OFFENCES

Defendants to whom Part II applies

1. Where the offence or every offence of which the defendant is accused or convicted in the proceedings is one which is not punishable with imprisonment the following provisions of this Part of this Schedule apply.

Exceptions to right to bail

2. The defendant need not be granted bail if—

(za) the defendant—

(i) is a child or young person, or

(ii) has been convicted in the proceedings of an offence;

(a) it appears to the court that, having been previously granted bail in criminal proceedings, he has failed to surrender to custody in accordance with his obligations under the grant of bail; and

(b) the court believes, in view of that failure, that the defendant, if released on bail (whether subject to conditions or not) would fail to surrender to custody.

3. The defendant need not be granted bail if the court is satisfied that the defendant should be kept in custody for his own protection or, if he is a child or young person, for his own welfare.

4. The defendant need not be granted bail if he is in custody in pursuance of a sentence of a court or a sentence imposed by an officer under the Armed Forces Act 2006.

5. The defendant need not be granted bail if—

(za) the defendant—

(i) is a child or young person, or

(ii) has been convicted in the proceedings of an offence;

(a) having been released on bail in or in connection with the proceedings for the offence, he has been arrested in pursuance of section 7 of this Act; and

(b) the court is satisfied that there are substantial grounds for believing that the defendant, if released on bail (whether subject to conditions or not) would fail to surrender to custody, commit an offence on bail or interfere with witnesses or otherwise obstruct the course of justice (whether in relation to himself or any other person).

6.—(1) The defendant need not be granted bail if—

(a) having been released on bail in, or in connection with, the proceedings for the offence, the defendant has been arrested in pursuance of section 7, and

(b) the court is satisfied that there are substantial grounds for believing that the defendant, if released on bail (whether subject to conditions or not), would commit an offence while on bail by engaging in conduct that would, or would be likely to, cause—

(i) physical or mental injury to an associated person, or

(ii) an associated person to fear physical or mental injury.

(2) In sub-paragraph (1) 'associated person' means a person who is associated with the defendant within the meaning of section 62 of the Family Law Act 1996.

PART IIA

DECISIONS WHERE BAIL REFUSED ON PREVIOUS HEARING

1. If the court decides not to grant the defendant bail, it is the court's duty to consider, at each subsequent hearing while the defendant is a person to whom section 4 above applies and remains in custody, whether he ought to be granted bail.

2. At the first hearing after that at which the court decided not to grant the defendant bail he may support an application for bail with any argument as to fact or law that he desires (whether or not he has advanced that argument previously).

3. At subsequent hearings the court need not hear arguments as to fact or law which it has heard previously.

PART III

[INTERPRETATION]

1. For the purposes of this Schedule the question whether an offence is one which is punishable with imprisonment shall be determined without regard to any enactment prohibiting or restricting the imprisonment of young offenders or first offenders.

2. References in this Schedule to previous grants of bail include—

(a) bail granted before the coming into force of this Act;

(b) as respects the reference in paragraph 2A of Part 1 of this Schedule (as substituted by paragraph 16 of Schedule 11 to the Legal Aid, Sentencing and Punishment of Offenders Act 2012), bail granted before the coming into force of that paragraph;

(c) as respects the references in paragraph 6 of Part 1 of this Schedule (as substituted by paragraph 17 of Schedule 11 to the Legal Aid, Sentencing and Punishment of Offenders Act 2012), bail granted before the coming into force of that paragraph;

(d) as respects the references in paragraph 9AA of Part 1 of this Schedule, bail granted before the coming into force of that paragraph;

(e) as respects the references in paragraph 9AB of Part 1 of this Schedule, bail granted before the coming into force of that paragraph;

(f) as respects the reference in paragraph 5 of Part 2 of this Schedule (as substituted by section 13(4) of the Criminal Justice Act 2003), bail granted before the coming into force of that paragraph;

(g) as respects the reference in paragraph 6 of Part 2 of this Schedule, bail granted before the coming into force of that paragraph.

3. References in this Schedule to a defendant's being kept in custody or being in custody include (where the defendant is a child or young person) references to his being kept or being in accommodation pursuant to a remand under section 91(3) or (4) of the Legal Aid, Sentencing and Punishment of Offenders Act 2012 (remands to local authority accommodation or youth detention accommodation).

4. In this Schedule-

'court', in the expression 'sentence of a court' includes a service court as defined in section 12(1) of the Visiting Forces Act 1952 and 'sentence', in that expression, shall be construed in accordance with that definition;

'default', in relation to the defendant, means the default for which he is to be dealt with under Part 2 of Schedule 8 to the Criminal Justice Act 2003 (breach of requirement of order).

TEXT OF THE BAIL (AMENDMENT) ACT 1993

Bail (Amendment) Act 1993, s. 1

(1) Where a magistrates' court grants bail to a person who is charged with or convicted of an offence punishable by imprisonment, the prosecution may appeal to a judge of the Crown Court against the granting of bail.

(1A) Where a magistrates' court grants bail to a person in connection with extradition proceedings, the prosecution may appeal to the High Court against the granting of bail.

(1B) Where a judge of the Crown Court grants bail to a person who is charged with, or convicted of, an offence punishable by imprisonment, the prosecution may appeal to the High Court against the granting of bail.

(1C) An appeal under subsection (1B) may not be made where a judge of the Crown Court has granted bail on an appeal under subsection (1).

(2) Subsections (1) and (1B) above apply only where the prosecution is conducted—
   (a) by or on behalf of the Director of Public Prosecutions; or
   (b) by a person who falls within such class or description of person as may be prescribed for the purposes of this section by order made by the Secretary of State.

(3) An appeal under subsection (1), (1A) or (1B) may be made only if—
   (a) the prosecution made representations that bail should not be granted; and
   (b) the representations were made before it was granted.

(4) In the event of the prosecution wishing to exercise the right of appeal set out in subsection (1), (1A) or (1B) above, oral notice of appeal shall be given to the court which has granted bail at the conclusion of the proceedings in which bail has been granted and before the release from custody of the person concerned.

(5) Written notice of appeal shall thereafter be served on the court which has granted bail and the person concerned within two hours of the conclusion of such proceedings.

(6) Upon receipt from the prosecution of oral notice of appeal from its decision to grant bail the court which has granted bail shall remand in custody the person concerned, until the appeal is determined or otherwise disposed of.

(7) Where the prosecution fails, within the period of two hours mentioned in subsection (5) above, to serve one or both of the notices required by that subsection, the appeal shall be deemed to have been disposed of.

(8) The hearing of an appeal under subsection (1), (1A) or (1B) above against a decision of the court to grant bail shall be commenced within forty-eight hours, excluding weekends and any public holiday (that is to say, Christmas Day, Good Friday or a bank holiday), from the date on which oral notice of appeal is given.

(9) At the hearing of any appeal by the prosecution under this section, such appeal shall be by way of re-hearing, and the judge hearing any such appeal may remand the person concerned in custody or may grant bail subject to such conditions (if any) as he thinks fit.

(10) In relation to a person under the age of 18—
   (a) the references in subsections (1) and (1B) above to an offence punishable by imprisonment are to be read as references to an offence which would be so punishable in the case of an adult; and
   (b) the references in subsections (6) and (9) above to remand in custody are to be read subject to the provisions of Chapter 3 of Part 3 of the Legal Aid, Sentencing and Punishment of Offenders Act 2012 (remands of children otherwise than on bail).

(11) [Rule-making power.]

(12) In this section—
   'extradition proceedings' means proceedings under the Extradition Act 2003;
   'magistrates' court' and 'court' in relation to extradition proceedings means a District Judge (Magistrates' Courts) designated in accordance with section 67 or section 139 of the Extradition Act 2003;
   'prosecution' in relation to extradition proceedings means the person acting on behalf of the territory to which extradition is sought.

Section D8   Assets Recovery

CIVIL RECOVERY AND TAXATION

D8.1 The Proceeds of Crime Act 2002 (POCA 2002) is the embodiment of the 'Assets Recovery Strategy' proposed two years earlier by the government's Performance and Innovation Unit (see 'Recovering the Proceeds of Crime' (June 2000)). The pursuit and recovery of criminal property is now a principal imperative of crime reduction policy.

The mechanisms of asset recovery may be broadly divided into seven separate categories:

(a) civil recovery of criminal property;
(b) taxation of criminal property;
(c) cash seizure and forfeiture;
(d) powers of investigation;
(e) restraint orders;
(f) seizure of realisable property other than cash (from a day to be appointed);
(g) post-conviction confiscation (see **E19**).

Abolition of the Assets Recovery Agency and the Serious Organised Crime Agency

D8.2 On 1 April 2008 the ARA and the office of Director were abolished (SCA 2007, s. 74(1); Assets Recovery Agency (Abolition) Order 2008 (SI 2008 No. 575)). The Serious Organised Crime Agency then assumed statutory responsibility for the overall conduct of the various forms of investigation and recovery procedures (SCA 2007, sch. 8). However, the CCA 2013 abolished the SOCA and transferred its powers to the National Crime Agency (NCA) from 7 October 2013. In addition, the DPP and the Director of the Serious Fraud Office (SFO) may pursue civil recovery proceedings. Powers of investigation and cash seizure continue to be exercisable by officers of various authorities (see **D8.3** and **D8.4**).

Accredited Financial Investigators

D8.3 The SCA 2007, ss. 78 to 81 and sch. 11, extend the investigative powers of 'accredited financial investigators'. An accredited financial investigator is someone who has been trained and accredited under s. 3 of the POCA 2002. The Home Secretary has made various orders under s. 453 of the POCA 2002 identifying authorities which may provide financial investigators such as the Department of Works and Pensions, the Department of Business, Innovation and Skills and local authorities (see the Proceeds of Crime Act 2002 (References to Financial Investigators) Order 2009 (SI 2009 No. 975, as amended by SI 2009 No. 2707)).

Civil Recovery Orders and Taxation

D8.4 An 'enforcement authority' may apply to the High Court for a civil recovery order under part 5 of the POCA 2002. An enforcement authority may be the Director General of the NCA, the DPP or the Director of the SFO. If the enforcement authority proves to the civil standard the existence of 'property obtained through unlawful conduct' ('recoverable property') or property that represents it, the court may make an order vesting the property in a trustee for civil recovery. (The meaning of 'unlawful conduct' is the same as that applicable to cash forfeiture — see D8.14.) This will be a receiver who has wide powers to realise the property for the benefit of the authority. The Home Secretary has by order set a minimum threshold of £5,000. Proceedings may not be taken in respect of cash alone. Without notice applications may be made for 'freezing orders' and 'interim recovery orders'. For the reciprocal recognition and execution of freezing orders by EU States, see the Council Framework Decision 2003/577/HJA. The Limitation Act 1980, ss. 27A and 27B, has been amended to extend the limitation period for recovery from 12 years to 20 years from the date upon which the cause of action accrued (PACA 2009, s. 62). The SOCPA 2005, s. 98, inserted new ss. 245A to 245G into the POCA 2002 which provided a new power to make a freezing order and regulated the use of that power. In principle, a freezing order prohibits 'any person to whose property the order applies from in any way dealing with the property' (s. 245A(2)). However, as in the case of interim recovery orders, an order may be varied to 'exclude' permitted ways of dealing with the property from the general prohibition under s. 245C. Under s. 282A, inserted by the CCA 2013, s. 48, the court may make orders in defined circumstances in relation to property outside England and Wales, thereby rectifying the Supreme Court decision to the contrary in *SOCA v Perry* [2013] 1 AC 182.

Under part 6 of the POCA 2002, the Director General of the NCA may take over the tax collection functions of the Inland Revenue in cases where the Director has reasonable grounds to suspect that taxable income, gains or profits are the proceeds of crime.

Neither of these procedures is conditional upon a successful criminal prosecution. Proceedings **D8.5** are increasingly brought or tax levied whether or not there has been a connected criminal case. Moreover, even an acquittal is no bar to civil recovery proceedings in respect of the very same conduct. In *SOCA v Namli* [2013] EWHC 1200 (QB), Males J stated (at [41]) that 'an acquittal whether here or abroad is not conclusive of the defendant's innocence'. It was, however, evidence on which he could rely, though it did not have the status of a formal presumption, and its weight was a matter to be determined, taking account of the circumstances as a whole. The weight of an acquittal could be affected by the reason for it: e.g., if it was prompted by procedural defects rather than an assessment of the merits, it might carry 'very little weight'. In *SOCA v Gale* [2011] 2 All ER 1 the Supreme Court held that there is nothing in the 'confusing' jurisprudence of the European Court that supports a conclusion that the criminal standard must apply to proof of criminal conduct in civil recovery proceedings — in that case, the appellant had been acquitted in Portuguese criminal proceedings. Thus, in serious criminal cases, legal advice should include the possibility that, even if acquitted, the defendant's assets (including property that he may have sold or given away) could be pursued through the High Court or become the subject of a tax demand. Mortgage providers are advised to spell out in their application forms that a deliberate misstatement could lead to a civil recovery order (*SOCA v Pelekanos* [2009] EWHC 2307 (QB)). Although civil recovery proceedings are barred in respect of property which has been taken into account for the purposes of a confiscation order under s. 308(9), that will not preclude proceedings for civil recovery where the confiscation order is quashed on appeal (*Director of the ARA v Singh* [2005] 1 WLR 3747). Moreover, the admission of evidence that has been ruled inadmissible in criminal proceedings on the basis that it was obtained unlawfully is not an abuse of process. The civil court applies different criteria for the exclusion of evidence under r. 32.1 of the Civil Procedure Rules 1998, namely, that the proceedings are fair and that the case is dealt with justly. While the exclusion of the evidence in the criminal proceedings is relevant, what matters are the circumstances (*Olden v SOCA* [2010] EWCA Civ 143). The A-G and Home Secretary have issued *Guidance to Prosecuting Bodies on their Asset Recovery Powers* (5 November 2009), available via www.attorneygeneral.gov.uk. A civil settlement would not be appropriate for those who committed such serious crimes as corruption of senior foreign government officials and they should not be viewed or treated in any different way to other criminals. It would be inconsistent with basic principles of justice for

D

Part D Procedure

the criminality of corporations to be glossed over by a civil, as opposed to a criminal, sanction (*Innospec Ltd* (26 March 2010 unreported, Southwark CC, Thomas LJ). See also *R (Director of ARA) v He* [2004] EWHC 3021 (Admin).

For a more detailed treatment of these procedures, see E. Rees, R. Fisher and R. Thomas, *Blackstone's Guide to the Proceeds of Crime Act 2002* (5th edn). It will be interesting to see how judicial attitudes develop when confronted with deferred prosecution agreements under the CCA 2013.

MAGISTRATES' COURTS: CASH SEIZURE AND FORFEITURE

Search and Seizure

D8.6   Proceeds of Crime Act 2002, s. 289

(1) If a customs officer, a constable or an accredited financial investigator is lawfully on any premises and has reasonable grounds for suspecting that there is on the premises cash—
  (a) which is recoverable property or is intended by any person for use in unlawful conduct, and
  (b) the amount of which is not less than the minimum amount,
  he may search for the cash there.

(2) If a customs officer, a constable or an accredited financial investigator has reasonable grounds for suspecting that a person (the suspect) is carrying cash—
  (a) which is recoverable property or is intended by any person for use in unlawful conduct, and
  (b) the amount of which is not less than the minimum amount,
  he may exercise the following powers.

(3) The officer, constable or accredited financial investigator may, so far as he thinks it necessary or expedient, require the suspect—
  (a) to permit a search of any article he has with him,
  (b) to permit a search of his person.

(4) An officer, constable or accredited financial investigator exercising powers by virtue of subsection (3)(b) may detain the suspect for so long as is necessary for their exercise.

(5) The powers conferred by this section—
  (a) are exercisable only so far as reasonably required for the purpose of finding cash,
  (b) are exercisable by a customs officer only if he has reasonable grounds for suspecting that the unlawful conduct in question relates to an assigned matter (within the meaning of the Customs and Excise Management Act 1979),
  (c) are exercisable by an accredited financial investigator only in relation to premises or (as the case may be) suspects in England, Wales or Northern Ireland.

(6) Cash means—
  (a) notes and coins in any currency,
  (b) postal orders,
  (c) cheques of any kind, including travellers' cheques,
  (d) bankers' drafts,
  (e) bearer bonds and bearer shares,
  found at any place in the United Kingdom.

(7) Cash also includes any kind of monetary instrument which is found at any place in the United Kingdom, if the instrument is specified by the Secretary of State by an order made after consultation with the Scottish Ministers.

(8) This section does not require a person to submit to an intimate search or strip search (within the meaning of section 164 of the Customs and Excise Management Act 1979).

When the PACA 2009, s. 63, is brought into force, s. 289 will be amended by the insertion of new subsections (1A) to (1E) and related alterations to subsections (4) and (5). See **D8.8**.

D8.7 **General** Chapter 3 of part 5 of the POCA 2002 provides for powers of search, seizure and forfeiture of cash. 'Cash' includes postal orders, all forms of cheque, bankers' drafts, bearer bonds (and any kind of monetary instrument specified by the Home Secretary) 'found at any place in the United Kingdom' (s. 289(6) and (7)).

Searches   Searches may be conducted by constables, officers of Revenue and Customs, accred-   **D8.8**
ited financial investigators and immigration officers. Premises or persons may be searched for cash
'which is recoverable property or is intended by any person for use in unlawful conduct' (s. 289(1)).
In the case of customs officers, searches are permitted only if the officer has reasonable grounds for
suspecting that the unlawful conduct relates to an 'assigned matter' as defined by the Customs and
Excise Management Act 1979 — essentially any matter in relation to which the Commissioners are
'for the time being required in pursuance of any enactment to perform any duties'. For immigration
officers, unlawful conduct means an offence under the Immigration Acts or any offence listed in the
Asylum and Immigration (Treatment of Claimants, etc.) Act 2004, s. 14(2).

From a day to be appointed there will be a power to search vehicles which are in a public place or
'place to which at that time people have ready access but which is not a dwelling' where 'it appears
to the officer... that the vehicle is under the control of a person (the suspect) who is in or in the
vicinity of the vehicle' (s. 289(1A)–(1E)). 'Recoverable property' is a phrase used throughout the
Act and is simply property 'obtained through unlawful conduct' (s. 304(1)). If such property has
been disposed of, property that represents 'the original property' is also deemed to be 'recoverable
property' (s. 305(1)). Thus, if stolen goods are sold for cash, the cash itself is recoverable property.
In broad terms, unlawful conduct means crime wherever it is committed; more precisely, it is
conduct that is unlawful under UK criminal law or, if it occurs in another country or territory,
that is contrary to the criminal law of that country and would be unlawful if it occurred in the
UK (s. 241). A person obtains property through unlawful conduct if he obtains it 'by or in return
for the conduct' (s. 242(1)). The unlawful conduct need not be his own.

Section 164A of the Customs and Management Act 1979 supposedly 'clarifies' search powers at
the border and is intended to comply with the European Council Cash Control Regulation on
controls of cash entering and leaving the Community (No. 1889/2005).

An officer exercising powers under the POCA 2002, s. 289, must have reasonable grounds for   **D8.9**
suspecting (a) that such cash is on the premises or is being carried by the person, and (b) that the
amount of cash is not less than £1,000 (Proceeds of Crime Act 2002 (Recovery of Cash in Summary
Proceedings: Minimum Amount) Order 2006 (SI 2006 No. 1699)). Where individuals hold less
than the minimum amount, but together hold £1,000 or more, the amounts can be aggregated if
there are grounds for suspecting that they have a common source or destination (*Commissioners of
Customs and Excise v Duffy* (2002) *The Times*, 5 April 2002). The whole of a cash amount may be
seized if it is not reasonably practicable to sever it from a suspected amount (s. 294(2)).

Where premises are to be searched, the officer must be on the premises lawfully. The powers
are exercisable 'only so far as reasonably required for the purpose of finding cash'. Involuntary
'intimate' or 'strip searches' within the meaning of the Customs and Excise Management Act
1979, s. 164, are not permitted (s. 289(8)). Searches are governed by a Code of Practice (see the
Proceeds of Crime (Cash Searches: Code of Practice) Order 2008 (SI 2008 No. 947)).

Searches need prior approval from a magistrate or from a police officer of at least the rank of
inspector (or a designated customs officer or accredited financial investigator) unless 'in the
circumstances it is not practicable to obtain that approval' beforehand (s. 290). If a search is
conducted without the authority of a magistrate, and no cash is recovered or any cash is released
within 48 hours, a written report must be completed specifying the reasons for the search and
why prior approval was not practicable (s. 290(6) and (7)).

Applications to magistrates' court are governed by the Magistrates' Courts (Detention and
Forfeiture of Cash) Rules 2002 (SI 2002 No. 2998); applications may be made to any magistrates' court wherever situated.

Seizure   Constables, officers of Revenue and Customs, financial investigators or immigration   **D8.10**
officers may go on to seize cash if they have reasonable grounds for suspecting that it is recoverable property or is intended by any person for use in unlawful conduct (s. 294(1)). The whole
of a cash amount may be seized if it is not reasonably practicable to sever it from a suspected

amount (s. 294(2)). Cash seized under the powers of seizure in the PACE 1984 (see **D1.176**) may be re-seized under these provisions. Section 294 imposes no time-limit for doing so. The authority is allowed a reasonable period of grace between the expiry of PACE powers (e.g., where criminal proceedings are abandoned) and re-seizure under s. 294 (*R (Iqbal) v Luton and South Bedfordshire Magistrates' Court* [2011] EWHC 705 (Admin)). The initial 48-hour limit on detention of the cash (see **D8.11**) commences only on the re-seizure under s. 294 (*Chief Constable of Merseyside v Hickman* [2006] EWHC 451 (Admin)).

Detention of Cash

D8.11   Once seized, cash may be retained for investigation. The initial time-limit for retention is 48 hours, although this may be extended by a magistrate for a further period of six months (extended from three months by the PACA 2009, s. 64), and thereafter by further order(s) up to a maximum of two years (s. 295). Weekends, Christmas Day, Good Friday and bank holidays are excluded from the 48-hour calculation (s. 295(1A) and (1B)). There are two conditions under s. 295(5) and (6) for continued detention of cash: first, that the reasonable suspicion is maintained and, secondly, that either (a) the derivation of the cash is still being investigated, or (b) consideration is being given to bringing 'in the United Kingdom or elsewhere' proceedings against 'any person' for an offence with which the cash is 'connected', or (c) such proceedings have commenced but have not concluded. The cash must be deposited in an interest bearing account.

In order to succeed, an application for the return of any part of the cash requires the court to be satisfied that the above conditions no longer apply (s. 297(3)). The burden of proving otherwise lies upon the person from whom the cash has been seized. It is an abuse of process to seek a High Court declaration of ownership while proceedings continue (*Capper v Chaney and Commissioner of Metropolitan Police* (2010) 174 JP 377).

A constable, customs officer or accredited financial investigator may release the whole or part of the cash, after notifying the court or justice, which made the order, if satisfied that its retention is no longer justified (s. 297).

D8.12   From a day to be appointed, a 'senior officer' who is satisfied that the cash is recoverable property or is intended for use in unlawful conduct may serve a forfeiture notice which, if no objection is made, results in the forfeiture of the cash (see **D8.18**).

Section 75(1)–(3) of the SCA 2007 amended s. 341 of the POCA 2002 to introduce the notion of the 'detained cash investigation' permitting further investigation into the derivation or destination of detained cash. The Crown Court may issue a production order under s. 345 of the POCA 2002 (see **D8.22**) where there are reasonable grounds for suspecting that the cash which is the subject of the 'detained cash investigation' is recoverable property or is intended to be used in unlawful conduct.

Forfeiture
D8.13

Proceeds of Crime Act 2002, s. 298

(1) While cash is detained under section 295, an application for the forfeiture of the whole or any part of it may be made—
   (a) to a magistrates' court by the Commissioners of Customs and Excise, an accredited financial investigator or a constable,
   (b) (in Scotland) to the sheriff by the Scottish Ministers.
(2) The court or sheriff may order the forfeiture of the cash or any part of it if satisfied that the cash or part—
   (a) is recoverable property, or
   (b) is intended by any person for use in unlawful conduct.
(3) But in the case of recoverable property which belongs to joint tenants, one of whom is an excepted joint owner, the order may not apply to so much of it as the court thinks is attributable to the excepted joint owner's share.
(4) Where an application for the forfeiture of any cash is made under this section, the cash is to be detained (and may not be released under any power conferred by this chapter) until any proceedings in pursuance of the application (including any proceedings on appeal) are concluded.

From a day to be appointed, s. 298(1) is amended by the PACA 2009, s. 65(2), so as to add a reference to ss. 297C and 297D (further powers for forfeiture of detained cash: see **D8.18**).

The Power   Cash may be forfeited where the court is satisfied that it is 'recoverable property' **D8.14** or 'is intended by any person for use in unlawful conduct' (POCA 2002, s. 298(2)). Forfeiture proceedings are civil rather than criminal in nature. The standard of proof is 'the balance of probabilities' (s. 241(3)). A magistrates' court may order the forfeiture of all or part of any cash if satisfied that it is either recoverable property or was intended for use by any person in criminal conduct (s. 298). Procedure is governed by the Magistrates' Courts (Detention and Forfeiture of Cash) Rules 2002 (SI 2002 No. 2998); proceedings are in the nature of a complaint and, as such, are regulated under the MCA 1980, ss. 51 to 74. Magistrates assume effective service of documents unless the contrary is shown but may treat notice of the proceedings as ineffective if the respondent demonstrates that he did not receive the notice (2002 Rules, r. 9, as amended by SI 2012 No. 1275). The power to exclude evidence under the PACE 1984, s. 78, is not available in forfeiture proceedings (*Revenue and Customs Commissioners v Pisciotto* [2009] EWHC 1991 (Admin)). The admission of hearsay evidence is governed by the Magistrates' Courts (Hearsay Evidence in Civil Proceedings) Rules 1999 (SI 1999 No. 681).

'Recoverable property' is property 'obtained through unlawful conduct' (s. 304(1)). A person obtains property through unlawful conduct if he obtains it 'by or in return for the conduct' (s. 242(1)). The unlawful conduct need not be his own. In *R (Chief Constable of the Greater Manchester Police) v City of Salford Magistrates' Court* [2009] 1 WLR 1023 the cash consisted of the proceeds of sale of otherwise legitimate goods which had been manufactured by a company whose workforce included unlawful immigrant workers. They were 'people whom it was a criminal offence to employ' who had made a 'material contribution' to the manufacture of the goods. Certainly at the detention stage of the proceedings, the circumstances were capable of supporting a reasonable suspicion that the cash was obtained through unlawful conduct. See also *Xu* [2008] EWCA Crim 2372. However, in *Nuro v Home Office* [2014] EWHC 462 (Admin), the Divisional Court held that it is perverse and unlawful to find that earnings from work done by an illegal entrant who had entered the UK without leave were recoverable property. It is not an offence for an illegal immigrant to work (unless in breach of conditions) and there was insufficient causal nexus to justify forfeiture.

While there is no need to prove specific criminal conduct, the Administrative Court in *Angus v UKBA* [2011] EWHC 461 (Admin) and the Court of Appeal in *Director of the ARA v Szepietowski* [2008] Lloyd's Rep FC 10 and in *Olupitan v Director of the ARA* [2008] Lloyd's Rep FC 253 have held that there is no difference in the test to be applied under the POCA 2002, s. 242(2)(b), for civil recovery of property and that for cash forfeiture, namely that the applicant must at least show that the cash was obtained through conduct of one of a number of kinds, each of which would have been unlawful (preferring *Director of the ARA v Green* [2005] EWHC 3168 (Admin) to *Muneka v Commissioners of Customs and Excise* [2005] EWHC 495 (Admin); see also *Wiese v UK Border Agency* [2012] EWHC 2549 (Admin)). According to Moore-Bick LJ in *Szepietowski* (at [107]), the prosecutor:

> ... need not prove the commission of any specific criminal offence, in the sense of proving that a particular person committed a particular offence on a particular occasion. Nonetheless, I think it is necessary for her to prove that specific property was obtained by or in return for a criminal offence of an identifiable kind (robbery, theft, fraud or whatever) or, if she relies on section 242(2), by or in return for one or other of a number of offences of an identifiable kind.

A pleading that the respondent 'has committed immigration offences, acquisitive criminal offences, mortgage fraud and laundered the proceeds of these (and possible other offences) in addition to cheating the public revenue' may be 'sufficient indication of the alleged "kinds" of conduct to satisfy the requirements of the statute' (Carnwath LJ in *Olupitan* at [24]).

In *Director of the ARA v Green* [2005] EWHC 3168 (Admin), Sullivan J explained that, by contrast with civil recovery of tangible assets, greater latitude in inference was reasonable in cash forfeiture cases in the context of society's abandonment of cash as a lawful medium for large transactions:

. . . conduct consisting in the mere fact of having a very large sum of cash in the form of banknotes in one's possession in certain circumstances (eg at an airport) may well provide reasonable grounds for suspicion and demand an answer. By contrast, conduct consisting of the mere fact of being in possession of other types of property, expensive jewellery, houses, cars and so forth, or the mere fact of having a lavish lifestyle or of living beyond one's apparent means, do not, without anything more, provide reasonable grounds for suspicion demanding an explanation.

D8.15 The evidence in support of an application may include evidence that the cash has been hidden and untruthful or inconsistent explanation(s) offered for its possession. It has been held that a court which finds that the defendant has lied in the context of formal questioning as to the source or destination of cash is entitled to infer that it is related to unlawful conduct (*Muneka v Commissioners of Customs and Excise* [2005] EWHC 495 (Admin)). The background circumstances may be relevant: e.g., that the suspected person was travelling to a well-known centre for the supply of drugs. The cash itself may be contaminated with traces of drugs which are not explicable in terms of normal contamination of notes in circulation (*Pruijsen v Customs and Excise Commissioners* (18 October 1999 unreported)). Moreover, there may be specific evidence to associate the carrier of cash with illegal activity on a previous occasion. Previous convictions are admissible (*Ali v Best* (1997) 161 JP 393; *Isleworth Crown Court, ex parte Morland* (1998) 162 JP 251). In certain circumstances, the applicant may even rely upon a previous acquittal. In *Customs and Excise Commissioners v Thorpe* (18 November 1996 unreported), the defendant was stopped at an airport en route to Spain in possession of £12,500 in cash which was seized under the powers under the Drug Trafficking Act 1994. On a previous occasion, four and a half years earlier, the same man had been seen to go to a helicopter that had just landed and take a holdall that contained cannabis and amphetamines to a waiting car. Proceedings against him for drugs offences were later withdrawn and his acquittal was directed. In applying for forfeiture of the cash, the Customs were not precluded from relying on the facts of the earlier incident, it being held by the Divisional Court that his argument as to issue estoppel had no application. (See also *Commissioners of Customs and Excise v T* (1998) 162 JP 162; as to whether forfeiture following an acquittal is ECHR compliant, see *Scottish Ministers v Doig* 2009 SLT 1106.)

In *Begum v West Midlands Police* [2013] 1 All ER 1261 a woman had been found with £7,000 cash that she had not declared in her application for state benefits. This did not amount to 'use' of the cash in unlawful conduct. Cash was lawfully forfeited where an innocent person had found and handed to the police a large sum of concealed cash in circumstances in which the court was entitled to infer on the balance of probabilities that the money had been obtained through unlawful conduct of an unidentifiable kind, that the hider had not abandoned his intention to recover the cash and that he intended to use it in unlawful conduct since any further use by the hider would almost inevitably involve him in committing a criminal offence. Section 298 cannot be interpreted as applying only when money is intended for use in further criminal activities as opposed to use of the money itself being criminal conduct (*Fletcher v Chief Constable of Lancashire Constabulary* [2013] EWHC 3357 (Admin)).

Where an application for forfeiture is made, the cash is to be detained and may not be released until any proceedings in pursuance of the application (including any proceedings on appeal) are concluded (s. 295(4)). In *R (Chief Constable of Lancashire Constabulary) v Burnley Magistrates' Court* [2003] EWHC 3308 (Admin), magistrates had refused an application to extend the initial 48-hour detention on the basis that the police did not have reasonable grounds to detain the cash. However, the magistrates omitted to order the release of the cash under s. 297(2). Before the 48 hours expired, the police applied for forfeiture. The Administrative Court held that it was not possible to characterise the Chief Constable's decision as an abuse without having considered carefully the proper ambit of the exercise of his duty to the public. The Chief Constable was at liberty to make the application he did. The statutory provision permitted it and the decision of the justices did not prevent it. There was no suggestion or evidence of *mala fides*. There was no evidence that the Chief Constable's purpose was to detain rather than forfeit. Had the justices wished, they could have brought an end to the period of detention under s. 295(1). There is no statutory requirement that all available evidence should be in place before the forfeiture application is made.

Where a parallel prosecution is brought, it may be appropriate to detain the cash but not to commence a forfeiture application until the criminal proceedings are concluded. 'It is ... important that care is taken to ensure that the fair trial of a defendant is not prejudiced by anything arising in civil proceedings in the magistrates' court and steps should be taken accordingly. Liaison between police acting under part 5 of the 2002 Act and the prosecuting authority is essential' (*Payton* [2006] EWCA Crim 1226).

Third Parties Third parties may lay claim to the cash in the course of detention or forfeiture **D8.16** proceedings 'or at any other time' (POCA 2002, s. 301). Thus, the true owner may apply in circumstances where he can show (a) that he was deprived of the cash or of property that it represents by unlawful conduct and (b) that it was not 'recoverable property' immediately before he was deprived of it. From a day to be appointed, if he is not the person from whom the cash was seized, the cash may be released to him or to the person from whom it was seized if it appears to belong to him and the court is satisfied that it is no longer recoverable property and no objection is made by the person from whom the cash was seized (POCA 2002, s. 301(5)).

Compensation and Costs Where no forfeiture order is made, the person from whom the cash **D8.17** was seized or the person to whom it belongs may apply for compensation (POCA 2002, s. 302). An application is a complaint within the meaning of the MCA 1980, s. 127, and, accordingly, a six-month time-limit runs from the date when the money was returned (*Davis v Chief Constable of Leicestershire* [2012] EWHC 3388 (Admin)). Once the forfeiture notice provisions of the PACA 2009 come into force, there will be a similar entitlement where the cash is not forfeited (PACA 2009, sch. 7, para. 109). Compensation will normally be no more than the accrued interest but, if the court is satisfied that the person has suffered loss as a result of the detention and 'the circumstances are exceptional', it may order reasonable additional compensation. In exercising its power under the MCA 1980, s. 64(1), to make 'such order as to costs ... as it thinks just and reasonable' to a successful respondent, a magistrates' court should not start from the presumption that costs followed the event but from the presumption that no order should be made against a police or regulatory authority that has acted honestly, reasonably, properly and on grounds that reasonably appeared to be sound unless an order was justified by other factors relevant to the magistrates' discretion such as hardship or the fact that the conduct of the public authority had been unreasonable or in some other way open to criticism (*R (Perinpanathan) v City of Westminster Magistrates' Court* [2010] 4 All ER 680, where *R (Orton) v Truro Magistrates' Court* [2009] EWHC 168 (Admin) was doubted, but note that an appeal to the Supreme Court in *Perinpanathan* is pending). In *R (Stone) v Camberwell Green Magistrates' Court* (2010) 174 JP 567, forfeiture proceedings were resolved by agreement where part of the detained cash was transferred to HMRC in settlement of unpaid tax and the balance was forfeited. The Divisional Court declined to determine whether the MCA 1980, s. 64, or the Courts Act 1971, s. 52, was the appropriate costs provision; s. 52 allows the court to award 'just and reasonable' costs where 'a complaint ... is not proceeded with'.

Any party aggrieved by the making or non-making of a forfeiture order may appeal to the Crown Court (POCA 2002, s. 299). The application must be made within 30 days of the forfeiture order.

Forfeiture Notices From a day to be appointed, a 'senior officer' who is satisfied that detained **D8.18** cash is recoverable property or is intended for use in unlawful conduct may serve a forfeiture notice which, if no objection is made, results in the forfeiture of the cash (POCA 2002, ss. 297A to 297G, as amended by the PACA 2009, s. 65(1)). The notice must specify, *inter alia*, the period for objecting which 'must be at least 30 days starting with the day after the notice is given' (s. 297B). The notice lapses if an objection is made within that period (s. 297C(4)) but the cash may be detained for a further 48 hours (s. 297D). A person aggrieved by the forfeiture may apply to the magistrates' court to set aside the forfeiture within 30 days of the end of the objection period (s. 297E).

POWERS OF INVESTIGATION

General

D8.19 Part 8 of the POCA 2002 contains an armoury of judicial orders for the purposes of the investigation and pursuit of criminal property:

(a) production orders;
(b) search and seizure warrants;
(c) disclosure orders;
(d) customer information orders;
(e) account monitoring orders.

The exercise of these functions is now governed by two Codes of Practice (Proceeds of Crime Act 2002 (Investigative Powers of Prosecutors in England, Wales and Northern Ireland: Code of Practice) Order 2008 (SI 2008 No. 1978) and Proceeds of Crime Act 2002 (Investigations in England, Wales and Northern Ireland: Code of Practice) Order 2008 (SI 2008 No. 946)). The CrimPR, part 6, also applies (see Supplement, **R-55** *et seq.*).

The Codes are admissible in evidence and a court 'may take account of any failure to comply with its provisions in determining any question in the proceedings' (s. 377(7)). However, failure to comply with any provision of the Codes will not *of itself* render a person liable to criminal or civil proceedings.

D8.20 All of the orders may be made on *ex parte* application. The conditions for the making of the various orders differ according to the type of investigation involved.

The first type of investigation is a 'confiscation investigation', which is an investigation into whether a person has benefited from his criminal conduct or the extent or whereabouts of his benefit from his criminal conduct (s. 341(1)): see **E19**. Such measures may be used after a confiscation order has been made, provided the true and dominant purpose is indeed an investigation into the true extent or whereabouts of the benefit and not merely to locate realisable property (*R (Horne) v Central Criminal Court* [2012] 1 WLR 3152).

The second type is a 'civil recovery investigation', which is an investigation into whether property 'is recoverable property or associated property, who holds the property or its extent or whereabouts' (s. 341(2)). By s. 341(3), an investigation does not qualify as a civil recovery investigation if proceedings for a recovery order in respect of the property have started, if an interim receiving or administration order applies, or if the property is detained under the cash detention provisions (see **D8.11**).

Thirdly, a 'detained cash investigation' is an investigation for the purposes of cash seizure into the derivation of seized cash and into whether it is intended to be used in unlawful conduct (s. 341(3A)).

Fourthly, a 'money laundering investigation' is an investigation into 'whether a person has committed a money laundering offence' (s. 341(4)).

Fifthly, an 'exploitation proceeds investigation' is an investigation under part 7 of the CAJA 2009 (criminal memoirs etc.) (s. 341(5)).

Only a High Court judge may make an order as part of a civil recovery investigation or exploitation proceeds investigation or, until the PACA 2009, s. 66, is brought into force, a detained cash investigation; orders that are part of any other form of investigation may be granted by a judge of the Crown Court (s. 343).

The Proceeds of Crime Act 2002 (External Investigations) Order 2013 (SI 2013 No. 2605) makes detailed provision for the use of the investigatory powers by the Director of the NCA, the DPP or the Director of the SFO in assisting an 'external investigation'. The POCA 2002, s. 447(3) defines an external investigation as:

> …an investigation by an overseas authority into—
> (a) whether property has been obtained as a result of or in connection with criminal conduct,…
> (aa) the extent or whereabouts of property obtained as a result of or in connection with criminal conduct, or
> (b) whether a money laundering offence has been committed.

For general guidance on mutual assistance, see *Van der Pijl v Secretary of State for the Home Department* [2014] EWHC 281 (Admin) and *R (Secretary of State for the Home Department) v Southwark Crown Court* [2013] EWHC 4366 (Admin).

Prejudicing an Investigation

A person commits an offence if, knowing or suspecting that an investigation is being, or is about **D8.21** to be conducted, he makes a disclosure that is likely to prejudice it (s. 342(2)(a)) or 'falsifies, conceals, destroys or otherwise disposes of' relevant documents or causes or permits another to do so (s. 342(2)(b)). See **B21.31** for details.

Production Orders

Proceeds of Crime Act 2002, ss. 345 and 346   **D8.22**

345.—(1) A judge may, on an application made to him by an appropriate officer, make a production order if he is satisfied that each of the requirements for the making of the order is fulfilled.
(2) The application for a production order must state that—
  (a) a person specified in the application is subject to a confiscation investigation, a civil recovery investigation, an exploitation proceeds investigation or a money laundering investigation, or
  (b) property specified in the application is subject to a civil recovery investigation or a detained cash investigation.
(3) The application must also state that—
  (a) the order is sought for the purposes of the investigation;
  (b) the order is sought in relation to material, or material of a description, specified in the application;
  (c) a person specified in the application appears to be in possession or control of the material.
(4) A production order is an order either—
  (a) requiring the person the application for the order specifies as appearing to be in possession or control of material to produce it to an appropriate officer for him to take away, or
  (b) requiring that person to give an appropriate officer access to the material,
within the period stated in the order.
(5) The period stated in a production order must be a period of seven days beginning with the day on which the order is made, unless it appears to the judge by whom the order is made that a longer or shorter period would be appropriate in the particular circumstances.
346.—(1) These are the requirements for the making of a production order.
(2) There must be reasonable grounds for suspecting that—
  (a) in the case of a confiscation investigation, the person the application for the order specifies as being subject to the investigation has benefited from his criminal conduct;
  (b) in the case of a civil recovery investigation—
    (i) the person the application for the order specifies as being subject to the investigation holds recoverable property or associated property,
    (ii) that person has, at any time, held property that was recoverable property or associated property at the time, or
    (iii) the property the application for the order specifies as being subject to the investigation is recoverable property or associated property;
  (ba) in the case of a detained cash investigation into the derivation of cash, the property the application for the order specifies as being subject to the investigation, or a part of it, is recoverable property;
  (bb) in the case of a detained cash investigation into the intended use of cash, the property the application for the order specifies as being subject to the investigation, or a part of it, is intended by any person to be used in unlawful conduct;

(c) in the case of a money laundering investigation, the person the application for the order specifies as being subject to the investigation has committed a money laundering offence;

(d) in the case of an exploitation proceeds investigation, the person the application for the order specifies as being subject to the investigation is within subsection (2A).

(2A) A person is within this subsection if, for the purposes of Part 7 of the Coroners and Justice Act 2009 (criminal memoirs etc), exploitation proceeds have been obtained by the person from a relevant offence by reason of any benefit derived by the person.

This subsection is to be construed in accordance with that Part.

(3) There must be reasonable grounds for believing that the person the application specifies as appearing to be in possession or control of the material so specified is in possession or control of it.

(4) There must be reasonable grounds for believing that the material is likely to be of substantial value (whether or not by itself) to the investigation for the purposes of which the order is sought.

(5) There must be reasonable grounds for believing that it is in the public interest for the material to be produced or for access to it to be given, having regard to—

(a) the benefit likely to accrue to the investigation if the material is obtained;

(b) the circumstances under which the person the application specifies as appearing to be in possession or control of the material holds it.

The CCA 2013, sch. 19 (not yet in force), amends the POCA 2002, ss. 345 and 346, so as to make further provision for civil recovery investigations; the sections are shown above as so amended.

D8.23 **Terms and Effect of the Order**   A production order requires the person appearing to be in possession or control of specified material to produce it to the appropriate officer for removal or for inspection normally within seven days of the order; the period may be lengthened or shortened as 'appropriate in the particular circumstances' (POCA 2002, s. 345(4) and (5)). Orders may be made in relation to material in the possession or control of a government department (s. 350).

A judge can supplement a production order by making an order requiring entry to premises to allow the appropriate officer to obtain access to the material (s. 347). Specific provisions apply to 'information contained in a computer' (s. 349). The production order has effect to require production of or access to the material in a form in which it is visible and legible. The material may be copied or retained for 'so long as is necessary to retain it' in connection with the relevant investigation and, in particular, until any proceedings are concluded.

An order does not require a person to produce or give access to privileged or excluded material (s. 348). 'Privileged material' is 'any material which the person would be entitled to refuse to produce on grounds of legal professional privilege in proceedings in the High Court' (s. 348(2)). Under s. 379 'excluded material' has the same meaning as in the PACE 1984, s. 11 (see **D1.148**). In broad terms it means material that is held in confidence and that falls into the following categories: (a) personal occupational or business records, (b) human tissue or tissue fluid taken for medical diagnosis or treatment, or (c) journalistic documents or records.

Production orders and orders to grant entry 'have effect as if they were orders of the court' (s. 351(7)). In other words, breaches of the orders are punishable as contempt of court.

D8.24 **Requirements**   A judge may grant a production order if satisfied that each of the necessary requirements is fulfilled (ss. 345 and 346). The first requirement varies according to the type of investigation: there must be reasonable grounds for 'suspecting' (a) that the subject of a confiscation investigation has benefited from his criminal conduct, (b) that the subject property of a civil recovery investigation is recoverable or associated property, (c) that the subject cash of a detained cash investigation is recoverable property or is intended by any person to be used in unlawful conduct or (d) that the subject of a money laundering investigation has committed a money laundering offence.

The remaining three requirements are common to all the forms of investigation mentioned above. There must be reasonable grounds for 'believing' (a) that the person specified in the application is in possession or control of the 'material' (s. 346(3)), (b) that the material 'is likely to be of substantial value (whether or not by itself) to the investigation' (s. 346(4)), and (c) that 'it is in the public interest for the material to be produced or for access to it to be given', having regard to the likely benefit if it is obtained and to the circumstances under which the specified person holds the material (s. 346(5)). The required state of mind is belief and not the lower standard of suspicion necessary for fulfilment of the first requirement. The application must specify the material and the person believed to be in possession or control of it (s. 345(3)).

Only an 'appropriate officer' may apply. The meaning of 'appropriate officer' varies according to the type of investigation (see s. 378): (a) in a confiscation investigation, it means an NCA officer, an accredited financial investigator, a constable, or a customs officer; (b) in a civil recovery investigation, it means an NCA officer or a member of the staff of the DPP or the Director of the SFO; (c) in a money laundering or detained cash investigation, it means an accredited financial investigator, a constable, or a customs officer; (d) in an exploitation proceeds investigation, it means an NCA officer.

Search and Seizure Warrants

Proceeds of Crime Act 2002, ss. 352 and 353

D8.25

352.—(1) A judge may, on an application made to him by an appropriate officer, issue a search and seizure warrant if he is satisfied that either of the requirements for the issuing of the warrant is fulfilled.

(2) The application for a search and seizure warrant must state that—
   (a) a person specified in the application is subject to a confiscation investigation, a civil recovery investigation, an exploitation proceeds investigation or a money laundering investigation, or
   (b) property specified in the application is subject to a civil recovery investigation or a detained cash investigation.

(3) The application must also state—
   (a) that the warrant is sought for the purposes of the investigation;
   (b) that the warrant is sought in relation to the premises specified in the application;
   (c) that the warrant is sought in relation to material specified in the application, or that there are reasonable grounds for believing that there is material falling within section 353(6), (7), (7A), (7B) or (8) on the premises.

(4) A search and seizure warrant is a warrant authorising an appropriate person—
   (a) to enter and search the premises specified in the application for the warrant, and
   (b) to seize and retain any material found there which is likely to be of substantial value (whether or not by itself) to the investigation for the purposes of which the application is made.

(5) An appropriate person is—
   (a) a constable, an accredited financial investigator or a customs officer, if the warrant is sought for the purposes of a confiscation investigation or a money laundering investigation;
   (b) a National Crime Agency officer or a member of the staff of the relevant Director, if the warrant is sought for the purposes of a civil recovery investigation;
   (c) a constable, an accredited financial investigator or an officer of Revenue and Customs, if the warrant is sought for the purposes of a detained cash investigation;
   (d) a National Crime Agency officer, if the warrant is sought for the purposes of an exploitation proceeds investigation.

(5A)   In this Part 'relevant Director'—
   (a) in relation to England and Wales, means the Director of Public Prosecutions or the Director of the Serious Fraud Office; and
   (b) in relation to Northern Ireland, means the Director of the Serious Fraud Office or the Director of Public Prosecutions for Northern Ireland.

(6) The requirements for the issue of a search and seizure warrant are—
   (a) that a production order made in relation to material has not been complied with and there are reasonable grounds for believing that the material is on the premises specified in the application for the warrant, or
   (b) that section 353 is satisfied in relation to the warrant.

(7) The reference in paragraph (a) or (c) of subsection (5) to an accredited financial investigator is a reference to an accredited financial investigator who falls within a description specified in an order made for the purposes of that paragraph by the Secretary of State under section 453.

353.—(1) This section is satisfied in relation to a search and seizure warrant if—
    (a) subsection (2) applies, and
    (b) either the first or the second set of conditions is complied with.
(2) This subsection applies if there are reasonable grounds for suspecting that—
    (a) in the case of a confiscation investigation, the person specified in the application for the warrant has benefited from his criminal conduct;
    (b) in the case of a civil recovery investigation—
        (i)   the person specified in the application for the warrant holds recoverable property or associated property,
        (ii) that person has, at any time, held property that was recoverable property or associated property at the time, or
        (iii) the property specified in the application for the warrant is recoverable property or associated property;
    (ba) in the case of a detained cash investigation into the derivation of cash, the property specified in the application for the warrant, or a part of it, is recoverable property;
    (bb) in the case of a detained cash investigation into the intended use of cash, the property specified in the application for the warrant, or a part of it, is intended by any person to be used in unlawful conduct;
    (c) in the case of a money laundering investigation, the person specified in the application for the warrant has committed a money laundering offence;
    (d) in the case of an exploitation proceeds investigation, the person specified in the application for the warrant is specified in s. 346(2A).
(3) The first set of conditions is that there are reasonable grounds for believing that—
    (a) any material on the premises specified in the application for the warrant is likely to be of substantial value (whether or not by itself) to the investigation for the purposes of which the warrant is sought,
    (b) it is in the public interest for the material to be obtained, having regard to the benefit likely to accrue to the investigation if the material is obtained, and
    (c) it would not be appropriate to make a production order for any one or more of the reasons in subsection (4).
(4) The reasons are—
    (a) that it is not practicable to communicate with any person against whom the production order could be made;
    (b) that it is not practicable to communicate with any person who would be required to comply with an order to grant entry to the premises;
    (c) that the investigation might be seriously prejudiced unless an appropriate person is able to secure immediate access to the material.
(5) The second set of conditions is that—
    (a) there are reasonable grounds for believing that there is material on the premises specified in the application for the warrant and that the material falls within subsection (6), (7), (7A), (7B), (8) or (8A),
    (b) there are reasonable grounds for believing that it is in the public interest for the material to be obtained, having regard to the benefit likely to accrue to the investigation if the material is obtained, and
    (c) any one or more of the requirements in subsection (9) is met.
(6) In the case of a confiscation investigation, material falls within this subsection if it cannot be identified at the time of the application but it—
    (a) relates to the person specified in the application, the question whether he has benefited from his criminal conduct or any question as to the extent or whereabouts of his benefit from his criminal conduct, and
    (b) is likely to be of substantial value (whether or not by itself) to the investigation for the purposes of which the warrant is sought.
(7) In the case of a civil recovery investigation, material falls within this subsection if it cannot be identified at the time of the application but it—
    (a) relates to the person or property specified in the application, or to any of the questions listed in subsection (7ZA), and
    (b) is likely to be of substantial value (whether or not by itself) to the investigation for the purposes of which the warrant is sought.

(7ZA) Those questions are—
   (a) where a person is specified in the application, any question as to—
      (i) what property the person holds or has held,
      (ii) whether the property is or has been recoverable property or associated property, or
      (iii) the nature, extent or whereabouts of the property, and
   (b) where property is specified in the application, any question as to—
      (i) whether the property is or has been recoverable property or associated property,
      (ii) who holds it or has held it,
      (iii) whether a person who appears to hold or to have held it holds or has held other property,
      (iv) whether the other property is or has been recoverable property or associated property, or
      (v) the nature, extent or whereabouts of the specified property or the other property.
(7A) In the case of a detained cash investigation into the derivation of cash, material falls within this subsection if it cannot be identified at the time of the application but it—
   (a) relates to the property specified in the application, the question whether the property, or a part of it, is recoverable property or any other question as to its derivation, and
   (b) is likely to be of substantial value (whether or not by itself) to the investigation for the purposes of which the warrant is sought.
(7B) In the case of a detained cash investigation into the intended use of cash, material falls within this subsection if it cannot be identified at the time of the application but it—
   (a) relates to the property specified in the application or the question whether the property, or a part of it, is intended by any person to be used in unlawful conduct, and
   (b) is likely to be of substantial value (whether or not by itself) to the investigation for the purposes of which the warrant is sought.
(8) In the case of a money laundering investigation, material falls within this subsection if it cannot be identified at the time of the application but it—
   (a) relates to the person specified in the application or the question whether he has committed a money laundering offence, and
   (b) is likely to be of substantial value (whether or not by itself) to the investigation for the purposes of which the warrant is sought.
(8A) In the case of an exploitation proceeds investigation, material falls within this subsection if it cannot be identified at the time of the application but it—
   (a) relates to the person specified in the application, the question whether exploitation proceeds have been obtained from a relevant offence in relation to that person, any question as to the extent or whereabouts of any benefit as a result of which exploitation proceeds are obtained or any question about the person's available amount, and
   (b) is likely to be of substantial value (whether or not by itself) to the investigation for the purposes of which the warrant is sought.
This subsection is to be construed in accordance with Part 7 of the Coroners and Justice Act 2009 (criminal memoirs etc).
(9) The requirements are—
   (a) that it is not practicable to communicate with any person entitled to grant entry to the premises;
   (b) that entry to the premises will not be granted unless a warrant is produced;
   (c) that the investigation might be seriously prejudiced unless an appropriate person arriving at the premises is able to secure immediate entry to them.
(10) An appropriate person is—
   (a) a constable, an accredited financial investigator or a customs officer, if the warrant is sought for the purposes of a confiscation investigation or a money laundering investigation;
   (b) a National Crime Agency officer or a member of the staff of the relevant Director, if the warrant is sought for the purposes of a civil recovery investigation;
   (c) a constable, an accredited financial investigator or an officer of Revenue and Customs, if the warrant is sought for the purposes of a detained cash investigation;
   (d) a National Crime Agency officer, if the warrant is sought for the purposes of an exploitation proceeds investigation.
(11) The reference in paragraph (a) or (c) of subsection (10) to an accredited financial investigator is a reference to an accredited financial investigator who falls within a description specified in an order made for the purposes of that paragraph by the Secretary of State under section 453.

The CCA 2013, sch. 19 (not yet in force), amends the POCA 2002, ss. 352 and 353, so as to make further provision for civil recovery investigations; the sections are shown above as so amended.

D8.26 **The Powers** A search and seizure warrant authorises an appropriate officer (see **D8.24**) to enter and search specified premises and to seize and retain any material 'which is likely to be of substantial value (whether or not by itself) to the investigation' (POCA 2002, s. 352(4)). Lord Thomas CJ stated in *R (Golfrate Property Management) v Southwark Crown Court* [2014] EWHC 840 (Admin) at [26]–[27] that the applicant:

> ...must make the necessary resources available so that the Resident Judge at the Crown Court can discharge his responsibility for ensuring that arrangements are in place for these difficult and important applications to be dealt with properly. Judges must therefore be provided with the papers promptly, be accorded the time required to read the papers, to hear the application and to provide written reasons...it is far, far better that time is afforded for an initial application to be subject to rigorous scrutiny in a complex case...the consequences of failing to accord the judge time is that much more time-consuming and expensive proceedings have to be undertaken by way of a review. At all events, a judge faced with such an application requires the presentation of a full and clear picture of what lies behind it and to be told of matters that might tell against it. The target of the application is entitled to expect such candour.

Essentially, a warrant is available only (a) where a production order has not been complied with and there are reasonable grounds for believing that the material is on the specified premises (s. 352) or (b), (i) where it is in the public interest to obtain the material and the material is likely to be of substantial value to the investigation but it is not appropriate to make a production order, notwithstanding that the requirements can be made out, because it is not practicable to communicate with the interested parties or because the investigation might be seriously prejudiced unless immediate access is obtained (s. 353(3) and (4)); or (ii) where the material is likely to be of substantial value to the investigation but cannot be identified in advance and it is not practicable to communicate with the interested parties or because the investigation might be seriously prejudiced unless immediate access is obtained (s. 353(5)). A warrant does not confer the right to seize 'privileged' or 'excluded' material (s. 354). Where property has been seized pursuant to a technically defective warrant, the Crown Court may authorise the retention of the property under the CJPA 2001, s. 59, on the ground that, were it to be returned, it would immediately become appropriate to issue a fresh warrant (*R (El-Kurd) v Winchester Crown Court* [2011] EWHC 1853 (Admin)).

D8.27 The control of search warrant powers under the PACE 1984 has been extended to embrace searches under a POCA warrant in confiscation and money laundering investigations (see the POCA 2002, s. 355, and the Proceeds of Crime Act 2002 (Application of Police and Criminal Evidence Act 1984 and Police and Criminal Evidence (Northern Ireland) Order 1989) Order 2003 (SI 2003 No. 174)). The PACE 1984 provisions that apply relate to search warrants (PACE 1984, s. 15), execution of warrants (s. 16), access and copying (s. 21) and retention (s. 22). For details of these provisions, see **D1.163** *et seq*. Certain modifications of the provisions are set out in the 2003 Order.

The POCA 2002 itself contains broadly similar but more limited controls on the execution of a warrant granted by a High Court judge in civil recovery investigations (s. 356).

Disclosure Orders

D8.28

Proceeds of Crime Act 2002, ss. 357 and 358

357.—(1) A judge may, on an application made to him by the relevant authority, make a disclosure order if he is satisfied that each of the requirements for the making of the order is fulfilled.

(2) No application for a disclosure order may be made in relation to a detained cash investigation or a money laundering investigation.

(2A) The relevant authority may only make an application for a disclosure order in relation to a confiscation investigation if the relevant authority is in receipt of a request to do so from an appropriate officer.

(3) The application for a disclosure order must state that—
  (a) a person specified in the application is subject to a confiscation investigation which is being carried out by an appropriate officer and the order is sought for the purposes of the investigation, or
  (b) a person specified in the application or property specified in the application is subject to a civil recovery investigation and the order is sought for the purposes of the investigation, or
  (c) a person specified in the application is subject to an exploitation proceeds investigation and the order is sought for the purposes of the investigation.

(4) A disclosure order is an order authorising an appropriate officer to give to any person the appropriate officer considers has relevant information notice in writing requiring him to do, with respect to any matter relevant to the investigation for the purposes of which the order is sought, any or all of the following—
  (a) answer questions, either at a time specified in the notice or at once, at a place so specified;
  (b) provide information specified in the notice, by a time and in a manner so specified;
  (c) produce documents, or documents of a description, specified in the notice, either at or by a time so specified or at once, and in a manner so specified.

(5) Relevant information is information (whether or not contained in a document) which the appropriate officer concerned considers to be relevant to the investigation.

(6) A person is not bound to comply with a requirement imposed by a notice given under a disclosure order unless evidence of authority to give the notice is produced to him.

(7) In this Part 'relevant authority' means—
  (a) in relation to a confiscation investigation, a prosecutor; and
  (b) in relation to a civil recovery investigation, a National Crime Agency officer or the relevant Director; and
  (c) in relation to an exploitation proceeds investigation, National Crime Agency officer.

(8) For the purposes of subsection (7)(a) a prosecutor is—
  (a) in relation to a confiscation investigation carried out by a National Crime Agency officer, the relevant Director or any specified person;
  (b) in relation to a confiscation investigation carried out by an accredited financial investigator, the Director of Public Prosecutions, the Director of Public Prosecutions for Northern Ireland or any specified person;
  (c) in relation to a confiscation investigation carried out by a constable, the Director of Public Prosecutions, the Director of Public Prosecutions for Northern Ireland, the Director of the Serious Fraud Office or any specified person; and
  (d) in relation to a confiscation investigation carried out by an officer of Revenue and Customs, the Director of Public Prosecutions, the Director of Public Prosecutions for Northern Ireland or any specified person.

(9) In subsection (8) 'specified person' means any person specified, or falling within a description specified, by an order of the Secretary of State.

358.—(1) These are the requirements for the making of a disclosure order.

(2) There must be reasonable grounds for suspecting that—
  (a) in the case of a confiscation investigation, the person specified in the application for the order has benefited from his criminal conduct;
  (b) in the case of a civil recovery investigation—
    (i) the person specified in the application for the order holds recoverable property or associated property,
    (ii) that person has, at any time, held property that was recoverable property or associated property at the time, or
    (iii) the property specified in the application for the order is recoverable property or associated property;
  (c) in the case of an exploitation proceeds investigation, the person specified in the application for the order is a person within section 346(2A).

(3) There must be reasonable grounds for believing that information which may be provided in compliance with a requirement imposed under the order is likely to be of substantial value (whether or not by itself) to the investigation for the purposes of which the order is sought.

(4) There must be reasonable grounds for believing that it is in the public interest for the information to be provided, having regard to the benefit likely to accrue to the investigation if the information is obtained.

The CCA 2013, sch. 19 (not yet in force), amends the POCA 2002, ss. 357 and 358, so as to make further provision for civil recovery investigations; the sections are shown above as so amended.

D8.29   **Effect of the Order**   A disclosure order under the POCA 2002, s. 357, enables an appropriate officer (see **D8.24**) to require any person considered to have relevant information to respond in any or all of three ways: to answer questions at a specified time and place; to provide information at a time and in a manner specified in the notice; and/or to produce documents or documents of a description by a time and in a manner specified in the notice. 'Relevant information' is defined as information the appropriate officer considers to be relevant to an investigation (s. 357(6)).

An application may be made by 'the relevant authority'. The relevant authority means, in a confiscation case, the DPP, the Director of the SFO (depending on who carries out the investigation) or any person specified by order of the Secretary of State. In respect of civil recovery investigations it may be one of those directors or an NCA officer. In confiscation cases, however, the authority must first have received a request from an appropriate officer. An order may not be granted in relation to money laundering and detained cash investigations. Notice may be given to anyone that the appropriate officer considers has relevant information. A disclosure order or notice (see **D8.31**) may not be addressed to persons who are not within the jurisdiction (*SOCA v Perry* [2013] 1 AC 182). There is no scope for a worldwide disclosure order (*King v Director of the SFO* [2009] 2 All ER 223).

The two conditions for the making of an order are essentially questions of fact, namely, whether there were reasonable grounds for believing that the material would likely be of substantial value and that it would be in the public interest that the material should be produced (*R (Malik) v Manchester Crown Court* [2008] 4 All ER 403).

An order does not confer the right to require persons to answer privileged questions, provide privileged information, produce privileged documents or produce 'excluded material' (s. 361). (See **D8.23** for the meaning of these terms.) 'A lawyer' may be required to provide a client's name and address.

D8.30   Generally, a statement made in response to a requirement of a disclosure order may not be used in evidence against the maker in criminal proceedings (s. 360(1)). Its use is permissible, however, in confiscation proceedings, in a prosecution for having failed without reasonable excuse to comply with the disclosure order, or in a prosecution for perjury. Moreover, an order may not be resisted on the basis that disclosure would breach the privilege against self-incrimination because it may lead to prosecution for an offence under s. 328 (entering or being concerned in a money laundering arrangement: see **B21.15**); the offence is a 'related' offence within the meaning of the Fraud Act 2006, s. 13, and no privilege applies (*JSC BTA Bank v Ablyazov* [2010] 1 WLR 976). More widely, the statement is admissible in any prosecution when the person 'in giving evidence' makes an inconsistent statement (s. 360(2)).

It is a summary offence to fail to comply with a requirement of a disclosure order without reasonable excuse (s. 359(1)) and it is an offence triable either way if, in purported compliance, a person knowingly or recklessly makes a false or misleading statement (s. 359(3)).

D8.31   **Disclosure Notices under the SOCPA 2005**   The SOCPA 2005, s. 62, confers powers on the DPP to issue 'disclosure notices' without any court order, requiring persons to answer questions, provide information and/or produce documents relevant to specific offences. The powers may be delegated to prosecutor level. The conditions are that there are reasonable grounds for suspecting that one of the offences has been committed and that the person has information that 'is likely to be of substantial value' to the investigation. If a notice is not complied with, a justice of the peace may grant a warrant to enter and seize documents. It is an offence not to comply with a notice or to provide false or misleading information.

Customer Information Orders

D8.32   Proceeds of Crime Act 2002, ss. 363 and 364

     363.—(1) A judge may, on an application made to him by an appropriate officer, make a customer information order if he is satisfied that each of the requirements for the making of the order is fulfilled.

(1A)   No application for a customer information order may be made in relation to a detained cash investigation.

(2)   The application for a customer information order must state that—
  (a)   a person specified in the application is subject to a confiscation investigation, a civil recovery investigation, an exploitation proceeds investigation or a money laundering investigation,
  (b)   [omitted by the CCA 2013, sch. 19].

(3)   The application must also state that—
  (a)   the order is sought for the purposes of the investigation;
  (b)   the order is sought against the financial institution or financial institutions specified in the application.

(4)   An application for a customer information order may specify—
  (a)   all financial institutions,
  (b)   a particular description, or particular descriptions, of financial institutions, or
  (c)   a particular financial institution or particular financial institutions.

(5)   A customer information order is an order that a financial institution covered by the application for the order must, on being required to do so by notice in writing given by an appropriate officer, provide any such customer information as it has relating to the person specified in the application.

(6)   A financial institution which is required to provide information under a customer information order must provide the information to an appropriate officer in such manner, and at or by such time, as an appropriate officer requires.

(7)   If a financial institution on which a requirement is imposed by a notice given under a customer information order requires the production of evidence of authority to give the notice, it is not bound to comply with the requirement unless evidence of the authority has been produced to it.

364.—(1)   'Customer information', in relation to a person and a financial institution, is information whether the person holds, or has held, an account or accounts at the financial institution (whether solely or jointly with another) and (if so) information as to—
  (a)   the matters specified in subsection (2) if the person is an individual;
  (b)   the matters specified in subsection (3) if the person is a company or limited liability partnership or a similar body incorporated or otherwise established outside the United Kingdom.

(2)   The matters referred to in subsection (1)(a) are—
  (a)   the account number or numbers;
  (b)   the person's full name;
  (c)   his date of birth;
  (d)   his most recent address and any previous addresses;
  (e)   the date or dates on which he began to hold the account or accounts and, if he has ceased to hold the account or any of the accounts, the date or dates on which he did so;
  (f)   such evidence of his identity as was obtained by the financial institution under or for the purposes of any legislation relating to money laundering;
  (g)   the full name, date of birth and most recent address, and any previous addresses, of any person who holds, or has held, an account at the financial institution jointly with him;
  (h)   the account number or numbers of any other account or accounts held at the financial institution to which he is a signatory and details of the person holding the other account or accounts.

(3)   The matters referred to in subsection (1)(b) are—
  (a)   the account number or numbers;
  (b)   the person's full name;
  (c)   a description of any business which the person carries on;
  (d)   the country or territory in which it is incorporated or otherwise established and any number allocated to it under the Companies Act 2006 or corresponding legislation of any country or territory outside the United Kingdom;
  (e)   any number assigned to it for the purposes of value added tax in the United Kingdom;
  (f)   its registered office, and any previous registered offices, under the Companies Act 2006 (or corresponding earlier legislation) or anything similar under corresponding legislation of any country or territory outside the United Kingdom;
  (g)   its registered office, and any previous registered offices, under the Limited Liability Partnerships Act 2000 or anything similar under corresponding legislation of any country or territory outside Great Britain;
  (h)   the date or dates on which it began to hold the account or accounts and, if it has ceased to hold the account or any of the accounts, the date or dates on which it did so;

D

Part D Procedure

(i) such evidence of its identity as was obtained by the financial institution under or for the purposes of any legislation relating to money laundering;

(j) the full name, date of birth and most recent address and any previous addresses of any person who is a signatory to the account or any of the accounts.

(4) The Secretary of State may by order provide for information of a description specified in the order—

(a) to be customer information, or

(b) no longer to be customer information.

(5) Money laundering is an act which—

(a) constitutes an offence under section 327, 328 or 329 of this Act or section 18 of the Terrorism Act 2000, or

(aa) constitutes an offence under section 415(1A) of this Act; or

(b) would constitute an offence specified in paragraph (a) or (aa) if done in the United Kingdom.

The CCA 2013, sch. 19 (not yet in force), amends the POCA 2002, s. 363, so as to amend the provision for civil recovery investigations; the section is shown above as so amended.

D8.33 **Effect, Procedure and Requirements** A customer information order requires a 'financial institution' on written notice to provide 'customer information' to the 'appropriate officer' (see **D8.24**) (POCA 2002, s. 363(5)). 'Customer information' can amount to the most detailed information about financial accounts and account holders (s. 364).

Procedure is governed by the CrimPR, part 6 (see Supplement, **R-55** *et seq.*). Separate rules apply in civil recovery investigations. The office and rank required of an applicant is determined by the type of investigation (see s. 378 at **D8.24**).

As with the other types of order, the requirements for the making of an order vary according to the type of investigation. Thus, the nature of the grounds of reasonable suspicion or belief are different in different investigations. 'Public interest' and the 'substantial value (of an order) to the investigation' are constant criteria.

In keeping with the provisions relating to disclosure orders, a statement made by a financial institution in response to a customer information order cannot be used against it in criminal proceedings other than in confiscation proceedings, in a prosecution under s. 366 for non-compliance with the order itself or in any prosecution where the financial institution makes an inconsistent statement (s. 367). An application to vary or discharge the order may be made by the original applicant for the order or by 'any person affected by the order' (s. 369).

A financial institution commits an offence if it fails to comply with an order without reasonable excuse (s. 366(1)) or if, in purported compliance, it knowingly or recklessly makes a false or misleading statement (s. 366(3)). The latter is triable either way.

Account Monitoring Orders

D8.34 Proceeds of Crime Act 2002, ss. 370 and 371

370.—(1) A judge may, on an application made to him by an appropriate officer, make an account monitoring order if he is satisfied that each of the requirements for the making of the order is fulfilled.

(1A) No application for an account monitoring order may be made in relation to a detained cash investigation.

(2) The application for an account monitoring order must state that—

(a) a person specified in the application is subject to a confiscation investigation, a civil recovery investigation, an exploitation proceeds investigation or a money laundering investigation

(b) [omitted by the CCA 2013, sch. 19].

(3) The application must also state that—

(a) the order is sought for the purposes of the investigation;

(b) the order is sought against the financial institution specified in the application in relation to account information of the description so specified.

(4) Account information is information relating to an account or accounts held at the financial institution specified in the application by the person so specified (whether solely or jointly with another).

(5) The application for an account monitoring order may specify information relating to—
  (a) all accounts held by the person specified in the application for the order at the financial institution so specified,
  (b) a particular description, or particular descriptions, of accounts so held, or
  (c) a particular account, or particular accounts, so held.
(6) An account monitoring order is an order that the financial institution specified in the application for the order must, for the period stated in the order, provide account information of the description specified in the order to an appropriate officer in the manner, and at or by the time or times, stated in the order.
(7) The period stated in an account monitoring order must not exceed the period of 90 days beginning with the day on which the order is made.

371.—(1) These are the requirements for the making of an account monitoring order.
(2) In the case of a confiscation investigation, there must be reasonable grounds for suspecting that the person specified in the application for the order has benefited from his criminal conduct.
(3) [Substituted with s. 371(3A) by the CCA 2013, sch. 19.]
(3A) In the case of a civil recovery investigation, there must be reasonable grounds for suspecting that the person specified in the application holds recoverable property or associated property.
(4) In the case of a money laundering investigation, there must be reasonable grounds for suspecting that the person specified in the application for the order has committed a money laundering offence.
(5) In the case of any investigation, there must be reasonable grounds for believing that account information which may be provided in compliance with the order is likely to be of substantial value (whether or not by itself) to the investigation for the purposes of which the order is sought.
(6) In the case of any investigation, there must be reasonable grounds for believing that it is in the public interest for the account information to be provided, having regard to the benefit likely to accrue to the investigation if the information is obtained.

The CCA 2013, sch. 19 (not yet in force), amends the POCA 2002, ss. 370 and 371, so as to make further provision for civil recovery investigations; the sections are shown above as so amended.

Effect, Procedure and Requirements   An account monitoring order requires a financial insti-   **D8.35**
tution to provide an appropriate officer (see **D8.24**) with specified information 'relating to an account or accounts held' solely or jointly by a specified person ('account information') for the period stated in the order (POCA 2002, s. 370) which must not exceed 90 days from the date of the order. An order 'has effect in spite of any restriction on the disclosure of information (however imposed)' (s. 374); this appears to override any claim of confidentiality or data protection.

Procedure is governed by the CrimPR, part 6 (see Supplement, **R-55** *et seq.*). The requirements under s. 371 closely resemble those of the other orders. The general requirements for an order include reasonable belief in the likelihood of the account information being of substantial value to the investigation and that the provision of the information is in the public interest. There are restrictions similar to those relating to other orders on the use in criminal proceedings of a statement by a financial institution in response to an order (s. 372). An application to vary or discharge the order may be made by the original applicant for the order or by 'any person affected by the order' (s. 375).

RESTRAINT ORDERS

Proceeds of Crime Act 2002, ss. 40 and 41   **D8.36**

40.—(1) The Crown Court may exercise the powers conferred by section 41 if any of the following conditions is satisfied.
(2) The first condition is that—
  (a) a criminal investigation has been started in England and Wales with regard to an offence, and
  (b) there is reasonable cause to believe that the alleged offender has benefited from his criminal conduct.
(3) The second condition is that—
  (a) proceedings for an offence have been started in England and Wales and not concluded, and
  (b) there is reasonable cause to believe that the defendant has benefited from his criminal conduct.

(4) The third condition is that—
  (a) an application by the prosecutor has been made under section 19, 20, 27 or 28 and not concluded, or the court believes that such an application is to be made, and
  (b) there is reasonable cause to believe that the defendant has benefited from his criminal conduct.
(5) The fourth condition is that—
  (a) an application by the prosecutor has been made under section 21 and not concluded, or the court believes that such an application is to be made, and
  (b) there is reasonable cause to believe that the court will decide under that section that the amount found under the new calculation of the defendant's benefit exceeds the relevant amount (as defined in that section).
(6) The fifth condition is that—
  (a) an application by the prosecutor has been made under section 22 and not concluded, or the court believes that such an application is to be made, and
  (b) there is reasonable cause to believe that the court will decide under that section that the amount found under the new calculation of the available amount exceeds the relevant amount (as defined in that section).
(7) The second condition is not satisfied if the court believes that—
  (a) there has been undue delay in continuing the proceedings, or
  (b) the prosecutor does not intend to proceed.
(8) If an application mentioned in the third, fourth or fifth condition has been made the condition is not satisfied if the court believes that—
  (a) there has been undue delay in continuing the application, or
  (b) the prosecutor does not intend to proceed.
(9) If the first condition is satisfied—
  (a) references in this Part to the defendant are to the alleged offender;
  (b) references in this Part to the prosecutor are to the person the court believes is to have conduct of any proceedings for the offence;
  (c) section 77(9) has effect as if proceedings for the offence had been started against the defendant when the investigation was started.
41.—(1) If any condition set out in section 40 is satisfied the Crown Court may make an order (a restraint order) prohibiting any specified person from dealing with any realisable property held by him.
(2) A restraint order may provide that it applies—
  (a) to all realisable property held by the specified person whether or not the property is described in the order;
  (b) to realisable property transferred to the specified person after the order is made.
(2A) A restraint order must be made subject to an exception enabling relevant legal aid payments to be made (a legal aid exception).
(2B) A relevant legal aid payment is a payment that the specified person is obliged to make—
  (a) by regulations under section 23 or 24 of the Legal Aid, Sentencing and Punishment of Offenders Act 2012, and
  (b) in connection with services provided in relation to an offence which falls within subsection (5),
  whether the obligation to make the payment arises before or after the restraint order is made.
(3) A restraint order may be made subject to other exceptions, and an exception may in particular—
  (a) make provision for reasonable living expenses and reasonable legal expenses;
  (b) make provision for the purpose of enabling any person to carry on any trade, business, profession or occupation;
  (c) [omitted by the CCA 2013, s. 46].
(4) But where an exception to a restraint order is made under subsection (3), it must not make provision for any legal expenses which—
  (a) relate to an offence which falls within subsection (5), and
  (b) are incurred by the defendant or by a recipient of a tainted gift.
(5) These offences fall within this subsection—
  (a) the offence mentioned in section 40(2) or (3), if the first or second condition (as the case may be) is satisfied;
  (b) the offence (or any of the offences) concerned, if the third, fourth or fifth condition is satisfied.

(5A) A legal aid exception—
  (a) must be made subject to prescribed restrictions (if any) on—
    (i) the circumstances in which payments may be made in reliance on the exception, or
    (ii) the amount of the payments that may be made in reliance on the exception,
  (b) must be made subject to other prescribed conditions (if any), and
  (c) may be made subject to other conditions.
(5B) Any other exception to a restraint order may be made subject to conditions.
(6) Subsection (7) applies if—
  (a) a court makes a restraint order, and
  (b) the applicant for the order applies to the court to proceed under subsection (7) (whether as part of the application for the restraint order or at any time afterwards).
(7) The court may make such order as it believes is appropriate for the purpose of ensuring that the restraint order is effective.
(8) A restraint order does not affect property for the time being subject to a charge under any of these provisions—
  (a) section 9 of the Drug Trafficking Offences Act 1986;
  (b) section 78 of the Criminal Justice Act 1988;
  (c) Article 14 of the Criminal Justice (Confiscation) (Northern Ireland) Order 1990 (SI 1990 No. 2588);
  (d) section 27 of the Drug Trafficking Act 1994;
  (e) Article 32 of the Proceeds of Crime (Northern Ireland) Order 1996 (SI 1996 No. 1299).
(9) Dealing with property includes removing it from England and Wales.
(10) In this section 'prescribed' means prescribed by regulations made by the Secretary of State.

The CCA 2013, s. 46 (not yet in force), amends the POCA 2002, s. 41, so as to make provision for legal aid payments. Section 41 is shown above as so amended.

Power to make an Order   Under earlier legislation, restraint orders could be granted only by the High Court. Under the POCA 2002, part 2, the jurisdiction is transferred to the Crown Court. For a useful summary of the statutory scheme and procedure, see *Re Windsor* [2011] 1 WLR 1519.   **D8.37**

A restraint order prevents a person from dissipating or disposing of property that is potentially available for the satisfaction of any confiscation order that may be or has been made. A restraint order operates to prohibit 'any specified person from dealing with any realisable property held by him' (s. 41(1)). Realisable property is 'any free property' held by the defendant or by the recipient of a 'tainted gift' (s. 83). The reference to 'tainted gifts' ensures that criminal property can be preserved when it has been 'gifted' away into the hands of another. Property is 'free' unless it is subject to a recovery or forfeiture order or (when in force) a forfeiture notice (s. 82). Property is held by a person who has an 'interest' in it. This is not necessarily confined to the holding of a legal or equitable interest in the property. In the context of a VAT carousel fraud, all the conspirators may have a beneficial 'interest' in the proceeds of the conspiracy which may be the subject of a restraint order (*S* [2005] EWCA Crim 2919; but see also *Ahmad* [2012] 2 All ER 1204).

Ancillary to a restraint order, the court 'may make such order as it believes is appropriate for the purpose of ensuring that the restraint order is effective' (s. 41(7)). Frequently, defendants are required to provide statements disclosing their finances or to repatriate assets. From a day to be appointed, property that has been seized by or produced to 'an appropriate officer' (see **D8.24**) under a statutory power may be detained as part of the restraint order (s. 41A).

The Exercise of the Power   The underlying purpose of the legislation is to prevent the dissipation of assets in anticipation of an investigation or criminal proceedings. However, as a basic principle, 'if there is no [risk that property will be dissipated] ... or the risk is merely fanciful, the order ought not to be made since, *ex hypothesi*, it would not be necessary for the achievement of its only proper purpose' (*Re AJ and DJ* (9 December 1992 unreported) per Glidewell LJ). Since a restraint order amounts to an interference with the right to peaceful enjoyment of possessions under Article 1 of Protocol 1 to the ECHR, there can be no justification for an order unless such a risk exists (*Re B (Restraint Order)* [2009] 1 Cr App R 203). Where dishonesty is   **D8.38**

---

alleged, there will usually be reason to fear that assets will be dissipated. Prosecutors should be alive to the possibility that there may be no risk in fact and, where no dissipation has occurred over a long period, they should explain why dissipation is now feared. Where the respondent has had ample opportunity to dissipate assets but has not done so and has disclosed the existence of other assets, the prosecutor and judge must provide a reasoned explanation for an order (*Re B*). Prosecutors have a duty to make full and frank disclosure but, as they act in the public interest, a failure of disclosure should not result in the sanction of discharging the order save where their behaviour was appalling (*Jennings v CPS* [2006] 4 All ER 391). If the court considers that the prosecution have failed to consider the risk or failed to put relevant material before the court, but that the public interest still requires an order, the court may disallow the prosecution costs (*Stanford International Bank v SFO* [2011] Ch 33; *Jennings v CPS*).

D8.39   In the shape of s. 69, the POCA 2002 has its own 'legislative steer'. The powers of the court and of receivers must be exercised:

(a) with a view to securing the availability of the value of the property to satisfy any confiscation order;
(b) in a case where no order has yet been made, with a view to ensuring that the property does not decrease in value;
(c) 'without taking account of any obligation of the defendant or the recipient of a tainted gift if the obligation conflicts with the object of satisfying any confiscation order'.

The three objectives are subject to rules that:

(i) a person other than the defendant or a recipient of a tainted gift should be allowed to retain or recover the value of any interest held by him;
(ii) in respect of realisable property held by the recipient of a tainted gift, the powers should be exercised with a view to realising no more than the value for the time being of that gift;
(iii) where no confiscation order has yet been made, and the defendant or a recipient of a tainted gift makes an application, the court should not order the sale of property which cannot be replaced.

D8.40   Section 69(2)(c) of the POCA 2002 requires the courts to ignore any debt owed by the restrained person to an unsecured third-party creditor, so that the existence of such a debt would not empower the court to vary a restraint order unless there was no conflict with the object of satisfying any confiscation order that had been or might be made. The statutory provisions had changed significantly since the pre-2002 Act legislation (*Re X (Restraint Order: Variation)* [2005] QB 133, superseded by *Serious Fraud Office v Lexi Holdings* [2009] QB 376).

Where there are concurrent matrimonial proceedings, it may be possible to regularise the interests in shared property by ordering the transfer of the innocent partner's share as ancillary relief in those proceedings thus taking that share out of the calculation of the amount available for confiscation (*Webber v CPS* [2007] 1 WLR 1052; *Customs and Excise Commissioners v MCA* (2002) *The Times*, 25 July 2002; *CPS v Grimes; Grimes v Grimes* [2003] FLR 510; *Hedges* [2004] EWCA Crim 2133; *X v X* [2005] 2 FLR 487). This should not be regarded as 'open season to collusive agreements between dishonest former spouses'. 'As a matter of justice and public policy', where the family assets are themselves tainted, they should not be distributed to satisfy ancillary relief claims. 'The only decisive factor' is whether the assets are tainted as having been derived from crime (*CPS v Richards* [2006] 2 FLR 1220).

Restrictions on Restraint Orders

D8.41   No distress may be levied against any restrained property, nor may there be forfeiture for breach of a tenancy agreement without leave of the Crown Court (POCA 2002, s. 58(2) and (3)). Where other court proceedings are pending in respect of restrained property, the other court has a discretion whether or not to stay those proceedings once it has given an opportunity for the applicant for the restraint order and any receiver to make representations (s. 58(6)).

Basis for Making an Order

The satisfaction of any one of five 'conditions' in the POCA 2002, s. 40, provides the basis for **D8.42** a restraint order. The first three conditions are (a) that 'a criminal investigation has been started with regard to an offence' (s. 40(2)(a)), (b) that 'proceedings have been started' and (c) that there is an unconcluded application (or an application that the court believes is to be made) for reconsideration of confiscation or an application in respect of an absconded defendant and, in each case, that there is 'reasonable cause to believe that the alleged offender has benefited from his criminal conduct'.

Transitional provisions require that restraint orders may not be made under (a) above where an offence which is the subject of an investigation was committed before 24 March 2003 (Proceeds of Crime Act 2002 (Transitional Provisions, Savings and Amendment) Order (SI 2003 No. 333), art. 5). However, the applicant does not need to establish that all the offences under investigation occurred after that date. The judge should look at what offences were under investigation at the time of the application, not at the time when the investigation began. All that is required therefore, to establish jurisdiction, is that an offence that may, following conviction, give rise to a confiscation order is under investigation at the time of the application (*RCPO v Hill* [2005] EWCA Crim 3271).

The fourth and fifth conditions are that an application to reconsider the amount of benefit or the available amount determined in previous confiscation proceedings is not concluded (or that the court believes such an application is to be made) and there is reasonable cause to believe that the new amount will exceed the original amount. The last four conditions are not satisfied if the court believes that there has been undue delay in continuing the proceedings or that the prosecutor does not intend to proceed.

It appears that, for the purposes of the first two conditions, there need not necessarily be a con- **D8.43** nection between the current criminal investigation or proceedings and the 'criminal conduct' from which the person is believed to have benefited (*RCPO v Hill*). 'Criminal conduct' simply means any conduct that constitutes an offence in England and Wales or that would constitute an offence if it occurred here (s. 76). Accordingly, the conditions for a restraint order simply anticipate the twin components of a confiscation order — a conviction for an offence and a finding that the defendant has benefited from 'his criminal conduct'. In the case of someone found to have a 'criminal lifestyle', this means 'his general criminal conduct' whenever it occurred (see **E19.16**). It follows that a judge is entitled, in deciding on the terms of the restraint order, to have regard to the likelihood that the defendant, if convicted, would in due course be found to have 'a criminal lifestyle' and that the statutory assumptions of benefit in s. 10 would eventually apply (see **E19.34**). In those circumstances, the judge may make an unlimited restraint order (*Re K* [2005] EWCA Crim 619); where it is so made, a full duty of disclosure is borne by the applicant and the defendant must be given a note of the *ex parte* hearing (*Director of the ARA v Singh* [2005] 1 WLR 3747).

External Requests and Orders

A restraint order may be supported by a repatriation requirement in relation to liquid assets. **D8.44** In relation to overseas property generally, the prosecutor may send a letter of request, via the Secretary of State, to the relevant overseas authority requesting that the property be secured and, if a confiscation order has been made, realised.

The court may make an 'external order' prohibiting dealing with property which is the subject of an 'external request' (Proceeds of Crime Act 2002 (External Requests and Orders) Order 2005 (SI 2005 No. 3181) and s. 444). An external request 'is a request by an overseas authority to prohibit dealing with relevant property which is identified in the request' (s. 447(1)). An 'overseas authority' is an authority outside England and Wales which has responsibility for making such a request or for carrying out an investigation into whether property has been obtained as a result of or in connection with criminal conduct or into a money laundering offence (s. 447(11)). The 2005 Order has been amended by the Proceeds of Crime Act 2002 (External Requests and Orders) (Amendment) Order 2013 (SI 2013 No. 2604) so that an enforcement authority (see **D8.4**) may obtain a 'prohibition order'. A prohibition order operates to prevent any person to whose property the order applies from dealing with property in England and Wales or Northern Ireland subject to detailed exceptions. The enforcement authority may not apply for an order unless it believes that the aggregate value is not less than £10,000.

In September 2012, the Home Office published its 10th version of guidance for overseas authorities on 'Requests for Mutual Legal Assistance in Criminal Matters' (see www.gov.uk/government/uploads/system/uploads/attachment_data/file/269208/MLA_Guidelines_2014.pdf). Appeals are governed by the Proceeds of Crime Act 2002 (External Requests and Orders) Order 2005 (England and Wales) (Appeals under Part 2) Order 2012 (SI 2012 No. 138).

The 2005 Order confers jurisdiction to make orders only in respect of property in England and Wales. No machinery is provided for the exercise of the powers outside England and Wales. Notwithstanding that 'property' is defined in the Act as 'all property wherever situated' (s. 447(4)), its meaning depends upon the context which, by virtue of the Order, is limited to England and Wales.

Procedure

D8.45 The 'prosecutor', the Director General of the NCA or an accredited financial investigator may apply for a restraint order (POCA 2002, s. 42(1) and (2)). As the Financial Services Authority had power to bring a prosecution for money laundering (see **D3.64**), it could apply for an order (*Rollins* [2010] 4 All ER 880); this principle is likely to hold good for the Financial Conduct Authority.

Procedure is governed by the CrimPR, part 59 (see Supplement, **R-417**). An application may be made without notice.

Restraint proceedings are civil in nature (*Re S (Restraint Order: Release of Assets)* [2005] 1 WLR 1338 at [53]). Sections 2 to 4 of the Civil Evidence Act 1995, which deal with hearsay evidence, are applied. Indeed, hearsay evidence 'of whatever degree' is expressly admissible (s. 46(1)).

D8.46 The application must be made in writing and it must be supported by a witness statement, which must contain (CrimPR, r. 59.1(3)):

(a) the grounds for the application;
(b) details of the realisable property and of the person holding that property;
(c) the grounds for, and full details of, any application for an ancillary order; and
(d) where the application is made by an accredited financial investigator, a statement that he has been authorised to make the application.

An application to discharge the order may be made by the original applicant or by 'any person affected by the order' (s. 42(3)). The order must be discharged on the conclusion of the proceedings or, where the order was made for the purposes of an investigation, if proceedings are not started within a reasonable time (s. 42(7)). Note, however, that confiscation proceedings are not concluded until the confiscation order is satisfied or discharged (s. 85(5)).

A breach of an order may be dealt with by the Crown Court by committal for contempt of court (*M* [2009] 1 WLR 1179; Senior Courts Act 1981, s. 45(4)). Contempt in this context is civil and not criminal (*OB v Director of SFO* [2012] 3 All ER 999). Accordingly, the principle of speciality does not prevent an extradited person from being dealt with for such a contempt (*Director of the Serious Fraud Office v O'Brien* [2014] 2 All ER 798). A deterrent element is appropriate in the sentence (*Adewunmi* [2008] 2 Cr App R (S) 326). A breach is capable, without more illegality beyond the contempt itself, of constituting the offence of perverting the course of justice (*Kenny* [2013] 3 All ER 85). However, the Court added that '[i]n cases of breach of restraint orders, nothing we have said should encourage prosecutors to charge perverting the course of justice where it is unnecessary to do so; ordinarily the sanction of contempt of court will suffice'. The Court referred to *Sookoo* [2002] EWCA Crim 800 in reminding prosecutors that, in such cases the offence of perverting the course of justice 'should only be charged where there are serious aggravating features'.

The court has a discretion to exempt funds from the order to allow for reasonable living or **D8.47** legal expenses or 'for the purpose of enabling any person to carry on any trade, business, profession or occupation' (s. 41(3)). Paradoxically, the order must not make provision for legal expenses attributable to the investigation or proceedings to which the restraint order relates (see s. 41(4), *Re S (Restraint Order: Release of Assets)* [2005] 1 WLR 1338 and *CPS v Campbell* [2010] 1 WLR 650; this has been held to be compatible with the ECHR, see *A & U Ltd v CPS* [2008] 1 Cr App R 497). When in force, the CCA 2013, s. 46, will insert a new s. 41(2A) into the POCA 2002, allowing for monthly legal aid payments to be met. As a general rule the defendant is entitled to enjoy the standard of life he previously experienced and is entitled to meet continuing expenses as they arise, although this may not extend to keeping up an excessively 'Rolls Royce lifestyle' (*In re Peters* [1988] QB 871; *Re D* (28 October 1992 unreported)). No variation of the order is necessary to enable solicitors instructed by the defendant to transfer funds from his client account to its office account in satisfaction of legal fees incurred prior to the making of the order (*Irwin Mitchell v RCPO* [2009] 3 All ER 530). See also *SOCA v Azam* [2014] 1 All ER 206.

Receivers

If necessary, the court may order that property be managed by a management receiver (POCA **D8.48** 2002, s. 48). The court may confer specific powers upon the receiver that include powers to take possession of the property, commence and conduct legal proceedings, enter into contracts, employ agents and to 'take any other steps the court thinks appropriate'. The receiver may realise so much of the property as is necessary to meet his own remuneration and expenses (s. 49(2)(d)) and may do so even if the assets were beneficially owned by a third party, with the defendant having only the bare legal title to them (*Heath Sinclair v Glatt* [2009] 4 All ER 724).

Where a restraint order is discharged on the basis that the legal conditions are not met, there can be no subsequent order that the receiver's costs and expenses, previously incurred, should be met from the restrained property — nor is there any power to order the prosecutor to meet the receiver's costs and expenses (*CPS v Eastenders Cash and Carry plc* [2013] 2 All ER 437).

A court-appointed receiver is not an agent of either party but, in effect, an officer of the court (*Re Andrews* [1991] 3 WLR 1236). In cases of urgency, where it is feared that notice may result in dissipation of the property, the application to appoint a receiver may be made at the same time as an *ex parte* restraint application. The orders made must, however, be in the narrowest terms consistent with the need to act effectively, and ought not to include a general power of sale. In such circumstances, should it become necessary for the receiver to dispose of property, he should return to court on notice for further directions (*Re P* [2000] 4 All ER 473). The Act itself prevents the court from providing the receiver with power to 'manage or otherwise deal with the property' or to realise any of it for payments to the receiver, without first giving 'persons holding interests in the property a reasonable opportunity to make representations' (s. 49(8)).

Persons who are or who may be affected by the receiver's actions, as well as the receiver, may apply for such directions as the court believes are appropriate (s. 62) or for variation or discharge of the order (s. 63). No distress may be levied against any realisable property, nor may there be forfeiture for breach of a tenancy agreement without leave of the Crown Court (s. 58(2) and (3)). Where other proceedings are pending in respect of the property, the other court has a discretion whether or not to stay those proceedings once it has given an opportunity for the applicant for the restraint order and any receiver to make representations (s. 58(6)).

Self-incrimination

D8.49 Under the High Court jurisdiction, the privilege against self-incrimination was maintained by the inclusion of a prohibition on the use of any statement of assets in a criminal prosecution (*Re O (Disclosure Order: Disclosure of Assets)* [1991] 1 All ER 330). Orders drawn under the new procedures in the Crown Court should contain a clear and specific statement to this effect. This will not prevent the use of such statements in subsequent confiscation proceedings.

Variation, Discharge and Appeal

D8.50 There is no right to appeal directly against the making of a restraint order. A person affected by an order must first apply to vary or discharge the order (POCA 2002, s. 42(3)). Where such an application is made, both the original applicant and any person affected by the order has a right of appeal to the Court of Appeal, and thereafter to the Supreme Court (POCA 2002, ss. 43 and 44). From a day to be appointed, property may be detained until 'there is no further possibility' of an appeal (s.44A).

SEIZURE OF REALISABLE PROPERTY

D8.51 On a day to be appointed, the POCA 2002 will be amended to introduce wide new powers for 'an appropriate officer' to search premises, people and vehicles and to seize realisable property other than cash or 'exempt property' (ss. 47A to 47S).

'Exempt property' means (a) equipment, including vehicles, that is necessary for the defendant's personal use in his employment, business or vocation and (b) household items and furniture necessary 'for satisfying the basic domestic needs of the defendant and the defendant's family' (POCA 2002, s. 47C(4)). An 'appropriate officer' is an officer of Revenue and Customs, a constable or an accredited financial investigator.

The Secretary of State is required to issue a code of practice governing all the matters connected with the new powers (s. 47S).

Power to Seize Property

D8.52 In order to seize property, the officer must first be satisfied that one of the seven statutory conditions is met (s. 47B(1)). The first two conditions (s. 47B(2) and (3)) both require (a) that a criminal investigation into an indictable offence 'has been started' in England or Wales, (b) that a person has been arrested for the offence but (c) that proceedings have not yet been started. The first condition additionally requires that, where a restraint order is not in force, there is 'reasonable cause' to believe that the person has benefited from conduct constituting the offence. There is no such requirement under the second condition where a restraint order is in force.

The third and fourth conditions apply where proceedings have been started but not concluded (s. 47B(4) and (5)). Again, they are distinguished by whether a restraint order is in force. Where no order is in force, the third condition requires 'reasonable cause' for believing that the defendant has benefited.

The fifth condition (s. 47B(6)) operates where the prosecutor has made or where the officer believes the prosecutor will make an application under s. 19 or s. 20 (reconsideration of the case or benefit where no confiscation order has been made) or under s. 27 or s. 28 (confiscation order against an absconding defendant). There must be a reasonable belief that the defendant has benefited from criminal conduct. The sixth and seventh conditions relate to applications under ss. 21 and 22 for reconsideration of the benefit or available amount (see E19.49) where a confiscation order has been made (s. 47B(7) and (8))). For either condition to be met, there must be a reasonable belief that the court will raise the benefit or available amount figures respectively.

The power of seizure itself is contained in s. 47C. It is exercisable only where the officer is satis- **D8.53**
fied that there are reasonable grounds for suspecting that (a) the property may otherwise be
made unavailable for satisfying any confiscation order that has been or may be made against the
defendant or (b) the value of the property may otherwise be diminished as a result of conduct
by the defendant or any other person.

Use of the power to seize property requires 'appropriate approval' unless it is not practicable to
obtain approval beforehand (s. 47C(6)(a)). This means approval by a justice of the peace or, if
that is not practicable, a senior officer (s. 47G). In the case of a Revenue and Customs officer, the
power to seize may be exercised only if he has reasonable grounds for suspecting that the conduct constituting the offence relates to an assigned matter within the meaning of the Customs
and Excise Management Act 1979 (s. 47C(6)(b)).

Seized property may be detained initially for 48 hours (s. 47J). A magistrates' court may extend
the period (s. 47M). Thereafter, detention may continue while an application for a restraint
order or variation to include detention of the property is determined. The application must be
made during the initial or extended period.

Ancillary Powers

Complementary powers to search people, premises and vehicles are to be found in ss. 47D **D8.54**
to 47F. The exercise of these powers also requires 'appropriate approval' unless impracticable
(see **D8.53**).

Relevant Statutory Extracts

Proceeds of Crime Act 2002, ss. 47A to 47F and 47J to 47N **D8.55**

47A.—(1) In sections 47B to 47S 'appropriate officer' means—
  (a) an officer of Revenue and Customs,
  (b) a constable, or
  (c) an accredited financial investigator.
(2) In subsection (1)(c) the reference to an accredited financial investigator is a reference to an
accredited financial investigator who falls within a description specified in an order made for
the purposes of that provision by the Secretary of State under section 453.
47B.—(1) An appropriate officer may exercise the power conferred by section 47C if satisfied that
any of the following conditions is met.
(2) The first condition is that—
  (a) a criminal investigation has been started in England and Wales with regard to an indictable
offence,
  (b) a person has been arrested for the offence,
  (c) proceedings for the offence have not yet been started against the person in England
and Wales,
  (d) there is reasonable cause to believe that the person has benefited from conduct constituting the offence, and
  (e) a restraint order is not in force in respect of any realisable property.
(3) The second condition is that—
  (a) a criminal investigation has been started in England and Wales with regard to an indictable
offence,
  (b) a person has been arrested for the offence,
  (c) proceedings for the offence have not yet been started against the person in England and
Wales, and
  (d) a restraint order is in force in respect of any realisable property.
(4) The third condition is that—
  (a) proceedings for an indictable offence have been started in England and Wales and have not
been concluded,
  (b) there is reasonable cause to believe that the defendant has benefited from conduct constituting the offence, and
  (c) a restraint order is not in force in respect of any realisable property.

(5) The fourth condition is that—
   (a) proceedings for an indictable offence have been started in England and Wales and have not been concluded, and
   (b) a restraint order is in force in respect of any realisable property.
(6) The fifth condition is that—
   (a) an application by the prosecutor has been made under section 19, 20, 27 or 28 and not concluded, or the officer believes that such an application is to be made, and
   (b) there is reasonable cause to believe that the defendant has benefited from criminal conduct.
(7) The sixth condition is that—
   (a) an application by the prosecutor has been made under section 21 and not concluded, or the officer believes that such an application is to be made, and
   (b) there is reasonable cause to believe that the court will decide under that section that the amount found under the new calculation of the defendant's benefit exceeds the relevant amount (as defined in that section).
(8) The seventh condition is that—
   (a) an application by the prosecutor has been made under section 22 and not concluded, or the officer believes that such an application is to be made, and
   (b) there is reasonable cause to believe that the court will decide under that section that the amount found under the new calculation of the available amount exceeds the relevant amount (as defined in that section).
(9) The third or fourth condition is not met if the officer believes that—
   (a) there has been undue delay in continuing the proceedings, or
   (b) the prosecutor does not intend to proceed.
(10) If an application mentioned in the fifth, sixth or seventh condition has been made the condition is not met if the officer believes that—
   (a) there has been undue delay in continuing the application, or
   (b) the prosecutor does not intend to proceed.
(11) In relation to the first or second condition references in sections 47C to 47S to the defendant are to the person mentioned in that condition.
(12) In relation to the first or second condition section 77(9) has effect as if proceedings for the offence had been started against the defendant when the investigation was started.
47C.—(1) On being satisfied as mentioned in section 47B(1) an appropriate officer may seize any realisable property if the officer has reasonable grounds for suspecting that—
   (a) the property may otherwise be made unavailable for satisfying any confiscation order that has been or may be made against the defendant, or
   (b) the value of the property may otherwise be diminished as a result of conduct by the defendant or any other person.
(2) But the officer may not seize—
   (a) cash, or
   (b) exempt property.
(3) 'Cash' has the same meaning as in section 289.
(4) 'Exempt property' means—
   (a) such tools, books, vehicles and other items of equipment as are necessary to the defendant for use personally in the defendant's employment, business or vocation;
   (b) such clothing, bedding, furniture, household equipment, provisions or other things as are necessary for satisfying the basic domestic needs of the defendant and the defendant's family.
(5) In relation to realisable property which is free property held by the recipient of a tainted gift, references in subsection (4) to the defendant are to be read as references to the recipient of that gift. Section 47B(11) is subject to this subsection.
(6) The power conferred by this section—
   (a) may be exercised only with the appropriate approval under section 47G unless, in the circumstances, it is not practicable to obtain that approval before exercising the power, and
   (b) is exercisable by an officer of Revenue and Customs only if the officer has reasonable grounds for suspecting that conduct constituting the relevant offence relates to an assigned matter (within the meaning of the Customs and Excise Management Act 1979).
(7) 'Relevant offence' means—
   (a) in a case where the officer is satisfied that the first, second, third or fourth condition in section 47B is met, the offence mentioned in that condition,
   (b) in a case where the officer is satisfied that any of the other conditions in section 47B is met, the offence (or any of the offences) concerned.

47D.—(1) If an appropriate officer is lawfully on any premises the officer may search the premises for the purpose of finding any property which—

    (a) the officer has reasonable grounds for suspecting may be found there, and

    (b) if found there, the officer intends to seize under section 47C.

(2) The power conferred by this section may be exercised only with the appropriate approval under section 47G unless, in the circumstances, it is not practicable to obtain that approval before exercising the power.

(3) 'Premises' has the meaning given by section 23 of the Police and Criminal Evidence Act 1984.

47E.—(1) An appropriate officer may exercise the following powers if the officer has reasonable grounds for suspecting that a person is carrying property that may be seized under section 47C.

(2) The officer may, so far as the officer thinks it necessary or expedient for the purpose of seizing the property under that section, require the person—

    (a) to permit a search of any article with the person,

    (b) to permit a search of the person.

(3) An officer exercising a power under subsection (2) may detain the person for so long as is necessary for its exercise.

(4) A power conferred by this section may be exercised only with the appropriate approval under section 47G unless, in the circumstances, it is not practicable to obtain that approval before exercising the power.

(5) This section does not require a person to submit to an intimate search or strip search (within the meaning of section 164 of the Customs and Excise Management Act 1979).

47F.—(1) The powers specified in subsection (4) are exercisable if—

    (a) an appropriate officer has reasonable grounds for suspecting that a vehicle contains property that may be seized under section 47C, and

    (b) it appears to the officer that the vehicle is under the control of a person who is in or in the vicinity of the vehicle.

(2) The powers are exercisable only if the vehicle is—

    (a) in any place to which, at the time of the proposed exercise of the powers, the public or any section of the public has access, on payment or otherwise, as of right or by virtue of express or implied permission, or

    (b) in any other place to which at that time people have ready access but which is not a dwelling.

(3) But if the vehicle is in a garden or yard or other land occupied with and used for the purposes of a dwelling, the officer may exercise the powers under subsection (4) only if the officer has reasonable grounds for believing—

    (a) that the person does not reside in the dwelling, and

    (b) that the vehicle is not in the place in question with the express or implied permission of another who resides in the dwelling.

(4) The officer may, so far as the officer thinks it necessary or expedient for the purpose of seizing the property under section 47C, require the person to—

    (a) permit entry to the vehicle,

    (b) permit a search of the vehicle.

(5) An officer exercising a power under subsection (4) may detain the vehicle for so long as is necessary for its exercise.

(6) A power conferred by this section may be exercised only with the appropriate approval under section 47G unless, in the circumstances, it is not practicable to obtain that approval before exercising the power.

47J.—(1) This section applies if an appropriate officer seizes property under section 47C.

(2) The property may be detained initially for a period of 48 hours.

(3) The period of 48 hours is to be calculated in accordance with section 47H(7).

47K.—(1) This section applies if—

    (a) property is detained under section 47J, and

    (b) no restraint order is in force in respect of the property.

(2) If within the period mentioned in section 47J an application is made for a restraint order which includes provision under section 41A authorising detention of the property, the property may be detained until the application is determined or otherwise disposed of.

(3) If such an application is made within that period and the application is refused, the property may be detained until there is no further possibility of an appeal against—

    (a) the decision to refuse the application, or

    (b) any decision made on an appeal against that decision.

(4) In subsection (2) the reference to the period mentioned in section 47J includes that period as extended by any order under section 47M.

47L.—(1) This section applies if—

    (a) property is detained under section 47J,

    (b) a restraint order is in force in respect of the property, and

    (c) the order does not include provision under section 41A authorising the detention of the property.

(2) If within the period mentioned in section 47J an application is made for the order to be varied so as to include provision under section 41A authorising detention of the property, the property may be detained until the application is determined or otherwise disposed of.

(3) If such an application is made within that period and the application is refused, the property may be detained until there is no further possibility of an appeal against—

    (a) the decision to refuse the application, or

    (b) any decision made on an appeal against that decision.

47M.—(1) This section applies if—

    (a) property is detained under section 47J,

    (b) no restraint order is in force in respect of the property, and

    (c) no application has been made for a restraint order which includes provision under section 41A authorising detention of the property.

(2) A magistrates' court may by order extend the period for which the property or any part of it may be detained under section 47J if satisfied that—

    (a) any of the conditions in section 47B is met (reading references in that section to the officer as references to the court),

    (b) the property or part is realisable property other than exempt property (within the meaning of section 47C(4)), and

    (c) there are reasonable grounds for suspecting that—

        (i) the property may otherwise be made unavailable for satisfying any confiscation order that has been or may be made against the defendant, or

        (ii) the value of the property may otherwise be diminished as a result of conduct by the defendant or any other person.

(3) An application for an order may be made by—

    (a) the Commissioners for Her Majesty's Revenue and Customs,

    (b) a constable,

    (c) an accredited financial investigator, or

    (d) the prosecutor.

(4) If the property was seized in reliance on the first or second condition in section 47B, 'the prosecutor' means a person who is to have conduct of any proceedings for the offence.

(5) An order under this section must provide for notice to be given to persons affected by it.

(6) In this section 'part' includes portion.

47N.—(1) An order under section 47M may be discharged or varied.

(2) An application for variation or discharge of the order may be made by—

    (a) a person mentioned in section 47M(3), or

    (b) any person affected by the order.

(3) On an application under this section the court must discharge the order if—

    (a) the order was made on the ground that the first or second condition in section 47B was met but proceedings for the offence mentioned in that condition have not been started within a reasonable time,

    (b) the order was made on the ground that the third or fourth condition in section 47B was met but proceedings for the offence mentioned in that condition have now been concluded,

    (c) the order was made on the ground that the fifth, sixth or seventh condition in section 47B was met but the application mentioned in that condition has now been concluded or, as the case may be, has not been made within a reasonable time.

(4) An order made under section 47M lapses if a restraint order is made in respect of the property to which it relates (but provision authorising detention of the property may have been included in the restraint order by virtue of section 41A).

Section D9 Disclosure

INTRODUCTION

Types of Disclosure

An important issue in criminal procedure is the extent to which the prosecution and the defence **D9.1** must before trial disclose to each other the information pertaining to the case. Concentrating for the moment upon the prosecution, there is a central distinction between:

(a) the disclosure by the prosecution of its case, i.e. the evidence upon which it will rely at trial; and

(b) the disclosure of other material pertaining to the case, which it does not intend to use — 'unused material'.

As far as (a) is concerned, the position differs according to whether trial is taking place summarily or in the Crown Court. The extent to which the prosecution are under a duty to reveal their case is dealt with in **D15.71** *et seq.* (so far as trial on indictment is concerned), and in **D21.24** (for the more limited obligations relating to summary trial).

This section is concerned with the disclosure by the prosecution of unused material once proceedings have commenced. For disclosure of material pre-charge, see **D1**. It also covers the duty of the defence to make disclosure, not of unused material but of the case upon which they will rely at trial. The CJA 2003 made a number of important amendments to the law relating to disclosure, most of which are now in force (see **D9.4**).

The Scheme of the Legislation

The statutory regime governing the disclosure of unused material by the prosecution and the **D9.2** disclosure of the defence case by the defence is set out in the CPIA 1996, part I (ss. 1 to 21), as amended by the CJA 2003 and the CJIA 2008, and supplemented by the Code of Practice issued under the 1996 Act and the CrimPR, part 22.

The scheme of the legislation is as follows:

(a) there is a statutory duty upon the police officer investigating an offence to record and retain information and material gathered or generated during the investigation (see **D9.10**);

(b) the prosecution should inform the defence of certain categories of that material which they do not intend to use at trial (see **D9.13** to **D9.28**) — as mentioned above, there are separate obligations to inform the defence of material which they do intend to use;

(c) the defence then have a duty to inform the prosecution of the case which they intend to present at trial (**D9.29** to **D9.47**);

(d) the prosecution is under a continuing duty to disclose material which falls within the test for prosecution disclosure (**D9.24**).

The legislation makes provision for applications to be made to the court in certain circumstances where there is a dispute about whether the prosecution should disclose certain material (see **D9.26**); and there are sanctions laid down for defence failure to disclose or disclosure which is late, false or inconsistent (**D9.42**).

The categories of case to which this legislative scheme applies are laid down in s. 1. In summary, it is compulsory in relation to cases sent to the Crown Court to be tried on indictment. It may also apply on a voluntary basis to any summary trial, including those in the youth court (see **D9.37**).

D9.3   Criminal Procedure and Investigations Act 1996, s. 1

(1) This Part applies where—
   (a) a person is charged with a summary offence in respect of which a court proceeds to summary trial and in respect of which he pleads not guilty,
   (b) a person who has attained the age of 18 is charged with an offence which is triable either way, in respect of which a court proceeds to summary trial and in respect of which he pleads not guilty, or
   (c) a person under the age of 18 is charged with an indictable offence in respect of which a court proceeds to summary trial and in respect of which he pleads not guilty.

(2) This Part also applies where—
   (a) – (c) [repealed];
   (cc) a person is charged with an offence for which he is sent for trial,
   (d) a count charging a person with a summary offence is included in an indictment under the authority of section 40 of the Criminal Justice Act 1988 (common assault etc.),
   (e) a bill of indictment charging a person with an indictable offence is preferred under the authority of section 2(2)(b) of the Administration of Justice (Miscellaneous Provisions) Act 1933 (bill preferred by direction of Court of Appeal, or by direction or with consent of a judge),
   (f) a bill of indictment charging a person with an indictable offence is preferred under section 22B(3)(a) of the Prosecution of Offences Act 1985, or
   (g) following the preferment of a bill of indictment charging a person with an indictable offence under the authority of section 2(2)(ba) of the Administration of Justice (Miscellaneous Provisions) Act 1933 (bill of indictment preferred with consent of Crown Court judge following approval of deferred prosecution agreement), the suspension of the proceedings against the person under paragraph 2(2) of Schedule 17 to the Crime and Courts Act 2013 is lifted under paragraph 2(3) of that Schedule.

(3) This Part applies in relation to alleged offences into which no criminal investigation has begun before the appointed day.

(4) For the purposes of this section a criminal investigation is an investigation which police officers or other persons have a duty to conduct with a view to it being ascertained—
   (a) whether a person should be charged with an offence, or
   (b) whether a person charged with an offence is guilty of it.

The CCA 2013, sch. 17, para. 37, added s. 1(2)(g) so as to make provision for the application of part 1 of the CPIA 1996 following the lifting of a suspension of proceedings relating to a deferred prosecution agreement. The provision came into effect on 24 February 2014 (see **D12.106**).

D9.4   Commencement Dates   The disclosure provisions of part I of the CPIA 1996 apply to any alleged offence for which a criminal offence began on or after 1 April 1997. For the law prior to the introduction of the CJA 2003, see the 2005 edition of this work.

Most of the amendments contained in the CJA 2003 are now in force, the latest being the requirement to notify the prosecution of details of defence witnesses (s. 6C, inserted by the CJA 2003, s. 34), which was brought into effect on 1 May 2010. A number of amendments contained in the CJA 2003 have yet to be implemented, however. In summary, they are (references are to the relevant sections of the CPIA 1996):

(a) defence disclosure to co-accused (s. 5(5A), (5B) and (5D), inserted by the CJA 2003, s. 33(1));
(b) updated disclosure by the defence (s. 6B, inserted by the CJA 2003, s. 33(3));
(c) notification of names of experts instructed by the defence (s. 6D, inserted by the CJA 2003, s. 35);
(d) a further amendment to the sanctions for failure to disclose by the defence (s. 11(11), inserted by the CJA 2003, s. 39).

If an investigation commenced on or after 4 April 2005, the applicable law is the CPIA 1996 as amended by part V of the CJA 2003, and by the CJIA 2008, to the extent that amendments made by the Acts are in force. For a summary of the position in respect of investigations prior to that date, see the 2010 edition of this work.

In order to pinpoint when an investigation begins, it is necessary to look at the definition of criminal investigation contained in s. 1(4) and the Code of Practice, para. 2.1, which is set out at **D9.6**.

Secondary Sources   The legislative scheme is supplemented by a number of secondary sources: **D9.5**

(a) Part 22 of the CrimPR (see Supplement, **R-195**) and CPD IV, paras. 22A.1 and 22A.2 (see Supplement, **PD-37**).
(b) The Judicial Protocol on the Disclosure of Unused Material in Criminal Cases (the Judicial Disclosure Protocol) (see **appendix 4**).
(c) The A-G's Guidelines on Disclosure for investigators, prosecutors and defence practitioners (the A-G's Guidelines) (see **appendix 4**).
(d) The CPS/Police Disclosure Manual, a copy of which can be found online at www.cps.gov.uk/legal/d_to_g/disclosure_manual/.
(e) The Code of Practice for Arranging and Conducting Interviews of Witnesses Notified by the Accused (see **D9.34**).
(f) The 2013 Protocol and Good Practice Model on Disclosure of Information in Cases of Alleged Child Abuse and Linked Criminal and Care Directions Hearings (the Child Abuse Disclosure Protocol), which can be found online at www.judiciary.gov.uk/publications-and-reports/guidance/2013/protocol-good-practice-model-2013.

Part 22 of the CrimPR sets out the procedure to be followed on applications to the court for unused material and on public interest immunity applications and imposes requirements for giving notice to the court about prosecution and defence disclosure. CPD IV, para. 22A.1, states that all parties must be familiar with their obligations, in particular under the CPIA 1996 and the Code issued under that Act, and must comply with the Judicial Disclosure Protocol and the A-G's Guidelines on Disclosure.

The Judicial Disclosure Protocol was published in December 2013. The full text is to be found at **appendix 4**. It replaces the 2006 Disclosure Protocol and s. 4 of the Lord Chief Justice's Protocol for the Control and Management of Heavy Fraud and other Complex Cases. It sets out the principles to be applied to, and the importance of, disclosure; the expectations of the court and its role in disclosure, in particular in relation to case management; and the consequences if there is a failure of the prosecution or defence to comply with their obligations. Its emphasis is on prosecution-led disclosure, a constructive approach on both sides, supported by robust judicial case management. All requests by the defence for disclosure should now be made on the s. 8 application form, even if no hearing is sought in the first instance. There is extensive new guidance in the protocol on material held by third parties, and the Child Abuse Disclosure Protocol is commended as representing best practice in child abuse cases and should therefore be consulted in all cases of concurrent criminal and care proceedings.

Alongside the Judicial Disclosure Protocol, revised A-G's Guidelines on Disclosure for investigators, prosecutors and defence practitioners have been published and are set out at **appendix 4**. For ease of reference they are structured in the same way as the Judicial Disclosure Protocol and complement the messages in it. In particular, the guidelines emphasise the importance of prosecution-led disclosure and of applying the CPIA regime thoughtfully, tailored where appropriate to the type of investigation or prosecution in question. The A-G's Supplementary Guidelines on Digitally Stored Material (2011) are annexed to the new guidelines.

THE INVESTIGATION STAGE

The responsibilities of investigators in relation to unused material are set out in a variety of **D9.6** sources. The primary source is the CPIA Code of Practice which has been issued under s. 23 of the CPIA 1996. The code applies to criminal investigations carried out by police officers. By s. 26, those other than police officers charged with the duty of conducting criminal investigations must have regard to the code's provisions. The A-G's Guidelines deal with the duties of investigators and disclosure officers in paras. 15 to 27 (see **appendix 4**). For disclosure of material pre-charge, see **D1**.

The CPIA Code of Practice, para. 2.1, defines a criminal investigation as:

... an investigation conducted by police officers with a view to it being ascertained whether a person should be charged with an offence, or whether a person charged with an offence is guilty of it. This will include:

— investigations into crimes that have been committed;
— investigations whose purpose is to ascertain whether a crime has been committed, with a view to the possible institution of criminal proceedings; and
— investigations which begin in the belief that a crime may be committed, for example when the police keep premises or individuals under observation for a period of time, with a view to the possible institution of criminal proceedings [for an example, see *Uxbridge Magistrates' Court, ex parte Patel* (2000) 164 JP 209].

D9.7   Criminal Procedure and Investigations Act 1996, ss. 22 and 26

22.—(1) For the purposes of [part II] a criminal investigation is an investigation conducted by police officers with a view to it being ascertained—
(a) whether a person should be charged with an offence, or
(b) whether a person charged with an offence is guilty of it.
(2) In [part II] references to material are to material of all kinds, and in particular include references to—
(a) information and
(b) objects of all descriptions.
(3) In [part II] references to recording information are to putting it in a durable or retrievable form (such as writing or tape).
26.—(1) A person other than a police officer who is charged with the duty of conducting an investigation with a view to it being ascertained—
(a) whether a person should be charged with an offence, or
(b) whether a person charged with an offence is guilty of it,
shall in discharging that duty have regard to any relevant provision of a code which would apply if the investigation were conducted by police officers.
(2) A failure—
(a) by a police officer to comply with any provision of a code for the time being in operation by virtue of an order under section 25, or
(b) by a person to comply with subsection (1),
shall not in itself render him liable to any criminal or civil proceedings.
(3) In all criminal and civil proceedings a code in operation at any time by virtue of an order under section 25 shall be admissible in evidence.
(4) If it appears to a court or tribunal conducting criminal or civil proceedings that—
(a) any provision of a code in operation at any time by virtue of an order under section 25, or
(b) any failure mentioned in subsection (2)(a) or (b),
is relevant to any question arising in the proceedings, the provision or failure shall be taken into account in deciding the question.

Responsibilities of Investigation Officer and Disclosure Officer

D9.8 Every criminal investigation will involve an investigator and a disclosure officer, though in small cases this might be the same person. An investigator is any police officer involved in the conduct of a criminal investigation; a disclosure officer is the person responsible for examining material retained by the police during the investigation and for revealing material to the prosecutor and, at the request of the prosecutor, the accused (CPIA Code of Practice, para. 2.1). The CPIA Code of Practice, para 3.4, provides that the officer in charge of an investigation may delegate tasks to other persons participating in the investigation under arrangements for joint investigations. But the mere fact that suspicious documents are handed by an organisation to the police does not give rise to an inference that the subsequent investigation is a joint investigation between that organisation and the police (see *Khan* [2011] EWCA Crim 2240, involving a complaint by an electoral registration officer concerning false postal votes).

D9.9 There has been increasing emphasis on the need for the investigators and disclosure officers to improve their performance in relation to disclosure. The A-G's Guidelines require investigators and disclosure officers to be fair and objective and to work together with prosecutors on disclosure issues (para. 15). Investigators and disclosure officers must approach their duties in a 'thinking manner' and not as a box-ticking exercise and should be deployed on cases commensurate with their skills, training and experience (para. 16). Disclosure officers must specifically draw to the attention of the prosecutor any material where there is doubt as to whether it is disclosable (para. 26). An investigator who believes that a person may have information which satisfies the statutory test for disclosure cannot decline to make inquiries of that person in order to avoid the need to disclose what that person might say (*Joof* [2012] EWCA Crim 1475). In larger cases there may be a number of disclosure officers, but in such cases there must always be a lead officer (para. 18). Disclosure officers must inspect, view or listen to all relevant material. In some cases a detailed examination of all material seized may be required. In others, this would be virtually impossible and the Supplementary A-G's Guidelines (see **D9.10**), dealing with digitally stored material, may be applicable (para. 21). Relevant material must be retained but, if it later becomes apparent that it is incapable of impact, retention is no longer required (para. 25). Disclosure officers must seek the advice of prosecutors when in doubt as to their responsibilities (para. 26). In relation to digital material, investigators and prosecutors are to be transparent with the defence and the courts about how the prosecution has approached complying with its disclosure obligations, and the defence will be expected to play their part in defining the real issues in the case (Supplementary A-G's Guidelines, para. 3).

Duty to Record and Retain Material

D9.10 Investigators must record in a durable or retrievable form any material which may be relevant to the investigation and which is not already recorded. This will include negative information such as the fact that a number of people present at a particular place and time saw nothing unusual (CPIA Code of Practice, para. 4.1). The investigator is responsible for retaining material obtained in a criminal investigation which may be relevant to the investigation (para. 5.1). Material may be 'relevant to an investigation' if it appears to an investigator, or disclosure officer, that it has some bearing on any offence under investigation or any person being investigated, or on the surrounding circumstances of the case. 'Material' includes material gathered in the course of the investigation (e.g., documents seized in the course of searching premises) or generated by the investigation (e.g., interview records) (para. 2.1). The duty to retain material includes, for example, the following categories: crime reports, including crime report forms, relevant parts of incident report books and police officers' notebooks; final versions of witness statements; draft versions of witness statements where their content differs from the final version; interview records (written or taped); expert reports and schedules; any material casting doubt upon the reliability of a confession; and any material casting doubt on the reliability of a witness (see the list in para. 5.4). However, the duty to retain material does not extend to items purely ancillary to that in the above categories which possess no independent significance, such as duplicate copies of documents.

Digital material should be imaged where possible (Supplementary A-G's Guidelines, para. 17) and no more digital material may be seized than is justified (para. 20). It must be examined as soon as reasonably practicable and consideration should be given to allowing the person from whom it was seized or anyone with an interest in it to be present during the examination (para. 22). No digital material may be seized which an investigator has reasonable grounds to believe is subject to legal professional privilege, other than under the additional powers of seizure in the CJPA 2001 (para. 28). Guidance is also given in the A-G's Supplementary Guidelines as to retention of digital material (paras. 23 to 27), sifting (paras. 39 to 45), record keeping (paras. 46 to 49), scheduling (paras. 50 to 53) and third-party material (paras. 54 to 63).

D9.11 The Disclosure Manual states that reports, advices and other communications between the CPS and police in themselves will usually be of an administrative nature or derivative in that they contain professional opinion based on evidential material or material already subject to revelation. They will usually have no bearing on the case and thus will not be relevant.

The material must be retained at least until criminal proceedings are concluded. In the event of a conviction, material must be retained until the convicted person is released from custody or discharged from hospital (where the court imposes a custodial sentence or a hospital order) and, in any event, for at least six months from the date of conviction. Where an appeal against conviction is in progress when the release or discharge occurs, or at the end of the six months, the material must be retained until the appeal is determined. A similar rule applies where an application is being considered by the CCRC (paras. 5.8 and 5.9).

Duty to Reveal Material to the Prosecutor

D9.12 The CPIA Code of Practice, para. 6, requires that where the investigator believes that the person charged with an offence is likely to plead not guilty at a summary trial, or that the offence will be tried in the Crown Court, he must prepare a schedule listing material which has been retained and which does not form part of the case against the accused. This is known as the MG6C. If the investigator has obtained any 'sensitive material', this should be listed in a separate schedule or, in exceptional circumstances, disclosed to the prosecutor separately. Sensitive material is defined as material which the investigator believes would give rise to a real risk of serious prejudice to an important public interest if it were to be disclosed. (para. 2.1). Paragraph 6.12 gives a number of examples of such material, which range from material relating to national security to material given in confidence, and includes material relating to informants, undercover police officers, premises used for police surveillance, techniques used in the detection of crime, and material relating to a child witness (e.g., material generated by a local authority social services department). The A-G's Guidelines (see **appendix 4**) emphasise that descriptions by disclosure officers in non-sensitive schedules should be clear and accurate and must contain sufficient detail to enable the prosecutor to make an informed decision on disclosure (para. 23). Sensitive schedules must contain sufficient information to enable the prosecutor to decide whether the material itself should be viewed, bearing in mind its confidential nature (para. 24).

The investigator should draw the prosecutor's attention to any material which might satisfy the test for prosecution disclosure (see **D9.15**) including certain specified categories detailed in the CPIA Code of Practice, para. 7.3. The disclosure officer must certify that to the best of his knowledge and belief the duties imposed under the code have been complied with.

PROSECUTION DISCLOSURE

Responsibilities of Prosecutor to Review Material

D9.13 Prosecutors have a responsibility alongside that of the disclosure officer for making proper disclosure. The A-G's Guidelines require them to do all that they can to facilitate proper disclosure. This includes probing actions taken by disclosure officers, reviewing schedules and, if necessary, taking action to improve their quality and content (paras. 28 to 30). They should consider the defence statement, advise the investigator if any relevant lines of inquiry should be pursued and challenge the lack of, or inadequate, defence statements in writing (paras. 30 to 33). Prosecution advocates must ensure that all material which ought to be disclosed is disclosed to the defence, satisfy themselves that they are in possession of all relevant material and that they have been fully instructed as regards disclosure matters, and keep all disclosure decisions under review (paras. 35 to 37). In *Olu* [2011] 1 Cr App R 404, the disclosure schedule was deficient and late disclosure of material was made in the course of the trial. The Court of Appeal found that the conviction was not unsafe, but stated that it is the task of the CPS prosecutor to identify the issues in the case and for the disclosure officer to act under his guidance. In particular, it said that the disclosure regime will not work in practice unless the disclosure officer is directed by the prosecutor as to what is likely to be most relevant and important so that the officer approaches the matter through the exercise of judgement and not simply as a schedule-completing exercise.

Disclosure Post-charge but Prior to Statutory Obligation

The statutory scheme requires service of unused material at particular points (see **D9.23**), but **D9.14** the A-G's Guidelines require investigators and prosecutors to recognise that the interests of justice and fairness in the particular circumstances of any case may require disclosure of material after the commencement of proceedings but before the statutory duty arises (see paras. 14 and 44). This approach is in line with authority. In *DPP, ex parte Lee* [1999] 2 All ER 737, the Divisional Court considered whether the prosecution had a duty to disclose unused material in indictable-only offences prior to committal (prior to its abolition). The court found that there might well be circumstances in which it would be helpful to the defence to know of unused material at an earlier stage. For example:

(a) the previous convictions of the alleged victim when they might be expected to help the defence in a bail application;
(b) material to help an application to stay proceedings as an abuse of process;
(c) material to help the accused's arguments at committal;
(d) material to help the accused prepare for trial, e.g., eye-witnesses whom the prosecution did not intend to use.

Kennedy LJ said that a responsible prosecutor might recognise that fairness required that some of this material might be disclosed. The question was: what immediate disclosure (if any) did justice and fairness require in the circumstances of the case? It is submitted that this approach is consistent with the objective of ensuring that the legitimate rights of the accused are preserved. There has always been an ethical dimension to the duty to disclose, and the decision in *Ex parte Lee* is an indication that it survives the introduction of the CPIA 1996.

The Statutory Test for Disclosure

Section 3 of the CPIA 1996 requires the prosecutor to disclose previously undisclosed material **D9.15** to the accused if it 'might reasonably be considered capable of undermining the case for the prosecution against the accused, or of assisting the case for the accused'. The test is an objective one. If there is no such material, the accused must be given a written statement to that effect. The court officer must be informed by the prosecutor at the same time (CrimPR, r. 22.2). Prosecution material includes material which the prosecutor possesses or has been allowed to inspect under the provisions of the CPIA Code of Practice.

In determining whether unused material should be revealed to the defence as part of the disclosure process, the statutory test is whether it might reasonably be considered capable of:

(a) undermining the case for the prosecution against the accused; or
(b) assisting the case for the accused.

Something can be said to be undermined if it becomes more likely to fall (or fail) as a result. The prosecution case will be more likely to fail as a result of evidence which shows a defect, discrepancy or inconsistency in that case. Such evidence ought to be revealed as part of initial disclosure. In *Barkshire* [2011] EWCA Crim 1885 the Court of Appeal stated that the statutory test extends to anything available to the prosecution which might undermine confidence in the accuracy of evidence called by the prosecution, or which might provide a measure of support for the defence at trial. In that case, the failure of the prosecution to make proper disclosure of material relating to the role and activities of an undercover officer, as well as other material supportive of the defence case, where the materials were pertinent to a potential submission of abuse of process by way of entrapment and had the capacity to support the defence of necessity and justification, had rendered the trial unfair and the convictions unsafe. The prosecution case might also be undermined as a result of a particular defence, which the accused may or may not run. Clearly it is not possible to say at the stage of initial disclosure with certainty whether the defence will take a particular course. That will become clearer after defence disclosure, although it will actually only be entirely certain once the trial itself takes place. But the mere fact that material in the possession of the prosecution raises a new issue in the case which might reasonably be considered capable of assisting the defence is sufficient, it is submitted, to fulfil the statutory test.

D9.16   In *H* [2004] AC 134, the House of Lords stated that s. 3 does not require disclosure of material which is either neutral in effect or which is adverse to the accused, whether because it strengthens the prosecution or weakens the defence. However, the converse is that: 'Fairness ordinarily requires that any material held by the prosecution which weakens its case or strengthens that of the defendant... should be disclosed to the defence. Bitter experience has shown that miscarriages of justice may occur where such material is withheld from disclosure. The golden rule is that full disclosure of such material should be made.'

The Court of Appeal has made plain its view that there has been a wide range of serious misunderstandings as to the ambit of unused material to which the defence is entitled and as to the role to be played by the judge. Having quoted the above statement from *H and C*, the Judicial Disclosure Protocol states: 'However, it is also essential that the trial process is not overburdened or diverted by erroneous and inappropriate disclosure of unused prosecution material or by misconceived applications' (para. 3). It continues by stating that the 'overarching principle is that unused prosecution material will fall to be disclosed if, and only if, it satisfies the test for disclosure applicable to the proceedings in question, subject to any overriding public interest considerations' (para. 4). For examples of cases where material was rightly withheld because nothing in it served to exculpate the accused, see *Khan* [2007] EWCA Crim 2911 and *Yockney* [2012] EWCA Crim 2974. In *Khan,* the Court of Appeal found that a statement taken by the police from a defence witness, and which was later used by the prosecution to undermine his credibility in cross-examination, had not been disclosable under s. 3. The Court held that fairness did not require that the accused be provided with assistance from the Crown in the investigation of the defence case (applying *Brown* [1998] AC 367). In *Yockney,* the Court held that the conviction of Y for conspiracy to supply Class A drugs was not rendered unsafe by the Crown's failure to disclose evidence implicating his co-accused, L, in a second drugs conspiracy. While such evidence would have undermined the credibility of L's evidence to the effect that L was a drug addict and Y was his supplier, it would also have strengthened the case against Y, since it made it more likely that there had been a conspiracy between the two of them.

D9.17   In *Rowe and Davis v UK* (2000) 30 EHRR 1 (see **D9.53**), the ECtHR emphasised that the right to a fair trial means that the prosecution authorities should disclose to the defence all material evidence in their possession for and against the accused. Commenting on the case, the House of Lords in *H and C* noted that this had been the domestic law under the A-G's 1981 Guidelines on Disclosure but had ceased to be so in 1996 with the enactment of the CPIA. The A-G's Guidelines had required the disclosure of material which 'has some bearing on the offence(s) charged and the surrounding circumstances of the case'. The House of Lords appear therefore to have been saying in *H* that domestic law is now out of line with the Strasbourg jurisprudence, though they did not develop the point. If that is so, the position is that the CPIA must be read and given effect to in a way which is compatible with the ECHR (HRA 1998, s. 3), or the legislation is liable to be declared incompatible by a higher court (s. 4). See also **A7.66**.

D9.18   Some guidance for prosecutors on the *scope* of the duty of primary disclosure is contained in the A-G's Guidelines (see **appendix 4**). Paragraphs 6 to 8 state that, in deciding whether material satisfies the disclosure test, consideration should be given amongst other things to:

(a) the use that might be made of it in cross-examination;
(b) its capacity to support submissions that could lead to the exclusion of evidence, a stay of proceedings or a finding that any public authority had acted incompatibly with the accused's rights under the ECHR;
(c) its capacity to suggest an explanation or partial explanation of the accused's actions:
(d) the capacity of the material to have a bearing on scientific or medical evidence in the case.

In addition, material relating to the accused's mental or physical health, intellectual capacity, or to any ill-treatment which he may have suffered in custody is said to be likely to fall within the test for disclosure (para. 8).

For large and complex cases in the Crown Court, the A-G's Guidelines require that careful thought is given by prosecutors to prosecution-led disclosure from the very earliest stage (para. 50). A clear investigation and prosecution policy must be devised and the approach to disclosure set out in a Disclosure Management Document, tailored to the individual case, which sets out the prosecution's approach to disclosure, dealing with such matters as digital, video and third-party material, and reasonable lines of inquiry, as well as its understanding of the defence case (para. 51).

D9.19 Material must not be disclosed under the CPIA 1996, s. 3, if a court has concluded that it is not in the public interest that it be disclosed (s. 3(6) and see **D9.50** to **D9.68**). Material must not be disclosed to the extent that its disclosure is prohibited by the Regulation of Investigatory Powers Act 2000, s. 17 (CPIA 1996, s. 3(7)).

The disclosure of previous convictions of prosecution witnesses was considered by the Privy Council in *HM Advocate v Murtagh* [2011] 1 AC 731 in a decision which plainly applies to cases in England and Wales. Their lordships found that the disclosure of a previous conviction of a victim or a witness engages the rights of the witness under the ECHR, Article 8 (respect for private and family life). Nonetheless, material which has a possible bearing on a witness's credibility or character should be disclosed since the necessity to secure a fair trial justifies the disclosure as being necessary in a democratic society for the prevention of disorder or crime. See also **A7.64**.

D9.20

Criminal Procedure and Investigations Act 1996, s. 3

(1) The prosecutor must—
  (a) disclose to the accused any prosecution material which has not previously been disclosed to the accused and which might reasonably be considered capable of undermining the case for the prosecution against the accused, or of assisting the case for the accused, or
  (b) give to the accused a written statement that there is no material of a description mentioned in paragraph (a).
(2) For the purposes of this section prosecution material is material—
  (a) which is in the prosecutor's possession, and came into his possession in connection with the case for the prosecution against the accused, or
  (b) which, in pursuance of a code operative under Part II, he has inspected in connection with the case for the prosecution against the accused.
(3) Where material consists of information which has been recorded in any form the prosecutor discloses it for the purposes of this section—
  (a) by securing that a copy is made of it and that the copy is given to the accused, or
  (b) if in the prosecutor's opinion that is not practicable or not desirable, by allowing the accused to inspect it at a reasonable time and a reasonable place or by taking steps to secure that he is allowed to do so;
  and a copy may be in such form as the prosecutor thinks fit and need not be in the same form as that in which the information has already been recorded.
(4) Where material consists of information which has not been recorded the prosecutor discloses it for the purposes of this section by securing that it is recorded in such form as he thinks fit and—
  (a) by securing that a copy is made of it and that the copy is given to the accused, or
  (b) if in the prosecutor's opinion that is not practicable or not desirable, by allowing the accused to inspect it at a reasonable time and a reasonable place or by taking steps to secure that he is allowed to do so.
(5) Where material does not consist of information the prosecutor discloses it for the purposes of this section by allowing the accused to inspect it at a reasonable time and a reasonable place or by taking steps to secure that he is allowed to do so.
(6) Material must not be disclosed under this section to the extent that the court, on an application by the prosecutor, concludes it is not in the public interest to disclose it and orders accordingly.
(7) Material must not be disclosed under this section to the extent that it is material the disclosure of which is prohibited by section 17 of the Regulation of Investigatory Powers Act 2000.
(8) The prosecutor must act under this section during the period which, by virtue of section 12, is the relevant period for this section.

Service of Schedule

D9.21   Under the CPIA 1996, s. 4, non-sensitive disclosure schedules must be served on the defence at the same time unused material is served.

Criminal Procedure and Investigations Act 1996, s. 4

(1) This section applies where—
   (a) the prosecutor acts under section 3, and
   (b) before so doing he was given a document in pursuance of provision included, by virtue of section 24(3), in a code operative under Part II.
(2) In such a case the prosecutor must give the document to the accused at the same time as the prosecutor acts under section 3.

Summary Trials — Nature of Prosecution's Obligations

D9.22   By virtue of s. 1(1), the CPIA 1996 partially incorporates summary proceedings into the statutory disclosure scheme (see **D9.2**). The prosecution's duty of disclosure applies whenever the accused pleads not guilty and the court proceeds to summary trial. The Judicial Disclosure Protocol states that the principles relating to disclosure apply equally in the magistrates' courts. It follows that, whilst disclosure of unused material is undoubtedly essential in order to achieve justice, misconceived applications for disclosure, or inappropriate disclosure, must be avoided (see para. 30). Prosecutors are required to take into account information provided as to the defence case in the case-management forms when conducting any review of material (para. 33). The A-G's Guidelines require prosecutors to be alert to the possibility that material may exist which should be disclosed to the defence prior to the CPIA requirements applying to the case (para. 44 and see also **D9.14**).

Time-limits for and Method of Disclosure

D9.23   There are no statutory time-limits for disclosure of unused material. Provision was made in the legislation for a time-limit to be laid down by statutory instrument but no such instrument has ever been made. That being the case, the default position is set out in the CPIA 1996, s. 13(1): disclosure must be made as soon as reasonably practicable after the happening of a particular event, such as service of the prosecution case.

In Crown Court cases, the Judicial Disclosure Protocol requires that, if there is a preliminary hearing, the judge should seize the opportunity to impose an early timetable for disclosure and to identify any likely problems including as regards third-party material and material that will require an application to the Family Court (para. 9). The court should keep the timetable for prosecution and defence disclosure under review from the first hearing (para. 7). Large and complex cases will require robust case management by the judiciary, and the courts should be provided with an up-to-date timetable for disclosure whenever there are material changes as a result of difficulties that emerge (paras. 38 and 39). Unused material may be disclosed either by giving a copy to the defence or by allowing the defence to inspect the material at a reasonable time and place.

Continuing Duty to Review

D9.24   Under the CPIA 1996, s. 7A, the prosecutor remains under a continuing duty to review questions of disclosure. If, at any time before the accused is acquitted or convicted, the prosecutor forms the opinion that there is material which might undermine the prosecution case, or be reasonably expected to assist the accused's defence, it must be disclosed to the accused as soon as reasonably practicable (provided that the court has not ruled against disclosure in respect of that material). In practice this situation is most likely to arise either on service of the defence case statement or during the trial itself.

After service of the defence case statement, (see **D9.29**), the investigator must look again at the material retained, and draw the prosecutor's attention to any material which might reasonably be considered capable of undermining the prosecution case or of assisting the defence if it were to be disclosed. The disclosure officer must certify compliance with the duties imposed by the CPIA Code of Practice. If the investigator comes into possession of any new material after complying with the duties described above, then he must reveal it to the prosecutor (para. 8). This will then trigger a further requirement for disclosure by the prosecution (A-G's Guidelines, paras. 37 and 42).

This duty of continuous review will come into play during the trial when, e.g., a prosecution witness gives evidence which is materially inconsistent with a statement made earlier to the police. If the defence are unaware of the statement, prosecuting counsel should disclose it to his opposite number so that he can use it in cross-examination to discredit the testimony of the witness (*Clarke* (1931) 22 Cr App R 58 — although the case was many years before the 1996 Act, it is submitted that the principle still holds). Where the court has ruled against disclosure on public interest grounds, it must keep under review the question whether it is still in the public interest not to disclose the material affected by its order. The position so far as summary trial is concerned is dealt with in **D9.64**.

There is no general duty on the State through the police or CPS to investigate or provide disclosure post-conviction. Between conviction and sentence, there is a common-law duty to disclose any material that is not known to the accused but which may be relevant to sentence, such as information which might assist the accused in placing his role in the correct context vis-à-vis other offenders (*R (Nunn) v Chief Constable of Suffolk Constabulary* [2014] UKSC 37 and A-G's Guidelines, para. 71). Pending an appeal, the Crown's duty is to disclose any material, not previously disclosed, which is relevant to an identified ground of appeal. Once proceedings are complete, the Crown is still under a general duty to disclose any material which may cast doubt on the safety of conviction, unless there is good reason not to (*Nunn* and A-G's Guidelines, para. 72).

Criminal Procedure and Investigations Act 1996, s. 7A — D9.25

(1) This section applies at all times—
  (a) after the prosecutor has complied with section 3 or purported to comply with it, and
  (b) before the accused is acquitted or convicted or the prosecutor decides not to proceed with the case concerned.
(2) The prosecutor must keep under review the question whether at any given time (and, in particular, following the giving of a defence statement) there is prosecution material which—
  (a) might reasonably be considered capable of undermining the case for the prosecution against the accused or of assisting the case for the accused, and
  (b) has not been disclosed to the accused.
(3) If at any time there is any such material as is mentioned in subsection (2) the prosecutor must disclose it to the accused as soon as is reasonably practicable (or within the period mentioned in subsection (5)(a), where that applies).
(4) In applying subsection (2) by reference to any given time the state of affairs at that time (including the case for the prosecution as it stands at that time) must be taken into account.
(5) Where the accused gives a defence statement under section 5, 6 or 6B—
  (a) if as a result of that statement the prosecutor is required by this section to make any disclosure, or further disclosure, he must do so during the period which, by virtue of section 12, is the relevant period for this section;
  (b) if the prosecutor considers that he is not so required, he must during that period give to the accused a written statement to that effect.
(6) For the purposes of this section prosecution material is material—
  (a) which is in the prosecutor's possession and came into his possession in connection with the case for the prosecution against the accused, or
  (b) which, in pursuance of a code operative under Part 2, he has inspected in connection with the case for the prosecution against the accused.
(7) Subsections (3) to (5) of section 3 (method by which prosecutor discloses) apply for the purposes of this section as they apply for the purposes of that.
(8) Material must not be disclosed under this section to the extent that the court, on an application by the prosecutor, concludes it is not in the public interest to disclose it and orders accordingly.
(9) Material must not be disclosed under this section to the extent that it is material the disclosure of which is prohibited by section 17 of the Regulation of Investigatory Powers Act 2000.

Defence Applications for Disclosure from the Prosecution

D9.26 The defence can, under the CPIA 1996, s. 8, apply to the court for an order that the prosecutor should disclose any material which might reasonably be expected to assist the accused's defence. This applies to material held or inspected by the prosecutor (s. 8(3)), but also to any material which the disclosure officer must either supply to the prosecutor or allow the prosecutor to inspect if requested (s. 8(4)). Such an application may be made, however, only after the defence have served a defence statement (s. 8(1)).

In *DPP v Wood* (2006) 170 JP 177, it was held that disclosure of the material sought should have been refused by the magistrates' court as the defence statement served did not raise any issue to which the material was relevant. In the Judicial Disclosure Protocol, para. 26 (see **appendix** 4), it is emphasised that defence requests for specific disclosure of unused prosecution material which are not referable to any issue in the case identified by the defence case statement should be rejected.

The procedure for making an application under s. 8 is set out in the CrimPR, r. 22.5. In *K* [2006] 2 All ER 552, the Court of Appeal stated that the case management powers contained in the CrimPR permitted the judge to deal with issues of disclosure exclusively by reference to written submissions, and also to limit their length. The necessary public element of any hearing was sufficiently achieved if the accused, and any media present for the hearing, were supplied with copies of written submissions if they wished to see them. In *H* [2007] 2 AC 270, the House of Lords held that an application for defence disclosure under s. 8 can be made at the same time as the court deals with a preparatory hearing but the application cannot be held within the preparatory hearing.

D9.27   Criminal Procedure and Investigations Act 1996, s. 8

(1) This section applies where the accused has given a defence statement under section 5, 6 or 6B and the prosecutor has complied with section 7A(5) or has purported to comply with it or has failed to comply with it.

(2) If the accused has at any time reasonable cause to believe that there is prosecution material which is required by section 7A to be disclosed to him and has not been, he may apply to the court for an order requiring the prosecutor to disclose it to him.

(3) For the purposes of this section prosecution material is material—
   (a) which is in the prosecutor's possession and came into his possession in connection with the case for the prosecution against the accused,
   (b) which, in pursuance of a code operative under Part II, he has inspected in connection with the case for the prosecution against the accused, or
   (c) which falls within subsection (4).

(4) Material falls within this subsection if in pursuance of a code operative under Part II the prosecutor must, if he asks for the material, be given a copy of it or be allowed to inspect it in connection with the case for the prosecution against the accused.

(5) Material must not be disclosed under this section to the extent that the court, on an application by the prosecutor, concludes it is not in the public interest to disclose it and orders accordingly.

(6) Material must not be disclosed under this section to the extent that it is material the disclosure of which is prohibited by section 17 of the Regulation of Investigatory Powers Act 2000.

Consequences of Non-disclosure

D9.28 A failure on the part of the prosecution to make proper disclosure might result, in appropriate circumstances, in a defence application to stay proceedings as an abuse of process or in a successful appeal. In *R (L)* [2011] 3 All ER 969, the Court of Appeal upheld a decision of the trial judge to stay proceedings where the CPS had declined to obey a disclosure order under the CPIA 1996, s. 8, wrongly believing that to do so would open its employees up to prosecution for making copies of the indecent images in question. In *Hadley* [2006] EWCA Crim 2544 the prosecution failed to disclose videos relating to surveillance of the appellant's business premises and instead relied on summaries. The conviction was quashed. Moore-Bick LJ said that a conviction would be regarded as unsafe if the appellant showed that the material which was not disclosed was capable of affecting the jury's mind. His lordship went on to say that the Court of Appeal was likely to be slow to accept that the safety of a conviction was unaffected where a substantial volume of disclosable material had been withheld from the defence. However, where prosecution failures do not affect the fairness of the proceedings, appeals are unlikely to succeed. Recent authority has emphasised the importance of having regard to the overall objective of the CrimPR to deal with criminal cases justly and to treat the prosecution and defence fairly when making decisions on appeal points relating to non-disclosure. *DPP v Gowing* (2014) 178 JP 181 provides a good illustration. In *Gowing* the Divisional Court allowed an appeal against a decision by magistrates to stay a case on the ground that disclosure had not been served. The material had been sent in error to the wrong address. There was no suggestion of bad faith or failure to comply with the CPIA 1996, s. 3. The Court found that the magistrates had fallen into error by overlooking the overriding objective of the CrimPR; while proceedings should be efficient and expeditious, the power to stop them should not be used to punish the prosecution. *Brants v DPP* (2011) 175 JP 246 and *Prosecution Appeal: R v O* [2011] EWCA Crim 2854, both of which concerned late disclosure, are to similar effect. For consideration of the factors involved when an application for a stay is made, see **D3.70** *et seq.*, especially **D3.88**.

DEFENCE DISCLOSURE

The Defence Statement

By the CPIA 1996, s. 5, once the case is sent to the Crown Court and the prosecution case is served, the accused must give a defence statement to the court and the prosecutor. The defence statement is a written statement setting out the basis on which the case will be defended. The areas that the statement must cover are set out in s. 6A of the CPIA 1996, as amended by the CJA 2003, s. 33(2) and the CJIA 2008, s. 60(1). It must set out: the nature of the accused's defence, including any particular defences upon which he intends to rely; the matters of fact on which he takes issue with the prosecution, with the reasons why; particulars of the matters of fact on which he intends to rely for the purposes of his defence; and any points of law which he wishes to take, with any authorities on which he relies. It should be stressed that the duty of disclosure imposed on the defence is different to what is normally meant when one talks about 'the prosecution duty of disclosure'. It is a duty to reveal the case which will be presented at trial rather than, as in the case of the prosecution, unused material. **D9.29**

The degree of detail which is now required by the CPIA 1996 results from a perception among some prosecutors and members of the judiciary that defence lawyers were providing defence statements that were couched in too general terms, so that the intended benefits of their introduction in terms of improved case management were not being realised. In *Bryant* [2005] EWCA Crim 2079, the Court of Appeal had said that a defence statement consisting of a general denial of the counts in the indictment, accompanied by a statement that the accused took issue with any witness giving evidence contrary to his denial, was 'woefully inadequate'. Such a document did not meet the purposes of a defence statement. However, notwithstanding *Bryant*, if the accused raises no positive case at all in a defence statement and simply requires the Crown to prove its case, there is no failure to comply with the CPIA 1996, s. 6A, as long as the defence statement makes clear that this is the accused's position (*Rochford* [2011] 1 WLR 534, as explained in *Malcolm* [2011] EWCA Crim 2069). The distinction between the two cases rests on the difference between a positive but unspecified challenge to the evidence of a witness as against an approach which ensures the Crown proves its case. But suppose the evidence of the witness is tested by the defence in cross-examination without a positive alternative being put? *Rochford* suggests that there is no breach of s. 6A in such circumstances. **D9.30**

The Judicial Disclosure Protocol, para. 17 (see **appendix 4**), states: 'Judges expect a defence statement to contain a clear and detailed exposition of the issues of fact and law'. The Protocol requires judges to examine the defence statement with care to ensure that it complies with the formalities required by the CPIA (para. 19) and to investigate any failure by the defence to comply with its obligations (see para. 20). In appropriate circumstances the principle that there must be equality of arms will mean that the prosecution must spell out the inferences that it will be asking the trier of fact to draw from the primary facts adduced in its evidence, given that the defence is obliged to set out its reasoning for disputing issues of fact in that evidence. It follows that the scope of the defence statement should be viewed in the context of what might reasonably be required of the defence at a stage when they may not be clear about the way in which the prosecution put their case.

Legal professional privilege and the accused's privilege against self-incrimination survive s. 6A. The accused is required to disclose what is going to happen at the trial, but he is not required to disclose the confidential discussions with his lawyers, nor is he obliged to incriminate himself if he does not want to. But a lawyer cannot properly advise an accused not to file a defence statement or to omit from it something that is required to be there by s. 6A. For these propositions, see *Rochford and R (Kelly) v Warley Magistrates' Court* [2008] 1 WLR 2001.

In January 2011, the Bar Standards Board published revised guidance for counsel on the preparation of defence statements. The guidance states that counsel ought not to accept any instructions to draft or settle a defence statement unless given the opportunity and adequate time to gain proper familiarity with the case and to comply with fundamental requirements which are set out in the guidance.

D9.31 The position as regards disclosure between co-accused is at present governed by common law. In *Cairns* [2003] 1 WLR 796, the judge declined to order disclosure of the defence statements of C's co-accused, ruling that disclosure of such statements was only as between the accused and the Crown. The Court of Appeal held that the Crown should have disclosed the defence statements. Failing that, the judge should have ordered disclosure under s. 8. When s. 33 of the CJA 2003 comes fully into effect, this matter will be governed by s. 5(5A), (5B) and (5D) of the CPIA 1996. In a multi-accused case, the court will be able to order each of the accused to give copies of his defence statement to his co-accused. The court may act of its own motion, or in response to an application by any party, specifying the period within which the statement must be served.

A further amendment to the defence duty of disclosure is envisaged in the CPIA 1996, s. 6B, which is inserted by the CJA 2003, s. 33(3), but it is not yet in force. It applies where the accused has given a defence statement before the beginning of the relevant period. It requires the defence to provide an 'updated defence statement', or alternatively a statement that it has no changes to make to its initial defence statement.

D9.32 The question of the authorship of the defence statement (or an updating statement, or a statement that no updating is necessary) is dealt with in s. 6E(1), inserted by the CJA 2003, s. 36. It deems that, where an accused's solicitor purports to give such a statement on behalf of the accused, it is to be treated as given on behalf of the accused unless the contrary is proved. Of course, evidence can be adduced to show that it was not given with the accused's authority, but that may have adverse consequences where legal professional privilege is waived as a result (see **F9.68**).

At trial, the judge may direct that the jury receive a copy of any defence statement (whether initial or updated), edited to exclude any reference to inadmissible evidence. This can be done of the judge's own motion or on application, but only if it would help the jury to understand the case or resolve any issue in it (s. 6E(4)–(6)). A judge's conclusion that a defence statement should be shown to the jury to help it understand the case, exercising powers under s. 6E(5)(b), cannot be attacked on appeal unless it can be shown that his conclusion was unreasonable (*Sanghera* [2012] 2 Cr App R 196).

Alibi

D9.33 If the defence statement discloses an alibi, particulars of alibi must be given. This duty has been expanded as a result of the amendment to the CPIA 1996, s. 6A(2), brought about by the CJA 2003, s. 33(2). The names, addresses and dates of birth (or as much of this information as is known) of any alibi witnesses whom the accused intends to call must be contained within the defence statement. If the accused does not know any of these details, he must give any information in his possession that might assist in identifying or finding any such witness. Changes in relation to alibi witnesses, or the later discovery of the information required by statute, must be dealt with by the procedure for updated disclosure when this is in force. Alibi evidence continues to be defined as 'evidence tending to show that by reason of the presence of the accused at a particular place or in a particular area at a particular time he was not, or was unlikely to have been, at the place where the offence is alleged to have been committed at the time of its alleged commission' (see D17.15). The statutory obligation to provide the details of the witness is triggered by the accused's belief that the witness is able to assist; it is not necessary that the witness can give evidence or is willing to do so (*Re Joseph Hill & Co, Solicitors* [2014] 1 WLR 786).

Notification of Details of Defence Witnesses

D9.34 The defence are under a duty to notify the court and the prosecutor, separately from the defence statement, of any witnesses they intend to call at trial, other than the defendant himself and any alibi witnesses already notified (CPIA 1996, s. 6C). The defence must provide names, addresses, dates of birth or, if any such details are not known, other identifying information. Notice of intention to call a witness has to be given within 14 days (in the case of summary proceedings) and 28 days (in the case of Crown Court proceedings) from the date when the prosecutor complies, or purports to comply, with his initial duty to disclose under s. 3 (Criminal Procedure and Investigations Act 1996 (Defence Disclosure Time Limits) Regulations 2011 (SI 2011 No. 209), reg. 2). There is provision for applications for extensions of this period (reg. 3) and for treatment of weekends and bank holidays (reg. 2(4)). Any change in the plans to call witnesses (including a decision not to call a previously notified witness or to call a witness not previously notified) will have to be dealt with by way of an amended notice to the court and the prosecutor. It seems clear from *R (Kelly) v Warley Magistrates' Court* [2008] 1 WLR 2001 that these provisions override litigation privilege and legal professional privilege to the extent that such privileges are inconsistent with reasonable requirements for the proper working of the provisions (see F9.49 *et seq.*).

D9.35 The Code of Practice for Arranging and Conducting Interviews of Witnesses Notified by the Accused, made under s. 21A of the CPIA 1996, contains guidance to police officers and other persons charged with the duty of investigating offences in relation to interviews of witnesses notified by the accused (either to support an alibi or otherwise). Any such person must have regard to the Code (s. 21A(3)). Any provision of the Code or any failure to have due regard to the Code can be taken into account by a civil or criminal court or tribunal where relevant to deciding any question (s. 21A(13)). The Code deals with such matters as the information to be provided to the witness and the accused before any interview may take place, the arrangements for the interview, attendance of solicitors on behalf of the accused and the interviewee, and recording of the interview.

In *Rochford* [2011] 1 WLR 534, the case of *Penner* [2010] EWCA Crim 1155 was cited by the Court of Appeal as authority for the proposition that the combination of the provisions concerning notification of details of defence witnesses and the CrimPR have abolished, or at least are designed to abolish, trial by ambush.

In January 2011 the Law Society issued a practice note setting out the obligations and ethical considerations that defence solicitors should consider when conducting a case involving defence witnesses.

D9.36 ### Criminal Procedure and Investigations Act 1996, ss. 5, 6A, 6C and 6E

5.—(1) Subject to subsections (2) to (4), this section applies where—
    (a) [part I] applies by virtue of section 1(2), and
    (b) the prosecutor complies with section 3 or purports to comply with it.
(2) [Repealed.]
(3) [Repealed.]
(3A) Where [part I] applies by virtue of section 1(2)(cc), this section does not apply unless—
    (a) copies of the documents containing the evidence have been served on the accused under regulations made under para. 1 of Schedule 3 to the Crime and Disorder Act 1998; and
    (b) a copy of the notice under subsection (7) of section 51 of that Act has been served on him under that subsection.

(4) Where [part I] applies by virtue of section 1(2)(e), this section does not apply unless the prosecutor has served on the accused a copy of the indictment and a copy of the set of documents containing the evidence which is the basis of the charge.

(5) Where this section applies, the accused must give a defence statement to the court and the prosecutor.

(5A) [Not yet in force: see **D9.4**].

(5B) [Not yet in force: see **D9.4**].

(5C) A defence statement that has to be given to the court and the prosecutor (under subsection (5)) must be given during the period which, by virtue of section 12, is the relevant period for this section.

(5D) [Not yet in force: see **D9.4**].

6A.—(1) For the purposes of this Part a defence statement is a written statement—

(a) setting out the nature of the accused's defence, including any particular defences on which he intends to rely,

(b) indicating the matters of fact on which he takes issue with the prosecution,

(c) setting out, in the case of each such matter, why he takes issue with the prosecution,

(ca) setting out particulars of the matters of fact on which he intends to rely for the purposes of his defence [para (ca) was inserted by the CJIA 2008, s. 60(1): for commencement date, see **D9.4**], and

(d) indicating any point of law (including any point as to the admissibility of evidence or an abuse of process) which he wishes to take, and any authority on which he intends to rely for that purpose.

(2) A defence statement that discloses an alibi must give particulars of it, including—

(a) the name, address and date of birth of any witness the accused believes is able to give evidence in support of the alibi, or as many of those details as are known to the accused when the statement is given;

(b) any information in the accused's possession which might be of material assistance in identifying or finding any such witness in whose case any of the details mentioned in paragraph (a) are not known to the accused when the statement is given.

(3) For the purposes of this section evidence in support of an alibi is evidence tending to show that by reason of the presence of the accused at a particular place or in a particular area at a particular time he was not, or was unlikely to have been, at the place where the offence is alleged to have been committed at the time of its alleged commission.

(4) [Power to make regulations.]

6B.—[Not yet in force: see **D9.4**.]

6C.—(1) The accused must give to the court and the prosecutor a notice indicating whether he intends to call any persons (other than himself) as witnesses at his trial and, if so—

(a) giving the name, address and date of birth of each such proposed witness, or as many of those details as are known to the accused when the notice is given;

(b) providing any information in the accused's possession which might be of material assistance in identifying or finding any such proposed witness in whose case any of the details mentioned in paragraph (a) are not known to the accused when the notice is given.

(2) Details do not have to be given under this section to the extent that they have already been given under section 6A(2).

(3) The accused must give a notice under this section during the period which, by virtue of section 12, is the relevant period for this section.

(4) If, following the giving of a notice under this section, the accused—

(a) decides to call a person (other than himself) who is not included in the notice as a proposed witness, or decides not to call a person who is so included, or

(b) discovers any information which, under subsection (1), he would have had to include in the notice if he had been aware of it when giving the notice,

he must give an appropriately amended notice to the court and the prosecutor.

6E.—(1) Where an accused's solicitor purports to give on behalf of the accused—

(a) a defence statement under section 5, 6 or 6B, or

(b) a statement of the kind mentioned in section 6B(4),

the statement shall, unless the contrary is proved, be deemed to be given with the authority of the accused.

Defence Disclosure in Cases Tried Summarily

D9.37 In cases tried summarily there is no obligation on the defence to provide a defence statement. However, once the prosecutor has complied (or purported to comply) with its duty to disclose unused material (see **D9.15**), the accused may give the prosecutor and the court a defence statement (CPIA 1996, s. 6). In the absence of a defence statement, the accused cannot make an application for specific disclosure under s. 8, and the court cannot make any orders for disclosure of unused prosecution material (see s. 8(1) and **D9.26**).

Where the accused chooses to serve a defence statement he must do so within 14 days from the date when the prosecutor complies or purports to comply with his initial duty of disclosure (Criminal Procedure and Investigations Act 1996 (Defence Disclosure Time Limits) Regulations 2011 (SI 2011 No. 209), reg. 2: see **D9.40**). The court has power to extend this time-limit on the application of the accused (reg. 3).

If the accused provides a defence statement, the requirements in s. 6A as to the contents of the statement apply. The voluntary regime applies to summary trial, whether it is of a summary or an either-way offence or even (in the case of a juvenile) of an indictable-only offence (s. 1(1)). The Magistrates' Courts Protocol makes the following points in respect of defence statements:

(1) Defence advocates must give consideration at an early stage to whether to serve such a statement.
(2) Defence statements must contain a clear and detailed exposition of the issues of fact and law in the case and courts should examine them with care to ensure that they comply with the formalities required by the CPIA.
(3) Where late service of a defence statement results in potential delay to the proceedings, any application to adjourn for further disclosure or to make an application under s. 8 must be scrutinised carefully by the court.
(4) Any case which raises difficult issues of disclosure should be referred to a district judge, where one is available.

Notwithstanding the absence of a requirement to serve a defence statement, the defence must identify the real issues in a case in accordance with the overriding objective in the CrimPR, r. 1.1 (*Robinson v Abergavenny Magistrates' Court* (2007) 171 JP 683).

Criminal Procedure and Investigations Act 1996, s. 6 — D9.38

(1) This section applies where—
  (a) [part I] applies by virtue of section 1(1), and
  (b) the prosecutor complies with section 3 or purports to comply with it.
(2) The accused—
  (a) may give a defence statement to the prosecutor, and
  (b) if he does so, must also give such a statement to the court.
  . . .
(4) If the accused gives a defence statement under this section he must give it during the period which, by virtue of section 12, is the relevant period for this section.

Defence Admissions in Case Progression Forms

In *R (Firth) v Epping Justices* [2011] 4 All ER 326, judicial review was sought of the decision — **D9.39** — of a magistrates court to rely in committal proceedings upon the defence statement in a case progression form, made through the accused's counsel, which admitted contact with the victim of an assault but on the basis of self-defence. The contention was that admitting the document offended the principle that an accused could not be required to incriminate himself. The Divisional Court refused the application stating that it was repugnant to the new approach to criminal justice in the CrimPR whereby both sides disclosed the nature of their case. If the circumstances were such that an admission was tainted by unfairness, it could be excluded under the PACE 1984, s. 78. The rigour of this decision has now been mitigated by *Newell* [2012] 1 WLR 3142, where the Court of Appeal made clear that, while admissions by legal representatives in case progression forms are admissible in evidence, it will rarely be appropriate not to exercise discretion under s. 78 to exclude them.

Defence Disclosure in Cases Tried in the Crown Court — Time-limits

D9.40   By the Criminal Procedure Investigations Act 1996 (Defence Disclosure Time Limits) Regulations 2011 (SI 2011 No. 209), reg. 2, the defence statement must be served within 28 days of the prosecution's compliance (or purported compliance) with the duty of primary disclosure. The defence may apply for an extension, but the application must be made before the deadline expires (reg. 3). The application must not be granted unless the court is satisfied that it would not be reasonable to require the accused to give a defence statement within 28 days. There is no limit to the number of applications that may be made (reg. 3). Time runs from the date of service of a statement by the prosecution under the CPIA 1996, s. 3(1)(h), not from service of the scheduled unused material; however, the right to secondary disclosure is not lost if there is a short delay in serving the defence statement (*DPP v Wood* (2006) 170 JP 177; *Murphy v DPP* [2006] EWHC 1753 (Admin)).

In *Newell* [2012] 1 WLR 3142, the Court of Appeal noted that a typed defence statement has to be provided before the PCMH and that the PCMH should not proceed until this is done. The Judicial Disclosure Protocol notes that observation with approval but recognises that there may be some instances when there may be a well-founded defence application to extend the 28-day limit for serving a proper defence statement to enable an appropriate defence statement to be filed (para. 10). But extensions will not be granted lightly or as a matter of course. If an extension is sought, the application ought to be accompanied by an appropriate explanation (para. 12).

There is clearly a burden on defence representatives to embark on detailed preparation soon after receipt of the prosecution case. However, this responsibility cannot be discharged unless the prosecution makes timely disclosure of unused material. As it is put in the Judicial Disclosure Protocol, para. 10, 'the defence must have a proper opportunity to review the case papers and consider initial disclosure, with a view to preparing a properly completed defence statement which will inform the judge's conduct of the PCMH, and inform the prosecution of the matters required by sections 5, 6A and 6C of the CPIA'.

Given the early notification that the defence must now give of its legal arguments, which include those in relation to any alleged abuse of process and admissibility of evidence, there is a strong case for the prosecution to be compelled to give advance notice of its arguments and authorities on such points, if sought. Any failure to do so would seem to offend against the requirement that a fair trial should be based upon the principle of equality of arms.

D9.41   Criminal Procedure and Investigations Act 1996 (Defence Disclosure Time Limits)
                   Regulations 2011 (SI 2011 No. 209), regs. 2 and 3

   2.—(1) The relevant period for sections 5 (compulsory disclosure), section 6 (voluntary disclosure) and section 6C (notification of intention to call defence witnesses) begins with the day on which the prosecutor complies, or purports to comply, with section 3 (initial duty of prosecutor to disclose).

   (2) In a case where Part 1 applies by virtue of section 1(1) (application of Part 1 in respect of summary proceedings), the relevant period for section 6 and section 6C expires at the end of 14 days beginning with the first day of the relevant period.

   (3) In a case where Part 1 applies by virtue of section 1(2) (application of Part 1 in respect of Crown Court proceedings), the relevant period for section 5 and section 6C expires at the end of 28 days beginning with the first day of the relevant period

   (4) Where the relevant period would expire on a Saturday, Sunday, Christmas Day, Good Friday or any day that under the Banking and Financial Dealings Act 1971 is a bank holiday in England and Wales, the relevant period is treated as expiring on the next day that is not one of those days.

   (5) Paragraphs (2) and (3) are subject to regulation 3.

   3.—(1) The court may by order extend (or further extend) the relevant period by so many days as it specifies.

(2) The court may only make such an order—
    (a) on an application by the accused; and
    (b) if it is satisfied that it would be unreasonable to require the accused to give a defence state-
        ment under section 5 or section 6, or give notice under section 6C, as the case may be,
        within the relevant period.
(3) Such an application must—
    (a) be made within the relevant period;
    (b) specify the grounds on which it is made; and
    (c) state the number of days by which the accused wishes the relevant period to be extended.
(4) There is no limit on the number of applications that may be made under paragraph (2)(a).

Sanctions for Failure in Defence Disclosure

D9.42 Section 11 of the CPIA 1996 lays down sanctions for failure in defence disclosure which apply if the defence:

(a) fail to give the initial defence statement required under s. 5 in respect of Crown Court cases;
(b) in cases tried summarily or in the Crown Court, give the initial defence statement after the 14-day period during which it must be served;
(c) fail to provide an updated statement required under s. 6B(1) or a statement that no updating is necessary under s. 6B(4);
(d) fail to give notice of defence witnesses, as required by s. 6C;
(e) supply the documents in (c) or (d) outside the applicable time-limit;
(f) set out inconsistent defences in the defence statement;
(g) put forward a defence at trial that was not mentioned in the defence statement;
(h) rely on a matter that should have been mentioned in the defence statement to comply with s. 6A, but was not;
(i) give evidence of alibi or call a witness to give evidence in support of alibi without having complied with the provisions relating to notification of alibi witnesses;
(j) call a witness not included or adequately identified in the notice of defence witnesses.

The above list is a summary of s. 11(2) as amended by the CJA 2003, s. 39, and CJIA 2008, s. 60(2). The duty in (c) has not yet been brought into force.

D9.43 In the event that any of the above defence deficiencies applies, the court may comment upon the failure in question (s. 11(5)). Other parties (the prosecution and co-accused) may also comment upon any defect in disclosure, but in certain circumstances such comment requires the leave of the court. Those circumstances are where the defect that triggers the sanction is a failure to mention a point of law (including failure to mention a point about admissibility of evidence or abuse of process) or authority to be relied on, failure to give notice of or adequately identify a witness, or failure to give such notice in time (s. 11(6) and (7)).

If any of the above deficiencies applies, the court or jury may also draw such inferences as appear proper in deciding whether the accused is guilty of the offence concerned (s. 11(5)(b)). The accused may not, however, be convicted solely on the basis of such an inference (s. 11(10)). It would seem that the wording of s. 11(5)(b) would preclude the use of an inference from defective disclosure to bolster the prosecution case against a submission of no case to answer, since the phrase 'whether the accused is guilty of the offence concerned' is not apt to describe the decision which the court has to make on such a submission. The context in which such an inference can be drawn is therefore narrower than that applicable to inferences from silence under the CJPO 1994, s. 34 (see **F19.10**), which explicitly allows an inference to be drawn when the court determines whether there is a case to answer, reserving the wording replicated in s. 11(5)(b) of the 1996 Act to apply to the verdict.

If there is a failure of defence disclosure by breaching any of the requirements of the CPIA 1996, the only sanctions available to the court are those contained in s. 11. Therefore, the court cannot punish by way of contempt of court a failure to comply with its direction to amend (or provide) the defence statement (*Rochford* [2011] 1 WLR 534); it cannot rule as inadmissible the evidence of alibi witnesses on the basis that no defence statement had been served providing details of them (*R (Tinnion) v Reading Crown Court* [2010] RTR 263); and it cannot decline to allow the accused to put forward matters in cross-examination which go to a relevant issue because the material on which such cross-examination is based is produced at a very late stage with no advance notice (*T* [2012] EWCA Crim 2358). The appropriate sanction in all these instances is adverse comment and for the court or jury to be able to draw such inferences as may be proper. But, where a failure to provide a defence statement results in additional expense for the prosecution, a wasted costs order may be appropriate (*SVS Solicitors* [2012] EWCA Crim 319).

D9.44 Section 6E(2) of the CPIA 1996, inserted by the CJA 2003, s. 36, provides that where it appears to the judge at a pre-trial hearing (see **D15.39** *et seq.*) that the accused has failed to serve a defence statement, or to update it when required to do so, or to serve notice of intention to call defence witnesses, so that there may be comment made or inferences drawn under s. 11(5), he must warn the accused of that possibility. Curiously, this provision is fully in force even though the provision relating to updated statements (s. 6B) is not yet in force.

In *Essa* [2009] EWCA Crim 43, the court rejected the argument that the CPIA 1996, s. 11(5), is incompatible with the right to a fair trial under the ECHR, Article 6. The court said that the use of s. 11(5) is subject to judicial control. In particular the judge can interfere and stop the cross-examination if it is unfair, and, if unfair cross-examination has been embarked upon, it is open to the judge to tell the jury to disregard it. In those circumstances, s. 11(5) is compatible with the Convention.

D9.45 **Circumstances in which Comment may be Made** There is provision about the making of comments and drawing of inferences in three sets of circumstances:

(a) where the defect in question is that the accused put forward a defence different from that set out in his defence statement, the court must have regard to the extent of any difference, and whether there is any justification for it (s. 11(8));

(b) where the defect concerns failure to give notice of, or identify adequately, a defence witness, the court must have regard to whether there is any justification for the failure (s. 11(9));

(c) where the defect is that the accused issued a notice indicating that no updating is required to the defence statement, the question whether there has been a breach of the requirements for the contents of the defence statement or of the duty to supply particulars of alibi must be determined at the time when the statement under s. 6B(4) was made and as if the original defence statement had been made at that time (s. 11(11), which is not yet in force).

In cases where there is apparent inconsistency between the defence statement and the case run by the defence at trial, the judge needs to decide whether the jury should be permitted to draw an inference from the inconsistency, in accordance with the CPIA 1996, s. 11(5)(b). In *Wheeler* (2000) 164 JP 565, the accused was charged with knowingly importing cocaine from Jamaica. He had been arrested at Gatwick when drugs were found in his possession. In interview and later in evidence at his trial, he gave an explanation concerning his possession of the drugs which was inconsistent with his defence statement. In cross-examination, he said that the statement was a mistake. The trial judge gave no specific direction to the jury about the inconsistency. On appeal, it was the accused's case, and was accepted by his solicitors, that the defence statement did not reflect his instructions, and had not been approved by him. The appeal was allowed on the basis that the judge ought to have given the jury a specific direction on how to approach that inconsistency, given the fact that the accused's credibility had been crucial to his case. The Court of Appeal said that it would have been wise for the judge to have accepted that the fault lay with the solicitors, given that the conduct of the defence at trial was in accordance with the version of events that he gave in interview. There will inevitably be a proportion of cases in which defence disclosure is defective, whether due to errors by defence lawyers, a failure by the accused to be organised enough to attend to give instructions, or a lack of focus on the importance of the

issues involved. It is right to stress the need for judicial caution before allowing the jury to base
a verdict upon foundations which may turn out to be shaky.

There is now a presumption that a defence statement is issued with the authority of the accused, **D9.46**
subject to proof to the contrary (s. 6E(1), inserted by the CJA 2003, s. 36: see **D9.32**). It is submitted, however, that the reasoning of the Court of Appeal in *Wheeler* is still applicable in the
light of the new law. In *Wheeler* it was also suggested that defence statements should be signed,
to acknowledge their accuracy and avoid disputes. This issue arose in *R (Sullivan) v Crown
Court at Maidstone* [2002] 4 All ER 427. In that case the High Court found that a local practice
direction by the resident judge that all defence statements were to be signed by the accused was
unlawful, on the ground that there was no power to make it.

Where the judge decides to allow the jury to draw an inference in a case where there is apparent
inconsistency between the defence statement and the case run by the defence at trial, it is usually
unhelpful for the judge to give at the same time a direction as to lies in accordance with *Lucas*
[1981] QB 720; but if the factual context of the case is that the accused is entitled to the protection of a *Lucas* direction then that protection should be incorporated in the judge's direction to
the jury concerning the inference (see *Hackett* [2011] 2 Cr App R 35, the principles of which
appear to apply to situations in which comment is permissible under the CPIA 1996, s. 11,
discussed more fully at **F19.32**).

Criminal Procedure and Investigations Act 1996, s. 11 **D9.47**

(1) This section applies in the three cases set out in subsections (2), (3) and (4).
(2) The first case is where section 5 applies and the accused—
   (a) fails to give an initial defence statement,
   (b) gives an initial defence statement but does so after the end of the period which, by virtue
     of section 12, is the relevant period for section 5,
   (c) is required by section 6B to give either an updated defence statement or a statement of the
     kind mentioned in subsection (4) of that section but fails to do so,
   (d) gives an updated defence statement or a statement of the kind mentioned in section 6B(4)
     but does so after the end of the period which, by virtue of section 12, is the relevant period
     for section 6B,
   (e) sets out inconsistent defences in his defence statement, or
   (f) at his trial—
     (i) puts forward a defence which was not mentioned in his defence statement or is dif-
      ferent from any defence set out in that statement,
     (ii) relies on a matter (or any particular of any matter of fact) which, in breach of the
      requirements imposed by or under section 6A, was not mentioned in his defence
      statement [words in brackets added by CJIA 2008, s. 60(2): for commencement date,
      see **D9.4**],
     (iii) adduces evidence in support of an alibi without having given particulars of the alibi
      in his defence statement, or
     (iv) calls a witness to give evidence in support of an alibi without having complied with
      section 6A(2)(a) or (b) as regards the witness in his defence statement.
(3) The second case is where section 6 applies, the accused gives an initial defence statement, and
   the accused—
   (a) gives the initial defence statement after the end of the period which, by virtue of section
     12, is the relevant period for section 6, or
   (b) does any of the things mentioned in paras. (c) to (f) of subsection (2).
(4) The third case is where the accused—
   (a) gives a witness notice but does so after the end of the period which, by virtue of section 12,
     is the relevant period for section 6C, or
   (b) at his trial calls a witness (other than himself) not included, or not adequately identified,
     in a witness notice.
(5) Where this section applies—
   (a) the court or any other party may make such comment as appears appropriate;
   (b) the court or jury may draw such inferences as appear proper in deciding whether the
     accused is guilty of the offence concerned.

(6) Where—
  (a) this section applies by virtue of subsection (2)(f)(ii) (including that provision as it applies by virtue of subsection (3)(b)), and
  (b) the matter which was not mentioned is a point of law (including any point as to the admissibility of evidence or an abuse of process) or an authority,

comment by another party under subsection (5)(a) may be made only with the leave of the court.

(7) Where this section applies by virtue of subsection (4), comment by another party under subsection (5)(a) may be made only with the leave of the court.

(8) Where the accused puts forward a defence which is different from any defence set out in his defence statement, in doing anything under subsection (5) or in deciding whether to do anything under it the court shall have regard —
  (a) to the extent of the differences in the defences, and
  (b) to whether there is any justification for it.

(9) Where the accused calls a witness whom he has failed to include, or to identify adequately, in a witness notice, in doing anything under subsection (5) or in deciding whether to do anything under it the court shall have regard to whether there is any justification for the failure.

(10) A person shall not be convicted of an offence solely on an inference drawn under sub-section (5).

(11) Where the accused has given a statement of the kind mentioned in section 6B(4), then, for the purposes of subsections (2)(f)(ii) and (iv), the question as to whether there has been a breach of the requirements imposed by or under section 6A or a failure to comply with section 6A(2)(a) or (b) shall be determined—
  (a) by reference to the state of affairs at the time when that statement was given, and
  (b) as if the defence statement was given at the same time as that statement [not yet in force: see **D9.4**].

(12) In this section—
  (a) 'initial defence statement' means a defence statement given under section 5 or 6;
  (b) 'updated defence statement' means a defence statement given under section 6B;
  (c) a reference simply to an accused's 'defence statement' is a reference—
    (i) where he has given only an initial defence statement, to that statement;
    (ii) where he has given both an initial and an updated defence statement, to the updated defence statement;
    (iii) where he has given both an initial defence statement and a statement of the kind mentioned in section 6B(4), to the initial defence statement;
  (d) a reference to evidence in support of an alibi shall be construed in accordance with section 6A(3);
  (e) 'witness notice' means a notice given under section 6C.

Section 11 is shown as substituted by the CJA 2003, s. 39; s. 11(11) is not yet in force.

ROLE OF THE COURT

D9.48 The Judicial Disclosure Protocol clearly states that the disclosure process is to be 'led by the prosecution so as to trigger comprehensive defence engagement, supported by robust judicial management' (para. 6). While recognising that failure to disclose material to the defence remains the biggest single cause of miscarriages of justice, the Protocol also states that it is essential that the trial process is not overburdened or diverted by erroneous and inappropriate disclosure or by misconceived applications. The burden of disclosure must not be allowed to render the prosecution of cases impracticable. Accordingly, the Protocol emphasises the need for all involved to understand the statutory requirements and to undertake their roles with rigour, in a timely manner (paras. 1 to 3). The overarching principle to be applied is 'that unused material will fall to be disclosed if, and only if, it satisfies the test for disclosure applicable to the proceedings in question, subject to any overriding public interest considerations' (para. 4).

The courts are to:

(a) set realistic timetables for prosecution and defence disclosure (paras. 7, 9, 10 and 16);
(b) grant extensions only in response to an appropriate explanation for the request (para. 12);

(c) not allow the prosecution to abdicate their responsibility for reviewing unused material by allowing the defence to inspect everything on the schedule of non-sensitive unused material (para. 13);

(d) examine defence case statements with care to ensure that they comply with the formalities, investigate any failures and, if appropriate, give a warning about the possibility of an adverse inference being drawn (paras. 19 to 21);

(e) cease making blanket orders for disclosure and instead reject requests which are not referable to an issue identified in the defence case statement and which satisfy the test for disclosure (para. 26);

(f) allow adequate time to deal with disclosure issues at the plea and case management hearing (see paras. 28 to 29).

Particular issues affecting magistrates' courts are dealt with at paras. 30 to 37.

In *B* [2000] Crim LR 50, the Court of Appeal stressed that the decision as to whether primary disclosure should be made was for the prosecution. The assistance of the judge should be sought only if the questions could properly be decided by him, most obviously where there was an issue relating to public interest immunity. The conviction was quashed as unsafe and a retrial ordered, because the prosecution had asked the judge to read documents and consider whether they should be disclosed to the defence as undermining the prosecution case, thus transferring to him the responsibility for judging the weight and impact of the material. In fact, the defence would have been in a much better position to cross-examine the complainant if they had read the documents in question. **D9.49**

In *Stephenson* [2005] EWCA Crim 1778, the prosecution disclosed material to the defence which suggested that prosecution witnesses were significantly involved in drug-related offences. Prosecution counsel did not, however, place the material before the court, and sought in his closing speech to rely upon the credibility of his witnesses. The Court of Appeal held that the Crown was under a duty, in these circumstances, to place the material before the court. This should have been done as a concession by the Crown.

In *Olivier* [2007] EWCA Crim 2220, where the prosecution disclosed 8,000 pages of material within a few days of trial despite its being sought by the defence for about a year, the Court of Appeal found that the judge had been right to refuse an adjournment and to stay the proceedings on the basis that the accused would not receive a fair trial.

PUBLIC INTEREST IMMUNITY

Circumstances may arise in a case in which material held by the prosecution and tending to undermine the prosecution or assist the defence cannot be disclosed to the defence, fully or even at all, without the risk of prejudice to an important public interest. In such circumstances the courts may be justified in ordering that the material is withheld from disclosure, but they must only allow this to the minimum extent necessary to protect the public interest in question and must never imperil the overall fairness of the trial (*H* [2004] AC 134). Applications by the prosecution to the court to withhold material in these circumstances are known as public interest immunity applications. Although the 1996 Act generally disapplies the rules of common law in relation to the prosecution duty of disclosure (s. 21(1)), it preserves 'the rules of common law as to whether disclosure is in the public interest' (s. 21(2)). The provisions of the CPIA 1996 which provide for disclosure to the accused allow relevant material to be withheld on public interest grounds only if the court so decides (ss. 3(6), 7(5), 8(5) and 9(8)). **D9.50**

For the circumstances in which public interest immunity may be claimed, see **F9**. This section deals with the procedure in respect of such claims.

Background

The law concerning public interest immunity (previously known as Crown privilege) developed in civil proceedings: see *Duncan v Cammell Laird & Co Ltd* [1942] AC 624; and *Conway v* **D9.51**

Rimmer [1968] AC 910. Until the mid-1990s there were few reported cases concerning public interest immunity in criminal proceedings because it was left largely to the judgement of the prosecution as to whether material should be withheld and only exceptionally did courts make a ruling. That position changed with the case of *Ward* [1993] 2 All ER 577. Judith Ward had been convicted of multiple murder and explosives offences. The prosecution had failed to disclose material relevant to her alleged confessions and certain scientific evidence. In upholding her appeal, the Court of Appeal made it clear that the court, rather than the prosecution, had to be the final arbiter as to whether the prosecution was entitled to avoid disclosure on the basis of public interest immunity. It would be wrong to allow the prosecution to withhold material documents without giving notice of that fact to the defence. The court could then, if necessary, be asked to rule on the legitimacy of the prosecution's asserted claim. If the prosecution was not prepared to have the issue of public interest immunity determined by a court, they would inevitably have to abandon the case.

D9.52 The requirement set out in *Ward* to give notice to the defence of an application in every case seemed likely in some instances to lead to the material in question being compromised. Accordingly, some months after *Ward* was decided, the Court of Appeal laid down guidance as to the procedure to be followed in public interest immunity cases in the case of *Davis* [1993] 2 All ER 643. Lord Taylor CJ stated that:

(a) If the prosecution wish to rely on public interest immunity to justify non-disclosure then, in most cases, they must notify the defence that they are applying for a ruling by the court, and indicate to the defence at least the category of the material which they hold. The defence must then have the opportunity of making representations to the court.

(b) Where, however, the public interest would be injured if disclosure was made of the category of material, the prosecution should still notify the defence of the application, but need not specify the category of material. The defence would be able to address the court on the procedure to be adopted but the application itself would be *ex parte*. If the court on that application found that there should be an *inter partes* application it would so order. If not, it would rule on the *ex parte* application.

(c) In a highly exceptional case where even to reveal that an *ex parte* application was to be made would injure the public interest, the prosecution could apply to the court *ex parte* without notice. Again, if the court on hearing the application considered that notice should have been given to the defence, or even that the normal *inter partes* hearing should have been adopted, it would so order.

Lord Taylor emphasised the importance of the court keeping the situation under review.

Rule 22.3 of the CrimPR (see Supplement, **R-197**) in effect reproduces the procedure laid down in *Davis*: see **D9.59**.

Public Interest Immunity and Article 6

D9.53 The procedural fairness of public interest immunity has been examined in a number of decisions of the ECtHR.

In *Rowe and Davis v UK* (2000) 30 EHRR 1, the court gave an important ruling concerning the approach to be adopted by the court when public interest immunity issues have to be determined. The following points emerge from the court's unanimous decision.

(a) The right to a fair trial means that the prosecution authorities should disclose to the defence all material evidence in their possession for and against the accused.

(b) That duty of disclosure is not absolute, and 'in any criminal proceedings there may be competing interests, such as national security or the need to protect witnesses at risk of reprisals or keep secret police methods of investigation, which must be weighed against the rights of the accused'.

(c) But only such measures restricting the rights of the defence to disclosure as are strictly necessary are permissible under the ECHR, Article 6(1).

(d) Any difficulties caused to the defence by a limitation on its rights must be sufficiently counterbalanced by the procedure followed by the court.

(e) The task of the European Court is to ascertain whether the decision-making procedure applied in each case complies with the requirements of adversarial proceedings and equality of arms and incorporates adequate safeguards to protect the interest of the accused.

In *Rowe and Davis* it was necessary for the ECtHR to consider whether procedural failures at first instance could be remedied at a later stage. The judge at first instance had not considered material that had been withheld by the prosecution during the trial. On appeal the Court of Appeal had adopted an *ex parte* procedure to consider the material that had been withheld. The ECtHR found that this procedure did not remedy the unfairness of the judge at first instance in not considering the material. If he had considered the material he could have monitored the importance of the undisclosed evidence at a stage when it could have affected the course of the trial. Since the Court of Appeal hearing was *ex parte*, the court was reliant upon prosecution counsel and transcripts of the trial for an understanding of the possible relevance of the undisclosed material. The ECtHR reached the same conclusion in *Atlan v UK* (2002) 34 EHRR 833, a case in which the prosecution had repeatedly denied the existence of undisclosed material and the judge had not been informed of the true position. See also *Dowsett v UK* [2003] Crim LR 890.

The case of *Jasper v UK* (2000) 30 EHRR 441, established that an *ex parte* procedure at first **D9.54** instance would not necessarily breach Article 6(1). The ECtHR held (by a majority of nine to eight) that there was no breach because, although the application for an order permitting non-disclosure was heard on an *ex parte* basis, the defence were notified that the application had been made, the trial judge gave them as much information regarding the nature of the withheld evidence as possible without revealing what it was, and the defence were permitted to outline their case to the judge. The court reached the same conclusion in *Fitt v UK* (2000) 30 EHRR 480, which was decided on the same day on very similar grounds.

In *Botmeh* [2002] 1 WLR 531, it was argued that the *ex parte* procedure could not be followed in the Court of Appeal, but was confined to proceedings at first instance. The argument was rejected. There was nothing in the judgments *Rowe* and *Atlan* to suggest that *ex parte* examination of material by the Court of Appeal was of itself unfair.

In the light of these authorities, it appears that the procedures for handling public interest immunity applications in our domestic courts which are set out at **D9.55** to **D9.66** are currently compliant with Article 6 (see also para. 68 of the A-G's Guidelines which state that rigid adherence with the principles set out in *H* [2004] AC 134 is necessary to ensure compliance with Article 6).

Approach of the Courts to Public Interest Immunity

In the landmark decision of *H* [2004] AC 134, the House of Lords provided a template by **D9.55** which courts are to make public interest immunity decisions. Judges are to address a series of questions in sequential order:

(1) The court must first identify whether the material which the prosecution seeks to withhold is material that may weaken the prosecution case or strengthen that of the defence. If the material cannot be so described — because for instance it is neutral or damaging to the accused — then it should not be disclosed. If it can be so described, the golden rule is that disclosure should be made unless public interest immunity considerations prevent it.

(2) Next, in determining whether public interest immunity applies, the court is to apply the test of whether there is a real risk of serious prejudice to an important, and identified, public interest. If the material does not satisfy that test, it does not attract public interest immunity and must be disclosed.

(3) If the material does attract public interest immunity, the court must then consider whether the accused's interests can be protected without disclosure or whether disclosure can be ordered to an extent or in a way which will give adequate protection to the public interest in question and also afford adequate protection to the interests of the defence.

(4) In considering whether limited disclosure is possible, the court must give consideration to ordering the prosecution to make admissions, prepare summaries or extracts of evidence, or provide documents in an edited or anonymised form.

(5) If the court is minded to order limited disclosure of this kind, it must first ask whether it represents the minimum derogation necessary to protect the public interest in question. If not, then it must order more disclosure. If, however, the effect of limited disclosure may be to render the whole trial process unfair to the accused, fuller disclosure should be ordered even if this leads the prosecution to discontinue the proceedings.

(6) The issue of disclosure of the material should be reviewed as the trial unfolds, evidence is adduced and the defence advanced.

If material is capable of being disclosed in redacted or edited form or by way of summaries, it ought not to be necessary to place it before the court for a decision under (4) above. The A-G's Guidelines state that prosecutors should aim to disclose as much of the material as they properly can and should only seek a judicial ruling in truly borderline cases (para. 65). The Judicial Disclosure Protocol also encourages redactions, e.g., by removing personal details from a statement (para. 55(c)).

Practice and Procedure of Investigators

D9.56 Material which might in due course be made the subject of a public interest immunity application must be recorded by investigators in a 'sensitive schedule'. As to the contents of the schedule, see **D9.12**. Detailed guidance as to the assessment of sensitivity and the preparation of the schedule is contained in chapter 8 of the Disclosure Manual. Investigators are to specify the reasons why the material is sensitive, the degree of sensitivity attaching to the material, the consequences of revealing it to the defence, the significance of the material to the issues in the trial, the involvement of third parties in bringing the material to the attention of the police, the implications for continuance of the prosecution if disclosure is ordered, and whether it is possible to disclose the material without compromising its sensitivity. In considering the material, prosecutors are to consider the possibility of prejudice to the public interest through direct harm or indirectly through incremental or cumulative harm.

Inclusion of material upon a 'sensitive' schedule is of course in no way conclusive of the question of whether its disclosure is in the public interest. That question is quite clearly one to be answered by the court. The principle in *Ward* [1993] 2 All ER 577 (see **D9.51**), remains intact and is reinforced by the terms of the 1996 Act: the court, rather than the prosecutor (let alone the investigator) is the final arbiter as to whether disclosure can be avoided on the basis of public interest immunity. Further, it is clear that the categories of 'sensitive material' spelt out in the Code of Practice on Disclosure are wider than the types of material which the courts have been prepared to shield behind public interest immunity. The code gives as an example of sensitive material, 'material given in confidence'; but the fact that material has been given in confidence is not sufficient of itself to ensure that it attracts public interest immunity so as to enable the prosecution to avoid disclosing it (see **F9.30**). Nonetheless public interest immunity applications are likely to be founded on material which is contained in the 'sensitive' schedule.

Preparation of Applications

D9.57 The procedure that the prosecutor must follow in making an application for a public interest ruling is set out in the CrimPR, r. 22.3 (see Supplement, **R-197**). Detailed guidance is also contained in chapter 13 of the Disclosure Manual. The rules specify that applications must be in writing and must explain why it would not be in the public interest to disclose the material (r. 22.3(2)). The guidance emphasises that applications to the court will be rare and should be considered only if the other options of disclosing the material in a way that does not compromise the public interest in issue; or abandoning the case; or disclosing the material because it is in the overall public interest to do so, have been discounted or there is no agreement between the prosecutor, investigators or agencies, or the court's assistance is required to assess whether material should be disclosed. The CrimPR, r. 22.3(3)(a)(iii), complements this statement by requiring that the prosecutor must specify why no measure such as an admission of fact, or disclosure by summary, extract or edited copy would protect both the public interest and the defendant's right to a fair trial. Chapter 13 of the Disclosure Manual contains practical details about arranging the application and making the written submission to accompany it. The Judicial Disclosure Protocol also deals with the written submission. It discourages formulaic expressions and encourages the use of schedules in complex cases which set out the specific objection in relation to each item and leave a space for the decision (para. 55(d)).

The CrimPR, r. 22.3(2), makes provision for service of notices on the accused and interested parties where appropriate.

In *Menga* [1998] Crim LR 58, the Court of Appeal emphasised that prosecution counsel should ensure, as far as he can, that he has sight of all material in respect of which public interest immunity is to be claimed before the trial commences so that the applications can be made at the most convenient time. The CPS, said their lordships, had an obvious obligation to ensure that all such material was in their possession, and the police had a duty to pass the material on.

Categories of Hearing

D9.58 The CrimPR, r. 22.3(2)(b)(iii) and (4) (see Supplement, **R-197**), in effect reproduces the procedure laid down in *Davis* [1993] 2 All ER 643 (see **D9.52**). In Type 1 applications, a notice of application is served on the accused by the prosecutor. Type 2 applications arise where the prosecutor has reason to believe that to reveal to the accused the nature of the material to which the application relates would have the effect of disclosing that which the prosecutor contends should not in the public interest be disclosed. In such cases, the prosecutor is not to serve a notice but instead must notify the accused that a Type 2 application has been made. Type 3 applications arise where the prosecutor has reason to believe that to reveal to the accused the fact of an application being made would have the effect of disclosing that which the prosecutor contends should not in the public interest be disclosed. In such cases, no notice is required.

The Judicial Disclosure Protocol stipulates that in Type 1 and 2 applications proper notice to the defence is necessary to allow them to make focused submissions to the court. The notice should be as specific as possible, though it is accepted that in some cases only the generic nature of the material can properly be identified (para. 55(b)). To this end, the CrimPR, r. 22.3(4), provides that, where the prosecutor serves only part of the application on the defendant, the prosecutor must mark the other part to show that it is only for the court; and in that other part must explain why it has been withheld from the defendant. The judge should always ask the prosecution to justify the form of notice given or the decision not to give a notice (Judicial Disclosure Protocol, para. 55(b)). If the judge takes the view that the defence should have had notice of the application, or of the nature of the material, or that the application should be made *inter partes*, then it is plain that he should direct accordingly, as Lord Taylor CJ observed in *Davis* (see **D9.52**).

In *Smith* [1998] 2 Cr App R 1, the Court of Appeal stressed that no *ex parte* application should be made in circumstances where there was nothing to be said which could not be said in the presence of defence counsel.

Procedure in Court

D9.59 Hearings are to take place in private unless the court otherwise directs and may take place, wholly or in part, in the defendant's absence (CrimPR, r. 22.3(6): see Supplement, **R-197**).

Where the defendant is present, the court is to hear the prosecutor and any interested party first, then the defendant, in the presence of them all, and then once more the prosecutor and any interested party, but this time in the defendant's absence, unless it directs that other arrangements are to take place (r. 22.3(7)). The court is to determine the application only if satisfied that it has been able to take adequate account of such rights of confidentiality as apply to the material, and the defendant's right to a fair trial (r. 22.3(8)).

In *Jackson* [2000] Crim LR 377, the Court of Appeal stressed that it is imperative that in all cases the Crown is scrupulously accurate in the information provided in *ex parte* public interest immunity hearings. The judge must himself examine or view the evidence, so that he can have the facts of what it contained in mind. Only then can he be in a position to balance the competing interests of public interest immunity and fairness to the party claiming disclosure (*K (TD)* (1993) 97 Cr App R 342). In *Law* (1996) *The Times*, 15 August 1996, the Court of Appeal held that, in deciding whether to order the prosecution to disclose information, the judge was not restricted to considering only evidence admissible in a court of law. He was entitled to see additional material, even if it amounted to hearsay evidence.

In *Templar* [2003] EWCA Crim 3186, Latham LJ warned against frequent meetings between the judge and prosecuting counsel in chambers in order to consider public interest immunity issues, where the defendant and his lawyers were absent. In the instant case there were some 36 such meetings. Although there was in fact no impropriety, he warned of the danger that prosecuting counsel and judge might come to use the procedure as a 'mutual support mechanism', with the result that repeated visits to chambers might blur their appreciation of the respective tasks which they faced.

In *G* [2004] 1 WLR 2932, highly sensitive evidence was disclosed accidentally to the defence counsel and solicitor. The trial judge ordered them not to pass the information in question to anyone else, including their clients. It was held in the course of an interlocutory appeal that this order must be quashed as it would undermine the lawyer-client relationship.

D9.60   Applications must be recorded. The judge should give some short statement of reasons; this is often best done document by document as the hearing proceeds (Judicial Disclosure Protocol, para. 55(e)).

As to the procedure where the Court of Appeal reviews the conduct by the trial judge of a public interest immunity hearing, see **D27.32** and *McDonald* (2004) *The Times*, 8 November 2004.

Use of Special Advocates and Confidentiality Rings

D9.61   In *Rowe and Davis* (2000) 30 EHRR 1 (see **D9.53**), it was argued on behalf of the applicants in Strasbourg that the exclusion of the defence from the *ex parte* procedure conducted by the Court of Appeal should have been counterbalanced by the introduction of a special independent counsel who could argue the relevance of the undisclosed evidence, test the strength of the prosecution claim to public interest immunity, and safeguard against the risk of judicial error or bias. The court found a violation of the ECHR, Article 6, without the need to address this question but the issue arose again in *Edwards v UK* (2003) 15 BHRC 189. In that case, the tribunal of fact was the trial judge, who had to decide whether to exclude evidence because the accused had been entrapped. Material was produced to the trial judge in *ex parte* hearings. The defence was not aware of the material, and was unable to put forward an argument on it. The ECtHR found that the defence should have been given the opportunity to counter the evidence and show the judge that it was mistaken or unreliable. A procedure which denied the defence that opportunity on an issue which was so fundamental to a fair trial failed to comply 'with the requirements to provide adversarial proceedings and equality of arms' or to incorporate 'adequate safeguards to protect the interests of the accused'. During the course of the judgment, the role of special counsel was again canvassed, and mentioned with some approval by the court. Accordingly, in *H* [2004] 2 AC 134, the House of Lords were invited to state that special counsel should be appointed wherever material which the prosecution seeks to withhold is, or may be, relevant to a disputed issue of fact which the judge has to decide in order to rule on an application which will effectively determine the outcome of the proceedings. In particular, it was argued that such an appointment should be made whenever the defence relies on entrapment as a basis for staying the case as an abuse of process or excluding prosecution evidence. The House of Lords declined to hold that special counsel should always be appointed in such circumstances, saying that this would place the trial judge in a straitjacket. Lord Bingham did make it clear, however, that the appointment of special counsel may be a necessary step in appropriate cases to ensure that the contentions of the prosecution are tested and the interests of the accused protected. As to *H*, see further **D9.55**. In *Austin* [2009] EWCA Crim 1527, the Court of Appeal, citing *Ali and Hussain* (2008) 172 JP 516, held that, for the purposes of the appeal before it, it would assume the correctness of the proposition that if, in deciding a factual issue relating to the admissibility of evidence to be placed before a jury, a trial judge relies on material that has not been disclosed to the defence, then the principle of equality of arms is likely to be violated. Both cases appear to have proceeded on the basis that the material must either be disclosed to the defence or not be used for the purposes of determining the application.

No consideration was given to the use of a special advocate in *Austin* [2009] EWCA Crim 1527, but an issue involving the potential use of special counsel did arise in a later case involving the same accused: *Austin* [2014] 1 WLR 1045. In that case, the trial judge looked at the closed judgments of the Court of Appeal in the earlier case in order to see if there were any implications for the proceedings before him, including their fairness, but he did not inform the parties of his action. On appeal, the Court of Appeal found that the judge had been wrong. The right course would have been to raise the issue with the parties. It would also have been open to the judge to appoint special counsel, focused on the disclosure issue alone. On the facts, however, the conviction was safe since the closed material was not disclosable.

An alternative means of ensuring that the interests of the defendant are protected in cases where material cannot be disclosed to him was recognised in *R (Mohammed) v Secretary of State for Defence* [2013] 2 All ER 897, a claim for judicial review. Moses LJ held that there is no principle which prohibits a court considering whether to uphold or reject a claim for PII from ordering that, whilst the claim should not be upheld, nonetheless the documents or material should only be disclosed to those identified within a confidentiality ring on terms to be specified in an undertaking agreed by the parties. Provided legal advisers are satisfied that they can safely continue to act under a restriction, the inability to communicate with the client will not in such circumstances undermine the fundamental principles on which a fair application for judicial review depends. Moses LJ considered a wide range of authorities in reaching his judgment, including criminal cases. He specifically stated that he was proceeding on the assumption that there was no distinction between the principles applying to judicial review claims and civil claims. Equally, there is no reason to think that his reasoning cannot also apply to criminal cases.

Interventions of Third Parties

Section 16 of the CPIA 1996 provides for interventions by interested third parties when the **D9.62** court is considering the issue of public interest immunity.

Criminal Procedure and Investigations Act 1996, s. 16

Where—
  (a) an application is made under section 3(6), 7A(8), 8(5), 14(2) or 15(4),
  (b) a person claiming to have an interest in the material applies to be heard by the court, and
  (c) he shows that he was involved (whether alone or with others and whether directly or indirectly) in the prosecutor's attention being brought to the material,
the court must not make an order under section 3(6), 7A(8), 8(5), 14(3) or 15(5) (as the case may be) unless the person applying under paragraph (b) has been given an opportunity to be heard.

The nature of the duty of prosecutors towards informants was considered in *R (WV) v CPS* [2011] EWHC 2480 (Admin). The Divisional Court quashed a decision of the CPS to disclose the identity of an informant to the defence without having put the issue before a judge to consider. The court said it was of the highest importance to public confidence in the administration of justice that a decision to break an express or implied undertaking of confidence as to the identity of an informant or other provider of information, without informed consent from that individual, is made by a judge.

Categories of Public Interest Material

D9.63 For examples of circumstances in which the prosecution can successfully claim immunity from disclosure, see **F9.10** *et seq.*, especially **F9.14**.

Review of Public Interest Immunity Decisions

D9.64 Once a court has made a decision to exclude material from consideration on public interest immunity grounds, the approach that is taken with regard to reviewing the decision differs as between cases tried summarily and cases tried on indictment. In summary trials, it is necessary for the accused to apply for the decision to be reviewed, whereas in cases tried on indictment the court is under a duty to keep under review the question whether it is still not in the public interest to disclose the affected material. For an example of a case in the Crown Court where a judge ought to have reversed his original decision, see *Giles* [2011] EWCA Crim 2259. In that case the prosecution alleged that H and G were jointly engaged through companies in a missing trader fraud. The judge made public interest immunity rulings twice at a very early stage of the trial and once after the evidence in chief of H. G's defence was that he did not know the companies were engaged in fraud. The information that was withheld related to a separate investigation of H alone of money laundering involving another company of which G was company secretary. There was no suggestion that G was involved in wrongdoing in that other matter. The Court of Appeal, allowing G's appeal, held that whilst the early rulings by the judge could not be criticised, the effect of maintaining them was to deny G's counsel the possibility of putting allegations to H in cross-examination, and making a good deal of them in his closing speech. G's case was by no means hopeless and a jury might have reached a different verdict.

D9.65 The difference in approach between cases tried summarily and those tried on indictment stems from the dual role of the magistrates as triers of both fact and law, which was encountered in *South Worcester Justices, ex parte Lilley* [1995] 4 All ER 186. The problem is that, when the magistrates (in their role as triers of law) conduct a review of documents for which immunity is claimed, it may appear to prejudice them in their role as triers of fact. The problem is compounded when the review is conducted *ex parte*, in the absence of the accused and the defence lawyer. As a result, a new bench may be needed to try the case, after the old bench rules against disclosure. If that new bench were under a duty of continuous review, it would mean that it would be impossible ever to recruit a bench which was proof against the contamination which results from looking at the material. Hence the onus is put on the accused to make the application (see also *Stipendiary Magistrate for Norfolk, ex parte Taylor* (1997) 161 JP 773 and *R (DPP) v Acton Youth Court* [2001] 1 WLR 1828). The procedure for conducting a review is set out in the CrimPR, r. 22.6 (see Supplement, **R-200**), and is similar to the procedure used in the initial application (see **D9.58**).

D9.66   Criminal Procedure and Investigations Act 1996, ss. 14 and 15

14.—(1) This section applies where [part I] applies by virtue of section 1(1).

(2) At any time—

    (a) after a court makes an order under section 3(6), 7A(8) or 8(5), and

    (b) before the accused is acquitted or convicted or the prosecutor decides not to proceed with the case concerned,

the accused may apply to the court for a review of the question whether it is still not in the public interest to disclose material affected by its order.

(3) In such a case the court must review that question, and if it concludes that it is in the public interest to disclose material to any extent—

(a) it shall so order, and

(b) it shall take such steps as are reasonable to inform the prosecutor of its order.

(4) Where the prosecutor is informed of an order made under subsection (3) he must act accordingly having regard to the provisions of [part I] (unless he decides not to proceed with the case concerned).

15.—(1) This section applies where [part I] applies by virtue of section 1(2).

(2) This section applies at all times—

(a) after a court makes an order under section 3(6), 7A(8) or 8(5), and

(b) before the accused is acquitted or convicted or the prosecutor decides not to proceed with the case concerned.

(3) The court must keep under review the question whether at any given time it is still not in the public interest to disclose material affected by its order.

(4) The court must keep the question mentioned in subsection (3) under review without the need for an application; but the accused may apply to the court for a review of that question.

(5) If the court at any time concludes that it is in the public interest to disclose material to any extent—

(a) it shall so order, and

(b) it shall take such steps as are reasonable to inform the prosecutor of its order.

(6) Where the prosecutor is informed of an order made under subsection (5) he must act accordingly having regard to the provisions of [part I] (unless he decides not to proceed with the case concerned).

Intercept Material

D9.67 Section 17 of the RIPA 2000 prevents the fact of interception of a subject's communications and the product of that interception being relied upon or referred to by any party to criminal proceedings. It is given further effect by ss. 3(7), 7(6), 7A(9) and 9(9) of the CPIA 1996. However, s. 18 of the RIPA 2000 states that nothing in s. 17 is to prevent disclosure to a prosecutor to enable that person to determine what is required of him by his duty to secure the fairness of the prosecution. This duty may require the prosecutor to make admissions of fact, discontinue part of the case, not rely on certain evidence, or put his case in a different way. It may also require disclosure to the judge so that the judge may sum up the case in a particular way, give appropriate directions to the jury or require admissions of fact from the prosecution. The A-G's Section 18 RIPA Prosecutors Intercept Guidelines (see **appendix 2**) give detailed guidance on the approach to be taken by prosecutors.

In *Khyam* [2009] 1 Cr App R (S) 455 the Court of Appeal considered the interrelation of the RIPA 2000, ss. 17 and 18. It stated that the circumstances which might lead the court to depart from the prohibition in s. 17 must be highly unusual and material. In *Austin* [2009] EWCA Crim 1527, the Court of Appeal held that the CPIA 2006, s. 17, does not prevent the prosecution relying on intercepts and recordings made in a country outside the UK and in accordance with the laws of the other country concerned. Questions designed to elicit whether the intercepted system was a foreign system and whether its methodology produced evidence that was inadmissible were permissible.

D9.68 Since the prohibition in s. 17 affects both prosecution and defence, arguments concerning the right in the ECHR, Article 6(1), to equality of arms are not likely to be available. The position is different, however, with regard to non-disclosure of evidence. In *Khyam*, it was noted that the regulation of intercept material falls outside the normal disclosure process in criminal trials. Nonetheless the ECHR is applicable. In *Natunen v Finland* (2009) 49 EHRR 810, telephone intercept material had been destroyed by the investigating authorities in compliance with domestic law with the consequence that the accused was deprived of material which could have justified his defence. The ECtHR held that Article 6(3)(b) guaranteed the accused 'adequate time and facilities for the preparation of his defence' and therefore implied that the substantive defence activity on his behalf may comprise everything which was 'necessary' to prepare the main trial. Failure to disclose material evidence to the defence, where that material contained particulars which could enable the accused to exonerate himself or have his sentence reduced would constitute a refusal of facilities necessary for the preparation of the defence. Whilst the applicant had been able to put questions during the trial concerning all his conversations with the other parties, his argument had been rejected for lack of supporting evidence. The significance of the destroyed records was therefore plain.

DISCLOSURE OF EXPERT EVIDENCE

Experts and Content of Report

D9.69 Part 33 of the CrimPR (see Supplement, **R-256** *et seq.*) consolidates the rules on expert evidence. An expert has a duty to help the court to achieve the overriding objective by giving opinion which is objective and unbiased and within the expert's area or areas of expertise (CrimPR, r. 33.2(1)). This duty overrides any obligation to the client or person paying for his services (r. 33.2(2)). Part 33 goes on to provide explicit rules about the form in which expert evidence should be introduced, including such information as the court may need to decide whether the expert's opinion is reliable, about service of the evidence, and about the use of the court's case management powers to define what is in dispute between the experts. A failure to make timely disclosure of an expert's report entitles the judge to refuse to allow the report to go to the jury (*Ensor* [2010] 1 Cr App R 255).

Disclosure of Names and Addresses of Experts

D9.70 There is no obligation on the defence, either at common law or under the CPIA 1996, to reveal material which is not to be used at trial. However, there is a provision in s. 6D, inserted by the CJA 2003, s. 35, which might seem to run counter to this principle. The new provision (which is not yet in force) deals with any expert report commissioned by the accused. If he instructs a person with a view to providing any expert opinion for possible use at trial, he must give the court and the prosecutor the name and address of the expert in question. Potentially, such notification might open the door to the prosecution seeking evidence from the expert in question, as there is no property in a witness (see **F9.60**); however it will not be possible for the expert to provide evidence which involves a breach of privilege, e.g., information provided by the accused in privileged circumstances. No adverse inference may be drawn from failure of the defence to comply with s. 6D or from the fact that an expert has been consulted but not used as a witness.

THIRD-PARTY DISCLOSURE

D9.71 Sometimes the information which the accused needs for his defence will be in the hands of someone other than the prosecution — a 'third party' as far as the criminal case is concerned. In such cases, there may nonetheless be an obligation on the investigator to obtain the information. Alternatively, the third party may give up the information, voluntarily or under compulsion.

Obligations of Prosecutors

D9.72 Paragraph 3.5 of the CPIA Code of Practice requires investigators to pursue all reasonable lines of inquiry, whether these point towards or away from the suspect. The obligation to make disclosure under the CPIA 1996 and the A-G's Guidelines cannot be avoided by declining to make an inquiry which might produce disclosable material (see *Joof* [2012] EWCA Crim 1475 and **D9.9**). Where such investigation reveals the existence of material held by a third party which may be relevant to the investigation but such material is not obtained, the third party must be informed of the investigation and invited to retain the material in case a request for disclosure is made. But speculative inquiries of third parties are not required: there must be some reason to believe that they hold relevant material (see para. 3.6). In *DPP v Wood* (2006) 170 JP 177, the Administrative Court stated that a simple failure on the part of the prosecution to identify and obtain third-party material would not justify a stay of proceedings. A stay could be justified only if the material had significance in relation to a real issue which was damaging to the prosecution or helpful to the defence and the prosecutor had failed to act in accordance with the permissible limits of the A-G's Guidelines (as to which, see **D9.73**). The court also stated that there were circumstances where a third party's refusal to co-operate would require proceedings to be stayed even in the absence of any prosecutorial misconduct. In relation to the obtaining of relevant material from outside the European Union, the Court of Appeal in *Flook* [2010] 1 Cr App R 434 noted that the power of the courts to obtain third party material is limited. It stated that there cannot be an absolute obligation on the Crown to disclose such material since it does not hold the material; the obligation is to take reasonable steps to obtain it. This reasoning is adopted in the Judicial Disclosure Protocol at paras. 51 to 53, and reiterated in the A-G's Guidelines at paras. 59 to 64.

The obligation on a prosecutor to seek the disclosure from third parties of material which if in its hands would be disclosable was explored at first instance in *George* (December 2009 unreported). In that case the Office of Fair Trading had entered into a leniency agreement with employees of Virgin Atlantic Airways whereby, in exchange for immunity from prosecution, they were to co-operate fully with its investigation, to the extent if necessary of waiving any claim to legal professional privilege. On an application by the accused under the CPIA 1996, s. 8, for disclosure by the OFT of material over which legal professional privilege was claimed, Owen J, having become satisfied that the material was highly relevant, held that the OFT ought reasonably to press for disclosure of the material, notwithstanding the claim to privilege, on the basis that, failing a satisfactory response, it might revoke the immunity.

Voluntary Disclosure Route

There are a number of instances where special procedures have been evolved which will result in voluntary disclosure of material. **D9.73**

(a) *Material held by government departments and other Crown bodies.* The A-G's Guidelines, paras. 53 to 55, establish a procedure by which such material may be disclosed. The prosecution team are not to be regarded as being in constructive possession of such material but they must take reasonable steps to identify such material, including notifying the body of the nature of the prosecution case and of relevant issues. In turn government departments and other Crown bodies have a public law duty to co-operate with a criminal investigation. Statutory prohibitions on disclosure of material usually allow an exception for disclosure for the purposes of criminal proceedings, but questions of legal professional privilege or public interest immunity may nevertheless arise which may affect the willingness of Crown bodies to disclose information in their possession.

(b) *Material held by other agencies.* The A-G's Guidelines, para. 56, provide that the prosecution should take steps to obtain material or information in the possession of a third party (e.g., a local authority, social services department, hospital, doctor or school) if it might reasonably be considered capable of undermining the prosecution case or assisting the defence (i.e. to fulfil the test for primary or secondary disclosure). Paragraph 57 deals with the situation where the police or prosecutors meet with a refusal by the third party to supply such material or information. Such refusal might be made, for instance, if the third party considers that it owes a duty of confidentiality to a person in respect of whom the material relates, or that person's Article 8 right to privacy is engaged, and this overrides its duty to co-operate with the criminal investigation. If, despite the reasons put forward for refusal by the third party, it still appears reasonable to seek its production, and the provisions of the relevant statutes are satisfied, the prosecutor or investigator should apply for a witness summons requiring the third party to produce the material to the court. But there should be consultation with the agency before disclosure is made since there may be public interest reasons justifying withholding disclosure.

(c) *Others.* Third parties which are not public authorities have no public law responsibility to co-operate with an investigation. They may also owe duties of confidentiality arising out of a professional relationship such as a banking relationship. In such circumstances the third party may feel obliged to insist that he produces material in response to a summons (see D9.74).

Compulsory Disclosure Route

D9.74   Investigators have powers, under the PACE 1984, s. 8 and sch. 1, to compel third parties to disclose material for the purposes of a criminal investigation: see **D1.146** to **D1.168**. Where a person is charged and a third party is not prepared to hand over relevant material, the course of action available to the prosecution or the accused is to seek a witness summons. The procedure is laid down by the Criminal Procedure (Attendance of Witnesses) Act 1965, s. 2(1) (for the text, see **D15.96**), as far as Crown Court trial is concerned. In magistrates' courts, it is governed by the MCA 1980, s. 97 (see **D21.33**). The procedure involves issuing a witness summons to compel the third party to attend with the document(s) to give evidence, and/or to produce the document(s) in advance. The person seeking the witness summons must satisfy the court that the third party:

(a) is likely to be able to give or produce material evidence in the case; and
(b) will not voluntarily attend or produce the evidence.

D9.75   Under amendments introduced by the CPIA 1996, s. 66, there is a procedure for advance production whereby a summons which is issued under s. 2 may require the directed person to produce any document or thing at a place stated in the summons and at a time stated for inspection by the person applying for the summons. If on inspection the applicant for the summons concludes that he does not require the document or thing he can apply to the court for a direction that the summons is of no further effect (Criminal Procedure (Attendance of Witnesses) Act 1965, ss. 2A and 2B).

A common procedure for the Crown and magistrates' courts came into effect in 2007 with the introduction of a new CrimPR, part 28 (see Supplement, **R-208** *et seq.*). An application must be made by a party 'as soon as practicable after becoming aware of the grounds for doing so' (r. 28.3(1)). It may be made orally or in writing unless a document is required to be produced or confidential information is to be given in which case the application must be in writing and served on the proposed witness and, if the court so directs, a person to whom the evidence relates and another party (r. 28.5(3)). The application must identify the proposed witness and explain what evidence he can give or produce, why it is likely to be material, and why it would be in the interests of justice to issue a summons, warrant or order (r. 28.3(2)). At the hearing, the third party will be able to argue, for example, that there is no evidence held, or that it is not material, or that the duties and rights (including rights of confidentiality) of the proposed witness or person to whom the document or thing relates outweigh the reasons for issuing the summons.

In relation to banking material, either the prosecution or the defence may apply to magistrates or to the Crown Court for an order to inspect or take copies. See the Bankers' Books Evidence Act 1879 at **F8.35**.

D9.76   In *Brushett* [2001] Crim LR 471, the Court of Appeal considered a case where disclosure of reports held by social services departments was sought by the accused in a case of alleged sexual abuse of children. Their lordships characterised the principles governing disclosure by third parties as 'narrower' than those where the prosecution held such material. They indicated that disclosure should nevertheless be granted, for example, where there had been false accusations by the subject of the report in the past, or where there had been sexual activity with another adult.

In *Alibhai* [2004] EWCA Crim 681, Longmore LJ pointed out various unsatisfactory features of the procedure for disclosure of material held by third parties as follows:

(a) It is not possible to issue a witness summons to a person outside the jurisdiction.
(b) A witness summons to produce a 'document or thing' will not elicit information.
(c) The 'document or thing' must itself be likely to be material evidence, and a witness summons will not be issued for documents which will not themselves constitute evidence in the case but merely give rise to a line of inquiry which might result in evidence being obtained, still less for documents merely capable of use in cross-examination as to credit.
(d) There is no provision for the prosecution or defence, unless they so agree, to examine the documents before they are produced to the court as a result of the witness summons.

The Judicial Disclosure Protocol (see **appendix** 4) gives guidance as to the approach of the **D9.77** courts to requests for third-party material (see paras. 44 to 50). It states that speculative inquiries without any proper basis in relation to third-party material (whether by the prosecution or the defence) must be discouraged, and that, in appropriate cases, the court will consider making an order for wasted costs where the application is clearly unmeritorious and misconceived.

The possibility that the civil courts may be used as a means to compel the disclosure of information in criminal proceedings arises as a result of the decision of the Divisional Court in *R (Mohamed) v Secretary of State for Foreign and Commonwealth Affairs (No. 1)* [2009] 1 WLR 2579. In that case, the court made a *Norwich Pharmacal* order requiring disclosure by the Foreign Secretary of material which it considered was essential to a fair trial in criminal proceedings in the USA for terrorist offences. The case raises the interesting possibility that applications may be made for *Norwich Pharmacal* orders in future in circumstances in which the arguably stricter requirements of the witness summons procedure would prevent disclosure of information by a third party. For another instance, see *R (Omar) v Secretary of State for Foreign and Commonwealth Affairs* [2011] EWCA Civ 1587 in which the Court of Appeal (Civil Division) held that the information sought from the Foreign Secretary could potentially assist the applicant in defending a charge in Ugandan proceedings which, if proven against him, could result in the death penalty.

Section D10 Sending Cases from the Magistrates' Court to the Crown Court

INTRODUCTION

D10.1 All adult accused in criminal cases make their first appearance in the magistrates' court. If the offence is triable only in the Crown Court, the accused must be sent to that court for trial. If it is triable either way, the accused will be sent to the Crown Court for trial only if the accused indicates, or is deemed to indicate, a not guilty plea at the 'plea before venue' hearing and the mode of trial hearing that follows results in a decision in favour of Crown Court trial (either because the magistrates decline jurisdiction or because the accused elects Crown Court trial).

The case is sent for trial to the Crown Court under the CDA 1998, s. 51. Until 2012, s. 51 applied only to indictable-only offences; either-way offences were committed for trial in the Crown Court under the MCA 1980, s. 6. However, in 2012, s. 51 was made applicable to either-way offences in certain local justice areas; in 2013, the abolition of committal proceedings for either-way offences was extended throughout England and Wales (see the Criminal Justice Act 2003 (Commencement No. 31 and Saving Provisions) Order 2013 (SI 2013 No. 1103)). It follows that both indictable-only and either-way offences are now sent to the Crown Court for trial under s. 51.

There remains one other way of securing the Crown Court trial of an accused, namely the 'voluntary bill of indictment' (see **D10.44**).

The special rules relating to juveniles (i.e. defendants under the age of 18), in particular the CDA 1998, s. 51A, are considered in **D24**.

Need for a Formal Transfer to the Crown Court

D10.2 The necessity for a formal transfer of the case to the Crown Court for trial arises from the Administration of Justice (Miscellaneous Provisions) Act 1933, s. 2(2).

Administration of Justice Act (Miscellaneous Provisions) Act 1933, s. 2

(2) Subject as hereinafter provided no bill of indictment charging any person with an indictable offence shall be preferred unless either—

   (a)   the person charged has been sent for trial for the offence; or

   (b)   the bill is preferred by the direction of the Court of Criminal Appeal or by the direction or with the consent of a judge of the High Court . . .

   (ba) the bill is preferred with the consent of a judge of the Crown Court following a declaration by the court under paragraph 8(1) of Schedule 17 to the Crime and Courts Act 2013 (court approval of deferred prosecution agreement); or

   (c)   the bill is preferred under section 22B(3)(a) of the Prosecution of Offences Act 1985:
Provided that—

      (i)   where the person charged has been sent for trial, the bill of indictment against him may include, either in substitution for or in addition to any count charging an offence specified in the notice under section 57D(1) of the Crime and Disorder Act 1998, any counts founded on material which, in pursuance of regulations made under paragraph 1 of Schedule 3 to that Act, was served on the person charged, being counts which may lawfully be joined in the same indictment;

      (ii) a charge of a previous conviction of an offence may, notwithstanding that it was not included in such notice or in any such direction or consent as aforesaid, be included in any bill of indictment.

The phrase 'bill of indictment' in s. 2 means simply a draft indictment (which is the term now **D10.3** used in the CrimPR, part 14), prepared by or on behalf of the prosecution. It is 'preferred' by being sent to the Crown Court. It follows from s. 2 of the 1933 Act that a trial on indictment may not validly take place unless:

(a) the accused has been sent for trial under the CDA 1998, s. 51 or s. 51A;
(b) the Court of Appeal has directed the preferment of a bill of indictment (which occurs where the Court of Appeal quashes a conviction but then exercises its discretion, under the Criminal Appeal Act 1968, s. 7, to order that the successful appellant be retried); or
(c) the bill is preferred by the direction or with the consent of a High Court judge (a 'voluntary bill of indictment').

The effect of the proviso to s. 2(2) is that, provided the accused was validly sent for trial on a charge of an indictable offence, the indictment against him may include counts for other indictable offences, in respect of which he was not sent for trial, provided that those offences are disclosed by the evidence on the basis of which the case was originally sent to the Crown Court. See **D11** for detailed discussion of indictments.

Court of First Appearance

Whether the offence is triable either way or triable only on indictment, the accused will make **D10.4** his first appearance in a magistrates' court. The MCA 1980, s. 2(2), provides:

> A magistrates' court has jurisdiction under sections 51 and 51A of the Crime and Disorder Act 1998 in respect of any offence committed by a person who appears or is brought before the court.

Under the CDA 1998, s. 51(13), the functions of a magistrates' court under s. 51 may be discharged by a single justice.

SENDING CASES TO THE CROWN COURT UNDER THE CRIME AND DISORDER ACT 1998, s. 51

The CDA 1998, s. 51(1), provides that, where an adult appears or is brought before a magis- **D10.5** trates' court charged with an offence to which these provisions apply, the court 'shall send him forthwith' to the Crown Court for trial for the offence. This is, however, subject to the magistrates' power to adjourn (s. 52(5)), for example, where the case is under review and it may not be necessary to send the case to the Crown Court, or where the defence needs to muster the necessary information for a bail application.

By virtue of s. 51(2)(a) and (b), these provisions apply where the offence is triable only on indictment, or where the offence is triable either way and the mode of trial stage has resulted in a decision in favour of trial on indictment, in that either the magistrates have declined jurisdiction or the accused has refused the offer of summary trial. Under s. 51(2)(c), the magistrates must also send the accused forthwith to the Crown Court where notice has been given under s. 51B (serious fraud cases) or s. 51C (child witness cases) (see **D10.43**).

Either-way Offences under s. 51

The CDA 1998, s. 50A(3) sets out various steps which must be taken where the offence is triable **D10.6** either way (unless notice is given under s. 51B or 51C):

(a) 'plea before venue': the accused is asked to indicate whether he intends to plead guilty or not guilty;
(b) in the event of an indication of a not guilty plea (or no indication), mode of trial proce- dure: the prosecution and, if they wish, the defence make representations as to whether the

Part D Procedure

D

case is suitable for summary trial and the court then decides whether to accept jurisdiction and offer summary trial to the accused;

(c) if the magistrates decline jurisdiction, or if the accused elects trial on indictment, the case is sent for trial to the Crown Court under s. 51.

The procedure for determining mode of trial for either-way offences is considered in detail in **D6**.

The CDA 1998, s. 51(3), goes on to provide that, where the court sends an adult for trial under s. 51(1), it shall also send him to the Crown Court for trial for any either-way or summary offence with which he is charged and which appears to the court to be related to the offence being sent to the Crown Court under s. 51(1) (provided that, if the offence is a summary offence, it is punishable with imprisonment or disqualification from driving). Under s. 51E(c), an either-way offence is related to an indictable offence if the charge for the either-way offence could be joined in the same indictment as the charge for the indictable offence (applying the test for joinder set out in the CrimPR, r. 14.2(3)), and under s. 51E(d), a summary offence is related to an indictable offence if it arises out of circumstances that are the 'same as or connected with' those giving rise to the indictable offence.

One of the consequences of the provisions contained in s. 51(3) is that, if the accused is charged with an indictable-only offence, there will not be any question as to mode of trial in respect of any related either-way offences with which he is charged and to which he pleads not guilty (since any either-way offences will be sent for trial automatically alongside the indictable-only offence). If a summary offence is sent to the Crown Court under s. 51(3), it will be dealt with in accordance with the CDA 1998, sch. 3, para. 6 (see **D10.29**).

D10.7 If an adult has already been sent to the Crown Court for trial under s. 51(1) and then subsequently appears before a magistrates' court charged with an either-way or summary offence that appears to the court to be related to the offence sent for trial under s. 51(1), the court *may* send him forthwith to the Crown Court for trial for the either-way or summary offence (provided that, if the offence is a summary one, it is punishable with imprisonment or disqualification from driving) (s. 51(4)). Note that this is a discretionary power, not a mandatory duty. It follows from the discretionary nature of the power to send for trial under s. 51(4) that there will be a plea before venue and mode of trial hearing in respect of an either-way offence to which s. 51(4) applies.

Co-accused

D10.8 Section 51(5) of the CDA 1998 deals with the situation where there are co-accused. It applies where the court sends an adult for trial (under s. 51(1) or 51(3)), and another adult appears before the court, either on the same or a subsequent occasion, charged jointly with the first adult with an either-way offence, and that offence appears to the court to be related to an offence for which the first adult was sent for trial under s. 51(1) or (3). The court must (where it is the same occasion), or may (where it is a subsequent occasion), send the other adult forthwith to the Crown Court for trial for the either-way offence. Where the court sends an adult for trial under s. 51(5), it must (by virtue of s. 51(6)) at the same time send him to the Crown Court for trial for any either-way or summary offence with which he is charged and which appears to the court to be related to the offence for which he is sent for trial (provided that, if it is a summary offence, it is punishable with imprisonment or disqualification from driving).

D10.9 **Juvenile Co-accused** Section 51(7) covers the situation where an adult and a juvenile are jointly charged. It applies where the court sends an adult to the Crown Court for trial under s. 51(1), (3) or (5), and a child or young person (i.e. a person under the age of 18) appears before the court (on the same or a subsequent occasion) charged jointly with the adult with an indictable offence for which the adult is sent for trial under s. 51(1), (3) or (5), or charged with an indictable offence that appears to the court to be related to that offence. The court 'shall, if it considers it necessary in the interests of justice to do so, send the juvenile forthwith to the Crown Court for trial for the indictable offence'. Under s. 51(8), where the court sends a juvenile for trial under s. 51(7), it may at the same time send him to the Crown Court for trial for any indictable or summary offence with which he is charged and which appears to the court to be related to the offence for which he is sent for trial (again, if the offence is a summary one, it must be punishable with imprisonment or disqualification from driving). Section 51(9) makes it clear that these provisions are subject to the MCA 1980, ss. 24A and 24B (see **D24**).

Subsidiary Matters

Where a summary offence is sent to the Crown Court for trial under s. 51, it is to be regarded as having being adjourned by the magistrates *sine die* (s. 51(10)).   **D10.10**

Under s. 51(13), the functions of a magistrates' court under s. 51 may be discharged by a single justice.

Section 51A contains equivalent provisions to s. 51 for cases where defendants who are under the age of 18 are to be sent to the Crown Court for trial (see **D24**).

Presence of the Accused

The CDA 1998, s. 51(1), applies where the accused is 'before a magistrates' court'. If the accused does not appear in court for the s. 51 hearing, the court may issue a warrant for his arrest (see the MCA 1980, s. 1(6), and the Bail Act 1976, s. 7(1), which are applicable, respectively, where the accused fails to answer to a summons or requisition, or fails to answer to his bail, whether that bail was granted by the police or by a magistrates' court).   **D10.11**

Reporting Restrictions

Reporting restrictions in respect of allocation and sending proceedings are governed by the CDA 1998, s. 52A. The only details that may be published or broadcast are those permitted by s. 52A (s. 52A(1)).   **D10.12**

The purpose of the restrictions is to prevent potentially prejudicial reporting of the case prior to the conclusion of any trial. Therefore, s. 52A(6) makes it clear that the restrictions do not apply where the accused enters a plea of guilty at the 'plea before venue' hearing or after the conclusion of the accused's trial (or, where there is more than one defendant, the trial of the last to be tried).

Nature of Restrictions   The matters that may be reported are listed in the CDA 1998, s. 52A(7). They include the identity of the court and the name of the justice(s); the name, age, home address and occupation of the accused; the offence(s) with which the accused is or are charged; the names of counsel and solicitors engaged in the proceedings; arrangements regarding bail; and whether legal aid has been granted. Where notice has been given under s. 51B (serious fraud cases — see **D10.34**), the press may also report 'relevant business information' (defined in s. 52(9) to include the name and address of any business being carried on by the accused).   **D10.13**

Contravention of the reporting restrictions is an offence under s. 52B, punishable, on summary conviction, by a fine not exceeding level 5 on the standard scale (currently £5,000, but it will be an unlimited fine when the LASPO 2012, s. 85, comes into force). Proceedings may be brought only by, or with the consent of, the A-G.

Lifting the Restrictions   Under the CDA 1998, s. 52A(2), the magistrates can order that the restrictions do not apply to particular allocation or sending proceedings (in other words, they can lift the reporting restrictions). Where the accused (or any of the accused) objects to the lifting of the restrictions, the court may lift the restrictions only if it is satisfied, after hearing representations from (each of) the accused, that it is in the interests of justice to do so (s. 52A(3) and (4)).   **D10.14**

It is submitted that it should be very rare for the court to lift reporting restrictions other than upon an application by the accused, since the restrictions exist for the protection of the accused.

In *Leeds Justices, ex parte Sykes* [1983] 1 All ER 460, it was held (construing earlier legislation) that, in the event of disagreement between the defendants, the burden was on the accused who wanted reporting to show that it was in the interests of justice for the normal restrictions to be lifted. Griffiths LJ said (at pp. 134H–135B) that 'the interests of justice incorporate as a paramount consideration that the defendants should have a fair trial' and that, because Parliament has laid down a general rule against reporting, 'a powerful case' has to made out to lift the reporting restrictions. His lordship suggested, *obiter*, that an application for restrictions to be lifted on the ground that publicity might induce potential witnesses for the defendant making the application to come forward would 'merit really serious consideration by the justices' (*Ex parte Sykes*, at p. 137B).

The court must give all the co-accused a chance to make representations. Failure to do so is a serious breach of procedure and is likely to result in the quashing of the order lifting the reporting restrictions (*Wirral District Magistrates' Court, ex parte Meikle* (1990) 154 JP 1035).

D10.15   **Contempt of Court Act 1981**   The provisions dealing with cases where there are several accused and one of them wants to have the reporting restrictions lifted are necessary because, even if it were practicable to report only those parts of the proceedings relating to the accused who wants the restrictions lifted and omit everything relating to the others, the court has no power under the CDA 1998, s. 52A, to make an order to that effect. Construing earlier legislation, Griffiths LJ, in *Leeds Justices, ex parte Sykes* [1983] 1 All ER 460 (at p. 136A), said that 'If the reporting restrictions are to be lifted, then they are to be lifted . . . in their entirety. They cannot be lifted piecemeal'. The justices therefore cannot pick and choose which of the restrictions are lifted and which remain. However, it is submitted that they can achieve a similar result by first lifting reporting restrictions through an order under s. 52A and then making a further order under the Contempt of Court Act 1981, s. 4(2), postponing contemporaneous reporting of some of the evidence until after the trial on indictment (see *Horsham Justices, ex parte Farquharson* [1982] QB 762 and **D3.128**).

In *Sherwood, ex parte The Telegraph Group plc* [2001] 1 WLR 1983, Longmore LJ (at [22]) said that applications to postpone media coverage of court proceedings under the Contempt of Court Act 1981, s. 4(2), should be approached by way of a three-stage test:

(1) The first question is whether reporting would give rise to a 'not insubstantial' risk of prejudice to the administration of justice in the relevant proceedings. If not, that is the end of the matter.

(2) If such a risk is perceived to exist, then the second question arises: would a s. 4(2) order eliminate it? If not, there could clearly be no necessity to impose such a ban and that would be the end of the matter. On the other hand, even if the judge is satisfied that an order would achieve the objective, he still has to consider whether the risk could satisfactorily be overcome by some less restrictive means. If so, it could not be said to be 'necessary' to take the more drastic approach.

(3) If the judge concludes that there is no other way of eliminating the perceived risk of prejudice, it still does not follow necessarily that an order has to be made. The judge may still have to ask whether the degree of risk contemplated should be regarded as tolerable in the sense of being 'the lesser of two evils'. It is at this stage that value judgements might have to be made as to the priority between competing public interests.

This approach was cited with approval in *Re MGN Ltd* [2011] 1 Cr App R 387, where Lord Judge CJ summarised the approach, saying (at [15]) that 'an order under s. 4(2) of the 1981 Act should be regarded as a last resort'.

Effecting the Transfer: s. 51D

D10.16   Under the CJA 2003, s. 51D(1), the magistrates' court specifies, in a notice, the offence(s) for which the accused is being sent for trial and the location of the Crown Court where he is to be tried. A copy of the notice is served on the accused and a copy is sent to the Crown Court

(s. 51D(2)). The location of the Crown Court to which the accused is sent for trial is chosen by the magistrates having regard to the convenience of the defence, the prosecution and the witnesses; the desirability of expediting the trial (i.e. how soon a courtroom will become available); and any directions given by the Lord Chief Justice under the Senior Courts Act 1981, s. 75(1); CrimPR r. 9.3(3) (s. 51D(4)).

In *R (Bentham) v Governor of HM Prison Wandsworth* [2006] EWHC 121 (Admin), the accused argued that the notice failed to comply with the statutory requirements. The Divisional Court (anxious to discourage what Gross J described as a growth industry in unmeritorious complaints based on the drafting of such notices) ruled that the decision of substance is that of magistrates to send the accused to the Crown Court for trial. Only thereafter, and by way of an administrative act, is the notice prepared. No particular form is prescribed, nor is there any provision dealing with the consequences of a defective notice. It follows, said the court, that defects in the notice do not invalidate (or render ineffective) an otherwise valid (or effective) sending.

The various documents that the magistrates' court must send to the Crown Court are listed in the CrimPR, r. 9.5.

Each magistrates' court is informed of the location to which it should normally send defendants **D10.17** for trial, and (in the absence of any representations to the contrary by any of the parties) it will automatically send the accused to that location. Nonetheless, in some cases either the prosecution or the defence may invite the magistrates to send the case to a different location of the Crown Court. This may be appropriate if, for example, the offence with which the defendant is charged may have aroused such ill feeling locally that a fair trial at the nearest location of the Crown Court may not be possible. If the magistrates do not accede to a request to transfer the case to a particular location of the Crown Court, or if the location specified by the magistrates subsequently appears unsatisfactory to one of the parties, there are two other ways of moving the trial:

(a) the Senior Courts Act 1981, s. 76(2), empowers an officer of the Crown Court to alter the place of trial;

(b) if the transfer is not effected administratively, either party may make an application to the Crown Court, under s. 76(3) of the 1981 Act for the venue of the trial to be altered. Applications to vary the location of the trial under s. 76 are heard by a Crown Court judge, usually sitting in chambers.

Service of Evidence and Draft Indictment

Under the Crime and Disorder Act 1998 (Service of Prosecution Evidence) Regulations 2005 **D10.18** (SI 2005 No. 902), reg. 2, where a person is sent for trial under s. 51, copies of the documents containing the evidence on which the charge(s) are based must, within 70 days (50 days if the accused is in custody) from the date on which the accused was sent for trial, be served on the accused and on the Crown Court. Under reg. 3, the prosecutor may apply orally or in writing to the Crown Court for an extension (or further extension) of that period. Where the prosecutor wishes to make an oral application under reg. 3, written notice of the intention to do so must be given to the court and to the accused (reg. 4). Under reg. 5, any written application under reg. 3 must be sent to the court and to the accused, and must specify the grounds for the application. The accused may make written representations in response within three days of service of the application on him.

In *Fehily v Governor of Wandsworth Prison* [2003] 1 Cr App R 153, the Divisional Court held that failure by the prosecution to comply with the time-limit does not render the prosecution a nullity. Furthermore, the Crown Court has jurisdiction to extend time on an application by the prosecution even if the application is made after the expiry of the time-limit.

The draft indictment must be served on the Crown Court within 28 days of service on the **D10.19** accused of the copies of the documents containing the evidence on which the charge(s) are based

(CrimPR, r. 14.1(1)(a)). The indictment may contain any count that is supported by the evidence contained in the papers served by the prosecution, either in addition to or in substitution for the charges upon which the defendant was sent to the Crown Court by the magistrates' court (see the Administration of Justice (Miscellaneous Provisions) Act 1933, s. 2(2)). Any such counts must, however, be capable of being joined in the same indictment without breaching the CrimPR, r. 14.2(3), and so must be founded on the same facts or form (part of) a series of offences of the same or a similar character (see *Lombardi* [1989] 1 All ER 992 and **D11.14** *et seq.*).

Legal Aid

D10.20   The grant of legal aid for the Crown Court is governed by the LASPO 2012, ss. 16 to 20. See **D32** for discussion of legal aid.

Appearance in the Crown Court

D10.21   Under the CDA 1998, s. 52(1), the accused may be sent to the Crown Court in custody or on bail. It should be borne in mind that the presumption in favour of bail (under the Bail Act 1976, s. 4) continues to operate in favour of the accused, and so bail may be withheld only if one or more of the statutory grounds for withholding bail under sch. 1 to the 1976 Act are made out (see **D7.11** *et seq.*).

In appropriate cases, the first appearance at the Crown Court will be for a 'preliminary hearing'. However, a preliminary hearing is not required in every case sent for trial under the CDA 1998, s. 51. CPD I, para. 3A.9 (see Supplement, **PD-3**), states that a preliminary hearing should be ordered by the magistrates' court (or by the Crown Court) only where there are case management issues which call for such a hearing, the case is likely to last for more than four weeks or it would be desirable to set an early trial date, or the accused is a child or young person. If such a hearing is necessary, it should be held 14 to 21 days after the accused is sent to the Crown Court for trial.

Paragraph 3A.10 goes on to provide that, where the magistrates' court does not order a preliminary hearing, it should order a plea and case management hearing ('PCMH'), to be held approximately 13 weeks after the accused was sent for trial, if he was remanded in custody (16 weeks if he is on bail).

Early Guilty Plea Hearings

D10.22   CPD I, para. 3A.6 (see Supplement, **PD-3**), makes provision for early guilty plea hearings, to allow the Crown Court to deal promptly with a case where the accused wishes to plead guilty. This will be of relevance principally to indictable-only offences (since the accused can enter a guilty plea in the magistrates' court, at the plea before venue hearing, if the offence is triable either way). Sentence should normally be passed at an early guilty plea hearing (para. 3A.7), and any issues related to the basis of plea need to be sorted out beforehand, and a pre-sentence report (if required) obtained prior to the hearing.

Applications for Dismissal

D10.23   Under the CDA 1998, sch. 3, para. 2(1), the accused may (after the date when he is served with the documents containing the evidence on which the charge(s) are based, but before the date of the arraignment) apply orally or in writing to the Crown Court for the charge(s) to be dismissed. Where such an application is made, the judge must dismiss any charge (and quash any count relating to it in the indictment) if it appears to him that the evidence against the applicant 'would not be sufficient for him to be properly convicted' (para. 2(2)).

D10.24   **Procedure**   The accused may make an oral application for dismissal only if he gives written notice of intention to do so (CDA 1998, sch. 3, para. 2(3)). Paragraphs 2(4) and (5) formerly permitted oral evidence to be adduced, with the leave of the judge, but those paragraphs have been repealed. It follows that oral evidence cannot be adduced at an application for dismissal of a charge sent to the Crown Court under s. 51.

The procedure for an application to dismiss a charge is contained in the CrimPR, r.9.16 (see Supplement, R-113). Rule 9.16(2)(a) requires the accused to apply in writing not more than 28 days after service of the prosecution evidence. Copies of the application must be served on the prosecution and on any co-accused (r. 9.16(2)(b)). The application must 'explain why the prosecution evidence would not be sufficient for the defendant to be properly convicted'; ask for a hearing, if the accused wants one (and explain why a hearing is needed); identify any witnesses whom the accused wants to call to testify; and identify any material that the accused thinks will be needed to determine the application (r. 9.16(2)(c)). If the prosecution wish to oppose the application, they must serve notice to that effect not more than 14 days after service of the accused's notice, explaining their grounds of opposition, explaining why a hearing is needed if the prosecution are seeking one and identifying any witnesses and relevant material (r. 9.16(3)). Under r. 9.16(4), the court may determine the application at a hearing (in public or in private) or without a hearing. The court may shorten or extend the limits imposed by r. 9.16 (r. 9.16(5)(a)).

D10.25 Where a charge is dismissed under the CDA 1998, sch. 3, para. 2, further proceedings in respect of that charge may be brought only by means of the preferment of a voluntary bill of indictment (para. 2(6)). In *Arfan* (2012) 176 JP 682, Nicol J noted (at [23]) that, where an application to dismiss a case sent to the Crown Court has been successful, caution should be exercised before a High Court judge grants leave to prefer a voluntary bill of indictment, and went on to say:

> Without attempting to give an exhaustive list, there may be circumstances which would justify the granting of leave if the judge who had dismissed the charge had taken the decision without regard to a relevant statutory provision or judicial authority, or had otherwise erred in law, or if the Crown had new evidence which made a significant difference to its case, or if the decision to dismiss lacked a rational foundation.

Thus, an application for a voluntary bill 'will only succeed if the Crown can show that the circumstances are exceptional' (at [25]). This follows the approach taken in earlier cases, such as *Davenport* [2005] EWHC 2828 (QB), where Pitchers J said that an obvious example of where a voluntary bill would be appropriate 'would be if the judge had not had a crucial authority or statutory provision drawn to his attention' (at [23]), or where 'the prosecution can produce fresh cogent evidence which was not before the judge who dismissed the charges' (at [26]) (cited with approval by Griffith Williams J in *McGuiness* [2007] EWHC 1772 (QB), at [6]). The need for exceptional circumstances was emphasised again in *Dady* [2013] EWHC 475 (QB).

D10.26 **Challenging the Decision to Dismiss a Charge**   The accused cannot challenge the decision of the Crown Court judge not to dismiss a charge under the CDA 1998, sch. 3, para. 2, by way of judicial review. In *R (Snelgrove) v Woolwich Crown Court* [2005] 1 WLR 3223, the accused was charged with an indictable-only offence and made an application for the charge to be dismissed (under para. 2). The judge refused to dismiss the charge against the accused, who then applied for judicial review. The Divisional Court held that a decision under sch. 3 not to dismiss the charge is an order in a matter relating to trial on indictment for the purposes of the Senior Courts Act 1981, s. 29(3), and so judicial review is not available. The court reasoned that, following the sending of a case to the Crown Court, that court is seised of the matter and of all decisions concerning the issue between the accused and the Crown, and so those decisions necessarily relate to the trial on indictment; moreover, a decision whether to dismiss the charge affects the conduct of the trial, in that it determines whether or not the trial proceeds (per Auld LJ at [43]). The court ruled (at [44]) that *Central Criminal Court and Nadir, ex parte Director of Serious Fraud Office*, where the contrary decision had been reached, should be regarded as wrongly decided.

In *R (O) v Central Criminal Court* [2006] EWHC 256 (Admin), the Divisional Court re-affirmed that a judge's decision to refuse to dismiss a case under the CDA 1988, sch. 3, para. 2, was a matter relating to trial on indictment, and therefore not susceptible to judicial review.

In *Thompson* [2007] 2 All ER 205, it was held that the Crown's right of appeal under the CJA 2003, s. 58 (see **D16.74** *et seq.*), does not extend to a judge's ruling pursuant to the CDA 1998, sch. 3, para. 2, since that procedure can only lead to the dismissal of a charge or the quashing of an indictment, rather than the acquittal of the defendant. It follows that the only remedy for the prosecution in the face of the dismissal of a charge is to seek the preferment of a voluntary bill of indictment under sch. 3, para. 2(6).

D10.27   **Test on Dismissal Applications**   In *R (Inland Revenue Commissioners) v Crown Court at Kingston* [2001] 4 All ER 721, it was held that, on an application to dismiss (under earlier legislation), the judge was required to take into account the whole of the evidence against the accused, and that it was not appropriate for the judge to view any evidence in isolation from its context and other evidence (per Stanley Burnton J at [16]). The judge is not bound to assume that a jury would make every possible inference capable of being drawn against the accused but, where the case depends on the inferences or conclusions to be drawn from the evidence, the judge must assess the inferences or conclusions that the prosecution propose to ask the jury to draw, and decide whether it appears to him that the jury could properly draw those inferences and come to those conclusions (at [16]). It is submitted that the same principles would necessarily apply to applications to dismiss under the CDA 1998, sch. 3, para. 2. The decision in *R (Snelgrove) v Woolwich Crown Court* [2005] 1 WLR 3223 (see **D10.26**) means that the court in *R (Inland Revenue Commissioners) v Crown Court at Kingston* should not have entertained the application for judicial review of the decision of the Crown Court judge, but it is submitted that the Divisional Court's ruling about the test to be applied in such cases remains valid nonetheless.

D10.28   **Reporting Restrictions**   Reporting restrictions in relation to applications for the dismissal of charges are governed by the CDA 1998, sch. 3, para. 3. The restrictions apply automatically but can be lifted, under para. 3(2), by the judge dealing with the application. Under para. 3(8), reporting must be limited to details such as the identity of the judge, the names, ages, home addresses and occupations of the accused and witnesses; the offence(s) with which the defendant(s) are charged; the names of counsel and solicitors engaged in the proceedings; arrangements as to bail; whether legal aid has been granted. Contravention of these restrictions is a summary offence under para. 3(10), carrying a fine not exceeding level 5 (currently £5,000, but it will become an unlimited fine when the LASPO 2012, s. 85, is fully implemented). Where there is more than one defendant, and one of them objects to the making of an order lifting the restrictions, the judge is required to lift them if, and only if, he is satisfied (after hearing representations from the defendants) that it is in the interests of justice to do so (para. 3(3)).

Power of Crown Court to Deal with Summary Offence

D10.29   The CDA 1998, sch. 3, para. 6, sets out what happens when the accused is sent for trial for a related summary offence. If the accused is convicted on the indictment, the Crown Court judge has first to consider whether the summary offence is indeed related to the indictable offence(s) for which he was sent for trial. For these purposes, the summary offence is related to the indictable offence if it 'arises out of circumstances which are the same as or connected with those giving rise' to the indictable offence (para. 6(12)). If the judge is so satisfied, the accused is asked to enter a plea (para. 6(3)). If the accused pleads guilty, the Crown Court will pass sentence, but subject to the limitations on sentence applicable to a magistrates' court (para. 6(4)). If he pleads not guilty, para. 6(5) provides that the powers of the Crown Court cease in respect of the summary offence, save that the Crown Court may dismiss the charge if the prosecution indicate that they do not wish to proceed with the charge (para. 6(6)); if the prosecution wish to proceed with the charge, they have to do so in the magistrates' court.

Paragraph 6(8) makes it clear that the provisions of para. 6 do not apply where the summary offence in question is one to which the CJA 1988, s. 40, applies (see **D11.17**) and that offence has been added to the indictment.

The Courts Act 2003, s. 66, affects the power of the Crown Court to deal with summary-only offences in that it confers on Crown Court judges the 'powers of a justice of the peace who is a District Judge (Magistrates' Courts)'. It is submitted that the effect of this provision is that, if the Crown Court is left with a summary offence, the judge may, if the accused pleads not guilty, try the offence as if he were a magistrate instead of the accused being tried in a magistrates' court for the summary offence. It should be emphasised that this provision simply empowers the Crown Court judge to try the summary offence as if he were a magistrate, and so there is no obligation to do so. If the judge chooses not to try the offence, the trial will (assuming the prosecution wish to proceed with it) take place in the magistrates' court (the proceedings in the magistrates' court for the summary offence being treated, by virtue of the CDA 1998, s. 51(10), as if the court had adjourned them under the MCA 1980, s.10, without fixing the time and place for their resumption, when the summary offence was sent to the Crown Court under s. 51).

If the Court of Appeal quashes a conviction for the indictable offence to which a summary offence is related, that court must also set aside the conviction for the summary offence and may direct that no further proceedings in relation to the offence are to be undertaken (para. 6(9)). If the Court of Appeal does not so direct, it is open to the prosecution to proceed against the accused in the magistrates' court in respect of that summary offence.

In *Iles* (2012) 176 JP 601 the Court of Appeal considered a practice that had developed, whereby magistrates' courts adjourned summary-only matters, knowing the offender was due to appear at a Crown Court on other matters, and invited the Crown Court to enable the summary cases to be dealt with at the same time by the expedient of arranging for a circuit judge to sit as a district judge (under the Courts Act 2003, s. 66). Walker J said (at [3]) that such a practice has advantages, but there are also dangers, and so before this practice is followed, the magistrates' court must carefully consider whether it is in the interests of justice to do so, and ensure that there is power to do so. A Crown Court judge who is invited to deal with two sets of proceedings in this way must decide, in the light of submissions from both the prosecution and the defence, whether it is appropriate to do so. It must be borne in mind that: (1) the judge would, as regards the magistrates' court matters, be limited to the powers of a magistrates' court; and (2) sentences that the judge imposes when sitting as a district judge would have a different route of appeal from that applicable to sentences imposed by the judge when sitting as a Crown Court judge. If the invitation is accepted, consideration must again be given to these dangers at the stage of deciding what sentence should be imposed by the judge when sitting as a district judge.

Accused No Longer Facing an Offence Sent for Trial

The CDA 1998, sch. 3, para. 7, deals with the procedure to be adopted where the accused has **D10.30** been sent for trial for an indictable offence but, as a result of amendment of the indictment or because of a successful application for one or more charges to be dismissed, the indictment no longer includes a 'main offence'. The term 'main offence' is defined in para. 7(9) as either (a) an offence for which the accused has been sent to the Crown Court for trial under s. 51(1), or (b) an offence for which the accused has been sent for trial under s. 51(5) (which applies where there is a related either-way offence) or s. 51A(6) (which applies where there is a juvenile co-accused and an adult is charged with a related either-way offence), in respect of which the conditions for sending him to the Crown Court for trial under the relevant subsection continue to be satisfied.

If the accused still faces an allegation of an either-way offence, the Crown Court has to go through a mode of trial procedure, which preserves the accused's right to be tried summarily for an either-way offence only where he consents and also preserves the court's discretion to rule that the case is too serious for summary trial. First, he is asked to indicate whether he intends to plead guilty or not guilty (para. 7(5)). If he indicates a guilty plea, the Crown Court proceeds to the sentencing stage for that offence (para. 7(6)). If he indicates a not guilty plea, the court decides whether the case is more suitable for summary trial or for trial on indictment (para. 7(7)). Paragraph 8 enables the court to proceed under para. 7 in the absence of the accused where the accused is legally represented and the court considers that, because of his disorderly conduct before the court, it is not practicable to conduct the proceedings in his presence. In such a case, the representative is asked to give the indication as to plea.

Before deciding whether the case is more suitable for summary trial or for trial on indictment, the court must give the prosecution an opportunity to inform the court of the accused's previous convictions (if any) and must give the prosecution and the accused an opportunity to make representations as to whether summary trial or trial on indictment would be more suitable (para. 9(2)). In reaching its decision, the court has to consider whether the sentence that a magistrates' court would have power to impose for the offence(s) would be adequate, and must have regard to the allocation guidelines issued by the Sentencing Council under the CAJA 2009, s. 122 (para. 9(3)). Under para. 10, if the Crown Court considers that an offence is more suitable for summary trial, the accused is given the choice of trial on indictment or summary trial. If the Crown Court considers that the offence is more suitable for trial on indictment, the accused is informed that this is so (para. 11).

It should be noted that the special procedure for determining mode of trial for criminal damage where the value involved is less than £5,000 (see the MCA 1980, s. 22, at **D6.23**) is also applicable in this context (para. 14).

D10.31 These 'plea before venue' and mode of trial proceedings can be dealt with in the absence of the accused if the accused is legally represented, the legal representative signifies the accused's consent to the proceedings being conducted in his absence, and the court is satisfied that there is good reason for proceeding in the absence of the accused (para. 15(1)). If the court decides that the case is more suitable for summary trial and the legal representative indicates that the accused wishes to be tried summarily, the court will remit the accused for trial to the magistrates' court; otherwise, the trial will take place in the Crown Court (para. 15(3)).

In *Ashton* [2007] 1 WLR 181, the Court of Appeal held (at [55]) that a Crown Court judge exercising his powers to sit as a district judge under the Courts Act 2003, s. 66, may determine mode of trial and (assuming the accused pleads guilty or, following summary trial in front of the judge sitting as a district judge, is found guilty) then commit the defendant for sentence and then (sitting as a Crown Court judge) sit as the sentencing court.

D10.32 **Procedural Irregularities**   In *Haye* [2003] Crim LR 287, the accused was charged with robbery. He was sent for trial at the Crown Court pursuant to the CDA 1998, s. 51. At the plea and case management hearing in the Crown Court, the prosecution dropped the charge of robbery (an indictable-only offence) and replaced it with a charge of theft (triable either way). The accused pleaded not guilty to the theft charge. When the matter came on for trial, the accused was re-arraigned on the theft charge and entered a guilty plea. He subsequently appealed against conviction on the ground that the procedure set out in the CDA 1998, sch. 3, para. 7, had not been followed prior to the arraignment on the theft charge. In particular, he complained that proper consideration had not been given to the question of whether he should be tried summarily or whether the Crown Court should continue to deal with the case. He argued that the proceedings that followed the plea of guilty were, therefore, a nullity. The Court of Appeal agreed, holding that any failure to comply with the statutory procedure in relation to the right of an accused to make representations and/or to exercise choice as to mode of trial would have the consequence that, if the matter proceeded to trial, the hearing would be regarded as *ultra vires* and liable to be quashed. In the present case, the accused had been deprived of an opportunity of seeking to persuade the judge that summary trial would be more suitable. It followed that the proceedings in relation to the indictment alleging theft were a nullity.

However, *Haye* was considered by the Court of Appeal in *Ashton* [2007] 1 WLR 181. The Court said that, in the light of the decision of the House of Lords in *Soneji* [2006] 1 AC 340 and the earlier Court of Appeal decision in *Sekhon* [2003] 3 All ER 508, 'we are confident that if *Haye* was decided now the result would have been the other way' (per Fulford J at [69]). The Court reached this conclusion on the basis that, in the light of those two authorities and of the overriding objective in the CrimPR, and in the absence of a clear indication that Parliament intended jurisdiction automatically to be removed following a procedural failure, the decision of the court should be based on an assessment of the interests of justice and, in particular, on whether there is a real possibility that the prosecution or the defence might suffer prejudice. If there is a risk of prejudice, a court should go on to decide whether it is just to permit the proceedings to continue. In other words, procedural failings do not generally render the proceedings invalid, they merely give the court a discretion whether or not to proceed with the case (*Ashton* at [4] and [9]).

The approach laid down by *Ashton* was followed in *Thwaites* [2006] EWCA Crim 3235, where   **D10.33** the accused was sent for trial to the Crown Court charged with conspiracy to handle stolen goods. However, he was arraigned and tried on an indictment containing counts of burglary, but no indictable-only offence. During the course of the trial, it was discovered that the judge had failed to conduct the mode of trial procedure required by the CDA 1998, sch. 3, in respect of the either-way charges on the indictment. The trial judge ruled that, had the correct procedure been followed, the case would have been found as suitable only for trial on indictment, and so the accused had suffered no prejudice from the failure to conduct the mode of trial procedure. The Court of Appeal agreed, holding that earlier authorities such as *Haye* are no longer good law and that there was no unfairness or prejudice to the accused, who had received a fair trial.

The Court of Appeal revisited the consequences of failure to comply with para. 7 in *Gul* [2013] 1 WLR 1136. The accused had been sent for trial in respect of an indictable-only offence but the indictment as eventually drafted contained only either-way offences. The Crown Court did not go through the procedure laid down in para. 7, but instead simply took the accused's plea. The accused pleaded not guilty but was convicted by a jury. The Court of Appeal rejected the argument that the trial was a nullity. Lord Judge CJ (at [23]–[24]) said:

> The entitlement of the defendant is to make submissions in support of summary trial if he wishes to do so, but the defendant does not enjoy an unfettered entitlement to summary trial. The ultimate decision must be made by the court. If however the defendant wishes to be tried summarily and the court has failed to give him the opportunity to ask for it, there is nothing in the procedure which prevents an application by him to that effect…. If the decision is made by the Crown Court that the case is more suitable for summary trial, only then does the defendant have the right to elect trial by jury. He has no corresponding right to elect summary trial…the complaint here is no more and no less than that the defendant, like the prosecution, was not invited to make representations about the mode of trial. Thereafter no application to do so was made. The omission of that procedural step did not vitiate the indictment or the process before the Crown Court…What is more, any defect in the process, which meant that the defendant was not invited to make submissions about the possible suitability of summary trial was readily curable: the defendant could and should have made an appropriate application. In these circumstances, with a remedy available to the defendant, it is inconceivable that Parliament intended that the consequence of non-compliance would be to render subsequent proceedings in the Crown Court a nullity.

It is clear from this that the approach taken in *Thwaites* is to be preferred to that taken in *Haye*.

Notices in Serious or Complex Fraud Cases: s. 51B

The CDA 1998, s. 51B, replaces the CJA 1987, s. 4.   **D10.34**

Under the CDA 1998, s. 51B(1), a notice may be given in respect of an indictable offence if the prosecution are of the opinion (a subjective test) that the evidence in the case (a) is sufficient for the person charged to be put on trial for the offence, and (b) reveals a case of fraud 'of such seriousness or complexity that it is appropriate that the management of the case should without delay be taken over by the Crown Court'. This provision applies only where the prosecution is being brought by a 'designated authority' (or under s. 51B(7), one of its officers). The designated authorities are the DPP (this includes the CPS, since the DPP is head of the CPS and able to delegate his powers to Crown Prosecutors), the Director of the Serious Fraud Office, and the Secretary of State (s. 51B(9)). Where a notice has been given to the magistrates' court under s. 51B, the case must be sent forthwith to the Crown Court for trial, under s. 51(1). Under s. 51B(6), the effect of the notice under s. 51B is that, apart from ancillary matters such as granting bail and legal aid, the functions of the magistrates' court cease in relation to the case.

In the unlikely event that the magistrates accept jurisdiction at a mode of trial hearing in such a case, any such notice must be given before any summary trial begins (s. 51B(5)). The effect of the notice is that, apart from ancillary matters such as granting bail and legal aid, the functions of the magistrates' court cease in relation to the case (s. 51B(6)). A decision to give a notice under s. 51B is not subject to appeal and cannot be questioned in any court (s. 51B(8)).

The notice, which must be given to the magistrates' court at which the accused appears (s. 51B(4)), must specify the proposed place of trial; in selecting that place, s. 51B(3) provides that the designated authority must have regard to the same matters as magistrates have to take into account (under s. 51D(4)) when deciding where to send an accused for trial (see **D10.16**). The indictment must be preferred within 28 days of the giving of notice (subject to the power of the Crown Court to extend that time limit): see the CrimPR, r. 14.1.

D10.35   In *Wrench* [1996] 1 Cr App R 340 (decided under the 1987 Act), it was held that, if one of the charges is one to which the transfer provisions apply, then the procedure can also be used in respect of any other offences which can validly be joined on the same indictment. (This aspect of *Wrench* is not affected by the disapproval of that case in *T and K* [2001] 1 Cr App R 446.) It is submitted that the same principle would apply to transfers under s. 51B.

Because the case is sent to the Crown Court under s. 51, the ability to apply to the Crown Court for the charges to be dismissed (under the CDA 1998, sch. 3, para. 2) applies equally where a notice is given under s. 51B.

Notices in Certain Cases Involving Children: s. 51C

D10.36   The CDA 1998, s. 51C, replaces the CJA 1991, s. 53.

Under the CDA 1998, s. 51C(1), a notice may be given by the DPP (in practice, notice will usually be given by a Crown Prosecutor, since the DPP is able to delegate this function under s. 51C(5)) if he is of the opinion (a subjective test) that (a) the evidence in the case is sufficient for the person charged to be put on trial for the offence, (b) a child will be called as a witness at the trial and (c) in order to avoid any prejudice to the welfare of the child, the case 'should be taken over and proceeded with without delay by the Crown Court'. This provision applies only to the offences specified in s. 51C(3), which lists a number of specific sexual or violent offences but also includes any offence that involves an assault on, or injury or a threat of injury to, a person. Where a notice has been given to a magistrates' court under s. 51C, the case must be sent forthwith to the Crown Court for trial, under s. 51(1). A decision to give a notice under s. 51C is not subject to appeal and cannot be questioned in any court (s. 51C(6)).

For the purposes of s. 51C, 'child' is defined in s. 51C(7) as a person who is under the age of 17 or any person of whom a video recording (as defined in the YJCEA 1999, s. 63(1)) was made when he was under the age of 17 with a view to its admission as his evidence in chief in the trial.

D10.37   Under s. 51C(4), the effect of the notice under s. 51C is that, apart from ancillary matters such as granting bail and legal aid, the functions of the magistrates' court cease in relation to the case. The indictment must be preferred within 28 days of the giving of notice (subject to the power of the Crown Court to extend that time limit): see the CrimPR, r. 14.1.

Cases where notice has been served under s. 51C are sent for trial under s. 51, and so it is possible for the accused to apply to the Crown Court for the dismissal of the charge(s) under the CDA 1998, sch. 3, para. 2.

Juvenile Accused   In *Fareham Youth Court and Morey, ex parte CPS* (1999) 163 JP 812, it was held   D10.38
that in the case of a juvenile where the youth court has determined that he should be tried summarily,
the prosecution cannot reverse that decision by issue of a notice of transfer. In *T and K* [2001] 1 Cr
App R 446, Kay LJ (at [37]) said that, where the defendant is a juvenile, the DPP should not transfer
the case to the Crown Court unless satisfied that a magistrates' court would be likely to find that it
ought to be possible to sentence the defendant under the PCC(S)A 2000, s. 91 (see **D24.25** *et seq.*).

Depositions for Use in the Trial

The CDA 1998, sch. 3, para. 4, empowers a magistrate to issue a summons requiring a person to   D10.39
attend before a magistrate to have evidence taken in the form of a deposition. Under para. 4(1),
before issuing the summons, the magistrate must be satisfied that the person is likely to be able to
give material evidence (or to produce a relevant document or other exhibit) on behalf of the prosecution for an offence that has been sent to the Crown Court for trial, and that it is in the interests
of justice to issue a summons to secure the attendance of the witness. Under the CrimPR, part
28, the procedure for obtaining a witness summons under para. 4 is the same as in the case of
an application for a witness summons in the context of a summary trial or trial on indictment.

If the prosecutor makes the application on oath and the magistrate is satisfied that the summons would not result in the attendance of the witness, the magistrate may issue an arrest
warrant instead of a summons (para. 4(3)). If a summons is issued and the witness fails to
attend in answer to the summons, an arrest warrant may be issued (para. 4(5)) and the witness
is liable to be committed to custody for up to a month or be fined up to £2,500 (para. 4(7)).

Where evidence has been taken as a deposition under para. 4, para. 5(2) provides that the depo-   D10.40
sition may be read as evidence at the trial unless (under para. 5(3)) the trial judge orders that this
should not be so or a party to the proceedings objects to the use of the deposition.

The Divisional Court considered this power in *R (CPS) v Bolton Magistrates' Court* [2004] 2 All
ER 848, granting a declaration that the procedure of taking a deposition from a witness who
will not voluntarily make a statement is a 'proceeding in open court'. In the circumstances of a
particular case, however, the justices may exceptionally exclude persons from the taking of the
deposition or otherwise modify the procedure where that will assist in the reception of the evidence or is in the interests of justice to do so. There is, however, no basis for excluding the party
seeking the deposition, which will include the CPS and representatives of the investigating
authority. Kennedy LJ went on to hold (at [23]) that lawyers representing those sent for trial are
entitled to be present unless there is some special reason for excluding them. Nonetheless, anyone seeking to cross-examine the witness should normally be told to reserve cross-examination
for the Crown Court. However, in a case where the reluctant witness is likely to be unavailable
at the Crown Court, or can perhaps be spared attendance there if one or two questions are asked
at the earlier stage, it would be open to the justice to permit cross-examination.

This procedure is not available to the defence, since its object is to facilitate the gathering of
evidence for the prosecution.

Discontinuance of the Prosecution Case

The prosecution may discontinue the case against the accused not only in the magistrates' court,   D10.41
but also, in the case of offences sent up to the Crown Court under the CDA 1998, s. 51, at any
time before the indictment is preferred (Prosecution of Offences Act 1985, s. 23A: see **D3.65**).

Abuse of Process: the Discretion to Discharge an Accused

The fact that a magistrates' court has a duty under the CDA 1998, s. 51(1), to send the case to   D10.42
the Crown Court 'forthwith' does not necessarily preclude the court from exercising its jurisdiction to stay the proceedings as an abuse of process in an appropriate case, though such cases will
be very rare (*R (Salubi) v Bow Street Magistrates' Court* [2002] 1 WLR 3073, per Auld LJ at [20]).
For discussion of abuse of process, see **D3.70** *et seq.*

D

Part D Procedure

Statutory Materials

D10.43   Crime and Disorder Act 1998, ss. 50A, 51, 51B, 51C, 51D, 51E, 52, 52A and 52B and sch. 3

50A.—(1) Where an adult appears or is brought before a magistrates' court charged with an either-way offence (the 'relevant offence'), the court shall proceed in the manner described in this section.

(2) If notice is given in respect of the relevant offence under section 51B or 51C below, the court shall deal with the offence as provided in section 51 below.

(3) Otherwise—

   (a) if the adult (or another adult with whom the adult is charged jointly with the relevant offence) is or has been sent to the Crown Court for trial for an offence under section 51(2)(a) or 51(2)(c) below—

      (i) the court shall first consider the relevant offence under subsection (3), (4), (5) or, as the case may be, (6) of section 51 below and, where applicable, deal with it under that subsection;

      (ii) if the adult is not sent to the Crown Court for trial for the relevant offence by virtue of sub-paragraph (i) above, the court shall then proceed to deal with the relevant offence in accordance with sections 17A to 23 of the 1980 Act;

   (b) in all other cases—

      (i) the court shall first consider the relevant offence under sections 17A to 20 (excluding subsections (8) and (9) of section 20) of the 1980 Act;

      (ii) if, by virtue of sub-paragraph (i) above, the court would be required to proceed in relation to the offence as mentioned in section 17A(6), 17B(2)(c) or 20(7) of that Act (indication of guilty plea), it shall proceed as so required (and, accordingly, shall not consider the offence under section 51 or 51A below);

      (iii) if sub-paragraph (ii) above does not apply—

         (a) the court shall consider the relevant offence under sections 51 and 51A below and, where applicable, deal with it under the relevant section;

         (b) if the adult is not sent to the Crown Court for trial for the relevant offence by virtue of paragraph (a) of this sub-paragraph, the court shall then proceed to deal with the relevant offence as contemplated by section 20(9) or, as the case may be, section 21 of the 1980 Act.

(4) Subsection (3) above is subject to any requirement to proceed as mentioned in subsections (2) or (6)(a) of section 22 of the 1980 Act (certain offences where value involved is small).

(5) Nothing in this section shall prevent the court from committing the adult to the Crown Court for sentence pursuant to any enactment, if he is convicted of the relevant offence.

51.—(1) Where an adult appears or is brought before a magistrates' court ('the court') charged with an offence and any of the conditions mentioned in subsection (2) below is satisfied, the court shall send him forthwith to the Crown Court for trial for the offence.

(2) Those conditions are—

   (a) that the offence is an offence triable only on indictment other than one in respect of which notice has been given under section 51B or 51C below;

   (b) that the offence is an either-way offence and the court is required under section 20(9)(b), 21, 23(4)(b) or (5) or 25(2D) of the Magistrates' Courts Act 1980 to proceed in relation to the offence in accordance with subsection (1) above;

   (c) that notice is given to the court under section 51B or 51C below in respect of the offence.

(3) Where the court sends an adult for trial under subsection (1) above, it shall at the same time send him to the Crown Court for trial for any either-way or summary offence with which he is charged and which—

   (a) (if it is an either-way offence) appears to the court to be related to the offence mentioned in subsection (1) above; or

   (b) (if it is a summary offence) appears to the court to be related to the offence mentioned in subsection (1) above or to the either-way offence, and which fulfils the requisite condition (as defined in subsection (11) below).

(4) Where an adult who has been sent for trial under subsection (1) above subsequently appears or is brought before a magistrates' court charged with an either-way or summary offence which—

   (a) appears to the court to be related to the offence mentioned in subsection (1) above; and

   (b) (in the case of a summary offence) fulfils the requisite condition,

the court may send him forthwith to the Crown Court for trial for the either-way or summary offence.

(5) Where—
    (a) the court sends an adult ('A') for trial under subsection (1) or (3) above;
    (b) another adult appears or is brought before the court on the same or a subsequent occasion charged jointly with A with an either-way offence; and
    (c) that offence appears to the court to be related to an offence for which A was sent for trial under subsection (1) or (3) above,
the court shall where it is the same occasion, and may where it is a subsequent occasion, send the other adult forthwith to the Crown Court for trial for the either-way offence.

(6) Where the court sends an adult for trial under subsection (5) above, it shall at the same time send him to the Crown Court for trial for any either-way or summary offence with which he is charged and which—
    (a) (if it is an either-way offence) appears to the court to be related to the offence for which he is sent for trial; and
    (b) (if it is a summary offence) appears to the court to be related to the offence for which he is sent for trial or to the either-way offence, and which fulfils the requisite condition.

(7) Where—
    (a) the court sends an adult ('A') for trial under subsection (1), (3) or (5) above; and
    (b) a child or young person appears or is brought before the court on the same or a subsequent occasion charged jointly with A with an indictable offence for which A is sent for trial under subsection (1), (3) or (5) above, or an indictable offence which appears to the court to be related to that offence,
the court shall, if it considers it necessary in the interests of justice to do so, send the child or young person forthwith to the Crown Court for trial for the indictable offence.

(8) Where the court sends a child or young person for trial under subsection (7) above, it may at the same time send him to the Crown Court for trial for any indictable or summary offence with which he is charged and which—
    (a) (if it is an indictable offence) appears to the court to be related to the offence for which he is sent for trial; and
    (b) (if it is a summary offence) appears to the court to be related to the offence for which he is sent for trial or to the indictable offence, and which fulfils the requisite condition.

(9) Subsections (7) and (8) above are subject to sections 24A and 24B of the Magistrates' Courts Act 1980 (which provide for certain cases involving children and young persons to be tried summarily).

(10) The trial of the information charging any summary offence for which a person is sent for trial under this section shall be treated as if the court had adjourned it under section 10 of the 1980 Act and had not fixed the time and place for its resumption.

(11) A summary offence fulfils the requisite condition if it is punishable with imprisonment or involves obligatory or discretionary disqualification from driving.

(12) In the case of an adult charged with an offence—
    (a) if the offence satisfies paragraph (c) of subsection (2) above, the offence shall be dealt with under subsection (1) above and not under any other provision of this section or section 51A below;
    (b) subject to paragraph (a) above, if the offence is one in respect of which the court is required to, or would decide to, send the adult to the Crown Court under—
        (i) subsection (5) above; or
        (ii) subsection (6) of section 51A below,
the offence shall be dealt with under that subsection and not under any other provision of this section or section 51A below.

(13) The functions of a magistrates' court under this section, and its related functions under section 51D below, may be discharged by a single justice.

. . .

51B.—(1) A notice may be given by a designated authority under this section in respect of an indictable offence if the authority is of the opinion that the evidence of the offence charged—
    (a) is sufficient for the person charged to be put on trial for the offence; and
    (b) reveals a case of fraud of such seriousness or complexity that it is appropriate that the management of the case should without delay be taken over by the Crown Court.

(2) That opinion must be certified by the designated authority in the notice.

(3) The notice must also specify the proposed place of trial, and in selecting that place the designated authority must have regard to the same matters as are specified in paragraphs (a) to (c) of section 51D(4) below.

(4) A notice under this section must be given to the magistrates' court at which the person charged appears or before which he is brought.

(5) Such a notice must be given to the magistrates' court before any summary trial begins.

(6) The effect of such a notice is that the functions of the magistrates' court cease in relation to the case, except—

    (a) for the purposes of section 51D below;

    (b) as provided by regulations under section 19 of the Legal Aid, Sentencing and Punishment of Offenders Act 2012; and

    (c) as provided by section 52 below.

(7) The functions of a designated authority under this section may be exercised by an officer of the authority acting on behalf of the authority.

(8) A decision to give a notice under this section shall not be subject to appeal or liable to be questioned in any court (whether a magistrates' court or not).

(9) In this section 'designated authority' means—

    (a) the Director of Public Prosecutions;

    (b) the Director of the Serious Fraud Office;

    (c) [repealed]; or

    (e) the Secretary of State.

51C.—(1) A notice may be given by the Director of Public Prosecutions under this section in respect of an offence falling within subsection (3) below if he is of the opinion—

    (a) that the evidence of the offence would be sufficient for the person charged to be put on trial for the offence;

    (b) that a child would be called as a witness at the trial; and

    (c) that, for the purpose of avoiding any prejudice to the welfare of the child, the case should be taken over and proceeded with without delay by the Crown Court.

(2) That opinion must be certified by the Director of Public Prosecutions in the notice.

(3) This subsection applies to an offence—

    (a) which involves an assault on, or injury or a threat of injury to, a person;

    (b) under section 1 of the Children and Young Persons Act 1933 (cruelty to persons under 16);

    (c) under the Sexual Offences Act 1956, the Protection of Children Act 1978 or the Sexual Offences Act 2003;

    (d) of kidnapping or false imprisonment, or an offence under section 1 or 2 of the Child Abduction Act 1984;

    (e) which consists of attempting or conspiring to commit, or of aiding, abetting, counselling, procuring or [intentionally encouraging or assisting] the commission of, an offence falling within paragraph (a), (b), (c) or (d) above.

(4) Subsections (4), (5) and (6) of section 51B above apply for the purposes of this section as they apply for the purposes of that.

(5) The functions of the Director of Public Prosecutions under this section may be exercised by an officer acting on behalf of the Director.

(6) A decision to give a notice under this section shall not be subject to appeal or liable to be questioned in any court (whether a magistrates' court or not).

(7) In this section 'child' means—

    (a) a person who is under the age of 17; or

    (b) any person of whom a video recording (as defined in section 63(1) of the Youth Justice and Criminal Evidence Act 1999) was made when he was under the age of 17 with a view to its admission as his evidence in chief in the trial referred to in subsection (1) above.

51D.—(1) The court shall specify in a notice—

    (a) the offence or offences for which a person is sent for trial under section 51 or 51A above; and

    (b) the place at which he is to be tried (which, if a notice has been given under section 51B above, must be the place specified in that notice).

(2) A copy of the notice shall be served on the accused and given to the Crown Court sitting at that place.

(3) In a case where a person is sent for trial under section 51 or 51A above for more than one offence, the court shall specify in that notice, for each offence—

    (a) the subsection under which the person is so sent; and

    (b) if applicable, the offence to which that offence appears to the court to be related.

(4) Where the court selects the place of trial for the purposes of subsection (1) above, it shall have regard to—

    (a) the convenience of the defence, the prosecution and the witnesses;

    (b) the desirability of expediting the trial; and

    (c) any direction given by or on behalf of the Lord Chief Justice with the concurrence of the Lord Chancellor under section 75(1) of the Senior Courts Act 1981.

51E. For the purposes of sections 50A to 51D above—

    (a) 'adult' means a person aged 18 or over, and references to an adult include a corporation;

    (b) 'either-way offence' means an offence triable either way;

    (c) an either-way offence is related to an indictable offence if the charge for the either-way offence could be joined in the same indictment as the charge for the indictable offence;

    (d) a summary offence is related to an indictable offence if it arises out of circumstances which are the same as or connected with those giving rise to the indictable offence.

52.—(1) Subject to section 4 of the Bail Act 1976, section 41 of the 1980 Act, section 115(1) of the Coroners and Justice Act 2009, regulations under section 22 of the 1985 Act and section 25 of the 1994 Act, the court may send a person for trial under section 51 or 51A above—

    (a) in custody, that is to say, by committing him to custody there to be safely kept until delivered in due course of law; or

    (b) on bail in accordance with the Bail Act 1976, that is to say, by directing him to appear before the Crown Court for trial.

(2) Where—

    (a) the person's release on bail under subsection (1)(b) above is conditional on his providing one or more sureties; and

    (b) in accordance with subsection (3) of section 8 of the Bail Act 1976, the court fixes the amount in which a surety is to be bound with a view to his entering into his recognisance subsequently in accordance with subsections (4) and (5) or (6) of that section,

the court shall in the meantime make an order such as is mentioned in subsection (1)(a) above.

(3) The court shall treat as an indictable offence for the purposes of section 51 or 51A above an offence which is mentioned in the first column of Schedule 2 to the 1980 Act (offences for which the value involved is relevant to the mode of trial) unless it is clear to the court, having regard to any representations made by the prosecutor or the accused, that the value involved does not exceed the relevant sum.

(4) In subsection (3) above 'the value involved' and 'the relevant sum' have the same meanings as in section 22 of the 1980 Act (certain offences triable either way to be tried summarily if value involved is small).

(5) A magistrates' court may adjourn any proceedings under section 51 or 51A above, and if it does so shall remand the accused.

(6) Schedule 3 to this Act (which makes further provision in relation to persons sent to the Crown Court for trial under section 51 or 51A above) shall have effect.

52A.—(1) Except as provided by this section, it shall not be lawful—

    (a) to publish in the United Kingdom a written report of any allocation or sending proceedings in England and Wales; or

    (b) to include in a relevant programme for reception in the United Kingdom a report of any such proceedings,

if (in either case) the report contains any matter other than that permitted by this section.

(2) Subject to subsections (3) and (4) below, a magistrates' court may, with reference to any allocation or sending proceedings, order that subsection (1) above shall not apply to reports of those proceedings.

(3) Where there is only one accused and he objects to the making of an order under subsection (2) above, the court shall make the order if, and only if, it is satisfied, after hearing the representations of the accused, that it is in the interests of justice to do so.

(4) Where in the case of two or more accused one of them objects to the making of an order under subsection (2) above, the court shall make the order if, and only if, it is satisfied, after hearing the representations of the accused, that it is in the interests of justice to do so.

(5) An order under subsection (2) above shall not apply to reports of proceedings under subsection (3) or (4) above, but any decision of the court to make or not to make such an order may be contained in reports published or included in a relevant programme before the time authorised by subsection (6) below.

(6) It shall not be unlawful under this section to publish or include in a relevant programme a report of allocation or sending proceedings containing any matter other than that permitted by subsection (7) below—

   (a) where, in relation to the accused (or all of them, if there are more than one), the magistrates' court is required to proceed as mentioned in section 20(7) of the 1980 Act, after the court is so required;

   (b) where, in relation to the accused (or any of them, if there are more than one), the court proceeds other than as mentioned there, after conclusion of his trial or, as the case may be, the trial of the last to be tried.

(7) The following matters may be contained in a report of allocation or sending proceedings published or included in a relevant programme without an order under subsection (2) above before the time authorised by subsection (6) above—

   (a) the identity of the court and the name of the justice or justices;

   (b) the name, age, home address and occupation of the accused;

   (c) in the case of an accused charged with an offence in respect of which notice has been given to the court under section 51B above, any relevant business information;

   (d) the offence or offences, or a summary of them, with which the accused is or are charged;

   (e) the names of counsel and solicitors engaged in the proceedings;

   (f) where the proceedings are adjourned, the date and place to which they are adjourned;

   (g) the arrangements as to bail;

   (h) whether a right to representation funded by the Legal Services Commission as part of the Criminal Defence Service was granted to the accused or any of the accused.

(8) The addresses that may be published or included in a relevant programme under subsection (7) above are addresses—

   (a) at any relevant time; and

   (b) at the time of their publication or inclusion in a relevant programme.

(9) The following is relevant business information for the purposes of subsection (7) above—

   (a) any address used by the accused for carrying on a business on his own account;

   (b) the name of any business which he was carrying on on his own account at any relevant time;

   (c) the name of any firm in which he was a partner at any relevant time or by which he was engaged at any such time;

   (d) the address of any such firm;

   (e) the name of any company of which he was a director at any relevant time or by which he was otherwise engaged at any such time;

   (f) the address of the registered or principal office of any such company;

   (g) any working address of the accused in his capacity as a person engaged by any such company;

and here 'engaged' means engaged under a contract of service or a contract for services.

(10) Subsection (1) above shall be in addition to, and not in derogation from, the provisions of any other enactment with respect to the publication of reports of court proceedings.

(11) In this section—

'allocation or sending proceedings' means, in relation to an information charging an indictable offence—

   (a) any proceedings in the magistrates' court at which matters are considered under any of the following provisions—

      (i) sections 19 to 23 of the 1980 Act;

      (ii) section 51, 51A or 52 above;

   (b) any proceedings in the magistrates' court before the court proceeds to consider any matter mentioned in paragraph (a) above; and

   (c) any proceedings in the magistrates' court at which an application under section 25(2) of the 1980 Act is considered;

'publish', in relation to a report, means publish the report, either by itself or as part of a newspaper or periodical, for distribution to the public;

'relevant programme' means a programme included in a programme service (within the meaning of the Broadcasting Act 1990);

'relevant time' means a time when events giving rise to the charges to which the proceedings relate occurred.

52B.—(1) If a report is published or included in a relevant programme in contravention of section 52A above, each of the following persons is guilty of an offence—

(a) in the case of a publication of a written report as part of a newspaper or periodical, any proprietor, editor or publisher of the newspaper or periodical;

(b) in the case of a publication of a written report otherwise than as part of a newspaper or periodical, the person who publishes it;

(c) in the case of the inclusion of a report in a relevant programme, any body corporate which is engaged in providing the service in which the programme is included and any person having functions in relation to the programme corresponding to those of the editor of a newspaper.

(2) A person guilty of an offence under this section is liable on summary conviction to a fine not exceeding level 5 on the standard scale.

(3) Proceedings for an offence under this section shall not, in England and Wales, be instituted otherwise than by or with the consent of the Attorney General.

(4) Proceedings for an offence under this section shall not, in Northern Ireland, be instituted otherwise than by or with the consent of the Attorney General for Northern Ireland.

(5) Subsection (11) of section 52A above applies for the purposes of this section as it applies for the purposes of that section.

...

Schedule 3

1. [A-G's power to make regulations.]

Applications for dismissal

2.—(1) A person who is sent for trial under section 51 or 51A of this Act on any charge or charges may, at any time—

(a) after he is served with copies of the documents containing the evidence on which the charge or charges are based; and

(b) before he is arraigned (and whether or not an indictment has been preferred against him), apply orally or in writing to the Crown Court sitting at the place specified in the notice under section 51D(1) of this Act for the charge, or any of the charges, in the case to be dismissed.

(2) The judge shall dismiss a charge (and accordingly quash any count relating to it in any indictment preferred against the applicant) which is the subject of any such application if it appears to him that the evidence against the applicant would not be sufficient for him to be properly convicted.

(3) No oral application may be made under sub-paragraph (1) above unless the applicant has given to the Crown Court sitting at the place in question written notice of his intention to make the application.

...

(6) If the charge, or any of the charges, against the applicant is dismissed—

(a) no further proceedings may be brought on the dismissed charge or charges except by means of the preferment of a voluntary bill of indictment; and

(b) unless the applicant is in custody otherwise than on the dismissed charge or charges, he shall be discharged.

(7) [Power to make rules.]

Reporting restrictions

3.—(1) Except as provided by this paragraph, it shall not be lawful—

(a) to publish in the United Kingdom a written report of an application under paragraph 2(1) above; or

(b) to include in a relevant programme for reception in the United Kingdom a report of such an application,

if (in either case) the report contains any matter other than that permitted by this paragraph.

(2) An order that sub-paragraph (1) above shall not apply to reports of an application under paragraph 2(1) above may be made by the judge dealing with the application.

(3) Where in the case of two or more accused one of them objects to the making of an order under sub-paragraph (2) above, the judge shall make the order if, and only if, he is satisfied, after hearing the representations of the accused, that it is in the interests of justice to do so.

(4) An order under sub-paragraph (2) above shall not apply to reports of proceedings under sub-paragraph (3) above, but any decision of the court to make or not to make such an order may be contained in reports published or included in a relevant programme before the time authorised by sub-paragraph (5) below.

(5) It shall not be unlawful under this paragraph to publish or include in a relevant programme a report of an application under paragraph 2(1) above containing any matter other than that permitted by sub-paragraph (8) below where the application is successful.

(6) Where—

(a) two or more persons were jointly charged; and

(b) applications under paragraph 2(1) above are made by more than one of them,

sub-paragraph (5) above shall have effect as if for the words 'the application is' there were substituted the words 'all the applications are'.

(7) It shall not be unlawful under this paragraph to publish or include in a relevant programme a report of an unsuccessful application at the conclusion of the trial of the person charged, or of the last of the persons charged to be tried.

(8) The following matters may be contained in a report published or included in a relevant programme without an order under sub-paragraph (2) above before the time authorised by sub-paragraphs (5) and (6) above, that is to say—

(a) the identity of the court and the name of the judge;

(b) the names, ages, home addresses and occupations of the accused and witnesses;

(bb) where the application made by the accused under paragraph 2(1) above relates to a charge for an offence in respect of which notice has been given to the court under section 51B of this Act, any relevant business information;

(c) the offence or offences, or a summary of them, with which the accused is or are charged;

(d) the names of counsel and solicitors engaged in the proceedings;

(e) where the proceedings are adjourned, the date and place to which they are adjourned;

(f) the arrangements as to bail;

(g) whether a right to representation funded by the Legal Services Commission as part of the Criminal Defence Service was granted to the accused or any of the accused.

(9) The addresses that may be published or included in a relevant programme under sub-paragraph (8) above are addresses—

(a) at any relevant time; and

(b) at the time of their publication or inclusion in a relevant programme.

(9A) The following is relevant business information for the purposes of sub-paragraph (8) above—

(a) any address used by the accused for carrying on a business on his own account;

(b) the name of any business which he was carrying on on his own account at any relevant time;

(c) the name of any firm in which he was a partner at any relevant time or by which he was engaged at any such time;

(d) the address of any such firm;

(e) the name of any company of which he was a director at any relevant time or by which he was otherwise engaged at any such time;

(f) the address of the registered or principal office of any such company;

(g) any working address of the accused in his capacity as a person engaged by any such company;

and here 'engaged' means engaged under a contract of service or a contract for services.

(10) If a report is published or included in a relevant programme in contravention of this paragraph, the following persons, that is to say—

(a) in the case of a publication of a written report as part of a newspaper or periodical, any proprietor, editor or publisher of the newspaper or periodical;

(b) in the case of a publication of a written report otherwise than as part of a newspaper or periodical, the person who publishes it;

(c) in the case of the inclusion of a report in a relevant programme, any body corporate which is engaged in providing the service in which the programme is included and any person having functions in relation to the programme corresponding to those of the editor of a newspaper;

shall be liable on summary conviction to a fine not exceeding level 5 on the standard scale.

(11) Proceedings for an offence under this paragraph shall not, in England and Wales, be instituted otherwise than by or with the consent of the Attorney General.

(11A) [Northern Ireland.]

(12) Sub-paragraph (1) above shall be in addition to, and not in derogation from, the provisions of any other enactment with respect to the publication of reports of court proceedings.

(13) In this paragraph—

'publish', in relation to a report, means publish the report, either by itself or as part of a newspaper or periodical, for distribution to the public;

'relevant programme' means a programme included in a programme service (within the meaning of the Broadcasting Act 1990);

'relevant time' means a time when events giving rise to the charges to which the proceedings relate occurred.

Power of justice to take depositions etc.

4.—(1) Sub-paragraph (2) below applies where a justice of the peace for any commission area is satisfied that—

    (a) any person in England and Wales ('the witness') is likely to be able to make on behalf of the prosecutor a written statement containing material evidence, or produce on behalf of the prosecutor a document or other exhibit likely to be material evidence, for the purposes of proceedings for an offence for which a person has been sent for trial under section 51 or 51A of this Act by a magistrates' court for that area; and

    (b) it is in the interests of justice to issue a summons under this paragraph to secure the attendance of the witness to have his evidence taken as a deposition or to produce the document or other exhibit.

(2) In such a case the justice shall issue a summons directed to the witness requiring him to attend before a justice at the time and place appointed in the summons, and to have his evidence taken as a deposition or to produce the document or other exhibit.

(3) If a justice of the peace is satisfied by evidence on oath of the matters mentioned in sub-paragraph (1) above, and also that it is probable that a summons under sub-paragraph (2) above would not procure the result required by it, the justice may instead of issuing a summons issue a warrant to arrest the witness and to bring him before a justice at the time and place specified in the warrant.

(4) A summons may also be issued under sub-paragraph (2) above if the justice is satisfied that the witness is outside the British Islands, but no warrant may be issued under sub-paragraph (3) above unless the justice is satisfied by evidence on oath that the witness is in England and Wales.

(5) If—

    (a) the witness fails to attend before a justice in answer to a summons under this paragraph;

    (b) the justice is satisfied by evidence on oath that the witness is likely to be able to make a statement or produce a document or other exhibit as mentioned in sub-paragraph (1)(a) above;

    (c) it is proved on oath, or in such other manner as may be prescribed, that he has been duly served with the summons and that a reasonable sum has been paid or tendered to him for costs and expenses; and

    (d) it appears to the justice that there is no just excuse for the failure,

the justice may issue a warrant to arrest the witness and to bring him before a justice at the time and place specified in the warrant.

(6) Where—

    (a) a summons is issued under sub-paragraph (2) above or a warrant is issued under sub-paragraph (3) or (5) above; and

    (b) the summons or warrant is issued with a view to securing that the witness has his evidence taken as a deposition,

the time appointed in the summons or specified in the warrant shall be such as to enable the evidence to be taken as a deposition before the relevant date.

(7) If any person attending or brought before a justice in pursuance of this paragraph refuses without just excuse to have his evidence taken as a deposition, or to produce the document or other exhibit, the justice may do one or both of the following—

    (a) commit him to custody until the expiration of such period not exceeding one month as may be specified in the summons or warrant or until he sooner has his evidence taken as a deposition or produces the document or other exhibit;

    (b) impose on him a fine not exceeding £2,500.

(8) A fine imposed under sub-paragraph (7) above shall be deemed, for the purposes of any enactment, to be a sum adjudged to be paid by a conviction.

(9) If in pursuance of this paragraph a person has his evidence taken as a deposition, the designated officer for the justice concerned shall as soon as is reasonably practicable send a copy of the deposition to the prosecutor and the Crown Court.

(10) If in pursuance of this paragraph a person produces an exhibit which is a document, the designated officer for the justice concerned shall as soon as is reasonably practicable send a copy of the document to the prosecutor and the Crown Court.

(11) If in pursuance of this paragraph a person produces an exhibit which is not a document, the designated officer for the justice concerned shall as soon as is reasonably practicable inform the prosecutor and the Crown Court of that fact and of the nature of the exhibit.

(12) In this paragraph—
'prescribed' means prescribed by Criminal Procedure Rules;
'the relevant date' means the expiry of the period referred to in paragraph 1(1) above.

Use of depositions as evidence

5.—(1) Subject to sub-paragraph (3) below, sub-paragraph (2) below applies where in pursuance of paragraph 4 above a person has his evidence taken as a deposition.

(2) Where this sub-paragraph applies the deposition may without further proof be read as evidence on the trial of the accused, whether for an offence for which he was sent for trial under section 51 or 51A of this Act or for any other offence arising out of the same transaction or set of circumstances.

(3) Sub-paragraph (2) above does not apply if—
  (a) it is proved that the deposition was not signed by the justice by whom it purports to have been signed;
  (b) the court of trial at its discretion orders that sub-paragraph (2) above shall not apply; or
  (c) a party to the proceedings objects to sub-paragraph (2) above applying.

...

Power of Crown Court to deal with summary offence

6.—(1) This paragraph applies where a magistrates' court has sent a person for trial under section 51 or 51A of this Act for offences which include a summary offence.

(2) If the person is convicted on the indictment, the Crown Court shall consider whether the summary offence is related to the indictable offence for which he was sent for trial or, as the case may be, any of the indictable offences for which he was so sent.

(3) If it considers that the summary offence is so related, the court shall state to the person the substance of the offence and ask him whether he pleads guilty or not guilty.

(4) If the person pleads guilty, the Crown Court shall convict him, but may deal with him in respect of the summary offence only in a manner in which a magistrates' court could have dealt with him.

(5) If he does not plead guilty, the powers of the Crown Court shall cease in respect of the summary offence except as provided by sub-paragraph (6) below.

(6) If the prosecution inform the court that they would not desire to submit evidence on the charge relating to the summary offence, the court shall dismiss it.

(7) The Crown Court shall inform the designated officer for the magistrates' court of the outcome of any proceedings under this paragraph.

(8) If the summary offence is one to which section 40 of the Criminal Justice Act 1988 applies, the Crown Court may exercise in relation to the offence the power conferred by that section; but where the person is tried on indictment for such an offence, the functions of the Crown Court under this paragraph in relation to the offence shall cease.

(9) Where the Court of Appeal allows an appeal against conviction of an indictable offence which is related to a summary offence of which the appellant was convicted under this paragraph—
  (a) it shall set aside his conviction of the summary offence and give the clerk of the magistrates' court notice that it has done so; and
  (b) it may direct that no further proceedings in relation to the offence are to be undertaken;
and the proceedings before the Crown Court in relation to the offence shall thereafter be disregarded for all purposes.

(10) A notice under sub-paragraph (9) above shall include particulars of any direction given under paragraph (b) of that sub-paragraph in relation to the offence.

(11) ...

(12) An offence is related to another offence for the purposes of this paragraph if it arises out of circumstances which are the same as or connected with those giving rise to the other offence.

Procedure where no indictable-only offence remains

7.—(1) Subject to paragraph 13 below, this paragraph applies where—
  (a) a person has been sent for trial under section 51 or 51A of this Act but has not been arraigned; and

(b) the person is charged on an indictment which (following amendment of the indictment, or as a result of an application under paragraph 2 above, or for any other reason) includes no main offence.

(2) Everything that the Crown Court is required to do under the following provisions of this paragraph must be done with the accused present in court.

(3) The court shall cause to be read to the accused each remaining count of the indictment that charges an offence triable either way.

(4) The court shall then explain to the accused in ordinary language that, in relation to each of those offences, he may indicate whether (if it were to proceed to trial) he would plead guilty or not guilty, and that if he indicates that he would plead guilty the court must proceed as mentioned in sub-paragraph (6) below.

(5) The court shall then ask the accused whether (if the offence in question were to proceed to trial) he would plead guilty or not guilty.

(6) If the accused indicates that he would plead guilty the court shall proceed as if he had been arraigned on the count in question and had pleaded guilty.

(7) If the accused indicates that he would plead not guilty, or fails to indicate how he would plead, the court shall decide whether the offence is more suitable for summary trial or for trial on indictment.

(8) Subject to sub-paragraph (6) above, the following shall not for any purpose be taken to constitute the taking of a plea—

(a) asking the accused under this paragraph whether (if the offence were to proceed to trial) he would plead guilty or not guilty;

(b) an indication by the accused under this paragraph of how he would plead.

(9) In this paragraph, a 'main offence' is—

(a) an offence for which the person has been sent to the Crown Court for trial under section 51(1) of this Act; or

(b) an offence—

   (i) for which the person has been sent to the Crown Court for trial under subsection (5) of section 51 or subsection (6) of section 51A of this Act ('the applicable subsection'); and

   (ii) in respect of which the conditions for sending him to the Crown Court for trial under the applicable subsection (as set out in paragraphs (a) to (c) of section 51(5) or paragraphs (a) and (b) of section 51A(6)) continue to be satisfied.

8.—(1) Subject to paragraph 13 below, this paragraph applies in a case where—

(a) a person has been sent for trial under section 51 or 51A of this Act but has not been arraigned;

(b) he is charged on an indictment which (following amendment of the indictment, or as a result of an application under paragraph 2 above, or for any other reason) includes no main offence (within the meaning of paragraph 7 above);

(c) he is represented by a legal representative;

(d) the Crown Court considers that by reason of his disorderly conduct before the court it is not practicable for proceedings under paragraph 7 above to be conducted in his presence; and

(e) the court considers that it should proceed in his absence.

(2) In such a case—

(a) the court shall cause to be read to the representative each remaining count of the indictment that charges an offence triable either way;

(b) the court shall ask the representative whether (if the offence in question were to proceed to trial) the accused would plead guilty or not guilty;

(c) if the representative indicates that the accused would plead guilty the court shall proceed as if the accused had been arraigned on the count in question and had pleaded guilty;

(d) if the representative indicates that the accused would plead not guilty, or fails to indicate how the accused would plead, the court shall decide whether the offence is more suitable for summary trial or for trial on indictment.

(3) Subject to sub-paragraph (2)(c) above, the following shall not for any purpose be taken to constitute the taking of a plea—

(a) asking the representative under this section whether (if the offence were to proceed to trial) the accused would plead guilty or not guilty;

(b) an indication by the representative under this paragraph of how the accused would plead.

9.—(1) This paragraph applies where the Crown Court is required by paragraph 7(7) or 8(2)(d) above to decide the question whether an offence is more suitable for summary trial or for trial on indictment.

(2) Before deciding the question, the court—
  (a) shall give the prosecution an opportunity to inform the court of the accused's previous convictions (if any); and
  (b) shall give the prosecution and the accused an opportunity to make representations as to whether summary trial or trial on indictment would be more suitable.

(3) In deciding the question, the court shall consider—
  (a) whether the sentence which a magistrates' court would have power to impose for the offence would be adequate; and
  (b) any representations made by the prosecution or the accused under sub-paragraph (2)(b) above,
and shall have regard to any allocation guidelines (or revised allocation guidelines) issued as definitive guidelines under section 122 of the Coroners and Justice Act 2009.

(4) Where—
  (a) the accused is charged on the same occasion with two or more offences; and
  (b) it appears to the court that they constitute or form part of a series of two or more offences of the same or a similar character;
sub-paragraph (3)(a) above shall have effect as if references to the sentence which a magistrates' court would have power to impose for the offence were a reference to the maximum aggregate sentence which a magistrates' court would have power to impose for all of the offences taken together.

(5) In this paragraph any reference to a previous conviction is a reference to—
  (a) a previous conviction by a court in the United Kingdom, or
  (aa) a previous conviction by a court in another member State of a relevant offence under the law of that State, or
  (b) a previous conviction of a service offence within the meaning of the Armed Forces Act 2006.

(5A) For the purposes of sub-paragraph (5)(aa) an offence is 'relevant' if the offence would constitute an offence under the law of any part of the United Kingdom if it were done in that part at the time when the allocation decision is made.

10.—(1) This paragraph applies (unless excluded by paragraph 15 below) where the Crown Court considers that an offence is more suitable for summary trial.

(2) The court shall explain to the accused in ordinary language—
  (a) that it appears to the court more suitable for him to be tried summarily for the offence;
  (b) that he can either consent to be so tried or, if he wishes, be tried on indictment; and
  (c) in the case of a specified offence (within the meaning of section 224 of the Criminal Justice Act 2003), that if he is tried summarily and is convicted by the court, he may be committed for sentence to the Crown Court under section 3A of the Powers of Criminal Courts (Sentencing) Act 2000 if the committing court is of such opinion as is mentioned in subsection (2) of that section.

(3) After explaining to the accused as provided by sub-paragraph (2) above the court shall ask him whether he wishes to be tried summarily or on indictment, and—
  (a) if he indicates that he wishes to be tried summarily, shall remit him for trial to a magistrates' court acting for the place where he was sent to the Crown Court for trial;
  (b) if he does not give such an indication, shall retain its functions in relation to the offence and proceed accordingly.

11.—(1) If the Crown Court considers that an offence is more suitable for trial on indictment, the court—
  (a) shall tell the accused that it has decided that it is more suitable for him to be tried for the offence on indictment; and
  (b) shall retain its functions in relation to the offence and proceed accordingly.

...

13.—(1) This paragraph applies, in place of paragraphs 7 to 12 above, in the case of a child or young person who—
  (a) has been sent for trial under section 51 or 51A of this Act but has not been arraigned; and
  (b) is charged on an indictment which (following amendment of the indictment, or as a result of an application under paragraph 2 above, or for any other reason) includes no main offence.

(2) The Crown Court shall remit the child or young person for trial to a magistrates' court acting for the place where he was sent to the Crown Court for trial.

(3) In this paragraph, a 'main offence' is—

(a) an offence for which the child or young person has been sent to the Crown Court for trial under section 51A(2) of this Act; or

(b) an offence—

(i) for which the child or young person has been sent to the Crown Court for trial under subsection (7) of section 51 of this Act; and

(ii) in respect of which the conditions for sending him to the Crown Court for trial under that subsection (as set out in paragraphs (a) and (b) of that subsection) continue to be satisfied.

Procedure for determining whether offences of criminal damage etc. are summary offences

14.—(1) This paragraph applies where the Crown Court has to determine, for the purposes of this Schedule, whether an offence which is listed in the first column of Schedule 2 to the 1980 Act (offences for which the value involved is relevant to the mode of trial) is a summary offence.

(2) The court shall have regard to any representations made by the prosecutor or the accused.

(3) If it appears clear to the court that the value involved does not exceed the relevant sum, it shall treat the offence as a summary offence.

(4) If it appears clear to the court that the value involved exceeds the relevant sum, it shall treat the offence as an indictable offence.

(5) If it appears to the court for any reason not clear whether the value involved does or does not exceed the relevant sum, the court shall ask the accused whether he wishes the offence to be treated as a summary offence.

(6) Where sub-paragraph (5) above applies—

(a) if the accused indicates that he wishes the offence to be treated as a summary offence, the court shall so treat it;

(b) if the accused does not give such an indication, the court shall treat the offence as an indictable offence.

(7) In this paragraph 'the value involved' and 'the relevant sum' have the same meanings as in section 22 of the 1980 Act (certain offences triable either way to be tried summarily if value involved is small).

Power of Crown Court, with consent of legally-represented accused, to proceed in his absence

15.—(1) The Crown Court may proceed in the absence of the accused in accordance with such of the provisions of paragraphs 9 to 14 above as are applicable in the circumstances if—

(a) the accused is represented by a legal representative who signifies to the court the accused's consent to the proceedings in question being conducted in his absence; and

(b) the court is satisfied that there is good reason for proceeding in the absence of the accused.

(2) Sub-paragraph (1) above is subject to the following provisions of this paragraph which apply where the court exercises the power conferred by that sub-paragraph.

(3) If, where the court has decided as required by paragraph 7(7) or 8(2)(d) above, it appears to the court that an offence is more suitable for summary trial, paragraph 10 above shall not apply and—

(a) if the legal representative indicates that the accused wishes to be tried summarily, the court shall remit the accused for trial to a magistrates' court acting for the place where he was sent to the Crown Court for trial;

(b) if the legal representative does not give such an indication, the court shall retain its functions and proceed accordingly.

(4) If, where the court has decided as required by paragraph 7(7) or 8(2)(d) above, it appears to the court that an offence is more suitable for trial on indictment, paragraph 11 above shall apply with the omission of paragraph (a).

(5) Where paragraph 14 above applies and it appears to the court for any reason not clear whether the value involved does or does not exceed the relevant sum, sub-paragraphs (5) and (6) of that paragraph shall not apply and—

(a) the court shall ask the legal representative whether the accused wishes the offence to be treated as a summary offence;

(b) if the legal representative indicates that the accused wishes the offence to be treated as a summary offence, the court shall so treat it;

(c) if the legal representative does not give such an indication, the court shall treat the offence as an indictable offence.

D

Part D Procedure

VOLUNTARY BILLS OF INDICTMENT

D10.44 The Administration of Justice (Miscellaneous Provisions) Act 1933, s. 2(2)(b), provides that a bill of indictment may be preferred 'by the direction or with the consent of a judge of the High Court'.

Procedure for Obtaining a Voluntary Bill

D10.45 The procedure for obtaining a High Court judge's consent to the preferment of a bill of indictment is set out in the Indictments (Procedure) Rules 1971, rr. 6 to 10, and in CPD II, paras. 14B.1 to 14B.8 (see Supplement, **PD-20**). In summary, the procedure is as follows:

(a) An application must be made in writing, signed by the applicant (i.e. the prosecutor) or his solicitor (Indictments (Procedure) Rules 1971, r. 7).

(b) The application must state:
   (i)   whether there has been any previous application for a voluntary bill (r. 8(b));
   (ii)   whether there has been any sending for trial and any application for dismissal of the charge (under the CDA 1998, sch. 3, para. 2) and, if so, the result of any such application (r. 8(c)); and
   (iii) if there has been no sending for trial, why it is desired to prefer a voluntary bill instead (r. 9(1)).

(c) The application must be accompanied by the bill of indictment (i.e. draft indictment) that it is proposed to prefer (i.e. serve on the Crown Court) (r. 8(a)). The application must also be accompanied by a copy of any charges that have been sent for trial and any existing indictment that has been preferred in consequence of a sending for trial, together with a summary of the evidence in relation to each such count (CPD II, para. 14B.2).

(d) Where the accused has already been sent to the Crown Court for trial but the charge has been dismissed or withdrawn, the application must also be accompanied by a copy of the documents upon the basis of which the case was sent for trial, including any documentary exhibits (r. 9(2) and (3)). If there is any additional evidence the prosecutor intends to rely on which does not appear in the existing witness statements, documents or statements containing that evidence must also be sent. Where there has been no sending for trial, the applicant simply sends the witness statements of his proposed witnesses (r. 9(1)(a)). In each case, the application must contain a statement that the evidence contained in the application will be available at trial and that the case thereby disclosed is (to the best of the applicant's knowledge, information and belief) substantially a true case (r. 9(1)(a)).

(e) Except where the application is made by or on behalf of the DPP, it must also be accompanied by an affidavit verifying that the statements contained in the application are true to the best of the applicant's knowledge and belief (r. 8(a)). Where a Crown Prosecutor applies for a voluntary bill in exercise of the powers delegated to him by the DPP, the application is deemed to be made by or on behalf of the DPP and therefore does not have to be supported by an affidavit (see the Prosecution of Offences Act 1985, s. 1(6), and *Ex parte Bray* (1986) *The Times*, 7 October 1986). This is so even if the application was not expressly authorised by the DPP, but merely made by the Crown Prosecutor carrying out his general duties (ibid).

(f) Subject to a contrary direction by the judge, the application is determined without the attendance of the applicant or his witnesses. Should they be required to attend, their attendance is not in open court (r. 10). The judge's decision is signified in writing (r. 10).

(g) CPD II, para. 14B.6, states that the prospective defendant should be given notice that an application for a voluntary bill has been made, and that a copy of all the documents delivered to the judge should also be served on him. He should also be informed that he may make written submissions to the judge within nine working days of the date when notice of the application was given. These procedures should be followed unless there are 'good grounds' for not doing so, in which case prosecutors should inform the judge that the procedures have not been followed and seek leave to dispense with all or any of them. The judge should give leave only if 'good grounds' are shown (para. 14B.7). Paragraph 14B.8 states that, as well as considering any written submissions, the judge may invite oral submissions from either party, or accede to a request for an opportunity to make such oral submissions, if he considers it necessary or desirable to receive such oral submissions in order to make a sound and fair decision on the application. Any such oral submissions should be made on notice to the other party and in open court.

Note that the CCA 2013, sch. 17, para. 32, amended s. 2(2) of the 1933 Act so as to provide for deferred prosecution agreements (see **D12.106**). Once a deferred prosecution agreement has been approved, proceedings are commenced by seeking a voluntary bill of indictment from a Crown Court judge (not a High Court judge), without any involvement of a magistrates' court. Once the proceedings have been instituted in this way, they are automatically suspended. This suspension may only be lifted following the termination of the deferred prosecution agreement as a consequence of a breach of the agreement.

Finality of High Court Judge's Decision

Where a High Court judge directs the preferment of a voluntary bill of indictment under the   **D10.46**
Administration of Justice (Miscellaneous Provisions) Act 1933, s. 2(2)(b), the Court of Appeal will not inquire into the correctness or otherwise of his decision, so long as it is clear that he was acting within his jurisdiction (*Rothfield* (1938) 26 Cr App R 103 per Humphreys J at p. 106). The issuing of a voluntary bill of indictment is not subject to judicial review (*Manchester Crown Court, ex parte Williams* (1990) 154 JP 589). In *Rothfield*, the Court of Appeal also held that a High Court judge's authorisation for the preferring of a bill is binding on a trial judge, and the latter has no jurisdiction to quash the indictment simply on the basis that the former, according to the defence, made a mistake (at p. 106).

In *Rothfield*, Humphrey J went on (at p. 107) to add, *obiter*, that the court was specifically declining to say that the mere failure to comply with any of the procedural rules governing applications for voluntary bills will necessarily vitiate the discretion of a judge in granting leave to prefer a bill of indictment. It is apparent from this that procedural irregularities do not necessarily invalidate the judge's decision to grant a voluntary bill.

However, since only High Court judges have jurisdiction to direct preferment of a voluntary bill, a conviction on an indictment purportedly preferred on the direction of a circuit judge will inevitably have to be quashed (*Thompson* [1975] 2 All ER 1028).

Even though the decision of a High Court judge to issue a voluntary bill of indictment is not subject to judicial review, the decision of a prosecutor to seek a voluntary bill is susceptible to review, but only on very limited grounds, such as bad faith or personal malice on the part of the prosecutor (*Inland Revenue Commissioners, ex parte Dhesi* (1995) *Independent*, 14 August 1995).

In *Muse* [2007] EWHC 2924 (QB), on an application for a voluntary bill of indictment, the   **D10.47**
CPS had decided not to rely on certain evidence. The judge found that there was insufficient evidence to put the defendants on trial. The CPS subsequently reconsidered the matter, and sought a voluntary bill of indictment in respect of the same incident on the basis of the evidence that it had chosen not to use at the previous hearing. It was held by Openshaw J that it would be wrong in principle for the prosecution to be able to get round a decision that it did not like by inviting another judge to take a different view of the same material that had been before the judge who had dismissed the charges. However, a voluntary bill may be granted to correct a mistaken decision by the CPS or to reflect a change of mind within the CPS. The power to do so should be used sparingly, in truly exceptional cases. Relevant factors include the public interest in putting defendants on trial where there is sufficient evidence to justify doing so and the

offence is a serious one. On the other hand, given the desirability of finality in criminal matters, it would not usually be in the interests of justice that persons should have to face a second prosecution in relation to the same offence if the evidence relied on was in fact available at the earlier hearing, particularly when a deliberate decision had been taken not to rely on that evidence. Each case has to be decided on its own facts.

Circumstances in which it is Appropriate to Apply for a Voluntary Bill

D10.48 CPD II, para. 14B.4 (see Supplement, **PD-20**), makes the point that the preferment of a voluntary bill is 'an exceptional procedure' and goes on to say that this procedure should be used only where 'good reason to depart from the normal procedure is clearly shown' and only where 'the interests of justice, rather than considerations of administrative convenience, require it'.

Specific provision is made for the use of the voluntary bill procedure where a charge transferred to the Crown Court (under the CDA 1998, s. 51) has been dismissed (under the CDA 1998, sch. 3, para. 2) and the prosecution wish to seek a trial nonetheless; indeed, in such circumstances, further proceedings may be brought on the dismissed charge(s) only by means of the preferment of a voluntary bill of indictment (para. 2(6)).

D10.49 In *Davenport* [2005] EWHC 2828 (Admin), Pitchers J said (at [22]) that where a case is transferred to the Crown Court under the CJA 1987, s. 4 (now superseded by the CDA 1998, s. 51B), and an application to dismiss the charge is successful, it would be 'wrong in principle for the prosecution to be able to get round a decision that they do not like by inviting another judge to take a different view of the same material that was before the judge who dismissed the charges'. Such an application might, however, be appropriate 'if the judge had not had a crucial authority or statutory provision drawn to his attention' (at [23]) or 'where the prosecution can produce fresh cogent evidence which was not before the judge who dismissed the charges' (at [26]), though in that case it 'would still be necessary for the judge considering the voluntary bill to conclude that it was in the interests of justice for a voluntary bill to be preferred but he would be making a decision on new material and would not be being asked simply to take a different view from the one taken previously' (at [26]). In *McGuiness* [2007] EWHC 1772 (Admin), the same principles were applied to a case transferred to the Crown Court under the CDA 1998, s. 51; a voluntary bill was held to be appropriate in that case because the judge had made an error of law when dismissing the charge.

Section D11   The Indictment

INTRODUCTION

The indictment is the document containing the charges against the accused on which he is **D11.1** arraigned at the commencement of a trial on indictment. In terms of statutory authority, the law on indictments is contained principally in the Indictments Act 1915. The CrimPR, part 14 (see Supplement, **R-128** *et seq.*), amplifies the Act and part 14 is itself supplemented by CPD II, paras. 14A.1 to 14A9 (see Supplement, **PD-19**).

The content of this section can be divided into four categories:

(a) rules as to the form of an indictment, which includes rules as to the layout of an indictment, who is responsible for its drafting and the time-limits relevant to its preferment (**D11.2** to **D11.12**);

(b) rules as to the composition of an indictment, in terms of the charges included in an indictment and their wording (**D11.13** to **D11.62**);

(c) rules as to the alteration of an indictment, whether by joinder of charges or offenders, severance or amendment (**D11.63** to **D11.109**);

(d) rules for objecting to an indictment, whether by a motion to quash or as a ground of appeal (**D11.110** to **D11.117**).

REQUIREMENT THAT AN INDICTMENT BE SIGNED

The Rule

The CAJA 2009, s. 116, amended the Administration of Justice (Miscellaneous Provisions) Act **D11.2** 1933, s. 2(1), so that it reads:

(1) Subject to the provisions of this section, a bill of indictment charging any person with an indictable offence may be preferred by any person before the [Crown Court] and it shall thereupon become an indictment and be proceeded upon accordingly.

The effect of this amendment is to remove the statutory prerequisite that an indictment came into being only once it was signed by a proper officer of the Crown Court. In *Lord Chancellor v McCarthy* [2012] EWHC 2325 (Admin) it was emphasised, in the context of the determination of the class of offence for the purpose of payment, that an indictment that had been served pursuant to the CrimPR, r. 14, duly became 'the indictment' without the necessity for it to be signed.

The CrimPR, r. 14.1, still requires that a draft indictment should be served on the court and endorsed by a court officer; when the draft indictment is endorsed, the date of receipt should be added (r. 14.1(3)(a)). The officer of the Crown Court is required to endorse it, unless the court directs otherwise (r. 14.1(3)). Although not explicitly stated, it would appear that the officer ought to be satisfied that the requirements of s. 2(2) of the 1933 Act have been complied with. Section 2(2) (see **D10.2**), reflected in the CrimPR, r. 14.1(1), effectively provides that no draft indictment may be served unless:

(a) the accused has been sent for trial (pursuant to the CDA 1998, s. 51 or 51A);
(b) a High Court judge has directed or consented to the preferment of a voluntary bill of indictment;
(c) the Court of Appeal has ordered a retrial; or
(d) the accused has been transferred for trial.

Since 24 February 2014, special provision has provided for the preferring of the indictment in a case where there is a deferred prosecution agreement, which acts as the catalyst for the suspending of the proceedings pursuant to the terms of the agreement (see **D12.106**).

D11.3 **Problems with Compliance with this Rule**   Simple though the requirement to ensure that the indictment is signed may seem, the courts have had to grapple with the consequences of failure to comply with it. This was because, as the Court of Appeal emphasised in *Morais* [1988] 3 All ER 161 and the House of Lords reiterated in *Clarke* [2008] 2 All ER 665, the proper officer's signature is not 'a comparatively meaningless formality' but a 'necessary condition precedent to the existence of a proper indictment'. It may well be argued that the discretion of the court to dispense with this requirement, pursuant to r. 14.1(3), may have reduced its significance. In any event, the authorities demonstrated that the question was whether or not the failure to sign the indictment in the proper manner was actually more than a 'meaningless formality', or merely procedural. Examples of such procedural failures include:

(a) In *Jackson* [1997] 2 Cr App R 497, although the judge had directed in open court that the appropriate officer should sign the indictments, she had failed to comply with the judge's direction.
(b) In *Laming* (1989) 90 Cr App R 450, where the appropriate officer of the court signed the indictment on the front page rather than at the end, as was required by sch. 1 to the Indictment Rules 1971, the Court of Appeal held that it was nonetheless valid. The important fact was that the appropriate officer of the court had signed the indictment, intending thereby to validate it. The court added, however, that any departure from the normal practice of signing indictments at the end was to be strongly discouraged.

D11.4 **Consequences of an Unsigned Indictment**   In *Ashton* [2007] 1 WLR 181, the Court of Appeal held that the approach to procedural failures in relation to the indictment in cases such as *Morais* [1988] 3 All ER 161, had been superseded by the decision in the House of Lords in *Soneji* [2006] 1 AC 340. The same approach was followed by the Court of Appeal in *Clarke* [2006] EWCA Crim 1196. However, when the case of *Clarke* was considered by the House of Lords ([2008] 2 All ER 665), this approach was rejected and *Morais* affirmed. Applying the reasoning that had been adopted in *Soneji*, the questions to be asked, as identified by Lord Bingham, were as follows:

(a) What did Parliament intend to be the consequences of a failure to comply with the requirement in s. 2(1) that a draft indictment should be signed? Lord Bingham concluded (at [18]) that the answer was 'inescapable', namely that 'Parliament intended that the bill should not become an indictment unless and until it was duly signed by the proper officer'.
(b) What did Parliament intend to be the consequences of a trial proceeding on an unsigned draft indictment? Lord Bingham (at [19]) found the answer to be that 'Parliament intended that there could be no valid trial on indictment if there was no indictment'.

D11.5 The impact of the House of Lords' decision in *Clarke* was that proceedings on the basis of an unsigned indictment are invalid and represent a nullity (*Leeks* [2010] 1 Cr App R 87). However, failure to follow the correct procedure as to how the indictment should be signed, as opposed to whether it is signed at all, will not necessarily invalidate subsequent proceedings.

It may be that the impact of *Clarke* has been reduced by the CAJA 2009, s. 116(1)(c), which addressed the consequences of procedural failures by inserting subsections (6ZA) to (6ZC) into

s. 2 of the 1933 Act. The effect is that, where a draft indictment is served in accordance with s. 2(1) and (2), no objection may be taken to it after the commencement of the trial (i.e. after a jury is sworn or an accused pleads guilty) by reason of any failure to observe the rules relating to indictments. This, in combination with the discretion of the court (pursuant to the CrimPR, r. 14.1(3)) to dispense with the need for the indictment to be signed at all, may make technical objections based on the signing of the indictment less common.

RESPONSIBILITY FOR DRAFTING AN INDICTMENT

Ultimate Responsibility

Ultimate responsibility for the indictment rests with counsel for the prosecution, who must **D11.6** ensure that it is in proper form before arraignment. This principle was affirmed by Watkins LJ, giving the judgment of the Court of Appeal in *Newland* [1988] QB 402, who said (at p. 409):

> It was the responsibility of counsel to ensure that the indictment was in proper form before arraignment. A return to that practice — it seems not to be followed generally — may in our view be a salutary thing for everyone concerned, and moreover relieve the staff of the Crown Court of any responsibility it may be felt they have in that respect, and also to have the result of there being fewer appeals to this court based on defective indictments.

Mechanics of Drafting Indictments

Although at the time that Watkins LJ made the observations in *Newland* [1988] QB 402 (see **D11.7** D11.6) Crown Court staff drafted the bulk of indictments, invariably now the prosecuting authority prepares a schedule of charges drafted in the form of counts suitable for inclusion in an indictment. This schedule, in effect a draft indictment, is sent to the Crown Court, and all the Crown Court officer has to do is to check that there has been no contravention of the Administration of Justice (Miscellaneous Provisions) Act 1933, s. 2(2), and then to sign.

What has not changed, however, is the ultimate responsibility of counsel, once instructed, to ensure that the indictment is in proper form (*Moss* [1995] Crim LR 828).

TIME-LIMIT FOR SERVING A BILL OF INDICTMENT

The Rule

A draft indictment should be served on an appropriate officer of the Crown Court within **D11.8** 28 days of the date on which:

(a) a notice of transfer is given;
(b) a High Court judge has directed or consented to the preferment of a voluntary bill of indictment; or
(c) copies of documents are served where a person is sent for trial under the CDA 1998, s. 51 (CrimPR, r. 14.1).

CPD II, para. 14A.1 (see Supplement, **PD-19**), makes it clear that the draft indictment should be served more quickly than this 28-day period if the prosecution will be seeking to include counts on the indictment which differ from, or are additional to, the counts on the basis of which the accused was sent.

Extension of the Time-limit   The CrimPR, r. 14.1(2), permits the Crown Court to extend **D11.9** the time-limit, even after it has expired. Moreover, contrary to the position under the pre-2007 version of the Rules, there are no specific rules as to the means by which an application for an extension should be made, or what such an application should contain.

D

D11.10 **Breaches of the Rule** When r. 5 of the Indictments (Procedure) Rules 1971 still applied, it was held to be directory, not mandatory. Consequently, breach of the rule was not in itself a good ground of appeal, and the same principle applies to the CrimPR, r. 14.1. The effect of the Administration of Justice (Miscellaneous Provisions) Act 1933, s. 2(6ZA)–(6ZC), further underlines the lack of scope for an appeal based on such a breach. Case law under the old r. 5 is now of relevance only to the question of whether inordinate delay of a magnitude sufficient to prejudice the accused in the preparation of his defence might render a conviction unsafe or an application to extend the time-limit after its expiry ought to be granted.

Cases in relation to the form of the rule which simply provided that 'the bill of indictment must be preferred within 28 days of… committal or within such longer period as a judge of the Crown Court may allow' must now be considered in the light of these amendments.

D11.11 (a) In *Sheerin* (1976) 64 Cr App R 68, defence counsel moved to quash an indictment preferred 21 days out of time, no application for an extension of time having been made. The trial judge, finding that S had not suffered any prejudice by reason of the delay, gave leave for preferment of a late bill and rejected the motion to quash. On appeal, Lawton LJ held:

  (i) First, that the judge had had jurisdiction to grant the extension of time even though the application was not made until after the 28 days had elapsed (this is now expressly confirmed by r. 14.1).

  (ii) Secondly, as to the status of the rule, his lordship said (at p. 70): 'It is to be noted that the very title of the rules is "Procedure Rules" — that is rules for the guidance of courts in the administration of justice. They are not rules setting boundaries beyond which the courts cannot go.'

  (iii) Thirdly, the judge had properly exercised his discretion in allowing late preferment since preparation of the indictment would have taken longer than the usual period.

(b) In *Soffe* (1982) 75 Cr App R 133, the argument on appeal was that authorisation for an extension of time for preferment had been given by the chief clerk of the Crown Court concerned, not by a judge, and that the 28-day rule (as it then stood) had therefore been breached. Donaldson LJ, giving the Court of Appeal's judgment, said (at p. 136):

> There must be some doubt in this case whether the chief clerk in fact purported to extend the time limited by rule 5 or whether the bill was preferred out of time. So far as this application is concerned, it matters not which occurred. A breach of [the rules] does not constitute a material irregularity in the course of the trial or in any way invalidate the proceedings, and the applicant accordingly has no valid grounds of appeal.

(c) Similarly, when dismissing the appeal in *Farooki* (1983) 77 Cr App R 257, the court relied on the dicta in *Sheerin* and *Soffe*, and could find no valid distinction between the circumstances of the case before them (where an appropriate officer had apparently signed a late-preferred bill without consultation with or authorisation from a judge) and the circumstances of *Sheerin* and *Soffe*.

The approach in these three cases was specifically approved by the House of Lords in *Clarke* [2008] 2 All ER 665 (at [14]) (see **D11.4**).

D11.12 **The Need for Compliance** The lack of effective sanction for breach of the time-limit in CrimPR, r. 14.1, should not, however, be treated by prosecutors as a licence to take as long as they like to draft the indictment. In *Sheerin*, Lawton LJ gave this warning (at p. 71):

> If there is inordinate delay in preferring a bill of indictment, which clearly has caused, or clearly is likely to cause prejudice to accused persons, then the judge may very well not exercise his discretion and leave the prosecution to take such course as they think fit. Prosecutors should not assume that they will always be granted leave to prefer a voluntary bill of indictment.

Similarly, in *Soffe* (1982) 75 Cr App R 133, Donaldson LJ (at pp. 136–7), 'first and foremost', emphasised 'that it is the duty of all concerned to take all reasonable steps to ensure that bills of indictment are preferred within the 28-day period'.

COUNTS WHICH MAY BE INCLUDED IN AN INDICTMENT

Having identified who is responsible for drafting the indictment, and when that task needs to **D11.13** have been performed, the next question becomes which charges may be included in the indictment. This is a question of which charges may be included in the original draft of the indictment, rather than matters of joinder, severance or amendment to the indictment which may alter its content between the original drafting and the trial (which are dealt with below). The power to amend derives from the Indictment Act 1915, s. 5 (*Wells* (1995) 159 JP 243 and *Osieh* [1996] 1 WLR 1260; and see **D11.100**).

Charges Revealed by the Papers

The Administration of Justice (Miscellaneous Provisions) Act 1933, s. 2(2)(a), allows a bill of **D11.14** indictment charging an offence to be preferred if the person charged has been sent for trial, pursuant to the CDA 1998, s. 51 and sch. 3, in each case in conjunction with proviso (i) to the subsection. The proviso is: 'where the person charged has been sent for trial, the bill of indictment against him may include, either in substitution for or in addition to any count charging an offence specified in the notice under section 57D(1) of the Crime and Disorder Act 1998, any counts founded on material which, in pursuance of regulations made under paragraph 1 of schedule 3 to that Act, was served on the person charged, being counts which may lawfully be joined in the same indictment'. This position is reflected by the CrimPR, r. 14.2(5), and CPD II, para. 14A.1 (see Supplement, **PD-19**).

It follows that, subject to the rules on when counts and/or defendants are sufficiently closely linked to be properly joined in a single indictment (see **D11.63** and **D11.72**), a draft indictment may include charges for *any* indictable offence disclosed by the evidence served under the regulations for the service of the prosecution case after he has been sent. Usually the counts in the indictment simply follow the original charges.

Where the drafter chooses to include a count for an offence in respect of which the accused was not sent, he must be careful to ensure that the offence is in fact disclosed by the statements, so as to ensure compliance with the proviso to s. 2(2)(i). He must also ensure, pursuant to CPD II, para. 14A.1, that as much notice as possible of such charges is provided to the accused.

Application of the Proviso in s. 2(2)(i)　　Further points as to the effect of proviso (i) to the **D11.15** Administration of Justice (Miscellaneous Provisions) Act 1933, s. 2(2), are as follows.

(a) The prosecution may not rely on the proviso to s. 2(2) of the 1933 Act to prefer an indictment consisting *entirely* of counts for charges in respect of which the accused was not sent for trial, even where the accused has been sent on other charges and the offences charged in the indictment are disclosed by the evidence that was before the justices (*Lombardi* [1989] 1 All ER 992, which arose in the context of committal proceedings). The reasoning in *Lombardi* was that, in the absence of at least one count on the indictment for a 'committal' offence, the 'non-committal' counts cannot properly be said to be in addition to or in substitution for counts charging the offence in respect of which the accused was committed, as required by the terms of the proviso.

(b) The proviso may not be relied on to add counts to an indictment where that joinder in one indictment would have contravened the Indictment Rules 1971, r. 9 (now r. 14.2(3)), on the joinder of counts. This was demonstrated in *Lombardi*, in which Lord Lane CJ said (at p. 77):

> Section 2(2) is clearly restrictive. Its primary purpose is to prevent indictments being preferred save after committal or alternative judicial leave. The proviso allows some relaxation, which is itself restricted by the final words 'being counts which may lawfully be joined in the same indictment'.

It would, in our judgement, be contrary to the whole tenor of the section to allow the prosecution to prefer indictments in the way they here suggest without any reference to justices, judge or appellate court...

...charges in respect of which there has been no committal, even though based on evidence which was before the justices, can only be the proper subject of indictment where two conditions are satisfied. First, they must be in 'substitution' for or in addition to the counts in respect of which [the] defendant was committed...

The second condition which has to be satisfied is that the new counts 'may lawfully be joined in the same indictment'. That must...mean the same indictment as that containing the charges on which the appellant was committed. That is clear from the whole context and also from the use of the word 'include'...

In short, in the judgment of this court, the words of section 2(2) and its proviso are not apt to entitle the prosecution to prefer the second indictment.

(c) The proviso requires that any offence, other than one on which the accused was sent for trial, must be founded on the papers served under the regulations for the service of the prosecution case after he has been sent, but it does not require that such evidence must be conclusive (*Biddis* [1993] Crim LR 392, another case concerned with committal proceedings). In *Biddis*, it was argued that it was not permissible to add a count of possessing a firearm to the charge of robbery upon which the accused had been committed because a statement formally proving that it was a firearm within the meaning of the Firearms Act 1968, s. 57(1), was not included in the committal papers. The Court of Appeal held that evidence that the gun had been loaded and fired was sufficient evidence from which the jury could reasonably have inferred that it was an effective weapon.

D11.16 **Limitations to the Application of the Proviso** There are two important limitations to objections to indictments on the basis that there has not been compliance with the proviso.

(a) Insofar as an indictment consists of separate counts against several accused who are individually charged (i.e. there is no joint count), the counts against each accused should be treated for purposes of proviso (i) as a separate indictment. Therefore, if two accused, A1 and A2, were separately sent for trial (e.g., because, although their offences are linked, one was not arrested until after the other had been sent for trial) and the prosecution then prefer a single indictment against them both, neither can successfully argue that the counts were preferred without authority simply because the offence alleged against his co-accused happened not to be disclosed by the material served on himself (*Groom* [1977] QB 6): see **D11.22**. This principle is now embodied in CPD II, para. 14A.2 (see Supplement, **PD-19**).

(b) Section 2(2) and its proviso do not apply to the amendment of an indictment, being concerned with the question of what offences can be included in the bill of indictment when it is *preferred*. The power to amend derives from the Indictments Act 1915, s. 5 (*Wells* (1995) 159 JP 243 and *Osieh* [1996] 1 WLR 1260; and see **D11.100**).

Counts for Summary Offences

D11.17 In addition to being able to indict the accused for those offences for which he has been sent for trial together with any other indictable offences disclosed by the material served on the accused, the drafter of an indictment has a limited power to include counts for certain summary offences.

The power is contained in the CJA 1988, s. 40, and arises when (s. 40(1)):

(a) the accused has been sent for trial for an indictable offence; and
(b) a summary offence to which s. 40 applies is either:
  (i) 'founded on the same facts or evidence as a count charging an indictable offence', or
  (ii) 'is part of a series of offences of the same or similar character as an indictable offence which is also charged'; and
(c) the facts or evidence relating to the summary offence were disclosed 'to a magistrates' court inquiring into the offence as examining justices', or are disclosed by material served on the

accused as part of the procedure for sending indictable-only offences to the Crown Court under the CDA 1998, s. 51 and sch. 3 (see **D10**).

Where a count for a summary offence is included in an indictment by virtue of s. 40(1), it is tried exactly as if it were an indictable offence, but, if the accused is convicted, the maximum penalty that may be imposed is that which could have been imposed for the offence by a magistrates' court (s. 40(2)). In *Lewis* [2014] 1 Cr App R 345 (25) it was emphasised that an indictment including offences pursuant to s. 40 remained valid even if the accused was acquitted of the indictable offence.

Criminal Justice Act 1988, s. 40   **D11.18**

(1) A count charging a person with a summary offence to which this section applies may be included in an indictment if the charge—
   (a) is founded on the same facts or evidence as a count charging an indictable offence; or
   (b) is part of a series of offences of the same or similar character as an indictable offence which is also charged,
but only if (in either case) the facts or evidence relating to the offence are disclosed by material which, in pursuance of regulations made under paragraph 1 of Schedule 3 to the Crime and Disorder Act 1998 (procedure where person sent for trial under section 51 or 51A), has been served on the person charged.
(2) Where a count charging an offence to which this section applies is included in an indictment, the offence shall be tried in the same manner as if it were an indictable offence; but the Crown Court may only deal with the offender in respect of it in a manner in which a magistrates' court could have dealt with him.
(3) The offences to which this section applies are—
   (a) common assault;
   (aa) an offence under section 90(1) of the Criminal Justice Act 1991 (assaulting a prisoner custody officer);
   (ab) an offence under section 13(1) of the Criminal Justice and Public Order Act 1994 (assaulting a secure training centre custody officer);
   (b) an offence under section 12(1) of the Theft Act 1968 (taking motor vehicle or other conveyance without authority etc.);
   (c) an offence under section 103(1)(b) of the Road Traffic Act 1988 (driving a motor vehicle while disqualified);
   (d) an offence [of criminal damage etc.] which would otherwise be triable only summarily by virtue of section 22(2) of [MCA 1980]; and
   (e) any summary offence specified under subsection (4) below.

The Relevant Summary Offences   The summary offences to which the CJA 1988, s. 40,   **D11.19** applies are common assault, assaulting a prisoner custody officer or a secure training centre custody officer, taking a motor vehicle without the owner's consent, driving while disqualified and criminal damage where the value involved is the relevant sum or less (s. 40(3)).

For the purposes of s. 40(3), common assault includes the offence of battery (*Lynsey* [1995] 3 All ER 654), but common assault is not included as a lesser alternative to assault by beating unless added as a specific count (see *Nelson* [2013] 1 WLR 2861).

Although included within the scope of s. 40, criminal damage is not, strictly speaking, a summary offence, even when the value involved is less than the relevant sum. The MCA 1980, s. 22, merely provides that, where it is clear that the value does not exceed the relevant sum of £5,000, the court 'shall proceed *as if* the offence were triable only summarily' (*Fennell* [2000] 1 WLR 2011 and *Considine* (1980) 70 Cr App R 239). If the committing magistrates have not gone through the s. 22 procedure, the Court of Appeal has held that s. 40 will have no relevance, and the Crown Court is therefore not fettered by s. 40(2) to pass such sentence as could have been passed in a magistrates' court (*Alden* [2002] 2 Cr App R (S) 74).

However, the court came to the opposite view more recently in *Gwynn* [2003] 2 Cr App R (S) 41. The distinction between the two cases lies in the stage at which the criminal damage count was added to the indictment. In *Gwynn* the count had been on the indictment from the outset, and the court had applied its mind to the s. 22 consideration of the value of the criminal damage, whereas in *Alden* the count had been added once the case was in the Crown Court and s. 22 did not therefore arise.

D11.20 **The Preconditions in s. 40 of the Criminal Justice Act 1988** As to the preconditions for including a count for a summary offence, the CJA 1988, s. 40(1), does *not* require the magistrates actually to have committed the accused for trial for the summary matter, providing that the facts relating to the summary offence have been disclosed 'to a magistrates' court inquiring into the offence as examining justices'.

The phrases 'founded on the same facts *or evidence* as a count charging an indictable offence' and 'part of a series of offences of the same or similar character as an indictable offence', are taken almost verbatim from the Indictment Rules 1971, r. 9 (now r. 14.2(3)). The only significant difference between them is that r. 14.2(3) does not contain the words 'or evidence', and so to that extent the rule is narrower in ambit. This is borne out by *Plant* [2008] 2 Cr App R 386 (see **D16.70**).

The Court of Appeal has provided guidance as to interpretation of the phrase:

(a) In *Bird* [1996] RTR 22, B was charged on an indictment containing two counts: (1) possession of an offensive weapon (triable either way) which was found in his car when he was stopped and (2) driving while disqualified (summary only), in relation to the fact that he was driving at all. The Court of Appeal, rejecting the argument that charge (2) was improperly joined, held that the two offences were committed at the same time as he drove along and were 'founded on the same facts or evidence'.

(b) In *Smith* [1997] QB 837, the Court of Appeal held that offences of driving a conveyance taken without authority and driving while disqualified were not offences of a similar character to dangerous driving (which was the only indictable offence in the indictment on which the defendant was tried). Since the first two offences were not founded on the same facts as the third offence, they were improperly joined to the indictment, and the convictions in respect of them were quashed (see **D11.64**).

D11.21 Section 40 of the CJA 1988 should be read in conjunction with the CDA 1998, s. 51(3) (see **D10.6**), which requires a magistrates' court to send the accused for trial for any either-way or summary offence with which he is charged and which appears to the court to be related to the offence being sent to the Crown Court under the CDA 1998, s. 51(1) (provided that, if the offence is a summary offence, it is punishable with imprisonment or disqualification from driving). In the case of juveniles, the CDA 1998, s. 51A (see **D24.41**), has a similar effect.

DUPLICATION OF INDICTMENTS

D11.22 Closely linked with the questions of authority to prefer an indictment and counts that may be included in an indictment (see **D11.13**) is the question of whether there may be more than one indictment outstanding against an accused for the same offence. The effect of the somewhat intricate case law is as follows:

(a) Ordinarily, a single sending for trial may be used as authority to prefer several indictments (see, e.g., *Follett* [1989] QB 338 per Lord Lane CJ at p. 344H). Similarly, if several accused are all sent for trial on one occasion, the prosecution may choose to indict them separately if, for example, the offences are not sufficiently linked for a single trial to be in the interests of justice or they wish to use the evidence of one accused against the others.

(b) An accused may have two or more indictments outstanding against him for the same offence (*Poole* [1961] AC 223). Thus, if X has been sent for trial separately for offences A and B, if offences A and B are connected as required by the rules on joinder of counts, the prosecution may serve a joint indictment for both offences. The existence of a prior indictment for offence A by itself is no bar to the later joint indictment but the prosecution will be required to elect before trial on which of the two they wish to proceed (see **D11.95**).

(c) Similarly, where two accused are separately sent for trial and it is then wished to have them tried together, the prosecution may prefer a joint indictment regardless of whether separate indictments have already been preferred against the two accused individually (*Groom* [1977] QB 6 and CPD II, para. 14A.2 (see Supplement, **PD-19**)).

(d) Equally, the prosecution may, where counts in an indictment are improperly joined, ask the judge for leave to prefer two or more fresh indictments out of time and then elect to proceed on those instead of on the original. The consequent duplication of counts between the original and fresh indictments is irrelevant (*Follett* [1989] QB 338 at p. 345C–D). The prosecution must, however, ensure that the fresh indictments are preferred before the original one is quashed.

GENERAL FORM OF AN INDICTMENT

Layout

The layout of an indictment should substantially follow the form given in the CrimPR and the Indictments Act 1915. The form must be one of those set out in the CPD (r. 14.2(1)). The basic requirements as to the layout of an indictment are as follows: **D11.23**

(a) Each offence charged should be set out in a separate paragraph or *count* (r. 14.2(1)). If there is more than one count, they should be numbered (r. 14.2(4)).

(b) Each count should be divided into a statement of offence and particulars of offence (r. 14.2(1)(a) and (b)).

(c) The statement of offence describes the offence shortly in ordinary language, and, if the offence is statutory, should specify by section and subsection the provision contravened (Indictments Act 1915, s. 3(1), and r. 14.2(1)(a)).

(d) The particulars of offence should give 'such particulars as may be necessary for giving reasonable information as to the nature of the charge' (Indictments Act 1915, s. 3(1)). This is supplemented by r. 14.2(1)(b) which states that there should be included 'such particulars of the conduct constituting the commission of the offence as to make clear what the prosecutor alleges against the defendant'.

In short, the CrimPR, part 14 requires that the statement of offence makes clear what legislation underlies the charge, and that the particulars make clear what the accused is alleged to have done. It follows that the rules now require less than the Indictment Rules 1971, r. 6, which required all the essential elements of the offence to be disclosed (r. 6(b)), save that (a) it was not necessary to allege that the accused fell outside any 'exception, proviso, excuse or qualification' to liability, and (b) failure to disclose an essential element could be disregarded if the accused was not thereby 'prejudiced or embarrassed in his defence' (proviso to r. 6(b) and (c)). **D11.24**

Indictments Act 1915, s. 3

(1) Every indictment shall contain, and shall be sufficient if it contains, a statement of the specific offence or offences with which the accused person is charged, together with such particulars as may be necessary for giving reasonable information as to the nature of the charge.

(2) Notwithstanding any rule of law or practice, an indictment shall, subject to the provisions of this Act, not be open to objection in respect of its form or contents if it is framed in accordance with the rules under this Act.

Degree of Detail Required in the Particulars

D11.25   In normal circumstances, the particulars of offence are drafted in a short form. Such a course is encouraged as a means to avoid complex, lengthy or unmanageable trials (*Cohen* (1992) *Independent*, 29 July 1992).

Such brevity does not prejudice the defence since the way the prosecution put their case and the evidence they intend to call will sufficiently emerge from the documents served. For example, in *Teong Sun Chuah* [1991] Crim LR 463, the appellants were convicted of obtaining by deception. One of the grounds of appeal was that no particulars were given of the false representations relied on in support of the charges. The Court of Appeal said that, although it was advantageous for particulars to be given of the false representations in such cases, it was plain in the present case what the particulars were. No injustice was done by failing to spell them out in advance.

However, it is established practice to give extended particulars where the offence charged is complicated. For example, in *Warburton-Pitt* (1991) 92 Cr App R 136, the prosecution's failure to particularise the facts upon which they relied in support of allegations of recklessness formed the basis of a successful appeal. The Court of Appeal said that particulars of the allegations of recklessness were needed because the case was a complicated one; there were a number of possible explanations for the incident.

A comparison of *Teong Sun Chuah* and *Warburton-Pitt* demonstrates that the test is: do the particulars provided, whether in the indictment or elsewhere, meet the requirement in r. 14.2(1)(b) that there should be clarity as to the nature of the prosecution case?

This test was reaffirmed by the Court of Appeal in *K* [2005] 1 Cr App R 408. The particulars of the offence needed to provide reasonable information as to the nature of the charge and as to the principal matters on which the prosecution relied. In the case of a conspiracy charge, the indictment needed to spell out the agreement alleged, but such further information as is provided to assist the defence does not thereby become an ingredient of the offence that must be proved and on which the jury in due course have to be unanimous.

Moreover, it is open to the defence to ask for additional particulars. One of the purposes of doing so is to anchor the prosecution to a particular means by which the charge may be made out (see, e.g., *Landy* [1981] 1 All ER 1172 and *Hancock* [1996] 2 Cr App R 554).

Components of the Particulars

D11.26   Rule 5(2) of the Indictment Rules 1971 made provision for the rules to include specimen forms of counts approved by the Lord Chief Justice. No such specimens were provided under the 1971 Rules, and the 2007 redraft removed even reference to them. Such authority as there is on drafting counts for specific offences is therefore derived from decided cases. In addition, the CPS has issued guidance as to how particulars for certain offences should be drafted, and has drafted model forms for such counts (see www.cps.gov.uk/legal/index.html). A suggested form of count for the major offences will also be found in the section of this work dealing with the offence in question.

The standard components of particulars are:

(a) the names of the defendants charged in the count;

(b) the date of the offence (or the dates of the period within which it occurred if the precise date is not known);

(c) the act constituting the offence (e.g., 'stole' such and such an item of property, or 'inflicted grievous bodily harm' on such and such a person);

(d) the name of the victim of the offence (e.g., the owner of the property stolen or the person wounded or assaulted); and

(e) the state of mind on the part of the accused which the prosecution must establish in order to secure a conviction.

Points of drafting procedure which apply generally, whatever the specific offence alleged, are considered below.

Names   A person named in an indictment (whether as accused, victim or otherwise) should   **D11.27**
be described by his or her forenames and surname (see 2 Hale 175). Errors in stating names will not, however, affect the validity of the proceedings, provided that the misnamed person is identified with reasonable precision and the parties are not misled. Under r. 8 of the Indictment Rules 1971, it was sufficient where a person's name was not known to describe him as a 'person unknown'. There seems no reason to depart from that practice under the new rules. Trading companies may be described by their corporate name, whether or not they are incorporated.

Date of the Offence   The count should state the date on which the offence occurred insofar as   **D11.28**
it is known. Normal practice is to give the day of the month, followed by the month, followed by the year (e.g., 'on 1st day of January 2014'). If the precise date is unknown, it is sufficient to allege that the offence occurred 'on or about' a specified date, or 'on a day unknown' before a specified date, or 'on a date other than the date in count one'. Where the formula 'on or about' a date is used, the evidence must show the offence to have been committed 'within some period that has a reasonable approximation to the date mentioned in the indictment' (per Sachs LJ in *Hartley* [1972] 2 QB 1 at p. 7).

An alternative permitted formulation is 'on a day unknown between' two specified dates. If the last-mentioned formula is adopted, the days specified should be those immediately before the earliest and immediately after the latest days on which the offence could have been committed.

Thus, if the accused is found in possession of stolen goods on 31 December 2014 and the prosecution case is that the goods were stolen on 1 January 2013, a count for handling would allege that he received the goods 'on a day unknown between 31 December 2012 and 1 January 2015'. See also **D11.52** on duplicity in relation to this formulation.

Materiality of Date   If the evidence at trial as to date differs from that particularised in the   **D11.29**
count, that is not, as a rule, fatal to a conviction (*Dossi* (1918) 13 Cr App R 158; and see *Pritchett* [2007] EWCA Crim 586, in which *Dossi* was approved and it was held not to invalidate an indictment that the offence charged was in force for only part of the period mentioned in the indictment).

This position will be different where the allegation as to date is not merely procedural, but may determine the outcome of the case. For example, in some instances the date on which the act occurred will affect the age of the alleged victim, which may be material. This was the case in *Radcliffe* [1990] Crim LR 524, where, in a case of indecency with a child, the judge in summing-up said: 'The dates which are set out in the indictment . . . are immaterial. The prosecution do not have to prove that any particular act happened between those dates. What you have to prove is that it happened.' The Court of Appeal criticised this direction because the jury may have been left with the belief that her age was immaterial and that they could convict even if she was over 14 at the time.

Avoiding Prejudice as to Dates   The decision in *Wright v Nicholson* [1970] 1 All ER 12, pro-   **D11.30**
vides authority for the proposition that where the defence may have been prejudiced in the preparation of their case by a divergence during the evidence from the date specified in the count, the trial may be adjourned to allow them to respond to the altered situation. Alternatively, it might be necessary to discharge the jury and have a second trial on an amended indictment. Failure to allow an adjournment could result in the quashing of any resultant conviction as being unsafe or unsatisfactory.

However, some caution is necessary in applying that decision in the present context because (a) the appeal was not against conviction on indictment but against the dismissal by the Crown Court of an appeal against summary conviction, and (b) the Divisional Court's reasoning was

Part D Procedure

D

partly based on the faulty premise that the Crown Court had power to amend the information on which the magistrates had convicted the appellant.

D11.31   **Amendment of Dates**   Since divergence between a count and the evidence as to date is not in itself fatal to conviction, it may be unnecessary for the prosecution to apply for the indictment to be amended on such a divergence becoming apparent (*Dossi* (1918) 13 Cr App R 158; but see *Bonner* [1974] Crim LR 479, where the Court of Appeal apparently overlooked the point). However, as a matter of practice, it may be preferable to eliminate the divergence by an appropriate amendment, thus avoiding confusing the jury.

Continuous Offences

D11.32   In most instances, the rule against duplicity (i.e. each count may allege only one offence, see D11.45) requires that a count must allege that the offence occurred on *one* day, not on several days. Were it to be otherwise, the only sensible interpretation of such an allegation would be that the accused had committed several distinct offences on different days. Although, the prosecution is permitted to have one count for what are technically distinct criminal acts where those acts formed a single activity or transaction (e.g., pursuant to the CrimPR, r. 14.2(2)), the mention of more than one day (whether conjunctively or disjunctively) in the count is inconsistent with there having been a single activity on the accused's part.

The difference here is between an offence being committed once between a start and end date, and the offence having been committed repeatedly but separately on a number of days.

The exception to the general principle just stated is that where an offence is properly to be regarded as a continuing offence which may take place continuously or intermittently over a period of time, then a count may properly allege that it occurred on more than one day.

D11.33   **Enunciation of the Principle in *Hodgetts v Chiltern District Council***   The leading authority on drafting charges for continuous offences is *Hodgetts v Chiltern District Council* [1983] 2 AC 120, in which the House of Lords was concerned with the validity of an information under the Town and Country Planning Act 1971, s. 89(5), which created two offences, an initial one committed immediately where there was non-compliance with an enforcement notice requiring the subject of the notice to desist from a certain use of land, and a further offence committed by a person who had already been convicted of the initial offence and who still failed to desist from the prohibited use.

The argument for H was that s. 89(5) was separately breached on each day of the period during which an enforcement notice was ignored, and a separate information was required for each day. Rejecting this argument, Lord Roskill said (at p. 128, emphasis added):

> It is not an essential characteristic of a criminal offence that any prohibited act or omission, in order to constitute a single offence, should take place once and for all on a single day. It may take place, whether continuously or intermittently, over a period of time.
>
> ... as respects non-compliance with a 'desist' notice, it is in my view clear that the initial offence (as well as the further offence) though it too may take place over a period, whether continuously or intermittently (e.g., holding a Sunday market), is a single offence and not a series of separate offences committed each day that the non-compliance prior to the first conviction for non-compliance continues.
>
> ... in the instant case each information ... charged the offence 'on and since' a specified date ... I see no objection to [that wording], but it might be preferable if hereafter offences under the first limb of section 89(5) were charged as having been committed between two specified dates, the termini usually being on the one hand the date when compliance with the enforcement notice first became due and on the other hand a date not later than the date when the information was laid, or of course some earlier date if meanwhile the enforcement notice has been complied with. *Indictments frequently charge offences as having been committed between certain dates.* I see no reason in principle why the same practice should not be followed with these informations.

Application of the Principle   Other than in circumstances to which the CrimPR, r. 14.2(2),   **D11.34**
has application, the following points on drafting counts for continuous offences emerge from
the above decision:

(a) Although *Hodgetts v Chiltern District Council* [1983] 2 AC 120 concerned an information
    for a summary offence, the italicised words above make clear that the same principles apply
    to counts in an indictment.
(b) Determining whether an offence is properly to be treated as continuous will require detailed
    analysis of the offence-creating provision. In the absence of specific authority, the drafter of
    an indictment may have no means of knowing with certainty whether the offence for which
    he is indicting the accused is continuous or not. In such cases, it may be preferable to avoid
    potential complications by stating that the offence occurred on one day (not on several),
    unless the continuation of the misconduct significantly adds to the gravity of the case.
(c) That said, conspiracy is a clear example of a continuous indictable offence. The offence
    begins when any two or more parties enter into the unlawful agreement and continues until
    it comes to an end. See, e.g.:
    (i) *Greenfield* [1973] 3 All ER 1050 (and see **D11.46**), where a count for conspiring to cause
        explosions between 1 January 1968 and July 1971 was held not to be bad for duplicity;
    (ii) *Landy* [1981] 1 All ER 1172, where the Court of Appeal, in indicating how the pros-
        ecution should have drafted a count for conspiracy to defraud a bank, suggested that the
        particulars could have begun '[The defendants] *on divers days* between ... and ... con-
        spired together and with ...'.
(d) Theft is clearly not a continuous offence. However, where the evidence is that the accused,
    on numerous separate occasions over a lengthy period, stole small sums or items of property,
    but it is not possible to particularise the exact days on which the appropriations occurred,
    it is possible to have a single count alleging that, on a day within the overall period, the
    accused stole all the relevant money or property. The cases on this point (known as the
    general deficiency cases) are considered at **B4.3** (see also the discussion of sample counts at
    D11.36). This problem may also be cured by the CrimPR, r. 14.2(2).

Effect of the CrimPR, r. 14.2(2)   Rule 14.2(2) states: **D11.35**

> More than one incident of the commission of an offence may be included in a count if those inci-
> dents taken together amount to a course of conduct having regard to the time, place or purpose of
> commission.

Before this form of words was incorporated into the CrimPR, it had been argued that it was
usually possible to allege only one incident per count as to allege more than one incident in a
count fell foul of the rule against duplicity (see **D11.45**).

Circumstances in which it is suggested to be appropriate to use r. 14.2(2) to charge a 'multiple
offending count' are identified in CPD II, para. 14A.10 (see Supplement, **PD-19**):

> Rule 14.2(2) of the Criminal Procedure Rules allows a single count to allege more than one inci-
> dent of the commission of an offence in certain circumstances. Each incident must be of the same
> offence. The circumstances in which such a count may be appropriate include, but are not limited
> to, the following:
> (a) the victim on each occasion was the same, or there was no identifiable individual victim as, for
>   example, in a case of the unlawful importation of controlled drugs or of money laundering;
> (b) the alleged incidents involved a marked degree of repetition in the method employed or in
>   their location, or both;
> (c) the alleged incidents took place over a clearly defined period, typically (but not necessarily) no
>   more than about a year;
> (d) in any event, the defence is such as to apply to every alleged incident without differentiation.
>   Where what is in issue differs between different incidents, a single 'multiple incidents' count
>   will not be appropriate, though it may be appropriate to use two or more such counts accord-
>   ing to the circumstances and to the issues raised by the defence.

Counts which allege more than one incident can give rise to certain difficulties. One, which was identified in *Kidd* [1998] 1 All ER 42, is that the accused should be sentenced only for offences on which he has been indicted and of which he has been convicted. This is discussed further at **D20.52**.

In *Hartley* [2012] 1 Cr App R 91 Hughes LJ gave further guidance for multiple incident indictments. In particular:

(a) it is important to make clear where it is the case that what is charged is a course of conduct, and make clear the period over which it is charged;

(b) a verdict on the resultant charge must not be impossible to interpret, and so, where it is possible that there was one incident during the period encompassed by the course of conduct count, a count alleging that incident should also be included in the indictment (such a course may also avoid the difficulty of some jurors being sure of one incident and others being sure of another, a matter addressed in *Williams* [2012] EWCA Crim 2516);

(c) where specific incidents can be identified even 'exiguously' (e.g., 'the time the vase broke',) it is appropriate for such a single incident to be indicted and particularised in such terms (the same approach was encouraged in *Hobson* [2013] 1 WLR 3733);

(d) where the period of time over which the course of conduct is said to have occurred is long, it should be addressed by a series of counts covering the period (e.g., on a yearly basis).

Specimen or Sample Counts

D11.36 Where a person is accused of adopting a systematic course of criminal conduct, and where it is not appropriate to allege a continuous offence (see **D11.32**) or a multiple offending count (see **D11.35**), the prosecution sometimes proceeds by way of specimen or sample counts. For example, where dishonesty over a period of time is alleged, a limited number of sample counts are included so as to avoid too lengthy an indictment.

D11.37 **Procedure for Specimen Counts**   The practice which the prosecution ought to adopt in these circumstances is as follows:

(a) the defence should be provided with a list of all the similar offences of which it is alleged that those selected in the indictment are samples;

(b) evidence of some or all of these additional offences may in appropriate cases be led as evidence of system;

(c) in other cases, the additional offences need not be referred to until after a verdict of guilty upon the sample offence is returned (*DPP v Anderson* [1978] AC 964).

D11.38 **Potential Problems with Specimen Counts**   Potential problems arise with specimen counts in relation to sentencing because the accused should not thereby be denied his right to be tried by a jury for offending for which he may ultimately be sentenced. This is discussed at **D20.56** *et seq.*

In any event, it is crucial that the accused should know the case he has to meet (*Evans* [1995] Crim LR 245). In *Rackham* [1997] 2 Cr App R 222, the Court of Appeal emphasised that the indictment had to be drafted in such a way as to enable the accused to know, with as much particularity as the circumstances would admit, what case he had to meet.

D11.39 **Split Trials**   As an alternative to the use of specimen counts, ss. 17 to 21 of the DVCVA 2004 permit a court in certain circumstances to order that the trial of certain counts on an indictment take place before a jury in the normal way and that, if the jury convicts the accused on those counts, the remainder should then be tried before a judge alone. These provisions are set out and discussed at **D13.80**.

The procedure, drafting and service of indictments is set out at CPD II, paras. 14A.4 to 14A.9 (see Supplement, **PD-19**). The key points are:

(a) the prosecution must identify when drafting the indictment which counts should be tried by the jury and which should be held in reserve for the judge;

(b) when such an indictment is served, it should be accompanied by an application for a preparatory hearing, because it is only at such a hearing that such a mode of trial may be ordered (see
D15.49).

Place of the Offence

Provided the conduct alleged against the accused constitutes an offence regardless of where it **D11.40**
occurred, it is unnecessary for the particulars to specify venue. In *Wallwork* (1958) 42 Cr App R 153,
the particulars alleged that the offence, in that case of incest, had been committed 'in the county of
Sussex or elsewhere'. The Court of Criminal Appeal held that the indictment was not bad for duplicity as the venue need not have been mentioned at all. Lord Goddard CJ said (at pp. 156–7):

> So far as place is concerned, I think [counsel for the prosecution's] point is a perfectly good one, that
> incest is an offence wherever it is committed, and it matters not whether it is committed in one place
> or another, provided the prisoner knows the substance of the charge against him. It makes no differ-
> ence whether the incest in this case was committed in Sussex or Surrey or any other place…. There are
> cases…in which it is necessary to indicate a particular place in the indictment, and an illustration [is]
> the offence of larceny on a ship which was at the time of the larceny in a harbour or in a creek or other
> place of anchorage…where it would be necessary to show that the theft took place while the ship was in
> a harbour or some particular creek, and then it would be necessary to mention the name of the harbour
> or creek. But…it is not necessary to refer to any place in the indictment in an offence of this description.

The example given in the above passage of instances where the place of offence should be particularised may be anachronistic, but current examples of the same requirement are burglary
and dangerous driving. Counts for the former should state the building entered as a trespasser,
and counts for the latter the roads or other public places where the driving took place. The
reason, in both cases, is that, having regard to the definition of the offences, the place where the
prohibited conduct occurred is an essential ingredient of the crime (see, e.g., *Miller* [2011] 1 Cr
App R (S) 7, where it was held that the indictment for burglary should specify if it was committed on domestic premises as this had an impact on the maximum penalty).

Allegations as to Money and Property

The Criminal Procedure Act 1851, s. 18, provides that: **D11.41**

> In every indictment in which it shall be necessary to make any averment as to any money or any
> note of the Bank of England or any other bank, it shall be sufficient to describe such money or bank
> note simply as money, without specifying any particular coin or bank note; and such allegation, so
> far as regards the description of the property, shall be sustained by proof of any amount of coin or of
> any bank note, although the particular nature of the bank note shall not be proved.

Where the offence alleged is one against property, the count must give reasonable particulars
of the property concerned. This is normally done by stating what the property was, and who
owned it. If that is not known, the count may read 'belonging to a person unknown'. The value
of the property need not be stated.

Indicting Secondary Parties

When indicting a secondary party to an offence, namely an aider, abettor, counsellor or procurer, **D11.42**
there is no need to indicate, either in the statement of offence or particulars, that such was his role.
This convenient rule flows from the Accessories and Abettors Act 1861, s. 8, which provides that:

> Whosoever shall aid, abet, counsel, or procure the commission of any indictable offence, whether
> the same be an offence at common law or by virtue of any Act passed or to be passed, shall be liable
> to be tried, *indicted*, and punished as a principal offender [emphasis added].

The usual practice is to take advantage of the 1861 Act and employ the same form of words in
indicting a secondary party as would be used against a principal offender.

There is, however, no objection to an express allegation of aiding and abetting, and it may be
preferable so to draft if the circumstances are such that the accused could not possibly have

been guilty as a principal offender. In such cases, the precedent for a count against a principal offender may be adapted by prefixing the statement of offence with the words 'Aiding and abetting', and by inserting in the particulars 'aided and abetted [name of principal offender] to …'.

Where the prosecution are unsure of the precise role played by the accused, it is permissible to allege aiding, abetting, counselling or procuring in the alternative in one count (*Ferguson v Weaving* [1951] 1 KB 814).

D11.43   The normal practice of indicting secondary parties as if they were principals was criticised in *Maxwell* [1978] 3 All ER 1140, where the particulars for an offence of doing an act with intent, contrary to the Explosive Substances Act 1883, s. 3(a), alleged that M had planted a pipe bomb whereas in reality he had merely guided others to the scene where they planted it. The House of Lords dismissed M's appeal against conviction, but Viscount Dilhorne said, *obiter*, at p. 1352G:

> It is desirable that the particulars of the offence should bear some relation to the realities and where, as here, it is clear that the appellant was alleged to have aided and abetted the placing of the bomb and its possession or control, it would … have been better if the particulars of offence had made that clear.

Lords Hailsham of St Marylebone, Fraser and Edmund-Davies all commented to like effect; see, e.g., Lord Edmund-Davies at p. 1359G: 'However surprising and unreal such allegations might have sounded to a jury, … it has to be said that such wording [of the count] was strictly in accordance with section 8 of the Accessories and Abettors Act 1861' (but see *Montague* [2013] EWCA Crim 1781).

Consequences of Errors

D11.44   What if the particulars of offence are incorrect? In *Moses* [1991] Crim LR 617, the Court of Appeal observed that particulars of offence were not like the words of a statute, such that failure of the facts proved to fall precisely within them was fatal. It seems that the test to apply in relation to incorrect particulars is whether the defence were prejudiced by the erroneous description of the offence (see also *Hancock* [1996] 2 Cr App R 554).

THE RULE AGAINST DUPLICITY

The Rule

D11.45   The ordinary rule is that each count in an indictment must allege only one offence. If a count alleges more than one offence, it is said to be bad for duplicity and should be quashed before arraignment.

D11.46   **Duplicity Revealed by the Wording of the Count**   Whether or not a count is bad for duplicity is decided by looking at its wording without reference to the prosecution evidence as disclosed by the evidence served under the regulations for the service of the prosecution case after the accused has been sent for trial (*Greenfield* [1973] 3 All ER 1050, a case decided in the context of committal papers, followed in *Mintern* [2004] EWCA Crim 7).

This is illustrated by *Greenfield* itself, in which the appellants and others were charged in a count which alleged that they had conspired together to cause, by explosive substances, explosions in the UK. The prosecution relied on evidence of a series of explosions occurring in different parts of England which the jury were invited to conclude had all been the work of the same group.

On appeal, the defence argued that the conspiracy count was bad for duplicity because, as the trial progressed, the evidence was consistent with the existence of more than one conspiracy. The Court of Appeal held that, even if that were so, it did not affect the validity of the count, although it was essential that the jury should be directed to convict only if they found the offence charged proved. Lawton LJ said (at pp. 1155F–1156B):

> A conspiracy count is bad in law if it *charges* the defendants with having been members of two or more conspiracies. This is elementary law…. [Count 1] referred to one conspiracy only … judges may be in doubt as to what they should consider before deciding whether a conspiracy count is bad

for duplicity. They should look first at the count itself. In most cases it will be unnecessary to look at any other material. If particulars of the count have been requested and given, those too should be considered . . . . If the prosecution has been requested to give particulars and has refused to do so, the judge may have to look at the depositions to discover the nature of the charge.

Duplicity in a count is a matter of form; it is not a matter relating to the evidence called in support of the count.

D11.47 Thus, leaving aside the exceptional case of the defence having asked for and been refused additional particulars of a count, the only matters to be considered by a judge determining whether a count is bad for duplicity are the form (i.e. wording) of the count and any additional particulars supplied by the prosecution. The evidence as disclosed on the served documents is irrelevant. In *Ali* [2011] 3 All ER 1071 the Court of Appeal held that it was not appropriate to include two conspiracy charges in an indictment which were the same in law but factually different so as to gauge the jury's finding of fact for the purposes of sentence (see also **D19.83**).

If the evidence called at trial in fact establishes more than one offence but only one offence is charged in the count, then, subject to any possible amendment of the indictment, the accused will be entitled to an acquittal, not because the count was bad, but because the prosecution have failed to prove him guilty of the precise offence charged in the count, even though they may have proved him guilty of some other offence or offences (*Griffiths* [1966] 1 QB 589, which has been considered more recently in *Mehta* [2012] EWCA Crim 2824 and *Shillam* [2013] EWCA Crim 160).

D11.48 **Consideration of the Meaning of 'Offence'**   The proposition that a count must charge only one offence begs the question, what is an offence? The issue came before the House of Lords in *DPP v Merriman* [1973] AC 584. In that case two brothers (FM and JM) were charged in a joint count with wounding P with intent, where the evidence showed JM to have stabbed P both on his own and then with FM. In considering whether the judge had been correct to direct the jury that they should ignore any possibility that JM was acting in concert with FM, and should concentrate solely on whether he had personally stabbed P, the House of Lords considered the true import of the rule against duplicity. Lord Morris of Borth-y-Gest said (at p. 593A–E):

It is . . . a general rule that not more than one offence is to be charged in a count in an indictment . . . . The question arises — what is an offence? . . . I agree . . . that it will often be legitimate to bring a single charge in respect of what might be called one activity even though that activity may involve more than one act. It must, of course, depend upon the circumstances. In the present case, it was not at any time suggested, and in my view could not reasonably have been suggested, that count 1 was open to objection because evidence was to be tendered that the respondent stabbed [P] more than once.

In a similar vein, Lord Diplock said (at p. 607C):

The rule against duplicity, viz. that only one offence should be charged in any count of an indictment . . . has always been applied in a practical, rather than in a strictly analytical, way for the purpose of determining what constituted one offence. Where a number of acts of a similar nature committed by one or more defendants were connected with one another, in the time and place of their commission or by their common purpose, in such a way that they could fairly be regarded as forming part of the same transaction or criminal enterprise, it was the practice, as early as the 18th century, to charge them in a single count of an indictment. Where such a count was laid against more than one defendant, the jury could find each of them guilty of one offence only: but a failure by the prosecution to prove the allegation, formerly expressly stated in the indictment but now only implicit in their joinder in the same count, that the unlawful acts of each were done jointly in aid of one another, did not render the indictment *ex post facto* bad or invalidate the jury's verdict against those found guilty.

D11.49 **The Test Derived from *DPP v Merriman***   In summary, the conclusion in *DPP v Merriman* [1973] AC 584 was that a count is not to be held bad on its face for duplicity merely because its words are logically capable of being construed as alleging more than one criminal act. This applies whether a count is against one accused or several.

The test of whether it is proper to have a single count is: can the separate acts attributed to the accused fairly be said to form a single activity or transaction? (see **D11.57**). It follows from that test that, if the particulars of a count can sensibly be interpreted as alleging a single activity, it will not be bad for duplicity, even if a number of distinct criminal acts are implied.

This interpretation of the rule against duplicity clearly forms the basis for the rule permitting 'multiple offences' counts to be found in the CrimPR, r. 14.2(2). As the wording of that rule demonstrates, what is permitted is a count alleging a series of offences that amount to a course of conduct or, to use Lord Diplock's words, the same 'criminal enterprise' (see **D11.35**).

Practical Application of the Rule

D11.50   Thus, the rule against duplicity rests ultimately on common sense and pragmatic considerations of what is fair in all the circumstances. That being so, the rule is best understood in terms of past decisions on what is acceptable drafting practice, rather than by applying an artificial concept of what is a single offence. The guidelines below emerge from the cases.

D11.51   **Several Dates**   Unless the offence charged is properly to be construed as a continuing offence (see **D11.32**), a count alleging that the accused committed criminal acts on more than one day is bad for duplicity.

For example, in *Thompson* [1914] 2 KB 99, the count charged alleged the commission of incest 'on divers days between the month of January, 1909, and the 4th day of October, 1910'. Although the Court of Criminal Appeal dismissed the appeal because the appellant had had ample notice of the precise dates on which the acts of incest were said to have occurred, it was common ground that the count was 'irregular' because it patently alleged more than one offence.

However, in *DPP v McCabe* [1992] Crim LR 885, a charge alleging that M stole 76 library books from South Glamorgan Library between two specified dates was held not to be bad for duplicity. The Divisional Court held that where there is appropriation of a number of articles, but no evidence as to when the individual appropriations took place, the prosecution is entitled to charge the appropriation of the aggregate number within a specified period.

D11.52   **Several Items of Property**   A count for an offence against property may allege that several items were stolen, damaged, unlawfully possessed or otherwise subjected to the accused's criminal behaviour (per Lord Morris of Borth-y-Gest in the passage from *DPP v Merriman* [1973] AC 584, quoted at **D11.48**, and see *Wilson* (1979) 69 Cr App R 83). Provided there is nothing on the face of the count to indicate to the contrary, it will be presumed that, even if a separate criminal act is being alleged in respect of each item, those acts were so closely related as to form part of a single activity and are therefore properly charged in a single count.

A single count is appropriate if only one act is being alleged, albeit that the act was in respect of several items (e.g., *Thomas* (1800) 2 East PC 934, in which a count for uttering a number of forged receipts in one bundle was upheld). But the special circumstances of a case may make separate counts for each item necessary or desirable even if what is alleged against the accused is a single act or activity. For example, in *Bristol Crown Court, ex parte Willets* (1985) 149 JP 416, where the accused was charged with possession of five obscene videos, the Divisional Court said it would have been better to include five separate counts to allow the jury to consider the obscenity of each video individually (see also *Malhi* [1994] Crim LR 755).

D11.53   **Several Victims**   Old cases provide examples of a single count naming more than one person as the victim of the offence (see, e.g., *Giddins* (1842) Car & M 634). Modern practice, however, is in general to have a separate count per victim (see, e.g., *Mansfield* [1977] 1 All ER 134, in which M was charged, *inter alia*, with seven counts of murder, a different victim being named in each count, even though all seven deaths resulted from a single fire allegedly started by M).

Even so, what is appropriate must depend ultimately on the facts of each case. For example:

(a) In *Shillingford* [1968] 2 All ER 200, the Court of Appeal said it was unnecessary to have two separate counts where it was alleged that the appellant had administered a drug to enable both himself and another to have unlawful sexual intercourse with the victim. According to Salmon LJ: '…the essence of this offence consists in administering the drug, and…accordingly in this particular case there was only one offence under the section…In the view of this court, if there is only one administration there is only one offence, whether the administration was for the purpose of enabling one man or half a dozen men to have intercourse with the woman in question.'

(b) Similarly, in *Jemmison v Priddle* [1972] 1 QB 489, an information for taking and killing two red deer was held not to be bad for duplicity because the deer were shot within seconds of each other. In that case, however, there certainly could not have been any objection to two informations.

Count Alleging Acts or Omissions in the Alternative

D11.54 A separate question is raised where the statutory provision creating an offence indicates that it may be committed either by one of a number of positive acts or by a failure to act in one of a number of ways. This problem was specifically addressed by the Rules in their pre-April 2007 incarnation. Rule 7 of the Indictment Rules 1971 stated:

> Where an offence created by or under an enactment states the offence to be the doing or the omission to do any one of any different acts in the alternative, or the doing or the omission to do any act in any one of any different capacities, or with any one of any different intentions, or states any part of the offence in the alternative, the acts, omissions, capacities or intentions, or other matters stated in the alternative in the enactment or subordinate instrument may be stated in the alternative in an indictment charging the offence.

Although the CrimPR, part 14, does not replicate the Indictment Rules 1971, r. 7, the principle remains that a count containing particulars framed in the alternative is not necessarily bad for duplicity, as is recognised for example by the CrimPR, r. 14.2(2).

However, if an enactment creates several offences and it is desired to charge two or more of those offences in the alternative, the indictment must contain a separate count for each. Furthermore, it is plain that a single section, subsection or paragraph of a statute may be construed as creating more than one offence (see, e.g., *Naismith* [1961] 2 All ER 735 at **D11.55**). What is required, therefore, is a correct assessment of whether a statutory provision is creating one offence that may be committed in a number of alternative ways, or is creating several separate offences. If the former, these statutory alternatives may be particularised as alternatives in one count; if the latter, the rule against duplicity applies and each alternative the prosecution wish to put before the jury must go into a separate count.

D11.55 **Application of the Rule as to Alternative Acts or Omissions**   It follows from the discussion at D11.54 that decisions on whether an enactment creates one or several offences have consistently turned on whether, in defining the conduct prohibited, the enactment refers to a single act (or omission) or to several. If one act is referred to, the enactment will almost certainly be construed as creating one offence, even if the *mens rea* or other elements thereof are defined in the alternative; if more than one, it will be held that the enactment creates a separate offence for each separate act.

For example, in *Naismith* [1961] 2 All ER 735, Ashworth J, in determining whether an allegation under military law that N had 'caused grievous bodily harm to H with intent to do him grievous bodily harm or to maim, disfigure or disable him' was bad for duplicity, said (at p. 954):

> It seems to this court that the proposition with which [counsel for the Crown] started his argument is the right approach. That approach is to keep in mind the distinction between a section creating two or more offences and a section creating one offence but providing that that offence may be committed in more than one way…so far as the intents specified in section 18 are concerned, they are variations of method rather than creations of separate offences in themselves. It is probably true to say that the species of assault mentioned in that section, of which there are three, are each in themselves different offences, that is to say, wounding, causing grievous bodily harm and shooting, but that difference does not affect the result of this case in the least because the only act or species of assault alleged was causing grievous bodily harm.

Similarly, it was held in *Thomson v Knights* [1947] KB 336 that a count for being in charge of a motor vehicle when unfit through drink or drugs (contrary to what is now s. 4 of the Road Traffic

Act 1988) was valid because the section made criminal one act, namely being in charge of a vehicle, in two situations, namely when under the influence of drink or when under the influence of drugs.

D11.56 By contrast, in *Mallon v Allon* [1964] 1 QB 385, an information for admitting and allowing to remain in a licensed betting office a person apparently under 18 contrary to s. 5 of the Betting and Gaming Act 1960 (now repealed) was held bad because the enactment referred to two separate acts, first admitting a person on to licensed premises, and secondly allowing him to remain after he had got on to the premises.

Comparison of *Mallon v Allon* with *Thomson v Knights* indicates that the number of offences an enactment is held to create, whether one or several, turns on a fine analysis of the enactment in question, as well as on pragmatic considerations of whether one or several counts would be fairer (for further discussion of this topic see, e.g., **B4.163** and **B4.175**, and *Nicklin* [1977] 2 All ER 444, on the number of counts appropriate when the accused is charged with handling stolen goods); see also *Grout* [2011] 1 Cr App R 472, on the number of counts appropriate in the case of sexual offences.

'Quasi-duplicity'

D11.57 The foregoing discussion of the rule against duplicity demonstrates the distinction between an allegation that the accused has committed a number of distinct offences, which must always be put in separate counts, and an allegation merely that he committed a number of distinct criminal acts which formed part of one activity or transaction, which can properly go into a single count. The distinction was mentioned by both Lord Morris of Borth-y-Gest and Lord Diplock in their opinions in *DPP v Merriman* [1973] AC 584 (quoted at **D11.48**), but the leading authority is the Court of Appeal decision in *Wilson* (1979) 69 Cr App R 83, which incorporates the essential parts of the judgment of Lord Widgery CJ in *Jemmison v Priddle* [1972] 1 QB 489.

D11.58 **The Approach in *Wilson*** In *Wilson* (1979) 69 Cr App R 83, W was charged with theft. The issue was whether the indictment should have been split so as to have a separate count for the items allegedly stolen from different departments of two shops. Browne LJ (giving the judgment of the Court of Appeal) distinguished between duplicity in the full sense of the term and what he described as quasi-duplicity or divergence. He said (at p. 85):

> The word duplicity is used in a rather ambiguous sense ... First there is a case where it appears on the face of the indictment, or particulars of the indictment, that a count is charging more than one offence. It may sometimes be legitimate to look at the depositions in this context (see *Greenfield* [1973] 1 WLR 1151). That has been referred to in the course of the argument as true duplicity. Secondly, there is a case where, although the indictment is good on its face, it appears at the close of the prosecution case that the evidence establishes that more than one offence was committed on the occasion to which a particular count relates. Perhaps that is best described as divergence or departure, but it often seems to be called duplicity ... in whatever sense one uses the word duplicity, it is confined to those two situations. But even if a case is not within either the first or the second of those situations, there may be cases where, in the interests of justice, it may be right to make the prosecution split a count or elect on what particular charge they are going to proceed.

D11.59 In *Wilson* it was argued that the appellant's case fell within the second of the two situations outlined by Browne LJ (i.e. it was a case of divergence or departure rather than true duplicity). Having reviewed the authorities (especially *Jemmison v Priddle* [1972] 1 QB 489), Browne LJ adopted what Lord Widgery CJ had said in *Jemmison v Priddle* as correctly stating the law ((1979) 69 Cr App R 83 at pp. 86–7):

> Lord Widgery CJ said this ... 'What is the principle which distinguishes between [cases where one count is appropriate and cases where there should be several counts]? ... one finds that the explanation is given in somewhat inappropriate language, namely, that the test is whether the acts were all one transaction. That is a phrase hallowed by time, but not, in my judgment, of particular assistance in dealing with a particular problem. I find more assistance from somewhat different language used by Lord Parker CJ in *Ware v Fox* [1967] 1 WLR 379.' Then Lord Widgery CJ quotes

from what Lord Parker CJ had said at p. 381 ... and went on: 'I think perhaps that the phraseology of Lord Parker is more helpful to me than the phraseology often found in the text books, and I think that what it means is this, that it is legitimate to charge in a single information one activity even though the activity may involve more than one act. One looks at this case [i.e., *Jemmison v Priddle*] and asks oneself what was the activity with which the appellant was being charged. It was the activity of shooting red deer without a game licence, and although as a nice debating point it might well be contended that each shot was a separate act, indeed that each killing was a separate offence, I find that all these matters, occurring as they must have done within a very few seconds of time and all in the same geographical location are fairly to be described as components of a single activity, and that made it proper for the prosecution in this instance to join them in a single charge.'

Browne LJ concluded that: 'Whether there is one or more offence disclosed is really a question of fact and degree' ((1979) 69 Cr App R 83 at p. 88). On the facts of *Wilson*, the appellant 'entirely failed to satisfy' the court that the counts complained of disclosed more than one offence.

Application of the *Wilson* Principle   Thus, the principle emerging from *Wilson* (1979) 69   **D11.60**
Cr App R 83 and the earlier cases is simply that more than one criminal act may properly be alleged in one count if the acts formed a single activity. Whether there was one activity or several depends on the facts of each individual case.

This was illustrated in *Iaquaniello* [2005] EWCA Crim 2029, where the accused was charged on an indictment containing a count of doing an act or a series of acts tending and intended to pervert the course of public justice. The Court of Appeal held that it was not duplicitous for a count to state, in this context, 'act or acts'. Where the particulars of offence alleged that the accused did an act or a series of acts tending, and intended, to pervert the course of justice, it was not duplicitous to particularise the acts within one count on the indictment.

The *Wilson* principle is now reflected in the CrimPR, r. 14.2(2), save that the wording there used is that the acts 'amount to a course of conduct' rather than 'one activity'.

Charging Offences Conjunctively in an Effort to Avoid the Rule against Duplicity

It has so far been assumed that the rule against duplicity will apply whether separate offences   **D11.61**
are alleged in one count as alternatives or conjunctively. That assumption is in line with the overwhelming weight of authority (the only exception being *Clow* [1965] 1 QB 598, which was fact-specific and in any event distinguished in *Mallon v Allon* [1964] 1 QB 385 (see **D11.56**)). The same rule should therefore apply whether a count is framed conjunctively or disjunctively.

Effect of Breach of the Rule against Duplicity

Where a count is bad on its face for duplicity, the defence should move to quash it before the   **D11.62**
accused is arraigned. Although the objection can be taken at a later stage (*Johnson* [1945] KB 419), the Court of Appeal has disapproved of the defence postponing the application to quash for purely tactical reasons (*Asif* (1982) 82 Cr App R 123). It is open to the prosecution to defeat a motion to quash by asking the judge to allow a suitable amendment of the indictment (see the Indictments Act 1915, s. 5(1), for the power to amend indictments at **D11.100**).

The procedure of applying to quash a count will be available only if it is a case of 'true' duplicity, namely that the wording of the count shows that two or more offences are being alleged. Such a motion has to be determined solely by considering the wording of the indictment, without reference to the evidence. In a case of quasi-duplicity or divergence (see *Wilson* (1979) 69 Cr App R 83 and **D11.57**), which becomes apparent only after the evidence has been called, the defence should wait until the close of the prosecution case and then ask the judge to split the count.

Rejection by the trial judge of a motion to quash a count bad on its face for duplicity and/or rejection of an application to split a count open to objection for quasi-duplicity are plainly valid grounds of appeal. In *Donnelly* [1998] Crim LR 131, the Court of Appeal made it clear that cases of true duplicity and quasi-duplicity would be differently treated. In a case where the count was plainly duplicitous in form the appeal must be allowed, even if the point had not been taken at trial (though this does not necessarily follow, see *Thompson* [1914] 2 KB 99). In cases of 'quasi duplicity', a motion to quash the indictment should be moved before the trial judge. If it was not, the appeal would fail unless it was accompanied by an allegation of incompetence by counsel.

The approach taken by the House of Lords in *Clarke* [2008] 2 All ER 665 does not affect the principle that duplicity does not automatically result in the quashing of a count (*Marchese* [2009] 1 WLR 992).

JOINDER OF COUNTS IN AN INDICTMENT

The Rule

D11.63 The circumstances in which the prosecution may lawfully join two or more counts against one accused in a single indictment are prescribed by the CrimPR, r. 14.2(3), which replaces the test formerly contained in r. 9 of the Indictment Rules 1971 without any significant alteration to its content. It now states:

> An indictment may contain more than one count if all the offences charged—
> (a) are founded on the same facts; or
> (b) form or are a part of a series of offences of the same or a similar character.

An indictment containing counts which are not linked in either of the ways mentioned in r. 14.2(3) is invalid (although not a nullity), and any convictions returned on such an indictment are liable to be quashed on appeal. The procedure for such applications is set out in the CrimPR, rr. 3.21 and 3.22 (see Supplement, **R-28** and **R-29**).

Application of the Rule

D11.64 Unsurprisingly, cases in which the application of the rule have been considered relate to r. 9 of the Indictment Rules 1971 rather than the CrimPR, r. 14.2(3). There is no reason to anticipate that the slight changes to the wording of the rule would have any bearing on its application, and such cases are therefore still relevant.

In *Newland* [1988] QB 402, N was charged in an indictment containing counts relating to drugs offences and assaults, which were entirely unconnected. At trial, when counsel for N submitted that the indictment was invalid, the judge held that he had power under s. 5(3) of the Indictments Act 1915 (see **D11.76**) to sever the indictment. On appeal, the Court of Appeal held as follows.

(a) The power to sever under s. 5(3) applies only to a valid indictment. Watkins LJ, giving the court's judgment, said (at p. 406C–D):

> It was contended by counsel for the prosecution that the [trial judge] rightly derived the power he used from [Indictments Act 1915, s. 5(3)]. But we are in no doubt, in accepting the contrary submission of counsel for the appellant, that that subsection can only apply to a valid indictment. It states what the court may do by way of ordering separate trials of counts in a valid indictment in the interests of a fair trial for a defendant or defendants. The [trial judge] was wrong in his interpretation of that subsection.

(b) The trial judge could have amended the indictment so as to delete either the drugs count or the assault counts. That having been done, the trial could validly have proceeded on what remained (p. 406F). See also *Follett* [1989] QB 338.

(c) Given that no amendment had in fact been made, the unamended indictment was invalid by reason of the contravention of r. 9. Because it was capable of being rendered valid by an appropriate amendment, it was not a nullity (p. 408C–D applying *Bell* (1984) 78 Cr App R 305). But, even though the indictment itself was not a nullity, the fact of its being invalid was sufficient to render null the proceedings flowing from it (p. 408E).

(d) In the circumstances, no valid trial ever commenced and the court's powers under the Criminal Appeal Act 1968, s. 2(1), to quash a conviction and sentence therefore did not come into play. Having concluded that the proceedings against N were null, the court had no option but to exercise its inherent power at common law to quash the convictions (p. 408G–H).

In *Smith* [1997] QB 837, the Court of Appeal disapproved of *Newland* insofar as it related to the effect of misjoinder, as outlined in (c) above. Their lordships held that it was wrong to suggest that all proceedings flowing from an indictment containing a count improperly joined were a nullity (as opposed to the proceedings on the improperly joined count). *Smith* was approved and followed in *Lockley* [1997] Crim LR 455.

First Limb of the CrimPR, r. 14.2(3): Charges Founded on the Same Facts

The first limb of r. 14.2(3) is clearly satisfied if the offences alleged in counts joined in one **D11.65** indictment arose out of a single incident or an uninterrupted course of conduct (see, e.g., *Mansfield* [1977] 1 All ER 134, where the indictment against M was held to be properly joined where it contained counts for arson and murder relating to the same fire).

Joinder where One Offence is a Precondition of the Second   Rule 14.2(3) of the CrimPR, **D11.66** like its predecessor, is not restricted to offences that were committed contemporaneously or substantially contemporaneously with each other, as in *Mansfield* [1977] 1 All ER 134 (see D11.65), but extends to situations where later offences would not have been committed but for the prior commission of an earlier offence.

The leading authority is *Barrell* (1979) 69 Cr App R 250, where the appellants were charged jointly in counts 1 and 2 with affray and assault occasioning actual bodily harm, and W alone was charged in count 3 with attempting to pervert the course of justice. This third count related to an attempt by W to persuade the witness to counts 1 and 2 to 'modify' his evidence. On appeal it was submitted that count 3 did not arise from the same facts as counts 1 and 2. The argument was rejected by the Court of Appeal. Shaw LJ, giving the judgment of the court, said (at pp. 252–3):

> The phrase 'founded on the same facts' does not mean that for charges to be properly joined in the same indictment, the facts in relation to the respective charges must be identical in substance or virtually contemporaneous. The test is whether the charges have a common factual origin. If the charge described by counsel as the subsidiary charge is one that could not have been alleged but for the facts which give rise to what he called the primary charge, then it is true to say for the purposes of rule 9 that those charges are founded, that is to say have their origin, in the same facts and can legitimately be joined in the same indictment.

If W had not been involved in the violence which gave rise to the charges of assault and affray, he would have had no motive for offering the witness a bribe. It followed that all three counts had a common factual origin and were properly joined in one indictment.

A factual connection between the counts is established by a coincidence of time and place. It is irrelevant that the accused's explanation is different for each offence (*Roberts* [2009] 1 Cr App R 273).

Joinder of Mutually Destructive Counts   Difficulty has arisen over whether the principle in **D11.67** *Barrell* (1979) 69 Cr App R 250 can properly be extended to counts that are mutually destructive, that is, the prosecution evidence is such that, if their case on one count is accepted, the accused cannot have committed the offence alleged in the other count and vice versa.

The House of Lords settled the point in *Bellman* [1989] AC 836. The case centred on representations which B had made to obtain money. If they were false, he had obtained the property by deception. If they were true, he had conspired to evade the prohibition on the importation of controlled drugs. The indictment contained counts both for conspiracy and for obtaining by deception.

On appeal, B relied 'upon the more fundamental proposition that under our adversarial procedure of trial in which the burden of establishing the guilt of the accused is placed on the prosecution, it can never be right for mutually contradictory counts to be contained in one indictment. He submitted that to do so would be contrary to the prosecution's duty of proving the case, unfair to the accused and an embarrassment for the jury' (pp. 846H–847A). Lord Griffiths rejected the argument. There was nothing in the Indictments Act 1915 to support it; r. 9 of the Indictment Rules 1971 prima facie contradicted it, and no authority had been cited in which joinder had been refused on the ground that the facts of two counts were mutually destructive (p. 849B–D). On the other hand, it had long been the practice to include in one indictment counts for stealing and handling the same property even though a conviction for theft would necessarily preclude a conviction for handling and vice versa (see *Shelton* (1986) 83 Cr App R 379 for approval of the practice).

D11.68   Moreover, there will be occasions when justice can be done only by drafting mutually contradictory counts. An example is provided by the facts of *Barnes* (1985) 83 Cr App R 38, where the indictment contained counts for perjury and wounding with intent, the case being that Barnes was either telling the truth at an earlier trial and so was guilty of wounding, or he was telling lies, in which case he was guilty of perjury. The Court of Appeal dismissed the appeal on the ground that, whether or not the joinder of the mutually destructive counts was lawful, there had on the facts been no miscarriage of justice.

In *Bellman*, Lord Griffiths, *obiter*, confirmed the legality of the joinder because the factual origin of both counts was the attack on the victim (see p. 850F–G). Furthermore, the joinder was necessary in the interests of justice since, had Barnes been tried separately for the two offences, he might have 'played the system' by obtaining an acquittal for perjury through testifying that he had indeed wounded the victim and then, at his later trial for wounding, he could have reversed his evidence, secure in the knowledge that he could not be prosecuted again for perjury.

D11.69   **Application of the Decision in *Bellman***   Although the decision in *Bellman* [1989] AC 836 puts beyond doubt the propriety of joining mutually destructive counts in one indictment, the prosecution will rarely wish to prefer such an indictment in practice, since it leaves open the risk that a jury will not be able to reach a verdict on either. (Certain sexual offences provide one exception, see **B3.1** and **B3.94**.)

As a matter of evidence, it is clear that if, at the end of the prosecution case, it is established that the accused has committed a crime but it is impossible to say which, the judge must direct the jury to acquit. Similarly, if, as in *Bellman* itself, there is evidence on which the jury could properly convict of either count, they must nonetheless be directed in the summing-up that, should they be left in doubt about which of the two offences the accused has committed, they are under a duty to acquit of both, even though they are sure he committed one or other. The various evidential problems that may arise from mutually destructive counts are discussed by Lord Griffiths in *Bellman* at p. 847. See further **D16.63**.

Second Limb of the CrimPR, r. 14.2(3): Series of Offences of the Same or a Similar Character

D11.70   The circumstances in which two or more offences may be said to amount to a series of offences of the same or similar character within the meaning of the second limb of r. 14.2(3) were considered by the House of Lords in *Ludlow v Metropolitan Police Commissioner* [1971] AC 29. The indictment against L contained counts for (a) attempted theft at a public house in Acton on 20 August and (b) robbery at a different public house in Acton on 5 September. The trial judge refused an application that the two charges should be tried separately, and L was convicted on both counts. The case was considered by the House of Lords, where Lord Pearson delivered the leading opinion. The main points emerging from this opinion are as follows.

(a) Two offences are capable of constituting a 'series' for the purposes of r. 9 (see p. 38E–G confirming the Court of Appeal decision in *Kray* [1970] 1 QB 125).

(b) In deciding whether offences exhibit the similarity demanded by the rule, the court should take into account both their legal and their factual characteristics (p. 39B). The prosecution submission (that the phrase 'a similar character' means exclusively of a similar legal character) and the defence submission (that the phrase means exclusively of a similar factual character) were each rejected.

(c) To show the existence of a series of offences, the prosecution must be able to point to some nexus between them. This means 'a feature of similarity which in all the circumstances of the case enables the offences to be described as a series' (p. 39D). A nexus is clearly established if the offences are so connected that the evidence of one would be admissible to prove the commission of the other in accordance with the rules on similar fact evidence, but this is not essential (p. 39D–F, quoting with approval from *Kray* and *Clayton-Wright* [1948] 2 All ER 763).

(d) On the facts of *Ludlow*, the offences were similar in law in that they each had the ingredient of actual or attempted theft. They were also similar in fact because they involved stealing or attempting to steal in neighbouring public houses at a time interval of only 16 days. A sufficient nexus was therefore present to make the offences a series of a similar character within the meaning of r. 9, even though the similarity was not nearly striking enough to bring them within the similar fact evidence rule (p. 39H).

Application of the Principles in *Ludlow* The following cases are decisions on whether the degree of similarity between offences justified joinder under r. 9 of the Indictment Rules 1971, and thus by implication the CrimPR, r. 14.2(3): **D11.71**

(a) *Mansfield* [1977] 1 All ER 134, where three counts for arson were held to be properly joined since the offences were committed within a short space of time, and related to premises in the same geographical area, with each of which the accused had some connection.

(b) *Harward* (1981) 73 Cr App R 168, where it was held that an allegation relating to the handling of stolen goods could not be joined to an offence of conspiring to defraud banks by the use of stolen cheques and cheque cards. The only possible nexus between the charges, there being no factual similarity, was the element of dishonesty. However, the dishonesty in the conspiracy count related to H's involvement in fraudulent practices, whereas that in the handling count related to his state of mind when he received the goods. This was therefore insufficient.

(c) *McGlinchey* (1983) 78 Cr App R 282, where two counts for handling stolen goods were held to be properly joined. The only factual similarity between the offences seems to have been their closeness in time. (*McGlinchey* was applied in *Mariou* [1992] Crim LR 511.)

(d) *Marsh* (1985) 83 Cr App R 165, where the indictment included two pairs for criminal damage and reckless driving and a fifth count of assault occasioning actual bodily harm, relating to a wholly separate incident. The joinder was held to be improper because (i) there was no legal similarity between criminal damage and reckless driving on the one hand and assault on the other, and (ii) the common factual element of violence was insufficient by itself to provide a nexus.

(e) *Baird* [1993] Crim LR 778, where the indictment alleged two counts of indecent assault against two boys, the incidents having taken place nine years apart. Although there was no coincidence in time or place, there were similarities in the offences which, their lordships said, 'were truly remarkable'. They concluded that the judge was entitled to hold that the various counts could properly be joined under r. 9, and was justified in refusing to exercise his discretion to sever under the Indictments Act 1915, s. 5(3) (see **D11.76**).

(f) *C* (1993) *The Times*, 4 February 1993, where the accused was charged with rape and attempted rape. Although the counts were separated in time by 11 years, the victim in each case was the accused's daughter. It was held that the counts were properly joined.

(g) *Williams* [1993] Crim LR 533, where it was alleged that W had falsely imprisoned a girl of 13, having indecently assaulted her five days earlier. The Court of Appeal held that these were two separate incidents and the two offences were not of a similar character, despite an evidential nexus.

(h) *Ferrell* [2011] 1 All ER 95, where it was held that offences of supplying drugs and money laundering were correctly joined, even where the laundering offences pre-dated the possession of the drugs that were the subject of the supply counts, because it was proper for the jury to infer that the money that was laundered was the proceeds of drugs.

JOINDER OF ACCUSED

D11.72 Two or more accused may be joined in one indictment either as a result of being named together in one or more counts on the indictment, or as a result of being named individually in separate counts, albeit that there is no single count against them all.

Joint Counts

D11.73 All parties to a joint offence may be indicted for it in a single count. In drafting the count:

(a) There is no need to distinguish between principal offenders and secondary parties (Accessories and Abettors Act 1861, s. 8: see **D11.42**).

(b) The count need not expressly allege that the unlawful acts of each accused were done in aid of the others, as that allegation is implicit in the drafting of a single count (*DPP v Merriman* [1973] AC 584 per Lord Diplock at p. 607C).

Where the prosecution seek to join an accused to an indictment following an order that the accused in question be retried pursuant to the Criminal Appeal Act 1968, s. 7(2), then, in addition to the considerations of general application to an application for joinder, there is added the need to consider if the accused would be substantially adversely affected, so that joinder would represent an abuse of process (*Booker* [2011] 3 All ER 905). That said, there is no prohibition on the addition of counts to an indictment in such circumstances, where it is fair to do so (*Feeley* [2012] 1 WLR 3133).

D11.74 **Possible Verdicts on Joint Counts** Notwithstanding that the accused have been charged in a single count, the jury may convict all or any of them on the basis that they committed the offence charged independently of the others. For example, in *DPP v Merriman* [1973] AC 584, Lord Diplock said (at p. 607F):

> …whenever two or more defendants are charged in the same count of an indictment with any offence which men can help one another to commit it is sufficient to support a conviction against any and each of them to prove *either* that he himself did a physical act which is an essential ingredient of the offence charged *or* that he helped another to do such an act, *and*, that in doing the act or in helping the other defendant to do it, he himself had the necessary criminal intent.

In short, if two accused, A1 and A2, are charged in a joint count the jury may (a) acquit both, or (b) convict both, or (c) acquit one and convict the other.

Should they convict both it will usually be on the basis implicit in the joint count that they helped each other to commit the crime, but the jury may equally convict both where the evidence suggests that they acted independently of each other if they are satisfied that each accused committed the offence.

Similarly, if there is a split verdict, the verdict against the convicted accused is not open to challenge on the ground that the jury must have found that he acted alone without assistance either from his acquitted co-accused or anybody else. The argument that to uphold convictions on a single count in the absence of proof of joint enterprise contravenes the rule against duplicity was rejected in *DPP v Merriman*.

Despite this, the prosecution is well advised only to draft a joint count where the evidence reveals a joint enterprise. If the co-defendants were acting without reference to each other, separate counts are preferable.

Separate Counts

The joining of two or more accused in one indictment notwithstanding the absence of a joint **D11.75** count against them is governed by the decision in *Assim* [1966] 2 QB 249. In that case, the indictment against the two accused, A and C, contained two counts. The first alleged that A had maliciously wounded W, and the second alleged that C, on the same day, had caused actual bodily harm to L. A and C both worked at the premises where the two assaults had allegedly occurred, a nightclub of which both the victims were customers.

On appeal, A argued that it was bad in law to charge two different people in one indictment with two different offences. Offenders could properly be joined in one indictment only as principals said to have jointly committed one offence, or as principals and accessories (see p. 251F–G for counsel's argument). A five-judge Court of Appeal extensively reviewed the authorities, and (in a judgment given by Sachs J) reached the following conclusions:

(a) Questions of joinder, whether of offences or offenders, are 'matters of practice on which the court has, unless restrained by statute, inherent power both to formulate its own rules and to vary them in the light of current experience and the needs of justice' (p. 258F). On the assumption that the rule (now the CrimPR, r. 14.2(3)) covers only joinder of offences, the propriety of the joinder of offenders is unaffected either by the Indictments Act 1915 or by any other legislation, whether subordinate or primary, passed since then (p. 258E). Subsequently, Lord Widgery CJ in *Camberwell Green Stipendiary Magistrate, ex parte Christie* [1978] QB 602, said that *Assim* should be accepted as laying down a principle that joinder of offenders is a matter of the practice of the courts.

(b) Since joinder of offenders is merely a matter of practice, errors in the application of the relevant rules, though amounting to an irregularity in the proceedings, will not deprive the trial court of jurisdiction. Consequently, the Court of Appeal is entitled to dismiss an appeal against conviction advanced on this ground if there has been no miscarriage of justice (p. 259D–E), and especially where there has been a failure by the defence to object to the joint trial.

(c) Sachs J 'came to some general conclusions as to what would nowadays be an appropriate rule of practice on the basis that none of the rules of 1915 deal with the joinder of offenders'. In summary, joinder is appropriate if the offences separately alleged against the accused are, on the evidence, so closely related by time or other factors that the interests of justice are best served by a single trial. His lordship said (at p. 261B–F):

> As a general rule it is, of course, no more proper to have tried by the same jury several offenders on charges of committing individual offences that have nothing to do with each other than it is to try before the same jury offences committed by the same person that have nothing to do with each other. Where, however, the matters which constitute the individual offences of the several offenders are upon the available evidence so related, whether in time or by other factors, that the interests of justice are best served by their being tried together, then they can properly be the subject of counts in one indictment and can, subject always to the discretion of the court, be tried together. Such a rule, of course, includes cases where there is evidence that several offenders acted in concert but is not limited to such cases.
>
> Again, while the court has in mind the classes of case that have been particularly the subject of discussion before it, such as incidents which, irrespective of there appearing a joint charge in the indictment, are contemporaneous (as where there has been something in the nature of an affray), or successive (as in protection racket cases), or linked in a similar manner, as where two persons individually in the course of the same trial commit perjury as regards the same or a closely

connected fact, the court does not intend the operation of the rule to be restricted so as to apply only to such cases as have been discussed before it.

(d) It was conceded by the appellant and accepted by the court that, where there is a joint count against two accused, that count may be followed by a separate count or counts against one or more of the accused even in relation to a distinct matter, provided that there is no breach of what is now r. 14.2(3) (p. 257D, quoting *Cox* [1898] 1 QB 179). See also *Barrell* (1979) 69 Cr App R 250 at **D11.66**.

(e) On the facts of *Assim*, the joinder of A and C in one indictment was clearly proper, however narrowly any rule as to joinder of offenders might have been formulated (p. 260G). Having regard to the rule of practice Sachs J had stated, the counts they faced were so closely related by time and other factors that indicting the accused jointly was the correct course.

SEVERANCE

D11.76 The court has the power to order the separate trial of accused or of offences that are properly joined in one indictment, pursuant to the Indictments Act 1915, s. 5(3). This is supplemented by:

(a) s. 5(4), which requires the court, following an order for severance under s. 5(3), to make such order for postponement of the trial as appears necessary and expedient; and

(b) s. 5(5), which provides that the procedure on the separate trial of a count following an order under s. 5(3) shall be the same in all respects as if the count had been preferred in a separate indictment.

The power to sever an indictment contained in s. 5(3) was held to apply only to valid indictments in *Newland* [1988] QB 402. However, the decisions of the Court of Appeal in *Smith* [1997] QB 837 and *Lockley* [1997] Crim LR 455 have altered the effect upon the indictment where a count has been improperly joined (see **D11.64**). The procedure for such applications is set out in the CrimPR, r. 3.21 (see Supplement, R-28).

D11.77   Indictments Act 1915, s. 5

(3) Where, before trial, or at any stage of a trial, the court is of opinion that a person accused may be prejudiced or embarrassed in his defence by reason of being charged with more than one offence in the same indictment, or that for any other reason it is desirable to direct that the person should be tried separately for any one or more offences charged in an indictment, the court may order a separate trial of any count or counts of such indictment.

(4) Where, before trial, or at any stage of a trial, the court is of opinion that the postponement of the trial of a person accused is expedient as a consequence of the exercise of any power of the court under this Act to amend an indictment or to order a separate trial of a count, the court shall make such order as to the postponement of the trial as appears necessary.

(5) Where an order of the court is made under this section for the postponement of a trial—

(a) if such an order is made during a trial the court may order that the jury (if there is one) are to be discharged from giving a verdict on the count or counts the trial of which is postponed or on the indictment, as the case may be; and

(b) the procedure on the separate trial of a count shall be the same in all respects as if the count had been found in a separate indictment, and the procedure on the postponed trial shall be the same in all respects (if the jury has been discharged under para (a)) as if the trial had not commenced; and

(c) the court may make such order as to granting the accused person bail and as to the enlargement of recognisances and otherwise as the court thinks fit.

Severance of Counts on an Indictment

D11.78 The proper exercise of the power was considered by Lord Pearson in *Ludlow v Metropolitan Police Commissioner* [1971] AC 29 (see also **D11.70**). Having held that the joinder of the counts against L for attempted theft and robbery was lawful, his lordship dealt with the appellant's further argument that a single trial of the two offences inevitably prejudiced or embarrassed the accused in his defence since the jury heard evidence on count 1 that was inadmissible on count 2 and vice versa. Therefore, the trial judge should have ordered separate trials in exercise of the discretion given him by s. 5(3). In rejecting this argument Lord Pearson said (at pp. 40–2):

> Before the Indictments Act 1915, it was a tenable theory…to say that any joinder of counts relating to distinct alleged offences was necessarily so prejudicial to the accused that such joinder ought not to be permitted. [His lordship then reviewed pre-1915 cases lending support to the theory.]
>
> In my opinion, this theory — that a joinder of counts relating to different transactions is in itself so prejudicial to the accused that such a joinder should never be made — cannot be held to have survived the passing of the Indictments Act 1915. No doubt the juries of that time were much more literate and intelligent than the juries of the late 18th and 19th centuries, and could be relied upon in any ordinary case not to infer that, because the accused is proved to have committed one of the offences charged against him, therefore he must have committed the others as well. I think the experience of judges in modern times is that the verdicts of juries show them to have been careful and conscientious in considering each count separately. Also in most cases it would be oppressive to the accused, as well as expensive and inconvenient for the prosecution, to have two or more trials when one would suffice. *At any rate,…the manifest intention of the Act is that charges which either are founded on the same facts or relate to a series of offences of the same or a similar character properly can and normally should be joined in one indictment, and a joint trial of the charges will normally follow, although the judge has a discretionary power to direct separate trials under section 5(3).* If the theory were still correct, it would be the duty of the judge in the proper exercise of his discretion under section 5(3) to direct separate trials in every case where the accused was charged with a series of offences of the same or a similar character, and the manifest intention appearing from section 4 and [r. 9] would be defeated. *The judge has no duty to direct separate trials under section 5(3) unless in his opinion there is some special feature of the case which would make a joint trial of the several counts prejudicial or embarrassing to the accused and separate trials are required in the interests of justice.* In some cases the offences charged may be too numerous and complicated,…or too difficult to disentangle,…so that a joint trial of all the counts is likely to cause confusion and the defence may be embarrassed or prejudiced. In other cases objection may be taken to the inclusion of a count on the ground that it is of a scandalous nature and likely to arouse in the minds of the jury hostile feelings against the accused…

Application of this Principle   Thus, if counts for separate offences have validly been joined in one indictment, the normal consequence is that they will be tried together. The trial judge should exercise his discretion to order separate trials only if there is a special feature in the case which would make a single trial prejudicial or embarrassing. Although they are not intended to be exhaustive, examples of such special features might include the following.   **D11.79**

(a) *The scandalous nature of the evidence as to one of the counts.* For example in *Laycock* [2003] EWCA Crim 1477, the Court of Appeal warned that prosecutors should be careful not to charge counts that would prejudice an accused unless there was a real purpose to be served. In that case, the prosecution was criticised for including in a firearms indictment a count which showed that the accused had been sentenced to a previous sentence of imprisonment with the result that he was prohibited from possession of a firearm.
(b) *The number and/or complexity of the counts.* This may result in difficulties for a jury in disentangling evidence on one count from that on the other count or counts. In this regard, special considerations govern the trial of counts for sexual offences (see **D11.80**).

The fact that the accused wishes to give evidence in his own defence on one of the counts but not on the others is not, in the normal case, a sufficient reason for severance, even though non-severance will oblige him to choose between not testifying at all and exposing himself to cross-examination about all the charges (*Phillips* (1987) 86 Cr App R 18). See also *Lanford v General Medical Council* [1990] 1 AC 13.

Severance of Multi-count Indictments for Similar Offences, such as Sexual Offences

The CJA 2003, s. 101(1), created a number of gateways by which evidence of offences of a similar kind may be admissible as 'bad character' evidence in support of the offences charged   **D11.80** in the indictment. If such cross-admissibility between allegations is established, it follows that those allegations ought to be tried together. This arises most commonly in cases where there are a number of allegations of sexual offending. To understand the application of s. 101(1) in this context, it is of assistance to identify how the law has developed in relation to the joint trial of a number of sexual offences.

In *DPP v Boardman* [1975] AC 421, the indictment contained counts that B, the headmaster of a boarding-school, had (a) committed buggery on S, a 16-year-old pupil, and (b) had incited H, a 17-year-old pupil, to commit buggery on B. The primary question for the House of Lords was whether the trial judge correctly directed the jury that the evidence of one count was admissible as corroborative evidence in relation to the other. Resolution of this issue involved the answering of two essential questions.

D11.81 **Is the Other Allegation Admissible?** The CJA 2003, s. 101(1), now has a considerable bearing on this question. Some assistance is still provided by *DPP v Boardman* [1975] AC 421, where Lord Cross of Chelsea said that the first question is whether the evidence of one count is admissible supporting evidence of another: 'if it is decided that the evidence is inadmissible and the accused is being charged in the same indictment with offences against the other men the charges relating to the different persons ought to be tried separately' (p. 459D).

The reason why this approach was necessary is because '. . . it is asking too much of any jury to tell them to perform mental gymnastics of this sort. If the charges are tried together it is inevitable that the jurors will be influenced, consciously or unconsciously, by the fact that the accused is being charged not with a single offence against one person but with three separate offences against three persons.'

D11.82 **Has there been Contamination?** Even where the respective offences are otherwise admissible (e.g., as being mutually corroborative), the judge should consider whether there is material in the evidence served under the regulations for the service of the prosecution case after the accused has been sent for trial which suggests that the 'victims' colluded together to tell false stories. Again this should be considered as a preliminary issue.

If there is a real danger that that happened, separate trials should be ordered, but the judge should not use his imagination to invent a conspiracy to make false allegations where there is no evidence in the statements that such a conspiracy existed (see especially *Johannsen* (1977) 65 Cr App R 101, where it was held that the mere fact that four out of the five complainants knew each other gave rise to no more than a speculative possibility that they had collaborated, and there was accordingly no need to direct severance of the counts).

D11.83 **Limitations to the Impact of a Ruling on Severance in Such Cases** A decision as to severance does not represent a final decision on the admissibility of each incident alleged in the indictment as similar fact evidence to prove the others. Even where severance is refused, during the course of the ensuing trial it will still be necessary for the court to rule whether the evidence of one victim corroborates that of the other victims. If the court concludes, contrary to the provisional view taken at the application for severance stage, that each victim's evidence is relevant only to the offence against him, then either the jury must be directed accordingly in the summing-up or, more realistically, the jury should be discharged and severance ordered at that stage.

Conversely, if the court initially ordered severance, the prosecution could still ask to be allowed to lead evidence of the other incidents in support of whichever incident the jury is trying. Detailed guidance from Scarman LJ on how trial judges should approach applications for severance and problems of similar fact evidence in multi-count sexual cases will be found in *Scarrott* [1978] 1 QB 1016 at pp. 1027–8. See also *N (H)* [2011] EWCA Crim 730.

D11.84 **Application of *Boardman* beyond Indictments for Sexual Offences** It might have been thought that the arguments that Lord Cross used in *DPP v Boardman* [1975] AC 421 to justify his dictum that, in cases involving sexual offences, the indictment should be severed if the evidence of one victim could not be used as corroboration of the evidence of the other victims, would apply with equal force whatever the nature of the offence charged. However, the Court of Appeal in subsequent cases has refused to extend the principles stated in *Boardman* and *Scarrott* [1978] 1 QB 1016 beyond multi-count indictments for sexual offences.

Where there is a multi-count indictment for some other type of offence, the principles in *Ludlow v Metropolitan Police Commissioner* [1971] AC 29 apply (see **D11.70**). Accordingly, the judge should order separate trials only if there is a special feature in the case likely to cause the defence prejudice or embarrassment.

(a) In *McGlinchey* (1983) 78 Cr App R 282, the Court of Appeal held that two counts for handling stolen goods on dates approximately six weeks apart were properly joined in one indictment even though there was manifestly no striking similarity between the offences. The court approved the judge's exercise of discretion against severance, applying *Ludlow* and distinguishing *Boardman*.

(b) In *Cannan* (1991) 92 Cr App R 16, the Court of Appeal made it clear that, even where an indictment charged a series of sexual offences, the judge had a discretion whether to sever. This was so even though there was no striking similarity between the evidence on the various counts. The indictment in C's case included three sets of offences which were evidentially separate. The Court of Appeal rejected the submission that the judge should have followed 'the general modern practice in sexual cases', and severed the counts in the absence of striking similarity. Lord Lane CJ said (at p. 23):

> It may well be that often the judge in sexual cases will order severance... But the fact remains that the Indictments Act 1915 gives the judge a discretion, and... that is not a matter with which this Court will interfere, unless it is shown that the judge has failed to exercise his discretion upon the usual and proper principles...

Consideration of the *Boardman* Approach   In *DPP v P* [1991] 2 AC 447, Lord Mackay (at **D11.85** p. 462) made the following comment about the issue of whether, in the absence of striking similarity, there should have been joinder:

> ... the evidence referred to is admissible if the similarity is sufficiently strong, or there is other sufficient relationship between the events described in the evidence of the other young children of the family and the abuse charged, that the evidence, if accepted, would so strongly support the truth of that charge that it is fair to admit it notwithstanding its prejudicial effect. It follows that the answer to the second question is no, provided there is a relationship between the offences of a kind which I have just described.

On one interpretation, this could be taken to mean that the rule on joinder in cases of multiple sexual offences is the same as for admissibility, namely that the offences should constitute similar fact evidence in order to be tried together. However, in *Christou* [1997] AC 117, the House of Lords considered the words used by Lord Mackay, and stated that they were *obiter*. The approach to the question of severance in *Cannan* (1991) 92 Cr App R 16 was endorsed.

Consideration also has to be given to the cross-admissibility of different offences because the evidence of one is relevant to a 'matter in issue' with respect to another, pursuant to the CJA 2003, s. 101(1)(d) (*McAllister* [2009] 1 Cr App R 129, *Freeman* [2009] 2 All ER 18 and more recent decisions such as *AB* [2011] EWCA Crim 3331: see **F12.60**).

The court has a discretion as to severance, with which the appellate courts should interfere only on grounds of *Wednesbury* unreasonableness. In exercising his discretion, the essential task of the trial judge was to achieve a fair resolution of the issues. That required fairness to the accused but also to the prosecution and those involved in it. Among the factors which he might consider were:

(a) how discrete or interrelated were the facts giving rise to the counts;
(b) the impact of ordering two or more trials on the accused and his family, on the victims and their families, and on press publicity; and
(c) importantly, whether directions the judge could give to the jury would suffice to secure a fair trial if the counts were tried together.

(See also *Dixon* (1991) 92 Cr App R 43, *F* [1996] Crim LR 257, *O'Brien* [2000] Crim LR 863, *Thomas* [2006] EWCA Crim 2442 and *N (H)* [2011] EWCA Crim 730.)

Discretion to Order Separate Trials of Accused

D11.86 The court has a discretion to order separate trials of accused who have properly been joined in one indictment in accordance with the principles stated in *Ludlow v Metropolitan Police Commissioner* [1971] AC 29 (see **D11.70**). The existence of the discretion was acknowledged by Sachs J in *Assim* [1966] 2 QB 249. His lordship said at p. 261B–C:

> Where ... the matters which constitute the individual offences of the several offenders are upon the available evidence so related ... that the interests of justice are best served by their being tried together, then they can properly be the subject of counts in one indictment and can, *subject always to the discretion of the court*, be tried together [emphasis added].

Although that was said in the context of an indictment which did not contain a joint count, it has never been doubted that the discretion may be exercised as much in respect of accused charged in a joint count as in respect of those charged in separate counts on one indictment. The discretion may be attributed either to the court's inherent power to control its own proceedings or to the power to sever contained in the Indictments Act 1915, s. 5(3).

D11.87 **Guidance as to the Exercise of the Discretion** Because severance of the trial of jointly indicted accused is a matter of discretion, the way in which the discretion is exercised is unlikely to provide a successful ground of appeal (see **D11.114**). Guidance on ordering separate trials does, however, emerge from the decided cases. The following propositions summarise that guidance.

(a) Where the accused are charged in a joint count, the arguments in favour of a joint trial are very strong. These arguments include:
   (i) severance will necessitate much or all of the prosecution evidence being given twice before different juries and increase the risk of inconsistent verdicts;
   (ii) even if the accused are expected to blame each other for the offence (i.e. will run 'cut-throat' defences), the interests of the prosecution and the public in a single trial will generally outweigh the interests of the defence in not having to call each accused before the same jury to give evidence for himself which will incriminate the other (*Grondkowski* [1946] KB 369; *Moghal* (1977) 65 Cr App R 56; *Edwards* [1998] Crim LR 756; *Crawford* [1997] 1 WLR 1329).
(b) Where the prosecution case against one accused (A1) includes evidence that is admissible against him but not against his co-accused (A2), there is no obligation to order severance simply because the evidence in question might prejudice the jury against A2. However, the judge should balance the advantages of a single trial against the possible prejudice to A2, and should consider especially how far an appropriate direction to the jury is really likely to ensure that they take into account the evidence only for its proper purpose of proving the case against A1 (*Lake* (1976) 64 Cr App R 172; *B* [2004] 2 Cr App R 570; *Miah* [2012] 1 Cr App R (S) 47).
(c) Where a joint trial of numerous accused would lead to a very long and complicated trial, the judge should consider whether a number of shorter trials, each involving only some of the accused, might make for a fairer and more efficient disposition of the issues. This reason for severance is tied up with the rule against overloading indictments, which is considered at **D11.91**.

(d) There may be some distinction to be drawn between cases where the accused are jointly charged in a single count and those where they allegedly committed separate offences which were nonetheless sufficiently linked to be put in one indictment. In the latter situation, the cases against the accused are unlikely to be as closely intertwined as when a joint offence is alleged, and the public interest argument in favour of a single trial is correspondingly less strong. There should, therefore, be a greater willingness to order separate trials.

Presumption in Favour of Joint Trial The authorities cited above indicate that the decision **D11.88** whether or not to grant severance is one within the discretion of the trial judge, and that the decision should be in favour of joint trial unless the risk of prejudice is unusually great. Thus in *Josephs* (1977) 65 Cr App R 253, where the same issue arose as in *Lake* (1976) 64 Cr App R 172, Lord Widgery CJ said (at p. 255, emphasis added):

> ...it is a very rare thing for this court to interfere with the trial judge's decision about separate trials. Nothing is more peculiarly left to the trial judge as his concern with that particular point. *Of course we have jurisdiction to interfere where something has clearly gone wrong*, but it is very rare, and members of the court today cannot remember a case in which such an interference with the trial judge's decision was made.
>
> ...the fact that some of [a co-accused's] statements may rub off on the other accused...is just one of those things that happens in the course of a multiple criminal trial. The advantages of having co-defendants tried together is so great that the right to order a separate trial will not be granted unless there is good reason for it.

Refusal of Severance as a Ground of Appeal In general, the Court of Appeal will interfere with **D11.89** the exercise of a discretion only if it can be shown that the trial judge took into account irrelevant considerations, or ignored relevant ones, or arrived at a manifestly unreasonable decision. This was illustrated in *Moghal* (1977) 65 Cr App R 56, where the appeal failed even though the members of the court indicated strongly that, had they been trying the case, they would not have acted as the trial judge had done. The test of whether to intervene is usually stated simply as: did the trial judge's decision cause unacceptable prejudice to the appellant such as might have led to a miscarriage of justice? (*Grondkowski* [1946] KB 369 and *Moghal* (1977) 65 Cr App R 56).

In a suitable case, however, the Court of Appeal has shown that it is willing to exercise its power to intervene where, to use the words of Lord Widgery CJ in *Josephs* (1977) 65 Cr App R 253, 'something has clearly gone wrong'.

(a) In *O'Boyle* (1991) 92 Cr App R 202, O was charged with conspiracy to supply cocaine. His co-defendant R alleged that he had acted under duress from O. At trial, O's confession to US investigators was excluded, but counsel for R sought to cross-examine O on its contents. On appeal, the Court of Appeal held that the trial judge should have ordered severance. The court recognised that the trial judge had a discretion and that, generally, conspirators should be tried together. However, this was an exceptional case, where separate trials would have done little or no harm to the co-defendant or prosecution, while joint trial prejudiced the appellant. See also *Randle* [1995] Crim LR 331.

(b) In *Smith* (1966) 51 Cr App R 22, S and two others were prosecuted in relation to a large-scale theft. The evidence against the co-accused consisted largely of their admissions to the police, in which they also implicated S. The evidence directly admissible against S was scanty. The co-accused were acquitted and S alone convicted. Although the Court of Criminal Appeal accepted that the trial judge had correctly rejected an application for separate trials, the court nevertheless held that the only explanation for S alone being convicted was that the jury must have been prejudiced against him by the material in the co-accused's statements, notwithstanding the judge's direction that those statements were evidence only against the co-accused (see the discussion of *Smith* in *Lake* (1976) 64 Cr App R 172 at p. 177).

What the decisions in *Lake* and *Josephs* demonstrate is a distinction between ordinary prejudice **D11.90** occasioned by a joint trial and what Lord Widgery referred to as 'dangerous prejudice'. The

D

Part D Procedure

former is almost bound to arise when co-accused run inconsistent defences and does not in general justify severing the indictment. The latter, exemplified by *Smith*, should be dealt with by severance. See also *Miah* [2012] 1 Cr App R (S) 47.

Note that the situation may be different where the admissions made by one accused become admissible against another in the circumstances identified in *Hayter* [2005] 2 All ER 209.

Overloading Indictments

D11.91   In drafting indictments and in ruling on applications to sever indictments, both the drafter and the court should have regard not only to what is permitted by the rules on joinder (discussed from **D11.63**) but also to whether the interests of justice are best served by one long trial or several shorter ones.

If a single indictment, containing numerous counts and/or accused, would result in an unduly long or complicated trial and place an unfair burden on the jury, the prosecution should opt for however many shorter indictments are necessary to cover the same ground, notwithstanding that a single indictment would be within the rules. Similarly, if the prosecution have not taken the initiative in this regard, the court should intervene to order separate trials, whether of counts or accused.

In *Wright* [1995] Crim LR 251, it was made clear that the mere length of a trial is not sufficient in itself to characterise convictions as unsafe. (See also *Kellard* [1995] 2 Cr App R 134.) The issue is therefore not that a trial can never be both long and fair, but that no jury ought to be required to try an overloaded indictment.

There are various sources of guidance in this regard, including the observations of Lord Judge CJ in *N* [2010] 2 Cr App R 97 and the guidance related to cases of serious fraud (which are discussed in more detail in **D4** and **D15**).

D11.92   **Observations of the Court of Appeal**   Dicta on overloaded indictments are contained especially in *Novac* (1976) 65 Cr App R 107 and *Thorne* (1977) 66 Cr App R 6.

In *Novac*, there were some 19 counts against four accused (N, R, A-C and A). The major count was against N, R and A-C and alleged a conspiracy to procure males under 21 to commit acts of gross indecency. Further counts alleged specific offences such as living on the earnings of male prostitution, importuning in a public place and buggery or gross indecency with named persons. These had been committed both during the currency of the conspiracy and outside that period. The fourth accused (A) was not alleged to be a member of the conspiracy, but was charged with further indecency offences which had been uncovered during the police investigation.

D11.93   Bridge LJ, during the course of the judgment of the court, made observations about this complicated indictment (at p. 188):

> We cannot conclude this judgment without pointing out that…most of the difficulties which have bedevilled this trial, which have led in the end to the quashing of all convictions except on the conspiracy and related counts, arose directly out of the overloading of the indictment…the indictment of 19 counts against four defendants resulted…in a trial of quite unnecessary length and complexity. If the specific offence counts against [N, R and A-C] and all the counts against [A] had been tried separately, the main trial of the conspiracy and related counts would have been reasonably manageable and the four separate trials would have been short and straightforward. Quite apart from the question whether the prosecution could find legal justification for joining all these counts in one indictment and resisting severance, the wider and more important question has to be asked whether in such a case the interests of justice were likely to be better served by one very long trial, or by one moderately long and four short separate trials.
>
> We answer unhesitatingly that whatever advantages were expected to accrue from one long trial,…they were heavily outweighed by the disadvantages. A trial of such dimensions puts an

immense burden on both judge and jury. In the course of a four or five-day summing-up the most careful and conscientious judge may so easily overlook some essential matter. Even if the summing-up is faultless, it is by no means cynical to doubt whether the average juror can be expected to take it all in and apply all the directions given. Some criminal prosecutions involve consideration of matters so plainly inextricable and indivisible that a long and complex trial is an ineluctable necessity. But we are convinced that nothing short of the criterion of absolute necessity can justify the imposition of the burdens of a very long trial on the court.

Much the same sentiments were expressed in *Thorne*, where the trial was even longer. The indictment related essentially to three separate armed robberies. In addition, there were counts for related conspiracies to rob, handling some of the proceeds, and conspiracy to pervert the course of justice by making threats against a potential prosecution witness. In all, there were ten counts and 14 accused, and the trial lasted nearly seven months. The Court of Appeal (Lawton LJ) commented that the indictment was undoubtedly overloaded, and the trial placed 'a burden on the judge which he should never be asked to bear' (at p. 14). **D11.94**

A further aspect of not overloading indictments arises when the conduct of the accused may either be charged in a number of distinct offences or brought under one charge. In those circumstances, the prosecution should have just one count for the obviously appropriate offence, because nothing is gained and much is lost in terms of simplicity of presentation to the jury if the indictment contains counts for all the offences of which the accused might possibly be guilty (*Staton* [1983] Crim LR 190). This is the situation in which the CrimPR, r. 14.2(2), comes into its own (see **D11.35**).

Putting the Prosecution to its Election Both *Novac* (1976) 65 Cr App R 107 and *Thorne* (1977) 66 Cr App R 6 were cases in which the complexity of the indictment was in part attributable to the combination of conspiracy and substantive charges. CPD II, para. 14A.3 (see Supplement, **PD-17**), addresses this problem: **D11.95**

Criminal Practice Directions, para. 14A.3

14A.3 Save in the special circumstances described in the following paragraphs of this Practice Direction, it is undesirable that a large number of counts should be contained in one indictment. Where defendants on trial have a variety of offences alleged against them then, in the interests of effective case management, it is the court's responsibility to exercise its powers in accordance with the overriding objective... The prosecution may be required to identify a selection of counts on which the trial should proceed, leaving a decision to be taken later whether to try any of the remainder. Where an indictment contains substantive counts and one or more related conspiracy counts, the court will expect the prosecution to justify the joinder. Failing justification, the prosecution should be required to choose whether to proceed on the substantive counts or on the conspiracy counts. In any event, if there is a conviction on any counts that are tried, then those that have been postponed can remain on the file marked 'not to be proceeded with without the leave of the court or the Court of Appeal'. In the event that a conviction is later quashed on appeal, the remaining counts can be tried. Where necessary the court has power to order that an indictment be severed.

The 'special circumstances' alluded to in para. 14A.3 are where there is a split between a trial by jury and a trial by judge alone pursuant to the DVCVA 2004, ss. 17 to 21 (see **D11.39** and CPD II, paras. 14A.4 to 14A.9) and where multiple offending counts are used pursuant to the CrimPR, r. 14.2(2), (see **D11.35** and CPD II, paras. 14A.10 to 14A.13).

If a substantive count and a related conspiracy count are joined in the indictment, the prosecution will have to justify their inclusion. If their inclusion is not justified, the prosecution will have to decide on which counts they wish to proceed. It follows that a conspiracy count which adds nothing to the charge of a substantive offence has no place in the indictment (*Jones* (1974) 59 Cr App R 120; see *Watts* (1995) *The Times*, 14 April 1995). **D11.96**

If the prosecution elect to proceed upon the substantive charge, such an election is not necessarily irreversible. In *Findlay* [1992] Crim LR 372, for example, the prosecution, which had elected to proceed on substantive robbery counts, were permitted to reverse that election when the evidence necessary to sustain a conviction on those counts was later ruled inadmissible. The Court of Appeal dismissed the appeal, in view of the fact that there was no demonstrable prejudice to F.

D11.97 **Cases of Serious Fraud** The most striking instances of overloaded indictments have emerged in serious fraud cases.

One illustration is *Cohen* (1992) *Independent*, 29 July 1992 (the 'Blue Arrow' case), a case in which the indictment was long and complex, and in which the jury did not retire until the 184th day of the trial. The Court of Appeal said that the basic assumption that the jury determined guilt or innocence on evidence which they were able to comprehend and remember had been destroyed in that case. The prosecution had a heavy responsibility not to overload the indictment, but the ultimate responsibility lay with the trial judge, whose powers of severance should have been used at an early stage to overcome the problems of an overloaded indictment.

The prosecution's responsibility to ensure that the indictment was not overloaded was emphasised amongst the conclusions of the HM Crown Prosecution Service Inspectorate report, 'Review of the Investigation and Criminal Proceedings Relating to the Jubilee Line case', June 2006. At paras. 1.30 to 1.32, the Review emphasised that the lack of particularisation in the conspiracy to defraud allegation relied on by the prosecution, and its reliance on broad inferences which necessitated detailed examination of a very considerable number of documents, resulted in a considerable lengthening of the trial without any material effect on the overall level of criminality. The Review underlines the importance of the prosecution ensuring at the outset that their allegations are particularised, focused and aimed at keeping the evidence and length of trial within reasonable bounds.

D11.98 On 22 March 2005, 'A Protocol for the Control and Management of Heavy Fraud and other Complex Criminal Cases' was published. The Protocol is examined in more depth elsewhere (see **D15.50**); however, in the context of overloaded indictments it has the following to say, under the heading of 'consideration of the length of the trial' (para. 3(vi)):

(d) One course the judge may consider is pruning the indictment by omitting certain charges and/ or by omitting certain defendants. The judge must not usurp the function of the prosecution in this regard, and he must bear in mind that he will, at the outset, know less about the case than the advocates. The aim is to achieve fairness to all parties.

(e) Nevertheless, the judge does have two methods of pruning available for use in appropriate circumstances:

(i) Persuading the prosecution that it is not worthwhile pursuing certain charges and/or certain defendants.

(ii) Severing the indictment. Severance for reasons of case management alone is perfectly proper, although judges should have regard to any representations made by the prosecution that severance would weaken their case.... However, before using what may be seen as a blunt instrument, the judge should insist on seeing full defence statements of all affected defendants. Severance may be unfair to the prosecution if, for example, there is a cut-throat defence in prospect. For example, the defence of the principal defendant may be that the defendant relied on the advice of his accountant or solicitor that what was happening was acceptable. The defence of the professional may be that he gave no such advice. Against that background, it might be unfair to the prosecution to order separate trials of the two defendants.

D11.99 **Reopening an Application for Severance** An application to sever the indictment may be made on more than one occasion. Sometimes the second application will be before the same judge but not necessarily so (e.g., where the first application was made at a pre-trial review: see D15.46).

In *Wright* (1989) 90 Cr App R 325, Judge G at the pre-trial review refused to sever a conspiracy count from an indictment which also contained a series of counts relating to substantive offences. Before the trial itself began, defence counsel applied again to sever, this time before Judge C, who rejected the submission on the ground that the matter had been concluded by Judge G. The Court of Appeal held that the question for the second judge was whether there had been a sufficient change to justify reopening the question. If there had not, he was not obliged to hear the same point argued again.

AMENDING THE INDICTMENT

Statutory Provision

The power to amend an indictment, once it has been served, lies in the Indictments Act 1915, s. 5(1).   **D11.100**

Indictments Act 1915, s. 5

(1) Where, before trial, or at any stage of a trial, it appears to the court that the indictment is defective, the court shall make such order for the amendment of the indictment as the court thinks necessary to meet the circumstances of the case, unless, having regard to the merits of the case, the required amendments cannot be made without injustice.

Extent of the Power to Amend

The power to amend may be exercised both: **D11.101**

(a) in respect of formal defects in the wording of a count, for example when the statement of offence fails to specify the statute contravened or when the particulars do not disclose an essential element of the offence, and

(b) in respect of substantial defects such as divergences between the allegations in the count and the evidence foreshadowed in the material served under the regulations for the service of the prosecution case after the accused has been sent for trial or called at trial.

This was confirmed by the Court of Criminal Appeal in *Pople* [1951] 1 KB 53 at p. 54:

> The argument for the appellants appeared to involve the proposition that an indictment, in order to be defective, must be one which in law did not charge any offence at all and therefore was bad on the face of it. We do not take that view. In our opinion, any alteration in matters of description, and probably in many other respects, may be made in order to meet the evidence in the case so long as the amendment causes no injustice to the accused person.

It followed that the trial judge in *Pople* had been entitled to allow an amendment at the close of the prosecution case to make the property allegedly obtained by deception from a building society a cheque rather than the sum of money. Furthermore, there was no injustice to the accused because the matter in which the indictment was defective was 'the mere description of the thing obtained', while 'in substance, the charge was the same'.

Similarly, in *Radley* (1973) 58 Cr App R 394, Lord Widgery CJ quoted with approval the passage from *Pople* quoted above, and held that an indictment may be defective if it merely fails to allege an offence disclosed by the material served when sending for trial. 'Defective', in the context of s. 5(1), is not restricted to defects in form, but 'has got a very much wider meaning' (p. 401). Moreover, this wide meaning is acceptable because the power to amend is subject to the overriding limitation that it must not cause injustice (p. 402). See also *Booker* [2011] 3 All ER 905 for a recent restatement of the principle that the interests of justice should not be narrowly construed for these purposes.   **D11.102**

The power to amend may be exercised in respect of voluntary bills of indictment preferred on the direction of a High Court judge just as it may be exercised in respect of 'ordinary' indictments preferred on the authority of a sending for trial (*Allcock* [1999] 1 Cr App R 227; *Wells* [1995] 2 Cr App R 417 at p. 422; *Walters* (1979) 69 Cr App R 115 — all cases decided in the context of committal proceedings).

D11.103   **Limitation on Power to Amend**   If the indictment is so defective as to be a nullity, it is not capable of amendment and there is a mistrial. An indictment is invalid from the outset in this way where, for example, it alleges an offence unknown to law. Where a count describes a known offence inaccurately, however, it is capable of amendment, subject to the usual considerations of prejudice to the defendant (*McVitie* [1960] 2 QB 483, applied in *Tyler* (1992) 96 Cr App R 332).

D11.104   **Amendment by Insertion of a New Count**   As well as enabling amendments to be made to existing counts, s. 5(1) of the Indictments Act 1915 permits the insertion of an entirely new count into an indictment, whether in addition to or in substitution for the original counts (*Johal* [1973] QB 475), where Ashworth J said (at p. 481A), 'there is no rule of law which precludes amendment of an indictment after arraignment, either by addition of a new count or otherwise'.

The words 'after arraignment' appear in the sentence quoted because the main point at issue in that case was whether the amendment was made too late, but obviously the addition of a count before arraignment is even less open to objection than a subsequent addition. Where the addition is made after arraignment, it will be necessary to put the new counts to the accused for him to plead to them.

The amendment to an indictment can be so extensive that the question arises whether it amounts to the substitution of a fresh indictment. This was the issue in *Fyffe* [1992] Crim LR 442, where the Crown amended an 11-count indictment so that it contained 27 counts. It was submitted on appeal that the 27-count indictment was a fresh indictment and therefore the judge should have gone through the procedural steps of staying the 11-count indictment and granting the prosecution leave to prefer the 27-count indictment out of time, whereupon the defendants should have been arraigned once more. The appeal was dismissed since, for all material purposes, the 27 counts reproduced what had appeared in the 11 counts. No new allegations had been added; the amendments were of form rather than substance and it was not necessary to go through the process of re-arraignment.

D11.105   **The Evidential Basis for the New Count**   A further question arises as to whether it is necessary for the amendment to be founded on the material disclosed under the regulations for the service of the prosecution case after the accused has been sent for trial. According to the Court of Appeal in *Osieh* [1996] 1 WLR 1260, a case decided in the context of committal proceedings, it is not necessary. However, it was held in that case that the amendment *had* been founded on evidence disclosed at committal, and this approach ran counter to dicta in *Dixon* (1991) 92 Cr App R 43 and *Hall* [1968] 2 QB 788. In *Hall*, Lord Parker CJ said (at p. 792) that, granted that there was power to amend, the question is really 'whether the amendment asked for and granted was supported by evidence given at the committal proceedings'. The position has now been resolved in *Thompson* [2012] 4 All ER 408. The Court of Appeal approved and adopted the approach in *Osieh*. The power to amend under s. 5 was held not to be limited by the evidence served at committal, and the question to be assessed before permission to amend is granted is whether or not the accused will be unfairly prejudiced by the amendment. The fact that an amendment raises for the first time something not foreshadowed in the documents may be a ground for not permitting the amendment, or permitting it only together with an adjournment (see Professor J.C. Smith, 'Adding Counts to an Indictment' [1996] Crim LR 889).

Timing of Amendment

D11.106   The Indictments Act 1915, s. 5(1), makes clear that an indictment may be amended at any stage of a trial, whether before or after arraignment. This was demonstrated in the following cases:

    (a) in *Johal* [1973] QB 475, where the insertion of the new counts occurred after arraignment but before the empanelling of the jury;

(b) in *Pople* [1951] 1 KB 53, where the amendment took the form of an alteration in the description of the property obtained by deception and was granted after the close of the prosecution case;

(c) in *Collison* (1980) 71 Cr App R 249, where the amendment was made after the jury had been out considering their verdict for over three hours — on appeal, counsel for C accepted 'that the words in section 5(1) of the Indictments Act 1915 "at any stage of a trial" do permit amendment even after the jury have gone into retirement if the circumstances otherwise justify it and no injustice is caused to the defendant' (p. 253).

The later the amendment, the greater the risk of its causing injustice and therefore the less likely it is to be allowed. However, an indictment may be amended even at the stage of retrial, provided that no injustice is done (*Swaine* [2001] Crim LR 166; see also *B (JJ)* [2012] EWCA Crim 1440, adding an alternative count after the accused had given evidence was considered unfair, and *Feeley* [2012] 1 WLR 3133, adding counts to an indictment for a retrial was considered permissible). The procedure for amendment is contained in the CrimPR, rr. 3.21 and 3.22 (see Supplement, **R-28** and **R-29**).

Risk of Injustice

The main consideration for a judge deciding whether to allow an amendment is the risk of injustice. If the amendment cannot be made without injustice, it must not be made, as the last clause of s. 5(1) of the Indictments Act 1915 makes clear. The timing of the amendment is a major factor in determining whether there will be injustice. Thus, in *Johal* [1973] QB 475, the Court of Appeal rejected the view in *Harden* [1963] 1 QB 8 that an amendment that substantially substitutes another offence for that originally charged could *never* be made after arraignment, but agreed that such amendments would usually cause injustice. Ashworth J said (at pp. 480G–481C):   **D11.107**

> As a statement of principle, to be applied generally, this [i.e., the decision in *Harden*] is ... too wide. No doubt in many cases in which, after arraignment, an amendment is sought for the purpose of substituting another offence for that originally charged, or for the purpose of adding a further charge, injustice would be caused by granting the amendment. But in some cases (of which the present is an example) no such injustice would be caused and the amendment may properly be allowed ...
>
> In the judgment of this court there is no rule of law which precludes amendment of an indictment after arraignment, either by addition of a new count or otherwise ...
>
> On the other hand this court shares the view expressed in some of the earlier cases that amendment of an indictment during the course of a trial is likely to prejudice an accused person. The longer the interval between arraignment and amendment, the more likely it is that injustice will be caused, and in every case in which amendment is sought, it is essential to consider with great care whether the accused person will be prejudiced thereby.

Consideration of the Risk of Injustice Test   On the facts of *Johal* [1973] QB 475, there was no injustice because the amendment was made immediately after arraignment, and 'the situation was to all intents and purposes the same as if application to amend had been made before arraignment'. In *Collison* (1980) 71 Cr App R 249, where the amendment was made after the jury had retired, there was still no injustice because the amendment merely removed a technical impediment to the jury convicting of the lesser offence (see also *Teong Sun Chuah* [1991] Crim LR 463 for an example of amendment at a relatively late stage which was held to be acceptable since it caused no injustice).   **D11.108**

On the other hand, in *Gregory* [1972] 2 All ER 861, the Court of Appeal criticised a late amendment to the particulars by the deletion of the allegation as to ownership where that was the central issue in the case and it could not be said that the allegation that the motor belonged to a named person was 'mere surplusage'. In *O'Connor* [1997] Crim LR 516, similarly, there was held to be a risk of injustice where the effect of an amendment made at the close of the prosecution case was to allow the prosecution to shift its ground significantly. The Court of Appeal held that the amendment was unfair, because the Crown's case had changed very significantly, and the appellant had been confronted with a different and more difficult case. It was for the prosecution to decide how to put their case, and they could not rely on the court granting leave to change it as the trial progressed. (The same approach was adopted in *B (JJ)* [2012] EWCA Crim 1440, where it was held that the addition of an alternative count after the accused had given evidence could be unfair.)

Procedure on Amendment

D11.109 In *Moss* [1995] Crim LR 828, it was stated that, where counsel seeks an amendment, he ought to ensure that there is a properly amended form of indictment before the judge, and that any order of the court is clear and is complied with. When amendment is allowed, a note of the order must be endorsed on the indictment (Indictments Act 1915, s. 5(2)). It should be noted that failure to make a proper application to amend is fatal to the amendment, but failure to endorse an amendment is not (*Leeks* [2010] 1 Cr App R 87).

If necessary, an adjournment may be granted to allow the parties (in particular the defence) to deal with the altered position (s. 5(4)). Where the amendment comes during the course of a trial, there is power to discharge the jury from giving a verdict and order a retrial on the amended indictment (s. 5(5)(a)).

MOTION TO QUASH AN INDICTMENT

D11.110 Either party may move to quash either the whole indictment or a count thereof. The obvious time for doing so is before the accused is arraigned, although it would seem that the defence may make the application at any stage of the trial.

The effect of a successful application is that the accused may not be tried on the indictment (or particular count thereof to which the motion relates). However, this does not mean that the accused is thereby acquitted. Although the quashing of the indictment exhausts the effect of the sending on which it was founded (*Thompson* [1975] 2 All ER 1028), the prosecution may either institute fresh proceedings or apply for a voluntary bill of indictment.

D11.111 **Circumstances in which to Bring a Motion** A motion to quash may be brought in any of three circumstances.

(a) Where the indictment is bad on its face (e.g., for duplicity or because the particulars of a count do not disclose an offence known to law, as in *Yates* (1872) 12 Cox CC 233).

(b) Where the indictment (or a count thereof) has been preferred otherwise than in accordance with the provisions of the Administration of Justice (Miscellaneous Provisions) Act 1933, s. 2. Such an indictment must be quashed because it is preferred without authority (*Lombardi* [1989] 1 All ER 992).

(c) Where the indictment contains a count for an offence in respect of which the accused was not sent for trial and the material served under the regulations for the service of the prosecution case after he has been sent does not disclose a case to answer for that offence (*Jones* (1974) 59 Cr App R 120, a case decided in relation to committal documents).

D11.112 **Use of Such Motions by the Defence** Motions to quash are of little practical importance for the defence for three main reasons:

(a) the limited grounds on which they may be brought;

(b) the prosecution are often able to prevent a motion succeeding by making a suitable amendment to the indictment (e.g., splitting into two a count that the defence say should be quashed on grounds of duplicity);

(c) a successful motion results in the accused's discharge, not his acquittal.

However, such motions should not be ignored as a defence tool because failure to apply to quash may prejudice the chances of a successful appeal, since it may be argued that, if the defence at trial had felt themselves to be prejudiced by a defect in the indictment rendering it liable to be quashed, they would surely have made the appropriate application. The lack of a motion to quash may show that there was no miscarriage of justice (see, e.g., *Thompson* [1914] 2 KB 99 and *Donnelly* [1998] Crim LR 131).

Use of Such Motions by the Prosecution   Although motions to quash are most obviously a   **D11.113**
remedy available to the defence, the prosecution may wish to quash if they realise that an indictment they have preferred is invalid. The risk involved in adopting this course is that the committal on which the quashed indictment was founded may not be used as authority to prefer another indictment for the same offence (*Thompson* [1975] 2 All ER 1028 and dicta in *Newland* [1988] QB 402). The better course will usually be to ask the judge to stay (but not quash) the defective indictment and at the same time prefer a fresh indictment correcting the error in the original bill (*Follett* [1989] QB 338).

DEFECTS IN THE INDICTMENT AS A GROUND OF APPEAL

Where a trial proceeds on an unamended but defective indictment, there is an irregularity in the   **D11.114**
course of the trial which may result in the Court of Appeal finding that the conviction is unsafe (see, e.g., *Ayres* [1984] AC 447).

Decided cases do, however, show a marked reluctance on the part of the Court of Appeal to allow appeals on grounds of errors in the indictment. The precise reasoning varies. Sometimes it is said that the defect concerned a matter which was 'mere surplusage' (*Dossi* (1918) 13 Cr App R 158). Sometimes a distinction is drawn between an indictment which is a nullity and one which is merely defective (*McVitie* [1960] 2 QB 483 and *Nelson* (1977) Cr App R 119).

The most helpful approach is that adumbrated by Lord Bridge in *Ayres*. He said (at pp. 460G–461B):

> In a number of cases where an irregularity in the form of the indictment has been discussed in relation to the application of the proviso a distinction, treated as of crucial importance, has been drawn between an indictment which is 'a nullity' and one which is merely 'defective'. For my part, I doubt if this classification provides much assistance in answering the question which the proviso poses. If the statement and particulars of the offence in an indictment disclose no criminal offence whatever or charge some offence which has been abolished, in which case the indictment could fairly be described as a nullity, it is obvious that a conviction under that indictment cannot stand. But if the statement and particulars of offence can be seen fairly to relate to and to be intended to charge a known and subsisting criminal offence but plead it in terms which are inaccurate, incomplete or otherwise imperfect, then the question whether a conviction on that indictment can properly be affirmed under the proviso must depend on whether, in all the circumstances, it can be said with confidence that the particular error in the pleading cannot in any way have prejudiced or embarrassed the defendant.

The Test on Appeal   Normally, therefore, the crucial question is whether the defect has caused   **D11.115**
prejudice or embarrassment to the defence. This is illustrated by *Ayres* [1984] AC 447 itself. On the facts, the indictment faced by A 'did not charge him accurately with the only offence for which he could properly be convicted' (at p. 460C), because it charged a common-law conspiracy when he was in fact guilty of statutory conspiracy. Nonetheless, the House of Lords held that there had been no prejudice, because (at p. 462):

> The particulars of offence in this indictment left no one in doubt that the substance of the crime alleged was a conspiracy to obtain money by deception. The judge in summing up gave all the appropriate directions in relation to that offence ... the evidence amply proved that offence against the present appellant. The jury in returning a verdict of guilty must have been sure of his guilt of that offence. The judge passed a modest sentence comfortably below the maximum for that offence.

The misdescription of the offence in the statement of offence as a common-law conspiracy to defraud had in the circumstances not the slightest practical significance . . . there [cannot] possibly have been any actual miscarriage of justice.

Ayres was referred to in *Graham* [1997] 1 Cr App R 302, where the Court of Appeal made clear that a conviction would not be quashed because of a drafting or clerical error, or a discrepancy, omission or departure from good practice. A conviction would be unsafe only where the particulars did not support a conviction for the offence charged. See also *McKenzie* [2011] 1 WLR 2807 and *Wilson* [2014] 2 WLR 1780, in which the Court of Appeal repeated that, even where there was a material irregularity in the drafting of the indictment on which an appellant had been convicted, where the error constituted a mis-labelling of the offence (whether it be a misdescription in the statement or particulars of the offence as to the source of criminality), that would not result in the indictment being a nullity and a conviction based on that indictment would be safe unless there was unfairness occasioned to the appellant by the error.

D11.116   **Applications of the Test**   *Ayres* [1984] AC 447 is an extreme and somewhat questionable example of a defect in the indictment not resulting in a successful appeal. Appeals have also failed in the following cases notwithstanding the defects indicated below:

(a) *Thompson* [1914] 2 KB 99, where a count for incest was held to be bad for duplicity because it alleged offences 'on divers days' in a 21-month period;

(b) *McVitie* [1960] 2 QB 483, where the particulars omitted an essential ingredient of the offence charged (a breach of r. 5(1) of the Indictment Rules 1971);

(c) *Nelson* (1977) 65 Cr App R 119, where the statement of offence failed to specify the statute contravened (a breach of r. 6(a)(i) of the 1971 Rules);

(d) *Power* (1977) 66 Cr App R 159, where the statement of offence misdescribed the offence charged (a breach of r. 5(1) of the 1971 Rules);

(e) *Pritchett* [2007] EWCA Crim 586, where the indictment period commenced before the commencement date of the statute creating the offence.

In *Stocker* [2014] 1 Cr App R 247 (18), the statement of offence identified the wrong statute but the appeal failed on the basis that this was an error that could easily have been corrected at the time and occasioned no prejudice to the accused.

In each of the above, the reasoning of the court was essentially that the indictment, although defective, was not null as it described an offence known to the law albeit in inaccurate terms, and the accused, on the facts, had not been misled or prejudiced in the conduct of his defence by the error.

COURT'S DISCRETION TO PREVENT ABUSE OF PROCESS

D11.117   The Crown Court has an inherent power to protect its process from abuse. This includes the capacity to protect against delays in prosecution but other forms of abuse of process have been recognised. For a full discussion of abuse of process, see **D3.70** *et seq.*

Section D12   Arraignment and Pleas

INTRODUCTION

This section addresses the issues which arise at the stage in proceedings when the accused is **D12.1** normally asked to plead to the indictment. Normal practice is for the accused to enter a plea personally when arraigned by the clerk. There are a number of circumstances in which arraignment should not occur. Those addressed here are circumstances in which the defendant is unfit to plead, or where a claim to autrefois acquit or autrefois convict is raised. Two further bars to arraignment arise where the court has no jurisdiction to proceed (which is addressed at **D12.51** and at **A8.1 to A8.24**), or where the court orders a stay of proceedings before arraignment because the proceedings represent an abuse of the court's process (which is addressed at **D3.70** *et seq.*).

Where an accused is arraigned, there are then a number of pleas available to him (not guilty, guilty to the offence charged, guilty to a lesser offence etc.) and a variety of possible consequences that can follow from arraignment, including the prosecution offering no evidence or asking for counts to lie on the file. It is at this stage that plea bargains become relevant. There are also, finally, situations where a plea may change.

UNFITNESS TO PLEAD AND OTHER REASONS FOR FAILING TO PLEAD

An accused may fail to plead to the indictment when arraigned in three situations: **D12.2**

(a) because he is mentally incapable of doing so, i.e. he is unfit to plead;
(b) in the increasingly rare circumstances in which he is physically incapable, sometimes known as 'mute by visitation of God'; or
(c) because he wilfully chooses to stay silent, known as 'mute of malice'.

Unfitness to Plead

Whether or not an accused is fit to plead is determined in accordance with tests laid down by **D12.3** common law. The procedure to be followed when an accused might be unfit and the consequences of a finding of unfitness are contained in the Criminal Procedure (Insanity) Act 1964, ss. 4, 4A and 5. See also the CrimPR, r. 38.10 (see Supplement, **R-309**).

The Test of Unfitness to Plead   The leading case of *Pritchard* (1836) 7 C & P 303 concerned **D12.4** a deaf mute who was otherwise of sound mind. Alderson B's direction to the jury empanelled to determine whether P was fit to plead was in terms which Lord Parker CJ was later to say had become 'firmly embodied in our law' (*Podola* [1960] 1 QB 325 at p. 353). Alderson B said (7 C & P 303 at pp. 304–5):

> There are three points to be inquired into: First, whether the prisoner is mute of malice or not; secondly, whether he can plead to the indictment or not; thirdly, whether he is of sufficient intellect to comprehend the course of proceedings on the trial, so as to make a proper defence — to know that he might challenge [any jurors] to whom he may object — and to comprehend the details of the evidence . . . if you think that there is no certain mode of communicating the details of the trial to the prisoner, so that he can clearly understand them, and be able properly to make his defence to the charge; you ought to find that he is not of sane mind. It is not enough that he may have a general capacity of communicating on ordinary matters.

D12.5 There is considerable overlap between the issue of unfitness to plead and the issue of whether an accused is mute of malice or mute by visitation of God, as the factual position in *Pritchard* itself demonstrates. However, one would not today expect the issue of unfitness to be raised unless the accused is thought to be suffering from some degree of mental illness or deficiency, even if this may be exacerbated by physical problems. Nonetheless, Alderson B's direction in *Pritchard* remains the basis of the modern law, and the following points emerge from it:

(a) An accused may be unfit to plead even though he is not insane within the meaning of the M'Naghten rules. The point was expressly decided in *Governor of Stafford Prison, ex parte Emery* [1909] 2 KB 81 (and see also Lord Parker CJ's judgment in *Podola* [1960] 1 QB 325 at p. 353). It would logically follow that an accused may be unfit even though he is not suffering from any of the forms of mental disorder defined in s. 37(1) of the Mental Health Act 1983 that are a precondition for the making of a hospital order in the case of a convicted offender (see E22.1).

(b) The test of unfitness to plead is whether the accused will be able to comprehend the course of the proceedings so as to make a proper defence (*Pritchard*). Whether he can understand and reply rationally to the indictment is obviously a relevant factor, but the court must also consider whether he would be able to exercise his right to challenge jurors, understand details of the evidence as it is given, instruct his legal advisers and give evidence himself if he so desires.

(c) Assuming the accused can understand the course of the proceedings, he will be fit to plead even though he may act against his own best interests as a consequence of his mental condition (*Robertson* [1968] 3 All ER 557 — paranoiac who might have made irrational objections to potential jurors, held fit to plead). Similarly, a high degree of abnormality does not *ipso facto* render the accused unfit to plead (*Berry* (1977) 66 Cr App R 156 — finding of unfitness quashed because, although B was in a 'grossly abnormal mental state', the judge failed to direct the jury on the crucial issue of whether those abnormalities made him incapable of following the trial).

(d) Loss of memory through hysterical amnesia does not amount to unfitness to plead if the accused is otherwise normal at the time of trial (*Podola*). Such an accused will be able to comprehend the proceedings and communicate with his legal advisers, although his ability to give instructions as to the prosecution evidence will necessarily be limited.

But see also *Walls* [2011] 2 Cr App R 61.

D12.6 **Burden of Proof**   Following the evidence, the court must consider whether the accused is capable of understanding the proceedings so that he can:

(a) put forward his defence;
(b) challenge any juror to whom he has cause to object;
(c) give proper instructions to his legal representatives; and
(d) follow the evidence.

If the issue was raised by the defence, the burden of proof is on them to establish on a balance of probabilities that the accused is unfit (*Robertson* [1968] 3 All ER 557); if raised by the prosecution, they bear the burden of proof beyond reasonable doubt (*Podola* [1960] 1 QB 325). Whilst it will normally be raised by the defence, the prosecution might wish to assert that the accused is unfit to plead either because of the general principle that prosecuting counsel should act as a 'minister of justice' assisting the court, or because in certain circumstances (e.g., where the offence charged requires proof of a specific or ulterior intent on the part of the accused) it may in practice be difficult to establish guilt if, at the time of trial, the accused is manifestly suffering from mental illness.

Procedure for Determining Unfitness to Plead   In *Norman* [2009] 1 Cr App R 192 the Court   **D12.7**
of Appeal gave the following procedural guidance:

(a) Once the issue of fitness to plead has been raised, very careful case management is required to allow early resolution of the issue.
(b) Once full information is available, the court should consider carefully whether to postpone determination of the issue, or to proceed to an immediate determination.
(c) If the court determines the accused to be unfit, the court (pursuant to the Criminal Procedure (Insanity) Act, s. 4A(2)) is entitled to consider who is best placed to put the case for the accused. This is not necessarily the person who has been representing the accused until that point, as the responsibility of representing an unfit accused is different to that of representing an accused who is able to give instructions. The advocate instructed should be remunerated from central funds.

This procedural guidance is now supplemented by the CrimPR, r. 38.10 (see Supplement, **R-309**).

Timing of Raising the Issue   Subject to a special procedure contained in the Criminal   **D12.8**
Procedure (Insanity) Act 1964, s. 4(2) (set out in full at **D12.16**), the issue must be determined as soon as it arises (s. 4(4)). See also the CrimPR, r. 38.10 (see Supplement, **R-309**). Assuming the possibility of the accused being unfit is known to the parties before trial, it is submitted that the court should be informed of the situation before arraignment so that, if he is unfit, the accused will not be called on to plead.

Section 4(2) of the 1964 Act permits the court to postpone consideration of unfitness until any time up to the opening of the defence case. The court must be of the opinion that, having regard to 'the nature of the supposed disability', postponement is 'expedient' and 'in the interests of the accused'. Such a postponement would be appropriate where there is a reasonable chance that the prosecution evidence may be subject to successful challenge without the need for the defence to be called upon (*Webb* [1969] 2 QB 278; *Burles* [1970] 2 QB 191).

If an issue arises as to whether an accused is fit to be tried after the start of a trial, the jury already empanelled may determine whether he did the act alleged. This remains the case even where that jury is also determining the guilt or innocence of other accused. The same principle applies where the accused in question, who is charged with others, has been found unfit to plead before the start of the trial of those others (*B* [2009] 1 Cr App R 261).

The Issue of Fitness   Under the DVCVA 2004, s. 22, the decision whether the accused is unfit   **D12.9**
to plead is taken by a judge alone, rather than by a jury as had been the case before.

The Criminal Procedure (Insanity) Act 1964, s. 4(6), lays down that the court may not determine the question of unfitness except on the evidence (written or oral) of two or more registered medical practitioners, at least one of whom must have been approved by the Secretary of State as having special experience in the diagnosis or treatment of mental disorder (see **D20.73** for the power of the court to remand an accused for the preparation of reports on his mental condition under the Mental Health Act 1983, s. 35). Although such medical evidence is required, the judge is entitled to reject it. He must, however, keep the issue under review (*M* [2006] EWCA Crim 2391). Such medical evidence is required before a determination of unfitness is reached. It is not required before an accused is found to be fit to plead (*Ghulam* [2010] 1 WLR 891).

Trial of the Facts   Section 4A of the Criminal Procedure (Insanity) Act 1964 (which is set out   **D12.10**
in full at **D12.16**) applies where the court has determined that the accused is unfit to plead. It must then be determined by a jury whether the accused 'did the act or made the omission charged

against him as the offence' (s. 4A(2)). If they are satisfied that he did, they must find accordingly (s. 4A(3)). If they are not so satisfied, they must acquit. If the question of fitness to plead was determined on or before arraignment, a jury must be empanelled to try the issue of whether the accused did the act or made the omission. If it was postponed under s. 4(2), the jury by whom the accused was being tried should also determine whether he did the act or made the omission (s. 4A(5)).

The purpose of this 'trial of the facts' is to ensure that the case against an accused who has been found unfit to plead is tested. It aims in this way to avoid the detention of innocent persons in hospital, merely because they are mentally unfit. (It is also necessary to establish that the offence with which the unfit accused is charged is made out in law: *McKenzie* [2011] 1 WLR 2807.) Although the statute is silent on the standard of proof, it is clear that the test is 'beyond reasonable doubt' (*Chal* [2008] 1 Cr App R 247). The same rules of evidence apply to a trial of the facts as to a conventional criminal trial. Accordingly, the hearsay provisions of the CJA 2003 apply (*Chal*: see **F15.1**). See also *Creed* [2011] EWCA Crim 144 at **F12.1** as to the admissibility of evidence of bad character.

D12.11   **Relevance of the Mental Element of an Offence at the Trial of the Facts**   In *Antoine* [2001] 1 AC 340, the House of Lords held that, in this 'trial of the facts', the defence of diminished responsibility could not be raised. In their lordships' view, by using the word 'act' rather than 'offence' in the Criminal Procedure (Insanity) Act 1964, s. 4A(2), Parliament had made it clear that the jury was not to consider the mental ingredients of the offence. The defence could, however, rely on mistake, accident, self-defence or involuntariness.

Similarly in *Grant* [2002] QB 1030, it was held that provocation could not be raised at the s. 4A hearing, since it inevitably required examination of the accused's state of mind, rather than whether he 'did the act charged'.

In *Antoine*, the House of Lords (Lord Hutton) also observed that careful consideration would always have to be given to whether an accused found to be under a disability should be called to give evidence at the hearing under s. 4A(2). Applying that approach, the Court of Appeal in *Swinbourne* (2014) 178 JP 34 concluded that the interview under caution of such an accused should not be adduced at the s. 4A hearing, there being grounds to doubt that he would have understood the caution or the interview process.

Only exceptionally will it be possible for the intentions of the accused to be considered as part of the inquiry (e.g., see *R (Young) v Central Criminal Court* [2002] 2 Cr App R 178, where the *actus reus* of the offence was that the accused 'concealed' material facts contrary to the Financial Services Act 1986, s. 47(1) and *B* [2012] 3 All ER 1093, where the 'act' of voyeurism included the purpose of the voyeur).

D12.12   **The ECHR Perspective**   In *M* [2002] 1 WLR 824, the Court of Appeal considered the above procedures in the light of the ECHR, Article 6. The Court held that the criminal charge provisions of Article 6 do not apply to proceedings under ss. 4 and 4A of the 1964 Act, since those proceedings cannot result in a conviction. In any event, they concluded that the procedure under ss. 4 and 4A constituted a fair procedure, providing an opportunity for investigation of the facts on behalf of a disabled person, so far as possible. It fairly balanced the public interest and the interest of the person alleged to have committed the act. In addition, their lordships stated that the defence was able to make an application to stay proceedings for abuse of process when it appeared necessary, and this could be either before arraignment or before any question of disability fell to be determined.

This decision was endorsed by the House of Lords in *H* [2003] 1 All ER 497; any orders made following a finding that the accused did the act in question were said not to be punitive, but to be made only for the purpose of protecting the public.

Consequences of a Finding of Unfitness

D12.13   Under the Criminal Procedure (Insanity) Act 1964, s. 5 (set out in full at **D12.16**), if the accused is found unfit to plead, and the jury determines that he did the act or made the omission as charged, the court may make one of the following orders:

(a) a hospital order, for admission to such hospital as the Secretary of State specifies — such an order may be made the subject of a restriction order without limit of time (see **E22.1**);

(b) a supervision order; or

(c) an order for the accused's absolute discharge.

In *Grant* [2002] QB 1030, the Court of Appeal considered whether the procedure constituted a violation of the ECHR. The accused had been found unfit to plead to a charge of murder, with the result that the trial judge was compelled to make an order for admission to a hospital without limitation of time. The problem identified by their lordships was that the judge could not consider whether such an order was justified on the medical evidence, which was directed to the question of whether the accused was fit to plead.

In *Fairley* [2003] EWCA Crim 1625, it was emphasised that the only orders which the judge could make, following a finding that an accused who was unfit to plead had committed the act in question, were confined to those set out in the statute (although the specific restrictions referred to in *Fairley* no longer apply by virtue of the amendments made by the DVCVA 2004).

Rights of the Victim Under the DVCVA 2004, s. 38, the victim of a sexual or violent offence **D12.14** has certain rights where an offence is committed by a person who is found not guilty by reason of insanity or who is subject to a finding under the Criminal Procedure (Insanity) Act 1964, ss. 4 and 4A ('the patient'). Where the court makes a hospital order with a restriction order, the probation board for the area must take all reasonable steps to ascertain whether the victim wishes to make representations about any conditions to which the patient should be subject. The victim is also entitled to receive information about any conditions to which the patient is to be subject in the event of his discharge from hospital. This right was extended by the amendment of s. 38 by the Mental Health Act 2007, s. 48, so that the victim has the same entitlement to information from the hospital as from the probation board.

Reversing Such an Order In *R (Hasani) v Crown Court at Blackfriars* [2006] 1 All ER 817, **D12.15** the accused was found unfit to plead to serious offences against the person. A jury then determined that he had done the acts in question. The judge adjourned the matter to determine the issue of disposal. Before that issue could be determined, evidence was presented to show that the accused was capable of pleading. The judge then directed that the accused be arraigned. On judicial review, the judge's order was quashed, and the case was remitted to the Crown Court. The order to arraign was premature in that a fresh hearing on fitness to plead, in accordance with s. 4, had to be held first. There was nothing in the Criminal Procedure (Insanity) Act 1964 to preclude the holding of a second hearing on the issue of fitness to plead where the evidence justifies that course of action and there has been no final disposition of the case. In *McKenzie* [2011] 1 WLR 2807 it was recognised that, if a finding following a determination that an accused is unfit is later quashed by the Court of Appeal, it is not possible to return a guilty verdict of another offence or to order a retrial.

Procedure where Accused is Found Fit to Plead If the accused is found fit to plead before the **D12.16** calling of any prosecution evidence, he will thereafter be arraigned in the usual way and plead to the indictment.

Criminal Procedure (Insanity) Act 1964, ss. 4, 4A and 5

4.—(1) This section applies where on the trial of a person the question arises (at the instance of the defence or otherwise) whether the accused is under a disability, that is to say, under any disability such that apart from this Act it would constitute a bar to his being tried.

(2) If, having regard to the nature of the supposed disability, the court are of opinion that it is expedient to do so and in the interests of the accused, they may postpone consideration of the question of fitness to be tried until any time up to the opening of the case for the defence.

(3) If, before the question of fitness to be tried falls to be determined, the jury return a verdict of acquittal on the count or each of the counts on which the accused is being tried, that question shall not be determined.

(4) Subject to subsections (2) and (3) above, the question of fitness to be tried shall be determined as soon as it arises.

(5) The question of fitness to be tried shall be determined by the court without a jury.

(6) The court shall not make a determination under subsection (5) above except on the written or oral evidence of two or more registered medical practitioners at least one of whom is duly approved.

4A.—(1) This section applies where in accordance with section 4(5) above it is determined by a court that the accused is under a disability.

(2) The trial shall not proceed or further proceed but it shall be determined by a jury—
   (a) on the evidence (if any) already given in the trial; and
   (b) on such evidence as may be adduced or further adduced by the prosecution, or adduced by a person appointed by the court under this section to put the case for the defence,
   whether they are satisfied, as respects the count or each of the counts on which the accused was to be or was being tried, that he did the act or made the omission charged against him as the offence.

(3) If as respects that count or any of those counts the jury are satisfied as mentioned in sub-section (2) above, they shall make a finding that the accused did the act or made the omission charged against him.

(4) If as respects that count or any of those counts the jury are not so satisfied, they shall return a verdict of acquittal as if on the count in question the trial had proceeded to a conclusion.

(5) Where the question of disability was determined after arraignment of the accused, the determination under subsection (2) is to be made by the jury by whom he was being tried.

5.—(1) This section applies where—
   (a) a special verdict is returned that the accused is not guilty by reason of insanity; or
   (b) findings have been made that the accused is under a disability and that he did the act or made the omission charged against him.

(2) The court shall make in respect of the accused—
   (a) a hospital order (with or without a restriction order);
   (b) a supervision order; or
   (c) an order for his absolute discharge.

(3) Where—
   (a) the offence to which the special verdict or the findings relate is an offence the sentence for which is fixed by law, and
   (b) the court have power to make a hospital order,
   the court shall make a hospital order with a restriction order (whether or not they would have power to make a restriction order apart from this subsection).

(4) In this section—
   'hospital order' has the meaning given in section 37 of the Mental Health Act 1983;
   'restriction order' has the meaning given to it by section 41 of that Act;
   'supervision order' has the meaning given in Part 1 of Schedule 1A to this Act.

Muteness

D12.17 If an accused stays silent when arraigned, the issue arises whether he is silent for reasons beyond his control or by deliberate choice. In the former case, he is 'mute by visitation of God'; in the latter case, he is said to be 'mute of malice'.

D12.18 **Mute by Visitation of God**   If the finding of the jury is that the accused is 'mute by visitation of God', the court has the option of adjourning for a short period in order that means of communicating with him may be found (e.g., through bringing an expert in sign language or lip-reading to court, and see also *Harris* (1897) 61 JP 792, where the jury found that H was mute as a result of a self-inflicted wound to his throat and the case was simply adjourned for the wound to heal).

Alternatively, if it seems that the muteness will be permanent and cannot be overcome, the jury should be asked to go on to consider whether the accused is unfit to plead (see D12.4; see also *Pritchard* (1836) 7 C & P 303 and *Governor of Stafford Prison, ex parte Emery* [1909] 2 KB 81). Therefore, a finding that the accused is mute by visitation of God is likely to be merely a stage en route to a finding of unfitness to plead, rather than a final determination in itself — indeed, the classic direction of Alderson B in *Pritchard* required the jury to consider in turn whether P was (a) mute of malice, (b) able to plead, and (c) able to comprehend the course of the proceedings.

Mute of Malice   Section 6(1)(c) of the CLA 1967 provides that: **D12.19**

> Where a person is arraigned on an indictment... if he stands mute of malice or will not answer directly to the indictment, the court may order a plea of not guilty to be entered on his behalf, and he shall then be treated as having pleaded not guilty.

The court may not itself conclude that a silent accused is mute of malice but must empanel a jury to determine the issue (*Schleter* (1866) 10 Cox CC 409), the burden of proof being on the prosecution to establish malice beyond reasonable doubt (*Sharp* [1960] 1 QB 357). The accused has no right of challenge in respect of the jurors so empanelled (*Paling* (1978) 67 Cr App R 299).

If the accused is found mute of malice, there is no objection to the jury that has so found him going on to try the case, subject only to the general rule that a jury empanelled to try one issue may not try a second issue unless the trial of the latter commences within 24 hours of their empanelment to try the first (Juries Act 1974, s. 11).

In modern times, a silent accused will almost certainly be mute of malice. Should there be reasons beyond his control rendering him unable to answer to the indictment, that will have been realised long before arraignment and steps will have been taken to overcome the problem (e.g., by the provision of an interpreter). Alternatively, if he is or may be unfit to plead, either the prosecution or defence will raise that issue with the judge before the indictment is put, thus avoiding the question of muteness arising as a separate issue lest the accused should be found fit to plead and then stay silent when arraigned.

AUTREFOIS ACQUIT AND AUTREFOIS CONVICT

The pleas of autrefois acquit and autrefois convict, together with the plea of pardon (see **D12.52**),   **D12.20** are known as pleas in bar, because, if upheld, they bar any further proceedings on the indictment. The basic purpose of the two pleas is to protect the subject against repeated prosecutions for the same offence. Although a large body of case law has developed defining the precise circumstances in which the pleas may be relied on, in reality it will be very rare that a prosecution would occur where the proposed accused has already been acquitted or convicted of the offence that would be charged. In addition to domestic case law, it is relevant to consider the principle of double jeopardy enshrined in EU law by Article 54 of the Schengen Implementing Convention (CISA), which is one of the Schengen provisions which are binding on the UK. This is dealt with at **D12.30**.

There are a number of important statutory exceptions which will arise under the tainted acquittal provisions of the CPIA 1996, ss. 54 to 57, which are dealt with at **D12.38**, and the retrial provisions of the CJA 2003, ss. 75 to 97, which are dealt with at **D12.40**. Whilst not creating a form of autrefois, the CCA 2013, sch. 17, para. 11, provides that the prosecution will be prohibited from proceeding against an accused in respect of an offence that has been the subject of a deferred prosecution agreement (see **D12.106**) that has since expired.

Consideration of the pleas will involve asking: (a) what amounts to an acquittal or a conviction in this context? (b) precisely what is meant by being prosecuted twice for the same offence? and (c) what is the procedure to be followed on the pleas being raised?

Meaning of 'Acquittal' and 'Conviction' in Context of Autrefois Pleas

For an autrefois plea to succeed, the earlier conviction or acquittal relied on by the accused must   **D12.21** have been by a court of competent jurisdiction and the proceedings must not have been *ultra vires*. This is illustrated in respect of autrefois convict by *Kent Justices, ex parte Machin* [1952] 2 QB 355, in which the Divisional Court quashed M's conviction on the ground that the correct procedure for determining mode of trial had not been complied with and the magistrates therefore acted *ultra vires*. Lord Goddard CJ stated that the prosecution were entitled to recharge the accused as he 'has never been technically in peril and he could be tried again'. An autrefois plea does not arise where the accused has previously been cautioned in relation to conduct for which he is then prosecuted, though this might give rise to a claim of abuse of process (*DPP v Alexander* [2011] 1 WLR 653).

The same applies to *ultra vires* acquittals. For example, where magistrates purport to acquit an accused of an offence triable only on indictment, he cannot rely on the 'acquittal' to bar a trial on indictment (*West* [1964] 1 QB 15, and see also *Cardiff Magistrates' Court, ex parte Cardiff City Council* (1987) *The Times*, 24 February 1987). Similarly, in *DPP v Jarman* (2014) 178 JP 89 the Administrative Court found that the dismissal of proceedings for want of prosecution did not constitute an acquittal for the purposes of a plea of autrefois. The Court found on the facts of the case that the plea would have been unlikely to succeed even if it had been available because, at the hearing at which the court dismissed the case, it did not consider the merits of the evidence.

Scope of the Pleas

D12.22 **At Common Law**   The leading case is *Connelly v DPP* [1964] AC 1254, the facts of which are illustrative of the general principle. C and three others were jointly charged in two indictments, the first for murder and the second for armed robbery. The murder had occurred during the course of the indicted robbery and the issue considered by the House of Lords was whether, following C's acquittal for murder, his prosecution for robbery was precluded. At first instance, this plea was rejected, the jury following the judge's direction that the offence of murder could not be regarded as 'substantially or practically the same' as an offence of robbery with aggravation of a sum of money from a different employee. C was convicted of robbery, following a further trial.

D12.23 **The *Connolly* Nine Propositions**   C appealed against conviction on the ground that his plea of autrefois acquit should have been upheld. The House of Lords dismissed the appeal. The speech of Lord Morris of Borth-y-Gest reviewed at length the old authorities and summarised their effect in nine propositions ([1964] AC 1254 at pp. 1305–6), which may be further summarised as follows:

(a) *A man may not be tried for a crime in respect of which he has previously been acquitted or convicted.* This is the straightforward and obvious application of autrefois, and covers cases where the offence charged in a count is identical in law and on the facts to a crime of which the accused has previously been acquitted or convicted.

(b) *A man cannot be tried for a crime in respect of which he could on some previous indictment have been convicted.* This is the corollary of the power of a jury to return a verdict of not guilty as charged but guilty of a lesser offence. The reasoning is that, where the jury on a certain count could have convicted of a lesser offence but failed to do so, they have impliedly acquitted him both of the offence charged and of the lesser offence. This appears to be the case whether or not the lesser alternative was actually left to the jury. Consequently, their verdict can be relied on to bar a later indictment for either or both offences. Lord Morris traced the principle back to Hale's *Pleas of the Crown* (1778), giving the example of an acquittal for murder barring any later indictment for manslaughter ([1964] AC 1254 at p. 1311) (see *Old Street Magistrates' Court, ex parte Davies* [1995] Crim LR 629).

(c) *A man cannot be tried for a crime which is in effect the same, or is substantially the same, as a crime of which he has previously been acquitted or convicted (or could have been convicted by way of alternative verdict).* Lord Morris (see pp. 1310–28) undertook a detailed survey of the decided cases which relate to when a count is to be regarded as alleging a crime that is substantially the same as one of which the accused has previously been acquitted or convicted. One clear example of the test being satisfied is provided by an accused being indicted for murder after he has been acquitted of the alleged victim's manslaughter (*Wrote v Wigges* (1591) 4 Co Rep 45b; *Tancock* (1876) 34 LT 455).

   The same will apply whenever proof of an offence of which the accused has already been acquitted is a necessary step towards proving the offence now charged. The strictness of the test is, however, illustrated by *Salvi* (1857) 10 Cox CC 481, where S, after being acquitted on a charge of wounding with intent to murder, was indicted for murder after his victim's death. His plea of autrefois failed because murder could be committed without there being an intention to murder. Therefore, the evidence on the second indictment would not necessarily have to be such as to support a conviction on the first (it could show merely an intention to do the victim grievous bodily harm).

(d) What has to be considered is whether the crime or offence charged in the later indictment is the same, or is in effect or is substantially the same, as the crime charged in the former indictment and it is immaterial that the facts under examination or the witnesses being called in the later proceedings are the same as those in some earlier proceedings. The actual decision in *Connelly v DPP* provides the best illustration. The evidence called and facts relied on by the prosecution against C at the trial for robbery were precisely the same as they had called and relied on at the earlier trial for murder. But, despite the coincidence of prosecution facts and evidence at the two trials, the House of Lords were unanimous in holding that autrefois acquit did not avail.

Reconsideration of the Principles in *Beedie* The above analysis should now be considered in the light of the decision of the Court of Appeal in *Beedie* [1998] QB 356. B was prosecuted first for Health and Safety Act offences and then for manslaughter, both relating to the same death. At his trial for manslaughter, his counsel applied to stay the indictment, relying upon *Connelly*, but the judge refused. He was convicted and he appealed. The Court of Appeal considered the question of whether or not the second offence had to be the same as the first, or whether it was sufficient that it arose from the same facts, and stated the following principles: **D12.24**

(a) The House of Lords in *Connelly* had identified a narrow principle of autrefois. It was applicable only where the *same* offence was alleged in the second indictment. Rose LJ, delivering the judgment of the Court of Appeal in *Beedie*, quoted with approval Lord Devlin in *Connelly* (at p. 1340): 'For the doctrine to apply it must be the same offence both in fact and in law'.

(b) Importantly, however, judicial discretion should be exercised where the second offence arises out of the same or substantially the same set of facts as the first. In addition, there should be no sequential trials for offences on an ascending scale of gravity (relying on the principle in *Elrington* (1861) 1 B & S 688). As it was put in *Forest of Dean Justices, ex parte Farley* [1990] RTR 228 at p. 239, there is an 'almost invariable rule that when a person is tried on a lesser offence he is not to be tried again on the same facts for a more serious offence'.

(c) It was for the prosecution to show that there were special circumstances before the judge should allow the trial to proceed. In *Beedie*, a stay should have been ordered because the manslaughter allegation was based on substantially the same facts as the earlier summary prosecutions, it was a prosecution for an offence of greater gravity, and there were no special circumstances such as to allow the prosecution to proceed; the appeal was allowed (see also *South East Hampshire Magistrates' Court, ex parte CPS* [1998] Crim LR 422) and *Hartnett* [2003] Crim LR 719).

It follows that in such circumstances the plea of autrefois has in reality become a species of abuse of process. This was illustrated more recently, in *Cheong* [2006] EWCA Crim 524, in which it was held that, where an accused has not been acquitted or convicted in a foreign court but the prosecuting authority in that country has acted in some other way in relation to the charge now brought against him, the question for the court is whether the accused could not now receive a fair trial, or it would otherwise be unfair to try him. It was also illustrated by *Dwyer* [2012] EWCA Crim 10, where the Court of Appeal ruled that a conspiracy charge which relied in part on a substantive act to which D had pleaded guilty could not be stayed through a plea of autrefois convict, but could be stayed as an abuse of process.

Findings that Can Form Basis for Plea of Autrefois Acquit The following findings *do* amount to acquittals and therefore can found a plea of autrefois acquit: **D12.25**

(a) The quashing of a conviction by the Court of Appeal, provided it does not at the same time order a retrial (Criminal Appeal Act 1968, s. 2(3)).

(b) An acquittal by a foreign court of competent jurisdiction (*Aughet* (1919) 13 Cr App R 101). This was confirmed, *obiter*, by Lord Diplock in *Treacy v DPP* [1971] AC 537, when he said (at p. 562D) that the common-law doctrine of autrefois acquit and convict was 'a doctrine which has always applied whether the previous conviction or acquittal based on the same facts was by an English court or by a foreign court'.

D12.26 **Findings that Cannot Form Basis for Plea of Autrefois Acquit** The following findings do *not* amount to acquittals and therefore cannot found a plea of autrefois acquit:

(a) Discharge of the accused at committal proceedings (*Manchester City Stipendiary Magistrate, ex parte Snelson* [1977] 2 All ER 62).

(b) Quashing of an indictment following a motion to quash. This point would not seem to be covered by specific authority but follows inevitably from the nature of the remedy, which is to prevent any proceedings on the indictment in question and, *ex hypothesi*, prevent the returning of a verdict (*Newland* [1988] QB 402).

(c) The withdrawal of a summons by the prosecution in the magistrates' court prior to the accused having pleaded to it (*Bedford and Sharnbrook Justices, ex parte Ward* [1974] Crim LR 109). The reason for this, as Nolan J observed in *Grays Justices, ex parte Low* [1990] QB 54 at p. 59A–B is: '. . . there has been no adjudication upon the merits of the charge in the original summons, and the defendant has not been put in peril of conviction upon it'.

(d) The prosecution offering no evidence and laying an alternative charge as in *Brookes* [1995] Crim LR 630, where B pleaded not guilty to a charge under the OAPA 1861, s. 20, and the prosecution offered no evidence and laid a charge under s. 18. The Court of Appeal approved the rejection of his plea of autrefois acquit (see also *London Borough of Islington v Michaelides* [2001] Crim LR 843).

(e) The dismissal of an information under s. 15 of the MCA 1980 on account of the non-appearance of the prosecutor (*Bennett and Bond, ex parte Bennet* (1908) 72 JP 362 and *DPP v Jarman* (2014) 178 JP 89 (see **D12.21**)) or where the information is so faulty in form and content that the accused could never have been in jeopardy on it (*DPP v Porthouse* (1988) 89 Cr App R 21; *Dabhade* [1993] QB 329).

(f) The dismissal of a charge, pursuant to the CDA 1998, s. 51.

(g) The prosecution serving notice of discontinuance under the Prosecution of Offences Act 1985, s. 23.

(h) The jury being discharged from giving a verdict.

(i) Reliance on evidence of an offence of which the accused has been acquitted as similar fact evidence (*Z* [2000] 2 AC 483).

(j) Where the provisions relating to tainted acquittals in the CPIA 1996, ss. 54 to 57, apply (see **D12.38**).

In *Fawcett* [2013] EWCA Crim 1399 the Court of Appeal rejected the contention that it had been an abuse of process to prosecute the accused for burglary when he had earlier pleaded guilty to offences of handling stolen goods relating to the same conduct on an indictment that had been preferred in error. The Court found that the guilty pleas to that indictment could be vacated and the accused arraigned on the proper burglary indictment without any injustice.

D12.27 **Findings that Can Form Basis for Plea of Autrefois Convict** The following findings *do* amount to convictions and therefore can found a plea of autrefois convict:

(a) A conviction by a foreign court will found autrefois convict, subject to the qualification that if he who now relies on the foreign conviction was found guilty and sentenced in his absence and there is no likelihood of his ever returning to the country concerned to serve his sentence, the plea will fail (*Thomas* [1985] QB 604).

(b) A plea of autrefois convict could only be based upon a complete adjudication against the accused, including the final disposal of the case by passing sentence or some other order such as an absolute discharge. This was the conclusion of the Privy Council in *Richards v The Queen* [1993] AC 217. The underlying rationale of the plea was to prevent double punishment.

But, if a finding of guilt was all that was necessary to support the plea in bar, an accused might escape punishment altogether. The Privy Council thereby concluded that two earlier decisions to the contrary, *Sheridan* [1937] 1 KB 223 and *Grant* [1936] 2 All ER 1156, were wrongly decided.

Findings that Cannot Form Basis for Plea of Autrefois Convict   The following findings do **D12.28** *not* amount to convictions and therefore cannot found a plea of autrefois convict:

(a) The taking of an offence into consideration when passing sentence for other offences of which the offender has been convicted (*Nicholson* [1947] 2 All ER 535).
(b) A finding of guilt in disciplinary proceedings, albeit that the finding is followed by the imposition of a penalty (*Hogan* [1960] 2 QB 513).
(c) A finding of contempt of court in civil proceedings (*Green* [1993] Crim LR 46, but note that the position in relation to non-molestation orders has changed as a result of the DVCVA 2004, s. 1 (see **B14.130**)).

A Note on Issue Estoppel   A further question raised by the appeal in *Connelly v DPP* [1964] **D12.29** AC 1254, was whether the doctrine of issue estoppel applies in criminal cases, i.e. can either the prosecution or the defence prevent the other side reopening a question of fact if that question has already been decided in previous proceedings between the same parties? However, in *DPP v Humphrys* [1977] AC 1, it was held that issue estoppel has no place in criminal proceedings. There is a limited exception in the case of an application for habeas corpus: *Governor of Brixton Prison, ex parte Osman* [1991] 1 All ER 108. For full discussion of issue estoppel, see **F11.22** *et seq.*

Double Jeopardy in EU law

Allied to the concept of autrefois acquit is the principle of double jeopardy. The principle of **D12.30** double jeopardy in EU law, otherwise referred to as the *ne bis in idem* principle, is set out in Article 54 of the Schengen Implementing Convention (CISA), which is one of the Schengen provisions which are binding on the UK. Article 54 reads as follows:

> A person whose trial has been finally disposed of in one Contracting Party may not be prosecuted in another Contracting Party for the same acts provided that, if a penalty has been imposed, it has been enforced, is actually in the process of being enforced or can no longer be enforced under the laws of the sentencing Contracting Party.

A number of questions have arisen regarding the interpretation of Article 54, in particular on the definition of what constitutes 'same acts' and what is meant by a trial being 'finally disposed of'. The CJEU has adopted a purposive interpretation, emphasising the key aim of facilitating free movement in the Area of Freedom, Security and Justice as well as legal certainty for the accused.

'Finally Disposed of'   The CJEU has found that the *ne bis in idem* principle applies to: the **D12.31** termination of prosecutions by the Public Prosecutor following out-of-court settlements with the accused (Joined cases C-187/01 and C-385/01 *Gözütok and Brügge* [2003] ECR I-1345); final decisions acquitting the accused for lack of evidence (Case C-150/05 *Van Straaten* [2006] ECR I-9327); and time-barred prosecutions (Case C-467/04 *Gasparini* [2006] ECR I-9199). It is also applicable to criminal proceedings against an accused whose trial for the same acts as those for which he faces prosecution was finally disposed of in another Contracting State, even though, under the law of the State in which he was convicted, the sentence which was imposed on him could never, on account of specific features of procedure such as those referred to in the main proceedings, have been directly enforced (Case C-297/07 *Bourquain* [2008] ECR I-9425). However, *ne bis in idem* does not apply to a decision by which an authority of a Contracting State, after examining the merits of the case brought before it, makes an order (at a stage before the charging of a person suspected of a crime) suspending criminal proceedings, where the suspension decision does not, under the domestic law of that State, definitely bar further prosecution and therefore does not preclude new criminal proceedings in respect of the same acts in that State (Case C-491/07 *Turansky* [2008] ECR I-11039).

D12.32   **'Same Acts'**   In a consistent line of case law, the CJEU has interpreted the phrase 'same acts' as based on 'the identity of the material acts, understood as the existence of a set of facts which are inextricably linked together, irrespective of their legal classification given to them or the legal interest protected' (Case C-436/04 *Van Esbroek* [2006] ECR I-2333; Case C-150/05 *Van Straaten* [2006] ECR I-9327; Case C-288/0 *Kretzinger* [2007] ECR I-6641). In a case involving money laundering, the CJEU reiterated that the acts in question must make up 'an inseparable whole', but added that, if the acts do not make up an inseparable whole, the fact that they were committed with the same criminal intention does not suffice (Case C-367/05 *Kraajenbrink* [2007] ECR I-619 at [29]). The interpretation of the concept of 'same acts' under the CISA is equally valid for the purposes of the EAW Framework Decision (Case C-261/09 *Mantello* [2013] All ER (EC) 312).

D12.33   **'Enforced'**   In *Kretzinger* [2007] ECR I-6641 the CJEU confirmed that a penalty 'has been enforced' or is 'actually in the process of being enforced' if a suspended custodial sentence has been imposed.

Procedure on Autrefois Pleas

D12.34   The following procedural steps are involved in raising the plea of autrefois, although failure to observe the correct formalities in entering the plea does not prevent reliance on it (*Flatman v Light* [1946] KB 414).

(a) Under the Criminal Procedure Act 1851, s. 28, an accused may raise a plea of autrefois simply by stating that he has already been lawfully acquitted or convicted of the offence now charged. Where, however, he is legally represented, the correct procedure is for the plea to be entered in writing signed by counsel. A suggested form of words is, '[The accused] says that the Queen ought not further to prosecute the indictment against him because he has been lawfully acquitted/convicted of the offence charged therein'.

(b) The obvious time for pleading autrefois is before the indictment is put to the accused, but failure to do so then will not prevent the defence raising the issue at a later stage ('. . . the plea may be raised at any time either as a plea in bar to the second indictment or at any stage in the proceedings': per Lord Hodson in *Connelly v DPP* [1964] AC 1254 at p. 1331).

(c) The prosecution either admit that the plea is good (in which case the accused is discharged) or join issue in writing.

(d) Alternatively, the court may raise the plea of its own motion (*Cooper v New Forest District Council* [1992] Crim LR 877).

(e) Once the plea has been entered and issue joined by the prosecution, the burden of proof is on the accused to make good the plea on the balance of probabilities (*Coughlan* (1976) 63 Cr App R 33).

(f) The parties are not restricted to the formal record of the earlier proceedings (which will establish only the date and place of conviction or acquittal, the wording of the charges and the name of the accused), but may call relevant evidence. In the absence of dispute, counsel should shorten the proceedings by reading to the court a brief statement of the relevant facts from (a) the previous trial, and (b) the statements in the present case on which they respectively intend to rely in argument (*Coughlan*).

(g) The issue is determined by the judge without empanelling a jury (CJA 1988, s. 122).

(h) If a plea of autrefois convict or acquit succeeds, it is a bar to any further proceedings on the indictment. If the plea fails, the indictment is put and the accused is entitled to plead not guilty to the general issue notwithstanding his earlier unsuccessful reliance on autrefois (CLA 1967, s. 6(1): 'Where a person is arraigned on indictment . . . he shall in all cases be entitled to make a plea of not guilty in addition to any demurrer or special plea').

D12.35   **Statutory Provisions**   In addition to the procedure to deal with tainted acquittals (**D12.38**) and a procedure for the retrial of certain serious offences in the light of new evidence (**D12.40**), the common law on the ambit of autrefois is supplemented by two sets of statutory provisions.

D12.36   **Offences Against the Person Act 1861**   Sections 44 and 45 of the OAPA 1861 provide that, if justices, 'upon the hearing of any case of assault or battery upon the merits, *where the complaint was* *preferred by or on behalf of the party aggrieved*, shall deem the offence not to be proved, or shall find the assault or battery to have been justified, or so trifling as not to merit any punishment, and shall accordingly dismiss the complaint, they shall forthwith make out a certificate under their hands stating the fact of such dismissal and shall deliver such certificate to the party against whom the complaint was preferred' (s. 44, emphasis added). The obtaining of a s. 44 certificate of dismissal releases the party 'from all further or other proceedings, civil or criminal, *for the same cause*' (s. 45).

The italicised words indicate the main limitations on the scope of ss. 44 and 45. First, a certificate of dismissal may be granted only where the victim of the alleged offence is the prosecutor, rather than the police. Secondly, a certificate frees the recipient only from further proceedings 'for the same cause'.

Section 18 of the Interpretation Act 1978   Section 18 of the Interpretation Act 1978   **D12.37** states that:

> Where an act or omission constitutes an offence under two or more Acts, or both under an Act and at common law, the offender shall, unless the contrary intention appears, be liable to be prosecuted and punished under either or any of those Acts or at common law, but shall not be liable to be punished more than once for the same offence.

According to Humphreys J in *Thomas* [1950] 1 KB 26, the predecessor of s. 18 of the 1978 Act (s. 33 of the Interpretation Act 1889) 'added nothing and detracted nothing from the common law'. In particular, the prohibition on being punished more than once for the same offence did not protect an accused from being convicted and sentenced on successive occasions for different offences arising out of the same criminal act (conviction for wounding with intent no bar to later indictment for murder).

TAINTED ACQUITTALS

The provisions of the CPIA 1996, ss. 54 to 57, which relate to 'tainted acquittals', constitute   **D12.38** a major exception to the availability of autrefois acquit. They enable the prosecution of an accused for a second time for a crime of which he has already been acquitted at trial, provided certain conditions are met. Sections 54 and 55 (set out below) lay down a procedure relating to tainted acquittals where the following conditions are met:

(a) an accused has been acquitted of an offence (s. 54(1)(a)); and
(b) a person has been convicted of an administration of justice offence involving interference with or intimidation of a juror or a witness or potential witness (s. 54(1)(b)); and
(c) the court convicting of the administration of justice offence certifies that there is a real possibility that, but for the interference or intimidation, the acquitted person would not have been acquitted, and that it would not be contrary to the interests of justice to proceed against the acquitted person (s. 54(2) and (5)); and
(d) the High Court grants an order quashing the acquittal after deciding that the four conditions set out in s. 55 are satisfied (s. 55 is set out below).

The provisions of ss. 54 to 57 apply in relation to acquittals in respect of offences alleged to have been committed on or after 15 April 1997. It should be emphasised that it is the *original* offence of which the defendant was acquitted which must be alleged to have been committed on or after that date (s. 54(7)).

The formalities relating to the tainted acquittal procedure are set out in part 40 of the CrimPR (see Supplement, R-322). Part 40 makes it clear that the certification referred to in s. 54(2) must take place, at the latest, immediately after sentence (or committal for sentence, or remittal of a juvenile to the youth court to be dealt with for an offence).

Criminal Procedure and Investigations Act 1996, ss. 54 and 55   **D12.39**

54.—(1) This section applies where—
    (a) a person has been acquitted of an offence, and

(b) a person has been convicted of an administration of justice offence involving interference with or intimidation of a juror or a witness (or potential witness) in any proceedings which led to the acquittal.

(2) Where it appears to the court before which the person was convicted that—
  (a) there is a real possibility that, but for the interference or intimidation, the acquitted person would not have been acquitted, and
  (b) subsection (5) does not apply,
  the court shall certify that it so appears.

(3) Where a court certifies under subsection (2) an application may be made to the High Court for an order quashing the acquittal, and the Court shall make the order if (but shall not do so unless) the four conditions in section 55 are satisfied.

(4) Where an order is made under subsection (3) proceedings may be taken against the acquitted person for the offence of which he was acquitted.

(5) This subsection applies if, because of lapse of time or for any other reason, it would be contrary to the interests of justice to take proceedings against the acquitted person for the offence of which he was acquitted.

(6) For the purposes of this section the following offences are administration of justice offences—
  (a) the offence of perverting the course of justice;
  (b) the offence under section 51(1) of the Criminal Justice and Public Order Act 1994 (intimidation etc. of witnesses, jurors and others);
  (c) an offence of aiding, abetting, counselling, procuring, suborning or inciting another person to commit an offence under section 1 of the Perjury Act 1911.

(7) This section applies in relation to acquittals in respect of offences alleged to be committed on or after the appointed day.

55.—(1) The first condition is that it appears to the High Court likely that, but for the interference or intimidation, the acquitted person would not have been acquitted.

(2) The second condition is that it does not appear to the Court that, because of lapse of time or for any other reason it would be contrary to the interests of justice to take proceedings against the acquitted person for the offence of which he was acquitted.

(3) The third condition is that it appears to the Court that the acquitted person has been given a reasonable opportunity to make written representations to the Court.

(4) The fourth condition is that it appears to the Court that the conviction for the administration of justice offence will stand.

(5) In applying subsection (4) the Court shall—
  (a) take into account all the information before it, but
  (b) ignore the possibility of new factors coming to light.

(6) Accordingly, the fourth condition has the effect that the Court shall not make an order under section 54(3) if (for instance) it appears to the Court that any time allowed for giving notice of appeal has not expired or that an appeal is pending.

RETRIAL PROVISIONS OF THE CRIMINAL JUSTICE ACT 2003

D12.40 The CJA 2003 introduced a radical revision to the principles stated above. Sections 75 to 97 of the Act constitute the second major statutory exception to the rule against double jeopardy. In summary, they permit an accused to be retried for a 'qualifying' offence of which he has earlier been acquitted where there is new evidence of his guilt, following an order of the Court of Appeal quashing that acquittal.

Application

D12.41 As a starting point, the CJA 2003 defines the acquittals to which it has application.

(a) The new provisions apply to offences listed as 'qualifying offences' in the CJA 2003, sch. 5 (set out at **D12.48**). They are all serious offences, which in the main carry a maximum sentence of life imprisonment.

(b) The provisions apply to acquittals after trial on indictment in England and Wales (s. 75(1)) and to acquittals in proceedings outside the UK, of an offence that would have amounted to or included the commission of a qualifying offence in the UK or elsewhere (s. 75(4)).

(c) The meaning of 'acquittal' in s. 75(1) is extended by s. 75(2) so as to include any qualifying offence of which the accused could have been convicted on the original indictment as an alternative verdict (e.g., manslaughter where the original indictment was for murder). The implied acquittal of the alternative offence (manslaughter in the example) can be quashed by the same procedure as the express acquittal (for murder).

(d) Convictions, special verdicts of not guilty by reason of insanity and findings of unfitness to plead in alternative verdict offences are excluded from the procedure (s. 75(2)(a)–(c)).

By virtue of s. 75(6), the procedure, with its removal of the freedom from double jeopardy, is made fully retrospective. The provisions apply equally to acquittals before and after the passing of the CJA 2003. It is of course possible that the retrospective nature of this provision may be subject to challenge under the ECHR, Article 7.

Application for a Quashing Order   Section 76 of the CJA 2003 allows a prosecutor to apply to   **D12.42**
the Court of Appeal for an order to quash a person's acquittal for a qualifying offence or a lesser qualifying offence of which he could have been convicted at that time.

The application to the Court of Appeal to quash the acquittal requires the personal written consent of the DPP (s. 76(3)). Before giving his consent, the DPP must be satisfied (s. 76(4)):

(a) that there is evidence that meets the requirements of s. 78 (see **D12.45**);
(b) that it is in the public interest for the application to proceed; and
(c) that any trial would not run counter to our obligations under the Treaty on European Union relating to the principle of *ne bis in idem* (see **D12.30**).

The relevant Treaty obligations would appear to be apposite where a retrial is proposed for an offence already dealt with in another country of the EU. In such a case, the DPP would have to certify that such a course of action would not be contrary to the UK's obligations to the EU. In *Andrews* [2009] 1 Cr App R 347 the Court of Appeal approved the elucidation of the test by the then DPP, to the effect that consent would only be given to an application where the new evidence rendered a conviction highly probable. The Court also observed that the DPP's consent was not conclusive of the success of an application.

Notice   Notice of the application under the CJA 2003, s. 76(1) or (2), must be given to the   **D12.43**
Court of Appeal (s. 80(1)). The acquitted person must be served with a copy of the application within two days, and be charged with the offence in question. He is entitled to attend and be represented at the hearing in the Court of Appeal. The procedure is set out in the CrimPR, part 41 (see Supplement, **R-330**).

Criteria

The Court of Appeal must order a retrial if: **D12.44**

(a) 'there is new and compelling evidence in the case' (CJA 2003, s. 78); and
(b) 'it is in the interests of justice for an order to be made' (s. 79).

New Evidence   Under the CJA 2003, s. 78, evidence is 'new' if it was not adduced at the origi-   **D12.45**
nal trial of the acquitted person. This would include evidence that was available at the first trial, but not used. Reliance upon such evidence would raise questions about whether it would be in the interests of justice to order a retrial. Where the failure to use the evidence is because of a lack of diligence or expedition by the prosecutor, that is a factor relevant to the application of the interests of justice test (s. 79(2)(c)). But, as is pointed out in *Blackstone's Guide to the Criminal Justice Act 2003*, p.113, that formula is not apt to cover a tactical decision not to use the evidence

in question first time round. The A-G, however, gave to the House of Lords (*Hansard*, HL col. 710 (4 November 2003)), on behalf of the government:

> ...an undertaking, which I have agreed with the Director of Public Prosecutions, that where evidence was not adduced for tactical reasons, it would not be right to use it as a basis for an application...I hope that that will give some comfort. It will be reflected in guidance.

Section 78(5) makes clear that evidence that would have been inadmissible in the original proceedings could form the basis for an application for a retrial as 'new' evidence. It also applies to evidence that does not directly relate to the qualifying offence, but which would be admissible at a retrial of that offence, e.g., similar fact evidence (*Andrews* [2009] 1 Cr App R 347).

The evidence is 'compelling' if the Court of Appeal considers it to be reliable and substantial and highly probative of the case against the accused. What is compelling will depend on the context of the previous trial. For example, if the identity of the offender was not in issue in the original trial, new evidence as to identification would not fit the evidence criterion so as to justify a retrial.

In *Miell* [2008] 1 WLR 627, the new evidence upon which the prosecution sought to rely for the purposes of s. 78 was a confession which had been made after the accused had been convicted, and his subsequent conviction for perjury. The Court of Appeal carried out its own evaluation of the confession and, having concluded that it was unreliable, declined to treat it as 'new evidence'. See also *B and G* [2009] EWCA Crim 1077, where the Court of Appeal made clear that its assessment of whether evidence was compelling was different to a jury's assessment of whether it was persuasive, and *Dobson* [2011] 1 WLR 3230, where Lord Judge CJ made it clear that compelling evidence does not have to be irresistible.

D12.46 **Interests of Justice**   As to the interests of justice test in the CJA 2003, s. 79, the court will consider in particular whether a fair trial is unlikely (e.g., because of adverse publicity about the accused), the length of time since the alleged offence, and whether the police and prosecution have acted with due diligence and expedition with regard to the new evidence. The factors set out in s. 79 are not exhaustive, and the Court of Appeal can consider other relevant issues in determining whether a retrial would be in the interests of justice.

Dunlop [2007] 1 WLR 1567 is illustrative. D had been acquitted, but subsequently not only confessed to the offence but had pleaded guilty to perjury in relation to his evidence at the original trial. The Court of Appeal held that far from it being contrary to the 'interests of justice' to retry him, treating his plea and confession as new evidence (pursuant to s. 78), the public would have been rightly outraged if any other course were taken. By contrast, in *Miell* [2008] 1 WLR 627 (see **D12.45**), the Court of Appeal concluded that allowing the accused to be retried on the basis of his subsequent conviction for perjury would be contrary to the interests of justice, because in effect the burden would be on the accused to negate the impact of that conviction. In *Andrews* [2009] 1 Cr App R 347, the Court of Appeal observed that it would usually only be in the interests of justice to grant an application where the prospects of conviction were 'very good', but went on to observe that considerations of double jeopardy are irrelevant to the assessment of an application.

Procedural Issues

D12.47 Reporting restrictions may be imposed by the Court of Appeal in respect of matters surrounding the application for a retrial. The restrictions may last until the end of the retrial or to the point at which it is clear that the acquitted person can no longer be retried (CJA 2003, s. 82). The restrictions may apply to any information in respect of the investigation and to the republication of matters previously published. An application to order or refuse a retrial can be the subject of an appeal to the Supreme Court on a point of law (s. 81).

If a retrial is ordered, it must be on an indictment preferred by the direction of the Court of Appeal (s. 84). Arraignment must take place within two months of the date on which the Court of Appeal ordered a retrial, unless it specifies a longer period. The period can be extended only if the Court of Appeal is satisfied that the prosecutor has acted with due expedition since the order was made, and that there is still good and sufficient reason to hold the retrial despite any additional lapse of time.

The procedure in respect of the retrial provisions was considered in *Re D (Acquitted person: Retrial)* [2006] 1 WLR 1998.

Relevant Statutory Extracts

Criminal Justice Act 2003, ss. 75 to 80 and 82 to 84 and sch. 5, part 1   **D12.48**

75.—(1) This Part applies where a person has been acquitted of a qualifying offence in proceedings—
  (a) on indictment in England and Wales,
  (b) on appeal against a conviction, verdict or finding in proceedings on indictment in England and Wales, or
  (c) on appeal from a decision on such an appeal.
(2) A person acquitted of an offence in proceedings mentioned in subsection (1) is treated for the purposes of that subsection as also acquitted of any qualifying offence of which he could have been convicted in the proceedings because of the first-mentioned offence being charged in the indictment, except an offence—
  (a) of which he has been convicted,
  (b) of which he has been found not guilty by reason of insanity, or
  (c) in respect of which, in proceedings where he has been found to be under a disability (as defined by section 4 of the Criminal Procedure (Insanity) Act 1964), a finding has been made that he did the act or made the omission charged against him.
(3) References in subsections (1) and (2) to a qualifying offence do not include references to an offence which, at the time of the acquittal, was the subject of an order under section 77(1) or (3).
(4) This Part also applies where a person has been acquitted, in proceedings elsewhere than in the United Kingdom of an offence under the law of the place where the proceedings were held, if the commission of the offence as alleged would have amounted to or included the commission (in the United Kingdom or elsewhere) of a qualifying offence.
(5) Conduct punishable under the law in force elsewhere than in the United Kingdom is an offence under that law for the purposes of subsection (4), however it is described in that law.
(6) This Part applies whether the acquittal was before or after the passing of this Act.
(7) References in this Part to acquittal are to acquittal in circumstances within subsection (1) or (4).
(8) In this Part 'qualifying offence' means an offence listed in Part 1 of Schedule 5.
76.—(1) A prosecutor may apply to the Court of Appeal for an order—
  (a) quashing a person's acquittal in proceedings within section 75(1), and
  (b) ordering him to be retried for the qualifying offence.
(2) A prosecutor may apply to the Court of Appeal, in the case of a person acquitted elsewhere than in the United Kingdom, for—
  (a) a determination whether the acquittal is a bar to the person being tried in England and Wales for the qualifying offence, and
  (b) if it is, an order that the acquittal is not to be a bar.
(3) A prosecutor may make an application under subsection (1) or (2) only with the written consent of the Director of Public Prosecutions.
(4) The Director of Public Prosecutions may give his consent only if satisfied that—
  (a) there is evidence as respects which the requirements of section 78 appear to be met,
  (b) it is in the public interest for the application to proceed, and
  (c) any trial pursuant to an order on the application would not be inconsistent with obligations of the United Kingdom under Article 31 or 34 of the Treaty on European Union (as it had effect before 1 December 2009) or Articles 82, 83 or 85 of the Treaty on the Functioning of the European Union relating to the principle of *ne bis in idem*.
(5) Not more than one application may be made under subsection (1) or (2) in relation to an acquittal.

77.—(1) On an application under section 76(1), the Court of Appeal—
    (a) if satisfied that the requirements of sections 78 and 79 are met, must make the order applied for;
    (b) otherwise, must dismiss the application.
(2) Subsections (3) and (4) apply to an application under section 76(2).
(3) Where the Court of Appeal determines that the acquittal is a bar to the person being tried for the qualifying offence, the court—
    (a) if satisfied that the requirements of sections 78 and 79 are met, must make the order applied for;
    (b) otherwise, must make a declaration to the effect that the acquittal is a bar to the person being tried for the offence.
(4) Where the Court of Appeal determines that the acquittal is not a bar to the person being tried for the qualifying offence, it must make a declaration to that effect.

78.—(1) The requirements of this section are met if there is new and compelling evidence against the acquitted person in relation to the qualifying offence.
(2) Evidence is new if it was not adduced in the proceedings in which the person was acquitted (nor, if those were appeal proceedings, in earlier proceedings to which the appeal related).
(3) Evidence is compelling if—
    (a) it is reliable,
    (b) it is substantial, and
    (c) in the context of the outstanding issues, it appears highly probative of the case against the acquitted person.
(4) The outstanding issues are the issues in dispute in the proceedings in which the person was acquitted and, if those were appeal proceedings, any other issues remaining in dispute from earlier proceedings to which the appeal related.
(5) For the purposes of this section, it is irrelevant whether any evidence would have been admissible in earlier proceedings against the acquitted person.

79.—(1) The requirements of this section are met if in all the circumstances it is in the interests of justice for the court to make the order under section 77.
(2) That question is to be determined having regard in particular to—
    (a) whether existing circumstances make a fair trial unlikely;
    (b) for the purposes of that question and otherwise, the length of time since the qualifying offence was allegedly committed;
    (c) whether it is likely that the new evidence would have been adduced in the earlier proceedings against the acquitted person but for a failure by an officer or by a prosecutor to act with due diligence or expedition;
    (d) whether, since those proceedings or, if later, since the commencement of this Part, any officer or prosecutor has failed to act with due diligence or expedition.
(3) In subsection (2) references to an officer or prosecutor include references to a person charged with corresponding duties under the law in force elsewhere than in England and Wales.
(4) Where the earlier prosecution was conducted by a person other than a prosecutor, subsection (2)(c) applies in relation to that person as well as in relation to a prosecutor.

80.—(1) A prosecutor who wishes to make an application under section 76(1) or (2) must give notice of the application to the Court of Appeal.
(2) Within two days beginning with the day on which any such notice is given, notice of the application must be served by the prosecutor on the person to whom the application relates, charging him with the offence to which it relates or, if he has been charged with it in accordance with section 87(4), stating that he has been so charged.
(3) Subsection (2) applies whether the person to whom the application relates is in the United Kingdom or elsewhere, but the Court of Appeal may, on application by the prosecutor, extend the time for service under that subsection if it considers it necessary to do so because of that person's absence from the United Kingdom.
(4) The Court of Appeal must consider the application at a hearing.
(5) The person to whom the application relates—
    (a) is entitled to be present at the hearing, although he may be in custody, unless he is in custody elsewhere than in England and Wales or Northern Ireland, and
    (b) is entitled to be represented at the hearing, whether he is present or not.
(6) For the purposes of the application, the Court of Appeal may, if it thinks it necessary or expedient in the interests of justice—

(a) order the production of any document, exhibit or other thing, the production of which appears to the court to be necessary for the determination of the application, and

(b) order any witness who would be a compellable witness in proceedings pursuant to an order or declaration made on the application to attend for examination and be examined before the court.

(7) The Court of Appeal may at one hearing consider more than one application (whether or not relating to the same person), but only if the offences concerned could be tried on the same indictment.

...

82.—(1) Where it appears to the Court of Appeal that the inclusion of any matter in a publication would give rise to a substantial risk of prejudice to the administration of justice in a retrial, the court may order that the matter is not to be included in any publication while the order has effect.

(2) In subsection (1) 'retrial' means the trial of an acquitted person for a qualifying offence pursuant to any order made or that may be made under section 77.

(3) The court may make an order under this section only if it appears to it necessary in the interests of justice to do so.

(4) An order under this section may apply to a matter which has been included in a publication published before the order takes effect, but such an order—

(a) applies only to the later inclusion of the matter in a publication (whether directly or by inclusion of the earlier publication), and

(b) does not otherwise affect the earlier publication.

(5) After notice of an application has been given under section 80(1) relating to the acquitted person and the qualifying offence, the court may make an order under this section only—

(a) of its own motion, or

(b) on the application of the Director of Public Prosecutions.

(6) Before such notice has been given, an order under this section—

(a) may be made only on the application of the Director of Public Prosecutions, and

(b) may not be made unless, since the acquittal concerned, an investigation of the commission by the acquitted person of the qualifying offence has been commenced by officers.

(7) The court may at any time, of its own motion or on an application made by the Director of Public Prosecutions or the acquitted person, vary or revoke an order under this section.

(8) Any order made under this section before notice of an application has been given under section 80(1) relating to the acquitted person and the qualifying offence must specify the time when it ceases to have effect.

(9) An order under this section which is made or has effect after such notice has been given ceases to have effect, unless it specifies an earlier time—

(a) when there is no longer any step that could be taken which would lead to the acquitted person being tried pursuant to an order made on the application, or

(b) if he is tried pursuant to such an order, at the conclusion of the trial.

(10) Nothing in this section affects any prohibition or restriction by virtue of any other enactment on the inclusion of any matter in a publication or any power, under an enactment or otherwise, to impose such a prohibition or restriction.

(11) In this section—

'programme service' has the same meaning as in the Broadcasting Act 1990,

'publication' includes any speech, writing, relevant programme or other communication in whatever form, which is addressed to the public at large or any section of the public (and for this purpose every relevant programme is to be taken to be so addressed), but does not include an indictment or other document prepared for use in particular legal proceedings,

'relevant programme' means a programme included in a programme service.

83.—(1) This section applies if—

(a) an order under section 82 is made, whether in England and Wales or Northern Ireland, and

(b) while the order has effect, any matter is included in a publication, in any part of the United Kingdom, in contravention of the order.

(2) Where the publication is a newspaper or periodical, any proprietor, editor or publisher of the newspaper or periodical is guilty of an offence.

(3) Where the publication is a relevant programme—

(a) any body corporate or Scottish partnership engaged in providing the programme service in which the programme is included, and

(b) any person having functions in relation to the programme corresponding to those of an editor of a newspaper,

is guilty of an offence.

(4) In the case of any other publication, any person publishing it is guilty of an offence.

(5) If an offence under this section committed by a body corporate is proved—

(a) to have been committed with the consent or connivance of, or

(b) to be attributable to any neglect on the part of,

an officer, the officer as well as the body corporate is guilty of the offence and liable to be proceeded against and punished accordingly.

(6) In subsection (5), 'officer' means a director, manager, secretary or other similar officer of the body, or a person purporting to act in any such capacity.

(7) If the affairs of a body corporate are managed by its members, 'director' in subsection (6) means a member of that body.

(8) [Applies only to Scotland.]

(9) A person guilty of an offence under this section is liable on summary conviction to a fine not exceeding level 5 on the standard scale.

(10) Proceedings for an offence under this section may not be instituted—

(a) in England and Wales otherwise than by or with the consent of the Attorney General, or

(b) [applies only to Northern Ireland].

(11) [Applies only to Northern Ireland.]

84.—(1) Where a person—

(a) is tried pursuant to an order under section 77(1), or

(b) is tried on indictment pursuant to an order under section 77(3),

the trial must be on an indictment preferred by direction of the Court of Appeal.

(2) After the end of 2 months after the date of the order, the person may not be arraigned on an indictment preferred in pursuance of such a direction unless the Court of Appeal gives leave.

(3) The Court of Appeal must not give leave unless satisfied that—

(a) the prosecutor has acted with due expedition, and

(b) there is a good and sufficient cause for trial despite the lapse of time since the order under section 77.

(4) Where the person may not be arraigned without leave, he may apply to the Court of Appeal to set aside the order and—

(a) for any direction required for restoring an earlier judgment and verdict of acquittal of the qualifying offence, or

(b) in the case of a person acquitted elsewhere than in the United Kingdom, for a declaration to the effect that the acquittal is a bar to his being tried for the qualifying offence.

(5) An indictment under subsection (1) may relate to more than one offence, or more than one person, and may relate to an offence which, or a person who, is not the subject of an order or declaration under section 77.

(6) Evidence given at a trial pursuant to an order under section 77(1) or (3) must be given orally if it was given orally at the original trial, unless—

(a) all the parties to the trial agree otherwise,

(b) section 116 applies, or

(c) the witness is unavailable to give evidence, otherwise than as mentioned in subsection (2) of that section, and section 114(1)(d) applies.

(7) At a trial pursuant to an order under section 77(1), paragraph 5 of schedule 3 to the Crime and Disorder Act 1998 (use of depositions) does not apply to a deposition read as evidence at the original trial.

SCHEDULE 5

QUALIFYING OFFENCES FOR PURPOSES OF PART 10

PART 1

LIST OF OFFENCES FOR ENGLAND AND WALES

Offences Against the Person

Murder
    1. Murder.

Attempted murder

2. An offence under section 1 of the Criminal Attempts Act 1981 of attempting to commit murder.

Soliciting murder

3. An offence under section 4 of the Offences against the Person Act 1861.

Manslaughter

4. Manslaughter.

Corporate manslaughter

4A. An offence under section 1 of the Corporate Manslaughter and Corporate Homicide Act 2007.

Kidnapping

5. Kidnapping.

Sexual Offences

Rape

6. An offence under section 1 of the Sexual Offences Act 1956 or section 1 of the Sexual Offences Act 2003.

Attempted rape

7. An offence under section 1 of the Criminal Attempts Act 1981 of attempting to commit an offence under section 1 of the Sexual Offences Act 1956 or section 1 of the Sexual Offences Act 2003.

Intercourse with a girl under thirteen

8. An offence under section 5 of the Sexual Offences Act 1956.

Incest by a man with a girl under thirteen

9. An offence under section 10 of the Sexual Offences Act 1956 alleged to have been committed with a girl under thirteen.

Assault by penetration

10. An offence under section 2 of the Sexual Offences Act 2003 (c. 42).

Causing a person to engage in sexual activity without consent

11. An offence under section 4 of the Sexual Offences Act 2003 where it is alleged that the activity caused involved penetration within subsection (4)(a) to (d) of that section.

Rape of a child under thirteen

12. An offence under section 5 of the Sexual Offences Act 2003.

Attempted rape of a child under thirteen

13. An offence under section 1 of the Criminal Attempts Act 1981 of attempting to commit an offence under section 5 of the Sexual Offences Act 2003.

Assault of a child under thirteen by penetration

14. An offence under section 6 of the Sexual Offences Act 2003.

Causing a child under thirteen to engage in sexual activity

15. An offence under section 8 of the Sexual Offences Act 2003 where it is alleged that an activity involving penetration within subsection (2)(a) to (d) of that section was caused.

Sexual activity with a person with a mental disorder impeding choice

16. An offence under section 30 of the Sexual Offences Act 2003 where it is alleged that the touching involved penetration within subsection (3)(a) to (d) of that section.

Causing a person with a mental disorder impeding choice to engage in sexual activity

17. An offence under section 31 of the Sexual Offences Act 2003 where it is alleged that an activity involving penetration within subsection (3)(a) to (d) of that section was caused.

Drugs Offences

Unlawful importation of Class A drug

18. An offence under section 50(2) of the Customs and Excise Management Act 1979 alleged to have been committed in respect of a Class A drug (as defined by section 2 of the Misuse of Drugs Act 1971).

Unlawful exportation of Class A drug
19. An offence under section 68(2) of the Customs and Excise Management Act 1979 alleged to have been committed in respect of a Class A drug (as defined by section 2 of the Misuse of Drugs Act 1971).

Fraudulent evasion in respect of Class A drug
20. An offence under section 170(1) or (2) of the Customs and Excise Management Act 1979 alleged to have been committed in respect of a Class A drug (as defined by section 2 of the Misuse of Drugs Act 1971).

Producing or being concerned in production of Class A drug
21. An offence under section 4(2) of the Misuse of Drugs Act 1971 alleged to have been committed in relation to a Class A drug (as defined by section 2 of that Act).

Criminal Damage Offences

Arson endangering life
22. An offence under section 1(2) of the Criminal Damage Act 1971 alleged to have been committed by destroying or damaging property by fire.

Causing explosion likely to endanger life or property
23. An offence under section 2 of the Explosive Substances Act 1883.

Intent or conspiracy to cause explosion likely to endanger life or property
24. An offence under section 3(1)(a) of the Explosive Substances Act 1883.

War Crimes and Terrorism

Genocide, crimes against humanity and war crimes
25. An offence under section 51 or 52 of the International Criminal Court Act 2001.

Grave breaches of the Geneva Conventions
26. An offence under section 1 of the Geneva Conventions Act 1957.

Directing terrorist organisation
27. An offence under section 56 of the Terrorism Act 2000.

Hostage-taking
28. An offence under section 1 of the Taking of Hostages Act 1982.

Conspiracy
29. An offence under section 1 of the Criminal Law Act 1977 of conspiracy to commit an offence listed in this Part of this Schedule.

OTHER PLEAS THAT MAY BE TAKEN AT ARRAIGNMENT

D12.49 For convenience, three further objections that may be taken to the arraignment of the accused can briefly be addressed at this point.

Demurrer

D12.50 This is 'an objection to the form or substance of the indictment, apparent on the face of the indictment' (per Cantley J in *Inner London Quarter Sessions, ex parte Metropolitan Police Commissioner* [1970] 2 QB 80 at p. 83G). The guidance given in that case was to the following effect:

(a) the plea must be entered in writing, filed in the Crown Office, and a copy served on the opposite party, preferably prior to the accused being arraigned;
(b) on demurring, the defence are *not* entitled to refer the judge to the contents of the depositions and/or statements tendered at committal proceedings.

The scope of the remedy by demurrer is no wider than the scope of motions to quash. Lord Parker CJ said that he hoped that demurrer would now 'be allowed to die naturally' (at p. 85G). Similarly, Cantley J said that demurrers had been 'supplanted in practice by the safe and convenient procedures of motion to quash the indictment or motion in arrest of judgment' (a motion that the accused had been convicted of an offence not known to law) (at p. 83C). However, in *Cumberworth* (1989) 89 Cr App R 187, where the defence made a submission as to jurisdiction at the end of the prosecution evidence, the Court of Appeal stated, *obiter*, that it would have been more convenient procedurally to raise the point by way of demurrer at the outset of the trial, thus avoiding the necessity of hearing the evidence if the point were good.

The entry of a demurrer does not affect the accused's right to plead not guilty to the indictment should the demurrer fail (CLA 1967, s. 6(1)(a)).

Plea to the Jurisdiction

The purpose of this plea is to assert that the Crown Court has no jurisdiction to try the offence   **D12.51**
charged (e.g., because it is a summary offence or because it was committed abroad and does not come within the exceptional categories of 'foreign' offences that may be tried in England and Wales). Like a demurrer, the plea should be entered in writing prior to arraignment, although it is always open to the defence to take any jurisdictional point simply under a general not guilty plea (see, e.g., *Treacy v DPP* [1971] AC 537, where that was done, but see also *Cumberworth* (1989) 89 Cr App R 187 at **D12.50**, in which the court said that a jurisdiction point should be raised at the outset).

Pardon

This is the third special plea in bar (the other two being autrefois acquit and autrefois convict).   **D12.52**
It may be relied on where a pardon has been granted by the Crown on the advice of the Home Secretary in exercise of the royal prerogative of mercy. It must be pleaded at the first opportunity (i.e. before arraignment if the pardon has by then been granted). In modern times, the plea has become obsolete.

THE ARRAIGNMENT

Procedure on Arraignment

The procedure for arraignment is contained in the CrimPR, r. 3.24 (see Supplement, **R-31**).   **D12.53**
The arraignment consists of the clerk of the court reading the indictment to the accused and asking him whether he pleads guilty or not guilty to the counts contained therein. If there are several counts, a plea must be taken on each one separately immediately after it is read out (*Boyle* [1954] 2 QB 292); if, however, two counts are in the alternative and the accused pleads guilty to the first count, it is unnecessary to take a plea on the second (*Boyle*). If there is a joint indictment against several accused, normal practice is to arraign them together. Separate pleas must be taken from each of those named in any joint count. (As to the procedure to be adopted where an accused absents himself, see **D12.57** and **D12.70**.)

It is now standard practice to exclude the jurors in waiting from court until after the arraignment has been completed. This avoids the possibility of potential jurors being prejudiced by hearing the accused plead guilty to some but not all the counts on the indictment. After the jury have been sworn, they are told by the clerk the counts to which the accused has pleaded not guilty, no mention being made of any matters to which he has pleaded guilty nor of any co-accused who may have pleaded guilty.

Time for Arraignment

The Senior Courts Act 1981, s. 77(1), provides that rules of court are to prescribe the mini-   **D12.54**
mum and maximum periods which may elapse between a person being sent for trial and the

D

Part D Procedure

beginning of the trial (i.e. the arraignment). By s. 77(2), the trial of a person sent for trial shall not begin within the minimum period prescribed by the rules unless the defence and the prosecution consent, and shall not begin after the maximum period unless a Crown Court judge orders otherwise.

Section 77(3) defines the beginning of the trial as the time when the accused is arraigned. It should be noted, however, that the Crown Court has an unfettered discretion to adjourn proceedings, and there is thus no objection to the accused being arraigned within the eight weeks prescribed by the CrimPR, r. 39.1, and then the case being immediately adjourned to a later date if the parties are still not ready for trial.

Where the prosecution are seeking an order under the DVCVA 2004, s. 17 (see **D13.80**), for a trial of part of the indictment by a judge alone, they are required to prepare a split indictment with those charges which are to be tried by a jury in part one and the remaining counts in part two (CPD II, para. 14A.6: see Supplement, **PD-19**). At arraignment, the accused should be arraigned only on the counts in part one of the indictment, with arraignment on part two only to occur following conviction on part one (para. 14A.7).

D12.55 **Time-limits** In contrast to the former position on time limits, where cases are sent for trial under the CDA 1998, s. 51, no time-limits are laid down by the CrimPR as to the period between sending and arraignment.

D12.56 **Failure to Arraign within a Reasonable Period** While the absence of stated time limits creates a change, under the former regime, leave for late arraignment was readily given (see *Urbanowski* [1976] 1 All ER 679). The requirement under the ECHR, Articles 5(3) and 6(1), for a trial to be held within a reasonable period (see **A7.84**) is of obvious relevance.

Effect of Lack of Arraignment on the Validity of the Proceedings

D12.57 Failure by the court to have the accused arraigned does not necessarily render invalid subsequent proceedings on the indictment (*Williams* [1978] QB 373). Thus, the defence may waive the accused's right to be arraigned, either expressly or by simply remaining silent while the trial proceeds without arraignment. It was held in *K (John)* [2007] EWCA Crim 1339, where the accused absconded prior to arraignment, that by absenting himself he had waived his right to arraignment. It follows that the accused has also waived his right to be present for arraignment on an indictment which has been amended by the addition of a more serious count, even though he may have wished to plead guilty to the less serious alternative charge (*K (John)* at [19]).

A dictum of Edmund Davies LJ in *Ellis* (1973) 57 Cr App R 571 (at p. 575), that the 'only safe and proper course … is to say … that (apart from a few very special cases) it is an invariable requirement that the initial arraignment must be conducted between the clerk of the court and the accused person himself', should be understood in the context of the facts of that case, namely, the entry of a guilty plea.

On the facts of *Williams*, by contrast, W had always intended to plead not guilty and the trial proceeded in all respects as if he had so pleaded but in fact (through an administrative muddle) the indictment was never put. The pre-trial irregularity did not invalidate the proceedings and W's conviction was upheld despite lack of arraignment. This accords with the decisions of the Court of Appeal in *Ashton* [2007] 1 WLR 181 and of the House of Lords in *Clarke* [2008] 2 All ER 665, to the effect that a failure to follow the correct procedure as to arraignment is not necessarily fatal to proceedings thereafter. The question to be considered is whether Parliament intended non-compliance to be fatal to the validity of proceedings thereafter, and, if not, whether the accused has been prejudiced as a result of the failure.

Further, the decision in *Williams* is without prejudice to the principle that a plea of guilty must be entered by the accused personally, the corollary of which is that a conviction on a guilty plea will be valid only if the accused has been properly arraigned (see **D12.71**).

PLEAS THAT MAY BE ENTERED ON ARRAIGNMENT

In the great majority of cases, the plea entered by the accused will be simply one of guilty or not **D12.58** guilty. It is sometimes open to him to plead not guilty as charged but guilty of an alternative (lesser) offence.

The only alternatives to such a plea arise in the circumstances addressed above where it is submitted that it would not be appropriate for the accused to be arraigned at all, namely where the issue arises of whether he has previously been acquitted or convicted of the offence now charged (a plea of autrefois acquit or autrefois convict — see **D12.20**) or where there may be a plea to the jurisdiction (the defence wish to argue that the Crown Court does not have jurisdiction to deal with the case, e.g., because the offence was committed abroad).

PLEA BARGAINING

The issues that arise under this heading are: **D12.59**

(a) the extent to which the judge may properly influence the accused's decision as to plea by indicating the probable sentence, and
(b) the propriety of bargains between the prosecution and defence involving the offering of no evidence in respect of certain charges in return for the accused pleading guilty to others.

Judicial Indications of Sentence

A plea of guilty must be entered voluntarily. If the accused is deprived of a genuine choice as to **D12.60** plea and in consequence purports to plead guilty, the plea is a nullity and the conviction will be quashed on appeal (see **D12.101**).

This was stressed by the Court of Appeal in *Turner* [1970] 2 QB 321. In that case, the reason for holding the appellant's plea to be a nullity was that his counsel, during discussions about whether there should be a change of plea to guilty, went to see the judge, and, on returning to his client, stated that a conviction on a not guilty plea would entail a 'very real possibility' of a prison sentence whereas if T pleaded guilty it would be a 'fine or some other sentence not involving imprisonment'. In the circumstances, the Court of Appeal concluded that the promise of a non-custodial sentence in the event of a guilty plea, coupled with an implied threat of a custodial sentence should the not guilty plea be unsuccessfully maintained, took away T's free choice.

Having decided that the conviction must therefore be quashed, the Court of Appeal made certain observations designed to assist counsel and judges over what was referred to as 'the vexed question of plea bargaining' (at pp. 326E–327D). Those observations have now been superseded, following the decision in *Goodyear* [2005] 3 All ER 117, by CPD VII, Sentencing, part B (see Supplement, **PD-65**).

The *Goodyear* Approach

The correct approach to judicial indications of sentence is set out in *Goodyear* [2005] 3 All ER **D12.61** 117, restated in *Seddon* [2008] 2 Cr App R (S) 174 and *Ibori* [2014] 1 Cr App R (S) 73 (15), and endorsed in CPD VII, Sentencing, part C (see Supplement, **PD-66**). The CrimPR, r. 3.23 now sets out a detailed procedure for an application for an indication of the maximum sentence that would be passed if a guilty plea were entered (see Supplement, **R-30**). Proper roles in the process are identified for the court, and those responsible for prosecuting and defending. The guidelines also demonstrate the need to take into account the review of any sentence then passed, either by way of an appeal by the defendant or a reference on behalf of the A-G. The importance of following the procedure was again emphasised by the Court of Appeal in *Ali* [2014] EWCA Crim 542. In summary, the guidance is as follows.

D12.62 **Responsibilities of the Court**   (1)   A court should not give an indication of sentence unless one has been sought by the accused.

(2) However, the court remains entitled to exercise the power to indicate that the sentence, or type of sentence, on the accused would be the same whether the case proceeds as a plea of guilty or goes to trial, with a resulting conviction. Where the sentence will vary according to plea, the court should only give an indication as to the sentence following a guilty plea. An indication as to sentence following trial may put undue pressure on the accused to plead (*Clark* [2008] EWCA Crim 3221). The court is also entitled in an appropriate case to remind the defence advocate that the accused is entitled to seek an advance indication of sentence.

(3) Where an indication is sought, the court may refuse altogether to give an indication, or may postpone doing so, with or without giving reasons. The probability is that the judge would explain his reasons for deferral, and further indicate the circumstances in which, and when, he would be prepared to respond to a request for a sentence indication.

(4) Where the court has it in mind to defer an indication, the probability is that the judge would explain his reasons, and further indicate the circumstances in which, and when, he would be prepared to respond to a request for a sentence indication.

(5) If the court refuses to give an indication (as opposed to deferring it), it remains open to the defence to make a further request for an indication at a later stage. However, in such circumstances the court should not normally initiate the process, except where appropriate to indicate that the circumstances have changed sufficiently to permit a renewed application for an indication.

(6) Once an indication has been given, it is binding and remains binding on the judge who has given it, and it also binds any other judge who becomes responsible for the case. An indication may cease to be binding where guideline authority from the Court of Appeal alters the appropriate sentencing level (*Jalil* [2009] 2 Cr App R (S) 276) or where a new definitive sentencing guideline is issued by the Sentencing Council.

(7) If, after a reasonable opportunity to consider his position in the light of the indication, the accused does not plead guilty, the indication will cease to have effect.

(8) Where appropriate, there must be an agreed, written basis of plea, otherwise the judge should refuse to give an indication.

Additional guidance was given in *A-G's Ref (No. 80 of 2005)* [2005] EWCA Crim 3367, when the Court of Appeal stated that:

(a) the principal feature of an appropriate indication of sentence is that an advance indication should be sought by the defence, and not promulgated by the judge;

(b) an indication should not be given that a trial would result in a much longer sentence compared to the one offered if the accused pleads guilty.

D12.63 **Responsibilities of the Defence**   (1) Subject to the court's power to give an appropriate reminder to the advocate for the accused, the process of seeking a sentence indication should normally be started by the defence.

(2) Whether or not such a reminder has been given, the accused's advocate should not seek an indication without written authority, signed by his client, that he, the client, wishes to seek an indication.

(3) The advocate is personally responsible for ensuring that his client fully appreciates that (a) he should not plead guilty unless he is guilty, (b) any sentence indication given by the court remains subject to the entitlement of the A-G (where it arises) to refer an unduly lenient sentence to the Court of Appeal, (c) any indication given by the court reflects the situation at the time when it is given and if a guilty plea is not tendered in the light of that indication, the indication ceases to have effect, and (d) any indication which may be given relates only to the matters about which an indication is sought.

(4) An indication should not be sought while there is any uncertainty between the prosecution and the defence about an acceptable plea or pleas to the indictment, or the factual basis relating to any plea.

(5) Any agreed basis should be reduced into writing before an indication is sought.

(6) Where there is a dispute about a particular fact which counsel for the accused believes to be effectively immaterial to the sentencing decision, the difference should be recorded for the court to consider.

(7) The court should never be invited to indicate levels of sentence which depend on possible different pleas.

(8) In the unusual event that the accused is unrepresented, he would be entitled to seek a sentence indication of his own initiative, but it would be wrong for either the court or prosecuting counsel to take any initiative in this regard that might too readily be interpreted as or subsequently argued to have been improper pressure.

Responsibilities of the Prosecution (1) As the request for indication comes from the defence, **D12.64** the prosecution is obliged to react to, rather than initiate the process. In doing so, the prosecution should act in accordance with the CrimPR, r. 3.23(4) (see Supplement, **R-30**).

(2) If there is no final agreement about the plea to the indictment, or the basis of plea, and the defence nevertheless proceeds to seek an indication, which the court appears minded to give, prosecuting counsel should remind the court that an indication of sentence should normally not be given until the basis of the plea has been agreed, or the judge has concluded that he can properly deal with the case without the need for a *Newton* hearing (see **D20.8**).

(3) If an indication is sought, the prosecution should normally inquire whether the court is in possession of or has had access to all the evidence relied on by the prosecution, including any personal impact statement from the victim of the crime, as well as any information of relevant previous convictions recorded against the accused.

(4) If the process has been properly followed, it should not normally be necessary for counsel for the prosecution, before the court gives any indication, to do more than (a) draw the judge's attention to any minimum or mandatory statutory sentencing requirements, and, where applicable or where invited to do so (and as required by CPD VII, Sentencing, para. C.4: see Supplement, **PD-66**), to any definitive sentencing guidelines of the Sentencing Council or any relevant guideline cases, and (b) where it applies, to remind the judge that the entitlement of the A-G to refer any eventual sentencing decision as unduly lenient is not affected.

(5) In any event, counsel should not say anything which may create the impression that the sentence indication has the support or approval of the Crown.

Further guidance is given to prosecutors through the A-G's Guidelines on the Acceptance of Pleas (see **appendix 2**) as to their part in any discussion on plea and sentence in chambers.

Such discussions should take place only 'in the most exceptional circumstances'.

(a) Where they do take place, the prosecution advocate should if necessary remind the judge of the desirability of an independent record, and should himself make a full note, recording all decisions and comments. This note should be made available to the prosecuting authority.

(b) Where there is a discussion on plea and sentence and the prosecution advocate does not believe that the circumstances are exceptional, he should remind the judge of the relevant decisions of the Court of Appeal and disassociate himself from any discussion on sentence.

D

Part D Procedure

(c) He should not say or do anything which might be taken to agree, expressly or by implication, with a particular sentence.

(d) In cases where s. 35 of the CJA 1988 applies, he should indicate that the A-G may, if he sees fit, seek leave to refer any sentence as unduly lenient (see **D28.7**).

D12.65 **The Indication Process** (1) It is anticipated that any sentence indication would normally be sought at the plea and case management hearing, following a written application (see CrimPR, r. 3.23(2)).

(2) In accordance with *A-G's Ref (No. 80 of 2005)* [2005] EWCA Crim 3367, a hearing involving an indication of sentence should normally take place in open court with a full recording of the entire proceedings, and both sides represented, in the presence of the accused (one of the exceptions is where an accused is unaware that he is terminally ill).

(3) The court is most unlikely to be able to give an indication in complicated or difficult cases unless issues between the prosecution and the defence have been addressed and resolved. Therefore, in such cases, no less than seven days' notice of an intention to seek an indication should normally be given in writing to the prosecution and the court.

(4) If an application is made without notice when it should have been given, the court may conclude that any inevitable adjournment should have been avoided and that the discount for the guilty plea should be reduced accordingly.

(5) There should be very little need for the court to be involved in the discussions with the advocates, save to seek better information on any troubling aspect of the case. An opening by the Crown, or a mitigation plea by the defence, is not envisaged.

(6) The fact that notice has been given, and any reference to a request for a sentence indication, or the circumstances in which it was sought, would be inadmissible in any subsequent trial.

(7) Reporting restrictions should normally be imposed, to be lifted if and when the accused pleads or is found guilty.

It is clear from *Goodyear* [2005] 3 All ER 117 that the Court of Appeal did not envisage a process by which the judge should give some kind of preliminary indication, leading to comments on it by counsel for the Crown, with the judge then reconsidering his indication, and perhaps raising it to a higher level, with counsel for the accused then making further submissions to persuade the judge, after all, to reduce his indication. Any indication which has been given lapses if the accused does not then plead guilty and cannot later bind the court (*Patel* [2009] EWCA Crim 1161).

D12.66 **Indications where the Dangerous Offender Provisions Might Apply** In *Kulah* [2008] 1 All ER 16, the Court of Appeal provided guidance as to the approach a court should adopt when invited to give an indication in a case where the accused was charged with one or more specified offences within the CJA 2003, sch. 15, and might be liable to an indeterminate sentence pursuant to the CJA 2003, part 12, if he was determined to be a dangerous offender (see **E4**). The court should make clear that the accused was charged with a specified offence and that the necessary material for an assessment as to dangerousness was not available. It followed that if, in due course, he was assessed to be dangerous, the determinate sentence indicated would in fact become the notional determinate term, and the actual length of the sentence was beyond the judge's control. See also *Seddon* [2008] 2 Cr App R (S) 174.

D12.67 **Magistrates' Court** It would be impracticable for these new arrangements to be extended to proceedings in magistrates' courts. Accordingly, for the time being, magistrates should confine themselves to the statutory arrangements in the CJA 2003, sch. 3.

D12.68 **References and Appeals Against Sentence** If counsel for the prosecution has addressed his responsibilities, the discretion of the A-G to refer a sentence is wholly unaffected by the advance sentence indication process. In such circumstances, the fact that a judge has given an indication of sentence before plea will not bind the Court of Appeal if the A-G appeals on the basis that the sentence is unduly lenient (*A-G's Ref (No. 40 of 1996)* [1997] 1 Cr App R (S) 357: see **D28.10**).

The accused's entitlement to apply for leave to appeal against sentence if, for example, insufficient allowance has been made for matters of genuine mitigation, is similarly unaffected.

Arrangements between Prosecution and Defence

It is common practice for the prosecution and defence to agree through counsel prior to arraignment that, in the event of the accused pleading guilty to parts of the indictment, the Crown will not seek to prove him guilty as charged. Such an arrangement may take the form of accepting a plea of guilty to a lesser offence, or of offering no evidence on counts to which the accused pleads not guilty, or of asking the judge to allow some counts to remain on the file marked not to be proceeded with. This is addressed in more detail at **D12.79**, **D12.81** and **D12.82**. See also the A-G's Guidelines on Plea Discussions in Cases of Serious or Complex Fraud (see **appendix 2**). The CCA 2013, sch. 17, introduced deferred prosecution agreements (see **D12.106**) under which, with court approval, the accused and the prosecution may reach an agreement resulting in the suspension of an indictment before arraignment if the accused complies with the requirements specified in the agreement.

D12.69

PLEA OF NOT GUILTY

Entry of Plea of Not Guilty

Normal practice is for the accused to enter a plea of not guilty personally when arraigned by the clerk in the absence of any potential jurors (see **D12.1**). It is not, however, essential to the validity of a trial that he formally says the words 'not guilty' (*Williams* [1978] QB 373 at **D12.57**). If an accused wilfully stays silent when arraigned, or fails to give a direct answer to the charge, or enters a plea which purports to be one of guilty but is in fact ambiguous, the court may and should enter a plea of not guilty on his behalf (CLA 1967, s. 6(1)(c)).

D12.70

Effect of Plea of Not Guilty

A plea of not guilty puts the prosecution to proof of their entire case. The burden is therefore on them to satisfy the jury beyond reasonable doubt that the accused committed the *actus reus* of the offence (or aided, abetted, counselled or procured its commission), and that in doing so he had the necessary *mens rea*. Should the prosecution fail to adduce sufficient evidence as to *any* element of the offence, the accused is entitled to be acquitted on the judge's direction following a submission of no case to answer made at the close of the prosecution case.

D12.71

The defence statement should have indicated in advance of trial those parts of the prosecution case which are disputed (see **D9.29**). Nevertheless defence counsel is still entitled to take advantage of any deficiency in the prosecution evidence (e.g., a witness not coming up to proof) and submit that there is no case to answer, whether or not the element of the offence of which evidence is lacking would otherwise have been contested.

The only method by which the prosecution may be released from their obligation to prove each essential element of the offence is if the defence have made formal admissions under s. 10 of the CJA 1967, or where a fact is presumed (see **F3.61** *et seq.*) or judicially noticed (see **F1.4** *et seq.*).

PLEA OF GUILTY

Requirement that Accused Plead Personally

A plea of guilty must be entered by the accused personally. If counsel purports to plead guilty on behalf of an accused, the purported plea has no validity and the proceedings constitute a mistrial (*Ellis* (1973) 57 Cr App R 571). On appeal, the Court of Appeal will be obliged either to quash the conviction or to grant a writ of *venire de novo* (i.e. set the conviction aside but order that the

D12.72

D

Part D Procedure

accused be retried) (*Ellis*). In *Ellis*, defence counsel intervened during the arraignment to set out the basis on which the accused would plead guilty, and the judge proceeded to sentence. At no stage did the accused himself say he was guilty, although that was undoubtedly what he would have said had he been allowed to. On appeal, Edmund Davies LJ reviewed the authorities and then said (at pp. 574–5):

> . . . great mischief would ensue if a legal representative was generally regarded as entitled to plead on an accused's behalf. It would open the door to dispute as to whether, for example, counsel had correctly understood and acted upon the instructions which the accused had given him, and, if a dispute of that kind arose, the consequential embarrassment and difficulty could be difficult in the extreme.

> We think that the only safe and proper course accordingly is to say . . . that (apart from a few very special cases) it is an invariable requirement that the initial arraignment must be conducted between the clerk of the court and the accused person himself or herself directly.

Edmund Davies LJ's dicta do not expressly distinguish between cases where the accused intends to plead guilty and those where he intends to plead not guilty or refuses to plead. As regards the latter, it is possible for a valid trial to take place despite the absence of a personal plea from the accused (see **D12.57**). As regards guilty pleas, however, there can be no derogation whatsoever from the rule that the plea must come from the mouth of the accused. This is confirmed by *Williams* [1978] QB 373, where Shaw LJ, giving the judgment of the Court of Appeal, said (at p. 378G): 'No qualification of or deviation from the rule that a plea of guilty must come from him who acknowledges guilt is . . . permissible. A departure from the rule in a criminal trial would therefore necessarily be a vitiating factor rendering the whole procedure void and ineffectual.'

Effect of Plea of Guilty

D12.73 If the accused pleads guilty, the prosecution are released from their obligation to prove the case. There is no need to empanel a jury, and the accused stands convicted simply by virtue of the word that has come from his own mouth. The only evidence the prosecution then need call in the ordinary case is that of the accused's antecedents and criminal record (see **D20.45** to **D20.51**).

Exceptionally, there may be a dispute between the parties about the material facts of the offence. If the dispute is serious enough to have a significant effect on sentence, the prosecution will either have to call evidence in support of their own version at a so-called '*Newton* hearing' or allow sentence to be passed on the basis of the defence version (for *Newton* hearings, see **D20.8** to **D20.29**). However, even in such cases, the prosecution evidence goes to *how* the offence was committed, not whether it was committed, and the accused remains convicted by his own plea whatever the outcome of the *Newton* hearing. See *Padellec* [2012] EWCA Crim 1956 as to the need for the prosecution and court to be cautious about too readily accepting a basis of plea.

Adjournments Following Plea of Guilty

D12.74 Once a plea of guilty has been entered, the court may forthwith commence the procedure leading up to the passing of sentence (for which see **D20.2**). It may, on the other hand, take the plea and then adjourn. Whether or not to adjourn is entirely at the discretion of the court. Common reasons for an adjournment are to obtain reports on the accused or to await the outcome of other proceedings outstanding against him with a view to his being sentenced on one occasion for all matters (see *Bennett* (1980) 2 Cr App R (S) 96, for the desirability of linking up outstanding charges).

By virtue of the Senior Courts Act 1981, s. 81(1)(c), on adjourning, the court may either commit the accused to custody or grant him bail. Despite having been convicted, an accused who is remanded for inquiries or report at this stage still has a prima facie right to bail under the Bail Act 1976, s. 4, although in practice bail is usually withdrawn if the accused has pleaded guilty to a serious offence.

MIXED PLEAS

Three scenarios fall to be considered under the head of mixed pleas, namely where an accused **D12.75** pleads guilty to some charges but not others, where an accused pleads guilty and his co-accused do not, and where an accused pleads guilty and gives evidence against those co-accused who have not. The procedure is set out in the CPD VII, Sentencing, parts B to D (see Supplement, PD-65 *et seq*).

Mixed Pleas from an Accused

If an accused enters mixed pleas on a multi-count indictment and the prosecution are not **D12.76** prepared to accept those pleas, sentencing for the counts to which he has pleaded guilty should be postponed until after he has been tried on the not guilty counts. This is different from the situation of an accused who pleads guilty to a lesser offence, which is discussed at D12.79.

Mixed Pleas from Co-accused

Where there are co-accused, one of whom pleads guilty and the other not guilty, normal practice **D12.77** is to adjourn sentencing the former until after the trial of the latter. In the event of a conviction, they can then both be sentenced together. The desirability of co-accused being sentenced on one occasion by the same judge has frequently been stressed. Separate sentencing may lead to unacceptable disparity in the ways they are respectively treated. Also, the judge will hear, during the course of the trial of the accused pleading not guilty, evidence indicating the gravity of the offence charged and the extent of each accused's role in it, which information may ultimately assist him in sentencing the one pleading guilty.

The above principles were stated by Lord Goddard CJ in *Payne* [1950] 1 All ER 102, when he said:

> [Where several persons are indicted together, and one pleads guilty and the other or others not guilty] the proper course is to postpone sentence on the man who has pleaded guilty until the others have been tried and then to bring up all the prisoners to be dealt with together because by that time the court will be in possession of the facts relating to all of them and will be able to assess properly the degree of guilt of each.

A still stronger statement of the same principle occurs in the judgment of Boreham J in *Weekes* (1980) 74 Cr App R 161, where he said:

> Here are made manifest the difficulties that arise when persons involved with others are sentenced before the full facts have been heard, particularly where a trial is to take place, as it was to take place here.... There may be exceptions but generally it is clearly right, it is clearly fairer and it is better for both the public and all the defendants concerned, that all are sentenced at the same time by the same court whenever that is possible.

Practice where Accused Pleads Guilty and Gives Evidence for Prosecution against **D12.78** **Co-accused** It is now clear that an accused turning Queen's evidence should not be sentenced until after the co-accused's trial. This clarity resulted from 'difficulties' arising in *Weekes* (1980) 74 Cr App R 161, to which Boreham J referred in the passage quoted in **D12.77**, namely that W, one of four co-accused charged with armed robbery, was sentenced to seven years' imprisonment while a co-accused (S) had been given only 12 months, a term described by the Court of Appeal as 'ludicrously light', before W's trial by a different judge. At W's appeal, Boreham J criticised the decision to sentence S separately (at p. 166):

> It may be...that [S] was sentenced at that early stage by a different court because it had been made known that he was to give evidence on behalf of the Crown against the other three. If that was the reason...it is not sufficient reason.... it should be left to the judge who may sentence those who have pleaded not guilty to sentence all.

The clear statement in *Weekes* that an accused turning Queen's evidence should not be sentenced until after the co-accused's trial is in direct conflict with the dicta of Lord Goddard CJ in *Payne* [1950] 1 All ER 102. However, the reversal of the practice approved in *Payne* was signalled by two unreported cases in 1977, namely *Potter* (15 September 1977 unreported) and *Woods* (25 October 1977 unreported), before it was confirmed by *Weekes* and *Chan Wai-keung* [1995] 2 All ER 438. In *Coffey* (1976) 74 Cr App R 168, the principle that all should be sentenced at the end of any trial was held to apply when the accused who has pleaded guilty is going to testify for the co-accused, just as it applies when he is to testify for the prosecution. Even so, whether to sentence a co-accused pleading guilty forthwith or adjourn until after the co-accused's trial must, in the last resort, remain a question for the judge (*Palmer* (1994) 158 JP 138).

SOCPA 2005, ss. 73 to 75 (see **E1.13**), demonstrate that the court may take into account the assistance the accused is going to provide to the 'investigator or prosecutor', e.g., by giving evidence or intelligence, when determining his sentence, and should indicate that it has done so unless that would be contrary to the public interest (s. 73). However, if the accused then fails to provide the promised assistance, the prosecution may invite the court to review the sentence and the court may substitute a greater sentence for the sentence originally passed (s. 74, reversing *Stone* [1970] 2 All ER 594 on that point).

PLEA OF GUILTY TO A LESSER OFFENCE

D12.79   Where the indictment contains a count on which, if the accused were to plead not guilty, the jury could find him not guilty as charged but guilty of an alternative (hereafter referred to as 'lesser') offence, he may enter a plea to the same effect, namely not guilty to the offence charged but guilty only of the lesser offence (CLA 1967, s. 6(1)(b)).

If the plea is accepted, he is treated as having been acquitted of the offence actually charged and the court proceeds to sentence him for the lesser offence (CLA 1967, s. 6(5)). The circumstances in which a jury have the power to return a verdict of guilty of a lesser offence are defined by legislation, chiefly subsections (2) to (4) of s. 6 of the 1967 Act, which are considered in detail at **D19.41** to **D19.68**.

The considerations relevant to the decision by the prosecution to either accept or reject the plea are considered below.

The extent of the judge's control over the acceptance of a plea to a lesser offence is open to argument. In *Soanes* (1948) 32 Cr App R 136, Lord Goddard CJ said, '... it must always be in the discretion of the judge whether he will allow [a plea of guilty to a lesser offence] to be accepted'. However, it is doubtful whether the court can or should insist on one of the parties calling evidence, or call the witnesses itself. Therefore, if the prosecution refuse to call evidence to prove the accused guilty as charged, the court would have no real alternative but to accept the situation, subject to any proper question of professional misconduct.

Moreover, in the analogous situation of the accused pleading to some counts on the indictment in exchange for the prosecution offering no evidence on others, the rule seems to be that the prosecution are bound by the judge's views of the bargain if, and only if, they have expressly asked him to approve it in advance (see **D12.87**). If they choose not to seek his prior approval, they may accept the pleas even though the judge indicates in court that they ought to proceed on all counts (*Coward* (1979) 70 Cr App R 70 and *Broad* (1978) 68 Cr App R 281).

Status of Original Plea in Event of Verdict of Not Guilty

D12.80   In *Hazeltine* [1967] 2 QB 857, the accused, on being arraigned for wounding with intent contrary to s. 18 of the OAPA 1861, replied, 'Not guilty, but guilty to unlawful wounding'. The prosecution would not accept the plea, and a trial followed, during which H offered a defence of acting in reasonable self-defence. Although this was inconsistent with his original plea, almost no mention was made of it during the trial. When the jury then acquitted H, the judge proceeded to sentence H in accordance with his plea. That sentence had to be quashed on appeal as H had not been convicted of any offence. His original plea to unlawful wounding was impliedly withdrawn on the prosecution saying that it was not acceptable, and the jury's verdict implied an acquittal both in respect of the offence charged and in respect of the lesser included offence. Salmon LJ explained the purpose and effect of the then equivalent of s. 6(1) of the CLA 1967 (s. 39(1) of the Criminal Justice Administration Act 1914). His lordship said (at p. 861A–F):

> Prior to that statutory provision, it was not possible for an accused to plead guilty to unlawful wounding when charged with wounding with intent but it was and always has been possible for a jury, when a man is charged with wounding with intent, to return a verdict of unlawful wounding ...

> This court has no doubt but that section 39(1) of the Act of 1914 was introduced so as to remove this anomaly which resulted in the great waste of time and money to which I have referred. In the view of this court, however, that statutory provision did not get rid of the rule that there can be but one plea to one count should the trial proceed on that count. Accordingly if an accused pleads not guilty to wounding with intent but guilty to unlawful wounding and counsel for the prosecution or the judge takes the view that that plea ought not to be accepted and the trial proceeds, the plea of guilty to unlawful wounding is deemed to be withdrawn and the only plea is the plea of not guilty to wounding with intent. It is then for the jury to consider the evidence and at the end of the case to say either quite simply that the man is not guilty or that he is guilty of wounding with intent or that he is not guilty of wounding with intent but guilty to unlawful wounding.

Although couched in terms of wounding with intent and unlawful wounding, the above passage is obviously applicable whenever a plea of guilty to a lesser offence is rejected.

To avoid a repetition of the manifestly unsatisfactory result in *Hazeltine*, the Court of Appeal suggested that, in cases where the accused offers a defence that is inconsistent with his earlier plea to a lesser offence, the prosecution ought to call evidence of the plea and, if the accused testifies, cross-examine him about it (*Hazeltine* at p. 862F–G). There was no need to adopt a policy of always having separate counts for the greater and lesser offences. However, should the prosecution fail to adduce evidence of the plea, it is not open to the judge to repair the omission in his summing-up by informing the jury of what occurred (*Lee* [1985] Crim LR 798). Nor may the judge direct the jury to convict of the lesser offence as opposed to informing them that such a verdict is open to them (*Lee*, and see *Notman* [1994] Crim LR 518).

PROSECUTION OPTIONS ON PLEA OF NOT GUILTY OR MIXED PLEAS BEING ENTERED

Apart from the obvious course of proceeding to a contested trial, there are two options available   **D12.81** to the prosecution on the accused pleading not guilty, namely, to offer no evidence or to ask that the indictment remain on the court file. Similar responses are possible where an arraignment results in mixed pleas, with either only some of the accused pleading guilty, or with one accused entering guilty pleas to only some of the charges.

Each of these two options is addressed here. In addition, considerable guidance has been given, notably through guidelines handed down by the A-G and in the report of the Farquharson committee on the role of prosecuting counsel. This guidance is also addressed below.

Offering No Evidence

Criminal Justice Act 1967, s. 17   **D12.82**

Where a defendant arraigned on an indictment or inquisition pleads not guilty and the prosecutor proposes to offer no evidence against him, the court before which the defendant is arraigned may, if it thinks fit, order that a verdict of not guilty shall be recorded without the defendant being given in charge to a jury, and the verdict shall have the same effect as if the defendant had been tried and acquitted on the verdict of a jury.

The obvious situation for reliance on s. 17 is if the prosecution have reviewed their evidence since the accused was sent for trial, and have concluded that they cannot properly ask a jury to convict. Alternatively, offering no evidence on some counts in an indictment may be part of an agreement with the defence under which the accused pleads guilty to other counts.

Whilst the plain wording of s. 17 gives the court a discretion to decline to order a verdict of not guilty to be entered even though the prosecution intimate that they do not wish to proceed, in the last resort, the prosecution cannot be forced by the court to call evidence.

In *Renshaw* [1989] Crim LR 811, the Court of Appeal stressed the importance of the judge listening to the reasons given by the prosecution for proposing to offer no evidence. If he fails to heed what the prosecution say, he will deprive himself of a proper basis for approving or disapproving of their proposed course of action.

Letting Counts Lie on the File

D12.83 As an alternative to offering no evidence, the prosecution may ask the judge to order that an indictment (or counts thereof) shall lie on the file, marked not to be proceeded with without leave of the court or of the Court of Appeal. Such a course is particularly appropriate where the accused pleads guilty to the bulk of the charges against him (whether contained in one indictment or several) but not guilty to some subsidiary charges. Leaving the latter on the file avoids the necessity of a trial, but also avoids the accused actually being acquitted on the 'not guilty' counts, which might seem inappropriate if the evidence against him is in fact strong.

Contrary to what was previously understood to be the position, there is no objection to an entire indictment remaining on the file, as opposed to merely dealing with some counts of a multi-count indictment in that way (e.g., in *Central Criminal Court, ex parte Raymond* [1986] 2 All ER 379, as a result of R's conviction on one count of a severed 14-count indictment, the trial judge ordered that both the remaining counts of the original indictment and all counts of a completely separate indictment should lie on the file).

The use and practical effect of the order is helpfully summarised by Woolf LJ in *Ex parte Raymond* (at pp. 714H–715B):

> [It is important] to analyse the nature of the order that an indictment should lie on the file.
>
> It starts off by having the same effect as an order for an adjournment but an adjournment which it is accepted may never result in a trial. Frequently the order is made to safeguard the position of the prosecution and the defence in case a defendant, who has been convicted, should appeal, it being the intention of the court if there is no appeal or if the appeal is unsuccessful the defendant should never stand trial. That the defendant can still stand trial is indicated by the limits on the discretion of the court (laid down by the House of Lords in *Connelly v DPP* [1964] AC 1254) to prevent the Crown proceeding with a prosecution if it wishes to do so. However, in the majority of cases where such an order is made, there will be no trial and there will certainly come a stage when either the prosecution would not seek a trial or if it did seek a trial, the court would regard it as so oppressive to have a trial that leave to proceed would inevitably be refused.

D12.84 **Challenge to an Order to Lie on the File** Whether to order that counts lie on the file is a matter totally within the judge's discretion since there is no method by which either party can challenge his decision. There is no appeal to the Court of Appeal as that only arises once there has been a conviction. See *Mackell* (1981) 74 Cr App R 27, on the Court of Appeal's lack of jurisdiction to reverse an order that counts lie on the file, and Dunn LJ's dictum, quoted with approval in *Central Criminal Court, ex parte Raymond* [1986] 2 All ER 379, that 'there are certain matters upon which the trial judge should have the final say. It seems to us this is one of them'.

Moreover, it was made clear in *Ex parte Raymond* that there cannot be an application to the High Court for judicial review since a decision to leave counts on the file has been held to relate to a trial on indictment and so, by virtue of s. 29(3) of the Senior Courts Act 1981, is not eligible for review. The reasoning of the Court of Appeal was that an order to leave counts on the file effectively 'starts off by having the same effect as an order for an adjournment' (per Woolf LJ at p. 714H), and it was already recognised that decisions to adjourn were something on which 'the trial judge should have the final word' (per Lord Denning MR in *Sheffield Crown Court, ex parte Brownlow* [1980] QB 530).

The applicant in *Ex parte Raymond* argued that a Crown Court judge should not order that counts lie on the file unless the defence agree to that course, and, in the absence of such agreement, he ought to require the prosecution to elect between proceeding to trial and offering no evidence. The Court of Appeal ultimately refused to state its view or give any guidance on when orders to lie on the file are appropriate. This reticence was because of its primary decision that it did not in any event have jurisdiction to review the decision of the court below.

Circumstances in which an Order to Lie on the File May be Reversed The only situation in which the Crown Court or Court of Appeal is likely to give leave for a count or indictment ordered to lie on the file to be tried is if the accused's convictions on the other matters (i.e. the charges on the same or separate indictments to which he pleaded guilty or of which he was found guilty at the same time as the order to lie on the file was made) are quashed on appeal. **D12.85**

Accepting or Rejecting a Plea to a Lesser Offence

As was addressed at D12.79, it is possible for an accused to plead guilty to a lesser offence than that charged in the indictment. The prosecution may refuse to accept a plea of guilty to a lesser offence. If so, the plea is deemed to be withdrawn and the case proceeds as if the accused had simply pleaded not guilty (*Hazeltine* [1967] 2 QB 857). **D12.86**

Criteria to be Applied by the Prosecution

Guidelines The report of the Farquharson committee on the role of prosecuting counsel (May 1986), considered counsel's control over the acceptance of pleas. The committee discussed the authorities, and also made the point that, in the reverse situation of the judge thinking that the evidence on the depositions does not warrant a conviction or that further proceedings would be unfair, he has no power to prevent the prosecution calling their evidence save in the very exceptional case of the proceedings amounting to an abuse of the process of the court. **D12.87**

The principles set out by the Farquharson committee have in any event since been endorsed and developed by the CPS and the General Council of the Bar in a set of Guidelines jointly issued in 2002.

General Rule In accepting a plea of guilty to a lesser offence or guilty to some counts only on the indictment, prosecuting counsel is in reality making a decision to offer no evidence on a particular charge. Since the committee were of the opinion that counsel was undoubtedly entitled to offer no evidence on the indictment as a whole and could not be forced to call evidence against his will, it followed that he must also be entitled to decide to accept pleas to part only of the indictment. **D12.88**

The Three Qualifications This general rule is, however, subject to three qualifications: **D12.89**

(a) If prosecuting counsel expressly asks for the court's approval of his proposed acceptance of certain pleas, he must abide by the court's decision (*Broad* (1978) 68 Cr App R 281). There is no obligation on him to seek such approval, but he might feel it right to do so where either it is desirable to reassure the public at large that the course proposed is being properly taken, or he has been unable to reach agreement with his instructing solicitor about what ought to be done.

(b) In a case where the court's approval is not sought beforehand, it is nonetheless usual for counsel to explain in open court his reasons for accepting the plea. It is then open to the judge to express his views. If the judge, on the information available to him is 'of the opinion that the course proposed by counsel would lead to serious injustice, he may decline to proceed with the case until counsel has consulted with either the [DPP] or the [A-G] as may be appropriate' (Farquharson, para. k). However, in the final analysis and once those steps have been taken, the judge has no power to prevent counsel taking the course he thinks fit — 'any attempt by him to do so would give the impression that he was stepping into the arena and pressing the prosecution case'. However, the committee expressed the opinion that 'the occasions when counsel felt it right to resist the judge's views would be rare'.

(c) Should the decision to accept proposed pleas fall to be taken during the course of the trial, prosecuting counsel's position remains as in (b) above until the close of his case. Following the close of the prosecution case, however, if the judge has either found there is a case to answer or if no submission to the contrary has been made, there is, *ex hypothesi*, a case for the accused to answer, and 'it would be an abuse of process for the prosecution to discontinue without leave'. But, even though the judge can rule that the case shall proceed, 'it would not be the duty of counsel to cross-examine the defence witnesses or address the jury if he was of the view that it would not be proper to convict'.

D12.90   **Consideration in *Grafton***   The report of the Farquharson committee was referred to with approval in *Grafton* [1993] QB 101. In that case, there was a conflict of evidence between two prosecution witnesses. Having taken instructions, prosecution counsel said he would call no further evidence. However, the judge disagreed profoundly with this decision and proceeded to call the Crown's remaining witness himself. G was convicted, and appealed. The appeal was allowed on the basis that the decision whether to continue with the case or not had to be that of the prosecution. By proceeding as he did, the judge had ceased to appear impartial, but had become the adversary of the defendant. The Court of Appeal in *Grafton* also approved qualification (c) above. They added, however, that where the prosecution's case is complete, but the judge refuses leave to the Crown to discontinue, it was prosecution counsel's duty to remain in the case. If the prosecution's view later changed (perhaps as a result of hearing the accused testify), he would then be free to cross-examine witnesses or address the jury.

D12.91   **Acceptance of a Plea to a Lesser Offence**   As to the circumstances in which it is appropriate to accept a plea to a lesser offence, Lord Goddard in *Soanes* (1948) 32 Cr App R 136 declined to lay down a 'hard and fast rule' but expressed the view that, 'where nothing appears on the depositions which can be said to reduce the crime from the more serious offence charged to some lesser offence for which a verdict may be returned, the duty of counsel for the Crown would be to present the offence charged in the indictment'. The possible effect on the prosecution witnesses of testifying at a contested trial (e.g., where the offence charged is of a sexual nature) and/or the reaction of the victim to the charge being reduced may also have a bearing on counsel's ultimate decision (see, e.g., *Coward* (1979) 70 Cr App R 70).

D12.92   **The Attorney-General's Guidelines**   The A-G's Guidelines on the Acceptance of Pleas (see **appendix 2**) stress that justice should be conducted in public, save in the most exceptional circumstances, and that this includes the acceptance of pleas by the prosecution. Prosecutors are directed to the guidance contained in the Code for Crown Prosecutors, and told that they should be prepared to explain in open court the reasons for accepting pleas to a reduced number of charges or less serious charges.

CHANGE OF PLEA

D12.93   The final topic to be addressed in relation to the arraignment is the procedure to be followed, and criteria to be applied, where an accused seeks to change his plea thereafter. Where he wishes to change his plea from not guilty to guilty (see **D12.94**), this causes little difficulty. Where, however, he seeks to change his plea from guilty to not guilty (see **D12.95**) more difficult considerations arise, not least because such a change represents an assertion that an accused has realised that he did not commit the offence after all. The considerations in this category also include issues as to whether a plea was ambiguous (see **D12.100**) or involuntary (see **D12.101**). The topic is addressed procedurally by the CrimPR, r. 38.5 (see Supplement, **R-304**).

From Not Guilty to Guilty

The judge may allow the accused to change his plea from not guilty to guilty at any stage prior **D12.94** to the jury returning their verdict. The procedure is that the defence ask for the indictment to be put again and the accused then pleads guilty. If the change of plea comes after the accused has been put in the charge of a jury, the jury should be directed to return a formal verdict of guilty. This was emphasised in *Heyes* [1951] 1 KB 29, where the accused changed his plea in the jury's presence but they were not asked to return a verdict, and the judge proceeded forthwith to sentence. On appeal, Lord Goddard CJ said:

> Once the jury had heard the appellant say that he wished to withdraw his plea and admit his guilt, the proper proceeding was for the court to ask them to return a verdict. It appears that counsel did suggest to the learned recorder that this was the proper course; but the recorder thought that it did not matter. It does matter because, once a prisoner is in charge of a jury, he can only be either convicted or discharged by the verdict of the jury.

> As there was no verdict of the jury here, the trial was a nullity to such an extent that the court could set aside the proceedings and order a retrial or *venire de novo* [but, in the circumstances of this case we] will merely quash the conviction.

In *Poole* [2002] 1 WLR 1528, however, the accused changed her plea to guilty on the second day of the trial. The judge discharged the jury without entering any verdict, and proceedings continued as though the accused had pleaded guilty on arraignment, with an adjournment for reports. The accused then wished to vacate her plea of guilty and, when this was refused, appealed against conviction. The Court of Appeal held that the course taken was permissible and resulted in a valid conviction.

Although having the indictment put again with a view to a change of plea to guilty is a matter for the judge's discretion, it is difficult to envisage circumstances in which he would be unwilling to allow it to be done. Depending on the stage of the trial at which it comes, the change of plea will provide some mitigation for the accused when sentence is passed. As to the effect of such a change of plea upon the trial of a co-accused, see **D13.64** and the case of *Fedrick* [1990] Crim LR 403 dealt with there.

From Guilty to Not Guilty

Discretion to Allow a Change The judge has a discretion to allow the accused to withdraw **D12.95** a plea of guilty at any stage before sentence is passed. This was confirmed in *Plummer* [1902] 2 KB 339, where the major question for the court was whether P's conviction on a guilty plea in relation to a conspiracy charge could be sustained in view of the acquittal of his five alleged co-conspirators. P was not sentenced until after the acquittal of the others, and, prior to sentence, asked to withdraw his plea. Wright J said (at p. 347):

> Another point is raised in this case, namely, whether the court had power to allow the appellant to withdraw his plea of guilty. There cannot be any doubt that the court had such power at any time before, though not after, judgment [i.e. sentence] and, as we infer that but for the erroneous opinion that there was no such power the withdrawal would have been allowed, this might of itself be a ground for a *venire de novo*.

Similarly, Bruce J held that the first-instance court clearly had a discretion to allow the change of plea; that, if it had exercised its discretion against the appellant, the appellate court might have had no power to interfere; but, in fact, the discretion was never exercised one way or the other and that had deprived the appellant of a chance of an acquittal, with the consequence that the conviction could not stand (at p. 349).

The existence of the discretion was indirectly confirmed by the House of Lords in *S v Recorder of Manchester* [1971] AC 481, when it held that, in the context of change of plea, there is no conviction until sentence has been passed, and therefore magistrates (like the Crown Court) can allow a change to not guilty provided they have not yet passed sentence.

Finally, in *Dodd* (1981) 74 Cr App R 50, the Court of Appeal unhesitatingly accepted the three following propositions from counsel for D, namely that: (a) the court has a discretion to allow a defendant to change a plea of guilty to one of not guilty at any time before sentence; (b) the discretion exists even where the plea of not guilty is unequivocal; and (c) the discretion must be exercised judicially (see p. 57).

D12.96 **Application of the Discretion** The authorities make clear that the discretion now under consideration should be sparingly exercised in favour of the accused. Thus, in *McNally* [1954] 2 All ER 372, where the accused had indicated even in the magistrates' court an intention to plead guilty, could not possibly have misunderstood the nature of a straightforward charge and had unequivocally admitted guilt when the indictment was put to him, the Court of Criminal Appeal approved the trial judge's decision to refuse a change of plea. The same approach was more recently adopted in *Revitt v DPP* [2006] 1 WLR 3172 and *Brahmbhatt* [2014] EWCA Crim 573.

D12.97 **Unrepresented Accused** Even if the accused was unrepresented when he pleaded but instructs solicitors during an adjournment prior to sentencing and is advised by them that he has a defence, the court is not obliged to accede to a change of plea (*South Tameside Magistrates' Court, ex parte Rowland* [1983] 3 All ER 689).

In *Ex parte Rowland*, in considering such an application for a change of plea, the magistrates, 'rightly, balanced the instructions which the applicant had given to her solicitor after [the original plea] against the prospect that she was changing her story because of the possibility that she might be sentenced to a custodial sentence' (per Glidewell J at p. 692J). Furthermore, the magistrates 'were perfectly entitled to come to the conclusion to which they did come' (i.e. that fear of a custodial sentence was the real motivation for the change of plea), and thus were justified in exercising their discretion against R.

Glidewell J approved the advice given to the magistrates by their clerk that, 'to allow a change of plea was a matter for [the magistrates'] absolute discretion and that once an unequivocal plea had been entered the discretionary power should be exercised judicially, very sparingly and only in clear cases' (at p. 692A). However, the implication is that, had the magistrates thought the plea to have been entered under a misapprehension of law as to the nature of the offence, then their only proper course would have been to allow the application. Although *Ex parte Rowland* was a case concerning change of plea in the magistrates' court, there is no reason why the same principles should not apply in the Crown Court.

In *Revitt v DPP* [2006] 1 WLR 3172, the accused had been unrepresented, but had been advised by the court legal adviser of the nature and seriousness of the charges and of their right both to legal representations and to advance disclosure before plea. Where the accused proceeded to enter a guilty plea, the Administrative Court found the plea to be both informed and unequivocal.

D12.98 **Represented Accused** If the accused was represented when he entered his plea of guilty, there would seem to be no absolute bar to his applying to withdraw the plea, but it will obviously be very difficult to convince the court that the plea was entered by a genuine mistake. This was demonstrated in *Drew* [1985] 2 All ER 1061, where Lord Lane CJ said (at p. 923C): '...only rarely would it be appropriate for the trial judge to exercise his undoubted discretion in favour of an accused person wishing to change an unequivocal plea of guilty to one of not guilty. Particularly this is so in cases where, as here, the accused has throughout been advised by experienced counsel.'

Provided the court at first instance recognised that it had a discretion to allow a change of plea and applied the correct principles in determining the application, the Court of Appeal will not interfere with the trial judge's exercise of discretion (*Dodd* (1981) 74 Cr App R 50 (see **D12.95**); *Cantor* [1991] Crim LR 481; *Anjum* [2004] EWCA Crim 977; *Towers* [2004] EWCA Crim 1128).

Double Change of Plea

D12.99 Where the accused has changed his plea from not guilty to guilty, the judge still has a discretion to allow him to change back to not guilty (*Drew* [1985] 2 All ER 1061). The fact that the jury empanelled to try him as a result of the original not guilty plea formally found him guilty on hearing the change to guilty does not affect the existence of the judge's discretion. In *Drew*, Lord Lane CJ said (at p. 922C):

> There appears to this court no greater difficulty in altering the record following a jury's verdict than doing so upon a change of plea in any other situation. The jury's verdict where, as here, it is entered upon the direction of the judge, is essentially a formality. In our judgment, logic and good sense dictate that the trial judge should have the same power to allow a change of plea even where the verdict of guilty has been returned formally by the jury.

Ambiguous Pleas

D12.100 If an accused purports to enter a plea of guilty but, either at the time he pleads or subsequently in mitigation, qualifies it with words that suggest he may have a defence (e.g., 'Guilty, but it was an accident' or 'Guilty, but I was going to give it back'), then the court must not proceed to sentence on the basis of the plea but should explain the relevant law and seek to ascertain whether he genuinely intends to plead guilty.

If the plea cannot be clarified, the court should order a not guilty plea to be entered on the accused's behalf (CLA 1967, s. 6(1)(c): 'if [the accused] stands mute of malice *or will not answer directly to the indictment*, the court may order a plea of not guilty to be entered').

Should the court proceed to sentence on a plea which is imperfect, unfinished or otherwise ambiguous, the accused will have a good ground of appeal. Since the defect in the plea will have rendered the original proceedings a mistrial, the Court of Appeal will have the options either of setting the conviction and sentence aside and ordering a retrial (see, e.g., *Ingleson* [1915] 1 KB 512) or of simply quashing the conviction (see, e.g., *Field* (1943) 29 Cr App R 151). If the former course is chosen (i.e. there is to be a retrial), the court may either then and there direct that a not guilty plea be entered or order that the accused be re-arraigned in the court below (e.g., *Baker* (1912) 7 Cr App R 217).

Involuntary Pleas

D12.101 A plea of guilty must be entered voluntarily. If, at the time he pleaded, the accused was subject to such pressure that he did not genuinely have a free choice between 'guilty' and 'not guilty', his plea is a nullity (*Turner* [1970] 2 QB 321). On appeal, the Court of Appeal will have the same options as it has when a plea is adjudged ambiguous, namely that it must quash the conviction and sentence but will be able, in its discretion, to issue a writ of *venire de novo* for a retrial as the original proceedings constitute a mistrial.

Pressure to plead may come from a number of sources: the court, defence counsel or other factors. Whatever the source, the effect is the same.

D12.102 **The Court** An example of this principle is provided by *Barnes* (1970) 55 Cr App R 100, where the judge, during a submission of no case to answer made in the absence of the jury but in the presence of the accused, said that, having regard to the prosecution evidence, B was plainly guilty and was wasting the court's time by pleading not guilty. Despite this pressure, B did not change his plea. Allowing his appeal against conviction on other grounds, the court indicated that the judge's remarks were 'wholly improper', and, if B had pleaded guilty in consequence of them, the plea would have been null.

D12.103   **Defence Counsel**   It is the duty of counsel to advise his client on the strength of the evidence and the advantages of a guilty plea as regards sentencing (see, e.g., *Herbert* (1991) 94 Cr App R 233 and *Cain* [1976] QB 496). Such advice may, if necessary, be given in forceful terms (*Peace* [1976] Crim LR 119).

Where an accused is so advised and thereafter pleads guilty reluctantly, his plea is not *ipso facto* to be treated as involuntary (*Peace*). It will be involuntary only if the advice was so very forceful as to take away his free choice. Thus, in *Inns* (1974) 60 Cr App R 231, defence counsel, as he was then professionally required to do, relayed to the accused the judge's warning in chambers that, in the event of conviction on a not guilty plea, the accused would definitely be given a sentence of detention whereas if he pleaded guilty a more lenient course might be possible. This rendered the eventual guilty plea a nullity.

However, in the absence of a suggestion that counsel was acting as a conduit to pass on a threat or promise from the judge, it will be extremely difficult for an appellant to satisfy the court that he was deprived by counsel's advice of a voluntary choice when pleading. Thus, in *Hall* [1968] 2 QB 788, H was charged with burglary and, alternatively, with handling some of the items stolen during that burglary. The prosecution were willing to accept a plea to the latter. Counsel advised H that, if he pleaded not guilty to both counts, he ran the risk of being convicted of the burglary itself since his defence would involve attacks on the character of prosecution witnesses and thus the revelation of his own bad character. If so convicted, he could expect to receive up to 12 years' imprisonment, whereas if he pleaded guilty to handling the maximum sentence would be five years.

Dismissing H's appeal, Lord Parker CJ said (at pp. 534–7):

> What the court is looking to see is whether a prisoner in these circumstances has a free choice; the election must be his, the responsibility his, to plead guilty or not guilty. At the same time, it is the clear duty of any counsel representing a client to assist the client to make up his mind by putting forward the pros and cons, if need be in strong language, to impress upon the client what the likely results are of certain courses of conduct.

His lordship then paraphrased the advice given by counsel:

> [Defence counsel], in the opinion of this court, was only doing his duty in setting forth the dangers, even, as [he] said, in strong language.

> … anybody who has heard the evidence in this case and has understood the workings of the law and our procedure, could not fail to realise that the appellant has no grievance at all … and that his counsel performed his duty to the best of his ability. This court has no hesitation in those circumstances in dismissing the appeal.

The position will be different if the advice given by counsel is demonstrably wrong. For example, in *Sorhaindo* [2006] EWCA Crim 1429, the Court of Appeal held that, where an accused had erroneously been advised that his factual case afforded him no defence, he should have been permitted to vacate the guilty plea that he entered in reliance on this advice.

D12.104   **Guidance to Defence Counsel**   The Code of Conduct of the Bar, Written Standards for the Conduct of Professional Work, para. 12.3, confirms that defence counsel should explain to the accused the advantages and disadvantages of a guilty plea. It goes on to say that he must make it clear that the client has complete freedom of choice and that the responsibility for the plea is the accused's. It is common practice, endorsed by para. 12.5.1, to tell an accused that he should plead guilty only if he is guilty (see Lord Parker CJ's observation in *Turner* [1970] 2 QB 321 at p. 326F that: 'Counsel of course will emphasise that the accused must not plead guilty unless he has committed the acts constituting the offence charged'). However, it may be felt that, on occasions, realistic advice about the strength of the prosecution case and the sentencing discount for a guilty plea will effectively force an accused into a guilty plea however punctilious defence counsel may be in saying that he should plead guilty only if he is guilty.

Where an accused persists in pleading guilty notwithstanding telling counsel that he is in fact innocent, counsel may continue to act for him but must say nothing in mitigation that is inconsistent with the guilty plea (paras. 12.5.2 and 12.5.3). Counsel may thus be forced to confine his mitigation to the circumstances and background of the offender and any matters minimising the gravity of the offence which are apparent on the face of the prosecution statements; since his only instructions about the offence itself are that the accused is not guilty of it, counsel cannot explain (as he might otherwise do) the immediate temptations etc. that led to its commission.

Other Pressures   Apart from cases where pressure has been brought to bear on the accused to **D12.105** plead guilty, there may be other situations where his mind did not go with his plea and he is therefore entitled to have his conviction set aside. An example is *Swain* [1986] Crim LR 480, in which S changed his plea to guilty half-way through the prosecution case. He gave no coherent explanation to counsel at the time, but it was afterwards discovered that he had been under the influence of the drug LSD. Psychiatric evidence called before the Court of Appeal established that LSD can put the user into a state akin to schizophrenia where he drifts in and out of a delusional world and makes irrational decisions. The Court held the change of plea to have been a nullity.

DEFERRED PROSECUTION AGREEMENTS

The CCA 2013, sch. 17, introduced deferred prosecution agreements ('DPA') as an alternative **D12.106** to prosecution. These provisions were brought into force on 24 February 2014 by SI 2014 No. 258. Such an agreement, if complied with, involves an agreement between the accused and prosecution under which, if the accused abides by specified conditions during the currency of the agreement, the prosecution will be suspended and ultimately avoided.

The stages in the process are set out in sch. 17 and the CrimPR, part 12 (see Supplement, R-117). **D12.107** In summary, these are as follows:

(a) A designated prosecutor (identified in sch. 17, para. 3(1) as the DPP, Director of the SFO or any other prosecutor to be so designated) reaches an agreement with an accused (which may be a body corporate, partnership or unincorporated association but not an individual: para. 4(1)). The power of the prosecutor cannot be delegated (save in the circumstances set out in para. 3(3)). Pursuant to para. 6, a Code has been published by the DPP and the Director of the SFO to regulate the circumstances in which DPAs will be countenanced, which lists factors relevant to the prosecutor's decision to initiate negotiations for a DPA (the Code is available via the SFO web site). Such agreements are possible only where the accused is charged with an offence listed in sch. 17, part 2, and negotiations for such an agreement can only occur following the determination of the prosecutor that it is appropriate and after the prosecutor has communicated to this effect to the accused (see the Code, paras. 2.5 and 3.5).

(b) Under the terms of a DPA, the prosecutor will suspend the prosecution, with automatic effect from when the indictment is preferred in accordance with the Administration of Justice (Miscellaneous Provisions) Act 1933, s. 2(2)(a) (sch. 17, para. 2), if the accused will agree to comply with the requirements set out in para. 5(3) for the period identified (para. 5(2)). These requirements can include financial terms.

(c) Before a DPA can be agreed, the approval of the Crown Court must first be sought. It will be sought first in principle at a preliminary hearing conducted in private at which the court will be invited to agree that the draft DPA is 'likely to be in the interests of justice' and its terms are 'fair, reasonable and proportionate' (sch 17, para. 7, and the Code, para. 10). Thereafter, once the terms of the DPA are finally agreed between the parties, the court must again be asked for a declaration to the same effect. Only then, and once the DPA is published by the prosecution, will it take effect (sch. 17, para. 8, and the Code, para. 11) so that, when the bill of indictment is preferred, the proceedings are automatically suspended (sch. 17, para. 2(2)). The Code addresses the content of the application to the court and the terms of the agreement at paras. 6 and 7.

(d) There is provision to vary the terms of the DPA whilst it is operative (sch. 17, para. 10, and the Code, para. 13). If the accused breaches the requirements of the DPA, the prosecution can apply to the court (sch. 17, para. 9(1), and the Code, para. 12). Such an application, if made before the expiry of the DPA, prevents its expiry (sch. 17, para. 11(4)). If, on the balance of probabilities, the accused is found to be in breach, the court can either invite the prosecution to suggest a remedy or terminate the DPA (para. 9(3)). Whatever finding the court makes must be published by the prosecution. Similarly, the prosecution must publish its reasons for not applying to the court even though it believes the accused to be in breach (para. 9(8)).

(e) Otherwise, the DPA expires when its term comes to an end. Thereafter, the prosecution cannot institute fresh proceedings for the offence that was identified in the DPA unless it is later discovered that the accused had provided false information or otherwise misled the prosecution (para. 11).

The offences listed in sch. 17, part 2, in relation to which a DPA may be entered into, are as follows: conspiracy to defraud; cheating the public revenue; offences under the Theft Act 1968, ss. 1, 17, 20 and 24A; offences under the Customs and Excise Management Act 1979, ss. 68, 167 and 170; offences under the Forgery and Counterfeiting Act 1981, ss. 1 to 5; offences under the Companies Act 1985, s. 450; offences under the Value Added Tax Act 1994, s. 72; offences under the FSMA 2000, ss. 23, 25, 85, 346, 397 and 398; offences under the POCA 2002, ss. 327 to 330 and 333A; offences under the Companies Act 2006, ss. 658, 680 and 993; offences under the Fraud Act 2006, ss. 1, 6, 7 and 11; offences under the Bribery Act 2010, ss. 1, 2, 6 and 7; and offences under the Money Laundering Regulations 2007, reg. 45. A DPA may also be entered into in respect of any ancillary offence (as defined in para. 29) relating to a listed offence and the Secretary of State may amend the list by order.

Crime and Courts Act 2013, sch. 17

1.—(1) A deferred prosecution agreement (a 'DPA') is an agreement between a designated prosecutor and a person ('P') whom the prosecutor is considering prosecuting for an offence specified in Part 2 (the 'alleged offence').

(2) Under a DPA—

    (a) P agrees to comply with the requirements imposed on P by the agreement;

    (b) the prosecutor agrees that, upon approval of the DPA by the court (see paragraph 8), paragraph 2 is to apply in relation to the prosecution of P for the alleged offence.

2.—(1) Proceedings in respect of the alleged offence are to be instituted by the prosecutor in the Crown Court by preferring a bill of indictment charging P with the alleged offence (see section 2(2)(ba) of the Administration of Justice (Miscellaneous Provisions) Act 1933 (bill of indictment preferred with consent of Crown Court judge following DPA approval)).

(2) As soon as proceedings are instituted under sub-paragraph (1) they are automatically suspended.

(3) The suspension may only be lifted on an application to the Crown Court by the prosecutor; and no such application may be made at any time when the DPA is in force.

(4) At a time when proceedings are suspended under sub-paragraph (2), no other person may prosecute P for the alleged offence.

3.—(1) The following are designated prosecutors—

    (a) the Director of Public Prosecutions;

    (b) the Director of the Serious Fraud Office;

    (c) any prosecutor designated under this paragraph by an order made by the Secretary of State.

(2) A designated prosecutor must exercise personally the power to enter into a DPA and, accordingly, any enactment that enables a function of a designated prosecutor to be exercised by a person other than the prosecutor concerned does not apply.

(3) But if the designated prosecutor is unavailable, the power to enter into a DPA may be exercised personally by a person authorised in writing by the designated prosecutor.

4.—(1) P may be a body corporate, a partnership or an unincorporated association, but may not be an individual.

(2) In the case of a DPA between a prosecutor and a partnership—

    (a) the DPA must be entered into in the name of the partnership (and not in that of any of the partners);

    (b) any money payable under the DPA must be paid out of the funds of the partnership.

(3) In the case of a DPA between a prosecutor and an unincorporated association—

    (a) the DPA must be entered into in the name of the association (and not in that of any of its members);

    (b) any money payable under the DPA must be paid out of the funds of the association.

5.—(1) A DPA must contain a statement of facts relating to the alleged offence, which may include admissions made by P.

(2) A DPA must specify an expiry date, which is the date on which the DPA ceases to have effect if it has not already been terminated under paragraph 9 (breach).

(3) The requirements that a DPA may impose on P include, but are not limited to, the following requirements—

    (a) to pay to the prosecutor a financial penalty;

    (b) to compensate victims of the alleged offence;

    (c) to donate money to a charity or other third party;

    (d) to disgorge any profits made by P from the alleged offence;

    (e) to implement a compliance programme or make changes to an existing compliance programme relating to P's policies or to the training of P's employees or both;

    (f) to co-operate in any investigation related to the alleged offence;

    (g) to pay any reasonable costs of the prosecutor in relation to the alleged offence or the DPA.

The DPA may impose time limits within which P must comply with the requirements imposed on P.

(4) The amount of any financial penalty agreed between the prosecutor and P must be broadly comparable to the fine that a court would have imposed on P on conviction for the alleged offence following a guilty plea.

(5) A DPA may include a term setting out the consequences of a failure by P to comply with any of its terms.

6. [Requirement that the DPP and the Director of the SFO must jointly issue a Code of guidance for prosecutors.]

7.—(1) After the commencement of negotiations between a prosecutor and P in respect of a DPA but before the terms of the DPA are agreed, the prosecutor must apply to the Crown Court for a declaration that—

    (a) entering into a DPA with P is likely to be in the interests of justice, and

    (b) the proposed terms of the DPA are fair, reasonable and proportionate.

(2) The court must give reasons for its decision on whether or not to make a declaration under sub-paragraph (1).

(3) The prosecutor may make a further application to the court for a declaration under sub-paragraph (1) if, following the previous application, the court declined to make a declaration.

(4) A hearing at which an application under this paragraph is determined must be held in private, any declaration under sub-paragraph (1) must be made in private, and reasons under sub-paragraph (2) must be given in private.

8.—(1) When a prosecutor and P have agreed the terms of a DPA, the prosecutor must apply to the Crown Court for a declaration that—

    (a) the DPA is in the interests of justice, and

    (b) the terms of the DPA are fair, reasonable and proportionate.

(2) But the prosecutor may not make an application under sub-paragraph (1) unless the court has made a declaration under paragraph 7(1) (declaration on preliminary hearing).

(3) A DPA only comes into force when it is approved by the Crown Court making a declaration under sub-paragraph (1).

(4) The court must give reasons for its decision on whether or not to make a declaration under sub-paragraph (1).

(5) A hearing at which an application under this paragraph is determined may be held in private.

(6) But if the court decides to approve the DPA and make a declaration under sub-paragraph (1) it must do so, and give its reasons, in open court.

(7) Upon approval of the DPA by the court, the prosecutor must publish—

    (a) the DPA,

    (b) the declaration of the court under paragraph 7 and the reasons for its decision to make the declaration,

    (c) in a case where the court initially declined to make a declaration under paragraph 7, the court's reason for that decision, and

    (d) the court's declaration under this paragraph and the reasons for its decision to make the declaration,

unless the prosecutor is prevented from doing so by an enactment or by an order of the court under paragraph 12 (postponement of publication to avoid prejudicing proceedings).

9.—(1) At any time when a DPA is in force, if the prosecutor believes that P has failed to comply with the terms of the DPA, the prosecutor may make an application to the Crown Court under this paragraph.

(2) On an application under sub-paragraph (1) the court must decide whether, on the balance of probabilities, P has failed to comply with the terms of the DPA.

(3) If the court finds that P has failed to comply with the terms of the DPA, it may—
    (a) invite the prosecutor and P to agree proposals to remedy P's failure to comply, or
    (b) terminate the DPA.

(4) The court must give reasons for its decisions under sub-paragraphs (2) and (3).

(5) Where the court decides that P has not failed to comply with the terms of the DPA, the prosecutor must publish the court's decision and its reasons for that decision, unless the prosecutor is prevented from doing so by an enactment or by an order of the court under paragraph 12 (postponement of publication to avoid prejudicing proceedings).

(6) Where the court invites the prosecutor and P to agree proposals to remedy P's failure to comply, the prosecutor must publish the court's decisions under sub-paragraphs (2) and (3) and the reasons for those decisions, unless the prosecutor is prevented from doing so by an enactment or by an order of the court under paragraph 12 (postponement of publication to avoid prejudicing proceedings).

(7) Where the court terminates a DPA under sub-paragraph (3)(b), the prosecutor must publish—
    (a) the fact that the DPA has been terminated by the court following a failure by P to comply with the terms of the DPA, and
    (b) the court's reasons for its decisions under sub-paragraphs (2) and (3),
unless the prosecutor is prevented from doing so by an enactment or by an order of the court under paragraph 12 (postponement of publication to avoid prejudicing proceedings).

(8) If the prosecutor believes that P has failed to comply with the terms of the DPA but decides not to make an application to the Crown Court under this paragraph, the prosecutor must publish details relating to that decision, including—
    (a) the reasons for the prosecutor's belief that P has failed to comply, and
    (b) the reasons for the prosecutor's decision not to make an application to the court,
unless the prosecutor is prevented from doing so by an enactment or by an order of the court under paragraph 12 (postponement of publication to avoid prejudicing proceedings).

10.—(1) At any time when a DPA is in force, the prosecutor and P may agree to vary its terms if—
    (a) the court has invited the parties to vary the DPA under paragraph 9(3)(a), or
    (b) variation of the DPA is necessary to avoid a failure by P to comply with its terms in circumstances that were not, and could not have been, foreseen by the prosecutor or P at the time that the DPA was agreed.

(2) When the prosecutor and P have agreed to vary the terms of a DPA, the prosecutor must apply to the Crown Court for a declaration that—
    (a) the variation is in the interests of justice, and
    (b) the terms of the DPA as varied are fair, reasonable and proportionate.

(3) A variation of a DPA only takes effect when it is approved by the Crown Court making a declaration under sub-paragraph (2).

(4) The court must give reasons for its decision on whether or not to make a declaration under sub-paragraph (2).

(5) A hearing at which an application under this paragraph is determined may be held in private.

(6) But if the court decides to approve the variation and make a declaration under sub-paragraph (2) it must do so, and give its reasons, in open court.

(7) Where the court decides not to approve the variation, the prosecutor must publish the court's decision and the reasons for it, unless the prosecutor is prevented from doing so by an enactment or by an order of the court under paragraph 12 (postponement of publication to avoid prejudicing proceedings).

(8) Where the court decides to approve the variation the prosecutor must publish—
    (a) the DPA as varied, and
    (b) the court's declaration under this paragraph and the reasons for its decision to make the declaration,
unless the prosecutor is prevented from doing so by an enactment or by an order of the court under paragraph 12 (postponement of publication to avoid prejudicing proceedings).

11.—(1) If a DPA remains in force until its expiry date, then after the expiry of the DPA the proceedings instituted under paragraph 2(1) are to be discontinued by the prosecutor giving notice to the Crown Court that the prosecutor does not want the proceedings to continue.

(2) Where proceedings are discontinued under sub-paragraph (1), fresh criminal proceedings may not be instituted against P for the alleged offence.

(3) But sub-paragraph (2) does not prevent fresh proceedings from being instituted against P in a case where, after a DPA has expired, the prosecutor finds that, during the course of the negotiations for the DPA—

    (a) P provided inaccurate, misleading or incomplete information to the prosecutor, and

    (b) P knew or ought to have known that the information was inaccurate, misleading or incomplete.

(4) A DPA is not to be treated as having expired for the purposes of sub-paragraph (1) if, on the expiry date specified in the DPA—

    (a) an application made by the prosecutor under paragraph 9 (breach) has not yet been decided by the court,

    (b) following an application under paragraph 9 the court has invited the parties to agree proposals to remedy P's failure to comply, but the parties have not yet reached an agreement, or

    (c) the parties have agreed proposals to remedy P's failure to comply following an invitation of the court under paragraph 9(3)(a) but P has not yet complied with the agreement.

(5) In the case mentioned in sub-paragraph (4)(a)—

    (a) if the court decides that P has not failed to comply with the terms of the DPA, or that P has failed to comply but does not take action under paragraph 9(3), the DPA is to be treated as expiring when the application is decided;

    (b) if the court terminates the DPA, the DPA is to be treated as not having remained in force until its expiry date (and sub-paragraph (1) therefore does not apply);

    (c) if the court invites the parties to agree proposals to remedy P's failure to comply, the DPA is to be treated as expiring when the parties have reached such an agreement and P has complied with it.

(6) In the case mentioned in sub-paragraph (4)(b), the DPA is to be treated as expiring when the parties have reached an agreement and P has complied with it.

(7) In the case mentioned in sub-paragraph (4)(c), the DPA is to be treated as expiring when P complies with the agreement.

(8) Where proceedings are discontinued under sub-paragraph (1), the prosecutor must publish—

    (a) the fact that the proceedings have been discontinued, and

    (b) details of P's compliance with the DPA,

unless the prosecutor is prevented from doing so by an enactment or by an order of the court under paragraph 12 (postponement of publication to avoid prejudicing proceedings).

12. The court may order that the publication of information by the prosecutor under paragraph 8(7), 9(5), (6), (7) or (8), 10(7) or (8) or 11(8) be postponed for such period as the court considers necessary if it appears to the court that postponement is necessary for avoiding a substantial risk of prejudice to the administration of justice in any legal proceedings.

13.—(1) Sub-paragraph (2) applies where a DPA between a prosecutor and P has been approved by the Crown Court under paragraph 8.

(2) The statement of facts contained in the DPA is, in any criminal proceedings brought against P for the alleged offence, to be treated as an admission by P under section 10 of the Criminal Justice Act 1967 (proof by formal admission).

(3) Sub-paragraph (4) applies where a prosecutor and P have entered into negotiations for a DPA but the DPA has not been approved by the Crown Court under paragraph 8.

(4) Material described in sub-paragraph (6) may only be used in evidence against P—

    (a) on a prosecution for an offence consisting of the provision of inaccurate, misleading or incomplete information, or

    (b) on a prosecution for some other offence where in giving evidence P makes a statement inconsistent with the material.

(5) However, material may not be used against P by virtue of sub-paragraph (4)(b) unless evidence relating to it is adduced, or a question relating to it is asked, by or on behalf of P in the proceedings arising out of the prosecution.

(6) The material is—

    (a) material that shows that P entered into negotiations for a DPA, including in particular—

        (i) any draft of the DPA;

        (ii) any draft of a statement of facts intended to be included within the DPA;

        (iii) any statement indicating that P entered into such negotiations;

    (b) material that was created solely for the purpose of preparing the DPA or statement of facts.

D

Section D13   Juries

INTRODUCTION

D13.1   This section deals with the various stages of the process by which a jury is empanelled to try an accused, and the handling of that jury thereafter. The main source of the law on jurors is the Juries Act 1974. Regard must also be had to the CrimPR, rr. 38.6 to 38.9 and 39.1 to 39.4. Under the heading of the process for empanelment, this section addresses eligibility for jury service, the summoning of jurors, and the selection and empanelling of jurors for a particular case. Under the heading of jury management, this section addresses the conduct of jurors during a trial, and the judge's power to discharge the jury or individual jurors. The rules governing retirement of the jury while they consider their verdict and the verdicts they may return are considered in **D19**.

In addition, this section considers the extent to which errors in the formation of the jury may ground an appeal, and recent legislative measures designed to replace juries with trials by judge alone in certain categories of cases (see **D13.74** *et seq.*).

ELIGIBILITY FOR JURY SERVICE AND DISQUALIFICATION

D13.2   The basic rule is that all persons aged 18 to 70 who:

(a) are registered either as parliamentary or local government electors; and
(b) have been ordinarily resident in the UK for any period of at least five years since attaining the age of 13,

are eligible for jury service and are therefore under a duty to attend for service if summoned (Juries Act 1974, s. 1). CPD VI, para. 39B.1 (see Supplement, **PD-50**), states:

> The effect of section 321 of the Criminal Justice Act 2003 was to remove certain categories of persons from those previously ineligible for jury service (the judiciary and others concerned with the administration of justice) and certain other categories ceased to be eligible for excusal as of right, (such as members of Parliament and medical professionals). The normal presumption is that everyone, unless ineligible or disqualified, will be required to serve when summoned to do so.

There are a number of exceptions to this general rule. The first category is of those who are disqualified from serving by the provisions of the Juries Act 1974. The second category is of those who are able to excuse themselves from serving, either as of right under the Act, or at the discretion of the appropriate court officer in accordance with CPD VI, paras. 39B.2 and 39C.1 to 39C.10 and the *Guidance for summoning officers when considering deferral and excusal applications* published by HM Courts and Tribunals Service.

Ineligibility and Disqualification

D13.3   Parts I and II of sch. 1 to the Juries Act 1974 set out those persons who are disqualified for jury service.

The first group of disqualified persons, under sch.1, part I, consists of: (a) persons liable to be detained under the Mental Health Act 1983; (b) a person resident in a hospital on account of a mental disorder as defined in the 1983 Act (i.e. any disorder or disability of the mind); (c) those under a guardianship order or community treatment order under the 1983 Act; and (d) those who lack capacity within the meaning of the Mental Capacity Act 2005. The Mental Health (Discrimination) Act 2013, s. 2 amended the 1974 Act so as to remove the blanket ineligibility that previously applied to mentally disordered persons and replace it with a more limited disqualification.

The other persons disqualified (as defined by part II of sch.1), either for life or for ten years, are either disqualified by reason of previous convictions or by virtue of being on bail in criminal proceedings.

If a person serves on a jury knowing that he is disqualified from so doing, he commits a summary offence punishable with a fine of up to £5,000 (Juries Act 1974, s. 20(5)).

Juries Act 1974, s. 1 and sch. 1

D13.4

1.—(1) Subject to the provisions of this Act, every person shall be qualified to serve as a juror in the Crown Court, the High Court and the county court and be liable accordingly to attend for jury service when summoned under this Act if—
    (a) he is for the time being registered as a parliamentary or local government elector and is not less than eighteen nor more than seventy years of age;
    (b) he has been ordinarily resident in the United Kingdom, the Channel Islands or the Isle of Man for any period of at least five years since attaining the age of thirteen;
    (c) [omitted by the Mental Health (Discrimination) Act 2013, s. 2]; and
    (d) he is not disqualified for jury service.
(2) [Omitted by the Mental Health (Discrimination) Act 2013, s. 2.]
(3) The persons who are disqualified for jury service are those listed in Schedule 1.

SCHEDULE 1
PERSONS DISQUALIFIED FOR JURY SERVICE

PART 1
PERSONS SUBJECT TO MENTAL HEALTH ACT 1983 OR
MENTAL CAPACITY ACT 2005

1. A person for the time being liable to be detained under the Mental Health Act 1983.
1A. A person for the time being resident in a hospital on account of mental disorder as defined by the Mental Health Act 1983.
2. A person for the time being under guardianship under section 7 of the Mental Health Act 1983 or subject to a community treatment order under section 17A of that Act.
3. A person who lacks capacity, within the meaning of the Mental Capacity Act 2005, to act as a juror.
4. [Repealed].

PART 2
OTHER PERSONS DISQUALIFIED FOR JURY SERVICE

5. A person who is on bail in criminal proceedings (within the meaning of the Bail Act 1976).
6. A person who has at any time been sentenced in the United Kingdom, the Channel Islands or the Isle of Man—
    (a) to imprisonment for life, detention for life or custody for life,
    (b) to detention during her Majesty's pleasure or during the pleasure of the Secretary of State,
    (c) to imprisonment for public protection or detention for public protection,
    (d) to an extended sentence under section 227 or 228 of the Criminal Justice Act 2003 or section 210A of the Criminal Procedure (Scotland) Act 1995, or
    (e) to a term of imprisonment of five years or more or a term of detention of five years or more.
7. A person who at any time in the last ten years has—
    (a) in the United Kingdom, the Channel Islands or the Isle of Man—
      (i) served any part of a sentence of imprisonment or a sentence of detention, or
      (ii) had passed on him a suspended sentence of imprisonment or had made in respect of him a suspended order for detention,
    (b) in England and Wales, had made in respect of him a community order under section 177 of the Criminal Justice Act 2003, a community rehabilitation order, a community punishment order, a community punishment and rehabilitation order, a drug treatment and testing order or a drug abstinence order, or

(c) had made in respect of him any corresponding order under the law of Scotland, Northern Ireland, the Isle of Man or any of the Channel Islands or a service community order or overseas community order under the Armed Forces Act 2006.

8. For the purposes of this Part of this Schedule—

   (a) a sentence passed (anywhere) in respect of a service offence within the meaning of the Armed Forces Act 2006 is to be treated as having been passed in the United Kingdom, and

   (b) a person is sentenced to a term of detention if, but only if—

      (i) a court passes on him, or makes in respect of him on conviction, any sentence or order which requires him to be detained in custody for any period, and

      (ii) the sentence or order is available only in respect of offenders below a certain age,

and any reference to serving a sentence of detention is to be construed accordingly.

EXCUSAL FROM JURY SERVICE

Excusal as of Right

D13.5   Certain narrowly defined groups are entitled to be excused from jury service even though they are eligible to serve and have been duly summoned to attend for service under the Juries Act 1974, s. 2.

There are two main categories:

(a) Section 8 of the Juries Act 1974 deals with those excusable by virtue of having served in the recent past.

(b) Section 9(2A) sets out the position with regard to full-time serving members of the armed forces. The Crown Court officer should (within certain limits set out in s. 9A(2A) and (2B)) excuse such members if their commanding officer certifies that their absence would be prejudicial to the efficiency of the service.

If a member of an excusable group is summoned, the onus is on him to apply for excusal and satisfy an appropriate officer of the Crown Court that he does indeed belong to the group in question. Should he not ask to be excused, he (like anybody else who has been summoned) commits an offence by not attending for service. There is also provision for the court itself to excuse the juror without the application first going through an officer (see ss. 8(1) and 9(4)).

In addition, s. 9(3) provides that rules shall enable a juror refused excusal by an officer to appeal to the court against the refusal. Rule 39.1 of the CrimPR (see Supplement, **R-318**) requires the juror to give written notice of appeal to the appropriate officer, specifying the matters on which he relies as grounds for excusal. The juror must also be given an opportunity to make representations to the court. The appeal would normally be determined in chambers.

The courts have identified other categories of persons who, as a result of their occupation, qualify for excusal. These include those employed by the prosecuting authority (*Abdroikov* [2007] 1 All ER 315 (see **D13.27**) and CPD VI, para. 39C.9 (see Supplement, **PD-51**)) and those who have publicly expressed strong views on criminal issues, such as writers and journalists (*Cornwall* [2009] EWCA Crim 2458).

D13.6   Juries Act 1974, ss. 8 and 9

8.—(1) If a person summoned under this Act shows to the satisfaction of the appropriate officer, or of the court (or any of the courts) to which he is summoned—

   (a) that he has served on a jury, or duly attended to serve on a jury, in the prescribed period ending with the service of the summons on him, or

   (b) that the Crown Court or any other court has excused him from jury service for a period which has not terminated, the officer or court shall excuse him from attending, or further attending, in pursuance of the summons.

(2) In subsection (1) above 'the prescribed period' means two years or such longer period as the Lord Chancellor may prescribe...

9.—(1) [Repealed]

(2) If any person summoned under this Act shows to the satisfaction of the appropriate officer that there is good reason why he should be excused from attending in pursuance of the summons, the appropriate officer may, subject to section 9A(1A) of this Act, excuse him from so attending.

(2A) Without prejudice to subsection (2) above, the appropriate officer shall excuse a full-time serving member of Her Majesty's naval, military or air forces from attending in pursuance of a summons if—

(a) that member's commanding officer certifies to the appropriate officer that it would be prejudicial to the efficiency of the service if that member were to be required to be absent from duty, and

(b) subsection (2A) or (2B) of section 9A of this Act applies.

(2B) Subsection (2A) above does not affect the application of subsection (2) above to a full-time serving member of Her Majesty's naval, military or air forces in a case where he is not entitled to be excused under subsection (2A).

(3) Criminal Procedure Rules shall provide a right of appeal to the court (or one of the courts) before which the person is summoned to attend against any refusal of the appropriate officer to excuse him under subsection (2) above or any failure by the appropriate officer to excuse him as required by subsection (2A) above.

(4) Without prejudice to the preceding provisions of this section, the court (or any of the courts) before which a person is summoned to attend under this Act may excuse that person from so attending.

Discretionary Excusal

D13.7 Section 9(2) of the Juries Act 1974 permits a juror discretionary excusal wherever he can show to the satisfaction of the jury summoning officer that 'there is good reason why he should be excused from attending'. There is a right of appeal against the appropriate officer's refusal to excuse following the procedure set out in the CrimPR, r. 39.1. Excusal is dealt with in CPD VI, paras. 39B.3 and 39C.1 to 39C.10 (see Supplement, **PD-50** and **PD-51**). Excusal from service on a long trial is dealt with by the CrimPR, r. 39.4.

D13.8 **The Proper Approach to a Discretionary Excusal** The test identified in *Guildford Crown Court, ex parte Siderfin* [1990] 2 QB 683 for whether and, if so, in what circumstances conscientious and/or religious objection to serving on a jury should entitle a juror to be excused is whether the applicant has established a good reason for excusal. A conscientious objection arising out of religious belief is unlikely *on its own* to amount to a good reason, since it will not outweigh the necessity of the observance of the public duty to perform jury service. 'Adherence to some kind of religious belief cannot be regarded as an unchallengeable right to excusal from jury service' (p. 159F). But, where the applicant's belief would stand in the way of her fulfilling her duty as a juror 'properly, responsibly and honestly', then she should be excused.

As to procedure, although there is no right to be represented, the judge hearing the appeal has a discretion to allow it and, unless there is good reason to the contrary, an adjournment should be allowed for solicitors to be instructed (see p. 158G–H). Any application for excusal from jury service must first be independently considered by an appropriate officer; it is unacceptable for certain types of application to be automatically transferred to a judge.

SUMMONING FOR JURY SERVICE

D13.9 The procedure for summoning jurors is governed by s. 2 of the Juries Act 1974 and the CrimPR, r. 38.6. Responsibility for summoning jurors for service rests with the Lord Chancellor (s. 2(1)). In making arrangements for the discharge of that duty, the Lord Chancellor is to have regard to the convenience of the persons summoned and the desirability of selecting jurors who live within reasonable daily travelling distance of the Crown Court location they are summoned to attend (s. 2(2)). Subject to that, a person may be required to attend for service anywhere in England and Wales (s. 2(3)). The summons may be served by ordinary post (s. 2(4)).

The Basis for Selection

D13.10 To enable the Lord Chancellor to perform his duties in relation to the summoning of jurors, he must be provided with as many copies of published electoral registers as he requires (Juries Act

D

Part D Procedure

1974, s. 3). The copies must indicate those persons on the register who are either under 18 or over 70 (i.e. ineligible for jury service by reason of age). The choice of those to be summoned is made on a random basis from amongst those who are (a) on the register and (b) of an eligible age.

It follows that a summons may be sent to a person who is ineligible on a ground other than age or who is disqualified by reason of previous convictions. Therefore, s. 2(5) provides that the summons for service shall be accompanied by a notice informing the person summoned of the categories of ineligible person, the possibility of being prosecuted for serving when ineligible or disqualified, and the right to apply for excusal from or deferral of jury service.

Panels of those Summoned

D13.11 As well as summoning jurors, the Lord Chancellor is required to prepare panels (i.e. lists) of those persons who have been summoned (Juries Act 1974, s. 5(1)). The arrangement of and the information contained in the panels is a matter for his discretion (s. 5(1)). At present the only information given is the names and addresses of those summoned and the dates and place of attendance. Parties to a case which will or may be tried by jury are entitled to reasonable facilities for inspecting the panel from which their jurors will be drawn (s. 5(2)). The right must be exercised before the close of the trial (s. 5(3)).

Praying a Tales

D13.12 In the unlikely event that there will be insufficient jurors on the panel to form a complete jury to try an issue, the court may require any persons who are in the vicinity to be summoned without written notice for service (Juries Act 1974, s. 6(1)). This practice is known as *'praying a tales'*. The names of persons so summoned are added to the panel, and the court then proceeds as if they had been on the panel in the first instance (s. 6(2)). The reference in s. 6 to 'making up' a full jury by means of additional panellists suggests that the jury must always include at least one person who was on the original panel. This interpretation is consistent with the decision in *Solomon* [1958] 1 QB 203 (jury consisting of jurors not on the original panel was held to be no jury at all).

The Obligation Imposed by the Summons

D13.13 Unless the person summoned has been excused from jury service under the provisions described above, he commits an offence if he either fails to attend on a day covered by the summons, or, having attended, is then either not available when called on to serve or is unfit by reason of drink or drugs (Juries Act 1974, s. 20(1)). By s. 20(2), the offence is punishable either on summary conviction or as if it were a criminal contempt committed in the face of the court (i.e. the Crown Court judge may determine whether an offence has been committed without recourse to summary prosecution). The offence is punishable with a fine of up to £1,000. If the juror can show reasonable cause for his failure to attend etc. he is not liable to any penalty (s. 20(4): see *Andrews* [2008] EWCA Crim 2394 for a recent application of s. 20(4)).

D13.14 Juries Act 1974, ss. 2, 5 and 6

     2.—(1) Subject to the provisions of this Act, the Lord Chancellor shall be responsible for the summoning of jurors to attend for service in the Crown Court, the High Court and county courts and for determining the occasions on which they are to attend when so summoned, and the number to be summoned.

     (2) In making arrangements to discharge his duty under subsection (1) above the Lord Chancellor shall have regard to the convenience of the persons summoned and to their respective places of residence, and in particular to the desirability of selecting jurors within reasonable daily travelling distance of the place where they are to attend.

     (3) Subject to subsection (2) above, there shall be no restriction on the places in England and Wales at which a person may be required to attend or serve on a jury under this Act.

     [(4) Summons can be served either by post or by hand.]

(5) A written summons sent or delivered to any person under subsection (4) above shall be accompanied by a notice informing him—
  (a) of the effect of sections 1 [eligibility for jury service], 9(1) [excusal from jury service], 10 [reference of juror to judge with a view to discharge] and 20(5) [penalties for serving on a jury when disqualified etc.] of this Act; and
  (b) that he may make representations to the appropriate officer with a view to obtaining the withdrawal of the summons, if for any reason he is not qualified for jury service, or wishes or is entitled to be excused;
  and where a person is summoned under subsection (4) above . . . the appropriate officer may at any time put or cause to be put to him such questions as the officer thinks fit in order to establish whether or not the person is qualified for jury service.
[(6) Proof of service by post may be given by certificate.]
5.—(1) The arrangements to be made by the Lord Chancellor under this Act shall include the preparation of lists (called panels) of persons summoned as jurors, and the information to be included in panels, the court sittings for which they are prepared, their divisions into parts or sets, . . . their enlargement or amendment, and all other matters relating to the contents and form of the panels shall be such as the Lord Chancellor may from time to time direct.
(2) A party to proceedings in which jurors are or may be called on to try an issue, and any person acting on behalf of a party to such proceedings, shall be entitled to reasonable facilities for inspecting the panel from which the jurors are or will be drawn.
(3) The right conferred by subsection (2) above shall not be exercisable after the close of the trial by jury (or after the time when it is no longer possible for there to be a trial by jury).
(4) The court may, if it thinks fit, at any time afford to any person facilities for inspecting the panel, although not given the right by subsection (2) above.
6.—(1) If it appears to the court that a jury to try any issue before the court will be, or probably will be, incomplete, the court may, if the court thinks fit, require any persons who are in, or in the vicinity of, the court, to be summoned (without any written notice) for jury service up to the number needed (after allowing for any who may not be qualified under section 1 of this Act, and for excusals and challenges) to make up a full jury.
(2) The names of the persons so summoned shall be added to the panel and the court shall proceed as if those summoned had been included in the panel in the first instance.

Deferral of Jury Service

Section 9A of the Juries Act 1974 provides that, if a juror who has been summoned shows to the satisfaction of the appropriate officer that there is good reason why his attendance should be deferred, the officer shall vary the summons accordingly (s. 9A(1)). Obvious reasons for deferral are if the dates in the summons clash with the juror's holiday arrangements or business commitments. Attendance may be deferred only once in respect of one summons (s. 9A(2A)).   **D13.15**

An application for deferral may be made direct to the court (s. 9A(4)), and, in any event, there is a right of appeal against the appropriate officer's refusal to defer (s. 9A(3) and the CrimPR, r. 39.1).

Reference to the Judge for Discharge of a Summons

Should it appear to the appropriate officer of the court that a person attending for jury service in pursuance of a summons may be unable to act effectively as a juror on account of 'physical disability or insufficient understanding of English', that person may be brought before a judge who 'shall determine whether or not he should act as a juror and, if not, shall discharge the summons' (Juries Act 1974, s. 10).   **D13.16**

Furthermore, by s. 2(5), an officer may 'at any time put or cause to be put to [a person summoned for jury service] such questions as the officer thinks fit in order to establish whether or not the person is qualified for jury service'. Under s. 20(5), knowingly or recklessly providing false answers to such questions is a summary offence punishable with a fine of up to £1,000.

The Procedure   The procedure in relation to those who may be unable to act as jurors because of physical disability is governed by the Juries Act 1974, s. 9B. This states that the judge 'shall   **D13.17**

affirm the summons unless he is of the opinion that the person will not, on account of his disability, be capable of acting effectively as a juror, in which case he shall discharge the summons'.

In *Re Osman* [1996] 1 Cr App R 126, the Recorder of London, Sir Lawrence Verney, held at first instance that a person summoned to be a juror who was profoundly deaf should be discharged from jury service pursuant to s. 9B. The prospective juror could not follow the proceedings in court or the deliberations in the jury room without the assistance of an interpreter in sign language, and it would be an incurable irregularity in the proceedings for the interpreter to retire with the jury when they considered their verdict.

SELECTION OF JURY FOR A PARTICULAR CASE

D13.18 Once a jury panel has been selected by the process described above, the next stage is to select a jury for a particular case, pursuant to s. 11 of the Juries Act 1974. The procedure for selecting the jury is set out in the CrimPR, r. 38.6 (see Supplement, **R-305**). Normally, a jury will be called to try the issue of the accused's guilt or innocence. However, they might alternatively be asked to determine whether an accused whom the court has found to be unfit to plead did the act alleged, or to try the issues mute by visitation of God or of malice (for which see **D12.10** and **D12.17**).

Ballot in Open Court

D13.19
Juries Act 1974, s. 11

> (1) The jury to try an issue before a court shall be selected by ballot in open court from the panel, or part of the panel, of jurors summoned to attend at the place and time in question.

The 'ballot in open court' is conventionally conducted by the clerk of the court. Part of the jury panel which is sufficient to provide a full jury of 12, allowing for the possibility that some may be successfully challenged, is brought into the back of the court by an usher. These jurors are usually referred to as the 'jury in waiting'. The clerk is given the juror cards for each of the jurors in waiting (i.e. a card on which is printed the juror's name and address). He selects cards at random, and reads out the names on them, inviting the jurors in waiting to step into the jury-box should their names be called (see *Salt* [1996] Crim LR 517 and *Tarrant* [1998] Crim LR 342, on the need for selection to be random so far as practicable, however in *Jalil* [2009] 2 Cr App R (S) 276 it was held that a ballot remained valid where the prospective panel had been reduced by earlier challenges to other jurors to a final 12).

Under the CrimPR, r. 38.6(6), in the case of a trial expected to last more than four weeks, as many as 14 jurors may be selected initially to allow for potential discharges. The court will discharge any extra juror or jurors remaining by no later than the beginning of the prosecution evidence (r. 38.6(7)).

Once the jurors are in the box, the clerk informs the accused of his right to challenge jurors. He then reads out the names again, pausing after each name so that the juror may take the juror's oath (or affirm). The form of oath is: 'I swear by almighty God that I will faithfully try the defendant[s] and give [a] true verdict[s] according to the evidence'. That form is not set out in CPD VI, paras. 39E.1 to 39E.3 (see Supplement, **PD-53**), because the form may vary according to the faith indicated by the juror to the court (para. 39E.2), but para. 39E.3 states that a solemn affirmation shall be permitted if the juror objects to being sworn and sets out the form of that declaration. Each juror must take the oath or affirm separately (s. 11(3)).

D13.20 **Anonymity of Jurors** In *Comerford* [1998] 1 All ER 823, the Court of Appeal considered the decision of the trial judge that jurors should be identified by number not by name to reduce the risk of intimidation. Their lordships took the view that, as there was no mandatory requirement that names should be called, such a departure from the normal procedure did not render the trial a nullity, unless it made the proceedings unfair to the appellant. It was made clear, however, that the appellant could have exercised his right to ascertain the names of all the jurors forming the panel if he had so desired and it was said that it is 'highly desirable that in normal circumstances the usual procedure for empanelling a jury should be followed'.

Comerford [1998] 1 All ER 823 was considered in *Baybasin* [2014] 1 Cr App R 264 (19), in which complaint was made that the jury had been selected following a ballot by number, and other measures had been adopted to protect the jury. The Court of Appeal considered that the measures, such as collecting the jury from a city-centre pick-up point and requiring them to remain in their room when not in court, did not affect the fairness of the trial and that ballot by numbers had not inhibited the accused's right of challenge. The Court did, however, observe that the permissible measures for jury management and selection were now those promulgated by the Criminal Procedure Rules Committee, and that local initiatives ought to be referred to that committee for its approval.

Warnings to the Jury on Empanelment In the light of the decision of the House of Lords in   **D13.21**
Mirza [2004] 1 AC 1118 (see **D13.51**), the Court of Appeal issued *Practice Direction (Crown Court: Guidance to Jurors)* [2004] 1 WLR 665, which requires that the judge warn the jury that they should alert him to any concerns about the behaviour of fellow jurors at the time, rather than waiting until the conclusion of the case. That Practice Direction is consolidated in CPD VI, paras. 39G.1 to 39G.4 (see Supplement, **PD-55**). See also the *Crown Court Bench Book*, ch. 2, as supplemented and revised and the CrimPR, r. 39.3 (information provided for potential jurors).

As was restated in *Marshall* [2007] EWCA Crim 35, at the outset of the trial the judge should warn the jury: (a) that they must try the case on the evidence that they hear in court and on nothing else; (b) that they must not discuss the case with others outside court, such as members of their family; and (c) that they should not conduct their own private research, e.g., using the internet. See also *Thompson* [2011] 2 All ER 83 and *McDonnell* [2011] 1 Cr App R 347 for the special emphasis given to warnings on internet research and the collective responsibility of jurors. See also the approach of the Court of Appeal to a breach of the internet injunction to jurors in *A-G v Dallas* [2012] 1 WLR 991 (see **B14.103**). In *A-G v Davey* [2014] 1 Cr App R 1 (1), it was suggested that handing the jury a notice setting out what they must and must not do and the penal consequences of any breach might be advisable, so that no juror can subsequently claim that he did not understand what he should not do and what the consequences might be; this practice is now embodied in the CrimPR, r. 39.3.

CHALLENGING JURORS

It is fundamental to the jury process that the jurors who try an accused are selected at random.   **D13.22**
That said, however, it is recognised that there will be circumstances in which the interests of justice require some intervention in that random selection process. The methods of replacing one or more of the prospective jurors called into the box as a result of the clerk's ballot with others from the jury in waiting are:

(a) for either the prosecution or defence to challenge for cause;
(b) for the prosecution to ask a juror to stand by;
(c) for the judge to exercise his discretionary power to remove a juror.

The procedure for objecting to potential jurors is now contained in the CrimPR, r. 38.8 (see Supplement, **R-307**).

Challenges for Cause

A challenge for cause may be made by either the prosecution or defence. It is either a challenge   **D13.23**
to the whole panel of jurors, known as a challenge 'to the array', or to an individual juror, known as a challenge 'to the polls'.

Challenges to the Array At common law either party could challenge the whole panel sum-   **D13.24**
moned for their case on the ground that the person responsible for the summoning acted

improperly or was biased. Although this right is preserved by the Juries Act 1974, s. 12(6), it is now almost dormant.

Juries Act 1974, s. 12

(6) Without prejudice to subsection (4) above [right to challenge individual jurors], the right of challenge to the array, that is to say the right of challenge on the ground that the person responsible for summoning the jurors in question is biased or has acted improperly, shall continue to be unaffected by the fact that, since the coming into operation of section 31 of the Courts Act 1971 (which is replaced by this Act), the responsibility for summoning jurors for service in the Crown Court... has lain with the Lord Chancellor.

Historically, challenge to the array was made when the sheriff responsible for summoning the jury had an apparent interest in the outcome of the trial. More recently, such a challenge is more likely to relate to the racial or religious composition of the jury.

Specific malfeasance in the summoning was also a ground of challenge, as when jurors were summoned at the express request of prosecution or defence, or had been selected on grounds of their religion (see, e.g., *O'Doherty* (1848) 6 St Tr NS 831).

D13.25 **Racial or Religious Composition of the Jury**   In the absence of evidence of bias or improper conduct by the person responsible for summoning, the jury panel's being imbalanced racially or not reflecting the overall racial or religious composition of the catchment area from which jurors are summoned is *not* sufficient ground for challenge. See, for example, *Danvers* [1982] Crim LR 680 and *Broderick* [1970] Crim LR 155, which were both approved by the Court of Appeal in *Ford* [1989] QB 868 (analysed at **D13.40**). The principle of these decisions will apply equally to other apparent imbalances in the jury panel (e.g., as to the proportion of men to women).

D13.26 **Challenges to the Polls**

Juries Act 1974, s. 12

(4) The fact that a person summoned to serve on a jury is not qualified to serve shall be a ground of challenge for cause; but subject to that, and to the foregoing provisions of this section, nothing in this Act affects the law relating to challenge of jurors.

Thus, jurors who are too old or too young to be on a jury, or who have not been resident in the UK for a five-year period since attaining the age of 13, or who are not on the electoral roll, or who are disqualified by convictions may all be successfully challenged for cause (see **D13.3**).

In the absence of any challenge from the parties, a juror may in effect challenge himself by stating, if it be the case, that he is not qualified (*Cook* (1696) 13 St Tr 311). The summons sent to each juror is accompanied by a notice which sets out the ineligible and disqualified groups and warns him of his duty to inform the court if he comes within any of them.

D13.27

Police Officers and Employees of Prosecuting Authorities as Jurors   In *Abdroikov* [2007] 1 All ER 315, the House of Lords considered whether the Court of Appeal ([2005] 2 All ER 869), had been correct to hold that the presence on a jury of a police officer, or a prosecuting solicitor, did not offend against the requirement for a fair trial. The House of Lords identified the appropriate question to be whether a fair-minded observer would perceive a possibility of bias, albeit unconscious, as inevitable when a juror was professionally committed to only one side of an adversarial trial process. In the case of an employee of the prosecuting authority, their lordships concluded that such a perception of bias did arise, and it was therefore not appropriate for such an employee to form part of a jury trying a case brought by their employer. In the case of police officers, however, a fair-minded observer would not conclude that there was a real possibility that such a person would be biased as a juror simply because of his involvement in the administration of justice. The position would, however, be different if the juror had special knowledge either of the individuals involved or the facts of the case (as was the case in *Pintori* [2007] EWCA Crim 1700), or where the credibility or reliability of police evidence was a central issue (as was the case in one of the conjoined appeals in *Abdroikov* itself). The approach advocated by the House of Lords was applied in *Khan* [2008] 3 All ER 502, and approved by the ECtHR in *Hanif v UK* (2012) 55 EHRR 424. See also *Yemoh* [2009] EWCA Crim 930 and *LL* [2011] 1 Cr App R 338.

D13.28

Fear of Bias   At common law a qualified juror could be challenged *propter affectum*, i.e. on the ground of some presumed or actual bias which would make him unsuitable to try the case. This ground of challenge is preserved by the last clause of s. 12(4). Most authorities on challenges to the polls *propter affectum* are old, and reflect the very different social and legal conditions of their time. The broad thrust of the decisions is that a juror is challengeable if he has expressed hostility to one side or the other (*O'Coigley* (1798) 26 St Tr 1191), has expressed a wish as to the outcome of the case, is related to a party, or has some other connection with a party (e.g., was his servant or agent).

In *Kray* (1969) 53 Cr App R 412, the defence wished to object to any jurors who had read newspaper articles which had reported not only that two of the accused before the court charged with murder had been convicted at an earlier trial for murder but also included 'a number of facts which were not in evidence at the trial and which were discreditable of those to whom they referred'. Lawton J, having criticised the newspapers for publishing these additional facts, then said (at p. 415 emphasis added):

> This does, in my judgment, lead to a prima facie presumption that anybody who may have read that kind of information might find it difficult to reach a verdict in a fair-minded way. It is, however, a matter of human experience . . . first, that the public's recollection is short, and, secondly, that the drama . . . of a trial almost always has the effect of excluding from recollection that which went before. A person summoned for this case would not . . . disqualify himself merely because he had read any of the newspapers containing allegations of the kind I have referred to; but the position would be different if, as a result of reading what he had, *his mind had become so clogged with prejudice that he was unable to try the case impartially*.

Insofar as a general principle may be extracted from the above passage, it seems to be that a juror may be challenged for cause if his mind is so prejudiced that he is unable to try the case impartially, but merely having once been informed of matters discreditable to the accused will not necessarily occasion such prejudice.

Procedure for Challenging for Cause

D13.29

The Juries Act 1974, s. 12(1)(b), provides that 'any challenge for cause shall be tried by the judge before whom [the accused] is to be tried'.

D13.30

Timing   The challenge must be entered after the juror's name has been drawn by ballot and before he is sworn (s. 12(3)). Conventionally, a challenge is indicated simply by counsel for the challenging party saying the word 'challenge' as the juror is about to take the oath. Should the challenge not be made until after the juror has begun to take the oath the judge has a discretion to allow it but is not obliged to do so (*Harrington* (1977) 64 Cr App R 1).

It is clear from *Morris* (1991) 93 Cr App R 102, that the right to challenge for cause is limited to the time when the jury is sworn, and cannot be exercised during the course of the trial. M was accused of stealing from a Marks and Spencer store. During the trial, it was revealed that a juror was employed by that company. The judge refused to discharge the juror saying that the right way to deal with the matter was by a challenge for cause. The Court of Appeal, allowing the appeal, held that by the time the facts about the juror had emerged, it was too late for the defence to challenge for cause.

D13.31

Process   The burden of proof is on the challenging party, and the judge may order that the hearing be *in camera* or in chambers (CJA 1988, s. 118(2)). If the challenge is of any substance, it will be proper for it to be heard in the absence of the other jurors. The challenged juror should be kept outside the court except insofar as it is necessary to question him. The remaining jurors should leave the court, retiring to the jury room in the charge of the jury bailiff if they have already been sworn. A shorthand note of proceedings should in any event be taken, and the court's decision should be entered on the court record. The judge can hear evidence and question the juror concerned. Counsel may be allowed to ask questions directed to the ground on which the juror is challenged.

D13.32   After hearing the evidence and any submissions, the judge will decide whether to allow the challenge. If he does so, the juror is discharged and a fresh juror called to replace him. If the challenge is rejected, the judge should tell the juror not to disclose any of the matters dealt with during the challenge to other jurors, and not to allow the fact that the challenge was made to influence him.

Need for Prima Facie Evidence   The main difficulty in challenging for cause is that, in marked contrast to the practice adopted in the USA of conducting preliminary questioning of the jury panel to establish a prima facie ground of challenge, the challenging party must provide prima facie evidence of his grounds at the time that the challenge is made. It is only *after* this that a juror may be asked questions on the *voir dire* to determine whether the challenge is well founded.

The initial requirement of prima facie evidence from the challenger was stated in *Dowling* (1848) 7 St Tr NS 382, and was confirmed by Lord Parker CJ in *Chandler (No. 2)* [1964] 2 QB 322, in which his lordship said (at p. 338):

> ... before any right to cross-examine the juror arose, the defendant would have had to lay a foundation of fact in support of his ground of challenge. It is no good his saying, 'I think this man is antagonistic' .... There must be a foundation of fact creating a prima facie case before the juror can be cross-examined.

Similarly, in *Broderick* [1970] Crim LR 155, where defence counsel unsuccessfully sought to cross-examine each member of the panel to determine whether he or she might be biased against B on racial grounds, the Court of Appeal held that it had never been the practice to allow potential jurors to be paraded for cross-examination in a fishing expedition, seeking possible grounds on which a challenge might subsequently be made.

Kray (1969) 53 Cr App R 412 (see **D13.28**) represents a departure from this normal practice. Defence counsel was permitted to examine each juror who came into the box to be sworn on whether he had read certain newspaper articles discreditable to the accused. Although Lawton J stated that the production of the offending articles was in itself sufficient to raise a prima facie ground of challenge, in reality, the procedure adopted in *Kray* was justified by the wholly exceptional combination of circumstances that arose in that case.

D13.33
Standing Jurors By

The Right   This is a right possessed by the prosecution but not the defence (although in *Chandler (No. 2)* [1964] 2 QB 322 at p. 337, Lord Parker CJ observed that 'in an exceptional case the judge [could] in his discretion stand by a juror or allow the defendant to do so').

The CrimPR, r.38.8(3) provides that the prosecution must announce the exercise of its right before the juror completes the oath or affirmation.

Standing a juror by differs from challenging him for cause in that counsel need not give a reason for the stand-by. It differs from the peremptory challenges formerly available to the defence in that the juror is not conclusively removed from the jury but will be recalled to the jury-box should the entire jury panel be exhausted without a full jury being obtained, at which stage the prosecution must either accept him or show cause why he should not serve.

In the leading case of *Mason* [1981] QB 881, Lawton LJ, giving the Court of Appeal's judgment, summarised the position thus (at pp. 890H–891A):

> In our judgment, *Mansell* v *The Queen* (1857) 8 E & B 54 established beyond argument that prosecuting counsel have a right to request that a member of the jury panel shall stand by, and that this right can be exercised without there being a provable valid objection, until such time as the panel is exhausted; and when it is, if the Crown still wants to exclude a member of the jury from the panel, a valid objection must be shown.

Lawton LJ added the rider that he expected that prosecuting counsel would act responsibly and **D13.34** would not request a stand-by unnecessarily (p. 891C).

Guidance as to the Use of the Right   Since *Mason* [1981] QB 881 was decided, the defence right of peremptory challenge, which was perceived as a counterbalance to the prosecution right of stand-by, has been abolished. The A-G's guidelines on the exercise by the Crown of its right of stand-by (see **appendix 2**) affirm the general principles that:

(a) members of a jury should be selected at random from the panel subject to any rule of law as to right of challenge by the defence; and
(b) the Juries Act 1974 identifies those classes of persons who *alone* are disqualified from or ineligible for service on a jury, and no other class of person may be so treated (para. 2).

Responsibility for ensuring that an individual does not serve on a jury if he is not competent to discharge his duties properly rests, first, with the appropriate court officer and, ultimately, with the trial judge. In the context of that legislative background, para. 5 of the guidelines defines the two situations in which it is appropriate for prosecuting counsel to use his right of stand-by as follows:

(a) where a jury check authorised in accordance with the Attorney-General's guidelines on jury checks [see **D13.45** and **appendix 2**] reveals information justifying exercise of the right to stand by in accordance with para. 9 of the guidelines and the Attorney-General personally authorises the exercise of the right to stand by; or
(b) where a person is about to be sworn as a juror who is manifestly unsuitable and the defence agree that, accordingly, the exercise by the prosecution of the right to stand by would be appropriate. An example of the sort of *exceptional* circumstances which might justify stand-by is where it **D13.35** becomes apparent that ... a juror selected for service to try a complex case is in fact illiterate.

On the assumption that the guidelines are loyally followed, the importance of the right of stand-by has been vastly reduced. Counsel will exercise the right only in (a) the tiny minority of cases which involve national security or terrorism (para. 5(a)), or (b) 'ordinary' cases where a juror is obviously unsuitable *and the defence agree* (para. 5(b)). Thus, the chief function of the right now seems to be to avoid the clumsy mechanics of a challenge for cause where the parties concur that a juror should not serve.

In addition to the example given in para. 5(b) itself, subject to defence consent, jurors could properly be stood by if, e.g., counsel has been informed that they are in fact disqualified by previous convictions, or if they know the accused or any witnesses in the case. The guidelines are presumably not meant to inhibit prosecuting counsel from challenging for cause on grounds of bias if he considers that a juror's previous convictions or other involvement with the police might make him so prejudiced against the Crown as to be unable to try the case fairly. Whether such a challenge would succeed is open to question.

D13.36

The Court's Power to Exclude Jurors

Even in the absence of a formal challenge from either party, the trial judge has a residual discretion to exclude from the jury a juror selected by the initial ballot. Existence of the discretion can be traced back to Lord Campbell CJ's judgment in *Mansell v The Queen* (1857) 8 E & B 54, and has since been confirmed by Lord Parker CJ (*Chandler (No. 2)* [1964] 2 QB 322 at p. 327), by Lawton LJ (*Mason* **D13.37** [1981] QB 881 at p. 887G–H) and, most recently, by Lord Lane CJ in *Ford* [1989] QB 868.

Reasons for Exclusion   The discretion may and should be exercised where an individual juror is obviously incompetent to act but, for whatever reason, counsel do not challenge or exercise the right of stand-by. It is then the court's duty to prevent the 'scandal and perversion of justice which would arise from compelling or permitting such a juryman to be sworn' (per Lord Campbell CJ in *Mansell v The Queen* (1857) 8 E & B 54, who then gave as specific examples for the judge's intervention cases where the juror was mentally or physically infirm, or insane or drunk, or preoccupied with the dangerous illness of a relative).

Lawton LJ in *Mason* [1981] QB 881, succinctly described modern practice by saying (at p. 887G–H):

... trial judges, as an aspect of their duty to see that there is a fair trial, have had a right to intervene to ensure that a competent jury is empanelled. The most common form of judicial intervention is when a judge notices that a member of the panel is infirm or has difficulty in reading or hearing; and nowadays jurors for whom taking part in a long trial would be unusually burdensome are often excluded from the jury by the judge.

In *Jalil* [2009] 2 Cr App R (S) 276 the Court of Appeal found that a court was entitled to exclude jurors from the ballot who fell within criteria that had formed the basis of a challenge for cause that had been made and upheld in relation to other potential jurors.

D13.38 See also CPD VI, para. 39C.3 (see Supplement, **PD-51**).

Limitations However, judicial intervention should not extend beyond the kinds of situation mentioned above into a more systematic process which would undermine the random nature of jury selection or influence the overall composition of the jury (per Lord Lane CJ in *Ford* [1989] QB 868). In particular, the court has no power to discharge jurors on account of their religion, race or ethnic group in order to obtain a more diverse jury. Lord Lane said (at p. 872A) that the discretion to exclude a juror 'is to be exercised to prevent individual jurors who are not competent from serving. It has never been held to include a discretion to discharge a competent juror or jurors in an attempt to secure a jury drawn from particular sections of the community, or otherwise to influence the overall composition of the jury.' (See also the discussion of racially balanced juries at **D13.39**.)

D13.39 **Racial or Religious Balance of Jury**

From time to time judicial intervention has been sought to ensure that at least some members of the jury come from the same ethnic group as the accused. Although examples from the case law refer to the racial composition of the jury, the same principles have equal application to attempts to affect the religious composition of the jury. They include:

(a) *Binns* [1982] Crim LR 522 (trial of black accused on charges relating to racial riot in Bristol);
(b) *Bansal* [1985] Crim LR 151 (trial of Asians for offences of violence committed when protesting against a National Front march);
(c) *McCalla* [1986] Crim LR 335 (black accused alleging that his admissions to robbery were extracted from him by racially prejudiced white police officers);
(d) *Danvers* [1982] Crim LR 680 (accused at Nottingham Crown Court objected to the jury panel because it was entirely white and he was anxious that there should be a substantial representation of black people on the jury; challenge failed, even though the black population in Nottingham apparently represented about 10 per cent of the total);
(e) *Broderick* [1970] Crim LR 155 (black accused wished to be tried by an all-black jury).

The precise form of judicial aid sought has varied from case to case. In *Binns*, counsel asked the judge to exercise his right to stand jurors by until a jury representing 'the corporate good sense of the community' had been obtained; in *Bansal* the application was to move the venue of trial to a racially mixed area, while in *Broderick* the defence wished to have the jury panel paraded and asked 'fishing' questions about their possible racial prejudice.

Judicial response to the applications has been equally varied. The judges in *Binns* and *Bansal* were basically sympathetic to the defence request (although in doubt about how far they could go in ordering a certain racial mix on the jury or jury panel). By contrast, Judge Mander in *McCalla* ruled that he had no power to order that a jury be racially balanced and, even if he had such power, he would not have chosen to exercise it because a jury should be selected at random subject only to the law on disqualified jurors and challenges for cause. Moreover, to allow interference with jury selection on racial grounds would open the way to further manipulation, e.g.,
D13.40 on grounds of political view, sex, or religion, or for some similar reason.

Guidelines for Approaching the Issue It is the latter view which has found favour with the Court of Appeal. In *Ford* [1989] QB 868, F appealed against his convictions on the ground that the trial judge had refused an application for a racially balanced jury. The main points established by Lord Lane CJ's judgment are as follows:

(a) A challenge to the array of jurors summoned must be on the ground of bias or other irregularity on the part of the summoning officer. Therefore, the racial composition of the jury panel cannot of itself found a challenge or justify the judge in discharging the panel and ordering the summoning of a new one (see *Danvers* [1982] Crim LR 680 and **D13.25**).

(b) Summoning of jurors is the responsibility of the Lord Chancellor. It is not the judge's function to alter the composition of the jury panel or give directions about the area from which it should be drawn. Woolf J's direction in *Bansal* [1985] Crim LR 151, to the effect that the panel should be drawn from a part of the court's catchment area in which a high proportion of Asians lived, was made without benefit of full argument and was wrong.

(c) Nor should the judge consider a complaint that the jury panel is not truly random because it contains a lower proportion of persons of a certain race or ethnic group than live in the court's catchment area for jurors, unless, of course, the disproportion can be attributed to bias or impropriety on the part of the summoning officer. If the disproportion may be due to maladministration in the procedures for summoning jurors, that must be corrected by *administrative*, not judicial intervention.

(d) The mere fact that a juror is of a particular race or holds a particular religious belief cannot found a challenge for cause by a party on the ground of bias.

(e) The judge may not use his power to stand by or discharge individual jurors selected in the ballot from the jury panel for the purpose of securing a jury of a certain racial mix. To do so would conflict with the principle of random jury selection. In effect, the judge would be altering the composition of the jury panel when no irregularity on the part of the summoning officer had been shown and upholding a challenge when there was no ground in law for it. The judge's intervention should be restricted to the exceptional circumstances indicated in *Mansell v The Queen* (1857) 8 E & B 54 (see **D13.37**). Insofar as the judge in *Binns* [1982] Crim LR 522, had been prepared to stand jurors by until a balanced jury had been obtained, he was in error.

(f) In short, there is not (as had been suggested in *Frazer* [1987] Crim LR 418 and *Bansal*) any principle that a jury should be racially balanced, and it is impermissible for the judge to use his residual discretionary powers over the composition of the jury as a device for obtaining such a balance.

In *Smith* [2003] 1 WLR 2229, the Court of Appeal considered the standing of *Ford* in the light of the HRA 1998 and the ECHR, Article 6. It held that the approach in *Ford* had not been superseded by the HRA 1998. Pill LJ said:

> We do not accept that it was unfair for the appellant to be tried by a randomly selected all white jury or that the fair-minded and informed observer would regard it as unfair. We do not accept that, on the facts of this case, the trial could only be fair if members of the defendant's race were present on the jury. It was not a case where a consideration of the evidence required knowledge of the traditions or social circumstances of a particular racial group.

INVESTIGATION OF THE JURY PANEL

D13.41

Effective challenging of jurors depends on the amount of information about the jury panel available to the parties. Section 5(2) and (3) of the Juries Act 1974 entitles the parties to inspect the jury panel before or during trial but such inspection will inform them only of the names and addresses of the panel members. It will not of itself yield material capable of founding a challenge for cause.

D13.42

Proper Inquiries

There would seem to be no objection in theory to a party identifying the panellists summoned to the location of the Crown Court for the time when his case is listed to be heard and then making such inquiries as he sees fit into their employment, background, attitudes etc. on the off chance that grounds for a challenge for cause may emerge. He must, of course, take care not to infringe the general law on privacy or interfere with the jurors in a way which might amount to contempt of court or interference with the course of justice. In practice, the defence do not have the resources to conduct the kind of inquiries mentioned above.

D13.43 Checks for Previous Convictions

The one inquiry that the prosecution are likely to make is into the criminal records of the panellists. This practice was approved by the Court of Appeal in *Mason* [1981] QB 881. In that case, the police provided prosecution counsel with the results of checks as to whether the panellists summoned had convictions. Counsel stood by certain jurors, some but not all of whom were disqualified by their convictions, without informing defence counsel of the reason. Lawton LJ, giving the judgment of the Court of Appeal, justified the police action as being part of their usual function of preventing crime, it being an offence to serve on a jury when disqualified by convictions (see p. 891D–F).

Further, the court could see no reason why the information obtained should not be communicated to prosecuting counsel who could then make such use of it as he considered fit. 'The practice of supplying prosecuting counsel with information about potential jurors' convictions has been followed during the whole of our professional lives.... It is not unlawful, and has not until recently been thought to be unsatisfactory' (p. 891G). Prosecuting counsel is under no duty to transmit the information to the defence, although he may do so if he so wishes (p. 891B–D).

D13.44 Evolution since *Mason*

The decision in *Mason* that there is no objection to prosecution counsel standing a juror by if he has convictions but they are not such as to disqualify him, has been effectively reversed by the A-G's guidelines on the matter (see below). However, the case remains good authority to justify the practice of 'vetting' jurors by running a preliminary check on their criminal records.

Following the decision in *Mason*, the Association of Chief Police Officers (ACPO) issued recommendations on when the police 'should undertake a check of the names of potential jurors against records of previous convictions'. The recommendations are annexed to the A-G's guidelines on jury checks (see **appendix 2**). They identify three circumstances in which a check may be carried out.

(a) when 'there is reason to believe that attempts are being made to circumvent the statutory provisions excluding disqualified persons from service on a jury, including any case when there is reason to believe that a particular juror may be disqualified';

(b) when it is 'believed that in a previous related abortive trial an attempt was made to interfere with a juror or jurors'; and

(c) when, 'in the opinion of the DPP or the chief constable it is particularly important to ensure that no disqualified person serves on the jury'.

Save when authorised by the A-G's guidelines (see **D13.45**), no further checks on jurors should be carried out. Nor will the police check jurors on behalf of the defence unless requested to do so by the DPP. Should a jury check reveal that a juror, although not disqualified by his criminal record, may be unsuitable to sit as a member of the jury in a particular case, that information will be communicated to prosecuting counsel who will decide what use to make of it (recommendations (2) to (4)).

D13.45 Jury Vetting

In addition to the recommendations of ACPO, jury vetting by the police or prosecution is controlled by guidelines issued by the A-G (see **appendix 2**). In brief, they affirm that the provisions of the Juries Act 1974 on disqualified and ineligible jurors, combined with majority verdicts (which prevent one perverse juror stopping his colleagues from reaching a verdict) will, in all normal cases, be sufficient to ensure the proper administration of justice without recourse to any investigation of the jury panel going beyond that sanctioned by ACPO's recommendations on checking criminal records.

In two classes of case, however, the public interest may demand additional checks (para. 3). Those classes are (a) cases in which national security is involved and part of the evidence is likely to be heard in camera, and (b) terrorist cases (para. 4). In both types of case there is a risk that a juror's political views might be so extreme as to interfere with his fair assessment of the case or lead him to exert improper pressure on his fellow jurors, while in security cases there is the additional risk of the juror either voluntarily or under pressure making improper use of evidence given *in camera* (para. 5).

To ascertain whether a juror might be unsuitable for the above reasons, it may be necessary to investigate the panel by checking the records of Police Special Branches. In security (but not in terrorist) cases the investigation may additionally involve the security services (para. 6). Such checks may be made *only* on the personal authority of the A-G, and are therefore known as 'authorised checks' (para. 7). If a chief officer of police considers that an authorised check is likely to be desirable, he should refer the matter to the DPP, who will make the appropriate application to the A-G (para. 7).

The result of any authorised check will be sent to the DPP, who in turn will decide how much of the information should be passed on to prosecuting counsel (para. 8). In any event, no right of stand-by should be exercised by counsel on the basis of information derived from an authorised check unless he has the personal authority of the A-G and unless the information affords 'strong reason for believing that a particular juror might be a security risk, be susceptible to improper approaches or be influenced in arriving at a verdict for the reasons given [in the guidelines]' (para. 9).

Where a juror is stood by, prosecuting counsel may, in his discretion, disclose to the defence the information on which the stand-by was based, but he is under no duty to do so (para. 10). If an authorised check suggests that a juror might be biased against the accused, the defence should be informed of that in general terms although it may not be possible to give them precise details of the information revealed by the check (para. 11). It will be apparent that authorised checks are a possibility in only a tiny proportion of trials. In the general run of criminal cases, there will either be no check at all on the jury panel or there will be a check only of their criminal records.

COMPOSITION OF THE JURY AS A GROUND OF APPEAL   D13.46

The Juries Act 1974, s. 18, governs the extent to which the defence may use as a ground of appeal against conviction errors in the way the jury panel was summoned or the particular jury for their case was selected or empanelled. The overall effect is to prevent the verdict being challenged unless the irregularity complained of was raised but not remedied at trial. Moreover, s. 18 prevents lack of qualification or unfitness on the part of an individual juror being a ground of appeal.

Juries Act 1974, s. 18

(1) No judgment after verdict in any trial by jury in any court shall be stayed or reversed by reason—
  (a) that the provisions of this Act about the summoning or empanelling of jurors, or the selection of jurors by ballot, have not been complied with, or
  (b) that a juror was not qualified in accordance with section 1 of this Act, or
  (c) that any juror was misnamed or misdescribed, or
  (d) that any juror was unfit to serve.
(2) Subsection (1)(a) above shall not apply to any irregularity if objection is taken at, or as soon as practicable after, the time it occurs, and the irregularity is not corrected.
(3) Nothing in subsection (1) above shall apply to any objection to a verdict on the ground of personation.

It should be noted that the saving in s. 18(2) applies only to appeals based on contraventions of the Act's provisions as to the summoning or empanelling of jurors or their selection by ballot. If objection to such an irregularity was taken when or as soon as practicable after it occurred and the court did not correct it, it may be relied on as a material irregularity in the course of the trial justifying the quashing of a conviction by virtue of s. 2(1) of the Criminal Appeal Act 1968. Section 18(2) will not assist in a case where the defence did not know of the irregularity in summoning etc. until after conviction, since it will not have been possible to object until a stage at which the Crown Court was *functus officio*.

D13.47 **Unfitness of a Juror**

Save in the special case of impersonation of a juror, a juror's having been disqualified from or ineligible for jury service (Juries Act 1974, s. 18(1)(b)) or more generally unfit to serve (s. 18(1)(d)) cannot be a ground of appeal. The statutory provision follows the common law, for example:

(a) *Kelly* [1950] 2 KB 164, in which it was held that the only instances of convictions being quashed on account of a defect in a juror, that defect not having been raised at trial by means of a challenge for cause, were cases in which the juror actually summoned had been impersonated by another;

(b) *Tremearne* (1826) 5 B & C 254, in which the son of the juror called, who was not on the panel and was under age, answered for his father and served. The fact that the defence did not discover the defect in the juror until after conviction (and therefore could not have challenged for cause) is irrelevant to the application of s. 18 (see *Chapman* (1976) 63 Cr App R 75 and especially *Pennington* (1985) 81 Cr App R 217).

On a literal reading of s. 18 it is even possible to argue that, where a challenge was made at trial and wrongly rejected, the defence still cannot rely on the error on appeal. However, in such circumstances the proper ground of appeal would in fact be the judge's error of law in ruling against the challenge. Therefore, the appellant would not be caught by s. 18. See also *Tomar* [1997] Crim LR 682.

D13.48

The broad and somewhat draconian effect of s. 18 is illustrated by the leading case of *Chapman* (1976) 63 Cr App R 75. After conviction, the defence learnt that one of the jurors who tried the case was deaf and had heard only half the evidence. The defence were prevented from submitting on appeal that deafness rendered the juror unfit to serve, and that there had therefore been a material irregularity in the course of the trial (pursuant to the Criminal Appeal Act 1968, s. 2(1)(c) because s. 18(1)(d) expressly prevented any unfitness in a juror being used to reverse a verdict. Equally there had been no wrong decision on a question of law (for the purposes of s. 2(1)(b) of the 1968 Act), since no challenge had been made to the juror in the lower court. Accordingly, the only possible ground of appeal was the assertion that the verdict was unsafe (s. 2(1)(a)). On the facts of *Chapman*, the Court of Appeal concluded that the verdict was safe. The convictions were unanimous. Therefore, even on the assumption that, had he heard all the evidence, the deaf juror would have been for acquittal, the jury could and no doubt would have convicted by an 11–1 majority. Moreover, if the juror's incapacity had come to light during the course of the trial, the judge could simply have discharged him from the jury (see **D13.52**), allowing his colleagues to complete the trial and convict.

However, even though the argument failed on the facts, the Court of Appeal did indicate, *obiter*, that a juror's unfitness or lack of qualification was in principle a factor capable of rendering a conviction unsafe in conjunction with other circumstances.

D13.49 **Unfitness in General or in Particular**

It is unclear whether the terms of the Juries Act 1974, s. 18(1)(d), preventing a juror's unfitness to serve being used as the ground for reversing a verdict, apply only to an argument that the juror was unfit to serve on *any* jury or whether it extends to an argument that, although in general a qualified and competent juror, he was unfit to serve on the jury trying the appellant because of bias arising out of his knowledge of or previous dealings with him.

Whichever is the correct interpretation of s. 18 matters little, since common law, even before the passing of the 1974 Act, had made it virtually impossible to use subsequently discovered bias of a juror as a ground of appeal.

For example, in *Box* [1964] 1 QB 430, the foreman of the jury which had convicted the appellants gave evidence before the Court of Appeal that, at the time he served on the jury, he knew of the appellants' bad character. Neither the court nor the parties were aware that the juror possessed this knowledge when the jury was empanelled; nor did the juror ask to be excused as he plainly should have done. Considering the foreman's evidence, Lord Parker CJ adopted a dictum of Bankes J in *Syme* (1914) 10 Cr App R 284, to the effect that, unless the evidence shows the juror to have been determined *before* trial to come to a certain verdict regardless of the evidence, the court would not interfere. In the instant case, the foreman deposed that, when the trial commenced, he had had no views on the appellant's guilt or innocence but he formed very definite views as the case went along. Such evidence fell far short of that required by Bankes J, and the appeal failed.

Similarly, the foreman's knowledge of the appellant's bad character was not an automatic disqualification from serving on the jury, nor did it mean that he was unable to listen to the evidence and give the accused a fair trial in accordance with his oath. See also *Pennington* (1985) 81 Cr App R 217 and *Bliss* (1987) 84 Cr App R 1.

In practice it will be difficult if not impossible to satisfy the Court of Appeal that a juror was so biased against the accused before the case started that he was determined to convict whatever the evidence might turn out to be. These cases can be contrasted with decisions such as *Pintori* [2007] EWCA Crim 1700, in which a juror knew prosecution witnesses and this could justify a conclusion of bias on the part of the juror, thus rendering any resultant conviction unsafe.

D13.50

DISCHARGE OF JURORS OR ENTIRE JURY

The CrimPR, r. 38.7 sets out the procedure on the discharge of jurors (see Supplement, **R-306**). The judge has a discretion to discharge jurors from the jury and allow the trial to continue to verdict with the remainder, provided that at least nine jurors remain. He also has a discretion to discharge the entire jury from giving a verdict, in which case the accused is not acquitted but may be retried before a fresh jury. Once a jury has been discharged the general rule is that it is *functus officio* and cannot be reconvened to return a verdict, even if it is realised almost immediately after the order for discharge that the order was made in error (*Russell* (1984) 148 JP 765).

In *Follen* [1994] Crim LR 225, it was stated that there was no fixed rule of law that once the judge had discharged the jury he could not set aside that order, but it would be only in very rare circumstances that this should be done (see *S* [2005] EWCA Crim 1987, for an example of such circumstances). In *Aylott* [1996] 2 Cr App R 169, the Court of Appeal adopted a more flexible approach, and stated that the underlying principle was to ensure that proceedings were fair and to do justice in the particular case (see **D19.77** for more detail).

There are three situations that should be considered in this context. First, where the jury themselves identify a problem; secondly, where there is a problem with a particular juror; and, thirdly, where the problem extends to the jury as a whole.

In each of these situations the test to be applied is the same, either where there is or may be bias or prejudice against the accused, or misbehaviour that risks injustice to him. This approach is analysed below, together with consideration of how any alleged bias or misconduct can be investigated, and how any ultimate decision as to whether or not to discharge the jury can thereafter be reviewed on appeal. In November 2012 the President of the Queen's Bench Division issued a protocol for how jury irregularities should be investigated and addressed which is now embodied in CPD VI, paras. 39M.1 to 39M.26 (see Supplement, **PD-60**).

D13.51

Jury Monitoring Itself

The House of Lords in *Mirza* [2004] 1 AC 1118, decided in effect that if after verdict a juror raises a concern about a fellow juror's behaviour, the courts will not investigate such behaviour (see **D19.31**). As a result of the views expressed by Lord Hope and Lord Hobhouse, the Court of Appeal issued *Practice Direction (Crown Court: Guidance to Jurors)* [2004] 1 WLR 665, which is consolidated at CPD VI, paras. 39G.1 to 39G.4 (see Supplement, **PD-55**, and **D13.21**). Note especially para. 39G.3vi.

As was made clear in *Adams* [2007] 1 Cr App R 449, it is implicit in this approach that the Court of Appeal can hear evidence from jurors to resolve an issue of alleged jury bias when this is raised on appeal, although anyone seeking to interview jurors with a view to investigating such an issue should first obtain the Court of Appeal's leave. It was made clear that this course would only be countenanced in rare and exceptional cases (a recent example of such investigation is *Hambleton* [2009] EWCA Crim 13). Equally, a court at first instance would be entitled to question jurors in relation to any alleged impropriety. In *Thompson* [2011] 2 All ER 83 it was restated that an investigation of the jury was permissible only where there was a suggestion of a complete repudiation of the jury's oath, or a risk that extraneous material had entered the jury's deliberations (see *OKZ* [2010] EWCA Crim 2272 as an example of self-monitoring by a jury).

D13.52

Discharge of Individual Jurors

Juries Act 1974, s. 16

(1) Where in the course of a trial of any person for an offence on indictment any member of the jury dies or is discharged by the court whether as being through illness incapable of continuing to act or for any other reason, but the number of its members is not reduced below nine, the jury shall nevertheless...be considered as remaining for all the purposes of that trial properly constituted, and the trial shall proceed and a verdict may be given accordingly.

Section 16(1) is without prejudice to the judge's power to discharge the entire jury if he considers it preferable to do that (for which see **D13.56**), rather than continuing with reduced numbers (s. 16(3)). Discharge of jurors is *not* dependent on the consent of the parties.

D13.53 In a case where the jury has to consider more than one verdict, the judge retains the power to discharge a juror even after one or more of the verdicts has been given. The reasoning is that the trial (and the accompanying power to discharge) continues in respect of those counts on which the verdict has not been delivered (*Wood* [1997] Crim LR 229).

Judicial Discretion to Discharge a Juror Section 16(1) does not define the circumstances in which the judge may or should discharge a juror beyond implying that it may be on account of illness making the juror incapable of continuing to act or 'any other reason'. In *Hambery* [1977] QB 924, H's trial exceeded its estimate and was not likely to finish until after the weekend. The judge explained the position to the jury, one of whom indicated that she was due to go on holiday that weekend. After a short discussion with counsel, during which defence counsel raised no express objection, the judge discharged the juror in reliance on s. 16.

D13.54 On appeal, Lawton LJ held (p. 927D–H) that the extent of the jurisdiction to discharge a juror is a matter of common law, since s. 16 does not confer the power but merely sets out the consequences of exercising it. At common law a jury could be discharged 'in cases of evident necessity' (*Blackstone's Commentaries*, 1857 edn, and see also Erle CJ's judgment in *Winsor v R* (1866) LR 1 QB 390, where he refers (at p. 394) to 'a high degree of need...such as...might be denoted by the word necessity'). At that time and until 1925, if one juror had to be discharged then so had the whole jury (i.e. there was no power to continue with a reduced jury). Therefore, the present test for jurisdiction to discharge a juror must be the same as the old test for discharging the whole jury, namely, has an evident necessity for it arisen?

Although no specific guidance is given as to what may constitute an 'evident necessity', CPD VI, paras. 39H.1 to 39H.3 (see Supplement, **PD-56**), address the discharge of a juror for personal reasons, and the test set out at para. 39H.2 is that 'the judge must exercise his or her discretion according to the interests of justice and the requirements of each individual case'. It would seem to be a fairly elastic concept and is certainly not limited to illness or other cause making it literally impossible for the juror to continue to act.

Trial by jury depends on the willing co-operation of the public, and 'if the administration of justice can be carried on without inconveniencing jurors unduly it should be' (see *Winsor*, at p. 930C–G). Therefore, in the circumstances that had arisen in *Winsor*, the judge both had jurisdiction to discharge the juror and could not be criticised for the way he exercised his discretion. **D13.55**

In *S* [2009] EWCA Crim 104 the Court of Appeal described the test for discharge of a juror where there was potential for prejudice as being whether the presence of that juror might deprive the accused of a fair jury deliberation (see also *F* [2009] EWCA Crim 805).

Discharge for Misconduct Misconduct by a juror often necessitates discharge of the whole jury, however, it should be borne in mind that, depending on the precise circumstances, the judge might be able to deal with the problem by discharging only the juror guilty of the misconduct. **D13.56** See **D13.65** for fuller consideration of misconduct on the part of a juror.

Discharge of the Entire Jury

The judge has a discretion to discharge the whole jury from giving a verdict. If he does so, the accused is not acquitted but may be retried on the same indictment before a fresh jury (*Winsor v R* (1866) LR 1 QB 390). According to *Blackstone's Commentaries* (1857 edn), a jury should not be discharged unless an 'evident necessity' for it has arisen. In *Winsor v R*, Erle CJ gave some further limited guidance on the subject, which may be summarised as follows:

(a) a jury should not be discharged unless a high degree of need for it arises;
(b) whether to discharge is purely a matter for the judge's discretion; and
(c) if he exercises his discretion wrongly by discharging the jury when he ought not to have done so, the appellate courts are powerless to correct the error (the extent of appellate review of the discharge of a jury, or the refusal to accede to an application for discharge, is addressed at **D13.71**).

These points must be read subject to the authorities set out at **D13.57** and **D13.65** which identify the proper approach of the court to possible bias or prejudice by a juror or jury and to **D13.57** alleged misconduct on the part of jurors.

The Test for Bias or Prejudice

In *Sander v UK* [2000] Crim LR 767, the ECtHR emphasised the need for any allegation of bias to be looked at from an objective, as well as a subjective, standpoint. The question, in other words, is not only whether the jury which tried the accused can be shown to be biased, but also whether 'there were sufficient guarantees to exclude any objectively justified or legitimate doubts as to the impartiality of the court'.

S, a British national of Asian origin, had been tried in the Crown Court for conspiracy to defraud. During the trial, the judge received a note from a juror referring to racist remarks and jokes by other jurors. The judge directed the jury to disregard their prejudices and try the case solely on the evidence. The judge subsequently received a letter from the jury refuting the allegation of racial bias, and a letter from another juror apologising for making jokes and denying racial bias. The judge decided not to discharge the jury and S was found guilty. The appeal was dismissed by the Court of Appeal.

The ECtHR held that the allegations contained in the note were capable of causing objective **D13.58** legitimate doubts about the impartiality of the court, and these doubts were not dispelled by the jury's letter or the judge's directions. Article 6(1) of the ECHR had been violated. (See also *Montgomery v HM Advocate* [2001] 2 WLR 779.)

D

Part D Procedure

In *Porter v Magill* [2002] 2 AC 357, the House of Lords considered the question of bias in relation to the courts generally, and approved the test derived from *Re Medicaments and Related Classes of Goods (No. 2)* [2001] 1 WLR 700: would a fair-minded and informed observer conclude that there was a real possibility, or real danger (the two being the same) that the tribunal was biased (see **D3.33**).

This test, which is in accordance with that adopted by the ECtHR in *Sander*, was applied by the Court of Appeal in *Poole* [2002] 1 WLR 1528, *Brown* [2002] Crim LR 409 and *Mason* [2002] 2 Cr App R 628. In *Szypusz v UK* [2010] ECHR 1323 the ECtHR said that the impartiality of a jury must be subjectively and objectively beyond doubt. In some cases where an issue arose this could only be achieved by discharge, in others lesser safeguards might achieve the same objective.

In *Abdroikov* [2007] 1 All ER 315, it was held that a fair-minded and informed observer, in determining whether there was a real possibility of bias on the part of a juror, would draw a distinction between the unconscious bias to which any member of the public might be subject and a specific bias that would result from a particular juror being professionally committed to one party to the proceedings, or from having special knowledge either of individuals involved in the case or as to the facts of the case apart from those provided by the evidence (see also **D13.27**). In *Khan* [2008] 3 All ER 502, the Court of Appeal drew a distinction between partiality to a party and partiality to a witness. This distinction was approved and applied in *Cornwall* [2009] EWCA Crim 2458 and *A-G of Cayman Islands v Tibbetts* [2010] 3 All ER 95.

If an issue arises as to whether a member of the jury has knowledge which makes him unsuitable to sit on that jury, the test in *Porter v Magill* has to be applied in order to determine whether or not the requirements of fairness have been met and, in making that determination, there is no need to distinguish between the position under Article 6 and the position at common law (see *Burcombe* [2010] EWCA Crim 2818 and *LL* [2011] 1 Cr App R 338 as examples of the application of that test).

In *Hewgill* [2011] EWCA Crim 1778 the Court of Appeal applied the test for bias set out in *Re Medicaments* where there was evidence that an accused on bail had spoken to jurors during a luncheon adjournment. The Court concluded that, whilst undesirable, that would not have made a material difference to the jury's deliberations, and a fair-minded, independent and informed observer would conclude that the jury would have been able to reach their verdict without taking any such conversation into account. This approach was then followed in *Mears* [2011] EWCA Crim 2651, where the Court concluded that the independent observer could
D13.59 not come to such a view where a juror had been in contact with her fiancé, sitting in the public gallery, during the trial and thus aware of those aspects of the proceedings that took place in the absence of the jury. See also *Ahmed* [2014] EWCA Crim 619.

Grounds for Discharge

The decided cases deal with four main situations in which the question arises of the discharge of a jury, or in certain circumstances one juror. These are:

(a) when the jury cannot agree on their verdict (as discussed at **D19.84** *et seq.*);
(b) when they may have been inadvertently prejudiced against the accused;
(c) when one or more of their number has misconducted themselves; and
D13.60 (d) when they acquire or possess personal knowledge of the accused or his bad character.

D13.61 In addition, there is the related situation in which an application may be made for the discharge of the jury when the misconduct in question is that of the accused himself.

Accidental Prejudice

The way in which this most commonly arises is if a witness refers to the accused's bad character during a trial where character has not been put in issue.

The Principle   The leading authority is *Weaver* [1968] 1 QB 353, in which it was held that whether or not to discharge the jury is for the judge's discretion. Although it had been said in *Palmer* (1935) 25 Cr App R 97 that, once a jury was wrongly allowed to hear evidence of a previous conviction, it was very difficult for them to dismiss that evidence from their minds, that case should not now be treated as establishing a general rule that they must inevitably be discharged. How the judge should act will depend on the facts of the particular case, and the court 'will not lightly interfere with' what he does (see Sachs LJ's judgment in *Weaver* [1968] 1 QB 353 at p. 359G).

In *Weaver*, the accused's previous convictions were revealed during incautious cross-examination of the police officer who had interviewed him. Approving the judge's refusal to discharge and dismissing W's appeal against conviction, Sachs LJ said that every decision turned on its own facts and depended especially on 'the nature of what has been admitted into evidence, the circumstances in which it has been admitted and what, in the light of the circumstances of the case as a whole, is the correct course' (p. 360B). The factors which particularly weighed against discharge were (a) that defence counsel had himself been responsible for inviting the answers which he then complained of, and (b) the degree of prejudice had been minimised by the judge's **D13.62** wise summing-up.

Weaver may be contrasted with *Blackford* (1989) 89 Cr App R 239, in which the appellant was convicted of possessing cannabis with intent to supply after a police officer in cross-examination had gratuitously revealed that he had a previous conviction for a similar offence. The Court of Appeal concluded that this had been 'a deliberate attempt by the police to queer the appellant's pitch'. In those circumstances, the trial judge should have discharged the jury and ordered a retrial.

Revelation by a Co-accused   Should an improper indication that one accused may be of bad character come from his co-accused, the Court of Appeal will be particularly loath to interfere with the trial judge's exercise of discretion against discharging the jury. In *Sutton* (1969) 53 Cr App R 504, Fenton Atkinson LJ (giving the Court of Appeal's judgment) said (at pp. 512–3):

> We have considered this matter with some anxiety, but … in all the circumstances of this case the judge was justified in exercising his discretion in the manner in which he did, and we would certainly be slow to lay down as a general rule that where one co-defendant says something of this nature about his co-accused, a judge must automatically allow a fresh trial, because it would simply make it too easy if a trial is not going well for one co-accused to say something which would secure his co-accused the advantages, if they are advantages, of a new trial …. there was an exercise of discretion by the trial judge, and the court is always slow to interfere with such an exercise of discretion. **D13.63**

Similarly, the fact that one accused changes his plea during a trial does not necessarily require the discharge of the jury continuing to try his co-accused (*Sookram* [2011] UKPC 5).

Dealing with Prejudicial Revelation   Where the accused is represented by counsel and prejudicial matters are accidentally disclosed, it would seem that counsel must take the initiative and apply at trial for the jury to be discharged. If he fails to do so, any appeal is liable to be dismissed, even if the circumstances were such that, had an application for discharge been made, it would probably have been granted (*Wattam* [1942] 1 All ER 178). **D13.64**

It is different if the accused is unrepresented. Should circumstances then arise in which an application for discharge might succeed, the judge is under a duty so to inform the accused. Failure to do so will be a material irregularity in the course of the trial necessitating the quashing of any conviction (*Featherstone* [1942] 2 All ER 672). However, provided the accused is invited to consider applying for discharge, no complaint may be made if the judge, in the proper exercise of his discretion, then decides to rule against the application (*Featherstone*).

Other Forms of Accidental Prejudice   Other cases illustrate the same principle, namely that it is proper for a judge to exercise his discretion to discharge the jury when they inadvertently learn something to the accused's potential detriment. For example:

(a) Discovery that the accused faces further charges:
   (i) In *Dubarry* (1977) 64 Cr App R 7, while a jury trying D on one charge were considering their verdict, at least one member of the jury probably saw D being tried on another charge. The Court of Appeal held that the jury should have been discharged.
   (ii) In *Hutton* [1990] Crim LR 875, H was tried on charges of deception and obtaining credit whilst an undischarged bankrupt. Further trials were pending, so an order was made under the Contempt of Court Act 1981, s. 4(2), banning publication of the proceedings. Instead of a notice being pinned to the door, a copy of the order was attached, which published the fact that he faced further trials and which a juror was seen to read. The Court of Appeal held that as the juror who read the order might well have discussed it with his fellow jurors, potential prejudice resulted directly from the irregularity.
   (iii) In *Wilson* (1995) *The Times*, 24 February 1995, the Court of Appeal held that there was a real danger of bias where one of the jurors was the wife of a prison officer at the prison where the accused were held on remand.
(b) Where matters are heard during the trial which, albeit not evidence against the accused, cannot be ignored by the jury:
   (i) In *Fedrick* [1990] Crim LR 403, F's co-accused, S, changed his plea to guilty during the course of the trial. The prosecution had opened the case on the basis that F and S were 'in cahoots'. The judge emphasised to the jury that S's plea of guilty made no difference to F's position both at the time and in his summing-up. The Court of Appeal held that the jury could not properly consider F's case in isolation from S's. They should therefore have been discharged and a fresh trial held.
   (ii) In *Boyes* [1991] Crim LR 717, as the judge concluded his summing-up on charges of rape and indecent assault, the complainant's mother shouted from the public gallery, 'When is it going to come out about the other five girls he has attacked?' The judge told the jury not to pay any attention to the outburst. The Court of Appeal criticised the judge's failure to inquire of the jury whether they had heard the outburst. If they had, one could hardly think of more damaging and prejudicial evidence being taken to the jury room. It was only after such inquiry, with the help of counsel and a very careful contemplation by the judge, that he could decide what to do. He should have considered a fresh trial. His failure to do so was a serious irregularity.
   (iii) In *Maguire* [1997] 1 Cr App R 61, the judge told a defence witness who had refused to answer certain questions that he was to be arrested for contempt of court and would be dealt with at the end of the day. Defence counsel made an application to the judge to discharge the jury on the basis that M had been severely prejudiced. The judge refused, and directed the jury in due course that the arrest of the witness was not to affect their approach to the evidence, had nothing to do with M, and was to be ignored. The Court of Appeal held that the judge should have dealt with the witness in the absence of the jury; the direction given to the jury was not an adequate remedy as it could not have dispelled the inevitable prejudice which had been created.
   (iv) In *Brown* [2006] 2 Cr App R (S) 699, the Court of Appeal held that an assessment of the consequences of the jury hearing inadmissible material, whether by oversight or deliberate deployment, did not start with the presumption that the jury would be discharged. The same approach was taken in *Lawson* [2007] 1 Cr App R 277. See *Mitcham v R* [2009] UKPC 5 for the proper approach to the jury hearing inadmissible material.
   (v) Similarly, in *Tufail* [2006] EWCA Crim 2879, where the judge had inadvertently disclosed matters to the jury during his summing-up that had not been adduced during the trial, the Court of Appeal held that the factors to be considered in deciding whether

this necessitated the discharge of the jury were (a) the nature of the judge's actions to cure the slip, (b) the strength of the case against the accused, and (c) the degree to which the jury were or may have been influenced by it.

(c) Where publicity or comment on issues relating to the accused's case are reported at a time when they may have an effect on the jury. For example, in *McCann* (1991) 92 Cr App R 239, M and others were tried for conspiracy to murder Mr King, who was then Secretary of State for Northern Ireland, and others. They elected not to give evidence. During the closing stages of the trial, the Home Secretary announced in the House of Commons the government's intention of changing the law on the right to silence. That night, in televised interviews, Mr King himself and Lord Denning expressed in strong terms their view that in terrorist cases a failure to answer questions or give evidence was tantamount to guilt. Although the Court of Appeal afforded great weight to the trial judge's exercise of discretion, its powers to review were not confined to cases or error of principle or lack of material upon which the judge could properly have arrived at his decision. If necessary, it must examine anew the relevant facts and circumstances, and exercise a discretion by way of review if it considered that the failure to discharge the jury might have resulted in injustice. In this case there was a real risk that the jury had been influenced by the statements and the only way in which justice could be done and be seen to be done was by discharging the jury and ordering a retrial.

(d) Where there has been a material change in circumstances to the detriment of the accused which cannot otherwise be rectified:

(i) In *Ricketts* [1991] Crim LR 915, the trial judge gave leave for the statement of S to be read, on the basis that S's absence was caused by fear. After the jury had retired, S arrived, and the judge saw him in chambers, without informing counsel. Apparently S denied that he had failed to appear because he was frightened. The judge told S that his evidence had been read and was not in dispute and that he was free to go. The judge gave no indication to counsel that S had denied staying away through fear. R was convicted and appealed. The Court of Appeal held that S's evidence had been given prominence on a false basis, i.e. that it was so damning that R or someone on his behalf would seek violent revenge if he testified. In those circumstances, an application to discharge the jury could not properly have been resisted.

(ii) In *Robson* [1992] Crim LR 655, the trial judge decided to direct the jury on a different basis to that on which the parties had presented the evidence. The Court of Appeal found that the fresh issue raised by the judge did not merely introduce a new interpretation of the evidence. It opened up the possibility of conviction on a different factual basis from that put forward by the Crown, and one which had not been fully explored. That resulted in unfairness to the defence, and was a material irregularity. The best course would have been to discharge the jury.   **D13.65**

Misconduct by a Juror

The judge in his discretion may allow the jury to separate (Juries Act 1974, s. 13). It is standard practice to allow them to separate both for luncheon and overnight adjournments. The discretion of the judge to allow the jury to separate was extended by the CJPO 1994, s. 43, which allows the judge to permit separation even after the jury have retired to consider their verdict.

Inevitably the jury will have the opportunity to speak about the case with those who are not of their number. However, they should be warned on the first occasion they separate that that is something they must not do (see the guidance in the *Crown Court Bench Book Companion* and *A-G v Davey* [2014] 1 Cr App R 1 (1)). In *Prime* (1973) 57 Cr App R 632, Lord Widgery CJ said (at p. 637):   **D13.66**

> It is important in all criminal cases that the judge should on the first occasion when the jury separate warn them not to talk about the case to anybody who is not one of their number. If he does that and brings that home to them, then it is to be assumed that they will follow the warning and only

if it can be shown that they have misbehaved themselves does the opportunity of an application [for discharge] arise.

Most cases coming before the Court of Appeal on discharge of the jury due to misconduct concern allegations that, in defiance of the warning, one or more jurors spoke to prosecution witnesses or members of the public about the case. For example:

(a) In *Davis* [2001] 1 Cr App R 115, the foreman of the jury was found to have visited the scene of the crime during the trial, and the Court of Appeal held that this was a serious material irregularity.

(b) In *Karakaya* [2005] 2 Cr App R 77, the Court of Appeal stated that a juror should not conduct private research for material that might have a bearing on the trial. If such material were obtained or privately used, two fundamental linked rules were violated: the first was of open justice, and the second was that the prosecution and defence were entitled to a fair opportunity to address all material considered by the jury when reaching their verdict.

D13.67

(c) In *Marshall* [2007] EWCA Crim 35, the Court of Appeal recommended that the judge should warn the jury, at the outset of the trial, that they must try the case on the evidence that they heard in court and on nothing else, which meant that they should not conduct their own private research, e.g., using the internet.

See also *Thompson* [2011] 2 All ER 83, *A-G v Dallas* [2012] 1 WLR 991 and CPD VI, paras. 39M.2 to 39M.4 (see Supplement, PD-60).

Juror's Personal Knowledge of a Witness, the Accused or of the Accused's Bad Character

A further situation in which the judge will have to consider discharge either of the whole jury or of an individual juror is when it comes to light that a juror knows either the accused or a witness in the case. The problem is particularly acute where the juror may know the accused to be of bad character. The following propositions summarise the Court of Appeal's decisions relating to a juror's possible bias on account of his knowledge of the accused's character.

(a) A juror who knows the accused or who knows from hearsay of the accused's bad character ought not to sit on the jury, and should ask to be excused from service. Failure to disqualify himself on account of his knowledge of the accused is 'quite improper' (per Lord Parker CJ in *Box* [1964] 1 QB 430 at p. 435, for which see **D13.49**). Depending on the facts of the particular case, previous contact with a witness may not disqualify the juror, but in reality if the juror has any previous acquaintance with the accused, however slight, it is safer for him to be removed.

(b) If the defence are aware at the time the jury is empanelled that a juror is open to objection for the reasons stated in (a) they should obviously challenge for cause or (more simply) ask prosecuting counsel to stand the juror by. Although the Court of Appeal has stated that a juror is not automatically disqualified by knowledge of the accused's previous convictions (see per Lord Parker CJ in *Box*), those statements are in the context of cases where the relevant facts were not known to the defence until after the time for challenging had passed. They do not, it is submitted, cast doubt on the fundamental proposition that a person who knows facts detrimental to the accused should not be on the jury.

(c) Where a juror's possible knowledge of the accused is not brought to the court's attention until after the trial has commenced, the judge will have to consider discharging the individual juror and/or the entire jury. For example, in *Hood* [1968] 2 All ER 56, defence counsel informed the judge that H's wife, who had just given evidence for the defence, had recognised a jury member as a person who lived in the same road as her mother and would consequently know about her husband's previous convictions.

The Court of Appeal confirmed that (a) a juror is not automatically disqualified by knowledge of the accused's previous convictions, and (b) that the Court of Appeal will not inquire into what occurred in the jury room. Moreover, the judge was right not to address questions to the juror himself about the allegations but should have heard evidence from the wife.

D13.68

(d) If a juror's knowledge of or bias against the accused does not come to the defence's attention until after conviction, an appeal is most unlikely to succeed since the appellant will have to show that the juror had made up his mind before the trial started to convict the accused regardless of the evidence (*Box* [1964] 1 QB 430).

Misconduct of the Accused

In more recent times, the Court of Appeal has made clear that action by the accused, albeit that it may serve to prejudice the jury against him, will not, of itself, form the basis for the discharge of the jury. For example, in *Russell* [2006] EWCA Crim 470, the Court of Appeal considered whether misconduct by the accused during the course of the trial might result in the discharge of the jury. The accused, who was being tried for attempted murder, leapt from the dock and attacked the judge. Once the incident was over, the defence advocate asked the judge to discharge the jury on the basis that they had witnessed the attack and could no longer try the accused impartially. The judge refused to do so. The Court of Appeal dismissed the appeal. The accused's conduct was manipulative and intended to abort the trial. To continue with the trial was neither unfair, nor capable of being seen to be unfair.

D13.69

Investigation of Misconduct

Prior to deciding on the course of action which he will adopt in relation to alleged bias or misconduct, the judge will usually need to question one or more individual jurors, or the entire jury. Guidance is now provided by CPD VI, paras. 39M.5 to 39M.18 (see Supplement, **PD-60**).

In *Blackwell* [1995] 2 Cr App R 625, the Court of Appeal emphasised that the judge has a duty to investigate if there is any realistic suspicion that any juror has been approached or pressured or otherwise tampered with. Such investigation will probably include questioning of individual jurors or even the jury as a whole. Questioning must be directed to the possibility that the jury's independence has been compromised, rather than to their deliberations on the issues in the case (see also *Oke* [1997] Crim LR 898 and *Appiah* [1998] Crim LR 134, and the standard direction on the need to preserve the privacy of the jury room).

In *Orgles* [1994] 4 All ER 533, the point at issue was whether the recorder at trial had acted correctly in questioning individual jurors, who had complained of dissension in the jury room. The Court of Appeal held that the procedure adopted by the recorder of initially questioning the two jurors separately was wrong and amounted to an irregularity. The circumstances giving rise to an inference that an individual juror or jurors could not fulfil his duties normally arose externally. It was usual in that situation to question the individual juror in open court so that the trial judge might make inquiries without jeopardising the continued participation of the whole jury.

D13.70

Occasionally, however, the circumstances were internal to the jury, whether through individual characteristics or through interaction with fellow jury members. In the latter circumstances, the problem was not the capacity of one or more individuals to carry out their duties, but the capacity of the jury as a whole. The appropriate course therefore was for the jury as a whole to be asked in open court as to their capacity to continue with the trial. Thereafter, it would then be a matter for the judge's exercise of discretion as to whether he made no order, discharged the whole jury or discharged individual jurors up to three in number. See also *Farooq* [1995] Crim LR 169.

Consultation of the Parties   After making such inquiries as are appropriate, it is submitted that the judge should, as a matter of good practice, ask the parties for their views before discharging a juror. However, discharge is not dependent on their consent (see **D13.52**) and it is not absolutely essential even to consult them (see *Richardson* [1979] 3 All ER 247, where the court received a telephone message from a juror that her husband had died during an overnight adjournment and the judge discharged her without any consultation with counsel; the conviction was nonetheless upheld).

In *Bryan* [2002] Crim LR 240, members of the jury were overheard discussing the case on a bus, and referring to one elderly juror who had considered the accused guilty throughout the trial. The judge decided not to discharge the jury, but told them that the discussion was scandalous and a possible contempt of court, and directed them to return verdicts based on the evidence, and not on prejudice. The Court of Appeal suggested the following steps should be taken where there was a major crisis of that sort:

D13.71

(a) the judge should organise a pause for consideration — the jury could be told to cease deliberating and to await the ruling of the court as to when they would be asked to continue their deliberations;

(b) counsel and the judge should then adjourn for half-an-hour or so to allow proper consideration of the steps to take;

(c) the judge should then hear submissions from counsel, and, if necessary, rise to consider what to do.

In the circumstances arising in *Bryan*, it had been wrong to suggest that there was a possibility of contempt proceedings, since the jurors in question might have felt under threat. In the event, however, the jury had not been prevented from considering the case properly, and their verdicts were safe. See now also CPD VI, paras.39M.7 to 39M.11 (see Supplement, **PD-60**).

Appellate Review of the Exercise of the Discretion to Discharge

In *Winsor v R* (1866) LR 1 QB 390, it was made clear that the decision whether or not to discharge is purely a matter for the judge's discretion; and if he exercises his discretion wrongly by discharging the jury when he ought not to have done so, the appellate courts are powerless to correct the error.

In *Hambery* [1977] QB 924, Lawton LJ reviewed the earlier authorities (especially *Winsor v R*), and concluded that the view that discharge was solely a matter for the trial judge should be understood as referring only to discharge of the entire jury (pp. 928F–929E). A decision to discharge one juror and continue with the remainder is a matter that may be raised on appeal. If the judge acted capriciously, that would be a material irregularity in the course of the trial which could lead to the quashing of any conviction (p. 929F).

D13.72

However, that the decision to discharge the jury is unlikely to be interfered with on appeal was confirmed in *Gorman* [1987] 2 All ER 435. G, who was convicted at a retrial following the jury at his first trial being discharged, appealed on the ground that a note from the first jury to the judge was to the effect that they were deadlocked, with a split 9–3 in favour of acquittal. The judge simply told counsel that the jury were split and would be incapable of reaching a verdict, without revealing the numbers, and, with counsels' agreement, the jury were discharged. After G's conviction at the retrial, the defence discovered by chance the proportions in which the first jury had been split and argued on appeal that the judge had exercised his discretion to discharge the jury improperly. The Court of Appeal concluded that the law remained as stated in *Winsor v R*, namely that, if the first jury had as a matter of fact been discharged, a court hearing an appeal against the second jury's verdict had no power to review the propriety or otherwise of the discharge.

The position is different should the judge be invited to discharge the jury and refuse to do so. If the accused is then convicted, he may appeal on the basis that continuing with the original jury casts doubt on the safety of his conviction. Such cases have given rise to a considerable amount of authority on when judges ought to discharge juries, although, as it is a matter for discretion, the appellate court is unlikely to interfere save in extreme cases.

Risk of Contamination In *Barraclough* [2000] Crim LR 324, the jury were discharged because they had come to know, as a result of the evidence, of the fact that the accused had previous convictions, in circumstances in which that information should not have been revealed. The judge discharged the jury, who were in their first week of jury service, and a new jury were empanelled on the following day. On appeal it was argued that the retrial should have been delayed until there was an entirely new panel of jurors or that the first jury should have been discharged from further service. The Court of Appeal dismissed the appeal, in view of the fact that the court centre in question was a large one, with a panel of jurors at any one time of over 200, and in the light of the clear warning delivered by the trial judge.

D13.73

As to the general issue of contamination and retrials, their lordships took the view that in smaller court centres, where there was a greater likelihood of jurors meeting, the court might have to consider discharging the first jury from further attendance or delaying the retrial for, say, a fortnight. In larger court centres, there should be no such problem. Defence counsel should in any event raise any concerns about contamination at the time that the first jury was discharged. If he did not, it would not ordinarily be open to an accused to raise the point on appeal.

ISSUES THAT MAY BE TRIED BY ONE JURY

Subject to the exceptions mentioned below, a jury may try only one issue, that is, once it has brought in a verdict on the issue for which it was empanelled, it must be split up with the individual jurors going back into the pool of jurors in waiting with a view to being selected by ballot for further juries.

The exceptional cases in which a jury may be kept together to try a second issue are: (a) where the trial of the second issue begins within 24 hours from the time when the jury was constituted, and (b) where the trial of an issue of unfitness to plead has been postponed until the end of the prosecution evidence and the judge directs that the jury empanelled to try the general issue shall also try unfitness (Juries Act 1974, s. 11(5)). Even where it is decided that a jury shall try a second issue, the court may order individual members of it to be replaced by others selected by ballot from the jury panel (s. 11(6)).

Juries Act 1974, s. 11

(4) Subject to subsection (5) below, the jury selected by any one ballot shall try only one issue (but any juror shall be liable to be selected on more than one ballot).
(5) Subsection (4) above shall not prevent—
   (a) the trial of two or more issues by the same jury if the trial of the second or last issue begins within 24 hours from the time when the jury is constituted, or
...
   (c) in a criminal case beginning with a special plea, the trial of the accused on the general issue by the jury trying the special plea.
(6) In the cases within subsection (5)(a) [and (b)] above the court may, on the trial of the second or any subsequent issue, instead of proceeding with the same jury in its entirety, order any juror to withdraw, if the court considers that he could be justly challenged or excused, or if the parties to the proceedings consent, and the juror to replace him shall ... be selected by ballot in open court.

D13.74

An important corollary of the rule that a jury may try only one issue is that, if an accused is charged in two or more separate indictments, there must be a separate trial for each indictment (*Crane v DPP* [1921] 2 AC 299), and, subject to s. 11(5)(a), a fresh jury must be empanelled for each trial. A purported trial by one jury of two indictments is a nullity (*Crane*) and that is so even if the parties consented to the course adopted (*Dennis* [1924] 1 KB 867).

D13.75

JUDGE-ONLY TRIALS ON INDICTMENT

D13.76 The CJA 2003, ss. 43 to 50, introduced for the first time in England and Wales the concept of trial on indictment without a jury. There were two different sets of circumstances: fraud trials and jury tampering. In addition, the DVCVA 2004, introduced judge-only trials in the case of sample counts.

Fraud Trials

The CJA 2003, s. 43, gave the prosecution the right to apply for a trial in the Crown Court to take place without a jury (i.e. in front of a judge sitting alone) in the case of serious or complex fraud. However, s. 43 was never brought into force and has been repealed by the Protection of Freedoms Act 2012, s. 113 and sch. 10, part 10, without any replacement provision.

Jury Tampering

Where there is a danger of jury tampering, the prosecution will be able to apply for the trial to be conducted without a jury. Further, where the jury has been discharged in the course of a trial because of jury tampering, the prosecution will be able to apply for it to continue without a jury. 'Jury tampering' is likely to include threatened or actual harm to, or intimidation or bribery of, a jury or any of its members, or their family or friends or property. For the prosecution's application to be granted in respect of a trial which has yet to take place, the court must be satisfied that two conditions are fulfilled:

(a) that there is evidence of a real and present danger that jury tampering would take place (CJA 2003, s. 44(4)); and

(b) that there is so substantial a risk of jury tampering that it is necessary in the interests of justice for the trial to be conducted without a jury, notwithstanding any steps (e.g., police protection) that might reasonably be taken to prevent the risk (s. 44(5)).

D13.77 In *T* [2009] 3 All ER 1002 the Court of Appeal considered these provisions, concluding that they were 'unequivocal and unambiguous'. If the conditions are met, the court has no alternative to a non-jury trial. The court has to be satisfied that the conditions are met to the criminal standard. The risk to be considered in s. 44(4) may arise at any stage of the trial process and, in weighing up the steps that might be taken to avoid a risk of tampering for the purposes of s. 44(5), the court may have regard to the cost and feasibility of the measures and their impact on the jury subjected to them (see also *S (K)* [2010] 1 All ER 1084). See also *JSM* [2011] 1 Cr App R 42 and *S (K) (No. 2)* [2011] 1 Cr App R 46. There is no requirement that the material on the basis of which the court exercises its powers under s. 44 has to be disclosed to the accused. Equally there is no requirement that the eventual trial judge should have to consider all of that material (*Twomey* [2011] 1 Cr App R 356).

D13.78 **The Court's Decision**   Where the trial is already under way and the judge is minded to discharge the jury in accordance with his common-law powers because jury tampering appears to have occurred, he must hear representations from the defence and the prosecution as to how he should proceed. In *T* [2009] 3 All ER 1002 the Court of Appeal concluded that it would be appropriate for a court to reach its decision in reliance on sensitive material not disclosed to the defence. If the judge decides to discharge the jury, he may order that the trial shall continue without a jury if he is satisfied that this would be fair to the defendant. Alternatively, he may terminate the trial, and has the option of ordering that the retrial is to take place without a jury. Again, he must be satisfied that the danger of jury tampering is such as to make trial without jury necessary in the interests of justice, notwithstanding any steps that could be taken to prevent jury **D13.79** tampering (s. 46(5)). In *T* the Court of Appeal stressed that the preferred option would be for the judge to continue to hear the case alone, rather than to order a retrial. If a retrial is ordered, it does not have to be heard before the original judge who made that order (see also *S (K)* [2010] 1

All ER 1084). In *Guthrie* [2011] 2 Cr App R 260, Lord Judge CJ emphasised that the jurisdiction under s. 46 adds to, but does not replace, the court's existing powers to deal with jury difficulties.

Right of Appeal   There is a right of appeal to the Court of Appeal by both the defence and the prosecution against any decision made by the court at a preparatory hearing on any application for a trial without a jury (s. 45(5)). There is also a right of appeal against any order to continue a trial in the absence of a jury, or for a retrial to be conducted in the absence of a jury (s. 47).

Application   Where a court orders a trial to be conducted or continued without a jury, the trial will proceed in the usual way, except that functions which a jury would have performed will be performed by the judge alone. If the accused is convicted, the judge will have to give reasons for the conviction (s. 48).

Criminal Justice Act 2003, ss. 44 to 48

44.—(1) This section applies where one or more defendants are to be tried on indictment for one or more offences.

(2) The prosecution may apply to a judge of the Crown Court for the trial to be conducted without a jury.

(3) If an application under subsection (2) is made and the judge is satisfied that both of the following two conditions are fulfilled, he must make an order that the trial is to be conducted without a jury; but if he is not so satisfied he must refuse the application.

(4) The first condition is that there is evidence of a real and present danger that jury tampering would take place.

(5) The second condition is that, notwithstanding any steps (including the provision of police protection) which might reasonably be taken to prevent jury tampering, the likelihood that it would take place would be so substantial as to make it necessary in the interests of justice for the trial to be conducted without a jury.

(6) The following are examples of cases where there may be evidence of a real and present danger that jury tampering would take place—

  (a) a case where the trial is a retrial and the jury in the previous trial was discharged because jury tampering had taken place,

  (b) a case where jury tampering has taken place in previous criminal proceedings involving the defendant or any of the defendants,

  (c) a case where there has been intimidation, or attempted intimidation, of any person who is likely to be a witness in the trial.

45.—(1) This section applies—

  (a) [Repealed]

  (b) to an application under section 44.

(2) An application to which this section applies must be determined at a preparatory hearing (within the meaning of the 1987 Act or Part 3 of the 1996 Act).

(3) The parties to a preparatory hearing at which an application to which this section applies is to be determined must be given an opportunity to make representations with respect to the application.

(4) In section 7(1) of the 1987 Act (which sets out the purposes of preparatory hearings) for paragraphs (a) to (c) there is substituted—

  '(a) identifying issues which are likely to be material to the determinations and findings which are likely to be required during the trial,

  (b) if there is to be a jury, assisting their comprehension of those issues and expediting the proceedings before them,

  (c) determining an application to which section 45 of the Criminal Justice Act 2003 applies,'.

...

(10) In this section—

'the 1987 Act' means the Criminal Justice Act 1987,

'the 1996 Act' means the Criminal Procedure and Investigations Act 1996.

46.—(1) This section applies where—

  (a) a judge is minded during a trial on indictment to discharge the jury, and

  (b) he is so minded because jury tampering appears to have taken place.

(2) Before taking any steps to discharge the jury, the judge must—

    (a) inform the parties that he is minded to discharge the jury,

    (b) inform the parties of the grounds on which he is so minded, and

    (c) allow the parties an opportunity to make representations.

(3) Where the judge, after considering any such representations, discharges the jury, he may make an order that the trial is to continue without a jury if, but only if, he is satisfied—

    (a) that jury tampering has taken place, and

    (b) that to continue the trial without a jury would be fair to the defendant or defendants;

    but this is subject to subsection (4).

(4) If the judge considers that it is necessary in the interests of justice for the trial to be terminated, he must terminate the trial.

(5) Where the judge terminates the trial under subsection (4), he may make an order that any new trial which is to take place must be conducted without a jury if he is satisfied in respect of the new trial that both of the conditions set out in section 44 are likely to be fulfilled.

(6) Subsection (5) is without prejudice to any other power that the judge may have on terminating the trial.

(7) Subject to subsection (5), nothing in this section affects the application of section 44 in relation to any new trial which takes place following the termination of the trial.

47.—(1) An appeal shall lie to the Court of Appeal from an order under section 46(3) or (5).

(2) Such an appeal may be brought only with the leave of the judge or the Court of Appeal.

(3) An order from which an appeal under this section lies is not to take effect—

    (a) before the expiration of the period for bringing an appeal under this section, or

    (b) if such an appeal is brought, before the appeal is finally disposed of or abandoned.

(4) On the termination of the hearing of an appeal under this section, the Court of Appeal may confirm or revoke the order.

(5) Subject to rules of court made under section 53(1) of the Senior Courts Act 1981 (power by rules to distribute business of Court of Appeal between its civil and criminal divisions)—

    (a) the jurisdiction of the Court of Appeal under this section is to be exercised by the criminal division of that court, and

    (b) references in this section to the Court of Appeal are to be construed as references to that division.

48.—(1) The effect of an order under section 44 or 46(5) is that the trial to which the order relates is to be conducted—

    (a) without a jury, and

    (b) by a judge of the high Court exercising the jurisdiction of the Crown Court

(1A) The effect of an order under section 44 or 46(5) is that the trial to which the order relates is to be conducted without a jury.

(2) The effect of an order under section 46(3) is that the trial to which the order relates is to be continued without a jury.

(3) Where a trial is conducted or continued without a jury, the court is to have all the powers, authorities and jurisdiction which the court would have had if the trial had been conducted or continued with a jury (including power to determine any question and to make any finding which would be required to be determined or made by a jury).

(4) Except where the context otherwise requires, any reference in an enactment to a jury, the verdict of a jury or the finding of a jury is to be read, in relation to a trial conducted or continued without a jury, as a reference to the court, the verdict of the court or the finding of the court.

(5) Where a trial is conducted or continued without a jury and the court convicts a defendant—

    (a) the court must give a judgment which states the reasons for the conviction at, or as soon as reasonably practicable after, the time of the conviction, and

    (b) the reference in section 18(2) of the Criminal Appeal Act 1968 (notice of appeal or of application for leave to appeal to be given within 28 days from date of conviction etc.) to the date of the conviction is to be read as a reference to the date of the judgment mentioned in paragraph (a).

(6) Nothing in this Part affects—

    (a) the requirement under section 4 of the Criminal Procedure (Insanity) Act 1964 that a question of fitness to be tried be determined by a jury, or

    (b) the requirement under section 4A of that Act that any question, finding or verdict mentioned in that section be determined, made or returned by a jury.

D13.80

Sample Counts

A further avenue by which the prosecution can seek trial on indictment without a jury is opened up by the DVCVA 2004, s. 17. In essence, it is for the jury to try sample counts, with the remaining counts in the indictment capable of being tried by a judge sitting alone.

The application by the prosecution may be acceded to by the judge if the following conditions are fulfilled: **D13.81**

(a) that the number of counts in the indictment is such that a trial of them all by jury would be impracticable;

(b) that each count to be tried by the jury can be regarded as a sample of counts that could for their part be tried by a judge alone; and

(c) that it is in the interests of justice to grant the order sought.

The judge should have regard to any steps that might be taken to facilitate a jury trial, but not if that might result in the defendant receiving a lesser sentence.

Domestic Violence, Crime and Victims Act 2004, ss. 17 and 18

17.—(1) The prosecution may apply to a judge of the Crown Court for a trial on indictment to take place on the basis that the trial of some, but not all, of the counts included in the indictment may be conducted without a jury.

(2) If such an application is made and the judge is satisfied that the following three conditions are fulfilled, he may make an order for the trial to take place on the basis that the trial of some, but not all, of the counts included in the indictment may be conducted without a jury.

(3) The first condition is that the number of counts included in the indictment is likely to mean that a trial by jury involving all of those counts would be impracticable.

(4) The second condition is that, if an order under subsection (2) were made, each count or group of counts which would accordingly be tried with a jury can be regarded as a sample of counts which could accordingly be tried without a jury.

(5) The third condition is that it is in the interests of justice for an order under subsection (2) to be made.

(6) In deciding whether or not to make an order under subsection (2), the judge must have regard to any steps which might reasonably be taken to facilitate a trial by jury.

(7) But a step is not to be regarded as reasonable if it could lead to the possibility of a defendant in the trial receiving a lesser sentence than would be the case if that step were not taken.

(8) An order under subsection (2) must specify the counts which may be tried without a jury.

(9) For the purposes of this section and sections 18 to 20, a count may not be regarded as a sample of other counts unless the defendant in respect of each count is the same person.

18.—(1) An application under section 17 must be determined at a preparatory hearing.

(2) Section 7(1) of the 1987 Act and section 29(2) of the 1996 Act are to have effect as if the purposes there mentioned included the purpose of determining an application under section 17.

(3) Section 29(1) of the 1996 Act is to have effect as if the grounds on which a judge of the Crown Court may make an order under that provision included the ground that an application under section 17 has been made.

(4) The parties to a preparatory hearing at which an application under section 17 is to be determined must be given an opportunity to make representations with respect to the application.

(5) Section 9(11) of the 1987 Act and section 35(1) of the 1996 Act are to have effect as if they also provided for an appeal to the Court of Appeal to lie from the determination by a judge of an application under section 17.

(6) In this section—

'preparatory hearing' means a preparatory hearing within the meaning of the 1987 Act or Part 3 of the 1996 Act;

'the 1987 Act' means the Criminal Justice Act 1987;

'the 1996 Act' means the Criminal Procedure and Investigations Act 1996.

Section D14   Special Measures and Anonymity Orders

SPECIAL MEASURES FOR WITNESSES: GENERAL

Introduction

D14.1   Over recent decades there has been a sea-change in the courts' approach to child and other vulnerable witnesses such as those with physical or mental disabilities. The ethos now is that the orthodox procedures of the adversarial trial must be adapted to the needs of such witnesses, whether called by the prosecution or the defence (see *B* [2010] EWCA Crim 4 at [42] and CPD I, para. 3D.2 (see Supplement, **PD-6**)). The *Equal Treatment Bench Book 2013* emphasises that the Equality Act 2010 demands substantive equality for every person appearing in court to ensure their full participation, and that the court has safeguarding responsibilities in respect of children and vulnerable adults, often discharged through judicial discretion. The *Equal Treatment Bench Book's* comprehensive chapters on child, vulnerable and disabled witnesses are essential reading for advocates preparing any case involving such a witness.

Under the YJCEA 1999, s. 53(3) (see **F4.21** *et seq.*), all witnesses regardless of age (or disability) are presumed competent, and if that competence is put in issue, it need only be demonstrated that the witness can understand questions and give answers that can be understood, competence being 'witness, trial and issue specific' (*IA* [2013] EWCA Crim 1308 at [70]). This minimal competence test has resulted in many more young children and adults with mental disorders or severe impairments being witnesses in circumstances that would once have been unthinkable (see, e.g., *Watts* [2010] EWCA Crim 1824 and *F* [2013] 1 WLR 2143). The YJCEA 1999, ss. 16 to 30, are designed to modify the orthodox trial process for witnesses who are in fear, suffering from a physical or mental disability, or complainants of sexual offences, as well as witnesses aged under 18, so as to enable them to provide their best evidence. This section addresses the availability and use of special measures directions (SMDs) for child witnesses and vulnerable or intimidated adult witnesses. In general, the statutory regime of SMDs has been found to be compliant with the ECHR, Article 6; residual issues of compliance are noted below.

This section also considers witness anonymity orders made under the CAJA 2009 (see **D14.49** *et seq.*). For investigation anonymity orders, see **D1.197**.

The Court of Appeal has recently stressed that the overall responsibility of the court for the fairness of the trial has not been altered because of the wide range of special measures now available; trial judges are expected to deal with specific communication problems faced by any defendant or witness as part of their ordinary control of the judicial process (*Cox* [2012] 2 Cr App R 63 at [29]; *F* [2013] 1 WLR 2143). Thus, whilst the statutory regime is comprehensive in its application to non-defendant witnesses, it does not oust this residual inherent jurisdiction to make *ad hoc* modifications to the orthodox procedures for a particular non-eligible witness (e.g., as to screens and court dress), in the interests of justice (YJCEA 1999, s. 19(6)). This is the route to providing special measures for vulnerable defendants who are excluded from the statutory regime. However, that residual inherent jurisdiction has been viewed as limited, and the Court of Appeal has held that it does not extend to permitting a witness to testify by live link or by video-recorded interview in circumstances not covered by the YJCEA 1999 (*Ukpabio* [2008] 1 WLR 728; *H* [2003] EWCA Crim 1208).

D14.2   The litmus test of the special measures regime is to be found in s. 19(2), which requires the court to consider which measures will 'maximise the quality of the evidence'. For witnesses under 18, it is presumed that the test in s. 19(2) is satisfied by the playing of their recorded interviews with the police as their evidence in chief, and by cross-examination via video link (s. 21(2)). In certain circumstances this presumption can be displaced. In all other cases, s. 19(2) makes it clear that the measures should be tailored to the needs of the individual witness. The applicant should consider which SMDs, *if any*, would maximise the quality of the evidence *that particular witness* can give. The experience of those specialising in such cases is that the wording and spirit of s. 19(2) are widely ignored by police and prosecutors, who operate on assumptions that the presumptive measures must always be used, and so provide erroneous information to witnesses without evaluating their specific needs and preferences, and without considering early special measures strategy meetings. Conversely, sometimes witnesses are persuaded by prosecuting counsel to abandon measures which they need, such as the video link due to its perceived 'distancing effect'. This inflexibility of approach risks failing the witness as much as the position before SMDs were introduced. Such fears are also not borne out in a recent study of the effect of special measures on juror decision-making. (see L. Ellison and V.E. Munro, 'Do Special Measures Affect Jurors' Verdicts in Rape Cases?' (2013) 177 CL & J 103).

Range of Special Measures Available

The YJCEA 1999, part II, chapter I, ss. 16 to 33, as amended by the CAJA 2009, part 3, **D14.3** chapter 3 (ss. 98 to 104 and sch. 14, most of which came into force on 27 June 2011 by virtue of SI 2011 No. 1452) provide for a range of special measures which a court can direct in respect of vulnerable and intimidated witnesses. Additional measures to guarantee the anonymity of witnesses are in the CAJA 2009, part 3, chapter 2 (see **D14.60**), replacing the Criminal Evidence (Witness Anonymity) Act 2008. This package of measures is available in both the Crown Court and the magistrates' courts, including the youth court. Amendments providing access to intermediaries to child and vulnerable defendants (under the CAJA 2009, s. 104) have not yet been implemented, reportedly due to their resource implications.

The range of measures currently available is:

(a) *screening* the witness from the accused (YJCEA 1999, s. 23);
(b) giving evidence by *live link*, accompanied by a supporter (s. 24) (for other uses of live link, see **D15.97**);
(c) giving evidence in *private*, available for sex offence or human trafficking cases (included from 6 April 2013 by the Trafficking People for Exploitation Regulations 2013 (SI 2013 No. 554)) or where there is a fear that the witness may be intimidated (s. 25);
(d) ordering the *removal of wigs and gowns* while the witness gives evidence (s. 26);
(e) *video recording of evidence-in-chief* (s. 27);
(f) *video recording of cross-examination and re-examination* where the evidence in chief of the witness has already been video recorded (s. 28) (brought into force on a limited basis for pilot schemes; see **D14.46**);
(g) examination through an *intermediary* in the case of a young or incapacitated witness (s. 29);
(h) provision of *aids to communication* for a young or incapacitated witness (s. 30); and
(i) a *witness anonymity* order (CAJA 2009, part 3, chapter 2), which may be preceded by an *investigation anonymity* order applying to the police investigation and pre-trial procedures such as disclosure (part 3, chapter 1: see **D1.197**).

Practitioners should also bear in mind other protective procedures, such as: **D14.4**

- orders under the YJCEA 1999, s. 46, for restrictions on reporting and public access to protect a fearful or distressed adult witness's identity, where such an order is likely to improve the quality of that witness's testimony or cooperation (see **D3.140**);
- complainant anonymity in sex offence cases (Sexual Offences (Amendment) Act 1992, s. 1(1): see **D3.139**);
- the prohibition in the YJCEA 1999, ss. 34 to 38, on cross-examination by the accused in person of (i) child complainants of or witnesses to sexual offences, offences of violence,

cruelty, kidnapping, false imprisonment or abduction, and (ii) adult complainants in sexual offence cases (see **F7.2**); and
- the use of pre-trial depositions of children or young persons under the CYPA 1933, s. 43 (see **D14.46**).

Useful guidance can be found in *Achieving Best Evidence in Criminal Proceedings: Guidance on interviewing victims and witnesses, and guidance on using special measures* (March 2011), on the CPS and Ministry of Justice websites.

Eligibility Categories: General

D14.5   The measures apply with equal force to both prosecution and defence witnesses (YJCEA 1999, s. 19(1)). Different provisions apply in the case of an accused (see **D14.21**). The categories of eligibility are discussed in detail at **D14.13** *et seq*. In summary, they are:

- all witnesses under the age of 18 at the time of the hearing or video recording;
- vulnerable witnesses who are affected by a mental or physical impairment;
- witnesses in fear or distress about testifying;
- adult complainants of sexual offences, or offences under the Asylum and Immigration (Treatment of Claimants etc.) Act 2004, s. 4 (trafficking people for exploitation) (inserted by the Trafficking People for Exploitation Regulations 2013, with effect from 6 April 2013); and
- any witness in a case involving a 'relevant offence', currently defined to include homicide offences and other offences involving a firearm or knife.

For witnesses who are not automatically eligible (i.e. those affected by mental or physical impairment or in fear or distress about testifying), the court must determine whether the quality of the evidence would be diminished by the witness's condition (ss. 16(1)(b) and 17(1)), taking into account any views expressed by the witness (ss. 16(4) and 17(3)), before making a declaration of eligibility. Adult complainants of sexual offences (s. 17(4)) and witnesses in 'relevant offence' cases have an unqualified right to opt out of special measures (s. 17(5)). After the declaration of eligibility is made, the court must consider which special measures will maximise the quality of the witness's evidence; this is presumed to be the consequence of the 'primary rule' measures for all child witnesses (discussed at **D14.14**).

Testifying through an intermediary and aids to communication are not available for witnesses eligible only by reason of fear or intimidation.

Procedure relating to Special Measures Directions

D14.6   The ethos of active and effective case management (CrimPR, parts 3 and 9, and, especially, CPD I, para. 3A.13 (see Supplement, **PD-3**)) is crucial where young or vulnerable or intimidated witnesses are involved. An application for a SMD is required even for witnesses who are automatically eligible and entitled to a particular measure. If no application is made, a court can of its own motion raise whether a direction should be given (YJCEA 1999, s. 19(1)(b)).

Part 29 of the CrimPR (see Supplement, **R-216** *et seq*.) governs the procedure for applying for SMDs and witness anonymity orders in both the Crown Court and magistrates' courts. The procedure for applications for defendant's evidence directions is contained in rr. 29.14 to 29.17 (although rr. 29.3 to 29.7 also apply); the procedure is analogous to that described below but see also **D14.21**. The procedure on applications for witness anonymity orders (rr. 29.18 to 29.22) is dealt with at **D14.49** *et seq*.

D14.7   **Applications**   Applications must be in writing and made as soon as reasonably practicable, and in any event within 28 days after a not guilty plea is tendered in a magistrates' court, or 14 days after a not guilty plea is tendered in the Crown Court (CrimPR, r. 29.3: see Supplement, **R-218**). The time-limit applies to defence as well as to prosecution witnesses. Late applications must be accompanied by an explanation for the delay (r. 29.5); time-limits are expected to be respected and the parties must be fully prepared (CPD I, para. 3A.1: see Supplement, **PD-3**). Applications must not be made *ex parte* (r. 29.3(b)); if there is material which the applicant thinks ought not to be revealed to another party then the procedures for redaction in r. 29.12 must be followed.

Rule 29.10 requires the applicant for a SMD to:

(a)　explain the basis on which the witness is eligible for assistance;
(b)　explain (where the witness is not a child: r. 29.9) why special measures would be likely to improve the quality of his evidence;
(c)　set out the measure(s) sought;
(d)　report any views that the witness has expressed about the proposed measures; and
(e)　attach any other material relied upon, including any video-recorded evidence (r. 29.9(2)(c)).

An applicant seeking a hearing must explain why one is needed (r. 29.10(i)). In *Momodou (Practice Note)* [2005] 2 All ER 571 at [62], the Court of Appeal encouraged pre-trial arrangements to familiarise witnesses with the process of giving evidence and this is reflected in CPD I, para. 3G.2 (see Supplement, **PD-9**). For witnesses eligible for SMDs, it is strongly advisable that such visits take place *before* it is decided which SMD should be applied for, so that the witness and counsel can make an informed choice (see **D15.104**).

Opposed Applications　Any response opposing such an application, or variation or discharge **D14.8** of an order, must be in writing and served on all parties within 14 days of receipt of the application (CrimPR, r. 29.13); again material may be redacted under r. 29.12. Rule 29.13(4) requires that the respondent explain why issue is taken with:

(a)　the witness's eligibility for special measures; or
(b)　the effect of the proposed measure(s) on the quality of the evidence; or
(c)　their effect on the effective testing of that evidence.

The response should also indicate if an oral hearing is needed (r. 29.13(2)(c)).

The Ruling　If no opposition has been received within the prescribed time-limit, the court **D14.9** may decide the application without a hearing; opposed applications may be heard in public or private (CrimPR, r. 29.8). But the ruling granting, refusing, varying or discharging a SMD must be made at a hearing in public before the witness gives evidence (YJCEA 1999, s. 20(5); CrimPR, r. 29.4(2)). The decision may be taken in the absence of the applicant or any respondent who has had at least 14 days in which to make representations. The SMD has binding effect from the time it is made until the proceedings have been determined by a verdict, or abandoned, in relation to each accused (YJCEA 1999, s. 20(1)).

Procedure following the Ruling　The applicant is responsible for informing the witness of the **D14.10** court's decision as soon as reasonably practicable, and for explaining the arrangements which will be made (CrimPR, r. 29.4(1)).

Variation or Discharge of a Ruling　A party may apply in writing to discharge or vary a SMD, **D14.11** or to review a denial of a SMD, only if there has been a material change in circumstances since the order was granted (YJCEA 1999, s. 20(2)(a) and (3); CrimPR, r. 29.11), but the court may also so act of its own motion, without that constraint (usually after informal representations by a party). The SMD may be altered only if it is in the interests of justice to do so.

Jury Direction　Where a special measure has been used, the judge in a trial on indictment is **D14.12** required to give a warning to ensure that the measure does not prejudice the accused (YJCEA 1999, s. 32). The *Crown Court Bench Book* (3rd edn 2010 and 1st supp. Oct 2011) notes that the only adverse inference likely to occur to the jury is the possibility that the witness required protection from the accused or his associates. Important issues to be dealt with in the warning are: that special measures are now commonplace and are the way Parliament has decided such witnesses should give their evidence; that the use of special measures does not reflect on the accused or his case; and the importance of concentrating on the video-recorded evidence as it will not be repeated.

In *Brown* [2004] EWCA Crim 1620, the Court of Appeal made it clear that the judge is not required to repeat a special measures warning when summing-up if it was given when the witness gave evidence, when it was more likely to make an impression on the jury. An omission to give a direction altogether is not necessarily an error warranting quashing of a conviction (*R* [2010] EWCA Crim 2741).

It is inappropriate for counsel to undermine a SMD by suggesting to the jury that its use is relevant to weighing the witness's evidence (*Garland* [2008] EWCA Crim 3276).

ESTABLISHING ELIGIBILITY FOR SPECIAL MEASURES

Child Witnesses

D14.13   **Deemed Eligibility**   A child witness is defined as any person under the age of 18 at the time of the hearing or, if the witness has surpassed the maximum age by that date, who was under 18 when the video interview took place (YJCEA 1999, s. 22(1)(a)). As part of the implementation in England and Wales of Directive 2011/93/EU (replacing Counsel Framework Decision 2004/68/JHA) on combating the sexual abuse and exploitation of children and child pornography, the YJCEA 1999, s. 33(5) and (6), was amended by the Special Measures for Child Witnesses (Sexual Offences) Regulations 2013 (SI 2013 No. 2971) to extend the statutory presumption, that a complainant whose age is uncertain is under 18, so that it applies not only to human trafficking offences but also to sexual offences (as defined by the YJCEA 1999, s. 62), and offences under the Protection of Children Act 1978, s. 1, and the CJA 1988, s. 160 (both concerning indecent photographs of children).

It is vital to appreciate that all child witnesses are automatically eligible for special measures, including defence witnesses other than the child defendant, and so, subject to what is said at D14.15, it is generally not open to an opposing party to contend that a particular child does not need special procedures because they would not maximise the quality of his evidence. The House of Lords held in *Camberwell Green Youth Court, ex parte D* [2005] 1 All ER 999 that the deemed eligibility rule for child witnesses did not contravene the ECHR, Article 6.

Automatic eligibility does not mean that the child's specific needs must not be evaluated at the earliest opportunity in the investigation, using information from carers, teachers and others who know the child well. In complex cases and those involving very young children the police should seek early advice from the CPS, even before the *Achieving Best Evidence* interview is conducted, to consider whether an intermediary should evaluate the child's communication skills and to identify any possible issue about competence, and to identify topics to be covered to minimise the need for further interviews.

D14.14   **The 'primary rule'**   The 'primary rule' provides for the admission of any video interview and the use of live link for any non-video testimony. The regime previously included a category of children 'in need of special protection' (i.e. witnesses to charges of sexual or violent offences) for whom the primary rule was mandatory, but this rigidity created difficulties where the child preferred to testify in court. The CAJA 2009, s. 100, has abolished the special protection category whilst retaining the primary rule, but making it apply presumptively to *all* witnesses under 18, regardless of the nature of the offence charged.

D14.15   **Flexibility in Use of SMDs for Child Witnesses**   Following the implementation of the CAJA 2009, s. 100, the trial court now has greater flexibility in tailoring special measures to the needs of the individual child witness to facilitate his best evidence, and so this must now be the paramount consideration for the applicant. The court may disapply the primary rule where it is satisfied that compliance would be unlikely to maximise the quality of the child's evidence so far as practicable, in which case it should consider the other optional special measures (YJCEA 1999, s. 21(4)(c)). However, this flexibility carries a price, because this discretion implies that the admission of the video interview and live link can now be challenged for *every* child witness. Moreover, the subsistence of s. 21(2), deeming the primary rule measures to be likely to maximise the quality of the child's evidence, seems redundant since the court will already have decided this as an issue of fact in any case where the use of such measures has been challenged. Another reform introduced by the CAJA 2009, s. 100, enables the child to opt out of application of the primary rule in whole or in part (YJCEA 1999, s. 21(4)(ba)); the court must be satisfied that testifying in court would not diminish the quality of the child's evidence. The court must have regard to a non-exclusive set of factors. In practice the opt-out is most likely to be exercised regarding the live link (see **D14.38**).

Exactly what each measure entails should be explained and demonstrated to the witness and carers, ideally in a court visit which prosecuting counsel should consider attending if the witness has particular difficulties. If a visit is not possible in the limited time before an application has to be made, it may be necessary to apply to vary the measure already granted after the visit. In more complex cases, counsel should hold a special measures meeting with the witness, making full notes of the discussion for disclosure to the defence. Counsel calling the witness is responsible for communicating to the court at the PCMH the child's needs, such as the best time of day to schedule testimony, concentration span and other welfare concerns, and for checking that those circumstances have not changed by the trial. Consider also the use of an intermediary (see **D14.43**). No pressure to fit in with preconceived ideas of special measures (whether advantageous or disadvantageous) should be exerted on the witness.

If the child is giving evidence other than by way of the playing of a pre-recorded interview, the court must be alive to the needs of the witness and any difficulties the witness has (*Turner* [2013] 1 Cr App R 327 (25)). In *Turner*, the Court of Appeal approved the approach of the trial judge in circumstances where the witness was too embarrassed to vocalise what had happened to her; as there was no dispute that such sexual activity had taken place, that part of her statement was adduced under the CJA 2003, s. 114.

Adult Witnesses with Physical or Mental Impairment

The applicant for a declaration of eligibility under this category (YJCEA 1999, s. 16(2)) must **D14.16** provide the court with material establishing that the witness:

(a) is affected by a mental disorder within the meaning of the Mental Health Act 1983 (i.e. 'any disorder or disability of the mind' s. 1(2));
(b) otherwise has a significant impairment of intelligence and social functioning; or
(c) has a physical disability or is suffering from a physical disorder (not otherwise defined).

The *Equal Treatment Bench Book 2013* contains a useful glossary of physical and mental disabilities and illnesses.

The applicant must also satisfy the court that the quality of the evidence would be diminished by the witness's condition (s. 16(1)(b)). The court should also take into account, but is not bound by, the witness's wishes regarding eligibility (s. 16(4)).

Practitioners should be alert to the possibility that their witness may suffer from a mental impairment, as research shows that such people frequently are not detected by anyone in the criminal justice system as being in need of special measures. A useful set of prompts to identify such witnesses appears in *Vulnerable and Intimidated Witnesses: A police service guide* (March 2011). Police should seek advice from the CPS before the *Achieving Best Evidence* interview about areas to be covered and special measures used in the interview. In complex cases, an early special measures strategy meeting should be held with counsel and those who know the witness well to identify the difficulties and possible solutions, keeping full notes for disclosure purposes. If a witness suffers mental or physical impairment affecting communication, consideration should be given to using an intermediary. If issues of competence are likely to arise all necessary reports and statements identifying the specific difficulties and how they could be ameliorated during testimony must be collected at an early stage. Preconceived ideas of how a hypothetical witness with the same impairment as the actual witness should testify should be avoided (e.g., playing of the *Achieving Best Evidence* interview may be the best way to maximise such a witness's evidence-in-chief, but it may not). A court visit should also be arranged for the witness to test the measures in practice. Here again counsel calling the witness is responsible for communicating to the court at the PCMH the witness's needs, such as the best time of day to testify, concentration span and ways to detect its lapse, any medication or other care required, and other welfare concerns. The appropriateness of the measures ordered should be kept under review as circumstances may change and an application to vary them may be required. It is important to check at trial that the witness is still content to proceed with the special measures granted.

It might be easier for a physically disabled witness to testify by video link from a remote location (*Equal Treatment Bench Book 2013*, Physical Disability, para. 7).

Adult Complainants of Sexual Offences

D14.17   Such complainants are effectively *presumed* to be in fear or distress about testifying and are not subject to the threshold criteria for fearful adult witnesses. They are deemed to be eligible for special measures unless they decline to be so considered (YJCEA 1999, s. 17(4)). This applies to any offence under the SOA 2003, part 1, or any relevant superseded offence (YJCEA 1999, s. 62(1)). See also **D14.29**.

The special measures which are likely to maximise the quality of the evidence of complainants of sexual assault or intimidated witnesses vary widely in practice. The needs of each witness and how he can give his best evidence must be considered on an individual basis, with full consultation during a court visit, without making any assumptions. It may be that a sexual assault complainant can give evidence without the need for any special measures. Some complainants wish to see those they say assaulted them. Where a complainant's account was first taken by way of an *Achieving Best Evidence* interview this does not necessarily mean that it should be played as evidence in chief. Some witnesses will give their best evidence in court from behind a screen, whilst others need the protection of the video link room. A combination of measures is now possible after the CJA 2009 amendments, e.g., playing the video interview as evidence-in-chief with cross-examination of the witness in court behind a screen.

Complainants in Human Trafficking Cases

D14.18   By virtue of the Trafficking People for Exploitation Regulations 2013, complainants in relation to offences under the Asylum and Immigration (Treatment of Claimants, etc.) Act 2004, s. 4 (trafficking for exploitation: see **B22.36**) have the same status as adult complainants of sexual offences (see **D14.17**). They are deemed to be eligible for special measures unless they decline to be so considered (YJCEA 1999, s. 17(4)). See also **D14 .13** where there is doubt about the age of a witness, who might be under 18.

Intimidated and Other Special Witnesses

D14.19   **Witnesses in Fear or Distress about Testifying**   For a witness to be eligible for a SMD under the YJCEA 1999, s. 17(1), the court must be satisfied that the quality of the evidence is likely to be diminished by reason of fear or distress on the part of the witness in connection with testifying in the proceedings. The application must give details of the grounds on which the applicant states that the witness is intimidated or would be in fear or distress from testifying and should attach supporting evidence under the CrimPR, r. 29.10(a) and (h). The court is required by s. 17(2) to take into account the following factors:

(a) the nature and alleged circumstances of the offence;
(b) the age of the witness;
(c) so far as relevant, the witness's:
   • social and cultural background and ethnic origins,
   • domestic and employment circumstances, and
   • religious beliefs or political opinions;

(d) any behaviour towards a witness on the part of:
- the accused,
- the accused's family or associates, or
- any other person likely to be an accused or witness.

The court must also consider any views expressed by the witness (s. 17(3)).

On occasion, it may be appropriate to hold a *voir dire* and call the witness to testify to establish eligibility; it does not matter that other witnesses in the same circumstances are prepared to testify without special measures (*Brown* [2004] EWCA Crim 1620). In *Brown* it was also held that, although s. 17(2) required the court to consider the factors in s. 17(2)(a)–(d), it was entitled to find eligibility solely having regard to the nature and circumstances of the offence, regardless of the age of the witness or any particular vulnerability. The overall question for the trial court under s. 17 is fairness to the accused and to the witnesses, and the Court of Appeal is unlikely to interfere with its answer.

Witnesses to Relevant Offences Involving Knives or Guns   The CAJA 2009, s. 99, amends   **D14.20**
the YJCEA 1999, s. 17, so as to provide for automatic eligibility for special measures for witnesses in proceedings for 'any relevant offence'. A 'relevant offence' is an offence specified in sch. 1A to the YJCEA 1999 (set out in sch. 14 to the CAJA 2009). The categories of offences specified in sch. 1A are murder and manslaughter, offences under the OAPA 1861, ss. 18, 20, 38 and 47, the Prevention of Crime Act 1953, ss. 1 and 1A, the FA 1968, ss. 1 to 5, 16 to 21A and 24A, the CJA 1988, ss. 139, 139A and 139AA, and the VCRA 2006, ss. 28, 32 and 36; however, a number of these offences are to be treated as specified offences only if a knife or gun was involved. Note also the automatic eligibility of complainants of human trafficking (see **D14.18**).

Note that *all* witnesses involved in such cases, including police officers, are automatically eligible for a SMD unless they decline, without any proof of intimidation or other ground for concern about whether they can give their best evidence using the orthodox procedures.

Child and Other Vulnerable Defendants

The YJCEA 1999 expressly excluded the accused from access to special measures (ss. 16(1)   **D14.21**
and 17(1)). The resulting disparity in treatment between child defendants and other child witnesses was particularly evident in youth courts. After pressure from the House of Lords and the ECtHR (*Camberwell Green Youth Court, ex parte D* [2005] 1 All ER 999; *SC v UK* (2005) 40 EHRR 226), Parliament moved to give limited access to special measures to child and vulnerable adult defendants. In 2007 such defendants were given access to live link (YJCEA 1999, ss. 33A, 33B, 33C, inserted by the Police and Justice Act 2006, s. 47); under the CAJA 2009, s. 104 (inserting ss. 33BA and 33BB into the YJCEA 1999: not yet in force), they will have access to intermediaries for their testimony in the Crown Court and magistrates' courts. However, other special measures available to child witnesses are not made directly applicable to child defendants who give evidence, as YJCEA 1999, ss. 17(1) and 19(1), have not been repealed. This gives rise to questions about compliance with the ECHR, Article 6(3)(d).

CPD I, paras. 3G.1 to 3G.14 (see Supplement, **PD-9**), govern the treatment of vulnerable defendants in the Crown Court and magistrates' courts, adopting procedures analogous to those in use in youth courts. Its overriding principle states in part that all possible steps should be taken to assist a vulnerable defendant to understand and participate in the proceedings, adapting the ordinary trial process as necessary (see also CPD I, paras. 3D.2 and 3G.9). The welfare of a young defendant must be considered (CYPA 1933, s. 44), as must the CrimPR, parts 1 and 3 (the overriding objective and the court's powers of case management). Defence advocates should be fully familiar with CPD I, paras. 3A.1 to 3A.15 and CPD V, paras. 29A.1 and 29A.2, to enable them to assist the court in fulfilling its obligations to a child defendant or a defendant who is otherwise vulnerable.

The advice at **D14.15** and **D14.16** about handling witnesses applies equally to defendants. As to the inference which may be drawn, under the CJPO 1994, s. 35, from the failure of a vulnerable defendant to give evidence, see **F19.46**.

D14.22   **Eligibility of Defendant for Live Link**   The YJCEA 1999, s. 33A, allows the Crown Court or a magistrates' court, on application by the defence, to direct that the accused testify via a 'live link'. The court must be satisfied that it would be in the interests of justice, and also that the live link would enable the accused to participate more effectively as a witness, whether by improving the quality of his evidence or otherwise, because:

(a) if the accused is under the age of 18, his ability to participate effectively as a witness giving oral evidence is *compromised* by his 'level of intellectual ability or social functioning' (s. 33A(4)); or

(b) if the accused is aged 18 or over, he is *unable* to participate effectively in the proceedings as a witness giving oral evidence because he has a mental disorder (within the meaning of the Mental Health Act 1983) or a 'significant impairment of intelligence and social function' (s. 33A(5)).

Explanatory Notes accompanying the 2006 amendment stated that the presumption remains that adult defendants should give evidence in court. The Notes explained that 'the lower threshold for child defendants recognises that it may be more common for them to experience difficulties during the trial through limited intelligence and social development, than it would be for adults' but went on to emphasise that s. 33A(4) 'is aimed at juvenile defendants with a low level of intelligence or a particular problem in dealing with social situations, and is not intended to operate merely because an accused is a juvenile and is nervous, for example'.

D14.23   Under the CrimPR, r. 29.15, an applicant for a 'defendant's evidence direction' must explain how the proposed direction meets these prescribed conditions. An application for live link must identify a person to accompany the accused while testifying and explain why that person is appropriate. See also CPD I, para. 3G.11, and CPD V, paras. 29B.1 to 29B.5.

Section 33A(6) provides that the accused must give all his evidence in accordance with the live link direction, including any cross-examination. However, the court has discretion to discharge a direction if it is in the interests of justice (s. 33A(7)), such as where the accused finds that testifying via live link is more difficult than expected. Arrangements should be made for a vulnerable defendant to make a pre-trial familiarisation visit to the court, including practising using the live link, accompanied by an intermediary where one is to be used at trial (CPD I, paras. 3G.2 to 3G.4).

The Court of Appeal has held that live link cannot be made available under the court's inherent jurisdiction to defendants outside the statutory code (*Ukpabio* [2008] 1 WLR 728).

D14.24   **Eligibility for an Intermediary**   The Crown Court and magistrates' courts may deploy the inherent powers to direct that the defendant be assisted by an intermediary in giving his evidence (*R (C) v Sevenoaks Youth Court* [2010] 1 All ER 735 at [15]–[17]; *Head* [2009] EWCA Crim 1401; *R (P) v West London Youth Court* [2006] 1 All ER 477; CPD I, para. 3F.3). Sometimes the court orders that an intermediary accompany the defendant throughout the trial to assist him in understanding what is taking place. In September 2011, the Witness Intermediary Service adopted the practice of no longer assisting defence solicitors through their matching service in locating an appropriate intermediary for a defendant (although it would do so for other defence witnesses); operational guidance to HM Courts and Tribunal Service staff instructs them to direct solicitors to appropriate professional organisations (see *The Registered Intermediary Procedural Guidance Manual* (v. 2.0, February 2012) at paras. 1.4, 1.18 to 1.19 and 2.23). However, in *OP v Secretary of State for Justice* [2014] EWHC 1944 (Admin) the Divisional Court (Rafferty LJ) held (at [16]–[17]) that the withholding of access of vulnerable defendants to the Witness Intermediary Service, and to professionally regulated Registered Intermediaries acting in that capacity for their testimony, breached equality of arms with Crown witnesses under the ECHR, Article 6, so this situation is likely to change (although the Crown is to appeal that ruling).

Practitioners should be vigilant to identify defendants with comprehension difficulties which could justify an application for an intermediary. The need for special provision should be identified at the PCMH (see **D15.47**). In *R (AS) v Great Yarmouth Youth Court* [2011] EWHC 2059 (Admin), Mitting J held that magistrates had acted irrationally in ruling that a defendant with ADHD was not entitled to an intermediary. This judgment reinforces that a defendant with communication difficulties, like other vulnerable witnesses, is *entitled* to give his best evidence, if need be with the assistance of an intermediary, even where those difficulties do not make him wholly incapable of communicating his testimony. Where an appropriate intermediary is not available for a defendant assessed as being in need of one, the trial judge must make an informed assessment as to whether it is possible nonetheless to have a fair trial by adapting procedures, e.g., by taking frequent breaks to enable defence counsel to summarise the evidence for him and take instructions, and ensuring that all questions to all witnesses are phrased simply (*Cox* [2012] 2 Cr App R 63 at [21] and [29]–[30]).

The CAJA 2009, s. 104 (not yet in force), inserts new ss. 33BA and 33BB into the YJCEA 1999 to provide statutory authorisation for the defendant to testify assisted by an intermediary. Section 33BA sets out parallel criteria for eligibility for an intermediary as for the live link for adult and child defendants. A child defendant, unlike any other child witness, is not automatically eligible for an intermediary's assistance. A direction may be given only if and when the defendant gives evidence and only if it is necessary in order to ensure that the accused receives a fair trial — a separate and additional requirement from the incapacity criteria. Section 33BB provides for the discharge and variation of such directions. Implementation of these provisions has been postponed, apparently because of their resource implications; in many ways they will be more disadvantageous than the current *ad hoc* arrangements.

Compliance with the ECHR, Article 6   The differential eligibility criteria as between child **D14.25** defendants and ordinary child witnesses, and as between child and adult defendants, has been criticised as potentially contravening the ECHR, Article 6(3)(d) (see L. Hoyano, 'Coroners and Justice Act 2009 — (3) Special Measures Directions Take Two: Entrenching Unequal Access to Justice?' [2010] Crim LR 345).

THE SPECIAL MEASURES

Video-recorded Evidence-in-chief

Section 27 of the YJCEA 1999 permits the evidence-in-chief of an eligible witness to take the **D14.26** form of an interview with a police officer or social worker which is recorded on video before the trial, provided that the witness is available for cross-examination at trial. Specific issues relating to particular classes of witness are noted below.

ECHR Compliance   As the ECHR, Article 6, does not require face-to-face confrontation, it **D14.27** does not matter that the accused was not present during the recording of the video interview, provided that the defence has an adequate and proper opportunity to challenge and question the witness at some stage (*Camberwell Green Youth Court, ex parte D* [2005] 1 All ER 999 at [12]–[15] and [49]–[53]). The statutory discretion to exclude all or part of the video interview in the interests of justice adequately protects the defence's rights under Article 6 (*Camberwell Green Youth Court, ex parte D* at [33] and [45]–[46]). However, the YJCEA 1999, s. 27(4), contemplates the possibility that a video interview be admitted even where the witness does not appear at trial for cross-examination and, unless the hearsay provisions of the CJA 2003, ss. 114 to 117, apply (and subject to *Al-Khawaja and Tahery v UK* (2012) 54 EHRR 807: see **F16.33**), it is possible that this would breach Article 6. (See *Riat* [2013] 1 All ER 349 for the steps to be followed should such a hearsay application be made.)

Defence Witnesses   The use of video-recorded interviews as evidence-in-chief is available in prin- **D14.28** ciple to all vulnerable and intimidated witnesses apart from the accused, whether called by the prosecution or the defence. Since the primary rule *requires* that child witnesses testifying for the defence have their evidence-in-chief recorded on video, and this is expected to be conducted before trial (by an interviewer trained in *Achieving Best Evidence*), one of several logistical difficulties is that the prosecution might be able to improve its case if it were to have access to the defence video evidence before trial through the defence application for a SMD. This difficulty was met by the Crown Court (Special Measures Directions and Directions Prohibiting Cross-examination) Rules 2002 (SI 2002 No. 1688), r. 8(6) and (7), which provided that any video recording which the accused proposed to tender in evidence need not be sent to the prosecution until the close of the prosecution case at trial. Those provisions were not replicated in the CrimPR. However, r. 29.12 does provide for an applicant to withhold information relating to a special measures application from the other parties, and the Rules Committee apparently expected that this provision would apply to defence video interviews, if the conditions there identified were met. If the court concludes that they are, the normal sequence of events would follow and the prosecution would not see that defence evidence unless and until the defence decided to rely upon it as part of the defence case.

D14.29 **Adult Complainants of Sexual Offences** The measures available to adult complainants of sexual offences under the YJCEA 1999 included having a video-recorded interview admitted as evidence-in-chief where this was determined to be likely to maximise the quality of the complainant's evidence. The CAJA 2009 amendments make the video interview *presumptively* admissible in the Crown Court on the basis that it *will* maximise the quality of the witness's evidence so far as practicable (in the same way as child witnesses), unless the court is not satisfied of this, or otherwise concludes that its admission is not in the interests of justice (YJCEA 1999, ss. 22A(8) and (9)). Prosecutors should scrutinise the video interview to satisfy themselves that it provides the complainant's best direct evidence. In magistrates' courts however the original provisions continue to govern so that the prosecution must establish that the video interview is likely to maximise the quality of an adult complainant's evidence. Defence arguments that they are entitled to viva voce examination-in-chief so as to exploit any discrepancies with the video are likely to be given short shrift (*Davies* [2011] EWCA Crim 1177).

D14.30 **Availability for Cross-examination** A precondition to the admission of a recorded interview as evidence-in-chief is that the witness must be available for cross-examination at trial, whether in the ordinary way or with the use of special measures, unless the parties agree that it is unnecessary to call that witness (YJCEA 1999, s. 27(4) and (5)). It has become more common for the police to video interview prosecution witnesses with failing health or difficulties with memory retention, and if that witness is no longer able to testify by the time of trial, the video interview can be admitted under the CJA 2003, s. 116(2)(b) (see **F16.8** and, e.g., *Sed* [2005] 1 WLR 3218). This may also be relevant for an intimidated or otherwise reluctant witness who refuses to testify at trial (*Burton* (2011) 175 JP 385), but only if the court finds the admission of the video to be in the interests of justice having regard to its contents, the risk of unfairness to any party, and the availability of special measures at trial to assist that witness (CJA 2003, s. 116(2)(e) and (4)).

D14.31 **Witnesses Not Eligible for SMDs** The police may choose to record interviews with so-called 'significant witnesses', defined in police guidance such as the Murder Investigation Manual (ACPO 2006). But, unless the case involves a relevant offence within the meaning of the YJCEA 1999, sch. 1A (see **D14.20**), such witnesses are not entitled to special measures and there is no statutory provision for these interviews to be used as evidence-in-chief. However, the interview transcript can be used for the purposes of a statement under the CJA 1967 (see **D16.37**), and the defence might ask the court for permission to play some or all of the recording (see *Achieving Best Evidence*, paras. 1.25 to 1.28, 2.135 to 2.138 and 2.173 to 2.175).

D14.32 **Admissibility of the Video Interview** The conduct of an interview eligible to serve as evidence-in-chief is governed by *Achieving Best Evidence* (March 2011 edn; see in particular chs. 2 and 3). Any significant failure by an interviewer to comply with the guidance is a factor to be taken into account in deciding whether to exclude all or part of the recording in the interests of justice under s. 27(2) (*G v DPP* [1998] QB 919). The guidance is not intended to be a legally enforceable code, and most instances of non-compliance can be dealt with in summing-up as being relevant to weight; only if there is real prejudice to the defendant should an interview be ruled entirely inadmissible (*F* [2011] EWCA Crim 940 at [8] and [14]). The test is: 'could a reasonable jury properly directed be sure that the witness had given a credible and accurate account on the video tape, notwithstanding any breaches?' (*Hanton* [2005] EWCA Crim 2009; *K* [2006] 2 All ER 552). The same principle seems to apply to an intermediary assisting a witness in an *Achieving Best Evidence* interview, but the intermediary must be given latitude to tailor the guidance to the individual witness and the circumstances of the case, providing a full written record of intermediary involvement (*IA* [2013] EWCA Crim 1308 at [52]). Whilst it is possible for the trial judge to take into account other evidence which might corroborate the video evidence in ruling on its admissibility, considerable care should be taken in this regard (*K*, explaining dicta in *G v DPP*). Especially in the case of a very young child witness, or a vulnerable adult witness, it is not necessary that the witness have an independent recollection of events entirely apart from the video interview for it to be admitted, as that would defeat the purpose of the pre-trial recorded interview as a special measure (*R* [2010] EWCA Crim 2469 at [21]–[22]).

Editing the Interview   An application to tender a video interview as evidence-in-chief must **D14.33** specify, in addition to the information specified in the CrimPR, r. 29.10, whether all or only parts are to be adduced. In deciding under the YJCEA 1999, s. 27(2), whether to exclude part of a recording in the interests of justice, the court must consider whether any prejudice to the accused which might result from its admission is outweighed by the desirability of showing the whole, or substantially the whole, of the recording (s. 27(3)). Statements which are excised typically include hearsay, allegations of bad character against the suspect, answers to questions in breach of other rules of evidence or *Achieving Best Evidence* (see *C* [2012] EWCA Crim 2380, in which the Court of Appeal stated that a flawed identification by the child witness should have been excluded) and irrelevant material. However, frequently the interviews are rambling, lengthy and difficult to follow, and counsel should consider editing to remove irrelevant or repetitive material, as well as information which is no longer in issue, such as identity, so that the resulting evidence focuses on the issues. The recording must be edited in accordance with the court's ruling and the edited version is then served on the court officer and on the parties (CPD V, para. 27B.2). If at trial a problem with the editing of the video delays the proceedings, the court can consider making a wasted costs order (para. 27B.4). It is therefore incumbent on counsel before trial to check the edited videotape and transcript to ensure that the editing order has been complied with (see also *Achieving Best Evidence*, para. 5.6), and that the tape can be played on that courtroom's equipment.

Refreshing Memory from a Video Recording   The witness is entitled to and should view **D14.34** the (edited) video interview *before* trial (not on the same day) to refresh his memory (*R* [2010] EWCA Crim 2469 at [21]–[22]; CPD V, para. 29C.1 (see Supplement, **PD-44**)). See also **F4.26** and the CJA 2003, s. 139, and *Achieving Best Evidence*, paras. 4.48 to 4.53. The court should direct how and where refreshing will be done, on a case-by-case basis, requiring that any viewing is monitored by a person (usually the officer in the case) who will report to the court about anything said by the witness (CPD V, para. 29C.3). It is important that the witness's particular needs are considered in deciding when and where he will view the video, especially taking into account any issues regarding concentration span. An intermediary may advise the court as to how memory refreshment should take place, and may be present to facilitate communication but should not act as an independent person designated to take a note and report to the court if anything is said (CPD V, paras. 29C.1 and 29C.4). In exceptional circumstances, such as those involving very young children or children with learning disabilities, the prosecutor should consider making a video recording of the refreshment process (*Achieving Best Evidence*, para. 4.51); this was done in *Barker* [2010] EWCA Crim 4 where the complainant was then aged four. If the video is ruled inadmissible, or if the witness wishes to give viva voce evidence-in-chief, guidance should be sought from the court at the PCMH or pre-trial hearing on an acceptable alternative method of refreshing the witness's memory (CPD V, para. 29C.2).

Playing the Video Interview   Several practical matters arise. **D14.35**

(a) The prosecution must afford the defendant the opportunity to examine the video and any exhibits in circumstances which will allow him to have confidential discussion with his legal advisers (*R (L)* [2011] 3 All ER 969).

(b) Unless the parties otherwise agree, a recording adduced in Crown Court proceedings should be produced and proved by the interviewer or another witness who was present at the interview (CPD V, para. 27B.3).

(c) Where a video-recorded interview with a child aged 14 or over is admitted under the YJCEA 1999, s. 27, the oath should be administered before the start of any further questioning (see *Simmonds* [1996] Crim LR 816 at **F4.32**).

(d) The court may allow a jury to have a transcript of a video recording whilst it is being played if it will assist them to follow the evidence and they are instructed to use it only for that limited purpose (*Welstead* [1996] 1 Cr App R 59). Problems have arisen where the jury have been permitted, whether deliberately or inadvertently, to retain the transcripts during deliberations. Guidelines propounded in *Popescu* [2010] EWCA Crim 1230 and reiterated in *Sardar* [2012] EWCA Crim 134 require that transcripts be withdrawn from the jury once the video has been played except in very exceptional circumstances; if they are retained during cross-examination, then they must be retrieved at the conclusion of that testimony. The jury is not to be permitted to retire with the transcript unless the defence positively wants the jury to have them for very good reasons which the judge must explain to the jury, ensuring that the cross-examination and re-examination of the witness is fully summed up.

(e) Where the jury in the course of deliberations request that the video interview be replayed, the judge should ascertain the reasons for the request. If the jury wish to be reminded of the content of the testimony a summary from the judge's notes will likely suffice; however it may be appropriate to replay the recording where the jury wish to see the manner in which the witness testified (*Mullen* [2004] 2 Cr App R 290). The jury must be cautioned not to give the video interview disproportionate weight and be reminded of the oral cross-examination and re-examination of that witness (*Rawlings* [1995] 1 All ER 580; *W* [2011] EWCA Crim 1142).

D14.36   Supplementary Questions in Chief   The YJCEA 1999 imposed strict limitations on supplementary questions and evidence. The CAJA 2009, s. 103(2), relaxes these strictures; leave of the court will be required only where the matter has already been dealt with in the interview. Permission to ask the additional questions will be given if it is in the interests of justice.

D14.37   Issues related to Testimonial Competence   The trial judge will normally form a view as to the competence of the witness from the video recording, but if an issue is raised by the opponent of that evidence then the trial judge should investigate by asking the witness appropriate questions (*MacPherson* [2006] 1 Cr App R 459: see **F4.25**). See also **D14.13** about collecting evidence of competence for very young or mentally impaired witnesses.

Live Link Testimony

D14.38   A SMD for the use of a live link for the evidence of an eligible witness is authorised by the YJCEA 1999, s. 24. See also the CrimPR, rr. 29.23 to 29.26 (see Supplement, **R-238**) and CPD V, paras. 29B.1 to 29B.5 (see Supplement, **PD-43**). In this context, references to a live link are to 'a live television link or other arrangements whereby a witness, whilst absent from the courtroom or other place where the proceedings are being held, is able to see and hear a person there and to be heard and seen' by the judge, jury, justices, legal representatives, and interpreter for the accused (s. 24(8)). Whilst this list does not include the accused, this is possibly an unintended result of a cross-reference to screens in court (s. 23(2)(a)–(c)). Usually the witness testifies from a live link room in the same building where the trial is held, but a remote location is also permitted and should be considered for particularly young or vulnerable witnesses likely to be intimidated by the courthouse. Where a direction for a live link has been given, cross-examination must also be conducted by live link, unless the court directs otherwise because it is in the interests of justice and either there has been a material change in circumstances since the live link order was granted, or the court acts of its own motion (s. 24(2), (3) and (4)).

Dispensing with the Primary Rule for a Child Witness   The CAJA 2009 modifies the rigid **D14.39**
and mandatory 'primary rule' regime (see **D14.14**), enabling the child to opt out of application
of the primary rule in whole or in part (YJCEA 1999, s. 21(4)(ba)). This means that the child
can opt to testify in the courtroom, either with or without a screen, rather than using the live
link. The court must be satisfied that testifying in court would not diminish the quality of the
child's evidence (s. 21(4)(ba)). The court is likely to require evidence regarding the following
mandatory statutory factors (s. 21(4C)), as well as any other relevant factors in the particular
circumstances:

(a) the child's age and maturity;
(b) the child's ability to understand the consequences of giving evidence in court rather than
    through the live link;
(c) the child's relationship with the accused, if any;
(d) the child's social and cultural background and ethnic origins; and
(e) the nature and alleged circumstances of the offence charged.

Factor (b) will require careful handling of the witness familiarisation process (see **D14.10**),
especially as it may well be difficult for any first-time witness to predict how he will find the
experience of testifying.

Witness Supporters

The CAJA 2009, s. 102(1), amends the YJCEA 1999, s. 24(1A), so as to give statutory stand-   **D14.40**
ing to the routine practice of having a witness supporter in the live link room. The trial judge
is required to consider the witness's wishes in the choice of supporter, which should be stated
in the application (CrimPR, r. 29.24). There is now increased flexibility in the selection of a
supporter, which can be anyone known to or trusted by the witness who is not a party to the
proceedings and who has no detailed knowledge of the evidence in a case (CPD V, para. 29B.2).
Achieving Best Evidence, para. 4.19, states that any person present either during the investigative
interview or during the witness's memory refreshment should not support the witness pre-trial
or accompany the witness when giving evidence. The court usher should additionally be available to assist and to ensure that the judge's directions are complied with (CPD V, para. 29B.3).
The court has common-law powers to allow a witness supporter to be present if a child elects to
testify in the courtroom (now authorised by CPD V, para. 29B.5).

Screens

The use of a screen is permitted by the YJCEA 1999, s. 23. A screen allows the witness to give   **D14.41**
evidence in such a way that he cannot see the accused. He must be able to be seen by the judge,
jury or justices, the legal representatives and any interpreter or other person appointed to help him
(s. 23(2)). If there are two representatives, it is sufficient if the witness can be seen by one of them
(s. 23(3)). Occasionally a witness eligible for special measures has asked to use the screen rather
than the live link, because it would have the incidental effect of preventing the accused from seeing the witness testify; CPD V, para. 29A.2 provides that, if the witness wishes, the court may
authorise that the accused and the public be prevented from seeing the live link screen, in the
same way as would happen if the witness used a screen whilst testifying in the courtroom. Note,
however, that the Court of Appeal has held that the right of the accused to see his accusers should
be denied only in rare circumstances such as where the witness has been intimidated or where there
is an anonymity order (*Taylor* [1995] Crim LR 253; *Watford Magistrates' Court, ex parte Lenman*
[1993] Crim LR 388). Absent such circumstances, even where the witness testifies from behind
a screen, a video camera can be positioned so as to enable the accused to see the witness whilst the
screen prevents the witness from seeing the accused. The Court of Appeal has observed that, where
it is important that the accused be able to see the witness, e.g., to determine whether he recognises
her and whether she might have some motive or reason wrongly to implicate him in the offence
charged, then the live link rather than a screen should be used (*Pope* [2010] EWCA Crim 2113).

D

Removal of Wigs and Gowns

D14.42   It is customary to remove formal court dress where a child or vulnerable defendant is on trial, unless the court for good reason orders that they should be worn (CPD I, para. 3G.12). The court may be robed for sentencing in a grave case even though it has sat without robes for trial.

Intermediaries

D14.43   An intermediary is a neutral officer of the court. Experience has shown that one of the most useful functions of intermediaries is to assist the trial judge and counsel in establishing what types of questions are likely to cause misunderstanding, and thus avert them (cited with approval in *Cox* [2012] 2 Cr App R 63 at [28]). Even though the YJCEA 1999, s. 29, makes it clear that an intermediary can assist a witness to communicate by explaining questions and answers, this happens rarely in practice; questions are usually put directly to the witness, with the intermediary actively intervening only where miscommunication is likely to have occurred. The detailed procedural guidance and a case checklist in *The Registered Intermediary Procedural Guidance Manual* (February 2012) and especially the toolkit from 'The Advocate's Gateway' (www.theadvocatesgateway.org) help practitioners understand the roles of intermediaries at every step of their involvement. Intermediaries should not be asked to provide expert testimony or opinion regarding the reliability of a witness, or as to the defendant's fitness to plead, as their role is to assist communication of evidence as officers of the court. Appendix E of *Achieving Best Evidence* advises on how to elicit testimony from very young, disabled or psychologically disturbed children. An intermediary can be used at trial even if the *Achieving Best Evidence* interview was conducted without one.

D14.44   The Court of Appeal has approved the use of intermediaries for profoundly disabled witnesses incapable of speech (*Watts* [2010] EWCA Crim 1824). The use of an intermediary for the video-recorded interview must be approved by the court retrospectively. The intermediary's written assessment will greatly assist the 'ground rules' discussion between counsel and the trial judge, which the intermediary should also attend; however the ground rules will usually extend well beyond the communication issues involving the intermediary, such as timing of breaks, and these are for the trial judge to enforce. The intermediary can provide valuable assistance to all counsel in formulating appropriate questions, and it is appropriate for counsel to have a private consultation with the intermediary in preparing cross-examination. The intermediary must make a declaration before the video-recorded interview begins, and again before examination of the witness at trial, in the form prescribed by the CrimPR, r. 29.7. When an intermediary is used at trial, the judge or magistrates and at least one legal representative for both the prosecution and the defence must be able to see and hear the witness giving evidence and be able to communicate with the intermediary (s. 29(3)).

Responsibility for the Intermediary Register and the Witness Intermediary Scheme Matching Service has been moved to the NCA: the Register and the Service are available for defence as well as prosecution witnesses, but no longer for defendants.

Communication Aids

D14.45   Communication aids, such as sign and symbol boards or electronic communication devices, can be authorised under the YJCEA 1999, s. 30, to overcome physical difficulties with understanding or answering questions (for examples of use, see *Watts* [2010] EWCA Crim 1824). Communication aids usually will be used in conjunction with an intermediary to ensure accurate communication with the court. In cases of profound impairment it may be necessary to have a carer familiar with the witness interpret signals (*Watts* at [35]).

Video-recorded Cross-examination and Re-examination

D14.46   Section 28 of the YJCEA 1999 has finally been brought into force as of 30 December 2013 (SI 2013 No. 3236), but only for the purposes of Crown Court proceedings in Kingston-upon-Thames, Leeds and Liverpool, to enable six-month pilot schemes announced on 11 June 2013 by the Ministry of Justice to proceed. The Ministry of Justice will then consider how best to take this measure forward. While it was initially thought from the June 2013 announcement that s. 28 would be restricted to all child witnesses under 12 years, and to adult witnesses with severe communication difficulties, the limited implementation for the pilots applies to witnesses under 16 at the time of the hearing, and to witnesses eligible for assistance on grounds of incapacity which might diminish the quality of their evidence. Given recent Government statements referring to implementation of s. 28 in response to controversial cases concerning the cross-examination of adult complainants of sexual offences of normal capacity, it is possible that implementation will become much wider in scope. In the meantime, for criminal proceedings outside the pilot areas, the limited provision for pre-trial recorded evidence of a child complainant, including cross-examination, under the CYPA 1933, ss. 42 and 43, where attendance in court would involve 'serious danger to his life or health', remains available for charges of murder or manslaughter or complicity in suicide or other offences against the person (CYPA 1933, sch. 1); see also the Protection of Children Act 1978, s. 1(5), incorporating offences under s. 1(1)(a) of that Act, and the CJA 1988, sch. 15, incorporating offences under the Child Abduction Act 1984, part I. See also **D16.38**.

Evidence in Private for Sex and Intimidation Cases

Under the YJCEA 1999, s. 25, where the proceedings relate to a sexual offence (see **D14.17**), a   **D14.47** trafficking for exploitation case (see **D14.18**) or there are reasonable grounds to believe that a person other than the accused has sought or will seek to intimidate the witness, the court may permit a witness to give evidence in private. However, the accused, legal representatives and any interpreter or other person appointed to assist the witness cannot be excluded from the court under s. 25. Any order to close the court must provide for a nominated representative of a news gathering or reporting organisation to attend. The court retains inherent jurisdiction to close the court or to limit the numbers of people in the public gallery, e.g., in proceedings involving a vulnerable defendant (CrimPR, rr. 16.6 to 16.8, 17.3 and 29.1(iii)). In *Richards* (1999) 163 JP 246, the Court of Appeal held that s. 25 did not conflict with the ECHR, Article 6(1), because the latter expressly permits departure from the principle of trial in public where 'publicity would prejudice the interests of justice'.

BEST PRACTICE IN QUESTIONING CHILD AND VULNERABLE WITNESSES

There continues to be widely expressed criticism of the way in which counsel question young   **D14.48** children and other vulnerable witnesses, including adult complainants of sexual offences of normal capacity, damaging public confidence in the criminal justice system and potentially deterring valid complaints. Lord Judge CJ in *Barker* [2010] EWCA Crim 4 noted that 'the competency test is not failed because the forensic techniques of the advocate (in particular in relation to cross-examination) or the processes of the court (for example, in relation to the patient expenditure of time) have to be adapted to enable the child to give the best evidence of which he or she is capable' (see also *F* [2013] 1 WLR 2143 regarding how not to conduct a competency examination). Useful guidance may be found in 'The Advocate's Gateway' (www.theadvocatesgateway.org). This contains toolkits for questioning witnesses who are vulnerable for different reasons. It covers ground rules hearings (CPD I, paras. 3E.1 to 3E.6; *Equal Treatment Bench Book 2013*, Child and Vulnerable Adults, paras. 55 to 67), planning to question child and adult witnesses with communication needs, and effective participation by young defendants. See also annexes A and B to the NSPCC/Nuffield *Good Practice Guidance in Managing Young Witness Cases and Questioning Children* (July 2009), and *Achieving Best Evidence (2011)*, paras. 3.69 to 3.79, ch. 5 and app. E. Advocates can expect the court not to be tolerant of poor practice given the availability of these resources, as they are now endorsed by CPD I, paras. 3D.5 to 3D.8 and by the *Equal Treatment Bench Book 2013*, Children and Vulnerable Adults. Assessment by an intermediary should be

D

Part D Procedure

considered by the party calling the witness or by the trial judge if the witness seems unlikely to be able to recognise a problematic question or, even if able to do so, may be reluctant to say so to a questioner in a position of authority; the majority of young witnesses across all ages tend to fall into one or other or both categories. A deaf witness should always be assessed by an expert in deafness, and possibly also a suitably qualified intermediary (*Equal Treatment Bench Book 2013*, Children and Vulnerable Adults, para. 46).

In *Wills* [2012] 1 Cr App R 16 and again in *E* [2011] EWCA Crim 3028, the Court of Appeal stressed that compliance by defence counsel with agreed ground rules in cross-examining young and vulnerable witnesses does not prejudice their client's case, provided that the trial judge clearly explains to the jury the reasons why counsel have not conducted a detailed cross-examination of the witness about the defence case or engaged in robust questioning. Ramsey J noted that '[s]ome of the most effective cross-examination is conducted without long and complicated questions being posed in a leading or "tagged" manner' (*Wills* at [30]). CPD I, para. 3E.1, instructs the judiciary to stop over-rigorous or repetitive cross-examination of a child or vulnerable witness; para. 3E.5 states that advocates for multiple accused should be prevented from covering the same ground.

Partly in response to *Wills*, the Judicial College has issued a Bench Checklist for Young Witness Cases (www.judiciary.gov.uk/publications-and-reports/guidance/2012/jc-bench-checklist-young-wit-cases) which reiterates the need for instructions to all advocates at 'ground rules' discussions to adapt their questions to a child's developmental stage, 'enabling *this* child's "best evidence"' (emphasis in original). This guidance now has the force of CPD I, paras. 3D.3 and 3E.1 to 3E.6. The ground rules discussion must include how the defence case is to be put to the witness, bearing in mind the jury direction mandated by *Barker* that the defence case need not be addressed in detailed cross-examination of younger children. The Bench Checklist for Young Witness Cases cites *Wills* as authority for the duty on the court to enforce the ground rules in the course of cross-examination, and in particular to ensure that the tenor, tone, language and duration of the questioning is developmentally appropriate to the particular child, to prevent questioning that is irrelevant, repetitive, oppressive or intimidating, and to be alert to possible difficulties in understanding. The *Equal Treatment Bench Book 2013* guidance on child and vulnerable witnesses sets out even more detailed advice by which trial judges (and hence advocates) are expected to abide in managing cases to facilitate best evidence.

One particularly difficult issue is whether, and how, to put the defence case to a child complainant. In *Barker* Lord Judge CJ stated (at [42]):

> When the issue is whether the child is lying or mistaken in claiming that the defendant behaved indecently towards him or her, it should not be over-problematic for the advocate to formulate short, simple questions which put the essential elements of the defendant's case to the witness, and fully to ventilate before the jury the areas of evidence which bear on the child's credibility. Aspects of evidence which undermine or are believed to undermine the child's credibility must, of course, be revealed to the jury, but it is not necessarily appropriate for them to form the subject matter of detailed cross-examination of the child and the advocate may have to forego much of the kind of contemporary cross-examination which consists of no more than comment on matters which will be before the jury in any event from different sources. Notwithstanding some of the difficulties, when all is said and done, the witness whose cross-examination is in contemplation is a child, sometimes very young, and it should not take very lengthy cross-examination to demonstrate, when it is the case, that the child may indeed be fabricating, or fantasising, or imagining, or reciting a well rehearsed untruthful script, learned by rote, or simply just suggestible, or contaminated by or in collusion with others to make false allegations, or making assertions in language which is beyond his or her level of comprehension, and therefore likely to be derived from another source. Comment on the evidence, including a comment on evidence which may bear adversely on the credibility of the child, should be addressed after the child has finished giving evidence.

CPD I, para 3E.4, provides that the court may dispense with the normal practice of 'putting the case', imposing clearly defined restrictions on the advocate's cross-examination, where there is a risk of a young or otherwise vulnerable witness failing to understand, becoming distressed, or acquiescing to leading questions.

Another difficult issue is how to impeach such a witness's credibility through a previous inconsistent statement. Instead of the advocate commenting on inconsistencies during cross-examination, the advocate or judge, after discussing the matter, may point out important inconsistencies after (instead of during) the witness's testimony; the judge should also remind the jury of these during summing-up, disregarding any trivial inconsistencies (para. 3E.4). Body maps should be provided for the witness's use in sexual offence trials; advocates should never ask a witness (or intermediary) to point to his own body (para. 3E.4).

In *F (S)* [2012] QB 703 at [36]–[41], Lord Judge CJ reinforced the authority of *Galbraith* [1981] 2 All ER 1060 (see **D16.55** *et seq.*), with its emphasis on the constitutional primacy of the jury as the fact-finding body responsible for judging the credibility of the complainant, regardless of the nature of the case. These dicta are of particular force to child or vulnerable adult complainants (see also *Watts* [2010] EWCA Crim 1824 at [48]–[49], [54]). Therefore an application for a directed verdict is likely to succeed only where the complainant's evidence is so unsatisfactory, contradictory or transparently unreliable that no jury properly directed could convict (*F (S)* at [36]), which is likely to be a significantly higher threshold than heretofore. As was said in *Watts* (at [54]), 'the ordinary principles governing criminal trials require both the judge and the jury to face the realities which can sometimes arise where special measures are put in place, but these arrangements do not alter the principle that the primacy of the jury should be respected'.

WITNESS ANONYMITY ORDERS

One measure which has received considerable attention from both Parliament and the courts is the protection for a witness afforded by anonymity. **D14.49**

The House of Lords in *Davis* [2008] 1 AC 1128 unanimously held that the burgeoning practice of according anonymity to prosecution witnesses who claimed to be intimidated, which had been endorsed by the Court of Appeal in *Davis* [2006] 4 All ER 648, breached both the common law's and the ECHR's precepts of a fair trial.

Within a month Parliament responded to *Davis* with the Criminal Evidence (Witness Anonymity) Act 2008 (replaced by chapter 2 of part 3 of the CAJA 2009 as of 1 January 2010), which abolished the common law and introduced a new procedure for witness anonymity orders. **D14.50**

Sections 86 to 90 of the 2009 Act largely replicate ss. 2 to 5 and 7 of the 2008 Act, and thus decisions under the 2008 Act are still relevant. Lord Judge CJ comprehensively analysed the new statutory regime in *Mayers* [2009] 2 All ER 145. He stressed that 'an anonymity order should be regarded as the special measure of last practicable resort' (reiterated in CPD V, para. 29D.2), but that in such circumstances it represented Parliament's view as to how best to address the countervailing interests of the accused, the victim and the public, and concluded (perhaps dubiously) that such an order therefore complied with the ECHR, Article 6. A witness anonymity order protects the identity of the witness from disclosure in proceedings (CAJA 2009, s. 86), although (like a special measures direction) it cannot include screening of the witness from the judge or jury (s. 86(4)).

Procedure

An application for a witness anonymity order may be made by either the prosecution or defence pursuant to the CAJA 2009, s. 87, in a magistrates' court, the Crown Court and the Court of Appeal (s. 97). The procedure is set out in the CrimPR, rr. 29.18 to 29.22 (see **D14.51**

D

Part D Procedure

Supplement, **R-233** *et seq.*) and CPD V, paras. 29D.1 and 29D.2 (see Supplement, **PD-45**). In summary:

(a) The application must be served on all parties and contain nothing that might identify the witness (CrimPR, r. 29.19(1)). It should specify the measures proposed, explain how they comply with s. 88 and why no lesser measures will suffice (r. 29.19(1)(b)–(d)). The required supporting documentation is the statement of the witness whose anonymity is sought, any disclosure relating to that witness, and a defence statement or other available particulars of the defence case (r. 29.19(1)(e)). The Court of Appeal in *Mayers* [2009] 2 All ER 145 made clear that the prosecution's disclosure obligations in relation to an anonymous witness 'go much further than the ordinary duties of disclosure', adding that disclosure must be 'complete' and 'full and frank'. Any failures in disclosure will be very closely scrutinised (*Okuwa* [2010] EWCA Crim 832). Disclosure is now governed by the Judicial Protocol on Disclosure and the A-G's Guidelines on Disclosure (see **D9**) and the CrimPR, part 22. In the case of a defence application, the court should notify the DPP (r. 29.20).

(b) The accused (or other opposing party) is then afforded 14 days to respond to the application (r. 29.22(2)), and is required actively to assist the court (CPD V, para. 29D.7). In *Mayers* the Court of Appeal stressed the importance of detailed defence statements, both to anonymity applications and to disclosure in relation to anonymous witnesses: 'the defence statement provides the benchmark against which the disclosure process must be examined'. Where the application has been made by the defence, and the response is thus from the prosecution, additional disclosure obligations arise at that stage (r. 29.22(6)).

(c) At the hearing of the application, the applicant should provide the court, but not the other parties, with the information redacted from the application, and either identify the witness in question or set out reasons why it is not possible to identify him (r. 29.19(2)). An oral hearing will take place only where such a hearing has been sought (rr. 29.19(1)(f) and 29.22(2)(c)). If there is no such hearing, the applicant must reveal the witness's identity to the court before the witness gives evidence (r. 29.19(4)).

(d) Any hearing should normally take place in private, and can take place, in part, in the absence of the accused or his representative (r. 29.18(1)). Such an *ex parte* hearing must, in any event, take place after the court has heard or received in writing the parties' representations, so that the court can be addressed about, and give rigorous scrutiny to, the confidential material additional to the application (r. 29.19(3)). The court's overriding obligation is to ensure that the proceedings are fair (*Mayers* [2009] 2 All ER 145), and no order should be made without hearing representations of the parties (r. 29.18(2)), even if there is no hearing (r. 29.18(1)).

(e) The court may also use its common-law power to appoint a special advocate (*H* [2004] 2 AC 134 at [21]–[22]), adapting the procedures as needed from public interest immunity applications (*Mayers* at [10]). See now CPD V, para. 29D.14, which emphasises that such appointment would be exceptional and a course of last resort. For examples of the use of special advocates to cross-examine the witness claiming anonymity on a *voir dire*, see *Nazir* [2009] EWCA Crim 213 and *Chisholm* [2010] EWCA Crim 258.

(f) On a prosecutor's application, the court is likely to be assisted by the attendance of a senior investigator or other person of comparable authority who is familiar with the case (CPD V, para. 29D.12).

(g) In discharging the court's duty to test thoroughly the information supplied in confidence in order to satisfy itself that the three conditions prescribed by the Act are met, the court exceptionally may invite the applicant to present the proposed witness to be questioned by the court, ensuring that the arrangements prevent disclosure of his identity (para. 29D.13).

(h) In *C* [2008] EWCA Crim 3228 the Court of Appeal stressed that anonymity orders should not be made the subject of interlocutory appeals, as only at trial can their impact be assessed.

(i) During the trial the court and the parties (especially the applicant) are expected to keep under review the question of whether the conditions for making an anonymity order are met, and whether there is a case for discharge or variation (CPD V, paras. 29D.20 and 29D.21).

The A-G has issued guidelines arising from the Act: *The Prosecutor's Role in Applications for Witness Anonymity Orders* (30 November 2012) (see **appendix 2**), and the DPP has also issued guidance: *The Director's Guidance on Witness Anonymity* (December 2009, updated on 28 February 2013) available on the CPS website.

Criteria

An anonymity order can be granted only if three stipulated conditions are satisfied (CAJA 2009, s. 88) to the highest standard, probability not sufficing (*Mayers* [2009] 2 All ER 145 at [38]). These conditions require that the measures be necessary (Condition A), that in all the circumstances the order's effect would be consistent with the defendant receiving a fair trial (Condition B) and that the witness's testimony is so important that it is in the interests of justice for him to testify and he would not do so if the order was not made, or alternatively there would be real harm to the public interest if he were to testify without the order (Condition C). *In Mayers* Lord Judge CJ suggested that the proper starting point for trial judges is Condition C. It was stressed in *Mayers* that each of the three preconditions must be satisfied before an order can be made. However, the force of this admonition has arguably been undermined by *Willett* [2012] 2 Cr App R (S) 76, where the accused knew the identity of the witness as he was a cell-mate during a disclosed specified period, so Condition A (necessity) appeared not to be met. The Court of Appeal nevertheless held that the trial judge's direction 'was entirely apt to prevent the jury from holding [the witness's] anonymity against the appellant and to get them to concentrate on the evidence actually given by the witness'. If, as the Court of Appeal said, the standard directions ensure that no prejudice arises from the fact that the witness remains anonymous, then the stringent wording of the conditions themselves seem of little protection to the defence (see *Willett* at [45]–[46] and *Nazir* [2009] EWCA Crim 213).   **D14.52**

In relation to Condition A there are three bases on which an anonymity order may be necessary. **D14.53** The first two are based upon the necessity of protecting the safety of the witness or another person or to prevent serious damage to property (s. 88(3)(a) and (6)). It was held in *Mayers* that the oral evidence of the witness must be important, and the threat to his safety must be real; reluctance to give evidence is insufficient. The threat to the witness need not come from the accused. In *Powar* [2009] 2 Cr App R 120, the Court of Appeal rejected witness relocation as a practical alternative to anonymity in most cases. The ground of prevention of 'any serious damage to property' is controversial as it is contrary to the position of the Council of Europe (Committee of Experts, *Intimidation of Witnesses and the Rights of the Defence*, Recommendation No. R (97) 13, adopted by the Council of Europe Committee of Ministers on 10 September 1997). This ground may engage Article 6 issues since all of the ECtHR decisions approving witness anonymity were predicated on their rights to personal safety under Articles 2, 3 and 8. The Court of Appeal in *Mayers* interpreted this ground as requiring a 'serious risk' of serious damage to property (at [28]–[29]).

A third and distinct form of necessity is a generic ground of preventing 'real harm to the public interest, affecting any activities or safety of persons involved in them' (s. 88(3)(b)). This is less controversial, as before the Act there had been a regular practice for security, undercover and test purchase officers to testify using a pseudonym, with the benefit of a screen, and sometimes with modulation of their voices, but with the jury and defence fully aware that these witnesses were police officers acting in the course of their duties and that they were using a pseudonym (*Mayers* at [35] and *Jack* [1998] EWCA Crim 1206). A witness anonymity order for such vital intelligence and law-enforcement assets can usually be readily justified because it is not normally germane to the defence for the purposes of cross-examination to know the witness's true identity, and any matters of criticism can be directed to the witness using the name by which

Part D Procedure

the accused knew him (if at all) (*Mayers* at [30]–[35]). See also *Khan* [2010] EWCA Crim 1692 regarding Condition B.

D14.54 Section 89(2) provides guidance as to the considerations to which a court should have regard in assessing whether the three conditions are met:

(a) the defendant's general right to know the witness's identity;

(b) the extent to which the witness's credibility is in issue;

(c) whether the evidence might be the 'sole or decisive' evidence implicating the defendant (see the discussion of *Al-Khawaja v UK* (2012) 54 EHRR 807 at **D14.55**);

(d) whether the evidence could be properly tested without the witness's identity being disclosed (see *Donovan* [2012] EWCA Crim 2749, where the Court of Appeal held that the jury had been prevented from hearing admissible and substantive material relevant to the question whether either witness granted anonymity might have been lying);

(e) whether there is any reason to believe the witness has a tendency to be dishonest or any motive for dishonesty in the circumstances of the case, having regard to any relationship between the witness and the defendant or the defendant's associates, and any prior convictions; and

(f) whether it would be reasonably practicable to protect the witness by any other means (which seems to be an oblique reference to special measures directions as well as to witness protection programmes).

The weight to be given to any relevant factor is for the trial judge, and that decision can be challenged on appeal only in extreme cases (*Taylor* [2010] EWCA Crim 830). In *Mayers* it was emphasised that s. 89(1)(b) meant that the list was not exhaustive, and that no consideration outweighed the others. This is significant because the list includes the right of an accused to confront his accuser, *and* the status of the anonymous evidence as the 'sole and decisive' evidence against the accused, both being heavily stressed by the House of Lords in *Davis* [2008] 1 AC 1128.

D14.55 **Sole or Decisive Evidence**   In *Davis* [2008] 1 AC 1128 their lordships had carefully considered the consistent line of jurisprudence from the ECtHR that an accused could not have a fair trial under the ECHR, Article 6, where the evidence was based solely or to a decisive extent on the testimony of an anonymous witness (e.g., *Doorson v Netherlands* (1996) 22 EHRR 330 at [76]; *Kostovski v Netherlands* (1989) 12 EHRR 434 at [42], [44]; *Lucà v Italy* (2003) 36 EHRR 807 at [40]), a position adopted by the Council of Europe (Committee of Experts, *Intimidation of Witnesses and the Rights of the Defence*, Recommendation No. R (97) cl. 13). Lord Bingham (at [25]) and Lord Brown (at [64]) regarded the 'sole or decisive' test as a rule, whereas Lord Mance (at [89] and [96]–[97]) and Lord Carswell (at [59]) considered it to be a more flexible but nonetheless important principle to be weighed in the balance. The latter position was adopted by the Grand Chamber in *Al-Khawaja and Tahery v UK* (2012) 54 EHRR 807: whilst the cases before the Grand Chamber involved hearsay evidence, the majority's dicta make it clear that the reasoning also applies to anonymous witnesses (e.g., at [139] and [141]), and this was confirmed by the 4th Section of the ECtHR in *Ellis, Simms and Martin v UK* (2012) 55 EHRR 8 at [75]. The Grand Chamber described 'sole or decisive' as a 'rule' which should be applied flexibly, seemingly an oxymoron. That flexibility requires consideration of the strength of any corroborating evidence for that testimony, and strong procedural safeguards which permit a fair and proper assessment of its reliability. The Grand Chamber also elucidated the meaning of 'decisive', which Lord Phillips had found problematic in *Horncastle* [2010] 2 AC 373, as being narrowly understood as 'indicating evidence of such significance or importance as is likely to be determinative of the outcome of the case' (at [131]). It is therefore likely that the three conditions and enumerated factors in the English anonymous witness legislation would prima facie meet this test, and that the question of the fairness of any particular anonymous witness order must, like all other cases under Article 6, be considered in retrospect in the context of the whole trial as it unfolded. In *Ford* [2010] EWCA Crim 2250 and *Fox* [2010] EWCA Crim 1280, the Court of Appeal ruled inadmissible hearsay evidence from unidentified declarants. There must be adequate counterbalancing measures in place to protect the rights of the defence for the admission of the evidence to comply with Article 6 (*Pesukic v Switzerland* [2012] ECHR 2031).

Range of Protective Measures

Section 86(2) of the CAJA 2009 sets out a non-exclusive list of measures which may be taken to protect the identity of the witness, including withholding or redacting the witness's name or other identifying details, use of a pseudonym, screen, and voice modulation. In addition, no questions may be asked of the witness of any specified description which might lead to his identification; this prohibition can pose a major constraint on cross-examination. This means that the defence must anticipate what questions might be asked in cross-examination and make submissions at the application stage that the anonymity order would not be consistent with a fair trial, such that Condition B would not be satisfied. **D14.56**

Variation or Discharge of an Order

The court is required to keep any anonymity order under review. Any party may seek to discharge or vary it (CAJA 2009, s. 91), the procedure mirroring that employed for the original application (CrimPR, r. 29.21; see Supplement, **R-236**). A witness anonymity order may also be discharged or varied after the proceedings have come to an end (s. 92), or by an 'appeal court' in an appeal by the accused (s. 93). Such a variation or discharge may equally be ordered of the court's own motion (s. 91(2)(b)). The Court of Appeal has held that, where Condition C continues to be satisfied (see s. 88, and **D14.52**), it would be grossly unfair to a witness who has already testified to revoke the anonymity order because of what transpired later in the trial (*Taylor* [2010] EWCA Crim 830). **D14.57**

Jury Directions

Where testimony has been given anonymously, the judge in a trial on indictment is required to give a warning to ensure that the order does not prejudice the accused (CAJA 2009, s. 90). Directions endorsed in the *Crown Court Bench Book* have instructed jurors not to speculate as to the reasons why the witness testified under conditions of anonymity and, where the inference is almost inevitable, to deny specifically that the reason is attributable to the accused (*Nazir* [2009] EWCA Crim 213). It would seem difficult, however, for such admonitions to protect against adverse inferences, *a fortiori* because the *Crown Court Bench Book* provides that the direction should also explain how, if at all, the anonymity of the witness put the accused at a disadvantage in the conduct of his case; the more the disadvantage is emphasised, the more juries are likely to think that the risk to the witness must be very high indeed, and attribute that threat to the defence, to warrant the trial judge ordering a procedure which the judge acknowledges prejudices the defence's right to make full answer and defence. *Willett* [2012] 2 Cr App R (S) 76 (at [45]–[46]) shows the Court of Appeal's faith in the efficacy of jury directions to cure prejudice even where the original anonymous witness order was not warranted in the first place (see **D14.52**). **D14.58**

The Court of Appeal has suggested that a witness anonymity warning given when the witness gives evidence should be repeated when summing-up (*Okuwa* [2010] EWCA Crim 832).

SELECTED STATUTORY PROVISIONS

Statutory Provisions on Special Measures

Youth Justice and Criminal Evidence Act 1999, ss. 16 to 27, 29, 30 and 33A to 33C **D14.59**

16.—(1) For the purposes of this chapter a witness in criminal proceedings (other than the accused) is eligible for assistance by virtue of this section—

    (a) if under the age of 18 at the time of the hearing; or

D

Part D Procedure

    (b) if the court considers that the quality of evidence given by the witness is likely to be diminished by reason of any circumstances falling within subsection (2).

(2) The circumstances falling within this subsection are—

    (a) that the witness—

        (i) suffers from mental disorder within the meaning of the Mental Health Act 1983, or

        (ii) otherwise has a significant impairment of intelligence and social functioning;

    (b) that the witness has a physical disability or is suffering from a physical disorder.

(3) In subsection (1)(a) 'the time of the hearing', in relation to a witness, means the time when it falls to the court to make a determination for the purposes of section 19(2) in relation to the witness.

(4) In determining whether a witness falls within subsection (1)(b) the court must consider any views expressed by the witness.

(5) In this chapter references to the quality of a witness's evidence are to its quality in terms of completeness, coherence and accuracy; and for this purpose 'coherence' refers to a witness's ability in giving evidence to give answers which address the questions put to the witness and can be understood both individually and collectively.

17.—(1) For the purposes of this chapter a witness in criminal proceedings (other than the accused) is eligible for assistance by virtue of this subsection if the court is satisfied that the quality of evidence given by the witness is likely to be diminished by reason of fear or distress on the part of the witness in connection with testifying in the proceedings.

(2) In determining whether a witness falls within subsection (1) the court must take into account, in particular—

    (a) the nature and alleged circumstances of the offence to which the proceedings relate;

    (b) the age of the witness;

    (c) such of the following matters as appear to the court to be relevant, namely—

        (i) the social and cultural background and ethnic origins of the witness,

        (ii) the domestic and employment circumstances of the witness, and

        (iii) any religious beliefs or political opinions of the witness;

    (d) any behaviour towards the witness on the part of—

        (i) the accused,

        (ii) members of the family or associates of the accused, or

        (iii) any other person who is likely to be an accused or a witness in the proceedings.

(3) In determining that question the court must in addition consider any views expressed by the witness.

(4) Where the complainant in respect of a sexual offence or an offence under section 4 of the Asylum and Immigration (Treatment of Claimants, etc.) Act 2004 is a witness in proceedings relating to that offence (or to that offence and any other offences), the witness is eligible for assistance in relation to those proceedings by virtue of this subsection unless the witness has informed the court of the witness's wish not to be so eligible by virtue of this subsection.

(5) A witness in proceedings relating to a relevant offence (or to a relevant offence and any other offences) is eligible for assistance in relation to those proceedings by virtue of this subsection unless the witness has informed the court of the witness's wish not to be so eligible by virtue of this subsection.

(6) For the purposes of subsection (5) an offence is a relevant offence if it is an offence described in Schedule 1A.

(7) The Secretary of State may by order amend Schedule 1A.

18.—(1) For the purposes of this chapter—

    (a) the provision which may be made by a special measures direction by virtue of each of sections 23 to 30 is a special measure available in relation to a witness eligible for assistance by virtue of section 16; and

    (b) the provision which may be made by such a direction by virtue of each of sections 23 to 28 is a special measure available in relation to a witness eligible for assistance by virtue of section 17;

but this subsection has effect subject to subsection (2).

(2) Where (apart from this subsection) a special measure would, in accordance with subsection (1)(a) or (b), be available in relation to a witness in any proceedings, it shall not be taken by a court to be available in relation to the witness unless—

    (a) the court has been notified by the Secretary of State that relevant arrangements may be made available in the area in which it appears to the court that the proceedings will take place, and

(b) the notice has not been withdrawn.

(3) In subsection (2) 'relevant arrangements' means arrangements for implementing the measure in question which cover the witness and the proceedings in question.

(4) The withdrawal of a notice under that subsection relating to a special measure shall not affect the availability of that measure in relation to a witness if a special measures direction providing for that measure to apply to the witness's evidence has been made by the court before the notice is withdrawn.

(5) [Power of Secretary of State to amend so as to alter special measures available.]

19.—(1) This section applies where in any criminal proceedings—

    (a) a party to the proceedings makes an application for the court to give a direction under this section in relation to a witness in the proceedings other than the accused, or

    (b) the court of its own motion raises the issue whether such a direction should be given.

(2) Where the court determines that the witness is eligible for assistance by virtue of section 16 or 17, the court must then—

    (a) determine whether any of the special measures available in relation to the witness (or any combination of them) would, in its opinion, be likely to improve the quality of evidence given by the witness; and

    (b) if so—

        (i) determine which of those measures (or combination of them) would, in its opinion, be likely to maximise so far as practicable the quality of such evidence; and

        (ii) give a direction under this section providing for the measure or measures so determined to apply to evidence given by the witness.

(3) In determining for the purposes of this chapter whether any special measure or measures would or would not be likely to improve, or to maximise so far as practicable, the quality of evidence given by the witness, the court must consider all the circumstances of the case, including in particular—

    (a) any views expressed by the witness; and

    (b) whether the measure or measures might tend to inhibit such evidence being effectively tested by a party to the proceedings.

(4) A special measures direction must specify particulars of the provision made by the direction in respect of each special measure which is to apply to the witness's evidence.

(5) In this chapter 'special measures direction' means a direction under this section.

(6) Nothing in this chapter is to be regarded as affecting any power of a court to make an order or give leave of any description (in the exercise of its inherent jurisdiction or otherwise)—

    (a) in relation to a witness who is not an eligible witness, or

    (b) in relation to an eligible witness where (as, for example, in a case where a foreign language interpreter is to be provided) the order is made or the leave is given otherwise than by reason of the fact that the witness is an eligible witness.

20.—(1) Subject to subsection (2) and section 21(8), a special measures direction has binding effect from the time it is made until the proceedings for the purposes of which it is made are either—

    (a) determined (by acquittal, conviction or otherwise), or

    (b) abandoned,

in relation to the accused or (if there is more than one) in relation to each of the accused.

(2) The court may discharge or vary (or further vary) a special measures direction if it appears to the court to be in the interests of justice to do so, and may do so either—

    (a) on an application made by a party to the proceedings, if there has been a material change of circumstances since the relevant time, or

    (b) of its own motion.

(3) In subsection (2) 'the relevant time' means—

    (a) the time when the direction was given, or

    (b) if a previous application has been made under that subsection, the time when the application (or last application) was made.

(4) Nothing in section 24(2) and (3), 27(4) to (7) or 28(4) to (6) is to be regarded as affecting the power of the court to vary or discharge a special measures direction under subsection (2).

(5) The court must state in open court its reasons for—

    (a) giving or varying,

    (b) refusing an application for, or for the variation or discharge of, or

    (c) discharging,

a special measures direction and, if it is a magistrates' court, must cause them to be entered in the register of its proceedings.

(6) [Provision as to rules of court.]

21.—(1) For the purposes of this section—

(a) a witness in criminal proceedings is a 'child witness' if he is an eligible witness by reason of section 16(1)(a) (whether or not he is an eligible witness by reason of any other provision of section 16 or 17);

(b) [repealed]; and

(c) a 'relevant recording', in relation to a child witness, is a video recording of an interview of the witness made with a view to its admission as evidence-in-chief of the witness.

(2) Where the court, in making a determination for the purposes of section 19(2), determines that a witness in criminal proceedings is a child witness, the court must—

(a) first have regard to subsections (3) to (4C) below; and

(b) then have regard to section 19(2);

and for the purposes of section 19(2), as it then applies to the witness, any special measures required to be applied in relation to him by virtue of this section shall be treated as if they were measures determined by the court, pursuant to section 19(2)(a) and (b)(i), to be ones that (whether on their own or with any other special measures) would be likely to maximise, so far as practicable, the quality of his evidence.

(3) The primary rule in the case of a child witness is that the court must give a special measures direction in relation to the witness which complies with the following requirements—

(a) it must provide for any relevant recording to be admitted under section 27 (video recorded evidence-in-chief); and

(b) it must provide for any evidence given by the witness in the proceedings which is not given by means of a video recording (whether in chief or otherwise) to be given by means of a live link in accordance with section 24.

(4) The primary rule is subject to the following limitations—

(a) the requirement contained in subsection (3)(a) or (b) has effect subject to the availability (within the meaning of section 18(2)) of the special measure in question in relation to the witness;

(b) the requirement contained in subsection (3)(a) also has effect subject to section 27(2);

(ba) if the witness informs the court of the witness's wish that the rule should not apply or should apply only in part, the rule does not apply to the extent that the court is satisfied that not complying with the rule would not diminish the quality of the witness's evidence; and

(c) the rule does not apply to the extent that the court is satisfied that compliance with it would not be likely to maximise the quality of the witness's evidence so far as practicable (whether because the application to that evidence of one or more other special measures available in relation to the witness would have that result or for any other reason).

(4A) Where as a consequence of all or part of the primary rule being disapplied under subsection (4)(ba) a witness's evidence or any part of it would fall to be given as testimony in court, the court must give a special measures direction making such provision as is described in section 23 for the evidence or that part of it.

(4B) The requirement in subsection (4A) is subject to the following limitations—

(a) if the witness informs the court of the witness's wish that the requirement in subsection (4A) should not apply, the requirement does not apply to the extent that the court is satisfied that not complying with it would not diminish the quality of the witness's evidence; and

(b) the requirement does not apply to the extent that the court is satisfied that making such a provision would not be likely to maximise the quality of the witness's evidence so far as practicable (whether because the application to that evidence of one or more other special measures available in relation to the witness would have that result or for any other reason).

(4C) In making a decision under subsection (4)(ba) or (4B)(a), the court must take into account the following factors (and any others it considers relevant)—

(a) the age and maturity of the witness;

(b) the ability of the witness to understand the consequences of giving evidence otherwise than in accordance with the requirements in subsection (3) or (as the case may be) in accordance with the requirement in subsection (4A);

(c) the relationship (if any) between the witness and the accused;

(d) the witness's social and cultural background and ethnic origins;

(e) the nature and alleged circumstances of the offence to which the proceedings relate.

(5) to (7) [Repealed.]

(8) Where a special measures direction is given in relation to a child witness who is an eligible witness by reason only of section 16(1)(a), then—

(a) subject to subsection (9) below, and

(b) except where the witness has already begun to give evidence in the proceedings,

the direction shall cease to have effect at the time when the witness attains the age of 18.

(9) Where a special measures direction is given in relation to a child witness who is an eligible witness by reason only of section 16(1)(a) and—

(a) the direction provides—

(i) for any relevant recording to be admitted under section 27 as evidence-in-chief of the witness, or

(ii) for the special measure available under section 28 to apply in relation to the witness, and

(b) if it provides for that special measure to so apply, the witness is still under the age of 18 when the video recording is made for the purposes of section 28,

then, so far as it provides as mentioned in paragraph (a)(i) or (ii) above, the direction shall continue to have effect in accordance with section 20(1) even though the witness subsequently attains that age.

22.—(1) For the purposes of this section—

(a) a witness in criminal proceedings (other than the accused) is a 'qualifying witness' if he—

(i) is not an eligible witness at the time of the hearing (as defined by section 16(3)), but

(ii) was under the age of 18 when a relevant recording was made;

(b) [repealed]; and

(c) a 'relevant recording', in relation to a witness, is a video recording of an interview of the witness made with a view to its admission as evidence-in-chief of the witness.

(2) Subsections (2) to (4) and (4C) of section 21, so far as relating to the giving of a direction complying with the requirement contained in section 21(3)(a), apply to a qualifying witness in respect of the relevant recording as they apply to a child witness (within the meaning of that section).

22A.—(1) This section applies where in criminal proceedings relating to a sexual offence (or to a sexual offence and other offences) the complainant in respect of that offence is a witness in the proceedings.

(2) This section does not apply if the place of trial is a magistrates' court.

(3) This section does not apply if the complainant is an eligible witness by reason of section 16(1)(a) (whether or not the complainant is an eligible witness by reason of any other provision of section 16 or 17).

(4) If a party to the proceedings makes an application under section 19(1)(a) for a special measures direction in relation to the complainant, the party may request that the direction provide for any relevant recording to be admitted under section 27 (video recorded evidence in chief).

(5) Subsection (6) applies if—

(a) a party to the proceedings makes a request under subsection (4) with respect to the complainant, and

(b) the court determines for the purposes of section 19(2) that the complainant is eligible for assistance by virtue of section 16(1)(b) or 17.

(6) The court must—

(a) first have regard to subsections (7) to (9); and

(b) then have regard to section 19(2);

and for the purposes of section 19(2), as it then applies to the complainant, any special measure required to be applied in relation to the complainant by virtue of this section is to be treated as if it were a measure determined by the court, pursuant to section 19(2)(a) and (b)(i), to be one that (whether on its own or with any other special measures) would be likely to maximise, so far as practicable, the quality of the complainant's evidence.

(7) The court must give a special measures direction in relation to the complainant that provides for any relevant recording to be admitted under section 27.

(8) The requirement in subsection (7) has effect subject to section 27(2).

(9) The requirement in subsection (7) does not apply to the extent that the court is satisfied that compliance with it would not be likely to maximise the quality of the complainant's evidence

so far as practicable (whether because the application to that evidence of one or more other special measures available in relation to the complainant would have that result or for any other reason).

(10) In this section 'relevant recording', in relation to a complainant, is a video recording of an interview of the complainant made with a view to its admission as the evidence-in-chief of the complainant.

23.—(1) A special measures direction may provide for the witness, while giving testimony or being sworn in court, to be prevented by means of a screen or other arrangement from seeing the accused.

(2) But the screen or other arrangement must not prevent the witness from being able to see, and to be seen by—
  (a) the judge or justices (or both) and the jury (if there is one);
  (b) legal representatives acting in the proceedings; and
  (c) any interpreter or other person appointed (in pursuance of the direction or otherwise) to assist the witness.

(3) Where two or more legal representatives are acting for a party to the proceedings, subsection (2)(b) is to be regarded as satisfied in relation to those representatives if the witness is able at all material times to see and be seen by at least one of them.

24.—(1) A special measures direction may provide for the witness to give evidence by means of a live link.

(1A) Such a direction may also provide for a specified person to accompany the witness while the witness is giving evidence by live link.

(1B) In determining who may accompany the witness, the court must have regard to the wishes of the witness.

(2) Where a direction provides for the witness to give evidence by means of a live link, the witness may not give evidence in any other way without the permission of the court.

(3) The court may give permission for the purposes of subsection (2) if it appears to the court to be in the interests of justice to do so, and may do so either—
  (a) on an application by a party to the proceedings, if there has been a material change of circumstances since the relevant time, or
  (b) of its own motion.

(4) In subsection (3) 'the relevant time' means—
  (a) the time when the direction was given, or
  (b) if a previous application has been made under that subsection, the time when the application (or last application) was made.

(5) to (7) [Repealed.]

(8) In this chapter 'live link' means a live television link or other arrangement whereby a witness, while absent from the courtroom or other place where the proceedings are being held, is able to see and hear a person there and to be seen and heard by the persons specified in section 23(2) (a) to (c).

25.—(1) A special measures direction may provide for the exclusion from the court, during the giving of the witness's evidence, of persons of any description specified in the direction.

(2) The persons who may be so excluded do not include—
  (a) the accused,
  (b) legal representatives acting in the proceedings, or
  (c) any interpreter or other person appointed (in pursuance of the direction or otherwise) to assist the witness.

(3) A special measures direction providing for representatives of news gathering or reporting organisations to be so excluded shall be expressed not to apply to one named person who—
  (a) is a representative of such an organisation, and
  (b) has been nominated for the purpose by one or more such organisations, unless it appears to the court that no such nomination has been made.

(4) A special measures direction may only provide for the exclusion of persons under this section where—
  (a) the proceedings relate to a sexual offence or an offence under section 4 of the Asylum and Immigration (Treatment of Claimants, etc.) Act 2004; or
  (b) it appears to the court that there are reasonable grounds for believing that any person other than the accused has sought, or will seek, to intimidate the witness in connection with testifying in the proceedings.

(5) Any proceedings from which persons are excluded under this section (whether or not those persons include representatives of news gathering or reporting organisations) shall nevertheless be taken to be held in public for the purposes of any privilege or exemption from liability available in respect of fair, accurate and contemporaneous reports of legal proceedings held in public.

26. A special measures direction may provide for the wearing of wigs or gowns to be dispensed with during the giving of the witness's evidence.

27.—(1) A special measures direction may provide for a video recording of an interview of the witness to be admitted as evidence-in-chief of the witness.

(2) A special measures direction may, however, not provide for a video recording, or a part of such a recording, to be admitted under this section if the court is of the opinion, having regard to all the circumstances of the case, that in the interests of justice the recording, or that part of it, should not be so admitted.

(3) In considering for the purposes of subsection (2) whether any part of a recording should not be admitted under this section, the court must consider whether any prejudice to the accused which might result from that part being so admitted is outweighed by the desirability of showing the whole, or substantially the whole, of the recorded interview.

(4) Where a special measures direction provides for a recording to be admitted under this section, the court may nevertheless subsequently direct that it is not to be so admitted if—

(a) it appears to the court that—

(i) the witness will not be available for cross-examination (whether conducted in the ordinary way or in accordance with any such direction), and

(ii) the parties to the proceedings have not agreed that there is no need for the witness to be so available; or

(b) any Criminal Procedure Rules requiring disclosure of the circumstances in which the recording was made have not been complied with to the satisfaction of the court.

(5) Where a recording is admitted under this section—

(a) the witness must be called by the party tendering it in evidence, unless—

(i) a special measures direction provides for the witness's evidence on cross-examination to be given otherwise than by testimony in court, or

(ii) the parties to the proceedings have agreed as mentioned in subsection (4)(a)(ii); and

(b) the witness may not without the permission of the court give evidence in chief otherwise than by means of the recording as to any matter which, in the opinion of the court, is dealt with in the witness's recorded testimony.

(6) Where in accordance with subsection (2) a special measures direction provides for part only of a recording to be admitted under this section, references in subsections (4) and (5) to the recording or to the witness's recorded testimony are references to the part of the recording or testimony which is to be so admitted.

(7) The court may give permission for the purposes of subsection (5)(b) if it appears to the court to be in the interests of justice to do so, and may do so either—

(a) on an application by a party to the proceedings, or

(b) of its own motion.

(8) [Repealed.]

(9) The court may, in giving permission for the purposes of subsection (5)(b), direct that the evidence in question is to be given by the witness by means of a live link.

(9A) If the court directs under subsection (9) that evidence is to be given by live link, it may also make such provision in that direction as it could make under section 24(1A) in a special measures direction.

(10) A magistrates' court inquiring into an offence as examining justices under section 6 of the Magistrates' Courts Act 1980 may consider any video recording in relation to which it is proposed to apply for a special measures direction providing for it to be admitted at the trial in accordance with this section.

(11) Nothing in this section affects the admissibility of any video recording which would be admissible apart from this section.

[Section 28 is not yet in force and is not included here.]

29.—(1) A special measures direction may provide for any examination of the witness (however and wherever conducted) to be conducted through an interpreter or other person approved by the court for the purposes of this section ('an intermediary').

(2) The function of an intermediary is to communicate—

(a) to the witness, questions put to the witness, and

(b) to any person asking such questions, the answers given by the witness in reply to them, and to explain such questions or answers so far as necessary to enable them to be understood by the witness or person in question.

(3) Any examination of the witness in pursuance of subsection (1) must take place in the presence of such persons as Criminal Procedure Rules or the direction may provide, but in circumstances in which—

(a) the judge or justices (or both) and legal representatives acting in the proceedings are able to see and hear the examination of the witness and to communicate with the intermediary, and

(b) (except in the case of a video recorded examination) the jury (if there is one) are able to see and hear the examination of the witness.

(4) Where two or more legal representatives are acting for a party to the proceedings, subsection (3)(a) is to be regarded as satisfied in relation to those representatives if at all material times it is satisfied in relation to at least one of them.

(5) A person may not act as an intermediary in a particular case except after making a declaration, in such form as may be prescribed by Criminal Procedure Rules, that he will faithfully perform his function as intermediary.

(6) Subsection (1) does not apply to an interview of the witness which is recorded by means of a video recording with a view to its admission as evidence-in-chief of the witness; but a special measures direction may provide for such a recording to be admitted under section 27 if the interview was conducted through an intermediary and—

(a) that person complied with subsection (5) before the interview began, and

(b) the court's approval for the purposes of this section is given before the direction is given.

(7) Section 1 of the Perjury Act 1911 (perjury) shall apply in relation to a person acting as an intermediary as it applies in relation to a person lawfully sworn as an interpreter in a judicial proceeding; and for this purpose, where a person acts as an intermediary in any proceeding which is not a judicial proceeding for the purposes of that section, that proceeding shall be taken to be part of the judicial proceeding in which the witness's evidence is given.

30. A special measures direction may provide for the witness, while giving evidence (whether by testimony in court or otherwise), to be provided with such device as the court considers appropriate with a view to enabling questions or answers to be communicated to or by the witness despite any disability or disorder or other impairment which the witness has or suffers from.

...

33A.—(1) This section applies to any proceedings (whether in a magistrates' court or before the Crown Court) against a person for an offence.

(2) The court may, on the application of the accused, give a live link direction if it is satisfied—

(a) that the conditions in subsection (4) or, as the case may be, subsection (5) are met in relation to the accused, and

(b) that it is in the interests of justice for the accused to give evidence through a live link.

(3) A live link direction is a direction that any oral evidence to be given before the court by the accused is to be given through a live link.

(4) Where the accused is aged under 18 when the application is made, the conditions are that—

(a) his ability to participate effectively in the proceedings as a witness giving oral evidence in court is compromised by his level of intellectual ability or social functioning, and

(b) use of a live link would enable him to participate more effectively in the proceedings as a witness (whether by improving the quality of his evidence or otherwise).

(5) Where the accused has attained the age of 18 at that time, the conditions are that—

(a) he suffers from a mental disorder (within the meaning of the Mental Health Act 1983) or otherwise has a significant impairment of intelligence and social function,

(b) he is for that reason unable to participate effectively in the proceedings as a witness giving oral evidence in court, and

(c) use of a live link would enable him to participate more effectively in the proceedings as a witness (whether by improving the quality of his evidence or otherwise).

(6) While a live link direction has effect the accused may not give oral evidence before the court in the proceedings otherwise than through a live link.

(7) The court may discharge a live link direction at any time before or during any hearing to which it applies if it appears to the court to be in the interests of justice to do so (but this does not affect the power to give a further live link direction in relation to the accused).

The court may exercise this power of its own motion or on an application by a party.

(8) The court must state in open court its reasons for—
  (a) giving or discharging a live link direction, or
  (b) refusing an application for or for the discharge of a live link direction,
  and, if it is a magistrates' court, it must cause those reasons to be entered in the register of its proceedings.

33B.—(1) In section 33A 'live link' means an arrangement by which the accused, while absent from the place where the proceedings are being held, is able—
  (a) to see and hear a person there, and
  (b) to be seen and heard by the persons mentioned in subsection (2),
  and for this purpose any impairment of eyesight or hearing is to be disregarded.

(2) The persons are—
  (a) the judge or justices (or both) and the jury (if there is one),
  (b) where there are two or more accused in the proceedings, each of the other accused,
  (c) legal representatives acting in the proceedings, and
  (d) any interpreter or other person appointed by the court to assist the accused.
  [Sections 33BA and 33BB, inserted by the CAJA 2009, s. 104, are not yet in force and are not included here.]

33C. Nothing in this Chapter affects—
  (a) any power of a court to make an order, give directions or give leave of any description in relation to any witness (including an accused), or
  (b) the operation of any rule of law relating to evidence in criminal proceedings.

Statutory Provisions on Anonymous Witnesses

Coroners and Justice Act 2009, ss. 86 to 90   D14.60

86.—(1) In this Chapter a 'witness anonymity order' is an order made by a court that requires such specified measures to be taken in relation to a witness in criminal proceedings as the court considers appropriate to ensure that the identity of the witness is not disclosed in or in connection with the proceedings.

(2) The kinds of measures that may be required to be taken in relation to a witness include measures for securing one or more of the following—
  (a) that the witness's name and other identifying details may be—
    (i) withheld;
    (ii) removed from materials disclosed to any party to the proceedings;
  (b) that the witness may use a pseudonym;
  (c) that the witness is not asked questions of any specified description that might lead to the identification of the witness;
  (d) that the witness is screened to any specified extent;
  (e) that the witness's voice is subjected to modulation to any specified extent.

(3) Subsection (2) does not affect the generality of subsection (1).

(4) Nothing in this section authorises the court to require—
  (a) the witness to be screened to such an extent that the witness cannot be seen by—
    (i) the judge or other members of the court (if any), or
    (ii) the jury (if there is one);
  (b) the witness's voice to be modulated to such an extent that the witness's natural voice cannot be heard by any persons within paragraph (a)(i) or (ii).

(5) In this section 'specified' means specified in the witness anonymity order concerned.

87.—(1) An application for a witness anonymity order to be made in relation to a witness in criminal proceedings may be made to the court by the prosecutor or the defendant.

(2) Where an application is made by the prosecutor, the prosecutor—
  (a) must (unless the court directs otherwise) inform the court of the identity of the witness, but
  (b) is not required to disclose in connection with the application—
    (i) the identity of the witness, or
    (ii) any information that might enable the witness to be identified,
  to any other party to the proceedings or his or her legal representatives.

(3) Where an application is made by the defendant, the defendant—

    (a) must inform the court and the prosecutor of the identity of the witness, but

    (b) (if there is more than one defendant) is not required to disclose in connection with the application—

        (i) the identity of the witness, or

        (ii) any information that might enable the witness to be identified,

    to any other defendant or his or her legal representatives.

(4) Accordingly, where the prosecutor or the defendant proposes to make an application under this section in respect of a witness, any relevant material which is disclosed by or on behalf of that party before the determination of the application may be disclosed in such a way as to prevent—

    (a) the identity of the witness, or

    (b) any information that might enable the witness to be identified,

    from being disclosed except as required by subsection (2)(a) or (3)(a).

(5) 'Relevant material' means any document or other material which falls to be disclosed, or is sought to be relied on, by or on behalf of the party concerned in connection with the proceedings or proceedings preliminary to them.

(6) The court must give every party to the proceedings the opportunity to be heard on an application under this section.

(7) But subsection (6) does not prevent the court from hearing one or more parties in the absence of a defendant and his or her legal representatives, if it appears to the court to be appropriate to do so in the circumstances of the case.

(8) Nothing in this section is to be taken as restricting any power to make rules of court.

88.—(1) This section applies where an application is made for a witness anonymity order to be made in relation to a witness in criminal proceedings.

(2) The court may make such an order only if it is satisfied that Conditions A to C below are met.

(3) Condition A is that the proposed order is necessary—

    (a) in order to protect the safety of the witness or another person or to prevent any serious damage to property, or

    (b) in order to prevent real harm to the public interest (whether affecting the carrying on of any activities in the public interest or the safety of a person involved in carrying on such activities, or otherwise).

(4) Condition B is that, having regard to all the circumstances, the effect of the proposed order would be consistent with the defendant receiving a fair trial.

(5) Condition C is that the importance of the witness's testimony is such that in the interests of justice the witness ought to testify and—

    (a) the witness would not testify if the proposed order were not made, or

    (b) there would be real harm to the public interest if the witness were to testify without the proposed order being made.

(6) In determining whether the proposed order is necessary for the purpose mentioned in subsection (3)(a), the court must have regard (in particular) to any reasonable fear on the part of the witness—

    (a) that the witness or another person would suffer death or injury, or

    (b) that there would be serious damage to property,

    if the witness were to be identified.

89.—(1) When deciding whether Conditions A to C in section 88 are met in the case of an application for a witness anonymity order, the court must have regard to—

    (a) the considerations mentioned in subsection (2) below, and

    (b) such other matters as the court considers relevant.

(2) The considerations are—

    (a) the general right of a defendant in criminal proceedings to know the identity of a witness in the proceedings;

    (b) the extent to which the credibility of the witness concerned would be a relevant factor when the weight of his or her evidence comes to be assessed;

    (c) whether evidence given by the witness might be the sole or decisive evidence implicating the defendant;

    (d) whether the witness's evidence could be properly tested (whether on grounds of credibility or otherwise) without his or her identity being disclosed;

    (e) whether there is any reason to believe that the witness—

(i)   has a tendency to be dishonest, or

(ii) has any motive to be dishonest in the circumstances of the case,

having regard (in particular) to any previous convictions of the witness and to any relationship between the witness and the defendant or any associates of the defendant;

(f)   whether it would be reasonably practicable to protect the witness by any means other than by making a witness anonymity order specifying the measures that are under consideration by the court

90.—(1) Subsection (2) applies where, on a trial on indictment with a jury, any evidence has been given by a witness at a time when a witness anonymity order applied to the witness.

(2) The judge must give the jury such warning as the judge considers appropriate to ensure that the fact that the order was made in relation to the witness does not prejudice the defendant.

Section D15 Trial on Indictment: General Matters and Pre-trial Procedure

INTRODUCTION

D15.1   Once the accused has pleaded not guilty to the charges he faces (see **D12**), he places himself at the centre of a procedural framework, now governed by the CrimPR (see Supplement, **R-9**) and CPD I, part 3 (see Supplement, **PD-3**), and influenced by the strong recent emphasis on effective case management, that is designed to prepare the case for trial. This section addresses those matters of general preliminary application to trials on indictment, the conduct of hearings pre-trial, and the obligations and safeguards imposed by rules at the pre-trial stage. For special measures and anonymity of witnesses, see **D14**.

PLACE OF TRIAL

D15.2   The first issue that arises is the location in which the case is to be tried. Following on from this is the question of transfer of cases between Crown Court centres.

Venue of Trial

D15.3   This is primarily regulated by the Senior Courts Act 1981, s. 75, which empowers the Lord Chief Justice to regulate both the location of the Crown Court to which an accused is initially sent and the nature of the tribunal before which he is ultimately tried (i.e. High Court judge, circuit judge or recorder).

> **Senior Courts Act 1981, s. 75**
>
> (1) The cases or classes of cases in the Crown Court suitable for allocation respectively to a judge of the High Court, circuit judge, recorder or district judge (magistrates' court), and all other matters relating to the distribution of Crown Court business, shall be determined in accordance with directions given by or on behalf of the Lord Chief Justice with the concurrence of the Lord Chancellor.
>
> (2) Subject to section 74(1) [which requires that when hearing an appeal the Crown Court shall normally consist of a professional judge together with at least two justices of the peace], the cases or classes of cases in the Crown Court suitable for allocation to a court comprising justices of the peace (including those by way of trial on indictment which are suitable for allocation to such a court) shall be determined in accordance with directions given by or on behalf of the Lord Chief Justice with the concurrence of the Lord Chancellor.

In addition, the MCA 1980, s. 7, provides that, when specifying the particular location of the Crown Court to which an accused should be sent for trial, a magistrates' court must have regard, *inter alia*, to the directions given by the Lord Chief Justice under s. 75(1) of the Senior Courts Act 1981.

CPD XIII contains detailed guidance on listing; para. E deals with the allocation of business within the Crown Court (see Supplement, **PD-100**).

Transfer of Cases between Locations of the Crown Court

Section 76(1) of the Senior Courts Act 1981 provides that the Crown Court may give directions altering the place of any trial on indictment, varying either the venue specified in a notice under the CDA 1998, s. 51D(1), or any earlier decision of the Crown Court itself. Such a change can be brought about in a number of ways: **D15.4**

(a) an officer of the Crown Court may give such directions on behalf of the court (s. 76(2));
(b) either party, if dissatisfied with the place of trial that has been fixed, may apply to the Crown Court for a variation (s. 76(3)), such application to be heard in open court by a High Court judge (s. 76(4)).

The place of trial specified in notices of transfer under s. 4 of the CJA 1987 can be varied in the same way (s. 76(2A)); see also Supplement, **PD-101**.

Reasons for Transfer   Section 76 provides no assistance as to how the powers it gives are to be exercised. The power given to listing officers of the Crown Court by s. 76(2) to switch a trial from one court centre to another is exercised principally on administrative rather than judicial grounds. **D15.5**

Section 76(1) does contain the qualification that it is 'Without prejudice to the provisions of this Act about the distribution of Crown Court business'. It follows that, on an application by a party under s. 76(3) for variation of the venue, the High Court judge determining the application is entitled to consider any factors not originally taken into account. Such additional factors may include the possible prejudice to the accused of being tried in the area where the offence was allegedly committed if the nature of the charge has provoked exceptional public hostility.

However, in the light of the Court of Appeal's decision in *Ford* [1989] QB 868 (see **D13.40**), it would be inappropriate to vary the trial venue with a view to obtaining a multiracial jury panel (see also *Bansal* [1985] Crim LR 151).

Senior Courts Act 1981, s. 76   **D15.6**

(1) Without prejudice to the provisions of this Act about the distribution of Crown Court business, the Crown Court may give directions, or further directions, altering the place of any trial on indictment, whether by substituting some other place for the place specified in a notice under section 51D(1) of the Crime and Disorder Act 1998 (a 'section 51D notice') or by varying a previous decision of the Crown Court.
(2) Directions under subsection (1) may be given on behalf of the Crown Court by an officer of the court.
(2A) Where a preparatory hearing has been ordered under section 7 of the Criminal Justice Act 1987, directions altering the place of trial may be given under subsection (1) at any time before the time when the jury are sworn.
(2B) The reference in subsection (2A) to the time when the jury are sworn includes the time when the jury would be sworn but for the making of an order under Part 7 of the Criminal Justice Act 2003.
(3) The defendant or the prosecutor, if dissatisfied with the place of trial specified in a section 51D notice or as fixed by the Crown Court, may apply to the Crown Court for a direction, or further direction, varying the place of trial; and the court shall take the matter into consideration and may comply with or refuse the application, or give a direction not in compliance with the application, as the court thinks fit.
(4) An application under subsection (3) shall be heard in open court by a judge of the High Court.

CUSTODY TIME-LIMITS

D15.7   Section 22 of the Prosecution of Offences Act 1985 (set out at **D15.38**) was introduced to remedy the manifest inadequacy of the provisions then available to ensure that trials on indictment begin within a reasonable time. It empowers the Secretary of State to make regulations fixing:

    (a) the maximum period available to the prosecution to complete any preliminary (pre-trial) stage of proceedings for an offence; and/or

    (b) the maximum period for which an accused may be kept in custody while awaiting completion of such a stage.

Definition of Terms

D15.8   Inevitably the main concern of practitioners and the courts is the consequences of a time-limit expiring and applications being made to extend it. Before approaching these issues, however, it is of assistance to define some of the relevant terminology.

D15.9   **Committal**   References to 'committal' in this context should be taken to include the giving of a notice of transfer under the CJA 1987, s. 4, or under the CJA 1991, s. 53, and sending for trial under the CDA 1998, s. 51 (subject to specific variations in such cases).

Regulations under the Prosecution of Offences Act 1985, s. 22, have application not only to the time between committal and arraignment, but also to the time between the accused being charged and committal (for offences triable on indictment) or the time between charge and the commencement of summary trial (in other cases). Section 22 is thus relevant to the timing both of committal and summary trial, as well as to the timing of arraignment.

D15.10   **Preliminary Stage of Proceedings**   The general effect of s. 22 of the Prosecution of Offences Act 1985 is that the Secretary of State may by regulation impose time-limits in respect of any specified 'preliminary stage' of proceedings for an offence (s. 22(1)). The regulations may relate to any type of offence, whether triable only on indictment, triable either way or summarily. 'Preliminary stage' is defined as *not* including anything after the start of trial.

D15.11   **Start of a Trial on Indictment**   As far as trial on indictment is concerned, the 'start of trial' is defined as the point when a jury is sworn, or the court accepts a plea of guilty (Prosecution of Offences Act 1985, s. 22(11A)).

This is significant in cases where a preparatory hearing is held, whether for a long or complex case (in accordance with the CPIA 1996, s. 30: see **D15.51** *et seq.*) or for a serious or complex fraud (in accordance with the CJA 1987, s. 8: see **D15.60**). Under each of those sections, the beginning of the preparatory hearing is deemed to be the beginning of the trial, and therefore custody time-limits will cease to operate from that moment.

In *Re Kanaris* [2003] 1 All ER 593, the House of Lords considered the consequences of the removal of the protection of the custody time-limits regime where a preparatory hearing took place. Lord Hope said:

> . . . a judge who is minded to order a preparatory hearing in a long and complex case should be careful not to deprive an accused who is in custody of the protection of the statutory custody time-limit until it has become necessary for him to do so.

He indicated that the judge could, where appropriate, exercise powers under the CPIA 1996, s. 31(4)–(7) (see **D15.56**), before the preparatory hearing begins to permit effective case management whilst preserving the accused's right to the protection of the statutory custody time-limit.

Start of a Summary Trial　As far as summary trial is concerned, the start of trial is 'when the　**D15.12** court begins to hear evidence for the prosecution at trial' or accepts a plea of guilty (Prosecution of Offences Act 1985, s. 22(11B)). There is an exception where the court begins to consider whether to exercise its power, under the Mental Health Act 1983, s. 37(3), to make a hospital order without convicting the accused.

Meaning of Custody　As far as custody time-limits are concerned, 'custody' includes:　**D15.13**

(a) local authority accommodation to which a juvenile is committed by virtue of the CYPA 1969, s. 23 (Prosecution of Offences Act 1985, s. 22(11));
(b) the detention of a youth charged with an indictable offence — in *Stratford Youth Court, ex parte S* (1998) 162 JP 552, the Divisional Court held that the 56-day custody time-limit imposed for completion of preliminary stages in indictable offences applied to a young person charged with robbery because, in the case of a young person, it was an offence triable either way;
(c) where an accused remains in custody because he is unable to provide a surety, since he falls within the terms of the MCA 1980, s. 128 (*Re Ofili* [1995] Crim LR 880).

In *Peterborough Crown Court, ex parte L* [2000] Crim LR 470, the Divisional Court held that the whole period during which the accused was remanded in custody for the offence in question should be taken into account when calculating the relevant period for custody time-limits. There was no basis on which part of the period could be disregarded on the basis that the accused was also serving a custodial sentence for an unrelated matter.

Periods Applicable

The regulations may prescribe an *overall time-limit* within which the prosecution must com-　**D15.14** plete the stage of the proceedings in question (Prosecution of Offences Act 1985, s. 22(1)(a)). However, no overall time-limits currently apply.

Alternatively or additionally, the regulations may prescribe a *custody time-limit*, that being the maximum period for which the accused may be remanded in custody while the stage is being completed (s. 22(1)(b)).

Time-limits　The regulations in question, the Prosecution of Offences (Custody Time　**D15.15** Limits) Regulations 1987 (SI 1987 No. 299), only impose custody time-limits. These are as follows:

(a) *Between first appearance and committal.* By reg. 4(2) and (4), the maximum period for which an accused charged with an indictable offence may be held in the custody of the magistrates' court between his first appearance and committal proceedings is 70 days.
(b) *Between first appearance and summary trial.* If the offence is triable either way and the court determines to try the case summarily, the maximum period in custody between first appearance and the court beginning to hear evidence for the prosecution is again 70 days, unless the decision for summary trial is taken within 56 days, in which case the limit is reduced to 56 days (reg. 4(2) and (3)). In the case of a summary offence, the maximum period is 56 days (reg. 4(4A)).
(c) *Between committal and trial on indictment.* By reg. 5(3)(a), the maximum period for which an accused committed for trial to the Crown Court may be held in custody between 'committal' and the start of trial is 112 days.
(d) *Multiple committals.* If a single indictment is preferred containing counts in respect of which the accused was committed for trial on two or more different occasions, the 112-day limit applies separately in relation to each offence (reg. 6(4)). See also **D15.16**.
(e) *Voluntary bill.* Where proceedings are by way of a voluntary bill of indictment the 112-day period runs from the date of preferment of the bill (reg. 5(3)(b)).

(f) *Retrial directed by the Court of Appeal.* Where an indictment is preferred by direction of the Court of Appeal, following the ordering of a retrial, the 112-day limit applies from that preferment (reg. 5(2)(b) and (3)(b)). See also *Leeds Crown Court, ex parte Whitehead* (17 June 1999 unreported, DC).

(g) *Section 51 sending.* Where the accused has been sent for trial under the CDA 1998, s. 51, the maximum period is 182 days between the date on which he is sent to the Crown Court and the start of the trial. From this maximum must be deducted any period during which the accused was held in custody by the magistrates (reg. 5(6B)).

Separate Time-limits for Each Offence

D15.16 Each offence with which the accused is charged attracts its own time-limit (*Wirral District Magistrates' Court, ex parte Meikle* (1990) 154 JP 1035). In this case, M was charged with five different offences at different dates, being held in custody from the date of the first charge. In view of the fact that the 1987 Regulations repeatedly refer to 'offence' in the singular, the Divisional Court had no difficulty in concluding that each offence attracts its own custody time-limit. (See also *Great Yarmouth Magistrates, ex parte Thomas* [1992] Crim LR 116, *Waltham Forest Magistrates' Court, ex parte Lee* (1993) 157 JP 811, *Leeds Crown Court, ex parte Stubley* [1999] Crim LR 822 and *Wolverhampton Justices and Stafford Crown Court, ex parte Uppal* (1995) 159 JP 86.)

D15.17 **Meaning of Separate Offences**   In *R (Wardle) v Leeds Crown Court* [2001] 2 All ER 1, W was originally charged with murder, but the prosecution offered no evidence on that charge and preferred a charge of manslaughter on the day that the original custody time-limit was due to expire. On appeal, the House of Lords considered the question: what constitutes the charging of an offence, such as to trigger a fresh custody time-limit? It concluded:

(a) the word 'offence' in reg. 4 could not be read as including an alternative offence of which the accused could be found guilty under the CLA 1967;

(b) the situation would be different if the new charge was simply a restatement of the original charge with different particulars — it had to be a different offence in law to attract a fresh custody time-limit; and

(c) the bringing of a fresh charge would be an abuse of process if the prosecution could not demonstrate, on the facts of the case, that it was justified and had not been brought solely with a view to obtaining the substitution of a fresh custody time-limit.

Effect of Expiry of Custody Time-limit

D15.18 If a custody time-limit expires before completion of the stage of proceedings in question, the accused must be granted bail, in relation at least to the offence to which the limit relates. This is made clear by reg. 6(6), which states that, where the Crown Court is notified that the 112-day time-limit between 'committal' and the start of the trial is about to expire in a certain case, it must bail the accused as from the expiry of the limit, subject to a duty to attend for trial. The regulations do not expressly deal with the procedure for bailing an accused who has the benefit of the 70-day time-limit between charge and committal or summary trial.

D15.19 **The Grant of Bail**   The regulations may make provision for the Bail Act 1976 and the MCA 1980 to apply in cases where the accused is bailed as a result of a custody time-limit's expiry with such modifications as the Secretary of State considers necessary (Prosecution of Offences Act 1985, s. 22(2)(d)).

In the case of the Bail Act 1976, its application to accused persons in respect of whom custody time-limits have expired is modified in that:

(a) they are automatically entitled to bail;

(b) on granting bail, the court may not require sureties or the deposit of security; and

(c) following the grant of bail, they may not be arrested without warrant merely on the ground that a police officer believes they are unlikely to surrender to custody (reg. 8).

Other conditions, such as curfew, residence or reporting to a police station, may nevertheless be imposed as in other cases, and the rule that actual or feared breach of such conditions is a ground for arrest without warrant (Bail Act 1976, ss. 3(6) and 7(3)(b)) applies to an accused bailed on expiry of a time-limit just as it applies to an accused granted bail in any other circumstances (see also D7.42).

Procedure for Imposing Conditions   Regulation 6 requires the prosecution to give notice to   **D15.20**
the appropriate court and the accused stating whether they intend to ask the court to impose conditions on the bail of an accused in respect of whom a custody time-limit is about to expire. In response to such an indication, the defence must give either:

(a) written notice of a wish to be represented at the hearing of the application;
(b) written notice that the accused does not object to the proposed conditions; or
(c) a written statement of the accused's reasons for objecting.

It is the prosecution's duty to arrange for the accused to be brought before the court within the two days preceding expiry of a custody time-limit (reg. 6(1)(b)).

Where the accused acquires the right to bail as a result of the expiry of a custody time-limit, that right continues until the start of the trial. The decision to the contrary, *Croydon Crown Court, ex parte Lewis* (1994) 158 JP 886, no longer represents the law.

Limits on the Effect of Expiry   Beyond the grant of bail, the expiry of the custody time-limit   **D15.21**
otherwise has no effect on the proceedings. This was illustrated in *Sheffield Magistrates' Court, ex parte Turner* [1991] 2 QB 472. T had been unlawfully detained, contrary to the Prosecution of Offences Act 1985, s. 22, for a period culminating in his committal for trial. Although the Divisional Court granted a declaration relating to his period of unlawful detention, it was held that this had no effect on the validity of the committal, the fresh custody time-limit, laid down by reg. 5(3), which commenced on that date, or the lawfulness of his detention thereafter.

Consequences of Absconding

Escape from custody during the running of a custody time-limit automatically leads to the regu-   **D15.22**
lations imposing the time-limit being disregarded (Prosecution of Offences Act 1985, s. 22(5)). Similarly, if an accused has been released in consequence of the expiry of a custody time-limit and then fails to attend court in answer to his bail, the earlier expiry of the limit is disregarded and the question, once he has been arrested, of whether to bail him again or remand in custody is therefore entirely in the discretion of the court (s. 22(5)).

Procedure for Seeking an Extension of Time-limits

At any time before the expiry of a time-limit, the Crown Court, if the accused has already been   **D15.23**
committed for trial, or the magistrates' court, in other cases, may extend the limit if satisfied of two matters (Prosecution of Offences Act 1985, s. 22(3)):

(a) that 'the prosecution has acted with all due diligence and expedition', and
(b) that there is 'good and sufficient cause for doing so'.

Instances of 'good and sufficient cause' are given in s. 22(3)(a)(i) and (ii), but they are clearly meant to be no more than examples.

An already extended limit may be further extended (s. 22(3)).

The criteria for the extension of the time-limit are discussed in more detail below.

D15.24   **The Notice Requirement**   By reg. 7 of the Prosecution of Offences (Custody Time Limits) Regulations 1987, an application for extension may be made orally or in writing. Notice of the intention to make the application must be given to the defence and the court not less than five days before an application to the Crown Court and not less than two days before an application to a magistrates' court. Notice may, however, be dispensed with if the court is satisfied that it is not practicable for the prosecution to give it in the time specified (reg. 7(4)).

The effect of a failure by the prosecution to give proper notice was considered in *Governor of Canterbury Prison, ex parte Craig* [1991] 2 QB 195. It was held in that case that the justices still had a discretion under s. 22(3) of the Prosecution of Offences Act 1985 to extend a time-limit 'at any time before . . . expiry'. Hence they could extend the time-limit despite the prosecution's failure to show that it had been impracticable to give the accused two days' notice of an application for extension.

In *R (Haque) v Central Criminal Court* [2004] Crim LR 298, the Divisional Court considered the import of the opening words of s. 22(3): 'The appropriate court may, at any time before the expiry of a time-limit imposed by the regulations, extend, or further extend, that limit'. It was held that they had to be construed as meaning before the expiry of a time-limit imposed by the regulations *as extended, if appropriate* by the court. They did not mean that the application could only be made within the 182 days provided for in reg. 6B following the date on which the accused first appeared in the magistrates' court.

D15.25   **Use of a Chronology**   In *Chelmsford Crown Court, ex parte Mills* (2000) 164 JP 1, Lord Bingham CJ said that when a contested application was made for an extension, turning wholly or partly on whether the prosecution had acted with all due expedition, the judge should be given a detailed chronology (preferably agreed), showing the dates of all material events and orders. When the judge ruled on such an application, he should give reasons for his decision, which need not be long or elaborate.

Criteria for Extension

D15.26   The criteria for the extension of a custody time-limit, as set out in the Prosecution of Offences Act 1985, s. 22(3), are that the court must be satisfied (i) that there was good and sufficient cause, and (ii) that the Crown had acted with all due diligence and expedition (the need for 'diligence' was added by the CDA 1998). The authorities since 1985 have provided considerable assistance both in general terms as to the proper approach of the appropriate court to an application, and more specifically as to the proper meaning and ambit of the two criteria.

D15.27   **General Guidance**   In *Manchester Crown Court, ex parte McDonald* [1999] 1 All ER 805, Lord Bingham CJ set out the principles underlying the custody time-limit provisions in the Prosecution of Offences Act 1985, s. 22, and gave guidance upon the practicalities of interpreting the tests laid down by the statute. As far as the fundamental principles of the provisions are concerned, he emphasised the presumption of liberty set out in the ECHR, Article 5(3): 'Everyone arrested or detained [for trial] . . . shall be entitled to trial within a reasonable time or to release pending trial'. With that provision in mind, the overriding purposes of the statutory provisions were said to be:

(a) to ensure that the periods for which unconvicted defendants are held in custody are as short as is reasonably and practically possible;

(b) to oblige the prosecution to prepare cases for trial with due diligence and expedition; and

(c) to give the court power to control any extension of the maximum period for which any defendant may be held awaiting trial.

The main points of practical guidance which emerge from *Ex parte McDonald* are:

(1) It is for the prosecution to satisfy the court on the balance of probabilities that the statutory conditions are met.
(2) The necessary standard is that of a competent prosecutor conscious of his duty to bring the case to trial as quickly as is reasonably and fairly possible.
(3) In judging whether this standard was met, the court should consider the nature and complexity of the case, the preparation necessary, the conduct of the defence, the extent to which the prosecutor was dependent on others outside his control and other relevant factors.
(4) What amounts to good and sufficient cause is a matter for the court on the facts of the case.
(5) Staff shortages and sickness will be inadequate reasons for extension. The unavailability of a judge or a courtroom may be good and sufficient cause, but such cases should be approached with 'great caution'.
(6) The court should state the reasons for its decision.
(7) Once the court had heard full argument and decided, the Divisional Court would be most reluctant to disturb its decision, and would do so only on the familiar grounds which support an application for judicial review.

See also *R (Raeside) v Luton Crown Court* [2012] 4 All ER 1238.

Good and Sufficient Cause   Factors that have been held not to amount to a good and sufficient cause for the extension of a time-limit include the following.   **D15.28**

(1) *The seriousness of the offence charged.* For example, in *Governor of Winchester Prison, ex parte Roddie* [1991] 2 All ER 931, the Divisional Court held that the seriousness of the offence could not represent a good and sufficient cause, because Parliament had provided the same time-limit for all offences except treason. The more serious the charge, the more important it was for the police to get on with preparing the case.
(2) *Public protection.* For example, in *Central Criminal Court, ex parte Abu-Wardeh* [1997] 1 All ER 159, the Divisional Court held that the protection of the public was, in itself, an insufficient ground for the extension of a custody time-limit, disagreeing with *Luton Crown Court, ex parte Neaves* (1993) 157 JP 80. In *Birmingham Crown Court, ex parte Bell* [1997] 2 Cr App R 363, the Divisional Court accepted that, although protection of the public might not be enough in itself to constitute good and sufficient cause, where protection of prosecution witnesses was an issue, that might be capable in conjunction with other factors of giving rise to good and sufficient cause.
(3) *Factors that may be relevant to an application for bail.* For example, in *Sheffield Crown Court, ex parte Headley* [2000] Crim LR 374, the Divisional Court stated that it was wrong for a judge in considering an application to extend custody time-limits to take account of matters relevant to the grant of bail under the Bail Act 1976. The custody time-limits regime was a separate and additional safeguard for those in custody, over and above that provided by the Bail Act 1976. Parliament could not have intended that Bail Act considerations could be determinative of a custody time-limit application (see also *R (Eliot) v Reading Crown Court* [2001] Crim LR 811).

Unavailability of a Judge or Courtroom   Several cases have turned upon the question of   **D15.29**
whether the fact that there is no judge or courtroom in which a case may be tried can constitute good and sufficient cause for the grant of an extension. In *Norwich Crown Court, ex parte Cox* (1993) 97 Cr App R 145, the Divisional Court made it plain that, in appropriate circumstances, the lack of a judge and courtroom is capable of constituting the necessary 'good and sufficient cause'. Mann LJ stated that it 'must depend upon the facts of that instant case including, in particular, whether a trial date has been specified'. However, in *R (Miah) v Crown Court at Snaresbrook* [2006] EWHC 2873 (Admin), it was made clear that listing difficulties had to be

exceptional to justify an extension; difficulties caused by the pressure of work on a Crown Court in routine cases would not be sufficient.

The court must consider what measures had been taken to address the listing difficulties; if it was clear that the difficulties were systemic, rather than particular to the case, they would represent routine difficulties and would not therefore be sufficient (*Kalonji v Crown Court at Wood Green* [2007] EWHC 2804 (Admin)). It is incumbent on the court to make inquiries as to whether an earlier trial date is possible, either at that court centre or elsewhere (*Preston Crown Court, ex parte Barraclough* [1999] Crim LR 973). This involves the court in satisfying itself that the court staff responsible for fixing the date for trial have fulfilled their duties scrupulously (*Leeds Crown Court, ex parte Wilson* [1999] Crim LR 378).

The approach adopted in these cases culminated in the decision of the Divisional Court in *R (McAulay) v Coventry Crown Court* [2012] 3 All ER 519. The Court restated that unavailability of a court could only exceptionally represent a good and sufficient cause. However, the court went further. There is a need to keep court resources under review, and to take steps to address a shortfall in those resources. Such a shortfall will 'rarely, if ever' provide proper grounds for an extension of a custody time-limit, and detailed evidence will be required to establish the necessary 'good and sufficient cause' in such circumstances. See also *R (Raeside) v Luton Crown Court* [2012] 4 All ER 1238.

D15.30   **Convenience of Defence and Witnesses**   In *White v DPP* [1989] Crim LR 375, the Divisional Court found that the reason for the extension of the time-limit in W's case, namely that the defence had successfully applied for an adjournment to consider the prosecution statements that had only just been served on them, could permit an extension. The reasonable requirement of the defence to consider the papers was capable of being a good and sufficient cause for extension of time, although each case must turn on its own facts. Their lordships did not necessarily agree with the Crown Court judge's approach, namely, that he had to be satisfied beyond reasonable doubt of the existence of good cause before granting an extension (see **D15.35**). See also *O'Dowd v UK* (2012) 54 EHRR 187. The absence or illness of the accused is itself a ground for extension (s. 22(3)(a)(i)).

In *Central Criminal Court, ex parte Bennett* (1999) *The Times*, 25 January 1999, the illness of a prosecution witness, which prevented the trial from taking place, was held to amount to a good and sufficient cause. Likewise, the unexpected non-availability of a prosecution witness may suffice (*Leeds Crown Court, ex parte Redfearn* [1999] COD 437). The fact that a witness is a professional investigator does not make his convenience irrelevant (*Leeds Crown Court, ex parte Wilson* [1999] Crim LR 378).

D15.31   **Due Expedition**   In *Norwich Crown Court, ex parte Parker* (1992) 96 Cr App R 68, the Divisional Court said that all concerned with the prosecution were not required to act as though this were their only task at hand; 'all due expedition' meant the expedition appropriate in the circumstances, one of those circumstances being the custody time-limit. In *Governor of Winchester Prison, ex parte Roddie* [1991] 2 All ER 931, however, it was made clear that due expedition had to be measured against some objective yardstick or it would defeat the Act's objects. Therefore, the fact that the police were understaffed and suffered delays in the receipt of typing and scientific evidence did not mean there was due expedition.

The following factors have relevance to the assessment of this question.

D15.32   (a) *The stage of the proceedings to which the time-limit relates.* In considering whether the prosecution had acted with all due expedition, the judge ought to consider the matter by reference to the presence or absence of all due expedition at the stage to which the custody time-limit relates (*Birmingham Crown Court, ex parte Bell* [1997] 2 Cr App R 363). For example, in *Central Criminal Court, ex parte Behbehari* [1994] Crim LR 352, the Divisional Court held that, in determining whether the prosecution had acted with 'all due expedition', the court should take into account whether papers were served on the defence in time to allow adequate consideration of the type of committal. See also *R (CPS) v Ipswich Crown Court* [2010] EWHC 1515 (Admin).

By extension of the same principle, however, the due expedition of the prosecution should be assessed in relation to matters they were obliged to carry out, rather than additional burdens they had assumed (*Southwark Crown Court, ex parte DPP* [1999] Crim LR 394). The decision of the Divisional Court in *R (Hughes) v Woolwich Crown Court* [2006] EWHC 2191 (Admin) underlines the fact that the due expedition of the prosecution in complying with its duties of disclosure will be judged from the time that the obligation in fact arises, rather than necessarily when the formal requirements of the service of a defence statement have been completed (see also *R (Alexander) v Isleworth Crown Court* [2009] EWHC 85 (Admin) for consideration of due expedition in the context of obtaining psychiatric evidence on the issue of fitness to plead and *R (Clarke) v Lewes Crown Court* [2009] EWHC 805 (Admin) in relation to the obtaining of expert evidence more generally).

(b) *Who is responsible for any delay.* The other consideration to which the court should have **D15.33** regard is whether the lack of expedition is actually the fault of the prosecution, or whether it is caused by some third party and beyond the prosecution's control. The most obvious third party in this context is the independent science service. In *Central Criminal Court, ex parte Johnson* [1999] 2 Cr App R 51, the Divisional Court recognised that the prosecution would not have failed to show due expedition where delay had been caused by the independent science service, providing that all reasonable steps had been taken to ensure that the evidence in question was provided in proper time. This includes the obligation to make the laboratory aware of the trial date and time-limit. In *R (Holland) v Leeds Crown Court* [2003] Crim LR 272, failure to inform the laboratory of the time constraints was fatal to a claim to due expedition.

Similarly, delay occasioned by the non-availability of a prosecution witness will translate into a failure by the prosecution to act with due expedition only where it could not be shown that the prosecution had taken reasonable steps in the circumstances to ensure the attendance of the witness. However, the prosecution cannot be expected to 'nursemaid' their witnesses at all times (*Leeds Crown Court, ex parte Redfearn* [1999] COD 437).

Where the delay to proceedings is the result of, or substantially contributed to by, the conduct of the accused, the court is entitled to take that into account in weighing up whether the prosecution has acted with all due diligence (*O'Dowd v UK* (2012) 54 EHRR 187).

The Link between Due Expedition and the Need for an Extension In *Leeds Crown Court,* **D15.34** *ex parte Bagoutie* (1999) *The Times,* 31 May 1999, Lord Bingham CJ emphasised that the requirement of due expedition was not disciplinary in intention. It aimed to protect the accused from being kept in prison awaiting trial longer than was justifiable. Parliament had intended to insist that prosecutors could not seek extensions where the need for the extension was attributable to their own failure to act with due expedition. Hence, if the court was satisfied that there was good and sufficient cause for the extension, but was not satisfied that the prosecution had acted with all due expedition, it was not obliged to refuse the application if it concluded that the prosecution's failure had neither caused nor contributed to the need for the extension.

In *R (Gibson) v Winchester Crown Court* [2004] 3 All ER 475, the Divisional Court held that a judge may properly extend custody time-limits even where the prosecution had not acted with all due diligence, if the prosecution's failure is not itself a cause for the required extension.

Applying the Criteria

In *White v DPP* [1989] Crim LR 375, the Divisional Court expressed doubt over the Crown **D15.35** Court judge's approach to the extension of the custody time-limit in W's case, namely that he had to be satisfied beyond reasonable doubt of the existence of good cause before granting an extension. In *Governor of Canterbury Prison, ex parte Craig* [1991] 2 QB 195, Watkins LJ (giving the judgment of the Divisional Court) referred (at p. 132) to the doubt expressed in *White v DPP* and stated:

> In our view, the standard to be applied is that of the balance of probabilities. That is the standard for determining bail applications. It should apply equally, we think, to related interlocutory questions of the sort here in question.

The onus, then, is on the prosecution to satisfy the court as to the criteria for extension.

In *Wildman v DPP* (2001) 165 JP 453, the Divisional Court stated that the prosecution 'have to enable the defendant to test the matters which are relied upon by the Crown'. If the material on which they rely includes oral evidence, the defence must be given an opportunity to cross-examine (*R (DPP) v Havering Magistrates' Court* [2001] 3 All ER 997). However, it is for the prosecution to decide what evidence to call in support of their application, and the defence cannot insist on a witness being called purely to allow him to be criticised (*R (Rippe) v Chelmsford Crown Court* [2002] Crim LR 485).

Crown Court applications for extension of a time-limit may and normally would be determined by a Crown Court judge in chambers. In *Leeds Crown Court, ex parte Briggs (No. 1)* [1998] 2 Cr App R 413, the Divisional Court stated that the Crown Court judge dealing with an application should give reasons for granting an extension.

Appeals

D15.36 **From the Magistrates' Court to the Crown Court**   Following an application to a magistrates' court for extension of a time-limit, the party against whom the magistrates' decision goes may appeal to the Crown Court (Prosecution of Offences Act 1985, s. 22(7) and (8)). An appeal by the prosecution against refusal to extend must be commenced before the actual expiry of the limit, but, provided that is done, the limit is deemed not to have expired until after the determination of the appeal (s. 22(9)).

Rule 19.17 of the CrimPR sets out the procedure to be followed on such appeals, in particular, the requirement for notice to the court and the other party and the contents of the notice. Appeals against magistrates' decisions on applications to extend are matters that may and normally would be determined by a Crown Court judge in chambers.

D15.37 **From the Crown Court to the Divisional Court**   The mechanism of a challenge to the decision of the Crown Court to grant an extension of time-limits will depend on its basis.

(a) If it is on the basis that there was insufficient evidence to justify that decision, the challenge should be made by way of appeal by case stated to the Divisional Court. In that way, the Crown Court judge will be able to set out clearly the facts found and the material on which the findings were based (*Central Criminal Court, ex parte Behbehari* [1994] Crim LR 352).

(b) In other circumstances, it will be appropriate for a challenge to the decision to be by way of judicial review. In such a case, the requirement for promptness under the Civil Procedure Rules, part 54, will not always be satisfied by commencing proceedings within the three-month period set out therein, but will depend on the circumstances of the case. In *R (Siraju) v Crown Court at Snaresbrook* [2001] EWHC Admin 638, it was stated that a delay which makes it impossible for the matter to be reconsidered by the Crown Court before the original time-limit expires will normally be fatal to a judicial review application.

The exercise of the power to extend a time-limit cannot be used as a ground of appeal should the accused ultimately be convicted (s. 22(10)).

Statutes on Custody Time-limits

Prosecution of Offences Act 1985, ss. 22 and 22B

22.—(1) The Secretary of State may by regulations make provision, with respect to any specified preliminary stage of proceedings for an offence, as to the maximum period—

  (a) to be allowed to the prosecution to complete that stage;

  (b) during which the accused may, while awaiting completion of that stage, be—

    (i) in the custody of a magistrates' court; or

    (ii) in the custody of the Crown Court; in relation to that offence.

(2) [Permissible content of the regulations.]

(3) The appropriate court may, at any time before the expiry of a time limit imposed by the regulations, extend, or further extend that limit; but the court shall not do so unless it is satisfied—

  (a) that the need for the extension is due to—

    (i) the illness or absence of the accused, a necessary witness, a judge or a magistrate;

    (ii) a postponement which is occasioned by the ordering by the court of separate trials in the case of two or more accused or two or more offences; or

    (iii) some other good and sufficient cause; and

  (b) that the prosecution has acted with all due diligence and expedition.

(4) Where, in relation to any proceedings for an offence, an overall time limit has expired before the completion of the stage of the proceedings to which the limit applies, the appropriate court shall stay the proceedings.

(5) Where—

  (a) a person escapes from the custody of a magistrates' court or the Crown Court before the expiry of a custody time limit which applies in his case; or

  (b) a person who has been released on bail in consequence of the expiry of a custody time limit—

    (i) fails to surrender himself into the custody of the court at the appointed time; or

    (ii) is arrested by a constable on a ground mentioned in section 7(3)(b) of the Bail Act 1976 (breach, or likely breach, of conditions of bail);

the regulations shall, so far as they provide for any custody time limit in relation to the preliminary stage in question, be disregarded.

(6) Subsection (6A) below applies where—

  (a) a person escapes from the custody of a magistrates' court or the Crown Court; or

  (b) a person who has been released on bail fails to surrender himself into the custody of the court at the appointed time;

and is accordingly unlawfully at large for any period.

(6A) The following, namely—

  (a) the period for which the person is unlawfully at large; and

  (b) such additional period (if any) as the appropriate court may direct, having regard to the disruption of the prosecution occasioned by—

    (i) the person's escape or failure to surrender; and

    (ii) the length of the period mentioned in paragraph (a) above,

shall be disregarded, so far as the offence in question is concerned, for the purposes of the overall time limit which applies in his case in relation to the stage which the proceedings have reached at the time of the escape or, as the case may be, at the appointed time.

(6B) Any period during which proceedings for an offence are adjourned pending the determination of an appeal under Part 9 of the Criminal Justice Act 2003 shall be disregarded, so far as the offence is concerned, for the purposes of the overall time limit and the custody time limit which applies to the stage which the proceedings have reached when they are adjourned.

(7) Where a magistrates' court decides to extend, or further extend, a custody or overall time limit, or to give a direction under subsection (6A) above, the accused may appeal against the decision to the Crown Court.

(8) Where a magistrates' court refuses to extend, or further extend, a custody or overall time limit, or to give a direction under subsection (6A) above, the prosecution may appeal against the refusal to the Crown Court.

(9) An appeal under subsection (8) above may not be commenced after the expiry of the limit in question; but where such an appeal is commenced before the expiry of the limit the limit shall be deemed not to have expired before the determination or abandonment of the appeal.

(10) Where a person is convicted of an offence in any proceedings, the exercise, in relation to any preliminary stage of those proceedings, of the power conferred by subsection (3) above shall not be called into question in any appeal against that conviction.

(11) In this section—

'appropriate court' means—

(a) where the accused has been sent for trial or indicted for the offence, the Crown Court; and

(b) in any other case, the magistrates' court specified in the summons or warrant in question or, where the accused has already appeared or been brought before a magistrates' court, a magistrates' court for the same area;

'custody' includes local authority accommodation or youth detention accommodation to which a person is remanded under section 91 of the Legal Aid, Sentencing and Punishment of Offenders Act 2012, and references to a person being committed to custody shall be construed accordingly;

'custody of the Crown Court' includes custody to which a person is committed in pursuance of—

(a) section 43A of the Magistrates' Courts Act 1980 (magistrates' court dealing with a person brought before it following his arrest in pursuance of a warrant issued by the Crown Court); or

(b) section 52 of the Crime and Disorder Act 1998 (provisions supplementing section 51);

'custody of a magistrates' court' means custody to which a person is committed in pursuance of section 128 of the Magistrates' Courts Act 1980 (remand);

'custody time limit' means a time limit imposed by regulations made under subsection (1)(b) above or, where any such limit has been extended by a court under subsection (3) above, the limit as so extended;

'preliminary stage', in relation to any proceedings, does not include any stage after the start of the trial (within the meaning given by subsections (11A) and (11B) below);

'overall time limit' means a time limit imposed by regulations made under subsection (1)(a) above or, where any such limit has been extended by a court under subsection (3) above, the limit as so extended; and

'specified' means specified in the regulations.

(11ZA) For the purposes of this section, proceedings for an offence shall be taken to begin when the accused is charged with the offence or, as the case may be, an information is laid charging him with the offence.

(11A) For the purposes of this section, the start of a trial on indictment shall be taken to occur at the time when a jury is sworn to consider the issue of guilt or fitness to plead or, if the court accepts a plea of guilty before the time when a jury is sworn, when that plea is accepted; but this is subject to section 8 of the Criminal Justice Act 1987 and section 30 of the Criminal Procedure and Investigations Act 1996 (preparatory hearings).

(11AA) The references in subsection (11A) above to the time when a jury is sworn include the time when that jury would be sworn but for the making of an order under Part 7 of the Criminal Justice Act 2003.

(11B) For the purposes of this section, the start of a summary trial shall be taken to occur—

(a) when the court begins to hear evidence for the prosecution at the trial or to consider whether to exercise its power under section 37(3) of the Mental Health Act 1983 (power to make hospital order without convicting the accused), or

(b) if the court accepts a plea of guilty without proceeding as mentioned above, when that plea is accepted.

(12) For the purposes of the application of any custody time limit in relation to a person who is in the custody of a magistrates' court or the Crown Court—

(a) all periods during which he is in the custody of a magistrates' court in respect of the same offence shall be aggregated and treated as a single continuous period; and

(b) all periods during which he is in the custody of the Crown Court in respect of the same offence shall be aggregated and treated similarly.

(13) For the purposes of section 29(3) of the Senior Courts Act 1981 (High Court to have power to make prerogative orders in relation to jurisdiction of Crown Court in matters which do not relate to trial on indictment) the jurisdiction conferred on the Crown Court by this section shall be taken to be part of its jurisdiction in matters other than those relating to trial on indictment.

22B.—(1) This section applies where proceedings for an offence ('the original proceedings') are stayed by a court under section 22(4) or 22A(5) of this Act.

(2) If—

(a) in the case of proceedings conducted by the Director, the Director or a Chief Crown Prosecutor so directs;

(b) in the case of proceedings conducted by the Director of the Serious Fraud Office, the Commissioners of Inland Revenue or the Commissioners of Customs and Excise, that Director or those Commissioners so direct; or

(c) in the case of proceedings not conducted as mentioned in paragraph (a) or (b) above, a person designated for the purpose by the Secretary of State so directs,

fresh proceedings for the offence may be instituted within a period of three months (or such longer period as the court may allow) after the date on which the original proceedings were stayed by the court.

(3) Fresh proceedings shall be instituted as follows—

(a) where the original proceedings were stayed by the Crown Court, by preferring a bill of indictment;

(b) where the original proceedings were stayed by a magistrates' court, by laying an information.

(4) Fresh proceedings may be instituted in accordance with subsections (2) and (3)(b) above notwithstanding anything in section 127(1) of the Magistrates' Courts Act 1980 (limitation of time).

(5) Where fresh proceedings are instituted, anything done in relation to the original proceedings shall be treated as done in relation to the fresh proceedings if the court so directs or it was done—

(a) by the prosecutor in compliance or purported compliance with section 3, 4 or 7A of the Criminal Procedure and Investigations Act 1996; or

(b) by the accused in compliance or purported compliance with section 5 or 6 of that Act.

(6) Where a person is convicted of an offence in fresh proceedings under this section, the institution of those proceedings shall not be called into question in any appeal against that conviction.

PRE-TRIAL AND PLEA AND CASE MANAGEMENT HEARINGS

Since the introduction of the CrimPR, a considerably greater emphasis has been placed on case **D15.39** management (see **D4** for a full discussion). At the forefront of this development is the court's active role in ensuring that, by the time a case reaches trial, all necessary preparation has been completed, and completed as efficiently and expeditiously as possible. Nowhere is this approach better demonstrated than in relation to pre-trial hearings, the purpose of which is to reduce delay and focus on the key issues that are to occupy the court and jury at trial. This is very clearly shown by r. 3.9, which is entitled 'Case preparation and progression'.

Presence of the Accused at Preliminary Hearings

Sections 57A to 57E of the CDA 1998 permit an accused who is in police or prison custody to **D15.40** appear at any preliminary hearing via a live link. He is thereby deemed to be present at the hearing. These provisions apply nationally from 8 October 2012 (SI 2012 No. 2373).

The Impact of Automatic Directions

Such pre-trial hearings must now be viewed in the context of the automatic directions that are laid **D15.41** down under part 3 of the CrimPR (see Supplement, **R-9**) and CPD I, paras 3A.1 to 3A.15 and 3B.1 to 3B.5 (see Supplement, **PD-3** and **PD-4**). The directions are to be made automatically as part of the process of transferring the case to the Crown Court and are set out in the different versions of the case progression form set out in annex E of the Direction — which version is appropriate depends on the methods by which the case is transferred to the Crown Court.

The purpose of the automatic directions, which govern the preparation of the case by the parties, is to ensure that the matters set out have been addressed before the date of the plea and case management hearing at the Crown Court. All of the directions contained in the relevant form 'apply in every case unless the court otherwise orders' (CPD I, para. 3A.2).

In guidance provided by the Senior Presiding Judge on 22 April 2005, it was made clear that the magistrates' court must make the directions specified using the prescribed form. The guidance states:

> The standard directions are set out in the magistrates' court case progression forms for cases sent and committed to the Crown Court and *must* be made in every case: this is not discretionary. However, the magistrates' court may decide that additional or alternative directions are required in a particular case.

D15.42   **The Directions**   The deadline for activity by the parties formerly varied depending on the form of committal, transfer or sending. CPD I, para. 3A.2, makes it clear that generally the directions contained in the case progression form will apply whatever format has been used. A preliminary hearing is not always required but, if required, it should be held 'between 14 and 21 days after the case is sent for trial' (CPD I, para. 3A.9). With the removal of the need for preliminary hearings, the periods for the service of the case have now become (under the Crime and Disorder Act 1998 (Service of Prosecution Evidence) Regulations 2005 (SI 2005 No. 902): see **D10.18**) 50 days when the accused is in custody (8 days + 42 days) and 70 days when the accused is on bail (28 days + 42 days).

D15.43   **Inconsistent Time-limits**   The automatic directions for action that is required in response to the service of the case and completion of primary disclosure are culled from a variety of statutory provisions. Because the time-limits imposed by those statutory provisions have, in some cases, been decided in isolation, their combined effect can have unforeseen consequences. For example, the defence are required to provide a defence statement within 14 days of receipt of primary disclosure, because that is the time-limit imposed by the Criminal Procedure and Investigations Act 1996 (Defence Disclosure Time-limits) Regulations 1997 (SI 1997 No. 2680), but the prosecution do not have to prefer the indictment until 28 days after the service of their case, because that is the time-limit in the CrimPR, r. 14.1(1).

Early Guilty Plea Hearings and Preliminary Hearings

D15.44   Under CPD I, paras. 3A.6 to 3A.9 (see Supplement, **PD-3**), provision is made for two forms of Crown Court hearing to allow for the efficient management of the case in question at an early stage. The first is an early guilty plea hearing (para. 3A.6) where a guilty plea is anticipated. In such cases sentence would normally be passed at the hearing, and to that end para. 3A.7 states that the parties should prepare in advance by:

i)   addressing any issue arising from a basis of plea,
ii) making timely application for a presentence report and, if granted, ensuring that the Probation Service is provided with details of the offence(s) in respect of which the defendant intends to plead guilty, the details of any basis of plea(s) and of the defendant's current address and telephone number(s),
iii) obtaining medical or other material necessary for sentencing, and
iv) quantifying costs.

It is only in cases where no early guilty plea hearing is ordered that a preliminary hearing will be required. CPD I, para. 3A.9, provides that such a hearing should be ordered where:

(a) there are case management issues which call for such a hearing;
(b) the trial is likely to last for more than 4 weeks;
(c) it would be desirable to set an early trial date; or
(d) the defendant is a child or young person.

Where such a hearing is deemed appropriate, it should take place between 14 and 21 days after the case has been sent to the Crown Court.

Where a deferred prosecution agreement is proposed (see D12.106) then, under the CCA 2013, sch. 17, para. 7, a preliminary hearing must occur at which the court will be invited to declare that it is 'likely to be in the interests of justice' that the prosecution and accused enter into a deferred prosecution agreement and that the proposed terms of the agreement are 'fair, reasonable and proportionate'.

Pre-trial Hearings

The CPIA 1996, ss. 39 to 43, and especially ss. 39 and 40, provide reinforcement in statutory **D15.45** form for the various pre-trial procedures developed in the Crown Court in order to promote the efficient conduct of trials on indictment. They consolidate and bolster the rules for plea and case management hearings (see D15.47 and the CrimPR, r. 3.13).

Criminal Procedure and Investigations Act 1996, ss. 39 and 40

39.—(1) For the purposes of this Part a hearing is a pre-trial hearing if it relates to a trial on indictment and it takes place—
(a) after the accused has been sent for trial for the offence and
(b) before the start of the trial.
(2) For the purposes of this Part a hearing is also a pre-trial hearing if—
(a) it relates to a trial on indictment to be held in pursuance of a bill of indictment preferred under the authority of section 2(2)(b) or (ba) of the Administration of Justice (Miscellaneous Provisions) Act 1933 (bill preferred by direction of Court of Appeal or by direction or with consent of a judge), and
(b) it takes place after the bill of indictment has been preferred and before the start of the trial.
(3) For the purposes of this section the start of a trial on indictment occurs at the time when a jury is sworn to consider the issue of guilt or fitness to plead or, if the court accepts a plea of guilty before the time when a jury is sworn, when that plea is accepted; but this is subject to section 8 of the Criminal Justice Act 1987 and section 30 of this Act (preparatory hearings).
(4) The references in subsection (3) to the time when a jury is sworn include the time when that jury would be sworn but for the making of an order under Part 7 of the Criminal Justice Act 2003.
40.—(1) A judge may make at a pre-trial hearing a ruling as to—
(a) any question as to the admissibility of evidence;
(b) any other question of law relating to the case concerned.
(2) A ruling may be made under this section—
(a) on an application by a party to the case, or
(b) of the judge's own motion.
(3) Subject to subsection (4), a ruling made under this section has binding effect from the time it is made until the case against the accused or, if there is more than one, against each of them is disposed of; and the case against an accused is disposed of if—
(a) he is acquitted or convicted, or
(b) the prosecutor decides not to proceed with the case against him.
(4) A judge may discharge or vary (or further vary) a ruling made under this section if it appears to him that it is in the interests of justice to do so; and a judge may act under this subsection—
(a) on an application by a party to the case, or
(b) of the judge's own motion.
(5) No application may be made under subsection (4)(a) unless there has been a material change of circumstances since the ruling was made or, if a previous application has been made, since the application (or last application) was made.
(6) The judge referred to in subsection (4) need not be the judge who made the ruling or, if it has been varied, the judge (or any of the judges) who varied it.
(7) For the purposes of this section the prosecutor is any person acting as prosecutor, whether an individual or a body.

Procedure   As these are pre-trial hearings, they can therefore be conducted by a judge who will **D15.46** not be the eventual trial judge. They differ from preparatory hearings in long or complex cases (see **D15.51**) in this respect. Restrictions on the reporting of pre-trial rulings are contained in the CPIA 1996, ss. 41 and 42. There are no exemptions in respect of the publication of formal details, such as the name, address and occupation of the accused (again, in contrast with the position in relation to preparatory hearings).

In *Diedrick* [1997] 1 Cr App R 361, the appeal concerned the actions of the trial judge in questioning the accused about what he thought was a lie which the accused had told in the questionnaire. The Court of Appeal observed that what was said at the plea and directions hearing was not expected to form part of the material for trial, and it would rarely be appropriate to refer to it. Where the trial judge was considering the use of such material, counsel should be allowed to address the judge first.

Plea and Case Management Hearings

D15.47   Save in cases where a preparatory hearing is required (discussed at **D15.49**), the major pre-trial hearing will be the plea and case management hearing. The purpose of such hearings is to ensure that all steps necessary for the proper preparation of a case for trial have been taken or are properly timetabled for future attention. These hearings will occur within 13 weeks of sending where the accused is in custody or 16 weeks of sending where the accused is on bail (CPD I, para. 3A.10). That period is designed to give time for the matters listed in para. 3A.11 to have been completed. These include the service of the prosecution case, the preferring of the indictment, the service of a defence statement and the making of any application to dismiss (see Supplement, **PD-3**).

The rationale for such hearings is expressed at CPD I, para. 3A.13, as follows:

> Active case management at the PCMH is essential to reduce the number of ineffective and cracked trials and delays during the trial to resolve legal issues. The effectiveness of a PCMH hearing in a contested case depends in large measure upon preparation by all concerned and upon the presence of the trial advocate or advocate who is able to make decisions and give the court the assistance which the trial advocate could be expected to give. Resident Judges in setting the listing policy should ensure that list officers fix cases as far as possible to enable the trial advocate to conduct the PCMH and the trial.

D15.48   **The Form**   The form to be used at plea and case management hearings is that which appears in the CPD, Annex F, and is available via www.justice.gov.uk/courts/procedure-rules/criminal/formspage. In guidance provided by the Senior Presiding Judge on 22 April 2005, it was made clear that the new plea and case management hearing form is the only form that may be used at such hearings and this is emphasised in the form itself. The purpose of this is to ensure uniformity of forms across the country. The guidance went on to say that the 'discretionary element in respect of the PCMH form is the manner in which the form is used' and stresses the importance of there being a written record of all orders made at the plea and case management hearing which is made available to all concerned.

The matters of case preparation that are addressed in the form are also addressed in other parts of this book. These include:

(a) orders in relation to witnesses, such as special measures (see **D14.1**) and witness summonses (see **D15.94**);
(b) orders as to disclosure (see **D9** and **D15.71**); and
(c) outstanding legal issues, including applications under the bad character and hearsay provisions of the CJA 2003 (see **F12**, **F14** and **F16**).

CPD I, para. 3A.15, emphasises that further pre-trial hearings after the PCMH are to be discouraged, and should occur only where there is a compelling reason for them.

See *Newell* [2012] 1 WLR 3142 as to the status of the PCMH form. The Court of Appeal made clear that matters recorded on the form on behalf of the accused should not then ordinarily be used as evidence against him through the exercise of the court's discretion under the PACE, s. 78.

PREPARATORY HEARINGS

Preparatory hearings are a key pre-trial part of the criminal process in complex cases, the aims **D15.49**
of which are very much in keeping with the case management ethos described above, namely
the early identification of the issues and the tailoring of the trial process to those issues. Such
hearings may be held in long and complex cases (pursuant to the CPIA 1996: see **D15.51**)
and in serious fraud cases (pursuant to the CJA 1987: see **D15.60**).

The Fraud Protocol   At such hearings, it is important to consider the aspirations behind **D15.50**
the Protocol for the control and management of heavy fraud and other complex criminal
cases, issued on 22 March 2005 by the then Lord Chief Justice. The document is premised
on a general acceptance that trials of fraud and complex cases take too long, and need to be
controlled.

The Protocol seeks to achieve this, in conjunction with the CrimPR and CPD, by encouraging
continuous case management by judges presiding over trials which may last more than eight
weeks. The Protocol includes guidance covering the following areas.

(a) There should be initial consideration of the length of trial, requiring the prosecution team
    to justify the length of trial where it will exceed eight weeks (para. 1(iv)) and to notify the
    court and others where the case is likely to exceed that length (para. 1(v)). The trial judge is
    also expected to 'consider what steps should be taken to reduce the length of the trial, whilst
    still ensuring that the prosecution has the opportunity of placing the full criminality before
    the court' (para. 3(vi)(b)).
(b) Early appointment of a trial judge is required where the case will last more than four weeks,
    who will then 'manage the case from cradle to grave' (para. 2). The judge will require a more
    detailed knowledge of the case than would normally be the case (para. 3(i)(b)).
(c) Case management issues are highlighted, including the matters that should be addressed
    at directions hearings (para. 3(iii)), with a short preliminary hearing followed by a full case
    management hearing attended by trial counsel. Prior to that hearing, both prosecution and
    defence will have identified their cases and at the preliminary hearing there should be 'a real
    dialogue between the judge and all advocates for the purpose of identifying the focus of the
    prosecution case, the common ground and the real issues in the case' (para. 3(iv)(b)).
(d) On disclosure, there should be a timetable for structured disclosure which prevents the
    defence solicitors spending 'a disproportionate amount of time and incur[ring] dispropor-
    tionate costs trawling through a morass of documents' (para. 4(iii)).

Preparatory Hearings under the Criminal Procedure and Investigations Act 1996, ss. 28 to 38

Sections 28 to 38 of the CPIA 1996 contain provisions for preparatory hearings in long or com- **D15.51**
plex cases. They originate from the procedure established for serious fraud cases, which came
into force by virtue of the CJA 1987 (see **D15.60**).

Initiating a Preparatory Hearing   The decision to hold a preparatory hearing may be made by **D15.52**
a Crown Court judge at any time before a jury is sworn, on the application of any of the parties
or by the court of its own motion. The CrimPR rr. 3.14 to 3.18 (see Supplement, **R-21**) lay
down deadlines for the defence or prosecution to apply for a preparatory hearing and sets out
the procedure for determining any such application. Rule 3.16 also covers the situation where a
prosecutor seeks an order for a trial to be conducted with a judge sitting alone, within the terms
of the CJA 2003, s. 43 or s. 44 (see **D13.74** *et seq.*).

The Test for Holding a Hearing   A preparatory hearing can be held, within the scope of the **D15.53**
CPIA 1996, only if the case appears to the judge to be complex, serious or likely to lead to a lengthy
trial. Where there is no material upon which the judge can properly come to the conclusion that

D

Part D Procedure

the case will be complex, serious or lengthy, there is no power to hold a preparatory hearing. In such a case, there will be no jurisdiction to entertain an interlocutory appeal under these provisions (*Ward* [2003] 2 Cr App R 315). In *I* [2010] 1 WLR 1125 the Court of Appeal essentially concluded that preparatory hearings were only of value where such an interlocutory appeal might be required. On this basis, the real test for holding such a hearing is whether an issue of importance to the conduct of the trial ought to be resolved, on appeal if necessary, before the jury are sworn (however, see *VJA* [2010] EWCA Crim 2742, where the Court of Appeal said that the purposes of a preparatory hearing should be interpreted broadly and, in contrast. *Lawrence* [2014] 1 WLR 106 where the Court sought to restrict their availability).

D15.54   **The Status of a Preparatory Hearing**   The preparatory hearing is in fact a stage of the trial itself and may be used in order to settle various issues without requiring the jury to attend (s. 30). Since the trial begins with the preparatory hearing, the same judge must preside throughout, unless there is a compelling reason for a change of judge (see *I* [2010] 1 WLR 1125 and **D15.63**).

It is possible for a judge to conduct separate preparatory hearings in respect of different accused who are charged in the same indictment (*Re Kanaris* [2003] 1 All ER 593). Each accused is charged jointly and severally, and may thus be dealt with individually if the interests of justice so require.

D15.55   **Matters that May be Addressed during a Preparatory Hearing**   The purpose of a preparatory hearing is set out in the CPIA 1996, s. 29(2), and may be summarised as:

(a) identifying material issues for the jury;
(b) assisting them to understand those issues;
(c) expediting proceedings before them;
(d) helping the judge to manage the trial; and
(e) considering questions as to the severance or joinder of charges.

D15.56   **Disclosure**   Among the powers available to the court at a preparatory hearing is the power to order the prosecutor and the defence to make disclosure in advance of the hearing (CPIA 1996, s. 31(4)–(7)), in addition to any disclosure already made as a result of the general duties on the parties (see **D9**). In *H* [2007] 2 AC 270, the House of Lords held that an order or ruling in relation to disclosure under the CPIA, s. 8, did not fall within the purposes for which a preparatory hearing may be held, and therefore could not form the basis for an interlocutory appeal (see also **D15.64**).

D15.57   **Legal Rulings**   The court may also make rulings as to any question of law relating to the case, including questions as to the admissibility of evidence (CPIA 1996, s. 31(3)), but its powers in this respect may be circumscribed by the principle in *Re Gunawardena* [1990] 2 All ER 447. In that case, it was held that the power to make binding rulings in a preparatory hearing in a serious fraud case was limited by implication to the purposes for which preparatory hearings may be ordered, as set out in s. 29(2) (see **D15.55**).

Applications of this principle include the following.

(a) *Claydon* [2004] 1 WLR 1575, in which the Court of Appeal held that a judge had power to determine, at a preparatory hearing under s. 29, questions of admissibility of evidence under the PACE 1984, s. 78. His rulings on these matters were therefore subject to appeal under the CPIA 1996, s. 35.
(b) *R* (2000) *Independent*, 10 April 2000, in which, similarly, the Court of Appeal held that it had jurisdiction to hear an appeal brought pursuant to s. 35, in respect of evidence sought to be excluded under the PACE 1984, s. 78.
(c) *van Hoogstraaten* [2004] Crim LR 498, where the prosecution appealed against the ruling of the judge which was, in effect, to quash the indictment and, by contrast, the Court of Appeal held that the ruling in question lay outside the scope of the CPIA 1996, s. 29(2), and it therefore had no jurisdiction to entertain an appeal.

(d) *H* [2007] 2 AC 270, in which it was held that because an order as to disclosure, following an application under the CPIA 1996, s. 8, did not fall within the purposes of a preparatory hearing, it could not form the subject of an appeal. However, there was nothing to prevent a judge dealing with a preparatory hearing from addressing issues of disclosure at the same time and, in effect, in parallel.

(e) In *Shayler* [2001] 1 WLR 2206, the Court of Appeal held that the judge at a preparatory hearing could rule on whether a particular defence (in this case, duress/necessity) was available to an accused as a matter of law. See also *S Ltd and L Ltd* [2009] 2 Cr App R 171 as to the propriety of determining the availability of a defence at a preparatory hearing on the basis of his defence case statement.

Note however that in *H* considerable doubts were cast on the correctness of *Re Gunawardena,* **D15.58** *Claydon* and *van Hoogstraaten*. (See **D15.64** for a discussion of the effect that the House of Lords decision in *H* has in relation to rulings on abuse of process at preparatory hearings.) Applying that decision, in *VJA* [2010] EWCA Crim 2742 it was emphasised that the court should only make rulings that would serve a useful trial purpose and relating specifically to the matters identified in s. 29.

In addition, the CrimPR, part 3 addresses applications for a stay for abuse of process (r. 3.20) or the joinder or severance of the indictment (r. 3.21).

Where an order made pursuant to s. 29 is varied by the Court of Appeal following an interlocutory appeal (pursuant to s. 35) but the position is later altered by a subsequent decision of the Court of Appeal to the effect that its earlier decision was incorrect, the judge who originally made the order is entitled to vary it so as to accord with that second Court of Appeal decision (*Rowe* [2007] QB 975).

Reporting Restrictions   Restrictions on reporting preparatory hearings are contained in the **D15.59** CPIA 1996, s. 37, although certain formal details (e.g., the names, ages, home addresses and occupations of the accused and witnesses, and the offence(s) charged) may be published by virtue of s. 37(9). The court has power to lift the restrictions (s. 37(3)).

Criminal Procedure and Investigations Act 1996, ss. 29 to 32 and 34

29.—(1) Where it appears to a judge of the Crown Court that an indictment reveals a case of such complexity, a case of such seriousness or a case whose trial is likely to be of such length, that substantial benefits are likely to accrue from a hearing—
   (a) before the time when the jury are sworn, and
   (b) for any of the purposes mentioned in subsection (2),
   he may order that such a hearing (in this Part referred to as a preparatory hearing) shall be held.
(1A) A judge of the Crown Court may also order that a preparatory hearing shall be held if an application to which section 45 of the Criminal Justice Act 2003 applies (application for trial without jury) is made.
(1B) An order that a preparatory hearing shall be held must be made by a judge of the Crown Court in every case which (whether or not it falls within subsection (1) or (1A)) is a case in which at least one of the offences charged by the indictment against at least one of the persons charged is a terrorism offence.
(1C) An order that a preparatory hearing shall be held must also be made by a judge of the Crown Court in every case which (whether or not it falls within subsection (1) or (1A)) is a case in which—
   (a) at least one of the offences charged by the indictment against at least one of the persons charged is an offence carrying a maximum of at least 10 years' imprisonment; and
   (b) it appears to the judge that evidence on the indictment reveals that conduct in respect of which that offence is charged had a terrorist connection.
(2) The purposes are those of—
   (a) identifying issues which are likely to be material to the verdict of the jury;
   (b) assisting their comprehension of any such issues;
   (c) expediting the proceedings before the jury;
   (d) assisting the judge's management of the trial;
   (e) considering questions as to the severance or joinder of charges.

[(2) The purposes are those of—
   (a) identifying issues which are likely to be material to the determinations and findings which are likely to be required during the trial,
   (b) if there is to be a jury, assisting their comprehension of those issues and expediting the proceedings before them,
   (c) determining an application to which section 45 of the Criminal Justice Act 2003 applies,
   (d) assisting the judge's management of the trial,
   (e) considering questions as to the severance or joinder of charges.]

(3) In a case in which it appears to a judge of the Crown Court that evidence on an indictment reveals a case of fraud of such seriousness or complexity as is mentioned in section 7 of the Criminal Justice Act 1987 (preparatory hearings in cases of serious or complex fraud)—
   (a) the judge may make an order for a preparatory hearing under this section only if he is required to do so by subsection (1B) or (1C);
   (b) before making an order in pursuance of either of those subsections, he must determine whether to make an order for a preparatory hearing under that section; and
   (c) he is not required by either of those subsections to make an order for a preparatory hearing under this section if he determines that an order should be made for a preparatory hearing under that section;
and, in a case in which an order is made for a preparatory hearing under that section, requirements imposed by those subsections apply only if that order ceases to have effect.

(4) An order that a preparatory hearing shall be held may be made—
   (a) on the application of the prosecutor,
   (b) on the application of the accused or, if there is more than one, any of them, or
   (c) of the judge's own motion.

(5) The reference in subsection (1)(a) to the time when the jury are sworn includes the time when the jury would be sworn but for the making of an order under Part 7 of the Criminal Justice Act 2003.

(6) In this section 'terrorism offence' means—
   (a) an offence under section 11 or 12 of the Terrorism Act 2000 (offences relating to proscribed organisations);
   (b) an offence under any of sections 15 to 18 of that Act (offences relating to terrorist property);
   (c) an offence under section 38B of that Act (failure to disclose information about acts of terrorism);
   (d) an offence under section 54 of that Act (weapons training);
   (e) an offence under any of sections 56 to 59 of that Act (directing terrorism, possessing things and collecting information for the purposes of terrorism and inciting terrorism outside the United Kingdom);
   (f) an offence in respect of which there is jurisdiction by virtue of section 62 of that Act (extra-territorial jurisdiction in respect of certain offences committed outside the United Kingdom for the purposes of terrorism etc.);
   (g) an offence under Part 1 of the Terrorism Act 2006 (miscellaneous terrorist related offences);
   (h) conspiring or attempting to commit a terrorism offence;
   (i) incitement to commit a terrorist offence.

(7) For the purposes of this section an offence carries a maximum of at least 10 years' imprisonment if—
   (a) it is punishable, on conviction on indictment, with imprisonment; and
   (b) the maximum term of imprisonment that may be imposed on conviction on indictment of that offence is 10 years or more or is imprisonment for life.

(8) For the purposes of this section conduct has a terrorist connection if it is or takes place in the course of an act of terrorism or is for the purposes of terrorism.

(9) In subsection (8) 'terrorism' has the same meaning as in the Terrorism Act 2000 (see section 1 of that Act).

[*Note:* The version of s. 29(2) displayed in square brackets is in force only in respect of applications under the CJA 2003, s. 44 (jury tampering). Section 29(6)(i) is to be read as a reference to an offence under part 2 of the SCA 2007: see SCA 2007, s. 63 and sch. 6, para. 29.]

30. If a judge orders a preparatory hearing—
   (a) the trial shall start with that hearing, and

(b) arraignment shall take place at the start of that hearing, unless it has taken place before then.

31.—(1) At the preparatory hearing the judge may exercise any of the powers specified in this section.

(2) The judge may adjourn a preparatory hearing from time to time.

(3) He may make a ruling as to—
(a) any question as to the admissibility of evidence;
(b) any other question of law relating to the case;
(c) any question as to the severance or joinder of charges.

(4) He may order the prosecutor—
(a) to give the court and the accused or, if there is more than one, each of them a written statement (a case statement) of the matters falling within subsection (5);
(b) to prepare the prosecution evidence and any explanatory material in such a form as appears to the judge to be likely to aid comprehension by a jury and to give it in that form to the court and to the accused or, if there is more than one, to each of them;
(c) to give the court and the accused or, if there is more than one, each of them written notice of documents the truth of the contents of which ought in the prosecutor's view to be admitted and of any other matters which in his view ought to be agreed;
(d) to make any amendments of any case statement given in pursuance of an order under paragraph (a) that appear to the judge to be appropriate, having regard to objections made by the accused or, if there is more than one, by any of them.

(5) The matters referred to in subsection (4)(a) are—
(a) the principal facts of the case for the prosecution;
(b) the witnesses who will speak to those facts;
(c) any exhibits relevant to those facts;
(d) any proposition of law on which the prosecutor proposes to rely;
(e) the consequences in relation to any of the counts in the indictment that appear to the prosecutor to flow from the matters falling within paragraphs (a) to (d).

(6) Where a judge has ordered the prosecutor to give a case statement and the prosecutor has complied with the order, the judge may order the accused or, if there is more than one, each of them—

...

(b) to give the court and the prosecutor written notice of any objections that he has to the case statement;

...

(7) Where a judge has ordered the prosecutor to give notice under subsection (4)(c) and the prosecutor has complied with the order, the judge may order the accused or, if there is more than one, each of them to give the court and the prosecutor a written notice stating—
(a) the extent to which he agrees with the prosecutor as to documents and other matters to which the notice under subsection (4)(c) relates, and
(b) the reason for any disagreement.

(8) A judge making an order under subsection (6) or (7) shall warn the accused or, if there is more than one, each of them of the possible consequence under section 34 of not complying with it.

(9) If it appears to a judge that reasons given in pursuance of subsection (7) are inadequate, he shall so inform the person giving them and may require him to give further or better reasons.

(10) An order under this section may specify the time within which any specified requirement contained in it is to be complied with.

(11) An order or ruling made under this section shall have effect throughout the trial, unless it appears to the judge on application made to him that the interests of justice require him to vary or discharge it.

32.—(1) This section applies where—
(a) a judge orders a preparatory hearing, and
(b) he decides that any order which could be made under section 31(4) to (7) at the hearing should be made before the hearing.

(2) In such a case—
(a) he may make any such order before the hearing (or at the hearing), and
(b) section 31(4) to (11) shall apply accordingly.

34.—(1) Any party may depart from the case he disclosed in pursuance of a requirement imposed under section 31.

(2) Where—
   (a) a party departs from the case he disclosed in pursuance of a requirement imposed under section 31, or
   (b) a party fails to comply with such a requirement,
the judge or, with the leave of the judge, any other party may make such comment as appears to the judge or the other party (as the case may be) to be appropriate and the jury or, in the case of a trial without a jury, the judge may draw such inference as appears proper.

(3) In doing anything under subsection (2) or in do anything under it the judge shall have regard—
   (a) to the extent of the departure or failure, and
   (b) to whether there is any justification for it.

(4) Except as provided by this section, in the case of a trial with a jury no part—
   (a) of a statement given under section 31(6)(a), or
   (b) of any other information relating to the case for the accused or, if there is more than one, the case for any of them, which was given in pursuance of a requirement imposed under section 31,
may be disclosed at a stage in the trial after the jury have been sworn without the consent of the accused concerned.

Preparatory Hearings under the Criminal Justice Act 1987

D15.60   The CJA 1987 provides for special 'preparatory hearings' in serious cases of fraud. The relevant provisions are contained in ss. 7 to 11 of the Act, supplemented by the CrimPR, rr. 3.14 to 3.19 (see Supplement, **R-21**). The provisions are similar to those in the CPIA 1996, ss. 28 to 38 (see **D15.51**), and are therefore described in outline only.

D15.61   **Initiating such a Hearing, and its Purpose**   By s. 7(1) of the CJA 1987, if it appears to a Crown Court judge that the evidence on an indictment 'reveals a case of fraud of such seriousness or complexity that substantial benefits are likely to accrue from a [preparatory] hearing', then he may order such a hearing.

An order for a preparatory hearing may be made on the application of a party or of the judge's own motion (s. 7(2)). Again, the procedure to be employed in applying for such a hearing is set out in CrimPR, r. 3.15. The court's discretion should not be narrowly applied (*VJA* [2010] EWCA Crim 2742).

D15.62   **The Purpose of a Preparatory Hearing**   The purposes of the hearing are: (a) to identify the issues which are likely to be material to the verdict of the jury; (b) to assist their comprehension of those issues; (c) to expedite the proceedings before the jury; (d) to assist the judge's management of the trial; (e) the consideration of questions as to the severance or joinder of charges (CJA 1987, s. 7(1)(a)–(e): see **D15.55**).

D15.63   **The Status of a Preparatory Hearing**   The trial is deemed to begin with the preparatory hearing, the accused being arraigned at the start thereof (CJA 1987, s. 8). In *Southwark Crown Court, ex parte Commissioners for Customs and Excise* [1993] 1 WLR 764, the Divisional Court held that a change of judge after a preparatory hearing could only be accepted in exceptional circumstances, however the Court of Appeal in *I* [2010] 1 WLR 1125 made clear that it was sufficient that there was a compelling reason to change, rather than anything more exceptional.

D15.64   **Matters Addressed at Such a Hearing**   Any question as to the admissibility of evidence and any other question of law relating to the case may be determined at the preparatory hearing (CJA 1987, s. 9(3)). According to *Re Gunawardena* [1990] 2 All ER 447, however, that power is in fact confined to questions related to the purposes of the preparatory hearing, as now outlined in s. 7(1)(a)–(e) (see **D15.62**). See also the CrimPR, rr. 3.15 and 3.16.

Applications of this principle include the following:

(a) In *G* [2002] Crim LR 59, the trial judge at the preparatory hearing considered the management of the trial of three accused for conspiracy to cheat. He ruled that the indictment related only to one particular 'cell' of the alleged conspiracy, and therefore, only evidence which related to the narrower conspiracy would be admissible. It was held that the purpose of the ruling fell within s. 7(1)(a) since it was 'identifying issues which are likely to be material to the verdict of the jury'. Further, the judge's purpose was pro-active case management to ensure that the jury were not over-burdened.

(b) In *Claydon* [2004] 1 WLR 1575, the Court of Appeal held that the purpose of 'expediting the proceedings before the jury' must include 'questions of evidence such as typically arise under s. 78' of the PACE 1984. Following *Gunawardena*, however, his rulings as to abuse of process would not be subject to appeal because it did not come within the listed purposes of a preparatory hearing, but any resolution of the anomaly 'must be left to a higher court'. An attempt at such a resolution came in *H* [2007] 2 AC 270, in which at least some members of the Judicial Committee of the House of Lords concluded that a decision to stay or make other terminatory rulings came within the scope of s. 9. If the position set out in those speeches is followed, it has the potential to increase the ambit of rulings which may be appealed very dramatically (see also *VJA* [2010] EWCA Crim 2742).

Disclosure   Either before or at the preparatory hearing, the judge may, under the CJA 1987, **D15.65** s. 9(4), order the prosecution to do any or all of the following:

(a) supply the court and the accused with a 'case statement' specifying (i) the principal facts of the prosecution case; (ii) the witnesses who will speak to those facts; (iii) any exhibits relevant thereto; (iv) any proposition of law on which the prosecution propose to rely; and (v) the relevance of the aforementioned to any of the counts in the indictment;
(b) prepare their evidence and other explanatory material in a form that appears to the judge to be likely to aid comprehension by the jury (and to supply it in that form to the court and the accused);
(c) give the court and the accused notice of matters which, in their view, ought to be agreed (including, where appropriate, the truth of the contents of relevant documents);
(d) amend the case statement in the light of objections from the defence.

Once an order to the prosecution to supply a case statement has been complied with, the judge may, under s. 9(5), order the defence to do any or all of the following:

(a) give the court and the prosecution a written statement setting out in general terms the nature of the defence and indicating the principal matters on which they take issue with the prosecution;
(b) give the court and the prosecution notice of any objection they have to the prosecution case statement;
(c) inform the court and the prosecution of any point of law (including one of admissibility of evidence) which they wish to take and the authorities on which they will be relying; or
(d) give the court and the prosecution a notice stating the extent to which they are prepared to agree the documents and other matters which the prosecution have asked to have admitted, together with the reason for any refusal to agree.

Once the prosecution has received the defence case statement, it is entitled to make use of it by re-interviewing its own witnesses and asking them questions which arise from that statement. The judge has no power to forbid the prosecution from doing so or to prescribe the way in which they may carry out such re-interviews (*Nadir* [1993] 4 All ER 513).

Status of Rulings Made at a Preparatory Hearing   Subject to the possibility of being varied **D15.66** on appeal to the Court of Appeal (see D15.67), an order or ruling made at the preparatory hearing will have effect at the trial unless it then appears to the judge, on application by a party, that the interests of justice require him to vary or discharge it (CJA 1987, s. 9(10)). See D15.58 and *Rowe* [2007] QB 975 as to the effect of Court of Appeal decisions on such rulings.

The sanction for a party departing at trial from his case as disclosed at the preparatory hearing and/or failing to comply with an order made at the hearing is that the judge may comment on the departure or failure and the jury may draw such inferences as appear to them proper (s. 10(1)). The judge may also give leave to comment to any of the other parties, but, in deciding whether such leave is appropriate, must have regard to the extent of the departure from the case as earlier disclosed and the justification for it (s. 10(2)). Save as allowed under s. 10(1) and (2), no mention may be made to the jury of any information about the defence case disclosed at the preparatory hearing (s. 10(3)).

APPEALS FROM PREPARATORY HEARINGS

D15.67   There are provisions for appealing from rulings made by the judge at a preparatory hearing to the Court of Appeal and, ultimately, the Supreme Court (see the CPIA 1996, ss. 35 and 36, and the CJA 1987, s. 9(11)). Leave to appeal is required from either the judge or the court (ibid.).

Where leave to appeal has been granted, the preparatory hearing may continue, but it cannot be concluded until the appeal has been determined or abandoned (s. 35(2); s. 9(13)). The Court of Appeal may confirm, reverse or vary the decision appealed against (s. 35(3); s. 9(14)).

The Court of Appeal only has jurisdiction to entertain appeals from orders that the Crown Court was entitled to make within a preparatory hearing (though the pool of orders which may be appealed has potentially been dramatically increased by *H* [2007] 2 AC 270: see **D15.57** and **D15.64**).

The CrimPR, part 66 (see Supplement, **R-499** *et seq.*), contains the relevant procedural rules.

The Rules

D15.68   **Notice of Appeal**   An application for leave to the judge of the Crown Court who made the decision to be appealed should be made within two days of the relevant decision. Unless the application for leave is made on the same occasion that the relevant decision is given, the appellant must give written notice of the application (and specify the grounds upon which it is made) to the Crown Court officer and all the parties affected by the decision (r. 66.4(1)).

Under r. 66.2(1) and (2), notice of appeal or an application to the Court of Appeal for leave to appeal must be served on the Registrar, the Crown Court officer and all parties to the preparatory hearing affected by the order or ruling to be appealed. It must be served no later than five days after either the date of the decision to be appealed or the determination or withdrawal of any application for leave has been made to the judge of the Crown Court. If written notice of appeal was given to the Crown Court, a copy of it must accompany the notice or application for leave to appeal which is served on the Registrar (r. 66.3(2)(g)). The notice of appeal must (r. 66.3(2)):

(a) specify any question of law to which the appeal relates and must include any facts which are necessary for the consideration of that point of law;
(b) summarise the arguments to be advanced before the Court of Appeal;
(c) list any authorities which are to be cited in argument; and
(d) if the judge of the Crown Court has given leave to appeal against his ruling, the notice must refer to that and must set out the grounds on which leave was granted.

The notice should be accompanied by any documents or other things which are necessary for the proper determination of the appeal or application as the case may be (r. 66.3(2)(v)).

D15.69   **Response to a Notice of Appeal**   If the respondent wishes to oppose the appeal then, within five days of receipt of the notice, he must serve written notice to that effect in the form set out in the CPD. The notice must be served on the Registrar and must state the date on which he received the appellant's notice, summarise his response to the arguments to be advanced by the appellant and set out any authorities he proposes to rely on. Copies must also be served on the Crown Court officer, the appellant and any other parties directly affected by the decision (r. 66.5).

Role of the Court   The powers of a single judge of the Court of Appeal are set out in the **D15.70** CrimPR, r. 66.6, and may be exercised as though they were being exercised by the full court. Thus the single judge may give leave to appeal under the appropriate section, extend the time-limit for service of the notice of application and opposition, and give leave for a person in custody to attend a hearing. Any application refused by a single judge can be renewed before the full Court under r. 66.7 by means of service of a written notice.

Criminal Procedure and Investigations Act 1996, ss. 35 and 36

35.—(1) An appeal shall lie to the Court of Appeal from any ruling of a judge under section 31(3), from the refusal by a judge of an application to which section 45 of the Criminal Justice Act 2003 applies or from an order of a judge under section 43 or 44 of that Act which is made on the determination of such an application but only with the leave of the judge or of the Court of Appeal.

(2) The judge may continue a preparatory hearing notwithstanding that leave to appeal has been granted under subsection (1), but the preparatory hearing shall not be concluded until after the appeal has been determined or abandoned.

(3) On the termination of the hearing of an appeal, the Court of Appeal may confirm, reverse or vary the decision appealed against.

36. …

(2) The judge may continue a preparatory hearing notwithstanding that leave to appeal has been granted under Part II of the Criminal Appeal Act 1968, but the preparatory hearing shall not be concluded until after the appeal has been determined or abandoned.

Section 9(11), (13) and (14) of the CJA 1987, which creates a right of appeal in serious and complex fraud cases, is in identical terms to the CPIA 1996, s. 35.

PRE-TRIAL DISCLOSURE OF INFORMATION: PROSECUTION OBLIGATIONS

Regardless of whether the trial is preceded by a preliminary or preparatory hearing, certain **D15.71** obligations rest upon the parties to disclose information about the evidence they intend to call or other material which is in their possession but which they do not intend to use at trial.

Disclosure of Evidence to Be Called

The defence at trial on indictment are entitled to know in advance of trial the evidence the **D15.72** prosecution intend to call. Most if not all the evidence will in fact have been disclosed by the statements or depositions. If the prosecution wish to call additional evidence, they are under a duty to serve notice of it.

In *Owens and Owens* [2006] EWCA Crim 2206, the Court of Appeal held that, even where a court had ordered that evidence would only be admissible if served before a certain date, it retained the discretion to vary that order to admit evidence served later.

Disclosure of Information Not Intended to Be Used as Evidence

The prosecution's duty to be fair to the defence extends to disclosing information which will **D15.73** not be part of their case and might even contradict their case, and of which the defence might otherwise be unaware. This obligation is now set out in the CPIA 1996, part I (see **D9** for details).

Custody Record etc.

D15.74 By PACE Code C, para. 2.4, the defence are entitled to a copy of the custody record which the custody officer is required to keep in respect of each person detained at a police station (see **appendix** 1). Failure to supply a copy would be a breach of the Code and might lead to the exclusion of evidence through exercise of the court's discretion under the PACE 1984, s. 78 (see **F2.9**). Similarly, if the accused was stopped in the street and searched under the powers given to the police by the PACE 1984, s. 1, the defence are entitled to a copy of the record of search (see s. 2(9)).

PRE-TRIAL DISCLOSURE OF INFORMATION: DEFENCE OBLIGATIONS

D15.75 Historically, there was no general obligation on the defence to disclose the nature of their case, or the evidence they proposed to call before trial. The position altered radically with the implementation of the CPIA 1996, part I (see **D9** for details), which applies to alleged offences for which no criminal investigation began before 1 April 1997 (see **D9.4**) and is addressed in the Judicial Protocol on the Disclosure of Unused Material in Criminal Cases, issued in December 2013 (see **D9**).

Defence Statement of Case for a Preparatory Hearing

D15.76 Where a preparatory hearing is held in a case of serious fraud, the defence may be ordered to supply a written statement setting out in general terms the nature of the defence and indicating the principal matters on which they take issue with the prosecution (CJA 1987, s. 9(5)). This is very similar to the requirements in a defence statement as defined by the CPIA 1996, s. 6A (see **D9.29**).

Expert Evidence

D15.77 By the PACE 1984, s. 81, rules may require any party to proceedings before the court to disclose to the other parties any expert evidence which he proposes to adduce. Part 33 of the CrimPR (see Supplement, **R-256** *et seq.*) contains the rules that now apply under this power.

D15.78 **Application**   Nominally, the rules apply both to the prosecution and defence, but they have little relevance to the prosecution because prosecution expert evidence (like the ordinary prosecution evidence) will normally be disclosed by other means.

D15.79 **Content of the Rules**   The CrimPR, r. 33.3, sets out the procedure for a party to seek to have a summary of an expert's conclusions admitted as a fact and the steps to be taken where a party seeks to have expert evidence admitted when it is not agreed. On request, he must supply a copy of the record of any 'examination, measurement, test, or experiment' on which the finding or opinion is based or, if it is more practicable, he must allow reasonable opportunity to inspect such a record; the duty also applies to anything on which the procedure was carried out (r. 33.3(3)(d)). Once expert opinion has been served, the court may direct a meeting of experts to discuss the issues and to prepare a statement of those matters on which they agree and disagree (r. 33.6(2)). Alternatively, where several defendants give notice that they will seek to rely on expert opinion going to the same issue, the court may direct that only one expert should be instructed on their joint behalf (r. 33.7).

D15.80 **Breaches of the Rules**   Failure to comply with the rules means that the expert evidence will be admissible at trial only with leave of the court or agreement of every other party (CrimPR,

r. 33.3(4)). The court retains the power to extend time-limits for compliance with these rules, even after their expiry (r. 33.9(1)).

PRE-TRIAL DISCLOSURE OF THIRD-PARTY MATERIAL

Another important area of pre-trial disclosure relates to material in the possession of third parties. **D15.81** This will include records held by health and education authorities, or financial institutions. Although applications for such material may commonly be made on behalf of the accused, under para. 51 of the A-G's Guidelines: Disclosure of information for criminal proceedings (set out at **appendix 4**), the prosecution is placed under an obligation to obtain material in the hands of third parties which might be relevant to the prosecution case. Such disclosure is addressed in the Judicial Protocol on the Disclosure of Unused Material in Criminal Cases, issued in December 2013 (see **D9**).

In either event, the mechanism for securing disclosure of third-party material, unless it is volunteered, is through the issuing of a witness summons for the production of documents, pursuant to the Criminal Procedure (Attendance of Witnesses) Act 1965, s. 2A. These provisions are set out at **D15.96**, and this topic is addressed in more detail at **D9.71**.

PRIVATE MEETING BETWEEN JUDGE AND COUNSEL

Before or during the trial, counsel may, with the judge's agreement, see him privately about the **D15.82** case. The basic principles are contained in Lord Parker CJ's observations in *Turner* [1970] 2 QB 321 at p. 324, modified in the light of the decision of the five-judge Court of Appeal in *Goodyear* [2005] 3 All ER 117 (see also **D12.61** and CPD VI, para. 39N.1: see Supplement, **PD-61**). The guidance is as follows.

(a) Freedom of access between counsel and judge is essential. This is because there may be matters calling for communication or discussion which cannot, in the interests of the client, be mentioned in open court.
(b) It is imperative that so far as possible justice be administered in open court. Counsel should therefore ask to see the judge only when it is felt to be really necessary. Equally, the judge should be careful to treat communications made to him out of court as private only when fairness to the accused so requires. In *Llewellyn* (1978) 67 Cr App R 149, the Court of Appeal criticised a trial judge who had asked counsel to come to see him so that they could discuss whether the trial should proceed on a single count for conspiracy or on two conspiracy counts as in the indictment or on charges of substantive offences. The issues should have been aired publicly and a full shorthand note taken which, *inter alia*, might assist the Court of Appeal should the judge's decision later be challenged on appeal.
(c) Any private discussion that does take place should be between the judge and both prosecuting and defence counsel, regardless of who asked for the meeting. If the defence solicitor is in court he should also be allowed to attend if he wishes.
(d) In *Goodyear*, Lord Woolf CJ made it clear (at [67]) that private meetings between judge and counsel should not act as a vehicle for plea bargaining.

Recording the Meeting   Where such a meeting occurs it is essential that a record is made. In **D15.83** *Smith* [1990] 1 All ER 634, Russell LJ put it this way (at p. 1314B–C):

> Of course, on the authority of the well known case of *Turner* [1970] 2 QB 321, in some circumstances it is permissible for counsel to see the judge in his room to ascertain his reaction to possible sentencing options open to him. But that should never occur, as has been said on almost innumerable occasions in this court, in the absence of a shorthand note-taker or, alternatively, in the absence of some recording device.

His lordship went on to quote with approval the words of Mustill LJ in *Harper-Taylor* (1988) 138 NLJ 80 at pp. 80–1, which encapsulate the problems posed by 'unnecessary visits to the judge's room':

> A first principle of criminal law is that justice is done in public, for all to see and hear. By this standard a meeting in the judge's room is anomalous: the essence, and indeed the purpose, being that neither the defendant nor the jury nor the public are there to hear what is going on. Undeniably, there are circumstances where the public must be excluded. Equally, the jury cannot always be kept in court throughout. The withdrawal of the proceedings into private, without even the defendant being there, is another matter. It is true, as this court stated in *Turner* [1970] 2 QB 321 at p. 326, that there must be freedom of access between counsel and the judge when there are matters calling for communications or discussions of such a nature that counsel cannot in the interests of his client mention them in open court. Criminal trials are so various that a list of situations where an approach to the judge is permissible would only mislead; but it must be clear that communications should never take place unless there is no alternative.
>
> Apart from the question of principle, seeing the judge in private creates risks of more than one kind, as the present case has shown. The need to solve an immediate practical problem may combine with the more relaxed atmosphere of the private room to blur the formal outlines of the trial.... in particular, there is a risk that counsel and solicitors for the other parties may hear something said to the judge which they would rather not hear, putting them into a state of conflict between their duties to their clients, and their obligation to maintain the confidentiality of the private room.
>
> The absence of the defendant is also a potential source of trouble. He has to learn what the judge has said at second hand, and may afterwards complain (rightly or not) that he was not given an accurate account. Equally, he cannot hear what his counsel has said to the judge, and hence cannot intervene to correct a misstatement or an excess of authority...

PRESENCE OF THE ACCUSED AT TRIAL

The Principle

D15.84   As a general principle, an accused should be present throughout his trial. The attendance of the accused at the Crown Court is secured by the magistrates remanding him in custody or on bail when they send his case for trial. If, having been bailed, he fails to attend on the day notified to him as the day of trial, a bench warrant may be issued forthwith for his arrest under the Bail Act 1976, s. 7 (see **D7.98**).

The accused must be present at the commencement of a trial on indictment in order to plead. It is then the almost invariable practice for him to be present throughout his trial. The implication of this rule is that the accused must not only be physically present, but must have the proceedings interpreted to him if that is necessary (*Kunnath v The State* [1993] 4 All ER 30). The CrimPR, r. 38.2(1)(b) provides that the court must not proceed if the accused is absent, unless the court is satisfied that he has waived the right to attend and the trial will be fair despite his absence.

By extension, this also means that the judge ought not to deal with matters which constitute part of the trial proceedings in the absence of counsel for the defence. For example, in *Coolledge* [1996] Crim LR 748, an appeal was allowed because the judge inquired of a witness in chambers and in the absence of defence counsel as to the reason why he had failed to attend court to give evidence. The Court of Appeal held that counsel should not have been excluded since the procedure went beyond a mere inquiry, and affected the conduct of the trial itself, which was therefore tainted.

Exceptions to the Principle

D15.85   Notwithstanding this general rule, the accused's presence may be dispensed with in exceptional circumstances (per Lord Reading CJ in *Lee Kun* [1916] 1 KB 337 at p. 341). The situations in which the court may be justified in proceeding without the accused are as follows.

(a) as a result of the misbehaviour of the accused;
(b) where his absence is voluntary;

(c) when the accused is too ill to attend;
(d) following the death of the accused.

Each of these circumstances and various related matters is considered below.

Misbehaviour of the Accused   If the accused behaves in an unruly fashion in the dock, e.g., by   **D15.86**
shouting out, or if he is apparently trying to intimidate jurors or witnesses by his conduct, and
he thereby makes it impracticable for the hearing to continue in his presence, the judge may
order that he be removed from court and that the trial proceed without him (*Lee Kun* [1916] 1
KB 337). In practice, the judge would warn the accused before taking the extreme step of barring him from court, and it may be appropriate to allow him to return to the dock at a later stage
if he undertakes not to repeat his unruly behaviour. Unruly behaviour may also be deterred by
the threat of holding the accused to be guilty of a contempt in the face of the court (see **B14.85**).
An accused should not be handcuffed in the dock unless there is a real risk of violence or escape
and there is no alternative to visible restraint (*Horden* [2009] 2 Cr App R 406).

Voluntary Absence of the Accused   If the accused, having been present for the commence-   **D15.87**
ment of his trial, later voluntarily absents himself, either by escaping from custody or by failing
to surrender having been bailed by the court for the period of an adjournment, the judge has a
discretion to complete the trial in his absence (*Jones (No. 2)* [1972] 2 All ER 731). Should he be
convicted, sentence may also be passed in his absence (*Jones (No. 2)*).

Whether to proceed in the accused's absence must, however, be a matter for the judge's discretion. The alternative is to discharge the jury from giving a verdict, thus allowing a retrial to take
place before a different jury once the accused's presence has been secured. Whether or not the
court proceeds in the accused's absence, the judge may and almost certainly will issue a warrant
for his arrest under the Bail Act 1976, s. 7 (see **D7.98**).

The Principles to be Considered   In *Hayward* [2001] QB 862, the Court of Appeal consid-   **D15.88**
ered the principles which the trial judge ought to apply when dealing with an absent defendant,
and summarised them as follows.

(a) An accused has, in general, a right to be present at his trial and a right to be legally
    represented.
(b) Those rights can be waived, separately or together, wholly or in part, by the accused himself:
    (i) they may be wholly waived if, knowing or having the means of knowledge as to when
        and where his trial is to take place, he deliberately and voluntarily absents himself and/
        or withdraws instructions from those representing him;
    (ii) they may be waived in part if, being present and represented at the outset, the accused,
        during the course of the trial, behaves in such a way as to obstruct the proper course of
        the proceedings and/or withdraws his instructions from those representing him.
(c) The trial judge has a discretion as to whether a trial should take place or continue in the
    absence of an accused and/or his legal representatives.
(d) That discretion must be exercised with great care and it is only in rare and exceptional cases
    that it should be exercised in favour of a trial taking place or continuing, particularly if the
    accused is unrepresented.
(e) In exercising that discretion, fairness to the defence is of prime importance but fairness
    to the prosecution must also be taken into account. The judge must have regard to all the
    circumstances of the case including, in particular:
    (i) the nature and circumstances of the accused's behaviour in absenting himself from
        the trial or disrupting its continuation, and, in particular, whether his behaviour was
        deliberate, voluntary and such as plainly waived his right to appear;
    (ii) whether an adjournment might result in the accused being caught or attending volun-
        tarily and/or not disrupting the proceedings;
    (iii) the likely length of such an adjournment;

    (iv)   whether the accused, though absent, is, or wishes to be, legally represented at the trial or has waived his right to representation;

    (v)   the extent to which the absent accused's legal representatives are able to present his defence;

    (vi)   the extent of the disadvantage to the accused in not being able to give his account of events, having regard to the nature of the evidence against him;

    (vii)   the risk of the jury reaching an improper conclusion about the absence of the accused (but see (f) below);

    (viii)   the seriousness of the offence to the accused, victim and public;

    (ix)   the general public interest and the particular interest of victims and witnesses that a trial should take place within a reasonable time of the events to which it relates;

    (x)   the effect of delay on the memories of witnesses;

    (xi)   where there is more than one accused and not all have absconded, the undesirability of separate trials, and the prospects of a fair trial for the defendants who are present.

(f)   If the judge decides that a trial should take place or continue in the absence of an unrepresented accused, he must ensure that the trial is as fair as the circumstances permit. He must, in particular, take reasonable steps, both during the giving of evidence and in the summing-up, to expose weaknesses in the prosecution case and to make such points on behalf of the accused as the evidence permits. In summing-up he must warn the jury that absence is not an admission of guilt and adds nothing to the prosecution case.

D15.89   The clear emphasis in *Hayward* was on the need for caution before proceeding to try a defendant in his absence. In view of the need to ensure compliance with the ECHR, Article 6, that caution is entirely proper. For the same reason, it is entirely proper that the focus in determining whether to proceed should be upon the accused's right to attend the trial and be represented at it.

The principles outlined by the Court of Appeal in *Hayward* were considered and commended by the House of Lords in *Jones* [2003] 1 AC 1. Lord Bingham endorsed the Court of Appeal's guidelines with two reservations:

(1)   the seriousness of the offence should not be considered — the principles would be the same whether the offence was serious or minor; and

(2)   even if the accused absconded voluntarily, it would generally be desirable that he should be represented.

In *Lopez* [2013] EWCA Crim 1744, the Court of Appeal observed that the decision to proceed with a trial in the absence of an accused was one that had to be approached with the utmost care and that such a course should be adopted only in rare cases and only after consideration had been given to all relevant matters and in particular the fairness of the trial. Where the accused's defence involved the retraction of admissions made to the police in interview, his presence at his trial was of importance. CPD III, para 19E.3, also addresses trials in the absence of the accused (see Supplement, **PD-33**).

In *R (Drinkwater) v Solihull Magistrates' Court* (2012) 176 JP 401 the Administrative Court emphasised that expedition should not be a reason to continue a trial in the absence of the accused. See also *Rebihi* [2012] EWCA Crim 2481 for the proper direction that should be given to the jury if the trial is to continue in the absence of the accused.

D15.90   **Absent Defendant's Legal Representatives** The position of defence legal representatives when a trial continues in the absence of an accused who has absconded was considered in *Shaw* [1980] 2 All ER 433. The accused's instructions are not deemed to have been withdrawn and counsel and solicitor are not therefore automatically required to withdraw from the case. Whether counsel should continue to act and to what extent are essentially matters for him having regard to the guidance given in the Code of Conduct of the Bar (per Kilner Brown J in *Shaw* at p. 1529G). Counsel can advance existing instructions and even fresh instructions provided by the offender after he has absconded (*Pomfrett* [2010] 2 All ER 481).

The most the judge may do is invite counsel to assist the court in the manner suggested by what are now paras. 15.3.1 and 15.3.2 of the Written Standards for the Conduct of Professional Work in the Code (see also *O'Hare* [2006] EWCA Crim 471). In *Kepple* [2007] EWCA Crim 1339, however, the Court of Appeal said that counsel was entitled to cross-examine witnesses in the continuation of the trial of an absent accused, providing he considered that he had sufficient instructions to do so, as long as he did not suggest what the absent accused's account would have been.

Where an accused absconds and is convicted in his absence, the limited circumstances in which his legal representatives (assuming they have chosen not to withdraw) may give notice of appeal on his behalf are dealt with in **D26.13**.

Sickness of the Accused If the accused's absence from court is for reasons beyond his control, **D15.91** the trial may *not* continue in his absence unless he consents (see, e.g., the dicta of Williams J in *Abrahams* (1895) 21 VLR 343, adopted by Roskill LJ in *Jones (No. 2)* [1972] 2 All ER 731). The obvious and common example of involuntary absence is sickness. Thus, should the accused become ill during the course of his trial, the judge must either adjourn the case until he recovers or discharge the jury (*Howson* (1981) 74 Cr App R 172 and *Kaur* [2013] EWCA Crim 590).

One possible, though limited, exception to this proposition, mentioned in *Howson*, is that, if there are several accused and one falls sick, the trial may continue in that accused's absence provided that the evidence and proceedings in his absence relate entirely to the cases against his co-accused and have no possible bearing on his case.

The decision in *Howson* also indicates that it is not enough for an accused to be physically present if he is too unwell to pay proper attention to the proceedings and give instructions to his legal representatives.

Death of the Accused Where the accused dies before the trial is completed, formal evidence **D15.92** of death should be given, and endorsed upon the indictment. This may, e.g., be the evidence of the officer in the case that he has seen and identified the remains of the person named in the indictment. If such evidence is not available, other evidence such as a certified copy of the entry in the register of deaths will suffice. The endorsement of the indictment in such circumstances renders it of no legal effect.

ATTENDANCE OF WITNESSES

Securing the Attendance of Witnesses

In most cases, it is the responsibility of the police to secure the attendance of prosecution wit- **D15.93** nesses, and that of the defence solicitor to ensure that defence witnesses attend. The steps taken will depend on the sensitivity of the witness and whether there is a fixed date for trial, or whether the case is in a warned list in which case an accused, for example, would need to keep in daily contact with his solicitors during the period in which his case might be called on.

Compelling Attendance Where the prosecution or defence wish to secure the attendance of **D15.94** a witness but are not satisfied that he will attend voluntarily, they can apply for a witness summons. The procedure is set out in the Criminal Procedure (Attendance of Witnesses) Act 1965, ss. 2 to 4, which are set out at **D15.96**.

The same provisions are used to secure the production of documents, rather than the attendance of a witness, as evidence. The use of the provisions for this purpose is particularly pertinent to the disclosure of material in the possession of third parties, which is discussed at **D15.81** and **D9.72**.

Punishment for Failure to Attend A person who 'without just excuse' disobeys a witness **D15.95** order or summons requiring him to attend court is guilty of contempt of the court he fails to attend (Criminal Procedure (Attendance of Witnesses) Act 1965, s. 3(1)). He may be summarily punished as if he had committed a contempt in the court's face (ibid.); it is desirable

D

Part D Procedure

and appropriate for the judge who issued the warrant to deal in person with the witness (*Yusuf* [2003] 2 Cr App R 488). The maximum penalty is three months' imprisonment (s. 3(2)). It was stressed in *Popat* (2009) 172 JP 24 that it is disobedience of a summons which represents the contempt, and there is no requirement for an arrest warrant to have been issued in addition.

The existence of a 'just excuse' will not be lightly inferred. Witnesses are required to submit even to very substantial inconvenience in their business and private lives. Culpable forgetfulness can certainly never amount to a 'just excuse' (*Lennock* (1993) 97 Cr App R 228). However, the prosecution must prove beyond reasonable doubt that proper notification of the trial date was given (*Abdulaziz* [1989] Crim LR 717).

In *Wang* [2005] EWCA Crim 476, no witness summons had been issued at the time when the defendant was warned that he might be needed at the Crown Court on a particular date. The Court of Appeal quashed his conviction. Nevertheless, the court indicated that, if the defendant had been warned that the prosecution would obtain a witness summons, and had gone to ground to evade it, a conviction under s. 3 of the 1965 Act, or at common law, might have been sustainable. This approach was approved in *Popat*.

In *R (H) v Wood Green Crown Court* [2007] 2 All ER 259, it was made clear that a witness may be remanded for as long as there is a real possibility that he may be required to give evidence, or further evidence, as the case may be.

D15.96   Criminal Procedure (Attendance of Witnesses) Act 1965, ss. 2 to 3

2.—(1) This section applies where the Crown Court is satisfied that—
   (a) a person is likely to be able to give evidence likely to be material evidence, or produce any document or thing likely to be material evidence, for the purpose of any criminal proceedings before the Crown Court, and
   (b) it is in the interests of justice to issue a summons under this section to secure the attendance of that person to give evidence or to produce the document or thing.
(2) In such a case the Crown Court shall, subject to the following provisions of this section, issue a summons (a witness summons) directed to the person concerned and requiring him to—
   (a) attend before the Crown Court at the time and place stated in the summons, and
   (b) give the evidence or produce the document or thing.
(3) A witness summons may only be issued under this section on an application; and the Crown Court may refuse to issue the summons if any requirement relating to the application is not fulfilled.
(4) Where a person has been sent for trial, for any offence to which the proceedings concerned relate, an application must be made as soon as is reasonably practicable after service on that person, in pursuance of regulations made under paragraph 1 of Schedule 3 to the Crime and Disorder Act 1998, of the documents relevant to that offence.
(5) [Repealed.]
(6) Where the proceedings concerned relate to an offence in relation to which a bill of indictment has been preferred under the authority of section 2(2)(b) of the Administration of Justice (Miscellaneous Provisions) Act 1933 (bill preferred by direction of Court of Appeal, or by direction or with consent of judge) an application must be made as soon as is reasonably practicable after the bill was preferred.
(6A) Where the proceedings concerned relate to an offence that is the subject of a deferred prosecution agreement within the meaning of Schedule 17 to the Crime and Courts Act 2013, an application must be made as soon as reasonably practicable after the suspension of the proceedings is lifted under paragraph 2(3) of that Schedule.
(7) to (10) [Require compliance with the CrimPR and specify matters which may be covered by them.]
2A. A witness summons which is issued under section 2 above and which requires a person to produce a document or thing as mentioned in section 2(2) above may also require him to produce the document or thing—
   (a) at a place stated in the summons, and
   (b) at a time which is so stated and precedes that stated under section 2(2) above, for inspection by the person applying for the summons.
2B.—(1) If—
   (a) a document or thing is produced in pursuance of a requirement imposed by a witness summons under section 2A above,

(b) the person applying for the summons concludes that a requirement imposed by the summons under section 2(2) above is no longer needed, and

(c) he accordingly applies to the Crown Court for a direction that the summons shall be of no further effect,

the court may direct accordingly.

(2) and (3) [Require compliance with the CrimPR and specify matters which may be covered by them.]

2C. —(1) If a witness summons issued under section 2 above is directed to a person who—

(a) applies to the Crown Court,

(b) satisfies the court that he was not served with notice of the application to issue the summons and that he was neither present nor represented at the hearing of the application, and

(c) satisfies the court that he cannot give any evidence likely to be material evidence or, as the case may be, produce any document or thing likely to be material evidence,

the court may direct that the summons shall be of no effect.

(2) For the purposes of subsection (1) above it is immaterial—

(a) whether or not Criminal Procedure Rules require the person to be served with notice of the application to issue the summons;

(b) whether or not Criminal Procedure Rules enable the person to be present or represented at the hearing of the application.

(3) In subsection (1)(b) above 'served' means—

(a) served in accordance with Criminal Procedure Rules, in a case where such rules require the person to be served with notice of the application to issue the summons;

(b) served in such way as appears reasonable to the court to which the application is made under this section, in any other case.

(4) The Crown Court may refuse to make a direction under this section if any requirement relating to the application under this section is not fulfilled.

(5) to (7) [Require compliance with the CrimPR and specify matters which may be covered by them.]

(8) Where a direction is made under this section that a witness summons shall be of no effect, the person on whose application the summons was issued may be ordered to pay the whole or any part of the costs of the application under this section.

(9) [Taxation and payment of costs.]

2D. For the purpose of any criminal proceedings before it, the Crown Court may of its own motion issue a summons (a witness summons) directed to a person and requiring him to—

(a) attend before the court at the time and place stated in the summons, and

(b) give evidence, or produce any document or thing specified in the summons.

2E.—(1) If a witness summons issued under section 2D above is directed to a person who—

(a) applies to the Crown Court, and

(b) satisfies the court that he cannot give any evidence likely to be material evidence or, as the case may be, produce any document or thing likely to be material evidence,

the court may direct that the summons shall be of no effect.

(2) The Crown Court may refuse to make a direction under this section if any requirement relating to the application under this section is not fulfilled.

(3) and (4) [Require compliance with the CrimPR and specify matters which may be covered by them.]

3.—(1) Any person who without just excuse disobeys a witness summons requiring him to attend before any court shall be guilty of contempt of that court and may be punished summarily by that court as if his contempt had been committed in the face of the court.

(1A) Any person who without just excuse disobeys a requirement made by any court under section 2A above shall be guilty of contempt of that court and may be punished summarily by that court as if his contempt had been committed in the face of the court.

(2) No person shall by reason of any disobedience mentioned in subsection (1) or (1A) above be liable to imprisonment for a period exceeding three months.

The relevant rules are to be found in the CrimPR, part 28 (see Supplement, **R-208**).

Section 4 of the Act describes the powers available to ensure compliance with a witness summons.

Live Link

The use of a live link for the evidence of a witness is permitted by the YJCEA 1999, s. 24, the **D15.97** CJA 1988, s. 32, and the CJA 2003, s. 51.

In the context of the YJCEA 1999, references to live links are references to 'a live television link or other arrangements whereby a witness, whilst absent from the courtroom or other place where the proceedings are being held, is able to see and hear a person there and to be heard and seen' by the judge, jury, justices, legal representatives, and interpreter for the accused (s. 24(8)). As to live links under the YJCEA 1999, see **D14.38**.

The procedure relating to live link directions other than in the context of 'special measures' is now set out in the CrimPR, rr. 29.23 to 29.26 (see Supplement, **R-238** *et seq.*). The application must be made using part B of the prescribed form. Under the CrimPR, r. 29.23, the court may decide whether to give or discharge a direction at a hearing or without a hearing and in a party's absence if that party is the applicant or has had at least 14 days in which to make representations. Under r. 29.24, an applicant for a live link direction must identify the place from which the witness will give evidence and, if that place is in the UK, explain why it would be 'in the interests of the efficient or effective administration of justice for the witness to give evidence by live link'. If the applicant wants the witness to be accompanied by another person while giving evidence, that person must be named and the application must explain why it is appropriate for the witness to be accompanied. See also r. 29.10(f).

D15.98   **Live Links for Overseas Witnesses**   The CJA 1988, s. 32, provides for the use of live links for witnesses who are overseas.

Criminal Justice Act 1988, s. 32

(1) A person other than the accused may give evidence through a live television link in proceedings to which subsection (1A) applies if—
   (a) the witness is outside the United Kingdom;
   (b) [repealed];
   but the evidence may not be so given without the leave of the court.
(1A) This subsection applies—
   (a) to trials on indictment, appeals to the criminal division of the Court of Appeal and hearings of references under section 9 of the Criminal Appeal Act 1995;
   (b) to proceedings in youth courts, appeals to the Crown Court arising out of such proceedings and hearings of references under section 11 of the Criminal Appeal Act 1995 so arising.

Such links are now available at all trials in the Crown Court.

D15.99   **Further Use of Live Links in the Interests of Justice**   The CJA 2003, s. 51, allows a court to permit witnesses, other than the accused, to give evidence through a 'live link' from another location in the UK, rather than just from overseas. This will usually be via a closed circuit television link, but is defined in such a way as to include any technology with a similar effect, such as video conferencing facilities or the internet.

The court may authorise the use of a live link only if:

(a) it is in the interests of the efficient or effective administration of justice for the witness to give evidence in this way (e.g., because he works in a different part of the country and can give his evidence from his place of work via a live link); and
(b) notification has been received that the necessary facilities are available in the area where the criminal proceedings are to take place. (The assumption is that the parties will ensure that there are facilities in the location from which the witness will give evidence.)

Where a direction for a live link has been given, that means that the witness must give all his evidence in that way, so that cross-examination must also be conducted by live link. If it is in the interests of justice to do so, the court can rescind a direction for a live link.

Although the CJA 2003, s. 51, sought to increase the availability of live links, their availability remained under statutory control. Accordingly, it was not permissible for a court to permit a witness to give evidence by telephone where such a link was not available (*Hampson* [2014] 1 Cr App R 28 (4)).

CONTACT WITH WITNESSES, WITNESS COACHING AND FAMILIARISATION

An important aspect of the handling of witnesses is consideration of what contact it is appro-   **D15.100**
priate for counsel, and others involved in either the prosecution or defence team, to have with
them. This also involves consideration of the prohibition on witnesses being rehearsed by the
party that is to call them, which potentially competes with the need to ensure that a witness is
able to give his evidence in the best possible way, is not distracted by a lack of familiarity with
his surroundings in court, and receives proper support from those responsible for his welfare
through what can be a very stressful experience.

Contact between Counsel and Witnesses

Contact with witnesses was addressed in detail in the Code of Conduct. The Code has now been   **D15.101**
replaced by the Bar Standard Board's Handbook. Insofar as this addresses the issue, it may be
summarised as follows:

(a) There is no longer a general rule preventing a barrister from having contact with any witness.
Under the Written Standards that operated under the old Code, a barrister could have contact
with a witness whom he expected to call and examine in chief, with a view to introducing himself, explaining the court's procedure, and answering any questions about it which the witness
might have. CPS guidance still indicates that a prosecuting barrister has a positive responsibility
to ensure that a witness facing unfamiliar court procedures is put as much at ease as possible, particularly when that witness is nervous, vulnerable or apparently the victim of criminal conduct.

(b) Although the new Handbook provides only limited guidance, in a contested case in the
Crown Court it is generally inappropriate for a barrister to *interview* any potential witness.
Interviewing includes discussing the substance of the witness's evidence, or the evidence of
other witnesses. The practice set out in the Code for Pre-Trial Witness Interviews (Written
Standards, para. 6.3.2) remains useful (if not enforceable) guidance.

(c) To the extent that general disclosure obligations require (in the absence of any specific
requirement in the Handbook), where a barrister has interviewed a potential witness, that
fact should be disclosed to all the other parties in the case before the witness is called.

(d) Counsel must not rehearse, practise or coach any witness, in relation either to the evidence
itself or to the way in which to give it (Handbook, rC9.4), as was made clear in *Momodou
(Practice Note)* [2005] 2 All ER 571, where the extent of permissible witness familiarisation
was set out (see **D15.104**).

Prosecution Counsel   The proper handling of witnesses has become an important part of   **D15.102**
the role of the prosecutor, not least since the introduction of CPS Standards in this regard.
Prosecuting counsel should not confer with any investigator witness unless the latter has a supervisory responsibility in the investigation (e.g., as officer in the case), and should not confer with
or receive factual instructions directly from investigators on matters which may be in dispute.

Defence Counsel   The interlocking matters of conferences, counsel being attended at court   **D15.103**
by his professional client, and the seeing of witnesses are dealt with in various provisions of the
Code of Conduct of the Bar, which may be summarised as follows:

(a) Provided that the interests of justice and of the lay client will not be prejudiced, counsel
may agree with his professional client that attendance by the latter's representative may be
dispensed with (Handbook, rC17).

(b) Although, in general, counsel should not interview witnesses or discuss their evidence with
them, there may be extraordinary circumstances in which departure from this principle
is unavoidable. In *Fergus* (1994) 98 Cr App R 313 Steyn LJ stated (at p. 323) that, since
defence solicitors had failed to see the alibi witnesses in order to ask why they had remembered the events of the day in question, counsel should have seen them himself.

D

Part D Procedure

Witness Familiarisation

D15.104   In *Momodou (Practice Note)* [2005] 2 All ER 571, the Court of Appeal made clear that, while familiarisation of witnesses with the court and procedure is legitimate, it must be carefully regulated. Judge LJ stated (at [61] and [62]):

> There is a dramatic distinction between witness training or coaching, and witness familiarisation. Training or coaching for witnesses in criminal proceedings (whether for prosecution or defence) is not permitted. This is the logical consequence of well-known principle that discussions between witnesses should not take place, and that the statements and proofs of one witness should not be disclosed to any other witness. (See [*Richardson* [1971] 2 QB 484, *Arif* (1993) *The Times*, 17 June 1993, *Skinner* (1994) 99 Cr App R 212] and *Shaw* [2002] EWCA Crim 3004.) The witness should give his or her own evidence, so far as practicable uninfluenced by what anyone else has said, whether in formal discussions or informal conversations. The rule reduces, indeed hopefully avoids any possibility, that one witness may tailor his evidence in the light of what anyone else said, and equally, avoids any unfounded perception that he may have done so. These risks are inherent in witness training. Even if the training takes place one-to-one with someone completely remote from the facts of the case itself, the witness may come, even unconsciously, to appreciate which aspects of his evidence are perhaps not quite consistent with what others are saying, or indeed not quite what is required of him. An honest witness may alter the emphasis of his evidence to accommodate what he thinks may be a different, more accurate, or simply better remembered perception of events. A dishonest witness will very rapidly calculate how his testimony may be 'improved'. These dangers are present in one-to-one witness training. Where however the witness is jointly trained with other witnesses to the same events, the dangers dramatically increase. Recollections change. Memories are contaminated. Witnesses may bring their respective accounts into what they believe to be better alignment with others. They may be encouraged to do so, consciously or unconsciously. They may collude deliberately. They may be inadvertently contaminated. Whether deliberately or inadvertently, the evidence may no longer be their own. Although none of this is inevitable, the risk that training or coaching may adversely affect the accuracy of the evidence of the individual witness is constant. So we repeat, witness training for criminal trials is prohibited.
>
> This principle does not preclude pre-trial arrangements to familiarise witness with the layout of the court, the likely sequence of events when the witness is giving evidence, and a balanced appraisal of the different responsibilities of the various participants. Indeed such arrangements, usually in the form of a pre-trial visit to the court, are generally to be welcomed. Witnesses should not be disadvantaged by ignorance of the process, nor when they come to give evidence, taken by surprise at the way it works. None of this however involves discussions about proposed or intended evidence. Sensible preparation for the experience of giving evidence, which assists the witness to give of his or her best at the forthcoming trial is permissible. Such experience can also be provided by out of court familiarisation techniques. The process may improve the manner in which the witness gives evidence by, for example, reducing the nervous tension arising from inexperience of the process. Nevertheless the evidence remains the witness's own uncontaminated evidence. Equally, the principle does not prohibit training of expert and similar witnesses in, for example, the technique of giving comprehensive evidence of a specialist kind to a jury, both during evidence-in-chief and in cross-examination, and, another example, developing the ability to resist the inevitable pressure of going further in evidence than matters covered by the witnesses' specific expertise. The critical feature of training of this kind is that it should not be arranged in the context of nor related to any forthcoming trial, and it can therefore have no impact whatever on it.

D15.105   **Familiarisation by Outside Agency**   The Court of Appeal in *Momodou (Practice Note)* [2005] 2 All ER 571, went on to give guidance (at [63]–[65]) as to the way in which any familiarisation process ought to be regulated, where it was by an outside agency rather than, as is routine, through the Witness Service. The guidance was as follows:

(a) The CPS should be consulted where prosecution witnesses were involved, and the proposed programme should be put in writing.

(b) Where the defence engaged in such a process, counsel's advice should be sought and the trial judge should be informed.

(c) The familiarisation process should be supervised by a barrister or solicitor, preferably by an organisation accredited for the purpose by the Bar Council and Law Society.

(d) None of those involved should have personal knowledge of the matters in issue, and the material used should not bear any similarity to the issues in the case. Nothing should be done to play on or trigger the witnesses' recollection of events.

(e) Any discussion of the criminal proceedings in question must be stopped and advice given about why it is not permissible.

(f) Careful records should be kept of the programme, those present and those responsible for the process. The records should be handed to the CPS and, in relation to defence witnesses, to the court.

(g) Barristers and solicitors were professionally obliged to see that this guidance was followed.

Section D16   Trial on Indictment: The Prosecution Case

INTRODUCTION

D16.1   Following a plea of not guilty (see **D12**) and the empanelling of a jury (see **D13**), the trial proper commences with the prosecution case. This falls into two parts, namely (a) counsel's opening speech, and (b) the evidence.

Some evidence that forms the basis for the prosecution case is agreed by the accused, and may therefore be read or summarised in the form of admitted evidence. Other evidence is subjected to challenge on behalf of the accused, either through cross-examination of witnesses called or through objection being taken to the admissibility of evidence. The ultimate challenge to the validity of the prosecution case can be mounted at its conclusion, namely a submission of no case to answer.

Where evidence is excluded in such a way as to fundamentally undermine the prosecution case, or where the court upholds a submission of no case to answer, the prosecution now has a right of appeal, pursuant to the provisions of the CJA 2003, part IX. Because these provisions operate either during or at the conclusion of the prosecution case, they are addressed at the conclusion of this chapter.

First, however, it is important to consider the obligations that the law, and professional ethics, impose on those who prosecute.

DUTIES AND ROLE OF PROSECUTION COUNSEL

Introduction

D16.2   The manner in which prosecution counsel should conduct themselves in a criminal trial and the duties resting upon them are set out in dicta in Court of Appeal, the Code of Conduct of the Bar and the recommendations of the Farquharson committee on the role of prosecuting counsel, published in *Counsel*, Trinity 1986.

D16.3   **Ministers of Justice**   In *Puddick* (1865) 4 F & F 497, Crompton J said (at p. 499) that prosecution counsel 'are to regard themselves as ministers of justice, and not to struggle for a conviction' (see also per Avory J in *Banks* [1916] 2 KB 621 at p. 623). Some of the implications this has on the prosecutor's role are identified in the introductory paragraphs of the Farquharson report:

> There is no doubt that the obligations of prosecution counsel are different from those of counsel instructed for the defence in a criminal case or of counsel instructed in civil matters. His duties are wider both to the court and to the public at large. Furthermore, having regard to his duty to present the case for the prosecution fairly to the jury, he has a greater independence of those instructing him than that enjoyed by other counsel. It is well known to every practitioner that counsel for the

prosecution must conduct his case moderately, albeit firmly. He must not strive unfairly to obtain a conviction; he must not press his case beyond the limits which the evidence permits; he must not invite the jury to convict on evidence which in his own judgement no longer sustains the charge laid in the indictment. If the evidence of a witness is undermined or severely blemished in the course of cross-examination, prosecution counsel must not present him to the jury as worthy of a credibility he no longer enjoys.... Great responsibility is placed upon prosecution counsel and although his description as a 'minister of justice' may sound pompous to modern ears it accurately describes the way in which he should discharge his function.

In *Gonez* [1999] All ER (D) 674, the Court of Appeal endorsed the description of prosecuting counsel as a minister of justice, stating that it was incumbent on him not to be betrayed by personal feelings, not to excite emotions or to inflame the minds of the jury, and not to make comments which could reasonably be construed as racist and bigoted. He was to be clinical and dispassionate.

Relationship of Prosecution Counsel with those Instructing Him   As the Farquharson com-   **D16.4**
mittee stated in the passage quoted in **D16.3**, prosecution counsel is recognised as enjoying greater independence from those instructing him, whether it be the CPS or other prosecuting agency or private prosecutor, than does defence counsel from his solicitor or lay client.

The committee helpfully summarised their views in the following propositions:

(a) It is the duty of prosecution counsel to read the instructions delivered to him expeditiously and to advise or confer with those instructing him on all aspects of the case well before its commencement.
(b) A solicitor who has briefed counsel to prosecute may withdraw his instructions before the commencement of the trial up to the point when it becomes impracticable to do so, if he disagrees with the advice given by counsel or for any other proper professional reason.
(c) While he remains instructed it is for counsel to take all necessary decisions in the presentation and general conduct of the prosecution.
(d) Where matters of policy fall to be decided after the point indicated in (b) above (including offering no evidence on the indictment or on a particular count, or the acceptance of pleas to lesser counts), it is the duty of counsel to consult those instructing him, as their views at this stage are of crucial importance.
(e) In the rare case where counsel and his instructing solicitor are unable to agree on a matter of policy, it is (subject to (g) below) for prosecution counsel to make the necessary decisions.
(f) Where counsel has taken a decision on a matter of policy with which his instructing solicitor has not agreed, then it would be appropriate for the A-G to require counsel to submit to him a written report of all the circumstances, including his reasons for disagreeing with those who instructed him.
(g) When counsel has had the opportunity to prepare his brief and to confer with those instructing him, but at the last moment before trial unexpectedly advises that the case should not proceed or that pleas to lesser offences should be accepted, and his instructing solicitor does not accept such advice, counsel should apply for an adjournment if instructed so to do.
(h) Subject to the above, it is for prosecution counsel to decide whether to offer no evidence on a particular count or on the indictment as a whole and whether to accept pleas to a lesser count or counts.

Provisions of the Code of Conduct of the Bar Relating to Prosecuting Counsel

The CPS and the General Council of the Bar issued Guidelines in 2002 on the application of   **D16.5**
the Farquharson principles and, where appropriate, these have also been incorporated in the Written Standards for the Conduct of Professional Work in the Code of Conduct of the Bar (the 'Written Standards').

The status of the Code of Conduct of the Bar was explained as follows in *McFadden* (1975) 62 Cr App R 187, by James LJ (at p. 190):

> The Bar Council issues statements from time to time to give guidance to the profession in matters of etiquette and procedure. A barrister who conforms to the Council's rulings knows that he cannot be committing an offence against professional discipline. But such statements, although they have strong persuasive force, do not bind the courts. If therefore a judge requires a barrister to do, or refrain from doing, something in the course of a case, the barrister may protest and may cite any relevant ruling of the Bar Council, but since the judge is the final authority in his own court, if counsel's protest is unavailing, he must either withdraw or comply with the ruling or look for redress in a higher court.

D16.6   **Prosecution Counsel's Duties**   Until 6 January 2014, Written Standards issued under the 8th edition of the Code of Conduct addressed the duties of prosecuting counsel. The Code has now been replaced by the Bar Standards Board's Handbook which does not include comparable specific guidance, although the Written Standards are still available on the Bar Standards Board's web site. The observations of Avory J in *Banks* [1916] 2 KB 621, and the Farquharson committee (see **D16.3**) remain as guidance.

D16.7   **Core Obligations**   Under the new Code, the core obligations of counsel, including prosecution counsel, are set out at rC3:

1. you must not knowingly or recklessly mislead or attempt to mislead the *court*;
2. you must not abuse your role as an advocate;
3. you must take reasonable steps to avoid wasting the *court's* time;
4. you must take reasonable steps to ensure that the *court* has before it all relevant decisions and legislative provisions;
5. you must ensure that your ability to act independently is not compromised.

D16.8   **Documents Coming into Counsel's Possession**   The Written Standards sought to address (at paras. 7.2, 7.3.1 and 7.3.2) the problems which arose from counsel coming into possession of documents to which neither he nor his lay or professional clients are entitled.

Those provisions of the code were in part the consequence of what occurred in *Tompkins* (1977) 67 Cr App R 181. In that case, prosecution counsel used a note from the accused to defence counsel, which had been inadvertently dropped, as a previous inconsistent statement during cross-examination. The Court of Appeal upheld the conviction since, although the note was privileged as a communication between client and legal adviser, the doctrine of privilege merely protects a party from the obligation of producing a document and does not determine its admissibility or the use which may be made of it should it come into the hands of the other side. Moreover, even if the note had been inadmissible in itself, that would not have prevented counsel asking questions based upon it without directly revealing its contents to the jury.

D16.9   **Speaking to Witnesses**   The proper handling of witnesses has become an important part of the role of the prosecutor, not least since the introduction of CPS Standards in this regard. It is addressed in more detail at **D15.100**.

OPENING SPEECH

D16.10   There is little direct authority on what should or should not be said by prosecuting counsel in his opening address to the jury. By convention, it involves an outline of the evidence which the prosecution proposes to call. The following are matters that may affect the style and content of an opening speech.

Emotive Language

D16.11   In addressing the jury, prosecuting counsel must remember his role as a minister of justice who ought not to strive over-zealously for a conviction (see **D16.3**). He should therefore avoid using emotive language liable to prejudice the jury against the accused. Avory J's oft-quoted description in *Banks* [1916] 2 KB 621 was given in relation to observations by prosecution counsel 'calculated to prejudice the jury'. The use of emotive language was criticised by his lordship as being 'not in good taste or strictly in accordance with the character which prosecuting counsel should always bear in mind'.

Submissions as to Law

The extent to which the prosecutor deals with points of law that may arise during the trial or possible defences which the accused is likely to raise is a matter for his discretion, depending on the circumstances of the particular case. In *Lashley* [2005] EWCA Crim 2016, Judge LJ stated (at [13]):

D16.12

> The presumption should be that an opening address by counsel for the Crown should not address the law, save in cases of real complication and difficulty where counsel believes and the trial judge agrees that the jury may be assisted by a brief and well-focussed submission.

If counsel deals with a matter of law, it is usual to remind the jury that matters of law are ultimately for the judge, and that counsel's remarks should therefore be disregarded insofar as they differ from the judge's directions.

Omission of Evidence Objected to by Defence

If defence counsel has intimated that there is an objection to some of the prosecution evidence, no reference should be made to that evidence in opening. If the opening speech cannot be made coherently without reference to the disputed evidence, the judge should be invited to determine whether or not the evidence is admissible as a preliminary issue. See also **D16.43**.

D16.13

References to Inadmissible Evidence

Whether reference in opening to evidence which turns out to be inadmissible or which for any other reason is not called, represents a ground for quashing an accused's conviction depends on the extent to which the accused is prejudiced by it (*Jackson* [1953] 1 All ER 872). A relevant consideration is how the irregularity was dealt with in the summing-up.

D16.14

In fact, both defence counsel and the judge are likely to point out to the jury that what prosecuting counsel has said is simply not evidence. If the defence, as a result of prosecuting counsel's improper remarks, applied unsuccessfully for the jury to be discharged, the refusal to discharge may be used as a ground of appeal. However, the Court of Appeal is generally reluctant to interfere with a trial judge's exercise of discretion in respect of discharging a jury (see **D13.50** *et seq.*).

References to Plea of Guilty by Co-accused

Where the allegation against the accused on trial relates to his actions in concert with another who has pleaded guilty, presentation of the evidence against the accused on trial will involve reference to the actions of that other. To prevent speculation by the jury and provided the defence consent, the jury may be told in opening of the co-accused's plea. It has been implied that they may be told of it even if the defence do not consent. In *Moore* (1956) 40 Cr App R 50, Lord Goddard CJ said (at pp. 53–4):

D16.15

> When two people are indicted together for a criminal offence and one pleads guilty and the other does not, it is the commonest thing in the world to tell the jury, as was done in this case, 'You must not pay any attention to the fact that the other man has pleaded guilty'. Even if the plea has not been taken in the presence of the jury, it is very difficult to avoid telling the jury in some way that the other person has pleaded guilty.

The admissibility of convictions of persons other than the accused on trial (including guilty pleas by co-accused) is now governed by the PACE 1984, s. 74(1) (see **F11.6**), and is subject to s. 78 of the same Act (exclusion of evidence on grounds of unfairness) (see **F2.28**). Therefore, if it is necessary to address this issue in opening, it should be ventilated at the outset. Unless and until the judge rules the evidence of the co-accused's guilty plea to be admissible, his absence from the dock should be dealt with by a formula such as: 'X, of whom you may hear mention in the course of this case, is not before you and is none of your concern'.

Defence Statements

D16.16   Under s. 6E(4) of the CPIA 1996, the court has the power to provide a jury with copies of a defence statement served pursuant to that Act. This power is discussed in more detail at **D9**. In the context of the prosecution opening its case, or adducing evidence thereafter as part of its case, there will be circumstances, such as in relation to proving that notice had been given of a since rejected alibi, where the jury would be entitled to receive a copy of the defence statement to help them, using the wording of s. 6E(5), 'to understand the case or to resolve any issue in the case'.

WITNESSES THE PROSECUTION SHOULD CALL OR TENDER

General Rule: Witnesses on Back of Indictment

D16.17   Having opened his case, prosecuting counsel calls his witnesses and reads out any written statements admissible under exceptions to the rule against hearsay. As a matter of practice, he should call or read the statements of all witnesses whose statements have been served, or, to use the traditional phrase 'witnesses whose names are on the back of the indictment'.

Although counsel has a discretion not to call a witness on the back of the indictment, he must exercise his discretion in a proper manner and not for what Lord Thankerton in *Adel Muhammed El Dabbah v A-G for Palestine* [1944] AC 156 described as 'some oblique motive' (e.g., unfairly so as to surprise or prejudice the defence).

D16.18   **Rationale for the Rule**   The rationale for the above rule is that service of the statement of a witness is an indication that the prosecution will call that witness and will secure the attendance of the witness at trial, and therefore the defence do not need to approach that witness themselves for a statement. Thus, to avoid the defence being taken by surprise and prejudiced by the loss of evidence of potential value to their case, the prosecution are in general obliged to call him at the trial.

It follows that the rule has no application to witnesses whose statements have never formed part of the prosecution case, but were served upon the defence as unused material. The prosecution is under no duty to call such witnesses to give evidence (*Richardson* (1994) 98 Cr App R 174).

D16.19   **Exceptions to the Rule**   The general rule is subject to the following exceptions:

(a) *Witness to be read.* A witness on the back of the indictment need not be called or even brought to court if the prosecution anticipate being able to read his statement, e.g., by virtue of the CJA 1967, s. 9 (see **D22.38**), or the CJA 2003, ss. 116 and 117 (see **F16.7** *et seq.*).

(b) *Witness not credible.* Prosecuting counsel has a discretion not to call a witness whose name is on the back of the indictment if the witness no longer appears to counsel to be a credible witness, worthy of belief (*Oliva* [1965] 3 All ER 116). This exception presupposes that something has occurred between committal and trial to cast doubt on the witness's veracity. In *Oliva*, the prosecution declined to call the victim of an alleged offence who had made a statement to the police naming O as the culprit which he had later retracted. The Court of Criminal Appeal dismissed O's appeal, holding that the prosecution's duty extended only to calling witnesses who appeared capable of belief. As a result of his volte-face, the victim could no longer be regarded as creditworthy and, in the circumstances, prosecuting counsel had a discretion not to call him which he exercised properly.

(c) *Unhelpful but credible evidence.* The ruling of Park J in *Nugent* [1977] 3 All ER 662, and the Privy Council cases of *Seneviratne v R* [1936] 3 All ER 36 and *Adel Muhammed El Dabbah v A-G for Palestine* [1944] AC 156, have lent some support to the proposition that the prosecution need not call a witness, even though they regard him as capable of belief, if his anticipated evidence would be likely to confuse the jury about the nature of the prosecution case. However, in *Balmforth* [1992] Crim LR 825, the Court of Appeal held that, once the prosecution had decided that a witness on the back of the indictment was capable of belief, they must call him.

The Reality of the Prosecution's Obligation

D16.20 The problems which arose in *Nugent* [1977] 3 All ER 662, and earlier similar cases, over which side should call witnesses were the result of a misguided view that the prosecution at committal proceedings were under a duty to tender the evidence of *all* witnesses who appeared to be (a) credible and (b) capable of giving evidence relevant to the case. If the prosecution are not obliged to use all the evidence favouring their own case at the outset (*Epping and Harlow Justices, ex parte Massaro* [1973] QB 433), there can be no obligation to call evidence or tender statements helpful to the defence (see also **D16.25**).

The prosecution's duty is rather to inform the defence of all unused material, including statements containing evidence which contradicts the prosecution case and/or lays the foundation for a defence (see **D15.73**). Provided that is done, the defence will be able to interview the witnesses and arrange for them to be at the Crown Court to testify as defence witnesses if necessary (see also *Russell-Jones* [1995] 3 All ER 239 and *Brown* [1997] 1 Cr App R 112).

D16.21 **Mixed Statements** A grey area still remains where the prosecution have a number of statements broadly agreeing with each other but differing on points of detail, some being more helpful to the defence than others. In such cases, the better practice may be to include all the statements in the material served on the accused under the regulations for the service of the prosecution case after he has been sent, and, subject to any later doubts as to credibility, all the statement-makers should then be called by the prosecution at trial (see also *Witts* [1991] Crim LR 562). Where there is a duty on the prosecution to call or tender a witness, reading the statement of the witness may be an acceptable alternative (*Armstrong* [1995] Crim LR 831).

In *Cairns* [2003] 1 WLR 796, the issue was whether the Crown was entitled to call a witness, rather than whether it was obliged to do so. The Crown called a witness who, they submitted, was worthy of belief in respect of D1 and D2, but not in respect of D3 (their co-accused). The Court of Appeal held that there was no known principle requiring the prosecution to regard the whole of a witness's evidence to be reliable before calling him as a witness. It was not uncommon for part of a witness's evidence to be accepted by a jury and another part rejected. The Crown had acted properly, as had the judge, in admitting the evidence of the witness in question.

Duty to Have the Witnesses at Court

D16.22 Where the prosecution intend not to call a witness whose name appears on the back of the indictment, they nonetheless have a duty to ensure that he is present at court for the trial so that the defence may call him if they wish (per Lord Parker CJ in *Oliva* [1965] 3 All ER 116 at p. 1035: 'The prosecution must of course have in court the witnesses whose names are on the back of the indictment, but there is a wide discretion in the prosecution as to whether they should call them').

The above-stated rule as to attendance of witnesses does not apply if they are absent for reasons beyond the prosecution's control. The considerations relevant to the exercise of the judge's discretion in such cases were summarised by Geoffrey Lane J in giving the judgment of the Court of Appeal in *Cavanagh* [1972] 2 All ER 704. His lordship said (at p. 679B–F):

> The prosecution must take all reasonable steps to secure the attendance of any of their witnesses who are not the subject of a conditional witness order or whom the defence might reasonably expect to be present...

> If, however, it proves impossible, despite such steps, to have the witnesses present, the court may in its discretion permit the trial to proceed provided that no injustice will be done thereby. What considerations will affect the exercise of the court's discretion will vary infinitely from case to case. Would the defence wish to call the witness if the prosecution did not? What are the chances of securing the witness's attendance within a reasonable time? Are the prosecution prepared to proceed in his absence? If so, to what extent would the evidence of the absent witness have been likely to assist the defendant? If the absent witness can be procured, will other witnesses by then have become unavailable?

Does the Judge Have Power to Require the Prosecution to Call a Witness?

D16.23 The authorities on the prosecution's duty to call witnesses are inconclusive as to whether, in the last resort, the judge may force counsel to call a witness against his will. In *Oliva* [1965] 3 All ER 116 at p. 1036, Lord Parker CJ stated the position thus:

> If the prosecution appear to be exercising that discretion [not to call a witness] improperly, it is open to the judge of trial to interfere and in his discretion in turn to invite the prosecution to call a particular witness, and if they refuse there is the ultimate sanction in the judge himself calling that witness.

The implication of the dictum is that the judge can 'invite' rather than compel the calling of a witness by prosecution counsel. Counsel has the right to refuse the invitation, but must be aware that, if he does so, the judge could call the witness of his own motion.

A contrary view was taken in *Sterk* [1972] Crim LR 391, where the Court of Appeal held that the trial judge should have ordered the prosecution at least to tender a witness on the back of the indictment for cross-examination by the defence.

Tendering a Witness

D16.24 As an alternative to calling a witness and examining him in the normal way, it is open to prosecuting counsel to tender a witness for cross-examination. Counsel merely calls the witness, establishes his name and address, and then invites the defence to ask any questions they wish.

Additional Evidence

D16.25 The prosecution at trial on indictment are not confined to using solely the evidence that was included when its case was served pursuant to the Crime and Disorder Act 1998 (Service of Prosecution Evidence) Regulations 2005 (SI 2005 No. 902) (see **D10.18**). Under the old procedure (under the MCA 1980, s. 6), they were not obliged to use at committal all the evidence then available to them, and by extension they are not obliged to serve the whole of their case at the outset (*Epping and Harlow Justices, ex parte Massaro* [1973] QB 433; see **D16.20**). If, however, they intend to call evidence at trial additional to the evidence so served, whether that be evidence which was not then available or evidence which they simply chose not to adduce, they are required to give the defence notice of their intention.

They must also supply a copy of the statement of the additional witness or, as the case may be, a copy of the further statement made by a witness already relied upon, complying with the formal requirements of the CJA 1967, s. 9. If the defence do not object within seven days, it will then be possible to read the statement as evidence at the trial without calling the witness (see also the CrimPR, r. 27.4: Supplement, **R-207**).

Response to the Service of Additional Evidence In *Wright* (1934) 25 Cr App R 35, the **D16.26** ground of appeal was that the prosecution called a witness to produce two specimens of his writing, and then invited the jury to compare these specimens with the writing on a certain envelope in order to prove that the handwriting was his. Apart from objecting to the lack of evidence from a handwriting expert, the defence contended that they had not been notified of the intention to put the specimens into evidence. Avory J said (at p. 40):

> At most that is a grievance and cannot affect the admissibility of the evidence put before the jury, and, if the appellant or his counsel thought that he was being prejudiced by having had no notice and really desired to call expert evidence to deal with the question of handwriting, he could have applied for an adjournment, but he did not do so.

Thus, the sanction requiring the prosecution to give timely notice of additional evidence is the knowledge that, in the absence of such notice, the trial may have to be adjourned until it has been served and the defence have had time to consider their response to it. Alternatively, if an adjournment is undesirable in the circumstances, the judge could exercise his discretion and exclude the evidence under the PACE 1984, s. 78, on the ground that to admit it would be unfair in view of the lack of notice.

SUPPLYING INCONSISTENT STATEMENTS TO THE DEFENCE

As is clear from the discussion above, the prosecution is absolved from calling witnesses whose **D16.27** statements are inconsistent with the broad thrust of its case only if those statements have otherwise been made available to the defence. The prosecution's duty is now set out in the CPIA 1996 (see **D16.29**).

The prosecution duty of disclosure may cover (a) potential witnesses whom they do not intend to call, and (b) statements made by intended prosecution witnesses additional to the material served when the accused was sent for trial.

Common-law Duty

Whether or not the CPIA 1996 provisions apply, the common law has long identified cir- **D16.28** cumstances in which inconsistent statements should be disclosed. In *Clarke* (1930) 22 Cr App R 58, where the issue was whether an identification of the accused was correct, the Court of Appeal were critical of prosecution counsel's refusal to disclose an earlier description given by the witness. If there had been any serious discrepancy between the description and testimony, the court 'would have had seriously to consider whether any miscarriage of justice had been caused by this attitude which was unfortunately assumed by the learned counsel for the prosecution'.

Clarke was confirmed in *Liverpool Juvenile Court, ex parte R* [1988] QB 1, where the prosecution failed to disclose a previous inconsistent statement of the complainant. The Divisional Court held that the failure amounted to a breach of the rules of natural justice.

Disclosure where the Criminal Procedure and Investigations Act 1996 Applies

D16.29   Pursuant to the disclosure regime contained in the CPIA 1996, the prosecution must disclose material which is 'capable of undermining the case for the prosecution against the accused or of assisting the case for the accused' (s. 3(1)(a)). Beyond this, the prosecution have a continuing duty to keep disclosure under review (s. 9). If material becomes 'capable of undermining the case for the prosecution against the accused or of assisting the case for the accused', it must be disclosed 'as soon as reasonably practicable' (s. 9(2)).

Similar considerations apply to material which 'might be reasonably expected to assist the accused's defence as disclosed by the defence statement given under section 5' (s. 9(5)). For further details, see **D9**.

Use of a Witness Summons for a Disclosed Witness

D16.30   The defence are not entitled to a witness summons under s. 2 of the Criminal Procedure (Attendance of Witnesses) Act 1965 ordering its subject to attend court and produce statements in his possession made by anticipated prosecution witnesses, with a view to the contents of the statements being used in cross-examination of the witnesses at the accused's trial (*Cheltenham Justices, ex parte Secretary of State for Trade* [1977] 1 All ER 460). See **D15.96** for the text of s. 2 of the 1965 Act.

EXAMINATION AND CROSS-EXAMINATION
OF A WITNESS

Examination-in-Chief

D16.31   A variety of issues arise in relation to the calling of a witness by the prosecution. The first stage is for the witness to take the oath or affirmation (which is dealt with at **F4.32** *et seq.*). Thereafter, circumstances which may arise, and which are dealt with elsewhere, include:

(a) the use of the special measures provisions contained in the YJCEA 1999, part II, chapter 1 (see **D14**);

(b) the use of television live links where the witness is outside the UK, pursuant to the CJA 1988, s. 32 (see **D15.97**), or in the circumstances set out in the CJA 2003, s. 51 (see **D15.99**);

(c) the restriction on the use of leading questions (see **F6.13**);

(d) the rules in relation to memory refreshing, especially pursuant to the CJA 2003, s. 139 (see **F6.14**);

(e) the rules relating to the handling of hostile witnesses, as developed from the Criminal Procedure Act 1865, s. 3 (see **F6.55**).

The CrimPR, r. 38.11 (see Supplement, **R-310**) deals with live witness evidence, including arrangements for where the witness should wait before giving evidence and the sequence of evidence when a witness is called. A witness waiting to give evidence must not wait inside the courtroom, unless that witness is a party or an expert witness (r. 38.11(2)(a)). But see *Carty* (2011) 175 JP 424, where the presence of a witness in court in advance of her giving evidence was not of itself a reason to exclude her evidence).

D16.32   **Use of an Interpreter**   A decision whether an interpreter should be allowed to assist a witness to give evidence is a matter for the court to decide. The court is not bound to accept the assertion of a witness that an interpreter is necessary. It can investigate the need itself, and having been told that a witness has some command of English, the court may take the opportunity to assess the limits of the comprehension and fluency of the witness before permitting the use of an interpreter (*Sharma* [2006] 2 Cr App R (S) 416).

Cross-examination

Cross-examination of witnesses called by the prosecution on behalf of the accused gives rise   **D16.33**
to a number of issues. Limitations are imposed on the scope of proper cross-examination by a
number of sources, which include the following.

(a) The limitations imposed by statute, e.g., the restrictions on cross-examination by an
   accused in person, contained in the YJCEA 1999, ss. 34 and 35 (discussed at **F7.2**
   et seq.), and as to the sexual history of a complainant to whom s. 41 of that Act applies
   (see **F7.22**).
(b) The duty of the court to restrain lengthy cross-examination on matters not in issue, or
   which is otherwise unnecessarily prolonging the proceedings (*Kalia* (1974) 60 Cr App R
   200).
(c) The limitations imposed by the Code of Conduct of the Bar, discussed below.

Limits of Proper Cross-examination   Counsel is required to consider not only whether a pro-   **D16.34**
posed question is legally permissible but whether it is ethically justified. He must, therefore, 'not
make statements or ask questions which are merely scandalous or intended or calculated only to
vilify, insult or annoy either a witness or some other person' (Written Standards, para. 5.10(e)).
Moreover, it is for counsel to 'exercise personal judgment upon the substance and purpose of
questions asked and statements made', since he is 'personally responsible for the conduct and
presentation of his case' (para. 5.10(a)).

Counsel must not suggest that a witness or other person is guilty of crime, fraud or misconduct
or attribute to another person the crime or conduct of which his lay client is accused unless such
allegations go to a matter in issue (including the credibility of the witness) which is material to
his lay client's case, and appear to him to be supported by reasonable grounds (para. 5.10(h)).
A witness should never be impugned in a speech by counsel unless counsel has first given him
an opportunity in cross-examination to answer the allegation (para. 5.10(g)).

A limitation on defence counsel's unfettered discretion to cross-examine about the issues and
impugn the witness's character in the process was suggested by Lord Goddard CJ in *O'Neill*
(1950) 34 Cr App R 108, when he criticised defence counsel for his cross-examination, saying
that it was 'quite wrong and improper conduct on the part of counsel' to make charges against
the police (or any other prosecution witnesses) if he did not intend to call evidence in support of
those charges. A distinction had to be drawn between proper and temperate cross-examination
as to credit (where one was bound by the witness's answer) and the kind of allegations made by
counsel.

READING STATEMENTS AS EVIDENCE
AT THE TRIAL ON INDICTMENT

The subject-matter of this heading might equally be regarded as one of the exceptions to the rule   **D16.35**
against hearsay evidence and therefore be allocated to the evidence part of this work. However,
it is considered here as it also has crucial implications for the procedural question of which witnesses should attend at trial.

Statements Tendered at Committal

The CPIA 1996, sch. 2, provides for the statements tendered at committal by the prosecution to   **D16.36**
be read in evidence at the subsequent Crown Court trial. Identical provisions apply to a deposition taken under the MCA 1980, s. 97A, and tendered in evidence at committal. If the defence
wishes to prevent the statement or deposition in question being read at trial, it must give written

notification to the prosecutor and the Crown Court within 14 days of committal, stating that there is objection to the statement or deposition. The prosecution is obliged to give notice of the right to object when the statement is served (CrimPR, r. 10.4).

That does not, however, conclude the matter. According to sch. 2, para. 1(4), 'the court of trial may order that the objection shall have no effect if the court considers it to be in the interests of justice so to order'. This power is potentially most important; if the trial judge overrules the objection, the accused will have no opportunity to cross-examine the witness in question.

In the Parliamentary debate on the subject, it was stated by the government that it was antici-pated that the courts, in applying the 'interests of justice' test, would turn for guidance to the CJA 1988, s. 26 (see Baroness Blatch, *Hansard*, HL col. 951 (26 June 1996)). That section referred to the admissibility of certain hearsay statements under the CJA 1988, ss. 23 and 24 (now replaced by the CJA 2003, ss. 116 and 117). Although s. 26 itself has been repealed, the test under the CJA 2003 retains some of the features of the 1988 Act (see **F16.7**).

In considering whether the admission of such a statement under the 2003 Act would be in the interests of justice, the court must have regard to its contents, the risk of unfairness to the accused resulting from the inability to controvert the statement, and any other circumstances which may appear to be relevant. It would appear to have been the intention of Parliament, in the light of the statement of Baroness Blatch quoted above, that the court should consider the same factors in deciding whether to overrule a defence objection by virtue of the power con-tained in sch. 2, para. 1(4) of the 1996 Act.

In any event, a trial judge will no doubt be extremely wary about overruling the objections of the defence, and thus denying the accused the right to see those who are giving evidence against him, let alone the right to cross-examine them. Any suspicion that objections were overruled for reasons which were less than compelling would be contrary to well-established principle and, in addition to the normal channels for challenge, would be likely to lead to the prospect of a challenge based upon the ECHR, Article 6(3)(d) (see **A7** and **D30.9**).

Written Statements in Criminal Proceedings generally

D16.37 The CJA 1967, s. 9, provides for the admissibility of written statements in criminal proceedings other than committal proceedings (its terms are set out at **D22.38**). The CrimPR, r. 38.12 sets out the procedure (see Supplement, **R-311**).

In trials on indictment, it applies where the prosecution wish to adduce evidence additional to that which they used at committal proceedings. The party proposing to tender the statement in evidence must serve a copy of it on each of the other parties. If one of those parties, during the period of seven days from the date of service of the copy on him, serves notice on the party wishing to use the statement that he objects to it going into evidence, the statement cannot be read at the trial.

In effect, s. 9 statements are admissible only if all the parties agree. Even if a statement is admis-sible under s. 9, the court may require that the maker attend to give evidence, e.g., where the defence dispute the contents of the statement but failed to object through an oversight.

Depositions of Children or Young Persons

D16.38 Where a justice has taken a deposition out of court from a juvenile under the provisions of the CYPA 1933, s. 42, the deposition (subject to certain conditions) is admissible in any proceed-ings in respect of any of the offences mentioned in sch. 1 to the Act (s. 43). Schedule 1 lists numerous specific sexual offences, and also refers to 'any other offence involving bodily injury to a child or young person'. The juvenile may have been the victim of the offence but the power applies to depositions from juveniles other than victims.

The conditions of the admissibility of such a deposition are:

(a) that attendance at court would involve serious danger to the juvenile's life or health;
(b) that the deposition is signed by the justice by or before whom it purports to have been taken; and
(c) that, if the deposition is to be admitted against the accused, he was given reasonable notice of the intention to take it and he (or his legal representative) had the opportunity of cross-examining the deponent.

Evidence as to the effect of attending court on the juvenile's health must be provided by a duly qualified medical practitioner.

Address of Witness

In its 'Statement of National Standards of Witness Care in the Criminal Justice System' **D16.39** (1996) 161 JP 353, the Criminal Justice Consultative Council's Trial Issues Group proposed that, unless it was necessary for evidential purposes, witnesses should not be required to disclose their addresses in open court. The statement was approved by Lord Bingham CJ in July 1996, and is now contained in the CrimPR, r. 38(11)(2)(c). Where his address is relevant, the witness does not need to disclose it in open court, and can write it down for the record. Witnesses are informed by means of a 'Witness Pack' of their right to use this method if appropriate.

Formal Admissions

As an alternative to the reading of witness statements, facts derived from such witness state- **D16.40** ments or otherwise may be presented as agreed evidence. These facts, which are admitted by all parties to be true, are presented pursuant to the CJA 1967, s. 10 (see **F1.2**). Where such admissions have been reduced to writing, they should be provided to the jury providing they are relevant to the issues that they are to determine and do not contain inadmissible material (*Pittard* [2006] EWCA Crim 2028).

OBJECTIONS TO PROSECUTION EVIDENCE

Standard Procedure

Where the defence intend to object to the admissibility of prosecution evidence disclosed on **D16.41** the committal statements (hereafter referred to as 'disputed evidence'), the standard procedure is as follows.

(a) Defence counsel informs prosecution counsel of the objection before the latter opens his case to the jury. In his opening, prosecution counsel therefore makes no mention of the disputed evidence (as to circumstances where the admissibility issue ought to be resolved before the case starts, see **D16.43**).
(b) At the point at which the admissibility falls to be considered, the jury will withdraw to allow the matter to be resolved by the judge alone (see **D16.42**).
(c) If the admissibility of the disputed evidence raises collateral factual issues as to how it was obtained, it may be necessary to adduce evidence about those facts before the judge in the absence of the jury. This is known as a trial 'on the *voir dire*' because the witnesses testify on a special form of oath (see **F4.33**). Both prosecution and defence are entitled to call witnesses at this stage. However, their evidence (whether in chief or in cross-examination) should be limited to matters relevant to the admissibility of the disputed evidence. For the application of this rule to the admissibility of confessions, see the PACE 1984, s. 76(2), and *Brophy* [1982] AC 476 (see **F17.8** and **F17.62**).

Part D Procedure

(d) Whether or not there has been evidence on the *voir dire*, the parties make their representations to the judge about the admissibility of the disputed evidence.

(e) The judge then announces his findings on any factual issues arising on the *voir dire* and rules on whether the disputed evidence should be admitted or not, in the light of the findings of fact, the relevant law on admissibility of evidence and any discretionary power to exclude material which is legally admissible (considerations applicable to this determination are set out at **D16.48**).

(f) The jury return to court. If the judge ruled against the disputed evidence, the jury will know nothing about it (as to the editing of evidence consequent on such a ruling, see **D16.52**). If it is ruled admissible, the defence are still entitled to cross-examine on matters they raised on the *voir dire*, although at this stage the cross-examination goes to the weight, if any, that the jury should attach to the disputed evidence, not to its admissibility.

This procedure, and the extent to which it is appropriate to depart from it in certain circumstances, is discussed below.

Presence of Jury in Court during Determination of Question of Admissibility

D16.42   In *Hendry* (1988) 88 Cr App R 187, where the jury had retired for the *voir dire* contrary to the wishes of the defence, the Court of Appeal refused to follow earlier decisions in *Anderson* (1929) 21 Cr App R 178 and *Ajodha v The State* [1982] AC 204. It was held that the judge had the ultimate discretion as to whether or not the jury retired, as their presence could defeat one of the fundamental objectives of the *voir dire* procedure, namely, to prevent the jury knowing of potentially inadmissible evidence.

In *Mitchell* [1998] AC 695, the Privy Council stressed that the judge should give no explanation of the outcome of the *voir dire* to the jury, as to do so would risk unfair prejudice to the accused.

Determination of Question of Admissibility as a Preliminary Issue

D16.43   Where the evidence to which the defence indicate an objection is vital to the prosecution case, such that the prosecution case cannot sensibly be opened without reference to it, the question of admissibility may be determined as a preliminary issue.

In *Hammond* [1941] 3 All ER 318, the Court of Criminal Appeal, while stating that the appropriate time for determining admissibility of evidence is normally immediately prior to the evidence being called, also indicated that that practice should not be regarded as invariable. Humphreys J (giving the principal judgment) said (at p. 320, emphasis added):

> The ordinary practice in such a case, if there is any objection on the part of the counsel for the defence to the admissibility of a piece of evidence, is that he should inform the prosecution of that fact beforehand, and that that piece of evidence should not be opened to the jury. This court desires to reiterate that what was said by this court in *Cole* (1941) 28 Cr App R 43 is a good practice which should be adhered to, certainly in most cases. *The court cannot lay down as a rule of practice that in no case should the judge decide to hear in advance arguments as to the admissibility of evidence.* There may be cases in which it is convenient, and in which it cannot possibly result in any harm in its being done.

Although for some purposes a trial begins with the arraignment of the accused (see, e.g., the Senior Courts Act 1981, s. 77, which deals with time-limits for commencement of trial), it is arguable that, in general, there is no trial in being until a jury has been sworn and therefore no question connected with the trial (such as whether evidence is admissible) can validly be determined. In deference to this argument, it seems to be the practice to empanel a jury *before* considering objections to evidence (or any other question of law).

Circumstances in which a *Voir Dire* Hearing is Necessary

Most authorities on the procedure for objecting to evidence concern disputed confessions and **D16.44**
the holding of a trial on the *voir dire* to determine their admissibility. However, the procedure is
not limited to such circumstances. For example, in *Minors* [1989] 2 All ER 208, Steyn J stated
that the trial within a trial procedure ought to be adopted where there is a disputed issue as to
the admissibility of a computer printout (for further instances, see **F1.39**).

However, the Court of Appeal in *Flemming* (1987) 86 Cr App R 32, warned against resorting to
the procedure unnecessarily. F appealed against his conviction for robbery on the grounds that
(a) the identification evidence against him was unsatisfactory and should have been excluded,
and (b) the judge was wrong to conclude that he had signed notes of his interview with the police
on those pages which contained admissions. The Court of Appeal upheld the rulings of the trial
judge but stated that he should have made them without himself hearing evidence on the *voir
dire*. The issue of whether the accused had signed the relevant pages of the interview notes was
one solely for the jury, the question being whether a confession had been made at all, not whether
(assuming it had been made) it had been improperly obtained. As to the identification evidence,
the judge could consider the exercise of his discretion to exclude it by reading the depositions
and inviting argument from counsel. There was no need to call the witnesses before the judge.

Objecting to Evidence without a *Voir Dire*

The *voir dire* procedure is designed to assist the defence by preventing the jury hearing possibly **D16.45**
inadmissible evidence unless and until the judge rules it admissible. It therefore seems logical
that the defence should not be forced to adopt the procedure if they consider that the accused's
interests will be better served by having the possibly inadmissible evidence, and any evidence of
how it was obtained, adduced before both judge and jury as part of the general case.

The tactical reason sometimes advanced for not wanting a hearing on the *voir dire* is that, if
the judge in fact rules the disputed evidence admissible, the prosecution witnesses may have
to be asked the same questions before the jury as they were asked before the judge, albeit that
the cross-examination before the jury goes to the weight of the evidence, not its admissibility.
Having had a 'dry run' before the judge, the witnesses are likely to give a better account of themselves before the jury than they would have done had the questions come as a surprise.

In *Ajodha v The State* [1982] AC 204, the Privy Council affirmed the defence's right to have
evidence ruled inadmissible even though they do not seek to exclude it by means of the standard
voir dire procedure. See **F17.66** for details.

There are a number of qualifications of this general principle: **D16.46**

(a) If the defence elect not to have a *voir dire*, they are usually entitled to a ruling from the
    judge on the admissibility of the confession at the close of all the evidence, rather than at
    the end of the prosecution case (*Jackson* [1985] Crim LR 442). The judge should exclude a
    confession of his own motion only in a totally exceptional case where the prosecution's own
    evidence makes it quite clear that the confession was improperly obtained. Otherwise, the
    judge should not rule or be asked to rule on the confession's admissibility until the close of
    all the evidence, both prosecution and defence. This considerably reduces the attractiveness
    to the defence of forgoing the normal procedure, since their decision on whether or not to
    call evidence will have to be taken at a time when they still do not know whether the jury
    will ultimately be directed to ignore the accused's confession.
(b) In *Cunningham* [1985] Crim LR 374, the Court of Appeal took a liberal attitude to the
    prosecution being allowed to reopen their case when the defence evidence had raised matters
    relevant to the admissibility of a confession where there had not been a hearing on the *voir
    dire*. In that case, it was put to the police officers who had taken a confession statement from
    C that it was the result of earlier inducements by officers whom the prosecution chose not

to call. After C gave evidence repeating what had been put in cross-examination, the trial judge allowed the prosecution to reopen their case so as to call the officers named by C. The Court of Appeal held that it would have been an affront to the course of justice to have done otherwise.

D16.47 **Effect of the Police and Criminal Evidence Act 1984**   The above discussion has proceeded on the assumption that the enactment of ss. 76 and 78 of the PACE 1984 (admissibility of confessions and unfairly obtained evidence) has not affected the procedure for excluding confessions. However, Lord Lane CJ stated in *Sat-Bhambra* (1988) 88 Cr App R 55 at p. 62, that the wording of those two sections shows that, if it is sought to exclude evidence in reliance on them, the objection must always be made *before* the disputed evidence is adduced.

Lord Lane also drew attention to the PACE 1984, s. 82(3), under which the trial judge's general common-law powers to exclude evidence are preserved. Thus, if the defence do not ask for a *voir dire* but nonetheless evidence is adduced in the course of either the prosecution or defence cases which suggests that a confession was obtained in a manner prohibited by s. 76 or otherwise unfairly, the judge can be invited to exercise his residual common-law powers and either direct the jury to ignore the confession or discharge them from giving a verdict.

Guidance on *Voir Dire* Procedure where Objection to Evidence Taken under Police and Criminal Evidence Act 1984, s. 78

D16.48 Guidance has been given in *Keenan* [1990] 2 QB 54, on the appropriate procedure for asking the judge to rule under the PACE 1984, s. 78, that evidence obtained in breach of the PACE codes of practice should be excluded because its reception would have such an adverse effect on the fairness of the proceedings that it ought not to be admitted.

The Court of Appeal distinguished between three categories of case:

(a) Cases where a breach of the code is apparent from the custody record or statements of the prosecution witnesses, e.g., where (as in *Keenan* itself) there has been a breach of ss. 11 and 12 of PACE Code C relating to the contemporaneous noting of interviews with a suspect and/or showing him the officer's note. In this situation, it ought only to be necessary for prosecution counsel to make an admission as to the breach, after which there may be legal argument about the consequences for admissibility.

(b) Cases where there may be a prima facie breach which the prosecution seeks to justify, e.g., if access to a solicitor has been refused but the prosecution seek to justify that refusal on grounds such as the risk of interference with evidence if access had been allowed. In such cases, it will clearly be necessary for the prosecution to call evidence on the *voir dire* to explain away the prima facie breach, after which the accused may choose to testify in rebuttal.

(c) Alleged breaches which can be established only by evidence from the accused himself, e.g., cases of alleged oppression or where the accused claims that he was a person at risk not given the extra protection provided for in PACE Code C. Here, the accused will have to take the initiative by himself giving evidence on the *voir dire* to establish the breach.

In *Keenan*, Hodgson J thought that cases under (c) would be rare, and that in situations (a) and (b) it would be unlikely that the accused would want to testify in rebuttal. His lordship also said that the trial judge was obliged to give his ruling on whether admission of the evidence would be unfair in ignorance of what the defence's response to the evidence would be if it were admitted. That might seem unsatisfactory, but was simply a consequence of the overall structure of a criminal trial. The judgment helpfully summarises many of the earlier cases dealing with similar issues.

Reviewing a Determination as to Admissibility

D16.49 Prior to the enactment of the PACE 1984, the court was entitled to reconsider a ruling as to the admissibility of evidence where fresh evidence later emerged before the jury which cast doubt on its correctness. This was held in *Watson* [1980] 2 All ER 293, in which Cumming-Bruce LJ adopted the following passage from *Cross on Evidence* (5th edn, 1979, p. 720), as correctly stating the law:

> The judge retains his control over the evidence ultimately to be submitted to the jury through-out the trial. Accordingly, if, having admitted a confession as voluntary on evidence given in the absence of the jury, the judge concludes, in the light of subsequent evidence, that the confession was not voluntary, he may either direct the jury to disregard it, or, where there is no other sufficient evidence against the accused, direct an acquittal or, presumably, direct a new trial.

However, his lordship went on to say that 'the occasions on which a judge should allow counsel to invite him to reconsider a ruling already made are likely to be extremely rare' (p. 995D).

The Effect of the Police and Criminal Evidence Act 1984   The general principle stated in **D16.50**
Watson (i.e. that a trial judge may in exceptional circumstances be invited to reconsider his decision to admit disputed evidence) was no doubt intended to apply to any disputed evidence, whatever its nature, and not just to possibly inadmissible confessions. However, the position in respect of confession evidence has again been complicated by the wording of the PACE 1984, ss. 76 and 78.

In *Sat-Bhambra* (1988) 88 Cr App R 55, the Court of Appeal held that s. 76 (mandatory exclusion of a confession on grounds of oppression or unreliability) applies only *before* the confession has gone into evidence. There was consequently no statutory obligation on the judge to reconsider his earlier ruling. However, under s. 82(3) of the 1984 Act (preservation of discretionary powers to exclude evidence), the judge could still take whatever steps were necessary to prevent injustice, whether by directing the jury to disregard the evidence they had heard, commenting on its weight in the light of changed evidence, or even discharging them. But he was not, as the appellant contended, *obliged* to discharge them.

The relevant paragraphs from the Court of Appeal's judgment ((1988) 88 Cr App R 55 at p. 62) **D16.51**
are set out below:

> In *Watson* [1980] 1 WLR 991, decided before the 1984 Act, it was held that a judge who has second thoughts about the voluntariness of a statement which he has earlier ruled admissible upon the *voir dire* may, where it is appropriate so to do, change his opinion as to its admissibility, and may take such steps as are necessary to put matters right, by, for example, directing the jury to disregard it or discharging the jury.
>
> The words of section 76 are crucial: 'proposes to give in evidence' and 'shall not allow the confession to be given' are not . . . appropriate to describe something which has happened in the past. They are directed solely to the situation before the statement goes before the jury. Once the judge has ruled that it should do so, section 76 (and section 78, for the same reasons) ceases to have effect. The judge, whatever his change of mind may be, is no longer acting under section 76 as the appel-lant contends. To that extent the decision in *Watson* does not survive the wording of the 1984 Act.
>
> That does not mean that the judge is powerless to act. He has the power, if only under section 82(3), to take such steps as are necessary, depending on the circumstances, to prevent injustice. He may, if he thinks that the matter is not capable of remedy by a direction, discharge the jury; he may direct the jury to disregard the statement; he may by way of direction point out to the jury matters which affect the weight of the confession and leave the matter in their hands. He is not, as is the submis-sion here, obliged to discharge the jury and to order a new trial.
>
> If a defendant wishes under section 76 to exclude a confession, the time to make his submission to that effect is before the confession is put in evidence and not afterwards.

Editing of Prosecution Evidence

Where the prosecution evidence as foreshadowed in the committal statements contains mate-   **D16.52**
rial which is of such prejudicial effect that the jury clearly ought not to hear it, the practice is for the parties to 'edit' the evidence by agreement before it is called. This practice was recognised by the Court of Appeal in *Weaver* [1968] 1 QB 353. Sachs LJ indicated (at pp. 357G–358A)

that the best way for such editing to take place is for the evidence to appear 'unvarnished' in the committal statements. Counsel can then confer at trial to ensure that 'the editing is done in the right way and to the right degree'. If necessary the judge can also play a part in the process.

CPD V, paras. 27A.1 to 27A.6 (see Supplement, **PD-38**), contain detailed instructions on the treatment of statements served as part of the prosecution case where some of the material contained therein may be inadmissible or unduly prejudicial. Three options are set out:

(a) A composite statement can be prepared to replace several earlier statements made by a witness (para. 27A.2).
(b) A completely fresh statement can be prepared for a witness to sign, omitting those parts of the first statement which are inadmissible or prejudicial (para. 27A.3(b)). The circumstances in which this is the preferred option are set out at para. 27A.4.
(c) Where the prosecution decide that it is unnecessary to have a new statement, the procedure to be adopted is that the *original* of the witness's statement should be tendered to the court unmarked in any way but, on the *copies* served on the defence and provided to the court, the passages on which the prosecution do not propose to rely should either be bracketed or lightly struck out. The striking out should not be done in such a way as to obscure what is being deleted.

Paragraph 27A.3(a) states that the following note should be attached to the foot of the frontispiece or index to the bundle when served: 'The prosecution does not propose to adduce evidence of those passages of the attached copy statements which have been struck out and/or bracketed (nor will it seek to do so at the trial unless a notice of further evidence is served)'.

D16.53   A difficulty may arise where the jury ask to see the original of an edited document. They may be told that there are technical reasons why this cannot be permitted. Although this is not altogether satisfactory, it may be the only way of dealing with an inherent problem.

SUBMISSION OF NO CASE TO ANSWER

D16.54   After the prosecution has closed its case, the defence may submit that the evidence does not disclose a case to answer in respect of any or all the counts on the indictment. The procedure for the making of such an application is dealt with at **D16.67**, along with the consequences of such a submission (see **D16.70**). The first issue, however, is the test to be applied.

The Test to Be Applied

D16.55   The leading authority on the test a trial judge should apply in determining whether there is a case to answer is *Galbraith* [1981] 2 All ER 1060. In the course of his judgment in that case, Lord Lane CJ said (at p. 1042B–D):

> How then should the judge approach a submission of 'no case'? (1) If there is no evidence that the crime alleged has been committed by the defendant, there is no difficulty. The judge will of course stop the case. (2) The difficulty arises where there is some evidence but it is of a tenuous character, for example because of inherent weakness or vagueness or because it is inconsistent with other evidence. (a) Where the judge comes to the conclusion that the prosecution evidence, taken at its highest, is such that a jury properly directed could not properly convict upon it, it is his duty, upon a submission being made, to stop the case. (b) Where however the prosecution evidence is such that its strength or weakness depends on the view to be taken of a witness's reliability, or other matters which are generally speaking within the province of the jury and where on one possible view of the facts there *is* evidence upon which a jury could properly come to the conclusion that the defendant is guilty, then the judge should allow the matter to be tried by the jury ...

There will of course, as always in this branch of the law, be borderline cases. They can safely be left to the discretion of the judge.

The First Limb   As Lord Lane remarked, the first limb of the test set out in *Galbraith* [1981] 2   **D16.56**
All ER 1060, does not cause any conceptual problems. The test of there being 'no evidence that the crime alleged has been committed by the defendant' is intended to convey the same meaning as the words of Lord Parker CJ in his *Practice Direction (Submission of No Case)* [1962] 1 WLR 227, when he told magistrates that submissions of no case to answer at summary trial should be upheld, *inter alia*, if 'there has been no evidence to prove an essential element in the alleged offence'.

Such cases may arise, for example, where an essential prosecution witness has failed to come up to proof, or where there is no direct evidence as to an element of the offence and the inferences which the prosecution ask the court to draw from the circumstantial evidence are inferences which, in the judge's view, no reasonable jury could properly draw (see further **D22.49**). However, judges should take care to avoid taking into account defence evidence which is yet to be called and potential defences which have not yet been made out in assessing this limb of the test (*C* [2007] EWCA Crim 1862).

The Second Limb   The second limb of the test in *Galbraith* [1981] 2 All ER 1060, is far less   **D16.57**
straightforward, and has to be understood in the context of the practice that developed after the passing of the Criminal Appeal Act 1966, s. 4(1)(a) (now Criminal Appeal Act 1968, s. 2(1)), of inviting the judge to hold that there was no case to answer because a conviction on the prosecution evidence would be 'unsafe'. That form of submission reflected the power given to the Court of Appeal by first the 1966 and then the 1968 Act to quash a conviction on the basis that it was, in the court's opinion, 'unsafe or unsatisfactory' (but, since the Criminal Appeal Act 1995, part I, came into force, simply 'unsafe').

This approach inevitably involves the court considering the *quality* and *reliability* of the evidence, rather than its legal sufficiency, and therefore involved the court carrying out the assessment of evidence and witnesses that would otherwise be the exclusive prerogative of the jury. The judgment in *Galbraith* makes clear that it is no longer appropriate to argue on a submission of no case that it would be unsafe for the jury to convict, if only because that tempts the judge to impose his own views of the witnesses' veracity (see especially p. 1041B–C).

However, the second limb of the *Galbraith* test does leaves a residual role for the court as assessor of the reliability of the evidence. The court is empowered by the second limb of the *Galbraith* test to consider whether the prosecution's evidence is too inherently weak or vague for any sensible person to rely on it. Thus, if the witness undermines his own testimony by conceding that he is uncertain about vital points, or if what he says is manifestly contrary to reason, the court is entitled to hold that no reasonable jury properly directed could rely on the witness's evidence, and therefore (in the absence of any other evidence) there is no case to answer.

Reliability of Evidence under the Second Limb   It is often central to the application of the test   **D16.58**
in *Galbraith* [1981] 2 All ER 1060 to undertake an assessment of the reliability of the evidence adduced by the prosecution. This was illustrated in *Shippey* [1988] Crim LR 767, where the trial judge (Turner J) found there was evidence to support the prosecution's assertions, but that the evidence as a whole contained 'really significant inherent inconsistencies'. On a literal view of *Galbraith* and *Barker* (1975) 65 Cr App R 287, the case should therefore have gone to the jury for them to weigh the inconsistencies, but Turner J took a more robust view. He said that 'taking the prosecution case at its highest' did not mean 'taking out the plums and leaving the duff behind'. It was for the judge to assess the evidence and, if it was 'self-contradictory and out of reason and all common sense', then he could properly conclude that it was 'inherently weak and tenuous' within the meaning of the second limb of the *Galbraith* test.

However, it has since been emphasised, in *Pryer* [2004] EWCA Crim 1163, *Silcock* [2007] EWCA Crim 2176, and most recently and comprehensively in *Christou* [2012] EWCA Crim

450 that *Shippey* should not be elevated from a decision on specific facts into a legal principle. The proper test to be applied remains that enunciated in *Galbraith*, and the decision in *Shippey* merely illustrates the requirement that the court consider the evidence as a whole, including both its weaknesses and strengths.

D16.59   **The Proper Approach to a Submission of No Case to Answer**   The following propositions are advanced as representing the position that has now been reached on determining submissions of no case to answer:

(a) If there is no evidence to prove an essential element of the offence, a submission must obviously succeed.

(b) If there is some evidence which, taken at face value, establishes each essential element, the case should normally be left to the jury.

(c) If, however, the evidence is so weak that no reasonable jury properly directed could convict on it, a submission should be upheld. Weakness may arise from the sheer improbability of what the witness is saying, from internal inconsistencies in the evidence or from its being of a type which the accumulated experience of the courts has shown to be of doubtful value (especially in identification evidence cases, which are considered in **D16.60**).

(d) The question of whether a witness is lying is nearly always one for the jury, but there may be exceptional cases (such as *Shippey* [1988] Crim LR 767) where the inconsistencies are so great that any reasonable tribunal would be forced to the conclusion that the witness is untruthful, and that it would not be proper for the case to proceed on that evidence alone.

Having identified those general principles, it is appropriate to consider various particular types of evidence and categories of cases (For a striking example of a court's failure to follow proper procedure and an early intervention by the trial judge which led to the 'acquittal' being declared a nullity in the Court of Appeal, see *D* [2012] EWCA Crim 2181).

Identification Cases

D16.60   The correct approach to submissions of no case to answer in prosecutions turning upon identification evidence was laid down by the Court of Appeal in *Turnbull* [1977] QB 224 (see **F18.2** and **F18.18**), namely that, if the quality of the identification evidence on which the prosecution case depends is poor and there is no other evidence to support it, the judge should direct the jury to acquit (pp. 229H–230A). However, supporting evidence capable of justifying leaving a case to the jury, even where the identifying evidence is poor, need not be corroboration in the strict sense (p. 230B–D).

Although *Turnbull* predates *Galbraith* [1981] 2 All ER 1060, there is no suggestion that the principles in it have been affected by the later decision. In fact, the obligation on the trial judge to uphold a submission if the identifying evidence is poor and there is no supporting evidence may be regarded as the clearest example of the application of the second limb of the *Galbraith* test (*Daley v The Queen* [1994] 1 AC 117).

Confession Cases

D16.61   In *MacKenzie* (1992) 96 Cr App R 98, the Court of Appeal laid down special guidance for trial judges considering a submission of no case to answer in confession cases. Cases depending solely or mainly on confessions, like cases depending upon identification evidence, had given rise to miscarriages of justice. Accordingly, a court should, in the interests of justice, take the initiative and withdraw the case from the jury where the following conditions applied:

(a) the prosecution case depended wholly upon confessions;

(b) the accused suffered from a significant degree of mental handicap; and

(c) the confessions were unconvincing to a point where a jury properly directed could not properly convict upon them.

Confessions might be unconvincing, for example, because they lacked the incriminating details to be expected of a guilty and willing confessor, because they were inconsistent with other evidence, or because they were otherwise inherently improbable. See also *Wood* [1994] Crim LR 222.

Mutually Destructive Counts

Where two counts in an indictment are mutually destructive (e.g., alternative counts for theft and handling of the same goods), it may be possible to submit that no reasonable jury properly directed could be sure of which of the two counts the accused is guilty, and therefore they must be directed to acquit of both. **D16.62**

The problem arose in *Bellman* [1989] AC 836, a case chiefly important for the House of Lords' decision that mutually destructive counts may be joined in one indictment (see **D11.67**). In the course of reaching that conclusion, the House also considered whether in such cases the judge ought to have upheld a submission of no case in respect of all counts. Lord Griffiths said (at pp. 847G–848G):

> There are, of course, rare situations in which it is clear that the accused has committed a crime but the state of the evidence is such that it is impossible to say which crime he has committed. In such circumstances no prima facie case can be established to support either crime and neither crime can be left to the jury. The classic example arises where a man has given contradictory evidence on oath on two occasions. It is obvious that one statement must be false but in the absence of any evidence to indicate which statement was false it cannot be proved on which occasion the perjury was committed: see *Harris* (1822) 5 B & Ald 926 …

> An accused is always entitled to have the counts in the indictment considered separately by the judge at the end of the prosecution's evidence and if there is insufficient evidence to provide a prima facie case on any count to have that count withdrawn from the jury.

The situation in *Bellman* was different from that in the perjury example cited by Lord Griffiths. There being prima facie case sufficient in relation to both alternatives, it was a matter for the jury to decide at the end of all the evidence which of the two possible hypotheses based upon the prosecution evidence was the correct one. See also *Tsang Ping-nam v The Queen* [1981] 1 WLR 1462.

Prima Facie Case against Two Accused

Analogous problems to those discussed in **D16.62** arise where there are co-accused and the evidence establishes that one or other committed the offence charged but it is impossible to say which. **D16.63**

In such cases, and assuming there is no evidence of joint enterprise, both are clearly entitled to be acquitted on a submission of no case. Lord Griffiths stated the principle succinctly in his judgment in *Bellman* [1989] AC 836 (at p. 849A): 'It, of course, goes without saying that if the evidence shows that one of two accused must have committed a crime but it is impossible to go further and say which of them committed it, both must be acquitted: see *Lane* (1985) 82 Cr App R 5'. The same point had earlier been made by Lord Goddard CJ in *Abbott* [1955] 2 QB 497 at p. 503.

This approach was restated by the Court of Appeal in *Banfield* [2013] EWCA Crim 1394, which held that, where two accused were charged with murder, as opposed to conspiracy to murder, and the evidence was inconclusive as to whether the killing had been the responsibility of one, the other or both, the trial judge ought to have stopped the case against both. However, whether the evidence really does leave the question of which accused committed the offence in total doubt or whether there is evidence just capable of pointing to one or the other as the person responsible will depend on close analysis of the evidence in the particular case (compare *Gibson* (1984) 80 Cr App R 24, *Lane* (1986) 82 Cr App R 5, *Aston* (1992) 94 Cr App R 180 and *S* [1996] Crim LR 346, all of which involved injuries to young children where it was difficult to determine which of the two parents was responsible).

D

Part D Procedure

D16.64   The position in this regard has been significantly altered by the DVCVA 2004, which delays consideration of a submission of no case to answer in cases where, for example, one of two parents may have been responsible for the death of their child, until the conclusion of all the evidence (see **D16.69**).

A similar problem arises where evidence is as consistent with the guilt of a third party as with that of the accused. This was illustrated in *Grant* [2008] EWCA Crim 1890, where the only evidence against the accused was the presence of his DNA. The scientific analysis identified the DNA of the accused and of at least one other and was therefore as consistent with that other being responsible for the offence. The Court of Appeal concluded that the trial judge should have found that there was no case to answer.

Cases Based upon Inferences Drawn from Circumstantial Evidence

D16.65   There has been a degree of debate as to the proper approach to a submission of no case where the prosecution contends that guilt is proved, in whole or in part, by the drawing of certain inferences from circumstantial evidence. In the past, it was argued on the basis of *Moore* (20 August 1992 unreported) and *R (Inland Revenue Commissioners) v Crown Court at Kingston* [2001] 4 All ER 721, that a case to answer would only be made out where the prosecution could exclude any alternative inference being drawn from that circumstantial evidence. It is now clear that this is not the case.

On the proper application of the test in *Galbraith* [1981] 2 All ER 1060, the prosecution are not required to show that the jury could not reasonably reach any alternative inference contended for. The question is whether it is properly open to the jury to reach the inferences contended for by the prosecution.

This was the conclusion of Tuckey LJ, giving the judgment of the Court of Appeal in *Bokkum* (7 March 2000 unreported), at [32]:

> Read literally the passage in *Moore* would mean that in any case dependent on circumstantial evidence the judge would be required to withdraw the case from the jury if some inference other than guilt could reasonably be drawn from the facts proved. We do not think that the Court intended to say this and if it did it is contrary to what was said in *Galbraith*. The approach suggested may be appropriate in a case such as *Moore* where the inference of guilt is sought to be drawn from a single fact, but this is much more difficult in a case such as the instant case where the Crown rely on a combination of facts. The judge will, of course, withdraw the case if he considers that it would be unsafe for the jury to conclude that the defendant is guilty on the totality of the circumstantial evidence adduced, but if he concludes that it is open to them to convict then Galbraith requires the judge to leave the decision to them.

This statement of principle was specifically approved by the Court of Appeal in *Edwards* [2004] EWCA Crim 2102 at [84], and the same approach was adopted in *Jabber* [2006] EWCA Crim 2694 at [21] and *Goring* [2011] EWCA Crim 2, where it was emphasised that there was a case to answer where, on a reasonable assessment of the evidence, the jury were entitled (rather than bound) to reach conclusions consistent with guilt (see also *R (Boota) v Gwent Magistrates' Court* [2012] EWHC 3550 (Admin).

Silence in Interview

D16.66   The CJPO 1994, s. 34(2)(c), permits the court, in considering whether the accused has a case to answer, to take into account the fact that he failed to answer questions in interview. However s. 38(3) makes clear that a submission of no case cannot be rejected solely on the basis of such silence (see **F19.14**).

Moreover, as was demonstrated in *Broadhead* [2006] EWCA Crim 1705, care has to be taken to be sure that the accused is relying on facts he failed to mention in interview rather than simply putting the prosecution to proof before inferences can be relied upon at the close of the prosecution case, and therefore before he has given evidence.

Procedure on a Submission of No Case

Jury to be Kept in Ignorance of the Submission   Submissions of no case should be made **D16.67** in the absence of the jury, and should not be referred to in their presence thereafter if they are unsuccessful. This was made clear by the Court of Appeal in *Smith* (1986) 85 Cr App R 197. In that case, in which identification evidence was relied on, the judge told the jury during the summing-up that, if he had not thought there was sufficient evidence of identification, he would have withdrawn the case from them. Watkins LJ said (at p. 200 emphasis added):

> That is an improper observation for a judge to make to a jury. Submissions [of no case to answer] are made in the absence of the jury. There is very good reason for that as all who take part in trials know. The question as to whether or not there is a sufficiency of evidence is one which is exclusively for the judge following submissions made to him *in the absence of the jury*. His decision *should not be revealed* to the jury lest it wrongly influences them. There is a risk that they might convict because they think the judge's view is a sufficient indication that the evidence is strong enough for that purpose.

In *Crosdale v The Queen* [1995] 2 All ER 500, it was emphasised that a trial judge should ask a jury to withdraw during a submission of no case to answer since it was a matter for him alone whether there was sufficient evidence to go before the jury.

Timing of a Submission   Almost invariably, the proper time for making a submission of no **D16.68** case is after the prosecution have called their evidence (*Leadbeater* [1988] Crim LR 463). The only exceptions to this rule are cases where either (a) there is an objection to the jurisdiction of the court (see, e.g., *DPP v Doot* [1973] AC 807, in which the question was whether an offence of conspiracy had been committed inside or outside the jurisdiction), or (b) where there is an agreed statement of facts and the judge is effectively being asked whether what undoubtedly happened amounts to the offence charged. The trial judge cannot rule that there is no case to answer before the conclusion of the prosecution case unless all parties agree to his doing so (*N Ltd* [2008] 1 WLR 2684).

The Timing of a Submission: Special Provision under the Domestic Violence, Crime and Victims Act 2004   A different procedure is to be followed where the accused is charged in the **D16.69** same proceedings with an offence of murder or manslaughter and with an offence under the DVCVA 2004, s. 5 (causing or allowing the death of a child or a vulnerable adult: see B1.73), in respect of the same death. The question whether there is a case for him to answer on the charge of murder or manslaughter must not then be considered before the close of all the evidence. If the accused ceases to be charged with the offence under s. 5, then whether there is a case to answer on the murder or manslaughter charge is to be considered before he ceases to be so charged (s. 6). Although s. 6(4) changes the timing for a submission of no case to answer, it does not otherwise change the approach to such a submission (*Ikram* [2008] 4 All ER 253).

A similar procedure applies by virtue of the DVCVA 2004, s. 6A. The Domestic Violence, Crime and Victims (Amendment) Act 2012 amends the DVCVA 2004, s. 5, so as to extend it to cover causing or allowing a child or vulnerable adult to suffer serious physical harm. Where the accused is charged with such an offence and a relevant offence (i.e. an offence under the OAPA 1861, s. 18 or 20, or attempted murder), the question whether there is a case for him to answer on the relevant offence must not then be considered before the close of all the evidence.

Procedure Following a Successful Submission   As already indicated, the procedure upon the **D16.70** judge upholding a submission on all counts of the indictment is for the jury to return to court, so that one of their number can be asked to stand as foreman and, on the judge's direction, formally return a verdict of not guilty.

If the submission has succeeded on some counts but failed on others, the defendant should be regarded during the rest of the trial as no longer being charged on the former (*Plain* [1967] 1 All ER 614). However, in those circumstances no verdict is taken until the end of the trial when the

D

Part D Procedure

jury both announce their decision on the counts for which there was a case and, on the judge's direction, find the accused not guilty on the remainder of the indictment.

It was made clear in *Carson* (1990) 92 Cr App R 236, and restated in *Livesey* (2007) 1 Cr App R 462, that the court can direct a verdict of not guilty on the only charge indicted but permit the trial to continue in relation to any statutory alternative summary offence. In *Plant* [2008] 2 Cr App R 386, it was made clear that a successful submission in relation to the indictable offence on an indictment did not require the remaining summary offence, joined under the CJA 1988, s. 40, to be remitted to a magistrates' court.

D16.71   Initiative for a Submission   It is defence counsel's responsibility to make a submission of no case to answer should the circumstances warrant it (*Juett* [1981] Crim LR 113). In general, the trial judge is neither required nor even entitled to intervene if no submission is made. Exceptionally, however, the interests of justice may demand that the judge take the initiative and suggest that there may not be a case to answer. In such exceptional cases and assuming there was not in fact enough evidence to go to the jury at the end of the prosecution case, the Court of Appeal will quash the conviction, notwithstanding that defence counsel did not make a submission (*Juett*).

Stopping the Case before the End of the Trial

D16.72   Jury May Acquit at Any Time   At common law a jury are entitled to decide at any stage after the prosecution have closed their case that they do not need to hear any further evidence or argument but may wish to acquit forthwith. Although the judge may 'remind' them that this course is open to them, he should not go further and issue an invitation to them to acquit (*Kemp* [1995] 1 Cr App R 151, approving the observations of Roskill LJ in *Falconer-Atlee* (1973) 58 Cr App R 348 at p. 357). The judge must make it absolutely clear to the jury that, although they may acquit at this stage, they may not convict.

In *Speechley* [2005] 2 Cr App R (S) 75, counsel for the defence had, when opening the defence at trial, sought to remind the jury of their right to acquit. The judge ruled that he could not do so. The Court of Appeal held that the common-law right of the jury to acquit after the conclusion of the prosecution case was exercisable only where they had been invited to do so by the trial judge. If a jury was invited by counsel, or sought of its own motion, to return a verdict before the judge asked them to do so, he should direct the jury that it was his duty to ensure that justice was done and that it was not open to them to return a verdict until he had invited them to do so (see also *Collins* [2007] EWCA Crim 854 and *H (S)* [2011] 1 Cr App R 182).

D16.73   Submission at the Close of the Evidence   In *Boakye* (12 March 1992 unreported), Steyn LJ pointed out that, as a matter of principle, the judge was entitled to hold that there was no case to answer even at the end of the defence case:

> [Counsel for the Crown] has made a submission to us that it was not appropriate to make a submission of no case to answer at the end of the defence case. In our judgment a judge is entitled, even at that late stage, if no evidence is available on a count or if there is no evidence of that count upon which a reasonable jury could convict, to rule that there is no case to go before the jury. The contrary proposition would be a startling one. It would contemplate that the judge might be powerless to prevent a real miscarriage of justice in a case where there was a sudden change in the strength of the prosecution case as a result of cogent evidence emerging in the defence case. We rule without any doubt that it was within the power of the judge to make the ruling that was requested of him.

In *Anderson* (1998) *Independent*, 13 July 1998, the Court of Appeal, similarly, stated that, although it was more usual for defence counsel to make a submission of no case to answer at the close of the prosecution case, a trial judge is not precluded from entertaining and ruling on such a submission at the close of the defence case.

The reasoning of the Court of Appeal in *Brown* [1998] Crim LR 196, reinforces this approach. Their lordships stated that throughout the trial the judge has a duty not to allow a jury to consider evidence on which they could not safely convict. He should not invite them to acquit since, if they convicted, the accused would be left with a sense of grievance. But if, at the conclusion of the evidence, the trial judge is of the opinion that no reasonable jury properly directed could safely convict, he should raise the matter for discussion with counsel even if no submission of no case to answer is made. If, having heard submissions, he is of the same opinion, he should withdraw the case from the jury. See also *Brown* [2002] 1 Cr App R 46.

For the special rule where an accused is charged with murder/manslaughter or causing serious injury to a child, together with an offence under the DVCVA 2004, s. 5, see **D16.69**.

APPEALS BY THE PROSECUTION AGAINST ADVERSE RULINGS

Before the introduction of the CJA 2003, the prosecution's ability to challenge a ruling adverse **D16.74** to its position which either terminated a case entirely or excluded evidence in such a way as to fundamentally undermine its ability to continue was extremely limited. It had a right to appeal against rulings made at a preparatory hearing (see **D15.67**) and, after the termination of a prosecution, it was possible for the A-G to refer a point of law to the Court of Appeal, pursuant to the CJA 1977, s. 36, with a view to clarifying the law for the future.

Part 9 of the CJA 2003 (ss. 57 to 74) introduced provision for appeals by the prosecution against rulings of the Crown Court in relation to trial on indictment. These can be divided into two broad categories:

(a) appeals against terminating rulings (ss. 58 to 61);
(b) appeals against evidentiary rulings which significantly weaken the prosecution case (ss. 62 to 67).

Application

Pursuant to the Criminal Justice Act 2003 (Commencement No. 8 and Transitional and Saving **D16.75** Provisions) Order 2005 (SI 2005 No. 950), a terminating ruling may be the subject of a s. 58 appeal only where proceedings were committed or sent for trial after the date of its commencement (4 April 2005). The provisions relating to s. 62 evidentiary ruling appeals have not yet come into force.

Terminating Rulings

Section 58 of the CJA 2003 permits the prosecution to challenge rulings of the Crown Court **D16.76** which would otherwise bring proceedings in a particular case to an end, in such a way that, if the ruling in question was found to have been in error, it would be possible for the proceedings to continue. By virtue of s. 58(6), the prosecution may appeal in relation only to certain counts of the indictment. Moreover, s. 58(7) allows the prosecution to appeal other rulings made during the course of the trial in addition to the court's ruling in response to a submission of no case to answer. Such an appeal requires leave either from the trial judge or the Court of Appeal (s. 57(4)). Arguably the wording of s. 58 does not limit the use of such appeals only to terminatory rulings, but it was designed for such rulings.

The Court of Appeal has provided guidance on a number of occasions as to the scope of s. 58.

(a) In *Clarke* [2008] 1 Cr App R 403, the court accepted that the prosecution could appeal against the refusal of an adjournment to allow them to secure the attendance of the principal witness, without whose evidence the case was unsustainable.
(b) In *Y* [2008] 2 All ER 484, the court recognised that a ruling as to the admissibility of evidence was capable of both representing an evidential ruling (within the meaning of s. 62) and a terminating ruling (within s. 58) where its effect was to make the continuation of the case impossible.

(c) In *R* [2008] EWCA Crim 370, the court went one step further, and found that even a ruling as to the exclusion of evidence which was less obviously determinative of the prosecution case could be made the subject of an appeal under s. 58 if the prosecution chose to make it a terminating ruling by entering into an acquittal agreement, pursuant to s. 58(8). This approach was confirmed in *O* [2008] EWCA Crim 463 and *F* [2009] EWCA Crim 1639.

Consideration of an Appeal

D16.77   The rules applicable to appeals from both forms of preparatory hearing are contained in the CrimPR, part 67 (see Supplement, **R-507**). The process involves a series of stages, which are dealt with below.

The first step to be taken in relation to such an appeal is for the prosecution, pursuant to the CJA 2003, s. 58(4), either to inform the court that it intends to appeal or to request an adjournment (s. 58(4)(a)(ii)) to consider whether or not to appeal against the ruling of the court. In the latter event the prosecution must, in accordance with the CrimPR, r. 67.2, make the request to the judge of the court immediately following the relevant ruling. In *CPS v C* [2009] EWCA Crim 2614 the Court of Appeal underlined that these were the only options as to timing. See also *Mian* [2012] 3 All ER 661.

The court must grant the adjournment (s. 58(5)), which will be until the next business day (r. 67.2(2)). The provision for a longer adjournment where the interests of justice so required no longer applies.

D16.78   **Announcing the Decision to Appeal**   Following the adjournment (if any) or immediately after the ruling, the prosecutor must inform the judge whether he intends to appeal. If he does, he must either serve a notice of appeal on the court, the Registrar and the accused (which must take place either by the next day if the appeal is expedited or within five days if it is not (r. 67.3)) or apply orally to the judge for leave to appeal (CJA 2003, s. 57(4)). The judge must hear representations from the defence before deciding whether or not to grant leave, but must make the decision on the same day as the oral application for leave is made unless it is in the interests of justice to take longer (CrimPR, r. 67.5). In *Ali-Ali* [2009] 1 Cr App R 279 the Court of Appeal said that, before leave was granted, consideration should be given to whether the appeal was in the interests of justice, in the sense that the Court of Appeal would allow the prosecution of the accused to proceed.

Crucially, when appealing against a terminating ruling, the prosecution must undertake to offer no evidence against the accused in the event that the appeal is either abandoned or refused (s. 58(8)). In *Arnold* [2008] 1 WLR 2881 the Court of Appeal emphasised that the giving of this undertaking is an essential prerequisite of any appeal (see also *CPS v C* [2009] EWCA Crim 2614 and *T (N)* [2010] 4 All ER 545). A ruling that is to be subject to appeal ceases to have effect once notice has been given (s. 58(11)). In *H (S)* [2011] 1 Cr App R 182 the Court of Appeal criticised a judge at first instance for proceeding to invite the jury to acquit following notification that the prosecution sought to appeal against his ruling that there was no case to answer.

D16.79   **Expediting an Appeal**   Section 59 of the CJA 2003 permits an appeal to be expedited, in the discretion of the trial judge. When the prosecutor signals his intention to appeal, he must also make oral representations as to whether the appeal should be expedited. Before deciding the issue, the judge must hear representations from the defence and any interested party (CrimPR, r. 67.6). This decision is significant because, if the appeal is not expedited, the court may decide to discharge the jury rather than adjourn the case to allow the appeal to be heard (s. 59(3)).

Any decision by the judge to expedite an appeal may be reversed by him at any time before notice of appeal or application for leave to appeal is served on the Crown Court in accordance with the CrimPR, r. 67.6(3), or by the Court of Appeal thereafter. The reasons for the reversal of that decision must be provided in writing to the prosecutor, defence and any interested party.

Documentation   Usually a notice of appeal or application for leave to appeal must be served   **D16.80**
by the prosecutor on the Registrar, the Crown Court officer, the accused and any interested party. If the judge decides to expedite the appeal, that notice must be served on the day after the prosecutor states his intention to appeal. In any other case, the prosecutor has five days (CrimPR, r. 67.3). If the appeal or application is resisted, the necessary documentation must be served on the other parties on the next day if the appeal is expedited and otherwise within five days (r. 67.7). There are special rules for appeals which relate to rulings as to the disclosure of material over which public interest immunity is claimed in r. 67.8.

Conduct by the Court of Appeal   Rule 67.9 sets out the powers of a single judge in relation   **D16.81**
to such appeals. The options available to the Court of Appeal in relation to such an appeal are set out in the CJA 2003, s. 61, namely that it may either confirm the ruling at first instance (in which case it orders the acquittal of the accused), reverse it or vary it. If either of the latter options is taken, the orders that the Court of Appeal may then make are that (i) the Crown Court trial resume, (ii) a fresh trial take place, or (iii) if the defendant could not receive a fair trial if option (i) or (ii) is taken, the accused be acquitted (s. 61(4) and (5), as amended by the CJIA 2008, s. 44).

Evidentiary Rulings

Once the relevant provisions come into force, the prosecution may appeal one or more   **D16.82**
'qualifying' evidentiary rulings pursuant to the CJA 2003, s. 62. Such rulings are rulings as to the admissibility or exclusion of prosecution material (s. 62(9)), made at any time before the opening of the defence case (s. 62(2)) where the accused is charged with a 'qualifying offence'.

Qualifying Offences   These offences are defined in the CJA 2003, sch. 4, and can be sum-   **D16.83**
marised as follows:

(a) offences against the person, including murder, manslaughter, offences under the OAPA 1861, s. 18 and kidnap;
(b) sexual offences, including rape;
(c) drugs offences relating to Class A drugs;
(d) robbery with the use of a firearm or imitation firearm;
(e) arson endangering life and offences contrary to the Explosives Substances Act 1883, ss. 2 and 3;
(f) war crimes and terrorist offences.

Procedure   The CrimPR do not yet provide a procedural framework for such appeals,   **D16.84**
although it is likely to mirror that in part 66 which relates to s. 58 appeals. The first step, as with terminating ruling appeals, is for the prosecution to inform the court that it seeks to appeal against an identified ruling (CJA 2003, s. 62(5)). Leave to appeal, which may be granted by either the trial judge or the Court of Appeal (s. 57(4)), will be granted only if the ruling, or the rulings taken together, 'significantly weakens the prosecution's case' (s. 63). Again the issue of expedition of appeal is to be determined by the trial judge, and is subject to review (see **D16.79**).

Conduct of the Court of Appeal   The options available to the Court of Appeal in relation to   **D16.85**
such an appeal are set out in the CJA 2003, s. 61, namely that it may either confirm the ruling at first instance, reverse it or vary it. It may only reverse the ruling if the conditions in s. 67 are satisfied. The orders that it may make are those set out in s. 66(2). See *F* [2009] EWCA Crim 1639 as to the relationship between ss. 58 and 67.

Statutory Extracts on Prosecution Appeals

D16.86   Criminal Justice Act 2003, ss. 57 to 66

57.—(1) In relation to a trial on indictment, the prosecution is to have the rights of appeal for which provision is made by [part 9].

(2) But the prosecution is to have no right of appeal under this Part in respect of—
   (a) a ruling that a jury be discharged, or
   (b) a ruling from which an appeal lies to the Court of Appeal by virtue of any other enactment.

(3) An appeal under this Part is to lie to the Court of Appeal.

(4) Such an appeal may be brought only with the leave of the judge or the Court of Appeal.

58.—(1) This section applies where a judge makes a ruling in relation to a trial on indictment at an applicable time and the ruling relates to one or more offences included in the indictment.

(2) The prosecution may appeal in respect of the ruling in accordance with this section.

(3) The ruling is to have no effect whilst the prosecution is able to take any steps under sub-section (4).

(4) The prosecution may not appeal in respect of the ruling unless—
   (a) following the making of the ruling, it—
      (i) informs the court that it intends to appeal, or
      (ii) requests an adjournment to consider whether to appeal, and
   (b) if such an adjournment is granted, it informs the court following the adjournment that it intends to appeal.

(5) If the prosecution requests an adjournment under subsection (4)(a)(ii), the judge may grant such an adjournment.

(6) Where the ruling relates to two or more offences—
   (a) any one or more of those offences may be the subject of the appeal, and
   (b) if the prosecution informs the court in accordance with subsection (4) that it intends to appeal, it must at the same time inform the court of the offence or offences which are the subject of the appeal.

(7) Where—
   (a) the ruling is a ruling that there is no case to answer, and
   (b) the prosecution, at the same time that it informs the court in accordance with sub-section (4) that it intends to appeal, nominates one or more other rulings which have been made by a judge in relation to the trial on indictment at an applicable time and which relate to the offence or offences which are the subject of the appeal,
   that other ruling, or those other rulings, are also to be treated as the subject of the appeal.

(8) The prosecution may not inform the court in accordance with subsection (4) that it intends to appeal, unless, at or before that time, it informs the court that it agrees that, in respect of the offence or each offence which is the subject of the appeal, the defendant in relation to that offence should be acquitted of that offence if either of the conditions mentioned in subsection (9) is fulfilled.

(9) Those conditions are—
   (a) that leave to appeal to the Court of Appeal is not obtained, and
   (b) that the appeal is abandoned before it is determined by the Court of Appeal.

(10) If the prosecution informs the court in accordance with subsection (4) that it intends to appeal, the ruling mentioned in subsection (1) is to continue to have no effect in relation to the offence or offences which are the subject of the appeal whilst the appeal is pursued.

(11) If and to the extent that a ruling has no effect in accordance with this section—
   (a) any consequences of the ruling are also to have no effect,
   (b) the judge may not take any steps in consequence of the ruling, and
   (c) if he does so, any such steps are also to have no effect.

(12) Where the prosecution has informed the court of its agreement under subsection (8) and either of the conditions mentioned in subsection (9) is fulfilled, the judge or the Court of Appeal must order that the defendant in relation to the offence or each offence concerned be acquitted of that offence.

(13) In this section 'applicable time', in relation to a trial on indictment, means any time (whether before or after the commencement of the trial) before the time when the judge starts his summing-up to the jury.

(14) The reference in subsection (13) to the time when the judge starts his summing-up to the jury includes the time when the judge would start his summing-up to the jury but for the making of an order under Part 7.

59.—(1) Where the prosecution informs the court in accordance with section 58(4) that it intends to appeal, the judge must decide whether or not the appeal should be expedited.

(2) If the judge decides that the appeal should be expedited, he may order an adjournment.

(3) If the judge decides that the appeal should not be expedited, he may—
  (a) order an adjournment, or
  (b) discharge the jury (if one has been sworn).

(4) If he decides that the appeal should be expedited, he or the Court of Appeal may subsequently reverse that decision and, if it is reversed, the judge may act as mentioned in subsection (3)(a) or (b).

60.—(1) This section applies where the prosecution informs the court in accordance with section 58(4) that it intends to appeal.

(2) Proceedings may be continued in respect of any offence which is not the subject of the appeal.

61.—(1) On an appeal under section 58, the Court of Appeal may confirm, reverse or vary any ruling to which the appeal relates.

(2) Subsections (3) to (5) apply where the appeal relates to a single ruling.

(3) Where the Court of Appeal confirms the ruling, it must, in respect of the offence or each offence which is the subject of the appeal, order that the defendant in relation to that offence be acquitted of that offence.

(4) Where the Court of Appeal reverses or varies the ruling, it must, in respect of the offence or each offence which is the subject of the appeal, do any of the following—
  (a) order that proceedings for that offence may be resumed in the Crown Court,
  (b) order that a fresh trial may take place in the Crown Court for that offence,
  (c) order that the defendant in relation to that offence be acquitted of that offence.

(5) But the Court of Appeal may not make an order under subsection (4)(c) in respect of an offence unless it considers that the defendant could not receive a fair trial if an order were made under subsection (4)(a) or (b).

(6) Subsections (7) and (8) apply where the appeal relates to a ruling that there is no case to answer and one or more other rulings.

(7) Where the Court of Appeal confirms the ruling that there is no case to answer, it must, in respect of the offence or each offence which is the subject of the appeal, order that the defendant in relation to that offence be acquitted of that offence.

(8) Where the Court of Appeal reverses or varies the ruling that there is no case to answer, it must in respect of the offence or each offence which is the subject of the appeal, make any of the orders mentioned in subsection (4)(a) to (c) (but subject to subsection (5)).

62.—(1) The prosecution may, in accordance with this section and section 63, appeal in respect of—
  (a) a single qualifying evidentiary ruling, or
  (b) two or more qualifying evidentiary rulings.

(2) A 'qualifying evidentiary ruling' is an evidentiary ruling of a judge in relation to a trial on indictment which is made at any time (whether before or after the commencement of the trial) before the opening of the case for the defence.

(3) The prosecution may not appeal in respect of a single qualifying evidentiary ruling unless the ruling relates to one or more qualifying offences (whether or not it relates to any other offence).

(4) The prosecution may not appeal in respect of two or more qualifying evidentiary rulings unless each ruling relates to one or more qualifying offences (whether or not it relates to any other offence).

(5) If the prosecution intends to appeal under this section, it must before the opening of the case for the defence inform the court—
  (a) of its intention to do so, and
  (b) of the ruling or rulings to which the appeal relates.

(6) In respect of the ruling, or each ruling, to which the appeal relates—
  (a) the qualifying offence, or at least one of the qualifying offences, to which the ruling relates must be the subject of the appeal, and
  (b) any other offence to which the ruling relates may, but need not, be the subject of the appeal.

(7) The prosecution must, at the same time that it informs the court in accordance with sub-section (5), inform the court of the offence or offences which are the subject of the appeal.

(8) For the purposes of this section, the case for the defence opens when, after the conclusion of the prosecution evidence, the earliest of the following events occurs—

    (a) evidence begins to be adduced by or on behalf of a defendant,

    (b) it is indicated to the court that no evidence will be adduced by or on behalf of a defendant,

    (c) a defendant's case is opened, as permitted by section 2 of the Criminal Procedure Act 1865 (c. 18).

(9) In this section—

'evidentiary ruling' means a ruling which relates to the admissibility or exclusion of any prosecution evidence,

'qualifying offence' means an offence described in Part 1 of Schedule 4.

(10) [Secretary of State's power to amend part 1 of sch. 4.]

(11) Nothing in this section affects the right of the prosecution to appeal in respect of an evidentiary ruling under section 58.

63.—(1) Leave to appeal may not be given in relation to an appeal under section 62 unless the judge or, as the case may be, the Court of Appeal is satisfied that the relevant condition is fulfilled.

(2) In relation to an appeal in respect of a single qualifying evidentiary ruling, the relevant condition is that the ruling significantly weakens the prosecution's case in relation to the offence or offences which are the subject of the appeal.

(3) In relation to an appeal in respect of two or more qualifying evidentiary rulings, the relevant condition is that the rulings taken together significantly weaken the prosecution's case in relation to the offence or offences which are the subject of the appeal.

64.—(1) Where the prosecution informs the court in accordance with section 62(5), the judge must decide whether or not the appeal should be expedited.

(2) If the judge decides that the appeal should be expedited, he may order an adjournment.

(3) If the judge decides that the appeal should not be expedited, he may—

    (a) order an adjournment, or

    (b) discharge the jury (if one has been sworn).

(4) If he decides that the appeal should be expedited, he or the Court of Appeal may subsequently reverse that decision and, if it is reversed, the judge may act as mentioned in subsection (3)(a) or (b).

65.—(1) This section applies where the prosecution informs the court in accordance with section 62(5).

(2) Proceedings may be continued in respect of any offence which is not the subject of the appeal.

66.—(1) On an appeal under section 62, the Court of Appeal may confirm, reverse or vary any ruling to which the appeal relates.

(2) In addition, the Court of Appeal must, in respect of the offence or each offence which is the subject of the appeal, do any of the following—

    (a) order that proceedings for that offence be resumed in the Crown Court,

    (b) order that a fresh trial may take place in the Crown Court for that offence,

    (c) order that the defendant in relation to that offence be acquitted of that offence.

(3) But no order may be made under subsection (2)(c) in respect of an offence unless the prosecution has indicated that it does not intend to continue with the prosecution of that offence.

Section D17   Trial on Indictment: The Defence Case

INTRODUCTION

Assuming any submission of no case to answer has been rejected (see **D16.54**), the next stage following the close of the prosecution case is for the defence to call such evidence as they choose. This chapter briefly considers the various potential aspects of a defence case, from opening to the decision to call either the accused himself or any defence witnesses. Special considerations arise where the accused is representing himself (**D17.17**). First, however, it is necessary to assess briefly the professional duties of defence counsel.

D17.1

DUTIES AND ROLE OF DEFENCE COUNSEL

General Principle

Defence counsel is not subject to the constraints of impartiality that apply to prosecuting counsel (addressed at **D16.2**). Subject to the duty resting on any barrister not deliberately to mislead the court, and to the rules of professional conduct generally, he may use all proper means to secure the acquittal or lenient sentencing of his lay client (as is made clear at rC16 of the new Bar Standards Board's Handbook).

D17.2

In presenting the accused's defence, counsel should not be influenced by his personal opinion of its truth. This cardinal principle was restated by the Professional Conduct Committee of the Bar following the decision of the Court of Appeal in *McFadden* (1975) 62 Cr App R 187, which was to the effect that:

> It is the duty of counsel when defending an accused on a criminal charge to present to the court, fearlessly and without regard to his personal interests, the defence of that accused. It is not his function to determine the truth or falsity of that defence, nor should he permit his personal opinion of that defence to influence his conduct of it. No counsel may refuse to defend because of his opinion of the character of the accused nor of the crime charged. That is a cardinal rule of the Bar, and it would be a grave matter in any free society were it not. Counsel also has a duty to the court and to the public. This duty includes the clear presentation of the issues and the avoidance of waste of time, repetition and prolixity. In the conduct of every case counsel must be mindful of this public responsibility.

More recently, in *Ebanks v The Queen* [2006] 1 WLR 1827, the Privy Council stressed the duty of defence counsel to put his client's case irrespective of whether the accused would ultimately give evidence, that decision being one for the accused alone.

As the approach of the Court of Appeal in *Newell* [2012] 1 WLR 3142 illustrates, an advocate has authority to act, in the course of his profession, in a manner incidental to the execution of the express authority vested in the advocate by his client. This means that he is deemed to be his client's agent when he gives an undertaking, or identifies the issues in the case, e.g., on a plea and case management form, with the result that any such undertaking or statement is potentially admissible as evidence against his client.

Becoming a Witness

D17.3   Occasionally, the question will arise as to whether it is proper for defence counsel to be called as a witness on behalf of his client. In *Jaquith* [1989] Crim LR 563, the Court of Appeal provided guidance for the Bar Council and the Law Society as to the circumstances in which this should occur, which included the following:

(a) No advocate should give evidence in a criminal trial if doing so can possibly be avoided.

(b) If an advocate does give evidence, he should thereafter take no further part in the trial. It follows that, unless he has a leader, there must be a retrial.

(c) Counsel should be able to anticipate before the trial whether it will be necessary for him to give evidence. If it will be, he should withdraw.

(d) If the giving of evidence by an advocate causes real embarrassment or prevents proper cross-examination by other counsel, a retrial should be ordered.

In *Wood* [1996] 1 Cr App R 207, the Court of Appeal said that the rule should be enforced that a member of the Bar giving evidence could no longer act as counsel in the same case. The comment was made in response to a ground of appeal which concerned the tone of voice used by the trial judge and the physical expression of views by sighing, shrugging his shoulders and raising his eyebrows in a way that was said to be hostile to the defence. Their lordships' view was that they could not act on such information unless it was either agreed between counsel or supported by evidence.

Professional Embarrassment

D17.4   The Court of Appeal has identified other circumstances in which it would be inappropriate for counsel to act. These include the following:

(a) It is generally undesirable for husband and wife, or other partners living together, to appear as advocates against each other in a contested criminal matter (*Batt* [1996] Crim LR 910).

(b) It is undesirable for counsel to prosecute an accused whom he had previously defended. The Conduct Rules in the Bar Standards Board's Handbook refer (at rC21.4) to the risk that a barrister may have confidential information or special knowledge disadvantageous to a former client. In *Dann* [1997] Crim LR 46, it was made clear that it was the *risk* which was material.

Code of Conduct of the Bar

D17.5   Until 6 January 2014, the conduct of defence counsel was regulated by the written standards issued under the 8th edition of the Code of Conduct. Those are now superseded by the Conduct Rules in the Bar Standards Board's Handbook. Matters of relevance to defence counsel in the Conduct Rules include the following:

(a) He should satisfy himself, if he is briefed to represent more than one accused, that no conflict of interest is likely to arise (rC17).

(b) In the cross-examination of witnesses, rC7 is of central importance. It requires that the advocate 'must not make statements or ask questions merely to insult, humiliate or annoy a witness or any other person'. The advocate must put any 'serious allegation' to a witness and must not make a serious allegation against any person, or suggest that a person is guilty of a crime with which the accused is charged unless there are 'reasonable grounds for the allegation' and the other requirements in rC7.3 are met.

(c) The fact that the accused confesses to counsel that he did commit the offence charged does not bar counsel from appearing or continuing to appear for the defence on a not guilty plea (rC3.5 and gC9–10). Counsel may properly take objections to the competency of the court, the form of the indictment and the admissibility of any evidence, and may test the prosecution's evidence, but he may not himself call evidence or advance an affirmative defence inconsistent with the confession.

Other Issues

The interlocking matters of conferences, counsel being attended at court by his professional cli-   **D17.6** ent, and the seeing of witnesses are dealt with in various provisions of the Bar Standard Board's Handbook, and are summarised at **D15.100** *et seq*. See also *Anderson* [2010] EWCA Crim 2553, where the need for proper notes of all consultations between defence counsel and his client to be completed and retained was emphasised.

DEFENCE OPENING SPEECH

If the defence intend to call evidence as to the facts of the case other than, or in addition to, the   **D17.7** evidence of the accused, defence counsel has the right to an opening speech at the beginning of the defence case (*Hill* (1911) 7 Cr App R 1 and the CrimPR, r. 38.9(2)(f)). If, however, the only defence evidence is to come from the accused (or from the accused and character witnesses) then counsel does not have an opening speech. That is the implication of the Criminal Evidence Act 1898, s. 2. In an opening speech, defence counsel may both outline the anticipated defence case and criticise the evidence already given for the prosecution (*Randall* (1973) *The Times*, 11 July 1973). However, the speech should not make assertions of fact that are not to be proved by evidence that is to come.

THE DEFENCE CASE

Because the burden of proof is on the prosecution, the defence are never obliged to call   **D17.8** evidence, and more particularly the defence are not obliged to call the accused, since he is a competent but not compellable witness (Criminal Evidence Act 1898, s. 1(1)). Most defence witnesses are governed by the same rules and considerations as prosecution witnesses (discussed at **D16.31**). The only additional limitation is the duty of the court to stop evidence being given where it is irrelevant to the issues in the case (*Brown* [1998] 2 Cr App R 364), or where the court is being used as a political sounding board (*King* (1973) 57 Cr App R 696).

Order of Defence Evidence

The accused should normally be called before any other defence witnesses (PACE 1984, s. 79;   **D17.9** Criminal Evidence Act 1898, s. 2 and the CrimPR, r. 38.9(2)(g)). The rationale for this rule is that, whilst witnesses are normally kept out of court until they testify, the accused has the right to be present throughout his trial, and therefore would otherwise have the opportunity to adjust his evidence to accord with that of his witnesses. The court has a discretion to depart from this usual rule (PACE 1984, s. 79), for example to allow a witness whose evidence was not substantially disputed to testify out of the normal order if circumstances made that convenient (*Morrison* (1911) 6 Cr App R 159 and *Smith* [1968] 2 All ER 115, but see *Sutton* [2008] EWCA Crim 3129 as to the timing of psychiatric expert evidence). However, character witnesses must *always* be called after the accused unless there are other witnesses as to the facts (Criminal Evidence Act 1898, s. 2).

Part D Procedure

Police and Criminal Evidence Act 1984, s. 79

If at the trial of any person for an offence—

(a) the defence intends to call two or more witnesses to the facts of the case; and

(b) those witnesses include the accused, the accused shall be called before the other witness or witnesses unless the court in its discretion otherwise directs.

Criminal Evidence Act 1898, s. 2

Where the only witness to the facts of the case called by the defence is the person charged, he shall be called as a witness immediately after the close of the evidence for the prosecution.

A witness waiting to give evidence must not wait inside the courtroom, unless that witness is a party or an expert witness (CrimPR, r. 38.11(2)(a)). But see *Carty* (2011) 175 JP 424, where the Court of Appeal declined to exclude the potentially helpful evidence of a defence witness who had been in court during the prosecution case.

The Accused as a Witness

D17.10   The special evidential rules relating to the accused as a witness, for example, the application in his case of the rule against self-incrimination and the circumstances in which he may be cross-examined as to character, are fully discussed in **part F**. Mentioned below are some further points of a specifically procedural nature concerning evidence from the accused.

D17.11   **Evidence from the Witness Box**   Subject to a contrary direction from the court, an accused who chooses to testify should give his evidence from the witness-box, not the dock (Criminal Evidence Act 1898, s. 1(4), and see **F4.11**). The obvious situation in which the court might exercise its discretion against allowing the accused physically to enter the witness-box is when there is a perceived risk of violence from him that can be controlled more easily if he remains in the dock while testifying (*Symonds* (1924) 18 Cr App R 100). See also **D15.97** in relation to the use of live links for the accused, and CPD V, paras. 29A.1 to 29A.2 (see Supplement, **PD-42**).

D17.12   **The Decision to Call the Accused**   The decision whether to testify or not is for the accused himself.

The Court of Appeal has stated that, when the accused decides not to go into the witness box, it should be the invariable practice of counsel to have that decision recorded and to cause the accused to sign the record giving a clear indication (a) of the fact of his having, of his own accord, decided not to give evidence, and (b) that he has done that bearing in mind the advice, regardless of what it was, given to him by counsel (*Bevan* (1994) 98 Cr App R 354; *Ebanks v The Queen* [2006] 1 WLR 1827; *Anderson* [2010] EWCA Crim 2553). There is no right, even in cases to which the DVCVA 2004, s. 6, applies (**see B1.74**), for an accused to give evidence twice (*Ikram* [2008] 4 All ER 253).

Failure to advise the accused properly about the advisability of testifying may, in appropriate circumstances, constitute grounds for the Court of Appeal to decide that a conviction is unsafe and unsatisfactory (*Clinton* [1993] 2 All ER 998; for further detail, see **D26.23**).

D17.13   **Failure to Give Evidence**   Since s. 35 of the CJPO 1994 became law, it is particularly important that the accused should be advised whether to give evidence, since an inference may be drawn from his failure to do so. Section 35 is addressed at **F19.42**, and the procedure which the court should adopt is laid down in the CrimPR, r. 38.9(2)(e) and CPD VI, paras. 39P.1 to 39P.5 (see Supplement, **PD-62**).

In particular, para. 39P.2 states that, unless defence counsel has indicated that the accused will give evidence, the court is required to ask:

Have you advised your client that the stage has now been reached at which he may give evidence and, if he chooses not to do so or, having been sworn, without good cause refuses to answer any question, the jury may draw such inferences as appear proper from his failure to do so?

The approach of the court where the accused is unrepresented is addressed at **D17.17**.

ALIBI EVIDENCE

Prior to the commencement of the CPIA 1996, part I, alibi evidence and expert opinion evidence were the only types of evidence of which the defence were required to warn the prosecution in advance. That old regime, pursuant to the CJA 1967, s. 11, applies to offences for which the investigation commenced before 1 April 1997.

For later offences, the duty to give specific notice of alibi has been replaced by the wider duties placed on the defence by the CPIA 1996, ss. 5 to 6E (see **D9.29** *et seq.*). The consequences flowing from a defence failure to comply with its duty to notify an alibi now relate not to a potential impediment to the calling of alibi evidence, but to the fact that comment may be made or permitted or inferences drawn in relation to a notice of alibi that is served, or the failure to serve one. (Disclosure of expert evidence is addressed at **D9.69**.)

D17.14

The Meaning of 'Alibi'

The definition of 'alibi' in the CPIA 1996 is provided by s. 6A(3) (see **D9.33**), namely 'evidence tending to show that by reason of the presence of the accused at a particular place or in a particular area at a particular time he was not, or was unlikely to have been, at the place where the offence is alleged to have been committed at the time of its alleged commission'.

D17.15

It follows that it is only evidence putting the accused at a certain place at the time of the commission of the offence that creates an obligation on the defence to give particulars of alibi if he claims that he was elsewhere (*Lewis* [1969] 2 QB 1).

In *Fields* [1991] Crim LR 38, the Court of Appeal found that a letter from F's solicitor, claiming that F was 25 miles away from the scene of the crime at the time he was allegedly first seen by the witness who later identified him as a participant in the offence, did amount to a notice of alibi. This was because the letter contained a claim as to where F had been and that tended to show that F could not have been at the scene of the robbery when it took place.

Similarly, evidence may amount to an alibi even though it comes from the accused only and is to the effect that, at the relevant time, he was by himself at a location other than the scene of the crime (*Jackson* [1973] Crim LR 356).

However, the term 'alibi' presupposes that the offence alleged was committed at a particular place and time. Therefore, failure by the defence to notify the prosecution that the accused was not where they claimed him to be on one day during the period of three weeks over which the offence allegedly occurred did not mean that an alibi notice was necessary (*Hassan* [1970] 1 QB 423).

In *Johnson* [1995] 2 Cr App R 1, it was held that 'evidence in support of an alibi' must be evidence that the defendant was at some place or in a particular area other than the place where the offence was allegedly committed. J's instructions to his legal representatives were that he had not been present at the club where the offence was committed on the night in question. He was unable to say where he had been, since his arrest took place almost three months later. The Court of Appeal held that the trial judge was wrong to rule that an alibi notice was necessary in those circumstances.

The duty of defence disclosure under the CPIA 1996, s. 5, is addressed at **D9.29**.

D

Part D Procedure

Obligation to Consult Accused about Calling Alibi Evidence

D17.16 Defence counsel is under a duty to consult the accused before deciding not to call alibi evidence. In *Irwin* [1987] 2 All ER 1085, the accused's defence was alibi and at his first trial evidence of alibi was called. At the retrial, counsel decided, without consulting the accused, not to call those witnesses. On appeal, it was held that failure to consult the accused about the non-calling of the alibi witnesses was a material irregularity. According to Michael Davies J at p. 906, it is not necessarily vital to consult the client immediately before the alibi witnesses are or, as the case may be, are not called, but it is essential to have discussed the matter thoroughly at some stage. If the client declines to accept counsel's advice that the witnesses should not be called, then counsel should either act on his client's instructions or ask the judge to discharge him from the case (p. 905C–D). If the client accepts counsel's advice, it is preferable to have that confirmed by him in writing (p. 906C).

TREATMENT BY COURT OF UNREPRESENTED ACCUSED

D17.17 If an accused is not legally represented, the court will, as a matter of practice, seek to give him such assistance in conducting his defence as may seem appropriate.

Alternatively, where the accused dismisses his counsel and/or solicitors during the course of the trial (or they withdraw during trial) and the accused remains entitled to public funding, the judge should grant an adjournment for the accused to be represented (*Chambers* [1989] Crim LR 367 and *Sansom* [1991] 2 QB 130).

The Accused's Right to Give or Call Evidence

D17.18 The accused should always be told by the court at the end of the prosecution case of his right to give evidence himself, to call witnesses in his defence (whether or not he himself goes into the witness-box), or to stay silent and call no evidence. Failure to give the accused this information may lead to any conviction being quashed (*Carter* (1960) 44 Cr App R 225).

It is particularly important that an unrepresented accused should be informed of the inferences which may be drawn from a failure to give evidence, pursuant to the CJPOA 1994, s. 35 (see **F19.42**). The court is obliged to address the accused, pursuant to CPD VI, para. 39P.5 (see Supplement, **PD-62**), in the following terms:

> You have heard the evidence against you. Now is the time for you to make your defence. You may give evidence on oath, and be cross-examined like any other witness. If you do not give evidence or, having been sworn, without good cause refuse to answer any question, the jury may draw such inferences as appear proper. That means they may hold it against you. You may also call any witness or witnesses whom you have arranged to attend court. Afterwards you may also, if you wish, address the jury by arguing your case from the dock. But you cannot at that stage give evidence. Do you now intend to give evidence?

Restrictions on the Accused

D17.19 Since the YJCEA 1999, ss. 34 to 39 (see **F7.2**) came into effect, certain restrictions have applied. Unrepresented defendants are prohibited from cross-examining complainants and child witnesses in trials for certain offences. The courts also have the power to prohibit cross-examination of witnesses by unrepresented defendants if satisfied that the circumstances of the witness and the case merit it, and that a prohibition would not be contrary to the interests of justice. There are provisions for the appointment of representatives to conduct cross-examinations on behalf of unrepresented defendants.

For the position as to cross-examination by an unrepresented accused and related matters, see also *Brown* [1998] 2 Cr App R 364, which is dealt with at **F7.2**. The procedure on an application for a prohibition on cross-examination of a particular witness is specified by the CrimPR, r. 31.4 (see Supplement, **R-245**).

Section D18   Trial on Indictment: Procedure between Close of Defence Evidence and Retirement of Jury

INTRODUCTION

D18.1   This section addresses the progress of a trial on indictment following the closing of the defence case. This involves consideration of the potential reopening of either the defence or, more usually, the prosecution case thereafter, discussion between the court and counsel of the law relevant to the case, the closing speeches of counsel, and the judge's summing-up.

REOPENING OF PROSECUTION CASE

D18.2   The general principle is that once prosecuting counsel has stated that his case is closed he may not adduce any further evidence (see Tindal CJ in *Frost* (1839) 4 St Tr NS 85 at col. 386). The exceptions, described below, cannot be listed exhaustively, but as a general rule the court's discretion to admit fresh evidence after the close of the prosecution case must be exercised with great caution (*Munnery* (1991) 94 Cr App R 164). See also the CrimPR, r. 38.9(2)(h).

Matters which Arise *Ex Improviso*

D18.3   Where a matter arises *ex improviso* in the course of the defence case which no human ingenuity could have foreseen, the judge may allow the prosecution to adduce evidence on the point to rebut that which has been led by the defence (see also **F6.3** *et seq.*). This includes instances where matters are raised in defence counsel's closing submissions which had not been foreshadowed in the cross-examination of prosecution witnesses. The justification for this is that the CrimPR, r. 3.3, imposes a duty on the defence to identify the issues at an early stage; if they choose not to do so, the prosecution should be allowed to address them (*Malcolm v DPP* [2007] 3 All ER 578).

Evidence Becoming Available to the Prosecution Only after Close of Case

D18.4   If evidence unexpectedly becomes available to the prosecution between the close of their case and the judge's summing-up, they may exceptionally be given leave to call it even though the issue to which it relates does not arise *ex improviso* (*Doran* (1972) 56 Cr App R 429). For further discussion, see **F6.4**.

Evidence of a Purely Formal Nature Inadvertently Omitted

D18.5   It has been held that an omission to call evidence of a purely formal nature, the lack of which leaves a technical gap in the prosecution case, may be repaired by allowing them to reopen (*McKenna* (1956) 40 Cr App R 65). However, the circumstances in which this is appropriate are narrowly confined and should not be used as a device for rescuing the prosecution when they have failed to prepare or prove their case properly. *McKenna* should be contrasted with *Central Criminal Court, ex parte Garnier* [1988] RTR 42. See further **F6.5**.

Evidence to Rebut Answers in Cross-examination as to Credit

Although a witness's answers to questions going only to his credit are generally final, there are **D18.6** important exceptions to the rule, notably where the question related to a previous conviction, a previous inconsistent statement, possible bias or a reputation for untruthfulness (see **F7.42** *et seq.*). It follows that, where the accused or other defence witness is asked in cross-examination a question going to his credit and the question is such that the witness's answer is *not* final because it comes within one of these exceptions, the prosecution must be allowed to reopen their case to adduce evidence to rebut a denial given in cross-examination.

Time for Reopening Prosecution Case

As to the latest stage at which the prosecution may be permitted to reopen their case, assum- **D18.7** ing one of the exceptional situations applies, the majority of the decided cases contemplate the additional evidence being called either during or, more probably, at the end of the defence case. However, in *Flynn* (1957) 42 Cr App R 15, the judge gave the prosecution leave to call a witness to rebut an alibi raised *ex improviso* by the defence after closing speeches but before the summing-up (see also *Lawson v Stafford Magistrates' Court* [2007] EWHC 2490 (Admin), in which the prosecution were permitted an adjournment to obtain further evidence following the defence closing speech).

Use in Cross-examination of Unproved Material

The rule that the prosecution must adduce all the material on which they intend to rely as part **D18.8** of their case extends to the use they may make of statements or admissions not earlier proved in evidence in cross-examination.

For example in *Kane* (1977) 65 Cr App R 270, prosecuting counsel was criticised for cross-examining K about 'off the record' answers he had given to police officers, and which had not been adduced in evidence earlier. A distinction has been drawn between cases such as *Kane,* where the cross-examination on fresh material goes to the issues in the case, and cases where the cross-examination goes only to the credit of the defence witness (*Halford* (1978) 67 Cr App R 318). However, it will often be difficult, if not impossible, to determine the borderline between cross-examination as to credit and cross-examination on the issues. See also *Pershad* [2014] EWCA Crim 692.

REOPENING OF DEFENCE CASE

The judge may in his discretion allow the defence to reopen their case at any stage before the **D18.9** jury retire to consider their verdict. In *Morrison* (1911) 6 Cr App R 159, defence evidence which had only just then come to light was allowed after counsel's closing speeches. See also *Hussain* [2010] EWCA Crim 1327 as to considerations relevant to the re-opening of the defence case to call a latterly available witness. In *Sanderson* [1953] 1 All ER 485, the defence were allowed to call a witness even after the end of the summing-up. The Court of Appeal said that 'it was not a course one would wish to be taken often but, on the particular facts of this case, we think that there is no objection to what was done here. The learned recorder was fully justified in the course he took'. However, once the jury retires to consider its verdict, evidence must never be received, whether it is favourable to the defence or the prosecution (*Owen* [1952] 2 QB 362).

JUDGE CALLING OR RECALLING A WITNESS

The judge has a discretion to call a witness whom neither the prosecution nor defence have **D18.10** chosen to call (*Wallwork* (1958) 42 Cr App R 153). The power should be sparingly exercised (*Roberts* (1984) 80 Cr App R 89), and used only where it is necessary in the interests of justice.

D

Part D Procedure

Calling a Witness the Prosecution Fail to Call

D18.11   One appropriate situation for the judge taking such a course is where the prosecution have wrongly refused to call a witness whose name is on the back of the indictment (see dicta to that effect in *Oliva* [1965] 3 All ER 116). If the witness is likely to be adverse to the defence and the prosecution have already closed their case, the judge should not use his power so as to circumvent the restrictions on the prosecution reopening their case (*Cleghorn* [1967] 2 QB 584). If the defence want the judge to call such a witness, he has greater latitude in the exercise of his discretionary powers and any conviction is unlikely to be quashed even if the evidence turns out to be in some respects adverse to the defence (*Tregear* [1967] 2 QB 574).

Consequences of Such Action

D18.12   The parties require leave to cross-examine a witness called by the judge, but such leave should be given if the witness's evidence has been adverse to the party wishing to put questions (*Cliburn* (1898) 62 JP 232). Moreover, an adjournment may then be necessary to enable a cross- examining party to call his own evidence in rebuttal (*Coleman* (1987) *The Times*, 21 November 1987).

DISCUSSION OF THE RELEVANT LAW

D18.13   Prior to summing-up, it has become increasingly common for the court to invite counsel, in the absence of the jury, to make representations on how certain aspects of the case should be dealt with; the *Crown Court Bench Book* describes such discussions as routine. This is especially important where there might otherwise be misunderstanding or doubt as to how points of law and evidence which have arisen during the course of the case should be dealt with (*N* [1998] Crim LR 886; *Wright* [2000] Crim LR 510).

Such a discussion should, ideally, take place before speeches. Only in very exceptional circumstances would it be appropriate for the court to discuss the law with counsel after concluding his summing-up and before the jury's retirement (*Cocks* (1976) 63 Cr App R 79). The course adopted by the judge in *Charles* [1976] 1 WLR 248, of asking counsel to intervene in the course of the summing-up and correct any errors as they arose, was criticised by the Court of Appeal as it detracted from the authority of what the judge was saying.

Assisting the Court

D18.14   Counsel is under a duty to bring all relevant authorities to the court's attention even if some are unfavourable to his own argument. Further, he must bring any procedural irregularity to the attention of the court during the hearing and not reserve such matter to be raised on appeal (e.g., where a juror is seen speaking to a witness).

The duties outlined so far apply equally to prosecution and defence counsel (see Written Standards, para. 5.10(c)). In *Smith* [1994] Crim LR 458, one of the grounds of appeal was the fact that contact with a child witness during her evidence was alleged to be irregular. The Court of Appeal said that counsel should have raised the matter at the time with the judge, in the absence of the jury. Failure to do so was reprehensible.

A specific obligation is placed upon prosecuting counsel to assist the court at the conclusion of the judge's summing-up by drawing attention to any apparent errors or omissions of fact or law. No corresponding duty is placed upon defence counsel, but if he ignores a misdirection in the hope of using it as a ground of appeal, he runs a considerable risk. The Court of Appeal may dismiss the appeal on the basis that, if the error had been likely to make a difference to the verdict, counsel should have corrected it at the time (but see *Holden* [1991] Crim LR 478 at **D18.23**).

CLOSING SPEECHES

Subject to one exception, both the prosecution and defence have the right to a closing speech in **D18.15** which they may sum up their respective cases, criticise the opposition's case and comment upon the evidence. Final speeches are not normally recorded. Where it is apparent that exchanges of importance are likely to take place during final speeches, however, counsel should make this clear to the judge so that the presence of the shorthand writer can be ensured (*Osborne-Odelli* [1998] Crim LR 902). The court should intervene to seek clarification or correction of something said in a speech at its conclusion, or at a convenient break, rather than interrupting counsel in the presence of the jury (*Tuegel* [2000] 2 All ER 872).

Order of Speeches

The order of speeches is the result of extensive case law and statutory provisions stretching from **D18.16** the early 19th century to modern times. Those authorities are summarised by Watkins J in the course of his judgment in *Bryant* [1979] QB 108 at pp. 113–18. It is now clear that the prosecution speech is made first.

Restrictions on Prosecution Closing Speeches

In *Mondon* (1968) 52 Cr App R 695, the Court of Appeal held that the prosecution lost the **D18.17** right to make a closing speech where the accused was unrepresented and either called no evidence at all or was himself the only witness (apart from character witnesses). However, in *Stovell* [2006] EWCA Crim 27, the Court of Appeal concluded (per Rose LJ at [36]):

> ... in the light of the procedural and evidential changes which have taken place since the decision of this Court in *Mondon*, we are by no means satisfied that in all cases, particularly when a defendant has been represented substantially throughout the trial and there are issues arising during the defence upon which the jury would be assisted by comment from prosecuting counsel, it is necessarily inappropriate for prosecuting counsel to make a second speech.

Mondon was approved in *Rabani* [2008] EWCA Crim 2030. The position is now made clear in the CrimPR, r. 38.9(2)(i) (see Supplement, **R-308**), which provides that the prosecutor may make final representations where the accused is represented or has called at least one witness (other than himself) to give evidence in person about the facts of the case or where the court so permits.

Even where prosecuting counsel is entitled to make a closing speech, this does not mean that he should as a matter of course exercise the right. In particular, if the accused is legally represented but does not give or call any evidence, the normal practice is for prosecuting counsel *not* to sum up his case. This was confirmed by Watkins J in *Bryant* [1979] QB 108 at p. 117D, who said that the prosecution's right to make a speech in such circumstances:

> ... should only rarely be necessary to use save possibly in long and complex cases and whenever used should bear, as should the majority of speeches by prosecuting and defence counsel, the becoming hallmark of brevity.

In *Hoggard* [1995] Crim LR 747, it was emphasised that the prosecution had the statutory right, by virtue of the Criminal Procedure Act 1865, s. 2, to make a closing speech where the defendant was represented. The length of the speech should, however, be commensurate with the number and complexity of the issues. In a case where the defence relied on self-serving statements made in interviews, or allegations put in cross-examination to witnesses, it would generally be in order for the prosecution to make a closing speech in order to deal with them.

In *Tahir* [1997] Crim LR 837, the Court of Appeal held that prosecuting counsel should not be deprived of the right to make a closing speech in relation to a represented defendant where the co-defendant was unrepresented. In such circumstances, however, the speech must focus on the evidence relating to the represented defendant.

Limitations as to Content

D18.18   Neither counsel in a closing speech should allude to alleged facts or other matters which have not been the subject of evidence (see a resolution of the judges dated 26 November 1881, adopted in *Shimmin* (1882) 15 Cox CC 122). Neither should the jury be invited to add a recommendation of mercy to their verdict should it be one of guilty (*Black* [1963] 3 All ER 682).

D18.19   **Prosecution Counsel**   In *Gonez* [1999] All ER (D) 674, the Court of Appeal emphasised that prosecutors must remember their role as a minister of justice in relation to the terms in which they make their speeches (see **D16.3**). In *Ramdhanie* [2005] UKPC 47, the Privy Council upheld an appeal based upon an improper closing speech by the prosecutor, which contained emotive and unjustified comments on the defence case, insinuations of additional unadduced incriminating material and a number of passages where the prosecutor improperly vouched for the soundness of the prosecution's case.

Prosecuting counsel should not comment to the jury on the potentially serious consequences to police officers of their evidence being disbelieved, even where a police officer has raised the matter in evidence (*Gale* [1994] Crim LR 208).

Equally, prosecution counsel is not entitled to abandon or attack the credit of his own witness (unless he has been given leave to treat him as hostile) and he should not invite inferences contrary to the evidence he has called (*Pacey* (1994) *The Times*, 13 March 1994; *Cairns* [2003] 1 WLR 796).

Pursuant to the PACE 1984, s. 80A, the prosecution should not comment on the failure of the accused's spouse to give evidence. However, prosecution counsel is entitled to comment on the failure of the accused to answer questions in interview (see **F19.41**). Similarly, pursuant to the CPIA 1996, s. 11(5), the prosecution may make 'such comment as appears appropriate', providing that the court grants leave, about the failure of the accused to serve a defence statement, or as to divergence between that statement and his evidence (see **D9**).

D18.20   **Defence Counsel**   In delivering his closing speech defence counsel is not confined to putting forward his client's version of events. He may advance hypotheses which go beyond his client's version of events, always provided that other evidence has been called which supports such hypotheses (*Bateson* (1991) *The Times*, 10 April 1991).

Defence counsel should not refer to the likely consequences of a conviction in terms of punishment since sentencing is no concern of the jury (*A-G for South Australia v Brown* [1960] AC 432). See also *Edgington* [2014] 1 Cr App R 334 (24) (at [20]–[30]).

For the position as to comment by counsel on the defendant's failure to give evidence, see **F19.41**. Defence counsel is obviously entitled to comment upon his own client's not testifying. He is also, in a case where a co-accused runs a defence which conflicts with that of the accused he represents, entitled to comment upon the co-accused's not having entered the witness-box (*Wickham* (1971) 55 Cr App R 199). The judge has no power to prevent or restrict such comment, but may comment upon it himself if he considers it to have been unfair (*Wickham*).

SUMMING-UP

Preliminary and General Matters

D18.21   The trial judge's summing-up conventionally falls into two parts, namely, a direction on the law (see **D18.25**) and a summary of the evidence (see **D18.36**). The CrimPR, r. 38.14(2) sets out the appropriate steps to be followed on summing-up.

The Court of Appeal has discouraged courts from commencing a summing-up, or addressing an important aspect of one, at a late hour or just before the weekend (*Rimmer* [1983] Crim LR 250).

Both counsel should take as full a note of the summing-up as is possible. This is especially important where any sentence is likely to be short. A good note may avoid delay caused by waiting for
a transcript and thus expedite an appeal (*Campbell* [1976] Crim LR 508).

Correcting Errors   Where the judge discovers an error in his summing-up, whether as a result   **D18.22**
of representations by counsel (see **D18.23**) or otherwise, he should expressly acknowledge and
refer to the error, tell the jury to disregard it, and then go on to give the correct direction (*Cole*
[1993] Crim LR 300). In *Kilbane* [2003] EWCA Crim 607, the judge was alerted in the absence
of the jury to a misdirection as to the burden of proof in cases covered by the MDA 1971, s. 28.
When the jury returned, the judge gave a correct direction, but described it as an attempt to
'clarify' and 'repeat' what she had previously said. The Court of Appeal quashed the conviction,
quoting Salmon LJ in *Moon* [1969] 3 All ER 803:

> Such a misdirection could be corrected only in the plainest terms. The court must repeat the
> direction given, acknowledge that it was wrong, tell the jury to put out of their minds all they had
> heard from the court about the burden of proof… and then direct them on the law in clear terms
> incapable of being misunderstood.

Duties of Counsel in Relation to the Summing-up   Prosecuting counsel is under a duty to   **D18.23**
attend carefully to the summing-up and draw any possible errors (whether of fact or law) to the
judge's attention at its close (see *Donoghue* (1987) 86 Cr App R 267 and the Code of Conduct of
the Bar, Written Standards, para. 11.7). Moreover, the court is entitled to rely on such assistance
(*McVey* [1988] Crim LR 127).

Beyond the duties described at **D18.14**, defence counsel has traditionally been able to remain
silent, if he considered that to be in the best interests of his client (*Curtin* [1996] Crim LR
831, relying upon *Cocks* (1976) 63 Cr App R 79 and see also *Edwards* (1983) 77 Cr App R 5).
However, this position has been eroded more recently. For example:

(a)   It is the duty of both prosecution and defence counsel to alert the judge to evidence on which
      the jury could find provocation, before he sums up, and, if he agrees, remind him that he is
      required by statute to leave the remaining issues to the jury (*Cox* [1995] 2 Cr App R 513).
(b)   Defence counsel is under a duty to request a good character direction, if the accused was entitled
      to one, rather than making complaint later if one is not given (*Gilbert v R* [2006] 1 WLR 2108).

However, in *Holden* [1991] Crim LR 478, the Court of Appeal made it clear that the dismissal
of an appeal would not be automatic where defence counsel had failed to correct an error.

Written Directions

In an appropriate case, the judge may provide the jury with a written list of questions or directions to   **D18.24**
assist them in their task, setting out the legal issues which must be proved in order to reach their verdict, often described as the 'steps to verdict' (CrimPR, r. 38.14(3)). Before he does so, he should submit them to counsel, so that they can make suggestions and can base their closing speeches upon the
issues raised in the proposed directions. The jury should then be given the written list at the start of
the summing-up, so that the judge can take them through the directions one by one, as he deals with
each point. See *McKechnie* (1992) 94 Cr App R 51 and *Taxquet v Belgium* (2012) 54 EHRR 933.

The judge is, however, fully entitled to decline to provide the jury with written directions, even
where they have been requested (*Lawson* [1998] Crim LR 883); see the *Crown Court Bench Book*
and the *Crown Court Bench Book Companion* for more detail. Whilst failure by counsel to comment
on such draft directions is not necessarily fatal to an appeal based on any misdirection, such failure is
likely to affect the weight accorded to the deficiency (*Gammans* (13 November 1998 unreported)).

Standard Directions

As Lord Hailsham observed in *Lawrence* [1982] AC 510 (at p. 519), a summing-up should be   **D18.25**
'custom-built to make the jury understand their task in relation to a particular case'. Which legal

Part D Procedure

directions are necessary will therefore vary and what is set out here is a survey of the standard directions which may be required.

From the 1970s onwards, the Judicial Studies Board issued specimen directions in relation to the applicable law. The Court of Appeal encouraged the use of these standard forms of words by which directions on frequently recurring matters of law may or ought to be given. The specimen directions were suggested as guidelines only and judges were required to adapt them to the circumstances of particular cases. Their use was intended to 'help to reduce the flow of appeals against conviction' (*Jackson* [1992] Crim LR 214). In March 2010, the *Crown Court Bench Book* was first published. In its foreword Lord Judge CJ said that its 'objective has been to move away from the perceived rigidity of specimen directions towards a fresh emphasis on the responsibility of the individual judge, in an individual case, to craft directions appropriate to that case'. The *Bench Book* therefore provides bullet-pointed guidance, rather than scripted text for legal directions. It follows that the case law as to the appropriate form of directions on legal topics becomes more important. The previous directions are not withdrawn, but will not be updated. See also the guidance in the *Crown Court Bench Book Companion*.

In *Hayes* [2010] EWCA Crim 773, Hughes LJ, responding to a submission that the trial judge's direction did not conform to a Judicial Studies Board model direction, stated (at [12]):

> That...it needs to be said as clearly as possible, is not and never can be by itself a ground of appeal. The Judicial Studies Board does not issue directions or orders to judges. It is a forum within which they can compare their practices. The so-called model directions which are in any event about to be supplemented by additional sample directions are no more than that. They are examples which may be helpful to judges in framing a direction which is tailored to the individual case. It is fundamentally to misunderstand the nature of the Judicial Studies Board and the materials provided by it to treat any of its materials as carrying any force of law at all.... it is important that it should be understood what the significance is and more importantly what the significance is not of model directions issued by the Board.

D18.26   **Direction as to the Functions of Judge and Jury**   At the beginning of the summing-up, the judge ought to remind the jury of their respective roles and hence the different status of the two parts of the summing-up, that part relating to law, in relation to which he is the final arbiter, and that relating to fact (summarising the evidence before them). As regards the facts, the jury are the judges (*Wootton* [1990] Crim LR 201). Therefore, if, in the course of his summing-up, the judge expresses a certain view as to the facts or as to the significance of a piece of evidence but the jury disagree; or he has omitted to mention certain evidence which they consider important; or, conversely, he has stressed something which they consider unimportant — in all such eventualities, it is the *jury's* view which matters.

D18.27   **Burden and Standard of Proof**   Every summing-up must contain at least a direction to the jury as to the burden and standard of proof, and as to the ingredients of the offence or offences which the jury are called upon to consider (*McVey* [1988] Crim LR 127). Thus, if the judge fails properly to direct the jury as to the prosecution (a) having the burden of proof and (b) having to discharge that burden beyond reasonable doubt or so that the jury are sure, a conviction is liable to be quashed (see *Donoghue* (1987) 86 Cr App R 267 on the burden of proof and *Edwards* (1983) 77 Cr App R 5 on the standard of proof) (see also **F3.48**).

In *Bowditch* [1991] Crim LR 831, the Court of Appeal stressed that in cases involving injuries to a small child it was essential that a very clear direction should be given as to the burden of proof. This was to counteract any tendency on the part of the jury, albeit subconsciously, to succumb to their emotions. Where the statute under which an accused was being prosecuted imposed an evidential burden upon him, good sense dictated that in appropriate circumstances the court should seek agreement that this burden had been discharged so that only the prosecution's burden needed to be left to the jury (*Malinina* [2007] EWCA Crim 3228).

D18.28   **Separate Consideration of Counts and Defendants**   Where there is more than one count on the indictment, the jury should be directed to give separate consideration to each of them

(*Lovesey* [1970] 1 QB 352). For the same reason, the judge should also summarise the evidence on a count by count rather than a witness by witness basis (*Robson* [2007] EWCA Crim 3362).

Similarly, where there is more than one accused on trial, the jury should be directed to consider the case for and against each separately (*Smith* (1935) 25 Cr App R 119). Where the allegation against the accused is one of joint enterprise, a direction in accordance with the terms of *Powell and English* [1999] 1 AC 1 will be necessary (see **A4.10** *et seq.*).

Ingredients of Offence   Appellate decisions reveal a tension between the need for the trial   **D18.29** judge to direct the jury as to the ingredients of the offence charged on the one hand, and tailoring such directions to the actual issues in the particular case on the other.

The first of these approaches is exemplified in *McVey* [1988] Crim LR 127, in which the Court of Appeal made clear that it was insufficient for the judge simply to spell out the issue in the case. He was required to direct the jury as to the elements of the offence charged. The same approach was adopted in *James* [1997] Crim LR 598.

The second approach was advocated by Diplock LJ in *Mowatt* [1968] 1 QB 421, when he stated that the function of a summing-up was not to give a jury a general dissertation on some aspect of the criminal law, but to isolate the issues for the jury's consideration. Similarly, in *Lawrence* [1982] AC 510, Lord Hailsham of St Marylebone LC remarked (at pp. 519F–520A):

> The purpose of a direction to a jury is not best achieved by a disquisition on jurisprudence or philosophy or a universally applicable circular tour round the area of law affected by the case. The search for universally applicable definitions is often productive of more obscurity than light.... A direction to a jury should be custom built to make the jury understand their task in relation to a particular case. Of course it must include references to the burden of proof and the respective roles of jury and judge. But it should also include a succinct but accurate summary of the issues of fact as to which a decision is required, a correct but concise summary of the evidence and arguments on both sides, and a correct statement of the inferences which the jury are entitled to draw from their particular conclusions about the primary facts.

Failure to Answer Questions or Give Evidence   Pursuant to the CJPO 1994, ss. 34 and 35, the   **D18.30** jury are entitled to draw such inferences as they deem appropriate from the failure of the defendant to answer questions in interview (s. 34) or his failure to give evidence (s. 35). Guidance as to the proper form of direction that should be given was provided in *Cowan* [1996] QB 373 and by the Judicial Studies Board standard direction. Although the judge is not expected to identify every fact in relation to which an inference may be drawn, he is required to identify significant facts relied on and to remind the jury of any reason for silence advanced by the accused (*Lowe* [2007] EWCA Crim 833).

A number of limitations to the requirement for a s. 34 direction have been recognised:

(a) No inferences should be drawn from the silence in interview of an accused who does not give or call evidence, and has not advanced a positive case (*Moshaid* [1998] Crim LR 420).

(b) Where an accused's account had changed between interview and trial, this was a matter on which comment could be made without the need for a formal direction under s. 34 (*Maguire* (2008) 172 JP 417).

Where such inferences should not be drawn, the jury should be specifically directed to that effect (*McGarry* [1998] 3 All ER 805).

This topic is discussed in more detail at **F19.9**, **F19.24** and **F19.31**.

Failure to Call a Witness   In *Wright* [2000] Crim LR 510, the Court of Appeal emphasised the   **D18.31** dangers of comment on the failure of the defence to call certain witnesses in the summing-up, since such comments could so easily detract from the realisation that the burden of proof must be upon the prosecution. Such comment has been held to be justified, however, where the prosecution could have had no means of knowing that the witness could have any relevant evidence to give before the defence case (*Gallagher* [1974] 3 All ER 118) or the witness was one only the defence could have called, such as the accused's solicitor (*Wilmot* (1988) 89 Cr App R 341). See also *Khan* [2001] Crim LR 673 and the application of that decision in *Campbell* [2009] EWCA Crim 1076 and *Seaton* [2011] 1 All ER 932.

D18.32 **Other Standard Directions**   Other commonly given directions include ones concerning:

(a) the proper approach to circumstantial evidence (see **F1.18** and *Stephens and Clarke* (95/1758/S2 unreported);

(b) evidence of lies by the defendant (see **F1.21** for the direction set out in *Lucas* [1981] QB 720, and see also *Burge* [1996] 1 Cr App R 163);

(c) identification evidence (see **F18.9** for the direction set out in *Turnbull* [1977] QB 224), but note that such a direction is not required where the identifying witness retracts his identification (*Davis* [2006] EWCA Crim 2015) — see also *Ley* [2007] 1 Cr App R 325, in which the Court of Appeal held that a judge was not required to direct a jury to acquit if they rejected evidence which was potentially supportive of a weak identification;

(d) trial in the absence of the accused (see **D15.85**);

(e) the limited admissibility of interviews of co-defendants (see **F17.80** and the decisions in *Rhodes* (1959) 44 Cr App R 23 and *Hayter* [2005] 2 All ER 209) — see also *Knowlden* (1981) 77 Cr App R 94, in relation to the warning that should be given to the jury where one accused gives evidence adverse to another;

(f) pleas of co-accused (*Dixon* (2001) 164 JP 721: see **D12.77**);

(g) the need for corroboration and care warnings (see **F5.2** for the former and **F5.5**, the CJPO 1994, s. 32, and *Makanjuola* [1995] 3 All ER 730, for the latter);

(h) the need for a warning in relation to a witness who may be tainted by improper motives (see *Beck* [1982] 1 All ER 807 and **F5.14**);

(i) expert evidence (following *Stockwell* (1993) 97 Cr App R 260, the jury should be directed that they are not bound to accept expert opinion, see also **F10.41**); and

(j) the approach to evidence of good or bad character (see *Vye* (1993) 97 Cr App R 134, *Aziz* [1996] 1 AC 41 and in particular *Campbell* [2007] 1 WLR 2798, in which the Court of Appeal emphasised that the judge should explain the relevance of bad character evidence to the jury on the facts of the case, rather than by following any set direction) (see also **F12.36**).

See **D18.25** for the new approach to directions heralded by the *Crown Court Bench Book*.

Defences

D18.33 There is an obligation on the trial judge to give the legal directions which apply to the defence advanced on behalf of the accused. Common defences and partial defences to which this applies include:

(a) self-defence (see *Palmer* [1971] AC 814, *Lobell* [1957] 1 QB 547, *Harvey* [2009] EWCA Crim 469 and **A3.54**);

(b) alibi (see *Anderson* [1991] Crim LR 361 and **F3.45**) — where an alibi is demonstrated or accepted to be false, a *Lucas*-type direction is appropriate, see *Lesley* [1996] 1 Cr App R 39;

(c) provocation (*Stewart* [1995] 4 All ER 999) and loss of control; and

(d) diminished responsibility (see *Terry* [1961] 2 QB 314 and **B1.18**).

Where an accused is unrepresented, the judge should also remind the jury to bear in mind the difficulties for the accused of representing himself at trial (*De Oliveira* [1997] Crim LR 600, and see *Johnson* [2013] EWCA Crim 2001.

D18.34 **Alternative Defences**   The jury should not generally be directed on matters which are not issues in the case. Nonetheless, there are occasions when the jury should be directed as to a defence which has not been raised by the evidence or by counsel. The following cases provide examples:

(a) In *Watson* [1992] Crim LR 434, W was charged with buggery, which he denied. The Court of Appeal found that, although the defence of accident had not been raised, there was a duty

on the judge to spell out that penetration must have been deliberate (but see *Johnson* [1994] Crim LR 376, where the Court of Appeal concluded to the contrary).
(b) In *Phillips* [1999] All ER (D) 1372, P was charged with unlawful wounding contrary to the OAPA 1861, s. 20. The prosecution case was that P had deliberately attacked the victim with a knife and inflicted wounds upon her by way of retribution. P's case was that the wounding had been accidental. The trial judge summed up on the basis that the defence was accident, mentioning self-defence only to dismiss it. The Court of Appeal held that the judge ought to have left the defence of self-defence to the jury.

The Invisible Burden   This burden arises where a potential defence has not been raised on the   **D18.35**
accused's behalf, but there is a cogent, rather than speculative, evidential basis for its consideration (*Bonnick* (1978) 66 Cr App R 266). In such circumstances there is a burden upon the judge to raise such an alternative defence in his summing-up. Circumstances in which this may arise include cases where self-defence is lurking in the background (see *Kachikwu* (1965) 52 Cr App R 538 and S Doran, 'Alternative Defences: the "invisible burden" on the trial judge' [1991] Crim LR 878).

The Facts

In addition to directing the jury on the law, the judge should remind them of and comment   **D18.36**
upon the evidence. Despite suggestions to the contrary in *Attfield* [1961] 3 All ER 243, it is clear that a summary of the evidence is necessary in almost all cases. For example:

(a) In *Brower* [1995] Crim LR 746, it was made clear that in the majority of cases, it was necessary for the judge to sum up on the facts in order to assist the jury and ensure a fair trial. It was incumbent on the judge to define the issues and remind the jury of the evidence they had heard, albeit very recently.
(b) In *Amado-Taylor* [2000] 2 Cr App R 194, it was held to be a procedural irregularity for a judge to sum up without a review of the facts. There were exceptions where this was not required, such as where a case was short and simple. But the closing speeches of counsel were no substitute for a judicial and impartial view of the facts from the trial judge, whose duty it was to focus the attention of the jury upon the issues which he identified.

The Analysis Involved   In simple cases, it will suffice for the judge to sum up the facts by read   **D18.37**
ing out an abbreviated version of his note of the evidence. However, if the trial has been more complex, judges are exhorted to assist the jury by analysing the evidence and relating it to the various issues raised (*Gregory* [1993] Crim LR 623). Merely reading a note of the evidence in such cases has been criticised, not least because it 'must bore the jury to sleep' (see pp. 339–41 of Lawton LJ's judgment in *Charles* (1976) 68 Cr App R 334).

Similarly, in the passage from Lord Hailsham's speech in *Lawrence* [1982] AC 510 quoted at **D18.29**, reference is made to the desirability of the summing-up including a '*succinct* but accurate summary of the issues of fact as to which a decision is required, a correct but *concise* summary of the evidence and arguments on both sides, and a correct statement of the inferences which the jury are entitled to draw from their particular conclusions about the primary facts' (emphasis added). Such a succinct and focused summary of the evidence is of particular importance at the end of a long and complex trial, as it is required to provide the jury with a rational consideration of the evidence (*D, Potter and Heppenstall* [2007] EWCA Crim 2485).

Summarising the Defence Case   Crucially, in *Curtin* [1996] Crim LR 831, the Court of   **D18.38**
Appeal stated that as part of his duty the judge must identify the defence. The way in which he does so will depend on the circumstances of the case, however the following propositions apply:

(a) Where the accused has given evidence, it will be desirable to summarise that evidence.
(b) Where he has given evidence and answered questions in interview, it may be appropriate to draw attention to consistencies and inconsistencies between the two.
(c) When an accused is interviewed at length but does not give evidence, the judge has to decide how, fairly and conveniently, to place the interview before the jury.

D

Part D Procedure

(d) When the accused has done neither, it will usually be appropriate to remind the jury of counsel's speech.

Moreover, it is desirable for the judge to give an overview of the defence case, in addition to weaving the defence case into the chronology of the prosecution evidence (*Pomfrett* [2010] 2 All ER 481). As to the extent of the trial judge's duty to summarise the defence case where no evidence has been called for the defence, see *Singh-Mann* [2014] EWCA Crim 717.

On the question of whether defence counsel has a duty to draw the judge's attention to a failure to deal adequately with the defence, see **D18.23**.

D18.39 **Judicious Judicial Comment**   It is the judge's duty to state matters 'clearly, impartially and logically', and not to indulge in inappropriate sarcasm or extravagant comment (*Berrada* (1989) 91 Cr App R 131). Similarly, in *Marr* (1989) 90 Cr App R 154, the Court of Appeal stressed that observance of the accused's right to have his case presented fairly is never more important than when 'the cards seem to be stacked most heavily against the defendant' (p. 156). Lord Lane CJ added: 'however distasteful the offence, however repulsive the defendant, however laughable his defence, he is nevertheless entitled to have his case fairly presented to the jury both by counsel and by the judge' (p. 156).

However, provided he emphasises that the jury are entitled to ignore his opinions, the judge may comment on the evidence in a way which indicates his own views. Robust comments to the detriment of the defence case are permitted (e.g., *O'Donnell* (1917) 12 Cr App R 219, in which the judge described the accused's story as a 'remarkable one'), providing the judge is not so critical as effectively to withdraw the issue of guilt or innocence from the jury (*Canny* (1945) 30 Cr App R 143, in which the judge repeatedly told the jury that the defence case was absurd).

D18.40 **Advancing an Alternative Basis for Conviction**   The question sometimes arises whether the judge is confined, when summarising the case against the accused, to the same basis as that on which the prosecution has put its case. In *Japes* [1994] Crim LR 605, the Court of Appeal said that a judge was not bound by the way in which the Crown opened its case. As the evidence developed, it might become apparent that the offence may have been committed on a somewhat different factual basis. If so, the judge was not debarred from putting that basis before the jury to consider, so long as the accused was not disadvantaged or prejudiced by this course of action (see however *Falconer-Atlee* (1973) 58 Cr App R 348, where the judge was criticised for leaving the case to the jury on a new basis). In *Singh* [2011] EWCA Crim 2992 the Court of Appeal concluded that a trial judge had been entitled to advance a potential co-conspirator who was not particularised in the indictment, or advanced by the prosecution, where the jury would otherwise have been left with 'an incomplete range of options'.

Where the judge intends to direct the jury on a new legal basis, it is important that he should give the parties an opportunity to consider and if necessary to argue the point (*Ramzan* [1998] 2 Cr App R 328; see also *Taylor* [1998] Crim LR 582). In appropriate cases, the judge should give the defence the opportunity to call further evidence (*Powell* [2006] EWCA Crim 685).

As to leaving lesser alternative counts to the jury, see **D19.41**.

Summing-up Amounting to Direction

D18.41 Application of the principle that the judge should not dictate the jury's verdict through excessively robust comment during his summing-up (see **D18.39**) becomes difficult where the defence case amounts to an admission of guilt. Even in such circumstances, however, the judge must not take the issue of guilt away from the jury.

In *DPP v Stonehouse* [1978] AC 55, one of the issues was whether the admitted facts proved established an attempt to obtain property by deception or merely established acts which were preparatory to such an attempt. Having ruled as a matter of law that the facts proved did constitute an attempt, the judge so directed the jury. The majority of the House of Lords held that, even where any reasonable jury properly directed on the law must upon the facts reach a verdict of guilty, the trial judge should nevertheless leave the issues of fact to them.

The same approach was adopted in *Thompson* [1984] 3 All ER 565. The judge directed the jury that there 'could not be room for any doubt at all' about the elements of the offence being made out, and that he (the judge) had already ruled that the offence was within the jurisdiction of the court. The Court of Appeal held that the judge's direction amounted to an irregularity in the course of the trial.

In *Wang* [2005] 1 All ER 782, the House of Lords considered a number of authorities on the certified question of law: 'In what circumstances, if any, is a judge entitled to direct a jury to return a verdict of guilty?' Their lordships concluded unanimously that there were no such circumstances. This was the case even where a burden of proof lay on the defence. No matter how inescapable a judge might consider a conclusion to be, in the sense that any other conclusion would be perverse, it remained his duty to leave the decision to the jury, and not to dictate what the verdict should be.

The decision in *Wang* was applied in *Caley-Knowles* [2006] 1 WLR 3181 to two cases in which judges had directed the jury to convict. In each case the judge, in doing so, had made clear that he was taking the matter out of the hands of the jury. The Court of Appeal emphasised that it would be a significant misdirection and material irregularity for the decision to be taken away from the jury in that way. However, providing it is clear at all times that the verdict is the sole province of the jury, comment from the judge short of a direction to convict was permissible.

Appointment of a Foreman

At the end of the summing-up, the judge should advise the jury to appoint one of their number to be their foreman. The foreman will act as their spokesman and, in due course, announce their verdict. **D18.42**

Unanimity

Finally, the judge should invite the jury to retire and to seek to reach a unanimous decision. **D18.43**
However, a failure on the part of the judge to give the jury the direction that their verdicts must be unanimous will not necessarily render a conviction unsafe (*Georgiou* (1969) 53 Cr App R 428, see also *Daly* [1999] Crim LR 88).

To anticipate jury questions about the possibility of a majority verdict, the judge should direct the jury, at this stage, to try to reach a unanimous verdict. If the time should come when he can accept a verdict which is not the verdict of them all, he will give them a further direction (CPD VI, para. 39Q.1 (see Supplement, **PD-63**)). The judge should not, however, indicate the precise period which must elapse before a majority verdict becomes a possibility (*Thomas* [1983] Crim LR 745). If he does so, it will not necessarily be improper, e.g., where the effect is to alleviate anxiety or uncertainty which the jury may be feeling (*Guthrie* (1994) *The Times*, 23 February 1994 and *Porter* [1996] Crim LR 126). For the appropriate directions to be given in relation to majority verdicts and verdicts of guilt as to an alternative offence, see **D19.34** and **D19.41**.

Unanimity as to the Basis of a Guilty Verdict   Where the prosecution have put their case on **D18.44**
more than one basis, it may be necessary to tell the jury that, in order to convict, they must be unanimous not only as to the accused being guilty but also as to the basis on which he is guilty. For example, in *Brown* (1983) 79 Cr App R 115, the prosecution alleged the obtaining of property by the use of two different deceptions by B. The Court of Appeal held that the jury should have been directed that, if they were not unanimous that B used both deceptions, they should at least all agree as to which one he used.

In *Mitchell* [1994] Crim LR 66, the Court of Appeal stated that the following principles were to be derived from the cases:

(a) Where several matters were set out in a single count, the judge must consider whether to give the jury a direction that they must all be agreed on the particular ingredient which they rely on to find the accused guilty (*Brown*).

(b) Such a direction will be necessary only comparatively rarely. In the great majority of cases (particularly where dishonesty is alleged and where the allegations stand or fall together), it will be unnecessary and may serve only to confuse the jury (*Price* [1991] Crim LR 465 and *More* (1988) 86 Cr App R 234).

(c) In an appropriate case, where there was a realistic danger that the jury might return a verdict of guilty on the basis that some of them found one ingredient proved and others found another ingredient proved, a direction should be given that they must be unanimous as to the proof of the ingredient which demonstrated that offence.

D18.45   **Limitations to this Principle**   The Court of Appeal has sought to limit the need for a direction that the jury should be unanimous as to the ingredients that should be proved in a number of cases, examples of which are mentioned below:

(a) In *Jones* (1999) *The Times*, 17 February 1999, the Court of Appeal held that the considerations in *Brown* did not have any application to the circumstances where a verdict of manslaughter was returned as an alternative to murder. Provided a jury were agreed that an accused was guilty of manslaughter, in the sense that they were sure that he perpetrated an unlawful act which caused the death of the deceased, there was no need for unanimity as to the basis of that verdict (see **B1.35**).

(b) In *Giannetto* [1997] 1 Cr App R 1, the Court of Appeal stated that there were two cardinal principles involved in the proposition that a jury must find each essential element in an offence proved. First, the jury must be agreed upon the basis on which they found an accused guilty. Second, an accused must know what case he had to meet. Where the Crown alleged that on the evidence the accused must have committed the offence either as principal or as secondary offender, and made it equally clear that they could not say which, the basis on which the jury had to be unanimous was that the accused, having the necessary *mens rea*, by whatever means caused the result which was criminalised by the law (see *Smith* [1997] 1 Cr App R 14, about the application of these principles to an offence of affray; see also *Tirnaveanu* [2007] 4 All ER 301).

(c) In *D* [2001] 1 Cr App R 194, D was charged with indecent assaults on his daughter allegedly committed over a three-year period, in some instances in a variety of ways. The Court of Appeal held that where a number of different matters were set out in a single count, the judge should consider whether the jury should be given a direction that they should all be agreed upon the particular ingredient upon which they relied in order to find the accused guilty of the offence charged. Circumstances requiring such a direction would be rare but, where there was a realistic danger that the jury might not appreciate that they must all be agreed on the particular ingredient on which they relied to find their guilty verdict, a direction must be given that they should be unanimous as to the proof of that ingredient (see also *Carr* [2000] 2 Cr App R 149, *Boreman* [2000] Crim LR 409 and *Turner* [2000] Crim LR 325).

Section D19　Trial on Indictment: Procedure Relating to Retirement of the Jury and Verdict

INTRODUCTION

This chapter addresses the practices and procedures that are engaged with the retirement of the   **D19.1**
jury to consider its verdict. It also considers the different forms of verdict that can be reached,
the directions appropriate to them, and the consequences where the jury conclude that no
verdict can be reached.

RETIREMENT OF THE JURY

Basic Rules

The principle that governs the keeping of the jury during the period between the close of   **D19.2**
the judge's summing-up and their returning to court to announce their verdict was succinctly stated by James LJ in *Alexander* [1974] 1 All ER 539 at p. 426H: '. . . once the jury
retires to consider their verdict it should not separate, one from another and from the jury
bailiffs. They must remain in the charge of the court through the bailiffs throughout.' The
purpose of this is to ensure that nobody interferes with the jury while they are considering
their verdict.

The Need to Retire

In *Rankine* [1997] Crim LR 757, the Court of Appeal considered whether the judge was per-   **D19.3**
mitted to ask a jury if they wished to consider their verdict without retiring. Their lordships
held that there was nothing in the decided cases to render such an invitation wrong as a matter
of course, but stressed the danger that the jury might feel under pressure, and said that such a
course would be appropriate only in rare circumstances.

Timing of Retirement

If the summing-up concludes late in the day, the jury should not begin to consider their verdict   **D19.4**
until the following day. For example, in *Birch* (1992) *The Times*, 27 March 1992, the Court
of Appeal said that, in a serious case, especially one involving more than one defendant and a
number of verdicts, it was undesirable that a jury should be sent out after 3 p.m. unless there
were exceptional circumstances. However, see *Buttle* [2006] EWCA Crim 246, where it was
held proper for a jury to retire to consider its verdict on a Friday afternoon where there was a
reasonable prospect of their reaching a verdict that day.

The decision as to whether the jury should retire late in the afternoon, or wait until the next
morning, is one which the judge should take, and he should not leave it up to the jury to decide
(*Hawkins* (1994) 98 Cr App R 228). See also *Akano* (1992) *The Times*, 3 April 1992, where
retirements continuing until late in the evening were disapproved.

Custody of the Jury Bailiff

D19.5   Immediately before the jury retire, one or more court ushers takes an oath to escort the jurors to some 'private and convenient place' where [he] will not 'suffer anybody to speak to them about the trial this day, nor will [he] speak to them [himself] without leave of the court, except if it be to ask them if they are agreed upon their verdict'. An usher who has so sworn is thereafter referred to as a 'jury bailiff'.

At all times during their retirement the jury must be in the custody of a jury bailiff in the sense that the bailiff must be near enough to the room where they are to ensure that no non-juror enters the room or otherwise communicates with them.

D19.6   **Communication with the Jury**   Once the bailiff has escorted the jury to their room, he must not enter it 'unless he is expressly ordered by the court to make a communication to, or inquiry of, the jury, and except in special circumstances and at the express order of the court no other persons should have any communication with the jury' (see para. 4(29)(i) of the Court Manual issued by the Lord Chancellor's office on the creation of the Crown Court).

This wording was adopted by James LJ in his judgment in *Lamb* (1974) 59 Cr App R 196, finding it to have been a material irregularity for the clerk of court to have entered the jury room to tell the jury that they should continue to seek unanimity, they having sent a message via the bailiff asking if they could return a majority verdict. It was further stated that: 'If it be the practice in any Crown Court for directions of this kind between judge and jury to be communicated through the medium of court officers, that practice should cease'.

Similarly, in *Davis (No. 2)* (1960) 44 Cr App R 235, the introduction of a shorthand writer into the jury room and, in *Rose* [1982] 2 All ER 536, the clerk entering the jury room to deliver a message from the judge indicating how much longer the latter was prepared to give them to reach a verdict, were both material irregularities. The correct procedure for answering jury questions has been laid down by the Court of Appeal in, *inter alia*, *Gorman* [1987] 2 All ER 435, and is considered at **D19.18**. In *Szypusz v UK* [2010] ECHR 1323 it was held by the ECtHR that it was not a breach of proper procedure for a police officer to be present with a jury in retirement to control the operation of video equipment.

The jury bailiffs are themselves strictly limited in the communication which they can make with the jury. In *Brown* (1989) *The Times*, 25 October 1989, it was stressed that their fundamental duty was to prevent approaches by outsiders and preserve the integrity of the deliberative process. It followed that there was no impropriety, where a juror had indicated to the bailiff that he and his fellow jurors were intimidated by the atmosphere in court, in the bailiff asking him why. The bailiff had then reported the answer to the trial judge, who had addressed the jury as to their duty. As to an extraordinary breach of the limitation on communication between the jury bailiff and the jury in retirement, and the obstruction of communication between such a jury and the trial judge, see *Mole* [2013] EWCA Crim 2420.

D19.7   **Consequences of a Lapse of Custody**   If the jury leave the custody of the jury bailiff, it constitutes a material irregularity in the course of the trial which will almost certainly necessitate the quashing of any conviction. For example:

(a) In *Neal* [1949] 2 KB 590, the jury (with the judge's permission) left the court building in order to buy lunch at a restaurant. The conviction was quashed because, even assuming the circumstances justified the judge in allowing the jury to leave the court precincts, it was essential that the bailiff went with them. In his absence, there was no way of knowing who might have spoken to them about the case. It should be noted that the Juries Act 1974, s. 15, now permits the jury to purchase reasonable refreshment at their own expense during the course of their retirement.

(b) In *Ketteridge* [1915] 1 KB 467, where one of the jurors by mistake did not go to the jury room on retirement but left the court and was on his own for some 15 minutes before rejoining his colleagues, there was a breach both of the rule that the jury must not separate (see **D19.8**) and of the rule that the jurors must remain in a bailiff's custody.

Separation of Jury after Retirement   By the Juries Act 1974, s. 13, the judge may permit the   **D19.8**
jury to separate, even after they have retired to consider their verdict. In *Oliver* [1996] 2 Cr App R
514, the Court of Appeal considered the directions which the judge ought to give the jury when
allowing them to separate during consideration of their verdict, and stated that the jury ought to
be told:

(a) to decide the case on the evidence and the arguments seen and heard in court, and not on
     anything seen or heard outside the court;
(b) that the evidence had been completed and it would be wrong for any juror to seek or receive
     further evidence or information of any sort about the case;
(c) not to talk to anyone about the case save to the other members of the jury and then only
     when they were deliberating in the jury room;
(d) not to allow anyone to talk to them about the case unless that person was a juror and he or
     she was in the jury room deliberating about the case; and
(e) on leaving the court, to set the case on one side until they retired to the jury room to con-
     tinue the process of deliberating about their verdict.

Their lordships added that it was not necessary for the judge to use any precise form of words
provided the above points were properly covered. It would be desirable for the direction to be
given in full on the first dispersal by the jury, and for a brief reminder to be given at each subsequent dispersal. Further directions might be necessary in particular circumstances.

In *Edwards* [2004] All ER (D) 324 (Nov), the Court of Appeal made it clear that a failure by
the judge to direct a jury not to discuss the case with anyone or any outsider did not make a
subsequent conviction unsafe. The whole of the circumstances had to be considered, including
the absence of any suggestion that any such discussion had taken place, and the strength of the
evidence against the defendant.

Keeping the Jury in a Hotel   Rather than allowing the jury to separate and go home at the end   **D19.9**
of a court day, in appropriate cases arrangements can be made to keep them at a hotel overnight.
When this happens, the judge should direct the jury, before they leave court, that their deliberations should not continue at the hotel, but should await their return to court the next day
(*Tharakan* [1995] 2 Cr App R 368).

The 'Evident Necessity' Exception   Lord Goddard CJ in *Neal* [1949] 2 KB 590, stated that,   **D19.10**
by way of exception to the rule that the jury must not separate other than with the permission of
the judge, a juror could separate himself from the rest in a case of 'evident necessity'. The examples he gave of 'evident necessity' were if the juror required medical attention or wished to relieve
himself. It is submitted that the juror must remain in the custody of a jury bailiff throughout the
period that he is absent from the jury room.

Consequences of Improper Separation   The consequences of improper separation of the jury   **D19.11**
depend upon the extent to which the rule is breached. This is illustrated by a comparison of the
Court of Appeal's decisions in *Alexander* [1974] 1 All ER 539, on the one hand, and *Ketteridge*
[1915] 1 KB 467 and *Goodson* [1975] 1 All ER 760, on the other.

In *Alexander*, just after the jury had retired, one of them returned by himself to court in order to
collect the exhibits. Although the judge had by then risen, defence counsel was still in court, and
he told the juror to return to the jury room. Upon the judge being informed what had occurred,
the jury were brought back to court; the facts of the incident were confirmed, and they were
simply given the exhibits they wanted. James LJ acknowledged that whilst this constituted a
procedural irregularity, it did not amount to a *material* irregularity, and there was no possible
prejudice to the accused (see also *Farooq* [1995] Crim LR 169).

In *Ketteridge,* where the separation was for a much more substantial period and the separated
juror had been out of the control of the court, the conviction was quashed. Similarly, in *Goodson*
[1975] 1 All ER 760, a juror was allowed by the bailiff to leave the jury room and speak to

unidentified persons on the telephone. He was prevented from returning to the jury room and discharged. On appeal, it was held that what occurred was a material irregularity which had deprived the appellant of a potential voice in the jury room. The Court of Appeal did not rule on whether the judge had the power to discharge a juror even after the jury have retired (see also *Chandler* [1993] Crim LR 394).

Prohibition of Further Evidence Once Jury Enclosed

D19.12   It is generally said to be an absolute rule that once the jury have retired to consider their verdict no further evidence may be adduced before them. This was the conclusion of the Court of Appeal in *Owen* [1952] 2 QB 362, in which Lord Goddard CJ stated the law thus (at p. 369):

> ... we think it right to lay down that once the summing-up is concluded, no further evidence ought to be given. The jury can be instructed in reply to any question they may put on any matter on which evidence has been given, but no further evidence should be allowed.

Even where a pertinent request for further evidence is made, the jury 'ought to have been told that the prosecution had laid before them such evidence as they had thought fit and the evidence could not now be reopened' (p. 369). Whilst acknowledging the strength of the principle, the Court of Appeal in *Khan* [2008] EWCA Crim 1112 accepted that it had been subject to some relaxation, and upheld a conviction where evidence had been admitted late, by agreement with the defence. This echoed *Hallam* [2007] EWCA Crim 1495, where the court accepted that there were circumstances in which material would be put before the jury at the request of the accused on the basis that it advanced or purported to advance his case.

The prohibition only starts once the jury have actually retired. This was made clear in *Sanderson* [1953] 1 All ER 485, where the defence were allowed to call a witness who arrived while the judge was addressing the jury. In a case such as *Sanderson*, however, where evidence is available at the moment the judge finishes his remarks and before the jury have actually retired, there would seem to be no rule of law preventing further evidence, provided it is adduced before the jury retire, and subject to the judge's discretion.

The prohibition must be distinguished from the situation where the jury retires with exhibits, including CCTV material, to examine during their retirement, which is addressed by CPD VI, para. 39L.3 (see Supplement, **PD-59**).

D19.13   **Breach of the Prohibition**   Although the prohibition on the receipt of fresh evidence after the jury has retired is absolute, its breach will not invariably lead to the discharge of the jury. In *Kaul* [1998] Crim LR 135, the Court of Appeal observed that, although the introduction of fresh evidence after a jury had retired should almost invariably lead to the discharge of that jury, in certain circumstances the defence might properly invite the judge to continue with the trial. Where defence counsel took that risk, it did not necessarily bar the way to an appeal on the basis of the irregularity.

D19.14   **The Extent of the Prohibition**   The prohibition on evidence after retirement applies to documents as it does to oral evidence. For example:

(a) In *Davis* (1975) 62 Cr App R 194, it was a material irregularity for the jury to be supplied, inadvertently, with a copy of a police statement from a witness which had not been exhibited although it had been used by defence counsel in cross-examination.

(b) In *Hulme* [2007] 1 Cr App R 334, it had been an error to allow the jury to retire with a previous inconsistent statement from a hostile witness, even where it had been admitted in evidence pursuant to the CJA 2003, s. 119 (see also the CJA 2003, s. 122 at **F6.25**).

(c) In *Thomas* (3 February 1987 unreported) it was held to have been quite wrong to have provided the jury with a map during their retirement, no map having been exhibited in evidence.

Furthermore, if the jury asks to be supplied with tools or measuring equipment, great care must be taken to ensure that their intention is not to conduct a private experiment germane to the issues in the case. In *Stewart* (1989) 89 Cr App R 273, the Court of Appeal held that the trial judge had erred in permitting the jury, at their request but without asking them why, to have a pair of scales. The case was one in which the weight of a quantity of drugs allegedly concealed in a holdall was highly relevant. In *Maggs* (1990) 91 Cr App R 243 Lord Lane CJ agreed that equipment that was required or designed to enable a jury to carry out unsupervised scientific experiments, such as the scales in *Stewart*, was not permissible. However, a magnifying glass or a ruler or a tape-measure were the kind of objects which any person might normally have in his pocket when called to serve on a jury, and therefore there could be no objection to his using them in the jury room (see also *Crees* [1996] Crim LR 830).

In *Wallace* [1990] Crim LR 433, the usher supplied the jury in retirement with a dictionary, at their request, but without informing the judge. The jury had not understood what the judge had said about 'grievous' in 'grievous bodily harm'. After seeing the dictionary, they requested further guidance from the judge. The Court of Appeal held that it was an irregularity but not, in the circumstances, a material irregularity such as to lead to the quashing of the convictions.

In *McNamara* [1996] Crim LR 750, the Court of Appeal held that a request from the jury that the accused stand up in the dock and turn around (presumably so that they could perform a dock identification by comparison with video films seen during the trial) should have been treated as a request for further evidence, and was thus impermissible.

Jury's Own Specialist Knowledge or Researches　In *Fricker* (1999) *The Times*, 13 July 1999, **D19.15** the prohibition on new evidence after the jury's retirement was applied to specialist knowledge in the possession of one of the jurors. The Court of Appeal held that the trial judge had been wrong to rule that the jury had been entitled to take such specialist knowledge into account. It represented entirely new evidence, which neither party had had an opportunity to test. In these circumstances, it would have been appropriate to discharge the jury.

In *Marshall* [2007] EWCA Crim 35, evidence was found in the jury room, at the conclusion of the trial, which showed that at least one of the jurors had carried out research on the internet into the offences charged and the possible sentences they might attract. The Court of Appeal found this to be an irregularity but not, on the facts, a material one. However, Hughes LJ did observe (at [15]):

> ... the case underlines the importance of the direction which is conventionally given to jurors at the outset of the trial (and was given to this jury) to the general effect that the golden rule which they must apply is to try the case on the evidence alone which is what they hear in court and nothing else. That can, without drawing attention to any particular risks, conveniently be given in a form which reminds them first of the general rule, secondly of its application in a prohibition on discussion of the case with family, friends or anybody else, and quite often conveniently also with a reminder that private research, whether in the library or on the Internet, should be abjured.

See also the guidance in CPD VI, paras. 39M.3 to 39M.17 (see Supplement, **PD-60**) and the *Crown Court Bench Book Companion* for the approach to be adopted by the court; see also *A-G v Dallas* [2012] 1 WLR 991 for the penalties for disobedience by a juror of the injunction against research on the internet.

Repetition of Existing Evidence

It is, of course, only new evidence which the jury may not have after retirement. The jury may be pro- **D19.16** vided with items that have been exhibited in court. If the jury, after retirement, asks for any exhibits, the matter should be dealt with in open court. Counsel should be given an opportunity to ensure that the exhibits can properly go before the jury (*Ellis* (1991) 95 Cr App R 52; and see also *Devichand* [1991] Crim LR 446). In *Asgodom* [2012] EWCA Crim 2054 the fact that the electronic equipment in the jury room afforded a clearer CCTV image than the equipment used in court did not result in the jury having any new material in their retirement, and thus no unfairness flowed from this.

Application of this Rule to Tape Recordings　In *Emmerson* (1991) 92 Cr App R 284, com- **D19.17** plaint was made on appeal that the trial judge had refused to provide the jury with the tape of E's

Part D Procedure

interviews, which had been played at trial. The Court of Appeal held that the tape was evidence, becoming an exhibit on production by the officer, regardless of whether it was played during the trial. In *Riaz* (1991) 94 Cr App R 339, it was suggested that, if the jury ask to hear an exhibited tape, the better practice would be for the judge to order the court to reassemble, so that the jury could hear it in open court. The dictum to the contrary in *Emmerson* was disapproved. (For further detail on jury requests for tapes, see *Sardar* [2012] EWCA Crim 134 and **F8.56**.)

Questions from the Jury

D19.18   The jury are permitted to ask questions of the judge during their retirement. The normal method of so doing is to pass a note to the jury bailiff who takes it to the judge. The procedure to be adopted in answering such questions was set out in *Gorman* [1987] 2 All ER 435. The object of the procedures is: (a) to remove any suspicion of private or secret communication between the court and jury, and (b) to enable the judge to assist the jury properly on any matter of law or fact which appears to be troubling them (per Lord Lane CJ at p. 546C; for the facts, see **D13.71**).

Lord Lane set out three propositions to assist judges who receive a note from a jury who have retired to consider their verdict (at pp. 550H–551B):

> First of all, if the communication raises something unconnected with the trial, for example a request that some message be sent to a relative of one of the jurors, it can simply be dealt with without any reference to counsel and without bringing the jury back to court. [See *Connor* (1985) *The Times*, 26 June 1985 where that very situation seems to have arisen.]

> Secondly, in almost every other case a judge should state in open court the nature and content of the communication which he has received from the jury and, if he considers it helpful so to do, seek the assistance of counsel. This assistance will normally be sought before the jury is asked to return to court, and then, when the jury returns, the judge will deal with their communication.

> Exceptionally if, as in the present case, the communication from the jury contains information which the jury need not, and indeed should not, have imparted, such as details of voting figures... then, so far as possible the communication should be dealt with in the normal way, save that the judge should not disclose the detailed information which the jury ought not to have revealed.

D19.19   **Notes Not Relating to the Trial**   As to the first proposition, the implication is that, since the jury's note does not concern the trial itself, it need not even be read in open court. Presumably any answer which needs to be given may be conveyed via the jury bailiff. However, to avoid any possible complaint, it is as well to inform defence counsel of what has occurred (*Connor* (1985) *The Times*, 26 June 1985; *Brown* [1998] Crim LR 505). As to the proper approach to notes relating to problems in the jury room, see **D13.69**.

D19.20   **Notes Relating to the Trial**   Requiring notes connected with the trial to be read in open court, reflects a consistent line of authority going back to *Green* [1950] 1 All ER 38, in which Lord Goddard CJ said: '... any communication between a jury and the presiding judge must be read out in court, so that both parties, the prosecution and the defence, may know what the jury are asking and what is the judge's answer' (see also *Furlong* [1950] 1 All ER 636, *Townsend* [1982] 1 All ER 509 and *Rose* [1982] 2 All ER 536). In *Kachikwu* (1968) 52 Cr App R 538 at p. 541, it was further said by Winn LJ that, whenever a jury note is received, immediate steps should be taken to show it to counsel before it is put in the court archives. Whether to ask counsel for assistance about how the note should be answered is within the judge's discretion.

D19.21   **Answering a Note**   In *Gorman* [1987] 2 All ER 435 (see **D19.18**), it was envisaged that the jury should return to court to be given the answer to any note, however simple the answer. However, earlier authorities indicate that this is a matter for the judge's discretion, and that there is no objection in principle to an answer being communicated by a note taken in by the jury bailiff, provided he reads out in open court both the jury's note and the answer he is giving. Thus, in *Lamb* (1974) 59 Cr App R 196, James LJ said (at p. 199):

The practice should be that, on the court being informed by the jury bailiff of the jury's wish to make a request of the court or to communicate something to the court, the request or communication should either be delivered in writing to the court and the contents and any reply to be delivered through the bailiff, made known in public in court before delivery, or, the jury should be brought back into court to make the request themselves and the judge should answer their request in court.

Answering Only the Question Asked The jury's usual aim in asking a question of the judge **D19.22** will be to seek assistance on a matter which is troubling them. As *Gascoigne* [1988] Crim LR 317 shows, the judge's response should be within strict limits, particularly as far as any new issue is concerned. In that case the judge, in answering a jury note, proceeded spontaneously to give a direction as to an issue which the prosecution had never raised. The Court of Appeal observed that it would seldom be proper for a trial judge to open up spontaneously with a jury, after they had deliberated for some time, an issue which had not been referred to in the trial or the summing-up.

It might be proper to give a supplementary direction, where a matter canvassed at trial had accidentally been omitted from the summing-up. If this were done, it must be carried out with the utmost caution. It was very much more difficult to envisage any occasion where an entirely new basis for conviction should be volunteered at such a late stage. If, in a very exceptional case, such a direction were to be volunteered, counsel must be given an opportunity to make submissions.

Exceptions to this Requirement There are two exceptions to the rule that the judge should **D19.23** only answer the question which the jury has asked.

(1) Where the jury's question reveals that they have forgotten or failed to understand a crucial point, it is incumbent on the judge to remind them of it. In *Wickramaratne* [1998] Crim LR 565, it was apparent from the jury's question that they had failed to take the standard direction on the burden of proof on board. The Court of Appeal said that the trial judge should have reminded the jury in forcible terms of that important direction.
(2) Where the jury's question indicates that they are considering an irrelevant matter. The following cases provide examples:

  (a) Where the jury ask the judge if they are allowed to recommend leniency, the Court of Appeal have held that the judge must tell them that they must try the case on the evidence according to their oath and leave questions of penalty to the judge (*Sahota* [1979] Crim LR 678; *Langham* [1996] Crim LR 430). The reason for this is that the jury might have been influenced by the fact that they could add a rider recommending leniency to come to a verdict which they might not otherwise have done.
  (b) In *Thanki* (1991) 93 Cr App R 12, a note from the jury indicated that they suspected a diary, on which T relied, to be concocted. This had never been suggested by the prosecution. The court held that the accused should have been given an opportunity to meet this line of reasoning (presumably by means other than the production of evidence, in view of the prohibition on new evidence after the jury retires: see **D19.12**).

Notes Recording Voting Numbers Lord Lane CJ's third proposition (at **D19.18**) arose **D19.24** directly out of the ground of appeal in *Gorman* [1987] 2 All ER 435. The jury at G's first trial were discharged from giving a verdict after sending a note to the judge indicating that their 'voting' was split 9–3 for an acquittal. The judge simply told counsel that he had received a note that the jury were split, there was no prospect of them reaching a verdict, and, with counsels' agreement, the jury was discharged. The Court of Appeal concluded that there had been no irregularity in not revealing the content of the note, since the proportions in which the jury are split should not be revealed in open court, and the general rule that a jury note should be read out must therefore be qualified. In such circumstances, a judge should do as the judge did in *Gorman*, namely, give the gist of the note (i.e. the jury are split and unlikely to agree even if given more time) but keep secret that which the jury ought not to have communicated.

D

Part D Procedure

D19.25 **The Status of a Jury Note** A note from any juror is taken to be a note from the jury as a whole, and it was not appropriate to make inquiries as to which juror had written a particular note. This was stressed in *Obellim* [1997] 1 Cr App R 355. In that case a question from the jury caused the judge to suspect that its author might have previous convictions. The judge, without seeking the views of defence counsel, instigated inquiries into the identity of the juror in question, with a view to ascertaining whether he should have been disqualified from jury service. The Court of Appeal said that the only proper check the judge should have made was as to whether the proper inquiries had been made before the juror was called to jury service, and defence counsel should have been informed before even that check.

D19.26 **Consequences of Breach of the *Gorman* Procedure** The consequences of failing to observe the procedures described above depend upon the gravity of the breach. It will only represent a material irregularity if it 'goes to the root of the case'. This is illustrated by a comparison of the Court of Appeal's decisions in *Green* [1950] 1 All ER 38 and *Furlong* [1950] 1 All ER 636.

(a) In *Green*, the jury's question and the judge's answer were never read in court at any stage and the judge could not even remember what the question had been about. This was a material irregularity.

(b) In *Furlong* the respective communications were publicly read, albeit after the verdict, and the answer the judge had given was clearly correct. No such irregularity was found.

Investigation of the Jury's Retirement

D19.27 What occurs in the jury room during the course of the jury's deliberations is absolutely privileged, which is reinforced by the fact that the Contempt of Court Act 1981, s. 8, makes it an offence to disclose, obtain, publish etc. information about what took place in the jury room (see **B14.109**). It follows that alleged irregularities in the way the jury reached their verdict cannot be a ground of appeal.

D19.28 **Inquiries Covered by the Prohibition** In *Miah* [1997] 2 Cr App R 12, it was emphasised that the barrier to the Court of Appeal receiving material relating to the jury's deliberations was to be found in the common-law authorities (including *Ellis v Deheer* [1922] 2 KB 113 at p. 121) rather than in the Contempt of Court Act 1981.

Thompson [1962] 1 All ER 65 demonstrates strikingly the absolute nature of the rule that the Court of Appeal will not, metaphorically speaking, enter the jury room. The proposed ground of appeal was that the jury foreman had read to his colleagues a list of T's previous convictions which had somehow come into his possession. The Court of Criminal Appeal simply refused leave for the evidence of the irregularity to be adduced before them, because it would have breached the privacy of the jury room (see also *Scholfield* [1993] Crim LR 217).

The decision in *Box* [1964] 1 QB 430, where the complaint also related to a juror's prior knowledge of the accused's character, demonstrates that if the bias can be established without calling evidence of the juror's conduct in the jury room the appeal is not invalid *ab initio* (see also **D13.49** and **F9.22**).

The prohibition applies to attempts to obtain information about proceedings in the jury room by the defence (*Mickleburgh* [1995] 1 Cr App R 297), the prosecution (*McCluskey* (1994) 98 Cr App R 216), or the court (*Schot* [1997] 2 Cr App R 383). Inquiries may be embarked upon only with the consent of the court, which, as the trial judge is *functus officio* after sentence, means the Court of Appeal (*McCluskey*).

D19.29 **Inquiries outside the Prohibition** The prohibition does not extend to events outside the jury room, for example, in the hotel at which a jury is accommodated overnight. For example, in *Young* [1995] QB 324, some of the jurors met in a group and sought the assistance of a Ouija board as to the guilt of the accused. The Court of Appeal held that it could inquire into the incident, as it was not in the course of the jury's deliberation.

The Proper Approach to an Investigation

The issues surrounding the confidentiality of jury deliberations have been considered in detail **D19.30**
by the House of Lords in two cases: *Mirza* [2004] 1 AC 1118, and *Smith and Mercieca* [2005]
2 All ER 29 and are addressed in CPD VI, paras. 39M.1 to 39M.26 (see Supplement, **PD-60**).

The Approach in *Mirza* Their lordships considered two conjoined cases in which letters after **D19.31**
the trial indicated irregularities in the jury's deliberations. The Court of Appeal had dismissed
both appeals on the basis that evidence as to what had been said by the jurors in private was
inadmissible and contravened the Contempt of Court Act 1981, s. 8. Their lordships came to
the following conclusions.

(a) The common-law principle prohibiting intrinsic evidence of jury deliberations was in
    accordance with the ECHR, Article 6. In so doing, they looked at the rationale for the rule
    of confidentiality, and concluded that it underpinned the independence and impartiality of
    the jury as a whole.
(b) Consequently, confidentiality reinforced the values in Article 6, and provided essential
    assistance for the jury to operate as a collective body impartially, and independently of
    outside influences.
(c) Section 8 of the Contempt of Court Act 1981 did not affect the duty of the trial court and
    the Court of Appeal to investigate any irregularity in the conduct of the jury within the
    limits of the common law so as to ensure that the accused received a fair trial.

Their lordships went on to advise that certain measures should be taken to strengthen the
jury system. Jurors should be told to inform the court clerk or the judge in writing (either
individually or collectively) if anything improper came to their notice. They should be
reminded that what was said during their deliberations was confidential to them and could
not be repeated or discussed outside the jury room. Their duty of confidentiality continued
after the verdict. CPD VI, para. 39G.3 (see Supplement, **PD-55**), refers to the relevant
directions.

The Approach in *Smith and Mercieca* After the jury had retired and considered its verdict **D19.32**
over some period of time, one of its members alleged in some detail that some jurors were disregarding the judge's directions on the law, were indulging in speculation contrary to his instructions and were engaging in a process of horse-trading, whereby some jurors were being pressed
to return a guilty verdict on some counts in return for acquittal on others. The judge, with the
agreement of counsel, gave the jury a further direction.

On appeal, it was suggested, *inter alia*, that the judge should have carried out an investigation
into the alleged irregularities in the jury room. The Court of Appeal (prior to the judgment of
the House of Lords in *Mirza* [2004] 1 AC 1118) held that he was precluded from doing so by
the Contempt of Court Act 1981, s. 8(1). As a result, the judge was faced with the alternative of
discharging the jury or giving a further direction, and could not be criticised for choosing the
latter course, particularly since counsel had agreed to it.

On appeal to the House of Lords, it was held that the judge was not obliged as a matter of
law in these circumstances to investigate events in the jury room. The common-law prohibition against inquiring into such events certainly extended to matters connected with the
subject-matter of the jury's deliberations, and nothing in the opinions in *Mirza* casts doubt
upon that basic proposition. Further, their lordships were of the opinion that it would not have
been appropriate for the judge to question the jurors about the content of the letter, given that
such a course of action would have been likely to make the situation worse. The judge was left
with a choice of discharging the jury or giving them a further direction emphasising their duties.
He was entitled to adopt the latter course, providing that the direction given was sufficiently
comprehensive and emphatic.

D

Part D Procedure

In *Adams* [2007] 1 Cr App R 449, the Court of Appeal identified the approach that should be taken where, on appeal, it was necessary to make inquiries of the jury. It was stressed that such a course was exceptional (see also **D13.51**).

Relationship of Jury Room Restrictions to Freedom of Expression

D19.33   In *A-G v Scotcher* [2005] 3 All ER 1, the appellant was prosecuted under the Contempt of Court Act 1981, s. 8(1). He had served on a jury which convicted the defendants by a majority. The day after the end of the trial, he wrote to their mother informing her of the discussions which had taken place in the jury room, which he felt would show that the verdict was unsafe.

The Divisional Court held that it was not a defence for a juror to show that he had disclosed the jury's deliberations with the bona fide aim of preventing a miscarriage of justice. The House of Lords, which dismissed his appeal, held that he had been in contempt of court in writing to a third party but he would have been entitled to communicate with the Crown Court, the jury bailiff or the clerk of the court, or to have raised the matter directly with the Court of Appeal. Although the appellant's right to freedom of expression under the ECHR, Article 10(1), had been engaged, it was subject to a restriction which was prescribed by law and necessary in a democratic society for preventing the disclosure of information received in confidence. The rule governing the secrecy of jury deliberations was a crucial and legitimate feature of English trial law, with the result that the limitation placed on the juror's freedom of expression was justified.

TYPES OF VERDICT

D19.34   Before considering the method by which the jury return their verdict, it is necessary to consider the different types of verdict available to them. As was made clear at **D18.43**, CPD VI, para. 39K.1 (see Supplement, **PD-58**), instructs judges that they 'should' direct the jury on unanimous verdicts. In circumstances identified below, a jury may return a verdict that represents the view only of the majority (see **D19.35**), or return a verdict in relation to an offence in the alternative to the one charged (see **D19.41**). In *Hopkinson* [2014] 1 Cr App R 22 (3), the Court of Appeal repeated that the taking of special verdicts, by which the jury were required to indicate the basis for their finding of guilt, should only be used in the context of a trial for murder where there were a number of alternative defences, such as loss of control or diminished responsibility available, and even then only rarely.

MAJORITY VERDICTS

D19.35   At common law, the verdict of a jury had to be unanimous. This was qualified by what is now the Juries Act 1974, s. 17 (set out at the end of **D19.40**). By s. 17(1) some majority verdicts are permissible, subject to certain conditions being satisfied. The procedure for taking majority verdicts is set out in the CrimPR, r. 38.14(4) and CPD VI, paras. 39Q.1 to 39Q.9 (see Supplement, **PD-63**).

Time Requirement

D19.36   A majority verdict may not be accepted unless the jury have been considering their verdict for such period as the court considers reasonable having regard to the nature and complexity of the case, being in any event a period of not less than two hours (Juries Act 1974, s. 17(4)). Any period during which the jury return to court to ask a question of or receive a communication from the judge should be included when computing the two hours (*Adams* [1969] 3 All ER 437).

Time spent not actually deliberating, for example in making their way to the jury room and electing a foreman, is catered for by CPD VI, para. 39Q.3 (see Supplement, **PD-63**), which states that the jury should be allowed at least two hours and ten minutes for deliberation before the majority direction is given.

Application of the Time Requirement   It is unusual for judges to invite a majority verdict at D19.37
the earliest moment permitted. However, the time allowed before the majority verdict procedure is set in motion is a matter for the trial judge's discretion, depending largely on the complexity of the case. This is demonstrated by cases such as the following.

In *Wright* (1974) 58 Cr App R 444, following a five-day trial for murder, the judge had the jury
back after a bare two hours, told them he could now accept a majority verdict, and asked them
to retire for a short time to consider the matter. This was clearly a breach of the *Practice Direction*
guidance then applicable, but that is directory only, not mandatory (see **D19.40**). On appeal the
majority conviction was found to be lawful because (a) there had been no breach of the Juries Act
1974, s. 17, itself, and (b) the judge had not unjustifiably rushed the jury into a majority verdict.
Although the case had been relatively long, the issue was a very simple one, namely whether the
jury were satisfied that W's confession to the police had been genuine. In the circumstances,
allowing the jury a longer time to reach unanimity would not have helped.

In *Rose* [1982] 2 All ER 536, the Court of Appeal indicated that a period of two hours and 40 minutes was 'a little soon' for the majority verdict direction in a murder trial which had lasted for 15 days.

Minimum Number for Acceptable Majority

By the Juries Act 1974, s. 17(1), the minimum majorities permissible are 11–1 or 10–2, or (in D19.38
the case of a jury from which one or more of the original jurors have been discharged) 10–1 or
9–1. A jury reduced to nine must be unanimous.

Statement of Size of Majority and Minority in Open Court

If (and only if) the verdict is guilty, the foreman of the jury must state in open court the number D19.39
of jurors who respectively agreed to and dissented from the verdict (Juries Act 1974, s. 17(3)).

Since stating the size of a majority for conviction is expressed as a precondition of the court
accepting the verdict, failure to comply with s. 17(3) will result in any purported conviction
being quashed (*Barry* [1975] 2 All ER 760; *Austin* [2003] Crim LR 426). However, it is
sufficient for compliance with s. 17(3) if, as happened in *Pigg* [1983] 1 All ER 56, the foreman states the number in the majority leaving the size of the minority to be inferred by the
simplest of arithmetic. In *Pigg*, Lord Brandon of Oakbrook (with whose speech all the other
Law Lords concurred) stated the position thus (at p. 13G–H, emphasis added):

> …compliance with the requirement of section 17(3) of the Act of 1974 is mandatory before a
> judge can accept a majority verdict of guilty; but the precise form of words used by the clerk of the
> court when asking questions of the foreman of the jury, and the precise form of words used by the
> latter in answer to such questions, *as long as they make it clear to an ordinary person how the jury was
> divided*, do not constitute any essential part of that requirement.

Effect of Failure to Comply

The effect of non-compliance with the procedures described above varies depending on whether D19.40
the non-compliance amounts to a breach of the Juries Act 1974, s. 17, or is merely a breach of
CPD VI, paras. 39Q.1 to 39Q.9 (see Supplement, **PD-63**).

In the former case, since the court's power to accept a majority verdict depends entirely upon the
statutory provision, any conviction must be quashed (*Barry* [1975] 2 All ER 760; *Pigg* [1983]
1 All ER 56).

If, on the other hand, there has been failure to comply with paras. 39Q.1 to 39Q.9 and nothing
more, the conviction may stand since the direction is (as the name implies) directory not mandatory (*Wright* (1974) 58 Cr App R 444; *Shields* [1997] Crim LR 758). The Court of Appeal has,
however, stressed the importance of following the directions closely (*Georgiou* (1969) 53 Cr App
R 428). The Court of Appeal in *Arthur* [2013] EWCA Crim 1852 underlined the importance
of following the Judicial Studies Board wording for a majority direction, so that no pressure was

placed on, or perceived to be placed on, the jury when that direction was given. The trial judge had erroneously included words in his direction that had the effect of giving a partial *Watson* direction as part of the majority direction. Such a merging of the two directions was undesirable (but see *Scully* [2013] EWCA Crim 2288 where a contrary conclusion was reached).

Juries Act 1974, s. 17

(1) Subject to subsections (3) and (4) below, the verdict of a jury in proceedings in the Crown Court... need not be unanimous if—
    (a) in a case where there are not less than 11 jurors, 10 of them agree on the verdict; and
    (b) in a case where there are 10 jurors, nine of them agree on the verdict.

...

(3) The Crown Court shall not accept a verdict of guilty by virtue of subsection (1) above unless the foreman of the jury has stated in open court the number of jurors who respectively agreed to and dissented from the verdict.

(4) No court shall accept a verdict by virtue of subsection (1)... above unless it appears to the court that the jury have had such period of time for deliberation as the court thinks reasonable having regard to the nature and complexity of the case; and the Crown Court shall in any event not accept such a verdict unless it appears to the court that the jury have had at least two hours for deliberation.

VERDICT OF GUILTY OF AN ALTERNATIVE OFFENCE

D19.41 It is sometimes open to a jury to find the accused not guilty of the offence alleged in a count but guilty of some other alternative offence. This is commonly referred to as a verdict of guilty of a lesser offence.

At common law, a jury could find an accused guilty of a lesser offence if the definition of the greater offence charged necessarily included the definition of the lesser. However, the enactment of a number of statutory provisions has considerably broadened the situations in which alternative verdicts are now permitted. Although the decision of the House of Lords in *Saunders* [1988] AC 148, demonstrates that there is still a residual role for the common law to play, this discussion of alternative verdicts proceeds on the basis that the law is now to be found in statute.

The General Rule

D19.42 The general provision on the availability of alternative verdicts is contained in the CLA 1967, s. 6(3), which provides as follows:

Where, on a person's trial on indictment for any offence except treason or murder, the jury find him not guilty of the offence specifically charged in the indictment, but the allegations in the indictment amount to or include (expressly or by implication) an allegation of another offence falling within the jurisdiction of the court of trial, the jury may find him guilty of that other offence or of an offence of which he could be found guilty on an indictment specifically charging that other offence.

There are thus two principal situations covered by s. 6(3). One is where the offence charged *expressly* includes an allegation of another indictable offence; the other is where it *impliedly* includes such an allegation.

Express Allegation of Another Offence

D19.43 To determine whether a count expressly includes an allegation of another offence it is necessary to apply a 'blue-pencil test'. This involves striking from the particulars of the count in the indictment the allegations that the prosecution evidence cannot or may not be able to sustain and, if what remains is a valid count for another offence, that alternative may be left for the jury's consideration (*Lillis* [1972] 2 QB 236).

For example, in *Lillis*, the particulars of a count for burglary contrary to the Theft Act 1968, s. 9(1)(b), alleged that L, on a certain date, entered part of a building, and stole therein a lawnmower. However, the complaint of the owners was not that L had taken the mower in the first place but that he had failed to return it when he should have done. Although a submission of no case to answer on the charge of burglary inevitably succeeded, the judge held that there was a case to answer for theft by keeping, and he left that alternative verdict to the jury, who convicted. On appeal, the Court of Appeal applied the 'blue-pencil test', notionally striking from the count those allegations the prosecution could not prove. What remained were the particulars: 'L stole a lawn-mower'. As this was sufficient to satisfy the Indictment Rules 1971 for a count of theft, the alternative verdict had been open to the jury.

The *Lillis* test was approved by the House of Lords in their decision in *Metropolitan Police Commissioner v Wilson* [1984] AC 242.

Implied Allegation of Another Offence

There have been two distinct tests promulgated by the appellate courts for determining when a **D19.44** count impliedly includes an allegation of another offence. The first test was laid down by Sachs LJ in *Springfield* (1969) 53 Cr App R 608 ('the *Springfield* test'), and the second, less restrictive test was laid down by Lord Roskill in *Metropolitan Police Commissioner v Wilson* [1984] AC 242 ('the *Wilson* test').

The *Springfield* Test   Sachs LJ's test in *Springfield* (1969) 53 Cr App R 608, was that a count for **D19.45** offence A impliedly contains an allegation of offence B if, and only if, the commission of offence B is a necessary step towards committing offence A. There were two qualifications to this test:

(a) the court was entitled to look only at the wording of the count and the legal definitions of the offence in the count and the suggested alternative — therefore, if there was any possibility in law that the accused could have committed the 'count' offence without committing the alternative, the latter could not be left to the jury;
(b) it was irrelevant that the prosecution case was that the accused had in fact committed both offences.

Application of the *Springfield* Test   Since it has been overtaken by the *Wilson* test, applica- **D19.46** tions of the *Springfield* test are now of limited assistance. However, those cases which would still be decided the same way include the following.

(a) In *Hodgson* [1973] QB 565, it was held that a jury may, on a count of rape, convict of indecent assault. This is because the allegation of rape impliedly includes both an allegation of an assault and an allegation of indecency. This has application only where the victim is under 16 and the accused cannot rely on consent as a defence, otherwise consent would be a complete defence to the charge and no alternative would be needed.
(b) In *McCready* [1978] 3 All ER 967, it was held that, on a count for causing grievous bodily harm with intent contrary to the OAPA 1861, s. 18, the jury may not convict either of malicious wounding contrary to s. 20 of the Act or of any form of assault. This is because harm can be caused within the meaning of s. 18 without there having been either an application of force or a wounding. On the other hand, if the count under s. 18 is for wounding, the alternatives mentioned above would be open to the jury since an assault is a necessary step towards a wounding, while an allegation of wounding with intent to do grievous bodily harm expressly includes an allegation of malicious wounding.

The *Wilson* Test   The *Springfield* test was disapproved by Lord Roskill in *Metropolitan Police* **D19.47** *Commissioner v Wilson* [1984] AC 242. The question raised in that case was whether a count for inflicting grievous bodily harm impliedly includes an allegation of assault occasioning actual bodily harm. An allegation that grievous bodily harm occurred obviously and probably expressly includes an allegation that there was actual bodily harm (p. 259C). But do the words 'inflicting harm' impliedly include assault? The crucial passage from Lord Roskill's speech is at pp. 260H–261B:

> The critical question is, therefore, whether it being accepted that a charge of inflicting grievous bodily harm contrary to section 20 [of the Offences Against the Person Act 1861] may not necessarily

involve an allegation of assault, but may nonetheless do so, and in very many cases will involve such an allegation, the allegations in a section 20 charge 'include either expressly or by implication' allegations of assault occasioning actual bodily harm. If 'inflicting' can, as the cases show, include 'inflicting by assault', then even though such a charge may not necessarily do so, I do not for myself see why on a fair reading of section 6(3) these allegations do not at least impliedly *include* 'inflicting by assault'. That is sufficient for present purposes though I also regard it as also a possible view that those former allegations *expressly* include the other allegations.

Lord Roskill then held that the reasoning in *Springfield* should no longer be followed. Instead the test is that an allegation of the latter offence is impliedly included in the count where commission of the offence alleged in a count may involve commission of another offence, even if it is possible in law for the one offence to be committed without commission of the other.

D19.48   **Applications of the *Wilson* Test**   Applications of the *Wilson* test include:

(a) In *Metropolitan Police Commissioner v Wilson* [1984] AC 242 itself, the House of Lords restored W's conviction for assault occasioning actual bodily harm on a count alleging inflicting grievous bodily harm contrary to the OAPA 1861, s. 20 (the Court of Appeal, applying the *Springfield* test, had quashed the conviction).

(b) Similarly, in *Jenkins* (which was heard with *Wilson*), a conviction for actual bodily harm was restored on a count alleging burglary contrary to the Theft Act 1968, s. 9(1)(b), in that J, having entered a building as a trespasser, inflicted grievous bodily harm on a person therein.

(c) In *Savage* [1992] 1 AC 699, the House of Lords held that a verdict of assault occasioning actual bodily harm is a permissible alternative verdict on a count alleging unlawful wounding contrary to the OAPA 1861, s. 20.

(d) In *Whiting* (1987) 85 Cr App R 78, the Court of Appeal held that on a count for burglary contrary to the Theft Act 1968, s. 9(1)(b), where the allegation is that the accused, having entered as a trespasser, stole certain property, the jury may convict of entry as a trespasser with intent to steal contrary to s. 9(1)(a).

(e) In *Mandair* [1995] 1 AC 208, the House of Lords held that 'causing' grievous bodily harm contrary to the OAPA 1861, s. 18, was wide enough to include any action that could amount to inflicting grievous bodily harm under s. 20. *Metropolitan Police Commissioner v Wilson* was applied, and *Field* (1993) 97 Cr App R 357 overruled.

(f) In *Morrison* [2003] 1 WLR 1859, the Court of Appeal held that an allegation of attempted murder necessarily involves an allegation of attempt to cause grievous bodily harm, since the act of killing inevitably involves causing serious injury.

Specific Statutory Provisions Relating to Alternative Verdicts

D19.49   The CLA 1967, s. 6(3), is supplemented by a number of other provisions prescribing the alternative verdicts which may be returned on counts for certain specific offences.

D19.50   **Murder**   Section 6(2) of the CLA 1967 provides that:

> On an indictment for murder a person found not guilty of murder may be found guilty—
> (a) of manslaughter, or of causing grievous bodily harm with intent to do so; or
> (b) of any offence of which he may be found guilty under an enactment specifically so providing, or under section 14(2) of this Act; or
> (c) of an attempt to commit murder, or of an attempt to commit any other offence of which he might be found guilty; but may not be found guilty of any offence not included above.

Paragraph (b) of the subsection preserves the effect of the Infanticide Act 1938, s. 1(2) (upon the trial of a woman for murder or manslaughter of her newly born child the jury may convict of infanticide), and of the Infant Life (Preservation) Act 1929, s. 2(2) (upon a trial for, *inter alia*, murder of a child the jury may convict of child destruction). For s. 4(2) of the CLA 1967, see **D19.51**.

D19.51   **Assisting Offenders**   By the CLA 1967, s. 4(2), if the jury are satisfied that the offence with which the accused is charged (or some other offence of which he might be found guilty on that charge) has been committed by someone, but they find the accused himself not guilty of it, they may, by way of alternative verdict, find him guilty of assisting whoever the offender was contrary to s. 4(1) of the Act.

It has been held that, where it can be foreseen that a charge under s. 4(1) might be a proper way of dealing with the accused's case, the prosecution should not invoke s. 4(2) to put the matter before the jury but should have a separate count for assisting an offender (*Cross* [1971] 3 All ER 641). If, however, the possibility of a conviction under s. 4(1) only arises during the course of the case, then the prosecution are entitled to rely on s. 4(2), although they should still apply to amend the indictment to add an appropriate count before the evidence has been completed so that the defence have a fair opportunity of dealing with the new allegation (*Cross* and see also *Vincent* (1972) 56 Cr App R 281).

Attempts   By the CLA 1967, s. 6(4), 'any allegation of an offence shall be taken as including   **D19.52** an allegation of attempting to commit that offence'. It follows that, whenever a count charges the accused with a completed indictable offence, he may be convicted of an attempt to commit that offence. Moreover, when s. 6(3) is read in conjunction with s. 6(4), he may be convicted of an attempt to commit any other completed offence of which he could be found guilty on the count.

Conversely, under the second limb of s. 6(4), if the accused is charged merely with an attempt (or with any assault or other act preliminary to an offence, such as assault with intent to rob) but the evidence in fact establishes the completed offence, he may be convicted as charged. The court retains the discretion to discharge the jury or otherwise act with a view to the preferment of an indictment for the completed offence.

Driving Offences   The Road Traffic Offenders Act 1988, s. 24, makes provision for the alter-   **D19.53** native verdicts which may be returned where a person is tried for certain offences contrary to the Road Traffic Act 1988 (see **C2.8**).

Offences under the Public Order Act 1986   By the Public Order Act 1986, s. 7, if a jury find   **D19.54** the accused not guilty on a count for either violent disorder (contrary to s. 2 of the Act) or affray (contrary to s. 3), they may (without prejudice to the CLA 1967, s. 6(3)) find him guilty of the summary offence of threatening behaviour contrary to s. 4 of the 1986 Act.

In addition, because the offences under ss. 1, 2 and 3 of the 1986 Act (riot, violent disorder and affray) are in descending order of gravity, s. 6(3) of the CLA 1967 would have the result that a count under s. 1 will expressly or impliedly include an allegation of offences under the other two sections. Similarly, a count under s. 2 will include an allegation under s. 3.

Taking a Motor Vehicle without the Owner's Consent   If, on a count for theft, the jury are   **D19.55** not satisfied that the accused committed the offence charged, but it is proved that he commit- ted an offence under the Theft Act 1968, s. 12(1) (taking a motor vehicle without the owner's consent etc.), they may convict him of the latter offence (Theft Act 1968, s. 12(4)).

Common Assault   Until the CJA 1988, s. 40, came into force, a person charged under   **D19.56** the OAPA 1861, s. 47, with assault occasioning actual bodily harm could be convicted, as an alternative, of common assault. This followed from the CLA 1967, s. 6(3), and was the case whether or not there was a specific allegation of common assault as an alternative in the indictment.

By the CJA 1988, s. 40 (see **D11.17**), common assault becomes a summary offence. As a result, in *Mearns* [1991] 1 QB 82, it was held that common assault was not within the jurisdiction of the Crown Court, unless a specific count alleging that offence was added to the indictment. The position is now covered by the DVCVA 2004, s. 11 (see **D19.57**).

Other Offences Listed in the CJA 1988, s. 40   In *Mearns* [1991] 1 QB 82, it was suggested   **D19.57** that all the offences listed in s. 40 were excluded as alternative offences, unless specific counts were added. The position was altered, however, as a result of the DVCVA 2004, s. 11. This inserted subsections (3A) and (3B) in s.6 of the CLA 1967, which provide that an offence falls within the jurisdiction of the Crown Court if it is an offence to which s. 40 of the CJA 1988 applies, even if a count specifying it is not included in the indictment.

Judge's Discretion in Directing Jury as to Alternative Offences

D19.58 The judge in summing-up is not obliged to direct the jury about the option of finding the accused guilty of an alternative offence, even if that option is available to them as a matter of law. If, however, the possibility that the accused is guilty only of a lesser offence has been obviously raised by the evidence, the judge should, in the interests of justice, leave the alternative to the jury. This is the case even if neither prosecution nor defence counsel wishes the alternative offence to be left to the jury (*Coutts* [2006] 4 All ER 353, but see *Brown* [2011] EWCA Crim 1606). It is important for the court to leave an alternative which does not require proof of specific intent where such intent was required for the charge on the indictment (*Hodson* [2009] EWCA Crim 1590; *Foster* [2009] EWCA Crim 2214; *Johnson* [2013] EWCA Crim 2001). The court should not take the initiative to add an alternative charge after the accused has given evidence (*B (JJ)* [2012] EWCA Crim 1440).

D19.59 **Considerations Relevant to the Exercise of that Discretion** The judge's discretion in relation to alternative verdicts is usually invoked to protect the accused against being prejudiced by the unexpected introduction at a late stage of his trial of a suggestion that he is guilty on a charge that has never been expressly preferred against him and which he has not had a fair opportunity of countering in the course of his defence. Thus in *Metropolitan Police Commissioner v Wilson* [1984] AC 242, Lord Roskill rejected the defence argument that the extension of the availability of alternative verdicts implied in the abandonment of the *Springfield* test (see **D19.45**) might result in injustice by referring to the judge's discretion. His lordship said (at p. 261F):

> If it be said that [our conclusion in this case] exposes the defendant to the risk of conviction on a charge which would not have been fully investigated at the trial on the count in the indictment, the answer is that a trial judge must always ensure, before deciding to leave the possibility of conviction of another offence to the jury under section 6(3) [of the CLA 1967], that that course will involve no risk of injustice to the defendant and that he has had the opportunity of fully meeting that alternative in the course of his defence.

The proper approach to the exercise of the judge's discretion in this regard is further illustrated in a number of appellate decisions.

D19.60 **Exercise of the Discretion in** *Fairbanks* The exercise of the judge's discretion in relation to alternative verdicts was further considered by the Court of Appeal in *Fairbanks* [1986] 1 WLR 1202, in the context of the defence wanting the alternative of careless driving to be left to the jury at a trial for causing death by reckless driving. The judge had declined the request and the jury were directed to put out of their minds categories of bad driving other than recklessness. The jury, having sent a note indicating that they might have wanted to convict of careless driving, found H guilty as charged. On appeal, having reviewed the earlier authorities (*Vaughan* (1908) 1 Cr App R 25; *Naylor* (1910) 5 Cr App R 19; *Parrott* (1913) 8 Cr App R 186), Mustill LJ said that an alternative offence should be left to the jury 'only if that is in the interests of justice' (p. 1205H).

D19.61 The application of this test involved a number of possibilities:

(a) Since justice serves the interests of the public as well as those of the accused, there will be cases where, on the evidence, the accused *ought* to be convicted of at least the lesser offence and it would be wrong for the jury to acquit him entirely merely because they cannot be sure that he is guilty as charged (p. 1206D). In such cases the alternative should be left.

(b) Where, on the other hand, the lesser verdict simply did not arise given the way the case had been presented to the court (e.g., the defence was one of alibi), or where it might have arisen had a certain line of questioning been pursued but that had not in fact happened and the possible alternative had therefore ceased to be a live issue, it will be wrong to direct the jury about the alternative.

(c) Similarly, if the possible alternative is very trivial by comparison with the offence charged, introducing it will be an unnecessary and undesirable complication.

Applying those principles to the facts of *Fairbanks*, the judge erred by failing to direct the jury that they could return a verdict of careless driving. A verdict of not guilty of causing death by reckless driving but guilty of driving without due care and attention was a verdict at which a 'conscientious jury could properly arrive on the evidence', and it should have been available to them notwithstanding that they might use it as a bolt-hole to avoid facing up to the hard decision of whether the accused had been reckless.

Exercise of the Discretion in *Maxwell*   The decision in *Fairbanks* was approved by the House **D19.62** of Lords in *Maxwell* [1990] 1 All ER 801. M, who was charged with robbery, asserted that he was guilty of burglary, but denied that he had intended any violence to the victims. The prosecution declined to apply to amend the indictment to include a count of burglary and the judge directed the jury that they were not entitled to bring in a verdict in relation to burglary. The jury could have been directed that they were entitled to bring in a verdict of guilty to the even lesser charge of theft, but the judge did not deal with that possibility.

On appeal to the House of Lords, it was held that:

(a) the prosecution were entitled, on the evidence, to take the view that the jury should not be distracted by an inappropriate alternative count of burglary;
(b) the judge had been entitled to accept that view;
(c) the judge had been entitled to decline to leave the alternative of theft to the jury since it was relatively trifling, and the essential issue was: did M intend violence to be used?

Lord Ackner, with whose reasons the other Law Lords agreed, stated the test, in cases where the judge has failed to leave an alternative offence to the jury as follows (at p. 408F):

> ...the court, before interfering with the verdict, must be satisfied that the jury may have convicted out of a reluctance to see the defendant get clean away with what, on any view, was disgraceful conduct. If they are so satisfied then the conviction cannot be safe or satisfactory.

Maxwell has since been followed in *Cambray* [2007] RTR 128.

Exercise of the Discretion in *Coutts*   The Court of Appeal and House of Lords judgments in **D19.63** *Coutts* [2005] 1 WLR 1605 and [2006] 4 All ER 353 clash.

C was charged with murder. His defence was that the death had been a tragic accident. The parties agreed that it would be unfair to direct the jury on manslaughter, and the trial judge did not direct the jury on manslaughter. C was convicted, and appealed on the basis that the judge should have directed the jury on manslaughter. The House of Lords allowed the appeal.

Lord Bingham, with whom the other Law Lords agreed, stated that, while the murder count against the appellant was clearly a strong one, no appellate court could be sure that a jury to whom the alternative count had been left, would not have convicted of manslaughter. He stated the principle in this way:

> The public interest in the administration of justice is, in my opinion, best served if in any trial on indictment the trial judge leaves to the jury, subject to any appropriate caution or warning, but irrespective of the wishes of trial counsel, any obvious alternative offence which there is evidence to support. I would not extend the rule to summary proceedings since, for all their potential importance to individuals, they do not engage the public interest to the same degree. I would also confine the rule to alternative verdicts obviously raised by the evidence: by that I refer to alternatives which should suggest themselves to the mind of any ordinarily knowledgeable and alert criminal judge, excluding alternatives which ingenious counsel may identify through diligent research after the trial.

Application of this rule may in some cases benefit the defendant, protecting him against an excessive conviction. In other cases it may benefit the public, by providing for the conviction of a lawbreaker who deserves punishment. A defendant may, quite reasonably from his point of view, choose to roll the dice. But the interests of society should not depend on such a contingency... Nor, with respect, is it an objection that the jury's task would have been more complicated had a manslaughter direction been given. Compared with many directions given to juries, a manslaughter direction in this case would not have been complicated. But even if it would, that cannot be relied on as a reason for not leaving to the jury a verdict which they should on the facts have considered. If juries are to continue to command the respect of the public, they must be trusted to understand the issues raised even by a case of some complexity. For reasons already given, the wishes of counsel cannot override the judge's duty.

D19.64   Doubt was cast, in the course of the opinions delivered by members of the House of Lords in *Coutts*, on the test for an appellate court to apply, as set out in *Maxwell* [1990] 1 All ER 801 (see **D19.62**). Lord Hutton said that 'that approach is an unsatisfactory one and should no longer be taken'. As Lord Roger put it:

> Since the appeal court cannot inquire into what went on in the jury room, it is very far from clear how they are meant to satisfy themselves in any given case that a jury may have convicted out of a reluctance to see the defendant get clean away.

Coutts was applied by the Court of Appeal in *Foster* [2008] 2 All ER 597. It was emphasised that it would not always be appropriate for an alternative verdict to be left to the jury. It would depend on considerations of fairness, including the potential disadvantage to the accused if no alternative verdict was available, and the proportionality of the alternative verdict to the conduct alleged.

D19.65   **Consideration of the ECHR**   The need for the judge to exercise his discretion in such a way as to ensure that the accused is not prejudiced by the unexpected introduction of an alternative offence has been underlined by the ECtHR in *Pelissier and Sassi v France* (2000) 30 EHRR 715. In that case, the defendants, who had been acquitted of the substantive offence of criminal bankruptcy, were convicted on the prosecution's appeal of aiding and abetting the substantive offence. It was not contested that the French court had the power so to do, but it had violated the ECHR, Article 6, by doing so without the possibility having been properly raised in advance of the judgment.

D19.66   **Discussion in Advance with Counsel**   At the very least, a judge intending to leave an alternative verdict to the jury should warn counsel beforehand and should give them the opportunity of making representations about the propriety or otherwise of the proposed course (*Hazell* [1985] RTR 369). Counsel should also have an opportunity to address the jury about the alternative verdict, assuming it is to be left (*Hazell*).

In appropriate cases, giving the defence a fair opportunity to deal with an alternative verdict will involve drawing counsel's attention to the possibility of such a verdict before the close of defence evidence. In *Harris* (1993) *The Times*, 22 March 1993, for example, Steyn LJ in the Court of Appeal stated that it was appropriate to leave an alternative offence to the jury only if the accused had a full opportunity to meet the revised case against him so as to ensure that he was not prejudiced. See also *Griffiths* [2005] EWCA Crim 237.

It is generally assumed that, if the judge does not direct the jury about an alternative verdict or even (as in *Fairbanks* [1986] 1 WLR 1202) expressly tells them to ignore the possibility, they will be guided by him and either find the accused guilty as charged or acquit. However, in *Carter* [1964] 2 QB 1, a conviction for a lesser offence was upheld where prosecuting counsel had told the jury that the verdict was available but the judge made no reference to it in summing-up. In order to avoid criticism for flouting the judge's authority, it would seem advisable for counsel first to raise the issue in the absence of the jury after the close of the evidence.

Procedure where the Jury are Unable to Agree that the Accused is Not Guilty as Charged

D19.67 The CLA 1967, ss. 4(2) and 6(2) and (3), makes it a precondition of the jury convicting of an alternative offence that they should first find the accused not guilty of the offence specifically charged in the indictment. Where they cannot so agree, the clear wording of the legislation demonstrates that they are not entitled to return a verdict of guilty of the lesser offence. This could lead to the absurd result that the jury would be discharged from giving any verdict whatsoever when they are agreed that the accused is guilty of something.

The solution to this problem reached by the cases is by no means satisfactory. It was held in *Collison* (1980) 71 Cr App R 249 that if the possibility of an alternative verdict arose under the CLA 1967, s. 6(3) (the general provision), the judge, upon being informed that the jury cannot agree as to the greater offence but are agreed on the lesser, could and should amend the indictment by adding a separate count for the lesser offence. A verdict could then be taken on the added count and the jury discharged from giving a verdict on the other.

In *Foster* [2008] 2 All ER 597, the Court of Appeal considered the circumstances in which it would be appropriate to add counts to an indictment in relation to potential alternative verdicts. The Court observed that the indictment represented a statement of the charges on which the prosecution, rather than the court, sought a conviction, and that substantial amendment to the indictment at a very late stage in proceedings was liable to obscure the issues relied on by the parties and complicate the jury's task.

D19.68 **The Role of the Common Law in the Light of** *Saunders* In *Saunders* [1988] AC 148, in contrast to *Collison* (1980) 71 Cr App R 249, it was the effect of the CLA 1967, s. 6(2), that was in issue. The indictment charged murder only, but it became apparent towards the end of the jury's retirement that they had concluded that S was at least guilty of manslaughter. The judge took a verdict of guilty of manslaughter, although no separate count for manslaughter had been added, and discharged the jury from giving a verdict in respect of murder. The House of Lords held that an additional count of manslaughter was unnecessary. Prior to the enactment of the CLA 1967, alternative verdicts of manslaughter on a charge of murder had always been allowed by common law. The provisions of the Act did not abrogate the common law but were merely intended to deal with a procedural problem highlighted in *DPP v Nasralla* [1967] 2 AC 238, namely, whether the judge could ask for a verdict as to manslaughter if the jury had initially announced a verdict of not guilty *simpliciter*. Section 6(2) confirmed that he could. However, in situations not covered by s. 6(2), the common law continued to apply.

Although the interpretation of s. 6(2) adopted in *Saunders* [1988] AC 148, avoided the necessity of quashing S's conviction for manslaughter and ordering a retrial, it does seem surprising that the common law on alternative verdicts should have survived legislation which was apparently intended to define with some precision when such verdicts are, and when they are not, available. With respect, the decision in *Saunders* was convenient but ought to be confined to its special facts, and this appears to have been the view of the Court of Appeal in *Foster* [2008] 2 All ER 597.

Where problems similar to those in *Collison* arise, it is safer to deal with them by means of adding a count rather than invoking the court's purported residual powers at common law.

RETURNING THE VERDICT

General Procedure

D19.69 The jury's verdict is delivered in open court, in the presence of the accused. The invariable practice is for the person the jury have selected to be their foreman to state in response to questions from the clerk of court whether they find the accused guilty or not guilty.

The jury are entitled to return a partial verdict in the sense of finding an accused guilty on one count but not on others, or finding one accused guilty but another not. They are also entitled to find an accused guilty in respect of some only of the allegations set out in the particulars of a count, as when a count for theft specifies several items as the subject-matter of the charge and the jury are satisfied that the accused stole some of them but are left in doubt as to others (see *Furlong* [1950] 1 All ER 636, where the jury sent a note asking the judge if they could return such a verdict and the Court of Criminal Appeal held that the judge's affirmative answer was undoubtedly correct, even though the method by which he had communicated the answer was at fault).

D19.70   **Unanimity of the Verdict**   Unless a juror indicates dissent at the time, it is conclusively presumed that they all agree with the verdicts announced on their behalf, and the Court of Appeal will not breach the privacy of the jury room by hearing evidence that the necessary unanimity was lacking (*Roads* [1967] 2 QB 108, and see also *Lalchan Nanan v The State* [1986] AC 860, in which, on appeal from the Court of Appeal of Trinidad and Tobago in a capital case, the Privy Council held that the court below had rightly refused to read affidavits from four jurors to the effect that they had not realised the need for unanimity and had wished to acquit the appellant).

If the jury return to court apparently with a verdict prior to their having been given the majority verdict direction, the first question the foreman is asked is whether they have reached a verdict (or verdicts) on which they are all agreed (CPD VI, para. 39Q.2 (see **D19.73** and Supplement, **PD-63**)). If the foreman indicates that they have reached unanimous verdicts, he is then asked in respect of each count on the indictment and each accused charged in a count what the jury's verdict is.

D19.71   **Verdicts on Alternative Counts**   The general rule that there should be verdicts on each count is subject to the qualification that, where a jury wishes to convict on one of two counts which are in the alternative, it is preferable to take a verdict only on that count and discharge them from giving a verdict on the other. This is because the Court of Appeal will then, in appropriate circumstances, be able on appeal to substitute for the jury's verdict a verdict of guilty of the alternative count, whereas if the jury are allowed formally to acquit the accused of the alternative their verdict on that must stand, even though the conviction on the other count has to be quashed (see *Seymour* [1954] 1 All ER 1006, *Melvin* [1953] 1 QB 481 and *Roma* [1956] Crim LR 46, and also the Criminal Appeal Act 1968, s. 3, for the Court of Appeal's power to substitute for the actual verdict a conviction for another offence of which the jury could lawfully have convicted the appellant on the indictment).

Having regard to the above considerations, the procedure normally adopted where counts are in the alternative is for the clerk to ask the foreman whether the jury find the accused guilty on *either* of the counts. If the answer is yes, the foreman is asked on which count they wish to convict; a verdict is taken on that count, and the judge discharges them from giving a verdict on the other. If the answer is no, not guilty verdicts are taken on each count.

D19.72   **Verdicts on Counts of Descending Gravity**   A rather different problem arises where counts are not strict alternatives, but they arise out of the same facts and are of differing degrees of gravity (e.g., counts for wounding with intent to cause grievous bodily harm and malicious wounding contrary to ss. 18 and 20 of the OAPA 1861).

It is usual in such cases for the judge in summing-up to tell the jury to consider first the more serious count and only to go on to consider the lesser one if they are not satisfied as to the former. Similarly, when verdicts are taken, the foreman will be asked first for the verdict on the graver count. If it is guilty, the jury will be discharged from giving a verdict on the other; if it is not guilty, a verdict is also taken on the lesser count.

It would not be proper in such cases to allow the jury to convict on both counts because the lesser count really merges into the greater. For example in *Harris* [1969] 2 All ER 599, where H was convicted of both buggery and indecent assault on a boy of 14, the latter offence consisting in playing with the victim's private parts immediately prior to the act of buggery. Edmund Davies LJ (giving the Court of Appeal's judgment) said:

> There is no suggestion of any indecent assault upon [the victim] except that which formed the preliminary to and was followed very shortly thereafter by the commission of the full act of buggery. It does not seem to this court right or desirable that one and the same incident should be made the subject-matter of distinct charges, so that hereafter it may appear to those not familiar with the circumstances that two entirely separate offences were committed. Were this permitted generally, a single offence could frequently give rise to a multiplicity of charges and great unfairness could ensue. We accordingly allow the application for leave to appeal against the conviction of indecent assault, which really merges into the conviction for the graver charge.

Although his lordship appears to criticise even the formulating of distinct charges based on one incident, the actual mischief was in allowing the jury, once they had convicted of buggery, to go on to convict of the lesser charge also. They should simply have been discharged from giving a verdict in respect of indecent assault.

Where the jury were mistakenly asked for their verdict on the lesser count first, but this error was corrected and the proper procedure then followed, their conviction on the more serious count remained valid (*Fernandez* [1997] 1 Cr App R 123 and see *McEvilly* [2008] EWCA Crim 1162).

Procedure for Taking Majority Verdicts

D19.73 Majority verdicts are discussed at **D19.35**. The procedure for taking majority verdicts is set out at CPD VI, paras. 39Q.2 to 39Q.7 (see Supplement, **PD-63**). The main features of the procedure are as follows.

(a) If the jury return to court in a period in which it is considered that they should be trying to reach a unanimous verdict (and certainly where they return in less than two hours and ten minutes), the clerk of the court asks the foreman if they have reached a verdict on which they are all agreed. If the answer is yes, the verdict is taken; if the answer is no, they are sent back to their room with a direction to continue to try to achieve unanimity.

(b) If the jury return or are sent for after that period has elapsed, the clerk similarly asks the foreman if they have reached a verdict on which they are all agreed. If the answer at this stage is no, the judge directs the jury that he can now accept a majority verdict, and tells them the size of the permissible majorities. However, he must also tell them that, when they again retire, they should make a further attempt to reach a unanimous verdict, and only if that last attempt at unanimity fails should they come back with a majority decision.

(c) Upon the jury returning to court after the majority verdict direction has been given, the clerk asks the foreman whether they have reached a verdict on which the required majority of them are agreed. If the answer is yes, they are asked for the verdict. A verdict of not guilty should be accepted without more ado. If the verdict is guilty, the foreman should be further asked whether it was unanimous or by a majority and, if the latter, how many agreed and how many dissented.

Correcting a Verdict

D19.74 It occasionally happens that a jury return a verdict and then realise that they have been misunderstood.

D19.75 **Where the Verdict is Incorrect**   In such cases, the trial judge may allow them to correct their verdict (unless they have been discharged and have dispersed).

This was demonstrated in *Andrews* (1985) 82 Cr App R 148, in which the Court of Appeal held that a jury does have power to alter a verdict from not guilty to guilty provided it acts promptly

(*Parkin* (1824) 1 Mood CC 45; *Vodden* (1853) Dears CC 229). Whether such an alteration should be allowed is in the discretion of the trial judge, taking into account especially:

(a) the length of time which has elapsed between the original verdict and the moment when the jury express a wish to change;

(b) the apparent reason for the mistake, for example, as in *Andrews* itself, that the jury were mistakenly waiting for a further question from the court clerk; and

(c) the necessity to ensure that justice is done both to the prosecution and to the defence.

In *Andrews*, the accused had been discharged but this was *not* fatal to allowing a change of verdict. However, if the jury had been discharged, and certainly if they had been allowed to disperse, it would then have been too late to rectify the mistake.

Equally, if the jury had heard anything since returning the original verdict that might have affected their earlier thinking, that would preclude any alteration (*Tantram* [2001] Crim LR 824).

In *Austin* [2003] Crim LR 426, the Court of Appeal stated that, where a verdict was given in the sight and hearing of the entire jury without any dissent by any member of it, there was a presumption that they had all assented to it, albeit that such a presumption could be rebutted.

D19.76   **Correcting an Incomplete Verdict**   An alteration to the verdict may also be allowed where the original one was not so much incorrect as incomplete. For example, in *Carter* [1964] 2 QB 1 the jury, which had not been directed by the judge about the possibility of finding the accused guilty of a lesser offence (although prosecuting counsel had referred to it), initially found the accused simply not guilty. After the accused had been discharged, it became clear that the jury had wished to convict of the lesser offence and the accused were then recalled for the verdict to be completed and sentence passed. The conviction was upheld.

D19.77   **Otherwise Rectifying the Verdict**   Although the general rule is that, once the jury has been discharged, it is *functus officio* (see D13.50), there are circumstances in which it can be reconvened in order to rectify its verdict. Examples of such circumstances include the following cases.

(a) In *Aylott* [1996] 2 Cr App R 169, the judge discharged the jury because of a mistaken belief that they were unable to reach a verdict. When he received a further note from the jury which made it clear that they had already reached verdicts, he took the verdicts, as a result of which the appellant was convicted of murder. On appeal it was held that a judge was entitled in certain circumstances to set aside the discharge which he had ordered, for example, in *Aylott* the discharge had been based on a fundamental mistake. The underlying principle was to ensure that proceedings were fair and to do justice in the particular case.

(b) In *Maloney* [1996] 2 Cr App R 303, a guilty verdict was taken by the court on Friday afternoon, without asking how many jurors had agreed with the verdict and how many dissented. To rectify this mistake, the jury was reconvened the following Monday and asked about the figures. The Court of Appeal held that the discharge of the jury did not prevent the court carrying out the rectifying procedure. Nor were the lapse of time and the fact that the jury had dispersed fatal, in view of the CJPO 1994, s. 43, which permitted the jury to separate after retirement. There was no suggestion that they had deliberated further after the dispersal, nor that the numbers given as to the size of the majority were incorrect. The position would have been different if the jury had had to deliberate further, or, perhaps, if the verdict was being altered from not guilty to guilty.

Power of Judge to Refuse to Accept Verdict

D19.78   In general, a judge is obliged to accept the jury's verdict however much he may disagree with it (*Robinson* [1975] QB 508, following *Lester* (1938) 27 Cr App R 8). The exceptions to the general rule were succinctly stated by Lord Parker CJ in *Harris* [1964] Crim LR 54. The *Criminal Law Review*'s paraphrase of his lordship's judgment reads:

> Where a single verdict is ambiguous, or two verdicts are inconsistent, or the verdict is one which cannot on the indictment or in the circumstances be lawfully returned, the judge is entitled, unless the jury insist, to refuse to accept the first verdict and ask the jury to reconsider the matter and if they change their verdict to record only the second verdict.

Similarly, in *Robinson* [1975] QB 508, James LJ said (at p. 512F):

> ...once the jury has returned a verdict, then the judge cannot say 'I will not have it', provided, of course, it is a verdict that is not ambiguous and provided it is a verdict that can properly be returned upon the indictment they have been considering.

The Three Categories of Verdicts that a Judge can Refuse　Thus, there are three categories of　**D19.79**
case in which the first verdict need not be accepted:

(a) *The original verdict is one which the jury cannot lawfully return on the indictment*. An example would be a verdict of guilty of a lesser offence when such a verdict does not, in the circumstances of the case, come within any of the statutory provisions allowing a jury to convict the accused of something other than that with which he is expressly charged in the indictment (see **D19.41**).
(b) *The original verdict is ambiguous*. In such cases the judge should ask whatever questions are necessary to resolve the ambiguity (*Hawkes* (1931) 22 Cr App R 172) and may, if necessary, give a supplementary direction on the law before taking a final verdict (*Sweetland* (1957) 42 Cr App R 62). If the judge proceeds to sentence on a purported verdict of guilty which remains ambiguous, both conviction and sentence will have to be quashed (*Hawkes*).
(c) *Inconsistency in the verdict*. If the individual verdicts on a number of counts or in respect of several accused are inconsistent with each other, having regard to the nature of the evidence that has been adduced, the judge may ask the jury to reconsider their decision. He should only do so, however, if the verdicts are *necessarily* inconsistent. If there is a possible, albeit unlikely, view of the evidence on which the verdicts can be justified, the judge should accept them without further query. An example of this third category is the case of *Burrows* [1970] Crim LR 419. B, P and another were jointly charged with theft of a purse and P alone was charged in the alternative with handling it. The judge declined to accept the jury's initial verdict, acquitting all three of theft but convicting P of handling, because that acquittal implied that they were not satisfied that the goods in question had ever been stolen. Further discussion revealed a misunderstanding by the jury, and when this was corrected the jury found B guilty of theft. On appeal, it was held that the judge should have accepted the original verdicts, because they were not necessarily inconsistent *inter se* since the jury might have been sure that *either* B or the third co-accused had stolen the purse but the jury might have been unable to attribute responsibility to one or the other.

If the judge legitimately refuses to accept the jury's first verdict and in consequence they return a proper second verdict, it is the latter which is the operative decision. If the jury, notwithstanding the judge's intervention, persist in returning inconsistent verdicts, the inconsistency may be a good ground of appeal.

Supplementary Questions about the Verdict

It is not in general good practice to ask the jury questions about the basis on which they have　**D19.80**
returned a verdict of guilty (per Humphreys J in *Larkin* [1943] KB 174). Where the prosecution evidence is such that two or more views of the facts consistent with guilt are tenable, on one of which the accused's culpability is greater than on the other, it is the judge's responsibility to decide what the circumstances of the offence were for the purposes of sentencing (*Solomon* (1984) 6 Cr App R (S) 120 and *Stosiek* (1982) 4 Cr App R (S) 205). Asking the jury to refine their verdict may merely lead to confusion.

D19.81   **Circumstances in which Supplementary Questions May be Asked**   The one recognised exception to this principle is in cases where the accused is charged with murder and the jury have been left two or more alternative bases on which they might find the accused guilty of man-slaughter and not guilty of murder. This is because exactly why the accused was found guilty of manslaughter (whether it was on grounds of provocation or diminished responsibility and, if the latter, its cause) is of crucial importance to sentence (*Matheson* [1958] 2 All ER 87, *Frankum* (1983) 5 Cr App R (S) 259 and *Solomon* (1984) 6 Cr App R (S) 120 per Beldam J at p. 126).

There is, however, no absolute requirement to ask supplementary questions even in these cir-cumstances. In *Cawthorne* [1996] Crim LR 526, the Court of Appeal stressed that whether or not the judge asked the jury to indicate the basis of the verdict was a matter for his discretion; following the verdict, he was entitled to sentence on the basis of the facts which he had heard in evidence. In *Hopkinson* [2014] 1 Cr App R 22 (3), the Court of Appeal repeated that the taking of special verdicts should only be used in the context of a trial for murder where there were a number of alternative defences, and even then only rarely.

D19.82   **Procedure for Supplementary Questions**   Because the jury are entitled to decline to answer any supplementary question, beyond delivering its verdict, a judge who intends to ask a jury the basis of a guilty verdict should warn them of his intention before they retire (*Heckstall-Smith* [1989] Crim LR 742). After any such warning, if they convict, they should then be asked the supplementary question immediately after returning the main verdict and before they separate (*Heckstall-Smith*).

In complicated cases, it may be a 'sensible precaution' to write the questions down for the jury. In *Frankum* (1983) 5 Cr App R (S) 259, Dunn LJ approved the course adopted by the trial judge in the case who gave the jury a list of questions as follows: 'First, do you think it more probable than not that the accused was suffering from diminished responsibility? If so, you should find him guilty of manslaughter. If you find him guilty of manslaughter, you will be asked (1) is that on the ground of diminished responsibility, and (2) if so, do you think the abnormality (a) arose as a result of inherent causes, (b) was induced by injury from the toxic effects of [a drug F was taking for a peptic ulcer] or (c) was both?'

D19.83   **Factual Basis for Sentence**   Subject to the discussion above and **D19.41**, in general, if the judge has summed up the case to the jury on one factual basis, he is entitled to assume that they will acquit or convict on that basis and not on some alternative view of the facts which may theo-retically have been open on the evidence but was not a live issue during the trial (*Heckstall-Smith* [1989] Crim LR 742). Where the jury do attempt to indicate, while the judge is passing sen-tence, that the factual basis on which he is doing so is different from that which they found proved, the judge may refuse to hear what they wish to say (*Ekwuyasi* [1981] Crim LR 574).

JURY UNABLE TO AGREE ON A VERDICT

D19.84   If the jury cannot agree on a verdict, the judge discharges them from giving a verdict. As always when the jury are discharged, the accused is not acquitted but may be retried by a different jury. Whether to ask for a retrial is in the discretion of the prosecution. In the absence of exceptional reasons to the contrary, it is the practice to have a retrial following failure by one jury to agree. If a second jury also fail to agree, the prosecution would not usually seek a third trial but instead offer no evidence.

This convention was examined in *Henworth* [2001] 2 Cr App R 47, and it was stated that it should not be elevated into a proposition of law. In some cases, a further trial might be proper, e.g., if a jury had been tampered with, or some cogent piece of evidence for the Crown had since been discovered. Whether it was an abuse of process for the prosecution to seek a further trial must depend on the facts, including:

(a) the overall period of the delay and the reasons for it;
(b) the results of the previous trials;

(c) the seriousness of the offence; and (possibly)

(d) the extent to which the case against the defendant had changed since previous trials.

Jury Must Not Be Pressurised

The jury should be given as much time as they reasonably need to reach a verdict, and must not **D19.85**
be pressurised into agreeing against their better judgement. As Cassels J said in *McKenna* [1960]
1 QB 411 at p. 422: 'It is a cardinal principle of our criminal law that in considering their verdict . . . a jury shall deliberate in complete freedom, uninfluenced by any promise, unintimidated
by any threat'.

The pressure in *McKenna* itself was extreme, in that the jury were told by the judge that, if they
did not reach a verdict within the next ten minutes, they would have to be 'kept all night'. That
was at least capable of conveying the impression that they would be kept in their jury room.

Even a much gentler indication of a time-limit may result in unacceptable pressure on the jury.
In *Duggan* [1992] Crim LR 513, the jury made it known at 3.52 p.m. that, as some of them had
child care commitments, they wished to sit until they had reached a verdict. The judge said that
he was prepared to wait until 5 p.m. if it would help. The Court of Appeal held that the judge's
intimation of a time-limit was likely to put some of the jury under pressure, in view of their
earlier indication of commitments and the fact that it was clear that they would have to spend
the night in an hotel if they could not agree.

Proper Discussion of Timing with the Jury   Provided the principle in *McKenna* [1960] 1 **D19.86**
QB 411 is not breached, there is no objection to the jury being asked if there is any reasonable
prospect of their reaching agreement and being told that if there is not the judge will discharge
them, while if there is they may have as much time as they want (*Modeste* [1983] Crim LR 746).

Any communication between the judge and jury about the chances of a verdict being reached
should take place in open court and should not be conducted by, for example, the clerk going
into the jury room with a message (*Rose* [1982] 2 All ER 536). Where the jury request more time
to deliberate, the judge may be obliged to allow more time; in any event, he is fully justified in
permitting it (*Turner* [1994] Crim LR 287).

Wharton [1990] Crim LR 877 emphasises the importance of the judge inquiring of the jury in
open court as to the prospect of a verdict being reached. In that case, the jury retired to consider
their verdict at 3 p.m., received the majority direction at 5.34 p.m. and sent a note saying that
they had reached a verdict 9–3 at 6.10 p.m. The course then adopted by the judge, with counsel's concurrence, of sending the jury a message asking them to continue their deliberations, was
held to represent a material irregularity. Where the jury are unable to reach a verdict, the judge
should reassemble them in court and ascertain from the foreman in open court at first hand
what prospect there is of reaching a verdict.

When giving a majority direction, the judge should not refer to the possibility of another trial
taking place if the jury cannot agree, as to do so might put undue pressure on them to reach
agreement (*Boyes* [1991] Crim LR 717).

Saturday Sitting   In *Duffin* [2003] EWCA Crim 3064, the Court of Appeal considered the **D19.87**
circumstances in which the jury might be asked to consider their verdict on a Saturday. At the
trial of the defendant for possession with intent to supply Class A drugs, the jury was sent out
at 3.54 p.m. on the Friday of the last day of their scheduled sitting. At 6.07 p.m. the judge told
them they were under no pressure to deliver a verdict, and asked them to retire and consider
whether they wished to continue their deliberations or return the following day. Majority verdicts of guilty were returned at 7.31 p.m. The appeal of the accused on the ground that the jury
had been placed under improper pressure to deliver the verdicts was allowed. Occasionally a
Saturday sitting might be desirable and practicable but, if it was, the proper course was to determine whether the jury had commitments for the following day. Given the lateness of the hour

Part D Procedure

and the fact that the only options had been to stay late or return the following day, the jury had been put under pressure to deliver the verdicts.

Encouraging the Jury to Reach a Verdict

D19.88   *Watson* [1988] QB 690 raised the vexed question of whether a judge is entitled to use a form of words encouraging the jury to listen to each other's views and thus, if possible, reach agreement. In particular, the Court of Appeal considered the appropriateness in modern circumstances of a direction approved in *Walhein* (1952) 36 Cr App R 167, which drew attention to the cost and inconvenience caused by a jury not being able to agree. Lord Lane CJ's judgment in *Watson* starts from the proposition that (at p. 700A–B):

> ...a jury must be free to deliberate without any form of pressure being imposed upon them, whether by way of promise or of threat or otherwise. They must not be made to feel that it is incumbent upon them to express agreement with a view they do not truly hold simply because it might be inconvenient or tiresome or expensive for the prosecution, the defendant, the victim or the public in general if they do not do so.

Experience had shown that the *Walhein* direction potentially put too much pressure on jurors who happened to be in the minority to concur with the majority. There was, however, no reason why a jury should not be directed as follows (at p. 700F–G):

> Each of you has taken an oath to return a true verdict according to the evidence. No one must be false to that oath, but you have a duty not only as individuals but collectively. That is the strength of the jury system. Each of you takes into the jury-box with you your individual experience and wisdom. Your task is to pool that experience and wisdom. You do that by giving your views and listening to the views of the others. There must necessarily be discussion, argument and give and take within the scope of your oath. That is the way in which agreement is reached. If, unhappily, [ten of] you cannot reach agreement you must say so.

It is solely a decision for the trial judge, in the exercise of his discretion, whether or not to give the above direction at all and, if he does decide to give the direction, the time at which he does so (as was restated in *Pinches* [2010] EWCA Crim 2000).

D19.89   **The Timing of a 'Watson' Direction**   In *Watson* [1988] QB 690, it was held that the direction was probably best given as part of the summing-up or as a last resort should the jury have had the majority verdict direction but still be unable to reach the minimum majority required (pp. 700H–701A). The Court of Appeal have indicated, in any event, that, once a jury has retired, a *Watson* direction should never be given before the majority direction (*Atlan* [2005] Crim LR 63) but, equally, should not be given at the same time as a majority direction (*Buono* (1992) 95 Cr App R 338).

D19.90   **Form of the Direction**   If the direction is given, individual variations in its wording may prove dangerous and should if possible be avoided (*Watson* [1988] QB 690). In *Atlan* [2005] Crim LR 63, it was stressed that, if a *Watson* direction is given, it should be made clear that any 'give and take' should be within the scope of the juror's oath. The Court of Appeal suggested that it was just as dangerous to omit words from the *Watson* direction as to add them (see also *Morgan* [1997] Crim LR 593).

D19.91   **Retrial**   In *Bell* [2010] 1 Cr App R 407 the Court of Appeal confirmed that no rule of law forbids a second retrial in cases where juries in the first two trials have failed to reach a verdict. Where no verdict can be reached at a first retrial, it is initially for the prosecutor to judge whether, taking account of all relevant considerations, the public interest is better served by offering no evidence or by seeking a further retrial. The judge must then consider whether or not the proposed second retrial would be oppressive and unjust. A second retrial should be 'confined to the very small number of cases in which the jury is being invited to address a crime of extreme gravity which has undoubtedly occurred (as here) and in which the evidence that the defendant committed the crime (again, as here), on any fair minded objective judgment remains very powerful' (see also *Bowe v R* [2001] UKPC 19 and *Benguit* [2005] EWCA Crim 1953).

Section D20   Trial on Indictment: Sentencing Procedure

INTRODUCTION

D20.1   This section describes the procedure which applies following, as appropriate, a verdict or a plea of guilty, and which regulates the sentencing of the accused. First, there is a need to ascertain the basis of facts, which is of particular importance where the accused has pleaded guilty and the court has therefore not had the opportunity to form a view of the evidence at trial. Secondly, there is a need to consider the character of the accused, to obtain such pre-sentence reports as are appropriate about him, and to consider such mitigation as is advanced on his behalf, before either sentencing or adjourning sentence in one of a number of ways. This topic is addressed by the CrimPR, r. 38.16 (see Supplement, **R-315**).

Although sentencing procedure is essentially the same in both the Crown Court and magistrates' courts, it is the former that is considered here. For ways in which the summary procedure differs, see **D23**. See also **part E** as to the sentences that are available, and the procedures and guidelines that apply to them.

ASCERTAINING THE FACTS OF THE OFFENCE

D20.2   Where the accused pleads guilty, the first stage of the sentencing process is for prosecuting counsel to summarise the facts of the offence (CrimPR, r. 38.16(3)). As well as assisting the court, this informs the accused and the public of how the prosecution put their case.

It will normally be unnecessary for the facts to be opened at the conclusion of a contested trial. However, in the event of split pleas by co-accused, the sentencing of the accused who pleaded guilty will normally be adjourned until the conclusion of the trial of the accused who pleaded not guilty. If the latter is convicted, the facts will still have to be summarised for the benefit of the one who pleaded guilty.

The Duties of the Prosecutor in Relation to Sentencing

D20.3   By convention, the prosecution adopt a neutral attitude at the sentencing stage, not seeking to influence the court in favour of a heavy sentence. This is reflected in the Code of Conduct of the Bar, Written Standards, para. 11.8(a), which states:

> [Prosecuting counsel] should not attempt by advocacy to influence the court with regard to sentence: if, however, a defendant is unrepresented it is proper to inform the court of any mitigating circumstances about which counsel is instructed. [See also **D16.2** *et seq.*]

In addition to the general statements of principle just given, the following points may be made about the role of prosecution counsel at the sentencing stage.

(a) Prosecution counsel can only provide evidence of the impact on the victim of the offence for which the accused is to be sentenced if it accords with the relevant guidelines (see **D20.4**).

(b) Where the possibility arises of the court making an ancillary order in conjunction with the main sentence (e.g., compensation under the PCC(S)A 2000, s. 130, deprivation of property under s. 143 of the same Act, confiscation of the proceeds of crime, or forfeiture of prohibited articles such as drugs or offensive weapons), counsel has a duty to deal with the matter (Code of Conduct of the Bar, Written Standards, para. 11.8(d)).

(c) Prosecution counsel is under a general duty to assist the court to avoid appealable error. According to the standards applicable to criminal cases, this goes beyond ensuring that the judge does not exceed his maximum powers and extends to reminding him of (i) statutory provisions guiding him in his sentencing task and (ii) any relevant guidelines laid down by the Court of Appeal. The effect of para. 11.8(b) and (c) is that such assistance should be given either if requested by the court or on counsel's own initiative, if he considers that the judge has erred as a matter of sentencing law (see *Panayioutou* (1989) 11 Cr App R (S) 535 and **D20.6**).

(d) Prosecution counsel must prepare a 'plea and sentence document' which identifies the aggravating and mitigating factors of the offence and the relevant statutory provisions and sentencing guidelines (Addendum to the A-G's Guidelines on the Acceptance of Pleas and the Prosecutor's Role in the Sentencing Exercise).

Victim Impact Statements

D20.4   The court is frequently provided with an account from the victim of the offence for which the accused is to be sentenced, which can then be taken into account by the court when it passes sentence.

In *Hobstaff* (1993) 14 Cr App R (S) 632, the Court of Appeal stressed that allegations made by prosecuting counsel as to the effect of the offence upon the victim must be backed up by potentially admissible evidence. Such evidence should be made in a proper form, such as a witness statement, and served in advance on the defence and the court. Defence counsel could then deal with it in such a manner as he thought fit and the court would not be influenced by prosecution information alone (see also *A-G's Ref (No. 2 of 1995)* [1996] 1 Cr App R (S) 274).

In *H (Indecent Assault)* (1999) *The Times*, 18 March 1999, the Court of Appeal emphasised that where the prosecution does provide a statement from the victim, the sentencer should approach it with some care. Since it would ill-behove the accused to attempt to investigate such a statement, it would necessarily reflect one side of the case only.

In *Perks* [2001] 1 Cr App R (S) 66, the Court of Appeal laid down guidelines for the courts to take into account in considering 'victim personal statements' for the purpose of sentencing (see **E1.30** for details). The main points of *Perks* are now summarised in CPD VII, paras. F.1 to F.3 (see Supplement, **PD-69**).

Victim's Advocates and Victim Focus Scheme

D20.5   In the same regard a pilot scheme for the introduction of 'Victim's Advocates' was introduced in April 2006. In strict technical terms the scheme ended on 23 April 2008 and was replaced by the CPS Victim Focus Scheme. However, the five areas involved in piloting the Victim Advocate Scheme continue to operate the processes under that scheme for offences of murder, manslaughter, familial homicide and corporate manslaughter only. Under the Victim's Advocates Scheme, the court is permitted to hear from an advocate speaking on behalf of the victim's family. The procedure is set out in more detail in the Protocol for Pilot Courts on Victim's Advocates (available via www.judiciary.gov.uk/publications/criminal-protocol-4). The CPS Victim Focus Scheme applies in all other areas. It involves prosecutors offering to meet bereaved families.

Counsel's Duty to Assist the Court

Counsel must make himself aware of any legal limitations on the court's sentencing powers and **D20.6** any relevant guidelines as to sentence so as to be in a position to assist the judge if necessary (Code of Conduct of the Bar, Written Standards, para. 11.8(b)). This reflects dicta of the Court of Appeal (e.g., Lawton LJ in *Clarke* (1974) 59 Cr App R 298: '…counsel as a matter of professional duty to the court…should always before starting a criminal case satisfy themselves as to what the maximum sentence is', and *Kennedy* [1976] Crim LR 508: 'It is the duty of counsel to inform themselves what are the permissible sentences for the offences with which a defendant is charged, so as to be in a position to assist the judge if he makes a mistake').

In *Komsta* (1990) 12 Cr App R (S) 63, it was emphasised that there was a positive obligation on counsel, both for the prosecution and the defence, to ensure that no order is made which the court has no power to make. See also *Brown* [1996] Crim LR 134, *Johnstone* (1996) *The Times*, 18 June 1996, *A-G's Ref (No. 52 of 2003) (Webb)* [2004] Crim LR 306, and *Reynolds* [2008] 4 All ER 369.

In *Cain* [2007] 2 Cr App R (S) 135, the Lord Chief Justice observed:

> It is of course the duty of a judge to impose a lawful sentence, but sentencing has become a complex matter and a judge will often not see the papers very long before the hearing and does not have the time for preparation that advocates should enjoy. In these circumstances a judge relies on the advocates to assist him with sentencing. It is unacceptable for advocates not to ascertain and be prepared to assist the judge with the legal restrictions on the sentence that he can impose on their clients.

> This duty is not restricted to defence advocates. We emphasise the fact that advocates for the prosecution also owe a duty to assist the judge at the stage of sentencing. It is not satisfactory for a prosecuting advocate, having secured a conviction, to sit back and leave sentencing to the defence. Nor can an advocate, when appearing for the prosecution for the purpose of sentence on a plea of guilty, limit the assistance that he provides to the court to the outlining of the facts and details of the defendant's previous convictions.

> The advocate for the prosecution should always be ready to assist the court by drawing attention to any statutory provisions that govern the court's sentencing powers. It is the duty of the prosecuting advocate to ensure that the judge does not, through inadvertence, impose a sentence that is outside his powers. The advocate for the prosecution should also be in a position to offer to draw the judge's attention to any relevant sentencing guidelines or guideline decisions of this court.

The Factual Basis for Sentence

The great majority of summaries of the facts provided by the prosecution raise no procedural **D20.7** problems whatsoever. However, a considerable body of law has developed dealing with the proper approach to that minority of cases in which there is a dispute about the facts of the offence, in the sense that the prosecution version of how the offence was committed differs from that advanced by the defence in mitigation, albeit that the accused is clearly guilty on either version. This will arise in particular where the defence advance a written factual basis of plea which is not accepted by the prosecution or the court. Under the CrimPR, r. 38.16(4) (see Supplement, **R-315**), the court may give directions for determining the facts on the basis of which sentence must be passed; the principles to be applied are discussed at **D20.8** *et seq*.

DISPUTES ABOUT THE FACTS FOLLOWING A PLEA OF GUILTY

Newton Hearings

In *Newton* (1982) 77 Cr App R 13, although N pleaded guilty to sexual offences, there was **D20.8** considerable dispute between the prosecution and defence as to whether the sexual acts alleged had been consensual. The Court of Appeal indicated three ways in which the judge, in a case where there is such a sharp divergence on the facts of the offence, 'can approach his difficult task of sentencing'. Lord Lane CJ said (at p. 15):

> It is in certain circumstances possible to obtain the answer to the problem from a jury. For example, when it is a question of whether the conviction should be under section 18 or section 20 of the Offences against the Person Act 1861, the jury can determine the issue on a trial under section 18 by deciding whether or not the necessary intent has been proved by the prosecution...
>
> The second method which could be adopted by the judge in these circumstances is himself to hear the evidence on one side and another, and come to his own conclusion, acting so to speak as his own jury on the issue which is the root of the problem.
>
> The third possibility in these circumstances is for him to hear no evidence but to listen to the submissions of counsel and then come to a conclusion. But if he does that,...where there is a substantial conflict between the two sides, he must come down on the side of the defendant. In other words where there has been a substantial conflict, the version of the defendant must so far as possible be accepted.

The General Approach

D20.9   The basic propositions set out in *Newton* have since been analysed and refined. In particular, in *Underwood* [2005] 1 Cr App R 178, the Court of Appeal gave guidelines on the approach that the sentencer ought to take where an accused pleads guilty on a specific basis that the prosecution may not accept. In summary, and renumbered, they are as follows:

(1) The accused should be sentenced as far as possible on a basis that accurately reflects the facts of the individual case.

(2) If the resolution of the facts in dispute may matter to the sentencing decision, the responsibility for alerting the prosecutor to the areas of dispute rests with the defence (see also **D20.10**).

(3) The prosecution should not be taken by surprise and should if necessary take time to reflect, consult and consider their position and the interests of justice.

(4) Whatever view is formed by the prosecution on any proposed basis of plea is deemed to be conditional on the judge's acceptance of it.

(5) The prosecution may agree the accused's account of the disputed facts. If so, the agreement should be reduced to writing and signed by both advocates (see also **D20.14**).

(6) The agreement should be available to the judge before the prosecution's opening and if possible before he is invited to approve the acceptance of plea, or in any event before the sentencing hearing begins.

(7) If the agreed basis of plea is not signed by advocates for both sides, or it is not legible, the judge is entitled to ignore it.

(8) If the prosecution rejects the accused's version, the areas of dispute should be identified in a document that focuses the attention of the court on the precise facts which are in dispute.

(9) The most difficult situation arises when the prosecution lacks the evidence positively to dispute the accused's account. In many cases, for example, the matter in issue is outside the knowledge of the prosecution. The prosecution's position may be that they have no evidence to contradict the defence assertions, but that does not mean that the truth of matters outside their own knowledge should be agreed. In those circumstances, particularly if the facts relied upon by the accused arise from his personal knowledge and depend on his own account of the facts, the prosecution should only agree that account if it is supported by other material. Neither the prosecution nor the judge is bound to agree facts merely because the prosecution cannot gainsay the accused's account.

(10) Whether or not the basis of plea is agreed, the judge is not bound by any such agreement, and is entitled to insist that any evidence relevant to the facts in dispute should be called. The judge is responsible for the sentencing decision and may order a *Newton* hearing to ascertain the truth about disputed facts (see also **D20.15**).

(11) The prosecution and defence should call any relevant evidence. Where the issue arises from facts that are within the exclusive knowledge of the accused, the defence should be willing to call him. If he does not give evidence, the judge may draw such inferences as he thinks fit, subject to any explanation put forward.

(12) An adjournment for these purposes is often unnecessary.

(13) The judge should direct himself on the burden and standard of proof in accordance with ordinary principles.

(14) A *Newton* hearing has the following limitations:
  (a) some issues require a verdict from a jury, e.g., intent (see **D19.81**);
  (b) a judge cannot make findings of fact and sentence that are inconsistent with the pleas to the counts on the indictment;
  (c) where a number of persons are charged with a joint enterprise, the seriousness and context are always relevant;
  (d) matters of mitigation are not normally dealt with in a *Newton* hearing, but where there is no evidence to support an accused's account other than his contention, the judge is entitled to invite defence counsel to call his client;
  (e) where the impact of the dispute on the eventual sentencing decision is minimal, a *Newton* hearing is unnecessary — the judge will rarely be concerned with minute differences about events on the periphery (see also **D20.18**);
  (f) the judge is entitled to decline to hear evidence about disputed facts if the accused's case is absurd or obviously untenable, but he should explain why he has reached that conclusion (see also **D20.20**).

(15) If issues on a *Newton* hearing are resolved in the accused's favour, the credit due to him for a guilty plea should not be reduced.

(16) If the accused is disbelieved or obliges the prosecution to call evidence from a witness causing unnecessary and inappropriate distress, and conveys to the judge that he has no insight into the consequences of his offence and no genuine remorse for it, the judge may reduce the discount for a guilty plea, particularly if it has been tendered at a very late stage.

(17) There might be an exceptional case in which the normal entitlement to credit for a guilty plea is wholly dissipated by the *Newton* hearing, in which case the judge should explain his reasons.

Certain of the more important aspects of these guidelines are analysed below. *Underwood* was specifically endorsed by the Court of Appeal in *Temple* [2008] EWCA Crim 2511 and in *Nicholls v DPP* (2014) 178 JP 100.

In *Sheard* [2013] EWCA Crim 1161, the Court of Appeal expressed concern that the sentencing judge had been invited to resolve a factual dispute as to whether or not certain aggravating features of the seriousness of the offence were present without hearing any live evidence.

Duty of the Accused's Legal Representatives

It is the responsibility of defence solicitors and counsel to notify the prosecution that a plea of guilty will be put forward on the basis that the accused disputes the prosecution version of the facts (*Mohun* (1993) 14 Cr App R (S) 5). **D20.10**

As explained in *Gardener* [1994] Crim LR 301, this notification involves two stages. Where there was a dispute about relevant facts which might affect sentence, defence counsel should make that clear to the prosecution. The court should then be informed, ideally at the outset of the hearing and at the latest during mitigation, not merely that there is a dispute but that the defence wishes to see it resolved in a *Newton* hearing.

The Court of Appeal would not normally consider an argument that the sentencer had failed to order a hearing unless the possibility of such a hearing was raised unequivocally and expressly in the Crown Court (see also *A-G's Refs (Nos. 3 and 4 of 1996)* [1997] 1 Cr App R (S) 29 and *Hughes* [2011] EWCA Crim 556).

Power of Court to Direct a Hearing

D20.11 Ultimately, the decision as to whether or not a *Newton* hearing is required is for the court. As a result, such a hearing may arise even where prosecution and defence are agreed on the facts on which the plea is based. The judge is under a duty to hold a *Newton* hearing if an application of the principles stated in **D20.9** leads to that conclusion, even if the defence are against that course.

In *Smith* (1986) 8 Cr App R (S) 169, for example, the judge offered defence counsel a *Newton* hearing to resolve an important factual issue, but counsel declined. The judge then proceeded to sentence on a basis adverse to S. In the Court of Appeal, where the term was reduced, Peter Pain J quoted from Goff LJ in *Williams* (1983) 5 Cr App R (S) 134: '…the question whether an issue should be tried does not depend upon the consent of counsel for the appellant or the accused person as the case may be. It is entirely a matter for the decision of the court in any particular case, although the court may of course hear submissions from counsel on the propriety of ordering such an issue to be tried. The question whether counsel for a party agrees or does not agree to the trial of the issue is a matter of no materiality, the decision being entirely within the control of the court' (see also *Myers* [1996] 1 Cr App R (S) 187).

If the judge decides to hold a *Newton* hearing he should avoid giving the impression that he has made up his mind in advance that the defence version is implausible (*Satchell* [1997] 2 Cr App R (S) 258).

The Crown Court has the power to hold a *Newton* hearing even where such a hearing has already taken place in the magistrates' court which committed the accused for sentence. However, there ought to be good reason for it to reopen a factual dispute that has already been resolved elsewhere (*R (Gillan) v Crown Court at Winchester* [2007] 1 WLR 2214).

D20.12 **Factual Disputes Revealed by the Pre-sentence Report**   One way in which the court may be alerted to a factual dispute which may have a bearing on the eventual sentence is where the accused presents to the author of the pre-sentence report a factual account which is at variance with the prosecution case. In such circumstances, the court can initiate a *Newton* hearing (see, for example, *Oakley* [1998] 1 Cr App R (S) 100, where the Court of Appeal held that the sentencer should have heard evidence to resolve the conflict, whether or not the prosecution or defence asked for a *Newton* hearing). However, in *Tolera* [1999] 1 Cr App R 29, the Court of Appeal emphasised that the initiative rested with the defence where it was asking the court to sentence on a basis other than disclosed by the prosecution case. If the accused wished to rely on the account which he gave to the probation officer and which conflicted with the prosecution case, he should draw the relevant paragraphs to the attention of the court and ask that it be treated as the basis of sentence. The prosecution should be alerted to the fact that such a request would be made. A *Newton* hearing could then follow.

D20.13 **Dispute Arising in Ancillary Proceedings**   The court may also be alerted to a material factual dispute during proceedings ancillary to sentencing, such as confiscation. In *McNulty* [1994] Crim LR 385, for example, the court's inquiry as to whether a confiscation order should be made in respect of the proceeds of drug trafficking, raised doubts as to M's basis of plea of non-commercial supply. The judge therefore embarked on a *Newton* hearing, in which he found that M had been dealing commercially. The Court of Appeal held that it was proper to hold a *Newton* hearing in these circumstances, and upheld the sentence and the confiscation order. In such a situation, it is important to ensure that the *Newton* hearing is governed by the criminal rules of evidence and procedure, regardless of the assumptions and standard of proof which may govern an inquiry under the POCA 2002 (see **E19.10**).

Written Basis of Plea

D20.14 Where an accused pleads guilty on a particular basis (e.g., accepting only a limited version of the allegations made by the prosecution), he should set out the basis of the plea in a written form (*Tolera* [1999] 1 Cr App R 29). The Court of Appeal has indicated that it is reluctant to recognise that a plea was put forward on a particular basis unless there is such a written basis of plea, or the judge has accepted it expressly (*Kesler* [2001] 2 Cr App (S) 542). Where the court does not accept a basis of plea, it must make this clear before proceeding to sentence (*Lucien* [2009] EWCA Crim 2004). See also the CrimPR, r. 3.23 (see Supplement, **R-30**) as to applications for indications as to sentence.

Response to an Agreed Basis of Plea   In *Beswick* [1996] 1 Cr App R (S) 343, the Court of **D20.15** Appeal dealt with the situation where agreement had been reached between prosecution and defence counsel as to the facts upon which a plea of guilty was to be based, and the judge declined to give effect to that agreement.

Their lordships set out five principles for the guidance of the court in such cases:

(1) Whenever the court has to sentence an offender it should seek to do so on a basis which is true. The prosecution should not, therefore, lend itself to any agreement with the defence which was founded on an unreal and untrue basis.
(2) When that had happened, the judge was entitled to direct a *Newton* hearing in order to determine the true factual basis for sentence.
(3) Such a decision did not create a ground upon which an offender should be allowed to vacate his plea of guilty, provided he does admit his guilt of the offence to which he has pleaded guilty.
(4) The decision that there should be a trial of an issue meant that the judge was entitled to expect the assistance of prosecuting counsel in presenting evidence, and in testing any evidence called by the defence. The agreement which the prosecution has previously entered into with the defence must be viewed as conditional on the approval of the judge. If the judge's approval is not forthcoming, the defence cannot seek to hold the prosecution to the agreement.
(5) Before embarking on the trial of an issue, the judge might consider whether there is any part of the agreement by which the prosecution should be bound. Counsel should also consider which issues are to be tried, and which of the prosecution statements are relevant to them.

Guidance on the issues arising where the basis of a plea is the subject of an agreement between prosecution and defence is to be found in *Underwood* [2005] 1 Cr App R 178 (see **D20.9** and points (1), (4), (5), (6), (7), (8) and (10) in particular).

Longer-than-commensurate Sentence

In *Oudkerk* [1994] Crim LR 700, it was held that, where the imposition of a longer-than- com- **D20.16** mensurate sentence under the PCC(S)A 2000, s. 80(2)(b) (now repealed), was contemplated, the sentencing court must resolve by a *Newton* hearing any important issue going to the application of that provision. Similar situations may arise in relation to the application of the CJA 2003, ss. 224 to 236 (see **E4.1** *et seq.*).

Where *Newton* Hearing Unnecessary

Change of Plea   Some difficulty arises where the accused changes his plea to guilty after some **D20.17** evidence has been given by prosecution witnesses. In *Mottram* (1981) 3 Cr App R (S) 123, it was held that the judge should then hear evidence from the accused (and, presumably from any witnesses whom he wished to call), before deciding on the version of the facts which would form the basis for sentence. The totality of the evidence received on the point relevant to sentence can then be treated as a *Newton* hearing (see also *Archer* [1994] Crim LR 80).

Insignificant Disputes   The principles in *Newton* (1982) 77 Cr App R 13, apply only where **D20.18** the dispute between prosecution and defence is 'substantial' (see the words of Lord Lane's judgment quoted at **D20.8**). It follows that, where the judge's sentence would be the same whichever version of the facts he were to accept, there is no obligation on him to hear evidence but he can make up his mind one way or the other simply on the basis of counsels' representations.

This was illustrated in *Bent* (1986) 8 Cr App R (S) 19, where the factual dispute did not go to the gravamen of the charge. In cases such as *Bent*, a judge should sentence on the assumption that

Part D Procedure

the defence version is correct, and state that he is doing so (see dicta to that effect by Lincoln J in *Hall* (1984) 6 Cr App R (S) 321 at p. 324).

Further guidance on this topic is to be found in *Underwood* [2005] 1 Cr App R 178 (see **D20.9** and point (14)(e) in particular).

D20.19 **Extraneous Matters**   There is no requirement to hold a *Newton* hearing where the matter that is not accepted relates to extraneous mitigation which is outside the prosecution's knowledge (the 'reverse *Newton*' situation). For this see **D20.81** and *Underwood* [2005] 1 Cr App R 178 at **D20.9**, especially point (9).

D20.20 **Defence Version Manifestly Absurd**   The guidance in *Newton* (1982) 77 Cr App R 13 requires a sentencer either to hear evidence about a significant dispute as to the facts of the offence or to accept the defence version 'so far as possible'. The implication is that the defence story may be so implausible that a judge ought not to be obliged to waste time by hearing evidence before rejecting it.

Such an interpretation of *Newton* has been confirmed by subsequent decisions, in particular *Hawkins* (1985) 7 Cr App R (S) 351. In that case, H accepted that he had acted as the get-away driver in a joint offence of burglary but he only became aware of the full facts at a very late stage. The judge declined to hear evidence about the facts but sentenced on the prosecution version that H had been a knowing participant throughout. The Court of Appeal dismissed H's appeal because the suggestion that 'he was driving the car around to keep the engine warm or to look for a lavatory for himself, whilst unknown to him his colleagues were burgling a house was an incredible assertion'. The judge did not have to trouble himself with evidence.

The same approach was taken in *Bilinski* (1987) 86 Cr App R 146, and in *Walton* (1987) 9 Cr App R (S) 107 at p. 109 where Kennedy J said, '... the words used by this court in *Newton* (1982) 77 Cr App R 13 do not mean that in every case a judge must hear evidence before he rejects a version of the facts put forward in mitigation, but which for good reason he regards as untenable... The judge was fully entitled [in the circumstances of this case] to reject the submission that was put forward [in mitigation] out of hand during the course of argument'.

D20.21 **Evidence of the Accused Incredible**   Similar reasoning applies to the case where the accused gives an account on oath at the *Newton* hearing. The fact that the burden of proof is upon the prosecution does not inevitably lead to the conclusion that the accused's testimony must automatically be accepted in the absence of direct evidence to the contrary. If the accused's account on oath is incredible, the judge is entitled to reject it whether or not the prosecution call evidence. Thus, in *Kerr* (1980) 2 Cr App R (S) 54, K, who pleaded guilty to importing cannabis through Heathrow, gave evidence that, until almost the moment of leaving the plane, he had thought the packets in his luggage to be samples of marble, not drugs. It was held that the judge was entitled to reject that explanation even though the prosecution called no evidence and did not even cross-examine K.

D20.22 **Restrictions on the Court's Right to Reject the Accused's Account**   The judge's view that the defence version is manifestly absurd must, however, be in accordance with the facts. This was illustrated in *Costley* (1989) 11 Cr App R (S) 357. The prosecution alleged that C, who had pleaded guilty to inflicting grievous bodily harm, had used a piece of wood as a weapon. However, C claimed he had been provoked, and even then had only used his fists. In sentencing (without first hearing evidence), the judge said: 'I find as a fact that the attack was totally unprovoked by anything [V] said or did.... I reject your explanation for the use of violence as being wholly incredible'. The Court of Appeal held that it was not open to the judge to come to these conclusions, and upheld the appeal against sentence. In a case where the sentencer is faced with a substantial conflict on issues such as this, a *Newton* hearing should be held. Where the court feels unable to accept the defence account, it should make that clear, and indicate why (*Tolera* [1999] 1 Cr App R 29).

Procedure

Burden and Standard of Proof   In a *Newton* hearing, the burden of proof is on the prosecu-   **D20.23**
tion to satisfy the judge beyond reasonable doubt that their version of events is the correct one.
This was demonstrated in *Ahmed* (1984) 80 Cr App R 295, where the issue between prosecution and defence was whether A was a mere courier or a dealer. The trial judge, after hearing
evidence from the offender, decided against his account and sentenced accordingly. On appeal,
the defence argument that the judge had misdirected himself as to the standard of proof failed.
Parker LJ observed:

> If it be right that in the absence of evidence the submissions of the defence should be accepted and
> that the other two possible courses are to have the matter (where circumstances permit) determined
> by a jury or the judge, then it must in our view follow that the defence version of the facts must be
> accepted, unless a jury or the judge, as the case may be, is sure that it is wrong.

In *Kerrigan* (1993) 14 Cr App R (S) 179, it was said that it was better for the judge to direct
himself openly as to the relevant standard and onus of proof, although the failure to do so was
not fatal in every case.

Calling Evidence   Once the judge has decreed that there should be a *Newton* hearing, the   **D20.24**
hearing itself follows normal adversarial lines (per May LJ in *McGrath* (1983) 5 Cr App R
(S) 460 at p. 463). The parties are given the opportunity to call such evidence as they wish and
to cross-examine the witnesses called by the other side. The roles of the parties, and the court,
do require consideration.

Role of the Prosecution   Where the basic facts are not in dispute, the prosecution is not   **D20.25**
obliged to call any evidence, and the judge is then entitled to draw any appropriate inferences, provided that he directs himself properly as to the burden and standard of proof
(*Mirza* (1993) 14 Cr App R (S) 64). The prosecution is still required to participate, whether
or not they have material to dispute the defence account. In *Tolera* [1999] 1 Cr App R 29,
the Court of Appeal suggested that, in questioning the offender, the prosecutor should
adopt the role of *amicus curiae*, exploring matters which the court wished to be explored.
The prosecution should not leave the questioning to the judge.

Role of the Defence   On the other hand, the defence cannot be forced to call evidence or oth-   **D20.26**
erwise participate, but may simply observe while the prosecution seek to establish their version
to the judge's satisfaction. A defendant cannot, however, by declining to give evidence, frustrate
the exercise which the judge has undertaken so as to enable him subsequently to complain that
there has been no *Newton* hearing (*Mirza* (1993) 14 Cr App R (S) 64).

Role of the Court   In order to avoid giving the impression that he has made up his mind in   **D20.27**
advance, the judge should usually wait until the offender has been examined by his own counsel,
and cross-examined by counsel for the prosecution, before questioning him (*Myers* (1996) 1 Cr
App R (S) 187).

In assessing the evidence, the judge must, as the tribunal of fact, observe the directions which he
would have given the jury for their guidance. This was illustrated in *Gandy* (1989) 11 Cr App R
(S) 564. G had pleaded guilty to violent disorder. On the completion of the trial of his co-accused,
a *Newton* hearing was held to determine identification evidence relating to G's role. The Court
of Appeal held that, during that *Newton* hearing, it was important that the judge should have
approached the matter and directed himself as if he were a jury. In particular this required the court:

(a) to go through the steps which *Turnbull* [1977] QB 224 required the judge to set out when
    directing a jury;
(b) to consider the admissibility of identification evidence which breached the PACE 1984
    codes of practice; and
(c) to consider the reliability of other aspects of the evidence, e.g., discrepancies between the con-
    temporaneous descriptions and G's appearance.

D

Part D Procedure

Hence it appears that, in the context of a *Newton* hearing: (a) the rules of evidence should be strictly followed, and (b) the judge should direct himself appropriately as the trier of fact.

Consequences of a *Newton* Hearing

D20.28 **Loss of Mitigation for a Guilty Plea**   In *Underwood* [2005] 1 Cr App R 178 (see **D20.9**), the Court of Appeal set out guidance as to the extent to which the accused should receive credit for a guilty plea where a *Newton* hearing is necessary (see also *Stevens* (1986) 8 Cr App R (S) 291; *Jauncey* (1986) 8 Cr App R (S) 401; and *Williams* [1991] Crim LR 150). The main points are:

(a) if issues on a *Newton* hearing are resolved in the accused's favour, the credit due to him for a guilty plea should not be reduced;

(b) if the accused is disbelieved or obliges the prosecution to call evidence from a witness causing unnecessary and inappropriate distress, and conveys to the judge that he has no insight into the consequences of his offence and no genuine remorse for it, the judge may reduce the discount for a guilty plea, particularly if it has been tendered at a very late stage;

(c) there might be an exceptional case in which the normal entitlement to credit for a guilty plea is wholly dissipated by the *Newton* hearing, in which case the judge should explain his reasons.

If the judge mentions the prospect of loss of mitigation prior to holding a *Newton* hearing, he should be careful to avoid giving the impression that he has decided against the accused's version in advance (*Satchell* (1997) 2 Cr App R (S) 258). See also *Elicin* [2009] 1 Cr App R (S) 561.

Appeals in *Newton* Hearing Cases

D20.29 The Court of Appeal does have power to interfere with the decision of the sentencing judge as to the facts of the offence arrived at following a *Newton* hearing (*A-G's Refs (Nos. 3 and 4 of 1996)* (1997) 1 Cr App R (S) 29). However, there are important limitations (per Parker LJ in Ahmed (1984) 80 Cr App R 295):

(a) if the judge has properly directed himself as to the burden and standard of proof, the Court of Appeal will exercise its power only in 'exceptional cases' where 'no reasonable jury [properly] directed could have reached the judge's conclusion';

(b) if the accused himself gave evidence at the *Newton* hearing, the occasions on which interference is justified will be 'rare indeed', bearing in mind the trial judge's advantage in having seen the demeanour etc. of the accused when testifying.

In an appropriate case, however, the Court of Appeal will depart from findings of fact made by a judge in a *Newton* hearing (see, e.g., *Gandy* (1989) 11 Cr App R (S) 564, discussed in **D20.27**). In appropriate cases, the Court of Appeal can itself hold a *Newton* hearing (*Guppy* [1994] Crim LR 614).

DISPUTES ABOUT THE FACTS FOLLOWING A VERDICT OF GUILTY

General Principle

D20.30 Where the accused is convicted following a trial, it is for the sentencer to form his own view as to the facts of the offence established by the evidence, and to sentence accordingly. In general, the jury should not be asked to supplement a verdict of guilty by stating the factual basis on which they reached their decision (*Stosiek* (1982) 4 Cr App R (S) 205 and *Solomon* (1984) 6 Cr App R (S) 120).

There is a recognised exception to this principle, relating to a verdict of guilty of manslaughter (see **D19.81**). Although *Cranston* (1993) 14 Cr App R (S) 103 appears to give some encouragement to this becoming a wider practice, Dr. Thomas's commentary on that case at [1992] Crim

LR 831 correctly identifies the inevitable problems with such a course. A number of propositions emerge from the cases.

Court Not Bound to Accept the Version Most Favourable to the Accused

The court is not obliged to accept the version of events most favourable to the defence consistent **D20.31** with the jury's verdict. For example, in *Solomon* (1984) 6 Cr App R (S) 120, the court was held to be entitled, in a case where the appellant T was found not guilty of attempted murder but guilty of causing grievous bodily harm with intent, to sentence on the basis that T had deliberately caused grievous bodily harm with the shotgun, even though he had not intended to kill, despite the accused's evidence being to a contrary effect (see also *McGlade* (1990) 12 Cr App R (S) 105).

Giving the Accused the Benefit of the Doubt

The court should, however, be 'extremely astute' to give to the offender the benefit of any doubt **D20.32** about the facts of the offence (per Watkins LJ in *Stosiek* (1982) 4 Cr App R (S) 205). In *Stosiek*, S was sentenced for assaulting a plain-clothes police officer occasioning him actual bodily harm on the basis that S realised at the time of the assault that his victim was an officer. The Court of Appeal reduced the sentence because the alternative basis that S had over-reacted to what he took to be a minor assault by an ordinary member of the public was a 'reasonable possibility', and should therefore have been accepted in preference to the unfavourable alternative hypothesis.

In *Efionayi* (1995) 16 Cr App R (S) 380, the defendants were convicted of wilful neglect of a child over a 14-day period. The jury were directed that they could convict if satisfied that any neglect had occurred within the period specified in the count. After they convicted, the judge sentenced on the basis that the neglect covered the whole 14 days. The Court of Appeal allowed the appeal against sentence, stating that the judge should have taken the jury's verdict to relate to the shorter period and sentenced accordingly. The Court observed that, to prevent this problem, the indictment could easily have been amended to secure the jury's finding on the point.

The Basis Must be Consistent with the Verdict

The court must not adopt a view of the facts which is adverse to the offender and inconsistent **D20.33** with the jury's verdict, even if that verdict is difficult to understand. Thus, in *Hazelwood* (1984) 6 Cr App R (S) 52, H was acquitted of assault with intent to resist arrest but convicted of common assault in the alternative. His sentence was reduced: 'the court has . . . to have respect for the jury's verdict and must avoid concluding or indeed suspecting that the appellant was in fact resisting arrest' (per Stephen Brown LJ). This is really an aspect of the broader principle (see D20.41) that an offender must be sentenced only for those offences of which he has been found guilty or which he has admitted to the court whether by way of a guilty plea or by asking for them to be taken into consideration, or by otherwise agreeing that the indictment does not represent the full extent of his criminal conduct.

Impact of any Expressed Jury Opinion

If the jury indicate on their own initiative a view of the facts which is relevant to sentence, the **D20.34** judge is not bound by that view when he decides upon sentence. In *Mills* [2004] 1 Cr App R (S) 332, the offender was sentenced on the basis that he knew he was importing drugs with a high value, notwithstanding a note that had been submitted by the jury, stating that their verdict of guilty was based on a view that the offender genuinely believed that the goods he was importing were not drugs but were prohibited. The Court of Appeal agreed that the sentencing judge was not bound by the jury's finding, and dismissed the appeal.

Newton Hearing following a Trial

The court can hold a *Newton* hearing after the jury has returned a verdict of guilty (*Finch* **D20.35** (1993) 14 Cr App R (S) 226). This would be appropriate where an issue material to sentence was not properly canvassed during the trial because it was not relevant to guilt. In *Finch* itself, it was held that a *Newton* hearing should have been held to determine whether or not F had been entrapped, because it could, if true, amount to substantial mitigation, whilst not in law constituting a defence.

Ascertaining Facts by Verdict of Jury

D20.36 In *Newton* (1982) 77 Cr App R 13, the third alternative method of identifying the factual basis for sentence to which Lord Lane referred was to obtain the answer from a jury (see **D20.8**). The method for achieving this is to include a count on the indictment which will indicate how, in the jury's view, the primary offence to which the accused pleads guilty was committed. For example, in *Gandy* (1989) 11 Cr App R (S) 564 (see **D20.27** for the facts), where the issue was whether G, charged with violent disorder, had caused a particular injury, the Court of Appeal felt 'some regret that the Crown had not seen fit in the circumstances of this case to include a specific count against [the appellant] for either wounding with intent under section 18 of the Offences against the Person Act 1861 or alternatively under section 20 of that Act for unlawful wounding' (see also *Efionayi* (1995) 16 Cr App R (S) 380 and **D20.32**).

In *Dowdall* (1992) 13 Cr App R (S) 441, however, the Court of Appeal held that the jury should be used to decide the issue only where the difference in the versions of the facts alleged by the prosecution and the defence reflects different offences. In that case, in which D was charged with theft, the prosecution had amended the indictment to reflect two possible means of appropriation: finding and taking. On appeal, the Court held that the count should not have been split in two as the alternative averments added in each case were immaterial to guilt. The right course where sentence turned on which version was right was for the judge either to adopt D's version or to try the issue himself. Similarly, in *Ali* [2011] 3 All ER 1071, the Court of Appeal deprecated the suggestion of having two legally identical but factually different conspiracy charges on the same indictment as a means of identifying the factual basis for sentence.

ASCERTAINING THE FACTS OF THE OFFENCE WHERE ONE ACCUSED PLEADS GUILTY AND THE OTHER NOT GUILTY

D20.37 The rule that, if there has been a not guilty plea followed by a verdict of guilty, it is for the judge to decide for sentencing purposes how the offence was committed on the basis of the evidence he has heard during the course of the trial, and the rule that, if the accused pleads guilty, the judge must accept the defence version of the facts unless he is satisfied at a *Newton* hearing that the prosecution version is correct, come into conflict with each other when one accused pleads guilty and the co-accused not guilty.

The Court of Appeal has wavered in its approach to the problem. In *Taggart* (1979) 1 Cr App R (S) 144 and *Depledge* (1979) 1 Cr App R (S) 183, it was held that, when sentencing the accused who pleaded guilty, the judge could take into account the evidence he had heard at the co-accused's trial. However, in *Michaels* (1981) 3 Cr App R (S) 188, the judge was criticised for taking a view of the facts adverse to the appellants without having all the witnesses who had testified at the trial of their co-accused recalled for cross-examination. The Court of Appeal has since been afforded the opportunity of resolving the conflict between the earlier authorities on two occasions, namely in *Smith* (1988) 87 Cr App R 393 and *Mahoney* (1993) 14 Cr App R (S) 291.

The Approach in *Smith*

D20.38 In *Smith* (1988) 87 Cr App R 393, *Taggart* and *Depledge* were preferred to *Michaels*. S pleaded guilty to conspiracy to obtain property by deception. At their trial, certain of his co-accused offered the defence that they acted under duress stemming from S. When the time came to sentence, the judge indicated that he had taken a preliminary view that S was the ringleader in the enterprise, albeit that the jury had rejected the co-accused's claim that they had been subjected to duress by him. None of the evidence called at the trial was recalled but S was offered the opportunity to testify in his own defence that he was not the ringleader.

The Court of Appeal upheld the sentence and said that the judge had handled the procedural problem 'impeccably'. His primary task when sentencing was to decide what had been the facts of the conspiracy and, in doing that, he *was* entitled to take into account evidence he had heard at the trial of the co-accused and even witness statements. There was no need to have the witnesses recalled for cross-examination by the accused pleading guilty. To hold otherwise might have led to a situation where the judge felt constrained to sentence one conspirator on a view of the facts which he had rejected when sentencing a co-conspirator. It was, however, necessary for S himself to be offered the opportunity of giving evidence about the extent of his involvement. The judge had done that more than once, and the appeal was accordingly dismissed.

Difficulties with *Smith* The decision in *Smith* (1988) 87 Cr App R 393, while understand- **D20.39** able as a pragmatic solution to a difficult problem, may lead to a sense of unfairness being felt by an offender who is sentenced on a view of the facts which he disputes and which his counsel has not been able to test. In *Smith*, counsel was present in court during the trial of the co- accused, holding a noting brief. Thus, the defence at least knew what had been said against S. However, counsel had no standing to cross-examine the witnesses who impugned his client, and S himself never heard the evidence on the basis of which he was sentenced.

A further anomaly appears when one compares the approach outlined in *Smith* with that adopted in a case such as *Gandy* (1989) 11 Cr App R (S) 564 (see **D20.27**). In *Gandy*, a *Newton* hearing was held in relation to G, who had pleaded guilty, at the end of the trial of others. In that *Newton* hearing the judge was required to follow the rules which would govern the use of evidence in a jury trial. Clearly, there is no equivalent protection for the accused where the *Smith* procedure is concerned. The resultant distinction exacerbates the sense of unfairness already referred to (see also *Winter* [1997] Crim LR 66).

The Approach in *Mahoney*

In *Mahoney* (1993) 14 Cr App R (S) 291, the Court of Appeal favoured the approach suggested **D20.40** in *Michaels*, although neither that case nor *Taggart* nor *Depledge* was referred to. Twenty-one prisoners were indicted in relation to a prison riot. There were two trials, and M pleaded guilty to the lesser offence of violent disorder and was sentenced at the end of the second trial. The Court of Appeal reduced M's sentence, stating (Leonard J at p. 293):

> A further submission is made that in this case what happened was that the learned judge heard the evidence in the first trial and in the second trial which led to acquittal, and that in large part he passed sentence upon the appellant on the basis of that material. The problem about that was that the appellant was neither present at, nor represented at, either of those two trials. It was, in our view, wrong therefore, for the learned judge to pay regard to what he had heard in those trials when he was passing sentence upon the appellant.

> It is quite clear that the judge formed the view that the prosecution had been somewhat supine in accepting the pleas to violent disorder at the threshold of the second trial. That seems to be the point of his observation about his sentencing on the basis of the facts rather than the title of the offence. If there were matters which were in dispute, the learned judge should either have adopted the course which he indicated at the earlier stage and have sentenced on the basis of what the appellant through his counsel was accepting to be the appropriate facts of the case, or alternatively, if there was a need to resolve the dispute, it should have been resolved by means of a *Newton* hearing.

D

Part D Procedure

DUTY TO MAKE SENTENCE CONFORM TO FACTS
CONSISTENT WITH VERDICT

D20.41 The above heading may seem a statement of the obvious. It is, however, a cardinal principle of sentencing, confirmed by *Ralf* (1989) 11 Cr App R (S) 121. It has a number of implications for determining the facts of the offence, which are addressed below.

Respecting the Verdict

D20.42 First, as explained immediately above, the sentencer must respect the jury's verdict when determining the facts of the offence and not pass a sentence appropriate to a more serious charge of which the offender has been acquitted (*Gillespie* [1998] 2 Cr App R (S) 61). Similarly, if the prosecution accept a plea to a lesser offence or to one of several counts, the judge must be careful to sentence for that only and not for the more serious matters left on the file (*Booker* (1982) 4 Cr App R (S) 53). The Court of Appeal emphasised this in *Stubbs* (1988) 89 Cr App R 53, saying 'the court must abide loyally by the plea which had been tendered'.

Not Inflating the Offending

D20.43 Secondly, the judge must not sentence on the basis that the offender has committed other similar offences on other occasions, even if the circumstances of the offence charged or admissions made by the offender when being questioned by the police strongly indicate that it was not a 'one-off' occurrence (*Reeves* (1983) 5 Cr App R (S) 292 and *Ayensu* (1982) 4 Cr App R (S) 248). This is subject to the major exception that the defence may concede that the counts in the indictment are merely samples of a continuing course of conduct or ask for other offences to be taken into consideration (see **D20.52**).

Similarly, the judge must not, under the pretence of determining the facts of the offence at a *Newton* hearing, in effect find the accused guilty of an offence more serious than that with which he is charged (*Courtie* [1984] AC 463; *Druce* (1993) 14 Cr App R (S) 691).

Secondary Offending

D20.44 Difficult problems also arise where the prosecution version of the facts of the offence on the indictment (the primary offence) implies that the accused is guilty of an additional offence (the secondary offence) with which he is not charged.

There are some cases which seem to suggest that, provided the secondary offence is of no greater gravity than the primary offence, the judge may (subject to the need for a *Newton* hearing) sentence on the basis that the latter did indeed involve commission of the former as alleged by the prosecution. This is illustrated in the cases of *Ribas* (1976) 63 Cr App R 147 and *Rubinstein* (1982) 4 Cr App R (S) 202, which concerned, respectively, counts for importing controlled drugs and conspiracy to cultivate controlled drugs. The question arose whether the sentencers were right to reject the defence mitigation that the drugs were intended only for personal consumption, given that there was no count on either indictment for possession with intent to supply or conspiracy to supply. The Court of Appeal in both cases upheld the judges' approach.

These cases may be contrasted with *Lawrence* (1981) 3 Cr App R (S) 49, where L pleaded guilty to cultivating cannabis and the Court of Appeal held that the sentencer had to 'banish from his mind' the possibility that L was growing the cannabis in order to sell it. *Lawrence* was considered and applied in *O'Prey* [1999] 2 Cr App R (S) 83, where the Court of Appeal stressed that it was not permissible for the sentencer to sentence for criminality not reflected in the indictment (for the solution of adding a count to the indictment to reflect the secondary offence, see **D20.36**).

However, in other circumstances the Court of Appeal has positively exhorted sentencers to take into account other offences in this way. For example in *Boswell* [1984] 3 All ER 353, in the course of giving guidelines on sentencing for causing death by reckless driving, Lord Lane CJ said that an aggravating feature conclusive towards a custodial sentence was if the offender's driving had involved other offences. In *Khan* [2010] 1 Cr App R (S) 1, the Court of Appeal concluded that account could be taken of conduct relevant to the offence charged which had been scrutinised at trial.

EVIDENCE OF CHARACTER AND ANTECEDENTS

Requirement for Evidence of Character and Antecedents

After the prosecution summary of the facts, or immediately after the jury's verdict of guilty if **D20.45** it was a not guilty plea, it is the responsibility of the prosecution to adduce evidence about the offender's character and antecedents. The evidence is based upon a copy of written antecedents prepared in advance by the police according to a basic pattern prescribed at CPD II, paras. 10A.2 and 10A.6 to 10A.8 (see Supplement, **PD-18**).

Procedure for Giving Antecedents

Evidence of the offender's antecedents can either be presented through the calling of a police **D20.46** officer to give evidence on oath, or presented by prosecuting counsel, provided that the defence has agreed that the antecedents are not in dispute. Where the evidence is given by an officer, he takes the *voir dire* oath (see **F4.33**) and, in effect, reads from the antecedents and previous convictions forms. The normal rules of evidence are relaxed in that counsel may ask leading questions. Moreover, the antecedents will not necessarily have been prepared by the officer giving the evidence or contain matters within his personal knowledge. In fact, most of the information will have come from the offender himself, either on the occasion of his present arrest or in the course of his previous dealings with the police. Once the officer has completed his evidence in chief, he may be asked further questions by counsel for the defence.

Contents of Antecedents

The prosecution are not necessarily restricted to the basic and essentially uncontroversial form **D20.47** of antecedents specifically sanctioned by CPD II, paras. 10A.2 and 10A.6 to 10A.8. Further guidance has been provided as to what may or may not be included in the presentation of antecedents.

(a) It must not contain allegations of a generalised nature which are prejudicial to the offender and, by their very nature, incapable of proof (*Van Pelz* [1943] KB 157).
(b) In exceptional cases, it may be proper to adduce additional information about the offender's involvement in gangland crime and organised prostitution (*Wilkins* (1977) 66 Cr App R 49) or his position in a chain of criminals supplying drugs (*Robinson* (1969) 53 Cr App R 314). As to whether it is proper to adduce evidence of the offender's criminal associates, in *Bibby* [1972] Crim LR 513 the Court of Appeal ruled that it was unfair but Lord Goddard CJ in *Crabtree* [1952] 2 All ER 974 could see nothing wrong with such evidence provided that the officer could give it from first-hand knowledge.
(c) Such allegations are likely to be challenged by the defence, and, in the event of challenge, it is essential that the prosecution prove what they allege in accordance with the ordinary rules of criminal evidence.
(d) 'Evidence' from the antecedents officer based on hearsay is inadmissible, even if it takes the form of recounting information supplied to him by colleagues (*Wilkins*). This reflects a principle first stated in *Campbell* (1911) 6 Cr App R 131 that, whenever antecedents evidence is challenged by the defence, the onus is on the prosecution to prove their case by strict evidence. If they fail to do so, the judge should ignore the challenged allegation and state that he is ignoring it (see also *Sargeant* (1974) 60 Cr App R 74).

If the prosecution anticipate that the antecedents will be disputed by the defence, it is good practice to give the defence notice of the proposed evidence (see dicta in both *Robinson* and *Wilkins*).

Proof of the Offender's Convictions

D20.48 Like any other disputed part of the antecedents, if the offender disputes a previous conviction alleged against him at the antecedents stage, it must either be proved in accordance with the strict rules of evidence or ignored. For the methods of proving a previous conviction, see F11. If the offender has a long record, it is rare for it to be given in full. The judge will indicate which of the convictions he considers it necessary to read.

Spent Convictions

D20.49 The Rehabilitation of Offenders Act 1974, as applied to criminal proceedings by CPD V, paras. 35A.1 to 35A.3 (see Supplement, **PD-47**), restricts the circumstances in which it is proper to refer to 'spent convictions'.

The scheme of the 1974 Act is that, where an offender is sentenced to 48 months' imprisonment or less for an offence, his conviction becomes spent upon the expiry of the 'rehabilitation period'. That period runs from the date of completion of the sentence and varies in length depending upon the sentence imposed (e.g., 48 months for a prison sentence exceeding six months but not exceeding 30 months; 12 months for a community order). Commission of a further offence during the rehabilitation period for an earlier one usually means that neither conviction becomes spent until the rehabilitation date for the later one. Thus, recidivist offenders rarely enjoy the advantages of their convictions becoming spent. For further details of periods of rehabilitation, see E24; for evidential considerations, see F12.103.

D20.50 **The Proper Approach to Spent Convictions**   The main function of the Rehabilitation of Offenders Act 1974 is to protect a person with spent convictions from having to reveal his record in civil proceedings or when applying for a job. Indeed, s. 7(2) provides that the protection against questions relating to spent convictions afforded by s. 4(1) of the Act does *not* apply to evidence given in criminal proceedings. However, CPD V, paras. 35A.1 to 35A.3, give guidance on how the criminal courts should deal with spent convictions.

Breach of Court Orders

D20.51 If the offender's present conviction apparently puts him in breach of an existing court order such as a suspended sentence (for which see E6.11) or a conditional discharge (for which see E12.5), it will be necessary to put that breach to him. If he denies the breach, the matter must be proved by strict evidence. Upon the breach being admitted or proved, prosecuting counsel should, if possible, be able to give the court details of the offence in respect of which the order breached was made.

SENTENCING THE OFFENDER FOR MATTERS OF WHICH HE HAS NOT BEEN CONVICTED

D20.52 It is a basic principle of sentencing that the offender should be sentenced only for those crimes of which he has been convicted and not for anything else which the court may consider him to have done (see **D20.43**).

There are three identifiable exceptions to this principle where a sentencer may properly be influenced by other offences not officially before the court. These are as follows:

(a) taking into account a less serious secondary offence which has not been charged but the commission of which is implicit in, and represents an aggravating feature of, the more serious primary offence (see *Rubinstein* (1982) 4 Cr App R (S) 202 at **D20.44**);

(b) if the offender expressly asks for the other offences to be taken into consideration (see **D20.53**); and

(c) if the prosecution case is that the offences on the indictment are merely samples of a continuing course of conduct and the defence accept that to be so (see **D20.56**).

Taking Other Offences into Consideration

This is a common practice. It is based upon convention rather than statute or common law. It **D20.53** requires the co-operation of the police, the court and, most importantly, the offender himself. It operates to the benefit of both the police and the offender. The police are enabled to clear up numerous offences which might otherwise remain unsolved. The offender is able to 'wipe the slate completely clean' at a minimal cost in terms of increased sentence. The definitive sentencing guideline, *Offences Taken into Consideration*, applies in relation to all offenders whose cases are dealt with on or after 11 June 2012 (see Supplement, **SG-572**).

Normal Practice   The normal procedure involves the following stages. **D20.54**

(a) The police, having arrested a suspect for a certain offence and obtained admissions from him, will then invite him to tell them about other crimes they think he may have committed.

(b) Depending on the suspect's response, a list is then drawn up of the other offences.

(c) The suspect is charged with a limited number of offences, is prosecuted in the normal way, and pleads guilty.

(d) At some time before his court appearance, the offender is served with the list of the other offences and asked to sign it if he agrees that he committed them. He may, of course, accept some but not all of the offences.

(e) Copies of the list (the 't.i.c.s') are then given to the defence and included in prosecuting counsel's brief.

(f) At a convenient moment during counsel's summary of the facts of the offence to which the offender has pleaded guilty, the court is told that he wishes to have other offences taken into consideration. The court is given the original of the list, signed by the accused.

(g) The offender then confirms with the court that he does admit the offences and wants them taken into consideration.

(h) The court then decides whether to comply with the offender's request. Assuming that it does, prosecuting counsel gives brief details of the offences, and the sentencing process thereafter continues in the normal way. When passing sentence, the judge should state that he has taken so many other offences into consideration.

Although the t.i.c. procedure is geared for offenders expected to plead guilty, there is no objection to adapting it for an accused pleading not guilty. Thus, in anticipation of a guilty verdict, the police might prepare a t.i.c. list and then use an adjournment between conviction and sentence to invite the accused to sign the list.

Assessment of the Procedure   A number of matters arise in relation to the t.i.c. procedure. **D20.55**

(a) Since the offender is never charged with or convicted of the t.i.c.s, the court's powers of sentence are limited to the maximum for the offences on the indictment of which the offender has been convicted, whether by way of guilty plea or jury verdict (hereafter referred to as 'the conviction offences'). This is not a significant restriction since it is rare that a court would wish to impose a sentence nearing the maximum penalties. The exception to this limitation is that the court may order the offender to pay compensation for a matter taken into consideration, and to that extent may sentence directly for the offence (PCC(S)A 2000, s. 130(1)(a)).

(b) An offence should not be taken into consideration if it carries endorsement of the licence and discretionary or obligatory disqualification where the conviction offences are non-endorsable (*Collins* [1947] KB 560 and *Simons* (1953) 37 Cr App R 120). Otherwise, the offender would escape even endorsement whereas, had the t.i.c. offence been prosecuted in the normal way, the court would have been obliged to endorse in the absence of special reasons and might have chosen also to disqualify.

(c) Offences should not be taken into consideration unless the offender clearly requests the sentencer to do so and admits commission of the offences (*Griffiths* (1932) 23 Cr App R 153). In *Walsh* (8 March 1973 unreported), Scarman J stressed the importance of the offender understanding what is being done, admitting the offences and genuinely wanting them taken into consideration.

(d) It is not necessary to read the list out in full. It is sufficient if the judge confirms with the offender that he has signed the list containing a specified number of offences which he agrees that he committed, and confirms that he now wants them borne in mind when sentence is passed for the offences on the indictment. The request to take offences into consideration should come from the offender himself, not counsel (*Mortimer* (10 March 1970 unreported)).

(e) The judge always has a discretion whether or not to comply with a request to take an offence into consideration. He should not take into consideration an offence which the offender is willing to admit if the public interest requires that the offence be dealt with by indictment (*McLean* (1910) 6 Cr App R 26). Further, it would be bad practice to take offences into consideration which are either more serious than or of a completely different type from the conviction offences.

(f) The fact that an offence has been taken into consideration does not entitle the offender to rely on autrefois convict should he subsequently be prosecuted for it (*Nicholson* [1947] 2 All ER 535). However, in the absence of quite exceptional circumstances, the prosecution would not consider instituting proceedings for a matter that they know to have been taken into consideration by a court on a previous occasion.

(g) In passing sentence, the judge may increase the penalty somewhat because of the t.i.c.s. However, the amount of the increase will almost certainly be considerably less severe than it would have been had the offences taken into consideration been separately prosecuted.

As to the difficulties with which a court is presented where the offences to be taken into consideration are more serious than the offence on the indictment, see *Lavery* [2009] 3 All ER 295.

Sample Offences

D20.56   As an alternative to following strictly the procedure for taking other offences into consideration, the prosecution may invite the judge to treat the offences on the indictment of which the accused has been convicted, or to which he has pleaded guilty, as samples of a continuing course of conduct. (See **D11.36** for detail on the implications of sample counts when considering the indictment.)

This is an attractive course where the offender appears to have committed a large number of similar offences over a protracted period. Although there is no reason, in such a case, why a list of t.i.c.s should not be prepared as described in **D20.53**, the list can become inordinately long (see, e.g., *Sequeira* (1982) 4 Cr App R (S) 65, where, in respect of an offender who had claimed social security benefit for four years when ineligible, the t.i.c. procedure resulted in a list of 150 offences). See also CPD VII, Sentencing B (see Supplement, **PD-65**).

D20.57   **Sentencing for Sample Offences Following a Guilty Plea**   It is generally accepted, that where the accused pleads guilty and the defence agree with the prosecution that the offences on the indictment are merely samples, the court may sentence on that basis even though the offender does not formally ask for other offences to be taken into consideration.

Such an approach was approved in *Huchison* [1972] 1 All ER 936 per Phillimore LJ at p. 400C:

> Of course, there are cases where the prosecution puts forward a count as a sample count, and in those cases it is well understood that if that course is taken and the defence are notified, a judge is entitled to deal with the whole matter on the basis that the offence in fact was repeated more than once, or that there were other similar incidents.

If, however, the defence dispute the other occasions on which similar offences were allegedly committed, the judge should sentence the offender only for those occasions which he does admit, whether by way of guilty plea or by asking for a limited number of other occasions to be taken into consideration. This, again, was demonstrated in *Huchison*. The Court of Appeal held that where it became obvious that the defence denied the suggestion that the offence on the indictment was a sample one, the judge's options were either to sentence H strictly for the one act he had admitted, or to adjourn so that counts for the other occasions could be added to the indictment.

Huchison has been followed in *McKenzie* (1984) 6 Cr App R (S) 99 (sentence reduced for seven cheque card offences involving loss to the victims of £640 because the judge had apparently sentenced on the basis denied by the defence that the counts on the indictment were samples of continuing conduct in which £11,000 had been obtained), and *Ralf* (1989) 11 Cr App R (S) 121 (sentence for assault on a child reduced because the judge referred to the appellant having caused various injuries to the child over and above those she actually admitted).

Sentencing for Sample Offences Following a Trial   Where the accused pleads not guilty to **D20.58** the offences on the indictment but is found guilty, more recent authorities support the proposition that the accused should only be sentenced for offences which he has admitted to the court, whether by plea, by asking the court to take them into consideration, or in some other clear fashion (*Perkins* (1994) 15 Cr App R (S) 402).

Hence, the fact that the charges upon which the accused was found guilty were described by the prosecution as 'specimens' does not entitle the judge to sentence him as if he had been found guilty of other offences not included in the indictment. This is the view adopted in *Burfoot* (1990) 12 Cr App R (S) 252. The accused ought not to be deprived of his right to jury trial merely because offences are omitted from the indictment.

In *Clark* [1996] 2 Cr App R (S) 351, the Court of Appeal followed the reasoning in *Burfoot* and in *McKenzie* (1984) 6 Cr App R 99. Their lordships said that the weight of authority supported the proposition that, where an offender was convicted on a single count, the sentencer must not sentence him on the basis that he was guilty of further offences of a similar nature unless the offender admitted that this was so. Such authority as had been cited to the contrary (*Mills* (1979) 68 Cr App R 154 and *Singh* (1981) 3 Cr App R (S) 90) was rejected. The Court suggested that prosecutors should charge sufficient offences fairly to reflect the criminality of the offending.

A different conclusion was reached by the Court of Appeal in *Bradshaw* [1997] 2 Cr App R (S) 128. However, in *Canavan* [1998] 1 Cr App R 79, the Court of Appeal considered the conflict of authority and said that *Clark* was to be preferred to *Bradshaw*. Lord Bingham CJ stated in *Canavan* that a court could not base its decision as to sentence on the commission of offences not forming part of the offence for which the offender was to be sentenced. It is respectfully submitted that the decision in *Canavan*, upholding that in *Clark*, has resolved the question both authoritatively and in accordance with principle.

An alternative to the above procedure is now set out in the DVCVA 2004, s. 17. This allows the prosecution to apply for trial by jury on sample counts, with the judge trying the remaining counts alone (see **D13.80** for details).

REPORTS ON THE ACCUSED

D20.59   After the prosecution summary of the facts and antecedents evidence, the court considers any reports that have been prepared on the offender. These may include pre-sentence reports, medical and psychiatric reports and assessments for suitability for a community sentence. In many cases, it will have been necessary to delay sentencing to allow such reports to be prepared (see D20.62 and D20.111).

Judicial Promise of Non-custodial Sentence on Adjournment for Reports

D20.60   Where the court adjourns for reports in circumstances which justifiably lead the offender to expect that, if the report turns out to be favourable, the sentence will be non-custodial, the court is bound by the implied promise it has given. Consequently, if the report is indeed favourable, a custodial sentence should not be passed, and will be quashed on appeal, however deserved it would otherwise have been.

The principle was first stated in *Gillam* (1980) 2 Cr App R (S) 267. G, a serving prisoner, appeared to be sentenced for offences for which it was likely that he would receive a further prison term. However, the judge adjourned so that G's suitability for community service could be assessed, and ordered that, upon the expiry of his present sentence, G should be released on bail. The Court of Appeal's judgment observed that the main purpose of the adjournment was 'to ascertain whether community service was available for such a person as [G] and whether he was a fit subject to perform that service'. In the event, although G was assessed suitable for community service he received a sentence of imprisonment.

The Court of Appeal allowed the appeal for the following reasons (per Watkins LJ at p. 269, emphasis added):

> ...an important principle of sentencing is involved in this case. All the signs, when the appellant first appeared before the deputy circuit judge, ... pointed to the imposition of an immediate prison sentence. For reasons best known to himself he decided against that course but to request the production of a report with a view to considering whether or not this man should perform community service. There was, therefore, created in the appellant's mind an expectation, not unnaturally, of performing that service if the probation officer and others who were called upon to assist in the production of the report were disposed to recommend such a course to the court. It was recommended. *When a judge in these circumstances purposely postpones sentence so that an alternative to prison can be examined and that alternative is found to be a satisfactory one in all respects the court ought to adopt the alternative.* A feeling of injustice is otherwise aroused.

D20.61   **Application of the *Gillam* principle**   The decision in *Gillam* has been followed in a number of cases since, in which reports prepared on offenders during adjournments were favourable, and the custodial sentences ultimately imposed had to be quashed. These included:

(a) *Ward* (1982) 4 Cr App R (S) 103 (three-week adjournment so that W could stay at a probation hostel with a view to the making of a probation order with a condition of residence at the hostel);

(b) *McMurray* (1987) 9 Cr App R (S) 101 (four-week adjournment so that McM could attend a day assessment centre);

(c) *Wilkinson* (1988) 9 Cr App R (S) 468, the facts of which were similar to *Ward*, where the sentencing judge conceded that the judge who adjourned for social inquiry reports had, by so doing, more or less promised a non-custodial disposition, but said that the offence was so serious that he (the sentencing judge) was not prepared to incur public wrath by such a lenient course — the Court of Appeal held that, in the circumstances, he had no option but to honour the first judge's implied promise, whatever the public reaction.

D20.62   **Adjournment for Reports Not Binding the Judge**   However, there is no rule that adjourning for reports *inevitably* carries the implication that the sentence will be non-custodial if the report so recommends. The application of the *Gillam* principle depends upon 'there having been something in the nature of a promise, express or implied, that if a particular proposal is recommended, it will be adopted' (per Croom-Johnson J in *Moss* (1983) 5 Cr App R (S) 209).

Thus, if the judge makes it clear when adjourning that he is *not* committing himself to a non-custodial disposition even if the report is generally favourable and recommends such a course, the offender can have no complaints about the recommendation being rejected. That was held in *Horton* (1985) 7 Cr App R (S) 299, where the judge, on adjourning for reports, said that he thought that an immediate custodial sentence would be the likely conclusion. One reason for the judge adjourning in *Horton* was the fact that the offender was under 21 (there then being a statutory requirement for a report in respect of such offenders).

The combination of such a statutory requirement and the principle in *Gillam's* case creates a difficulty for the judge. He may well feel it necessary to obtain a report to comply with the statutory provisions. Silence about his ultimate intentions may be construed as an implied promise to pass a non-custodial sentence but equally he ought not to give the impression that a custodial sentence is inevitable. It may be thought that the judge in *Horton* steered a judicious middle course, indicating that custody was probable but leaving open the possibility that something truly exceptional in the reports might persuade him to change his mind. See also *Norton* (1989) 11 Cr App R (S) 143.

In *Renan* (1994) 15 Cr App R (S) 722, the Court of Appeal said that the silence of the judge when adjourning for a pre-sentence report should never be taken as an indication that a non-custodial sentence would be passed, even when the accused was granted bail. It was the duty of counsel in these circumstances to warn the defendant that the grant of bail did not mean that custody would be avoided.

Committal for Sentence   The *Gillam* principle also applies when the Crown Court is dealing **D20.63** with a committal for sentence or appeal from a magistrates' court. In both cases, if the ordering of reports by the court below created a reasonable expectation of a non-custodial sentence, the Crown Court is bound by the lower court's implied promise (*Rennes* (1985) 7 Cr App R (S) 343; *Gutteridge v DPP* (1987) 9 Cr App R (S) 279).

Effect of an Adjournment for Inquiries   It need not be an adjournment for reports which **D20.64** creates the expectation of a non-custodial sentence. In *McMillan* (1988) 10 Cr App R (S) 205, counsel addressed the Crown Court judge on the basis that sentence might be deferred in view of the fact that employment was available to M. The judge adjourned for an hour to allow confirmation that the employment was still open to be obtained. The Court of Appeal held that M's hopes had been raised by the judge's actions, resulting in a sense of grievance when a custodial sentence was nevertheless imposed. See also *Jackson* [1996] Crim LR 355.

Effect of Judicial Indications as to Sentence   Another situation in which the accused might **D20.65** have a legitimate expectation of a non-custodial sentence is where the judge has indicated that he will impose such a sentence. In *Turner* [1970] 2 QB 321 (see **D12.60**) the Court of Appeal held that any judicial indication of sentence must be given on the basis that it is irrespective of plea, and that an indication given on the basis that it applied only if the accused pleaded guilty bound the judge if the accused was convicted following a trial. That approach was considered in *Bird* (1978) 67 Cr App R 203, *Atkinson* [1978] 2 All ER 460 and more recently in *Keily* [1990] Crim LR 204. That approach has now to be read in the light of the guidance as to the correct approach to judicial indications of sentence enunciated in *Goodyear* [2005] 3 All ER 117, and now set out at CPD VII, para. C.1 (see Supplement, PD-66: see also **D12.61**). In particular, unless the same type of sentence would be passed irrespective of plea, only an indication as to sentence following a guilty plea should be given, and while such an indication remains binding both on the judge who gives it and any other judge with subsequent conduct of the case, the indication will cease to have effect if, after a reasonable period, the accused does not plead guilty. It follows that the proper approach is that set out in **D12**.

The fact that a judge gave an indication of sentence before plea will not bind the Court of Appeal if the A-G appeals against the sentence as unduly lenient (*A-G's Ref (No. 40 of 1996)* [1997] 1 Cr App R (S) 357: see **D28.10**).

Pre-sentence Report

D20.66   **Meaning**   The term 'pre-sentence report' is defined by the CJA 2003, s. 158(1), as a report which:

(a) with a view to assisting the court in determining the most suitable method of dealing with an offender, is made or submitted by an appropriate officer [defined in subsection (2)]; and

(b) contains information as to such matters, presented in such manner, as may be prescribed by rules made by the Secretary of State.

The report is usually in writing but, by s. 158(1A) and (1B) (as inserted by the CJIA 2008, s. 12), may be given orally in open court in certain circumstances.

D20.67   **Preparation of the Report**   Pre-sentence reports on adults are compiled by probation officers. In the cases of children under 13, reports are prepared by local authority social workers. In the cases of those aged 13 to 16 inclusive, responsibility is shared between the probation service and social services, precise arrangements varying from area to area (CYPA 1969, ss. 9 and 34(3)).

D20.68   **Circumstances in which a Report Must Be Obtained**   The CJA 2003 places an obligation on the court to obtain a pre-sentence report in two circumstances.

(a) Under s. 156(3)(a), the court 'shall obtain and consider a pre-sentence report' in determining whether a custodial sentence should be imposed. This is not obligatory, however, where the court is of the opinion that it is unnecessary and the accused is over 18. In the case of a juvenile, a pre-sentence report is obligatory unless the court considers it unnecessary (s. 156(4)) and in reaching that decision it has considered any existing pre-sentence report relating to the accused and takes account of the information therein (s. 156(5): see **E1.26**).

(b) Under s. 156(3)(b), the court is required to obtain and consider a pre-sentence report before forming an opinion as to the suitability of an offender for various types of community sentence (for further details, see **E8.7**).

D20.69   **Circumstances in which a Report May Be Prepared**   It is the duty of the probation service or, as the case may be, youth offending team to prepare a report if one is requested by the court. Alternatively, the probation service may take the initiative and prepare a report without being asked to do so if:

(a) it is anticipated that the accused will plead guilty and he is either aged 30 or less;

(b) the conviction will put him in breach of a suspended sentence or other court order; or

(c) he has recently been in contact with the probation service, or medical reports are also being prepared.

If the accused is female and pleading guilty, there will usually be a pre-trial report even if she does not fall within any of the aforementioned categories.

The probation service will be reluctant to prepare a report if the accused indicates a not guilty plea, both because it will be wasted effort in the event of an acquittal and also because one of the main purposes of a report is to assess the offender's attitude to his offence and that cannot be done if he denies having committed it. Where the court desires a report and one has not already been prepared, it will be necessary to adjourn. It may be made a condition of bail that the accused co-operates in the preparation of the report (Bail Act 1976, s. 3(6): see D7.63).

Procedure on Receiving Pre-sentence Report   A copy of the pre-sentence report must be   **D20.70**
given either to the offender or to his legal representative and to the prosecutor. In the case of an unrepresented offender aged under 18, the report need not be given to him personally but must be given to his parent or guardian if present. Where the offender is aged under 18 and disclosure to him or any parent or guardian would be likely to create a risk of significant harm to the offender, the copy provided need not be a complete copy of the report (CJA 2003, s. 159(2) and (3)).

A copy of the report may be withheld from the prosecutor if the prosecutor is not of a pre-scribed description and the court considers it inappropriate for him to be given it (s. 159(4)). The prescribed description of a prosecutor for these purposes is contained in the Pre-Sentence (Prescription of Prosecutors) Order 1998 (SI 1998 No. 191).

The probation officer who prepared the report is not usually present in court when the report is submitted, but the defence may require his attendance if they wish to challenge what has been written. The report is not read out in full in open court, but counsel may refer to passages of it in mitigation if he so desires.

New Disclosures in a Pre-sentence Report   In *Cunnah* [1996] 1 Cr App R (S) 393, the Court   **D20.71**
of Appeal stressed that when fresh and highly relevant material appeared in a pre-sentence report it must be discussed with counsel. This is particularly important, as was the case in *Cunnah,* where pleas had been entered on a limited basis.

Medical and Psychiatric Reports

It is a precondition of the making of a hospital order under the Mental Health Act 1983,   **D20.72**
s. 37(1) (or an interim hospital order under s. 38), that the court be satisfied on the written or oral evidence of two medical practitioners that the offender is suffering from a mental disorder within the meaning of the Act such as to warrant the making of an order (see **E22.1**). Equally, a report from at least one medical practitioner is required before a custodial sentence is passed on a mentally disordered offender (CJA 2003, s. 157).

Where a medical report is to be tendered in evidence under the provisions of the Mental Health Act 1983, s. 54(3)(a) requires that a copy be given to the offender's 'authorised person' (nor-mally his counsel or solicitor). If the accused is unrepresented, the gist of the report should be disclosed to him although he is not entitled to a copy; in the case of a juvenile, the substance of the report must be disclosed to any parent or guardian present in court (s. 54(3)(b)). The medical practitioner who made the report may be required to attend for cross-examination (s. 54(3)(c)).

Power to Remand to Obtain a Report   A magistrates' court has various powers in relation to   **D20.73**
obtaining such a report.

(a) When remanding an accused in custody the court may, in appropriate cases, request the prison medical service to prepare a report.
(b) If a magistrates' court is satisfied that the accused 'did the act or made the omission charged', it has the power to remand him for up to three weeks in custody or four weeks on bail for a medical examination to be made and report prepared (PCC(S)A 2000, s. 11(1) and (2)). A remand under s. 11(1) and (2) may be ordered notwithstanding that the accused is unconvicted. If the accused is granted bail, it *must* be made a condition of his bail that he co-operate in the preparation of the reports (s. 11(3)).

No specific provisions govern the obtaining of medical reports by the Crown Court. If none have been prepared as a result of proceedings in the court below, the court may exercise its inherent power to adjourn so as to give the opportunity for a report to be made.

D20.74   **Remand to Hospital**   The courts have been given the power, under the Mental Health Act 1983, s. 35, to remand an accused or convicted person to hospital, for the preparation of reports on his mental condition (see below). This may arise either on the court's own motion or at the initiative of defence solicitors. There are special requirements for medical evidence in the case of mentally disordered offenders.

Mental Health Act 1983, s. 35

(1) Subject to the provisions of this section, the Crown Court or a magistrates' court may remand an accused person to a hospital specified by the court for a report on his mental condition.

(2) For the purposes of this section an accused person is—

   (a) in relation to the Crown Court, any person who is awaiting trial before the court for an offence punishable with imprisonment or who has been arraigned before the court for such an offence and has not yet been sentenced or otherwise dealt with for the offence on which he has been arraigned;

   (b) in relation to a magistrates' court, any person who has been convicted by the court of an offence punishable on summary conviction with imprisonment and any person charged with such an offence if the court is satisfied that he did the act or made the omission charged or he has consented to the exercise by the court of the powers conferred by this section.

(3) Subject to subsection (4) below, the powers conferred by this section may be exercised if—

   (a) the court is satisfied, on the written or oral evidence of a registered medical practitioner that there is reason to suspect that the accused person is suffering from mental disorder; and

   (b) the court is of the opinion that it would be impracticable for a report on his mental condition to be made if he were remanded on bail;

but those powers shall not be exercised by the Crown Court in respect of a person who has been convicted before the court if the sentence for the offence of which he has been convicted is fixed by law.

(4) The court shall not remand an accused person to a hospital under this section unless satisfied, on the written or oral evidence of the approved clinician who would be responsible for making the report or of some other person representing the managers of the hospital, that arrangements have been made for his admission to that hospital and for his admission to it within the period of seven days beginning with the date of the remand; and if the court is so satisfied it may, pending his admission, give directions for his conveyance to and detention in a place of safety.

Other Reports

D20.75   Before passing a community sentence, the court must normally be satisfied, on the basis of a report from a probation officer (or social worker of a local authority social services department) that the offender is a suitable person to perform work under a community order (CJA 2003, s. 148 and s. 156: see **E8.2** and **E1.27**). An assessment for suitability for a community penalty is usually ordered in conjunction with a pre-sentence report.

Various other types of report may also be before the court. In particular, in the cases of juveniles, detailed reports by social workers may be prepared during the period of a remand in care prior to sentence. There may also be a report from the juvenile's school, dealing with his attendance, behaviour, performance etc. The CJA 2003, s. 161, permits the drug testing of offenders before any community penalty is imposed upon them.

MITIGATION OF SENTENCE

D20.76   The final stage in the sentencing process before the sentence is pronounced is the presentation of defence mitigation. The CrimPR, r. 38.16(6) (see Supplement, **R-315**) provides that before passing sentence the court must give the offender an opportunity to make representations and introduce evidence relevant to sentence and, where the offender is under 18, the court may give his parents, guardian or other supporting adult, if present, such an opportunity as well.

According to Comyn J in *Gross v O'Toole* (1982) 4 Cr App R (S) 283, the presentation of defence mitigation is 'purported to be the province of the most junior of counsel' but 'is in fact amongst the most difficult tasks any barrister can ever face'. The plea in mitigation usually consists solely of a speech by defence counsel. In his discretion, counsel may additionally call witnesses to speak to the offender's generally good character or to explain why, in their view, he acted as he did on the occasion in question.

Legal Representation at the Sentencing Stage

An unrepresented offender may, of course, put forward mitigation on his own behalf. However, **D20.77** if the court is considering a custodial disposition it is generally desirable that the mitigation should be professionally presented. This is especially so if the offender is either young or has not previously been given a custodial sentence.

Statutory Requirement for Representation   Section 83 of the PCC(S)A 2000, which applies **D20.78** to both the Crown Court and magistrates' courts, provides that (a) adult offenders who have not previously been sentenced to imprisonment and (b) offenders aged under 21 whether or not they have previously lost their liberty shall not be sentenced to imprisonment or, as the case may be, one of the custodial sentences available for the offenders aged under 21 unless they are legally represented. The exception to that requirement is where the accused was granted representation under the LASPO 2012, part 1, but it was withdrawn because of his conduct, or where it was withdrawn or refused because he was not financially eligible or where (having been informed of the right to apply for such representation and having the opportunity to do so) he has refused or failed to do so (s. 83(3)). See also the CrimPR, r. 38.2(1)(c) (see Supplement, **R-301**).

Section 83 extends to the passing of suspended sentences of imprisonment, but a suspended sentence which has not taken effect is ignored for purposes of deciding if an offender has previously had a prison sentence (s. 83(5)). Section 83(4) lays down that a person is to be treated as legally represented if he had legal assistance after conviction and before sentence.

Consequences of Breach   Failure to comply has been held to have differing consequences **D20.79** depending upon the court in error. If the failure occurred in the magistrates' court, the Crown Court, on appeal, must pass a sentence which the lower court could *lawfully* have passed, and therefore it must replace the custodial sentence with a non-custodial one (*Birmingham Justices, ex parte Wyatt* [1976] 3 All ER 897). If, however, the Crown Court was the sentencing court and the appeal is to the Court of Appeal, the latter may uphold the sentence below if they consider that it was the right one in all the circumstances (*McGinlay* (1975) 62 Cr App R 156; *Hollywood* (1990) 154 JP 705; *Wilson* [1995] Crim LR 510).

Powers of Criminal Courts (Sentencing) Act 2000, s. 83   **D20.80**

(1) A magistrates' court on summary conviction, or the Crown Court on committal for sentence or on conviction on indictment, shall not pass a sentence of imprisonment on a person who—
   (a) is not legally represented in that court, and
   (b) has not been previously sentenced to that punishment by a court in any part of the United Kingdom,
unless he is a person to whom subsection (3) below applies.
(2) A magistrates' court on summary conviction, or the Crown Court on committal for sentence or on conviction on indictment, shall not—
   (a) pass a sentence of detention under section 90 or 91 below,
   (b) pass a sentence of custody for life under section 93 or 94 below,
   (c) pass a sentence of detention in a young offender institution, or
   (d) make a detention and training order,
on or in respect of a person who is not legally represented in that court unless he is a person to whom subsection (3) below applies.
(3) This subsection applies to a person if either—
   (a) representation was made available to him for the purposes of the proceedings under Part 1 of the Legal Aid, Sentencing and Punishment of Offenders Act 2012 but was withdrawn

because of his conduct or because it appeared that his financial resources were such that he was not eligible for such representation;

(aa) he applied for such representation and the application was refused because it appeared that his financial resources were such that he was not eligible for such representation; or

(b) having been informed of his right to apply for such representation and having had the opportunity to do so, he refused or failed to apply.

(4) For the purposes of this section a person is to be treated as legally represented in a court if, but only if, he has the assistance of counsel or a solicitor to represent him in the proceedings in that court at some time after he is found guilty and before he is sentenced.

(5) For the purposes of subsection (1)(b) above a previous sentence of imprisonment which has been suspended and which has not taken effect under section 119 below . . . shall be disregarded.

(6) In this section 'sentence of imprisonment' does not include a committal for contempt of court or any kindred offence.

Requirement to Prove Mitigation

D20.81   Although normally a plea in mitigation consists solely of a speech by counsel, exceptionally, counsel may also decide to call evidence in order to establish the facts he is advancing in mitigation. Whether to call evidence and, if so, whether to call it before, in the middle or at the end of his speech is a matter for counsel (per Comyn J in *Gross v O'Toole* (1982) 4 Cr App R (S) 283). Having made his choice, he 'cannot . . . easily . . . go back on it' (*Gross v O'Toole* at p. 285).

The requirement to prove mitigation should not be confused with the resolution of a factual dispute as to the circumstances of the offence in a *Newton* hearing (see **D20.8** *et seq.*). The cases appear to draw a distinction between 'true *Newton*' situations, where the dispute is about the immediate circumstances of the offence, and what have been described by Dr. Thomas in his case commentaries in the *Criminal Law Review* as 'reverse *Newton*' situations. In the latter, the dispute is about extraneous matters about which the prosecution witnesses are unlikely to have any knowledge. Since these matters would not have formed part of the prosecution case, or be within the prosecution's knowledge, and may well be within the peculiar knowledge of the accused, the rule is that the onus of satisfying the judge rests on the defence.

D20.82   **Applicable Principles**   The general principles as to proving mitigation were stated by the Divisional Court in *Gross v O'Toole* (1982) 4 Cr App R (S) 283. G's mitigation, in relation to offering his services as a taxi driver, was that he had offered his services gratuitously. This mitigation was rejected by the court. The Divisional Court rejected the argument that the court ought not to have rejected a substantial part of the mitigation without giving an opportunity for affirmative evidence to be called. The decision whether to call evidence or rely solely on his own submissions was one for the defence advocate. Ormrod LJ said:

> . . . if an advocate is going to put forward in mitigation something which is, on the face of it, quite inconsistent with the other information that the magistrates have so far as sentence is concerned, e.g. the list of previous convictions, it really is for the defending advocate to indicate that he wishes to make good the submission . . . he takes the chance himself if he does not offer to call evidence . . .

> I do not think [the magistrates] were obliged to tell the defending advocate that they did not accept his mitigation, because I do not think anyone in court, least of all the defending advocate, could have supposed for a moment that they would accept his mitigation.

Comyn J, in a supplementary judgment, slightly qualified Ormrod LJ's remarks by stating that if, on a significant point on which there is room for some doubt, the magistrates do in fact doubt what the advocate is saying, they ought to tell him before he concludes his mitigation so he can try to remedy it. However, both their lordships clearly accepted the basic premise that it is for the defence to establish its own mitigation to the court's satisfaction, and whether they do that by a speech or evidence or both is essentially a matter for them, not the court.

D20.83   **Court's Discretion to Reject Such Evidence**   It follows from the principles stated in *Gross v O'Toole* (1982) 4 Cr App R (S) 283, that the court may reject matters advanced in mitigation even if the offender or other defence witnesses testify in support of those facts and no contradictory evidence is adduced by the prosecution (*Kerr* (1980) 2 Cr App R (S) 54).

This has been demonstrated in a number of cases.

(a) In *Ogunti* (1987) 9 Cr App R (S) 325, following O's guilty plea to possessing heroin with intent to supply, the court was held to be entitled to disbelieve counsel's mitigation to the effect that O had acted under duress. The Court of Appeal held that it was a 'reverse *Newton*' situation and the onus of proving the facts rested on the defence. The judge was entitled to draw reasonable inferences from the statements of the witnesses (e.g., as to the value of the drugs and the skilful way they were hidden in O's car), and therefore reject the defence account of the nature of O's involvement.

(b) In *Guppy* [1994] Crim LR 614, the Court of Appeal held that, where the offender raised extraneous matters of mitigation, a burden of proof rested upon him to the civil standard. Their lordships did state, however, that in the general run of cases the sentencer would readily accept the accuracy of defence counsel's statements.

(c) In *Broderick* (1993) 15 Cr App R (S) 476, it was held that the mitigation alleging duress went to matters outside the prosecution's knowledge so that *Newton* principles did not apply.

However, in *Tolera* [1999] 1 Cr App R 29, the Court of Appeal held that there was an onus on the prosecution to rebut the appellant's explanation that he had been under a degree of compulsion, falling short of duress, to carry the heroin which was the subject of the charge.

Content of Mitigation

D20.84 Guidance on matters of mitigation within the knowledge of the defence is provided by *Underwood* [2005] 1 Cr App R 178 (see **D20.9** and points (9), (11) and (14)(d) in particular). Guidance has similarly been provided in relation to other aspects of mitigation.

D20.85 **Mitigation Following Conviction** Where counsel delivers a plea in mitigation after a trial and a verdict of guilty, it is generally unrealistic for him to reiterate in strong terms his client's innocence and at the same time ask for leniency. It should not therefore be taken as an admission of guilt on his client's behalf, so as to undermine a subsequent appeal, if he accepts the jury's verdict and mitigates on that basis (*Wu Chun-piu v The Queen* [1996] 1 WLR 1113).

D20.86 **Citing of Authority** The Court of Appeal has encouraged the practice of counsel citing its previous decisions when mitigating at first instance (see *Ozair Ahmed* (1993) 15 Cr App R (S) 286, and *Johnson* [1994] Crim LR 537 and the commentary thereon). Reference should also be made, where appropriate, to Sentencing Council Guidelines. In circumstances where there are applicable guidelines it will be the exception rather than the rule to cite authorities which pre-date them (*Tongue* [2007] EWCA Crim 561).

D20.87 **Judicial Indications as to Sentence** Where the judge is contemplating imposing a sentence which defence counsel might not be anticipating, he is under a duty in fairness to the offender to give notice of what is in his mind so that defence counsel can then make submissions on that issue.

(a) In *Scott* (1989) 11 Cr App R (S) 249, the judge disqualified S for life without giving his counsel the opportunity to make submissions on that aspect of the sentence; the Court of Appeal reduced the disqualification.

(b) In *Woods* (1989) 11 Cr App R (S) 551, the Court of Appeal said that if the judge intended to impose a separate custodial sentence for an offence under the Bail Act 1976 he should invite submissions from counsel (see also *O'Brien* (1995) 16 Cr App R (S) 556).

(c) In *Metcalfe* [2009] 2 Cr App R (S) 568, it was indicated that where the court is minded not to make a direction in respect of time spent on remand in custody, pursuant to the CJA 2003, s. 240, submissions should be invited on behalf of the accused.

Derogatory Assertions in Mitigation

D20.88 There are two restrictions placed on the content of mitigation where that involved derogatory assertions, which in turn impose obligations on prosecution counsel. These are contained in the Bar Standards Board's Handbook Conduct Rules and the CPIA 1996.

D20.89   **Code of Conduct**   Defence counsel 'must not make statements or ask questions merely to insult, humiliate or annoy a witness or any other person' (Conduct Rules, rC7.1).

D20.90   **Criminal Procedure and Investigations Act 1996**   The CPIA 1996, ss. 58 to 61, allow the judge to impose reporting restrictions on false or irrelevant assertions made during a speech in mitigation. There is power to make a full order where there are substantial grounds for believing that the assertion is derogatory to a person's character, and either false or irrelevant to the proceedings. Whilst considering the matter, the court is empowered to make an interim order, provided that there is a real possibility that a full order will be made. The powers do not apply if the assertion has been made earlier in proceedings, e.g., at trial. Full orders may be revoked at any time by the court, and if not revoked will cease to have effect after one year. It is an offence to publish or broadcast in breach of a full or interim order, rendering the offender liable to a fine on summary conviction not exceeding level 5 on the standard scale.

D20.91

Criminal Procedure and Investigations Act 1996, s. 58

(1) This section applies where a person has been convicted of an offence and a speech in mitigation is made by him or on his behalf before—

     (a) a court determining what sentence should be passed on him in respect of the offence, or

     (b) a magistrates' court determining whether he should be committed to the Crown Court for sentence.

(2) This section also applies where a sentence has been passed on a person in respect of an offence and a submission relating to the sentence is made by him or on his behalf before—

     (a) a court hearing an appeal against or reviewing the sentence, or

     (b) a court determining whether to grant leave to appeal against the sentence.

(3) Where it appears to the court that there is a real possibility that an order under subsection (8) will be made in relation to the assertion, the court may make an order under subsection (7) in relation to the assertion.

(4) Where there are substantial grounds for believing—

     (a) that an assertion forming part of the speech or submission is derogatory to a person's character (for instance, because it suggests that his conduct is or has been criminal, immoral or improper), and

     (b) that the assertion is false or that the facts asserted are irrelevant to the sentence,

the court may make an order under subsection (8) in relation to the assertion.

(5) An order under subsection (7) or (8) must not be made in relation to an assertion if it appears to the court that the assertion was previously made—

     (a) at the trial at which the person was convicted of the offence, or

     (b) during any other proceedings relating to the offence.

(6) Section 59 has effect where a court makes an order under subsection (7) or (8).

(7) An order under this subsection—

     (a) may be made at any time before the court has made a determination with regard to sentencing;

     (b) may be revoked at any time by the court;

     (c) subject to paragraph (b), shall cease to have effect when the court makes a determination with regard to sentencing.

(8) An order under this subsection—

     (a) may be made after the court has made a determination with regard to sentencing, but only if it is made as soon as is reasonably practicable after the making of the determination;

     (b) may be revoked at any time by the court;

     (c) subject to paragraph (b), shall cease to have effect at the end of the period of 12 months beginning with the day on which it is made;

     (d) may be made whether or not an order has been made under subsection (7) with regard to the case concerned.

(9) For the purposes of subsections (7) and (8) the court makes a determination with regard to sentencing—

     (a) when it determines what sentence should be passed (where this section applies by virtue of subsection (1)(a));

     (b) when it determines whether the person should be committed to the Crown Court for sentence (where this section applies by virtue of subsection (1)(b));

(c) when it determines what the sentence should be (where this section applies by virtue of
subsection (2)(a));

(d) when it determines whether to grant leave to appeal (where this section applies by virtue
of subsection (2)(b)).

PRONOUNCEMENT OF SENTENCE

After the defence mitigation, the judge pronounces sentence. Normally he does so immediately   **D20.92**
upon the close of defence counsel's address, but there is no objection to his adjourning briefly
to consider his decision.

Giving Reasons

Section 174 of the CJA 2003 (see **E1.23** for the full text) creates an obligation on the judge   **D20.93**
to give reasons for, and explain the effects of, the sentence passed, save where the sentence is
fixed by law or is otherwise mandatory (s. 174(3)). See also the CrimPR, r. 38.16(7)(b) (see
Supplement, **R-315**). The information that the sentencer is required to give the offender is set
out in s. 174(1). In summary:

(a) The court must explain in non-technical terms its reasons for deciding on the sentence
passed, the structure of the sentence, what it requires the offender to do, what will
happen if it is not done, and any power which exists to vary or review the sentence
(s. 174(1)).

(b) In addition, the court must identify any relevant definitive sentencing guidelines and explain
how it has discharged its duty to follow those guidelines; where the court did not follow any
such guidelines because it was of the opinion that it would be contrary to the interests of
justice to do so, it must state why it was of that opinion (s. 174(2)(a) and (aa): see **E1.3**).

(c) If a custodial sentence is being passed, the court must explain why the offence is sufficiently
serious to warrant such a sentence (s. 174(2)(b)).

(d) Any reduction for a guilty plea must be mentioned in the reasons, together with any aggravating or mitigating factors which the court regarded as being of particular importance (s. 174(2)
(d)–(e)).

Statutory obligations to give reasons are also imposed by the following:

(a) PCC(S)A 2000, s. 130(3) — a court with power to make a compensation order in an
offender's case must explain its reasons for not doing so.

(b) RTOA 1988, s. 47(1) — where the court does not order disqualification or endorsement on
account of special reasons or hardship.

Pursuant to the CJA 2003, s. 240, the court is required to identify the allowance that it has
made to the sentence for the time spent by the accused in custody on remand. Where there is
no reliable information as to the relevant period, the court is entitled to adjourn the sentencing
hearing to allow such information to be obtained (*Annesley* [1976] 1 All ER 589). If an error is
made, correction can be made under the PCC(S)A 2000, s. 155 (see **D20.95**).

Court of Appeal Guidance   Even before the introduction of the CJA 2003, s. 174, the Court   **D20.94**
of Appeal had encouraged sentencers to give reasons, and had indicated that that should certainly be done if the sentence might seem unduly severe in the absence of explanation (*Newton*
(1979) 1 Cr App R (S) 252).

It has been held that failure by the sentencing court to give reasons when required to do so
does not invalidate the sentence (*McQueen* (1989) 11 Cr App R (S) 305), although the failure
may no doubt be taken into account by the appellate court should the offender appeal. Where
the sentencer does give reasons and what he says indicates an error of principle in the way he
approached his task, the Court of Appeal sometimes reduces the sentence even though the

penalty was not in itself excessive. A failure by the judge to state expressly that he is taking into account any guilty plea does not oblige the Court of Appeal to interfere with what is otherwise an appropriate sentence (*Wharton* (2001) *The Times*, 27 March 2001).

VARIATION OF SENTENCE

D20.95 By the PCC(S)A 2000, s. 155(1), a sentence imposed or other order made by the Crown Court when dealing with an offender may be varied or rescinded within 56 days of being passed or made. The judge who makes the variation must be the judge who originally passed sentence; if, however, he was accompanied by justices on the first occasion, they need not be present for the variation (s. 155(4) and see *Morrison* [2005] EWCA Crim 2705).

The power to vary may not be exercised in relation to any sentence or order if an appeal against it (or application for leave to appeal against it) has been determined (s. 155(1A)).

Extent of the Power to Vary

D20.96 The power in the PCC(S)A 2000, s. 155, may be used to replace one form of sentence with a quite different form. This was illustrated in:

(a) *Sodhi* (1978) 66 Cr App R 260, where the Crown Court, upon learning that S had been diagnosed by psychiatrists as suffering from paranoid psychosis and was dangerous, substituted for a six-month prison sentence a hospital order plus restriction order without time-limit; and

(b) *Iqbal* (1985) 7 Cr App R (S) 35, in which an unlawful sentence of 30 months' youth custody passed on a juvenile was replaced by an equivalent term of detention under what is now the PCC(S)A 2000, s. 91(3).

The Court of Appeal upheld both variations, saying in *Sodhi* that the word 'varied' in s. 155(1) has a wide meaning and the court's power is therefore not restricted to changing the length of a sentence. The section may also be used to add an extra order to the sentence already passed (*Reilly* [1982] QB 1208).

This provision may be used to make a correction to the period which the court has allowed for time spent in custody on remand pursuant to the CJA 2003, s. 240 (see **D20.93**).

Increasing the Sentence by Variation

D20.97 The obvious use of the power in the PCC(S)A 2000, s. 155, is to correct minor errors made by the court when passing sentence. It is also clear that the power may be used to benefit the offender by reducing his sentence if, on reflection, the judge considers that he was originally too harsh. Recent decisions also show that the power may be used to increase a sentence substantially in appropriate circumstances.

(a) In *Newsome* [1970] 2 QB 711, the sentencer had overlooked legislation then in force which obliged the court to suspend any sentence of imprisonment it passed on the appellants unless the term thereof exceeded six months. The Court of Appeal held that he had jurisdiction to increase the sentence to address this problem because he had always intended to pass a short, immediate custodial sentence, and the increase he ordered was virtually the minimum necessary to achieve his original object.

(b) In *Grice* (1977) 66 Cr App R 167, a more restrictive view was taken of the court's power to vary sentence. The sentencer had varied a suspended sentence to make the term one of immediate imprisonment where G had during the period for variation breached an undertaking given to the court pre-sentence. The Court of Appeal restored the original sentence, holding that only in exceptional circumstances (such as in *Newsome*) should s. 155 be used to make a substantial increase in penalty.

(c) In *Reilly* [1982] QB 1208, the sentencer initially declined to make a criminal bankruptcy order when he passed sentence. He was then persuaded to make the order, and varied the sentence accordingly. Kerr LJ, giving the Court of Appeal's judgment, held that *Grice* had to be considered in the light of *Sodhi* (1978) 66 Cr App R 260 and dicta of the House of Lords in *Menocal* [1980] AC 598, in which Lord Edmund-Davies said that, contrary to *Grice*, the statutory power to vary is not 'restricted to mere slips of the tongue or slips of the memory'. It was therefore clear 'almost beyond argument' that the judge in *Reilly* had jurisdiction to change his mind and add the criminal bankruptcy order.

(d) In *Hart* (1983) 5 Cr App R (S) 25, the sentencer became aware that he had been induced to pass a sentence of six months' imprisonment suspended for 18 months by a false story which H had invented to gain a lenient sentence. Unfortunately, the sentencer did not vary the sentence within the prescribed period. However, Lord Lane CJ said: '...the learned judge was absolutely correct...to take this opportunity to review the sentence, had he done it within the stipulated time. Where someone makes it known after the event that he, as this appellant put it, has "conned the court", in other words told lies to the court and has thereby escaped his just punishment, is one of the plain cases for which [section 155(1)] is designed'.

The Correct Approach to Upward Variation   General guidance was given in *McLean* (1988)   **D20.98**
10 Cr App R (S) 18, where the sentencer had passed a sentence of three years' imprisonment on the strength of M's promise that he had turned over a new leaf, but had varied his sentence to four years' imprisonment when he then promptly escaped from custody. The Court of Appeal held that the judge did have power to increase the sentence.

In the course of argument, McCullough J put to counsel that the proper approach of the court was to ask: (i) Did M's conduct create an exceptional situation? (ii) If it did, was the judge reasonably entitled to take the view that the exceptional situation undermined the whole basis upon which he passed sentence? If the answer to both questions was yes, then the judge could properly exercise the wide discretion given by the statute to increase the sentence. In delivering the court's judgment, Woolf LJ confirmed that this was the correct approach (at p. 22).

The upshot of the above cases seems to be that the Crown Court may increase sentence by a variation under s. 155(1), even to the extent of substituting an immediate custodial sentence for a suspended one, where additional argument put before the court (as in *Reilly* [1982] QB 1208) or information that the original sentence was passed on an incorrect factual basis (as in *Hart* (1983) 5 Cr App R (S) 25 and *McLean*) justifies such variation. It is clear from *McLean* that the principle advanced in *Grice* (1977) 66 Cr App R 167 remains good law: namely, that variations to the detriment of the offender are justified only in exceptional circumstances.

More recently, in *Reynolds* [2008] 4 All ER 369, the Court of Appeal held that the power to vary could be used within the variation period to increase sentence when the impact of chapter 5 of the CJA 2003 (in that the offence was a 'specified' offence, or that a 'specified' offence was a 'serious' offence) had not originally been appreciated. If a sentence is rescinded in such circumstances, the court may then adjourn sentence, e.g., to allow a report to be prepared to address the question of dangerousness, even if that results in sentencing finally occurring after the end of the period.

Procedure for Variation of Sentence

Presence of the Offender   In both *May* (1981) 3 Cr App R (S) 165 and *Cleere* (1983) 5 Cr App   **D20.99**
R (S) 465, it was held that the offender has a right to be present when his sentence is varied, and variations made in the absence of the respective appellants and without their having the benefit of legal representation were quashed.

This was slightly qualified in *Shacklady* (1987) 9 Cr App R (S) 258, where Rose J, quoting a sentence from Watkins LJ's judgment in *Cleere*, stated the principle to be that 'the defendant or his counsel must have an opportunity to address the court' (p. 261). Accordingly, a variation made in the absence of the offender but with counsel in attendance on his behalf was upheld.

In *McLean* (1988) 10 Cr App R (S) 18 (see **D20.98**), M's sentence was increased from three to four years after his escape from custody and hence in his absence (voluntary on his part, unavoidable from the court's point of view). The judge heard representations from M's counsel on the occasion when he varied sentence. With the obvious exception of such circumstances, it is submitted that a genuine increase by variation should not be made unless both the offender and counsel are present.

D20.100 **Hearing in Open Court**   In *Dowling* (1988) 88 Cr App R 88, it was stressed that any variation of sentence should take place in open court. In that case, the judge purported to vary the sentence, as a result of a query from his clerk, without returning to court, or discussing the matter with counsel. The Court of Appeal emphasised that where the 'judge is minded to vary a sentence he has passed or even to clarify a doubt or ambiguity as to the effect of it, he should do so in open court'. Only in this manner would all those concerned hear the final decision from the judge directly, and in such a way that a shorthand note would be available. The court may rescind a sentence on one occasion, and then resentence at a later date, provided that the whole process is completed within the variation period (*Dunham* [1996] 1 Cr App R (S) 438).

Variations outside the 56-day Period

D20.101 A sentence may not be varied outside the period specified in the PCC(S)A 2000, s. 155(1) (*Menocal* [1980] AC 598, where the House of Lords quashed an order which was not added to the original sentence until after the expiry of the time for variation). *Menocal* was followed in *Hart* (1983) 5 Cr App R (S) 25 and *Hudson* [2011] 2 Cr App R (S) 666. The period cannot be extended by rescinding the original sentence within the time-limit, and then not sentencing until after the time-limit has expired (*Stillwell* (1991) 94 Cr App R 65).

D20.102 **Correcting Rather than Varying**   A distinction is drawn, however, between varying the sentence by changing its length, adding an order to it or replacing it with a different type of disposition and merely correcting a technical defect in the sentence as originally announced. For example, in *Saville* [1981] QB 12, the Court of Appeal upheld the correction of the terms of a criminal bankruptcy order because the Crown Court has an inherent jurisdiction, apart from the statutory jurisdiction, to remedy mistakes in its record and the correction or variation was of such a minor nature that it was appropriate to exercise the inherent jurisdiction. Correcting technical defects does not include varying the reference to the legislation under which a confiscation order has been made (*Bukhari* [2009] 2 Cr App R (S) 113).

DEFERRING SENTENCE

Purpose of Deferring Sentence

D20.103 Under the PCC(S)A 2000, ss. 1 to 1D (set out at **D20.110**), the purpose for which sentence may be deferred is to enable the court, when it does deal with the offender, to have regard to:

(a) his conduct after conviction (including, where appropriate, the making by him of reparation for his offence), or

(b) any change in his circumstances (s. 1(1)).

The court must fix the date to which sentence is deferred, the maximum period allowed being six months (s. 1(4)). Subject to an exception mentioned below, sentence may be deferred only once (s. 1(4)).

Deferment requires the offender's consent and the court must be satisfied that exercise of the power would be in the interests of justice (s. 1(3)). The court dealing with the offender after the period of deferment may deal with him in any way the deferring court could have done (s. 1D(2)(a)). By s. 1D(2)(b), that includes, where sentence was deferred by a magistrates' court, committing the offender for sentence under s. 3. Where a magistrates' court defers sentence and then commits under s. 3, the Crown Court may also defer sentence, that being the exception to the rule that sentence may be deferred only once (s. 1D(3)).

Where there is a requirement to make a referral order on a young offender (see **E10.5**), the court may not defer passing sentence on him.

Requirements that May be Imposed The most important requirement imposed on an offender when his sentence is deferred is to return on the specified day. Upon deferring sentence, the court does not bail the offender but, if he should fail to appear on the deferment date, a warrant may be issued for his arrest (PCC(S)A 2000, s. 1(7)). **D20.104**

The requirements imposed by the court when deferring sentence may include reparative and other activity to be undertaken during the period of deferment. When the court comes to impose sentence at the end of the period of deferment, it is able to have regard to the conduct of the offender and any change in his circumstances. In this context, 'conduct' includes reference to how well the offender has complied with any requirements imposed by the court. The CJA 2003, s. 204(3), allows a curfew to be imposed as a condition of a deferred sentence; the court may include a further curfew as a condition of a community order imposed at the conclusion of the deferred period, although it ought then to take the earlier period of curfew into account (*Ali* (2012) 176 JP 1).

The court may appoint a supervisor to monitor the offender's compliance with the requirements imposed, who may be a probation officer. Those requirements may include one as to residence (s. 1A). If the court is satisfied that the offender has failed to comply with one or more requirements, it may deal with him before the end of the period of deferment (s. 1B). He may in any event be dealt with before the end of the period of deferment if he commits another offence (s. 1C).

Challenge to a Deferred Sentence A deferred sentence may, in appropriate circumstances, be referred by the A-G to the Court of Appeal for review (see **D28.11**), where he considers that it constitutes an unduly lenient sentence (*A-G's Ref (No. 22 of 1992)* (1993) 97 Cr App R 275; *A-G's Ref (No. 101 of 2006)* [2006] EWCA Crim 3335). **D20.105**

Appropriate Circumstances for Deferring

In *George* [1984] 3 All ER 13, Lord Lane CJ gave some indication of when it may be appropriate to defer sentence. He referred especially to cases where the improvement in the offender's conduct or steps which the court wants him to take are not sufficiently specific to be made the subject of a requirement in a probation order, but nonetheless the court wishes to see what progress he makes before sentencing (p. 1085G–H). However, deferment should not be used either as an easy option when the sentencer's intentions could in fact be achieved by other means (*George*, at p. 1086A) or where it imposes such a restriction on the offender's freedom of action that another order was more appropriate (*Skelton* [1983] Crim LR 686). **D20.106**

Recommended Procedure when Deferring Sentence

Lord Lane CJ in his judgment in *George* [1984] 3 All ER 13, gave guidance on the procedure which should be adopted when deferring sentence. The chief points to be noted are: **D20.107**

(a) When deferring sentence the court must make it clear to the offender the particular purposes under the PCC(S)A 2000, s. 1(1), that it has in mind, and the conduct that is expected of him during deferment. The court should also make it clear that it is deferring sentence as opposed to merely adjourning (*Fairhead* [1975] 2 All ER 737).

(b) A careful note should be made by the court of what the offender is told. Ideally, the offender himself should also be given a written note of the conduct expected of him.

(c) The court eventually passing sentence should:

(i) ascertain the purpose of the deferment and any requirement as to conduct then imposed;

(ii) determine whether the offender has substantially conformed (or attempted to conform) with the proper expectations of the deferring court.

(d) In order to decide whether the offender has lived up to expectations, the sentencing court will almost certainly require an up-to-date pre-sentence report. To avoid unnecessary delay, it may be appropriate to order the report when sentence is deferred. If the offender has conformed with the sentencing court's expectations, he may expect a non-custodial sentence; if he has not, the sentencing court should state with precision in what respects he has failed. Failure to do so may lead to any custodial sentence being quashed because of the appearance given that the sentencing court merely disagrees with the original decision to defer as opposed to being genuinely disappointed in the offender's conduct (*Glossop* (1981) 3 Cr App R (S) 347).

The above procedure is recommended in part because the judge who passes sentence need not necessarily be the judge who deferred sentence, and it is therefore necessary to ensure as far as possible that the former knows how the latter was thinking. However, whenever possible, both the judge who deferred sentence and counsel who then represented the offender should make themselves available for the eventual sentencing (*Gurney* [1974] Crim LR 472 and *Ryan* [1976] Crim LR 508).

(e) Every effort should be made to sentence the offender on the date to which sentence was deferred (per Lord Lane CJ in *Anderson* (1983) 78 Cr App R 251). In exceptional circumstances, however, the court may adjourn to a later date, even if that is more than six months after the original deferment (*Ingle* [1974] 3 All ER 811). In *Anderson* the Court of Appeal held that the Crown Court had not been deprived of its jurisdiction to sentence by reason of the delay, but the sentence eventually passed should reflect how stale the offence had become.

Custodial Sentence after Deferment

D20.108 As indicated by Lord Lane CJ in *George* [1984] 3 All ER 13, the tacit understanding between the court and the offender when sentence is deferred is that, if he substantially conforms (or, at least, tries to conform) with the deferring court's proper expectations, the sentencing court will pass a non-custodial sentence. It follows that, although conviction for further offences during a deferment period will almost certainly lead to a custodial sentence (see, e.g., *Hope* (1980) 2 Cr App R (S) 6), merely staying out of trouble does not guarantee the opposite. For example, in *Smith* (1976) 64 Cr App R 116, where sentence was deferred to see if S could (a) work regularly and (b) reduce his alcohol consumption, the Court of Appeal upheld an eventual custodial sentence because he had done neither of those things, even though he had avoided further offending.

There are qualifications to this approach:

(a) where the offender falls short of the deferring court's expectations in only a minor way, this should not be used as a justification for a custodial sentence (*Smith* (1979) 1 Cr App R (S) 339);

(b) offences which were allegedly committed during the period of deferment but which are unresolved by the time the period expires should not influence the sentencer in any way unless and until the offender has been convicted of the later alleged offences (*Aquilina* [1990] Crim LR 134).

Sentencing before the End of the Deferment Period

D20.109 Once sentence has been deferred, the court may not proceed to sentence until the deferment period has expired, unless either it revokes the order for deferment within 56 days by virtue of the PCC(S)A 2000, s. 155(1) (see **D20.95**), or s. 1C applies (*McQuaide* (1974) 60 Cr App R 239).

The effect of the latter provisions is that, if an offender is convicted of an offence (the subsequent offence) during a deferment period, the court passing sentence on him for the subsequent offence may also sentence for the deferment offence (s. 1C(3)). This does not apply if sentence was deferred by the Crown Court and the sentencing court for the subsequent offence is a magistrates' court (proviso (a) to s. 1C(3)).

In the converse case of the Crown Court sentencing for the subsequent offence, sentence having been deferred by a magistrates' court, the Crown Court's powers in respect of the deferment offence are limited to those of a magistrates' court (proviso (b)). Apart from the possibility of the court that sentences an offender for a subsequent offence also sentencing him for the deferment offence, conviction for a subsequent offence during a deferment period always entitles the *deferring* court to sentence forthwith for the deferment offence, even though the deferment period has not expired (s. 1C(1)).

Powers of Criminal Courts (Sentencing) Act 2000, ss. 1 to 1D   D20.110

1.—(1) The Crown Court or a magistrates' court may defer passing sentence on an offender for the purpose of enabling the court, or any other court to which it falls to deal with him, to have regard in dealing with him to—

    (a) his conduct after conviction (including, where appropriate, the making by him of reparation for his offence); or

    (b) any change in his circumstances;

but this is subject to subsections (3) and (4) below.

(2) Without prejudice to the generality of subsection (1) above, the matters to which the court to which it falls to deal with the offender may have regard by virtue of paragraph (a) of that subsection include the extent to which the offender has complied with any requirements imposed under subsection (3)(b) below.

(3) The power conferred by subsection (1) above shall be exercisable only if—

    (a) the offender consents;

    (b) the offender undertakes to comply with any requirements as to his conduct during the period of the deferment that the court considers it appropriate to impose; and

    (c) the court is satisfied, having regard to the nature of the offence and the character and circumstances of the offender, that it would be in the interests of justice to exercise the power.

(4) Any deferment under this section shall be until such date as may be specified by the court, not being more than six months after the date on which the deferment is announced by the court; and, subject to section 1D(3) below, where the passing of sentence has been deferred under this section it shall not be further so deferred.

(5) Where a court has under this section deferred passing sentence on an offender, it shall forthwith give a copy of the order deferring the passing of sentence and setting out any requirements imposed under subsection (3)(b) above—

    (a) to the offender,

    (b) where an officer of a local probation board has been appointed to act as a supervisor in relation to him, to that board,

    (ba) where an officer of a provider of probation services has been appointed to act as a supervisor in relation to him, to that provider, and

    (c) where a person has been appointed under section 1A(2)(b) below to act as a supervisor in relation to him, to that person.

(6) Notwithstanding any enactment, a court which under this section defers passing sentence on an offender shall not on the same occasion remand him.

(7) Where—

    (a) a court which under this section has deferred passing sentence on an offender proposes to deal with him on the date originally specified by the court, or

    (b) the offender does not appear on the day so specified,

the court may issue a summons requiring him to appear before the court at a time and place specified in the summons, or may issue a warrant to arrest him and bring him before the court at a time and place specified in the warrant.

(8) Nothing in this section or sections 1A to 1D below shall affect—

    (a) the power of the Crown Court to bind over an offender to come up for judgment when called upon; or

(b) the power of any court to defer passing sentence for any purpose for which it may lawfully do so apart from this section.

1A.—(1) Without prejudice to the generality of paragraph (b) of section 1(3) above, the requirements that may be imposed by virtue of that paragraph include requirements as to the residence of the offender during the whole or any part of the period of deferment.

(2) Where an offender has undertaken to comply with any requirements imposed under section 1(3)(b) above the court may appoint—

(a) an officer of a local probation board or an officer of a provider of probation services, or

(b) any other person whom the court thinks appropriate,

to act as a supervisor in relation to him.

(3) A person shall not be appointed under subsection (2)(b) above without his consent.

(4) It shall be the duty of a supervisor appointed under subsection (2) above—

(a) to monitor the offender's compliance with the requirements; and

(b) to provide the court to which it falls to deal with the offender in respect of the offence in question with such information as the court may require relating to the offender's compliance with the requirements.

1B.—(1) A court which under section 1 above has deferred passing sentence on an offender may deal with him before the end of the period of deferment if—

(a) he appears or is brought before the court under subsection (3) below; and

(b) the court is satisfied that he has failed to comply with one or more requirements imposed under section 1(3)(b) above in connection with the deferment.

(2) Subsection (3) below applies where—

(a) a court has under section 1 above deferred passing sentence on an offender;

(b) the offender undertook to comply with one or more requirements imposed under section 1(3)(b) above in connection with the deferment; and

(c) a person appointed under section 1A(2) above to act as a supervisor in relation to the offender has reported to the court that the offender has failed to comply with one or more of those requirements.

(3) Where this subsection applies, the court may issue—

(a) a summons requiring the offender to appear before the court at a time and place specified in the summons; or

(b) a warrant to arrest him and bring him before the court at a time and place specified in the warrant.

1C.—(1) A court which under section 1 above has deferred passing sentence on an offender may deal with him before the end of the period of deferment if during that period he is convicted in Great Britain of any offence.

(2) Subsection (3) below applies where a court has under section 1 above deferred passing sentence on an offender in respect of one or more offences and during the period of deferment the offender is convicted in England and Wales of any offence ('the later offence').

(3) Where this subsection applies, then (without prejudice to subsection (1) above and whether or not the offender is sentenced for the later offence during the period of deferment), the court which passes sentence on him for the later offence may also, if this has not already been done, deal with him for the offence or offences for which passing of sentence has been deferred, except that—

(a) the power conferred by this subsection shall not be exercised by a magistrates' court if the court which deferred passing sentence was the Crown Court; and

(b) the Crown Court, in exercising that power in a case in which the court which deferred passing sentence was a magistrates' court, shall not pass any sentence which could not have been passed by a magistrates' court in exercising that power.

(4) Where a court which under section 1 above has deferred passing sentence on an offender proposes to deal with him by virtue of subsection (1) above before the end of the period of deferment, the court may issue—

(a) a summons requiring him to appear before the court at a time and place specified in the summons; or

(b) a warrant to arrest him and bring him before the court at a time and place specified in the warrant.

1D.—(1) In deferring the passing of sentence under section 1 above a magistrates' court shall be regarded as exercising the power of adjourning the trial conferred by section 10(1) of the Magistrates' Courts Act 1980, and accordingly sections 11(1) and 13(1) to (3A) and (5) of that Act (non-appearance of the accused) apply (without prejudice to section 1(7) above) if the offender does not appear on the date specified under section 1(4) above.

(2) Where the passing of sentence on an offender has been deferred by a court ('the original court') under section 1 above, the power of that court under that section to deal with the offender at the end of the period of deferment and any power of that court under section 1B(1) or 1C(1) above, or of any court under section 1C(3) above, to deal with the offender—

    (a) is power to deal with him, in respect of the offence for which passing of sentence has been deferred, in any way in which the original court could have dealt with him if it had not deferred passing sentence; and

    (b) without prejudice to the generality of paragraph (a) above, in the case of a magistrates' court, includes the power conferred by section 3 below to commit him to the Crown Court for sentence.

(3) Where—

    (a) the passing of sentence on an offender in respect of one or more offences has been deferred under section 1 above, and

    (b) a magistrates' court deals with him in respect of the offence or any of the offences by committing him to the Crown Court under section 3 below,

the power of the Crown Court to deal with him includes the same power to defer passing sentence on him as if he had just been convicted of the offence or offences on indictment before the court.

(4) Subsection (5) below applies where—

    (a) the passing of sentence on an offender in respect of one or more offences has been deferred under section 1 above;

    (b) it falls to a magistrates' court to determine a relevant matter; and

    (c) a justice of the peace is satisfied—

        (i) that a person appointed under section 1A(2)(b) above to act as a supervisor in relation to the offender is likely to be able to give evidence that may assist the court in determining that matter; and

        (ii) that that person will not voluntarily attend as a witness.

(5) The justice may issue a summons directed to that person requiring him to attend before the court at the time and place appointed in the summons to give evidence.

(6) For the purposes of subsection (4) above a court determines a relevant matter if it—

    (a) deals with the offender in respect of the offence, or any of the offences, for which the passing of sentence has been deferred; or

    (b) determines, for the purposes of section 1B(1)(b) above, whether the offender has failed to comply with any requirements imposed under section 1(3)(b) above.

ADJOURNMENTS

Apart from its power under the PCC(S)A 2000, s. 1, to defer passing sentence for up to six **D20.111** months, the Crown Court has inherent jurisdiction at common law to adjourn before sentencing an offender. In other words, it need not sentence on the occasion on which an offender pleads guilty or is found guilty.

Although there are no express limitations on the grounds for adjourning or the length of the adjournment, by analogy with the decision in *Arthur v Stringer* (1986) 84 Cr App R 361, it would be improper to adjourn solely because the offender is slightly too young for the form of sentence the court considers desirable in his case and adjourning will allow him to attain the minimum age necessary. The discretion vested in the court to adjourn has to be exercised judicially. It cannot be said to have been exercised judicially if the only reason for exercising it was to ensure that the offender had reached the age of 21 by the time he was sentenced, thus enabling the court to pass a sentence of imprisonment.

During the period of the adjournment, the offender may be remanded in custody or granted bail at the court's discretion (see the Senior Courts Act 1981, s. 81(1)(c), for the power to grant bail).

Maximum Length

D20.112   As to the maximum period for an adjournment, analogous guidance is provided by the MCA 1980, s. 10(3), which restricts an adjournment after conviction to a maximum of three weeks at a time if the offender is remanded in custody, four weeks if he is granted bail. Although the subsection does not directly apply to the Crown Court when dealing with an offender convicted on indictment, it is an indication of the kind of periods Parliament considers appropriate for post-conviction adjournments, at least where the ultimate sentence is likely to be relatively short.

Where the Crown Court is dealing with an offender who has appealed against his conviction and/or sentence in the magistrates' court, the higher court is directly bound by the provisions of s. 10(3) since the appeal takes the form of a rehearing, and the Crown Court's powers are therefore no greater than those of the magistrates (*Arthur v Stringer* (1986) 84 Cr App R 361).

Binding Over

D20.113   A final power possessed by the Crown Court, analogous to adjourning, is to bind the offender over to come up for judgment if called upon to do so. Although in form a postponement of sentence, this is used more as a means of avoiding sentencing an offender if, exceptionally, the court does not want to impose a penalty but the ordinary alternatives to a penalty (such as a conditional discharge or a probation order) are inappropriate to meet the court's concerns in the particular circumstances of the case. The understanding is that, if the offender does not reoffend and complies with any conditions the court imposes when binding him over, he will not in fact be required to return before the court.

Section D21   Summary Trial: General and Preliminary Matters

INTRODUCTION

This section and the two sections which follow examine the procedure for summary trial, concentrating on those respects in which it differs from trial on indictment. It should be read in conjunction with **D5** and **D6** which deal with the proceedings in a magistrates' court prior to the commencement of trial (or the sending of the case to the Crown Court). **D21.1**

JURISDICTION TO TRY CASES SUMMARILY

Basis of Jurisdiction

The jurisdiction of a magistrates' court to try cases summarily is set out in the MCA 1980, s. 2. **D21.2**
See also **D3.23** and **D3.24**. Under s. 2:

(a) A magistrates' court has jurisdiction to try any summary offence (s. 2(1)).

(b) A magistrates' court has jurisdiction to try an either-way offence provided only that the procedure for determining mode of trial contained in the MCA 1980, ss. 18 to 22A, has resulted in a decision for summary trial (s. 2(3)).

Magistrates' Courts Act 1980, s. 2 **D21.3**

(1) A magistrates' court has jurisdiction to try any summary offence.

(2) A magistrates' court has jurisdiction under sections 51 and 51A of the Crime and Disorder Act 1998 in respect of any offence committed by a person who appears or is brought before the court.

(3) Subject to—
   (a) sections 18 to 22A, and
   (b) any other enactment (wherever contained) relating to the mode of trial of offences triable either way,
a magistrates' court has jurisdiction to try summarily any offence which is triable either way.

Determining the Place of the Trial

The Courts Act 2003, s. 30(3), empowers the Lord Chancellor (with the concurrence of the **D21.4**
Lord Chief Justice) to give directions as to the distribution and transfer of magistrates' courts business. Where a person is charged with an offence, the prosecution decide which court that person should appear before and this decision will have to take account of any such directions (s. 30(4)).

The approach usually adopted is that a case should normally be heard either at a magistrates' court in the local justice area where the offence is alleged to have been committed, or where the person charged with the offence resides.

Transfer of Cases between Magistrates' Courts

D21.5   It sometimes proves necessary, or desirable, to transfer cases from one magistrates' court to another. The MCA 1980, s. 27A, contains a general power to effect such a transfer at any stage in the proceedings. This power may be exercised by the court of its own motion, or on the application of one of the parties to the case. Where the court is minded to transfer a case, it should invite representations from all parties before doing so. There is to be no appeal from a decision on transfer.

> **Magistrates' Courts Act 1980, s. 27A**
>
> (1) Where a person appears or is brought before a magistrates' court—
>   (a) to be tried by the court for an offence, ...
>   the court may transfer the matter to another magistrates' court.
> (2) The court may transfer the matter before or after beginning the trial. ...
> (3) But if the court transfers the matter after it has begun to hear the evidence and the parties, the court to which the matter is transferred must begin hearing the evidence and the parties again.
> (4) The power of the court under this section to transfer any matter must be exercised in accordance with any directions given under section 30(3) of the Courts Act 2003.

D21.6   In addition to the general power conferred by s. 27A, there are specific statutory provisions relevant to sentencing hearings and remand hearings:

(a) By virtue of the PCC(S)A 2000, s. 10(1), where a magistrates' court has convicted an offender of an offence (the 'instant offence') and is then informed that he also stands convicted in another magistrates' court of another offence for which he is yet to be sentenced, it may remit him to that other court to be dealt with for the instant offence. This power applies only if (i) the offender is aged 18 or over, (ii) the other court consents to the case being remitted, and (iii) the instant offence is either imprisonable or punishable with disqualification from driving (s. 10(1) and (2)). The provisions of the MCA 1980, s. 128 (power to remand in custody or on bail and maximum period for remands in custody), apply where a case is remitted to another court just as they would apply if the court were adjourning with a view to the offender being brought back before itself (PCC(S)A 2000, s. 10(3)(a)). Once the case has been remitted, the other court may deal with the case as if all the proceedings before the convicting court had in fact taken place before itself (s. 10(3)(b)). This includes the power to remit the offender to a third magistrates' court (s. 10(4)) or even to remit him back to the original convicting court (s. 10(5)). It will be noted that s. 10 applies only if the person to be remitted has already been convicted (though not sentenced or committed for sentence) in *both* the courts concerned.

(b) To avoid inconveniently long journeys from prison to court for remand hearings, a magistrates' court may order that, for any subsequent remands, the accused is to be brought before an alternate magistrates' court nearer to the prison where he is on remand (s. 130(1)). While the order under s. 130(1) is in force, the alternate court exercises all the powers relating to any further remand (whether in custody or on bail) and the granting of legal aid which would otherwise fall to be exercised by the original court (s. 130(3)). The order ceases to have force when either the alternate court — upon making a further remand in custody — orders that the accused be brought before the original court at the end of the remand, or it grants the accused bail (s. 130(4)). The alternate court would no doubt remand the accused to be brought back before the original court on the occasion of the last remand before it is anticipated that a substantive step will be taken in the proceedings (e.g., it will ensure that the accused appears in the original court for the commencement of a summary trial or the determination of mode of trial).

THE INFORMATION OR WRITTEN CHARGE

Contents of the Information or Written Charge

D21.7   D5.1 *et seq.* set out the various ways of commencing criminal proceedings, including the written charge and requisition (for public prosecutions) and the information and summons (private prosecutions); **D5.12** *et seq.* discuss the content of the written charge or information.

Part 7 of the CrimPR (see Supplement, **R-91** *et seq.*) deals with the procedure on starting a prosecution in a magistrates' court.

Rule against Duplicity

An information or written charge should allege only one offence. However, under the CrimPR, **D21.8** r. 7.2(4), a single document may contain more than one information or more than one written charge. This means that an accused who appears before a magistrates' court may face more than one charge.

In *Carrington Carr v Leicestershire County Council* (1994) 158 JP 570, it was said that there are five situations where informations (or written charges) may be duplicitous:

(a) where two or more discrete offences are charged conjunctively in one information (for example, where a single information alleges both dangerous driving and careless driving);
(b) where two offences are charged disjunctively or in the alternative in one information (for example, where a single information alleges dangerous driving or careless driving);
(c) where an offence was capable of being committed in more ways than one (for example, driving under the influence of drink or drugs) and both ways are referred to in one information;
(d) where a single offence was charged in respect of an activity but the activity involved more than one act; and
(e) where a single activity was charged but a number of particulars are relied on by the prosecution to prove the offence (for example, a single act of obtaining by deception where the deception involved several misrepresentations).

In the latter two situations, it is submitted that a single information or written charge may well be appropriate. However, if the accused wishes to admit some, but not all, of the allegations (or wishes to raise different defences to different allegations), separate informations or charges will be necessary.

The rule against duplicity was considered in *Euro Foods Group v Cumbria County Council* (2013) 177 JP 614. However, it is respectfully submitted that the case should not be regarded as authoritative as the court mistakenly applied r. 12 of the Magistrates' Courts Rules 1981, rather than the CrimPR, r. 7(3).

See also **D11.45** *et seq.* for discussion of the rule against duplicity in the context of indictments.

Whether One or More than One Act is Being Alleged Under the CrimPR, r. 7.3(2), more **D21.9** than one incident of the commission of the offence may be included in the allegation if those incidents, taken together, amount to a course of conduct (having regard to the time, place or purpose of commission). This mirrors r. 14.2(2), which applies to indictments. Whether more than one offence is being alleged in a single charge depends on the facts of the particular case. There are many decided cases on the point, of which the following are merely examples.

(a) *Anderton v Cooper* (1980) 72 Cr App R 232: the charge concerned alleged management of a brothel between specified dates. This was held not to amount to duplicity, as the charge was alleging a single continuing offence.
(b) *Cullen v Jardine* [1985] Crim LR 668: a single charge alleging the unlawful felling of 90 trees without a licence was held not to be bad for duplicity. Even though the felling had taken place over a three-day period and there might have been separate defences advanced in respect of different trees, it was still possible to regard the felling as one activity. The magistrates were perfectly capable on the information as drafted of determining how many trees the accused had illegally felled and adjusting the penalty accordingly.
(c) *Heaton v Costello* (1984) 148 JP 688: the charge alleged theft of a bottle of cider, a pair of trousers and a cardigan from a supermarket. It was held that the appropriate test in such cases is whether the various acts can properly and fairly be described, having regard to all the circumstances of the case, as forming part of one activity. The present charge was held not to be bad for duplicity, since all the items were stolen on one visit to the supermarket. The case goes a little

beyond the leading authority of *Wilson* (1979) 69 Cr App R 83 (concerning the equivalent rules on indictments), since the theft of the cider was effected by switching price labels and the theft of the clothing by walking through the checkouts without paying. Thus, one theft had been completed within the store, while the other remained incomplete until the accused had passed the checkout. Nevertheless, the Divisional Court held that there was a single activity.

(d) *Barton v DPP* (2001) 165 JP 779: a single charge alleged theft of a total of £1,338.23. The prosecution case was that on 94 separate occasions, the accused had taken small amounts of cash from the till. The accused gave no specific explanation for the individual takings and put forward the same defence for all. The charge was held not be duplicitous. Indeed, to bring 94 separate charges would rightly have been regarded as oppressive. See also *Tovey* [2005] 2 Cr App R (S) 606 (a case on indictments).

(e) *Ministry of Agriculture, Fisheries and Food v Nunn Corn (1987) Ltd* [1990] Crim LR 268: a charge was held to be duplicitous because it alleged more than one victim of the offence (in this case, different purchasers of seeds). It is submitted that this should not be seen as an invariable rule. In most cases the fact that there are separate victims will indeed mean that there were separate offences (e.g., theft of an item belonging to A and theft of an item belonging to B will necessarily be separate offences). However, there may be circumstances where a single offence can be committed against more than one victim (for example, where the accused is charged with stealing property that is owned jointly by A and B or where a single unlawful act on the part of the accused causes loss to more than one victim, as where a single act of fraud causes property in which several people have an interest to lose value).

D21.10 **Whether a Statutory Provision Creates One or More than One Offence** An important issue that may arise when the question of duplicity is under consideration is whether the statutory provision in question creates a single offence or more than one offence. This is a matter of statutory interpretation, but case law may serve as a guide to the approach taken by the courts. Again, there are many cases on this point, of which the following are examples:

(a) *Surrey Justices, ex parte Witherick* [1932] 1 KB 450: a single charge alleged driving without due care and attention or without reasonable consideration (contrary to what is now the Road Traffic Act 1988, s. 3). It was held to be duplicitous because the section creates two separate offences, one of driving without due care and the other of driving without reasonable consideration. Accordingly, they must be alleged in separate charges, not as alternatives in a single charge.

(b) *Thomson v Knights* [1947] KB 336: a single charge alleged driving when unfit through drink or drugs (contrary to what is now the RTA 1988, s. 4). This charge was held not to be duplicitous, since the section creates a single offence of driving when in a 'self-induced state of incapacity, whether that incapacity was due to drink or drugs', not two separate offences of driving while unfit through drink, and driving while unfit through drugs.

(c) *Amos v DPP* [1988] RTR 198: a single charge alleging that a bus driver was guilty of 'failing to behave in a civil and orderly manner and to take all reasonable precautions to ensure the safety of passengers alighting from the vehicle', contrary to regulations governing the conduct of drivers, was held to be defective. The structure of the regulation in question, with its division of different types of misconduct into separate paragraphs, showed that it was creating a number of separate offences (one per paragraph), not a single compendious offence of misconduct.

(d) *Mohindra v DPP* [2005] RTR 95: this case concerned the RTA 1988, s. 172(3) (see **C2.12** for details); the court rejected the argument that the subsection creates two separate offences, one based on the obligation created by s. 172(2)(a) and the other based on s. 172(2)(b). It follows that a charge that simply refers to s. 172(3) is not bad for duplicity. In holding that s. 172(3) creates only one offence, the Divisional Court observed that whether the failure to comply with the requirement is a breach of an obligation under s. 172(2)(a) or (2)(b) is not an issue unless and until the addressee asserts that he was not the keeper or, as a keeper, he seeks to rely on the defence in s. 172(4).

AMENDMENT OF INFORMATION OR WRITTEN CHARGE

Before (or during the course of) a summary trial it may become apparent that the information **D21.11** or written charge is defective, either in the sense that it does not comply with the CrimPR, part 7 (see **D21.7**), or in the sense that there is a discrepancy between the particulars alleged in it and the prosecution evidence adduced at trial. The MCA 1980, s. 123, greatly limits the extent to which any such defect may be used as a ground for objecting to the proceedings, but at the same time requires the court to grant an adjournment if variation between the information (or written charge) and the evidence adduced may have misled the defence.

Magistrates' Courts Act 1980, s. 123

(1) No objection shall be allowed to any information or complaint, or to any summons or warrant to procure the presence of the defendant, for any defect in it in substance or in form, or for any variance between it and the evidence adduced on behalf of the prosecutor or complainant at the hearing of the information or complaint.

(2) If it appears to a magistrates' court that any variance between a summons or warrant and the evidence adduced on behalf of the prosecutor or complainant is such that the defendant has been misled by the variance, the court shall, on the application of the defendant, adjourn the hearing.

If read literally, the wording of s. 123 requires the magistrates to ignore any defect in an information (or written charge), however gross it might be, save to the extent of granting the defence an adjournment in the circumstances set out in s. 123(2). The appellate courts have not, however, allowed the section to have such a sweeping effect. Lord Widgery CJ in *Garfield v Maddocks* [1974] QB 7, at p. 12, summarised the correct approach thus:

> Those extremely wide words, which on their face seem to legalise almost any discrepancy between the evidence and the information, have in fact always been given a more restricted meaning, and in modern times the section is construed in this way, that if the variance between the evidence and the information is slight and does no injustice to the defence, the information may be allowed to stand notwithstanding the variance which occurred. On the other hand, if the variance is so substantial that it is unjust to the defendant to allow it to be adopted without a proper amendment of the information, then the practice is for the court to require the prosecution to amend in order to bring their information into line. Once they do that, of course, there is provision in [s. 123(2)] whereby an adjournment can be ordered in the interests of the defence if the amendment requires him to seek an adjournment.

In *New Southgate Metals Ltd v London Borough of Islington* [1996] Crim LR 334, the Divisional Court held that there are three types of error which can occur in an information (or written charge):

(a) an error 'so fundamental that it cannot be rescued by any appropriate and reasonable amendment': this will cause the prosecution to fail without more;

(b) a 'defect that is substantial enough to require amendment': the magistrates have power to allow amendment (subject to granting an adjournment if the defence are placed at any disadvantage by the amendment) — if such an error is not corrected, any conviction obtained upon the defective information is at risk of being quashed by the Divisional Court;

(c) an error that is 'so trivial that no amendment is required' where the defence were always aware of the true basis of the complaint: the conviction may be upheld even without amendment of the charge.

In *New Southgate Metals Ltd*, the charge referred to the wrong statute. The Divisional Court **D21.12** held that this error was capable of amendment, since the factual particulars of the offence were accurately set out in the charge, and the error to be one that was 'trivial in nature and in no way misled or disadvantaged the defence'.

Minor Defects which Do Not Require Amendment

D21.13 In *Sandwell Justices, ex parte West Midlands Passenger Transport Executive* [1979] RTR 17, the Divisional Court held that a variation between the information (which alleged that the company had put a vehicle on the road with a defective rear nearside tyre) and the evidence (which was that it was a defective rear offside tyre) was so trivial that, even in the absence of the amendment which was in fact made, the conviction would have been upheld. It was clear that the company was always aware of which tyre was the subject of the complaint, and had in fact brought it to court for inspection at the hearing.

Defects which Require Amendment but which Are Not Incurable

D21.14 In such cases, if an amendment is sought and allowed, the court must go on to consider whether the defence have been misled by the original error and, if they have, it should grant an adjournment. Failure by the prosecution to ask for the amendment, or failure by the court to grant an adjournment, may lead to any conviction being quashed by the Divisional Court. In the case of summary offences, an important question is whether or not the six-month time-limit for commencing a prosecution (see the MCA 1980, s. 127) has expired: if it has not, there is nothing to stop the prosecution simply starting the proceedings again, and this is a strong factor in favour of allowing an amendment to the existing charge. However, the fact that the time-limit has expired is not necessarily fatal to an application to amend the existing charge. The following cases serve as examples of the scope of the power to amend under s. 123:

(a) *Meek v Powell* [1952] 1 KB 164: the charge referred to a repealed section of an Act which had later been re-enacted in identical terms; it was held that the justices could have allowed the charge to be amended (granting an adjournment if sought), or they could have dismissed it, allowing the prosecution to commence fresh proceedings under the correct Act, but it was not open to them to convict in the absence of such an amendment.

(b) *Newcastle-upon-Tyne Justices, ex parte John Bryce (Contractors) Ltd* [1976] 2 All ER 611: the justices permitted the amendment of a charge which had originally alleged *permitting* the use of an overladen lorry so as to allege its actual use. It was held that, even though the amendment was more than six months from the date of the alleged offence (cf. the MCA 1980, s. 127) and even though it substituted a different offence for that originally charged ('use' and 'permitting use' were two separate offences), nonetheless the amendment was permissible. The defence were not misled or taken by surprise, since the nature of the prosecution case had always been apparent from the statement of facts on the summons.

(c) *Scunthorpe Justices, ex parte McPhee* (1998) 162 JP 635: the accused had been charged with robbery, but the CPS subsequently agreed to accept pleas of guilty to theft and common assault. The justices granted an application to amend the charge to allege theft, but refused to allow an amendment to charge common assault (since the six-month time-limit (under the MCA 1980, s. 127) for the summary offence of common assault had elapsed). Dyson J, giving the judgment of the Divisional Court, said:

> (1) The purpose of the six-month time limit imposed by s 127 of the 1980 Act is to ensure that summary offences are charged and tried as soon as reasonably practicable after their alleged commission.
> (2) Where an information has been laid within the six-month period it can be amended after the expiry of that period.
> (3) An information can be amended after the expiry of the six-month period, even to allege a different offence or different offences provided that:
>   (i)   the different offence or offences allege the 'same misdoing' as the original offence; and
>   (ii) the amendment can be made in the interests of justice.
>
> ...The phrase 'same misdoing'...should not be construed too narrowly. I understand it to mean that the new offence should arise out of the same (or substantially the same) facts as gave rise to the original offence...

Once they are satisfied that the amended offence or offences arise out of the same or substantially the same facts as the original offence, the justices must go on to consider whether it is in the interests of justice to allow the amendment. In exercising their discretion the justices should pay particular regard to the interests of the defendant. If an amendment will result in a defendant facing a significantly more serious charge, that should weigh heavily — perhaps conclusively — against allowing the amendment after the six-month time limit has expired.

These conditions were met in the instant case, and the information could have been amended accordingly.

(d) *Thames Magistrates' Court, ex parte Stevens* (2000) 164 JP 233: the accused was charged with assault occasioning actual bodily harm (OAPA 1861, s. 47). The prosecution subsequently indicated that they wished to withdraw the s. 47 charge and replace it with a charge alleging the summary offence of common assault (CJA 1988, s. 39) instead. However, it was more than six months since the commission of the offence. The Divisional Court held that the magistrate had correctly concluded that what was being sought by the prosecution was an amendment of the original charge rather than the laying of a new charge. The MCA 1980, s. 127, therefore did not prevent the court from dealing with the charge of common assault. The magistrate, in considering whether the amendment was in the interests of justice, had taken proper account of the fact that: (i) the case against the accused was, to all intents and purposes, the same after the amendment as before; (ii) the accused had not been misled or prejudiced by the amendment; (iii) she knew the case against her; (iv) she had not been deprived by the amendment of any defence; (v) the evidence to be adduced by the prosecution was not different after the amendment; and (vi) the effect of the amendment was in fact to reduce the gravity of the original charge.

(e) *DPP v Short* (2002) 166 JP 474: the charge alleged that the defendant 'used' a vehicle with excess alcohol (rather than 'drove') under the RTA 1988, s. 5. At the end of the evidence, the prosecution invited the justices to exercise their power under the MCA 1980, s. 123, to amend the information to substitute 'drove' for 'used', thus bringing the information within the wording of the RTA 1988, s. 5. The magistrates refused to allow the information to be amended. The Divisional Court said that, taking account of the express reference to s. 5 of the 1988 Act, it could not be said that the information disclosed an offence not known to law. The court went on to say that the MCA 1980, s. 123, confers a wide discretion on justices to amend a charge, and that discretion should ordinarily be exercised in favour of amendment unless so amending would result in injustice to an accused. In the present case, no injustice would have been caused to the accused by the proposed amendment, since he was fully aware of the case against him. It followed that the justices had erred in refusing the prosecution amendment.

(f) *R (James) v DPP* (2004) 168 JP 596: the accused was charged with supplying a Class B drug. At the close of her case, it was submitted on her behalf that the evidence, although demonstrating an attempt to supply the drug, did not demonstrate an actual supply. The prosecution, relying on s. 123, applied to amend the information to allege an offence of attempting to supply a Class B drug (contrary to the Criminal Attempts Act 1981). Issues arose as to whether the justices were right to allow the amendment after the close of the defence case and whether they were right not to hold fresh mode of trial proceedings after allowing the amendment. The Divisional Court held that there is no fetter on the justices relying on the very wide wording of s. 123 to substitute a different offence, even where that offence arises under a different Act of Parliament, provided that no injustice is caused to the accused in so doing. There is, said the court, no reason why magistrates' courts should apply different principles to the Crown Court, which has the power to make such amendments. In the present case, the court decided that the accused had suffered no prejudice and went on to hold that, where there is no such injustice to the accused, there is no requirement on the magistrates to restart the mode of trial procedure when the charge is amended to substitute one offence for another.

(g) *Shaw v DPP* (2007) 171 JP 254: the justices allowed a charge to be amended to allege a different offence. The new offence carried imprisonment, whereas the original one did not. Significantly, the amendment introduced the new charge outside the six-month time-limit imposed by s. 127 of the 1980 Act. The Divisional Court held that the substitution of a new offence with a significantly heavier penalty, especially one where the accused faces the possibility of a custodial sentence, should have led the justices to reach the conclusion that it was not in the interests of justice to allow such an amendment.

(h) In *Foster v DPP* (2014) 178 JP 15, the accused was charged with an offence allegedly committed on 18 April. In fact, the offence with which he was charged was such that it could not have been committed before the period of 28 days from 28 March had expired. It followed that the accused could not be guilty of the offence charged. Wilkie J said (at [23]) that:

> ...a discrepancy of [this] nature...where the information on the basis of which the defendant before the magistrates had been brought to court does not disclose any offence at all, must be of sufficient substance that it requires amendment in order for the magistrates properly then to try the information. It would be an extremely odd set of circumstances if the magistrates could lawfully try a case and convict someone of an offence where the statement of the offence does not in fact, on the evidence, on any view, disclose the commission of the offence of which they convict the defendant.

Fundamental Defects that Cannot be Rescued by Amendment

D21.15   In *Atterton v Browne* [1945] KB 122, Humphreys J said: 'There have been...many decisions [under the predecessor of s. 123] which show that the section does not operate to prevent an objection being effective where the error alleged is fundamental, such as, for instance, where one offence is charged in the information and a different offence is found in the conviction recorded by the justices, even though the two matters may seem to be very much the same thing'. Similarly, it has been held that a charge which names the wrong person (e.g., the company secretary when it should have been the company itself) is so flawed that amendment cannot assist (*City of Oxford Tramway Co. v Sankey* (1890) 54 JP 564). In *Marco (Croydon) Ltd v Metropolitan Police* [1984] RTR 24, it was held that magistrates were not entitled to allow the amendment of the name of the defendant company from 'A J Bull Ltd' to the correct name of 'Marco (Croydon) Ltd, trading as A & J Bull Containers'. Similarly, in *R (J Sainsbury plc) v Plymouth Magistrates' Court* (2006) 170 JP 690, the charge named the defendant company as 'J Sainsbury plc (trading as Sainsburys Supermarket Ltd)'. J Sainsbury plc asserted that it was not the proper defendant, since the relevant store was operated by J Sainsbury Supermarkets Ltd. The prosecution applied under the MCA 1980, s. 123, to substitute J Sainsbury Supermarkets Ltd as defendant. The district judge acknowledged that the two companies were two separate legal entities, but allowed the amendment notwithstanding that the time-limit for bringing a prosecution had since expired. The Divisional Court, however, held that the proper defendant had not been before the court and so the effect of the decision of the district judge was impermissibly to prefer a charge out of time.

Where the correct defendant is not before the court, the only remedy for the prosecution in the case of an irremediable defect is to start the proceedings afresh (which, in the case of a summary offence, is possible only if less than six months have elapsed since the commission of the offence). There must then be an adjournment so that a fresh summons or requisition can be served on the new defendant (*Greater Manchester Justices, ex parte Aldi GmbH & Co KG* (1995) 159 JP 717). However, where the accused is misnamed but nonetheless appears before the court, this may have the effect of waiving the error and rendering amendment permissible (see *Allan v Wiseman* [1975] RTR 217, where the wrong surname was used but the right person was nonetheless before the court).

D21.16   Where the effect of the amendment would be to replace one offence with a different one, a key question is how similar those offences are. In *Williams v DPP* [2009] EWHC 2354 (Admin), the accused was suspected of drink-driving. At the police station, he failed to give an adequate breath sample and was asked for a blood or urine sample. He refused to give a blood sample, on the basis that he was scared of needles, and also failed to provide a urine sample. However, he was charged with failure to provide a breath specimen. On the day of the trial (some nine months later), the magistrates acceded to an application by the CPS to amend the charge to allege failure to provide a urine sample. The Divisional Court ruled that this amendment would have been permissible but for the fact that the magistrates also allowed a further adjournment of four months. The same approach was taken in *Wyllie v CPS* [1988] Crim LR 753, where a charge under what is now the RTA 1988, s. 7 (failure to provide a specimen of urine for analysis), was amended to allege failure to provide a specimen of blood; the Divisional Court said the amendment was permissible because, on the facts of the particular case, the evidence would have been the same under whichever limb of the section the case was prosecuted. In *R (Thornhill) v Uxbridge Magistrates' Court* (2008) 172 JP 297, on the other hand, the accused had been asked to provide a specimen of urine, it being accepted that a medical reason precluded him from providing a specimen of breath; he refused to comply and was charged with failing to provide a specimen of breath. The prosecution later sought to amend the charge to allege failure to provide a specimen of urine. The six-month time-limit for commencing proceedings in respect of the failure to supply a specimen of urine had expired. Silber J held that there is a distinct difference between a failure to provide a specimen of urine and one of breath, and so the decision of the justices to permit the amendment of the charge was quashed. However, in *Williams*, Thomas LJ noted (at [19]) that the CPS did not appear and were not represented in *Thornhill*, and so it is of limited value as an authority; in any event, the question whether the offence arises out of the same or substantially the same facts is a factual question. On this basis, it is submitted that *Thornhill* should not be followed. In *Crann v CPS* [2013] EWHC 552 (Admin), Foskett J pointed out (at [23]) that '[e]very case depends upon its won facts, the essential question being whether the principles appropriate to the question of whether the discretionary exercise involved in deciding whether to grant the amendment to the charge were observed'.

TIME WITHIN WHICH SUMMARY TRIAL SHOULD TAKE PLACE

General Rule

A magistrates' court may not try an accused for a *summary* offence unless the information was **D21.17** laid (i.e. served on the magistrates' court) within six months of the time when the offence was allegedly committed (MCA 1980, s. 127(1)). Section 127(2)(a) makes it clear that s. 127(1) does not apply to indictable offences (which term includes either-way offences).

Section 127 refers to the laying of an information but does not make it clear when time starts to run in the case of proceedings brought by the written charge and requisition procedure established by the CJA 2003, s. 29 (see **D5.4**). The possibilities are either the date of the issue of the written charge and requisition, or the date when they are received by the accused (or deemed to be received under the CrimPR, r. 4.10). It is submitted that the relevant date ought to be the date when the written charge and requisition are issued. This would be consistent with the position in the case of proceedings brought by the laying of an information and issue of a summons, where time starts to run when the information is laid (not when the summons is received by the accused).

In *Atkinson v DPP* [2005] 3 All ER 971, it was held (following *Lloyd v Young* [1963] Crim LR 703) that, where there is uncertainty as to whether proceedings were started in time, the question should be determined according to the criminal standard of proof and the magistrates should decline to hear the matter unless satisfied so that they are sure that the proceedings were commenced within the statutory time-limit.

As regards either-way offences, there is no time-limit within which proceedings must be started **D21.18** (*Kemp v Liebherr (Great Britain) Ltd* [1987] 1 All ER 885) unless it is one of the exceptional offences for which there is statutory limitation on the time for taking proceedings on indictment, in which case that limitation applies equally to summary proceedings (s. 127(2) and (4)).

Even where a statute creates an either-way offence and then appears to impose a time-limit in respect of summary proceedings (but not proceedings on indictment), the limitation is overridden by the MCA 1980, s. 127(2). In *Kemp v Liebherr (Great Britain) Ltd*, a prosecution under the Health and Safety at Work etc. Act 1974 was commenced more than six months after evidence justifying a prosecution had become available to the prosecutor. By s. 34(3) of the Act, summary proceedings for contravening the Act apparently had to be commenced within six months of obtaining the evidence. The Divisional Court held that the proceedings were nonetheless within time since, on a true construction of the Act, the offence charged was triable either way and, therefore, s. 34(3) was effectively negated by the MCA 1980, s. 127(2). It should be noted, however, that this case involved a statute that pre-dated the MCA 1980. It is submitted that the same result would not occur in the case of a statute that was enacted after the MCA 1980, since Parliament would be taken as overriding s. 127(2) in the later Act if it chose to place a time-limit on the commencement of summary proceedings, but not proceedings on indictment.

Start of Time-limit

D21.19   The time-limit begins to run from the commission of the offence, rather than the date alleged in the charge. Hence, where there is an application to amend the date in the charge to a later date, so that it falls within the six-month time-limit, the fact that six months had elapsed from the date alleged in the charge is not in itself a valid objection to the amendment (*Blackburn Justices, ex parte Holmes* (2000) 164 JP 163).

Where a statute creates a *continuing* summary offence, a prosecution can be brought at any time until six months have elapsed from the date when the offence ceased to be committed (*British Telecommunications plc v Nottinghamshire County Council* [1999] Crim LR 217; *Hertfordshire County Council v National Grid Gas plc* [2008] 1 All ER 1137).

Some statutes which create offences specify different periods within which the prosecution must be commenced, or different starting points for that period; some statutes specify alternative periods, usually one with a start date based on the date of the commission of the offence and the other based on the date when the commission of the offence came to light or when the prosecuting authority has sufficient evidence on which to proceed. Where the prosecution is brought by an organisation and the start date depends on knowledge, there is 'no principle of law that knowledge in a prosecutor begins immediately any employee of that prosecutor has the relevant knowledge'; whilst 'prosecutors are not entitled to shuffle papers between officers or sit on information so as to extend a time limit' there is a 'degree of judgment involved in bringing a prosecution', and so knowledge 'involves an opportunity for those with appropriate skills to consider whether there is sufficient information to justify a prosecution' (*RSPCA v Johnson* [2009] EWHC 2702 (Admin), per Pill LJ at [33]).

Such statutes usually require the prosecutor to certify the date when the requisite evidence came to their attention. In *Haringey Magistrates' Court, ex parte Amvrosiou* [1996] EWHC 14 (Admin), it was held that it was not possible to go behind a certificate under the RTOA 1988, s. 6(3), stating the date on which evidence sufficient in the prosecutor's opinion to warrant the proceedings came to his knowledge, since that subsection said that the certificate 'should be conclusive evidence of that fact', save possibly in two exceptional cases: where it is plain that there has been fraud or where the certificate is wrong or arguably wrong on its face. In *Burwell v DPP* (2009) 173 JP 351, Keene LJ (at [20]) said that the first of these exceptions would 'encompass the situation where the certificate is plainly (even if honestly) inaccurate'; however, the certificate 'would have to be plainly wrong'. This is because the prosecutor 'is entitled to a degree of judgment as to when there is sufficient evidence available to warrant a prosecution'.

In *Azam v Epping Forest District Council* [2009] EWHC 3177 (Admin), Cranston J set out (at [25]) a number of general principles, including the following, relating to such certificates:

(1) If no certificate is issued, or if the certificate is defective, the court must decide whether the prosecution is in fact brought within the period specified.

(2) To decide that issue, the court must address the issue of when sufficient evidence in the opinion of the prosecutor to justify a prosecution came to his knowledge...[A] margin of judgment

is conferred on prosecutors to form an opinion about the sufficiency of the evidence to justify a prosecution. Any additional time taken to decide whether notwithstanding the evidence a prosecution is in the public interest must be ignored. Moreover, prosecutors cannot prevent time running by not applying their mind to the case; they cannot avoid forming an opinion and any such period is to be discounted.

(3) To be effective a certificate must comply exactly with the statutory requirements. For example, it must state the date. Deficiencies cannot be remedied by reference to extrinsic evidence.

(4) A valid certificate is determinative of the matter unless the certificate is inaccurate on its face, or can be shown to be fraudulent.

(5) The exception for a certificate inaccurate on its face applies only when the certificate is plainly, even if honestly, wrong. It must be patently misleading.

In *Lamont-Perkins v RSPCA* (2012) 176 JP 369 the court had to consider a certificate issued under the Animal Welfare Act 2006, s. 31(2), certifying 'the date on which evidence came to the Prosecutor's knowledge, such that the Prosecutor thinks it is sufficient to justify criminal proceedings'. Wyn Williams J (at [35]) said that such a certificate can be challenged on only two bases: 'First, it can be challenged on the basis that it constitutes a fraud; second, it can be challenged on the basis that it is plainly wrong'. His lordship went on to say (at [46] and [47]) that a magistrates' court has no jurisdiction to hear a summons alleging offences under the 2006 Act if the information upon which the summons is based was laid outside the time-limit permitted by the Act. If the s. 31(2) certificate is plainly wrong, 'it has no effect and the magistrates must disregard it. They will then be left to determine whether or not the prosecutor has initiated proceedings within the time limit permitted by s. 31(1) and if he has not the magistrates will have no jurisdiction to hear the summons in question'. Thus there is no need to seek judicial review or to challenge the prosecution as an abuse of process. Rather, as his lordship points out at [50], in most cases a challenge to the jurisdiction of the magistrates can be taken as a preliminary point; if necessary, evidence relevant to determining the issue of jurisdiction can be adduced within the preliminary hearing.

For the position where the charge is amended after the expiry of the time-limit so as to allege a different offence, see *Scunthorpe Justices, ex parte McPhee* (1998) 162 JP 635 at **D21.14**.

Magistrates' Courts Act 1980, s. 127   **D21.20**

(1) Except as otherwise expressly provided by any enactment and subject to subsection (2) below, a magistrates' court shall not try an information...unless the information was laid...within six months from the time when the offence was committed...

(2) Nothing in—
   (a) subsection (1) above; or
   (b) subject to subsection (4) below, any other enactment (however framed or worded) which, as regards any offence to which it applies, would but for this section impose a time-limit on the power of a magistrates' court to try an information summarily or impose a limitation on the time for taking summary proceedings,
shall apply in relation to any indictable offence.

(3) Without prejudice to the generality of paragraph (b) of subsection (2) above, that paragraph includes enactments which impose a time-limit that applies only in certain circumstances (for example, where the proceedings are not instituted by or with the consent of the Director of Public Prosecutions or some other specified authority).

(4) Where, as regards any indictable offence, there is imposed by any enactment (however framed or worded, and whether falling within subsection (2)(b) above or not) a limitation on the time for taking proceedings on indictment for that offence no summary proceedings for that offence shall be taken after the latest time for taking proceedings on indictment.

DISCRETION NOT TO PROCEED ON ACCOUNT OF DELAY

Effect of Delay

Even where proceedings were commenced within time, a magistrates' court has a discretion to   **D21.21**
refuse to try a case, and so to acquit the accused without trial, if there has been delay amounting

to an abuse of the process of the court (*Brentford Justices, ex parte Wong* [1981] QB 445). Delay as a possible abuse of process is dealt with fully at **D3.77** *et seq*.

Where the delay is deliberate, it is likely to amount to an abuse of process, as in *Brentford Justices, ex parte Wong*, where the prosecutor deliberately delayed in effecting service of the summons in order to gain more time in which to decide whether or not to continue the case against the accused.

Where deliberate delay in bringing the case to court cannot be shown, the defence may nonetheless apply for the magistrates to exercise their discretion not to proceed if (i) there has been inordinate or unconscionable delay due to the prosecution's inefficiency, and (ii) prejudice to the defence from the delay is either proved or to be inferred (per Lloyd LJ in *Gateshead Justices, ex parte Smith* (1985) 149 JP 681). It is clear that where there is an element of deliberate delay on the part of the prosecution, the courts are more willing to stay the prosecution than if there has been mere inefficiency. Conversely, if the delay was in part attributable to the accused's own conduct, an application to stay is unlikely to succeed.

D21.22   **Delay in Service of Summons or Requisition**   There is no specific time-limit within which the summons (or requisition) must be served once the information has been laid (or the written charge issued). However, excessive delay in effecting service could amount to an abuse of process giving the court the power to dismiss the case. For example, in *Watford Justices, ex parte Outrim* [1983] RTR 26, the summons was served almost two years after issue. It was held that when service of the summons is delayed so long as to produce substantial prejudice to an accused or to be unconscionable, the justices have a discretion to decline to proceed to hear the case. Where the accused has not tried to evade service or in any way contributed to the failure to serve him (e.g., by giving a wrong address or by failing to leave a forwarding address), there is a clear inference that something had gone wrong with the process serving procedures, and in such circumstances the justices are entitled and, in appropriate cases, bound to refuse to proceed with the case.

D21.23   **Application to Summary Offences and Either-way Offences**   The discretion to halt the proceedings applies both to proposed trials of summary offences and to summary trials of offences triable either way. However, it is submitted that the discretion to stay the proceedings is more likely to be exercised in the former class of case since Parliament, by enacting the MCA 1980, s. 127, has indicated that proceedings for summary offences should take place within a reasonably short period, and delays in bringing the accused before the court effectively thwart Parliament's intention.

DISCLOSURE BY THE PROSECUTION

Advance Warning of the Prosecution Case

D21.24   **A-G's Guidelines on Disclosure**   The A-G's Guidelines on Disclosure (set out in **appendix 4**) give the accused a right to pre-trial disclosure of the prosecution case. Paragraph 57 provides that, in the case of summary trial:

> The prosecutor should... provide to the defence all evidence upon which the Crown proposes to rely in a summary trial. Such provision should allow the accused or their legal advisers sufficient time properly to consider the evidence before it is called.

The effect of this is to put an accused who is being tried in the magistrates' court in the same position as an accused who is being tried in the Crown Court as regards obtaining copies of the statements of the persons to be called as prosecution witnesses. The provisions in the A-G's Guidelines are in addition to the requirement on the prosecution to disclose 'initial details' of their case under the CrimPR, part 21 (see **D5.18**).

D21.25   **Advance Disclosure and the Right to a Fair Trial**   In *Stratford Justices, ex parte Imbert* [1999] 2 Cr App R 276, the Divisional Court considered whether the possibility of an accused being tried summarily without having had sight of the witness statements of the prosecution witnesses was a violation of the right under the ECHR, Article 6(3)(a), 'to be informed promptly... and in detail, of the nature and cause of the accusation against him'. The Divisional Court held that it was not, although their lordships recognised that their decision was *obiter* (doubly so when it came to their view that it would still not be a violation after the implementation of the HRA 1998). It is submitted that the absence of advance information about the prosecution case might in certain circumstances be a violation of Article 6(3)(b), which lays down the accused's right 'to have adequate time and facilities for his defence', as well as a violation of Article 6(3)(a). In order that the trial should be fair, it is necessary that the defence should be able to consider the prosecution evidence, and prepare upon the basis of knowledge rather than guesswork. Sometimes the nature of that evidence will be predictable, and the defence advocate will be able to respond with the necessary agility of thought. But in other instances, the defence may be ambushed by an unexpected line of evidence. Given the undesirability of adjournments, it is submitted that the requirement of disclosure set out in para. 57 of the A-G's Guidelines should be regarded as necessary in order to accord the accused the rights guaranteed by the Convention.

Disclosure of Unused Prosecution Material

The position relating to disclosure under the CPIA 1996 in summary trials is dealt with at **D21.26** D9.37. The main difference between disclosure under the CPIA in the magistrates' court, as against the Crown Court, is that in the magistrates' court the provision of a 'defence statement' is voluntary, not mandatory (CPIA 1996, s. 6). If, however, the defence choose to serve a defence statement, it must fulfil the requirements that are applicable to defence statements (set out in s. 6A), and adverse inferences can be drawn (under s. 11) if it does not comply with those requirements or if, for example, the accused serves the defence statement late or puts forward a different case at trial. The only advantage of serving a defence statement in the magistrates' court is that it triggers a further check by the prosecution (under s. 7A) to see if they have any previously undisclosed material which might assist the accused's defence as set out in the defence statement. If the defence statement would not add anything to what the accused said when interviewed by the police (and so the prosecution are already aware of the nature of the defence case), it is submitted that there is little to be gained from serving a defence statement where the case is to be heard by a magistrates' court.

SECURING THE ATTENDANCE OF WITNESSES: WITNESS SUMMONSES

The attendance of witnesses for purposes of criminal proceedings in magistrates' courts may be **D21.27** secured by the issue of a summons or warrant under the MCA 1980, s. 97, which applies equally to proposed prosecution and proposed defence witnesses. It provides that, where a magistrate is satisfied that:

(a) any person within the jurisdiction is likely to be able to give material evidence, or produce any document or thing likely to be material evidence, for purposes of a summary trial, and
(b) it is in the interests of justice to issue a summons to secure the attendance of that person to give evidence or produce the document or thing,

the magistrate may issue a summons requiring the person to attend before the court on the date specified in the summons (s. 97(1)). A similar power is given to justices' clerks by the Justices' Clerks Rules 2005 (SI 2005 No. 545), sch. 1, para. 2.

If a magistrate (but not a clerk) is also satisfied by evidence on oath that it is probable that a summons issued under s. 97(1) would not procure the witness's attendance, he may issue a warrant (s. 97(2)).

Should a person summoned under s. 97(1) fail to attend as required, the court may issue a war- **D21.28** rant (s. 97(3)). It must, however, be satisfied that:

(a) the witness is indeed likely to be able to give material evidence or produce a material document or thing;

(b) he has been duly served with the summons and been paid or tendered a reasonable sum for costs and expenses; and

(c) there is no just excuse for the failure to attend.

Requirement (a) must be established by evidence on oath; requirement (b) may be established either by evidence on oath or in such other manner as is prescribed. By virtue of the CrimPR, part 4 (see Supplement, **R-34** *et seq.*), a witness summons may be served in one of the following ways:

(a) by handing it to individual (r. 4.3(1)(a));

(b) by leaving it at, or sending it by first class post to, an address where it is reasonable to believe that the individual will receive it (r. 4.4(1) and r. 4.4(2)(a)).

Material Evidence

D21.29   The power to issue a witness summons is conditional upon the magistrate being satisfied that the witness will be able to give or produce material evidence. In *Peterborough Magistrates' Court, ex parte Willis* (1987) 151 JP 785, it was held that a witness summons should not be issued to enable someone to find out whether the witness can give any material evidence, as there has to be material before the court on which it may be satisfied that the witness is likely to be able to give material evidence. The Divisional Court added that, when it reviews a s. 97 order, it will consider only the material before the magistrates who issued the summons.

Similarly, where the summons is to produce a document or thing, the applicant must be able to show that the item to be produced would be admissible evidence and not, for example, material subject to legal professional privilege (*Derby Magistrates' Court, ex parte B* [1996] AC 487). Moreover, the court will not allow s. 97 to be used for 'fishing expeditions'. In the context of drink-driving prosecutions, for example, the court in *R (Cunliffe) v Hastings Magistrates' Court* [2006] EWHC 2081 (Admin) quashed witness summonses to produce documents relating to the functioning and design of the breath-testing instruments, since the requests had amounted to a 'fishing expedition' and because the documents were not admissible *per se* because they would need an expert witness to interpret them.

In *Reading Justices, ex parte Berkshire County Council* [1996] 1 Cr App R 239, Simon Brown LJ summarised the key principles governing such applications as follows (at pp. 246–7):

(i) to be material evidence documents must be not only relevant to the issues arising in the criminal proceedings, but also documents admissible as such in evidence;

(ii) documents which are desired merely for the purpose of possible cross-examination are not admissible in evidence and, thus, are not material for the purposes of s. 97;

(iii) whoever seeks production of documents must satisfy the justices with some material that the documents are 'likely to be material' in the sense indicated, likelihood for this purpose involving a real possibility, although not necessarily a probability;

(iv) it is not sufficient that the applicant merely wants to find out whether or not the third party has such material documents. This procedure must not be used as a disguised attempt to obtain discovery.

Procedure

D21.30   Part 28 of the CrimPR deals with witness summonses, warrants and orders (see Supplement, **R-208** *et seq.*). Rule 28.2, provides that the court may issue (or withdraw) a witness summons, warrant or order with or without a hearing, and that any hearing under part 28 must be in private unless the court otherwise directs. Under r. 28.3(1), a party seeking a witness summons (or warrant) must apply as soon as practicable after becoming aware of the grounds for doing so. It should also be noted that, under the MCA 1980, s. 97(2B), an application for a witness summons (whether made by the defence or the prosecution) may be refused if the magistrate or clerk is not satisfied that the application has been made as soon as reasonably practicable after the accused pleaded not guilty. Rule 28.3(2) requires the applicant to explain:

(i) what evidence the proposed witness can give or produce;

(ii) why it is likely to be material evidence; and

(iii) why it would be in the interests of justice to issue a summons... or warrant...

The application may be made orally (unless r. 28.5 applies — see below) except where the court directs otherwise (r. 28.3(3)). Where the application is in writing, it has to be in the prescribed form (r. 28(4)).

Rule 28.5 applies where the application is for a witness summons requiring the proposed witness to produce in evidence a document or thing, or to give evidence about information apparently held in confidence, that relates to another person. Under r. 28.5(4), the court must not issue a witness summons in such a case unless everyone served with the application has had at least 14 days in which to make representations, and the court is satisfied that it has been able to take adequate account of the duties and rights, including rights of confidentiality, of the proposed witness and of any person to whom the proposed evidence relates.

Under r. 28.6, a person served with an application for a witness summons requiring production **D21.31** of a document or thing may object to its production on the ground that either it is not likely to be material evidence, or the duties or rights (including rights of confidentiality) of the proposed witness or of any person to whom the document or thing relates outweigh the reasons for issuing a summons. Under r. 28.6(2), the court may require the proposed witness to make the document or thing available for the objection to be assessed.

Rule 28.7 makes provision for the withdrawal of a witness summons or warrant. The party who applied for it may seek its withdrawal on the ground that it no longer is needed; the witness (or any person to whom the evidence relates) may seek its withdrawal on the grounds that he was not aware of the application for it, and either he cannot give or produce evidence likely to be material evidence, or his duties or rights (including rights of confidentiality) outweigh the reasons for the issue of the summons or warrant (r. 28.7(1)).

Failure to Testify

If a witness attends the magistrates' court but refuses without just excuse to take the oath (or **D21.32** affirm) or to give evidence (or to produce a document or thing), he may be imprisoned for up to one month and/or fined up to £2,500 (MCA 1980, s. 97(4)). This applies whether the witness attended court voluntarily or in answer to a summons or was brought there following execution of a warrant.

Statutory Provision on Witness Summonses and Warrants

Magistrates' Courts Act 1980, s. 97   **D21.33**

(1) Where a justice of the peace is satisfied that—
   (a) any person in England or Wales is likely to be able to give material evidence, or produce any document or thing likely to be material evidence, at the summary trial of an information … by a magistrates' court, and
   (b) it is in the interests of justice to issue a summons under this subsection to secure the attendance of that person to give evidence or produce the document or thing,
the justice shall issue a summons directed to that person requiring him to attend before the court at the time and place appointed in the summons to give evidence or to produce the document or thing.
(2) If a justice of the peace is satisfied by evidence on oath of the matters mentioned in subsection (1) above, and also that it is probable that a summons under that subsection would not procure the attendance of the person in question, the justice may instead of issuing a summons issue a warrant to arrest that person and bring him before such a court as aforesaid at a time and place specified in the warrant …
(2A) A summons may also be issued under subsection (1) above if the justice is satisfied that the person in question is outside the British Islands but no warrant shall be issued under subsection (2) above unless the justice is satisfied by evidence on oath that the person in question is in England or Wales.
(2B) A justice may refuse to issue a summons under subsection (1) above in relation to the summary trial of an information if he is not satisfied that an application for the summons was made by a party to the case as soon as reasonably practicable after the accused pleaded not guilty.

(2C)   In relation to the summary trial of an information, subsection (2) above shall have effect as if the reference to the matters mentioned in subsection (1) above included a reference to the matter mentioned in subsection (2B) above.

(3)   On the failure of any person to attend before a magistrates' court in answer to a summons under this section, if—

(a)   the court is satisfied by evidence on oath that he is likely to be able to give material evidence or produce any document or thing likely to be material evidence in the proceedings; and

(b)   it is proved on oath, or in such other manner as may be prescribed, that he has been duly served with the summons, and that a reasonable sum has been paid or tendered to him for costs and expenses; and

(c)   it appears to the court that there is no just excuse for the failure, the court may issue a warrant to arrest him and bring him before the court at a time and place specified in the warrant.

(4)   If any person attending or brought before a magistrates' court refuses without just excuse to be sworn or give evidence, or to produce any document or thing, the court or justice, as the case may be, may commit him to custody until the expiration of such period not exceeding one month as may be specified in the warrant or until he sooner gives evidence or produces the document or thing or impose on him a fine not exceeding £2,500 or both.

(5)   A fine imposed under subsection (4) above shall be deemed, for the purposes of any enactment, to be a sum adjudged to be paid by a conviction.

PRE-TRIAL HEARINGS

Early Administrative Hearings

D21.34   The CDA 1998, s. 50, makes provision for pre-trial hearings. It provides that where the accused has been charged with an offence at a police station, the magistrates' court before whom he appears for the first time in relation to that charge may consist of a single justice (s. 50(1)). At a hearing under s. 50, the accused is asked whether he wishes to be provided with legal aid (s. 50(2)(a)); if he indicates that he does, the necessary arrangements must be made for him to apply for it and, where appropriate, obtain it (s. 50(2)(b)) and, if necessary, the hearing may be adjourned for this purpose under s. 50(4A)(a). On adjourning the hearing, the magistrate may remand the accused in custody or on bail (s. 50(3)(b)). Under s. 50(4), an early administrative hearing may be conducted by a justices' clerk (or an assistant clerk who has been specifically authorised by the justices' clerk for that purpose), but the clerk is not empowered to remand the accused in custody or, without the consent of the prosecutor and the accused, to remand the accused on bail on conditions other than those (if any) previously imposed.

Section 50(1) makes it clear that s. 50 applies only where the accused was charged at the police station, and so does not apply where the accused is granted police bail and is then charged by the CPS using the written charge and requisition procedure. However, there is nothing to prevent magistrates' courts operating a system of early administrative hearings in all cases where a not guilty plea is expected.

Pre-trial Hearings and Pre-trial Rulings

D21.35   The MCA 1980, s. 8A, applies to cases that are to be tried summarily where the accused has entered a not guilty plea (s. 8A(1)). For these purposes, a pre-trial hearing is a hearing that takes place before the court begins to hear evidence from the prosecution at the trial (or, in those cases where fitness to plead is an issue, before the court considers whether to exercise its power under the Mental Health Act 1983, s. 37(3), to make a hospital order without convicting the accused (s. 8A(2)). At a pre-trial hearing, the magistrates may decide any question as to the admissibility of evidence and any other question of law relating to the case (s. 8A(4)). Such rulings may be made only if the court has given the parties an opportunity to be heard and it appears to the court that it is in the interests of justice to make the ruling (s. 8A(3)(b) and (c)). If the accused is unrepresented, he must be given the chance to apply for legal aid (s. 8A(5)). Pre-trial rulings may be made on the application of the defence or prosecution, or of the court's own motion (s. 8A(6)).

Under s. 8B(1), a pre-trial ruling is binding until the case against the accused (or, where there is more than one, against each of them) is disposed of. The case is disposed of if the accused is acquitted or convicted, or the prosecutor decides not to proceed with the case, or the case is dismissed (s. 8B(2)). However, under s. 8B(3), the court may (on application by a party or of its own motion) discharge or vary a pre-trial ruling provided it appears to the court that it is in the interests of justice to do so, and the court has given the parties an opportunity to be heard. A party can apply for the ruling to be discharged or varied only if there has been a material change of circumstances since the ruling was made or, if there has been a previous application under s. 8B, since that application was made (s. 8B(5)). In *R (CPS) v Gloucester Justices* (2008) 172 JP 506, MacKay J, considering the power of the magistrates' court to vary the pre-trial ruling of its own motion, made the point that it is difficult to accept that it could be in the interests of justice for the court to annul or discharge its own ruling without a compelling reason to do so, such as changed circumstances or fresh evidence; it is not sufficient that a different bench reaches a different conclusion on the same material (at [12]). In *Jones v South East Surrey Local Justice Area* (2010) 174 JP 342, Cranston J noted (at [11]) that, before the introduction of ss. 8A and 8B into the MCA 1980, *Newham Juvenile Court, ex parte F (a minor)* [1986] 3 All ER 17 had recognised a similar rule in common law. That case concerned the power of one bench to review the decision of another bench about the mode of trial for a juvenile accused. Cranston J quoted from the judgment of Simon Brown LJ in *Newham* (at p. 946B): 'Once a decision has been made after proper inquiry and consideration of all relevant factors, it cannot be reversed merely by re-examining the case afresh on the same material'. In *Newham*, McCullough J (at p. 947D–E) had said that review of a decision 'will be permissible if a change of circumstances has occurred since the original decision was taken' or 'if circumstances are brought to the attention of the court which, although existing when the original decision was taken, were not then drawn to the attention of the court'. Cranston J also referred to *Acton Youth Court, ex parte DPP* [2002] Crim LR 75, where Laws LJ (at [25] and [26]) had said that it is 'necessary for the efficacious administration of justice to take a strict approach to the power of a lower court to revisit and revoke an order earlier made by itself' but that 'there must be some power to do so in the interests of justice'; that power arises where there is 'a change of relevant circumstances' but 'cases in which an earlier existing circumstance, not drawn to the attention of the court at the first hearing, would justify the court in later overturning its first decision would be most infrequent'. Cranston J (at [24] and [25]) assumed (having heard no argument to the contrary) that the common-law rule remains, but would be relevant only to those cases where ss. 8A and 8B do not apply (they 'bite' only once the decision has been made that a summary trial will occur).

D21.36 Under the MCA 1980, s. 25, where the magistrates have accepted jurisdiction in the case of an either-way offence, the prosecution may ask the magistrates (before the start of the summary trial) to reconsider that decision (on the ground that the magistrates' sentencing powers are inadequate to deal with the offence if the accused is convicted); under the MCA 1980, s. 8B(6)(a), any pre-trial ruling in respect of such an offence is discharged when the case is sent to the Crown Court for trial (so, unsurprisingly, the Crown Court would not be bound by that ruling).

Statutory Provisions on Pre-trial Hearings and Rulings

D21.37 Magistrates' Courts Act 1980, ss. 8A and 8B

8A.—(1) For the purposes of this section a hearing is a pre-trial hearing if—
    (a) it relates to an information—
        (i) which is to be tried summarily, and
        (ii) to which the accused has pleaded not guilty, and
    (b) it takes place before the start of the trial.

(2) For the purposes of subsection (1)(b), the start of a summary trial occurs when the court begins—

    (a) to hear evidence from the prosecution at the trial, or

    (b) to consider whether to exercise its power under section 37(3) of the Mental Health Act 1983 (power to make hospital order without convicting the accused).

(3) At a pre-trial hearing, a magistrates' court may make a ruling as to any matter mentioned in subsection (4) if—

    (a) the condition in subsection (5) is met,

    (b) the court has given the parties an opportunity to be heard, and

    (c) it appears to the court that it is in the interests of justice to make the ruling.

(4) The matters are—

    (a) any question as to the admissibility of evidence;

    (b) any other question of law relating to the case.

(5) The condition is that, if the accused is not legally represented—

    (a) the court must ask whether he wishes to be provided with representation for the purposes of the proceedings under Part 1 of the Legal Aid, Sentencing and Punishment of Offenders Act 2012, and

    (b) if he does, the necessary arrangements must be made for him to apply for it and, where appropriate, obtain it.

(6) A ruling may be made under this section—

    (a) on an application by a party to the case, or

    (b) of the court's own motion.

(7) For the purposes of this section and section 8B, references to the prosecutor are to any person acting as prosecutor, whether an individual or body.

8B.— (1) Subject to subsections (3) and (6), a ruling under section 8A has binding effect from the time it is made until the case against the accused or, if there is more than one, against each of them, is disposed of.

(2) The case against an accused is disposed of if—

    (a) he is acquitted or convicted,

    (b) the prosecutor decides not to proceed with the case against him, or

    (c) the information is dismissed.

(3) A magistrates' court may discharge or vary (or further vary) a ruling under section 8A if—

    (a) the condition in section 8A(5) is met,

    (b) the court has given the parties an opportunity to be heard, and

    (c) it appears to the court that it is in the interests of justice to do so.

(4) The court may act under subsection (3)—

    (a) on an application by a party to the case, or

    (b) of its own motion.

(5) No application may be made under subsection (4)(a) unless there has been a material change of circumstances since the ruling was made or, if a previous application has been made, since the application (or last application) was made.

(6) A ruling under section 8A is discharged in relation to an accused if—

    (a) the magistrates' court sends him to the Crown Court for trial for the offence charged in the information, or

    (b) a count charging him with the offence is included in an indictment by virtue of section 40 of the Criminal Justice Act 1988.

Reporting Restrictions applicable to Pre-trial Hearings

D21.38   Section 8C of the MCA 1980 imposes restrictions on reporting of pre-trial hearings in order to avoid prejudicing the right to a fair trial. The publishing of anything other than the basic factual information permitted by s. 8C(7) is prohibited — unless the court orders that reporting restrictions should not apply — until such time as the case against the defendant is disposed of. Section 8C(7) permits the publication of the identity of the court and the names of the justices; the names, ages, home addresses and occupations of the accused and witnesses; the offence(s) with which the accused is charged; the names of counsel and solicitors in the proceedings; where the proceedings are adjourned, the date and place to which they are adjourned; any arrangements as to bail; whether legal aid was granted.

The power to lift the reporting restrictions is conferred by s. 8C(3). Where the court is minded to order that the reporting restrictions do not apply and the accused (or one of the accused) objects to the making of an order removing the restrictions, the court may make the order if (and only if) satisfied, after hearing representations from (each of) the accused, that it is in the interests of justice to do so (s. 8C(4)(a) and (5)(a)).

Breach of these reporting restrictions is a summary offence punishable, under s. 8D, with a level 5 fine (currently £5,000, but it will become an unlimited fine when the LASPO 2012, s. 85, is fully implemented). Under s. 8D(6), proceedings for this offence require the consent of the A-G.

CASE MANAGEMENT

D21.39 CPD I, para. 3A.3, says that, in all cases to be tried in a magistrates' court or youth court, the 'trial preparation form' authorised for use must be used, adding that the form, and the notes which accompany it, provide a timetable for the effective preparation of a case and a list of all the matters that the court should consider in giving directions for trial. Where the accused intends to plead not guilty, the defence must normally complete the relevant parts of the form before (or, with the court's permission, during) the first hearing. The form requires the parties (in particular, the defence) to identify, with a significant level of detail, the issues in the case. When a defendant indicates a not guilty plea but has not completed the relevant sections of the trial preparation form, the justices' legal adviser must either ensure that the form is completed or, in appropriate cases, assist the court to obtain and record the essential information on the form (CPD VI, para. 37A.10).

The contents of such forms are, in principle, admissible if they contain admissions by the accused. In *R (Firth) v Epping Justices* [2011] 4 All ER 326, for example, it was held that the magistrates were entitled to treat an assertion of self-defence in the case management form as an admission by the defence that the accused was present at the scene of the offence. However, this decision must be seen in the light of *Newell* [2012] 1 WLR 3142. In that case, the issue was whether the trial judge was right to admit as evidence a previous inconsistent statement in the PCMH form. The Court of Appeal held that the statement in the PCMH form was prima facie admissible, but the judge ought to have excluded it under the PACE 1984, s. 78. Sir John Thomas P considered the position in the magistrates' courts and said (at [35]), that:

> The Trial Preparation Form . . . should be completed at the first hearing. It provides for the making of admissions or the acknowledgement that matters are not in issue. Where admissions are made in that way they will be admissible at the trial. Where statements are made on the form which are not made under the section relating to admissions, such statements should be made without the risk that they would be used at trial as statements of the defendant admissible in evidence against the defendant, provided the advocate follows the letter and the spirit of the Criminal Procedure Rules.

It is likely that the same view would be taken (subject to the power to exclude evidence under the PACE 1984, s. 78) if the prosecution were to seek to adduce the contents of such a form at trial.

D21.40 **Essential Case Management: Applying the Criminal Procedure Rules** In December 2009, Leveson LJ (then Senior Presiding Judge for England and Wales) issued guidance to magistrates' courts in a document entitled *Essential Case Management: Applying the Criminal Procedure Rules*. Where the accused pleads not guilty, the parties must, from the start, identify the disputed issues and tell the court what they are; if the parties do not supply this information, the court must require them to do so. The 'live' evidence at the trial should be confined to those issues, and so only witnesses 'who are really needed in relation to genuinely disputed, relevant issues should be required to attend'. Moreover, the court's directions must include a timetable for the progress of the case, and the parties are required to warn the court 'promptly' if any problems (e.g., relating to witnesses) are anticipated.

In *R (Drinkwater) v Solihull Magistrates' Court* (2012) 176 JP 401, Sir John Thomas P said (at [49]) that 'in any case in the magistrates' court where a trial is likely to be other than a short one, it should be the ordinary practice for a timetable for the conduct of a trial to be set at the time the trial date is fixed and the estimate made'. His lordship went on to say (at [50]) that, in setting the timetable:

> ... the court should scrutinise the reasons why it is said a witness is necessary and the time examination and cross-examination would take. It is also important in setting a timetable to have regard to the nature of the issues and the fact that the trial is a summary trial; any estimate of more than a day in the Magistrates' Courts should be scrutinised with the utmost rigour. Parties must realise that a summary trial requires a proportionate approach. If a timetable for the trial is not set, it is difficult to have any real confidence that the estimate is accurate.

Standard Case Preparation Time-limits

D21.41   The Preparation for Trial form contains a summary of applicable time-limits (some of which are not in fact prescribed by the CrimPR but are regarded as standard directions). Those time-limits are as follows:

Written admissions (under the CJA 1967, s. 10; CrimPR, r. 37.6): the parties must serve any written admissions of agreed facts within 14 days of the date when the accused pleads not guilty.

Defence statement (under the CPIA 1996, s. 6): any defence statement must be served within 14 days of the prosecutor complying (or purporting to comply) with the duty of disclosure imposed by the CPIA 1996, s. 3 (Criminal Procedure and Investigations Act 1996 (Defence Disclosure Time Limits) Regulations 2011 (SI 2011 No. 209), reg. 2(2)).

Details of defence witnesses (under the CPIA 1996, s. 6C): details of any defence witness must be notified within 14 days of the prosecutor complying (or purporting to comply) with the duty of disclosure imposed by the CPIA 1996, s. 3 (Criminal Procedure and Investigations Act 1996 (Defence Disclosure Time Limits) Regulations 2011 (SI 2011 No. 209), reg. 2(2)).

Application for disclosure (under the CPIA 1996, s. 8): the accused must serve any application for prosecution disclosure when serving any defence statement; the prosecutor must serve any representations in response within 14 days thereafter (CrimPR, r. 22.5(5)(b)).

D21.42   *Witness statements* (under the CJA 1967, s. 9): the accused must serve any defence witness statement to be read at trial before the trial, and any objection to a witness statement being read at trial must be made within seven days of service of the statement.

Measures to assist a witness or defendant to give evidence (under the CrimPR, part 29): any application for special or other measures must be served within 28 days of the date when the accused pleads not guilty (r. 29.3(a)(i)), and any representations in response must be served within 14 days after that (r. 29.13(2)(b)).

Cross-examination where defendant not represented (under the YJCEA 1999, ss. 34 to 36; CrimPR, part 31): the accused must serve notice of any representative appointed to cross-examine within seven days of the date when the accused pleads not guilty (r. 31.1(3)); the prosecutor must serve any application to prohibit cross-examination by the defendant in person as soon as reasonably practicable, and any representations in response must be served within 14 days thereafter (r. 31.4(6)(a)).

Expert evidence (under the CrimPR, part 33): if either party relies on expert evidence, the expert's report must be served within 28 days of the date when the accused pleads not guilty (although r. 33.4(1)(b)(i) merely says 'as soon as practicable'); a party who wants that expert to attend the trial must give notice within seven days thereafter, and a party who relies on expert evidence in response then has 14 days in which to serve it. There must be a meeting of experts (under r. 33.6) within 14 days of that, and the parties must notify the court immediately after the meeting if the length of the trial is affected by the outcome of the meeting.

Hearsay evidence (under the CrimPR, part 34): the prosecutor must serve any notice to intro-   **D21.43**
duce hearsay evidence within 28 days of the date when the accused pleads not guilty, and the accused must serve any notice to introduce hearsay evidence as soon as reasonably practicable (r. 34.2(3)(a)). Any application to determine an objection to hearsay evidence must be served within 14 days of service of the notice or evidence (r. 34.3(2)(c)(i)).

Bad character evidence (under the CrimPR, part 35): the prosecutor must serve any notice to introduce evidence of the defendant's bad character within 28 days of the date when the accused pleads not guilty (r. 35.4(3)(a)), and any application to determine an objection to that notice must be served within 14 days after that. Any application to introduce evidence of a non-defendant's bad character must be served within 14 days of prosecution disclosure, and any notice of objection to that evidence must be served within 14 days after that (r. 34.4(5)(b)).

Previous sexual behaviour evidence (under the YJCEA 1999, s. 41; CrimPR, part 36): the accused must serve any application for permission to introduce evidence of a complainant's previous sexual behaviour within 28 days of prosecution disclosure (r. 36(2)(b)), and the prosecutor must serve any representations in response within 14 days thereafter (r. 36.5(a)).

Points of law: any skeleton argument must be served at least 14 days before the trial, and any skeleton argument in reply must be served within seven days thereafter.

Trial readiness: the parties must certify readiness for trial at least 14 days before the trial, confirming which witnesses will give evidence in person, and the trial time estimate.

TRIAL OF INFORMATIONS AND WRITTEN CHARGES

Discretion Not to Try an Information

Save in cases where there has been inordinate delay amounting to an abuse of the process of the   **D21.44**
court (see **D21.21**), magistrates are almost always obliged to hear the prosecution evidence.
In *Birmingham Justices, ex parte Lamb* [1983] 3 All ER 23, the Divisional Court held that the justices erred in refusing to try charges for reasons such as the relative triviality of the charge, the apparent frailty of the prosecution evidence insofar as it had been disclosed, and the long period that would elapse before the court would have time to hear the case on the basis of a not guilty plea. McNeill J said (at p. 344D):

> [T]he law does not permit cases, on grounds of supposed injustice, to be dismissed out of hand without hearing any evidence. The justices can reflect their sense of injustice at the end of the prosecution case if they are not satisfied that the offence has been made out. They can reflect it at the end of the whole of the evidence by acquitting the defendant or, if they feel obliged to convict, they can reflect it by imposing such a penalty as reflects their view of the case.

It is submitted that this statement may be too wide insofar as it suggests that magistrates may *never* dismiss a charge without a hearing, since they may do so where there has been unconscionable delay or where the proceedings otherwise amount to an abuse of process (*Horseferry Road Magistrates' Court, ex parte Bennett* [1994] 1 AC 42). However, this jurisdiction is confined to cases where the accused could not receive a fair trial, or it would be unfair for him to be tried (*R (CPS) v City of London Magistrates' Court* [2006] EWHC 1153 (Admin) at [28]). See **D3.75**.

Apparent bad faith on the part of the prosecutor has also been held sufficient to justify dismissal   **D21.45**
without hearing (see *Sherwood v Ross* [1989] Crim LR 576, where a private prosecution was brought apparently as a bargaining counter in negotiations over a civil claim).

In *Watford Justices, ex parte DPP* [1990] RTR 374, a magistrates' court refused to hear evidence and dismissed two charges of burglary. The decision was taken on the basis that the accused had spent time in custody, and the charges were rather trivial. The Divisional Court granted a declaration that the magistrates had acted contrary to the MCA 1980, s. 9(2), which required them to hear evidence before convicting an accused or dismissing the information. Thus, if the prosecution wish to adduce evidence, the magistrates must hear that evidence unless the information can be dismissed on the basis that the prosecution have been guilty of abuse of process.

Discretion to Try Informations Separately

D21.46   Where an accused faces several charges, or there are several accused charged with separate offences, the decision whether the charges or accused should be tried together or separately is one for the magistrates (*Chief Constable of Norfolk v Clayton* [1983] 2 AC 473). In *Clayton*, Lord Roskill set out the practice which should be adopted in such cases. His lordship said (at pp. 491G–492E):

> ...I see no compelling reason why your lordships should not say that the practice in magistrates' courts in these matters should henceforth be analogous to the practice prescribed in *Assim* [1966] 2 QB 249 in relation to trials on indictment. Where a defendant is charged on several informations and the facts are connected..., I can see no reason why those informations should not, if the justices think fit, be heard together. Similarly, if two or more defendants are charged on separate informations but the facts are connected, I can see no reason why they should not, if the justices think fit, be heard together...Of course, when this question arises, justices will be well advised to inquire both of the prosecution and of the defence whether either side has any objection to all the informations being heard together. If consent is forthcoming on both sides, there is no problem. If such consent is not forthcoming, the justices should then consider the rival submissions and...rule as they think right in the overall interests of justice...Absence of consent, either express where the defendant is present or represented and objects or necessarily brought about by his absence or the absence of representation, should no longer in practice be regarded as a complete and automatic bar to hearing more than one information at the same time or informations against more than one defendant charged on separate informations at the same time when in the justices' view the facts are sufficiently closely connected to justify this course and there is no risk of injustice to defendants by its adoption. Accordingly, the justices should always ask themselves whether it would be fair and just to the defendant or defendants to allow a joint trial. Only if the answer is clearly in the affirmative should they order joint trial in the absence of consent by or on behalf of the defendant.

The above passage implies that where all parties (including the prosecution) are in favour of a joint trial, the court should automatically agree to that course. In the case of both prosecution and defence being *against* a joint trial, the ultimate decision is still with the magistrates, but they should be slow to exercise their discretion in favour of ordering a joint trial when all the parties want separate trials (*Highbury Corner Magistrates' Court, ex parte McGinley* (1986) 150 JP 257, per Lloyd LJ).

Successive Trials by Same Bench

D21.47   If an accused who is charged with two or more offences applies successfully for the offences to be tried separately, the question then arises whether the bench that decided in favour of separate trials may properly hear any or all of the cases. This is part of the broader question of whether knowledge that the accused faces more than one charge in their court should disqualify magistrates on the ground of possible bias (see also **D3.38**). The proper approach is to apply the usual test for bias, namely whether the fair-minded and informed observer, having considered the facts, would conclude that there was a real possibility that the tribunal was biased (per Lord Hope in *Porter v Magill* [2002] 2 AC 357 at [103]). In *Sandwich Justices, ex parte Berry* (1982) 74 Cr App R 132, Donaldson LJ, at p. 134, said that the question whether an accused who is to be tried by justices in more than one trial is entitled to a fresh bench of justices for each trial is essentially a matter for the discretion of the justices. However, his lordship observed that '[t]here may well be cases in which there would be real problems in the justices approaching a subsequent information in a proper and impartial manner or, alternatively, at least of their appearing to do so. In such a case the magistrates ought to refuse to adjudicate upon the second or subsequent informations and put it to another bench.'

Alternative Charges

It is possible for an accused to be charged with offences which are alternatives, in the sense that **D21.48** the two charges are based on the same facts and the prosecution seek a conviction on one or the other. One offence will be more serious than the other, and the prosecution present their case on the basis that the accused is guilty of the more serious offence or, alternatively, if he is not guilty of that offence then he is guilty of the lesser offence. In such a case, the accused should not be convicted of both offences, since that would effectively mean that he has been convicted twice for the same wrong, which is unfair (per Laws LJ in *R (Dyer) v Watford Magistrates' Court* (2013) 177 JP 265, at [11]). See **D22.69**.

Charges against Two or More Defendants Jointly

A single charge may be brought against two or more defendants who allegedly committed an **D21.49** offence jointly. The principles governing such cases are analogous to those governing trial of joint counts in a trial on indictment. The justices may convict either or both, whether on the basis that they did indeed commit the offence jointly or on the basis that they acted independently of each other. The acquittal of one does not prevent the conviction of the other (see, e.g., *Barsted v Jones* (1964) 124 JP 400). As at trial on indictment (see **D11.86**), there is a discretion to order separate trials where two or more defendants are jointly charged in an information. However, it is submitted that a joint trial will generally be preferable.

SPECIAL PLEAS IN THE CONTEXT OF SUMMARY TRIALS

Double Jeopardy

There is no special procedure for pleading autrefois acquit or autrefois convict at summary trial. **D21.50** However, a previous acquittal or conviction for the same matter is as much a bar to summary proceedings as it is to proceedings on indictment (*Connelly v DPP* [1964] AC 1254, per Lord Morris of Borth-y-Gest at p. 1320). The issue may be raised simply on a not guilty plea. For detailed discussion of the autrefois doctrine, see **D12.20** *et seq.*

The question most frequently raised by autrefois arising out of summary proceedings is whether there has been a genuine acquittal or, as the case may be, conviction by magistrates acting properly within their jurisdiction. If there has not, the accused is said never to have been in jeopardy and therefore unable to rely on autrefois. The withdrawal of a charge before a plea is entered does *not* found autrefois, whereas the dismissal of the charge following a not guilty plea and the offering of no evidence normally does. However, a distinction is drawn between cases where, for whatever reason, no evidence is offered and those where the proceedings in the magistrates' courts are so flawed that the accused was never in danger of a valid conviction. In the latter type of case, a purported acquittal (or conviction) does not prevent the magistrates re-trying the accused for the same offence (see *Dabhade* [1993] QB 329, where it was confirmed that fresh proceedings may be brought if (but only if) the accused was never in jeopardy of a valid conviction). Thus, where magistrates purport to acquit the accused without giving the prosecution the opportunity to call evidence, the purported acquittal is liable to be quashed and the autrefois doctrine will not prevent fresh proceedings for the same offence being instituted (*Dorking Justices, ex parte Harrington* [1984] AC 743). For example, in *Holmes v Campbell* (1998) 162 JP 655, a magistrates' court dismissed the charge against the accused when the prosecutor failed to appear at the hearing. The prosecutor subsequently brought fresh proceedings (making the same allegations) but the magistrates' court declined to try the case on the ground that it would be an abuse of process. The Divisional Court held that, by virtue of the MCA 1980, s. 15, the accused could not have been convicted at a hearing where the prosecutor was absent, and so had not been in jeopardy of conviction at that hearing. It followed that the doctrine of autrefois acquit did not prevent the hearing of the fresh charge.

A similar situation, with the same result, arose in *DPP v Jarman* (2014) 178 JP 89, where the prosecutor failed to attend and the magistrates dismissed the case for want of prosecution under s. 15. Fresh proceedings were then instituted. Griffith Williams J (at [30]) reiterated that the scope of autrefois acquit 'is narrowly confined to those cases where the accused is put in peril of conviction for the same offence as that with which he is then charged'. This requires that 'the court must be in a position to conduct a hearing and so it follows that there must be a prosecutor to prosecute and a defendant to defend unless, of course, the defendant has wilfully absented himself or herself and so the trial proceeds in his or her absence' (at [31]). In *Jarman*, the accused 'was in no way in peril because, while the court was competent to try him and there was a valid charge upon which he was to be tried, the dismissal was not on the merits; there was no prosecutor and the magistrates had heard no evidence' (at [32]).

In *J (JF)* [2013] 2 Cr App R 97 (10), the Court of Appeal undertook a detailed analysis of the scope of the autrefois doctrine. After consideration of *Connelly v DPP*, Sir John Thomas P (at [23]) concluded that 'the scope of autrefois is narrow and the offence, as well as the facts, must be the same for the plea of autrefois to apply'. Moreover, a key question is whether the accused was ever 'in peril' of being convicted on the earlier occasion. So far as magistrates' court cases are concerned, his lordship gave an example (at [45]) of where an accused would be at peril for the purposes of autrefois, namely a case where the court sets a date for trial, the accused attends, the prosecutor unsuccessfully applies for an adjournment of the trial (with the effect that the magistrates are entitled to proceed with the trial), and the prosecution then offer no evidence, with the result that the accused is acquitted by the magistrates. His lordship went on (at [50]) to rule that the accused can be 'in peril' only when the magistrates' court hearing is for the purpose of determining whether he is guilty (which can be the first hearing when the plea is put, but is more likely to be the date fixed for the summary trial).

Where the prosecution have preferred two charges in the alternative arising out of the same facts and the court puts the prosecution to their election as to the one on which they wish to proceed, the immediate dismissal of the information on which they are not proceeding does not enable the accused to rely on autrefois in respect of the other (*Broadbent v High* [1985] RTR 359).

Unfitness to Plead

D21.51 There is no specific procedure by which a person's fitness to plead may be determined in the magistrates' court (and the Criminal Procedure (Insanity) Act 1964, s. 4 and s. 4A, apply only to trial on indictment). If the accused is thought to be suffering from a mental disability such as to render him unable to comprehend the course of the proceedings or make a proper defence to the charge (i.e. he would be found unfit to plead if he were facing trial on indictment — see D12.2 *et seq.*), the defence have the following options:

(a) Assuming the offence is triable either way, the accused may elect trial on indictment and have the question of fitness determined by a jury in the Crown Court. Indeed, it would be open to the justices to decline jurisdiction on the basis that the Crown Court is the more appropriate forum for a case where fitness to plead is an issue.

(b) Assuming there is to be a summary trial, the accused may plead not guilty (or a not guilty plea may be entered on his behalf), thereby putting the prosecution to proof of their case. If the definition of the offence requires the prosecution to prove *mens rea*, and especially if the offence involves a specific intent, the accused's mental condition may make it difficult for the prosecution to discharge their burden. The common-law defence of insanity is available to an accused in a summary trial (*Horseferry Road Magistrates' Court, ex parte K* [1997] QB 23 at p. 46; *R (Singh) v Stratford Magistrates' Court* [2007] 4 All ER 407).

(c) They may invite the court to make a hospital order under the Mental Health Act 1983, s. 37(3) (as amended by the Mental Health Act 2007), without convicting the accused. Section 37(3) enables magistrates to achieve a result very similar to that which follows upon an accused being found unfit to plead to an indictment: if the court is satisfied that the accused did the act or made the omission charged, the court may, if it thinks fit, make such a hospital order without convicting him. This provision should be read in conjunction with the PCC(S)A 2000, s. 11(1), which provides that if, on the summary trial of an offence punishable with imprisonment, the court is satisfied that the accused did the act or made the omission charged, but thinks that there ought to be an inquiry into his physical or mental condition before the method of dealing with him is decided, the court must adjourn the case to enable a medical examination and report to be made.

The same principles are to be followed in respect of a young person facing trial in the youth   **D21.52**
court (*R (P) v Barking Youth Court* [2002] 2 Cr App R 294; *G v DPP* [2012] EWHC 3174 (Admin)). For detailed guidance on the approach to be taken, see *CPS v P* [2008] 4 All ER 628 (see **D24.99**).

In *R (Singh) v Stratford Magistrates' Court*, the Divisional Court considered the effect of the Mental Health Act 1983, s. 37(3). Hughes LJ (at [39]–[41]) said that a magistrates' court has the power, in an appropriate case, to try the issue of insanity and pronounce its conclusion upon it, without convicting or acquitting the accused, provided that the conditions for making an order under s. 37(3) are met. However, if satisfied that there is no purpose in resolving the issue of insanity, and if a s. 37(3) order is going to be made, the court can deal with the case without trying that issue. If it is clear that no s. 37(3) order is going to be possible on the medical evidence whatever happens then, in the absence of some other compelling factor, the case must proceed to trial. Before embarking on a case in which s. 37(3) may be applied, magistrates should make it clear that it is a possibility and should invite submissions from the parties upon the course to be adopted. In particular, careful consideration must be given to any reason advanced why the issue of insanity should be tried. Such an application should be resolved having regard to the interests of justice, which include, but are not limited to, justice to the accused.

Powers of Criminal Courts (Sentencing) Act 2000, s. 11   **D21.53**

(1) If, on the trial by a magistrates' court of an offence punishable on summary conviction with imprisonment the court—
  (a) is satisfied that the accused did the act or made the omission charged, but
  (b) is of the opinion that an inquiry ought to be made into his physical or mental condition before the method of dealing with him is determined,
  the court shall adjourn the case to enable a medical examination and report to be made, and shall remand him.
(2) An adjournment under subsection (1) above shall not be for more than three weeks at a time where the court remands the accused in custody, nor for more than four weeks at a time where it remands him on bail.
(3) Where on an adjournment under subsection (1) above the accused is remanded on bail, the court shall impose conditions under paragraph (d) of section 3(6) of the Bail Act 1976 and the requirements imposed as conditions under that paragraph shall be or shall include requirements that the accused—
  (a) undergo medical examination by a registered medical practitioner or, where the inquiry is into his mental condition and the court so directs, two such practitioners; and
  (b) for that purpose attend such an institution or place, or on such practitioner, as the court directs and, where the inquiry is into his mental condition, comply with any other directions which may be given to him for that purpose by any person specified by the court or by a person of any class so specified.

D21.54

Mental Health Act 1983, s. 37

(3) Where a person is charged before a magistrates' court with any act or omission as an offence and the court would have power, on convicting him of that offence, to make a [hospital order], then, if the court is satisfied that the accused did the act or made the omission charged, the court may, if it thinks fit, make such an order without convicting him.

D21.55 **Adjournment for Reports**   It will be noted that the power to order medical reports under the PCC(S)A 2000, s. 11(1), and the power to make a hospital order under the Mental Health Act 1983, s. 37(3), both depend merely upon the court being satisfied that the accused committed the *actus reus* of the offence with which he is charged. Therefore, in a case where the accused is apparently suffering from mental illness or impairment, the court may cause a not guilty plea to be entered on his behalf and hear the prosecution evidence. Assuming that evidence establishes the *actus reus*, the court may then adjourn for reports. If, on the basis of those reports, the medical criteria for the making of a hospital order are satisfied, the court may make such an order *without convicting the accused*. For details about the preconditions for a hospital order and, in particular, the need for reports from medical practitioners confirming that the accused is suffering from a mental disorder as defined by the Mental Health Act 1983, see **E22.1**.

D21.56 **Either-way Offences**   Where the accused is charged with an either-way offence a further difficulty arises, namely that the magistrates' court will not have jurisdiction to commence summary trial of the offence unless the accused consents to summary trial. *Ex hypothesi*, he is unlikely to be in a fit state to give his consent. In *Lincoln (Kesteven) Justices, ex parte O'Connor* [1983] 1 All ER 901, the accused was charged with assault occasioning actual bodily harm. His mental state was such that he was incapable of consenting to summary trial. The Divisional Court held that a trial is *not* a necessary precondition of the court being satisfied for the purposes of s. 37(3) that the accused committed the *actus reus* of the offence. In an exceptional case such as the instant one, where the accused was legally represented and everybody agreed that he had assaulted the victim, the justices could conclude without evidence that the offence had occurred. Therefore, they had jurisdiction to make a hospital order. It is, however, clear that the magistrates have no jurisdiction under s. 37(3) to make a hospital order in respect of a person charged with an indictable-only offence (*Chippenham Magistrates' Court, ex parte Thompson* (1996) 160 JP 207).

Section D22   Summary Trial: The Course of the Trial

PLEAS WHICH MAY BE TENDERED TO THE INFORMATION/WRITTEN CHARGE

Pleas that May Be Tendered

D22.1 A summary trial begins with the taking of the plea from the accused (MCA 1980, s. 9(1)). The justices' legal adviser (or the court) reads the allegation of the offence to the accused, explains what the procedure at the hearing will be, asks whether the accused has been advised about the potential effect on sentence of a guilty plea, and then asks whether the accused pleads guilty or not guilty (CrimPR, r. 37.2(2)).

If the accused pleads guilty, the court may convict him without hearing evidence (s. 9(3); CrimPR, r. 37.7); if he pleads not guilty, the court will proceed to try the case (or adjourn to a later date for the trial to take place. If a plea of not guilty was entered on a previous occasion, the justices' legal adviser or the court must ask the accused to confirm that plea (r. 37.3(2)).

The requirement to record a conviction following a guilty plea is without prejudice to the requirement to hold a *Newton* hearing (*Newton* (1982) 77 Cr App R 13) if there is a substantial variation between the prosecution and defence versions of the facts of the offence (see **D23.7**).

D22.2 In the absence of a guilty plea, the court is under a duty to hear evidence and either convict the accused or dismiss the charge (s. 9(2)).

Magistrates' Courts Act 1980, s. 9

(1) On the summary trial of an information, the court shall, if the accused appears, state to him the substance of the information and ask him whether he pleads guilty or not guilty.
(2) The court, after hearing the evidence and the parties, shall convict the accused or dismiss the information.
(3) If the accused pleads guilty, the court may convict him without hearing evidence.

Alternative Offences

D22.3 The only pleas which may be entered to an information are those of guilty or not guilty. Unlike the Crown Court, a magistrates' court has no power to return a verdict of not guilty as charged but guilty of a lesser offence (see *Lawrence v Same* [1968] 2 QB 93, overruled on a different point in *Chief Constable of Norfolk v Clayton* [1983] 2 AC 473), and it follows that a plea to like effect is not an option available to the accused even if the prosecution would be willing to accept it. However, in a case where a plea to something other than the offence charged would be acceptable to the parties, the procedural difficulty may be overcome simply by charging the accused with the lesser offence (assuming, if it is a summary offence, the six-month time-limit under the MCA 1980, s.127, has not expired). The accused may then plead guilty to the new charge in exchange for the prosecution offering no evidence on the original one (see also **D22.8**).

Whether or not a new charge should be added is a matter for the prosecution; the court has no power to add a charge if that course of action is opposed by the prosecution (*R (Morales) v Kettering Magistrates' Court* (2014) 178 JP 22).

Plea of Guilty

D22.4 The same basic principles govern guilty pleas at summary trial as govern such pleas at trial on indictment (see **D12.72** *et seq.*). It is essential that the plea be *unequivocal*. The CrimPR, r. 37.7(1)(b), says that the court must be satisfied that the guilty plea 'represents a clear acknowledgement of guilt'. If, when the charge is put, the accused does not answer directly or qualifies what purports to be a guilty plea with words suggesting that he is really putting forward a defence, then the court must try to resolve the ambiguity. If the plea remains ambiguous, the court must reject it and hear evidence before convicting or acquitting. The concept of an equivocal plea has been extended to pleas which, although unambiguous when made, are thrown into doubt by something which occurs between plea and sentence (e.g., the presentation of mitigation which is inconsistent with guilt, as in *Durham Quarter Sessions, ex parte Virgo* [1952] 2 QB 1). It has also been extended to pleas entered under duress (*Huntingdon Crown Court, ex parte Jordan* [1981] QB 857). One reason why justices must be careful to ensure that a purported plea of guilty is unequivocal is that if they convict and sentence on an equivocal plea the accused may appeal to the Crown Court against conviction, notwithstanding the general rule in the MCA 1980, s.108, that a person who pleads guilty in the magistrates' court may appeal only against sentence (see **D29.4**). If the Crown Court finds the plea to have been equivocal, it remits the case to the lower court with a binding direction to hear the evidence on a not guilty plea (*Plymouth Justices, ex parte Hart* [1986] QB 950).

D22.5 If the accused attends court, the plea must come from him personally and may not be entered by his counsel or solicitor on his behalf (*Wakefield Justices, ex parte Butterworth* [1970] 1 All ER 1181). This accords with the judgment in *Williams* [1978] QB 373 where Shaw LJ (at p. 378G) said that: 'No qualification of or deviation from the rule that a plea of guilty must come from him who acknowledges guilt is . . . permissible. A departure from the rule in a criminal trial would therefore necessarily be a vitiating factor rendering the whole procedure void and ineffectual.' While that was said in the context of an appeal against conviction on indictment, the Court of Appeal appears to have been laying down a general principle of application to *all* criminal proceedings. However, a special difficulty arises in magistrates' courts when the accused does not appear in person but is deemed to be present because he is legally represented (under the MCA 1980, s. 122). It is submitted that, in the light of *Williams*, it is doubtful whether a legal representative can enter a binding guilty plea in the absence of the accused.

Where the accused is a corporation, however, a duly appointed 'representative' of the corporation may, *inter alia*, consent to summary trial (where the offence is triable either way) and enter a plea of guilty or not guilty (MCA 1980, sch. 3, para. 2(b) and (c)).

Plea of Not Guilty

D22.6 A not guilty plea to an information will normally be entered by the accused personally. If, however, he is absent and the court decides to proceed in his absence, or he remains silent when asked to plead, or enters an ambiguous plea, then the court simply hears the evidence in accordance with the requirement of the MCA 1980, s. 9(2), as if there had been a not guilty plea.

The options open to the prosecution (other than proceeding to summary trial) where an accused does not plead guilty are as follows.

D22.7 **Withdrawal of Summons** The prosecution may, with the leave of the court, withdraw the summons (*Redbridge Justices, ex parte Sainty* [1981] RTR 13). If the prosecution are not in a position to prove guilt on the day appointed for the hearing, or for any other reason do not wish to proceed forthwith to trial, they may prefer to withdraw the summons (rather than offering no evidence or asking for an adjournment), since such withdrawal avoids there being a verdict of not guilty.

Consequently, a fresh summons may later be obtained in respect of the same offence, and the accused will not be able to rely upon autrefois acquit to prevent the trial on that summons proceeding.

That withdrawal of a summons is not equivalent to an acquittal was confirmed in *Grays Justices, ex parte Low* [1990] 1 QB 54. Nolan J said (at p. 59A–B):

> [T]he withdrawal of a summons with the consent of the justices will not of itself operate as a bar to the issue of a further summons in respect of the same charge where there has been no adjudication upon the merits of the charge in the original summons, and the defendant has not been put in peril of conviction upon it.

It is submitted that the same principles will apply to prosecutions commenced by way of charge at the police station and to prosecutions brought under the written charge and requisition procedure: the prosecution can avert a not guilty verdict by withdrawing the charge and then re-prosecute.

Offering No Evidence   Once the accused has entered a plea of not guilty, the option of asking   **D22.8** for the summons to be withdrawn ceases to be open to the prosecution. Therefore, if they are not ready to proceed on the date that has been fixed for trial, the only course available to them is to ask for an adjournment. If the adjournment is refused, they must either call whatever evidence they do have at court or, if that evidence would plainly be insufficient for a conviction, offer no evidence.

Other situations where it may be appropriate for the prosecution to offer no evidence are where the accused has pleaded guilty to one offence and the prosecution do not wish to proceed with another (related) charge, or where new evidence exonerating the accused has come to light, or where the CPS have reviewed the evidence and have decided that there is insufficient prospect of securing a conviction to merit continuing the proceedings.

Where the charge is dismissed following the prosecution deciding to offer no evidence, this   **D22.9** counts as an acquittal for the purpose of the doctrine of autrefois acquit. In *R (A) v South Staffordshire Youth Court* (2007) 171 JP 36, the accused was charged with assault occasioning actual bodily harm. He pleaded not guilty. The prosecution subsequently preferred the more serious charge of inflicting grievous bodily harm and offered no evidence in respect of the lesser charge, which was formally dismissed by the court. During the trial of the grievous bodily harm charge, the prosecutor concluded that he would not be able to establish that charge and offered the accused the opportunity to plead guilty to the original lesser charge. The question at issue was whether the court had jurisdiction to reopen the case on the charge of occasioning actual bodily harm. It was held that, in a case where a not guilty verdict is entered in the Crown Court under the CJA 1967, s. 17 (which provides that where the prosecutor offers no evidence, the court may order that a verdict of not guilty be recorded without the need for a verdict from a jury), an accused is entitled to rely on the defence of autrefois acquit if charged again with that offence. This principle applies equally where a magistrates' court dismisses a charge pursuant to the MCA 1980, s. 27 (which provides that where on the summary trial of an either-way offence the court dismisses the information, the dismissal shall have the same effect as an acquittal on indictment), since s. 27 is, for all practical purposes, the same as s. 17. The court was therefore *functus officio* and the decision to proceed on the lesser charge was wrong.

Change of Plea

A magistrates' court may allow an accused to change his plea from guilty to not guilty at any   **D22.10** stage before sentence is passed (*S (an infant) v Recorder of Manchester* [1971] AC 481). Lord Upjohn, at p. 507, observed that 'this discretionary power is one which should only be exercised in clear cases and very sparingly'.

The procedure for seeking permission to change plea is set out in the CrimPR, r. 37.9 (see Supplement, **R-291**). The accused must apply, in writing (unless the court directs otherwise), as soon as practicable after becoming aware of the reasons for making an application to change plea, explaining why it would be unjust not to allow him to withdraw the guilty plea, and identifying any evidence he wishes to call. The application must also say whether the accused is waiving legal professional privilege.

Whether to accede to an application for a change of plea is in the court's discretion and there is no automatic rule that an accused who was unrepresented when he entered his plea is entitled to change it upon obtaining legal representation during the period of an adjournment before sentence (*South Tameside Magistrates' Court, ex parte Rowland* [1983] 3 All ER 689). The question for the bench is whether the original plea was unequivocal and entered with a proper understanding of what the charge entailed. If it was, then the magistrates are entitled to refuse any application to change.

D22.11 In *Revitt v DPP* [2006] 1 WLR 3172, the Divisional Court applied the guidance given in *S v Recorder of Manchester*, holding that if, after an unequivocal plea of guilty has been made, it becomes apparent that the accused did not appreciate the elements of the offence to which he was pleading guilty, then it is likely to be appropriate to permit him to withdraw his plea (per Lord Phillips CJ (at [17])). Similarly, if the facts relied upon by the prosecution do not add up to the offence charged, justice will normally demand that the accused be permitted to withdraw his plea (at [18]). His lordship added (at [19]) that the onus lies on a party seeking to vacate a guilty plea to demonstrate that justice requires that this should be permitted.

If the court permits a change of plea from guilty to not guilty in the case of an either-way offence, it must go on to allow the accused to consider afresh whether to consent to summary trial and so he should be put to his election again (*Bow Street Magistrates' Court, ex parte Welcombe* (1992) 156 JP 609; see also **D6.34**).

Once the court has passed sentence, it is *functus officio*, although a conviction based upon a guilty plea may be set aside by appealing to the Crown Court on the basis that the plea was equivocal.

A magistrates' court has an unfettered discretion to allow a change of plea from not guilty to guilty at any time before a verdict is returned.

FAILURE OF PARTIES TO APPEAR

Failure of an Accused to Appear

D22.12 These paragraphs should be read in conjunction with **D5**, which deals with adjournments and with the options available to a magistrates' court upon non-appearance in answer to a summons or requisition, and **D7**, which deals with bail.

D22.13 **Trial in the Absence of the Accused: Powers and Procedure** Under the MCA 1980, s. 11(1), if the accused is under 18 years of age, the court *may* proceed in his absence (s. 11(1)(a)), and, if the accused has attained the age of 18, the court must proceed in his absence unless it appears to the court to be contrary to the interests of justice to do so (s. 11(1)(b)). Thus, where the accused is absent, assuming he is aged 18 or over, the general rule is that the court will proceed as if he were present and, unless a plea was entered on an earlier occasion, had pleaded not guilty (CrimPR, r. 37.11(3)(a)(i)). However, where proceedings were commenced by summons or by written charge and requisition, then (unless the accused has appeared on a previous occasion in answer to the summons or requisition) it must be proved to the satisfaction of the court that the summons (or requisition) was served on him a reasonable time before the hearing (MCA 1980, s. 11(2); CrimPR r. 37.11(3)(c)(i)). Proof of service of a summons or requisition is governed by the CrimPR, part 4 (see **D5.14**).

Where the case has previously been adjourned (under the MCA 1980, s. 10(1)), it is necessary to satisfy the court that the accused has had 'adequate notice' of the adjournment date (MCA 1980, s. 10(2)) or, as it is expressed in the CrimPR, r. 37.11(3)(c)(ii), 'reasonable notice' of when and where the hearing would resume. Rule 4.7(2)(g) has the effect of requiring service of such an adjournment notice to be proved in the same way as service of a summons or requisition.

If the accused does not appear and the conditions for proceeding in his absence are satisfied, a not guilty plea is entered on his behalf (CrimPR, r. 37.11(3)(a)(ii)). The burden is then on the prosecution to prove the case to the normal criminal standard, whether by calling oral evidence or by reading statements served on the accused under the CJA 1967, s. 9 (such statements are admissible in the absence of objection from the defence — positive consent is not required: see s. 9(2)(d)). Should the prosecution evidence turn out to be insufficient, the court is obliged to acquit the accused, notwithstanding his absence. Assuming, however, that the case is proved, the court may either proceed immediately to sentence or, in certain circumstances, it may adjourn to give the accused notice that he should attend for sentencing (MCA 1980, s. 10(3)).

D22.14 Where the proceedings were instituted by means of an information or by the issue of a written charge and requisition, the MCA 1980, s. 11(3) and (4), restrict the power of the court to pass a custodial sentence, or impose a disqualification, upon an offender who is absent (see **D23.10**).

D22.15 **Either-way Offences**   The power to conduct a trial in the absence of the accused applies both to either-way and summary offences. However, if the proceedings are for an either-way offence, the trial cannot proceed in the absence of the accused unless, at an earlier hearing, he consented to summary trial. It will normally be necessary for the accused to have attended in person for the determination of mode of trial (see **D6.9**). Assuming he has done so and consented to summary trial, the actual trial may then take place in his absence.

D22.16 **Determining whether to Proceed to Trial in Accused's Absence**   Section 11(2A) makes it clear that 'the court shall not proceed in the absence of the accused if it considers that there is an acceptable reason for his failure to appear'; however, s. 11(6) provides that the court is not required to inquire into the reasons for the accused's failure to appear before deciding whether to proceed in his absence. Section 11(7) requires the court to state in open court its reasons for not proceeding in the absence of an accused who has attained the age of 18 (see also the CrimPR, r. 37.11(3)(a)).

Despite the statutory presumption in favour of trying an absent accused as if he were present, the power to proceed in the absence of the accused has to be exercised with some caution. In *Dewsbury Magistrates' Court, ex parte K* (1994) *The Times*, 16 March 1994, the Divisional Court quashed the conviction in his absence of a juvenile aged 16, for burglary of a dwelling-house. Their lordships held that the convenience of the court in processing the case could not possibly outweigh the facts that he was 16, on a very serious charge entailing the risk of a custodial sentence if convicted, and had no record of non-attendance.

D22.17 **Adjournment Sought on Medical Grounds**   In *Bolton Magistrates' Court, ex parte Merna* (1991) 155 JP 612, the Divisional Court considered the position where the accused is absent, and seeks an adjournment on medical grounds. Bingham LJ (at p. 622) said that if the court suspects the grounds to be spurious or believes them to be inadequate, it should ordinarily express its doubts, giving the defendant an opportunity to seek to resolve them. The court may call for better evidence, require further inquiries to be made or adopt any other expedient that is fair to both parties. His lordship added that a claim of illness with apparently responsible professional support should not be rejected without the court satisfying itself that it is proper to reject it and that no unfairness would result. McCullough J, at p. 616C–G, said the discretion to proceed in the absence of the accused under s. 11 should be exercised judicially and with proper regard to the principle that the accused is entitled to a fair trial (including a fair opportunity to be present to hear the evidence given against him and, should he want to do so, to give evidence in his own defence and call witnesses). Where there is a medical certificate but the court is not satisfied with it, the sensible course in many cases will be to adjourn long enough for a court official or police officer to make a telephone call to the doctor to provide confirmation that the accused is indeed unfit to attend court. If the justices, after such a short adjournment, are still not satisfied, 'it may be the only reasonable thing to do will be to adjourn again to enable some further approach to be made'.

It is clear from this that the fact that a medical certificate has been received from the accused is not conclusive. In *Ealing Magistrates' Court, ex parte Burgess* (2001) 165 JP 82, the Divisional

Court reaffirmed that justices have a discretion to reject an accused's medical certificate, refuse an adjournment and proceed to hear the case in his absence. That discretion has to be exercised with proper regard to the principle that an accused has a right to a fair trial and a fair opportunity to be present. However, Tuckey LJ emphasised that the accused is entitled to a 'fair opportunity', not 'unlimited opportunity'.

D22.18   The principles applicable to such cases were helpfully summarised by Sharp J in *R (Killick) v West London Magistrates' Court* [2012] EWHC 3864 (Admin) (at [17]):

1. The overriding principle is that the court should not proceed to hear a case in the defendant's absence without satisfying itself that the claim for an adjournment may properly be rejected and that no unfairness will thereby be done . . .

2. The discretion to commence a trial in the absence of a defendant should be exercised with the utmost care and caution. Where a defendant to a criminal charge wishes to resist it and is shown by medical evidence to be unfit to attend court to do so, either as a result of involuntary illness or incapacity, it would be very rarely, if indeed ever, right for the court to exercise its discretion in favour of commencing the trial, or to proceed to hear the case in his absence, at any rate unless the defendant is represented and asks that the trial should begin . . .

3. If a court asked for an adjournment on medical grounds, suspects the grounds to be spurious or believes them to be inadequate, the court should ordinarily express its doubts and thereby give the defendant an opportunity to resolve those doubts . . .

4. A court considering an application to adjourn will need carefully to distinguish between genuine reasons for the defendant not being present and those reasons which are spuriously advanced or designed to frustrate the process. However, if the court comes to the conclusion that either of the latter is the case, it should say so. It cannot simply be inferred that a court has come to that conclusion unless that is clearly stated by the magistrates . . .

5. If a conclusion is open to the court reasonably on the material before it either to the effect that an excuse given is spurious or there is a truly compelling and exceptional reason for proceeding notwithstanding a good excuse for non-attendance, the court has the power to do so. This however will be an exceptional case . . .

CPD I, para. 5C.3 (see Supplement, **PD-15**), emphasises that the court 'is not absolutely bound by a medical certificate' and may require the medical practitioner who provided the certificate to give evidence or may exercise its discretion to disregard a certificate which it finds 'unsatisfactory'. Paragraph 5C.4 goes on to state that the circumstances in which the court may find a medical certificate 'unsatisfactory' include cases where the certificate indicates that the accused is unfit to attend work (rather than to attend court), where the nature of the his ailment (e.g., a broken arm) does not appear to be capable of preventing his attendance at court, or where the accused is certified as suffering from stress, anxiety, or depression and there is no indication of him recovering within a realistic timescale. Paragraph 5C.5 stipulates that a medical certificate should set out the 'exact nature' of the ailment from which the accused is suffering and (unless it is self-evident) why that ailment prevents him from attending court; the certificate must also give an indication as to when the accused is likely to be able to attend court, or a date when the certificate expires.

D22.19   **Involuntary Absence of Accused**   In *R (R (a Juvenile)) v Thames Youth Court* (2002) 166 JP 613, the accused was a juvenile. On the day his trial was listed for hearing before the youth court, he was arrested in connection with an unrelated offence and so was unable to attend the youth court. The district judge decided to try the case in his absence. Pitchford J said (at [29]) that in cases where an accused has plainly not absented himself from his trial voluntarily, but fully expected to be present, the threshold of prejudice and fairness that the accused has to demonstrate for the purposes of establishing that a guilty verdict might be unsafe is a comparatively low one, particularly where he is a juvenile. It is an important consideration that a juvenile might not have the same level of understanding as an adult. However, it is submitted that it would be wrong in principle for an accused to be tried in his absence in any case where the court is aware that the absence is unavoidable and out of the accused's control. Some support for this view may be derived from the decision in *Jones* [2003] 1 AC 1 (see **D15.89**), where the House of Lords held (in the context of trial on indictment) that a judge has a discretion to commence a trial in the absence of the accused, but this discretion should be exercised with great caution; if the absence is attributable to involuntary illness or incapacity it would be very rarely, if ever, right to do so, at any rate unless the accused was represented and asked that the trial should begin (per Lord Bingham at [13]). These principles were applied to summary trial by Beatson J in *R (Drinkwater) v Solihull Magistrates' Court* (2012) 176 JP 401, at [32]–[35]. In particular, his lordship applied the dictum of Hughes LJ in *Armouchi* [2007] EWCA Crim 3019, at [10], that proceeding in the absence of an accused is 'a step which ought normally to be taken only if it is unavoidable'. In the instant case, the magistrates were held to have erred in refusing to grant an adjournment (with the effect that the trial took place in the absence of the accused) because they did not give adequate consideration to the factors militating against trial in the absence of the accused. It is submitted that this also needs to be put in the context of the effect of the presumption created by the MCA 1980, s. 11, that the court must proceed in the absence of the accused if he does not attend, unless it appears to the court to be contrary to the interests of justice to do so, and the proviso that the court cannot proceed in the absence of the accused if it considers that there is an 'acceptable reason' for his failure to appear.

Thames Youth Court was followed in *R (Davies) v Solihull Justices* [2008] EWHC 1157 (Admin). After his case had been called on, it was discovered that the accused had been excluded from the court building by the security staff because of disorderly behaviour. The justices ruled that the accused had, by virtue of his conduct, voluntarily absented himself from the hearing of his case, and that he should be tried in his absence. Underhill J (at [9]) said that it is only in 'very rare circumstances' that a criminal trial may proceed in the absence of the accused. In general, a trial may only proceed in his absence where either the accused disrupts the proceedings in court to such an extent that it is necessary to remove him so that the case can proceed, or where he had absconded or deliberately absented himself from the hearing. In the present case, the accused's misbehaviour did not justify excluding him from his own trial. Moreover, the justices erred in treating him as being voluntarily absent, since he had wanted to be in court but was prevented by the exclusion. Whilst it could be said that the exclusion was his own fault, that was not the same as it being his own choice; the position was no different than if he had committed an offence on the way to court and then been arrested. Moreover, the court had taken no steps to see if attendance could be secured. A pragmatic approach would have been for the court to issue a warning to the accused that if he misbehaved in court he would be removed and that his trial would proceed in his absence.

Adjournments   Another option open to the court if it does not try the accused in his absence is **D22.20** simply to adjourn the case (under the MCA 1980, s. 10(1)). Under s. 10(2), the court may either set the date for the hearing to resume when it adjourns the case or, unless it remands the accused (in which case a date must be fixed), leave the time and place to be determined. The trial can resume only where the court is satisfied that the parties have had adequate notice; if the accused was not present when the case was adjourned, it will therefore be necessary to send an adjournment notice to him.

Warrant for Arrest   Under the MCA 1980, s. 13(1), where the court, instead of proceeding in **D22.21** the absence of the accused, adjourns or further adjourns the trial, it has the option of issuing a warrant for his arrest, provided that the offence in question is punishable with imprisonment, or the court, having convicted the accused, proposes to impose a disqualification on him (s. 13(3) (adults) and s. 13(3A) (juveniles)). For this provision to apply, it must be proved to the satisfaction of the court that the summons or requisition was served on the accused within a reasonable time before the trial (s. 13(2A)), unless the present adjournment is a second or subsequent adjournment of the trial, the accused was present on the last occasion when the trial was adjourned and the date for the present hearing was fixed then (s. 13(2B)).

If the accused appears to be evading service of the summons or requisition, and the offence is an indictable one, it is open to the prosecution to start proceedings again by seeking an arrest warrant. The MCA 1980, s. 1(6), provides that, 'Where the offence charged is an indictable offence, a warrant under this section may be issued at any time notwithstanding that a summons has, or a written charge and requisition have, previously been issued'.

If the accused is currently on bail and fails to attend court, a warrant for his arrest may, in any event, be issued under the Bail Act 1976, s. 7(1).

Declaration that the Accused Did Not Know of the Proceedings

D22.22 The provisions as to service of a summons or requisition, and the possibility of trial in absence, make it possible for an accused to be tried and sentenced when, in fact, he knew nothing of the proceedings (e.g., if the summons was left for him with someone else at his address who failed to pass it on). The MCA 1980, s. 14(1), therefore provides a procedure by which a conviction in absence may be set aside. The accused must make a statutory declaration that he did not know of the summons (or requisition) or of the proceedings until a date after the court had begun to try the case. The declaration must specify the date on which he first had knowledge of the proceedings, and must be served on the court within 21 days thereof. The effect of a timely statutory declaration is to make void the summons (or requisition) and all subsequent proceedings, although the information (or written charge) itself is unaffected. Consequently, the prosecution may serve a fresh summons (or requisition) for the same offence, even if it is a summary offence and more than six months have elapsed since the date of commission. Under s. 14(3), the court may allow a statutory declaration to take effect even though it is served out of time if, in the circumstances, it appears to the court that it was not reasonable for the accused to serve the declaration within the 21 days permitted. The accused may appear before the court in person to make a statutory declaration, or he may send the declaration to the clerk's office by registered letter or recorded delivery (s. 14(2)). The procedure established by s. 14 is summarised in the CrimPR, r. 37.16 (see Supplement, **R-298**).

D22.23
Magistrates' Courts Act 1980, s. 14

(1) Where a summons has been issued under section 1 above and a magistrates' court has begun to try the information to which the summons relates, then, if—
  (a) the accused, at any time during or after the trial, makes a statutory declaration that he did not know of the summons or the proceedings until a date specified in the declaration, being a date after the court has begun to try the information; and
  (b) within 21 days of that date the declaration is served on the designated officer for the court, without prejudice to the validity of the information, the summons and all subsequent proceedings shall be void.
(2) For the purposes of subsection (1) above a statutory declaration shall be deemed to be duly served on the designated officer if it is delivered to him, or left at his office, or is sent in a registered letter or by the recorded delivery service addressed to him at his office.
(3) If on the application of the accused it appears to a magistrates' court (which for this purpose may be composed of a single justice) that it was not reasonable to expect the accused to serve such a statutory declaration as is mentioned in subsection (1) above within the period allowed by that subsection, the court may accept service of such a declaration by the accused after that period has expired; and a statutory declaration accepted under this subsection shall be deemed to have been served as required by that subsection.
(4) Where any proceedings have become void by virtue of subsection (1) above, the information shall not be tried again by any of the same justices.

Plea of Guilty by Post

D22.24 To avoid the inconvenience of putting the prosecution to proof in cases where the accused does not wish to contest the charge but is unwilling to attend court to plead guilty, the MCA 1980, s. 12, sets out a procedure allowing the accused to plead guilty by post.

D22.25 **Procedure** The procedure applies to proceedings for summary offences started by means of summons or requisition in a magistrates' court (s. 12(1)) or, where the accused is aged 16 or 17, in a youth court (s. 12(2)). Whether to give the accused the option of pleading by post is at the discretion of the prosecutor. The main steps in the procedure are:

(a) With the summons (or requisition), the prosecutor serves (i) a notice summarising the effect of s. 12, (ii) a concise statement of the facts of the offence or a copy of the written statements under the CJA 1967, s. 9, and (iii) a notice setting out any information relating to the accused which will, or may, be placed before the court by or on behalf of the prosecutor (s. 12(3)). If the witness statements are served, they are admissible as evidence unless the accused objects. If the accused fails to plead guilty by post or to attend court to plead not guilty, and so fails to object to the use of the witness statements as evidence, the court can proceed to try him in his absence, the prosecution case being based upon the witness statements already served on him. In *Rymer v DPP* [2011] 1 WLR 188, Hooper LJ (at [68]) expressed the view that failure to use the form prescribed is unlikely to result in a conviction based on a postal plea of guilty being quashed, provided that the notice contains a sufficient statement of the effect of s. 12.

(b) The prosecutor notifies the court that the above documents have been served (s. 12(1)(b)).

(c) Assuming he wishes to take advantage of the procedure, the accused (or his solicitor) must notify the court in writing that he desires to plead guilty without attending court (s. 12(4)). A form is normally enclosed with the summons for the purpose. On the form (or in an accompanying letter), the accused may state any mitigating circumstances that he wants brought to the court's attention. Provided the notification is received before the actual hearing, it does not matter that it arrives after the return date specified in the summons or requisition (*Norham and Islandshire Justices, ex parte Sunter Bros Ltd* [1961] 1 All ER 455). If the offence is endorsable, he must also send his driving licence, plus a statement of his date of birth and sex (RTOA 1988, ss. 7 and 8).

(d) If the court is satisfied that all the above has been done, it may proceed to hear and dispose of the case as if the accused had appeared and pleaded guilty (MCA 1980, s. 12(5)). The prosecutor may, but need not, be present (s. 12(5)). The notification of a guilty plea, the statement of facts served by the prosecution or (unless the court otherwise directs) the written statement or statements under the CJA 1967, s. 9, and any statement submitted in mitigation must be read out by the clerk in open court (s. 12(7)–(7B)). Failure to do so will render the proceedings a nullity. In *Epping and Ongar Justices, ex parte Breach* [1987] RTR 233, for example, the Divisional Court quashed a company's conviction and sentence for using an overloaded goods vehicle because, although the company had entered a plea of guilty by post, its statement in mitigation had not been read out. Moreover, such errors cannot be remedied by the bench reconsidering its decision within 28 days under the provisions of the MCA 1980, s. 142(2), since that subsection applies only where the accused has been *found* guilty, not where he has given notice of intention to plead guilty (see *Ex parte Breach*). It is also a strict rule that the only statement about the facts of the offence allowed to be given by or on behalf of the prosecution is that which they served on the accused with the summons (s. 12(8)). Thus, when he pleads guilty by post, the accused knows exactly how the case against him will be put.

(e) The court is not obliged to hear and dispose of the case on a plea of guilty by post simply because the parties have chosen to adopt the procedure. The magistrates may, in their discretion, decide that the case is not appropriate for such disposal. If so, they must adjourn so that (at the resumed hearing) the case may be dealt with as if the plea had never been notified (s. 12(9)). The adjournment notice sent to the accused must state the reason for the adjournment (s. 12(10)). Alternatively, the magistrates may accept the plea, hear the statement of facts and mitigation, and then decide that the accused ought to be given an opportunity to attend before sentence is pronounced. If so, they adjourn after convicting. Again the notice of adjournment must specify the reason for it (s. 12(10) and see *Mason* [1965] 2 All ER 308, where a disqualification from driving imposed in the absence of the accused after he had been convicted on a plea of guilty by post at an earlier hearing was quashed because the adjournment notice failed to state that the reason why the magistrates adjourned on the first occasion was because they were considering disqualification). Indeed it should be borne in mind that a sentence of imprisonment, or disqualification from driving, cannot be imposed in the absence of the accused. If the court is minded to impose such a sentence, the accused will be summoned to attend on a later occasion (MCA 1980, s. 11(3) and (4)).

(f) At any time before the hearing, the accused may withdraw his plea of guilty by post simply by giving written notice to that effect to the clerk (s. 12(6)). The magistrates have jurisdiction at the hearing itself to allow a change of plea, enabling an accused who earlier pleaded guilty by post to contest the matter (*Bristol Justices, ex parte Sawyers* [1988] Crim LR 754).

Part D Procedure

D

This procedure is summarised in the CrimPR, rr. 37.8 and 37.14(4) (see Supplement, **R-290** and **R-296**).

D22.26 **Where Accused Attends Court after Plea of Guilty by Post**   The MCA 1980, s. 12A, makes provision for the application of s. 12 where the accused appears in court. If the accused has indicated that he wishes to plead guilty by post but nevertheless appears before the court, the court may (if the accused consents) proceed as if the accused were absent. Similarly, if the accused has not indicated that he wishes to plead guilty by post but, when he attends court, indicates that he wishes to plead guilty, the court may (if he consents) proceed as if he were absent and he had indicated an intention to plead guilty by post. Where the court proceeds as if the accused were absent, the prosecution summary of the facts of the case must not go beyond the statement served on the accused when he was given the option of pleading guilty by post. However, if the accused is in fact present in court, he must be given the opportunity to make an oral submission with a view to mitigation of sentence.

In *Rymer v DPP* [2011] 1 WLR 188, the accused chose to plead guilty by post, his written plea of guilty was accepted at a hearing in his absence, and a conviction was recorded; the court then adjourned the case to consider whether he should be disqualified from driving. At the adjourned hearing, before sentence had been passed, the accused informed the court that he wished to plead not guilty. The Divisional Court held that he had no automatic right to plead not guilty; rather, he had to show a good reason why he should be allowed to change his plea.

D22.27 **DVLA Printout**   The 'pleading guilty by post' system is used most commonly for driving offences, and so the RTOA 1988, s. 13, makes provision for a printout from the DVLA to be admissible as evidence of previous convictions for traffic offences without the need to give the defendant advance notice of intention to refer to these previous convictions (see **C2.20**).

Statutory Material

D22.28   Magistrates' Courts Act 1980, s. 12

(1) This section shall apply where—
    (a) a summons has been issued requiring a person to appear before a magistrates' court, other than a youth court, to answer to an information for a summary offence, not being—
        (i) [repealed]
        (ii) an offence specified in an order made by the Secretary of State by statutory instrument; and
    (b) the designated officer for the court is notified by or on behalf of the prosecutor that the documents mentioned in subsection (3) below have been served upon the accused with the summons.
(2) The reference in subsection (1)(a) above to the issue of a summons requiring a person to appear before a magistrates' court other than a youth court includes a reference to the issue of a summons requiring a person who has attained the age of 16 at the time when it is issued to appear before a youth court.
(3) The documents referred to in subsection (1)(b) above are—
    (a) a notice containing such statement of the effect of this section as may be prescribed;
    (b) either of the following, namely—
        (i) a concise statement of such facts relating to the charge as will be placed before the court by the prosecutor if the accused pleads guilty without appearing before the court, or
        (ii) a copy of such written statement or statements complying with subsections (2)(a) and (b) and (3) of section 9 of the Criminal Justice Act 1967 (proof by written statement) as will be so placed in those circumstances; and
    (c) if any information relating to the accused will or may, in those circumstances, be placed before the court by or on behalf of the prosecutor, a notice containing or describing that information.
(4) Where the designated officer for the court receives a notification in writing purporting to be given by the accused or by a legal representative acting on his behalf that the accused desires to plead guilty without appearing before the court—
    (a) the designated officer for the court shall inform the prosecutor of the receipt of the notification; and
    (b) the following provisions of this section shall apply.

(5) If at the time and place appointed for the trial or adjourned trial of the information—
  (a) the accused does not appear; and
  (b) it is proved to the satisfaction of the court, on oath or in such manner as may be prescribed, that the documents mentioned in subsection (3) above have been served upon the accused with the summons,
the court may, subject to section 11(3) and (4) above and subsections (6) to (8) below, proceed to hear and dispose of the case in the absence of the accused, whether or not the prosecutor is also absent, in like manner as if both parties had appeared and the accused had pleaded guilty.

(6) If at any time before the hearing the designated officer for the court receives an indication in writing purporting to be given by or on behalf of the accused that he wishes to withdraw the notification—
  (a) the designated officer for the court shall inform the prosecutor of the withdrawal; and
  (b) the court shall deal with the information as if the notification had not been given.

(7) Before accepting the plea of guilty and convicting the accused under subsection (5) above, the court shall cause the following to be read out before the court by the clerk of the court, namely—
  (a) in a case where a statement of facts as mentioned in subsection (3)(b)(i) above was served on the accused with the summons, that statement;
  (aa) in a case where a statement or statements as mentioned in subsection (3)(b)(ii) above was served on the accused with the summons and the court does not otherwise direct, that statement or those statement;
  (b) any information contained in a notice so served, and any information described in such a notice and produced by or on behalf of the prosecutor;
  (c) the notification under subsection (4) above; and
  (d) any submission received with the notification which the accused wishes to be brought to the attention of the court with a view to mitigation of sentence.

(7A) Where the court gives a direction under subsection (7)(aa) above the court shall cause an account to be given orally before the court by the clerk of the court of so much of any statement as is not read aloud.

(7B) Whether or not a direction under paragraph (aa) of subsection (7) above is given in relation to any statement served as mentioned in that paragraph the court need not cause to be read out the declaration required by section 9(2)(b) of the Criminal Justice Act 1967.

(8) If the court proceeds under subsection (5) above to hear and dispose of the case in the absence of the accused, the court shall not permit—
  (a) any other statement with respect to any facts relating to the offence charged; or
  (b) any other information relating to the accused,
to be made or placed before the court by or on behalf of the prosecutor except on a resumption of the trial after an adjournment under section 10(3) above.

(9) If the court decides not to proceed under subsection (5) above to hear and dispose of the case in the absence of the accused, it shall adjourn or further adjourn the trial for the purpose of dealing with the information as if the notification under subsection (4) above had not been given.

(10) In relation to an adjournment on the occasion of the accused's conviction in his absence under subsection (5) above or to an adjournment required by subsection (9) above, the notice required by section 10(2) above shall include notice of the reason for the adjournment.

(11) No notice shall be required by section 10(2) above in relation to an adjournment—
  (a) which is for not more than 4 weeks; and
  (b) the purpose of which is to enable the court to proceed under subsection (5) above at a later time.

Failure of Prosecutor to Appear

If the prosecutor does not appear for the trial or adjourned trial (but the accused is present), **D22.29** the court may at its discretion either (a) dismiss the information, or (b) adjourn the trial, or (c) proceed in the prosecutor's absence (MCA 1980, s. 15(1)). Section 15 is supplemented by the CrimPR, r. 37.11(2), which provides that, where the prosecutor is absent, the court may, if it has already received evidence, deal with the case as if the prosecutor were present; otherwise, the court should inquire into the reasons for the prosecutor's absence and, if satisfied there is no good reason, may exercise its power to dismiss the allegation.

The option of proceeding in the absence of the prosecutor is available only if the court has received evidence on a previous occasion (i.e. the case was adjourned part-heard after prosecution evidence sufficient to raise a case to answer had been adduced — if that has not been done, the court obviously cannot proceed in the prosecutor's absence because there will be no one with standing to call the evidence).

Should the court decide to adjourn, it may not remand the accused in custody unless (a) he has been brought from custody or (b) he cannot be remanded on bail because of his failure to find sureties (s. 15(2)).

The power to dismiss the charge has not been conferred for punitive purposes. The justices must not, therefore, exercise their power to dismiss where they know that a prosecutor is on the way to court, and that the case is otherwise ready to be presented (*Hendon Justices, ex parte DPP* [1994] QB 167); nor should the power be invoked where the prosecutor is present but unable to proceed because of the absence of the prosecution file (*DPP v Shuttleworth* (2002) 166 JP 417). In *DPP v Jarman* (2014) 178 JP 89, the prosecutor failed to attend and the magistrates dismissed the case for want of prosecution under the MCA 1980, s. 15. Griffith Williams J said (at [36]) that:

> While the overriding objective [in the CrimPR, part 1] includes... the requirement to deal with cases efficiently and expeditiously, the... power to dismiss proceedings pursuant to s 15 of the Act must not... be used, save in the most exceptional cases, to, in effect, punish the prosecution for its inefficiency.

Where a magistrates' court dismisses a charge under s. 15 without consideration of the merits of the case because of the non-attendance of the prosecutor, there is no rule of law which prevents the court dealing with an identical charge subsequently preferred against the same accused; the question to be decided is whether the new charge amounts to an abuse of process, and so the court must consider what prejudice would be caused by the preferment of that new charge (*Holmes v Campbell* (1998) 162 JP 655).

Failure of Both Parties to Appear

D22.30 Should neither the prosecutor nor the accused appear for the trial (or adjourned trial) of an information, the court may either dismiss the information or — if evidence has been received on a previous occasion — proceed in their absence (MCA 1980, s. 16).

Appearance by Legal Representative

D22.31 The parties to proceedings in magistrates' courts may be represented by legal representatives (MCA 1980, s. 122(1)). Alternatively, they may conduct their case in person. It is not the practice to grant persons other than the parties or their legal representatives a right of audience, unless statute expressly allows for alternative representation in a particular category of case. However, where a party wishes to have the assistance of a friend, the friend may sit by the party, advise during the course of the hearing, suggest questions or points for argument etc., although he will not be permitted actually to ask questions of witnesses himself or address the court (*McKenzie v McKenzie* [1971] P 33). See D3.118.

The nature of the assistance permitted was examined by the Court of Appeal in *Leicester City Justices, ex parte Barrow* [1991] 2 QB 260. Watkins LJ, giving the judgment of the court, confirmed that a party was entitled to have someone attend as a friend, to take notes, to quietly make suggestions, and to give advice. His lordship said (at p. 289), that a litigant has the right to present his own case and, in doing so, to arm himself with such assistance as he thought necessary, subject to the right of the court to intervene; he did not have to seek the leave of the court to exercise that right. Nevertheless, the court should be informed of the fact that a party would have his adviser with him; and, if the assistance was unreasonable in nature or degree, was provided for an improper purpose or was in any way inimical to the administration of justice, the court could restrict him in the use of that assistance.

D22.32 Where a party does not attend court but is represented by a legal representative, he is deemed not to be absent (s. 122(2)). The prosecution is customarily conducted by a Crown Prosecutor, or counsel or a solicitor acting on behalf of the CPS. If the accused chooses not to attend but to be legally represented, his representative may cross-examine the prosecution witnesses, make submissions and speeches, and even call witnesses other than the accused, exactly as if his client were present. Furthermore, the effect of s. 122(2) is that the presence of the legal representative precludes the issue of a warrant for the accused's arrest under s. 13 (warrants for arrest where the court adjourns instead of proceeding in the absence of the accused). However, s. 122(3) limits the effect of this deeming provision to the extent that a represented party is *not* deemed to be present if his presence was required to 'satisfy any provision of any enactment or any condition of a recognizance expressly requiring his presence'. Consequently, an accused who fails to surrender to custody in answer to his bail may have a warrant issued for his arrest whether or not he is legally represented in court (see the Bail Act 1976, s. 3(1), which provides that a person granted bail in criminal proceedings shall be under a duty to surrender to custody, and s. 7(1) which empowers the court to issue a bench warrant if he does not do so). Similarly, the terms of the MCA 1980, s. 23, make it clear that proceedings to determine mode of trial require the actual presence of the accused save in the exceptional circumstances defined in the section.

Magistrates' Courts Act 1980, s. 122   D22.33

(1) A party to any proceedings before a magistrates' court may be represented by a legal representative.
(2) Subject to subsection (3) below, an absent party so represented shall be deemed not to be absent.
(3) Appearance of a party by a legal representative shall not satisfy any provision of any enactment or any condition of a recognisance expressly requiring his presence.

THE COURSE OF THE TRIAL

Active Case Management: Applying the Criminal Procedure Rules

In *Essential Case Management: Applying the Criminal Procedure Rules* (December 2009) the point is   D22.34
made that, on the day of the trial, the court should begin by establishing what disputed issues the parties intend to explore. The court may also require the parties to provide a 'timed "batting order" of live witnesses', details of any formal admissions and written evidence, 'warning of any point of law', and 'a timetable for the whole case'. Moreover, during the trial, 'the court must ensure that "live" evidence, questions, and submissions are strictly directed to the relevant disputed issues'.

In *R (Drinkwater) v Solihull Magistrates' Court* (2012) 176 JP 401 (Admin), Sir John Thomas P said (at [47]) that it is 'self-evident that proceedings in the magistrates' courts ought to be simple, speedy and summary. That requires close attention to the Criminal Procedure Rules and active case management before *and during* the trial' (emphasis added). His lordship went on to emphasise the importance of setting a timetable (see **D21.40**) and added that, at the commencement of the trial, the court 'should check with the parties that the timetable and the estimates remain valid. If there is any variation which lengthens the estimate, the court should make every effort to see if the trial can still be accommodated that day by sitting late or otherwise' (at [51]). Moreover, once the trial has started, 'the court must actively manage the trial, keeping an eye on progress in relation to the timetable' (at [52]). His lordship noted (at [54]) that if a magistrates' court case cannot be concluded on time, the magistrates may not be available to continue the hearing the following day. The consequential delay is 'plainly inimical to the principles of speedy and summary justice', making it 'essential that the closest attention is paid to timetabling, that the case is actively managed and concluded within the estimate'.

CPD VI, para. 37A.11 (see Supplement, **PD-48**), states that, immediately prior to the commencement of the trial, the justices' legal adviser must summarise for the court the agreed and disputed issues, together with the way in which the parties propose to present their cases. This will usually be based on the contents of the trial preparation form. If it is done by way of a 'pre-court briefing', it should be confirmed in court or agreed with the parties.

The stages of the summary trial itself are set out in the CrimPR, r. 37.3.

Witnesses Waiting to Testify

D22.35   The CrimPR, r. 37.4(2)(a), stipulates that, in the absence of a direction to the contrary, a witness who is waiting to give evidence must (unless he is either a party to the proceedings or an expert witness) wait outside the courtroom.

In *Carty* (2011) 175 JP 424, it was held that there is no rule of law which compels the exclusion of factual witnesses from a trial prior to their giving evidence, although it is good practice for witnesses to be excluded in the normal course of things (per Mackay J (at [10])). His lordship noted that, while the PACE 1984, s. 78, might operate so as to give the court a discretion to exclude the evidence of a prosecution witness if his earlier presence in court might lead to the creation of an adverse effect on the fairness of the trial, this provision would not apply in the case of a witness called by a co-accused (as had occurred in that case).

THE PROSECUTION CASE

Opening Speech

D22.36   Assuming the accused pleads not guilty, the prosecution representative has the right to make an opening speech, summarising the prosecution case and identifying the relevant law and facts, before calling his evidence (CrimPR, r. 37.3(3)(a)). The opening is usually kept short and, in straightforward cases, may be dispensed with completely.

In *L and B v DPP* [1998] 2 Cr App R 69, the case had been adjourned for a month after the main prosecution witnesses had given evidence. At the resumed hearing, the justices invited the prosecutor to deliver a second speech in order to remind them of evidence which they were having difficulty remembering. On appeal to the Divisional Court, the appellants contended that the prosecution should not have been allowed to address the justices again. The Divisional Court dismissed the appeal. There was nothing unfair in the prosecutor being asked to remind the court of evidence which had been given, subject to the safeguard that the defence should invariably be asked to address the court in reply, to correct any errors or draw attention to any differences of recollection.

Witnesses whom the Prosecution Must Call

D22.37   After the opening speech (if any), the prosecutor must call evidence (CrimPR, r. 37.3(3)(b)). Where a prosecution witness attends court to give evidence in a summary trial, the prosecutor is obliged to call him to give evidence if the defence so requests, or at least tender him for cross-examination (*Wellingborough Magistrates' Court, ex parte Francois* (1994) 158 JP 813). If the prosecutor serves a bundle of witness statements on the defence prior to summary trial, the prosecution must call as witnesses all the people whose statements have been served, unless any of the exceptions which relate to Crown Court trials are applicable (see **D16.20**). Otherwise, the prosecutor retains an unfettered discretion until the case starts, and the outline of the evidence is given to the court in the opening speech. If the prosecution choose not to call a particular witness and the court is satisfied that the interests of justice require that he should give evidence and that it would be unfair to the defence that he should not do so, they should so rule, although the court cannot compel the prosecutor to call a witness. In an appropriate case, the justices may call the witness themselves (*Haringey Justices, ex parte DPP* [1996] QB 351, per Stuart-Smith LJ at pp. 358–9).

WRITTEN EVIDENCE AT SUMMARY TRIAL: CRIMINAL JUSTICE ACT 1967, s. 9

D22.38   A party wishing to tender a written statement as evidence at a summary trial rather than calling the maker of the statement may make use of the provisions of the CJA 1967, s. 9. Part 27 of the

CrimPR (see Supplement, **R-204** *et seq.*) governs the use of witness statements under the CJA 1967, s. 9. The main points about s. 9 are that:

(a) The statement must be signed by the maker, and must contain a declaration that it is true to the best of his knowledge and belief, and that he made it knowing that if it were tendered in evidence he might be prosecuted for wilfully stating in it anything he knew to be false or did not believe to be true (s. 9(2)(a) and (b)). In *Wood v DPP* (2010) 174 JP 562, Mitting J ruled that the fact that the statutory declaration on the statement referred to two pages, when there were in fact three, did not render the statement inadmissible.

(b) A copy of the statement (together with a copy of any documentary exhibit it refers to) must be served on each of the other parties (s. 9(2)(c)). If, within seven days of service, any of them serves a counter-notice objecting to the statement being put in evidence, it may not be used (s. 9(2)(d)). It follows that a party wishing to avail himself of s. 9 should serve the copy statement at least seven days before the proposed hearing date. The onus is then on his opponent to object to the statement within the week. However, the strict requirements of service of the copy statement may be waived by the opposing party (proviso to s. 9(2)). Conversely, even where the copy statement was served more than a week before the hearing and no objection to its being read was indicated, the court may, of its own volition or on the application of a party, require the maker of the statement to attend and give oral evidence (s. 9(4)(b)). In practice, where a s. 9 statement has been served on the defence but, by inadvertence, no notice objecting it was given within the statutory time, the court is likely to adjourn for the witness to be called rather than insisting upon the strict letter of s. 9(2). This is particularly so where the accused is unrepresented. In *Wood v DPP*, the accused had received an unsigned copy of the original statement of a prosecution witness. Mitting J held that the court was nonetheless entitled to admit the (signed) original statement, the contents of which were identical to those of the unsigned copy served on the defence.

(c) The CrimPR, r. 27.1, requires that written statements to be tendered in evidence under s. 9 must be in the prescribed form. There is also a prescribed form to accompany the statements, indicating the intention of the prosecutor to tender those statements in evidence in the absence of objection from the defence.

(d) Where a statement is admitted in evidence under s. 9, it is either read in full to the court or, at the court's discretion, parts of it may be summarised (s. 9(6); CrimPR, r. 37.5). Rule 27.1(6), provides that where a written statement is tendered in accordance with s. 9, the name of the maker of the statement must be read aloud unless the court otherwise directs. Rule 27.1(7) requires that where, under s. 9(6), any part of the evidence is read out aloud (or summarised), the evidence shall be read (or summarised) by or on behalf of the party who has tendered the evidence.

Under r. 27.3, if the statement refers to a document or object as an exhibit, it must describe that exhibit so as to identify it clearly, and the exhibit must be labelled or marked (with the label or mark being signed by the maker of the statement). Rule 27.4(1) provides that a party wanting to introduce in evidence a written statement must serve a copy on the court and each other party before the hearing and must serve the statement or an authenticated copy on the court at or before that hearing. Where a party relies on only part of a statement, the copy must be marked in such a way as to make that clear (r. 27.4(2)). Under r. 27.4(3), where a prosecutor serves a copy of a statement on the defence, the defence must be informed of their right, within seven days of service, to object to the introduction of the statement in evidence (rather than the witness giving evidence in person). By virtue of r. 27.4(4), the court may require the witness to give evidence in person either on application by a party to the proceedings or on its own initiative.

A s. 9 statement is *not* to be taken conclusively to be true, but is merely 'admissible as evidence to the like extent as oral evidence to the like effect by [the maker]' would be admissible (s. 9(1)). It follows that if the defence fail to serve a notice objecting to the admissibility of the statement, they are not precluded at trial from adducing evidence inconsistent with it (*Lister v Quaife* [1983] 2 All ER 29). The position is then analogous to that which arises when a prosecution witness is called in person but significant differences between his evidence and the anticipated defence evidence are not put to him in cross-examination as they ought to be. Although the court may then treat the defence case on the disputed areas with some scepticism, it is not entitled to reject it out of hand and — if left in doubt by the combined effect of the defence evidence and the formally unchallenged prosecution evidence — would be obliged to give the benefit of the doubt to the defence. However, the defence should not use the reasoning in *Lister v Quaife* as a tactical device so as to avoid the necessity of putting the defence case to a prosecution witness in person (per May LJ at p. 55B). If there are differences between the defence case and the contents of a proposed s. 9 statement, then a notice should be served objecting to the statement. In the event of failure to give such notice and defence witnesses then contradicting the statement, the prosecution should ask for an adjournment so that the maker of the statement can be called. The court ought not only to agree to the adjournment but should also consider ordering that the costs thrown away be paid by the defence whatever the eventual outcome of the case (*Lister v Quaife* at pp. 54H–55A). In any event, the prosecution should hesitate before making use of the s. 9 procedure in respect of evidence that is central to their case (per Stephen Brown J, at p. 55E).

(e) CPD V, para. 27A.5 (see Supplement, **PD-38**), notes that, where statements are to be tendered under s. 9 in the course of summary proceedings and the statement contains evidence which is inadmissible or prejudicial, that evidence should not be excised by means of striking out or bracketing (a method that would otherwise be permissible) and so there will be a need to prepare fresh statements excluding any inadmissible or prejudicial material.

D22.39   Criminal Justice Act 1967, s. 9

(1) In any criminal proceedings a written statement by any person shall, if such of the conditions mentioned in the next following subsection as are applicable are satisfied, be admissible as evidence to the like extent as oral evidence to the like effect by that person.
(2) The said conditions are—
   (a) the statement purports to be signed by the person who made it;
   (b) the statement contains a declaration by that person to the effect that it is true to the best of his knowledge and belief and that he made the statement knowing that, if it were tendered in evidence, he would be liable to prosecution if he wilfully stated in it anything which he knew to be false or did not believe to be true;
   (c) before the hearing at which the statement is tendered in evidence, a copy of the statement is served, by or on behalf of the party proposing to tender it, on each of the other parties to the proceedings; and
   (d) none of the other parties or their solicitors, within seven days from the service of the copy of the statement, serves a notice on the party so proposing objecting to the statement being tendered in evidence under this section:
   Provided that the conditions mentioned in paragraphs (c) and (d) of this subsection shall not apply if the parties agree before or during the hearing that the statement shall be so tendered.
(3) The following provisions shall also have effect in relation to any written statement tendered in evidence under this section, that is to say—
   (a) if the statement is made by a person under the age of 18, it shall give his age;
   (b) if it is made by a person who cannot read it, it shall be read to him before he signs it and shall be accompanied by a declaration by the person who so read the statement to the effect that it was so read; and
   (c) if it refers to any other document as an exhibit, the copy served on any other party to the proceedings under paragraph (c) of the last foregoing subsection shall be accompanied by a copy of that document or by such information as may be necessary in order to enable the person on whom it is served to inspect that document or a copy thereof.
(3A) In the case of a statement which indicates in pursuance of subsection (3)(a) of this section that the person making it has not attained the age of fourteen, subsection (2)(b) of this section shall have effect as if for the words from 'made' onwards there were substituted the words 'understands the importance of telling the truth in it'.
(4) Notwithstanding that a written statement made by any person may be admissible as evidence by virtue of this section—
   (a) the party by whom or on whose behalf a copy of the statement was served may call that person to give evidence; and

    (b) the court may, of its own motion or on the application of any party to the proceedings, require that person to attend before the court and give evidence.

[(5) and (5A) Applications before trial under subsection (4)(b) above to courts other than a magistrates' court.]

    (6) So much of any statement as is admitted in evidence by virtue of this section shall, unless the court otherwise directs, be read aloud at the hearing and where the court so directs an account shall be given orally of so much of any statement as is not read aloud.

    (7) Any document or object referred to as an exhibit and identified in a written statement tendered in evidence under this section shall be treated as if it had been produced as an exhibit and identified in court by the maker of the statement.

    (8) A document required by this section to be served on any person may be served—

        (a) by delivering it to him or to his solicitor; or

        (b) by addressing it to him and leaving it at his usual or last known place of abode or place of business or by addressing it to his solicitor and leaving it at his office; or

        (c) by sending it in a registered letter or by the recorded delivery service or by first class post addressed to him at his usual or last known place of abode or place of business or addressed to his solicitor at his office; or

        (d) in the case of a body corporate, by delivering it to the secretary or clerk of the body at its registered or principal office or sending it in a registered letter or by the recorded delivery service or by first class post addressed to the secretary or clerk of that body at that office; and in paragraph (d) of this subsection references to the secretary, in relation to a limited liability partnership, are to any designated member of the limited liability partnership.

Formal Admissions

Where a party introduces into evidence a fact admitted by another party or the parties jointly admit a fact (e.g., where a formal admission is made — usually by the accused — under the CJA 1967, s. 10 (see **F1.2**)), a written record must, unless the court otherwise directs, be made of the admission (CrimPR, r. 37.6).   **D22.40**

OBJECTIONS TO PROSECUTION EVIDENCE

The procedure to be followed where the defence object, during the course of a summary trial, to proposed prosecution evidence (or have some other preliminary point of law to argue before the magistrates) raises the difficulty that the magistrates are the judges of both fact and law. Especially if the issue is one of admissibility of evidence, there is a danger that the magistrates will learn the nature of the evidence in the course of hearing arguments about its admissibility. Should they then rule it inadmissible, they may have difficulty in ignoring it when reaching a verdict. This problem is mitigated to some extent by the availability of pre-trial rulings (see **D21.35**) but these will not avail where issues of admissibility are raised for the first time during the course of trial itself.   **D22.41**

The stage of the trial at which the magistrates rule upon a question of admissibility of evidence (or other incidental issue) is a matter for their discretion (per Lord Lane CJ's judgment in *F v Chief Constable of Kent* [1982] Crim LR 682). However, delaying the determination of a question of admissibility of a confession until after the conclusion of the prosecution evidence may be unfair to the defence, in that the accused will not be able to give evidence about alleged irregularities in the obtaining of the confession unless he testifies in his own defence, which will expose him to cross-examination about the general issues. Moreover, in taking the decision what evidence to call, the defence advocate ought to know whether crucial evidence, such as a confession, is to be part of the case against his client. These special considerations were recognised by Lord Lane in the following passage from his judgment in *F v Chief Constable of Kent* (quoted in *Epping and Ongar Justices, ex parte Manby* [1986] Crim LR 555 and *A v DPP* (2000) 164 JP 317), where the admissibility of a confession was at issue:

> It is impossible to lay down any general rule as to when magistrates should announce their decision on this type of point, and indeed when the point itself should be taken. Every case will be different.

> Some sort of preliminary point, for instance with regard to the admissibility of a document or something like that, can plainly, with the assistance of the clerk, be decided straight away. Other points … may require a decision at a later stage of the case, possibly after further argument. It may be that in some cases the defendant will be entitled to know what the decision of the justices with regard to the admissibility of a confession is at the close of the prosecution case in order to enable him to know what proper course he should take with regard to giving evidence and calling evidence and so on.

D22.42   It is submitted that, where a confession is the main evidence against the accused, so that without it there might not be a case to answer, the interests of justice dictate that admissibility should be determined as a preliminary issue. In *ADC v Chief Constable of Greater Manchester* (14 March 1983 unreported, DC), quoted in *Halawa v Federation against Copyright Theft* [1995] 1 Cr App R 21 at p. 27, Goff LJ said:

> The proper approach of magistrates is to proceed in accordance with the justice of the case. I recognise that in very many cases it would indeed be proper for magistrates to deal with the issue of admissibility of a confession before the close of the prosecution case. To give a very simple and perhaps extreme example, if the only evidence before magistrates is the evidence of a confession and nothing else, then as a matter of common justice, the magistrates ought to deal with the issue of the admissibility of that confession as a preliminary point, before the close of the prosecution case, so that the defendant can then decide whether to make a submission of no case to answer.

Police and Criminal Evidence Act 1984, s. 78

D22.43   Whereas under the PACE 1984, s. 76 (see **D22.44**), the court is obliged to hear evidence about the obtaining of the confession (as the prosecution have to prove that the confession was not obtained in the manner forbidden by s. 76), where the admissibility of prosecution evidence falls to be considered under the general exclusionary discretion in s. 78, the court has a discretion to hear evidence on the issue of admissibility but is not obliged to do so (and so may rule on the matter following submissions on behalf of the parties). In the latter type of case, it is still a matter for the justices' discretion when they determine admissibility. In *Vel v Chief Constable of North Wales* (1987) 151 JP 510, Lloyd LJ said that in some cases the justices should deal with an application to exclude evidence when it arises, but in other cases they may leave the decision until the end of the hearing. Nonetheless, his lordship said that it was impossible to lay down any general rule, other than that 'the object should always be to secure a trial which is fair and just to both sides'. In *Halawa v Federation Against Copyright Theft* [1995] 1 Cr App R 21, the Divisional Court said that, in most cases, it is generally better for the magistrates to hear all the prosecution evidence (including the disputed evidence) before considering an application to exclude evidence under s. 78 (per Gibson LJ at p. 34). This does of course leave the justices with the very difficult (some might say impossible) task of putting from their minds prejudicial evidence that they have heard but then decide is inadmissible.

Police and Criminal Evidence Act 1984, s. 76

D22.44   Where the defence object to the admissibility of a confession on the basis of the PACE 1984, s. 76, the terms of s. 76 require that the court shall not admit the confession unless satisfied that it was not obtained by oppression or by words or conduct likely to render it unreliable. It follows that magistrates (just like the Crown Court) are obliged to determine such an issue as soon as it is raised and, if necessary, hear evidence on the obtaining of the confession. In *Liverpool Juvenile Court, ex parte R* [1988] QB 1 at pp. 10–11, Russell LJ summarised the position regarding s. 76 as follows:

> 1. The effect of section 76(2) of the Police and Criminal Evidence Act 1984 is that in summary proceedings justices must now hold a trial within a trial if it is represented to them by the defence that a confession was or may have been obtained by either of the improper processes appearing in subparagraphs (a) or (b) of section 76(2).
>
> 2. In such a trial within a trial the defendant may give evidence confined to the question of admissibility and the justices will not be concerned with the truth or otherwise of the confession.

3. In consequence of paragraphs 1 and 2 above, the defendant is entitled to a ruling upon admissibility of a confession before, or at, the end of the prosecution case.

4. There remains a discretion open to the defendant as to the stage at which an attack is to be made upon an alleged confession. A trial within a trial will only take place before the close of the prosecution case if it is represented to the court that the confession was, or may have been, obtained by one or other of the processes set out in subparagraphs (a) or (b) of section 76(2). If no such representation is made the defendant is at liberty to raise admissibility or weight of the confession at any subsequent stage of the trial. For the avoidance of doubt, I consider that 'representation' is not the same as, nor does it include, cross-examination. Thus the court is not required to embark upon, nor is the defence bound to proceed upon, a *voir dire* merely because of a suggestion in cross-examination that the alleged confession was obtained improperly.

5. It should never be necessary to call the prosecution evidence relating to the obtaining of a confession twice.

In his fourth proposition, Russell LJ would seem to be encouraging defence advocates to delay formally objecting to a confession until their own case, at which stage the magistrates may still exclude the confession if the accused's evidence raises a reasonable possibility that there was a breach of s. 76(2). This suggestion would seem to be at odds with the case law on challenging confessions at trials on indictment (see **D16.47** and **F17.63** and especially *Sat-Bhambra* (1988) 88 Cr App R 55, where it was held that, once a confession had been adduced by the prosecution, it is too late for the defence to represent that it was obtained by oppression or in circumstances likely to render it unreliable).

'Dock Identifications'

One particular element of some prosecution cases is the use of the so-called 'dock identification' **D22.45** (see **F6.45** and **F18.6**). Where the identity of the accused as the person who committed the offence is in issue, asking a witness who has not previously identified the accused at an identification parade or video identification procedure 'do you see the person who committed the offence in court today?' is undesirable. This is because the safeguards built into the out-of-court identification procedures are not available when the witness is asked to identify the accused in the dock at his trial, and because the accused is at a great disadvantage — the eyes of the witness are bound to go to the person sitting in the dock. Whether a dock identification should be admitted in the exercise of discretion is for the justices to decide (*North Yorkshire Trading Standards Department v Williams* (1995) 159 JP 383, per Rose LJ). In *Barnes v DPP* [1997] 2 Cr App R 505, the accused was charged with failing to provide a breath specimen. There had been no identification procedure and the only evidence that the accused was the person who refused to provide a specimen was a 'dock identification' by a police officer. The Divisional Court confirmed that the justices had a discretion in such cases to allow an accused to be identified in court even if there had not been a previous identification procedure.

In *Karia v DPP* (2002) 166 JP 753, the accused appealed against conviction for a number of **D22.46** motoring offences on the ground that the magistrates should not have allowed the police officer who had stopped the vehicle to make a 'dock identification' of him, and that an identification parade should have been held. He argued that the decision in *Barnes v DPP* permitting dock identifications in such cases was incompatible with the HRA 1998. Stanley Burnton J said (at [29]) that the aim of a dock identification in such cases is usually to avoid an unmeritorious dismissal of a prosecution case resulting from a failure to make a purely formal identification of the accused. Moreover, in *Karia* the accused had not notified the prosecution that identity was in issue, and so the dock identification was not unfair because there was no basis on which the police could have considered that it would be useful to hold an identification procedure (at [33]). As far as the human rights point was concerned, his lordship said (at [40]) that a requirement that the issues should be made known to the court before or during the proceedings cannot infringe the ECHR, Article 6; moreover, a requirement that an accused should indicate before or at his trial what are the issues in the trial does not infringe his right to silence. On this

Part D Procedure

D

basis, it would appear that dock identifications are to be ruled out only where the accused has already indicated that identity is in issue in the case. In *Holland v HM Advocate* [2005] HRLR 25, the Privy Council confirmed that there is no basis, except perhaps in an extreme case, for regarding dock identifications as inadmissible *per se*.

'SPECIAL MEASURES' DIRECTIONS

D22.47   The court has power to make arrangements for vulnerable witnesses and accused both under its inherent jurisdiction and under the YJCEA 1999. These powers include powers to protect witness anonymity and are dealt with fully at **D14**.

The special measures available under the YJCEA 1999, s. 19, which are those most commonly used in the magistrates' court, include:

(a) screening the witness from the accused (s. 23);

(b) giving evidence by live link (s. 24), although the significance of this provision is reduced by the CJA 2003, s. 51, which enables a court to authorise witnesses, other than the accused, to give evidence through a live link in criminal proceedings;

(c) giving evidence in private, in a sexual case, or where there are reasonable grounds for believing that someone other than the accused has sought, or will seek, to intimidate the witness (s. 25);

(d) video recording of evidence-in-chief (s. 27) — again, this provision will be made less relevant once the CJA 2003, s. 137, which extends the circumstances in which evidence-in-chief can take the form of a video-recorded statement, is brought fully into force;

(e) video recording of cross-examination and re-examination where the evidence-in-chief of the witness has been video recorded (s. 28);

(f) examination through an intermediary (s. 29);

(g) provision of aids to communication to enable the witness to testify despite any disability, disorder or other impairment (s. 30).

In *R (S) v Waltham Forest Youth Court* [2004] 2 Cr App R 335, the accused (who was aged 13) wanted to testify in her own defence but said that she was too scared to do so because of the physical presence in court of her co-accused. The Divisional Court held that there is no power to make a direction under the 1999 Act in relation to the evidence of the accused. However, the effect of this authority has been reversed to the extent that one special measure (namely, testifying via a 'live link') is available for the accused under the YJCEA 1999, s. 33A.

The procedure for making (and opposing) applications for special measures directions is set out in the CrimPR, part 29 (see Supplement, **R-216**).

Position of Justices Following Application

D22.48   Justices who have ruled on an application for special measures are not disqualified from hearing the case against the accused. In *KL and LK v DPP* (2002) 166 JP 369, the prosecution made an application for the use of screens in relation to a prosecution witness, on the grounds that she would feel intimidated having to give evidence in the accused's presence and had been intimidated. The question to be decided was whether the justices should withdraw from the case after hearing the application. Richards J said (at [13]) that:

> . . . there can be no objection in principle to justices continuing to hear a case after listening to and ruling on an application for the witness to be screened from a defendant. The fact that evidence or submissions adverse to the defendant are advanced in support of such an application does not necessarily prevent fair-minded consideration of the case after the application has been determined, whether it has been allowed or refused.

It is submitted that the same approach would be taken with regard to any other applications for special measures.

SUBMISSION OF NO CASE TO ANSWER

Under the CrimPR, r 37.3(c), the magistrates may acquit the accused on the ground that the **D22.49** prosecution evidence is insufficient for any reasonable court properly to convict. They may do so following an application by the defence or on their own initiative but, in either case, the prosecutor must be given an opportunity to make representations. Thus, at the close of the prosecution evidence, the defence may submit that there is no case to answer (see **D16.54** for the position in trial on indictment).

Rule 37.3(c) sets out the basis for the decision, namely that no reasonable court could properly convict. Thus, the decision depends not on whether the justices would at that stage convict or acquit but on whether the evidence is such that a reasonable tribunal might convict. If a reasonable tribunal might convict on the evidence so far laid before it, there is a case to answer. The submission should succeed if a conviction would be perverse, in the sense that no reasonable bench could convict.

There is no obligation on justices to give reasons for rejecting a submission of no case to answer (*Moran v DPP* (2002) 166 JP 467, per Maurice Kay LJ at [16]).

Credibility of Prosecution Witnesses

An important issue is the extent to which justices may have regard to the credibility of prosecu- **D22.50** tion witnesses when considering a submission of no case to answer. In the Crown Court, the test to be applied by the judge when ruling on a submission of no case is set out in *Galbraith* [1981] 2 All ER 1060: is the prosecution evidence so tenuous that, even taken at its highest, a jury properly directed could not properly convict on it? The requirement that the Crown Court judge should 'take the prosecution evidence at its highest' is intended to leave questions of credibility to the jury. In *Barking and Dagenham Justices, ex parte DPP* (1995) 159 JP 373, the Divisional Court said that questions of credibility should, except in the clearest of cases, not normally be taken into account by justices considering a submission of no case. Nonetheless, it is submitted that some justices may well take the pragmatic view that it would be inappropriate for them to go through the motions of hearing defence evidence if they have already formed the view that the prosecution evidence is so unconvincing that they will not be able to convict on it in any event. However, the general principle remains that, so long as the necessary minimum amount of prosecution evidence has been adduced so as to raise a case on which a reasonable tribunal *could* convict, the justices should allow the trial to run its course rather than acquitting on a submission.

Prosecution Right of Reply

When the justices are provisionally minded to uphold the submission of no case to answer, they **D22.51** should first call on the prosecution to address them (*Barking and Dagenham Justices, ex parte DPP* (1995) 159 JP 373), so that the prosecutor has an opportunity to address the court to show why the case should not be dismissed. This means that the prosecution have the right to reply to the defence submission that there is no case to answer unless, having heard the defence submission, the magistrates decide to rule against the defence and indicate this fact to the prosecutor.

Reopening the Case following a Submission

In some cases, the deficiency in the prosecution case which is highlighted by the defence submis- **D22.52** sion of no case to answer may be cured by allowing the prosecution to reopen their case, rather than upholding the submission of no case to answer and acquitting the accused. In *Hughes v DPP* (2003) 167 JP 589, Stanley Burnton J said (at [16]) that when, on a submission of no case to answer, a point is raised which has no bearing on the merits of the prosecution, and the defect in the prosecution case is one of omission (and probably oversight), the advocate acting for the

Part D Procedure

prosecution should request leave to recall the relevant witness to supplement the prosecution evidence. His lordship added that, in such a case, the magistrates should normally exercise their discretion to permit the prosecution to reopen their case so that such evidence can be given, particularly where the fact in question is likely to be uncontroversial. Indeed, if necessary, the magistrates should consider inviting the prosecution to recall the relevant witness. It is submitted that it may well be appropriate for the justices to allow the prosecution to reopen their case, and thus adduce evidence that was inadvertently omitted, even if the missing evidence has a more direct bearing on the merits of the prosecution case. If the defect in the prosecution case is one that could be cured simply and speedily by allowing them to reopen their case and recall a witness, it may well be that the interests of justice require that the prosecution be given the chance to remedy the defect. It is difficult to see how the defendant would be prejudiced by this decision. However, if the reopening of the prosecution case would require an adjournment, and thus cause delay in the disposal of the case, the balance of the interests of justice might require that the submission be upheld and the defendant acquitted.

In *Tuck v Vehicle Inspectorate* [2004] EWHC 728 (Admin), the Divisional Court considered another case in which magistrates had permitted the prosecution to repair omissions in their evidence after they had closed their case, following a submission of no case to answer. MacKay J, in a judgment with which Kennedy LJ agreed, summarised the principles applicable as follows (at [15]):

(1) The discretion to allow the case to be reopened is not limited to matters arising *ex improviso* or mere technicalities, but is a more general discretion.
(2) The exercise of this discretion should not be interfered with by a higher court unless its exercise was wrong in principle or perverse.
(3) The general rule remains that the prosecution must finish its case once and for all and the test to be applied is narrower than consideration of whether the additional evidence would be of value to the tribunal. The discretion will only be exercised on the rarest of occasions.
(4) The discretion must be exercised carefully having regard to the need to be fair to the defence, and giving consideration to the question of whether any prejudice will be caused.
(5) The courts have in the past differed as to whether the mere loss of a tactical advantage can constitute such prejudice.
(6) Criminal procedure while adversarial is not a game, and the overall interests of justice include giving effect to the requirement that a prosecution should not fail through inefficiency, carelessness or oversight.
(7) Of particular significance is the consideration of whether there is any risk of prejudice to the accused.

D22.53 In *Smith v DPP* [2008] EWHC 771 (Admin), following a submission of no case to answer, a district judge permitted the prosecution to recall their main witness. Dyson LJ (at [5]) said that 'Prosecuting authorities should not be encouraged to believe that they can reopen a case to adduce evidence which was available to them but which they did not adduce before a case was closed. Sloppiness would result if it were thought that omissions could routinely be made good by the Crown at a later stage in the proceedings. On the other hand, the interests of the defendant must be balanced against the public interest in ensuring that those who have committed crimes should be convicted.' In the instant case, the judge's decision to allow the Crown to reopen their case was not a 'plainly wrong' exercise of his discretion. The witness in question had already given evidence that the person who committed the offence was the accused, and the judge was entitled to permit the prosecution to strengthen their case by allowing the witness to give evidence to meet a point made in the course of the submission of no case to answer.

R (Payne) v South Lakeland Magistrates' Court (2011) 175 JP 357 provides another example of a case where the prosecution were permitted to reopen their case. The accused was charged with driving a motor vehicle on a road at a speed in excess of the speed limit but, through an oversight on the part of the prosecution, no evidence of the speed of the vehicle was adduced. The magistrates adjourned the hearing to enable the prosecutor to cure this deficiency in the prosecution evidence. On appeal, Pitchford LJ said (at [38]–[40]) that no prejudice would be caused to the accused by such an adjournment 'because he had not attended trial and had no intention of giving evidence, and accordingly of contesting the matter on the merits'. Moreover, '[i]t is not in the public interest that cases should be decided upon the vagaries of forensic mistakes made by lawyers, provided no prejudice is done by delay or for other specific reasons'.

Ambushes Not Permitted   From the perspective of professional conduct and ethics, it is also **D22.54** noteworthy that in his judgment in *Hughes v DPP* (2003) 167 JP 589 (see **D22.52**), Stanley Burnton J said (at [16]) (echoing comments made by Auld LJ in *Gleeson* [2004] 1 Cr App R 406) that 'Ambushes of the kind attempted in this case are to be discouraged and discountenanced. Criminal proceedings are not a game: their object is to achieve a fair determination of the innocence or guilt of the defendant'. A similar point was made in *R (DPP) v Chorley Justices and Andrew Forrest* [2006] EWHC 1795 (Admin), where Thomas LJ gave a warning (at [26]) that the defence must raise issues as early as possible in the case:

If a defendant refuses to identify what the issues are, one thing is clear: he can derive no advantage from that or seek, as appears to have happened in this case, to attempt an ambush at trial. The days of ambushing and taking last-minute technical points are gone. They are not consistent with the overriding objective of deciding cases justly, acquitting the innocent and convicting the guilty.

In *R (CPS) v Norwich Magistrates' Court* [2011] EWHC 82 (Admin), the prosecution opened the case (a charge of assault) by stating that identification was not in dispute (the section of the case management form completed by the defence raised the issue of self-defence). At the close of the prosecution case, the defence made a submission of no case to answer based on the lack of adequate identification. The prosecution sought to call additional evidence, but the magistrates refused to allow this. The Divisional Court said that the decision of the magistrates was wrong. Richards LJ said (at [22]):

... if the defence was going to take a positive point on identification, it was incumbent on it to flag the point at an early stage, not to wait until the close of the prosecution case before raising it for the first time in a submission of no case. It should have been expressed during the case management process and included in terms in the trial information form. That is all the more obvious in the environment in which the parties now operate by reference to the Criminal Procedure Rules and the overriding objective. Even if there had been an omission to deal with it at that earlier stage, it ought to have been raised very clearly when the prosecuting advocate opened the case by telling the magistrates that there was no issue over identification. It was not appropriate, as it seems to me, simply to sit tight and to raise it at the end of the prosecution case by way of a submission of no case.

His lordship concluded, at [25], that 'the decision to refuse the prosecution application to re-open ran counter to the overriding objective . . ., was plainly contrary to the interests of justice and lacked any reasonable basis'.

Reconsidering the Decision   In *Steward v DPP* [2004] 4 All ER 1105, the justices acceded to **D22.55** a submission of no case to answer. The prosecutor then pointed out that the reasons given by the magistrates contained an error of fact. The justices reviewed their decision, and concluded that there was a case to answer. The accused, who was subsequently convicted, appealed by way of case stated on the basis that the justices had been acting *functus officio* by proceeding to hear the case after reaching a finding of no case to answer. The Divisional Court held that the justices were entitled to reopen a case, despite having acceded to a submission of no case to answer, where an error in the reasons has been identified by the prosecution and the accused agrees that there was an error. In those circumstances, the process of adjudication has not been completed and the justices are not *functus officio*. The case was said to be distinguishable from *Essex Justices, ex parte Final* [1963] 2 QB 816 (where it was held that justices should not reopen a case once they have reached their decision), as that case had been reopened in order to hear further submissions on the evidence, whereas in the present case the error was identified immediately, and the justices admitted it and rectified it; also, the earlier case was decided at a time when it was less common for justices to give reasons for accepting a submission of no case to answer, and so errors in their reasoning were less likely to be immediately apparent (per Maurice Kay J at [10] and [11]).

DEFENCE CASE AND SPEECHES

D22.56   If a submission of no case to answer is not made, or is unsuccessful, the defence then have the opportunity to present evidence to the court. The CrimPR, r. 37.3, makes no reference to an opening speech by the defence, and established practice is that the defence have no right to make an opening speech prior to calling their evidence. After the close of the prosecution case (and after any submission of no case to answer has been rejected), the accused may introduce evidence (r. 37.3(e)).

The CJPOA 1994, s. 35(2) (and the CrimPR, r. 37.3(d)), requires the justices' legal adviser (or the court) to explain that the accused is entitled to give evidence and to point out the potential effect, namely adverse inferences being drawn, under s. 35 (see **F19.42**), if he does not testify or if he refuses to answer any questions while testifying. In *Radford v Kent County Council* (1998) 162 JP 697, however, the magistrates failed to warn an accused that adverse inferences could be drawn if he failed to testify. Nonetheless, in their stated case, the justices said that 'we drew no inferences whatsoever from the failure of the appellant to give evidence, but simply were aware that the evidence for the prosecution was not rebutted by evidence from or on behalf of the appellant'. The Divisional Court held that, although the warning of the consequences of not testifying is very important, the failure to give the warning in the particular case did not render the appellant's conviction unsafe.

D22.57   It should be also be borne in mind that the restrictions on an accused cross-examining witnesses in cases involving alleged sexual offences (YJCEA 1999, ss. 34 to 39) apply equally in magistrates' courts. The procedural aspects are contained in the CrimPR, part 31. See **D17.19**.

If the accused is going to call other witnesses as well as giving evidence himself, the accused should give evidence first unless the court otherwise directs (PACE 1984, s. 79).

Evidence in Rebuttal

D22.58   Rule 37.3(3)(f) of the CrimPR provides that, after any evidence called by the defence, 'a party may introduce further evidence if it is then admissible', for example to rebut evidence that has already been adduced. Although this provision refers to 'a party', it is submitted that it is generally the prosecution who will seek to adduce rebuttal evidence (bearing in mind that the defence will have adduced any evidence on which they wish to rely after the close of the prosecution case).

Rebuttal evidence may be appropriate if something has arisen *ex improviso* (i.e. something that could not reasonably have been foreseen) during the course of the defence case (see **F6.2**), or where the evidence which the prosecution seek to adduce is intended to remedy a technical deficiency in their case. In those circumstances, the justices may allow the prosecution case to be reopened (*Price v Humphries* [1958] 2 QB 353; *Hammond v Wilkinson* (2001) 165 JP 786). However, the power to allow the prosecution to reopen their case can go beyond such technical difficulties. For example, in *James v South Glamorgan County Council* (1994) 99 Cr App R 321, the main prosecution witness had not arrived but the trial proceeded nonetheless; after the prosecution case had been closed and while the defendant was giving evidence, the witness arrived. It was accepted by the magistrates that the witness had a good reason for being late and the prosecution were allowed to call him as a witness. It was held by the Divisional Court that, since the evidence had not been available at the proper time and there was no unfairness to the defendant (not least because there was no suggestion that the accused's case would have been differently conducted had the evidence of the witness been given when it ought to have been), the decision of the magistrates was correct.

Similarly, in *Khatibi v DPP* (2004) 168 JP 361, Nelson J said (at [17]) that the discretion to **D22.59** admit evidence after the close of the prosecution case is not confined to the well-established exceptions of rebuttal and mere formality. The discretion must, however, be exercised with great caution. The magistrates should bear in mind the strictly adversarial nature of the English criminal process, whereby the cases for the prosecution and the defence are presented consecutively in their entirety. The normal order of events should not be departed from substantially unless justice really demands such a course of action. His lordship added (at [18]) that, in deciding whether to exercise their discretion to permit the calling of evidence after the close of the prosecution case, the magistrates must look carefully at the interests of justice overall, and in particular the risk of any prejudice to the defendant.

In *R (Lawson) v Stafford Magistrates' Court* [2007] EWHC 2490 (Admin), the accused was charged with driving in excess of the speed limit. During his closing submissions, defence counsel raised for the first time the issues that the prosecution had to satisfy the court that the signs indicating the limit complied with the relevant regulations and that the speed measuring device should be tested. The justices invited the prosecution to apply for the case to be adjourned part-heard so that these evidential issues could be addressed. The defence contended that the justices erred in encouraging an adjournment. The Divisional Court held that the accused had sought to ambush the prosecution and the magistrates were entitled to adjourn the case to receive further evidence. Aikens J (at [32]) pointed out that, in a pre-trial hearing before magistrates, an accused or his lawyer should be specifically asked what issues are being taken by the defence. His lordship went on to say (at [34]) that 'magistrates have a jurisdiction to adjourn a trial to permit the prosecution to rectify a deficiency in evidence which is only identified by the defence at a very late stage, after the close of the prosecution case'. His lordship explained (at [39]) that:

> [T]he courts' power to allow a case to be re-opened is a power which must be exercised rarely and having regard to the need to be fair to the defendant. A court must bear in mind the question of whether any prejudice to the defendant will be caused by a case being re-opened. However those points do not detract from the legal proposition that justices are entitled to hear evidence after the case has been closed where special circumstances exist.

Rebuttal Evidence after Magistrates have Retired to Consider Verdict In *Khatibi* (2004) 168 **D22.60** JP 361, Nelson J pointed out (at [20]) that it has 'generally been accepted that an application to call further evidence cannot succeed after the bench has retired to consider its verdict'. It is therefore only in the rarest of cases that further evidence may be adduced once the justices have retired to consider their verdict. In *Webb v Leadbetter* [1966] 2 All ER 114, one of two prosecution witnesses failed to arrive. The one available witness was called. The prosecution case closed. The accused gave evidence and his case closed. The justices had retired to consider their decision when they were informed that the second prosecution witness, whose car had broken down, had arrived. They returned to court and allowed the prosecution to call him. His evidence corroborated that of the first prosecution witness. The accused was convicted. The Divisional Court held that, although justices have a discretion to allow further evidence to be called in particular circumstances, the manner of the exercise of that discretion depends on the stage of the case. In the absence of 'special circumstances' (per Lord Parker CJ) or even 'very special circumstances' (per Winn LJ), they should not allow evidence to be called after they have retired. In the instant case, such circumstances were absent and so the further evidence had been wrongly admitted.

This decision was followed in *R (Traves) v DPP* (2005) 169 JP 421, where the accused was charged with driving whilst disqualified. At the trial, the prosecution failed to produce the memorandum of conviction which was necessary in order to prove that the accused had been disqualified. The defence made a submission of no case to answer. The justices retired to consider their decision but, before they returned to court to announce their decision, they were informed that the prosecution now had the evidence that had been lacking. The prosecution sought, and were granted, leave to reopen their case. The prosecution produced evidence of the disqualification and the defendant was convicted. The Divisional Court held that the moment of retiring to consider the decision is a critical point, after which only very special circumstances could allow further evidence to be called. In the instant case, there existed no such very special circumstances and so the conviction was quashed.

D22.61 However, in *Malcolm v DPP* [2007] 3 All ER 578, the Divisional Court took a broader of view of what would amount to 'special circumstances', enabling the case to be reopened even after the justices had retired to consider their verdict. The accused had been charged with driving with excess alcohol. In her final speech, defence counsel submitted that there had been no warning, as required by the RTA 1988, s. 7(7), that a failure to provide a specimen might render the accused liable to prosecution and that, accordingly, there was no admissible evidence of the analysis of alcohol in her breath. The magistrates retired to consider the submissions. They returned to court and gave their conclusions that the case would have to be dismissed because of the lack of admissible evidence of the proportion of alcohol in the appellant's breath. Before they formally dismissed the case, however, counsel for the prosecution requested leave to recall the officer in charge of the breath test procedure. The Divisional Court reiterated the test established by *Webb v Leadbetter*, that special circumstances are required before they can receive further evidence after they have retired to consider their verdict. However, Stanley Burnton J, with whom Maurice Kay LJ agreed, said (at [31]):

> [Counsel for the appellant's] submissions, which emphasised the obligation of the prosecution to prove its case in its entirety before closing its case, and certainly before the end of the final speech for the defence, had an anachronistic, and obsolete, ring. Criminal trials are no longer to be treated as a game, in which each move is final and any omission by the prosecution leads to its failure. It is the duty of the defence to make its defence and the issues it raises clear to the prosecution and to the court at an early stage... Even in a relatively straightforward trial such as the present, in the magistrates' court (where there is not yet any requirement of a defence statement or a pre-trial review), it is the duty of the defence to make the real issues clear at the latest before the prosecution closes its case. In *Pydar Justices, ex parte Foster* [1995] 160 JP 87 at 90B Curtis J. commented on the submission that a defending advocate was entitled to 'keep his powder dry'. He said:
>
>> Without any doubt whatsoever, it is the duty of a defending advocate properly to lay the ground for a submission, either by cross examination or, if appropriate, by calling evidence.
>
> That was not done in this case.

The court concluded that there were, therefore, special circumstances entitling the magistrates to allow the case to be reopened. Moreover, Stanley Burnton J added (at [39]) that, 'I respectfully disagree with the decision of Bean J in *Traves*. In my judgment it was wrongly decided'. His lordship appears to be saying that Bean J should have decided that the facts in that case did, in fact, disclose 'special circumstances'.

Closing Speeches

D22.62 The CrimPR, r. 37.3(g), provides that (after the defence have adduced any evidence they wish and after any rebuttal evidence), the prosecutor 'may make final representations in support of the prosecution case' if the accused is represented or (whether represented or not) the accused has called evidence other than his own testimony. Under r. 37.3(h), the accused may then 'make final representations in support of the defence case' (in other words, make a closing speech). Thus, if any prosecution representations are made, the accused is given the chance to reply, and so will always have the last word before the magistrates consider their verdict.

The CrimPR, r. 37.3(4), makes it clear that, if a party wishes to introduce evidence or make representations after the specified opportunity to do so under r. 37.3(3), the court is entitled to refuse to receive any such evidence or representations. It is submitted that the court should refuse to receive additional evidence or representations save in the most exceptional circumstances.

Rule 37.3(4)(b) makes it clear that the court must not receive additional evidence or representations after it has announced its verdict, thus preserving the principle of finality.

SEEING THE MAGISTRATES IN CHAMBERS

The bench has an inherent discretion to hear representations in chambers during the course **D22.63** of a trial (*Nottingham Magistrates' Court, ex parte Furnell* (1996) 160 JP 201). However, given the magistrates' role as fact finders, the discretion has to be exercised with even greater caution than in the case of Crown Court trial. In any event, all parties should be made aware of what is happening and be represented in chambers (except where there is an issue of public interest immunity to be heard on an *ex parte* basis) and a contemporaneous note should be taken, normally by the justices' legal adviser.

DECISION ON THE ISSUE OF GUILT

Manner of Arriving at and Announcing Decision

Adverse Inferences   The adverse inference provisions of the CPIA 1996, s. 11 (see **D9.47**), **D22.64** apply to summary trials. An adverse inference may be drawn if the accused decides to serve a defence statement (which is voluntary, under s. 6) but does so late, or (for example) presents at trial a case that is inconsistent with the case set out in the defence statement, or relies on a matter that was not disclosed in the defence statement. Similarly, the adverse inference provisions contained in the CJPO 1994, s. 34 (see **F19.10**), apply to summary trials where the accused failed to mention when questioned matters on which he subsequently relies in his defence. In *T v DPP* (2007) 171 JP 605, the Divisional Court summarised the approach to be taken in a case where a magistrates' court is considering whether to draw adverse inferences in such a case. The justices should ask themselves three questions (per Hughes LJ at [26]):

(1) Has the defendant relied in his defence on a fact which he could reasonably have been expected to mention in his interview, but did not? If so, what is it?
(2) What is his explanation for not having mentioned it?
(3) If that explanation is not a reasonable one, is the proper inference to be drawn that he is guilty?

Use of Personal Knowledge   In reaching their decision on a question of fact, it is open to mag- **D22.65** istrates to use their personal local knowledge. However, they should inform the prosecution and the defence that they are doing so, so that those representing the parties have the opportunity of commenting upon the knowledge which the magistrates claim to have (*Bowman v DPP* [1991] RTR 263; *Norbrook Laboratories (GB) Ltd v Health and Safety Executive* [1998] EHLR 207). In *Gibbons v DPP* (12 December 2000 unreported), the appellants were charged with assault. They said they had been acting in self-defence. An eye-witness gave evidence that the appellants were responsible. After the closing speeches had been made, the district judge had cause to visit the place where the alleged offence had occurred. While there, he checked the site of the assault, the distance the witness was located from the attack and whether her view would have been obstructed. The Divisional Court held that the matters checked were all critical issues at the trial. At the very least, the district judge should have informed the parties of his intention of taking a view, so that they could have had the opportunity to make submissions as to where the witness had actually been located. It followed that there had been a defect in the trial process; the convictions were quashed and a retrial ordered.

Connected with this is the possibility of the justices visiting the scene of the crime as part of the trial process. In *M v DPP* [2009] 2 Cr App R 1181, it was said (per Leveson LJ at [31]) to be critical that, before a court embarks on a 'view', it is determined with absolute clarity what will happen on the view, who should stand where, what objects (if any) should be placed where, and who should do what.

D22.66 **Majority Decisions** In the event of disagreement, a lay bench reaches its decisions (including a decision to acquit or convict) by a majority. Where the bench is even-numbered, the chairman does *not* have a casting vote. Therefore, in the event of the justices being equally divided, it will be necessary for the case to be adjourned for rehearing before a differently constituted court (*Redbridge Justices, ex parte Ram* [1992] QB 384).

Assuming there is the possibility of a majority, justices are under a duty to reach a decision. In both *Bridgend Justices, ex parte Randall* [1975] Crim LR 287 and *Bromley Justices, ex parte Haymills (Contractors) Ltd* [1984] Crim LR 235, benches of three magistrates pronounced themselves unable to decide on the charge against the accused and remitted the case for rehearing by another bench. In each case, the Divisional Court ordered the original justices to reach a decision, saying that if two of them were unhappy about convicting then the prosecution had failed to prove its case and the finding would have to be one of not guilty.

When the decision is announced in open court by the chairman, he does not state whether it is unanimous or by a majority.

D22.67 **Duty to Give Reasons** The CrimPR, r. 37.3(5), provides that the court, if it convicts the accused (or makes a hospital order instead of doing so), must give 'sufficient reasons to explain its decision'. However, the justices are not required to state their reasons in the form of a judgment or to give reasons in any elaborate form (*McKerry v Teesdale and Wear Valley Justices* (2000) 164 JP 355, per Lord Bingham, at [23]). If a party wishes to obtain more detailed reasons, a request can be made to the magistrates to state a case. In *R (McGowan) v Brent Justices* (2002) 166 JP 29, the Divisional Court confirmed that *McKerry v Teesdale and Wear Valley Justices* is still good law following the coming into force of the HRA 1998. Tuckey LJ (at [18]), said that 'the essence of the exercise in a criminal case such as this is to inform the defendant why he has been found guilty. That can usually be done in a few simple sentences.'

If the court acquits the accused, it may (but is not required to) give an explanation of its decision (CrimPR, r. 37.3(6)(a)).

Guilty of a Lesser Offence

D22.68 The justices are restricted to reaching a decision of guilty or not guilty on the charge actually before them. They have no power to find an accused not guilty as charged but guilty of a lesser offence (*Lawrence v Same* [1968] 2 QB 93). This applies even when a jury, on an equivalently worded count for an either-way offence, would be entitled (under the CLA 1967, s. 6(3)) to return an alternative verdict. Thus, in *Lawrence v Same* a purported summary conviction for common assault on a charge of unlawful wounding was quashed. It would have been otherwise had there been two separate charges, and the court had decided to convict only on the lesser offence.

There are, however, a number of exceptions to this rule. For example, the RTOA 1988, s. 24, enables magistrates, whenever trying certain driving offences, to find the accused not guilty of the offence charged, but guilty of another specified driving offence (e.g., convicting the accused of careless driving instead of dangerous driving, even though the only charge before the court is one of dangerous driving; see also C2.8). Similarly, the Theft Act 1968, s. 12A(5), provides that where an accused is charged with aggravated vehicle taking, he may instead be convicted of the lesser offence of vehicle taking contrary to s. 12; s. 12A(5) applies to summary trials as well as to trials on indictment (*R (H) v Liverpool City Youth Court* [2001] Crim LR 487).

D22.69 **Alternative Offences** If the accused is charged with alternative offences at the outset and pleads not guilty to both, the magistrates should not convict him of both offences. In *R (Dyer) v Watford Magistrates' Court* (2013) 177 JP 265, the accused was charged with an offence under the POA 1986, s. 4, and also with the racially aggravated version of the offence under the CDA 1998, s. 31(1)(a). Before trial, he offered to plead guilty to the s. 4 offence, but that offer was rejected by the prosecution. Following trial, he was convicted of both offences. The Divisional

Court declined to follow its earlier decisions in *DPP v Gane* (1991) 155 JP 846 and *R (CPS) v Blaydon Youth Court* (2004) 168 JP 638 (where it had been held that it was open to the magistrates' court to convict the accused of both offences in similar circumstances), and quashed the conviction on the lesser charge. The Court held that it was 'unfair and disproportionate' for an accused to be convicted twice for a single wrong, since a person's criminal record should record what he had done, no more and no less (per Laws LJ, at [11]). In such a case, the magistrates should adjourn the lesser charge at the end of the trial but before conviction so that, if an appeal succeeded against conviction on the greater charge, a conviction on the lesser offence might thereafter properly be recorded against the accused (at [12]); in other words, the court gives no verdict on the lesser alternative and adjourns that lesser charge *sine die* under the MCA 1980, s. 10, so that the lesser charge can be brought back, if appropriate, if the accused appeals successfully against the conviction for the more serious offence (per Hickinbottom J at [14]).

SETTING ASIDE A CONVICTION FOR REHEARING BEFORE DIFFERENTLY CONSTITUTED BENCH

General

The MCA 1980, s. 142(2), enables an accused who was convicted in a magistrates' court **D22.70** (whether he pleaded guilty or was found guilty) to ask the magistrates to set the conviction aside. This application can be considered by the same magistrates who convicted the accused or by a different bench. If the conviction is set aside, the case is reheard by different magistrates from those who convicted.

An application under s. 142(2) may be appropriate if, for example, the magistrates made an error of law or there was some defect in the procedure which led to the conviction. In *Croydon Youth Court, ex parte DPP* [1997] 2 Cr App R 411 at p. 416, McCowan LJ said that the purpose of s. 142(2) is most accurately described as a 'power to rectify mistakes', and that it is generally and correctly regarded as a slip rule. Similarly, in *Zykin v CPS* (2009) 173 JP 361, Bean J quoted from *R (Holme) v Liverpool Magistrates' Court* (2005) 169 JP 306, and said (at [16]) that s. 142 'does not confer a wide and general power on a magistrates' court to re-open a previous decision on the grounds that it is in the interests of justice to do so'; rather, it is 'a power to be used in a relatively limited situation, namely one which is akin to mistake or the slip rule'.

The limited scope of s. 142(2) was emphasised in *DPP v Chajed* [2013] 2 Cr App R 60 (6). Hickinbottom J, with whom Laws LJ agreed, said (at [26]) that, where there has been a simple mistake (or something akin to such), s. 142 enables a magistrates' court to rectify it, if necessary by directing the case be reheard by different justices. However, once a guilty verdict has been pronounced by magistrates, it does not enable a convicted accused to make further submissions with a view to persuading the bench to change its mind and substitute a not guilty verdict. If the magistrates have reached the wrong decision on the merits of submissions which have been made to them, the appropriate course for the accused is to appeal to the Crown Court or by way of case stated to the High Court.

The CrimPR, r. 37.17(2), provides that the court may exercise its power to set aside a conviction under s. 142 on application by a party, or on its own initiative. An application under s. 142 may be dealt with in a public or private hearing, or without a hearing. Under r. 37.17(3), the court must not exercise its power in the absence of a party unless the court makes a decision proposed by that party, or the party has agreed in writing to that decision, or the party has had an opportunity to make representations at a hearing. Rule 37.17(4) states that an application for a conviction to be set aside should be made in writing as soon as reasonably practicable after the conviction, and should be served on the court and on each other party. The application must explain why the conviction should be set aside, and must identify any witness that the defendant wants to call, and any other proposed evidence.

Accused Convicted in Absence

D22.71   In *Gwent Magistrates' Court, ex parte Carey* (1996) 160 JP 613, the Divisional Court held that magistrates have a broad discretion in deciding whether or not to reopen a case under the MCA 1980, s. 142, when an accused has been convicted in his absence. They are entitled to have regard to the fact that the accused failed to attend the original hearing through his own fault and that witnesses would be inconvenienced if a retrial were to be ordered. Henry LJ also said that the magistrates were entitled to take account of the apparent strength of the prosecution case, although little weight should be given to it, since an apparently strong case can collapse during the course of a trial. His lordship also pointed out that the magistrates, by refusing to reopen the case, were not 'finally shutting out the defendant from the judgment seat' because he still had his unfettered right of appeal to the Crown Court under s. 108.

In *Dewsbury Magistrates, ex parte K* (1994) *The Times*, 16 March 1994, the accused was convicted in his absence, but his failure to attend court was not intentional. He sought a rehearing but the justices refused. This refusal was quashed by the Divisional Court, which said that any inconvenience to the court or to the prosecution should not outweigh the right of the accused to have an opportunity of defending himself. Similarly, in *R (Killick) v West London Magistrates' Court* [2012] EWHC 3864 (Admin), it was held that a magistrates' court erred in refusing to set aside a conviction under s. 142 where the accused had been tried in his absence despite medical evidence which suggested that he was unfit to attend court.

D22.72   In *R (Morsby) v Tower Bridge Magistrates' Court* (2008) 172 JP 155, the accused had been remanded in custody and so failed to attend his trial for another offence, of which he was convicted in his absence. He applied under s. 142 to rescind his conviction and reopen the trial. It was held that the magistrates' court had placed substantially too much weight on the accused's failure to communicate with the court from prison. The interests of justice clearly required the rescission of the claimant's conviction and a retrial in his presence. Similarly, in *R (Blick) v Doncaster Magistrates' Court* (2008) 172 JP 651, notice of the trial date was sent to the last known address of the accused. In the meantime, she had moved address but had not informed the magistrates' court of her change of address. She was convicted in her absence. The refusal by the magistrates' court to reopen the case was quashed by the Divisional Court because the magistrates' court had been wrong to take the question of whether the accused had acted with 'all due diligence' as the primary test of whether or not to make the order under s. 142(2) and had also erred in taking account of the cost to the 'public purse'.

Use of s. 142 where Accused Pleaded Guilty

D22.73   In *R (Williamson) v City of Westminster Magistrates' Court* [2012] 2 Cr App R 299, the accused pleaded guilty in the magistrates' court but subsequently said that he did so on the basis of incompetent advice from his solicitor. Burnett J said (at [31]) that the purpose of the MCA 1980, s. 142, as originally enacted, was to enable the magistrates' court itself to correct mistakes so as to avoid the need for parties to appeal to the Crown Court, or to the High Court by way of case stated, or to bring judicial review proceedings; despite subsequent amendment, the power 'remains rooted in the concept of correcting mistakes and errors. It is not a power equivalent to an appeal to the Crown Court or the High Court, nor is it a general power of review'. His lordship noted that, in *Croydon Youth Court, ex parte DPP*, McCowan LJ had said (at p. 417) that, 'It would be wholly wrong...for it to be possible to employ s. 142(2) as a method of a defendant obtaining a re-hearing as a substitute for an appeal to the Crown Court which he cannot pursue because he has unequivocally pleaded guilty'. However, Burnett J said (at [36]) that the court accepted 'that there may be circumstances in which s. 142(2) could be used to allow an unequivocal guilty plea to be set aside'. His lordship suggested that a case in which a guilty plea was entered to an offence unknown to law would be an example, since it would 'fall comfortably within the language of mistake'. Other examples 'include cases where a jurisdictional bar was not appreciated by the defendant relating, for example, to a time limit or the identity of a prosecutor'. His lordship added that the court would not exclude the possibility that s. 142(2) 'would be apt to deal with a case in which circumstances developed after a guilty plea and sentence which led the prosecution to conclude that the conviction should not be sustained'. Nonetheless, the Court went on to hold that the circumstances relied upon by Williamson, even if they were established, did not bring the case within the ambit of s. 142(2).

Delay

There is no time-limit for making an application under s. 142. However, where an accused **D22.74** applies under s. 142(2) for the trial to be reheard, delay in making the application is a relevant consideration for the magistrates in deciding whether or not to grant that application (*Ealing Magistrates' Court, ex parte Sahota* (1998) 162 JP 73).

Prosecution Role

Where a magistrates' court sets aside a conviction under the MCA 1980, s. 142, the court **D22.75** cannot require the Crown to pursue a prosecution (*R (Rhodes-Presley) v South Worcestershire Magistrates' Court* [2008] EWHC 2700 (Admin)). If the prosecution do not wish to proceed with a retrial, it may be necessary to list the matter before the magistrates; the prosecution will offer no evidence and the magistrates will then have no option but to dismiss the case with a verdict of not guilty (per Ouseley J at [9] and [10]).

Statutory Basis for Setting Aside for Rehearing

Magistrates' Courts Act 1980, s. 142   D22.76

(2) Where a person is convicted by a magistrates' court and it subsequently appears to the court that it would be in the interests of justice that the case should be heard again by different justices, the court may so direct.

(2A) The power conferred on a magistrates' court by subsection (2) above shall not be exercisable in relation to a conviction if—

(a) the Crown Court has determined an appeal against—

(i) the conviction; or

(ii) any sentence or order imposed or made by the magistrates' court when dealing with the offender in respect of the conviction; or

(b) the High Court has determined a case stated for the opinion of that court on any question arising in any proceeding leading to or resulting from the conviction.

(3) Where a court gives a direction under subsection (2) above—

(a) the conviction and any sentence or other order imposed or made in consequence thereof shall be of no effect; and

(b) section 10(4) above shall apply as if the trial of the person in question had been adjourned.

THE ROLE OF THE JUSTICES' CLERK/LEGAL ADVISER

Introduction

The qualifications and appointment of justices' clerks are described at **D3.29**. There is a distinc- **D22.77** tion between 'clerks' in the strict sense of the word and the 'legal advisers' who form part of the court staff. The function of a clerk in court is the same whether he is a court legal adviser or the actual clerk to the justices, although a legal adviser may (and ought) to seek assistance from *the* clerk if a point of difficulty arises on which the adviser does not feel qualified to advise the magistrates.

A justices' clerk must perform his legal functions independently. He is not subject to the directions of the Lord Chancellor or any other person when performing such legal functions, e.g., giving advice to the justices (Courts Act 2003, s. 29). An assistant clerk is similarly independent save that he is subject to the directions of the justices' clerk (s. 29(2)).

The statutory functions of the clerk are set out in the Courts Act 2003, s. 28, which provides: **D22.78**

(4) The functions of a justices' clerk include giving advice to any or all of the justices of the peace to whom he is clerk about matters of law (including procedure and practice) on questions arising

in connection with the discharge of their functions, including questions arising when the clerk is not personally attending on them.

(5) The powers of a justices' clerk include, at any time when he thinks he should do so, bringing to the attention of any or all of the justices of the peace to whom he is clerk any point of law (including procedure and practice) that is or may be involved in any question so arising.

The CrimPR, r. 37.14 (see Supplement, **R-296**), provides a further summary of the duties of the justices' legal adviser. These include: drawing the court's attention, before the hearing begins, to the prosecution allegations, what is agreed and what is in dispute, and what the parties have said about how they expect to present their cases; whenever necessary, giving the court legal advice (and, if necessary, attending the members of the court outside the courtroom to give such advice, so long as the parties are informed of any advice given outside the courtroom); assisting the court in the formulation of its reasons and the recording of those reasons; assisting the accused if he is unrepresented; and assisting the court by making a note of the substance of any oral evidence or representations, marking as inadmissible any parts of written statements introduced in evidence that are ruled inadmissible; ensuring that a record is kept of the court's decisions and the reasons for them, and making any announcement (other than of the verdict or sentence).

CPD VI, para. 37A.5 (see Supplement, **PD-48**), provides a list of matters on which the clerk or legal adviser may legitimately advise the magistrates:

(a) questions of law;
(b) questions of mixed law and fact;
(c) matters of practice and procedure;
(d) the process to be followed at sentence and the matters to be taken into account, together with the range of penalties and ancillary orders available, in accordance with the relevant sentencing guidelines;
(e) any relevant decisions of the superior courts or other guidelines;
(f) the appropriate decision-making structure to be applied in any given case; and
(g) other issues relevant to the matter before the court.

The justices' legal adviser is also required to assist the court, where appropriate, as to the formulation of reasons and the recording of those reasons (para. 37A.6). The clerk may also ask questions of witnesses and the parties in order to clarify the evidence and any issues in the case, and must ensure that every case is conducted justly (para. 37A.13).

Duties of Clerk with Regard to Questions of Law

D22.79 The role of the clerk (or justices' legal adviser) is to *advise* on law, practice and procedure. Since the magistrates are the ultimate arbiters of both law and fact there is no obligation on them to adopt the clerk's advice on law, but it is accepted practice that they should in fact do so. Thus, in *Jones v Nicks* [1977] RTR 72 at p. 76, Lord Widgery CJ strongly criticised magistrates for rejecting the clerk's advice that mitigation advanced by a motorist in respect of an offence of speeding could not amount to special reasons for not endorsing his licence. His lordship said: 'Justices really must accept legal advice from their clerk in circumstances like this; if they do not, all that happens is that a great deal of time and money is wasted in bringing the matter up here to be put right.'

If the clerk forms the view that the justices are wrong, however, he has no power to ignore their order and treat it as a nullity (*Liverpool Magistrates' Court, ex parte Abiaka* (1999) 163 JP 497). In those circumstances, he should refer the matter back to the same bench, or to a different bench if the original bench is unavailable, so that they can consider his fresh legal advice and alter the original order, or he should arrange for the matter to go to the Crown Court or the High Court.

When a point of law arises during the course of proceedings, any advice given by the clerk to the magistrates should be given publicly in open court. Moreover, CPD VI, para. 37A.14 (see Supplement, **PD-48**), requires that the clerk must provide the parties with an opportunity to respond to any advice given.

In *Chichester Justices, ex parte DPP* [1994] RTR 175 at p. 178, Morland J said that, if the clerk who advises the justices is not the clerk who was present in court when the parties made their submissions on the point of law at issue, it is essential that the clerk should hear informal submissions on the relevant law from the parties before advising the justices.

Advice on law will certainly include advice on the elements of the offence charged and on questions of admissibility of evidence. So far as sentencing is concerned, the clerk should be careful not to go beyond advising on the range of penalties available and any relevant guidelines; he should certainly not advocate a certain type of disposal, as this would be to interfere with a decision which is for the bench alone.

Clerk to Play No Part in Decisions on Questions of Fact

CPD VI, para. 37A.12 (see Supplement, **PD-48**), makes it clear the clerk or legal adviser must **D22.80** play no part in making findings of fact (but may assist the bench by reminding them of the evidence, and clarifying the issues which are to be determined). Contravention of this rule may lead to judicial review of the court's decision (see, e.g., *Stafford Justices, ex parte Ross* [1962] 1 All ER 540, where the conviction was quashed because, while the accused was giving evidence in his own defence, the clerk handed the bench a note which, in effect, argued that the evidence ought not to be believed).

Retirement of Clerk with Bench

The CrimPR, r. 37.14(2), says that the justices' legal adviser must give the court legal advice and **D22.81** may, if necessary, attend the members of the court outside the courtroom to give such advice; however, the parties must be informed of any advice given outside the courtroom.

The clerk should not leave the courtroom with the justices when they retire to consider their verdict. If the magistrates require assistance from the clerk, he should join them only when asked to do so and should return to the courtroom once the advice has been given, so as to avoid giving the impression that he is participating improperly in the decision-making process (*Eccles Justices, ex parte Farrelly* (1993) 157 JP 77). CPD VI, para. 37A.15, states that, where the justices request their adviser to join them in the retiring room, this request should be made in the presence of the parties in court. Moreover, any legal advice given to the justices in their retiring room should be regarded as provisional, and the adviser should then repeat the substance of the advice in open court and give the parties an opportunity to make representations on the correctness of that provisional advice; the legal adviser should state in open court whether the provisional advice is confirmed or if he has varied it (and, if so, how). The same point was made in *Clark v Kelly* [2004] 1 AC 681 (a case which concerned the role of the clerk to the justices in the district court (the Scottish equivalent of the magistrates' court)), where the Privy Council said that, subject to such safeguards, the role of the clerk is compatible with the accused's right to a fair trial under the ECHR, Article 6.

It is submitted, however, that this procedure may legitimately not be followed if the substance **D22.82** of the clerk's advice is simply repeating advice he has already given in open court, and on which the parties have already had the chance to make submissions. However, if the clerk advises the justices after they have retired to consider their decision and the clerk cites authority which was not cited in open court, he should inform the advocates in the case and give them the opportunity to make further submissions to the magistrates (*W v W* (1993) *The Times*, 4 June 1993).

In *R (Murchison) v Southend Magistrates' Court* (2006) 170 JP 230, the justices had retired to consider their verdict. They reached their decision and then invited the court legal adviser to assist in the compilation of reasons. After the legal adviser had done so, she informed the justices of the accused's antecedents. The justices then returned to court and gave their verdict. The accused was convicted. Immediately afterwards, the justices announced that they had seen the antecedents and were minded to adjourn sentence for a pre-sentence report. Judicial review of the conviction was sought on the ground that the justices had been made aware of the accused's antecedents before they had announced their decision in open court. The Divisional Court

Part D Procedure

D

dismissed the appeal because the magistrates had not known of the accused's previous convictions until after they had concluded their deliberations and had reached a reasoned decision. However, it was said that, as a matter of procedure, 'no advice should be offered by a legal adviser, provisional or otherwise, on sentence until the magistrates have returned to court, announced their decision on conviction, heard about the accused's antecedents and listened to counsel's submissions' (per Hallett LJ at [20]). Her ladyship added that 'legal advisers should only attend upon the bench . . . when called upon to do so; and then only to assist with matters arising at that stage' and that (given the possibility that in the instant case the legal adviser went into the retiring room with a copy of the appellant's previous convictions in her hand) legal advisers should ensure that any such documentation is left elsewhere when they retire to give the justices legal advice (at [21]).

Noting the Evidence

D22.83   The CrimPR, r. 37(3)(b)(i), says that the justices' legal adviser must assist the court by making a note of the substance of any oral evidence or representations. The importance of note-taking was emphasised in *L v DPP* [2008] 1 Cr App R 131, where Collins J (at [27]) said that, 'it is desirable that a note should be taken by someone — whether the clerk or someone deputised by the clerk — which is capable of being used as a formal note of the evidence if there is any later dispute as to what was or was not said in the course of evidence at the hearing'. Auld LJ echoed this sentiment (at [37]), saying, 'It is clearly important that adequate notes are made, even in comparatively minor cases . . ., going, albeit briefly, to the basis upon which the prosecution case is opened, the salient features of the evidence on both sides, and to any submissions as to law . . .'.

It is desirable that the defence should be supplied with a copy of the clerk's note if they are appealing against conviction to the Crown Court (*Clerk to Highbury Corner Justices, ex parte Hussein* [1986] 1 WLR 1266 (per Lord Lane CJ at p. 1271)).

Role of Justices' Legal Adviser where Accused is Unrepresented

D22.84   Under the CrimPR, r. 37.2(2)(b) (see Supplement, **R-284**), the justices' legal adviser (or the justices themselves) must explain the allegation, and what procedure will be adopted at the hearing, in terms the accused can understand. Moreover, r. 37.4(6) states that the justices' legal adviser (or the court) may ask a witness questions and, in particular, where the accused is not represented, ask any question necessary in the accused's interests. Rule 37.14(3)(a) provides that the justices' legal adviser must 'assist' an unrepresented defendant. However, the legal adviser must discharge the duty to assist unrepresented parties to present their case without appearing to become an advocate for the party concerned (CPD VI, para. 37A.16: see Supplement, **PD-48**). In *Simms v Moore* [1970] 2 QB 327 at pp. 332–3, Lord Parker CJ gave guidance which may be summarised as follows:

(1) In general neither the court nor the justices' legal adviser should take an active part in the proceedings except to clear up ambiguities in the evidence.
(2) So far as examining witnesses is concerned, this should never be done if the party concerned is legally represented or where a party, even though unrepresented, is competent to and desires to examine the witnesses himself.
(3) Where an unrepresented party is not competent, through a lack of knowledge of court procedure or rules of evidence or otherwise, to examine the witnesses properly, the court can at its discretion permit the justices' legal adviser to do so.
(4) When this is permitted, there is no reason why the justices' legal adviser should not do so by reference to a proof of evidence or statement handed in to him, provided always that an opportunity is given to the other side to see it or to have a copy.
(5) Where notes of evidence have to be or are taken, care should be taken not to use the proof or statement as the basis of the notes. The best course is for it to be arranged that someone else, possibly a member of the court itself, should take the note.

(6) Generally, the discretion in the court should be so exercised that examination of witnesses by the clerk should be permitted only when there are reasonable grounds for thinking that thereby the interests of justice would be best promoted, care being taken to see that nothing is done which conflicts with the rules of natural justice or the principle that justice must manifestly be seen to be done.

Thus, it is common practice for the justices' legal adviser to explain to an unrepresented accused the purpose of cross-examination and, if the accused himself still seems incapable of doing it properly, to frame suitable questions on his behalf. Moreover, under r. 37.3(3)(d), at the close of the prosecution case, the justices' legal adviser (or the justices) must explain to the accused that he has the right to give evidence, and also the potential effect of not doing so at all, or of refusing to answer a question while doing so (namely the drawing of adverse inferences).

Section D23   Sentencing in the Magistrates' Court

INTRODUCTION

D23.1   The procedure to be followed between a plea or verdict of guilty and the court pronouncing sentence in the Crown Court is described in section **D20**. Sentencing procedure in the magistrates' courts follows the same basic pattern. The following paragraphs, which should be read in conjunction with section **D20** and with **part E** (which deals with sentencing generally), focus on topics of particular relevance to magistrates' courts. The duty on the court, under the CAJA 2009, s. 125, to follow any relevant sentencing guidelines, unless satisfied that it would be contrary to the interests of justice to do so, applies to all courts, including magistrates' courts. The Magistrates' Court Sentencing Guidelines (see Supplement, **SG-225** *et seq.*), which are updated regularly, cover most of the offences that are regularly encountered in magistrates' courts, together with some very useful general explanatory material.

ADJOURNMENTS PRIOR TO SENTENCE

D23.2   *Magistrates' Courts Act 1980, s. 10*

(3) A magistrates' court may, for the purpose of enabling inquiries to be made or of determining the most suitable method of dealing with the case, exercise its power to adjourn after convicting the accused and before sentencing him or otherwise dealing with him; but, if it does so, the adjournment shall not be for more than four weeks at a time unless the court remands the accused in custody and, where it so remands him, the adjournment shall not be for more than three weeks at a time.

It is apparent from the words 'at a time' that, although the maximum period for adjournment after conviction is four weeks on bail or three weeks in custody, the court is not obliged to sentence at the end of the first such adjournment but may, if necessary, adjourn again. A common reason for adjourning the case prior to passing sentence will be to enable the preparation of a pre-sentence report, especially if the court is considering a custodial sentence or a community order (since a report will normally be required in such cases by virtue of the CJA 2003, s. 156). Where an offender is granted bail for a post-conviction adjournment, the court may impose a condition that he make himself available for the purpose of enabling inquiries or a report to be made to assist the court in dealing with him for the offence (Bail Act 1976, s. 3(6)(d)), provided that it appears to be necessary to do so for the purpose of enabling inquiries or a report to be made (BA 1976, sch. 1, part 1, para. 8(1A)).

D23.3   There is some overlap between the MCA 1980, s. 10(3), and the PCC(S)A 2000, s. 11, which empowers magistrates to adjourn for medical reports once they are satisfied that the accused committed the *actus reus* of the offence. If magistrates have convicted, they must *ex hypothesi* be satisfied as to the *actus reus*, and may therefore adjourn under s. 11. However, the chief value of s. 11 is not so much at the post-conviction stage (as the magistrates may adjourn for medical reports under the general powers of the MCA 1980, s. 10(3)) but before conviction when the obtaining of suitable reports and recommendations may enable the court to make a hospital or guardianship order without finding the accused guilty. Where the court adjourns under the PCC(S)A 2000, s. 11, and grants bail to the accused, it *must* make it a condition of bail that he undergo a medical examination by either one or two duly qualified medical practitioners (s. 11(3)).

In December 2009, Leveson LJ (then Senior Presiding Judge for England and Wales) issued **D23.4** guidance to magistrates' courts in a document entitled *Essential Case Management: Applying the Criminal Procedure Rules* (see also D21.40). That document says that where the accused pleads guilty, the court should (unless committing for sentence) pass sentence on the same day 'if at all possible'. Where a pre-sentence report is needed, 'it may be that a report prepared for earlier proceedings will be sufficient or a "fast delivery" report (oral or written) may be prepared that day'. Moreover, where a *Newton* hearing is needed, the court should identify the disputed issue and 'if possible, determine it there and then or, if it really cannot be decided, give directions . . . to ensure that the next hearing is the last'. The importance of avoiding delay is emphasised by the CrimPR, r. 37.10(9)(a), which says that once account has been taken of all relevant information, and any report that may be available, the court must, as a general rule, pass sentence there and then.

Keeping Sentencing Options Open   In *Nottingham Magistrates' Court, ex parte Davidson* **D23.5** [2001] 1 Cr App R (S) 167, Lord Bingham CJ (at p. 169), set out the following principle:

> If a court at a preliminary stage of the sentencing process gives to a defendant any indication as to the sentence which will or will not be thereafter passed upon him, in terms sufficiently unqualified to found a legitimate expectation in the mind of the defendant that any court which later passes sentence upon him will act in accordance with the indication given, and if on a later occasion a court, without reasons which justify departure from the earlier indication, and whether or not it is aware of that indication, passes a sentence inconsistent with, and more severe than, the sentence indicated, the court will ordinarily feel obliged, however reluctantly, to adjust the sentence passed so as to bring it into line with that indicated.

This dictum was cited with approval in *Thornton v CPS* [2010] 2 Cr App R (S) 434. In that case, Aikens LJ went on to say (at [49]) that:

> . . . it is imperative that magistrates do not put themselves in a position which binds the hands of another bench on the question of sentence unless they are absolutely certain that it is the right course to take. Forms can be used, and forms of words used, to ensure that no expectation about sentence, legitimate or otherwise, is engendered in the mind of defendants or their advisers. If those forms and words are used correctly, then unnecessary and expensive expeditions to this court will be avoided.

His lordship also referred to the dictum of Wilkie J in *Nicholas v Chester Magistrates' Court* (2009) 173 JP 542 (at [13]), that the court would 'thoroughly deprecate the practice, if such it be, of one bench to adjourn sentencing for reports and in so doing giving an indication as to the type of sentence which it would be appropriate to pass where that bench is not reserving sentence to itself'. He explained that, by so doing, the effect (save in an exceptional case) is to fetter the discretion of the sentencing court and that 'should only be done where the bench reserves to itself the sentence, or in a case where it is absolutely obvious that a certain type of sentence should be considered or should not be considered'.

PRESENTING THE FACTS, CHARACTER AND ANTECEDENTS

The procedure to be followed before sentence is passed in a magistrates' court is basically the **D23.6** same as in the Crown Court. The CrimPR, r. 37.10(2), requires the prosecutor to summarise the prosecution case, if the sentencing court has not heard evidence (i.e. if the offender has pleaded guilty, or there has been an adjournment after the offender was convicted following a trial); r. 37.10(3) then requires the prosecutor to identify any offence(s) to be taken into consideration, and to provide information relevant to sentence (including any aggravating or mitigating factors, relevant legislative provisions, and any guidelines or guideline cases). The prosecutor also has to draw the court's attention to any statement of the effect of the offence on the victim, the victim's family or others (i.e. any victim personal statement).

Under r. 37.10(4), the offender must provide details of financial circumstances. Rule 37.10(7) requires the court, before passing sentence, to give the offender an opportunity to make representations and introduce evidence relevant to sentence. Thus there will be an opportunity for a plea in mitigation to be made on behalf of the offender.

The court which passes sentence need not be composed of the justices who convicted the offender (or who sat at an earlier post-conviction hearing when the case was adjourned) but, where the court which is to pass sentence consists of, or includes, justices who were not sitting when the offender was convicted, the court must 'make such inquiry into the facts and circumstances of the case as will enable the justices who were not sitting when the offender was convicted to be fully acquainted with those facts and circumstances' (MCA 1980, s. 121(7)). This will invariably be done through the summary of the relevant facts presented by the prosecutor (prior to any plea in mitigation by the defence).

Newton Hearings

D23.7   Under the CrimPR, r. 37.10(5), where the accused pleads guilty but wants to be sentenced on a different basis to the facts put forward by the prosecution, he must set out that basis in writing (identifying exactly what is in dispute). The court may invite the parties to make representations about whether the dispute is material to sentence (in the sense that the sentence would differ depending on whether it is based on the prosecution version or the defence version of the facts). If the court decides that it is a material dispute, the court will invite 'such further representations or evidence as it may require' and then decide the dispute. Although the CrimPR appear to suggest that, where the difference in versions put forward by the parties is significant (in that it would make a difference to the sentence passed), the court has a choice of hearing further representations or evidence, it is submitted that magistrates should follow the procedure laid down in *Newton* (1982) 77 Cr App R 13, and (if they are unwilling simply to accept the defence version of events) hear evidence (i.e. hold a *Newton* hearing) and then make findings of fact and sentence accordingly. Indeed, cases where it is possible to resolve such a factual dispute without hearing evidence are likely to be very rare, since the decision is likely to involve the court assessing the credibility of the evidence adduced by the parties. *Newton* hearings are considered in more detail in **D20.8**.

In *Warley Magistrates' Court, ex parte DPP* [1999] 1 All ER 251, Kennedy LJ (at p. 224) said that where there is a significant difference between the prosecution and defence versions of the facts of the offence:

(a) if the magistrates think that their sentencing powers will be adequate however the dispute is resolved, they should follow the *Newton* procedure and either accept the defence version or hear evidence and then make findings of fact;
(b) if they think that their sentencing powers will not be adequate however the dispute is resolved, they should simply commit for sentence, leaving the Crown Court to follow the *Newton* procedure;
(c) if the decision whether or not to commit for sentence turns or may turn on which version is found to be correct, the magistrates should follow the *Newton* procedure.

ADJUDICATION ON AND PRONOUNCEMENT OF SENTENCE

Majority Decision

D23.8   As with any adjudication of a magistrates' court, the decision as to sentence may be by a majority of those sitting. In the event of an equal division, the court could adjourn under the MCA 1980,

s. 10 (adjournments after conviction and before sentence), for the matter to be reconsidered at the resumed hearing.

Reasons and Explanation

The CrimPR, r. 37.10(9)(b), requires that, when passing sentence, the court must (unless nei- **D23.9** ther the offender nor any member of the public is present) explain the reasons for deciding on that sentence. Unless the offender is absent, or his ill-health or disorderly conduct makes it impracticable to do so, the court must also explain the effect of the sentence, the consequences of failing to comply with any requirements imposed, and any power that the court has to vary or review the sentence (r. 37.10(9)(c)). The court must also consider exercising any power it has to make a costs or other order (r. 37.10(9)(e)). It should also be noted that the CJA 2003, s. 174(1), imposes a duty to give reasons for, and explain the effect of, any sentence (see **E1.23**). In the case of a custodial sentence or a community sentence, the court must explain why it regards the offence as being sufficiently serious to warrant such a sentence (s. 174(2)(b) and (c)). The court must also mention any aggravating or mitigating factors which it regarded as being of particular importance (s. 174(2)(e)). The court must identify any relevant definitive sentencing guidelines and explain how it has discharged its duty to follow those guidelines; where the court did not follow any such guidelines because it was of the opinion that it would be contrary to the interests of justice to do so, it must state why it was of that opinion (s. 174(2)(a) and (aa)). The court is also required to record the reason for passing a custodial sentence in the warrant of commitment and in the court register (s. 174(5)).

SENTENCING IN ABSENCE

The power in the MCA 1980, s. 11(1), to proceed in the accused's absence extends to passing **D23.10** sentence without him there, once the court has found the case proved. However, this is qualified by s. 11(3)–(5):

Magistrates' Courts Act 1980, s. 11

(3) In proceedings to which this subsection applies, the court shall not in a person's absence sentence him to imprisonment or detention in a young offender institution or make a detention and training order or an order under paragraph 8(2)(a) or (b) of Schedule 12 to the Criminal Justice Act 2003 that a suspended sentence shall take effect.

(3A) But where a sentence or order of a kind mentioned in subsection (3) is imposed or given in the absence of the offender, the offender must be brought before the court before being taken to a prison or other institution to begin serving his sentence (and the sentence or order is not to be regarded as taking effect until he is brought before the court).

(4) In proceedings to which this subsection applies, the court shall not in a person's absence impose any disqualification on him, except on resumption of the hearing after an adjournment under section 10(3) above; and where a trial is adjourned in pursuance of this subsection the notice required by section 10(2) above shall include notice of the reason for the adjournment.

(5) Subsections (3) and (4) apply to—
    (a) proceedings instituted by an information, where a summons has been issued; and
    (b) proceedings instituted by a written charge.

The effect of these provisions is that, where the proceedings were started by written charge and requisition (or, in the case of a private prosecution, by information and summons), the court must adjourn the sentencing hearing if the offender is absent and either (a) the court is considering the imposition of a custodial sentence, or (b) the court is considering the imposition of a disqualification and the hearing has not previously been adjourned to give the offender an opportunity to attend (see also the CrimPR, r. 37.10(10)(a)). Although the prohibition in s. 11(4) will, in the majority of cases, be relevant to proposed disqualification from driving, it extends to any form of disqualification that a magistrates' court may order (see **E21**). Although s. 11(3) appears to prohibit the imposition of a custodial sentence if the offender is absent,

s. 11(3A) goes on to provide that, if the court does pass a custodial sentence in the absence of the offender, that sentence cannot take effect until he has been brought before the court. In any event, these provisions do not apply where the proceedings were started by the offender being charged at a police station, and so do not apply where the accused was bailed to return to the court (see s. 11(5)).

A disqualification imposed in contravention of s. 11(4) will be a nullity and liable to be quashed (*Llandrindod Wells Justices, ex parte Gibson* [1968] 2 All ER 20).

D23.11   Where an accused is represented by counsel or solicitor, the deeming provision in the MCA 1980, s. 122 (see **D22.31**), presumably has the effect of allowing the normally prohibited sentences to be passed even though the offender is not physically present, but in practice the court would almost certainly adjourn rather than proceed in the absence of the offender.

Where an absent offender is being sentenced for a summary offence, the court may take account of any previous convictions that he may have, provided notice of intention to cite the convictions was served on him at least seven days prior to the hearing (MCA 1980, s. 104). This restriction on the use of previous convictions does not apply to sentencing for either-way offences or to sentencing in a youth court.

As regards sentencing for endorsable offences, an accused who does not intend to attend court is under a duty to send in his licence before the hearing date, and the court may then take account of any endorsements on the licence when sentencing. If the licence is not duly delivered, the court may adjourn for production of it. Alternatively, if the prosecution have obtained from the DVLA a printout of the details recorded there in respect of the accused, the court may proceed to sentence on the basis of the printout.

Warrants

D23.12   Depending on the penalty they have in mind, magistrates may consider it undesirable to proceed to sentence in the offender's absence. If so, they will adjourn. They may also be able to issue a warrant for the offender's arrest. The power to issue a warrant upon adjourning is contained in the MCA 1980, s. 13(1). The same basic conditions apply to issuing a warrant at the post-conviction stage as apply before conviction (i.e. where the proceedings were commenced by way of summons or written charge and requisition, it must be proved that the summons or requisition was served on the accused a reasonable time before the trial or adjourned trial, or else the accused was present in court when the case was adjourned to the present date). However, following conviction, the powers of the court are widened in that it may issue a warrant even though the offence is non-imprisonable, provided it is proposing to impose a disqualification on the offender (s. 13(3)(b)).

In cases where the accused has entered a plea of guilty by post, there is no power to issue a warrant if either the magistrates decide to adjourn rather than accept the plea, or, having convicted, they adjourn before sentence (e.g., because they are considering disqualification) (s. 13(4)). However, if the court has adjourned once without issuing a warrant in such a case and the accused fails to appear for the adjourned hearing, then (subject to proof that the adjournment notice was duly served) a warrant may be issued.

Attendance at Sentencing Hearings via Live Link

D23.13   The CDA 1998, ss. 57D and 57E, enable the court to direct that an accused in custody may appear at sentencing hearings via a 'live link' from the place at which he is being held. Section 57D deals with preliminary hearings which turn into sentencing hearings because the accused pleads guilty (see **D5.38**). Section 57E deals with other sentencing hearings. Under s. 57E(2), where it is likely that an offender who has been convicted will be held in custody during the sentencing hearing, the court may direct that the offender attend via a live link. Under s. 57E(4), such a direction may be given by the court of its own motion or following an application from either party, and may include subsequent sentencing hearings in relation to that offence. A direction may be given only if the court is satisfied that it is not contrary to the interests of justice to do so (s. 57E(5)). The court may, if it is in the interests of justice to do so, rescind the live link direction, either of its own motion or on the application of either party (s. 57E(6)). Under s. 57E(7), the offender can give oral evidence via the live link under s. 57E only if the court is satisfied that it is not contrary to the interests of justice for him to give his evidence in that way. If the court refuses an application for (or for the rescission of) a live link direction under s. 57E, it must state its reasons in open court and, in the case of a magistrates' courts, must record the reasons in the court register (s. 57E(8)).

RESTRICTIONS ON MAGISTRATES' COURTS' POWERS OF SENTENCE

Offences Triable Either Way

The maximum sentence that magistrates may currently impose upon an offender summarily convicted of an either-way offence listed in the MCA 1980, sch. 1, is six months' imprisonment and/or a fine of up to £5,000. Where an offence is made triable either way by the statute creating it, the maximum sentence on summary conviction is six months' imprisonment or the term prescribed by the statute, whichever is the less, and/or a fine of up to £5,000 or the amount prescribed by the statute, whichever is the greater (PCC(S)A 2000, s. 78, and MCA 1980, s. 32(1) and (2)).   **D23.14**

The six-month ceiling on magistrates' powers of imprisonment contained in s. 78(1) may be expressly excluded. Thus, if an offence-creating enactment simply provides that the maximum term on summary conviction for an offence triable either way shall be nine months' imprisonment, the effect of s. 78(1) is to reduce the maximum to six months, but, if it provides that 'notwithstanding anything in section 78(1) of the PCC(S)A 2000, the maximum term shall be nine months', then s. 78(1) is overridden and the maximum is indeed nine months.

The CJA 2003, s. 154(1) (not yet in force), empowers a magistrates' court to impose up to 12 months' imprisonment for a single offence and s. 282 increases the maximum penalty on summary conviction for an either-way offence from six months to 12 months.

The rule that the maximum fine for an either-way offence is £5,000 does not apply if the offence-creating enactment is a 'relevant enactment' (i.e. one passed after 1977), and so the maximum fine in such cases is whatever the statute prescribes, whether more or less than £5,000. Nor does the £5,000 maximum apply to fines for continuing offences where the court may impose a penalty for each day on which the offence is continued after a specified date, or to certain specified either-way offences under the Misuse of Drugs Act 1971 (see the MCA 1980, s. 32(4) and (5), qualifying the effect of s. 32(2)).   **D23.15**

By virtue of the MCA 1980, s. 34(3), if the statute creating the offence empowers the court to impose a custodial sentence on the offender but makes no mention of a fine, then (unless this provision is expressly excluded), the court may, instead of imposing a custodial sentence, impose a fine of up to £5,000 if the offence is triable either way, or £1,000 (level 3) if the offence is a summary one.

The LASPO 2012, s. 85 (not yet in force), proposes the removal of the limit in respect of relevant offences (defined in a way that includes the vast majority of criminal offences) where, on 'commencement day', the offence is punishable by a fine or maximum fine of £5,000 or more. The court will then be able to impose 'a fine of any amount'.

Summary Offences

The maximum sentence of imprisonment (if any) for a summary offence is six months or that prescribed by the statute creating the offence, whichever is the less (PCC(S)A 2000, s. 78(1)).   **D23.16**

Again this is subject to the six-month ceiling in s. 78(1) being expressly overridden by any other enactment. The maximum fine for a summary offence is whatever the offence-creating provision specifies. Nearly always, the enactment will fix the fine by reference to a level on the standard scale of fines rather than by reference to a specific sum of money (see E15.9 for the standard scale of fines). The offence-creating provision will indicate whether a fine may be imposed in addition to any sentence of imprisonment or only as an alternative thereto.

The CJA 2003, s. 281(4) and (5) (not yet in force), provides for all summary offences contained in Acts passed before or in the same Session as the 2003 Act with a maximum penalty of six months' imprisonment to have this maximum penalty raised automatically to 51 weeks. The CJA 2003, sch. 26 (also not yet in force), increases the penalty for a number of specific summary offences to 51 weeks.

Aggregate Prison Terms

D23.17 Magistrates sentencing an offender for several offences and imposing imprisonment for two or more of them may make the terms concurrent or consecutive (MCA 1980, s. 133(1)). This is subject to the maximum *aggregate* term that a magistrates' court may impose on one occasion for several offences, which is six months, unless it is sentencing for two or more either-way offences, in which case it is 12 months (proviso to s. 133(1) and (2)). Where magistrates have power to deal with an offender for breach of a suspended sentence, they may (if they choose to activate part or all of the suspended term) make it run consecutively to any term of imprisonment they impose for the offences that put the offender in breach (CJA 2003, sch. 12, para. (9)(1)(b)). In such a case, the aggregate of the suspended term and the terms for the present offences may exceed the aggregate normally permitted by s. 133(1) and (2) (*Chamberlain* (1992) 13 Cr App R (S) 525).

The CJA 2003, s. 155(2) (not yet in force), amends the MCA 1980, s. 133(1), to empower a magistrates' court to impose a maximum aggregate term of 65 weeks.

Aggregate Fines

D23.18 When magistrates are dealing with an offender for several offences (whether summary or triable either way), they may fine him up to the statutory maximum for each offence. In other words, there is no restriction on the aggregate fine that may be imposed.

Criminal Damage Cases

D23.19 Where magistrates deal with a charge of criminal damage under the special procedure in the MCA 1980, s. 22, as if it were a summary offence (see D6.22) and the accused is convicted, their powers of sentencing are restricted to three months' imprisonment or to a fine at level 4 (currently £2,500, see E15.9). If, on the other hand, they conclude that the value involved in the offence exceeded the relevant sum (£5,000) and therefore adopt the usual procedure for determining mode of trial, the maximum sentence, should there be a decision for summary trial and conviction, is that which may be imposed for any other either-way offence listed in sch. 1 to the MCA 1980 (i.e. six months' imprisonment and/or a fine of £5,000). When the CJA 2003, sch. 32, para. 27, comes into force, the maximum sentence of imprisonment for criminal damage where the value does not exceed the relevant sum will be increased to 51 weeks.

Compensation Orders

D23.20 The maximum amount of compensation that a magistrates' court may order in respect of any one offence (whether summary or triable either way) is £5,000 (PCC(S)A 2000, s. 131(1)). Where an offender is convicted of several offences there is no restriction on the aggregate sum of compensation (i.e. he may be ordered to pay £5,000 for each offence).

Where the offender asks for offences to be taken into consideration, compensation may be ordered in respect of offences taken into consideration but the total amount ordered must not exceed the maximum which could be ordered for the offence(s) of which the offender has actually been convicted (s. 131(2)). Thus, if the offender is convicted of three offences and asks for six others to be taken into consideration, the maximum compensation order is £15,000.

Custody for Young Offenders

A magistrates' court may impose a sentence of detention in a young offender institution on an **D23.21** offender aged 18 to 20. The court's powers are limited to the same extent as are their powers to imprison offenders who have attained the age of 21.

A youth court may impose a detention and training order, for which the maximum duration is 24 months (12 months' custody and 12 months' supervision in the community). See E7.15.

Other Sentencing Powers

Magistrates are also entitled to suspend a prison sentence, although the term suspended must **D23.22** not exceed that which they could have imposed as a sentence of immediate imprisonment.

As to the various non-custodial sentencing options, these are all at the disposal of magistrates' courts to the same extent and in the same circumstances as they are at the disposal of the Crown Court.

Provisions of the Magistrates' Courts Act 1980 and the Powers of Criminal Courts (Sentencing) Act 2000 relating to Magistrates' Sentencing Powers

Magistrates' Courts Act 1980, ss. 32, 33 and 133 **D23.23**

32.—(1) On summary conviction of any of the offences triable either way listed in Schedule 1 to this Act a person shall be liable to imprisonment for a term not exceeding six months or to a fine not exceeding the prescribed sum or both, except that—

(a) a magistrates' court shall not have power to impose imprisonment for an offence so listed if the Crown Court would not have that power in the case of an adult convicted of it on indictment;

...

(2) For any offence triable either way which is not listed in Schedule 1 to this Act, being an offence under a relevant enactment, the maximum fine which may be imposed on summary conviction shall by virtue of this subsection be the prescribed sum unless the offence is one for which by virtue of an enactment other than this subsection a larger fine may be imposed on summary conviction.

(3) Where, by virtue of any relevant enactment, a person summarily convicted of an offence triable either way would, apart from this section, be liable to a maximum fine of one amount in the case of a first conviction and of a different amount in the case of a second or subsequent conviction, subsection (2) above shall apply irrespective of whether the conviction is a first, second or subsequent one.

(4) Subsection (2) above shall not affect so much of any enactment as (in whatever words) makes a person liable on summary conviction to a fine not exceeding a specified amount for each day on which a continuing offence is continued after conviction or the occurrence of any other specified event.

(5) Subsection (2) above shall not apply on summary conviction of any of the following offences:—

(a) offences under section 5(2) of the Misuse of Drugs Act 1971 (having possession of a controlled drug) where the controlled drug in relation to which the offence was committed was a Class B or Class C drug;

(b) offences under the following provisions of that Act, where the controlled drug in relation to which the offence was committed was a Class C drug, namely—

(i) section 4(2) (production, or being concerned in the production, of a controlled drug);

(ii) section 4(3) (supplying or offering a controlled drug or being concerned in the doing of either activity by another);

(iii) section 5(3) (having possession of a controlled drug with intent to supply it to another);

(iv) section 8 (being the occupier, or concerned in the management, of premises and permitting or suffering certain activities to take place there);

(v) section 12(6) (contravention of direction prohibiting practitioner etc. from possessing, supplying etc. controlled drugs); or

(vi) section 13(3) (contravention of direction prohibiting practitioner etc. from prescribing, supplying etc. controlled drugs).

[(6) Any power by subordinate instrument to restrict the amount of fine which may be imposed on summary conviction for an either-way offence shall not be affected by subsection (2) above.]

(7) [Repealed.]

(8) In subsection (5) above 'controlled drug', 'Class B drug' and 'Class C drug' have the same meaning as in the Misuse of Drugs Act 1971.

(9) In this section—

'fine' includes a pecuniary penalty but does not include a pecuniary forfeiture or pecuniary compensation;

'the prescribed sum' means £5,000 or such sum as is for the time being substituted in this definition by an order in force under section 143(3) below;

'relevant enactment' means an enactment contained in the Criminal Law Act 1977 or in any Act passed before, or in the same session as, that Act.

33.—(1) Where in pursuance of subsection (2) of section 22 above a magistrates' court proceeds to the summary trial of an information, then, if the accused is summarily convicted of the offence—

(a) subject to subsection (3) below the court shall not have power to impose on him in respect of that offence imprisonment for more than three months or a fine on level 4 on the standard scale; and

(b) section 3 of the Powers of Criminal Courts (Sentencing) Act 2000 (committal to Crown Court for sentence) shall not apply as regards that offence.

(2) In subsection (1) above 'fine' includes a pecuniary penalty but does not include a pecuniary forfeiture or pecuniary compensation.

(3) Paragraph (a) of subsection (1) does not apply to an offence under section 12A of the Theft Act 1968 (aggravated vehicle-taking).

133.—(1) Subject to section 265 of the Criminal Justice Act 2003, a magistrates' court imposing imprisonment or a sentence of detention in a young offender institution on any person may order that the term of imprisonment or detention in a young offender institution shall commence on the expiration of any other term of imprisonment or detention in a young offender institution imposed by that or any other court; but where a magistrates' court imposes two or more terms of imprisonment or detention in a young offender institution to run consecutively the aggregate of such terms shall not, subject to the provisions of this section, exceed six months.

(2) If two or more of the terms imposed by the court are imposed in respect of an offence triable either way which was tried summarily otherwise than in pursuance of section 22(2) above [criminal damage triable only summarily if the value involved was less than £5,000], the aggregate of the terms so imposed and any other terms imposed by the court may exceed six months but shall not, subject to the following provisions of this section, exceed 12 months.

(2A)   In relation to the imposition of terms of detention in a young offender institution subsection (2) above shall have effect as if the reference to an offence triable either way were a reference to such an offence or an offence triable only on indictment.

(3) The limitations imposed by the preceding subsections shall not operate to reduce the aggregate of the terms that the court may impose in respect of any offences below the term which the court has power to impose in respect of any one of those offences.

(4) Where a person has been sentenced by a magistrates' court to imprisonment and a fine for the same offence, a period of imprisonment imposed for non-payment of the fine, or for want of sufficient [goods] to satisfy the fine, shall not be subject to the limitations imposed by the preceding subsections.

(5) For the purposes of this section a term of imprisonment shall be deemed to be imposed in respect of an offence if it is imposed as a sentence or in default of payment of a fine adjudged to be paid by the conviction or for want of sufficient [goods] to satisfy such a sum.

Powers of Criminal Courts (Sentencing) Act 2000, ss. 78 and 131

78.—(1) A magistrates' court shall not have power to impose imprisonment, or detention in a young offender institution, for more than six months in respect of any one offence.

(2) Unless expressly excluded, subsection (1) above shall apply even if the offence in question is one for which a person would otherwise be liable on summary conviction to imprisonment or detention in a young offender institution for more than six months.

(3) Subsection (1) above is without prejudice to section 133 of the Magistrates' Courts Act 1980 (consecutive terms of imprisonment).

(4) Any power of a magistrates' court to impose a term of imprisonment for non-payment of a fine, or for want of sufficient distress to satisfy a fine, shall not be limited by virtue of subsection (1) above.

(5) In subsection (4) above 'fine' includes a pecuniary penalty but does not include a pecuniary forfeiture or pecuniary compensation.

(6) In this section 'impose imprisonment' means pass a sentence of imprisonment or fix a term of imprisonment for failure to pay any sum of money, or for want of sufficient distress to satisfy any sum of money, or for failure to do or abstain from doing anything required to be done or left undone.

(7) Section 132 of the Magistrates' Courts Act 1980 contains provision about the minimum term of imprisonment which may be imposed by a magistrates' court.

131.—(1) The compensation to be paid under a compensation order made by a magistrates' court in respect of any offence of which the court has convicted the offender shall not exceed £5,000.

(2) The compensation or total compensation to be paid under a compensation order or compensation orders made by a magistrates' court in respect of any offence or offences taken into consideration in determining sentence shall not exceed the difference (if any) between—

(a) the amount or total amount which under subsection (1) above is the maximum for the offence or offences of which the offender has been convicted; and

(b) the amount or total amounts (if any) which are in fact ordered to be paid in respect of that offence or those offences.

VARIATION OF SENTENCE UNDER THE MAGISTRATES' COURTS ACT 1980, s. 142

The MCA 1980, s. 142(1), allows a magistrates' court to vary or rescind its decision as to sentence if it is in the interests of justice to do so. The power is similar to that in respect of setting aside a conviction (see D22.70). The magistrates can reopen the case under s. 142 regardless of whether the accused pleaded guilty or was found guilty. However, s. 142 cannot operate where the accused was acquitted (see *Coles v East Penwith Justices* (1998) 162 JP 687, where the Divisional Court held that there was no power under s. 142(1) to revoke a defendant's costs order where the prosecution had withdrawn the charges).   **D23.24**

Guidance on the use of s. 142(1) was given in *Holme v Liverpool City Justices* (2005) 169 JP 306. The accused pleaded guilty to dangerous driving, a pedestrian having sustained serious injuries. A community sentence was imposed. The magistrates agreed to a request from CPS to reopen the case under s. 142, on the basis that the original counsel for the prosecution had not addressed the extent of the pedestrian's injuries and that the difference between the sentence imposed and the custodial sentence that would probably have been imposed had the court known all the facts offended the principles of justice. On appeal to the Divisional Court, Collins J (at [30]) said that: **D23.25**

> ... the power under s. 142 is to be used in a relatively limited situation, namely one which is akin to mistake or, as the court says, the slip rule. But there is no reason, on the face of it, to limit it further. It seems to me that if a court has been misled into imposing a particular sentence, and it is discovered that it has been so misled, then the sentence may properly be said to have been imposed because of a mistake; the mistake being the failure of the court to appreciate a relevant fact. That may well give power to the court to exercise the jurisdiction conferred by s. 142, but it does not indicate that that power should necessarily be used.

It follows that s. 142 can be used to increase sentence only in exceptional circumstances. His lordship went on (at [33]) to say that the sort of case which is appropriate for use of the power under s. 142 is one 'where the mistake is quickly identified and it is accepted on all sides that a mistake had been made'. At [42]–[43], his lordship said that it was possible to envisage circumstances in which the failure of the court to be aware of factors which would be relevant to sentence could properly mean that it would be appropriate to resort to s.142, but:

> ... it would only be in very rare circumstances that it would be appropriate to resort to s. 142 to consider an increase in sentence, particularly if that increase ... brought the possibility of custody as opposed to another form of disposal.

The facts of the instant case, said the court, did not come anywhere near justifying such a use of s. 142.

D23.26 In *Zykin v CPS* (2009) 173 JP 361, Bean J quoted from *Holme* and said (at [16]) that s. 142 'does not confer a wide and general power on a magistrates' court to reopen a previous decision on the grounds that it is in the interests of justice to do so'; rather, it is 'a power to be used in a relatively limited situation, namely one which is akin to mistake or the slip rule'. In *R (Williamson) v City of Westminster Magistrates' Court* [2012] 2 Cr App R 299 (see **D22.73**), Burnett J said (*obiter*), at [31], that it could be contended that it would be in the interests of justice to substitute a new sentence on the ground that the one originally imposed was manifestly excessive. However, his lordship said that s. 142(1) 'cannot be read as conferring a power to substitute a new sentence in the same way as an appellate court might'.

D23.27 The power under s. 142 should not be used to punish an offender who has misbehaved in the dock after pronouncement of sentence by increasing what was first announced (*Powell* (1985) 7 Cr App R (S) 247, a case which in fact concerned misbehaviour by an offender at the Crown Court).

In *R (Trigger) v Northampton Magistrates' Court* (2011) 175 JP 101, it was held to have been inappropriate for the magistrates to exercise their powers under s. 142 to increase a sentence originally imposed some 20 months earlier. Ramsey J said (at [33]) that the 'wide power and absence of any time limit in s. 142 must however be exercised taking account of the principle of finality of sentencing'. Moreover, although s. 142 gives the magistrates jurisdiction to vary or rescind the sentence so as to impose a sentence that could have been imposed at the date of the original sentence, 'it must be borne in mind that it would not usually be in the interests of justice to increase a sentence imposed earlier unless the power is exercised speedily after the date of the original sentence'.

D23.28 The CrimPR, r. 42.4(2) (see Supplement, **R-349**), states that the court may exercise its power to vary or rescind a sentence on application by a party, or on its own initiative. An application under s. 142 may be dealt with in a public or private hearing, or without a hearing. Under r. 42.4(3), a party seeking a variation in sentence under s. 142 must apply in writing as soon as reasonably practicable after the sentence has been passed, explaining why that sentence should be varied and specifying the variation that the applicant proposes. The application must be served on the court and on each other party. Under r. 42.4(4), the court cannot vary the sentence in the absence of the defendant unless the court is making the variation which he has proposed, or the effect of the variation is that he is not dealt with more severely under the sentence as varied than before, or he has been given the opportunity to make representations at a hearing.

D23.29   Magistrates' Courts Act 1980, s. 142

(1) A magistrates' court may vary or rescind a sentence or other order imposed or made by it when dealing with an offender if it appears to the court to be in the interests of justice to do so; and it is hereby declared that this power extends to replacing a sentence or order which for any reason appears to be invalid by another which the court has power to impose or make.

(1A) The power conferred on a magistrates' court by subsection (1) above shall not be exercisable in relation to any sentence or order imposed or made by it when dealing with an offender if—

(a) the Crown Court has determined an appeal against—
   (i) that sentence or order;
   (ii) the conviction in respect of which that sentence or order was imposed or made; or
   (iii) any other sentence or order imposed or made by the magistrates' court when dealing with the offender in respect of that conviction (including a sentence or order replaced by that sentence or order); or

(b) the High Court has determined a case stated for the opinion of that court on any question arising in any proceeding leading to or resulting from the imposition or making of the sentence or order.

[(2), (2A) and (3) Relate to setting aside a conviction: see **D22.76**.]

(4) [Repealed.]

(5) Where a sentence or order is varied under subsection (1) above, the sentence or other order, as so varied, shall take effect from the beginning of the day on which it was originally imposed or made, unless the court otherwise directs.

COMMITTAL FOR SENTENCE

Powers to Commit for Sentence

As an alternative to passing sentence themselves, magistrates may in some circumstances com- **D23.30**
mit the offender to the Crown Court to be sentenced. The major powers to commit for sentence
are as follows:

(a) PCC(S)A 2000, s. 3: general power to commit an adult offender who is summarily con-
    victed of an either-way offence.
(b) PCC(S)A 2000, s. 3A: power to commit an adult offender who is summarily convicted of
    an either-way offence in a case where the 'dangerous offender' provisions of the CJA 2003
    are applicable.
(c) PCC(S)A 2000, s. 4: power to commit an adult offender who indicates a guilty plea at a plea
    before venue hearing and who is being sent for trial for one or more related offences.
(d) CJA 2003, sch. 12, paras. 8(6) and 11(2): power to commit an offender who is in breach of
    a requirement under a Crown Court suspended sentence and power to commit an offender
    convicted of an offence committed during the operational period of a Crown Court sus-
    pended sentence, respectively.
(e) PCC(S)A 2000, s. 13(5): power to commit an offender convicted of an offence committed
    during the period of Crown Court conditional discharge.
(f) CJA 2003, sch. 8, para. 9(6): power to commit an offender who is in breach of a Crown
    Court community order to be dealt with for that breach.
(g) PCC(S)A 2000, s. 6: supplementary power to commit offenders who are being commit-
    ted under the PCC(S)A 2000, ss. 3 to 4A, or 13(5) or the CJA 2003, sch. 12, para. 11(2),
    to be sentenced also for other matters that would otherwise fall to be dealt with by the
    magistrates.

Committal under the Powers of Criminal Courts (Sentencing) Act 2000, s. 3

The PCC(S)A 2000, s. 3, applies where a magistrates' court has convicted an offender of one **D23.31**
or more either-way offences and the court takes the view that the seriousness of the offence(s) is
such that its sentencing powers are inadequate. In such a case, the magistrates' court may commit the offender (in custody or on bail) to the Crown Court to be sentenced. The Crown Court
can then pass sentence on the offender as if he had been convicted on indictment, and so the
limitations on the magistrates' sentencing powers do not apply (s. 5).

Limitations on the Power to Commit under s. 3

Scope of s. 3   Although the PCC(S)A 2000, s. 3(1), refers to an adult being convicted of an **D23.32**
either-way offence 'on the summary trial' of that offence, it is submitted that this includes not
just cases where the accused pleads not guilty but is found guilty by the court, but also cases
where the accused indicates a plea of guilty at the plea before venue hearing. Support for this
interpretation can be found in the wording of the MCA 1980, s. 17A(6), which provides that, if
the accused (at a plea before venue hearing) indicates that he would plead guilty, the court shall
proceed as if the proceedings constituted from the beginning the summary trial of the information, and he pleaded guilty to it.

Nature of the Offence   The offender must have been convicted of an either-way offence (not **D23.33**
a summary offence). Furthermore, the MCA 1980, s. 17D(2)(b), provides that the power to
commit for sentence contained in the PCC(S)A 2000, s. 3 (or s. 4), does not apply when an
offender is convicted of an offence of criminal damage which the magistrates dealt with as if it
were a summary offence because the value involved did not exceed £5,000 (see **D6.22** for the
special procedure for criminal damage charges).

Reason for Committal under s. 3

D23.34   In order to commit to the Crown Court for sentence under the PCC(S)A 2000, s. 3, the magistrates must be of the opinion that the offence(s) are so serious that the proper punishment exceeds their powers. The circumstances which usually give rise to a committal based upon s. 3 are:

(a) the accused is revealed as having a record of relevant previous convictions (the CJA 2003, s. 143, indicates that each previous conviction may be treated as an aggravating factor); or

(b) the accused asks for further offences to be taken into consideration ('t.i.c.s' may result in an increase in the sentence eventually passed).

So far as committals for sentence in other circumstances is concerned, the Divisional Court has considered on several occasions whether the magistrates have an unfettered discretion to commit for sentence under s. 3 where the accused is convicted following trial, or are bound (in the absence of new material) by their original acceptance of jurisdiction. In *Manchester Magistrates' Court, ex parte Kaymanesh* (1994) 15 Cr App R (S) 838, it was held that, if nothing further came to light after the decision to try the case summarily had been made, the magistrates should not normally commit for sentence to the Crown Court. However, the court took a different view in *Sheffield Crown Court, ex parte DPP* (1994) 15 Cr App R (S) 768 and *Dover Justices, ex parte Pamment* (1994) 15 Cr App R (S) 778. In both of these cases, the Divisional Court held that the power of the magistrates to commit for sentence under what is now s. 3 is unfettered. The court held that there was nothing unreasonable or illogical about permitting a court to form one view at the stage of deciding on summary trial, and a different view at the stage of deciding to commit for sentence. In *North Sefton Magistrates' Court, ex parte Marsh* (1995) 16 Cr App R (S) 401, the Divisional Court came down firmly in favour of a broad interpretation of s. 3, and stated that *Ex parte Kaymanesh* was wrongly decided. The decision to commit for sentence under s. 3 does not have to be based on information received by the court after the decision to try the accused summarily. However, the Divisional Court in both *Ex parte Marsh* and *Ex parte Pamment* did stress that magistrates should think carefully when deciding to accept jurisdiction because normally an offender should be able to conclude that, once jurisdiction had been accepted, he would not on the same facts be committed for sentence. In *Southampton Magistrates' Court, ex parte Sansome* [1999] 1 Cr App R (S) 112, the Divisional Court confirmed that the correct approach was that taken in *Marsh* and *Pamment*.

D23.35   It is submitted that, as a matter of good practice, magistrates should not normally commit an offender for sentence under s. 3 unless new information has come to light since the mode of trial decision was taken. However, if magistrates do commit for sentence on the basis of information which was already known to the court when the decision to try the case was reached, judicial review will not be granted since the magistrates have not acted beyond their powers. It should also be borne in mind that the question of whether a s. 3 committal can only be triggered by new information, or whether the magistrates can, in effect, simply change their minds about the adequacy of their sentencing powers, is now relevant only in those cases where the accused indicates an intention to plead not guilty (or gives no indication as to plea) at the 'plea before venue' hearing and is subsequently convicted by the magistrates. Where the accused indicates an intention to plead guilty, he will do so in the magistrates' court, and so will be convicted by the magistrates, however serious the offence is and before the magistrates are given any information about the seriousness of the offence.

In *Wirral Magistrates' Court, ex parte Jermyn* [2001] 1 Cr App R (S) 137, it was held that a decision to commit for sentence is not the sort of decision for which reasons have to be given, as any person so committed has the opportunity to make full representations to the sentencing court in due course as to the appropriate penalty (per Penry-Davey J at [39]).

D23.36   **Legitimate Expectation**   The discretion of the magistrates to commit for sentence is subject to the general principle of 'legitimate expectation'. If the offender has been led to believe, whether expressly or by implication, that he will be sentenced by the magistrates, he should not subsequently be committed for sentence, whether by the same or a differently constituted bench. In *Nottingham Magistrates' Court, ex parte Davidson* [2000] 1 Cr App R (S) 167 at p. 169, Lord Bingham CJ summarised the 'legitimate expectation' principle as follows:

> ... if a court at a preliminary stage of the sentencing process gives to a defendant any indication as to the sentence which will or will not be thereafter passed upon him, in terms sufficiently unqualified to found a legitimate expectation in the mind of the defendant that any court which later passes sentence upon him will act in accordance with the indication given, and if on a later occasion a court, without reasons which justify departure from the earlier indication, and whether or not it is aware of that indication, passes a sentence inconsistent with, and more severe than, the sentence indicated, the court will ordinarily feel obliged, however reluctantly, to adjust the sentence passed so as to bring it into line with that indicated.

It follows that where the offender had received an indication when the case was adjourned for a pre-sentence report that there would be no committal for sentence, he could not subsequently be committed for sentence. Similarly, in *Wirral Magistrates' Court, ex parte Jermyn* [2001] 1 Cr App R (S) 137, it was clear that the offender was warned of the court's power to commit, but the warning gave the impression that the court was satisfied, on the material that it had, that the matter should remain in the magistrates' court and that would change only if new material emerged; no such material did emerge and so the offender had a legitimate expectation that he would be sentenced in the magistrates' court.

D23.37   The burden is on the offender to show that there was a 'clear and unequivocal representation' that sentence would be determined by the magistrates (*Sheffield Magistrates' Court, ex parte Ojo* (2000) 164 JP 659).

Moreover, the expectation must be a legitimate one. In *R (Harrington) v Bromley Magistrates' Court* [2007] EWHC 2896 (Admin), the magistrates indicated that the accused would not be committed to the Crown Court for sentence provided that the pre-sentence report did not disclose that he was a danger to the public. Although the report stated that he was not, he was nonetheless subsequently committed for sentence. He argued that his committal was unlawful, being contrary to a legitimate expectation engendered by the indication that had been given by the justices. It was held that, whether the challenge is to the original or subsequent decision, it is the rationality and lawfulness of the first decision which ultimately determines the issue. Mitting J (at [12]) said that he could not conceive of circumstances in which a *properly given* (emphasis added) indication could be gone back on by a subsequent decision without that decision being held to be irrational or unlawful.

D23.38   Magistrates sometimes use the phrase 'keeping all options open' when adjourning for a pre-sentence report, in an effort to avoid arousing the expectations of the accused. In *Norwich Magistrates' Court, ex parte Elliott* [2000] 1 Cr App R(S) 152, Otton LJ said (at p. 159) that:

> ... care should be taken that nothing is said or done which might indicate to the accused that committal has been ruled out. If the court wishes to retain the discretion to commit to the Crown Court it should say so. For the court properly to retain the discretion to commit for sentence in such circumstances, it is necessary for it to make absolutely clear to the accused that the decision whether or not to commit for sentence has not been taken, and would only be taken at the adjourned hearing ... [However,] the mere fact of adjourning for pre-sentence reports, without more, cannot amount to a promise by the court that the subsequent justices will not commit the defendant to the Crown Court for sentence.

However, in *Feltham Justices, ex parte Rees* [2001] 2 Cr App R (S) 1, the justices invited the accused's solicitor to mitigate before them and then adjourned for the preparation of a pre-sentence report; at the time of the adjournment they stated that they were leaving 'all options open' but did not say that committal to the Crown Court was one of those options. This was held to have given rise to a legitimate expectation that the justices themselves would pass sentence (and that the phrase 'all options open' meant that a custodial sentence was a possibility). Rose LJ (at [12]) said that, 'if justices have in mind that one of the options which is open to them is to commit for sentence, they should specifically say so'. Elias J, in a short concurring judgment, said (at [14]–[15]):

> If the legitimate expectation is not to be created in those circumstances, it is incumbent on the justices to make it absolutely clear to the accused that the decision whether or not to commit for sentence has not been taken, and that he might yet be sent for sentence before the Crown Court. The simple issue in this case is whether the words 'all options open' did make it absolutely clear that the defendant might be sent to the Crown Court for sentence. In my judgment, they did not…

If the Crown Court does pass sentence on an offender who has been committed for sentence despite the magistrates having adjourned for reports in circumstances giving rise to a legitimate expectation that the sentence would be non-custodial if the reports should be favourable, the Crown Court on committal for sentence is as much precluded from imposing a custodial sentence as the magistrates would have been (*Rennes* (1985) 7 Cr App R (S) 343, applying the general principle in *Gillam* (1980) 2 Cr App R (S) 267).

Inadequacy of Maximum Fine

D23.39   The PCC(S)A 2000, s. 3, is usually invoked because the offence merits a longer custodial sentence than the magistrates can impose. However, it also allows the magistrates to commit for sentence because of the limitations on the amount of the fine which they can impose. In *North Essex Justices, ex parte Lloyd* [2001] 2 Cr App R (S) 15, the magistrates committed for sentence on the basis that, even though imprisonment was not appropriate, a larger fine should be imposed than the £5,000 to which they were restricted. The Divisional Court held that there was no reason why they should not commit for sentence if they considered that the appropriate punishment was a fine but, given the statutory limit on the amount of the fine they could impose, the maximum fine at their disposal would be a figure which was too low a punishment for the particular circumstances of the case before them (per Lord Woolf CJ at [9]). His lordship added that, in such a case, it would be helpful if the justices spell out the reason for their decision to commit. Although the Crown Court judge would not be bound by their statement, it would be extremely valuable for him to know the basis on which the committal had been made (at [10]).

When the LASPO 2012, s. 85, is brought fully into force, the limit on the maximum fine which may be imposed by a magistrates' court will be removed and this basis for committal for sentence will no longer apply.

Guilty Plea at 'Plea before Venue' and Committal for Sentence

D23.40   Guidance on several issues that may arise in this context was given by the Divisional Court in *Warley Magistrates' Court, ex parte DPP* [1999] 1 All ER 251. The Court held as follows:

(a) The magistrates must have regard to the discount to be granted on a plea of guilty when deciding whether the punishment which they would have power to inflict would be adequate.

(b) Where the gravity of the offence is such that, even when allowance has been made for the indicated plea, it is obvious that whatever may be the mitigation the punishment should be greater than the magistrates' court has power to impose, then the court should be prepared to commit the offender to the Crown Court for sentence without seeking any pre-sentence report or hearing in full any mitigation which he may wish to advance. However, if that course is to be adopted, the offender should be told what the court has in mind, and he or his legal representative should be allowed to make brief submissions in opposition to that course. If the court is persuaded by the submission to change its mind, it should invite the prosecutor to make any submission he may wish to make in reply.

(c) In other cases (i.e. where, after allowance has been made for the plea of guilty, it appears that the court sentencing powers are or may be adequate), the hearing should proceed as usual. If a court, initially minded to commit at an early stage of the proceedings, is persuaded not to adopt that course at that stage, it can keep the option open by saying that the option of committal remains available, and then arranging for the preparation of a pre-sentence report. If, at the end of the hearing, whether or not to commit for sentence remains a live issue, the court should seek assistance from the prosecution and from the offender or his representative in relation to that issue.

(d) If the accused indicates a plea of guilty but there is a dispute as to the facts which must be resolved before sentence can be passed, necessitating a *Newton* hearing (see **D20.8** *et seq.*):

(i) if the magistrates consider that, whatever the outcome of the *Newton* hearing, they will have adequate powers of sentencing, they should proceed to hold a *Newton* hearing;

(ii) if the magistrates consider that, whatever the outcome, the offender will have to be committed for sentence, it is clearly preferable to leave the Crown Court to conduct the *Newton* hearing;

(iii) if the decision as to whether or not to commit for sentence turns, or may turn, on the outcome of the *Newton* hearing, the magistrates' court should proceed to conduct the *Newton* hearing.

(e) If a magistrates' court does conduct a *Newton* hearing and then commits to the Crown Court, it should record its findings for the benefit of the Crown Court, but it is open to the offender to seek to challenge those findings in the Crown Court (which may conduct a fresh *Newton* hearing) if he can point to some significant development, such as the discovery of important further evidence, having occurred since the magistrates' court reached its conclusion.

Bail   In *Rafferty* [1999] 1 Cr App R 235, the Court of Appeal considered the question whether   **D23.41**
a committal for sentence should be on bail or in custody where the accused indicates a plea of guilty in the 'plea before venue' procedure. Thomas J said (at p. 237) that:

> . . . in most cases where a plea of guilty is made at the plea before venue, it will not be usual to alter the position as regards bail or custody. In the usual case, when a person who has been on bail pleads guilty at the plea before venue, the usual practice should be to continue bail, even if it is anticipated that a custodial sentence will be imposed by the Crown Court, unless there are good reasons for remanding the defendant in custody. If the defendant is in custody, then after entering a plea of guilty at the plea before venue, it would be unusual, if the reasons for remanding him in custody remained unchanged, to alter the position.

It should be borne in mind, however, that there is no statutory presumption in favour of bail, since the BA 1976, s. 4, does not apply where an offender is being committed for sentence. Nonetheless, it is submitted that *Rafferty* has effectively modified the principle, which dated back to *Coe* [1968] 1 All ER 65, that an offender committed for sentence should normally be committed in custody, since he faces a relatively long custodial sentence.

Challenging the Decision to Commit or to Refuse to Commit

If an offender is aggrieved at a decision to commit him for sentence to the Crown Court, there   **D23.42**
is little that can be done about it. The Crown Court only has power to remit the case back to the magistrates' court if the committal is plainly invalid (e.g., s. 3 is invoked by the magistrates in respect of an offence which is triable only summarily); in any other case, the committal can be challenged only by means of an application for judicial review before the Divisional Court (*Sheffield Crown Court, ex parte DPP* (1994) 15 Cr App R (S) 768). However, such a challenge would succeed only if the committal were perverse in the *Wednesbury* sense that no reasonable bench of magistrates could have decided to commit the defendant for sentence (for example, where the committal defeated a legitimate expectation that there would be no committal for sentence — see above).

However, two points should be noted. First, it is by no means inevitable that the Crown Court will in fact impose a sentence which is more severe than the sentence which the magistrates' court could have imposed. Secondly, there is the option of appealing to the Court of Appeal against the sentence imposed by the Crown Court (under the Criminal Appeal Act 1968, s. 10) if that sentence is in fact excessive.

If the prosecution are unhappy with a decision *not* to commit for sentence, judicial review may be available. However, the Divisional Court will interfere with such decisions only where they are properly categorised as 'truly astonishing' (*Warley Magistrates' Court, ex parte DPP* [1999] 1 All ER 251 at 225, per Kennedy LJ and *R (DPP) v Devizes Magistrates' Court* [2006] EWHC 1072 (Admin), per Maurice Kay LJ at [25]).

D23.43   Powers of Criminal Courts (Sentencing) Act 2000, s. 3

(1) Subject to subsection (4) below, this section applies where on the summary trial of an offence triable either way a person aged 18 or over is convicted of the offence.
(2) If the court is of the opinion—
    (a) that the offence or the combination of the offence and one or more offences associated with it was so serious that the Crown Court should, in the court's opinion, have the power to deal with the offender in any way it could deal with him if he had been convicted on indictment,
    (b) [repealed]
    the court may commit the offender in custody or on bail to the Crown Court for sentence in accordance with section 5(1) below.
(3) Where the court commits a person under subsection (2) above, section 6 below (which enables a magistrates' court, where it commits a person under this section in respect of an offence, also to commit him to the Crown Court to be dealt with in respect of certain other offences) shall apply accordingly.
(4) This section does not apply in relation to an offence as regards which this section is excluded by section 17D or 33 of the Magistrates' Courts Act 1980 (certain offences where value involved is small).
(5) The preceding provisions of this section shall apply in relation to a corporation as if—
    (a) the corporation were an individual aged 18 or over; and
    (b) in subsection (2) above, paragraph (b) and the words 'in custody or on bail' were omitted.

Committal for Sentence under the Powers of Criminal Courts (Sentencing) Act 2000, s. 4

D23.44 The PCC(S)A 2000, s. 4(1) and (2), provides that, where the accused has indicated that he will plead guilty to an either-way offence (and so is deemed to have pleaded guilty to it) and he is also sent for trial for one or more related offences, the magistrates may commit him to the Crown Court for sentence in respect of the either-way offence to which he has pleaded guilty. For the purposes of these provisions, one offence is related to another if the charges for them could be joined (under the CrimPR, r. 14.2(3): see **D11.63**) in the same indictment if both were to be tried in the Crown Court (s. 4(7)). Thus, the two charges must be founded on the same facts or must be, or be part of, a series of offences of the same or a similar character.

Section 4(4) provides that, where the justices have committed an offender for sentence pursuant to s. 4(2), the Crown Court can exceed the sentencing powers of the magistrates' court in respect of the either-way offence so committed only if either:

(a) the magistrates stated that they considered their sentencing powers were inadequate to deal with the offender for that offence (and so they also had power to commit him for sentence under s. 3); or
(b) he is also convicted by the Crown Court of one or more of the related offences.

D23.45 If the magistrates take the view that their sentencing powers are adequate to deal with the offence in respect of which the offender has indicated a guilty plea, then only s. 4 allows the justices to commit him to the Crown Court for sentence for that offence. On the other hand, if the magistrates take the view that their sentencing powers are not adequate to deal with that offence, they have two options: they can either commit him for sentence for that offence under s. 3, or they can commit him for sentence under s. 4 but indicate that they took the view that their sentencing powers were inadequate and so could have invoked s. 3. When committing an offender for sentence the court should state whether it is doing so under s. 3 or s. 4. If the magistrates commit under s. 4 but do not consider that their sentencing powers are adequate to deal with the offence, they should state (under s. 4(4)) that they also had the power to commit the defendant for sentence under s. 3, so as to avoid inadvertently fettering the powers of the Crown Court when dealing with the offence.

In *S* [2012] EWCA Crim 2031 Thirlwall J said (at [21]) that where an accused is committed for sentence under s. 4, the magistrates must consider whether their powers would be sufficient in respect of the matter which is being committed for sentence. If they do not consider that their sentencing powers would be sufficient, it is imperative that they observe the requirements of the statute and state in open court that the court has power to commit him under s. 3. If that is not done, the Crown Court will be able to exceed the powers of a magistrates' court in respect of the offence committed for sentence under s. 4 only where there is a conviction in the Crown Court in respect of at least one matter which was sent for trial.

It is submitted that the best practice is to use s. 3 where the magistrates' sentencing powers are not adequate and to use s. 4 where their powers are adequate.

Powers of Criminal Courts (Sentencing) Act 2000, s. 4   D23.46

(1) This section applies where—
  (a) a person aged 18 or over appears or is brought before a magistrates' court ('the court') on an information charging him with an offence triable either way ('the offence');
  (b) he or (where applicable) his representative indicates under section 17A, 17B or 20(7) of the Magistrates' Courts Act 1980 that he would plead guilty if the offence were to proceed to trial; and
  (c) proceeding as if section 9(1) of that Act were complied with and he pleaded guilty under it, the court convicts him of the offence.

(1A) But this section does not apply to an offence as regards which this section is excluded by section 17D of that Act (certain offences where value involved is small).

(2) If the court has sent the offender to the Crown Court for trial for one or more related offences, that is to say, one or more offences which, in its opinion, are related to the offence, it may commit him in custody or on bail to the Crown Court to be dealt with in respect of the offence in accordance with section 5(1) below.

(3) If the power conferred by subsection (2) above is not exercisable but the court is still to determine to, or to determine whether to, send the offender to the Crown Court for trial under section 51 or 51A of the Crime and Disorder Act 1998 for one or more related offences—
  (a) it shall adjourn the proceedings relating to the offence until after it has made those determinations; and
  (b) if it sends the offender to the Crown Court for trial for one or more related offences, it may then exercise that power.

(4) Where the court—
  (a) under subsection (2) above commits the offender to the Crown Court to be dealt with in respect of the offence; and
  (b) does not state that, in its opinion, it also has power so to commit him under section 3(2) or, as the case may be, section 3A(2) above,
  section 5(1) below shall not apply unless he is convicted before the Crown Court of one or more of the related offences.

(5) Where section 5(1) below does not apply, the Crown Court may deal with the offender in respect of the offence in any way in which the magistrates' court could deal with him if it had just convicted him of the offence.

(6) Where the court commits a person under subsection (2) above, section 6 below (which enables a magistrates' court, where it commits a person under this section in respect of an offence, also to commit him to the Crown Court to be dealt with in respect of certain other offences) shall apply accordingly.

(7) For the purposes of this section one offence is related to another if, were they both to be prosecuted on indictment, the charges for them could be joined in the same indictment.

(8) In reaching any decision under or taking any step contemplated by this section—

(a) the court shall not be bound by any indication of sentence given in respect of the offence under section 20 of the Magistrates' Courts Act 1980 (procedure where summary trial appears more suitable); and

(b) nothing the court does under this section may be challenged or be the subject of any appeal in any court on the ground that it is not consistent with an indication of sentence

Hearing in the Crown Court following a Committal under the Powers of Criminal Courts (Sentencing) Act 2000, s. 3 or s. 4

D23.47 **Procedural Issues** Committal under the PCC(S)A 2000, s. 3, will be to the most convenient location of the Crown Court, having regard to any relevant local direction on the matter. The Crown Court, when hearing a s. 3 committal, comprises a circuit judge or recorder (the presence of lay justices is required only for appeals from magistrates' courts (Senior Courts Act 1981, s. 74)).

Before proceeding to hear the case, the Crown Court should confirm that the person before it has indeed been committed for sentence by the magistrates' court. This is usually done by asking the offender if he admits that fact. In the absence of such admission, the prosecution must prove the committal by formal evidence. The evidence might come from a certified copy of the magistrates' court register or from someone present in the magistrates' court at the time of the committal. Once the committal has been admitted or proved, the procedure before sentence is passed is exactly the same as when there is a guilty plea, with a prosecution summary of the facts and a plea in mitigation on behalf of the offender.

Where the offender indicates that he is appealing against his conviction in the lower court, the sentencing proceedings should be adjourned until the conclusion of the appeal (*Faithful* [1950] 2 All ER 1251). If, however, the court inadvertently disposes of the committal for sentence in ignorance of the fact that the offender is appealing against conviction, the appeal should be heard nonetheless and, if it succeeds, the sentence passed on the committal will simply fall with the conviction (*Croydon Crown Court, ex parte Bernard* [1981] 3 All ER 106).

Where the offender asked the lower court to take other offences into consideration, he is not bound to take the same course in the Crown Court (i.e. the normal procedure for taking offences into consideration should be followed in the Crown Court and, in the absence of a request to consider the other matters, they must be ignored (*Davies* (1981) 72 Cr App R 262).

D23.48 **Powers of Crown Court** The PCC(S)A 2000, s. 5, provides that, following a committal for sentence under s. 3 or (subject to the restrictions discussed above) s. 4, the Crown Court may deal with the offender as if he had just been convicted on indictment.

Powers of Criminal Courts (Sentencing) Act 2000, s. 5

(1) Where an offender is committed by a magistrates' court for sentence under section 3, 3A or 4 above, the Crown Court shall inquire into the circumstances of the case and may deal with the offender in any way in which it could deal with him if he had just been convicted of the offence on indictment before the court.

(2) In relation to committals under section 4 above, subsection (1) above has effect subject to section 4(4) and (5) above.

(3) Section 20A(1) of the Magistrates' Courts Act 1980 (which relates to the effect of an indication of sentence under section 20 of that Act) shall not apply in respect of any specified offence (within the meaning of section 224 of the Criminal Justice Act 2003)—

(a) in respect of which the offender is committed under section 3A(2) above; or

(b) in respect of which—

(i) the offender is committed under section 4(2) above; and

(ii) the court states under section 4(4) above that, in its opinion, it also has power to commit the offender under section 3A(2) above.

D23.49 *Newton* **hearings** If a *Newton* hearing took place at the magistrates' court, the Crown Court should adopt the outcome. In *Warley Justices, ex parte DPP* [1999] 1 All ER 251,

Kennedy LJ said (at p. 224) that it may be that the offender will seek to challenge the magistrates' findings in the Crown Court, but added 'I would not expect him to be allowed to do so unless he could point to some significant development, such as the discovery of important further evidence, having occurred since the magistrates' court reached its conclusion'. A similar point was made in *Gillan v DPP* [2007] 1 WLR 2214, where the court considered the question: 'Where magistrates have determined the factual basis for sentencing at a *Newton* hearing, and then commit the defendant for sentence in the Crown Court, does the duty of the Crown Court to inquire into the circumstances of the case include a power to hear evidence in a second *Newton* hearing to determine afresh the factual basis on which the defendant shall be sentenced?' Forbes J, giving the judgment of the Divisional Court said (at [28]–[29]):

> I am completely satisfied that the Crown Court does have jurisdiction to hold a further *Newton* hearing if it is in the interests of fairness and justice to do so... However, the fact that the Crown Court has jurisdiction or a power to hold a further *Newton* hearing does not mean, ipso facto, that it should accede to an application to do so in any case where it is apparent that the magistrates have already conducted such a hearing and made clear findings of fact as part of their perfectly proper decision-making with regard to committing the defendant to the Crown Court for sentence. Essentially, the matter is a question for the discretion of the judge, in the proper exercise of which he or she must be fully mindful of his or her obligation to carry out a proper inquiry into the circumstances of the case... I would not expect the judge in the Crown Court to exercise his discretion in favour of allowing a defendant to re-open the magistrates' findings of fact unless the defendant was able to point to some significant development or matter, such as (but not confined to) the discovery of important further evidence having occurred since the Magistrates' Court reached its conclusion on the facts. In saying that, I would not wish it to be thought that I was laying down any absolute or strict formula as to how the judge should exercise his or her discretion in any particular case. Everything will depend upon the facts and circumstances of the particular case; each case must be considered individually.

If the divergence between prosecution and defence versions becomes apparent for the first time at the Crown Court (or no *Newton* hearing was held at the magistrates' court), the Crown Court should, of course, hold a *Newton* hearing to determine the issue (*Munroe v DPP* (1988) 152 JP 657).

Age of Offender   In *Robson* [2007] 1 All ER 506, the Court of Appeal considered the position where the offender has attained an age of relevance to sentencing powers during the period between the magistrates' court and Crown Court proceedings. In that case, a 17-year-old offender was convicted of sexual assault and was committed to the Crown Court for sentence under the PCC(S)A 2000, s. 3C (part of the 'dangerous offender' provisions established by the CJA 2003). When he appeared for sentencing, he had attained the age of 18. The Court of Appeal considered whether the age of an offender committed to the Crown Court for sentence is to be treated, for the purpose of sentence, differently from the age of an offender convicted after trial. The latter has to be sentenced on the basis of his age at the date of his conviction, whether he is convicted following a guilty plea or a guilty verdict (*Danga* [1992] QB 476 and *Robinson* [1993] 2 All ER 1). The court held that, at least for the purposes of the sentencing regime created for dangerous offenders by the CJA 2003, (see **E4**), the matter should be decided on the basis of the wording of the relevant statutory provisions. For dangerous offenders, these refer to age at the date of conviction (not sentence), and so the relevant date for sentence purposes is the date of the conviction, not the date of the Crown Court appearance following committal for sentence. Given that the PCC(S)A 2000, s. 89(1), provides that a sentence of imprisonment may not be passed on a person 'if he is aged under 21 when *convicted* of the offence', it would seem that the use of the word 'convicted' requires the court to pass a sentence appropriate to the age at the date of conviction, not the date of sentence, and so an offender who attains the age of 21 between conviction in the magistrates' court and appearance in the Crown Court for sentence should be sentenced as if he were under 21, and therefore is not eligible for a sentence of imprisonment.

D23.50

D

Part D Procedure

Other Committal Powers

D23.51   **Dangerous Offenders**   The PCC(S)A 2000, s. 3A, enables a magistrates' court which convicts an adult defendant to commit him to the Crown Court for sentence when the criteria for an extended sentence under the 'dangerous offender' provisions of the CJA 2003, as amended by the LASPO 2012, would appear to be met (see E4). It is submitted that s. 3A applies both following an indication of a guilty plea at a plea before venue hearing and where the accused is found guilty following a summary trial.

Powers of Criminal Courts (Sentencing) Act 2000, s. 3A

(1) This section applies where on the summary trial of a specified offence triable either way a person aged 18 or over is convicted of the offence.

(2) If, in relation to the offence, it appears to the court that the criteria for the imposition of a sentence under section 226A of the Criminal Justice Act 2003 would be met, the court must commit the offender in custody or on bail to the Crown Court for sentence in accordance with section 5(1) below.

(3) Where the court commits a person under subsection (2) above, section 6 below (which enables a magistrates' court, where it commits a person under this section in respect of an offence, also to commit him to the Crown Court to be dealt with in respect of certain other offences) shall apply accordingly.

(4) In reaching any decision under or taking any step contemplated by this section—

    (a) the court shall not be bound by any indication of sentence given in respect of the offence under section 20 of the Magistrates' Courts Act 1980 (procedure where summary trial appears more suitable); and

    (b) nothing the court does under this section may be challenged or be the subject of any appeal in any court on the ground that it is not consistent with an indication of sentence.

(5) Nothing in this section shall prevent the court from committing an offender convicted of a specified offence to the Crown Court for sentence under section 3 above if the provisions of that section are satisfied.

(6) In this section, references to a specified offence are to a specified offence within the meaning of section 224 of the Criminal Justice Act 2003.

Committal for Sentence in Respect of Breach of a Crown Court Order

D23.52   An offender can be committed to the Crown Court to be dealt with if he is in breach of certain Crown Court orders, and an offender who has been convicted in a magistrates' court of an offence committed during the currency of certain Crown Court orders can also be committed for sentence.

Conditional Discharge

D23.53   The PCC(S)A 2000, s. 13(5), provides that where an offender is convicted by a magistrates' court of an offence committed during the period of conditional discharge imposed by the Crown Court, the magistrates' court may commit him (in custody or on bail) to the Crown Court to be dealt with.

Community Order

D23.54   The CJA 2003, sch. 8, para. 9(6), provides that, where a community order was made by the Crown Court and a magistrates' court would otherwise have the power to deal with the offender for breach of the order (because, under para. 7(1)(b), the order included a direction that any failure to comply with the requirements of the order was to be dealt with by a magistrates' court), it may instead commit him (in custody or on bail) to be dealt with by the Crown Court.

Suspended Sentence Order

D23.55   The CJA 2003, sch. 12, para. 8(6), deals with failure to comply with community order requirements under a suspended sentence order. It provides that, where a suspended sentence order was made by the Crown Court and a magistrates' court would otherwise have the power to deal with the offender for breach of the order (because, under para. 6(1)(b), the order included a direction that any failure to comply with the community requirements of the order was to be dealt with by a magistrates' court), it may instead commit him (in custody or on bail) to be dealt with by the Crown Court.

The CJA 2003, sch. 12, para. 11(2), deals with offences committed during the operational period of a suspended sentence. It provides that, where an offender is convicted by a magistrates' court of any offence and the court is satisfied that the offence was committed during the operational period of a suspended sentence passed by the Crown Court, the magistrates' court may, if it thinks fit, commit him (in custody or on bail) to the Crown Court. If it does not do so, it must inform the Crown Court of the conviction.

Guidance on the effect of some of the committal powers under the CJA 2003 was given by the **D23.56** Court of Appeal in *Majury* [2007] EWCA Crim 2968. The Court emphasised that the CJA 2003, sch. 12, para. 8(6), applies only to a breach of a suspended sentence order with which the magistrates themselves can deal (in the case of a suspended sentence order made by the Crown Court, where the breach comprises a failure to comply with a community requirement and the Crown Court directed when the sentence was passed that failures to comply should be dealt with by the magistrates' court); para. 8(6) does not apply to breach of a suspended sentence when the sentence was passed by the Crown Court and the breach is comprised in the commission of a further offence. Furthermore, para. 11(2) does not apply to the 'new' offences committed in breach of the suspended sentence. If the offender is committed to the Crown Court, the Crown Court can deal with the breach under sch. 12, para. 8(1)(b) (see para. 11(1)). If the offender is not committed to the Crown Court, but the Crown Court receives notice of the breach, it can take its own enforcement proceedings by issuing a summons or a warrant for his arrest under para. 12(1). Paragraph 11(2) does not of itself give the Crown Court power to deal with the offences committed during the operational period of the suspended sentence; rather, it is the means by which the breach of the suspended sentence is brought before the Crown Court to be dealt with under para. 8(1)(b). If the justices want the Crown Court to deal with the original offence and the 'new' offences, and the latter are triable either way, the justices should decide whether the powers of the Crown Court to sentence for the new offences should be those of the Crown Court or of the magistrates' court. If the former, the committal of those offences would take place under the PCC(S)A 2000, s. 3; if the latter, committal would be under s. 6 of that Act (see **D23.57**).

Committal under the Powers of Criminal Courts (Sentencing) Act 2000, s. 6

The PCC(S)A 2000, s. 6, gives a power to commit for sentence which may be used to supple- **D23.57** ment a committal under the provisions listed in s. 6(4), which include committal for sentence under the PCC(S)A 2000, ss. 3 to 4A; committal for sentence in respect of the breach of a conditional discharge imposed by the Crown Court (under the PCC(S)A 2000, s. 13(5)); and committal to be dealt with for breach of a suspended sentence imposed by the Crown Court (under the CJA 2003, sch. 12, para. 11(2)).

These committal powers are referred to below as 'primary' committal powers.

By virtue of the PCC(S)A 2000, s. 6(2), when a magistrates' court exercises a primary committal power in respect of an indictable offence (in this context, an either-way offence), it may also commit the offender to the Crown Court to be dealt with in respect of any other offence of which he stands convicted (whether summary or indictable) that the magistrates' court has jurisdiction to deal with as regards sentence. Section 6(2) expressly states that, provided the committing court would be able to deal with the matter if it were not to commit, the power to commit arises even if the conviction was by a different court.

To take the example of a magistrates' court which has decided to commit an offender under s. 3, for one either-way offence, a committal under s. 6 might (for instance) relate to:

(a) another, less serious, either-way offence of which the magistrates have convicted the
offender on the same occasion;

(b) a summary offence of which they have convicted the offender on the same occasion.

The reason a committal under s. 3 for the secondary offence would be inappropriate in situation
(a) is that, because the offence is not sufficiently serious, the magistrates' powers of sentencing
for it are adequate. In situation (b), a committal under s. 3 would be inappropriate simply
because that section does not extend to summary offences.

D23.58   By virtue of s. 6(3), where the offence in respect of which the 'primary' power of committal
arises is a *summary* offence, the magistrates may also commit the offender for sentence in respect
of (a) any other offence carrying imprisonment or disqualification from driving of which their
court has convicted the offender, or (b) breach of a suspended sentence passed on the offender
by that or another magistrates' court. In *Qayum* [2010] EWCA Crim 2237, the Court of Appeal
noted that s. 6(3) gives the magistrates a 'secondary' power to commit for sentence in respect
of a breach of a suspended sentence order, but only where the 'relevant offence' (i.e. the offence
in respect of which the 'primary' power of committal is being exercised) is itself summary only.
In fact, the primary power of committal will, in practice, nearly always relate to an indictable
offence, and so s. 6(3) is of little practical significance.

D23.59   The other use of s. 6 is where a summary conviction puts the offender in breach of a suspended
sentence passed by the Crown Court and the magistrates consider that, although the breach
should be committed to the Crown Court under the CJA 2003, sch. 12, para 11(2), the offence
giving rise to the breach is not in itself serious enough to warrant committal under s. 3. The
court should then commit the offender under para. 11(2), for possible activation of the suspended sentence, and under s. 6, for sentence for the present offence (*Majury* [2007] EWCA
Crim 2968).

D23.60   It should be noted that s. 6 applies only where the committal is under one of the enactments
specified in s. 6(4). In *Ayhan* [2012] 1 WLR 1775, the offender was committed for sentence to
the Crown Court in respect of three offences, one of which was triable either way and two of
which were summary only. The memorandum of conviction stated that all three committals
were made under the PCC(S)A 2000, s. 3. However, s. 3 applies only to either-way offences. In
fact, the summary offences had been committed under s. 6 (see **D23.57**). The Court of Appeal
held that 'the essential question is not what power the memorandum of conviction records the
justices to have used, but the power they actually used' (per Lord Judge CJ, at [16]). The correct approach 'was to examine the question whether the magistrates' court was vested with the
necessary jurisdiction to commit to the Crown Court. If it was, then an omission from, or an
inaccuracy in, the memorandum of conviction about the statutory powers which were exercised, or which were available to be exercised, did not affect the validity of the committal' (at
[18]). His lordship went on to hold (at [22]) that 'provided the power of the magistrates' court
to commit for sentence was properly exercised in respect of one or more either-way offences in
accordance with s. 3 of the 2000 Act, a mistake in recording the statutory basis for a committal
of summary-only offences does not invalidate the committal. The principle is that thereafter
the Crown Court must abide by the sentencing powers available to the magistrates' court in
relation to the summary only offences. If that principle is not followed, then the sentences must
be reduced to sentences which fall within the jurisdiction of the magistrates.' The Court in so
holding declined to follow *Stockton* [2009] EWCA Crim 354 and *Buisson* [2011] EWCA Crim
1841, where the Court had reached a contrary conclusion as regards the validity of the committal.
Ayhan was followed in *Luff* [2013] EWCA Crim 1958, where the committal purported to be
under s. 6, but the Court of Appeal held that the reference to s. 6 was a mistake, and that the
committal should be treated as having been under s. 4.

It should also be noted that the power to commit for sentence under s. 6 does not apply where
the offender has been committed for trial, rather than sentence, in respect of another offence
(*Abouderbala* [2012] EWCA Crim 1458).

Powers of Crown Court following Committal for Sentence under the Powers of Criminal Courts (Sentencing) Act 2000, s. 6

Following a committal under the PCC(S)A 2000, s. 6, the Crown Court may deal with the **D23.61** offender in respect of the offence(s) so committed in any way the magistrates' court might have done (s. 7). The Crown Court's sentencing powers for an offence committed under s. 6 are thus identical to those of the magistrates' court. This limitation on the Crown Court's powers reveals the basic purpose of a committal under s. 6, namely to enable one court to deal with an offender for all matters outstanding against him rather than have the sentencing function split between the Crown Court and the magistrates' court. The purpose of s. 6 is *not* to expose the offender to risk of greater punishment than the lower court could inflict.

In *Morgan* (2012) 176 JP 633, Irwin J tentatively raised the possibility (at [23]) that, when a person is committed to the Crown Court for breach of a suspended sentence, the effect of s. 7(2) might be to give that court untrammelled powers of sentence in respect of all matters committed to it, including any offences constituting the breach of that suspended sentence. However, his lordship regarded that as doubtful. The Court of Appeal went on to reject this suggestion even more emphatically in *Bateman* [2013] 1 WLR 1710, where Moore-Bick LJ said (at [20]) that, when considering the proper interpretation of s. 7(2), it had to be borne in mind that s. 7(1) and (2) are both concerned with committals under s. 6 (committal of a person to the Crown Court to be dealt with in respect of an associated offence), and that subsection (2) must be read in the context of subsection (1), to which it provides an exception. His lordship noted that committal to be dealt with for breach of a suspended sentence imposed by the Crown Court takes place under the CJA 2003, sch. 12, para. 11(2), not under the PCC(S)A 2000, s. 6. It follows that, when s. 7(2) refers to committal under s. 6 to be dealt with by the Crown Court in respect of a suspended sentence, it must be referring to a suspended sentence previously imposed by a magistrates' court. This provision enables the Crown Court to exercise the powers under sch. 12, paras. 8 and 9, which could otherwise have been exercised by the magistrates themselves, and ensures that, on committal to the Crown Court under s. 6, a person is not exposed to a more severe penalty than could have been imposed on him by the magistrates.

Where the offender is in breach of a suspended sentence imposed by the Crown Court, and **D23.62** the breach is because of the commission of an either-way offence, the magistrates' court should consider carefully whether its sentencing powers are adequate in respect of the offence which constituted the breach. As Irwin J said in *Morgan* (at [26]), if the magistrates consider that the gravity of the offence which constitutes the breach, together with any associated matters, is such as to justify committal under s. 3 (on the basis that their sentencing powers are inadequate), then the offence(s) should be committed pursuant to s. 3, rather than s. 6, so that the Crown Court powers are those contained in s. 5, not those contained in s. 7 (a point echoed by Moore-Bick LJ in *Bateman*, at [31]).

Powers of Criminal Courts (Sentencing Act), 2000, ss. 6 and 7   **D23.63**

6. (1) This section applies where a magistrates' court ('the committing court') commits a person in custody or on bail to the Crown Court under any enactment mentioned in subsection (4) below to be sentenced or otherwise dealt with in respect of an offence ('the relevant offence').
   (2) Where this section applies and the relevant offence is an indictable offence, the committing court may also commit the offender, in custody or on bail as the case may require, to the Crown Court to be dealt with in respect of any other offence whatsoever in respect of which the committing court has power to deal with him (being an offence of which he has been convicted by that or any other court).
   (3) Where this section applies and the relevant offence is a summary offence, the committing court may commit the offender, in custody or on bail as the case may require, to the Crown Court to be dealt with in respect of—
   (a) any other offence of which the committing court has convicted him, being either—
   (i) an offence punishable with imprisonment; or

(ii) an offence in respect of which the committing court has a power or duty to order him to be disqualified under section 34, 35 or 36 of the Road Traffic Offenders Act 1988 (disqualification for certain motoring offences); or

(b) any suspended sentence in respect of which the committing court has under paragraph 11(1) of Schedule 12 to the Criminal Justice Act 2003 power to deal with him.

(4) The enactments referred to in subsection (1) above are—

(a) the Vagrancy Act 1824 (incorrigible rogues);

(b) sections 3 and 4 [3 to 4A] above (committal for sentence for offences triable either way);

(c) section 13(5) below (conditionally discharged person convicted of further offence);

...and

(e) paragraph 11(2) of Schedule 12 to the Criminal Justice Act 2003 (committal to Crown Court where offender convicted during operational period of suspended sentence).

7. (1) Where under section 6 above a magistrates' court commits a person to be dealt with by the Crown Court in respect of an offence, the Crown Court may after inquiring into the circumstances of the case deal with him in any way in which the magistrates' court could deal with him if it had just convicted him of the offence.

(2) Subsection (1) above does not apply where under section 6 above a magistrates' court commits a person to be dealt with by the Crown Court in respect of a suspended sentence, but in such a case the powers under paragraphs 8 and 9 of Schedule 12 to the Criminal Justice Act 2003 (power of court to deal with suspended sentence) shall be exercisable by the Crown Court.

(3) Without prejudice to subsections (1) and (2) above, where under section 6 above or any enactment mentioned in subsection (4) of that section a magistrates' court commits a person to be dealt with by the Crown Court, any duty or power which, apart from this subsection, would fall to be discharged or exercised by the magistrates' court shall not be discharged or exercised by that court but shall instead be discharged or may instead be exercised by the Crown Court.

(4) Where under section 6 above a magistrates' court commits a person to be dealt with by the Crown Court in respect of an offence triable only on indictment in the case of an adult (being an offence which was tried summarily because of the offender's being under 18 years of age), the Crown Court's powers under subsection (1) above in respect of the offender after he attains the age of 18 shall be powers to do either or both of the following—

(a) to impose a fine not exceeding £5,000;

(b) to deal with the offender in respect of the offence in any way in which the magistrates' court could deal with him if it had just convicted him of an offence punishable with imprisonment for a term not exceeding six months.

Section D24   Trial of Juveniles

INTRODUCTION

The Aims of the Youth Justice System

The CDA 1998, s. 37(1), provides that: 'It shall be the principal aim of the youth justice system **D24.1** to prevent offending by children and young persons'. Section 37(2) goes on to require that: 'In addition to any other duty to which they are subject, it shall be the duty of all persons and bodies carrying out functions in relation to the youth justice system to have regard to that aim'. However, the CYPA 1933, s. 44(1), provides that 'every court in dealing with a child or young person who is brought before it, either as an offender or otherwise, shall have regard to the welfare of the child or young person'. Also relevant in this context are the purposes of sentencing in the case of young offenders, set out in the CJA 2003, s. 142A(3), namely the punishment of offenders, the reform and rehabilitation of offenders, the protection of the public, and the making of reparation by offenders to persons affected by their offences.

Terminology: 'Juvenile', 'Adult', 'Child' and 'Young Person'   **D24.2**

(a) *Juvenile.* This term is convenient shorthand for a person who has not attained the age of 18. The word 'juvenile' is used in this sense throughout this section.
(b) *Adult.* In the context of criminal procedure and mode of trial, an 'adult' is any person aged 18 or over. In the context of sentencing, however, 'adult' is sometimes used to mean those aged 21 or over, since it is at that age that an offender currently becomes liable to imprisonment rather than detention in a young offender institution.
(c) *Child.* By the CYPA 1933, s. 107(1), 'child' (when used in that Act) means a person under the age of 14 years. The CYPA 1969, s. 70(1), contains a similar provision in respect of the majority of the provisions of that Act, while the CYPA 1963, s. 65(3), provides that the 1963 Act shall be construed 'as one with' the 1933 Act.
(d) *Young person.* The definition sections referred to in (c) above also define 'young person' as a 'person who has attained the age of 14 years and is under the age of 18 years'. Thus, juveniles divide into children (aged under 14) and young persons (aged 14 to 17 inclusive).

Youth Offending Teams

Pursuant to the CDA 1998, s. 39, each local authority has to establish a youth offending team **D24.3** (YOT). The YOT has to comprise:

(a) a probation officer;
(b) a person with experience of social work in relation to children, nominated by the director of children's services appointed by the local authority;
(c) a social worker;
(d) a police officer;

D

Part D Procedure

(e) a person nominated by a Clinical Commissioning Group, Primary Care Trust or Local
    Health Board any part of whose area lies within the local authority's area; and
(f) a person with experience in education nominated by the director of children's services.

Other people may be co-opted on to the YOT (for example, housing officers and people with
experience of dealing with drugs and alcohol misuse). The functions of the YOT are to co-ordinate
the provision of youth justice services for all those in the authority's area who need them, and to
carry out such functions as are assigned to it in the local authority's 'youth justice plan'. The plan
(made under the CDA 1998, s. 40) sets out how youth justice services in the area are to be provided
and funded, and the functions of the YOTs in that area. The YOT is able to ascertain the needs of
each young offender, identifying the specific problems that make that young person offend and
measuring the risk that the young person poses to others. This enables the YOT to identify suitable programmes to address the needs of the young person in order to prevent further offending.

Prosecuting Young Defendants

D24.4 Detailed guidance (entitled *The CPS: Youth Offenders*) on prosecuting young defendants
from the perspective of the CPS is to be found on its web site (www.cps.gov.uk/legal/v_
to_z/youth_offenders/). That guidance makes reference to *Chief Constable of Kent, ex parte
L* (1991) 93 Cr App R 416, where it was held that the discretion of the CPS to continue or
to discontinue criminal proceedings against a juvenile is reviewable by the Divisional Court,
but only where it can be demonstrated that the decision was made regardless of or clearly
contrary to a settled policy of the DPP evolved in the public interest (see generally **D2.20**).
This means that Crown Prosecutors have to be careful to follow the guidance contained in
the Code for Crown Prosecutors and, in particular, the guidance on 'youth offenders'. In *R
(E) v DPP* [2012] 1 Cr App R 68, the Divisional Court considered a decision to prosecute a
14-year-old girl for the alleged sexual abuse by her of her two younger sisters and emphasised
the importance of the decision-maker considering, in a case where the alleged offender and
the victim are both under 18, what is in the best interests and welfare both of the accused and
of the victim.

D24.5 **Age of Criminal Responsibility**   There is an irrebuttable presumption that a person who is
under the age of 10 cannot be guilty of a criminal offence (CYPA 1933, s. 50). There used to be
a rebuttable presumption that a child aged between 10 and 14 was incapable of committing an
offence. This presumption was, however, abolished by the CDA 1998, s. 34. In *JTB* [2009] 1
AC 1310 the House of Lords ruled that, by enacting s. 34, Parliament intended to abolish both
the presumption and the defence of *doli incapax*. The trial judge's ruling, that the accused (aged
12) was precluded by s. 34 from raising the issue of *doli incapax*, was therefore upheld.

Court of First Appearance

D24.6 The juvenile's first court appearance in respect of an offence will be in the youth court unless the
case is one of the exceptional ones where the first appearance is in the adult magistrates' court.
Those exceptional cases are where:

(a) the juvenile is jointly charged with an adult; or
(b) the juvenile is charged with aiding and abetting an adult to commit an offence (or vice
    versa); or
(c) the juvenile is charged with an offence which arises out of circumstances which are the same
    as (or connected with) those which resulted in the charge faced by an adult accused.

Bail

D24.7 The Bail Act 1976 (with the presumption in favour of bail in s. 4) applies to juveniles (i.e.
persons under the age of 18 (s. 2(2)). The criteria for granting bail are virtually the same as for

adults. There are a number of important differences. First, a juvenile can be refused bail where this is necessary for his own 'welfare', not just if necessary for his own 'protection', as is the case with adults (BA 1976, sch. 1, part 1, para. (3)). Secondly, a parent or guardian may be asked to act as a surety not only for the juvenile's attendance at court (the function of the surety in the case of adult defendants) but also for compliance with any other conditions of bail which the court may impose (BA 1976, s. 3(7)). In *R (B) v Brent Youth Court* [2010] EWHC 1893 (Admin), Wilkie J ruled that the requirement imposed by the CYPA 1933, s. 44, to have regard to the 'welfare' of a defendant under the age of 18, requires the court to consider whether, notwithstanding the restrictions on repeated bail applications contained in the BA 1976, sch. 1, part IIA (see **D7.70**), it should nonetheless consider substantively a further bail application in order to have regard to the welfare of the juvenile.

The most significant difference between adults and juveniles is in what happens to a juvenile under the age of 18 if bail is withheld, whether before or after conviction. Where juveniles are refused bail, they are remanded to local authority accommodation or to youth detention accommodation under the LASPO 2012, ss. 91 to 107 (see **D7.132**).

Mode of Trial

The normal rules governing mode of trial are modified to a large extent in the case of juveniles. **D24.8** The great majority of juveniles are tried and sentenced in *youth courts*. By virtue of the CYPA 1933, s. 45, youth courts are magistrates' courts. It follows that trial in the youth court is merely a form of summary trial (even though there are special rules relating to the constitution and proceedings of youth courts). However, the youth court has jurisdiction to try offences which, in the case of an adult, are triable only on indictment (with the exception of homicide and certain firearms offences). Whereas an adult may never be tried summarily for an offence triable only on indictment and always has the right to elect trial on indictment for an offence triable either way, a juvenile may be (and normally is) tried summarily for an indictable offence, whatever his wishes as to mode of trial may be. In other words, he has no right to elect a Crown Court trial. If a juvenile is sent to the Crown Court for trial, it is because the *magistrates* have decided that they should not accept jurisdiction — the most the juvenile may do is to make representations for or against staying in the youth court.

In summary, a juvenile either may or must be tried in an adult court if he is charged:

(a) with homicide, or
(b) with an offence to which the PCC(S)A 2000, s. 91, applies (offences carrying at least 14 years' imprisonment in the case of an adult, together with those specified in s. 91 itself), or
(c) with certain offences to which mandatory minimum sentence provisions (e.g. the Firearms Act 1968, s. 51A) apply, or
(d) with an offence which falls within the ambit of the 'dangerous offender' provisions of the CJA 2003 (see **E4**), or
(e) alongside an adult defendant.

The procedure for determining where the juvenile will be tried in those cases where mode of trial is an issue is discussed in **D24.20** *et seq.*

TRIAL OF JUVENILES IN THE YOUTH COURT

As we have seen, the youth court has jurisdiction to try offences which would be triable **D24.9** only on indictment in the case of an adult. Most juveniles are therefore tried in the youth court.

Constitution and Operation of the Youth Court

D24.10   The CYPA 1933, s. 45, sets out the framework under which lay magistrates and district judges are authorised to hear youth court cases. Under s. 45(2), a justice of the peace is not qualified to sit as a member of a youth court unless authorised to do so under s. 45(3). Under s. 45(3), authorisation is given by the Lord Chief Justice, with concurrence of the Lord Chancellor. These personal authorisations are valid throughout England and Wales. A magistrate can be given authorisation for particular proceedings (set out in the authorisation) or for all youth court proceedings (s. 45(3)). This is to ensure that, given the specific knowledge and understanding that is required in youth court cases, only trained and suitable magistrates sit in youth courts.

Under the Youth Courts (Constitution of Committees and Right to Preside) Rules 2007 (SI 2007 No. 1611), r. 3, there has to be a committee, known as a 'youth panel' for each local justice area. The panel consists of the youth justices (i.e. the justices authorised to sit as members of a youth panel) for that local justice area. Its functions include liaison with other bodies to share information and represent the views of youth justices.

D24.11   Composition of the Youth Court   The composition of the youth court is governed by the Youth Courts (Constitution of Committees and Right to Preside) Rules 2007, r. 10(1). This requires a youth court to consist of either (a) a district judge (magistrates' courts) sitting alone, or (b) not more than three justices, including a man and a woman.

Under r. 10(2) and (3), if no male justice or (as the case may be) no female justice is available due to circumstances that were unforeseen when the justices to sit were chosen, or if the only male (or female) justice present cannot properly sit as a member of the court, then the court may be constituted without a male (or female) justice if the other members of the youth court think it 'inexpedient in the interests of justice for there to be an adjournment'.

In *Birmingham Justices, ex parte F* (2000) 164 JP 523, the juvenile was tried by a youth court which consisted of two male magistrates. No point as to the absence of a female magistrate was taken by prosecution, defence or the clerk. The juvenile was found guilty, and sought judicial review on the ground that there should have been at least three magistrates, including a man and a woman, in accordance with the requirement for a mixed bench. The Divisional Court granted judicial review, and ordered a retrial, holding that what is now r. 10(1) is mandatory unless the justices decide in their discretion to proceed under what is now r. 10(2) and (3). Such discretion has to be exercised publicly and with submissions from the parties (per Laws J at [14]). In the present case, it had not been exercised in that way. This issue might be reopened in the light of *Ashton* [2007] 1 WLR 181, where it was held that, where there has been a procedural failure in the exercise of a statutory power, the court should first ask itself whether the intention of the legislature was that any act done following that procedural failure should be invalid. The decision in *Birmingham Justices, ex parte F* would, of course, stand if it were to be held that Parliament did intend the particular irregularity to be fatal (cf. *Clarke* [2008] 2 All ER 665)

D24.12   Under r. 11(1), a youth court (unless it consists of a district judge sitting alone) must be chaired by a district judge (if he is sitting as a member of the court) or by a youth justice who is on the list of approved youth court chairmen. Rule 11(2) provides that a youth justice may preside before he has been included on a list of approved youth court chairmen only if he is under the supervision of a youth justice who is on a list of approved chairmen and has completed the necessary training course. Rule 12 deals with the exceptional situation where no youth justice entitled to preside at the hearing is present. Rule 12(1) states that the youth justices present may appoint one of their number to preside provided that they are satisfied as to the suitability of the justice they propose as chair and (unless the absence of a qualified chairman arises because of illness, circumstances unforeseen when the youth justices to sit were chosen or some other emergency) the justice in question has completed, or is undergoing, a chairman training course.

Exclusion of Public   The public are excluded from the courtroom of a youth court. The CYPA   **D24.13**
1933, s. 47(2), stipulates that the only persons permitted to be present in the youth court are:

(a) members and officers of the court;
(b) parties to the case before the court and their legal representatives;
(c) witnesses and other persons directly concerned in that case;
(d) bona fide representatives of news gathering or reporting organisations; and
(e) such other persons as the court may specially authorise to be present.

These restrictions also appear in the CrimPR, r. 37.2(c). The only persons entitled to be present in the youth court apart from the accused, the parents and the justices and their clerk are:

(a) the lawyers representing the juvenile or the prosecution in the case (lawyers cannot enter the courtroom if a case they are appearing in is not yet being dealt with);
(b) court officials (for example, the usher);
(c) reporters (but note the reporting restrictions set out below);
(d) probation officers and social workers involved in the case;
(e) witnesses giving evidence (they are allowed to remain in court once they have given evidence);
(f) anyone else directly involved in the case;
(g) anyone whom the magistrates specifically allow to be present.

Under the VCRA 2006, s. 11(7), where the youth court is dealing with proceedings for an offence under s. 11(1) (breach of a drinking banning order), one person authorised to be present by a relevant authority may be in the courtroom.

The position in the youth court should be contrasted with those cases where a juvenile is appearing as an accused, or as a witness, in the adult magistrates' court or the Crown Court — in those courts, the public has the right to be present unless the court takes the exceptional step of sitting '*in camera*'.

Media Reports

Restrictions on what can be reported are contained in the CYPA 1933, s. 49 (which is   **D24.14**
prospectively amended by the YJCEA 1999, sch. 2, para 3). Under s. 49(1), no report of proceedings in a youth court may be published or broadcast which reveals the name, address or other identifying detail of any juvenile concerned in the proceedings, whether he be concerned as a party or merely as a witness. The overarching test is whether the particulars in question are likely to lead to the juvenile being identified as someone concerned in the proceedings.

These automatic restrictions on publishing or broadcasting identifying details of a juvenile   **D24.15**
involved in youth court proceedings apply only while that person remains a juvenile. In *T v DPP; North East Press Ltd* (2004) 168 JP 194, during the course of youth court proceedings, the accused attained the age of 18. The justices ruled that the CYPA 1933, s. 49, no longer applied. It was held by the Divisional Court that an accused in proceedings before the youth court ceases to benefit from the reporting restrictions contained in s. 49 as soon as he attains the age of 18, because the specific purpose of s. 49 is to protect children and young persons from adverse publicity. The fact that a person had been a young person at the commencement of proceedings could not justify such a person continuing to benefit from s. 49 once he has ceased to be a young person. When the amendments to s. 49 made by the YJCEA 1999 come into force, the matter will be put beyond doubt, as the amended s. 49(1) will read, 'No matter relating to any child or young person concerned in proceedings to which this section applies shall *while he is under the age of 18* be included in any publication if it is likely to lead members of the public to identify him as someone concerned in the proceedings' (emphasis added).

D24.16 **Lifting the Restrictions** The court may lift the ban on publicity to the extent it considers necessary either to avoid injustice to the juvenile himself (CYPA 1933, s. 49(5)(a)) or, in the case of a juvenile who is unlawfully at large, where it is necessary to do so for the purpose of apprehending him (s. 49(5)(b)). However, s. 49(5)(b) applies only to a juvenile who is charged with, or convicted of, a violent or sexual offence or an offence punishable in the case of an adult with imprisonment for 14 years or more; moreover, the power conferred by s. 49(5)(b) may be exercised only upon the application of the DPP (this includes Crown Prosecutors), and notice of the application must be given to the juvenile's legal representative (s. 49(7)). The power to lift the reporting restrictions may be exercised by a single justice (s. 49(8)).

The court may also lift the ban on publicity where a juvenile has been convicted of an offence, if it is satisfied that it is in the public interest to do so (s. 49(4A)). Before doing so, it must afford an opportunity to the parties to make representations (s. 49(4B)). In *McKerry v Teesdale and Wear Valley Justices* (2000) 164 JP 355, the Divisional Court recognised that there was a tension between the young person's right to privacy and the 'hallowed principle that justice is administered in public, open to full and fair reporting of the proceedings in court' (per Lord Bingham CJ at [17]). His lordship stressed that the power to dispense with anonymity under s. 49(4A), had to be exercised with very great care, caution and circumspection (at [29]). His lordship said (at [17]) that it would be wholly wrong for any court to dispense with a young person's prima facie right to anonymity as an additional punishment, and that it was also very difficult to see any place for 'naming and shaming'. The court must be satisfied that the statutory criterion, that it was in the public interest to dispense with the reporting restrictions, is satisfied. His lordship observed that this will very rarely be the case, and justices making an order under s. 49(4A) must be clear *why* it is in the public interest to dispense with the restrictions (at [17]). His lordship added that, in weighing up the public interest, it is entirely proper for the justices to ask a reporter present in court if he wishes to say anything.

It should be borne in mind that the rule on publicity in the youth court is the reverse of that which applies in the adult magistrates' court and the Crown Court, where the media are permitted to identify a juvenile concerned in proceedings unless an order to the contrary is made under s. 39 of the 1933 Act (see D24.84). In the youth court, on the other hand, the juvenile must not be identified unless the court gives permission.

Attendance of Parent or Guardian

D24.17 The CYPA 1933, s. 34A(1), provides that if the juvenile is aged under 16 the court *must* (and if the juvenile is aged 16 or 17, the court *may*) require a parent or guardian to 'attend at the court during all the stages of the proceedings, unless and to the extent that the court is satisfied that it would be unreasonable to require such attendance, having regard to the circumstances of the case'. 'Guardian' is defined as any person who, in the opinion of the court, has for the time being 'the care of the child or young person' (CYPA 1933, s. 107). 'Parent' is not defined in the 1933 Act, but, by the Adoption Act 1976, s. 39, includes the adopter of an adopted child. In cases where the local authority has parental responsibility, their representative, rather than, or in certain cases as well as, the parent must (or may) be required to attend (CYPA 1933, s. 34A(2)).

Course of the Trial in a Youth Court

D24.18 The course of a trial in the youth court is essentially the same as the course of a trial in an adult magistrates' court. The CrimPR, part 37 (see Supplement, R-283), which applies to trials in both adult magistrates' courts and youth courts, governs the procedure.

As a matter of terminology, the words 'conviction' and 'sentence' are not to be used in connection with juveniles tried summarily (CYPA 1933, s. 59). They are replaced by, respectively, the terms 'finding of guilt' and 'order made on a finding of guilt' (CrimPR, r. 37.1(2)). This applies both to proceedings in the youth court and to proceedings against juveniles in the adult magistrates' court. It does not, however, apply to proceedings on indictment.

The procedure in the youth court is intended to be less formal than in the adult magistrates' court. So, for example, the accused sits on a chair, not in a dock, and usually has a parent or guardian sitting nearby; the accused and any juvenile witnesses are addressed by their first names; the oath taken by witnesses is to 'promise' (not 'swear') to tell the truth (CYPA 1963, s. 28(1)).

Statutory Provisions Relating to Youth Court Procedure

Children and Young Persons Act 1933, ss. 34A, 47, 49 and 59   D24.19

34A.—(1) Where a child or young person is charged with an offence or is for any other reason brought before a court, the court—
(a) may in any case; and
(b) shall in the case of a child or a young person who is under the age of sixteen years, require a person who is a parent or guardian of his to attend at the court during all the stages of the proceedings, unless and to the extent that the court is satisfied that it would be unreasonable to require such attendance, having regard to the circumstances of the case.
(2) In relation to a child or young person for whom a local authority have parental responsibility and who—
(a) is in their care; or
(b) is provided with accommodation by them in the exercise of any functions (in particular those under the Children Act 1989) which are social services functions within the meaning of the Local Authority Social Services Act 1970,
the reference in subsection (1) above to a person who is a parent or guardian of his shall be construed as a reference to that authority or, where he is allowed to live with such a person, as including such a reference.
In this subsection 'local authority' and 'parental responsibility' have the same meanings as in the Children Act 1989.
47.—(1) Youth courts shall sit as often as may be necessary for the purposes of exercising any jurisdiction conferred on them by or under this or any other Act.
(2) No person shall be present at any sitting of a youth court except—
(a) members and officers of the court;
(b) parties to the case before the court, their legal representatives, and witnesses and other persons directly concerned in that case;
(c) bona fide representatives of newspapers or news agencies;
(d) such other persons as the court may specially authorise to be present.
…
49.—(1) The following prohibitions apply (subject to subsection (5) below) in relation to any proceedings to which this section applies, that is to say—
(a) no report shall be published which reveals the name, address or school of any child or young person concerned in the proceedings or includes any particulars likely to lead to the identification of any child or young person concerned in the proceedings; and
(b) no picture shall be published or included in a programme service as being or including a picture of any child or young person concerned in the proceedings.
(2) The proceedings to which this section applies are—
(a) proceedings in a youth court;
(b) proceedings on appeal from a youth court (including proceedings by way of case stated);
(c) proceedings in a magistrates' court under Schedule 2 to the Criminal Justice and Immigration Act 2008 (proceedings for breach, revocation or amendment of youth rehabilitation orders); and
(d) proceedings on appeal from a magistrates' court arising out of any proceedings mentioned in paragraph (c) (including proceedings by way of case stated).
(3) The reports to which this section applies are reports in a newspaper and reports included in a programme service; and similarly as respects pictures.
(4) For the purposes of this section a child or young person is 'concerned' in any proceedings whether as being the person against or in respect of whom the proceedings are taken or as being a witness in the proceedings.
(4A) If a court is satisfied that it is in the public interest to do so, it may, in relation to a child or young person who has been convicted of an offence, by order dispense to any specified extent

with the requirements of this section in relation to any proceedings before it to which this section applies by virtue of subsection (2)(a) or (b) above, being proceedings relating to—

(a) the prosecution or conviction of the offender for the offence;

(b) the manner in which he, or his parent or guardian, should be dealt with in respect of the offence;

(c) the enforcement, amendment, variation, revocation or discharge of any order made in respect of the offence;

(d) where an attendance centre order is made in respect of the offence, the enforcement of any rules made under section 221(1)(d) or (e) of the Criminal Justice Act 2003; or

(e) where a detention and training order is made, the enforcement of any requirements imposed under section 103(6)(b) of the Powers of Criminal Courts (Sentencing) Act 2000.

(4B) A court shall not exercise its power under subsection (4A) above without—

(a) affording the parties to the proceedings an opportunity to make representations; and

(b) taking into account any representations which are duly made.

(5) Subject to subsection (7) below, a court may, in relation to proceedings before it to which this section applies, by order dispense to any specified extent with the requirements of this section in relation to a child or young person who is concerned in the proceedings if it is satisfied—

(a) that it is appropriate to do so for the purpose of avoiding injustice to the child or young person; or

(b) that, as respects a child or young person to whom this paragraph applies who is unlawfully at large, it is necessary to dispense with those requirements for the purpose of apprehending him and bringing him before a court or returning him to the place in which he was in custody.

(6) Paragraph (b) of subsection (5) above applies to any child or young person who is charged with or has been convicted of—

(a) a violent offence,

(b) a sexual offence, or

(c) an offence punishable in the case of a person aged 21 or over with imprisonment for fourteen years or more.

(7) The court shall not exercise its power under subsection (5)(b) above—

(a) except in pursuance of an application by or on behalf of the Director of Public Prosecutions; and

(b) unless notice of the application has been given by the Director of Public Prosecutions to any legal representative of the child or young person.

(8) The court's power under subsection (5) above may be exercised by a single justice.

(9) If a report or picture is published or included in a programme service in contravention of subsection (1) above, the following persons, that is to say—

(a) in the case of publication of a written report or a picture as part of a newspaper, any proprietor, editor or publisher of the newspaper;

(b) in the case of the inclusion of a report or picture in a programme service, any body corporate which provides the service and any person having functions in relation to the programme corresponding to those of an editor of a newspaper,

shall be liable on summary conviction to a fine not exceeding level 5 on the standard scale.

(10) In any proceedings under schedule 7 to the Powers of Criminal Courts (Sentencing) Act 2000 (proceedings for varying or revoking supervision orders) before a magistrates' court other than a youth court or on appeal from such a court it shall be the duty of the magistrates' court or the appellate court to announce in the course of the proceedings that this section applies to the proceedings; and if the court fails to do so this section shall not apply to the proceedings.

(11) In this section—

'legal representative' means an authorised advocate or authorised litigator, as defined by section 119(1) of the Courts and Legal Services Act 1990;

'programme' and 'programme service' have the same meaning as in the Broadcasting Act 1990;

'sexual offence' means an offence listed in part 2 of Schedule 15 to the Criminal Justice Act 2003;

'specified' means specified in an order under this section;

'violent offence' means an offence listed in part 1 of Schedule 15 to the Criminal Justice Act 2003;

and a person who, having been granted bail, is liable to arrest (whether with or without a warrant) shall be treated as unlawfully at large.

59. The words 'conviction' and 'sentence' shall cease to be used in relation to children and young persons dealt with summarily and any reference in any enactment...to a person convicted, a conviction or a sentence shall, in the case of a child or young person, be construed as including a reference to a person found guilty of an offence, a finding of guilt or an order made upon such finding, as the case may be.

Substantial amendments to s. 49 are made by the YJCEA 1999, sch. 2; however, these amendments are not yet in force.

DETERMINING MODE OF TRIAL OF JUVENILES

Most trials involving juvenile defendants take place in the youth court. However, there are cases **D24.20** where a juvenile may, or must, be tried in an adult court (either an adult magistrates' court or the Crown Court). The law on mode of trial for juveniles is to be found (somewhat confusingly) in a combination of statutory sources, including the CYPA 1933, s. 46, the CYPA 1963, s. 18, and the MCA 1980, ss. 24 and 29. In summary, there are five circumstances in which the trial of a juvenile may or must take place in the Crown Court:

(a) where the juvenile is accused of homicide (i.e. murder or manslaughter); or
(b) where the juvenile is charged with a firearms offence where the Firearms Act 1968, s. 51A, applies (or using someone to mind a weapon under the VCRA 2006, s. 29(3)); or
(c) where the juvenile is accused of an offence to which the PCC(S)A 2000, s. 91, applies (i.e. an offence carrying at least 14 years' imprisonment in the case of an adult or one specified in s. 91 itself); or
(d) where the juvenile is charged with a 'specified' offence as defined by the CJA 2003, s. 224 (and so falls within the ambit of the 'dangerous offender' provisions of that Act, as amended by the LASPO 2012); or
(e) where the juvenile is charged alongside an adult.

There is only one situation where the trial of a juvenile may take place in an adult magistrates' court, namely where the juvenile is charged alongside an adult.

Trial on Indictment   The MCA 1980, s. 24(1), provides that, unless a juvenile is sent to the **D24.21** Crown Court for trial, he must be tried summarily.

Magistrates' Courts Act 1980, s. 24

(1) Where a person under the age of 18 years appears or is brought before a magistrates' court on an information charging him with an indictable offence he shall, subject to sections 51 and 51A of the Crime and Disorder Act 1998 and to sections 24A and 24B below, be tried summarily.

The MCA 1980, s. 24(1), has to be read in conjunction with the CDA 1998, ss. 51 and 51A. Section 51(7) deals with cases where there is an adult co-accused. Section 51A deals with those cases in which either a juvenile must be tried on indictment or else the magistrates have a discretion to send him to the Crown Court for trial. Section 51A(2) and (3) require the court to send the juvenile forthwith to the Crown Court for trial where the juvenile is charged with:

(a) homicide; or
(b) a firearms offence where there is a mandatory minimum sentence (Firearms Act 1968, s. 51A), or an offence under the VCRA 2006, s. 29(3) (minimum sentences in certain cases of using someone to mind a weapon);
(c) an offence to which the provisions of the PCC(S)A 2000, s. 91, apply and the court considers that it ought to be possible to sentence the juvenile to detention under that section in the event of his being convicted of the offence; or
(d) the offence is a 'specified' offence (under the CJA 2003, s. 224) and it appears to the court that, if he is found guilty of the offence, the criteria for the imposition of a sentence under

D

Part D Procedure

the CJA 2003, s. 226B (extended sentence for certain violent or sexual offences) would be met.

The functions of the court under s. 51A can be exercised by a single justice (s. 51A(11)).

D24.22   **Homicide Cases**   The term 'homicide' is not defined but obviously includes murder and manslaughter; however, it does not include causing death by dangerous driving, as that offence falls within the ambit of the PCC(S)A 2000, s. 91 (see **D24.25**). Under the DVCVA 2004, s. 6(5), an offence under s. 5 of that Act of causing or allowing a person's death is an offence of homicide for these purposes. Where a juvenile is charged with homicide, there is no determination of mode of trial, since the case has to be sent to the Crown Court.

D24.23   **Firearms Offences**   Under the CDA 1998, s. 51A(2) and (3), a juvenile must be sent to the Crown Court for trial on any charge where, if convicted, he would be subject to the mandatory minimum sentence under the Firearms Act 1968, s. 51A (see **E5.9**). These minimum sentence provisions apply only where the offender had attained the age of 16 when he committed the offence (FA 1968, s. 51A(1)(b)). The court has to impose a term of detention of at least three years if the offender was under 18 at the date of the offence (s. 51A(5)(a)(ii)), unless the court is of the opinion that there are exceptional circumstances relating to the offence or to the offender which justify its not doing so (s. 51A(2)). Where these requirements would be satisfied if the juvenile were to be convicted, he will be sent to the Crown Court for trial. If he pleads guilty or is found guilty in the Crown Court, the sentence imposed by virtue of the FA 1968, s. 51A, takes the form of a sentence of long-term detention under the PCC(S)A 2000, s. 91. The position is similar where the juvenile is charged with an offence to which the VCRA 2006, s. 29(3) (using someone to mind a weapon), is applicable. Again, the minimum age is 16 (at the date of the offence) and the minimum sentence, in the absence of exceptional circumstances, is three years in the case of an offender who is under the age of 18 at the date of conviction.

D24.24   **Mandatory Sentences Generally**   It should be noted that the mandatory minimum sentences for a third class A drug trafficking conviction (PCC(S)A 2000, s. 110) or third domestic burglary (s. 111) do not apply to juveniles as the third offence must be committed after the offender has attained the age of 18.

Cases Falling within the Powers of Criminal Courts (Sentencing) Act 2000, s. 91

D24.25   The CDA 1998, s. 51A, must be read in conjunction with the PCC(S)A 2000, s. 91, which provides for the punishment of juveniles convicted on indictment of certain serious offences. Section 91 empowers the Crown Court to order that a juvenile be detained for a period not exceeding the maximum sentence of imprisonment which may be imposed on an adult offender for the offence in question. It applies only in the following cases:

(a) where a juvenile who has attained the age of ten is convicted of an offence which carries at least 14 years' imprisonment in the case of an adult offender;

(b) where a juvenile who has attained the age of ten is convicted of an offence under the Sexual Offences Act 2003, ss. 3, 13, 25 or 26.

This provision is necessary because of the relatively limited ambit of the normal custodial sentence for young offenders, namely the detention and training order: this order is limited to a total of 24 months (12 months' custody, followed by 12 months' supervision); where the offender is under the age of 15, a detention and training order can be imposed only if he is a 'persistent offender'; moreover, a detention and training order is not available where the offender is under the age of 12. Section 91 achieves two key objectives: (a) it enables the Crown Court to pass a longer term of detention than would otherwise be possible (given the 24-month limit on the duration of the detention and training order); and (b) it enables the Crown Court to impose a term of detention where otherwise no detention would be possible (in the case of an offender under the age of 12, or an offender under the age of 15 who is not a persistent offender).

Scope of s. 91   The power to impose a sentence under s. 91 applies where a juvenile indicates   **D24.26**
a guilty plea, at the 'plea before venue' hearing, to an offence to which s. 91 applies, and is then
committed to the Crown Court for sentence under the PCC(S)A 2000, s. 3B (see **D24.61**),
and it also applies where a juvenile is sent for trial, under the CDA 1998, s. 51A(2) and (3)(b),
in respect of an offence to which s. 91 applies, and is then convicted of that offence. This means
that if the juvenile, at the 'plea before venue' hearing, indicates a not guilty plea to such an
offence, the magistrates have to consider whether, if he is found guilty of the offence, it 'ought
to be possible' to sentence him under s. 91; if so, he must be sent to the Crown Court for trial.

In *AM* [1998] 1 All ER 874 at p. 372, Lord Bingham CJ confirmed that, where a juvenile is
charged with more than one offence, and the PCC(S)A 2000, s. 91, applies to one or some,
but not all, of those offences, the court may, when considering the seriousness of the offence(s)
to which s. 91 applies, consider the seriousness of the combination of all offences, since they
are 'associated offences' within the meaning of the PCC(S)A 2000, s. 161(1). However, in the
event of conviction, the Crown Court may order long-term detention only in respect of those
offences to which s. 91 applies.

Where a juvenile appears before a youth court charged with a number of offences and is sent
to the Crown Court in respect of some (but not all) of them, the youth court is not required to
adjourn proceedings in respect of the other offences (MCA 1980, s. 10(3A)).

Deciding Mode of Trial where s. 91 Applies

Where the appropriateness of summary trial is canvassed in a case falling within the ambit of   **D24.27**
the PCC(S)A 2000, s. 91, the court should hear representations from both the prosecution
and defence, but *evidence* about the gravity of the offence (as opposed to representations) is not
appropriate at this stage (*South Hackney Juvenile Court, ex parte RB and CB* (1983) 77 Cr App
R 294).

When a youth court is deciding whether or not to send a juvenile to be tried in the Crown Court
in a case where s. 91 applies, the court is entitled to know about any previous findings of guilt
recorded against the juvenile (*R (Tullet) v Medway Magistrates' Court* (2003) 167 JP 541).

It must be emphasised that the juvenile has no right to elect Crown Court trial. Where he is
tried is a matter for the magistrates, who will take account of the representations made by the
prosecution and defence in coming to their decision. In *R (W) v Brent Youth Court* (2006) 170
JP 198, the Divisional Court observed that if the youth court is to make a satisfactory decision it must have all the necessary information before it. The facts of the case as alleged, which
must be assumed to be true unless manifestly not, should be put accurately before the court.
It is the duty of both advocates to ensure that the summary of the facts is scrupulously fair and
balanced. The court should also be told of any undisputed mitigation that will be available
to the accused including (where applicable) an indication of an intention to plead guilty. The
accused's previous record must, said the Court, be accurately described (per Smith LJ at [6]).
Smith LJ also pointed out (at [9]) that, where several defendants are charged together and all
are under 18, the court must consider the position of each defendant separately 'even if this
results in one defendant being tried in the youth court and others in the Crown Court'. It
follows that one juvenile cannot be sent to the Crown Court for trial merely because a juvenile co-accused is being sent there (*R (W and M) v Oldham Youth Court* [2010] EWHC 661
(Admin)).

Guidance on the Decision-making Process in s. 91 Cases

In *R (D) v Manchester City Youth Court* [2002] 1 Cr App R (S) 573, Gage J said (at [22]) that   **D24.28**
the effect of s. 24 is that a magistrates' court should not decline jurisdiction unless 'the offence
and the circumstances surrounding it and the offender are such as to make it more than a
vague or theoretical possibility that a sentence of detention for a long period may be passed'.

This necessarily means that the justices must take into account the sentencing practice of the Crown Court (and the Court of Appeal) in relation to s. 91. As Stanley Burnton J observed in *R (D) v Sheffield Youth Court* (2003) 167 JP 159, 'in deciding whether it considers that it ought to be possible to sentence a defendant pursuant to s. 91, the youth court must consider the sentencing powers of the Crown Court and the guidance that has been given as to their exercise. If, on the basis of that guidance, there is no real possibility of such a sentence, [sending the juvenile to the Crown Court] is inappropriate' (at [39]). His lordship added (at [40]) that, in making its decision, the youth court should take into account any undisputed facts put forward as mitigation (such as the good character of the accused). However, contentious mitigation should be ignored: if the case is sent to the Crown Court and the accused convicted, mitigation will be a matter for that court.

D24.29 In *R (W) v Thetford Youth Court* [2003] 1 Cr App R (S) 323, Gage J said that, where an offence is likely to attract a sentence of less than two years' custody, the appropriate sentence will be a detention and training order. In the case of an offender under 15 who is not a persistent offender, or a child under 12, the most likely sentence will be a non-custodial sentence. It follows that, in most cases, the appropriate place of trial will be the youth court (at [29]). However, his lordship went on to say (at [30]) that there may be cases where, despite the fact that the offender is under 15 and no detention and training order can be made, the only appropriate sentence is a custodial sentence pursuant to s. 91, possibly for a period of less than two years. However, such cases would rarely call for a sentence pursuant to s. 91, particularly if the court is dealing with an offender under the age of 12. He emphasised that the mere fact that a youth court, unable to make a short detention and training order, considers that the option to pass a short custodial sentence should be available, does not mean that it should decline jurisdiction:

> It seems to me that in such circumstances the fact that a detention and training order is not available indicates that Parliament intended that generally a non-custodial sentence should be passed... [C]ases involving offenders under 15 for whom a detention and training order is not available will only rarely attract a period of detention, under s. 91; the more rarely if the offender is under 12.

In *R (C) v Balham Youth Court* [2004] 1 Cr App R (S) 143, Scott Baker LJ (at [33]) adopted a similar view:

> ...the fact than an offender...does not qualify for a detention and training order...is not an exceptional circumstance to justify passing a sentence of less than two years under section 91 of the 2000 Act.

His lordship went on to say (at [34]) that the relevant question in that case was whether it was such a serious case that detention above two years would or might realistically be required.

D24.30 In *R (M and W) v West London Youth Court* [2004] EWHC 1144 (Admin), Leveson J (at [16]) expressed the test in slightly different terms:

> Whether there is a real prospect that a custodial sentence of, or in excess of, 2 years might be required, or is there any unusual feature of this case which might justify a sentence of less than two years, pursuant to section 91(3), for which purpose the absence of a power to impose a detention and training order because the offender is under the age of 15 is not an unusual feature?

In *R (H) v Southampton Youth Court* [2005] 2 Cr App R (5) 171, it was emphasised that offenders under 18, and in particular those under 15, should be tried in the youth court, with Crown Court jurisdiction being reserved for the most serious crimes. It would only be in exceptional cases that an offender aged between 12 and 14 should be sent for trial to the Crown Court. Leveson J summarised the relevant principles as follows (at [33]–[35]):

> The general policy of the legislature is that those who are under 18 years of age, and in particular children of under 15 years of age, should, wherever possible, be tried in the youth court. It is that court which is best designed to meet their specific needs. A trial in the Crown Court with the inevitably greater formality and greatly increased number of people involved (including a jury and the public) should be reserved for the most serious cases.

It is a further policy of the legislature that, generally speaking, first-time offenders aged 12 to 14 and all offenders under 12 should not be detained in custody and decisions as to jurisdiction should have regard to the fact that the exceptional power to detain for grave offences should not be used to water down the general principle. Those under 15 will rarely attract a period of detention and, even more rarely, those who are under 12.

In each case the court should ask itself whether there is a real prospect, having regard to his or her age, that this defendant whose case they are considering might require a sentence of, or in excess of, two years or, alternatively, whether although the sentence might be less than two years, there is some unusual feature of the case which justifies declining jurisdiction, bearing in mind that the absence of a power to impose a detention and training order because the defendant is under 15 is not an unusual feature.

D24.31 In *R (B) v Norfolk Youth Court* [2013] EWHC 1459 (Admin), Cox J said (at [50]) that 'a trial in the Crown Court should be reserved for those most serious and...exceptional cases, which truly merit the description "grave crimes"'. Her ladyship added that to fall within that definition an offence would have to be 'so serious that it necessitated the exceptional course of declining jurisdiction for such crimes. The exceptional power to detain for grave crimes should not be used to water down the general principle that a child...should stand trial in the youth court, which is, for him, the appropriate place of trial'.

In *CPS v Newcastle-upon-Tyne Youth Court* [2010] EWHC 2773 (Admin), the youth court had retained jurisdiction in a case involving a charge of rape. It was held that the District Judge had taken the 'wrong approach'. Langstaff J said (at [18]) that this was because he:

> ...should not have asked what sentence was likely. He should have asked what sentence was realistically possible bearing in mind the range. He should not, as he appears to have done, have taken every feature which bore on the level of sentence at its most favourable to the defendant. That might ultimately be a conclusion of the court but it could not be said there was no real prospect that a court's decision might be otherwise.

His lordship based this view on the line of cases which had considered the principles governing the exercise of the power to commit a juvenile to the Crown Court for trial in a case to which the PCC(S)A 2000, s. 91, applies. The effect of that case law (at [8]):

> ...is that the decision maker should not decide what sentence he or she would consider appropriate, nor predict the actual sentence which would be passed, but ask whether there is a real prospect that the case may attract a sentence to which section 91 would apply. Thus, what the court should have in mind is what is within the available range of sentences which are not manifestly excessive, not attempting to establish where within the range a sentence will necessarily be. Plainly, regard must be had to the particular facts of a case in forming an appropriate assessment of what the sentencing range might be.

Suitability of Crown Court Trial Not a Relevant Factor If the accused before the youth **D24.32** court is charged with an offence to which s. 91 applies, the only question for the youth court is whether it considers that, if he is found guilty of the offence, it ought to be possible to sentence him pursuant to s. 91. Once it so considers, the youth court has no discretion in the matter. Questions of the suitability of the Crown Court for the trial of the offender are irrelevant to the decision to be made by the youth court. In *Devizes Youth Court, ex parte A* (2000) 164 JP 330, the Divisional Court specifically ruled out the argument that the Crown Court is not a suitable place to deal with a case against a youth, holding that the relevant provisions of international conventions (such as the United Nations' Standard Minimum Rules for the Administration of Juvenile Justice, the United Nations' Convention on the Rights of the Child) affect the way in which the trial is conducted, not the decision as to whether the case is dealt with in the Crown Court or the youth court: if the justices form the judgement that, if the accused is found guilty of the offence, it ought to be possible to sentence him to detention under s. 91, they are bound to send the juvenile to the Crown Court for trial (see the judgment of Brooke LJ at p. 334).

This view seemed to be doubted in *R (W) v Southampton Youth Court* [2003] 1 Cr App R (S) 455. Lord Woolf (sitting with Kay LJ) said (at [16] and [18]):

> While the need to impose the appropriate sentence is important, so is the need to ensure that wherever possible the trial should take place in the appropriate setting. That is more satisfactorily achieved in a youth court than in a Crown Court... [J]ustices should start off with a strong presumption against sending young offenders to the Crown Court unless they are satisfied that that is clearly required, notwithstanding the fact that the forum for trial will not be so appropriate as the youth court.

However, in *R (D) v Sheffield Youth Court* (2003) 167 JP 159, Stanley Burnton J said that he did not think that Lord Woolf intended to suggest that a youth court which considers that it ought to be possible to sentence the accused pursuant to s. 91 nonetheless has a discretion whether or not to commit him to the Crown Court (at [38]):

> If he did, his observation was inconsistent with the decision in *Devizes*, where the point was the basis of its decision, and I should follow *Devizes*. In any event, in my judgment, *Devizes* was correctly decided. Section 24(1) unambiguously requires the youth court to commit to the Crown Court if the conditions for the exercise of the power to commit are satisfied: the words are 'the Court shall commit the accused for trial'. Parliament has decided that the Crown Court is the suitable venue for the trial of persons under the age of 18 if the conditions expressly laid down by section 24(1) are satisfied.

D24.33   In *R (W) v Brent Youth Court* (2006) 170 JP 198, Smith LJ (at [44]) rejected the view that a youth court should *never* accept jurisdiction in the case of a minor charged with rape, saying that she doubted whether there should be any such hard and fast rule. Her ladyship said that there may well be some cases where the accused is under 14 in which it will not be appropriate to commit him to the Crown Court and so 'in the case of very young defendants it may be appropriate [for the youth court] to accept jurisdiction'. A Protocol issued in November 2007 by Leveson LJ (Senior Presiding Judge) and entitled 'Rape Cases in the Youth Court', provides (in para. 8) that '[i]n considering whether the youth court should retain jurisdiction in a rape case, the court will need to consider: (a) the suitability of the youth court as a venue; (b) the desirability of the case being heard by a circuit judge authorised to try serious sexual cases'. The Protocol thus envisages a circuit judge sitting in the youth court as a District Judge (made possible by the Courts Act 2003, s. 66). In *W v Warrington Magistrates' Court* (2009) 173 JP 561, the Divisional Court upheld just such a decision. Nonetheless, Pill LJ (at [34]) emphasised that the court must apply the statutory test in the MCA 1980, s. 24(1)(a), adding that 'Parliament has seen fit to grant a right to a Crown Court hearing (including trial by jury) to young offenders in certain circumstances and that cannot be defeated administratively. There will be alleged sexual offences involving very young defendants where committal to the Crown Court is the correct decision'.

D24.34   **Summary of Approach to be Taken in s. 91 Cases**   The relevant law was restated in *R (CPS) v Redbridge Youth Court* (2005) 169 JP 393, where the court (at (11)) adopted counsel's summary of the legal framework. Although it is not necessary, in order to invoke the PCC(S)A 2000, s. 91, that the crime be one of exceptional gravity, the power to make an order for detention is a long-stop reserved for very serious offences. When considering the MCA 1980, s. 24, the youth court should start with a strong presumption against sending a young defendant to the Crown Court unless it is satisfied that it is clearly required (since the general policy of the legislature is that those under 18 years of age and, in particular, children under 15 years of age, should, wherever possible, be tried in the youth court). It follows that a trial in the Crown Court should be reserved for the most serious cases. A magistrates' court should not decline jurisdiction unless the offence and the circumstances surrounding it and the offender are such as to make it more than a vague or theoretical possibility that a sentence of detention for a long period might be passed under s. 91. Section 91 is primarily applicable to cases of such gravity that the court is or might be considering a sentence of at least two years, and there has to be a real possibility or a real prospect of such a sentence.

It is stated in the definitive sentencing guideline *Overarching Principles — Sentencing Youths* (at para. 12.11: see Supplement, **SG-527**) that:

i) a young person aged 10 or 11 (or aged 12–14 but not a persistent offender) should be committed to the Crown Court…only where charged with an offence of such gravity that, despite the normal prohibition on a custodial sentence for a person of that age, a sentence exceeding two years is a realistic possibility;

ii) a young person aged 12–17 (for which a detention and training order could be imposed) should be committed to the Crown Court…only where charged with an offence of such gravity that a sentence substantially beyond the 2 year maximum for a detention and training order is a realistic possibility.

CPD XIII, Annex 2, states that, where possible, cases involving sexual offences which fall within the ambit of s. 91 should be listed before a District Judge who has been authorised to hear cases involving serious sexual offences, to decide whether the case should be sent to the Crown Court for trial. If the case is retained in the youth court, and the offence involves actual or attempted penetrative activity, the case must be tried by an authorised District Judge; in other cases, the District Judge must consider whether the case is so serious and/or complex that it should be tried by an authorised District Judge, or whether it can be heard by any District Judge or any youth court bench.

Challenging the Decision to Send a Juvenile to the Crown Court

The appropriate means of challenging a decision to send a juvenile to the Crown Court is by way of judicial review. In *AH* (2003) 167 JP 30, an application to stay the proceedings as an abuse of process was made at the start of the trial, on the ground that the case should not have been sent for trial. It was held that the appropriate forum for challenging the decision to commit for trial is the Divisional Court (by way of an application for judicial review) rather than by making an abuse of process application in the Crown Court (per Mance LJ at [13]). **D24.35**

It might be thought that the Divisional Court would apply the well-known *Wednesbury* 'perversity' test to any challenge to a decision to send for trial. However, it is clear from *R (W) v Thetford Youth Court* [2003] 1 Cr App R (S) 323, *R (W) v Southampton Youth Court* [2003] 1 Cr App R (S) 455 and *R (D) v Sheffield Youth Court* (2003) 167 JP 159 that the test is less restrictive than that. As Stanley Burnton J put it in the latter case (at [41]):

The test to be applied by the High Court on judicial review of a decision of a youth court under s. 24(1) is: in the judgment of the High Court, was the decision of the youth court wrong?…It is not sufficient for the High Court to consider that it would have made a different decision under s. 24(1) to that of the youth court. Only if the High Court is satisfied that the original decision was wrong may it interfere.

Where a youth court intends to send a juvenile to the Crown Court for trial with a view to the imposition of a sentence of detention under the PCC(S)A 2000, s. 91, in the event of conviction the court should give reasons for its decision (*R (C) v Balham Youth Court* [2004] 1 Cr App R (S) 143, per Scott Baker LJ at [14]).

It should be noted that, even if a juvenile is tried and convicted in the Crown Court, the Crown Court is not obliged to pass a sentence of detention under s. 91. The Crown Court retains the power to deal with the offender in any way that the youth court could have done. It would, however, generally be undesirable for the Crown Court to remit the case to the youth court for sentence under s. 8 of the 2000 Act (see **D24.109**), since the youth court will already have expressed the view that the case is too serious for its powers (*Allen* (1999) 163 JP 841).

Challenging a Refusal to Send a Juvenile to the Crown Court

If the justices refuse to send the juvenile to the Crown Court in a case where a sentence under s. 91 of the 2000 Act would be available, the procedure to be used to challenge that decision should be an application for judicial review (and not the seeking of a voluntary bill of indictment). In *R (DPP) v Camberwell Youth Court* [2005] 4 All ER 699, the Divisional Court said that, in order that the matter can be dealt with within the sort of timescale that would be **D24.36** involved in seeking a voluntary bill of indictment, an expedited hearing of the application for judicial review should be sought (by completing Form N463). It follows that if, without adequate explanation, an application for a voluntary bill is made, the court will probably refuse consent on the basis that no good reason has been shown to depart from the normal procedure, and the interests of justice do not require it (per Kennedy LJ at [36]).

Powers of Criminal Courts Sentencing Act 2000, s. 91

(1) Subsection (3) below applies where a person aged under 18 is convicted on indictment of—
    (a) an offence punishable in the case of a person aged 21 or over with imprisonment for 14 years or more, not being an offence the sentence for which is fixed by law; or
    [(b) an offence under section 3 of the Sexual Offences Act 2003 (in this section, 'the 2003 Act') (sexual assault); or
    (c) an offence under section 13 of the 2003 Act (child sex offences committed by children or young persons); or
    (d) an offence under section 25 of the 2003 Act (sexual activity with a child family member); or
    (e) an offence under section 26 of the 2003 Act (inciting a child family member to engage in sexual activity)].
(1A) Subsection (3) below also applies where—
    (a) a person aged under 18 is convicted on indictment of an offence—
        (i) under subsection (1)(a), (ab), (aba), (ac), (ad), (ae), (af) or (c) of section 5 of the Firearms Act 1968 (prohibited weapons), or
        (ii) under subsection (1A)(a) of that section,
    (b) the offence was committed after the commencement of section 51A of that Act and for the purposes of subsection (3) of that section at a time when he was aged 16 or over, and
    (c) the court is of the opinion mentioned in section 51A(2) of that Act (exceptional circumstances which justify its not imposing required custodial sentence).
(1B) Subsection (3) below also applies where—
    (a) a person aged under 18 is convicted on indictment of an offence under the Firearms Act 1968 that is listed in section 51A(1A)(b), (e) or (f) of that Act and was committed in respect of a firearm or ammunition specified in section 5(1)(a), (ab), (aba), (ac), (ad), (ae), (af) or (c) or section 5(1A)(a) of that Act;
    (b) the offence was committed after the commencement of section 30 of the Violent Crime Reduction Act 2006 and for the purposes of section 51A(3) of the Firearms Act 1968 at a time when he was aged 16 or over; and
    (c) the court is of the opinion mentioned in section 51A(2) of the Firearms Act 1968.
(1C) Subsection (3) below also applies where—
    (a) a person aged under 18 is convicted of an offence under section 28 of the Violent Crime Reduction Act 2006 (using someone to mind a weapon);
    (b) section 29(3) of that Act applies (minimum sentences in certain cases); and
    (c) the court is of the opinion mentioned in section 29(6) of that Act (exceptional circumstances which justify not imposing the minimum sentence).
(2) ...
(3) If the court is of the opinion that neither a youth rehabilitation order nor a detention and training order is suitable, the court may sentence the offender to be detained for such period, not exceeding the maximum term of imprisonment with which the offence is punishable in the case of a person aged 21 or over, as may be specified in the sentence.
(4) Subsection (3) above is subject to (in particular) section 152 and 153 of the Criminal Justice Act 2003.
(5) Where—
    (a) subsection (2) of section 51A of the Firearms Act 1968, or
    (b) subsection (6) of section 29 of the Violent Crime Reduction Act 2006,
requires the imposition of a sentence of detention under this section for a term of at least the term provided for in that section, the court shall sentence the offender to be detained for such period, of at least the term so provided for but not exceeding the maximum term of imprisonment with which the offence is punishable in the case of a person aged 18 or over, as may be specified in the sentence.

Dangerous Offenders

D24.37 **Extended Sentences**   The CDA 1998, s. 51A(2) and (3)(d), stipulate that, where the offence is a 'specified offence' (within the meaning of the CJA 2003, s. 224) and it appears to the court that, if the juvenile is found guilty of the offence, the criteria for the imposition of an extended sentence under s. 226B of that Act would be met, the court must send him forthwith to the Crown Court for trial for that offence.

Offences that come within the definition of 'specified offence' for these purposes are listed in the CJA 2003, sch. 15. Section 226B applies where the court takes the view 'that there is a significant risk to members of the public of serious harm occasioned by the commission by the offender of further specified offences'. If the appropriate custodial term for the present offence is at least four years, the court may impose an extended sentence, so that the juvenile is under licence, following release from custody, for an extended period for the purpose of protecting members of the public from serious harm occasioned by the commission by him of further specified offences (see E4). Where a juvenile is charged with an offence to which these provisions apply, the court has to consider whether the criteria for imposing a sentence under s. 226B are likely to be met and, if so, send the juvenile to the Crown Court for trial.

In *R (DPP) v East Surrey Youth Court (Ghanbari, interested party)* [2006] 2 All ER 444, the **D24.38** Divisional Court considered the guidance on the dangerous offender provisions of the CJA 2003, given by the Court of Appeal in *Lang* [2006] 2 All ER 410. Rose LJ emphasised (at [17]) the need highlighted in *Lang*, in relation to those under 18, to be 'particularly rigorous before concluding that there is a significant risk of serious harm by the commission of further offences': such a conclusion is unlikely to be appropriate in the absence of a pre-sentence report following assessment by a youth offending team. The advice given in *R (B) v Barking Youth Court* [2006] EWHC 2121 (Admin) that 'those advising young offenders should make shift to obtain material by which the magistrates may be informed of the degree of their client's dangerousness on the first occasion of his appearance before the court' (per Laws LJ, at [11]) would seem to conflict with *Lang* on this point. It is submitted that the view of the Court of Appeal in *Lang* is to be preferred, given the importance of ensuring that the 'dangerous offender' provisions are invoked only when it is appropriate to do so.

The definitive sentencing guideline *Overarching Principles — Sentencing Youths* suggests (at para. 12.14: see Supplement, **SG-527**) that, because a young offender should normally be dealt with in a youth court, where a young person charged with a specified offence would not otherwise be sent to the Crown Court for trial, it is generally preferable for the decision whether to commit under these provisions to be made after conviction.

The CPS guidance on 'youth offenders' (see D24.4) similarly suggests that there will be few cases **D24.39** in which it will be appropriate to exercise the power conferred by the CDA 1998, s. 51(3)(d), and that such power should be exercised only where (a) there is sufficient information (which will usually include a risk assessment in a recent pre-sentence report) about the nature and circumstances of the offender, the offence and any pattern of behaviour of which the offence forms part, to enable the court to assess the offender as dangerous, and (b) it is in the interests of justice for the youth to be tried on indictment. The guidance goes on to say that 'prosecutors should usually recommend summary trial on the basis that the youth court is the appropriate tribunal for youth trials' and that trial on indictment is unnecessary as the youth can be committed for sentence under the PCC(S) A 2000, s. 3C (see D24.64), if (having heard all the facts about the offence and the offender) the court decides that a sentence under the dangerous offender provisions may be necessary. On this basis, sending a juvenile to the Crown Court for trial is described as an 'exceptional' course of action.

Thus, even if the juvenile is charged with a 'specified offence', the case should be tried in the youth court unless it is clearly a case where the juvenile is likely to be found to be 'dangerous', or a sentence under the PCC(S)A 2000, s. 91 (where applicable), is a real possibility. In other cases involving a 'specified offence', the youth court should try the case and rely on its power to commit for sentence under the PCC(S)A 2000, s. 3C, if appropriate.

Life Sentences The CJA 2003, s. 226, provides that, if a person under the age of 18 is con- **D24.40** victed of a serious offence (defined by s. 224 as an offence which is listed in sch. 15 and which carries a life sentence), and the court is of the opinion that there is a significant risk to members of the public of serious harm occasioned by the commission by him of further specified offences, and considers that the seriousness of the offence, or of the offence and any associated offences, is such as to justify the imposition of a sentence of detention for life, then the court must impose a sentence of detention for life under the PCC(S)A 2000, s. 91. Determination of mode of trial in such cases therefore takes place in the way as other cases which fall within the ambit of s. 91.

Related Offences

D24.41   The CDA 1998, s. 51A(4), provides that, where a magistrates' court sends a juvenile to the Crown Court for trial under s. 51A(2), the court may also send him for trial for any other related indictable or summary offence with which he is charged. Where the related offence is a summary one, it can be sent to the Crown Court only if it is punishable with imprisonment or disqualification from driving.

D24.42   The CDA 1998, sch. 3, para. 13, applies where a juvenile has been sent to the Crown Court for trial under s. 51A (or, in a case where there is an adult co-accused, under s. 51(7)) but, as a result of an amendment to the indictment or a successful application (under para. 2) for the main charge to be dismissed, the indictment includes no main offence (i.e. an offence for which the juvenile was sent to the Crown Court for trial under s. 51A(2), or an offence for which he was sent for trial under s. 51(7) (adult co-accused)). In such a case, the Crown Court must remit the juvenile 'to a magistrates' court acting for the place where he was sent to the Crown Court for trial'.

D24.43   Crime and Disorder Act 1998, s. 51A

(1)   This section is subject to sections 24A and 24B of the Magistrates' Courts Act 1980 (which provide for certain offences involving children or young persons to be tried summarily).

(2)   Where a child or young person appears or is brought before a magistrates' court ('the court') charged with an offence and any of the conditions mentioned in subsection (3) below is satisfied, the court shall send him forthwith to the Crown Court for trial for the offence.

(3)   Those conditions are—
   (a)   that the offence falls within subsection (12) below;
   (b)   that the offence is such as is mentioned in subsection (1) of section 91 of the Powers of Criminal Courts (Sentencing) Act 2000 (other than one mentioned in paragraph (d) below in relation to which it appears to the court as mentioned there) and the court considers that if he is found guilty of the offence it ought to be possible to sentence him in pursuance of subsection (3) of that section;
   (c)   that notice is given to the court under section 51B or 51C below in respect of the offence;
   (d)   that the offence is a specified offence (within the meaning of section 224 of the Criminal Justice Act 2003) and it appears to the court that if he is found guilty of the offence the criteria for the imposition of a sentence under section 226B of that Act would be met.

(4)   Where the court sends a child or young person for trial under subsection (2) above, it may at the same time send him to the Crown Court for trial for any indictable or summary offence with which he is charged and which—
   (a)   (if it is an indictable offence) appears to the court to be related to the offence mentioned in subsection (2) above; or
   (b)   (if it is a summary offence) appears to the court to be related to the offence mentioned in subsection (2) above or to the indictable offence, and which fulfils the requisite condition (as defined in subsection (9) below).

(5)   Where a child or young person who has been sent for trial under subsection (2) above subsequently appears or is brought before a magistrates' court charged with an indictable or summary offence which—
   (a)   appears to the court to be related to the offence mentioned in subsection (2) above; and
   (b)   (in the case of a summary offence) fulfils the requisite condition,
   the court may send him forthwith to the Crown Court for trial for the indictable or summary offence.

(6)   Where—
   (a)   the court sends a child or young person ('C') for trial under subsection (2) or (4) above; and
   (b)   an adult appears or is brought before the court on the same or a subsequent occasion charged jointly with C with an either-way offence for which C is sent for trial under subsection (2) or (4) above, or an either-way offence which appears to the court to be related to that offence,

the court shall where it is the same occasion, and may where it is a subsequent occasion, send the adult forthwith to the Crown Court for trial for the either-way offence.

(7) Where the court sends an adult for trial under subsection (6) above, it shall at the same time send him to the Crown Court for trial for any either-way or summary offence with which he is charged and which—

    (a) (if it is an either-way offence) appears to the court to be related to the offence for which he was sent for trial; and

    (b) (if it is a summary offence) appears to the court to be related to the offence for which he was sent for trial or to the either-way offence, and which fulfils the requisite condition.

(8) The trial of the information charging any summary offence for which a person is sent for trial under this section shall be treated as if the court had adjourned it under section 10 of the 1980 Act and had not fixed the time and place for its resumption.

(9) A summary offence fulfils the requisite condition if it is punishable with imprisonment or involves obligatory or discretionary disqualification from driving.

(10) In the case of a child or young person charged with an offence—

    (a) if the offence satisfies any of the conditions in subsection (3) above, the offence shall be dealt with under subsection (2) above and not under any other provision of this section or section 51 above;

    (b) subject to paragraph (a) above, if the offence is one in respect of which the requirements of subsection (7) of section 51 above for sending the child or young person to the Crown Court are satisfied, the offence shall be dealt with under that subsection and not under any other provision of this section or section 51 above.

(11) The functions of a magistrates' court under this section, and its related functions under section 51D below, may be discharged by a single justice.

(12) An offence falls within this subsection if—

    (a) it is an offence of homicide; or

    (b) each of the requirements of section 51A(1) of the Firearms Act 1968 would be satisfied with respect to—

        (i) the offence; and

        (ii) the person charged with it,

    if he were convicted of the offence; or

    (c) section 29(3) of the Violent Crime Reduction Act 2006 (minimum sentences in certain cases of using someone to mind a weapon) would apply if he were convicted of the offence.

Crime and Disorder Act 1998, sch. 3, para. 13

D24.44

(1) This paragraph applies, in place of paragraphs 7 to 12 above, in the case of a child or young person who—

    (a) has been sent for trial under section 51 or 51A of this Act but has not been arraigned; and

    (b) is charged on an indictment which (following amendment of the indictment, or as a result of an application under paragraph 2 above, or for any other reason) includes no main offence.

(2) The Crown Court shall remit the child or young person for trial to a magistrates' court acting for the place where he was sent to the Crown Court for trial.

(3) In this paragraph, a 'main offence' is—

    (a) an offence for which the child or young person has been sent to the Crown Court for trial under section 51A(2) of this Act; or

    (b) an offence—

        (i) for which the child or young person has been sent to the Crown Court for trial under subsection (7) of section 51 of this Act; and

        (ii) in respect of which the conditions for sending him to the Crown Court for trial under that subsection (as set out in paragraphs (a) and (b) of that subsection) continue to be satisfied.

'Plea before Venue' Procedure for Juveniles The MCA 1980, ss. 24A to 24D, apply a procedure similar to that contained in ss. 17A to 17C of that Act (the 'plea before venue' hearing) to cases involving an accused who is under the age of 18. **D24.45**

The plea before venue procedure set out in s. 24A applies where the court would otherwise be required to send a juvenile to the Crown Court for trial by virtue of the CDA 1998, s. 51(7) or

(8) (cases where there is an adult co-accused) or s. 51A(3)(b), (4), or (5) (cases falling within the ambit of the PCC(S)A 2000, s. 91). However, s. 24A does not apply where a juvenile is charged with an offence listed in the CDA 1998, s. 51A(12), namely homicide or cases where the requirements of the Firearms Act 1968, s. 51A(1), or the VCRA 2006, s 29(3), would apply if he were convicted of the offence. It follows that, except in the cases which fall within s. 51A(12), a plea before venue hearing has to take place where there is a possibility of the juvenile being tried in the Crown Court because he is charged jointly with an adult or where the offence is one to which the PCC(S)A 2000, s. 91, applies.

In those cases, the juvenile is invited to indicate whether he intends to plead guilty or not guilty (s. 24A(6)). If he indicates that he intends to enter a guilty plea, he is deemed to have pleaded guilty at that point (s. 24A(7)). The magistrates then proceed to the sentencing stage; if the offence is one to which the PCC(S)A 2000, s. 91, applies, the magistrates may commit the juvenile to the Crown Court for sentence under the PCC(S)A 2000, s. 3B (see **D24.61**), if they take the view that their sentencing powers are insufficient. If the juvenile indicates a not guilty plea (or gives no indication as to intended plea), the magistrates proceed to determine mode of trial (s. 24A(8) and (9)). Thus, if the case is one to which s. 91 of the 2000 Act applies, the magistrates go on to consider whether it ought to be possible to impose a sentence of detention under that section if the juvenile is found guilty of it; if the case is one where the juvenile is charged alongside an adult who is to be tried in the Crown Court, the magistrates go on to consider whether it is necessary in the interests of justice for the juvenile to be sent to the Crown Court for trial as well.

D24.46   Section 24B enables the plea before venue procedure to be determined in the absence of the juvenile if he is legally represented, and the court considers that, because of the juvenile's disorderly conduct before the court, it is not practicable for proceedings to be conducted in his presence, and the court considers that it should proceed in his absence. In such cases, the legal representative is invited to enter a plea on behalf of the juvenile (and an indication by the representative of an intended guilty plea is deemed to be a plea of guilty under s. 24B(2)(c)).

Proceedings under s. 24A or 24B can be adjourned. Where the accused is present, the adjournment may take the form of a remand, either in custody or on bail (s. 24C). The functions of the magistrates' court under ss. 24A to 24C may be exercised by a single justice (s. 24D(1)).

D24.47   Magistrates' Courts Act 1980, ss. 24A to 24D

24A.—(1) This section applies where—
  (a) a person under the age of 18 years appears or is brought before a magistrates' court on an information charging him with an offence other than one falling within section 51A(12) of the Crime and Disorder Act 1998 ('the 1998 Act'); and
  (b) but for the application of the following provisions of this section, the court would be required at that stage, by virtue of section 51(7) or (8) or 51A(3)(b), (4) or (5) of the 1998 Act to determine, in relation to the offence, whether to send the person to the Crown Court for trial (or to determine any matter, the effect of which would be to determine whether he is sent to the Crown Court for trial).
  (2) Where this section applies, the court shall, before proceeding to make any such determination as is referred to in subsection (1)(b) above (the 'relevant determination'), follow the procedure set out in this section.
  (3) Everything that the court is required to do under the following provisions of this section must be done with the accused person in court.
  (4) The court shall cause the charge to be written down, if this has not already been done, and to be read to the accused.
  (5) The court shall then explain to the accused in ordinary language that he may indicate whether (if the offence were to proceed to trial) he would plead guilty or not guilty, and that if he indicates that he would plead guilty—
    (a) the court must proceed as mentioned in subsection (7) below; and
    (b) (in cases where the offence is one mentioned in section 91(1) of the Powers of Criminal Courts (Sentencing) Act 2000) he may be sent to the Crown Court for sentencing under section 3B or (if applicable) 3C of that Act if the court is of such opinion as is mentioned in subsection (2) of the applicable section.

(6) The court shall then ask the accused whether (if the offence were to proceed to trial) he would plead guilty or not guilty.

(7) If the accused indicates that he would plead guilty, the court shall proceed as if—

(a) the proceedings constituted from the beginning the summary trial of the information; and

(b) section 9(1) above was complied with and he pleaded guilty under it,

and, accordingly, the court shall not (and shall not be required to) proceed to make the relevant determination or to proceed further under section 51 or (as the case may be) section 51A of the 1998 Act in relation to the offence.

(8) If the accused indicates that he would plead not guilty, the court shall proceed to make the relevant determination and this section shall cease to apply.

(9) If the accused in fact fails to indicate how he would plead, for the purposes of this section he shall be taken to indicate that he would plead not guilty.

(10) Subject to subsection (7) above, the following shall not for any purpose be taken to constitute the taking of a plea—

(a) asking the accused under this section whether (if the offence were to proceed to trial) he would plead guilty or not guilty;

(b) an indication by the accused under this section of how he would plead.

24B.—(1) This section shall have effect where—

(a) a person under the age of 18 years appears or is brought before a magistrates' court on an information charging him with an offence other than one falling within section 51A(12) of the Crime and Disorder Act 1998;

(b) but for the application of the following provisions of this section, the court would be required at that stage to make one of the determinations referred to in paragraph (b) of section 24A(1) above ('the relevant determination');

(c) the accused is represented by a legal representative;

(d) the court considers that by reason of the accused's disorderly conduct before the court it is not practicable for proceedings under section 24A above to be conducted in his presence; and

(e) the court considers that it should proceed in the absence of the accused.

(2) In such a case—

(a) the court shall cause the charge to be written down, if this has not already been done, and to be read to the representative;

(b) the court shall ask the representative whether (if the offence were to proceed to trial) the accused would plead guilty or not guilty;

(c) if the representative indicates that the accused would plead guilty the court shall proceed as if the proceedings constituted from the beginning the summary trial of the information, and as if section 9(1) above was complied with and the accused pleaded guilty under it;

(d) if the representative indicates that the accused would plead not guilty the court shall proceed to make the relevant determination and this section shall cease to apply.

(3) If the representative in fact fails to indicate how the accused would plead, for the purposes of this section he shall be taken to indicate that the accused would plead not guilty.

(4) Subject to subsection (2)(c) above, the following shall not for any purpose be taken to constitute the taking of a plea—

(a) asking the representative under this section whether (if the offence were to proceed to trial) the accused would plead guilty or not guilty;

(b) an indication by the representative under this section of how the accused would plead.

24C.—(1) A magistrates' court proceeding under section 24A or 24B above may adjourn the proceedings at any time, and on doing so on any occasion when the accused is present may remand the accused.

(2) Where the court remands the accused, the time fixed for the resumption of proceedings shall be that at which he is required to appear or be brought before the court in pursuance of the remand or would be required to be brought before the court but for section 128(3A) below.

24D.—(1) The functions of a magistrates' court under sections 24A to 24C above may be discharged by a single justice.

(2) Subsection (1) above shall not be taken as authorising—

(a) the summary trial of an information (other than a summary trial by virtue of section 24A(7) or 24B(2)(c) above); or

(b) the imposition of a sentence,

by a magistrates' court composed of fewer than two justices.

D

Where Juvenile is Charged with an Adult

D24.48 The CDA 1998, s. 51(7), applies where an adult is sent for trial under s. 51 and a juvenile appears before the court (whether on the same or a subsequent occasion) charged jointly with an adult who has been sent for trial for the same or a related offence. It provides that the court shall, if it considers it necessary in the interests of justice to do so, send the child or young person forthwith to the Crown Court for trial for the indictable offence. By virtue of s. 51(8), the juvenile may also be sent for trial for any related offences (though if a related offence is a summary offence this provision will apply only if it is punishable with imprisonment or involves obligatory or discretionary disqualification from driving).

Crime and Disorder Act 1998, s. 51

(7) Where—
  (a) the court sends an adult ('A') for trial under subsection (1), (3) or (5) above; and
  (b) a child or young person appears or is brought before the court on the same or a subsequent occasion charged jointly with A with an indictable offence for which A is sent for trial under subsection (1), (3) or (5) above, or an indictable offence which appears to the court to be related to that offence,
  the court shall, if it considers it necessary in the interests of justice to do so, send the child or young person forthwith to the Crown Court for trial for the indictable offence.
(8) Where the court sends a child or young person for trial under subsection (7) above, it may at the same time send him to the Crown Court for trial for any indictable or summary offence with which he is charged and which—
  (a) (if it is an indictable offence) appears to the court to be related to the offence for which he is sent for trial; and
  (b) (if it is a summary offence) appears to the court to be related to the offence for which he is sent for trial or to the indictable offence, and which fulfils the requisite condition.
(9) Subsections (7) and (8) above are subject to sections 24A and 24B of the Magistrates' Courts Act 1980 (which provide for certain cases involving children and young persons to be tried summarily).

D24.49 Determining Mode of Trial   The court will invite representations from the prosecution and defence on the issue of whether or not it is 'necessary in the interests of justice' to send the juvenile to the Crown Court.

In coming to their decision on this question, the justices have to balance what may well be conflicting interests. On one hand, it is desirable that there should be a joint trial (to avoid prosecution witnesses having to give their evidence twice, to avoid the risk of inconsistent verdicts, and to avoid the risk of disparity in the sentences which are passed in the event of conviction). On the other hand, a juvenile may well find appearing in the Crown Court an unduly traumatic experience. It is submitted that the younger the juvenile and the less serious the charge, the more reluctant the justices should be to send the juvenile to the Crown Court. Also relevant are the likely plea of the juvenile, and the degree of his involvement in the offence: if the juvenile is likely to plead guilty and it is accepted by the prosecution that he played only a minor role in the offence, it is likely to be more appropriate to deal with him separately.

In *R (DPP) v East Surrey Youth Court (Ghanbari, interested party)* [2006] 2 All ER 444, the Divisional Court said that, when deciding whether or not to send a juvenile for trial in the Crown Court, justices should bear in mind the policy of the legislature is that those who are under 18 should, wherever possible, be tried in a youth court, which is designed for their specific needs. When an accused under the age of 18 is jointly charged with an adult, an exercise of judgement is called for by the youth court when assessing the competing presumptions in favour of (i) joint trial of those jointly charged, and (ii) the trial of young defendants in the youth court. Factors relevant to that judgement will include the age and maturity of the young defendant, the comparative culpability in relation to the offence and the previous convictions of the two and whether the trial can be severed without either injustice or undue inconvenience to witnesses (per Rose LJ at [17]).

The definitive sentencing guideline *Overarching Principles — Sentencing Youths* states (at **D24.50** para. 12.16: see Supplement, **SG-527**) that any presumption in favour of sending a juvenile to the Crown Court to be tried jointly with an adult must be balanced with the general presumption that juveniles should be dealt with in the youth court. Paragraph 12.17 indicates that, when deciding whether to separate the juvenile and adult defendants, the court must consider:

(a) the young age of the offender, particularly where the age gap between the adult and youth is substantial,
(b) the immaturity and intellect of the youth,
(c) the relative culpability of the youth compared with the adult and whether or not the role played by the youth was minor, and
(d) any lack of previous convictions on the part of the youth compared with the adult offender.

Paragraph 12.18 adds that a 'very significant factor' will be whether the trial of the adult and the juvenile could be severed 'without inconvenience to witnesses or injustice to the case as a whole', and notes the benefit in the same tribunal sentencing all offenders. The guidance concludes that, in 'most circumstances, a single trial of all issues is likely to be most in the interests of justice'.

Similar points are made in the CPS guidance on 'youth offenders', where the relevant factors **D24.51** are said to include:

(a) the respective ages of the adult and youth;
(b) the respective roles of the youth and adult in the commission of the offence;
(c) the likely plea;
(d) whether there are existing charges against the youth before the youth court;
(e) the need to deal with the youth as expeditiously as possible consistent with the interests of justice; and
(f) the likely sentence upon conviction.

The definitive sentencing guideline *Allocation* (see Supplement, **SG-590**) gives some examples of factors that should be considered when deciding whether to separate the juvenile and the adult. Those factors include: whether separate trials can take place without causing undue inconvenience to witnesses or injustice to the case as a whole; the age of the juvenile, particularly if there is a substantial gap between his age and the adult's; the immaturity of the juvenile; the relative culpability of the juvenile compared with the adult (e.g., whether the role played was minor); and the lack of previous findings of guilty recorded against the juvenile.

No Power to Remit to Youth Court In *R (W (a minor)) v Leeds Crown Court* [2012] 1 Cr App **D24.52** R 162, the Divisional Court ruled that, where an adult and a juvenile are charged together and the adult is to be tried in the Crown Court, and the magistrates decide that it is necessary in the interests of justice for the juvenile to be tried in the Crown Court as well, the Crown Court has no power to remit the juvenile back to the youth court for trial even if, for example, the adult pleads guilty in the Crown Court and so the juvenile will be tried alone in the Crown Court.

Procedure where Juvenile is Not Sent with Adult to the Crown Court for Trial If the juve- **D24.53** nile indicates a plea of guilty, and is thereby deemed to have pleaded guilty, the magistrates will consider whether their sentencing powers in respect of the juvenile are adequate. Those powers are to make any one or more of the following orders (PCC(S)A 2000, s. 8(8)):

(a) absolute discharge;
(b) conditional discharge;
(c) a fine (up to £1,000 for a juvenile who has attained the age of 14; up to £250 for one who has not: PCC(S)A 2000, s. 135);
(d) requiring the juvenile's parents to enter into a recognizance to keep proper control of him.

An adult magistrates' court is also able to make a referral order under the PCC(S)A 2000, s. 16(1).

If the powers contained in the PCC(S)A 2000, s. 8(8), are not sufficient, the justices will remit the juvenile to the youth court to be sentenced (under the PCC(S)A 2000, s. 8(6)).

If the case is one where, in the youth court, a referral order would be mandatory under the PCC(S)A 2000, s. 16(2), the adult magistrates' court may, but is not obliged to, remit the case to the youth court (s. 8(7)).

If, on the other hand, the juvenile pleads not guilty, the adult magistrates' court may try him or remit him for trial to the youth court (under the MCA 1980, s. 29(2)). In the absence of a good reason to the contrary (e.g. the prosecution wishing to offer no evidence), it is submitted that he should normally be remitted to the youth court for trial.

D24.54   **Procedure where Adult Co-accused is Tried Summarily**   Where the juvenile is jointly charged with an adult who is to be tried summarily (i.e. the offence is a summary one, or an either-way offence where the adult defendant and the justices both agreed to summary trial), the procedure is as follows. If the juvenile indicates a plea of not guilty at the plea before venue hearing, the adult court *must* try him (CYPA 1933, s. 46(1)(a)). If he indicates a guilty plea at the plea before venue hearing, or if he is subsequently found guilty, the magistrates will remit him to the youth court for sentence if the sentences which the adult court can impose (see **D24.53**) are inappropriate. If the adult pleads guilty and the juvenile pleads not guilty, the adult magistrates' court *may* try him under the MCA 1980, s. 29(2), or else remit him to the youth court for trial. Although the magistrates could theoretically try the juvenile (even though the adult has pleaded guilty, so that there will be no trial of the adult), it is much more likely that they will remit him to the youth court for trial. There is little justification for trying a juvenile on his own in the adult magistrates' court. If the juvenile pleads guilty (or the adult court does try him and he is found guilty), the adult court will remit him to the youth court if none of the sentences which the adult court can impose are appropriate.

Where the juvenile is charged with aiding and abetting the adult or the adult is charged with aiding and abetting the juvenile, the adult magistrates' court has a discretion to try them both if they both plead not guilty (CYPA 1933, s. 46(1)(b); CYPA 1963, s. 18(a)). If the adult and juvenile are charged with offences which arise out of the same circumstances and both plead not guilty, the adult magistrates' court may either try the juvenile or remit him to the youth court for trial (CYPA 1963, s. 18(b)). If the adult pleads guilty and the juvenile not guilty, the magistrates are likely to remit the juvenile to the youth court for trial; if the adult magistrates' court tries the juvenile and convicts him, he will be remitted to the youth court for sentence if the magistrates' sentencing powers (see above) are inappropriate.

D24.55   **Where the PCC(S)A 2000, s. 91, Applies and there is an Adult Co-accused**   There will be cases where a juvenile and an adult are charged with an offence to which the PCC(S)A 2000, s. 91, applies, and so the CDA 1998, ss. 51(7) and 51A(2), are both relevant. If the adult is sent to the Crown Court for trial, the question of whether a sentence under s. 91 would be appropriate in the event of the juvenile being convicted of the offence will be highly relevant to the decision whether to send the juvenile to the Crown Court for trial. As both defendants will be appearing in the adult magistrates' court, it will be that court which takes the decision on where the juvenile is to be tried. The adult court has no power to remit the juvenile to the youth court for that court to decide mode of trial (*Tottenham Youth Court, ex parte Fawzy* [1999] 1 All ER 365).

D24.56   **Severance**   CPD I, para. 3G.1 (see Supplement, **PD-9**), says that if a 'vulnerable defendant, especially one who is young, is to be tried jointly with one who is not, the court should consider at the plea and case management hearing, or at a case management hearing in a magistrates' court, whether the vulnerable defendant should be tried on his own'; however, the court should only so order 'if satisfied that a fair trial cannot be achieved by use of appropriate special measures or other support for the defendant'. If a vulnerable defendant is tried jointly with one who is not, the court should consider modifications to the trial process to accommodate the needs of the vulnerable defendant.

If the offence with which the adult and juvenile are charged is one which falls within the ambit of the PCC(S)A 2000, s. 91, or the 'dangerous offender' provisions of the CJA 2003, but the court orders that the adult and the juvenile be tried separately, the juvenile would still be tried in the Crown Court (with its procedures modified as appropriate). However, if the offence does not fall within the scope of these provisions, it seems anomalous that the juvenile should still be tried in the Crown Court even though he is being tried separately from the adult. Nevertheless, this is inevitable, as there is currently no statutory power enabling the Crown Court to remit the juvenile to the youth court for trial in such a case.

Varying the Decision on Mode of Trial

The MCA 1980, s. 25, which enables the prosecution to apply to the magistrates' court to reverse a decision in favour of summary trial, applies only where the accused has attained the age of 18, and so is inapplicable in the case of juveniles. **D24.57**

Challenging the Decision to Try a Case Summarily

Where the decision of the justices to try the case summarily is alleged to be unreasonable, the appropriate remedy for the prosecution is to seek judicial review (*Inner London Youth Court, ex parte DPP* (1997) 161 JP 178). **D24.58**

In *R (D) v Sheffield Youth Court* (2008) 172 JP 576, the accused (a juvenile) appeared in an adult magistrates' court charged with offences falling under the PCC(S)A 2000, s. 91, and he was jointly charged with adults. The magistrates' court allowed the accused to enter pleas of guilty to all charges against him and then remitted him to the youth court for the accused to be dealt with there. Richards LJ said (at [18]) that he did not think that it was Parliament's intention that failure to consider the matters set out in what is now the CDA 1998, ss. 51(7) and 51A(2), should render subsequent steps invalid. It followed that, despite the failure of the court to consider the relevant statutory provisions, there had been a valid acceptance of summary jurisdiction by the magistrates' court; equally, the subsequent decision to remit the case to the youth court was valid. His lordship added that the failure of the magistrates' court to proceed in the way that it should have done did not empower the youth court subsequently to reopen the matter under the MCA 1980, s. 142; it was too late for the matter to be reopened in that way.

COMMITTAL FOR SENTENCE

Three powers of committal for sentence under the PCC(S)A 2000 are relevant to juveniles: s. 3B (which applies where a juvenile gives an indication of a guilty plea to an offence to which s. 91 applies); s. 3C (which applies where a juvenile pleads guilty to, or is found guilty of, an offence for which an extended sentence under the CJA 2003, s 226B, may be imposed); and s. 4A (which applies where a juvenile is sent for trial for one or more offences but also indicates a guilty plea for one or more other offences). **D24.59**

Committal under the Powers of Criminal Courts (Sentencing) Act 2000, s. 3B

The PCC(S)A 2000, s. 3B, provides that, where a juvenile (or his representative) indicates a guilty plea at the plea before venue hearing (under the MCA 1980, s. 24A, or s. 24B, as the case may be), and the court is of the opinion that the offence (together with any associated offences) is such that the Crown Court should have power to deal with the offender under the PCC(S)A 2000, s. 91, then the court may commit him (in custody or on bail) to the Crown Court for sentence. **D24.60**

Section 3B(3) provides that, where a juvenile is committed for sentence under s. 3B(2), s. 6 of the 2000 Act (which enables a magistrates' court to commit the offender to the Crown Court to be dealt with in respect of other offences) is applicable.

It should be noted that s. 3B does not apply where the young defendant indicates an intention to plead not guilty (or gives no indication) and is convicted after summary trial; in such cases, the youth court must pass sentence itself.

D24.61   Powers of Criminal Courts (Sentencing) Act 2000, s. 3B

(1) This section applies where—
   (a) a person aged under 18 appears or is brought before a magistrates' court ('the court') on an information charging him with an offence mentioned in subsection (1) of section 91 below ('the offence');
   (b) he or his representative indicates under section 24A or (as the case may be) 24B of the Magistrates' Courts Act 1980 (child or young person to indicate intention as to plea in certain cases) that he would plead guilty if the offence were to proceed to trial; and
   (c) proceeding as if section 9(1) of that Act were complied with and he pleaded guilty under it, the court convicts him of the offence.
(2) If the court is of the opinion that—
   (a) the offence; or
   (b) the combination of the offence and one or more offences associated with it, was such that the Crown Court should, in the court's opinion, have power to deal with the offender as if the provisions of section 91(3) below applied, the court may commit him in custody or on bail to the Crown Court for sentence in accordance with section 5A(1) below.
(3) Where the court commits a person under subsection (2) above, section 6 below (which enables a magistrates' court, where it commits a person under this section in respect of an offence, also to commit him to the Crown Court to be dealt with in respect of certain other offences) shall apply accordingly.

Committal for Sentence: Related Offences Sent for Trial

D24.62   The PCC(S)A 2000, s. 4A, applies where a juvenile is charged with an offence to which s. 91 of the 2000 Act applies and, at the 'plea before venue' hearing, the juvenile (or his representative) indicates an intention to plead guilty to that offence. Under s. 4A(2), if the court has sent the offender to the Crown Court for trial for one or more offences that are related to the s. 91 offence, it may commit him (in custody or on bail) to the Crown Court to be dealt with in respect of the s. 91 offence. Under s. 4A(4), if the magistrates commit the s. 91 offence to the Crown Court for sentence but do not state that, in their opinion, the case is one where it ought to be possible to impose detention under s. 91, the Crown Court cannot impose detention under s. 91 for that offence (and so is limited to the sentences that could be imposed by the youth court) unless the juvenile is convicted by the Crown Court of one or more of the related offences. This provision thus mirrors the PCC(S)A 2000, s. 4, which is applicable to adult offenders.

Powers of Criminal Courts (Sentencing) Act 2000, s. 4A

(1) This section applies where—
   (a) a person aged under 18 appears or brought before a magistrates' court ('the court') on an information charging him with an offence mentioned in subsection (1) of section 91 below ('the offence');
   (b) he or his representative indicates under section 24A or (as the case may be) 24B of the Magistrates' Courts Act 1980 (child or young person to indicate intention as to plea in certain cases) that he would plead guilty if the offence were to proceed to trial; and
   (c) proceeding as if section 9(1) of that Act were complied with and he pleaded guilty under it, the court convicts him of the offence.
(2) If the court has sent the offender to the Crown Court for trial for one or more related offences, that is to say one or more offences which, in its opinion, are related to the offence, it may commit him in custody or on bail to the Crown Court to be dealt with in respect of the offence in accordance with section 5A(1) below.
(3) If the power conferred by subsection (2) above is not exercisable but the court is still to determine to, or to determine whether to, send the offender to the Crown Court for trial under section 51 or 51A of the Crime and Disorder Act 1998 for one or more related offences—
   (a) it shall adjourn the proceedings relating to the offence until after it has made those determinations; and

(b) if it sends the offender to the Crown Court for trial for one or more related offences, it may then exercise that power.

(4) Where the court—
  (a) under subsection (2) above commits the offender to the Crown Court to be dealt with in respect of the offence; and
  (b) does not state that, in its opinion, it also has power so to commit him under section 38(2) or, as the case may be, section 3C(2) above,

section 5A(1) below shall not apply unless he is convicted before the Crown Court of one or more of the related offences.

(5) Where section 5A(1) below does not apply, the Crown Court may deal with the offender in respect of the offence in any way in which the magistrates' court could deal with him if it had just convicted him of the offence.

(6) Where the court commits a person under subsection (2) above, section 6 below (which enables a magistrates' court, where it commits a person under this section in respect of an offence, also to commit him to the Crown Court to be dealt with in respect of certain other offences) shall apply accordingly.

(7) Section 4(7) above applies for the purposes of this section as it applies for the purposes of that section.

Committal for Sentence: Dangerous Offenders

The PCC(S)A 2000, s. 3C, enables committal for sentence of dangerous young offenders. **D24.63** Where a juvenile is convicted of an offence specified in the CJA 2003, s. 224, and it appears to the court that the criteria for the imposition of a sentence under s. 226B would be met, the court must commit the offender (in custody or on bail) to the Crown Court for sentence (s. 3C(2)). The power to commit for sentence under s. 3C can be exercised whether the accused pleaded guilty or was found guilty. According to Pitchford LJ in *R (BW) v Caernarfon Youth Court* (2013) 177 JP 534 (at [18]–[19]), this is to take account of the fact that:

> ...there may become available to the court, either in the course of evidence or upon the production of pre-sentence reports, information which drives the tribunal to alter its opinion as to the seriousness of the offences committed, and the risk for the future of repetition. For that reason, the court is given a residual power in very exceptional circumstances to commit to the Crown court for sentence, notwithstanding the original acceptance of summary jurisdiction.

The offender can also be committed (under the PCC(S)A 2000, s. 6) to be sentenced for other offences that the magistrates would otherwise be dealing with (s. 3C(3)). Section 3C(4) makes it clear that s. 3C does not prevent the court from committing a specified offence to the Crown Court for sentence under s. 3B if the provisions of that section are satisfied.

Powers of Criminal Courts (Sentencing) Act 2000, s. 3C **D24.64**

(1) This section applies where on the summary trial of a specified offence a person aged under 18 is convicted of the offence.

(2) If, in relation to the offence, it appears to the court that the criteria for the imposition of a sentence under section 226B of the Criminal Justice Act 2003 would be met, the court must commit the offender in custody or on bail to the Crown Court for sentence in accordance with section 5A(1) below.

(3) Where the court commits a person under subsection (2) above, section 6 below (which enables a magistrates' court, where it commits a person under this section in respect of an offence, also to commit him to the Crown Court to be dealt with in respect of certain other offences) shall apply accordingly.

(4) Nothing in this section shall prevent the court from committing a specified offence to the Crown Court for sentence under section 3B above if the provisions of that section are satisfied.

(5) In this section, references to a specified offence are to a specified offence within the meaning of section 224 of the Criminal Justice Act 2003.

Powers of Crown Court Following Committal for Sentence

The PCC(S)A 2000, s. 5A, provides that, where an offender is committed for sentence under **D24.65** s. 3B, 3C or 4A, the Crown Court may deal with the offender in any way in which it could deal with him if he had just been convicted of the offence on indictment. It should be noted, however, that in *Robson* [2007] 1 All ER 506, the Court of Appeal ruled that the Crown Court is required to pass sentence on the basis of the age of the offender at the date of conviction (not the age of appearance before the Crown Court).

Powers of Criminal Courts (Sentencing) Act 2000, s. 5A

(1) Where an offender is committed by a magistrates' court for sentence under section 3B, 3C or 4A above, the Crown Court shall inquire into the circumstances of the case and may deal with the offender in any way in which it could deal with him if he had just been convicted of the offence on indictment before the court.

(2) In relation to committals under section 4A above, subsection (1) above has effect subject to section 4A(4) and (5) above.

Relationship between the Powers of Criminal Courts (Sentencing) Act 2000 and Dangerous Offender Provisions

D24.66 The existence of the power of committal for sentence conferred by the PCC(S)A 2000, s. 3C, necessitates consideration of the relationship between s. 91 of that Act and the dangerous offender provisions (CJA 2003, s. 226B). If the offence is a 'specified offence' (as defined by the CJA 2003, s. 224(1) — i.e. an offence specified in sch. 15 of that Act), the youth court must send the juvenile to the Crown Court (under the CDA 1998, s. 51A(3)(d)) if the justices are of the opinion that the Crown Court will take the view that there is a significant risk to members of the public of serious harm occasioned by the commission by the offender of further specified offences. If the offence is a 'serious offence' (as defined by s. 224(2) — i.e. an offence specified in sch. 15 and punishable with a life sentence), the youth court must similarly send the juvenile to the Crown Court for trial (under the CDA 1998, s. 51A(3)(b)) if the justices are of the opinion that it ought to be possible to sentence him under the PCC(S)A 2000, s. 91 (in this case to a sentence of detention for life pursuant to the CJA 2003, s. 226) because the Crown Court would take the view that there is a significant risk to members of the public of serious harm occasioned by the commission by the offender of further specified offences.

D24.67 There are, essentially, three categories of offence:

(a) offences which fall within s. 91 but which are not 'specified offences' under s. 224: the court follows the plea before venue procedure (under the MCA 1980, s. 24A), and may commit the juvenile to the Crown Court for sentence, under the PCC(S)A 2000, s. 3B, if he indicates a guilty plea.

(b) offences which are 'specified offences' but which do not fall within s. 91: the justices must decide whether it appears to them that the criteria for the imposition of a sentence under the CJA 2003, s. 226B, are satisfied. If the justices take the view that the criteria are satisfied, they must send the juvenile to the Crown Court for trial. If the justices take the view that the criteria are not satisfied, they will try the case summarily. If they try the case and convict the juvenile, and decide at that stage that the criteria are, in fact, satisfied (they will, of course, have much more information by that stage), they must commit the juvenile to the Crown Court for sentence under the PCC(S)A 2000, s. 3C(2).

(c) offences that are both 'specified' offences and fall within s. 91: the justices will go through the 'plea before venue' procedure. If the juvenile indicates a guilty plea, he may be committed for sentence either under s. 3B, on the basis that the justices are of the opinion that the Crown Court should have power to impose detention under s. 91 (a test that depends on the seriousness of the offence), or under s. 3C, on the basis that it appears to the court that the criteria for the imposition of a sentence under s. 226B would be met (a test that depends largely on there being a significant risk of future serious harm). If the juvenile indicates an intention to plead not guilty (or gives no indication), the justices have to decide whether to try the case summarily or to send the juvenile for trial in the Crown Court. If the justices take the view that the Crown Court ought to be able to pass a sentence under s. 91 or that the defendant is likely to satisfy the criteria for a sentence under

s. 226B, they must send the juvenile for trial in the Crown Court. If the justices decide to try the case themselves and they find the juvenile guilty, they will be able to commit him to the Crown Court for sentence under s. 3C (if they decide, at that stage, that the criteria for a sentence under s. 226B are met) but not under s. 3B (which applies only to guilty pleas). If the juvenile is committed for sentence under s. 3C, the Crown Court has power (under s. 5A) to impose a sentence under s. 91 if it decides that the criteria for a sentence under s. 226B are not in fact met.

MODE OF TRIAL AND PROCEDURE FOR PERSONS CLOSE TO 18TH BIRTHDAY

This part of the section deals with the various provisions relevant to persons whose age at the time of proceedings against them places them on the borderline between being a juvenile or an adult (i.e. close to their 18th birthday). Some of the relevant case law was decided at a time when the determining event was the accused's 17th birthday, and so it needs to be borne in mind that the coming into force of the CJA 1991, s. 68, made the 18th birthday the watershed at which a juvenile becomes an adult.   **D24.68**

Determining Age

By the CYPA 1933, s. 99(1), where a person apparently under 18 is brought before a court, the court is to make 'due inquiry' as to his age and must take into account such evidence on the matter as may be forthcoming at the hearing of the case. However, any order or judgment of the court is not to be invalidated by subsequent proof that the person's age was incorrectly stated, and he is deemed for purposes of the 1933 Act to be whatever age he is presumed or declared to be by the court (s. 99(1)). The court is entitled to accept what he (or his parent or guardian, if present) says on the matter, although in cases of doubt it may ask for further inquiries to be undertaken. The MCA 1980, s. 150(4), makes similar provision in respect of age-dependent powers granted to magistrates by that Act. For the purposes of the PCC(S)A 2000, a person's age 'shall be deemed to be that which it appears to the court ... after considering any available evidence' (s. 164(1)).   **D24.69**

Children and Young Persons Act 1933, s. 99   **D24.70**

(1) Where a person, whether charged with an offence or not, is brought before any court otherwise than for the purposes of giving evidence, and it appears to the court that he is a child or young person, the court shall make due inquiry as to the age of that person, and for that purpose shall take such evidence as may be forthcoming at the hearing of the case, but an order or judgment of the court shall not be invalidated by any subsequent proof that the age of that person has not been correctly stated to the court, and the age presumed or declared by the court to be the age of the person so brought before it shall, for the purposes of this Act, be deemed to be the true age of that person, and, where it appears to the court that the person so brought before it has attained the age of 18 years, that person shall for the purposes of this Act be deemed not to be a child or young person.

[(2) to (4) deal with proof of age of the victim of an offence where the charge alleges that he was a child or young person.]

Magistrates' Courts Act 1980, s. 150

(4) Where the age of any person at any time is material for the purposes of any provision of this Act regulating the powers of a magistrates' court, his age at the material time shall be deemed to be or to have been that which appears to the court after considering any available evidence to be or to have been his age at that time.

Discovery of True Age during Proceedings

The statutory presumption in the MCA 1980, s.150(4), that an accused is whatever age he is declared to be by the court, prevents judgments or orders of the court (in particular, findings of guilt and sentences) being disturbed should it be discovered, after the conclusion of the proceedings, that the court was misled as to age. The presumption cannot assist   **D24.71** where it emerges during the course of the proceedings that the court's initial view about age was erroneous. However, proviso (c) of the CYPA 1933, s. 46(1), gives an adult magistrates' court which has embarked upon the trial of an accused in the belief that he was an adult the discretion to complete the hearing even if it should appear to the court during the course of the proceedings that he is in fact a juvenile. Conversely, s. 48(1) of the 1933 Act provides that:

> A youth court sitting for the purpose of hearing a charge against a person who is believed to be a child or young person may, if it thinks fit to do so, proceed with the hearing and determination of the charge notwithstanding that it is discovered that the person in question is not a child or young person.

Mode of Trial where Accused Attains the Age of 18 during Proceedings

D24.72 **Relevant Date**   In *Islington North Juvenile Court, ex parte Daley* [1983] 1 AC 347, the House of Lords had to consider at what stage of the proceedings an accused charged with an either-way offence must attain the relevant age (then 17, now 18) in order to entitle him to elect to be tried by a jury. Lord Diplock, with whom the other Law Lords agreed, held (at p. 364) that 'the only appropriate date at which to determine whether an accused person has attained an age which entitles him to elect to be tried by jury for offences which . . . are triable either way is the date of his appearance before the court on the occasion when the court makes its decision as to the mode of trial'. In *Ex parte Daley*, the accused was 16 when he made his first appearance in the juvenile court (when the case was simply adjourned). By the time he next appeared, he had attained the age of 17 and so had ceased to be a juvenile according to the law at the time. The effect of the decision of the House of Lords was that he was entitled to elect trial by jury, because he became an adult before mode of trial was determined. Thus, in *Nottingham Justices, ex parte Taylor* [1992] QB 557, the accused was aged 16 when he pleaded not guilty to charges of robbery. He attained the age of 17 (and hence, according to the law at the time, became an adult) before the court was ready to try the case. The Divisional Court held that the material date was that at which the mode of trial was determined, when he was still aged 16, and so he had to be tried summarily in the youth court. Similarly, in *Uxbridge Youth Court, ex parte H* (1998) 162 JP 327, the accused was 17 (and so a juvenile) when arrested and charged but, by the time he made his first appearance at the youth court, he had turned 18. The Divisional Court held that the youth court did not have jurisdiction to deal with the accused, since he had attained the age of 18 (and so was an adult) by the time of his first court appearance.

D24.73 The reference by Lord Diplock in *Ex parte Daley* to the moment when the youth court 'makes its decision as to the mode of trial' is unhelpful to the extent that the only situations in which the court has to choose between summary trial and trial on indictment are when either the juvenile is jointly charged with an adult who is being sent for trial or when the juvenile is charged with an offence which falls within the ambit of the PCC(S)A 2000, s. 91, or where the offence falls within the 'dangerous offender' provisions of the CJA 2003. In all other cases, there is no choice, since the juvenile *must* be tried summarily whether the magistrates like it or not (save when homicide is alleged or in the case of the other exceptions (see **D24.22**), in which case he must be tried on indictment). Thus, in the great majority of cases, there is no separate occasion on which mode of trial for a juvenile is determined — he is simply asked to plead guilty or not guilty. Therefore, it is submitted that Lord Diplock must be taken as having meant that the right of a person who attains the relevant age during the currency of proceedings against him to be tried on indictment for an indictable offence depends either upon his age when mode of trial is determined, or — if there is no express determination of mode of trial — upon his age when the court is ready for the charge to be put. If he is under that age on the occasion of entering a plea, he had no right to elect trial on indictment, even if the matter is forthwith adjourned for trial at a later date and he attains the age before any evidence is heard.

D24.74 The corollary of *Ex parte Daley* is that, where the offence charged is triable only on indictment in the case of an adult, an erstwhile juvenile must go to the Crown Court for trial if he attains the age of 18 before a plea is taken. In *Vale of Glamorgan Juvenile Justices, ex parte Beattie* (1986) 82 Cr App R 1, the youth court was held to have no power or discretion to proceed summarily on a charge of robbery because, even though the accused was 16 when he first appeared before the court, he had had his 17th birthday (and, according to the law at the time, then became an adult) before the court was ready to take a plea. The Divisional Court held that the material date for determining the mode of trial was the date when the charge was put to him and the proceedings were ready to be commenced.

It must also follow that, in cases where the sequence of events is as in *Ex parte Beattie* but the offence is triable either way, the 'juvenile', if he wants to be dealt with summarily, can only make representations to that effect, the court being entitled to refuse jurisdiction if it considers that the charge is too serious for summary disposal. Moreover, any summary trial would take place in the adult magistrates' court, not the youth court.

Additional Charges after Accused Attains the Age of 18

Where an accused against whom proceedings have properly been commenced in the youth **D24.75** court attains the age of 18 and is then charged with an additional matter, the latter charge may not be heard in the youth court (*Chelsea Justices, ex parte DPP* [1963] 3 All ER 657). That applies regardless of whether the youth court is able to retain jurisdiction over the original charge. Accordingly, in *Chelsea Justices, ex parte DPP*, the Divisional Court issued an order prohibiting the youth court from hearing a charge of attempted murder first preferred when the accused was 17 (and hence, at that time, an adult), even though it arose out of the same facts as a charge of wounding with intent preferred when he was 16.

Deliberate Delay until Accused Becomes 18

The position where the prosecution deliberately delays the issue of process, so that the accused **D24.76** is no longer a juvenile when he appears in court, was considered in *Rotherham Justices, ex parte Brough* [1991] Crim LR 522. The prosecution wanted the juvenile to be tried for an offence under s. 18 of the OAPA 1861, which would be triable only on indictment in the case of an adult. In order to avoid any possibility that the youth court might try him, his first court appearance was fixed for a date after his 17th birthday, which at that time was when he became an adult. The Divisional Court held that the accused had not been prejudiced since the delay was under a week, and the justices would probably have sent the case to the Crown Court for trial anyway. It is submitted, however, that this sort of manipulation of procedure could easily be held to amount to an abuse of process, particularly if there were any evidence of bad faith on the part of the prosecution or if the accused could point to particular prejudice from the delay in instituting proceedings.

TRIAL OF JUVENILES ON INDICTMENT

The procedure for trying a juvenile on indictment is identical to that for trying an adult, subject **D24.77** to certain modifications, which are discussed below.

Reporting Restrictions

Under the CYPA 1933, s. 39(1), a court may direct that no newspaper report of proceedings **D24.78** before it shall reveal the name, address, or school, or any particulars calculated to lead to the identification of any juvenile concerned in the proceedings. A direction may also be given that no picture of the juvenile shall be published. Section 39 applies to sound and television broadcasts just as it applies to reports in newspapers (CYPA 1963, s. 57(4)). However, as Tugendhat J pointed out in a civil case, *MXB v East Sussex Hospitals NHS Trust* (2013) 177 JP 31 (at [4]), there has been no extension of s. 39 to apply to any other form of report, such as one made via social media or published on the internet.

Section 39 applies to any court — Crown Court, adult magistrates' court or civil courts. It is otiose in respect of youth courts, since publicity for such proceedings is governed by s. 49 (see

D24.14). Under s. 39, the onus is on the court to make an order restricting publicity. If no order is made, the media are at liberty to report the names etc. of juveniles just as they are at liberty to report the names of adults. The protection of s.39 may be extended not just to a juvenile accused but to any juvenile involved in the proceedings (e.g., as a witness).

In *Jolleys* [2014] 1 Cr App R 215 (15), Leveson LJ confirmed (at [12]–[13]) that a person is 'concerned in the proceedings' for the purposes of the CYPA 1933, s. 39, if, and only if, he is the person by or against or in respect of whom the proceedings are taken, or a witness in those proceedings. In relation to criminal proceedings, this can only include a child or young person who is the victim of an alleged offence, or the defendant or a witness. It does not extend to children or young persons simply on the basis that they may be concerned in the more general sense of being affected by the offence or the proceedings.

In *JC v Central Criminal Court* (2014) 178 JP 188, it was held that an order made under s. 39 cannot extend to reports of the proceedings after the subject of the order has reached the age of majority at 18 (per Sir Brian Leveson P, at [39]).

D24.79 Publication of matter in contravention of a direction given under s. 39(1) is a summary offence punishable with a fine of up to £5,000 (s. 39(2)). Where an order under s. 39 is breached, the proper course is for the judge to report the matter so that proceedings for the summary offence created by s. 39 may be taken, not to treat it as a contempt of court (*Tyne Tees Television Ltd* (1997) *The Times*, 20 October 1997).

D24.80 **Criteria for Making an Order**   In *Central Criminal Court, ex parte S* (1999) 163 JP 776, the Divisional Court held that there has to be a good reason for making an order under s. 39 preventing identification of a juvenile who appears before an adult court. The Court said that in deciding whether or not to make such an order, the weight which the court should attach to the various factors relevant to the decision might be different at differing stages of the proceedings. For example, after the juvenile has been convicted, it might be appropriate to place greater weight on the interest of the public in knowing the identity of those who have committed serious crimes.

In considering the range of factors that may be considered by a court when determining whether or not to make a direction under s. 39, some useful guidance comes from the judgment of Simon Brown LJ in *Winchester Crown Court, ex parte B* [1999] 4 All ER 53 at p. 790 (that decision was not followed in *Manchester Crown Court, ex parte H and D* [2000] 2 All ER 166, but this was on a point that does not affect what is said below). His lordship identified a set of principles which should be considered when determining whether or not to make a s. 39 direction:

> (i) In deciding whether to impose or thereafter to lift reporting restrictions, the court will consider whether there are good reasons for naming the defendant. (ii) In reaching that decision, the court will give considerable weight to the age of the offender and to the potential damage to any young person of public identification as a criminal before the offender has the benefit or burden of adulthood. (iii) By virtue of s. 44 of the Act of 1933, the court must 'have regard to the welfare of the child or young person.' (iv) The prospect of being named in court with the accompanying disgrace is a powerful deterrent and the naming of a defendant in the context of his punishment serves as a deterrent to others. These deterrents are proper objectives for the court to seek. (v) There is a strong public interest in open justice and in the public knowing as much as possible about what has happened in court, including the identity of those who have committed crime. (vi) The weight to be attributed to the different factors may shift at different stages of the proceedings and, in particular, after the defendant has been found, or pleads, guilty and is sentenced. It may then be appropriate to place greater weight on the interest of the public in knowing the identity of those who have committed crimes, particularly serious and detestable crimes. (vii) The fact that an appeal has been made may be a material consideration.

In *R (Y) v Aylesbury Crown Court* [2012] EWHC 1140 (Admin), Hooper LJ discussed the operation of s. 39 (at [39]–[48]). His lordship said that, where there is an application by an accused to restrict publication under s. 39, he will have to satisfy the court that there is a 'good reason' to impose that restriction. This reason will usually be based on the accused's welfare (since this has to be taken into account under the CYPA 1933, s. 44). The court must also have regard to the public interest, and to the ECHR, Article 10. This includes the possible public interest in 'knowing the outcome of proceedings in court' and in the 'valuable deterrent effect that the identification of those guilty of at least serious crimes may have on others'. So far as Article 10 is concerned, the Court adopted the words of the document entitled 'Reporting Restrictions in the Crown Court' (published in October 2009, by what is now the Judicial College, the Newspaper Society, the Society of Editors and Times Newspapers Ltd), namely that 'any order restricting publication must be necessary, proportionate and there must be a pressing social need for it'. The Court went on to say that, prior to conviction, the accused's welfare is likely to take precedence over the public interest but, after conviction, the age of the accused and the seriousness of the crime of which he has been convicted will be particularly relevant; the judge may permit the publication of some details but not all. His lordship concluded that where the factors favouring a restriction on publication and the factors favouring publication are very evenly balanced, the court should make an order restricting publication.

In *R (A) v Lowestoft Magistrates' Court* [2014] 1 WLR 1489, Kenneth Parker J noted (at [10]) that s. 39:

> ...engages important, and competing, principles, namely, on the one hand, the private and family life of a child, and the best interests of that child, and, on the other hand, the freedom of the media to publish, and of the public to receive, information or comment, and the requirements of open justice. These principles are enshrined on one side in Article 8 of the ECHR, and in the jurisprudence recognising the best interests of the child as a primary consideration, and on the other in Articles 6 and 10 of the ECHR...The rights under Articles 8 and 10 are qualified, and neither the best interests of the child nor the principle of open justice necessarily dictate the conclusion in any particular case, so that in many, if not most, instances a balance has to be struck between a number of weighty claims.

Drafting Orders under the CYPA 1933, s. 39   Orders under s. 39 must be drafted with some **D24.81** care. In *Briffet and Bradshaw v DPP* (2002) 166 JP 66, it was held that a person would be guilty of an offence under s. 39 only if the terms of the order imposing reporting restrictions are clear and unambiguous: the order must leave no doubt in the mind of a reasonable reader as to precisely what it is that is prohibited (per Laws LJ at [13]).

In *R (Gazette Media) v Teesside Crown Court* [2005] EWCA Crim 1983 the Court of Appeal declined an invitation to modify the approach taken in *Southwark Crown Court, ex parte Godwin* [1992] QB 190, where it was held that a court has no power, when making an order under s. 39, to order in terms that the name of a defendant is not to be published in any report of the proceedings, since an order under s. 39 has to be restricted to the terms of the section, either using the words of the section or words to the like effect and no more.

Lifting the Restrictions   The court has the power to lift the restrictions imposed under s. 39. **D24.82** In *Central Criminal Court, ex parte S*, the Divisional Court declined to follow *Leicester Crown Court, ex parte S* [1993] 2 All ER 659 and held that it is not the case that a s. 39 order, once given, should be discharged only in 'rare and exceptional circumstances'. Sullivan J said that this would place 'an unwarranted gloss upon the broad discretion conferred by the statute'.

Appeals Against Orders   In *Lee* [1993] 2 All ER 170 at pp. 110–11 (per Lloyd LJ), the Court **D24.83** of Appeal summarised the position in relation to appeals against a decision under s. 39 as follows:

(a) a member of the press who is aggrieved by an order under s. 39 should go back to the Crown Court in the event of a change of circumstances, or should appeal to the Court of Appeal (under the CJA 1988, s. 159);
(b) an accused who is aggrieved by the withholding or discharging of an order under s. 39 should go back to the Crown Court in the event of a change of circumstances or challenge the validity of the order by seeking judicial review;
(c) if an accused indicates that he is intending to apply to the Divisional Court, the Crown Court has power under s. 39 to make a temporary order or grant a stay of the order discharging the direction, pending a decision of the Divisional Court.

D24.84   **Children and Young Persons Act 1933, s. 39**

(1) In relation to any proceedings in any court the court may direct that—

   (a) no newspaper report of the proceedings shall reveal the name, address, or school, or include any particulars calculated to lead to the identification, of any child or young person concerned in the proceedings, either as being the person by or against or in respect of whom the proceedings are taken, or as being a witness therein;

   (b) no picture shall be published in any newspaper as being or including a picture of any child or young person so concerned in the proceedings as aforesaid; except insofar (if at all) as may be permitted by the direction of the court.

(2) Any person who publishes any matter in contravention of any such direction shall on summary conviction be liable in respect of each offence to a fine not exceeding level 5 on the standard scale.

D24.85   Replacement of s. 39   The YJCEA 1999, s. 45 (not yet in force), replaces s. 39 of the 1933 Act and provides that, in proceedings formerly covered by s. 39 (i.e. proceedings other than in the youth court), the court may direct that no matter relating to the accused or a witness shall, while he is under the age of 18, be included in any publication if it is likely to lead members of the public to identify him as a person concerned in the proceedings (s. 45(3)). The court may make an 'excepting direction', which dispenses, to the extent specified in the direction, with the restrictions imposed by a direction under s. 45(3) if it is satisfied that it is necessary in the interests of justice to do so (s. 45(4)) or if satisfied that the effect of the restrictions is to impose a 'substantial and unreasonable restriction' on the reporting of the proceedings, and that it is in the public interest to remove or relax that restriction (s. 45(5)). The mere fact that the proceedings have been determined or abandoned is not sufficient in itself (ibid.). In deciding whether to impose reporting restrictions or to make an excepting direction, the court must have regard to the welfare of the juvenile in question (s. 45(6)). The restrictions apply to any identifying details, but include (in particular) the juvenile's name and address, the identity of any school or other educational establishment attended by him, the identity of any place of work, and any still or moving picture of him (s. 45(8)).

Attendance of Parent or Guardian

D24.86   The CYPA 1933, s. 34A (power of court to order that the juvenile's parent or guardian attend), applies to proceedings in the Crown Court and adult magistrates' court in the same way as it applies in proceedings in the youth court (see **D24.17**).

TRIAL OF JUVENILES IN ADULT MAGISTRATES' COURTS

D24.87   The exceptional circumstances in which a juvenile is to be tried summarily in an adult magistrates' court rather than a youth court are set out in the CYPA 1933, s. 46, and the CYPA 1963, s. 18. Their effect is as follows:

(a) Where an adult and juvenile are charged jointly with an offence, and both plead not guilty to that offence, the trial must take place in the adult magistrates' court (first proviso to the CYPA 1933, s. 46(1)). If, however, the juvenile has pleaded not guilty and either (i) the adult has pleaded guilty, or (ii) the adult is sent to the Crown Court for trial but the magistrates decide that it is not necessary in the interests of justice for the juvenile to be sent to the Crown Court as well, then the juvenile may be remitted to the youth court for trial (by virtue of the MCA 1980, s. 29(2)). Whether to remit the juvenile in these circumstances is a matter for the adult court's discretion, but it is submitted that it would normally be appropriate to remit the juvenile for trial in the youth court.

(b) Where an adult is charged with aiding, abetting, causing, procuring, allowing or permitting a juvenile to commit an offence, and at the same time the juvenile is charged with the offence as principal offender, the adult magistrates' court may, in its discretion, hear the charge against the juvenile (second proviso to the CYPA 1933, s. 46(1)). The same applies in the reverse situation (where a juvenile is charged with aiding, abetting etc. an adult: CYPA 1963,

s. 18). The normal practice, however, is simply to join aiders and abettors with the principal offender in a single charge (i.e. as if they are all principal offenders, as permitted by the Accessories and Abettors Act 1861, s. 8), in which event the first proviso to the CYPA 1933, s. 46(1), applies. Thus, the situation envisaged by the second proviso will rarely arise.

(c) Where a juvenile is charged separately from but at the same time as an adult, and the charge against one arises out of circumstances which are the same as or linked with the charge against the other, then the adult court may try the charge against the juvenile (CYPA 1963, s. 18). It is not entirely clear whether, when referring to a juvenile and adult being charged at the same time, the second proviso to the CYPA 1933, s. 46(2), and the CYPA 1963, s. 18, are referring to the moment when proceedings are commenced or to the time when the accused appear before the court. The latter construction would, however, appear more appropriate.

(d) Where it becomes apparent during the course of proceedings before an adult magistrates' court that an accused who had been thought to be over 18 is in fact a juvenile, the adult court may, if it thinks fit, complete the hearing (third proviso to the CYPA 1933, s. 46(1)). Similarly, the CYPA 1933, s. 46(1A), provides that, where a plea of guilty by post is received from a person who is in fact a juvenile but the court has no reason to be aware of his true age, then he shall be deemed to be an adult.

It will be noted that in situation (a) the adult magistrates' court is obliged to try both the juvenile and adult together unless the MCA 1980, s. 29, comes into play, whereas in situations (b) to (d), whether to try the juvenile or remit him to the youth court is in the court's discretion. It should also be noted that the fact that a juvenile will ultimately have to be tried before the youth court does not prevent him being brought before an adult court for purposes of a bail application and remand (CYPA 1933, s. 46(2)).

Summary Trial Procedure for Juveniles Tried in an Adult Magistrates' Court

The procedure in an adult magistrates' court when a juvenile is being tried is the same as the procedure for trial of an adult, subject to the application of the CYPA 1933, ss. 34A and 39 (see **D24.19** and **D24.84**). Indeed, the CrimPR, part 37, applies to all summary trials, whether in a youth court or an adult magistrates' court. **D24.88**

Where a juvenile is tried in an adult magistrates' court, the automatic reporting restrictions contained in the CYPA 1933, s. 49, do not apply. However, the court has a discretion to impose reporting restrictions under the CYPA 1933, s. 39, to prevent identifying details of the juvenile being published or broadcast (see **D24.78**).

Under the CYPA 1933, s. 34A(1), a parent or guardian must (if the juvenile is under 16), or may (if the juvenile is 16 or 17) be ordered to attend each hearing in the case unless, and to the extent that, it would be unreasonable to require such attendance (see **D24.17**).

Children and Young Persons Act 1933, s. 46   **D24.89**

(1) Subject as hereinafter provided, no charge against a child or young person, and no application whereof the hearing is by rules made under this section assigned to youth courts, shall be heard by a magistrates' court which is not a youth court: Provided that—

  (a) a charge made jointly against a child or young person and a person who has attained the age of 18 years shall be heard by a magistrates' court other than a youth court, and

  (b) where a child or young person is charged with an offence, the charge may be heard by a magistrates' court which is not a youth court if a person who has attained the age of 18 years is charged at the same time with aiding, abetting, causing, procuring, allowing or permitting that offence; and

  (c) where in the course of any proceedings before any magistrates' court other than a youth court it appears that the person to whom the proceedings relate is a child or young person, nothing in this subsection shall be construed as preventing the court, if it thinks fit so to do, from proceeding with the hearing and determination of those proceedings.

(1A) If a notification that the accused desires to plead guilty without appearing before the court is received by the designated officer for a court in pursuance of section 12 of the Magistrates' Courts Act 1980 and the court has no reason to believe that the accused is a child or young person, then, if he is a child or young person he shall be deemed to have attained the age of 18 for the purposes of subsection (1) of this section in its application to the proceedings in question.

(2) No direction, whether contained in this or any other Act, that a charge shall be brought before a youth court shall be construed as restricting the powers of any justice or justices to entertain an application for bail or for a remand, and to hear such evidence as may be necessary for that purpose.

D24.90   Children and Young Persons Act 1963, s. 18

Notwithstanding section 46(1) of [the CYPA 1933]...a magistrates' court which is not a youth court may hear an information against a child or young person if he is charged—

(a) with aiding, abetting, causing, procuring, allowing or permitting an offence with which a person who has attained the age of 18 is charged at the same time; or

(b) with an offence arising out of circumstances which are the same as or connected with those giving rise to an offence with which a person who has attained the age of 18 is charged at the same time.

D24.91   Magistrates' Courts Act 1980, s. 29

(1) Where—

(a) a person under the age of 18 ('the juvenile') appears or is brought before a magistrates' court other than a youth court on an information jointly charging him and one or more other persons with an offence; and

(b) that other person, or any of those other persons, has attained that age,

subsection (2) below shall have effect notwithstanding proviso (a) in section 46(1) of the Children and Young Persons Act 1933 (which would otherwise require the charge against the juvenile to be heard by a magistrates' court other than a youth court).

In the following provisions of this section 'the older accused' means such one or more of the accused as have attained the age of 18.

(2) If—

(a) the court proceeds to the summary trial of the information in the case of both or all of the accused, and the older accused or each of the older accused pleads guilty; or

(b) the court—

(i) in the case of the older accused or each of the older accused, proceeds to inquire into the information as examining justices and either commits him for trial or discharges him; and

(ii) in the case of the juvenile, proceeds to the summary trial of the information,

then, if in either situation the juvenile pleads not guilty, the court may before any evidence is called in his case remit him for trial to a youth court acting for the same place as the remitting court or for the place where he habitually resides.

(3) A person remitted to a youth court under subsection (2) above shall be brought before and tried by a youth court accordingly.

(4) Where a person is so remitted to a youth court—

(a) he shall have no right of appeal against the order of remission; and

(b) the remitting court may give such directions as appear to be necessary with respect to his custody or for his release on bail until he can be brought before the youth court.

(5) The preceding provisions of this section shall apply in relation to a corporation as if it were an individual who has attained the age of 18.

VULNERABLE DEFENDANTS: ADAPTATIONS TO NORMAL TRIAL PROCESS

D24.92 Various adaptations to the trial process are applicable which, subject to exceptions, apply whether the trial of a juvenile is to take place in the Crown Court or in a magistrates' court.

Ensuring Fairness of the Trial Process

D24.93 In *V v UK* (2000) 30 EHRR 121, the ECtHR scrutinised the procedure adopted for the murder trial of two juveniles in the Crown Court. At the opening of the trial, the judge made an order under the CYPA 1933, s. 39, that there should be no publication of the names, addresses or other identifying details of the accused, or publication of their photographs. Nevertheless, the trial took place in the full glare of national and international publicity. The ECtHR held that the right of the two accused to a fair trial under the ECHR, Article 6(1), had been violated.

The ECtHR stated that it is essential that a young child charged with a serious offence attracting high levels of media interest should be tried in such a way as to reduce as far as possible any feelings of intimidation. It considered that the formality and ritual of the Crown Court must at times have seemed incomprehensible and intimidating for a child aged 11. Moreover, there was evidence that certain of the modifications to the courtroom, in particular the raised dock which was designed to enable the accused to see what was going on, had the adverse effect of increasing their sense of discomfort during the trial, since they felt exposed to the scrutiny of the press and public. Further, there was evidence that the post-traumatic stress disorder suffered by the accused, combined with the lack of any therapeutic work since the offence, had limited their ability to instruct lawyers or testify in their own defence. The ECtHR found that they were unable to follow the trial or take decisions in their own best interests. They were therefore unable to participate effectively in the criminal proceedings against them and were, in consequence, denied a fair hearing in breach of Article 6(1).

It should be emphasised that the ECtHR did not find that trial of juveniles in the Crown Court is necessarily unfair, only that appropriate adaptations to the procedure have to be made to accommodate the needs of the young defendant.

CPD I, paras. 3G.7 to 3G.14 (see Supplement, **PD-9**), set out the special arrangements which should be made where a vulnerable defendant is being tried; this includes a juvenile being tried in the Crown Court or in an adult magistrates' court.

Possible modifications include: **D24.94**

(a) arranging for the accused to visit, out of court hours and before the trial, the courtroom in which that hearing is to take place, so that he can familiarise himself with it;

(b) if the possibility of the accused testifying via a live link is being considered, he should have an opportunity to have a practice session;

(c) putting appropriate reporting restrictions in place;

(d) ensuring, so far as possible, that all the participants are on the same, or almost the same, level;

(e) allowing the accused to sit with members of his family and with another suitable supporting adult such as a social worker, and in a place which permits easy, informal communication with his legal representatives;

(f) ensuring that each step of the trial is explained in language that the accused can understand;

(g) conducting the trial according to a timetable which takes full account of the accused's ability to concentrate, including frequent and regular breaks;

(h) ensuring that the trial is conducted in simple, clear language that the accused can understand and that examination-in-chief and cross-examination are conducted using questions that are short and clear;

(i) in the Crown Court, not wearing robes and wigs;

(j) having no recognisable police presence in the courtroom save for good reason;

(k) if necessary, restricting attendance by members of the public in the courtroom to a small number (e.g., those with an immediate and direct interest in the outcome of the case) and restricting the number of reporters attending in the courtroom to such number as is judged practicable and desirable.

Additionally, in cases where there is a young or vulnerable defendant (or witness), it may be necessary to hold a 'ground rules' hearing to lay down rules for the questioning of that defendant or witness (CPD I, paras. 3E1 to 3E.6). It may also be necessary to make use of an intermediary (paras. 3F.1 to 3F.6).

Similar points were made by Scott Baker LJ in *R (P) v West London Youth Court* [2006] 1 All ER   **D24.95** 477 (at [26]), where his lordship observed that the defendant's 'effective participation' in the trial could be aided by measures such as:

    i) keeping the claimant's level of cognitive functioning in mind;

    ii) using concise and simple language;

iii) having regular breaks;
iv) taking additional time to explain court proceedings;
v)   being proactive in ensuring the claimant has access to support;
vi) explaining and ensuring the claimant understands the ingredients of the charge;
vii) explaining the possible outcomes and sentences;
viii) ensuring that cross-examination is carefully controlled so that questions are short and clear and frustration is minimised.

D24.96   In *SC v UK* (2005) 40 EHRR 226, the applicant, who was aged 11 years at the time, challenged the fairness of his Crown Court trial. The ECtHR held that there had been a breach of the applicant's right to a fair trial. The ECtHR said that the right of an accused to effective participation in his criminal trial generally includes not only the right to be present, but also the right to hear and follow the proceedings. In the case of a child, it is essential that he be dealt with in a manner which takes full account of his age, level of maturity and intellectual and emotional capacities, and that steps are taken to promote his ability to understand and participate in the proceedings, including conducting the hearing in such a way as to reduce as far as possible his feelings of intimidation and inhibition (at [28]). In the present case, two experts had assessed the juvenile as having a very low intellectual level for his age. The ECtHR said that it could not conclude that the juvenile was capable of participating effectively in his trial. The ECtHR considered that, when the decision is taken to deal with a child who risks not being able to participate effectively because of his young age and limited intellectual capacity, by way of criminal proceedings rather than some other form of disposal directed primarily at determining the child's best interests and those of the community, it is essential that he be tried in a specialist tribunal which is able to give full consideration to and make proper allowance for the handicaps under which he labours and adapt its procedure accordingly (at [35]). The trial in this case took place before the measures now set out in CPD I came into effect but it is unlikely that those measures would have brought about a different result. However, the effect of the decision of the ECtHR would seem to be confined to children whose intellectual level is unusually low.

D24.97   *SC v UK* was considered in *R (P) v West London Youth Court* [2006] 1 All ER 477, in which the main issue was whether the intellectual capacity of the accused (who was aged 15 but had a mental age of eight) was such that he could not effectively participate in the proceedings. It was held that neither youth nor limited intellectual capacity necessarily leads to a breach of Article 6. What is crucial is whether the tribunal hearing the case (in the instant case, a youth court) is able to adapt its procedures so that the defendant can effectively participate in the proceedings. Scott Baker LJ ruled (at [7]) that the district judge had correctly directed himself that the minimum requirements for a fair trial for the accused were:

> (i) he had to understand what he is said to have done wrong; (ii) the court had to be satisfied that the juvenile when he had done wrong by act or omission had the means of knowing that was wrong; (iii) he had to understand what, if any, defences were available to him; (iv) he had to have a reasonable opportunity to make relevant representations if he wished; (v) he had to have the opportunity to consider what representations he wished to make once he had understood the issues involved. He had therefore to be able to give proper instructions and to participate by way of providing answers to questions and suggesting questions to his lawyers in the circumstances of the trial as they arose.

D24.98   In a similar vein, Openshaw J said in *R (C) v Sevenoaks Youth Court* [2010] 1 All ER 735 (at [17]):

> . . . when trying a young child, and most particularly a child. . .with learning and behavioural difficulties, . . . the Youth Court has a duty under its inherent powers and under the Criminal Procedure Rules to take such steps as are necessary to ensure that he has a fair trial, not just during the proceedings, but beforehand as he and his lawyers prepare for trial. He must be given such help as he needs to understand the case against him; he must be helped to give his own side of the story as his proof of evidence is drawn up; it may be that he needs help to speak to his lawyers, let alone to the court; he will need help to follow the case as it proceeds. . .he will need particular help to decide if he is to give evidence, and if so he will need help to do so. It is in the highest degree unlikely that this level of help can be given by a lawyer, however kind and sympathetic she may be. He needs someone to

befriend and to help him, both during the trial itself and in preparation for it. In short, he needs an intermediary…. Moreover, the court will have to adapt its procedures to ensure that the hearing is fair…by using simple language, by taking breaks, by taking any and all such steps as are necessary. Experienced justices sitting in youth courts are well able to ensure the fairness of the proceedings.

In *Dixon* [2013] 3 All ER 242, Treacy LJ emphasised (at [85]) the importance of ensuring that, where there is a vulnerable defendant, proper allowance was made for his difficulties in order to ensure effective participation in the trial process and (at [97]) the need for the judge to take an active role throughout the proceedings to ensure that the accused is actively participating in the proceedings.

For the range of special measures available for young defendants, see **D14.26** *et seq*.

FITNESS TO PLEAD

In *CPS v P* [2008] 4 All ER 628, the Divisional Court considered the procedure to be adopted **D24.99** in cases where a youth court has to consider the question of the juvenile's capacity to stand trial on the basis that he may not be fit to plead. In particular, Smith LJ considered whether there should ever be a stay before evidence is heard, saying (at [51]):

> [N]otwithstanding the fact that the youth court is a creature of statute (like any other magistrates' court) it has an inherent jurisdiction to stay proceedings as an abuse of process at any stage. The jurisdiction is limited to matters directly affecting the fairness of the trial of the particular defendant concerned and does not extend to the wider supervisory jurisdiction for upholding the rule of law, which is vested in the High Court…However…it will be in only exceptional cases that it should be exercised, on the ground of one or more of the capacity issues, before any evidence is heard.

Her ladyship then addressed the weight to be accorded to medical evidence in such cases (at [52] and [53]):

> Medical evidence…will rarely provide the whole answer to the question of whether the child ought to be tried for a criminal offence. This is an issue which the court has to decide, not the doctors, although of course the medical evidence may be of great importance. But, the medical evidence must almost always be set in the context of other evidence relating to the child, which may well bear upon the issues of his understanding, mental capacity and ability to participate effectively in a trial…The court must be willing, in an appropriate case, to disagree with and reject the medical opinion. It is the court's opinion of the child's level of understanding which must determine whether a criminal trial proceeds.

> …[I]n most cases, the medical evidence should be considered as part of the evidence in the case and not as the sole evidence on a freestanding application. Although the medical evidence might on its own appear quite strong, when other matters are considered the court might conclude that the defendant's understanding and ability to take part in the trial are greater than were suggested by the doctors and that, with proper assistance from his legal adviser and suitable adjustments to the procedure of the court, the trial can properly proceed to a conclusion.

Smith LJ also emphasised (at [54]–[57]) the need to keep the issue of capacity under review **D24.100** and, as part of that review process, to consider whether the case was one where the court should simply make a finding of fact whether the juvenile committed the *actus reus* of the offence (thus enabling a disposal under the Mental Health Act 1983 rather than convicting the accused):

> [T]he court has a duty to keep under continuing review the question of whether the criminal trial ought to continue. If at any stage the court concludes that the child is unable to participate effectively in the trial, it may decide to call a halt. However, the court may consider that it is in the interests of the child that the trial should continue…

> If the court decides that it should call a halt to the criminal trial on the ground that the child cannot take an effective part in the proceedings, it should then consider whether to switch to a consideration of whether the child has done the acts alleged…That process is part of the protective jurisdiction contemplated by the 1983 Act and the child's article 6 rights are not even engaged.

The decision as to whether or not to switch to fact-finding is one for the discretion of the court . . . I consider that proceedings should be stayed as an abuse of process before fact-finding only if no useful purpose at all could be served by finding the facts.

If the court decides to find the facts and finds that the defendant did the acts alleged, it would then consider whether to seek further medical evidence with a view to making an order under the Mental Health Act 1983. If the court finds that the defendant did not do the acts alleged, the proceedings would be brought to an end by a finding of not guilty.

In *G v DPP* [2012] EWHC 3174 (Admin), Pitchford LJ emphasised (at [31]) that the discretion as to whether or not to conduct an inquiry as to whether the accused was guilty of the facts of which he was charged, without making a finding of guilt, depends upon the court's assessment of whether it is necessary to do so in the particular circumstances of the case.

SENTENCING POWERS AND PROCEDURE IN THE YOUTH COURT

Sentencing Powers Generally

D24.101 All the sentences and other orders provided for by statute for use in respect of juvenile offenders are at the disposal of the youth court following conviction of a juvenile, with the exception of long-term detention under the PCC(S)A 2000, which is available only to the Crown Court. There is detailed discussion of the sentencing options available in respect of young offenders in **part E** of this work. In brief, the principal sentences are as follows:

(a) detention and training orders (see **E7.15** for details);
(b) fines (see **E15**) — in the case of juveniles, fines are limited by virtue of the MCA 1980, s. 24(3) and (4), to a maximum of £1,000 in the case of offenders who are aged 14 to 17, and a maximum of £250 where the offender is aged 10 to 13 (or the maximum specified for the offence, if less);
(c) youth rehabilitation orders under the CJIA 2008, s. 1 (see **E9.2**);
(d) referral orders and reparation orders (see **E10** and **E11** for details); and
(e) absolute and conditional discharges (see **E12** for details).

The youth court is also empowered to make certain orders against the parents of a juvenile whom it has convicted, namely binding the parents over or making a parenting order (see **E14** for details).

Procedure before Sentence in the Youth Court

D24.102 Under the CrimPR, r. 37.10(7), before the court passes sentence on a young offender, it must give his parent, guardian or other supporting adult, if present, an opportunity to make representations and introduce evidence relevant to sentence (as well as giving the offender an opportunity to do so).

D24.103 **Preparation of Reports**   The responsibility for preparing reports on juveniles rests primarily on the local authority in whose area the juvenile resides (CYPA 1969, s. 9), although in the cases of juveniles who have attained the age of 13, the task may be undertaken by probation officers (see s. 34(3) of the 1969 Act and SI 1970 No. 1882).

Children and Young Persons Act 1969, s. 9

(1) Where a local authority bring proceedings for an offence alleged to have been committed by a [juvenile] or are notified that any such proceedings are being brought, it shall be the duty of the authority, unless they are of opinion that it is unnecessary to do so, to make such investigations and provide the court before which the proceedings are heard with such information relating to the home surroundings, school record, health and character of the person in respect of whom the proceedings are brought as appear to the authority likely to assist the court.

(2) If the court mentioned in subsection (1) of this section requests the authority aforesaid to make investigations and provide information or to make further investigations and provide further information relating to the matters aforesaid, it shall be the duty of the authority to comply with the request.

Children and Young Persons Act 1969, s. 34

(3) In the case of a person who has attained such age as the Secretary of State may by order specify, an authority shall, without prejudice to subsection (2) of section 9 of this Act, not be required by virtue of subsection (1) of that section to make investigations or provide information which it does not already possess with respect to his home surroundings if, by direction of the justices or local probation board acting for any relevant area, arrangements are in force for information with respect to his home surroundings to be furnished to the court in question by an officer of a local probation board.

Sending to Another Youth Court

Instead of itself sentencing a juvenile who pleads or is found guilty before it, a youth court may **D24.104** remit him to the youth court for the area where he habitually resides, which court may then deal with him as if it had just convicted him (PCC(S)A 2000, s. 8(2) and (3)). The receiving court also has all the powers of jurisdiction that it would have had if it had dealt with the matter in the first place. It can, for example, accept a change of plea during the course of proceedings (*Stratford Youth v Court, ex parte Conde* [1997] 1 WLR 113).

Sentencing Powers where Accused Attains the Age of 18 after Finding of Guilt

Children and Young Persons Act 1963, s. 29 **D24.105**

Where proceedings in respect of a young person are begun for an offence and he attains the age of 18 before the conclusion of the proceedings, the court may deal with the case and make any order which it could have made if he had not attained that age.

Prima facie, s. 29 could be interpreted as permitting the youth court to retain jurisdiction to try an indictable offence even where the 'juvenile' attains the age of 18 before mode of trial is determined, provided the proceedings were commenced when he was still 17. In the light of *Islington North Juvenile Court, ex parte Daley* [1983] 1 AC 347 (see **D24.72**), however, such a broad interpretation is clearly untenable.

Section 29 is, nonetheless, relevant to sentencing. Where an accused pleads or is found guilty when still a juvenile but attains the age of 18 during an adjournment before sentence, the court may deal with him as if he remained under that age. In *Aldis v DPP* [2002] 2 Cr App R (S) 400, the accused attained the age of 18 before conviction and sentence. It was held that the justices were entitled, pursuant to s. 29, to sentence the offender to a detention and training order even though he had attained the age of 18 prior to the sentencing hearing, provided he was under 18 at the date when the court decided whether they were obliged to try him summarily. This should be seen in light of the fact that the relevant age for determining the type of sentence is the date of conviction, not the date when sentence is passed (*Danga* [1992] QB 476; *Robson* [2007] 1 All ER 506), and so the effect of the CYPA 1963, s. 29, is not as anomalous as it may at first seem.

Remission to an Adult Magistrates' Court The PCC(S)A 2000, s. 9(1), gives the youth court **D24.106** a discretionary power to remit a juvenile to an adult magistrates' court once he reaches the age of 18. The adult magistrates' court may then 'deal with the case in any way in which it would have power to deal with it if all proceedings relating to the offence which took place before the youth court had taken place before [the adult court]' (s. 9(2)(b)). There is no right of appeal against the order of remission (s. 9(4)).

In *R (Denny) v Acton Youth Court* [2004] 2 All ER 961, a 17-year-old was charged with attempted robbery. He entered a plea of not guilty at the youth court. By the time the matter came on for trial and he was found guilty, he was 18. The justices in the youth court adjourned sentence and remitted him to the adult magistrates' court pursuant to s. 9. The Divisional Court held that the order remitting the case to the adult court was unlawful: youth courts should never remit an offender to a magistrates' court for sentence in relation to an offence which, in the case of an adult, is triable only on indictment (per Maurice Kay LJ at [9]). It was also held (at [14]) that, provided the adult court has not reached the stage of considering sentence, it is possible for the youth court to rescind a remittal to an adult magistrates' court under the MCA 1980, s. 142(1), since a remittal under s. 9 is an 'order made when dealing with an offender'.

Powers of Criminal Courts (Sentencing) Act 2000, s. 9

(1) Where a person who appears or is brought before a youth court charged with an offence subsequently attains the age of 18, the youth court may, at any time after conviction and before sentence, remit him for sentence to a magistrates' court (other than a youth court).

D24.107 **Determining Sentence Available where Offender Attains Age of 18**   The *type* of sentence is generally fixed by the offender's age at the date of conviction (*Danga* [1992] QB 476). This was confirmed in *Robson* [2007] 1 All ER 506, where the accused was aged 17 when he was convicted of sexual assault. The youth court committed him to the Crown Court for sentence under the PCC(S)A 2000, s. 3C. When he appeared for sentencing, he had attained the age of 18. The Court of Appeal held that, as a matter of statutory construction, the age of the offender for the purpose of determining which of the statutory regimes under the CJA 2003, ss. 224 to 236 (dangerous offenders: see E4), applies to him is his age at the date of conviction. The court reached this conclusion on the basis that the relevant provisions refer to cases where 'a person aged 18 or over is *convicted*' and where 'a person aged under 18 is *convicted*'. The use of the word 'convicted', rather than 'sentenced', was held to be determinative of the question of which date is relevant. Where appropriate, however, the court should have regard to the offender's age at the date when the offence was committed when considering the severity of the penalty to impose.

Where an offender crosses a relevant age threshold between the date of commission of the offence and the date of conviction, the starting point is the sentence that he would have been likely to receive if he had been sentenced at the date of the commission of the offence (*Ghafoor* [2003] 1 Cr App R (S) 428, per Dyson LJ at [31]). In *Bowker* [2008] 1 Cr App R (S) 412, the Court of Appeal again considered the approach to be taken where an offender who has attained the age of 18 is convicted of an offence committed whilst under the age of 18. The court emphasised that the principle that his culpability should be judged by reference to his age at the time of the offence is only a starting point. The sentence that would have been imposed at the time of the commission of the offence is a 'powerful' factor, not the sole or determining factor. The sentencer also has to take account of the matters set out in the CJA 2003, s. 142, including deterrence.

SENTENCING PROCEDURE AND POWERS IN THE CROWN COURT

Sentencing Powers Generally

D24.108 The Crown Court has the same powers as the youth court when sentencing a young offender (see **D24.101**) save that:

(a) the Crown Court may impose a sentence of detention under the PCC(S)A 2000, s. 91;
(b) the MCA 1980, s. 24(3) and (4), do not apply to the Crown Court, and so there is no limitation on the maximum amount of a fine that the Crown Court may impose.

Remission to the Youth Court

D24.109 Save in cases of homicide, where a juvenile has been convicted on indictment, the Crown Court 'shall unless satisfied that it would be undesirable to do so', remit the case to a youth court acting for the place where the offender was sent for trial' (PCC(S)A 2000, s. 8(2)). The youth court may then deal with the offender as if he had been tried and found guilty by itself (s. 8(3)). There is no appeal against the order of remission, although the sentence eventually passed by the youth court may be appealed to the Crown Court (or the Divisional Court, if wrong in law) in the usual way (s. 8(5)). The Crown Court may remit the offender to the youth court in custody or on bail (s. 8(4)(a)).

The obligation imposed on the Crown Court by s. 8(2) to remit a juvenile convicted before it to the youth court for sentence 'unless satisfied that it would be undesirable to do so' might seem to be a major fetter on the power of the Crown Court to deal with juveniles. However, s. 8(2) has been interpreted so as to give the Crown Court an almost unfettered discretion to retain the sentencing function for itself if it so wishes, and, in practice, the great majority of juveniles convicted in the Crown Court are also sentenced there. Guidance on the application of s. 8 was given by Lord Lane CJ in *Lewis* (1984) 79 Cr App R 94 at p. 99. His lordship indicated that reasons for *not* remitting include:

(a) that, in a case where the juvenile pleaded not guilty and was convicted, the Crown Court judge who presided at the trial will be better informed about the facts of the offence and general nature of the case than the youth court could hope to be;
(b) that, in a case where an adult and juvenile have been jointly tried on indictment and both convicted, sentencing the juvenile in the Crown Court will avoid the risk of unacceptable disparity in sentencing that would arise if he were to be remitted to the youth court;
(c) that remitting would cause delay, unnecessary duplication of proceedings and extra expense.

Lord Lane did suggest (ibid.) that it may become desirable to remit the case where a report has to be obtained and the Crown Court judge will be unable to sit when the report becomes available, but added that this situation should be avoided wherever possible. It is submitted that, in virtually any case, the Crown Court will be able to justify a decision not to remit on the basis of one or other of the reasons put forward by Lord Lane.

Paragraph 12.19 of the definitive sentencing guideline *Overarching Principles — Sentencing*   **D24.110**
Youths (see Supplement, **SG-527**) notes that when considering whether remittal is 'undesirable' the court 'should balance the need for expertise in the sentencing of young offenders with the benefits of sentence being imposed by the court which had determined guilt'. Paragraph 12.20 goes on to make the specific point that a referral order (see **E10**) is not available in the Crown Court (since the PCC(S)A 2000, s. 16, applies only where a youth court or other magistrates' court is dealing with a person aged under 18 for an offence).

Cases where the Powers of Criminal Courts (Sentencing) Act 2000, s. 91, Applies

Where the juvenile was sent to the Crown Court because he was charged with an offence to which   **D24.111**
the PCC(S)A 2000, s. 91, applies, the Crown Court is not obliged to pass a sentence of detention under s. 91. The Crown Court retains the power to deal with the offender in any way that the youth court could have done. It will generally be undesirable for the Crown Court to remit the case to the youth court for sentence under the PCC(S)A 2000, s. 8(2), since the youth court will already have expressed the view that the case is too serious for its powers (*Allen* (1999) 163 JP 841).

Powers of Criminal Courts (Sentencing) Act 2000, s. 8   **D24.112**

(1) Subsection (2) below applies where a child or young person (that is to say, any person aged under 18) is convicted by or before any court of an offence other than homicide.
(2) The court may and, if it is not a youth court, shall unless satisfied that it would be undesirable to do so, remit the case—
  (a) if the offender was sent to the Crown Court for trial under section 51 or 51A of the Crime and Disorder Act 1998, to a youth court acting for the place where he was committed for trial or sent to the Crown Court for trial;
  (b) in any other case, to a youth court acting either for the same place as the remitting court or for the place where the offender habitually resides;
but in relation to a magistrates' court other than a youth court this subsection has effect subject to subsection (6) below.

(3) Where a case is remitted under subsection (2) above, the offender shall be brought before a youth court accordingly, and that court may deal with him in any way in which it might have dealt with him if he had been tried and convicted by that court.

(4) A court by which an order remitting a case to a youth court is made under subsection (2) above—

   (a) may, subject to section 25 of the Criminal Justice and Public Order Act 1994 (restrictions on granting bail), give such directions as appear to be necessary with respect to the custody of the offender or for his release on bail until he can be brought before the youth court; and

   (b) shall cause to be transmitted to the designated officer for the youth court a certificate setting out the nature of the offence and stating—

      (i) that the offender has been convicted of the offence; and

      (ii) that the case has been remitted for the purpose of being dealt with under the preceding provisions of this section.

(5) Where a case is remitted under subsection (2) above, the offender shall have no right of appeal against the order of remission, but shall have the same right of appeal against any order of the court to which the case is remitted as if he had been convicted by that court.

SENTENCING PROCEDURE AND POWERS IN THE ADULT MAGISTRATES' COURT

D24.113 The powers of the adult magistrates' court to deal with a juvenile offender are restricted by the PCC(S)A 2000, s. 8(6)–(8). Under s. 8(6), the magistrates must remit the juvenile to the youth court to be sentenced unless the case is one where the court is required by the PCC(S)A 2000, s. 16(2), to refer the offender to a youth offender panel (in which event the court may, but need not, remit the case to the youth court) or where the magistrates' court's very limited sentencing powers are appropriate. Those powers are:

(a) absolute or conditional discharge;

(b) a fine (the maximum fine that an adult magistrates' court may impose on a juvenile is restricted in the same way as the maximum fine that may be imposed by a youth court (see **D24.101**));

(c) binding over the juvenile's parents;

(d) ancillary orders (such as disqualification from driving, endorsement of the driving licence and orders ancillary to the sentence proper such as orders to pay compensation or costs).

Where the juvenile is remitted to the youth court, the remission must be either to the youth court acting for the same place as the remitting court or to the court for the place where the juvenile habitually resides (see s. 8(2)). The remitting court may grant the juvenile bail (s. 8(4)(a)).

D24.114   Powers of Criminal Courts (Sentencing) Act 2000, s. 8

(6) Without prejudice to the power to remit any case to a youth court which is conferred on a magistrates' court other than a youth court by subsections (1) and (2) above, where such a magistrates' court convicts a child or young person of an offence it must exercise that power unless the case falls within subsection (7) or (8) below.

(7) The case falls within this subsection if the court would, were it not so to remit the case, be required by section 16(2) below to refer the offender to a youth offender panel (in which event the court may, but need not, so remit the case).

(8) The case falls within this subsection if it does not fall within subsection (7) above but the court is of the opinion that the case is one which can properly be dealt with by means of—

   (a) an order discharging the offender absolutely or conditionally, or

   (b) an order for the payment of a fine, or

   (c) an order (under section 150 below) requiring the offender's parent or guardian to enter into a recognisance to take proper care of him and exercise proper control over him,

with or without any order that the court has powers to make when absolutely or conditionally discharging an offender.

Section D25   Civil Behaviour Orders: ASBOs, Closure Orders, SCPOs and VOOs

ANTI-SOCIAL BEHAVIOUR, CRIME AND POLICING ACT 2014

The ABCPA received Royal Assent on 13 March 2014. Provisions of relevance to this section **D25.1** include part 1, which is entitled 'Injunctions' and introduces a new injunction to prevent nuisance and annoyance (IPNA) and part 2, which is entitled 'Criminal behaviour orders' and introduces the CBO. The IPNA is intended to replace the 'stand alone' ASBO and the CBO is intended to replace the 'post-conviction' ASBO. Chapter 3 of part 4 is entitled 'Closure of premises associated with nuisance or disorder etc.' and is intended to replace closure orders under parts 1 and 1A of the ASBA 2003; chapter 1 of part 4 creates community protection notices (CPN) and chapter 2 of part 4 creates public spaces protection orders (PSPO). None of these provisions are yet in force. What follows is a consideration of the background to the introduction of these reforms and an overview of the new IPNAs, CBOs and closure orders.

Background

In February 2011, the government published a consultation document that sought views on **D25.2** the replacement of the current tools for tackling anti-social behaviour with a new suite of powers. In May 2012, the Home Office published a White Paper, entitled *Putting victims first: more effective responses to anti-social behaviour*, which built on the responses to the consultation and called for the introduction of IPNAs and CBOs amongst a range of other measures. The draft Anti-social Behaviour Bill followed on 13 December 2012. The subsequently re-titled Anti-social Behaviour, Crime and Policing Bill was introduced into the House of Commons on 9 May 2013.

The Explanatory Notes state that of the 14 parts to the Bill, part 1 'makes provision for a civil injunction to prevent nuisance and annoyance', part 2 'makes provision for an order on conviction to prevent behaviour which causes harassment, alarm or distress' and part 4 'covers the new powers to deal with community protection and makes provision for a community protection notice, a public spaces protection order and provisions to close premises associated with nuisance and annoyance'.

In October 2013, the Home Office published *Draft guidance for frontline professionals*, which stated that IPNAs would be available '[t]o stop or prevent individuals engaging in anti-social behaviour quickly, nipping problems in the bud before they escalate' and that CBOs would be '[i]ssued by any criminal court against a person who has been convicted of an offence to tackle the most persistently anti-social individuals who are also engaged in criminal activity'.

As to IPNAs, the draft guidance goes on to state that the important differences between the new injunctions and ASBOs are (a) the range of potential applicants is much wider, (b) the standard of proof for obtaining an IPNA will be the civil standard rather than the criminal standard for obtaining an ASBO, (c) the anti-social behaviour test is lower for an IPNA than for an ASBO, (d) there is no 'necessity' requirement for an IPNA whereas there is for an ASBO, (e) breaching an IPNA will not be a criminal offence, whereas breaching an ASBO is, and (f) positive require-ments can attach to an IPNA whereas an ASBO can only contain negative requirements.

As to CBOs, the draft guidance states that unlike an ASBO, there will be no need to establish 'necessity' as a pre-condition to making an order and it will be possible for the court to include positive requirements just as in an IPNA.

Injunctions to Prevent Nuisance and Annoyance

D25.3   The provisions of part 1 of the ABCPA 2014 (ss. 1 to 21) concern the IPNA. An application for an IPNA must be made to a youth court where the respondent is under 18 years of age (s. 1(8)(a)) or to the High Court or the county court in any other case (s. 1(8)(b)). An application for an injunction can be made only by a local authority, a housing provider, the chief officer of police for a police area, the chief constable of the British Transport Police Force, Transport for London, the Environment Agency, the Natural Resources Body for Wales, the Secretary of State (in certain defined circumstances) and the Welsh Ministers (also in certain defined circumstances) (s. 5(1)). Applications can be made on notice or without notice (s. 6(2)). If the latter, the court can make an interim IPNA pending the determination of the full application (s. 7).

On an application for an IPNA under s. 1, the court may grant an injunction against a person aged ten or over (the respondent) if two conditions are met. The first condition is that the court is satisfied, on the balance of probabilities, that the respondent has engaged or threatens to engage in anti-social behaviour (s. 1(2)). The second condition is that the court considers it just and convenient to grant the injunction for the purpose of preventing the respondent from engaging in anti-social behaviour (s. 1(3)). The meaning of 'anti-social behaviour' is set out in s. 2. It means (a) conduct that has caused, or is likely to cause, harassment, alarm or distress to any person, (b) conduct capable of causing nuisance or annoyance to a person in relation to that person's occupation of residential premises (but only where the applicant is a housing provider, a local authority, or the chief officer of police) or (c) conduct capable of causing housing-related nuisance or annoyance to any person. An IPNA can contain terms that both prohibit the respondent from doing anything described in the injunction and require the respondent to do anything described in the injunction (s. 1(4)). The prohibitions and requirements that comprise the IPNA must, so far as is practicable, be such as to avoid (a) any interference with the times, if any, at which the respondent normally works or attends school or other educational establishment, and (b) any conflict with the requirements of any other court order or injunc-tion to which the respondent may be subject (s. 1(5)). Before the court can make an IPNA that includes a requirement (as opposed to a prohibition), the person who would be responsible for supervising the respondent's compliance with that requirement must provide evidence about the suitability and enforceability of the requirement (s. 3(2)). Moreover, where the court is considering making two requirements, it must consider their compatibility with each other first (s. 3(3)).

The IPNA must either specify the period for which it has effect or state that it has effect until further order; where the IPNA is granted before the respondent turns 18, the period of the IPNA must be specified and it must be no more than 12 months (s. 1(6)). Particular prohibitions or requirements can be effective for different periods, and the IPNA may specify what those periods are (s. 1(7)). A court granting an IPNA may attach a power of arrest to a prohibition or requirement if the court thinks that either the anti-social behaviour in which the respondent has engaged or threatens to engage consists of or includes the use or threatened use of violence against other persons, or there is a significant risk of harm to other persons from the respondent (s. 4(1)). A power of arrest can apply for a shorter period than the prohibitions or requirements in the order to which it relates (s. 4(2)).

D25.4   The court that granted the injunction (save where that was a youth court and the respondent is now over 18, in which case the 'court' means the county court) can vary or discharge an IPNA on the application of either the original applicant or the respondent (s. 8(1)). The power to vary an IPNA includes the power (a) to add a prohibition or requirement to the order, or to extend the period during which an existing prohibition or requirement has effect, and (b) to attach a power of arrest or to extend the time during which an existing power of arrest has effect (s. 8(3)).

Where a power of arrest attaches to an IPNA, a constable may arrest a respondent without warrant if the constable has reasonable cause to suspect that the respondent is in breach of a term of the order (s. 9(1)). In most cases, the arrested respondent will have to be brought before the court that made the order to be dealt with within 24 hours (s. 9(3)). If there is no power of arrest attached to the IPNA, the applicant who thinks that the respondent is in breach of the order's terms may apply to the court that granted the IPNA for a warrant for the respondent's arrest (s. 10(1)). A warrant can be issued by the court in these circumstances only if the judge or justice has reasonable grounds for believing that the respondent is in breach of a term of the injunction (s. 10(2)). The youth court's powers for dealing with respondents under the age of 18 who are found to have breached the terms of an IPNA are set out in sch. 2, and include making supervision orders or detention orders.

Criminal Behaviour Orders

The provisions of part 2 of the ABCPA 2014 (ss. 22 to 33) concern CBOs. Where an offender **D25.5** has been convicted of a criminal offence, the court may make a CBO against the offender if two conditions are met. The first condition is that the court is satisfied, beyond reasonable doubt, that the offender has engaged in behaviour that caused or was likely to cause harassment, alarm or distress to any person. The second condition is that the court considers that making the order will help in preventing the offender from engaging in such behaviour (s. 22(1)–(3)). The court can make a CBO only on the application of the prosecution (s. 22(7)): it cannot do so of its own motion. Further, the court can make a CBO only if it is made in addition to a sentence imposed in respect of the offence or an order that the offender be conditionally discharged (s. 22(6)).

Like an IPNA, a CBO can contain both prohibitions and requirements (s. 22(5)). The prohibitions and requirement that comprise the CBO must, so far as is practicable, be such as to avoid (a) any interference with the times, if any, at which the respondent normally works or attends school or other educational establishment, and (b) any conflict with the requirements of any other court order or injunction to which the respondent may be subject (s. 22(9)). Before the court can make a CBO that includes a requirement (as opposed to a prohibition), the person who would be responsible for supervising the respondent's compliance with that requirement must provide evidence about the suitability and enforceability of the requirement (s. 24(2)). Moreover, where the court is considering making two requirements, it must consider their compatibility with each other first (s. 24(3)).

In deciding whether to make a CBO, the court can consider evidence led by the prosecution **D25.6** and the offender (s. 23(1)). It does not matter whether the evidence would have been admissible in the proceedings that led to the offender's conviction (s. 23(2)). The court can adjourn the decision whether to make a CBO, even if the adjournment is sought after the offender has been sentenced (s. 23(3)). If the court adjourns the decision whether to make a CBO, it can make an interim CBO to last until the final hearing (s. 26(1)). Where an offender fails to attend any adjourned proceedings, instead of adjourning the proceedings again, the court can either issue a warrant for the offender's arrest or make a CBO in his absence (s. 23(4)).

A CBO takes effect on the day it is made (s. 25(1)) unless the offender is already subject to a CBO in which case the new order may be made to follow on from the expiry of the earlier order (s. 25(2)). A CBO must specify the period for which it has effect (s. 25(3)). For offenders who have not reached the age of 18 when the order is made, that period must be a fixed period of not less than one year and not more than three years (s. 25(4)). For offenders who have reached the age of 18, that period must be either a fixed period of not less than two years or an indefinite period (s. 25(5)). Like the IPNA, prohibitions and requirements can take effect for different periods (s. 26(6)).

A CBO may be varied or discharged by the court that made it on the application of either the offender or the prosecution (s. 27(1)). If an application for variation or discharge is dismissed, the losing party can apply again under s. 27(1) only if either the court or the other party consents (s. 27(2) and (3)). The power to vary or discharge a CBO includes a power to add additional prohibitions or requirements or to extend the period for which a prohibition or requirement has effect (s. 27(4)). Further, s. 28 provides that, where the offender will still be under the age of 18 at the end of a period of 12 months beginning with the date when the CBO was made and the terms of the CBO run beyond that 12-month period, the court must review the operation of the CBO, taking into account, in particular, the extent to which the offender has complied with the CBO, in order to consider whether an application should be made to vary or discharge the order.

An offender who, without reasonable excuse, does anything he is prohibited from doing by a CBO, or fails to do anything he is required to do by a CBO, commits an offence (s. 30(1)). The offence of breaching a CBO is triable either way. The maximum sentence on indictment is imprisonment for a period not exceeding five years or a fine or both (s. 30(2)). An offender who is convicted of breaching the terms of a CBO cannot be conditionally discharged (s. 30(3)).

Closure of Premises

D25.7   The provisions of chapter 3 of part 4 of the ABCPA 2014 (ss. 76 to 93) concern closure notices and closure orders. A police officer of at least the rank of inspector, or the local authority, may issue a closure notice if satisfied on reasonable grounds (a) that the use of particular premises has resulted, or (if the notice is not issued) is likely soon to result, in nuisance to members of the public, or (b) that there has been, or (if the notice is not issued) is likely soon to be, disorder near those premises associated with the use of those premises, and that the notice is necessary to prevent the nuisance or disorder from continuing, recurring or occurring (s. 76(1)). A closure notice prohibits access to the premises for either 24 hours (extendable by a further 24 hours) (s. 77(1)) or, where the notice is issued by a police officer of at least the rank of superintendent or is issued by a local authority and signed by its chief executive officer or his delegate, for 48 hours (s. 77(2)). A closure notice cannot prohibit access to the premises by people who habitually live on the premises or the owner of the premises (s. 76(4)). A closure notice must identify the premises, explain the effect of the notice, state that failure to comply with the notice is an offence, state that an application will be made for a closure order under s. 80, specify when and where the application will be heard, explain the effect of a closure order and give information about the names of, and means of contacting, persons and organisations in the area that provide advice about housing and legal matters (s. 76(5)). A closure notice may be issued only if reasonable efforts have been made to inform people who live on the premises (whether habitually or not) and any person who has control of or responsibility for the premises or who has an interest in them, that the notice is going to be issued (s. 76(6)). If, during the effective period of the closure notice, the relevant police officer or the local authority is no longer satisfied that either of the two conditions necessary for the issuing of the notice is met, then the officer or authority must issue a cancellation notice (cancelling the closure notice) or a variation notice (altering the closure notice so that it does not apply to a part of the premises) (s. 78(1)–(3)). Section 79 sets out the provisions governing the service of closure notices on those affected by them.

Whenever a closure notice has been issued and not cancelled, an application must be made to a magistrates' court for a closure order (s. 80(1)). The application must be heard not later than 48 hours after service of the closure notice (s. 80(3)). The court may make a closure order if it is satisfied (a) that a person has engaged, or (if the order is not made) is likely to engage, in disorderly, offensive or criminal behaviour on the premises, (b) that the use of the premises has resulted, or (if the order is not made) is likely to result, in serious nuisance to members of the public, or (c) that there has been, or (if the order is not made) is likely to be, disorder near those premises associated with the use of those premises, and that the order is necessary to prevent the behaviour, nuisance or disorder from continuing, recurring or occurring (s. 80(5)). The period of a closure order must not exceed three months (s. 80(6)). A closure order may prohibit access to the premises by anyone, at any time and in any circumstances (s. 80(7)). Further, a closure order may be made in respect of the whole or any part of the premises and may include provision about access to a part of the building or structure of which the premises form part (s. 80(8)).

The magistrates' court may adjourn the hearing of an application for a closure order for a maximum of 14 days to enable those who would be affected by the making of a closure order to show that such an order should not be made (s. 81(3)). In circumstances where an adjournment for that purpose is granted, the court may order that the closure notice remains in force until the final hearing (s. 81(4)).

D25.8 Where a closure order is made, an application for an extension of the order may be made at any time before the order is due to expire (s. 82(1)). A police officer or local authority may make an application for an extension only if satisfied on reasonable grounds that it is necessary for the period of the order to be extended to prevent the occurrence, recurrence or continuance of (a) disorderly, offensive or criminal behaviour on the premises, (b) serious nuisance to members of the public resulting from the use of the premises, or (c) disorder near the premises associated with the use of the premises, and if also satisfied that either the police (where the applicant is the local authority) or the local authority (where the applicant is a police officer) has been consulted about the intention to make an application (s. 82(3)). Just as a closure order can be extended before it expires, so an application can be made for it to be discharged before it expires (s. 83(1)). The magistrates' court may not make an order discharging the closure order unless satisfied that the closure order is no longer necessary to prevent the occurrence, recurrence or continuance of (a) disorderly, offensive or criminal behaviour on the premises, (b) serious nuisance to members of the public resulting from the use of the premises, or (c) disorder near the premises associated with the use of the premises (s. 83(7)).

Under s. 84, an appeal to the Crown Court lies against a decision of the magistrates' court either to make a closure order or not to make a closure order.

An 'authorised person' may enter premises in respect of which a closure order is in force and do anything necessary to secure the premises against entry (s. 85(1)); a person may be authorised for this purpose, in the case of a closure order made on an application by the police, by the chief officer of police for the area or, in the case of a closure order made on a local authority application, by that authority (s. 85(2)). Such a person may use reasonable force to achieve his objectives under s. 85(1) (s. 85(3)).

D25.9 A person who, without reasonable excuse, remains on or enters premises in contravention of a closure notice (including a notice continued in force under s. 81) commits an offence (s. 86(1)). A person who, without reasonable excuse, remains on or enters premises in contravention of a closure order also commits an offence (s. 86(2)). A person who, without reasonable excuse, obstructs a person acting under s. 79 (service of closure notices) or s. 85(1) (entering or securing premises subject to a closure order) also commits an offence (s. 86(3)). A person who is convicted under s. 86(1) or (3) is liable to imprisonment for a period not exceeding three months or to a fine or to both (s. 86(4)). A person who is convicted under s. 86(2) is liable to imprisonment for a period not exceeding six months or to a fine or both (s. 86(5)).

Transitional Provisions and Procedural Provisions

D25.10 Parts 1 and 2 and chapter 3 of part 4 of the ABCPA 2014 each have saving and transitional provisions (ss. 21, 33 and 93 respectively) that will need to be considered as and when the relevant provisions are brought into force.

The CrimPR, part 50 (see Supplement, R-361), now includes CBOs in the list of behaviour orders to which it applies. Thus, when part 2 of the ABCPA 2014 is brought into force, the provisions of part 50 will apply to any applications made for a CBO.

ANTI-SOCIAL BEHAVIOUR ORDERS

D25.11 The CDA 1998, s. 1, provides for anti-social behaviour orders (usually referred to as ASBOs). ASBOs are to be replaced by the range of orders available under the ABCPA 2014 (see

D25.1). Section 1 now provides for three different types of ASBOs: 'stand-alone' (s. 1(1)), post-conviction (s. 1C) and county court (s. 1B) (the latter being outside the scope of this book). An ASBO is an order that 'prohibits the defendant from doing anything described in the order' (CDA 1998, s. 1(4)). Under the CDA 1998, s. 1(6), the prohibitions that may be imposed under an ASBO are those necessary for 'protecting persons...from further anti-social acts by the defendant'. Detailed guidance on ASBOs may be found in *A Guide to Anti-social Behaviour Orders* (Home Office, 2006) as well as in *Anti Social Behaviour Orders: A Guide for the Judiciary* (2007) plus supplements.

'Stand-alone' ASBOs

D25.12   **Nature of the Offending Behaviour**   'Stand-alone' ASBOs are brought by complaint to a magistrates' court (CDA 1998, s. 1(3)). Section 1(1) provides that a 'relevant authority' (see D25.15) may apply for an ASBO if it appears to the authority that two conditions are fulfilled in respect of any person aged ten or over:

(a) the person has acted in an anti-social manner, i.e. 'in a manner that caused or was likely to cause harassment, alarm or distress to one or more persons not of the same household as himself' (s. 1(1)(a)); and

(b) 'such an order is necessary to protect relevant persons from further anti-social acts by him' (s. 1(1)(b)).

'Anti-social behaviour' is not described in the Act beyond the broad definition in s. 1(1)(a) above. In *R (Mills) v Birmingham Magistrates' Court* (2006) 170 JP 237 an ASBO imposed upon an habitual shoplifter from chain stores was quashed as her conduct did not cause harassment, alarm or distress nor was it likely to. In *Perry v Humberside Police* [2012] EWHC 3226 (Admin) a former journalist had begun an online blog about his local community. He claimed that various figures in his village had been guilty of corruption and perverting the course of justice. The police applied for a 'stand-alone' ASBO against him and the magistrates' court imposed a ten-year order. The Divisional Court quashed the ASBO. The Court held that the mere fact that a blog may contain material that is untrue or even defamatory may justify the civil courts in granting an injunction but, in deciding whether or not the statutory criteria for the purposes of imposing an ASBO were made out, the District Judge put far too much weight upon the fact that the allegations made in the blog were uncorroborated. The Court found that:

> ...the District Judge far too readily accepted the assertion made by each of the complainants that they had suffered harassment, alarm or distress. More is required than repeating this mantra in each witness statement...the entries on the blog and the physical contacts such as there were between the appellant and those whom he targeted were offensive and tiresome, it is even possible that they could properly be described as amounting to anti-social behaviour but I do not think that the high threshold set by the statutory criteria was met at all.

The Court also found that the District Judge had not properly worked out the relevant considerations under the ECHR, Article 10. Further, a duration of ten years was neither reasonable nor necessary.

D25.13   In *R (Gosport Borough Council) v Fareham Magistrates' Court* [2007] 1 WLR 634, the Divisional Court held that, in order to show that behaviour 'caused' harassment, alarm or distress within the meaning of s. 1(1)(a), it would probably be necessary for a court to hear evidence from one of the harassed, alarmed or distressed victims. In contrast, the alternative formulation in s. 1(1)(a), 'or was likely to cause', enables police witnesses to demonstrate that there were potential victims present, who it was likely were caused harassment, alarm or distress (per Bean J at [20]). 'Likely' in this context means more probable than not (*Chief Constable of Lancashire v Potter* [2003] EWHC 2272 (Admin)).

As to the question of necessity in s. 1(1)(b), in *R (Cooke) v DPP* (2008) 172 JP 596, the Divisional Court held that an ASBO should not be made where an individual's mental impairment meant he did not have the capacity to understand the order, or that he could not comply with it, as the order would not be necessary for the protection of the public. Similarly, in *Pender v DPP* (2013) 177 JP 662, the Divisional Court held that an ASBO should not have been made against a repeat offender who had begged for money for cigarettes because his severe nicotine addiction meant that he did not have the mental capacity to comply with the order (see also **D25.29**). For a case where the offender's learning difficulties did not render the making of an ASBO unnecessary, see *Fairweather v Commissioner of Police of the Metropolis* [2008] EWHC 3073 (Admin).

Standard of Proof   In *R (McCann) v Crown Court at Manchester* [2003] 1 AC 787, the House **D25.14** of Lords held that ASBOs under the CDA 1998, s. 1, are preventative not punitive and therefore civil not criminal in nature. Nonetheless, their lordships went on to hold that there are good reasons for applying the higher, criminal, standard when allegations are being made which, if proved, would have serious consequences for the defendant. It follows that, when applying s. 1(1)(a), the court must be sure that the defendant acted in the manner specified in that provision. In other words, the proceedings are civil in nature but the court must apply the criminal standard of proof. Their lordships also said that the inquiry under s. 1(1)(b), namely that such an order is necessary to protect persons from further anti-social acts by the defendant, does not involve a standard of proof: it is an exercise of judgement or evaluation.

Under the CDA 1998, s. 1(5), the court is required to 'disregard any act of the defendant which he shows was reasonable in the circumstances'. The burden is on the defendant to show this on the balance of probabilities.

'Relevant Authority'   An application for an ASBO may be made only by a 'relevant authority'. **D25.15** This term is defined by s. 1(1A), and includes local authorities, the police (including the British Transport Police), social landlords (registered under the Housing Act 1996, s. 1), and housing action trusts (established under the Housing Act 1988, s. 62). The CDA 1998, s. 1A(2), enables the Secretary of State to add to the list of 'relevant authorities' that may apply for anti-social behaviour orders. The Crime and Disorder Act 1998 (Relevant Authorities and Relevant Persons) Order 2006 (SI 2006 No. 2137) added the Environment Agency and Transport for London to the list of bodies that are 'relevant authorities'. In magistrates' courts, applications are most commonly made by the police or a local authority.

'Relevant Persons'   The court has to be satisfied that 'relevant persons' are in need of protec- **D25.16** tion by an ASBO. This term is defined by the CDA 1998, s. 1(1B). Broadly, relevant persons are people who are within the government area of the applicant body. Where the British Transport Police apply for an ASBO, 'relevant persons' means 'persons who are within or likely to be within a place specified in s. 31(1)(a)–(f) of the Railways and Transport Safety Act 2003 (that is, on the track, on the network, in a station, in a light maintenance depot, on other land used for purposes of or in relation to a railway, or on other land in which a person who provides railway services has a freehold or leasehold interest); or persons who are within or likely to be within such a place'. Where the applicant is the Environment Agency, relevant persons are those on or in the vicinity (or likely to be on or in the vicinity) of land in respect of which the Agency has a statutory function. In the case of Transport for London (TfL), it connotes persons who are on or in the vicinity (or likely to be on or in the vicinity) of land or vehicles used in connection with TfL services.

Application Procedure   The application for an ASBO has to be made to the magistrates' court **D25.17** that serves the area concerned (CDA 1998, s. 1(3)). The magistrates' court will be sitting in its civil capacity. Hearsay is admissible and the Civil Evidence Act 1995 and the Magistrates' Courts (Hearsay Evidence in Civil Proceedings) Rules 1999 (SI 1999 No. 681) must be complied with. As to the weight to be attached to hearsay evidence, see *Moat Housing Group–South Ltd v Harris* [2006] QB 606.

In *Birmingham City Council v Shafi* [2009] 3 All ER 127, the Court of Appeal made plain that the specific requirements of the ASBO legislation, including the standard of proof, should not be circumvented by local authorities applying for injunctions in the civil courts to prohibit conduct of the kind that an ASBO is designed to prevent. In *Birmingham City Council v James* [2014] 1 WLR 23, the Court of Appeal held that *Shafi* did not establish a 'closest fit' principle whereby a local authority is required to apply only for the injunctive order that most closely fits the facts. Accordingly, in that case, where the local authority could have applied for an ASBO instead of an injunction in restraint of gang-related violence (IRGV) under the PACA 2009, s. 34, that was no reason to hold that the making of an IRGV had been unnecessary.

In *R (Chief Constable of West Mercia Constabulary) v Boorman* (2005) 169 JP 669, it was held that evidence of events that took place more than six months before an application for an ASBO (i.e. outside the time-limit under the MCA 1980, s. 127, for commencing a prosecution in the case of summary offences) may be admissible both for the purposes of proving that a person acted in an anti-social manner during the relevant period and to show that such an order is necessary. However, it should also be noted that the VCRA 2006, s. 59, amends the CDA 1998, s. 1, by adding a s. 1(5A), which provides that nothing in s. 1 affects the operation of the MCA 1980, s. 127. It follows that some conduct within the six-month period preceding the application is necessary to obtain an ASBO.

In *Birmingham City Council v Dixon* [2010] 1 WLR 32, the High Court held that evidence of an individual's post-complaint behaviour could be relevant as to whether his behaviour during a period that formed the basis of a complaint was anti-social. However, it had to be stressed that, in order to make good the complaint, it was necessary to prove the allegations in the complaint itself; whilst evidence of post-complaint behaviour might assist in proving the complaint, it did not enlarge the complaint itself. Further, the admission of post-complaint behaviour was also relevant as to whether an ASBO was necessary to protect the public in a local authority's area, e.g., an individual might have 'turned over a new leaf', become ill or had an accident so that the ASBO was no longer necessary.

D25.18   Where an ASBO is being sought by a local authority, failure by the local authority to consult the person against whom they are seeking the ASBO during the decision-making process is not a breach of that person's rights under Article 6 or 8 of the ECHR, since he can resist the application in court (*Wareham v Purbeck District Council* (2005) 169 JP 217). There is, however, a statutory duty upon an applicant body to consult other relevant authorities before applying for an ASBO. For example, the police must consult the relevant local authority and vice versa (CDA 1998, s. 1(E)).

In *R (M) v Sheffield Magistrates' Court* [2005] 1 FLR 81, the Divisional Court gave detailed guidance on cases where a local authority applies for an ASBO against a child in its care, to ensure that the interests of the child are protected properly.

D25.19   As the youth court has no civil jurisdiction, all stand-alone ASBOs are applied for in the adult magistrates' court. *Practice Direction (Magistrates' Courts: Composition)* [2006] 1 WLR 636 stipulates that, where there is an application to a magistrates' court for an ASBO (or for an ASBO to be varied or discharged) and the person against whom the order is sought is under 18, the justices constituting the court should normally be qualified to sit in the youth court. However, applications for interim orders under s. 1D (see **D25.25**), including those made without notice, may be listed before justices who are not so qualified. If it is not practicable to constitute a bench in accordance with the direction, in particular where to do so would result in a delayed hearing, para. 3 provides that 'this direction does not apply'.

Section 40 of the Crime and Security Act 2010 (not yet in force) inserts a new s. 1(1C) into the CDA 1998, which requires the relevant authority to prepare a report on the family circumstances of a person under the age of 16 before making an application for a stand-alone ASBO.

For permissible terms of an ASBO, see **D25.32**.

For breach of an ASBO, see **D25.39**.

D25.20   **Duration of an ASBO**   An ASBO has effect for the period specified in the order (which must be at least two years) or until further order of the court (CDA 1998, s. 1(7)). Under s. 1(9), except with the consent of both parties, an ASBO cannot be discharged before the end of the period of two years beginning with the date of service of the order. In *R (Lonergan) v Crown Court at Lewes* [2005] 2 All ER 362, Kay LJ (at [13]) said that, just because the ASBO must run for a minimum of two years, it does not follow that each and every prohibition within the ASBO (such as a curfew) must endure for the life of the order. A prohibition which prevented a defendant from using the railways for ten years was disproportionate and unnecessary to provide protection to those whose job it is to operate the railway network and was reduced to three years on appeal (*Ball* [2010] EWCA Crim 1740). See also *Perry v Humberside Police* [2012] EWHC 3226 (Admin) at **D25.12**. For an example of the rare circumstances in which an indefinite order may be appropriate, see *Avery* [2010] 2 Cr App R (S) 209, where 'a group had pursued a course of reprehensible conduct where they were messianic in their fervour about the cause of animal rights and where they had shown no real remorse at any stage and were likely to repeat their offending'. For an example where an indefinite order was held to be inappropriate, see *West* [2013] EWCA Crim 1309.

For reviews of youth ASBOs, see **D25.21**.

Variation, Discharge and Reviews of an ASBO   Subject to the proviso that the order cannot **D25.21** be discharged before two years have elapsed unless both parties consent, s. 1(8) of the CDA 1998 enables the applicant or the defendant to apply to the magistrates' court for the order to be varied or discharged.

Under the Magistrates' Courts (Anti-Social Behaviour Orders) Rules 2002 (SI 2000 No. 2784), r. 6(2), an application to vary or discharge an ASBO must be made in writing to the magistrates' court which made the order, or, in the case of an application under s. 1C (see **D25.27**), to any magistrates' court in the same local justice area, specifying the reason why the court should vary or discharge the order. If the court considers that there are no grounds upon which it might conclude that the order should be varied or discharged, it may determine the application without a hearing (r. 6(3)). Otherwise, a hearing of the application takes place under r. 6(4).

In *Leeds City Council v RG* [2007] 4 All ER 652, it was held that the duration of an ASBO made under s. 1(1) can be extended on an application to vary its terms under s. 1(8). However, Latham LJ said (at [11]) that an application to impose more stringent obligations (including greater length) on a defendant can succeed only if the applying authority can put before the justices material which justifies the extension as necessary in order to achieve the statutory objective (and the usual burden and standard of proof apply to the determination of that question). In the case of an application to extend the length of the ASBO by variation, the applying authority has to persuade the court that it is appropriate to do so rather than make an application for a new ASBO. There would be a clear rationale for example, for asking for an extension of an ASBO for *less* than two years, on the basis that the authority did not consider that it was necessary to have a further period as long as the minimum period of two years which applies if a fresh ASBO is ordered. In *James v Birmingham City Council* (2010) 174 JP 250 the High Court considered whether the local authority was required to establish a fresh act of anti-social behaviour before any variation of an ASBO, or at least any variation by extension, could take effect. The court held that there was no basis for saying that a variation required the establishment of a fresh anti-social act. However, applying *Leeds City Council v RG*, it said that there would have to be cogent evidence to show that it was necessary to extend the terms of the order. No doubt that evidence was likely in most cases to involve some additional anti-social acts. However, this was not necessarily so and whether a variation is necessary is ultimately a question for the court.

The CDA 1998, s. 1J, creates an obligation to carry out a one year review of all ASBOs issued **D25.22** to persons aged under 17. A review may result in variation or discharge (s. 1J(5)(c)). Section 1K sets out which agencies are responsible for the reviews. Under s. 1J(2), if the subject of the ASBO will be under the age of 18 at the end of the 'review period' (defined in s. 1J(3)) and the term of the ASBO runs until the end of that period or beyond, then, before the end of that period, a review of the operation of the order must be carried out. Full details of how such reviews should be conducted are contained in *A Guide to Reviewing Anti-social Behaviour Orders given to Young People and Individual Support Orders* (2009), issued pursuant to s. 1J(7).

D25.23   **Appeals**   The CDA 1998, s. 4(1), provides for an appeal to the Crown Court against the making of an ASBO or interim ASBO by a magistrates' court. The fact that s. 4(1) refers to an appeal against the *making* of an order does not prevent a defendant from appealing against the *terms* of the order itself (*R v Manchester Crown Court, ex parte Manchester City Council* [2001] ACD 53). The appeal is by way of full rehearing and remains civil in character. In *R (Langley) v Preston Crown Court* [2009] 3 All ER 1026, Scott Baker LJ said that, on true construction of s. 4, there is no right of appeal against the decision of a magistrates' court to vary or discharge an ASBO. In *R (Birmingham City Council) v Birmingham Crown Court* [2009] EWHC 3329 (Admin), the High Court considered out-of-time appeals to the Crown Court against 'stand-alone' ASBOs. It held that appellants should indicate their proposed grounds of appeal briefly and, where possible, indicate the merits of the appeal, also briefly. In doing so, they should bear in mind the need not to say so much at an interlocutory stage that the tribunal of fact considering the appeal (if permission is granted) might be prejudiced. Secondly, they should say why time should be extended, giving the reasons for delay and, if they are able to, why the proposed respondent would not be prejudiced by an extension of time. The grounds of appeal must be stated in any notice of appeal against an ASBO made in civil proceedings in a magistrates' court (Crown Court Rules 1982 (SI 1982 No. 1109), as amended by SI 2009 No. 3361).

D25.24   Under s. 4(2)(a), the Crown Court may make 'such orders as may be necessary to give effect to its determination of the appeal'. In addition, it may make any incidental or consequential order as it considers just (s. 4(2)(b)). Any order of the Crown Court made on an appeal under s. 4 (other than one directing that an application be reheard by a magistrates' court) shall, for the purposes of variation, be treated as if it were an order of the magistrates' court from which the appeal was brought and not an order of the Crown Court (s. 4(3)).

It is also possible to seek judicial review of the making of an ASBO (or a refusal to make one) or to appeal by way of case stated. However, in *R (W) v Acton Youth Court* (2006) 170 JP 31, the Divisional Court held that, in a claim for judicial review, it is not enough for the claimant to demonstrate that there were some errors in procedure, or that the terms of the order can be criticised (since the remedy for such complaints where the order is made by a magistrates' court is by way of appeal to the Crown Court); to succeed in having the order quashed by judicial review the claimant must demonstrate that the process before the magistrates was so flawed that the making of the order amounted to an excess of jurisdiction (per Pitchers J at [26]).

In *Samuda v DPP* [2008] EWHC 205 (Admin), it was held that the MCA 1980, s. 142 (the power to reopen cases: see **D22.70**), does not apply to ASBOs since such orders are civil in nature.

D25.25   **Interim ASBOs**   The CDA 1998, s. 1D(2), enables an interim ASBO to be made if the court considers that it is just to do so pending the determination of the main application. The effect of the order is to prohibit the defendant from doing anything described in the order (s. 1D(3)). Under s. 1D(4), an interim order has to be for a fixed period; it may be varied, renewed or discharged; and, if it has not previously ceased to have effect, it will cease to have effect on the determination of the main application. An appeal lies against the making of an interim order in the same way as it does for a final ASBO (s. 4(1)) (see **D25.23**).

The Magistrates' Court (Anti-Social Behaviour Orders) Rules 2002 (SI 2002 No. 2784), r. 5(1), provides that an application for an interim ASBO may, with leave of the justices' clerk, be made without notice being given to the defendant. The justices' clerk may grant such leave only if satisfied that it is 'necessary for the application to be made without notice being given to the defendant' (r. 5(2)). In *R (Manchester City Council) v Manchester Justices* [2005] EWHC

253 (Admin), Henriques J said (at [34]) that, in deciding whether the clerk is satisfied that it is necessary for the application to be made without notice being given to the defendant, he should have regard, *inter alia*, to:

(a) the likely response of the defendant on receiving notice of such an application;
(b) whether such a response was liable to prejudice the complaint having regard to the complainant's vulnerability;
(c) the gravity of the conduct complained of within the scale tackled by ASBOs in general as opposed to the locality of the magistrates' court;
(d) the urgency of the matter;
(e) the nature of the prohibitions sought;
(f) the right of the defendant to know about the proceedings; and
(g) the counterbalancing protections in the defendant's favour, namely (i) the ineffectiveness of the order until served, (ii) the limited period of time for which the order would be effective, and (iii) the defendant's right to apply to vary or discharge the order.

His lordship made the point (at [23]) that the test in r. 5(2) is less stringent than the test applied **D25.26** by the justices following the granting of leave (for which see *R (Kenny) v Leeds Magistrates' Court* [2004] 1 All ER 1333).

Where an interim order is granted, the interim order and the application, together with a summons giving a date for the defendant to attend court, must be served on the defendant, in person, as soon as practicable after the making of the interim order (r. 5(3)). Under r. 5(4), an interim order made without notice does not take effect until it has been served on the defendant. Moreover, if it is not served on the defendant within seven days of being made, it ceases to have effect (r. 5(5)). An interim order also ceases to have effect if the application for an ASBO is withdrawn (r. 6(6)).

Under r. 5(7), where the court refuses to make an interim order without notice being given to the defendant, it may direct that the application be made on notice. Rule 5(8) stipulates that, if an interim order is made without notice, and the defendant subsequently applies to the court for the order to be discharged or varied, his application cannot be dismissed without his being given the opportunity to make oral representations to the court.

Given the fact that the defendant can seek a review of the interim ASBO, the power to make an interim order without notice is not inconsistent with the ECHR, Article 6 (*R (M) v Secretary of State for Constitutional Affairs* [2004] 2 All ER 531).

Section 1D(1)(c) and (d) enable interim orders to be made where a request is made by the prosecution for an order under s. 1C (see **D25.27**) or the court is minded to make an order under s. 1C of its own motion. There is thus a power to grant an interim ASBO following conviction, pending a full hearing.

Post-conviction ASBOs

An ASBO may also be imposed following a conviction. **D25.27**

Crime and Disorder Act 1998, s. 1C

(2) If the court considers—
   (a) that the offender has acted, at any time since the commencement date [1 April 1999], in an anti-social manner, that is to say in a manner that caused or was likely to cause harassment, alarm or distress to one or more persons not of the same household as himself, and
   (b) that an order under this section is necessary to protect persons in any place in England and Wales from further anti-social acts by him,
   it may make an order which prohibits the offender from doing anything described in the order.

The first limb of the test is identical to that in 'stand-alone' ASBOs (see cases cited at **D25.12**).

D25.28   Post-conviction ASBOs in relation to young people will be applied for in the court that convicted them (either the youth court or the Crown Court). Section 1C(4) provides that an ASBO can be made only in addition to a sentence imposed in respect of the offence of which the offender has been convicted, or in addition to an order for a conditional discharge. Under s. 1C(5), the starting point of an ASBO can be suspended until an offender has been released from a custodial sentence. With orders on conviction, an additional factor has to be considered, namely the impact of the sentence on the necessity for an order, since the one may make the other unnecessary (see, e.g., *P (Shane Tony)* [2004] 2 Cr App R (S) 343, *Thomas* [2008] EWCA Crim 2151, *Belaid* [2008] EWCA Crim 2153 and *Boyce* [2009] EWCA Crim 2306). In *R (F) v Bolton Crown Court* [2009] EWHC 240 (Admin) the High Court quashed a post-conviction ASBO imposed on a 13-year-old boy on the basis that his sentence of a two-year supervision order plus a curfew order, which incorporated structured sessions to address the root causes of his offending behaviour (including his difficult home circumstances), undermined the conclusion that an ASBO was necessary. (For the duration of ASBOs generally, see **D25.20**.) In *Dyer* [2010] EWCA Crim 2096, Thomas LJ said (at [7]) that it was always desirable when an ASBO is sought post-conviction for a judge to consider the publication *Anti Social Behaviour Orders: A Guide for the Judiciary* (see **D25.11**) and that it 'should always be consulted before an ASBO' is made post-conviction. The Guide suggests that relevant considerations will be: (1) the nature and length of the sentence, (2) its likely effect on the defendant, (3) the nature, length and effect (if any) of previous sentences, and (4) the duration, conditions and likely effect of any period of licence. On the facts of *Dyer*, the Court of Appeal upheld a post-conviction ASBO imposed in addition to a four-year sentence for 'street-dealing' of cannabis. In *Barclay* [2011] 2 Cr App R (S) 385 (following *Dyer*) the Court of Appeal upheld the imposition of ASBOs in addition to sentences ranging from three and a half to five years as it found that there was a basis for concluding in relation to three of the four appellants that the custodial sentences might not deter future offending. Moreover, it held that the ASBOs were not simply directed at future drugs offending but also at the defendants' involvement in the anti-social behaviour associated with the open street dealing of drugs and their contribution to making that particular geographical area a 'no go' area. For an example of an ASBO that was considered unnecessary and disproportionate in addition to a sentence of three and a half years' imprisonment, see *Stewart* [2012] EWCA Crim 1231.

D25.29   As to the question of necessity generally, in *R (Cooke) v DPP* (2008) 172 JP 596 the Divisional Court held that an ASBO should not be made where an individual's mental impairment meant he did not have the capacity to understand the order, or that he could not comply with it, as the order would not be necessary for the protection of the public. In *Pender v DPP* (2013) 177 JP 662, the Divisional Court, applying *Cooke*, quashed an ASBO against a 63-year-old man convicted of a number of offences of begging in a public place. A doctor had given uncontradicted evidence that the defendant suffered learning difficulties, schizophrenia and severe nicotine addiction and that his begging behaviour was the manifestation of his addiction. The doctor concluded that the defendant lacked capacity to understand the prohibition in the ASBO and the consequences of its breach. The judge in the Crown Court concluded that the defendant *did* understand the nature and consequences of the ASBO. However, the Divisional Court found that the judge had not set out the reasons for reaching that factual conclusion and, while a fact-finder was entitled to disagree with an expert, there must be a basis for it and the basis must be set out.

In *Gowan* [2008] 1 Cr App R (S) 50, the offender was convicted of threatening to kill his wife. The judge made an ASBO prohibiting him from having any contact with the complainant or going within 200 metres of the house where she lived, the terms of the order to be suspended until the defendant was released from custody. The Court of Appeal held that s. 1C(2) is directed at protecting members of the general public from an offender's conduct and so could not be used to protect a wife with whom an offender had been and would in the future be cohabiting (since she would be in the same household as the offender). The judge therefore had no power to make the order.

Section 1C(9A) allows a local authority, where a person subject to an ASBO resides in its area, to prosecute for breach of an ASBO made under s. 1C.

Section 1C(4A) empowers the court to adjourn any proceedings in relation to an order under s. 1C, even after sentencing the offender. If the offender does not appear for any adjourned proceedings, the court may further adjourn the proceedings or (if satisfied that he has had adequate notice of the time and place of the adjourned proceedings) issue a warrant for his arrest (s. 1C(4B) and (4C)).

D25.30 Section 1CA makes provision for the variation and discharge of ASBOs made under s. 1C (see also **D25.21**). The application for variation or discharge may be by the offender (s. 1CA(1)), the DPP (s. 1CA(3)), or a relevant authority (s. 1CA(4)) (see **D25.15**). By virtue of s. 1CA(7), an order under s. 1C cannot be discharged within two years of the date when the order was made unless (if the offender is the applicant) the DPP consents or (if the application is made by the DPP or by a relevant authority) the offender consents. A relevant authority may apply for variation of the order only if the protection of relevant persons from anti-social acts by the person subject to the order would be more appropriately effected by a variation of the order, and may apply for discharge of the order only if it is no longer necessary to protect relevant persons from anti-social acts by him by means of such an order (s. 1CA(4)).

The obligation to carry out a one year review of all ASBOs issued to persons aged under 17 applies (s. 1J: see **D25.21**).

D25.31 **Applications for ASBOs under s. 1C** Section 1C(3) of the CDA 1998 stipulates that the court may make an ASBO either if the prosecutor asks it to do so, or of its own volition. Where a court does make an order of its own motion, such an order may be quashed if the making of the order breached the requirement for procedural fairness. The court is required to put precisely to the defendant the concerns in relation to his anti-social behaviour that it proposes to address and it should invite submissions on the proposal to make an order and the contents of such an order (*R (McGarrett) v Kingston Crown Court* [2009] EWHC 1776 (Admin)). Under s. 1C(3A), the court may, for the purpose of deciding whether to make an ASBO under s. 1C, consider evidence led by the prosecution and the defence. It is immaterial whether such evidence would have been admissible in the proceedings in which the offender was convicted (s. 1C(3B)).

In *R (W) v Acton Youth Court* (2006) 170 JP 31, the Divisional Court confirmed that proceedings under s. 1C are civil, not criminal, in nature. It follows that hearsay is admissible. However, as Pitchers J put it (at [24]), a court 'must distinguish between hearsay which, on examination, they find to be cogent and what is more properly to be regarded as unreliable tittle tattle'. In *W and F* [2007] 3 All ER 562, the civil nature of the proceedings was endorsed, as was the admissibility of hearsay. But Aikens J indicated (at [41]) that a court must be satisfied to a criminal standard that the defendant has acted in the anti-social manner alleged (see **D25.14**). Detailed procedural rules are set out in the CrimPR, part 50, governing 'civil behaviour orders', including ASBOs under the CDA 1998, s. 1C, and interim ASBOs under s. 1D (see Supplement, **R-361** *et seq.*). In *Lima* [2010] EWCA Crim 284 a failure to comply with the CrimPR, part 50, resulted in procedural unfairness and was one of the reasons the Court of Appeal quashed the ASBO. Mackay J said at [8]: 'This case illustrates in our judgment the need for observance of such rules where an order significantly restricting the liberty of a person is envisaged'.

D25.32 **Terms of ASBOs** General guidance in respect of the terms of any ASBO was provided by the Court of Appeal in *P (Shane Tony)* [2004] 2 Cr App R (S) 343. Giving the judgment of the court, Henriques J said (at [34]):

(1) The test for making an order is one of necessity to protect the public from further anti-social acts by the offender.
(2) The terms of the order must be precise and capable of being understood by offender.
(3) The findings of fact giving rise to the making of the order must be recorded.
(4) The order must be explained to the offender.

(5) The exact terms of the order must be pronounced in open court and the written order must accurately reflect the order as pronounced.

D25.33 In *Boness* [2006] 1 Cr App R (S) 690, the Court of Appeal gave detailed guidance on the nature and purpose of ASBOs:

(1) An ASBO must be precise and capable of being understood by the offender. It follows that the court should ask itself before making an order: 'Are the terms of this order clear so that the offender will know precisely what it is that he is prohibited from doing?' (at [19]). See also *Delaney v Calderdale Magistrates' Court* [2009] EWHC 3635 (Admin).

(2) Following a finding that the offender has acted in an anti-social manner (whether or not the act constituted a criminal offence), the test for making an order that prohibits the offender from doing something is one of necessity. Each separate order prohibiting a person from doing a specified thing has to be necessary to protect persons from further anti-social acts by him. Accordingly, any order has to be tailor-made for the individual offender (at [28]).

(3) Given the requirement that the order has to be necessary to protect persons from further anti-social acts by the offender, the purpose of an ASBO is not to punish. It follows that the use of an ASBO to punish an offender is unlawful (at [29]).

(4) A court should not impose an ASBO as an alternative to prison or other sanction; rather, the court should decide the appropriate sentence and then move on to consider whether an ASBO should be made after sentence has been passed (at [29]).

(5) It also follows from the requirement that the order has to be necessary to protect persons from further anti-social acts by the offender that the court should not impose an order which prohibits an offender from committing a specified criminal offence, if the sentence which can be passed following conviction for the offence should be a sufficient deterrent (at [30]). An ASBO should not be used merely to increase the sentence of imprisonment which an offender is liable to receive (at [32]).

(6) As well as considering whether an order is necessary to protect persons from further anti-social acts by him, the court must ensure that the terms of the order are proportionate, in the sense that they must be commensurate with the risk to be guarded against. This is particularly important where an order may interfere with an ECHR right, e.g., Articles 8, 10 and 11 (at [38]).

ASBOs should contain terms which are prohibitions directed to the anti-social behaviour. Negative terms which are in truth mandatory orders to do something specific are not permissible (*R (M) v Sheffield Magistrates' Court* [2005] 1 FLR 81). In *N v DPP* (2007) 171 JP 393, the Divisional Court quashed an ASBO term that prohibited a 15-year-old from 'congregating in groups of three or more in a public place other than with adults over the age of 21'. Applying *Boness*, the court stated that this would prevent him from attending a sporting event or even standing in a bus queue. The term was replaced with a somewhat inelegantly drafted one preventing N from 'congregating in a public place in a group of two or more persons in a manner causing or likely to cause any person fear for their safety'. In *M v DPP* (2007) 171 JP 457 the Divisional Court quashed a term ('not to knowingly associate with a person or persons while such person or persons are engaged in attempting or conspiring to commit any criminal offence in England and Wales') on the basis that the clause involved the exercise of a value judgement on the part of the defendant who might have to take an instant decision as to whether those with whom he was associated were about to commit a crime and that could not be right.

D25.34   **Prohibition of Conduct Amounting to an Offence**   The question of whether an ASBO may include a term prohibiting the defendant from committing a specific criminal offence has vexed the courts. In *Kirby* [2006] 1 Cr App R (S) 151, the offender pleaded guilty to driving offences. The judge imposed an ASBO because it effectively increased the penalty that the court could impose for further similar offences to five years' custody. The Court of Appeal held that the power to make an ASBO should not normally be exercised where the underlying objective is to give the court higher sentencing powers in the event of future similar offending (per Clarke J at [9]). His lordship added (at [11]) that the making of an ASBO should not be a normal part of a sentencing process, particularly in cases which do not in themselves specifically involve intimidation, harassment and distress. Rather, it is an exceptional course to be taken in particular circumstances. *Kirby* was approved in *Williams* [2006] 1 Cr App R (S) 305.

In *Morrison* [2006] 1 Cr App R (S) 488, the Court of Appeal held that, if a breach of an ASBO consists of no more than the commission of an offence for which a maximum penalty is prescribed by statute, it is wrong in principle to pass a sentence for that breach calculated by reference to the five-year maximum for breach of an ASBO; the tariff is determined by the statutory maximum for the offence in question. There may, however, be exceptional cases in which it can properly be said that the vice of the breach of an ASBO, although it amounts to an offence, goes beyond that offence, e.g., repeated offences of criminal damage directed against a particular and perhaps vulnerable victim or group of victims. However, in *Lamb* [2006] 2 Cr App R (S) 84, Leveson J said (at [16]) that the view expressed in *Morrison* 'appears to ignore the impact of anti-social behaviour on the wider public which was the purpose of the legislation in the first place' and also 'means that anti-social behaviour short of a criminal offence could be more heavily punished than anti-social behaviour that coincidentally was also a criminal offence'. He said that the contrary approach taken in *Tripp* [2005] EWCA Crim 2253 and *Braxton* [2005] 1 Cr App R (S) 167 was to be preferred. In *Tripp*, Clarke J (at [7]) had said that, where breach of an ASBO consists of conduct which is itself a criminal offence, the potential sentence may be far longer than the maximum for that basic offence; in *Braxton*, Leveson J had made the point (at [17]) that the offender in that case had to understand that misconduct that the offender might consider trivial was, because of the persistence of that conduct, now to be treated seriously, specifically to protect the public.

It is submitted that the following principles can be derived from this body of case law: **D25.35**

(a) it is permissible to include in an ASBO a clause which prohibits the offender from committing a specific criminal offence (or which prohibits the offender from engaging in conduct which also amounts to a specific criminal offence);
(b) however, this should not be done solely in order to increase the penalty which can be imposed on the offender if he commits that offence;
(c) if the offender breaches that term of the ASBO, the court dealing with the breach should have regard to the maximum penalty applicable for the specific criminal offence but may, if it is just and proportionate to do so, impose a sentence for the breach of the ASBO which exceeds the maximum sentence for the specific criminal offence (subject of course to the maximum sentence available for breach of an ASBO).

In *Heron v Plymouth City Council* [2009] EWHC 3562 (Admin), the Divisional Court found that the condition that prevented the appellant from causing 'harm, alarm or distress' to any person was too imprecise and simply a replication of offences contained in the Public Order Act 1986.

Prohibitions that are Too Wide What if the terms of an ASBO are drafted too widely? In *R* **D25.36** *(W) v DPP* (2005) 169 JP 435, it was held that a term of the order prohibiting the defendant from committing any criminal offence was plainly too wide. It is, said the court, well established that a person subject to a restraining order is entitled to know what he can and cannot do (*B v Chief Constable of Avon and Somerset Constabulary* [2001] 1 All ER 562). The court went on to hold that the clause in question was plainly invalid and, therefore, unenforceable (i.e. breach proceedings could not follow). In *M v DPP* (2007) 171 JP 457, the Divisional Court reiterated that, where a clause is too broad, it cannot stand.

The question of the raising of arguments as to the validity of clauses in an ASBO in the context of **D25.37** proceedings for breach (rather than on appeal from the making of the order) was revisited in *DPP v T* [2007] 3 All ER 471. On the particular facts the Divisional Court ruled that the wide provision 'not to act in an anti-social manner' without further definition or limitation should never again be included in an ASBO (see also *Heron v Plymouth City Council* [2009] EWHC 3562 (Admin) at **D25.35**). It held that the normal rule in relation to an order of the court is that it must be treated as valid and be obeyed unless and until it is set aside. Even if the order should not have been made in the first place, a person may be liable for any breach of it committed before it is set aside. Moreover, the person against whom an ASBO is made has a full opportunity to challenge that order on appeal or to apply to vary it. Accordingly, insofar as any question does arise as to the validity of such an order, there is no obvious reason why the person against whom the order was made should be allowed to raise that issue as a defence in subsequent breach proceedings rather than by way of appeal against the original order (per Richards LJ at [27]). His lordship went on to say (at [35]):

> ...although it is alleged that the relevant provision of the ASBO is unduly wide and uncertain and unnecessary for the purpose of protecting against further anti-social acts, we very much doubt whether that could be said to go to the validity of the order. The magistrates' court plainly had jurisdiction under the Crime and Disorder Act 1998 to make an ASBO. It seems to us that if the court was in error in including a provision in these terms... that did not have the consequence of taking the order outside the court's jurisdiction; and if the order was within the court's jurisdiction, it would remain valid even if there were errors in it that were open to correction on appeal. With great respect to the Divisional Court in *R (W)*, we do not accept that because an order is 'plainly too wide' it is also 'plainly invalid'.

Where the court is concerned that one or more of the terms of the ASBO is drafted too widely, Richards LJ indicated (at [37]) that the court may:

> ...consider whether the relevant provision lacked sufficient clarity to warrant a finding that the respondent's conduct amounted to a breach of the order; whether the lack of clarity provided a reasonable excuse for non-compliance with the order; and whether, if a breach was established, it was appropriate in the circumstances to impose any penalty for the breach.

D25.38 **Appeals**   The CDA 1998, s. 4, does not on the face of it give a right of appeal to the Crown Court against the making of a post-conviction ASBO in the magistrates' court. However, there is a right of appeal to the Crown Court by reason of s. 108 (3) of the MCA 1980. An appeal against the ruling of the Crown Court will be by an application for judicial review or by way of case stated. Appeals against post-conviction ASBOs made in the Crown Court are to the Court of Appeal, Criminal Division, despite the civil nature of the order (*P (Shane Tony)* [2004] 2 Cr App R (S) 343). See also **D25.23**.

Breach of an ASBO and Sentencing

D25.39 The CDA 1998, s. 1(10), provides that if, without reasonable excuse, a person does anything that he is prohibited from doing by an ASBO (either an interim or final order), he commits an offence, which is triable either way. Those aged 18 or over will be brought before a magistrates' court and those aged under 18 will be brought before a youth court, irrespective of which court originally made the order. The maximum penalty for an adult in the magistrates' court is six months' imprisonment and/or a fine up to £5,000. On conviction on indictment, the maximum penalty for an adult is five years' imprisonment and/or a fine. In the youth court, the maximum penalty for those aged between 12 and 17 is a two-year detention and training order. If the person is aged between 12 and 14 at conviction, the court must also be of the opinion that he is a persistent offender before it can pass such a sentence. Where a person aged under 16 is convicted of breaching an ASBO, the court will be required, once the Crime and Security Act 2010, s. 41, comes into force, to make a parenting order (see **D25.48**).

Section 1(11) stipulates that the court cannot grant a conditional discharge when it convicts a defendant under s. 1(10).

A copy of the original order, certified as such by the proper officer of the court which made it, is admissible as evidence of its having been made and of its contents to the same extent that oral evidence of those things is admissible (s. 1(10)(c)). Whether an order has been breached is a question of fact, having regard to the actual terms of the order (*Doughan* (2007) 171 JP 397).

'Reasonable Excuse'   The meaning of the phrase 'reasonable excuse' in this context was consid- **D25.40**
ered by the Court of Appeal in *Nicholson* [2006] 1 WLR 2857. The court ruled that forgetfulness
on the part of the accused, or a misunderstanding on his part of the terms of the ASBO, *may* be
capable of constituting a defence of reasonable excuse (per Auld LJ at [15]). Where the accused
appears before the Crown Court (the offence under s. 1(10) is triable either way) and raises such
a defence, it is a matter for the jury to resolve (at [17]). In *Charles* [2010] 4 All ER 553, the Court
of Appeal considered the question of where the burden lies when the defence raise 'reasonable
excuse' and said that it cannot have been intended by Parliament to place any burden of proof
on the defendant under s. 1(10) which criminalises conduct that Parliament itself has not criminalised and has not prescribed the terms in which that can be done. The Court held that the
burden of disproving reasonable excuse rests on the Crown where the defendant has raised the
issue on the evidence before the court and that the Act is perfectly workable on the basis that it
imposes only an evidential burden on the defendant, but leaves the legal burden on the Crown.
The question of what is the nature of the mental element that a prosecutor must prove when a
defendant is prosecuted for beach of an ASBO was considered in *B v DPP* [2012] 1 WLR 2357.
The Divisional Court found that s. 1(10) does not require the Crown to prove a specific mental
element on the part of a defendant at the time he committed the acts which constitute the breach
of an ASBO. However, if the issue of reasonable excuse arises in any given case, a defendant can
raise his state of mind at the time of the alleged breach since the state of mind will usually be
relevant to the issue of reasonable excuse. Applying *Nicholson*, the court held that, as the effect
of s. 1(10) is to criminalise conduct that would otherwise not be criminal, it would not be right,
on principle, to exclude matters that go to a defendant's state of mind (such as forgetfulness or a
misapprehension about the meaning of the order or an accidental breach).

Sentencing   In *Lamb* [2006] 2 Cr App R (S) 84, Leveson J said (at [19]) that, where breaches **D25.41**
of ASBOs do not involve harassment, alarm or distress, community penalties, rather than custody, should be considered in order to help the offender learn to live within the terms of the
ASBO to which he is subject. In those cases when there is no available community penalty (as
where the offender refuses to co-operate), custodial sentences which are necessary to maintain
the authority of the court should be kept as short as possible.

In *Stevens* [2006] 2 Cr App R (S) 453, the Court of Appeal did not consider it was wrong in
principle for a sentence of imprisonment to be imposed in respect of breach of an ASBO, where
the conduct amounting to that breach constituted an offence for which the statutory maximum
sentence was a fine.

The definitive sentencing guideline for breach of an ASBO (see Supplement, **SG-458**) applies
to adult and young offenders, although very different principles are set out in respect of each.
Seriousness is determined in the same way for both categories of offender: two aspects of culpability need to be considered, namely the degree to which the offender intended to breach
the order and the degree to which he intended to cause the harm that resulted or could have
resulted. The original conduct that led to the making of the ASBO is also a relevant consideration. Offender mitigation is relevant, particularly if the offender has a low level of understanding due to mental health issues or learning disabilities. The sentencing ranges and starting
points apply to first time offenders convicted after a trial. Importantly, in this context, 'first time
offender' means somebody who does not have a conviction for breach of an ASBO.

The guideline identifies three starting points for adults according to the nature of the failure and harm, each starting point having a defined range, which is adjusted according to the
non-exhaustive list of aggravating and mitigating features. Offender mitigation is considered
after the court has reached a provisional sentence based on its assessment of offence seriousness. The range is a Band B fine to two years' custody. For a recent application of the guideline
where there were repeated breaches of the ASBO which did not involve harassment, alarm or
distress, see *Savage* [2012] EWCA Crim 1678, where the Court of Appeal reduced a sentence
of 18 months to one of 12 months.

The sentencing framework for persons aged under 18 is significantly different and is summarised at annex C of the guideline. A youth without any previous convictions will usually be subject to a referral order. In most other cases, the appropriate sentence will be a community sentence, although a fine or reparation order may be appropriate where the breach involved no harassment, etc. Custody should be used only as a measure of last resort and, even where the custody threshold is crossed, the court should normally impose a community penalty. Where a custodial sentence is considered to be unavoidable, the starting point is a four-month detention and training order, with a range of up to 12 months. But see also the definitive sentencing guideline *Overarching Principles — Sentencing Youths* (Supplement, **SG-515**) which post-dates the guideline on ASBOs.

Reporting Restrictions

D25.42   Where the offender is under the age of 18, the CDA 1998, s. 1C(9B) and (9C), removes, in the case of ASBOs made under s. 1C (i.e. post-conviction), the automatic reporting restrictions (which would normally apply, pursuant to the CYPA 1933, s. 49 (see **D24.14**), to prevent reporting of the identity of the juvenile), although the court retains a discretion, under s. 39 of the 1933 Act (see **D24.78**), to apply reporting restrictions. The same provision is made in respect of proceedings for breaches under s. 1(10) of the Act: by virtue of s. 1(10D) and (10E), the CYPA 1933, s. 49, does not apply to such proceedings, but s. 39 of the 1933 Act does apply. (Note that s. 39 will be replaced by the YJCEA 1999, s. 45, if it is brought into force.)

Section 39 was considered in the context of ASBOs in *R (T) v St. Albans Crown Court* [2002] EWHC 1129 (Admin). Elias J was of the view that where an ASBO has been imposed, that is a factor which reinforces the general public interest in the public disclosure of court proceedings for two reasons. First, disclosure of the identity of the individuals may make an order efficacious; secondly, the very purpose of ASBOs is to protect the public from individuals who have committed acts of anti-social behaviour. In each case the balance has to be struck between the desirability of public disclosure and the need to protect the welfare of the child. In *R (K) v Knowsley MBC* (2004) 168 JP 461, the Divisional Court endorsed Elias J's approach and said it applied equally to interim ASBOs. However, the court recognised the fact that the order was an interim one meant that the allegations against the defendant were unproven (and might or might not be proven at a full hearing) and that was a very important consideration in deciding where the balance lies.

D25.43   In *R (Stanley, Marshall and Kelly) v Metropolitan Police Commissioner* (2004) 168 JP 623, the Divisional Court gave guidance on post-ASBO publicity and its dissemination. When questions of publicity arise in such cases, the police and local authorities should recognise that those subject to the orders might have their rights under the ECHR, Article 8(1), infringed; they should consider whether the publicity that is envisaged is necessary and proportionate to the authorities' legitimate aims. Whether publicity is intended to inform, to reassure, to assist in enforcing the existing orders by policing, to inhibit the behaviour of those against whom the orders have been made or to deter others, it is unlikely to be effective unless it includes photographs, names and at least partial addresses. Those responsible for publicity must therefore leave no room for misidentification. As to the remainder of the content of any publicity, that has to depend upon the facts of the case. If residents have been exposed to criminal behaviour for years and orders have been obtained by reference to that behaviour and in order to bring it to an end, there is no reason why publicity material should not say so. It must not assert that those against whom orders have been made have been convicted of any crime, since ASBO proceedings are civil, not criminal (per Kennedy LJ at [40]).

As a result of the *Stanley* case, the Home Office issued detailed guidance, *Publicising Anti-social Behaviour Orders*, in October 2005. This guidance makes the point that, 'each individual case should be judged on its merits as to whether or not to publicise the details of an individual subject to an ASBO' and that the decision-making process should aim to consider and record several key factors:

(a) the need for publicity;
(b) a consideration of the human rights of the public;

(c) a consideration of the human rights of those against whom ASBOs are made;
(d) what the publicity should look like and whether it is proportionate to the aims of the publicity.

Special Measures in ASBO Cases

The CDA 1998, s. 1I, makes provision for 'special measures' for witnesses in proceedings for **D25.44** ASBOs. It applies to magistrates' court proceedings for a 'stand-alone' ASBO, magistrates' court or Crown Court proceedings for an ASBO under s. 1C (i.e. after conviction) and to applications in the magistrates' court for an interim ASBO under s. 1D. It applies to such proceedings the special measures provisions contained in the YJCEA 1999 (with the omission of those that are applicable only in the context of criminal proceedings). For discussion of special measures, see **D14** and **D22.47**.

Individual Support Orders

Individual support orders (ISOs), made under the CDA 1998, ss. 1AA and 1AB, are aimed **D25.45** at preventing further anti-social behaviour where a 'stand-alone' ASBO has already been made against a person under the age of 18. ISOs are available in respect of post-conviction ASBOs (as well as county court ASBOs). ISOs can also be applied for by the relevant authority carrying out a review of the post-conviction ASBO pursuant to s. 1K of the CDA 1998 (see **D25.21**).

ISOs can be made more than once and can be made *subsequent* to the making of the ASBO, provided that, at the time an application for an ISO is made, the ASBO is still in force and the defendant is still a child or young person and the application is made by the same relevant authority that applied for the ASBO. Further, by the CDA 1998, s. 1AB(5A), the ISO cannot be made to last beyond the lifetime of the original ASBO.

Section 1AA(1B) stipulates that the court must make an ISO if three conditions are fulfilled. **D25.46** Those conditions (set out in s. 1AA(3)) are:

(a) that an ISO 'would be desirable in the interests of preventing any repetition of the kind of behaviour which led to the making of (i) the anti-social behaviour order, or (ii) an order varying that order (in a case where the variation is made as a result of further anti-social behaviour by the defendant)';
(b) that the defendant is not already subject to an ISO; and
(c) that arrangements for implementing ISOs are available in the area in which the defendant resides or will reside.

The effect of an ISO is set out in s. 1AA(2): it requires the defendant to comply, for a period not exceeding six months, with such requirements as are specified in the order, and to comply with any directions given by the responsible officer (who supervises the defendant under the order) with a view to the implementation of those requirements.

The requirements specified under s. 1AA(2) must be ones 'that the court considers desirable in the interests of preventing any repetition of the kind of behaviour' mentioned in s. 1AA(3) (s. 1AA(5)). Under s. 1AA(6), the defendant may be required to participate in specified activities, present himself at specified times to a person or persons and comply with any arrangements for his education. The offender cannot be required to attend a place (or different places) on more than two days per week (s. 1AA(7)). Section 1AA(8) obliges the court, when imposing requirements, to avoid (as far as practicable) any conflict with the defendant's religious beliefs and any interference with the times, if any, at which he normally works or attends school or any other educational establishment. Under s. 1AA(9), the court is required to obtain and consider information from a local authority social worker or a member of a youth offending team in order to determine whether the individual support conditions are fulfilled and, if so, what requirements should be included in the order.

D25.47   Section 1AB(1) requires the court to explain to the defendant, in ordinary language and in open court, the effect of the order, the consequences of failure to comply with its requirements, and the court's power to review the order. Under s. 1AB(3), failure without reasonable excuse to comply with any of the requirements included in the ISO is a summary offence, punishable with a fine of up to £1,000 (where the offender is aged 14 to 17), or £250 (where the offender is aged 10 to 13). Section 1AB(4) stipulates that a referral order cannot be made in respect of a conviction under s. 1AB(1).

Under s. 1AB(5), an ISO ceases to have effect (if it has not already expired) when the ASBO to which it is linked ceases to have effect. Section 1AB(6) allows the defendant or the responsible officer to apply to the court for the order to be varied or discharged; s. 1AB(7) allows a court to vary or discharge an ISO if it is varying the ASBO to which it is linked.

The CDA 1998, s. 4(1), enables an appeal to the Crown Court against the making of an ISO by a magistrates' court.

Parenting Orders

D25.48   The CDA 1998, s. 9(1B), provides that, where a court makes an ASBO against a person under the age of 16, it must also make a parenting order (see **E14.1**) against the parents of that child if it is satisfied that the parenting order would be desirable in the interests of preventing any repetition of the kind of behaviour that led to making of the ASBO. Before making such an order a court shall obtain and consider information including any report prepared under s. 1(1C) about the person's family circumstances (see **D25.17**) and the likely effect of the order on those circumstances.

Section 41 of the Crime and Security Act 2010 (not yet in force) inserts a new s. 8A into the CDA 1998. When in force, s. 8A will require the court to make a parenting order when a young person under the age of 16 is convicted of breaching an ASBO (see **D25.39**). The making of the order will be mandatory unless the court is of the opinion that there are exceptional circumstances that would make a parenting order inappropriate (s. 8A(2)). If the court does not make a parenting order because it is of the opinion that there are exceptional circumstances that would make it inappropriate, it must state in open court that it is of that opinion and what those circumstances are (s. 8A(4)). The court should ensure that the terms of the parenting order are adequate to prevent (a) 'any repetition of the kind of behaviour' which led to the court making the ASBO in the first place; or (b) the commission of further offences (s. 8A(3)). The majority of the requirements of the CDA 1998, ss. 8 and 9 (see **E14.2**) apply to s. 8A; the court must ensure that the parenting order does not conflict with 'religious beliefs, work or education' (s. 8A(6)(b)), and must explain the effect of a parenting order (s. 8A(6)(a)). The right of appeal under s. 10(4) is extended to the provisions of s. 8A (Crime and Security Act 2010, s. 41(5)).

For breach of a parenting order, see **E14.5**.

Intervention Orders

D25.49   Intervention orders, which may be sought by a relevant authority (see **D25.15**), may be attached to a 'stand-alone' ASBO by virtue of the CDA 1998, s. 1G. Their purpose is to tackle anti-social behaviour resulting from drug abuse. Intervention orders are available only where the court is making an ASBO in respect of a defendant who has attained the age of 18, a report from an appropriately qualified person shows that the individual's anti-social behaviour is linked to misuse of drugs, and the court is satisfied that a number of conditions are satisfied, namely:

(a)   an intervention order is desirable in the interests of preventing a repetition of the behaviour which led to the behaviour order being made (the 'trigger behaviour');

(b)   appropriate activities relating to the trigger behaviour or its cause are available for the defendant;

(c)   the defendant is not currently subject to another intervention order or to any other treatment relating to the trigger behaviour or its cause (whether on a voluntary basis or by virtue of a requirement imposed by a court);

(d) arrangements for implementing intervention orders are available in the area in which the defendant resides or will reside.

The intervention order requires the defendant to comply, for a period not exceeding six months, with such requirements as are specified in the order, and with any directions given by a person authorised to do so under the order. The defendant may be required to participate in specified activities or to present himself to a specified person at specified times. Failure without reasonable excuse to comply with the intervention order is an offence under s. 1H(3), punishable with a fine on level 4 (currently £2,500).

By virtue of s. 1H(4), the intervention order ceases to have effect (if it has not already done so) when the ASBO as a result of which it was made ceases to have effect.

Section 1H(5) enables the applicant or the relevant authority to apply to the court for the intervention order to be varied or discharged.

CLOSURE ORDERS

The ASBA 2003, part 1, and the Crime and Courts Act 2013 (Application and Modification **D25.50** of Certain Enactments) Order 2014 (SI 2014 No. 1704), govern the 'crack house' closure order regime. The ASBA 2003, part 1A, governs closure orders in relation to premises associated with persistent disorder and nuisance. Part 1A mirrors part 1.

The SOA 2003, part 2A, creates a third form of closure order available in relation to premises used for activities related to specified prostitution offences or pornography offences. The specified prostitution offences are those contained in the SOA 2003, ss. 47, 48, 49, 50, 52 and 53, and the specified pornography offences are those contained in ss. 48, 49 and 50 of the same Act (see **B3**). The provisions in part 2A are very similar to those in the ASBA 2003, parts 1 and 1A. Closure orders are civil orders, issued under the civil jurisdiction of a magistrates' court. There are two stages to the closure process: the initial issue of a closure notice and the making of a closure order.

The Home Office has published 'Notes of Guidance' on the ASBA 2003, part 1, last revised in **D25.51** August 2005; caution is merited when using the Notes of Guidance because an earlier version of the part 1 Guidance has been criticised by the High Court for containing errors and has been departed from in two cases. The Guidance does not have a particular legal status but is capable of being persuasive authority (*Chief Constable of Cumbria Constabulary v Wright* [2007] 1 WLR 1407).

In addition to the obvious kinds of premises, the part 1 Guidance anticipates that the process may apply to common areas adjacent to houses or flats, factories, public buildings, community centres or halls, car parks and even hospitals or schools. Section 1(9) provides for the Secretary of State to exempt certain premises, but he has yet to do so.

The Home Office has published 'Notes of Guidance' on part 1A orders, which describe the new form of order as 'an order of last resort'. Unlike under part 1, there is an obligation on those discharging functions under part 1A to have regard to the Guidance (ASBA 2003, s. 11K). Home Office guidance on SOA 2003, part 2A, orders is also available. There is an obligation on those discharging functions under part 2A to have regard to any such guidance (SOA 2003, s. 136P(2)).

Closure Notices

The authorisation for the issue of a closure notice under part 1 must be given by a designated per- **D25.52** son not below grade 2 (which means a NCA officer designated as a person having the powers and privileges of a constable under the CCA 2013, ss. 9(2)(a) and 10(1)(a)) (ASBA 2003, s. 1(1)) who has reasonable grounds for believing 'that at any time during the relevant period the premises have been used in connection with the unlawful use, production or supply of a Class A controlled drug' *and* that 'the use of the premises is associated with the occurrence of disorder or serious nuisance to members of the public'. The 'relevant period' is the three months preceding the date upon which the relevant officer comes to make the authorisation decision (s. 1(10)).

Before such authorisation can be issued, the officer must be satisfied that there has been consultation with the local authority and that reasonable steps have been taken to establish the identity of any person who lives on the premises or who has control of or responsibility for or an interest in the premises (s. 1(2)). The notice should contain confirmation of the above.

There is no statutory requirement on the part of the police and relevant housing authority to demonstrate that they have considered and tried other less draconian measures before applying for a crack house closure order so that such a closure order is one of last resort (*Leary v Chief Constable of West Midlands Police* [2012] EWHC 639 (Admin)).

The notice must contain various other details, including the date, time and place of the hearing in the magistrates' court and the fact that access to the premises by any person other than a person who habitually resides in the premises or the owner of the premises is prohibited (s. 1(4)).

The making of a closure order is not contingent on the original closure notice being valid, although defects in the notice 'would affect the validity of the notice so as to make it impossible to maintain criminal proceedings under section 4(1) or (2) insofar as they depended upon the validity of the notice' (*R (Errington) v Metropolitan Police Authority* (2006) 171 JP 89 at [23]: for criminal proceedings see **D25.68**). See also *R (Byrne) v Commissioner of Police of the Metropolis* [2010] EWHC 3656 (Admin) as to the impropriety of mounting a collateral challenge on public law grounds to the validity of the closure notice in the magistrates' court or the Crown Court on appeal. As to service of the notice, see s. 1(6).

D25.53 Closure notices under part 1A can be authorised by a police officer not below the rank of a superintendent *or* the local authority if either has reasonable grounds for believing 'that at any time during the relevant period a person has engaged in anti-social behaviour on the premises' *and* 'that the use of the premises is associated with significant and persistent disorder or persistent serious nuisance to members of the public' (ASBA 2003, s. 11A(1)). 'Anti-social behaviour', as under the ASBO regime (see **D25.12**), is defined as 'behaviour by a person which causes or is likely to cause harassment, alarm or distress to one or more other persons not of the same household as the person' (s. 11L). The notice must contain various details, including the date, time and place of the hearing in the magistrates' court and the fact that access to the premises by any person other than a person who habitually resides in the premises or the owner of the premises is prohibited (s. 11A(5)). As to service of the notice, see s. 11A(7).

D25.54 Closure notices under the new part 2A can be authorised by a police officer not below the rank of a superintendent if three conditions are satisfied. First, he must have reasonable grounds for believing either that 'during the relevant period, the premises were used for activities related to one or more specified prostitution offences' (but not if only one person obtained all of the sexual services in question, whether or not on a single occasion) (SOA 2003, s. 136B(3)) or 'during the relevant period, the premises were used for activities related to one or more specified pornography offences' (s. 136B(4)) or both (s. 136B(2)). 'The relevant period' means the period of three months ending with the day on which the officer is considering whether to authorise the issue of the notice (s. 136B(5)). Secondly, the officer must have reasonable grounds for believing that the making of a closure order is necessary to prevent the premises being used for activities related to one or more specified prostitution or pornography offences (s. 136B(6)). Premises are being used for activities related to a specified prostitution offence in the case of an offence under the SOA 2003, s. 47 (obtaining sexual services from a child), at any time when the sexual services are being provided on the premises, and in the case of any other specified prostitution offence, at any time when the person in respect of whom the offence is committed is providing sexual services as a prostitute on the premises (SOA 2003, s. 136A(4)). Premises are being used for activities related to a specified pornography offence at any time when the person in respect of whom the offence is committed is doing anything on the premises which enables an indecent image of himself or herself to be recorded (s. 136A(5)). It does not matter whether the officer believes that the offence or offences in question have been committed or that they will be committed (or will be committed unless a closure order is made) (s. 136B(8)). Thirdly, the officer must be satisfied that the local authority for the area in which the premises are situated has been consulted *and* that reasonable steps have been taken to establish the identity of any person who resides on the premises or who has control of or responsibility for or an interest in the premises (s. 136B(7)). Importantly, the issue of a closure notice may be authorised whether or not a person has been convicted of any specified prostitution or pornography offence that the authorising officer believes has been committed (s. 136B(10)). The notice has effect until the application for a closure order is determined (s. 136C(7)). If the closure order hearing is adjourned, the notice will cease to have effect unless the court orders that it continue in effect until the end of the period of the adjournment (s. 136C(8)). The notice must contain various details, including on which specified offence(s) the officer's reasonable grounds are based, the date, time and place of the hearing in the magistrates' court, and the fact that access to the premises by any person other than a person who regularly resides in the premises or the owner of the premises is prohibited (s. 136C(1)). As to service of the notice, see s. 136C(3).

Applications for Closure Orders

The Statutory Test   Once a closure notice has been issued, a constable must apply to a magistrates' court for a closure order. The application must be heard no later than 48 hours after the notice was served (ASBA 2003, ss. 2(2) and 11B(3); SOA 2003, s. 136D(3)). A closure order is an order that the premises in respect of which the order is made are closed to all persons for such period (not exceeding three months) as the court decides (ss. 2(4) and 11B(5); s. 136D(2)). It may be made in respect of all or any part of the premises in respect of which the notice was issued (ss. 2(8) and 11B(9); s. 136E(4)).

D25.55

The court may make a part 1 order only if it is satisfied of the following three conditions pursuant to s. 2(3):

(a) the premises in respect of which the closure notice was issued have been used in connection with the unlawful use, production or supply of a Class A controlled drug;
(b) the use of the premises is associated with the occurrence of disorder or serious nuisance to members of the public; and
(c) the making of the order is necessary to prevent the occurrence of such disorder or serious nuisance for the period specified in the order.

In determining whether the terms of s. 2(3)(b) are satisfied, the Divisional Court in *Dumble v Commissioner of Police of the Metropolis* [2009] EWHC 351 (Admin) held that it would be helpful for magistrates' courts to bear in mind these principles: (a) if the disorder or nuisance had permanently ceased then the terms of s. 2(3)(b) would not be satisfied, (b) a pattern of disorderly use and disturbance was likely to be material and (c) a temporary hiatus from the required state of affairs would not deprive the court of the power to make a closure order.

It is immaterial whether any person has been convicted of an offence relating to the use, production or supply of a controlled drug (s. 2(9)). In *Chief Constable of Cumbria Constabulary v Wright* [2007] 1 WLR 1407, the Divisional Court made plain that the justices would have to be satisfied of each of the three matters specified in s. 2(3) and that the disorder or serious nuisance must have some connection with the Class A drug use, production or supply. Whilst there was no time bar on incidents relied upon, the magistrates' court may make an order only if satisfied that the use of the premises in connection with the unlawful use, production or supply of a class A controlled drug is currently associated with the occurrence of disorder or serious nuisance to members of the public and that the making of the order is necessary to prevent its occurrence in the future.

D25.56 The statutory test for a part 1A closure order requires the magistrates' court to be satisfied of the following three conditions pursuant to s. 11B(4):

(a) a person has engaged in anti-social behaviour on the premises in respect of which the part 1A closure notice was served;

(b) the use of the premises is associated with significant and persistent disorder or persistent serious nuisance to members of the public; and

(c) the making of the order is necessary to prevent the occurrence of such disorder or nuisance for the period specified in the order.

For the definition of 'anti-social behaviour', see **D25.53**.

D25.57 The statutory test for a part 2A closure order requires the magistrates' court to be satisfied of the following three conditions pursuant to the SOA 2003, s. 136D(5)–(7) and (10):

(a) during the relevant period, the premises were used for activities related to one or more specified prostitution offences (but not if only one person obtained all of the sexual services in question, whether or not on a single occasion) *or* during the relevant period, the premises were used for activities related to one or more specified pornography offences;

(b) the court is satisfied that the making of the closure order is necessary to prevent the premises being used for activities related to one or more specified prostitution or pornography offences during the period to be specified in the order; and

(c) before the issue of the closure notice was authorised, reasonable steps were taken to establish the identity of any person who resides on the premises or who has control of or responsibility for or an interest in the premises, and that he was given a copy of the closure notice.

'The relevant period' means the period of three months ending with the day on which the issue of the closure notice was authorised (s. 136D(8)).

D25.58 Even if a closure order is made, it may include such provision as the court thinks appropriate relating to access to any other part of the building or structure of which the premises form part (ASBA 2003, ss. 2(5) and 11B(6); SOA 2003, s. 136E(3)).

In *Dumble v Commissioner of Police for the Metropolis* [2009] EWHC 351 (Admin), the Divisional Court held that a hiatus of 16 days between the service of the closure notice and the making of the order was not sufficient to conclude that the conduct had permanently ceased.

D25.59 **Burden and Standard of Proof**   The burden of proof is on the police (*R (Cleary) v Highbury Corner Magistrates' Court* [2007] 1 All ER 270). The standard of proof is the normal civil standard. In *Chief Constable of the Merseyside Police v Harrison* [2007] QB 79 the High Court distinguished closure orders from ASBOs, which require a criminal standard of proof (see **D25.14**), describing them as 'less adverse to the interests' of individuals than ASBOs. However, in *Cleary* (at [7]), the court emphasised that, since a closure order may dispossess a person from his home, Article 8 of the ECHR is of central importance, and a court must be satisfied that it is necessary and proportionate to make such an order. The civil standard of proof is plainly coloured by these considerations. It should be borne in mind, however, that the ECHR, Article 8, does not require the police to have considered less draconian measures before seeking a closure order (*Leary v Chief Constable of West Midlands* [2012] EWHC 639 (Admin)).

D25.60 **Application Procedure**   An application for a closure order is a civil matter and, as with ASBO hearings, hearsay is admissible. Consequently, the Civil Evidence Act 1995 and the Magistrates' Courts (Hearsay Evidence in Civil Proceedings) Rules 1999 (see **D25.17**) apply.

In *R (Cleary) v Highbury Corner Magistrates' Court* [2007] 1 All ER 270 the Divisional Court emphasised the importance of a fair hearing in compliance with the ECHR, Article 6, recognising that the first hearing held within 48 hours may well not be effective in order to achieve that aim (see **D25.61** for the power to adjourn). The evidence relied upon by the police ought to be served before the first hearing and, if it is not fully served by then, the court made plain that fairness requires that it is served well in advance of an adjourned hearing.

The court in *Cleary* also reiterated the dangers of relying upon hearsay evidence, identified in *Moat Housing Group-South Limited v Harris* [2006] QB 606, and pointed out that the statutory timetable in the ASBA 2003 was at odds with the usual entitlement to 21 days' notice of reliance on hearsay under the Magistrates' Courts (Hearsay Evidence in Civil Proceedings) Rules 1999. The Rules do provide for a shortening of that notice period but they certainly could not be complied with in the case of the first hearing. The court suggested that, if hearsay evidence was to be relied upon, the police should make any application to reduce the notice period at the first hearing.

Adjournment   The magistrates' court has a statutory jurisdiction under the ASBA 2003,   **D25.61**
ss. 2(6) (part 1) and 11B(7) (part 1A), and the SOA 2003, s. 136E(1) (part 2A), to adjourn the hearing of an application for 14 days to allow the occupier of the premises, or the person who has control or responsibility for the premises, or any other person with an interest, to show why a closure order should not be made. A magistrates' court may order the closure notice to continue in effect until the end of the adjournment (ss. 2(7) and 11B(7); s. 136E(2)).

In *Commissioner of the Metropolitan Police v Hooper* [2005] 4 All ER 1095 it was held that a further adjournment was possible under s. 54 of the MCA 1980, but the power should be exercised in exceptional circumstances since the notice will lapse if any adjournment beyond the 14-day period is allowed. See also *R (Turner) v Highbury Corner Magistrates' Court* [2006] 1 WLR 220.

Duration

As mentioned at **D25.55**, a closure order can be made for any period of up to three months in   **D25.62**
the first instance. If such an application is made by the police (or the local authority), the court has power to extend the order under s. 5(1) of the ASBA 2003 (part 1) and s. 11E(1) (part 1A) (and the SOA 2003, s. 136H(1)) at any time before a closure order's designated period ends, for a period of up to three months (ss. 5(4) and 11E(5); s.136I(3)), but the overall length of the order must not exceed six months (ss. 5(5) and 11E(6); s. 136I(4)).

An application to extend a part 1 order is made by complaint and must be authorised by a designated person not below grade 2 (see **D25.52**) and he must have reasonable grounds for believing that it is necessary to extend the order (s. 5(2)(a)). Additionally, the officer must be satisfied that the local authority has been consulted (s. 5(2)(b)). Under part 1A, the application must be authorised by a police officer not below the rank of superintendent or the local authority, as appropriate, and such a person must have reasonable grounds for believing that it is necessary to extend the order for the purpose of preventing the occurrence of significant and persistent disorder or persistent serious nuisance. The relevant person must be satisfied that the local authority has consulted the appropriate chief officer or vice versa (s. 11E(2) and (3)). Before a court can make such an extension, it must be satisfied 'that the order is necessary to prevent the occurrence of disorder or serious nuisance for a further period' (s. 5(4)) or 'that the order is necessary to prevent the occurrence of significant and persistent disorder or persistent serious nuisance to members of the public for a further period' (s. 11E(5)). The part 1 Home Office Guidance states at para. 10.2.1 that extensions after three months should not be routine (the same is said in the part 1A Guidance at para. 11.1.1). For the proper approach to part 1 extensions, see *R (Smith) v Crown Court at Snaresbrook* [2009] 1 All ER 547.

An application to extend a part 2A order is made by complaint and must be authorised by a   **D25.63**
police officer not below the rank of superintendent (SOA 2003, s. 136H(2)). The officer must have reasonable grounds for believing that it is necessary to extend the period for which the order has effect to prevent the premises being used for activities related to any of the specified

prostitution or pornography offences in respect of which the original order was made and the officer must be satisfied that the local authority has been consulted about the intention to make a complaint (s. 136H(4) and (5)). Before a court can make such an extension, it must be satisfied 'that the extension is necessary to prevent the premises being used for activities related to any of the specified prostitution or pornography offences' in respect of which the original order was made (s. 136I(2)). An order to extend may include such provision as the court thinks appropriate relating to access to any other part of a building or other structure in which the premises are situated (s. 136I(5)).

In *R (Longato) v Camberwell Green Magistrates' Court* [2009] EWHC 691 (Admin), the High Court held that a defendant had a right to be on notice of a hearing to extend an order and that such notice is required by the MCA 1980, s. 55(3), and the Magistrates' Courts Rules 1981, r. 99. A failure to do so was an irregularity and a real injustice and the claimant was entitled to have the order quashed by way of judicial review.

Discharge

D25.64 An application for the discharge of a closure order is made by way of complaint to a magistrates' court; it may be made by a constable, the local authority, a person on whom the closure notice was served or a person who has an interest in the closed premises but upon whom a notice was not served (ASBA 2003, ss. 5(6) and 11E(7); SOA 2003, s. 136J(1)). The court must not make an order discharging a closure order unless it is satisfied that the closure order is no longer necessary to prevent the occurrence of disorder or serious nuisance (s. 5(8)) or significant and persistent disorder or persistent serious nuisance (s. 11E(9)) to members of the public. Under the SOA 2003, part 2A, the court may not make an order discharging a closure order unless it is satisfied that the order is no longer necessary to prevent the premises being used for activities related to any of the specified prostitution or pornography offences in respect of which the original order was made (s. 136J(3)).

Appeals

D25.65 The ASBA 2003, ss. 6(1) and 11F(1), confer a right of appeal to the Crown Court against a decision to make, extend or discharge an order. An appeal is also available against a decision not to make those orders. An appeal against the making of an order or the extension of an order may be brought either by someone who was served with the notice, or someone who has an interest in the premises but was not served with the notice (ss. 6(3) and 11F(3)). Conversely, either a local authority or a constable may appeal against the decision of a court not to make or extend an order. Under the SOA 2003, part 2A, an appeal to the Crown Court is available against a decision to make an order, to extend an order and not to discharge an order (s. 136K(1)) as well as a decision not to make an order, not to extend an order and to discharge an order (s. 136K(2)). The former can be brought by a person on whom the closure notice relating to the closed premises was served, or any other person who has an interest in the closed premises but on whom the closure notice was not served (s. 136K(1)) and the latter by a local authority or a constable (s. 136K(2)). On appeal the Crown Court may make such order as it thinks appropriate (ASBA 2003, ss. 6(5) and 11F(5); SOA 2003, s. 136K(4)).

Such appeals are 'as of right' and by way of full rehearing, do not require permission and, as such, do not require the appellant to specify the grounds upon which he appeals. An appeal must be brought before the Crown Court within 21 days beginning on the day of decision (ASBA 2003, ss. 6(2) and 11(2); SOA 2003, s. 136K(3)). In *R (Errington) v Metropolitan Police Authority* (2007) 171 JP 89, Collins J said that Crown Courts should give such appeals priority and hear them in a matter of days. In *Hampshire Police Authority v Smith* [2010] 4 All ER 316 the Divisional Court held that the appeal notice must be issued within 21 days, not that it must be heard within that period. The primary issue on appeal was whether the time for service of the notice could be extended in accordance with r. 7(5) of the Crown Court Rules

1982 (which continues to apply in relation to appeals from the magistrates' court which relate to civil cases, notwithstanding their general replacement by the CrimPR). The court said that r. 7(5) does not apply to a notice of appeal issued under the ASBA 2003, s. 6(2). There was a clear and unqualified statutory time-limit which provides an appellant with a significant period of time in which to issue a notice of appeal and the statute makes no provision for extension. In *R (Longato) v Camberwell Green Magistrates' Court* [2009] EWHC 691 (Admin) it was held that Parliament had intentionally not given a general power to magistrates to reopen hearings in civil cases (MCA 1980, s. 142 did not apply) and no such power existed at common law (see also **D25.23**).

Access to Other Premises

Under the ASBA 2003, ss. 7 and 11G, and the SOA 2003, s. 136L, anyone who either lives in or owns any part of a building or structure in which closed premises are situated and in respect of which the closure order does not have effect may apply to the magistrates' court (or the Crown Court where an order was made on appeal) to obtain access. It is immaterial whether any provision for access has been made pursuant to s. 2(5) or s. 11B(6) or s. 136E(3) (see **D25.55**) or s. 136I(5) (see **D25.62**). **D25.66**

Powers of Entry

A constable (or another authorised person) and, for part 1A purposes, a constable or a person authorised by the local authority ('a relevant person') have a power under the ASBA 2003, s. 3(2) and s. 11C(2) and the SOA 2003, s. 136F(2), to enter the premises in respect of which an order has been made and to do anything reasonably necessary to secure the premises against entry by any person. An authorised person is a person authorised by the chief officer of police for the area in which the premises are situated (ASBA 2003, ss. 3(6) and 11C(6); SOA 2003, s. 136F(6)). That person may use reasonable force. A similar power exists in relation to premises in respect of which a closure notice has been served (ss. 1(7A) and 11A(9); s. 136C(5)) but is limited to constables (parts 1 and 2A only) and is for the sole purpose of effecting service of a notice. A relevant person may also enter closed premises to carry out essential maintenance or repairs (s. 11C(5)) as can a police constable or an authorised person (s. 3(5); s. 136F(5)). **D25.67**

Criminal Offences

Section 4 of the ASBA 2003 provides that a person commits an offence if he remains on or enters premises in contravention of either a closure notice (s. 4(1)) or a closure order (s. 4(2)(b) and (c)), obstructs a constable or an authorised person seeking to enter and secure the closure of premises in accordance with s. 3(2) or obstructs a constable seeking to effect the service of a closure notice under s. 1(6) (s. 4(2)(a)). An authorised person is a person authorised by the chief officer of police for the area in which the premises are situated (ASBA 2003, s. 3(6)). Section 11D creates parallel offences in respect of part 1A and s. 136G does the same in relation to the SOA 2003, part 2A. **D25.68**

A person guilty of an offence under s. 4 is liable on summary conviction to imprisonment for a period not exceeding six months, or to a fine not exceeding level 5 on the standard scale, or to both. The parallel offences under part 1A and the SOA 2003, part 2A, attract the same penalties.

Defences

There is a statutory defence of reasonable excuse for remaining on or entering premises (ASBA 2003, ss. 4(4) and 11D(4); SOA 2003, s.136G(3)). **D25.69**

In *R (Errington) v Metropolitan Police Authority* (2007) 171 JP 89, Collins J expressed the view (at [23]) that an invalid notice may afford a defence to any criminal charge under s. 4(1) or (2) (see **D25.52** as to the validity of closure notices).

Reimbursement of Costs

D25.70   Under the ASBA 2003, ss. 8 and 11H, and the SOA 2003, s. 136M, either the police or a local authority which incurs expenditure for the purpose of clearing, securing or maintaining the closed premises may apply to the court that made the closure order for an order that the owner reimburse those costs. The limitation period for applications is three months, starting with the day on which the closure order ceases to have effect.

As for costs of proceedings, *R (Taylor) v Commissioner for the Metropolitan Police* (2009) 173 JP 121, which was an appeal against a decision to refuse to make an order for costs against the police following the dismissal of their application for a part 1 closure order, confirmed that the MCA 1980, s. 64, which gives a magistrates' court power to award costs in matters brought by complaint (i.e. civil proceedings), applied to the closure order regime.

Compensation

D25.71   Pursuant to the ASBA 2003, ss. 10 and 11J, and the SOA 2003, s. 136O, anyone who suffers financial loss as a result of either a closure notice or a closure order may apply to the court where it was made or extended for compensation from central funds. The limitation period here is three months starting with the day the court decided not to make a closure order, or the day the Crown Court dismissed an appeal, or the day an order ceases to have effect (whichever is latest) (ss. 10(3) and 11J(3); s. 136O(3)). In order for compensation to be granted under part 1, the court must be satisfied that the person had no connection with the use of the premises or, if he is the owner or occupier of the premises, that he took reasonable steps to prevent the use, and that the person has incurred financial loss and it is appropriate to do so (s. 10(4)). Under part 1A, in order for compensation to be granted, the court must be satisfied that the person had no association with the significant and persistent disorder or the persistent serious nuisance or, if that person is the owner or occupier of the premises, that he took reasonable steps to prevent such use of the premises, and that he has incurred financial loss and it is appropriate to grant it (s. 11J(4)). Under the SOA 2003, part 2A, the court must be satisfied that the person was not associated with the use of the premises for the activities related to the specified offences and, if the person is the owner or occupier of the premises, that the person took reasonable steps to prevent that use and that the person has incurred financial loss as mentioned in subsection (1), and having regard to all the circumstances it is appropriate to order payment of compensation in respect of that loss (s. 136O(5)). 'The owner' is defined at s. 11(10) (part 1), s. 11L(9) (part 1A) and s. 136R(11) (part 2A) and includes certain leaseholders.

SERIOUS CRIME PREVENTION ORDERS

D25.72   The SCA 2007, part 1, introduced the serious crime prevention order (SCPO). These orders are civil orders available upon application to the High Court (SCA 2007, s. 1) and upon conviction for a 'serious offence' in the Crown Court (s. 19). They are designed to protect the public by preventing, restricting or disrupting involvement in serious crime. SCPOs can include extensive restrictions and requirements (see s. 5). An order may endure for a period of up to five years (SCA 2007, s. 16). Prohibitions, restrictions and requirements can also be placed on bodies corporate, partnerships and unincorporated associations (SCA 2007, s. 5(3)). The SCA 2007 provides for general safeguards (ss. 6 to 10) as well as information safeguards (ss. 11 to 15).

Powers of the High Court

D25.73   In order to impose an SCPO, the High Court (a) must be satisfied (see **D25.80** as to standard of proof) that a person ('the respondent') has been involved in serious crime (whether in England and Wales or elsewhere); and (b) must have reasonable grounds to believe that the order would protect the public by preventing, restricting or disrupting involvement by the person in serious crime in England and Wales (SCA 2007, s. 1(1) (a) and (b)). When the court is considering such an order, it is concerned with future risk. There must be a real, or significant risk (not a bare possibility) that the defendant will commit further serious offences (*Hancox* [2010] 4 All ER 537 at [9]).

An order under s. 1 may contain such prohibitions, restrictions or requirements, and such other terms, as the court considers appropriate for the purpose of protecting the public by preventing, restricting or disrupting involvement by the person concerned in serious crime in England and Wales (s. 1(3)). In *Hancox* the Court of Appeal indicated that, although not couched in terms of necessity, this phrase is no different in practice. Hughes LJ said (at [10]) 'that it is not enough that the order *may* have some public benefit in preventing, restricting or disrupting involvement by the defendant in serious crime; the interference which it will create with the defendant's freedom of action must be justified by the benefit; the provisions of the order must be commensurate with the risk'. Further, his lordship said that much of what the Court of Appeal said in relation to ASBOs in *Boness* [2006] 1 Cr App R (S) 690 (see **D25.33**) applies to SCPOs, in particular the test of proportionality, the emphasis on the order being practicable and enforceable, the test of precision and certainty and the fact that the order is preventative not punitive. See *Silk* [2010] EWCA Crim 3140 for an example of a requirement that the Court of Appeal found was too widely framed and consequently capable of being unjust or leading to unintended breaches. The powers of the court in respect of an order under s. 1 are subject to the safeguards set out in ss. 6 to 15 (s. 1(4): see **D25.76** for the safeguards).

Involvement in Serious Crime   A person is treated as 'involved in serious crime' in any of three **D25.74** circumstances. First, if he has a conviction for a serious offence (SCA 2007, s. 2(1)(a) and (2)(a)). A list of serious offences is set out in part 1 of sch. 1 to the Act and includes drug trafficking, drug importation, people trafficking, arms trafficking, prostitution and child sex, money laundering, fraud, public revenue offences, blackmail, armed robbery, bribery, copyright offences and environmental offences. An offence can be treated as if it were specified in sch. 1 if, in the particular circumstances of the case, the court considers it to be sufficiently serious to be so treated (s. 2(2)(b)). In *Batchelor* [2011] 1 Cr App R (S) 169 the Court of Appeal said 'serious crime' is not restricted to offences committed by multiple offenders in the context of organised crime or offences committed with a high degree of sophistication: there is nothing in the Act which suggests that the restrictions cannot be applied to a single offender (in this case a man convicted of numerous offences of dishonesty). The single test is whether there are reasonable grounds to believe that the order would prevent, restrict or disrupt the offender's involvement in serious crime. See also *Mangham* [2013] 1 Cr App R (S) 62 (11).

Secondly, a person can be involved in serious crime if he has facilitated the commission by another person of such an offence (s. 2(1)(b)).

Thirdly, a person is involved if 'he has conducted himself in a way that was likely to facilitate the commission by himself or another person of a serious offence in England and Wales (whether or not such an offence was committed)' (s. 2(1)(c)). In applying s. 2(1)(c), the court must ignore acts that the respondent can show to be reasonable and, subject to that exception, it must also ignore his intention or any other aspect of his mental state at the time the offence was committed (s. 4(2) and (3)).

Criminal conduct which takes place outside the jurisdiction may be taken into account (ss. 1(1)(a) and 2(4) and (5)).

Prohibitions, etc.   Non-exhaustive examples of the type of provision that may be made by **D25.75** an SCPO are contained in the SCA 2007, s. 5. An SCPO may include, *inter alia*, prohibitions or restrictions on an individual's financial dealings, working arrangements, access to premises (including his dwelling) and travel arrangements. It may also regulate the means by which an individual communicates or associates with others, and may require the individual to answer certain questions and produce certain documents.

D25.76 **Safeguards** The SCA 2007 provides general safeguards in relation to the making of SCPOs in ss. 6 to 10.

By s. 6, individuals under the age of 18 may not be the subject of an order. By s. 8, an order whether in the Crown Court or High Court may be made only on an application by the DPP or the Director of the SFO. The High Court must, on an application by a third party, give that person an opportunity to make representations in the proceedings about the decision it is making, if the making, varying or discharging of an order (or a decision not to vary or discharge an order) would be likely to have a significant adverse effect on that person (s. 9(1)–(3)); a similar duty applies to the Crown Court under s. 9(4) but this does not extend to the discharge of an SCPO (it has no power to discharge). A court which is considering an appeal against an order must also, on application by a person, give that person an opportunity to make such representations, if that person was given an opportunity to make representations in the proceedings which are the subject of the appeal (s. 9(5)).

A person is bound by an order (or a variation of an order) if he is represented at the proceedings at which the order (or the variation) is made or if a notice setting out the terms of the order has been served on him (s. 10).

Information safeguards are created by ss. 11 to 15. A person may not be required by an SCPO to answer questions, or provide information, orally (s. 11). An order cannot override legal professional privilege, except it does not prevent an order that requires a lawyer to provide the name and address of one of his clients (s. 12).

Powers of the Crown Court

D25.77 The Crown Court has a power to impose an SCPO where a person has been convicted of a serious offence in England and Wales either in the Crown Court or in a case where a magistrates' court has committed the matter for sentence (SCA 2007, s. 19(1)). The Crown Court may impose an order on the same basis as the High Court (see **D25.73**). It can make an order in addition to sentencing the person in relation to the offence or conditionally discharging him (s.19(7)). In accordance with s. 19(6), such an order is also subject to the safeguards in ss. 6 to 15 (see **D25.76**). Proceedings in relation to SCPOs can be adjourned even after sentencing (s. 36(1)(b)).

Duration and Discharge

D25.78 An SCPO may not be in force for more than five years from the date it is specified to come into force, although different provisions of the order can come into force at different times (s. 16(1)–(4)). The court is not prevented from making a new order to the same or similar effect, either after an order or any of its provisions has expired or in anticipation of an earlier order or provision ceasing to be in force (s. 16(5) and (6)).

The High Court, unlike the Crown Court, also has the power, on application, to discharge an order in certain circumstances (s. 18).

Variation

D25.79 The High Court has the power, on application, to vary an order, if it has reasonable grounds to believe that such a variation would protect the public by preventing, restricting or disrupting involvement by the person in serious crime in England and Wales (s. 17(1)). An application to vary (which includes a power to extend the order, subject to the overriding five-year limit) may be made by the authority which applied for the original order (s. 17(3)(a)). The subject of the order may apply to vary only if there has been a change of circumstances (s. 17(3)(b)(i) and (4)). A person significantly adversely affected by the order may apply to vary only if he has had or applied to have an opportunity to make representations in earlier proceedings and there has been a change of circumstances, or if he has not so applied but it was reasonable for him not to have done so (s. 17(3)(b)(ii), (5), (6) and (7)); such a person cannot make an application for the order to be more onerous (s. 17(5)(c)).

The Crown Court also has power, on application, to vary an order already in existence when it is dealing with a person convicted of a serious crime (SCA 2007, s. 20(2)). Section 21 gives it a similar power of variation when it is dealing with a person convicted of an offence under s. 25 (failing to comply with an SCPO). Further, the Crown Court may vary an order made or varied by the High Court (s. 22(1)) and the High Court may vary or discharge an order made or varied by the Crown Court (s. 22(2)). A decision by the Crown Court not to make or vary an order under s. 19 does not prevent a subsequent application to the High Court to make or vary an order in relation to the same offence (s. 22(4)).

As to the interrelationship between orders made in the High Court and the Crown Court, see s. 22.

Standard of Proof

Proceedings in the High Court and the Crown Court are civil proceedings (SCA 2007, ss. 35   **D25.80** and 36). These sections also make plain that the standard of proof is the civil standard. This is in stark contrast with the House of Lords' decision in *R (McCann) v Crown Court at Manchester* [2003] 1 AC 787 (see **D25.14**). However, given the undoubted engagement of the ECHR, Article 8 (the right to private and family life), in relation to some or all of the envisaged prohibitions, restrictions and requirements, the civil standard of proof will be affected by such considerations (*R (AN) v Mental Health Tribunal (Northern Region)* [2006] QB 468; *Chief Constable of the Merseyside Police v Harrison* [2007] QB 79).

Application Procedure

The Civil Procedure Rules 1998 (SI 1998 No. 3132), part 77, make provision for applications   **D25.81** in the High Court for or relating to SCPOs.

The Crown Court, when exercising its jurisdiction in relation to SCPOs, is a criminal court for the purposes of procedure rules and practice directions (s. 36(4)). The CrimPR, part 50 ('Civil Behaviour Orders after Verdict or Finding'), applies to SCPOs by virtue of r. 50.1 (see Supplement, **R-361** *et seq.*).

Appeals

An appeal from a High Court decision relating to an SCPO is to the Court of Appeal (SCA   **D25.82** 2007, s. 23). Section 24 makes provision for appeals from the Crown Court; such appeals require the leave of the Court of Appeal or to be certified fit for appeal by the sentencing judge.

Criminal Offences

A failure, without reasonable excuse, to comply with an SCPO is an either-way offence (SCA   **D25.83** 2007, s. 25). A person guilty of such an offence is liable, on summary conviction, to imprisonment for a term not exceeding six months, a fine not exceeding the statutory maximum or both and, on conviction on indictment, to imprisonment for a term not exceeding five years, a fine or both (s. 25(1) and (2) and sch. 13, para. 4). *Koli* [2013] 1 Cr App R (S) 39 (6), described by the Court of Appeal as 'a ground-breaking case', was the first case to consider the appropriate sentence for breach of an SCPO. The Court set out the following as relevant factors:

(a) the lapse of time between the imposition of the original order and the date of the breach;
(b) any history of non-compliance and the issue as to whether non-compliance has been repeated and has come in the face of warnings and requests for information;
(c) whether the non-compliance was inadvertent or deliberate;

(d) whether the breach was related to the commission of further serious offences and might lead to the conclusion that the failure to comply added to the risk that the particular subject of the order was likely to commit further offences; and

(e) any harm caused by non-compliance for breach.

On the particular facts, the concurrent two-year sentences of imprisonment for two convictions for failure to notify in relation to possession of mobile phones and a motor vehicle, following a trial, were reduced to 12 months concurrent. The Court held that recall to prison following breach of the offender's licence conditions (mirroring the terms of his SCPO) relating to the original sentence for money laundering offences did not obviate the need for a criminal court to impose a punishment upon breach of an SCPO imposed at the time of the original sentence.

The court before which a person is convicted of an offence under s. 25 may also order the forfeiture of anything in his possession at the time of the offence which the court considers to have been involved in the offence (s. 26). Where a company, partnership, etc. has been convicted of this offence, the DPP or the Director of the SFO may, if he considers it to be in the public interest, petition for its winding up under the Insolvency Act 1986 (s. 27).

VIOLENT OFFENDER ORDERS

D25.84   The CJIA 2008, part 7, introduced another civil order, the violent offender order (VOO), which can be applied for by a chief officer of police by way of complaint in a magistrates' court (s. 100). The person to whom an application relates must be given notice of any such application and of the hearing a reasonable time before the hearing (s. 105). The Magistrates' Courts (Violent Offender Orders) Rules 2009 (SI 2009 No. 2197) require that an application for a VOO must be in the form set out in sch. 1. *A Guide to Violent Offender Orders* (2009) has been published by the Home Office.

The Statutory Test

D25.85   A VOO can be made only if the court is satisfied that the person is a 'qualifying offender' *and* that he has since the relevant conviction acted in such a way as to make it necessary to make a VOO for the purpose of protecting the public from the risk of serious violent harm caused by him (CJIA 2008, s. 101(3)). In deciding whether an order is necessary, the court is specifically required by s. 101(4) to have regard to whether the person would be subject to any other measure which operated to protect the public.

The risk of serious violent harm may be to the public in general or specified members of it and must be a *current* risk of serious physical or psychological harm caused by that person committing one or more specified offences (s. 98(2): see **D25.86** for the meaning of 'specified offence'). A VOO made under s. 101 must be in the form set out in sch. 2 to the Magistrates' Courts (Violent Offender Orders) Rules 2009.

Qualifying Offenders

D25.86   A 'qualifying offender' means a person who is aged 18 or over who comes within the CJIA 2008, s. 99(2) *or* (4). A person comes within s. 99(2) if he has been convicted of a specified offence, regardless of whether the conviction occurred before or after the commencement of part 7; he must also have either received a custodial sentence of at least 12 months for that offence or received a hospital order (with or without a restriction order). A person also comes within s. 99(2) if (i) he has been found not guilty of a specified offence by reason of insanity *and* received a hospital order (with or without a restriction order) or a supervision order (s. 99(2)(b) and (3)) or (ii) if he has been found to have been under a disability and to have done the act charged in relation to a specified offence *and* has received a hospital order (with or without a restriction order) or a supervision order (s. 99(2)(c) and (3)).

The term 'specified offence' is defined in s. 98(3) to mean manslaughter, soliciting murder, wounding with intent to cause grievous bodily harm, malicious wounding, attempted murder, conspiracy to murder and relevant service offences (specified at s. 98(4)).

Under s. 99(4), a person could still qualify for a VOO if the conviction for the equivalent of a specified offence was obtained outside England and Wales, i.e. the offence would have to have constituted an offence in the country in question as well as have constituted a specified offence or an offence of murder if it had been committed in England and Wales (a 'relevant offence') (s. 99(5)). An offence is an act punishable under the law of the particular country, however it is described in that law (s. 99(6)). Additionally, just as with convictions in England and Wales, the offender would either have to have received a sentence of imprisonment of at least 12 months or the equivalent of a hospital order (s. 99(4)(a)) or the court would have had to have made the equivalent findings and disposals in relation to insanity and fitness to plead (s. 99(4)(b) and (c)). Rule 4 of the Magistrates' Courts (Violent Offender Orders) Rules 2009 provides that a defendant who wishes to serve a notice under s. 99(7) (denying that an act done outside England and Wales would have constituted a specified offence if it had been done in England and Wales) must do so no later than three days before the hearing date for the application under s. 100.

Terms of a VOO

A qualifying offender may be made subject to such prohibitions, restrictions or conditions (as authorised by the CJIA 2008, s. 102), 'as the court making the order considers necessary for the purpose of protecting the public from the risk of serious violent harm caused by the offender' (s. 98(1)(a)). Section 102(1) authorises prohibitions, etc. that prevent the offender from going to a particular place or premises (the person can be prevented altogether or have specified access); from attending a specified event (e.g., a wedding or a football match); from having any contact or a specified description of contact with an individual (a person could therefore, for example, be prohibited from face-to-face contact but not be restricted in relation to telephone contact). The Secretary of State has power to amend s. 102(1) by order. **D25.87**

Any of the provisions, etc. in a VOO may also relate to conduct in Scotland or Northern Ireland (s. 102(2)). Presumably a court would have to find it necessary for a prohibition, etc. to so extend and so specify.

Duration

A VOO cannot be made so as to come into force when a person is in custody for any offence, is on licence or is subject to a hospital order or a supervision order (CJIA 2008, s. 101(5)). VOOs can be made for a period of not less than two years and not more than five years, unless renewed or discharged (s. 98(1)(b)). The minimum term of a VOO is two years from the date it came into force, unless discharged. Either the offender or the chief officer of police that applied for the VOO (or, if different, the chief officer of police for the area in which the offender resides or is intending to reside) can apply to the appropriate court to vary, renew or discharge a VOO (s. 103). An order can be renewed for a period of up to five years (s. 103(1)(b)). Reading s. 98(1)(b) together with s. 103(1)(b) suggests that a VOO is indefinitely renewable, as long as each period of renewal is for no more than five years. However, before a court can renew or vary so as to impose *additional* prohibitions etc., it must be satisfied of the necessity in accordance with s. 103(5). Each prohibition etc. must be necessary for the purpose specified and can only be of a kind authorised by s. 102. **D25.88**

VOOs are available on an interim basis (IVOOs) (s. 104) if it appears to the court that the person to whom the application relates is a qualifying offender and that it would be likely to make a VOO if it was determining the full application and that it is 'desirable' to act before the full application is heard 'with a view to securing the immediate protection of the public from the risk of serious violent harm caused by P' (s. 103(3)). There is no specific limit on the duration of an IVOO but it will have effect 'only for such period as is specified in the order' (s. 104(6)(a)).

Section 104(8) makes the VOO variation and discharge powers in s. 103 applicable to IVOOs, but not the renewal powers. An application for an IVOO must be in the form set out in sch. 1 to the Magistrates' Courts (Violent Offender Orders) Rules 2009 (see r. 2) and an interim IVOO must be in the form set out in sch. 3. Under r. 3, an application for the variation, discharge or renewal of a VOO (or an interim VOO) must be made in writing and must specify the reason why the applicant believes the court should vary, discharge or renew the order, as the case may be.

Notification Requirements

D25.89 Any person subject to a VOO will also be subject to complex notification requirements, broadly similar to the requirements which apply to offenders convicted of sex offences (CJIA 2008, ss. 107 to 122). These requirements are automatic once a VOO or IVOO is in force (s. 107(1)), although those subject to IVOOs are not subject to the periodic notification requirements in s. 110. See the Criminal Justice and Immigration Act 2008 (Violent Offender Orders) (Notification Requirements) Regulations 2009 (SI 2009 No. 2019).

Appeals

D25.90 A person subject to a VOO or an IVOO can appeal against the making of the order to the Crown Court (CJIA 2008, s. 106(1)). Such a person can also appeal to the Crown Court against the making or refusal to make an order under s. 103 (namely, the variation, renewal or discharge of a VOO) (s. 106(2)). As s. 103 applies in relation to the variation or discharge of an IVOO (s. 104(8)), an appeal will also lie to the Crown Court against the variation or discharge, or refusal to vary or discharge, an IVOO.

The Crown Court has wide powers on appeal. It can make such orders as may be necessary to give effect to its determination as well as such incidental or consequential orders as appear to it to be just (s. 106(3)). Any order made by the Crown Court on appeal from a magistrates' court is treated, for the purposes of any application to vary, renew or discharge, as an order of the magistrates' court from which the appeal was brought (s. 106(4)).

Criminal Offences

D25.91 There are three types of offences provided for by the CJIA 2008, s. 113, all of which attract the same penalty. A failure, without reasonable excuse, to comply with any prohibition, restriction or condition contained in a VOO or failure, without reasonable excuse, to comply with various notification requirements is an either-way offence as is knowingly providing false information in relation to notification requirements (s. 113(1)–(3)).

A person guilty of any of these offences is liable, on summary conviction, to imprisonment for a term not exceeding six months or a fine not exceeding the statutory maximum or both and, on conviction on indictment, to imprisonment for a term not exceeding five years or a fine or both (s. 113(7) and sch. 27, para. 31).

Section D26   Appeal to the Court of Appeal
(Criminal Division) Following Trial on Indictment

BASES OF JURISDICTION OF THE COURT OF APPEAL
(CRIMINAL DIVISION)

Statutory Bases

The vast majority of appeals against conviction and sentence are disposed of by the Court of   **D26.1**
Appeal (Criminal Division) under its statutory jurisdiction. Section 15(2) of the Senior Courts
Act 1981 enables the exercise of the statutory powers conferred under the following legislative
provisions:

Criminal Appeal Act 1968, ss. 1 and 2	Jurisdiction to determine appeals against conviction on indictment.
Criminal Appeal Act 1968, ss. 9 and 11	Jurisdiction to determine appeals against sentence passed following conviction on indictment.
Criminal Appeal Act 1968, ss. 10 and 11	Jurisdiction to determine appeals against sentence passed on a committal for sentence.
Criminal Justice Act 1982, s. 36	Jurisdiction to give an opinion on a point of law referred to the court by the A-G following an acquittal on indictment.
Criminal Justice Act 1987, s. 9(11)–(14)	Jurisdiction to determine appeals against rulings made at preparatory hearings in serious fraud cases.
Criminal Justice Act 1988, ss. 35 and 36	Jurisdiction to increase sentence on a reference by the A-G following an unduly lenient sentence for an offence triable only on indictment.
Criminal Appeal Act 1995, s. 13	Jurisdiction to determine appeals on a reference by the CCRC.

There is no power for the Court of Appeal (Criminal Division) to hear an appeal against a
refusal to make a football banning order (*Boggild* [2012] 4 All ER 1285: see **E21.7**).

Venire de Novo

D26.2   In addition to its statutory jurisdiction, the Court of Appeal retains the power to deal with appeals by way of a writ of *venire de novo*. The power has its origins in the jurisdiction of the Court for Crown Cases Reserved, a forerunner of the modern Court of Appeal (Criminal Division). In essence, the power is exercised when there has been such a fundamental irregularity in procedure that no valid trial has taken place. In *Rose* [1982] AC 822, the House of Lords referred with approval to an article by Sir Robin Cooke (published at (1955) 71 LQR 100) in which he identified categories of procedural irregularity which had been found sufficient to ensure that the trial was in effect a nullity and hence justify the issue of a writ of *venire de novo*. The categories identified were as follows:

(a) where there was error as to the true plea of the defendant or some doubt about the nature of his plea, whether guilty or not guilty;

(b) where there was misjoinder of defendants (*Crane v DPP* [1921] 2 AC 299);

(c) where there was failure to take the verdict of the jury on a change of plea from not guilty to guilty (*Hancock* (1931) 23 Cr App R 16);

(d) where there was some irregularity in the committal proceedings (*Gee* [1936] 2 KB 442);

(e) where there was personation of a juror (*Wakefield* [1918] 1 KB 216);

(f) where there was denial of the right to challenge a juror (*Williams* (1925) 19 Cr App R 67); and

(g) where the judge was unqualified to act as such.

When *Rose* was before the Court of Appeal, Lord Lane CJ added an eighth category of case in which retrials had historically been ordered, namely when the verdict of the jury was so ambiguous or ill-expressed that no judgment could properly be given on it. His reasoning was approved in the House of Lords.

The effect of the procedure is that the Court orders a retrial and the prosecution prefers a fresh indictment against the accused.

ALLOCATION OF BUSINESS

Matters Dealt with by the Full Court

D26.3   Under the Senior Courts Act 1981, s. 55, a court consisting of an uneven number of judges no fewer than three is required to determine (a) an appeal against conviction, (b) a review of a sentence under the CJA 1988, part IV (A-G's references), (c) an appeal against a finding under the Criminal Procedure (Insanity) Act 1964, s. 4 (unfitness to plead), that a person is under a disability, (d) an application for leave to appeal a verdict of not guilty by reason of insanity or a finding under s. 4 of the 1964 Act which has not previously been refused by a single judge, and (e) an application for leave to appeal to the Supreme Court.

Ordinarily, a court sitting to deal with any of the above hearings will comprise just three judges. But, exceptionally, five or even seven judges will sit when the matter to be decided is very important and would benefit from the authority of such a court or where there have been conflicting decisions of the Court of Appeal on the same point (*Newsome* [1970] 2 QB 711).

Matters Dealt with by a Two-judge Court

D26.4   By virtue of s. 55(4) of the Senior Courts Act 1981, a court comprised of two judges may deal with any matter other than those mentioned at **D26.3**.

Matters Dealt with by a Single Judge

D26.5   Sections 31 and 44 of the Criminal Appeal Act 1968 set out the matters which may be dealt with by a single judge. Rule 65.5 of the CrimPR sets out the procedure governing the renewal before the full court of any application refused by the single judge (see **D27.10** and, for the full text, see Supplement, **R-489**).

DECIDING OUTCOME OF APPEAL AND GIVING JUDGMENT

The Court of Appeal may determine an appeal by majority decision. If a two-judge court is **D26.6** equally divided then, under the Senior Courts Act 1981, s. 55(5), the case must be reargued before a reconstituted court comprised of an uneven number of judges. A case is finally determined once the decision has been announced in open court, even if no reasons have yet been given, as it is then properly binding on the judges (*Coates* [2004] 4 All ER 1150). Consequently in *Steele* [2007] 1 WLR 222, it was held that when the Court circulated the transcript of its judgment in advance of handing it down, the appeal was determined even though, when the judgment was handed down, not all members of the original constitution were present. The handing down of the judgment was merely its formal promulgation.

APPEAL AGAINST CONVICTION

Statutory Basis of Appeal against Conviction

Criminal Appeal Act 1968, s. 1   **D26.7**

(1) Subject to subsection (3) below a person convicted of an offence on indictment may appeal to the Court of Appeal against his conviction.
(2) An appeal under this section lies only—
    (a) with the leave of the Court of Appeal; or
    (b) if, within 28 days of the date of the conviction, the judge of the court of trial grants a certificate that the case is fit for appeal.

Unless the trial judge certifies that a case is fit for appeal, leave to appeal to the Court of Appeal is required (see **D26.8**). CPD III, paras. 19H.1 to 19H.4 (see Supplement, **PD-36**), give guidance as to the circumstances in which a certificate of fitness to appeal should be granted. Such a certificate of fitness to appeal against conviction or sentence should be issued only in exceptional circumstances. The certificate removes the need for leave to appeal to be granted by the Court of Appeal but it does not commence the appeal; advocates still need to follow the procedure under the CrimPR, part 68.

Appeal against Conviction with Leave

Unless the trial judge has granted a certificate that the case is fit for appeal, any would-be appel- **D26.8** lant needs leave to appeal. Written grounds of appeal must be submitted within 28 days of the conviction. The initial decision either to grant or refuse leave is usually taken on the papers by the single judge (Criminal Appeal Act 1968, s. 31(2)(a)), but sometimes the decision as to leave may be made by a two-judge or full court at the discretion of the Registrar of Criminal Appeals ('the Registrar'). The need for expedition is sometimes a reason for holding such a leave hearing. Such a hearing will also often take place when an unlawful sentence has been passed and the sentence will inevitably need adjusting.

If leave is refused by the single judge, the applicant is entitled to renew his application before a two-judge or full court under s. 31(3).

Appeal against Conviction following a Plea of Guilty

The fact that a plea of guilty has been entered does not preclude an appeal against the result- **D26.9** ant conviction. If the conviction is found to be unsafe despite the plea of guilty (see **D26.14**), it will be quashed. However, the fact that an appellant was fit to plead, had received expert advice, had been aware of what he was doing and had intended to plead guilty would be highly relevant to the consideration of the safety of the conviction (*Lee* [1984] 1 All ER 1080). The most common basis upon which an unequivocal plea of guilty is challenged is where there has been an incorrect ruling on a point of law by the trial judge which allows the appellant no escape from a guilty verdict. But if an appellant has simply been influenced to enter a plea of guilty because of a decision to admit evidence which meant that his prospects of acquittal were hopeless, the conviction would not normally be held to be unsafe (*Chalkley* [1998] QB 848). That aspect of the judgment in *Chalkley* was approved in *Togher* [2001] 3 All ER 463, and has found reflection in *Hanson* [2005] 1 WLR 3169, where Rose V-P observed that it was highly unlikely that an appeal would be entertained when a defendant pleaded guilty following a decision to admit evidence of bad character.

The Court of Appeal may also quash a conviction arising from a guilty plea following the admission of fresh evidence on appeal under the Criminal Appeal Act 1968, s. 23 (*Swain* [1986] Crim LR 480).

A conviction may also be held to be unsafe when the guilty plea which led to it flowed from inappropriate legal advice. The Court of Appeal considered one such case in *Sadighpour* [2013] 1 WLR 2725. S had pleaded guilty to an offence of possessing a false identity document contrary to the Identity Documents Act 2010, s. 4, without being advised as to a possible defence under the Immigration and Asylum Act 1999, s. 31. The Court observed that in *Boal* (1992) 95 Cr App R 272 it was indicated that a guilty plea might be set aside on appeal in such a situation if the circumstances are such that the Court regards the conviction as unsafe. But it was an exceptional course to be taken only when the Court believes that the overlooked defence would quite probably have succeeded and therefore concludes that an injustice has been done. The approach in *Boal* was adopted in *Dastjerdi* [2011] EWCA Crim 365. The Court in *Sadighpour* noted that in *Mohamed* [2011] 1 Cr App R 432, the Court of Appeal had cited *Boal* but spoken in terms of there being 'no reasonable prospect of a defence under section 31 succeeding'. The Court concluded that if it asked itself whether the defence would quite probably succeed or whether it put the question in terms of there being a reasonable prospect of a s. 31 defence succeeding, it was quite satisfied that the appellant would not satisfy either test.

Single Right of Appeal

D26.10 If an appeal is unsuccessful (either because leave is refused or leave is granted and the appeal is dismissed), there is usually no opportunity for a further appeal even if the point to be argued is that new or fresh evidence has arisen (*Pinfold* [1988] QB 462).

Two minor caveats to that rule were acknowledged in *Pinfold*:

(a) where the appeal has been abandoned, the Court of Appeal may in exceptional circumstances treat the abandonment as a nullity (*Medway* [1976] QB 779); and

(b) if the dismissal of the first appeal involved some procedural irregularity which led to injustice for the appellant, the court may treat the dismissal as a nullity.

Unless either of those caveats apply, an unsuccessful appellant's only remedy is to ask the CCRC to refer his case back to the Court of Appeal (see **D28.1**). See also *Mohammed* [2004] EWCA Crim 2889.

Right of Appeal Vests only in the Convicted Person

D26.11 Section 1(1) of the Criminal Appeal Act 1968 confers a right of appeal only on a person convicted on indictment. However, s. 44A provides that the Court of Appeal may allow an approved person to begin or continue an appeal on behalf of a deceased appellant (see, e.g., *Whelan* [1997] Crim LR 659).

Directions Concerning Loss of Time and Frivolous and Vexatious Appeals

Section 29 of the Criminal Appeal Act 1968 enables the Court of Appeal to direct that all or **D26.12**
part of the time an applicant for leave to appeal has spent in custody since the commencement
of the appeal proceedings shall not count in relation to the sentence he is required to serve. CPD
X, paras. 68E.1 and 68E.2 (see Supplement, **PD-86**), govern the procedure for directions in
relation to loss of time served after service of the notice of appeal and include a reminder of the
warning given by the Court of Appeal in *Hart* [2007] 1 Cr App R 412 that it may order that
time be lost even where counsel has advised that there are good grounds for appeal. In *Fortean*
[2009] EWCA Crim 437, the Court of Appeal ordered that six weeks of the time spent by an
applicant in custody should not count towards his sentence after he had renewed his application for leave to appeal against conviction following the refusal of leave by the single judge. It
was emphasised that the fact that counsel or solicitors have associated themselves with such a
renewal will be relevant, but it will not necessarily avoid such an order if there was no justification for continuing the case. A single judge refusing permission under s. 31 is now asked to
identify on Form SJ cases without merit where the court should consider using the power under
s. 29 should the refused application be renewed to the full court. There is also a box for the
applicant to indicate why such an order should not be made, whether or not an indication has
been given by the single judge. In *Brind* [2008] EWCA Crim 934, the Court of Appeal listed
five renewed applications for leave to appeal together in order to reiterate its powers under s. 29.
The Vice-President stated that, where the single judge had indicated on Form SJ that the application was without merit, the would-be applicant must expect that the court will order that the
time served should not count.

By virtue of s. 20 of the 1968 Act, the Court may summarily dismiss an appeal or application for
leave to appeal without either of the parties being called on to attend if it considers the appeal
to be frivolous or vexatious. A ground of appeal is 'frivolous or vexatious' if it is so unmeritorious that there is no realistic prospect of it succeeding after full argument (*Taylor* [1979] Crim
LR 649). In *Achogbuo* [2014] 2 Cr App R 94 (7) Lord Thomas CJ emphasised that the Court
of Appeal would consider exercising the power under s. 20 more frequently if unmeritorious
cases were appealed. *Achogbuo* was thought to be an example of an appeal being brought, based
on alleged incompetence of the lawyers acting at trial, without 'due diligence' and involved the
Court referring the circumstances to the Solicitors Regulation Authority.

Appellant who Absconds

The Court of Appeal may consider and determine the appeal of a person who has absconded. **D26.13**
In *Charles* [2001] 2 Cr App R 233, the Court expressed the view that it might be contrary to
the ECHR, Article 6, if the appeal of a person was shut out solely because he had absconded.

The approach taken in Charles was approved in *Okedare* [2014] EWCA Crim 228 where
Hallett V-P said (at [31]–[33]):

> . . . we are satisfied that the practice should be: applications from absconders should not be treated
> as ineffective per se. If there are grounds for believing an absconder has given authority to appeal,
> expressly or impliedly, or the case is one where the Court might wish to intervene in the interests of
> justice, the Court should proceed as normal. The application should be put before the single judge.
> The single judge may adjourn the application for more information, grant/refuse leave or refer the
> application to the full Court as usual.
>
> If the single judge is satisfied there is no authority to pursue an application for leave and the applica-
> tion is not one the Court would wish to entertain, she or he has the power to treat the application
> as ineffective and time will continue to run. However, we would expect orders declaring an applica-
> tion ineffective and orders staying applications brought on behalf of absconders to be the exception
> rather than the norm at this stage.
>
> However, it remains the professional responsibility of the lawyer to highlight the fact their client
> has absconded for the benefit of the Criminal Appeal Office and the single judge. He must provide

a full account of the circumstances of the absconding (with updates if necessary) coupled with an explanation for the basis for the assertion of authority and/or any reason why the Court would wish to entertain the application.

In approving such an approach, the Court saw no reason to distinguish between appeals against conviction and sentence. Moreover, if leave to appeal has been granted, it is a matter for the full Court to decide whether to hear the case on the merits or stay the appeal.

DETERMINATION OF APPEALS AGAINST CONVICTION

Statutory Basis of Determination of Appeal

D26.14   Criminal Appeal Act 1968, s. 2

(1) Subject to the provisions of this Act, the Court of Appeal—
   (a) shall allow an appeal against conviction if they think that the conviction is unsafe; and
   (b) shall dismiss such an appeal in any other case.

The Safety Test

D26.15   By virtue of s. 2 of the Criminal Appeal Act 1968, the principal question for the Court of Appeal in the determination of an appeal against conviction is whether or not the conviction is unsafe.

Prior to the amendment of s. 2 by the Criminal Appeal Act 1995, it provided that the Court of Appeal should allow an appeal if it was of the view that the conviction was unsafe or unsatisfactory, or that the judgment of the court of trial should be set aside because of an error of law, or that there had been a material irregularity in the course of the trial. Even if the point in issue concerning a point of law or material irregularity was decided in favour of the appellant, the Court could exercise the proviso and dismiss the appeal if it was satisfied that no miscarriage of justice had occurred. Despite the change in wording, the authorities which developed in relation to the application of the earlier version of s. 2 are relevant to the operation of the provision as now amended and the consideration of the ultimate question of the safety of the conviction.

D26.16   The classic analysis of the Court's powers under the old s. 2 was set out in *Cooper* [1969] 1 QB 267, where Lord Widgery said (at p. 271C–G):

> [This is] a case in which every issue was before the jury and in which the jury was properly instructed, and, accordingly, a case in which this court will be very reluctant indeed to intervene. It has been said over and over again throughout the years that this court must recognise the advantage which a jury has in seeing and hearing the witnesses, and if all the material was before the jury and the summing-up was impeccable, this court should not lightly interfere. Indeed, until the passing of the Criminal Appeal Act 1966 [which somewhat widened the court's powers to quash a conviction] it was almost unheard of for this court to interfere in such a case.

> However, now our powers are somewhat different, and we are indeed charged to allow an appeal against conviction if we think that the verdict of the jury should be set aside on the ground that under all the circumstances of the case it is unsafe or unsatisfactory. That means that in cases of this kind the court must in the end ask itself a subjective question, whether we are content to let the matter stand as it is, or whether there is not some lurking doubt in our minds which makes us wonder whether an injustice has been done. This is a reaction which may not be based strictly on the evidence as such; it is a reaction which can be produced by the general feel of the case as the court experiences it.

Despite the comments by the Court in *F* [1998] Crim LR 307 to the effect that there was no need to add to the simple words of the new section and the concept of lurking doubt was inappropriate, *Cooper* is still regularly used as guidance for the approach to be taken in relation to the issue of whether or not a conviction is safe, and the Court has continued to refer to the test (see, e.g., *Litchfield* [1998] Crim LR 507). As Professor Sir John Smith points out in his commentary on *F*, the repealed words 'or unsatisfactory' played no part in the decision in *Cooper*, and that case has not been overruled. The scope of the continuing applicability of the concept of 'lurking doubt' was considered in *Pope* [2013] 1 Cr App R 214 (14), where Lord Judge CJ observed (at [14]):

> As a matter of principle, in the administration of justice when there is trial by jury, the constitutional primacy and public responsibility for the verdict rests not with the judge, nor indeed with this court, but with the jury. If therefore there is a case to answer and, after proper directions, the jury has convicted, it is not open to the court to set aside the verdict on the basis of some collective, subjective judicial hunch that the conviction is or may be unsafe. Where it arises for consideration at all, the application of the 'lurking doubt' concept requires reasoned analysis of the evidence or the trial process, or both, which leads to the inexorable conclusion that the conviction is unsafe. It can therefore only be in the most exceptional circumstances that a conviction will be quashed on this ground alone, and even more exceptional if the attention of the court is confined to a re-examination of the material before the jury.

It follows from *Pope* (and other cases) that the Court of Appeal (unlike its continental European counterparts) is concerned with the safety of the conviction and not with innocence. If there is a case to answer and if the jury, after proper directions, has convicted (on admissible evidence) then, in the absence of material not considered by the jury, an appeal against conviction will not succeed save in the most exceptional circumstances. The public responsibility for the verdict rests with the jury. It follows that the trial judge's role in deciding whether there is sufficient admissible evidence upon which a jury could properly convict of a count charged in the indictment is vital if miscarriages of justice are to be avoided. Likewise if, on any count, there is more than one factual route to verdict, the trial judge's role in deciding whether there is sufficient admissible evidence to convict on each of those routes is similarly vital. The approach taken in *Pope* was followed in *Davies* [2013] EWCA Crim 1592.

In *Mullen* [2000] QB 520, an appeal was based upon the circumstances in which the appellant was brought to trial. The English authorities had colluded with their Zimbabwean counterparts to ensure M's deportation from Zimbabwe to England in a manner which amounted to an abuse of process. The Court held that abuse of process could still amount to a ground for the quashing of a conviction under the new wording of s. 2. Any safe conviction must of necessity be lawful and, if a trial should never have taken place, the conviction could not be safe.

D26.17   In *Smith* [1999] 2 Cr App R 238, the Court dealt with an appeal which was based on a contention that the trial judge had been wrong to reject a submission of no case to answer. After the judge had rejected the submission, the accused gave evidence and admitted his guilt. Prior to the amendment of s. 2, the Court could have quashed the conviction if it thought that the rejection of the submission of no case was erroneous. Faced with the question of whether the change in the wording had changed that position, the Court held that it had not and, even though the appellant had admitted his guilt, the conviction was quashed.

The test applied by the Court is different to that applied by the trial judge on a submission of no case to answer (*Arobieke* [1988] Crim LR 314).

D26.18   So far as 'fresh evidence' cases are concerned, the classic statement relating to the old s. 2 is to be found in *Stafford v DPP* [1974] AC 878 where Lord Kilbrandon approved *Cooper* and summarised the test to be applied by each member of the appellate court as: 'Have I a reasonable doubt, or perhaps even a lurking doubt, that this conviction may be unsafe or unsatisfactory?' Their lordships rejected the central submission by the appellants that the consideration by the Court should be of the likely effect that the fresh evidence would have had on the minds of the jury; the test was no different in a fresh evidence case than in any other appeal against conviction.

In *Ahmed* [2010] EWCA Crim 2899, the Court restated its role in deciding whether fresh evidence renders a conviction unsafe. Hughes LJ emphasised that the responsibility for deciding whether fresh material renders a conviction unsafe is on the Court, which must make up its own mind. It must consider the nature of the issue before the jury and such information as it can gather as to the reasoning process through which the jury will have been passing. The Court is likely to ask itself by way of check what impact the fresh material might have had on the jury. But Hughes LJ observed that, in most cases of arguably relevant fresh evidence, it will be impossible to be 100 per cent sure that it might not possibly have had *some* impact on the jury's deliberations, since *ex hypothesi* the jury have not seen the fresh material. The most important question for the Court is whether the fresh material causes it to doubt the safety of the guilty verdict. Hughes LJ pointed out that the Court had had the advantage of seeing the analysis of *Pendleton* [2002] 1 All ER 524 and *Dial* [2005] 1 WLR 1660 made by a different constitution of the Court in *Burridge* [2011] 2 Cr App R (S) 148 (at [99]–[101]) and agreed with it. In *Dial* it was held that where fresh evidence is under consideration the primary question is for the Court itself and is not what effect the fresh evidence would have had on the mind of the jury. Moreover, both in *Stafford v DPP* and in *Pendleton*, the House of Lords rejected the proposition that the jury impact test was determinative, explaining that it was only a mechanism in a difficult case for the Court to 'test its view' as to the safety of a conviction. See also *S* [2012] EWCA Crim 1433, where the Court of Appeal heard fresh evidence from expert witnesses which cast doubt on expert evidence given years before in a series of cases of alleged sexual abuse, 'when diagnostic criteria were not as now they are'.

D26.19   The Criminal Evidence (Witness Anonymity) Act 2008 provides (in s. 11) that, where a court is considering an appeal in a case where the trial ended before commencement (21 July 2008), it may not treat the conviction as unsafe solely on the ground that the trial court had no power to make an anonymity order in relation to a witness. It must, however, treat the conviction as unsafe if the anonymity order was not one that the trial court could have made had the 2008 Act (or its successor provision in the CAJA 2009, part 3, chapter 2: see the CAJA 2009, sch. 22, para. 17) been in force and, as a result of the order, the accused did not receive a fair trial. (See D14.49 for witness anonymity orders generally.)

APPROACH OF COURT OF APPEAL TO COMMONLY OCCURRING ERRORS IN THE COURSE OF A TRIAL

D26.20   Exhaustive consideration of the many errors and irregularities which can found a successful appeal against conviction is not possible within this section and regard should be had to other parts of this work dealing with matters of procedure and substantive law. Nevertheless, it is possible to identify commonly occurring errors, some of which are dealt with below.

Wrongful Admission or Exclusion of Evidence

D26.21   The wrongful exclusion of admissible evidence or wrongful inclusion of inadmissible evidence will lead to the quashing of a conviction if the error means that the conviction is unsafe. That remains true even if the appellant's advocate failed to object to the admission of the evidence when it was adduced. But the fact that the advocate did not object to the evidence will be a factor in determining whether its admission was sufficiently prejudicial to render the conviction unsafe (*Stirland v DPP* [1944] AC 315; *Mustafa* (1977) 65 Cr App R 26). See also *T* [2012] EWCA Crim 2358.

Erroneous Exercise of Discretion

D26.22   The Court of Appeal has often said that it will not interfere to quash a conviction on the basis of an erroneous exercise of discretion save in very limited circumstances (*Grondkowski* [1946] KB

369; *Selvey v DPP* [1970] AC 304; *Moghal* (1977) 65 Cr App R 56). The prospects of an appeal succeeding in relation to a matter in the judge's discretion are much improved if there has been a failure to exercise the discretion or a failure to take relevant factors into account, or the judge has taken irrelevant factors into account in the exercise of his discretion (*Sullivan* [1971] 1 QB 253; *Quinn* [1996] Crim LR 516). Occasionally, the Court of Appeal has suggested a wider approach to its function of reviewing the exercise of the judge's discretion. In *McCann*(1991) 92 Cr App R 239, the Court said that the review was not limited to cases in which a trial judge had erred in principle or where there was no material on which the decision he reached could properly have been arrived at. If necessary, the Court could examine afresh the relevant facts and circumstances in order to exercise a discretion by way of review where the judge's ruling may have resulted in injustice to the appellants.

Conduct of Lawyers

D26.23 Errors on the part of advocates may lead to a conviction being found to be unsafe. If the decision of the advocate is taken in good faith, having weighed the competing considerations and having consulted his client where appropriate, the Court of Appeal is much less likely to interfere than where the decision is taken in defiance of instructions and without reference to the client (*Clinton* [1993] 2 All ER 998).

A number of formulations of the test for determining when an advocate's conduct is sufficient to lead to the quashing of a conviction have found favour at different times. That the advocate's conduct must be flagrantly incompetent was said to be necessary in *Ensor* [1989] 2 All ER 586, whilst in *Richards* [2000] All ER (D) 900, the court held that the test to be applied in relation to the conduct of the lawyer was that contained in *Associated Provincial Picture Houses Ltd v Wednesbury Corporation* [1948] 1 KB 223, i.e. the *Wednesbury* unreasonableness test.

The Court of Appeal has recognised the difficulties associated with such tests and, in *Clinton*, stressed that the real test to be applied was not the extent or quality of the advocate's incompetence but whether the conduct affected the safety of the conviction in accordance with s. 2(1) of the Criminal Appeal Act 1968. In *Scollan* [1999] Crim LR 566, the Court approved that approach and said that the position had been unaffected by the amendment of s. 2(1) by the Criminal Appeal Act 1995 (see **D26.15**). Similarly in *Nangle* [2001] Crim LR 506, the Court emphasised that a test requiring flagrant incompetence might not be appropriate in the light of the ECHR, Article 6. What mattered was whether the appellant had had a fair trial; if the conduct of his lawyers was such that that requirement had not been met, the Court might have to intervene. In *Boodram v State of Trinidad and Tobago* [2002] 1 Cr App R 103, the Privy Council observed that, if the conduct of an appellant's lawyers was such that he had been denied due process, the conclusion would be that he had not had a fair trial and the conviction should be quashed without the need for an investigation of the impact of the lawyers' failings on the outcome of the trial.

D26.24 Guidance as to the procedure to be followed by an advocate when dealing with an appeal involving criticism of counsel was issued by the Bar Council and approved by Lord Taylor CJ in December 1995. The guidance was quoted with approval by Judge LJ in *Doherty* [1997] 2 Cr App R 218, and the importance of advocates following that guidance was emphasised in *Nasser* (1998) *The Times*, 19 February 1998. Paragraph A2-72 of the *Guide to Commencing Proceedings in the Court of Appeal Criminal Division* (2008) describes the waiver procedure which is required of an applicant when grounds of appeal criticising the conduct of lawyers are advanced. See also *Achogbuo* [2014] 2 Cr App R 94 (7), where Thomas LJ stated (at [16]):

> Before applications are made to this court alleging incompetent representation which is based upon
> an account given by a convicted criminal, we expect lawyers to take proper steps to ascertain by
> independent means, including contacting the previous lawyers, as to whether there is any objective
> and independent basis for the grounds of appeal.

See also *Kanu* [2014] EWCA Crim 67.

Rejection of Submission of No Case to Answer

D26.25 The wrongful rejection of a submission of no case to answer at the close of the prosecution case will lead to the conclusion that a conviction is unsafe (*Abbott* [1955] 2 QB 497). That can be so even when the appellant has given evidence and admitted his guilt in cross-examination (*Smith* [1999] 2 Cr App R 238). The failure of an experienced advocate to make a submission of no case will not preclude the quashing of a conviction on the basis that there was in fact no case to answer, but the Court of Appeal will presume that the advocate had reason to not make the submission and will look at the whole of the evidence in making its decision. The court will not ordinarily interfere if a submission would have succeeded but was not made, and evidence of guilt emerged later in the trial (*Juett* [1981] Crim LR 113).

Defects in the Indictment

D26.26 There are a number of different challenges to the safety of a conviction which can be made by reference to defects in the indictment.

Where the indictment charges an offence not known to law, the conviction will be quashed (*DPP v Bhagwan* [1972] AC 60). That will be the case even if the accused pleads guilty or no point is taken at trial (*Whitehouse* (1977) 65 Cr App R 33).

Where the indictment is preferred and signed without jurisdiction, the proceedings will be a nullity (*Thompson* (1975) 61 Cr App R 108, but see *Ashton* [2007] 1 WLR 181). A bill of indictment must be duly signed by the proper officer of the court for it to be a valid indictment. Without such an indictment, there could be no valid trial on indictment (*Clarke* [2008] 2 All ER 665). But see **D11.4** and the CAJA 2009, s. 116.

Where an indictment is duplicitous, a conviction may be quashed if the duplicity results in the conviction being unsafe (*Cain* [1983] Crim LR 802; *Levantiz* [1999] 1 Cr App R 465). That is so whether objection was taken at trial or not (*Molloy* [1921] 2 KB 364).

When counts are improperly joined or included in an indictment contrary to r. 14.2 of the CrimPR, s. 2(2) of the Administration of Justice (Miscellaneous Provisions) Act 1933, or s. 40 of the CJA 1988, the conviction may be quashed. If the joinder of counts falls foul of s. 2(2) of the 1933 Act, the conviction will be quashed subject to the caveat that application must be made at trial to quash the indictment. In *Morry* [1946] KB 153, the appellant had been unrepresented at trial but the trial judge raised the point and that was held to be sufficient. In *Nisbet* [1972] 1 QB 37, the Court of Appeal expressed the *obiter* view that it had inherent jurisdiction to quash added or substituted counts if they might result in injustice even though they were founded on the committal papers and no objection was taken at trial. If counts are improperly joined contrary to r. 14.2 or s. 40, the conviction in relation to the wrongly joined count will be quashed (*Smith* [1997] 1 Cr App R 390).

Inconsistent Verdicts

D26.27 The Court of Appeal will quash a conviction based on apparently inconsistent verdicts only if those verdicts are such that no reasonable jury applying its mind to the evidence could have reached the conclusions that it did (*Durante* [1972] 3 All ER 962, adopting the judgment of Devlin J in *Stone* (13 December 1954 unreported)). For examples of the importance of the scrutiny of the facts of a case in the application of this rule, see *Drury* (1971) 56 Cr App R 104; *Kirby* (1972) 56 Cr App R 758; *Grizzle* [1991] Crim LR 553; *McKechnie* (1991) 94 Cr App R 51; *Harrison* [1994] Crim LR 859; *Aldred* [1995] Crim LR 160; *Malashev* [1997] Crim LR 587; *G* [1998] Crim LR 483; *Hayward* [2000] Crim LR 189; *B & Q plc* [2005] EWCA Crim 2297; *Burke* [2006] EWCA Crim 3122; *W* [2009] EWCA Crim 476; and *S* [2014] EWCA Crim 927. In *Ahmadzai* [2009] EWCA Crim 2031 the Court of Appeal reiterated that, where such a ground is advanced, it is for the appellant to show a logical inconsistency between the verdicts criticised and then to demonstrate that it is not possible to postulate a legitimate chain of reasoning which could explain the apparent inconsistency.

The Court of Appeal held in *Gilmartin* [2013] EWCA Crim 2631 that a jury had not given inconsistent verdicts by acquitting two offenders of possession of an offensive weapon but convicting them of an affray during which they were said to have threatened the victims with weapons. The jury must have been sure that they had used weapons, but could have been unsure about the nature of the weapons and which offender had used which weapon.

In *Formhals* [2014] 1 WLR 2219, the Court of Appeal considered whether there could be inconsistent verdicts when verdicts were reached on some counts whilst a jury failed to agree on others. Though the Court dismissed the appeal, Davis LJ said (at [28]–[29]):

> ...what the Court of Appeal ultimately has to consider is whether or not a conviction is safe. The failure of a jury to agree on a verdict is, as we have said, self-evidently not a verdict. But in our view, in a context such as the present, linguistics should not be allowed to triumph over justice. It thus may be that where a jury fails to reach a verdict that cannot be said to give rise, strictly, to an inconsistent verdict when set against another verdict. But that is labelling; and in our view, the principles applicable to inconsistent verdicts are capable of applying by analogy where it simply is logically inexplicable as to how a jury could not reach a verdict on one count when set against a verdict of guilt they had reached on another count. We thus think it would be going too far to preclude a defendant in such a situation from even being permitted to argue that the resulting situation gives rise to an unsafe conviction...
>
> It will be a rare case indeed where a failure to reach a verdict can be said to be logically inexplicable when contrasted with or set against a verdict or verdicts which have been reached. If such an argument is to be run, it will have to be run in cases which will call for the closest scrutiny by the court. Moreover, such an argument has to be run in circumstances where the principles applicable to inconsistent verdicts (in the true sense of the words) are — as has long been established — themselves very tightly prescribed...The bar is thus set high for the application of the principle of inconsistent verdicts. It can be set no less high, and perhaps is set higher, where the attempt is to compare and contrast a verdict of guilt with a failure by the jury to agree.

Conduct of the Trial Judge

Excessive judicial intervention during the course of the evidence of the accused has sometimes led to the quashing of a conviction. In *Hulusi* (1974) 58 Cr App R 378, Lawton LJ summed up the principle underlying such appeals (at p. 385): **D26.28**

> It is a fundamental principle of an English trial that, if an accused gives evidence, he must be allowed to do so without being badgered and interrupted. Judges should remember that most people go into the witness-box, whether they be witnesses for the Crown or the defence, in a state of nervousness. They are anxious to do their best. They expect to receive a courteous hearing, and when they find, almost as soon as they get into the witness-box and are starting to tell their story, that the judge of all people is intervening in a hostile way, then, human nature being what it is, they are liable to become confused and not to do as well as they would have done had they not been badgered and interrupted.

Conduct other than interruption which prevents justice being done to the defence case can also give rise to a successful ground of appeal against conviction (*Barnes* (1970) 55 Cr App R 100). In *Alves* [1997] 1 Cr App R 78, the Court of Appeal held that dismissive remarks about the prospects of acquittal, albeit in the absence of the jury, when the accused was in the course of giving evidence, would have the same inhibiting effect on an accused as interruption, and quashed the conviction. In *Cordingley* [2007] EWCA Crim 2174, the Court expressed the view that exchanges between the judge and counsel betrayed a rudeness and discourtesy on the judge's part of which he should be ashamed. The judge had also delayed a change of clothes for the accused after he had withdrawn his bail. The Court observed that the safety of a conviction does not simply depend on the strength of evidence the jury hears, but also on the observance of due process. It was an inescapable effect of the judge's conduct that the appellant must have been inhibited in the course of his defence. In *Cole* [2008] EWCA Crim 3234, the Court quashed a conviction for dangerous driving when the trial judge had not only made inappropriate interventions, but had treated defence counsel's questions and submissions with hostility. It culminated in his sending a note to defence counsel headed '6P's'. The 6P's were explained in bold as 'Prior Planning Prevents Piss Poor Performance'. See also *Lashley* [2005] EWCA Crim 2015, *Harirbafan* [2008] EWCA Crim 1967, *Copsey* [2008] EWCA Crim 2043 *Michel* [2010] 1 WLR 879, *Malcolm* [2011] EWCA Crim 2069 and *Meall* [2011] EWCA Crim 2526.

APPROACH OF COURT OF APPEAL TO COMMONLY OCCURRING ERRORS IN SUMMING-UP

D26.29   Plainly, errors in the summing-up may found a successful appeal against conviction if the error leads to the conclusion that the conviction is unsafe.

Misdirection on Law

D26.30   A misdirection as to law will lead to the quashing of a conviction only if that misdirection causes the conviction to be unsafe. Thus, in *Edwards* (1983) 77 Cr App R 5 and *Donoghue* (1987) 86 Cr App R 267, the Court of Appeal dismissed the appeals despite the judge having failed to direct the jury as to the standard and burden of proof respectively. In each case the Court observed that the evidence against the defendant was very strong and justified the exercise of the proviso which then applied under s. 2(1) of the Criminal Appeal Act 1968. By contrast, in *James* [1997] Crim LR 598, the Court quashed a conviction for robbery where the trial judge had failed to direct the jury that it was necessary for the force used to be for the purpose of stealing. That direction was crucial to distinguish between robbery and theft. See also *Vinall* [2012] 1 Cr App R 400.

Wrongful Withdrawal of Issues from the Jury

D26.31   In *Sheaf* (1925) 19 Cr App R 46, Avory J said 'When we once arrive at the conclusion that a vital question of fact has not been left to the jury, the only ground on which we can affirm a conviction is that there has been no miscarriage of justice, on the ground that if the question had been left to the jury, they must necessarily have come to the conclusion that the appellant was guilty'. Thus, if a judge fails to direct a jury as to an issue of fact going to an element of the offence, the conviction may be quashed if it is, as a result, unsafe.

Where the evidence on a particular issue is agreed, it can be appropriate for a judge to direct a jury that they may draw an adverse inference against the accused on that issue. But if the judge removes all issues of fact and law from the jury so that they are effectively directed to convict, the conviction is highly likely to be quashed (*Stonehouse* [1978] AC 55). That is not inevitably so if a not guilty verdict from a properly directed jury would have been perverse (*Thompson* [1984] 3 All ER 565).

Misdirection on Facts

D26.32   A misstatement or omission of a fact in the course of the summing-up may lead to the quashing of a conviction if the fact was of such importance that, if it had been correctly stated, the jury may not have reached the same verdict. In *Bateson* [1969] 3 All ER 1372, the Court of Appeal quashed the conviction where the judge told the jury that the accused had first mentioned his defence when the trial had commenced. The Court took the view that it was at least 'on the cards' that the jury would have acquitted if the facts had been correctly stated to them. Conversely in *Wright* [1974] 58 Cr App R 444, the Court dismissed an appeal when the misdirection as to facts was not sufficiently central. Scarman LJ said (at p. 452):

> At the end of the day, when the appellant's case is not that the judge erred in law but that the judge erred in his handling of the facts, the question must be, first of all, was there error, and secondly, if there was, was it significant error which might have misled the jury? If this court has a lurking doubt it is its duty to quash the conviction as unsafe, but this court…has reached the clear conclusion that this verdict was safe and satisfactory.

Improper Comment on Facts or Defence Case

D26.33 A judge is entitled to comment on the facts and express an opinion as to those facts, so it is rare that an appeal will be successful when it is based on such judicial comments. It is only when a judge exhibits blatant unfairness and pro-prosecution bias that the conviction will be imperilled. In *Canny* (1945) 30 Cr App R 143, the conviction was quashed when the judge repeatedly described the defence case as absurd. Similarly, in *Berrada* (1989) 91 Cr App R 131, the conviction was quashed when the judge described allegations put by the defence to a prosecution witness as 'really monstrous' and 'wicked'.

Comment on Failure of Accused to Testify

D26.34 A direction on the failure of an accused to testify is an important one and an error as to that direction may give rise to an arguable ground of appeal. Detailed consideration of the appropriate direction to the jury can be found at **F19.41**.

Comment on the Accused's Character

D26.35 Detailed consideration of the elements of directions as to character may be found at **F12**. An inappropriate direction may lead to the quashing of a conviction.

EFFECT OF SUCCESSFUL APPEAL AGAINST CONVICTION

D26.36

Criminal Appeal Act 1968, ss. 2 and 7

2.—(2) In the case of an appeal against conviction the court shall, if they allow the appeal, quash the conviction.

(3) An order of the Court of Appeal quashing a conviction shall, except when under section 7 below the appellant is ordered to be retried, operate as a direction to the court of trial to enter, instead of the record of conviction, a judgment and verdict of acquittal.

7.—(1) Where the Court of Appeal allow an appeal against conviction and it appears to the court that the interests of justice so require, they may order the appellant to be retried.

(2) A person shall not under this section be ordered to be retried for any offence other than—

    (a) the offence of which he was convicted at the original trial and in respect of which his appeal is allowed as mentioned in subsection (1) above;

    (b) an offence of which he could have been convicted at the original trial on an indictment for the first mentioned offence; or

    (c) an offence charged in an alternative count of the indictment in respect of which no verdict was given in consequence of his being convicted of the first-mentioned offence.

Decision to Order a Retrial

D26.37 Under s. 2(2) of the Criminal Appeal Act 1968, the Court of Appeal may quash a conviction and order that the court of trial enter a verdict of not guilty against the accused. Alternatively, the court may order a retrial of the successful appellant under s. 7.

The factors which the Court will take into account when deciding whether or not to order a retrial will include the length of time which has elapsed between the appellant's original conviction and the successful appeal and the extent to which any fresh evidence received undermines the strength of the case against the appellant (*Saunders* (1974) 58 Cr App R 248; *Flower* [1966] 1 QB 146; *McIlkenny* (1991) 93 Cr App R 287).

Occasionally, a retrial will not be ordered because of considerable publicity surrounding the alleged offences which is adverse to the defendant (*Taylor* (1994) 98 Cr App R 361). But, it is submitted, an application that the appellant should not be retried because of prejudicial publicity is highly unlikely to succeed. The Court of Appeal will allow such an application only if it is satisfied on the balance of probabilities that, as a result of the publicity, one or all of the verdicts returned by a jury would be unsafe. The Court may take account of the time between the publicity and the retrial and can seek to minimise its effect by a change of trial venue and suitable questions to the jury (*Stone* [2001] Crim LR 465).

In *Maxwell* [2011] 4 All ER 941, a case involving serious prosecutorial misconduct, the Supreme Court ruled (by a majority) that the Court of Appeal was entitled to order a retrial notwithstanding the abuse of process that had been revealed to have taken place prior to the original trial. The 'interests of justice' test in s. 7 called for an exercise of judgment and in the instant case (involving a grave crime and an admission of guilt) it would be wrong to override the exercise by the Court of Appeal of its discretion.

D26.38   Section 8 includes a number of procedural requirements to be followed when a retrial is ordered. The most important of those requirements are as follows:

(a)   a new indictment must be preferred by the Court of Appeal;

(b)   arraignment must be within two months of the quashing of the conviction unless the Court allows longer;

(c)   at any time after the two months has elapsed, the appellant may apply for the order for retrial to be set aside and for a verdict of not guilty to be entered;

(d)   upon receipt of such an application, the Court may quash the order for retrial or may allow late arraignment — the Court will allow late arraignment only if the prosecution has acted with due expedition and there is good and sufficient cause that the retrial take place despite the delay following the order for a retrial.

In *Horne* [1992] Crim LR 304, the prosecution papers were lost and, as a result, the accused was not arraigned within the two-month time-limit. The prosecution was held not to have acted with due expedition despite an early trial date being set down. In *Jones* [2003] 1 Cr App R 313, an adjourned date for the arraignment was set down outside the two-month period without the prosecution noticing the difficulties that listing would produce. The Court of Appeal held that the prosecution had acted with due expedition but if the applicable test had been of due diligence (as in relation to custody time-limits), the position would have been different. Defence lawyers were also criticised for failing to draw the difficulties to the attention of the prosecution in order that they could comply with the order of the court.

The procedure to be followed when making an application to arraign more than two months after the Court ordered a retrial, or when the accused wants such an order to be set aside more than two months after that order, is set out in the CrimPR, r. 68.14 (see Supplement, R-531).

Partially Successful Appeal: Substituting Verdict

D26.39   Criminal Appeal Act 1968, s. 3

(1)   This section applies on an appeal against conviction, where the appellant has been convicted of an offence to which he did not plead guilty and the jury could on the indictment have found him guilty of some other offence, and on the finding of the jury it appears to the Court of Appeal that the jury must have been satisfied of facts which proved him guilty of the other offence.

(2)   The Court may, instead of allowing or dismissing the appeal, substitute for the verdict found by the jury a verdict of guilty of the other offence, and pass such sentence in substitution for

the sentence passed at the trial as may be authorised by law for the other offence, not being a sentence of greater severity.

Section 3 allows the Court of Appeal to substitute a verdict of guilty for an offence other than that of which the appellant was convicted if it appears to the court that:

(a) the jury could on the indictment have found the appellant guilty of the substituted offence, the allegation of which was expressly or impliedly included in the allegation in the particular count in the indictment, and

(b) the jury must have been satisfied of facts which proved the appellant guilty of the substituted offence (*Graham* [1997] 1 Cr App R 302).

Section 3 applies to two broad categories of cases. The first is where the appellant was tried and convicted on a single count but the evidence was such that the jury could have convicted of the substituted offence. For example, in *Spratt* [1980] 2 All ER 969, following a conviction for murder, fresh evidence as to diminished responsibility allowed the substitution of a conviction for manslaughter.

The second category of case is where there are counts charged in the alternative and the jury have convicted on a count which is not supported by the evidence. The Court may substitute the alternative count provided the jury have not already entered a not guilty count in relation to that count (*Seymour* [1954] 1 All ER 1006; but see also *Smythe* (1980) 72 Cr App R 8 for a minor variation of the rule).

For illustration of the care that must be taken with the application of s. 3 in practice, see *Shields* [2012] 1 Cr App R 113.

Section 3A provides that, if the Court quashes a conviction produced by a guilty plea, in circumstances where the appellant could have pleaded guilty to or been convicted of another offence and it appears to the court that his plea of guilty indicates an admission by him of acts which would make him guilty of the other offence, the court may substitute a plea of guilty to that offence without allowing or dismissing the appeal. The court may then proceed to sentence for that offence but may not pass a more grave sentence than that originally passed.

In *Lawrence* [2014] 1 WLR 106, the Court of Appeal said that s. 3A has to be construed strictly; its operation must be confined to cases where the guilty plea inevitably involves an admission to the alternative offence. Any other approach would involve the Court in making a decision as to whether a defence was available and that could not be permitted given the importance of the right to jury trial. In *Lawrence*, a wrongly entered guilty plea to possession of a prohibited weapon could not be substituted with a conviction for possessing a firearm without a certificate contrary to the FA 1968, s. 1(1)(a), as the indictment alleging possession of the prohibited weapon did not, and did not need to, allege the absence of a firearm certificate so there could not have been a conviction on that indictment of the offence sought to be substituted. However, in *White* [2014] EWCA Crim 714 the Court of Appeal allowed substitution of conviction for appropriate offences notwithstanding that the indictment on which the appellant had been convicted was wholly flawed.

Sentence when Appeal Allowed on Part Only of an Indictment

If an appellant has been convicted in the Crown Court of a number of offences and the **D26.40** Court of Appeal quashes some of the convictions but not others, the court is entitled to resentence the offender on the counts on which he remains convicted. The power, which arises under the Criminal Appeal Act 1968, s. 4, is limited to the extent that the court may not pass a sentence of greater totality or severity than that which was originally passed by the Crown Court. The Court of Appeal may resentence even on those counts for which the Crown Court imposed no separate penalty (*O'Grady* (1941) 28 Cr App R 33; *Dolan* (1975) 62 Cr App R 36).

RIGHT OF APPEAL AGAINST SENTENCE

Statutory Basis of Appeal against Sentence

D26.41   The right to appeal against sentence is statutory and derives from the Criminal Appeal Act 1968. Section 9 governs appeals against sentence following conviction on indictment. Appeals from sentences imposed in the Crown Court following summary conviction are covered by s. 10. The definition of sentence for the purposes of the sections is to be found in s. 50.

Whether the appeal lies under s. 9 or s. 10, the appellant must, by virtue of s. 11, either have leave to appeal from the Court of Appeal or the sentencing judge must certify that the case is fit for appeal against sentence. CPD III, paras. 19H.1 to 19H.4 (see Supplement, **PD-36**), deal with the certification of fitness for appeal against sentence. Paragraph 19H.3 directs that a sentencing judge should not certify an appeal against sentence 'merely in the light of mitigation to which, in his opinion, he has given due weight'. The reality in practice is that certificates of appeal against sentence are rarely applied for and are even less seldom granted. Paragraphs 19H.5 and 19H.6 govern the grant of bail pending appeal following the issue of a certificate of fitness for appeal. Bail can only be granted in the Crown Court within 28 days of the conviction or sentence which is to be the subject of the appeal and may not be granted if an application for bail has already been made to the Court of Appeal. The procedure for bail to be granted by a judge of the Crown Court pending an appeal is governed by the CrimPR, part 19. The length of time likely to elapse before the appeal is heard is not relevant to the decision as to the grant of a certificate. However, if a judge issues a certificate, it may be one factor to take into account in deciding whether to grant bail. If the judge does grant bail, he should consider a condition of residence in line with the practice of the Court of Appeal (CPD III, para. 19H.6).

Sentence Following Conviction on Indictment

D26.42   Criminal Appeal Act 1968, ss. 9 and 50

9.—(1) A person who has been convicted of an offence on indictment may appeal to the Court of Appeal against any sentence (not being a sentence fixed by law) passed on him for the offence, whether passed on his conviction or in subsequent proceedings.

(1A)   In subsection (1) of this section, the reference to a sentence fixed by law does not include a reference to an order made under subsection (2) or (4) of section 269 of the Criminal Justice Act 2003 in relation to a life sentence (as defined in section 277 of that Act) that is fixed by law.

(2) A person who on conviction on indictment has also been convicted of a summary offence under paragraph 6 of Schedule 3 to the Crime and Disorder Act 1998 (power of Crown Court to deal with summary offence where person sent for trial for indictable-only offence) may appeal to the Court of Appeal against any sentence passed on him for the summary offence (whether on his conviction or in subsequent proceedings) under subsection (7) of that section or sub-paragraph (4) of that paragraph.

50.—(1) In this Act, 'sentence', in relation to an offence, includes any order made by a court when dealing with an offender including, in particular—

(a)   a hospital order under Part III of the Mental Health Act 1983, with or without a restriction order;

(b)   an interim hospital order under that Part;

(bb)   a hospital direction and a limitation direction under that Part;

(c)   a recommendation for deportation;

(ca)   a confiscation order under Part 2 of the Proceeds of Crime Act 2002;

(cb)   an order which varies a confiscation order made under Part 2 of the Proceeds of Crime Act 2002 if the varying order is made under section 21, 22 or 29 of that Act (but not otherwise);

(cc)   a direction under section 20(3) or 21(3) of the Crime (Sentences) Act 1997 (extended supervision for sexual or violent offenders);

(d)   a confiscation order under the Drug Trafficking Act 1994 other than one made by the High Court;

    (e)   a confiscation order under Part VI of the Criminal Justice Act 1988;

    (f)   an order varying a confiscation order of a kind which is included by virtue of paragraph (d) or (e) above;

    (g)   an order made by the Crown Court varying a confiscation order which was made by the High Court by virtue of section 19 of the Act of 1994;

    (h)   a declaration of relevance within the meaning of section 23 of the Football Spectators Act 1989; and

    (i)   an order under section 129(2) of the Licensing Act 2003 (forfeiture or suspension of personal licence).

(1A) Section 14 of the Powers of Criminal Courts (Sentencing) Act 2000 (under which a conviction of an offence for which an order for conditional or absolute discharge is made is deemed not to be a conviction except for certain purposes) shall not prevent an appeal under this Act, whether against conviction or otherwise.

(2) Any power of the Criminal Division of the Court of Appeal to pass a sentence includes a power to make a recommendation for deportation in cases where the court from which the appeal lies had power to make such a recommendation.

(3) An order relating to a requirement to make a payment under regulations under section 23 or 24 of the Legal Aid, Sentencing and Punishment of Offenders Act 2012 is not a sentence for the purposes of this Act.

D26.43 A person convicted on indictment may appeal to the Court of Appeal against *any* sentence passed on him for the offence, unless it is one fixed by law (i.e. the life sentence for murder) (s. 9(1)). Under s. 9(2) as it applied prior to the abolition of committals, if an offender is convicted on indictment and pleads guilty to an additional offence which was committed or transferred to the Crown Court by the magistrates under the CJA 1988, s. 41, his right of appeal extended to his sentence for that matter also. The appeal is available if the sentence is passed at the time of the conviction or later. Thus, the right of appeal exists if an offender is resentenced for an offence following subsequent offending. Equally, if an offender is convicted of drug trafficking offences and is subsequently made the subject of a confiscation order, the offender may appeal against the confiscation order (*Neal* [1999] Crim LR 509).

Section 50(1) of the 1968 Act states that 'sentence' includes any order made by a court when dealing with an offender'. The definition therefore covers not only the penalty but also many orders made ancillary to that sentence. Thus an order to pay costs (*Hayden* [1975] 2 All ER 558) or compensation (see the numerous cases such as *Vivian* [1979] 1 All ER 48) may be the subject of appeal to the Court of Appeal. Other ancillary orders which have been held to be part of the sentence for the purposes of an appeal are restitution orders under the Theft Act 1968, s. 28 (*Parker* [1970] 2 All ER 458); orders binding an offender over to come up for judgment if required to do so (*Williams* [1982] 3 All ER 1092); and orders revoking a parole licence (*Welch* [1982] 2 All ER 824). Section 50(1) also specifically provides that hospital orders under part III of the Mental Health Act 1983 (whether with or without a restriction order) and recommendations for deportation are part of the sentence.

Although by virtue of s. 9(1) it is not possible to appeal against the mandatory life sentence for murder, it is possible to appeal against the minimum term set by the court or against a whole life term (s. 9(1A)). Moreover, the period specified in respect of a discretionary life sentence under s. 82A of the PCC(S)A 2000 is susceptible to appeal. An appeal can be instituted against either the failure of a sentencer to specify a period (*Hollies* (1995) 16 Cr App R (S) 463), or against the actual period which the sentencer fixes (*D* (1995) 16 Cr App R (S) 564). (For details of s. 82A, see **E4.16**.)

Sentence Following Summary Conviction and Crown Court Disposal

Criminal Appeal Act 1968, s. 10

D26.44

(1) This section has effect for providing rights of appeal against sentence when a person is dealt with by the Crown Court (otherwise than on appeal from a magistrates' court) for an offence of which he was not convicted on indictment.

(2) The proceedings from which an appeal against sentence lies under this section are those where an offender convicted of an offence by a magistrates' court—

    (a) is committed by the court to be dealt with for his offence at the Crown Court; or

    (b) having been made the subject of an order for conditional discharge or a youth community order within the meaning of the Powers of Criminal Courts (Sentencing) Act 2000 or a community order within the meaning of the Criminal Justice Act 2003 or given a suspended sentence, appears or is brought before the Crown Court to be further dealt with for his offence.

(3) An offender dealt with for an offence at the Crown Court in a proceeding to which subsection (2) of this section applies may appeal to the Court of Appeal against any sentence passed on him for the offence by the Crown Court.

D26.45   The right of appeal against a sentence imposed by the Crown Court for which the offender was summarily convicted is governed by s. 10. The appeal arises when (a) an offender is committed for sentence (e.g., under the PCC(S)A 2000, s. 3 or s. 6), or (b) having been made the subject of an order for conditional discharge or a community order or given a suspended sentence of imprisonment, he breaches the order or suspended sentence by a subsequent conviction and falls to be dealt with by the Crown Court for the breach (s. 10(2)(a) and (b)). Although such cases are dealt with relatively infrequently, there are two main situations in which such matters come before the Crown Court, namely:

(a) the offender is summarily convicted of an offence which puts him in breach of an order mentioned in s. 10(2)(b) that was made by a magistrates' court and the convicting magistrates' court decides to commit him for sentence in respect of the subsequent offence and also decides to commit him to be dealt with for the breach;

(b) the offender is summarily convicted of an offence which puts him in breach of a relevant order previously made against him by the Crown Court when dealing with him following committal for sentence for a summary conviction. In such a case, the magistrates' court may either commit the offender to be dealt with for the breach or may decline to commit him but, in the latter case, the Crown Court may secure the attendance of the offender before it by the appropriate process.

The previous limitation of the right of appeal to a sentence imposing a term of imprisonment of six months or more has been removed by the CJA 2003, s. 319. Thus any offender committed to the Crown Court for sentence may institute an appeal against the sentence imposed upon him.

Powers of the Court of Appeal when Determining an Appeal against Sentence

D26.46   Criminal Appeal Act 1968, s. 11

(1) Subject to subsection (1A) below, an appeal against sentence, whether under section 9 or section 10 of this Act, lies only with the leave of the Court of Appeal.

(1A)   If, within 28 days of the date on which sentence was passed, the judge who passed it grants a certificate that the case is fit for appeal under section 9 or 10 of this Act, an appeal lies under this section without the leave of the Court of Appeal.

(2) Where the Crown Court, in dealing with an offender either on his conviction on indictment or in a proceeding to which section 10(2) of this Act applies, has passed on him two or more sentences in the same proceeding..., being sentences against which an appeal lies under section 9(1) or section 10, an appeal or application for leave to appeal against any one of those sentences shall be treated as an appeal or application in respect of both or all of them.

(2A)   Where following conviction on indictment a person has been convicted under section 41 of the Criminal Justice Act 1988 of a summary offence an appeal or application for leave to appeal against any sentence for the offence triable either way shall be treated also as an appeal or application in respect of any sentence for the summary offence and an appeal or application for leave to appeal against any sentence for the summary offence shall be treated also as an appeal or application in respect of the offence triable either way.

(2B) If the appellant or applicant was convicted on indictment of two or more offences triable
either way, the references to the offence triable either way in subsection (2A) above are to be
construed, in relation to any summary offence of which he was convicted under section 41
of the Criminal Justice Act 1988 following the conviction on indictment, as references to the
offence triable either way specified in the notice relating to that summary offence which was
given under subsection (2) of that section.

(3) On an appeal against sentence the Court of Appeal, if they consider that the appellant
should be sentenced differently for an offence for which he was dealt with by the court below
may—

(a) quash any sentence or order which is the subject of the appeal; and

(b) in place of it pass such sentence or make such order as they think appropriate for the
case and as the court below had power to pass or make when dealing with him for the
offence;

but the court shall so exercise their powers under this subsection that, taking the case as a
whole, the appellant is not more severely dealt with on appeal than he was dealt with by the
court below.

(3A) Where the Court of Appeal exercise their power under paragraph (a) of subsection (3) to
quash a confiscation order, the Court may, instead of proceeding under paragraph (b) of
that subsection, direct the Crown Court to proceed afresh under the relevant enactment.

(3B) When proceeding afresh pursuant to subsection (3A), the Crown Court shall comply with
any directions the Court of Appeal may make.

(3C) The Court of Appeal shall exercise the power to give such directions so as to ensure that any
confiscation order made in respect of the appellant by the Crown Court does not deal more
severely with the appellant than the order quashed under subsection (3)(a).

(3D) [Defines confiscation order and relevant enactment by reference to the Drug Trafficking
Offences Act 1986, the CJA 1988, the Drug Trafficking Act 1994 and the POCA 2002.]

(4) [Repealed.]

(5) [Concerns the position where the Court of Appeal quashes an interim hospital order but does
not replace it with its own sentence.]

(6) [Repealed.]

(7) For the purposes of this section, any two or more sentences are to be treated as passed in the
same proceeding if—

(a) they are passed on the same day; or

(b) they are passed on different days but the court in passing any one of them states that it is
treating that one together with the other or others as substantially one sentence.

D26.47 Upon appeal against sentence, the Court of Appeal may quash the sentence and substitute any
other sentence or order that it deems appropriate, provided that the substituted sentence could
lawfully have been passed by the Crown Court and provided also that the appellant is not dealt
with more severely when the case is viewed as a whole. The Court may not impose a mandatory
sentence where a Crown Court has failed to impose or if it would mean treating the appellant
more severely (*Reynolds* [2008] 4 All ER 369).

As the Court must look at the position as a whole when deciding whether the substituted sentence would constitute treating the appellant more severely, it follows that, if the offender was
sentenced for two or more matters, the Court may increase the sentence for one of them and
adjust the others accordingly. See, e.g., *McKenna* (1985) 7 Cr App R (S) 348.

D26.48 Infrequently, the relative severity of a substituted sentence to the original sentence is not immediately obvious. Examples of such situations include:

(a) 'Taking the case as a whole' means taking together the totality of the matters in respect of
which the appellant was being dealt with in the court below on the day he was sentenced' (per
Glidewell J in *Sandwell* (1984) 80 Cr App R 78 at p. 81). In *Sandwell*, S pleaded guilty on
the same day to two offences charged in separate indictments, and was sentenced for each to,
inter alia, 12 months' disqualification to run consecutively. There is no power to impose consecutive disqualifications and so those disqualifications fell to be quashed, but the Court of
Appeal varied the sentence to two years' disqualification for each offence to run concurrently.

(b) A sentence of life imprisonment may not be substituted for a sentence of imprisonment for a fixed term of years (*Whittaker* [1967] Crim LR 431).

(c) An immediate custodial term may not be imposed in place of a suspended sentence (*Peppard* (1990) 12 Cr App R (S) 88, following *McCabe* (1988) 10 Cr App R (S) 134).

(d) A hospital order coupled with a restriction order for an indefinite period has been held to be no more severe than a sentence of three years' imprisonment (*Bennett* [1968] 2 All ER 753, cited with approval in *Crozier* (1990) 12 Cr App R (S) 206). Furthermore, a hospital order without restriction has been substituted for a sentence of Borstal training (*Marsden* [1968] 2 All ER 341). It would appear that the rationale underlying those decisions is that, in contrast to a custodial term, a hospital order is intended to be a remedial treatment and not a punishment.

(e) A fine in combination with a custodial term may properly be substituted for a reduced custodial term (*Walton* (29 August 1989 unreported)). W had been sentenced by the court below to four months' imprisonment. He served 11 days in custody and was then released on bail. At the appeal, such term of imprisonment as would allow immediate release was substituted, with the addition of a fine of £1,000.

(f) A period of disqualification from driving may be imposed or increased where a sentence of imprisonment is reduced (*Ardani* (1983) 77 Cr App R 302). Conversely, in *McLaren* (1983) 5 Cr App R (S) 332, the appellant's fine was increased but his period of disqualification was reduced.

Commonly Occurring Grounds of Appeal against Sentence

D26.49   From the existing case law, it is possible to identify a number of heads of appeal against sentence which have emerged. What follows is a summary of the more conspicuous of those heads of appeal.

D26.50   **Sentence Wrong in Law**   The Court of Appeal will intervene when the sentence imposed on an appellant could not legally be passed. A simple example is *Corcoran* (1986) 8 Cr App R(S) 118, in which a youth convicted summarily was sentenced to three years' detention, ostensibly in accordance with s. 53(3) of the CYPA 1933 but following committal for sentence. As s. 53(3) detention could be imposed only following conviction on indictment, the Court of Appeal was forced to substitute the maximum available sentence in the youth court of 12 months' youth custody, despite observing that a sentence of three years was richly deserved.

D26.51   **Sentence Wrong in Principle or Manifestly Excessive**   The Court of Appeal will interfere with a sentence if it is of the view that it was outside the broad range of appropriate penalties. The fact that a sentence is merely severe will not be sufficient. In *Nuttall* (1908) 1 Cr App R 180, Channell J said, 'This court will ... be reluctant to interfere with sentences which do not seem to it to be wrong in principle, though they may appear heavy to individual judges'. Likewise, in *Gumbs* (1926) 19 Cr App R 74, Lord Hewart CJ stated:

> ... this court never interferes with the discretion of the court below merely on the ground that this court might have passed a somewhat different sentence; for this court to revise a sentence there must be some error in principle.

If a sentence is not of the appropriate form (because for example an offender was not eligible for the custodial sentence imposed upon him), the more appropriate description is that the sentence is 'wrong in principle'. Equally, an inappropriate combination of sentences can be most appropriately described as 'wrong in principle' (see *Socratous* (1984) 6 Cr App R (S) 33, in which the imposition of a short custodial term combined with a probation order was held to be wrong in principle).

D26.52   That a sentence passed is 'manifestly excessive' is the basis that is most commonly used in the modern appeal process. An appeal will succeed only if the sentence was excessive in the sense of being outside the appropriate range for the offence and offender in question, as opposed to being merely more than the Court of Appeal itself would have passed. For example in *Withers* [1983] Crim LR 339, the principal submission was that a sentence of nine months' imprisonment for stealing £1,000 from employers was too long by three months. The Court held that a sentence of six months would not have been wrong, but to reduce the sentence by such a small amount would have been 'tinkering' with the judge's decision and the appeal was dismissed. Although the sentence was 'excessive' in one sense, it was not so excessive as to be outside the appropriate range. Equally, where a sentence was not manifestly excessive at the time that it was passed, the Court of Appeal will not interfere with the level of that sentence just because the 'tariff' for that offence is reduced after the sentence is passed or legislation alters the level of sentence to be imposed (*Graham* [1999] 2 Cr App R (S) 312).

By virtue of the CAJA 2009, s. 125(1), a judge must follow sentencing guidelines (see **E1.3**).

Judge's Remarks when Sentencing   If the judge's sentencing remarks tend to reveal that   **D26.53** he has taken irrelevant factors into account in deciding the appropriate sentence to impose on the appellant, the Court of Appeal may allow the appeal and substitute a different sentence. But if the Court takes the view that the sentence was appropriate despite the flaws in the decision-making by the judge, it may nonetheless uphold the sentence. Examples of circumstances in which the judge's sentencing remarks might lead to a reduction in sentence include where the judge implies that he has increased the sentence because the offender elected trial on indictment, pleaded not guilty, or made attacks on the character of prosecution witnesses (*Skone* (1966) 51 Cr App R 165; *Scott* (1983) 5 Cr App R (S) 90; *Doab* [1983] Crim LR 569).

Procedural Errors   The failure of a judge to follow the correct procedure may lead to a vari-   **D26.54** ation in the sentence by the Court of Appeal. But that is by no means necessarily the case. The failure of a sentencing judge to secure a pre-sentence report before passing sentence in circumstances where one was required will not necessarily lead to a reduction in sentence, but the Court of Appeal will secure such a report before dealing with the appeal. Similarly, where information about an offender's antecedents has been inappropriately given to the court of sentence, the Court may either reduce the sentence or maintain it as the correct sentence in all the circumstances (*Wilkins* (1977) 66 Cr App R (S) 49; *Van Pelz* [1943] KB 157). The failure of the judge to hold a *Newton* hearing when asked to do so is more likely to result in a reduction in sentence, as the sentencing judge may well have proceeded on a basis adverse to the defendant (see *Costley* (1989) 11 Cr App R (S) 357 and **D20.22**).

Sense of Grievance   The Court of Appeal will intervene when the appellant has a justifiable   **D26.55** sense of grievance at the sentence imposed upon him following events preceding sentence. In practice, this principle applies most often when a sentencing judge orders pre-sentence reports and indicates that, if the reports are satisfactory, a non-custodial sentence will be passed, but then proceeds to send the offender into custody despite positive reports (*Gillam* (1980) 2 Cr App R (S) 267; *Ward* (1982) 4 Cr App R (S) 103). Moreover, if an indication of a non-custodial sentence is given privately to an advocate and a guilty plea follows, any subsequent judge will be bound by the indication of the first judge (*Moss* (1983) 5 Cr App R (S) 209). But if a judge indicates that the fact of his ordering reports should not be taken as any indication that he would eventually pass a non-custodial sentence, or indicates that he is 'making no promises', then obviously the court will not be moved to vary the sentence imposed if a custodial sentence follows, as the appellant's hopes could not be said to have been legitimately raised (*Horton* (1985) 7 Cr App R (S) 299).

Disparity of Sentence   There has been some inconsistency in the approach taken by the   **D26.56** Court of Appeal to the question of the circumstances in which a difference in sentence between co-accused can form a ground of appeal against sentence. In *Stroud* (1977) 65 Cr App R 150, Scarman LJ stated that disparity can never in itself be a sufficient ground of appeal. Instead, the question for the Court of Appeal is simply whether the sentence received by the appellant was wrong in principle or manifestly excessive. If it was not, the appeal should be dismissed, even though a co-offender was, in the Court's view, treated with undue leniency. To reduce the heavier sentence would simply result in two, rather than one, over-lenient penalties. Decisions in the same vein include *Brown* [1975] Crim LR 177, *Hair* [1978] Crim LR 698 and *Weekes* (1980) 74 Cr App R 161.

By contrast, in *Fawcett* (1983) 5 Cr App R (S) 158, the Court held that, where an offender had received a sentence which in and of itself was not objectionable but, for no apparent good reason, was more severe than that of his co-accused, the Court could intervene if the disparity was serious. Lawton LJ said that the question to be asked is:

> ...would right-thinking members of the public, with full knowledge of all the relevant facts and circumstances, learning of this sentence consider that something had gone wrong with the administration of justice?

(See also *Wood* (1983) 5 Cr App R (S) 381 and *Sigston* [2004] EWCA Crim 1548.)

In more recent cases the Court has followed the approach in *Fawcett* (but see *Tate* (2006) 150 SJ 1192, for an example of a case following the line of reasoning in *Stroud*).

The fact that offenders who are sentenced at roughly the same time as an appellant in the same Crown Court have received more lenient sentences for comparable offences can never be relied on as a ground of appeal. The court will not allow such comparisons to be made (*Large* (1981) 3 Cr App R (S) 80).

D26.57   **Failure to Distinguish between Offenders**   The failure of the court of sentence to distinguish between offenders when one has powerful mitigation and the other does not can give rise to a successful ground of appeal against sentence. See, e.g., *Fraser* (1982) 4 Cr App R (S) 254.

APPEAL AGAINST VERDICT OF NOT GUILTY BY REASON OF INSANITY

D26.58   Criminal Appeal Act 1968, ss. 12 and 13

12.—(1) A person in whose case there is returned a verdict of not guilty by reason of insanity may appeal to the Court of Appeal against the verdict—
   (a) with the leave of the Court of Appeal; or
   (b) if, within 28 days of the date of the verdict, the judge of the court of trial grants a certificate that the case is fit for appeal.
13.—(1) Subject to the provisions of this section, the Court of Appeal—
   (a) shall allow an appeal under section 12 of this Act if they think that the verdict is unsafe; and
   (b) shall dismiss such an appeal in any other case.
(2) [Repealed.]
(3) Where apart from this subsection—
   (a) an appeal under section 12 of this Act would fall to be allowed; and
   (b) none of the grounds for allowing it relates to the question of the insanity of the accused,
   the Court of Appeal may dismiss the appeal if they are of opinion that, but for the insanity of the accused, the proper verdict would have been that he was guilty of an offence other than the offence charged.
(4) Where an appeal under section 12 of this Act is allowed, the following provisions apply—
   (a) if the ground, or one of the grounds, for allowing the appeal is that the finding of the jury as to the insanity of the accused ought not to stand and the Court of Appeal are of opinion that the proper verdict would have been that he was guilty of an offence (whether the offence charged or any other offence of which the jury could have found him guilty), the court—
      (i) shall substitute for the verdict of not guilty by reason of insanity a verdict of guilty of that offence; and

(ii) shall, subject to subsection (5) below, have the like powers of punishing or otherwise dealing with the appellant, and other powers, as the court of trial would have had if the jury had come to the substituted verdict; and

(b) in any other case, the Court of Appeal shall substitute for the verdict of the jury a verdict of acquittal.

As with appeals against other findings in the Crown Court, leave is required to appeal a finding **D26.59** of not guilty by reason of insanity unless the judge certifies that the case is fit for appeal. Equally, just as s. 2 of the 1968 Act stipulates that the Court of Appeal will allow an appeal against conviction only if the verdict is unsafe, the court takes the same approach under s. 12 to any appeal against a finding of not guilty by reason of insanity.

If the basis for allowing the appeal is that the appellant is not insane, the court will substitute a finding of guilt of the appropriate offence and sentence accordingly. If the court reaches the view that the appeal should be allowed on grounds which are not related to the insanity of the appellant, but which grounds undermine the safety of the conviction (such as fresh evidence showing that the appellant did not commit the offence), a verdict of not guilty will be recorded. If the court reaches the view that a verdict of not guilty would not have been appropriate, but findings that the appellant did the act or omission charged and was under a disability were appropriate, it may make any of the orders which could have been made by the court of sentence (s. 14).

The *Guide to Commencing Proceedings in the Court of Appeal Criminal Division* (2008) provides valuable guidance as to the procedure to be followed upon an appeal against a verdict of not guilty by reason of insanity (see D9 of the guide).

APPEAL AGAINST FINDING OF UNFITNESS TO PLEAD

Criminal Appeal Act 1968 s. 15   **D26.60**

(1) Where there has been a determination under section 4 of the Criminal Procedure (Insanity) Act 1964 of the question of a person's fitness to be tried, and there have been findings that he is under a disability and that he did the act or made the omission charged against him, the person may appeal to the Court of Appeal against either or both of those findings.

(2) An appeal under this section lies only—
    (a) with the leave of the Court of Appeal; or
    (b) if, within 28 days from the date of the finding that the accused did the act or made the omission charged, the judge of the court of trial grants a certificate that the case is fit for appeal.

Section 15 enables the Court of Appeal to quash a finding of unfitness to plead. If the finding was made after arraignment and the court is of the view that the appellant should have been acquitted, the court may order the acquittal of the appellant. In other cases, following the finding that the appellant is fit to plead, the court will ensure that the appellant is brought to trial. See also *Norman* [2009] 1 Cr App R 192. Guidance as to the procedure to be followed on an appeal against a finding of unfitness to plead or that the accused did the act or made the omission charged is set out at D8 of the *Guide to Commencing Proceedings in the Court of Appeal Criminal Division* (2008).

APPEAL AGAINST CONVICTION: SUBSTITUTION OF FINDING OF INSANITY OR UNFITNESS TO PLEAD

Under s. 6 of the Criminal Appeal Act 1968, the Court of Appeal may quash a conviction on the **D26.61** basis that the offender should have been found not guilty by reason of insanity or unfit to plead. In such circumstances, the court may then make any appropriate order which would have been available to the court of sentence.

D

Part D Procedure

JUDICIAL REVIEW OF ORDERS RESTRICTING OPEN JUSTICE

D26.62   Section 159 of the CJA 1988 allows for appeals to the Court of Appeal (Criminal Division) against orders made by the Crown Court restricting reporting in relation to a trial on indictment (or public access to the trial (see **D3.122** *et seq.*)).

It appears that the Court of Appeal has no power to grant an order which would act to restrict reporting or access when the Crown Court has refused to make such an order (*Lee* [1993] 2 All ER 170).

Section D27   Procedure on Appeal to the Court of Appeal (Criminal Division)

THE RULES AND THE GUIDE

D27.1 The procedure for appealing to the Court of Appeal (Criminal Division) is governed by relevant sections of the Criminal Appeal Act 1968 combined with the CrimPR, parts 65 to 73 (see Supplement, **R-485** *et seq.*). Part 65 sets out general rules applicable to appeals to the Court of Appeal (Criminal Division); in parts 66 to 73 the same general framework forms the basis for the procedure adopted in the different types of appeal dealt with in those parts. The rules also provide for the forms to be used. Part 68, read in conjunction with part 65, deals with appeals against conviction and sentence under the Criminal Appeal Act 1968. Appeals under the POCA 2002 are dealt with under the Proceeds of Crime Act 2002 (Appeals under Part 2) Order 2003 (SI 2003 No. 82). Appeals under the CJA 2003, sch. 22 are dealt with under the Criminal Justice Act 2003 (Mandatory Life Sentences: Appeals in Transitional Cases) Order 2005 (SI 2005 No. 2798).

The *Guide to Commencing Proceedings in the Court of Appeal Criminal Division* ('the Guide') was issued in October 2008. The Guide provides a good deal of useful practical advice.

This section deals with the procedure for appealing against conviction and the procedure for appealing against sentence.

NOTICE OF APPEAL AND NOTICE OF APPLICATION FOR LEAVE TO APPEAL

D27.2 **Criminal Appeal Act 1968, s. 18**

(1) A person who wishes to appeal under this Part of this Act to the Court of Appeal, or to obtain the leave of that court to appeal, shall give notice of appeal or, as the case may be, notice of application for leave to appeal, in such manner as may be directed by rules of court.

(2) Notice of appeal, or of application for leave to appeal, shall be given within 28 days of the conviction, verdict or finding appealed against, or in the case of appeal against sentence, from the date on which sentence was passed or, in the case of an order made or treated as made on conviction, from the date of the making of the order.

(3) The time for giving notice under this section may be extended, either before or after it expires, by the Court of Appeal.

D27.3 Notice of appeal (if the trial judge has granted a certificate that the case is fit for appeal) or notice of application for leave to appeal (required in all other cases) must be lodged in the prescribed manner. Under s. 18(2), the notice must be lodged within 28 days of either conviction or sentence, depending on which is being appealed. By virtue of s. 18A, the same rule applies in respect of cases of contempt of court. If a conviction is the subject of appeal, then time runs from the date of conviction and not sentence (if the sentence hearing takes place at a later date) (*Long* (1997) 161 JP 769). Rule 68.2(1) of the CrimPR (see Supplement, **R-519**) requires an applicant to serve the relevant notice on an officer of the Crown Court. That service will be on an officer of the Crown Court that convicted and sentenced the applicant. Rule 68.3 sets out the numerous required contents of a notice of appeal.

The Crown Court forwards the notice and grounds of appeal to the office of the Registrar of Criminal Appeals. CPD X, paras. 68A.1 to 68A.6 (see Supplement, **PD-82**), govern the provision of notice of appeal to the prosecuting authority and the giving of notice by the prosecuting authority should it wish to be heard.

The Guide encourages prompt action on the part of counsel and solicitors in the event of a conviction. At para. A1-1, the Guide states that, immediately following the conclusion of the case, the legal representatives should see the convicted accused and counsel should orally express his view as to the prospects of an appeal against conviction and/or sentence. If there are no reasonable grounds of appeal, that should be confirmed in writing and a copy of the document be provided then or as soon as practicable thereafter. If there are reasonable grounds of appeal, they should be drafted, signed and sent to the accused's solicitors as soon as possible. The solicitors should then immediately send a copy to the accused.

D27.4   CPD X, para. 68B.6 (see Supplement, **PD-83**), specifies target times within which appeals should be heard. The target times run from when the case is received by the listing officer; for an appeal against sentence the target time is 28 days, whilst for an appeal against conviction it is 63 days rising to 80 days where a witness is to attend.

Paragraph II.2.2 stipulates that the listing of matters before the Court of Appeal takes precedence over all lower courts and, wherever possible, the Crown Court should have regard to that when arranging to release an advocate to attend the Court of Appeal.

GROUNDS OF APPEAL

Drafting and Contents of Grounds of Appeal

D27.5   At para. A2-2 of the Guide, it is stated that grounds of appeal should be sufficiently detailed to enable the Registrar and the Court of Appeal to identify clearly the matters relied on. Paragraph A2-3 reminds the reader of the level of detail in the grounds which is required by the CrimPR, r. 68.3. At para. A2-5, the Guide stipulates that any document mentioned in the grounds should be clearly identified by exhibit number or otherwise.

Advice with Grounds

D27.6   Paragraph A2-4 of the Guide points out that the Court of Appeal requires the grounds of appeal and relevant facts to be set out in one document. Counsel should not submit separate grounds and advice. The purpose of the document is to enable the single judge easily to identify the facts and issues in the case, and its intended readership is not the lay or professional client.

Perfection and Variation

D27.7   The grounds of appeal first lodged may be varied or amplified within such time as the Court of Appeal will allow (CrimPR, r. 65.3: see Supplement, **R-487**). Section A5 of the Guide deals with the process of perfection of grounds of appeal. When grounds of appeal are lodged, it is necessary to identify any transcripts which are needed to perfect the grounds of appeal. If the Registrar agrees, the transcripts are secured and sent to counsel. When the Registrar's office sends the transcripts to counsel, he has 14 days within which to perfect his grounds. In the absence of any response from counsel, the grounds are placed before the single judge. If counsel does not wish to perfect his grounds, the transcript should be returned with a note to that effect (para. A5-3). If counsel is not able to perfect the grounds within 14 days, it is advisable that he contact the office of the Registrar as soon as possible. The purpose of perfection of the grounds is two-fold: first, to save judicial time by enabling the court to identify the relevant parts of the transcript; secondly, to enable counsel to reconsider his grounds in the light of the transcript. Paragraph A5-1 suggests that the perfected grounds should comprise a fresh document which includes references to the appropriate part of the transcript by page number and letter. If, having read the transcript, the advocate forms the view that the appeal is no longer arguable, he should inform his solicitors of that in an appropriate advice (para. A5-4). He should also inform the Registrar but should not send him a copy of the advice. If the advocate advises abandonment and the applicant for leave continues with the appeal, he is at risk of a direction that time served does not count (see **D26.12**).

Duty of Counsel with Regards to Grounds of Appeal

D27.8

Paragraph A2-6 of the Guide states that 'Counsel should not settle or sign grounds unless they are reasonable, have some real prospect of success and are such that he is prepared to argue before the court'. Counsel should not settle grounds he is unable to support just because he is 'instructed' to do so by his lay client. It is not unknown for counsel to be criticised for grounds of appeal which the Court of Appeal considers improper. In *Morson* (1976) 62 Cr App R 236, grounds of appeal drafted by counsel suggested that the summing-up was unfair and amounted to a direction to convict. Scarman LJ said that the description of the summing-up was a travesty and that the court deplored the fact that that ground of appeal was put forward.

Appellant Drafting Notice and Grounds of Appeal

D27.9

An appeal may be conducted in person, without the benefit of legal representation. The necessary forms are available to prospective appellants in custody as well as those who are at liberty. However, the unrepresented applicant who has had the benefit of negative advice as to the prospects of success of his appeal runs an increasing risk of a direction that any time he has served in custody between the commencement of appeal proceedings and their conclusion not count towards time served (see **D26.12**).

LEAVE TO APPEAL

Procedure for Obtaining Leave to Appeal

D27.10

Ordinarily, once the grounds have been perfected, the case is referred to a single judge for the consideration of whether leave to appeal should be granted. In determining whether or not to grant leave, the single judge may be assisted by having the prosecution's response to the grounds. Consequently, under the CrimPR, r. 68.6 (see Supplement, **R-523**), the Registrar or single judge may direct that the prosecution respond to the grounds within Form RN. The A-G and the Registrar have agreed guidance on the types of cases and/or issues where the Registrar should consider either directing or inviting a party to serve a response in Form RN before leave is considered (para. A6-2 of the Guide). As examples, the Registrar might direct a response within Form RN in cases where the grounds advanced concern issues of public interest immunity, allegations of jury irregularity, criticism of the conduct of the judge and complex frauds. The Registrar might invite a response from a party in cases concerning, for example, homicide, serious sexual crimes, violence or domestic violence and cases with a national profile or high media interest.

Sometimes, the single judge or Registrar may refer the case to a full court to determine the issues of leave and the prosecution will be asked to attend. If the full court grants leave, the court may then forthwith proceed to a substantive hearing of the appeal. Such a course may be taken, for example, when there is a novel point of law or because, in a sentence case, the sentence passed is unlawful and must be amended (para. A11-3 of the Guide).

The far more usual procedure is for the single judge to consider the issue of leave on the papers. If the application for leave is refused, the applicant has 14 days to notify his intention to renew the application before the court (r. 65.5). The time for notification may be extended either before or after that 14-day period has expired upon application by the applicant (rr. 65.3 and 65.4), but the applicant must have good reason for not being able to comply with the deadline. That reason cannot be to do with the merits of the case. If the applicant has received misleading advice as to the need to notify his renewal from the prison in which he is held, that is capable of being sufficient (*Doherty* [1971] 3 All ER 622).

D27.11 If the single judge grants leave on a particular ground without deciding the issue of leave in respect of the other grounds, the appellant is free to argue the other grounds at the substantive hearing of the appeal. But if the single judge grants leave on one ground but refuses leave on others, the appellant must renew his application for leave in relation to those other grounds, having previously informed the respondents and the Registrar's office of his intention, before he is allowed to argue them at the substantive hearing (*Cox* [1999] 2 Cr App R 6).

A renewed application for leave to appeal is heard by the court. The court will be comprised of at least two judges and usually three. The applicant has no right to attend, so if he is in custody he will not be present. Even though legal aid is not available for representation at such hearings, it is common for counsel to provide their services free of charge (and for applications to be fully argued) and for counsel to submit written skeleton arguments for renewed applications for leave to appeal. If counsel is to appear on behalf of an applicant at a renewed application for leave, whether on a privately paid or pro bono basis, the Court of Appeal Office should be informed of that in writing as soon as possible (para. A12-3 of the Guide). Where counsel does not appear, renewed applications for leave to appeal are often placed in a 'non-counsel list'. Such hearings then simply involve the calling on of the case followed by one member of the court giving judgment in the case.

Extension of Time for Leave to Appeal

D27.12 Although the time period for lodging the notice of application for leave to appeal is 28 days, that period may be extended either before or after its expiry (Criminal Appeal Act 1968, s. 18(3)). The period may be extended either by the Registrar's office or the single judge; its extension is a matter of discretion. An appellant is usually required to show good reason for the extension of time to be granted (*Ramsden* [1972] Crim LR 547; *Burley* (1994) *The Times* 9 November 1994). Any application for an extension of time in which to serve an application for leave to appeal or notice of appeal must be supported with reasons as to why the application or notice was not served in time. It is not sufficient simply to tick the relevant box requesting an extension of time. Paragraph A3-4 of the Guide stipulates that any application for an extension of time must be made at the time of the serving of the application or notice and not before. In exceptional circumstances, the Court of Appeal will allow an extension even where the period of delay is inordinate and unexplained because, if the appeal has merit, the refusal might lead to a reference to the CCRC, with all the attendant delay and cost associated (*King* [2000] Crim LR 835). There is no incompatibility with the ECHR in imposing time-limits on appeal proceedings provided that they are not too short or too rigorously enforced (*Ballinger* [2005] 2 Cr App R 433). If the appellant has commenced an appeal against sentence and subsequently seeks to commence an appeal against conviction, the court will usually allow an extension of time so as to avoid any difficulties associated with resolving an appeal against sentence before the conviction appeal is resolved (*Mitchell* [1977] 2 All ER 168).

TRANSCRIPTS

D27.13 By virtue of the CrimPR, r. 68.3(2) (see Supplement, **R-520**), the notice of appeal is now required to indicate which transcripts will be required for the resolution of the appeal. Those transcripts may include, for example, the evidence of particular witnesses and rulings on issues of law. The Registrar will usually provide those transcripts; if there is any disagreement as to the need for them, the Registrar may refer the matter to the single judge for resolution (para. A4-2 of the Guide). Given the cost associated with the provision of a transcript, counsel should request one only if it is essential for the conduct of the appeal (*Flemming* (1987) 86 Cr App R 32 and para. A4-2 of the Guide). In *Lifely* (1990) *The Times*, 16 July 1990, the Court of Appeal said that transcripts of submissions made by counsel to the trial judge were costly and time-consuming to prepare and were usually unnecessary. At para. A4-1 of the Guide it is pointed out that, in conviction cases, a transcript of the summing-up and proceedings up to and including verdict are invariably obtained. In sentence cases which follow a guilty plea, a transcript of the prosecution opening of the facts is usually obtained. Paragraph A4-3 points out that the cost of unnecessary transcripts may be ordered to be paid by the appellant.

BAIL PENDING APPEAL

Bail by the Court of Appeal

Criminal Appeal Act 1968, s. 19   **D27.14**

(1) The Court of Appeal may, subject to section 25 of the Criminal Justice and Public Order Act 1994, if they think fit,—
   (a) grant an appellant bail pending the determination of his appeal; or
   (b) revoke bail granted to an appellant by the Crown Court under paragraph (f) of section 81(1) of the Senior Courts Act 1981 or paragraph (a) above; or
   (c) vary the conditions of bail granted to an appellant in the exercise of the power conferred by either of those paragraphs.
(2) The powers conferred by subsection (1) above may be exercised—
   (a) on the application of an appellant; or
   (b) if it appears to the registrar of criminal appeals of the Court of Appeal ... that any of them ought to be exercised, on a reference to the court by him.

The Court of Appeal may grant bail to an appellant under s. 19 and an application about **D27.15** bail and any conditions may be made by either the appellant or respondent. Rule 68.8(2) of the CrimPR requires that any application must be by way of Form B and must be served on the Registrar (unless the application is with the notice of appeal) and the other party at least 24 hours before the application is to take place to enable the Crown to make representations about the application and any conditions (para. A8-2 of the Guide). If bail is granted, it is the practice of the Court of Appeal to require a condition of residence (para. A8-4).

An urgent application should normally be made first to the Crown Court judge under the Senior Courts Act 1981, s. 81 (see **D27.17**) and the Court of Appeal may decline to treat the application as urgent if that was not done.

In *Watton* (1978) 68 Cr App R 293, the Court of Appeal said that the question that the court **D27.16** should ask itself is whether there are exceptional circumstances which drive the court to the conclusion that justice can only be done with the granting of bail. The strength of the grounds of appeal will be a relevant factor in the decision as to whether to grant bail. Equally, the likely length of time before the appeal is heard will be relevant depending on how long the appellant has to serve. If an appellant is granted bail but his appeal is unsuccessful, he will be returned to custody.

Rules 68.9 and 68.10 of the CrimPR (see Supplement, **R-526** and **R-527**) contain detailed provisions as to the imposition of conditions of bail and the forfeiture of any sureties. Under s. 19(1)(b) and (c) the court may vary or revoke bail previously granted by the Court of Appeal or the Crown Court.

The Registrar may vary bail in certain circumstances (see **D27.35**).

Bail Granted by the Crown Court

D27.17   Senior Courts Act 1981, s. 81

(1) The Crown Court may, subject to section 25 of the Criminal Justice and Public Order Act 1994, grant bail to any person—

  (a) [bail following sending to the Crown Court: see D7];

  (b) who is in custody pursuant to a sentence imposed by a magistrates' court, and who has appealed to the Crown Court against his conviction or sentence; or

  (c) who is in the custody of the Crown Court pending the disposal of his case by that court; or

  (d) who, after the decision of his case by the Crown Court, has applied to that court for the statement of a case for the High Court on that decision; or

  (e) who has applied to the High Court for a quashing order to remove proceedings in the Crown Court in his case into the High Court, or has applied to the High Court for leave to make such an application; or

  (f) to whom the Crown Court has granted a certificate under section 1(2) or 11(1A) of the Criminal Appeal Act 1968 or under subsection(1B) below; or

  (g) who has been remanded in custody by a magistrates' court on adjourning a case under section 11 of the Powers of Criminal Courts (Sentencing) Act 2000 (remand for medical examination), section 52(5) of the Crime and Disorder Act 1998 (adjournment of proceedings under section 51 etc) or—

    (i)   [repealed];

    (ii)   section 10 (adjournment of trial);

    (iia)   section 17C (intention as to plea: adjournment);

    (iii)   section 18 (initial procedure on information against adult for offence triable either way); or

    (iiia) section 24C (intention as to plea by child or young person: adjournment);
    of the Magistrates' Courts Act 1980;

  (h) in respect of whom a judge of the Crown Court is required to make a decision pursuant to section 115(3) of the Coroners and Justice Act 2009 (bail decisions in murder cases to be made by Crown Court judge);
and the time during which a person is released on bail under any provision of this subsection shall not count as part of any term of imprisonment or detention under his sentence.

(1A) The power conferred by subsection (1)(f) does not extend to a case to which section 12 or 15 of the Criminal Appeal Act 1968 (appeal against verdict of not guilty by reason of insanity or against findings that the accused is under a disability and that he did the act or made the omission charged against him) applies.

(1B) A certificate under this subsection is a certificate that a case is fit for appeal on a ground which involves a question of law alone.

(1C) The power conferred by subsection (1)(f) is to be exercised—

  (a) where the appeal is under section 1 or 9 of the Criminal Appeal Act 1968, by the judge who tried the case; and

  (b) where it is under section 10 of that Act, by the judge who passed the sentence.

(1D) The power may only be exercised within twenty-eight days from the date of the conviction appealed against, or in the case of appeal against sentence, from the date on which sentence was passed or, in the case of an order made or treated as made on conviction, from the date of the making of the order.

(1E) The power may not be exercised if the appellant has made an application to the Court of Appeal for bail in respect of the offence or offences to which the appeal relates.

(1F) It shall be a condition of bail granted in the exercise of the power that, unless a notice of appeal has previously been lodged in accordance with subsection (1) of section 18 of the Criminal Appeal Act 1968—

  (a) such a notice shall be so lodged within the period specified in subsection (2) of that section; and

  (b) not later than 14 days from the end of that period, the appellant shall lodge with the Crown Court a certificate from the registrar of criminal appeals that a notice of appeal was given within that period.

(1G) If the Crown Court grants bail to a person in the exercise of the power, it may direct him to appear—
  (a) if a notice of appeal is lodged within the period specified in section 18(2) of the Criminal Appeal Act 1968 at such time and place as the Court of Appeal may require; and
  (b) if no such notice is lodged within that period, at such time and place as the Crown Court may require.
(1H) Where the Crown Court grants a person bail under subsection (1)(g) it may direct him to appear at a time and place which the magistrates' court could have directed and the recognisance of any surety shall be conditioned accordingly.
(1J) The Crown Court may only grant bail to a person under subsection(1)(g) if the magistrates' court which remanded him in custody has certified under section 5(6A) of the Bail Act 1976 that it heard full argument on his application for bail before it refused the application.
(2) Provision may be made by rules of court as respects the powers of the Crown Court relating to bail, including any provision—
  (a) except in the case of bail in criminal proceedings (within the meaning of the Bail Act 1976), allowing the court instead of requiring a person to enter into a recognisance, to consent to his giving other security;
  (b) allowing the court to direct that a recognisance shall be entered into or other security given before a magistrates' court or a justice of the peace, or, if the rules so provide, a person of such other description as is specified in the rules;
  (c) prescribing the manner in which a recognisance is to be entered into or other security given, and the persons by whom and the manner in which the recognisance or security may be enforced;
  (d) authorising the recommittal, in such cases and by such courts or justices as may be prescribed by the rules, of persons released from custody in pursuance of the powers;
  (e) making provision corresponding to sections 118 and 119 of the Magistrates' Courts Act 1980 (varying or dispensing with requirements as to sureties, and postponement of taking recognisances).
(3) Any reference in any enactment to a recognisance shall include, unless the context otherwise requires, a reference to any other description of security given instead of a recognisance, whether in pursuance of subsection (2)(a) or otherwise.
(4) The Crown Court, on issuing a warrant for the arrest of any person, may endorse the warrant for bail, and in any such case—
  (a) the person arrested under the warrant shall, unless the Crown Court otherwise directs, be taken to a police station; and
  (b) the officer in charge of the station shall release him from custody if he, and any sureties required by the endorsement and approved by the officer, enter into recognisances of such amount as may be fixed by the endorsement:
  Provided that in the case of bail in criminal proceedings (within the meaning of the Bail Act 1976) the person arrested shall not be required to enter into a recognisance.
(5) A person in custody in pursuance of a warrant issued by the Crown Court with a view to his appearance before that court shall be brought forthwith before—
  (a) if the person is charged with murder or with murder and one or more other offences, the Crown Court, and
  (b) in any other case, either the Crown Court or a magistrates' court.
(6) A magistrates' court shall have jurisdiction, and a justice of the peace may act, under or in pursuance of rules under subsection (2) whether or not the offence was committed, or the arrest was made, within the court's area, or the area for which he was appointed.

Section 81(1) of the Senior Courts Act 1981 provides that the Crown Court may grant bail to any person to whom it has granted a certificate under ss. 1(2) or 11(1A) of the Criminal Appeal Act 1968. **D27.18**

Section 81 also provides for the means by which the Crown Court may exercise the power. The Court of Appeal may revoke or vary bail granted by the Crown Court (Criminal Appeal Act 1968, s. 19(1)(b) and (c)). CPD III, paras. 19H.1 to 19H.4, give guidance both on the granting of certificates that a case is fit for appeal and on the consequent granting of bail (see

D26.7). Bail can only be granted in the Crown Court within 28 days of the conviction or sentence which is to be the subject of the appeal and may not be granted if an application for bail has already been made to the Court of Appeal. The procedure for bail to be granted by a judge of the Crown Court pending an appeal is governed by the CrimPR, part 19. The Crown Court judge should use the Criminal Appeal Office Form BC (Crown Court Judge's Order granting bail). The length of the period which might elapse before the hearing of any appeal is not relevant to the granting of a certificate but, if the judge does decide to grant a certificate, it is one factor in the decision whether also to grant bail (CPD III, para. 19H.6). In *Harries* [2007] EWCA Crim 820, the Court of Appeal cautioned that a Crown Court judge should grant a certificate of appeal only where there was an unresolved issue of law or where there were clear reasons for considering that an appeal would be allowed. In the instant case, the judge expressly declined to give any view as to the substance of the grounds of appeal when granting a certificate; if he had sought the assistance of the prosecution as to the grounds advanced, he might have realised that the appeal was extremely unlikely to succeed.

Suspension of Other Sentences Pending Appeal

D27.19   The Court of Appeal may suspend the disqualification of a driver pending appeal (RTOA 1988, s. 40(2)). By virtue of s. 30(1) and (2) of the Criminal Appeal Act 1968, an order for the restitution of property to a person made by the Crown Court under the PCC(S)A 2000, s. 148, shall, unless the Court of Appeal directs to the contrary in a case in which, in its opinion, title to the property is not in dispute, be suspended until there is no further possibility of an appeal which might result in the order being varied or set aside. In determining whether there is any possibility of an appeal, the power of a court to give leave to appeal out of time is to be disregarded. Thus, a restitution order will take effect 28 days from sentence if no notice of application for leave to appeal is given but, if notice is given, it will be suspended until determination of the appeal unless the Court of Appeal gives a direction to the contrary because title to the property does not appear to be disputed. The Court may annul or vary the order for restitution even though the conviction is not quashed (s. 30(2)). Under the PCC(S)A 2000, s. 132(1), compensation orders are treated for the purposes of the Criminal Appeal Act 1968, s. 30, in the same way as restitution orders. The enforcement of any fine the appellant was ordered to pay is suspended upon notice of appeal or application for leave to appeal being given.

PRESENCE OF THE APPELLANT AT THE APPEAL

D27.20   Criminal Appeal Act 1968, s. 22

(1) Except as provided by this section, an appellant shall be entitled to be present, if he wishes it, on the hearing of his appeal, although he may be in custody.

(2) A person in custody shall not be entitled to be present—

   (a) where his appeal is on some ground involving a question of law alone; or

   (b) on an application by him for leave to appeal; or

   (c) on any proceedings preliminary or incidental to an appeal; or

   (d) where he is in custody in consequence of a verdict of not guilty by reason of insanity or of a finding of disability,

   unless the Court of Appeal give him leave to be present.

(3) The power of the Court of Appeal to pass sentence on a person may be exercised although he is for any reason not present.

(4) The Court of Appeal may give a live link direction in relation to a hearing at which the appellant is expected to be in custody but is entitled to be present (by virtue of subsection (1) or leave given under subsection (2)) at any time before the beginning of that hearing.

(5) For this purpose—
    (a) a 'live link direction' is a direction that the appellant (if he is being held in custody at the time of the hearing) is to attend the hearing through a live link from the place at which he is held; and
    (b) 'live link' means an arrangement by which the appellant is able to see and hear, and to be seen and heard by, the Court of Appeal (and for this purpose any impairment of eyesight or hearing is to be disregarded).

(6) The Court of Appeal—
    (a) must not give a live link direction unless the parties to the appeal have had the opportunity to make representations about the giving of such a direction; and
    (b) may rescind a live link direction at any time before or during any hearing to which it applies (whether of its own motion or on the application of a party).

D27.21 An appellant who is not in custody has the right to be present at his appeal. The position in respect of appellants in custody is governed by the CrimPR, r. 68.11 (see Supplement, **R-528**). An appellant has the right to attend a hearing in public unless either (a) the hearing is preliminary or incidental to an appeal (including an application for permission) or (b) the party is in custody by virtue of a verdict of not guilty by reason of insanity or a finding of disability. An appellant may be present for the purposes of s. 22 via live link (s. 22(4)–(6)).

If an appellant is not in custody or bailed to appear at the hearing, he is not required to be present at the hearing. If he is not present, but has been given notice of the hearing, the Court of Appeal may proceed in his absence. If an appellant absconds before the hearing of his appeal, the Court may adjourn the appeal, find against the appellant in his absence or, exceptionally, agree to hear the appeal on its merits (*Flower* [1966] 1 QB 146; *Carter* (1994) 98 Cr App R 106).

By virtue of the CrimPR, r. 68.12, if the Court decides an appeal affecting sentence in a party's absence, it may vary that decision if it failed to take account of something because of that party's absence. A party who seeks such a variation must serve a written application on the Registrar no more than seven days after the decision (if the party was represented at the appeal hearing) or no more than seven days after the Registrar serves the decision (if the party was not represented at the hearing).

HEARING OF AN APPEAL

Practice in Usual Case

D27.22 Rule 65.7 of the CrimPR requires the Registrar to give as much notice as reasonably practicable of the date on which the court will hear any appeal or application. The notice must be served on (a) the parties (b) any party's custodian, and (c) any other party the court requires to be notified. As is made plain in r. 65.7(3), notice should not ordinarily be given of public interest immunity hearings. If a representation order is to be granted for an appellant for any hearing, it is normally granted either by the Registrar or by the single judge at the same time as he gives leave to appeal. In most cases, a representation order will be granted only if the single judge grants leave. The representation order is usually limited to an advocate, but if necessary it will be extended to provide for the services of a solicitor. The Registrar will forward the necessary papers to counsel and will try to agree a date for the hearing with counsel's clerk. It is usual for various dates to be offered to counsel's clerk. The respondent is not usually represented at an appeal against sentence. At an appeal against conviction, the respondent is invariably represented. CPD X, paras. 68B.1 to 68B.4, govern the usual procedure for the listing of an appeal against conviction or sentence (see Supplement, **PD-83**).

The use of case summaries by the Criminal Appeal Office is governed by CPD X, paras. 68G.1 to 68G.7 (see Supplement, **PD-88**). Under para. 68F.1, advocates must ensure that the court and any other party has a single document containing all of the points that are to be argued. On an appeal against conviction, a skeleton argument must be served if the appeal notice 'does not sufficiently outline the grounds of the appeal, particularly where a complex or novel point of law has been raised'. On a sentencing appeal, a skeleton argument 'may be helpful if a complex issue is raised'.

The service of skeleton arguments is governed by para. 68F.2: the 'appellant's skeleton argument, if any, must be served no later than 21 days before the hearing date, and the respondent's skeleton argument, if any, no later than 14 days before the hearing date', unless otherwise directed. Any skeleton argument should contain a numbered list of the points the advocate intends to argue and should be as succinct as possible (para. 68F.3).

D27.23 In *Erskine* [2010] 1 All ER 1196, Lord Judge CJ referred to the aphorism of Viscount Falkland in 1641 to the effect that if it is not *necessary* to refer to a previous decision of the court, it is *necessary* not to refer to it. Similarly, if it is not *necessary* to include a previous decision in the bundle of authorities, it is *necessary* to exclude it. He stated that that approach would be rigidly enforced and gave guidance as to the citation of authorities in relation to appeals against conviction and sentence. On appeal against conviction, the advocate must be prepared to justify the citation of each authority relied on in the bundle. The court is most unlikely to be prepared to look at an authority which does no more than illustrate or restate an established proposition. It is good practice for advocates to agree a list of authorities and prepare a joint bundle. For appeals against sentence, the advocate must again be ready to justify the citation of any authority. If a definitive sentencing guideline is available, it will rarely be the case that there is any advantage to citing an authority which pre-dates the issue of that guideline. Authorities which post-date the issue of the guideline but do not refer to it will, similarly, rarely be of assistance. Where an authority involves no more than the court upholding a sentence imposed at the Crown Court, the advocate must be ready to justify how it can assist the court in deciding whether a sentence is wrong in principle or manifestly excessive.

The Registrar has issued guidance on the citation of authorities by advocates. From 1 October 2012, all advocates are required to provide a list of authorities upon which they wish to rely in their written or oral submissions. That list of authorities should be annexed to, but not form part of, the grounds of appeal or appeal notice or respondent's notice. If, exceptionally, it is not annexed to the appeal notice or respondent's notice it should be annexed to any skeleton argument. The Registrar refers to the comments of Lord Judge CJ in *Erskine*. If the list needs to be amended, a complete new list should be created in order that only one definitive list is in existence. There is further guidance as to the contents of the list to be submitted. The previous practice whereby advocates were asked to fax copies of their list of authorities to the head usher is discontinued and the fax number will no longer be in use. The guidance as to citation of authority set out in *Erskine* is now embodied in CPD XII, paras. D.2 to D.13 (see Supplement, **PD-93**).

Receipt of Evidence by the Court of Appeal

D27.24   Criminal Appeal Act 1968, s. 23

(1) For purposes of an appeal or an application for leave to appeal under this part of this Act [appeals against conviction and/or sentence and references to the Court of Appeal by the Home Secretary] the Court of Appeal may, if they think it necessary or expedient in the interests of justice—

    (a) order the production of any document, exhibit or other thing connected with the proceedings, the production of which appears to them necessary for the determination of the case;

    (b) order any witness to attend for examination and be examined before the Court (whether or not he was called in the proceedings from which the appeal lies); and

    (c) receive any evidence which was not adduced in the proceedings from which the appeal lies.

(1A) The power conferred by subsection (1)(a) may be exercised so as to require the production of any document, exhibit or other thing mentioned in that subsection to—

    (a) the Court;

    (b) the appellant;

    (c) the respondent.

(2) The Court of Appeal shall, in considering whether to receive any evidence, have regard in particular to—

    (a) whether the evidence appears to the Court to be capable of belief;

(b) whether it appears to the Court that the evidence may afford any ground for allowing the appeal;
(c) whether the evidence would have been admissible in the proceedings from which the appeal lies on an issue which is the subject of the appeal; and
(d) whether there is a reasonable explanation for the failure to adduce the evidence in those proceedings.
(3) Subsection (1)(c) above [power to receive evidence of any witness if tendered] applies to any evidence of a witness (including the appellant) who is competent but not compellable, and applies also to the appellant's husband or wife where the appellant makes an application for that purpose and the evidence appeal lies except on such an application.

At any appeal against conviction, the Court of Appeal may admit evidence which is relevant **D27.25** to that appeal by virtue of s. 23. Section 23(1)(b) has been amended by the CJIA 2008, sch. 8, so as to extend the power of the Court (or a judge or the Registrar) to issue a witness order to anyone whom it is thought may be able to give relevant evidence. The former qualification that the witness was compellable in the proceedings below has been repealed. The principal effect of this amendment is that both jurors and, subject to waiver of privilege, legal representatives can be compelled to appear at the hearing of an appeal. In appropriate cases, evidence may be introduced in the interests of justice at the request of the respondents and is not limited to rebuttal of fresh evidence adduced by the appellant (*Hanratty* [2002] 3 All ER 534). However, it will not be admitted where its purpose is to advance a basis for conviction not argued previously and not put before the jury (*Fitzgerald* [2006] EWCA Crim 1565). The admission of evidence under s. 23 is a matter of discretion. The Court will admit evidence if it is necessary or expedient in the interests of justice (s. 23(1)). The factors listed in s. 23(2) are not preconditions for the admission of evidence, but are merely factors to take into account in deciding whether evidence should be received. As Lord Judge CJ observed in *Erskine* [2010] 1 All ER 1196 (at [39]), '[v]irtually by definition, the decision whether to admit fresh evidence is case and fact specific. The discretion to receive fresh evidence is a wide one focussing on the interests of justice.' For observations on the relevance of s. 23 to the admissibility of psychiatric reports on appeal against sentence, see *Beesley* [2012] 1 Cr App R (S) 71. For the applicability of s. 23 to applications for third-party disclosure on appeal, see *Doski* [2011] EWCA Crim 987. In *Cleobury* [2012] EWCA Crim 17, the Court of Appeal restated its view on the role of expert evidence on appeal. The renewed application for permission to appeal was based upon the contents of a report from an expert which was secured post-conviction and sought to criticise the way in which DNA evidence was dealt with at trial. The Court observed (at [15]) that it has become not uncommon to try to persuade the Court to reconsider the DNA evidence given at trial by adducing a new report. While there are occasions when this is justified, such as where there has been an advance in DNA science, it is for the defence to call their expert evidence at trial and it is not the function of the Court of Appeal to permit expert evidence to be re-litigated on appeal. For a summary of the principles to be applied by the Court of Appeal when deciding whether or not to receive expert evidence under s. 23, and an example of the application of those principles, see *Chattoo* [2012] EWCA Crim 190. See also *Meachen* [2009] EWCA Crim 1701.

The Court may also receive fresh evidence under s. 23 on an appeal against sentence and may even do so when considering an appeal against the findings of a *Newton* hearing. If the Court is of the view, in the light of that fresh evidence, that the findings of the *Newton* hearing were wrong, it must proceed to hold the hearing again as there is no power to remit the issue for rehearing in the Crown Court (*Malook* [2011] 3 All ER 373).

In *Smith* [2014] 2 Cr App R 1 (1) the Court of Appeal strongly criticised 'a growing and unwelcome tendency of convicted defendants to dismiss their original counsel and then to bring in new counsel to criticise their predecessors'. The Court described this as an attempt to circumvent the restriction on calling fresh evidence contained in s. 23 and deplored this strategy.

Capable of Belief The Court of Appeal will often make a judgement as to whether the evi- **D27.26** dence is capable of belief before actually hearing it. Thus the court gives an indication as to whether or not the evidence appears to be capable of belief. Matters which will be important in

Part D Procedure

that consideration will include the contents of any statement produced and the compatibility of those contents with the evidence at trial, along with any explanation as to how the evidence came to light. In *Sale* [2000] 2 Cr App R 431, Rose LJ said that fresh evidence falls into three categories. First, evidence which is plainly capable of belief; there is no difficulty with such evidence and the court will ordinarily receive it. Second, evidence which is plainly incapable of belief; such evidence again presents no difficulty and the court will usually not receive such evidence. The third type of evidence is that which is possibly capable of belief; it may be necessary for the court to hear the witness *de bene esse* in order to determine whether the evidence is capable of belief, and that course is frequently followed. See *Patel* [2010] EWCA Crim 1858 for a practical application of the test in respect of an application to admit affidavits as fresh evidence.

D27.27   **Capable of Founding a Ground of Appeal**   Even if fresh evidence potentially fulfils all the other criteria in the Criminal Appeal Act 1968, s. 23, it is necessary that it is capable of founding an arguable ground of appeal before it can be admitted. For example, an appellant may produce evidence of a statement by the complainant which was inconsistent with his evidence at trial. Unless the inconsistency of the statement is of sufficient magnitude to be capable of disturbing the safety of the conviction, it will not be admissible. See *Aslam* [2014] EWCA Crim 1292 and *Kingston* [2014] EWCA Crim 1420.

D27.28   **Admissible in the Proceedings from which the Appeal Lies**   Plainly, evidence which would not have been admissible at the trial proceedings cannot form the basis of a successful appeal against conviction. The importance of that point has been most keenly felt in appeals involving misconduct by police officers which only comes to light after conviction (*Twitchell* [2000] 1 Cr App R 373).

D27.29   **Reasonable Explanation for the Failure to Adduce the Evidence**   In *Stafford and Luvaglio (No. 1)* (1969) 53 Cr App R 1, Edmund-Davies LJ said 'public mischief would ensue and legal process could become indefinitely prolonged were it the case that evidence produced at any time will generally be admitted by this court when verdicts are being reviewed'. That warning against the potential dangers of admitting fresh evidence is indicative of a general reluctance on the part of the Court of Appeal to admit evidence without a reasonable explanation for the failure to adduce the evidence at trial. Nevertheless, it should always be borne in mind that the ultimate test for admission of evidence under the Criminal Appeal Act 1968, s. 23, is whether it is in the interests of justice. In exceptional circumstances, the Court will admit fresh evidence even when there is no reasonable explanation for the failure to adduce it at trial. For a highly unusual and stark example of the admission of such evidence leading to the quashing of a conviction, see *Solomon* [2007] EWCA Crim 2633. For an example of the operation of this factor in relation to the receipt of fresh medical evidence, see *Moyle* [2008] EWCA Crim 3059.

An appellant will not have a reasonable explanation for failing to adduce evidence at trial if he has taken a decision not to call particular evidence following advice from his lawyers (*Hampton* (2004) *The Times*, 13 October 2004). Similarly, it will not assist an appellant that alibi witnesses have not been called because his lawyers had been unable to trace them, if the appellant could have made his lawyers aware of information which would have enabled them to trace the witnesses in good time (*Beresford* (1971) 56 Cr App R 143). If witnesses could genuinely not be found in time for trial, that may amount to a reasonable explanation. But before the Court will admit the evidence, it is likely to be necessary for each person involved in the process of finding and taking a proof of evidence from the witnesses to serve a statement of truth about their role in that process (*Gogana* (1999) *The Times*, 12 July 1999; *James* [2000] Crim LR 571). The statement of truth is commonly known amongst practitioners as a 'Gogana affidavit'.

Procedure for Calling Evidence

D27.30   Rule 68.3 of the CrimPR requires that an appellant who wishes the Court of Appeal to exercise its power to receive evidence should so indicate within the notice of appeal. An order for a witness to attend may be made only if the witness would have been a compellable witness before the Crown Court (Criminal Appeal Act 1968, s. 23(1)(b)). It may be made by a single judge (s. 31(2); see **D27.34**). The decision to receive the evidence is for a court and not a single judge or the Registrar. Indeed, even an order under s. 23(4) that the witness be examined by an officer of the court prior to determination of the appeal is one that only a court can make.

By virtue of s. 23(4), if the Court of Appeal thinks it necessary or expedient in the interests of justice, the court may order that the examination of any compellable witness be conducted before any judge, officer of the court or other person appointed by the court for the purpose. The deposition may then be admitted as evidence before the Court, so avoiding the need for oral evidence (s. 23(4)). By virtue of s. 23(1)(c) and (3), whilst the power to order a witness to attend and to order that his evidence be taken in deposition form before an examiner is exercisable only in respect of compellable witnesses, the discretion to receive evidence tendered by the appellant applies not only to compellable witnesses but also to those who are merely competent. Sometimes, the Court can rely on the written statement or affidavit of the witness without hearing oral evidence.

D27.31 Whilst the rules do not specify the precise way in which a witness's evidence should be given, the usual route is the same as that adopted in first instance proceedings. The witness is examined in chief by the party tendering his evidence, cross-examined by the opposite party and then, if need be, re-examined and questioned directly by the court. The procedure followed by the Court of Appeal will more often than not be a matter for the court, and so it may commence the questioning of the witness and allow the parties to ask any additional questions they see fit. Where the appellant is allowed to call evidence, the prosecution may be allowed to call their own evidence in rebuttal. See *Lee* [1984] 1 All ER 1080, for a case where the court contemplated hearing virtually the whole of the prosecution and defence cases in order to determine an appeal against conviction where the appellant had pleaded guilty at the Crown Court. The Court of Appeal noted that there were exceptional circumstances and stipulated that it was not to provide a precedent for the hearing of such extensive evidence.

REVIEW OF PUBLIC INTEREST IMMUNITY

D27.32 In *McDonald* (2004) *The Times*, 8 November 2004, the Court of Appeal set out the principles that applied to a review of a trial judge's conduct of a public interest immunity hearing.

(a) The approach was to be the same whether the hearing had been on notice or not. The principles regarding the appointment of special counsel or the need for a judge to recuse himself are the same in both cases.
(b) The Court of Appeal would have to review all the material with the prosecution present. A prosecution summary by itself is not sufficient. However, such a summary is usually desirable, especially where the material is voluminous.
(c) The review of the material should be carried out by a court of the same constitution as hears the substantive appeal.
(d) The review is to take place sufficiently in advance of the substantive hearing to permit special counsel to be appointed and prepared if the need arises.
(e) In the majority of cases where the material can be read in an hour or two and where there are no listing difficulties, the review should take place in the first week of that constitution of the court sitting, with the substantive hearing following in the third week.
(f) Where the public interest immunity material is unusually voluminous, special listing arrangements have to be made over a longer time-scale.

ABANDONING AN APPEAL

D27.33 Rule 65.13 of the CrimPR (see Supplement, **R-497**) governs the abandonment of an appeal. An appellant may abandon an appeal without permission before a hearing by serving a notice of abandonment on the Registrar and any respondent, but at any hearing may only abandon an appeal or application with the permission of the court (r. 65.13(2)). The appellant must serve the notice of abandonment (Form A) on the Registrar's office and any respondent. The form must be signed by, or on behalf of, the appellant (r. 65.13(3)). The Registrar must date the form and serve it on the appellant, the custodian of the appellant, the officer of the Crown Court and any other party upon whom the notice of appeal was served. The proceedings are then deemed to have been dismissed or refused (r. 65.13(4)). Abandonment of the appeal does not preclude the making of a loss of time order or the award of costs against the appellant. Once an appeal has commenced, the appellant may still abandon the appeal but needs the leave of the Court of Appeal (*De Courcy* [1964] 3 All ER 251).

If an appellant abandons his appeal, he may reinstate it with the leave of the Court. Any application for the reinstatement of an abandoned appeal or application must be made in writing to the Registrar, setting out the reasons for the application (r. 65.13(5)). The Court will allow such a reinstatement if it is of the view that the abandonment was a nullity because, for example, of fraud, mistake or erroneous advice. The important question will be whether the appellant's mind goes with the abandonment. If he cannot show that it did not, the abandonment will not be held to be a nullity. In *Grant* [2005] EWCA Crim 2018, correspondence between G and his lawyers culminated in his lawyers advising that if they did not hear from him within seven days they would abandon the appeal. Because of a delay in the post, caused by G being transferred between prisons, he had no opportunity to communicate a change of mind about his appeal. The Court held that by virtue of G's original letter his mind had gone with the notice and the abandonment was therefore not a nullity.

In *Smith* [2014] 2 Cr App R 1 (1), the Court of Appeal revisited the question of when an abandonment of appeal was a nullity because it came about as a result of wrong legal advice. Following a review of relevant authorities, the Court observed (at [58]) that:

> From this review of the law we derive four propositions which are relevant to the present case:
> i) A notice of abandonment of appeal is irrevocable, unless the Court of Appeal treats that notice as a nullity.
> ii) A notice of abandonment is a nullity if the applicant's mind does not go with the notice which he signs.
> iii) If the applicant abandons his appeal after and because of receiving incorrect legal advice, then his mind may not go with the notice which he signs. Whether this is the case will depend upon the circumstances.
> iv) Incorrect legal advice for this purpose means advice which is positively wrong. It does not mean the expression of opinion on a difficult point, with which some may agree and others may disagree.

APPLICATIONS TO A SINGLE JUDGE

D27.34

Criminal Appeal Act 1968, ss. 31 and 44

31.—(1) There may be exercised by a single judge in the same manner as by the Court of Appeal and subject to the same provisions—
  (a) the powers of the Court of Appeal under this Part of this Act specified in subsection (2) below;
  (aa) the power to give leave under section 14(4B) of the Criminal Appeal Act 1995;
  (b) the power to give directions under section 4(4) of the Sexual Offences (Amendment) Act 1976; and
  (c) the powers to make orders for the payment of costs under sections 16 to 18 of the Prosecution of Offences Act 1985 in proceedings under this Part of this Act.
(2) The powers mentioned in subsection (1)(a) above are the following—
  (a) to give leave to appeal;
  (b) to extend the time within which notice of appeal or of application for leave to appeal may be given;
  (c) to allow an appellant to be present at any proceedings;
  (ca) to give a live link direction under section 22(4);
  (d) to order a witness to attend for examination;

(e) to exercise the powers conferred by section 19 of this Act [bail pending determination of appeal];
(f) to make orders under section 8(2) of this Act and discharge or vary such orders [orders relating to procedure on a retrial];
[(g) repealed];
(h) to give directions under section 29(1) of this Act [directions for loss of time];
(i) to make orders under s. 23(1)(a).

(2ZA) The power of the Court of Appeal to renew an interim hospital order made by them by virtue of any provision of this part may be exercised by a single judge in the same manner as it may be exercised by the Court.

(2A) The power of the Court of Appeal to suspend a person's disqualification under section 40(2) of the Road Traffic Offenders Act 1988 may be exercised by a single judge in the same manner as it may be exercised by the court.

(2B) The power of the Court of Appeal to grant leave to appeal under section 159 of the Criminal Justice Act 1988 [appeals against orders restricting publicity] may be exercised by a single judge in the same manner as it may be exercised by the court.

(2C) The power of the Court of Appeal, under section 130 of the Licensing Act 2003, to suspend an order under section 129 of that Act may be exercised by a single judge in the same manner as it may be exercised by the Court.

(2D) The power of the Court of Appeal to grant leave to appeal under section 9(11) of the Criminal Justice Act 1987 may be exercised by a single judge in the same manner as it may be exercised by the Court.

(2E) The power of the Court of Appeal to grant leave to appeal under section 35(1) of the Criminal Procedure and Investigations Act 1996 may be exercised by a single judge in the same manner as it may be exercised by the Court.

(2F) The powers of the Court of Appeal to make, discharge or vary a witness anonymity order under Chapter 2 of Part 3 of the Coroners and Justice Act 2009 may be exercised by a single judge in the same manner as they may be exercised by the Court.

(3) If the single judge refuses an application on the part of an appellant to exercise in his favour any of the powers above specified, the appellant shall be entitled to have the application determined by the Court of Appeal.

44.—(1) There may be exercised by a single judge—
(a) the powers of the Court of Appeal under this Part of this Act—
  (i) to extend the time for making an application for leave to appeal;
  (ii) to make an order for or in relation to bail; and
  (iii) to give leave for a person to be present at the hearing of any proceedings preliminary or incidental to an appeal; and
(b) their powers to make orders for the payment of costs under sections 16 and 17 of the Prosecution of Offences Act 1985 in proceedings under this Part of this Act,
but where the judge refuses an application to exercise any of the said powers the applicant shall be entitled to have the application determined by the Court of Appeal.

(2) The power of the Court of Appeal to suspend a person's disqualification under section 40(3) of the Road Traffic Offenders Act 1988 may be exercised by a single judge, but where the judge refuses an application to exercise that power the applicant shall be entitled to have the application determined by the Court of Appeal.

The single judge may be either a judge of the High Court or a Lord Justice of Appeal (s. 44). The functions of the single judge are ordinarily carried out by a High Court judge. By virtue of ss. 31 and 44, a single judge may exercise a number of powers in the same manner as the Court of Appeal. It should be noted that the single judge may order a witness to attend for examination, but it is a matter for the court as to whether the evidence will be received (*Ahmed* [1996] Crim LR 339).

APPLICATIONS TO THE REGISTRAR

Criminal Appeal Act 1968, s. 31A D27.35

(1) The powers of the Court of Appeal under this Part of this Act which are specified in subsection (2) below may be exercised by the registrar.
(2) The powers mentioned in subsection (1) above are the following—
  (a) to extend the time within which notice of appeal or of application for leave to appeal may be given;

(aa) to give a live link direction under section 22(4);
(b) to order a witness to attend for examination;
(c) to vary the conditions of bail granted to an appellant by the Court of Appeal or the Crown Court;
(d) to make orders under section 23(1)(a).

(3) No variation of the conditions of bail granted to an appellant may be made by the registrar unless he is satisfied that the respondent does not object to the variation; but, subject to that, the powers specified in that subsection are to be exercised by the registrar in the same manner as by the Court of Appeal and subject to the same provisions.

(4) If the registrar refuses an application on the part of an appellant to exercise in his favour any of the powers specified in subsection (2) above, the appellant shall be entitled to have the application determined by a single judge.

(5) In this section 'respondent' includes a person who will be a respondent if leave to appeal is granted.

The powers exercisable by the Registrar in connection with appeals are set out in s. 31A of the Criminal Appeal Act 1968. Under r. 65.2 of the CrimPR, the Registrar must fulfil the duty of active case management under r. 3.2 (see **D4.6**). In fulfilling that duty, the Registrar may exercise (subject to the direction of the court) any of the powers of case management in rr 3.5 (the court's general powers of case management), 3.9(3) (requiring a certificate of readiness) and 3.10 (requiring a party to identify intentions and anticipated requirements).

Section D28   Reference to the Court of Appeal (Criminal Division) Following Trial on Indictment

REFERENCE BY THE CRIMINAL CASES REVIEW COMMISSION

The 'CCRC' was created by the Criminal Appeal Act 1995. Under s. 9, the CCRC may at any time refer a conviction on indictment or any sentence imposed in relation to that conviction (unless it is a sentence fixed by law) to the Court of Appeal. Under s. 11, the CCRC may refer any summary conviction or associated sentence to the Crown Court. For the CCRC to refer a case, there must be a real possibility that the Court of Appeal or Crown Court will quash the original conviction or sentence. The reference will ordinarily only be made in respect of an argument or information not available in the court of first instance or on appeal (s. 13). However, in exceptional circumstances, the CCRC may refer a case without any such development in the proceedings (s. 14). **D28.1**

Under the CrimPR, r. 68.5, when a reference is made, the Registrar must serve the reference on the appellant and must treat it as the notice of appeal unless a notice of appeal is given under r. 68.2 (see D27.3). The reference or notice must then be served on the respondent. The respondent may then serve a respondent's notice and must do so if it wishes to make representations or is directed to serve a respondent's notice by the court or Registrar (r. 68.6(2)).

Sections 17 to 21 set out the investigative powers of the CCRC. Under s. 17, the CCRC may require any public body to produce any document or information.

In *R (Director of Revenue and Customs Prosecutions) v Criminal Cases Review Commission* [2007] 1 Cr App R 395 the Divisional Court held that, when deciding whether to refer a case, the CCRC is not required to have regard to, let alone follow, a practice of the Court of Appeal operating at a stage with which the CCRC is not concerned. Thus, whilst it may be the usual practice of the Court of Appeal to refuse applications for extension of time to appeal when the appeal is based on a change in the law, the CCRC is not required to adopt the same practice. By contrast, the CCRC is required to have regard to the way in which the Court of Appeal Criminal Division approaches the 'unsafe' test when deciding whether to refer a case. That guidance to the CCRC on the relevance of the practice of the Court of Appeal in relation to extensions of time in change of law cases was forcefully overturned in *Cottrell* [2007] 1 WLR 3262. The President said that it is not open to the CCRC lawfully to apply a policy based on the decision in *R (DRCP) v CCRC*. The practice of the court must be addressed and evaluated in every case. Just as the court will not normally allow an application for an extension of time for leave to appeal in a change of law case, a conviction should not normally be referred on the basis of a change of law. In the final analysis, however, it is for the CCRC to exercise its own independent and fact specific judgement whether to refer a case, provided it gives proper weight to the law and practice of the court. Section 16C of the Criminal Appeal Act 1968, inserted by the CJIA 2008, s. 42, now empowers the Court of Appeal to dismiss an appeal following a reference by the CCRC if (i) the only ground for allowing it would be that there has been a change in the law since the date of the conviction; and (ii) had the reference not been made but the appellant had sought an extension of time within which to seek leave to appeal on the ground of the development of the law, the court would not think such an extension appropriate. Giving the judgment of the **D28.2** court in *Tierney* [2009] EWCA Crim 2220, Lord Judge CJ respectfully invited the CCRC to continue to have regard to *Cottrell* in respect of appeals based on a change in law.

D28.3   A distinction between 'change of law' cases, and those involving a subsequent definition of an aspect of the law (where previously there had been none) was drawn by the Court of Appeal in *Rowe* (2008) 172 JP 585. In the latter type of case, the issues dealt with in *Cottrell* did not arise. The appellant in *Rowe* had been convicted of the possession of indecent images of children. His conviction was prior to the judgment of the Court of Appeal in *Porter* [2006] 1 WLR 2633 and followed a summing-up by the trial judge which was inconsistent with *Porter* in respect of the possession of deleted images on a computer. Giving the judgment of the court, Lord Judge CJ explained (at [21]):

> Before the decision in *Porter* this court had not addressed the problem of possession of indecent images of children in the context of items deleted from a computer or computers in a defendant's possession. *Porter* explained the principles. It is binding upon us. It is not suggested that it was wrongly decided or decided per incuriam. If, following his application, the appellant had been granted leave to appeal, whether by the single judge, or, following refusal by the single judge, if he had applied to this court, we must assume that the principles now explained in *Porter* would have been decided in this case some time before *Porter* was decided. Until *Porter* was decided, however, the law had simply not been defined.

The CCRC was therefore justified in referring the conviction.

D28.4   In *R (Dowsett) v Criminal Cases Review Commission* [2007] EWCA Crim 1923, the Divisional Court held that the CCRC is not required to refer a case to the Court of Appeal Criminal Division simply because the Strasbourg court has ruled that there has been a breach of the ECHR. The Court of Appeal does not automatically quash convictions in such cases and so the CCRC should apply the test set out in the Criminal Appeal Act 1995, s. 13(1)(a), and refer a case only if there is a real possibility that the conviction would not be upheld.

By the CJA 2003, s. 315, leave from the Court of Appeal is required if an appellant is to argue any grounds additional to those upon which the CCRC has referred his case to the Court of Appeal.

See *Siddall* [2006] EWCA Crim 1353, for the timetable suggested by the Court of Appeal for the progress of an appeal referred by the CCRC.

The CCRC publishes a wide range of policy and procedure guidance which may be accessed via www.justice.gov.uk/about/criminal-cases-review-commission.

REFERENCES BY THE ATTORNEY-GENERAL

Reference on a Point of Law Following Acquittal

D28.5   Criminal Justice Act 1972, s. 36

(1) Where a person tried on indictment has been acquitted (whether in respect of the whole or part of the indictment) the Attorney-General may, if he desires the opinion of the Court of Appeal on a point of law which has arisen in the case, refer that point to the court, and the court shall, in accordance with this section, consider the point and give their opinion on it.

(2) For the purpose of their consideration of a point referred to them under this section the Court of Appeal shall hear argument—

(a) by, or by counsel on behalf of, the Attorney-General; and

(b) if the acquitted person desires to present any argument to the court, by counsel on his behalf or, with the leave of the court, by the acquitted person himself.

(3) Where the Court of Appeal have given their opinion on a point referred to them under this section, the court may, of their own motion or in pursuance of an application in that behalf, refer the point to the Supreme Court if it appears to the court that the point ought to be considered by the Supreme Court.

(4) If a point is referred to the Supreme Court under subsection (3) of this section, the Supreme Court shall consider the point and give its opinion on it accordingly.

(5) Where, on a point being referred to the Court of Appeal under this section or further referred to the Supreme Court, the acquitted person appears by counsel for the purpose of presenting any argument to the Court of Appeal or the Supreme Court, he shall be entitled to his costs, that is to say to the payment out of central funds of such sums as are reasonably sufficient to compensate him for expenses properly incurred by him for the purpose of being represented on the reference or further reference; and any amount recoverable under this subsection shall be ascertained, as soon as practicable, by the registrar of criminal appeals or, as the case may be, such officer as may be prescribed by [Supreme Court Rules].

...

(7) A reference under this section shall not affect the trial in relation to which the reference is made or any acquittal in that trial.

Section 36 provides for the reference of a point of law to the Court of Appeal by the A-G. The **D28.6** use of the power is confined to circumstances following the acquittal of an accused where the A-G requires the opinion of the Court of Appeal on a point of law. There is no provision for the referral of points of law which do not arise from proceedings resulting in an acquittal. In *A-G's Reference (No. 1 of 1975)* [1975] QB 773, Lord Widgery stated that the procedure should not be used simply for very heavy questions of law but should be used for short but important points requiring a quick ruling.

Whatever the opinion of the Court of Appeal, the acquittal is unaffected. Nevertheless, the acquitted defendant is entitled to be represented at the hearing (s. 36(5)).

The process of referral of a point of law by the A-G is governed by the CrimPR, part 70 (see Supplement, **R-541** *et seq.*).

The *Guide to Commencing Proceedings in the Court of Appeal Criminal Division* (2008) provides valuable guidance as to the procedure to be followed upon an A-G's reference of a point of law on an acquittal (see D7 of the Guide).

Section 36 provides for the further referral of the point of law to the Supreme Court following the judgment of the Court of Appeal. The point may be referred to the Supreme Court upon application by the parties or on the Court of Appeal's own motion. The procedure for the making of an application for a reference to the Supreme Court is governed by the CrimPR, part 74 (see Supplement, **R-569** *et seq.*).

Reference for Review of Sentence

Criminal Justice Act 1988, part IV (ss. 35 and 36) **D28.7**

35.—(1) A case to which this part of this Act applies may be referred to the Court of Appeal under section 36 below.

(2) Subject to rules of court, the jurisdiction of the Court of Appeal under section 36 below shall be exercised by the criminal division of the Court, and references to the Court of Appeal in this part of this Act shall be construed as references to that division.

(3) This part of this Act applies to any case—
   (a) of a description specified in an order under this section; or
   (b) in which sentence is passed on a person—
      (i) for an offence triable only on indictment; or
      (ii) for an offence of a description specified in an order under this section.

(4) and (5) [Order-making power and procedure.]

(6) In this part of this Act 'sentence' has the same meaning as in the Criminal Appeal Act 1968, except that it does not include an interim hospital order under part III of the Mental Health Act 1983, and 'sentencing' shall be construed accordingly.

36.—(1) If it appears to the Attorney-General—

Part D Procedure

D

     (a) that the sentencing of a person in a proceeding in the Crown Court has been unduly leni-
ent; and

     (b) that the case is one to which this part of this Act applies,

he may, with the leave of the Court of Appeal, refer the case to them for them to review the
sentencing of that person; and on such a reference the Court of Appeal may—

       (i) quash any sentence passed on him in the proceeding; and

       (ii) in place of it pass such sentence as they think appropriate for the case and as the court
below had power to pass when dealing with him.

(2) Without prejudice to the generality of subsection (1) above, the condition specified in paragraph (a) of that subsection may be satisfied if it appears to the Attorney-General that the
judge—

     (a) erred in law as to his powers of sentencing; or

     (b) failed to pass a sentence required by—

       (zi) section 1A(5) of the Prevention of Crime Act 1953;

       (i) section 51A(2) of the Firearms Act 1968;

       (ia) section 139AA(7) of this Act;

       (ii) section 110(2) or 111(2) of the Powers of Criminal Courts (Sentencing) Act 2000;

       (iii) section 224A, 225(2) or 226(2) of the Criminal Justice Act 2003; or

       (iv) under section 29(4) or (6) of the Violent Crime Reduction Act 2006.

(3) For the purposes of this part of this Act any two or more sentences are to be treated as passed in
the same proceeding if they would be so treated for the purposes of section 11 of the Criminal
Appeal Act 1968.

(3A) Where a reference under this section relates to a case in which the judge made an order specified in subsection (3B), the Court of Appeal shall not, in deciding what sentence is appropriate for the case, make any allowance for the fact that the person to whom it relates is being
sentenced for a second time.

(3B) The orders specified in this subsection are–

     (a) an order under section 269(2) of the Criminal Justice Act 2003 (determination of mini-
mum term in relation to mandatory life sentence);

     (b) an order under section 82A(2) of the Powers of Criminal Court (Sentencing) Act 2000
(determination of minimum term in relation to discretionary life sentences and certain
other sentences).

(4) No judge shall sit as a member of the Court of Appeal on the hearing of, or shall determine
any application in proceedings incidental or preliminary to, a reference under this section of a
sentence passed by himself.

(5) Where the Court of Appeal have concluded their review of a case referred to them under this
section the Attorney-General or the person to whose sentencing the reference relates may refer
a point of law involved in any sentence passed on that person in the proceeding to the Supreme
Court for its opinion, and the Supreme Court shall consider the point and give its opinion on
it accordingly, and either remit the case to the Court of Appeal to be dealt with or itself deal
with the case.

(6) A reference under subsection (5) above shall be made only with the leave of the Court of
Appeal or the Supreme Court; and leave shall not be granted unless it is certified by the Court
of Appeal that the point of law is of general public importance and it appears to the Court
of Appeal or the Supreme Court (as the case may be) that the point is one which ought to be
considered by the Supreme Court.

(7) For the purpose of dealing with a case under this section the Supreme Court may exercise any
powers of the Court of Appeal.

D28.8   The scope of the power to refer now extends beyond indictable-only offences to include a number of offences, and combinations of offences, set out in the Criminal Justice Act 1988 (Reviews
of Sentencing) Order 2006 (SI 2006 No. 1116), sch. 1 (see **D28.11**). An offence is deemed to be
triable only on indictment for the purposes of s. 35 if it is so for an adult and it is irrelevant that
a youth can be tried summarily on such an allegation (*W* (1993) *The Times*, 16 March 1993).
It is for the A-G personally to consider whether leave should be sought for a reference to the
Court of Appeal on the basis that the sentence was unduly lenient and if appropriate to apply
for leave. The procedure to be followed is set out in the CJA 1988, sch. 3, supplemented by the
CrimPR, part 70 (see Supplement, **R-541**). If leave is granted, the reference proceeds according

to the facts before the sentencing judge, and the Court of Appeal will not alter the sentence on the grounds of new material that was not before the sentencing judge, but will decide whether the sentence was unduly lenient on the basis of what was before the sentencing judge (*A-G's Ref (No. 19 of 2005)* [2006] EWCA Crim 785). However, if the Court concludes that the sentence was unduly lenient, it may receive fresh material, either favourable or adverse to the offender, in reaching its conclusions as to the correct new sentence (*A-G's Ref (No. 74 of 2010)* [2011] EWCA Crim 873).

Guidance as to the procedure to be followed on an A-G's reference of an unduly lenient sentence is set out at D6 of the *Guide to Commencing Proceedings in the Court of Appeal Criminal Division* (2008).

Double Jeopardy   When the Court of Appeal increases a sentence under the reference procedure, its practice has often been to allow some discount on the sentence it would consider appropriate because of what is usually termed the 'double jeopardy' of an offender having to wait before knowing if his sentence is to be increased. In *A-G's Refs (Nos. 14 and 15 of 2006)* [2007] 1 All ER 718, the Court gave some guidance as to the relevance and applicability of such double jeopardy. The effect of the principle will vary significantly according to the circumstances. Where an offender has a substantial part of a long determinate sentence remaining to be served or is serving a discretionary life sentence, the principle has limited effect, if any, because the anxiety occasioned by the process will consequently be less keenly felt. Where, however, an offender had completely served a custodial sentence, was close to release, had a custodial sentence substituted for a non-custodial sentence or was very young, the discount for double jeopardy should be near the upper end of the range, at about 30 per cent. **D28.9**

Additional Matters Taken into Account on Reference   The following additional points apply to references under the CJA 1988, s. 35. **D28.10**

(a) If an indication of sentence is given to an offender by the sentencing judge, the Court of Appeal will take that into account but is not necessarily bound by it. In *A-G's Refs (Nos. 86 and 87 of 1999)* [2001] 1 Cr App R (S) 505, an indication was given by the judge before trial that a non-custodial sentence would be imposed whether the accused pleaded guilty or proceeded to a contested trial. The indication was repeated after a finding of guilty. That indication plainly could have had no effect on any decision made by the offender as to plea and so would be no bar to the increase of sentence under the reference procedure (cf. *A-G's Ref (No. 44 of 2000)* [2001] Cr App R 416, relevance of prosecution representations to the accused).

(b) By virtue of s. 35(6), a 'sentence' for the purposes of the reference procedure has the same meaning as in the Criminal Appeal Act 1968, s. 50 (see **D26.42**) (except that it does not include an interim hospital order under part III of the Mental Health Act 1983) and thus is any order made by a court when dealing with an offender.

(c) The Court of Appeal will act in relation to a sentence only if it is unduly lenient and not simply lenient. The test to be applied is whether the sentence was outside the range which the judge, applying his mind to all relevant factors, could reasonably consider appropriate (*A-G's Ref (No. 4 of 1989)* [1990] 1 WLR 41).

(d) The Court of Appeal's decision following the reference may be the subject of appeal to the Supreme Court by the A-G or the offender. That appeal must be by leave of either the Court of Appeal or the Supreme Court and must concern a point of law of public importance.

Reviewable Sentences and Procedure: Statutory Provisions

Criminal Justice Act 1988 (Reviews of Sentencing) Order 2006 (SI 2006 No. 1116), sch. 1 **D28.11**

1. Any case tried on indictment—
    (a) following a notice of transfer given under section 4 of the Criminal Justice Act 1987 (notices of transfer and designated authorities) by an authority designated for that purpose under subsection (2) of that section; or

(b) in which one or more of the counts in respect of which sentence is passed relates to a charge which was dismissed under section 6(1) of the Criminal Justice Act 1987 (applications for dismissal) and on which further proceedings were brought by means of preferment of a voluntary bill of indictment.

1A. Any case tried on indictment—

    (a) following a notice given under section 51B of the Crime and Disorder Act 1998 (notices in serious or complex fraud cases); or

    (b) following such a notice, in which one or more of the counts in respect of which sentence is passed relates to a charge—

        (i) which was dismissed under paragraph 2 of Schedule 3 to the Crime and Disorder Act 1998 (applications for dismissal); and

        (ii) on which further proceedings were brought by means of the preferment of a voluntary bill of indictment.

2. Any case in which sentence is passed on a person for one of the following offences:

    (a) an offence under section 16 of the Offences against the Person Act 1861 (threats to kill);

    (b) an offence under section 5(1) of the Criminal Law Amendment Act 1885 (defilement of a girl between 14 and 17);

    (c) an offence under section 1 of the Children and Young Persons Act 1933 (cruelty to persons under 16) or section 20 of the Children and Young Persons Act (Northern Ireland) 1968 (cruelty to persons under 16);

    (d) an offence under section 6 of the Sexual Offences Act 1956 (unlawful sexual intercourse with a girl under 16), section 14 or 15 of that Act (indecent assault on a woman or on a man), section 52 of the Offences against the Person Act 1861 (indecent assault upon a female), or Article 21 of the Criminal Justice (Northern Ireland) Order 2003 (indecent assault on a male);

    (e) an offence under section 1 of the Indecency with Children Act 1960 or section 22 of the Children and Young Persons Act (Northern Ireland) 1968 (indecent conduct with a child);

    (f) an offence under section 4(2) or (3) (production or supply of a controlled drug), section 5(3) (possession of a controlled drug with intent to supply) or section 6(2) (cultivation of cannabis plant) of the Misuse of Drugs Act 1971;

    (g) an offence under section 54 of the Criminal Law Act 1977 or Article 9 of the Criminal Justice (Northern Ireland) Order 1980 (inciting a girl under 16 to have incestuous sexual intercourse);

    (h) an offence under section 50(2) or (3), section 68(2) or section 170(1) or (2) of the Customs and Excise Management Act 1979, insofar as those offences are in connection with a prohibition or restriction on importation or exportation of either:

        (i) a controlled drug within the meaning of section 2 of the Misuse of Drugs Act 1971, such prohibition or restriction having effect by virtue of section 3 of that Act; or

        (ii) an article prohibited by virtue of section 42 of the Customs Consolidation Act 1876 but only insofar as it relates to or depicts a person under the age of 16;

    (i) offences under sections 29 to 32 of the Crime and Disorder Act 1998 (racially or religiously aggravated assaults; racially or religiously aggravated criminal damage; racially or religiously aggravated public order offences; racially or religiously aggravated harassment etc);

    (j) an offence under section 4 of the Asylum and Immigration (Treatment of Claimants, etc.) Act 2004 (trafficking people for exploitation);

    (k) an offence under section 71 of the Coroners and Justice Act 2009 (slavery, servitude and forced or compulsory labour).

3. To the extent that part IV of the Criminal Justice Act 1988 does not apply by virtue of section 35(3)(b)(i), any case in which sentence is passed on a person for an offence under one of the following sections of the Sexual Offences Act 2003:

    (a) section 3 (sexual assault);

    (b) section 4 (causing a person to engage in sexual activity without consent);

    (c) section 7 (sexual assault of a child under 13);

    (d) section 8 (causing or inciting a child under 13 to engage in sexual activity);

    (e) section 9 (sexual activity with a child);

    (f) section 10 (causing or inciting a child to engage in sexual activity);

    (g) section 11 (engaging in sexual activity in the presence of a child);

    (h) section 12 (causing a child to watch a sexual act);

(i)   section 14 (arranging or facilitating commission of a child sex offence);
(j)   section 15 (meeting a child following sexual grooming etc);
(k)   section 25 (sexual activity with a child family member);
(l)   section 47 (paying for sexual services of a child);
(m) section 48 (causing or inciting child prostitution or pornography);
(n)   section 49 (controlling a child prostitute or a child involved in pornography);
(o)   section 50 (arranging or facilitating child prostitution or pornography);
(p)   section 52 (causing or inciting prostitution for gain);
(q)   section 57 (trafficking into the UK for sexual exploitation);
(r)   section 58 (trafficking within the UK for sexual exploitation);
(s)   section 59 (trafficking out of the UK for sexual exploitation);
(sa) section 59A (trafficking people for sexual exploitation);
(t)   section 61 (administering a substance with intent).

4.—(1) Any case in which sentence is passed on a person for—
(a)   attempting to commit a relevant offence;
(b)   inciting the commission of a relevant offence; or
(c)   an offence under section 44 or 45 of the Serious Crime Act 2007 (encouraging or assisting an offence) in relation to a relevant offence.

(2) In this paragraph, 'a relevant offence' means an offence set out in paragraph 2(a) to (h), (j) or (k) or paragraph 3.

Criminal Justice Act 1988, sch. 3

D28.12

REVIEWS OF SENTENCING — SUPPLEMENTARY

1. Notice of an application for leave to refer a case to the Court of Appeal under section 36 above shall be given within 28 days from the day on which the sentence, or the last of the sentences, in the case was passed.

2. If the registrar of criminal appeals is given notice of a reference or application to the Court of Appeal under section 36 above, he shall—
   (a) take all necessary steps for obtaining a hearing of the reference of application; and
   (b) obtain and lay before the court in proper form all documents, exhibits and other things which appear necessary for the proper determination of the reference or application.

3. Rules of court may enable a person to whose sentencing such a reference or application relates to obtain from the registrar any documents or things, including copies or reproductions of documents, required for the reference or application and may authorise the registrar to make charges for them in accordance with scales and rates fixed from time to time by the Treasury.

4. An application to the Court of Appeal for leave to refer a case to the Supreme Court under section 36(5) above shall be made within the period of 14 days beginning with the date on which the Court of Appeal conclude their review of the case; and an application to the Supreme Court for leave shall be made within the period of 14 days beginning with the date on which the Court of Appeal conclude their review or refuse leave to refer the case to the Supreme Court.

5. The time during which a person whose case has been referred for review under section 36 above is in custody pending its review and pending any reference to the Supreme Court under subsection (5) of that section shall be reckoned as part of the term of any sentence to which he is for the time being subject.

6. Except as provided by paragraphs 7 and 8 below, a person whose sentencing is the subject of a reference to the Court of Appeal under section 36 above shall be entitled to be present, if he wishes it, on the hearing of the reference, although he may be in custody.

7. A person in custody shall not be entitled to be present—
   (a) on an application by the Attorney-General for leave to refer a case; or
   (b) on any proceedings preliminary or incidental to a reference,
   unless the Court of Appeal give him leave to be present.

8. The power of the Court of Appeal to pass sentence on a person may be exercised although he is not present.

9. A person whose sentencing is the subject of a reference to the Supreme Court under section 36(5) above and who is detained pending the hearing of that reference shall not be entitled to be present on the hearing of the reference or of any proceeding preliminary or incidental thereto except where an order of the Supreme Court authorises him to be present, or where the Supreme Court of Appeal, as the case may be, give him leave to be present.

10. The term of any sentence passed by the Court of Appeal or Supreme Court under section 36 above shall, unless they otherwise direct, begin to run from the time when it would have begun to run if passed in the proceeding in relation to which the reference was made.

11. Where on a reference to the Court of Appeal under section 36 above or a reference to the Supreme Court under subsection (5) of that section the person whose sentencing is the subject of the reference appears by counsel for the purpose of presenting any argument to the Court of Appeal or the Supreme Court, he shall be entitled to his costs, that is to say to the payment out of central funds of such funds as are reasonably sufficient to compensate him for expenses properly incurred by him for the purpose of being represented on the reference; and any amount recoverable under this paragraph shall be ascertained, as soon as practicable, by the registrar of criminal appeals or, as the case may be, under Supreme Court Rules.

12. [Northern Ireland.]

Section D29   Challenging Decisions of Magistrates' Courts and of the Crown Court in its Appellate Capacity

ROUTES OF CHALLENGE OF DECISIONS OF MAGISTRATES' COURTS

D29.1 A person aggrieved by a decision of the magistrates' court has three means of challenge to that decision available to him. They are as follows:

(a) appeal to the Crown Court;
(b) appeal to the High Court by way of case stated;
(c) application to the High Court for judicial review.

Any person convicted by a magistrates' court may appeal against either the conviction and/or sentence. If the offender pleaded guilty in the magistrates' court then he may also appeal against conviction (in the limited circumstances set out in **D29.4**) and sentence to the Crown Court. An appeal to the High Court by way of case stated or an application for judicial review is available to either party in the magistrates' court if they are aggrieved at the outcome of proceedings. An appeal by way of case stated or application for judicial review is heard by a Divisional Court of the Queen's Bench Division of the High Court.

APPEAL TO THE CROWN COURT

Magistrates' Courts Act 1980, s. 108

D29.2

(1) A person convicted by a magistrates' court may appeal to the Crown Court—
  (a) if he pleaded guilty, against his sentence;
  (b) if he did not, against the conviction or sentence.
(1A) Section 14 of the Powers of Criminal Courts (Sentencing) Act 2000 (under which a conviction of an offence for which a conditional or absolute discharge is made is deemed not to be a conviction except for certain purposes) shall not prevent an appeal under this section, whether against conviction or otherwise.
(2) A person sentenced by a magistrates' court for an offence in respect of which an order for conditional discharge has been previously made may appeal to the Crown Court against the sentence.
(3) In this section 'sentence' includes any order made on conviction by a magistrates' court, not being—
  (a) [repealed by Criminal Justice Act 1982, sch. 16]
  (b) an order for the payment of costs;
  (c) an order under section 37(1) of the Animal Welfare Act 2006 (which enables a court to order the destruction of an animal); or
  (d) an order made in pursuance of any enactment under which the court has no discretion as to the making of the order or its terms;

and also includes a declaration of relevance, within the meaning of section 23 of the Football Spectators Act 1989.

(4) Subsection (3)(d) above does not prevent an appeal against a surcharge imposed under section 161A of the Criminal Justice Act 2003.

Appeals against Conviction and Sentence

D29.3   Appeals to the Crown Court are governed by the MCA 1980, s. 108, and the CrimPR, part 63. Appeals from the youth court are governed by the same provisions (as a youth court is part of the magistrates' court) but an important difference between an appeal from a youth court and one from an adult magistrates' court lies in the composition of the court. Ordinarily an appeal from the youth court must be heard by a judge or recorder of the Crown Court sitting with two lay justices (one man and one woman) who are authorised to sit in the youth court. Exceptionally, the Crown Court may include only one justice of the peace and need not include both a man and a woman if the presiding judge decides that the hearing of the appeal will otherwise be unreasonably delayed or one or more of the justices who started hearing the appeal is absent (r. 63.10).

The broad definition of 'sentence' contained within s. 108(3) mirrors that in the equivalent provision for the Court of Appeal Criminal Division in s. 50 of the Criminal Appeal Act 1968.

Appeal against Conviction Following Plea of Guilty

D29.4   Generally, if a plea of guilty is entered in the magistrates' court, no appeal against the resulting conviction is available to the Crown Court. There are exceptions to that rule as follows:

(a) *When a plea is equivocal when made.* A plea is equivocal when made if a defendant enters a plea of guilty but, by additional comment following the plea, suggests that he is not guilty and has a defence. For example, if on a charge of assault a defendant pleads guilty but adds that he was only defending himself, then the plea is equivocal. The usual practice would then be for the clerk of the court to explain any necessary matters of law to the defendant and retake the plea. If the defendant then unambiguously pleads guilty the court may proceed to sentence, but if the plea remains equivocal, the court enters a not guilty plea. If the court does not follow that procedure and the Crown Court is satisfied on appeal that the plea was equivocal, the case will be remitted back to the magistrates' court for a fresh plea to be entered. The magistrates' court is required to co-operate with any investigation by the Crown Court into whether or not the plea is equivocal. Such co-operation extends to the provision of affidavits explaining the circumstances in which the guilty plea came to be entered (*Rochdale Justices, ex parte Allwork* [1981] 3 All ER 434). If, having conducted a proper inquiry into whether or not the initial plea was equivocal, the Crown Court remits the proceedings with a direction that a trial take place, the magistrates' court must comply with that direction (*Plymouth Justices, ex parte Hart* [1986] QB 950).

(b) *When a plea is subsequently shown to be equivocal.* The usual circumstances in which an unambiguous plea of guilty subsequently becomes equivocal are when material emerges in mitigation which undermines the unambiguous nature of the plea. On appeal on such a basis, the Crown Court should remit the case for trial (*Durham Quarter Sessions, ex parte Virgo* [1952] 2 QB 1; *Blandford Justices, ex parte G* [1967] 1 QB 82).

(c) *When a plea is entered under duress.* Plainly, any plea entered under duress is not a true plea and the Crown Court may remit a case back to the magistrates' court for trial if a plea of guilty has been entered under duress. In *Huntingdon Justices, ex parte Jordan* [1981] QB 857, J had pleaded guilty to shoplifting under duress from her husband. Her defence to the shoplifting allegations would similarly have been one of duress. The Divisional Court held that the Crown Court had jurisdiction to remit the case for trial in such circumstances if they were made out.

(d) *When autrefois convict or acquit arises.* The Crown Court in its appellate capacity may examine a plea in bar of autrefois convict or acquit even where the defendant has pleaded guilty in an entirely unambiguous way in the magistrates' court (*Cooper v New Forest District Council* [1992] Crim LR 877).

(e) *When a reference is made by the CCRC.* Under s. 11 of the Criminal Appeal Act 1995, the CCRC may refer any conviction in the magistrates' court to the Crown Court irrespective of whether the conviction arose from a plea of guilty or following a trial. Thus all of the bases of challenge to a conviction following a guilty plea in the Crown Court are available through the CCRC.

Appeal against Binding Over

Under s. 1(1) of the Magistrates' Courts (Appeals from Binding Over Orders) Act 1956, any **D29.5** person who feels aggrieved at being bound over by the magistrates may appeal that binding over order to the Crown Court. The appeal is by way of rehearing, and so if the facts which led to the binding over are not accepted by the appellant, they must be proved to the satisfaction of the court (*Shaw v Hamilton* [1982] 2 All ER 718).

Procedure on Appeal to the Crown Court

Rule 63.2(1) and (3) of the CrimPR (see Supplement, **R-471**) requires notice of appeal to be **D29.6** given in writing to the relevant magistrates' court officer and every other party within 21 days of sentence being passed or sentence being deferred. The appellant has 21 days from the date of sentence, even if that is after the date of conviction, if he is appealing only against conviction. The time-limit is also 21 days where the appeal is against an order, or failure to make an order. That is to be contrasted with the position in respect of an appeal against conviction from the Crown Court to the Court of Appeal Criminal Division (see **D27.2**). The notice should state whether the appeal is against conviction or sentence or an order or failure to make an order. The notice of appeal must also summarise the issues and in an appeal against conviction must specify the witnesses whom the appellant will want to question and state how long the trial lasted in the magistrates' court and how long the appeal is likely to take. In an appeal against a finding that the appellant insulted someone or interrupted proceedings in the magistrates' court, the magistrates' court's written findings of fact and the appellant's response to those findings must be attached to the notice. Any notice must also stipulate whether the appellant has asked the magistrates' court to reconsider the case and identify all those upon whom the notice has been served. Under r. 63.9(d), the Crown Court may allow an appeal notice to be in a form other than the specified form, or to be presented orally. If a notice is served within time, no leave to appeal is required. By virtue of r. 63.3 an application for an extension of time must be served with the appeal notice and must explain why the appeal notice is late. Under r. 63.9(a), the Crown Court may shorten or extend (even after it has expired) any time-limit under part 63.

Bail pending appeal is dealt with at **D29.16**.

An appeal is heard by a circuit judge or recorder who must normally sit with two lay magistrates who were not involved with the original proceedings (Senior Courts Act 1981, s. 74). Prior to the hearing, the defence may request a copy of the clerk's notes of evidence of the summary trial. Any request the appellant might make for a copy should be 'viewed sympathetically' (per Lord Lane CJ in *Clerk to Highbury Corner Justices, ex parte Hussein* [1986] 1 WLR 1266).

Hearing   Under s. 79(3), the appeal proceeds by way of complete rehearing. Thus, at an appeal **D29.7** against conviction, counsel for the respondent (i.e. the prosecution) makes an opening speech and calls evidence, after which counsel for the appellant may make a submission of no case to answer. If that fails, defence evidence is called, counsel makes a closing speech, and the court announces its decision. The parties may call evidence which has only become available to them since the trial, or evidence they decided not to use in the magistrates' court. The information on which the appellant was convicted may not be amended by the Crown Court (*Garfield v*

Maddocks [1974] QB 7). In *Swansea Crown Court, ex parte Stacey* [1990] RTR 183, it was held that the judge erred in allowing a prosecution application to amend the information in respect of the date of the alleged offences. Equally, the Crown Court cannot strike out an amendment made by the magistrates (*Fairgrieve v Newman* (1985) 82 Cr App R 60).

An appeal against sentence is, in essence, a fresh sentencing hearing. The prosecution opens the facts and antecedents of the appellant, and defence counsel then mitigates. The court then decides the sentence to be imposed. When dealing with an appeal against sentence, the Crown Court should not ask itself whether the sentence was within the discretion of the magistrates (as would be the appropriate question in judicial review proceedings) but should consider whether, in the light of all the matters which the Crown Court had heard, the sentence passed by the magistrates was the correct one. If what the court thinks is the appropriate sentence differs significantly from the sentence imposed by the magistrates, the appeal should be allowed and the sentence of the Crown Court substituted for that of the magistrates *(Swindon Crown Court, ex parte Murray* (1998) 162 JP 36). The Crown Court is not entitled to increase the sentence on appeal from the magistrates' court on the basis that the magistrates ought to have committed the offender to the Crown Court for sentence in the first place (*R (Lees-Sandey) v Chichester Crown Court* (2004) *The Times*, 15 October 2004).

D29.8   If a defendant pleads guilty in the magistrates' court but disputes the version of events put forward by the prosecution, and the magistrates decide to accept the defendant's version of events without hearing evidence, the Crown Court hearing an appeal against sentence is not bound by that action. As the appeal is a rehearing, the court may determine the appeal and hence pass a different sentence on a different factual basis to that which formed the basis of the sentence imposed by the magistrates' court. However, if the Crown Court intends to decide the appeal on a different factual basis, the court should inform the appellant of that intention in clear terms and allow him the opportunity of a *Newton* hearing (*Bussey v DPP* [1999] 1 Cr App R (S) 125).

D29.9   **Reasons for Decision**   Reasons for the decision of the Crown Court should be given by the judge presiding over the hearing. The reasons should include a statement of the main contentious issues in the case and how the court had resolved them. A refusal to give reasons might amount to a denial of natural justice (*Harrow Crown Court, ex parte Dave* [1994] 1 All ER 315). The duty to provide reasons exists whether the court allows or dismisses the appeal against conviction (*Inner London Crown Court, ex parte Lambeth London Borough Council* [2000] Crim LR 303). If reasons are not given the decision of the Crown Court will usually be vitiated, but that is not an unqualified rule. If, for example, the reasons are obvious, the failure to set them out will not necessarily be fatal (*Kingston Crown Court, ex parte Bell* (2000) 164 JP 633). In *Snaresbrook Crown Court, ex parte Input Management Ltd* (1999) 163 JP 533, the Divisional Court defined the obligation to give reasons, holding that the reasons given by the Crown Court should enable the defendant: (i) to see the nature of the criminality found to exist by the court; and (ii) to properly consider whether there are grounds for a further appeal to the Divisional Court by way of case stated.

Powers of the Crown Court on Appeal

D29.10   The powers of the Crown Court when disposing of an appeal are set out in the Senior Courts Act 1981, s. 48. The decision of the Crown Court may be a majority decision. This means that the lay justices can out-vote the judge. The lay justices must, however, accept any decisions on questions of law made by the judge.

Section 48(2) provides that, following an appeal from the magistrates' court, the Crown Court:

(a) may confirm, reverse or vary any part of the decision appealed against, including a determination not to impose a separate penalty in respect of an offence; or

(b) may remit the matter with its opinion thereon to the authority whose decision is appealed against; or

(c) may make such other order in the matter as the court thinks just, and by such order exercise any power which the said authority might have exercised.

Section 48(4) and (5) further provide that:

(4) ...if the appeal is against a conviction or a sentence, the preceding provisions of this section shall be construed as including power to award any punishment, whether more or less severe than that awarded by the magistrates' court whose decision is appealed against, if that is a punishment which that magistrates' court might have awarded.

(5) This section applies whether or not the appeal is against the whole of the decision.

Thus, s. 48 allows the Crown Court to:

(a) quash the conviction;

(b) remit the case to the magistrates' court (for example, in the case of an equivocal plea);

(c) vary the sentence imposed by the magistrates (this includes the power to increase the sentence, but not beyond the maximum sentence which the magistrates' court could have passed: s. 48(4)).

Under the Criminal Appeal Act 1995, s. 11(5), if a reference to the Crown Court is made by the **D29.11** CCRC, the Crown Court has no power to increase the sentence.

If a defendant's hopes of a non-custodial sentence are legitimately raised as a result of an indication given by magistrates that favourable pre-sentence reports would be likely to result in a non-custodial sentence, the Crown Court should not impose or uphold a custodial sentence. Whilst the appeal proceedings constitute a complete rehearing, the expectation created in the appellant should be respected (*Isleworth Crown Court, ex parte Irvin* [1992] RTR 281).

In *Portsmouth Crown Court, ex parte Ballard* (1989) 154 JP 109, it was held that the Crown Court had no power to impose a sentence consecutive to one imposed *after* the date of imposition of the sentence being appealed.

An unsuccessful appellant may be required to pay the prosecution's costs (Prosecution of Offences Act 1985, s. 18(1)(b) (see **D33.20**) and CrimPR, r. 78.1(2)). A successful appellant may be awarded his costs (s. 16(3)) as may a private prosecutor (s. 17(1) and (2)), but there is no provision for a public prosecutor to be awarded costs from the public purse.

Abandonment of Appeal

Magistrates' Courts Act 1980, s. 109   **D29.12**

(1) Where notice to abandon an appeal has been duly given by the appellant—
  (a) the court against whose decision the appeal was brought may issue process for enforcing that decision, subject to anything already suffered or done under it by the appellant; and
  (b) the said court may, on the application of the other party to the appeal, order the appellant to pay to that party such costs as appear to the court to be just and reasonable in respect of expenses properly incurred by that party in connection with the appeal before notice of the abandonment was given to that party.

(2) In this section 'appeal' means an appeal from a magistrates' court to the Crown Court, and the reference to a notice to abandon an appeal is a reference to a notice shown to the satisfaction of the magistrates' court to have been given in accordance with rules of court.

Rule 63.8 of the CrimPR (see Supplement, **R-477**) sets out the procedure for abandonment of **D29.13** an appeal under the MCA 1980, s. 109. The appellant may abandon his appeal by giving notice in writing to that effect to the magistrates' court, to the appropriate officer of the Crown Court and to the prosecution and to any other party to the appeal (r. 63.8(1)(a)). The appeal may be abandoned without permission if it is done before the hearing commences. Once the hearing has started, the appeal may be abandoned only with the permission of the Crown Court. As with a notice of appeal, under r. 63.9(d), the Crown Court may allow the notice of abandonment to be given in a form other than that specified or to be given orally. The Crown Court has a discretion to award costs in an appeal from a magistrates' court in all cases (even where a timely notice of abandonment has been served).

An appeal cannot be abandoned simply by an appellant failing to attend or failing to instruct an advocate. Upon the abandonment of an appeal, the Crown Court has no power to increase sentence (*Gloucester Crown Court, ex parte Betteridge* (1997) 161 JP 721). Once an appeal has been abandoned, the Crown Court has no power to reinstate the appeal unless the abandonment was a nullity (*Knightsbridge Crown Court, ex parte Commissioners of Customs and Excise* [1986] Crim LR 324).

Proceeding in the Absence of the Parties

D29.14   If an appellant fails to attend at the appeal hearing when required but is represented by an advocate, the Crown Court should hear the appeal. It is not open to the Crown Court to treat the non-attendance as an effective abandonment of the appeal (*R (Hayes) v Chelmsford Crown Court* (2003) 167 JP 65).

Where neither party appears or is represented, the proper course is to dismiss the appeal (*Croydon Crown Court, ex parte Clair* [1986] 2 All ER 716).

Enforcement of Orders of Crown Court on Appeal

D29.15   Magistrates' Courts Act 1980, s. 110

After the determination by the Crown Court of an appeal from a magistrates' court the decision appealed against as confirmed or varied by the Crown Court, or any decision of the Crown Court substituted for the decision appealed against, may, without prejudice to the powers of the Crown Court to enforce the decision, be enforced—
  (a) by the issue by the court by which the decision appealed against was given of any process that it could have issued if it had decided the case as the Crown Court decided it;
  (b) so far as the nature of any process already issued to enforce the decision appealed against permits, by that process;
the decision of the Crown Court shall have effect as if it had been made by the magistrates' court against whose decision the appeal is brought.

Bail Pending Appeal

D29.16   Under the MCA 1980, s. 113, bail may be granted pending appeal to the Crown Court in respect of either conviction or sentence. The Bail Act 1976 does not apply so there is no right to bail. Under the Senior Courts Act 1981, s. 81(1), an appellant refused bail by the magistrates may apply to the Crown Court for bail. It is no longer possible to apply to the High Court for bail pending appeal if the Crown Court refuses bail.

APPEAL TO DIVISIONAL COURT BY WAY OF CASE STATED

Principles of Appeal by way of Case Stated

D29.17   Magistrates' Courts Act 1980, ss. 111 to 114

111.—(1) Any person who was a party to any proceeding before a magistrates' court or is aggrieved by the conviction, order, determination or other proceeding of the court may question the proceeding on the ground that it is wrong in law or is in excess of jurisdiction by applying to the justices composing the court to state a case for the opinion of the High Court on the question of law or jurisdiction involved; but a person shall not make an application under this section in respect of a decision against which he has a right of appeal to the High Court or which by virtue of any enactment passed after 31st December 1879 is final.
  (2) An application under subsection (1) above shall be made within 21 days after the day on which the decision of the magistrates' court was given.
  (3) For the purpose of subsection (2) above, the day on which the decision of the magistrates' court is given shall, where the court has adjourned the trial of an information after conviction, be the day on which the court sentences or otherwise deals with the offender.

(4) On the making of an application under this section in respect of a decision any right of the applicant to appeal against the decision to the Crown Court shall cease.

(5) If the justices are of opinion that an application under this section is frivolous, they may refuse to state a case, and, if the applicant so requires, shall give him a certificate stating that the application has been refused; but the justices shall not refuse to state a case if the application is made by or under the direction of the Attorney-General.

(6) Where justices refuse to state a case, the High Court may, on the application of the person who applied for the case to be stated, make an order of mandamus requiring the justices to state a case.

112.—(1) Any conviction, order, determination or other proceeding of a magistrates' court varied by the High Court on an appeal by case stated, and any judgment or order of the High Court on such an appeal, may be enforced as if it were a decision of the magistrates' court from which the appeal was brought.

(2) [Family court variations.]

113.—(1) Where a person has given notice of appeal to the Crown Court against the decision of a magistrates' court or has applied to a magistrates' court to state a case for the opinion of the High Court, then, if he is in custody, the magistrates' court may, subject to section 25 of the Criminal Justice and Public Order Act 1994, grant him bail.

(2) If a person is granted bail under subsection (1) above, the time and place at which he is to appear (except in the event of the determination in respect of which the case is stated being reversed by the High Court) shall be—

   (a) if he has given notice of appeal, the Crown Court at the time appointed for the hearing of the appeal;

   (b) if he has applied for the statement of a case, the magistrates' court at such time within 10 days after the judgment of the High Court has been given as may be specified by the magistrates' court;

and any recognisance that may be taken from him or from any surety for him shall be conditioned accordingly.

(3) Subsection (1) above shall not apply where the accused has been committed to the Crown Court for sentence under section 37 above or section 3 of the Powers of Criminal Courts (Sentencing) Act 2000.

(4) Section 37(6) of the Criminal Justice Act 1948 (which relates to the currency of a sentence while a person is released on bail by the High Court) shall apply to a person released on bail by a magistrates' court under this section pending the hearing of a case stated as it applies to a person released on bail by the High Court under section 22 of the Criminal Justice Act 1967.

114. Justices to whom application has been made to state a case for the opinion of the High Court on any proceeding of a magistrates' court shall not be required to state the case until the applicant has entered into a recognisance, with or without sureties, before the magistrates' court, conditioned to prosecute the appeal without delay and to submit to the judgment of the High Court and pay such costs as that court may award; and (except in any criminal matter) a justices' clerk shall not be required to deliver the case to the applicant until the applicant has paid him the fees payable for the case and for the recognisances to the designated officer for the court.

Appeal from the magistrates' court by way of case stated is provided for in the MCA 1980,   **D29.18** s. 111(1), and the procedure is governed by ss. 111 to 114 of that Act, part 64 of the CrimPR (see Supplement, R-480 *et seq.*), and the Civil Procedure Rules, part 52. The appeal is to a Divisional Court of the Queen's Bench Division of the High Court. The essence of the procedure is an appeal on a point of law which is identified in a document known as the 'case'. The case is initially drafted by the justices' clerk in conjunction with the bench whose decision is being appealed.

Features of the 'case stated' process which emerge from s. 111 include:

(a) The remedy is available to both the prosecution and defence.

(b) The remedy operates only in relation to an error of law or a decision taken in excess of jurisdiction. A decision as to a question of fact will ordinarily not give rise to an appeal by way of case stated but may do so if the finding of fact is alleged to be such that no reasonable bench could have properly reached that factual conclusion on the evidence (*Bracegirdle v Oxley* [1947] KB 349; *Braintree District Council v Thompson* [2005] EWCA Civ 178). In *Oladimeji v DPP* [2006] EWHC 1199 (Admin), the court stated that any defendant who believes that the justices should not have arrived at a finding for which there was evidence because, for example, it was against the weight of the evidence, has his remedy in an appeal to the Crown Court and not to the High Court. Under s. 111(4), any appellant who employs the case stated procedure forfeits his right to appeal to the Crown Court. In *K v CPS* [2013] EWHC 1678 (Admin) the Divisional Court observed that questions framed by a District Judge such as 'Was I right to assert that criminal proceedings are about a search for the truth?' should never form part of a case stated as they are not the proper subject of s. 111.

(c) The remedy is available only after the final determination of proceedings in the magistrates' court. If trial proceedings are adjourned the procedure cannot be employed during the period of adjournment (*Streames v Copping* [1985] QB 920).

(d) The remedy is available in respect of errors made in relation to sentence as well as conviction. Such appeals have often been successfully established by the prosecution where the court has wrongly held that there were 'special reasons' for not disqualifying a driver (see, e.g., *Haime v Walklett* [1983] RTR 512). On a defendant's part, he may use the case stated procedure if the bench has passed a sentence which is so far beyond the usual level of sentence for such an offence that it is 'harsh and oppressive' (*Tucker v DPP* [1992] 4 All ER 901).

Procedure on Appeal by way of Case Stated

D29.19 By virtue of the MCA 1980, s. 111(2) and (3), an application to state a case must be made within 21 days of the 'day on which the court sentences or otherwise deals with the offender'. The CrimPR, part 64 (see Supplement, **R-480**), provides a more uniform procedure for an application to state a case whether it be from the magistrates' court or from the Crown Court under the Senior Courts Act 1981, s. 28 (see **D29.37**). Rule 64.2 governs the initial application for the court to state a case for the opinion of the High Court. The application must made be in writing no more than 21 days after the decision sought to be appealed. The only substantial change effected by the revision of part 64 in the practice to be adopted in magistrates' courts is that, by virtue of r. 64.2(1)(b), notice must now be given to the other parties as well as the court officer of the intention to apply to state a case. The other parties may then make representations. Notice to the other parties as well as the court officer was always previously required when applying to the Crown Court to state a case. Rule 64.2(2) requires that the application must specify the decision in issue, as well as the proposed question(s) of law or jurisdiction on which the opinion of the High Court will be sought. It must also indicate the proposed grounds of appeal and include any application for bail pending appeal and the suspension of any disqualification pending appeal (where such suspension can be ordered). Under r. 64.2(3), any party wishing to make representations on the application must serve them on the court officer and any other parties within 14 days of service of the application for a case to be stated. The court may determine the application without a hearing (r. 64.2(4)).

The bench may refuse to state a case on the basis that it is frivolous. Frivolous, in this context, has been defined as 'futile, misconceived, hopeless or academic' and it should be rare that the magistrates' court reach such a conclusion (*Mildenhall Magistrates' Court, ex parte Forest Heath District Council* (1997) 161 JP 401). If the court refuses to state a case, it must serve notice of the decision on each party. If the applicant asks for written reasons, those written reasons must be served on each party no more than 21 days after the request (CrimPR, r. 64.2(5)).

The applicant may challenge the decision to refuse to state a case by way of judicial review. Upon the applicant doing so, the Divisional Court may quash the decision to refuse to state a case and decide to proceed to a substantive hearing of the case stated application, using the affidavit evidence provided by the parties as the 'case stated'. Such procedure has the advantage that the Divisional Court does not have to wait for the case to be returned to the magistrates' court for a case to be stated before quashing a conviction (*Reigate Justices, ex parte Counsell* (1983) 148 JP 193; *Ealing Justices, ex parte Woodman* [1994] Crim LR 372). In *Blackfriars Crown Court, ex parte Sunworld Ltd* [2000] 2 All ER 837, the Divisional Court said that if the court below has given a reasoned judgment which contains all the necessary findings of fact and identifies the points of law in question in its refusal to state a case, the single judge should grant permission for judicial review if it considers the point to be arguable. In that way, the need for a case to be stated is obviated.

Under s. 114 of the MCA 1980, if a magistrates' court does state a case, it may require an applicant to enter into a recognizance that he will prosecute the appeal without delay and pay any costs ultimately awarded against him by the High Court.

Preparation of Case Stated   If the court decides to state a case then, unless a magistrates' court **D29.20** directs otherwise or the court includes a District Judge, a justices' legal adviser must give the court legal advice and, if the court so requires, assist it by preparing and amending a draft case (CrimPR, r. 64.4). Rule 64.3(4) (see Supplement, **R-482**), provides that the draft case must specify the decision in issue as well as the question(s) of law or jurisdiction on which the opinion of the High Court will be sought. It must also include a succinct summary of the nature and history of the proceedings, the court's relevant findings of fact and the relevant contentions of the parties. If a question to be asked of the High Court is whether there was sufficient evidence on which the court reasonably could reach a finding of fact, the draft case must specify the relevant finding of fact and include a summary of the evidence on which the court reached that finding. The draft case must not include any further account of the evidence received by the court (r. 64.3(5)).

Service and Representations   The CrimPR, r. 64.3(2) requires the court officer to serve notice **D29.21** of a decision to state a case on each party as well as notice of any recognizance ordered by the court. That notice having been given then, unless the court directs otherwise, the court officer must serve a draft case on each party no more than 21 days after the court's decision to state a case (r. 64.3(3)). Any party wishing to make representations about the content of the draft case, or proposing a revised draft, must serve its representations or revised draft on each party and the court officer no more than 21 days after the service of the draft case. As with the drafting of a case, the court may require the justices' legal adviser to amend and complete the case (r. 64.4(2)). By virtue of r. 64.3(7), the court must state the case not more than 21 days after the time for service of representations has expired. The case stated must identify the court that stated it and the court office for that court (r. 64.3(8)). The court officer must serve the case stated on each party (r. 64.3(9)). A failure to comply with the time-limits set out for the various participants is not necessarily fatal to an application. Rule 64.5 provides that the court may extend a time-limit even after it has expired. Any party seeking such an extension must make an application when serving either the application or representations for which the extension is needed and explain the delay. Within ten days of receiving the case, under para. 18.4 of the *Civil Procedure Rules Part 52 Practice Direction*, the applicant or his legal representative must lodge it at the Administrative Court Office. Paragraph 18.6 requires the applicant to serve the appellant's notice and accompanying documents on the respondents within four days of their being lodged at the Divisional Court. The time for lodging the case may be extended by the Divisional Court, but without such an extension the claim may be struck out if the applicant fails to lodge within ten days.

Whilst the time-limits applying after an application for the magistrates to state a case has been made may be extended (or shortened), the initial 21-day time-limit within which an application must be made cannot be varied as it is prescribed by statute. If the application arrives late when sent by post, the 21-day time-limit is met if the application would have arrived on time in the normal course of events (*P and M Supplies (Essex) Ltd v Hackney London Borough Council* (1990) 154 JP 814).

Amendment of Case   Where there is a difference between an earlier draft of the case and the **D29.22** final version, the Divisional Court will act on the final version (*Thomas* [1990] Crim LR 269). On an appeal by way of case stated, the court is confined to the facts set out in the case. Thus if any party wishes to add any evidential matter to the case, he should seek to have the case amended either by agreement with the other party and the lower court or by application to the Divisional Court under the Senior Courts Act 1981, s. 28A(2) (*Skipaway Ltd v Environment Agency* [2006] EWHC 983 (Admin)).

Bail Pending Appeal

D29.23 An appellant by way of case stated who has been sentenced to a term of immediate custody may be granted bail pending appeal by the magistrates' court under the MCA 1980, s. 113. If granted bail, he must surrender to the magistrates' court no later than ten days after the final determination of the appeal. The exact date on which he must surrender will be fixed by the magistrates' court after the appeal. If refused bail, he may apply to a judge in chambers in the High Court under the CJA 1967, s. 22. The procedure for an application for bail to the High Court in such circumstances is set out in the Rules of the Supreme Court, ord. 79, r. 9.

Determination by Divisional Court of an Appeal by way of Case Stated

D29.24 The Divisional Court which hears an application by way of case stated will be comprised of at least two judges, and often three. If a two-judge court cannot agree, the appeal is unsuccessful (see the *obiter* remarks of Scrutton LJ in *Flannagan v Shaw* [1920] 3 KB 96 at p. 107). No evidence is called at the hearing as all evidence which needs to be referred to will be contained in the stated case (see **D29.17**). Instead the appeal is conducted by way of submissions from the parties. If the facts contained within the case give rise to a point of law which was not argued before the magistrates but would have provided the defendant with a defence, the court may consider the point provided no further evidence is necessary (*Whitehead v Haines* [1965] 1 QB 200).

Under s. 28A(3) of the Senior Courts Act 1981, the court may 'reverse, affirm or amend' the decision of the magistrates' court, or remit the case with its opinion, or make any other order (including an order as to costs) as it sees fit. Thus the Divisional Court may quash an acquittal with a direction that the magistrates' court convicts and sentences. Alternatively, the court may simply substitute a conviction for the previous acquittal and proceed to sentence. Similarly, if the appeal concerns sentence only, the court may substitute the appropriate sentence.

An appellant may abandon an appeal by way of case stated without leave (*Collet v Bromsgrove District Council* (1996) 160 JP 593).

The Divisional Court is entitled to order a retrial before the same bench or a different bench where a fair trial is still possible (*Griffith v Jenkins* [1992] 2 AC 76).

APPLICATION FOR JUDICIAL REVIEW

Prerogative Orders Generally

D29.25 The High Court polices the decision-making of inferior public bodies by way of judicial review. Consequently, decisions of the magistrates' court and some of those of the Crown Court (those which are not concerned with matters relating to trial on indictment) are susceptible to review. The High Court does so by means of prerogative orders, foremost of which are quashing orders, mandatory orders and prohibiting orders.

The application for judicial review is dealt with by a Divisional Court of the Queen's Bench Division of the High Court.

The granting of prerogative orders is discretionary and the Divisional Court will sometimes withhold relief despite it being open to the court to grant it where fairness and the due administration of justice demand it. Undue delay on behalf of the applicant for judicial review may sometimes result in the withholding of relief. In *Neath and Port Talbot Justices, ex parte DPP* [2000] 1 WLR 1376, the Divisional Court identified the principal factors to be taken into account in considering whether delay should lead to a refusal of relief. They are:

(a) the seriousness of the offence;
(b) the nature of the evidence in the case (and in particular the extent to which the quality of the evidence would be affected by delay);
(c) the extent of any contribution by the defendant to the error of the magistrates' court;
(d) the extent of any contribution by the defendant to any delay in the review process;
(e) the extent to which the complainant would be justifiably aggrieved by the abandonment of the proceedings;
(f) the extent to which the defendant would be justifiably aggrieved by the continuation of the proceedings.

D29.26 Rule 54.5(1) of the Civil Procedure Rules provides that a claim form must be filed promptly and, in any event, not later than three months after the grounds to make the claim first arose. But a judicial review claim will not necessarily be regarded as being in time merely because it is made within a three-month period. Instead, the claim form must be lodged promptly, and applications for judicial review have been rejected as being out of time where delay has occurred within the three-month period (see, e.g., *Independent Television Commission, ex parte TV NI Ltd* (1991) *The Times*, 30 December 1991).

The Divisional Court has also refused relief when the defendant had an appeal to the Crown Court available to him (*Peterborough Justices, ex parte Dowler* [1996] 2 Cr App R 561). But in *Hereford Magistrates' Court, ex parte Rowlands* [1998] QB 110, Lord Bingham CJ emphasised the importance of the supervisory jurisdiction of the High Court in ensuring continued high standards in magistrates' courts, and concluded that the existence of a right to appeal to the Crown Court, particularly if unexercised, should not ordinarily preclude permission for judicial review, nor substantive relief in a proper case.

D29.27 The principal grounds upon which judicial review may be sought are:

(a) error of law on the face of the record — i.e. an error disclosed by the court records;
(b) excess of jurisdiction;
(c) breach of natural justice.

The concept of breach of natural justice has frequently been litigated and has been widely drawn. It has been held to include:

(i) failing to give the accused adequate time to prepare a defence (*Thames Magistrates' Court, ex parte Polemis* [1974] 2 All ER 1219);
(ii) failing to grant an adjournment to allow for the attendance of a witness (*Bracknell Justices, ex parte Hughes* [1990] Crim LR 266);
(iii) the prosecution failing to call or disclose the statement of a witness who might assist the defence (*Leyland Justices, ex parte Hawthorn* [1979] QB 283);
(iv) the prosecution failing to disclose the previous convictions of prosecution witnesses (*Knightsbridge Crown Court, ex parte Goonatilleke* [1986] QB 1);
(v) making an order as to costs against a defendant without inquiring as to his means (*Newham Justices, ex parte Samuels* [1991] COD 412).

D29.28 The proceedings in the magistrates' court must ordinarily be concluded before any application for judicial review. Interlocutory decisions by the magistrates' court are not generally amenable to review (*Greater Manchester Justices, ex parte Aldi GmbH & Co KG* [1995] RTR 207), but it is possible to review a decision as to whether proceedings should commence (*R (Hoar-Stevens) v Richmond-upon-Thames Magistrates* [2004] Crim LR 474; *Rochford Justices, ex parte Buck* (1979) 68 Cr App R 114).

D

Whilst it is possible to challenge a sentence by way of judicial review, it is not usually appropriate and the defendant should seek his remedy through appeal to the Crown Court unless there are clear and substantial grounds for proceeding by way of review (*Allen v West Yorkshire Probation Service* (2001) 165 JP 313; *Tucker v DPP* [1992] 4 All ER 901). Both of these cases were appeals by way of case stated but the court made it clear that judicial review was also inappropriate.

Quashing Orders

D29.29   Quashing orders are used to nullify decisions and orders made by the magistrates' court, such as decisions to commit for sentence and convictions. Its use in respect of acquittals is more limited than in the case stated procedure because of the double jeopardy principle. Even if the prosecution are prejudiced to the extent that, had the defence had been similarly prejudiced it would have required the quashing of the conviction, review will still not be available. That principle was reaffirmed by the House of Lords in *Dorking Justices, ex parte Harrington* [1984] AC 743, but an important exception to the rule was established. In simple terms, the rule will not apply where the magistrates acquit where they have no jurisdiction to do so. If that occurs, the acquittal is a nullity and a quashing order may be made. Such a situation may come about when the magistrates acquit in respect of an indictable-only offence (*West* [1964] 1 QB 15) or a defendant is acquitted of an either-way offence when the correct mode of trial procedures have not been followed (*Cardiff Magistrates' Court, ex parte Cardiff City Council* (1987) *The Times,* 24 February 1987), or the magistrates' court, in the absence of good reason, acquits without listening to any of the prosecution witnesses available at court (*Hendon Justices, ex parte DPP* [1994] QB 167).

D29.30   **Excess of Jurisdiction**   When a magistrates' court acts in excess of jurisdiction, the Divisional Court may issue a quashing order. In *Kent Justices, ex parte Machin* [1952] 2 QB 355, a conviction was quashed when magistrates failed to explain to a defendant the possibility that he could be committed for sentence before he consented to summary trial.

Judicial review is rarely the most appropriate means of challenge to a sentence imposed by the magistrates but it can in very limited circumstances be used to challenge a sentence passed in excess of jurisdiction. In *St Albans Crown Court, ex parte Cinnamond* [1981] QB 480, the Divisional Court extended the concept of excess of jurisdiction to include a sentence that was so harsh that no reasonable tribunal, properly understanding its powers, could have passed it. Not surprisingly, the courts have repeatedly sought to confine the applicability of *Ex parte Cinnamond* to very limited circumstances. In *Croydon Crown Court, ex parte Miller* (1986) 85 Cr App R 152, it was said that the sentence would have to appear in all the circumstances to be, by any acceptable standard, truly astonishing. Whilst in *Truro Crown Court, ex parte Adair* [1997] COD 296, Lord Bingham CJ questioned whether the sentence needed to be truly astonishing but asserted that it needed to fall clearly outside the broad area of the lower court's sentencing discretion.

D29.31   **Breach of Rules of Natural Justice**   A number of decisions of magistrates' courts have been quashed where a magistrate or clerk has an interest of either a pecuniary or non-pecuniary nature such as to give rise to a reasonable suspicion of bias. In addition, procedural irregularities have often led to the quashing of decisions on the grounds of breach of natural justice (see **D29.25**).

D29.32   **Error of Law**   An error of law made by a magistrates' court is amenable to review. As an example, in *Southampton Justices, ex parte Green* [1976] QB 11, the Court of Appeal quashed an order made by the magistrates that G should forfeit the surety provided as the decision-making process was wrong in law. So far as the exercise of discretion on questions of law is concerned, the court will apply the test in *Associated Provincial Picture Houses Ltd v Wednesbury Corporation* [1948] 1 KB 223 (*Re Proulx* [2001] 1 All ER 57).

Mandatory Orders

A mandatory order is issued to compel a magistrates' court to comply with its obligations and usually flows from an order quashing the original decision. One may be issued where the magistrates' court has wrongly refused jurisdiction (*Rochford Justices, ex parte Buck* (1978) 68 Cr App R 114; *Wells Street Stipendiary Magistrate, ex parte Seillon* [1978] 3 All ER 257). In matters of discretion, if the magistrates' court overlooked the fact that it had a discretionary power, or applied the wrong principles in deciding whether or not to exercise it, the Divisional Court will issue a mandatory order requiring the court to consider or reconsider the matter, applying the correct principles as stated by the High Court (*Highgate Justices, ex parte Lewis* [1977] Crim LR 611). The court will not be required to exercise the power in a particular way unless it is clear that that would be the only conclusion to which a reasonable tribunal directing itself properly could come.

D29.33

Prohibiting Orders

A prohibiting order prevents a magistrates' court from taking a particular course of action which would be in excess of its jurisdiction (*Hatfield Justices, ex parte Castle* [1981] 3 All ER 509).

D29.34

Procedure on Application for Judicial Review

The procedure to be followed on an application for judicial review is governed by the Senior Courts Act 1981, s. 31, along with part 54 of the Civil Procedure Rules and the *Part 54 Practice Direction*. The Judicial Review Pre-Action Protocol usually requires that a claimant for judicial review write to the proposed defendant explaining the basis of the challenge. Such a letter gives the decision-maker an opportunity to reverse the decision before proceedings are started. But a decision by a court will normally be a final decision and so the court will not be able to reverse that decision as it will often be *functus officio*. The Protocol recognises that in such circumstances a letter before claim is not necessary. If an interim decision of a court is to be challenged, the court will not be *functus officio* and the court should be put on notice that an application for judicial review will be made. The claimant should then apply for an adjournment in order to bring the judicial review proceedings (*Streames v Copping* [1985] QB 920). If the application for an adjournment is refused, the Administrative Court may stay the magistrates' court proceedings as interim relief under para. 6.4 of the Pre-Action Protocol.

D29.35

Any claimant for judicial review requires permission to pursue the claim. The issue of permission is usually resolved on the papers by the single judge. If permission is granted, the matter proceeds to a substantive hearing.

(a) The first stage of the process is to submit a claim form. As well as the matters that normally have to appear in a claim form (see the Civil Procedure Rules, r. 8.2), r. 54.6 provides that the claimant has to identify interested parties and must state the remedy sought. The claim form has to be accompanied by the documents required by the *Part 54 Practice Direction* which supplements part 54. Paragraph 5.6 of the *Practice Direction* provides that the claim form must include or be accompanied by a detailed statement of the claimant's grounds for bringing the claim for judicial review, a statement of the facts relied upon, and a time estimate for the hearing. The statement of facts and the grounds to be relied on are usually drafted by counsel if the claimant is legally represented. The claim form must also be accompanied by any written evidence in support of the claim (or in support of any application to extend time), a copy of any order that the claimant seeks to have quashed, an approved copy of the lower court's reasons for reaching the decision under challenge, copies of any documents on which the claimant proposes to rely, copies of any relevant statutory material, and a list of essential documents for reading in advance by the court (with page references to the passages relied on) (para. 5.7). The prosecution must always be named as an interested party where the claim is for judicial review of a decision of a magistrates' court or the Crown Court (para. 5.2). Not more than 21 days after the service of the claim form the defendant must file an acknowledgement of service. The acknowledgement

D

Part D Procedure

of service must be served on the claimant, and on any other person named in the claim form, not later than seven days after it is filed. If the person serving it intends to contest the claim, the acknowledgement of service must set out a summary of the grounds for contesting the claim, known as 'summary grounds of resistance', and must state the name and address of anyone whom the person filing it considers to be an interested party.

(b) The court will generally consider the question of permission without a hearing (para. 8.4) Where there is a hearing, neither the defendant nor any other interested party need attend the hearing unless the court directs otherwise (para. 8.5). The court will not usually make an order for costs where the defendant or any interested party does attend a hearing (para. 8.6). The single judge will grant permission if the claimant's application for judicial review discloses an arguable case. Rule 54.12 provides that, if the court (without a hearing) refuses permission to proceed or gives permission that is subject to conditions or on certain grounds only, the court will serve its reasons for making the order along with the order itself. Under r. 54.12, 'the claimant may not appeal but may request the decision to be reconsidered at a hearing' (and must file a request for such a hearing within seven days of the service of the court's reasons for the decision). The renewed application will be before a Divisional Court in a criminal cause or matter. Neither the defendant, nor anyone else served with the claim form, may apply to set aside an order giving the claimant permission to proceed (r. 54.13).

(c) Once permission has been granted, the defendant (and anyone else served with the claim form who wishes to contest the claim or support it on additional grounds) must serve detailed grounds for resisting the claim (or supporting it on additional grounds), and any written evidence, within 35 days after the service of the order granting permission.

(d) The court may decide the claim for judicial review without a hearing where all the parties agree (r. 54.18). In all other circumstances, the claimant must file and serve a skeleton argument not less than 21 working days before the date of the hearing of the judicial review claim (para. 15.1 of the *Practice Direction*). Under para. 15.2, the defendant (and any other party wishing to make representations at the hearing) must file and serve a skeleton argument not less than 14 working days before the date of the hearing. The skeleton arguments must contain a list of issues, a list of the legal points to be taken (together with any relevant authorities), a chronology of events, a list of essential reading by the court in advance of the hearing and a list of persons referred to.

(e) The claimant must have the court's permission if he is to rely on grounds other than those for which the court gave permission to proceed (r. 54.15). The claimant must give notice no later than seven clear days before the hearing to any person served with the claim form if he intends to rely on additional grounds at the hearing of the claim for judicial review.

(f) The usual procedure followed at the hearing is one of legal argument supported by affidavits or witness statements. However, it is possible for oral evidence to be called if necessary.

Bail Pending Judicial Review

D29.36   In contrast to the position in respect of appeals by way of case stated, the magistrates' court has no power to grant bail pending an application for judicial review. Bail may be secured through an application to a judge in chambers under s. 37(1)(d) of the CJA 1948.

ROUTES TO CHALLENGE DECISIONS OF THE CROWN COURT ACTING IN ITS APPELLATE CAPACITY

Appeal by way of Case Stated

D29.37   Senior Courts Act 1981, s. 28

(1) Subject to subsection (2), any order, judgment or other decision of the Crown Court may be questioned by any party to the proceedings, on the ground that it is wrong in law or is in excess

of jurisdiction, by applying to the Crown Court to have a case stated by that court for the opinion of the High Court.

(2) Subsection (1) shall not apply to—

    (a) a judgment or other decision of the Crown Court relating to trial on indictment; or

    (b) any decision of that court under the Local Government (Miscellaneous Provisions) Act 1982 which, by any provision of any of those Acts, is to be final.

(3) Subject to the provisions of this Act and to rules of court, the High Court shall, in accordance with section 19(2), have jurisdiction to hear and determine—

    (a) any application, or any appeal (whether by way of case stated or otherwise), which it has power to hear and determine under or by virtue of this or any other Act; and

    (b) all such other appeals as it had jurisdiction to hear and determine immediately before the commencement of this Act.

(4) In subsection (2)(a) the reference to a decision of the Crown Court relating to trial on indictment does not include a decision relating to a requirement to make a payment under regulations under section 23 or 24 of the Legal Aid, Sentencing and Punishment of Offenders Act 2012.

D29.38 In common with applications by way of case stated from the magistrates' court, an application to appeal by way of case stated from the Crown Court may be made in respect of an error of law or where it is alleged that the Crown Court acted in excess of jurisdiction. There can be no challenge on the basis that a decision is against the weight of the evidence. Similarly, as with appeals by way of case stated from the magistrates' court, the proceedings in the Crown Court must have been finally decided before the case stated procedure may be employed (*Loade v DPP* [1990] 1 QB 1052). By virtue of s. 28(1)(a), no appeal by way of case stated is possible in respect of matters relating to trial on indictment (see **D29.40** for the meaning of 'relating to trial on indictment'). The means of challenge is plainly available in respect of any decision of the Crown Court relating to an appeal against conviction or sentence from the magistrates' court.

The procedure to be followed upon an application to the Crown Court to state a case is governed by the CrimPR, part 64 (see Supplement, **R-480**). Rule 64.2 governs the initial application for the court to state a case for the opinion of the High Court. The application must be made in writing no more than 21 days after the decision sought to be appealed and must be served on each party and the court officer. In contrast to the position when applying to the magistrates' court to state a case (see **D29.21**), an extension to the 21 days allowed for the application may be made at the time of the application (r. 64.2(2)(d)(i)). In common with the procedure in the magistrates' court, r. 64.2(2) requires that the application must specify the decision in issue as well as the proposed question(s) of law or jurisdiction on which the opinion of the High Court will be sought. It must also indicate the proposed grounds of appeal and include any application for bail pending appeal and the suspension of any disqualification pending appeal (where such suspension can be ordered). Under r. 64.2(3), a party wishing to make representations on the application must serve them on the court officer and any other parties within 14 days of service of the application for a case to be stated. The court may determine the application without a hearing (r. 64.2(4)). If the court refuses to state a case, it must serve notice of the decision on each party. If the applicant asks for written reasons, those written reasons must be served on each party no more than 21 days after the request (r. 64.2(5)).

D29.39 If the court decides to state a case then r. 64.3(2) requires the court officer to serve notice of that decision on each party as well as notice of any recognizance ordered by the court. In contrast to the position in the magistrates' court, the applicant must then serve a draft case on each party and the court officer no more than 21 days after the court's decision to state a case (r. 64.3(3)). The draft case must specify the decision in issue as well as the question(s) of law or jurisdiction on which the opinion of the High Court will be sought. It must also include a succinct summary of the nature and history of the proceedings, the court's relevant findings of fact and the relevant contentions of the parties (r. 64.3(4)). Any party wishing to make representations about the content of the draft case, or proposing a revised draft, must serve its representations or revised draft on each party and the court officer no more than 21 days after the service of the draft case.

By virtue of r. 64.3(7), the court must state the case no more than 21 days after the time for service of representations has expired. The court officer must serve the case stated on each party (r. 64.3(9)). Time-limits may be shortened or extended in accordance with r. 64.5.

Under s. 81(1)(d) of the Senior Courts Act 1981, bail pending appeal by way of case stated from the Crown Court may be granted by a judge in chambers.

Application for Judicial Review

D29.40   By virtue of s. 29(3) of the Senior Courts Act 1981, it is possible to challenge a decision of the Crown Court by way of judicial review provided that that decision does not concern a matter relating to trial on indictment. In *Re Smalley* [1985] AC 622, the House of Lords held that the phrase 'relating to trial on indictment' covered all decisions relating to the conduct of the trial. It has thus been held that the decision to stay any part of an indictment as an abuse of process is a matter relating to trial on indictment (*Ashton* [1994] AC 9), as is an order that counts should lie on the file in the usual way (*Central Criminal Court, ex parte Raymond* [1986] 2 All ER 379), a decision as to the order in which indictments are tried (*Southwark Crown Court, ex parte Ward* [1996] Crim LR 123) and decisions as to disclosure (*Chester Crown Court, ex parte Cheshire County Council* [1996] Crim LR 336). It has also been held that the decision to hold a trial on the issue of fitness to plead is a matter relating to trial on indictment (*Bradford Crown Court, ex parte Bottomley* [1994] Crim LR 753) as is the imposition of a mandatory life sentence (*R (Lichniak) v Secretary of State for the Home Department* [2002] QB 296).

Matters which do not relate to trial on indictment include forfeiture of a surety (*Re Smalley*), forfeiture of property used in the course of an offence belonging to a third party (*Maidstone Crown Court, ex parte Gill* [1986] 1 All ER 129), binding over of an acquitted accused (*Inner London Crown Court, ex parte Benjamin* (1986) 85 Cr App R 265) and restrictions on the publication of the identity of a convicted youth (*Leicester Crown Court, ex parte S (A Minor)* [1993] 2 All ER 659).

Under s. 81(1)(e) of the 1981 Act, bail may be granted pending judicial review of a decision of the Crown Court.

If a defendant convicted in the magistrates' court appeals to the Crown Court, any further appeal to the High Court on a point of law should be by way of case stated and not judicial review (*Gloucester Crown Court, ex parte Chester* [1998] COD 365).

NO POWER OF JUDICIAL REVIEW OVER DECISIONS OF THE HIGH COURT

D29.41   There is no power available to the High Court to judicially review the decisions of the High Court. In that vein, the decision of a judge of the High Court on an application for leave to prefer a voluntary bill of indictment is not amenable to judicial review (*Manchester Crown Court, ex parte Williams* (1990) 154 JP 589).

THE CHOICE BETWEEN JUDICIAL REVIEW AND CASE STATED

D29.42   Both judicial review and the case stated procedure set aside the decision of the court below, and a choice must be made as to which route to pursue. In *R (P) v Liverpool City Magistrates* (2006) 170 JP 453, Collins J stated:

(a)   the normal route for an appeal against a decision of justices where it is alleged there has been an error of law is by way of case stated;

(b) it would be wrong to seek judicial review where case stated was appropriate, merely in order to avoid the more stringent time-limit;

(c) however, judicial review is more appropriate where there is an issue of fact to be raised and decided which the justices did not decide themselves;

(d) judicial review may also be appropriate where it is alleged that there has been unfairness or bias in the conduct of the case by the justices but, where it is alleged that there has been a misdirection or an error of law, case stated is the appropriate remedy.

In *North Essex Justices, ex parte Lloyd* [2001] 2 Cr App R (S) 86, the Divisional Court said that judicial review should be pursued where the inferior court has acted in excess of jurisdiction.

Judicial review is the only remedy available where the defence wish to challenge a committal for trial or sentence, as the case stated procedure is not available where there has not been a final determination of the case.

In *Essen v DPP* [2005] EWHC 1077 (Admin), Sedley LJ said that the authorities restricting **D29.43** appeal by way of case stated to those where there has been a final determination 'could usefully be revisited'. This was borne partly out of a concern that an appellant might be left without a remedy. If the interlocutory decision had been made more than 21 days before the final determination of the case, the case stated procedure would not be available. In addition, on one view, the court lacks jurisdiction to undertake judicial review of interlocutory decisions of justices (a view based on *Rochford Justices, ex parte Buck* (1979) 68 Cr App R 114). But it is submitted that the rule is not without exception. In *R (Watson) v Dartford Magistrates' Court* [2005] EWHC 905 (Admin), it was held that the normal rule is that the High Court should not interfere with interlocutory rulings made by justices; but if the prosecution would say at the end of the trial that it was too late for the defendant to complain, there is no fetter on the High Court intervening.

APPEAL FROM THE DIVISIONAL COURT

Any appeal from the High Court in a criminal cause or matter, either in relation to an appeal by **D29.44** way of case stated or a judicial review, is direct to the Supreme Court (see **D30.5**).

Section D30   Appeals to the Supreme Court and the Role of the European Court of Justice and the European Court of Human Rights

APPEAL TO THE SUPREME COURT

D30.1   From 1 October 2009, the Supreme Court, established under the Constitutional Reform Act 2005, s. 23, replaced the House of Lords as the highest court of the UK.

The Supreme Court Rules (SI 2009 No. 1603) govern practice and procedure.

From the Court of Appeal (Criminal Division)

D30.2   Criminal Appeal Act 1968, ss. 33 and 34

   33.—(1) An appeal lies to the Supreme Court, at the instance of the defendant or the prosecutor, from any decision of the Court of Appeal on an appeal to that court under part I of this Act or part 9 of the Criminal Justice Act 2003 or section 9 (preparatory hearings) of the Criminal Justice Act 1987 or section 35 of the Criminal Procedure and Investigations Act 1996 or section 47 of the Criminal Justice Act 2003.

   (1A) [Repealed by the SCA 2007, sch. 8, para. 144.]

   (1B) An appeal lies to the Supreme Court, at the instance of the acquitted person or the prosecutor, from any decision of the Court of Appeal on an application under section 76(1) or (2) of the Criminal Justice Act 2003 (retrial for serious offences).

   (2) The appeal lies only with the leave of the Court of Appeal or the Supreme Court; and leave shall not be granted unless it is certified by the Court of Appeal that a point of law of general public importance is involved in the decision and it appears to the Court of Appeal or the Supreme Court (as the case may be) that the point is one which ought to be considered by the Supreme Court.

   (3) Except as provided by this part of this Act and section 13 of the Administration of Justice Act 1960 (appeal in cases of contempt of court), no appeal shall lie from any decision of the criminal division of the Court of Appeal.

   (4) In relation to an appeal under subsection (1B), references in this Part to a defendant are references to the acquitted person.

   34.—(1) An application to the Court of Appeal for leave to appeal to the Supreme Court shall be made within the period of 28 days beginning with the relevant date; and an application to the Supreme Court for leave shall be made within the period of 28 days beginning with the date on which the application for leave is refused by the Court of Appeal.

   (1A)   In subsection (1), 'the relevant date' means—

   (a) the date of the Court of Appeal's decision, or

   (b) if later, the date on which the Court gives reasons for its decision.

   (2) The Supreme Court or the Court of Appeal may, upon application made at any time by the defendant or, in the case of an appeal under section 33(1B), by the prosecutor, extend the time within which an application may be made by him to the Supreme Court or the Court of Appeal under subsection (1) above.

   (3) An appeal to the Supreme Court shall be treated as pending until any application for leave to appeal is disposed of and, if leave to appeal is granted, until the appeal is disposed of; and for purposes of this part of this Act an application for leave to appeal shall be treated as disposed of at the expiration of the time within which it may be made, if it is not made within that time.

D30.3   Sections 33 and 34 of the Criminal Appeal Act 1968 allow either the prosecution or defence to appeal a decision of the Court of Appeal to the Supreme Court, but only if the Court of

Appeal or the Supreme Court itself considers that the appeal involves a point of law of general public importance which should be considered by the Supreme Court. In addition, the Court of Appeal must certify that the appeal involves a question concerning a point of law of general public importance. An application to the Court of Appeal for leave to appeal to the Supreme Court must be made by the party seeking to appeal no more than 28 days after the court gives the reasons for its decision.

Part 74 of the CrimPR (see Supplement, **R-569** *et seq.*) governs the making of an application to the Court of Appeal for permission to appeal or refer a case to the Supreme Court.

Where the Court of Appeal is of the view that the prospective appeal raises no point of law of public importance, it may decide so on the papers (*Daines* [1961] 1 All ER 290). A refusal to allow oral submissions will not amount to a violation of a person's rights under the ECHR, Article 6 (*Steele* [2007] 1 WLR 222). A refusal by the Court of Appeal to certify a question cannot be appealed. In *Dunn* [2011] 1 WLR 958, the Court of Appeal concluded that the fact that whether an appeal that has failed before it raises a point of law of public importance is decided by the Court itself does not offend either Article 6 or Article 14 of the ECHR.

If the Court of Appeal certifies a question but leave to appeal to the Supreme Court is refused, the party may apply for leave to the Supreme Court within 28 days of the refusal by the Court of Appeal. **D30.4**

If the Court of Appeal decides an appeal on one ground but leaves others undecided and the Supreme Court hears the appeal of that decision, the Supreme Court may either rule on those grounds as if it were the Court of Appeal or may remit them back to the Court of Appeal for its decision. In *Mandair* [1995] 1 AC 208, the House of Lords stated that the undecided grounds of appeal should be identified and written submissions should be made as to whether and how the House of Lords should dispose of them and the principle is equally applicable to appeals to the Supreme Court.

In *Practice Statement (House of Lords: Appearance of Counsel)* [2008] 1 WLR 1143, the House of Lords reminded the Bar that counsel instructed to appear before the highest court in the land are expected to be present at and throughout the hearing. That stricture no doubt continues to apply.

From a Divisional Court of the Queen's Bench Division

Section 1(1)(a) of the Administration of Justice Act 1980 provides that any appeal from a Divisional Court of the Queen's Bench Division in a criminal cause or matter is direct to the Supreme Court, leapfrogging the Court of Appeal. In a similar leave process to that operating in the Court of Appeal (see **D30.2**), the Divisional Court must certify that the appeal involves a point of law of general public importance and leave to appeal must be granted by either the Divisional Court or the Supreme Court. **D30.5**

THE COURT OF JUSTICE OF THE EUROPEAN UNION

Treaty on the Functioning of the European Union (TFEU), Article 267   D30.6

(1) The Court of Justice of the European Union shall have jurisdiction to give preliminary rulings concerning:
  (a) the interpretation of the Treaties;
  (b) the validity and interpretation of acts of the institutions, bodies, offices or agencies of the Union;
(2) Where such a question is raised before any court or tribunal of a Member State, that court or tribunal may, if it considers that a decision on the question is necessary to enable it to give judgment, request the Court to give a ruling thereon.
(3) Where any such question is raised in a case pending before a court or tribunal of a Member State against whose decisions there is no judicial remedy under national law, that court or tribunal shall bring the matter before the court.

(4) If such a question is raised in a case pending before a court or tribunal of a Member State with regard to a person in custody, the Court of Justice of the European Union shall act with the minimum of delay.

D30.7 The CJEU assumes in principle full jurisdiction to give preliminary rulings in the field of EU criminal law, with the limits to its jurisdiction set out by Article 35(2) of the EU Treaty (under the old third pillar) being abolished. This means that the avenue for UK courts to bring references to Luxembourg is now open. The only exception is Article 276 of the TFEU, according to which the Court will have 'no jurisdiction to review the validity or proportionality of operations carried out by the police or other law-enforcement services of a Member State or the exercise of the responsibilities incumbent upon Member States with regard to the maintenance of law and order and the safeguarding of internal security'. Article 267 is more fully discussed at **A9.9**.

D30.8 In *Plymouth Justices, ex parte Rogers* [1982] QB 863, it was held that a magistrates' court has the power to make a reference to the CJEU and the Divisional Court will not interfere with the exercise of the justices' discretion to make such a reference unless they act unreasonably in doing so, or misdirect themselves. Nevertheless, the Divisional Court advised that justices should exercise considerable caution before making such a reference. If a magistrates' court erred in the interpretation of community law, that could always be corrected by the higher courts. When making a reference, the form of the question to be answered is very important and the higher courts will normally be in a better position to assess the appropriateness of the question and assist in formulating it appropriately.

So far as the Crown Court is concerned, the House of Lords stated in *Henn* [1981] AC 850 (per Lord Diplock at p. 904):

> ...in a criminal trial upon indictment it can seldom be a proper exercise of the presiding judge's discretion to seek a preliminary ruling before the facts of the alleged offence have been ascertained, with the result that the proceedings will be held up for nine months or more in order that at the end of the trial he may give to the jury an accurate instruction as to the relevant law, if the evidence turns out in the event to be as was anticipated at the time the reference was made — which may not always be the case. It is generally better, as the judge himself put it, that the question be decided by him in the first instance and reviewed thereafter if necessary through the hierarchy of the national courts.

The procedure to be adopted in an application for a reference by the Crown Court is set out in the CrimPR, part 75 (see Supplement, **R-573** *et seq.*). It is supplemented by CPD X, paras. 75A.1 to 75A.7 (see Supplement, **PD-89**), which set out the relevant persons to whom the order for reference should be addressed, as well as the required contents of any backsheet to the order. In addition, the matters which need to be included within any application for the Court to apply its urgent preliminary ruling procedure are identified.

THE EUROPEAN COURT OF HUMAN RIGHTS

D30.9 An individual has the power to petition the ECtHR if he feels that his human rights under the ECHR have been violated (see **A7**).

In order that a complaint be admissible before the ECtHR, the applicant must have exhausted all domestic remedies. The applicant is not required, however, to have pursued points which have no chance of success. Thus in *V v UK* (2000) 30 EHRR 121, the Court was concerned with the case of two boys convicted of the murder of James Bulger. The Court ruled that Article 6 requires a specially adapted procedure for the trial of juveniles in the Crown Court which promotes the welfare of the young defendant, respects his right to privacy and enables him to understand and take part fully in the proceedings. The Court rejected an argument by the UK government that the complaint was inadmissible because the boys had not exhausted all domestic remedies as they had failed to argue in the domestic courts that their inability to understand and participate fully in the proceedings meant that they were in effect unfit to plead. The Court observed that the government could not point to one example where such an application had been successful.

In addition, the petition must raise an issue which is not substantially the same as one upon which the Commission or Court has already ruled and, equally, the petition cannot have been submitted to another 'procedure of international investigation or settlement'.

Under Article 35, the petition must be brought within six months of the date when the final decision is taken. That date was defined in *Greenock Ltd v UK* (1985) 42 DJR 33, as the date of a final decision taken in the exhaustion of an effective and sufficient domestic remedy, or from the date of the act or decision complained of where that act or decision finally determines the applicant's position in the domestic jurisdiction. Since the beginning of 2014, the ECHR has required strict adherence to formalities of the application process required under r. 47 of the Court's rules (see www.echr.coe.int/Documents/Rules_Court_ENG.pdf).

D30.10

The Court sits in committees of three judges, chambers of seven judges and, exceptionally, in Grand Chambers of 17 judges. The parties are required to file written evidence within certain time-limits and, if the Court considers it necessary, an oral hearing at which the applicant is represented takes place. The decision of the Court may be by way of majority. The Court can compel any State which is in breach of the ECHR to make 'just satisfaction', and if it finds that the State's laws are incompatible with the Convention, can impose a duty on the State to rectify the position.

D

Part D Procedure

Section D31 Extradition

INTRODUCTION

D31.1 Extradition involves one territory making a request to another for the surrender of a person accused or convicted of an offence to stand trial, be sentenced or serve a custodial sentence. Extradition is governed by the Extradition Act 2003.

A foreign territory can be designated as a category 1 or category 2 territory by order of the Secretary of State (ss. 1 and 69). Part 1 of the Act governs requests from a category 1 territory and part 2 governs requests from a category 2 territory. Part 3 governs requests made by the UK and is not dealt with in this section.

Part 1 Warrants

D31.2 Part 1 (ss. 1 to 68) implements the Framework Decision of the EU on the European Arrest Warrant (EAW) and the surrender procedures between Member States (2002/584/JHA). (See also **A9.13**.) It applies to requests received from a category 1 territory (currently only EU Member States and Gibraltar) and is intended to allow surrender based on the mutual recognition of arrest warrants issued by Member States (*Office of the King's Prosecutor, Brussels v Cando Armas* [2006] 2 AC 1). The EAW form is in the annex to the Framework Decision.

If questions of interpretation arise in dealing with EAWs, the Extradition Act 2003 must be read subject to the common-law presumption that it was intended to give effect to the UK's obligations under the Framework Decision, but this is subject to the language of the Act (*Assange v Swedish Prosecution Authority* [2012] 2 AC 471 at [217]). There are a number of decisions of the CJEU on its interpretation (see **A9.13**). The Act should not be read so as to import undue technicalities into the extradition process (*Dabas v High Court of Justice, Madrid* [2007] 2 AC 31).

The National Crime Agency has been designated as the authority to receive part 1 warrants which it will certify if the requirements in s. 2 are met (see **D31.13**); when the ABCPA 2014, s. 157, comes into force, the NCA must not issue a certificate in an accusation case if it is clear that a judge would find extradition to be disproportionate (as to proportionality, see **D31.33**).

Part 2 Requests

D31.3 Part 2 (ss. 69 to 141) applies to requests from category 2 territories. It simplifies the previous rules governing the admissibility of foreign documents (s. 202). Article 3 of the Extradition Act 2003 (Designation of Part 2 Territories) Order 2003 (SI 2003 No. 3334) designates certain category 2 territories so that they do not have to provide evidence to justify the issue of an arrest warrant or evidence of a case to answer.

The Secretary of State must issue a certificate under s. 70 (certifying the request has been made in the approved way) if he receives a valid request for the extradition to a category 2 territory of a person who is in the UK, unless s. 70(2) applies (s. 70(1)). Where (i) there are competing requests for extradition, (ii) the person requested is a refugee or (iii) the person requested has been granted leave to enter or remain because removal to the requesting territory would be a breach of the ECHR, Article 2 or 3, he may refuse to issue a certificate (s. 70(2)). The question of whether a request is valid is dealt with in s. 70(3)–(7) (see **D31.16**). Once the Secretary of State has issued a certificate (which must identify the Order designating the territory as a category 2 territory), he must send the request and the certificate to the appropriate judge and is not thereafter to consider whether the extradition is compatible with rights under the ECHR (s. 70(9)–(11)).

First instance extradition hearings in England and Wales will only be dealt with at Westminster Magistrates' Court by an 'appropriate judge' who is designated by the Lord Chief Justice (ss. 67 and 139). The CPS ordinarily acts on behalf of the requesting territory.

ARREST AND INITIAL HEARING

Part 1

A person wanted on a certified EAW may be arrested under s. 3. At an initial hearing the judge **D31.4** must decide if the arrested person has been given a copy of the EAW and may discharge him if this has not happened (s. 4(2) and (4)). The judge must also find as a question of fact whether the person has been brought before him as soon as practicable; if this test is failed, the person must be discharged (s. 4(3) and (5): see *Nikonovs v Governor of HM Prison Brixton* [2006] 1 All ER 927 at [21] as to the meaning of 'practicable').

Section 5 deals with provisional arrest when a EAW has not yet been issued or certified and it is rarely used in practice; it requires production before the appropriate judge within 48 hours of arrest (s. 6(2)). A certified part 1 warrant must be produced at the hearing unless an extension of a further 48 hours is granted. The provisions on discharge are similar to those for a certified EAW (ss. 6(6) and (7)).

At the hearing, the judge must decide on the balance of probabilities whether the person produced before him is the person named in the EAW (s. 7(2) and (3); see *Lumenica v Government of Albania* [2012] EWHC 3802 (Admin)). If not so satisfied, the judge must order his discharge (s. 7(4)). The judge has the same powers as when hearing a summary trial; there can be an adjournment to allow further evidence or legal advice or representation to be obtained. Delays in the grant of legal aid which are not the fault of the person produced or his legal advisers cannot be held against the requested person (*Stopyra v District of Lublin, Poland* [2013] 1 All ER 187 at [46]).

The judge's powers under s. 7(6) do not include the power under the MCA 1980, s. 142 (see **D22.70**), to re-open cases to correct mistakes (*R (Klimeto) v City of Westminster Magistrates' Court* [2013] 1 WLR 420).

Issues arising under ss. 4, 6 and 7 cannot be reopened after the initial hearing (*Stanczyk v Circuit* **D31.5** *Court in Katowice* [2010] EWHC 3651 (Admin)).

If the person is not discharged, the consent procedure is explained and consent to extradition is requested. A person may consent at any time (s. 45). Consent is irrevocable and must be given before the judge in writing (ss. 8(3)(c) and 45). Consent results in an immediate extradition order and the loss of any right of appeal and the protection of speciality (i.e. he can be dealt with for any matters on return to the requesting territory and not just those specified in the warrant). This position will alter once the ABCPA 2014, s. 163, comes into force. Once consent is given, a person should be removed within ten days but this period can be extended (s. 47; see **D31.46**).

Once consent has been dealt with, the judge will ordinarily ask if there are any issues regarding the **D31.6** validity of the warrant, the extradition offence, bars or human rights to be raised at the extradition hearing; when the ABCPA 2014, s. 157, comes into force, the judge must also inquire about proportionality (see **D31.12**). If no issues are raised, the case will proceed immediately to an uncontested extradition hearing, which is currently required to protect the requested person's speciality rights (this will not be required once the speciality protection is retained following consent: see **D31.5**).

If the case is to be contested, the hearing must be set within 21 days of the arrest (s. 8(1)(a) and (4)). It is not unusual for the extradition hearing to open immediately before adjourning to a future date. If the extradition hearing does not begin within 21 days, the person may apply to be discharged or the judge may order discharge of his own motion unless reasonable cause is shown for the delay (s. 8(7) and (8); see also *Asliturk v HM Prison Wandsworth* [2010] EWHC 1720 (Admin)). Section 8(5) allows a party to apply to the judge for the period to be extended; an application to fix a later date for the extradition hearing may be made on the day on which the hearing is set to begin.

Part 2

D31.7   Under part 2 an arrest may take place on a warrant issued by an appropriate judge (s. 71) if the Secretary of State has certified a request and sent the required documents to the judge (s. 70) or under a provisional warrant (s. 74). A person arrested under part 2 must be brought before the appropriate judge and given a copy of the warrant for his arrest as soon as practicable (ss. 72 and 74). Discharge for failing to produce the person as soon as practicable is mandatory but discharge for failure to serve the warrant is discretionary. Provisional arrest is more common under part 2 than under part 1.

The question of identity is decided at the extradition hearing. The person must be informed either of the contents of the request for extradition (s. 72(7)(a)) or that he is accused of an offence or alleged to be unlawfully at large after conviction if arrested provisionally (s. 74(7)(a)). The consent procedure is explained and consent to extradition is requested. The procedure is the same as for part 1 (see **D31.5**), except that a person who consents has his case sent to the Secretary of State (ss. 127 and 128: see **D31.40**).

D31.8   If the arrest is under a provisional warrant, the judge must fix a date by which the certified extradition request must be received, failing which the person's discharge must be ordered (s. 74(10) and (11)). Most category 2 territories have 45 days in which to send the request but territories designated by article 4 of the Extradition Act 2003 (Designation of Part 2 Territories) Order 2003 (SI 2003 No. 3334) have longer. The extradition hearing must begin within two months of the first appearance of a person arrested under s. 71 or two months from the day on which the certified extradition request is received by the judge following provisional arrest (s. 76). If the extradition hearing has not begun within the required period and no extension has been granted, the requested person can apply for discharge (ss. 75(4), 76(4) and (5)). It is common practice for the judge to open the hearing before the end of the required period and then adjourn; he has the same power to adjourn as when hearing a summary trial (see **D31.4**).

Bail

D31.9   Once the initial hearing is completed, the requested person must be remanded on bail or in custody. Normal considerations in relation to bail apply (see **D7**). There is no presumption in favour of bail for a convicted person (s. 198(5)). A person denied bail by a magistrates' court or granted bail subject to conditions may seek bail or seek to vary the conditions in the High Court (CJA 1967, s. 22(1A)). The High Court may be reluctant to allow an application unless there have been two unsuccessful applications in the magistrates' court. The CPS, on behalf of the requesting territory, may appeal a decision to grant bail to the High Court provided that it opposed the grant of bail before the magistrates (Bail (Amendment Act) 1993, s. 1(1A) and (3)).

Request for Temporary Transfer or Contact with Prosecutor

D31.10   The ABCPA 2014, s. 159 (not yet in force), inserts a new s. 21B into the 2003 Act. In part 1 accusation cases, s. 21B provides a mechanism to allow the temporary transfer of a requested person to the requesting territory or for him to speak with the prosecutor or investigator. This process requires the consent of the requested person and requesting territory.

Domestic Criminal Proceedings

If a person arrested under part 1 or part 2 is charged with an offence in the UK and the judge is aware of this before the extradition hearing begins, he must adjourn proceedings until the UK proceedings have concluded (ss. 8A, 76A and 214). Where the judge becomes aware of such a charge after the extradition hearing has begun, he must adjourn the hearing until the UK proceedings have concluded (ss. 22 and 88).   **D31.11**

If a person arrested under part 1 or part 2 is serving a sentence of imprisonment in the UK, the proceedings may be adjourned for up to six months until the person is released (ss. 8B, 23, 76B and 89). Under the ABCPA 2014, s. 161 (not in force), which inserts new ss. 36A, 36B, 118A and 118B into the 2003 Act, if the court is informed after the extradition hearing that a person has been charged with an offence or is serving a sentence in the UK then similar provisions will apply so that the court may order that extradition is not to be carried out.

THE EXTRADITION HEARING

Order of Consideration of Issues

Part 1 and part 2 hearings involve similar steps. Issues to be considered include the following: **D31.12**

- any challenge to the validity of the EAW or request (see **D31.13** and **D31.16**) — the issue of identity is also dealt with for part 2 requests (see **D31.17**);
- whether the conduct identified in the warrant or request amounts to an extradition offence or offences (see **D31.18**) and, if it does, what bars arise (see **D31.21**);
- whether extradition is compatible with the person's rights under the ECHR and, (once the ABCPA 2014, s. 157, comes into force) for part 1 accusation cases, whether it is proportionate (see **D31.33**);
- whether the requested person is entitled to an adjournment or discharge on the basis that extradition would be unjust or oppressive due to his physical or mental condition (see **D31.36**);
- whether, in a part 2 accusation case, the evidence is sufficient to require an answer by the person (a prima facie case: see **D31.32**), unless the requesting territory has been designated by the Secretary of State (see **D31.3**);
- in a conviction case, whether the person was present when convicted and, if not, whether he was deliberately absent — if he was not deliberately absent, he must be entitled to a retrial and for a part 2 request the evidence must provide a prima facie case unless the requesting territory has been designated (see **D31.31** and **D31.32**).

If any of these requirements are not met or if a bar is made out, the person will be discharged. Otherwise, at the conclusion of the extradition hearing, extradition is ordered for a part 1 case (s. 21(3); *Zubkovs v Court in Riga, Latvia* [2012] EWHC 3331 (Admin) confirms that the extradition hearing finishes when extradition is ordered) or a part 2 case is sent to the Secretary of State (s. 87(3)). At the extradition hearing the judge has the same powers as a magistrates' court hearing a summary trial, including the power to adjourn (ss. 9(1) and 77). The judge's powers under ss. 9(1) and 77(1) do not include the power under the MCA 1980, s. 142 (see **D22.70**), to re-open cases to correct mistakes (*R (Klimeto) v City of Westminster Magistrates' Court* [2013] 1 WLR 420). The requesting territory must prove that the warrant or request is valid, contains conduct which amounts to an extradition offence and that the prima facie case requirement (if applicable) and provisions relating to convictions in absence are satisfied. Unless otherwise specified, matters must be proved to the criminal standard (s. 206).

Validity of Part 1 Warrant

D31.13　A warrant which does not satisfy the requirements of s. 2 is not a valid part 1 warrant, and the judge must order the person's discharge (*Cando Armas, Lacorre v High Instance Court of Paris* [2008] EWHC 2871 (Admin)). A warrant is valid only if issued by a judicial authority. The NCA, as the designated authority, must certify that the foreign judicial authority has the function of issuing EAWs in the category 1 territory (s. 2(7) and (8); *Ministry of Justice, Republic of Lithuania v Bucnys* [2014] 2 All ER 235 at [33]).

It is for the judge to determine whether the person or body that has issued the EAW has the quality of being a 'judicial authority'; 'judicial authority' embraces courts, judges, magistrates and public prosecutors (*Bucnys* at [34]) and, in a conviction case, a Ministry of Justice could be a judicial authority if certain conditions are satisfied (at [66]). *Ziri v Head of the International Police Cooperation Division National Police Board* [2012] EWHC 3329 (Admin) considered the position of police authorities.

The contents of the warrant are to be assessed at the time the warrant is certified by the designated authority and any defects can be remedied before this time (*Dhar v National Office of the Public Prosecution Service, The Netherlands* [2012] EWHC 697 (Admin)).

A warrant must contain a statement that the person is accused of an offence and sought for prosecution or is convicted and sought for the execution or imposition of a sentence (s. 2(2), (3) and (5)).

A part 1 warrant may deal with both accusations and convictions (*Pomiechowski v District Court in Legnica, Poland* [2013] 1 WLR 2653). Part 1 warrants cannot be supplemented by further information in order to meet the requirements in s. 2(2) (*Dabas v High Court of Justice, Madrid* [2007] 2 AC 31 at [50]; *Pinnick v Court of First Instance No. 2 of La Linea de la Conception, Spain* [2013] EWHC 1034 (Admin)). A warrant which seeks the person's return for questioning and not prosecution is invalid (*Vey v Office of the Public Prosecutor of the County of Montlucon* [2006] EWHC 760 (Admin): see also **D31.22**). Whether a person is wanted for prosecution is a question of fact, requiring a purposive construction and a 'cosmopolitan' approach rather than a parochial English one (*Re Ismail* [1999] 1 AC 320). The prosecution process may allow questioning to occur after surrender or for the investigation to continue (*R (Miguel Meizoso-Gonzales) v Juzgado de Instruccion Cinco de Palma de Mallorca* [2010] EWHC 3655 (Admin)). The purpose for which extradition is requested must be clear from an examination of the EAW as a whole and only if the wording of the warrant is equivocal should the court consider other evidence as a last resort (*Asztaslos v Szekszard City Court Hungary* [2011] 1 All ER 1027).

D31.14　In an accusation case the warrant must contain sufficient particulars of the circumstances in which the offence was committed, including the time and place at which the offence was committed and the provisions of law of the requesting territory that have been contravened (s. 2(4)(c)). The level of detail regarding the underlying offences that must be provided by a conviction warrant is not necessarily the same as that required in an accusation warrant (*Sandi v Craiova Court, Romania* [2009] EWHC 3079 (Admin) at [32]). There is no need for the warrant to provide particulars of an offence which has led to the activation of a suspended sentence of imprisonment if the person is not being extradited for this offence (*Zawadzki v Regional Court in Warsaw, Poland* [2013] EWHC 433 (Admin)). A conviction warrant must contain particulars of the conviction (s. 2(6)(b)) but this need not include the date of conviction (*R (Bader) v Penal Division of the Veszprem County Court Hungary* [2011] EWHC 436 (Admin)). The level of detail that must be provided in a warrant will depend on the circumstances and complexity of the conduct alleged; a broad omnibus description, such as 'conspiracy to defraud' will not suffice (*Von der Pahlen v Government of Austria* [2006] EWHC 1672 (Admin)).

A warrant must contain particulars of the sentence that may be imposed on conviction or sentence for each offence (s. 2(4)(d) and (6)(d)) or particulars of the sentence that has been imposed if the person has been sentenced (s. 2(6)(e)). See *Taylor v Public Prosecutors Office Berlin Germany* [2012] EWHC 475 (Admin) at [15] for an illustration of a failure in this respect. If the warrant deals with more than one sentence, it may provide the aggregate sentence (*Pilecki v Circuit Court of Legnica, Poland* [2008] 4 All ER 445: see also speciality at **D31.27**). If the sentences are aggregated after the EAW is issued, this does not affect the validity of the warrant (*Zakrzewski v Regional Court in Lodz, Poland* [2013] 2 All ER 93).

The Supreme Court has stated that the validity of a part 1 warrant depends on whether it contains the particulars required by s. 2 and not whether these particulars are correct (*Zakrzewski v Regional Court in Lodz, Poland* at [8]). Therefore the validity is also unaffected if particulars which are initially correct become incorrect. However, if the particulars required by s. 2 are or have become incorrect, the court can consider whether this amounts to an abuse of process (at [11]–[13], see **D31.37**). The Court considered that the jurisdiction described in *Criminal Court at the National High Court, 1st Division v Murua* [2010] EWHC 2609 (Admin) at [58]–[59] should be more properly characterised as abuse of process rather than considering the validity of the warrant. First, this jurisdiction is exceptional and the s. 2 particulars must be wrong or incomplete in some respect which is misleading (although not necessarily intentionally). Second, the true facts required to correct the error or omissions must be clear and beyond legitimate dispute. Third, the error or omission must be material to the operation of the statutory scheme. **D31.15**

If the warrant is a valid part 1 warrant, the judge will decide whether the offence in the warrant is an extradition offence (s. 10: see **D31.18**). If so, then bars to extradition are considered (s. 11: see **D31.21**).

Part 2 Requests

Section 70 governs the validity of requests under part 2 (see **D31.3**). Section 70 requires that a request contain similar statements to those required for a part 1 warrant (see **D31.13**), i.e. that a person is accused and wanted for prosecution or convicted and sought for the imposition or service of a sentence. The request must be made by an appropriate authority or representative of that territory (s. 70(5)–(7)). **D31.16**

Part 2 imposes additional requirements for the initial stages of the extradition hearing (s. 78(2)). The judge must decide if the documents sent to him include:

(a) the request and certificate;
(b) particulars of the person whose extradition is requested;
(c) particulars of the offence specified in the request;
(d) a warrant for the arrest of an accused person; or
(e) a certificate of conviction and sentence, if already sentenced, for a person alleged to be unlawfully at large after conviction.

A discharge must be granted if the judge has not been provided with these documents or if they do not include the required information. The level of detail required in a part 2 request is the same as for a part 1 warrant (*Dudko v Government of the Russian Federation* [2010] EWHC 1125 (Admin): see **D31.14**).

If the judge is satisfied on the balance of probabilities that the person before the court is the person who is the subject of the request (s. 78(4)(a) and (5)), he goes on to consider if the offence in the request is an extradition offence (s. 78(4)(b): see **D31.18**). A part 2 request can be supplemented by further information to establish an extradition offence (*Norris v Government of the USA* [2008] 1 AC 920 at [85]). Finally, the judge must decide if the request and certificate have been served on the requested person (s. 78(4)(c)). **D31.17**

If any of these conditions is not met, s. 78(6) demands a discharge. Otherwise the bars to extradition are considered under s. 79 (see **D31.21**).

EXTRADITION OFFENCE

D31.18   An extradition offence is a criminal offence (*Director of the Serious Fraud Office v O'Brien* [2014] 2 All ER 798 at [34]) and is defined in ss. 64 and 65 for part 1 and ss. 137 and 138 for part 2; these sections will be amended by the ABCPA, s. 164, when it comes into force. There are separate but similar definitions for accusation and conviction cases. There are a number of categories of extradition offence and conduct may satisfy more than one category. The judge is not concerned with the criminal law or the ingredients of the offence in the requesting territory.

In most part 1 cases, extradition offences fall within s. 64(2) and (3) or s. 65(2) and (3).

For an offence to fall within s. 64(2) or 65(2):

(a) the conduct must have occurred within the requesting territory;
(b) no part of it can have occurred within the UK;
(c) the framework list on the EAW (which has 32 categories of offences: see *Jama v Senior Public Prosecutor Gera, Germany* [2014] 1 WLR 1843 for the approach when considering the categories) must be ticked (*Dabas v High Court of Justice, Madrid* [2007] 2 AC 31) or a separate certificate provided; and
(d) the conduct must be punishable under the law of the requesting territory with at least three years' imprisonment in an accusation case or a sentence of at least 12 months' imprisonment must have been imposed in a conviction case (this will be reduced to a minimum requirement of four months' imprisonment once the ABCPA 2014, s. 164, comes into force).

There is no equivalent category for part 2 as dual criminality is required in all circumstances.

For an offence to fall within s. 64(3) or 65(3):

(a) the conduct must have occurred within the requesting territory;
(b) the conduct must have constituted an offence if it had taken place in the UK ('the dual criminality requirement'); and
(c) it must be punishable under the law of the requesting territory with at least 12 months' imprisonment in an accusation case or a sentence of at least four months' imprisonment must have been imposed in a conviction case.

Sections 137(2) and 138(2) make similar provision for accused and convicted persons in part 2 cases if the conduct would have constituted an offence if it had taken place in the UK. There is an additional requirement for part 2 in that the conduct must also be punishable with imprisonment for 12 months in the UK.

D31.19   If conduct which takes place outside the requesting territory brings about an intended effect within that territory then it will be treated as having occurred in the requesting territory (*Cando Armas, Lacorre v High Instance Court of Paris* [2008] EWHC 2871 (Admin) and *Tesler v Government of the USA* [2011] EWHC 52 (Admin)).

The court should approach the document issued by the judicial authority benevolently and without undue formality (*Beriro v Public Prosecutor at the Bordeaux County Court, France* [2010] EWHC 2071 (Admin)). It must be shown that the conduct would, if it had taken place in the UK, have constituted the *actus reus* of a UK offence (*Hertel v Government of Canada* [2010] EWHC 2305 (Admin)). If necessary, the *mens rea* of the UK offence can be inferred from the conduct described in the warrant or request (*Zak v Regional Court of Bydgoszcz, Poland* [2008] EWHC 470 (Admin)), but only if it impels the inference rather than merely enabling it (*Assange v Swedish Prosecution Authority* [2011] EWHC 2849 (Admin) at [57]). The information in a warrant may be supplemented by further information provided by the requesting territory (*Dabas v High Court of Justice, Madrid* [2007] 2 AC 31 at [49]). However, when considering dual criminality the court cannot take into account evidence put forward by the requested person contradicting the extradition request but it can do so if considering whether the fairness or accuracy of the description of the extradition offence gives rise to an abuse of process (*Government of the USA v Shlesinger* [2013] EWHC 2671 (Admin): see **D31.15** and **D31.37**).

There are additional definitions of extradition offence in ss. 64, 65, 137 and 138 which deal **D31.20** with extra-territorial offences or International Criminal Court offences.

The Extradition Act 2003 (Multiple Offences) Order 2003 (SI 2003 No. 3150) amends the Act to deal with warrants or requests for more than one offence; unless the context requires otherwise, any reference in the Act to an offence is to be construed as a reference to offences.

BARS TO EXTRADITION

Section 11 in part 1 and s. 79 in part 2 require the judge to decide if there are any bars to extradi- **D31.21** tion. The bars most frequently relied on are double jeopardy, extraneous considerations and the passage of time. A new bar for part 1, if there is no prosecution decision, will be added when the ABCPA 2014, s. 156, comes into force.

No Prosecution Decision

For part 1 cases, under s. 12A (inserted by the ABCPA 2014, s. 156, which is not yet in force), **D31.22** the judge will decide if there are reasonable grounds to believe that the competent authorities in the requesting territory have made decisions to charge and try the requested person. If those decisions have not been made and this is not solely because of the requested person's absence then extradition will be barred unless the requesting territory can prove the decisions have been made or that any failure is solely caused by the requested person's absence.

Double Jeopardy

By virtue of ss. 12 and 80, double jeopardy will bar extradition if any rule of law in this juris- **D31.23** diction, including the abuse of process jurisdiction, would result in the requested person's discharge (see **A9.22** and **D12.30**). *Hamburg Public Prosecutor's Office v Altun* [2011] EWHC 397 (Admin) and *Osaikhwuwuomwan v Court of Ancona, Italy* [2012] All ER (D) 25 (Oct) involve a successful invocation of this bar.

Extraneous Considerations

Extraneous considerations will bar extradition by virtue of ss. 13 and 81 if: **D31.24**

(a) the warrant or request is issued for the purpose of prosecuting or punishing the requested person on account of his race, religion, nationality, gender, sexual orientation or political opinions (to be proved on the balance of probabilities); or
(b) there is a 'reasonable chance' that if extradited he might be prejudiced at his trial or punished, detained or restricted in his personal liberty for one of the same reasons (*Fernandez v Government of Singapore* [1971] 2 All ER 691).

The requested person must show a causal link between the issue of the warrant or request or the specific harm that he asserts he will suffer and one of the extraneous considerations.

Passage of Time

Passage of time will bar extradition if it would make the person's extradition unjust or oppressive **D31.25** (ss. 14 and 82). Any delay caused by the requested person cannot, except in the most exceptional circumstances, be relied upon by him and the whole period which follows this delay will ordinarily be considered to be caused by the person (*Gomes v Government of Trinidad and Tobago*

[2009] 3 All ER 549 at [26]–[29]). However, a requested person can become unlawfully at large and therefore a fugitive only if he knew that he was required to serve a sentence; it was not enough that he knew that a suspended sentence might be activated (*Pinto v Judicial Authority of Portugal* [2014] EWHC 1243 (Admin)). Injustice under ss. 14 and 82 relates to prejudice at trial on return. The requesting territory is presumed to be able to protect against an unjust trial and the requested person must prove a fair trial is impossible (*Gomes* at [35]–[36]). Oppression relates to changes in a person's circumstances. It requires more than hardship, which is a common result of extradition, and the seriousness of the offence is relevant (*Kakis v Government of the Republic of Cyprus* [1978] 2 All ER 634).

Age

D31.26 Age is a bar in relation to a part 1 warrant only. Section 15 makes it clear that age acts as a bar only where the person has not attained the age required in the UK for the conduct complained of to be a criminal offence (e.g., he was under the age of ten at the time).

Speciality

D31.27 Speciality is dealt with in s. 17, for part 1 warrants, and by the Secretary of State for part 2 cases. It is very difficult to argue as a bar for part 1 cases because all category 1 territories are signatories to the Framework Decision which provides for speciality protection under Article 27. See *Brodziak v Circuit Court in Warsaw, Poland* [2013] EWHC 3394 (Admin), where whether aggregate sentences imposed for extradition and non-extradition offences would breach the speciality protection was considered.

Forum

D31.28 Extradition will be barred if a substantial measure of the alleged criminal conduct occurred in the UK and if the judge decides, taking account only of the matters specified in s. 19B (for part 1 warrants) or s. 83B (for part 2 warrants), that it would not be in the interests of justice. However, if the judge receives a prosecutor's certificate then he must not find extradition is barred (ss. 19C and 83C).

Additional Potential Bars

D31.29 By virtue of ss. 16 and 83, hostage-taking considerations may act as a bar to extradition in respect of both part 1 warrants (although this will cease to be the case when the ABCPA 2014, s. 158, comes into force) and part 2 requests. Sections 18, 19 and 19A provide that extradition may be barred in the case of part 1 warrants where the person to whom the EAW refers has previously been extradited to or transferred to the UK and the consent of the territory from which he was previously extradited is required for further onward extradition and has not been given.

Procedure where No Bars to Extradition

D31.30 For part 1 cases, if there are no bars to extradition and the person has not been convicted, human rights must be considered next (s. 11(5); see **D31.33**); when the ABCPA 2014, s. 157, comes into force, the court will also have to consider proportionality. If the requested person has been convicted, the judge must consider s. 20 (see **D31.31**).

For part 2 cases, if there are no bars to extradition and the person has not been convicted, the judge will consider whether there is a prima facie case (see **D31.32**). If the requested person has been convicted, the judge must consider s. 85 (see **D31.31**).

The existence of a previous warrant does not preclude action under a new warrant in respect of the same conduct (*Mihociu v Central Court of the District Court of Pest Hungary* [2010] EWHC 708 (Admin)).

CONVICTION IN ABSENCE

For part 1 cases, if the person has been convicted the judge must proceed under s. 20. If **D31.31** the person was not convicted in his presence, the judge will consider if the person was deliberately absent. If the person was convicted in his presence then he does not also need to be present at any subsequent hearing to allow a suspended sentence to be enforced or activated (*Brodka v Military District Court in Warsaw, Poland* [2011] EWHC 1262 (Admin)). If the requesting territory proves, to the criminal standard, that the requested person was deliberately absent, s. 20(4) provides that the judge will proceed to consider human rights under s. 21 (see **D31.33**). See also *Mitoi v Government of Romania* [2006] EWHC 1977 (Admin).

If the person was not deliberately absent, the judge must decide if he has the right to a retrial or review amounting to a retrial with the features set out in s. 20(8) (s. 20(5)). That right must be automatic and not involve any exercise of discretion (*Bohm v Romanian Judicial Authority* [2011] EWHC 2671 (Admin)). However, it can involve the application of the law to the facts in a case in accordance with a criminal code which requires a requested person to make an application for a retrial on return in order to obtain it (*Nastase v Office of the State Prosecutor, Trento, Italy* [2012] EWHC 3671 (Admin)). If there is no right to a retrial, the person must be discharged. Otherwise the judge will go on to consider human rights (see **D31.33**).

For part 2 cases, if the requested person has been convicted, the questions in s. 85 (which is identical to s. 20) must be considered. If the person has been convicted in his presence or was deliberately absent from his trial, the judge will continue to consider human rights (see **D31.33**). Otherwise, if the requested person is not discharged, the judge will continue to consider the prima facie case under s. 86 (which is similar to s. 84: see **D31.32**).

PRIMA FACIE CASE

Under s. 84(1), in a part 2 case, the judge must consider if there is sufficient evidence to make **D31.32** a case requiring an answer if the requested person was appearing at a summary trial, unless the requesting territory has been designated under the Extradition Act 2003 (Designation of Part 2 Territories) Order 2003 (SI 2003 No. 3334), art. 4 (see **D31.3**). See also *Governor of Pentonville Prison, ex parte Alves* [1993] AC 284. The procedure is akin to a contested committal. Section 84(2)–(4) deal with the admissibility of evidence (*Tudor v United Arab Emirates* [2012] EWHC 1098 (Admin), *Patel v India* [2013] EWHC 819 (Admin) and *Shankaran v India* [2014] EWHC 957 (Admin), which also confirms that on appeal the High Court should form its own assessment as to whether a prima facie case is made out (at [18])). If there is a prima facie case or the judge is not required to consider this because the requesting territory has been designated then he will consider human rights under s. 87 (see **D31.33**).

HUMAN RIGHTS AND PROPORTIONALITY

The final consideration at an extradition hearing is whether a person's extradition would be com- **D31.33** patible with his Convention rights as defined by the HRA 1998, s. 1 (ss. 21 and 87). See **A7** for human rights generally. For part 1 accusation cases, once the ABCPA 2014, s. 157, which inserts a new s. 21A into the 2003 Act, comes into force, the court will also have to consider proportionality. Section 21A sets out a number of specified matters which the judge must take into account when deciding whether extradition would be disproportionate: the seriousness of the conduct, the likely penalty if convicted and the possibility of the requesting territory taking less coercive measures.

It is often alleged that violations will take place following extradition and the approach for these prospective violations differs in some respects from that which is applied in the domestic context. Articles 3, 5, 6 and 8 of the ECHR are those most commonly relied on in extradition cases to show a prospective violation.

There is a rebuttable presumption that States designated as part 1 territories will fulfil their obligations under the ECHR. This may be rebutted only by clear and cogent evidence (*Agius v Malta* [2011] EWHC 759 (Admin). Diplomatic assurances may be given by a requesting territory to try and establish that there is no risk of a violation of a Convention right. In *Othman (Abu Qatada) v UK* (2012) 55 EHRR 1 the ECtHR considered the detailed process which a court should go through to assess the quality of any diplomatic assurances which are given and whether they can be relied upon (see *Aleksynas v Minister of Justice, Republic of Lithuania* [2014] EWHC 437 (Admin), in which the court accepted assurances, and *Badre v Court of Florence, Italy* [2014] EWHC 614 (Admin), in which it did not).

D31.34   A requested person must demonstrate substantial grounds for believing that there is a real risk that he will receive treatment which would breach Article 3 if extradited (*Harkins v UK* (2012) 55 EHRR 561) but does not have to prove that a person sent to any prison in the requesting State would suffer a violation of Article 3 (*Lutsyuk v Government of Ukraine* [2013] EWHC 189 (Admin) at [22]; and see *Badre v Court of Florence, Italy* [2014] EWHC 614 (Admin), which considered systemic issues affecting the Italian prison service, and *Government of Ghana v Gambrah* [2014] EWHC 1569 (Admin), which concerned detention on death row). A successful claim that detention in a Polish prison would constitute a breach of Article 3 will require new factual issues with extremely strong evidence providing 'something approaching an international consensus' (*Krolik v Regional Court in Czestochwa, Poland* [2013] 1 WLR 490 at [6]–[7]). Country guidance issued in an asylum case should be treated as an authoritative starting point (*Lutsyuk v Government of Ukraine*, at [15]–[16] and [24]). However, not every form of ill-treatment will be sufficient to reach the minimum level of severity necessary to bar extradition (*Harkins* at [129]–[131]). Article 3 may be violated if a person who is ill could be detained after his extradition and would not receive appropriate medical care (*Aswat v UK* (2014) 58 EHRR 1 at [50]). Alleged or feared Article 3 ill-treatment by non-State actors in the requesting territory will prevent extradition only where it can be shown that the requesting State will fail to provide reasonable protection (*R (Bagdanavicius) v Secretary of State for the Home Department* [2005] 2 AC 668).

In *Othman (Abu Qatada)*, the ECtHR confirmed that Article 5 could be relied on to prevent extradition if there was a real risk of a flagrant violation which might involve, for example, arbitrary detention for many years without any intention to bring a person to trial (at [232]–[233]).

It must normally be assumed that the EU Member States will be capable of providing the sufficient minimum safeguards for a fair trial required by Article 6 (*Symeou v Public Prosecutor's Office at the Court of Appeals Patras, Greece* [2009] 1 WLR 2384). Extradition will violate Article 6 if the requested person has suffered or there is a real risk he will suffer a flagrant denial of justice. A flagrant denial of justice means a trial which is manifestly contrary to the provisions of Article 6 or the principles it embodies. This must be more than the mere irregularities or lack of safeguards in the trial procedures such as might result in a breach of Article 6 if occurring within a Contracting State itself (*Othman (Abu Qatada)* at [258]–[261]).

D31.35   It is very difficult to show that extradition will involve a violation of Article 8; hardship alone will not suffice. It is only if there is some quite exceptionally compelling feature or combination of features that interference with the private and family life which results from extradition will be disproportionate to the objective that extradition serves (*Norris v Government of USA (No. 2)* [2010] 2 All ER 267 at [56]). The Court may consider the gravity of the offence (*Norris* at [63]), the potential violation of the Article 8 rights of other family members (*Norris* at [64]) and the length of any sentence left to serve (*Wysocki v Polish Judicial Authority* [2010] EWHC 3430 (Admin)). The Supreme Court considered the Article 8 rights of children, which would be affected by the extradition of a parent in *HH v Deputy Prosecutor of the Italian Republic, Genoa*

[2013] 1 AC 338. The Court found that delay since offences had been committed is relevant as are the circumstances in which the offender left the requesting jurisdiction. The Court reiterated that the rights of the children are a primary consideration to be taken into account as part of a balancing exercise.

If the judge finds that extradition is compatible with the requested person's rights under the ECHR, he will order extradition (part 1 case) or the case will be sent to the Secretary of State (part 2 case) (see **D31.3**).

PHYSICAL OR MENTAL CONDITION

D31.36

Extradition may be barred or the proceedings adjourned if the requested person's physical or mental condition makes it unjust or oppressive to extradite him (ss. 25 and 91). Unjust and oppressive have the same meanings as for the passage of time bar (*Government of the Republic of South Africa v Dewani* [2013] 1 WLR 82 at [74]: see **D31.25**). Adequate medical evidence must be provided (*Jervis v Office of the Public Prosecutor of the Court of Appeals, Rennes* [2008] EWHC 2011 (Admin)). Only a very high risk that the requested person will commit suicide whatever steps are taken will be sufficient to bar extradition (*Mazurkiewicz v Rzeszow Circuit Court* [2011] EWHC 659 (Admin)). Amongst the factors to be considered is what might happen to a requested person after extradition (*Government of South Africa v Dewani* [2014] EWHC 153 (Admin) at [50]). If there is a genuine and legitimate dispute between medical experts as to a requested person's fitness to plead or stand trial then this is normally an issue which the court in the requesting State should determine as part of the trial process, although the English court can consider whether in a particular case this would result in unjustness or oppression (*Edwards v Government of the USA* [2013] 4 All ER 871 at [54]–[58]). However, it might be unjust and oppressive to order the extradition of a person who was agreed to be unfit to stand trial at the time of the extradition proceedings if there was a prospect he might remain permanently unfit. In these circumstances the court would need to consider whether an undertaking to allow his return, if after a reasonable time for further treatment he was still likely to remain unfit, should be required from the requesting territory (*Dewani* at [60]).

ABUSE OF PROCESS

D31.37

Courts have an implied jurisdiction to order a person's discharge if his extradition would constitute an abuse of process (see also asylum discussed at **D31.38**). In *R (Government of the USA) v Bow Street Magistrates' Court* [2007] 1 WLR 1157 the Divisional Court set out the steps to be followed where abuse of process is alleged as the judge should be alert to the possibility of it being raised as a delaying tactic:

(a) no steps should be taken to investigate an alleged abuse of process unless the judge is satisfied that there is proper reason to believe that an abuse may have taken place — this requires the acts of alleged abuse to be identified with particularity;

(b) the judge must consider whether that conduct, if established, could amount to an abuse of process;

(c) he must consider whether there are reasonable grounds for believing that such conduct may have occurred.

If the judge is satisfied that these preliminary criteria are fulfilled, he should not accede to extradition unless he has satisfied himself that such abuse has not occurred.

The requested person must prove the abuse on the balance of probabilities and the judge may ask for whatever information or evidence he requires from the requesting territory to determine this issue.

Misconduct or bad faith by the police of the requesting State in the investigation of the case or the preparation of evidence for trial will not amount to an abuse (*Symeou v Public Prosecutor's Office at the Court of Appeals Patras, Greece* [2009] 1 WLR 2384). If the statements in a part 1 warrant are inaccurate or incomplete, this may amount to an abuse of process (see **D31.15**).

If the requested person had a valid reason for being absent from his trial then extradition proceedings which are based on a conviction in his absence may amount to an abuse of process (*Campbell v Public Prosecutor of the Grande Instance Tribunal of St Malo, France* [2013] EWHC 1288 (Admin)).

ASYLUM

D31.38 Extradition cannot take place until the final determination of any asylum claim which is made between the issue of a certificate and the extradition of the person (ss. 39 and 121). For part 1 cases, extradition can take place if it is to a safe third country (s. 40). An asylum claim made outside the relevant period may not stop extradition, although it will depend on the facts of the asylum application in question (*R (Dos Santos) v Cascais Court 2nd Criminal Chamber, Portugal* [2010] EWHC 1815 (Admin)). Once the ABCPA 2014, s. 162, comes into force the same protection will apply for asylum claims made before the extradition process commences. Where a person has refugee status in respect of the requesting territory, his extradition would constitute an abuse of process (*District Court in Ostroleka v Dytlow* [2009] EWHC 1009 (Admin)).

PROCEDURAL MATTERS

D31.39 If extradition is contested, a short adjournment may be allowed by the judge for the case to be prepared (for delays arising from the processing of legal aid applications, see **D31.4**). The CrimPR, part 17, makes specific provision for extradition proceedings. The court will case manage proceedings, requiring early identification of issues by the defence who will be expected to particularise the issues to be raised and any evidence to be relied on (*R (Government of the USA) v Bow Street Magistrates' Court* [2007] 1 WLR 1157 at [77]). If a person is remanded in custody, and is not serving a sentence in the UK, the case will be reviewed every 28 days.

Section 202 provides for the admission of documents in authenticated or unauthenticated form (s. 202(5)). Evidence may be given through a television link by witnesses who are outside the UK (see the Evidence Through Television Links (England and Wales) Order 2013 (SI 2013 No. 1598)).

The rules of disclosure in criminal proceedings do not apply to extradition cases. In part 1 cases, the only documents ordinarily served are the EAW and certificate, a witness statement from the arresting police officer and antecedents. In part 2 cases, the certificate and request will be served which should contain more detail and must include evidence if the territory is not designated. When acting for the requesting territory, the CPS has a duty of candour to disclose evidence or information that severely undermines or destroys its case (*R (Raissi) v Secretary of State for the Home Department* [2008] QB 836).

SECRETARY OF STATE

D31.40 Where a judge sends a part 2 case to the Secretary of State, he must consider if any of the bars under ss. 94 to 96A apply (death penalty, speciality or earlier extradition or transfer to the UK). A requested person has four weeks from the day his case is sent to the Secretary of State to make representations indicating that any of these bars apply (s. 93(5) and (6)). If the Secretary of State finds none apply, he will make an order for extradition under s. 93(4).

APPEALS

Sections 26 to 34 govern appeals under part 1 and ss. 103 to 116 govern appeals under part 2.   **D31.41**
The CrimPR, part 17 (see Supplement, **R-140**) governs the procedure on extradition appeals.
An appeal to the High Court may be on a question of law or fact and can be brought by the
requesting territory or the requested person. Permission is not required but it will be once the
ABCPA 2014, s. 160, comes into force; the CrimPR, r. 17.17(4) states that permission will be
granted if the court finds a ground of appeal to be reasonably arguable; r. 17.22 will deal with
renewing an application. For part 2 cases, an appeal by the requested person cannot be heard
until after the Secretary of State has made his decision and can be against the decision of the
judge or the Secretary of State or both.

Orders made by the High Court for the filing of evidence, skeleton arguments and joint bundles
must be complied with or an application made for a variation in advance of the time for compliance. If this does not occur then the court may not permit evidence to be relied on or arguments
that should have been included in a skeleton to be advanced at a hearing (*McIntyre v Government
of the USA* [2014] EWHC 1886 (Admin) at [66]).

Notice of Appeal

In *Mucelli v Government of Albania* [2009] 3 All ER 1035 the House of Lords confirmed that   **D31.42**
notices of appeal must be filed at the High Court and served on the respondent (and any interested
party) within seven days for part 1 and 14 days for part 2 (ss. 26(4) and 103(9)). In *Lukaszewski
v District Court in Torun, Poland* [2012] 4 All ER 667, it was held (at [33]–[34]) that a power
to extend these periods for British Citizens had to be implied, given that the protection of the
ECHR, Article 6(1), was engaged in relation to the determination of the civil right to enter and
remain in the UK which would be affected by the extradition proceedings. Once the ABCPA
2014, s. 160, comes into force, permission to appeal will be required and, if the notice of application for leave to appeal is given after the prescribed period, the High Court must still allow the
application to be dealt with if the person has done everything reasonably possible to ensure that
the notice was given as soon as it could be given. The Act provides that the notice must be given
in accordance with the rules of court and these permit breaches of the requirements in the rules
to be remedied (*R (Aldhouse) v Royal Government of Thailand* [2012] EWHC 191 (Admin)). The
14-day period for part 2 begins from the date the Secretary of State informs the person sought, or
his solicitors, of the extradition order. The Secretary of State is entitled to assume that any person
will be informed of the contents of a letter, e-mail or fax on the same day as its delivery regardless
of whether it is in fact read (*Salazaar-Duarte v USA* [2010] EWHC 3150 (Admin)).

In part 2 cases, the High Court has indicated that it intends to fix a date for a case management
conference 35 days after the appeal notice is lodged. Applications for any matters which require
the permission of the court, such as interpreters, experts or representation orders, must be
provided no later than five days before the conference (*R (Jaffar) v Government of Spain* [2012]
EWHC 3692 (Admin)).

If the recipient's office is closed during the whole of the last day of service, the notice will be validly
filed or served if given at any time during the next business day (*Mucelli*). The same strict time-
limits apply to appeals brought by the requesting territory against discharge (ss. 28(5) and 105(5)).

A valid notice of appeal must identify the appellant and identify the decision under appeal.
However, a generous view should be taken of any notice of appeal which is not in accordance
with the rules, given the shortness of the permitted period for the filing of a notice (*Lukaszewski
v District Court in Torun, Poland* at [18]).

If an appellant is unrepresented and in custody, the advocate last representing the appellant
should make the appellant aware of the time-limits and procedure for lodging a valid appeal
(*Dunne v High Court of Dublin, Ireland* [2009] EWHC 2003 (Admin)).

Fresh Evidence

D31.43   In order to adduce fresh evidence on appeal, that evidence must not have been available at the extradition hearing and it must be decisive (*Szombathely City Court v Fenyvesi* [2009] 4 All ER 324). 'Not available' means that it was not at the disposal of the party wishing to adduce it and it could not have been obtained with reasonable diligence. The admissibility of fresh evidence does not extend to situations where the appellant seeks expert evidence more favourable to him (*Undrits v Northern Circuit Prosecutor's Office, Estonia* [2009] EWHC 3430 (Admin)). It may be possible to admit evidence that was available in order to avoid a breach of rights under the ECHR, but only if this new evidence would be decisive (*Plotkowski v Regional Court in Elblag, Poland* [2012] EWHC 375 (Admin)).

New Issue

D31.44   If an issue was available to be raised by a requested person on the evidence adduced at the extradition hearing, the requested person will, in general if not always, be entitled to raise that issue on appeal even though it was not raised at that hearing (*Hoholm v Government of Norway* [2009] EWHC 1513 (Admin); *R (Adedeji) v Public Prosecutor's Office, Germany* [2012] EWHC 3237 (Admin) at [10]). However, the authorities on this point are not settled; see *Khan v Government of the USA* [2010] EWHC 1127 (Admin) and *Koziel v District Court in Kielce, Poland* [2011] EWHC 3781 (Admin). *Jones v Government of the USA* [2012] EWHC 2332 (Admin) considered whether an issue which was abandoned in the magistrates' court could be revived on appeal. If it is asserted on appeal that arguments were not made or evidence was not adduced because of misconduct by legal representatives, the appellant should be formally invited to waive privilege, and the legal representatives should be invited to respond (*Sondy v CPS* [2010] EWHC 108 (Admin)).

Further Appeal or Remedy

D31.45   An appeal under part 1 or part 2 from the decision of the High Court lies to the Supreme Court, with leave (ss. 32 and 114) and only if the High Court has certified a point of law of public importance (ss. 32(4) and 114(1)). The Court's residual discretion to reopen a final determination of an appeal under the Civil Procedure Rules, r. 52.17, can be used in a part 1 case as there is no other means of protecting against the risk of a breach of the ECHR because of a material change in circumstances after the requested person's appeal rights have been exhausted (*Taylor v Governor of HM Prison Wandsworth* [2009] EWHC 1020 (Admin); see *Government of South Africa v Dewani* [2014] EWHC 153 (Admin) at [50] for the court using this power in a part 2 case). See also the CrimPR, r 17.27 as to the procedure (see Supplement, **R-166**). An appeal under s. 108 can be brought on human rights grounds at any time before physical removal. The High Court will consider the appeal only if it is necessary to do so to avoid real injustice and the circumstances are exceptional and make it appropriate to consider the appeal (s. 108(7)). For guidance as to how applications will be dealt with, see *McIntyre v Government of the USA* [2014] EWHC 1886 (Admin) at [11].

The time within which the appeal must be heard (ss. 31 and 113) can be extended in the interests of justice, and does not require exceptional circumstances (*Wright v City of Westminster Magistrates' Court* [2011] EWHC 515 (Admin)).

POST-HEARING MATTERS

Time-limit for Removal

D31.46   If a person does not appeal an order for his extradition under part 1, he must be removed within ten days of the expiry of the seven-day period allowed for giving notice of appeal or any later date fixed by the judge after an application by the requesting territory (s. 35(3)). If the person is not removed within this period, he can seek to be discharged, unless reasonable cause is shown for the delay (s. 35(5)). Human error in computing the days for removal can amount to reasonable cause (*Owens v Westminster Magistrates' Court* [2010] 1 WLR 17). The requesting territory can seek an extension of time from the judge (s. 35(4)(b)). Similar provisions apply under s. 36 following unsuccessful appeals to the High Court or Supreme Court. Any application for discharge under s. 35 or 36 must be made to the appropriate judge in the magistrates' court (*Kasprzak v Warsaw Regional Court, Poland* [2011] EWHC 100 (Admin)).

Part 2 makes similar provision for removal and a right to seek discharge if not removed within 28 days following the expiry of the 14-day period allowed to lodge an appeal against the Secretary of State's order for extradition where none is brought (s. 117), or following an unsuccessful appeal (s. 118; see *R (Tajik) v City of Westminster Magistrates' Court* [2013] 2 All ER 602).

Section D32   Public Funding

INTRODUCTION

D32.1   The primary source of the law on public funding in criminal matters is the LASPO 2012, as supplemented by various statutory instruments. The LASPO provisions apply to any representation order dated on or after 1 April 2013. Any order dated before 1 April 2013 continues throughout the life of the case (which may include long delayed confiscation proceedings) under the previous law as set out in earlier editions of this work.

Grant of legal aid in most criminal cases is authorised by Her Majesty's Courts Service, operating under a service level agreement on behalf of the Legal Aid Agency (LAA).

REPRESENTATION ORDERS

Grant of Right to Representation

D32.2   The LAA funds individuals and other legal persons who are granted the right to representation in accordance with the LASPO 2012, s. 16. The provisions for legal persons who are not individuals are contained in part 6 of the Criminal Legal Aid (General) Regulations 2013 (SI 2013 No. 9) and in the Legal Aid (Financial Resources and Payment for Services) (Legal Persons) Regulations 2013 (SI 2013 No. 512).

Section 16 of the LASPO 2012 provides for representation to be made available to an individual, including in relation to any kind of criminal proceedings, enabling him to resist an appeal to the Crown Court otherwise than in an official capacity. Where the right is granted, it includes representation for any related bail or other preliminary or incidental proceedings (s. 16(3)). Under s. 14 the term 'criminal proceedings' is defined as including:

(a) proceedings before a court for dealing with an individual accused of an offence,
(b) proceedings before a court for dealing with an individual convicted of an offence, including proceedings in respect of a sentence or order,
(c) proceedings for dealing with an individual under the Extradition Act 2003,
(d) proceedings for binding an individual over to keep the peace or to be of good behaviour under s. 115 of the Magistrates' Courts Act 1980 and for dealing with an individual who fails to comply with an order under that section,
(e) proceedings on an appeal brought by an individual under s. 44A of the Criminal Appeal Act 1968 (appeal in case of death of appellant),
(f) proceedings on a reference under s. 36 of the Criminal Justice Act 1972 on a point of law following the acquittal of an individual on indictment,
(g) proceedings for contempt committed, or alleged to have been committed, by an individual in the face of a court, and
(h) such other proceedings, before any court, tribunal or other person, as may be prescribed.

Section 14 enables other proceedings to be brought within the ambit of legal funding by deeming those proceedings to be criminal proceedings.

The Criminal Legal Aid (General) Regulations 2013, reg. 9, prescribes certain proceedings as **D32.3** criminal proceedings for the purposes of s. 14(h).

Criminal Legal Aid (General) Regulations 2013, reg. 9

(a) civil proceedings in a magistrates' court arising from a failure to pay a sum due or to obey an order of that court where such failure carries the risk of imprisonment;

(b) proceedings under sections 14B, 14D, 14G, 14H, 21B and 21D of the Football Spectators Act 1989 in relation to banning orders and references to a court;

(c) proceedings under section 5A of the Protection from Harassment Act 1997 in relation to restraining orders on acquittal;

(d) proceedings under sections 1, 1D and 4 of the Crime and Disorder Act 1998 in relation to anti-social behaviour orders;

(e) proceedings under sections 1G and 1H of the Crime and Disorder Act 1998 in relation to intervention orders, in which an application for an anti-social behaviour order has been made;

(f) proceedings under section 8(1)(b) of the Crime and Disorder Act 1998 in relation to parenting orders made where an anti-social behaviour order or a sex offender order is made in respect of a child;

(g) proceedings under section 8(1)(c) of the Crime and Disorder Act 1998 in relation to parenting orders made on the conviction of a child;

(h) proceedings under section 9(5) of the Crime and Disorder Act 1998 to discharge or vary a parenting order made as set out in sub-paragraph (f) or (g);

(i) proceedings under section 10 of the Crime and Disorder Act 1998 in relation to an appeal against a parenting order made as set out in sub-paragraph (f) or (g);

(j) proceedings under Part 1A of Schedule 1 to the Powers of Criminal Courts (Sentencing) Act 2000 in relation to parenting orders for failure to comply with orders under section 20 of that Act;

(k) proceedings under sections 2, 5 and 6 of the Anti-social Behaviour Act 2003 in relation to closure orders;

(l) proceedings under sections 20, 22, 26 and 28 of the Anti-social Behaviour Act 2003 in relation to parenting orders—
    (i) in cases of exclusion from school; or
    (ii) in respect of criminal conduct and anti-social behaviour;

(m) proceedings under sections 97, 100 and 101 of the Sexual Offences Act 2003 in relation to notification orders and interim notification orders;

(n) proceedings under sections 104, 108, 109 and 110 of the Sexual Offences Act 2003 in relation to sexual offences prevention orders and interim sexual offences prevention orders;

(o) proceedings under sections 114, 118 and 119 of the Sexual Offences Act 2003 in relation to foreign travel orders;

(p) proceedings under sections 123, 125, 126 and 127 of the Sexual Offences Act 2003 in relation to risk of sexual harm orders and interim risk of sexual harm orders;

(q) proceedings under sections 3, 5, 9 and 10 of the Violent Crime Reduction Act 2006 in relation to drinking banning orders and interim drinking banning orders;

(r) proceedings under section 13 of the Tribunals, Courts and Enforcement Act 2007 on appeal against a decision of the Upper Tribunal in proceedings in respect of—
    (i) a decision of the Financial Conduct Authority;
    (ia) a decision of the Prudential Regulation Authority
    (ii) a decision of the Bank of England; or
    (iii) a decision of a person in relation to the assessment of any compensation or consideration under the Banking (Special Provisions) Act 2008 or the Banking Act 2009;

(s) proceedings before the Crown Court or the Court of Appeal in relation to serious crime prevention orders under sections 19, 20, 21 and 24 of the Serious Crime Act 2007;

(t) proceedings under sections 100, 101, 103, 104 and 106 of the Criminal Justice and Immigration Act 2008 in relation to violent offender orders and interim violent offender orders;

(u) proceedings under sections 26, 27 and 29 of the Crime and Security Act 2010 in relation to—
    (i) domestic violence protection notices; or
    (ii) domestic violence protection orders; and

(v) any other proceedings that involve the determination of a criminal charge for the purposes of Article 6(1) of the European Convention on Human Rights.

Regulation 19 deals with incidental proceedings, defined as:

(a) proceedings in the Crown Court, following committal for sentence by a magistrates' court;

(b) proceedings to quash an acquittal under the CPIA 1996, s. 54 (tainted acquittals: see **D12.38**); and

(c) proceedings for confiscation and forfeiture in connection with criminal proceedings.

Regulation 20 deals with proceedings that are not to be regarded as incidental and so justify a separate representation order, defined as:

(a) proceedings for applications for judicial review or habeas corpus in relation to criminal proceedings; and

(b) proceedings for dealing with an individual who is alleged to have failed to comply with an order of the magistrates' court or the Crown Court.

D32.4   The decision whether or not to grant a representation order is to be determined by a two-stage test, incorporating an assessment of means and 'according to the interests of justice'

Legal Aid, Sentencing and Punishment of Offenders Act 2012, s. 17

(2) In deciding what the interests of justice consist of for the purposes of such a determination, the following factors must be taken into account—

(a) whether, if any matter arising in the proceedings is decided against the individual, the individual would be likely to lose his or her liberty or livelihood or to suffer serious damage to his or her reputation,

(b) whether the determination of any matter arising in the proceedings may involve consideration of a substantial question of law,

(c) whether the individual may be unable to understand the proceedings or to state his or her own case,

(d) whether the proceedings may involve the tracing, interviewing or expert cross-examination of witnesses on behalf of the individual, and

(e) whether it is in the interests of another person that the individual be represented.

In respect of proceedings in the Crown Court on indictment (Criminal Legal Aid (General) Regulations 2013, reg. 24(1)) or following a committal for sentence (reg. 19(2)), the interests of justice test is deemed met. Appeals to the Crown Court are not automatically covered (reg. 24(2)). In assessing whether the accused is likely to lose his liberty, regard must be had to the facts alleged by the prosecution, rather than the maximum penalty that could theoretically be imposed (*Highgate Justices, ex parte Lewis* [1977] Crim LR 611). So it is not enough that the offence carries a custodial sentence: the court must consider whether a custodial sentence might be imposed in the particular case. In *Liverpool City Magistrates, ex parte McGhee* [1993] Crim LR 609, the Divisional Court rejected the contention that what is now called an unpaid work requirement could be regarded as a sentence which deprives the accused of liberty. However, Rose LJ did add that the list of criteria (in what is now the LASPO 2012, s. 17) is not exhaustive, and so the possibility of a community punishment order (now a community order with a relevant requirement) may be a factor in deciding whether or not to make a representation order.

In *R (Punatar) v Horseferry Road Magistrates' Court* [2002] EWHC 1196 (Admin), an application for representation submitted at the end of court proceedings was refused because the prosecution substituted a charge for a non-imprisonable offence in place of an imprisonable one. The Divisional Court held that representation should have been granted due to the fact that when the solicitor decided to attend court the offence that was charged at that time merited representation. It was wrong to apply hindsight.

D32.5   The factor which includes expert cross-examination of witnesses (see s. 17(2)(d) at **D32.4**) means expert cross-examination of witnesses, not cross-examination of expert witnesses (*Liverpool City Magistrates, ex parte McGhee*). In *Scunthorpe Justices, ex parte S* (1998) *The Times*, 5 March 1998, the Divisional Court considered that refusal of legal aid to an accused aged 16 who sought to challenge whether a police officer had acted in the execution of his duty was irrational. The expertise needed to cross-examine police witnesses, and to find, select and proof defence witnesses, was beyond an accused aged 16.

In *R (GKR Law Solicitors) v Liverpool Magistrates' Court* [2008] EWHC 2974 (Admin) the Divisional Court held that it was appropriate to grant representation to a defendant in relation to a special reasons hearing, where a witness in the case was the defendant's 12-year-old son. The child was a witness entitled to and requiring special measures and consideration would need to be given to video-interviewing the young witness in order to ensure best evidence is given; such measures would be outside the competence and resources of the defendant.

In *R (Matara) v Brent Magistrates' Court* (2005) 169 JP 576, the accused was charged with failure to provide a specimen of breath. He made an application for legal aid. It was argued that he would be unable to understand the court proceedings because his understanding of English was inadequate; the court's response was that an interpreter would be provided. On appeal, it was held that at least one of the 'interests of justice' criteria in what is now s. 17 of the LASPO 2012 was met, making the refusal of legal aid unreasonable to a degree which entitled the Divisional Court to intervene. The availability of an interpreter did not meet the point that it was the claimant's case that he was unable to understand what was being said at the time of his arrest, a point which lay at the heart of his defence. It went to his ability to state his own case and the overall fairness of the trial. The decision to refuse legal aid was therefore quashed and the case remitted to a differently constituted bench for reconsideration.

In *Chester Magistrates' Court ex parte Ball* (1999) 163 JP 813 it was indicated that any defendant of previous good character pleading not guilty to a charge equal to, or more significant than, s. 5 of the Public Order Act 1986 in terms of nature and seriousness might be granted legal aid regardless of his social or professional standing, because there might be damage to the defendant's reputation. It is unlikely that this principle will assist in relation to applications for legal aid in respect of non-imprisonable road traffic or regulatory offences.

In *Oates* [2002] 1 WLR 2833, it was held that legal assistance by way of a representation order will not, save in exceptional circumstances, be granted on a renewed application for permission to appeal against conviction following refusal by the single judge; this is not contrary to the right of an accused to defend himself through legal assistance of his own choosing under the ECHR, Article 6(3)(c).

Applying for a Representation Order in a Magistrates' Court and the Crown Court

D32.6 Section 17 of the LASPO 2012 provides for the determination by the LAA of applications for a representation order in a magistrates' court and (save in exceptional circumstances) in the Crown Court.

This responsibility has been delegated to court officials at the appropriate magistrates' court centre under a service level agreement. Magistrates have no power to grant representation, save when considering an appeal against the refusal of representation. Representation is applied for using the prescribed form (CRM14) and submitting it to the representation authority, along with any proof of means required for those who are not passported (form CRM15).

The Crown Court has very limited power to grant a representation order and may do so only on oral application under the Criminal Legal Aid (Determinations by a Court and Choice of Representative) Regulations 2013 (SI 2013 No. 614). Regulation 6 states that a representation order may only be granted in proceedings:

(a) which are described in the LASPO 2012, s. 14(g) (contempt in the face of the court);
(b) which arise out of an alleged failure to comply with an order of the Crown Court and it appears to the court that there is no time to instruct a provider; or

(c) where the individual is brought before the court under the Senior Courts Act 1981, s. 81, in pursuance of a Crown Court warrant.

Any other order of the Crown Court will be invalid (Criminal Legal Aid (General) Regulations 2013, reg. 3).

D32.7   Financial eligibility for a grant of representation is determined under part 3 of the Criminal Legal Aid (Financial Resources) Regulations 2013 (SI 2013 No. 471), as amended by SI 2013 No. 2791 in relation to the magistrates' court and, in relation to applications made on or after 27 January 2014, the Crown Court. A means assessment is carried out following submission of information on form CRM15. Applicants who fall into one or more of the following categories will automatically pass the means test assessment:

(i) under the age of 18;
(ii) directly or indirectly in receipt of a 'qualifying benefit'.

A qualifying benefit means any of the following (or their equivalent benefit payable in Northern Ireland):

(a) income support;
(b) income-based jobseeker's allowance;
(c) guarantee credit;
(d) income-related employment and support allowance; and
(e) universal credit.

An individual granted representation for the Crown Court may be called upon to pay contributions from income and, if convicted, from capital under the Criminal Legal Aid (Contribution Orders) Regulations 2013 (SI 2013 No. 483), as amended by SI 2013 No. 2792. If the individual is acquitted, contributions are returned with interest.

For those refused legal aid in the Crown Court to recover, on acquittal, from central funds, an application for legal aid must have been made and refused (Costs in Criminal Cases (Legal Costs) (Exceptions) Regulations 2014 (SI 2014 No. 130). This is the case however inevitable such a refusal may be.

There are duties of disclosure upon providers (overriding legal privilege) contained in reg. 5 of the Criminal Legal Aid (General) Regulations 2013 where there is a failure by a client without good reason to comply with the requirements to provide information or documents, or a statement is made which the client knows or believes to be false. This confirms the Legal Aid (Disclosure of Information) Regulations 2013 (SI 2013 No. 457). The LAA must not disclose privileged information for the purposes of criminal investigations or proceedings if it relates to the defence of an individual or legal person.

Applying for a Representation Order in the Courts above the Crown Court

D32.8   Provision for the grant of legal aid in the High Court, Court of Appeal and Supreme Court is made by the Criminal Legal Aid (Determinations by a Court and Choice of Representative) Regulations 2013. The merits test is deemed to be satisfied in these courts under reg. 21 of the Criminal Legal Aid (General) Regulations 2013 save in the relation to appeals to the Crown Court.

> **Criminal Legal Aid (Determinations by a Court and Choice of Representative)**
> **Regulations 2013, regs. 7 and 8**
>
> 7.—(1) On the application of an individual, the High Court may make a determination under section 16 of the Act as to whether an individual qualifies for representation for the purposes of criminal proceedings before the High Court in relation to an appeal by way of case stated from a decision of the magistrates' court or the Crown Court.
>
> (2) On the application of an individual, or of its own motion, the High Court may make a determination under section 16 of the Act as to whether an individual qualifies for representation for the purposes of proceedings before the High Court, or proceedings before the Supreme Court on appeal from the High Court, described in—

    (a) section 14(a) to (g) of the Act, other than proceedings under paragraph (1); or.

    (b) regulation 9(r) of the General Regulations

8.—(1) On the application of an individual, or of its own motion, the Court of Appeal may make a determination under section 16 of the Act as to whether an individual qualifies for representation for the purposes of any criminal proceedings before the Court of Appeal, or criminal proceedings before the Supreme Court on appeal from the Court of Appeal.

(2) A determination made in accordance with paragraph (1)—

    (a) must not be made until service of an appeal notice in respect of the proceedings has taken place; and.

    (b) may specify the stage of the proceedings at which the determination is to take effect.

The duties of the higher courts to make costs orders are contained in the Criminal Legal Aid (Recovery of Defence Costs Orders) Regulations 2013 (SI 2013 No. 511). In the Court of Appeal there is no means test as to financial eligibility and legal aid, albeit, when appropriate, with a contribution, will always be available, However, as a consequence, a successful appellant paying privately cannot recover his costs from central funds.

In *K* (2005) *The Times*, 15 February 2005, the Court of Appeal emphasised that (under earlier **D32.9** provisions) when a court grants a representation order for an appeal, the representation order only covers work on, and attendance or appearance at, the hearing in respect of the grounds upon which the court has granted leave to appeal. It does not cover any work, preparation or time in court that is done or spent in respect of any renewed application in respect of a ground on which leave to appeal has been refused. If, on a renewed application made at the same time as an appeal, leave is granted, the practice of the court is exactly the same as applies when a renewed application is made separately.

Nature of Representation

The Criminal Legal Aid (Determinations by a Court and Choice of Representative) Regulations **D32.10** 2013 (SI 2013 No. 614), part 3, sets out the details of:

- which litigator may be chosen and the procedure where a person appearing in proceedings heard at the same time has already chosen a litigator (reg. 13);
- whether there may be a transfer of the case to another litigator (regs. 14 and 15 and see **D32.14**);
- whether and when an advocate may be chosen (regs. 16 to 28);
- the number of advocates that may be chosen (regs. 19 to 23).

Criminal Legal Aid (Determinations by a Court and Choice of Representative) Regulations 2013, regs. 10 to 23

10. This Part makes provision in relation to the right, conferred by section 27(4) of the Act (choice of provider of services etc), of an individual who qualifies for representation for the purposes of criminal proceedings by virtue of a determination under section 16 of the Act (representation for criminal proceedings), in accordance with Part 2 of these Regulations or Part 5 of the General Regulations, to select a representative.

11.—(1) The relevant court may make a determination under this Part only if it has considered an application made in accordance with paragraph (2)

(2) For the purposes of paragraph (1), an application must—

    (a) be made by the individual seeking the determination;

    (b) be in writing; and

    (c) specify what the relevant court is being asked to determine and the grounds upon which it is being asked to do so.

(3) When it makes a determination under this Part, the relevant court must give reasons.

12. In relation to any criminal proceedings described in section 14(a) to (f) and (h) of the Act (criminal proceedings), the right of an individual conferred by section 27(4) of the Act does not include the right to select a provider unless the provider—

    (a) is employed by the Lord Chancellor to provide criminal legal aid;

    (b) is permitted to provide criminal legal aid to the individual under the arrangements the Lord Chancellor has made with the provider; or

    (c) is representing the individual before the Court of Appeal in an appeal against a decision of the Upper Tribunal in proceedings in respect of a decision of—

        (i)   the Financial [Conduct] Authority;

        (ii) the Bank of England; or

        (iii) a person in relation to the assessment of any compensation or consideration under the Banking (Special Provisions) Act 2008 or the Banking Act 2009.

[Note that reg. 12 requires amendment to take account of the abolition of the FSA and the creation of the Financial Conduct Authority and the Prudential Regulation Authority.]

13.—(1) Subject to paragraph (2), in relation to any criminal proceedings involving co-defendants, the right of an individual conferred by section 27(4) of the Act does not include the right to select a provider who is not also instructed by the individual's co-defendant (or by one of the individual's co-defendants, if there are more than one) unless the relevant court or the Director determines that—

    (a) there is a conflict of interest between the individual and that co-defendant; or.

    (b) there is likely to be a conflict of interest between the individual and that co-defendant.

(2) Paragraph (1) does not apply where the provider selected by the individual is an advocate.

(3) In this regulation 'co-defendants' means defendants whose cases are to be heard together.

14.—(1) Subject to paragraph (2), where an individual has selected a provider in criminal proceedings, the right conferred by section 27(4) of the Act does not include a right to select a provider in place of the original provider.

(2) The relevant court may determine that the individual can select a provider in place of the original provider in the circumstances set out in paragraphs (3) or (4).

(3) The circumstances are that the relevant court determines that—

    (a) there has been a breakdown in the relationship between the individual and the original provider such that effective representation can no longer be provided by the original provider; or

    (b) there is some other compelling reason why effective representation can no longer be provided by the original provider.

(4) The circumstances are that the relevant court determines that—

    (a) the original provider—

        (i)   considers there to be a duty to withdraw from the case in accordance with the provider's professional rules of conduct; or

        (ii) is no longer able to represent the individual through circumstances outside the provider's control; and

    (b) the original provider has supplied the relevant court with details as to—

        (i)   the nature of any such duty to withdraw from the case; or

        (ii) the particular circumstances that render the provider unable to represent the individual.

15.—(1) Paragraph (2) applies where, in relation to an individual—

    (a) a determination is withdrawn in accordance with regulation 26 of the General Regulations or regulation 9 of these Regulations; and

    (b) a subsequent determination under section 16 of the Act that the individual qualifies for representation is made in respect of the same proceedings.

(2) Subject to paragraph (3), the right of an individual conferred by section 27(4) of the Act does not include a right to select a provider other than the provider named in the original representation order.

(3) The relevant court may determine that the individual can select a provider other than the provider named in the original representation order if that court determines that there are good reasons why a different provider should be selected.

16.—(1) Subject to paragraph (2), in relation to any criminal proceedings before a magistrates' court, the right of an individual conferred by section 27(4) of the Act does not include a right to select an advocate.

(2) The relevant court may determine that the individual can select an advocate if—

    (a) the proceedings relate to an extradition hearing under the Extradition Act 2003 or an indictable offence; and

    (b) the relevant court determines that because there are circumstances which make the proceedings unusually grave or difficult, representation by an advocate would be desirable.

17.—(1) Subject to paragraph (2), where an individual is entitled to select an advocate in accordance with regulation 16, the right of an individual conferred by section 27(4) of the Act does not include a right to select a Queen's Counsel or more than one advocate.

(2) The relevant court may determine that the individual can select a Queen's Counsel or more than one advocate if the individual is—

    (a) the subject of an extradition hearing under the Extradition Act 2003; and

(b) the relevant court determines that the individual could not be adequately represented except by a Queen's Counsel or more than one advocate.

18.—(1) Subject to paragraphs (2) to (6), in relation to any criminal proceedings that are not before a magistrates' court, the right of an individual conferred by section 27(4) of the Act does not include a right to select a Queen's Counsel or more than one advocate.

(2) The relevant court may determine that an individual can select a Queen's Counsel if that individual's case involves substantial novel or complex issues of law or fact which could not be adequately presented except by a Queen's Counsel, and either—
  (a) the exceptional condition is met; or
  (b) the counsel condition is met.

(3) The relevant court may determine that an individual can select two junior advocates if that individual's case involves substantial novel or complex issues of law or fact which could not be adequately presented by a single advocate, including a Queen's Counsel alone, and either—
  (a) the exceptional condition is met; or
  (b) the prosecution condition is met.

(4) The relevant court may determine that an individual can select a Queen's Counsel and a junior advocate if that individual's case involves substantial novel or complex issues of law or fact which could not be adequately presented except by a Queen's Counsel assisted by a junior advocate and either—
  (a) the exceptional condition is met; or
  (b) the counsel condition and the prosecution condition are met.

(5) The relevant court may determine that an individual can select three advocates if the proceedings relate to a prosecution brought by the Serious Fraud Office and the relevant court determines that three advocates are required to represent the individual.

(6) If the proceedings described in paragraph (5) are in the Crown Court, that court must also determine that the individual's case involves substantial novel or complex issues of law or fact which could not be adequately presented by two junior advocates, or by a Queen's Counsel assisted by a junior advocate, and either—
  (a) the exceptional condition is met; or
  (b) the prosecution condition is met.

(7) In this regulation—

'the counsel condition' means, in relation to particular criminal proceedings, that a Queen's Counsel or senior Treasury Counsel has been instructed on behalf of the prosecution;

'the exceptional condition' means, in relation to particular criminal proceedings, that the individual's case is exceptional compared with the generality of cases involving similar offences;

'the prosecution condition' means, in relation to particular criminal proceedings, any of the following circumstances—
  (a) two or more advocates have been instructed on behalf of the prosecution and the relevant court is satisfied that the individual will be, or will be likely to be, prejudiced if they too are not represented by two or more advocates;
  (b) the number of prosecution witnesses exceeds 80;
  (c) the number of pages of prosecution evidence exceeds 1000;
  and

'prosecution evidence' means all witness statements, documentary and pictorial exhibits and records of interview with the individual and with any other defendants which form part of the committal or served prosecution documents or are included in any notice of additional evidence.

19.—(1) A determination that an individual is entitled to select a Queen's Counsel or more than one advocate under regulation 18 may only be made by the following judges—
  (a) subject to paragraph (2), in the course of a trial or a preliminary hearing, pre-trial review or plea and directions hearing, the judge who has been assigned as the trial judge;
  (b) where a trial judge has not been assigned, by—
    (i) a High Court judge; or
    (ii) subject to paragraph (2), a resident judge of the Crown Court or, in the absence of a resident judge, a judge nominated by a resident judge of the Crown Court for the purpose of making such a determination; or
  (c) where the proceedings are in the Court of Appeal, by the Registrar of Criminal Appeals, a High Court judge or a judge of the Court of Appeal.

(2) A determination made by a judge referred to in paragraph (1)(a) or (b)(ii) does not take effect unless it is approved by a presiding judge of the circuit or by a judge nominated by a presiding judge of the circuit for the purpose of giving such approval.

20. Nothing in regulation 18 permits an individual to select more than one Queen's Counsel.

21. For the purposes of making a determination under regulation 18, the relevant court may require from any advocate already assigned to the individual a written opinion on the representation needed to adequately present the case.

22.—(1) The Director may, upon the committal, transfer or sending for trial of an individual, determine that the individual can select a Queen's Counsel without a junior advocate if the proceedings are a trial for murder.

(2) The Director may, upon receipt of a notice of transfer of an individual's case under section 4 of the Criminal Justice Act 1987, determine that the individual can select a Queen's Counsel with one junior advocate if the prosecution is brought by the Serious Fraud Office.

23.—(1) The right of an individual conferred by section 27(4) of the Act does not include a right to select—

(a) two junior advocates, unless the relevant court determines that the individual could not be adequately represented by a junior advocate and a noting junior;

(b) a Queen's Counsel assisted by a junior advocate, unless the relevant court determines that the individual could not be adequately represented by a Queen's Counsel assisted by a noting junior;

(c) three junior advocates, unless the relevant court determines that the individual could not be adequately represented by two junior advocates and a noting junior;

(d) two junior advocates and a noting junior, unless the relevant court determines that the individual could not be adequately represented by a junior advocate and two noting juniors;

(e) a Queen's Counsel assisted by two junior advocates, unless the relevant court determines that the individual could not be adequately represented by a Queen's Counsel assisted by a junior advocate and a noting junior; or

(f) a Queen's Counsel assisted by a junior advocate and a noting junior, unless the relevant court determines that the individual could not be adequately represented by a Queen's Counsel assisted by two noting juniors.

(2) In this regulation 'noting junior' means a junior advocate whose instructions include (but are not limited to) taking a note of the proceedings.

A representation order for failure to pay a confiscation order may not be extended to assigned counsel under reg. 16(2) as it is not an indictable offence (*Taylor v City of Westminster Magistrates' Court* (2009) 173 JP 405).

An individual who faces proceedings that fall within the definition of very high cost criminal cases ('VHCC') does not have the absolute right to choose a representative to act for him. Only litigators, and in most cases advocates, who are accredited to carry out VHCC work may act in such proceedings. There is an obligation to report possible VHCC cases to the LAA under the Criminal Legal Aid (Remuneration) Regulations 2013 (SI 2013 No. 435), reg. 12, which also provides a sanction.

Notification of Very High Cost Cases

D32.11   Criminal Legal Aid (Remuneration) Regulations 2013, reg. 12

(1) A litigator who has conduct of a case which is, or is likely to be classified as, a Very High Cost Case, must notify the Lord Chancellor in writing as soon as practicable.

(2) Where a litigator fails to comply with this regulation without good reason, and as a result there is a loss to public funds, the Lord Chancellor may refuse payment of the litigator's costs up to the extent of such loss.

(3) The Lord Chancellor must not refuse payment under paragraph (2) unless the litigator has been given a reasonable opportunity to show why the payment should not be refused.

The Criminal Legal Aid (Remuneration) Regulations 2013, reg. 2, defines a very high cost case as:

...a case in which a section 16 determination has been made and which the Director classifies as a Very High Cost Case on the grounds that—

(a) in relation to fees claimed by litigators—

(i) if the case were to proceed to trial, the trial would in the opinion of the Director be likely to last for more than 40 days and the Director considers that there are no exceptional circumstances which make it unsuitable to be dealt with under an individual case contract for Very High Cost Cases made by the Lord Chancellor under section 2(1) of the Act; or

    (ii) if the case were to proceed to trial, the trial would in the opinion of the Director be likely to last no fewer than 25 and no more than 40 days and the Director considers that there are circumstances which make it suitable to be dealt with under an individual case contract for Very High Cost Cases made by the Lord Chancellor under section 2(1) of the Act;

(b) in relation to fees claimed by advocates, if the case were to proceed to trial, the trial would in the opinion of the Director be likely to last for more than 60 days and the Director considers that there are no exceptional circumstances which make it unsuitable to be dealt with under an individual case contract for Very High Cost Cases made by the Lord Chancellor under section 2(1) of the Act.

Certificate for Two Counsel

In *Z* (9 October 2008 unreported, Leeds Crown Court), general guidance was given in relation to the grant of a certificate for two counsel in criminal cases.   **D32.12**

(a) The fact that the prosecution were represented by two counsel had little bearing on whether the defence ought to have the same number.

(b) It is not enough that a case should involve substantial, complex or novel issues of law; the fundamental question for the court was why the case could not be presented by a single advocate.

(c) The identity of the proposed second advocate is not relevant.

(d) It will not usually be appropriate to decide on the level of representation until the prosecution case and defence case statement have been served.

(e) The application should state with some precision the work to be done by the second advocate and the reason why it cannot be done by a single advocate alone.

(f) The court expects both advocates to be present throughout the entire case, save where the trial judge grants a leave of absence.

(g) It is imperative that defendants receive the most appropriate representation; in cases where the criteria are met for leading counsel and junior that is the application that should be made. The financial benefit that comes from being a leading junior should not cloud that decision-making. The same principles apply to the use of inexperienced juniors.

(h) The court has the power to keep the need for two counsel under review and can amend the certificate at any time should it be appropriate to do so.

In *A-G's Ref (No. 82a of 2000)* [2002] 2 Cr App R 342, the Court of Appeal held that the principle of equality of arms does not require that, where the Crown instructs leading counsel and the defence is being funded at public expense, the accused is entitled to be represented by leading counsel as well.

Appeals against Refusal of Representation

Where an applicant for the grant of a representation order is refused, the provisions for appeal are contained in the Criminal Legal Aid (General) Regulations 2013.   **D32.13**

Criminal Legal Aid (General) Regulations 2013, regs. 28 to 30

28. Where an individual remains dissatisfied following a review under regulation 27, that individual may appeal to a court in accordance with regulations 29 and 30 against the decision that the interests of justice do not require, or no longer require, representation to be made available.

29.—(1) In relation to a determination by the Director under section 16 of the Act that the interests of justice do not require, or no longer require, representation to be made available before the magistrates' court, the appeal lies to the magistrates' court.

(2) The court must either—

    (a) affirm the determination; or

    (b) decide that the interests of justice require representation to be made available, or to continue to be made available, to an individual for the purposes of criminal proceedings.

(3) Where the court makes a decision under paragraph (2)(b), the individual may apply to the Director for a determination.

(4) Where an individual applies to the Director under paragraph (3)—

    (a) if the individual states in writing, verified by a statement of truth, that the individual's financial resources have not changed since the date of the individual's original application for a determination, so as to make the individual financially ineligible for representation under section 21 of the Act (financial resources) and regulations made under that section, the Director must make a determination that the individual qualifies for representation; or

    (b) if the individual's financial resources may have so changed since the date of the individual's original application, the Director—

        (i) must determine whether the individual qualifies for representation in accordance with section 21 of the Act and regulations made under that section; and

        (ii) if the individual does so qualify, must make the determination accordingly.

(5) In this regulation—

'magistrates' court' means the magistrates' court in which the proceedings in respect of which an individual is seeking a determination under section 16 of the Act are taking place, or are to take place, and includes a single justice and a District Judge (magistrates' court); and

'statement of truth' means a declaration provided in accordance with regulations made under section 21 of the Act (financial resources).

30.—(1) In relation to a determination by the Director that the interests of justice do not require, or no longer require, representation to be made available in a case in the Crown Court, the appeal lies to an officer of the Crown Court ('the officer').

(2) The officer may refer the appeal to a judge of the Crown Court.

(3) The officer or the judge may—

    (a) affirm the determination; or

    (b) decide that the interests of justice require representation to be made available, or to continue to be made available, to an individual for the purposes of criminal proceedings.

(4) Where the officer or a judge makes a decision under paragraph (3)(b), the Director must make a determination reflecting that decision and record the determination in a representation order.

Transfer of Representation

D32.14   The rules on transfer of representation orders distinguish between the situations where the client wishes to transfer and the litigator is under a professional duty to withdraw.

Criminal Legal Aid (Determinations by a Court and Choice of Representative) Regulations 2013, regs. 14 and 15

14.—(1) Subject to paragraph (2), where an individual has selected a provider in criminal proceedings, the right conferred by section 27(4) of the Act does not include a right to select a provider in place of the original provider.

(2) The relevant court may determine that the individual can select a provider in place of the original provider in the circumstances set out in paragraphs (3) or (4).

(3) The circumstances are that the relevant court determines that—

    (a) there has been a breakdown in the relationship between the individual and the original provider such that effective representation can no longer be provided by the original provider; or

    (b) there is some other compelling reason why effective representation can no longer be provided by the original provider.

(4) The circumstances are that the relevant court determines that—

    (a) the original provider—

        (i) considers there to be a duty to withdraw from the case in accordance with the provider's professional rules of conduct; or

        (ii) is no longer able to represent the individual through circumstances outside the provider's control; and

    (b) the original provider has supplied the relevant court with details as to—

        (i) the nature of any such duty to withdraw from the case; or

        (ii) the particular circumstances that render the provider unable to represent the individual.

15.—(1) Paragraph (2) applies where, in relation to an individual—

    (a) a determination is withdrawn in accordance with regulation 26 of the General Regulations or regulation 9 of these Regulations; and

    (b) a subsequent determination under section 16 of the Act that the individual qualifies for representation is made in respect of the same proceedings.

(2) Subject to paragraph (3), the right of an individual conferred by section 27(4) of the Act does not include a right to select a provider other than the provider named in the original representation order.

(3) The relevant court may determine that the individual can select a provider other than the provider named in the original representation order if that court determines that there are good reasons why a different provider should be selected.

In *Ashgar Khan* (10 July 2001 unreported, Birmingham Crown Court), the court emphasised the requirement to satisfy the Criminal Defence Service (General) (No. 2) Regulations 2001, reg. 16(2), and in particular the need to show good cause for the transfer (reflected in similar terms in the current regulations):

> It will not generally be sufficient to allege a lack of care or competence of existing representatives. As from 2nd April 2001 only those solicitors who have obtained a criminal franchise contract with the Legal Services Commission are able to undertake work and obtain a representations order in criminal proceedings. Those franchises are only obtained after rigorous audit, inspection and control by the Legal Services Commission, the Commission thereby satisfying itself that the professional standard of solicitors with franchises is of a high order. The court will infer from that fact that such solicitors do provide representation or good quality. Only in extremely rare circumstances, and where full particulars are given in the application, will a general ground of loss of confidence or incompetence be entertained. It must be further pointed out that it will not be sufficient simply to say that there is a breakdown in the relationship between solicitor and client. Many breakdowns are imagined rather than real or as the result of proper advice. This court will want to look to see what the cause of that is.

FUNDING OF JUDICIAL REVIEW AND APPEAL BY WAY OF CASE STATED

D32.15 Work undertaken in relation to judicial review of criminal proceedings is not treated as being incidental to those proceedings. However, appeals by way of case stated are covered within the definition of criminal proceedings. Verbal or written advice following conviction and, if appropriate, an application for representation in the High Court is treated as incidental to the proceedings and should be claimed as part of representation in those proceedings.

If there is no representation order in force, advice and assistance can be given in the appeals and review class of work under the terms of the standard crime contract 2010 (as amended)

FUNDING OF CERTAIN CIVIL PROCEEDINGS

D32.16 The POCA 2002 contains a range of civil measures designed to deprive criminals of the proceeds from criminal conduct. Cases involving earlier legislation continue to have effect in appropriate cases. Limited funding under civil legal aid is available and can be undertaken by providers working under the standard crime contract as 'Associated Civil Work'.

To be eligible for civil legal aid, the type of work must appear in sch. 1 to the LASPO 2012 and not be excluded. Judicial review and habeas corpus are covered subject to exclusions but only work related to the following sections of the POCA 2002 is covered: ss. 41, 47M, 54(3), 62, 67A, 72, 73, 361, 362, 369 and 375 (public funding is no longer available in relation to cash forfeiture).

Section D33   Costs

POWER TO AWARD COSTS

D33.1 The power of the courts to award costs in criminal proceedings is contained in ss. 16 to 21 of the Prosecution of Offences Act 1985, supplemented by the Costs in Criminal Cases (General) Regulations 1986 (SI 1986 No. 1335). The Prosecution of Offences Act 1985, s. 16, deals with costs out of central funds in favour of an acquitted accused, known as 'defendant's costs orders'; s. 17 deals with prosecution costs out of central funds; s. 18 with orders that a convicted accused pay prosecution costs; s. 19 with awards of costs in other circumstances (such as in relation to witnesses, intermediaries and certain advocacy services); s. 19A with orders that a party guilty of improper acts or omissions in the course of the proceedings pay any costs thrown away by his opponent in consequence; and s. 19B with awards of costs against third parties. A detailed commentary on the costs in criminal cases is contained in the *Practice Direction (Costs in Criminal Proceedings)* [2013] 1 WLR 3255.

Costs as a Sanction

D33.2 Rule 3.5(6) of the CrimPR (see Supplement, **R-12**) provides for sanctions in respect to breach of the rules:

> If a party fails to comply with a rule or a direction, the court may—
> (a) fix, postpone, bring forward, extend, cancel or adjourn a hearing;
> (b) exercise its powers to make a costs order; and
> (c) impose such other sanction as may be appropriate.

Costs of a Witness Summons

D33.3 Under the Criminal Procedure (Attendance of Witnesses) Act 1965, s. 2, there is a power to award costs to a person who successfully applies to set aside an order for a witness summons. This power was considered in *DLA Piper UK LLP v BDO LLP* [2013] EWHC 3970 (Admin). The Divisional Court held that the statute had a lacuna: no costs could be awarded to a party who successfully resists the original application for a summons but costs may be awarded to a successful applicant to set aside such an order provided that person was not notified of the original application. The Court stated that there is no inherent jurisdiction to make a costs order and no order could be made against the solicitors acting as they had not been guilty of any act or omission that would have justified a wasted costs order.

DEFENDANT'S COSTS ORDERS

Jurisdiction to Make a Defendant's Costs Order

D33.4 In any of the situations listed below the appropriate court may make a defendant's costs order in favour of a successful accused or, as the case may be, appellant. The effect of a defendant's costs order is that the defence costs are paid out of central funds. The LASPO 2012 radically alters the position in relation to defendant's costs orders. The powers of the court to make defence costs orders under the Prosecution of Offences Act 1985, s. 16, are substantially reduced, as is the value of the orders which continue to be available.

The new provisions described in this edition apply to proceedings in the magistrates' court commenced on or after 1 October 2012 and to determinations in the Crown Court in relation to legal aid applications (which are required to be refused before a central funds order can be made) made on or after 27 January 2014 (see the Costs in Criminal Cases (General) (Amendment) (No. 2) Regulations 2013 (SI 2013 No. 2830)).

Proceedings in the magistrates' court begin with the issue of a warrant requisition or summons; an appeal to the Crown Court begins when the notice of appeal is served; other proceedings in the Crown Court begin when they are sent; in the High Court, proceedings begin when an application for leave to appeal by way of case stated is made or other notice is given; proceedings in the Court of Appeal begin when an application for leave to appeal is given or other notice of appeal is given; proceedings in the Supreme Court begin when an application for leave to appeal is made (LASPO 2012, sch. 7, part 4).

These changes also apply to applications by the A-G to the Court of Appeal, extradition proceedings and Courts Martial.

Under the Prosecution of Offences Act 1985, s. 16(1), but subject to the LASPO 2012, where an information is not proceeded with, or the accused is acquitted after a trial, the court with the power to make a defendant's costs order is the court which acquits the accused. The fact that the court would not have tried the case because the information was laid out of time does not prevent the court from making a defendant's costs order (*Patel v Blakey* [1988] RTR 65). The phrase 'not proceeded with' is wide enough to encompass proceedings that have been stayed as an abuse of process (*R (R E Williams and Sons) v Hereford Magistrates' Court* [2008] EWHC 2585 (Admin)). This would also extend to proceedings that were discontinued as a result of the defendant receiving a police caution (*R (Stoddard) v Oxford Magistrates' Court* (2005) 169 JP 683), or being bound over to keep the peace (*Emohare v Thames Magistrates' Court* (2009) 179 JP 303). There is power to award costs in relation to pre-charge work, e.g., in relation to providing advice and assistance at a police station provided that the advice was related to the proceedings (*R (Hale) v North Sefton Justices* [2002] EWHC 257 (Admin)). There is no power to award defence costs in relation to breach proceedings brought in respect of community orders and the like; any order, assuming there to be jurisdiction, would need to be applied for under the MCA 1980, s. 64.

The LASPO 2012, sch. 7, paras. 2 and 3, limit the award of costs in respect of legal fees (in magistrates' courts and the Crown Court) and cap these at the legal aid rates prescribed by the Lord Chancellor. This limitation also applies to experts' fees in those proceedings.

Under the LASPO 2012 costs will be awarded only to individuals (and not to companies or other bodies), except in Supreme Court proceedings.

Under s. 16(2) of the Prosecution of Offences Act 1985, where an accused is not tried for an offence for which he has been sent for trial (or in respect of which notice of transfer has been given), or he is tried on indictment and acquitted on any count in the indictment, the Crown Court has jurisdiction to make a defendant's costs order, not only to allow for costs during those proceedings but also in respect of proceedings in the lower court.

D33.5

Under s. 16(3) of the 1985 Act, where an accused convicted in the magistrates' court appeals against conviction and it is set aside by the Crown Court, or he appeals against sentence and is awarded a less severe punishment by the Crown Court, the Crown Court may make a defendant's costs order (subject to the cap that the LASPO 2012, sch. 7, imposes).

Under the LASPO 2012, sch. 7, para. 3, the Court of Appeal has no power to make a defendant's costs order in respect of legal costs save in limited circumstances relating to a defendant who has been found not guilty by reason of insanity, or has been found unfit to stand trial, or having been found unfit to stand trial, has been found to have done the act or made the omission alleged against him. The Court can award an amount in respect of legal costs in relation to the costs of

Part D Procedure

an individual defendant in proceedings in the court below. On an appeal under the CJA 1987, s. 9(11) (appeals against orders or rulings at preparatory hearings), the Court of Appeal may no longer make an order for payment of costs from central funds. Personal costs may be awarded (Prosecution of Offences Act 1985, s. 16(4A)).

D33.6   There is no power to award costs under the Prosecution of Offences Act 1985, s. 16, in respect of proceedings commenced by way of complaint (as opposed to charge or information), such as alleged breaches of community orders or civil proceedings under the POCA 2002. Costs in those proceedings, when properly claimable, are governed by the MCA 1980, s. 64.

In *Liverpool Magistrates' Court, ex parte Abiaka* (1999) 163 JP 497, the Divisional Court held that s. 16(1) gave power to any constitution of the magistrates' court to make a defendant's costs order, and was not confined to the same constitution of justices who had dismissed the case.

Proper Approach to Making of a Defendant's Costs Order

D33.7   The Prosecution of Offences Act 1985, s. 16, merely empowers courts to make defendants' costs orders but gives no guidance on when and how the power should be exercised. Such guidance is, however, provided by the *Practice Direction (Costs in Criminal Proceedings)* [2013] 1 WLR 3255.

The *Practice Direction* applies whenever a magistrates' court, the Crown Court, Divisional Court or the Court of Appeal considers an award of costs in criminal proceedings. Paragraph 2.1.1 makes it clear that magistrates' courts may make defendant's costs orders, whether sending the proceedings to the Crown Court for trial or dealing summarily with an offence. In deciding whether to make an order, magistrates' courts should take into account the same factors as the Crown Court (see below).

Paragraphs 2.1.1 (magistrates' courts) and 2.2.1 (Crown Court) of the *Practice Direction* stipulate that, where s. 16 of the Act applies, an order should normally be made 'unless there are positive reasons for not doing so'. An example for not making an order is that 'the defendant's own conduct has brought suspicion on himself and has misled the prosecution into thinking that the case against him was stronger than it was'; in such a case, 'the defendant can be left to pay his own costs'. In *R (Rees) v Snaresbrook Crown Court* [2012] EWHC 3879 (Admin) the Divisional Court expressed the view *obiter* that this was not an exclusive list and thought an order might also be refused if, though acquitted, the defendant had committed perjury or relied on an ambush defence. Paragraph 2.1.1 (magistrates' courts) makes it clear that the decision whether to make an order under s. 16 'is a matter in the discretion of the court in the light of the circumstances of each particular case', effectively reducing the scope for challenging a refusal to make an order under s. 16. Paragraphs 2.1.1 and 2.2.1 state that the court, if it declines to make a costs order, should explain that the reason for not making an order does not involve any suggestion that the defendant is guilty of any criminal conduct but that the order is being refused because of a particular positive reason, which should be specifically identified. Paragraph 2.4.3 of the *Practice Direction* provides that where the Court of Appeal has jurisdiction to make an order under s. 16, it will have in mind the principles applied by the Crown Court in relation to acquitted defendants.

D33.8   When considering whether the defendant brought the prosecution on himself, the court is entitled to rely on a statement of facts from the prosecution. Thus, the court does not have to hear oral evidence on this matter (*Mooney v Cardiff Justices* (2000) 164 JP 220).

In *R (Stoddard) v Oxford Magistrates' Court* (2005) 169 JP 683, the defendants were charged with selling alcohol to an under-age purchaser. After considerable delay, the prosecution indicated that they were willing to conclude the proceedings by way of a formal caution, and the defendants accepted that offer. The charges were subsequently dismissed, with the prosecution offering no evidence. The defendants applied for a defendant's costs order under s. 16, but the application was refused. The Divisional Court held that a caution is not to be equated with a conviction. Although by accepting a formal caution a defendant is acknowledging that he has committed the alleged offence, and the existence of the caution can be drawn to the attention of a court on a subsequent occasion, it can be distinguished from a conviction since a defendant does not receive a criminal record, there is no penalty, and no risk of publicity. It follows that, where a prosecution is withdrawn following the acceptance by the accused of a caution, the defendant stands acquitted for the purposes of the making of a defendant's costs order under s. 16.

In *R (Spiteri) v Basildon Crown Court* (2009) 173 JP 327 the applicant successfully reviewed a **D33.9** refusal to make a defendant's costs order on the grounds that he was acquitted on a 'technicality'. It was held that a costs order could not be refused on the sole ground that the applicant had brought the proceedings upon himself, as more was required, such as the defendant having misled the prosecution as to the strength of the case against him. A similar point arose in *Dowler v MerseyRail* (2009) 173 JP 332, where the Divisional Court ruled that courts should give reasons for a refusal contemporaneously with the ruling.

In *R (Harry A Coff Ltd) v Environment Agency* [2003] EWHC 1305 (Admin), a district judge declined to make a defendant's costs order under s. 16 on the ground that the amount sought was unreasonable on its face and the court should not allow costs that reflect extravagance. The Divisional Court held that the district judge was wrong to refuse to make a defendant's costs order on this basis. What had been asked for was an order for costs to be assessed. It would therefore be for the person subsequently assessing the costs to determine whether the costs claimed were excessive. Where the Crown would not accept a proposal from the defence to be bound over to keep the peace until it became apparent, on the day of trial, that the complainant would not give evidence, it was wrong for the judge to limit the amount of the defendant's costs order to the cost of that day alone (*Newcombe v CPS* [2013] EWHC 2160 (Admin)).

Costs should not be denied merely because the prosecution acted properly in bringing the case. See, e.g., *Birmingham Juvenile Court, ex parte H* (1992) 156 JP 445, where the defence solicitor admitted that the prosecution was not malicious, but the Divisional Court held that this was no reason for the justices to refuse to make a defendant's costs order.

The ECHR can also be relevant to the way in which costs applications are dealt with. In *Hussain* **D33.10** *v UK* (2006) 43 EHRR 437, counsel for the Crown informed the court that a key witness did not want to give evidence and that the prosecution did not feel that she ought to be compelled to give evidence; accordingly, they offered no evidence. The applicant was duly acquitted. He made an application for a defendant's costs order under s. 16. The trial judge stated that there was compelling evidence against the defendant on the court papers and that he was not going to exercise his discretion to make an order for costs in his favour. The ECtHR noted that the presumption of innocence enshrined in the ECHR, Article 6(2), is one of the elements of a fair criminal trial required by Article 6 and will be violated if a statement of a public official concerning a person charged with a criminal offence reflects an opinion that he is guilty unless he has been proved so according to law. The Court observed that, although the ECHR does not guarantee a defendant who had been acquitted the right to reimbursement of his costs, there was no question of any conduct by the applicant which could have brought him within the sort of cases in which a costs order might be refused, and no suggestion that he was in any way responsible for the non-attendance of the witness. The only natural interpretation which could be put on the trial judge's words was that he was refusing the order because he was of the view that, although the applicant had been acquitted, he was in fact guilty of the offence. That was incompatible with the presumption of innocence, and it followed that there had been a violation of Article 6(2). For a detailed review of the ECHR jurisprudence, see *Ashendon v UK* (2011) 54 EHRR 433.

Partial Acquittal Paragraphs 2.1.1 and 2.2.2 of the *Practice Direction* deal with the situa- **D33.11** tion where an accused is acquitted on some but not all charges or counts. The Prosecution of Offences Act 1985, s. 16(2)(b), expressly allows a defendant's costs order to be made in such cases. Paragraph 2.2.2 provides that the court may order that only part of the costs incurred be paid (see also s. 16(7) of the Act). The court 'should make whatever order seems just having regard to the relative importance of the two charges and the conduct of the parties generally'. The same approach applies in magistrates' courts (see para. 2.1.1). No doubt the court's decision will in practice depend on whether the accused was acquitted on the major part of the indictment or only on subsidiary counts. Whether a plea to the matters of which he was ultimately convicted was offered to the prosecution but rejected will also be of importance.

D33.12 **Costs on Crown Court Appeal**   Paragraph 2.2.3 of the *Practice Direction* points out that the Crown Court may make a defendant's costs order in favour of a successful appellant. In *R (Barrington) v Preston Crown Court* [2001] EWHC Admin 599, the accused was convicted in the magistrates' court of failing to provide a breath specimen. She appealed to the Crown Court. At the Crown Court, the prosecution offered no evidence after a crucial witness failed to attend. The conviction was quashed. However, the judge refused an application for a defendant's costs order. On review, it was held that, having regard to the fact that the case collapsed not because of anything the accused had said or done, or any misleading behaviour on her part, but simply because a prosecution witness had failed to attend court, an application for a defendant's costs order should have been successful. Similarly, in *R (Cunningham) v Exeter Crown Court* [2003] 2 Cr App R (S) 374, the Divisional Court reiterated that, where the Crown Court allows an appeal from the magistrates' court, the successful defendant should be awarded his costs under s. 16 unless there are positive reasons for not doing so. Where the court takes the view that there are such reasons for not awarding costs, it should set out its reasons for coming to that view (albeit briefly, but in sufficient detail that the defendant can see the basis for the decision). In *R (Pluckrose) v Snaresbrook Crown Court* (2009) 173 JP 492 the Divisional Court ruled it appropriate to deny costs to a successful appellant whose appeal had been allowed as an act of mercy.

Effect of Defendant's Costs Order: the General Rule

D33.13 The effect of a defendant's costs order is that the accused or appellant is paid his costs out of central funds. 'Proceedings' include any there may have been in a court below that making the costs order (see the definition of 'proceedings' in s. 21(1)). Thus, where the Crown Court on trial on indictment or appeal from the magistrates makes a defendant's costs order, the order will cover the costs of the sending proceedings or summary trial. Paragraph 1.3.1 of the *Practice Direction (Costs in Criminal Proceedings)* [2013] 1 WLR 3255 provides that, where the court is sitting in an appellate capacity, the order 'will include the costs incurred in the proceedings in the lower courts unless for good reason the court directs that such costs are not included in the order'.

The term 'costs' covers only expenses properly incurred in the proceedings; it cannot include expenses that do not relate directly to the proceedings themselves, such as loss of earnings (see para. 1.3.1 of the *Practice Direction*). Paragraph 1.3.1 goes on to note that where the party in whose favour the costs order is made is funded by legal aid, he will only recover his 'personal costs' (Prosecution of Offences Act 1985, s. 21(4A)(a)).

D33.14 If the accused agrees, the amount payable under s. 16(6) may be fixed forthwith, or it may be taxed (Practice Direction (Costs in Criminal Proceedings) [2013] 1 WLR 3255, para. 1.4.1). Courts will generally decline to award a fixed sum with respect to costs unless it is both modest and not contentious. In either case the claim must be determined in accordance with regulations made by the Lord Chancellor (s. 16(9)(b)). The relevant provisions are part III (regs. 4 to 13) of the Costs in Criminal Cases (General) Regulations 1986 (SI 1986 No. 1335). These provide in essence that the 'appropriate authority' (or officers appointed to act on his behalf) shall consider the claim for costs submitted by or on behalf of the accused, and shall allow costs not exceeding prescribed maximums in respect of work that appears to have been actually and reasonably done and disbursements that have been actually and reasonably incurred (reg. 7). Regulation 7(6), which applies to legal proceedings where not all individuals are eligible for legal aid, provides that, in such proceedings, if the amount of an award out of central funds is not fixed by the court, any amount payable in respect of legal costs must be calculated in accordance with rates or scales or other provision made by the Lord Chancellor, whether or not that results in the fixing of an amount that the appropriate authority considers reasonably sufficient or necessary to compensate the person. The amount payable is calculated at the current appropriate legal aid rates. The 'appropriate authority' is (a) the Registrar in the case of Court of Appeal proceedings; (b) the Master of the Crown Office in the case of Divisional Court proceedings; (c) an officer appointed by the Lord Chancellor in the case of Crown Court and magistrates' court proceedings. Save in relation to magistrates' court proceedings, an applicant (i.e. any person in whose favour an order for costs out of central funds has been made) who is dissatisfied with the appropriate authority's decision as to the amount of the costs payable may first apply for redetermination by the authority. If the result of that is unsatisfactory, there is an appeal to a costs judge, and a further appeal from him to the High Court if a point of principle of general importance is involved (regs. 9 to 12). The procedure on appeal to the High Court against the decision of a costs judge is governed by the Civil Procedure Rules, part 52. The above provisions for redetermination and appeal do not apply where the costs determined are in respect of magistrates' courts proceedings (see reg. 9), but the decision of the justices' clerk may be challenged by judicial review in accordance with the usual principles governing such applications.

A claim for costs which exceeds that quoted to an insurer would not in principle be disallowed if **D33.15** that quotation was significantly lower than market rates, nor would full recovery of costs in such circumstances offend the indemnity principle (*Orrow* [2011] 3 Costs LR 34).

R (McCormick) v Liverpool City Magistrates' Court [2001] 2 All ER 705 concerned costs incurred before legal aid was granted. The accused did not have the means to pay those costs. It was held that costs are incurred by an accused for the purpose of s. 16(6) if he is contractually obliged to pay for them; there is no requirement to prove that he had in fact paid, or was likely to pay, those costs.

There are conflicting decisions in relation to the payment of agency fees. If these are claimed as a disbursement a reasonable payment can be recovered, subject to the statutory limits now in place. However, if the time spent is charged to profit costs, *Murray* [2013] Costs LR 867 suggests that, where an agent is instructed, it is not possible to recover an amount greater than that charged to the principals by the agent. However, that decision is inconsistent with a series of earlier decisions (*Duxbury* [1997] Costs LR (Core Vol) 423; *Pullum* [1997] Costs LR (Core Vol) 413; *Smith and Graham v Lord Chancellor* [1999] All ER (D) 957). The decision in *Murray* fails to acknowledge that the issue is the contractual liability accepted by the client to the principal firm and not the liability incurred by that firm.

Murray confirms that a former senior solicitor, requalified as a barrister, may recover hourly remuneration at the rate appropriate to a senior solicitor.

Orders for Less than the Full Costs Incurred

By the Prosecution of Offences Act 1985, s. 16(6A), where the court making a defendant's costs **D33.16** order is of the opinion that there are circumstances making it inappropriate for the accused to recover the full amount of the costs that would otherwise be assessed payable under s. 16(6), it shall assess what amount would be just and reasonable and specify it in the order. One obvious situation for fixing the costs at less than the full amount is where an accused is acquitted on some but not all the counts on the indictment.

In *Dudley Magistrates' Court, ex parte Power City Stores Ltd* (1990) 154 JP 654, where the defendant wanted to recover the cost of employing leading counsel, the Divisional Court held that, in calculating the amount of costs to be paid under s. 16, the officer doing the assessment has to carry out a two-stage test. First, he has to consider whether the expenses claimed were properly incurred by the defendant. If so, the second step is to ask what amount would be reasonably sufficient to compensate the defendant for those costs. The test is whether the defendant acted reasonably in instructing the counsel he did. There are cases in which junior counsel or a solicitor could conduct the case, but in which it is reasonable to instruct leading counsel. In *R (Hale) v North Sefton Justices* [2002] EWHC 257 (Admin) it was held that the question was whether the accused had acted reasonably in the circumstances by instructing a solicitor at a particular hourly rate, not whether he could have instructed a more junior solicitor. In that case, the justices' clerk had applied the statutory criterion of reasonable sufficiency in s. 16(6) to the wrong issue, namely the quality of representation, rather than the costs incurred.

Order in Favour of a Publicly Funded Accused

D33.17 By the Prosecution of Offences Act 1985, s. 21(4A)(a), the costs of a publicly funded accused shall *not* — for purposes of a defendant's costs order — be taken to include any costs of representation under the LASPO 2012, part 1 (legal aid). It follows that a defendant's costs order will generally be pointless in the case of such an accused since all the legal costs properly incurred on his behalf will have been defrayed out of legal aid, and there will be nothing left on which the order can bite. A costs order will, however, be appropriate if, for example, the accused was not aided until a late stage of the proceedings and paid for the costs of his early representation privately, or if there were unusual expenditures incurred on his behalf which were not authorised by the Legal Aid Agency. Similarly, he can, as a result of a defendant's costs order, become entitled to an allowance for travelling and subsistence, as if he had been a witness. The upshot of s. 21(4A)(a) is that, save in a minority of exceptional cases, defendant's costs orders are relevant only to accused who have paid for their defences privately. In *Lamb* [2011] 6 Costs LR 1092 a defendant was allowed costs even though a representation order, held by his previous solicitors, had in error not been formally discharged. However, where the same firm continues to act privately for a client who has the benefit of a representation order, the effect of the Criminal Legal Aid (Remuneration) Regulations 2013, reg. 9, is that payment cannot be recovered from central funds for legal expenses incurred until the representation order is withdrawn notwithstanding the agreement of the client (*McCatty* [2013] Costs LR 863).

In *Brewer v Secretary of State for Justice* [2009] 3 All ER 861 the court held that a publicly funded defendant was able to recover payments made to a third party for professional services as out-of-pocket expenses. Whether such payments would be recoverable depended upon (i) the profession of the person instructed and the services provided, (ii) the reason why it was necessary and reasonable to incur the expenditure, and (iii) why the work was not paid for under the representation order in force. In cases where the expenditure claimed was outside the norm, the person claiming should assist the court by providing full details of the heads of expenditure.

Appeals and Reviews in relation to Defence Costs Orders

D33.18 If a magistrates' court refuses to make a defence costs order, an application may be made by way of judicial review. This will also apply to a Crown Court appeal from the lower court. However in *Hunter v Newcastle Crown Court* [2014] QB 94 it was held that the High Court had no jurisdiction to review a refusal to make such an order when it related to a trial on indictment and there is no right of appeal to the Court of Appeal.

PROSECUTION COSTS

Power to Make Order for Prosecution Costs

D33.19 Subject to what follows, the Prosecution of Offences Act 1985, s. 17(1), provides that the court may award a prosecutor such amount out of central funds as it considers reasonably necessary to compensate him for any expenses properly incurred by him in the proceedings. This applies whether or not the accused is convicted, but applies only to proceedings in respect of an indictable offence (whether tried summarily or on indictment) and proceedings before a Divisional Court in respect of a summary offence (s. 17(1)(a) and (b)). An important restriction on the ambit of s. 17(1) is that no order may be made in favour of a public authority (s. 17(2)), which term is defined by s. 17(3) as comprising a police force, the CPS, local authorities and any other authority appointed by the Crown or financed by money voted by Parliament. Thus, s. 17(1) is of potential value only in that tiny proportion of prosecutions brought by private individuals or organisations. Where the subsection does potentially apply, an order *should* be made unless there is good reason for not doing so — e.g., the proceedings have been instituted or continued without good cause (see para. 2.6.1 of the *Practice Direction (Costs in Criminal Proceedings)* [2013] 1 WLR 3255). Even so, an express application must be made, rather than assuming that the court will automatically order costs of its own motion (para. 2.6.1).

Regulations 4 to 13 of the Costs in Criminal Cases (General) Regulations 1986 apply to assessment of prosecutors' costs out of central funds as they apply to costs under defendant's costs orders. Under earlier regulations, it was held that a private prosecutor could not claim for the time he had spent in preparation and presentation of the prosecution, although he was entitled to recover travelling and secretarial expenses (*Stockport Magistrates' Court, ex parte Cooper* (1984) 149 JP 261) and legal expenses can be recovered when a private prosecutor is represented; these are paid at private client rates.

In *Murphy v Media Protection Services Ltd* [2013] Costs LR 16 a private prosecutor was denied costs recovery as the prosecution was essentially advanced to protect commercial interests (satellite broadcast of football matches) and the litigation had been conducted in a manner indistinguishable from litigation in the civil courts where a substantial sum of money is involved. This was an exceptional case where the civil costs regime should apply, and because the prosecutor had been unsuccessful it would have to bear its own costs. A further consequence of the ruling was that the appellant's costs were not recoverable from central funds as would normally have been the case, but fell onto the respondent on 'loser pays' principles.

Order that the Accused Pay Prosecution Costs

D33.20 The Prosecution of Offences Act 1985, s. 18(1) and (2), authorise the making of orders that a convicted accused or unsuccessful appellant shall pay costs to the prosecutor, or where the appellant is unsuccessful in the Court of Appeal to the prosecutor or other named third party. In addition, reg. 14 of the Costs in Criminal Cases (General) Regulations 1986 provides, *inter alia*, that the Prosecution of Offences Act 1985, s. 18, is to apply to proceedings in the Crown Court on committals for sentence (including committals to be dealt with for breach of a suspended sentence, probation order or conditional discharge) just as it applies to trials on indictment. In short, the Crown Court when dealing with the committed offender may order him to pay costs.

In *Hamilton-Johnson v RSPCA* [2002] 2 Cr App R (S) 390, the issue was whether the Crown Court had jurisdiction to order a defendant who appealed unsuccessfully from the magistrates' court to the Crown Court to pay to the prosecutor sums by way of costs which the magistrates had refused to award to the prosecutor. The Court of Appeal (Civil Division) concluded that the Crown Court had the requisite jurisdiction to make such an order, but should hesitate before doing so as the magistrates would be far better placed to decide the issue.

D33.21 In *Constantine* [2011] 3 All ER 767 the Court of Appeal held that prosecution costs ought not to be ordered until any issue of confiscation under the POCA 2002 had been resolved.

Amount of Order for Prosecution Costs

D33.22 When a court makes an order under the Prosecution of Offences Act 1985, s. 18, for the payment of prosecution costs, it orders the payment of an amount that it considers 'just and reasonable'. That sum must be specified in the order (s. 18(3)). The court may not delegate (e.g., to a justices' clerk or Crown Court officer) the duty of determining what the accused should pay (*Bunston v Rawlings* [1982] 2 All ER 697). See also para. 1.4.1 of the *Practice Direction (Criminal Proceedings: Costs)* [2013] 1 WLR 3255. Therefore, the prosecution should, if possible, be able to inform the court of the costs that have been incurred at each stage of the relevant proceedings, thus enabling the court to make an appropriate order. Where the prosecution are unable to provide a figure forthwith, the court should adjourn for inquiries to be made by an appropriate officer.

When seeking an order for costs against a defendant, the prosecution must give notice to the defendant of its intention to apply for such an order (*Emmett* (1999) *The Times*, 15 October 1999).

In *Associated Octel Ltd* [1997] 1 Cr App R (S) 435, the Court of Appeal held that the costs of the prosecution for the purposes of s. 18(1) might include the costs of the prosecuting authority in carrying out investigations. In *Octel*, the offence was both investigated and prosecuted by the Health and Safety Executive. It is submitted that the position would be different where different bodies investigated and prosecuted (e.g., the police and the CPS respectively). It would not seem to be 'just and reasonable' for the court to order the defendant to pay the prosecution in respect of costs for which it was not liable. As to the procedure to be adopted in cases where the prosecution seeks an order requiring the defendant to pay costs, the Court of Appeal observed that:

(a) the prosecution should serve on the defence, at the earliest time, full details of its costs, so as to give the defence a proper opportunity to consider them and make representations on them, if appropriate;

(b) if the defendant, once served with a schedule of the prosecution's costs, wished to dispute the whole or any part of the schedule, he should give proper notice to the prosecution of the objections which it was proposed to make and should at least make it clear to the court what the objections were — in some exceptional cases, a full hearing would need to be held for the objections to be resolved, as there was no provision for the taxation of the prosecution's costs in a criminal case.

In *Balshaw v CPS* [2009] 1 WLR 2301 the Court of Appeal held that the proposition in *Associated Octel Ltd* [1997] 1 Cr App R (S) 435 should not be taken too far and that the CPS need not show a contractual liability to the third party to pay costs. In that case the prosecution made clear that it was intended that they would be reimbursing the police for costs occasioned in relation to a forensic accountant's report. The Court held:

> Since the CPS was, thereby, acknowledging its obligation to pay any award of those fees to the police in respect of the report and the report formed an important part of the CPS's presentation of the case, the judge was correct to conclude that the order was just and reasonable.

D33.23 In *Bow Street Stipendiary Magistrate, ex parte Multimedia Screen Ltd* (1998) *The Times*, 28 January 1998, the defendant sought judicial review of a costs order requiring him to pay £15,000 although he had made only a tiny profit from the offence of which he was convicted. The Divisional Court held that the prosecution had had to do a lot of research and so the order was appropriate. In most cases, precise assessment of prosecution costs will be irrelevant, since the principles discussed below as to the exercise of the court's discretion in the making of orders will result in the amount the accused is required to pay being well below the actual costs, however restrictively interpreted.

Section 18(1) is subject to two specific qualifications. First, where a person is, on summary conviction, fined £5 or less, no order for costs may be made 'unless in the particular circumstances of the case [the court] considers it right to do so'. Secondly, where a juvenile is convicted before a magistrates' court, the amount of any costs he is ordered to pay shall not exceed the amount of any fine imposed on him (s. 18(5)). It is submitted that, where a juvenile is dealt with by means other than a fine, the costs that may be awarded against him are entirely discretionary and not subject to any statutory upper limit.

Proper Approach to Orders that the Accused Pay Prosecution Costs

Paragraph 3.4 of the *Practice Direction (Costs in Criminal Proceedings)* [2013] 1 WLR 3255 states **D33.24** that an order should be made under the Prosecution of Offences Act 1985, s. 18, where the court is satisfied that the offender or appellant has the means and ability to pay. This is the fundamental principle governing costs against the accused and merely confirms pre-existing case law; see, e.g., *Mountain* (1978) 68 Cr App R 41, where the Court of Appeal varied orders that M and K pay the entire prosecution costs as assessed (probably £1,000) to orders that they pay £150 and £250 respectively, Lawton LJ saying that when imposing financial penalties, including costs, the court must have regard to the means of a convicted person. Similarly, in *Nottingham Justices, ex parte Fohmann* (1986) 84 Cr App R 316, the Divisional Court quashed an order by magistrates that F pay a fine of £400 (for offences of obtaining by deception by turning back the odometers on cars he was selling at auction) and prosecution costs of £600, since he was in receipt of benefit and, even if able to maintain the rate of £10 per week ordered by the court, would have taken two years to pay the combined fine and costs. Glidewell LJ indicated that the amount of costs ordered should not exceed that which the offender can reasonably pay within a year. The case also illustrates that the propriety or otherwise of the decision on costs must be viewed in the light of the overall financial orders made by the court, in particular, any fines or compensation the offender is required to pay. This principle was clearly stated by Phillimore LJ in *Whalley* (1972) 56 Cr App R 304 at p. 305: 'This Court takes the view that whenever a court is imposing a financial penalty, or making an order in regard to costs, it must have regard to the means of the individual'.

To make an order such that a sale would be required of a matrimonial home being used by an adult child with Asperger's syndrome was unreasonable (*Pegley* [2012] EWCA Crim 2583).

Although *Ex parte Fohmann* remains important for its statement of principle, the suggested time-limit of a year for payment of costs may no longer be appropriate in view of the Court of Appeal having held that fines and compensation may now be fixed at amounts requiring payment by instalments over a two or even three-year period (see **E15.21** and **E16.8**). In deciding whether the offender has sufficient means to pay an order for costs, mortgage debts should be taken into account (*Ghadami* [1998] 1 Cr App R (S) 42).

In *Northallerton Magistrates' Court, ex parte Dove* (1999) 163 JP 657, the Divisional Court gave the following series of guidelines on the imposition of costs.

(1) The order to pay costs should never exceed the sum which the offender is able to pay, and which it is reasonable to expect him to pay, having regard to his means and any other financial order imposed on him.
(2) Nor should it exceed the sum which the prosecutor has actually and reasonably incurred.
(3) The purpose of such an order is to compensate the prosecutor and not to punish the offender, e.g., for exercising his constitutional right to defend himself.
(4) Any costs ordered should not in the ordinary way be grossly disproportionate to any fine imposed. Where the fine and the costs exceeded the sum which the offender could reasonably be ordered to pay, the costs should be reduced, rather than the fine.
(5) An offender facing a fine or an order as to costs should disclose to the magistrates the data relevant to his financial position, so that they can assess what he can reasonably afford to pay. Failure to make such disclosure could lead the court to draw reasonable inferences as to his means.
(6) The court should give the offender a fair opportunity to adduce any relevant financial information and make submissions prior to the determination of any financial order.

In *Nuthoo* [2011] 1 Costs LR 87 the Court of Appeal added the following guideline (at [12]):

> . . . a costs order is to be enforced as if it had been adjudged to be paid on conviction in the magistrates' court . . .; that it is the duty of the court to consider the defendant's means . . .; that it is the court that has the power to allow an individual to pay by instalments . . .; that in default of payment, imprisonment will be imposed, in this case up to a maximum of six months . . .; and that therefore,

in order to avoid sending an offender to prison by the back door, and to ensure that the length of time over which the order would be paid is not oppressive, the amount and length of time for payment must be just, albeit that a period of up to three years for payment in an appropriate case is not necessarily too long.

D33.25 **Plea** A plea of guilty certainly does not preclude the making of an order for costs. However, combined with other factors such as the offender's limited means, it may persuade the court not to make an order or to make one for considerably less than the actual costs (see O'Connor LJ's judgment in *Maher* [1983] QB 784 at p. 789D–H). The weight to be attached to the plea in this context will depend, *inter alia*, on the stage at which it was entered and the gravity of the case. Thus, in *Maher*, the Court of Appeal (distinguishing the earlier case of *Matthews* (1979) 1 Cr App R (S) 346) ordered that the three appellants should pay a total of £180,000 costs, even though they had all eventually pleaded guilty and one of them had done so at the earliest possible opportunity. The costs orders were justified, *inter alia*, because the offences were exceptionally serious — murder and a major conspiracy to import heroin.

D33.26 **Remainder of the Sentence** Where the offender is given an immediate custodial sentence it is unusual to impose an order for costs, if only because he will for the time being have no income out of which to make the required payments. But, again, it is ultimately a matter for the court's discretion. Thus, if there is good reason to suppose that he has substantial capital assets (in particular if they are the proceeds of crime), an order may properly be made (see, e.g., *Maher* [1983] QB 784). Where the sentence is non-custodial, one line of authority suggests that any order for costs should not be out of proportion to the penalty proper. The Court of Appeal has considered on a number of occasions the question whether the court should make an order for the payment of prosecution costs which is larger than the fine imposed for the offence itself. For example, in *Whalley* (1972) 56 Cr App R 304, an order to pay the whole costs of prosecuting a drink-driving offence, for which W had been disqualified and fined £20, was reduced to an order to pay costs not exceeding £50. Similarly, in *Firmston* (1984) 6 Cr App R (S) 189, costs of £400 ordered following F's conviction on indictment for theft from a shop were reduced to £100 because he had been given an absolute discharge for the offence itself. These cases were cited in *Boyle* [1995] Crim LR 514, in which the Court of Appeal nonetheless decided to follow instead the case of *Bushell* (1980) 2 Cr App R (S) 77. Their lordships upheld an order to pay £1,000 prosecution costs where the offender had been fined £250 after electing trial on indictment when the case could conveniently have been tried summarily; in such a case, which was otherwise appropriate for an order for him to pay prosecution costs, the offender could properly be ordered to pay costs on the Crown Court scale. In a level 1 fine case a costs order for £6,871 was grossly disproportionate notwithstanding the complexity of prosecuting the case and a late guilty plea (*R (Middleton) v Cambridge Magistrates' Court* (2012) 176 JP 569).

D33.27 **Conduct of the Defence** At least in theory, an offender who is found guilty on indictment of an either-way offence should not be punished in costs for having exercised his constitutional right to trial by jury (*Hayden* [1975] 2 All ER 558). However, any order made will inevitably reflect the fact that he has chosen the more expensive method of trial (*Hayden*, and see also *Bushell* (1980) 2 Cr App R (S) 77 where orders to pay £250 costs against each of two accused were upheld because, even though the offence was merely one of obtaining services worth £21 and the fines imposed were only £100, they had elected Crown Court trial in a matter eminently suitable for summary disposition and thus greatly increased the costs incurred by the prosecution). The exercise of the court's discretion may also be affected by the accused having chosen to plead not guilty when the prosecution case against him was manifestly strong and he must have known all along that he was guilty (see dicta in *Singh* (1982) 4 Cr App R (S) 38 where an order of £400 costs against S following his conviction on indictment for a minor assault occasioning actual bodily harm was upheld partly because he had 'extravagantly' elected trial on indictment when there was 'really no need in the circumstances' for him to do so). The relevance of the reasonableness of the defence (albeit disbelieved) to costs was also referred to, *obiter*, by Lawton LJ in *Mountain* (1978) 68 Cr App R 41 (at pp. 43–4, emphasis added):

> In many cases at the trial the accused says, as he is entitled to say and frequently is justified in saying, that there has been some mistake on the part of the prosecution witnesses; that they have confused themselves in thinking that they saw something which they did not see, that their memories have failed them or that the accused has some explanation for what at first sight seems to be criminal conduct. *In that class of case it may be unfair to make an order that the accused should pay the costs of the prosecution.* But there are other kinds of cases which come before the Crown Court where the defence is that everybody except the accused is telling lies and that the prosecution's case is virtually a concocted one. . . .
>
> It is in that kind of case that courts are entitled to make an order that the accused should pay the costs of the prosecution.

Conduct of the Prosecution   Where a minor case is in the Crown Court through the prosecu-   **D33.28**
tion's choice, they cannot expect to recover their full costs from the accused. In *Hall* (1988) 10 Cr App R (S) 456, H was willing to plead guilty to careless driving. The case went to the Crown Court because the prosecution insisted on a charge of reckless (now 'dangerous') driving. In the Crown Court, H pleaded guilty to careless driving, and the Crown offered no evidence on the reckless driving charge. H was conditionally discharged and ordered to pay £372 prosecution costs. On appeal, the order was reduced to £25 (the amount appropriate to a guilty plea in the magistrates' court at the time). See also *Clark* (1993) 14 Cr App R (S) 360.

Apportionment between Co-defendants   Where there is more than one accused, each should   **D33.29**
be liable only for that portion of the prosecution's costs which is attributable to him. In *Ronson* [1991] Crim LR 794, the appellant and two co-defendants were each ordered to pay a third of the prosecution costs (£440,000 each). The fourth defendant was unable to pay. On appeal, the Court of Appeal held that the right approach was to see what would be a reasonable estimate of the cost of trying each defendant alone. That could not be done here. It was not right that the three defendants who could pay should bear the burden of the fourth. Hence the costs of each defendant were reduced from a third to a quarter. Thus, the court should divide the total amount payable between the number of defendants (not just those who are able to pay) so that each defendant pays only his own share of the costs and does not subsidise a defendant who cannot pay. However, in *Harrison* (1993) 14 Cr App R (S) 419, the Court of Appeal upheld an order made against only one of a number of defendants: he was the principal offender (the other defendants having played relatively minor roles in the offences) and he had the means to pay the amount ordered. In *Durose* [2004] EWCA Crim 2188, it was argued by counsel that the court had power to make an order for costs which imposed joint and several liability. The court did not hear full argument on the point but said that their 'instinctive reaction' was that that is not an appropriate kind of order to make in a criminal case. The point was left open for decision in a later case. That the correct question was to ask, in relation to each defendant, what would have been the costs had he been tried alone was confirmed in *R (Gray) v Aylesbury Crown Court* [2014] 1 WLR 818, but subject to an overriding discretion if no figures could easily be identified.

APPEALS ON COSTS

Neither party has a right of appeal to the Crown Court in respect of a costs order made by a mag-   **D33.30**
istrates' court: the prosecution have no right of appeal to the Crown Court, and the MCA 1980, s. 108(3)(b), precludes a defence appeal to the Crown Court against a costs order. However, it was held in *Hamilton-Johnson v RSPCA* [2002] 2 Cr App R (S) 390, that the Crown Court does have jurisdiction to make an order as to costs incurred before the conclusion of the magistrates' court proceedings (either under the Prosecution of Offences Act 1985, s. 18(1), or the Senior Courts Act 1981, s. 48(2)). Usually, following an unsuccessful appeal against conviction, the Crown Court should hesitate to modify the magistrates' costs order. If the prosecutor wishes

to seek an increase in the costs the defendant has to pay, he should give written notice to this effect to the defendant, so that the defendant is aware of the possible consequences of pursuing an appeal against conviction.

ORDERS TO PAY COSTS THROWN AWAY

D33.31   The Prosecution of Offences Act 1985, s. 19(1) and (2), empowered the Lord Chancellor to make regulations by virtue of which a party to criminal proceedings may be ordered to pay costs thrown away as a result of his 'unnecessary or improper act or omission'. Regulation 3 of the Costs in Criminal Cases (General) Regulations 1986 provides that, before making such an order, the court shall hear the parties concerned, and shall take into account any other order as to costs which has been made in the proceedings (reg. 3(2)). Conversely, when the time comes to make a general order as to costs, the court shall take into account any order that has already been made under reg. 3 (reg. 3(4)). The amount to be paid by the 'guilty' party must be specified in the order (reg. 3(3)). In the case of a juvenile who has been convicted of an offence, any sum he is ordered to pay by a magistrates' court under reg. 3 shall not exceed the amount of any fine imposed on him (reg. 3(5)). If, during the period of an adjournment, the prosecution serves a notice of discontinuance, the court retains jurisdiction to determine applications for costs (*DPP v Denning* [1991] 2 QB 532). For an order as to costs to be made under reg. 3, there must be a causal relationship between the unnecessary or improper act, and the incurring of the costs to be paid under the order (*Wood Green Crown Court, ex parte DPP* [1993] 2 All ER 656). The court in *DPP V Denning* defined an act as unnecessary or improper if events would not have occurred if the party had conducted itself properly. A mere mistake without repetition can be grounds for a costs order under s. 19. If additional costs arise from the prosecution not conducting the case properly, it is not an answer to be unsure whether the fault lies with the CPS or the police as the prosecution's responsibility is indivisible. However, s. 19 contains a direction not a duty and, where there is a satisfactory explanation, no order should be made (*R (Singh) v Ealing Magistrates' Court* (2014) 178 JP 253).

D33.32   Regulation 3 is the only provision under which the prosecution may be ordered to pay costs to the accused personally. According to para. 4.1.1 of the *Practice Direction (Costs in Criminal Proceedings)* [2013] 1 WLR 3255, an order is appropriate only where the improper act or omission which has caused costs to be thrown away is that of the accused or prosecutor personally, not where it is that of the legal representatives. For orders that legal representatives pay costs, see **D33.34**.

In *Leicester Crown Court, ex parte Commissioners of Customs and Excise* (2001) *The Times*, 23 February 2001, the prosecution had refused to disclose some documents and there was an application to stay the trial as an abuse of process. The prosecution offered no evidence and the judge ordered verdicts of not guilty to be recorded. The judge ordered the prosecution to pay the defence costs incurred. The question to be decided was whether the costs order was a matter relating to trial on indictment and so excluded from judicial review by the Senior Courts Act 1981, s. 29. The Divisional Court held that, under reg. 3 of the Costs in Criminal Cases Regulations 1986, the judge has to consider first whether there had been an unnecessary or improper act or omission by, or on behalf, of the prosecution. Secondly, he has to determine whether the costs that were incurred by the defendants were as a result of that unnecessary or improper act or omission. Thirdly, he has to decide whether he would, as a matter of discretion, order all or part of the costs to be paid by the party in default. It is implicit in the last stage that, before an order can be made, the judge is required to identify the costs incurred as a result of the unnecessary or improper act or omission. Having performed those exercises, the judge has to specify the amount to be paid. In the present case, the judge had not complied with reg. 3. However, that was not a decision made without jurisdiction, since the judge was entitled to make a costs order once he was seised of the issue of whether the relevant documents had been disclosed. In those circumstances, the High Court had no jurisdiction to reconsider the judge's decision on an application for judicial review.

In *DPP v Bury Magistrates' Court* [2007] EWHC 3256 (Admin) the Divisional Court considered the position of a party to proceedings who had failed, in accordance with the duty under the CrimPR, part 3, to report the opposing party for breach of the rules. An adjournment could have been avoided if the breach had been reported. The Court held that, when assessing the quantum of any loss, a court would consider taking into account the failings of the party seeking to claim a loss.

See also *R (DPP) v Sheffield Crown Court* [2014] EWHC 2014 (Admin), where the Divisional Court quashed an order made under the Prosecution of Offences Act 1985, s. 19, requiring an acquitted defendant's costs to be paid by the CPS, rather than out of central funds. The trial judge considered that the CPS had acted improperly in prosecuting the defendant, this being in his view, 'an unnecessary or improper act or omission'.

Lord Thomas CJ indicated that a judge has no jurisdiction to use s. 19 as a means of impugning the prosecutorial discretion given to the DPP.

WITNESS EXPENSES AND FEES FOR COURT-APPOINTED LAWYERS

Section 19(3) of the Prosecution of Offences Act 1985 empowers the Lord Chancellor to make reg- **D33.33** ulations authorising the payment out of central funds of (a) witness expenses, (b) the cost of obtaining medical reports, (c) the fees of an interpreter, (d) the proper fee or costs of a person appointed under the Criminal Procedure (Insanity) Act 1964, s. 4A, to put the case for the defence and (e) the fees, costs and expenses of a legal representative appointed under the YJCEA 1999, s. 38(4), to cross-examine a witness where the Act prevents a defendant undertaking that cross-examination in person. Part V of the Costs in Criminal Cases (General) Regulations 1986 (regs. 15 to 25) deals with such payments. By reg. 16(1), the expenses properly incurred by the witness or, as the case may be, maker of a medical report or interpreter are to be allowed out of central funds unless the court directs otherwise. This applies whatever the outcome of the proceedings and regardless of whether the witness etc. is required by the prosecution or defence. A non-expert witness (other than police or prison officers) is entitled to travelling expenses, a subsistence allowance and a loss allowance (e.g., for loss of earnings) (see reg. 18). Payment of professional witnesses, experts, suppliers of medical reports and interpreters is dealt with in regs. 19 and 20. If a defendant's costs order is made in favour of the accused, he may also be allowed a subsistence allowance and travelling expenses, but he is not entitled to compensation for loss of earnings (reg. 23). See also paras. 2.5.1 and 2.5.2 of the *Practice Direction (Costs in Criminal Proceedings)* [2013] 1 WLR 3255.

The costs of court- appointed lawyers are paid from central funds at private client rates.

COSTS AGAINST LEGAL REPRESENTATIVES

An order to pay costs may be made against a legal representative (as distinct from a party) by **D33.34** virtue of the inherent jurisdiction of the Crown Court (in the case of a solicitor) or under the Prosecution of Offences Act 1985, s. 19A (in respect of a solicitor or a barrister).

The Crown Court has inherent jurisdiction to order that a solicitor pay personally any costs thrown away by his or his staff's improper act or omission (see para. 4.6.1 of the *Practice Direction (Costs in Criminal Proceedings)* [2013] 1 WLR 3255). Such an order may not be made unless reasonable notice is given to the solicitor and he has a reasonable opportunity of being heard in reply (para. 4.6.2). This power should be used only in exceptional circumstances and not where a statutory power would be available (para. 4.6.3). In *Holden and Co. v CPS* [1990] 2 QB 261, it was held that mistake, error of judgement or mere negligence were not sufficient to trigger such an order. The court's jurisdiction arose only where there was a serious dereliction of the solicitor's duty to the court. The primary object of such an order was to reimburse a litigant for costs incurred because of the solicitor's default, but there were also punitive and deterrent elements in the order.

The power to order legal representatives to pay costs has been extended by the Prosecution of Offences Act 1985, s. 19A. A magistrates' court, the Crown Court or the Court of Appeal may disallow costs or order the legal representative concerned to meet the whole or part of any wasted costs. Wasted costs are costs which are incurred as a result of any improper, unreasonable or negligent act or omission by the representative or his employee, or which the court considers it unreasonable to expect a party to pay in the light of such act or omission occurring after the costs were incurred (s. 19A(3)). The test is therefore extended to cover negligence, in addition to improper or unreasonable acts or omissions.

Procedure and Practice in Making Order

D33.35 The procedure for the exercise of the power is laid down in regs. 3A to 3D of the Costs in Criminal Cases (General) Regulations 1986. These require the court to specify the amount of the wasted costs order, and allow the representative and any party to the proceedings to make representations. The hearing should normally be in chambers, with a shorthand writer present. The court should give reasons for its order, which it may announce in public. Paragraph 4.2.2 of the *Practice Direction* says that judges in criminal cases have more direct responsibility for costs than their civil counterparts and so should keep the question of costs in the forefront of their mind at every stage of the case. They ought to be prepared to take the initiative themselves without any prompting from the parties. Paragraph 4.2.4 provides that judges contemplating making a wasted costs order should bear in mind the guidance given by the Court of Appeal in *Re a Barrister (Wasted Costs Order) (No. 1 of 1991)* [1993] QB 293, and para. 4.2.5 goes on to refer to the additional guidance given by the Court of Appeal in *Re P (a Barrister) (Wasted Costs Order)* [2002] 1 Cr App R 207.

In *Re a Barrister (Wasted Costs Order) (No. 1 of 1991)*, the Court of Appeal considered an order made against defence counsel in the Crown Court. The trial judge purported to 'disallow such part of the brief fee which would otherwise have been payable on the partial trial as exceeds what would be the proper enhanced refresher for the retrial'. His order was based upon his finding that the barrister was guilty of an 'unreasonable act or omission'. On appeal by the barrister, the Court of Appeal held that the order was *ultra vires* and fatally flawed, since it did not specify the amount of the wasted costs. In any event, the barrister was not, their lordships held, guilty of any unreasonable act or omission such as could found a wasted costs order. They went on to lay down the following guidelines as to the practice to be adopted in deciding upon a wasted costs order:

1 There is a clear need for any judge or court intending to exercise the wasted costs jurisdiction to formulate carefully and concisely the complaint and grounds upon which such an order might be sought. Those measures were draconian, and, as in contempt proceedings, the grounds had to be clear and particular.

2 Where necessary a transcript of the relevant part of the proceedings under discussion should be available. And, in accordance with the rules, a transcript of any wasted costs hearing had to be made.

3 A defendant involved in a case where such proceedings were contemplated should be present if, after discussion with counsel, it was thought that his interests might be affected. And he should certainly be present and represented if the matter might affect the course of his trial. Regulation 3B(2) [of the Costs in Criminal Cases (General) Regulations 1986: see **D33.42**] furthermore required that before a wasted costs order was made 'the court shall allow the legal or other representative and any party to the proceedings to make representations'. There might be cases where it might be appropriate for counsel for the Crown to be present.

4 A three-stage test or approach is recommended when a wasted costs order was contemplated:
   (i) Had there been an improper, unreasonable or negligent act or omission?
   (ii) As a result, had any costs been incurred by a party?
   (iii) If the answers to (i) and (ii) were yes; should the court exercise its discretion to disallow or order the representative to meet the whole or any part of the relevant costs, and if so what specific sum was involved?

5 It was inappropriate to propose any deal or settlement, such as was suggested in the present case, that the representative might forgo fees. The judge should formally state his complaint, in chambers, and invite the representative to make his own comments. After any other party had been heard the judge should give his formal ruling. Discursive conversations such as took place in the present case might be unfair and should certainly not take place.

6 As was indicated above the judge had to specify the sum to be disallowed or ordered. Alternatively, the relevant available procedure should be substituted, should it be impossible to fix the sum.

Further guidance was given in *Re P (a Barrister) (Wasted Costs Order)*, where the Court of Appeal reiterated that the crucial questions in determining whether to make a wasted costs order were those set out in 4(i)–(iii) above, and stated that the standard of proof to be applied was on the balance of probability. Generally, it would be appropriate for any application in respect of costs to be heard by the trial judge. It was, however, open for the trial judge to decline to consider such an application if, for example, he was personally embarrassed by the appearance of bias. It was only in the most exceptional circumstances that it would be appropriate to pass the matter to another judge, and the fact that, in the proper exercise of judicial functions, a judge had expressed views in relation to the conduct of a lawyer against whom an order was sought did not of itself normally constitute bias or the appearance of bias so as to necessitate a transfer.

If criticism is made by the court of a litigator, not only must an amount in issue be specified, but notice of the wasted costs hearing must be given to the litigator. An advocate instructed to represent a defendant is not thereby instructed to represent the litigator in question (*Reeves & Co. Solicitors* [2011] 4 Costs LR 616).

In *Ridehalgh v Horsefield* [1994] Ch 205, the Court of Appeal gave guidance on the discretion to **D33.36** make a wasted costs order in favour of one party to litigation against the legal representative of the other. Sir Thomas Bingham MR made it clear that the judgment was applicable to criminal as well as civil courts, and made the following points.

(a) 'Improper' covered, but was not confined to, conduct which would ordinarily justify serious professional penalty. It was not limited to significant breach of the relevant code of professional conduct. It included conduct which was improper according to the consensus of professional, including judicial, opinion, whether it violated the letter of a professional code or not.

(b) 'Unreasonable' described conduct which was vexatious, i.e. designed to harass the other side rather than advance the resolution of the dispute. Conduct could not be described as unreasonable simply because it led to an unsuccessful result, or because other more cautious legal representatives would have acted differently. The acid test was whether the conduct permitted of a reasonable explanation. If it did, the course adopted might be regarded as optimistic and reflecting on a practitioner's judgment, but it was not unreasonable.

(c) 'Negligent' should be understood in an untechnical way to denote failure to act with the competence reasonably expected of ordinary members of the profession. It was not a term of art and did not necessarily involve an actionable breach of the legal representative's duty to his own client.

(d) A legal representative was not acting improperly, unreasonably or negligently simply because he acted for a party who pursued a claim or defence which was plainly doomed to fail.

(e) However, a legal representative could not lend his assistance to proceedings which were an abuse of process, and was not entitled to use litigious procedures for purposes for which they were not intended, for example, by issuing proceedings for reasons unconnected with success in the action, pursuing a case which was known to be dishonest or knowingly conniving at incomplete disclosure of documents.

(f) Any judge considering making a wasted costs order must make full allowance for the fact that an advocate in court often had to make decisions quickly and under pressure.

(g) Legal professional privilege might be relevant. If so, the privilege was the client's which he alone could waive. Judges should make full allowance for the inability of respondent lawyers to tell the whole story. Where there was room for doubt, the respondent lawyers were entitled to the benefit of it. It was only when, with all allowance made, a lawyer's conduct of proceedings was quite plainly unjustifiable, that it would be appropriate to make the order.

(h) When a solicitor sought the advice of counsel, he did not abdicate his own professional responsibility. He had to apply his mind to the advice received. But the more specialised the advice, the more reasonable it was likely to be for him to accept it.

(i) A threat to apply for a wasted costs order should not be used as a means of intimidation. However, if one side considered that the conduct of the other was improper, unreasonable or negligent and likely to cause a waste of costs, it was not objectionable to alert the other side to that view.

(j) In the ordinary way, such applications were best left until after the end of the trial.

(k) As to procedure, the respondent lawyer should be told very clearly what he was said to have done wrong. No formal process of discovery would be appropriate. Elaborate pleadings should in general be avoided. The Court of Appeal could not imagine circumstances in which the applicant could interrogate the respondent lawyer or vice versa. The legal representative must have opportunity to show cause why an order should not be made, but this did not mean that the burden was on the legal representative to exculpate himself.

Paragraph 4.2.7 of the *Practice Direction* says that the court may postpone the making of a wasted costs order to the end of the case if it appears more appropriate to do so, e.g., where there may be conflict between the legal representatives as to the apportionment of blame, or the legal representative concerned is unable to make full representations because of a possible conflict with his duty to the client.

In Re Joseph Hill Solicitors (Wasted costs order) [2014] 1 WLR 786 the Court of Appeal emphasised that 'the power to make a wasted costs order can be valuable but this case, and others recently before this Court, demonstrate that it should be reserved only for the clearest cases otherwise more time, effort and cost goes into making and challenging the order than was alleged to have been wasted in the first place'. The Court declined to make an order because, although the solicitors had failed to lodge an alibi notice in good time, they had been acting in accordance with the standard, now identified as mistaken, practice of the profession.

D33.37 The reference to 'criminal proceedings' in the Prosecution of Offences Act 1985, s. 19A(1), is wide enough to include proceedings relating to the issue of a witness summons. A local authority attending to answer an application for disclosure of social services files relating to the complainant in a criminal case is a party to criminal proceedings, and can be the beneficiary of a wasted costs order (*Re A Solicitor (Wasted Costs Order)* [1996] 1 FLR 40).

Paragraph 4.2.8 of the *Practice Direction* stipulates that a wasted costs order should normally be made regardless of the fact that the client of the legal representative concerned is funded by Criminal Legal Aid. However, where the court is minded to disallow substantial costs arising from criminal legal aid, it may, instead of making a wasted costs order, make observations to the determining authority that work may have been unreasonably done in accordance with para. 4.3.1.

Paragraph 4.5.1 notes that the Administrative Court is governed by a different regime, namely making a wasted costs order under the Senior Courts Act 1981, s. 51(6), and has to comply with the Civil Procedure Rules, r. 46.8 (which contains similar provisions as to giving the legal representative a reasonable opportunity to attend a hearing to give reasons why the court should not make such an order).

In *R (Hide) v Staffordshire County Council* [2007] EWHC 2441 (Admin) the Divisional Court declined to order wasted costs when the effect of the order being made would be the bankruptcy of the advocate.

Examples of Conduct Justifying Order for Wasted Costs

D33.38 In *Re a Barrister (Wasted Costs Order) (No. 4 of 1992)* (1994) *The Times*, 15 March 1994, the Court of Appeal held that a barrister who practised at home without a clerk must not rely wholly on instructing solicitors to notify him of the dates and times of his cases. He was responsible for keeping abreast of listing details and should have adopted a system which enabled him to do so.

In *Rodney (Wasted Costs Order)* (9 December 1996 unreported), counsel failed to appear before the Court of Appeal due to an error by a junior clerk. He was liable for the actions of a clerk in chambers in the same way as a solicitor was vicariously liable on a wasted costs order for the actions of a clerk in his firm.

In *Re A Barrister (Wasted Costs Order No. 4 of 1993)* (1995) *The Times*, 21 April 1995, the Court of Appeal held that a judge should not impose such a draconian penalty as a wasted costs order without taking into account the daily demands of practice and the difficulties associated with time estimates.

In *Re a Firm of Solicitors (Wasted Costs Order)* [1999] All ER (D) 728, Q, who was on trial in the Crown Court, was unhappy with his barrister and wished to dispense with her services. Defence counsel suggested that this should be put in writing, and when the court had risen, the experienced solicitor's clerk took a statement from Q to that effect. Whilst the clerk was reading the statement back to Q, the usher brought the jury past them. It was later contended that some of them must have heard what was said, and the jury had to be discharged. The judge made a wasted costs order, which was upheld by the Court of Appeal. The question was whether taking those instructions at a place where he knew the jury was likely to appear and then being oblivious to their appearance constituted negligence on the part of the clerk. In the circumstances, he had been negligent.

In *Re Boodhoo (Wasted Costs Order)* [2007] 4 All ER 762, the Court of Appeal held that it was not unreasonable for a solicitor to withdraw from proceedings in circumstances where a client had warned in advance that he would not attend the trial, and no instructions in relation to continuing to act in the client's absence had been obtained.

In *SVS Solicitors* [2012] Costs LR 502 the Court of Appeal upheld a wasted costs order made against solicitors who were complicit in their client's breach of the CrimPR and manipulation of the criminal process to suit his own ends. The Court observed that in such circumstances a solicitor should withdraw from the case in the event that a client refuses to comply properly with the obligations imposed by rules governing criminal procedure.

It is not negligent, but perfectly proper, for the defence to withhold from the Crown relevant documents undermining the prosecution case until after the Crown has established that there is a case to answer (*Reeves & Co. Solicitors* [2011] 4 Costs LR 616).

In *Henrys Solicitors* [2012] EWCA Crim 1480 the requirements for a wasted costs order were met where an advocate accepted instructions in two cases on the same day in geographically distant Crown Courts when there was a real risk that a hold-up at the first court might result in wasted costs being incurred in the second. However, Pitchford LJ did remark (at [9]) that it was not the case that 'because an advocate fails to appear at the listed time on the listed day that a wasted costs order will follow'.

A wasted costs order cannot be made in favour of defence solicitors as they are not a party to the proceedings. The effect is that, while a privately paying client may recover wasted costs, a firm with the benefit of a representation order cannot do so (*R (CPS) v Bolton Crown Court* [2013] EWHC 3570 (Admin)).

AWARDS OF COSTS AGAINST THIRD PARTIES

The Prosecution of Offences Act 1985, s. 19B enables costs to be awarded against third parties where there has been serious misconduct by a third party. See also para. 4.7 of the *Practice Direction (Costs in Criminal Proceedings)* [2013] 1 WLR 3255. **D33.39**

The Costs in Criminal Cases (General) Regulations 1986, reg. 3F(1), provides that if (a) there has been serious misconduct (whether or not constituting a contempt of court) by a third party; and (b) the court considers it appropriate, having regard to that misconduct, to make a third-party costs order against him, the court may order the third party to pay all or part of the costs incurred or wasted by any party as a result of that misconduct. Under reg. 3F(2), the court may make a third-party costs order at any time during or after the proceedings, either on the application of any party or of its own initiative. This is qualified by reg. 3F(3), which stipulates that the court may make a third-party costs order during the proceedings only if it decides that there are good reasons to do so, rather than making the order after the proceedings; the parties to the proceedings, and the third party, must be allowed to make representations on the issue of the timing of the order.

D33.40 Regulation 3F(4) requires the court, before making a third-party costs order, to allow the third party, and any party to the proceedings, to make representations; the court is also empowered to hear evidence.

Under reg. 3G, where a party applies to the court for a third-party costs order or the court decides that it might make a third-party costs order of its own initiative, the third party must receive written notice of the application; this written notice must include details of the alleged misconduct of the third party. If the third party or any other party does not attend the hearing, the court may proceed in his absence if satisfied that he have been duly served with notice of the hearing; if an order is made, it can be set aside if it is later shown that the third party did not receive notice (reg. 3G(8)).

Regulation 3H makes provision for appeals against third-party costs orders. In the case of an order made by a magistrates' court, the appeal lies to the Crown Court; in the case of an order made at first instance by the Crown Court, the appeal lies to the Court of Appeal. The appeal has to be instituted (with written notice to the court that made the order, stating the grounds of appeal) within 21 days of the order being made. This time-limit may be extended where there is good reason (reg. 3H(4)). Under reg. 3H(6), the appeal court may affirm, vary or revoke the order, as it thinks fit.

The Regulations were considered in *Allied Language Solutions* [2013] 1 WLR 3820 following difficulties in obtaining interpreters. The Court of Appeal held that, for there to be serious misconduct, there must be a history of failure to address an underlying issue.

STATUTES AND REGULATIONS RELATING TO COSTS

D33.41   **Prosecution of Offences Act 1985, ss. 16 to 21.**

 16.—(1) Where—
  (a) an information laid before a justice of the peace for any area, charging any person with an offence, is not proceeded with;
  (b) [repealed];
  (c) a magistrates' court dealing summarily with an offence dismisses the information;
  that court or, in a case falling within paragraph (a) above, a magistrates' court for that area, may make an order in favour of the accused for a payment to be made out of central funds in respect of his costs (a 'defendant's costs order').
 (2) Where—
  (a) any person is not tried for an offence for which he has been indicted or sent for trial; or
  (b) any person is tried on indictment and acquitted on any count in the indictment;
  the Crown Court may make a defendant's costs order in favour of the accused.
 (3) Where a person convicted of an offence by a magistrates' court appeals to the Crown Court under section 108 of the Magistrates' Courts Act 1980 (right of appeal against conviction or sentence) and, in consequence of the decision on appeal—
  (a) his conviction is set aside; or
  (b) a less severe punishment is awarded;
  the Crown Court may make a defendant's costs order in favour of the accused.
 (4) Where the Court of Appeal—
  (a) allows an appeal under Part I of the Criminal Appeal Act 1968 against—
   (i) conviction;
   (ii) a verdict of not guilty by reason of insanity; or

(iii) a finding under of the Criminal Procedure (Insanity) Act 1964 that the appellant is under disability that he did the act or made the omission charged against
him; or

(aa) directs under section 8(1B) of the Criminal Appeal Act 1968 the entry of a judgment and
verdict of acquittal;

(b) on an appeal under that Part against conviction—
(i) substitutes a verdict of guilty of another offence;
(ii) in a case where a special verdict has been found, orders a different conclusion on the
effect of that verdict to be recorded; or
(iii) is of the opinion that the case falls within paragraph (a) or (b) of section 6(1) of that
Act (cases where the court substitutes a finding of insanity or unfitness to plead);

(c) on an appeal under that Part against sentence, exercises its powers under section 11(3) of
that Act (powers where the court considers that the appellant should be sentenced differently for an offence for which he was dealt with by the court below); or

(d) allows, to any extent, an appeal under section 16A of that Act (appeal against order made
in cases of insanity or unfitness to plead);
the court may make a defendant's costs order in favour of the accused.

(4A) The court may also make a defendant's costs order in favour of the accused on an appeal under
section 9(11) of the Criminal Justice Act 1987 (appeals against orders or rulings at preparatory
hearings) or section 35(1) of the Criminal Procedure and Investigations Act 1996 (appeals
against orders or rulings at preparatory hearings) or under Part 9 of the Criminal Justice Act
2003.

(5) Where—
(a) any proceedings in a criminal cause or matter are determined before a Divisional Court of
the Queen's Bench Division;
(b) the Supreme Court determines an appeal, or application for leave to appeal, from such a
Divisional Court in a criminal cause or matter;
(c) the Court of Appeal determines an application for leave to appeal to the Supreme Court
under Part II of the Criminal Appeal Act 1968; or
(d) the Supreme Court determines an appeal, or application for leave to appeal, under Part II
of that Act;
the court may make a defendant's costs order in favour of the accused.

(6) A defendant's costs order shall, subject to the following provisions of this section, be for the
payment out of central funds, to the person in whose favour the order is made, of such amount
as the court considers reasonably sufficient to compensate him for any expenses properly
incurred by him in the proceedings.

(6A) Where the court considers that there are circumstances that make it inappropriate for the
accused to recover the full amount mentioned in subsection (6), a defendant's costs order must
be for the payment out of central funds of such lesser amount as the court considers just and
reasonable.

(6B) Subsections (6) and (6A) have effect subject to—
(a) section 16A, and
(b) regulations under section 20(1A)(d).

(6C) When making a defendant's costs order, the court must fix the amount to be paid out of
central funds in the order if it considers it appropriate to do so and—
(a) the accused agrees the amount, or
(b) subsection (6A) applies.

(6D) Where the court does not fix the amount to be paid out of central funds in the order—
(a) it must describe in the order any reduction required under subsection (6A), and
(b) the amount must be fixed by means of a determination made by or on behalf of the court
in accordance with procedures specified in regulations made by the Lord Chancellor.

(7) to (9) [Repealed.]

(10) Subsection (6) above shall have effect, in relation to any case falling within subsection (1)(a)
or (2)(a) above, as if for the words 'in the proceedings' there were substituted the words 'in or
about the defence'.

(11) Where a person ordered to be retried is acquitted at his retrial, the costs which may be ordered
to be paid out of central funds under this section shall include—
(a) any costs which, at the original trial, could have been ordered to be so paid under this section if he had been acquitted; and

D

Part D Procedure

(b) if no order was made under this section in respect of his expenses on appeal, any sums for the payment of which such an order could have been made.

16A.—(1) A defendant's costs order may not require the payment out of central funds of an amount that includes an amount in respect of the accused's legal costs, subject to the following provisions of this section.

(2) Subsection (1) does not apply where condition A, B, C or D is met.

(3) Condition A is that the accused is an individual and the order is made under—

    (a) section 16(1),

    (b) section 16(3), or

    (c) section 16(4)(a)(ii) or (iii) or (d).

(4) Condition B is that the accused is an individual and the legal costs were incurred in proceedings in a court below which were—

    (a) proceedings in a magistrates' court, or

    (b) proceedings on an appeal to the Crown Court under section 108 of the Magistrates' Courts Act 1980 (right of appeal against conviction or sentence).

(5) Condition C is that the legal costs were incurred in proceedings in the Supreme Court.

(5A) Condition D is that—

    (a) the accused is an individual,

    (b) the order is made under section 16(2),

    (c) the legal costs were incurred in relevant Crown Court proceedings, and

    (d) the Director of Legal Aid Casework has made a determination of financial ineligibility in relation to the accused and those proceedings

(and condition D continues to be met if the determination is withdrawn).

(6) [Power to make regulations.]

(7) Regulations under subsection (6) may not remove or limit the exception provided by condition C.

(8) Where a court makes a defendant's costs order requiring the payment out of central funds of an amount that includes an amount in respect of legal costs, the order must include a statement to that effect.

(9) Where, in a defendant's costs order, a court fixes an amount to be paid out of central funds that includes an amount in respect of legal costs incurred in proceedings in a court other than the Supreme Court, the latter amount must not exceed an amount specified by regulations made by the Lord Chancellor.

(10) In this section—

    'legal costs' means fees, charges, disbursements and other amounts payable in respect of advocacy services or litigation services including, in particular, expert witness costs;

    'advocacy services' means any services which it would be reasonable to expect a person who is exercising, or contemplating exercising, a right of audience in relation to any proceedings, or contemplated proceedings, to provide;

    'expert witness costs' means amounts payable in respect of the services of an expert witness, including amounts payable in connection with attendance by the witness at court or elsewhere;

    'litigation services' means any services which it would be reasonable to expect a person who is exercising, or contemplating exercising, a right to conduct litigation in relation to proceedings, or contemplated proceedings, to provide.

(11) In subsection (5A)—

    'determination of financial ineligibility', in relation to an individual and proceedings, means a determination under section 21 of the Legal Aid, Sentencing and Punishment of Offenders Act 2012 that the individual's financial resources are such that the individual is not eligible for representation under section 16 of that Act for the purposes of the proceedings;

    'Director of Legal Aid Casework' means the civil servant designated under section 4(1) of the Legal Aid, Sentencing and Punishment of Offenders Act 2012;

    'relevant Crown Court proceedings' means any of the following—

    (a) proceedings in the Crown Court in respect of an offence for which the accused has been sent by a magistrates' court to the Crown Court for trial;

    (b) proceedings in the Crown Court relating to an offence in respect of which a bill of indictment has been preferred by virtue of section 2(2)(b) of the Administration of Justice (Miscellaneous Provisions) Act 1933;

(c) proceedings in the Crown Court following an order by the Court of Appeal or the Supreme Court for a retrial.

17.—(1) Subject to subsection (2) and (2A) below, the court may—

(a) in any proceedings in respect of an indictable offence; and

(b) in any proceedings before a Divisional Court of the Queen's Bench Division or the Supreme Court in respect of a summary offence;

order the payment out of central funds of such amount as the court considers reasonably sufficient to compensate the prosecutor for any expenses properly incurred by him in the proceedings.

(2) No order under this section may be made in favour of—

(a) a public authority; or

(b) a person acting—

(i) on behalf of a public authority; or

(ii) in his capacity as an official appointed by such an authority.

(2A) Where the court considers that there are circumstances that make it inappropriate for the prosecution to recover the full amount mentioned in subsection (1), an order under this section must be for the payment out of central funds of such lesser amount as the court considers just and reasonable.

(2B) When making an order under this section, the court must fix the amount to be paid out of central funds in the order if it considers it appropriate to do so and—

(a) the prosecutor agrees the amount, or

(b) subsection (2A) applies.

(2C) Where the court does not fix the amount to be paid out of central funds in the order—

(a) it must describe in the order any reduction required under subsection (2A), and

(b) the amount must be fixed by means of a determination made by or on behalf of the court in accordance with procedures specified in regulations made by the Lord Chancellor.

(3) to (4) [Repealed.]

(5) Where the conduct of proceedings to which subsection (1) above applies is taken over by the Crown Prosecution Service, that subsection shall have effect as if it referred to the prosecutor who had the conduct of the proceedings before the intervention of the Service and to expenses incurred by him up to the time of intervention.

(6) In this section 'public authority' means—

(a) a police force within the meaning of section 3 of this Act;

(b) the Crown Prosecution Service or any other government department;

(c) a local authority or other authority or body constituted for purposes of—

(i) the public service or of local government; or

(ii) carrying on under national ownership any industry or undertaking or part of an industry or undertaking; or

(d) any other authority or body whose members are appointed by Her Majesty or by any Minister of the Crown or government department or whose revenue consist wholly or mainly of money provided by Parliament.

18.—(1) Where—

(a) any person is convicted of an offence before a magistrates' court;

(b) the Crown Court dismisses an appeal against such a conviction or against the sentence imposed on that conviction; or

(c) any person is convicted of an offence before the Crown Court;

the court may make such order as to the costs to be paid by the accused to the prosecutor as it considers just and reasonable.

(2) Where the Court of Appeal dismisses—

(a) an appeal or application for leave to appeal under Part I of the Criminal Appeal Act 1968; or

(b) an application by the accused for leave to appeal to the Supreme Court under Part II of that Act;

(c) an appeal or application for leave to appeal under section 9(11) of the Criminal Justice Act 1987; or

(d) an appeal or application for leave to appeal under section 35(1) of the Criminal Procedure and Investigations Act 1996;

it may make such order as to the costs to be paid by the accused, to such person as may be named in the order, as it considers just and reasonable.

(2A) Where the Court of Appeal reverses or varies a ruling on an appeal under Part 9 of the Criminal Justice Act 2003, it may make such order as to the costs to be paid by the accused, to such person as may be named in the order, as it considers just and reasonable.

D

Part D Procedure

(3) The amount to be paid by the accused in pursuance of an order under this section shall be specified in the order.

(4) Where any person is convicted of an offence before a magistrates' court and—

    (a) under the conviction the court orders payment of any sum as a fine, penalty, forfeiture or compensation; and

    (b) the sum so ordered to be paid does not exceed £5;

the court shall not order the accused to pay any costs under this section unless in the particular circumstances of the case it considers it right to do so.

(5) Where any person under the age of 18 is convicted of an offence before a magistrates' court, the amount of any costs ordered to be paid by the accused under this section shall not exceed the amount of any fine imposed on him.

(6) Costs ordered to be paid under subsection (2) or (2A) above may include the reasonable cost of any transcript of a record of proceedings made in accordance with rules of court made for the purposes of section 32 of the Act of 1968.

19. [Lord Chancellor's power to make regulations empowering courts to make an order as to costs where a party incurs costs as a result of an unnecessary act or omission by another party.]

19A.—(1) In any criminal proceedings—

    (a) the Court of Appeal;

    (b) the Crown Court; or

    (c) a magistrates' court,

may disallow, or (as the case may be) order the legal or other representative concerned to meet, the whole of any wasted costs or such part of them as may be determined in accordance with regulations.

(2) Regulations shall provide that a legal or other representative against whom action is taken by a magistrates' court under subsection (1) may appeal to the Crown Court and that a legal or other representative against whom action is taken by the Crown Court under subsection (1) may appeal to the Court of Appeal.

(3) In this section—

'legal or other representative', in relation to any proceedings, means a person who is exercising a right of audience, or a right to conduct litigation, on behalf of any party to the proceedings;

'regulations' means regulations made by the Lord Chancellor; and

'wasted costs' means any costs incurred by a party—

    (a) as a result of any improper, unreasonable or negligent act or omission on the part of any representative or any employee of a representative; or

    (b) which, in the light of any such act or omission occurring after they were incurred, the court considers it is unreasonable to expect that party to pay.

19B.—(1) The Lord Chancellor may by regulations make provision empowering magistrates' courts, the Crown Court and the Court of Appeal to make a third party costs order if the condition in subsection (3) is satisfied.

(2) A 'third party costs order' is an order as to the payment of costs incurred by a party to criminal proceedings by a person who is not a party to those proceedings ('the third party').

(3) The condition is that—

    (a) there has been serious misconduct (whether or not constituting a contempt of court) by the third party, and

    (b) the court considers it appropriate, having regard to that misconduct, to make a third party costs order against him.

(4) to (6) [Specify what the regulations may and must provide.]

20. [The Lord Chancellor may make regulations for carrying this part of the Act into effect.]

Interpretation, etc.

21.—(1) In this Part—

'accused' and 'appellant', in a case where section 44A of the Criminal Appeal Act 1968 (death of convicted person) applies, include the person approved under that section;

'defendant's costs order' has the meaning given in section 16 of this Act;

'legally assisted person', in relation to any proceedings, means a person for whom advice, assistance or representation is provided under arrangements made for the purposes of Part 1 of the Legal Aid, Sentencing and Punishment of Offenders Act 2012;

'proceedings' includes—

(a) proceedings in any court below; and

(b) in relation to the determination of an appeal by any court, any application made to that court for leave to bring the appeal; and

'witness' means any person properly attending to give evidence, whether or not he gives evidence or is called at the instance of one of the parties or of the court, but does not include a person attending as a witness to character only unless the court has certified that the interests of justice required his attendance.

(2) Except as provided by or under this Part no costs shall be allowed on the hearing or determination of, or of any proceedings preliminary or incidental to, an appeal to the Court of Appeal under Part I of the Criminal Appeal Act 1968.

(3) Subject to rules of court made under section 53(1) of the Senior Courts Act 1981 (power by rules to distribute business of Court of Appeal between its civil and criminal divisions), the jurisdiction of the Court of Appeal under this part, or under regulations made under this part, shall be exercised by the Criminal Division of that court; and references in this Part to the Court of Appeal shall be construed as references to that division.

(4) For the purposes of sections 16, 16A and 17 of this Act, the costs of any party to proceedings shall be taken to include the expense of compensating any witness for the expenses, trouble or loss of time properly incurred in or incidental to his attendance.

(4A) Where one party to any proceedings is a legally assisted person then—

(a) for the purposes of sections 16, 16A and 17 of this Act, his costs shall be taken not to include the cost of advice, assistance or representation provided to the person under arrangements made for the purposes of Part 1 of the Legal Aid, Sentencing and Punishment of Offenders Act 2012; and

(b) for the purposes of sections 18 to 19B of this Act, his costs shall be taken to include the cost of such advice, assistance or representation.

(5) Where, in any proceedings in a criminal cause or matter or in either of the cases mentioned in subsection (6) below, an interpreter is required because of the accused's lack of English, the expenses properly incurred on his employment shall not be treated as costs of any party to the proceedings.

(6) The cases are—

(a) where an information charging the accused with an offence is laid before a justice of the peace for any area but not proceeded with and the expenses are incurred on the employment of the interpreter for the proceedings on the information; and

(b) where the accused is sent for trial but not tried and the expenses are incurred on the employment of the interpreter for the proceedings in the Crown Court.

Costs in Criminal Cases (General) Regulations 1986 (SI 1986 No. 1335), regs, 3 to 25   D33.42

3.—(1) Subject to the provisions of this regulation, where at any time during criminal proceedings—

(a) a magistrates' court,

(b) the Crown Court, or

(c) the Court of Appeal

is satisfied that costs have been incurred in respect of the proceedings by one of the parties as a result of an unnecessary or improper act or omission by, or on behalf of, another party to the proceedings, the court may, after hearing the parties, order that all or part of the costs so incurred by that party shall be paid to him by the other party.

(2) When making an order under paragraph (1), the court may take into account any other order as to costs which has been made in respect of the proceedings.

(3) An order made under paragraph (1) shall specify the amount of costs to be paid in pursuance of the order.

(4) Where an order under paragraph (1) has been made, the court may take that order into account when making any other order as to costs in respect of the proceedings.

(5) No order under paragraph (1) shall be made by a magistrates' court which requires a person under the age of 17 who has been convicted of an offence to pay an amount by way of costs which exceeds the amount of any fine imposed on him.

3A.—This Part of these regulations applies to action taken by a court under section 19A of the Act and in this Part of these regulations:—

'wasted costs order' means any action taken by a court under section 19A of the Act; and 'interested party' means the party benefiting from the wasted costs order and, where he was receiving services funded for him as part of the Criminal Defence Service, or an order for the payment of costs out of central funds was made in his favour, shall include the authority responsible for determining costs payable in respect of work done under the representation order or out of central funds as the case may be.

General

3B.—(1) A wasted costs order may provide for the whole or any part of the wasted costs to be disallowed or ordered to be paid and the court shall specify the amount of such costs.

(2) [Revoked.]

(3) When making a wasted costs order the court may take into account any other order as to costs in respect of the proceedings and may take the wasted costs order into account when making any other such order.

(4) [Revoked.]

Appeals

3C.—(1) A legal or other representative against whom the wasted costs order is made may appeal—

(a) in the case of an order made by a magistrates' court, to the Crown Court, and

(b) in the case of an order made at first instance by the Crown Court, to the Court of Appeal.

(2) to (5) [Revoked.].

(6) The appeal court may affirm, vary or revoke the order as it thinks fit.

3D.—Where the person required to make a payment in respect of sums due under a wasted costs order fails to do so, the payment may be recovered summarily as a sum adjudged to be paid as a civil debt by order of a magistrates' court by the party benefiting from the order, save that where he was receiving services funded for him as part of the Criminal Defence Service or an order for the payment of costs out of central funds was made in his favour, the power to recover shall be exercisable by the Lord Chancellor.

3E.—(1) This Part of these Regulations applies where there are, or have been criminal proceedings in a magistrates' court, the Crown Court or the Court of Appeal.

(2) In this Part of these Regulations—

'court' means the court in which the criminal proceedings are taking, or took, place;

'interested party' means the party benefiting from the third party costs order and, where he was receiving services funded for him as part of the Criminal Defence Service or an order for the payment of costs out of central funds was made in his favour, shall include the authority responsible for determining costs payable in respect of work done under the representation order or out of central funds as the case may be;

'party' means a party to the criminal proceedings;

'third party' means a person who is not a party;

'third party costs order' means an order as to the payment, by a third party, of costs incurred by a party in accordance with regulation 3F.

3F.—(1) If—

(a) there has been serious misconduct (whether or not constituting a contempt of court) by a third party; and

(b) the court considers it appropriate, having regard to that misconduct, to make a third party costs order against him

the court may order the third party to pay all or part of the costs incurred or wasted by any party as a result of the misconduct.

(2) to (5) [Revoked.]

(6) A third party costs order shall specify the amount of costs to be paid in pursuance of the order.

(7) When a third party costs order has been made the court shall notify the third party and any interested party of the order and the amount ordered to be paid.

3G. [Revoked.]

Appeals

3H.—(1) A third party against whom a third party costs order is made may appeal—

(a) in the case of an order made by a magistrates' court, to the Crown Court; and

(b) in the case of an order made at first instance by the Crown Court, to the Court of Appeal.

(2) to (5) [Revoked.]

(6) The appeal court may affirm, vary or revoke the order as it thinks fit.

31. Where the person required to make a payment in respect of sums due under a third party costs order fails to do so, the payment may be recovered summarily as a sum adjudged to be paid as a civil debt by order of a magistrates' court by the party benefiting from the order, save that where he was receiving services funded for him as part of the Criminal Defence Service or an order for the payment of costs out of central funds was made in his favour, the power to recover shall be exercisable by the Lord Chancellor.

[**4. to 13.** Prescribe the procedure to be followed by a person in whose favour an order for costs out of central funds has been made; define the 'appropriate authority' to whom the claim for costs should be submitted; prescribe the manner in which the appropriate authority should determine and authorise payment of costs, and provide for redetermination of the costs or an appeal to the taxing master and ultimately the High Court where the applicant for costs is dissatisfied with the appropriate authority's decision.]

[**13A. to 13C.** Provide for modifications of the regulations to allow for payment of court appointees, acting under the Criminal Procedure (Insanity) Act 1964, s. 4A, or the YJCEA 1999, s. 38.]

14.—(1) Sections 17 and 18 of the Act [orders for private prosecutors' costs out of central funds and orders that accused pay prosecution costs] shall apply to proceedings in the Crown Court in respect of a person committed by a magistrates' court to that Court—

(a) with a view to his being sentenced for an indictable offence in accordance with [the PCC(S)A 2000, ss. 3 and 4]; or

(b) with a view to his being sentenced by the Crown Court under section 6(6) or 9(3) of the Bail Act 1976 [committal where magistrates consider that an offence of absconding is too serious to be punished adequately by them etc.]; or

(c) with a view to the making of a hospital order with an order restricting his discharge under Part III of the Mental Health Act 1983,

as they apply where a person is convicted in proceedings before the Crown Court.

[(2) Section 18 of the Act to apply to certain committals and appeals under the Vagrancy Act 1824 — incorrigible rogues etc.]

[(3) Section 18 to apply to proceedings in either a magistrates' court or the Crown Court when the proceedings concern breach of conditional discharge and certain community orders.]

15. In this Part of these regulations—

'expenses' include compensation to a witness for his trouble or loss of time and out of pocket expenses;

'proceedings in a criminal cause or matter' includes any case in which—

(a) an information charging the accused with an offence is laid before a justice of the peace for any area but not proceeded with; or

(b) the accused is sent for trial but not tried;

'professional witness' means a witness practising as a member of the legal or medical profession or as a dentist, veterinary surgeon or accountant who attends to give professional evidence as to matters of fact;

'private prosecutor' means any person in whose favour an order for the payment of costs out of central funds could be made under section 17 of the Act;

'the relevant amount' has the meaning assigned to it by regulation 17;

'witness' means any person properly attending to give evidence, whether or not he gives evidence or is called at the instance of one of the parties or of the court, but does not include—

(a) a person attending as a witness to character only unless the court has certified that the interests of justice required his attendance;

(b) a member of a police force attending court in his capacity as such;

(c) a full-time officer of an institution to which the Prison Act 1952 applies attending court in his capacity as such; or

(d) a prisoner in respect of any occasion on which he is conveyed to court in custody.

General

16.—(1) Where, in any proceedings in a criminal cause or matter in a magistrates' court, the Crown Court, a Divisional Court of the Queen's Bench Division, the Court of Appeal or the Supreme Court—

(a) a witness attends at the instance of the accused, a private prosecutor or the court; or

(b) an interpreter is required because of the accused's lack of English; or

(ba) a witness called by the defendant is examined through an intermediary under section 29 of the Youth Justice and Criminal Evidence Act 1999; or

(bb) an intermediary is required to assist the defendant; or
(c)   a medical practitioner makes a report otherwise than in writing,
the expenses properly incurred by a witness referred to in sub-paragraph (a) or by that interpreter, intermediary or medical practitioner shall be allowed out of central funds in accordance with this Part of these regulations, unless the court directs that the expenses are not to be
allowed out of central funds.

(2) Subject to paragraph (3), any entitlement to an allowance under this Part of these regulations
shall be the same whether the witness, interpreter, intermediary or medical practitioner attends
on the same day in one case or more than one case.

(3) Paragraph (2) shall not apply to allowances under regulation 25.

Determination of rates or scales of allowances payable out of central funds

17.—(1) The Lord Chancellor shall, with the consent of the Treasury, determine the rates or scales
of allowances payable out of central funds to witnesses, interpreters, intermediaries or medical
practitioners and a reference in this Part of these regulations to an allowance not exceeding
the relevant amount means an amount calculated in accordance with the rates or scales so
determined.

[18.—(1) Witnesses other than professional or expert witnesses may be allowed (a) a loss allowance not exceeding the relevant amount in respect of (i) expenditure to which he would not
otherwise have been subject or (ii) any loss of earnings or of State benefit, and (b) a subsistence
allowance not exceeding the relevant amount (para. (1)). This also applies to persons who
necessarily attend for the purposes of the proceedings but not to give evidence (para. (2)).
It does not apply to police officers, prison officers or prisoners conveyed to court in custody
(para. (3)).]

Professional witnesses

[19. A professional witness may be allowed a professional witness allowance not exceeding the
relevant amount.]

Expert witnesses etc.

20.—(1) The court may make an allowance in respect of an expert witness for attending to give
expert evidence and for work in connection with its preparation of such an amount as it may
consider reasonable having regard to the nature and difficulty of the case and the work necessarily involved.

(2) Paragraph (1) shall apply, with the necessary modifications, to—
(a) an interpreter or intermediary, or
(b) a medical practitioner who makes a report otherwise than in writing for the purpose of
[the PCC(S)A 2000, s. 11],
as it applies to an expert witness.

[21. and 22. Deal respectively with night allowances for professional and expert witnesses, and
allowances for seamen detained on shore.]

Prosecutors and defendants

23. A person in whose favour an order is made under section 16, 17 or 19(4) of the Act may be
allowed the same subsistence allowance and travelling expenses as if he attended as a witness
other than a professional or expert witness.

[24. Detailed provisions as to the travelling expenses a witness may be allowed.]

[25. Concerns payment for medical reports requested by the court under the PCC(S)A 2000,
s. 11, or with a view to making a hospital order or a probation order with a condition of
treatment.]

Section E1   Sentencing: General Provisions

PURPOSES OF SENTENCING

The CJA 2003, s. 142, sets out a list of the purposes of sentencing.   **E1.1**

Criminal Justice Act 2003, s. 142

(1) Any court dealing with an offender in respect of his offence must have regard to the following
    purposes of sentencing—
    (a) the punishment of offenders,
    (b) the reduction of crime (including its reduction by deterrence),
    (c) the reform and rehabilitation of offenders,
    (d) the protection of the public, and
    (e) the making of reparation by offenders to persons affected by their offences.

Section 142(2) limits the scope of this by stating that s. 142(1) does not apply in relation to an offender who is aged under 18 at the time of conviction. Section 142A of the 2003 Act specifies the purposes of sentencing in relation to offenders aged under 18, but is not in force. The relevant provisions for young offenders are the CDA 1998, s. 37, which states that the principal purpose of the youth justice system 'is to prevent offending by children and young persons', and the statutory duty under the CYPA 1933, s. 44, to 'have regard to the welfare of the child or young person'. Section 142(1) does not apply where the offence is fixed by law (murder), where the sentence falls to be imposed under the Prevention of Crime Act 1953, s. 1A(5), the PCC(S)A 2000, s. 110(2) or 111(2), the FA 1968, s. 51A(2), the CJA 1988, s.139AA(7), or the VCRA 2006, s. 29 (all prescribed minimum sentences: see E5): or under the CJA 2003, ss. 224A, 225(2) or 226(2) (dangerous offenders: see E4), or in relation to the making of a hospital order (with or without restriction), an interim hospital order, a hospital direction or a limitation direction (as to which, see E22). Section 142(3) states that 'sentence' includes any order made by a court when dealing with an offender in respect of his offence, and so would clearly extend to ancillary orders as well as custodial, community, and financial penalties. The Court of Appeal in *Sellafield Ltd* [2014] EWCA Crim 49 made it clear that the purposes of sentencing listed in s. 142 are equally applicable to corporate offenders.

The definitive sentencing guideline, *Overarching Principles: Seriousness* (see Supplement,   **E1.2**
SG-21), states that 'The Act does not indicate that any one purpose should be more important than any other and in practice they may all be relevant to a greater or lesser degree in any individual case — the sentencer has the task of determining the manner in which they apply' (para. 1.2). In *Wilkinson* [2010] 1 Cr App R (S) 628 the Court of Appeal endorsed the general approach of the guideline, but said that, in cases of gun crime, protection of the public is the paramount consideration.

SENTENCING GUIDELINES

The CAJA 2009, part 4 (ss. 118 to 136 and sch. 15), created a Sentencing Council for England   **E1.3**
and Wales and abolished the Sentencing Guidelines Council and the Sentencing Advisory Panel.

E

Part E Sentencing

2159

Section 120 requires the Council to prepare sentencing guidelines, which may be general in nature or limited to a particular offence, particular category of offence, or particular category of offender. By s. 121, the sentencing guidelines should specify the 'offence range' appropriate for a court to impose on an offender convicted of that offence and, if the guidelines describe different categories of case, specify for each category a 'category range' within the offence range. The guidelines should also specify the 'starting point' within the offence range or within each category range.

Coroners and Justice Act 2009, s.125

(1) Every court —
    (a) must, in sentencing an offender, follow any sentencing guidelines which are relevant to the offender's case, and
    (b) must, in exercising any other function in relation to the sentencing of offenders, follow any sentencing guidelines which are relevant to the exercise of that function,
    unless the court is satisfied that it would be contrary to the interests of justice to do so.

E1.4 Where a court is deciding what sentence to impose, and there are in place applicable 'offence-specific guidelines' structured in the way described in s. 121, the duty imposed on the court under s. 125(1)(a) includes in all cases a duty to impose a sentence which is within the offence range, and a duty to decide which of the categories most resembles the offender's case in order to identify the sentencing starting point, but nothing in s. 125 imposes on the court a duty to impose a sentence which is within the category range (s. 125(2) and (3)). The duty to decide which category most resembles the offender's case does not apply if none of the categories sufficiently resembles the offender's case (s. 125(4)). The duty on the court to impose a sentence which is within the offence range is subject to the CJA 2003, s. 144 (reduction in sentence for guilty pleas), the SOCPA 2005, ss. 73 and 74 (assistance by defendants: reduction of sentence), and any rule of law as to the totality of sentences (s. 125(5)). The duty imposed by s. 125(1) is also subject to the CJA 2003, ss. 148(1) and (2), 152, 153, 164(2), 224A and 269 and sch. 21 and the various statutory provisions prescribing specific sentences considered in E5). Finally, nothing in s. 125 is to be taken as restricting any power which enables a court to deal with a mentally disordered offender in the manner it considers to be most appropriate in all the circumstances. Section 125(2)–(5) applies for the purposes of determining the notional determinate term in relation to an offence (s. 126).

On the face of it the requirement that 'every court… must follow any sentencing guidelines' is a tighter requirement than the pre-existing obligation on the court under the CJA 2003 to 'have regard to' the guidelines. However, the duty to follow the guidelines is applicable to the whole of the 'offence range' and not to the 'category range' (arguably this is less prescriptive than before). Also, a court may choose not to follow the guideline if to do so would be 'contrary to the interests of justice'. In *Thornley* [2011] 2 Cr App R (S) 361 Lord Judge CJ said that the 'interests of justice' required a court considering a sentencing guideline to take into account subsequent statutory change and appellate case law: 'guidelines are not tramlines — nor are they ring-fenced'. In *Dyer* [2013] EWCA Crim 2114 Leveson LJ said that the role of the Court of Appeal was to interpret the guidelines and provide practical illustrations of their operation, including examples where departure from them might be appropriate. His lordship further observed that an appeal against sentence on the basis of alleged disparity with a sentence imposed on a co-defendant, or on a defendant sentenced in a different case, was effectively precluded where the relevant guideline(s) had been followed and applied. In *Blackshaw* [2012] 1 WLR 1126 the Court of Appeal considered a number of sentences imposed in the context of widespread public disorder across cities and towns which occurred during the summer of 2011. Lord Judge CJ said that the sentencing guidelines in place at that time had not contemplated the exceptional context of such disorder and that sentences above the normal ranges indicated in the guidelines had been appropriate and inevitable. It is not open to a judge to ignore, or to depart from, a definitive sentencing guideline because in the judge's view the guideline is 'out of touch' (*Heathcote-Smith* [2012] 2 Cr App R (S) 133; *Taylor* [2012] 2 Cr App R (S) 581) or because earlier appellate authority is to be preferred (*Healey* [2013] 1 Cr App R (S) 176 (33); *Dyer*).

The CAJA 2009, sch. 22, part 4, contains transitional provisions following the setting up of the **E1.5** Sentencing Council. In particular, para 28(2) refers to 'existing guidelines', which means any definitive guideline of the Sentencing Guidelines Council or any guidelines issued by the Court of Appeal before the SGC came into being and which have not been superseded. By art. 7 of the commencement order (SI 2010 No. 816), 'existing guidelines' are to be treated as guidelines issued by the Sentencing Council under s. 120 of the 2009 Act.

The SGC definitive guidelines and the Sentencing Council definitive guidelines are all set **E1.6** out in edited form in the Supplement. Under the statutory provisions that existed before the CJA 2003, the Court of Appeal had issued sentencing guidelines on the court's own initiative since the 1980s and, since 1999, subject to the advice of the Sentencing Advisory Panel. Such guidelines have always been regarded as authoritative, but not strictly binding, in that a sentencer may, having given reason, depart from them (*Johnson* (1994) 15 Cr App R (S) 827).

Appellate judges have stressed that it is the duty of counsel to bring any sentencing guidelines to the attention of the sentencer, in case they might otherwise be overlooked. An example is *Panayioutou* (1989) 11 Cr App R (S) 535.

In *Valentas* [2010] 2 Cr App R (S) 477 the Court of Appeal said that the duty to 'have regard' (as it was expressed at that time) to sentencing guidelines was limited to definitive guidelines. While it may on occasions be useful to look at other documents, such as a consultation paper, these documents did not carry the same statutory requirement, and judges should not seek to guess what form the final version might take. Under the CAJA 2009, the same principle applies since, by s. 125(8), sentencing guidelines are defined as 'definitive sentencing guidelines'. An on-going Sentencing Council Crown Court Survey which requires judges to complete a statistical return after each occasion on which sentence is passed has no relevance to the sentencing decision itself (*DG* [2010] EWCA Crim 2813).

Sentencing guidelines are not retrospective in effect and, if a guideline reduces sentencing levels for a particular category of offence, no right of appeal lies for an offender sentenced before that guideline came into effect (*Boakye* [2013] 1 Cr App R (S) 6 (2)). Conversely, if the guideline increases sentencing levels, and an offender is sentenced for an offence committed before that guideline came into effect, the ECHR, Article 7, is not engaged because sentencing guidelines are instruments of practice rather than law (*Bao* [2008] 2 Cr App R (S) 61).

The decision of the Court of Appeal in *A-G's Refs (Nos. 15, 16 and 17 of 2012)* [2013] 1 Cr App R (S) 289 (52) provides a summary of the proper judicial approach to Sentencing Council guidelines. According to Hallett LJ, the guidelines set out a series of eight steps for the sentencing process, not all of which will be necessary in every case but which should be followed sequentially. Step One is the determination of the offence category, to which there are two aspects: culpability and harm. The court should determine culpability and harm by reference *only* to the factors listed there. The judge must do his best to reach a fair assessment of the overall offending, namely culpability and harm, before proceeding to Step Two. The judge should declare his conclusions on Step One in his sentencing remarks, for the benefit of the offender, those advising the offender, and in the event of appeal. At Step Two, the judge should use the corresponding starting point to reach a sentence within the category ranges which follow. The starting point applies to all offenders irrespective of plea or previous convictions. The judge should then factor in any aggravating or mitigating features and adjust the sentence within the range. The Council emphasises that the list of aggravating and mitigating factors is non-exhaustive. In some cases, having considered these factors it may be appropriate to move outside the identified category range. If that is so, the judge should explain the reasoning (*Datsun* [2014] 1 Cr App R (S) 137 (25)). In cases where the offender is regarded as being at the very top of the highest range it may be justifiable for the court to depart from the guideline.

E

Part E Sentencing

SERIOUSNESS OF OFFENCE

Determining the Seriousness of an Offence

E1.7   Criminal Justice Act 2003, s. 143

(1) In considering the seriousness of any offence, the court must consider the offender's culpability in committing the offence and any harm which the offence caused, was intended to cause or might foreseeably have caused.

The definitive sentencing guideline, *Overarching Principles: Seriousness* (see Supplement, **SG-21**), states that 'The sentencer must start by considering the *seriousness* of the offence, the assessment of which will determine which of the sentencing thresholds has been crossed, indicate whether a custodial, community or other sentence is the most appropriate, be a key factor in determining the length of a custodial sentence, the onerousness of the requirements to be incorporated in a community sentence and the amount of any fine imposed' (para. 1.3 at **SG-22**).

REQUIRED REDUCTIONS IN SENTENCE

Reduction in Sentence for Guilty Plea

E1.8   Criminal Justice Act 2003, s. 144

(1) In determining what sentence to pass on an offender who has pleaded guilty to an offence in proceedings before that or another court, a court must take into account—
   (a) the stage in the proceedings for the offence at which the offender indicated his intention to plead guilty, and
   (b) the circumstances in which this indication was given
(2) In the case of an offence the sentence for which falls to be imposed under a provision mentioned in subsection (3), nothing in that provision prevents the court, after taking into account any matter referred to in subsection (1) of this section, from imposing any sentence which is not less than 80 per cent of that specified in that provision.
(3) The provisions referred to in subsection (2) are—
   section 1A(6)(a) of the Prevention of Crime Act 1953;
   section 110(2) of the Sentencing Act;
   section 111(2) of the Sentencing Act;
   section 139AA(8)(a) of the Criminal Justice Act 1988.
(4) In the case of an offence the sentence for which falls to be imposed under a provision mentioned in subsection (5), nothing in that provision prevents the court from imposing any sentence that it considers appropriate after taking into account any matter referred to in subsection (1) of this section.
(5) The provisions referred to in subsection (4) are—
   section 1A(6)(b) of the Prevention of Crime Act 1953;
   section 139AA(8)(b) of the Criminal Justice Act 1988.

The definitive sentencing guideline, *Reduction in Sentence for a Guilty Plea* (see Supplement, **SG-1**), explains that a reduction in sentence in such circumstances 'is appropriate because a guilty plea avoids the need for a trial (thus enabling other cases to be disposed of more expeditiously), shortens the gap between charge and sentence, saves considerable cost, and, in the case of an early plea, saves victims and witnesses from the concern about having to give evidence' (para. 2.2). Reduction for plea is a separate matter from remorse and other aspects of mitigation, and is separate from any reduction which may be appropriate to reflect assistance to the prosecuting or enforcement authorities (para. 2.3).

The guideline makes it clear that the principle of a reduction applies in the Crown Court, a magistrates' court, and, whenever practicable, in a youth court (para. 1.1). It should be applied to any of the punitive elements of a sentence, but not to the rehabilitative elements, nor to any ancillary order including a disqualification from driving (para. 2.5). The effect of the plea may, in an appropriate case, be to change a custodial sentence to a community one, in which case the change in form of the sentence incorporates the reduction for plea (para. 2.6).

The guideline indicates that the level of reduction should be a proportion of the total sentence **E1.9** imposed, calculated by reference to the circumstances in which the guilty plea was indicated, in particular the stage in the proceedings. The greatest reduction (recommended one-third) will be given where the plea was indicated at the 'first reasonable opportunity', reducing to a recommended one-quarter (where a trial date has been set) to a recommended one-tenth (for a guilty plea entered at the 'door of the court' or after the trial has begun (para. 4.2)). In each case there is a presumption that the recommended reduction will be given unless there are good reasons for a different amount. In *Caley* [2013] 2 Cr App R (S) 305 (47) the Court of Appeal said that when the 'first reasonable opportunity' arose was a matter for the sentencing judge. It would not normally be at the police station, although a frank admission at that stage would normally mitigate. The Court noted the widespread use of 'early guilty plea schemes' and said that the first reasonable opportunity for most offenders who appear in the Crown Court was at the magistrates' court or immediately on arrival at the Crown Court. It would *not* normally be at the plea and case management hearing. Leaving aside those few cases where the offender genuinely could not know whether he was guilty before receiving legal advice or disclosure of prosecution evidence, it was usually open to an offender to admit his guilt (or at least to admit what he had done) prior to receiving advice from his lawyer. In *Girma* [2010] 1 Cr App R (S) 172, the Court of Appeal said (at [103]) that, in a multi-handed trial likely to last many months, at great public expense, a guilty plea entered shortly before trial when savings can still be made might attract a reduction in the order of 20 per cent rather than the recommended 10 per cent. The Court in *Caley* agreed that such cases did arise, but that larger discounts must not become routine. Even in complex cases there may be no real obstacle to an offender admitting guilt at an early stage. In cases where the prosecution case is overwhelming, it may not be appropriate to give the full reduction that would otherwise be given (guideline, para. 5.3). Where a court is satisfied that a lower reduction should be given for this reason, a recommended reduction of 20 per cent is likely to be appropriate where the guilty plea was indicated at the first reasonable opportunity (para. 5.4 and *Caley*). See also *Wilson* [2012] 2 Cr App R (S) 441, referred to with approval in *Caley*. It was held in *Birt* [2011] 2 Cr App R (S) 82 that a pre-trial offer to plead guilty is not the same as a plea of guilty and no credit should normally be given for it, but in *Caley* the Court said that an offender may 'indicate a plea of guilty' by notifying the Crown that he would admit a lesser charge or would invite discussion to do so, provided that the position taken by him was a reasonable one. An offender should not benefit from the recommended reduction for plea if he has deliberately delayed the criminal justice process by absconding (*Ward* [2014] 1 Cr App R (S) 466 (74)).

The guideline says that, if an offender is being sentenced as a dangerous offender, any specified minimum custodial term should be reduced in the normal way to reflect the guilty plea (para. 5.1). A sentencer cannot remedy a perceived defect in the law, such as where a maximum penalty appears to be too low, by refusal of the appropriate discount (para. 5.6). If after pleading guilty there is a *Newton* hearing and the offender's version of the facts is rejected, some or all of the recommended reduction for plea may be lost (para. 4.3(iv)). In *Caley* the Court said that this was 'common sense'. The scale of the loss of reduction was a matter for the judge, but would depend on all the circumstances including the extent of the issue determined, whether witnesses were required, and the additional time and effort involved. For the application of a guilty plea to setting the minimum term in murder cases, see part F of the guideline (at **SG-6**) and **E3.2**, and for application of the guilty plea to setting the specified period under the PCC(S)A 2000, s. 82A, see part G (at **SG-7**) and **E4.30**.

The CJA 2003, s. 174(7), states that where, as a result of taking into account any matter referred to in s. 144(1), the court imposes a punishment on the offender which is less severe than it otherwise would have imposed, it must state that fact.

In *Fearon* [1996] 2 Cr App R (S) 406 the Court of Appeal stressed that the sentencing judge **E1.10** should always make it clear that a reduction for the guilty plea had been made. The guideline further requires that 'when pronouncing sentence the court should usually state what the sentence would have been if there had been no reduction as a result of the guilty plea' (para. 3.1).

Section 144(2) and (3) refer to various minimum required custodial sentences which are considered at **E5**. In those circumstances the reduction for guilty plea must not produce a final sentence which is less than 80 per cent of the required minimum sentence (and see *Gray* [2007] 2 Cr App R (S) 494). It is clear from *Darling* [2010] 1 Cr App R (S) 420 that if the judge has found that it would be unjust in all the circumstances to impose the minimum required sentence then the limited reduction permissible under s. 144(2) no longer applies. Section 144(2) and (3) make no reference to minimum sentences for certain firearm offences under the FA 1968, s. 51A. The Court of Appeal decided in *Jordan* [2005] 2 Cr App R (S) 266 that s. 51A did not permit any reduction to reflect a guilty plea (see further **E5.13**).

Reduction in Sentence for Assistance by Offender

E1.11   The SOCPA 2005, s. 73, makes provision for reduction in an offender's sentence to reflect assistance given or offered to the authorities by that offender. Any reduction on this ground is separate from and additional to the appropriate discount for pleading guilty (*Wood* [1997] 1 Cr App R (S) 347). These two matters require consideration at Steps 3 and 4 in the Sentencing Council guidelines. A helpful overview of the provisions and general guidance on their practical effect is provided by the Court of Appeal in *P* [2008] 2 Cr App R (S) 16.

Serious Organised Crime and Police Act 2005, s. 73

(1) This section applies if a defendant—
   (a) following a plea of guilty is either convicted of an offence in proceedings in the Crown Court or is committed to the Crown Court for sentence, and
   (b) has, pursuant to a written agreement made with a specified prosecutor, assisted or offered to assist the investigator or prosecutor in relation to that or any other offence.
(2) In determining what sentence to pass on the defendant the court may take into account the extent and nature of the assistance given or offered.
(3) If the court passes a sentence which is less than it would have passed but for the assistance given or offered, it must state in open court—
   (a) that it has passed a lesser sentence than it would otherwise have passed, and
   (b) what the greater sentence would have been.
(4) Subsection (3) does not apply if the court thinks that it would not be in the public interest to disclose that the sentence has been discounted; but in such a case the court must give written notice of the matters specified in paragraphs (a) and (b) of subsection (3) to both the prosecutor and the defendant.
(5) Nothing in any enactment which—
   (a) requires that a minimum sentence is passed in respect of any offence or an offence of any description or by reference to the circumstances of any offender (whether or not the enactment also permits the court to pass a lesser sentence in particular circumstances), or
   (b) in the case of a sentence which is fixed by law, requires the court to take into account certain matters for the purposes of making an order which determines or has the effect of determining the minimum period of imprisonment which the offender must serve (whether or not the enactment also permits the court to fix a lesser period in particular circumstances),
   affects the power of a court to act under subsection (2).
(6) If, in determining what sentence to pass on the defendant, the court takes into account the extent and nature of the assistance given or offered as mentioned in subsection (2), that does not prevent the court from also taking account of any other matter which it is entitled by virtue of any other enactment to take account of for the purposes of determining—
   (a) the sentence, or
   (b) in the case of a sentence which is fixed by law, any minimum period of imprisonment which an offender must serve.

E1.12   Section 73(7) provides that, where a court thinks that it would not be in the public interest to state in open court that a discount has been given, the CJA 2003, s. 174 (which requires the court to explain its reasons), does not apply to the extent that the explanation would reveal that a discount has been given for that reason. Further, the CJA 2003, s. 270, which requires the court to give reasons for its selection of the minimum term in a case of murder, is qualified to the same extent.

Section 74 provides for a subsequent review of a sentence passed (a) on an offender who received a discounted sentence under s. 73 on the basis of a promise to assist which he did not fulfil, or (b) on an offender who received a discounted sentence at the time, but has since given or offered to give further assistance, or (c) on an offender who did not receive a discounted sentence within s. 73(2) but has subsequently given or offered to give assistance.

Extent of Discount   Sections 73 and 74 of the SOCPA 2005 are silent as to the appropriate   E1.13
extent of any reduction to reflect actual or promised assistance by the offender. There are a number of long-standing Court of Appeal authorities which, according to *P* [2008] 2 Cr App R (S) 16, are still relevant despite the introduction of the statutory scheme. The decision in *Sinfield* (1981) 3 Cr App R (S) 258 establishes that, where an offender has given significant assistance to the police or prosecuting authorities, especially where it leads to the apprehension of other offenders or the prevention of other offences, he may expect a discount, possibly a substantial one, from his sentence. The level of discount will depend on the quality, quantity, accuracy and timeliness of the information given, the offender's willingness to testify if required, and the extent to which his co-operation with the authorities has put himself or his family at serious risk of reprisal. In general, the greater the nature of the criminality revealed by the offender, the greater the consequent risks to the offender and his family. The discount should be set at a level appropriate to show to offenders that it was worthwhile to provide such assistance (*Sivan* (1988) 10 Cr App R (S) 282). This created a difficulty in *Dougall* [2011] 1 Cr App R (S) 227, where the offender had provided very considerable assistance in the context of offences involving large-scale corruption. In view of the relatively low custodial sentence which would have been appropriate on a guilty plea without such assistance, the Court of Appeal said that it was appropriate in this case to reward the co-operation by suspending the sentence. While it was said in *Wood* (1987) 9 Cr App R (S) 238 that, in a case where a discount had been given for assistance, that fact should be made clear in open court, there are many cases where such a course would put the informant in greater danger. The statutory scheme in s. 73(4) preserves the possibility of dealing with a difficult and sensitive matter other than in open court. In *A and B* [1999] 1 Cr App R (S) 52, the Court of Appeal reviewed earlier authorities and restated the applicable general principles. It was there noted that the Court of Appeal might on occasion increase the level of discount which had been granted by the trial judge, on the basis of later information which showed that the material provided by the offender had turned out to be of greater value to the authorities than initially had been thought. Section 74 provides for any such adjustment to be carried out by bringing the matter back before the sentencer, rather than by way of an appeal against sentence. For consideration of sentence reviews under s. 74, see *Blackburn* [2008] 2 Cr App R (S) 16 and D [2011] 1 Cr App R (S) 424.

AGGRAVATING FACTORS

Previous Convictions

Criminal Justice Act 2003, s. 143   E1.14

(2) In considering the seriousness of an offence ('the current offence') committed by an offender who has one or more previous convictions, the court must treat each previous conviction as an aggravating factor if (in the case of that conviction) the court considers that it can reasonably be so treated having regard, in particular, to—

(a) the nature of the offence to which the conviction relates and its relevance to the current offence, and

(b) the time that has elapsed since the conviction.

The Sentencing Council's definitive guidelines list previous convictions as an aggravating feature. Although relevant and recent previous convictions clearly aggravate the offence, it is wrong to impose a sentence wholly disproportionate to the seriousness of the latest offence purely on the basis of a bad record (*Byrne* [2012] EWCA Crim 418; *Bailey* [2013] EWCA Crim 1779). In any case, a clean record, or a record of few convictions, will often be regarded as a significant mitigating factor and may be taken into account under the CJA 2003, s. 166(1) (see **E1.20** and *Seed* [2007] 2 Cr App R (S) 436). The various definitive sentencing guidelines issued by the Sentencing Council specify sentence starting points which make no assumption as to the offender's criminal record, and may well require adjustment upwards or downwards to take account of the presence or absence of relevant recent convictions. All sentencing guidelines issued prior to those of the Sentencing Council specified starting points which were based upon the offender being a 'first time offender'.

Section 143(4) makes it clear that 'previous conviction' in this context means a previous conviction by a court in the UK or a previous conviction of a service offence within the meaning of the Armed Forces Act 2006 or a previous conviction in another EU Member State of a 'relevant offence'. By s. 143(5), this does not prevent the court from treating a previous conviction by a court outside the UK as an aggravating factor in any case where the court considers it appropriate to do so.

The provision of information on antecedents in the Crown Court and magistrates' courts is dealt with in CPD II, paras. 10A.1 to 10A.8 (see Supplement, **PD-18**).

Offending on Bail

E1.15 The CJA 2003, s. 143(3), states: 'In considering the seriousness of any offence committed while the offender was on bail, the court must treat the fact that it was committed in those circumstances as an aggravating factor'. This is particularly so where the offence committed on bail is of the same type as the offence for which bail was granted (*Jeffrey* [2004] 1 Cr App R (S) 179).

While s. 143(3) is expressed in mandatory terms, it has to be set against the established sentencing principle that consecutive sentences are appropriate where one offence is committed while the offender is on bail in respect of another (see **E2.19**). Operation of these rules together might result in a disproportionately severe sentence.

Increase in Sentences for Racial or Religious Aggravation and for Offences with a Terrorist Connection

E1.16 The CJA 2003, s. 145, states that where a court is considering the seriousness of an offence other than one under the CDA 1988, ss. 29 to 32, if the offence was racially or religiously aggravated, the court must treat that fact as an aggravating factor on sentence and must state in open court that the offence was so aggravated.

For the definition of 'racial or religious aggravation', see **B11.149**. In *Morrison* [2001] 1 Cr App R (S) 12, the Court of Appeal said that the appropriate additional punishment to reflect racial aggravation would depend on all the circumstances, but in that case approved the enhancement by two years of a nominal sentence of four and a half years for burglary committed in circumstances of racial aggravation.

Section 145 is of general application in sentencing, except that it does *not* apply where the court is imposing sentence for one of the racially or religiously aggravated offences under the CDA 1998, ss. 29 to 32 (certain aggravated assaults, aggravated criminal damage, certain aggravated public order offences, or aggravated harassment: see **B11.149**). The racially or religiously aggravated forms of these offences carry higher maximum penalties. The cases of *Saunders* [2000] 1 Cr App R (S) 548 and *Kelly* [2001] 2 Cr App R (S) 341 provide sentencing guidelines for cases involving racial aggravation. They are both cases of racially aggravated actual bodily harm and are considered at **B2.33**. Nor does s. 145 apply where the offender has been convicted of the basic offence where a racially or religiously aggravated version exists. In *McGillivray* [2005] 2 Cr App R (S) 366, the offender pleaded guilty to assault occasioning actual bodily harm. The racially aggravated version of that offence had originally been charged as well, but no evidence was adduced on that count and a verdict of not guilty was entered. The judge passed a sentence of three years' imprisonment on the basis that the assault had been racially aggravated. The Court of Appeal said that it had not been open to the judge to sentence on that basis, since the offender had not been convicted of the racially aggravated form of the offence. The sentence was reduced to two years, a sentence appropriate for the basic offence.

Under the C-TA 2008, s. 30, where an offence of a kind specified in sch. 2 to that Act appears to the sentencing court to have a terrorist connection that fact will be treated as an aggravating factor. See **B10.111**.

Increase in Sentences for Aggravation Related to Disability, Sexual Orientation or Transgender Identity

The CJA 2003, s. 146, applies where the court is considering the seriousness of an offence com-   **E1.17**
mitted in any of the following circumstances:

(a) that, at the time of committing the offence, or immediately before or after doing so, the offender demonstrated towards the victim of the offence hostility based on—
   (i) the sexual orientation (or presumed sexual orientation) of the victim, or
   (ii) a disability (or presumed disability) of the victim, or
   (iii) the victim being (or being presumed to be) transgender

or

(b) that the offence is motivated (wholly or partly)—
   (i) by hostility towards persons who are of a particular sexual orientation, or
   (ii) by hostility towards persons who have a disability or a particular disability, or
   (iii) by hostility towards persons who are transgender.

The court must treat the fact that the offence was committed in any of those circumstances as an aggravating factor, and must state in open court that the offence was committed in such circumstances (s. 146(1)–(3)). It is immaterial whether or not the offender's hostility is based, to any extent, on any other factor (s. 146(4)). 'Disability' means 'any physical or mental impairment' (s. 146(5)). References to being transgender include references to being transsexual, or undergoing, proposing to undergo or having undergone a process or part of a process of gender reassignment (s. 146(6)). It was held in *B* [2013] 2 Cr App R (S) 443 (69) that an assault committed because the offender believed the victim to be a paedophile was not an offence aggravated by hostility towards the 'sexual orientation (or presumed sexual orientation) of the victim'; s. 146 was not designed to cover such a case.

General Aggravating Factors

Criminal Justice Act 2003, s. 156   **E1.18**

(1) In forming any such opinion as is mentioned in section 148(1) or (2)(b), section 152(2) or section 153(2), or in section 1(4)(b) or (c) of the Criminal Justice and Immigration Act 2008 (youth rehabilitation orders with intensive supervision and surveillance or fostering), a court must take into account all such information as is available to it about the circumstances of the offence or (as the case may be) of the offence and the offence or offences associated with it, including any aggravating or mitigating factors.
(2) In forming any such opinion as is mentioned in section 148(2)(a), the court may take into account any information about the offender which is before it.

The definitive sentencing guideline, *Overarching Principles: Seriousness* (see Supplement, **SG-21**), sets out a list of aggravating factors relevant to sentencing. Some of these reflect higher culpability on the part of the offender, others reflect a more than usually serious degree of harm. It is submitted that aggravating factors affecting the seriousness of the offence should always be taken into account when deciding, *inter alia*, whether an offence is 'serious enough' to warrant a community sentence (CJA 2003, s. 148(1)) or 'so serious that neither a fine alone nor a community sentence can be justified' (CJA 2003, s. 152(2)). Each of the Sentencing Council's definitive guidelines sets out a non-exhaustive list of aggravating factors to be taken into account when sentencing for the particular offence.

Lies told by the offender, whether at police interview or during trial, are not an aggravating factor for sentence (*Scott* (1983) 5 Cr App R (S) 90; *Lowndes* [2014] 1 Cr App R (S) 471 (75)).

MITIGATION

General Mitigating Factors

E1.19   See the CJA 2003, s. 156(2), set out at **E1.18**.

The definitive sentencing guideline, *Overarching Principles: Seriousness* (see Supplement, **SG-21**), sets out a list of mitigating factors relevant to sentencing. Some of these reflect significantly lower culpability on the part of the offender, others that the harm caused by the offence is less than usually serious. Each of the Sentencing Council's definitive guidelines sets out at Step Two a non-exhaustive list of mitigating factors to be taken into account when sentencing for the particular offence.

Personal Mitigation

E1.20   The CJA 2003, s. 166(1), makes provision for a sentencer to take account of any matters that 'in the opinion of the court, are relevant in mitigation of sentence'. Whether to take account of personal mitigation is a matter within the discretion of the court (see Scarman LJ in *Inwood* (1974) 60 Cr App R 70) and, in particular, the serious nature of the offence may mean that little weight can be given to what would otherwise be regarded as significant personal mitigation.

The CJA 2003, s. 166(2), states that even though the offence, or the combination of the offence and one or more offences associated with it, was so serious that a community sentence could not normally be justified for the offence, the court may, after taking matters of personal mitigation into account, pass a community sentence. In *Seed* [2007] 2 Cr App R (S) 436, the Court of Appeal stressed that good character and a clean record can be important personal mitigation. Other standard features of personal mitigation include remorse, youth/immaturity, old age, serious illness of the offender (*Bernard* [1997] 1 Cr App R (S) 135; *Hall* [2013] 2 Cr App R (S) 434 (68)), lapse of time since the offence where this is not the fault of the offender, significant pressure on the offender (short of duress) to commit the offence (*Lingu* [2014] 1 Cr App R (S) 120 (21)), determination to address addiction or offending behaviour, and meritorious conduct unrelated to the offence (see, e.g., *Alexander* [1997] 2 Cr App R (S) 74). Serious adverse impact of a custodial sentence on persons other than the offender (such as young children of a single parent) may be taken into account in the discretion of the court (*Petherick* [2013] 1 WLR 1302; *Humphries* [2013] EWCA Crim 1748).

Criminal Justice Act 2003, s. 166

(1) Nothing in—

    (a) section 148 (imposing community sentences),

    (b) section 152, 153 or 157 (imposing custodial sentences),

    (c) section 156 (pre-sentence reports and other requirements),

    (d) section 164 (fixing of fines),

    (e) paragraph 3 of Schedule 1 to the Criminal Justice and Immigration Act 2008 (youth rehabilitation order with intensive supervision and surveillance), or

    (f) paragraph 4 of Schedule 1 to that Act (youth rehabilitation order with fostering),

prevents a court from mitigating an offender's sentence by taking into account any such matters as, in the opinion of the court, are relevant in mitigation of sentence.

TOTALITY PRINCIPLE

The CJA 2003, s. 166(3), states that nothing prevents a court: **E1.21**

(a) from mitigating any penalty included in an offender's sentence by taking into account any other penalty included in that sentence, and
(b) in the case of an offender who is convicted of one or more other offences, from mitigating his sentence by applying any rule of law as to the totality of sentences.

The CAJA 2009, s. 125(5)(c), states that the duty on a court to follow sentencing guidelines (see E1.3) is 'subject to any rule of law as to the totality of sentences'.

The definitive sentencing guideline, *Totality* (see Supplement, **SG-578**), restates general principles set out in earlier case law, providing:

> ...all courts, when sentencing for more than a single offence, should pass a total sentence which reflects all the offending behaviour before it and is just and proportionate. This is so whether the sentences are structured as concurrent or consecutive. Therefore, concurrent sentences will ordinarily be longer than a single sentence for a single offence.

> ...it is usually impossible to arrive at a just and proportionate sentence for multiple offending simply by adding together notional single sentences. It is necessary to address the offending behaviour, together with the factors personal to the offender as a whole.

PREVALENCE

The definitive sentencing guideline, *Overarching Principles: Seriousness* (see Supplement, **E1.22** **SG-21**), states (at paras. 1.38 and 1.39) that the seriousness of an individual case should be judged on its own dimensions of harm and culpability, rather than as part of a collective social harm. It is legitimate for the overall approach to sentencing levels for particular offences to be guided by their cumulative effect. However, it would be wrong to further penalise individual offenders by increasing sentence length for committing an individual offence of that type. In respect of increasing sentence levels across the board for offences involving the carrying of weapons, see *Povey* [2009] 1 Cr App R (S) 228 and **B12.142**.

There may be exceptional circumstances that lead a court to decide that local prevalence should influence sentencing levels. The issue in such cases is the harm being caused to the community. It is essential that sentencers both have supporting evidence from an external source to justify claims that a particular crime is prevalent in their area and are satisfied that there is a compelling need to treat the offence more seriously than elsewhere. Such evidence may be supplied by the local Criminal Justice Board or emerge from a 'community impact statement' prepared by the police (see CPD VII, para. H.6: see Supplement, **PD-71**). An example is *Wicks* [2014] 1 Cr App R (S) 355 (57).

The principle set out in the guideline was endorsed by the Court of Appeal in *Oosthuizen* [2006] 1 Cr App R (S) 385, *Lanham* [2009] 1 Cr App R (S) 592, *Moss* [2011] 2 Cr App R (S) 199 and *McDonagh* [2014] EWCA Crim 478.

DUTY TO GIVE REASONS FOR, AND EXPLAIN EFFECT OF, SENTENCE

Criminal Justice Act 2003, s. 174 **E1.23**

(1) A court passing sentence on an offender has the duties in subsections (2) and (3).
(2) The court must state in open court, in ordinary language and in general terms, the court's reasons for deciding on the sentence.
(3) The court must explain to the offender in ordinary language—
  (a) the effect of the sentence,

E

Part E Sentencing

(b) the effects of non-compliance with any order that the offender is required to comply with and that forms part of the sentence,

(c) any power of the court to vary or review any order that forms part of the sentence, and

(d) the effects of failure to pay a fine, if the sentence consists of or includes a fine.

(4) [Matters which may be covered by the CrimPR.]

(5) Subsections (6) to (8) are particular duties of the court in complying with the duty in subsection (2).

(6) The court must identify any definitive sentencing guidelines relevant to the offender's case and

(a) explain how the court discharged any duty imposed on it by section 125 of the Coroners and Justice Act 2009 (duty to follow guidelines unless satisfied it would be contrary to the interests of justice to do so);

(b) where the court was satisfied it would be contrary to the interests of justice to follow the guidelines, state why.

(7) Where, as a result of taking into account any matter referred to in section 144(1) (guilty pleas), the court imposes a punishment on the offender which is less severe than the punishment it would otherwise have imposed, the court must state that fact.

(8) Where the offender is under 18 and the court imposes a sentence that may only be imposed in the offender's case if the court is of the opinion mentioned in—

(a) section 1(4)(a) to (c) of the Criminal Justice and Immigration Act 2008 and section 148(1) of this Act (youth rehabilitation order with intensive supervision and surveillance or with fostering), or

(b) section 152(2) of this Act (discretionary custodial sentence),

the court must state why it is of that opinion.

E1.24 Some provisions, which require a court to explain why it has *not* taken a particular course of action in sentencing the offender, have not been brought within s. 174. Examples are the duty imposed by the PCC(S)A 2000, s. 130(3), to give reasons on passing sentence if the court does not make a compensation order; the duty imposed under the CJPA 2001, s. 33, to give reasons for not imposing a travel restriction order when the court has power to do so; the duty imposed under the Football Spectators Act 1989 where the offender is convicted of a relevant offence for the court to give reasons why it is not making a football banning order; and the duty imposed under the CDA 1998, s. 9, to impose a parenting order on the parent of a young offender aged under 16 unless the court is not satisfied that such an order would be desirable in the interests of preventing offending by the young offender (in which case the sentencer must give reasons in open court that this criterion is not satisfied, and why not).

Failure to Comply

E1.25 No consequence of any failure to comply with these requirements is specified in the CJA 2003, s. 174. Lord Taylor CJ said in *Baverstock* (1993) 14 Cr App R (S) 471 (at p. 475) that the statutory provisions were 'not to be treated as a verbal tightrope for judges to walk' and that even if judges made a mistake and failed to explain something they should have explained, the Court of Appeal would not interfere with the resultant sentence 'unless it is wrong in principle or excessive'. In *Giga* [2008] 2 Cr App R (S) 638, where the judge made a mistake when explaining to the offender how long he could expect to serve in custody, the Court of Appeal said that such an error did not make the sentence unfair, nor did it found the basis for an appeal. The decision in *Bright* [2008] 2 Cr App R (S) 578 is to the same effect.

REPORTS

Pre-sentence Reports

E1.26   Criminal Justice Act 2003, ss. 156 and 158

156.—(1) [See E1.18.]

(2) [See E1.18.]

(3) Subject to subsection (4), a court must obtain and consider a pre-sentence report before—

    (a) in the case of a custodial sentence, forming any such opinion as is mentioned in section 152(2), section 153(2), section 225(1)(b), section 226(1)(b), section 226A(1)(b) or section 226B(1)(b), or

    (b) in the case of a community sentence, forming any such opinion as is mentioned in section 148(1) or (2)(b), or in section 1(4)(b) or (c) of the Criminal Justice and Immigration Act 2008, or any opinion as to the suitability for the offender of the particular requirement or requirements to be imposed by the community order or youth rehabilitation order.

(4) Subsection (3) does not apply if, in the circumstances of the case, the court is of the opinion that it is unnecessary to obtain a pre-sentence report.

(5) In a case where the offender is aged under 18, the court must not form the opinion mentioned in subsection (4) unless—

    (a) there exists a previous pre-sentence report obtained in respect of the offender, and

    (b) the court has had regard to the information contained in that report, or, if there is more than one such report, the most recent report.

(6) No custodial sentence or community sentence is invalidated by the failure of a court to obtain and consider a pre-sentence report before forming an opinion referred to in subsection (3), but any court on an appeal against such a sentence—

    (a) must, subject to subsection (7), obtain a pre-sentence report if none was obtained by the court below, and

    (b) must consider any such report obtained by it or by that court.

(7) Subsection (6)(a) does not apply if the court is of the opinion—

    (a) that the court below was justified in forming an opinion that it was unnecessary to obtain a pre-sentence report, or

    (b) that, although the court below was not justified in forming that opinion, in the circumstances of the case at the time it is before the court, it is unnecessary to obtain a pre- sentence report.

(8) In a case where the offender is aged under 18, the court must not form the opinion mentioned in subsection (7) unless—

    (a) there exists a previous pre-sentence report obtained in respect of the offender, and

    (b) the court has had regard to the information contained in that report, or, if there is more than one such report, the most recent report.

(9) References in subsections (1) and (3) to a court forming the opinions mentioned in sections 152(2) and 153(2) include a court forming those opinion for the purposes of section 224A(3).

(10) The reference in subsection (1) to a court forming the opinion mentioned in section 153(2) includes a court forming that opinion for the purposes of section 226A(6) or 226B(4).

158.—(1) In this Part 'pre-sentence report' means a report which—

    (a) with a view to assisting the court in determining the most suitable method of dealing with an offender, is made or submitted by an appropriate officer, and

    (b) contains information as to such matters, presented in such manner, as may be prescribed by rules made by the Secretary of State.

(1A) Subject to any rules made under subsection (1)(b) and to subsection (1B), the court may accept a pre-sentence report given orally in open court.

(1B) But a pre-sentence report that—

    (a) relates to an offender aged under 18, and

    (b) is required to be obtained and considered before the court forms an opinion mentioned in section 156(3)(a),

    must be in writing.

(2) In subsection (1) 'an appropriate officer' means—

    (a) where the offender is aged 18 or over, an officer of a local probation board or an officer of a provider of probation services, and

    (b) where the offender is aged under 18, an officer of a local probation board or an officer of a provider of probation services, a social worker of a local authority or a member of a youth offending team.

The normal requirement (as stated in s. 156(3)) is that the court should obtain a pre-sentence **E1.27** report before making a decision to impose a custodial or community sentence. The court has discretion to dispense with that requirement whenever it appears to the court to be 'unnecessary' to obtain one (s. 156(4)). This discretion is, however, subsequently narrowed (in s. 156(5)) in respect of offenders who are under the age of 18. Section 156(6) provides that no sentence shall be invalidated by failure of the court to comply with these requirements, but, on appeal against a custodial or community sentence passed without the court having obtained and considered a pre-sentence report, the appellate court must obtain and consider one unless, in accordance with s. 156(7), the appellate court is of the opinion that the court below was justified in not calling for a report or that the court below was not so justified but, in the circumstances of the case at the time when it is before the appellate court, it is unnecessary to obtain a pre-sentence report. The appellate court cannot, however, take this line in respect of an offender who is under the age of 18. In such a case the appellate court must order a pre-sentence report, or at least have sight of the most recent previous pre-sentence report prepared on the offender (s. 156(8)).

In *Armsaramah* [2001] 1 Cr App R (S) 467, the Court of Appeal approved the decision of the sentencer to impose a custodial sentence of five years on an adult offender convicted of kidnapping and robbery, without the benefit of a pre-sentence report. The Court of Appeal noted that the defence had not called for a report, the offender had been convicted after a trial, and the judge had made every possible assumption in favour of the defendant in light of the information available.

E1.28   The CJA 2003, s. 159, deals with disclosure of a pre-sentence report, other than a report given orally in court, (a) to the offender or his legal representative, (b) if the offender is under 18, to any parent or guardian of his who is present in court (unless information in the report would be likely to create a significant risk of harm to the offender, in which case a complete copy of the report need not be given to the offender, or to his parent or guardian) and (c) to the prosecutor (unless the court considers that it would be inappropriate for the prosecutor to be given it).

Other Reports

E1.29   The CJA 2003, s. 160, applies where a report (other than a pre-sentence report) is made by an officer of a local probation board (or an officer of a provider of probation services) or a member of the youth offending team with a view to assisting the court (except a youth court) in deciding how best to deal with an offender. It provides for disclosure of the contents of the report to the defence.

Victim Personal Statements

E1.30   CPD VII, paras. F.1 to F.3 (see Supplement, **PD-69**), and the decisions of the Court of Appeal in *Perks* [2001] 1 Cr App R (S) 66 and *Perkins* [2013] 2 Cr App R (S) 460 (72) together provide guidance on the relevance of victim personal statements placed before the sentencer on the impact which the offence had on the victim or, in a case where the victim had died, the impact on his surviving close family. According to Lord Judge CJ in *Perkins*, properly formulated statements provide real assistance for the court. They provide a practical way of ensuring that the court will consider the evidence of the victim about the personal impact of the offence. The process is not an opportunity for the victim to suggest, or discuss, the type or level of sentence to be imposed. The distinction is important. Victims must be provided with information which makes it clear that they *may* make a statement but are under no obligation to do so.

E1.31   Further guidance is as follows:

   (a) Except where inferences can properly be drawn from the nature of, or circumstances surrounding, the offence, the court must not make assumptions unsupported by evidence about the effects of an offence on the victim (*Perkins* at [5]).

(b) If an offence has had a particularly damaging or distressing effect upon the victim, this should be made known to and be taken into account by the court when passing sentence (said to be an 'elementary principle of sentencing' in *Nunn* [1996] 2 Cr App R (S) 136; see also *Doe* (1995) 16 Cr App R (S) 718).

(c) The statement constitutes evidence and must be treated as such. It must be in a formal witness statement, served on the offender's legal advisors in time for his instructions to be taken, and for any objection to the use of the statement, or part of it, if necessary, to be prepared. Responsibility for presenting it lies with the prosecution. The statement may be challenged in cross-examination and it may give rise to disclosure obligations. It may be used after conviction to deploy an argument that the credibility of the victim is open to question (*Perkins* at [9]).

(d) Evidence of the victim alone should be approached with care, the more so if it related to matters which the defence could not realistically be expected to investigate.

(e) The opinions of the victim and the victim's close relatives on the appropriate level of sentence should not be taken into account (see also *Perkins*). The court must pass what it judged to be the appropriate sentence having regard to the circumstances of the offence and of the offender. It could not accede to a plea for vengeance by the relatives, and had to be very cautious about paying attention to pleas for mercy. This was, however, subject to two exceptions:

(i) where the sentence passed on the offender was aggravating the victim's distress, the sentence might be moderated to some degree 'as an act of mercy' (examples are *Nunn* and *Roche* [1999] 2 Cr App R (S) 105); and

(ii) where the victim's forgiveness or unwillingness to press charges provided evidence that his physical or mental suffering must be very much less than would normally be the case (examples are *Hutchinson* (1994) 15 Cr App R (S) 134 and *Mills* [1998] 2 Cr App R (S) 229). (In *A-G's Ref (No. 36 of 2013) (Hall)* [2014] 1 Cr App R (S) 394 (61) some victims of sexual offences committed by the offender wrote to the Court of Appeal to say that they were content with the original sentence(s). Lord Judge CJ said that these views could not determine what was appropriate, and the total sentence was increased from 15 months to 30 months.)

(f) The court should consider whether it is desirable in its sentencing remarks to refer to the evidence provided on behalf of the victim. In selecting any passages for quotation in open court the advocate and judge must be very sensitive to the position of the victim, and the need to respect the victim's privacy (*Perkins* at [11]).

(g) Where the author of a victim personal statement wishes to read out that statement in open court that wish should be complied with wherever possible. The matter was for the court to decide, however, and there should not be delay or adjournment in order to accede to the victim's request (CPD VII, para. F.3).

E1.32 CPD VII, paras. G.1 to G.3 (see Supplement, **PD-70**), deal with sentencing issues arising in relation to the proper treatment of bereaved families. CPD VII, paras. I.1 to I.10 (see Supplement, **PD-72**), deal with impact statements tendered on behalf of a business rather than an individual.

Mentally Disordered Offenders

E1.33 The CJA 2003, s. 157(1), states that in any case where an offender is or appears to be mentally disordered, the court must obtain and consider a medical report before passing a custodial sentence other than one fixed by law. This is subject to s. 157(2), which states that the court need not order such a report if, in the circumstances of the case, it is of the opinion that it is unnecessary to do so. Section 157(6) defines 'medical report'. A medical report is distinct from a pre-sentence report, and s. 157(7) clearly states that the ordering of a medical report does not displace the need to order a pre-sentence report under s. 156.

E

Part E Sentencing

Section 166(5) provides that nothing in the sections mentioned in s. 166(1)(a)–(d) (see **E1.20**) is to be taken as requiring a court to pass a custodial sentence, or any particular custodial sentence, on a mentally disordered offender, or as restricting any power (under the Mental Health Act 1983 or otherwise), which enables a court to deal with such an offender in the manner it considers to be the most appropriate in all the circumstances. 'Mentally disordered', in relation to a person, means suffering from a mental disorder within the meaning of the Mental Health Act 1983 (s. 166(6)).

Section E2 Custodial Sentences: General Provisions

AVAILABLE CUSTODIAL SENTENCES

By the PCC(S)A 2000, s. 76(1), the term 'custodial sentence' means (a) a sentence of impris- **E2.1**
onment, (b) a sentence of detention under the PCC(S)A 2000, s. 90 or 91, (c) a sentence of
detention under the CJA 2003, s. 226, 226B or 228, (d) a sentence of custody for life under the
PCC(S)A 2000, s. 93 or 94, (e) a sentence of detention in a young offender institution, or (f) a
detention and training order. The term 'sentence of imprisonment' does not include a committal for contempt of court or any kindred offence (s. 76(2)).

Offenders aged under 21 at the date of conviction cannot be sentenced to imprisonment
(PCC(S)A 2000, s. 89(1)). Those under 21 cannot be committed to prison for any reason,
such as non-payment of a fine, but if a person under 21 is remanded in custody, committed in
custody for sentence, or sent in custody for trial under the CDA 1998, s. 51 or 51A, he may
be committed to prison for the period before his case is disposed of (PCC(S)A 2000, s. 89(2)).

MAXIMUM CUSTODIAL SENTENCES

Maximum prison terms for indictable offences and offences triable either way are almost always **E2.2**
laid down by statutes creating those offences. Maximum terms are indicated in respect of each
of the offences dealt with in **part B**. Where a person is convicted on indictment and is liable to
be sentenced to imprisonment, but the sentence is not limited to a specified term or life by any
enactment, the maximum prison sentence available is two years (PCC(S)A 2000, s. 77). This
provision does not apply to common-law offences, for which the penalty which may be imposed
by the Crown Court is not subject to any limitation except that it must not be disproportionate
to the actual offence committed (*Higgins* [1952] 1 KB 7). For sentencing by magistrates' courts,
and by the Crown Court when exercising the powers of a magistrates' court, see **E2.5**.

There are special rules in respect of statutory conspiracies and attempts, as to which see **A5.41**
and **A5.69** respectively.

Changes to Maximum Sentences The effect of statutory changes to maximum sentences is as **E2.3**
follows. Unless there is clear provision to the contrary, where an offender falls to be sentenced
for an offence committed before an increase in the relevant maximum sentence, he should be
sentenced on the basis of the old maximum. Article 7 of the ECHR states that no heavier penalty shall be imposed than the one applicable at the time the offence was committed (*Welch v
UK* (1995) 20 EHRR 247). When the offence is charged as having been committed on a day
unknown between specified dates and the maximum sentence was increased between those
dates, the lower maximum applies (*Street* [1997] 2 Cr App R (S) 309; *Cairns* [1998] 1 Cr App
R (S) 434). If the maximum penalty is reduced between the time of commission of the offence
and the date of conviction then, in the absence of guidance from the relevant provision or commencement order, it seems that the sentencing court should infer the intention of Parliament in
a common-sense way (*A-G's Ref (No. 48 of 1994)* (1995) 16 Cr App R (S) 980; *Shaw* [1996] 2
Cr App R (S) 278). The Court of Appeal in *H* [2012] 2 All ER 340 issued important guidance
on the proper approach to sentencing of 'historic' or 'cold' cases, especially sexual offences committed many years ago but only recently brought to conviction. Lord Judge CJ said that while

E

Part E Sentencing

sentence must be limited to the maximum sentence at the date when the offence was committed it was wholly unrealistic to attempt an assessment of what sentence would have been passed for the offence if it had come to light at or shortly after the time it was committed (see also **B3.4**).

E2.4   **Abiding by the Maximum**   In *Carroll* (1995) 16 Cr App R (S) 488, the Court of Appeal said that sentencers must abide loyally by the maximum sentence provided, that the maximum sentence should be reserved for the most serious examples of that offence and that an appropriate discount (such as for a guilty plea: see **E1.8**) should be made. In considering whether a particular offence is one of the worst examples of its kind, sentencers should have regard to the range of cases which is actually encountered in practice, 'and ask themselves whether the particular case they are dealing with comes within the broad band of that type' but 'should not use their imaginations to conjure up unlikely worst possible kinds of case' (per Lawton LJ in *Ambler* (1975) CSP A1–4C01, followed and applied in *Bright* [2008] 2 Cr App R (S) 578). The statutory maximum should not normally be imposed where there is significant mitigation. An example is *Pinto* [2006] 2 Cr App R (S) 579, where the maximum sentence of ten years imposed for an offence of cruelty to a child was reduced to eight years on appeal.

Limits on Imposition of Imprisonment: Magistrates' Courts

E2.5   General limits on the power of magistrates' courts to impose imprisonment are specified by the PCC(S)A 2000, s. 78, and the MCA 1980, s. 32. The minimum prison sentence which may be imposed is one of five days (MCA 1980, s. 132) and the maximum is six months in respect of any one offence (PCC(S)A 2000, s. 78(1)) unless a shorter maximum term is provided by statute. The six-month limit does not, however, apply to imprisonment for non-payment of a fine (see **E15.11**). The maximum aggregate term which magistrates can impose is six months, unless two of the terms are imposed for offences triable either way, in which case the maximum aggregate term is 12 months (MCA 1980, s. 133). These provisions also apply to the sentence of detention in a young offender institution but not to the detention and training order. For more detailed treatment of the sentencing powers of a magistrates' court, see **D23**. Magistrates' courts are, of course, subject to the criteria for determining both the imposition and length of a custodial sentence (see **E2.7** and **E2.9**).

A magistrates' court having power to imprison a person may instead order him to be detained within the precincts of the court-house or at any police station until such hour, not later than 8 p.m. on the day on which the order is made, as the court directs (MCA 1980, s. 135(1)). Such order shall not operate to deprive the person of a reasonable opportunity of returning home on the same day (s. 135(2)).

RESTRICTIONS ON IMPOSING CUSTODIAL SENTENCES

Persons Not Legally Represented

E2.6   The PCC(S)A 2000, s. 83(1), states that a magistrates' court on summary conviction, or the Crown Court on committal for sentence or on conviction on indictment shall not pass a sentence of imprisonment on a person who (a) is not legally represented in that court, and (b) has not been previously sentenced to that punishment by a court in any part of the UK unless he is a person to whom s. 83(3) applies. Section 83(3) applies to a person if either (a) representation was made available to him for the purposes of the proceedings under the LASPO 2012 but was withdrawn because of his conduct or because it appeared that his financial resources were such that he was not eligible for such representation, or (b) having been informed of his right to apply for such representation and having had the opportunity to do so, he refused or failed to apply (s. 83(3)).

Section 83(2) extends the effect of these provisions to custodial sentences other than imprisonment: (a) detention under the PCC(S)A 2000, s. 91, (b) custody for life, (c) detention in a young offender institution and (d) the detention and training order.

For the purposes of s. 83, a person is to be treated as legally represented if, but only if, he has the assistance of counsel or a solicitor to represent him in the proceedings in that court at some time after he is found guilty and before he is sentenced (s. 83(4)).

A custodial sentence passed contrary to the provisions of s. 83 is unlawful, but may be substituted by a lawful sentence on appeal (*Howden* [2007] 1 Cr App R (S) 164; *Henry* [2014] 1 Cr App R (S) 347 (55)).

General Restrictions

Criminal Justice Act 2003, s. 152   **E2.7**

(1) This section applies where a person is convicted of an offence punishable with a custodial sentence other than one—
   (a) fixed by law, or
   (b) falling to be imposed under section 1A(5) of the Prevention of Crime Act 1953, under section 51A(2) of the Firearms Act 1968, under section 139AA(7) of the Criminal Justice Act 1988, under section 110(2) or 111(2) of the Sentencing Act, under section 29(4) or (6) of the Violent Crime Reduction Act 2006 or under section 224A, 225(2) or 226(2) of this Act.
(2) The court must not pass a custodial sentence unless it is of the opinion that the offence, or the combination of the offence and one or more offences associated with it, was so serious that neither a fine alone nor a community sentence can be justified for the offence.

The sentencer may turn to a custodial sentence only when all other sentencing options have been considered and rejected. Custody is a last resort. As Lord Woolf CJ observed in *Kefford* [2002] 2 Cr App R (S) 495, 'the message is imprisonment only when necessary and for no longer than necessary'. The message was reinforced in *Seed* [2007] 2 Cr App R (S) 436, when Lord Phillips CJ noted that at times of prison overcrowding the custodial regime would be more punitive and the opportunities for rehabilitative intervention in prison would be restricted.

The definitive sentencing guideline, *Overarching Principles: Seriousness* (see Supplement, SG-21), states that the clear intention of this 'threshold test' is to reserve prison as a punishment for the most serious offences, but that it is impossible to determine definitively which features of a particular offence make it serious enough to merit a custodial sentence (para. 1.32).

Section 152(3) deals with the exceptional situation where a court may pass a custodial sentence on an offender who has failed to express his willingness to comply with a requirement proposed to be included in a community order and where the requirement requires an expression of such willingness. Requirements which require the offender's expression of willingness to comply are a mental health treatment requirement (s. 207(3)(c)), a drug rehabilitation requirement (s. 209(2)(d)), and an alcohol treatment requirement (s. 212(3)).

Two or More Offences   Where the offender stands convicted of two or more offences the   **E2.8** court, in deciding whether custody is justified under s. 152(2), must consider the seriousness of the sum of the offences, provided that these are 'associated' with one another. Section 161(1) of the 2000 Act specifies when one offence is to be regarded as associated with another.

Powers of Criminal Courts (Sentencing) Act 2000, s. 161

(1) For the purposes of this Act, an offence is associated with another if—
   (a) the offender is convicted of it in the proceedings in which he is convicted of the other offence, or (although convicted of it in earlier proceedings) is sentenced for it at the same time as he is sentenced for that offence; or
   (b) the offender admits the commission of it in the proceedings in which he is sentenced for the other offence and requests the court to take it into consideration in sentencing him for that offence.

In *Baverstock* [1993] 2 All ER 32 the offender was dealt with for two offences; the second having been committed while the offender was on bail in respect of the first. The offender was sentenced for the two offences on the same occasion; hence, they were 'associated' for the purposes of s. 161(1). It is clear from the case of *Godfrey* (1993) 14 Cr App R (S) 804 that, where a sentencer is sentencing for a new offence and at the same time revokes a community sentence which had earlier been passed on the offender and re-sentences for that offence, or where the sentencer passes a sentence for an offence in respect of which a conditional discharge had earlier been granted, the new offence and the earlier offence are associated offences. In *Godfrey* itself, however, the judge imposed 'no separate penalty' for a breach of conditional discharge. This meant that the earlier offence was not being sentenced on the same occasion as the new offence, and thus the two offences could not be regarded as associated. In *Crawford* (1993) 98 Cr App R 297, it was held that, where the offender had been committed to the Crown Court in respect of an offence of theft which placed him in breach of a suspended sentence imposed for an earlier offence of theft, the two offences were not associated offences. *Crawford* was followed and applied in *Cawley* (1994) 15 Cr App R (S) 25. Where an offender has been convicted in respect of a number of charges which are represented as 'sample counts', offences which are not included in the indictment, nor formally taken into consideration, are not associated offences (*Canavan* [1998] 1 Cr App R (S) 79; *Hartley* [2012] 1 Cr App R (S) 166). See further **D20.56**.

LENGTH OF SENTENCE

General Provision

E2.9   **Criminal Justice Act 2003, s. 153**

(1) This section applies where a court passes a custodial sentence other than one fixed by law or imposed under section 224A, 225 or 226.

(2) Subject to section 1A(5) of the Prevention of Crime Act 1953, section 51A(2) of the Firearms Act 1968, section 139AA(7) of the Criminal Justice Act 1988, sections 110(2) and 111(2) of the Sentencing Act, section 29(4) or (6) of the Violent Crime Reduction Act 2006 and sections 226A(4) and 226B(2) of this Act, the custodial sentence must be for the shortest term (not exceeding the permitted maximum) that in the opinion of the court is commensurate with the seriousness of the offence, or the combination of the offence and one or more offences associated with it.

The wording in s. 153(2) is a clear reflection of the well-established principle that, when it is necessary to impose a custodial sentence, that sentence should be as short as possible to achieve the goals of that sentence.

Section 153(2) states that the court may have regard to 'the combination of the offence and one or more offences associated with it' when determining the length of a custodial sentence. The PCC(S)A 2000, s. 161(1) (see **E2.8**), defines when one offence may be regarded for these purposes as 'associated with' another.

E2.10   Dealing with Several Offences   Where the offender is being sentenced for several offences, this approach could lead to a total sentence which is disproportionate to the overall seriousness of the offending behaviour. The CJA 2003, s. 166(3)(b), declares that nothing shall prevent a court 'in a case of an offender who is convicted of one or more other offences, from mitigating his sentence by applying any rule of law as to the totality of sentences'. This provision gives statutory recognition to the totality principle. For discussion of that principle, see **E1.21**.

Where a court is dealing with an offender for several offences, one (or more) of which is (or are) so serious that only custody can be justified but the remainder of which are not so serious, the court is not precluded from passing custodial sentences for the lesser offences. However, those sentences should normally be ordered to run concurrently with the sentences for the more serious offences and should not increase the length of the overall term (*Oliver* [1993] 2 All ER 9).

E2.11   Considering Shorter Period   The Court of Appeal in *Ollerenshaw* [1999] 1 Cr App R (S) 65 said that, when a court is considering imposing a custodial sentence of about 12 months or less, it should ask itself (especially where this will be the offender's first prison sentence) whether a shorter period might be equally effective. Six months may be just as effective as nine, or two months may be just as effective as four. In *Kefford* [2002] 2 Cr App R (S) 495, Lord Woolf CJ said that the overcrowding of the prison system was a matter of grave concern and that all courts should heed the message, which was 'imprisonment only when necessary and for no longer than necessary'. See also *Mills* [2002] 2 Cr App R (S) 229, with respect to the female prison population, and *Seed* [2007] 2 Cr App R (S) 436.

Time Remanded in Custody to Count as Time Served

Criminal Justice Act 2003, s. 240ZA   E2.12

(1) This section applies where—
   (a) an offender is serving a term of imprisonment in respect of an offence, and
   (b) the offender has been remanded in custody (within the meaning given by section 242) in connection with the offence or a related offence.
(2) It is immaterial for that purpose whether, for all or part of the period during which the offender was remanded in custody, the offender was also remanded in custody in connection with other offences (but see subsection (5)).
(3) The number of days for which the offender was remanded in custody in connection with the offence or a related offence is to count as time served by the offender as part of the sentence.
But this is subject to subsections (4) to (6).
(4) If, on any day on which the offender was remanded in custody, the offender was also detained in connection with any other matter, that day is not to count as time served.
(5) A day counts as time served—
   (a) in relation to only one sentence, and
   (b) only once in relation to that sentence.
(6) A day is not to count as time served as part of any period of 28 days served by the offender before automatic release (see section 255B(1)).
(7) For the purposes of this section a suspended sentence—
   (a) is to be treated as a sentence of imprisonment when it takes effect under paragraph 8(2)(a) or (b) of schedule 12, and
   (b) is to be treated as being imposed by the order under which it takes effect.

Section 240ZA, inserted by the LASPO 2012, s. 108, has the effect of crediting periods of **E2.13** remand in custody automatically, so that it is no longer necessary (as it was under the former s. 240) for sentencers to give any direction that time served on remand in custody should count towards sentence. The section applies to offenders sentenced on or after 3 December 2012, irrespective of the date of the offence. As from a date to be appointed, s. 240ZA is amended by the ORA 2014, s. 9.

Section 240ZA applies to sentences of imprisonment, detention in a young offender institution, detention under the PCC(S)A 2000, s. 91, and extended sentences of imprisonment or detention. It should also be noted, however, that s. 240ZA does not apply to the detention and training order, so it remains necessary when imposing a detention and training order to take into account any period spent in custody on remand (PCC(S)A 2000, s. 101(8): see **E7.23**).

The reference in s. 240ZA(6) to the period of 28 days is to the case where an offender has been released from a custodial sentence and then recalled. Section 255B(1) (referred to in s. 240ZA(6)) has the effect that a recalled prisoner must serve at least 28 days before being re-released. Time served on remand does not count towards those 28 days.

Of course, in cases where the offender has spent a substantial period in custody on remand, that matter may still be relevant to the court when deciding whether a short custodial sentence is justified or whether, in effect, the offender has already served his sentence in custody on remand. See, for example, *Barrett* [2010] 2 Cr App R (S) 551 and *Maughan* [2011] 2 Cr App R (S) 493 at **E6.4**. If the appropriate sentence is one of six months' imprisonment and the offender has spent three months on remand, the sentence of six months should be imposed but no further punishment is necessary. To this extent, at least, it remains important for accurate information to be before the court as to the number of days spent on remand, so that an explanation can be given in open court as to the sentence passed and its practical effect.

In respect of other sentences where the law requires the setting of a specified period under the PCC(S)A 2000, s. 82A (life sentence where that sentence is not fixed by law), s. 82A(3)(b) of that Act requires the court when fixing the specified minimum period to take into account any direction which it would have given under s. 240ZA (see **E4.16**). In fixing the minimum term applicable in a case of murder, the court is required by s. 269(3)(b) to take into account the effect of s. 240ZA (see **E3.2**).

E2.14   Section 242(2) explains that 'remanded in custody' means 'remanded in or committed to custody by order of a court', or 'remanded to youth detention accommodation' under the LASPO 2012, s. 91(4), or 'remanded, admitted or removed to hospital' under the Mental Health Act 1983. It does not apply to any committal in default of payment of any sum of money, other than one adjudged to be paid on a conviction (s. 242(1)). It does not include time spent in police detention but, according to the Court of Appeal in *Al Daour* [2011] EWCA Crim 2392, although police detention did not come within the terms of s. 242(2), it was not necessarily wrong to adjust sentence length to take account of an extended period in police detention (in that case under the Terrorism Act 2000). Section 242(2) appears to provide a closed list of what can amount to 'remanded in custody'. In *Watson* [2000] 2 Cr App R (S) 301, the Court of Appeal said that it was right to take into account a period of 11 months that the offender had spent on remand in a bail hostel under restrictive conditions, although the Court clearly stated that a period in a bail hostel was not to be equated with a period on remand in custody. It is submitted that these decisions are still good law, and that a judge retains discretion, notwithstanding s. 240ZA, to adjust the length of a custodial sentence to take account of such periods falling outside the terms of s. 242.

E2.15   **Extradited Prisoners**   The CJA 2003, s. 243, relates to extradited prisoners. Section 243, as amended by the LASPO 2012, s. 110, provides that in the case of an extradited prisoner the court must specify in open court the number of days for which the prisoner was kept in custody while awaiting extradition, and that s. 240ZA applies to days specified in this way as if they were days for which the prisoner was remanded in custody.

Crediting Periods of Remand on Bail

E2.16   The CJA 2003, s. 240A, states that, where an offender has been remanded on bail and that bail was subject both to a 'qualifying curfew condition' (requiring that person to remain at one or more specified places for a total of not less than nine hours in any given day) and an 'electronic monitoring condition' (imposed under the Bail Act 1976, s. 3(6ZAA)), the court must normally direct that the 'credit period' is to count as time served by the offender as part of the sentence. It is the responsibility of the court to make this direction, unlike the adjustment for time spent on remand in custody, which under s. 240ZA does not require an order of the court. The credit period under s. 240A is calculated by taking the following five steps, as set out in s. 240A(3) (amended by the LASPO 2012, s. 109 and sch. 16). Step 1 is to add the day on which the offender's bail was first subject to the relevant conditions (even if these did not apply for the whole day) and the number of other days on which the offender's bail was subject to these conditions (excluding the last day if part of that day was spent in custody). Step 2 is to deduct the number of days on which the offender was also subject to any requirement of electronic monitoring of a curfew requirement, or was on temporary release under the Prison Act 1952, s. 47. Step 3 is to deduct any days during which the offender broke either or both of the conditions. Step 4 is to divide the result by two, and Step 5 is to round up the figure to the nearest whole number, if necessary. Subject to s. 240A(3A) and (3B), the court must direct that the credit period is to count as time served. Subsection (3A) states that a day of the credit period counts as time served in relation to only one sentence, and only once in relation to that sentence, and subsection (3B) says that a day of the credit period is not to count as time served as part of any period of 28 days served by the offender before automatic release (s. 244B(1)). The sentencer should state in open court the number of days on which the offender was subject to the conditions and the number of days which the court deducted under each of Steps 2 and 3 (s. 240A(8)). As with s. 240ZA, the term 'imprisonment' must be taken to apply to sentences of detention in a young offender institution, extended sentences of imprisonment or detention in a young offender institution, and determinate sentences of detention under the PCC(S)A 2000, s. 91. Again in line with s. 240ZA, a suspended sentence counts as a sentence of imprisonment for these purposes if it takes effect in consequence of breach. As from a date to be appointed, s. 240A is amended by the ORA 2014, s. 9.

Guidance on the operation of s. 240A was provided by the Court of Appeal in *Monaghan* **E2.17**
[2010] 2 Cr App R (S) 343. The Court indicated that a period of time spent by the offender subject to an electronically monitored curfew of *less* than nine hours should not normally occasion a reduction but that in those circumstances the court should consider giving some modest credit where the offender had spent a significant or substantial period of time subject to those conditions. Whether such credit should be given, and how much credit should be given, was a matter for the sentencing judge. The Court of Appeal in *Hoggard* [2014] 1 Cr App R (S) 239 (42), decided after s. 240A was amended by the LASPO 2012, said that, in a case where the judge intends to direct that the full credit period during which an offender has been on bail subject to a qualifying curfew condition should count as time served but where there is uncertainty over the number of days involved, the judge may adapt and apply the approach recommended in *Nnaji* [2009] 2 Cr App R (S) 700: 'The defendant will receive credit for half the time spent under curfew qualified under the provisions of section 240A. On the information before me the total period is XX days (subject to the deduction of XX days that I have directed under Step(s) 2 and /or (3) making a total of XX days), but if this period is mistaken this court will order an amendment of the record for the correct period to be recorded.' Sweeney J said that it was essential that every court which imposed a curfew and tagging condition used the relevant Court Service form which was required to follow the defendant from court to court. Solicitors and counsel were required to ask the defendant whether he had been subject to curfew and tagging and, if the answer was 'yes', to find out, from the court record, for which periods. It was the responsibility of the CPS to have a system for ensuring that such information was available. In *Hoggard* itself, under Step 1 there was a period of 94 days. There was nothing to require a reduction from that period under Step 2. Under Step 3 the probation service said that the defendant had broken either or both of the relevant conditions on a total of eight of the 94 days. The breaches were denied. The net period in dispute was therefore four days. To resolve the dispute would have required an adjournment, the attendance of the prosecution, and probably the calling of evidence. The Court concluded that, in the circumstances of this case, such proceedings would amount to a disproportionate use of time and expense. Accordingly the issue was resolved in the defendant's favour. Having applied Steps 4 and 5 the Court ordered that 47 days should count towards the service of the sentence. If the above form of words is used, any error can be corrected in the court office even after the expiry of the 56 days allowed under the slip rule. The Court of Appeal in *Hoggard* also noted that in future it will scrutinise with great care applications for extension of time for appeal where the sole complaint is an error of calculation relating to s. 240A. See also *Leacock* [2013] EWCA Crim 1994.

Effect of Time on Remand on Suspended Sentence or Community Sentence   For the rel- **E2.18**
evance of time spent on remand to the imposition of a suspended sentence, see **E6.4**. Section 240ZA does not deal with the situation where an offender has been remanded in custody for a period of time before being sentenced to a community sentence. This is dealt with in the CJA 2003, s. 149, which states that the court *may* have regard to any such period in determining the restrictions on liberty to be imposed by a community order or by a youth rehabilitation order. See **E8.3**.

Concurrent and Consecutive Custodial Sentences

Where an offender is convicted on more than one count, the court should impose separate **E2.19**
sentences on each count. Prison sentences may run concurrently or consecutively. The court

E

Part E Sentencing

should make it clear which sentence relates to which count and whether the sentences are concurrent or consecutive. If it fails to do so, it is presumed that the sentences are concurrent. Where a court passes a prison sentence on a person who is already serving one or more sentences of imprisonment, it must make clear whether the fresh sentence is to be served concurrently with or consecutively to the existing sentence or sentences. It is unlawful to pass a sentence partly concurrent with and partly consecutive to another sentence (*Salmon* [2003] 1 Cr App R (S) 414). There is no power to antedate the commencement of a sentence (PCC(S)A 2000, s. 154; *Whitfield* [2002] 2 Cr App R (S) 186; *AJ* [2013] EWCA Crim 908), so the new sentence takes effect from the date on which it is imposed, unless the sentencer specifies a later date. A court imposing a prison sentence must not direct that the new sentence shall commence on the expiration of any other prison sentence from which the offender has been released on licence under the CJA 2003 or the CJA 1991 (CJA 2003, s. 265). See further *Costello* [2010] 2 Cr App R (S) 608, which holds (after considering earlier authorities) that it is wrong in principle in such a case to pass a sentence disproportionate to the most recent offence in an attempt to ensure that the offender serves more than the remainder of the licence period of the original offence.

Terms of imprisonment may be ordered to run consecutively even where that results in a total term greater than the maximum which could have been imposed for any of the offences (e.g., *Prime* (1983) 5 Cr App R (S) 127).

E2.20   General Rule on Concurrent Sentences   For guidance on the imposition of concurrent sentences, see the definitive sentencing guideline on *Totality* in the Supplement at **SG-496**. Where offences arise out of the same incident, sentences should be concurrent. Concurrent sentences should be imposed where multiple deaths arise from a single act of dangerous driving (*Noble* [2003] 1 Cr App R (S) 312) or where convictions for dangerous driving and for inflicting grievous bodily harm relate to the same incident (*Bain* [2005] 2 Cr App R (S) 319) or where digital and then penile penetration of the victim by the offender has occurred during the same sexual assault (*Tamby* [2008] 2 Cr App R (S) 366). In *Cosco* [2005] 2 Cr App R (S) 405, where the offender committed three offences of indecent exposure during the course of one afternoon, the Court of Appeal said that the three offences were part of a single course of conduct and concurrent sentences were appropriate. Occasionally, however, consecutive sentences are upheld for offences committed on the same occasion. An example is *Hardy* [2006] 2 Cr App R (S) 47, where the Court of Appeal upheld consecutive sentences totalling two years' imprisonment for dangerous driving, driving while disqualified and failing to provide a specimen. Steel J said that, while the offence of dangerous driving carried the main custodial sentence, it would be bizarre to add no further custodial term for the other matters. There was well established authority, deriving from *Wheatley* (1983) 5 Cr App R (S) 417, that consecutive sentences should usually be imposed in such circumstances.

E2.21   Guidance on Use of Consecutive Sentences   For guidance on the imposition of consecutive sentences, see the definitive sentencing guideline on *Totality* in the Supplement at **SG-496**. Consecutive sentences should normally be imposed where an offender has used violence to resist arrest for another offence (*Wellington* (1988) 10 Cr App R (S) 384) or has used violence to make good his escape (*Edwards* [2009] EWCA Crim 602). In the case of robbery involving the use of a real or imitation firearm, earlier decisions such as *French* (1982) 4 Cr App R (S) 57, *McGrath* (1986) 8 Cr App R (S) 372 and *Greaves* [2004] 2 Cr App R (S) 41 indicate that consecutive sentences are generally appropriate. In *A-G's Refs (Nos. 21 and 22 of 2003)* [2004] 2 Cr App R (S) 63, however, the Court of Appeal said that, in many cases of robbery, the possession or use of the firearm was intrinsic to the seriousness of the robbery itself, and concurrent sentences would not be inappropriate so long as the sentence as a whole reflected the overall criminality in the case. The Court of Appeal also said that, if the offender is in possession of a firearm at the time of committing another offence, such as criminal damage or dealing in drugs, it will often be appropriate to impose consecutive sentences for the firearms offence and the other offence. There is authority that consecutive sentences should normally be imposed where the offender commits an offence on bail which was granted in respect of the other offence (*Whittaker* [1998] 1 Cr App R (S) 172), but it is not clear how the principle squares with the CJA 2003, s. 143(3): see **E1.15**. A custodial sentence imposed for a failure to surrender to bail should normally be ordered to be served consecutively (*White* [2003] 2 Cr App R (S) 133 and **D7.119**). A custodial sentence imposed for escape from lawful custody should run consecutively to the sentence being served at the time of the escape (*Clarke* (1994) 15 Cr App R (S) 825) as should a custodial sentence for offences committed within prison by a serving prisoner (*Ali* [1998] 2 Cr App R (S) 123). Where an offender has attempted to interfere with the course of justice in relation to an offence committed by him, sentence for the interference offence should normally be consecutive to the sentence for the other offence (*A-G's Ref (No. 1 of 1990)* (1990) 12 Cr App R (S) 245).

Totality Principle Consecutive sentences are always subject to the totality principle: see **E1.21**. In *Raza* [2010] 1 Cr App R (S) 354 the Court of Appeal said that where consecutive sentences are imposed, and one is a prescribed minimum sentence, the principle of totality must not be applied in a way that undermines the intention of Parliament in setting the minimum sentence. See, however, *Sparkes* [2011] 2 Cr App R (S) 614, where the Court of Appeal, in order to preserve totality, chose to adjust a prescribed minimum sentence, rather than consecutive sentences imposed for other offences. See further the definitive sentencing guideline on *Totality* in the Supplement at **SG-496**. **E2.22**

Relevance to Sentence of Early Release Provisions

In *Round* [2010] 2 Cr App R (S) 292 the Court of Appeal confirmed the long-standing principle that matters of early release, licence and home detention curfew should normally be left out of account when imposing sentence. A sentencer may, however, wish to adjust sentence length to avoid an unusual, adverse effect upon an offender's release date (*Waite* (1992) 13 Cr App R (S) 26; *Cozens* [1996] 2 Cr App R (S) 321; *Harrison* [1998] 2 Cr App R (S) 174). These decisions do not require a sentencer to pass an unduly lenient sentence to avoid that result (*Parker* [2000] 2 Cr App R (S) 295). Nothing should be taken to detract from the principle that a sentencer should not increase sentence length merely to bring an offender within a different early release category (*Kenway* (1985) 7 Cr App R (S) 457). **E2.23**

In *Al-Buhairi* [2004] 1 Cr App R (S) 496, and in *Alkazraji* [2004] 2 Cr App R (S) 295, the Court of Appeal held that it was not proper for a judge to adjust sentence to take account of the fact that the offender may be released early on the home detention curfew scheme.

In *Bright* [2008] 2 Cr App R (S) 578 and in *Giga* [2008] 2 Cr App R (S) 638 the Court of Appeal has said that a trial judge's error, when explaining in open court the effect of early release provisions upon the offender's sentence, in no way invalidated that sentence or provided grounds for saying that the sentence was wrong in principle.

Relevance to Sentence of Allocation to Particular Custodial Regime

The sentencer should not recommend that an offender serve a custodial sentence at a specified prison, since it may not always be possible for this to be arranged (*Lancaster* (1995) 16 Cr App R (S) 184). The fact that a prisoner will be required to serve his sentence in isolation for his own protection is not normally a relevant consideration when passing sentence (*Kay* (1980) 2 Cr App R (S) 284; *Parker* [1996] 2 Cr App R (S) 275). An exceptional case is *Holmes* (1979) 1 Cr App R (S) 233. **E2.24**

Sentences of 12 Months or More: Licence Conditions

By the CJA 2003, s. 238, where the court imposes a determinate sentence of imprisonment or detention in a young offender institution (but not a sentence of detention under the PCC(S) A 2000, s. 91, or the CJA 2003, s. 226B) of 12 months or more on an offender for any offence, the part of the sentence to be served after release from custody will be subject to prescribed **E2.25**

standard conditions, and may be made subject to further conditions similar to the requirements applicable to the community sentence. The conditions to be imposed on licence will be
determined shortly before release of the offender by the Secretary of State, but the court, at the
time of passing sentence, may make recommendations as to the content of those conditions (s.
238(1)), and the Secretary of State must have regard to any such recommendation (s. 238(2)).
The conditions that the Secretary of State may attach to a licence are to be prescribed by order
(s. 250), and the sentencer will wish to bear these in mind when making a recommendation
at the point of sentence. A recommendation made by the sentencer as to licence conditions is
not to be treated as part of the sentence (s. 238(3)), and so cannot be the subject of an appeal
against sentence.

The definitive sentencing guideline, *New Sentences: CJA 2003* (see Supplement, **SG-9**), states
that a court 'may sensibly suggest interventions that could be useful when passing sentence, but
should only make specific recommendations about the requirements to be imposed on licence
when announcing short sentences and where it is reasonable to anticipate their relevance at the
point of release.' (para. 2.1.14).

Breach of Supervision Requirement

E2.26   As from a date to be appointed, where an offender is released from a sentence of imprisonment
or a sentence of detention in a young offender institution of less than two years, the offender
will be made subject to a supervision period which will begin at the expiry of the sentence and
end on the expiry of the period of 12 months beginning immediately after the offender has
served the requisite custodial period (CJA 2003, s. 256AA, inserted by the ORA 2014, s. 2). If
the offender breaches a requirement of supervision imposed under s. 256AA, he will be brought
before the appropriate magistrates' court to be dealt with for the breach (s. 256AC, inserted
by the ORA 2014, s. 3). If it is proved to the satisfaction of the court that the person has failed
without reasonable excuse to comply with a supervision requirement, the court may:

(a) order the person to be committed to prison (or in the case of a person under the age of 21,
     to a young offender institution) for a period not exceeding 14 days;
(b) order the person to pay a fine not exceeding level 3 on the standard scale; or
(c) make an order (a 'supervision default order'), imposing on the person (i) an unpaid work
     requirement (as defined by the CJA 2003, s. 199) or (ii) a curfew requirement (as defined
     by the CJA 2003, s. 204).

A person dealt with under s. 256AC may appeal to the Crown Court. The ORA 2014, sch.
19A, makes provision about requirements of supervision default orders and about the breach,
revocation and amendment of supervision default orders.

Section E3   Mandatory Life Sentences

INTRODUCTION

An offender aged 21 and over who is convicted of murder (but not related offences such as **E3.1** attempted murder or conspiracy to murder) must be sentenced to imprisonment for life (Murder (Abolition of Death Penalty) Act 1965, s. 1(1)). For an offender aged under 21 on the date of conviction, the equivalent sentence is custody for life (see the PCC(S)A 2000, s. 93, and **E3.11**). If, however, the offender who is convicted of murder was aged under 18 when the offence was committed, the sentence is one of detention at Her Majesty's pleasure (see the PCC(S)A 2000, s. 90, and **E3.12**).

MURDER: LIFE IMPRISONMENT

The CJA 2003, ss. 269 to 277 and schs. 21 and 22, provide a statutory scheme for the set- **E3.2** ting of minimum terms in murder cases. These provisions apply to all cases in which a court passes a mandatory life sentence for murder. This applies to sentences of life imprisonment for murder, detention at Her Majesty's pleasure under the PCC(S)A 2000, s. 90, and custody for life imposed for murder committed by an 18, 19 or 20-year-old offender under the PCC(S) A 2000, s. 93. By the CJA 2003, s. 269(2), the court must normally make an order that the early release provisions of the C(S)A 1997, s. 28(5)–(8), are to apply to the offender as soon as he has served the part of his sentence which is specified in the order. That part is to be such as the court considers appropriate, taking into account (a) the seriousness of the offence, or the combination of the offence and any one or more offences associated with it, and (b) the effect of any direction which it would have given under the CJA 2003, s. 240ZA (crediting periods of remand in custody) or of any direction which it would have given under s. 240A (crediting of periods of remand on certain types of bail), if it had sentenced him to a term of imprisonment (s. 269(3)). If the offender was aged 21 or over when he committed the offence, the court may, however, because of the seriousness of the offence, order that the early release provisions are not to apply to the offender (s. 269(4)). An order under s. 269(4) would have the effect of impos-ing a 'whole life' minimum term. A judge fixing the minimum term to be served as part of the mandatory life sentence for murder is concerned with the seriousness of the offence and not the dangerousness of the offender. The element of public protection is provided by the inde-terminate nature of the life sentence itself and becomes the responsibility of the Parole Board once the minimum term has been served (*Leigers* [2005] 2 Cr App R (S) 654; *Jones* [2006] 2 Cr App R (S) 121). In considering the seriousness of an offence under s. 269(3) or (4), the court must have regard to (a) the 'general principles' set out in sch. 21 and (b) any guidelines relating to offences in general which are relevant to the case and are not incompatible with the provisions of sch. 21 (s. 269(5)). Any court making an order under s. 269(2) or (4) must, in compliance with the duty under s. 174(2) to state its reasons for deciding on the order made, state in open court, in ordinary language, its reasons; in particular, which of the starting points in sch. 21 it has chosen and its reasons for doing so and its reasons for any departure from that starting point (s. 270). See further CPD VII, paras. M.1 to M.14 (see Supplement, **PD-76**).

Schedule 21 Principles

E3.3 Schedule 21 sets out a detailed scheme of 'general principles' for determination of the minimum term in relation to mandatory life sentences. It should be noted that, for the purposes of sch. 21, 'child' means a person under 18 years of age, 'minimum term' means the part of the sentence to be specified by the sentencer under s. 269(2), and 'whole life order' means an order under s. 269(4). Section 28 of the CDA 1998 (meaning of 'racially or religiously aggravated') applies for the purposes of sch. 21 as it does for ss. 29 to 32 of the 1998 Act (see **B11.149**), and for the purposes of sch. 21 an offence is aggravated by sexual orientation if it is committed in circumstances mentioned in the CJA 2003, s. 146(2)(a)(i) or (b)(i), is aggravated by disability if it is committed in circumstances mentioned in s. 146(2)(a)(ii) or (b)(ii) and, an offence is aggravated by transgender identity if it is committed in circumstances mentioned in s. 146(2)(a)(iii) or (b)(iii) (see **E1.17**).

In *Oakes* [2013] 2 All ER 30, a five-strong Court of Appeal, confirming earlier decisions including *Bieber* [2009] 1 WLR 223, and having regard to the decision of the ECtHR in *Vinter v UK* (2012) 55 EHRR 1003, said that a whole life order is not incompatible with the ECHR, Article 3. The Grand Chamber of the ECtHR held in *Vinter v UK* [2013] ECHR 645 that for a sentence of life imprisonment to be compatible within Article 3 there must be provision for the possibility of review and release. A five-strong Court of Appeal in *A-G's Ref (No. 69 of 2013)* [2014] 23 All ER 73, however, found that the power of the Secretary of State conferred by the C(S)A 1997, s. 30, to release any life sentence prisoner exceptionally on compassionate grounds satisfied that requirement, so that English law was compliant with the ECHR and judges should continue to impose the whole life order in the rare circumstances in which it was appropriate to do so.

E3.4   **Criminal Justice Act 2003, sch. 21, paras. 4 to 11**

Starting points

4.—(1) If—
    (a) the court considers that the seriousness of the offence (or the combination of the offence and one or more offences associated with it) is exceptionally high, and
    (b) the offender was aged 21 or over when he committed the offence,
    the appropriate starting point is a whole life order.
  (2) Cases that would normally fall within sub-paragraph (1)(a) include—
    (a) the murder of two or more persons, where each murder involves any of the following—
      (i) a substantial degree of premeditation or planning,
      (ii) the abduction of the victim, or
      (iii) sexual or sadistic conduct,
    (b) the murder of a child if involving the abduction of the child or sexual or sadistic motivation,
    (c) a murder done for the purpose of advancing a political, religious, racial or ideological cause, or
    (d) a murder by an offender previously convicted of murder.
5.—(1) If—
    (a) the case does not fall within paragraph 4(1) but the court considers that the seriousness of the offence (or the combination of the offence and one or more offences associated with it) is particularly high, and
    (b) the offender was aged 18 or over when he committed the offence,
    the appropriate starting point, in determining the minimum term, is 30 years.
  (2) Cases that (if not falling within paragraph 4(1)) would normally fall within sub-paragraph (1)(a) include—
    (a) the murder of a police officer or prison officer in the course of his duty,
    (b) a murder involving the use of a firearm or explosive,
    (c) a murder done for gain (such as a murder done in the course or furtherance of robbery or burglary, done for payment or done in the expectation of gain as a result of the death),
    (d) a murder intended to obstruct or interfere with the course of justice,
    (e) a murder involving sexual or sadistic conduct,
    (f) the murder of two or more persons,
    (g) a murder that is racially or religiously aggravated or aggravated by sexual orientation, disability or transgender identity, or

(h) a murder falling within paragraph 4(2) committed by an offender who was aged under 21 when he committed the offence.

5A.—(1) If—

(a) the case does not fall within paragraph 4(1) or 5(1),

(b) the offence falls within sub-paragraph (2), and

(c) the offender was aged 18 or over when the offender committed the offence,

the offence is normally to be regarded as sufficiently serious for the appropriate starting point, in determining the minimum term, to be 25 years.

(2) The offence falls within this sub-paragraph if the offender took a knife or other weapon to the scene intending to—

(a) commit any offence, or

(b) have it available to use as a weapon,

and used that knife or other weapon in committing the murder.

6. If the offender was aged 18 or over when he committed the offence and the case does not fall within paragraph 4(1), 5(1) or 5A(1), the appropriate starting point, in determining the minimum term, is 15 years.

7. If the offender was aged under 18 when he committed the offence, the appropriate starting point, in determining the minimum term, is 12 years.

Aggravating and mitigating factors

8. Having chosen a starting point, the court should take into account any aggravating or mitigating factors, to the extent that it has not allowed for them in its choice of starting point.

9. Detailed consideration of aggravating or mitigating factors may result in a minimum term of any length (whatever the starting point), or in the making of a whole life order.

10. Aggravating factors (additional to those mentioned in paragraph 4(2), 5(2)) and 5A(2) that may be relevant to the offence of murder include—

(a) a significant degree of planning or premeditation,

(b) the fact that the victim was particularly vulnerable because of age or disability,

(c) mental or physical suffering inflicted on the victim before death,

(d) the abuse of a position of trust,

(e) the use of duress or threats against another person to facilitate the commission of the offence,

(f) the fact that the victim was providing a public service or performing a public duty; and

(g) concealment, destruction or dismemberment of the body.

11. Mitigating factors that may be relevant to the offence of murder include—

(a) an intention to cause serious bodily harm rather than to kill,

(b) lack of premeditation,

(c) the fact that the offender suffered from any mental disorder or mental disability which (although not falling within section 2(1) of the Homicide Act 1957) lowered his degree of culpability,

(d) the fact that the offender was provoked (for example by prolonged stress),

(e) the fact that the offender acted to any extent in self-defence or in fear of violence,

(f) a belief by the offender that the murder was an act of mercy, and

(g) the age of the offender.

The starting points in sch. 21 are set out as amended by the Criminal Justice Act 2003 (Mandatory Life Sentence: Determination of Minimum Term) Order 2010 (SI 2010 No. 197), which inserted para. 5A (in force from 2 March 2010); para. 5A applies in relation to a sentence imposed for an offence of murder committed on or after that day. The CAJA 2009, sch. 21, para. 52, made amendments to para. 11 consequential on the changes in the law on provocation which apply only in relation to offences committed on or after 4 October 2010. The LASPO 2012, s. 65(9), amended para. 5(2)(g) by the insertion after 'aggravated by sexual orientation' of the phrase 'disability or transgender identity', and is applicable to sentences for murder committed on or after 3 December 2012.

Paragraph 12 states that nothing in sch. 21 restricts the application of the CJA 2003, s. 143(2) (previous convictions: see **E1.14**), s. 143(3) (commission of an offence while on bail: see **E1.15**) or s. 144 (reduction in sentences for guilty pleas: see **E1.8**). Detailed guidance as to the procedure for passing a mandatory life sentence under s. 269 and sch. 21 can be found in CPD VII, paras. M.1 to M.14 (see Supplement **PD-76**). The definitive sentencing guideline, *Reduction in*

E3.5

Sentence for a Guilty Plea (see **E1.8** and, for the text, see Supplement, **SG-1**), is applicable when setting the minimum term to be served in a mandatory life sentence. In *Jones* [2006] 2 Cr App R (S) 121, the Court said that while the reduction for guilty plea could have no direct effect on a whole life minimum term, the offender's guilty plea was one among many factors to bear in mind when considering whether a whole life minimum term was appropriate. If it was not a borderline case, a whole life minimum term would be appropriate despite a guilty plea. In *Peters* [2005] 2 Cr App R (S) 627, endorsed on this point in *Caley* [2013] 2 Cr App R (S) 305 (47) (see **E1.9**), the Court said that where the offender makes it clear that he accepts responsibility for the killing, in considering whether the offender has pleaded guilty at the first reasonable opportunity, there are some cases where that opportunity would not arise until the accused has obtained advice on possible defences from leading counsel.

Appeal

E3.6   Since the sentence for murder is a mandatory sentence, there is no appeal against it. By the Criminal Appeal Act 1968, s. 9(1A), however, an offender may appeal against an order specifying a minimum term made under the CJA 2003, s. 269(2), or against an order under s. 269(4) that the early release provisions are not to apply. The A-G may refer an order specifying a minimum term under s. 269(2) to the Court of Appeal under the CJA 1988, s. 36(3A), which states that the Court of Appeal 'shall not, in deciding what order under that section is appropriate for the case, make any allowance for the fact that the person to whom it relates is being sentenced for a second time'. This is a reference to the normal recognition on an A-G's reference for review of a sentence on the basis that it was unduly lenient, that some reduction from the increased sentence is appropriate to reflect the fact that the offender has had to face the prospect of being sentenced twice over (see **D28.9**). Subsection (3A) is an exception to that principle.

Court of Appeal Guidance

E3.7   Guidance on the operation of these provisions for the setting of minimum terms in murder cases can be found in a series of Court of Appeal decisions, the most prominent of which are *Last* [2005] 2 Cr App R (S) 381, *Peters* [2005] 2 Cr App R (S) 627, *Jones* [2006] 2 Cr App R (S) 121 and *Height* [2009] 1 Cr App R (S) 656. See also *A-G's Ref (No. 106 of 2004)* [2005] 1 Cr App R (S) 682, *Warsame* [2005] 1 Cr App R (S) 699, and *Reid* [2005] 2 Cr App R (S) 60. Taken together, these cases show that while judges must pay close attention to the scheme of sch. 21, to identify the correct starting point and relevant aggravating and mitigating factors, there is considerable flexibility within the scheme, which requires the exercise of judicial discretion. In *Jones*, the Court of Appeal pointed out the huge gap which exists between the specified starting points, which could only provide 'a very broad framework' for the sentencing exercise. In *A-G's Ref (No. 12 of 2008)* [2009] 1 Cr App R (S) 97, where the murder involved a prolonged and very violent attack on an elderly man, the case was before the Court of Appeal on the question whether the murder was committed in the furtherance of gain, and hence attracted a 30-year starting point. The Court of Appeal criticised the way in which the sentencing hearing had adopted a somewhat 'mechanistic or arithmetical approach', and said that looking at the seriousness of the case as a whole, the appropriate minimum term was 22 years. On the other hand, it was held in *Davies* [2009] 1 Cr App R (S) 79 that, if the presence of a particular feature of the murder (such as whether it involved sexual or sadistic conduct, attracting a 30-year rather than a 15-year starting point) is in issue, that circumstance must be proved according to the criminal standard. See also *Healy* [2009] 2 Cr App R (S) 10. In *M* [2010] 2 Cr App R (S) 117 the Court of Appeal said that the starting point for a murder involving use of a knife should not normally be the same as a murder involving a firearm or explosive, but that the use of a knife would always constitute an aggravating factor. For offences committed on or after 2 March 2010, see the CJA 2003, sch. 21, para. 5A, which came into effect on that day.

E3.8   Care must be taken not to 'double count' an aggravating factor which is already catered for in a specified starting point. The list of aggravating and mitigating features is not exhaustive. In *Blue*

[2009] 1 Cr App R (S) 6 it was accepted by the Court of Appeal that the judge had been entitled to find that the murder had been aggravated by a racial element but not sufficient to make the 'huge leap' from a 15-year to a 30-year starting point. The relative weight to be accorded to each, or to any particular combination, of those features, will vary greatly, depending on the circumstances of the case, and sch. 21, para. 9, indicates that 'detailed consideration' of aggravating and mitigating factors may result in a final minimum term of any length. In *Peters*, it was noted that, although sch. 21, para. 11(a), treats as a mitigating factor an intention to cause grievous bodily harm rather than to kill, there would be circumstances where the absence of that intention would provide little or no mitigation (a very clear example of this is *Cameron* [2011] 1 Cr App R (S) 163). The same was true of para. 11(e), where the offender had, to some extent, acted in self-defence.

In upholding a whole life minimum term in *Coonan* [2011] EWCA Crim 5 the Court of Appeal E3.9 considered para. 11(c) and said that, even though an element of mental disturbance was intrinsic to the murders committed, the jury had rejected the defence of diminished responsibility at trial and the sentencing judge should not impose a sentence which reflected a defence that had been rejected. In *Inglis* [2011] 1 WLR 1110 the Court considered a case of 'mercy killing', where the relevant aggravating features included para. 10(a), (b) and (d) factors but where specific mitigating features included para. 11(f) factors. Lord Judge CJ said that the 'prescriptive statutory regime' in relation to murder had on occasions caused difficulty and dilemma, and that on the facts the specific aggravating factors should not be taken to aggravate the murder. If it were otherwise the express mitigating factor would be deprived of any practical effect. The minimum term was reduced from nine years to five years. In *Height* [2009] 1 Cr App R (S) 656 the offenders were implicated in the murder of Anderson's wife. Anderson had recruited Height to carry out the murder. The judge imposed a 30-year starting point on Height, since his motive for murder was financial gain, while Anderson's motive was not financial but, rather, to dispose of his wife. The Court of Appeal said that, taken literally, para. 6 seems to suggest that any case falling outside the specified criteria attracts a 15-year starting point. However, according to Lord Judge CJ, the scheme was not to be interpreted rigidly in that way. It was hard to imagine a case in which one offender, acting for gain, should be subject to a different starting point to the offender who agreed to pay him. The appropriate starting point for each offender was 30 years.

In *Malasi* [2009] 1 Cr App R (S) 276 the Court of Appeal considered the principles applicable E3.10 when sentencing an offender, aged 16, for two murders committed 15 days apart. It was held that the judge should have regard to the provisions of sch. 21 in respect of each murder, assessing all relevant factors, aggregate the minimum terms arrived at and then make an appropriate adjustment for totality. There should not be consecutive minimum terms.

Guidance on the meaning and application of para. 5A was provided by the Court of Appeal in *Kelly* [2012] 4 All ER 687, where the Court dealt with several appeals in relation to it. The Court considered the phrase 'took the knife or other weapon to the scene', as well as particular problems arising from a joint enterprise where only one of the offenders carried a knife.

MURDER: OFFENDERS UNDER 21

For an offender convicted of murder who is aged under 21 at the date of conviction, the manda- E3.11 tory sentence is custody for life under the PCC(S)A 2000, s. 93, unless the offender was under 18 when the offence was committed, in which case the mandatory sentence is detention at Her Majesty's pleasure.

Guidance on the setting of a minimum term for the sentence of custody for life is now set out in the CJA 2003, ss. 269 to 277 and schs. 21 and 22 (see E3.2). It should be noted that an offender aged 18, 19 or 20 cannot attract a 'whole life' starting point but may, in a case where the seriousness of the offence is 'particularly high' attract a starting point of 30 years. Otherwise, the starting point is 15 years. In *Martin* [2010] 1 Cr App R (S) 226 the Court of Appeal said that there should be no sudden escalation of sentence as soon as an offender crossed a particular age threshold. It is not the case that as soon as an offender attains the age of 18 the minimum term will automatically be 15 years. A balancing exercise is required, taking into account offence seriousness and offender culpability as well as age.

MURDER: DETENTION AT HER MAJESTY'S PLEASURE

E3.12   The PCC(S)A 2000, s. 90, prescribes a mandatory sentence of detention at Her Majesty's pleasure for murder committed by an offender who was under 18 at the time of the offence. It is confined to murder cases (*Abbott* [1964] 1 QB 489). A person so sentenced will be detained in such place and under such conditions as the Secretary of State may direct or may arrange (s. 92).

Guidance on the setting of a minimum term for the sentence of detention at Her Majesty's pleasure is now set out in the CJA 2003, ss. 269 to 277 and schs. 21 and 22 (see **E3.2**). See *M* [2006] 1 Cr App R (S) 293, *Malasi* [2009] 1 Cr App R (S) 276 and *Patterson* [2009] 1 Cr App R (S) 103. It should be noted that an offender who was aged under 18 when he committed the offence cannot attract a 'whole life' starting point or a starting point of 30 or 15 years. The starting point is always 12 years.

Section E4   Dangerous Offenders

OVERVIEW OF PROVISIONS

General

Sections 224 to 236 of and schs. 15 and 15B to the CJA 2003, as amended by the LASPO 2012, **E4.1**
provide measures for sentencing 'dangerous offenders'. In any case where the sentence for the
offence would otherwise fall within the provisions for the sentencing of dangerous offenders,
nothing shall prevent the sentencing court from imposing a hospital or guardianship order
under the Mental Health Act 1983 instead (CJA 2003, sch. 32, para. 38: see **E22**).

Sentence Indications

Where a defendant is charged with a specified offence to which the dangerous offender provi-   **E4.2**
sions may apply, the judge should be cautious about giving a sentence indication in accordance
with the guidelines laid down in *Goodyear* [2005] 3 All ER 117 (see **D12.61**). That case did
not address this particular issue, but there are obvious practical difficulties in giving such an
indication where relevant reports are not available and the issue of dangerousness has still to
be determined by the judge. In *Kulah* [2008] 1 All ER 16 the Court of Appeal said that there
would be some cases where the assessment of dangerousness would be manifest based on the
nature of the offence and the antecedent history, but the great majority of cases would not be
clear cut. A judge who had not been provided with reports might well feel disinclined to give an
indication. The court deprecated what had happened in *Kulah* itself, where the first judge had
quite properly refused to give an indication, but the request had been renewed before a second
judge who had not been informed about the first application.

Offence Classification

Section 224 of the CJA 2003 defines 'specified offence', 'serious offence', and 'serious harm' for   **E4.3**
the purposes of these provisions. 'Specified offences' are those sexual offences or violent offences
which are listed in sch. 15 (s. 224(1)). All of the 'sexual offences' or 'violent offences' in sch. 15
carry a maximum penalty of two years' imprisonment or more. A 'serious offence' is defined
as a specified sexual or violent offence which (apart from s. 224A) is punishable in the case of
a person aged 18 or over by (i) imprisonment for life, or (ii) imprisonment for a determinate
period of ten years or more (s. 224(2)). 'Serious harm' means death or serious personal injury,
whether physical or psychological (s. 224(3)).

Offences Listed in sch. 15   The specified violent offences are manslaughter; kidnapping, false   **E4.4**
imprisonment and offences under the following enactments: OAPA 1861, ss. 4, 16, 18, 20
to 23, 27 to 32, 35, 37, 38, and 47; Explosive Substances Act 1883, ss. 2 and 3; Infant Life
(Preservation) Act 1929, s. 1; CYPA 1933, s. 1; Infanticide Act 1938, s. 1; FA 1968, ss. 16,
16A, 17(1), 17(2) and 18; Theft Act 1968, ss. 8 and 9 (where the burglary is committed with
intent to inflict grievous bodily harm, or to do unlawful damage), 10 and 12A (involving an
accident which caused the death of any person); Criminal Damage Act 1971, s. 1 (arson) and
1(2); Taking of Hostages Act 1982, s. 1; Aviation Security Act 1982, ss. 1 to 4; Mental Health
Act 1983, s. 127; Prohibition of Female Circumcision Act 1985, s. 12; POA 1986, ss. 1 to 3;

CJA 1988, s. 134; RTA 1988, ss. 1 and 3A; Aviation and Maritime Security Act 1990, ss. 1 and 9 to 13; Channel Tunnel (Security) Order 1994 (SI 1994 No. 570), part II; Protection from Harassment Act 1997, s. 4 or 4A; CDA 1998, ss. 29, 31(1)(a) and 31(1)(b); Terrorism 2000, ss. 54, 56, 57 and 59; International Criminal Court Act 2001, ss. 51 and 52; A-tCSA 2001, ss. 47, 50 and 113; Female Genital Mutilation Act 2003, ss. 1 to 3; DVCVA 2004, s. 5; TA 2006, ss. 5, 6, 9, 10 and 11. Paragraph 64 of sch. 15 also makes it clear that aiding, abetting, counselling, procuring, conspiring or attempting to commit any of the specified violent offences or encouraging or assisting them within the meaning of the SCA 2007 are also covered. Attempt to commit murder and conspiracy to commit murder are also listed.

The specified sexual offences include offences under the Protection of Children Act 1978, s. 1, the CJA 1988, s. 160 and the SOA 2003, ss. 1 to 19, 25, 26, 30 to 41, 47 to 50, 52, 53, 57 to 59A, 61 to 67, 69 and 70. Paragraph 153 of sch. 15 makes it clear that aiding, abetting, counselling, procuring, conspiring or attempting to commit any of the specified sexual offences or encouraging or assisting them within the meaning of the SCA 2007 are also covered.

Schedule 15 is unaffected by the LASPO 2012 but it should be noted that sch. 15A has been repealed.

IMPRISONMENT OR DETENTION FOR LIFE FOR SERIOUS OFFENCE

Life Sentence for Serious Offence

E4.5   Criminal Justice Act 2003, s. 225

(1) This section applies where—
  (a) a person aged 18 or over is convicted of a serious offence committed after the commencement of this section, and
  (b) the court is of the opinion that there is a significant risk to members of the public of serious harm occasioned by the commission by him of further specified offences.
(2) If—
  (a) the offence is one in respect of which the offender would apart from this section be liable to imprisonment for life, and
  (b) the court considers that the seriousness of the offence, or of the offence and one or more offences associated with it, is such as to justify the imposition of a sentence of imprisonment for life, the court must impose a sentence of imprisonment for life.
  [(3), (3A) to (3C) and (4) repealed.]
(5) An offence the sentence for which is imposed under this section is not to be regarded as an offence the sentence for which is fixed by law.

E4.6 For the meaning of 'serious offence' and 'serious harm', see **E4.3**.

The statutory criteria in the CJA 2003 for determining whether the imposition of a custodial sentence is justified and, if so, for fixing its length (set out at **E2.7** and **E2.9**) apply to discretionary life sentences. In *MJ* [2012] 2 Cr App R (S) 416, Lord Judge CJ stressed that the decision whether to impose an indeterminate sentence was made at sentencing, and at that point the court must form its opinion whether there was a significant risk to members of the public of serious harm occasioned by the offender committing any further specified offences. On the issue of public safety the decision made at sentencing was required to address the future. Nothing in the decision of the Supreme Court in *Smith* [2011] 4 All ER 661 (which dealt with the special case of the imposition of an indeterminate sentence upon an offender who had reoffended following release on life licence) was inconsistent with that approach.

Prior to the changes made by the LASPO 2012, guidance on the choice between a life sentence and the closely similar sentence of imprisonment for public protection was provided in *Wilkinson* [2010] 1 Cr App R (S) 100. In that case Lord Judge CJ said that a life sentence should come into consideration where the seriousness of the offence is such that a life sentence would have a denunciatory value over and above imprisonment for public protection to reflect the public abhorrence of the particular crime. Following abolition of the sentence of imprisonment for public protection by the LASPO 2012, initial guidance on the future use of the discretionary life sentence was given by the Court of

Appeal in *Saunders* [2014] 1 Cr App R (S) 258 (45). Lord Judge CJ said that, in cases which, prior to the implementation of the LASPO 2012, would have required a sentence of imprisonment for public protection, the discretionary life sentence will arise for consideration where the necessary level of public protection cannot be achieved by the new extended sentence. The 'denunciatory' element, previously identified to distinguish between the circumstances in which a life sentence rather than imprisonment for public protection should be imposed, is no longer apposite. Although the denunciatory element of the sentencing decision may continue to justify the passing of a discretionary life sentence, its absence does not preclude such an order. As every judge appreciates, however, the life sentence remains the sentence of last resort. The Court of Appeal in *A-G's Ref (No. 27 of 2013) (Burinskas)* [2014] EWCA Crim 334 endorsed what was said in *Saunders*. Lord Thomas CJ said that although the provisions of s. 225 remained the same, the statutory context was fundamentally changed by the LASPO 2012, and it was inevitable that life sentences under s. 225 would be imposed more frequently than before. Cases decided before 2012 were now of limited value.

The Court in *Saunders* confirmed that a court retains power to impose a sentence of life imprisonment for any offence which carries that maximum penalty if the offence in question is not listed in sch. 15 to the CJA 2003 and the court is therefore not required to pass a life sentence under s. 225. Neither the CJA 2003, nor the LASPO 2012, removed that power. The occasions on which a court might impose a discretionary life sentence on an offender who did not fall within the dangerous offender provisions of the CJA 2003 would be rare, but one example might be an offender who had committed repeated offences of very serious drug supply. **E4.7**

Detention for Life for Serious Offence

Criminal Justice Act 2003, s. 226 **E4.8**

(1) This section applies where—
  (a) a person aged under 18 is convicted of a serious offence committed after the commencement of this section, and
  (b) the court is of the opinion that there is a significant risk to members of the public of serious harm occasioned by the commission by him of further specified offences.
(2) If—
  (a) the offence is one in respect of which the offender would apart from this section be liable to a sentence of detention for life under section 91 of the Sentencing Act, and
  (b) the court considers that the seriousness of the offence, or of the offence and one or more offences associated with it, is such as to justify the imposition of a sentence of detention for life, the court must impose a sentence of detention for life under that section.
[(3), (3A) and (4) repealed.]
(5) An offence the sentence for which is imposed under this section is not to be regarded as an offence the sentence for which is fixed by law.

For the meaning of 'serious offence' and 'serious harm', see E4.3.

In *Lang* [2006] 2 All ER 410, the Court of Appeal said that when sentencing young offenders it was important to bear in mind that they may change and develop in a shorter time than an adult. This, together with their level of maturity, may be highly relevant when assessing future conduct and whether that may give rise to a significant risk of serious harm. See further *Frota* [2007] EWCA Crim 2602 and *Kehoe* [2009] 1 Cr App R (S) 41. **E4.9**

EXTENDED SENTENCE

Extended Sentence: Persons 18 or Over

Criminal Justice Act 2003, s. 226A **E4.10**

(1) This section applies where—
  (a) a person aged 18 or over is convicted of a specified offence (whether the offence was committed before or after this section comes into force),
  (b) the court considers that there is a significant risk to members of the public of serious harm occasioned by the commission by the offender of further specified offences,

Part E Sentencing

   (c) the court is not required by section 224A or 225(2) to impose a sentence of imprisonment for life, and

   (d) condition A or B is met.

(2) Condition A is that, at the time the offence was committed, the offender had been convicted of an offence listed in Schedule 15B.

(3) Condition B is that, if the court were to impose an extended sentence of imprisonment, the term that it would specify as the appropriate custodial term would be at least 4 years.

(4) The court may impose an extended sentence of imprisonment on the offender.

(5) An extended sentence of imprisonment is a sentence of imprisonment the term of which is equal to the aggregate of—

   (a) the appropriate custodial term, and

   (b) a further period (the 'extension period') for which the offender is to be subject to a licence.

(6) The appropriate custodial term is the term of imprisonment that would (apart from this section) be imposed in compliance with section 153(2).

(7) The extension period must be a period of such length as the court considers necessary for the purpose of protecting members of the public from serious harm occasioned by the commission by the offender of further specified offences, subject to subsections (7A) to (9).

(7A) The extension period must be at least 1 year.

(8) The extension period must not exceed—

   (a) 5 years in the case of a specified violent offence, and

   (b) 8 years in the case of a specified sexual offence.

(9) The term of an extended sentence of imprisonment imposed under this section in respect of an offence must not exceed the term that, at the time the offence was committed, was the maximum term permitted for the offence.

E4.11 For the meaning of 'serious offence' and 'serious harm', see **E4.3**. Section 226A was inserted by the LASPO 2012, s. 124, with effect from 3 December 2012; it is set out above as amended, from a date to be appointed, by the ORA 2014, s. 8 (insertion of s. 226A(7A) and consequential amendment to s. 226A(7)). It is irrelevant whether the offence was committed before or after s. 226A came into force. Note that, by virtue of the LASPO, 2012, sch. 21, para. 36, s. 226A is modified so that, in the case of an offender aged at least 18 but under 21, the reference in s. 226A(1)(c) to imprisonment for life is to be read as a reference to custody for life and other references to imprisonment are to be read as references to detention in a young offender institution.

The offender must pass the 'dangerousness test' (see **E4.19**). An extended sentence of imprisonment (or detention in a young offender institution if the offender is aged 18, 19 or 20) can only be passed where (Condition A) the offender has previously been convicted of an offence listed in sch. 15B, or (Condition B) the appropriate custodial term, proportionate to the seriousness of the offence, is at least four years. Clearly, if the offender qualifies for an extended sentence by virtue of Condition A the custodial term imposed may be for less than four years. To the custodial term there must always be added the appropriate extension period. The total term of an extended sentence of imprisonment (or detention in a young offender institution) must not exceed the maximum penalty for the offence. An extended sentence of eight years' imprisonment was therefore held to be unlawful in *Oldfield* [2012] 1 Cr App R 211 where the maximum penalty for the offence was five years.

E4.12 According to the Court of Appeal in *Saunders* [2014] 1 Cr App R (S) 258 (45), the new extended sentence is 'much more onerous' than the version originally created by the CJA 2003, but it cannot be treated as a direct replacement for the old sentence of imprisonment for public protection. Under the version of the extended sentence in place prior to the implementation of the LASPO 2012, release from the sentence was at the half way point of the custodial term. For the new post-LASPO extended sentence under s. 226A, however, release is normally at the two-thirds point of the custodial term, unless the custodial term is ten years or more, or the sentence is imposed for an offence listed in sch. 15B. If either (or both) of these conditions apply, the case will be referred at the two-thirds point to the Parole Board, which will consider whether it is no longer necessary for the protection of the public for the offender to be detained (CJA 2003, s. 246A). It follows that in all cases the post-LASPO extended sentence for an offender aged 18 or over is more onerous in its effect than before, and that in some cases the precise date of release from the extended sentence cannot be known at point of sentence. In *A-G's Ref (No. 27 of 2013) (Burinskas)*

[2014] EWCA Crim 334, Lord Thomas CJ said that s. 226A is, in effect, a new form of extended sentence. Imposition of the sentence is discretionary, so that if there is a finding of dangerousness a life sentence or an extended sentence will usually be appropriate but the option of a determinate sentence should not be forgotten. It is the extended period of licence which provides protection to the public. The Court considered argument before it that the changes made to early release from an extended sentence created an anomaly in that the first opportunity for release occurred sooner for a life sentence prisoner than for a prisoner serving an extended sentence. In one of the appeals before the court, the sentencing judge had reduced the custodial term in the extended sentence by one year to reflect the fact that time to be served had been increased. The Court said that this adjustment should not have been made since, other than when fixing the minimum term in a life sentence case under s. 82A, a judge should disregard early release provisions.

Extended Sentence: Persons under 18

Criminal Justice Act 2003, s. 226B   E4.13

(1) This section applies where—
   (a) a person aged under 18 is convicted of a specified offence (whether the offence was committed before or after this section comes into force),
   (b) the court considers that there is a significant risk to members of the public of serious harm occasioned by the commission by the offender of further specified offences,
   (c) the court is not required by section 226(2) to impose a sentence of detention for life under section 91 of the Sentencing Act, and
   (d) if the court were to impose an extended sentence of detention, the term that it would specify as the appropriate custodial term would be at least 4 years.
(2) The court may impose an extended sentence of detention on the offender.
(3) An extended sentence of detention is a sentence of detention the term of which is equal to the aggregate of—
   (a) the appropriate custodial term, and
   (b) a further period (the 'extension period') for which the offender is to be subject to a licence.
(4) The appropriate custodial term is the term of detention that would (apart from this section) be imposed in compliance with section 153(2).
(5) The extension period must be a period of such length as the court considers necessary for the purpose of protecting members of the public from serious harm occasioned by the commission by the offender of further specified offences, subject to subsections (5A) to (7).
(5A) The extension period must be at least 1 year.
(6) The extension period must not exceed—
   (a) 5 years in the case of a specified violent offence, and
   (b) 8 years in the case of a specified sexual offence.
(7) The term of an extended sentence of detention imposed under this section in respect of an offence may not exceed the term that, at the time the offence was committed, was the maximum term of imprisonment permitted for the offence in the case of a person aged 18 or over.

For the meaning of 'specified offence' and 'serious harm', see **E4.3**. Section 226B was inserted   E4.14
by the LASPO 2012, s. 124, with effect from 3 December 2012; it is set out above as amended, from a date to be appointed, by the ORA 2014, s. 8 (insertion of s. 226B(5A) and consequential amendment to s. 226B(5)). Note that, by virtue of the LASPO, 2012, sch. 21, para. 36, s. 226B is modified so that the reference in s. 226B to '18' is to be read as a reference to '21'. It should be noted that it is irrelevant whether the offence was committed before or after s. 226B came into force.

The offender must pass the 'dangerousness test' (see **E4.19**). An extended sentence of detention can be passed only where the appropriate custodial term, proportionate to the seriousness of the offence, is at least four years. There is no equivalent provision in s. 226B to that of Condition A in s. 226A, so it follows that the custodial term under s. 226B must always be for at least four years. To the custodial term there must always be added the appropriate extension period. The total term of an extended sentence of detention must not exceed the maximum penalty for the offence. A person sentenced to be detained under s. 226B is liable to be detained in such place as may be determined by the Secretary of State (s. 235).

Although s. 226B was not directly in issue in either *Saunders* [2014] 1 Cr App R (S) 258 (45) or *A-G's Ref (No. 27 of 2013) (Burinskas)* [2014] EWCA Crim 334, the early release provisions in respect of ss. 226A and 226B are identical, and it is submitted that those two decisions (considered at E4.12) are equally applicable to s. 226B, subject of course to the adjustments which need to be made to sentencing when dealing with offenders aged under 18.

Life Sentence for Second Listed Offence

E4.15   The CJA 2003, s. 224A (inserted by the LASPO 2012, s. 122), provides for the sentence of life imprisonment for the second listed offence.

Criminal Justice Act 2003, s. 224A

(1) This section applies where—
    (a) a person aged 18 or over is convicted of an offence listed in Part 1 of Schedule 15B,
    (b) the offence was committed after this section comes into force, and
    (c) the sentence condition and the previous offence condition are met.

(2) The court must impose a sentence of imprisonment for life unless the court is of the opinion that there are particular circumstances which—
    (a) relate to the offence, to the previous offence referred to in subsection (4) or to the offender, and
    (b) would make it unjust to do so in all the circumstances.

(3) The sentence condition is that, but for this section, the court would, in compliance with sections 152(2) and 153(2), impose a sentence of imprisonment for 10 years or more, disregarding any extension period imposed under section 226A.

(4) The previous offence condition is that—
    (a) at the time the offence was committed, the offender had been convicted of an offence listed in Schedule 15B ('the previous offence'), and
    (b) a relevant life sentence or a relevant sentence of imprisonment or detention for a determinate period was imposed on the offender for the previous offence.

(5) A life sentence is relevant for the purposes of subsection (4)(b) if—
    (a) the offender was not eligible for release during the first 5 years of the sentence, or
    (b) the offender would not have been eligible for release during that period but for the reduction of the period of ineligibility to take account of a relevant pre-sentence period.

(6) An extended sentence imposed under this Act (including one imposed as a result of the Armed Forces Act 2006) is relevant for the purposes of subsection (4)(b) if the appropriate custodial term imposed was 10 years or more.

(7) Any other extended sentence is relevant for the purposes of subsection (4)(b) if the custodial term imposed was 10 years or more.

(8) Any other sentence of imprisonment or detention for a determinate period is relevant for the purposes of subsection (4)(b) if it was for a period of 10 years or more.

(9) An extended sentence or other sentence of imprisonment or detention is also relevant if it would have been relevant under subsection (7) or (8) but for the reduction of the sentence, or any part of the sentence, to take account of a relevant pre-sentence period.

(10) For the purposes of subsections (4) to (9)—
    'extended sentence' means—
        (a) a sentence imposed under section 85 of the Sentencing Act or under section 226A, 226B, 227 or 228 of this Act (including one imposed as a result of section 219A, 220, 221A or 222 of the Armed Forces Act 2006), or
        (b) an equivalent sentence imposed under the law of Scotland, Northern Ireland or a member state (other than the United Kingdom);
    'life sentence' means—
        (a) a life sentence as defined in section 34 of the Crime (Sentences) Act 1997, or
        (b) an equivalent sentence imposed under the law of Scotland, Northern Ireland or a member state (other than the United Kingdom);
    'relevant pre-sentence period', in relation to the previous offence referred to in subsection (4), means any period which the offender spent in custody or on bail before the sentence for that offence was imposed;
    'sentence of imprisonment or detention' includes any sentence of a period in custody (however expressed).

(11) An offence the sentence for which is imposed under this section is not to be regarded as an offence the sentence for which is fixed by law.

E4.16 For offences listed in sch. 15B, see below. Section 224A came into force on 3 December 2012 and so this sentence is available for offenders whose offence was committed on or after that date. The relevant sentence is life imprisonment if the offender is aged 21 and over, and custody for life if he is aged 18, 19 or 20. Section 224A(10) incorporates the definition of 'life sentence' which is to be found in the Crime (Sentences) Act 1997, s. 34, which defines life sentence to include imprisonment for public protection. There are probably very few examples of offenders who would fall within the criteria in s. 224A but who would not attract a discretionary life sentence for the new offence in any event. However, to qualify for a discretionary life sentence the offender must pass the 'dangerousness' test. This is *not* a requirement for the life sentence under s. 224A. It is clear that the new 'life sentence for the second listed offence' is *not* a straight replacement for the sentence of imprisonment for public protection, but provides a new route to imposing a life sentence, albeit one which is unlikely to be used very often. Even if all the conditions in s. 224A apply, the court may still avoid passing the 'life sentence for second listed offence' if there are particular circumstances relating to either the current offence or the past offence, or to the offender, which 'would make it unjust to do so in all the circumstances'. This formula is the same as that which applies in the prescribed minimum sentences in relation to drug trafficking and domestic burglary (PCC(S)A 2000, ss. 110 and 111): see E5.1 and E5.4.

E4.17 The offences listed in part 1 of sch. 15B are: manslaughter; offences under the OAPA 1861, ss. 4 and 18, the FA 1968, ss. 16, 17(1) and 18, the Theft Act 1968, s. 8 (where at some time during the commission of the offence the offender had in his possession a firearm or imitation firearm), the Protection of Children Act 1978, s. 1, the TA 2000, ss. 56, 57 and 59, the A-tCSA 2001, ss. 47, 50 and 113, the SOA 2003, ss. 1, 2, 4 to 12, 14, 15, 25 and 26 (if D is over 18), 47 to 50 and, where the offence is punishable with life imprisonment, 30, 31, 34, 35 and 62, the DVCVA 2004, s. 5, the TA 2006, ss. 5, 9, 10 and 11. Also included are attempts to commit any of these offences, conspiracy to commit a listed offence or murder, incitement to commit a listed offence or murder, an offence under the SCA 2007 in relation to which a listed offence or murder is the offence which the person intended or believed would be committed, and aiding, abetting, counselling or procuring the commission of a listed offence.

The offences listed in part 2 of sch. 15B are murder, and any offence that was abolished before the coming into force of sch. 15B and which would, if committed on the relevant day, have constituted an offence specified in part 1.

It should be noted that the new offence must be listed in *part 1* of sch. 15B, while the previous offence can be listed anywhere in the schedule. This is to allow for the inclusion within the previous conviction of the offence of murder and repealed offences (such as under the Sexual Offences Act 1956) which have been replaced with broadly equivalent offences.

E4.18 Several of the offences in part 1 are not punishable with life imprisonment *per se*, but only become so as one of the two relevant offences under s. 224A. Many of the sexual offences carry maximum terms of ten or 14 years. The offence under the Protection of Children Act 1978, s. 1, is included and has a maximum of ten years. The offence of robbery (which does carry life imprisonment) is included, but only where, at some time during the commission of the offence, the offender had in his possession a firearm or imitation firearm within the meaning of the FA 1968. This particular formulation has caused difficulty under earlier provisions. In *Gore* [2010] 2 Cr App R (S) 590 the Court of Appeal held that the offence of robbery committed in the circumstances so described included involvement by the offender in a joint enterprise robbery in the course of which one of his co-defendants had been in possession of a firearm.

The Court of Appeal in *A-G's Ref (No. 27 of 2013) (Burinskas)* [2014] EWCA Crim 334 provided guidance in respect of this sentence. Lord Thomas CJ said (at [43]) that, where s. 224A might be relevant, it could be tempting for the judge to move straight to consideration of that provision before deciding whether the offender qualifies as a dangerous offender. That temptation should be resisted. The proper approach is:

(a) Consider the issue of dangerousness. If the offender is *not* dangerous, and s. 224A does not apply, a determinate sentence should be passed. If the offender is *not* dangerous, but the

E

Part E Sentencing

conditions in s. 224A are satisfied, then (subject to s. 224A(2)(a) and (b)) a life sentence for the second listed offence *must* be imposed.

(b) If the offender *is* dangerous, consider whether the seriousness of the offence(s) justifies a discretionary life sentence. If a life sentence is justified then it *must* be passed. If s. 224A also applies, the judge should record that fact, in open court. If a life sentence is not imposed then the judge should consider s. 224A. If it applies then (subject to the terms of that section) a life sentence *must* be imposed under that section.

ASSESSMENT OF DANGEROUSNESS

E4.19 Section 229 of the CJA 2003 deals with the necessary evidence base for the assessment of dangerousness required for the court to establish whether, under any of ss. 225, 226, 226A and 226B, the offender poses a 'significant risk to members of the public of serious harm occasioned by the commission by him of further specified offences'. Section 229 is not relevant where the court is considering the application of s. 224A (life sentence for the second listed offence).

Section 229 applies where (a) a person has been convicted of a specified offence; and (b) it falls to a court to assess whether there is a significant risk to members of the public of serious harm occasioned by the commission by him of further such offences. In making that assessment, the court:

    (a) must take into account all such information as is available to it about the nature and circumstances of the offence,

    (aa) may take into account all such information as is available to it about the nature and circumstances of any other offences of which the offender has been convicted by a court anywhere in the world,

    (b) may take into account any information which is before it about any pattern of behaviour of which any of the offences mentioned in paragraph (a) or (aa) forms part, and

    (c) may take into account any information about the offender which is before it.

E4.20 In the leading case of *Lang* [2006] 2 All ER 410, Rose LJ said that the requirement that a risk be 'significant' means more than a possibility — it must be 'noteworthy, of considerable amount or importance'. A wide variety of information will need to be considered before such an assessment is made by the court. The court will rely upon the pre-sentence report and the details of the offender's previous convictions, where relevant. A psychiatric report would be appropriate in some cases, but should be clearly directed to the issue of dangerousness. In *Pluck* [2007] 1 Cr App R (S) 43 the Court of Appeal commented that reports before the courts were not binding on the sentencer but, if the judge was minded to depart from the conclusion set out in a report, counsel should be warned in advance. It would only rarely be appropriate for a judge to permit cross-examination of the author of a pre-sentence report on the assessment of risk (*S* [2006] 2 Cr App R (S) 224). Wherever possible the prosecution should be in a position to describe to the court the facts of any previous specified offences on the record. If there is doubt over the accuracy of the facts or circumstances of previous convictions of the offender, it may be necessary, according to *Samuels* (1995) 16 Cr App R (S) 856, to adjourn to investigate the context of an earlier offence, but it may be possible to proceed on the information before the court or to infer the seriousness of past offences from the sentences which had been imposed for them. It is clear that in the assessment of dangerousness it is not just previous *specified* offences which are relevant. The court may have regard to offences on the record which are not specified offences, especially where they indicate an escalating pattern of seriousness. Indeed, it is not a prerequisite to a finding of dangerousness that the offender has any previous convictions. A first offender might qualify. Nor is it necessary that serious harm (or indeed any harm) has been caused by the offender in the course of past offences, since that may have been simply a matter of good fortune — a public protection sentence may properly be imposed where there is a significant risk of serious harm from such offences in the future (see further *Johnson* [2007] 1 All ER 1237). The Court of Appeal in *Pedley* [2009] 1 WLR 2517 said that there was no justification for trying to redefine the 'significant risk of serious harm' test in terms of numerical probability. Each case must be determined on its own facts, but that did not mean that the sentence was too uncertain to comply with the ECHR, Article 5(1).

In *Lang*, Rose LJ said that since the CJA 2003 defines 'serious harm' as 'death or serious personal **E4.21** injury, whether physical or psychological', and that was a phrase familiar to courts from earlier legislation, earlier guidance might be helpful. His lordship said that the fact that the further offence that is foreseen is a 'serious offence' does not automatically mean that commission of such an offence would result in 'serious harm', and if the offence foreseen is not a 'serious offence', it will be rare that there is a 'significant risk of serious harm'. In *Terrell* [2008] 2 All ER 1065, a case where the offender had pleaded guilty before the magistrates to making indecent photographs of a child and had been committed to Crown Court for sentence, the Court of Appeal said that, although there was a clear risk that the offender might reoffend in a similar way in future, there was no evidence that his offending would escalate to photographing children or to child abuse. It could not therefore be shown that the offender represented a 'significant risk…of serious harm', where 'serious harm' meant death or serious personal injury, the latter phrase being deliberately coloured by the associated word 'death'. The Court of Appeal in *Lang* confirmed that risk to 'members of the public' was a general term, and should not be construed so as to exclude any particular group, such as prison officers or staff in mental hospitals. It seems safe to assume that such a risk could properly be made out where the risk is specific to a small group of individuals, or just to one potential victim (applying the pre-Act authorities of *Hashi* (1995) 16 Cr App R (S) 121 and *S* (1994) 15 Cr App R (S) 765).

In applying s. 229 the court will be relying upon the facts of the offence (especially where these have emerged in some detail during the course of a contested trial), the contents of a pre-sentence report, and the contents of any other relevant report, such as a psychiatric report. The Court of Appeal confirmed in *Lavery* [2009] 3 All ER 295 that the sentencer was entitled to have regard to offences which the offender had asked to have taken into consideration. Other material may be taken into account, as in *Hillman* [2006] 2 Cr App R (S) 565, where the judge properly had regard to a synopsis of material prepared by the prosecution containing details of earlier alleged misconduct by the offender which had resulted in the making of an anti-social behaviour order against him. The Court of Appeal said that although the incidents referred to in the synopsis had not been tested in adversarial judicial proceedings, they could be regarded as 'hard information' and could be relied upon. In *Considine* [2008] All ER 621 the Court of Appeal confirmed that the word 'information' in s. 229 was not restricted in its meaning to 'evidence', and that relevant information bearing on the offender's dangerousness in a particular case might include material adverse to the offender but which had not been proved by criminal conviction. For consideration of the circumstances in which the Court of Appeal might consider new reports on an offender attempting to challenge an assessment of dangerousness made by a sentencing judge, see *Beesley* [2012] 1 Cr App R (S) 71.

Multiple Offences and Concurrent Terms   In *Pinnell* [2011] 2 Cr App R (S) 168 it was held **E4.22** that, where a person has been convicted of a specified offence and the court had concluded that there was a significant risk to members of the public of serious harm occasioned by the commission by him of further such offences, but that none of the associated offences for which the offender was been sentenced would justify a four-year custodial term, the seriousness of the aggregate offending must be considered. If a four-year custodial term results from aggregating the shortest terms commensurate with the seriousness of each offence, then that four-year term can be imposed in relation to the specified offence.

In *Brown* [2007] 1 Cr App R (S) 468, the Court of Appeal said that the passing of consecutive extended sentences, or the passing of an extended sentence followed by a consecutive determinate sentence, was undesirable and should be avoided, but in *Pinnell* the Court said that the position had changed by virtue of the 2008 amendments to the extended sentence provisions. Since (according to the early release provisions as they were at that time) release from the custodial term of the extended sentence had to occur at the half-way point of the custodial term and would therefore have been known at the time of passing sentence, consecutive extended sentences, or the passing of an extended sentence followed by a consecutive determinate sentence, was permissible provided that there was a particular reason for doing so.

E

Part E Sentencing

E4.23 The LASPO 2012, s. 125(3), amended the provisions on early release for the extended sentence under the CJA 2003, ss. 226A and 226B (see **E4.10**). It is submitted that the decision in *Pinnell* now needs to be reconsidered by the Court of Appeal. If, at the time of imposing the extended sentence it is clear that the offender will be released by law at the two-thirds point of the custodial term, the position adopted in *Pinnell* continues to apply. If, however, it is clear at the time of imposing the extended sentence that the date of the offender's early release will depend upon a decision to be made in the future by the Parole Board then the position adopted in *Pinnell* can no longer apply. The Court of Appeal in *Saunders* [2014] 1 Cr App R (S) 258 (45) noted the problem, but declined to give guidance, since the point did not arise in that case.

Giving of Reasons and Correcting Errors

E4.24 In *Lang* [2006] 2 All ER 410, the Court of Appeal said that the sentencer should be careful to give reasons for all conclusions, particularly for the finding of whether or not there is a significant risk. Reasons should include reference to the information which has been taken into account. If the sentencer is minded to come to a different conclusion from the report(s) presented, it would be wise to alert counsel so that representations can be made on the issue.

In *Reynolds* [2007] 2 Cr App R (S) 553 the Court of Appeal dealt with eight cases in which errors had been made by trial judges in applying the dangerousness provisions of the 2003 Act, mainly caused by the complexity of the legislation. The Court noted that if a mistake was identified quickly enough, the sentencing court could exercise its power under the 'slip rule' (i.e. under the PCC(S)A 2000, s. 155(1): see **D20.95**). This would include where a judge had failed to note that an offence was a 'specified' offence, or that a specified offence was a 'serious' specified offence. If the period of 56 days under that provision had elapsed, it was likely that the only other remedy for a mistake was correction by way of an appeal but, provided the original sentence was rescinded within 56 days, the sentencer could if necessary adjourn (e.g., for preparation of reports) to pass sentence on a day more than 56 days from the day when the rescinded sentence had been imposed.

PERIOD SPECIFIED UNDER THE POWERS OF CRIMINAL COURTS (SENTENCING) ACT 2000, s. 82A

E4.25   Powers of Criminal Courts (Sentencing) Act 2000, s. 82A

(1) This section applies if a court passes a life sentence in circumstances where the sentence is not fixed by law.

(2) The court shall, unless it makes an order under subsection (4) below, order that the provisions of section 28(5) to (8) of the Crime (Sentences) Act 1997 (referred to in this section as the 'early release provisions') shall apply to the offender as soon as he has served the part of his sentence which is specified in the order.

(3) The part of his sentence shall be such as the court considers appropriate taking into account—
   (a) the seriousness of the offence, or of the combination of the offence and one or more offences associated with it;
   (b) the effect of any direction which it would have given under section 240ZA of the Criminal Justice Act 2003 (crediting periods of remand in custody) or under section 246 of the Armed Forces Act 2006 (equivalent provision for service courts) or under section 240A of that Act of 2003 (crediting periods of remand on bail subject to certain types of condition) if it had sentenced him to a term of imprisonment; and
   (c) the early release provisions as compared with section 244(1) of the Criminal Justice Act 2003.
   In Case A or Case B below, this subsection has effect subject to, and in accordance with, subsection (3C) below.

(3A) Case A is where the offender was aged 18 or over when he committed the offence and the court is of the opinion that the seriousness of the offence, or the combination of the offence and one or more other offences associated with it,—
   (a) is exceptional (but not such that the court proposes to make an order under subsection (4) below), and
   (b) would not be adequately reflected by the period which the court would otherwise specify under subsection (2) above.

(3B) Case B is where the court is of the opinion that the period which it would otherwise specify under subsection (2) above would have little or no effect on time spent in custody, taking into account all the circumstances of the particular offender.

(3C) In Case A or Case B above, in deciding the effect which the comparison required by subsection (3)(c) above is to have on reducing the period which the court determines for the purposes of subsection (3)(a)(and before giving effect to subsection (3)(b) above), the court may, instead of reducing that period by one-half,—

(a) in Case A reduce it by such lesser amount (including nil) as the court may consider appropriate according to the seriousness of the offence, or

(b) in Case B above, reduce it by such lesser amount (but not by less than one-third) as the court may consider appropriate in the circumstances.

(4) If the offender was aged 21 or over when he committed the offence and the court is of the opinion that, because of the seriousness of the offence or of the combination of the offence and one or more offences associated with it, no order should be made under subsection (2) above, the court shall order that the early release provisions shall not apply to the offender.

Section 82A(3)(b) is reproduced as amended by the CJIA 2008, s. 19 (which inserted the last **E4.26** sentence in subsection (3) and the whole of subsections (3A) to (3C)). These provisions are *not* in force. For discussion of these subsections, see E4.31. The LASPO 2012, s. 110 and sch. 21, also amended s. 82A.

The imposition of a life sentence is designed to protect the public from the offender, whereas the period specified under s. 82A is meant to reflect the degree of punishment, retribution and deterrence appropriate for the offence, aside from the question of public protection (*Wheaton* [2005] 1 Cr App R (S) 425). The specified period should not be lengthened with a view to protecting the public (*Adams* [2000] 2 Cr App R (S) 274). The effect of specifying part of the sentence under s. 82A is that the life sentence prisoner will not become eligible to be considered for early release until the expiry of that period. If the court is of the view that because of the seriousness of the offence or offences no order should be made under s. 82A(2), it should make an order under s. 82A(4) to the effect that the early release provisions shall not apply to the offender. In *Oakes* [2013] 2 All ER 30 the Court of Appeal said that such an order (referred to in the judgment as a 'whole life order') is reserved for the most exceptional discretionary life sentence cases. While stopping just short of saying that a whole life order was limited to cases of murder, the Court said that whole life orders outside the context of murder would be 'very rare indeed'.

Some of the cases referred to below relate to earlier versions of these provisions but, it is submitted, still represent the law.

Procedure

CPD VII, para. L.1 (see Supplement, **PD-75**) indicates that the sentencer should specify the **E4.27** relevant period, save in the very exceptional case where he considers that the offence is so serious that imprisonment for life is justified by that alone, irrespective of the risk to the public. In that case, he should state this in open court when passing sentence. A decision not to specify might be the subject of an appeal (*Hollies* (1995) 16 Cr App R (S) 463). When specifying the relevant period, the judge should have regard to the specific terms of the section, and should indicate the reasons for the decision. Before specifying the relevant period, the sentencer should permit counsel for the defence to address the court on the appropriate length of the relevant part. An order under s. 82A may be the subject of an appeal (*McBean* [2002] 1 Cr App R (S) 430) or might constitute an unduly lenient sentence (*A-G's Ref (No. 82 of 2000)* [2001] 2 Cr App R (S) 289).

Section 82A(3)(a)

In *A-G's Ref (No. 3 of 2004)* [2005] 1 Cr App R (S) 230, the Court of Appeal emphasised that, **E4.28** when having regard to the seriousness of the offence (or the combination of the offence and other offences associated with it), the section permitted the sentencer to look at the totality of the associated offences, rather than just the offence for which the indeterminate sentence was being passed, and to consider whether the sentences for the associated offences would have been consecutive to the main sentence if an indeterminate sentence had not been given. In a case where the offender falls to be sentenced on the same occasion for more than one serious specified offence, or for one or more serious specified offence and one or more specified offence, such sentences should take effect concurrently rather than consecutively but the seriousness of the totality of the offences should be reflected in the length of the period selected by the judge under s. 82A (*Edwards* [2007] 1 Cr App R (S) 646 and *Meade* [2007] 1 Cr App R (S) 762).

Section 82A(3)(b)

E4.29   This subsection refers to the CJA 2003, ss. 240ZA and 240A (effect of time spent in custody on remand or under qualifying curfew: see **E2.12**). Section 82A(3)(b) is oddly worded, given that a court (following the implementation of s. 240ZA) can no longer 'give a direction' under that section, but it is submitted that s. 82A(3)(b) must be taken to mean that the court when setting the period under s. 82A should make an appropriate adjustment for both of the matters referred to in s. 82A(3)(b), even though s. 240ZA operates automatically to deduct time spent in custody on remand from a determinate custodial sentence. According to the Court of Appeal in *Marklew* [1999] 2 All ER 939, the sentencer should normally give full credit under s. 82(3)(b) for the period spent by the defendant on remand. *Marklew* also indicates, however, that there may be some circumstances in which the giving of full credit to the offender would not be appropriate. In *McKenzie* [2011] EWCA Crim 2278 the Court of Appeal allowed an appeal where the offender had spent 216 days on remand but the judge refused an application for those days to count towards the minimum term of four years in a sentence of imprisonment for public protection. Since remand time is deducted from the minimum term, and not from the notional determinate sentence, the number of days served on remand should *not* be doubled (*Taylor* [2008] 2 Cr App R (S) 480). It is submitted that these decisions still represent the law, notwithstanding s. 240ZA.

Section 82A(3)(c)

E4.30   A sentencer exercising power under s. 82A is required to take into account the fact that under the CJA 2003, s. 244, a prisoner who has received a determinate sentence is entitled to be released after serving one half of his sentence. In *Marklew* the Court of Appeal issued guidance on the setting of the period to be specified under s. 82A; Thomas J stated that henceforth sentencers should make clear what the determinate sentence would have been and should then normally fix the specified period at *one-half* of the notional term. In fixing the notional determinate sentence, allowance should be made for a guilty plea (*Meek* (1995) 16 Cr App R (S) 1003). The principle of setting the specified period at *one-half* of the notional determinate sentence has been followed and applied in many subsequent cases. The rationale, according to Pill LJ in *West* [2001] 1 Cr App R (S) 103, is that an indeterminate sentence prisoner should be in no worse a position on an application for early release than a determinate sentence prisoner.

Section 82A(3A) to (3C)

E4.31   These subsections will, when brought into force, permit the sentencer to reduce the notional determinate sentence by some lesser period than one half when fixing the specified period. This is permissible in two cases, referred to as case A and case B. Case A is where the offender was aged 18 or over when he committed the offence and the court is of the opinion that the seriousness of the offence, or of the combination of the offence and one or more other offences associated with it, is 'exceptional' (but not as to justify an order under s. 82A(4)), and would not be adequately reflected by the period which the court would otherwise specify under s. 82A(2). In case A the court may reduce the notional determinate sentence by such lesser amount (including nil) as the court may consider appropriate according to the seriousness of the case. Case B is where the court is of the opinion that the period which it would otherwise specify under s. 82A(2) would have little or no effect on time spent in custody, taking into account all the circumstances of the particular offender. In case B the court may reduce the notional determinate sentence by such lesser amount (but not by less than one-third) as the court may consider appropriate in the circumstances.

Section E5 Prescribed Custodial Sentences

MINIMUM CUSTODIAL SENTENCES FOR CLASS A DRUG OFFENCES

Section 110 of the PCC(S)A 2000 provides that where: **E5.1**

(a) a person is convicted of a Class A drug trafficking offence committed after 30 September 1997,
(b) at the time when that offence was committed he was aged 18 or over and had been convicted in any part of the UK of two other Class A drug trafficking offences (or equivalent offence in another EU Member State committed after 15 August 2010), and
(c) one of those offences was committed after he had been convicted of the other,

the Crown Court shall impose a custodial sentence for a term of at least seven years, unless the court is of the opinion that there are particular circumstances which relate to any of the offences or to the offender which would make it unjust to do so in all the circumstances (s. 110(2) and (2A)).

For the purposes of s. 110, 'Class A drug trafficking offence' means a drug trafficking offence **E5.2** committed in respect of a Class A drug (see **B19.7**); s. 110(5) defines 'drug trafficking offence' by reference to the POCA 2002, sch. 2 (see **E19.17**) (s. 110(5)); and 'custodial sentence' means imprisonment or detention in a young offender institution (s. 110(6)). Nothing in s. 110 prevents a hospital order being imposed on an offender in an appropriate case (Mental Health Act 1983, s. 37(1A)). In *Harvey* [2000] 1 Cr App R (S) 368, the Court of Appeal upheld a sentence of seven years' imprisonment on an offender imposed under this power. Lord Bingham CJ said that the object of the provision plainly was to require courts to impose a sentence of at least seven years in cases where otherwise they would not, or might not, have done so. His lordship declined to indicate what might amount to circumstances 'which would make it unjust' to impose the prescribed sentence, but for subsequent examples see *Pearce* [2005] 1 Cr App R (S) 364, *Turner* [2006] 1 Cr App R (S) 565, *McDonough* [2006] 1 Cr App R (S) 647, *Reid* [2008] 2 Cr App R (S) 383 and *Lucas* [2012] 2 Cr App R (S) 57.

In a case where either of the earlier Class A drug trafficking offences was dealt with by way of an absolute or conditional discharge (admittedly rather unlikely) or, before 1 October 1992, by way of a probation order, and the offender was not subsequently sentenced for the offence, the conviction for that offence is a conviction for limited purposes only (see the PCC(S)A 2000, s. 14, and **E12.6**) and would not count as a qualifying conviction for the purposes of s. 110.

For consecutive sentences where one sentence is a prescribed custodial sentence, see *Raza* [2010] 1 Cr App R (S) 354 at **E5.10**.

Guilty Plea

Where the offender has pleaded guilty, the sentencing court is required to take into account the **E5.3** stage at which he indicated his intention to plead guilty and the circumstances in which this indication was given (CJA 2003, s. 144). Section 144(2) states that in the case of an offence coming within s. 110 the court may not impose a sentence which would be less than 80 per cent of the minimum sentence specified (and see *Gray* [2007] 2 Cr App R (S) 494). Eighty per cent of seven years produces a sentence slightly less than five years and eight months. It is desirable for the judge to explain how the final sentence has been arrived at (*Brown* [2000] 2 Cr App R (S) 435). If the sentencer has taken a starting point above the minimum sentence, a sentence reduction to reflect the guilty plea of, say, 30 per cent, may be perfectly appropriate on the facts provided that the final sentence is not less than 80 per cent of the minimum sentence (*Gray*). In *Darling* [2010] 1 Cr App R (S) 420 the Court of Appeal held that, where the sentencing judge is of the opinion that there are particular circumstances which would make it unjust to impose the minimum sentence, the limited reduction permissible for a guilty plea no longer applies and the judge may in an appropriate case reduce sentence to reflect a guilty plea to a sentence which is less than 80 per cent of the minimum sentence specified.

MINIMUM CUSTODIAL SENTENCES FOR DOMESTIC BURGLARY

E5.4 Section 111 of the PCC(S)A 2000 provides that where:

(a) a person is convicted of a domestic burglary committed after 30 November 1999;

(b) at the time when the domestic burglary was committed he was aged 18 or over and had been convicted in England and Wales of two other domestic burglaries; and

(c) one of those other burglaries was committed after he had been convicted of the other, and both of them were committed after 30 November 1999,

the Crown Court shall impose a custodial term of at least three years except where the court is of the opinion that there are particular circumstances which relate to any of the offences or the offender which would make it unjust to do so in all the circumstances.

The CAJA 2009, sch. 17, para. 10(3), amended s. 111 so as to provide for the treatment of previous convictions elsewhere in the UK or in another EU Member State. The amendment took effect from 15 August 2010. A previous domestic burglary which took place outside England and Wales is a relevant offence for the purposes of s. 111 only if it was committed after that date.

E5.5 For the purposes of s. 111, 'domestic burglary' means a burglary committed in respect of a building or part of a building which is a dwelling (s. 111(5)), and it must always be established that each of the relevant burglaries was in fact a domestic burglary (*Miller* [2011] 1 Cr App R (S) 7). For these purposes s. 111 and the Theft Act. s. 9, should be read together and as a whole (*Coleman* [2013] 2 Cr App R (S) 514 (79)). People who live in narrow boats or caravans should attract the same protection conferred by s. 111 as people who live in more conventional housing. In *Flack* [2013] 2 Cr App R (S) 366 (56) the Court of Appeal said that if, on the current charge of burglary, it was in dispute whether the property was a dwelling or not, the matter should be resolved by a jury asked to consider alternative counts on the indictment, and not by a *Newton* hearing after conviction.

An attempt to commit a domestic burglary is not a qualifying offence (*Maguire* [2003] 2 Cr App R (S) 40, in which the Court of Appeal agreed with the view expressed in a previous edition of this work). 'Custodial sentence' means imprisonment or detention in a young offender institution (s. 110(6)). Nothing in s. 111 prevents a hospital order being imposed on an offender in an appropriate case (Mental Health Act 1983, s. 37(1A)).

E5.6 In *Andrews* [2013] 2 Cr App R (S) 26 (5), and again in *Silvera* [2013] EWCA Crim 1764, the Court of Appeal has stressed that, when a judge is sentencing a 'three-strikes' burglary case, the three-year prescribed sentence in s. 111 should not be adopted as the sentencing starting point. The proper approach was to apply the Sentencing Council definitive guideline in the usual way, but then to cross-check that the resulting sentence did not infringe the rule in s. 111 (or, if it did, to consider whether there were particular circumstances relating to any of the offences or to the offender which would make imposition of the minimum sentence unjust).

In *McInerney* [2003] 1 All ER 1089, Lord Woolf CJ said at [16]:

> It may be helpful to give examples of the type of situation where a three year sentence may be unjust. The sentence could be unjust if two of the offences were committed many years earlier than the third offence, or if the offender has made real efforts to reform or conquer his drug addiction, but some personal tragedy triggers the third offence, or if the first two offences were committed when the offender was not yet 16. As we read s. 111 it gives the sentencer a fairly substantial degree of discretion as to the categories of situations where the presumption can be rebutted.

The prescribed sentence was found to be unjust in *Stone* [2012] 2 Cr App R (S) 50, where the offender reached through an open window and stole a box containing items worth £60. He had two previous convictions for domestic burglary, committed 11 years and six years earlier, and there was personal mitigation. His sentence was reduced to eight months' imprisonment, to permit his immediate release.

In *Gibson* [2004] 2 Cr App R (S) 451, the Court of Appeal held that, where the judge had adjourned for an assessment of the offender's suitability for a community penalty in circumstances where that gave rise to an expectation on the offender's part that, if the report was positive, he would receive such a sentence, it was unjust then to impose the prescribed sentence under s. 111. In *Sparkes* [2011] 2 Cr App R (S) 614 where the offender was subject to the prescribed sentence, properly imposed consecutively to a sentence of five years for other offences, it was held to be unjust to pass the prescribed sentence because the overall sentence would infringe totality. The case of *Raza* [2010] 1 Cr App R (S) 354 (see **E5.10**), however, suggests that the other sentences should be adjusted rather than the prescribed sentence.

Sequence of Offences

The key considerations in the PCC(S)A 2000, s. 111, are the dates on which the qualifying **E5.7** offences were committed and the dates on which the offender was convicted. The sequence must be (a) commission, then conviction, (b) commission, then conviction, (c) commission, then conviction; s. 111 would not bite in a case where the offender commits a third domestic burglary before being convicted of the second (*Hoare* [2004] 2 Cr App R (S) 261). 'Convicted' must be distinguished from 'sentenced'. So, commission of a third domestic burglary at a time when the offender is on bail awaiting sentence for a second domestic burglary does trigger the operation of the section (*Webster* [2004] 2 Cr App R (S) 126). Section 111 can operate in an uneven way, so that one offender will infringe the provision after having been convicted of just three domestic burglaries, while another might have been convicted of (or had taken into consideration) many more such offences without yet having infringed it.

A finding of guilt in a youth court is equivalent to a conviction and counts for these purposes (*Frost* [2001] 2 Cr App R (S) 124). It is unclear whether an earlier spent conviction for domestic burglary counts as a qualifying conviction. It is submitted that such a conviction does count, but that the fact that the conviction was spent may be a particular circumstance relating to that offence making the imposition of the prescribed sentence unjust in all the circumstances.

Guilty Plea

Where the offender has pleaded guilty, the sentencing court is required to take into account **E5.8** the stage at which he indicated his intention to plead guilty and the circumstances in which this indication was given (CJA 2003, s. 144: see **E1.8**). Section 144(2) states that in the case of an offence coming within s. 111, the court may not impose a sentence which would be less than 80 per cent of the minimum sentence specified (and see *Gray* [2007] 2 Cr App R (S) 494, *Darling* [2010] 1 Cr App R (S) 420, and the discussion at E5.3). Eighty per cent of three years produces a sentence of just less than two years and five months. It would seem, by analogy with

E

Part E Sentencing

Brown [2002] 2 Cr App R (S) 435, that where discount has been given for plea the sentencer should explain how the final sentence has been arrived at. In *Nelson* [2013] EWCA Crim 2410 the offender fell within the provisions of s. 111, but had availed himself of the early guilty plea scheme at the Crown Court. The Court of Appeal said that, in all the circumstances of the case, the proper starting point was four years and three months, from which a full one-third discount for plea could be given without infringing the rule in s. 144(2). Had a lower starting point (close to three years) been appropriate, then there would have been a clash between s. 144(2) and the offender's expectation of a full discount under the early guilty plea scheme. In such circumstances, it is submitted that the statutory provision must take precedence.

MINIMUM CUSTODIAL SENTENCES FOR FIREARMS OFFENCES

E5.9   Section 51A of the FA 1968 provides for minimum custodial sentences for certain firearms offences committed on or after 22 January 2004. For details of the offences listed in s. 51A, see **B12.56**, **B12.85** *et seq.* and **B13.83**.

Firearms Act 1968, s. 51A

(1) This section applies where—
- (a) an individual is convicted of
   - (i)   an offence under s. 5(1)(a), (ab), (aba), (ac), (ad), (ae), (af) or (c) of this Act, or
   - (ii) an offence under s. 5(1A)(a) of this Act, or
   - (iii) an offence under any of the provisions of this Act listed in subsection (1A) in respect of a firearm or ammunition specified in section 5(1)(a), (ab), (aba), (ac), (ad), (ae), (af), or (c) or section 5(1A)(a) of this Act, and
- (b) the offence was committed after the commencement of this section and at a time when he was aged 16 or over.

(1A)   The provisions are—
- (a) section 16 (possession of firearm with intent to injure);
- (b) section 16A (possession of firearm with intent to cause fear of violence);
- (c) section 17 (use of firearm to resist arrest);
- (d) section 18 (carrying firearm with criminal intent);
- (e) section 19 (carrying a firearm in a public place);
- (f) section 20(1) (trespassing in a building with firearm).

(2) The court shall impose an appropriate custodial sentence (or order for detention) for a term of at least the required minimum term (with or without a fine) unless the court is of the opinion that there are exceptional circumstances relating to the offence or to the offender which justify its not doing so.

(3) Where an offence is found to have been committed over a period of two or more days, or at some time during a period of two or more days, it shall be taken for the purposes of this section to have been committed on the last of those days.

Subsections (1)(a)(iii) and (1A) apply only in relation to offences committed on or after 6 April 2007 (VCRA 2006, s. 30).

In *A-G's Ref (No. 114 of 2004)* [2005] 2 Cr App R (S) 24, the Court of Appeal made it clear that s. 51A applies only where one of the specific offences listed there is proved or admitted. Although the offender in the case considered by the court might properly have been charged with an offence under the FA 1968, s. 5, no such count had been included on the indictment and so the minimum sentence could not apply. In *A-G's Ref (Nos. 48 and 49 of 2010)* [2011] 1 Cr App R (S) 706 it was held that, although s. 51A did not extend to a conspiracy or an attempt to commit any of the offences there set out, the specified minimum sentence was a highly relevant though not determining factor in sentencing for an inchoate offence.

E5.10   The minimum sentences specified in s. 51A are five years' imprisonment (or detention in a young offender institution for those aged 18 to 20) in the case of an offender aged 18 or over when convicted, and three years' detention under the PCC(S)A 2000, s. 91 (long-term detention), for any offender aged at least 16 but under 18 at the time he committed the offence (s. 51A(4)). The specified minimum sentence on an offender aged under 18 is the sentence of long-term detention under the PCC(S)A 2000, s. 91. Nothing in s. 51A prevents a hospital order being imposed on an offender in an appropriate case (Mental Health Act 1983, s. 37(1A)). See *McEneaney* [2005] 2 Cr App R (S) 531.

In *Raza* [2010] 1 Cr App R (S) 354 the Court of Appeal said that, where an offender was being sentenced for a number of offences, one of which is subject to a prescribed minimum custodial sentence, the principle of totality applies and the sentencer must pass an overall term which is proportionate to the overall offending, but that principle must not be applied in such a way that it undermines the intention of Parliament.

The Exceptional Circumstances Proviso

The 'exceptional circumstances' proviso in the FA 1968, s. 51A(2), is differently worded from the   **E5.11**
'particular circumstances' proviso in the PCC(S)A 2000, ss. 110 (see **E5.1**) and 111 (see **E5.4**).
It is important to note, however, that the minimum sentence for the firearms offences listed in
the FA 1968, s. 51A, applies to *all* such offences, whereas ss. 110 and 111 apply only to repeat
offenders.

The Court of Appeal has given some indication of the factors which might amount to 'exceptional circumstances' in respect of this provision, building on the early declaration in *Jordan* [2005] 2 Cr App R (S) 266 that such cases would be 'rare'. General guidance was given in *Rehman* [2006] 1 Cr App R (S) 404. The Court of Appeal said that, in determining whether the case involved 'exceptional circumstances', it was necessary to look at the case as a whole. Sometimes there would be a single isolated factor that would amount to an exceptional circumstance, but in other cases it would be the collective impact of all the relevant circumstances. The court said that, so far as it could identify a rationale for this sentencing provision, it was to do with deterrence, rather than public protection. Lord Woolf CJ said that s. 51A was capable of causing considerable injustice, especially bearing in mind that possession of a prohibited firearm was an absolute offence. Reading s. 51A in the light of the HRA 1998, s. 3, his lordship said that the circumstances would be 'exceptional' if it would mean that to impose the minimum sentence would result in an arbitrary and disproportionate sentence. Unless a judge was clearly wrong in *not* identifying exceptional circumstances when they were present, the Court of Appeal would not readily interfere with the trial judge's decision.

In *Rehman* itself, the Court of Appeal held that the judge had erred in not finding exceptional   **E5.12**
circumstances in the case, where the offender's background (in particular his previous good character), his early plea of guilty, his ignorance of the unlawfulness of the weapon (he had purchased it as a collector's model), and the fact that there was just one weapon, taken together amounted to exceptional circumstances. The sentence was reduced from five years to one year, allowing the offender's immediate release. Exceptional circumstances were found in *Stoker* [2014] 1 Cr App R (S) 286 (47), where the offender, a man of good character, admitted possession of a stun gun disguised as a mobile phone. The weapon could not be fired, and the offender was unaware that its possession was illegal. The sentence of five years' imprisonment was reduced to two years. In *Boateng* [2011] 2 Cr App R (S) 697 the Court of Appeal found exceptional circumstances in the fact that the 20-year-old offender, of previous good character, had not known that the bag left at her flat a few days earlier by a friend contained a prohibited firearm and ammunition, although she did admit at a *Newton* hearing that she realised the bag contained something 'dodgy'. The five-year sentence was reduced to two years. In *Ocran* [2011] 1 Cr App R (S) 223, however, the 24-year-old offender was a single mother of previous good character, who admitted that she had known of the presence of two weapons hidden under a wardrobe in her flat, apparently placed there by others who had access to the flat. Despite strong personal mitigation the five-year sentence was upheld. In *A-G's Ref (No. 37 of 2013) (Culpeper)* [2014] 1 Cr App R (S) 411 (62), the Court of Appeal increased a sentence of two years' imprisonment to five years. The offender was

in possession of a Browning self-loaded pistol containing ammunition. It was accepted that he had stored the gun for a few days because he owed money to his drug suppliers, who had forced him to store the gun, as well as drugs, at his home. The Court of Appeal said the factors in this case fell 'well short' of exceptional. Being subjected to pressure of that kind was not unusual. In *Evans* [2006] 1 Cr App R (S) 346, the offender's obsessive compulsive symptoms, which had apparently led him to hoard guns, did not amount to exceptional circumstances. It was relevant in this case that the offender was a civilian reception officer at a police station, who had abused his position to steal ammunition which had been handed in. Exceptional circumstances were found in *Shaw* [2011] 2 Cr App R (S) 376, where the 76-year-old offender, a man in poor health, pleaded guilty to two counts of possessing a prohibited weapon (a sawn-off shotgun). The Court of Appeal said that there were no exceptional circumstances relating to the offence but his poor health tipped the balance, sentence being reduced from five years to three years.

Guilty Plea

E5.13 In contrast to the PCC(S)A 2000, ss. 110(2) and 111(2), there is no provision in the FA 1968, s. 51A, limiting the extent to which the offender's guilty plea can affect the sentence imposed. The Court of Appeal in *Jordan* [2005] 2 Cr App R (S) 266 held that, in respect of s. 51A, Parliament must have intended to exclude the normal principles of reduction of sentence to reflect a guilty plea. No discount was available for plea. The rigour of s. 51A was mitigated by the possibility of exceptional circumstances being found. Such cases would be rare, but if the judge had properly identified exceptional circumstances the sentence would then be at large.

MINIMUM CUSTODIAL SENTENCES FOR USING SOMEONE TO MIND A WEAPON

E5.14 The VCRA 2006, s. 28, creates an offence where the offender uses another person to look after, hide or transport a dangerous weapon for him under arrangements or in circumstances that facilitate, or are intended to facilitate, the weapon's being available to the offender for an unlawful purpose. It is set out at **B12.198**. Where at the time of the offence the offender was aged 18 or over and the dangerous weapon in respect of which the offence was committed was a firearm mentioned in s. 5(1)(a)–(af) or (c) or s. 5(1A)(a) of the FA 1968 (firearms possession of which attracts a minimum sentence), the court must impose a term of imprisonment (or detention in a young offender institution) of not less than five years, unless it is of the opinion that there are exceptional circumstances relating to the offence or to the offender which justify its not doing so. If the offender is aged under 18 at the time of conviction, the court must impose a sentence of detention under the PCC(S)A 2000, s. 91, of not less than three years, unless it is of the opinion that there are exceptional circumstances relating to the offence or to the offender which justify its not doing so.

Statutory Aggravating Factor

E5.15 Where a court is considering the seriousness of an offence under the VCRA 2006, s. 28, the fact that the offender was aged 18 or over and used a person to look after etc. the weapon who was under 18, the court must treat that fact as increasing the seriousness of the offence (s. 29(11)). The judge should state in open court that the offence was so aggravated (s. 29(12)).

Guilty Plea

E5.16 In contrast to the PCC(S)A 2000, ss. 110(2) and 111(2), there is no reference in the CJA 2003, s. 144 (reduction of sentence on plea of guilty), to the VCRA 2006, s. 28, as limiting the extent to which the offender's guilty plea can affect the sentence imposed. The Court of Appeal in *Jordan* [2005] 2 Cr App R (S) 266 held that, in respect of s. 51A, Parliament must have intended to exclude the normal principles of reduction of sentence to reflect a guilty plea. No discount was available for plea. It is submitted that the same applies to the VCRA 2006, s. 28. The rigour of s. 51A was said in *Jordan* to be mitigated by the possibility of exceptional circumstances being found. Such cases would be rare, but if the judge had properly identified exceptional circumstances the sentence would then be at large.

MINIMUM CUSTODIAL SENTENCE FOR THREATENING WITH OFFENSIVE WEAPON IN PUBLIC

Section 1A(1) of the Prevention of Crime Act 1953 provides that a person is guilty of an offence   **E5.17** if that person (a) has an offensive weapon with him in a public place, (b) unlawfully and intentionally threatens another person with the weapon, and (c) does so in such a way that there is an immediate risk of serious physical harm to that other person. For consideration of this offence, see **B12.165**.

Prevention of Crime Act 1953, s. 1A

(4) A person guilty of an offence under this section is liable—
  (a) on summary conviction, to imprisonment for a term not exceeding 12 months or to a fine not exceeding the statutory maximum, or to both;
  (b) on conviction on indictment, to imprisonment for a term not exceeding 4 years or to a fine, or to both.
(5) Where a person is aged 16 or over is convicted of an offence under this section, the court must impose an appropriate custodial sentence (with or without a fine) unless the court is of the opinion that there are particular circumstances which—
  (a) relate to the offence or to the offender, and
  (b) would make it unjust to do so in all the circumstances.
(6) In this section 'appropriate custodial sentence' means—
  (a) in the case of a person who is aged 18 and over when convicted, a sentence of imprisonment for a term of at least 6 months;
  (b) in the case of a person who is aged at least 16 but under 18 when convicted, a detention and training order of at least 4 months.
(7) In considering whether it is of the opinion mentioned in subsection (5) in the case of a person aged under 18, the court must have regard to its duty under section 44 of the Children and Young Persons Act 1933.

This provision was inserted by the LASPO 2012, s. 142. Where sentence is imposed under s. 1A(6)(a) and the offender has pleaded guilty, the sentencing court is required to take into account the stage at which he indicated his intention to plead guilty and the circumstances in which this indication was given (CJA 2003, s. 144: see **E1.8**). Section 144(3) states that, in the case of an offence coming within s. 1A(6)(a), the court may not impose a sentence which would be less than 80 per cent of the minimum sentence specified (and see *Gray* [2007] 2 Cr App R (S) 494, *Darling* [2010] 1 Cr App R (S) 420 and the discussion at **E5.3**). It would seem, by analogy with *Brown* [2002] 2 Cr App R (S) 435, that where discount has been given for plea the sentencer should explain how the final sentence has been arrived at. Where sentence is imposed under s. 1A(6)(b), however, it is clear from s. 144(4) that the normal principles applicable to reduction for a guilty plea apply. For the CYPA 1933, s. 44, see **E1.1**. It should be noted that, under s. 1A(6)(b), a detention and training order of four months is the shortest term which may lawfully be imposed. The 'particular circumstances' proviso at s. 1A(5)(a) and (b) is very similarly worded to the equivalent provisions in the PCC(S)A 2000, ss. 110 and 111 (see **E5.1** and **E5.4**).

MINIMUM CUSTODIAL SENTENCE FOR THREATENING WITH ARTICLE WITH BLADE OR POINT OR OFFENSIVE WEAPON

Section 139AA(1) of the CJA 1988 provides that a person is guilty of an offence if that person   **E5.18** (a) has an offensive weapon with him in a public place or on school premises, (b) unlawfully and intentionally threatens another person with the weapon, and (c) does so in such a way that there is an immediate risk of serious physical harm to that other person. For consideration of this offence, see **B12.180**.

Criminal Justice Act 1988, s. 139AA

(6) A person guilty of an offence under this section is liable—

   (a) on summary conviction, to imprisonment for a term not exceeding 12 months or to a fine not exceeding the statutory maximum, or to both;

   (b) on conviction on indictment, to imprisonment for a term not exceeding 4 years or to a fine, or to both.

(7) Where a person is aged 16 or over is convicted of an offence under this section, the court must impose an appropriate custodial sentence (with or without a fine) unless the court is of the opinion that there are particular circumstances which—

   (a) relate to the offence or to the offender, and

   (b) would make it unjust to do so in all the circumstances.

(8) In this section 'appropriate custodial sentence' means—

   (a) in the case of a person who is aged 18 and over when convicted, a sentence of imprisonment for a term of at least 6 months;

   (b) in the case of a person who is aged at least 16 but under 18 when convicted, a detention and training order of at least 4 months.

(9) In considering whether it is of the opinion mentioned in subsection (7) in the case of a person aged under 18, the court must have regard to its duty under section 44 of the Children and Young Persons Act 1933.

This provision was inserted by the LASPO 2012, s. 142. Where sentence is imposed under s. 139AA(8)(a) and the offender has pleaded guilty, the sentencing court is required to take into account the stage at which he indicated his intention to plead guilty and the circumstances in which this indication was given (CJA 2003, s. 144: see **E1.8**). Section 144(3) states that, in the case of an offence coming within s. 139AA(8)(a), the court may not impose a sentence which would be less than 80 per cent of the minimum sentence specified (and see *Gray* [2007] 2 Cr App R (S) 494, *Darling* [2010] 1 Cr App R (S) 420 and the discussion at **E5.3**). It would seem, by analogy with *Brown* [2002] 2 Cr App R (S) 435, that where discount has been given for plea the sentencer should explain how the final sentence has been arrived at. Where sentence is imposed under s. 139AA(8)(b), however, it is clear from s. 144(4) that the normal principles applicable to reduction for a guilty plea apply. For the CYPA 1933, s. 44, see **E1.1**. It should be noted that, under s. 139AA(8)(b), a detention and training order of four months is the shortest term which may lawfully be imposed. The 'particular circumstances' proviso at s. 139AA(7)(a) and (b) is very similarly worded to the equivalent provisions in the PCC(S)A 2000, ss. 110 and 111 (see **E5.1** and **E5.4**).

Section E6   Suspended Sentences

POWER TO IMPOSE SUSPENDED SENTENCES

The power to impose a suspended sentence under the CJA 2003 applies to sentences of impris- **E6.1**
onment and to sentences of detention in a young offender institution. The suspended sentence
is available to the Crown Court where that court imposes a determinate custodial sentence of
imprisonment or detention in a young offender institution of not more than two years or where
a magistrates' court imposes a determinate custodial sentence of not more than six months.
Sentences of less than 14 days cannot be suspended. Detention and training orders cannot be
suspended.

Criminal Justice Act 2003, s. 189 **E6.2**

(1) If a court passes a sentence of imprisonment for a term of at least 14 days but not more than
    2 years, it may make an order providing that the sentence of imprisonment is not to take effect
    unless—
    (a) during a period specified in the order for the purposes of this paragraph ('the operational
        period') the offender commits another offence in the United Kingdom (whether or not
        punishable with imprisonment), and
    (b) a court having power to do so subsequently orders under paragraph 8 of schedule 12 that
        the original sentence is to take effect.
(1A) An order under subsection (1) may also provide that the offender must comply during a
    period specified in the order for the purposes of this subsection ('the supervision period') with
    one or more requirements falling within section 190(1) and specified in the order.
(1B) Where an order under subsection (1) contains provisions under subsection (1A) it must
    provide that the sentence of imprisonment will also take effect if—
    (a) during the supervision period the offender fails to comply with a requirement imposed
        under subsection (1A), and
    (b) a court having power to do so subsequently orders under paragraph 8 of Schedule 12 that
        the original sentence is to take effect.
(2) Where two or more sentences imposed on the same occasion are to be served consecutively,
    the power conferred by subsection (1) is not exercisable in relation to any of them unless the
    aggregate of the terms of the sentences does not exceed 2 years.
(3) The supervision period (if any) and the operational period must each be a period of not less
    than six months and not more than two years beginning with the date of the order.
(4) Where an order under subsection (1) imposes one or more community requirements, the
    supervision period must not end later than the operational period.
(5) A court which passes a suspended sentence on any person for an offence may not impose a
    community sentence in his case in respect of that offence or any other offence of which he is
    convicted by or before the court or for which he is dealt with by the court.
(6) Subject to any provision to the contrary contained in the Criminal Justice Act 1967, the
    Sentencing Act, or any enactment or instrument made under any enactment after 31st
    December 1967, a suspended sentence which had not taken effect under paragraph 8 of
    Schedule 12 is to be treated as a sentence of imprisonment for the purposes of all enactments
    and instruments made under enactments.
(7) In this Part—
    (a) 'suspended sentence order' means an order under subsection (1),
    (b) 'suspended sentence' means a sentence to which a suspended sentence order relates, and
    (c) 'community requirements' in relation to a suspended sentence order means a requirement
        imposed under subsection (1A).

E6.3   Section 189 is set out as substituted by the LASPO 2012, s. 68, with effect from 3 December 2012. The two main changes are (i) to extend the length of the term of imprisonment or detention in a young offender institution which may be suspended, from one year to two years, and (ii) to remove the need for a suspended sentence to include at least one community requirement.

A suspended sentence cannot be ordered unless all the statutory provisions as to the imposition of a sentence of immediate imprisonment have been observed. Before a suspended sentence can be passed, the court must take account of the relevant provisions of the CJA 2003, ss. 152 and 153, which must be complied with before any custodial sentence is passed (see **E2.7** and **E2.9**). The power to impose a suspended sentence in a magistrates' court is limited in the same way in which magistrates' powers to impose prison sentences are limited (see **E2.5**).

The definitive sentencing guideline, *New Sentences: CJA 2003* (see Supplement, **SG-9**), provides that, while there are many similarities between the suspended sentence and the community order, the crucial difference is that the suspended sentence is a prison sentence (or a sentence of detention in a young offender institution) and is only appropriate for an offence that crosses the custody threshold, and for which custody is the only option (para. 2.2.10). As far as the length of the sentence is concerned, before making the decision to suspend, the court must first have decided that a prison sentence (or sentence of detention in a young offender institution) is justified and should also have decided the length of that sentence, which should be the shortest term commensurate with the seriousness of the offence if it were to be imposed immediately. The decision to suspend the sentence should not lead to a longer term being imposed than if the sentence were to take effect immediately (para. 2.2.12). It is submitted that these points continue to apply to the suspended sentence as amended by the LASPO 2012, but that in other respects the guideline is now out of date and requires revision. In *Seferi* [2013] 1 Cr App R (S) 350 (63) the Court of Appeal upheld the decision of the judge to impose an immediate custodial sentence on one co-defendant and to suspend sentence on another, in light of personal mitigation relevant to the latter.

E6.4   The CJA 2003, s. 240ZA (time remanded in custody to count as time served), provides, by s. 240ZA(7), that a suspended sentence:

   (a) is to be treated as a sentence of imprisonment when it takes effect under paragraph 8(2)(a) of (b) of schedule 12, and
   (b) is to be treated as being imposed by the order under which it takes effect.

Where an offender has spent time on remand in custody prior to the imposition of a suspended sentence, the law is that he should be given credit for those days at such time when the suspended sentence is activated, rather than at the time the suspended sentence is imposed (see **E6.13**). In some cases, however, the Court of Appeal has taken the view that, if an offender has spent a considerable period in custody on remand, and has in fact served the equivalent of a short custodial sentence, it would be wrong to pass a custodial sentence at all, whether immediate or suspended. Thus in *Barrett* [2010] 2 Cr App R (S) 551 the Court of Appeal varied a sentence of 12 weeks' imprisonment suspended for 12 months to a conditional discharge, since the maximum available sentence was six months and the offender had spent almost four months in custody on remand. In *Maugham* [2011] 2 Cr App R (S) 493 the Court said that where the offender had spent 198 days on remand (the equivalent of a 13-month sentence) it was wrong to pass a sentence of six months' imprisonment suspended for two years. The sentence should have been constructed in a way which would have given the offender the benefit of the time served on remand. It is submitted that these cases remain good law after the changes to the suspended sentence made by the LASPO 2012.

Consecutive Terms

E6.5   Section 189(2) of the CJA 2003 (as amended) states that where two or more sentences imposed on the same occasion are to be served consecutively, the power to suspend sentence is not exercisable in relation to any of the sentences unless the aggregate of the terms does not exceed two years.

Combining with Other Sentences or Orders

It is submitted that an immediate prison sentence and a suspended sentence should not be imposed **E6.6**
on the same occasion (by analogy with *Sapiano* (1968) 52 Cr App R 674), nor should a suspended
sentence be imposed on an offender currently serving a term of imprisonment (by analogy with
Butters (1971) 55 Cr App R 515). A court which passes a suspended sentence on an offender
must not on the same occasion impose a community sentence in respect of that offence or any
other offence for which he is dealt with by the court (CJA 2003, s. 189(5)). It is submitted that
a suspended sentence cannot be combined with a discharge when sentencing for a single offence
(see **E12.4**) but a discharge could be given for one offence when a suspended sentence was passed
in respect of another offence sentenced on the same occasion. A fine may be combined with a suspended sentence, but it is improper to combine them when a fine standing alone would have been
the proper sentence. A fine may be added to a suspended sentence, but a suspended sentence should
not be added to a fine. There is no restriction on imposing ancillary provisions such as compensation orders, restitution orders, or deprivation orders, at the same time as a suspended sentence.

IMPOSITION OF REQUIREMENTS

Section 190(1) of the CJA 2003 lists the requirements with which the court may order the **E6.7**
offender to comply during the supervision period of the suspended sentence. These are:

(a)   an unpaid work requirement (as defined by s. 199),
(aa) a rehabilitation activity requirement (s. 200A),
(b)   an activity requirement (s. 201),
(c)   a programme requirement (s. 202),
(d)   a prohibited activity requirement (s. 203),
(e)   a curfew requirement (s. 204),
(f)   an exclusion requirement (s. 205),
(g)   a residence requirement (s. 206),
(h)   a mental health requirement (s. 207),
(i)   a drug rehabilitation requirement (s. 209),
(j)   an alcohol treatment requirement (s. 212),
(ja) an alcohol abstinence and monitoring requirement (s. 212A),
(k)   a supervision requirement (s. 213),
(l)   in a case where the offender is aged under 25, an attendance centre requirement (s. 214), and
(m)   an electronic monitoring requirement (s. 215).

The alcohol abstinence and monitoring requirement is being piloted in the South London local
justice area with effect from 31 July 2014 (see SI 2014 No. 1777) and is not available in all parts
of the country. The electronic monitoring requirement will become available as a free-standing
requirement (in addition to its former role as a means of securing compliance with one or more
other requirements) when the CCA 2013, s. 44 and sch. 16, part 4, is brought into force. As
from a date to be appointed, s. 201 (the activity requirement referred to in (b)) and s. 213 (the
supervision requirement referred to in (k)) are repealed and are replaced by the rehabilitation
activity requirement referred to in (aa), inserted by the ORA 2014, s. 15 and sch. 5.

For details of these requirements, see **E8.12** to **E8.29**.

Since the amendment of the CJA 2003, s. 189, by the LASPO 2012 (i.e. since 3 December **E6.8**
2012), it is now lawful to impose a suspended sentence without including a community requirement. It seems likely, however, that in the great majority of cases suspended sentence orders will
continue to include at least one community requirement. The definitive sentencing guideline,
New Sentences: CJA 2003 (see Supplement, **SG-9**), says that, while the offence for which a
suspended sentence is imposed is generally likely to be more serious than one for which a community sentence is imposed, the imposition of the custodial sentence is a clear punishment and

deterrent and it is likely that the requirements to be undertaken during the supervision period would be less onerous than if a community sentence had been imposed. This principle was approved and applied in *Jarman* [2008] EWCA Crim 810.

Whenever the court passes a suspended sentence which contains two or more different requirements, it must consider whether, in the circumstances of the case, the requirements are compatible with each other (s. 190(5)). Power to insert such requirements is made subject to the court ensuring, so far as possible, that they avoid any conflict with the offender's religious beliefs, or with the requirements of any other relevant order to which he may be subject, and avoid interference with the times, if any, at which he normally works or attends school or any other educational establishment (s. 217). The court must also be satisfied that local facilities exist, and that local arrangements are in place, for the carrying out of relevant requirements (s. 218). A suspended sentence must specify the local justice area in which the offender will reside (s. 216(1)).

E6.9   **Restrictions on Imposition of Requirements**   The court cannot make an unpaid work requirement unless satisfied that the offender is a suitable person to perform such work (CJA 2003, s. 199(3)). The court cannot make a rehabilitation activity requirement (when power to make that requirement is in force) unless the responsible officer obtains the agreement of any person other than the offender whose co-operation is necessary to comply with the requirement (s. 200A(10)). The court cannot impose an activity requirement unless it has consulted an officer of a provider of probation services and is satisfied that it is feasible to secure compliance with the requirement (s. 201(3)) and has secured the agreement of any person other than the offender and the responsible officer whose co-operation is required (s. 201(4)). The court cannot insert a programme requirement unless the relevant programme has been accredited by the Secretary of State and is to be carried out at a place approved by a provider of probation services (s. 202(2) and (7)). As from a date to be appointed, the limitation upon the place where the requirement is to be carried out, is removed (ORA 2014, s. 16). The court cannot insert a prohibited activity requirement unless it has consulted an officer of a provider of probation services (s. 203(2)). The court cannot insert a mental health requirement unless the court is satisfied that the mental condition of the offender is such as requires and is susceptible to treatment and does not warrant the making of a hospital or guardianship order, that arrangements have been made for the treatment to be carried out, and that the offender has consented to the inclusion of the mental health requirement into the suspended sentence (s. 207(3)). The court may not insert a drug rehabilitation requirement unless it is satisfied that the offender is dependent on, or has a propensity to misuse, a controlled drug and that his dependency or propensity is such as requires and may be susceptible to treatment, that arrangements can be made for the treatment to be carried out, that the requirement has been recommended by the responsible officer, and that the offender has expressed his willingness to comply with the requirement (s. 209(2)). The court may not impose an alcohol treatment requirement unless it is satisfied that the offender is dependent on alcohol, that his dependency is such as requires and may be susceptible to treatment, that arrangements can be made for the treatment to be carried out, and that the offender has expressed his willingness to comply with the requirement (s. 212(2)). The court may not include an alcohol abstinence and monitoring requirement unless the consumption of alcohol by the offender is an element of the offence, or the consumption of alcohol contributed to the commission of the offence and the court is satisfied that the offender is not dependent on alcohol, the court does not include in the order an alcohol treatment requirement, and the court has been notified that arrangements for monitoring of such a requirement are locally available (s. 212A(9)–(12)).

If the suspended sentence contains a curfew requirement or an exclusion requirement, the court *must* also require the licence to contain an electronic monitoring requirement, as defined by s. 215 of the Act, *unless* the court is unable to do so because there is some person, other than the offender, whose co-operation is required but who does not consent (s. 215(2)), or because electronic monitoring arrangements are not available in the local area (s. 218(4)), or because, in the particular circumstances of the case, the court considers it inappropriate to do so.

If the suspended sentence contains an unpaid work requirement, an activity requirement, a programme requirement, a prohibited activity requirement, a residence requirement, a mental health treatment requirement, a drug rehabilitation requirement, an alcohol treatment requirement, an alcohol abstinence and monitoring requirement, a supervision requirement or an attendance centre requirement, the court *may* also require the licence to contain an electronic monitoring requirement, unless the court is unable to do so because there is some person, other than the offender, whose co-operation is required but who does not consent (s. 215(2)), or because electronic monitoring arrangements are not available in the local area (s. 218(4)).

POWER TO PROVIDE FOR REVIEW

E6.10 Section 191(1) of the CJA 2003 confers a discretion on the court to provide that a suspended sentence that imposes one or more community requirements is made subject to periodic review, at review hearings, at specified intervals of time. The court may order the offender to attend those hearings, and it may order an officer of a provider of probation services, before each review, to provide to the court a report on the offender's progress under the suspended sentence. If the offender is subject to a suspended sentence which contains a drug rehabilitation requirement, such requirement will already be subject to court review hearings under the CJA 2003, s. 210, so s. 191(2) provides that in those circumstances the suspended sentence cannot be subject to review under s. 191(1). A review hearing is conducted by the court responsible for the order, and s. 191(3)–(5) specifies which court is responsible for review of the suspended sentence in particular situations.

Section 192 describes what is to happen at the review hearings. Section 192(1) permits the court to amend any community requirement of the suspended sentence order, after consideration of the report from the review officer. This is limited by s. 192(2) which explains that the court cannot amend the order by adding a requirement of a different kind unless the offender consents to that new requirement, but it can impose a requirement of the same kind. The offender's consent is always required before the court amends a drug rehabilitation requirement, an alcohol treatment requirement, or a mental health treatment requirement (s. 192(2)(b)). The court may also extend the supervision period, but not so that it infringes the normal rules on suspended sentences in s. 189(3) or (4), by lasting for longer than two years from the date of the original order or ending later than the operational period.

Under s. 192(4), if on the basis of the report from the review officer the court is of the opinion that the offender is making satisfactory progress, it can dispense with the next pending review hearing, or may amend the order so that subsequent reviews can be held by considering the papers rather than by a full hearing. The court may order the offender to attend a review hearing if progress is no longer satisfactory, or it may adjust the intervals of time between review hearings (s. 192(5) and (7)).

BREACH, COMMISSION OF FURTHER OFFENCE AND AMENDMENT

General

E6.11 Section 193 refers to the CJA 2003, sch. 12, which contains provisions relating to the breach, revocation and amendment of the community requirements of suspended sentence orders, and to the effect of the offender being convicted of a further offence.

By para. 4, if the responsible officer is of the opinion that the offender has failed without reasonable excuse to comply with any of the community requirements of the suspended sentence, the officer must give a *warning* describing the circumstances of the failure, stating that the failure is unacceptable, and informing the offender that if within the next 12 months he again fails to comply with any requirement of the order, he will be brought back before the court. The responsible officer need not give a warning if a previous warning was given within the preceding 12 months or if he refers the matter to an enforcement officer. By para. 5, if there has been a warning, and within 12 months there is a further failure without reasonable excuse to comply, the responsible officer must refer the matter to an enforcement officer. The enforcement officer is then under a duty 'to consider the matter and, where appropriate, to cause an information to be laid' in respect of the failure to comply (para. 5A). Paragraphs 6 and 7 deal in detail with the arrangements for issue of a summons or warrant by a magistrates' court or by the Crown Court.

Powers Available to Deal with Breach

E6.12   Paragraph 8 of sch. 12 to the CJA 2003 describes the powers of the court when it deals with an offender who has failed without reasonable excuse to comply with any of the community requirements of the suspended sentence order (under para. 8(1)(a)), or an offender convicted of an offence committed during the operational period of a suspended sentence order (under para. 8(1)(b)).

Criminal Justice Act 2003, sch. 12, para. 8

(2) The court must consider [the offender's] case and deal with him in one of the following ways—
   (a)   the court may order that the suspended sentence is to take effect with the original term unaltered,
   (b)   the court may order that the suspended sentence is to take effect with the substitution for the original term of a lesser term,
   (ba) the court may order the offender to pay a fine of an amount not exceeding £2,500,
   (c)   in the case of a suspended sentence order that imposes one or more community requirements, the court may amend the order by doing any one or more of the following—
         (i)   imposing more onerous community requirements which the court could include if it were then making the order,
         (ii)   subject to subsections (3) and (4) of section 189, extending the supervision period, or
         (iii) subject to subsection (3) of that section, extending the operational period[,]
   (d)   in the case of a suspended sentence order that does not impose any community requirements, the court may, subject to section 189(3), amend the order by extending the operational period.
(3) The court must make an order under sub-paragraph (2)(a) or (b) unless it is of the opinion that it would be unjust to do so in view of all the circumstances, including the matters mentioned in sub-paragraph (4); and where it is of that opinion the court must state its reasons.
(4) The matters referred to in sub-paragraph (3) are-
   (a) the extent to which the offender has complied with any community requirements of the suspended sentence order, and
   (b) in a case falling within sub-paragraph (1)(b) the facts of the subsequent offence.

As from a date to be appointed, para. 8 is amended by the ORA 2014, s. 18(7), so as to omit para. 8(4A), which deals with the powers of magistrates' courts to amend on change of residence; the ORA 2014, s. 18 inserts a new s. 220A into the CJA 2003, which creates a duty on the offender to obtain permission from the responsible officer or a court before changing residence. Paragraph 8(2)–(4) is set out as amended by the LASPO 2012, in particular by the insertion of sub-paragraph 8(2)(ba). The power to impose a fine has effect in relation to breach of suspended sentence orders where the order was made on or after 3 December 2012. Prior to that date, there was no power to impose a fine for breach. It should be noted that, where the offender is before the court in respect of breach of a suspended sentence order, the court *must* deal with him in one of the ways listed in para. 8; it is not permissible simply to revoke the order or to make no order with respect to it. There is no power under para. 8(2) for the court dealing with a breach to impose a custodial term longer than that originally suspended (a point noted in *Cassidy* [2011] 2 Cr App R (S) 240). In *Phipps* [2008] 2 Cr App R (S) 114 the Court of Appeal observed that the power of the court to impose custody when dealing with breach of a requirement attached to a suspended sentence was thereby more restricted than its power when dealing with breach of a requirement in a community order. The Court of Appeal in *Levesconte* [2012] 2 Cr App R (S) 80 held that, where the offender had committed a further offence and the suspended sentence was activated in full, it was wrong to impose a longer sentence for the new offence simply by virtue of its having been committed in breach of the suspended sentence. To do so would be to punish the offender twice for the same matter.

The CJA 2003, s. 240ZA (time remanded in custody to count as time served) provides, by **E6.13** s. 240ZA(7), that:

(7) For the purposes of this section a suspended sentence—
    (a) is to be treated as a sentence of imprisonment when it takes effect under paragraph 8(2)(a) of (b) of schedule 12, and
    (b) is to be treated as being imposed by the order under which it takes effect.

That is consistent with the previous statutory provision in the CJA 2003, s. 240(7)(a) and (b), and the case law in *Carruthers v Hampshire Probation Service* (2010) 174 JP 553 and *Hewitt* [2011] 2 Cr App R (S) 633. Under s. 240ZA, however, the days spent by the offender on remand before the suspended sentence was imposed are deducted automatically in the event of activation of the suspended sentence following breach, rather than (as before) requiring an order of the court. It is clear that it is no longer possible for a judge passing a suspended sentence to indicate to the offender that the sentence has been suspended because of the time spent on remand, but that those days will not count in the event of breach. This is because the judge activating the suspended sentence now has no power to prevent the days on remand being deducted automatically. See *Archer v Governor of Low Newton Prison* (1 April 2014 unreported, DC).

The definitive sentencing guideline, *New Sentences: CJA 2003* (see Supplement, SG-9), pro-   **E6.14** vides that where an offender is near the end of the operational period (having complied with the requirements imposed) and commits another offence, it may be more appropriate to amend the order rather than activate it (para. 2.2.19). If a new offence committed is of a less serious nature than the offence for which the suspended sentence was passed, it may justify activating the sentence with a reduced term or amending the terms of the order (para. 2.2.20). It is expected that any activated suspended sentence will be consecutive to the sentence imposed for the new offence (para. 2.2.21). While it will often be appropriate when deciding whether to activate the suspended sentence, or whether to activate it in full or in part, to have regard to the successful completion (or part-completion) by the offender of one or more community requirements in the order (see, for example, *Pash* [2014] 1 Cr App R (S) 14 (4)), it will not always be appropriate to do so. It was held to be appropriate to activate a suspended sentence in full in *Sheppard* [2008] 2 Cr App R (S) 524 and in *Zeca* [2009] 2 Cr App R (S) 460 where compliance with the order had been reluctant and there had been repeated breaches. In *Finn* [2012] 2 Cr App R (S) 569 the Court of Appeal upheld the judge's decision to activate the suspended sentence in full despite the offender completing 140 hours of unpaid work, because he had breached the order on six occasions in a 'wholesale failure' to comply with the supervision requirement.

Amendment of Requirements

Paragraphs 13 to 19 of sch. 12 to the CJA 2003 deal with various forms of amendment to com-   **E6.15** munity requirements in a suspended sentence order which may be made by an appropriate court on application by the offender or an officer of a provider of probation services, or as to change of residence and other matters.

E

Part E Sentencing

Section E7 Custodial Sentences: Detention and Custody of Offenders under 21

INTRODUCTION

E7.1   For the restriction on imposing imprisonment on persons aged under 21, see **E2.1**. The custodial sentences which are available for offenders under the age of 21 are detention in a young offender institution (determinate custodial sentence for those aged 18 to 20 inclusive: see **E7.4**), custody for life (indeterminate custodial sentence for those aged 18 to 20 inclusive; see **E7.7**), detention under the PCC(S)A 2000, s. 91 (see **E7.9**) and the detention and training order (determinate custodial sentence for those aged under 18: see **E7.15**).

The PCC(S)A 2000, s. 83(2), prohibits the passing of any of these custodial sentences on an offender aged under 21 who is not legally represented. This prohibition does not apply, however, if representation was made available to him for the purposes of the proceedings under the LASPO 2012, part 1 (legal aid), but was withdrawn because of his conduct or if his financial resources are such that he was not eligible for such representation or if, having been informed of his right to apply for legal representation and having had the opportunity to do so, he has refused or failed to apply (s. 83(3)). A person is to be treated as 'legally represented' for these purposes if, but only if, he has the assistance of counsel or a solicitor to represent him in that court at some time after he is found guilty and before he is sentenced (s. 83(4)).

DETERMINING THE AGE OF THE OFFENDER

E7.2   Powers of Criminal Courts (Sentencing) Act 2000, s. 164

(6) For the purposes of any provision of this Act which requires the determination of the age of a person by the court or the Secretary of State, his age shall be deemed to be that which it appears to the court or (as the case may be) the Secretary of State to be after considering any available evidence.

When a court imposes a sentence on an assumption of the offender's age made under s. 164(1), the sentence is not rendered unlawful when it is discovered subsequently that the assumption was incorrect (*Brown* (1989) 11 Cr App R (S) 263). If there is a dispute about the offender's age, the best course may be to adjourn until the matter can be resolved (*Steed* (1990) 12 Cr App R (S) 230).

In *Danga* [1992] QB 476, where the offender was aged 20 when convicted but aged 21 when sentenced, it was held that the relevant age of the offender, for the purposes of the PCC(S)A 2000, s. 96(1), was the age at the date of conviction. In *Robinson* [1993] 2 All ER 1 it was held, following *Danga*, that, in determining whether an offender was eligible for a sentence under s. 91, the relevant age was the age of the offender at the time of conviction rather than his age at the time of sentence.

E7.3   In *Ghafoor* [2003] 1 Cr App R (S) 428, the offender, who was 17 when the offence was committed but 18 when convicted, pleaded guilty to riot. It was noted that the maximum penalty for the offence was ten years' detention in a young offender institution but, had the offender

2218

been convicted when still 17, the maximum penalty would have been a detention and training order of 24 months, less an appropriate discount for guilty plea. The Court of Appeal stated that, when fixing the appropriate term of detention in a young offender institution, a powerful factor (although not a sole or determining factor) would be the term which the offender would have been likely to receive if he had been sentenced at the date of the commission of the offence. The sentence of four and a half years' detention in a young offender institution was reduced to 18 months. *Ghafoor* was followed and applied in *Jones* [2004] 1 Cr App R (S) 126, *Britton* [2007] 1 Cr App R (S) 745, *Bowker* [2008] 1 Cr App R (S) 412 and *Y* [2014] 1 Cr App R (S) 228 (39). In *Bowker* it was held that there was no infringement of the ECHR, Article 7(1), in a case where the sentence imposed on an 18-year-old offender was greater than the maximum sentence which could have been imposed on him at the time of the offence (when he was aged 17).

The definitive sentencing guideline, *Sentencing Youths* (see Supplement, **SG-515**), provides further guidance on sentencing in cases where the young offender has crossed a significant age threshold between commission of an offence and date of sentence.

DETENTION IN A YOUNG OFFENDER INSTITUTION

Power to Order Detention

Powers of Criminal Courts (Sentencing) Act 2000, s. 96

    E7.4

(1) Subject to sections 90, 93 and 94 above, where—
    (a) a person aged at least 18 but under 21 is convicted of an offence which is punishable with imprisonment in the case of a person aged 21 or over, and
    (b) the court is of the opinion that either or both of paragraphs (a) and (b) of section 79(2) above apply or the case falls within section 79(3),
the sentence that the court is to pass is a sentence of detention in a young offender institution.

It should be noted that the procedural provisions which must be complied with before a custodial sentence may lawfully be imposed upon an adult offender must also be complied with in respect of an offender aged under 21 (see **E2.7** and **E2.9**).

A sentence of detention in a young offender institution may be suspended, in accordance with the provisions of the CJA 2003, s. 189. To be eligible for suspension the sentence of detention in a young offender institution must be for at least 14 days and not more than two years in the Crown Court and for at least 14 days but not more than six months in the magistrates' court. See **E6.1**.

Time spent in custody on remand is deducted automatically from the term of detention in a young offender institution (CJA 2003, s. 240ZA: see **E2.12**). Time spent on bail subject to qualifying curfew and electronic monitoring conditions will normally be deducted by the sentencing court from a sentence of detention in a young offender institution (CJA 2003, 240A: see **E2.16**).

As from a date to be appointed, where an offender is released from a sentence of detention in a young offender institution of less than two years, he will be made subject to a supervision period which will begin at the expiry of the sentence and end on the expiry of the period of 12 months beginning immediately after he has served the requisite custodial period (CJA 2003, s. 256AA, inserted by the ORA 2014, s. 2). If the offender breaches a requirement of supervision imposed under s. 256AA, he will be brought before the appropriate magistrates' court to be dealt with for the breach (s. 256AC, inserted by the ORA 2014, s. 3). The court's powers on breach are set out at **E2.26**.

Minimum and Maximum Terms

The PCC(S)A 2000, s. 97, provides for minimum and maximum terms for this sentence.   **E7.5**

Powers of Criminal Courts (Sentencing) Act 2000, s. 97

(1) The maximum term of detention in a young offender institution that a court may impose for an offence is the same as the maximum term of imprisonment that it may impose for that offence.

(2) Subject to subsection (3) below, a court shall not pass a sentence for an offender's detention in a young offender institution for less than 21 days.

(3) A court may pass a sentence of detention in a young offender institution for less than 21 days for an offence under section 65(6) of the Criminal Justice Act 1991 (breach of requirement imposed on young offender on his release from detention).

In *Dover Youth Court, ex parte K (A Minor)* [1999] 4 All ER 24, the Divisional Court held that, on a proper construction of the word 'sentence', s. 97(2) should be taken to refer to the sentence imposed for a particular offence, rather than to the total sentence produced by aggregating more than one custodial term.

Concurrent and Consecutive Sentences of Detention

E7.6   Powers of Criminal Courts (Sentencing) Act 2000, s. 97

(4) Where—
  (a) an offender is convicted of more than one offence for which he is liable to a sentence of detention in a young offender institution, or
  (b) an offender who is serving a sentence of detention in a young offender institution is convicted of one or more further offences for which he is liable to such a sentence,
  the court shall have the same power to pass consecutive sentences of detention in a young offender institution as if they were sentences of imprisonment.

(5) Subject to section 84 above (restriction on consecutive sentences for released prisoners) where an offender who—
  (a) is serving a sentence of detention in a young offender institution, and
  (b) is aged 21 or over,
  is convicted of one or more further offences for which he is liable to imprisonment, the court shall have the power to pass one or more sentences of imprisonment to run consecutively upon the sentence of detention in a young offender institution.

For concurrent and consecutive custodial sentences, see **E2.19**.

The sentence of detention in a young offender institution is subject to the statutory criteria for determining whether a custodial sentence should be imposed (see **E2.7**) and for determining custodial sentence length (see **E2.9**).

Although the statutory criteria are equally applicable to sentences of detention in a young offender institution as they are to imprisonment, the authorities suggest that it is often appropriate to pass a shorter custodial sentence on an offender who has not yet attained the age of 21 than the term which would be imposed on an adult who has committed the same offence, although this may be outweighed by other factors in the case. Comment to this effect can be found in *A-G's Ref (No. 42 of 1996)* [1997] 1 Cr App R (S) 388 and in *Howells* [1999] 1 All ER 50.

The length of a sentence of detention in a young offender institution is normally reduced following a plea of guilty. The relevant statutory provision and guidelines are set out at **E1.8**.

CUSTODY FOR LIFE

E7.7   Powers of Criminal Courts (Sentencing) Act 2000, s. 94

(1) Where a person aged at least 18 but under 21 is convicted of an offence—
  (a) for which the sentence is not fixed by law, but
  (b) for which a person aged 21 or over would be liable to imprisonment for life,
  the court shall, if it considers that a sentence for life would be appropriate, sentence him to custody for life.

The criteria for the imposition for the sentence of custody for life, where it is imposed as a discretionary sentence, are those contained in the CJA 2003, ss. 152 and 153 (see **E2.7** and **E2.9**). Where a person aged 18, 19 or 20 on the date of conviction for an offence which is a 'serious offence' satisfies the requirements of the CJA 2003, s. 225 (see **E4.5**), the court must impose a sentence of custody for life. The PCC(S)A 2000, s. 82A, provides that a sentencer imposing a sentence of custody for life as a discretionary life sentence under s. 94, may specify that part of the sentence which must expire before the offender becomes eligible for consideration for early release. The sentencer should start by deciding what determinate sentence would have been appropriate if custody for life had not been imposed, and then specify a period which will normally be one half of that notional sentence as the part to be specified under s. 82A (*Marklew* [1999] 2 All ER 939). Credit should be given for relevant mitigating factors, such as the youth of the offender.

The Court of Appeal has stressed that custody for life is reserved for exceptional cases and should **E7.8** not be passed on the assumption that it is a more merciful disposal than a fixed-term sentence (*Hall* (1986) 8 Cr App R (S) 458 and *Lynas* (1992) 13 Cr App R (S) 363). It appears that the criteria applicable to the use of discretionary life imprisonment in the case of an adult should also be applied in relation to custody for life, while having regard to the relative youth of the offender.

A sentence of custody for life was upheld in *Busby* (1992) 13 Cr App R (S) 291, where the offender, aged 18, pleaded guilty to rape of a girl aged three. He was not suffering from any mental illness but was described as 'flat and detached' and showed no remorse. He had committed two earlier assaults on young children and, in the light of that, it was held that the primary responsibility of the court was to protect the public.

DETENTION UNDER THE PCC(S)A 2000, s. 91

Powers of Criminal Courts (Sentencing) Act 2000, s. 91 **E7.9**

(1) Subsection (3) below applies where a person aged under 18 is convicted on indictment of—
   (a) an offence punishable in the case of a person aged 21 or over with imprisonment for 14 years or more, not being an offence the sentence for which is fixed by law; or
   (b) an offence under section 3 of the Sexual Offences Act 2003 (in this section, 'the 2003 Act') (sexual assault); or
   (c) an offence under section 13 of the 2003 Act (child sex offences committed by children or young persons); or
   (d) an offence under section 25 of the 2003 Act (sexual activity with a child family member); or
   (e) an offence under section 26 of the 2003 Act (inciting a child family member to engage in sexual activity).
(1A)   Subsection (3) below also applies where—
   (a) a person aged under 18 is convicted on indictment of an offence—
      (i)   under subsection (1)(a), (ab), (aba), (ac), (ad), (ae), (af) or (c) of section 5 of the Firearms Act 1968 (prohibited weapons), or
      (ii) under subsection (1A)(a) of that section,
   (b) the offence was committed after the commencement of section 51A of that Act and at a time when he was aged 16 or over, and
   (c) the court is of the opinion mentioned in section 51A(2) of that Act (exceptional circumstances which justify its not imposing required custodial sentence).
(1B)   Subsection (3) below also applies where—
   (a) a person aged under 18 is convicted on indictment of an offence under the Firearms Act 1968 that is listed in section 51A(1A)(b), (e) or (f) of that Act and was committed in respect of a firearm or ammunition specified in section 5(1)(a), (ab), (aba), (ac), (ad), (af) or (c) or section 5(1A)(a) of that Act;
   (b) the offence was committed after the commencement of section 30 of the Violent Crime Reduction Act 2006 and for the purposes of section 51A(3) of the Firearms Act 1968 at a time when he was aged 16 or over; and
   (c) the court is of the opinion mentioned in section 51A(2) of the Firearms Act 1968.
(1C)   Subsection (3) below also applies where—
   (a) a person aged under 18 is convicted of an offence under section 28 of the Violent Crime Reduction Act 2006 (using someone to mind a weapon);
   (b) section 29(3) of that Act applies (minimum sentences in certain cases); and
   (c) the court is of the opinion mentioned in section 29(6) of that Act (exceptional circumstances which justify not imposing the minimum sentence).
(2) [Repealed]

(3) If the court is of the opinion that neither a youth rehabilitation order nor a detention and training order is suitable, the court may sentence the offender to be detained for such period, not exceeding the maximum term of imprisonment with which the offence is punishable in the case of a person aged 21 or over, as may be specified in the sentence.

(4) Subsection (3) above is subject to (in particular) sections 152 and 153 of the Criminal Justice Act 2003.

(5) Where—

(a) subsection (2) of section 51A of the Firearms Act 1968, or

(b) subsection (6) of section 29 of the Violent Crime Reduction Act 2006,

requires the imposition of a sentence of detention under this section for a term of at least the required minimum term (within the meaning of that section), the court shall sentence the offender to be detained for such period, of at least that term but not exceeding the maximum term of imprisonment with which the offence is punishable in the case of a person aged 18 or over, as may be specified in the sentence.

E7.10   It should be noted that s. 91 is not available in respect of burglary of commercial premises, where the maximum penalty is ten years' imprisonment (*Brown* (1995) 16 Cr App R (S) 932). In *Ganley* [2001] 1 Cr App R (S) 60 the Court of Appeal noted that the power to impose detention under s. 91 was unaffected by the introduction of detention and training orders. If detention for two years or less is called for, it will normally be appropriate to make a detention and training order rather than an order under s. 91. It should be noted, however, that the detention and training order may be imposed on an offender aged under 15 only where he is a 'persistent offender'. There is no such restriction in relation to detention under s. 91. In *S J-R and DG* [2001] 1 Cr App R (S) 377, two boys aged 14 were convicted of robbery. Neither qualified as a persistent offender, but the Court of Appeal endorsed sentences of 15 months and 30 months' detention under s. 91. Further, in *Q* [2012] 2 Cr App R (S) 309 sentences of 18 months' detention under s. 91 were upheld in the case of three offenders aged 13 and 14 who had committed a robbery at a corner shop while armed with a handgun. Since none of the offenders was a persistent offender, the Court of Appeal agreed with the judge that a detention and training order was not available, and also agreed that a youth rehabilitation order would have been inappropriate on the facts.

Powers under s. 91 are limited to conviction in the Crown Court; a youth court may not exercise them. In a case where the offence merits a greater penalty than is permitted by the scheme of maximum penalties for the detention and training order (see E7.15), the proper course is for the magistrates to commit to the Crown Court for trial to allow for the possibility of an order under s. 91 being made. In *AM* [1998] 1 All ER 874, the Court of Appeal again reminded magistrates of the need to commit for trial any case which might merit detention under s. 91. In *R (D) v Manchester City Youth Court* [2002] 1 Cr App R (S) 573, however, the Divisional Court quashed a committal for a trial of a boy aged 13 charged with indecent assault. The boy was not a 'persistent offender', and so a detention and training order could not be imposed. Gage J said that committal with a view to sentence under s. 91 should normally be ordered only where a custodial sentence in excess of two years was envisaged by the youth court. That approach was endorsed by the Divisional Court in *R (W) v Southampton Youth Court* [2003] 1 Cr App R (S) 455, where Lord Woolf CJ said that the general policy of the legislation was that young offenders should, wherever possible, be tried by a youth court. If an offender did not qualify for a detention and training order because he was under 15 and not a persistent offender, the most likely outcome was a non-custodial penalty. Only exceptionally, if the appropriate sentence would be 24 months or thereabouts, would committal to Crown Court with a view to sentence under s. 91 be appropriate. See also *R (C) v Balham Youth Court* [2004] 1 Cr App R (S) 143.

E7.11   Time spent in custody (or local authority secure accommodation) is deducted automatically from a sentence imposed under s. 91 (see the CJA 2003, s. 240ZA, at E2.12), and time on remand or on bail subject to qualifying curfew and electronic monitoring conditions will normally be deducted by the sentencing court from a sentence imposed under s. 91 (CJA 2003, s 240A). The PCC(S)A 2000, s. 83 (restriction on imposing sentence where offender not legally represented), applies (see E2.6). As to an order of detention under s. 91 imposed upon an offender serving a detention and training order, and vice versa, see the PCC(S)A 2000, s. 106A.

Sentencing Principles

Where a young offender has been convicted of more than one offence, and power to sentence **E7.12**
the offender under s. 91 is available in respect of one of the offences but not the other(s),
Fairhurst [1986] 1 All ER 46 established that it was wrong to pass a sentence under s. 91 for
an offence which did not warrant such a sentence to compensate for the inability to pass such
a sentence for an offence which did justify a longer term of detention but which did not carry
power to sentence under s. 91. In *Walsh* [1997] 2 Cr App R (S) 210 there were five offenders,
all girls aged 14 or 15. They pleaded guilty to false imprisonment and unlawful wounding,
committed while carrying out a sustained violent attack on another girl aged 14. Sentences of
detention under s. 91 were imposed, for terms varying between three and a half years and three
years 11 months. It was argued on appeal that the sentences were wrong since the real gravamen
of the offending lay in respect of the unlawful wounding, an offence for which s. 91 is not available. The Court of Appeal, however, held that the two offences were associated with each other
and s. 91 was available for the offence of false imprisonment. Sentence lengths were, however,
reduced in this case for other reasons. The approach taken in *Walsh* was endorsed in *AM* [1998]
1 All ER 874. See also *R* [2013] 1 Cr App R (S) 327 (58).

General guidance on the use of the PCC(S)A 2000, s. 91, was provided by Lord Lane CJ in
Fairhurst, in which his lordship commented that it was not necessary, in order to invoke the
provisions of s. 91, that the crime committed should be one of exceptional gravity, such as
attempted murder, manslaughter, wounding with intent, armed robbery or the like but, on
the other hand, that it was not good sentencing practice to pass a sentence of detention under
s. 91 simply because the maximum available sentence of youth custody (now a detention and
training order) appeared to be on the low side for the particular offence committed. These
comments were endorsed by Lord Bingham CJ in *AM*. Lord Bingham also stated that, while a
Crown Court sentencer should not exceed the 24-month limit without much careful thought,
if it was concluded that a longer (even if not much longer) sentence was called for then the court
should impose whatever it considered the appropriate period of detention under s. 91 to be.
The definitive sentencing guideline *Sentencing Youths* provides further guidance on sentencing
young offenders under s. 91 (see Supplement, **SG-526**).

In *Ratcliffe* [2008] 2 Cr App R (S) 441, seven and a half years' detention under s. 91 was reduced **E7.13**
to six years on appeal in respect of a youth aged 17 on a plea of guilty to criminal damage being
reckless whether life would be endangered. He dropped a block of masonry on to a train, with
the result that the driver was seriously injured and the train ran out of control for some distance.
In *Z* [2008] 2 Cr App R (S) 623, 42 months' detention under s. 91 was upheld on a 14-year-old
boy who pleaded guilty to causing death by dangerous driving. The offender had taken a vehicle and driven it erratically around a residential estate in the afternoon. He lost control of the
car, which mounted a pavement and hit a tree. The tree snapped and crushed a 19-month-old
child in a baby buggy. The offender left the scene but was eventually traced. In *Jephson* [2001]
1 Cr App R (S) 18, a 17-year-old young woman pleaded guilty to taking part in an attempted
robbery at a bank in which an imitation firearm had been produced. The offender was of previous good character and from a stable home. She was not the instigator of the offence and had
expressed remorse. The Court of Appeal reduced a term of five years' detention to one of four
years. In *P* [2006] 1 Cr App R (S) 659, a sentence of three years' detention under s. 91 was
upheld on a 12-year-old boy who pleaded guilty to kidnapping a boy aged eight and subjecting him to violence and abuse. The offender was assessed as being of very low intelligence and
as having special educational needs. After giving 'anxious consideration' to the case, the Court
of Appeal concluded that although the sentence was long for an offender of this age, it was
justified and not excessive. In *SP* [2010] 1 Cr App R (S) 186 a sentence of six years' detention
under s. 91 was upheld on a 13-year-old boy convicted after a trial of the manslaughter of two
people by setting fire to a building in which they were sleeping. The boy, who acted alongside
his 17-year-old brother, was described as being of low intelligence, and his parents had shown

little interest in him. The Court of Appeal said that the case had presented 'an extraordinarily difficult sentencing exercise'.

DETENTION FOR LIFE UNDER THE PCC(S)A 2000, s. 91

E7.14   If the offence carries imprisonment for life as the maximum penalty in respect of an adult, then detention for life may be ordered under s. 91. Where a person aged under 18 on the date of conviction for an offence which is a 'serious offence' satisfies the requirements of the CJA 2003, s. 226 (see E4.8), the court must impose a sentence of detention for life.

The PCC(S)A 2000, s. 82A, provides that a sentencer imposing a sentence of detention for life may specify what part of the sentence must expire before the offender becomes eligible for consideration for early release. The sentencer should start by deciding what determinate sentence would have been appropriate if detention for life had not been imposed, and then specify a period which will normally be one half of that notional sentence as the part to be specified under s. 82A (*Marklew* [1999] 2 All ER 939). Credit should be given for relevant mitigating factors.

In *Carr* [1996] 1 Cr App R (S) 191, the offender was a 15-year-old girl who pleaded guilty to causing grievous bodily harm with intent, having stabbed another schoolgirl in the back with a knife. She asked for two other offences, in which she had tried to strangle other schoolgirls, to be taken into consideration. Reports revealed other instances of disturbed and aggressive behaviour and indicated that the defendant was 'exceptionally dangerous'. An indeterminate sentence under s. 91 was imposed. In *JM* [2003] 1 Cr App R (S) 245, a sentence of detention for life was upheld in the case of a boy of 14 convicted of causing grievous bodily harm with intent, who had a history of violent and disturbed behaviour. He had struck a man on the back of the head with a wooden stake, fracturing his skull and causing long-lasting injuries. It was accepted that the offender was likely to remain a serious danger to the community for the foreseeable future, and no confident prediction of improvement could be made. Taking a notional determinate sentence of seven years, a period of three and a half years was specified under the PCC(S)A 2000, s. 82A.

DETENTION AND TRAINING ORDERS

E7.15   Sections 100 to 107 of the PCC(S)A 2000 provide for the detention and training order. The detention and training order is available to youth courts and to the Crown Court in respect of offenders aged under 18 who have been convicted of an offence punishable with imprisonment in the case of an adult. Where an offender is aged 17 at the date of conviction but is aged 18 when sentenced, the sentence takes effect as a detention and training order rather than a sentence of detention in a young offender institution (*Danga* (1992) 13 Cr App R (S) 408; *Hahn* [2003] 2 Cr App R (S) 636).

Powers of Criminal Courts (Sentencing) Act 2000, s. 100

(1) Subject to sections 90 and 91 above, sections 226 and 226B of the Criminal Justice Act 2003, and subsection (2) below, where—

    (a) a child or young person (that is to say, any person aged under 18) is convicted of an offence which is punishable with imprisonment in the case of a person aged 21 or over, and

    (b) the court is of the opinion that subsection (2) of section 152 of the Criminal Justice Act 2003 applies or the case falls within subsection (3) of that section, the sentence that the courts is to pass is a detention and training order.

(1A) Subsection (1) applies with the omission of paragraph (b) in the case of an offence the sentence for which falls to be imposed under these provisions—

    (a) section 1A(5) of the Prevention of Crime Act 1953 (minimum sentence for offence of threatening with offensive weapon in public);

    (b) section 139AA(7) of the Criminal Justice Act 1988 (minimum sentence for offence of threatening with article with blade or point or offensive weapon).

(2) A court shall not make a detention and training order—
    (a) in the case of an offender under the age of 15 at the time of the conviction, unless it is of the opinion that he is a persistent offender;
    (b) in the case of an offender under the age of 12 at that time, unless—
        (i) it is of the opinion that only a custodial sentence would be adequate to protect the public from further offending by him; and
        (ii) the offence was committed on or after such date as the Secretary of State may by order appoint.
(3) A detention and training order is an order that the offender in respect of whom it is made shall be subject, for the term specified in the order, to a period of detention and training followed by a period of supervision.

For s. 90 (detention at Her Majesty's pleasure), see E3.12; for s. 91 (long-term detention), see E7.14. No day has yet been appointed for the purposes of s. 100(2)(b); it follows that a detention and training order cannot be imposed on an offender aged 10 or 11.

Power to pass a detention and training order on a young offender aged under 15 at the time of conviction is limited to cases in which the offender qualifies as a 'persistent' offender. Section 100(4) states that, where the court makes a detention and training order on an offender aged under 15, it must state in open court that it is of the opinion mentioned in s. 100(2)(a) and, where applicable, (b)(i). This is in addition to the normal obligations on the sentencer to give reasons for imposing a custodial sentence. In *AD* [2001] 1 Cr App R (S) 202, it was held that formal cautions on the record are relevant in determining persistence. Formal cautions for juveniles were replaced by reprimands and warnings under the CDA 1998, and by youth cautions under the LASPO 2012, but it is clear that these are to be regarded as relevant in the same way. The definitive sentencing guideline, *Sentencing Youths*, provides guidance on the meaning of 'persistent offender' (see Supplement, SG–521). It indicates that a finding of persistence may be derived from previous convictions and from orders which require an admission or finding of guilt, such as reprimands and final warnings, but not penalty notices for disorder. The guideline suggests that a young offender is likely to be found to be persistent if he has been so dealt with in relation to imprisonable offences on at least three occasions in the past 12 months. A number of earlier decisions on the meaning of 'persistent offender' were considered in *L* [2013] 1 Cr App R (S) 317 (56), although unfortunately without reference to the relevant guideline. The 14-year-old offender pleaded guilty to three offences of street robbery committed within a few minutes of each other, on the basis that he had aided and abetted the offences rather than taking an active part. The offences were committed in the company of slightly older youths. L had two previous reprimands, one for theft of a bicycle and one for possession of an imitation firearm (no factual details available). The Court quashed a detention and training order for ten months on the basis that this could not be described as 'persistent'. A youth rehabilitation order was substituted.

E7.16

Duration of Order and Consecutive Orders

Powers of Criminal Courts (Sentencing) Act 2000, s. 101

E7.17

(1) Subject to subsections (2) and (2A) below, the term of a detention and training order made in respect of an offence (whether by a magistrates' court or otherwise) shall be 4, 6, 8, 10, 12, 18 or 24 months.
(2) The term of a detention and training order may not exceed the maximum term of imprisonment that the Crown Court could (in the case of an offender aged 21 or over) impose for the offence.
(2A) Where—
    (a) the offence is a summary offence,
    (b) the maximum term of imprisonment that a court could (in the case of an offender aged 18 or over) impose for the offence is 51 weeks,
the term of a detention and training order may not exceed six months.
(3) Subject to subsections (4) and (6) below, a court making a detention and training order may order that its term shall commence on the expiry of the term of any other detention and training order made by that or any other court.
(4) A court shall not make in respect of an offender a detention and training order the effect of which would be that he would be subject to detention and training orders for a term which exceeds 24 months.

E

Part E Sentencing

(5) Where the term of the detention and training orders to which an offender would otherwise be subject exceeds 24 months, the excess shall be treated as remitted.

(6) A court making a detention and training order shall not order that its term shall commence on the expiry of the term of a detention and training order under which the period of supervision has already begun (under section 103(1) below).

(7) Where a detention and training order ('the new order') is made in respect of an offender who is subject to a detention and training order under which the period of supervision has begun ('the old order'), the old order shall be disregarded in determining—

 (a) for the purposes of subsection (4) above whether the effect of the new order would be that the offender would be subject to detention and training orders for a term which exceeds 24 months; and

 (b) for the purposes of subsection (5) above whether the term of the detention and training orders to which the offender would (apart from that subsection) be subject exceeds 24 months.

Subsection (2A) and the reference to it in subsection (1) are inserted by the CJA 2003, s. 298, which is not in force. As from a date to be appointed, s. 101 is amended by the ORA 2014, s. 6.

E7.18   By s. 101(1), the term of a detention and training order must be for one of the specified periods set out in that subsection, the minimum period being four months and the maximum period 24 months. It follows that in a case where the court would otherwise have imposed a detention and training order for four months but there is a guilty plea or other significant mitigation (or the offender has spent a period of time on remand in custody: see E7.23), then the court cannot impose a detention and training order at all. It was noted by the Divisional Court in *Inner London Crown Court, ex parte N and S* [2001] 1 Cr App R (S) 343, that one effect of the introduction of detention and training orders had been to raise the custody threshold for young offenders. In *Ganley* [2001] 1 Cr App R (S) 60, the Court of Appeal said that terms of less than four months could not be aggregated so as to reach the four-month minimum. Individual terms of less than four months would not comply with s. 101(1). Section 101(1) is expressed as being 'subject to' s. 101(2), which explains that when imposing such a sentence the court may not exceed the maximum term of imprisonment which the Crown Court could have imposed on an adult for that offence. It follows from this that, if the maximum sentence for an offence is three months' imprisonment, a detention and training order cannot be imposed at all. An example is the offence of interfering with a motor vehicle (see B4.137). Where a court is sentencing for a summary-only offence, the longest detention and training order it may impose is normally six months, because that is the maximum term which the Crown Court could impose for that offence (see the CJA 1988, s. 40(2), at D11.18, and s. 41(7)). An exception is the offence of absconding, under the Bail Act 1976, s. 6, where the maximum penalty in the Crown Court is 12 months. Otherwise, the maximum sentence of 24 months is available to the youth court as well as to the Crown Court, since the restrictions on the imposition of imprisonment and detention in a young offender institution by magistrates' courts (see E2.5) are not applicable to the detention and training order.

E7.19   In accordance with general principles, the maximum sentence of 24 months should not normally be imposed where the offender has pleaded guilty or there is other significant mitigation (*Kelly* [2002] 1 Cr App R (S) 40 and *Dalby* [2006] 1 Cr App R (S) 216, but for an exceptional case see *T* [2011] EWCA Crim 2345). If, however, the offence for which the offender is being sentenced is one which would have attracted a sentence of long-term detention under PCC(S) A 2000, s. 91, for a term in excess of 24 months, it is possible that (making due allowance for mitigation) the proper sentence would be a detention and training order for 24 months. This approach was taken in *Fieldhouse* [2001] 1 Cr App R (S) 361, where there was a guilty plea and a significant period in custody. See also *S (A)* [2001] 1 Cr App R (S) 62), where the maximum sentence may be explicable on the same basis. Restricting the sentencing courts to the specific terms identified in s. 101(1) has given rise to practical difficulty. If the appropriate duration of a detention and training order would otherwise be, say, 18 months, but the offender enters a timely guilty plea and/or there is other significant mitigation, the court must reduce the term, at least to 12 months, to take such matters into account. There is no stopping point between 18 and 12 months (*Pitt* [2002] 1 Cr App R (S) 195).

The definitive sentencing guideline, *Sentencing Youths*, says that when a court is considering the duration of a detention and training order where the offender is aged 15, 16 or 17, and there is no specific offence guideline, it may be appropriate, depending on the young offender's maturity as well as age, to consider a starting point from half to three-quarters of that which would have been identified for an adult offender. For offenders younger than 15, greater flexibility will be required to reflect the wide range of culpability (see Supplement, **SG-525**).

Consecutive Orders   As far as consecutive detention and training orders are concerned, it is **E7.20** clear that the terms of each order must comply with the PCC(S)A 2000, s. 101(1) and (2), but the Court of Appeal has held in *Norris* [2001] 1 Cr App R (S) 401 that it is not necessary for the total term to add up to one of the periods listed. This point was overlooked in *C* [2009] EWCA Crim 446. When imposing consecutive detention and training orders for two summary-only offences, the youth court may exceed a total term of six months, although that is the maximum aggregate term of imprisonment which the Crown Court can impose, by virtue of the MCA 1980, s. 133 (*C v DPP* [2002] 1 Cr App R (S) 189).

A detention and training order cannot run consecutively to an order under s. 91 (*Hayward* [2001] 2 Cr App R (S) 149) nor vice versa (*Lang* [2001] 2 Cr App R (S) 175). As to a detention and training order imposed upon an offender serving a sentence under s. 91, and vice versa, see the PCC(S)A 2000, s. 106A.

Imposition of Excessive Term   If a term, or aggregate term, longer than 24 months is imposed **E7.21** by the court, the excess is automatically remitted (PCC(S)A 2000, s. 101(5)). The period of 24 months was formerly the maximum aggregate term of detention in a young offender institution which might be imposed on an offender aged 15, 16 or 17, in which context there was a similar rule relating to automatic remission of sentence length over 24 months. That rule frequently caused difficulty for sentencers and in *AM* [1998] 1 All ER 874 the Court of Appeal reminded sentencers once again of the need to make it clear whether the sentence being imposed on the offender was one of detention in a young offender institution (now a detention and training order) or one of long-term detention under the PCC(S)A 2000, s. 91. See further *GF* [2000] 2 Cr App R (S) 364 and commentary.

Early Release   Ordinarily, the period of detention and training shall be one-half of the full term **E7.22** of the order, although the Secretary of State retains a discretion to release a person under such an order at a somewhat earlier date (PCC(S)A 2000, s. 102). The second half of the order is the period of supervision, although again the Secretary of State retains power to provide by order that the period of supervision shall be curtailed (s. 103). Supervision will be carried out by an officer of a local probation board, a social worker of a local authority, or a member of a youth offending team. As from a date to be appointed, where an offender serving a detention and training order is aged 18 or over at the half-way point of the order and the order is for less than 24 months, he will be made subject to a supervision period which will begin at the expiry of the term of the detention and training order and end on the expiry of the period of 12 months beginning immediately after the half-way point of the order (PCC(S)A 2000, s. 106B, inserted by the ORA 2014, s. 6).

Requirement to Take into Account Period Spent on Remand

Powers of Criminal Courts (Sentencing) Act 2000, s. 101   **E7.23**

(8) In determining the term of a detention and training order for an offence, the court shall take account of any period for which the offender has been remanded—
(a) in custody, or
(b) on bail subject to a qualifying curfew condition and an electronic monitoring condition (within the meaning of section 240A of the Criminal Justice Act 2003),
in connection with the offence, or any other offence the charge for which was founded on the same facts or evidence.

(9) Where a court proposes to make detention and training orders in respect of an offender for two or more offences—

    (a) subsection (8) above shall not apply; but

    (b) in determining the total term of the detention and training orders it proposes to make in respect of the offender, the court shall take account of the total period (if any) for which he has been remanded in custody in connection with any of those offences, or any other offence the charge for which was founded on the same facts or evidence.

(10) Once a period of remand has, under subsection (8) or (9) above, been taken account of in relation to a detention and training order made in respect of an offender for any offence or offences, it shall not subsequently be taken account of (under either of those subsections) in relation to such an order made in respect of the offender for any other offence or offences.

E7.24 It is important to note that, with respect to the detention and training order, the court *must* take into account any period for which the offender has been remanded in custody or was subject to a qualifying curfew. The CJA 2003, ss. 240ZA and 240A (see **E2.12** *et seq.*), do not apply to the detention and training order. Where a young offender has spent time on remand or subject to a qualifying curfew prior to the imposition of a detention and training order, in order to achieve the same effect which the operation of s. 240ZA or 240A would have, it will be necessary for the sentencer to double the number of days spent on remand before deducting that total from the length of the order imposed (*Eagles* [2007] 1 Cr App R (S) 612, followed and applied in *J* [2013] 1 Cr App R (S) 412 (74)). The requirement on the court to make such reduction has caused difficulty in relation to the specified duration of a detention and training order, which must be for one of the seven periods set out in the PCC(S)A 2000, s. 101(1). In *Inner London Crown Court, ex parte I* (2000) *The Times*, 12 May 2000, the Divisional Court stated that the duty imposed by s. 101(8) was to 'take account' of the time spent on remand in custody, but this did not require the sentencer to make a 'one-for-one discount'. This general approach was confirmed by the Court of Appeal in *B* [2001] 1 Cr App R (S) 89 and by the Divisional Court in *Inner London Crown Court, ex parte N and S* [2001] 1 Cr App R (S) 343.

Breach of Order

E7.25 Section 104 of the PCC(S)A 2000 provides powers in relation to breach of supervision requirements in a detention and training order. By s. 104(3), if it is proved to the satisfaction of a youth court acting for the relevant local justice area that the offender has failed to comply with supervision requirements specified in the order, the court may:

    (a) order the offender to be detained in youth detention accommodation not exceeding the maximum period found under subsection (3A) below as the court may specify;

    (aa) order the offender to be subject to such period of supervision, not exceeding the maximum period found under subsection (3A) below, as the court may specify; or

    (b) impose on the offender a fine not exceeding level 3 on the standard scale.

Subsection (3A) states that the relevant maximum period is the shorter of three months, and the period beginning with the date of the offender's failure and ending with the last day of the term of the detention and training order. A failure occurring over two or more days is taken to have occurred on the first of those days (s. 104(3B)). The court may make an order under s. 104(3) before or after the end of the term of the detention and training order (s. 104(3C)), and a period of detention or supervision ordered under s. 104(3) begins on the date the order is made and may overlap to any extent with the period of supervision under the detention and training order.

Subsections (3A) to (3D) were inserted by the LASPO 2012 and were included to reverse the effect of the decision of the Divisional Court in *H v Doncaster Youth Court* (2009) 173 JP 162, where it was held that the 'remainder of the term' of the order meant the period of the order outstanding at the date when the court dealt with the breach, and not the period outstanding from the date of the breach itself.

Section 105 relates to the commission of a further imprisonable offence by the offender during the currency of a detention and training order. The court, whether or not it passes any other sentence on the offender, may order him to be detained in youth detention accommodation from the date of the new order for the whole or part of the period between the date of commission of the new offence and the date at which the full term of the original order would have come to an end. Such an order may be made even where the offender is convicted of the new offence after the full term of the original order has come to an end, as long as the offence was committed within the supervision part of the order. The reinstated part of the sentence may be served before any sentence imposed for the new offence, or it may be served concurrently with that sentence, but the reinstated period shall be disregarded in determining the appropriate length of the new sentence.

Section 106 deals with the effect of imposing a detention and training order on a person already subject to a term of detention in a young offender institution, and vice versa. Section 106A deals with the effect of imposing a sentence of detention under the PCC(S)A 2000, s. 91, on an offender already subject to a detention and training order, and vice versa. As from a date to be appointed, a new s. 106B (further supervision after end of term of detention and training order) is inserted by the ORA 2014, s. 6.

Section E8   Community Orders

POWER TO MAKE A COMMUNITY ORDER

E8.1   If the offender is aged 18 or over at the date of the offence, and the offence was committed on or after 4 April 2005, the appropriate community sentence is a community order under the CJA 2003.

Criteria for the Imposition of Community Order

E8.2   By the CJA 2003, s. 147, a 'community sentence' means a sentence that consists of or includes a 'community order' (as defined by s. 177) or 'a youth rehabilitation order'. By s. 177, a 'community order' is an order imposed on an offender aged 18 or over in respect of an offence committed on or after 4 April 2005. The order will contain one or more requirements imposed by the court. These requirements are considered in detail at **E8.9**. A number of general provisions apply to the imposition of all community sentences. These are dealt with now, before turning to the details of the individual requirements.

Criminal Justice Act 2003, s. 148

(1) A court must not pass a community sentence on an offender unless it is of the opinion that the offence, or the combination of the offence and one or more offences associated with it, was serious enough to warrant such a sentence.

(2) Where a court passes a community sentence—
   (a) the particular requirement or requirements forming part of the community order, or, as the case may be, youth rehabilitation order, comprised in the sentence must be such as, in the opinion of the court, is, or taken together are, the most suitable for the offender, and
   (b) the restrictions on liberty imposed by the order must be such as in the opinion of the court are commensurate with the seriousness of the offence, or the combination of the offence and one or more offences associated with it.

(2A)   Subsection (2) is subject to section 177(2A) (community orders: punitive elements) and to paragraph 3(4) of Schedule 1 to the Criminal Justice and Immigration Act 2008 (youth rehabilitation order with intensive supervision and surveillance).

(3) [Repealed]

(4) Subsections (1) and (2)(b) have effect subject to section 151(2).

(5) The fact that by virtue of any provision of this section—
   (a) a community sentence may be passed in relation to an offence; or
   (b) particular restrictions on liberty may be imposed by a community order or youth rehabilitation order.
   does not require a court to pass such a sentence or to impose those restrictions.

E8.3   Section 149 deals with the situation where an offender was remanded in custody in connection with the offence (or any other offence the charge for which was founded on the same facts or evidence) before being convicted of, or pleading guilty to, it. It states that the sentencing court 'may have regard' to any such period of remand when determining the restrictions on liberty to be imposed by a community order or youth rehabilitation order. This clearly confers a discretion to take account of such period, rather than requiring the court to do so. 'Remanded in custody' has the meaning given in s. 242(2) (see **E2.16**). The definitive sentencing guideline, *New Sentences: CJA 2003*, states at para. 1.1.37 (see Supplement, **SG-11**) that: 'The court should seek to give credit for time spent on remand (in custody or equivalent status) in all cases. It should make clear, when announcing sentence, whether or not credit for time on remand has been given.' In *Hemmings* [2008] 1 Cr App R (S) 623, the offender, after spending 99 days on remand, pleaded guilty to battery and criminal damage. The maximum available penalty was six months, and the offender had spent the equivalent of that time on remand. The Court of Appeal quashed the community order imposed on sentence, saying that a community order was a form of punishment and, given the period spent on remand, further punishment was inappropriate. A conditional discharge was substituted. However, in *Rakib* [2012] 1 Cr App R (S) 1 the Court of Appeal doubted *Hemmings*, and that case may now be regarded as confined to its particular facts. The Court in *Rakib* said that there were circumstances where a judge might properly make a community order on an offender who had spent perhaps a substantial period of time on remand (173 days in that case) because there were strong rehabilitative or public protection reasons for a community disposal. The Court agreed with the relevant paragraphs of the guideline. See further *Bodman* [2011] 2 Cr App R (S) 249 at **E8.33**.

E8.4   Section 150(1) provides that the power to make a community order or youth rehabilitation order is not available where the sentence for the offence:

(a)   is fixed by law (murder);
(b)   falls to be imposed under the FA 1968, s. 51A(2) (required custodial sentence for certain firearms offences);
(c)   falls to be imposed under the PCC(S)A 2000, s. 110(2) or 111(2);
(ca) falls to be imposed under the VCRA 2006, s. 29(4) or (6) (required custodial sentence in certain cases of using someone to mind a weapon);
(cb) falls to be imposed under the CJA 2003, s. 224A (life sentence for second listed offence); or
(d)   falls to be imposed under the CJA 2003, ss. 225 to 228 (requirement to impose custodial sentences for certain offences committed by offenders posing risk to public).

Section 150(2) provides that the power to make a community order is not exercisable in respect of an offence for which the sentence:

(a) falls to be imposed under the Prevention of Crime Act 1953, s. 1A(5) (minimum sentence for offence of threatening with offensive weapon in public), or

(b) falls to be imposed under the CJA 1988, s. 139AA(7) (minimum sentence for offence of threatening with article with blade or point in public or on school premises or with offensive weapon on school premises).

Section 150 needs to be read in the light of the PCC(S)A 2000, s. 164, which makes it clear that any reference in that Act to a sentence falling to be imposed under these provisions is to be read in accordance with s. 305(4) of the CJA 2003. That subsection, in turn, says that a sentence falls to be imposed under s. 150(1)(b), (c) or (ca) or s. 150(2)(a) or (b) where it is required by the relevant provision but the court is *not* of the opinion mentioned therein. A sentence falls to be imposed under the CJA 2003, s.224A or s. 225(2), if the court is obliged to pass a sentence of imprisonment for life, or, under s. 226(2), if the court is obliged to pass a sentence of detention for life. See further *Burns* [2009] EWCA Crim 1907.

E8.5   Section 150A restricts the power to make a community order by limiting it to (a) cases where the offence is punishable with imprisonment, or (b) in any other case, where s. 151 confers power to make such an order.

E8.6   Section 151 will, *when brought into force*, allow the sentencer to impose a community order on certain offenders aged 18 or over when convicted, instead of imposing a fine, if the offender is a 'persistent offender previously fined'. This status requires that the offender has, on three or more previous occasions since attaining the age of 16, been convicted and had passed on him a sentence consisting only of a fine.

E

Part E Sentencing

E8.7 **Reports** Section 156 of the CJA 2003 deals with pre-sentence reports and other requirements, with respect to community sentences. It is set out at E1.26. Whenever a court is
considering whether to impose a community sentence, and what restrictions to put on the
offender's liberty as part of that sentence, the court must take into account all the information available to it, including information about the offence and about the offender. Before
imposing a community sentence, the sentencing court must normally obtain a pre-sentence
report but the court need not obtain such a report if it considers it 'unnecessary' to do so.
Given the information and specialist advice contained in pre-sentence reports, it would
surely be rare for a court to impose a community sentence without first considering such a
report.

Section 159 deals with disclosure of pre-sentence reports to the defence and the prosecution
(see E1.28).

Section 160 applies where a report (other than a pre-sentence report) is made by an officer of
a local probation board with a view to assisting any court in deciding how best to deal with an
offender. This section provides for disclosure of the contents of that report to the defence (but
not the prosecution).

E8.8 **Drug Testing** Section 161 of the CJA 2003 provides for pre-sentence drug testing, but is not
in force. In any case where the court is considering imposing on an offender a community sentence or a suspended sentence, it may make an order that the offender undergo pre-sentence
drug testing, to ascertain whether the offender has any specified Class A drug in his body.
Failure without reasonable excuse to comply with the testing as required by the court is punishable by a fine of an amount not exceeding level 4 (currently £2,500). If s. 161 is brought into
force, it will replace the PCC(S)A 2000, s. 36A, which is applicable only in respect of offenders
aged 18 or over where the court is considering passing a community sentence.

Community Order Requirements

E8.9 Section 177 lists the requirements with which the court may order an offender aged 18 or over
to comply during the course of a community sentence. They are:

(a) an unpaid work requirement (as defined in s. 199),
(aa) a rehabilitation activity requirement (s. 200A),
(b) an activity requirement (s. 201),
(c) a programme requirement (s. 202),
(d) a prohibited activity requirement (s. 203),
(e) a curfew requirement (s. 204),
(f) an exclusion requirement (s. 205),
(g) a residence requirement (s. 206),
(ga) a foreign travel prohibition order requirement (s. 206A),
(h) a mental health treatment requirement (s. 207),
(i) a drug rehabilitation requirement (s. 209),
(j) an alcohol treatment requirement (s. 212),
(ja) an alcohol abstinence and monitoring requirement (s. 212A),
(k) a supervision requirement (s. 213),
(l) in a case where the offender is aged under 25, an attendance centre requirement (s. 214), and
(m) an electronic monitoring requirement (s. 215).

The alcohol abstinence and monitoring requirement is being piloted in the South London local
justice area with effect from 31 July 2014 (see SI 2014 No. 1777) and is not available in all parts
of the country. The electronic monitoring requirement will become available as a free-standing
requirement (in addition to its former role as a means of securing compliance with one or more
other requirements) when the CCA 2013, s. 44 and sch. 16, part 4, are brought into force. As from
a date to be appointed, s. 201 (the activity requirement referred to in (b)) and s. 213 (the supervision

requirement referred to in (k)) are repealed and are replaced by the rehabilitation activity requirement referred to in (aa), inserted by the ORA 2014, s. 15 and sch. 5.

A number of general provisions apply, which are dealt with now, before turning to the details of the **E8.10** individual requirements. The CJA 2003, s. 177(2A), requires that, where the court makes a community order, the court must (a) include in the order at least one requirement imposed for the purpose of punishment, or (b) impose a fine for the offence in respect of which the community order is made, or (c) do both of those things, unless (by s. 177(2B)) there are exceptional circumstances which relate to the offence or to the offender which would make it unjust in all the circumstances for the court to impose punishment in the particular case and would make it unjust in all the circumstances to impose a fine for the offence concerned. Any community order must specify the local justice area in which the offender resides or will reside (s. 216(1)). The court must ensure, so far as practicable, that any requirement imposed in a community order is such as to avoid (a) any conflict with the offender's religious beliefs, or with the requirements of any other relevant order to which the offender may be subject, and (b) any interference with the times, if any, at which the offender normally works, attends school or any other educational establishment (s. 217(1)). The court which makes the relevant order must forthwith provide copies of the order to the offender and to the appropriate responsible officer (s. 219(1)), and to certain other persons affected by the order (s. 219(2) and sch. 14). There is also a general duty on the offender made subject to a community order to keep in touch with the responsible officer in accordance with such instructions as he may from time to time be given by that officer, and the offender must notify the officer of any change of address (s. 220). As from a date to be appointed, the ORA 2014, s. 18, amends the CJA 2003, s. 220, and inserts a new s. 220A, which creates a general duty on the offender to obtain permission before changing residence. A community order must specify a date (the 'end date'), not more than three years after the date of the order, by which all the requirements in it must have been complied with, but if a community order imposes two or more different requirements the order may specify a date by which each of those requirements must have been complied with, and the last of those days must be the same as the end date (s. 177(5) and (5A)). A community order ceases to be in force on the end date, but that is subject to s. 200(3) (duration of community order imposing unpaid work requirement): see **E8.12**. Before making a community order which contains two or more requirements, the court must consider whether, in the circumstances of the case, the requirements are compatible with each other (s. 177(6)).

The definitive sentencing guideline, *New Sentences: CJA 2003* (see **SG-9**), provides that, in **E8.11** many cases, a pre-sentence report will be pivotal in helping a sentencer decide whether to impose a custodial sentence or whether to impose a community order and, if so, whether particular requirements, or combinations of requirements, are suitable for an individual offender. The court must always ensure (especially where there are multiple requirements) that the restriction on liberty placed on the offender is proportionate to the seriousness of the offence committed. The court must also consider the likely effect of one requirement on another, and that they do not place conflicting demands upon the offender (para. 1.1.15). Having reached the provisional view that a community sentence is the most appropriate disposal, the sentencer should request a pre-sentence report, indicating which of the three sentencing ranges is relevant and the purpose(s) of sentencing that the package of requirements is designed to fulfil (para. 1.1.16).

Unpaid Work Requirement

The number of hours of unpaid work which may be ordered by the court under the CJA 2003, **E8.12** s. 199, must be not less than 40 and not more than 300 (s. 199(2)). Before inserting an unpaid work requirement into a community order, the court must, if it thinks necessary, hear from an appropriate officer that the offender is a suitable person to perform work under the requirement (s. 199(3)) and that local arrangements exist for the requirement to be carried out (s. 218(1)). The appropriate officer is an officer of the local probation board or an officer of a provider of probation services.

If the court makes community orders on the offender in respect of two or more offences of which the offender has been convicted on the same occasion and includes unpaid work requirements in each of them, the court may direct that the hours of work may run concurrently or consecutively, but the total number of hours must not exceed 300 (s. 199(5)). The work required should normally be completed within 12 months (s. 200(2)) but, unless revoked, a community order imposing an unpaid work requirement remains in force until the offender has worked under it for the number of hours specified (s. 200(3)). It was held in *Davison* [2009] 2 Cr App R (S) 76 (departing from *Odam* [2009] 1 Cr App R (S) 120) that where a community order contained a single requirement of unpaid work, to be completed within 12 months, it was a 'community sentence of at least 12 months' for the purposes of the notification requirements of the SOA 2003 (see **E23**).

Rehabilitation Activity Requirement

E8.13 The CJA 2003, s. 200A, which is inserted by the ORA 2014, s. 15 (not yet in force), provides for the rehabilitation activity requirement which replaces both the activity requirement and the supervision requirement (see **E8.14** and **E8.27**). A rehabilitation activity requirement is a requirement that, during the relevant period, the offender must comply with any instructions given by the responsible officer to attend appointments or participate in activities or both. By s. 200A(11), the 'relevant period' means (i) in relation to a community order, the period for which the community order is in force, and (ii) in relation to a suspended sentence, the supervision period. Appointments and activities can take place at any time during the order. The maximum number of days for which the offender may be instructed to participate in activities must be specified in the order. The activities include those which form part of an accredited programme (as set out in s. 202) and those whose purpose is reparative, such as restorative justice. 'Restorative justice' activities are defined in s. 200A(8) and (9). The responsible officer must obtain the agreement of any person other than the offender whose co-operation is necessary to comply with the requirement.

Activity Requirement

E8.14 Section 201(1) of the CJA 2003 defines an activity requirement as a requirement that the offender must either present himself to a specified person, at a specified place such as a community rehabilitation centre, for a certain number of days, and/or take part in specified activities for a certain number of days. The aggregate number of days must not exceed 60 (s. 201(5)). An activity requirement may include such tasks as receiving help with employment, or group work on social problems. Reparative activities, involving contact between offenders and persons affected by their offences, are also within the compass of this requirement (s. 201(2)). Before inserting an activity requirement into a community sentence, the court must consult an officer of a local probation board or an officer of a provider of probation services, be satisfied that it is feasible to secure compliance with the requirement (s. 201(3)), and be satisfied that local arrangements exist for persons to participate in such activities (s. 218(2)). If the activity requirement would involve the co-operation of a person other than the offender and the responsible officer, the consent of that other person must be obtained before the requirement can be inserted into the order (s. 201(4)). As from a date to be appointed, s. 201 is repealed by the ORA 2014, s. 15.

Programme Requirement

E8.15 Section 202(1) of the CJA 2003 defines a programme requirement as a requirement that the offender must participate in an accredited programme at a specified place on a certain number of days. Section 202(3) and (6) provide that 'programme' means a systematic set of activities, and a programme requirement operates to require the offender, in accordance with instructions given by the responsible officer, to participate in the accredited programme as specified, on the number of days specified, and to comply with instructions given by the person in charge of that programme. Such programmes include those which address offending behaviour and cover topics such as anger management, sex offending, substance misuse and so on. Section 202(4) and (5) have been repealed. It was held in *Price* [2014] 1 Cr App R (S) 216 (36) that, while the responsible officer has a wide discretion as to the appropriate programme to follow and the place where it must be undertaken, the court is not relieved of the duty to specify that an accredited programme needs to be undertaken; failure to specify that a programme needed to be complied with, and to specify the number of days rendered the order unlawful. As from a date to be appointed, s. 202 is amended by the ORA 2014, s. 16, by repealing s. 202(7) (approval by the probation service of place specified).

Prohibited Activity Requirement

Section 203(1) of the CJA 2003 defines a prohibited activity requirement. The court can **E8.16** require an offender to refrain from taking part in certain activities, on a specified day or days (such as attending football matches), or over a specified period of time. The requirement may include forbidding him to contact a certain person, and may be that the offender does not possess, use or carry a firearm (s. 203(3)). Before inserting a prohibited activity requirement into a community sentence, the court must consult an officer of a local probation board or an officer of a provider of probation services. Since the primary purpose of a prohibited activity requirement is to prevent, or at least reduce the risk of, further offending, such a requirement should be proportionate to the risk of further offending (*J* (2008) 172 JP 513).

Curfew Requirement

By the CJA 2003, s. 204, a curfew requirement is a requirement that the offender remain at a **E8.17** place specified by the court for certain periods of time. These periods of time must not be less than two hours and not more than six hours in any given day (s. 204(2)). An order might require the offender to be indoors at home between 5 p.m. and 9 a.m. A curfew requirement within a community order may not specify periods which fall outside the period of 12 months beginning with the date on which the order was made (s. 204(3)). Before inserting a curfew requirement into a community order, the court must obtain and consider information about the place proposed to be specified in the order, including information as to the attitude of persons likely to be affected by the enforced presence there of the offender (s. 204(6)). Where the court makes a community sentence which includes a curfew requirement, it *must* normally also impose an electronic monitoring requirement unless the court considers it inappropriate to do so (s. 177(3)).

Exclusion Requirement

Under the CJA 2003, s. 205, an exclusion requirement is a requirement which prohibits an **E8.18** offender from entering a specified place, or places, or area (such as a specified town centre), during a period specified in the order. The order can exclude the offender from different places for different periods of time. It may also be used as a means of keeping the offender away from a specified person, in which case the person for whose protection the order is made should be given a copy of the requirement made by the court (s. 219 and sch. 14). An exclusion requirement cannot last longer than two years. The Secretary of State may by order amend the periods of time which can be specified in an exclusion requirement (s. 223(3)(b)). Where the court makes a community order which includes an exclusion requirement, it *must* normally also impose an electronic monitoring requirement unless the court considers it inappropriate to do so (s. 177(3)). Since the primary purpose of an exclusion requirement is to prevent, or at least reduce the risk of, further offending, such a requirement should be proportionate to the risk of further offending (*J* (2008) 172 JP 513).

Residence Requirement

A residence requirement is a requirement that the offender resides at a place specified in the **E8.19** order for a specified period of time (CJA 2003, s. 206(2)). Before making such a requirement, the court must consider the home surroundings of the offender (s. 206(3)). A court may not specify residence at a hostel or other institution except on the recommendation of an officer of a local probation board or an officer of a provider of probation services (s. 206(4)).

E

Part E Sentencing

Foreign Travel Prohibition Requirement

E8.20 By inserting a foreign travel prohibition requirement into a community order, the court will be able to prohibit the offender from travelling, on a day or days specified in the order, for a period specified, to any country or territory outside the British Islands, or to any specified country. A day so specified must not fall outside the period of 12 months from the date of the order, and a period so specified must not exceed 12 months from the date of the order.

Mental Health Treatment Requirement

E8.21 The mental health treatment requirement in the CJA 2003, s. 207, is a requirement that the offender must, during a period or periods specified in the order, submit to mental health treatment, by or under the direction of a registered medical practitioner or registered psychologist. The treatment may take the form of treatment as a resident patient in a hospital or care home within the meaning of the Care Standards Act 2000, treatment as a non-resident patient, or treatment under the direction of such registered medical practitioner or registered psychologist as may be specified (s. 207(2)). Before the court can insert a mental health treatment requirement, it must be satisfied that the mental condition of the offender (a) is such as requires and may be susceptible to treatment but (b) is not such as to warrant the making of a hospital order or a guardianship order. The court must also be satisfied that arrangements have been made or can be made for the treatment to be specified in the order, and that the offender has expressed his willingness to comply with such an order (s. 207(3)). The supervising officer will supervise the offender only to the extent necessary for revoking or amending the order (s. 207(4)).

Section 208 deals with provision for the registered medical practitioner or chartered psychologist subsequently to change the place at which the offender is to receive treatment to a place where treatment can be better or more conveniently given. The registered medical practitioner or registered psychologist must notify in writing the responsible officer in advance, and the offender must consent to any such change.

Drug Rehabilitation Requirement

E8.22 By the CJA 2003, s. 209, the court may insert into a community sentence a drug rehabilitation requirement, which includes drug treatment and testing. It requires that, during a period specified in the order (the treatment and testing period), the offender must submit to treatment by or under the direction of a specified person having the necessary qualifications or experience and must provide samples, at such times and in such circumstances as are requested, to determine whether he has any drug in his body during that period (s. 209(1)).

Before imposing a drug rehabilitation requirement, the court must be satisfied that the offender is dependent on, or has a propensity to misuse, any controlled drug (as defined by the MDA 1971, s. 2) and that his dependency or propensity is such as requires and may be susceptible to treatment (s. 209(2)(a)). The court must also be satisfied that arrangements have been made or can be made for the proposed treatment (s. 209(2)(b)), and that the insertion of a drug rehabilitation requirement has been recommended to the court as being suitable for the offender by an officer of the local probation board or an officer of a provider of probation services (s. 209(2)(c)). The offender must express his willingness to comply with the requirement (s. 209(2)(d)). There is no minimum period for the treatment and testing requirement. It may take the form of treatment as a resident in a specified institution or place, or treatment as a non-resident (s. 209(4)). The Secretary of State may by order amend the periods of time which can be specified in a drug rehabilitation requirement (s. 223(3)(c)).

E8.23 It is submitted that Court of Appeal authorities relating to drug treatment and testing orders under the PCC(S)A 2000 provide useful guidance as to the appropriate use of the drug rehabilitation requirement in a community order. In *A-G's Ref (No. 64 of 2003)* [2004] 2 Cr App R (S) 106 the Court of Appeal said that (a) judges should be alert to pass sentences which had a realistic prospect of reducing drug addiction whenever it was possible sensibly to do so; (b) many offences were committed by an offender under the influence of drugs, but the fact that the offender was so acting was not itself a reason for making a DTTO; (c) a necessary pre-requisite of the making of a DTTO was clear evidence that the offender was determined to free himself from drugs; (d) a DTTO was likely to have a better prospect of success earlier rather than later in a criminal career, but there would be exceptional cases; (e) it would be very rare for a DTTO to be appropriate for an offence involving serious violence or threat of violence with a lethal weapon; (f) the type of offence for which a DTTO would generally be appropriate would be an acquisitive offence carried out to obtain money for drugs; (g) a DTTO might be appropriate even when a substantial number of offences had been committed; (h) a DTTO was unlikely to be appropriate for a substantial number of serious offences which either involved violence or had a particularly damaging effect on the victim(s), and there must be a degree of proportionality between offence and sentence so that excessive weight was not given to the prospect of rehabilitation; (i) material about the offender which became available between sentencing and appeal might be of particular significance as to the propriety of a DTTO, so that an up-to-date assessment of the offender might be ordered at that stage.

Section 210 states that the court may (and must if the treatment and testing period is more than **E8.24** 12 months) provide for the drug rehabilitation requirement to be reviewed periodically at intervals of not less than one month, provide for these reviews to be held by the court responsible for the order (a review hearing) and require the offender to attend each review hearing. An officer of a provider of probation services will provide a written report, which will include the results of the offender's drug tests, on the offender's progress under the requirement in advance of each review hearing (s. 210(1)). Section 211 sets out what is to happen at each review of a drug rehabilitation requirement. The court, after considering the review officer's report, may amend the requirement, but cannot do so unless the offender consents. If the offender does not consent to the proposed amendment to the requirement, the court may revoke the order and resentence the offender as if he had just been convicted (s. 211(3)). If it does so, the court must take into account the extent to which the offender has complied with the requirements of the order. If the court wishes it may impose a custodial sentence on the offender, provided the offence was punishable with imprisonment (s. 211(4)). If the offender's progress is satisfactory, the court can state that in future reviews can be on paper and without a hearing (s. 211(6)). If the offender's progress then becomes unsatisfactory and he is not present, the court can require him to attend in future (s. 211(7)). The court may also amend the order to provide for future review hearings (s. 211(8)). As from a date to be appointed ss. 210 and 211 are amended by the ORA 2014, sch. 4, paras. 4 and 5.

Alcohol Treatment Requirement

By the CJA 2003, s. 212, the court may insert into a community order an alcohol treatment **E8.25** requirement. It requires that, during a period specified in the order, the offender must submit to treatment by or under the direction of a specified person having the necessary qualifications or experience with a view to the reduction or elimination of the offender's dependency on alcohol.

Before imposing an alcohol treatment requirement, the court must be satisfied that the offender is dependent on alcohol and that his dependency is such as requires and may be susceptible to treatment (s. 212(2)). The court must also be satisfied that arrangements have been made or can be made for the proposed treatment. The offender must express his willingness to comply with the requirement (s. 212(3)). There is no minimum period for the alcohol treatment requirement. Treatment may take the form of treatment as a resident in a specified institution or place, or treatment as a non-resident or treatment by or under the direction of such person having the necessary qualification or experience (s. 212(5)).

Alcohol Abstinence and Monitoring Requirement

Section 212A provides for a new alcohol abstinence and monitoring requirement, although **E8.26** initially these requirements are subject to a pilot scheme operating in the South London local justice area with effect from 31 July 2014 (LASPO 2012, ss. 76 and 77 and SI 2014 No. 1777).

E

Part E Sentencing

An alcohol abstinence and monitoring requirement may be imposed only if (i) the consumption of alcohol is an element of the offence for which the offender was convicted or was a factor that contributed to its commission, (ii) the offender is *not* dependent on alcohol, and (iii) an alcohol treatment requirement is not also imposed.

Supervision Requirement

E8.27 A supervision requirement is a requirement that, during the relevant period, the offender must attend appointments with the responsible officer or another person determined by the responsible officer at such time and place as may be determined by the officer (CJA 2003, s. 213(1)), with a view to promoting the offender's rehabilitation (s. 213(2)). The 'relevant period' in this context means the full duration of the community order. As from a date to be appointed, s. 213 is repealed by the ORA 2014, s. 15.

Attendance Centre Requirement

E8.28 Section 214 of the CJA 2003 provides for an attendance centre requirement to be inserted into a community order. An attendance centre requirement is available only in respect of offenders aged under 25 years (see s. 177 and the cross-heading before s. 214).

Under an attendance centre requirement in a community sentence, the offender must attend at an attendance centre specified in the relevant order for a specified number of hours which must be not less than 12 nor more than 36 (s. 214(2)). The offender must not be required to attend more than once on any single day or for more than three hours on any occasion (s. 214(6)). The court cannot make an attendance centre requirement unless satisfied that there is an attendance centre available locally (s. 218(3)) and that the attendance centre order specified is reasonably accessible to the offender (s. 214(3)). The responsible officer will notify the offender of the date and time required for the first attendance, and subsequent hours are fixed by the officer in charge of the attendance centre (s. 214(5) and (6)). Sections 221 and 222 set out the powers of the Secretary of State to continue to provide attendance centres and to regulate a number of aspects of their provision. As from a date to be appointed, s. 214 is amended by the ORA 2014, s. 17, by inserting s. 214(3A) and (3B), which make further provision as to the selection of an attendance centre suitable for the offender.

Electronic Monitoring Requirement

E8.29 Section 215 of the CJA 2003 provides that the court passing a community sentence can order the electronic monitoring of the offender's compliance with any of the other requirements in the sentence. When the CCA 2013, s. 33 and sch. 16, part 4, are brought into force, the CJA 2003, s. 215, will also provide for the use of an electronic monitoring requirement for monitoring the offender's whereabouts (other than for the purpose of monitoring his compliance with other requirements in the order) during a period specified in the order. Where the court makes a community order which includes a curfew requirement or an exclusion requirement, it *must* also impose an electronic monitoring requirement, unless the court considers it inappropriate to do so (s. 177(3)), and it *may* do so in respect of any other requirement (s. 177(4)). The periods of electronic monitoring can be specified by the court in the order, or set by the responsible officer (s. 215(1)). If the court is proposing to include such a requirement but there is a person, other than the offender, without whose co-operation it will not be practicable to secure the monitoring, the requirement cannot be included without that person's consent (s. 215(2)). The court must ensure that electronic monitoring arrangements are available in the local area and that the necessary provision can be made under those arrangements (s. 218(4)). An electronic monitoring requirement may not be included in the order for the purposes of monitoring compliance with an alcohol abstinence and monitoring programme, unless the electronic monitoring requirement is in place for the purpose of monitoring compliance with a different requirement in the order or (when the CCA 2013, s. 44 and sch. 16, part 4, are brought into force) an electronic monitoring requirement is imposed as a free-standing requirement in the order (s. 215(5) and (6)).

ENFORCEMENT OF COMMUNITY ORDERS

Section 179 of the CJA 2003 introduces sch. 8 to that Act, which contains provisions dealing **E8.30**
with breach, revocation and amendment of community orders, and the effect of the offender
being convicted of a further offence. Schedule 8 is amended by the ORA 2014, sch. 4, para. 6;
new paras. 1A and 6A are inserted and paras. 5, 6, 13, 14, 17 to 20 and 24 are amended; these
changes define the role of the enforcement officer and make it clear that the relevant enforcement officer must be an officer of a provider of probation services. Section 18 of the 2014 Act
substitutes para. 16, inserts a new para. 16A and includes a minor amendment to para. 9. The
changes made by the ORA 2014, sch. 4 have effect from 1 June 2014 (SI 2014 No. 1287); s. 18
of that Act is not yet in force.

Breach of Community Order

By the CJA 2003, sch. 8, para. 5, if the responsible officer is of the opinion that the offender **E8.31**
has failed without reasonable excuse to comply with any of the requirements of a community
order, the officer must give a *warning* describing the circumstances of the failure, stating that the
failure is unacceptable, and informing the offender that if within the next 12 months he again
fails to comply with any requirement of the order, he will be brought back before the court. The
responsible officer need not give a warning if a previous warning was given within the preceding 12 months or if he refers the matter to an enforcement officer. By para. 6, if there has been a
warning, and within 12 months there is a further failure without reasonable excuse to comply,
the responsible officer must refer the matter to an enforcement officer. The enforcement officer
is then under a duty 'to consider the matter and, where appropriate, to cause an information to
be laid' in respect of the failure to comply (para. 6A). Paragraphs 7 and 8 deal in detail with the
arrangements for issue of summons or warrant by the justice of the peace or by the Crown Court.

In *West Yorkshire Probation Board v Robinson* [2010] 4 All ER 1110 the Divisional Court said
that the plain purpose of the warning provisions was to provide the probation officer with a
discretion which could be exercised just once. If there is a further breach within the 12-month
period, the matter must come back before the court. The court also noted that when the information is laid there is nothing in the legislation to prevent the probation service from setting
out details of the breach which prompted the warning as well as details of the second breach.
The mere fact that a defendant has lodged an appeal against conviction or against sentence does
not amount to a reasonable excuse for non-compliance with a community order (*West Midlands
Probation Board v Sadler* [2008] 3 All ER 1193).

Paragraph 9 describes the powers of a magistrates' court when dealing with a breach of a com- **E8.32**
munity order. If it is proved to the satisfaction of the court before which the offender is brought
that he has failed without reasonable excuse to comply with any of the requirements of the community order, the court *must* deal with him in one of the following ways (set out in para. 9(1)):

(a) by amending the terms of the community order so as to impose more onerous requirements
which the court could include if it were then making the order;

(aa) by ordering the offender to pay a fine of an amount not exceeding £2,500;

(b) where the community order was made by a magistrates' court, by dealing with him, for the
offence in respect of which the order was made, in any way in which the court could deal with
him if he had just been convicted by it of the offence;

(c) where—

(i) the community order was made by a magistrates' court,

(ii) the offence in respect of which the order was made was not an offence punishable by
imprisonment,

(iii) the offender is aged 18 or over, and

(iv) the offender has wilfully and persistently failed to comply with the requirements of the order,
by dealing with him, in respect of that offence, by imposing a sentence of imprisonment for
a term not exceeding 6 months.

E

The LASPO 2012 contained provision to amend para. 9(1) so as to change the duty of the court to deal with the breach in one of the ways set out into a power to do so; that provision in the LASPO was repealed (without having been brought into force) by the CCA 2013, and so it remains the case that the court *must* deal with the breach in one of the ways specified. When dealing with the offender under para. 9(1), the magistrates' court must take into account the extent to which the offender has complied with the requirements of the community order (para. 9(2)). In dealing with an offender under para. 9(1)(a), the court may extend the duration of particular requirements (subject to statutory limitations on the maximum duration of particular requirements) but may not exceed the original end date of the order (para. 9(3)). The court may extend the duration of the order for up to six months beyond the original end date even if that involves the total duration of the order exceeding three years. Such an extension may be exercised only once (para. 9(3ZA), (3ZB) and (3ZC)). If the community order was made by the Crown Court, the magistrates' court may commit the offender in custody or release him on bail to appear before the Crown Court (para. 9(6)).

E8.33   Paragraph 10 describes the powers of the Crown Court when dealing with a breach of a community order. If it is proved to the satisfaction of the court before which the offender is brought that he has failed without reasonable excuse to comply with any of the requirements of the community order, the court must deal with him in one of the following ways (set out in para. 10(1)):

(a) by amending the terms of the community order so as to impose more onerous requirements which the Crown Court could impose if it were then making the order; or

(aa) by ordering the offender to pay a fine of an amount not exceeding £2,500;

(b) by dealing with him, for the offence in respect of which the order was made, in any way in which he could have been dealt with for that offence by the court which made the order if the order had not been made; or

(c) where—
   (i)   the offence in respect of which the order was made was not punishable with imprisonment,
   (ii)   the offender is aged 18 or over,
   (iii) the offender has wilfully and persistently failed to comply with the requirements of the order,
   by dealing with him, in respect of that offence, by imposing a sentence of imprisonment or, in the case of a person aged at least 18 but under 21, detention in a young offender institution for a term not exceeding 6 months.

The LASPO 2012 contained provision to amend para. 10(1) so as to change the duty of the court to deal with the breach in one of the ways set out into a power to do so; that provision was repealed (without having been brought into force) by the CCA 2013, and so it remains the case that the court *must* deal with the breach in one of the ways specified. When dealing with the offender under para. 10(1), the Crown Court must take into account the extent to which the offender has complied with the requirements of the community order (para. 10(2)). In dealing with an offender under para. 10(1)(a), the court may extend the duration of particular requirements (subject to statutory limitations on the maximum duration of particular requirements). The court may extend the duration of the order for up to six months beyond the original end date even if that involves the total duration of the order exceeding three years. Such an extension may be exercised only once (para. 10(3ZA), (3ZB) and (3ZC)). If the Crown Court proceeds under para. 10(1)(b) or (c), it must revoke the community order if it is still in force (para. 10(5)).

In *Bodman* [2011] 2 Cr App R (S) 249 the offender pleaded guilty to burglary and was sentenced to a community order. In making that order the judge made it clear that he had taken account of 114 days spent by the offender on remand, and further indicated that, if the offender was resentenced for the burglary, a custodial sentence was inevitable and the remand time would not count. The offender committed a further burglary and the judge passed a custodial sentence without credit for the 114 days. On appeal, the Court of Appeal said that on resentencing the judge should give credit unless it would be unjust to do so, and that required evaluation of the situation as it was at the time of resentencing. On the particular facts of this case, where the judge had made the position clear at the time of the original sentence, he had not been wrong to decline to give credit. The decision in *Stickley* [2008] 2 Cr App R (S) 191 took too narrow a view of the law by suggesting that the resentencing exercise was entirely separate from what had gone before. See also *Whitehouse* [2011] 1 Cr App R (S) 567. These decisions pre-date the statutory change made by the CJA 2003, s. 240ZA, whereby time served on remand is now deducted automatically from a custodial sentence. It may be that the judge dealing with an offender for breach of a community order by imposing custody has no power to direct that the time spent on remand shall not count.

Revocation of Community Order

Paragraphs 13 to 15 of sch. 8 to the CJA 2003 deal with revocation of a community order where, **E8.34** on application by the offender or an officer of a provider of probation services, having regard to changed circumstances since the order was made, it is in the interests of justice to revoke the order or to deal with the offender for the offence in some other way. These circumstances would include the offender making good progress under the order or responding satisfactorily to the requirements in the order.

Paragraphs 21 to 23 deal with the powers of a magistrates' court and the Crown Court in circumstances where an offender subject to a community order has been convicted of a further offence. If a magistrates' court is dealing with the subsequent offence, and the community order was made by a magistrates' court, the magistrates' court may revoke the community order, or revoke it and deal with the offender for that original offence in any way in which he could have been dealt with by the court for that offence (para. 21(2)). When dealing with the offender under para. 21(2), the magistrates' court must take into account the extent to which the offender has complied with the requirements of the community order (para. 21(3)). If the community order was made by the Crown Court, the magistrates' court may instead commit the offender in custody or release him on bail to appear before the Crown Court (para. 22(1)). If the Crown Court is dealing with the subsequent offence, it may revoke the community order, or revoke it and deal with the offender for that original offence in any way in which he could have been dealt with for the offence by the court which made the order (para. 23(2)). When dealing with the offender under para. 23(2), the Crown Court must take into account the extent to which the offender has complied with the requirements of the community order (para. 23(3)).

Amendment of Community Order

Paragraphs 16 to 20 of sch. 8 to the CJA 2003 deal with various forms of amendment to require- **E8.35** ments in a community order which may be made by an appropriate court, on application by the offender or an officer of a provider of probation services, as to change of residence, change of circumstances of the offender, overall duration of the order, and other matters.

E

Part E Sentencing

Section E9   Youth Rehabilitation Orders

INTRODUCTION

E9.1   By the CJA 2003, s. 147, a 'community sentence' means a sentence which consists of or includes a 'community order' or a 'youth rehabilitation order'. For the general provisions relating to the imposition of any community sentence, especially the CJA 2003, ss. 148, 149 and 150, see **E8.2**.

E9.2   **Criminal Justice and Immigration Act 2008, s. 1**

(1) Where a person aged under 18 is convicted of an offence, the court by or before which the person is convicted may in accordance with Schedule 1 make an order (in this part referred to as a 'youth rehabilitation order') imposing on the person any one or more of the following requirements—
   (a) an activity requirement (see paragraphs 6 to 8 of Schedule 1),
   (b) a supervision requirement (see paragraph 9 of that Schedule),
   (c) in a case where the offender is aged 16 or 17 at the time of the conviction, an unpaid work requirement (see paragraph 10 of that Schedule),
   (d) a programme requirement (see paragraph 11 of that Schedule),
   (e) an attendance centre requirement (see paragraph 12 of that Schedule),
   (f) a prohibited activity requirement (see paragraph 13 of that Schedule),
   (g) a curfew requirement (see paragraph 14 of that Schedule),
   (h) an exclusion requirement (see paragraph 15 of that Schedule),
   (i) a residence requirement (see paragraph 16 of that Schedule),
   (j) a local authority residence requirement (see paragraph 17 of that Schedule),
   (k) a mental health treatment requirement (see paragraph 20 of that Schedule,
   (l) a drug treatment requirement (see paragraph 22 of that Schedule),
   (m) a drug testing requirement (see paragraph 23 of that Schedule),
   (n) an intoxicating substance treatment requirement (see paragraph 24 of that Schedule), and
   (o) an education requirement (see paragraph 25 of that Schedule).
(2) A youth rehabilitation order—
   (a) may also impose an electronic monitoring requirement (see paragraph 26 of Schedule 1), and
   (b) must do so if paragraph 2 of that Schedule so requires.
(3) A youth rehabilitation order may be—
   (a) a youth rehabilitation order with intensive supervision and surveillance (see paragraph 3 of Schedule 1), or
   (b) a youth rehabilitation order with fostering (see paragraph 4 of that Schedule)
(4) But a court may only make an order mentioned in subsection (3)(a) or (b) if—
   (a) the court is dealing with the offender for an offence which is punishable with imprisonment,
   (b) the court is of the opinion that the offence, or the combination of the offence and one or more offences associated with it, was so serious that, but for paragraph 3 or 4 of Schedule 1, a custodial sentence would be appropriate (or, if the offender was aged under 12 at the time of conviction, would be appropriate if the offender had been aged 12), and
   (c) if the offender was aged under 15 at the time of conviction, the court is of the opinion that the offender is a persistent offender.
(5) Schedule 1 makes further provision about youth rehabilitation orders.
(6) This section is subject to—
   (a) sections 148 and 150 of the Criminal Justice Act 2003 (restrictions on community sentences etc.), and
   (b) the provisions of parts 1 and 3 of Schedule 1.

Section 4 of the CJIA 2008 defines 'the responsible officer' in relation to a YRO. Section 5 sets **E9.3** out the duties of the responsible officer and the duties of the offender in respect of whom a YRO is in force.

Schedule 1 makes further provision about YROs. Paragraph 30(1) of sch. 1 states that a YRO takes effect on the day on which it is made, but that is subject to para. 30(1A) which provides that the court may order that the YRO takes effect instead on a later date. Further, by para. 30(2), if ('in particular') a detention and training order is in force in respect of an offender, the court may order the YRO to take effect (a) when the period of supervision begins or (b) upon expiry of the term of the detention and training order. The phrase 'in particular' envisages that there are other (unspecified) circumstances in which a court may wish to order the YRO to take effect at a later date.

A court must not make a YRO in respect of an offender at a time when another YRO or a reparation order is in force without revoking the earlier order (para. 30(4)). Paragraph 31 deals with concurrent and consecutive YROs. A YRO must specify a date (the 'end date'), not more than three years after the date on which it is made, by which all the requirements in it must have been complied with (para. 32). Where a YRO imposes two or more different requirements, the YRO may specify a date by which each of those requirements must have been complied with, and the last of those days must be the same as the end date of the order. A YRO ceases to be in force at the end date, subject to para. 10(7), which creates an exception for a YRO with an unpaid work requirement (see **E9.8**). In the case of a YRO with intensive supervision and surveillance, the date by which that requirement must have been complied with must not be earlier than six months from the date of the making of the order.

Paragraph 33 states that the order must specify the local justice area in which the offender **E9.4** resides or will reside. Paragraph 34 deals with provision of copies of the order. Paragraph 36 states that, where the Crown Court makes a YRO, it may include in the order a direction that further proceedings relating to the order be in a youth court, whether (a) in respect of breach or (b) on application for amendment or revocation of the order.

REQUIREMENTS

Prior to making a YRO, a court must obtain and consider information about the family cir- **E9.5** cumstances of the young person and the effect that a YRO would be likely to have on those circumstances (sch. 1, para. 28). Any requirement must (so far as practicable) avoid conflict with the young person's religious beliefs and avoid interference with times at which the young person would normally work or attend an educational establishment. Where an order contains more than one requirement (or more than one YRO is being made), the court must consider whether the requirements are compatible with each other (para. 29).

The definitive sentencing guideline, *Sentencing Youths*, sets out a recommended approach to fixing the nature and extent of requirements in a YRO. The guideline indicates (at paras. 10.9 to 10.22: see Supplement, **SG-525**) that there are three 'intervention levels' — standard, enhanced and intensive. The sentencing court will consider a pre-sentence report prepared by a member of the youth offending team, who will identify a level of intervention for the court to consider. The consideration process that the court should follow is (a) what requirements are most suitable for the offender? (b) what overall period is necessary to ensure that all requirements may be satisfactorily completed? and (c) are the restrictions on liberty that result from those requirements commensurate with the seriousness of the offence?

Activity Requirement

The CJIA 2008, sch. 1, paras. 6 to 8, provide that an activity requirement means a requirement **E9.6** that the offender must participate in an activity or activities, including residential exercises, at a place specified and for a number of days specified which (subject to one exception) must not exceed 90 days in total. The exception is where the court has made a YRO with intensive supervision and surveillance in which case an activity requirement may specify a number of days greater than 90 but not more than 180 (an extended activity requirement) (para. 3). A court may include an activity requirement only if it has consulted an appropriate officer and is satisfied both that it is feasible to secure compliance and that provision for the activities can be made (para. 8(3)). Where compliance with an activity requirement would involve the co-operation of a person other than the offender and the responsible officer, the court may not include such a requirement unless that other person consents.

Supervision Requirement

E9.7   By sch. 1, para. 9, a supervision requirement is a requirement to attend appointments as required by the responsible officer. This requirement lasts for the length of the order, which may not be for more than three years.

Unpaid Work Requirement

E9.8   By sch. 1, para. 10, an unpaid work requirement is a requirement for an offender aged 16 or 17 on the date of conviction to work a specified number of hours between 40 and 240. The work should normally be completed within 12 months. Paragraph 10(7) states that, unless revoked, a YRO with an unpaid work requirement remains in force until the offender has worked under it for the number of hours specified in it. The court must not impose such a requirement unless after hearing (if the court thinks necessary) from an appropriate officer it is satisfied that the offender is a suitable person to perform work under such a requirement and that provision can be made to perform work under such a requirement in the local area in which the offender resides or is to reside (para. 10(3)).

Programme Requirement

E9.9   By sch. 1, para. 11, a programme requirement is a requirement to participate in a programme, i.e. a systematic set of activities, at a specified place on a specified number of days. Where appropriate, this may include a requirement to reside at a specified place for a specified period. A court may include a programme requirement only if it is recommended by the appropriate officer and the court is satisfied that the programme is available to the offender at the place or places proposed. Where compliance with that requirement would involve the co-operation of a person other than the offender and the responsible officer, the court may not include such a requirement unless that other person consents.

Attendance Centre Requirement

E9.10   By sch. 1, para. 12, an attendance centre requirement is a requirement to attend an attendance centre for the specified period. This requires the young person to attend at the beginning of the period and then, during the period, to engage in an occupation or receive instruction as directed. For a young person aged 16 or over at the time of conviction, the minimum length is 12 hours and the maximum is 36 hours; at age 14 or 15, the minimum is 12 hours and the maximum is 24 hours; at age 13 or below, the maximum is 12 hours. A court may include an attendance centre requirement only where it has been notified that a place at a centre is available for the young person and it is satisfied that the centre is reasonably accessible to him. The first time at which the offender is required to attend is fixed by the responsible officer and subsequent hours are fixed by the officer in charge of the centre, but attendance must not involve attendance on more than one occasion in any one day or for more than three hours on any occasion.

Prohibited Activity Requirement

E9.11   By sch. 1, para. 13, a prohibited activity requirement is a requirement to refrain from specified activities on a specified day or days, or during a specified period. A court may include a prohibited activity requirement only if it has consulted an appropriate officer. The requirements that may be included include a requirement that the offender does not possess, use or carry a firearm.

Curfew Requirement

By sch. 1, para. 14, a curfew requirement is a requirement to remain at a specified location **E9.12** for specified periods between two and 16 hours in any day. The periods may not fall outside 12 months beginning with the day on which the requirement is made. Before making a curfew requirement, a court must obtain and consider information about the place to be specified, and this must include information about the attitude of people likely to be affected by the enforced presence there of the offender. The court must also make an electronic monitoring requirement (see E9.21) unless the court considers it to be inappropriate or electronic monitoring is not available.

Exclusion Requirement

By sch. 1, para. 15. an exclusion requirement is a prohibition on entering a specified place dur- **E9.13** ing a specified period that must not exceed three months. The requirement may operate for different places on different days. The court must also make an electronic monitoring require- ment (see E9.21) unless the court considers it to be inappropriate or electronic monitoring is not available.

Residence Requirement

By sch. 1, para. 16, a residence requirement is a requirement that the young person live with **E9.14** a specified person or in a specified place. The person named in the order must consent. If the court specifies a place where the offender must live, this is referred to as a 'place of residence requirement' and may be imposed only if the offender is aged 16 or over at the time of convic- tion. Before making a place of residence requirement the court must consider the home sur- roundings of the young person. It may not specify a hostel or institution as a place where an offender must reside except on the recommendation of an appropriate officer. Where the order requires residence at a specified place, it may also provide that it does not prohibit residence elsewhere with the prior approval of the responsible officer.

Local Authority Residence Requirement

By sch. 1, para. 17, a local authority residence requirement is a requirement to reside in accom- **E9.15** modation provided by a local authority for a specified period. The period must not exceed six months, nor may it apply to a young person once that person attains the age of 18. The requirement may also state that the young person is *not* to reside with a specified person. This requirement may not be included unless the court is satisfied that the behaviour which consti- tuted the offence was due to a significant extent to the circumstances in which the young person was living and that the requirement will assist in his rehabilitation. Further, by para. 19, the young person must be legally represented when the court is considering whether to include this requirement, or representation was made available for the purposes of the proceedings under the LASPO 2012, part 1 (legal aid), but was withdrawn because of the offender's conduct, or the offender has been informed of his right to apply for representation but has refused or failed to apply. Before a local authority residence requirement can be made the court must consult a parent or guardian of the offender (unless this is impracticable), and the local authority which is to receive the offender (para. 17(4)).

Mental Health Treatment Requirement

By sch. 1, para. 20, a mental health treatment requirement is a requirement for residential or **E9.16** non-residential treatment by or under the direction of a registered medical practitioner or a chartered psychologist, for a period or periods specified in the order. A court must be satisfied that the offender's condition requires and may be susceptible to treatment, but is not such as to warrant the making of a hospital order or guardianship order. The court must be satisfied also that the necessary arrangements have or can be made and that the offender is willing to comply. Paragraph 21 provides for the possibility that, by arrangement of the medical practitioner or psychologist, and with the consent of the offender, the treatment may be provided or continued at an institution or place different from that specified in the order.

Drug Treatment Requirement

E9.17   By sch. 1, para. 22, a drug treatment requirement is a requirement for residential or non-residential treatment with a view to reducing or eliminating the offender's dependency on (or propensity to misuse) controlled drugs as defined by the MDA 1971, s. 2. This requirement may be included only if arrangements can be made for the treatment, it has been recommended to the court by an appropriate officer and the young person has expressed willingness to comply. The court must be satisfied that the young person is dependent on (or has a tendency to misuse) controlled drugs and that the dependency is susceptible to treatment.

Drug Testing Requirement

E9.18   By sch. 1, para. 23, a drug testing requirement is a requirement to provide samples as directed, in order to find out whether there is a controlled drug in the young person's body during any treatment period. This requirement will operate alongside the drug treatment requirement. The court must specify the minimum number of samples in each month and may specify when, how, and what type of sample must be provided. As with the drug treatment requirement, it may be included only where the court has been notified that arrangements are in place to enable the testing to take place and the young person has expressed willingness to comply.

Intoxicating Substance Treatment Requirement

E9.19   By sch. 1, para. 24, an intoxicating substance treatment requirement is a requirement for residential or non-residential treatment with a view to reduce or eliminate the offender's dependency on (or propensity to misuse) intoxicating substances (i.e. alcohol and any other substance or product (but not a controlled drug), capable of being inhaled or otherwise used for the purpose of causing intoxication). This requirement may be included only if arrangements can be made for the treatment, it has been recommended to the court by an appropriate officer and the young person has expressed willingness to comply. The court must be satisfied that the young person is dependent on (or has a tendency to misuse) intoxicating substances and that the dependency is susceptible to treatment.

Education Requirement

E9.20   By sch. 1, para. 25, an education requirement is a requirement to comply during a period or periods specified in the order with 'approved education arrangements'. This means arrangements for the education of the offender which are made by the parent or guardian of the young person and approved by the local authority specified in the order. The court must consult the local authority and must be satisfied both that, in the view of the authority, suitable arrangements exist to provide full-time education suited to the young person and that such a requirement is necessary to secure the good conduct of the young person or to prevent further offending.

Electronic Monitoring Requirement

E9.21   By sch. 1, para. 26, an electronic monitoring requirement is a requirement for electronic monitoring in order to secure compliance with another requirement in a YRO. The court must have been notified that arrangements are in place in the area and that provision can be made for the monitoring being proposed. Where compliance with the electronic monitoring requirement would involve the co-operation of a person other than the offender and the responsible officer, the court may not include such a requirement unless that other person consents.

Youth Rehabilitation Order with Intensive Supervision and Surveillance

The CJIA 2008, s.1(3)(a), states that a YRO may be with intensive supervision and surveillance, **E9.22** but (by s. 1(4)) only if (a) the court is dealing with an offender for an offence which is punishable with imprisonment, (b) the court is of the opinion that the offence, or the combination of the offence and one or more offences associated with it was so serious that, but for para. 3 or 4 of sch. 1, a custodial sentence would be appropriate (or if the offender was aged under 12 at the time of conviction, would have been appropriate if the offender had been aged 12), and (c) if the offender was aged under 15 at the time of conviction, the court is of the opinion that the offender is a persistent offender. By sch. 1, para. 3, a YRO with intensive supervision and surveillance may include an activity requirement, the maximum number of days being at least 90 but not more than 180. This is described as an extended activity requirement and the court must then also include a supervision requirement and a curfew requirement. The curfew must be accompanied by electronic monitoring unless the exceptions apply. Other requirements (but not the fostering requirement) may also be included subject to the general duty regarding compatibility and the statutory obligation to ensure that restrictions on liberty are commensurate with the seriousness of the offence(s). For an example of the application of these provisions, see *L* [2013] 1 Cr App R (S) 317 (56).

As to the YRO with intensive supervision and surveillance, see the definitive sentencing guideline *Sentencing Youths*, paras. 10.23 to 10.27 (see Supplement, **SG-525**).

Youth Rehabilitation Order with Fostering

The CIJA 2008, s. 1(3)(b), states that a YRO may be with fostering, but only if the conditions set out in s. 1(4) are satisfied (see **E9.22**). In addition, by sch. 1, para. 4, the court must **E9.23** be satisfied that the behaviour which constituted the offence was due to a significant extent to the circumstances in which the young person was living and that the imposition of a fostering requirement would assist in the rehabilitation of the young person. The requirement may be included only where the court has been notified that arrangements are available in the area of the relevant local authority. Further, by para. 19, the young person must be legally represented when the court is considering whether to include this requirement, or representation was made available for the purposes of the proceedings under the LASPO 2012, part 1 (legal aid), but was withdrawn because of the offender's conduct, or the offender has been informed of his right to apply for representation but has refused or failed to apply. Before a fostering requirement can be made the court must consult a parent or guardian of the offender (unless this is impracticable), and the local authority which is to receive the offender (para. 17(4)). A supervision requirement must also be made. The court must specify the period during which the young person must reside with a foster parent, which must not exceed 12 months nor operate after the young person has attained the age of 18.

See further on the YRO with fostering, the definitive sentencing guideline *Sentencing Youths*, paras. 10.23, 10.24 and 10.28 to 10.31 (see Supplement, **SG-525**).

BREACH, REVOCATION AND AMENDMENT OF ORDER

Provisions on breach, revocation and amendment of community rehabilitation orders are to be **E9.24** found in the CJIA 2008, sch. 2. By para. 3, if the responsible officer is of the opinion that the offender has failed without reasonable excuse to comply with any of the community requirements of the suspended sentence, the officer must give a *warning* describing the circumstances of the failure, stating that the failure is unacceptable, and informing the offender that if within the next 12 months he again fails to comply with any requirement of the order, he will be brought back before the court. By para. 4, if there has been a warning, and within 12 months there is a further failure without reasonable excuse to comply, the responsible officer may issue a second warning. If there is a further failure within the original 12 months then the officer must cause an information to be laid before a magistrate, or before the Crown Court. Breach of a YRO is dealt with by the 'appropriate court', which is the Crown Court if the order was made by that court and no direction has been made under para. 36 of sch. 1 (para. 5(2) of sch. 2), or if the breach has been committed to the Crown Court by the magistrates' court (para. 7). Otherwise the appropriate court is a youth court if the offender is aged under 18 or a magistrates' court if the offender is aged 18 or over (para. 5(3)). Any breach should either be admitted by the offender or be formally proved to the criminal standard of proof (*West Yorkshire Probation Board v Boulter* [2006] 1 WLR 232) and the prosecution should be in a position to put before the court the facts of the original offence, at least in outline, as well as the facts of the breach (*Clarke* [1997] 2 Cr App R (S) 163). These two cases relate to community orders under earlier provisions, but it is submitted that they are equally applicable to the YRO.

E9.25   The magistrates have power to deal with the offender on breach (para. 6(2)):

(a) by ordering payment of a fine not exceeding £2,500; or
(b) by amending the terms of the YRO so as to impose any requirement which could have been included in the order when it was made, in addition to, or in substitution for, any requirement or requirements already included in the order; or
(c) by dealing with the offender, for the offence in respect of which the order was made, in any way in which the court could have dealt with the offender for that offence (had the offender been before that court to be dealt with for it).

If the court proceeds under para. 6(2)(b), it must take into account the extent to which the offender has complied with the order (para. 6(4)). If the court is inserting an unpaid work requirement, and the order did not previously contain such a requirement, the minimum number of hours which may be specified is 20 (rather than 40 (para. 6(7)). If the original order did not contain an extended activity requirement or a fostering requirement, the court may not insert one upon breach. The court has power under para. 9(6A)–(6D) to amend the order, by extending its duration beyond three years, but not for a period of more than six months beyond the original end date. Such extension may be exercised only once.

If the court deals with the offender under para. 6(2)(c), it must revoke the original order (para. 6(11)). If the court is proceeding under para. 6(2)(c) and the offender has wilfully and persistently failed to comply with the YRO, the court may impose a YRO with intensive supervision and surveillance (para. 6(13)). If the original order is a YRO with supervision and surveillance and the offence was punishable with imprisonment, the court may impose a custodial sentence (para. 6(14)).

The powers of the Crown Court when dealing with breach are set out in para. 8, and they are closely similar to those applicable in the magistrates' court.

E9.26   By paras. 11 and 12 (dealing with the youth court and Crown Court respectively), if it appears to the appropriate court to be in the interests of justice to do so, having regard to circumstances which have arisen since the order was made, the appropriate court may on application by the offender or the responsible officer:

(a) revoke the order, or
(b) both revoke the order and deal with the offender, for the offence in respect of which the order was made, in any way in which it could have dealt with the offender for that offence (had the offender been before that court to be dealt with for it).

Circumstances in which the order may be revoked include where the offender has made good progress under the order.

An application for the amendment of the order may be made to the appropriate court by the offender or by the responsible officer (para. 13 in respect of the youth court and para. 14 in respect of the Crown Court). By para. 16A, the appropriate court may, on application by the offender or the responsible officer, amend the YRO by substituting a later date than the 'end date' originally specified under sch. 1, para. 32. The new date may fall more than three years after the date on which the order originally took effect, but must not fall outside the period of six months from the original end date. The appropriate court may, in the interests of justice and taking account of circumstances which have arisen since the order was made, extend beyond 12 months the period within which an unpaid work requirement must be completed (para. 17).

See further the definitive sentencing guideline, *Sentencing Youths*, paras. 10.32 to 10.42 (see Supplement, **SG-525**), especially the guidance on breach at para. 10.42.

E

Section E10   Referral Orders

INTRODUCTION

E10.1   Under part III of the PCC(S)A 2000, a youth court or, exceptionally, an adult magistrates' court, dealing with an offender under the age of 18 for whom this is his first conviction, is in certain circumstances required to sentence the young offender by ordering him to be referred to a youth offender panel. In other circumstances the court has a discretion to deal with the young offender in that way. The youth offender panel is composed of people with an interest or expertise in dealing with young people. The panel agrees a 'contract' with the offender and his family which is aimed at tackling the offending behaviour and its causes. The contract sets out certain requirements, which may include the young offender being required to apologise to, and carry out some form of reparation for, the victim of the offence, or to carry out community work, or to take part in family counselling or drug rehabilitation. These requirements are specified by the youth offender panel rather than the sentencing court, and are not dealt with further here. The provisions referred to below set out the law as amended by the LASPO 2012 in relation to offences committed on or after 3 December 2012.

REQUIREMENT TO REFER AND POWER TO REFER

E10.2   The circumstances which must exist before the court is *required* to make a referral order are set out in the PCC(S)A 2000, ss. 16 and 17(1). In respect of s. 16, they are as follows:

(a) that the youth court (or other magistrates' court) is dealing with an offender under the age of 18 where neither the offence nor any connected offence is one for which the sentence is fixed by law;

(b) the court is not proposing to pass a custodial sentence or make a hospital order in respect of the offence or any connected offence;

(c) the court is not proposing to grant an absolute or conditional discharge in respect of the offence;

(d) the compulsory referral conditions set out in s. 17 are satisfied; and

(e) the court has been notified by the Secretary of State that arrangements for the implementation of referral orders are available in the area in which the young offender resides or will reside.

E10.3   The compulsory referral conditions referred to are set out in s. 17. They are satisfied in relation to an offence if the offence is punishable with imprisonment and the offender:

(a) pleaded guilty to the offence and to any connected offence;

(b) has never been convicted by or before a court in the UK of any offence other than the offence and any connected offence, nor convicted by or before a court in another Member State of any offence.

E10.4   The circumstances which must exist before a court has *power* to make a referral order, but is not under a requirement to do so, are set out in ss. 16 and 17(2) and are satisfied in relation to an offence if:

(a) the offender is being dealt with by the court for the offence and one or more connected offences, whether or not any of them is an offence punishable with imprisonment;

(b) he pleaded guilty to at least one of the offences mentioned in (a) above, whether or not he has been previously found guilty of an offence.

Making of Referral Orders

The referral order must specify the relevant youth offending team responsible for implementing the order, require the offender to attend each of the appropriate meetings of the panel, and specify the period (the 'compliance period') during which the youth offender contract is to have effect. The minimum compliance period is three months and the maximum period is one year (s. 18(1)). The definitive sentencing guideline, *Sentencing Youths*, provides guidance on the duration of a referral order (see Supplement, **SG-523**). Paragraphs 8.4 and 8.5 state that a court should be prepared to use the whole range of periods permitted, and that in general orders of ten to 12 months should be made only for the more serious offences. When making the order, the court must explain to the young offender in ordinary language the effect of the order and the consequences which may follow if there is a failure to agree the terms of the contract or if the young offender breaches the terms of the contract (s. 18(3)). Where the court is dealing with the young offender for connected offences and is passing more than one referral order, the court may order that the specified periods of the orders shall run concurrently or consecutively to one another, but the total period shall not exceed 12 months (s. 18(4)–(7)).

E10.5

In the case of a young offender who is under the age of 16 when the order is made, the court must, and in any other case may, make an order requiring the parent or guardian of the young offender (or a representative of a local authority where that local authority has parental responsibility and the young offender is in the authority's care or is provided by them with accommodation under any statutory provision) to attend the relevant meetings of the youth offender panel (s. 20(1) and (2)). This does not apply if the court is satisfied that in the circumstances of the case it would be unreasonable to require such attendance (s. 20(3)).

Mixing Referral Orders with Other Sentences or Orders

There are very strict limitations on the mixing of a referral order with other sentences or orders. A referral order cannot be made where the court imposes a custodial sentence or hospital order on the offender for the offence or for any connected offence, or where it grants an absolute or conditional discharge for the offence (PCC(S)A 2000, s. 16(1)). Where the court makes a referral order for an offence, it must not at the same time deal with the offender for that offence in any of the 'prohibited ways', which are to impose any community sentence, fine, reparation order or conditional discharge or any requirement to attend a meeting under s. 1(2A) of the Street Offences Act 1959 (s. 19(4)). Where the court makes a referral order for an offence, it is required to deal with any associated offence either by making a referral order or by passing an absolute discharge, and it must not deal with any connected offence in any of the 'prohibited ways' (s. 19(3)). Whether in respect of the offence for which the referral order is made or for any connected offence, the court must not make an order binding over the young offender to keep the peace or binding over the parent or guardian of the young offender under s. 150. Finally, where there is a requirement rather than a power to make a referral order, the court may not defer passing sentence on the young offender, although other specified powers of adjournment, remand, remission for sentence and committal for sentence are unaffected (s. 19(7)). Notwithstanding all these restrictions, it would still be permissible for the court, at the same time as making a referral order, in an appropriate case to make a compensation order under s. 130, a restitution order under s. 148 (see **E17**) or a deprivation order under s. 143 (see **E18**). By the CJA 2003, s. 324 and sch. 34, a court sentencing a young offender by referral order may at the same time make a parenting order under the CDA 1998, s. 8 (see **E14.1**).

E10.6

E

Part E Sentencing

BREACH, REVOCATION AND AMENDMENT OF REFERRAL ORDERS

E10.7   Provisions for dealing with a young offender who is referred back to court in breach of a referral order, or is convicted while subject to a referral order, are set out in the PCC(S)A 2000, sch. 1. In the case of a young offender who is under the age of 18 when he appears in court having been referred back, the appropriate court is the youth court acting for the relevant local justice area and, if he is 18 or over at that time, it is a magistrates' court acting for that area (para. 1).

Under the PCC(S)A 2000, ss. 27A and 27B, there is power to revoke referral orders and power to extend the contract period.

If it is proved to the satisfaction of the court that the youth offender panel was entitled to make the finding of breach of the referral order which resulted in the young offender being referred back to court, or that any discretion of the panel in that respect was exercised reasonably, the court may (provided that the young offender is present before it) revoke the referral order and may deal with the young offender in any other manner in which he could have been dealt with for that offence by the court which made the order (para. 5(5)(a)). The court must have regard to the circumstances of his referral back to court and, where a contract has taken effect, the extent of his compliance with it (para. 5(5)(b)). The court may, on the other hand, decide not to revoke the referral order, either because the court does not endorse the decision of the panel to refer the order back to the court or for any other reason (para. 7).

E10.8   Where an offender who is subject to a referral order is convicted of an offence, the court dealing with the offence may, if that offence was committed before the referral order was made, sentence the offender for the new offence by extending the compliance period of the referral order (para. 11). The court may adopt a similar course even where the offence was committed after the referral order was made, but only if the court is satisfied that 'exceptional circumstances' exist, and states in open court why it is so satisfied (para. 12). In neither of these situations, however, can the compliance period be extended so as to exceed 12 months. Apart from cases falling within paras. 11 or 12, the court will deal with the commission of a further offence under para. 14, which states that, unless the court sentencing for the new offence deals with the case by way of absolute discharge, the effect of dealing with the offender for the further offence is to revoke the referral order. The court may, if it is in the interests of justice, deal with the offender for the original offence in any other manner in which the offender could have been dealt with for that offence by the court which made the referral order (para. 14(3)). The court must have regard, where a contract has taken effect, to the extent to which the young offender has complied with its terms (para. 14(4)).

The court which made the referral order may vary the youth offending team specified in the order because of the young offender's change of residence (s. 21(5)).

Section E11   Reparation Orders

POWER TO MAKE A REPARATION ORDER

Under ss. 73 and 74 of the PCC(S)A 2000, the Crown Court and youth courts have power to **E11.1** impose a reparation order on an offender aged under 18 who is convicted of any offence except murder.

A reparation order is *not* a 'community sentence' within the meaning of the CJA 2003, s. 147.   **E11.2**

Powers of Criminal Courts (Sentencing) Act 2000, ss. 73 and 74

73.—(1) Where a child or young person (that is to say, any person aged under 18) is convicted of an offence other than one for which the sentence is fixed by law, the court by or before which he is convicted may make an order requiring him to make reparation specified in the order—
   (a) to a person or persons so specified; or
   (b) to the community at large;
   and any person so specified must be a person identified by the court as a victim of the offence or a person otherwise affected by it.
(2) An order under subsection (1) above is in this Act referred to as a 'reparation order'.
(3) In this section and section 74 below 'make reparation', in relation to an offender, means make reparation for the offence otherwise than by the payment of compensation; and the requirements that may be specified in a reparation order are subject to section 74(1) to (3).
(4) The court shall not make a reparation order in respect of the offender if it proposes—
   (a) to pass on him a custodial sentence; or
   (b) to make in respect of him a youth rehabilitation order.
(4A) The court shall not make a reparation order in respect of the offender at a time when a youth rehabilitation order is in force in respect of him unless when it makes the reparation order it revokes the youth rehabilitation order.
(4B) Where a youth rehabilitation order is revoked under subsection (4A), paragraph 24 of Schedule 2 to the Criminal Justice and Immigration Act 2008 (breach, revocation or amendment of youth rehabilitation order) applies to the revocation.
(5) Before making a reparation order, a court shall obtain and consider a written report by an officer of a local probation board, an officer of a provider of probation services, a social worker of a local authority or a member of a youth offending team indicating—
   (a) the type of work that is suitable for the offender; and
   (b) the attitude of the victim or victims to the requirements proposed to be included in the order.
(6) The court shall not make a reparation order unless it has been notified by the Secretary of State that arrangements for implementing such orders are available in the area proposed to be named in the order under section 74(4) below and the notice has not been withdrawn.
(7) [Repealed]
(8) The court shall give reasons if it does not make a reparation order in a case where it has power to do so.
74.—(1) A reparation order shall not require the offender—
   (a) to work for more than 24 hours in aggregate; or
   (b) to make reparation to any person without the consent of that person.
(2) Subject to subsection (1) above, requirements specified in a reparation order shall be such as in the opinion of the court are commensurate with the seriousness of the offence, or the combination of the offence and one or more offences associated with it.
(3) Requirements so specified shall, as far as practicable, be such as to avoid—
   (a) any conflict with the offender's religious beliefs or with the requirements of any youth community order to which he may be subject; and

E

Part E Sentencing

    (b) any interference with the times, if any, at which he normally works or attends school or any other educational establishment.

  (4) A reparation order shall name the local justice area in which it appears to the court making the order (or to the court amending under Schedule 8 to this Act any provision included in the order in pursuance of this subsection) that the offender resides or will reside.

  (5) In this Act 'responsible officer', in relation to an offender subject to a reparation order, means one of the following who is specified in the order, namely—

    (a) an officer of a local probation board or an officer of a provider of probation services (as the case may be);

    (b) a social worker of a local authority;

    (c) a member of a youth offending team.

    ...

  (8) Any reparation required by a reparation order—

    (a) shall be made under the supervision of the responsible officer; and

    (b) shall be made within a period of three months from the date of the making of the order.

E11.3   The wording of s. 73(2) indicates that the court may require reparation to be made to a person who is the victim of the offence, or to someone 'otherwise affected' by it. In a case of assault, this might include not just the victim of the assault but, instead or in addition, a bystander who suffered shock as a result of witnessing the assault. Since the reparation order is not a community order, it should only be used where the offender has committed an offence which is not serious enough to justify imposing a youth rehabilitation order (s. 73(4)). Section 74(2) makes it clear that the number of hours of work required of the young offender and, presumably, the nature of that work, must be such as in the opinion of the court are commensurate with the seriousness of the offence committed. A reparation order may be imposed without the court first obtaining a pre-sentence report but, by s. 73(5), before making a reparation order the court must obtain and consider a report from a probation officer, a social worker or a member of a youth offending team indicating the type of work which is suitable for the young offender, and the attitude of the victim, or victims, to the requirements to be included in the order. Before making a reparation order, the court must explain to the offender in ordinary language the effect of the order and of the requirements proposed to be included in it, the consequences which may follow if he fails to comply with any of those requirements, and that the order may be reviewed by the court on the application either of the offender or of the responsible officer (s. 73(7)). The consent of the offender to the making of the order is not required. Section 73(8) requires the court to give reasons why it has not made a reparation order in a case where it had power to do so.

Mixing Reparation Orders with Other Sentences or Orders

E11.4   A reparation order cannot be combined with a custodial sentence, a youth rehabilitation order or a referral order, either for the same offence or, it is submitted, for different offences sentenced at the same time (s. 73(4) and (4A)). There is nothing to prevent a reparation order being combined with ancillary orders such as a compensation order or a deprivation order under s. 143.

BREACH AND REVOCATION OF REPARATION ORDERS

E11.5   Arrangements for dealing with the offender's failure to comply with the terms of a reparation order are set out in the PCC(S)A 2000, sch. 8.

Section E12   Absolute and Conditional Discharges

POWER TO GRANT ABSOLUTE AND CONDITIONAL DISCHARGES

Powers of Criminal Courts (Sentencing) Act 2000, s. 12

E12.1

(1) Where a court by or before which a person is convicted of an offence (not being an offence the sentence for which is fixed by law or falls to be imposed under section 110(2) or 111(2) below, section 1A(5) of the Prevention of Crime Act 1953, section 51A(2) of the Firearms Act 1968, section 139AA(7) of the Criminal Justice Act 1988, section 224A, 225(2) or 226(2) of the Criminal Justice Act 2003 or section 29(4) or (6) of the Violent Crime Reduction Act 2006) is of the opinion, having regard to the circumstances including the nature of the offence and the character of the offender, that it is inexpedient to inflict punishment, the court may make an order either—
   (a) discharging him absolutely; or
   (b) if the court thinks fit, discharging him subject to the condition that he commits no offence during such period, not exceeding three years from the date of the order, as may be specified in the order.
(2) Subsection 1(b) above has effect subject to section 66ZB(6) of the Crime and Disorder Act 1998 (youth cautions).
(3) An order discharging a person subject to such a condition as is mentioned in subsection (1)(b) above is in this Act referred to as 'an order for conditional discharge'; and the period specified in any such order is in this Act referred to as 'the period of conditional discharge'.
(4) [Repealed.]
(5) If (by virtue of section 13 below) a person conditionally discharged under this section is sentenced for the offence in respect of which the order for conditional discharge was made, that order shall cease to have effect.

A discharge is *not* a community sentence within the meaning of the CJA 2003, s. 147.

In *Wehner* [1977] 3 All ER 553, it was held that while it was 'sound practice' for the court to explain the effect of a conditional discharge to the offender personally, the delegation of the task of explanation to the offender's lawyer is not prohibited, provided that the court is satisfied that the explanation has been made and understood before it makes the order. By s. 12(6), any court may, on making an order for conditional discharge, allow any person who consents to do so to give security for the good behaviour of the offender. Where a conditional discharge has been imposed on appeal, it shall be deemed, if made on appeal from a magistrates' court, to have been imposed by that court and, if made on appeal from the Crown Court or the Court of Appeal, to have been made by the Crown Court (s. 15(2)).

Use of Absolute Discharge

The power to grant an absolute discharge is available to all criminal courts whatever the age **E12.2** of the offender and, apart from the exceptional cases in which the PCC(S)A 2000, s. 12(1), applies, whatever the offence committed. Its imposition may reflect the triviality of the offence, the circumstances in which it came to be prosecuted, or special factors relating to the offender. Cases in which the Court of Appeal has advocated the use of the absolute discharge include *Smedleys Ltd v Breed* [1974] AC 839 and *King* [1977] Crim LR 627.

Use of Conditional Discharge

E12.3 The power to grant a conditional discharge is available to all criminal courts whatever the age of the offender. The conditional discharge cannot be used in any of the cases set out in the PCC(S) A 2000, s. 12(1) (see **E12.1**), nor where the offender has been convicted of doing something which he is prohibited from doing by an anti-social behaviour order without reasonable excuse (CDA 1998, s. 1(11)), nor where the offender has been convicted of without reasonable excuse doing anything which he is prohibited from doing by a sex offender order (CDA 1998, s. 2(9)). By the CDA 1998, s. 66ZB(5) and (6), where (a) a person who has received two or more youth cautions is convicted of an offence committed within two years of the date of the last of those cautions or (b) a person who has received a youth conditional caution followed by a youth caution is convicted of an offence within two years of the date of the youth caution, the court must not deal with the offence by way of conditional discharge unless it is of the opinion that there are exceptional circumstances relating to the offence or the person that justify its doing so. By the LASPO 2012, s. 135(5), a reprimand or warning of a person under the CDA 1998, s. 65 (repealed by the LASPO 2012), 'is to be treated for the purposes of any enactment...as a youth caution'.

When a discharge is conditional, the sole condition is that the offender should commit no further offence during the period of the conditional discharge. No other condition or requirement may be inserted. The period of the conditional discharge is fixed by the court but must not exceed three years. Cases in which the Court of Appeal has advocated the use of the conditional discharge include *Whitehead* (1979) 1 Cr App R (S) 187 and *Watts* (1984) 6 Cr App R (S) 61.

Combining Discharge with Other Sentences or Orders

E12.4 A discharge cannot be combined with a punitive measure for the same offence (*Savage* (1983) 5 Cr App R (S) 216) except where permitted by statute. Thus a discharge cannot be combined with a custodial sentence, a community order or a fine (*Sanck* (1990) 12 Cr App R (S) 155). If, however, an offender is given a discharge for one of a number of offences, the court is free to exercise its normal powers of sentence with respect to his other offences (*Bainbridge* (1979) 1 Cr App R (S) 36). There are restrictions on the use of the discharge where the court is proposing to make a referral order (see **E10.6**). Section 12(7) of the PCC(S)A 2000 states that:

> (7) Nothing in this section shall be construed as preventing a court, on discharging an offender absolutely or conditionally in respect of any offence, from making an order for costs against the offender or imposing any disqualification on him or from making in respect of the offence an order under section 130, 143 or 148 below (compensation orders, deprivation orders and restitution orders) or from making in respect of the offence an unlawful profit order under section 4 of the Prevention of Social Housing Fraud Act 2013.

The Prevention of Social Housing Fraud Act 2013 came into force on 15 October 2013 in England and on 5 November 2013 in Wales.

For s. 130 (compensation orders), see **E16.15**; for s. 143 (deprivation orders), see **E18.6**; and for s. 148 (restitution orders), see **E17.4**. The wording of s. 12(7) permits the combination of a discharge with 'any disqualification'. Thus, for example, a discharge may be combined with an order for disqualification from driving. A discharge may be combined with an order to disqualify a person from acting as a company director (reversing the decision in *Young* (1990) 12 Cr App R (S) 262) or with a recommendation for deportation (*Akan* [1973] 1 QB 491).

Section 12(7) makes no mention of confiscation orders (see **E19**). In *Varma* [2013] 1 AC 463 the Supreme Court reversed the decision of the Court of Appeal in *Magro* [2011] QB 309 and held that a confiscation order can be made on discharging an offender absolutely or conditionally in respect of any offence.

BREACH OF CONDITIONAL DISCHARGE

A conditional discharge can be breached only by the conviction of the offender of a further **E12.5**
offence committed during the period of the discharge (PCC(S)A 2000, s. 13(1)). A court dealing with the breach (the Crown Court if it made the conditional discharge, or the magistrates'
court if it made it) may sentence the offender for the original offence in any manner in which
it could have dealt with him if he had just been convicted before the court for that offence (s.
13(6)), but the Crown Court dealing with a person conditionally discharged by a magistrates'
court is limited to the lower court's powers (s. 13(7)). One magistrates' court may deal with
breach of a conditional discharge imposed by a different magistrates' court, but only with the
consent of the original magistrates' court (s. 13(8)). Where an offender aged under 18 has
been conditionally discharged by a magistrates' court in respect of an offence triable only on
indictment in the case of an adult, and the offender has now attained the age of 18, the powers
exercisable by the court under s. 13(6), (7) or (8) are to impose a fine not exceeding £5,000 for
the original offence, or to deal with the offender in any way in which a magistrates' court could
deal with him if it had just convicted him of an offence punishable with imprisonment for a
term not exceeding six months (s. 13(9)). Sentencing for the original offence always terminates
the conditional discharge itself, but any order for compensation or costs made at the time of the
discharge remains valid (*Evans* [1963] 1 QB 979).

LIMITED EFFECT OF CONVICTION

Powers of Criminal Courts (Sentencing) Act 2000, s. 14

E12.6

(1) Subject to subsection (2) below, a conviction of an offence for which an order is made under
section 12 above discharging the offender absolutely or conditionally shall be deemed not to
be a conviction for any purpose other than the purposes of the proceedings in which the order
is made and of any subsequent proceedings which may be taken against the offender under
section 13 above.
(2) Where the offender was aged 18 or over at the time of his conviction of the offence in question
and is subsequently sentenced (under section 13 above) for that offence, subsection (1) above
shall cease to apply to the conviction.
(3) Without prejudice to subsections (1) and (2) above, the conviction of an offender who is discharged absolutely or conditionally under section 12 above shall in any event be disregarded
for the purposes of any enactment or instrument which—
(a) imposes any disqualification or disability upon convicted persons; or
(b) authorises or requires the imposition of any such disqualification or disability.
(4) Subsections (1) to (3) above shall not affect—
(a) any right of any offender discharged absolutely or conditionally under section 12 above to
rely on his conviction in bar of any subsequent proceedings for the same offence; or
(b) the restoration of any property in consequence of the conviction of any such offender; or
(c) …

An offender who has been discharged by the Crown Court or a magistrates' court may appeal
against his conviction, or sentence or any other ancillary order made in conjunction with the
discharge (s. 14(6)).

A conviction in respect of which a discharge is granted does not count for the purpose of s. 110
or 111 of the 2000 Act. Nor did it count as a conviction of a new offence within the operational
period so as to justify activation of an old-style suspended sentence under the 2000 Act (*Moore*
[1995] QB 353). It is submitted that the position remains the same with respect to activation of
a suspended sentence for a new offence under the CJA 2003.

Section E13   Binding Over

INTRODUCTION

E13.1 This section deals with the court's power to bind over a person to keep the peace and the Crown Court's power to bind a person over to come up for judgment. The power to bind over a parent or guardian of an offender aged under 18 is dealt with at E14.6.

BINDING OVER TO KEEP THE PEACE

Power to Bind Over to Keep the Peace

E13.2 Powers of a magistrates' court to bind over a person to keep the peace arise either on complaint (under the MCA 1980, s. 115) or of the court's own motion under common-law powers and pursuant to various statutes, most importantly the Justices of the Peace Act 1361. While an order under s. 115 can be made only after a full hearing of the complaint, where the court binds over of its own motion it may do so at any time before the conclusion of criminal proceedings, on withdrawal of the case by the prosecution, on a decision by the prosecution to offer no evidence, on an adjournment, or upon acquittal of the defendant, where a justice considers that the person's conduct is such that there might be a breach of peace in the future, whether committed by him or by others. These powers, which are exercisable 'not by reason of any offence having been committed, but as a measure of preventive justice' (*Veater v Glennon* [1981] 2 All ER 304), may be used in a wide variety of situations, including as a sentencing option against a convicted offender. A person bound over to keep the peace may be made subject to a condition that he shall not possess, use, or carry a firearm (Firearms Act 1968, s. 52(1)).

E13.3 The power to bind over is frequently used as a method of disposal in cases involving minor assaults or minor incidents of public disorder, where the prosecution are prepared not to proceed, provided that the defendant agrees to be bound over. The person bound over is required to enter into a recognizance in an amount which will be forfeited if he fails to keep the peace for a specified period.

> **Justices of the Peace Act 1968, s. 1**
>
> (7) It is hereby declared that any court of record having a criminal jurisdiction has, as ancillary to that jurisdiction, the power to bind over to be of good behaviour, a person who or whose case is before the court, by requiring him to enter into his own recognisances or to find sureties or both, and committing him to prison if he does not comply.

The Crown Court is a court of record (Senior Courts Act 1981, s. 45), so that both magistrates' courts and the Crown Court have powers to bind over offenders and others who are before the court. The Court of Appeal (Criminal Division) also possesses these powers (*Sharp* [1957] 1 QB 552). Those who may be bound over include an acquitted defendant (*Inner London Crown Court, ex parte Benjamin* (1986) 85 Cr App R 267), a defendant before the court in respect of whom the prosecution has been unable to proceed (*Lincoln Crown Court, ex parte Jude* [1998] 3 All ER 737), a witness before the court (*Sheldon v Bromfield Justices* [1964] 2 QB 573), and a complainant (*Wilkins* [1907] 2 KB 380). On the other hand, the victim of an assault who is not a party to the proceedings and has not been called to give evidence against the assailant, who has pleaded guilty, cannot be bound over (*Swindon Crown Court, ex parte Pawitter Singh* [1984]

1 All ER 941), nor can a person who is the subject of an unconditional witness order, but who is in the event not required to give evidence (*Kingston-upon-Thames Crown Court, ex parte Guarino* [1986] Crim LR 325).

Bind Over: Procedural Requirements

Where a court contemplates exercising its power against a person who has not been charged **E13.4** with an offence, it should ensure that the person concerned understands what the court has in mind and give him the opportunity to make representations (*Hendon Justices, ex parte Gorchein* [1973] 1 All ER 168). It is also good practice to allow an acquitted defendant, upon whom the court proposes to make a bind over, an opportunity to address the court on the matter (*Woking Justices, ex parte Gossage* [1973] QB 448). In *Middlesex Crown Court, ex parte Khan* (1997) 161 JP 240, the Divisional Court stated that before binding over an acquitted defendant the judge should be satisfied beyond reasonable doubt that the defendant posed a potential threat to other persons and was a man of violence. A mere belief that the acquitted person might pose such a threat was not enough. In the case of a disturbance in the face of the court, natural justice does not require that the person concerned be given a warning or a chance to make representations before being bound over (*North London Metropolitan Magistrate, ex parte Haywood* [1973] 3 All ER 50). Where the court proposes to bind over a person who has been convicted, in anything other than a trivial sum, his means and other personal circumstances should be investigated, and representations allowed in respect of them (*Central Criminal Court, ex parte Boulding* [1984] QB 813). It was held in *Lincoln Crown Court, ex parte Jude* [1998] 3 All ER 737 that a sum of £500 was not so trivial an amount as to dispense with the requirement of a means inquiry. The court should fix the period of the recognizance and the sum of money to be forfeited upon breach at the time when it orders the bind over. There is no upper limit to the amount, save that it must be reasonable. A person may, therefore, be bound over in a sum which exceeds the maximum fine which could be exacted for the relevant offence (*Sandbach Justices, ex parte Williams* [1935] 2 KB 192).

The period for which the order may run is entirely within the discretion of the court. Although an order to bind over may name a person or persons for whose special protection it is made (e.g., *Wilson v Skeock* (1949) 65 TLR 418), there is no power to insert specific conditions in an order binding a person over to keep the peace or to be of good behaviour (*Randall* (1986) 8 Cr App R (S) 433). Under the Magistrates' Courts (Appeals from Binding Over Orders) Act 1956, there is a right of appeal to the Crown Court against an order by a magistrates' court to enter into recognizances to keep the peace. See, further, *Preston Crown Court, ex parte Pamplin* [1981] Crim LR 338. Where the bind over is made by the Crown Court on sentence, an appeal lies to the Court of Appeal by virtue of Criminal Appeal Act 1968, s. 50(1).

Requirement for Additional Penalty

It is unclear whether a convicted offender may be bound over to keep the peace without the **E13.5** passing of some other sentence. The wording of the Justices of the Peace Act 1968, s. 1(7) (see E13.3), indicates that the bind over is 'ancillary' to the court's criminal jurisdiction, and this may mean that a court should determine the penalty for the offence before the ancillary power of binding over to keep the peace is considered. There is evidence, however, that bind overs are sometimes imposed on sentence without any additional penalty.

Refusal or Failure to Enter into Recognizance

The sanction available to a magistrates' court in the case of a failure or a refusal to enter into a **E13.6** recognizance is imprisonment. This may be for a maximum period of six months or until the person complies with the order, if sooner (MCA 1980, s. 115(3)). Imprisonment cannot be imposed on a person who is under the age of 21 (PCC(S)A 2000, s. 89). Such a person may properly consent to be bound over even though his refusal to consent could not lead to imprisonment

(*Conlan v Oxford* (1983) 5 Cr App R (S) 237). A person aged between 18 and 20 inclusive who refuses to consent to be bound over by a magistrates' court may be detained under the PCC(S) A 2000, s. 108 (see *Howley v Oxford* (1985) 81 Cr App R 246 and **E15.5**). There is no power in these circumstances to order the detention of a person who is under the age of 18, but a magistrates' court may order such a person to attend at an attendance centre (see s. 60(1)(b)). It seems that the Crown Court may deal with a refusal to be bound over as a contempt of court.

Failure to Comply with Conditions of Order

E13.7   If a person who has been bound over by the Crown Court is adjudged to have failed to comply with the conditions of the order, the court may forfeit the whole or part of the recognizance in its discretion, allow time for payment, direct payment by instalments or reduce or discharge the recognizance (PCC(S)A 2000, s. 139(1)), but it is not empowered to impose a prison term (*Finch* (1962) 47 Cr App R 58, *Gilbert* (1974) CSP D10–3A01). The Crown Court, when forfeiting a recognizance, must fix a term of imprisonment or detention, to be served in default (PCC(S)A 2000, s. 139(2)). See further **E13.4** and **E13.5**.

In a magistrates' court, a recognizance can be declared to be forfeit only by way of an order on complaint (MCA 1980, s. 120), by virtue of whichever power originally imposed the bind over. Such proceedings are civil in character, and require only the civil standard of proof (*Marlow Justices, ex parte O'Sullivan* [1984] QB 381), but the person concerned should be told the nature of the breach alleged and be given an opportunity to present evidence, call witnesses or give an explanation (*McGregor* [1945] 2 All ER 180). There is no right of appeal against an adjudication of forfeiture (*Durham Justices, ex parte Laurent* [1945] KB 33).

BINDING OVER TO COME UP FOR JUDGMENT

Powers to Bind Over to Come Up for Judgment

E13.8   The common-law power (*Spratling* [1911] 1 KB 77) to bind over to come up for judgment, which can be exercised only by the Crown Court, may be exercised in respect of any offence except one where the penalty is fixed by law. The effect of such an order is that the offender is bound over on recognizance on specified conditions. If he breaks one or more of the conditions, he will be brought back before the court for sentence but, if he does not break any of the conditions during the specified period, he will either not be sentenced for the offence, or will receive a nominal penalty.

A bind over to come up for judgment is in lieu of sentence, and it is therefore wrong to impose it in addition to a sentence for the offence (*Ayu* [1958] 3 All ER 636). An offender must consent to the making of the order, though consent would not be vitiated by a realistic expectation of a custodial sentence in the alternative (*Williams* [1982] 3 All ER 1092). Where the judge proposes to call an offender to come up for judgment, notice shall be given to him (*David* (1939) 27 Cr App R 50).

If the offender is in breach of the order, he may forfeit the recognizance as well as being sentenced for the original offence. Where a person is brought back before the court on the ground that a recognizance entered into by him has been broken, the facts against him must be proved beyond reasonable doubt (*McGarry* (1945) 30 Cr App R 187). The order is a 'sentence' made on conviction on indictment (*Abrahams* (1952) 36 Cr App R 147) and an appeal lies to the Court of Appeal (Criminal Appeal Act 1968, s. 50(1); *Williams* [1982] 3 All ER 1092).

Section E14   Orders Against Parents

PARENTING ORDERS

Under ss. 8 to 10 of the CDA 1998, the Crown Court and youth courts have power to impose **E14.1** a parenting order on a parent or guardian of a child or young person where, *inter alia*, that child or young person has been convicted of any offence (s. 8(1)(c)). The court must be notified by the Secretary of State that local arrangements for implementation have been made. Section 8(1)(a), (b) and (d) allow for the imposing of parenting orders in consequence of the making of a child safety order in the case of a child, an anti-social behaviour order or sex offender order in the case of a child or young person, or where a parent is convicted of an offence involving failure to comply with a school attendance order or failure to secure the regular attendance at school of a registered pupil.

Section 8A, inserted by the Crime and Security Act 2010, s. 41, but never brought into force, would have made it mandatory for the court to make a parenting order when a young person under 16 has breached an ASBO. As from a date to be appointed, s. 8A is repealed by the ABCPA 2014, s. 181.

Power to Make Parenting Order

Crime and Disorder Act 1998, s. 8

E14.2

(4) A parenting order is an order which requires the parent—
   (a) to comply, for a period not exceeding twelve months, with such requirements as are specified in the order; and
   (b) subject to subsection (5) below, to attend, for a concurrent period not exceeding three months, such counselling or guidance sessions as may be specified in directions given by the responsible officer.

(5) A parenting order may, but need not, include such a requirement as is mentioned in subsection (4)(b) above in any case where a parenting order under this section or any other enactment has been made in respect of the parent on a previous occasion.

(6) The relevant condition is that the parenting order would be desirable in the interests of preventing—
   ...
   (b) in a case falling within paragraph (c) of that subsection, the commission of any further offence by the child or young person;
   ...

(7) The requirements that may be specified under subsection (4)(a) above are those which the court considers desirable in the interests of preventing any such repetition or, as the case may be, the commission of any such further offence.

(7A) A counselling or guidance programme which a parent is required to attend by virtue of subsection (4)(b) above may be or include a residential course but only if the court is satisfied—
   (a) that the attendance of the parent at a residential course is likely to be more effective than his attendance at a non-residential course in preventing any such repetition or, as the case may be, the commission of any such further offence, and
   (b) that any interference with family life which is likely to result from the attendance of the parent at a residential course is proportionate in all the circumstances.

(8) [Meaning of 'responsible officer'.]

Requirements specified in s. 8(4)(a) might commonly include that the parent ensure that the child is accompanied to and from school each day, and is indoors by a certain hour in the evening. It is clear from s. 8(4)(b) and (5) that the court has no discretion to dispense with the requirement of attendance at counselling sessions, unless the parent has been the subject of a parenting order on a previous occasion. While s. 8 creates a power to pass a parenting order where the young offender is aged under 18, s. 9 goes further and places a duty on the court to make a parenting order where the young offender is aged under 16. If, however, the court is not satisfied that the 'relevant condition' is fulfilled (i.e. that the making of a parenting order would be desirable in the interests of preventing the commission of any further offence by the child or young person under 16) then the court must state in open court that it is not so satisfied, and why it is not (s. 9(1)). A similar duty, and similar exception, apply where the offender has been made subject to an anti-social behaviour order (s. 9(1B)).

By the CJA 2003, s. 324 and sch. 34, a youth court has power to make a parenting order at the same time as sentencing the young offender by referral order (see **E10**). This combination was formerly not permitted. If the offender is aged under 16, such that the youth court would normally be under a duty to impose a parenting order unless not satisfied that the 'relevant condition' is fulfilled, such a duty does *not* extend to cases where the youth court is considering whether to make a parenting order at the same time as sentencing the young offender by referral order.

E14.3   Before making a parenting order the court need not obtain a pre-sentence report, but, by s. 9(2), before making a parenting order in a case where the young offender is aged under 16, the court must obtain and consider information about the young offender's family circumstances and the likely effect of the order on those circumstances. By s. 9(2A), which does not apply in respect of any offence to which s. 8A applies (see **E14.1**), if the court proposes to make a parenting order at the same time as sentencing the young offender by referral order, the court must obtain and consider a report by an appropriate officer indicating the requirements proposed to be included in the parenting order and indicating their desirability in preventing the commission of further offences by the young offender. Section 9(3) requires that before making a parenting order the court must explain to the parent in ordinary language the effect of the order and of the requirements proposed to be included in it, the consequences which may follow if he fails to comply with any of those requirements, and that the court has power to review the order on the application either of the parent or of the responsible officer. Requirements specified in, and directions given under, a parenting order shall, as far as practicable, be such as to avoid any conflict with the parent's religious beliefs and any interference with the times, if any, at which he normally works or attends an educational establishment (s. 9(4)). In *R (M) v Inner London Crown Court* [2003] EWHC 301 (Admin), the Divisional Court held that the making of parenting orders did not contravene the ECHR, Article 8, guaranteeing respect for private and family life.

Variation and Appeal

E14.4   If, while the parenting order is in force, application is made to the court either by the responsible officer or by the parent, the court may, where appropriate, make an order discharging the parenting order or varying it by cancelling any provision included within it or by inserting in it any provision which could have been included in the order if the court had then the power to make it and were exercising that power (s. 9(5)). If an application is made for the discharge of a parenting order and that application is dismissed, no fresh application for discharge can be made without the consent of the court which made the order (s. 9(6)).

A person in respect of whom a parenting order has been made by virtue of s. 8(1)(c) (commission of offence by offender aged under 18) has the same right of appeal against that order as if the offence that led to the making of the order were an offence committed by him and the order were a sentence passed on him for the offence (s. 10(4)).

Breach of Parenting Order

If while a parenting order is in force the parent without reasonable excuse fails to comply with **E14.5** any requirement included in the order or specified in directions given by the responsible officer, he shall be liable on summary conviction to a fine not exceeding level 3 on the standard scale (s. 9(7)). It would appear that in the absence of such failure to comply by the parent, commission of a further offence by the child does not constitute a breach of the parenting order.

BINDING OVER OF PARENT OR GUARDIAN OF OFFENDER AGED UNDER 18

By the PCC(S)A 2000, s. 150(1), where a child or young person (a person aged under 18) is **E14.6** convicted of an offence the court may exercise its power to bind over his parent or guardian. Where the offender is aged under 16 when sentenced it shall be the duty of the court to bind over the parent or guardian of the young offender if it is satisfied that to do so would be desirable in the interests of preventing the commission by the young offender of further offences. If the court is not satisfied of that on the particular facts of the case, it should state in open court that it is not, and give reasons. Such an order cannot be made where the young offender has been sentenced by way of referral order (see **E10**).

By s. 150(2) and (3), the court is empowered to order the parent or guardian to enter into a recognizance (in a sum not exceeding £1,000) to take proper care of the offender and exercise proper control over him. Entry into the recognizance requires the consent of the parent or guardian, but if consent is refused and the court considers that refusal unreasonable, the parent or guardian may be punished by a fine not exceeding £1,000. A court which has passed a sentence which consists of or includes a youth rehabilitation order may include in the recognizance a provision that the young offender's parent or guardian ensure that the young offender complies with the requirements of that sentence. The maximum duration of the recognizance is until the offender reaches the age of 18, or for a period of three years, whichever is the shorter period (s. 150(4)).

In fixing the level of the recognizance, the court shall take into account, among other things, the means of the parent or guardian, whether doing so has the effect of increasing or reducing the level of the recognizance (s. 150(7)).

As far as forfeiture of the recognizance is concerned, s. 150(5) states that the MCA 1980, s. 120, shall apply in relation to a recognizance under s. 150 as it does to a recognizance to keep the peace (see **E13.7**). The court may order forfeiture of the whole, or part, of the recognizance, together with costs. A right of appeal against an order under s. 150 made by a magistrates' court is created by s. 150(8) and where the order is made by the Crown Court, a similar right applies under s. 150(9). A court may subsequently vary or revoke an order made under s. 150 on application by the parent or guardian, if it appears to be in the interests of justice to do so, having regard to any change in circumstances since the order was made (s. 150(10)).

FINE, COSTS, COMPENSATION OR SURCHARGE TO BE PAID BY PARENT OR GUARDIAN

The parent or guardian of a juvenile may be ordered by the court to pay the fine, costs or order **E14.7** for compensation imposed upon a juvenile by virtue of the PCC(S)A 2000, s. 137.

Powers of Criminal Courts (Sentencing) Act 2000, s. 137

(1) Where—
    (a) a child or young person (that is to say, any person aged under 18) is convicted of any offence for the commission of which a fine or costs may be imposed or a compensation order may be made, and

(b) the court is of opinion that the case would best be met by the imposition of a fine or costs or the making of such an order, whether with or without any other punishment, the court shall order that the fine, compensation or costs awarded be paid by the parent or guardian of the child or young person instead of by the child or young person himself, unless the court is satisfied—

(i) that the parent or guardian cannot be found; or

(ii) that it would be unreasonable to make an order for payment, having regard to the circumstances of the case.

Section 137(1A), provides that any surcharge (see E15.24) must be paid by the parent or guardian unless he cannot be found or it is unreasonable to require him to pay. Section 137(2) further provides that where a person under 18 would otherwise be required to pay a fine in respect of breach of a youth rehabilitation order, reparation order, an attendance centre order, attendance centre rules, or supervision requirements under a detention and training order, the court shall order the fine to be paid by the parent or guardian, subject to the same qualifications as appear in s. 137(1). The court may make a financial circumstances order with respect to the parent or guardian (s. 136(1)).

Section 137(3) states that in the case of a young person who has attained the age of 16 years, subsections (1) and (2) shall have effect as if, instead of imposing a duty, they conferred a power to make such an order. While an order under s. 137 may be made against a parent or guardian who has failed to attend court after having been required to do so, apart from such case no order should be made without giving the parent or guardian an opportunity of being heard (s. 137(4)). An appeal against an order made by a magistrates' court under s. 137 lies to the Crown Court (s. 137(6)) and an appeal against an order made by the Crown Court under s. 137 lies to the Court of Appeal (s. 137(7)).

E14.8   The court should not make an order under s. 137 against a parent or guardian without first considering the means of that parent or guardian (*Lenihan v West Yorkshire Metropolitan Police* (1981) 3 Cr App R (S) 42). It may be 'unreasonable' for the court to make an order under s. 137 in a case where the parent or guardian has done all that he or she reasonably could to prevent the offending (*Sheffield Crown Court, ex parte Clarkson* (1986) 8 Cr App R (S) 454; *TA v DPP* [1997] 1 Cr App R (S) 1; *J-B* [2004] 2 Cr App R (S) 211). Assessment of the means of the parent or guardian, or assessment of the extent to which the parent or guardian has been neglectful of the offender, should be made on the basis of properly admissible evidence and not simply assumed from the pre-sentence report prepared upon the offender.

Section 137(8) provides that where a local authority has parental responsibility for a child or young person, and the child or young person is in the care of a local authority, or is being provided with accommodation by them in the exercise of their social services functions, references to 'parent or guardian' should be construed as references to that local authority. In *D v DPP* (1995) 16 Cr App R (S) 1040, the Divisional Court held that a court should not make an order against the local authority in a case where the authority had done all that it reasonably and properly could to protect the public from the young offender and to keep the young offender from criminal ways; where the local authority so contends, it should be ready to provide evidence to the court of the steps which it has taken. In *Bedfordshire County Council v DPP* [1996] 1 Cr App R (S) 322 the Divisional Court further held that, before an order for payment by a local authority could be made, a causative link should normally be established between any fault proved on the part of the council and the offences committed. If no such causative fault was shown to the satisfaction of the court, it would be unreasonable to order compensation. 'Local authority' and 'parental responsibility' have the same meaning as in the Children Act 1989 (s. 137(9)).

Section E15   Fines

IN THE CROWN COURT

Powers of Crown Court to Impose Fines

Criminal Justice Act 2003, s. 163

E15.1

> Where a person is convicted on indictment of any offence, other than an offence for which the
> sentence is fixed by law or falls to be imposed under section 110(2) or 111(2) of the Sentencing Act
> or under section 224A, 225(2) or 226(2) of this Act, the court, if not precluded from sentencing the
> offender by its exercise of some other power, may impose a fine instead of or in addition to dealing
> with him in any other way in which the court has power to deal with him, subject however to any
> enactment requiring the offender to be dealt with in a particular way.

Section 163 deals with the general power of the Crown Court to impose a fine on an offender
convicted on indictment. In general the Crown Court can impose a fine on an offender either
instead of, or in addition to, dealing with him in any other way. There are some sentences
which cannot be combined with a fine. A fine cannot be combined with a hospital order
(Mental Health Act 1983, s. 37(8)), nor with a discharge when sentencing for a single offence
(*McClelland* [1951] 1 All ER 557). There are also the exceptional cases, referred to in s. 163,
where a fine is not available as a penalty.

There is no statutory limit to the amount of fine which may be imposed by the Crown Court   **E15.2**
(see also the Criminal Law Act 1977, s. 32(1)), and this includes a case where an offender is
committed for sentence under the PCC(S)A 2000, s. 3, following conviction in a magistrates'
court of an offence triable either way. If, however, the magistrates' court commits a person
to the Crown Court under s. 6 (see D23.57), the Crown Court must observe all the limitations on sentencing powers which would have applied in the magistrates' court with regard,
for example, to the limitations on magistrates' powers to imprison and financial limitations
on fines (see E15.8) or compensation orders. These limitations apply even where the offence
is triable either way and the magistrates' court might have committed to the Crown Court
under s. 3.

Powers of Criminal Courts (Sentencing) Act 2000, s. 139

> (1) Subject to the provisions of this section, if the Crown Court imposes a fine on any person or
>   forfeits his recognisance, the court may make an order—
>   (a) allowing time for the payment of the amount of the fine or the amount due under the
>   recognisance;
>   (b) directing payment of that amount by instalments of such amounts and on such dates
>   respectively as may be specified in the order;
>   (c) in the case of a recognisance, discharging the recognisance or reducing the amount due
>   under it.
> (2) Subject to the provisions of this section, if the Crown Court imposes a fine on any person or
>   forfeits his recognisance, the court shall make an order fixing a term of imprisonment or of
>   detention under section 108 above (detention of persons aged 18 to 20 for default) which he
>   is to undergo if any sum which he is liable to pay is not duly paid or recovered.

Power and Duty of Court to Fix Term in Default

Although a term of imprisonment or detention to be served in default must be fixed in every   **E15.3**
case where the Crown Court imposes a fine or forfeits a recognizance (unless the offender is

under 18 years of age), it seems that a failure to fix such a term does not invalidate the fine itself (*Hamilton* (1980) 2 Cr App R (S) 1). For the PCC(S)A 2000, s. 108, see E15.5, and for the table of maximum periods of imprisonment or detention in a young offender institution which may be fixed in default, see E15.7. The term which is fixed should relate to the whole sum, rather than to any instalment (*Power* (1986) 8 Cr App R (S) 8). Where fines are imposed in respect of more than one offence, the terms to be served in default may be ordered to run concurrently or consecutively (*Savundranayagan* [1968] 3 All ER 439), and the court may order that the term(s) to be served in default may run concurrently or consecutively to any term of imprisonment or detention in a young offender institution to which the offender is sentenced at that time by the court or which he is currently serving (s. 139(5)). A term of imprisonment in default may be imposed consecutively to a maximum prison sentence imposed for the same offence (*Carver* [1955] 1 All ER 413). Consecutive custodial terms are, however, subject to the totality principle (*Savundranayagan* [1968] 3 All ER 439). See, further, *Benmore* (1983) 5 Cr App R (S) 468.

Where the Crown Court imposes a fine on committal for sentence from a magistrates' court, in circumstances where the powers of the Crown Court are limited to those of the magistrates' court, the Crown Court must specify the term to be served in default (s. 139(7)).

E15.4   **Powers of Criminal Courts (Sentencing) Act 2000, s. 139**

(3) No person shall on the occasion when a fine is imposed on him or his recognisance is forfeited by the Crown Court be committed to prison or detained in pursuance of an order under subsection (2) above unless—
  (a) in the case of an offence punishable with imprisonment, he appears to the court to have sufficient means to pay the sum forthwith;
  (b) it appears to the court that he is unlikely to remain long enough at a place of abode in the United Kingdom to enable payment of the sum to be enforced by other methods; or
  (c) on the occasion when the order is made the court sentences him to immediate imprisonment, custody for life or detention in a young offender institution for that or another offence, or so sentences him for an offence in addition to forfeiting his recognisance, or he is already serving a sentence of custody for life or a term—
    (i)   of imprisonment
    (ii) of detention in a young offender institution; or
    (iii) of detention under section 108 above.

E15.5   **Powers of Criminal Courts (Sentencing) Act 2000, s. 108**

(1) In any case where, but for section 89(1) above, a court would have power—
  (a) to commit a person aged at least 18 but under 21 to prison for default in payment of a fine or any other sum of money, or
  (b) to make an order fixing a term of imprisonment in the event of such a default by such a person, or
  (c) to commit such a person to prison for contempt of court or any kindred offence,
the court shall have power, subject to subsection (3) below, to commit him to be detained under this section or, as the case may be, to make an order fixing a term of detention under this section in the event of default, for a term not exceeding the term of imprisonment.
(2) For the purposes of subsection (1) above, the power of a court to order a person to be imprisoned under section 23 of the Attachment of Earnings Act 1971 shall be taken to be a power to commit him to prison.
(3) No court shall commit a person to be detained under this section unless it is of the opinion that no other method of dealing with him is appropriate; and in forming any such opinion, the court—
  (a) shall take into account all such information about the circumstances of the default or contempt (including any aggravating or mitigating factors) as is available to it; and
  (b) may take into account any information about that person which is before it.
(4) Where a magistrates' court commits a person to be detained under this section, it shall—
  (a) state in open court the reason for its opinion that no other method of dealing with him is appropriate; and

(b) cause that reason to be specified in the warrant of commitment and to be entered in the register.

There is no power to fix a term of detention under s. 108 in relation to an offender aged under 18 (*Basid* [1996] 1 Cr App R (S) 421; *Byas* (1995) 16 Cr App R (S) 869). It should be noted that, although s. 108(3) states that no court shall commit an offender to be detained unless 'no other method of dealing with him is appropriate', a sentence of detention under s. 108, is not a 'custodial sentence' for the purposes of the PCC(S)A 2000: s. 76(1) (see **E2.1**). The obligation in s. 83 (restriction on imposing custodial sentence on persons under 21 not legally represented), also does not apply in the present context.

Where a court has power to commit a person aged at least 21 but under 25 to prison in default **E15.6** of payment of any sum of money, or a court would have power (but for the restrictions on imprisonment of young offenders and defaulters), to commit a person aged under 21 to prison in default of payment of any sum of money, or for failing to do or abstain from doing anything required to be done or left undone, the court may make an attendance centre order, requiring the offender to attend at an attendance centre for such number of hours as may be specified (PCC(S)A 2000, s. 60(1)(b) and (c)). The aggregate number of hours of attendance must not be less than 12, except where the offender is aged under 14 and the court is of the opinion that 12 hours would be excessive having regard to his age or other circumstances. The aggregate number of hours shall not exceed 12, except where the court is of the opinion, having regard to all the circumstances, that 12 hours would be inadequate, and in that case shall not exceed 24 hours (where the person is aged under 16) or 36 hours (where the person is aged 16 or over but under 21 or, where s. 60(1)(c) applies, under 25) (s. 60(3) and (4)). A person shall not be required to attend at an attendance centre more than once a day or for more than three hours on any occasion (s. 60(10)). If the defaulter pays the whole sum outstanding, the attendance centre order ceases to have effect, and payment of the sum outstanding shall reduce the number of hours proportionately (s. 60(12)).

Table of Maximum Periods in Default

The periods set out in the following table are the maximum periods of imprisonment or deten- **E15.7** tion to be served in default, applicable to the corresponding fine values (PCC(S)A 2000, s. 139(4)):

Not exceeding £200	7 days
Over £200, not exceeding £500	14 days
Over £500, not exceeding £1,000	28 days
Over £1,000, not exceeding £2,500	45 days
Over £2,500, not exceeding £5,000	3 months
Over £5,000, not exceeding £10,000	6 months
Over £10,000, not exceeding £20,000	12 months
Over £20,000, not exceeding £50,000	18 months
Over £50,000, not exceeding £100,000	2 years
Over £100,000, not exceeding £250,000	3 years
Over £250,000, not exceeding £1 million	5 years
Over £1 million	10 years

These are maximum periods, and the Crown Court has discretion to fix a shorter term within the appropriate bracket (*Szrajber* (1994) 15 Cr App R (S) 821). Where more than one fine is imposed, consecutive terms may be fixed. Where, exceptionally, a magistrates' court is empowered to fix a term in default of payment of a fine, the same periods apply, except that a default term in excess of 12 months cannot be exceeded (MCA 1980, sch. 4).

IN THE MAGISTRATES' COURT

Powers of Magistrates' Court to Impose Fines

E15.8 Where an offender has been summarily convicted of an offence triable either way which is listed in the MCA 1980, sch. 1, the magistrates may fine him an amount not exceeding the 'prescribed sum' (MCA 1980, s. 32(1)). By s. 32(9) of that Act, 'the prescribed sum' means £5,000. Where, however, the offender has been summarily convicted of an offence triable either way, and the statute creating the offence prescribes a particular maximum penalty upon summary conviction, the magistrates may fine him an amount not exceeding the maximum penalty indicated in the statute creating the offence or the prescribed sum, whichever is the greater (s. 32(2)), and subject to the exception of certain drug offences listed in s. 32(5). Where the maximum penalty indicated in the statute creating the offence is expressed to be 'the statutory maximum', that maximum is the prescribed sum (i.e. £5,000). The effect of the LASPO 2012, s. 85 (not yet in force), will be that such an offence is punishable by a fine of any amount rather than being limited to a maximum of £5,000, and this removal of the limit will apply to any 'relevant offence' which is 'punishable on summary conviction by a fine or maximum fine of £5,000 or more (however expressed)' (s. 85(1)). In the case of an offender under 18 years of age, a lower maximum fine applies (see **E15.10**).

The maximum fine which may be imposed for a summary offence is nearly always prescribed in the statute which creates the offence. If the statute refers only to punishment by means of imprisonment, power to impose a fine at level 3 is nonetheless included (MCA 1980, s. 34(3)).

Standard Scale of Maximum Fines for Summary Offences and Guideline Fines in Magistrates' Courts

E15.9 The 'standard scale' of maximum fines for summary offences is contained in the CJA 1982, s. 37(2). This scale applies to summary offences only; for offences triable either way dealt with summarily, see **E15.8**. For offenders under 18, a special maximum fine applies (see **E15.10**).

Level on the scale	Amount of fine
1	£200
2	£500
3	£1,000
4	£2,500
5	£5,000

The *Magistrates' Court Sentencing Guidelines* provide guideline fines for magistrates' courts expressed as one of three fine bands (A, B or C). For the applicable principles for fixing the level of a fine in a particular case, set out in the Explanatory Material in part 5 of those Guidelines, see Supplement, **SG-356** *et seq.*

Fining Juveniles

E15.10 Under the PCC(S)A 2000, s. 135, where a person under 18 years of age is found guilty by a magistrates' court of an offence in respect of which the court would normally be empowered to impose a fine exceeding £1,000, the amount of the fine imposed shall not exceed £1,000. Section 135 also provides that, if the offender is under the age of 14 and the court could otherwise have imposed a fine exceeding £250, the amount of the fine imposed shall not exceed £250.

There is no limit upon the fine which may be imposed by a Crown Court upon a juvenile convicted on indictment.

See **E14.7** for the court's power to order that a fine be paid by a parent or guardian.

The definitive sentencing guideline, *Sentencing Youths*, says that in practice many young people who offend have few financial resources. It will rarely be appropriate to take an education maintenance allowance or similar provision into account as a resource from which a financial penalty may be paid, especially where the recipient is a young person who is living independently or as part of a household primarily dependent upon state benefits (paras. 9.2 and 9.3: see Supplement, **SG-524**).

Enforcement of Fines

Enforcement of all fines is carried out by magistrates' courts, whether the fine was imposed in a magistrates' court or in the Crown Court. The procedure for enforcement of fines is contained in the MCA 1980, ss. 75 to 91, and the Courts Act 2003. By virtue of the definition of 'fine' in s. 150 of the 1980 Act, the same procedures also apply to the enforcement of compensation orders, surcharges, the recovery of recognizances which the court has ordered to be forfeited and any other 'sum adjudged to be paid by a conviction or order of a magistrates' court', subject to certain exceptions which are indicated where appropriate below. The magistrates' court which is responsible for enforcement is that court which imposed the fine or, if the fine was imposed by the Crown Court, the court specified in the fine order or, if none was specified, the court which committed the offender for trial or sentence to the Crown Court. If the offender is now residing in a different local justice area, a transfer of fine order may be made (MCA 1980, s. 89). When ordering a fine, the Crown Court must fix a term to be served in default (see **E15.3**) but a magistrates' court should not normally do so (ss. 82(3) and 77(2)). **E15.11**

When a fine is imposed it becomes due for payment immediately. The magistrates' court may, however, instead of requiring immediate payment, allow time for payment or order payment by instalments (s. 75(1)). Subsequently, further time may be given (s. 75(2)). If the court orders payment by instalments, default in any one instalment is taken to be a default in payment of all instalments then unpaid (s. 75(3)). By the Courts Act 2003, sch. 5, para. 12, the court must make a collection order in every case in which a fine or compensation order is imposed unless this would be impracticable or inappropriate. If an offender defaults on a collection order and is not already subject to an attachment of earnings order or application for benefit reduction, a fines officer must make an attachment of earnings order or application for benefit reduction. A court must in any event, unless it would be impracticable or inappropriate to do so, make an attachment of earnings order or application for benefit reduction whenever a compensation order has been imposed (sch. 5, para. 7A) or the court concludes that the offender is an existing defaulter and that the existing default cannot be disregarded (para. 8). In other cases, the court may make an attachment of earnings order or application for benefit reduction with the offender's consent. (para. 9).

If the offender fails to pay the whole or any part of the sum within the time allowed by the court, the magistrates' court may issue a summons or warrant requiring the offender to appear or issue a warrant to arrest him and bring him before the court to conduct a means inquiry to investigate the offender's ability to pay (MCA 1980, s. 83). The court may require that the offender produce evidence of his income and outgoings. If the court orders the offender to produce a statement of means and the offender fails to do so, such failure is an offence punishable by a fine up to level 3 (s. 84(2)). If the offender knowingly or recklessly furnishes a statement which is false in a material particular, or knowingly fails to disclose any material fact, this is an offence punishable with imprisonment not exceeding four months, a fine not exceeding level 3, or both (s. 84(3)). **E15.12**

In the light of information received by the court at the means inquiry, the magistrates may grant further time to the offender for payment of the fine, or arrange payment by instalments, or reduce the amount of each instalment (s. 75). The court may remit the whole or any part of the fine having regard to any change in the offender's circumstances since his conviction (s. 85(1)). This requirement may be satisfied where the defaulter's means have changed since the fine was imposed, or arrears have accumulated by the imposition of additional fines to the point where repayment of the total amount within a reasonable time becomes unlikely, or the defaulter is serving a period of imprisonment. There is no power to remit excise penalties, which include fines and back duty for using an untaxed vehicle. The court may also remit or reduce the fine where the fine was imposed in the absence of adequate information about the offender's means, either because he was convicted in his absence or failed to comply with an order to furnish information concerning his means. If the Crown Court imposed the fine, the magistrates may remit the fine in whole or in part only if they first obtain the consent of the Crown Court. It should be noted that the power to remit is restricted to fines and there is no equivalent power in respect of compensation orders (s. 85(4)).

E15.13   The court may order the offender's *immediate imprisonment*, (or, in the case of an offender aged 18 or over but under 21, detention under the PCC(S)A 2000, s. 108), for the term originally specified as being the time to be served in default or, if no such time was specified, a term specified by the court having regard to the table in the MCA 1980, sch. 4. This table corresponds to the first seven entries listed in the PCC(S)A 2000, s. 139(4), which is set out at E15.7. The period of commitment should be the shortest which in the view of the court is likely to succeed in obtaining payment, and the periods prescribed are to be regarded as maxima rather than the norm. The period of imprisonment may be suspended on condition that regular payments are made. Where such payments are not made the defaulter should be brought back before the court for consideration of whether the period of imprisonment should be implemented. An immediate committal to custody can be ordered only where the defaulter is already serving a custodial sentence (MCA 1980, s. 82(3)), if a means inquiry establishes that the defaulter has the means to pay immediately and the offence was punishable by imprisonment (s. 82(4)(a)), or where there has been a means inquiry and the court is satisfied that the default is due to wilful refusal or culpable neglect, and has considered or tried all other methods of enforcing payment and concluded that they are inappropriate or unsuccessful (s. 82(4)(b)). The other methods that the court is required to have considered or tried are money payment supervision order (s. 88), application for deduction from benefit, attachment of earnings order, distress warrant, the taking of civil proceedings, and, if the offender is aged under 25, an attendance centre order.

The requirement that the court must have 'considered or tried' all other methods of enforcement must be complied with and allows no room for the exercise of discretion (*Norwich Magistrates' Court, ex parte Tigger (formerly Lilly)* (1987) 151 JP 689). The warrant of commitment should state the grounds on which the court was satisfied that it was undesirable or impracticable to use the other methods of enforcement (*Oldham Justices, ex parte Cawley* [1997] QB 1). For an offender aged over 18 but under 21, the PCC(S)A 2000, s. 108(4), further requires the justices to specify in the warrant their reasons for concluding that detention is the only appropriate method of dealing with the defaulter (see E15.5). 'Wilful refusal', which means a deliberate defiance of the court order, or 'culpable neglect', which means a reckless disregard of the court order, must be established by proof beyond reasonable doubt (*South Tyneside Justices, ex parte Martin* (1995) *The Independent*, 20 September 1995).

FINES: SENTENCING PRINCIPLES

E15.14   The CJA 2003, s. 162, provides that, where an individual has been convicted of an offence, the court may, before sentencing him, make a 'financial circumstances order' with respect to him. Both magistrates' courts and the Crown Court may make such an order. Where a magistrates' court has been notified in accordance with the MCA 1980, s. 12(4), that an individual wishes to plead guilty without appearing before the court, the court also has power to make a financial circumstances order (s. 162(2)). A 'financial circumstances order' is an order requiring the relevant individual 'to give to the court, within such period as may be specified in the order, such a statement of his assets and other financial circumstances as the court may require' (s. 162(3)). An individual who, without reasonable excuse, fails to comply with a financial circumstances order is liable on summary conviction to a fine not exceeding level 3 (s. 162(4)), and if such individual makes, in pursuance of a financial circumstances order, a statement which he knows to be false in a material particular, is reckless as to its falsity or knowingly fails to disclose any material fact he is liable on summary conviction to a fine not exceeding level 4 (s. 162(5)).

Under the CJA 2003, s. 164, the following statutory principles are applicable to the fixing of **E15.15** fines, both in the Crown Court and in magistrates' courts.

Criminal Justice Act 2003, s. 164

(1) Before fixing the amount of any fine to be imposed on an offender who is an individual, a court must inquire into his financial circumstances.

(2) The amount of any fine fixed by a court must be such as, in the opinion of the court, reflects the seriousness of the offence.

(3) In fixing the amount of any fine to be imposed on an offender (whether an individual or other person), a court must take into account the circumstances of the case including, among other things, the financial circumstances of the offender so far as they are known, or appear, to the court.

(4) Subsection (3) above applies whether taking into account the financial circumstances of the offender has the effect of increasing or reducing the amount of the fine.

(4A) In applying subsection (3), a court must not reduce the amount of a fine on account of any surcharge it orders the offender to pay under section 161A, except to the extent that he has insufficient means to pay both.

(5) Where—

(a) an offender has been convicted in his absence in pursuance of section 11 or 12 of the Magistrates' Courts Act 1980 (non-appearance of accused), or

(b) an offender—

   (i) has failed to furnish a statement of his financial circumstances in response to a request which is an official request for the purposes of section 20A of the Criminal Justice Act 1991 (offence of making false statement as to financial circumstances).

   (ii) has failed to comply with an order under section 162(1) above, or

   (iii) has otherwise failed to cooperate with the court in its inquiry into his financial circumstances,

and the court considers that it has insufficient information to make a proper determination of the financial circumstances of the offender, it may make such determination as it thinks fit.

For the MCA 1980, ss. 11 and 12, see **D22.13** and **D22.24** respectively. Section 164 is an important section concerned with fixing the amount of a fine. The court must inquire into the financial circumstances of an offender before fixing the amount of a fine. When determining the amount of the fine, the court must take into account the financial circumstances of the offender, the seriousness of the offence, and the circumstances of the case.

Proportionality to Gravity of Offence

The first principle in relation to the use of the fine, whether in the Crown Court or in mag- **E15.16** istrates' courts, is that the selection of the fine as a sentence, and the determination of the appropriate level of any fine, should reflect the seriousness of the offence. A fine is an inappropriate penalty where the seriousness of the offence requires an immediate custodial sentence. An example is *A-G's Ref (No. 41 of 1994)* (1995) 16 Cr App R (S) 792, where fines totalling £350 had been imposed on the offender who had pleaded guilty to wounding with intent to cause grievous bodily harm. The Court of Appeal held that the sentence was 'absurd', and unduly lenient and substituted a custodial term of 30 months. On the other hand, there are cases which are not so serious as to justify a fine. In *Jamieson* (1975) 60 Cr App R 318 the offender, who had a clean record and substantial personal mitigation, was convicted of theft of a half bottle of whisky from a supermarket and fined £300. The Court of Appeal varied the sentence to a conditional discharge.

It is clear from the CJA 2003, s. 164(2), that the level of the fine imposed should reflect the seriousness of the offence. The imposition of the maximum available fine should be reserved for the most serious instances of the offence which are reasonably likely to occur. The existence of significant mitigation, such as the offender's guilty plea, should normally preclude the imposition of the maximum fine. In *Universal Salvage v Boothby* (1983) 5 Cr App R (S) 428 a company was fined for breach of regulations requiring it to have in its lorry proper equipment to record the journeys made. It was accepted that, in reliance on a letter from the relevant government department, the company had reasonably believed that the regulations were not applicable to them. Liability for the offence was strict, but the Divisional Court held that the circumstances provided considerable mitigation and that the imposition of the maximum fine on the company by the magistrates' court constituted an error of law. In all cases involving fines it is the 'first duty' of the sentencer to 'measure that fine against the gravity of the offence' (per Kenneth Jones LJ in *Messana* (1981) 3 Cr App R (S) 88), having regard to all relevant matters in aggravation and mitigation.

Sellafield Ltd and Network Rail Infrastructure [2014] EWCA Crim 49 and *Southern Water Services* [2014] EWCA Crim 120 provide good examples of the approach which a court should take to sentencing corporations (in these cases for breaches of environmental or health and safety regulations). Familiar issues of harm and culpability of the corporation determine the matter of offence seriousness. Culpability includes previous similar breaches of relevant regulations.

The court should not calculate the level of the fine on the basis of the compensation which would have been received if the victim had made application to the Criminal Injuries Compensation Board (*Roberts* (1980) 2 Cr App R (S) 121).

In *Warden* [1996] 2 Cr App (S) 269, the Court of Appeal observed that, where an offender had spent time on remand in custody but had subsequently received a fine as the appropriate sentence for the offence, some credit should normally be given for the time spent in custody. The amount of the credit was a matter for the discretion of the sentencer.

E15.17   Helpful guidance on the proper use of fines when imposed for several different offences was provided by the Court of Appeal in *Yorkshire Water Services* [2002] 2 Cr App R (S) 37, where the defendant company pleaded guilty to 17 counts of supplying water unfit for human consumption. The counts related to four separate incidents in which contaminated water was supplied, and a large number of households were affected. In reducing the total fine imposed from £119,000 to £80,000, Rougier J stated that the relevant considerations in setting the fine in a case of this sort were (1) the degree of culpability involved in the commission of the offence, (2) the damage done, considering both its spacial and temporal ambit together with the physical and economic ill effects, (3) the offender's previous record, including failure to heed warnings, (4) the need to strike a balance between a fitting punishment and avoiding counter-productive effects on the offending organisation, (5) the offender's plea, attitude, and performance after the event. In determining the appropriate fine, the court should determine the penalty for any one incident rather than 'tot up' the various manifestations of that incident. In *Chelmsford Crown Court, ex parte Birchall* (1989) 11 Cr App R (S) 510, the Divisional Court said that the application of a 'rigid formula' to the calculation of a fine was incorrect, even for a single offence, and it was wrong to apply it to each of ten offences and add the figures up: the courts had to consider all the circumstances and apply the principles of sentencing which were well known. The main importance of this decision is its clear endorsement of the application to fines of the totality principle (see, in relation to custodial sentences, **E1.21**). When fining in respect of a number of offences, the sentencer must review the total sentence and ensure that it remains proportionate to the totality of the offending, as well as being within the offender's capacity to pay. The CJA 2003, s.166(3), reinforces this sentencing principle by stating that the court may mitigate the overall sentence 'by applying any rule of law as to the totality of sentences'.

Further guidance on the appropriate level of fines for particular offences may be obtained from the *Magistrates' Court Sentencing Guidelines* (see Supplement, **SG-237** *et seq.*).

Taking into Account Means of Offender

E15.18   It is well established that while a fine is meant to be a punishment and it is perfectly proper for the offender to have to endure a degree of hardship in paying the fine, since 'one of the objects of the fine is to remind the offender that what he has done is wrong' (per Lord Lane CJ in *Olliver*

(1989) 11 Cr App R (S) 10), the imposition of a fine which is quite beyond the means of the offender is wrong in principle.

Where the offender lacks the means to pay the level of fine which is proportionate to the seriousness of the offence, it is contrary to principle to impose a custodial sentence instead. According to Roskill LJ in *Reeves* (1972) 56 Cr App R 366, where the offender had pleaded guilty to obtaining £600 by deception and had received a prison sentence of nine months, the comments made by the sentencer 'must plainly have indicated to the appellant...that he was being sent to prison not because the offence itself merited a sentence of immediate imprisonment but because he had not the financial wherewithal to pay a substantial fine. That...is, of course, completely wrong.'

Where the offender is well-off and paying the fine proportionate to the offence would cause **E15.19** him little inconvenience, it is contrary to principle to impose a custodial sentence instead (*Gillies* [1965] Crim LR 64). It is, however, right to raise the level of the fine in such a case, so as to increase its impact on the offender, although the Court of Appeal in *Jerome* [2001] 1 Cr App R (S) 316 said that there must remain some proportionality between the offence and the fine. In that case a fine of £10,000 imposed on a relatively affluent offender for handling stolen goods worth £2,739 was said to be manifestly excessive, and was reduced to £6,000. It should be noted that the CJA 2003, s. 164(4), makes it clear that the level of a fine should be adjusted upwards or downwards to take account of the offender's ability to pay. This does not, of course, affect the principle that an offender who is well-off should not be dealt with by financial penalty where the offence itself merits custody and an offender who is less well-off would have gone to prison (*Markwick* (1953) 37 Cr App R 125). The principle that a rich offender must not be permitted to 'buy his way out of prison' is a fundamental one, and it applies equally where the offender has family or friends who are able to meet a substantial fine (*Curtis* (1984) 6 Cr App R (S) 250).

The requirement that the court should adjust the level of the fine in accordance with the offender's means entails that the court should not assume that someone other than the offender will be paying the fine. In *Charambous* (1984) 6 Cr App R (S) 389, where a fine was imposed on a married woman who had limited income of her own, the Court of Appeal stressed that the fine must reflect the offender's means and was not a fine on the family.

In the case of a corporate offender, the court must take into account whether the corporation **E15.20** operates primarily for the purpose of making a profit for its shareholders, or whether a fine would have to be met from public funds and so might be said to harm the public. *Sellafield Ltd and Network Rail Infrastructure* [2014] EWCA Crim 49 provides a helpful analysis of how this issue should impact on sentence.

If a defendant company wishes to make a submission as to its ability to pay a fine, it should supply copies of its accounts and other financial information to the court. Where such information has been withheld, the court is entitled to assume that the company is able to pay any fine it is minded to impose (*F Howe and Sons (Engineers) Ltd* [1999] 2 All ER 249). The definitive sentencing guideline, *Corporate Manslaughter and Health and Safety Offences Causing Death*, provides guidance, in paras. 12 to 26 and Annex A (see Supplement, **SG-531** *et seq.* and **SG-538**), as to the appropriate financial information which should be provided to the court by a corporate defendant convicted of one of the offences within the guideline and the approach which should be taken by the court in setting the appropriate level of fine.

Instalments Should Require Payment within a Reasonable Time

Where a fine is ordered to be paid by instalments, it should normally be capable of being paid **E15.21** off by the offender within 12 months (*Nunn* (1983) 5 Cr App R (S) 203). In *Olliver* (1989) 11 Cr App R (S) 10, however, it was held by the Court of Appeal that the maximum time is not limited to 12 months. Lord Lane CJ said (at p. 15):

> ...there is nothing wrong in principle in the period of payment being longer, indeed much longer than one year, providing it is not an undue burden and so too severe a punishment having

regard to the nature of the offence and the nature of the offender. Certainly it seems to us that a two-year period will seldom be too long, and in an appropriate case three years will be unassailable, again of course depending on the nature of the offender and the nature of the offence.

The *Magistrates' Court Sentencing Guidelines* states that 'normally a fine should be of an amount that is capable of being paid within 12 months' (see Supplement, **SG-357**).

There is an exception in relation to corporate defendants, where the fine may be payable over a substantially longer period than for an individual (*Rollco Screw and Rivet Co.* [1999] 2 Cr App R (S) 436).

Combining Fines with Other Sentences or Orders

E15.22 For restrictions imposed by statute on combining a fine with certain custodial sentences see the CJA 2003, s. 163, at **E15.1**. Apart from those cases, there is no statutory general restriction on combining fines with imprisonment or other custodial sentences, whether in respect of the same offence or different offences sentenced on the same occasion, though this will not often be a desirable combination, since incarceration may well deprive the offender of the means to pay the fine. In any event, a fine and a custodial sentence will be an inappropriate combination where the offender lacks the means to pay the fine, and hence will serve the term fixed in default of payment (*Maund* (1980) 2 Cr App R (S) 289), or where the offender will be saddled with a significant financial burden on his release from prison.

A fine may be combined with an immediate custodial sentence, exceptionally where the custodial term imposed is considered to be inadequate and additional punishment is required (*Garner* [1986] 1 All ER 78, per Hodgson J) but also where the fine is being used as a means of removing an offender's profit from his offending. A more sophisticated approach to the removal of substantial proceeds of offending, which was not available to the courts at the time of this decision, is to make a confiscation order (see **E19**).

E15.23 It is possible, whether sentencing for a single offence or for different offences sentenced on the same occasion, to combine a fine with a community order or a reparation order. A fine cannot, however, be combined with a discharge when sentencing for a single offence (*McClelland* [1951] 1 All ER 557), although it may be combined with a discharge when sentencing for different offences sentenced on the same occasion. A fine cannot be combined with a hospital order (Mental Health Act 1983, s. 37(8)).

A fine and a compensation order may be combined. The PCC(S)A 2000, s. 130(12), provides that, where the offender has insufficient means to pay both an appropriate fine and appropriate compensation, the court shall give preference to compensation. In a particular case this will mean that the level of the fine is reduced to enable the full compensation order to stand, or that no fine is ordered and the compensation order stands alone. Fines may be combined with other financial orders, such as an order to pay the costs of the prosecution, though the court must consider the total effect of the orders it is making, and should ensure that the whole sum the offender has to pay is not beyond his means. A fine may also be combined with a restitution order under the PCC(S)A 2000, s. 148(1), with a deprivation order under s. 143, and with a disqualification order, where the vehicle was used for the purposes of crime, under s. 147.

Surcharge

E15.24   Criminal Justice Act 2003, s. 161A

(1) A court when dealing with a person for one or more offences must also (subject to subsections (2) and (3)) order him to pay a surcharge.
(2) Subsection (1) does not apply in such cases as may be prescribed by an order made by the Secretary of State.
(3) Where a court dealing with an offender considers—
  (a) that it would be appropriate to make a compensation order or an unlawful profit order (or both), but

   (b) that he has insufficient means to pay both the surcharge and appropriate compensation (or both the surcharge, appropriate compensation and an appropriate amount under the unlawful profit order),

the court must reduce the surcharge accordingly (if necessary to nil).

(4) For the purposes of this section a court does not 'deal with' a person if it—

   (a) discharges him absolutely, or

   (b) makes an order under the Mental Health Act 1983 in respect of him.

(5) In this section 'unlawful profit order' means an unlawful profit order under section 4 of the Prevention of Social Housing Fraud Act 2013.

Section 161B states that the surcharge payable under s. 161A is such amount as the Secretary of State may specify by order. The Criminal Justice Act 2003 (Surcharge) Order 2012 (SI 2012 No. 1696) specifies the amount of the surcharge applicable. It revokes the Criminal Justice Act 2003 (Surcharge No. 2) Order 2007 (SI 2007 No. 1079), but only in relation to offences committed on or after 1 October 2012. For an offence committed before that date, or when dealing with an offender for more than one offence any of which was committed before that date, the 2007 Order continues to apply. By the 2007 Order, a surcharge of £15 is payable in relation to a fine, but is not payable in respect of any other disposal.

In *Stone* [2013] EWCA Crim 723 the Court of Appeal quashed a surcharge order where the judge had imposed a surcharge of £100 on the basis that the 2012 Order applied, but the offences were committed before 1 October 2012 and had not been dealt with by way of a fine. See also *Swallow* [2013] EWCA Crim 719, where the surcharge imposed under the 2012 Order had to be quashed because some of the offences were committed before 1 October 2012 and, again, the 2007 Order did not apply because the offender had not been fined. In *Bailey* [2014] 1 Cr App R (S) 376 (59) the Court held that where an offence was committed at some time shortly before or shortly after 1 October 2012 the court should take a view on the evidence but not engage in lengthy (and costly) analysis. In the absence of a clear answer the defendant should be given the benefit of the doubt. In *Stone* the Court of Appeal said that a surcharge order may be the subject of an appeal by the offender, the definition of 'sentence' in the Criminal Appeal Act 1968, s. 50(1), being wide enough to cover it. In the case of an application for leave to appeal a surcharge, the matter should be considered by the single judge on the papers. If leave to appeal on other grounds is given, the appeal will be listed before the full court. If the only ground upon which leave is given is the wrongful making of a surcharge order, then the case will be listed as a non-counsel hearing. Pitchford LJ also pointed out that, if there is a failure by the sentencing court to impose a surcharge order when it should have done so, the Court of Appeal will normally be unable to remedy that omission since to do so would normally involve treating the offender more severely overall on sentence. If the court has overlooked the need to impose a surcharge that omission can, of course, be remedied within 56 days under the 'slip rule'. The Court in *Bailey* said that it was the duty of the advocates at the sentencing hearing to make sure that the correct surcharge sum was imposed, and this should be confirmed with the clerk if necessary. If there was a doubt the matter should be referred back to the court. If an error is made it should be possible for the record to be corrected well within the 56 days.

The appropriate form of wording for judges to use in relation to the surcharge when making their sentencing remarks has been a matter of concern and debate. It was agreed at a meeting of the Council of Circuit Judges in December 2012 that it was desirable for an agreed form of words to be produced. In particular, any reference to 'victim' surcharge should be avoided, lest it be thought that the modest sum payable by way of surcharge somehow reflects the injury done to the injured party in the case. At the beginning, or end, of the sentencing remarks the following form of words could be used:

    The surcharge provisions apply to this case and the order can be drawn up accordingly.

This form of words is said to be appropriate for use in all cases. If this form of words is used it should not be necessary for the judge to state the relevant amount in open court. Unfortunately, in *Stone*, the Court of Appeal referred throughout to the 'victim surcharge order'.

The 2012 Order states that a surcharge will not be payable in cases where the offender is dealt with by way of a disposal not set out in the schedule to the Order. Articles 3 to 6 of the Order and the schedule set out the amounts payable as follows.

(Table 1) *If the offender was under 18 when the offence was committed*: conditional discharge, £10; fine, youth rehabilitation order, referral order or community order, £15; suspended sentence, £20; custodial sentence imposed by the Crown Court, £20. It should be noted that for offenders aged under 18, the PCC(S)A 2000, s. 137(1A), provides that any surcharge must be paid by the young offender's parent or guardian unless he cannot be found or it is unreasonable to require him to pay.

(Table 2) *If the offender was aged 18 or over when the offence was committed*: conditional discharge, £15; fine—10 per cent of the value of the fine, rounded up or down to the nearest pound, which must be no less than £20 and no more than £120; community order, £60; suspended sentence where the term suspended is six months or less, £80; suspended sentence where the term suspended is more than six months, £100; imprisonment or detention in a young offender institution imposed by the Crown Court of up to and including six months, £80; imprisonment or detention in a young offender institution imposed by the Crown Court for more than six months and up to and including 24 months, £100; imprisonment or detention in a young offender institution exceeding 24 months, £120; imprisonment or custody for life, £120.

(Table 3) *If the offender is not an individual (i.e. a corporate offender)*: conditional discharge, £15; fine, 10 per cent of the value of the fine, rounded up or down to the nearest pound, which must be no less than £20 and no more than £120.

If the offender is sentenced for more than one offence: (i) the offender is only subject to the under 18 surcharge rate if all the offences were committed when he was under 18; (ii) in any case where the offender is made subject to two or more disposals of the same form the surcharge is paid once; (iii) if the offender is made subject to two or more different forms of disposal, the surcharge to be imposed is the higher or highest applicable amount.

No surcharge is payable in respect of an absolute discharge or a hospital order (s. 161A(4)). Applying the provisions of the 2012 Order, no surcharge is payable in respect of any immediate custodial sentence imposed in a magistrates' court (including a youth court), or in respect of a reparation order or a bind-over to keep the peace.

There is no power in the Crown Court to fix a default term when imposing a surcharge. The PCC(S)A 2000, s.139, which empowers the fixing of a default term for a fine has not been amended to include the surcharge. There is, however, power to give the offender time to pay the surcharge, by virtue of the PCC(S)A 2000, s.141, as amended. See further *Holden* [2013] EWCA Crim 2017.

Section E16 Compensation Orders

POWER TO MAKE COMPENSATION ORDERS

The power of the court to make compensation orders is governed by the PCC(S)A 2000, ss. **E16.1**
130 to 134.

Powers of Criminal Courts (Sentencing) Act 2000, s. 130

(1) A court by or before which a person is convicted of an offence, instead of or in addition to
dealing with him in any other way, may, on application or otherwise, make an order (in this
Act referred to as a 'compensation order') requiring him—
  (a) to pay compensation for any personal injury, loss or damage resulting from that offence
  or any other offence which is taken into consideration by the court in determining sentence; or
  (b) to make payments for funeral expenses or bereavement in respect of a death resulting from
  any such offence, other than a death due to an accident arising out of the presence of a
  motor vehicle on a road;
  but this is subject to the following provisions of this section and to section 131 below.

(2) Where the person is convicted of an offence the sentence for which is fixed by law or falls to
be imposed under section 110(2) or 111(2) above, section 1A(5) of the Prevention of Crime
Act 1953, section 51A(2) of the Firearms Act 1968, section 139AA(7) of the Criminal Justice
Act 1988, section 224A, 225(2) or 226(2) of the Criminal Justice Act 2003 or section 29(4)
or (6) of the Violent Crime Reduction Act 2006, subsection (1) above shall have effect as if the
words 'instead of or' were omitted.

(2A) A court must consider making a compensation order in any case where this section empowers
it to do so.

(3) A court shall give reasons, on passing sentence, if it does not make a compensation order in a
case where this section empowers it to do so.

(4) Compensation under subsection (1) above shall be of such amount as the court considers
appropriate, having regard to any evidence and to any representations that are made by or on
behalf of the accused or the prosecutor.

The victim does not have to apply to the court before a compensation order can be made. In **E16.2**
Holt v DPP [1996] 2 Cr App R (S) 314, the Divisional Court held that a compensation order
could be made in respect of a victim of theft who had died before sentence was passed. There is
no limit to the amount of compensation which the Crown Court or a magistrates' court may
order, except that a compensation order shall not exceed £5,000 where a magistrates' court
imposes such an order on an offender aged under 18 (s. 131(1) and (1A), as amended by the
CCA 2013, s. 44, with effect from 11 December 2013). Nor is there a limit to the compensation (or total compensation) to be ordered for offences taken into consideration, except that a
magistrates' court dealing with an offender aged under 18 cannot make a total compensation
order in respect of the offences taken into consideration which exceeds £5,000 (s. 131(2), as
amended by the CCA 2013, s.44). In *Crutchley* (1994) 15 Cr App R (S) 627, followed in *Hose*
(1995) 16 Cr App R (S) 682, the Court of Appeal held that where an offender pleads guilty on
the basis of specimen counts, the amount of compensation is limited to the losses resulting from
the offences charged. *Crutchley* was distinguished in *Revenue and Customs Prosecutions Office v
Duffy* [2008] 2 Cr App R (S) 593.

The court should make clear which amounts of compensation relate to which offences: the **E16.3**
fixing of a 'global figure' is inappropriate (*Oddy* [1974] 2 All ER 666), unless the offences

2277

E

Part E Sentencing

were committed against the same victim (*Warton* [1976] Crim LR 520). Where there are competing claimants for available funds, the total compensation available should normally be apportioned on a pro rata basis (*Miller* [1976] Crim LR 694), though in *Amey* [1983] 1 All ER 865 the court selected some claimants for compensation and excluded others. Where there are co-defendants, it is preferable to make separate orders against each of them (*Grundy* [1974] 1 All ER 292). It may be appropriate in a case of assault to reduce the compensation order to reflect a degree of provocation by the victim (*Flinton* [2008] 1 Cr App R (S) 575).

A compensation order is part of the sentence of the court, and a decision by the trial judge not to make a compensation order, in accordance with s. 130(3), is a matter relating to trial on indictment and so not amenable to judicial review (*R (Faithfull) v Crown Court at Ipswich* [2008] 3 All ER 749).

Nature of Payment

E16.4   **Liability for, and Evidence of, Injury, Loss or Damage**   'Any personal injury, loss or damage': it is not a prerequisite of making a compensation order that the offender would be civilly liable for the loss (*Chappell* (1984) 80 Cr App R 31), though this will generally be the case. The court may compensate distress and anxiety (*Bond v Chief Constable of Kent* [1983] 1 All ER 456, *Godfrey* (1994) 15 Cr App R (S) 536). 'Loss' may include a sum by way of interest (*Schofield* [1978] 2 All ER 705). An award may be made whenever it can fairly be said that a particular loss results from the offence (*Rowlston v Kenny* (1982) 4 Cr App R (S) 85), without having regard to technical issues of causation (*Thomson Holidays Ltd* [1974] QB 592). Thus in *Taylor* (1993) 14 Cr App R (S) 276 it was held to be appropriate to require the offender to pay £50 compensation to a man who had been kicked in the course of an affray in which the offender and four others had accosted another group of men and a fight had developed. It could not be established that Taylor had kicked the victim, but it was said to be 'artificial and unjust to look narrowly at the physical acts of each defendant'. A case which fell on the other side of the line was *Derby* (1990) 12 Cr App R (S) 502, where the offender had threatened the victim with a knife and his co-accused had seriously injured the victim by attacking him with a piece of wood. It was held that a compensation order for £4,000 made against the offender was improper, since the offender had clearly not been responsible for inflicting the injuries. This approach was followed in *Denness* [1996] 1 Cr App R (S) 159. See also *Deary* (1994) 14 Cr App R (S) 648.

E16.5   Where there has been no damage or loss (e.g., where a stolen article is recovered and returned undamaged), no compensation order can be made (*Hier* (1976) 62 Cr App R 233, *Tyce* (1994) 15 Cr App R (S) 415); the issue is the loss to the victim rather than the benefit to the offender. Conversely, where there has been damage or loss to the victim, a compensation order is not precluded by the fact that the offender has made no profit from the offence. The amount of the victim's loss should either be agreed by the offender or established by evidence. The case of *Vivian* [1979] 1 All ER 48 is clear authority for this point. In *Horsham Justices, ex parte Richards* [1985] 2 All ER 1114, Neill LJ said (at p. 993): '. . . in my judgment the court has no jurisdiction to make a compensation order without receiving any evidence where there are real issues raised as to whether the claimants have suffered any, and if so what, loss'. The court should, however, hesitate to embark on a complex inquiry into the scale of loss, since compensation orders are designed to be used only in clear, straightforward cases (see **E16.14**).

In the case of an offence under the Theft Act 1968 or the Fraud Act 2006, where the property in question is recovered, any damage to the property occurring while it was out of the owner's possession is treated as having resulted from the offence, however and by whomsoever it was caused (PCC(S)A 2000, s. 130(5); *Quigley v Stokes* [1977] 2 All ER 317).

Motor Accidents   A compensation order may only be made in respect of injury, loss or damage (other than loss suffered by a person's dependants in consequence of his death) which was due to an accident arising out of the presence of a motor vehicle on a road, if:

(a) it is damage which falls within s. 130(5); or

(b) it is in respect of injury, loss or damage for which the offender is uninsured in relation to the use of the vehicle, and compensation is not payable under any arrangements to which the Secretary of State is a party (i.e. the Motor Insurers' Bureau Agreement) (s. 130(6)).

In the case of property damage, the Agreement does not cover the first £300 of the damage, and a compensation order up to that amount may be made in an appropriate case (*DPP v Scott* (1995) 16 Cr App R (S) 292). See further *Austin* [1996] 2 Cr App R (S) 191. If a compensation order is made in respect of such an accident, the compensation can include a sum representing the whole or part of any loss of or reduction in preferential rates of insurance attributable to the accident ('no claims' bonus) (s. 130(7)). A vehicle which is exempted from insurance (Road Traffic Act 1988, s. 144) is not uninsured for these purposes (s. 130(8)). In a motor accident case where there are real issues as to liability and quantum, the court should adhere to the general principle (see **E16.14**) that a compensation order should be made only in a clear case (*Stapylton* [2013] 1 Cr App R (S) 68 (12)).

Compensation for Loss Arising from Death   A compensation order in respect of funeral expenses may be made for the benefit of anyone who incurred the expenses (s. 130(9)). A compensation order in respect of bereavement may only be made for the benefit of a person who could claim damages for bereavement under the Fatal Accidents Act 1976, s. 1A (i.e. the spouse of the deceased or, in the case of a deceased minor, his parents, or mother if the minor is illegitimate), and the amount of that compensation shall not exceed the sum specified in the Fatal Accidents Act 1976, s. 1A(3) (£12,980 where the cause of action arises after 1 April 2013) (s. 130(10)).

E16.6

E16.7

Offender's Means and Parental Liability

In determining whether to make a compensation order, and in determining the amount to be paid, it is the duty of the court to have regard to the offender's means so far as they appear or are known to the court (s. 130(11), and see further, **E16.12**). The court may allow the offender time to pay the sum due under the compensation order, or direct payment of the sum by instalments of such amounts and on such dates as the court may specify (PCC(S)A 2000, s. 141, and the MCA 1980, s. 75(1)).

E16.8

Where a child or young person is convicted of an offence and the court makes an order for compensation, it should, under the PCC(S)A 2000, s. 137, normally order the parent or guardian of the child or young person to pay the compensation order (see **E14.7**).

Payment, Discharge and Review

The victim of the offence shall not receive the compensation until there is no further possibility of an appeal on which the order could be varied or set aside (s. 132(1)). By s. 133, at any time before the offender has paid into court the whole of the money under the order, the magistrates' court having power to enforce the order may, on the application of the offender, discharge the order or reduce it, on the ground that:

E16.9

(a) the injury, loss or damage in respect of which the order was made has been held in civil proceedings to be less than it was taken to be for the purposes of the order;

(b) that property, the loss of which was the subject of the order, has now been recovered;

(c) the means of the offender are insufficient to satisfy both the compensation order and a confiscation order made against him in the same proceedings under the CJA 1988, part IV, or the POCA 2002, part 2, or an unlawful profit order under the Prevention of Social Housing Fraud Act 2013, s. 4 (or both); or

(d) the offender's means have suffered a substantial reduction, which was unexpected at the time of making the order.

E

Part E Sentencing

Before the magistrates can act to discharge or reduce the order under (c) or (d), they must have the consent of the Crown Court if the Crown Court made the order.

Enforcement of Compensation Orders

E16.10   Enforcement of compensation orders is the function of the magistrates' courts. The maximum terms of imprisonment which a magistrates' court may impose in default of payment of compensation orders are specified in the MCA 1980, sch. 4. These are the same periods which apply in the case of fines, and which are set out in the table at E15.7, except that the magistrates have no power to specify a term in default in excess of 12 months. These are maximum terms, and the magistrates have discretion to fix a lower term. The Crown Court is not empowered to make an order fixing the term to be served in default of payment of a compensation order (in contrast to its duty to do so in respect of fines: *Komsta* (1990) 12 Cr App R (S) 63, and see E15.3). The maximum terms indicated in sch. 4 will thus normally also apply in default of compensation orders imposed by the Crown Court. Exceptionally, however, if the Crown Court makes a compensation order for an amount in excess of £20,000 and considers that a maximum default term of 12 months is inadequate, it may fix a longer period, not exceeding the term specified for the equivalent amount in the PCC(S)A 2000, s. 139(4). As with fines, part payment of the compensation order will result in a proportionate reduction in the term to be served in default.

COMPENSATION ORDERS: SENTENCING PRINCIPLES

Compensation Order Not Alternative to Sentence

E16.11   In *Inwood* (1974) 60 Cr App R 70, Scarman LJ said (at p. 73): 'Compensation orders were not introduced into our law to enable the convicted to buy themselves out of the penalties for crime. Compensation orders were introduced into our law as a convenient and rapid means of avoiding the expense of resort to civil litigation when the criminal clearly has means which would enable the compensation to be paid.' It follows from this important principle that the imposition of a compensation order should not affect the punishment imposed for the offence and, in particular, should not 'permit the offender to buy his way out of a custodial sentence'.

This principle is, however, subject to the PCC(S)A 2000, s. 130(12), which gives priority to the imposition of a compensation order over a fine. This, to some extent, permits the offender to 'buy his way out of the penalties for crime', by reducing the fine in order for compensation to be paid, but s. 130(12) does not affect sentences other than fines. Some watering down of the principle in *Inwood* (1974) 60 Cr App R 70 may be detected in other decisions of the Court of Appeal such as *Huish* (1985) 7 Cr App R (S) 272, but its importance was re-emphasised by Lord Taylor CJ in *A-G's Ref (No. 5 of 1993)* (1994) 15 Cr App R (S) 201.

Taking into Account Means of Offender

E16.12   It is the responsibility of the offender to inform the court of his resources, and not for the sentencer to initiate inquiries into the matter (*Bolden* (1987) 9 Cr App R (S) 83). It is not the duty of the prosecutor to establish the offender's means (*Johnstone* (1982) 4 Cr App R (S) 141), but where the offender's lawyer advances mitigation on the basis that the offender will pay substantial compensation, the lawyer is under an obligation to ensure that the necessary means exist (*Coughlin* (1984) 6 Cr App R (S) 102; *Huish* (1985) 7 Cr App R (S) 272; *Bond* (1986) 8 Cr App R (S) 11). If the offender misleads the court into believing that he has the means to pay compensation, a subsequent appeal by the offender against the compensation order will not succeed (*Hayes* (1992) 13 Cr App R (S) 454; *Dando* [1996] 1 Cr App R (S) 155). He must pay the compensation, or serve the appropriate term in default of payment. If an offender 'has suffered a substantial reduction in his means which was unexpected at the time the order was made', the order may be reduced or discharged by a magistrates' court under the PCC(S)A 2000, s. 133. If the order was made by the Crown Court, the magistrates must obtain the consent of the Crown Court before proceeding (*Favell* [2010] EWCA Crim 2948).

It is generally wrong to make a compensation order which will require the sale of the offender's home (*Harrison* (1980) 2 Cr App R (S) 313), but it is not unreasonable to expect the offender to sell other items to pay the compensation (*Workman* (1979) 1 Cr App R (S) 335). In such a case the court must ascertain the value of the asset (*Chambers* (1981) 3 Cr App R (S) 318). An order should not be made on the basis of the sale of an asset where it is not certain that the offender will be able to dispose of that asset (*Hackett* (1988) 10 Cr App R (S) 388: family home, in joint names).

Co-defendants may be required to pay different sums by way of compensation if their capacity to pay is different. See *Beddow* (1987) 9 Cr App R (S) 235, where the offender was one of two defendants who pleaded guilty to being carried in a vehicle taken without consent by a third defendant, who had fallen asleep at the wheel, causing the van to crash. The offender was conditionally charged and ordered to pay £300 in compensation. The other two defendants received a suspended sentence and a conditional discharge respectively, but neither was required to pay compensation. The Court of Appeal approved the sentences on the basis that the offender was the only one of the defendants who was in work and could afford to pay. See also *Stapleton* [1977] Crim LR 366. A compensation order should not be imposed on the assumption that persons other than the offender will pay, or contribute to, the order (*Hunt* [1983] Crim LR 270).

Compensation Should be Payable within Reasonable Time

In *Webb* (1979) 1 Cr App R (S) 16, Cantley J observed (at p. 18) that: 'It is no use making a compensation order (particularly one with a sentence of imprisonment in default of compliance) if there is no realistic possibility of the compensation order being complied with'. This may be because the offender has very limited means (as in *Webb*) or because the offender is serving a custodial sentence with no immediate prospect of work (e.g., *Grafton* (1979) 1 Cr App R (S) 305). A compensation order should not be made which involves payments by instalment over an unreasonable length of time. In *Bradburn* (1973) 57 Cr App R 948, Lord Widgery CJ said that, in general, compensation orders 'should be sharp in their effect rather than protracted' and that an order which would take four years to complete was 'unreasonably long'. In *Olliver* (1989) 11 Cr App R (S) 10, the Court of Appeal indicated that a fine (or compensation order) might properly be repaid over a period of up to three years. Lord Lane CJ said (at p. 15) that: 'Certainly it seems to us that a two-year period will seldom be too long, and in an appropriate case three years will be unassailable'. See also *Yehou* [1997] 2 Cr App R (S) 48.

E16.13

Compensation Order Should be Made Only in Clear Case

In *Donovan* (1981) 3 Cr App R (S) 192, the offender pleaded guilty to taking a conveyance, having hired a car for two days and failed to return it. The car had suffered no damage. The offender was fined £250, with £100 costs and £1,388 compensation, on the basis of the hire company's loss of use. Eveleigh LJ said that: 'A compensation order is designed for the simple, straightforward case where the amount of the compensation can be readily and easily ascertained'. Since the amount of damages in a civil case of loss of use 'is notoriously open to argument', the compensation order was quashed, and the hire company left to pursue its civil remedy if it wished to do so. In *Hyde v Emery* (1984) 6 Cr App R (S) 206 the offender pleaded guilty to three charges of obtaining unemployment benefit by false representation. There was a dispute over whether the sum claimed in compensation by the DHSS should be reduced by the amount of supplementary benefit which he could legitimately have claimed. Watkins LJ said in the Divisional Court that the magistrates should have declined to deal with the matter. See also *Briscoe* (1994) 15 Cr App R (S) 699, *White* [1996] 2 Cr App R (S) 58 and *Stapylton* [2013] 1 Cr App R (S) 68 (12).

E16.14

A slightly different line was taken in *James* [2003] 2 Cr App R (S) 574. The offender pleaded guilty to 20 counts of false accounting. The total sum involved was in dispute, but there was an agreed minimum loss of £8,000 to the victim. The Court of Appeal said that it was proper for a compensation order in that sum to be ordered, bearing in mind that the only realistic chance for the victim to receive any compensation from the offender was through the criminal court. In *Pola* [2010] 1 Cr App R (S) 32 the Court of Appeal upheld a compensation order in the sum of £90,000 made against a man convicted of failing to discharge a duty pursuant to the Health and Safety etc. at Work Act 1974, where a workman had been severely injured by the collapse of a wall. The Court noted that criminal courts had now developed more expertise in financial assessment from the experience of confiscation proceedings, and it might be that the very cautious approach adopted in the earlier authorities to the making of compensation orders needed some modification.

Combining Compensation Orders with Other Sentences or Orders

E16.15 Compensation orders may be imposed on an offender 'instead of or in addition to dealing with him in any other way' (PCC(S)A 2000, s. 130(1): see **E16.1**). It is expressly provided that a compensation order may be combined with a discharge (s. 12(7)).

While a compensation order may be combined with a sentence of immediate custody where the offender is clearly able to pay or has good prospects of employment on his release from custody (*Love* [1999] 1 Cr App R (S) 484), it is often inappropriate to impose a compensation order as well as a custodial sentence. It may well be undesirable for a compensation order to be hanging over the offender's head after release, and the order may be 'counterproductive, and force him back into crime to find the money' (*Inwood* (1974) 60 Cr App R 70). See also *Morgan* (1982) 4 Cr App R (S) 358, *Clark* (1992) 13 Cr App R (S) 124 and *Jorge* [1999] 2 Cr App R (S) 1. While it is not wrong to combine a compensation order with a suspended sentence, and, indeed, that combination is positively encouraged by s. 118(5), regard should be had to the fact that if the offender is in breach of the suspended sentence, its activation may bring to an end any prospect of the payment of compensation (*McGee* [1978] Crim LR 370). It is contrary to principle to suspend a custodial sentence merely because of the offender's ability to pay compensation.

Where it would be appropriate both to impose a fine and to make a compensation order, but the offender has insufficient means to pay both, the court shall give preference to compensation, though it may impose a fine as well (s. 130(12)). This means that the fine should be reduced or, if necessary, dispensed with altogether, to enable the compensation to be paid. A compensation order may, thus, stand alone on sentence.

Guidelines for Compensation

E16.16 Starting points for compensating physical and mental injuries commonly encountered in a magistrates' court are set out in the *Magistrates' Court Sentencing Guidelines* (see Supplement, SG-387).

Section E17   Restitution Orders

POWER TO MAKE RESTITUTION ORDERS

A restitution order is designed to restore to a person entitled to them goods which have been sto- **E17.1**
len or otherwise unlawfully removed from him, or to restore to him a sum of money representing the proceeds of the goods, out of money found in the offender's possession on apprehension.
Either the Crown Court or a magistrates' court may make such an order.

Powers of Criminal Courts (Sentencing) Act 2000, s. 148

(1) This section applies where goods have been stolen, and either—
   (a) a person is convicted of any offence with reference to the theft (whether or not the stealing
       is the gist of his offence); or
   (b) a person is convicted of any other offence, but such an offence as is mentioned in para-
       graph (a) above is taken into consideration in determining his sentence.
(2) Where this section applies, the court by or before which the offender is convicted may on the
    conviction (whether or not the passing of sentence is in other respects deferred) exercise any of
    the following powers—
   (a) the court may order anyone having possession or control of the stolen goods to restore
       them to any person entitled to recover them from him; or
   (b) on the application of a person entitled to recover from the person convicted any other
       goods directly or indirectly representing the stolen goods (as being the proceeds of any
       disposal or realisation of the whole or part of them or of goods so representing them), the
       court may order those other goods to be delivered or transferred to the applicant; or
   (c) the court may order that a sum not exceeding the value of the stolen goods shall be paid,
       out of any money of the person convicted which was taken out of his possession on his
       apprehension, to any person who, if those goods were in the possession of the person con-
       victed, would be entitled to recover them from him;
   and in this subsection 'the stolen goods' means the goods referred to in subsection (1) above.

For the purposes of s. 148, 'stealing' is very widely construed to include not just theft and **E17.2**
offences where theft is a constituent element, such as robbery and burglary, but also where the
goods were obtained by blackmail or fraud (or deception where the act in question was prior
to the commencement of the Fraud Act 2006), or were stolen goods handled following any of
these offences (Theft Act 1968, s. 24(4)). A restitution order should not be made unless the
evidence on which it is based (including available documents) is clear and has been given before
sentence is imposed (PCC(S)A 2000, s. 148(5); *Church* (1970) 55 Cr App R 65). A restitution
order should not be made where the question of title to goods is unclear. According to Woolf J:

> . . . the criminal courts are not the appropriate forum in which to satisfactorily ventilate complex
> issues as to the ownership of such money or goods. In cases of doubt it is better to leave the victim
> to pursue his civil remedies or, alternatively, to apply to the magistrates' court under the Police
> (Property) Act 1897. On the other hand, in appropriate cases where the evidence is clear, it is
> important that the court should make proper use of the power to order restitution since this can
> frequently avoid unnecessary expense and delay in the victim receiving the return of his property.
> (*Calcutt* (1985) 7 Cr App R (S) 385, at p. 390)

For obvious reasons, there is no requirement under these provisions that account should be
taken of the offender's means: contrast compensation orders at **E16.12**.

If an order is made under s. 148(2)(a), it will be inappropriate to order restitution under
s. 148(2)(b) or (c) in addition, since the person will thereby recover more than the value of the

goods (*Parsons* (1976) CSP J3–2F01). Under s. 148(2)(a), the person in 'possession or control' need not be the offender, but may be an innocent purchaser. Where a person has, in good faith, bought the goods from the convicted person, or has, in good faith, lent money to the convicted person on the security of the goods, the court may order payment of compensation to that person out of money taken from the offender under s. 148(2)(c) (s. 148(4)). Such an order may be made with or without that person's application (s. 149(2)).

E17.3   Under s. 148(2)(b), an application must be made by the person claiming, and may not relate to goods held by a third party. Where the offender is no longer in possession of the goods, orders may be made under both s. 148(2)(b) and (c), with reference to the same goods, providing that the person does not thereby recover more than the value of the goods (s. 148(3)).

An order may be made under s. 148(2)(c) with or without an application being made (s. 149(2)). Again, where the offender is no longer in possession of the goods, orders may be made under both s. 148(2)(b) and (c), with reference to the same goods, providing that the person does not thereby recover more than the value of the goods (s. 148(3)).

Money seized from the offender after he has been arrested may be the subject of an order (*Ferguson* [1970] 2 All ER 820, where £2,000, taken from the offender's safe deposit box 11 days after his arrest, was held to have been in his possession at the time of his apprehension). But it seems that money seized prior to his arrest may not (*Hinde* (1977) 64 Cr App R 213, a case decided in relation to forfeiture orders but applicable by analogy here). There is no need to show that the money is the proceeds of the relevant offence; all that is necessary is that it be shown that the money belongs to the offender (*Lewis* [1975] Crim LR 353). It was also established in *Lewis* that under s. 148(2)(c), a restitution order may be made against an offender for a greater sum than he received from the offence, provided that it is not for a sum greater than the total loss occasioned by the offence (in contrast to *Grundy* [1974] 1 All ER 292, which established that joint and several liability should not apply in relation to a compensation order).

An offender may appeal against a restitution order as against any other sentence. Such an order is, however, where made on conviction on indictment, subject to an automatic suspension for 28 days from the date of conviction (unless the trial court directs to the contrary on the ground that 'the title to the property is not in dispute': Criminal Appeal Act 1968, s. 30(1)) or, further, until the determination of any appeal. Where made by a magistrates' court, s. 149(4) provides that it is subject to an automatic suspension for 21 days from the date of conviction or, further, until the determination of any appeal (unless the court directs to the contrary as above).

COMBINING RESTITUTION ORDERS WITH OTHER SENTENCES OR ORDERS

E17.4   A restitution order may be made in combination with any other sentence passed by the court.

Section E18   Deprivation and Forfeiture Orders

POWERS TO MAKE DEPRIVATION ORDERS UNDER THE PCC(S)A 2000, s. 143

Nature and Effect of Order

The main power of the courts to order the forfeiture of property connected with the commis-   **E18.1**
sion of an offence is created by the PCC(S)A 2000, s. 143(1). Other powers of forfeiture under
specific statutes are considered at **E18.7**. The power under s. 143 may be exercised by the Crown
Court or a magistrates' court, in respect of any offence.

Powers of Criminal Courts (Sentencing) Act 2000, s. 143

(1) Where a person is convicted of an offence and the court by or before which he is convicted is
satisfied that any property which has been lawfully seized from him, or which was in his possession or under his control at the time when he was apprehended for the offence or when a
summons in respect of it was issued—
   (a) has been used for the purpose of committing, or facilitating the commission of, any
       offence, or
   (b) was intended by him to be used for that purpose,
the court may (subject to subsection (5) below) make an order under this section in respect of
that property.

(2) Where a person is convicted of an offence and the offence, or an offence which the court has
taken into consideration in determining his sentence, consists of unlawful possession of property which—
   (a) has been lawfully seized from him, or
   (b) was in his possession or under his control at the time when he was apprehended for the
       offence of which he has been convicted or when a summons in respect of that offence was
       issued,
the court may (subject to subsection (5) below) make an order under this section in respect of
that property.

(3) An order under this section shall operate to deprive the offender of his rights, if any, in the
property to which it relates, and the property shall (if not already in their possession) be taken
into the possession of the police.

(4) Any power conferred on a court by subsection (1) or (2) above may be exercised—
   (a) whether or not the court also deals with the offender in any other way in respect of the
       offence of which he has been convicted; and
   (b) without regard to any restrictions on forfeiture in any enactment contained in an Act
       passed before 29th July 1988.

(5) In considering whether to make an order under this section in respect of any property, a court
shall have regard—
   (a) to the value of the property; and
   (b) to the likely financial and other effects on the offender of the making of the order (taken
       together with any other order that the court contemplates making).

(6) Where a person commits an offence to which this subsection applies by—
   (a) driving, attempting to drive, or being in charge of a vehicle, or
   (b) failing to comply with a requirement made under section 7 or 7A of the Road Traffic Act
       1988 (failure to provide specimen for analysis or laboratory test or to give permission for
       such a test) in the course of an investigation into whether the offender had committed an
       offence while driving, attempting to drive or being in charge of a vehicle, or

     (c) failing, as the driver of a vehicle, to comply with subsection (2) or (3) of section 170 of the Road Traffic Act 1988 (duty to stop and give information or report accident),
the vehicle shall be regarded for the purposes of subsection (1) above (and section 144(1)(b) below) as used for the purpose of committing the offence (and for the purpose of committing any offence of aiding, abetting, counselling or procuring the commission of the offence).

    (7) Subsection (6) above applies to—

      (a) an offence under the Road Traffic Act 1988 which is punishable with imprisonment;

      (b) an offence of manslaughter; and

      (c) an offence under section 35 of the Offences Against the Person Act 1861 (wanton and furious driving).

    (8) Facilitating the commission of an offence shall be taken for the purposes of subsection (1) above to include the taking of any steps after it has been committed for the purpose of disposing of any property to which it relates or of avoiding apprehension or detection.

E18.2   The effect of an order under s. 143 is to deprive the offender of his rights, if any, in the property (s. 143(3)), but it does not affect the rights of any other person, who may apply for recovery of the property (see **E18.3**). The power does not extend to real property, such as the offender's home (*Khan* (1982) 4 Cr App R (S) 298). Nor should an order be made where the property is subject to joint ownership (*Troth* (1980) 71 Cr App R 1, where it was said that deprivation orders should be confined to 'simple, uncomplicated cases'). This was the problem in *Kearney* [2011] 2 Cr App R (S) 608, where the offender had committed six offences of making off without payment by filling his car with fuel and driving away without paying. The judge dealt with the matter by a community order together with an order depriving the offender of his rights in the vehicle. The deprivation order was quashed on appeal, it now having emerged that the car had been purchased on a hire purchase agreement. The power does not extend to property which was associated with an offence committed by some person other than the offender: s. 143(1)(a)(i) should be read as if the words 'by him' rather than 'by anyone' appeared after the word 'offence' (*Slater* [1986] 3 All ER 786; *Neville* (1987) 9 Cr App R (S) 222). The phrase 'facilitating the commission of, any offence' in s. 143 includes the taking of any steps after it has been committed for the purpose of disposing of any property to which it relates or of avoiding apprehension or detection (s. 143(8)). Section 143(6) and (7) make it clear that an offender's vehicle *shall* be regarded as having been used for the purpose of any offence specified therein. Section 143(6) and (7), however, in no way limit the courts' power to order forfeiture of an offender's car in respect of other offences under the general provision in s. 143(1). See also the important sentencing principle as to totality at **E18.5**. Where the making of a deprivation order is being considered by the court, *Pemberton* (1982) 4 Cr App R (S) 328 requires that evidence be laid before the judge on the issue and that 'full and proper investigation' must be made into the prosecution's application. In *Trans Berckx BVBA v North Avon Magistrates' Court* (2012) 176 JP 28, the Divisional Court granted an application for judicial review in a case where the magistrates had made a deprivation order under s. 143 without considering the criteria specified in s. 143(5). See also *Ball* [2003] 2 Cr App R (S) 92.

Dealing with Property

E18.3   The property shall normally be taken into the possession of the police, if not in their possession already, and the Police (Property) Act 1897 shall apply to such property. However, no application can be made by a claimant after six months from the date of the deprivation order. And no such order can be made unless the claimant satisfies the court either that he had not consented to the offender having possession of the property or, where the order was made under the PCC(S)A 2000, s. 143(1)(a), that he did not know, and had no reason to suspect, that the property was likely to be used for the purpose mentioned in s. 143(1) (s. 144(1): see also *Kearney* [2011] 2 Cr App R (S) 608). The police have power under the 1897 Act to dispose of property where its ownership has not been ascertained and no court order has been made in respect of it. In relation to s. 143, the police have similar powers where no application has been made within six months or no such application has succeeded (s. 144(2)). By s. 25(1) of the UK Borders Act 2007, a court making an order under s. 143 of the PCC(S)A 2000 may order that the property be taken into the possession of the Secretary of State (rather than the police) where the court thinks that the offence relates to immigration or asylum or was committed for a purpose connected therewith.

E18.4

Powers of Criminal Courts (Sentencing) Act 2000, s. 145

(1) Where a court makes an order under section 143 above in a case where—
   (a) the offender has been convicted of an offence which has resulted in a person suffering personal injury, loss or damage, or
   (b) any such offence is taken into consideration by the court in determining sentence,
   the court may also make an order that any proceeds which arise from the disposal of the property and which do not exceed a sum specified by the court shall be paid to that person.
(2) The court may only make an order under this section if it is satisfied that but for the inadequacy of the offender's means it would have made a compensation order under which the offender would have been required to pay compensation of an amount not less than the specified amount.

No order can be made under this provision before the expiry of the six-month period mentioned above, or where a successful application has been made under the Police (Property) Act 1897 in respect of the property (s. 145(3)).

DEPRIVATION ORDERS: SENTENCING PRINCIPLES

Deprivation Order Affects Totality of Sentence

See the PCC(S)A 2000, s. 143(5), at **E18.1**. In *Buddo* (1982) 4 Cr App R (S) 268, the offender pleaded guilty to burglary and assault. In addition to a total prison sentence of two years, the offender was deprived of his rights in a motor caravan in which he had driven to commit the burglary. The Court of Appeal was of the view that such an order could properly be made on the facts but that sentencers were 'not required to make such an order in every case in which a vehicle is used in the commission of a crime'. In this case, according to Park J, the deprivation order was 'overdoing the punishment', and the order was quashed. See also *Scully* (1985) 7 Cr App R (S) 119, *Priestley* [1996] 2 Cr App R (S) 144 and, in relation to deprivation of a computer, *Townsend-Johnson* [2010] EWCA Crim 1027.

E18.5

Where the order would have a disproportionately severe impact upon the offender, it is also inappropriate. In *Tavernor* [1976] RTR 242, an order depriving the offender of his rights in a car, imposed in addition to a suspended prison sentence and a fine, was quashed in view of the offender's physical disability. See also *Highbury Corner Metropolitan Stipendiary Magistrate, ex parte Di Matteo* [1991] 1 All ER 102.

In a case where several offenders are equally implicated and receive comparable sentences, it is wrong to impose in addition a deprivation order upon one of them (*Ottey* (1984) 6 Cr App R (S) 163; but see *Burgess* [2001] 2 Cr App R (S) 5, where it was said that the principle can be taken so far but no further). This may be contrasted with the principle applicable to compensation orders, the object of which is to compensate the victim, rather than to punish the offender (see **E16.11**).

Combining Deprivation Orders with Other Sentences or Orders

A deprivation order may be combined with a compensation order, and provision is made under the PCC(S)A 2000, s. 145, to allow the sale of property connected with the offence in order to finance compensation for the victim where the means of the offender would otherwise have been inadequate to meet a compensation order. A deprivation order may be combined with a discharge (s. 12(7)).

E18.6

OTHER STATUTORY POWERS TO MAKE
FORFEITURE ORDERS

E18.7 Many other statutes contain their own forfeiture provisions relating to offences committed under those statutes, or to property regulated under those statutes. The Misuse of Drugs Act 1971 includes a commonly used provision.

Misuse of Drugs Act 1971, s. 27

(1) Subject to subsection (2) below, the court by or before which a person is convicted of an offence under this Act or an offence falling within subsection (3) below or an offence to which section 1 of the Proceeds of Crime (Scotland) Act 1995 relates or a drug trafficking offence, as defined in Article 2(2) of the Criminal Justice (Confiscation) (Northern Ireland) Order 1990 may order anything shown to the satisfaction of the court to relate to the offence, to be forfeited and either destroyed or dealt with in such other manner as the court may order.

(2) The court shall not order anything to be forfeited under this section, where a person claiming to be the owner of or otherwise interested in it applies to be heard by the court, unless an opportunity has been given to him to show cause why the order should not be made.

(3) An offence falls within this subsection if it is an offence which is specified in—
   (a) paragraph 1 of Schedule 2 to the Proceeds of Crime Act 2002 (drug trafficking offences), or
   (b) so far as it relates to that paragraph, paragraph 10 of that Schedule.

E18.8 Any personal property which relates to the offence may be forfeited, including money (*Beard* [1974] 1 WLR 1549), but s. 27 does not extend to intangibles, or to property situated outside the jurisdiction of the English courts (*Cuthbertson* [1981] AC 470). Nor, apparently, does s. 27 permit the forfeiture of real property such as a house (*Pearce* [1996] 2 Cr App R (S) 316). The property must be shown to relate to the offence of which the offender has been convicted; its relation to intended offences is insufficient (*Morgan* [1977] Crim LR 488; *Ribeyre* (1982) 4 Cr App R (S) 165; *Llewellyn* (1985) 7 Cr App R (S) 225; *Cox* (1986) 8 Cr App R (S) 384). Thus, where the offender was convicted of possession of cocaine, which was hidden in his car, a forfeiture order under s. 27 could not be made in respect of £1,489 also found in his possession and accepted to be the proceeds of drug dealing, since this was the proceeds of drugs other than those to which the conviction related (*Boothe* (1987) 9 Cr App R (S) 8). In *Boothe* an order made under the predecessor to the PCC(S)A 2000, s. 143 (see **E18.1**), for forfeiture of a car was upheld. It is clear that an order in relation to the car might have been made under s. 27 of the 1971 Act (*Bowers* (1994) 15 Cr App R (S) 315). If the offender disputes that property is related to the offence of which he has been convicted, he must be permitted to call evidence (*Churcher* (1986) 8 Cr App R (S) 94). Under s. 27(2), it seems that the court may order forfeiture notwithstanding such an application: contrast the position under the PCC(S)A 2000, s. 143, at **E18.1**. It may be assumed that the sentencing principles listed in relation to the PCC(S)A 2000, s. 143, also apply here. There is, however, under s. 27, no power to sell property to generate compensation.

For the power of forfeiture under the Firearms Act 1968 and power of seizure of offensive weapons, see **B12**. For powers of forfeiture in terrorism cases, see **B10.112**.

Section E19   Confiscation Orders

GENERAL

Part 2 of the Proceeds of Crime Act (POCA) 2002 provides for the making of confiscation   **E19.1**
orders following conviction in criminal cases (other than for certain terrorist offences which
have separate legislation). (See **D8** for all other methods of asset recovery under the POCA
2002.) The basic framework is a merger and extension of the two similar but separate schemes
contained in the Drug Trafficking Act 1994 for drug offences and in the CJA 1988 for other
offences (see the 2002 edition of this work). The Act came into force on 24 March 2003. The
transitional arrangements specify that part 2 shall not have effect where the index offence, or
any of the offences, was committed before that date — in which case the earlier legislation
should be applied. Where an offence occurs over a period, it is taken to have occurred on
the earliest day in the period (Proceeds of Crime Act 2002 (Transitional Provisions, Savings
and Amendment) Order (SI 2003 No. 333)). A defendant charged with a conspiracy which
straddled the commencement date and who pleaded guilty on the basis that his first admitted
act was after that date, but who did not suggest that the conspiracy dates were wrong, fell to
be dealt with under the earlier legislation (*Evwierhowa* [2011] 2 Cr App R (S) 442). Where
offences in an indictment do straddle the material date and the prosecutor bases the confiscation application only upon offences committed after the date, it is permissible to proceed
under the POCA 2002 (*Stapleton* [2009] 1 Cr App R (S) 209; see also *Simpson* [2004] QB 118
and *Aslam* [2005] 1 Cr App R (S) 660). Similarly, in a mixed indictment, where the defendant
is convicted only of offences occurring after the relevant date, the appropriate regime is that
of the POCA 2002 (*Onuigbo* [2014] EWCA Crim 65). Where there are two indictments, one
relating to offences committed before 24 March 2003 and the other relating to offences all
committed after that date, the court must treat them as separate proceedings and apply separate confiscation regimes (*Moulden* [2009] 1 Cr App R 362). For substitution of the correct
legislation on appeal see *Boughton-Fox* [2014] EWCA Crim 227 and *Bukhari* [2009] 1 Cr App
R (S) 113.

The Assets Recovery Agency and the Serious Organised Crime Agency were abolished on 1
April 2008 and 1 October 2013 respectively. Part 2 of the Act now refers solely to 'the prosecutor', i.e. the legal person that has brought the criminal prosecution out of which the confiscation
proceedings arise or that has assumed conduct of those proceedings. It means 'a person entitled
to prosecute'. Accordingly, a private prosecutor is entitled to bring confiscation proceedings
even where that person has no financial or personal interest in the outcome (*R (Virgin Media
Ltd) v Zinga* [2014] 1 Cr App R 382 (27)). In *Zinga*, in return for police assistance in prosecuting a company which had sold equipment allowing free access to Virgin products, Virgin Media
had undertaken to donate 25 per cent of any compensation to the police in return for assistance
in the investigation of the offence. It did not matter that private prosecutors could not conduct
financial investigations into a defendant's circumstances and supply the statement of information required by the POCA 2002. The 2002 Act distinguished between those who could investigate and those who could prosecute. The fact that a prosecutor may not possess investigative
powers did not impair the ability to participate fully in confiscation proceedings provided that
an appropriate officer, as defined by s. 378(1), assisted by exercising the investigatory powers.
As the confiscation proceedings were for the sole benefit of the State, it could not be said that
the agreement between Virgin Media and the police was an abuse of process, but it did run the

risk of providing an incentive for the police to devote resources to assisting Virgin in its claim for compensation and gave rise to a perception of compromised police independence. It was not appropriate for the Court to comment upon the circumstances in which the police should assist in confiscation proceedings brought by private prosecutors. Such issues were for careful and very urgent consideration by the Association of Chief Police Officers, the Association of Police and Crime Commissioners, and the Home Office.

A confiscation hearing is mandatory in all cases if the prosecution applies for a determination. A finding that a defendant has a 'criminal lifestyle' triggers an unlimited review of all property that he holds at the time of the order or has received or expended in the previous six years, in which the court is required to make assumptions that the property stems from his 'general criminal conduct' unless he proves otherwise or it is not in the interests of justice to make the assumption.

Human Rights Act 1998

E19.2 **Article 6**   Viewed overall, the process of confiscation amounts to the 'determination of a criminal charge' and 'a defendant enjoys full benefit of all the rights conferred by Article 6(1) of the ECHR in all aspects of confiscation proceedings' including the guarantee of a hearing within a reasonable time. Article 6(1) is engaged, for example, in late enforcement proceedings to commit a defaulting defendant to prison (*Lloyd v Bow Street Magistrates' Court* [2004] 1 Cr App R 132; *Crowther v UK* (2005) *The Times*, 11 February 2005; *R (Minshall) v Marylebone Magistrates' Court* [2010] 2 All ER 806; *R (Syed) v City of Westminster Magistrates' Court* [2010] EWHC 1617 (Admin)), and in a late prosecution application for reconsideration of the available amount (*Re Saggar* [2005] 1 WLR 2693). There is an entitlement to a 'public hearing' (*Saccoccia v Austria* (2010) 50 EHRR 243).

Perhaps paradoxically, it has also been held that confiscation proceedings are part of the sentencing process and that the defendant is not at that point 'charged with a criminal offence' within the meaning of Article 6(2). Once he is convicted, Article 6(2) has no application in relation to allegations made about the defendant's character and conduct as part of the sentencing process, unless such accusations are of such a nature and degree as to amount to the bringing of a new 'charge' within the autonomous Convention meaning (*Benjafield* [2003] 1 AC 1099; *McIntosh v Lord Advocate* [2003] 1 AC 1078; *Van Offeren v Netherlands* (2005) Appln. No. 19581/04, 5 July 2005; *Phillips v UK* (2001) 11 BHRC 280: see also **A7.105**). Accordingly, the use of the mandatory assumptions of fact and reverse burdens of proof in the determination of benefit (see **E19.30**) and of the realisable amount do not engage, let alone breach, the specific protections of Article 6(2), including the presumption of innocence (*Grayson v UK* (2008) 48 EHRR 722). (Note, however, the Supreme Court decision in *Waya* [2013] 1 AC 294, which has introduced liberalisation of the regime in the form of 'proportionality': see **E19.6** and **E19.30**).

E19.3 There remains some opacity as to whether the fairness requirements of Article 6(1) nevertheless require proof to the criminal standard where the evidence of a particular benefit derives solely from evidence of the commission of other offences. In *Geering v Netherlands* (2007) 46 EHRR 1212, a confiscation order was made on the basis of other offences having been committed despite an acquittal on appeal in other proceedings. The ECtHR held that the defendant was entitled to the presumption of innocence because he was 'charged with a criminal offence' in the sense that the confiscation hearing was a redetermination of his guilt of the offences of which he had been acquitted. In *Briggs-Price* [2009] 1 AC 1026 the House of Lords thought that *Geering* 'needs to be approached with some care': 'What the Court in *Geering* found objectionable was that neither the commission of the offences nor the alleged benefits had been proved.' In *Briggs-Price* the trial evidence had included allegations that the defendant had committed drug offences other than those for which he was indicted. In the confiscation proceedings, the judge calculated the benefit on the basis that he was 'sure' that the defendant had committed those offences. That approach was approved. In keeping with earlier decisions, the House of Lords continued to hold that the Article 6(2) presumption of innocence does not apply to confiscation proceedings (Lord Brown dissenting) with the qualification that, where the only evidence of a particular benefit is the commission of other offences, the general right to a fair trial under Article 6(1) in 'the determination of a criminal charge' necessarily implies a requirement that those offences must be proved to the criminal standard. Subsequently, some uncertainty has followed from the decision of the Supreme Court in *SOCA v Gale* [2011] 2 All ER 1, in which Lord Phillips described the Strasbourg jurisprudence as 'confusing' and concluded that overall there was nothing that lent support to the conclusion that the criminal standard must be applied to proof of criminal conduct under the POCA 2002. However, *Gale* concerns civil recovery and the full implications for criminal confiscation are not easy to deduce. In *Bagnall* [2013] 1 WLR 204, the Court of Appeal held that, in an assumed benefit case, the prosecution were not required to prove the source of that benefit to the criminal standard, albeit that this involved allegations and evidence of other offences. *Briggs-Price* was distinguished on the basis that the 'issue in that case concerned the logically prior question of whether the defendant had been in possession of property in the past' and not its source (see also *Whittington* [2010] 1 Cr App R (S) 545 and see further **E19.12**). Putting all this together, the legal reality appears to be that the civil standard is universal.

Article 7   Article 7 of the ECHR prohibits, *inter alia*, the imposition of 'a heavier pen-   **E19.4** alty…than the one that was applicable at the time the criminal offence was committed' (see **A7.104**). Confiscation orders and imprisonment in default are, for these purposes, penalties (*Welch v UK* (1995) 20 EHRR 247; *Jamil v France* (1996) 21 EHRR 65). However, there is no breach of Article 7 simply because the determination of the defendant's benefit or of the available amount includes property acquired by the defendant before the legislation came into force, provided that the offence giving rise to the confiscation proceedings was committed after that date (*Welch v UK*; *Taylor v UK* (1998) Appln. 31209/96, 10 September 1997). Discrete historical points of retrospectivity may continue to arise from the sequential toughening of confiscation legislation from the Drug Trafficking Offences Act 1986 onwards. See, e.g., *Togher v Revenue and Customs Prosecutions Office* [2008] QB 476, which concerned the change brought about by the Drug Trafficking Act 1994 (and continued in the POCA 2002) in maintaining the liability to pay the confiscation order irrespective of the fact that the period of imprisonment in default has been served. It was held that, where the index offence had occurred before the 1994 Act was passed, the requirement was incompatible with Article 7.

Article 8   Article 8 guarantees the rights to respect for private and family life, home and cor-   **E19.5** respondence. Any interference in those rights must be 'necessary in a democratic society…for the prevention of disorder or crime'. Similar provisions in earlier confiscation legislation have been held to achieve a proportionate balance between the private interests of the defendant and those of the public (*Benjafield* [2003] 1 AC 1099). Hardship is not a consideration in the determination of the amount of the confiscation order. 'The court is merely concerned with the arithmetic exercise of computing what is, in effect, a statutory debt' (*Ahmed* [2005] 1 All ER 128). However, following *Waya* [2013] 1 AC 294, while the provisions themselves may not be necessarily disproportionate in principle, their application may in practice be held to result in disproportionate and unlawful consequences (see **E19.6**).

Article 8 is not engaged when the value of the family home is accounted as part of the 'available amount' (see **E19.49**). 'The extent of the relevance' of a partner's interest in the family home is 'within the appreciation' of the Contracting State (*Danison v UK* (1998) Appln. 45042/98, 7 September 1999). However, consideration of the interests of third parties, including partners, under Article 8 and consequent issues of proportionality may become relevant in restraint proceedings (see **D8.36**) or at the enforcement stage of a confiscation order (see **E19.66**) if, for example, the prosecutor attempts to realise the value of the family home in order to meet an unpaid confiscation order (*Ahmed*).

Protocol 1, Article 1   Article 1 encodes an entitlement to peaceful enjoyment of one's posses-   **E19.6** sions and states that 'No one shall be deprived of his possessions except in the public interest and subject to the conditions provided for by law and by the general principles of international law', but preserves 'the right of a State to enforce such laws as it deems necessary to control the use of property in accordance with the general interest or to secure the payment of taxes or other contributions or penalties'.

In a ground-breaking decision, the Supreme Court has now followed the lead of the ECtHR (see, e.g., *Ismayilov v Russia* (2008) Appln. 30352/03, 6 November 2008) in holding that, in limited circumstances, the more literal applications of the legislation are capable of leading to disproportionate results and, consequently, breaches of Article 1 (*Waya* [2013] 1 AC 294: see further E19.30).

The Process: A Summary

E19.7   Proceeds of Crime Act 2002, s. 6

(1) The Crown Court must proceed under this section if the following two conditions are satisfied.

(2) The first condition is that a defendant falls within any of the following paragraphs—

(a) he is convicted of an offence or offences in proceedings before the Crown Court;

(b) he is committed to the Crown Court for sentence in respect of an offence or offences under section 3, 3A, 3B, 3C, 4, 4A or 6 of the Sentencing Act;

(c) he is committed to the Crown Court in respect of an offence or offences under section 70 below (committal with a view to a confiscation order being considered).

(3) The second condition is that—

(a) the prosecutor asks the court to proceed under this section, or

(b) the court believes it is appropriate for it to do so.

(4) The court must proceed as follows—

(a) it must decide whether the defendant has a criminal lifestyle;

(b) if it decides that he has a criminal lifestyle it must decide whether he has benefited from his general criminal conduct;

(c) if it decides that he does not have a criminal lifestyle it must decide whether he has benefited from his particular criminal conduct.

(5) If the court decides under subsection (4)(b) or (c) that the defendant has benefited from the conduct referred to it must—

(a) decide the recoverable amount, and

(b) make an order (a confiscation order) requiring him to pay that amount.

(6) But the court must treat the duty in subsection (5) as a power if it believes that any victim of the conduct has at any time started or intends to start proceedings against the defendant in respect of loss, injury or damage sustained in connection with the conduct.

(6A) The court must also treat the duty in subsection (5) as a power if—

(a) an order has been made, or it believes an order may be made, against the defendant under section 4 (criminal unlawful profit orders) of the Prevention of Social Housing Fraud Act 2013 in respect of profit made by the defendant in connection with the conduct, or

(b) it believes that a person has at any time started or intends to start proceedings against the defendant under section 5 (civil unlawful profit orders) of that Act in respect of such profit.

(7) The court must decide any question arising under subsection (4) or (5) on a balance of probabilities.

(8) The first condition is not satisfied if the defendant absconds (but section 27 may apply).

(9) References in this Part to the offence (or offences) concerned are to the offence (or offences) mentioned in subsection (2).

E19.8   A confiscation order does not itself confiscate any property but, instead, requires the offender to pay over a sum of money: 'the recoverable amount'. This will be either (a) the full amount of what the court has found to be his 'benefit' from his 'criminal conduct' or (b) the value of all his assets at the time of the order (including tainted gifts), if he can prove that amount to be less: 'the available amount'.

Under s. 6(2) an order may be made in the Crown Court against anyone (a) convicted of an offence in the Crown Court; (b) committed to the Crown Court for sentence; or (c) committed to the Crown Court for specific consideration of a confiscation order. When either (a) the prosecutor asks the Crown Court to proceed, or (b) the court itself considers that it is appropriate to do so (s. 6(3)), the court *must* proceed towards the making of a confiscation order.

The POCA 2002 abolished the power of magistrates to make confiscation orders. At present, magistrates must commit a convicted defendant to the Crown Court 'with a view to a confiscation order being considered' if the prosecution so requests (s. 70). This includes summary offences (*Sumal and Sons (Properties)* [2013] 1 WLR 2078).

Procedure is governed by the CrimPR, parts 57 and 58 (see Supplement, **R-389** *et seq.*).

The confiscation order may be made before sentence; however, the court may postpone the confiscation hearing for up to two years from the date of conviction and proceed instead to sentence the defendant or to order compensation (although not other monetary penalties). In 'exceptional circumstances' longer postponements are possible.

A strict order of events must be followed after conviction or committal (the following text has been expressly approved by the Court of Appeal as 'a useful guide' (*Whittington* [2010] 1 Cr App R (S) 545):   **E19.9**

(a) The process starts when the prosecution asks for an inquiry or when 'the court believes it is appropriate' to hold one.
(b) The court must then decide whether the defendant has a 'criminal lifestyle'. This depends solely upon the nature of the offence or offences of which he has been convicted in the current or earlier proceedings.
(c) The judge must then determine whether the defendant has benefited from 'criminal conduct'. There are two alternatives:
   (i) if the defendant has been found to have a criminal lifestyle, the court must determine whether he has benefited from 'his *general* criminal conduct';
   (ii) if, on the other hand, the defendant does not have a criminal lifestyle, the court must determine whether he has benefited from 'his *particular* criminal conduct' (i.e. from the particular offence(s) of which he has been convicted or has had taken into consideration).
(d) Next, the judge must determine the value of the defendant's proceeds of crime or benefit — 'the recoverable amount'. In calculating benefit from 'general criminal conduct', the judge must apply the relevant assumptions as to income and expenditure in the previous six years and as to property 'held' by the defendant on conviction (unless the defendant can show an assumption to be incorrect or that 'there would be a serious risk of injustice if an assumption were made').
(e) Lastly, the judge must make a confiscation order in that sum *unless* the defendant can prove that the value of all his existing assets, known as 'the available amount' (including artificial or 'tainted' gifts to others), is less than the value of the benefit. If so, the 'available amount' becomes the 'recoverable amount' and, therefore, is the amount of the confiscation order.

Information, Evidence and Proof

Proceeds of Crime Act 2002, ss. 16 to 18   **E19.10**

16.—(1) If the court is proceeding under section 6 in a case where section 6(3)(a) applies, the prosecutor must give the court a statement of information within the period the court orders.
(2) If the court is proceeding under section 6 in a case where section 6(3)(b) applies and it orders the prosecutor to give it a statement of information, the prosecutor must give it such a statement within the period the court orders.
(3) If the prosecutor believes the defendant has a criminal lifestyle the statement of information is a statement of matters the prosecutor believes are relevant in connection with deciding these issues—
   (a) whether the defendant has a criminal lifestyle;
   (b) whether he has benefited from his general criminal conduct;
   (c) his benefit from the conduct.
(4) A statement under subsection (3) must include information the prosecutor believes is relevant—
   (a) in connection with the making by the court of a required assumption under section 10;
   (b) for the purpose of enabling the court to decide if the circumstances are such that it must not make such an assumption.

(5) If the prosecutor does not believe the defendant has a criminal lifestyle the statement of information is a statement of matters the prosecutor believes are relevant in connection with deciding these issues—

(a) whether the defendant has benefited from his particular criminal conduct;

(b) his benefit from the conduct.

(6) If the prosecutor gives the court a statement of information—

(a) he may at any time give the court a further statement of information;

(b) he must give the court a further statement of information if it orders him to do so, and he must give it within the period the court orders.

(7) If the court makes an order under this section it may at any time vary it by making another one.

17.—(1) If the prosecutor gives the court a statement of information and a copy is served on the defendant, the court may order the defendant—

(a) to indicate (within the period it orders) the extent to which he accepts each allegation in the statement, and

(b) so far as he does not accept such an allegation, to give particulars of any matters he proposes to rely on.

(2) If the defendant accepts to any extent an allegation in a statement of information the court may treat his acceptance as conclusive of the matters to which it relates for the purpose of deciding the issues referred to in section 16(3) or (5) (as the case may be).

(3) If the defendant fails in any respect to comply with an order under subsection (1) he may be treated for the purposes of subsection (2) as accepting every allegation in the statement of information apart from—

(a) any allegation in respect of which he has complied with the requirement;

(b) any allegation that he has benefited from his general or particular criminal conduct.

(4) For the purposes of this section an allegation may be accepted or particulars may be given in a manner ordered by the court.

(5) If the court makes an order under this section it may at any time vary it by making another one.

(6) No acceptance under this section that the defendant has benefited from conduct is admissible in evidence in proceedings for an offence.

18.—(1) This section applies if—

(a) the court is proceeding under section 6 in a case where section 6(3)(a) applies, or

(b) it is proceeding under section 6 in a case where section 6(3)(b) applies or it is considering whether to proceed.

(2) For the purpose of obtaining information to help it in carrying out its functions the court may at any time order the defendant to give it information specified in the order.

(3) An order under this section may require all or a specified part of the information to be given in a specified manner and before a specified date.

(4) If the defendant fails without reasonable excuse to comply with an order under this section the court may draw such inference as it believes is appropriate.

(5) Subsection (4) does not affect any power of the court to deal with the defendant in respect of a failure to comply with an order under this section.

(6) If the prosecutor accepts to any extent an allegation made by the defendant—

(a) in giving information required by an order under this section, or

(b) in any other statement given to the court in relation to any matter relevant to deciding the available amount under section 9,

the court may treat the acceptance as conclusive of the matters to which it relates.

(7) For the purposes of this section an allegation may be accepted in a manner ordered by the court.

(8) If the court makes an order under this section it may at any time vary it by making another one.

(9) No information given under this section which amounts to an admission by the defendant that he has benefited from criminal conduct is admissible in evidence in proceedings for an offence.

E19.11   **Exchange of Information**   The procedure has its own form of pleadings now governed by the CrimPR, r. 58.1 (see Supplement, **R-405**). First, the prosecution must serve a 'Statement of Information' outlining the matters that it believes are relevant to the various stages of the inquiry (POCA 2002, s. 16).

In return, the defendant may be ordered to 'indicate . . . in a manner ordered by the court' the extent to which he accepts the allegations in the statement and, if he does not accept any allegation, 'to give particulars of any matters he proposes to rely on' (s. 17). If the defendant fails 'in any respect' to comply with such an order, he can be treated as having accepted 'every allegation' in the statement apart from (a) those to which he has responded and (b) the basic allegation that he has benefited from criminal conduct (*Crutchley* (1994) 15 Cr App R (S) 627). If it was clear from the terms on which a defendant consented that he accepted facts which justified the making of an order, a judge, provided that he was satisfied there had been an unambiguous acceptance of those facts from which the defendant should not be permitted to resile, would be entitled to rely on the consent. This is not simply because the defendant has consented but because his acceptance constitutes evidence upon which the judge is entitled to rely. Nevertheless, 'judges should be astute to ensure that agreements on the amount to be recovered were soundly based' (*Mackle* [2014] 2 WLR 267; *M* [2009] 2 Cr App R (S) 66).

In addition, the court has a free-standing power at any time to order the defendant to provide written information 'to help it in carrying out its functions' (s. 18). Failure to comply without reasonable excuse entitles the court to draw adverse inferences. The judge cannot order a third party such as a solicitor to provide information (*R (Dechert Solicitors) v Southwark Crown Court* [2001] EWHC Admin 477).

Evidence and Proof   The standard of proof is that of 'the balance of probabilities' (POCA **E19.12** 2002, s. 6(7)). (There may be one exception: where the prosecution can prove the obtaining of benefit *only* by proof of criminal offences outside the indictment, the criminal standard may apply (*Briggs-Price* [2009] 1 AC 1026: see further below and **E19.3**). The prosecution carry the burden of proving both the fact that the defendant has benefited from criminal conduct and the amount of his benefit. However, in lifestyle cases, once the prosecution establish any income, expenditure or interest in property, there are mandatory assumptions as to benefit. The defendant carries the burden of proving that the available amount is less than the value of the benefit.

It has been held that 'the ordinary rules of criminal evidence [do] not apply' to confiscation hearings (*Silcock* [2004] 2 Cr App R (S) 323). The hearsay provisions of the CJA 2003, while not strictly applicable, provide an appropriate framework for the determination of admissibility issues (*Clipston* [2011] 2 Cr App R (S) 569). Where the hearing has been preceded by a contested trial, the judge is entitled to form his own view from the evidence (*Threapleton* [2003] 2 All ER 458). However, in the confiscation proceedings, a defendant is still entitled to challenge the evidence. This is so even where the defendant has pleaded guilty and has declined a *Newton* hearing. The court must act with scrupulous fairness in making its assessment for the purposes of a confiscation order, and such proceedings were designed to be fully adversarial, affording the accused every opportunity to challenge evidence against himself and to call witnesses (*Knaggs* [2010] 1 WLR 435; *HM Advocate v McIntosh (No. 1)* [(2003] 1 AC 1078; *Jenkins* (1990) 12 Cr App R (S) 582). Even so, an unqualified plea of guilty with no challenge to the prosecution opening on the basis of which a defendant was content to be sentenced are circumstances that the judge is fully entitled to regard as powerful evidence contradicting assertions made in the confiscation proceedings. The judge may take account of discrepancies between a defendant's evidence in the trial and his evidence in the confiscation hearing (*O'Connell* [2005] EWCA Crim 1520). The judge may make additional and more extensive findings of fact than those upon which the verdict was based and is entitled to take into account all of the evidence he had heard in the confiscation hearing provided that he acts consistently with the verdict and its factual basis (*Sangha* [2009] 2 Cr App R (S) 94). This could include trial evidence of other offences.

It remains arguable on the authority of *Briggs-Price* that, where the *only* proof that the defendant has obtained a particular benefit from criminal conduct derives from the commission of offences outside the indictment, the judge must be satisfied of the defendant's guilt to the criminal standard to be compliant with the ECHR, Article 6(1). However, in *SOCA v Gale* [2011] 2 All ER 1, a civil recovery case, the Supreme Court concluded that there was nothing in the Strasbourg jurisprudence that lent support to the conclusion that the criminal standard must apply to prove criminal offences under the POCA 2002. In *Bagnall* [2013] 1 WLR

204, the Court of Appeal held that, in an assumed benefit case, the prosecution were not required to prove the source of that benefit to the criminal standard, albeit that this involved allegations and evidence of other offences. *Briggs-Price* was distinguished on the basis that the 'issue in that case concerned the logically prior question of whether the defendant had been in possession of property in the past' and not its source (see also *Whittington* [2010] 1 Cr App R (S) 545 and **E19.3**).

E19.13   **The Effect of the Basis of a Guilty Plea**   The agreed basis of a guilty plea, while relevant to sentence, will not necessarily limit the ambit of the confiscation inquiry. The prosecution should consider whether any sentencing concession might conflict with the assumptions of benefit which must ordinarily be applied in subsequent confiscation proceedings (see **E19.30**). 'What is unacceptable is for the concession to be made for part of the sentencing process, without qualification, but for reliance to be placed, tacitly, on the assumptions when it comes to the confiscation hearing' (*Lunnon* [2005] 1 Cr App R (S) 111). In *Lunnon*, it had been accepted by the Crown that the defendant had no prior involvement in drug trafficking. In those circumstances, to apply a mandatory assumption that the defendant had previously benefited from drug trafficking would amount to 'injustice' and allow the court to disapply the assumption. The determining feature is the extent of the concession made by the prosecution rather than the fact that the defendant's plea has been entered on a limited basis. In *Lazarus* [2005] 1 Cr App R (S) 552, the prosecution accepted a guilty plea to a drugs offence on the basis of limited involvement in the offence. The Court of Appeal nevertheless upheld a confiscation order that 'assumed' that monies passing through a bank account in previous years were the proceeds of drug trafficking. It held that the basis of the plea was not inconsistent with prior drug trafficking; the prosecution had never been invited to agree, as they had in *Lunnon*, that there had been no previous trafficking and the defendant had known shortly after the acceptance of his plea that the prosecution were seeking to rely on the statutory assumptions and had the opportunity to rebut them. See also *Green* [2007] 3 All ER 751 and *McCarry* [2008] EWCA Crim 1587. In *Bakewell* [2006] 2 Cr App R (S) 277, the prosecution accepted a written basis of plea limiting the amount of the defendant's payment for participation in a fraudulent evasion of duty. Significantly, they were not prepared to accept the defendant's assertion that this was the extent of his benefit. Without that concession, the payment was merely to be regarded as his 'reward'; correctly applying s. 76(5), his benefit, in contrast to his reward, was the whole value of the pecuniary advantage obtained in the evasion of duty.

E19.14   In most cases the prosecution are best advised to say no more than that they do not dispute a defence assertion for the purposes of sentence but that they cannot say what information may arise in the course of the confiscation inquiry (*Lazarus*).

E19.15   **Special Counsel**   Frequently, the judge will have seen and reviewed material which has not been disclosed for reasons of public interest immunity. The material may be highly adverse to a defendant in subsequent confiscation proceedings and, in particular, damaging to his credibility — e.g., information that he has been a highly successful criminal for many years. In such a situation, the appointment of special counsel should be considered (*May* [2005] 3 All ER 523).

MAKING OF CONFISCATION ORDER

Stage One — Determining Criminal Lifestyle

E19.16   Proceeds of Crime Act 2002, s. 75

(1) A defendant has a criminal lifestyle if (and only if) the following condition is satisfied.
(2) The condition is that the offence (or any of the offences) concerned satisfies any of these tests—
    (a) it is specified in Schedule 2;
    (b) it constitutes conduct forming part of a course of criminal activity;
    (c) it is an offence committed over a period of at least six months and the defendant has benefited from the conduct which constitutes the offence.

(3) Conduct forms part of a course of criminal activity if the defendant has benefited from the conduct and—
 (a) in the proceedings in which he was convicted he was convicted of three or more other offences, each of three or more of them constituting conduct from which he has benefited, or
 (b) in the period of six years ending with the day when those proceedings were started (or, if there is more than one such day, the earliest day) he was convicted on at least two separate occasions of an offence constituting conduct from which he has benefited.
(4) But an offence does not satisfy the test in subsection (2)(b) or (c) unless the defendant obtains relevant benefit of not less than £5000.
(5) Relevant benefit for the purposes of subsection (2)(b) is—
 (a) benefit from conduct which constitutes the offence;
 (b) benefit from any other conduct which forms part of the course of criminal activity and which constitutes an offence of which the defendant has been convicted;
 (c) benefit from conduct which constitutes an offence which has been or will be taken into consideration by the court in sentencing the defendant for an offence mentioned in paragraph (a) or (b).
(6) Relevant benefit for the purposes of subsection (2)(c) is—
 (a) benefit from conduct which constitutes the offence;
 (b) benefit from conduct which constitutes an offence which has been or will be taken into consideration by the court in sentencing the defendant for the offence mentioned in paragraph (a).

E19.17 The court must first decide whether the defendant has a 'criminal lifestyle' (s. 6(4)(a)). This is a purely formulaic exercise in which the defendant qualifies if one of the offences of which he has been convicted falls within the statutory catalogue in s. 75 (see also the Proceeds of Crime Act 2002 (Commencement No. 5) (Amendment of Transitional Provisions) Order (SI 2003 No. 531)). There are three sub-divisions:

(a) Offences specified in sch. 2 (including their inchoate forms and encouraging or assisting the commission of such an offence under the SCA 2007, s. 44). The specified offences fall under the following broad headings: (i) drug trafficking; (ii) money laundering; (iii) directing terrorism; (iv) people trafficking; (v) arms trafficking; (vi) counterfeiting; (vii) intellectual property; (viii) prostitution and child sex; (ix) blackmail. An offence under the Gangmasters (Licensing) Act 2004, s. 12, is also specified.
(b) An offence that 'constitutes conduct forming part of a course of criminal activity'. To qualify, a defendant must have been convicted of:
 (i) three or more other offences in the current proceedings, each of which was committed on or after 24 March 2003 and which constitutes conduct from which he has benefited (i.e. at least four offences in all), or
 (ii) such an offence on at least two separate occasions in the six years before the current proceedings were started.
 A conviction for these purposes includes an offence taken into consideration. The total benefit from the offences or offences taken into consideration must be at least £5,000.
(c) An offence committed over a period of at least six months resulting in benefit of not less than £5,000. (It is wrong to hold it as sufficient where a conspiracy lasted for over six months but the individual defendant participated for a shorter period: *Bajwa* [2012] 1 All ER 348; see also *Odamo* [2014] 1 Cr App R (S) 252 (44).)

Stage Two — Determination of Benefit from Criminal Conduct

E19.18 Proceeds of Crime Act 2002, s. 76

(1) Criminal conduct is conduct which—
 (a) constitutes an offence in England and Wales, or
 (b) would constitute such an offence if it occurred in England and Wales.
(2) General criminal conduct of the defendant is all his criminal conduct, and it is immaterial—
 (a) whether conduct occurred before or after the passing of this Act;
 (b) whether property constituting a benefit from conduct was obtained before or after the passing of this Act.

(3) Particular criminal conduct of the defendant is all his criminal conduct which falls within the following paragraphs—
(a) conduct which constitutes the offence or offences concerned;
(b) conduct which constitutes offences of which he was convicted in the same proceedings as those in which he was convicted of the offence or offences concerned;
(c) conduct which constitutes offences which the court will be taking into consideration in deciding his sentence for the offence or offences concerned.

(4) A person benefits from conduct if he obtains property as a result of or in connection with the conduct.

(5) If a person obtains a pecuniary advantage as a result of or in connection with conduct, he is to be taken to obtain as a result of or in connection with the conduct a sum of money equal to the value of the pecuniary advantage.

(6) References to property or a pecuniary advantage obtained in connection with conduct include references to property or a pecuniary advantage obtained both in that connection and some other.

(7) If a person benefits from conduct his benefit is the value of the property obtained.

Criminal conduct is conduct that either constitutes an offence in England and Wales or which would constitute an offence if it occurred here (s. 76(1)). Managing etc. property prior to the service of a planning enforcement notice is not 'criminal conduct' absent a finding of an attempt or conspiracy to commit an offence (*Ali* [2014] EWCA Crim 1658).

E19.19 If the defendant does not have a criminal lifestyle, the court must nevertheless determine the benefit of 'his *particular* criminal conduct' (s. 6(4)(a)). The inquiry is restricted to the offences that are proved or admitted in the current proceedings, including offences taken into consideration (s. 76(3)). The assumptions do not apply.

If, on the other hand, he does have a criminal lifestyle, the court must determine his benefit from 'his general criminal conduct' (s. 6(4)(b)). General criminal conduct is all of the defendant's criminal conduct regardless of when it occurred (s. 76(2)). In determining benefit from general criminal conduct in the previous six years, the court must apply the required assumptions (see **E19.34**). Note, however, that, where a confiscation order has been made in earlier proceedings, no account may be taken in a subsequent application of any benefit obtained prior to the earlier order (*Chahal* [2014] EWCA Crim 101).

E19.20 Obtaining A person benefits from criminal conduct 'if he obtains property as a result of or in connection with the conduct' (POCA 2002, s. 76(4)). Property is all property wherever situated and includes (a) money, (b) all forms of real or personal property, (c) things in action and other intangible or incorporeal property. Property held or obtained abroad is nevertheless benefit, notwithstanding that no offence has been committed in that jurisdiction (*McKinnon* [2004] 2 Cr App R (S) 234). The benefit to the 'defendant is the value of the property obtained' (s. 76(7)). Property is 'obtained' by a person 'if he obtains an interest in it' (s. 84(2)(b)). An interest in land includes 'any legal estate or equitable interest or power' (s. 84(2)(f)); an interest in property other than land includes a right including a right to possession (s. 84(2)(h)). Where the defendant has obtained a pecuniary advantage, the benefit is an amount equal to the value of the advantage (s. 76(5)). The burden of proving that the defendant has obtained property and the amount of that property lies upon the prosecution to the civil standard of proof. There may possibly be an exception requiring proof to the criminal standard where the prosecution can *only* establish that the defendant had obtained property in the past by proof of criminal offences other than those charged on the indictment (*Briggs-Price* [2009] 1 AC 1026: see **E19.3** and **E19.12**). However, even if this is a correct statement of law, this does not mean that, whenever the evidence upon which the prosecution rely to prove the obtaining of property implies the commission of offences, the prosecution must then necessarily prove the fact of the obtaining to the criminal standard: 'If the prosecution can prove that the defendant has obtained assets in the past other than by proof of previous criminal offences then the prosecution may do so on a balance of probabilities' (*Whittington* [2010] 1 Cr App R (S) 545).

E19.21 In an important review of confiscation principles, the House of Lords in *May* [2008] 1 AC 1028 set out the now-famous 'three questions': (a) Has the defendant (D) benefited from the relevant criminal conduct, (b) if so, what is the value of the benefit D has so obtained and (c) what sum is recoverable from D? In addressing these questions, the court must first establish the facts as best it can. In very many cases the factual findings will be decisive. In the context of the first question, the House in *May* and in the simultaneous decision in *Jennings v DPP* [2008] 1 AC 1046 held that the phrase 'obtains' necessarily connotes 'a power of disposition or control'. Their lordships set out 'broad principles' which include the following:

> D ordinarily obtains property if in law he own it, whether alone or jointly, which will ordinarily connote a power of disposition or control, as where a person directs a payment or conveyance of property to someone else. He ordinarily obtains a pecuniary advantage if (among other things) he evades a liability to which he is personally subject. Mere couriers or custodians or other very minor contributors to an offence, rewarded by a specific fee and having no interest in the property or the proceeds of sale, are unlikely to be found to have obtained that property. It may be otherwise with money launderers.

In *Jennings v DPP*, the House applied *May* holding that a defendant 'cannot and should not be deprived of what he has never gained or its equivalent, because that is a fine; in particular, it is not sufficient that a person is instrumental in the property being obtained as his acts may contribute significantly to property being obtained without his obtaining it'.

The Court of Appeal has since applied the *May* approach to various sets of facts. In *Sivaraman* [2009] 1 Cr App R (S) 469, where the manager of a service station accepted delivery of fuel on behalf of his employer without excise duty being paid, his benefit was the amount he was paid as he had acted as an employee, not as a joint trader. Similarly, in *Clark* [2011] 2 Cr App R (S) 319 the defendant had assisted in the shipment of stolen cars abroad but, although an integral facilitator of the overall conspiracy, he was a bailee of the cars with nothing to link him to the original thefts or proceeds (see also *Mitchell* [2009] 2 Cr App R (S) 463). In *Worrall* [2012] EWCA Crim 1150 a brothel-keeper was not liable for payments made independently to the prostitutes themselves. In *Allpress* [2009] 2 Cr App R (S) 399 a five-judge court considered the 'full value' approach in five conjoined appeals. These respectively involved drug trafficking couriers, a shopkeeper who had allowed the storage of cash at his shop knowing it was criminal property, and a partner in a law firm who had used a firm account to transfer funds obtained by another's criminal conduct,. The Court rejected the prosecution argument that money laundering cases constitute a 'special category'. The legislation refers not to de facto possession but to a 'right to possession'. Whether a person was intended to be regarded as holding an interest in property by mere manual possession, or whether something more was required, was put beyond doubt by those words. Moreover, even if a mere custodian of property were held to have a limited interest in the property, the relevant value would be the value of that interest, which if the property was being held purely for another would be nil. However, in relation to the law firm, the account concerned was an account of the defendant and his partners with their bank. Payment of money into that account gave rise to a thing in action in his favour, jointly with his partners. The starting point was therefore that that was his property (applying *Sharma* [2006] 2 Cr App R (S) 416). He had assisted another to retain control of the proceeds of that person's criminal conduct but, with that ultimate objective, had received funds in respect of which he had legal ownership and practical control. Note also *Ilyas v Aylesbury District Council* [2009] 1 Cr App R (S) 316, where the defendant, albeit a cipher, had allowed the transfer of a house into her name as part of a fraudulent scheme by her family in which she subsequently transferred it back to the family. It was held that, where the legal title to real property is transferred as a result of or in connection with a fraudulent scheme, especially where the transferee is himself party to the scheme, he is generally in sufficient control of the title to meet the *May* test and is liable for the full value of the property.

E19.22

In *Frost* [2010] 1 Cr App R (S) 485 a school business manager created false invoices which resulted in the local authority reclaiming VAT which was credited to the school bank account. Although he had been able to bring about the transfer into the school account dishonestly, the transfers did not create a thing in action against the bank in his favour and, therefore, did not give him an

E19.23

interest in the property until he successfully extracted the money from that account. One should not 'confuse criminal liability and resulting benefit'. In *Wilkinson* [2009] EWCA Crim 2733 the defendant was observed by police officers getting into a stolen car. He admitted suspecting that the car was stolen but explained that he had been test driving it and had decided not to purchase it. A confiscation order for the full value of the car was quashed on the basis that he never had any right to possess the car. He had obtained the property for a limited time and a limited purpose and had no more control over the property than a courier or custodian would have had. Unless and until he had chosen to purchase the car, he was plainly obliged to return it. Accordingly, it seems clear that cases such as *Simpson* [1998] 2 Cr App R (S) 111, disapproved in *May*, which held that a courier of cash obtains the whole amount that he has carried, are no longer good law.

Obtaining state benefits or evading tax on the basis of a false declaration or failure to declare a change in circumstances will amount to obtaining a pecuniary advantage (i.e. of the amount of the state benefits or tax). However, legitimate trading profit which has not been declared for tax or national insurance purposes does not *per se* amount to criminal property (*Gabriel* [2007] 1 WLR 2272; see also *A-G's Ref (No. 25 of 2001) (Moran)* [2002] 1 WLR 253). Even so, 'these words do not mean more than that profits from legitimate trading can never without more give rise to criminal property' (*K (I)* [2007] 1 WLR 2262). Where the defendant has been proved to have cheated the Revenue, legitimate but undeclared cash profits may amount to criminal property in that they represent 'in part' the tax of which the Revenue has been cheated.

A pecuniary advantage can be obtained by deferment of a debt or by temporary evasion of payable duty. There has been considerable litigation respecting excise duty on imported goods. In *Smith* [2002] All ER 366 the defendant fraudulently imported cigarettes by sea, sailing past Customs houses at Immingham and Hull without paying the excise duty. The boat was intercepted before the cigarettes could be offloaded and sold. The House of Lords upheld a confiscation order in the amount of the duty temporarily evaded. The Supreme Court has ruled that the decision in *Smith* does not fall foul of principles of proportionality (*Waya* [2013] 1 AC 294; see **E19.30**): in *Smith*, their lordships were not considering property held momentarily and returned but the pecuniary advantage of avoiding duty. (See also *Dimsey* [2000] 2 All ER 142 and *Edwards* [2005] 2 Cr App R (S) 160.) It is irrelevant that cigarettes are counterfeit (*Varsani* [2011] 1 Cr App R (S) 575).

E19.24   In keeping with the decision in *May*, a person obtains a pecuniary advantage only if he evades a liability to which he is personally subject. Accordingly, the defendant only obtains:

> ...a benefit by way of a pecuniary advantage in the form of the evasion of excise duty if he was himself under a liability for the payment of that duty which he dishonestly evaded. To help somebody else to evade the payment of duty payable by that other person, within intent to defraud, is no less criminal, but in confiscation proceedings the focus is on the benefit obtained by the relevant offender. An offender may derive other benefits from helping a person who is under a liability for the payment of duty to avoid that liability, e.g. by way of payment for the accessory's services, but that is another matter. In order to decide whether the offender has obtained a benefit in the form of the evasion of a liability, it is necessary to determine whether the offender had a liability which he avoided... that turns on whether the appellant was liable for the payment of excise duty on the relevant goods under the relevant Regulations (*Chambers* [2008] EWCA Crim 2467).

The various regulations that impose joint and several liability for duty upon a person who causes or has caused goods to reach an excise point are not to be construed as necessarily catching all those who assist with the dispatch or transport of the goods. A person who causes or has caused goods to reach an excise point will not be liable for duty unless he retains a connection with the goods at the duty point — which, in tobacco smuggling cases, is at the time the ship enters the port limits (*White* [2010] EWCA Crim 978). Thus the loader of the lorry does not benefit to the full amount of the duty evaded (*Mitchell* [2009] 2 Cr App R (S) 463 and *Khan* [2009] EWCA Crim 588) nor does a person who handles smuggled cigarettes after importation (*Bell* [2011] EWCA Crim 6; see also *Tatham* [2014] EWCA Crim 226). In order to obtain the goods for the purposes of the legislation it had to be established by the evidence or reasonable inferences that the person had actually obtained a benefit. Playing an active part in the handling of goods to assist in their commercial realisation did not alone establish that a person had benefited from his criminal activity (*Mackle* [2014] 2 WLR 267). Persons who had arranged for cigarettes to be fraudulently imported into the UK 'held' the cigarettes at the excise duty point within the meaning of the Tobacco Products Regulations 2001, reg. 13(1), despite their innocent agents having been in physical possession of the cigarettes, as they were the persons who had exercised control over the cigarettes (*Taylor* [2013] EWCA Crim 1151). A salaried manager at a tobacco factory 'held' the tobacco at the time that duty became payable and 'caused' it to reach the duty point while retaining a connection with the goods thus making him personally liable for the duty, but he had not personally obtained a pecuniary advantage (*James* [2012] 1 WLR 2641). As to holders of bills of lading, see *Bajwa* [2011] 1 All ER 348. For the evasion of VAT in such circumstances, see *Redmond* [2011] EWCA Crim 203. The decision in *Waller* [2009] 1 Cr App R (S) 149, in which the Court of Appeal held that the benefit includes the value of the goods themselves, was 'clearly wrong' (see *Ahmad* [2012] 2 All ER 1137; *Bagnall* [2013] 1 WLR 204 and **E19.29**).

No pecuniary advantage is obtained by a temporary and unrealised increase in the value of shares (*Rigby* [2006] 1 WLR 3067).

Generally, much depends on the particular circumstances and whether the defendant has obtained an overall pecuniary advantage from his activities. Where, for example, he has cheated the Revenue by diverting company income into a secret account for his own use, he may be liable for the whole amount and not just the amount of the evaded tax (*Foggon* [2003] 2 Cr App R (S) 507).

Difficult questions of fact can arise where unlawful conduct has contributed in part to the profit-making of otherwise legitimate companies. Where a disqualified director has continued to operate a legitimate company, the turnover of the company may be relevant to ascertaining the benefit obtained by the director but it is not necessarily correct to equate the turnover with the benefit obtained by the offender (*Seager* [2010] 1 WLR 815; *Hill v Department for Business, Innovation and Skills* [2011] EWHC 3436 (Admin)). Insofar as it suggests otherwise, *Neuberg* [2008] 1 Cr App R (S) 481 is no longer good law. See also *Del Basso* [2011] 1 Cr App R (S) 268. Where a taxpayer cheated the Revenue by falsely representing the turnover of a business, he obtained a pecuniary advantage equal to the tax due on the undeclared turnover. Moreover, the property obtained was the entirety of the undeclared turnover, not merely the tax due (*William* [2013] EWCA Crim 1262). In *Xu* [2008] EWCA Crim 2372 a Chinese restaurant was found to have obtained a benefit from the employment of illegal immigrants, 'which might be looked at either in terms of receipts generated by their employment or expenses avoided'. However, 'it is not realistic or just to conclude that the entirety of the receipts from each and every customer flowed from the employment of these illegal immigrants'. Accordingly, as the illegal workers made up a quarter of the workforce, the Court of Appeal reduced the benefit figure to one quarter of the overall receipts. See also *R (Chief Constable of the Greater Manchester Police) v City of Salford Magistrates' Court* [2009] 1 WLR 1023. There are three situations where the benefit obtained by a company may be treated as a benefit obtained by the individual criminal, namely (a) if an offender attempts to shelter behind a corporate veil, (b) where an offender does an act in the name of the company that constitutes a criminal offence, and (c) where the business structure constitutes a device, cloak or sham in an attempt to disguise the true nature of a transaction (*Sale* [2014] 1 WLR 663). Rental income from a property obtained through mortgage fraud constitutes benefit (*Wootton* [2013] EWCA Crim 2522; *Oyebola* [2014] 1 Cr App R (S) 359 (58)). **E19.25**

It is not necessary for the property to pass to the defendant. As long as he does actually obtain the property, he need only do so momentarily. In *Patel* [2000] 2 Cr App R (S) 10 the defendant was a dishonest postmaster who had taken cash from the till and given half of it to an accomplice as part of a benefit book racket. The fact that he paid over a share was irrelevant as he had obtained all the property. Technically speaking, the burglar caught in the act obtains what he has momentarily taken: 'Success or otherwise is irrelevant' (*Wilkes* [2003] 2 Cr App R (S) 625;

see also *Alagobola* [2004] 2 Cr App R (S) 248 and *Roisseter* [2004] EWCA Crim 1827). Note, however, that in *Wilkes* the prosecutor did not assert that the benefit should include the value of the stolen goods. An order which did include their value would be disproportionate (*Waya* [2013] 1 AC 294: see E19.6 and E19.30).

E19.26 **Joint Enterprise and Individual Benefit**   In strict theory the prosecution must prove that the defendant has, in fact, obtained property or a pecuniary advantage himself and not simply that it has been obtained by others, e.g., co-conspirators. Accordingly, no benefit is obtained if the defendant withdraws from a conspiracy to rob before any robbery occurs and he has not been 'instrumental in obtaining the cash in any realistic way' (*Byatt* [2006] 2 Cr App R (S) 779). In *Davy* [2003] 2 Cr App R (S) 603, the defendant had conspired to obtain and sell on fake ecstasy tablets. The tablets were seized in transit and, accordingly, he had neither obtained any property nor derived any pecuniary advantage. In *Olubitan* [2004] 2 Cr App R (S) 70, the defendant joined the conspiracy on the day that police action brought it to an end. The Court of Appeal stated (at [25]):

> We reject [the] extreme submission...that, where there is a conspiracy, anyone who joins the conspiracy as a matter of law becomes liable for his proportion of the total amount by which the conspirators as a whole may have benefited. [The Act requires] findings of fact...the court may often be entitled to make robust inferences if convicted defendants remain unhelpful as to which of them obtained what benefit as defined by the Act. In many cases, an equal division of the benefit which the conspirators as a whole obtained between the defendants before the court may constitute a fair and reasonable inference. But, in our judgement, the section is not to be construed so that a person may be held to have obtained property or derived a pecuniary advantage when a proper view of the evidence demonstrates that he has not in fact done so.

E19.27   An order cannot be made jointly and severally against defendants. There must be individual orders. In *May* [2008] 1 AC 1028 the House of Lords revisited principles of apportionment and determined that a 'division of the spoils' approach is not appropriate when the benefit consists of property that is jointly obtained by defendants; in other words, where the benefit has been jointly controlled, separate orders for the full amount may be made against each defendant (see also *Fields* [2014] 2 WLR 233, *Lambert* [2012] 2 Cr App R (S) 535, *Green* [2008] 1 AC 1053 and *Houareau* [2006] 1 Cr App R (S) 509). In *Ahmad* [2014] UKSC 36, the Supreme Court indicated (at [51]) that judges should be ready to investigate and make findings as to whether there were separate obtaining; while this may sometimes be too difficult or impossible, although a court 'should never make a finding that there has been a joint obtaining from convenience, or worse, laziness'. Moreover, at the enforcement stage, a payment by one offender of an amount due under the confiscation order should go to reduce the amount payable by the others (*Ahmad* at [72]): 'To take the same proceeds more than once would not serve the aim of the legislation', would be disproportionate, and would violate the ECHR, Protocol 1, Article 1. Where there had been a joint obtaining, confiscation orders had to be made against each defendant for the whole of the benefit obtained. However, each had to provide that it was not to be enforced to the extent that any sum had been recovered in satisfaction of another confiscation order in respect of the same joint benefit (*Ahmad* at [74]).

Classically, in drugs cases where payment is obtained by one defendant on behalf of several defendants jointly, others who have joint control may be liable for the whole of the common pool. 'It does not matter that proceeds of sale may have been received by one conspirator who retains his share before passing on the remainder; what matters is the capacity in which he received them' (*Green* [2007] 3 All ER 751). Whether proceeds of sale were initially received on the individual's own personal behalf or on behalf of the conspirators as a whole is a question of fact for the judge to decide on the evidence before him.

As Cranston J stated (at [19]–[20]), giving the judgment of the Court of Appeal in *Mahmood* [2013] 1 WLR 3146:

> Mere couriers or custodians and other minor contributors to a conspiracy who had been rewarded by a specific fee and had no interest in the property or proceeds of sale are unlikely to be found to have obtained the property...even a person who played a more substantial role in a conspiracy could be

found not to have obtained it . . . conversely, a person does not have to be at the top of a conspiracy in order to have obtained the full value of the property . . . what matters is the capacity in which a conspirator received the property, whether for his own personal benefit or on behalf of others or jointly on behalf of himself and others. The issue is not resolved by attaching a label to the person's position in the conspiracy, although the role a person played might assist in evaluating the available evidence.

Where one defendant receives the benefit and then shares it with other members of the enter-   **E19.28**
prise, for example by passing it through a bank account of which he is the sole signatory, that
defendant is treated as having obtained the whole amount of the benefit. The amount of his
benefit is not reduced by the share that he passes to the other members, as Newman J held in
Sharma [2006] 2 Cr App R (S) 416 at [19]–[25]:

> Where the proceeds of crime are concerned, there is no room for the application of trust
> principles and the application of the normal legal consequences which flow from the
> receipt of money for others. Nor in this area of the law would the purpose of the statute,
> namely to deprive criminals of the benefits of their criminal enterprise, be assisted by the
> introduction of collateral inquiries on an issue as to whether, when the benefit or part
> of the benefit is paid on to another criminal or other person participating in the crime,
> the original recipient is to be regarded as having never held the benefit for himself and to
> have obtained no fresh or continuing benefit from making the disposal to another . . . The
> amount of money which might be recovered pursuant to a confiscation order is irrel-
> evant. In every case, at the time a confiscation order is made, there can be no certainty that
> the amount to be paid will be paid and thus, where more than one confiscation order is
> made in respect of a victim's loss, the question of double recovery may not arise.

Connection with Criminal Conduct   The full definition of 'benefit' goes beyond property   **E19.29**
which has been obtained '*as a result of* ' criminal conduct. The Act also catches property which
has been obtained '*in connection with*' the defendant's criminal conduct (s. 76(4)). However, this
does not mean property which has been purchased simply in order to obtain the benefit — 'the
cost of committing the offence' (unless in a criminal lifestyle case that expenditure is assumed
to have been funded from previous criminal conduct (see **E19.34**)). In *Ahmad* [2014] UKSC
36 the two appellants were directors of second line buffer companies in a carousel MTIC fraud.
The Supreme Court upheld identical orders against each for the full amount of the VAT loss to
HMRC (£12.6 million) applying the principles in *May* [2008] 1 AC 1028 (subject to individual
enforcement: see **E19.27**). However, the Court of Appeal ([2012] 2 All ER 1137) earlier held
that their benefit could not include the value of the goods bought and sold in order to spin the
carousel and, therefore, did not include the total amount of monies that passed through company bank accounts over which they had control (£92 million). On a proper construction of the
Act, that was not property obtained 'in connection with' the criminal conduct: 'if the appellants
had obtained the goods by theft or by fraud and sold them on, the resulting sale price would be
a benefit. In this case the offence was cheating the revenue of the VAT, the selling or purported
selling of the goods was a mechanism by which the fraud was committed and the necessary costs
involved in the selling or purported selling were the costs of committing the offence.'

Whether benefit can arise from the commission of a 'regulatory offence' will depend upon the
terms of the relevant statute or regulations. In *Sumal and Sons (Properties)* [2013] 1 WLR 2078
a company was convicted of owning rental property without a licence contrary to the Housing
Act 2004. That Act did not affect the validity of a tenancy or licence and the right to recover
rent remains enforceable. Accordingly, a confiscation order was quashed as the company was
not unlawfully obtaining rent 'as a result of or in connection with' the statutory breach.

Where property received by a defendant through his criminal conduct generates an income
without his interest in the property itself being diminished, such as investment interest or
rent, the income is obtained in connection with the criminal conduct (*Pattison* [2008] 1
Cr App R (S) 287). The obtaining of the property need not be exclusively connected with
or result from the criminal conduct as long as it has some 'connection' with it (*Osei* (1998)

E

10 Cr App R (S) 289: an airline ticket and money given to a drugs courier for showing to an immigration officer in order to obtain entry; *Finch* (1993) 14 Cr App R (S) 226: money obtained by 'ripping-off' a drug dealer; *Randle and Pottle* [1991] COD 369: profits from the sale of a book about the prison escape of the spy, George Blake, in which the defendants had participated).

In *Paulet* [2009] EWCA Crim 288 P had pleaded guilty to obtaining a pecuniary advantage by deception. He was living unlawfully in the UK and had no entitlement to seek or find employment but he had obtained work using a counterfeit French passport and a false national insurance number. A confiscation order was made in respect of monies in UK bank accounts into which he had deposited his wages. He argued that the money that he had earned from his employment was too remote from the criminal act to amount to a benefit under the Act, but the court was inclined to follow *Carter* [2006] EWCA Crim 416 and *King* [1987] QB 547 and to apply the test: 'Was the deception an operative cause of the obtaining of benefit'? There must now be some uncertainty as to the correctness of this outcome as a result of *obiter dicta* in the Supreme Court's approach to 'proportionality' in *Waya* [2013] 1 AC 294 (see **E19.30**). (See also *Paulet v UK* (2014) *The Times*, 19 May 2014).

E19.30   **Proportionality and Abuse of Process**   Before the iconoclastic decision of a nine-judge Supreme Court in *Waya* [2013] 1 AC 294, the Court of Appeal had occasionally had tentative recourse to the discretionary abuse of process jurisdiction in order to ameliorate some of the more 'draconian' features of benefit calculation. The Supreme Court has, instead, chosen the different, and arguably sounder, juridical route of 'proportionality'. It has construed the terms of the ECHR, Protocol 1, Article 1, as applied by the HRA 1998, s. 3, so that, in limited circumstances, 'the judge should, if confronted by an application for an order which would be disproportionate, refuse to make it but accede only to an application for such sum as would be proportionate' (at [16]: see **E19.6**). The judgment further addresses this issue thus (at [12], [20]–[21] and [24]):

> It is clear law, and was common ground between the parties, that this imports, via the rule of fair balance, the requirement that there must be a reasonable relationship of proportionality between the means employed by the State in, inter alia, the deprivation of property as a form of penalty, and the legitimate aim which is sought to be realised by the deprivation...

> The difficult question is when a confiscation order sought may be disproportionate. The clear rule as set out in the Strasbourg jurisprudence requires examination of the relationship between the aim of the legislation and the means employed to achieve it. The first governs the second, but the second must be proportionate to the first. Likewise, the clear limitation on the domestic court's power to read and give effect to the statute in a manner which keeps it Convention compliant is that the interpretation must recognise and respect the essential purpose, or 'grain' of the statute.

> ...The purpose of the legislation is plainly, and has repeatedly been held to be, to impose upon convicted defendants a severe regime for removing from them their proceeds of crime.... It does not, however, follow that its deterrent qualities represent the essence (or the 'grain') of the legislation. They are, no doubt, an incident of it, but they are not its essence. Its essence, and its frequently declared purpose, is to remove from criminals the pecuniary proceeds of their crime.

> ...it must clearly be understood that the judge's responsibility to refuse to make a confiscation order which, because disproportionate, would result in an infringement of the Convention right under...(Article 1)...is not the same as the re-creation by another route of the general discretion once available to judges but deliberately removed. An order which the judge would not have made as a matter of discretion does not thereby ipso facto become disproportionate. So to treat the jurisdiction would be to ignore the rule that the Parliamentary objective must, so long as proportionately applied, be respected.

The Court accepted the potential for disproportionate outcomes in abuse of process cases such as *Morgan* [2008] 4 All ER 890 and *Shabir* [2009] 1 Cr App R (S) 497, while stating (at

[18]): 'the better analysis of such situations is that orders such as those there considered ought to be refused by the judge on the grounds that they would be wholly disproportionate and a breach of [Article 1]. There is no need to invoke the concept of abuse of process.' In *Morgan*, (a) the defendant's crimes were limited to offences causing loss to one or more identifiable losers, (b) his benefit was limited to those crimes, (c) the loser had neither brought nor intended to bring civil proceedings to recover the loss, but (d) the defendant either had repaid the loser or was ready, willing and able immediately to repay him the full amount of the loss. However, the Court of Appeal in *Morgan* opined (at [31]) that the position may be different:

> ...where the defendant, even if he has repaid the victim or is ready to do so, has significantly profited through use of the stolen money whilst it was in his hands and thus has obtained a benefit beyond the loss inflicted on the victim; examples include the defendant who invests the money profitably, or gambles with it successfully, or who buys or obtains property which is let out... [or] where although repayment in full is offered, it is uncertain that it will be accomplished... and prosecutors might properly be cautious about accepting promises to pay in the future from defendants whose dishonesty forms the basis of their crimes; indeed we anticipate that it may be difficult to establish abuse... unless the defendant has either already made restitution in full or is in a position to tender it immediately in a guaranteed form, such as a banker's draft or funds in a solicitor's hands.

In *Shabir* a pharmacist had inflated prescription claims. It was accepted that his illicit proceeds amounted to £464, whereas, applying the 'criminal lifestyle' provisions of the POCA 2002, the benefit figure reached £212,464.

The Supreme Court in *Waya* went further: to value stolen goods as benefit when they are returned intact to the owner where the burglar or handler is caught in the act would be disproportionate (see, e.g., *Wilkes* [2003] 2 Cr App R (S) 625), stating (at [32]): **E19.31**

> If... an order were sought independently of the lifestyle provisions and the concomitant assumptions, and to the extent that it were based solely on the momentary benefit of obtaining goods which had been restored intact to the true owners, that order would be disproportionate and ought not to be made: it would not serve the aim, or go with the grain, of the legislation. Such a defendant's proceeds of crime would already have been restored to the loser in their entirety. An order in the same sum again would simply impose an additional financial penalty upon him. If such a defendant deserves an additional financial penalty, as in some cases he may, it ought to be imposed openly by way of fine, and whether or not he is also sent to prison, providing he has the means to pay.

Moreover, their lordships stated (at [34]):

> There may be other cases of disproportion analogous to that of goods or money entirely restored to the loser. That will have to be resolved case by case as the need arises. Such a case might include, for example, the defendant who, by deception, induces someone else to trade with him in a manner otherwise lawful, and who gives full value for goods or services obtained. He ought no doubt to be punished and, depending on the harm done and the culpability demonstrated, maybe severely, but whether a confiscation order is proportionate for any sum beyond profit made may need careful consideration. Counsel's submissions also touched very lightly on cases of employment obtained by deception, where it may well be that difficult questions of causation may arise, quite apart from any argument based upon disproportion. Those issues were not the subject of argument in this case and must await an appeal in which they directly arise; moreover related issues are understood to be currently before the Strasbourg court.

The Court of Appeal has since quashed confiscation orders for the value of a stolen vehicle which was subsequently recovered intact — albeit in Ibiza (*Axworthy* [2012] EWCA Crim 2889). Note, however, that, if a defendant obtained chattels as a result of his criminal conduct and used them for a substantial period, thereby materially reducing their value, and the chattels were ultimately restored to their true owners, the court should not give credit for the residual value of those chattels. The court had to focus on the property that the defendant originally obtained. There was nothing in the wording of the POCA 2002 or the ECHR which required the court to deduct the residual value. A confiscation order based on the original value of the property would not be disproportionate (*Harvey* [2014] 1 WLR 124).

An order was also quashed for the amount of property obtained by the forgery of a will where, although probate had been granted to the defendant, the estate had yet to be distributed (*Hursthouse* [2013] EWCA Crim 517). In *Sale* [2014] 1 WLR 663 the defendant had corruptly given gifts to a Network Rail employee in order to procure contracts. An order in the sum of the total value of the contacts obtained was disproportionate. A proportionate order would be one which took account of the profit gained under the relevant contracts together with the value of the pecuniary advantage gained by obtaining a market share, excluding competitors and saving on the costs of preparing proper tenders. Unfortunately, the value of that pecuniary advantage had not been assessed: 'In cases of this nature in the future, it was to be hoped that prosecutors would be alert to this aspect of the case, so that the real benefit or pecuniary advantage derived by the wrongdoer could be identified' (see also *Morgan* [2014] 1 All ER 1208). There is a 'clear distinction' between cases in which goods or services are provided by way of a lawful contract but the transaction is tainted by associated illegality and cases where the entire undertaking is unlawful, as in *King* [2014] EWCA Crim 621 where an order for the business turnover was upheld against a commercial car trader posing as a private seller in breach of consumer protection regulations, as the 'entire enterprise was characterized by deliberate misrepresentation'. On the other hand, the fact that defendants had not acted dishonestly or in bad faith in committing, for example, an offence under the Trade Marks Act 1964, a lifestyle offence, did not mean that an order applying the assumption of benefit to their gross profits was disproportionate: 'It is the proceeds that matter, not the blame' (*Hampshire County Council v Beazley* [2013] 1 WLR 3331). Where smuggled cigarettes are seized by HM Revenue and Customs, there has not been restoration to HMRC of the lost duty and, accordingly, an order for the value of the cigarettes is not disproportionate (*Louca* [2013 EWCA Crim 2090).

For the correct approach to a confiscation order that includes an amount that is also the subject of a compensation order, see *Jawad* [2013] 1 WLR 3861 and **E19.62**.

E19.32   The mandatory nature of the process makes the prosecution decision to invoke it critical and there must be an individual exercise of judgement in each case. As the Supreme Court noted in *Waya*, 'the Crown has an important preliminary function in ensuring that a disproportionate order is not sought. But the safeguard of the defendant's Convention right under [Article 1] not to be the object of a disproportionate order does not, and must not, depend on prosecutorial discretion.'

Dicta may need to be revisited in cases such as *CPS v Nelson* [2010] QB 678; *Del Basso* [2011] 1 Cr App R (S) 268; *Wilkinson* [2009] EWCA Crim 2733; *Mahmood* [2006] 1 Cr App R (S) 570 and *Farquhar* [2008] 2 Cr App R (S) 601.

In *R (Secretary of State for Work and Pensions) v Croydon Crown Court* [2011] 1 Cr App R (S) 1 the Divisional Court upheld a judge's refusal to make an order following an earlier unequivocal representation by the judge (to which the prosecution did not object) that confiscation proceedings would not follow if voluntary repayment was made. For the court to give an offender an inducement and then renege after she had acted to her disadvantage would damage the integrity of the criminal justice process.

E19.33   In *R (BERR) v Lowe* [2009] 2 Cr App R (S) 544 the Court held that an abuse did not arise from the making of an order where the property had been recovered by a liquidator following its fraudulent transfer by a defendant company director during winding-up proceedings: 'the suggestion of abuse could not remotely arise since the defendant made no effort to restore the property of his own accord and his criminal conduct was not limited to one or more identifiable loser'.

E19.34   **The Role of the Assumptions**   Where the court determines that the defendant has a criminal lifestyle, all the assumptions in the POCA 2002, s. 10, are mandatory. The first three assumptions, relating to property transferred or held by a defendant and to expenditure made by him, cover the six-year period ending on the day when proceedings were started. However, where an earlier confiscation order has been made on the basis of general criminal conduct (or where the court was 'entitled' to make an extended order under earlier legislation), the relevant period commences on 'the day when the defendant's benefit was calculated for the purposes of the last such confiscation order' (POCA 2002, ss. 8(8) and 10(8) and (9); *Chahal* [2014] EWCA Crim 101; *Barnett* [2011] EWCA Crim 2936). The assumptions are not triggered unless and until the prosecution has proved that the defendant obtained the property (or incurred expenditure) which the prosecution contends goes towards the valuation of the defendant's benefit' (*Whittington* [2010] 1 Cr App R (S) 545).

Proceeds of Crime Act 2002, s. 10

(1) If the court decides under section 6 that the defendant has a criminal lifestyle it must make the following four assumptions for the purpose of—
  (a) deciding whether he has benefited from his general criminal conduct, and
  (b) deciding his benefit from the conduct.
(2) The first assumption is that any property transferred to the defendant at any time after the relevant day was obtained by him—
  (a) as a result of his general criminal conduct, and
  (b) at the earliest time he appears to have held it.
(3) The second assumption is that any property held by the defendant at any time after the date of conviction was obtained by him—
  (a) as a result of his general criminal conduct, and
  (b) at the earliest time he appears to have held it.
(4) The third assumption is that any expenditure incurred by the defendant at any time after the relevant day was met from property obtained by him as a result of his general criminal conduct.
(5) The fourth assumption is that, for the purpose of valuing any property obtained (or assumed to have been obtained) by the defendant, he obtained it free of any other interests in it.
(6) But the court must not make a required assumption in relation to particular property or expenditure if—
  (a) the assumption is shown to be incorrect, or
  (b) there would be a serious risk of injustice if the assumption were made.
(7) If the court does not make one or more of the required assumptions it must state its reasons.
(8) The relevant day is the first day of the period of six years ending with—
  (a) the day when proceedings for the offence concerned were started against the defendant, or
  (b) if there were two or more offences and proceedings for them were started on different days, the earliest of those days.
(9) But if a confiscation order mentioned in section 8(3)(c) has been made against the defendant at any time during the period mentioned in subsection (8)—
  (a) the relevant day is the day when the defendant's benefit was calculated for the purposes of the last confiscation order;
  (b) the second assumption does not apply to any property which was held by him on or before the relevant day.
(10) The date of conviction is—
  (a) the date on which the defendant was convicted of the offence concerned, or
  (b) if there are two or more offences and the convictions were on different dates, the date of the latest.

E19.35 The first assumption is that any property transferred to the defendant within the six-year period that preceded the start of the proceedings was obtained by him (a) 'as a result of his general criminal conduct', and (b) at the earliest time he appears to have held it (s. 10(2)). Proceedings start when a summons or warrant is issued or when a defendant is charged following arrest without warrant or when a voluntary bill of indictment is preferred (s. 85). Property is transferred if 'an interest' in it is transferred or granted by another (s. 84(2)(c)).

E19.36 The second assumption is that any property held by the defendant at any time after the date of conviction was obtained as a result of his general criminal conduct at the earliest time he appears to have held it (s. 10(3)). It is irrelevant when he acquired the property (*Chrastny (No. 2)* [1991] 1 All ER 189). Where the defendant establishes that he holds property which has been purchased partly by means of a legitimate mortgage (i.e. not one fraudulently obtained), only the value of the equity should be treated as representing criminal proceeds (*Roach* [2008] EWCA Crim 2649).

E19.37 The third assumption is that any expenditure incurred by the defendant at any time after the start of the six-year period was met from property obtained by him as a result of his general criminal conduct (s. 10(4)). In other words, once some expenditure is proved, the court must assume it was funded from property obtained as a result of earlier criminal conduct. The fact of expenditure, classically in drugs cases, may be inferred from the circumstances:

> This is a perfectly proper inference to make, as a matter of common sense... In relation to a large quantity of drugs of this sort, approaching the matter on the balance of probabilities where there is no alternative credible explanation, the inference is obvious: money would be required to pay for the drugs. Those who traffic in the drugs trade do not normally extend credit or trust to others involved (*Dellaway* [2001] 1 Cr App R (S) 77).

Dellaway was explained in *Green* [2007] 3 All ER 751 (at [25]–[26]):

> In a case such as *Dellaway*, in which the defendants were found in possession of one parcel of drugs and there was no direct evidence of the source of the funds used to purchase them, to make the assumption... produces no injustice. However, if there is evidence which the court accepts, as there was in this case, that the proceeds of sale were regularly reinvested in new stock, the position is different. If a defendant has purchased and sold drugs continuously over a long period of time, it will often be the case that the funds used to purchase each new parcel of drugs will have been derived in whole or in part from the proceeds of sale of the previous parcel. In such a case the money received from the sale of the drugs clearly does represent the proceeds of drug trafficking and an assumption (were it necessary to make one) that the expenditure required in order to purchase the next consignment was met out of payments received in connection with drug trafficking would clearly be correct. It is equally clear, however, that the proceeds of sale and the money used to buy the new stock is the same money and that it would be wrong to treat the defendant as having received two separate sums of money when in fact he has received only one...

E19.38 Arguably the legitimate boundaries of inference have been stretched on occasions. In *Barnham* [2006] 1 Cr App R (S) 83, the defendant was convicted of two conspiracies to import drugs but no importation had actually occurred. The judge was entitled to infer, 'provided he keeps well in mind that the risk of serious injustice must be avoided', that the defendant had in fact available to him quantities of drugs intended for importation and that those drugs had been paid for out of earlier trafficking. Moreover, where the judge concluded that the defendant was the lead organiser, he was entitled to discount the possibility that other conspirators had contributed to the cost of the drugs. In *Odesanya* [2005] All ER (D) 221 (Oct), the defendant had been convicted of a drugs importation. In the confiscation proceedings he could be linked to an earlier importation of drugs, although there was no evidence proving the amount or value of the earlier drugs. The Court of Appeal nevertheless upheld an inference that the amount and value of the first importation were identical with those of the second, noting that there was no evidence from the defendant on the point.

The limits of the exercise were illustrated in *Williams* [2001] 2 Cr App R (S) 44. The judge properly calculated drugs expenditure of nearly £500,000. However, treating this sum as profit from a notional earlier transaction, he then purported to work out the gross amount of *that* transaction. Deciding arbitrarily that the expenditure represented a 25 per cent profit on the earlier transaction, he multiplied the expenditure by four, making nearly £2 million, to which he then added the net benefit, making a total of nearly £2.5 million. The Court of Appeal quashed the order, observing:

> The mistake... was to take the figure produced by the application of the proper approach, £484,437, and then to subject it to a series of further hypotheses for which there was no evidential basis, namely:
> (i)   that it was the product of a particular form of drug trafficking i.e. wholesale supply,
> (ii) that it represented net profits of such activity and

(iii) that a hypothetical quantity and value of drugs must have been required to be purchased during the preceding 6 years to enable such a net profit to be realised.

A finding or concession that a minder or courier had no beneficial interest in property such as drugs or that it is the defendant's first such offence, should prevent any inference that he paid for the property (*J* [2001] 1 Cr App R (S) 273; *Butler* (1993) 14 Cr App R (S) 537; *Johannes* [2002] 2 Cr App R (S) 109). As Cranston J stated in *Mahmood* [2013] 1 WLR 3146 (at [26]):

> The section 10(4) assumption does not mean that, unless he can prove otherwise, each conspirator is treated as having incurred all of the expenditure. It may be that in the circumstances of a particular case the court can draw inferences that a particular member of the conspiracy met an expense of its operation. In other, and perhaps many cases, the natural inference will be that the conspirators will have contributed equally to such expenses. But without a finding that the defendant in question spent something, the section 10(4) assumption is not triggered.

The fourth assumption is that the defendant is or was the only person with an interest in any property which he is proven or assumed to have obtained (s. 10(5)). (For the deduction of third-party interests from the available amount, see **E19.56**.)   **E19.39**

Defeating the Assumptions   An assumption may not be made if the defendant proves on the   **E19.40**
balance of probabilities that it is 'incorrect', e.g., by evidence of legitimate income (s. 10(6)(a)) (see, e.g., *Hesketh* [2006] EWCA Crim 2596). If the court finds an assumption to be incorrect, it must give reasons for its conclusion (s. 10(7)). It has been held by the ECtHR that the defence burden of proving that assets are probably legitimate is not incompatible with the ECHR, Article 6 (*Grayson v UK* (2008) 48 EHRR 722).

It is to be noted that the first assumption is that the property was obtained as a result of 'his [i.e. the defendant's] general criminal conduct' (s. 10(2)(a)). Therefore, it may be sufficient for the defendant to show that the property was obtained as a result of offences committed by persons other than the defendant.

An assumption can be avoided when 'there would be a serious risk of injustice if the assumption   **E19.41**
were made' (s. 10(6)(b)). 'It is putting it too high' to require the defendant to prove injustice on the balance of probabilities; 'the judge must avoid any real risk of injustice'; the court 'should step back and determine whether there is or might be a risk of serious or real injustice and, if there is or might be, then such an order should not be made' (*Benjafield* [2003] 1 AC 1099).

In *Jones* [2007] 1 WLR 7 the Court of Appeal expressly approved the following statement from an earlier edition of this work: the risk of injustice must arise from the operation of the assumptions in the calculation of benefit and not from eventual hardship in the making of a confiscation order (see also *Dore* [1997] 2 Cr App R (S) 152; *Neuberg* [2008] 1 Cr App R (S) 481; *Ahmed* [2005] 1 All ER 128). What is contemplated is some unjust contradiction in the process of assumption and an agreed factual basis for sentence (see **E19.13** and *Lunnon* [2005] 1 Cr App R (S) 111, *Lazarus* [2005] 1 Cr App R (S) 552 and *Bakewell* [2006] 2 Cr App R (S) 277) or in the process of assumption itself, e.g., in the double counting of income and expenditure.

There is no double penalty when drugs are both forfeited under the Misuse of Drugs Act 1971, s. 27 (see **E18.7**), and their value is counted as expenditure (*Dore*). In the case of cash, there should be no double counting if the Act is properly applied. The court must make the confiscation order before making any forfeiture order under any other statutory provisions and once the confiscation order is made there is no cash left to forfeit (*Barker* (15 December 1996 unreported)).

If the court is satisfied of a serious risk of injustice 'in an appropriate case', it may temper the   **E19.42**
full force of the assumptions by making a percentage discount to guard against 'a remote possibility that a small part of the property . . . had a legitimate source' (*Deprince* [2004] 2 Cr App R (S) 463).

E

Part E Sentencing

Stage Three — Determination of the Recoverable Amount

E19.43
Proceeds of Crime Act 2002, ss. 7 and 80

7.—(1) The recoverable amount for the purposes of section 6 is an amount equal to the defendant's benefit from the conduct concerned.

(2) But if the defendant shows that the available amount is less than that benefit the recoverable amount is—

(a) the available amount, or

(b) a nominal amount, if the available amount is nil.

(3) But if section 6(6) or (6A) applies the recoverable amount is such amount as—

(a) the court believes is just, but

(b) does not exceed the amount found under subsection (1) or (2) (as the case may be).

(4) In calculating the defendant's benefit from the conduct concerned for the purposes of subsection (1), any property in respect of which—

(a) a recovery order is in force under section 266, or

(b) a forfeiture order is in force under section 298(2),

must be ignored.

(5) If the court decides the available amount, it must include in the confiscation order a statement of its findings as to the matters relevant for deciding that amount.

80.—(1) This section applies for the purpose of deciding the value of property obtained by a person as a result of or in connection with his criminal conduct; and the material time is the time the court makes its decision.

(2) The value of the property at the material time is the greater of the following—

(a) the value of the property (at the time the person obtained it) adjusted to take account of later changes in the value of money;

(b) the value (at the material time) of the property found under subsection (3).

(3) The property found under this subsection is as follows—

(a) if the person holds the property obtained, the property found under this subsection is that property;

(b) if he holds no part of the property obtained, the property found under this subsection is any property which directly or indirectly represents it in his hands;

(c) if he holds part of the property obtained, the property found under this subsection is that part and any property which directly or indirectly represents the other part in his hands.

(4) The references in subsection (2)(a) and (b) to the value are to the value found in accordance with section 79.

Section 7 is prospectively amended by the PACA 2009, sch. 7, para. 100, so as to add any property which has been forfeited in pursuance of a forfeiture notice under s. 297A (see **D8.18**).

E19.44 **The Amount of Benefit** The first rule is that 'the recoverable amount... is an amount equal to the defendant's benefit from the conduct concerned' (POCA 2002, s. 7(1)). The amount of the defendant's benefit is literally 'the value of the property obtained' (s. 76(7)). It follows that benefit does not mean profit. In other words, all of the property obtained in accordance with the principles in *May* [2008] 1 AC 1028 (see **E19.20**) is to be accounted and not merely the profit element (see also *Smith* (1989) 11 Cr App R (S) 290; *Del Basso* [2011] 1 Cr App R (S) 268; *Simons* (1994) 15 Cr App R (S) 126; *Banks* [1997] 2 Cr App R (S) 110; *Simpson* [1998] 2 Cr App R (S) 111; *Currey* (1995) 16 Cr App R (S) 42; *Carter* [2006] EWCA Crim 416). Note that, according to the Court of Appeal, although *Waya* suggested that *Del Basso* was correctly decided, 'the final decision does seem excessively harsh and may arguably be characterised as disproportionate' (*Harvey* [2014] 1 WLR 124 at [65]). As a general rule, the recoverable amount should not be reduced to reflect, for example, the notional outlay of expenses in the acquisition of controlled drugs (*Versluis* [2005] 2 Cr App R (S) 144).

No discount can be given to reflect income which the defendant would have derived from the loser had there been no misconduct — e.g., where a defendant had falsely claimed income support, no account was to be taken of working families tax credit to which he would have been entitled but for his misrepresentations (*Richards* [2005] 2 Cr App R (S) 583).

Notwithstanding authorities to the contrary under earlier legislation, it seems to be accepted **E19.45** that s. 79(3) expressly allows the deduction of a mortgage advance from the market value of property purchased with a combination of monies from criminal conduct and innocent monies (*Nadarajah* [2007] EWCA Crim 2688; see also *Moulden* [2005] 1 Cr App R (S) 691; *Johnson* [1991] 2 QB 249; *Ginwalla* [2005] EWCA Crim 3553; *Pattison* [2008] 1 Cr App R (S) 287; *Olupitan v Director of Assets Recovery Agency* [2008] EWCA Civ 104).

In *Waya* [2013] 1 AC 294, the Supreme Court distinguished the mechanics and legal implications of obtaining a loan from those of a normal mortgage transaction. In the latter, the advance is paid by the mortgage lender into the purchaser's solicitor's client account in trust for and to the order of the lender until paid over to the vendor's solicitor. The advance remains in the beneficial ownership of the lender until completion. The purchaser himself has no control over the disposal of the advance and it never comes into his possession. The appellant had obtained a £465,000 mortgage (60 per cent of the value) by false representations as to his means (but continued to meet the repayments); he had contributed £310,000 of his own funds towards the purchase (40 per cent of the value). The Court stated (at [53] and [78]):

> Mr Waya never in fact acquired anything but an equity of redemption, . . . the equity of redemption corresponding in value (at that point) to his untainted down-payment of £310,000. To conclude . . . .that Mr Waya obtained £465,000 is a legally inaccurate account of the transaction, because the loan sum never became his or came into his possession. Under the tripartite contractual arrangements between vendor, purchaser and mortgage lender Mr Waya obtained property in the form of a thing in action which was an indivisible bundle of rights and liabilities, and it cannot be correct to fasten onto the rights and ignore the liabilities (the analysis would of course be different if the loan had ever been at the defendant's free disposal . . .) In short, what Mr Waya obtained was the right to have the mortgage advance applied in the acquisition of his flat, subject from the moment of completion to the mortgage lender's security, which ensured the repayment of the advance. This thing in action had no market value at or immediately after completion, as the equity of redemption (or in everyday speech, the equity) represented Mr Waya's down-payment. There will no doubt be other mortgage fraud cases in which this thing in action does have a value. One example would be the common case where false representations as to income and status of the borrower are accompanied by a dishonestly inflated valuation of the property which is being purchased. In such a case the fraud may not only have induced a larger loan than would otherwise have been made, but may well have induced a loan which is not fully secured as the lender believes. Another example might be the case where the property which the defendant is purporting to purchase does not exist, or is not really being purchased at all. In both these cases the thing in action has a real value to the defendant.

> . . . we consider that the benefit obtained by Mr Waya from his criminal behaviour was a thing in action with no immediate market value. It was an item of property but it had a very short life, since on completion it immediately came to be represented by a fractional 60 per cent share of the leasehold interest in the flat, subject to (the whole of) the mortgage, with the remaining 40% representing the untainted contribution.

In *Waya* the property had increased in value: 'In economic terms, his benefit was so much of any appreciation in value *as was attributable to the mortgage obtained by his dishonesty*. Immediately after completion this value was nil, but as the market value of the flat increased the benefit came to have a significant value, that is 60 per cent of the appreciation in the net value of the flat, *subject to the mortgage*' (emphasis added).

Valuation of Benefit   Secondly, 'the basic rule' of valuation throughout the POCA 2002 is **E19.46** that the value of any property is its market value at the material time (s. 79(2)). If the defendant and another person both hold interests in the same property, then it is the value of the defendant's limited interest which is to be taken for the purposes of calculating his benefit (s. 79(3); *Waya* [2013] 1 AC 294; *Rose* [2008] 3 All ER 315). This does not mean that the value of a true owner's interest in property wipes out its benefit value when obtained by the defendant.

The material time for valuing benefit 'is the time the court makes its decision' (s. 80(1)). Its value at that time is the *greater* of the following:

(a) its (market) value at the time it was obtained by the defendant (adjusted for subsequent inflation); or

(b) if he still holds the property, its current market value or, if he no longer holds the property, the market value of any property that 'directly or indirectly represents' it, or a combination of both if he has converted only part of the property which he originally obtained (s. 80(2)).

Thus, if the market value of the property has declined since the defendant obtained it, his benefit is its original market value adjusted upwards for inflation (*Foxley* (1995) 16 Cr App R (S) 879). It is generally appropriate to apply the Retail Price Index rather the Consumer Price Index (*Shepherd* [2014] EWCA Crim 179). The Court of Appeal has held that a defendant is not entitled to discount an increase in the market value of a property as a result of home improvements — 'value is the predominant approach' (*X* [2007] EWCA Crim 2498).

The fraudulent purchase and subsequent sale of vehicles is a single process leading to a single benefit for these purposes. The judge should first look at the value of the vehicle when the defendant obtained it and then go on to see whether there were any proceeds of sale in his hands that exceeded (or were less than) the value of the vehicle when he obtained it. The benefit is the greater of the two values (*Scragg* [2006] EWCA Crim 2916 and see *X* [2007] EWCA Crim 2498).

Market value may vary according to whether goods have been obtained wholesale, e.g., by theft from containers in transit, or from a retail outlet (*Ascroft* [2004] 1 Cr App R (S) 326). The market value of property obtained by a thief or handler is the amount it would have cost the defendant to obtain the property legitimately or the economic value to the loser, rather than what the defendant could get for the property if he sold it (*Rose* [2008] 3 All ER 315).

E19.47   Overruling previous authority, the House of Lords held in *Islam* [2009] 1 AC 1076 that it is consistent with both the language and the spirit of the statutory scheme to take account of the black market value of drugs when valuing the benefit obtained by a defendant from their illegal importation, although such drugs had a nil market value after seizure for the purposes of assessing the amount available for confiscation. *Mejia* [2009] EWCA Crim 1940 concerned the importation of cocaine-impregnated fibre board which had been fashioned into ornate doors. It was argued that no market of any kind had been established for cocaine-impregnated doors and, in the absence of evidence as to the cost of extraction of the cocaine, there was no basis on which to determine the price that would be paid by a willing buyer. The Court of Appeal held that, had it been argued at trial that the relevant property was cocaine-impregnated doors, or that the true value was the invoice value of the doors or the purchase cost of the cocaine, the judge could have made relevant findings of fact. However, it was absurd to suggest that no value was to be attached to a product containing pure cocaine brought into the UK for the very purposes of extracting the cocaine and selling it on. The value of the cocaine was a reasonable indicator of the value of the doors. The relevant question was the market value of the property in the UK, not its cost at source. Even so, it may equally be argued on the basis of some of the dicta in *Islam* that, in drugs cases, the relevant market value will vary according to the position occupied by the defendant in the supply chain. In other words, the market value of drugs held by a wholesale dealer will be their value 'at that time' and not their subsequent and greater street value. However, where a court is satisfied that the dealer intends to cut the drugs in his possession and to supply them at street level, the benefit is the retail value (*Elsayed* [2014] EWCA Crim 333).

A worthless cheque has no value (*Johnson* (1990) 91 Cr App R 332).

E19.48   **Effect of Recovery or Forfeiture Order, Forfeiture Notice or Claim by Victim**   In calculating benefit, the court must ignore any property over which there is a recovery or forfeiture order or forfeiture notice in force (s. 7(4), as prospectively amended by the PACA 2009, sch. 7, para. 100: see **E19.43**). The effect of the subsection does not appear to have been considered in *Chatha* [2008] EWCA Crim 2597 where cash that was likely to be forfeited was included in the benefit, and, in the case of general criminal conduct, the court must deduct any previous confiscation orders (s. 8(3)). A court need not calculate the recoverable amount and make an order 'if it believes that any victim of the conduct has at any time started or intends to start proceedings against the defendant in respect of loss, injury or damage sustained in connection with the conduct' (s. 6(6): see E19.7). If it does decide to do so, the benefit is 'such amount as the court believes just'. Subsequent civil proceedings, e.g. a claim by Revenue and Customs for the recovery of the balance of unpaid duty not fully met by a confiscation order, will not necessarily amount to an abuse of process merely because Revenue and Customs did not disclose in the confiscation proceedings that they would or might institute civil action (*Revenue and Customs Commissioners v Crossman* [2008] 1 All ER 483).

Stage Four — Determination of the Available Amount

Proceeds of Crime Act 2002, s. 9　　　　　　　　　　　E19.49

(1) For the purposes of deciding the recoverable amount, the available amount is the aggregate of—

   (a) the total of the values (at the time the confiscation order is made) of all the free property then held by the defendant minus the total amount payable in pursuance of obligations which then have priority, and

   (b) the total of the values (at that time) of all tainted gifts.

(2) An obligation has priority if it is an obligation of the defendant—

   (a) to pay an amount due in respect of a fine or other order of a court which was imposed or made on conviction of an offence and at any time before the time the confiscation order is made, or

   (b) to pay a sum which would be included among the preferential debts if the defendant's bankruptcy had commenced on the date of the confiscation order or his winding up had been ordered on that date.

(3) 'Preferential debts' has the meaning given by section 386 of the Insolvency Act 1986.

This is the 'bottom line' of confiscation. A court cannot confiscate more than a defendant is worth — 'the available amount'. The assessments, first of the amount of benefit, and then of the available amount, are entirely separate exercises. The calculation of the available amount is simply a computation of the defendant's realisable assets (including tainted gifts), regardless of their origins, illegitimate or not. Where an asset is jointly owned by defendants, the court has to determine the extent of each owner's beneficial interest (*Gangar* [2012] 4 All ER 972). The value is the market value. Costs of sale may be deducted (*Cramer* (1992) 13 Cr App R (S) 390). If the offender proves on the balance of probabilities that he is worth less than the amount of his benefit, the 'available amount' becomes the 'recoverable amount' and, therefore, the amount of the order (s. 7(2)(a); see *Summers* [2008] 2 Cr App R (S) 569; *A-G's Ref (No. 2 of 2008) (Winters)* [2008] EWCA Crim 2953). Where he fails to do so, it is not necessary for the judge to have to make a specific finding that there are hidden assets (*Smith* [2011] EWCA Crim 2029). Where the judge is satisfied that there are hidden assets, it is for the defendant to prove that their value is less than the benefit figure (*Siddique* [2005] EWCA Crim 1812; *Barnham* [2006] 1 Cr App R (S) 83; *Valentine* [2006] EWCA Crim 2717). That was so even if his inability arose not from his deceitfulness but simply from his inability to satisfy the court of his true means. However, there was a balance to be struck. While the courts were right to treat with some scepticism assertions made by a defendant whose credibility, given his offending, might be deeply suspect, the absence of independent and credible corroborating evidence was not fatal as a proposition of law (despite the oft-cited dictum in *Walbrook* (1993) 15 Cr App R (S) 783 that generalised assertions will rarely be sufficient). While it might well prove fatal as a matter of fact, that was something that the judge had to decide when considering the facts (*Glaves v CPS* [2011] EWCA Civ 69; *Lee* [2013] EWCA Crim 657). Where the court concludes that the defendant has not revealed the true extent of his assets, it is not bound to make an order in the full amount of the benefit figure — it must adopt 'a just and proportionate view of the facts as a whole' (*McIntosh* [2011] 4 All ER 917). 'A confiscation order which, due to its magnitude, exceeds by far the likely assets of the defendant may operate as a disincentive to cooperate' (*Ahmad* [2012] 2 All ER 1137). Where a defendant asserts that assets have been disposed of, he must provide positive evidence to that effect (*Druce* [2013] EWCA Crim 40). In drugs importation cases,

E19.50

notwithstanding that the benefit figure is calculated on wholesale values, when assessing what may be available, the court is entitled to have regard to the fact that drugs which had been successfully imported and sold had a higher retail value (*Soutter* [2011] EWCA Crim 3160).

E19.51 The ECtHR has held that the defendant's burden of proving that the realisable assets are less than the benefit finding is not incompatible with Article 6 (*Grayson v UK* (2008) 48 EHRR 722, approving the respective Court of Appeal decisions in *Ripley* [2005] EWCA Crim 1453 and *Barnham* [2006] 1 Cr App R (S) 83).

The 'available amount' is the aggregate of:

(a) the total value at the time of the order of 'all the free property then held by the defendant' (minus the total amount of any priority obligations), *and*
(b) the total value of all 'tainted gifts' (s. 9(1)).

Property is 'held' by a person 'if he holds an interest in it' (s. 84). Property, therefore, includes a beneficial interest in a deceased's estate under a will or upon intestacy, administered or not. This is so notwithstanding that the market value at the time of the confiscation order may be negligible where there have been no probate or letters of administration and no information as to the extent of the assets, it being open to the prosecutor to apply for a revaluation once the extent of the interest becomes established (*Walbrook*; *Re Maye* [2008] 1 WLR 315).

When valuing a defendant's beneficial interest in shared property, the fact that his interest in the property cannot be realised without a court order or the consent of others does not mean that it has a nominal value only. Where property is subject to a trust, the court must proceed on the basis that the defendant will, if necessary, obtain an order under the Trusts of Land and Appointment of Trustees Act 1996 for the sale of the whole property and that he will receive his due proportion of the proceeds (*Modjiri* [2010] 4 All ER 837). Free property will include an entitlement under a trust where trustees have an administrative power (such as a power of investment) which cannot preclude the defendant's entitlement to such income as there is when income is produced by the invested assets, but it does not include a benefit under a trust where there is, by distinction, a dispositive power, such as the power of accumulation, which precludes any right to income at all until the trustees decide not to accumulate (*W* [2011] 2 Cr App R (S) 309). A beneficial interest under a 'Friends Provident Children's Trust' is free property (*Walker* [2012] 1 WLR 173).

E19.52 Whether or not a pension fund has any realisable value depends upon whether or not the policy is capable of being surrendered before maturity. If it is not, the fund has no value as a realisable asset — bearing in mind, however, that the prosecution may apply for a reconsideration under s. 22 when the policy matures (*Chen* [2010] 2 Cr App R (S) 221; *Cornfield* [2007] 1 Cr App R (S) 771: see also, in respect of company pensions, *Silvester* [2009] EWCA Crim 2182). In *Chen*, the Court of Appeal distinguished *Ford* [2009] 1 Cr App R (S) 68, which had held that, where a fund does have a surrender value, the available amount is the full value of the fund notwithstanding that the surrender value may be considerably less. The preferred view of the court in *Chen* was that the available amount is the sum that the defendant can actually realise, namely the surrender value.

Commission that had arisen from illegal conduct and was owed to an offender could not be treated as a realisable asset (*Najafpour* [2010] 2 Cr App R (S) 245).

The fact that a bankruptcy order had been made against an offender when all his assets were in the hands of his trustee in bankruptcy did not affect the judge's power to make a confiscation order. Whilst it might affect the enforcement of the confiscation order it would not affect the making of it. Under s. 102(8), property held by a defendant included property held by a trustee in bankruptcy and it was therefore impossible to say that an order could not be made against a bankrupt. If the public interest was relevant, it would not be served if the defendant was able to avoid an order by applying for his own bankruptcy when he was aware of the likelihood that a confiscation order would be made against him (*Shahid* [2009] 2 Cr App R (S) 687).

Realisable property may be recovered from any trust or company irrespective of any legal obstacles or protections that might arise under company or trust law (*RCPO v May* [2009] EWHC 1826 (QB)). Where a defendant controls a company and the company controls property which represents the benefit, the corporate veil may be lifted and company assets treated as those of the defendant (*Omar* [2005] 1 Cr App R (S) 446). **E19.53**

Property is 'free' unless there is already a forfeiture or deprivation order in force (s. 82). Cash which is merely the subject of an application for summary forfeiture under s. 298(4) remains 'free property'. If the cash is then included in the recoverable amount, further forfeiture under s. 308(9) is prevented. The purpose of s. 308(9) is plainly to ensure that money that has been seized is not deployed in a unfair way, so that it is both used to make up the quantum of a recoverable amount *and* the amount available for forfeiture (*Weller* [2009] EWCA Crim 810, where Moses LJ said (at [19]) that a 'decision has to be made as to which process is going to be used').

The process of calculation is as follows:

(a) identify the free property in which the defendant has an interest at the time of the order;
(b) calculate the total current market value of his beneficial interests in that property;
(c) deduct the amount of his priority obligations (i.e. fines, etc., and preferential debts);
(d) lastly, add the total value of any 'tainted gifts'.

In Customs and Excise cases, seizure of the instruments of crime, such as motor vehicles, results in their immediate forfeiture so that they no longer form part of the available amount (*Thacker* (1995) 16 Cr App R (S) 461).

The available amount must be reduced by the amount of any outstanding fine or other order made following a conviction at any time before the confiscation order is made (s. 9(2)(a)). A further discount must be given for any sum 'which would be included among the preferential debts' if the defendant's bankruptcy had commenced or his winding-up been ordered on the date of the confiscation order (s. 9(2)(b)). 'Preferential debt' has the same meaning as in s. 386 of the Insolvency Act 1986 and includes remuneration of employees and pension scheme contributions.

Tainted Gifts The total value of 'all tainted gifts' must be added to the available amount (s. 9(1)(b)). Any difficulty that the defendant may have in retrieving the actual gift is immaterial (*Smith* [2014] 1 WLR 898; *Tighe* [1996] 1 Cr App R (S) 314). A defendant makes a gift if he transfers property to another for 'significantly less' consideration than its value at the time he obtained it (s. 78(1)). The discharge by payment of a lump sum as part of a divorce settlement, which was itself intended to discharge a mortgage, does not amount to a gift (*Rastelli* [2008] EWCA Crim 373). **E19.54**

The process of then identifying whether a gift is 'tainted' varies according to whether or not the defendant has been found to have a criminal lifestyle. Where a defendant has a criminal lifestyle or where 'no court has made a decision', a gift is tainted if it was made since the start of the six-year period preceding the commencement of the proceedings (s. 77(2) and (9)). Alternatively, a gift is tainted, regardless of when it was made, if it is proved to consist of property obtained by the defendant 'as a result of or in connection with his general criminal conduct' or of property in his hands which represented such property 'in whole or part... directly or indirectly' (s. 77(3)). If the defendant does not have a criminal lifestyle, any gift is tainted if made 'after the date on which the offence concerned was committed' (s. 77(5)). Under the POCA 2002, a continuing offence is deemed to be committed 'on the first occasion when it is committed' (s. 77(6)).

The value of the tainted gift is the value of 'the property given' so that in a transaction for consideration, the property given is the proportion of the whole that represents the gift element (s. 78(2)). The value of the property given is its market value. The market value is the greater of the following: (a) its value at the time it was given (adjusted for subsequent inflation); or (b) its value at the time of the confiscation order. If the recipient of the gift has retained none or only **E19.55** part of the property, its value is that of 'any property which directly or indirectly represents it in his hands' or a combination of the value of what he has retained and such property (s. 81).

It appears that, where a defendant has made a tainted gift to another defendant without real ownership or control passing, the value of the property should not be accounted simultaneously as part of the first defendant's available amount and as the second defendant's benefit (*Richards* [2008] EWCA Crim 1841).

E19.56 **Third-party Interests** The court should first determine whether the defendant himself has any beneficial interest in the property. Ordinary principles of property and trust law, including separate corporate identity, the doctrine of 'sham' and the presumption that a registered owner is the beneficial owner of real property, apply in determining whether the defendant 'holds an interest' in the property. See *Alom* [2012] EWCA Crim 736 at [23] ('where legal ownership is clearly expressed, it will be a rare outcome that beneficial ownership does not follow the same pattern'), *Jones v Kernott* [2012] 1 AC 776, *Re Ali* [2013] 1 FLR 1061, *CPS v Piper* [2011] EWHC 3570 (Admin), *Larkfield Ltd v RCPO* [2010] 3 All ER 1173 and *RCPO v Johnson* [2011] EWCA Crim 1950. If the court does determine that the defendant has such an interest, it should then go on to consider whether any other party's share is genuinely beneficial or whether it is a tainted gift (*Buckman* [1997] 1 Cr App R (S) 325). The genuineness of an encumbrance, such as a mortgage, is a question of fact to be determined on the evidence (*Ghori* [2012] EWCA Crim 1115; *Rowsell* [2011] EWCA Crim 1894; *Harvey* [1999] 1 Cr App R (S) 354). It is 'self-evident' that, in order to establish a third-party interest, there must be some evidence of when and how it was acquired (*Perrey* [2011] EWCA Crim 2316). The balance of a negative equity cannot be set off against the available amount (*Ghadami* [1998] 1 Cr App R (S) 42).

Frequently, the defendant's share in the value of the family home will be included in the available amount. At this stage the fact that the home may need to be sold to meet the order, and innocent family members suffer hardship as a result, is irrelevant to 'the arithmetic exercise' of calculating the defendant's worth (*Ahmed* [2005] 1 All ER 128). The provisions are compatible with the ECHR (*Danison v UK* (1998) Appln. 45042/98, 7 September 1999).

However, an innocent partner or third party may be able to temper the harshness of the process in three ways. First, the position may be very different at the enforcement stage (see **E19.66**). If the order is not met and the prosecutor applies for permission to realise the property through the appointment of an enforcement receiver, the court is obliged to receive representations from affected third parties (POCA 2002, s. 51(8)), which may include subsequent applications by them for recognition of their beneficial interest in the property (*Re Norris* [2001] 3 All ER 961). The rights under the ECHR, Article 8, of those affected are engaged and the court must consider whether, for example, the loss of the home is proportionate (*Ahmed*).

E19.57 A tenant protected by contract or statute is not a 'person who has possession of realisable property' and may not be ordered to give up possession of property to the receiver under s. 51(5) (*Brittain (as Enforcement Receiver) v Noskova* [2009] EWHC 2884 (Admin)).

Secondly and similarly, where a management receiver has been appointed in the context of a restraint order over the property and the receiver wishes, for example, to realise part of the property to meet expenses, the court must give persons holding interests in the property a reasonable opportunity to make representations (s. 49(8)).

Lastly, where there are concurrent matrimonial proceedings, it may be possible to regularise the interests in shared property by ordering the transfer of the innocent partner's share as ancillary relief in those proceedings thus taking that share out of the calculation of the available amount. In *Customs and Excise Commissioners v MCA* [2003] 2 WLR 210, the prosecution sought to enforce an order by realising the home. The wife, who had filed for divorce before the offences occurred, sought their transfer to her as ancillary relief under the Matrimonial Causes Act 1973. It was held that it would be disproportionate to any legitimate public interest to force a sale of the home and that the appropriate course in these circumstances is to order the transfer of the defendant's entire beneficial and legal interests to the wife (see also *CPS v Grimes*; *Grimes v Grimes* [2003] 2 FLR 510; *Hedges* [2004] EWCA Crim 2133; *X v X* [2005] 2 FLR 487). Since the abolition by the POCA 2002 of the High Court jurisdiction over restraint and enforcement, there is no longer any dual procedure under which confiscation and matrimonial ancillary relief can be combined. The proper course is for the matrimonial aspects to be dealt with first (*Webber v CPS* [2007] 1 WLR 1052). This should not be regarded as 'open season to collusive agreements between dishonest former spouses'. 'As a matter of justice and public policy', where the family assets are themselves tainted, they should not be distributed to satisfy ancillary relief claims. In *CPS v Richards* [2006] 2 FLR 1220, the Court stated that, when conducting the discretionary balancing exercise in the family proceedings, 'the only decisive factor' is whether the assets are tainted as having been derived from crime. However, in *Stodgell v Stodgell* [2009] 2 FLR 244 (where, significantly, the ancillary application was for a lump sum and not a transfer of the family home) it was said that 'while non-complicity in the crime is a necessary condition for the wife to succeed in an ancillary relief claim as a matter of discretion where she is in competition with a confiscation order, such non-complicity is not a sufficient condition'.

E19.58 So far as the enforcement of the actual confiscation order is concerned, there is 'no legal principle under which a person could be deprived of the benefit of illegally obtained property on the grounds of public policy' (*Gibson v RCPO* [2009] 2 WLR 471). In that case, the family home had been purchased in joint names before the offences began but, to the knowledge of the defendant's wife, mortgage payments were met from their proceeds. Nevertheless, the court declined to hold that this aspect displaced her beneficial interest. The payments were not gifts as she had provided consideration by bringing up the children and looking after the home. The case could not be equated with the principle in *Richards* which involved the discretionary transfer of property; what the prosecution had sought here was for the court to take property from a person who already owned it.

Confiscation Orders and Sentence

Proceeds of Crime Act 2002, ss. 13 to 15   **E19.59**

13.—(1) If the court makes a confiscation order it must proceed as mentioned in subsections (2) and (4) in respect of the offence or offences concerned.

(2) The court must take account of the confiscation order before—
  (a) it imposes a fine on the defendant, or
  (b) it makes an order falling within subsection (3).

(3) These orders fall within this subsection—
  (a) an order involving payment by the defendant, other than an order under section 130 of the Sentencing Act (compensation orders) or an order under section 4 of the Prevention of Social Housing Fraud Act 2013 (unlawful profit orders);
  (b) an order under section 27 of the Misuse of Drugs Act 1971 (forfeiture orders);
  (c) an order under section 143 of the Sentencing Act (deprivation orders);
  (d) an order under section 23 or 23A of the Terrorism Act 2000 (forfeiture orders).

(4) Subject to subsection (2), the court must leave the confiscation order out of account in deciding the appropriate sentence for the defendant.

(5) Subsection (6) applies if—
  (a) the Crown Court makes—
    (i) both a confiscation order and a compensation order under section 130 of the Sentencing Act,
    (ii) both a confiscation order and an unlawful profit order under section 4 of the Prevention of Social Housing Fraud Act 2013, or
    (iii) a confiscation order, a compensation order and an unlawful profit order,
  against the same person in the same proceedings, and
  (b) the court believes he will not have sufficient means to satisfy all the orders in full.

(6) In such a case the court must direct that so much of the compensation or amount payable under the unlawful profit order (or both) as it specifies is to be paid out of any sums recovered under the confiscation order; and the amount it specifies must be the amount it believes will not be recoverable because of the insufficiency of the person's means.

14.—(1) The court may—
    (a) proceed under section 6 before it sentences the defendant for the offence (or any of the offences) concerned, or
    (b) postpone proceedings under section 6 for a specified period.

(2) A period of postponement may be extended.

(3) A period of postponement (including one as extended) must not end after the permitted period ends.

(4) But subsection (3) does not apply if there are exceptional circumstances.

(5) The permitted period is the period of two years starting with the date of conviction.

(6) But if—
    (a) the defendant appeals against his conviction for the offence (or any of the offences) concerned, and
    (b) the period of three months (starting with the day when the appeal is determined or otherwise disposed of) ends after the period found under subsection (5),
the permitted period is that period of three months.

(7) A postponement or extension may be made—
    (a) on application by the defendant;
    (b) on application by the prosecutor;
    (c) by the court of its own motion.

(8) If—
    (a) proceedings are postponed for a period, and
    (b) an application to extend the period is made before it ends,
the application may be granted even after the period ends.

(9) The date of conviction is—
    (a) the date on which the defendant was convicted of the offence concerned, or
    (b) if there are two or more offences and the convictions were on different dates, the date of the latest.

(10) References to appealing include references to applying under section 111 of the Magistrates' Courts Act 1980 (statement of case).

(11) A confiscation order must not be quashed only on the ground that there was a defect or omission in the procedure connected with the application for or the granting of a postponement.

(12) But subsection (11) does not apply if before it made the confiscation order the court—
    (a) imposed a fine on the defendant;
    (b) made an order falling within section 13(3);
    (c) made an order under section 130 of the Sentencing Act (compensation orders);
    (d) made an order under section 4 of the Prevention of Social Housing Fraud Act 2013 (unlawful profit orders).

15.—(1) If the court postpones proceedings under section 6 it may proceed to sentence the defendant for the offence (or any of the offences) concerned.

(2) In sentencing the defendant for the offence (or any of the offences) concerned in the postponement period the court must not—
    (a) impose a fine on him,
    (b) make an order falling within section 13(3),
    (c) make an order for the payment of compensation under section 130 of the Sentencing Act, or
    (d) make an unlawful profit order under section 4 of the Prevention of Social Housing Fraud Act 2013.

(3) If the court sentences the defendant for the offence (or any of the offences) concerned in the postponement period, after that period ends it may vary the sentence by—
    (a) imposing a fine on him,
    (b) making an order falling within section 13(3),
    (c) making an order for the payment of compensation under section 130 of the Sentencing Act, or
    (d) making an unlawful profit order under section 4 of the Prevention of Social Housing Fraud Act 2013.

(4) But the court may proceed under subsection (3) only within the period of 28 days which starts with the last day of the postponement period.

(5) For the purposes of—
    (a) section 18(2) of the Criminal Appeal Act 1968 (time limit for notice of appeal or of application for leave to appeal), and

(b) paragraph 1 of Schedule 3 to the Criminal Justice Act 1988 (time limit for notice of application for leave to refer a case under section 36 of that Act),

the sentence must be regarded as imposed or made on the day on which it is varied under subsection (3).

(6) If the court proceeds to sentence the defendant under subsection (1), section 6 has effect as if the defendant's particular criminal conduct included conduct which constitutes offences which the court has taken into consideration in deciding his sentence for the offence or offences concerned.

(7) The postponement period is the period for which proceedings under section 6 are postponed.

The judge may make a confiscation order before sentence or postpone the determination **E19.60** and proceed to sentence (s. 14(1)). When sentence follows the confiscation proceedings the most basic principle of sentencing must still prevail — that a person cannot be sentenced for offences of which he has not been convicted (or had taken into consideration), unless he accepts that the offences are specimen examples of a wider course of conduct (*Bragazon* (1998) 10 Cr App R (S) 258; *Ayensu* (1982) 4 Cr App R (S) 248). It is, therefore, wrong to deny credit for having no previous convictions where the application of the assumptions has resulted in a finding of previous involvement in drug trafficking (*Callan* (1994) 15 Cr App R (S) 574). Even so, the sentencer may 'pay some regard to the evidence placed before him...in the same way as he might pay regard to general evidence placed before him' to find, for example, that this was not the first occasion on which the defendant had offended (*Harper* (1989) 11 Cr App R (S) 240; *Thompson* [1997] 1 Cr App R (S) 289). Where the outcome of a confiscation inquiry does result in a conflict with other features of the case, the judge is entitled to hold a *Newton* hearing to resolve the conflict (*McNulty* (1994) 15 Cr App R (S) 606).

Relationship with Other Orders

The interaction between confiscation orders and other sentencing powers is regulated by the **E19.61** POCA 2002, s. 13. The effect of the confiscation order on the sentence varies according to the type of sentencing order. A distinction is made between the principal financial orders (but not including compensation and unlawful profit orders) and other orders. The court cannot make certain financial orders (fines, deprivation orders or forfeiture orders under the Misuse of Drugs Act 1971 or the Terrorism Act 2000) without taking account of the confiscation order and reducing the defendant's available means accordingly (s. 13(2) and (3)). Generally, however, the judge must 'leave the confiscation order out of account in deciding the appropriate sentence' (s. 13(4)), e.g., in deciding whether to impose a custodial sentence (*Rogers* [2002] 1 Cr App R (S) 337; *Andrews* [1997] 1 Cr App R (S) 279). A fine is not appropriate when a court has sentenced a defendant to imprisonment and made a confiscation order (*Hedley* (1989) 11 Cr App R (S) 298). The duty to make a confiscation order continues where the court makes an absolute or conditional discharge (*Varma* [2013] 1 AC 463). The POCA 2002 has particular rules to ensure the primacy of compensation for victims over confiscation. The court must still go through the process of making the confiscation order, then fixing the amount of compensation without regard to the existence of the confiscation order. If 'the court (then) believes... [the defendant] will not have sufficient means to satisfy both the orders in full', it must order the shortfall in compensation to be paid out of the confiscated sum (s. 13(5) and (6); see also *Mitchell* [2001] 2 Cr App R (S) 141; *Williams* [2001] 1 Cr App R 500). If the defendant does have the means, he can be ordered to pay the money twice over both as confiscation and compensation (*Brazil* (12 January 1995 unreported); *Williams* and *Mitchell*). However, the Court of Appeal in *Jawad* [2013] 1 WLR 3861, applying the approach of the Supreme Court in *Waya* [2013 1 AC 294, has held that, before doing so, the court should now consider whether a confiscation order that includes the amount of the compensation amounts to disproportionate double-counting and, accordingly, to an infringement of the ECHR, Protocol 1, Article 1 (see further **E19.30**). Even so, as Hughes LJ stated (at [21]:

> ...we do not agree that the mere fact that a compensation order is made for an outstanding sum due to the loser, and thus that the money *may* be restored, is enough to render disproportionate a

POCA confiscation order which includes that sum. What will bring disproportion is the certainty of double payment.

Accordingly, the mere making of a compensation order did not mean that the confiscation order had to be reduced by that amount. Hughes LJ outlined a series of practical points (at [23]):

(a) If the defendant has control of his assets, he ought to be able to make repayment in the knowledge that, once he proves he has done so, credit would be given for it against a confiscation order. Repayment through solicitors on notice to the Crown should be sufficient.

(b) If repayment has not been made before the confiscation hearing, proof that his solicitors were in funds and willing to give an undertaking to repay on his behalf is likely to suffice.

(c) Where the defendant is not in control of his assets, similar principles should apply. If the assets are in the hands of the Crown, he can request repayment. If the assets are subject to a restraint order, he can apply for a variation of it for the purpose of repayment.

(d) In very few cases there might be occasion for a brief adjournment of a confiscation hearing for immediate arrangements for payment to be made but the court should not entertain a defendant's well-meaning intentions not backed by assurance of repayment.

An order for costs ought not to be made where the judge has assessed the available amount to be less than the benefit figure. The implication of such an assessment is that no further funds are available (*Ahmed* [1997] 2 Cr App R (S) 8; *Szrajber* [1994] 15 Cr App R (S) 821; *Hopes* (1989) 11 Cr App R (S) 38).

Postponement

E19.62 Either the prosecution or defence may apply for a postponement or the court may order a postponement of its own motion (POCA 2002, s. 14(7)). The court has an unfettered discretion to postpone the determination for specified periods up to a maximum of two years from the date of conviction (or longer in exceptional circumstances) (s. 14(4) and (5)). If a determination is postponed, the judge may sentence in the meantime so long as he does not impose a fine or make a compensation, forfeiture or deprivation order (s. 15(2)); these orders may be imposed after a postponed determination but only in the 28 days immediately following. Even so, a postponed confiscation order is not invalidated by the making of such orders beforehand (*Parvinta-Taylor* [2010] 2 Cr App R (S) 420; *Donohoe* [2007] 1 Cr App R (S) 548). Costs should not be awarded before making the confiscation order (*Threapleton* [2003] 3 All ER 458; *Smart* [2003] 2 Cr App R (S) 384).

It appears however that, once the confiscation proceedings have started, there is no statutory requirement to complete them within a particular period or before sentence. Where the trial judge had directed the prosecutor to provide statements of information and then proceeded to sentence, the direction should be treated as a decision to proceed under s. 6 before sentence and not a decision to postpone proceedings for a specified period (*CPS Swansea v Gilleeney* [2009] 2 Cr App R (S) 538).

E19.63 Numerous problems arose under earlier legislation when judges misapplied the postponement provisions. It is now unlikely that a procedurally incorrect order would sustain a subsequent appeal as orders are not to be quashed only on the ground that 'the procedure connected with the application for or the granting of a postponement' was defective (s. 14(11)).

In *Knights* [2006] 1 AC 368 the House of Lords held that flaws in the postponement procedure under the CJA 1988 would not invalidate a subsequent confiscation order if the judge has acted in good faith (see also *Ashton* [2007] 1 WLR 181). Even so, the Court of Appeal has since held that, where there had been an order for postponement but no return date set and the confiscation application was not then revived until after the expiry of the permitted two-year period, there was no jurisdiction to proceed (*Iqbal* [2010] 1 WLR 1985). A decision to postpone need not be expressed in any particular form of words. The fact that the judge has so decided may be inferred from the circumstances; e.g., where he has made plain his intention to sentence first and it was understood by all concerned that confiscation would be dealt with at a later date (*Tahir* [2006] EWCA Crim 792). Listing is a judicial function and listing officers make the necessary arrangements on behalf of the judiciary. A decision by the judge to put the date back because of his unavailability constitutes a postponement. The decision is effected by the judge giving instructions to the list officer who fixes a new date (*Neish* [2010] 1 WLR 2395).

The two-year period may be exceeded in 'exceptional circumstances' (s. 14(4)). The phrase **E19.64** 'must take its colour from the setting in which it appears' should not be strictly construed (*Soneji* [2006] 1 AC 340). A judge had not erred in finding that there were 'exceptional circumstances' where there had been late filing of statements by the Crown and the defence, listing difficulties, and adverse weather conditions. Parliament had intended a broad interpretation of 'exceptional circumstances' and the failure to specify the period of postponement was not a bar to recovery as it was a procedural error (*Johal* [2014] 1 WLR 146).

The failure to refer expressly to 'exceptional circumstances' will not invalidate a postponement if it can be inferred that the court made an appraisal of the circumstances and had the appropriate test in mind, and if the order can be justified (*Chuni* [2002] 2 Cr App R (S) 371; *Gadsby* [2002] 1 Cr App R (S) 423). It is only if the timetable initially set makes it likely that the two-year period will be exceeded that the court must on the first occasion address itself to 'exceptional circumstances' (*Knights* [2006] 1 AC 368). Listing difficulties are capable of amounting to exceptional circumstances (*Soneji*; *Young* [2004] 2 All ER 63; *Groombridge* [2004] 1 Cr App R (S) 84).

The court may postpone the determination while the defendant appeals against conviction. If the appeal takes more than two years, postponement for up to three months after the appeal is permitted (s. 14(6)). The court may grant a postponement without a hearing — presumably only where the parties agree (CrimPR, r. 58.2).

Form of Order and Payment of Amount

The court must fix the recoverable amount. An order confiscating the equity of a particular **E19.65** property 'valued at not less than £26,000' is defective (*Jubb* [2002] 2 Cr App R (S) 8).

The ordinary principle is that the order must be satisfied immediately (s. 11(1)). However, if the defendant shows that he needs time to pay, he can be allowed a specified period of up to six months to meet the order. If he applies before the end of that period, it can be extended in exceptional circumstances to a maximum of 12 months from the date of the order. There is no inherent jurisdiction to extend time to pay further (*Revenue and Customs Prosecution Service v Kearney* [2007] EWHC 640 (Admin)).

From a date to be appointed, a magistrates' court may order the release for the satisfaction of a confiscation order of money which has been seized under the PACE 1984, s. 19, and is held in a bank account or which has been produced to an appropriate officer under a production order (POCA 2002, s. 67A).

ENFORCEMENT, RECONSIDERATION AND APPEALS

Enforcement

An order is effectively treated as a fine to be collected and enforced by a specified magistrates' **E19.66** court or, if none is specified, by the committing magistrates' court (POCA 2002, s. 35(2)). If the amount of the order is not paid in time, interest accrues on the unpaid amount for the period for which it remains unpaid (s. 12). A payment by one offender of an amount due under the confiscation order should go to reduce the amount payable by the others. To take the same proceeds more than once would not serve the aim of the legislation, would be disproportionate, and would violate the ECHR, Protocol 1, Article 1. Where there had been a joint obtaining, confiscation orders had to be made against each defendant for the whole of the benefit obtained. However, each had to provide that it was not to be enforced to the extent that any sum had been recovered in satisfaction of another confiscation order in respect of the same joint benefit (*Ahmad* [2014] UKSC 36).

E19.67 The mechanism for imposing terms of imprisonment or detention for default is almost identical to that used in the enforcement of fines and many of the provisions of the PCC(S)A 2000 are expressly incorporated in the POCA 2002. Thus, the Crown Court must fix a default term in accordance with the scale set out in the PCC(S)A 2000, s. 139(4) (see **E15.7**). Failure to do so, however, will not invalidate the order (*Ellis* [1996] 2 Cr App R (S) 403). The scale ranges from seven days for an amount not exceeding £200 up to ten years for anything over £1 million. These are maximum terms and the court has a discretion up to the maximum period in the band. A number of principles emerge from the authorities, enumerated by Laws LJ in *Castillo* [2012] 2 Cr App R (S) 201 at [12]:

1. All the circumstances of the case have to be considered.
2. It is of the first importance to have in mind that the purpose of the default term is to secure payment of the confiscation order.
3. It is not the court's function to find an arithmetical match between the amount of the order and the length of the term, such that for any given band or bracket prescribed in the statute an order at the bottom of the band should attract a default term likewise at the bottom of the band, an order in the middle of the band should attract a term in the middle or an order at the top should attract a term at the top.
4. The court is not to be influenced by the overall totality of the sentence passed for the crime plus the default term.
5. But for any given band the court should have regard to the maxima: the maximum amount of a confiscation order within the band and the maximum default term within the band.
6. Given principle (5), and especially in a case...falling within the top band where there is no maximum confiscation order but only a maximum default term, regard must be had to the requirement of proportionality.
   ...The purpose of the default term is not punishment for the achievement of retributive justice. It is rather to secure satisfaction of the confiscation order and so deprive the criminal of the fruits of his crime. In that endeavour, the demands of proportionality are much weaker than where the court is punishing the offender. Although retributive justice is by no means the only aim of sentencing, it remains a first condition of criminal punishment that the offender should get no more than his just deserts. Proportionality is thus at the centre of the process. By contrast, the ancillary regime of asset recovery is established on an altogether different footing. Its first condition is effectiveness.

In that case, the Court of Appeal substituted a nine-year term for the ten-year maximum where the defendant was found to have £3 million in hidden assets. See further *Szrajber* (1994) 15 Cr App R (S) 821; *French* (1996) 16 Cr App R (S) 841; *Qema* [2006] EWCA Crim 2806; *Howard* [2007] EWCA Crim 1489; *Liscott* [2007] EWCA Crim 1706; *Pigott* [2010] 2 Cr App R (S) 91; *Smith* [2009] EWCA Crim 344; and *Price* [2010] 2 Cr App R (S) 283.

The default period is served consecutively but 'serving that term does not prevent the confiscation order from continuing to have effect so far as any other method of enforcement is concerned' (s. 38(5)). Once he has served half of the default period, the defendant must be released unconditionally (CJA 2003, s. 258). Default imprisonment is remitted if payment is made. If the non-imprisoned defendant does default, the magistrates must summons the defendant. The length of the default term actually ordered to be served is then calculated according to the outstanding amount including interest 'at the time the period of detention is imposed' and not according to the amount at the time of the original confiscation order (MCA 1980, s. 79(2); *R (Gibson) v Secretary of State for Justice* [2013] EWHC 2481 (Admin)). The magistrates may not allow payment by instalments or hold a further means inquiry (POCA 2002, s. 35(3)). It appears, however, that they need not necessarily commit him to serve the default period immediately but may 'postpone the issue of the warrant until such time and on such conditions, if any, as the court thinks just' (MCA 1980, s. 77; see *DPP v Greenacre* [2008] 1 WLR 438 and *Revenue and Customs Prosecution Service v Kearney* [2007] EWHC 640 (Admin)). Magistrates may postpone the issue of a warrant of commitment for a default term until after the expiry of a sentence imposed for separate offences (*RCPO v Taylor* [2010] EWHC 715 (Admin)).

The court should be satisfied that no alternative means of enforcement are available before committing an offender; it may be unreasonable to do so when the sale of property has fallen through but the property remains saleable and the offender is co-operating in efforts to sell it (*Barnett v DPP* [2009] EWHC 2004 (Admin); *R (Joyce) v Dover Magistrates' Court* [2008] EWHC 1448 (Admin)). However, the provision in the MCA 1980, s. 82(4) (see **E15.13**), that the court 'has considered or tried all other methods of enforcing payment of the sum and it appears to the court that they are inappropriate or unsuccessful' must be 'read with care... It is enough for the court to have regard to other methods... it is not a requirement before an order can be made that all other methods should have been tried and failed' (*Johnson v Birmingham Magistrates' Court* (2012) 176 JP 298). A refusal to adjourn where the defendant faces lengthy imprisonment and is unrepresented may be contrary to common law and ECHR principles of fairness (*R (Agogo) v North Somerset Magistrates' Court* [2011] EWHC 518 (Admin)).

Proceedings to enforce an order by commitment to prison are part of the determination of a **E19.68** criminal charge within the meaning of the ECHR, Article 6(1), and must be determined 'within a reasonable time' (*Lloyd v Bow Street Magistrates' Court* [2004] 1 Cr App R 132; *Crowther v UK* (2005) *The Times*, 11 February 2005; *R (Syed) v City of Westminster Magistrates' Court* [2010] EWHC 1617 (Admin)). However, this must take account of where the delay has been caused by the defendant's decision to pursue 'every avenue of appeal available to him' (*R (Minshall) v Marylebone Magistrates' Court* [2010] 2 All ER 806) or where he has failed to engage with the process knowing that the prosecution intend to enforce the order (*Marsden v Leicester Magistrates' Court* [2013] EWHC 919 (Admin)). Where enforcement by way of a warrant for committal is stayed as a result of delay, it may not be appropriate to stay all enforcement action such as civil sanctions or compensation (*R (CPS) v Derby and South Derbyshire Magistrates' Court* [2010] EWHC 370 (Admin); *R (Joyce) v Dover Magistrates' Court* [2008] EWHC 1448 (Admin)).

Enforcement proceedings do not amount to the bringing of a fresh charge so as to breach the principle of speciality in extradition law (*R (Woolley) v Birmingham Magistrates' Court* [2010] EWHC 12 (Admin)).

If the order is not satisfied, the prosecution may ask the Crown Court to appoint an enforcement receiver (s. 50). The court may then confer powers on the receiver to: (a) take possession of realisable property; (b) manage 'or otherwise deal with' the property; (c) realise the property 'in such manner as the court may specify'; (d) bring, continue or defend legal proceedings (s. 51(2)). The offender is a party to the proceedings and is able to make appropriate applications, e.g., in relation to delay (*Re Dahner* [2010] EWHC 3397 (Admin)). For third-party rights and representations, see **E19.56**.

Where the prosecutor believes that realisable property is situated outside the UK, a Request **E19.69** for Assistance may be sent to the Home Secretary who may, in turn, forward the request to the relevant government (s. 74). A Request for Assistance asks the receiving country to apply the various co-operation treaties and, in particular, to prohibit anyone from dealing in the property and to ensure that the proceeds 'are applied in accordance with the law of the receiving country'. If property is realised abroad, the amount which the defendant has been ordered to pay under the order is reduced accordingly.

A financial reporting order under the SOCPA 2005, s. 76(2) (see **E21.32**), should not be imposed for the purpose of facilitating enforcement of a confiscation order. Such an order could be appropriate in the case of a 'master criminal' sentenced to a lengthy term who would be able nevertheless to use 'loyal acolytes' to manipulate, conceal and deploy his substantial hidden assets (*Wright* [2009] 2 Cr App R (S) 313).

Reconsideration

Confiscation orders may be varied within 56 days under the general 'slip-rule', particularly where **E19.70** further information comes to light (PCC(S)A 2000, s. 155; see *Miller* (1990) 12 Cr App R

(S) 519). However, the POCA 2002 itself anticipates that the full extent of the defendant's assets may not emerge for some considerable time or, alternatively, that his assets actually amount to less than originally thought. Accordingly, the court retains powers to vary findings (a) as to the existence or amount of benefit for up to six years from conviction or (b) indefinitely as to the available amount. Procedure is governed by the CrimPR, rr. 58.3 and 58.4 (see Supplement, **R-407**).

The prosecutor has six years from the date of conviction in which to ask the court to consider evidence of benefit which was 'not available' to it at the time of conviction or when the court decided not to proceed with a determination (ss. 19 to 21). The court may fix the recoverable amount as such amount that 'the court believes is just'. It may not apply the s. 10 assumptions to property obtained or expenditure made after that date. Accordingly, it is extremely unlikely that such an order would be so disproportionate as to infringe the ECHR, Protocol 1, Article 1. The judge should consider the amount outstanding, the additional amount available, the passage of time since the original confiscation order and the impact on the defendant, together with the legislative policy in favour of maximising the recovery of the proceeds of crime, and legitimately after-acquired assets. The correct test on appeal is whether the new order is wrong in principle or manifestly excessive and not whether it is '*Wednesbury* unreasonable' (*Padda* [2014] 1 WLR 1920).

Secondly, the prosecutor (or a receiver) may apply at any point for reconsideration of the available amount (s. 22). Section 22 even catches property that has accrued to the defendant after the date of the confiscation order and regardless of whether the prosecution can prove that it is the result of crime (*Tivnan* [1999] 1 Cr App R (S) 92; *Re Peacock* [2010] EWCA Civ 1465; *Bates* [2007] 1 Cr App R (S) 9). Note that the ECHR entitlement to 'a hearing within a reasonable time' applies to reconsideration of the available amount notwithstanding that Parliament has stipulated no statutory time-limit. The issue of delay must be determined by reference to the entirety of the proceedings and not on the basis that the reconsideration proceedings are distinct and separate (*Re Saggar* [2005] 1 WLR 2693). The court may extend the time available for payment (*Escobar v DPP* [2009] 1 WLR 64).

E19.71   The defendant (or an appointed receiver) may apply to the Crown Court for the amount of the order to be reduced if the available amount is inadequate for payment in full (s. 23). An application does not provide an opportunity to try and make good deficiencies in the case presented at the time of the confiscation order (*Gokal v Serious Fraud Office* [2001] EWCA Civ 368; *Re McKinsley* [2006] 1 WLR 3420; *R v Liverpool Magistrates' Court, ex parte Ansen* [1998] 1 All ER 692; *Rooney* [2007] EWCA Crim 236).

The procedure is intended to be used only where there had been a genuine change in a defendant's financial circumstances: it is a safety net intended to provide for post-confiscation order events. In *Najafpour* [2010] 2 Cr App R (S) 245, Elias LJ stated (at [12]):

> A typical example is where property is sold for less than its anticipated value. The intention of this provision is clear: it is to ensure that a defendant does not serve the period in default where it turns out that he is in fact unable to raise the money which the court anticipated he would be able to do when it imposed the confiscation order.

It is not open to a defendant to challenge an earlier finding in the confiscation proceedings that he had hidden assets (*Younis* [2009] 2 Cr App R (S) 247). However, there is no rule of law that the court cannot be persuaded that a defendant was unable to pay the outstanding amount because of a worsening of his financial circumstances unless he gives full disclosure of what had happened to his assets, including previously unidentified assets. In a case involving previously unidentified assets, a defendant had to be allowed to try to persuade the court that his identified assets had shrunk in value and that as a result he was unable to pay the amount outstanding. What the court made of his evidence would be a matter of judgement and much would depend on the nature of the case (*Glaves v CPS* [2011] EWCA Civ 69; *Re O'Donoghue* [2004] EWCA Civ 1800; *Telli v RCPO* [2008] 3 All ER 405).

E19.72   The scheme was not intended to include a tainted gift in a confiscation order only for a defendant to be able to obtain a reduction because he could not realise it as an asset. That did not mean that a defendant would face a term of imprisonment in default if he was unable to satisfy a confiscation order solely as a result of his inability to realise a gift. Enforcing magistrates were bound to consider all methods of enforcement, particularly when the value of remaining realisable property was still sufficient to satisfy the order (*L* [2010] EWHC 1531 (Admin)).

The clarification of a third party's interest in property might be a post-confiscation order event, and the extent of such interest might have to be decided (*Re Norris* [2001] 3 All ER 961). However, a defendant is not entitled to rely on the fact that he has failed to recover funds which he had placed with a third party in order to hide them; their irrecoverability could not, in the circumstances, be classed as a post-confiscation order event (*Re B* [2008] EWHC 3217 (Admin)).

Appeals

A confiscation order or variation (apart from variations based upon inadequacy of the available amount — see *Ward* [2011] 1 WLR 766) constitutes a sentence for the purposes of appeal (Criminal Appeal Act 1968, s. 50(1): see **D26.42**). Accordingly, the defendant may appeal against the making or the amount of an order with the leave of the Court of Appeal. The Court may confirm, quash or vary the order.

Where a defendant has pleaded guilty on the basis of incorrect legal advice (e.g., as to the implications of admitting a 'lifestyle' offence), the order should be set aside on appeal only 'in the most exceptional circumstances' and 'there would need to be a well-founded submission that the whole process was unfair' (*Ayankoya* [2011] EWCA Crim 1488; *Hirani* [2008] EWCA Crim 1463; *Kirman* [2010] EWCA Crim 614; *Perkes* [2010] EWCA Crim 101). However, consent to an order under a mistake of law is not binding. Consent does not confer jurisdiction to make an order; it requires a deliberation by the judge. It would be manifestly unfair for a defendant to be bound by consent when the only possible explanation was that it was given under a mistake of law (*Mackle* [2014] 2 WLR 267).

Where the Court quashes an order, it may, instead of substituting its own order, direct the Crown Court to proceed afresh so long as the appellant is not dealt with more severely than under the order which is quashed (Criminal Appeal Act 1968, s. 11(3A)). Procedure is governed by the Proceeds of Crime Act 2002 (Appeals under Part 2) (Amendment) Order 2013 (SI 2013 No. 24). There is a single time-limit of 28 days for giving notice of appeal from the date of the decision sought to be appealed. This may be extended. The rules bring the procedural aspects broadly in line with the Criminal Appeal Act 1968 and the rules that formerly applied under the 1968 Act (CrimPR, parts 71 to 73: see Supplement, **R-549** *et seq.*). The prosecutor has a general right of appeal under the POCA 2002 itself 'in respect of' the making of an order and against a decision not to make an order. This requires leave. The prosecutor cannot appeal against refusals to reconsider whether to proceed, to reconsider the amount of benefit or to hold an inquiry for an absconder (s. 31). The parties may appeal further to the Supreme Court (s. 33).

MISCELLANEOUS

Absent Defendants

Inability to Attend There is in principle no reason why in an appropriate case the common-law principle that the judge has a discretion to continue proceedings in the absence of a defendant who is unable to attend (e.g., because of a long-standing illness) does not apply to confiscation proceedings (*Jones* [2003] 1 AC 1; *Bhanji* [2011] EWCA Crim 1198). In the case of a person who is unwell and absent, if no order is made because of the absence of the defendant on account of illness, the effect of the POCA 2002, ss. 19 and 20 is that, when the case is reconsidered after his recovery, it will only be possible to deploy the assumptions in relation to evidence which was not available to the prosecutor at the earlier time (*Ali* [2014] EWCA Crim 1658). In *Gavin and Tasie* [2011] 1 Cr App R (S) 73, in separate cases, G and T had been removed from the UK between the commencement and conclusion of confiscation proceedings; T was removed under a voluntary

E19.73

E19.74

Part E Sentencing

E

facilitated return scheme (the Home Office was unaware of the proceedings and he did not inform his solicitors of his pending removal) and G was unwillingly deported notwithstanding Home Office awareness of the proceedings. In T's case, the confiscation order was upheld on the basis that he had by implication consented to be absent. However, where, as in G's case, inability to attend arises because an arm of the State has prevented his attendance, the proceedings should not be continued: 'It cannot…be in accordance with the [ECHR] for the State to deny a right to be present. It is an important safeguard in securing a fair trial, even in circumstances where his presence is not, on the facts, essential to secure that fairness. We consider this was a breach of Article 6.'

E19.75 **Absconding**   Wilful absconding triggers a specific scheme under the POCA 2002. Note, however, that the scheme does not apply where a defendant is voluntarily absent (*Ali* [2014] EWCA Crim 1658). Once a *convicted* defendant absconds, the prosecution cannot proceed in the normal way (s. 6(8)). They may, instead, apply to proceed under s. 27 but the court has a discretion rather than a duty to do so and the price is a more limited form of inquiry. The court may proceed if it 'believes it is appropriate for it do so' (s. 27(3)) and the prosecution have taken reasonable steps to contact the defendant. The court then proceeds as if the defendant were present but the required assumptions and the provisions requiring defence disclosure must be ignored (s. 27(5)). 'Any person the court believes is likely to be affected by an order' is entitled to appear and to make representations; if the defendant reappears following the making of an order, he can then do little other than to apply for a variation on the basis that the available amount is inadequate (s. 23). Nice questions of construction could arise where the absconding does not occur, for example, until after the benefit has been calculated using the assumptions. Arguably, the court may exercise its common-law discretion to continue as normal. If the prosecution applied to proceed under s. 27 in the defendant's absence but 'no court has proceeded' under that section, the prosecution may make a second attempt within six years if it has fresh evidence.

There is a similar discretion to proceed where an unconvicted defendant absconds before the proceedings for the index offence(s) have been concluded (s. 28). Once two years have elapsed from the day that 'the court believes he absconded', a similarly modified form of inquiry can take place. If he then reappears before the proceedings for the offence(s) are concluded, the court may discharge the order if it finds either that there has been 'undue delay' in continuing the prosecution or that the prosecutor does not intend to continue with the prosecution (s. 30(4)). (It has also been held that s. 28 operates to permit the court may make an order under s. 6 where the defendant has been convicted in his absence (Okedare [2014] EWCA Crim 1173.) However, if on his reappearance the defendant is 'tried and acquitted', the order must be discharged (s. 30(2)).

Compensation

E19.76 There are detailed provisions under which the court may order 'such compensation it believes is just' where there has been a 'serious default' by the prosecuting authorities (POCA 2002, s. 72). In order to qualify for compensation three conditions must be met: (a) a criminal investigation has been started but has not resulted in conviction (or the conviction is quashed on appeal); (b) there has been a serious default without which the investigation would not have continued; and (c) a person who held realisable property suffered loss in consequence of an order under part 2. Procedures are governed by the CrimPR, r. 58.10 (see Supplement, **R-414**). Where an order has been quashed out of time but monies have previously been paid to a receiver, the Courts Service has no liability to repay those monies (*R (Seago) v Her Majesty's Courts and Tribunal Service* [2012] EWHC 3490 (Admin)).

Confiscation and EU Law

E19.77 EU law has established a system of mutual recognition of confiscation orders. Under this system, a competent authority in one Member State is obliged in principle to recognise and execute a confiscation order issued by an authority in another Member State (see **A9.17**).

Section E20 Recommendation for Deportation

POWER TO RECOMMEND FOR DEPORTATION

E20.1 The Secretary of State is empowered under the Immigration Act 1971 to order the deportation from the UK of persons who are not British citizens. A court may, on sentencing an offender, make a recommendation that the offender be deported, by virtue of that Act and the British Nationality Act 1981. The final decision on deportation is taken by the Home Secretary, who is able to take account of a wider range of considerations than is the court, such as the political situation in the country to which the offender will go (*Nazari* [1980] 3 All ER 880).

Sections 32 to 39 of the UK Borders Act 2007 place the Secretary of State under a duty to make a deportation order in respect of a 'foreign criminal' unless certain exceptions apply. 'Foreign criminal' is defined in s. 32 as a person who is not a British citizen, is convicted in the UK of an offence, and who has either been sentenced to imprisonment for at least 12 months or who has committed an offence specified by the Secretary of State under the Nationality, Immigration and Asylum Act 2002 and who is subject to a period of imprisonment. The reference to 'imprisonment' for these purposes includes detention in a young offender institution and extends to any indeterminate sentence provided that it may last for at least 12 months. A suspended sentence does not count. It is also clear from s. 38 that there must be a single term of imprisonment of at least 12 months — it does not apply to a case in which two or more shorter terms run consecutively to total more than 12 months. The 2007 Act makes no changes to the court's power to recommend deportation as such, but in practice the power is now greatly curtailed, being applicable only to cases in which a short custodial sentence, or a non-custodial penalty, has been imposed on the offender. It was held by the Court of Appeal in *Kluxen* [2011] 1 WLR 218 that the issue of making a recommendation is now likely to arise only in the case of an offender receiving a short custodial sentence who has a long record of minor offending, or in cases involving the misuse of identity documents. A good example, in which *Kluxen* was followed and applied, is *Junab* [2013] 2 Cr App R (S) 159 (23). See also *Gheorghiu* [2013] 2 Cr App R (S) 497 (74) and *Ul Haq* [2014] 1 Cr App R (S) 307 (52). The Court in *Mintchev* [2011] 2 Cr App R (S) 465 held that, as a matter of principle, it would be wrong to reduce to below 12 months an otherwise appropriate sentence so as to avoid the provisions of the UK Borders Act 2007; however, one case suggests that an otherwise appropriate sentence can be structured by way of shorter consecutive terms, thereby avoiding the provisions of the Act (*Hakimzadeh* [2010] 1 Cr App R (S) 49). In *Gebru* [2011] EWCA Crim 3321, the Court of Appeal noted the judge's sentencing remark that there was 'no point in considering the need for an extended sentence . . . because you will be deported automatically'; Hallett LJ said that the provisions described as 'automatic deportation' may not necessarily lead to deportation in every case, and so judges should not alter their sentence on that assumption. *Gebru* was considered and approved in *A-G's Ref (No. 41 of 2013) (M)* [2014] 1 Cr App R (S) 493 (80); Pitchford LJ pointed out that an offender could be released from prison before a deportation order was made and executed and so the sentencing court should make its decision on the risk posed by the offender without regard to the possibility that he would one day be deported.

E20.2 By the Immigration Act 1971, s. 3(6), a recommendation may be made in respect of any person who is not a British citizen, who is aged 17 or over, and who is convicted of an offence punishable with imprisonment as an adult. A 'British citizen' is a person who has a right of abode in the UK (see, for the definition, the British Nationality Act 1981, part I), but, in addition, a

2327

Commonwealth citizen or a citizen of the Irish Republic shall not be recommended for deportation if that person was resident in the UK when the 1971 Act came into force, and has been ordinarily resident in the UK for at least the five years immediately prior to the date of conviction (s. 7(1)) (for the definition of 'Commonwealth citizen' see the British Nationality Act 1981, s. 37 and sch. 3). Section 6(2) provides that a court shall not make a recommendation for deportation unless the offender has been given at least seven days' written notice. This may require adjournment after conviction. If the court is considering making a recommendation for deportation, the defence should be given an opportunity to address the court on that matter (*Antypas* (1973) 57 Cr App R 207).

In the past it has been possible to make a recommendation for deportation against a person protected by the EEC Treaty, Article 48, only if the conditions specified in Articles 3 and 9 of Directive 64/221 were satisfied. These were considered in *Bouchereau* [1978] QB 732, and the principles which emerged have been followed in subsequent cases. The principles applicable here appear to be the same as those which apply in respect of any other non-British subject who does not come within one of the exceptions in the Immigration Act 1971 (*Kluxen* [2011] 1 WLR 218).

E20.3 Before making a recommendation for deportation the sentencing court should always give careful consideration to the circumstances of the case, and full reasons for the decision to recommend deportation should always be given, in fairness to the offender and also to provide assistance to the Secretary of State who would have to make the final decision (*Nazari* [1980] 3 All ER 880; *Rodney* [1996] 2 Cr App R (S) 230). The Court of Appeal in *Bozat* [1997] 1 Cr App R (S) 270, while endorsing these requirements, said that a failure to give reasons did not necessarily mean that a recommendation should be quashed; the Court of Appeal could provide its own reasons if it considered deportation to be appropriate. See also *Ul Haq* [2014] 1 Cr App R (S) 307 (52).

The Crown Court's common-law power to bind over an offender to come up for judgment has on occasion been used as a means of requiring an offender to leave the country indefinitely (see E13). Such power is not restricted by the Immigration Act 1971.

RECOMMENDATION FOR DEPORTATION:
SENTENCING PRINCIPLES

Whether the Accused's Continued Presence in UK to Detriment of Community

E20.4 The principles set out below must now be read in light of the changes made by the UK Borders Act 2007, ss. 32 to 39 (see **E20.1**).

In *Nazari* [1980] 3 All ER 880, Lawton LJ said (at p. 1373):

> This country has no use for criminals of other nationalities, particularly if they have committed serious crimes or have long criminal records. That is self-evident. The more serious the crime and the longer the record the more obvious it is that there should be an order recommending deportation. On the other hand, a minor offence would not merit an order.

The Court of Appeal in *Benabbas* [2006] 1 Cr App R (S) 550 reviewed a large number of authorities on the power to recommend deportation, and affirmed the continuing importance of the principles set out in *Nazari*. It was said that the required 'detriment to the community' had to be judged by reference to the public interest and the requirements of public policy. See also *Carmona* [2006] 1 WLR 2264 at **E20.6**.

Harshness of Foreign Regime Not to Be Considered

E20.5 In *Nazari* [1980] 3 All ER 880, Lawton LJ said (at p. 1373): '... the courts are not concerned with the political systems which operate in other countries.... The court has no knowledge of those matters over and above that which is common knowledge; and that may be wrong.... It is for the Home Secretary to decide in each case whether an offender's return to his country of origin would have consequences which would make his compulsory return unduly harsh.' The principle in *Nazari* was reaffirmed in *Ukoh* [2005] 2 Cr App R (S) 231.

Likely Impact on Third Parties

Formerly it had been thought that the decision over whether to recommend deportation must **E20.6** engage with Convention rights, including the right to family life under Article 8 (*Boultif v Switzerland* (2001) 33 EHRR 1179 and *Mokrani v France* (2005) 40 EHRR 123). In the important case of *Carmona* [2006] 1 WLR 2264, however, the Court of Appeal preferred the view that, since the sentencing court was involved only in making a recommendation, and the final decision on deportation rested with the Home Secretary, the issue of engagement with Article 8, as well as the offender's rights under Articles 2 and 3, were for the Home Secretary and not the court.

Combining Recommendation with Other Sentences or Orders

A recommendation for deportation is ancillary to sentence. There is no statutory restriction **E20.7** upon combining a recommendation for deportation with any other sentence or order. Although a conviction followed by a discharge is treated as a conviction for limited purposes only (see E12.6), the Immigration Act 1971, s. 6(3), provides that, for the purposes of a recommendation for deportation, a person who has been found to have committed an offence 'shall ... be regarded as a person convicted of the offence'.

Section E21   Exclusions and Disqualifications

ALCOHOL-RELATED

Licensed Premises Exclusion

E21.1
Licensed Premises (Exclusion of Certain Persons) Act 1980, s. 1

(1) Where a court by or before which a person is convicted of an offence committed on licensed premises is satisfied that in committing that offence he resorted to violence or offered or threatened to resort to violence, the court may, subject to subsection (2) below, make an order (in this Act referred to as an 'exclusion order') prohibiting him from entering those premises or any other specified premises, without the express consent of the licensee of the premises or his servant or agent.

(2) An exclusion order may be made either—
   (a) in addition to any sentence which is imposed in respect of the offence of which the person is convicted; or
   (b) where the offence was committed in England or Wales, notwithstanding the provisions of sections 12 and 14 of the Powers of Criminal Courts (Sentencing) Act 2000 (cases in which absolute and conditional discharges may be made, and their effect), in addition to an order discharging him absolutely or conditionally; or
   (c) [Scotland];
   but not otherwise.

(3) An exclusion order shall have effect for such period, not less than three months or more than two years, as is specified in the order, unless it is terminated under section 2(2) below.

Such order may be made by the court either of its own motion, on the application of the victim or prosecutor or on the application of an interested third party made by way of representation to the prosecutor (*Penn* [1996] 2 Cr App R (S) 214).

The expression 'licensed premises' means premises in respect of which there is in force a justices' on-licence. In *Grady* (1990) 12 Cr App R (S) 152, the offender pleaded guilty to assault occasioning actual bodily harm, after having been involved in an altercation in a public house, during which she pushed or punched the landlady, causing bruising to her back. The Court of Appeal quashed an order excluding the offender from entering licensed premises within the county of Norfolk for 12 months. It was said that exclusion orders were designed for those who might be described as making a nuisance of themselves in public houses, to the annoyance of other customers and possible danger to the licensee; it was inappropriate to make such an order in the case of a woman of mature years with a clean record. In *Arrowsmith* [2003] 2 Cr App R (S) 301, the offender had head-butted a man in a public house, breaking his nose. The sentencer, in addition to passing a sentence of 12 months' imprisonment for the offence, made an exclusion order relating to 165 specified licensed premises within the Borough of Crewe and Nantwich, where the offender resided. The Court of Appeal upheld the order on the particular facts of the case, but said that courts should not regard the decision as an invitation to draft overly wide exclusion orders.

Section 2 of the Act states that anyone who enters premises in breach of an exclusion order shall be guilty of an offence punishable on summary conviction with a fine not exceeding £200, or to imprisonment for one month or both. At the time of such conviction, the court shall consider whether the exclusion order should continue in force, and may terminate it, or vary it by deleting the name of any specified premises, if it thinks fit. There is no power to extend the order. By s. 4, a copy of any exclusion order, or order terminating or varying an exclusion order, shall be sent by the court to the licensee of the premises concerned.

Drinking Banning Orders

The VCRA 2006, chapter 1, provides power for a court to make a 'drinking banning order' **E21.2** where the court is satisfied that the offender has engaged in criminal or disorderly conduct while under the influence of alcohol and that such an order is necessary to protect other persons from further conduct by him of that kind while he is under the influence of alcohol. The power to make such an order on conviction in criminal proceedings (ss. 6 to 8) is in force only in magistrates' courts in the areas specified in the Violent Crime Reduction Act 2006 (Commencement No. 8) Order 2010 (SI 2010 No. 469), from 1 April 2010, and the (Commencement No. 9) Order (SI 2010 No. 2541), from 1 November 2010. It was expected that, when the 2006 Act powers to make orders on conviction were fully in force, they would replace the powers under the Licensed Premises (Exclusion of Certain Persons) Act 1980 (see **E21.1**). However, as from a date to be appointed, the power to impose a drinking banning order upon conviction of a criminal offence will be repealed and replaced by the power under the ABCPA 2014, part 2, to impose a criminal behaviour order (see **D25.5**).

Powers to make a drinking banning order on an application to a magistrates' court (s. 3) and by way of an order in county court proceedings (s. 4) were brought into force on 31 August 2009, together with powers of variation and supplementary provisions, by the Violent Crime Reduction Act 2006 (Commencement No. 7) Order 2009 (SI 2009 No. 1840). Such an order may impose any prohibition which is necessary for the purpose of protecting others from criminal or disorderly conduct by the subject of the order while he is under the influence of alcohol (s. 1(2)) and must be for not less than six months nor more than two years (s. 2(1)). A drinking banning order may include provision for the prohibition to cease if the subject of the order satisfactorily completes an approved course (s. 2(3)), and if an order does not contain such a provision the court must give its reasons why not (s. 2(8)). Breach of a drinking banning order is a summary offence punishable with a fine not exceeding level 4 on the standard scale (s. 11). Provisions relating to the making of an application for a drinking banning order and to procedure in relation to breach of such an order are set out in the Magistrates' Courts (Drinking Banning Order) Rules 2009 (SI 2009 No. 2937).

FOOTBALL BANNING ORDERS

There are powers contained in the Football Spectators Act 1989 to exclude offenders who have **E21.3** been convicted of 'a relevant offence' from attendance at football matches. Where the court is satisfied that there are reasonable grounds to believe that a banning order would help to prevent violence or disorder at or in connection with any regulated football match(es), it *must* make a banning order (s. 14A(2)). Where these criteria are established, there is no discretion not to make an order (*Allen* [2011] EWCA Crim 3076). The order prohibits the offender from attending a regulated football match in the UK, and requires him to report when required to a police station when matches are being played outside the UK (s. 14(4)). It is not possible to make an order limited to particular matches or particular teams. A banning order may include other requirements, and must require the offender to surrender his passport in connection with any match played outside the UK (s. 14E(3)). A banning order takes effect on the day when the order is made (s. 14F(1)). If the offender is sentenced to immediate imprisonment (including any form of detention), the banning order must be for at least six years and not more than ten years; if the offender is not sentenced to custody, the banning order must be for at least three years and not more than five years (s. 14F(3) and (4)). In *Gough v Chief Constable of*

Derbyshire [2002] QB 459, the Divisional Court held that football banning orders were a lawful and proportionate restriction on a national citizen's freedom of movement under European Community law. The court also held that such an order imposed after conviction was not a 'penalty' and accordingly there could be no infringement of the ECHR, Article 7, when, after conviction for a public order offence, the criminal court had imposed a ban for six years (twice the maximum ban available when the offence was committed).

Relevant Offences

E21.4   The 'relevant offences' are listed in sch. 1 to the 1989 Act. A wide range of offences involving violence, possession of an offensive weapon, drunkenness, public disorder, damage to property and road traffic offences are 'relevant offences', but only if they were committed at or in connection with a football match, or when travelling to or from a football match (whether or not the match was actually attended by the offender). This is an important requirement, but much turns on the particular facts. Banning orders made under the Act were quashed in *Elliott* [2007] 2 Cr App R (S) 430, where a group of men who had attended a football match were later involved in violence in a public house but the violence was itself unrelated to the match. On the other hand, banning orders were upheld in *Parkes* [2011] 2 Cr App R (S) 54 even though some of those involved were supporters of neither club involved in the match in question. The applicable principles and case law are helpfully summarised in *Doyle* (2012) 176 JP 337. The offences listed extend to any attempt or conspiracy, aiding, abetting, counselling or procuring the commission of such an offence and to encouraging or assisting such an offence within the meaning of the SCA 2007, part 2.

Declaration of Relevance

E21.5   In respect of a number of the offences listed in the Football Spectators Act 1989, sch. 1, before making a banning order the court is required to make a 'declaration that the offence related to a particular football match or matches' (a 'declaration of relevance'), which ordinarily requires that the prosecutor shall have given notice to the accused, at least five days before the first day of the trial, that it was proposed to show that the offence charged did relate to a particular football match or matches. Exceptionally, however, the court may make such a declaration in a case where the required notice has not been given, but only if the accused consents to waive the giving of full notice or the court is satisfied that the interests of justice do not require further notice to be given (s. 23). In *DPP v Beaumont* [2008] 2 Cr App R (S) 549, it was suggested that a failure formally to state a declaration of relevance is not fatal to the proper making of a football banning order, provided that the court had the relevant considerations in mind before making the order.

Regulated Football Match

E21.6   The provisions as amended now relate to any 'regulated football match', which means 'an association football match (whether in the United Kingdom or elsewhere) which is a prescribed match or a match of a prescribed description' (Football Spectators Act 1989, s. 14(2)).

Miscellaneous Matters

E21.7   A magistrates' court or the Crown Court has power to make a banning order. Such an order can only be made in addition to a sentence imposed in respect of the relevant offence, or in addition to a conditional discharge for that offence (s. 14A(4)). A banning order may be made in combination with a conditional discharge notwithstanding the PCC(S)A 2000, s. 14 (s. 14A(5) and see E12.6). A banning order cannot be made where the offender has received an absolute discharge for the offence.

It is clear that a banning order may on the facts be justified on the basis of a single offence, without further evidence of repetition or propensity (*Hughes* [2006] 1 Cr App R (S) 632), and in making such an order a court is entitled to take into account the potential deterrent effect of the order on persons other than the offender (*R (White) v Blackfriars Crown Court* [2008] 2 Cr App R (S) 542), followed in *Curtis* [2010] 1 Cr App R (S) 193).

For the purposes of deciding whether to make an order and whether the condition in s. 14A(2) (see **E21.3**) is satisfied, the court may consider evidence led by the prosecution and the defence (s. 14A(3A)) and it is immaterial whether that evidence would have been admissible in the proceedings (s. 14A(3B)). In *Boggild* [2012] 4 All ER 1285, Hughes LJ stated (at [20]) that 'it is palpably not the scheme of the Act to make a football banning order the inevitable consequence of a football related conviction'. But where the court is not satisfied as to the need to make an order in respect of a relevant offence, it must state that fact in open court and give its reasons (s. 14A(3)). On making a banning order, the court must explain the effect of that order to the offender in ordinary language (s. 14E(1)). The order requires the person to report initially at a specified police station within five days of the order being made (s. 14E(2)). There is power whereby the court may impose additional requirements on the person subject to the order in relation to any regulated football matches (s. 14G(1)). In particular, the court may make an order under the POA 1986, s. 35, requiring the offender to attend at a police station within seven days of the making of the order to have his photograph taken (s. 35(1)). This particular requirement, however, can be made by the court only where it has been requested by the prosecutor (s. 35(3)).

If a banning order has been in force for at least two-thirds of the period of the order, the person subject to it may apply to the court by which it was made to terminate it early (s. 14H).

A person subject to a banning order who fails to comply with any requirement imposed by the order is guilty of an offence punishable on summary conviction with imprisonment for a term not exceeding six months, or a fine not exceeding level 5, or both (s. 14J).

DISQUALIFICATION OF COMPANY DIRECTOR

By the Company Directors Disqualification Act 1986, ss. 1 and 2, a court may make a disquali- **E21.8**
fication order against an offender, wherever he is convicted of an indictable offence, whether tried on indictment or summarily, in connection with the promotion, formation, management or liquidation or striking off of a company ('liquidation' was widely construed in *Georgiou* (1988) 87 Cr App R 207 and *Goodman* (1993) 14 Cr App R (S) 147, approving *Corbin* (1984) 6 Cr App R (S) 17), or in connection with the receivership or management of a company's property. This has the effect that the offender must not act as an insolvency practitioner nor, without the leave of the court, be a director of a company, a liquidator or administrator of a company, a receiver or manager of a company's property, or in any way, directly or indirectly, be concerned or take part in the promotion, formation or management of a company, for a speci-fied period beginning with the date of the order. Such a disqualification has general effect; a court has no power to limit the order to a particular type of company (*Ward* (2001) *The Times*, 10 August 2001). The purpose of the order is to protect the public from those who, for reasons of dishonesty, or naivety or incompetence, abuse their role and status as director (per Potter LJ in *Edwards* [1998] 2 Cr App R (S) 213).

Length of Disqualification

The maximum period of disqualification which may be imposed by a magistrates' court is **E21.9**
five years, and the maximum for the Crown Court is 15 years. There is no minimum period. In *Millard* (1994) 15 Cr App R (S) 445, the Court of Appeal identified an 'upper bracket' or disqualification for more than ten years, which should be reserved for particularly serious cases (including those where the director has been disqualified previously), and a 'middle bracket' of six to ten years. The decision in *Edwards* appears to recognise a third bracket, of between two and five years, reflecting the distinctions drawn in the civil case of *Re Sevenoaks Stationery (Retail)* [1991] Ch 164, but this may overlook the fact that in a criminal case there is no equiva-lent to the two-year minimum disqualification period which applies in a civil case. Relevant sen-tencing factors include the duration of the offending, whether the offender had been dishonest

throughout or had traded for a considerable period legitimately, the amount involved, the previous character of the offender, and whether there had been a prompt admission of guilt (*Cadman* [2012] 2 Cr App R (S) 525).

Disqualification for 15 years was appropriate in *Vanderwell* [1998] 2 Cr App R (S) 439 for a 'thoroughly dishonest fraudster' who pleaded guilty to managing a company while an undischarged bankrupt, obtaining property by deception and failing to keep proper accounts, and who had served an earlier prison sentence for fraud and received an earlier disqualification. See also *Atterbury* [1996] 2 Cr App R (S) 151, when disqualification for 12 years was imposed on the offender who had acted as a company director in contravention of an earlier disqualification order. Ten years' disqualification was upheld in *Sheikh* [2011] 1 Cr App R (S) 99 for sophisticated dishonest activity carried out over a number of years. Seven years' disqualification was upheld in *Bott-Walters* [2005] 2 Cr App R (S) 438, where the offender, the managing director of a company, had obtained £200,000 from another company by deception. Disqualification for five years was appropriate in *Theivendran* (1992) 13 Cr App R (S) 601 (managing a company whilst an undischarged bankrupt and obtaining excessive credit contrary to the Insolvency Act 1986) and in *Ashby* [1998] 2 Cr App R (S) 37. In *Victory* [1999] 2 Cr App R (S) 102, two years' disqualification was reduced to 12 months in the case of a director who was 'careless to the point of incompetence' in keeping accounting records.

Contravention

E21.10   A contravention of a disqualification order is, in itself, a criminal offence punishable on indictment with up to two years' imprisonment, a fine, or both, and on summary conviction with up to six months or a fine (Company Directors Disqualification Act 1986, s. 13). Where a disqualification order is made against a person who is already subject to one, the periods specified shall run concurrently (s. 1(3) and *Johnson* [1996] 2 Cr App R (S) 228).

DRIVING

Disqualification from Driving on Commission of an Offence

E21.11   By s. 146 of the PCC(S)A 2000, a court by or before which a person is convicted of an offence may, instead of or in addition to dealing with him in any other way, order him to be disqualified, for such period as it thinks fit, from holding or obtaining a driving licence (s. 146(1)). The power is made available to the Crown Court and magistrates' courts and applies in relation to any offence.

On a literal reading of s. 146, conviction for an offence may, without more, attract a period of disqualification from driving for such period as the court thinks fit. In *Cliff* [2005] 2 Cr App R (S) 118, the offender was convicted of affray. He was sentenced to 15 months' imprisonment together with a disqualification under s. 146 for two years. The Court of Appeal upheld the disqualification, saying that it was not necessary for the offence of conviction to be related in any way to the use of a motor vehicle. The court added, however, that an order under s. 146 could not be made arbitrarily, and there must be sufficient reason for it. In this case, the offender had admitted that before the incident of affray he had driven his car while affected by drink or drugs or both. In *Bye* [2006] 1 Cr App R (S) 157, disqualification for 12 months under s. 146 in conjunction with a prison sentence of eight months was upheld by the Court of Appeal in a case where the offender got out of his car and attacked another motorist; in *Waring* [2006] 1 Cr App R (S) 56, disqualification for 18 months in conjunction with a prison sentence of four months for escape from lawful custody was upheld. In the latter case the offender had been stopped by the police, provided a positive breath test but, in the process of being taken to the police station, had jumped from the police car and escaped. He thereby avoided a second breath test and any possibility of being prosecuted for driving with excess alcohol. In *Sofekun*

[2009] 1 Cr App R (S) 460 an order under s. 146 was upheld where the offender had cannabis concealed within the bonnet of his car in small bags ready for supply. The Court of Appeal said that nothing in *Cliff* should be taken to have created any restrictions on the exercise of the power which cannot be found in the statutory provision itself. There is no power under s. 146 to order an offender to take an extended driving test on the expiry of the disqualification under the RTOA 1988, s. 36.

Totality   It is unclear whether an order made under s. 146 affects the totality of the sentence   **E21.12** (by analogy with the power to order forfeiture of the offender's property under s. 143: see **E18.5**) or whether it should be regarded as an ancillary order (by analogy with compensation orders: see **E16.11**) imposition of which should not affect the punishment imposed for the offence. In *Sofekun* the disqualification was viewed alongside the custodial sentence imposed in that case as 'part of an overall punitive sentence', and it is respectfully submitted that this is the better view.

Power to Extend   The CAJA 2009, s. 137 and sch. 18, provide for the extension of any driving   **E21.13** disqualification imposed under s. 146 in cases where the court also passes a custodial sentence. The new provisions (PCC(S)A 2000, ss. 147A and 147B) provide that the period of disqualification is extended by the period which is actually spent in custody by the offender. These provisions come into force on a day to be appointed.

Disqualification from Driving where Motor Vehicle Used for Committing or Facilitating Commission of an Offence

Section 147 of the PCC(S)A 2000 provides that the Crown Court may disqualify an offender   **E21.14** from holding or obtaining a licence to drive a motor vehicle in cases where a motor vehicle has been used for the purpose of committing, or facilitating the commission of, the offence. This power is available:

(a) where a person is convicted before the Crown Court of an offence punishable on indictment with imprisonment for a term of two years or more, or where the offender has been convicted by a magistrates' court of such an offence and he is committed under s. 3 of the 2000 Act to the Crown Court for sentence (s. 147(1)), or

(b) where he is convicted before any court of common assault or any other offence involving assault (including an offence of aiding, abetting, counselling or procuring the commission of such an offence, or encouraging or assisting such an offence within the meaning of the SCA 2007, part 2) (s. 147(2)),

and the Crown Court is satisfied that the motor vehicle was used (whether by the person convicted or by anyone else) for the purpose of committing, or facilitating the commission of the offence in question (s. 147(3)). Section 147(6) provides that facilitating the commission of an offence includes the taking of any steps after it has been committed for the purpose of disposing of any property to which it relates or of avoiding apprehension or detection.

In a case falling within s. 147, the Crown Court may order the person convicted to be disqualified, for such period as the court thinks fit, from holding or obtaining a licence (s. 147(3) and (4)), but there is no power under s. 147 to order the defendant to take an extended driving test on the expiry of the disqualification under the RTOA 1988, s. 36.

It should be noted that there is no requirement under s. 147 that the person convicted was the driver of the vehicle (*Matthews* [1975] RTR 32; *Skitt* [2005] 2 Cr App R (S) 122), nor that the vehicle was directly involved in the commission of the offence, although use of the vehicle must at least have facilitated its commission (*Patel* (1994) 16 Cr App R (S) 756). If there is no causal link at all, an order under s. 147 cannot be made (*Parrington* (1985) 7 Cr App R (S) 18, although disqualification might now be ordered instead under s. 146 (see **E21.11**).

Duty to Warn and Consider Effects   Before disqualifying the offender, the court must   **E21.15** warn counsel of the possibility of disqualification under s. 147, and counsel should be given an opportunity to address the court on that matter. Failure to warn may result in the disqualification being quashed on appeal (*Powell* (1984) 6 Cr App R (S) 354). A court imposing a disqualification under s. 147 should take account of its likely effects on the offender's employment prospects (*Liddey* [1999] 2 Cr App R (S) 122; *Bowling* [2009] 1 Cr App R (S) 122).

E21.16 **Power to Extend**   The CAJA 2009, s. 137 and sch. 18, provide for the extension of any driving disqualification imposed under s. 146 in cases where the court also passes a custodial sentence. The new provisions (PCC(S)A 2000, ss. 147A and 147B) provide that the period of disqualification is extended by the period which is actually spent in custody by the offender. These provisions come into force on a day to be appointed.

CHILDREN AND VULNERABLE ADULTS

Disqualification from Working with Children

E21.17 The CJCSA 2000, ss. 26 to 34, provided a power for, and in certain cases a duty on, the Crown Court to impose a disqualification order on a person who had committed an offence against a child and who had received a qualifying sentence. Where an order was made, its effect was to disqualify the person concerned from working with children in the future.

E21.18 With effect from 17 June 2013, the court's power to disqualify offenders from working with children was abolished in all cases. This change was brought about by the Protection of Freedoms Act 2012, s. 83, and the Protection of Freedoms Act 2012 (Commencement No. 6) Order 2013 (SI 2013 No. 1180). By the Safeguarding Vulnerable Groups Act 2006 (Commencement No. 8 and Saving) Order 2012 (SI 2012 No. 2231), the remaining provisions of the 2000 Act were repealed on that date. This was a confusing way of changing the sentencing provisions, given that on its face s. 83 of the 2012 Act has nothing to do with disqualification orders made by a court. However, although the implementation process might have been unusual, it is submitted that the effect is clear.

Barring Offenders from Regulated Activity Relating to Children and Vulnerable Adults

E21.19 By virtue of the Safeguarding Vulnerable Groups Act 2006 and the Safeguarding Vulnerable Groups Act 2006 (Commencement No. 3) Order 2009 (SI 2009 No. 39), there has been, since 20 January 2009, a duty on a court to inform an offender that the Disclosure and Barring Service will bar him from working with children and/or vulnerable adults in any case where the court (a) disqualifies him under the CJCSA 2000 (see **E21.17**), (b) imposes a risk of sexual harm order under the SOA 2003, or (c) convicts him of a specified offence involving harm or a risk of harm to children or vulnerable adults. The power of the court to disqualify under (a) above was abolished from 17 June 2013, so from that date only the powers under (b) and (c) remain.

E21.20 The reason for the requirement on the court is said to be to avoid a possible defence to a charge under s. 7(1) of the 2006 Act (offence of seeking to engage in, offering to engage in or engaging in a regulated activity from which barred), that he did not know he was barred from that activity (s. 7(3)).

E21.21 Judges are required to inform the offender, in a case where the offender has been convicted of a specified offence, or has been made subject to an order of a specified description (namely, a risk of sexual harm order) that he either *will* be barred or (depending upon the offence of conviction) *may be* barred from working with children or with vulnerable adults, or both. The offender either '*will* or *may be*' barred because (depending upon the offence for which he is convicted) some offenders are barred without the right to make representations and some are barred with the right to make representation.

The specified offences can be found in the schedule to the Safeguarding Vulnerable Groups Act   **E21.22**
2006 (Prescribed Criteria and Miscellaneous Provisions) Regulations 2009 (SI 2009 No. 37).
The four paragraphs in the schedule list the offences which will result in automatic inclusion on
one or other (or both) lists, either with or without the right to make representations. It should
be noted that the original list of specified offences has been amended by SI 2009 No. 2610, SI
2010 No. 1146 and SI 2012 No. 2160.

While the task of judges is to inform the offender, the Court of Appeal in *Smith* [2012] 1 All ER   **E21.23**
451 pointed out that a court making a sexual offences prevention order should avoid duplicating or interfering with the prohibitions placed upon the offender by virtue of the 2006 Act. It
is unclear how much detail judges need to provide when informing the offender of the implication of the conviction. Currently the CrimPR, r. 42.3, simply states that the court 'must tell the
defendant that the notification requirements apply, and under what legislation'. It is submitted
that an agreed form of words might usefully be drawn up for judges to employ in these cases,
and that a notice in agreed form could then be handed to the offender.

SEXUAL OFFENCES PREVENTION ORDERS

The SOA 2003, ss. 104 to 113, provide powers for the courts to impose a sexual offences pre-   **E21.24**
vention order (SOPO). Whenever a prosecution application is made for a SOPO the appropriate procedure as set out in the CrimPR, part 50 (Civil Behaviour Orders after Verdict or
Finding: see Supplement, **R-361**) should be complied with. A court may make a SOPO under
the SOA 2003, s. 104, where the court deals with an offender in respect of a sexual offence
listed in sch. 3 (see **E23.3**, although by the CJIA 2008, s. 141, any conditions there relating to
the way in which the offender is dealt with, or to the age of any person, are to be disregarded)
or one of the offences listed in sch. 5 to the SOA 2003 where the context of the offence gives
rise to concern over the risk of future sexual offending (both schedules are amended by SI 2007
No. 296 to cover a wider range of offences), or where the offender is found not guilty of such
an offence by reason of insanity, or where there is a finding that he is under a disability and has
done the act charged against him in respect of such an offence. The court must be satisfied that
it is necessary to make such an order, for the purpose of 'protecting the public or any particular
members of the public from serious sexual harm from the defendant' (s. 104(1)–(3)). This
phrase means 'protecting the public in the United Kingdom or any particular members of that
public from serious physical or psychological harm, caused by the defendant committing one
or more offences listed in schedule 3' (s. 106(3)). Acts, behaviour, convictions and findings
include those occurring before the commencement date (s. 106(4)), which was 1 May 2004.
An order may also be made following a conviction on an application by a chief officer of police
in respect of a qualifying offender (s. 104(1) and (4)–(6)). As to the standard of proof required
when a chief officer of police applies for a SOPO, see *R (Chief Constable of Cleveland Police) v
Haggas* [2010] 3 All ER 506. A SOPO may be imposed in conjunction with any sentence. As
from a date to be appointed, the power to make a SOPO following conviction or following
application is repealed by the ABCPA 2014, s. 113 and sch. 5. The order will be replaced by a
closely similar provision enabling the making of a sexual harm prevention order.

A SOPO prohibits the offender from doing anything described in the order, and has effect for a   **E21.25**
fixed period (not less than five years) specified in the order or until further order (s. 107(1)). An
order for less than five years is unlawful (*Roberts* [2010] EWCA Crim 907). The only prohibitions that may be included in the order are those necessary for the purpose of protecting the
public or any particular members of the public from serious sexual harm from the defendant
(s. 107(2)). Where (a) the order is made in respect of an offender who was a relevant offender
immediately before the making of the order, and (b) the offender would otherwise cease to
be subject to the notification requirements (see **E23**) while the order has effect, the offender
remains subject to the notification requirements (s. 107(3)). Where an order is made in respect
of an offender who was not a relevant offender immediately before the making of the order, the

order causes the offender to become subject to the notification requirements from the making of the order until the order (as renewed from time to time) ceases to have effect (s. 107(4)). In *Hammond* [2008] EWCA Crim 1358, and again in *Smith* [2012] 1 All ER 451, the Court of Appeal said that it would often though not always be appropriate to align the duration of a SOPO with the applicable notification period set by the SOA 2003.

Provisions relating to the variation, renewal and discharge of SOPOs are set out in s. 108, and provisions relating to appeals against SOPOs are set out in s. 110. On the relationship between these sections, see *Hoath* [2011] 4 All ER 306.

If an offender who is subject to a SOPO without reasonable excuse does anything which he is prohibited from doing by that order, he commits an offence which is punishable on summary conviction with imprisonment for a term not exceeding six months or a fine not exceeding the statutory maximum or both, or on conviction on indictment with imprisonment for a term not exceeding five years. Where a person is convicted of such an offence, it is not open to the court to make a conditional discharge in respect of the offence (s. 113).

E21.26   A SOPO is designed for those who present an ongoing risk of danger to the public in general, or any particular member of the public, from serious sexual harm. An order under the section can impose a significant restriction on the liberty of the offender and should be construed as authorising no more severe interference with that liberty than is proportionate to the risk. In *Roberts* [2010] EWCA Crim 907 the Court of Appeal said that the statutory criteria must always be made out, and such orders must not be made as a matter of course, or 'on the hoof'; judges must be given the opportunity to consider a draft proposed order in advance. In *Smith*, Hughes LJ indicated (at [26]) that a draft should be served on the court and the offender not less than two days before the hearing and should be provided in electronic form to facilitate amendment. If counsel invite the judge to make such an order, appropriate material should be placed before the judge to show that the statutory requirements have been met. In *Hemsley* [2010] 3 All ER 965 the Court of Appeal said that SOPOs should be clear on their face, capable of being complied with by the offender without unreasonable difficulty and/or the assistance of a third party, and free of the risk of unintentional breach. Such orders must be carefully drafted and, bearing in mind that they are often made against those of limited education, simplicity is a virtue. In *Pelletier* [2012] EWCA Crim 1060 the Court of Appeal said that the final version of the order must be approved and initialled by the judge and that it was sensible for a copy of the order to be given to the offender and that he should sign for it. In *Smith*, Hughes LJ stated (at [4]) that the SOPO:

> . . . offers a flexibility in drafting which is in one sense welcome because it enables the order to be tai-lored to the exact requirements of the case. That flexibility, however, must not lead draftsmen to an inventiveness which stores up trouble for the future. It will do this if it creates a provision which is, or will become, unworkable. That may be because it is too vague or because it potentially conflicts with other rules applicable to the defendant, or simply because it imposes an impermissible level of restriction on the ordinary activities of life. The SOPO must meet the twin tests of necessity and clarity. The test of necessity brings with it the subtest of proportionality.

E21.27   In *Mortimer* [2010] EWCA Crim 1303 the Court of Appeal deleted or amended a number of prohibitions in an order relating to the offender's access to the internet, on the basis that the prohibitions were disproportionate and/or very difficult to enforce. The Court substituted pro-visions which prohibited owning any device with access to the internet without first notifying the monitoring officer, and prohibiting the offender from deleting from that device its history of internet use or refusing to show such history to a police officer on request. In *Thompson* [2009] EWCA Crim 3258 the Court of Appeal struck down a requirement purporting to allow the police unannounced access to the defendant's home to check his computer equipment and internet use. In *Smith* the Court suggested that probably the best approach is one which requires the preservation of readable internet history coupled with a submission to inspection on request.

The relationship between the SOPO and the dangerous offender regime was considered in *Terrell* [2008] 2 All ER 1065, where the 21-year-old offender pleaded guilty before the magistrates' courts to four offences of making indecent photographs of a child and was committed to Crown Court for sentence. The Court of Appeal concluded that the dangerous offender provisions did not apply in this case. The Court noted that the court's discretion to make a SOPO is prescribed by the SOA 2003 without reference to the dangerous offender provisions. Those provisions required that imprisonment is appropriate, while the prevention order does not. The person on whom a sentence of imprisonment for public protection is imposed is released only when safety permits, and subject to licence provisions indefinitely. Restrictions imposed during a prevention order may be onerous, or may be no greater than those which normally operate during a licence period after release from custody. The threshold of dangerousness for a sentence of imprisonment for public protection (where 'serious harm' means 'death or serious personal injury') is higher than that required for a prevention order. The Court concluded that the restrictions which a court could impose under a prevention order would affect the question whether the dangerousness provisions had to be invoked in a particular case. It may be possible to avoid imposing such a sentence by imposing instead apt and effective conditions within a prevention order. While the sentence of imprisonment for public protection was repealed by the LASPO 2012, it is submitted that the observations in *Terrell* remain relevant where the court is considering the imposition of an extended sentence.

Following an earlier division of views in the authorities as to whether an indeterminate sentence and a SOPO are mutually exclusive, it is now clear from *Smith* that the 'usual rule' is that an indeterminate sentence needs no SOPO. The Court in that case also noted that a SOPO should not duplicate or interfere with restrictions imposed by the sex offender notification provisions or with prohibitions placed on the offender by the Independent Barring Service. Terms in SOPOs prohibiting the offender from activities likely to bring him into contact with children can be justified only as required beyond the restrictions placed upon him by the IBS. What is covered by the Safeguarding Vulnerable Groups Act 2006 needs to be considered by the judge in each case. The prosecution should be in a position to supply that information, and to make the case for any additional SOPO requirements.

RESTRAINING ORDERS UNDER THE PROTECTION FROM HARASSMENT ACT 1997

A court which is sentencing or otherwise dealing with a person convicted of an offence may, **E21.28** as well as dealing with the offender in any other way, make a restraining order under s. 5 of the Protection from Harassment Act 1997. A restraining order may also be made if appropriate under s. 5A whenever an offender has been convicted of any offence, rather than (as was formerly the case) only following a conviction under s. 2 or s. 4 of the 1977 Act. Moreover, under s. 5A, courts can now make a restraining order against a person who has been acquitted of an offence, provided that the court believes that a restraining order is necessary to protect another person from harassment, but a person against whom such an order is made under s. 5A has the same right of appeal against the order as if he had been convicted of the offence in question before the court which made the order (s. 5A(5)).

These changes do not apply to convictions or acquittals recorded prior to 30 September 2009, but may apply where conduct complained of occurred before that date (SI 2009 No. 2616). Whenever a prosecution application is made for a SOPO the appropriate procedure as set out in the CrimPR, part 50 (Civil Behaviour Orders after Verdict or Finding: see Supplement, **R-361**) should be complied with.

For the purpose of protecting the victim of the offence (or any other person mentioned in the **E21.29** order) from further conduct which amounts to harassment, or will cause a fear of violence, the order may prohibit the offender from doing anything described in the order. An order may be made for the protection of an individual, a group of individuals provided that the group was sufficiently clearly defined, or a limited company (*Buxton* [2011] 1 WLR 857). The order is a civil order and the civil standard of proof applies (*Major* [2011] 1 Cr App R 322). In *James* [2013] 2 Cr App R (S) 542 (85) the offender was convicted of assault upon his adult stepdaughter but the Court of Appeal quashed a restraining order which had been imposed in addition to a community order on the basis that it was clear from the jury's verdict that much of the complainant's evidence had been rejected, and it was not fair to impose a restraining order where most of the trouble was attributable to the complainant. The order must be drafted in clear and precise terms so that there is no doubt as to its conditions, and may make reference to specific roads or addresses from which the offender is prohibited, if necessary by the inclusion of a map (*Debnath* [2006] 2 Cr App R (S) 169). In considering the terms and extent of the restraining order, the court should have regard to proportionality with the seriousness of the offence. The order has effect for a specified period or until further order.

There is no principle that a restraining order made following an acquittal can be made only on uncontested facts, or can be used only rarely; the relevant evidence will usually have emerged at the trial, but additional evidence can be heard on the matter (*Major*). A restraining order following an acquittal was upheld in *Thompson* [2011] 2 Cr App R (S) 131, where the offender was acquitted of assaulting a woman with whom he had a relationship, but the judge formed the view on the basis of evidence given at the trial, that the order was necessary to protect the complainant from harassment. By contrast, in *K* [2012] 1 Cr App R (S) 523 a similar order was quashed on appeal, it being found that the prosecution had offered no evidence in respect of the charges against the defendant and the limited information available to the judge did not provide a sound evidential basis for making the order. See also *Brough* [2012] 2 Cr App R (S) 30 and *Jose* [2013] EWCA Crim 939.

The prosecutor, the defendant or any other person mentioned in the order may apply to the court which made the order for it to be varied or discharged by a further order. The Court of Appeal may decline to interfere with the terms of a restraining order if the appropriate remedy was an application to the court to vary or discharge the order (*Debnath*).

If without reasonable excuse the offender does anything which he is prohibited from doing under the order, he is guilty of an offence punishable, on conviction on indictment, with imprisonment for a term not exceeding five years, or a fine, or both; or on summary conviction to imprisonment for a term not exceeding six months, or a fine not exceeding the statutory maximum, or both.

As for the approach to sentence in case of breach of a restraining order, see the definitive sentencing guideline *Breach of a Protective Order* (see Supplement, **SG-45**). The earlier decision in *Liddle* [1999] 3 All ER 816 is also of assistance, where Curtis J observed that relevant sentencing factors would be the relative seriousness and persistence of the offender's conduct, whether there was a history of disobedience to court orders, and the actual impact of the harassment on the victim. The attitude of the offender was also relevant, such as whether he had pleaded guilty, expressed remorse, and was willing to receive appropriate treatment or help. A sentence of two years' imprisonment was appropriate in *Lindsey* [2013] EWCA Crim 1829 for serious repeated breaches of an order, including breach of a suspended sentence imposed for earlier breach. See also *Moore* [2013] EWCA Crim 474.

TRAVEL RESTRICTION ORDERS: DRUG TRAFFICKING OFFENDERS

E21.30   By the CJPA 2001, ss. 33 to 37, any criminal court (but, in practice, the Crown Court) is given power to impose a travel restriction order on an offender who is convicted of a drug trafficking offence committed after that date, and who has been sentenced by that court to a term of imprisonment for four years or more (s. 33(1)). The effect of the order is to restrict the offender's freedom to leave the UK for a period specified by the court, and it may require delivery up of his passport (or 'travel authorisation'). The minimum duration of a travel restriction order is two years, starting from the date of the offender's release from custody. There is no maximum period prescribed in the legislation. The court must always consider whether such an order should be made and must give reasons where it does not consider such an order to be appropriate (s. 33(2)). According to Leveson LJ in *Shaw* [2011] EWCA Crim 98, given the terms of the statute it is not sufficient for the judge simply to assert that the offences did not contain a foreign element.

'Drug trafficking offence' is defined by s. 34. It may be noted that this is a different definition from that provided by the POCA 2002, sch. 2. Possession of a Class A drug with intent to supply is not within the section (*Whittle* [2007] 2 Cr App R (S) 578; *Boland* [2012] EWCA Crim 1953). Section 35 provides for revocation and suspension of travel restriction orders. Section 36 creates various offences in relation to contravention of these orders.

Guidance on the imposition of travel restriction orders was given by the Court of Appeal in *Mee* **E21.31** [2004] 2 Cr App R (S) 434. The order was designed to prevent or reduce the risk of offending after the offender's release from prison. It was not confined to cases involving importation, but those were the cases in which it was most likely to be appropriate. The restriction on a person's freedom to travel was a significant restriction and should not be taken away for a number of years unless there were grounds for doing so. The length of the order should be that which was required to protect the public in the light of the assessment of risk of reoffending, taking into account the offender's age, previous convictions, family contacts and employment considerations. *Mee* was followed and applied in *Fuller* [2006] 1 Cr App R (S) 52, where a travel restriction order, imposed on a woman aged 25 who had pleaded guilty to importation of cocaine, was quashed on the basis that there was no significant risk of reoffending and that the order would prevent contact between the offender's child and his grandparents in Jamaica for a period of seven years. See also *Onung* [2007] 2 Cr App R (S) 9. If the travel restriction order is for four years or less it is open to the offender to apply to revoke or suspend the order after a period of two years. If the order is for a period between four and ten years, four years must elapse before such application is made.

FINANCIAL REPORTING ORDERS

Under the SOCPA 2005, s. 76(1) and (2), a court sentencing an offender for an offence listed **E21.32** in s. 76(3) may also make a financial reporting order in respect of that offender, provided that it is satisfied that the risk of the person's committing another offence of the kind mentioned in s. 76(3) is sufficiently high to justify the making of the order. The relevant offences include offences under the Theft Act 1968, ss. 15, 15A, 16 and 20(2); under the Theft Act 1978, ss. 1 and 2; offences under the Fraud Act 2006, ss. 1 and 11, conspiracy to defraud; any of the 'lifestyle offences' specified in the POCA 2002, sch. 2; offences of false accounting under the Theft Act 1968, s. 17; offences under the Bribery Act 2010, ss. 1, 2 and 6 and offences under the Terrorism Act 2000, s. 15, 16, 17 or 18.

The purpose of a financial reporting order is to require the person on whom the order is imposed to make a report to a person specified in the order as to such particulars of his financial affairs as may be specified in the order (s. 79(3)). The report may relate to a specified period of time beginning with the date on which the order comes into force and to subsequent specified periods of time, each beginning immediately after the end of the previous one (s. 79(2)). Each report must be made within a number of days after the end of the period in question, as specified in the order (s. 79(5)).

A financial reporting order comes into force when it is made and has effect for the period specified in the order, beginning with the date in which it is made. If made by a magistrates' court, the period must not exceed five years (s. 76(6)). If made by the Crown Court, the period must not exceed 20 years, where the person has been sentenced to imprisonment for life, or 15 years, in any other case (s. 76(7)).

E21.33   In *Adams* [2009] 4 All ER 574 the Court of Appeal said that a financial reporting order was not a 'penalty' for the purposes of the ECHR, Article 7, so an order imposed on an offender whose offences had been committed before financial reporting orders came into existence did not amount to a retrospective penalty. The Court of Appeal in *Wright* [2009] 2 Cr App R (S) 313 said that a financial reporting order should not be made to facilitate the enforcement of a confiscation order, and that in every case judges should consider carefully whether a financial reporting order would achieve anything when financial investigators have much the same powers. See also *Bell* [2012] 2 Cr App R (S) 15.

A person who without reasonable excuse includes false or misleading information in a report, or who otherwise fails to comply with any requirement of s. 79, is guilty of an offence and liable on summary conviction to imprisonment for a term not exceeding six months, or to a fine not exceeding level 5 on the standard scale, or to both (s. 79(10)).

Section 80 provides for the variation and revocation of financial reporting orders by the court which made the order, and s. 81 provides for verification and disclosure of such orders.

RELATED ORDERS

Orders under the Crime and Disorder Act 1998 (ASBOs)

E21.34   The CDA 1998 applies, *inter alia*, where an offender is convicted of an offence and the court considers that the offender has acted in an anti-social manner. These orders are discussed at **D25.11**.

Serious Crime Prevention Orders

E21.35   The SCA 2007, ss. 19 to 22, provide that the Crown Court has power to make an order known as a serious crime prevention order on a person aged 18 or over convicted of a serious offence (whether convicted in the Crown Court or committed for sentence) in addition to sentencing the person or conditionally discharging him (s. 19). See **D25.72** for a full discussion of such orders.

Section E22   Mentally Disordered Offenders

HOSPITAL ORDERS

An admission to a hospital by means of a hospital order has the same effect for most purposes **E22.1** as a compulsory civil commitment under part II of the Mental Health Act 1983. The order lapses after six months, but may be renewed for a further six months and then at yearly intervals thereafter, where the responsible medical officer considers further detention necessary for the protection of the public or in the interests of the patient's health or safety (Mental Health Act 1983, s. 20 and sch. 1). There is no limit to the number of renewals which might subsequently be made, but the patient may be discharged from hospital by way of various powers exercised by the responsible medical officer, the hospital managers, or a mental health review tribunal.

Mental Health Act 1983, s. 37

(1) Where a person is convicted before the Crown Court of an offence punishable with imprisonment other than an offence the sentence for which is fixed by law, or is convicted by a magistrates' court of an offence punishable on summary conviction with imprisonment, and the conditions mentioned in subsection (2) below are satisfied, the court may by order authorise his admission to and detention in such hospital as may be specified in the order or, as the case may be, place him under the guardianship of a local social services authority or of such other person approved by a local social services authority as may be so specified.

(1A) In the case of an offence the sentence for which would otherwise fall to be imposed—
   (za) under section 1A(5) of the Prevention of Crime Act 1953,
   (a) under section 51A(2) of the Firearms Act 1968,
   (aa) under section 139AA(7) of the Criminal Justice Act 1988,
   (b) under section 110(2) or 111(2) of the Powers of Criminal Courts (Sentencing) Act 2000,
   (ba) under section 224A of the Criminal Justice Act 2003,
   (c) under any of section 225(2) or 226(2) of the Criminal Justice Act 2003, or
   (d) under section 29(4) or (6) of the Violent Crime Reduction Act 2006 (minimum sentences in certain cases of using someone to mind a weapon)
nothing in those provisions shall prevent a court from making an order under subsection (1) above for the admission of the offender to a hospital.

(1B) References in subsection (1A) above to a sentence falling to be imposed under any of the provisions mentioned in that subsection are to be read in accordance with section 305(4) of the Criminal Justice Act 2003.

(2) The conditions referred to in subsection (1) above are that —
   (a) the court is satisfied, on the written or oral evidence of two registered medical practitioners, that the offender is suffering from mental disorder and that either—
     (i) the mental disorder from which the offender is suffering is of a nature or degree which makes it appropriate for him to be detained in a hospital for medical treatment and appropriate medical treatment is available for him; or
     (ii) in the case of an offender who has attained the age of 16 years, the mental disorder is of a nature or degree which warrants his reception into guardianship under this Act; and
   (b) the court is of the opinion, having regard to all the circumstances including the nature of the offence and the character and antecedents of the offender, and to the other available methods of dealing with him, that the most suitable method of disposing of the case is by means of an order under this section.

At least one of the two medical practitioners referred to in s. 37(2) must be approved, for the **E22.2** purposes of s. 12, by the Secretary of State, as having special experience in the diagnosis or treatment of mental disorder (s. 54(1)). A hospital order may be appropriate, even though no causal link is established between the offender's mental disorder and the offence in respect of which the order is made (*McBride* (1972) CSP F2–2A01). In *Blackwood* (1974) 59 Cr App R 170, the Court of Appeal said that a court should not normally make a hospital order if the offender was not legally represented. Only a youth court may make a hospital order or guardianship order on a juvenile (PCC(S)A 2000, s. 8(6)).

Section 37(3) of the Mental Health Act 1983 deals with the power of a magistrates' court to make a hospital order, where the court is satisfied that the person did the act or made the omission charged, without proceeding to conviction. This power is to be very sparingly used (*Lincoln (Kesteven) Justices, ex parte O'Connor* [1983] 1 All ER 901).

E22.3   A hospital order or guardianship order cannot be made unless the court is satisfied, on the written or oral evidence of the approved clinician who would be in charge of the offender's treatment, or of some other person representing the managers of the hospital, that arrangements have been made for the offender's admission to that hospital within 28 days of the date of the order (s. 37(4)). The health authorities are under no legal obligation to accept offenders from the courts (see, e.g., the comments of Field J in *Barker* [2003] 1 Cr App R (S) 212). They are, however, under a legal obligation to supply information to the courts about the availability of beds in their regions for the admission of persons under hospital orders (s. 39). In an emergency or other special situation arising within that 28 days, the Secretary of State may give directions for the admission of the offender to a hospital different from that specified in the order (s. 37(5)).

The decision whether to make a hospital order under s. 37 or impose a sentence of imprisonment is within the discretion of the court (*Khelifi* [2006] 2 Cr App R (S) 650). The fact that the conditions in s. 37(2) are all made out does not compel the making of a hospital order, or give rise to a presumption that one will be made. The welfare of the offender is always an important consideration, but must be assessed in light of the seriousness of the offence.

By s. 37(8), when a hospital order or a guardianship order is made, the court shall not pass a sentence of imprisonment, make an order for detention, impose a fine, make a community order or a youth rehabilitation order in respect of the offence, or require a parent of a juvenile so dealt with to enter into a recognizance (see **E14.6**). A hospital order cannot be combined with a referral order (see **E10**). The court may, however, 'make any other order which the court has power to make apart from this section': this would include ancillary orders such as a compensation order.

Interim Hospital Orders

E22.4   Section 38 provides for the making of an 'interim hospital order' for the purposes of establishing whether a convicted person is suitable to be the subject of a hospital order. The qualifying conditions are virtually the same as for the making of a hospital order under s. 37 (see **E22.1**), but the interim order is available to the court 'before making a hospital order or dealing with him in some other way'. One difference in the powers is that an interim order can be made only where one of the registered medical practitioners who give evidence is employed at the hospital where the person is to be detained. An interim hospital order is not a final disposal of the case; such an order may last for up to 12 weeks, renewable for further periods of not more than 28 days at a time, though in no case may it last for more than a total of 12 months. No minimum period is specified. Power to make an interim hospital order under s. 38 may also be exercised for the purposes of determining whether a person should be made subject to a hospital direction or a limitation direction under s. 45A (s. 45A(8): see **E22.12**). At the end of the interim period the court must make a final disposal of the case, and the interim order comes to an end. In a case where a court renews an interim hospital order, or where it finally disposes of the case by making a hospital order under s. 37, the offender need not appear before the court, provided that he is legally represented and his representative has had an opportunity of being heard (s. 38(2) and (6)).

GUARDIANSHIP ORDERS

Guardianship orders are made under the Mental Health Act 1983, s. 37 (see **E22.1**). By s. 40(2) **E22.5** a guardianship order shall confer on the authority or person named in the order as guardian, the same powers as a guardianship application made and accepted under part II of the 1983 Act. These powers, in outline, are to determine place of residence, require attendance for treatment, occupation, education or training, and to require access to the patient in any place of residence for a doctor, social worker or other specified person (Mental Health Act 1983, s. 8).

The relevant statutory provisions are the same as those which relate to the courts' powers to make hospital orders, except that there is no requirement in respect of the making of a guardianship order that the mental disorder must be treatable, and see the requirement in s. 37(2)(a)(ii) (see **E22.1**). In addition, by s. 37(6), a guardianship order cannot be made unless the relevant authority or person is willing to receive the offender into guardianship. Section 39A empowers a court which is minded to make a guardianship order to request the local social services authority to inform the court whether it would be willing to comply with the order and, if so, to give information about how it would exercise its powers under s. 40(2). A guardianship order lasts for six months, but may be renewed for a further six months and thereafter annually (s. 20).

RESTRICTION ORDERS

Power to Make Restriction Orders

Mental Health Act 1983, s. 41   E22.6

(1) Where a hospital order is made in respect of an offender by the Crown Court, and it appears to the court, having regard to the nature of the offence, the antecedents of the offender and the risk of his committing further offences if set at large, that it is necessary for the protection of the public from serious harm so to do, the court may, subject to the provisions of this section, further order that the offender shall be subject to the special restrictions set out in this section; and an order under this section shall be known as 'a restriction order'.

(2) A restriction order shall not be made in the case of any person unless at least one of the registered medical practitioners whose evidence is taken into account by the court under section 37(2)(a) above has given evidence orally before the court.

For hospital orders, see **E22.1**.

The special restrictions applicable to a patient under a restriction order are set out in s. 41(3). **E22.7** In particular, powers under the 1983 Act to transfer or discharge the patient are exercisable only with the consent of the Secretary of State. Only the Crown Court may make a restriction order, though magistrates may commit an offender to the Crown Court, provided the offender is aged 14 or over, with a view to such a disposal (s. 43 and see *Avbunudje* [1999] 2 Cr App R (S) 189). If the magistrates' court commits the offender to the Crown Court, but the Crown Court decides not to make a restriction order, the Crown Court's powers of sentence are limited to those which the magistrates could have imposed, unless there is also in effect a general committal for sentence.

A restriction order cannot be made unless there is evidence that it is necessary to protect the public from serious harm (*Courtney* (1987) 9 Cr App R (S) 404; *Kearney* [2003] 2 Cr App R (S) 85). A court is not bound to accept medical evidence for or against restricting discharge when a hospital order is made (*Royse* (1981) 3 Cr App R (S) 58, *Birch* (1989) 11 Cr App R (S) 202). There is no requirement for a causal connection between the disorder and the offence (*Hatt* [1962] Crim LR 647, approved in *Birch*).

Unlike a hospital order under s. 37, a restriction order does not lapse in the ordinary way unless renewed, but continues for as long as the restriction order is in place. If the restriction order is for a fixed period, at the end of that period the restrictions no longer apply but the hospital order continues in effect (s. 41(5)). Neither the responsible medical officer nor the hospital managers may discharge the patient without the Secretary of State's consent. The Secretary of State or a mental health review tribunal may release a patient who is subject to a restriction order at any time, either absolutely or conditionally (s. 42(1) and (2)). If the patient is discharged conditionally, the restriction order remains in force and the patient may be recalled to hospital.

Sentencing Principles

E22.8   In *Birch* (1989) 11 Cr App R (S) 202, the Court of Appeal gave important guidance upon the selection of sentence for mentally disordered offenders generally, and in particular the appropriate use of restriction orders under the Mental Health Act 1983, s. 41. The following general points emerge:

(a) In a case involving a degree of mental disorder, the sentencer should consider whether a period of compulsory detention is apposite.

(b) If such an order is inappropriate, the sentencer must consider whether the conditions contained in s. 37, for the making of a hospital order (see E22.1), are satisfied. If in doubt, he may wish to make an interim hospital order, giving the court and the doctors further time to decide. If the conditions in s. 37 are satisfied, he will consider whether to make a hospital order or impose a custodial sentence.

(c) The sentencer should then consider whether the conditions of s. 41 are satisfied.

E22.9   Hughes LJ in *A-G's Ref (No. 54 of 2011)* [2012] 1 Cr App R (S) 635 gave a detailed explanation of the relevant powers and difficult choices which a judge is required to make in this area of law. In making the choice between an indeterminate custodial sentence or a hospital order with restrictions, the 'absolutely crucial difference' between the two regimes is that under the former regime release is conditional upon the responsible authority being satisfied that the offender is no longer a risk to the public, while under the latter regime the responsible authority must be satisfied that the offender presents no danger arising from his medical condition. Release from the former regime is on licence and the offender can be recalled if his behaviour shows that he is still a danger. On release from hospital, recall is available but only if the offender's medical condition relapses. The Court in this case preferred custody to the hospital order imposed by the judge, partly because the offender had been living a criminal lifestyle and there was a clear risk that he would resume it on release. The decision in *Fort* [2013] EWCA Crim 2332, where the 18-year-old offender had been sentenced to custody for life after pleading guilty to diminished responsibility manslaughter, went the other way. The Court in this case felt that the offender would not continue to pose a significant risk of serious harm to members of the public once his mental disorder had been cured.

If the sentencer decides on a restriction order, he must then choose an unlimited order, or one for a fixed term. It is regarded as imprudent in any but the most exceptional circumstances to impose a restriction for a fixed rather than an unlimited period (*Gardiner* [1967] 1 All ER 895; *Birch* and *Nwohia* [1996] 1 Cr App R (S) 170).

E22.10   If the criteria within the Mental Health Act 1983, s. 41, are established, the sentencer may, but is not obliged to, make a restriction order. The decision is that of the judge, and a restriction order may be made even though not recommended by the medical evidence (*Royce* (1981) 3 Cr App R (S) 58). The alternative sentences are life imprisonment, an extended sentence, or a fixed-term sentence. The cases make it clear that an indeterminate sentence is to be preferred to a fixed-term sentence where the offender is subject to a degree of mental instability which makes it probable that he will continue to offend unless detained for an indefinite period (*Pither* (1979) 1 Cr App R (S) 209). Where the conditions for a restriction order under the Mental Health Act 1983 are made out, a bed in an appropriate hospital is available, and the medical evidence is that the mental disorder is treatable and that successful treatment will greatly diminish the risk posed by the offender, a restriction order should normally be imposed in preference to a life sentence (*Mbatha* (1985) 7 Cr App R (S) 373; *Hutchinson* [1997] 2 Cr

App R (S) 60; *Mitchell* [1997] 1 Cr App R (S) 90). In the decision of the House of Lords in *Drew* [2004] 2 Cr App R (S) 65, however, it was noted that offenders subject to hospital orders (with or without restriction) are entitled to release when their medical condition has been successfully treated, while release from a life sentence is a matter for the Parole Board, which can take into account all relevant matters of risk rather than just mental health. A life sentence thereby provided a greater degree of control over the offender. See further *IA* [2006] 1 Cr App R (S) 521 and *Welsh* [2011] 2 Cr App R (S) 399.

Mustill LJ in *Birch* also gave guidance (at p. 215) on the choice between a restriction order and **E22.11** a custodial sentence, suggesting that this choice may arise in two distinct situations:

(a) 'If the offender is dangerous and no suitable secure hospital accommodation is available: here the judge will be driven to impose a prison sentence.' A number of earlier cases indicate that where a determinate custodial sentence is imposed rather than a hospital order, it must be proportionate to the offence committed (*Clarke* (1975) 61 Cr App R 320; *Hook* (1980) 2 Cr App R (S) 353; *Fisher* (1981) 3 Cr App R (S) 112). In other cases, however, the Court of Appeal has upheld a disproportionate term of custody, on the grounds of the protection of the public, on an offender for whom no place was available in a hospital (*Scanlon* (1979) 1 Cr App R (S) 60; *Gouws* (1981) 3 Cr App R (S) 325).

(b) 'Where the sentencer considers that notwithstanding the offender's mental disorder there was an element of culpability in the offence which merits punishment. This may happen where there is no connection between the mental disorder and the offence, or where the defendant's responsibility for the offence is "diminished" but not wholly extinguished.' In *Nafei* [2005] 2 Cr App R (S) 127 the Court of Appeal upheld a sentence of imprisonment on an offender who was suffering from schizophrenia and for whom a hospital order was recommended, but where there was no causal connection between the mental condition and the offence and in *Welsh* [2011] 2 Cr App R (S) 399, where the offender bore substantial responsibility for the offence, public confidence required the passing of a life sentence rather than a restriction order. See also *Wood* [2010] 1 Cr App R (S) 6.

HOSPITAL AND LIMITATION DIRECTIONS

Sections 45A and 45B of the Mental Health Act 1983 are designed to apply where the court has **E22.12** heard evidence that the offender is suffering from a mental disorder and the making of a hospital order is appropriate, but the court wishes to ensure that the offender upon completion of his period of treatment will thence be transferred to prison for the remainder of the sentence rather than being released from hospital.

Section 45A applies where a person is convicted before the Crown Court of an offence the **E22.13** sentence for which is not fixed by law and the court considers making a hospital order before deciding to impose a sentence of imprisonment (s. 45A(1)). It was held by the Court of Appeal in *Fort* [2013] EWCA Crim 2332 that 'sentence of imprisonment' in this context does not include the sentence of detention in a young offender institution, so that the power under s. 45A is limited to offenders aged 21 and over. The Court could find no good reason why the power was so limited, and recommended that it should be extended by Parliament to include young adult offenders. By s. 45A(2), the court must be satisfied on the written or oral evidence of two registered medical practitioners (at least one of whom must give oral evidence: s. 45A(4)) that:

(a) the offender is suffering from a mental disorder;
(b) the mental disorder from which the offender is suffering is of a nature or degree which makes it appropriate for him to be detained in a hospital for medical treatment; and
(c) appropriate medical treatment is available for him.

In these circumstances the court may make a 'hospital direction', which is a direction that, instead of being detained in prison, the offender be detained in a specified hospital. The court may also make a 'limitation direction', which is a direction that the offender also be made subject to the restrictions set out in s. 41 of the 1983 Act (see **E22.6**). The court must also be satisfied on the written or oral evidence of the approved clinician who would have overall charge of his case, or of some other person representing the managers of the hospital, that arrangements have been made for the offender's admission to that hospital and for his admission within the period of 28 days from the making of the order. The court may, pending admission within that period, give directions for the offender's detention in a place of safety (s. 45A(5)). A hospital direction and a limitation direction given in respect of an offender have effect not only as regards the sentence of imprisonment imposed but also as regards any other sentence of imprisonment imposed on the same or a previous occasion (s. 45A(9)).

E22.14 Section 45B provides that with respect to any person a hospital direction shall have effect as a transfer direction and a limitation direction shall have effect as a restriction direction. While a person is subject to a hospital direction and a limitation direction the responsible medical officer must supply to the Secretary of State a report on the offender at least every 12 months.

In *Cooper* [2010] EWCA Crim 2335 the offender pleaded guilty to diminished responsibility manslaughter. Although he had no history of mental disorder he was substantially in the grip of serious mental disorder at the time of the offence. The judge imposed imprisonment for public protection with a minimum term of six years together with a hospital and restriction order, directing that the offender was to remain at specified secure accommodation for treatment. The Court of Appeal upheld the sentence, noting that if and when the offender's treatment was successful the Mental Health Review Tribunal would make a recommendation to the Parole Board for release. The offender would remain in hospital until the Board made its decision. The offender on release would be subject to recall for breach of his life licence. See also *Staines* [2006] 2 Cr App R (S) 376.

Section E23   Notification Requirements under the Sexual Offences Act 2003

INTRODUCTION

A person is subject to the notification requirements of the SOA 2003 if he is convicted of an **E23.1** offence listed in sch. 3 to that Act, or is found not guilty of such an offence by reason of insanity, or is found to be under a disability and to have done the act charged against him in respect of such an offence, or is cautioned in respect of such an offence (SOA 2003, s. 80). A person subject to the notification requirements is referred to in the Act as a 'relevant offender'. The notification requirements are set out in s. 83. They are that the offender must, within the period of three days of the conviction, finding or caution, notify to the police the offender's date of birth, national insurance number, name (and any aliases), home address and any other address at which he regularly stays and provide any other information prescribed in regulations made by the Secretary of State. Subsequent changes to these details must also be notified to the police (s. 84). The Secretary of State has power to add further requirements. Additional requirements imposed by the Sexual Offences Act 2003 (Notification Requirements) (England and Wales) Regulations 2012 (SI 2012 No. 1876), that offenders should provide details of their bank, debit and credit card accounts, were upheld by the Divisional Court in *R (Prothero) v Secretary of State for the Home Department* [2014] 1 WLR 1195. Persons who were formerly subject to registration under the Sex Offenders Act 1997 are now made subject to the notification requirements under the SOA 2003 (s. 81).

The retrospective element in the notification requirements under the Sex Offenders Act 1997 was held by the European Commission on Human Rights not to breach the ECHR, Article 7(1), since registration under that Act was not a 'penalty' within the meaning of Article 7 (*Ibbotson v UK* (1999) 27 EHRR CD332). Although the requirements of the 1997 Act did not extend to offenders conditionally discharged (according to the House of Lords in *Longworth* [2006] 1 All ER 887) the requirements of the 2003 Act do apply to such offenders from 1 May 2004 (see **E23.4**). The Supreme Court held in *R (F (A Child)) v Secretary of State for the Home Department* [2011] 1 AC 331 that the indefinite notification requirement under the Act, which contained no provision for review, was disproportionate and infringed Article 8. The Sexual Offences (Remedial) Order 2012 (SI 2012 No. 1883) inserted ss. 91A to 91E into the SOA 2003, to provide for the review of indefinite notification requirements.

The requirements of the 2003 Act are not an additional form of punishment, and so should **E23.2** not be taken into account when determining the sentence to be passed. See *A-G's Ref (No. 50 of 1997)* [1998] 2 Cr App R (S) 155. The provisions of the Act are automatic in their effect and, in principle, do not require the sentencer dealing with a case involving one of the listed offences to make reference to them, although informing the offender is now required by the CrimPR, r. 42.3 (see Supplement, **R-348**). The SOA 2003, s. 92, provides that, where a sentencer states in open court that an offender has been convicted of a listed offence and certifies those facts, the certificate shall be sufficient evidence of those facts.

LISTED OFFENCES

Offences listed in sch. 3 to the SOA 2003 are offences under: **E23.3**

SOA 1956, s. 1 (rape);

SOA 1956, s. 5 (intercourse with a girl under 13);

SOA 1956, s. 6 (intercourse with a girl under 16) if the offender was 20 or over;

SOA 1956, s. 10 (incest by a man) if the victim or other party was under 18;

SOA 1956, s. 12 (buggery) if the offender was 20 or over and the victim or other party was under 18;

SOA 1956, s. 13 (indecency between men) if the offender was 20 or over and the victim or other party was under 18;

SOA 1956, s. 14 (indecent assault on a woman) if the victim was under 18 or the offender was sentenced to at least 30 months' imprisonment or was admitted to hospital and subject to a restriction order;

SOA 1956, s. 15 (indecent assault on a man) if the victim was under 18 or the offender was sentenced to at least 30 months' imprisonment or was admitted to hospital subject to a restriction order;

SOA 1956, s. 16 (assault with intent to commit buggery) if the victim or other party was under 18;

SOA 1956, s. 28 (causing or encouraging the prostitution of, intercourse with, or indecent assault on, a girl under 16);

Indecency with Children Act 1960, s. 1 (indecent conduct towards young child);

Criminal Law Act 1977, s. 54 (inciting girl under 16 to have incestuous sexual intercourse);

Protection of Children Act 1978, s. 1 (indecent photographs of children) if the photographs showed persons under 16 and subject to age of offender and sentence imposed;

Customs and Excise Management Act 1979, s. 170 (penalty for fraudulent evasion of duty) in relation to indecent or obscene articles, if the prohibited goods included indecent photographs of persons under 16 and the offender was 18 or over or received a sentence of at least 12 months' imprisonment

CJA 1988, s. 160 (possession of indecent photograph of child) if the indecent photograph showed persons under 16 and the offender was 18 or over or received a sentence of at least 12 months' imprisonment;

SO(A)A 2000 (abuse of position of trust) if the offender was 20 or over;

SOA 2003, s. 1 or s. 2 (rape, assault by penetration);

SOA 2003, s. 3 (sexual assault) subject to age of offender and sentence imposed;

SOA 2003, s. 4, 5 or 6 (causing sexual activity without consent, rape of child under 13, assault of child under 13 by penetration);

SOA 2003, s. 7 (sexual assault of child under 13) where the offender was aged 18 or over or was sentenced to at least 12 months' imprisonment;

SOA 2003, ss. 8 to 12 (causing or inciting a child under 13 to engage in sexual activity; child sex offences committed by adults);

SOA 2003, s. 13 (child sex offences committed by children or young persons), if the offender was sentenced to at least 12 months' imprisonment;

SOA 2003, s. 14 (arranging or facilitating the commission of a child sex offence), where the offender was aged 18 or over or was sentenced to at least 12 months' imprisonment;

SOA 2003, s. 15 (meeting a child following sexual grooming);

SOA 2003, ss. 16 to 19 (abuse of a position of trust), if the offender is imprisoned, detained in a hospital or receives a community sentence of at least 12 months;

SOA 2003, s. 25 or s. 26 (familial child sex offences) where the offender was aged 18 or over or was sentenced to at least 12 months' imprisonment;

SOA 2003, ss. 30 to 37 (offences against persons with a mental disorder impeding choice);

SOA 2003, ss. 38 to 41 (care workers for persons with mental disorder) subject to age of offender and sentence imposed;

SOA 2003, s. 47 (paying for sexual services of a child) where the victim was under 16 and where the offender was aged 18 or over or was sentenced to at least 12 months' imprisonment;

SOA 2003, s. 48 (causing or inciting child prostitution or pornography) where the offender was aged 18 or over or was sentenced to at least 12 months' imprisonment;

SOA 2003, s. 49 (controlling a child prostitute or child involved in pornography) where the offender was aged 18 or over or was sentenced to at least 12 months' imprisonment;

SOA 2003, s. 50 (arranging or facilitating child prostitution or pornography) where the offender was aged 18 or over or was sentenced to at least 12 months' imprisonment;

SOA 2003, s. 61 (administering a substance with intent);

SOA 2003, s. 62 or s. 63 (committing an offence, or trespassing, with intent to commit a sexual offence) subject to age of offender and sentence passed and subject to age of intended victim;

SOA 2003, s. 64 or s. 65 (sex with an adult relative) subject to age of offender and sentence imposed;

SOA 2003, s. 66 (exposure), subject to age of offender, age of victim and sentence imposed;

SOA 2003, s. 67 (voyeurism), subject to age of offender and sentence imposed;

SOA 2003, s. 69 or s. 70 (intercourse with animal or sexual penetration of corpse), subject to age of offender and sentence imposed;

CJIA 1998, s. 63 (possession of extreme pornographic images) where the offender was aged 18 or over and is sentenced in respect of the offence to imprisonment for a term of at least two years;

CAJA 2009, s. 62(1) (possession of prohibited images of children) where the offender was aged 18 or over and is sentenced in respect of the offence to imprisonment for a term of at least two years.

An attempt or conspiracy to commit the relevant offences or to encourage or assist the commission of such an offence within the meaning of the SCA 2007, part 2 (sch. 3, para. 94).

NOTIFICATION PERIOD

The length of the notification period depends on the sentence which was imposed, and is set out in a table in s. 82(1) of the SOA 2003, which can be summarised as follows: **E23.4**

Description of relevant offender	*Notification period*
A person sentenced to imprisonment for life, imprisonment for public protection, imprisonment for a term of 30 months or more, or admitted to a hospital subject to a restriction order	Indefinite period
A person sentenced to imprisonment for a term of more than six months but less than 30 months	10 years
A person sentenced to imprisonment for a term of six months or less or admitted to hospital without being subject to a restriction order	7 years
A person cautioned	2 years
A person conditionally discharged	The period of the conditional discharge
A person of any other description	5 years

This table applies to sentences of detention in a young offender institution, detention and training order, long-term detention under the PCC(S)A 2000, s. 91, and a sentence of custody for life, as it does to imprisonment (SOA 2003, s. 131). It should be noted that, if the person is under 18 on the relevant date, this table has effect as if for the periods of ten years, seven years, five years and two years there were substituted a reference to one half of those periods (s. 82(1)). There are special provisions for determining the notification period where consecutive or partly concurrent custodial terms have been imposed (s. 82(2)). A person sentenced to a detention and training order for 12 months is to be treated as if he had been sentenced to a custodial term of six months (*Slocombe* [2006] 1 All ER 670).

UNREASONABLE FAILURE TO COMPLY

E23.5   Unreasonable failure to comply with notification requirements or the deliberate provision of false information is an offence punishable on summary conviction with imprisonment for a term not exceeding six months, or a fine not exceeding the statutory maximum, or both; on conviction on indictment, the maximum penalty is five years' imprisonment (SOA 2003, s. 91). See *B* [2005] 2 Cr App R (S) 403, *Bowman* [2006] 2 Cr App R (S) 268, *Daly* [2008] 1 Cr App R (S) 105 and *Grosvenor* [2010] 2 Cr App R (S) 648.

Section E24   Rehabilitation of Offenders

GENERAL PRINCIPLE

Under the Rehabilitation of Offenders Act 1974, after the passage of time convictions may become **E24.1** 'spent' and a convicted person may consider himself 'rehabilitated'. When a conviction is spent, the offender is treated for a range of purposes as if he had never been convicted of the offence concerned. While s. 7(2) of the Act excludes from its scope the operation of criminal proceedings, CPD V, paras. 35A.1 to 35A.3 (see Supplement, **PD-47**), nonetheless require that spent convictions which appear on an offender's record should be marked as such, and that nobody should refer in open court to such spent convictions without the authority of the judge, which should only be given where the interests of justice so require. When passing sentence, the sentencer should make no reference to spent convictions unless it is necessary to do so to explain the sentence being passed. The guidance in CPD V applies in magistrates' courts, suitably adapted.

The Act's protection applies to all convictions, except those which result in an excluded sentence (see **E24.2**). 'Conviction' is given a broad meaning in the Act, but would not extend to cover the imposition of a bind over to keep the peace which has been imposed at any time except at sentence. It is unclear whether the Act applies to a recommendation for deportation. Offences in respect of which a conditional discharge is made do not count as convictions for a variety of purposes, but s. 1(4) of the Act provides that these are convictions which may be the subject of rehabilitation.

SENTENCES FALLING OUTSIDE THE SCOPE OF REHABILITATION

Certain sentences fall outside the scope of the Rehabilitation of Offenders Act 1974, and an **E24.2** offender who has received such a sentence can never become rehabilitated with respect to that conviction. Those sentences include:

(a) life imprisonment;
(b) imprisonment or detention in a young offender institution for a term exceeding 48 months;
(c) detention during Her Majesty's pleasure;
(d) detention under the PCC(S)A 2000, s. 91, for life or for a term exceeding 48 months;
(e) custody for life;
(f) imprisonment for public protection under the CJA 2003, s. 225, detention for public protection under the CJA 2003, s. 226, or an extended sentence under the CJA 2003, s. 227 or 228.

REHABILITATION PERIODS

Rehabilitation periods in respect of sentences not specified in the Rehabilitation of Offenders **E24.3** Act 1974, s. 5(1) (see **E24.2**), are set out in a Table in s. 5(2). The Act was subject to substantial amendment when the LASPO 2012, s. 139, came into force on 10 March 2014. The original

E

Part E Sentencing

periods set out in the 1974 Act are replaced with the following periods. These periods have retrospective effect so that all convictions, whenever they were acquired by an offender, are now subject to the following rehabilitation periods. In contrast to the original rehabilitation periods, which all ran for a specified period from the date when sentence was imposed, the revised periods for the most part finish at the expiry of a period which runs from the completion of the sentence. Completion, in the case of a custodial sentence, means completion of the whole sentence including the licence period and not the date of release from the custodial part of the sentence.

Sentence	End of rehabilitation period for adult offenders	End of rehabilitation period for offenders under 18 at date of conviction
A custodial sentence of more than 30 months and up to, or consisting of, 48 months	The end of the period of 7 years beginning with the day on which the sentence (including any licence period) is completed	42 months beginning with the day on which the sentence (including any licence period) is completed
A custodial sentence of more than 6 months and up to, or consisting of, 30 months	The end of the period of 48 months beginning with the day on which the sentence (including any licence period) is completed	The end of the period of 24 months beginning with the day on which the sentence (including any licence period) is completed
A custodial sentence of 6 months or less	The end of the period of 24 months beginning with the day on which the sentence (including any licence period) is completed	The end of the period of 18 months beginning with the day on which the sentence (including any licence period) is completed
A fine	The end of the period of 12 months beginning with the date of the conviction in respect of which the sentence is imposed	The end of the period of 6 months beginning with the date of the conviction in respect of which the sentence is imposed
A compensation order	The date on which the payment is made in full	The date on which the payment is made in full
A community or youth rehabilitation order	The end of the period of 12 months beginning with the day provided for by or under the order as the last day on which the order is to have effect	The end of the period of 6 months beginning with the day provided for by or under the order as the last day on which the order is to have effect
A relevant order	The day provided for by or under the order as the last day on which the order is to have effect	The day provided for by or under the order as the last day on which the order is to have effect

A 'relevant order' means a conditional discharge, a bind over to keep the peace (where imposed on conviction), a hospital order with or without restrictions, a referral order or any order which imposes a disqualification, disability, prohibition or other penalty, but not a reparation order (s. 2(8)). It should be noted that, where no provision is made by or under a community or youth rehabilitation order or a relevant order for the last day on which the order is to have effect, the rehabilitation period for the order is to be the period of 24 months beginning with the date of conviction (s. 2(3)).

There is no rehabilitation period for: (a) an order discharging a person absolutely for an offence, or (b) any other sentence in respect of a conviction where the sentence is not dealt with in the

Table, and, in such cases, references in the Act to any rehabilitation period are to be read as if the period of time were nil.

For the purposes of the Act, a suspended sentence of imprisonment counts as a sentence of immediate imprisonment of the same length. Two consecutive custodial sentences are aggregated for the purposes of the Act (s. 5(9)(b)). Where an offender receives more than one sentence or order in respect of a single offence, the relevant rehabilitation period is the longest of those applicable (s. 6(2)).

Effect of Further Conviction

A person who has been convicted can only become rehabilitated under the Rehabilitation of **E24.4** Offenders Act 1974 if he is not reconvicted within the relevant rehabilitation period (s. 6(4)). If he is reconvicted of anything other than a summary offence (s. 6(6)), the rehabilitation period for the first offence continues to run until the expiry of the period for the second offence. If an excluded sentence (see E24.2) is passed for the second offence, this excludes both convictions permanently from the possibility of rehabilitation.

The Protection of Freedoms Act 2012, ss. 92 to 101, provide for certain convictions and cautions to be disregarded and sch. 9, para. 134, amends s. 1 of the 1974 Act to provide that the 1974 Act has no application to them. Convictions and cautions within the scope of the Act are those that criminalised consensual homosexual acts between men over the age of consent, namely the SOA 1956, ss. 12 and 13. The provisions also cover corresponding offences which applied before the 1956 Act had effect as well as equivalent offences in service law.

Exceptions to the Act

The Rehabilitation of Offenders Act 1974 (Exceptions) Order 1975 (SI 1975 No. 1023) cre- **E24.5** ates a large number of exceptions to the scope of the Act. It provides that, in respect of a range of occupations, any applicant seeking employment in the relevant occupation must declare any spent conviction. A decision of the Court of Appeal that the 1975 Order was *ultra vires* since it was incompatible with the ECHR, Article 8, was reversed by the Supreme Court in *R (T) v Chief Constable of Greater Manchester Police* [2014] UKSC 35. Prior to the decision of the Supreme Court, however, amendments were made to the 1975 Order by the Rehabilitation of Offenders Act 1974 (Exceptions) Order 1975 (Amendment) Order (SI 2013 No. 1198). The Order now provides that for employment purposes a conviction falls within the scope of the 1974 Act if it was imposed for an offence other than one listed in art. 2A(5), it did not result in a custodial sentence, the person has not been convicted of any other offence at any time, and that 11 years have passed since the date of conviction (five and a half years if the offender was then under 18). Even if all these conditions apply, spent convictions must still be disclosed for a few specified forms of employment.

Section F1   General Principles of Evidence in Criminal Cases

FACTS IN ISSUE

The facts in issue comprise: (a) the facts which the prosecution bear the burden of proving or **F1.1** disproving (in order to establish the guilt of the accused) and (b) the facts which, in exceptional cases, the accused bears the burden of proving (in order to succeed in his defence). '[W]henever there is a plea of not guilty, everything is in issue and the prosecution have to prove the whole of their case, including the identity of the accused, the nature of the act and the existence of any necessary knowledge or intent' (*Sims* [1946] KB 531, per Lord Goddard CJ at p. 539). Thus the nature of the facts in issue in any given case is determinable by reference to the legal ingredients of the offence charged and any defence raised. Any fact which is formally admitted under the CJA 1967, s. 10, ceases to be in issue — it must be taken to have been proved and is not open to contradictory proof. Under s. 10(1) of the Act, a formal admission may be made of 'any fact of which oral evidence may be given in any criminal proceedings', words which make it clear that the section cannot be used to admit what would otherwise fall to be excluded because, say, it is inadmissible hearsay (*Coulson* [1997] Crim LR 886). Although it has been held that s. 10(1) covers only facts and therefore cannot apply to the opinion of an expert (*Naylor* [2010] EWCA Crim 1188), a party who accepts another party's expert's conclusions may admit them as fact under s. 10 (CrimPR, r. 33.3: considered at **F10.44**).

FORMAL ADMISSIONS

Criminal Justice Act 1967, s. 10   **F1.2**

(1) Subject to the provisions of this section, any fact of which oral evidence may be given in any criminal proceedings may be admitted for the purpose of those proceedings by or on behalf of the prosecutor or defendant, and the admission by any party of any such fact under this section shall as against that party be conclusive evidence in those proceedings of the fact admitted.

(2) An admission under this section—
   (a) may be made before or at the proceedings;
   (b) if made otherwise than in court, shall be in writing;
   (c) if made in writing by an individual, shall purport to be signed by the person making it and, if so made by a body corporate, shall purport to be signed by a director or manager, or the secretary or clerk, or some other similar officer of the body corporate;
   (d) if made on behalf of a defendant who is an individual, shall be made by his counsel or solicitor;
   (e) if made at any stage before the trial by a defendant who is an individual, must be approved by his counsel or solicitor (whether at the time it was made or subsequently) before or at the proceedings in question.

(3) An admission under this section for the purpose of proceedings relating to any matter shall be treated as an admission for the purpose of any subsequent criminal proceedings relating to that matter (including any appeal or retrial).

(4) An admission under this section may with the leave of the court be withdrawn in the proceedings for the purpose of which it is made or any subsequent criminal proceedings relating to the same matter.

F1.3   Ordinarily, written admissions should be put before the jury, provided at least that they are relevant to an issue before the jury and do not contain any material which should not go before the jury (*Pittard* [2006] EWCA Crim 2028). In court, a formal admission may be made by counsel or a solicitor *orally* (see s. 10(2)(b) and (d), and *Lewis* [1989] Crim LR 61). Whatever the manner of making a formal admission under s. 10 of the 1967 Act, it should be such that what has been admitted should appear clearly on the shorthand note (*Lennard* [1973] 2 All ER 831). It is also important that the jury are clear as to what has been formally admitted. In *Lewis* (1971) 55 Cr App R 386, in which counsel for the accused formally admitted every fact alleged in the prosecution's opening speech and the prosecution called no evidence, relying solely on admissions, leave to appeal against conviction was refused. The court added, however, that such a procedure should be adopted only rarely and with caution, because jurors, when considering the opening speech, might find it difficult to distinguish between law, mixed fact and law, and comment. Where a party introduces in evidence a fact admitted by another party, or parties jointly admit a fact, then unless the court otherwise directs, a written record must be made of the admission (CrimPR, rr. 37.6 (magistrates' court) and 38.13 (Crown Court)).

Formal admissions made with the benefit of advice are an important and cogent part of the evidence in a trial. If it is sought to resile from them, leave to withdraw them is unlikely to be given under s. 10(4) without cogent evidence from the accused and those advising him that the admissions were made by reason of mistake or misunderstanding (*Kolton* [2000] Crim LR 761).

JUDICIAL NOTICE

Introduction

F1.4   Generally speaking, the doctrine of judicial notice allows the tribunal of fact to treat a fact as established, notwithstanding that no evidence has been adduced to establish it. The doctrine, however, takes three distinct forms. The first two, judicial notice without inquiry and judicial notice after inquiry, were defined and distinguished by Lord Sumner in *Commonwealth Shipping Representative v Peninsular and Oriental Branch Service* [1923] AC 191, at p. 212: 'Judicial notice refers to facts, which a judge can be called upon to receive and to act upon, either from his general knowledge of them, or from inquiries to be made by himself for his own information from sources to which it is proper for him to refer'. The phrase 'judicial notice' is also used, in a third sense, to refer to the use which may be made by jurors or magistrates of their personal knowledge of facts in issue or relevant to the facts in issue. This has been referred to as jury or magistrate notice. These three forms of judicial notice require separate analysis.

Judicial Notice without Inquiry at Common Law

F1.5   If a fact is sufficiently notorious or of such common knowledge that it requires no proof, the judge, without recourse to any extraneous sources of information, may take judicial notice of it and direct the jury to treat it as established, notwithstanding that it has not been established by evidence. Examples include: the fact that a fortnight is too short a period for human gestation (*Luffe* (1807) 8 East 193); the fact that the streets of London are full of traffic (*Dennis v A.J. White & Co.* [1916] 2 KB 1, at p. 6); the fact that reconstructed trials with a striking degree of realism are among the popular forms of modern television entertainment (*Yap Chuan Ching* (1976) 63 Cr App R 7); and the fact that cocaine hydrochloride is a form of cocaine (*A-G for the Cayman Islands v Roberts* [2002] 1 WLR 1842). In criminal cases, foreign law, being a question of fact generally calling for the evidence of an appropriately qualified expert, cannot be the subject of judicial notice (*Ofori* (1994) 99 Cr App R 223). There is one exception: the common law of Northern Ireland (*Re Nesbitt* (1844) 14 LJ MC 30 at p. 33).

Judicial Notice without Inquiry Pursuant to Statute

Judicial notice of a fact may be required by statute. The most important examples are the Evidence **F1.6**
Act 1845, s. 2, and the Interpretation Act 1978, s. 3. Section 2 of the 1845 Act requires judicial
notice to be taken of the fact that a judicial or official document purporting to have been signed
by a judge was signed by that judge.

Evidence Act 1845, s. 2

All courts, judges, justices, masters in Chancery, masters of courts, commissioners judicially acting,
and other judicial officers, shall henceforth take judicial notice of the signature of any of the equity
or common law judges of the superior courts at Westminster, provided such signature be attached
or appended to any decree, order, certificate, or other judicial or official document.

Section 3 of the Interpretation Act 1978, as supplemented by s. 22(1) and sch. 2, para. 2,
requires judicial notice to be taken of statutes of the UK (whether general, local and personal,
or private) passed after 1850.

Interpretation Act 1978, s. 3

Every Act is a public Act to be judicially noticed as such, unless the contrary is expressly provided
by the Act.

Thus in the absence of express provision to the contrary, evidence is not required to prove
either the contents of an Act passed after 1850 or that such an Act has been duly passed by both
Houses of Parliament. At common law, the courts are bound to take judicial notice of Public
Acts passed before 1850. Private Acts passed before 1850 require to be proved by the produc-
tion of a Queen's Printer's or Stationery Office copy (see the Evidence Act 1845, s. 3, and the
Documentary Evidence Act 1882, s. 2).

Statutory instruments may be proved by Queen's Printer's or Stationery Office copies (see *Ashley*
(1967) 52 Cr App R 42 and the Documentary Evidence Act 1868, s. 2, at **F8.17**). There is
no equivalent to the Interpretation Act 1978, s. 3, for judicial notice to be taken of statutory
instruments, although some instruments have acquired such notoriety that judicial notice may
be taken of them (*Jones* (1968) 54 Cr App R 63).

Judicial Notice after Inquiry

In a number of cases, judges have taken judicial notice of a fact only after referring to extraneous **F1.7**
sources of information, such as certificates from ministers or officials, learned treatises, works
of reference and expert witnesses. Such a judicial inquiry is distinct from proof by evidence in
the normal way: the rules of evidence are inapplicable; the result of the inquiry is not open to
evidence in rebuttal; and the result, except in the case of facts lacking constancy (e.g., the status of a foreign government), constitutes a legal precedent. The justification for judicial notice
after inquiry is that some facts, although not sufficiently notorious to be the subject of judicial
notice without inquiry, are readily demonstrable by reference to sources of virtually indisputable
authority, or arise so frequently that proof in the normal way is undesirable because of the cost
and the need for uniformity of decision. Judicial notice after inquiry has been taken of the following three kinds of fact:

(a) Facts of a political nature, such as relations between the government of the UK and a
foreign state, the status of foreign sovereigns or governments, the membership of diplomatic suites, and the extent of territorial sovereignty. The source of information is usually
a minister, whose certificate will be treated as an indisputably accurate source for reasons
of public policy, namely the desirability of avoiding conflict between the courts and the
executive. In *Bottrill, ex parte Kuechenmeister* [1947] KB 41, the Court of Appeal, treating
as conclusive the certificate of the Foreign Secretary that Germany still existed as a State
and German nationality as a nationality, and that His Majesty was still in a state of war with
Germany, held that the applicant for a writ of *habeas corpus* was still an enemy alien. See also

Duff Development Co. Ltd v Government of Kelantan [1924] AC 797; *Engelke v Musmann* [1928] AC 433; and *Carl Zeiss Stiftung v Rayner and Keeler Ltd (No. 2)* [1967] 1 AC 853.

(b) Facts which are readily demonstrable after reference to appropriate authoritative works of reference or learned treatises. Illustrations would be the day of the week on which a certain date fell, after reference to an almanac or diary; the longitude and latitude of a certain place, after reference to an atlas or other geographical work; and the date and location of a well-known historical event, after reference to an appropriate authoritative history. See *Read v Bishop of Lincoln* [1892] AC 644 and *R (HRH Sultan of Pahang) v Secretary of State for the Home Department* [2011] EWCA Civ 616.

(c) Customs and professional practices, after consultation with suitably qualified experts. See *Brandao v Barnett* (1846) 12 Cl & F 787 (the custom of bankers' lien); *Re Rosher* (1884) 26 Ch D 801 (conveyancers' practices); *Davey v Harrow Corporation* [1958] 1 QB 60 (ordnance surveyors' practices); and *Heather v P-E Consulting Group Ltd* [1973] 1 Ch 189 (accountants' practices).

PERSONAL KNOWLEDGE OF COURT OR JURY

Judges

F1.8   It has been held that a judge may use personal knowledge of matters within the common knowledge of people in the locality, a principle which derives from cases decided under the Workmen's Compensation Acts, under which county court judges sat as arbitrators and took into account, in assessing compensation, personal knowledge of the labour market, conditions of work, and wages (see, e.g., *Keane v Mount Vernon Colliery Co. Ltd* [1933] AC 309 and *Reynolds v Llanelly Associated Tinplate Co. Ltd* [1948] 1 All ER 140). See also, *sed quaere, Mullen v Hackney London Borough Council* [1997] 2 All ER 906.

Magistrates

F1.9   In *Wetherall v Harrison* [1976] QB 773 the issue was whether the accused had a reasonable excuse for failure to give a blood sample. The accused said that he had had a sort of fit, which the prosecution alleged had been simulated. One of the justices, a practising registered medical practitioner, gave his professional view on the matter to the other justices, who also drew on their own experience of wartime inoculations and the fear that they could create in certain cases. Dismissing the appeal, the Divisional Court held that justices, unlike judges, lack the ability to exclude certain factors from their consideration. In particular, if a magistrate is a specialist, whether doctor, engineer or accountant, it is not possible for him to approach the decision in the case as though he did not have that training, and it would be a very bad thing if he had to. One of the advantages of justices is that they bring a lot of varied experience into the court-room, and use it. Although it would be quite wrong for a justice to give evidence to himself or the other justices in contradiction of that which had been heard in court, he can employ his basic knowledge, for the benefit of himself and the other justices, in considering, weighing up and assessing the evidence given before the court.

'It has always been recognised that justices may and should — after all, they are local justices — take into consideration matters which they know of their own knowledge, and particularly matters in regard to the locality' (*Ingram v Percival* [1969] 1 QB 548 per Lord Parker CJ at p. 555). The appellant had been convicted of unlawfully using a net secured by anchors for taking salmon or trout in tidal waters. It was held that the justices were fully entitled to make use of their own knowledge that the place where the net was fixed was in tidal waters. See also *Paul v DPP* (1989) 90 Cr App R 173 concerning a charge of soliciting a woman for the purposes of prostitution from a motor vehicle in a street in such manner or in such circumstances as to be likely to cause nuisance to other persons in the neighbourhood, contrary to the Sexual Offences Act 1985, s. 1(1). It was held that the justices, who had no evidence before them that anyone had actually been caused nuisance, were entitled to take into account two matters within their local knowledge: first, that the area in question was often frequented by prostitutes and that there was a constant procession of cars driving around the area at night; and secondly, that it was a heavily populated residential area. In *Field, ex parte White* (1895) 64 LJ MC 158, the issue being whether cocoa necessarily contains foreign ingredients, no evidence was adduced. The justices, relying on their own knowledge of the subject, found for the accused. Although Wills J observed that perhaps in future evidence should be heard on such a matter, the Divisional Court refused to disturb the justices' finding.

Jurors

The doctrine of judicial notice also applies to jurors in relation to matters coming within the sphere of their everyday knowledge and experience (*Rosser* (1836) 7 C & P 648, approved in *Jones* [1970] 3 All ER 1559). In *Jones* it was argued that it had not been proved that the accused had been given an opportunity to provide a specimen of breath for a breath test, because there had been no evidence to show that the device used, the Alcotest R80, was 'of a type approved by the Secretary of State' for the purposes of the Road Safety Act, 1967, s. 7. Rejecting this argument, Edmund-Davies LJ said, at p. 20: '...the number of decided cases in which it has been proved that the Alcotest R80 device is of an approved type has by now become so large and so widely reported that, in our judgment, a court (including the jury) is entitled to take judicial notice of that fact, and its formal proof is accordingly no longer necessary'.

F1.10

However, although jurors may use their *general* knowledge, they may not use their *personal* knowledge to supplement or contradict the evidence given in the case. The older authorities suggest that a juror with particular knowledge of a matter should be sworn as a witness and give evidence in the normal way (*Rosser* (1836) 7 C & P 648; *Manley v Shaw* (1840) Car & M 361; *Antrim Justices* [1895] 2 IR 603). A preferable solution, it is submitted, is the course adopted in *Blick* (1966) 50 Cr App R 280. In that case a juror passed a note to the judge to the effect that his own local knowledge contradicted the alibi evidence given by the accused. In consequence the judge allowed the prosecution to call evidence, relating to the matters contained in the note, to rebut the alibi. This decision was upheld by the Court of Criminal Appeal.

It should also be explained to the jury that their verdict must be reached solely upon the evidence adduced at trial and that they should not, for example, undertake internet searches for additional material (see the *Crown Court Bench Book*, ch. 2, and **D13.21**).

RELEVANCE

Introduction

The cardinal rule of the law of evidence is that, subject to the exclusionary rules, all evidence which is sufficiently relevant to the facts in issue is admissible, and all evidence which is irrelevant or insufficiently relevant to the facts in issue should be excluded. As to the former, however, evidence which is relevant may nonetheless be excluded if it is such that no reasonable jury, properly directed as to its defects, could place any weight on it (*Robinson* [2006] 1 Cr App R 221, a case concerning voice recognition evidence). As to the latter, inasmuch as an offence of strict liability involves no proof of *mens rea*, evidence of motive, intention or knowledge is inadmissible, being irrelevant to what the Crown has to prove and merely prejudicial to the accused (*Sandhu* [1997] Crim LR 288; and see also *Byrne* [2002] 2 Cr App R 311). The classic formulation of relevance is to be found in Article 1 of Stephen's *Digest of the Law of Evidence* (12th edn, 1936), according to which the word signifies that 'any two facts to which it is applied are so related to each other that according to the common course of events one either taken by itself or in connection with other facts proves or renders probable the past, present or future existence or non-existence of the other'. *Nethercott* [2002] Cr App R 117 provides an example of a fact which was relevant to the past existence of another fact. N's defence was that he had

F1.11

acted under duress as a result of threats by his co-accused G. Evidence of the fact that G had subsequently attacked N with a knife was relevant to the defence because it made it more likely that N, at the time of the offence, had genuinely feared for his safety.

On the question of relevance, Lord Simon of Glaisdale has said:

> Evidence is relevant if it is logically probative or disprobative of some matter which requires proof. I do not pause to analyse what is involved in 'logical probativeness', except to note that the term does not of itself express the element of experience which is so significant of its operation in law, and possibly elsewhere. It is sufficient to say, even at the risk of etymological tautology, that relevant (i.e., logically probative or disprobative) evidence is evidence which makes the matter which requires proof more or less probable. (*DPP v Kilbourne* [1973] AC 729, at p. 756.)

The question of relevance is typically a matter of degree to be determined, for the most part, by common sense and experience (*Randall* [2004] 1 All ER 467, per Lord Steyn at [20]).

Evidence of the good character of a prosecution witness is generally inadmissible to bolster his credibility, because it amounts to 'oath-helping' (see *Robinson* [1994] 3 All ER 346 at **F7.57**), but may be admissible if relevant to an issue in the case, for example in a case of rape, the defence being consent, evidence of the complainant's disposition to resist any form of pre-marital sexual intimacy (*Amado-Taylor* [2001] EWCA Crim 1898) and, in a case of inflicting grievous bodily harm, the defence being self-defence accompanied by evidence that the complainant had started the violence making racially abusive comments, evidence to show that the complainant was not a racist (*Lodge* [2013] EWCA Crim 987).

For some of the more frequently recurring examples of relevant evidence, see **F1.18** *et seq*.

Strict Application of the Test

F1.12   There is a long-standing practice on the part of the prosecution to make admissions in relation to facts that may point to a third party having committed the crime with which the accused is charged, such admissions being relevant and admissible material to weigh in the scales in deciding whether it might have been the third party and not the accused who committed the offence (*Greenwood* [2005] 1 Cr App R 99). Such admissions were made in *Blastland* [1986] AC 41, but the test of 'logical probativeness' was strictly applied to exclude additional evidence relating to the state of mind of the third party. The appellant, B, was convicted of the buggery and murder of F, a boy. At the trial, B admitted that he had met F and engaged in homosexual activity with him (including attempted buggery), but said that shortly afterwards he saw another man nearby and, fearing that he had been observed committing a serious offence, panicked and ran away. B's description of the other man corresponded closely to one M. B said that M must have committed both offences charged. There were formal admissions by the prosecution showing M to have been known to engage in the past in homosexual activities with adults but not with children. There were also both formal admissions and evidence relating to M's movements on the evening of F's murder. The defence sought leave to call a number of witnesses to give evidence that before F's body had been found, M had made statements to them that a boy had been murdered. The trial judge ruled that this evidence was inadmissible. Before the House of Lords, the appellant submitted that the statements made by M were admissible as original evidence to show M's state of mind, i.e. his knowledge of the murder before the body had been found. Lord Bridge, giving the judgment of the House, held that such evidence would only have been admissible if M's state of mind had been either directly in issue itself or of direct and immediate relevance to an issue arising at the trial. The evidence had been properly rejected because the issue at the trial was whether B had committed the crimes, and what was relevant to that was not the fact of M's knowledge but how he had come by it; since he might have come by that knowledge in a number of different ways, there was no rational basis on which the jury could be invited to draw an inference as to the source of that knowledge. To do so would have been mere speculation. The evidence of what M said, therefore, could not be put before the jury to support the conclusion that he, rather than B, may have been the criminal. See also *Kearley* [1992] 2 AC 228 at **F15.17**, *Williams* [1998]

Crim LR 494 and *Akram* [1995] Crim LR 50. However, in *Gadsby* [2006] EWCA Crim 3206, it was held, *obiter*, that evidence may be relevant if it is capable of increasing or diminishing the probability of facts indicating that some other person committed the crime (e.g., evidence that a person with the opportunity of committing the crime had a propensity to do so).

The strict approach taken in *Blastland* was also adopted in *T (AB)* [2007] 1 Cr App R 43. The complainant alleged that she had been sexually abused by the appellant, who was her uncle, and by her grandfather and her step-grandfather, but it was not alleged that they were acting in concert. The grandfather admitted the allegations against him but died before the matter reached court. The step-grandfather pleaded guilty to counts of indecently assaulting the complainant. It was held that evidence of the grandfather's admission and of the step-grandfather's guilty plea should not have been admitted, because it was not relevant, in itself, to the issue whether the appellant abused the complainant; and that while it was 'tempting' to say that it was relevant to the issue of her credibility, that would amount to a form of 'oath helping' which has never been permissible as a ground for admitting evidence.

Relevance of Demeanour of Victim

In *Keast* [1998] Crim LR 748 (applied in *Venn* [2003] EWCA Crim 236) it was held that **F1.13** unless there is some concrete basis for regarding long-term demeanour and state of mind of a victim of sexual abuse as confirming or disproving the occurrence of such abuse, it cannot assist a jury bringing their common sense to bear on who is telling the truth. However, demeanour witnessed close in time to the event in question may have probative value, by analogy with the principle of *res gestae* (*Townsend* [2003] EWCA Crim 3173).

Relevance in Drug Cases

Concerning the offence of possession of drugs with intent to supply, evidence which is arguably **F1.14** relevant to the question of intent may fall to be excluded because of its prejudicial effect in indicating dealing in drugs in the past or generally. This principle and the following cases will need to be read subject to the provisions in the CJA 2003, ss. 98 to 113, relating to the accused's bad character (see **F12**) notwithstanding the suggestion that, if the evidence would have been admissible before the 2003 Act, there would be 'something highly artificial' in the prosecution having to make an application under the Act (*Graham* [2007] EWCA Crim 1499). Under the principle, it has been held that evidence of the possession of weights and scales on which there are traces of the drug in question will be admitted (*Batt* [1994] Crim LR 592), but not evidence of past deposits in and withdrawals from savings accounts, because that can only found an inference of past drug dealing (*Gordon* [1995] 2 Cr App R 61). In *Batt* it was also held that evidence of the discovery of £150 in an ornamental kettle in B's house was inadmissible because it had nothing to do with intent to supply in future the drugs found, but had a highly prejudicial effect as evidence of propensity to supply or of past or future supplying generally. *Batt*, however, has not laid down a general principle that evidence of possession of money is never admissible (*Nicholas* [1995] Crim LR 942; *Okusanya* [1995] Crim LR 941). On one view the decision in *Batt* turned on the fact that the trial judge had failed to direct the jury as to how they could properly use the evidence of the money found (*Morris* [1995] 2 Cr App R 69). Alternatively *Batt* should be seen as a case strictly confined to its own facts, bearing in mind that £150 was too small, and its hiding place too unremarkable, to be the hallmark of present drug dealing (*Okusanya*). In *Wright* [1994] Crim LR 55, it was held that drug traders needed to keep by them large sums of cash and therefore evidence of the discovery of £16,000 was capable of giving rise to an inference of dealing and tended to prove that the drugs found were for supply. In *Gordon* [1995] 2 Cr App R 61, it was held that evidence of the discovery of £4,200 was admissible subject to an appropriate direction. Similarly in *Smith* [1995] Crim LR 940, it was held that evidence that in recent months £9,000 had been deposited in S's account, £2,100 of which could not be explained by legitimate transactions, was admissible, subject to an appropriate direction. The jury should be directed (a) that evidence of the discovery of money is relevant only if they reject any innocent explanation for it advanced by the accused, (b) that if there is any possibility of the money having been in the accused's possession for reasons other than drug dealing, then the evidence is not probative, but (c) that if they conclude that it indicates not merely past dealing but an on-going dealing in drugs, they may take into account the finding of it, together with the drugs, in considering the issue of intent to supply (*Grant* [1996] 1 Cr App R 73 and *Green* [2009] EWCA Crim 1688, where a similar direction was given on a charge of conspiracy to supply drugs; cf. *Antill* [2002] EWCA Crim 2114). The same principles apply where the prosecution relies on a list of names or drugs paraphernalia (*Lovelock* [1997] Crim LR 821 and *Haye* [2002] EWCA Crim 2476). Such a direction, however, will not always need to be given in terms (*Malik* [2000] 2 Cr App R 8). The jury should also be directed not to treat it as evidence of propensity, i.e. not to pursue the line of reasoning that because of the past dealing the accused is likely to be guilty (*Simms* [1995] Crim LR 304 and *Lucas* [1995] Crim LR 400). In *Guney* [1998] 2 Cr App R 242, the Court of Appeal declined to follow earlier authorities to the effect that, where possession of the drugs is in issue, evidence of possession of money or drugs paraphernalia can never be relevant to that issue (*Halpin* [1996] Crim LR 112; *Richards* [1997] Crim LR 499). It was held that, although evidence of possession of a large sum of cash or enjoyment of a wealthy lifestyle does not, on its own, prove possession, there are numerous sets of circumstances in which it may be relevant to that issue, not least to the issue of knowledge as an ingredient of possession. The real issue in the case was whether G was knowingly in possession of nearly five kilos of heroin or whether it had been 'planted', the defence having conceded that, if possession were to be proved, then it would be open to the jury to infer intent to supply. It was held that, in all the circumstances, evidence of the finding of nearly £25,000 in cash in the wardrobe of G's bedroom and in close proximity to the drugs was relevant to the issue of possession. *Guney* was applied in *Griffiths* [1998] Crim LR 567. See also *Edwards* [1998] Crim LR 207 and *Scott* [1996] Crim LR 652.

F1.15 **Illegal Importation Cases**   In cases of illegal importation of controlled drugs in which the accused denies any knowledge of how the drugs came to be in his possession, evidence of finding drugs in his home is relevant and admissible because the jury are entitled to consider such a coincidence, which may go to rebut the defence raised (*Willis* (29 January 1979 unreported) and *Peters* [1995] 2 Cr App R 77). The principle is not confined to couriers, but extends to those who claim to have been unknowingly involved in the importation of drugs, such as those meeting couriers at airports (*Groves* [1998] Crim LR 200). Evidence admissible to rebut such a defence includes evidence of the possession of drugs or drugs paraphernalia, and evidence suggesting a pattern of the accused having been involved in previous importations: see, as to the latter, *Ilomuanya* [2005] EWCA Crim 58, where the evidence relied on was held to be irrelevant because it neither established nor tended to suggest any such pattern.

Evidence of Marginal Relevance

F1.16 Although it has been said that relevance is typically a matter of degree (*Randall* [2004] 1 All ER 467, per Lord Steyn at [20]), it is probably more accurate to say that evidence is either relevant or not and, if relevant, has differing degrees of probative force. For example, evidence of facts which supply a motive for an accused to have committed a particular crime is generally admissible to show that it is more likely that he committed that crime (*Ball* [1911] AC 47, per Lord Atkinson at p. 68 and *Phillips* [2003] 2 Cr App R 528; but see also, in the case of offences of strict liability, *Sandhu* [1997] Crim LR 288). However, evidence of motive will be excluded if it is so remote from the offence charged that it can be said to be without any probative value at all (*Berry* (1986) 83 Cr App R 7). Similarly, on a charge of manslaughter against a doctor, although expert evidence of his skill as shown by his treatment of the case under investigation is admissible, expert evidence as to his skilful treatment of patients on other occasions is inadmissible (*Whitehead* (1848) 3 Car & Kir 202). On a charge of causing death by dangerous driving, evidence that the accused used cocaine shortly before the accident is relevant, even in the absence of evidence as to the amount of cocaine used (*Pleydell* [2006] 1 Cr App R 212, applied in *Ashworth* [2012] EWCA Crim 1064; contrast, in the case of alcohol consumed, *Woodward* [1995] 2 Cr App R 388).

Evidence of marginal relevance may be excluded on the grounds that it would lead to a multiplicity of subsidiary issues, involving the court in a protracted investigation and distracting it from the main issue (*A-G v Hitchcock* (1847) 1 Exch 91 per Rolfe B at p. 105 and *Patel* [1951] 2 All ER 29, per Byrne J at p. 30). Similarly, questioning of a witness may be disallowed if it relates to matters too far removed from the issues in the case and is in the nature of a fishing expedition (*Haddock* [2011] EWCA Crim 303). On occasions, the effect of evidence which is technically admissible is so slight that it is wiser not to adduce it, especially if there is any danger of a contravention of the PACE 1984, s. 78 (see **F2.9**), i.e. where its admission would have such an adverse effect on the fairness of the proceedings that the court ought not to admit it (*Robertson* [1987] QB 920, per Lord Lane CJ at p. 928; and see also *Williams* [1990] Crim LR 409).

Evidence of Earlier Trial

Where two trials arise out of the same transaction, evidence of the outcome of the first is gener-   **F1.17**
ally inadmissible at the second, because the verdict in the first, whether reached on the same or different evidence, is usually irrelevant; some exceptional feature is needed before it will be considered relevant (*Hui Chi-ming v The Queen* [1992] 1 AC 34). The principle applies *a fortiori* if the first trial arose out of a different transaction (*Terry* [2005] QB 996 at [34]). On one view, the rationale of the principle is that the evidence amounts to nothing more than evidence of the opinion of the first jury (*Hui-chi Ming v The Queen*), but by itself that would be a reason for never admitting evidence of a previous verdict. The true rationale, in the case of an earlier acquittal, is that in most cases it is impossible to be certain why a jury acquitted (*D* [2007] EWCA Crim 684), although the principle appears also to apply in the case of an acquittal following a ruling by a trial judge that there was insufficient evidence to go to the jury (see *Hudson* [1994] Crim LR 920 and cf. *Colman* [2005] QB 996). The cases indicate that the 'exceptional feature' arises where there is a clear inference from the verdict that the jury rejected a witness's evidence because they did not believe him and his credibility is directly in issue in the second trial, as when it is alleged that an officer has fabricated an admission, the officer having given evidence of an admission in an earlier trial resulting in an acquittal by virtue of which his evidence can be shown to have been disbelieved (*Edwards* [1991] 2 All ER 226). See also *Hay* (1983) 77 Cr App R 70, *Cooke* (1986) 84 Cr App R 286 and *Deboussi*. As to the relevance (and admissibility) of previous convictions or acquittals as evidence of the facts on which they were based, see **F11.6** *et seq*.

CIRCUMSTANTIAL EVIDENCE

Introduction

Circumstantial evidence is to be contrasted with direct evidence. Direct evidence is evidence of   **F1.18**
facts in issue. In the case of testimonial evidence, it is evidence about facts in issue of which the witness claims to have personal knowledge, for example, 'I saw the accused strike the victim'. Circumstantial evidence is evidence of *relevant facts*, i.e. facts from which the existence or non-existence of facts in issue may be inferred. It does not necessarily follow that the weight to be attached to circumstantial evidence will be less than that to be attached to direct evidence. For example, the tribunal of fact is likely to attach more weight to a variety of individual items of circumstantial evidence, all of which lead to the same conclusion, than to direct evidence to the contrary coming from witnesses lacking in credibility.

Circumstantial evidence 'works by cumulatively, in geometrical progression, eliminating other possibilities' (*DPP v Kilbourne* [1973] AC 729 per Lord Simon at p. 758). Pollock CB, likening circumstantial evidence to a rope comprised of several cords, said:

> One strand of the cord might be insufficient to sustain the weight, but three stranded together may be quite of sufficient strength.

Thus it may be in circumstantial evidence — there may be a combination of circumstances, no one of which would raise a reasonable conviction, or more than a mere suspicion; but the whole, taken together, may create a strong conclusion of guilt, that is, with as much certainty as human affairs can require or admit of. (*Exall* (1866) 4 F & F 922, at p. 929.)

However, although circumstantial evidence may sometimes be conclusive, it must always be narrowly examined, if only because it may be fabricated to cast suspicion on another. For this reason, it has been said that: 'It is also necessary before drawing the inference of the accused's guilt from circumstantial evidence to be sure that there are no other co-existing circumstances which would weaken or destroy the inference' (*Teper v The Queen* [1952] AC 480, per Lord Normand at p. 489). Nonetheless, there is no requirement, in cases in which the prosecution's case is based on circumstantial evidence, that the judge direct the jury to acquit unless they are sure that the facts proved are not only consistent with guilt but also inconsistent with any other reasonable conclusion (*McGreevy v DPP* [1973] 1 All ER 503).

Presumption of Fact

F1.19   Certain varieties of circumstantial evidence have arisen so frequently in practice as to attract the label 'presumption of fact'. For the presumption of continuance of life, see **F3.62**; for the presumption of intention, see **F3.63**; and for the presumption of guilty knowledge in cases of handling, theft etc., see **F3.64**. Other frequently recurring examples of circumstantial evidence include evidence of plans and acts preparatory to the commission of an offence (to show intention to commit the offence); evidence of opportunity; evidence of lack of opportunity, which may assist the accused, e.g., alibi evidence, or the prosecution, e.g., evidence that after his arrest the accused had no opportunity to commit further offences and no offences similar to those with which he is charged were committed in the same area (*Wilson* [2008] EWCA Crim 1754); and evidence of identity, including evidence of physical idiosyncrasy, manner of vocal or written expression, fingerprints, DNA and tracker dog evidence (*Haas* (1962) 35 DLR (2d) 172 (British Columbia), *Pieterson* [1995] 1 WLR 293 and *Sykes* [1997] Crim LR 752). Other typical examples of circumstantial evidence are dealt with below.

F1.20   **Motive**

Surely in an ordinary prosecution for murder you can prove previous acts or words of the accused to show that he entertained feelings of enmity towards the deceased, and this is evidence not merely of the malicious mind with which he killed the deceased, but of the fact that he killed him.... it is more probable that men are killed by those who have some motive for killing them than by those who have not. (*Ball* [1911] AC 47 per Lord Atkinson (during argument) at p. 68, affirmed in *Williams* (1986) 84 Cr App R 299.)

This classic statement remains good law and any doubt that may have been cast upon it in *Berry* (1986) 83 Cr App R 7 should be disregarded (*Phillips* [2003] 2 Cr App R 528 at [26]). Evidence of motive may be admissible notwithstanding that the motive is irrational and *Berry*, insofar as it suggests otherwise, has been disapproved (*Phillips* at [30]). Evidence of motive may also be admissible notwithstanding that it reveals the accused's criminal disposition. In *Williams* W was charged with making a threat to kill E, intending that she would fear that the threat would be carried out. Evidence was admitted of previous acts of violence by W against E, including an assault in respect of which he had been convicted and sentenced to a term of imprisonment which had come to an end six weeks before the time of the present offence. The prosecution case was that: (a) the threat had been made because of resentment arising from the imprisonment; and (b) the previous acts of violence tended to show that W intended his threat to be taken seriously. In the same way, evidence that the accused lacked a motive to commit the crime charged may be admissible to show the comparative improbability of his having committed it (*Grant* (1865) 4 F & F 322). He may also adduce evidence that someone else had such a motive, as in *Greenwood* [2005] 1 Cr App R 99 where, in the case of an undisputed murder, it was held that the accused was entitled to adduce evidence to show that the victim's ex-boyfriend was near the murder scene and appeared to have a motive. It does not follow from the foregoing, however, that evidence of motive (or its absence) is necessarily relevant to the facts in issue on a particular charge (see, e.g., *Graham-Kerr* (1989) 88 Cr App R 302 (the indecency of a photograph), applied in *Rowley* (1991) 94 Cr App R 95 (an act outraging public decency), and *H* [2005] 2 All ER 859 at **B3.48**; and compare *Court* [1989] AC 28).

Lies

Lies told by the accused, on their own, do not make a positive case of any crime (*Strudwick* (1994)   **F1.21**
99 Cr App R 326 at p. 331). However, they may indicate a consciousness of guilt and in appropriate circumstances may therefore be relied upon by the prosecution as evidence supportive of guilt, as in *Goodway* [1993] 4 All ER 894 where the accused's lies to the police as to his whereabouts at the time of the offence were used in support of the identification evidence adduced by the prosecution. In that case it was held that, whenever a lie told by an accused is relied on by the Crown or may be used by the jury to support evidence of guilt, as opposed merely to reflecting on his credibility (and not only when it is relied on as corroboration or as support for identification evidence), a threefold *Lucas* ([1981] QB 720) direction should generally be given to the jury:

(a) The lie must be deliberate and must relate to a material issue.
(b) They must be satisfied that there was no innocent motive for the lie, reminding them that people sometimes lie, for example, in an attempt to bolster up a just cause, or out of shame or a wish to conceal disgraceful behaviour.
(c) The lie must be established by evidence other than that of the witness who is to be corroborated.

See also the *Crown Court Bench Book* at pp. 242 *et seq.* and *Taylor* [1994] Crim LR 680. In *Taylor* [1998] Crim LR 822, a trial for murder in which the only issue was provocation and T admitted that he had lied in saying that he had never had any contact with the victim, it was held that the jury should have been directed that the lies could support the case of murder only if they were sure that they were told to conceal the fact that T had murdered the victim, rather than merely to conceal his connection with the death, i.e. to avoid responsibility for deliberate murder rather than a provoked killing. Similarly, in *Reszpondek* [2010] EWCA Crim 2358 at [19], a murder trial in which there was evidence that R had told many lies and had been involved in acts of concealment of the death, it was held that this evidence could be used by the jury to support an inference of murder, provided that they were cautioned that the evidence could be accounted for by the fact that the victim's death might have resulted from manslaughter. See also *Bullen* [2008] 2 Cr App R 364.

In *Goodway* it was also held that a direction need not be given where it is otiose as indicated in *Dehar* [1969] NZLR 763, i.e. where the rejection of the explanation given by the accused almost necessarily leaves the jury with no choice but to convict as a matter of logic. For an example, see *Barsoum* [1994] Crim LR 194 and cf. *Wood* [1995] Crim LR 154. See also *Gordon* [1995] Crim LR 306. Nor, it seems, does a judge need to give a *Lucas* direction where the accused has offered an explanation for his lies and the judge has dealt with that explanation fairly in his summing-up (*Saunders* [1996] 1 Cr App R 463 at pp. 518–19).

The Four *Burge* Situations   In *Burge* [1996] 1 Cr App R 163, the Court of Appeal held that a   **F1.22**
Lucas direction is usually required in four situations, which may overlap (Kennedy LJ at p. 173):

1. Where the defence relies on an alibi.
2. Where the judge considers it desirable or necessary to suggest that the jury should look for support or corroboration of one piece of evidence from other evidence in the case, and amongst that other evidence draws attention to lies told, or allegedly told, by the defendant.
3. Where the prosecution seek to show that something said, either in or out of the court, in relation to a separate and distinct issue was a lie, and to rely on that lie as evidence of guilt in relation to the charge which is sought to be proved.
4. Where although the prosecution have not adopted the approach to which we have just referred, the judge reasonably envisages that there is a real danger that the jury may do so.

The Court of Appeal held that the direction (if given) should, so far as possible, be tailored to the circumstances of the case, but that it will normally suffice to make two points: first that the lie must be admitted or proved beyond reasonable doubt, and secondly that the mere fact that the accused lied is not in itself evidence of guilt since defendants may lie for innocent reasons, so only if the jury is sure that the accused did not lie for an innocent reason can a lie support the prosecution case. The court also stressed that the need for the direction arises only in cases where the prosecution say, or the judge envisages that the jury may say, that the lie is evidence against the accused, in effect using it as an implied admission of guilt. The direction is not needed in run-of-the-mill cases where the defence case is contradicted by the evidence of prosecution witnesses in such a way as to make it necessary for the prosecution to say that, insofar as the two sides are in conflict, the accused's account is untrue. Equally, a *Goodway* direction is not required simply because the jury may reject the evidence of an accused about a central issue in the case, because that situation is covered by the general direction on the burden and standard of proof (*Hill* [1996] Crim LR 419).

F1.23   As to the first situation identified in *Burge*, in *Lesley* [1996] 1 Cr App R 39 it was held that where evidence is adduced in support of an alibi, the Judicial Studies Board specimen direction (which then ended with the words 'An alibi is sometimes invented to bolster a genuine defence': see now the *Crown Court Bench Book*) should routinely be given. It was also held, however, that whether failure to do so renders a conviction unsafe depends on the facts of each case and the strength of the evidence. The accused had served an alibi notice but did not call the person named in it and gave no evidence himself. The prosecution inferentially invited the jury to conclude that the alibi was false and therefore evidence of guilt. Taking account of the fact that the chief prosecution witness was not altogether satisfactory, it was held that failure to give the direction rendered the verdict unsafe (cf. *Drake* [1996] Crim LR 109, in which the proviso was applied). See also *Peacock* [1998] Crim LR 681, in which P, when first interviewed, said that he had spent the evening of the robbery with his girlfriend, but at trial gave evidence that he had spent the evening with his former girlfriend and that what he had said initially was not a lie but a mistake. *Lesley* was distinguished in *Harron* [1996] 2 Cr App R 457, where it was held that the judge had not erred in failing to direct the jury that an alibi is sometimes falsified to bolster a genuine defence because the central issue in the case was whether the prosecution witnesses were lying or whether H was. Lies had not played a part in the way the Crown had put their case nor constituted a matter which the jury might have taken into account separate from their determination of the main issue, which turned upon the truthfulness of the witnesses. If they accepted the evidence for the Crown it necessarily involved a conclusion that the evidence of the accused was untrue, and that he was lying. See also *Gultutan* [2006] EWCA Crim 207 and *House* [1994] Crim LR 682.

F1.24   As to the third situation identified in *Burge*, in *Genus* [1996] Crim LR 502, where the accused claimed to have been acting under duress and the prosecution case was that the accused had told lies to the police and in evidence on collateral issues (i.e. on issues not directly relevant to the question of duress) and that the jury should, by reason of those lies, disbelieve their account of acting under duress, it was held that the case cried out for a *Lucas* direction. In *Robinson* [1996] Crim LR 417, where the judge in his summing-up gave considerable prominence to the issue whether R had lied about when his defence was first made known to the police, it was held that the case fell clearly within the fourth situation identified in *Burge*.

F1.25   As to the fourth situation identified in *Burge*, the Court of Appeal is unlikely to be persuaded that there was a real danger of the jury treating a particular lie as evidence of guilt if defence counsel at the trial did not alert the judge to that danger and ask him to consider whether a direction should be given to meet it (per Kennedy LJ in *Burge* [1996] 1 Cr App R 163 at p. 174). The failure of defence counsel to raise the matter at the trial may also be taken into account in cases in which both the third and the fourth situations identified in *Burge* arise, and may lead the Court of Appeal to conclude that the matter was not a large or important feature of the case and that the absence of the usual direction did not make the conviction unsafe (*McGuinness* [1999] Crim LR 318).

Situations where a *Lucas* Direction is Unnecessary   A *Lucas* direction is required only where   **F1.26** lies are directly related in some way to the offence charged, for example a lie which amounts to a false alibi (*Smith* [1995] Crim LR 305), but not a lie concerning some matter which is relevant only to the credibility of the accused (*Landon*) [1995] Crim LR 338). However, even if a lie is relied on merely to attack credibility, a *Lucas* direction is appropriate in exceptional circumstances, for example where the lie figures largely in the case and there is a risk that the jury may think that the accused must be guilty because he lied (*Tucker* [1994] Crim LR 683).

In *Middleton* [2001] Crim LR 251, it was said *per curiam* that if the question arises at trial whether a *Lucas* direction is required, it will generally be more useful to consider the application to the facts of the case of the principles derived from the many cases on the point, rather than to trawl through the cases themselves. The court stressed that the point of a *Lucas* direction is to warn against the 'forbidden reasoning' that lies necessarily demonstrate guilt. Where there is no risk of such forbidden reasoning on the part of the jury, a direction is unnecessary. See also, applying *Middleton, W* [2012] EWCA Crim 2516, where there was no risk of the forbidden reasoning and a *Lucas* direction might have advanced an aspect of the case against the accused which had not previously been put forward. According to *Middleton*, a direction is also generally unnecessary in relation to lies told by an accused in evidence, because the position is covered by the general directions on the burden and standard of proof. In cases where a direction could be given about a lie told in evidence, a judge may not be obliged to give a direction, especially if it would do more harm than good (*Nyanteh* [2005] EWCA Crim 686).

A *Lucas* direction is not likely to be required in the many cases of handling stolen goods in which the accused denies knowledge or belief that the goods were stolen, including those in which the accused gives different and inconsistent versions as to how he came by the goods, and the Crown's case is that he is not telling the truth (*Barnett* [2002] 2 Cr App R 168).

It is usually unhelpful to give both a *Lucas* direction and a direction as to possible inferences under the CJPO 1994, s. 34 (see **F19.9** *et seq.*). The judge should select and adapt the direction more appropriate to the facts and issues in the case. If the explanation given by an accused for his failure to mention a fact is said to be a lie, a s. 34 direction alone will suffice. The explanation should be incorporated into that direction. In such a case, it would be unnecessary, confusing and unduly favourable to the defence for the judge to give the usual *Lucas* examples of innocent reasons for lying (*Hackett* [2011] 2 Cr App R 35, applying *Rana* [2007] EWCA Crim 2261).

Continuance of Events over Period of Time

Evidence of the speed at which someone was driving at a particular point in time may be admitted to prove the speed at which he was driving a short time earlier or, as the case may be, later (see, respectively, *Dalloz* (1908) 1 Cr App R 258 and *Beresford v St Albans Justices* (1905) 22 TLR 1).   **F1.27**

MULTIPLE ADMISSIBILITY

Evidence which is admissible in law for one purpose cannot be excluded because it is inadmissible for some other purpose (although if it is tendered by the prosecution it may be excluded as a matter of discretion). '[I]t often happens, both in civil and criminal cases, that evidence is tendered on several alternative grounds, and yet it is never objected that if on any ground it is admissible, that ground must not prevail, because on some other ground it would be inadmissible and prejudicial' (*Bond* [1906] 2 KB 389, per Jelf J at pp. 411–2). The principle has attracted the somewhat misleading label of 'multiple admissibility' (J.H. Wigmore, *Evidence in Trials at Common Law*, vol. 1 (revised by Peter Tillers) (1983), sect. 13). A typical example would be a case in which evidence of a confession which implicates both its maker and a co-accused is   **F1.28** admitted in evidence against its maker, having been ruled inadmissible evidence against the co-accused. As to confessions implicating co-accused, see further **F17.80** and **F16.41**.

Where the principle applies, it has been said that 'it is usual for the judge (not always very successfully) to caution the jury against being biased by treating the evidence in the objectionable sense' (*Bond* [1906] 2 KB 389 per Jelf J at p. 412). Nowadays such a warning is often mandatory: see, e.g., *Gunewardene* [1951] KB 600 (a confession admissible for use only against its maker and not against any co-accused); *Flicker* [1995] Crim LR 493 (statements in which a confession is inextricably linked with material relating to the accused's propensity to offend); and *Norman* [2006] EWCA Crim 1662 (evidence of the discovery of drugs on a previous occasion inadmissible on the issue of intention to supply drugs subsequently found in the same place). Where evidence of the bad character of an accused, D1, is relevant to an issue between the Crown and a co-accused, D2, as when D2 adduces evidence of D1's bad character in support of D2's defence of having acted under duress, although the judge may direct the jury to ignore the evidence when considering the case against D1, such a direction need not be given if, in the circumstances of the case, it would needlessly perplex the jury and require them to indulge in mental gymnastics for very little, if any, benefit to D1 (*Randall* [2004] 1 All ER 467 at [35] and *Robinson* [2006] 1 Cr App R 480); as to the admissibility of such evidence, see **F12.67** *et seq*. In the case of a confession tendered by the prosecution and implicating both its maker and his co-accused, one solution is to edit the confession by omitting references to the co-accused or by replacing their names with letters of the alphabet or expressions such as 'another person' (see *Rogers* [1971] Crim LR 413; *Silcott* [1987] Crim LR 765; and generally **F17.90**). Alternatively, but only in exceptional circumstances, the judge may find it necessary to order separate trials for the accused (*Lake* (1976) 64 Cr App R 172).

CONDITIONAL ADMISSIBILITY

F1.29   The relevance of a particular item of evidence may become apparent only if considered together with other evidence. However, because evidence is given in order and by one witness at a time, it often happens that the other evidence can only be adduced at a later stage. Prima facie, therefore, the first item of evidence is irrelevant, and for that reason inadmissible. In these circumstances, upon an undertaking by counsel to demonstrate the relevance of the first item by introducing the further evidence, the court may allow the first item of evidence to be admitted conditionally or *de bene esse*. If, notwithstanding the introduction of the further evidence, the first item remains irrelevant, the judge will direct the jury to disregard it. For example, in the case of a conspiracy, if the judge is satisfied that a statement was made by one conspirator that is reasonably open to the interpretation that it was made in furtherance of the common design, it is admissible in evidence against another party to the conspiracy, provided that the judge is also satisfied that there is sufficient further evidence beyond the statement itself to show that the other party was a party to the conspiracy. Admitting evidence of such a statement may be conditional upon the adduction of the further evidence. If it transpires that there is insufficient further evidence, or no such evidence, the statement should be disregarded (see generally **F16.76** *et seq.*). See also the cases on accusations made in the presence of the accused, the relevance of which depends on evidence of the accused's reaction to them (see Lords Atkinson and Reading in *Christie* [1914] AC 545 at pp. 554 and 565 respectively and **F17.99**). In an extreme case, where great prejudice may be caused to an accused, a warning by the judge may be insufficient, and it may be necessary for the judge to discharge the jury.

THE BEST EVIDENCE RULE

As an Inclusionary Rule

F1.30   In *Omychund v Barker* (1745) 1 Atk 21, in which depositions of Hindu witnesses were admitted in evidence, notwithstanding that they did not accept the authority of the Gospel, Lord

Hardwicke said (at p. 49): '...there is but one general rule of evidence, the best that the nature of the case will admit'. This case suggests an inclusionary rule permitting the admission of the best evidence available in the circumstances of the case, but under the modern law of evidence, there exists no general rule to this effect.

As an Exclusionary Rule

The best evidence rule is now all but defunct. In *Francis* (1874) LR 2 CCR 128, in which **F1.31** the accused was indicted for false pretences, in that he falsely represented a ring to be a diamond ring, evidence was admitted of his attempts on other occasions to obtain money on a cluster ring in order to prove guilty knowledge. Rejecting an argument that because the cluster ring itself was not produced in court, evidence of witnesses who saw it and swore to its being false had been improperly admitted, Lord Coleridge CJ said: 'No doubt if there was not admissible evidence that this ring was false it ought not to have been left to the jury; but though the non-production of the article may afford ground for observation more or less weighty, according to circumstances, it only goes to the weight, not to the admissibility, of the evidence'.

However, very occasionally reliance is placed upon the rule. In *Quinn* [1962] 2 QB 245, on a charge of keeping a disorderly house, arising out of the performance of allegedly indecent striptease acts, one of the accused sought to put in evidence a film made three months after the events complained of and purporting to depict the acts performed, together with evidence that the acts depicted in the film were identical to the acts performed. It was held that the evidence had been properly rejected. Ashworth J said (at p. 257): '...it was admitted that some of the movements in the film (for instance, that of a snake used in one scene) could not be said with any certainty to be the same movements as were made at the material time. In our judgment, this objection goes not only to weight, as was argued, but to admissibility: it is not the best evidence.' Compare *Thomas* [1986] Crim LR 682, a case of reckless driving in which a video recording of the route taken by the accused was ruled admissible to remove the need for maps and photographs and to convey a more accurate picture of the roads in question. The reasoning in *Quinn* [1962] 2 QB 245 is difficult to reconcile with the clear statement of Lord Denning MR in *Garton v Hunter* [1969] 2 QB 37. Referring to the best evidence rule, his lordship said (at p. 44):

> That old rule has gone by the board long ago. The only remaining instance of it that I know is that if an original document is available in your hands, you must produce it. You cannot give secondary evidence by producing a copy. Nowadays we do not confine ourselves to the best evidence. We admit all relevant evidence. The goodness or badness of it goes only to weight, and not to admissibility.

See also Ackner LJ in *Kajala v Noble* (1982) 75 Cr App R 149 at p. 152 and *Governor of Pentonville Prison, ex parte Osman* [1990] 3 All ER 701 at p. 308; and cf. *Springsteen v Masquerade Music Ltd* [2001] EWCA Civ 563, discussed at **F8.4**. As to proof of the contents of documents, see **F8**.

QUESTIONS OF LAW AND FACT

In a Trial on Indictment: General Principles

As a general rule, questions of law (including practice) are for the judge, and questions of fact **F1.32** for the jury. In trials on indictment without a jury, the judge decides all questions of both law and fact and, if the accused is convicted, must give a judgment which states the reasons for the conviction (CJA 2003, s. 48(3) and (5)). Lay magistrates, when sitting with a judge in the Crown Court, are also judges of the court (Senior Courts Act 1981, ss. 8 and 73); they should participate in all questions to be determined by the court, including the factual aspect of any question relating to the admissibility of evidence, but must accept the ruling of the judge on any question of law (*Orpin* [1975] QB 283). In jury trials, questions of law for the judge include those relating to:

(a) challenges to jurors — see **D13.22** *et seq.*;
(b) the discharge of a juror or the whole jury — see **D13.50** *et seq.*;
(c) the competence of persons to give sworn or unsworn evidence — see **F4.2** *et seq.*;
(d) the admissibility of evidence;
(e) the withdrawal of an issue from the jury;
(f) submissions of no case to answer — see **D16.54** *et seq.*;
(g) the numerous issues on which the jury should be directed in the summing-up, such as the substantive law governing the charge, the burden and standard of proof, the use which the jury is entitled to make of the evidence adduced, the operation of any presumptions, the nature of, and any requirement for, corroboration, etc. — see further **D18.21** *et seq.* and **F5**; and
(h) matters ancillary to the trial itself, such as questions of bail, costs and leave to appeal.

Questions of fact for the jury include:

(a) whether the accused stands mute of malice or by visitation of God;
(b) the credibility of the witnesses called and the weight of the evidence adduced; and
(c) whether, applying the burden and standard of proof applicable to the case, they are satisfied as to the existence or non-existence of the facts in issue.

In jury trials, questions of fact which fall to be determined by the *judge* are the existence or non-existence of preliminary facts, i.e. facts which must be proved as a condition precedent to the admissibility of certain types of evidence; the sufficiency of evidence (in deciding whether an issue should be withdrawn from the jury); and the evaluation of evidence adduced by the parties (for the purpose of commenting on its weight in his summing-up to the jury). There are also a number of special cases, dealt with below, in which questions of fact fall to be determined, either wholly or in part, by the judge.

F1.33 **Construction of Words**   As a general rule, the construction of ordinary words in a statute is a question for the tribunal of fact (*Cozens v Brutus* [1973] AC 854 — 'insulting behaviour' under the Public Order Act 1936, s. 5; *Chambers v DPP* [1995] Crim LR 896 — 'disorderly behaviour' under the Public Order Act 1986, s. 5; *Feely* [1973] QB 530 — 'dishonestly' under the Theft Act 1968, s. 1(1); *Harris* (1968) 84 Cr App R 75 — 'knowledge or belief' under the Theft Act 1968, s. 22(1); *Garwood* [1987] 1 All ER 1032 — 'menaces' under the Theft Act 1968, s. 21(1); *Howard* [1993] Crim LR 213 — an 'explosive substance' under the OAPA 1861, s. 29; and *Kirk* [2006] EWCA Crim 725 — 'indecent or obscene' under the Postal Services Act 2000, s. 85(4)). Thus, although a judge is perfectly at liberty to direct a jury that it is not open to them to give to a word a particular meaning (being a meaning so unreasonable that if it were adopted and the accused convicted, the Court of Appeal would treat the verdict as perverse), normally he should not direct the jury as to the meaning of an ordinary word. The exception to this rule is where the word has been used in a context which indicates that it is being used in an unusual sense or has acquired a special meaning as a result of the authorities, as happened in relation to the word 'fraudulently' under the Larceny Act 1916, s. 1(1) — see Lawton LJ in *Feely* [1973] QB 530. In *Brutus v Cozens* [1973] AC 854, Lord Reid said (at p. 861C–E):

> The meaning of an ordinary word of the English language is not a question of law. The proper construction of a statute is a question of law. If the context shows that a word is used in an unusual sense the court will determine in other words what that unusual sense is. But here there is in my opinion no question of the word 'insulting' being used in any unusual sense.... It is for the tribunal which decides the case to consider, not as law but as fact, whether in the whole circumstances the words of the statute do or do not as a matter of ordinary usage of the English language cover or apply to the facts which have been proved. If it is alleged that the tribunal has reached a wrong decision then there can be a question of law but only of a limited character. The question would normally be

whether their decision was unreasonable in the sense that no tribunal acquainted with the ordinary use of language could reasonably reach that decision.

When a statutory provision is dealing with a technical subject and can only be understood with the assistance of an expert, then the words used must be given their ordinary and natural meaning to a person qualified to understand them, and evidence as to that meaning may be received from an appropriate expert (*Couzens* [1992] Crim LR 822).

As to the construction of *documents*, this is generally a matter of fact for determination by the jury, with the exception of binding agreements between parties and all forms of parliamentary and local government legislation, which are for the judge to construe as a matter of law. The City Code on Take-overs and Mergers sufficiently resembles legislation as to require construction of its provisions by a judge (*Spens* [1991] 4 All ER 421). However, if the legislation contains straightforward words which can be given their ordinary meaning, there will be nothing requiring any judicial interpretation as to their meaning and effect (*Pouladian-Kari* [2013] EWCA Crim 158).

Foreign Law Questions relating to the law of any jurisdiction other than that of England **F1.34** and Wales are questions of fact to be determined, on the evidence adduced, by the judge alone.

Administration of Justice Act 1920, s. 15

Where for the purpose of disposing of any action or other matter which is being tried by a judge with a jury in any court in England or Wales, it is necessary to ascertain the law of any other country which is applicable to the facts of the case, any question as to the effect of the evidence given with respect to that law shall, instead of being submitted to the jury, be decided by the judge alone.

Section 15 of the 1920 Act applies to criminal proceedings (*Hammer* [1923] 2 KB 786). As to the proof of foreign law, see **F8.22** and **F10.27**.

Autrefois Acquit or Convict Where an accused pleads autrefois acquit or convict, it shall be **F1.35** for the judge, without the presence of a jury, to decide the issue (CJA 1988, s. 122). See also **D12.20** *et seq*.

Perjury The question whether a statement on which perjury is assigned was 'material' in the **F1.36** judicial proceeding in which it was made is a question of law to be determined by the court of trial (Perjury Act 1911, s. 11(6)).

Duty of Care in Cases of Manslaughter In a case of manslaughter by gross negligence, the **F1.37** existence of a duty of care or a duty to act, if in dispute, is a question of law, but the question whether the facts establish the existence of the duty is for the jury (*Evans* [2009] 1 All ER 13). The position is the same, in respect of a duty of care, in a case of corporate manslaughter.

In Summary Trials

In the case of proceedings presided over by lay justices, the justices decide all questions of both **F1.38** law and fact, but on questions of law, including the law of evidence, should seek and accept the advice of the clerk. As to the proper role of the justices' clerk in a summary trial, see CPD VI, paras. 37A.1 to 37A.18 (see Supplement, **PD–48**), and **D22.77** *et seq*. In theory, District Judges (Magistrates' Courts) are in the same position as lay justices. In practice, however, the District Judge will be the more experienced lawyer, so that the occasions for asking for advice will be quite rare.

HEARINGS ON THE *VOIR DIRE*

General Principles

The hearing on the *voir dire*, or trial within a trial, is the procedure whereby the court deter- **F1.39** mines disputed preliminary facts, i.e. facts which must be established as a condition precedent

F

Part F Evidence

to the admission of certain items of evidence. The procedure is set out at **D16.41** to **D16.53** (trial on indictment) and **D22.41** (summary trial).

Concerning what evidence is admissible for the purpose of proving or disproving disputed preliminary facts, there is some authority to suggest that the judge is bound by the exclusionary rules of evidence which apply in relation to the admissibility of evidence at the trial proper. Thus, at common law, it has been held that it is wrong for a judge to determine the admissibility of a confession on the basis of the depositions (*Chadwick* (1934) 24 Cr App R 138). Most of the decisions concern specific statutory provisions governing the admissibility of evidence. In *O'Loughlin* [1988] 3 All ER 431, a decision on the conditions of admissibility imposed by the CJA 1925, s. 13(3) (now repealed), Kenneth Jones J ruled that in a criminal statute, unless other methods of proof are specified (e.g., 'by information or belief'), 'proof' means proof by admissible evidence. Preliminary facts under the CJA 1988, s. 23 (repealed — see now the CJA 2003, s. 116, at **F16.8**), called for proof by admissible evidence (*Neill v North Antrim Magistrates' Court* [1992] 4 All ER 846, *obiter* but applied in *Belmarsh Magistrates' Court, ex parte Gilligan* [1998] 1 Cr App R 14 and *Wood* [1998] Crim LR 213; and *Case* [1991] Crim LR 192 and *Mattey* [1995] 2 Cr App R 409, at **F16.14**). However, it was also held that a written statement could be admitted under the CJA 1988, s. 23(3)(b), on the basis of the *unsworn* evidence of its maker that he was not giving oral evidence through fear (*Greer* [1998] Crim LR 572; *Jennings* [1995] Crim LR 810). As regards the preliminary facts set out in s. 24(1)(i) and (ii) of the CJA 1988 (now repealed), it was held that, although evidence was often desirable, it was not always essential, because in appropriate circumstances the judge could infer the facts from the document sought to be admitted under s. 24 and the method or route by which it had been produced before the court (*Foxley* [1995] 2 Cr App R 523 and *Ilyas* [1996] Crim LR 810). See also *O'Connor* [2010] EWCA Crim 2287 at **F16.26**, a decision under the CJA 2003, s. 117.

F1.40   In trials on indictment, the various matters which may fall to be determined in a hearing on the *voir dire* include the following:

(a) the competence of a witness (see **F4.2** and **F4.25**);

(b) the admissibility of a confession (see **F17.62** to **F17.74**) or some other variety of admissible hearsay, such as a *res gestae* statement (see, e.g., *Jenkins* (1869) LR 1 CCR 187) or a statement made by someone who does not give evidence 'through fear' (see the CJA 2003, s. 116(2)(e), **F16.17** and *Shabir* (2013) 177 JP 271);

(c) the admissibility of a tape recording (see *Robson* [1972] 2 All ER 699 and **F8.53**);

(d) the admissibility of a statement contained in a document produced by a computer (see **F8.49**); and

(e) the admissibility of a plea of guilty against an accused who subsequently changes his plea to not guilty (*Rimmer* [1972] 1 All ER 604 at **F17.3** and cf. *Hetherington* [1972] Crim LR 703).

Cases in which a Hearing on Voir Dire Usually Not Required

F1.41   A hearing on the *voir dire* is not normally required to determine the admissibility of evidence relating to an identification parade. In *Walshe* (1980) 74 Cr App R 85 Boreham J said (at p. 87):

> . . . those representing the applicant drew some close analogy between the admissibility of evidence of an identification parade and the admissibility of a voluntary statement. But those are very different matters. As soon as a statement is challenged the law places on the Crown the burden of showing that it is admissible by proving that it was voluntarily made. [See now the PACE 1984, s. 76(2).] That is a separate and different matter. Here there was no burden on the Crown to prove the admissibility of the evidence relating to the identification parade and what flowed from it. It was clearly admissible evidence and should have been admitted. Its quality is, of course, another matter, to be considered by the jury.

In *Beveridge* (1987) 85 Cr App R 255, it was argued on appeal that in the light of the PACE 1984, s. 78, *Walshe* could no longer stand. It was held, dismissing the appeal, that where a question arises under s. 78 as to the admissibility of identification parade evidence, although there may be rare occasions when it will be desirable to hold a trial within a trial, in general the judge should decide on the basis of the depositions, statements and submissions of counsel.

In *Flemming* (1987) 86 Cr App R 32, a decision under the law prior to the 1984 Act, the appel- **F1.42** lant argued that identification evidence was inadmissible on the grounds, *inter alia*, that the identification at the police station was carried out in circumstances which contravened Home Office Circular No. 109 of 1978. It was submitted that the result was that the probative value of the evidence was minimal compared to its prejudicial effect, so that it would be unfair for the evidence to be admitted. The Court of Appeal held that it was quite unnecessary to hold a trial within a trial for this purpose. Woolf LJ (referring to one of the guidelines laid down by Lord Widgery CJ in *Turnbull* [1977] QB 224, at p. 229, namely that when, in the opinion of the judge, the quality of the identifying evidence is poor, the judge should withdraw the case from the jury unless there is other evidence which goes to support its correctness) said, at pp. 36–7:

> In the normal way the trial judge will make his assessment whether he needs to take the action referred to by the Lord Chief Justice either at the end of the case for the prosecution or after all the evidence in the case has been called. There may be exceptional cases where the position is so clear on the depositions that he can give a ruling at an earlier stage. However, the trial judge should not decide the matter by holding a preliminary trial, as in this case, before the evidence for the prosecution has been placed before the jury.
>
> It is, of course, true that the trial judge has a residual discretion to exclude evidence which is strictly admissible if he comes to the conclusion that its probative value is outweighed by its prejudicial effect, so that its admission would be unfair to the defendant. However, this residual discretion cannot justify the holding of trials within a trial as occurred here. Issues of this sort can be satisfactorily dealt with by the judge perusing the depositions, together with any facts that are common ground between the prosecution and the defence.

See also *Martin* [1994] Crim LR 218.

Application to Summary Trial

There can be no question of a trial within a trial in proceedings before magistrates, because **F1.43** the function of the *voir dire* is to allow the tribunal of law to decide a point of law in the absence of the tribunal of fact, and magistrates are judges of both fact and law. Thus, if the admissibility of a confession is in dispute, and the magistrates decide that matter as a separate issue by hearing evidence as to the preliminary facts and ruling in favour of admissibility, it is unnecessary to repeat the evidence about the confession in the trial proper. See generally **D22.41**.

It is impossible to lay down any general rule as to when the question of admissibility should be determined by magistrates, or as to when their decision on it should be announced, every case being different (*F v Chief Constable of Kent* [1982] Crim LR 682). These principles, insofar as they relate to confessions, are subject to the statutory constraint of the PACE 1984, s. 76(2), and the decision in *Liverpool Juvenile Court, ex parte R* [1988] QB 1. However, subject to this and other similar statutory constraints, there is still no general rule as to when admissibility should be determined and the decision on it announced. In *Epping and Ongar Justices, ex parte Manby* [1986] Crim LR 555 the applicant, convicted as the proprietor of a firm on whose behalf an overweight vehicle had been driven, contested the admissibility of a certificate of a police officer to the effect that the applicant had admitted responsibility for the vehicle (see **C2.17**), and sought leave to have the question resolved as a preliminary issue. It was held that the justices had not erred in refusing the application and admitting the evidence as providing a prima facie case for the applicant to deal with later, if he saw fit.

Admissibility of Confession If, during the course of a summary trial, the defence challenge **F1.44** the admissibility of a confession under the PACE 1984, s. 76(2) (see **F17.8**), the magistrates are bound by the terms of that subsection to hold a trial within a trial. In *Liverpool Juvenile Court, ex parte R* [1988] QB 1, Russell LJ held as follows:

(a) During the course of a summary trial, if the defence, before the close of the prosecution case, make a representation to the court that a confession made by the defendant was or may have been obtained by either of the improper methods set out in s. 76(2), the magistrates must hold a trial within a trial and make a ruling on the admissibility of the confession during or at the end of the prosecution case. (If the defence make an alternative submission based on the PACE 1984, s. 78, this should be examined at the same trial within a trial at the same time: *Halawa v Federation against Copyright Theft* [1995] 1 Cr App R 21.)

(b) In such a trial within a trial, the defendant may give evidence confined to the question of admissibility.

(c) At this stage, the magistrates will not be concerned with whether or not the confession is true.

(d) If the defence do not make a representation before the close of the prosecution case, the defendant may raise the question of the admissibility or weight of the confession at any subsequent stage at the trial.

(e) At this later stage, however, although the court retains an inherent jurisdiction to exclude the confession, as well as the power to exclude by virtue of the PACE 1984, s. 78 (see **F2.28**), it is not required to embark on a trial within a trial.

Nothing in the court's judgment was intended to lay down guidance as to the trial of indictable offences in the Crown Court.

F1.45   **Challenging Admissibility under the PACE 1984, s. 78**   Where the defence make a submission that the magistrates should exercise their discretion to exclude evidence under s. 78, they are not entitled to have that issue settled as a preliminary issue in a trial within a trial (*Vel v Chief Constable of North Wales* (1987) 151 JP 510). In *Halawa v Federation against Copyright Theft* [1995] 1 Cr App R 21, it was held that the duty of a magistrate, on an application under s. 78, is either to deal with the issue when it arises or to leave the decision until the end of the hearing, the objective being to secure a trial that is fair and just to both parties. Thus in some cases the accused will be given the opportunity to exclude the evidence before giving evidence on the main issues, because if denied that opportunity his right to remain silent on the main issues will be impaired, but in most cases it is better for the whole of the prosecution case, including the disputed evidence, to be heard first, because under s. 78 regard should be had to 'all the circumstances' and fairness to the prosecution requires that the whole of its case, in this regard, be before the court. In deciding, the court may take account of the extent of the issues to be raised by the evidence of the accused in the trial within a trial. A trial within a trial may be appropriate if the issues are limited, but not if it is likely to be protracted and to raise issues which will need to be re-examined in the trial itself.

Where there is a s. 78 challenge to evidence of statements made by an accused, it is normally desirable in the interests of justice for the court to hear the evidence in question and to have canvassed in questioning any circumstances which it is said would render its admission unfair. Where the justices resolve to exclude it, they should then consider, after seeking the views of the parties, whether the substantive hearing should be conducted by a differently constituted bench (*DPP v Lawrence* [2008] 1 Cr App R 147).

Section F2   The Discretion to Exclude Evidence; Evidence Unlawfully, Improperly or Unfairly Obtained

THE DISCRETION TO EXCLUDE AT COMMON LAW

General Principles

Although there is no common-law authority to suggest that a criminal court has any power to **F2.1** *admit* as a matter of discretion evidence which is inadmissible under an exclusionary rule of law, it is well established that a judge, as part of his inherent power and overriding duty in every case to ensure that the accused receives a fair trial, always has a discretion to *exclude* otherwise admissible prosecution evidence if, in his opinion, its prejudicial effect on the minds of the jury outweighs its true probative value. The classic description of the discretion is that of Lord du Parcq, delivering the reasons of the Board in *Noor Mohamed v The King* [1949] AC 182. Referring to cases in which the prosecution seek to admit similar-fact evidence, his lordship said (at p. 192):

> . . . in all such cases the judge ought to consider whether the evidence which it is proposed to adduce is sufficiently substantial, having regard to the purpose to which it is professedly directed, to make it desirable in the interest of justice that it should be admitted. If, so far as that purpose is concerned, it can in the circumstances of the case have only trifling weight, the judge will be right to exclude it. To say this is not to confuse weight with admissibility. The distinction is plain, but cases must occur in which it would be unjust to admit evidence of a character gravely prejudicial to the accused even though there may be some tenuous ground for holding it technically admissible.

The first clear statements as to the existence of this exclusionary discretion are to be found in **F2.2** the speeches of Lord Moulton and Lord Reading CJ in *Christie* [1914] AC 545, at pp. 559 and 564 respectively. Thereafter, the discretion developed on a case-by-case basis in relation to particular and different types of otherwise admissible evidence. In relation to similar fact evidence, for example, see *Harris v DPP* [1952] AC 694, at p. 707 (in which Viscount Simon cited and applied the passage from *Noor Mohamed v The King* set out above) and *DPP v Boardman* [1975] AC 421, at pp. 438, 441, 453, and 463. In relation to evidence otherwise admissible under the Theft Act 1968, s. 27(3), see *List* [1966] 3 All ER 710; *Herron* [1967] 1 QB 107; *Perry* [1984] Crim LR 680; and generally **F12.99** *et seq.* Concerning exercise of the discretion in relation to identification evidence, see **F18**. See also *Eatough* [1989] Crim LR 289.

In *Sang* [1980] AC 402, the House of Lords was firmly of the opinion that, notwithstanding **F2.3** its case-by-case development, under the modern law the discretion is a general one. The cases, therefore, are not to be treated as a closed list of the situations in which the discretion may be exercised (see Viscount Dilhorne and Lord Salmon, at pp. 438 and 445 respectively). The cases are nothing more than examples of a single discretion founded on the duty of the judge to ensure that every accused person has a fair trial (per Lords Scarman and Fraser, at pp. 452 and 447 respectively). Lord Salmon said (at p. 445):

> I recognise that there may have been no categories of cases, other than those to which I have referred, in which technically admissible evidence proffered by the Crown has been rejected by the court on the ground that it would make the trial unfair. I cannot, however, accept that a judge's undoubted duty to ensure that the accused has a fair trial is confined to such cases. In my opinion the category of such cases is not and never can be closed except by statute.

F

Part F Evidence

F2.4   **Discretion to Exclude Only Prosecution Evidence**   The discretion may only be exercised to exclude evidence on which the prosecution, as opposed to any co-accused, proposes to rely. In *Lobban v The Queen* [1995] 2 All ER 602 (at p. 887), the Privy Council cited with approval the following description of this principle in Keane, *The Modern Law of Evidence* (3rd edn, 1994) at p. 36:

> There is no discretion to exclude, at the request of one co-accused, evidence tendered by another. Thus although…there is a discretion to exclude similar fact evidence tendered by the prosecution, such evidence, when tendered by an accused to show the misconduct on another occasion of a co-accused is, if relevant to the defence of the accused, admissible whether or not it prejudices the co-accused (see per Devlin J in *Miller* [1952] 2 All ER 667 (Winchester Assizes), approved in *Neale* (1977) 65 Cr App R 304). Similarly, there is no discretion to prevent an accused from cross-examining a co-accused about his previous convictions and bad character when, as a matter of law, he becomes entitled to do so…

See, in the case of evidence of bad character adduced by a co-accused, the CJA 2003, s. 101(1)(e), and *Musone* [2007] 1 WLR 2467 at **F12.67** *et seq.*

F2.5   In *Lobban v The Queen* itself, it was held that there is no discretion to exclude the exculpatory part of a 'mixed' statement (see **F17.93**) on which one co-accused wishes to rely on the grounds that it implicates another. R made a statement containing admissions as well as an exculpatory explanation, an integral part of which implicated L, his co-accused. The prosecution tendered the statement against R; it was no evidence against L. Counsel for L submitted that the trial judge should have exercised his discretion to edit the statement to exclude the parts implicating L. The Privy Council held that no such discretion existed. The discretionary power applies only to evidence on which the prosecution proposes to rely. Although the prosecution had *tendered* the statement, they could not rely on it as evidence against L and the disputed material supported R's defence. There was therefore no discretionary power to exclude the disputed material. However in *Thompson* [1995] 2 Cr App R 589, at pp. 596–7, Evans LJ observed that where evidence is inadmissible against and prejudicial to an accused, but relevant to and therefore admissible for a co-accused, the only safeguard is the cumbersome device of separate trials, and it might be preferable to allow a discretion to exclude where the prejudice to the accused is substantial and the evidence of only limited benefit to the co-accused.

F2.6   **Admissions, Confessions and Evidence Obtained Improperly or Unfairly**   The discretion founded on the duty of the judge to ensure that every accused has a fair trial is not limited to excluding evidence which is likely to have prejudicial value out of proportion to its probative value, but extends to other evidence which might operate unfairly against the accused, namely admissions, confessions and other evidence obtained from the accused after the commission of the offence by improper or unfair means (*Sang* [1980] AC 402 per Lords Diplock, Fraser and Scarman, at pp. 436, 450 and 456 respectively). The discretion, in its extended form, merits discrete analysis: as to admissions and confessions, see **F2.14**; as to evidence obtained from the accused by improper or unfair means, see generally **F2.12** *et seq.*

Exercise of Discretion as Basis of Appeal

F2.7   Exercise of the discretion is a subjective matter, and each case has to be decided in the context of its own particular facts (*Sang* [1980] AC 402, per Lords Fraser and Scarman, at pp. 450 and 456 respectively). In *Selvey v DPP* [1970] AC 304 Lord Guest went so far as to say (at p. 352): 'If it is suggested that the exercise of this discretion may be whimsical and depend on the individual idiosyncrasies of the judge, this is inevitable where it is a question of discretion'. It follows from this that the Court of Appeal will not lightly interfere with judicial exercise of the discretion. It was held that the Court of Appeal will not interfere unless:

(a) the judge has failed even to consider exercise of the discretion, in which case the appeal court may exercise its own discretion (*Cook* [1959] 2 QB 340); or

(b) he has erred in principle, or there is no material on which he could properly have arrived at his decision (*Cook* per Devlin J, at p. 348, approved by Viscount Dilhorne in *Selvey v DPP* at p. 342 and applied in *Burke* (1985) 82 Cr App R 156).

Application to Summary Trial

In *Sang* [1980] AC 402, Lord Scarman made the following *obiter* observations relating to summary trials (at p. 456):

> The development of the discretion has, of necessity, been largely associated with jury trial. In the result, legal discussion of it is apt to proceed in terms of the distinctive functions of judge and jury. No harm arises from such traditional habits of thought, provided always it be borne in mind that the principles of the criminal law and its administration are the same, whether trial be (as in more than 90 per cent of the cases it is) in the magistrates' court or on indictment before judge and jury. The magistrates are bound, as is the judge in a jury trial, to ensure that the accused has a fair trial according to law; and have the same discretion as he has in the interests of a fair trial to exclude legally admissible evidence. No doubt, it will be rarely exercised. And certainly magistrates would be wise not to rule until the evidence is tendered and objection is taken. . . . They must wait and see what is tendered; and only then, if objection be taken, rule. When asked to rule, they should bear in mind that it is their duty to have regard to legally admissible evidence, unless in their judgment the use of the evidence would make the trial unfair.

F2.8

THE DISCRETION TO EXCLUDE: STATUTORY PROVISIONS

Police and Criminal Evidence Act 1984, s. 78

The common-law discretion founded on the duty of the judge or magistrates to ensure that every accused person has a fair trial has now been buttressed by statute. The PACE 1984, s. 78(1), provides that in any criminal proceedings 'the court may refuse to allow evidence on which the prosecution propose to rely to be given if it appears to the court that, having regard to all the circumstances, including the circumstances in which the evidence was obtained, the admission of the evidence would have such an adverse effect on the fairness of the proceedings that the court ought not to admit it'. Section 78 applies to 'evidence on which the prosecution *proposes* to rely' and therefore applications to exclude evidence under the section should be made before the evidence is adduced (and, if reference is to be made to it in the prosecution opening speech, before that speech): see, in the case of a confession, *Sat-Bhambra* (1988) 88 Cr App R 55, considered at **F17.67**, and, in the case of identification evidence, *Lashley* [2005] EWCA Crim 2016.

F2.9

Section 78(1) is generally regarded as conferring a discretionary power, but strictly speaking it does not involve an exercise of discretion because if a court decides that admission of the evidence in question would have such an adverse effect on the fairness of the proceedings that it ought not to admit it, it cannot logically exercise a discretion to admit it (per Auld LJ in *Chalkley* [1998] QB 848 at p. 874). Either way, the Court of Appeal has been loath to interfere with the decisions of trial judges under s. 78. It has been said that the Court of Appeal will intervene only if the judge has not exercised his discretion under s. 78 at all or has done so but in a *Wednesbury* unreasonable manner (*Associated Provincial Picture Houses Ltd v Wednesbury Corporation* [1948] 1 KB 223) and that where the Court of Appeal does intervene, it will exercise its own discretion (*O'Leary* (1988) 87 Cr App R 387 per May LJ at p. 391; *Quinn* [1995] 1 Cr App R 480 at p. 498; *Christou* [1992] QB 979; *Khan* [1997] Crim LR 508; *Dures* [1997] 2 Cr App R 247). However, it is submitted that the true test for the Court of Appeal should be whether the admission of the evidence in question renders the conviction unsafe, since that is now the only ground on which it may allow an appeal against conviction (see the Criminal Appeal Act 1968, s. 2(1) at **D26.14** *et seq.*, and generally A. Clarke, 'Safety or Supervision' [1999] Crim LR 108).

F2.10 The subsection may be used to attempt to exclude *any* evidence on which the prosecution propose to rely (see, e.g., *O'Loughlin* [1988] 3 All ER 431 (depositions and documentary records); information provided by the defence on a Plea and Case Management Hearing Form (see *Newell* [2012] 1 WLR 3142, considered at **F16.73**); *Mason* [1988] 3 All ER 481 (confessions); *Beveridge* (1987) 85 Cr App R 255 (identification parades); *Deenik* [1992] Crim LR 578 (voice identifications); and *McGrath v Field* [1987] RTR 349 (intoximeter readings)). Thus in the case of (a) any admissible evidence which is likely to have a prejudicial effect out of proportion to its probative value, and (b) admissions, confessions and other evidence obtained from the accused after the commission of the offence by improper or unfair means, and which might operate unfairly against the accused (*Sang* [1980] AC 402), the court may now exclude *either* under its powers at common law *or* pursuant to s. 78. In *Matto v Wolverhampton Crown Court* [1987] RTR 337 Woolf LJ said (at p. 346): 'Whatever is the right interpretation of s. 78, I am quite satisfied that it certainly does not reduce the discretion of the court to exclude unfair evidence which existed at common law. Indeed, in my view in any case where the evidence could properly be excluded at common law, it can certainly be excluded under s. 78.' An example is *O'Connor* (1986) 85 Cr App R 298. A and B were jointly charged with having conspired to commit an offence. A pleaded guilty and B not guilty. At the trial of B the prosecution sought to admit the conviction of A under the PACE 1984, s. 74. The prejudicial effect of this evidence clearly outweighed its probative value, because A's admission of the offence charged might have led the jury to infer that B must have conspired with A, and therefore the common-law discretion to exclude could have been invoked. Instead, the Court of Appeal held that the evidence should have been excluded under s. 78. See also *Kempster* [1989] 1 WLR 1125 and *Mattison* [1990] Crim LR 117, which are considered at **F11.14** and **F11.13** respectively. In *Daniels* [2011] 1 Cr App R 228, on the other hand, it was held that the fact that an accused has entered into an agreement pursuant to the SOCPA 2005, s. 73 (see **E1.13**) will not in itself call for exclusion of his evidence under s. 78, even if it is of central importance; the dangers inherent in giving evidence against accomplices are met by giving the jury a proper warning (see **F5.14**).

The primary importance of s. 78, however, is not the degree of overlap with the common law, but the fact that it extends the common-law powers by reason of its potential for the exclusion of evidence obtained by improper or unfair means. Concerning evidence improperly or unfairly obtained, the common-law powers are restricted to admissions, confessions and other evidence obtained from the accused after the commission of the offence (*Sang* [1980] AC 402). In *Sang*, their lordships, despite their apparent unanimity, were neither clear nor in agreement as to the precise meaning of the phrase 'evidence obtained from the accused after the commission of the offence'. Section 78, however, is capable of application to *any* evidence obtained by improper or unfair means and on which the prosecution seek to rely. The application of s. 78 to such evidence is considered separately at **F2.28**.

Other Statutory Provisions

F2.11 Unlike the PACE 1984, s. 78(1), which is of general application, other statutory provisions empower the court, in the exercise of its discretion, to exclude specific types of otherwise admissible evidence. Thus the CJA 2003, s. 101(3), confers a discretion to exclude otherwise admissible evidence of the bad character of the accused, having regard to the particular factors set out in s. 101(4) (see **F12.15**) and appears to provide a protection *additional* to the PACE 1984, s. 78(1) (see *Highton* [2005] 1 WLR 3472 at **F12.19**). Similarly, the CJA 2003, s. 126, confers a discretion to exclude otherwise admissible hearsay statements, whether adduced by the prosecution or defence; and, in the case of evidence adduced by the prosecution, expressly preserves the power to exclude such evidence under s. 78(1) (see **F16.93** and s. 126(2) at **F16.94**).

ADMISSIBILITY OF EVIDENCE OBTAINED UNLAWFULLY, IMPROPERLY OR UNFAIRLY

General Rule of Admissibility

Where evidence has been obtained illegally, the court may exercise its power, in appropriate   **F2.12**
circumstances, to stay proceedings (see *Warren v A-G for Jersey* [2012] 1 AC 22, considered at
D3.108). However, where proceedings have not been stayed then, subject to the exceptions
considered in **F2.13** to **F2.17**, evidence obtained unlawfully, improperly or unfairly is admissible as a matter of *law*. (Concerning the existence and extent of the *discretion* to exclude evidence
thus obtained, see **F2.18** *et seq*.) In *Kuruma, Son of Kaniu v The Queen* [1955] AC 197, Lord
Goddard CJ, on behalf of the Board, said (at p. 203):

> ...the test to be applied in considering whether evidence is admissible is whether it is relevant to
> the matters in issue. If it is, it is admissible and the court is not concerned with how the evidence
> was obtained. While this proposition may not have been stated in so many words in any English
> case there are decisions which support it, and in their lordships' opinion it is plainly right in
> principle.

Referring to this pronouncement in *Jeffrey v Black* [1978] QB 490, Lord Widgery CJ said (at
p. 497): 'I have not the least doubt that we must firmly accept the proposition that an irregularity in obtaining evidence does not render the evidence inadmissible'. Evidence is admissible,
therefore, if it has been obtained by any of the following means:

(a) Theft (*Leatham* (1861) 8 Cox CC 498 per Crompton J at p. 501).
(b) Unlawful search of persons (*Jones v Owen* (1870) 34 JP 759; *Kuruma, Son of Kaniu v The
    Queen* [1955] AC 197).
(c) Unlawful search of premises (*Jeffrey v Black* [1978] QB 490).
(d) The use of *agents provocateurs* (*Sang* [1980] AC 402).
(e) Eavesdropping (*Stewart* [1970] 1 All ER 689; *Keeton* (1970) 54 Cr App R 267; *Maqsud Ali*
    [1966] 1 QB 688; *Senat* (1968) 52 Cr App R 282).
(f) Invasion of privacy (*Khan* [1997] AC 558, in which evidence of an incriminating conversa-
    tion was obtained by means of a secret electronic surveillance device). See also the RIPA
    2000 at **D1.187** *et seq*. and **F2.51**.

Procedures for Obtaining Evidence Prescribed by Statute

Although in general the court is not concerned with how evidence is obtained, where it is a   **F2.13**
necessary step towards procuring a conviction for an offence that the evidence be obtained in
accordance with a procedure prescribed by statute, evidence obtained other than in accordance
with that procedure will not be admissible. See *Scott v Baker* [1969] 1 QB 659 (the procedure for
providing a specimen in relation to an offence of drink driving), approved in *Spicer v Holt* [1977]
AC 987 and distinguished in *Public Prosecution Service of Northern Ireland v Elliott* [2013] 2 Cr
App R 180 (17) (see **F3.71**); and contrast *Trump* (1979) 70 Cr App R 300 (see **F2.24**), *Adams*
[1980] QB 575 and *Tunbridge Wells Borough Council v Quietlynn Ltd* [1985] Crim LR 594.

Confessions

If it is represented to the court that a confession made by an accused person was or may have been   **F2.14**
obtained by the means set out in the PACE 1984, s. 76(2), the court shall not allow the confession to be given in evidence against him, except to the extent that the prosecution prove to the
court beyond reasonable doubt that the confession was not so obtained. Concerning the admissibility of both confessions and facts discovered in consequence of inadmissible confessions, see
generally **F17**.

F

Evidence Obtained by Torture or Inhuman or Degrading Treatment

F2.15   If it is represented to the court that a confession made by an accused was or may have been obtained by oppression, which is defined to include torture, the court shall not allow the confession to be given in evidence against him except insofar as the prosecution proves to the court beyond reasonable doubt that the confession (notwithstanding that it may be true) was not so obtained (see **F17.8** to **F17.10**). At common law, however, there is a broader general principle, established in *A v Secretary of State for the Home Department (No. 2)* [2006] 2 AC 221, that evidence obtained by torture is inadmissible. In that case, according to Lord Bingham, as a matter of constitutional principle, evidence obtained by torturing another human being may not lawfully be admitted against a party to proceedings in a British court, irrespective of where, or by whom, or on whose authority the torture was inflicted. His lordship said (at [52]):

> The principles of the common law, standing alone … compel the exclusion of third party torture evidence as unreliable, unfair, offensive to ordinary standards of humanity and decency and incompatible with the principles which should animate a tribunal seeking to administer justice. But the principles of the common law do not stand alone. Effect must be given to the European Convention, which itself takes account of the all but universal consensus embodied in the Torture Convention.

The House of Lords did not clearly define torture for these purposes, but Lord Hoffmann (at [97]) expressed a preference for the definition adopted by Parliament in the CJA 1988, s. 134, namely the infliction of severe pain or suffering on someone by a public official in the performance or purported performance of his official duties. The House also held that a conventional approach to the burden of proof was inappropriate in the context of a hearing before the Special Immigration Appeals Commission (SIAC) (in which, for example, the appellant may not see the statement or know what it says and may not know the name or identity of its author) and, by a majority, that the SIAC should refuse to admit the evidence if it concludes, on a balance of probabilities, that it was obtained by torture. However, it is submitted that in a criminal trial, if the defence can establish a prima facie case that evidence on which the prosecution seeks to rely was obtained by torture, the burden will be on the prosecution to prove beyond reasonable doubt that it was not so obtained.

F2.16   Evidence obtained by inhuman or degrading treatment contrary to the ECHR, Article 3, and in breach of the privilege against self-incrimination, may also fall to be excluded (*Jalloh v Germany* (2007) 44 EHRR 667). Incriminating real evidence recovered as a direct result of torture should never be admitted, but evidence secured as an indirect result of statements made and obtained by inhuman treatment may be admitted if it is only accessory in securing a conviction and its admission does not compromise defence rights (*Gäfgen v Germany* (2009) 48 EHRR 253). See also **A7.98**. It is arguable that evidence should be excluded if obtained as a result of secret detention, but the argument for exclusion is not as strong as in relation to torture, there being no equivalent of the Torture Convention, Article 15, in relation to secret detention (*XX v Secretary of State for the Home Department* [2012] 4 All ER 692 at [39], *obiter*).

Privileged Documents

F2.17   If a document protected by legal professional privilege (or secondary evidence of it) has been obtained by the opponent of the party entitled to assert the privilege, then the document (or secondary evidence of it) will be admissible in evidence. This principle applies whether the document was obtained by the inadvertence of the party entitled to assert the privilege or by the wrongful act of his opponent (*Calcraft v Guest* [1898] 1 QB 759; *Tompkins* (1977) 67 Cr App R 181). In civil proceedings, the party in whom the privilege is vested may apply for an injunction to restrain his opponent from making any use of the confidential information obtained in the document (*Lord Ashburton v Pape* [1913] 2 Ch 469). However, the principle of *Lord Ashburton v Pape* cannot be used to prevent the prosecution from tendering relevant evidence in a public prosecution (see *Butler v Board of Trade* [1971] Ch 680, a decision which is consistent with the general rule that criminal courts are not concerned with the method by which the evidence they consider has been obtained).

In *ITC Film Distributors Ltd v Video Exchange Ltd* [1982] Ch 431, one party to civil proceedings obtained by a trick in court privileged documents belonging to the other party. By that stage in the case there were difficulties in the way of granting injunctive relief under the principle established in *Lord Ashburton v Pape* [1913] 2 Ch 469. Warner J held that the public interest that litigants should be able to bring their documents into court without fear that they might be filched by their opponents required an exception to the rule in *Calcraft v Guest* [1898] 1 QB 759; and he observed that to obtain documents in such circumstances is probably a contempt of court which the court should not countenance by admitting the documents in evidence. It is submitted that if the same facts were to arise in a public prosecution rather than civil proceedings, then, notwithstanding the principles established in *Calcraft v Guest* and *Butler v Board of Trade* [1971] Ch 680, the result, on the reasoning employed by Warner J, would be the same.

DISCRETIONARY EXCLUSION OF EVIDENCE OBTAINED UNLAWFULLY, IMPROPERLY OR UNFAIRLY

Cases before *Sang*

Prior to *Sang* [1980] AC 402, the cases revealed an unbroken chain of dicta to the effect that in **F2.18** criminal proceedings the court has a general discretion to exclude otherwise admissible prosecution evidence which has been obtained by improper or unfair means, e.g.:

(a) Evidence obtained 'by a trick' (*Kuruma, Son of Kaniu v The Queen* [1955] AC 197, per Lord Goddard CJ at p. 204.

(b) Evidence obtained 'oppressively, by false representations, by a trick, by threats, by bribes' (*Callis v Gunn* [1964] 1 QB 495, per Lord Parker CJ at pp. 501–2).

(c) Evidence obtained 'by conduct of which the Crown ought not to take advantage' (*King v The Queen* [1969] 1 AC 304, per Lord Hodson at p. 319).

(d) In the context of an illegal search, exceptional cases in which 'not only have the police officers entered without authority, but they have been guilty of trickery or they have misled someone, or they have been oppressive or they have been unfair, or in other respects they have behaved in a manner which is morally reprehensible' (*Jeffrey v Black* [1978] QB 490, per Lord Widgery CJ at p. 498).

Despite these various dicta as to the existence of a discretion to exclude evidence which has been **F2.19** obtained oppressively, improperly or unfairly, there were very few cases in which such a discretion was in fact exercised. It was exercised in *Ameer* [1977] Crim LR 104 to exclude evidence which had been obtained as a result of the activities of an *agent provocateur*, and a similar course was taken in *Foulder* [1973] Crim LR 45 and in *Burnett* [1973] Crim LR 748; but all three cases were overruled in *Sang* [1980] AC 402. The only other case in which the discretion was exercised was *Payne* [1963] 1 All ER 848. P was charged with drunken driving. He had been induced to submit himself to examination by a doctor to see if he was suffering from any illness or disability, on the understanding that the doctor would not examine him for the purpose of seeing whether he was fit to drive; but at the trial the doctor gave evidence of P's unfitness to drive based on his symptoms and behaviour in the course of that examination. The conviction was quashed on the ground that the judge should have exercised his discretion to exclude the doctor's evidence. In *Sang* [1980] AC 402, however, *Payne* was regarded as analogous to cases in which an accused is unfairly induced to confess to an offence, and the judgment of the Court of Criminal Appeal was therefore seen to be based on the maxim *nemo tenetur se ipsum prodere* (no man is to be compelled to incriminate himself). In *McDonald* [1991] Crim LR 122, a decision under the PACE 1984, s. 78, it was held that it was not unfair to adduce evidence of a damaging admission, made by the accused in the course of a psychiatric examination, on a non-medical issue. See also *Gayle* [1994] Crim LR 679 and, in the case of confessions made to probation officers, *Elleray* [2003] 2 Cr App R 165.

Sang

F2.20   In *Sang* [1980] AC 402, the House of Lords held that, whatever the ambit of the judicial discretion to exclude admissible evidence, it does not extend to excluding evidence of a crime on the grounds that it was instigated by an *agent provocateur*, because if it did so extend it would amount to a procedural device whereby the trial judge could avoid the substantive law, under which it is clearly established that there is no defence of entrapment (*McEvilly* (1973) 60 Cr App R 150 and *Mealey* (1974) 60 Cr App R 59). The point of law of general importance certified by the Court of Appeal, however, went beyond the issue of *agents provocateurs* and raised a much wider question, namely: 'Does a trial judge have a discretion to refuse to allow evidence, being evidence other than evidence of an admission, to be given in any circumstances in which such evidence is relevant and of more than minimal probative value?' Although it was not strictly necessary for their lordships to answer the certified question in its full breadth, they proceeded to do so, and the primary importance of *Sang* is the *obiter* answer given. Treating the certified question as if it were not confined to trial by jury but concerned the existence of the discretion in any criminal trial, whether in the Crown Court or in a magistrates' court, their lordships, by way of answer, agreed on the following form of words suggested by Viscount Dilhorne (at p. 437):

> (1) A trial judge in a criminal trial has always a discretion to refuse to admit evidence if in his opinion its prejudicial effect outweighs its probative value. (2) Save with regard to admissions and confessions and generally with regard to evidence obtained from the accused after commission of the offence, he has no discretion to refuse to admit relevant admissible evidence on the ground that it was obtained by improper or unfair means. The court is not concerned with how it was obtained. It is no ground for the exercise of discretion to exclude that the evidence was obtained as the result of the activities of an *agent provocateur*.

The first of the above propositions is considered at **F2.1** to **F2.8**.

F2.21   As to the second proposition, despite the apparent unanimity, their lordships expressed various differing views, especially as to the meaning to be ascribed to the words 'and generally with regard to evidence obtained from the accused after commission of the offence', as the following extracts from the speeches illustrate:

(a) Lord Diplock (at p. 436) treated the phrase as referring to 'evidence tantamount to a self-incriminatory admission which was obtained from the defendant, after the offence had been committed, by means which would justify a judge in excluding an actual confession which had the like self-incriminating effect', and cited, by way of illustration, *Barker* [1941] 2 KB 381 (in which fraudulently prepared documents produced to a tax inspector were held to stand on precisely the same footing as an oral or written confession brought into existence as the result of a promise, inducement or threat) and *Payne* [1963] 1 All ER 848 (see **F2.19**). Lord Diplock said (at p. 436):

> The underlying rationale of this branch of the criminal law...is...now to be found in the maxim *nemo debet prodere se ipsum*.....That is why there is no discretion to exclude evidence discovered as the result of an illegal search but there is discretion to exclude evidence which the accused has been induced to produce voluntarily if the method of inducement was unfair.

(b) Lord Salmon, taking a less restrictive view as to the meaning of the phrase, said (at p. 444) 'In my opinion, the decision as to whether evidence may be excluded depends entirely on the particular facts of each case and the circumstances surrounding it — which are infinitely variable'. The category of cases in which evidence may be rejected on the grounds that it would make a trial unfair was not closed and could never be closed except by statute (at p. 445).

(c) Lord Fraser of Tullybelton, who agreed with Lord Diplock that the decision in *Payne* [1963] 1 All ER 848 was based, at least in part, on the maxim *nemo tenetur se ipsum accusare*, concluded that the phrase under discussion applied 'only to evidence and documents obtained from an accused person or from premises occupied by him' and would 'leave judges with a discretion to be exercised in accordance with their individual views of what is unfair or oppressive or morally reprehensible' (at p. 450).

(d) Lord Scarman (at pp. 456–7) treated the phrase as referring exclusively to the obtaining of evidence from the accused.

Cases after *Sang*

Much of the case law subsequent to *Sang* [1980] AC 402 has neither clarified nor refined the principles laid down in that case; see, e.g., *Winter v Barlow* [1980] RTR 209; *Doyle v Leroux* [1981] RTR 438; *Clarke* (1984) 80 Cr App R 344; and *Morris v Beardmore* [1981] AC 446, in which Lord Roskill said (at p. 469) that in *Sang* the House had carefully defined the limits of judicial discretion to exclude evidence otherwise clearly admissible, setting at rest many doubts which had previously existed as to its existence and scope, and that it would be a retrograde step to enlarge upon its now narrow limits or to engraft an exception, merely in order to meet the situation under discussion in that case. However, other authorities, such as *Khan* [1997] AC 558, *Trump* (1979) 70 Cr App R 300, *Adams* [1980] QB 575 and *Apicella* (1985) 82 Cr App R 295, are illustrative of what evidence is and is not capable of being treated as 'evidence tantamount to a self-incriminatory admission'; and *Fox* [1986] AC 281 has put a major gloss on the principles established in *Sang* [1980] AC 402, to the effect that where evidence has been unlawfully obtained from the accused after the commission of the offence, the discretion will not be exercised if those who obtained the evidence did so on the basis of a bona fide mistake as to their powers. In this regard, see also *Trump* (1979) 70 Cr App R 300. These cases are considered below. **F2.22**

Khan   In *Khan* [1997] AC 558, the House of Lords, relying upon the dictum of Lord Diplock in *Sang* set out at **F2.21**, held that evidence of an incriminating conversation obtained by means of a secret electronic surveillance device was not subject to the discretion recognised in *Sang* to exist in the case of admissions and confessions, because the accused had not been 'induced' to make the admissions recorded. **F2.23**

Trump   In *Trump* (1979) 70 Cr App R 300, the appellant was convicted of driving while unfit through drink. He was given a breathalyser test which proved positive. The officer administering the test then arrested him unlawfully. The appellant was taken to the police station and given a statutory warning that he might be prosecuted if he failed to provide a specimen. Under the relevant procedures, no such warning was required. As a result of the warning, the accused consented to the provision of a specimen of blood which was found to contain a proportion of alcohol above the prescribed limit. He appealed on the ground that the specimen of blood had been unlawfully obtained and that the result of its analysis should have been excluded. It was conceded by the appellant that after the breath test had proved positive, the officer had a statutory power of arrest (but not under the statutory provision which the officer purported to use) and that had he exercised that power the result of the analysis of blood would have been admissible as evidence. The Court of Appeal held that: **F2.24**

(a) the giving of blood by the accused was very close to his making an admission that he had consumed an excessive amount of alcohol, and therefore was subject to the discretion recognised in *Sang* [1980] AC 402 to exist in cases analogous to improperly obtained admissions; but
(b) the judge would have erred if he had excluded the evidence because, although the blood was given as the result of a threat, the officer was acting in good faith and the evidence could not have undermined the fairness of the trial.

Apicella   In *Apicella* (1985) 82 Cr App R 295 the appellant was convicted on three counts of rape. Each of the victims had contracted an unusual strain of gonorrhoea. The appellant, whilst held on remand, was suspected by the prison doctor to be suffering from gonorrhoea. The doctor, for solely therapeutic reasons, called in a consultant physician who, on the assumption that the appellant was consenting, took a sample of body fluid in order to make a diagnosis. In fact, the appellant submitted because he had been told by a prison officer that, being a prisoner, he had to submit. The sample showed that the appellant was suffering from the same strain of gonorrhoea as the victims, and the prosecution called evidence to that effect. On appeal, although no reference to *Trump* (1979) 70 Cr App R 300 appears to have been made, the Court of Appeal rejected a submission that the body **F2.25** fluid taken without consent was the physical equivalent of an oral confession. Lawton LJ, giving the judgment of the court, held that the pertinent question was whether the intended use of the evidence was likely to make the trial unfair; that the appellant was not tricked into submitting to the examination in the way which led the court in *Payne* [1963] 1 All ER 848 (see **F2.19**) to exclude evidence; and that the prosecution's use of the evidence was not unfair.

F2.26 *Adams*   In *Adams* [1980] QB 575 the accused was charged with offences under the Obscene Publications Act 1959, s. 2. On 6 April 1977, the police, acting under a search warrant issued under s. 3(1) of the 1959 Act, entered and searched the accused's bookshop and seized certain articles. On 12 April 1977, officers purporting to act under the same warrant, entered and searched the shop and seized further articles. The Court of Appeal held that since a warrant issued under s. 3(1) authorised only one entry, search and seizure of premises, and was spent once that had been carried out, the entry, search and seizure on 12 April was unlawful. On the question whether the judge should have exercised his discretion to exclude the articles seized on 12 April, it was held that there was no material suggesting that the error of the police as to the continuing validity of the warrant after the search on 6 April was oppressive in the sense that the adjective was used in *Sang* [1980] AC 402. This assumes, contrary to the view of Lord Diplock in *Sang* (see **F2.21**), that evidence discovered as a result of an illegal search *is* subject to the discretion recognised in that case and, in appropriate circumstances, may be excluded.

F2.27 *Fox*   In *Fox* [1986] AC 281 the appellant was convicted under the Road Traffic Act 1972, s. 6(1), on the basis of the proportion of alcohol in a breath specimen which he had been required to provide at a police station following his wrongful arrest. Officers had entered the appellant's house without his consent and without statutory authority, and required him to provide a specimen of breath. He refused. He was then arrested and taken to the police station where he was required to provide the specimen of breath which was the crucial item of evidence which led to his conviction. The requirement to provide a specimen in the appellant's house was not valid and the appellant had committed no offence by failing to comply with it. Consequently, his arrest for failure to provide a specimen was unlawful. On appeal, it was submitted that the evidence of the specimen obtained at the police station, although relevant and admissible, ought to have been excluded by the justices in the exercise of their discretion. This submission was rejected by both the Divisional Court and the House of Lords. Lord Fraser of Tullybelton said (at p. 293): 'Of course, if the appellant had been lured to the police station by some trick or deception, or if the police officers had behaved oppressively towards the appellant, the justices' jurisdiction to exclude otherwise admissible evidence recognised in *Sang* might have come into play. But there is nothing of that sort suggested here. The police officers did no more than make a bona fide mistake as to their powers.' This passage was cited and applied by McNeill J in *Gull v Scarborough* [1987] RTR 261. See also *DPP v Wilson* [1991] RTR 284, a decision under the PACE 1984, s. 78.

Police and Criminal Evidence Act 1984, s. 78

F2.28   (1) In any proceedings the court may refuse to allow evidence on which the prosecution proposes to rely to be given if it appears to the court that, having regard to all the circumstances, including the circumstances in which the evidence was obtained, the admission of the evidence would have such an adverse effect on the fairness of the proceedings that the court ought not to admit it.
        (2) Nothing in this section shall prejudice any rule of law requiring a court to exclude evidence.

The importance of s. 78(1) is reflected in the large volume of reported cases in which it has arisen for consideration. It is important to stress at the outset, however, the salutary warning given by Auld J in *Jelen* (1989) 90 Cr App R 456 at pp. 464–5:

> ... the decision of a judge whether or not to exclude evidence under section 78 of the 1984 Act is made as a result of the exercise by him of a discretion based upon the particular circumstances of the case and upon his assessment of the adverse effect, if any, it would have on the fairness of the proceedings. The circumstances of each case are almost always different, and judges may well take different views in the proper exercise of their discretion even when the circumstances are similar. This is not an apt field for hard case law and wellfounded distinctions between cases.

The following paragraphs make a number of general observations. The cases concerning confessions and identification evidence are also considered separately and in more detail at **F17** and **F18** respectively.

Procedure As to procedure, the issue of unfairness may be raised by counsel for any accused **F2.29** against whom the evidence may be used (by the prosecution). Section 78(1) applies not to evidence which the prosecution have adduced, but to evidence on which the prosecution *propose* to rely. In *Harwood* [1989] Crim LR 285, in which a submission that evidence should be excluded under s. 78 was made *after* the evidence had been given, the Court of Appeal doubted whether s. 78 could in any circumstances entitle the judge to withdraw the evidence or to direct the jury to acquit when the judge had not been invited to refuse to allow the evidence to be given. However, where a judge has excluded evidence on which the prosecution propose to rely but, at some later stage in the trial, in his opinion the balance of fairness shifts, he then has a discretion to reconsider his ruling and admit the evidence (*Allen* [1992] Crim LR 297).

It seems reasonable to suppose that if the court is prepared to entertain a submission that a particular item would have such an adverse effect on the fairness of the proceedings that the court ought not to admit it, argument should take place in the absence of the jury and, in cases in which evidence needs to be called as to the circumstances in which the evidence was obtained (because they are in dispute), there should be a hearing on the *voir dire*. In *Manji* [1990] Crim LR 512 the accused denied that he had made certain damaging admissions in a conversation with police officers and alleged that he had not been cautioned. On a defence application under s. 78 to exclude this evidence as having been obtained in breach of the Codes of Practice under the PACE 1984, the trial judge refused to hold a trial within a trial on the issue of whether the accused had been cautioned. It was held that the judge had erred. However, where a question arises under s. 78(1) as to the admissibility of identification parade evidence, it has been held that, although there may be rare occasions when it will be desirable to hold a trial within a trial, in general the judge should decide on the basis of the depositions, statements and submissions of counsel (*Beveridge* (1987) 85 Cr App R 255). See **F1.41**.

In *Anderson* [1993] Crim LR 447 it was acknowledged, *per curiam*, that it is not entirely clear **F2.30** under s. 78(1) where the burden of proof lies. It is submitted that, if there is no dispute as to the circumstances in which the evidence was obtained, there will be no issue of fact and no question of burden of proof will arise; if there is such a dispute, evidence is called for and, in accordance with the general rule, the burden should be on the prosecution to disprove beyond reasonable doubt the circumstances on which the accused relies. However, in *R (Saifi) v Governor of Brixton Prison* [2001] 4 All ER 168, which concerned the application of s. 78 in extradition proceedings, it was held that the absence from s. 78 of any suggestion that facts are to be proved to any particular standard is deliberate; that a magistrate may simply evaluate the evidence tendered both by the government and the accused as to the circumstances in which the evidence was obtained and may decide, on that evidence, the question of adverse effect on the fairness of the proceedings; and therefore that there is no need for a magistrate to make a specific finding in relation to every issue raised.

As to the procedure in summary trials, see **F1.43**.

The Test for Exclusion Section 78(1) of the PACE 1984 directs the court, in deciding whether **F2.31** to exercise the statutory discretion, to have regard to all the circumstances, including those in which the evidence was obtained. In some cases, of course, the submission to exclude under the subsection will *not* be based on the circumstances in which the evidence was obtained; see, e.g., the cases in which an application has been made under s. 78(1) to exclude evidence of the conviction of a person otherwise admissible under s. 74 of the 1984 Act, which are considered at **F11.6**.

In other cases, however, counsel will be fully justified in basing a submission to exclude on the circumstances in which the evidence was obtained, because it is implicit in the subsection that there can be circumstances in which the evidence was obtained which makes it have such an adverse effect on the fairness of the proceedings that the court ought not to admit it (*Matto v*

Wolverhampton Crown Court [1987] RTR 337 per Woolf LJ). Thus, the court may have regard to any unlawful, improper or unfair conduct by means of which the evidence was obtained, including, in particular, conduct in breach of the ECHR or the provisions of the 1984 Act (or the codes of practice issued under the Act) relating to such matters as search, seizure, arrest, detention, treatment, questioning and identification. Even where the evidence in question was obtained by someone who is not 'charged with the duty of investigating offences' for the purposes of s. 67(9) of the 1984 Act, the principles underlying Code C may be of assistance in considering the discretion to exclude under s. 78(1) (*Smith* [1994] 1 WLR 1396). Useful guidance can be found in *Achieving Best Evidence in Criminal Proceedings: Guidance on interviewing victims and witnesses, and guidance on using special measures* (March 2011): see *Dunphy* (1993) 98 Cr App R 393, a decision on an earlier version of the guidance. However, breach of the ECHR, the 1984 Act or the PACE codes etc. will not necessarily result in exclusion: every case has to be determined on its own particular facts (*Parris* (1988) 89 Cr App R 65, per Lord Lane CJ at p. 72; *Khan* [1995] QB 27; *Keenan* [1990] 2 QB 54 per Hodgson J at p. 69). Equally, the fact that evidence has been obtained by 'oppressive' conduct will not automatically result in exclusion, because oppressive conduct, depending on its degree and actual or possible effect, may or may not affect the fairness of admitting particular evidence (*Chalkley* [1998] QB 848 at p. 874).

F2.32   **'The Fairness of the Proceedings'**   In cases in which the court takes the view that there was serious or reprehensible conduct, and this results in exclusion, the decision should not be taken in order to discipline the police (*Mason* [1988] 3 All ER 481 per Watkins LJ; *Delaney* (1988) 88 Cr App R 338 per Lord Lane CJ at p. 341). The critical test under s. 78 is whether any impropriety affects the fairness of the proceedings: the court cannot exclude evidence under the section simply as a mark of its disapproval of the way in which it was obtained (per Auld LJ in *Chalkley*).

Thus if a sample of hair is obtained by an assault and not in accordance with the PACE 1984 and is then used to prepare a DNA profile which implicates the accused, the evidence will be admitted on the basis that the means used to obtain it have done nothing to cast doubt on its reliability and strength (*Cooke* [1995] 1 Cr App R 318 and cf. *Nathaniel* [1995] 2 Cr App R 565). The same reasoning may also justify the admission in evidence of the fruits of an improper search (see *Stewart* [1995] Crim LR 500, where the entry involved a number of breaches of Code B; and see also *McCarthy* [1996] Crim LR 818). The evidence should be excluded, however, where there is a real risk that the improper means used to obtain it have affected its reliability, and therefore the fairness of the trial, e.g., a case involving a complete flouting of Code B in which the accused claims that the property allegedly found must have been planted. (But see *Wright* [1994] Crim LR 55 at **F2.50**.) Equally, where officers are justified in delaying taking a suspect to a police station in order that a search may be conducted with his assistance, but abuse that opportunity to circumvent Code C by asking a series of questions, beyond those necessary to the search, on matters which properly ought to be asked under the rules of the Code applying at a police station, the answers may be excluded on the grounds of unfairness (*Khan* [1993] Crim LR 54, applied in *Raphaie* [1996] Crim LR 812).

F2.33   In *Quinn* [1990] Crim LR 581 Lord Lane CJ said:

> The function of the judge is therefore *to protect the fairness of the proceedings*, and normally proceedings are fair if a jury hears *all* relevant evidence which either side wishes to place before it, but proceedings may become unfair if, for example, one side is allowed to adduce relevant evidence which, for one reason or another, the other side cannot properly challenge or meet, or where there has been an abuse of process, e.g. because evidence has been obtained in deliberate breach of procedures laid down in an official code of practice.

In *Quinn*, identification evidence had come into existence abroad as a result of arrangements made by a foreign police force. A police officer went to a criminal court in Dublin, where the accused was on trial in respect of other offences committed in the Republic of Ireland, and identified the accused. It was held that, in the circumstances of the case, the judge had to have regard to such factors as (a) the possible cross-examination handicap to the defence; (b) the possibility of mistake being increased because of the way in which the identification was arranged and the fact that both the judge himself and the defence could warn the jury of the disadvantages of the procedure adopted and the consequent danger of relying upon the evidence; (c) the fact that the accused was deprived of the opportunity to stand on an identification parade or to consult a solicitor or to record what happened when the identification was carried out; (d) that the accused was not told of the identification at the time; and (e) the fact that the identification evidence did not stand alone but could be tested by other evidence. The Court of Appeal could find nothing to indicate that the trial judge had misdirected himself, had regard to irrelevant matters or failed to have regard to relevant matters. In *Konscol* [1993] Crim LR 950, the trial judge admitted evidence of an interview with K, containing lies, conducted by a Belgian customs officer. There was no dispute that K had said what was recorded, and the interview was conducted fairly according to Belgian law, but K was neither cautioned nor advised that he could have a lawyer present. The Court of Appeal dismissed the appeal and declined to lay down guidelines as to when a court should admit a statement made overseas according to rules which did not coincide with the provisions of the PACE 1984. See also *McNab* [2002] EWCA Crim 1605.

In *Mason* [1988] 3 All ER 481 the accused was convicted of arson. After arrest, the accused and **F2.34** his solicitor were told by police officers that a fingerprint of the accused had been identified on glass from a bottle found at the scene of the crime. This was a deliberate falsehood designed to elicit a confession. The solicitor advised the accused to explain any involvement on his part in the incident, whereupon the accused confessed. There was no other prosecution evidence. Quashing the conviction, the Court of Appeal held that had the judge, in the exercise of the statutory discretion, taken into account the deceit practised on the solicitor, which he had failed to do, he would have been driven to exclude the confession. See also *Samuel* [1988] QB 615. *Mason* was distinguished in *DPP v Marshall* [1988] 3 All ER 683. On a charge of selling intoxicating liquor without a licence, evidence was adduced that officers, wearing plain clothes, and without announcing their office, had purchased liquor from the premises in question. It was held that this evidence could not have any effect on the fairness of the trial and therefore was not to be excluded under the PACE 1984, s. 78.

Scope of s. 78(1) As regards the scope of the PACE 1984, s. 78(1), in *Mason* [1988] 3 All ER **F2.35** 481 Watkins LJ said that it 'does no more than to restate the power which judges had at common law before the 1984 Act was passed'. It is submitted that this view is erroneous in principle and inconsistent with the authorities to date.

(a) Concerning the provisions of part VIII of the PACE 1984, s. 82(3) expressly preserves the discretion to exclude which the court possessed at common law prior to the coming into force of the Act, and therefore Parliament, in enacting s. 78, must be taken to have extended the pre-existing discretion.

(b) Section 78(1), insofar as it may be used to exclude evidence obtained by improper or unfair means, is not confined, as is the common-law power described in *Sang* [1980] AC 402 (at p. 437), to 'admissions, confessions and generally with regard to evidence obtained from the accused after the commission of the offence', but extends to any evidence on which the prosecution propose to rely.

(c) Nor, in relation to evidence obtained improperly or unfairly, is s. 78(1) necessarily confined, in the way that the common-law power apparently is, to cases in which those who obtained the evidence acted *mala fide* (*Fox* [1986] AC 281, see F2.27). See further F2.45.

Section 78(1) *may* be used to exclude evidence obtained illegally, improperly or unfairly. Insofar as it may be used in this way to exclude admissions, confessions and evidence obtained from the accused after the commission of the offence, it overlaps with the common-law discretion as defined in *Sang*. The subsection, however, has the potential for the exclusion of *any* evidence on which the prosecution propose to rely, whether obtained from the accused, his premises, or from any other source. Thus, in *Gaynor* [1988] Crim LR 242, evidence that a witness had picked out the accused at a group identification was excluded under s. 78 on the basis of a breach of PACE Code D.

F2.36   **Prosecutions Founded on Entrapment**   The leading authority on the application of the PACE 1984, s. 78(1), to a prosecution founded on entrapment is the decision of the House of Lords in *Loosely* [2001] 4 All ER 897, from which the following propositions derive.

(a)   Although in English law entrapment is not a substantive defence, where an accused can show entrapment, the court may stay the proceedings as an abuse of the court's process or it may exclude evidence pursuant to s. 78.

(b)   Of these two remedies, the grant of stay, rather than the exclusion of evidence at the trial, should, as a matter of principle, normally be regarded as the appropriate response. A prosecution founded on entrapment would be an abuse of the court's process. Police conduct which brings about state-created crime is unacceptable and improper. To prosecute in such circumstances would be an affront to the public conscience.

(c)   A decision on whether to stay criminal proceedings is distinct from a decision on the forensic fairness of admitting evidence (*Chalkley* [1998] 2 Cr App R 79 at p. 105). Thus if the court is not satisfied that a stay should be granted and the trial proceeds, the question under s. 78 is not whether the proceedings should have been brought but whether the fairness of the proceedings will be adversely affected by, for example, admitting the evidence of the *agent provocateur* or evidence which is available as a result of his activities (*Shannon* [2001] 1 WLR 51 at p. 68). However, if an application to exclude evidence under s. 78 is in substance a belated application for a stay, it should be treated as such and decided according to the principles appropriate to the grant of a stay.

(d)   In deciding whether conduct amounts to state-created crime, the existence or absence of a predisposition on the part of the accused to commit the crime is not the criterion by which the acceptability of police conduct is to be decided, because predisposition does not make acceptable what would otherwise be unacceptable conduct on the part of the police or other law enforcement agencies. (But cf. *Moon* [2004] EWCA Crim 2872, where absence of disposition on the part of M to deal with or supply heroin was regarded as a critical factor.) A useful guide is to consider whether the police did no more than present the defendant with an unexceptional opportunity to commit a crime. The yardstick for the purposes of this test is, in general, whether the police conduct preceding the commission of the offence was no more than might have been expected from others in the circumstances. McHugh J had this approach in mind in *Ridgeway v The Queen* (1995) 184 CLR 19 at p. 92, when he said:

> The State can justify the use of entrapment techniques to induce the commission of an offence only when the inducement is consistent with the ordinary temptations and stratagems that are likely to be encountered in the course of criminal activity. That may mean that some degree of deception, importunity and even threats on the part of the authorities may be acceptable. But once the State goes beyond the ordinary, it is likely to increase the incidence of crime by artificial means.

Of its nature, the technique of providing an opportunity to commit a crime is intrusive. The greater the degree of intrusiveness, the closer will the courts scrutinise the reason for using it. On this, proportionality has a role to play. Whether a police officer can be said to have caused the commission of the offence, rather than merely providing an opportunity for the accused to commit it with a police officer instead of in secrecy with someone else, will usually be a most important factor, but not necessarily decisive. See also *Jones* [2010] 3 All ER 1186.

(e)   Ultimately, the overall consideration is always whether the conduct of the police or other law enforcement agency was so seriously improper as to bring the administration of justice into disrepute. In applying this test, the court has regard to all the circumstances of the case.

The following circumstances are of particular relevance. (For an illustration of how account may be taken of them, see *Moore* [2013] EWCA Crim 85.) (i) The nature of the offence. The use of proactive techniques is more appropriate in the case of some offences, e.g., dealing in unlawful substances, offences with no immediate victim (such as bribery), offences which victims are reluctant to report and conspiracies. The secrecy and difficulty of detection, and the manner in which the particular criminal activity is carried on, are relevant considerations. (ii) The reason for the particular police operation and supervision. The police must act in good faith. Having reasonable grounds for suspicion is one way good faith may be established. It is not normally considered a legitimate use of police power to provide people not suspected of being engaged in any criminal activity with the opportunity to commit crimes. (See, e.g., *Ramanauskas v Lithuania* (2010) 51 EHRR 303, where an officer acted on no more than *rumours* about a prosecutor's openness to bribery.) The principle is that the police should prevent and detect crime, not create it. Closely linked with the question whether the police were creating or detecting crime is the supervision of their activities. To allow police officers or controlled informers to undertake entrapment activities unsupervised carries great danger, not merely that they will try to improve their performances in court, but of oppression, extortion and corruption. The need for reasonable suspicion and proper supervision were both stressed in the Undercover Operations Code of Practice, issued jointly by all UK police authorities and HM Customs and Excise in response to the HRA 1998 (see now the Code of Practice for the Use of Human Intelligence Sources). However, the requirement of reasonable suspicion does not necessarily mean that there must have been suspicion of the accused. The police may, in the course of a bona fide investigation into suspected criminality, provide an opportunity for the commission of an offence which is taken by someone to whom no suspicion previously attached (see, e.g., *Williams v DPP* [1993] 3 All ER 365). Sometimes random testing may be the only practicable way of policing a particular trading activity. (iii) The nature and extent of police participation in the crime. The greater the inducement held out by the police, and the more forceful or persistent the police overtures, the more readily may a court conclude that the police overstepped the boundary. (In the absence of persuasion or pressure or the offer of a significant inducement, it will not generally amount to an abuse of process for an officer to so insinuate himself into the confidence of the accused as to offer an opportunity to commit a crime: see *M* (2011) 175 JP 273.) In assessing the weight to be attached to the police inducement, regard is to be had to the defendant's circumstances, including his vulnerability. For the police to behave as would an ordinary customer of a trade, whether lawful or unlawful, being carried on by the accused will not normally be regarded as objectionable. (iv) The accused's criminal record. This is unlikely to be relevant unless it can be linked to other factors grounding reasonable suspicion that the accused is currently engaged in criminal activity.

(f) Neither the judicial discretion conferred by s. 78, nor the court's power to stay proceedings as an abuse of the court, has been modified by the ECHR, Article 6, and the jurisprudence of the ECtHR. There is no appreciable difference between the requirements of Article 6, or the Strasbourg jurisprudence on Article 6, and the English law as it has developed in recent years. There is nothing in either the general principle applied by the ECtHR in *Teixeira de Castro v Portugal* (1998) 28 EHRR 101 or in the cluster of factors to which it attached importance which suggests any difference from the current English approach to entrapment.

Undercover Operations   Where evidence has been obtained by illegal undercover operations, **F2.37** the court may, in appropriate circumstances, stay the proceedings (see *Warren v A-G for Jersey* [2012] 1 AC 22, considered at **D3.108**). But where proceedings have not been stayed, the question arises whether to exclude the evidence obtained by the undercover operations. In *Smurthwaite* [1994] 1 All ER 898 it was held that the relevant factors, in deciding whether to exclude under the PACE 1984, s. 78, evidence obtained as a result of police undercover operations, *include* whether the undercover officer was acting as an *agent provocateur* in the sense that he was enticing the accused to commit an offence he would not otherwise have committed; the nature of any entrapment; whether the evidence consists of admissions to a completed offence or relates to the actual commission of an offence; how active the officer's role was in obtaining the evidence; whether there is an unassailable record of what occurred or whether it is strongly corroborated; and whether the officer abused his role to ask questions which ought properly to have been asked as a police officer and in accordance with the codes (see *Christou* [1992] QB 979 and *Bryce* [1992] 4 All ER 567 at **F2.44**). It was held that if in all the circumstances the evidence would have the adverse effect described in s. 78(1) then the judge will exclude it. The factors recited in *Smurthwaite* also apply in the case of evidence obtained by undercover journalists acting not on police instructions, but on their own initiative (*Shannon* [2001] 1 WLR 51; *Shannon v UK* (2006) 42 EHRR 660). Section 78(1) cannot be circumvented by the police using, as *agents provocateurs*, informants who will not be called as witnesses. Thus if an informant, acting on police instructions, entraps an accused into committing an offence and the accused is then approached by an undercover police officer in whose presence the offence is committed, a submission may be made under s. 78(1) to exclude the officer's evidence notwithstanding that his behaviour throughout cannot be criticised having regard to the relevant factors in *Smurthwaite* (*Smith* [1995] Crim LR 658; cf. *Mann* [1995] Crim LR 647). However, entrapment, whether direct or indirect, is not in itself sufficient to require exclusion under s. 78. The facts and circumstances amounting to entrapment may be taken into account (and in an appropriate case may prove decisive), but the principal focus must be the procedural fairness of the proceedings, the nature and reliability of the prosecution evidence and the fullness and fairness of the opportunity available to the accused to deal with it (per Potter LJ in *Shannon* [2001] 1 WLR 51 at [38]; and see also *Governor of Pentonville Prison, ex parte Chinoy* [1992] 1 All ER 317).

F2.38 In *Smurthwaite*, the two appellants, S and G, had been tried for soliciting to murder. In each case the person solicited was an undercover police officer posing as a contract killer, and the prosecution case depended upon secret tape recordings of meetings held between the undercover officer and the accused. In S's case, the Court of Appeal was not persuaded that the officer was an *agent provocateur*. There was an element of entrapment and a trick, but (a) the tapes recorded not admissions about some previous offence but the actual offence being committed, (b) the tapes showed that S made the running and that the officer had taken a minimal role in the planning and had used no persuasion towards S, (c) the tapes were an accurate and unchallenged record and (d) the officer had not abused his role to ask questions which ought properly to have been asked as a police officer. In these circumstances, the judge's decision not to exclude the evidence was upheld. The outcome was the same in G's case: the facts were very similar and, although the first meeting between G and the officer was not recorded and there was a stark conflict of evidence as to what was said at that meeting, the existence of a total record was only one factor, and both the contents of the subsequent taped conversations and statements made by G in her formal police interviews supported the officer's account of the first meeting. In *Latif* [1996] 1 All ER 353, the accused was convicted of being knowingly concerned in the importation of drugs which had been brought into the country by an undercover customs officer. Although the accused had been lured into England by the deceit of an informer and both he and the undercover officer had possibly committed the offence of possessing heroin in Pakistan, the House of Lords upheld the trial judge's refusal to exclude the informer's evidence under s. 78. See also *Pattemore* [1994] Crim LR 836 and *Morley* [1994] Crim LR 919.

F2.39 In *Williams v DPP* [1993] 3 All ER 365 plain-clothes officers, as part of an investigation into thefts from vehicles in Essex, which was not directed at any specific individual, parked an insecure and unattended van, which appeared to contain a valuable load of cigarettes, in a busy street. Concealed officers later observed the accused removing cartons from the van. It was held that magistrates were entitled, in exercising their discretion under s. 78, to admit the police evidence. The officers were not acting as *agents provocateurs* and, following *DPP v Marshall* [1988] 3 All ER 683 (see **F2.34**) and the reasoning in *Christou* [1992] QB 979 (see **F2.44**), the trick was not applied to the accused: they voluntarily applied themselves to the trick. The argument that *Christou* could be distinguished, because in that case the police were seeking to obtain evidence of offences which had already been committed, was rejected. See also *Ealing London Borough Council v Woolworths plc* [1995] Crim LR 58, where a boy aged 11, acting on the instructions of trading standards officers, had purchased an 18-category video film. In *Nottingham City Council v Amin* [2000] 2 All ER 946, a taxi driver who was not licensed to ply for hire in a certain district, was flagged down there by plain-clothes officers who were then taken to their destination. A stipendiary magistrate used s. 78 to exclude the officers' evidence, having regard to the HRA 1998 and decisions of the ECtHR. On appeal, the respondent relied on *Teixeira de Castro v Portugal* (1998) 28 EHRR 101. In that case two undercover agents had instigated an offence and, since there was nothing to suggest that without their intervention it would have been committed, it was held that the intervention and use made of it at the trial amounted to a violation of the right to a fair trial under Article 6. (See also *Barkshire* [2011] EWCA Crim 1885.) Lord Bingham CJ distinguished the case on the basis that 'the facts...simply cannot lend themselves to the construction that this respondent was in any way prevailed upon or overborne or persuaded or pressured or instigated or incited to commit the offence'. Lord Bingham said (at pp. 1076–7):

> On the one hand it has been recognised as deeply offensive to ordinary notions of fairness if a defendant were to be convicted and punished for committing a crime which he only committed because he had been incited, instigated, persuaded, pressurised or wheedled into committing it by a law enforcement officer. On the other hand, it has been recognised that law enforcement agencies have a general duty to the public to enforce the law and it has been regarded as unobjectionable if a law enforcement officer gives a defendant an opportunity to break the law, of which the defendant freely takes advantage, in circumstances where it appears that the defendant would have behaved in the same way if the opportunity had been made by anyone else.

In *Loosely*, Lord Hoffmann made two important comments on this passage. First (at [54] and **F2.40** [55]), it was observed in relation to the final sentence that Lord Bingham obviously did not mean only that the accused would have responded in the same way to someone who was not a policeman, because the accused in such cases *ex hypothesi* has no knowledge that he is dealing with a policeman, and therefore such a condition would invariably be satisfied:

> What he meant was that the policemen behaved like ordinary members of the public in flagging the taxi down. They did not wave £50 notes or pretend to be in distress. The test of whether the law enforcement officer behaved like an ordinary member of the public works well and is likely to be decisive in many cases of regulatory offences committed with ordinary members of the public, such as selling liquor in unlicensed quantities (*DPP v Marshall* [1988] 3 All ER 683) ... But ordinary members of the public do not become involved in large scale drug dealing, conspiracy to rob...or hiring assassins (...*Smurthwaite* [1994] 1 All ER 898). The appropriate standards of behaviour are in such cases more problematic. And even in the case of offences committed with ordinary members of the public, other factors may require a purely causal test to be modified.

Secondly (at [70]), Lord Hoffmann observed that when Lord Bingham said that the accused should not be 'incited, instigated, persuaded, pressurised or wheedled' into committing the offence he was not intending each of those verbs to be given a disjunctive and technical meaning, but was intending to evoke a more general concept of conduct which causes the accused to commit the offence as opposed to giving him the opportunity to do so. 'No doubt a test purchaser who asks someone to sell him a drug is counselling and procuring, perhaps inciting the commission of an offence...But the fact that his actions are technically unlawful is not regarded in English law as a ground for treating them as an abuse of power: see *R v Latif* [1996] 1 All ER 353....' See also *Jones* [2010] 3 All ER 1186 and *East Riding of Yorkshire Council v Dearlove* [2012] RTR 388.

Undercover Operations after Commission of the Offence   As to evidence obtained by under- **F2.41** cover operations *after* commission of the offence, although the PACE 1984, s. 78(1), does apply, each case must be decided on its own facts. In *Jelen* (1989) 90 Cr App R 456, D, J and K were charged with conspiracy to commit false accounting. D pleaded guilty and after he was sentenced gave evidence for the prosecution in the case against J and K. D had been the first to be arrested. He made admissions and implicated J. That was the first that the police had heard of J's involvement and their view was that they would have had to caution J if they had sought to question him then but that they had insufficient evidence upon which they could have arrested and charged him. They accordingly asked D if he would obtain some corroboration of what he had told them by arranging to have a recorded conversation with J without J knowing that it was being recorded. D then held such a conversation with J in the course of which D lied to J, telling him that he had not said anything to the police. During the conversation, J made remarks from which his guilt could have been inferred. The trial judge admitted the evidence and the Court of Appeal held that although there was an element of entrapment, it could see no reason to disagree with the judge's conclusion. Cf. *H* [1987] Crim LR 47, which the court distinguished.

F2.42 In *Bailey* [1993] 3 All ER 513, two co-accused exercised their right to silence when interviewed by the police. They were charged, remanded in police custody and placed together in a bugged cell by officers who, in order to lull them into a false sense of security, pretended that they had been forced to put them in the same cell by an unco-operative custody officer. It was held that evidence of incriminating conversations between them, obtained by this police subterfuge, was admissible. Although the police were not entitled to question the accused further, they did not have to protect them from any opportunity to hold incriminating conversations, if they chose to do so, and there was nothing in the 1984 Act or Code of Practice C to prohibit them from bugging a cell, even after an accused had been charged and had exercised his right to silence. The judge was therefore entitled to admit the evidence. See also *Shaukat Ali* (1991) *The Times*, 19 February 1991, *Roberts* [1997] 1 Cr App R 217, *Mason* [2002] 2 Cr App R 628 and *Turner* [2013] EWCA Crim 642.

Similarly, although the deliberate flouting of the PACE 1984, s. 30 (see **D1.20**), for the sole purpose of creating an opportunity for a covert recording before an interview under caution, may, depending upon the circumstances, result in exclusion under s. 78, the fairness of the proceedings will not be affected where, as in *King* [2012] EWCA Crim 805, the officers neither engaged the accused in conversation nor tricked them into believing that they must make some response to their arrest, but merely gave them an opportunity to speak together in the belief that they were not being overheard. See also *Plunkett* [2013] 1 WLR 3121, where it was held that, even if there had been a breach of the RIPA 2000 or the PACE 1984, s. 30(1A), admissions covertly recorded were admissible because the breaches would have been minor given the seriousness of the crimes (aggravated burglary, false imprisonment and possession of a firearm) and the need to protect the victims of the crimes.

F2.43 In *Khan* [1997] AC 558 the police made a recording of an incriminating conversation relating to the importation of heroin, by means of a secret electronic surveillance device. The House of Lords held that the fact that evidence has been obtained in apparent or probable breach of the right to privacy set out in the ECHR, Article 8, or for that matter the law of a foreign country, is relevant to exercise of the s. 78 power, but the significance of such conduct is its effect, if any, upon the fairness of the proceedings. It therefore upheld the decision of the trial judge that the circumstances in which the evidence had been obtained, even if they constituted a breach of Article 8, did not require exclusion. In *Khan v UK* (2001) 31 EHRR 1016, the ECtHR held that, although the recording was obtained in breach of Article 8, its use at the trial did not violate the right to a fair hearing under Article 6. The court, repeating what it had said in previous judgments such as *Schenk v Switzerland*, held that the central question was whether the proceedings as a whole were fair. Noting that the accused had had the opportunity to challenge the admissibility of the evidence under s. 78, as well as its authenticity, the court found that the use of the evidence did not conflict with the requirements of fairness guaranteed by Article 6(1). Similar conclusions have also been reached by the ECtHR in respect of evidence obtained in breach of Article 8 by the unlawful installation of a listening device in the applicant's home (*Chalkley v UK* (2003) 37 EHRR 680) and by the unlawful use of covert listening devices at a police station (*PG* *and JH v UK* (2008) 46 EHRR 1272). See also *Mason* [2002] 2 Cr App R 628 and *Khan* [2013] EWCA Crim 2230, involving a breach of both the RIPA 2000 and Article 8. In *Perry v UK* (2004) 39 EHRR 76 there are dicta (at [40]) to suggest that where personal data is recorded in breach of Article 8, its use at trial in a public court-room may also constitute a breach of Article 8. However, in *Button* [2005] EWCA Crim 516, where video evidence had been obtained in breach of Article 8, the proposition that the court was bound to exclude such evidence because otherwise it would act unlawfully was rejected on the basis that the court played no part in the covert surveillance, which had already occurred, and breach of Article 8 was subsumed by the Article 6 duty to ensure a fair trial. As to covert filming, see also *Loveridge* [2001] 2 Cr App R 591 in which the accused was covertly and unlawfully filmed at court; *Marriner* [2002] EWCA Crim 2855, in which undercover journalists had made secret videos (as well as tape-recordings) of the accused; and *Rosenberg* [2006] EWCA Crim 6, where both R and the police were aware of surveillance carried out by the complainant but neither initiated nor encouraged by the police.

Khan v UK was distinguished in *Allan v UK* (2003) 36 EHRR 143, in which it was held that the use of statements obtained in a way which effectively undermines a suspect's right to make a meaningful choice whether to speak to the authorities or remain silent infringed procedural rights inherent in the ECHR, Article 6. A was convicted of murder. He had been interviewed by officers on several occasions, but acting on legal advice had consistently refused to answer questions. H, an experienced informer, who had undergone coaching by police officers, was fitted with recording devices and placed in A's cell for the specific purpose of questioning him to obtain information about the murder. At the trial H gave evidence that A had admitted his presence at the scene of the murder. However, this conversation, which proved to be decisive evidence at trial, was not recorded on tape. The court acknowledged that whether the right to silence is undermined to such an extent as to invoke Article 6 depends on the circumstances of the case, but was satisfied that evidence of the conversations with H had been obtained without sufficient regard to fair trial guarantees. The admissions allegedly made formed decisive evidence against him. They were not spontaneous but induced by persistent questioning of H who, at the instigation of the police, in effect interrogated A, but without any of the safeguards of a formal interview, including the issuing of a caution and the attendance of a solicitor. Compare *Bykov v Russia* [2010] ECHR 1517. When the case returned to the Court of Appeal (*Allan* [2004] EWCA Crim 2236), the conviction was quashed. It was held that H was a 'police stooge', an agent of the state carrying out the equivalent of interrogation after A had exercised a right of silence. The use of H to obtain admissions impinged on A's common-law right of silence and privilege against self-incrimination. The admission of H's evidence was in effect to allow the subversion of the provisions of PACE Code C serving to give procedural effect to the right to silence.

In *Christou*, the police set up a shop staffed by two undercover officers who purported to be **F2.44** willing to buy stolen jewellery. Transactions in the shop were recorded (on tape and video) in order to recover stolen property and obtain evidence against thieves and receivers. The accused, charged in consequence of the operation, sought to exclude evidence on the grounds that it had been obtained, without administering a caution in accordance with para. 10.1 of Code of Practice C, by a trick designed to deprive them of their privilege against self-incrimination. The Court of Appeal, distinguishing *Payne* [1963] 1 All ER 848 (see **F2.19**) and *Mason* [1988] 3 All ER 481 (see **F2.34**), held that the accused had voluntarily applied themselves to the trick and this had resulted in no unfairness. It was further held that although the officers had grounds to suspect the accused of having committed an offence, para. 10.1 of Code of Practice C was not intended to apply to the facts in question. It was designed to protect suspects who are vulnerable to abuse or pressure from officers, or who may believe themselves to be so. Where a suspect, even if not in detention, is being questioned by an officer acting as such, for the purpose of obtaining evidence, the parties are not on equal terms; the officer is perceived to be in a position of authority and the suspect may be intimidated or undermined. The accused, however, were not questioned by officers acting as such, conversation was on equal terms and there was no question of pressure or intimidation. *Christou* was applied in *Maclean* [1993] Crim LR 687, a very similar case in which a person suspected of the illegal importation of drugs 'applied himself to the trick', which was the opportunity of holding a conversation with a car salvage operator, who was in reality a customs officer. In *Cadette* [1995] Crim LR 229 a suspected drug courier, at the request of customs officers, telephoned C, pretended that she had not been arrested and tried to persuade C to come to the airport. Evidence of their conversation was admitted. It was held that although there comes a point when officers may move from following up available lines of inquiry in order to obtain evidence to a stage where they seek in effect to deprive a suspect of the protection afforded by the 1984 Act and Codes, the officers had not crossed the line. See also *Mason* [2002] 2 Cr App R 628.

In *Christou*, Lord Taylor CJ further held that it *would* be wrong for the police to adopt an under-cover pose or disguise to enable them to ask questions about an offence uninhibited by Code of Practice C and with the effect of circumventing it, and a judge could then exclude under s. 78. In that case, however, questions asked by the officers about the origin of the goods formed a part of their undercover pose as receivers — such information would prevent them from reselling the goods in the area from which they were stolen. See also *Lin* [1995] Crim LR 817, where an undercover officer was introduced to the accused not for the purpose of obtaining evidence about a past offence involving a stolen Inland Revenue cheque, but to discover the future plans of the accused in relation to an on-going conspiracy to handle stolen cheques. It was held that a conversation about the Inland Revenue cheque was a necessary part of establishing the officer's credentials as a 'criminal'. The position was different in *Bryce* [1992] 4 All ER 567, where an undercover officer, in conversations with the accused about a car, asked how recently it had been stolen. The accused replied 'two to three days' and added 'we are having two a week away. Would you be interested in any others?' The Court of Appeal, quashing the conviction for handling, held that the evidence of these conversations should have been excluded. The questions were not necessary to the maintenance of the undercover pose. They went directly to the issue of guilty knowledge, they were disputed, there was no caution and there were no contemporary records.

F2.45 **Bad Faith** The common-law discretion to exclude evidence obtained unlawfully will not be exercised if those who obtained the evidence made a bona fide mistake as to their powers; but it may be exercised if such persons resorted to trickery, deception or oppression (*Fox* [1986] AC 281). Some of the authorities on the PACE 1984, s. 78, draw the same distinction, laying great stress on whether the police acted *mala fide*, *knowingly* exceeding their powers. In *Matto v Wolverhampton Crown Court* [1987] RTR 337, the accused was convicted of driving with excess alcohol. Police officers, when requesting a specimen of breath on the accused's property, realised that they were acting illegally. The specimen proved positive. The accused was then arrested and, at the police station, provided another positive specimen. The appeal was allowed on the grounds that, the officers having acted *mala fide* and oppressively, the Crown Court, had it directed itself properly, could have exercised its discretion under s. 78 to exclude the evidence. See also *Mason* [1988] 3 All ER 481, in which a *deliberate* deceit was practised on both the accused and his solicitor and *Canale* [1990] 2 All ER 187, in which it was held that had the trial judge directed his mind to breaches of the interview rules under Code of Practice C which were 'flagrant', 'deliberate' and 'cynical', he would and should have concluded that the interviews should be excluded under s. 78.

F2.46 Other authorities, however, adopting an approach designed to protect the suspect from being denied his civil rights, make it clear that the statutory discretion may be exercised even in the absence of *deliberate* or *wilful* misconduct. Thus, in *DPP v McGladrigan* [1991] RTR 297, the Divisional Court held that the argument on *mala fides* originated from *Fox*, a case decided before the PACE 1984 came into force, and that s. 78(1) of the 1984 Act gave the courts a new and considerably wider discretion. The court relied upon *Samuel* [1988] QB 615 to reject the argument that *mala fides* had to be established before the statutory discretion could be exercised. The court also pointed out that, insofar as *Matto v Wolverhampton Crown Court* suggested that in breathalyser cases *Fox* still applied, it should be noted that the case was not only a successful appeal by the accused, but also preceded *Samuel*. See also *Brine* [1992] Crim LR 123. In *Foster* [1987] Crim LR 821, where no contemporaneous record of an interview had been made, there was no record of a reason for not having made such a record and the accused was not given the opportunity to read and sign the record of the interview, it was ruled that it was irrelevant whether the breaches were wilful or merely ignorant; in the absence of a contemporaneous record at the trial, the accused was deprived of the opportunity to demonstrate that his denial of the offence was not an afterthought but a denial which he made at the time of his arrest.

In *Alladice* (1988) 87 Cr App R 380, a case in which the accused had been improperly denied the **F2.47** right of access to a solicitor pursuant to the PACE 1984, s. 58, Lord Lane CJ, giving the reserved judgment of the Court of Appeal, held that if the police had acted in bad faith, the court would have little difficulty in ruling any confession inadmissible under s. 78; but that if the police, albeit in good faith, had nevertheless fallen foul of s. 58, it was still necessary for the court to decide whether admission of the evidence would adversely affect the fairness of the proceedings to such an extent that the confession ought to be excluded. (On the facts, however, it was held that had the trial judge considered s. 78, he would not have been obliged to exclude the evidence because the accused was well able to cope with the interviews, understood the cautions that he had been given — at times exercising his right to silence — and was aware of his rights. Thus if the solicitor had been present, his advice would have added nothing to the knowledge of his rights which the accused already had.) See also *Dunford* (1990) 91 Cr App R 150; *Parris* (1988) 89 Cr App R 68; *Walsh* (1989) 91 Cr App R 161; and *Anderson* [1993] Crim LR 447. In *Walsh*, Saville J, referring to breaches of s. 58 or the provisions of the Codes of Practice, said (at p. 163):

> …although bad faith may make substantial or significant that which might not otherwise be so, the contrary does not follow. Breaches which are themselves significant and substantial are not rendered otherwise by the good faith of the officers concerned.

Significant and Substantial Breaches In *Quinn* [1990] Crim LR 581, *Walsh* (1989) 91 Cr **F2.48** App R 161 and *Keenan* [1990] 2 QB 54 were referred to with approval as authority for the general proposition that a significant and substantial breach of a PACE Code may well result in the exclusion of evidence obtained in consequence, even in the absence of bad faith. Whether a breach is 'significant and substantial' for these purposes is clearly a question of fact and degree. In *Sparks* [1991] Crim LR 128 (in which the proviso to s. 2(1) of the Criminal Appeal Act 1968 was applied), breaches of Code C (failure to caution and failure to keep a proper interview record) were held to be substantial. See also *Okafor* [1994] 3 All ER 741 (failure to caution, to remind of the right to legal advice and to make a contemporaneous record of interview); *Coelho* [2008] EWCA Crim 627 (failure to record in the original language a statement made other than in English and failure to provide an opportunity to the suspect to read a record and check its accuracy) and *Joseph* [1993] Crim LR 206 (failure to make contemporaneous record of interview), but cf. *Watson v DPP* (2004) 168 JP 116. In *Pall* (1992) 156 JP 424, it was held that the absence of a caution was bound to be significant in most circumstances. In *Ibrahim* [2008] 2 Cr App R 311, where guidance was given on the application of s. 78 to 'safety interviews' carried out under the TA 2000, sch. 8, it was said that much will turn on the nature of the warning or caution given, if any. See also, concerning breaches of Code D, *Samms* [1991] Crim LR 197 (identification by confrontation: failure to show that it was impracticable to hold a parade or a group identification), *Marcus* [2004] EWCA Crim 3387 (failure in a video identification procedure to use images of persons bearing a sufficient resemblance to the accused) and *Preddie* [2011] EWCA Crim 312 (improper street identification that rendered valueless a subsequent video identification procedure). Contrast *Rajakuruna* [1991] Crim LR 458, where a breach of Code C (failure to inform a person not under arrest that he is not obliged to remain with the officer) was held to be not significant or substantial. In appropriate circumstances, breach of the right to legal advice in the PACE 1984, s. 58, and in the ECHR, Article 6(3)(c), may result in the exclusion of evidence (see generally **F17.30**). However, in the case of drink-driving offences the public interest requires that the obtaining of breath specimens should not be delayed to any significant extent in order to enable a suspect to take legal advice (*Campbell v DPP* (2002) 166

JP 742; *Kennedy v CPS* (2003) 167 JP 267); and it is a question of fact and degree in any given case whether the custody officer acted without delay to secure the provision of legal advice and whether the person held in custody was permitted to consult a solicitor as soon as was practicable (*Kirkup v DPP* (2004) 168 JP 255; *Whitley v DPP* (2004) 168 JP 350). Similarly, in the case of juveniles, there is no reason to delay the obtaining of specimens in order for an appropriate adult to be present (*R (DPP) v B* (2003) 167 JP 144).

F2.49   It is important to stress that the test for exclusion is not the seriousness of the breach *per se*, but the extent of any unfairness caused thereby (see **F2.31**). In *Ryan* [1992] Crim LR 187, it was argued that the judge's conclusion that there had been a major breach of the identification code (Code of Practice D) should have sufficed to exclude the evidence. Rejecting this argument, the Court of Appeal pointed out that there had been occasions when there had been quite serious breaches but, it being established that this had not caused unjust prejudice to the accused, the judge had quite properly allowed the evidence in. In *Hoyte* [1994] Crim LR 215 a confession was admitted, despite a failure to caution, on the basis that the police had acted in good faith and, in the circumstances, there could have been no unfairness under s. 78. The outcome was the same in *Senior* [2004] 3 All ER 9, where customs officers had asked a series of preliminary 'routine' questions without first cautioning the accused, and also in *Devani* [2008] 1 Cr App R 65, where the accused was a solicitor and the questioning, which was not oppressive, took place in the presence of her principal. See also, applying *Senior*, *Rehman* [2006] EWCA Crim 1900. Similarly in *Gill* [2004] 4 All ER 681 evidence obtained in a 'Hansard' interview was admitted, despite a failure to caution, on the basis that the interviewers had not acted in bad faith and the interviewees knew that criminal proceedings were in prospect and must have known that they were not obliged to answer questions. See also *Law-Thompson* [1997] Crim LR 674 (confessions made by a mentally disordered accused in the absence of an appropriate adult).

F2.50   In *Wright* [1994] Crim LR 55, evidence of a search was admitted notwithstanding that a record of the search had not been made in W's custody record (contrary to s. 18(8) of the 1984 Act) and that there were said to have been breaches of PACE Code B (no communication had been made with W, he was not present at the search and no proper list had been made of the property). Noting that there had been no deliberate breach of Code B, it was held that the judge had taken into account the breach of s. 18(8) and the other matters could not have placed W at any disadvantage. See also *Khan* [1997] Crim LR 508 and *Sanghera* [2001] 1 Cr App R 299.

Telephone Interceptions

F2.51   Chapter 1 of part I of the RIPA 2000 replaced the Interception of Communications Act 1985 and regulates the interception of communications in the course of their transmission by a public postal service or by a public or private telecommunications service. A conversation between two people face-to-face which is overheard by means of a listening device does not constitute a conversation in the course of a transmission (*Allsop* [2005] EWCA Crim 703). Interception of communications without authorisation under the Act is an offence (s. 1(1) and (2) and see **B9.84**) and may also be a tort (s. 1(3)).

F2.52   Certain interceptions may be lawfully carried out without a warrant (ss. 3 and 4). Under s. 3(2), interception of a communication that is sent by, or intended for, a person who has consented to the interception is lawful provided that it is authorised as a directed surveillance. Other than interceptions under ss. 3 and 4, interceptions require a warrant issued by the Secretary of State (s. 5). The grounds for issuing a warrant are set out in s. 5(2) and (3). Substantial restrictions apply to the use of intercepted material. In general, no evidence shall be adduced, questions asked, assertion or disclosure made, or other things done, in, for the purposes of, or in connection with legal proceedings, which would tend to show that an offence under s. 1(1) or (2) was or may have been committed or that an application for an interception warrant has been made (s. 17, and see *A-G's Ref (No. 5 of 2002)* [2005] 1 AC 167). This is subject to exceptions specified in s. 18. It is not contrary to s. 17 for evidence to be adduced as to whether an interception was of a public or private telecommunications system (*A-G's Ref (No. 5 of 2002) (W)* [2003] 1 WLR 2902). The restrictions do not apply to evidence of interceptions conducted outside the jurisdiction. In *P* [2002] 1 AC 46, the House of Lords rejected an argument that the admissibility of telephone interceptions made overseas, in accordance with both the laws of the country in question and the ECHR, would infringe Article 6. It was held that (1) the criterion of fairness under Article 6 is the same as that to be applied by a judge under the PACE 1984, s. 78; (2) the fair use of interception evidence at a trial is not a breach of Article 6 even if the evidence was unlawfully obtained; (3) it is a cogent factor in favour of the admission of such evidence that one of the parties to the conversation is to be a witness and give evidence of what was said during it; and (4) there is no principle of exclusion of interception evidence in English law independent of the Interception of Communications Act 1985 (see now the RIPA 2000). In *Sargent* [2003] 1 AC 347, a decision under the 1985 Act, it was held that there is no rule prohibiting the use of inadmissible interceptions at police interviews and that, subject to the PACE 1984, s. 78, such use will not render the interview evidence inadmissible.

In *Mahmood* [2014] 1 Cr App R 434 (31), it was held that a blanket interception and recording   **F2.53** of the telephone calls of prisoners at two prisons did not constitute a breach of the RIPA 2000. Under s. 4(4) of the Act, interception of a communication is authorised if it is in exercise of a power conferred by or under rules made under the Prison Act 1952, s. 47. It was held that under the Prison Rules 1999, rr. 34 and 35A, the Secretary of State is empowered to impose restrictions and conditions on the telephone calls made by prisoners either across the entire prison estate or in relation to particular prisoners or classes of prisoners.

Section F3 Burden and Standard of Proof and Presumptions

BURDEN OF PROOF

Legal and Evidential Burdens

F3.1 There are two principal kinds of burden, the legal burden and the evidential burden. The legal burden is a burden of proof, i.e. a burden imposed on a party to prove a fact or facts in issue. In some cases the legal burden in relation to some of the facts in issue will be on one party, and the legal burden in relation to another (or others) will be on the other party. For example, if insanity is raised by way of defence, the legal burden on that issue is on the defence, whereas the legal burden on the other facts in issue is on the prosecution (*M'Naghten's Case* (1843) 10 Cl & F 200; *Smith* (1910) 6 Cr App R 19). Any statutory provision imposing a legal burden on the accused may be open to challenge on the basis of incompatibility with Article 6(2) of the ECHR (see **F3.18**). Questions of construction are questions of law in respect of which no burden lies on either party (*Scott v Martin* [1987] 2 All ER 813).

F3.2 **The Legal Burden** The legal burden is sometimes referred to as the persuasive burden or the risk of non-persuasion, phrases which indicate that a party bearing the legal burden on a fact in issue will lose on that issue if the burden is not discharged to the required standard of proof. The standard of proof required to discharge the legal burden varies according to whether the burden is borne by the prosecution or defence. If the legal burden is borne by the prosecution, the standard required is proof beyond reasonable doubt (*Woolmington v DPP* [1935] AC 462 — see further **F3.49**). If the legal burden is borne by the accused, the standard required is proof on a balance of probabilities (*Carr-Briant* [1943] KB 607); the accused never bears the heavier burden of proof beyond reasonable doubt — see further **F3.54**). The question whether a party has discharged a legal burden borne by him is decided by the tribunal of fact, whether jury or magistrates, at the end of the trial after all the evidence has been presented.

F3.3 **The Evidential Burden** The evidential burden is not a burden of proof but the burden of adducing evidence or 'the duty of passing the judge', in other words the burden imposed on a party to adduce sufficient evidence on a fact or facts in issue to satisfy the judge that such issue or issues should be left before the tribunal of fact. In some cases, the evidential burden on some of the facts in issue will be on one party and the evidential burden on another (or others) will be on the other party. Very often a party bearing the legal burden on an issue also bears the evidential burden on that issue. However, in the case of many defences (including, for example, self-defence), the evidential burden in relation to the defence is on the accused and the legal burden in relation to the defence is on the prosecution. Thus, if there is no evidence sufficient to justify a jury concluding that the defence is established, the issue will be withdrawn from them, and such withdrawal will not amount to a breach of the ECHR, Article 6 (*Bianco* [2001] EWCA Crim 2516 at [15], approved in *Batchelor* [2013] EWCA Crim 2638). However, if there is sufficient evidence for the defence to be put before the jury, the legal burden of disproving it will be on the prosecution (see, e.g., *Lobell* [1957] 1 QB 547 and see generally **F3.37** to **F3.47**) and this will be the case even if the judge takes the view that the evidence is most unlikely to be of sufficient cogency or strength to be accepted by the jury (*Hammond* [2013] EWCA Crim 2709 at [6]).

Although normally a judge will not leave a particular defence to the jury until the conclusion of the evidence, in rare cases in which the precise nature of the evidence to be called is clear it may be appropriate for the judge to indicate at an earlier stage what his ruling is likely to be (*Pommell* [1995] 2 Cr App R 607 at p. 612). If, during a trial, a judge indicates that he will leave a particular defence to the jury, but later changes his view, he should inform the defence, because they may then wish to give more evidence on the matter and defence counsel may wish to seek to persuade the judge not to withdraw the issue (*Wright* [1992] Crim LR 596).

Discharge of Burdens Borne by the Prosecution   If the evidential burden on a particular issue   **F3.4** is borne by the prosecution, it is discharged by the adduction of sufficient evidence to justify as a possibility a finding by the tribunal of fact that the legal burden on the same issue has been discharged, in other words 'such evidence as, if believed and if left uncontradicted and unexplained, could be accepted by the jury as proof' (*Jayasena v The Queen* [1970] AC 618, per Lord Devlin at p. 624). If the prosecution bear both the evidential and legal burden on a particular issue and discharge the evidential burden, it does not necessarily follow that they will succeed on that issue — the issue in question will go before the jury for them to determine whether or not the legal burden has been discharged. However, if the prosecution bear both the legal and evidential burden on an issue and fail to discharge the evidential burden, they will necessarily fail on that issue, since the judge will withdraw that issue from the jury. Questions relating to the sufficiency of the evidence adduced by the prosecution may be raised by the judge of his own motion, but usually arise on a defence submission of no case to answer after the prosecution have closed their case. As to submissions of no case to answer more generally, see **D16.54** *et seq.*

Discharge of Burdens Borne by the Defence   If the accused bears both the evidential and the   **F3.5** legal burden on a particular issue, e.g. insanity, the evidential burden is discharged by the adduction of such evidence as might satisfy the jury on the probability of that which the accused is called upon to establish (*Carr-Briant* [1943] KB 607, per Humphreys J at p. 612). If the accused bears the evidential but not the legal burden on a particular issue, e.g. self-defence, the evidential burden is discharged by the adduction of such evidence as 'might leave a jury in reasonable doubt' (*Bratty v A-G for Northern Ireland* [1963] AC 386, per Lord Morris at p. 419). In no case is the accused called upon to prove a fact beyond reasonable doubt: the standard of proof is proof on the balance of probabilities (*Carr-Briant*).

Incidence of Legal Burden: General Rule

The general rule is that the prosecution bear the legal burden of proving all the elements in the   **F3.6** offence necessary to establish guilt (*Woolmington v DPP* [1935] AC 462). See also *Mancini v DPP* [1942] AC 1, per Lord Simon at p. 11. In *Woolmington*, W was charged with the murder of his wife, who had left him to return to her mother. He visited her with a sawn-off shotgun concealed under his coat, and when they met she was killed by a shot from the gun. W said that while attempting to induce his wife to return to him by threatening to kill himself, the gun went off accidentally. Swift J directed the jury that, once it was proved that W shot his wife, W bore the burden of disproving malice aforethought. The House of Lords held this to be a misdirection. Viscount Sankey LC said, at pp. 481–2:

> But while the prosecution must prove the guilt of the prisoner, there is no such burden laid on the prisoner to prove his innocence and it is sufficient for him to raise a doubt as to his guilt; he is not bound to satisfy the jury of his innocence....

> Throughout the web of the English criminal law one golden thread is always to be seen, that it is the duty of the prosecution to prove the prisoner's guilt subject to what I have already said as to the defence of insanity and subject also to any statutory exception....No matter what the charge or where the trial, the principle that the prosecution must prove the guilt of the prisoner is part of the common law of England and no attempt to whittle it down can be entertained....It is not the law of

F

Part F Evidence

England to say, as was said in the summing-up in the present case: 'if the Crown satisfy you that this woman died at the prisoner's hands then he has to show that there are circumstances to be found in the evidence which has been given from the witness-box in this case which alleviate the crime so that it is only manslaughter or which excuse the homicide altogether by showing it was a pure accident'.

F3.7   The prosecution bear the burden of proving all the elements in the offence, even if this involves proving negative averments. Thus, in a case of rape the prosecution bear the burden of proving that the complainant did not consent (*Horn* (1912) 7 Cr App R 200). Similarly, the prosecution bear the burden of proving absence of consent on a charge of assault (*Donovan* [1934] 2 KB 498). Furthermore, if capacity to consent is in issue, the prosecution will also bear the burden of proving incapacity (*A (G)* [2014] 2 Cr App R 73 (5)). For the former offence of obtaining by deception, the prosecution bore the burden of proving the falsity of the statement, even if that involved proving a negative (*Mandry* [1973] 3 All ER 996, in which the statement, made by street traders selling scent for £1, was 'You can go down the road and buy it for two guineas in the big stores'). *Mandry* also illustrates that there is a limit to what can reasonably be required of the prosecution when seeking to prove a negative. A constable gave evidence that he had visited four shops in the area and that the scent was not sold at any of them. In cross-examination, he admitted that he had not visited a well-known department store. The judge directed the jury that the police could not be expected to visit every shop in London in order to prove that the scent was not being sold for two guineas in any shop; and that if the accused knew of any shop where it could be bought at that price, they were perfectly entitled to adduce such evidence. The Court of Appeal held that no criticism could be made of this direction. In many cases, however, because of the difficulties of proving a negative proposition, statute may, exceptionally, require the accused to bear the burden of proving certain facts (see **F3.9** to **F3.17**).

There are only three categories of exception to the general rule as laid down in *Woolmington v DPP* [1935] AC 462:

(a) insanity;
(b) express statutory exceptions; and
(c) implied statutory exceptions.

Statutory exceptions are sometimes referred to as reverse onus provisions.

F3.8   **Exception in Case of Defence of Insanity**   If the accused raises the defence of insanity, he will bear the burden of proving it (on a balance of probabilities) (*M'Naghten's Case* (1843) 10 Cl & F 200; *Smith* (1910) 6 Cr App R 19; *Sodeman v The King* [1936] 2 All ER 1138). Under the Criminal Procedure (Insanity) Act 1964, s. 6, if the accused is charged with murder and raises one of two issues, either insanity or diminished responsibility, the court shall allow the prosecution to adduce evidence tending to prove the other of those issues. The burden on the prosecution will be to prove the other of those issues beyond reasonable doubt (*Grant* [1960] Crim LR 424, per Paul J).

Criminal Procedure (Insanity) Act 1964, s. 6

Where on a trial for murder the accused contends—
(a) that at the time of the alleged offence he was insane so as not to be responsible according to law for his actions; or
(b) that at that time he was suffering from such abnormality of mental functioning as is specified in subsection (1) of section 2 of the Homicide Act 1957 (diminished responsibility),
the court shall allow the prosecution to adduce or elicit evidence tending to prove the other of those contentions, and may give directions as to the stage of the proceedings at which the prosecution may adduce such evidence.

If an accused is alleged to be under a disability rendering him unfit to plead and stand trial on indictment, the issue may be raised by either the prosecution or defence (see the Criminal Procedure (Insanity) Act 1964, s. 4, and generally **D12.2** *et seq.*). If the prosecution contend that the accused is under such a disability and this is disputed by the defence, the burden of proof is on the prosecution to satisfy the court beyond reasonable doubt (*Robertson* [1968] 3 All ER 557). If the defence contend that the accused is under such a disability, the burden is on the defence on a balance of probabilities (*Podola* [1960] 1 QB 325).

Express Statutory Exceptions   Statute may expressly cast on the accused the burden of prov-   **F3.9**
ing a particular issue or issues. The legal burden in relation to all other issues in such cases will
remain on the prosecution, in accordance with the general rule as laid down in *Woolmington
v DPP* [1935] AC 462. Prior to the coming into force of the HRA 1998, it could be said with
confidence that statutory provisions which put on the accused an obligation to 'prove' a particular matter, had thereby cast a legal burden on the defence. However provisions of this kind
and the decisions pertaining to them must now be read subject to the decision of the House of
Lords in *Lambert* [2002] 2 AC 545 (discussed at **F3.19**) that in appropriate circumstances the
words 'to prove' may be read down under the HRA 1998, s. 3, so as to impose on an accused no
more than an evidential burden.

An example of an express statutory exception is the Homicide Act 1957, s. 2.

Homicide Act 1957, s. 2

(2) On a charge of murder, it shall be for the defence to prove that the person charged is by virtue
of this section not liable to be convicted of murder.

Where the defence of diminished responsibility is raised, the onus is on the defence to prove
it on a balance of probabilities (*Dunbar* [1958] 1 QB 1; *Grant* [1960] Crim LR 424). Section
2(2) does not contravene the ECHR, Article 6(2), and should not be read down as imposing on
the defence only an evidential burden (*Lambert* [2001] 1 All ER 1014, affirmed in *Foye* (2013)
177 JP 449).

Section 2(2) leaves it to the defence to decide whether the issue of diminished responsibility
should be raised; if, therefore, the judge detects evidence of diminished responsibility but the
defence do not raise the issue, the judge is not bound to direct the jury to consider the matter,
but, at most, should in the absence of the jury draw the matter to the attention of the defence so
that they may decide whether they wish the issue to be considered by the jury (*Campbell* (1986)
84 Cr App R 255, per Lord Lane CJ, *obiter*).

Another example of an express statutory exception is the Prevention of Crime Act 1953, s. 1   **F3.10**
(see **B12.138**). In the case of an offensive weapon *per se*, the prosecution are not required to
prove that the accused had it with him with the intention of using it to cause injury to the person; if possession in a public place is proved, the onus is on the accused to prove on a balance
of probabilities lawful authority or reasonable excuse for the possession (*Davis v Alexander*
(1970) 54 Cr App R 398). In the case of an article not made or adapted for use for causing
injury to the person, the onus is on the prosecution to prove that the accused carried it with
the intention of using it to injure; and if the jury are satisfied as to this, and the issue of lawful
authority or reasonable excuse has been raised, the onus is on the accused to prove on a balance of probabilities such authority or excuse (*Petrie* [1961] 1 All ER 466; *Brown* (1971) 55
Cr App R 478).

A final example is the Homicide Act 1957, s. 4(2) ('Where it is shown that a person charged
with the murder of another killed the other or was a party to his...being killed, it shall be for
the defence to prove that the person charged was acting in pursuance of a suicide pact between
him and the other').

Implied Statutory Exceptions   A statute can place the legal burden of proof on the accused   **F3.11**
not only expressly but also by implication, i.e. on its true construction. In summary trials, the
matter is governed by the MCA 1980, s. 101. Concerning trials on indictment, the leading
authorities are *Edwards* [1975] QB 27 and *Hunt* [1987] AC 352; in the latter it was made clear
that when, in *Woolmington v DPP* [1935] AC 462, Viscount Sankey LC referred to 'any statutory exception' (see **F3.6**), he was referring to statutory exceptions in which Parliament had
placed the burden of proof on the accused *either* expressly *or* by implication (per Lords Griffiths
and Ackner).

Magistrates' Courts Act 1980, s. 101

> Where the defendant to an information or complaint relies for his defence on any exception, exemption, proviso, excuse or qualification, whether or not it accompanies the description of the offence or matter of complaint in the enactment creating the offence or on which the complaint is founded, the burden of proving the exception, exemption, proviso, excuse or qualification shall be on him; and this notwithstanding that the information or complaint contains an allegation negativing the exception, exemption, proviso, excuse or qualification.

The cases, in the ensuing commentary, in which statutory provisions have been so construed as to place a legal burden on the accused, must now be read subject to the HRA 1998 and the decisions discussed at **F3.18** *et seq*. Any implied statutory exception must now be open to challenge on the basis of incompatibility with the ECHR, Article 6(2). As to summary trials, it is submitted that 'the burden of proving' to which the MCA 1980, s. 101, refers always means the legal burden and therefore any implied statutory exception is capable of derogating from Article 6(2). It follows that for each such exception the question of compatibility will need to be considered by reference to the three-stage test set out in *Lambert* [2002] 2 AC 545, discussed at **F3.19** (cf. per Clarke LJ in *R (Grundy & Co Excavations Ltd) v Halton Division Magistrates' Court* (2003) 167 JP 387 at [60] and [61]).

F3.12 Concerning the construction of s. 101, the following matters of general importance should also be noted:

(a) On its wording, s. 101 applies to summary trials. However, it is now established that where a statute, on its true construction, places the legal burden of proof on an accused, the burden is on the accused whether the case be tried summarily or on indictment; s. 101 reflects and applies to summary trials the common-law rule relating to the incidence of the burden of proof evolved by judges on trials on indictment (*Hunt* [1987] AC 352).

(b) The section applies where the words of exception etc. amount to a defence.

(c) In *Nimmo v Alexander Cowan & Sons Ltd* [1968] AC 107, Lord Pearson gave the following *obiter* guidance (at p. 135) as to the construction of the Scottish equivalent of s. 101. An exemption, exception or proviso is easily recognisable from the wording of the enactment — an exception would naturally begin with the word 'except' and a proviso with the words 'Provided always that'. The addition of the words 'excuse' and 'qualification' showed an intention to widen the provision. There is no usual formula for an 'excuse'. A 'qualification', if understood in a grammatical sense, might cover any adjective, adverb or adjectival or adverbial phrase. More probably it means some qualification, such as a licence, for doing what would otherwise be unlawful. There is no usual formula for 'qualification' in that sense. The court should look at the substance and effect of the enactment in question, as well as its form, in order to ascertain whether it contains an 'excuse or qualification'.

F3.13 In a case of driving without a licence, it is for the accused driver to prove that he has a current driving licence (*John v Humphreys* [1955] 1 All ER 793). Similarly, in cases of driving without insurance, it is for the accused driver to prove that he is insured (*Williams v Russell* (1933) 149 LT 190; *Philcox v Carberry* [1960] Crim LR 563). In *Gatland v Metropolitan Police Commissioner* [1968] 2 QB 279, the accused had left a skip on the road with which a car had collided. They were charged with an offence under the Highways Act 1959, s. 140(1), which provided that 'if a person, without lawful authority or excuse, deposits anything whatsoever on a highway in consequence whereof a user of the highway is injured or endangered, that person shall be guilty of an offence'. The Divisional Court held that it was for the prosecution to prove that a thing had been deposited on the highway and that in consequence a user of the highway had been injured or endangered; but that it was for the accused to prove lawful authority or excuse. Contrast, *Westminster City Council v Croyalgrange* [1986] 2 All ER 353. See also, construing Environmental Protection Act 1990, s. 33(1)(a), *Environment Agency v M.E. Foley Contractors Ltd* [2002] 1 WLR 1756.

Nimmo v Alexander Cowan & Sons Ltd   *Nimmo v Alexander Cowan & Sons Ltd* [1968] AC   **F3.14**
107 was a Scottish civil action brought by a workman under the Factories Act 1961, s. 29(1)
(now repealed). Section 29(1) provided that every place at which any person has at any time
to work 'shall, so far as is reasonably practicable, be made and kept safe for any person working
there'. The question before the House of Lords was whether the burden of proving that it was not
reasonably practicable to make the working place safe lay on the defendant or the pursuer. The
same question could have arisen in a criminal action: s. 155(1) of the 1961 Act made a breach of
s. 29(1) a summary offence. Both Lord Pearson (at p. 134) and Lord Reid (at p. 115) observed
that the incidence of the burden of proof would be the same whether the proceedings were civil or
criminal. The House divided on the construction of the section. The majority held that it was for
the pursuer (or prosecution) to prove that the working place was not safe, and for the defendant
(or accused) to excuse himself by proving that it was not reasonably practicable to make it safe.
Their lordships were in agreement, however, that if the linguistic construction of a statute does
not clearly indicate on whom the burden should lie, the court should look to other considerations to determine the intention of Parliament, such as the mischief at which the Act was aimed
and the ease or difficulty that the respective parties would encounter in discharging the burden.

Edwards   The MCA 1980, s. 101, sets out in statutory form the common-law rule which   **F3.15**
applies to trials on indictment. This was established in *Edwards* [1975] QB 27. Prior to *Edwards*
there was a rule of statutory interpretation that 'if a negative averment be made by one party
which is peculiarly within the knowledge of the other, the party within whose knowledge it lies,
and who asserts the affirmative, is to prove it and not he who asserts the negative' (*Turner* (1816)
5 M & S 206, per Bayley J at p. 211). This approach was followed in *Oliver* [1944] KB 68 and
Ewens [1967] 1 QB 322.

In *Edwards* [1975] QB 27, the accused was convicted on indictment of selling intoxicating
liquor without a licence, contrary to the Licensing Act 1964, s. 160(1)(a). He appealed on the
ground that the prosecution had failed to adduce any evidence to show that he was not the
holder of a licence. It was submitted that at common law the burden of proving an exception,
exemption and the like is borne by the accused only if the facts constituting such exception or
exemption are peculiarly within the accused's own knowledge which, in the instant case, they
were not, because the police had access to the public register of local licences. The Court of
Appeal, dismissing the appeal, held that it was for the accused to prove that he was the holder of
a licence. Referring to the common-law exception to the fundamental rule that the prosecution
must prove every element of the offence charged, Lawton LJ said, at p. 40:

> It is limited to offences arising under enactments which prohibit the doing of an act save in specified
> circumstances or by persons of specified classes or with specified qualifications or with the licence
> or permission of specified authorities. Whenever the prosecution seeks to rely on this exception,
> the court must construe the enactment under which the charge is laid. If the true construction is
> that the enactment prohibits the doing of acts, subject to provisos, exemptions and the like, then
> the prosecution can rely upon the exception.
>
> In our judgment its application does not depend upon either the fact, or the presumption, that the
> defendant has peculiar knowledge enabling him to prove the positive of any negative averment.

Hunt   In *Hunt* [1987] AC 352, the House of Lords held that: **F3.16**

(a) *Edwards* was decided correctly, subject to one qualification. The formula given by Lawton
    LJ was 'a helpful approach' and 'an excellent guide to construction' but was not intended
    to be, and is not, exclusive in its effect — on rare occasions a statute will be construed as
    imposing the legal burden on the accused although outside the ambit of the formula (see
    the speech of Lord Griffiths, with which Lords Keith and Mackay agreed, at p. 365 and that
    of Lord Ackner at p. 379).
(b) In the final analysis each case must turn on the construction of the particular legislation
    to determine whether the defence is an exception within the meaning of the MCA 1980,
    s. 101, which reflects the rule for trials on indictment (per Lord Griffiths at p. 375).

(c) In construing an enactment in order to ascertain where the burden of proof lies, the court is not restricted to the form or wording of the statutory provision but is entitled to have regard to matters of policy. The court must look at the substance and effect of the enactment and practical considerations affecting the burden of proof, particularly the ease or difficulty that the respective parties would encounter in discharging the burden (per Lord Griffiths at p. 375 and per Lord Ackner at pp. 380 and 382). However, Parliament can never lightly be taken to have intended to impose an onerous duty on an accused to prove his innocence in a criminal case, and a court should be very slow to draw any such inference from the language of a statute (per Lord Griffiths at p. 374).

F3.17   In *Hunt*, the appellant was found to be in possession of a powder containing morphine mixed with two other substances which were not controlled drugs. He was convicted of the unlawful possession of morphine, contrary to the Misuse of Drugs Act 1971, s. 5(2). Under the Misuse of Drugs Regulations 1973, sch. 1, para. 3, any preparation of morphine containing not more than 0.2 per cent of morphine compounded with other ingredients was excepted from the prohibition on possession contained in s. 5 of the 1971 Act. The question, on appeal, was whether it was for the prosecution to prove that the accused did not come within the exception contained in para. 3, or for the accused to prove that he did come within it. Quashing the conviction, the House of Lords held that:

(a) The case did not come within the formula, laid down by Lawton LJ in *Edwards* [1975] QB 27, as to when the legal burden is on the accused.

(b) On the true construction of the provisions, it was for the prosecution to prove not only that the powder contained morphine, but also that it was not morphine in the form permitted by para. 3. This would not place an undue burden on the prosecution. In the normal case the substance in question would be analysed for the police, and there would be no difficulty in producing evidence to show that it did not fall within sch. 1 to the 1973 Regulations. However, if the burden were to be placed on the accused, he would be faced with very real difficulties in discharging it, because the suspected substance is usually seized by the police and there is no statutory provision entitling the accused to a portion of it. Often there is very little of the substance, and it may have been destroyed in the process of analysis on behalf of the prosecution.

(c) Since the question of construction was obviously one of real difficulty, regard should be had to the fact that offences involving the misuse of hard drugs are among the most serious in the criminal calendar, and in these circumstances any ambiguity should be resolved in favour of the accused by placing the burden of proving the nature of the substance involved on the prosecution.

See also, in similar vein, *Makuwa* [2006] 1 WLR 2755: where the language of a statute does not make it clear whether the defence has to be established by the accused or negatived by the prosecution, the court should consider the mischief at which the statute was aimed and practical considerations affecting the burden of proof, in particular the ease or difficulty that the respective parties would encounter in discharging the burden. See also *DPP v Wright* [2010] QB 224.

The ruling in *Hunt* that regard may be had to the ease or otherwise that the respective parties will encounter if required to discharge the legal burden, gives an added validity, it is submitted, to a number of cases decided prior to *Edwards* [1975] QB 27 and difficult to reconcile with it. See, e.g., *Curgerwen* (1865) LR 1 CCR 1 and *Putland* [1946] 1 All ER 85.

Incidence of the Legal Burden: the Human Rights Act 1998

F3.18   Any reverse onus provision is open to challenge on the basis of incompatibility with the ECHR, Article 6(2), which provides that 'everyone charged with a criminal offence shall be presumed innocent until proved guilty according to the law'. However, a reverse onus provision will not inevitably give rise to a finding of incompatibility (per Lord Hope in *Lambert* [2002] 2 AC

545 at [87]). It is now well settled that, in deciding the issue, the court should focus on the particular circumstances of the case and strike a reasonable balance between the general interest of the community and the protection of the fundamental rights of the individual. The relevant principles to be found in the jurisprudence of the ECtHR were summarised by Lord Bingham in *Sheldrake v DPP* [2005] 1 AC 264 at [21].

> The overriding concern is that a trial should be fair, and the presumption of innocence is a fundamental right directed to that end. The Convention does not outlaw presumptions of fact or law but requires that these should be kept within reasonable limits and should not be arbitrary. It is open to states to define the constituent elements of a criminal offence, excluding the requirement of *mens rea*. But the substance and effect of any presumption adverse to a defendant must be examined, and must be reasonable. Relevant to any judgment on reasonableness or proportionality will be the opportunity given to the defendant to rebut the presumption, maintenance of the rights of the defence, flexibility in application of the presumption, retention by the court of a power to assess the evidence, the importance of what is at stake and the difficulty which a prosecutor may face in the absence of a presumption. Security concerns do not absolve member states from their duty to observe basic standards of fairness. The justifiability of any infringement of the presumption of innocence cannot be resolved by any rule of thumb, but on examination of all the facts and circumstances of the particular provision as applied in the particular case.

The obvious drawback to a test so reliant on notions of fairness, reasonableness and proportionality is that views may reasonably differ so that in many cases it will be as possible to reach a rational conclusion of compatibility as incompatibility. A good example, in this respect, is furnished by *Keogh* [2007] 3 All ER 789, where the Court of Appeal, reversing the decision of Aikens J, held that the Official Secrets Act 1989, ss. 2(3) and 3(4), could be 'read down' so as to impose only an evidential burden on the accused, on the basis that a reverse burden was not a necessary element in the operation of ss. 2 and 3, it being 'practicable' to require the prosecution to prove that the accused knew or had reasonable cause to believe that the information that he disclosed related to such matters as 'defence', and that its disclosure would be damaging.

The leading domestic authorities are *Johnstone* [2003] 3 All ER 884 and *Sheldrake v DPP*, but it is useful to consider first the decision in *Lambert* and the subsequent cases in which it has been followed or distinguished.

Lambert: **Misuse of Drugs Act 1971, s. 28**   In *Lambert* [2002] 2 AC 545, the accused was **F3.19** charged with possession of cocaine with intent to supply contrary to the Misuse of Drugs Act 1971, s. 5(3). In his defence, he relied on s. 28 of the 1971 Act (see **B19.96**), asserting that he did not believe or suspect or have reason to suspect that the bag which he had carried contained cocaine. The trial judge directed the jury that under s. 28 the legal burden was on the accused. The Court of Appeal dismissed the appeal against conviction. One of the principal issues before the House of Lords was whether s. 28 as applied by the trial judge contravened Article 6(2) or could be interpreted, under the HRA 1998, s. 3(1), as placing on the accused an evidential burden only, i.e. in a way which would be compatible with Article 6. The House of Lords held (Lord Steyn dissenting) that, since the trial had taken place before the coming into force of the 1998 Act, the accused was not entitled to rely in an appeal after the Act had come into force on an alleged breach of his rights under the ECHR by the trial judge. On the question of compatibility with Article 6, the House was of the view (Lord Hutton dissenting) that s. 28 is not compatible with Article 6(2) but, under s. 3 of the 1998 Act, may be read as imposing only an evidential burden on the accused. The words 'to prove' in s. 28(2) (and 'if he proves' in s. 28(3)) can be taken to mean 'to give sufficient evidence' (see per Lord Steyn at [42] and Lord Hope at [94]).

In his judgment, Lord Steyn approached the question of compatibility in three stages by ask- **F3.20** ing first whether s. 5(3) of the 1971 Act, read with s. 28, interfered with Article 6(2) and, if so, secondly whether there was an objective justification for such interference and thirdly whether it was proportionate, i.e. no greater than was necessary. As to the first question, it was held that s. 28 was an ingredient of the offence under s. 5(3) in that knowledge of the existence and control of the contents of the container is the gravamen of the offence, taking into account that s. 28 deals directly with the situation where the accused is denying moral blameworthiness and the fact that the maximum prescribed penalty is life imprisonment, and therefore s. 28 derogates from the presumption of innocence. Lord Steyn also reached this conclusion on broader grounds. He held that the answer should not turn on the distinction between constituent elements of the crime and defensive issues, which will sometimes be unprincipled and arbitrary. Lord Steyn said (at [35]; cf. Lord Hutton at [185]):

> After all, it is sometimes simply a matter of which drafting technique is adopted: a true constituent element can be removed from the definition of the crime and cast as a defensive issue whereas any definition of an offence can be reformulated so as to include all possible defences within it. It is necessary to concentrate not on technicalities and niceties of language but rather on matters of substance.

Lord Steyn (at [35]) adopted the reasoning of Dickson CJC, giving the judgment of the Canadian Supreme Court in *Whyte* (1988) 51 DLR (4th) 481: 'If an accused is required to prove some fact on the balance of probabilities to avoid conviction, the provision violates the presumption of innocence because it permits a conviction in spite of a reasonable doubt in the mind of the tribunal of fact as to the guilt of the accused'. As to the second question, Lord Steyn was satisfied that there was an objective justification for interference with the burden of proof in the 1971 Act. Sophisticated drug smugglers, dealers and couriers typically secrete drugs in some container, enabling the person in possession to say that he was unaware of the contents. Such defences are commonplace and pose real difficulties for the police and prosecuting authorities. Turning to the third question, the principle of proportionality required the House to consider whether it was necessary to impose a legal rather than an evidential burden on the accused. Lord Steyn noted that to put a legal burden on the accused had a far-reaching consequence, that a guilty verdict may be returned in respect of an offence punishable by life imprisonment even though the jury may consider that it is reasonably possible that the accused had been duped. The burden of showing that *only* a reverse legal burden can overcome the difficulties of the prosecution in drugs cases was a heavy one. A 'new realism' had significantly reduced the problems faced by the prosecution in drugs cases. First, the relevant facts usually being peculiarly within the knowledge of the possessor of the container, such possession presumptively suggests, in the absence of exculpatory evidence, knowledge of the contents. Secondly, the judge can now comment on an accused's failure to mention facts when questioned or charged under the CJPO 1994, s. 34 (see **F19.10**). Thirdly, in cases where a 'mixed statement' is received in evidence, the judge may direct that excuses do not have the same weight as the incriminating part of the statement (see **F17.95**). For these reasons, s. 28 did not satisfy the criterion of proportionality but was a disproportionate reaction to the perceived difficulties facing the prosecution in drugs cases. However, under s. 3 of the HRA 1998, the words 'to prove' in s. 28(2) (and 'if he proves' in s. 28(3)) could be read as placing only an evidential burden on the accused.

F3.21 *L v DPP*: CJA 1988, s. 139(4)   *Lambert* [2002] 2 AC 545 was distinguished in *L v DPP* [2003] QB 137, a case of being in possession of a lock-knife contrary to the CJA 1988, s. 139 (see **B12.165**), in relation to s. 139(4), whereby it is a defence for an accused 'to prove that he had good reason or lawful authority for having the article with him in a public place'. Striking 'a fair balance', it was held that s. 139(4) does not conflict with the ECHR, Article 6. Six reasons were given. (1) Under s. 139 it is for the prosecution to prove that the accused knowingly had the article in his possession. (2) There is a strong public interest in bladed articles not being carried in public without good reason. (3) The accused is proving something within his own knowledge. (4) Notwithstanding the adversarial nature of English proceedings, an accused, whether he gives evidence or not, is entitled, under Article 6, to expect the court to scrutinise the evidence with a view to deciding if a good reason exists. (5) In the great majority of cases the tribunal of fact makes a judgment as to whether there was a good reason without the decision depending on whether it has to be proved that there is a good reason. (6) Limited weight should be given, in striking the balance, to the much more restricted power of sentence for an offence under s. 139 than for an offence under the MDA 1971, s. 28. See also *Mathews* [2004] QB 690, applying *L v DPP* in relation to both s. 139(4) and (5) of the 1988 Act.

***Drummond*: RTOA 1988, s. 15** *Lambert* [2002] 2 AC 545 was also distinguished in   **F3.22**
Drummond [2002] 2 Cr App R 352, in relation to the 'hip flask' defence in the RTOA 1988, s. 15, whereby it is for the accused to prove that he consumed alcohol before providing a specimen and after the offence (see **C5.52**). The court noted that the offence of driving while over the limit does not require the court to ascertain the accused's intent; that conviction follows a scientific test which is intended to be as exact as possible; that if an accused drinks after the event, it is he who defeats the aim of the legislature by making the test potentially unreliable; and that the relevant scientific evidence to set against the specimen result is within the knowledge or means of access of the accused. For these reasons it was held that the legislative interference with the presumption of innocence in s. 15 was not only justified, but was no greater than was necessary.

***DPP v Barker*: RTOA 1988, s. 37(3)** In *DPP v Barker* (2004) 168 JP 617, B was charged with   **F3.23**
driving while disqualified and relied on the RTOA 1988, s. 37(3), whereby a person disqualified from driving is entitled to hold a provisional licence and to drive a vehicle in accordance with its conditions. It was held that the MCA 1980, s. 101, applied (see **F3.11**) and therefore the burden was on B to show that he had a provisional licence and was driving in accordance with its conditions. The burden was held to be wholly proportionate; as to being the holder of a provisional licence, the burden could easily be discharged by producing the licence; and as to the conditions of the licence, in some cases, in the absence of any information from the accused as to the identity of a passenger, it would be impossible for the prosecution to establish his identity and that he was the holder of a licence and therefore qualified to be supervising the driver.

***Johnstone*: Trade Marks Act 1994, s. 92(5)** *Johnstone* [2003] 3 All ER 884 concerned the   **F3.24**
Trade Marks Act 1994, s. 92(5), whereby it is a defence for a person charged with an offence under s. 92 (unauthorised use of a trade mark) to show that he believed on reasonable grounds that use of a sign was not an infringement of the trade mark. The House of Lords, approving the decision of the Court of Appeal in *S* [2003] 1 Cr App R 602, was of the unanimous *obiter* view that s. 92(5) should be interpreted as imposing on the accused the legal burden and that this interpretation was compatible with Article 6(2). According to Lord Nicholls (at [50] and [51]):

> A sound starting point is to remember that if an accused is required to prove a fact on the balance of probability... this permits a conviction in spite of the fact-finding tribunal having a reasonable doubt as to the guilt of the accused... This consequence of a reverse burden of proof should colour one's approach when evaluating the reasons why it is said that, in the absence of a persuasive burden on the accused, the public interest will be prejudiced to an extent which justifies placing a persuasive burden on the accused. The more serious the punishment which may flow from conviction, the more compelling must be the reasons. The extent and nature of the factual matters required to be proved by the accused, and their importance relative to the matters required to be proved by the prosecution, have to be taken into account. So also does the extent to which the burden on the accused relates to facts which, if they exist, are readily provable by him as matters within his own knowledge or to which he has ready access.

> In evaluating these factors the court's role is one of review. Parliament, not the court, is charged with the primary responsibility for deciding, as a matter of policy, what should be the constituent elements of a criminal offence... The court will reach a different conclusion from the legislature only when it is apparent the legislature has attached insufficient importance to the fundamental right of an individual to be presumed innocent until proved guilty.

In relation to s. 92, it was held that two particular factors constituted compelling reasons why   **F3.25**
s. 92(5) put a legal burden on the accused. First, those who trade in brand products are aware of the need to be on guard against counterfeit goods. They are aware of the need to deal with reputable suppliers and to keep records and of the risks they take if they do not. Secondly, that whereas the s. 92(5) defence relates to facts within the accused's own knowledge and his sources of supply are known to him, by and large it is to be expected that those who supply

traders with counterfeit products, if traceable at all by outside investigators, are unlikely to be co-operative. So, in practice, if the prosecution must prove that a trader acted dishonestly, there would be fewer investigations and prosecutions. Among the other factors considered was an important policy consideration: to protect consumers and honest manufacturers and traders. Counterfeiting is a serious contemporary problem with adverse economic effects on genuine trade and on consumers, in terms of quality of goods, and, sometimes, on health or safety.

F3.26 *A-G's Ref (No. 1 of 2004)*: **Insolvency Act 1986**   In *A-G's Ref (No. 1 of 2004)* [2004] 4 All ER 457, a five-judge Court of Appeal was convened to hear five appeals. The first two appeals concerned the same statutory provisions in the Insolvency Act 1986, namely s. 353(1), whereby a bankrupt is guilty of an offence if he does not inform the official receiver of a disposal of property comprised in his estate (see **B7.59**), s. 357(1), whereby a bankrupt is guilty of an offence if he makes, or in the five years before the start of the bankruptcy made, any gift or transfer of, or any charge on, his property (see **B7.63**) and s. 352, under which a person is not guilty of an offence under either s. 353(1) or s. 357(1), among others, if he had no intent to defraud or to conceal the state of his affairs (see **B7.58**). It was held that: (1) s. 352, if interpreted as imposing a legal burden on the accused for the purposes of s. 353(1), does not breach Article 6, and (2) s. 352, if interpreted as imposing a legal burden on the accused for the purposes of s. 357(1), does breach Article 6 but can be read down so as to impose only an evidential burden. The reason given for the conclusion in (1) was that the proper working of insolvency law depends on the inclusion in the assets of an insolvent company, and in the estate of a bankrupt, of all the assets that should be comprised in them; that concealment or disposal of such assets to the disadvantage of the creditors can be done alone and in private; and that whether there has been fraud will often be known only to the individuals in question. These considerations normally justify the imposition on an accused who is proved to have deliberately acted in a manner that gives rise to an inference that he sought to defraud his creditors, of the burden of proving that he did not intend to do so. It was further held that the decision in *Carass* [2002] 1 WLR 1714 cannot stand with *Johnstone* [2003] 3 All ER 884 and must be treated as impliedly overruled.

F3.27 In *Carass* it was held that s. 206(4) of the 1986 Act, whereby, in relation to various offences of fraud in anticipation of winding up, it is a defence for an accused to prove that he had no intent to defraud (see **B7.45**), must be regarded as imposing only an evidential burden. Thus the burden under s. 206(4) of the 1986 Act is a legal burden compatible with Article 6(2) and the same conclusion has also been reached in relation to the defence in s. 208(4) of the 1986 Act (see **B7.49**), which has some parallel with s. 206 (*R (Griffin) v Richmond Magistrates' Court* [2008] 1 Cr App R 453). The reason given for the conclusion in (2) above was the very wide ambit of s. 357. For example, it applies to disposals made long before the commencement of bankruptcy, and possibly at a time when there was no indication of insolvency, and the prosecution does not have to prove that the bankrupt was aware of the possibility of his insolvency. In these circumstances, to require the bankrupt to prove that he had no intent to defraud is not justified and infringes Article 6.

F3.28 *A-G's Ref (No. 1 of 2004)*: **Protection from Eviction Act 1977**   The third appeal in *A-G's Ref (No. 1 of 2004)* [2004] 4 All ER 457 concerned the Protection from Eviction Act 1977, s. 1(2), whereby if a person unlawfully deprives the residential occupier of any premises of his occupation or the premises, he shall be guilty of an offence 'unless he proves that he believed, and had reasonable cause to believe, that the residential occupier had ceased to reside in the premises' (see **B13.1**). It was held that this reverse burden was justified for three reasons. First, the essence of the offence is unlawfully depriving the occupier of his occupation of the premises, and the defence is only available if the accused can bring himself within a narrow class of exception. Secondly, the circumstances relied upon by the accused are peculiarly within his own knowledge. Thirdly, the imposition of a criminal penalty is designed to regulate conduct in the public interest and there is a strong public interest in deterring landlords from ejecting tenants unlawfully.

A-G's Ref (No. 1 of 2004): **Homicide Act 1957, s. 4(2)**   The fourth appeal in *A-G's Ref (No. 1* **F3.29** *of 2004)* [2004] 4 All ER 457 concerned the Homicide Act 1957, s. 4(2), which provides that 'Where it is shown that a person charged with the murder of another killed the other it shall be for the defence to prove that the person charged was acting in pursuance of a suicide pact between him and the other'. It was held that the legal burden is on the accused. The defence only arises once the prosecution has proved all the elements of murder and therefore the burden to justify the reverse burden of showing that it is proportional is more readily discharged. The penalty for murder is of the harshest kind, but in the Homicide Act 1957 Parliament singled out the defences of diminished responsibility and suicide pacts as requiring proof by an accused. Parliament no doubt had in mind the fact that in many cases the only evidence of a suicide pact would emanate from the survivor. The facts to establish the defence lie within the accused's knowledge and the reverse burden provides protection for society from murder disguised as a suicide pact killing.

A-G's Ref (No. 1 of 2004): **CJPO 1994, s. 51(7)**   The fifth appeal in *A-G's Ref (No. 1 of 2004)* **F3.30** [2004] 4 All ER 457 concerned the CJPO 1994, s. 51(7), whereby if it is proved that the accused did an act which intimidated or was intended to intimidate another person ('the victim'), and that he did so knowing or believing that the victim was assisting in the investigation of an offence or was a witness or potential witness or a juror or potential juror in proceedings for an offence, he shall be presumed, 'unless the contrary is proved', to have done the act with the intention of thereby causing the investigation or the course of justice to be obstructed, perverted or interfered with (see **B14.46**). It was held that although the reverse burden involved an ingredient of the offence, not a special defence, the imposition of a legal burden on the accused was both justified and proportional. Witness and jury intimidation is a very serious threat to the administration of criminal justice which has substantially increased and continues to do so and it is understandable that Parliament should wish to take strong measures to stamp it out. Once all the matters that give rise to the presumption are proved, it is entirely reasonable that the burden of proving lack of intention should rest with the accused. In balancing the potential detriment to the accused and the mischief Parliament is seeking to eradicate, the balance comes down firmly in favour of the prosecution.

Sheldrake v DPP: **General**   In *A-G's Ref (No. 1 of 2004)* [2004] 4 All ER 457 Lord Woolf CJ, **F3.31** giving the judgment of the court, saw the need to simplify the task of lower courts when faced with reverse onus provisions by providing them with guidance on the relevant principles to be applied. The court noted the large number of authorities on the subject and the conflicting messages some of them gave. In particular the court noted the significant difference in emphasis between the approaches of Lord Steyn in *Lambert* [2002] 2 AC 545 and Lord Nicholls in *Johnstone* [2003] 3 All ER 884, and that 'few provisions will be left as imposing a legal burden on Lord Steyn's approach' (at [38]). It was suggested that until clarification by a further decision of the House of Lords, the lower courts, if in doubt as to what should be the outcome of a challenge to a reverse burden, should follow the approach of Lord Nicholls rather than that of Lord Steyn. Lord Woolf also set out 'General Guidance' in the form of ten general principles. However, in *Sheldrake v DPP* [2005] 1 AC 264, the House of Lords held that both *Lambert* and *Johnstone*, unless or until revised or supplemented, should be regarded as the primary domestic authorities on reverse burdens; that nothing said in *Johnstone* suggested an intention to depart from or modify *Lambert*, which should not be treated as superseded or implicitly overruled; and that the differences in emphasis were explicable by the difference in the subject-matter of the two cases. The House also expressly declined to endorse Lord Woolf's 'General Guidance', save to the extent that it was in accordance with the opinions of the House in *Lambert* and *Johnstone*. Lord Bingham said that the task of the court is never to decide whether a reverse burden should be imposed on an accused, but always to assess whether a burden enacted by Parliament unjustifiably infringes the presumption of innocence, and questioned Lord Woolf's assumption that Parliament would not make an exception without good reason. Such an assumption, it was held, may lead the court to give too much weight to the enactment under review and too little

F

Part F Evidence

weight to the presumption of innocence and the obligation imposed on the court by s. 3. See also, applying these principles, *DPP v Wright* [2010] QB 224: to construe the Hunting Act 2004, s. 1 and sch. 1, as imposing a legal burden on the accused would be an oppressive, disproportionate, unfair and unnecessary intrusion upon the presumption of innocence.

F3.32   *Sheldrake v DPP*: **RTA 1988, s. 5(2)**   In *Sheldrake v DPP* [2005] 1 AC 264, the House heard two conjoined appeals. The first concerned the RTA 1988, s. 5(2) (see C5.35), whereby it is a defence for a person charged with an offence of being in charge of a motor vehicle on a road or other public place after consuming excess alcohol to prove that, at the time of the alleged offence, the circumstances were such that there was no likelihood of his driving the vehicle whilst the proportion of alcohol in his breath, blood or urine remained likely to exceed the prescribed limit. It was held that even on the assumption that s. 5(2) infringes the presumption of innocence, it was directed to the legitimate object of preventing death, injury and damage caused by unfit drivers and met the tests of acceptability identified in the Strasbourg jurisprudence. It was not objectionable to criminalise conduct in these circumstances without requiring the prosecutor to prove criminal intent. The accused has a full opportunity to show that there was no likelihood of his driving, a matter so closely conditioned by his own knowledge at the time as to make it much more appropriate for him to prove the absence of a likelihood of his driving on the balance of probabilities than for the prosecutor to prove such a likelihood beyond reasonable doubt. The imposition of a legal burden did not go beyond what was necessary. Counsel had submitted that all burdens on the defence should be evidential only. It was held that such a fundamental change was not mandated by Strasbourg authority and remained a matter for Parliament and not the House of Lords.

F3.33   *Sheldrake v DPP*: **Terrorism Act 2000, s. 11(2)**   The second appeal in *Sheldrake v DPP* [2005] 1 AC 264 concerned the TA 2000, s. 11(1) and (2).

Terrorism Act 2000, s. 11

(1) A person commits an offence if he belongs or professes to belong to a proscribed organisation.
(2) It is a defence for a person charged with an offence under subsection (1) to prove—
    (a) that the organisation was not proscribed on the last (or only) occasion on which he became a member or began to profess to be a member, and
    (b) that he has not taken part in the activities of the organisation at any time while it was proscribed.

The House was of the unanimous opinion that the ingredients of the offence are set out fully in s. 11(1) and that s. 11(2) adds no further ingredient. The House also held, by majority, that s. 11(2) is incompatible with Article 6 and should be read and given effect as imposing on the accused an evidential burden only. Six reasons were given for the conclusion of incompatibility.

(1) The extraordinary breadth of s. 11(1) and the uncertain scope of the word 'profess' are such that some of those liable to be convicted and punished under s. 11(1) may be guilty of no conduct that can reasonably be regarded as blameworthy or such as should properly attract criminal sanctions. As to the breadth of the subsection, it covers, for example, a person who joined an organisation when it was not a terrorist organisation or not a proscribed organisation, or when, if it was, he did not know that it was. There would be a clear breach of the presumption of innocence and a real risk of unfair conviction if such a person could exonerate himself only by establishing the defence provided and it was the clear duty of the courts to protect an accused against such a risk.
(2) As to s. 11(2)(b), it may be all but impossible for an accused to show that he has not taken part in the activities of the organisation. Terrorist organisations do not generate minutes or records on which he can rely and although he can assert his non-participation, his evidence may well be discounted as unreliable.
(3) If s. 11(2) imposes a legal burden and the accused fails to prove the matters specified, there is no room for the exercise of discretion — the court must convict him.

(4) The penalty for the offence, imprisonment for up to ten years, is severe.

(5) Security considerations carry weight, but they do not absolve Member States from their duty to ensure that basic standards of fairness are observed.

(6) Little significance can be attached to the requirement in s. 117 that the DPP gives his consent to a prosecution because Article 6 is concerned with the procedure relating to the trial of a criminal case and not the decision to prosecute.

As to the reading down of s. 11(2), there could be no doubt that Parliament intended it to impose a legal burden on the accused, because s. 118 of the Act lists a number of sections that are to be understood as imposing an evidential burden only and s. 11(2) is not among those listed. However, the majority held that s. 11(2) should be treated as if s. 118 applied to it, on the basis that, although that was not the intention of Parliament when enacting the 2000 Act, it was the intention of Parliament when enacting the HRA 1998, s. 3.

Makuwa: **Immigration and Asylum Act 1999, s. 31(1)**   *Makuwa* [2006] 1 WLR 2755 con- **F3.34** cerned the Immigration and Asylum Act 1999, s. 31(1), whereby it is a defence to various offences, including using a false instrument contrary to the Forgery and Counterfeiting Act 1981, s. 3, for a refugee to show that, having come to the UK directly from another country where his life was threatened, he (a) presented himself to the UK authorities without delay, (b) showed good cause for his illegal entry or presence, and (c) made a claim for asylum as soon as was reasonably practicable after his arrival in the UK. The accused was charged with using a false instrument — a false passport — contrary to s. 3 of the 1981 Act and relied upon s. 31(1) of the 1999 Act. The Court of Appeal held that the accused bore the legal burden in relation to all the matters in s. 31(1) except the issue of refugee status and that the infringement of the ECHR, Article 6(2), was justifiable as a proportionate way of achieving the legitimate objective of maintaining proper immigration controls by restricting the use of forged passports, one of the principal means by which they were likely to be overcome.

Williams: **Firearms Act 1982, s. 1(5)**   *Williams* [2013] 2 All ER 787 concerned the FA 1982, **F3.35** s. 1(5), whereby it is a defence for the accused to show that he did not know and had no reason to suspect that an imitation firearm was so constructed or adapted as to be readily convertible into a firearm to which the FA 1968, s. 1, applies (see **B12.34**). It was held that s. 1(5) imposes a legal burden on the accused and can be justified as a necessary and proportionate derogation from the presumption of innocence: firearms offences are a very serious problem and the need for protection of the public is obvious; the question of knowledge or lack of it involves facts readily available to the accused, whereas it could be very difficult for the prosecution to disprove absence of knowledge and reason to suspect; the prosecution must have first proved to the criminal standard that the accused was in possession of an imitation firearm readily convertible into a lethal firearm; and the maximum sentence for the offence is ten years.

Regulatory Offences   According to Lord Clyde in *Lambert* [2002] 2 AC 545 the imposition **F3.36** of a legal burden on the accused may be acceptable in the case of statutory offences which are concerned to regulate the conduct of some particular activity in the public interest. Lord Clyde said at [154]: 'The requirement to have a licence in order to carry on certain kinds of activity is an obvious example. The promotion of health and safety and the avoidance of pollution are among the purposes to be served by such controls. These kinds of cases may properly be seen as not truly criminal. Many may be relatively trivial and only involve a monetary penalty. Many may carry with them no real social disgrace or infamy'. This line of reasoning has been relied upon in subsequent cases, including *S* [2003] 1 Cr App R 602 in which the Court of Appeal (at [48]) regarded the Trade Marks Act 1994, s. 92, as being in the nature of a regulatory offence with a degree of moral obloquy rather less than the 'truly criminal' cases. *Davies v Health and Safety Executive* (2002) *The Times*, 27 December 2002 concerned the Health and Safety at Work etc. Act 1974, ss. 3(1) and 33(1), which together make it an offence for an employer to fail to discharge the duty to conduct his undertaking in such a way as to ensure, so far as is reasonably practicable, that persons not in his employment who may be affected thereby are not exposed to risks to their health and safety, and s. 40 of the Act whereby, for these purposes, 'it shall be for the accused to prove...that it was not reasonably practicable to do more than was in fact done to satisfy the duty'. It was held that since s. 40 related to an ingredient of the offence under ss. 3 and 33, it did make some inroad into the presumption of innocence, but that the imposition of a legal burden on the accused was justified, necessary and proportionate. Important reasons given for reaching this conclusion included the fact that the Act was regulatory, its purpose to secure the health, safety and welfare of employees and others, that the offences in question involved no risk of imprisonment and that the moral obloquy was less than that of truly criminal offences. In *Chargot Ltd (t/a Contract Services)* [2009] 2 All ER 645, a case involving charges under ss. 33 and 37 of the 1974 Act, *Davies v Health and Safety Executive* was followed, on essentially the same reasoning, and notwithstanding that the penalties for individuals had since been increased to up to two years' imprisonment and an unlimited fine when convicted on indictment (Health and Safety (Offences) Act 2008, s. 1(1) and (2) and sch. 1). See also *R (Grundy & Co Excavations Ltd) v Halton Division Magistrates' Court* (2003) 167 JP 387, in relation to the exceptions from the necessity for a licence for the felling of trees in the Forestry Act 1967, s. 9, and the relevant regulations. In that case it was held that the offence of tree felling was a classic regulatory offence, designed to protect the nation's trees, which involved only a monetary penalty, and carried no real social disgrace, infamy, or moral stigma or obloquy.

Incidence of the Evidential Burden: General Rule

F3.37   Generally speaking, a party bearing the legal burden on a particular issue will also bear the evidential burden on that issue. Thus, as a general rule, the prosecution bear both the legal and evidential burden in relation to all the elements in the offence necessary to establish guilt; and where the defence bear the legal burden of proving insanity or, by virtue of an express or implied statutory exception, some other issue, they will also bear the evidential burden in that regard (although, concerning insanity, in rare and exceptional cases the judge may of his own motion raise the issue and leave it to the jury: *Thomas* [1995] Crim LR 314). In relation to numerous common-law and statutory defences, however, the evidential burden is on the defence, and, if it is discharged so that the defence in question is put before the jury, the legal burden is then on the prosecution to disprove such defence. Although it is said in these cases that the evidential burden is on the defence, that burden will be discharged *whenever* there is sufficient evidence in relation to the defence to leave it to the jury; the evidence may be adduced by the defence (or elicited by them in cross-examination), *or* it may be given by a prosecution witness (or a co-accused) giving his evidence in chief *or* it may be given in any other way (*Bullard v The Queen* [1957] AC 635). Where such a defence arises upon the evidence called by any party, then whether or not it has been mentioned by the defence, the judge must leave it to the jury (*Palmer v The Queen* [1971] AC 814 at p. 823). See also *Bonnick* (1978) 66 Cr App R 266, *Hopper* [1915] 2 KB 431 at p. 435 and *DPP (Jamaica) v Bailey* [1995] 1 Cr App R 257; and cf. *Groark* [1999] Crim LR 669, considered at F3.44. If there is no evidence to support the defence upon which an accused seeks to rely, the judge is entitled to withdraw the case from the jury (*Hill* (1988) 89 Cr App R 74 and *Pommell* [1995] 2 Cr App R 607). However it has been said that even if there is no evidence in support of a defence and it is not raised by defence counsel (perhaps for tactical reasons), if there is a reasonable possibility on one interpretation of the evidence adduced that the accused may have that defence, the judge should put it to the jury (*Watson* [1992] Crim LR 434). The defences to which the foregoing principles relate are as follows.

F3.38   **Provocation and Loss of Self-control**   If sufficient evidence is adduced to raise an issue with respect to the statutory defence of loss of control, which has replaced the common-law defence of provocation (see B1.24), the jury must assume that the defence is satisfied unless the prosecution proves beyond reasonable doubt that it is not (CAJA 2009, s. 54(5)). Sufficient evidence is adduced to raise an issue with respect to the statutory defence if evidence is adduced on which, in the opinion of the trial judge, a jury, properly directed, could reasonably conclude that the defence might apply (s. 54(6)).

It is submitted that the following principles, which applied in the case of the common-law **F3.39** defence of provocation, will also apply in the case of loss of control under the CAJA 2009, s. 54(6). A judge is under no duty to put before the jury strained and implausible inferences for the purpose of creating a defence of provocation for which, in truth, there is no basis (*Walch* [1993] Crim LR 714; see also *Wellington* [1993] Crim LR 616). The judge is required to leave the defence to the jury only if there is some evidence, from whatever source, suggestive of the reasonable possibility that the accused might have lost his self-control. If there is no such evidence, but merely a speculative possibility of an act of provocation, the issue does not arise, and suggestions in cross-examination cannot by themselves raise the issue (*Acott* [1997] 1 All ER 706; see also *Kromer* [2002] EWCA Crim 1278, *Miao* (2003) *The Times*, 26 November 2003 and *Serrano* [2007] EWCA Crim 3182; and cf. *Stewart* [1995] 4 All ER 999).

In *Jewell* [2014] EWCA Crim 414, a decision under s. 54(6), in which the evidence of a planned execution was described as 'overwhelming', it was held that a bare assertion by the accused that the reason for the killing was loss of control could not, on its own, amount to sufficient evidence to leave the defence before the jury.

In *Dawes* [2013] 3 All ER 308, it was held that, if there is evidence sufficient for the purposes of s. 54(6), it must be left to the jury, whatever forensic tactical decisions may have been made by the defence and that, in this respect, long-standing principles are unchanged. In *Hopper* [1915] 2 KB 431, it was held that provocation should have been left to the jury in a murder trial at which the defence had been accident. See also *Dhillon* [1997] 2 Cr App R 104 and *Rossiter* [1994] 2 All ER 752, in which the issue of provocation was not raised by the defence, the accused maintaining that she was defending herself. It was held that whenever there is material, on a charge of murder, which is capable of amounting to provocation, however tenuous it may be, the judge should leave that issue to the jury.

This principle also applies if the defence do not rely on provocation but rely instead on accident (*Dhillon*), or maintain that the accused was not at the scene of the crime, or that he was there but that the crime was committed by someone else (*Cambridge* [1994] 2 All ER 760, also explaining that the word 'tenuous', as used in *Rossiter*, described the provocative acts and words, not the evidence of their existence). The principle also applies even if the defence have conveyed to the judge that in their opinion the issue should *not* be left to the jury (*Burgess* [1995] Crim LR 425).

However, it is most unsatisfactory that where the defence do not rely on provocation at the **F3.40** trial, the judge's failure to direct the jury on it can found an appeal against conviction. For this reason, in *Cox* [1995] 2 Cr App R 513 it was held that if it appears to *either* counsel that there is evidence on which the jury could find provocation, they should regard it as their duty to point it out to the judge before he sums up. There are compelling grounds, it is submitted, for extending this duty so that it applies in relation to other defences. Where there is sufficient evidence of provocation, but the trial judge fails to leave the issue before the jury, the Court of Appeal may nonetheless conclude that the conviction is safe (*Van Dongen* [2005] 2 Cr App R 632).

Self-defence In *Lobell* [1957] 1 QB 547 the appellant was convicted of wounding with intent **F3.41** to cause grievous bodily harm. There was some evidence to support his defence of self-defence. The trial judge directed the jury that it was for the defence to establish that plea to their satisfaction. The conviction was quashed on the grounds that this was a misdirection. Although the prosecution are not obliged to give evidence in chief to rebut a suggestion of self-defence before the issue is raised, once there is sufficient evidence to leave the issue before the jury, it is for the prosecution to disprove it beyond reasonable doubt. See also *Wheeler* [1967] 3 All ER 829 at p. 830 and *Abraham* [1973] 3 All ER 694 at p. 1273. There may be evidence of self-defence even if the defence of the accused is one of alibi. In *Bonnick* (1978) 66 Cr App R 266, a case of stabbing in which the defence was one of alibi, it was held, rejecting the contention that the evidence of the Crown witnesses had raised the issue of self-defence, that the question whether there was sufficient evidence to leave an issue before the jury was a question for the trial judge to answer by applying common sense to the evidence; but when there was sufficient evidence to raise a prima facie case, the issue should be left to the jury. In *Dickens* [2005] EWCA Crim 2017,

Part F Evidence

it was held that since, in the particular circumstances of the case, it was extremely difficult to disentangle the defences of self-defence and accident and unwise to approach the facts as if they fell within mutually exclusive compartments, both defences should have been left to the jury.

F3.42 **Duress**   The Crown are not called upon to anticipate a defence of duress and destroy it in advance, but if the accused places before the court such material as makes duress a live issue, fit and proper to be left to the jury, it is for the Crown to destroy that defence in such a manner as to leave in the jury's mind no reasonable doubt that the accused cannot be absolved on the grounds of the alleged compulsion (*Gill* [1963] 2 All ER 688, per Edmund Davies J at p. 846). See also *Bone* [1968] 2 All ER 644, per Lord Parker CJ at p. 985. As to duress of circumstances, see also *Pommell* [1995] 2 Cr App R 607.

F3.43 **Non-insane Automatism**   Although the onus is on the defence to prove insanity on a balance of probabilities, where there is evidence on which a jury could find automatism not due to a disease of the mind, the onus is on the prosecution to disprove such automatism beyond reasonable doubt: the *obiter* view of the majority in *Bratty v A-G for Northern Ireland* [1963] AC 386. See also *Stripp* (1978) 69 Cr App R 318 and *Pullen* [1991] Crim LR 457. Where the defence of automatism is raised by an accused, two questions fall to be decided by the judge before the defence can be left to the jury: (1) whether a proper evidential foundation for the defence has been laid and (2) whether the evidence shows the case to be one of insane automatism, i.e. a case which falls within the M'Naghten Rules, or one of non-insane automatism. If the judge rules that the case is one of insanity, the jury then has to decide, on the basis of the judge's direction, whether the accused is guilty or not guilty by reason of insanity (*Burgess* [1991] 1 QB 92). Where the issues of both insanity and non-insane automatism arise in the same case, the judge should distinguish between them in his summing-up and explain that, whereas it is for the defence to prove insanity, it is not for them to prove automatism; it is for the prosecution to negative it once the defence lay a foundation for it (*Burns* (1973) 58 Cr App R 364, per Stephenson LJ at p. 374).

F3.44 **Intoxication**   Insofar as intoxication may constitute a defence, once there is evidence before the court to support it, the onus of disproof rests on the prosecution (*Kennedy v HM Advocate* 1944 JC 171; *Foote* [1964] Crim LR 405). However, in *Groark* [1999] Crim LR 669 it was held that if, in a case of wounding with intent, there is evidence of drunkenness which might give rise to the issue whether the accused did form the specific intent, but the defence is that the accused knew what was happening but acted in self-defence, defence counsel is not obliged to seek a direction on self-induced intoxication in relation to intent; the judge may ask him if he has any objection to such a direction and, if he does object, then the direction need not be given. As to mistake due to voluntary intoxication, see further *Hatton* [2006] 1 Cr App R 247 (see **A3.60**) and the CJIA 2008, s. 76(5) (see **A3.57**).

F3.45 **Alibi**   Although there is no general rule of law that in every case where alibi is raised the judge must specifically direct the jury, quite apart from the general direction on burden and standard of proof, that it is for the prosecution to negative the alibi, it is the clear duty of the judge to give such a direction if there is a danger of the jury thinking that an alibi, because it is called a defence, raises some burden on the defence to establish it (*Wood (No. 2)* (1967) 52 Cr App R 74 per Lord Parker CJ). It is a common and good *practice* to give such a specific and additional direction in any event (*Preece* (1992) 96 Cr App R 264); and ideally it should be given (*Anderson* [1991] Crim LR 361; *Johnson* [1995] Crim LR 242). In *Mussell* [1995] Crim LR 887, it was held that a special direction is necessary if the nature of the alibi is that the accused was at a specific place elsewhere, raising the question why he did not call witnesses in support, but is unnecessary if the evidence amounts to little more than a denial that he committed the crime.

F3.46 **Mistaken Belief in Consent**   Where a case involves a charge of rape under the SOA 1956 (i.e. brought before 1 May 2004), if there is evidence before the court that the accused mistakenly believed that the complainant had consented, the onus of disproof lies on the prosecution (*Thomas* (1983) 77 Cr App R 63; *Gardiner* [1994] Crim LR 455). For the position on consent under the SOA 2003, see **B3.29** *et seq*.

Statutory Defences The principles set out above also apply in relation to a huge variety of **F3.47** statutory defences. Thus where an accused puts forward an explanation for his conduct based on the Criminal Law Act 1967, s. 3 (see **A3.54**; and see also the CJIA 2008, s. 76, at **A3.57**), the jury should be clearly directed that it is for the Crown to destroy the validity of such an explanation and that it is not for the accused to establish it (*Cameron* [1973] Crim LR 520; *Khan* [1995] Crim LR 78). In some cases, the statute expressly imposes a burden on the Crown to disprove beyond reasonable doubt a defence in respect of which the accused has discharged an evidential burden (see, e.g., the TA 2000, s. 118 (at **B10.29**), and *G* [2010] 1 AC 43).

STANDARD OF PROOF

General Rule

The standard of proof means the degree to which proof must be established by a party bearing **F3.48** a burden of proof. The standard required of the prosecution before the tribunal of fact can find the accused guilty is proof such that the jury is sure of his guilt. However, in a prosecution under the Mental Capacity Act 2005, s. 44, for ill-treatment or neglect of a person who lacks capacity (see **B2.146**), the prosecution has to prove lack of capacity only on a balance of probabilities (s. 2(4) of the 2005 Act, *Hopkins* [2011] EWCA Crim 1513 and *Dunn* [2011] 1 Cr App R 425). Where the legal burden on a particular issue is borne by the accused, the standard required of the defence before the tribunal of fact can find in favour of the accused on that issue is proof on a balance of probabilities.

Usual Direction where Legal Burden on Prosecution

It is the duty of the judge in the summing-up to make it clear to the jury what standard of proof **F3.49** the prosecution are required to meet. It is not a matter of some precise formula or particular form of words being used; what matters is the effect of the summing-up (*Allan* [1969] 1 All ER 91, per Fenton Atkinson LJ at p. 36).

However, though the law requires no particular formula, judges are wise, as a general rule, to adopt one. The time-honoured formula is that the jury must be satisfied beyond reasonable doubt (*Ferguson v The Queen* [1979] 1 WLR 94 per Lord Scarman), a phrase approved by the House of Lords (*Woolmington v DPP* [1935] AC 462; *Mancini v DPP* [1942] AC 1), but the favoured phrase now is that before the jury can return a verdict of guilty, they must be sure that the accused is guilty (see the *Crown Court Bench Book*, p. 16). This direction is designed to avoid the difficulties juries encounter with the concept of beyond reasonable doubt (*Majid* [2009] EWCA Crim 2563). Where the phrase beyond reasonable doubt has been used in the trial, e.g., by counsel in their speeches, the jury should be directed that it is the same as being sure (*Adey* (unreported, 97/5306/W2)).

Directions using the words 'reasonably sure', 'pretty sure', 'pretty certain' and 'sure, which **F3.50** is less than being certain' have all been disapproved (*Head* (1961) 45 Cr App R 225, *Woods* [1961] Crim LR 324, *Law* [1961] Crim LR 52 and *Stephens* (2002) *The Times*, 27 June 2002 respectively). As to the last, a judge should not draw a distinction between being sure and being certain, because this is likely only to confuse (*Majid*; *Stephens*). It is inadequate merely to direct the jury that they must be 'satisfied' without any indication of the degree of satisfaction required (*Hepworth* [1955] 2 QB 600; *Allan* [1969] 1 All ER 91, per Fenton Atkinson LJ). It was held to be proper to direct that 'You, the jury, must be completely satisfied' or 'You must feel sure of the prisoner's guilt' (*Hepworth* [1955] 2 QB 600, per Lord Goddard CJ at p. 603).

In *McGreevy v DPP* [1973] 1 All ER 503, it was argued on the basis of *Hodge* (1838) 2 Lew CC 227, that if the case against the accused depends wholly or substantially on circumstantial evidence, the judge should direct the jury that not only must they be satisfied that the circumstances are consistent with the accused having committed the offence, but also they must be satisfied that the circumstances are inconsistent with any other rational conclusion than that

F

the accused is the guilty person. The House of Lords held that there is no rule of law requiring such a direction. It suffices, in such a case, to give the usual direction that they, the jury, must be satisfied of the guilt of the accused beyond reasonable doubt.

Cases Requiring Explanation of Usual Direction

F3.51   Judges have used a variety of expressions with a view to explaining to the jury the meaning of 'reasonable doubt', some of which have suggested too low a standard of proof and resulted in a conviction being quashed. For example, in *Gray* (1973) 58 Cr App R 177 the trial judge defined a reasonable doubt as 'a doubt based upon good reason and not a fanciful doubt' and as 'the sort of doubt which might affect you in the conduct of your everyday affairs'. The Court of Appeal, quashing the conviction, held that if the judge had referred to the sort of doubt which may affect the mind of a person in the conduct of important affairs, there could have been no criticism, but the reference to everyday affairs might have suggested too low a standard. See also *Stafford* (1968) 53 Cr App R 1, in which Edmund-Davies LJ said (at p. 2): 'We do not...agree with the trial judge when, directing the jury upon the standard of proof he told them to "Remember that a reasonable doubt is one for which you could give reasons if you were asked", and we dislike such a description or definition.' It was against a background of cases of this kind that in *Ching* (1976) 63 Cr App R 7 Lawton LJ, delivering the judgment of the court, said (at p. 11): 'We point out and emphasise that if judges stopped trying to define that which is almost impossible to define there would be fewer appeals. We hope that there will not be any more for some considerable time.' Earlier, his lordship said (at p. 10):

> ...in most cases...judges would be well advised not to attempt any gloss upon what is meant by 'sure' or what is meant by 'reasonable doubt'. In the last two decades there have been numerous cases before this court, some of which have been successful, some of which have not, which have come here because judges have thought it helpful to a jury to comment on what the standard of proof is. Experience in this court has shown that such comments usually create difficulties. They are more likely to confuse than help. But the exceptional case does sometimes arise.

F3.52   *Ching* itself illustrates the kind of exceptional case in which a judge should explain to a jury what is meant by reasonable doubt. In that case the judge, in his summing-up, had directed the jury on the standard of proof by using the two classic formulations, 'sure' and 'beyond reasonable doubt', and had explained that these were two ways of saying the same thing. After retirement the jury returned to court, and the judge understood the foreman to ask for a further direction on the standard of proof. The judge said:

> A reasonable doubt...is a doubt to which you can give a reason as opposed to a mere fanciful sort of speculation such as 'Well, nothing in this world is certain, nothing in this world can be proved'...It is sometimes said the sort of matter which might influence you if you were to consider some business matter. A matter, for example, of a mortgage concerning your house, or something of that nature.

The Court of Appeal held that:

(a) in the light of the foreman's request, the case was an exceptional one, calling for a further direction; and

(b) although it disliked that part of the additional direction in which the judge had defined a reasonable doubt as one to which you can give a reason, taking the effect of both the summing-up and the additional direction together, the judge was right in what he did.

F3.53   In exceptional cases in which the jury do ask for an explanation of 'reasonable doubt', a suitable form of words is provided by *Walters v The Queen* [1969] 2 AC 26. There, the Privy Council, while of the opinion that it is a matter of discretion for the judge to choose the most appropriate set of words to enable the particular jury in question to understand the standard of proof, upheld the following direction of the trial judge: 'A reasonable doubt is that quality and kind of doubt which, when you are dealing with matters of importance in your own affairs, you allow to influence you one way or the other.' The decision was affirmed in *Gray* (1973) 58 Cr App R 177.

If the jury ask whether unlikely possibilities preclude a finding of guilt, the judge should tell the jury to exclude fanciful possibilities and act only on realistic possibilities (*Majid* [2009] EWCA Crim 2563).

Direction where Legal Burden on Defence

In the exceptional cases in which the legal burden of proving an issue is borne by the defence (see F3.54 F3.8 *et seq.*), it is discharged by proof on a balance of probabilities. See, in the case of insanity, *Sodeman v The King* [1936] 2 All ER 1138; in the case of the Prevention of Crime Act 1953, s. 1, an express statutory exception, *Brown* (1971) 55 Cr App R 478; in the case of the Homicide Act 1957, s. 2(2), another express statutory exception, *Dunbar* [1958] 1 QB 1; and in the case of implied statutory exceptions under the MCA 1980, s. 101, *Islington London Borough Council v Panico* [1973] 3 All ER 485. In *Carr-Briant* [1943] KB 607, the accused, who was convicted of an offence under the Prevention of Corruption Acts 1906 and 1916 (now repealed), was considered at that time to bear the legal burden of proving that money given or lent to an employee of a government department was not paid or given corruptly. The trial judge directed the jury that the burden on the accused was as heavy as that normally resting on the prosecution. Humphreys J, quashing the conviction, said (at p. 612) that 'the jury should be directed that . . . the burden of proof required is less than that required at the hands of the prosecution in proving the case beyond a reasonable doubt, and that the burden may be discharged by evidence satisfying the jury of the probability of that which the accused is called upon to establish'.

The classic definition of proof on a 'balance of probabilities' is that of Denning J in *Miller v Minister of Pensions* [1947] 2 All ER 372, at p. 374: 'If the evidence is such that the tribunal can say: "We think it more probable than not", the burden is discharged, but, if the probabilities are equal, it is not.'

BURDEN OF PROOF ON FACTS AFFECTING ADMISSIBILITY OF EVIDENCE

When the admissibility of a particular item of evidence is in dispute, the burden of proving F3.55 preliminary facts, that is those facts which must be proved as a condition precedent to the admission of the disputed evidence, lies on the party seeking to admit that evidence. Thus, at common law the prosecution bore the burden of proving the facts constituting the condition precedent to the admissibility of confessions, a rule which has now been put on a statutory basis (*Thompson* [1893] 2 QB 12 and the PACE 1984, s. 76(2): see F17.8. The burden of proving the competence of a witness is on the party seeking to call that witness (YJCEA 1999, s. 54(2): see F4.2 and F4.29). As to the requirement to satisfy the judge of the originality and genuineness of a tape recording, see *Robson* [1972] 2 All ER 699, *Stevenson* [1971] 1 WLR 1, *Rampling* [1987] Crim LR 823, and the Code of Practice for Tape Recording of Police Interviews (Code E).

STANDARD OF PROOF ON FACTS AFFECTING ADMISSIBILITY OF EVIDENCE

When the burden of proving the admissibility of a particular item of evidence is borne by F3.56 the prosecution, the standard to be met is proof beyond reasonable doubt. See, in the case of confessions at common law, *Sartori* [1961] Crim LR 397, *Cave* [1963] Crim LR 371 and *DPP v Ping Lin* [1976] AC 574, at p. 580 (a rule now put on a statutory basis by the PACE 1984, s. 76(2)); and on the issue of the genuineness of samples of writing which it is sought to admit under the Criminal Procedure Act 1865, s. 8, for the purposes of comparison with a disputed writing, *Ewing* [1983] QB 1039. In *Ewing*, the Court of Appeal held that since s. 8 of the 1865 Act did not itself deal with the standard of proof required to satisfy the judge as to the genuineness of the sample writing, the matter was governed by the common law, and accordingly, if the prosecution sought to admit such a sample, they should prove genuineness beyond reasonable doubt. The court was of the opinion that the earlier decision of the Court of Appeal in *Angeli* [1979] 3 All ER 950, that the standard was the civil one, must have been reached *per incuriam*.

Although there is little authority on the point, as a matter of principle, when the burden of proving the admissibility of a particular item of evidence is borne by the defence, the standard to be met should be proof on a balance of probabilities. See, in the case of a defence application under the CJA 1988, s. 23 (now repealed), *Mattey* [1995] 2 Cr App R 409. See also the PACE 1984, s. 76A(2) and (3), at **F17.28**.

PRESUMPTIONS

Presumptions without Basic Facts: Generally

F3.57   Presumptions without basic facts come into operation without the need for proof or admission of any basic or primary fact — they are merely rules that a certain conclusion must be drawn by the court in the absence of any evidence in rebuttal. Thus, although referred to as 'presumptions', in fact they are indistinguishable from the other rules relating to the incidence of the legal or evidential burden. Three examples are considered: the presumption of innocence, the presumption of sanity, and the presumption that mechanical and other instruments of a kind that are usually in working order, were in working order at the time of their use.

Presumption of Innocence

F3.58   The phrase 'the presumption of innocence' is often used as a convenient abbreviation of the common-law rule that, generally speaking, the prosecution bears the burden of proving all the elements in the offence necessary to establish guilt (see *Woolmington v DPP* [1935] AC 462 and generally **F3.6**).

Presumption of Sanity

F3.59   The presumption of sanity is a convenient abbreviation of the common-law rule that if the accused raises the defence of insanity, he will bear the burden of proving it (on a balance of probabilities) (see *Layton* (1849) 4 Cox CC 149, *M'Naghten's Case* (1843) 10 Cl & F 200, and generally **F3.8**). The phrase is to be distinguished from 'the presumption of mental capacity' which has been used to refer to the common-law rule that the evidential burden in relation to automatism not due to a disease of the mind is borne by the accused (see *Bratty v A-G for Northern Ireland* [1963] AC 386 at **F3.43**).

Presumption as to Working of Mechanical and Other Instruments

F3.60   There is a presumption that mechanical and other instruments of a kind that are usually in working order, were in working order at the time of their use. The party against whom the presumption operates bears an evidential burden to adduce some evidence to the contrary. The presumption has been applied in the case of speedometers (see *Nicholas v Penny* [1950] 2 KB 466, in which it was held that justices were entitled to convict of speeding on the evidence of one officer as to the speedometer reading of a police car driven at an even distance behind the accused's car, notwithstanding that no evidence had been adduced as to the accuracy of the speedometer). Traffic lights have likewise been presumed to be in working order: in *Tingle Jacobs & Co. v Kennedy* [1964] 1 All ER 888, Lord Denning MR said (at p. 639) 'when you have a device of this kind set up for public use in active operation . . . the presumption should be that it is in proper working order unless there is evidence to the contrary'. See also, in the case of a public weighbridge, *Kelly Communications Ltd v DPP* (2003) 167 JP 73.

As to representations of fact made otherwise than by a person but that depend for their accuracy on information supplied by a person, see also the CJA 2003, s. 129 (see **F15.28**).

PRESUMPTIONS OF FACT

General Principles

The phrase 'presumption of fact' has been used to describe certain frequently recurring varie-   **F3.61**
ties of circumstantial evidence, i.e. evidence of relevant facts from which the existence of some
fact which is in issue *may* be inferred. Thus, presumptions of fact, sometimes referred to as
provisional presumptions, operate in the following manner: on the proof or admission of a
basic or primary fact, another fact may be presumed in the absence of sufficient evidence to the
contrary. The party against whom the presumption operates bears neither a legal nor an evidential burden in relation to the presumed fact; if he adduces no evidence to the contrary, he runs
a risk of losing on that issue, but he is not *bound* to lose on that issue. The following examples
are considered: the presumption of continuance of life, the presumption of intention, and the
presumption of guilty knowledge in cases of handling, theft, etc.

Continuance of Life

On the proof or admission of the basic fact that a person was alive on a certain date, it may be   **F3.62**
presumed, in the absence of sufficient evidence to the contrary, that he was still alive on some
subsequent date (*MacDarmaid v A-G* [1950] P 218; *Re Peete* [1952] 2 All ER 599). Whether
or not such an inference should be drawn is a question for the jury, and is entirely dependent
upon the facts of the case. Thus, if there is proof that a person was in good health on one day,
there would be a strong, almost irresistible, inference that he was alive on the next day, and the
jury would in all probability find that he was so; if, on the other hand, it were proved that he was
in a dying condition on the first day and nothing further was proved, the jury would probably
decline to draw the inference that he was alive on the following day (*Lumley* (1869) LR 1 CCR
196, per Lush J at p. 198, on the question of whether a husband was alive at the date of his wife's
allegedly bigamous second marriage, approved in *Morrison* (1938) 27 Cr App R 1).

Intention

Criminal Justice Act 1967, s. 8   **F3.63**

A court or jury, in determining whether a person has committed an offence—
(a) shall not be bound in law to infer that he intended or foresaw a result of his actions by reason
    only of its being a natural and probable consequence of those actions; but
(b) shall decide whether he did intend or foresee that result by reference to all the evidence, draw-
    ing such inferences from the evidence as appear proper in the circumstances.

Section 8 of the 1967 Act puts on a statutory basis the common-law presumption of fact that
a person intends the natural consequences of his acts, and reverses the decision in *DPP v Smith*
[1961] AC 290 that in certain circumstances the presumption is a presumption of law (*Wallett*
[1968] 2 QB 367 and *Moloney* [1985] AC 905). As to jury directions on intention, see the
authorities considered at **A2.4**.

Guilty Knowledge in Cases of Handling, Theft etc.

In cases of handling and theft, on proof or admission of the fact that the accused was   **F3.64**
found in possession of property so shortly after it was stolen that it can fairly be said that
he was in recent possession of it, the jury should be directed that such possession calls for
explanation, and if none is given, or one is given which they are convinced is untrue, they
are entitled to infer, according to the circumstances, that the accused is either the handler
or the thief and to convict accordingly (*Schama* (1914) 84 LJ KB 396; *Garth* [1949] 1 All
ER 773; *Aves* [1950] 2 All ER 330; *Williams* [1962] Crim LR 54). It is desirable in most
cases to direct the jury that the burden of proof remains on the prosecution, and if, therefore, the explanation given by the accused leaves them in doubt as to whether he came by

the property honestly, the prosecution have not proved their case and they should acquit (*Aves* and *Hepworth* [1955] 2 QB 600, applied in *Moulding* [1996] Crim LR 440). See also *Aubrey* (1915) 11 Cr App R 182, *Brain* (1918) 13 Cr App R 197 and *Sanders* (1919) 14 Cr App R 11.

F3.65   The doctrine of recent possession applies not only in the case of 'receiving', but also in the case of a charge under the second limb of the Theft Act 1968, s. 22 (*Ball* [1983] 2 All ER 1089). Apart from handling and theft, the doctrine may also apply to other offences with a theft ingredient, as when the accused is charged with burglary contrary to s. 9(1)(b), and it is proved that shortly after the premises were entered and property stolen therefrom, the accused was found in possession of the property (*Loughlin* (1951) 35 Cr App R 69 and *Seymour* [1954] 1 All ER 1006). There is no general rule of law to the effect that the doctrine has no application in cases in which there is some evidence of the circumstances in which the accused came into possession of the stolen goods (see per Stocker LJ in *Raviraj* (1986) 85 Cr App R 93, commenting on *obiter* remarks made in *Bradley* (1979) 70 Cr App R 200). However, the doctrine cannot be relied upon where the accused failed to give an explanation *after* he was cautioned (*Raviraj*).

F3.66   'Recent'   Whether possession is 'recent' is a question of fact and degree dependent on all the circumstances of the case in question. Relevant factors include the nature of the property, its saleability, and any evidence, other than that of the accused's possession of the goods, connecting him with the offence charged. In *Smythe* (1980) 72 Cr App R 8, Kilner Brown J said (at p. 11): 'Nearly every reported case is merely a decision of fact as an example of what is no more than a rule of evidence'. The precedents, therefore, are of somewhat limited value.

It is instructive, however, to note that in *Cash* [1985] QB 801, in which the goods were found in the possession of the appellant, C, on 25 February 1983, and none of the property was stolen more recently than 16 February 1983, the Court of Appeal, upholding C's conviction for handling, said that it was not properly open to the jury to infer that C was the burglar or thief. In that case two others were charged in the same indictment: A, who was convicted of burglary and handling offences; and E, who pleaded guilty to burglary and obtaining property by deception. The prosecution case was that C handled goods taken, by A, E and other persons unknown, in the course of a number of separate burglaries which took place between July and October 1982 and January and 16 February 1983. Some of the proceeds of the burglaries were recovered from C's flat on 25 February 1983. A was a lodger in the flat. When arrested, C declined to answer questions, and at the trial elected to give no evidence. In *Smythe* (1980) 72 Cr App R 8 the Court of Appeal said that it would be quite unsafe to infer positive proof of participation in a series of burglaries and robberies from the mere fact of possession, between two and three months after the robberies, of articles stolen in the course of them. See also *Marcus* (1923) 17 Cr App R 191: a period of eight months between the theft and the time when the goods were first seen in the possession of the accused was too long a period for the doctrine to apply.

F3.67   'Otherwise than in the course of stealing'   In ordinary cases of handling, the prosecution are not required to adduce affirmative proof that the goods were handled 'otherwise than in the course of the stealing' (see the Theft Act 1968, s. 22(1)). This remains the position in recent possession cases, because if the jury draws the inference that the accused is guilty of handling, this includes the inference that he was not the actual thief. However, where the accused is in possession of stolen goods so recently after they are stolen that the inevitable inference is that he is the thief, as when he is found within a few hundred yards of the scene of the theft and minutes after the theft took place, then if he is only charged with handling, the Crown can prove that offence only if it proves affirmatively that the accused was not the thief, and the judge should direct the jury that they must acquit the accused of handling if they take the view that he was the thief (*Cash* [1985] QB 801, applied in *A-G of Hong Kong v Yip Kai-Foon* [1988] AC 642; *Ryan v DPP* (1994) 158 JP 485).

IRREBUTTABLE PRESUMPTIONS OF LAW

General Principles

Irrebuttable presumptions of law, or conclusive presumptions, operate in the following way: on **F3.68** the proof or admission of a basic or primary fact another fact must be presumed which no evidence is admissible to rebut. Such presumptions are nothing more than rules of substantive law, as the following example illustrates. (See also the SOA 2003, s. 76, considered at **B3.32**.)

Presumption that Children under Ten Cannot be Guilty of Offence

The CYPA 1933, s. 50, provides that: 'It shall be conclusively presumed that no child under the **F3.69** age of 10 years can be guilty of an offence'. It follows from this that a person over the age of ten who receives property dishonestly acquired by a person under the age of ten cannot be guilty of receiving stolen property, although if he has the necessary *mens rea*, he may be guilty of theft (*Walters v Lunt* [1951] 2 All ER 645; *McGregor v Benyon* [1957] Crim LR 608).

REBUTTABLE PRESUMPTIONS OF LAW

General Principles

Rebuttable presumptions of law operate in the following manner: on the proof or admission of **F3.70** the basic or primary facts, another fact must be presumed in the absence of sufficient evidence to the contrary. If the defence rely upon a rebuttable presumption of law and adduce prima facie evidence of the basic facts, a legal burden is placed on the prosecution requiring them to disprove or negative the presumed fact beyond reasonable doubt. If the prosecution rely upon a rebuttable presumption of law and adduce prima facie evidence of the basic facts, an evidential burden is placed on the defence which may be discharged by the adduction of such evidence as might leave a jury in reasonable doubt; and if the defence do discharge the evidential burden, the effect is as if the presumption had never come into play — the prosecution are still required to prove the presumed fact beyond reasonable doubt (*Kay* (1887) 16 Cox CC 292 and *Willshire* (1881) 6 QBD 366 (the presumption of marriage)).

The foregoing relates to common-law presumptions. As to the statutory presumptions which operate to place on the defence a legal burden requiring them to disprove or negative a presumed fact by the adduction of such evidence as will satisfy the jury on a balance of probabilities, see **F3.9** *et seq*. As to the statutory presumptions arising under the PACE 1984, s. 74, see **F11.6**. Presumptions relating to the due execution of documents are considered at **F8.43**. The rebuttable presumptions of law that now fall to be considered are the presumptions of regularity, marriage and death.

Presumption of Regularity

The presumption of regularity, expressed in the maxim *omnia praesumuntur rite esse acta*, oper- **F3.71** ates as follows: on proof or admission of the basic or primary fact that a person has acted in a public or official capacity, it is presumed, in the absence of sufficient evidence to the contrary, that that person was regularly and properly appointed and that the act was regularly and properly performed. The presumption cannot be rebutted merely by challenging the presumed fact — evidence must be adduced (*Campbell v Wallsend Slipway and Engineering Co. Ltd* [1978] ICR 1015). Typical examples concern the validity of an official appointment. Thus, on a charge of assaulting a police officer in the course of his duty, evidence that the officer acted in that capacity is sufficient proof of his due appointment (*Gordon* (1789) 1 Leach 515; and see *Cooper v Rowlands* [1971] RTR 291). See also *Borrett* (1833) 6 C & P 124 (a person acting as an officer of the Post Office), *Roberts* (1878) 38 LT 690 (a deputy county court judge), and *Campbell v*

Part F Evidence

Wallsend Slipway and Engineering Co. Ltd (an inspector of the Health and Safety Executive). In *Langton* (1876) 2 QBD 296, the presumption operated to establish the due incorporation of a company which had acted as such. In *Cresswell* (1873) 1 QBD 446, evidence that a marriage had been celebrated in a building in which other marriages had also been celebrated was sufficient to establish that the building was duly consecrated.

The presumption must be applied with caution in cases where commission of an offence is dependent upon compliance with formal statutory conditions. Thus, the Divisional Court has held that it is wrong to presume, on the basis of evidence that a breath test device has been issued to the police, that it was officially approved by the Secretary of State (*Scott v Baker* [1969] 1 QB 659, approved in *Withecombe* [1969] 1 All ER 157). See also *Swift v Barrett* (1940) 163 LT 154, in which the Divisional Court required strict proof that a road sign complied with regulations. Such authorities, it is submitted, are not easily reconciled with *Gibbins v Skinner* [1951] 2 KB 379, in which it was held that evidence that speed-limit signs had been erected on a road was sufficient to establish that the local authority had performed its statutory duties pursuant to the Road Traffic Acts and given a direction justifying the erection of the signs. *Scott v Baker* was distinguished in *Public Prosecution Service of Northern Ireland v Elliott* [2013] 2 Cr App R 180 (17) in relation to fingerprints taken using an electronic reader that had not been officially approved by the Secretary of State. The Supreme Court held that the well-established rule of law that evidence which is relevant is admissible, even if obtained illegally, extends to evidence created by an unlawful process. It was also held that the statutory requirement for approval of an electronic fingerprint reader is not analogous to the approval requirements in the case of breath test or speed gun devices, because whereas the latter devices are means of measuring something that cannot subsequently be re-measured, fingerprints can be reproduced subsequently and the accuracy of the initial readings, if disputed, can be checked by the provision of more samples.

Presumptions of Marriage

F3.72   The civil authorities, although not explicit on the point, suggest that there are three different presumptions of marriage:

(a) a presumption of formal validity (i.e. a presumption of compliance with the formal requirements of the *lex loci celebrationis*, e.g., the requirement, in the case of a Church of England marriage under English law, to obtain a common or special licence);

(b) a presumption of essential validity (i.e. a presumption that each of the parties had the capacity to marry and was not, for example, under the age of 16 or already married); and

(c) a presumption of marriage arising from cohabitation.

Although there is a dearth of criminal authority, it is submitted that the presumptions of formal and essential validity apply in criminal as well as civil proceedings. The presumption of marriage arising from cohabitation, however, would appear to be of limited utility in criminal proceedings; the authorities show that if the prosecution bear the burden of proving the existence of a marriage, the presumption by itself is insufficient to discharge even the evidential burden. Thus in a case of bigamy, the prosecution, in seeking to prove a valid first marriage which subsisted at the date of the second marriage, must adduce some evidence of the celebration of the first marriage; evidence of acknowledgement, cohabitation or repute will not suffice (*Morris v Miller* (1767) 4 Burr 2057). It will suffice, however, if there is not only evidence that the accused had cohabited with a woman and spoken of her as his wife, but also proof from the register of marriages that a person of the same name as the accused married that woman (*Birtles* (1911) 6 Cr App R 177). See also *Umanski* [1961] VR 242.

F3.73 Presumption of Death

By virtue of a long sequence of judicial statements, which either assert or assume such a rule, it appears accepted that there is a convenient presumption of law applicable to certain cases of seven years' absence where no statute applies. That presumption in its modern shape takes effect (without examining its terms too exactly) substantially as follows. Where as regards 'A.B' there is no acceptable affirmative evidence that he was alive at some time during a continuous period of seven years or more, then if it can be proved first, that there are persons who would be likely to have heard of him over that period, secondly that those persons have not heard of him, and thirdly that all due inquiries have been made appropriate to the circumstances, 'A.B.' will be presumed to have died at some time within that period. (*Chard v Chard* [1956] P 259, per Sachs J at p. 272)

The authorities conflict as to the date on which the fact of death may be presumed; it is either the date of the proceedings in question or the date at the end of the period of absence for seven years (*Lal Chand Marwari v Mahant Ranrup Gir* (1925) 42 TLR 159, at p. 160, and contrast *Re Westbrook's Trusts* [1873] WN 167 and *Chipchase v Chipchase* [1939] P 31).

Under the Presumption of Death Act 2013, s. 1, an application may be made to the High Court for a declaration that a missing person is presumed to be dead. Under s. 2(1), the court must make the declaration if satisfied that the missing person has died or has not been known to be alive for a period of at least seven years. Under s. 2(2), the court must include in the declaration a finding as to the date and time of the missing person's death, a matter to be determined in accordance with s. 2(3) and (4). Under s. 3, a declaration under the Act is conclusive of the missing person's presumed death and time of the death and is effective against all persons and for all purposes. Sections 1 to 3 came into force on 1 October 2014 (see SI 2014 No. 1810).

Concerning the proviso to the OAPA 1861, s. 57 ('persons [charged with bigamy] marrying a second time whose husband or wife shall have been continually absent for the space of seven years then last past, and shall not have been known by such person to be living within that time'), see **B2.131**.

CONFLICTING PRESUMPTIONS

There is civil authority that where two presumptions of equal strength apply in a case with the **F3.74** result that two facts are presumed, the one in conflict with the other, the presumptions neutralise each other and the case falls to be determined without the application of either (*Monckton v Tarr* (1930) 23 BWCC 504). *Willshire* (1881) 6 QBD 366 is often cited in support of this proposition, although there was no true conflict in that case, which involved two presumptions of unequal strength, a rebuttable presumption of law and a presumption of fact. W was charged with bigamously marrying D in the lifetime of C. W had gone through four ceremonies of marriage, with A in 1864, with B in 1868, with C in 1879, and with D in 1880. The prosecution relied upon the presumption of essential validity in seeking to establish the validity of the marriage of 1879. W sought to show that the marriage of 1879 was void, and accordingly relied upon his previous conviction, in 1868, for marrying B during the lifetime of A: A was alive in 1868 and under the presumption of continuance of life could be presumed to have been alive in 1879, in which case the marriage of 1879 was void. The trial judge did not leave the issue of whether A was alive in 1879 to the jury, directing them that the onus was on W to adduce evidence of her existence on that date. The conviction was quashed. Lord Coleridge CJ, referring to a 'conflict' of presumptions, held that the accused was not bound to do more than set up A's life in 1868, which would be presumed to continue, and it was then for the prosecution to disprove her existence on that date. It is submitted that there was no real conflict of presumptions in this case. The decision reached was correct. The onus of proving the validity of the 1879 marriage was on the prosecution. Their reliance on the presumption of validity placed nothing more than an evidential burden on W, which he had successfully discharged in reliance upon the presumption of continuance of life. The onus remained on the prosecution to establish the validity of the 1879 marriage.

Section F4 Competence and Compellability of Witnesses and Oaths and Affirmations

GENERAL

Meaning of Competence and Compellability

F4.1 A witness is competent if he may lawfully be called to testify, and is compellable if, being competent, he may lawfully be compelled by the court to testify. As to securing the attendance of a witness, whether by witness order or witness summons, see **D15.93** *et seq*. and **D22.28** *et seq*.

Determining Competence

F4.2 The question whether a witness is competent to give evidence in criminal proceedings must be determined by the court in accordance with the YJCEA 1999, s. 54 (set out at **F4.29**). It is for the party calling the witness to satisfy the court on a balance of probabilities that the witness is competent (s. 54(2)) and expert evidence may be received on the question (s. 54(5)). In deciding the question, the court must treat the witness as having the benefit of any special measures directions which the court has given or proposes to give in relation to the witness (s. 54(3)). Equally, the competency test is not failed because the forensic techniques of the advocates have to be adapted to enable a witness to give the best evidence of which he is capable (*F* [2013] 1 WLR 2143). Any proceedings held to decide the question of competence shall take place in the absence of the jury (s. 54(4)) and any questioning of the witness shall be conducted by the court in the presence of the parties (s. 54(6)). See also, in the case of children and persons of unsound mind, **F4.25**. As regards statements made by unavailable witnesses, see the CJA 2003, s. 123(4), at **F16.8**.

There are some common-law authorities as to the time for determining the competence of a witness. In the case of a prosecution witness, it has been held that the question should be raised and decided at the beginning of the trial (*Yacoob* (1981) 72 Cr App R 313). An objection to the competence of a witness should be made before the witness has been examined in chief (*Wollaston v Hakewill* (1841) 3 Man & G 297; *Bartlett v Smith* (1843) 11 M & W 483), unless the incompetence only becomes apparent during examination-in-chief (*Jacobs v Layborn* (1843) 11 M & W 685). If, at this stage, the witness is ruled incompetent, the judge should direct the jury to ignore his evidence (*Whitehead* (1866) LR 1 CCR 33).

Witnesses who Refuse to Take the Oath or Testify

F4.3 Judges of the Crown Court may exercise their power to punish summarily for contempt of court (Senior Courts Act 1981, s. 45(4)) any compellable witness who refuses to take an oath or make an affirmation (*Hennegal v Evance* (1806) 12 Ves Jr 201). Likewise, but subject to public policy or a claim to privilege which the court upholds, a witness who refuses to answer a proper question may be found to be in contempt of court and face the penalty of imprisonment (*Ex parte Fernandez* (1861) 10 CB NS 13). A witness who refuses to testify and runs the risk of committal to prison as a contemnor should be given the opportunity of legal representation (*K* (1984) 78 Cr App R 82). In *Phillips* (1983) 78 Cr App R 88, it was stressed that, on a finding of contempt, sentence need not be passed immediately; the witness may change his mind. See further **B14.89** and **B14.103**.

Wards of Court as Witnesses

The leave of the wardship court is not required to call a ward to give evidence at a criminal **F4.4**
trial. This is so irrespective of whether (a) the child is interviewed and has made witness
statements before or after becoming a ward, (b) it is the prosecution or defence who wish to
call the child or (c) the child's failure to give evidence would prevent the prosecution taking place (*Re K (Minors) (Wardship: Criminal Proceedings)* [1988] Fam 1; *Re R (A Minor)
(Wardship: Criminal Proceedings)* [1991] 2 All ER 193, per Lord Donaldson MR at p. 917).
Concerning interviews with wards, see CPD V, paras. 28A.1 to 28A.8 (see Supplement,
PD–41), *Re R (Minors)* [1990] 2 All ER 633 and *Re R (A Minor) (Wardship: Criminal
Proceedings)* [1991] 2 All ER 193.

General Rule as to Competence and Compellability

The general rule relating to the competence and compellability of witnesses has two limbs: **F4.5**

(a) The first is that any person is a competent witness in any proceedings. The exceptions to this
limb relate to the accused, children, and persons with a disorder or disability of the mind.
(b) The second is that all competent witnesses are compellable. The exceptions to this limb
relate to the accused and his or her spouse or civil partner.

The first limb of the general rule has been put on a statutory basis. Under the YJCEA 1999,
s. 53(1), which has effect subject to s. 53(3) and (4), 'At every stage in criminal proceedings
all persons are (whatever their age) competent to give evidence'. Under s. 53(3), a person is
not competent to give evidence if it appears to the court that he is not a person who is able to
(a) understand questions put to him as a witness and (b) give answers to them which can be
understood (see **F4.21**). Section 53(4) provides that a person charged is not competent to give
evidence for the prosecution (see **F4.8**).

Deaf and Speech Impaired Witnesses

A person who can neither hear nor speak is competent as a witness, provided that the court is **F4.6**
satisfied that he understands the nature of an oath (*Ruston* (1786) 1 Leach 408; *O'Brien* (1845)
1 Cox CC 185). Such a person may take an oath (or make an affirmation) and be examined and
cross-examined, through an interpreter, using sign language. The interpreter should also take an
oath (or make an affirmation). A witness who cannot speak may be allowed to give his evidence
in written form. See also the 'special measures' of examination through an intermediary, which
the court can direct under the YJCEA 1999, s. 29, and *F* [2013] 1 WLR 2143.

No Property in the Evidence of a Witness

No party has any property in the evidence of a witness, so that even if there is a contract between **F4.7**
a witness and a party, whereby the latter binds himself not to testify on a matter on which the
court can compel him to give evidence, such a contract is contrary to public policy and unenforceable (*Harmony Shipping Co. SA v Saudi Europe Line Ltd* [1979] 3 All ER 177). However,
once a witness in a criminal case has testified on behalf of the prosecution, he cannot be compelled to testify on behalf of the defence (*Kelly* (1985) *The Times*, 27 July 1985). As to expert
witnesses, see also **F9.60**.

THE ACCUSED

As a Witness for the Prosecution

An accused is not competent as a witness for the prosecution. Under the YJCEA 1999, s. 53(4), **F4.8**
'A person charged in criminal proceedings is not competent to give evidence in the proceedings
for the prosecution (whether he is the only person, or is one of two or more persons, charged in

the proceedings)'. A co-accused may only give evidence for the prosecution if he ceases to be a co-accused. Section 53(5) provides that: 'In subsection (4) the reference to a person charged in criminal proceedings does not include a person who is not, or is no longer, liable to be convicted of any offence in the proceedings (whether as a result of pleading guilty or for any other reason)'. 'Other reasons' why a co-accused may not, or may no longer, be liable to be convicted, are that he has been acquitted or is to be tried separately or that the A-G has entered a *nolle prosequi*. If an accused pleads guilty, he is competent for the prosecution even if he suggests in his evidence that he was not a participant in the offence, unless the plea is set aside (*McEwan* [2011] EWCA Crim 1026).

F4.9 There is a rule of practice, not law, that an accomplice against whom proceedings are pending but who is not an accused in the proceedings in which the prosecution seek to call him, should only be called by the prosecution if they have undertaken to discontinue the proceedings against him. In *Pipe* (1967) 51 Cr App R 17, Pipe was charged with housebreaking and larceny. He was alleged to have stolen a safe and its contents. Swan was called to prove that he had helped Pipe to break open the safe. Swan, before the commencement of Pipe's trial, had been charged with complicity in Pipe's crime in relation to the safe. Swan was not indicted with Pipe. It was intended to try him later. The Court of Criminal Appeal held that it was 'wholly irregular' to have called Swan in these circumstances.

In *Turner* (1975) 61 Cr App R 67 it was argued that for some time past there had been a practice for judges not to admit the evidence of accomplices who could still be influenced by continuing inducements, and that in *Pipe* the Court of Appeal had adjudged that this practice had become a rule of law. Rejecting this argument, Lawton LJ said, at p. 78:

> There is nothing in either the arguments [in *Pipe*] or the judgment itself to indicate that the court thought it was changing a rule of law as to the competency of accomplices to give evidence which had been followed ever since the 17th century. The facts of that case must be closely examined....
>
> [*Pipe's*] *ratio decidendi* is confined to a case in which an accomplice, who has been charged, but not tried, is required to give evidence of his own offence in order to secure the conviction of another accused. *Pipe* on its facts was clearly a right decision. The same result could have been achieved by adjudging that the trial judge should have exercised his discretion to exclude Swan's evidence on the ground that there was an obvious and powerful inducement for him to ingratiate himself with the prosecution and the court and that the existence of this inducement made it desirable in the interests of justice to exclude it. See *Noor Mohamed v The King* [1949] AC 182 per Lord du Parcq at p. 192 and followed in *Harris v DPP* [1952] AC 694 per Viscount Simon at p. 707.

As a Witness on his Own Behalf

F4.10 The accused is a competent witness for the defence pursuant to the YJCEA 1999, s. 53(1), whereby 'At every stage in criminal proceedings all persons are...competent to give evidence'. The phrase 'at every stage in criminal proceedings' allows the accused to give evidence not only in the trial itself, but also after conviction, in mitigation of sentence (see *Wheeler* [1917] 1 KB 283, a decision construing a similar phrase used in the Criminal Evidence Act 1898, s. 1, prior to its amendment by the YJCEA 1999). There is some old authority to the effect that the accused is not entitled as of right to give evidence on the *voir dire* (*Baldwin* (1931) 23 Cr App R 62) but that the court may in its discretion allow the accused to give evidence at this stage if the justice of the case makes this desirable (*Cowell* [1940] 2 KB 49). The wording of s. 53(1), however, supports the current practice, which is for the accused to elect whether to give evidence on the *voir dire*.

The accused is not a compellable witness for the defence. Under the Criminal Evidence Act 1898, s. 1(1), 'A person charged in criminal proceedings shall not be called as a witness in the proceedings except upon his own application'.

Giving Evidence from the Witness Box

F4.11 The Criminal Evidence Act 1898, s. 1(4), provides that 'Every person charged in criminal proceedings who is called as a witness in the proceedings shall, unless otherwise ordered by the court, give his evidence from the witness box or other place from which other witnesses give their evidence'. Concerning the statutory precursor to s. 1(4) (s. 1(g) of the 1898 Act), it was held that the intention was that the accused should 'have an opportunity of giving evidence on his own behalf in the same way and from the same place as the witnesses for the prosecution'. Thus the accused should give his evidence from the witness-box unless, for example, he is too infirm to walk there or too violent to be controlled there (*Symonds* (1924) 18 Cr App R 100, per Swift J at p. 101). Section 1(4) does not confer on justices a discretion to direct where evidence should be given from but allows them, in exceptional circumstances of the kind described in *Symonds*, to deny the accused the right he would otherwise have to give evidence from the witness box. To offer the accused a choice as to whether he wishes to give evidence from the dock or the witness stand is also to fetter that right and any such practice should cease (*Farnham Justices, ex parte Gibson* [1991] RTR 309, where the conviction of a defendant required to give evidence from the dock was quashed, applying the principle that justice must not only be done but must also be seen to be done).

Requirement to Give Evidence on Oath and Liability to Cross-examination   If **F4.12** the accused elects to testify, he must give his evidence on oath and will be liable to cross-examination.

Criminal Justice Act 1982, s. 72

(1) Subject to subsections (2) and (3) below, in any criminal proceedings the accused shall not be entitled to make a statement without being sworn, and accordingly, if he gives evidence he shall do so (subject to sections 55 and 56 of the Youth Justice and Criminal Evidence Act 1999) on oath and be liable to cross-examination; but this section shall not affect the right of the accused, if not represented by counsel or a solicitor, to address the court or jury otherwise than on oath on any matter on which, if he were so represented, counsel or a solicitor could address the court or jury on his behalf.

(2) Nothing in subsection (1) above shall prevent the accused making a statement without being sworn—

    (a) if it is one which he is required by law to make personally; or

    (b) if he makes it by way of mitigation before the court passes sentence upon him.

The qualification in s. 72(1) relating to the YJCEA 1999, ss. 55 and 56, has the effect that the evidence of an accused who is competent to give evidence but who is not permitted to be sworn shall be given unsworn. Sections 55 (determining whether a witness should give sworn evidence) and 56 (the reception of unsworn evidence) are set out at **F4.29**.

If the accused does testify, he is liable to cross-examination by the prosecution and, whether or not he has given evidence against a co-accused, by counsel for any co-accused (*Hilton* [1972] 1 QB 421). Subject to the CJA 2003, s. 101 (defendant's bad character), considered at **F12.15**, and to the Criminal Evidence Act 1898, s. 1(4) (see **F4.11**), he will be treated like any other witness. His evidence will be evidence for all the purposes of the case, including the purpose of being evidence against any co-accused (*Rudd* (1948) 32 Cr App R 138, per Humphreys J at p. 140). In *Paul* [1920] 2 KB 183, in which an accused had confined his evidence in chief to an admission of his own guilt, it was held that the prosecution had properly been allowed to cross-examine him and thereby elicit evidence which undermined the defence of his co-accused.

As a Witness for a Co-accused

An accused is a competent witness for any co-accused by virtue of the YJCEA 1999, s. 53(1)   **F4.13** (see **F4.29**). An accused, however, is not a compellable witness for a co-accused because, under the Criminal Evidence Act 1898, s. 1(1), a person charged in criminal proceedings shall not be called as a witness 'except upon his own application' (see **F4.10**). An accused who does give evidence for a co-accused may be cross-examined to show his own guilt of the offence charged (*Rowland* [1910] 1 KB 458).

A co-accused who ceases to be 'a person charged', and therefore ceases to be on trial, is both competent and compellable as a witness for any 'co-accused'. This may happen in the following ways:

(a) the co-accused pleads guilty;

(b) the co-accused, at the end of the prosecution case, makes a successful submission of no case to answer; or

(c) the co-accused is tried separately as the result of a successful application to sever the indictment.

THE SPOUSE OR CIVIL PARTNER OF THE ACCUSED

General

F4.14 The competence and compellability of the spouse or civil partner of an accused is governed by the YJCEA 1999, s. 53(1) (see **F4.29**), and the PACE 1984, s. 80.

Police and Criminal Evidence Act 1984, s. 80

(2) In any proceedings the spouse or civil partner of a person charged in the proceedings shall, subject to subsection (4) below, be compellable to give evidence on behalf of that person.

(2A) In any proceedings the spouse or civil partner of a person charged in the proceedings shall, subject to subsection (4) below, be compellable—

(a) to give evidence on behalf of any other person charged in the proceedings but only in respect of any specified offence with which that other person is charged; or

(b) to give evidence for the prosecution but only in respect of any specified offence with which any person is charged in the proceedings.

(3) In relation to the spouse or civil partner of a person charged in any proceedings, an offence is a specified offence for the purposes of subsection (2A) above if—

(a) it involves an assault on, or injury or a threat of injury to, the spouse or civil partner or a person who was at the material time under the age of 16;

(b) it is a sexual offence alleged to have been committed in respect of a person who was at the material time under that age; or

(c) it consists of attempting or conspiring to commit, or of aiding, abetting, counselling, procuring or inciting the commission of, an offence falling within paragraph (a) or (b) above.

(4) No person who is charged in any proceedings shall be compellable by virtue of subsection (2) or (2A) above to give evidence in the proceedings.

(4A) References in this section to a person charged in any proceedings do not include a person who is not, or is no longer, liable to be convicted of any offence in the proceedings (whether as a result of pleading guilty or for any other reason).

(5) In any proceedings a person who has been but is no longer married to the accused shall be compellable to give evidence as if that person and the accused had never been married.

(5A) In any proceedings a person who has been but is no longer the civil partner of the accused shall be compellable to give evidence as if that person and the accused had never been civil partners.

(6) Where in any proceedings the age of any person at any time is material for the purposes of subsection (3) above, his age at the material time shall for the purposes of that provision be deemed to be or to have been that which appears to the court to be or to have been his age at that time.

(7) In subsection (3)(b) above 'sexual offence' means an offence under the Protection of Children Act 1978 or Part 1 of the Sexual Offences Act 2003.

The reference in s. 30(3)(c) to incitement has effect as a reference to (or to conduct amounting to) the offences of encouraging or assisting crime under part 2 of the SCA 2007 (SCA 2007, s. 63(1) and sch. 6, para. 9).

As a Witness for the Prosecution

F4.15 The spouse or civil partner of an accused is competent to give evidence for the prosecution (YJCEA 1999, s. 53(1): see **F4.29**), unless also 'a person charged' in the criminal proceedings (YJCEA 1999, s. 53(4) and (5), considered at **F4.8**). A spouse or civil partner is competent under s. 53(1) irrespective of whether the evidence to be given will be directed against the accused or any co-accused.

As to compellability, the rule, subject to one exception, is that the spouse or civil partner shall be compellable to give evidence for the prosecution, but only in respect of any 'specified offence' with which any person is charged in the proceedings (PACE 1984, s. 80(2A)(b)). The exception is where the spouse or civil partner is also charged in the proceedings (see s. 80(4) and (4A)).

It is submitted that the words 'spouse' and 'civil partner' used in s. 80 refer to persons whose marriage or civil partnership (wherever celebrated) would be recognised by English law. In *Khan* (1987) 84 Cr App R 44, a decision on the common law before the 1984 Act came into force, it was held that a woman who had gone through a Muslim ceremony of marriage with an accused already married under English law to another woman, was in the same position as a mistress, a woman who had not gone through a ceremony of marriage at all or one who had gone through a ceremony of marriage which was void because bigamous. See also *Yacoob* (1981) 72 Cr App R 313. In *Pearce* [2002] 1 WLR 1553 it was held that the words 'wife or husband of the accused' which appeared in s. 80 prior to its amendment by the YJCEA 1999, do not cover a cohabitee of an accused who is not married to the accused, and that proper respect for family life, as envisaged by the ECHR, Article 8, does not require that such a cohabitee should not be compelled to give evidence. See also *Der Heijden v The Netherlands* [2013] 1 FCR 123: compelling a cohabitee, in a relationship of 18 years duration and out of which two children were born, to give evidence against her partner would interfere with her right to respect for family life under Article 8, but under Article 8(2) would be 'necessary...for the prevention of...crime'.

'Compellable' Offences   Section 80(3) specifies the offences in respect of which the spouse or civil partner of the accused shall be compellable to give evidence for the prosecution. A spouse or civil partner is compellable if the offence charged 'involves' an assault on, or injury or a threat of injury to, the spouse or civil partner of the accused or a person who was at the material time under the age of 16. *A (B)* [2012] 1 All ER 280 addressed the question, posed in earlier editions of this work, whether the 'involvement' must be legal (as a matter of legal definition the offence charged requires an assault on, or injury or a threat of injury to, one of the types of person described in s. 80(3)(a)) or can be factual (as a matter of legal definition the offence charged does not require an assault on or injury or a threat of injury to one of the types of such person but in fact it did involve, or is alleged to have involved, an assault on or injury or a threat of injury to one of the types of such person). In *BA*, the accused, who had shouted to his wife that he was going to burn their house down with the children in it, was charged under the Criminal Damage Act 1971, s. 2(a) with the offence of making a threat to another, intending that that other would fear it would be carried out, to destroy or damage any property belonging to that other or a third person. It was held that: under the PACE 1984, s. 80(3)(a), the 'involvement' must be legal; the offence itself does not have to have as one of its ingredients 'an assault on or injury or threat of injury' — it is sufficient if the offence encompasses the real possibility of an assault etc.; the offence under s. 2(a) of the 1971 Act is directed at property and does not encompass the real possibility of an assault etc.; and therefore the wife of the accused was not compellable to give evidence against him. The phrase 'a threat of injury' may cover not only an uttered threat, but also a threat by conduct, as in *Verolla* [1963] 1 QB 285, where the accused was charged with attempting to murder his wife by poisoning her. A case of that kind, however, is now covered by s. 80(3)(c).

Procedural Issues   There is no requirement to tell a wife who is competent but not compellable for the prosecution that she is not compellable before interviewing her, e.g., where a wife is interviewed about a crime of which her husband is suspected. If the issue arises whether it is in the interests of justice to admit as hearsay a statement made voluntarily by her, the prosecution's hand is likely to be strengthened if it can be shown that she was told that she was under no obligation to make the statement, but failure to give such a warning will not necessarily prevent

F4.16

F4.17

admissibility (*L* [2009] 1 WLR 626 and *Horsnell* [2012] EWCA Crim 227: see **F16.43**). The same principles apply of course in the case of a husband or civil partner.

The following propositions, relating to a spouse who is competent but not compellable for the prosecution, derive from *Pitt* [1983] QB 25, at pp. 65–6:

(a) The choice whether to give evidence is that of the spouse, and is not lost because that spouse made a witness statement or gave evidence at the committal proceedings. The spouse retains the right of refusal up to the point when, with full knowledge of that right, he or she takes the oath in the witness-box. Waiver of the right is effective only if made with full knowledge of the right of refusal.

(b) If the spouse waives the right of refusal, he or she becomes an ordinary witness. It follows that if the nature of the evidence then given justifies it, an application may be made to treat the spouse as a hostile witness.

(c) Although not a rule of either law or practice, it is desirable that where a spouse, being competent but not compellable for the prosecution, is called for the prosecution, the judge should explain to the spouse, in the absence of the jury, that before taking the oath, he or she has the right to refuse to give evidence, but that if he or she chooses to give evidence, he or she may be treated like any other witness (but failure to give such an explanation does not necessarily justify interfering with a guilty verdict: *Nelson* [1992] Crim LR 653).

The same principles would apply, of course, in the case of a civil partner.

As a Witness for the Accused

F4.18   The spouse or civil partner of an accused is competent to give evidence for the accused (YJCEA 1999, s. 53(1): see **F4.29**); and shall be compellable to give evidence for the accused (PACE 1984, s. 80(2)), unless also charged in the proceedings (see s. 80(4) and (4A)).

As a Witness for a Co-accused

F4.19   The spouse or civil partner of an accused is competent to give evidence on behalf of any other person charged in the proceedings, whether or not the accused consents (YJCEA 1999, s. 53(1): see **F4.29**). As to compellability, the rule, subject to one exception, is that the spouse or civil partner shall be compellable to give evidence on behalf of any such other person, but only in respect of any 'specified offence' with which any person is charged in the proceedings (PACE 1984, s. 80(2A)(a)). The exception is where the spouse or civil partner is also charged in the proceedings (see s. 80(4) and (4A)).

Competence and Compellability of Former Spouse or Civil Partner of the Accused

F4.20   In any proceedings, a person who has been but is no longer married to the accused shall be compellable to give evidence as if they had never been married (PACE 1984, s. 80(5)). The same principle applies to a former civil partner (s. 80(5A)). Such a person, therefore, is compellable on behalf of the prosecution, the accused or any co-accused, whether the evidence relates to events which occurred before, during or after the terminated marriage. The phrase 'is no longer married' covers the situation where the parties have been divorced and where a voidable marriage has been annulled; but not the situation where the parties have been judicially separated or are merely not cohabiting (whether or not in consequence of an informal arrangement, formal agreement or non-cohabitation order). If the marriage of the parties was void *ab initio*, there never was a legally valid marriage, and accordingly a party to such a union will be both competent and compellable on behalf of the accused (the other party to that union), any co-accused or the prosecution. The phrase 'in any proceedings' means any proceedings which take place after s. 80(5) came into effect (1 January 1986); and therefore an ex-wife or an ex-husband is competent and compellable to give evidence in such proceedings about any matter, whether it took place before or after that date (*Cruttenden* [1991] 2 QB 66).

OTHER WITNESSES

Children and Persons with a Disorder or Disability of the Mind

The competence of a child (or person with a disorder or disability of the mind) to give evidence **F4.21**
in criminal proceedings, and the question whether he or she should give sworn or unsworn
evidence, are governed by the YJCEA 1999, ss. 53 to 56, which are set out at **F4.29**.

As to competence, the rule is that all persons are (whatever their age) competent to give evidence (s. 53(1)); but a person is not competent if it appears to the court that he is not a person
who is able to (a) understand questions put to him as a witness and (b) give answers to them
which can be understood (s. 53(2) and (3)). In *MacPherson* [2006] 1 Cr App R 459, it was held
that the words 'put to him as a witness' mean the equivalent of 'being asked of him in court'.
Accordingly, an infant who can only communicate in baby language with its mother will not
ordinarily be competent, but a child who can speak and understand basic English with strangers
will be competent. It was also held that there is no requirement that the witness be aware of his
status as a witness and that questions of credibility and reliability are not relevant to competence
but go to the weight of the evidence and may be considered, if appropriate, on a submission of
no case to answer. Equally, a person who has no recollection of an event may be a perfectly competent witness (*DPP v R* [2007] EWHC 1842 (Admin)). The following propositions relating
to s. 53 derive from *Barker* [2010] EWCA Crim 4.

(a) In each case, the question under s. 53 is whether the individual witness or child is compe-
    tent to give evidence in the particular trial. The question is entirely witness or child specific.
(b) There are no presumptions or preconceptions.
(c) The witness does not need to understand the special importance of telling the truth in court
    and does not need to understand every single question or give a readily understood answer
    to every question (applied in *IA* [2013] EWCA Crim 1308). Dealing with it broadly and
    fairly, provided the witness can understand the questions put to him and can also provide
    understandable answers, he is competent.
(d) Questions, of course, come from both sides. If the child is called as a witness by the pros-
    ecution, he should have the ability to understand the questions put to him by the defence
    as well as the prosecution and to provide answers to them which are understandable.
(e) Section 53 requires not the exercise of a discretion, but the making of a judgment on
    whether the witness fulfils the statutory criteria.

Clearly the younger the child, the more likely it is that he will be unable to understand questions **F4.22**
put and give answers to them which can be understood. However, a court cannot properly conclude
that a child is incapable of satisfying the test on the basis of the child's age alone (*MacPherson*; *Powell*
[2006] 1 Cr App R 468). The fact that a child under ten years of age cannot be prosecuted for the
offence of wilfully giving false evidence contrary to the YJCEA 1999, s. 57 (see **B14.18**), is not a
reason for excluding the unsworn evidence of a competent child witness (*N* (1992) 95 Cr App R
256, a decision under the CYPA 1933, s. 38(2), the statutory precursor to s. 57 of the 1999 Act).

Sworn Evidence Whether a child (or person of unsound mind) may be sworn for the purpose **F4.23**
of giving evidence on oath is governed by the YJCEA, s. 55. A witness may not be sworn for this
purpose unless he has attained the age of 14 and 'has a sufficient appreciation of the solemnity
of the occasion and of the particular responsibility to tell the truth which is involved in taking an
oath' (s. 55(2)). If the witness is able to give intelligible testimony, i.e. if he is able to understand
questions put to him as a witness and give answers to them which can be understood (s. 55(8)),
he is presumed to have a sufficient appreciation of those matters unless any party adduces evidence tending to show the contrary (s. 55(3)). If any such evidence is adduced, it is for the party
seeking to have the witness sworn to satisfy the court, on a balance of probabilities, that he has
attained the age of 14 and has a sufficient appreciation of the matters in question (s. 55(4)).

F4.24   **Unsworn Evidence**   The evidence of a person (of any age) who is competent to give evidence in criminal proceedings but who is not permitted to be sworn for the purpose of giving evidence on oath shall be given unsworn and shall be received in evidence by the court (s. 56(1), (2) and (4)). A deposition of unsworn evidence given by such a person may also be taken for the purposes of criminal proceedings and shall also be received in evidence (s. 56(3) and (4)).

Determining the Competence of Children and Persons with a Disorder or Disability of the Mind

F4.25   If a judge has reason to doubt whether a child (or person with a disorder or disability of the mind) is able to understand questions put to him as a witness, or to give answers to them which can be understood, because he has difficulty in comprehension or expression, the judge will conduct a preliminary investigation under s. 54 (considered at **F4.2**). Such an inquiry should be recorded by the shorthand writer so that it appears in the official transcript (*Khan* (1981) 73 Cr App R 190). The issue of competence should be determined in the ordinary way, i.e. before the witness is sworn, usually as a preliminary issue at the start of the trial, when the judge should watch the video-taped interview of the child and/or ask the child appropriate questions (*MacPherson* [2006] 1 Cr App R 459). Where there is material such as an ABE interview and reports from intermediaries that proceed on the basis that a witness is competent subject to the use of special measures, a competence hearing may be unnecessary at the initial stage and serve only to cause delay, increase expense and put unnecessary strain on the witness (*F* [2013] 1 WLR 2143 at [39]). In *Hampshire* [1996] QB 1, which was not a decision under s. 54, it was held as follows:

(a) The issue of competence should be dealt with at the earliest possible moment, not as an act of 'ratification' after the evidence has been given.

(b) The judge should conduct the investigation. It is a matter of his perception of the child's understanding as demonstrated in ordinary discourse, not an issue to be resolved by him in response to an adversarial examination and cross-examination.

(c) If there has been an application to use video-recorded evidence (see **F16.87**), the judge's pre-trial view of the recording, if the interview has been properly conducted, will normally enable him to form a view on competence, but if it leaves him in doubt, he should conduct an investigation.

F4.26   **Time to Determine Competence**   The question of a child's competence to give evidence must be decided at the time of the trial, but should be kept under review, and may need to be revisited when the child's evidence is complete. Thus although at the start of the trial a video-taped interview may indicate competence, a ruling to that effect should be reversed if the child is unable to understand questions at the trial, or to give answers to them which can be understood, which may be the result of lapse of time and lack of memory (*Powell* [2006] 1 Cr App R 468, applied in *Malicki* [2009] EWCA Crim 365). If a child is unable to provide intelligible answers to questions in cross-examination, or a meaningful cross-examination is impossible, the first decision on competence will not produce a fair trial and the evidence admitted will fall to be excluded. Questions of credibility should not be addressed when conducting the second test any more than they should be addressed when conducting the first. There will be case specific occasions when undue delay may render a trial unfair and lead to the exclusion of the evidence of a child on competency grounds. However, it does not follow from *Powell* and *Malicki* that, in cases involving very young children, delay on its own automatically requires the court to prevent or stop the evidence of the child from being considered by the jury (*Barker* [2010] EWCA Crim 4). Furthermore, in *R* [2010] EWCA Crim 2469 it was doubted that *Malicki* supported the proposition that a child's evidence should be excluded under the PACE 1984, s. 78, where she no longer has a reliably independent memory of the events upon which her allegations were based. That proposition, it was said, could seriously undermine the statutory reforms introduced to deal with the evidence of children and other vulnerable witnesses. It was also pointed out that it is not infrequent for witnesses to have no independent recollection of events and to say no more than that their statement is accurate.

If the defence are of the opinion that the judge should consider the issue of a child's competence and, if the child is thought to be competent, should keep the matter under review, they should challenge the child's competence or make an application to exclude the child's evidence under the PACE 1984, s. 78; failure to do so will count against an argument, on appeal, that the judge improperly failed to consider the issue of competence and to keep the matter under review (*Edwards* [2011] EWCA Crim 3028 at [28]).

Evidence of Competence and Procedural Issues   Prior to the enactment of the YJCEA 1999, **F4.27** it was held that the question whether a child is capable of giving 'intelligible testimony' does not require any input from experts such as child psychiatrists, because it is a simple test well within the capability of a judge or magistrate (*G v DPP* [1997] 2 All ER 755). It is submitted that s. 54(5), whereby expert evidence may be received on the question, should be invoked only where necessary.

If a judge conducts an inquiry into the competence of a person with a disorder or disability of the mind, it is not normally necessary to call that person to give evidence on the subject: the proper course is to adduce expert medical evidence (*Barratt* [1996] Crim LR 495).

Any proceedings held for the determination of the question whether a witness may be sworn for the purpose of giving evidence on oath should take place in the absence of the jury (s. 55(5)). Expert evidence may be received on the question (s. 55(6)) and any questioning of the witness shall be conducted by the court in the presence of the parties (s. 55(7)).

The Weight to be Attached to Evidence Given by Persons with a Disorder or Disability of the Mind

Where a person with a learning disability gives evidence, it is left to the jury to attach to his **F4.28** evidence such weight as they see fit. If his evidence is so tainted as to be unworthy of credit, it is the proper function of the jury to disregard it and not to act upon it (*Hill* (1851) 2 Den CC 254). However, a person suffering from a mental disorder or disability may be a reliable witness. In *Barratt* [1996] Crim LR 495, in which the witness was suffering from the psychiatric condition known as fixed belief paranoia and held bizarre beliefs about certain aspects of her private life, the Court of Appeal could see no reason for supposing that on matters not affected by her condition, her evidence was not as reliable as that of any other witness. See also *R (B) v DPP* [2009] 1 WLR 2072.

Youth Justice and Criminal Evidence Act 1999, Part II, Chapter V

Youth Justice and Criminal Evidence Act 1999, ss. 53 to 56   F4.29

53.—(1) At every stage in criminal proceedings all persons are (whatever their age) competent to give evidence.
(2) Subsection (1) has effect subject to subsections (3) and (4).
(3) A person is not competent to give evidence in criminal proceedings if it appears to the court that he is not a person who is able to—
(a) understand questions put to him as a witness, and
(b) give answers to them which can be understood.
(4) A person charged in criminal proceedings is not competent to give evidence in the proceedings for the prosecution (whether he is the only person, or is one of two or more persons, charged in the proceedings).
(5) In subsection (4) the reference to a person charged in criminal proceedings does not include a person who is not, or is no longer, liable to be convicted of any offence in the proceedings (whether as a result of pleading guilty or for any other reason).

54.—(1) Any question whether a witness in criminal proceedings is competent to give evidence in the proceedings, whether raised—

(a) by a party to the proceedings, or

(b) by the court of its own motion,

shall be determined by the court in accordance with this section.

(2) It is for the party calling the witness to satisfy the court that, on a balance of probabilities, the witness is competent to give evidence in the proceedings.

(3) In determining the question mentioned in subsection (1) the court shall treat the witness as having the benefit of any directions under section 19 [special measures directions in the case of vulnerable and intimidated witnesses] which the court has given, or proposes to give, in relation to the witness.

(4) Any proceedings held for the determination of the question shall take place in the absence of the jury (if there is one).

(5) Expert evidence may be received on the question.

(6) Any questioning of the witness (where the court considers that necessary) shall be conducted by the court in the presence of the parties.

55.—(1) Any question whether a witness in criminal proceedings may be sworn for the purpose of giving evidence on oath, whether raised—

(a) by a party to the proceedings, or

(b) by the court of its own motion,

shall be determined by the court in accordance with this section.

(2) The witness may not be sworn for that purpose unless—

(a) he has attained the age of 14, and

(b) he has a sufficient appreciation of the solemnity of the occasion and of the particular responsibility to tell the truth which is involved in taking an oath.

(3) The witness shall, if he is able to give intelligible testimony, be presumed to have a sufficient appreciation of those matters if no evidence tending to show the contrary is adduced (by any party).

(4) If any such evidence is adduced, it is for the party seeking to have the witness sworn to satisfy the court that, on a balance of probabilities, the witness has attained the age of 14 and has a sufficient appreciation of the matters mentioned in subsection (2)(b).

(5) Any proceedings held for the determination of the question mentioned in subsection (1) shall take place in the absence of the jury (if there is one).

(6) Expert evidence may be received on the question.

(7) Any questioning of the witness (where the court considers that necessary) shall be conducted by the court in the presence of the parties.

(8) For the purposes of this section a person is able to give intelligible testimony if he is able to—

(a) understand questions put to him as a witness, and

(b) give answers to them which can be understood.

56.—(1) Subsections (2) and (3) apply to a person (of any age) who—

(a) is competent to give evidence in criminal proceedings, but

(b) (by virtue of section 55(2)) is not permitted to be sworn for the purpose of giving evidence on oath in such proceedings.

(2) The evidence in criminal proceedings of a person to whom this subsection applies shall be given unsworn.

(3) A deposition of unsworn evidence given by a person to whom this subsection applies may be taken for the purposes of criminal proceedings as if that evidence had been given on oath.

(4) A court in criminal proceedings shall accordingly receive in evidence any evidence given unsworn in pursuance of subsection (2) or (3).

(5) Where a person ('the witness') who is competent to give evidence in criminal proceedings gives evidence in such proceedings unsworn, no conviction, verdict or finding in those proceedings shall be taken to be unsafe for the purposes of any of sections 2(1), 13(1) and 16(1) of the Criminal Appeal Act 1968 (grounds for allowing appeals) by reason only that it appears to the Court of Appeal that the witness was a person falling within section 55(2) (and should accordingly have given his evidence on oath).

The Sovereign and Diplomats

F4.30 The Sovereign is a competent but not a compellable witness. Total or partial immunity from compellability to give evidence is also enjoyed by heads of other sovereign states; diplomatic agents; members of the family of a diplomatic agent forming part of his household; members of the administrative and technical staff of a diplomatic mission and members of their families; persons connected with consular posts; and members of the staff of international organisations. See:

(a) Diplomatic Privileges Act 1964, s. 2(1) and sch. 1, arts. 1, 31, 37, 38(2) and 39;
(b) Consular Relations Act 1968, s. 1(1) and sch. 1, arts. 1(1), 44 and 58(2);
(c) International Organisations Act 1968;
(d) State Immunity Act 1978; and
(e) International Organisations Act 1981.

Bankers

Subject to a variety of safeguards, a copy of an entry in a banker's book shall in all legal proceedings be received as prima facie evidence of such entry, and of the matters, transactions and accounts therein recorded (Bankers' Books Evidence Act 1879, ss. 3 and 9). In any legal proceeding to which the bank is not a party, bank personnel cannot be compelled to produce the originals of such books or to give evidence to prove the matters recorded therein, unless specifically ordered to do so by a judge (see the Bankers' Books Evidence Act 1879, s. 6, at **F8.36**). **F4.31**

OATHS AND AFFIRMATIONS

General Rule and Exceptions

Unless legislation otherwise provides, before giving evidence a witness must take an oath or affirm (CrimPR, r. 38.11(3)). The evidence of a person who is competent to give evidence but who is not permitted to be sworn, shall be given unsworn (see **F4.24**); and at common law a witness called merely for the purpose of producing a document need not be sworn (*Perry v Gibson* (1934) 1 A & E 48). As to the latter situation, the witness, if not sworn, is not liable to cross-examination. However, if the identity of the document is disputed, and must be established, this must be done by sworn evidence. **F4.32**

Where a video recording of an interview with a child is admitted under the YJCEA 1999, s. 27, and the child is then aged 14 or over, the oath should be administered before the start of the cross-examination (*Simmonds* [1996] Crim LR 816, a decision under the CJA 1988, s. 32A, the statutory precursor to s. 27). Where the oath is administered at some later stage, the judge should warn the jury that the earlier answers were not evidence until given subsequent ratification. Without such an explanation, an appeal would be unanswerable (*Simmonds*, applying *Lee* [1988] Crim LR 525). Under the YJCEA 1999, s. 56(5), where a witness who is competent to give evidence in criminal proceedings has given evidence unsworn, no conviction, verdict or finding in those proceedings shall be taken to be unsafe for the purposes of the grounds of appeal in the Criminal Appeal Act 1968, s. 2(1), 13(1) or 16(1), by reason only that he was a person falling within s. 55(2) of the 1999 Act and therefore should have given his evidence on oath.

Form and Manner of Oath: Christians and Jews

Oaths Act 1978, s. 1 **F4.33**

(1) Any oath may be administered and taken in England, Wales or Northern Ireland in the following form and manner:—
    The person taking the oath shall hold the New Testament, or, in the case of a Jew, the Old Testament, in his uplifted hand, and shall say or repeat after the officer administering the oath the words 'I swear by Almighty God that...', followed by the words of the oath prescribed by law.
    ...
(4) In this section 'officer' means any person duly authorised to administer oaths.

The words of s. 1 are directive; therefore failure to comply with them will not necessarily invalidate the taking of an oath, because the efficacy of an oath depends upon it being taken in a way binding, and intended to be binding, upon the conscience of the intended witness (*Chapman* [1980] Crim LR 42, where leave to appeal was refused, the witness in question having failed to take the Testament in his hand).

In the case of a witness in the trial proper, 'the words of the oath prescribed by law', approved by a resolution of the judges of the King's Bench Division on 11 January 1927, are 'the evidence which I shall give shall be the truth, the whole truth and nothing but the truth'. When a witness gives evidence in a trial within a trial, the oath is 'I swear by Almighty God that I will true answer make to all such questions as the Court shall demand of me'. In relation to any oath administered to and taken by any person before a youth court, or administered to and taken by any child or young person before any other court, s. 1 of the Oaths Act 1978 shall have effect as if the words 'I promise before Almighty God' were set out instead of the words 'I swear by Almighty God that' (CYPA 1963, s. 28(1)). Where, in any oath otherwise duly administered and taken, either of the forms mentioned in s. 28 of the CYPA 1963 is used instead of the other, the oath shall nevertheless be deemed to have been duly administered and taken (s. 28(2)).

Form and Manner of Oath: Other Religious Beliefs

F4.34   Oaths Act 1978, s. 1

(2) The officer shall (unless the person about to take the oath voluntarily objects thereto, or is physically incapable of so taking the oath) administer the oath in the form and manner aforesaid without question.
(3) In the case of a person who is neither a Christian nor a Jew, the oath shall be administered in any lawful manner.
(4) In this section 'officer' means any person duly authorised to administer oaths.

Section 1(2) makes it clear that it is incumbent upon a person who is neither a Christian nor a Jew to object to the taking of an oath in the form and manner prescribed by s. 1(1). Such a person may affirm or may take the oath upon such holy book as is appropriate to his or her religious belief. Muslims are sworn on the Koran (*Morgan* (1764) 1 Leach 54). Hindus are sworn on the Vedas or other sacred books. Parsees are sworn on the Zendavesta. The modern practice is to inquire what oath a witness accepts as binding and swear him accordingly.

Whether an oath is administered 'in a lawful manner' for the purposes of s. 1(3) does not depend on what may be the considerable intricacies of the particular religion adhered to by the witness but on (a) whether the oath appears to the court to be binding on the conscience of the witness and (b) whether it is an oath which the witness himself considers to be binding on his conscience (*Kemble* [1990] 3 All ER 116, where a Muslim, who had taken the oath using the New Testament, was held to have been properly sworn).

It is improper to cross-examine a Muslim who has affirmed as to whether he thinks that he is bound to tell the truth (*Majid* [2009] EWCA Crim 2563). However, in cases in which the ground is properly laid for an expectation that a witness will take the oath on a particular holy book, but he affirms, and the matter is raised in the absence of the jury, the judge has a discretion to allow sensitive questions on the reason for not taking the oath on the holy book (*Mehrban* [2002] 1 Cr App R 561, where a Muslim witness for the prosecution who had taken the oath on the Koran had challenged one of the accused, also a Muslim, to do likewise).

Swearing with Uplifted Hand

F4.35   Oaths Act 1978, s. 3

If any person to whom an oath is administered desires to swear with uplifted hand, in the form and manner in which an oath is usually administered in Scotland, he shall be permitted to do so, and the oath shall be administered to him in such form and manner without further question.

Validity of Oaths

F4.36

Oaths Act 1978, s. 4

(1) In any case in which an oath may lawfully be and has been administered to any person, if it has been administered in a form and manner other than that prescribed by law, he is bound by it if it has been administered in such form and with such ceremonies as he may have declared to be binding.

(2) Where an oath has been duly administered and taken, the fact that the person to whom it was administered had, at the time of taking it, no religious belief, shall not for any purpose affect the validity of the oath.

Affirmations

F4.37

Oaths Act 1978, ss. 5 and 6

5.—(1) Any person who objects to being sworn shall be permitted to make his solemn affirmation instead of taking an oath.

(2) Subsection (1) above shall apply in relation to a person to whom it is not reasonably practicable without inconvenience or delay to administer an oath in the manner appropriate to his religious belief as it applies in relation to a person objecting to be sworn.

(3) A person who may be permitted under subsection (2) above to make his solemn affirmation may also be required to do so.

(4) A solemn affirmation shall be of the same force and effect as an oath.

6.—(1) Subject to subsection (2) below, every affirmation shall be as follows:—

'I, [name] do solemnly, sincerely and truly declare and affirm,'

and then proceed with the words of the oath prescribed by law, omitting any words of imprecation or calling to witness.

(2) Every affirmation in writing shall commence:—

'I, [name] of [address], do solemnly and sincerely affirm,'

and the form in lieu of the jurat shall be 'Affirmed at this day of 20, Before me.'

Section F5 Corroboration and Care Warnings

GENERAL RULE

F5.1 The general rule is that there is no requirement that evidence be corroborated and no require-ment that the tribunal of fact be warned of the danger of acting on uncorroborated evidence. This section concerns two categories of exception to the general rule:

(a) where corroboration is required by statute; and
(b) where the tribunal of fact should be warned to exercise care before acting on the evidence of certain types of witness, if unsupported.

There is a third category of exception, made up of four cases — confessions by men-tally handicapped persons, identification evidence, sudden unexplained infant deaths and unconvincing hearsay evidence — in all of which there is a special need for caution which has led to requirements analogous to but different from those relating to the first two categories. These requirements are considered at **F17.56**, **F18.9** *et seq.*, **F5.18** and **F16.93** respectively.

CORROBORATION REQUIRED BY STATUTE

Introduction

F5.2 Corroboration is required by statute in four cases: treason; perjury (see **B14.16**); offences of speeding (see **C6.58**); and attempts to commit any such offences. As to treason, the Treason Act 1795, s. 1, provides that a person charged with the offence of treason by compassing the death or restraint of the Queen or her heirs shall not be convicted except on the oaths of two lawful and credible witnesses. As to the last case, under the Criminal Attempts Act 1981, s. 2(2)(g), any provision whereby a person may not be convicted or committed for trial on the uncorroborated evidence of one witness (including any provision requiring the evidence of not less than two credible witnesses) shall have effect with respect to an offence under s. 1 of the Act of attempting to commit an offence (see **A5.69**) as it has effect with respect to the offence attempted. Where corroboration is required by statute, a conviction should not be based on uncorroborated evi-dence and, if it is, will be open to successful appeal. Thus, in the absence of corroboration, the judge should direct an acquittal.

The Meaning of Corroboration

F5.3 In the case of perjury, corroboration bears the technical meaning it once bore at common law (*Hamid* (1979) 69 Cr App R 324). Corroboration in this technical sense is probably also required in the case of the other three statutory provisions (see per Lord Reading CJ in *Baskerville* [1916] 2 KB 658 at p. 667). Evidence, to be capable of being corroboration in the strict or technical sense, must:

(a) be relevant and admissible (*Scarrott* [1978] QB 1016 at p. 1021);
(b) be credible (*DPP v Kilbourne* [1973] AC 729 at p. 746 and *DPP v Hester* [1973] AC 296 at p. 315);

(c) be independent, i.e. emanate from a source other than the witness requiring corroboration (*Whitehead* [1929] 1 KB 99 and *Cooper* [2010] 2 Cr App R 92, considered at **B14.16**); and
(d) implicate the accused.

Corroboration Direction

Where a judge directs a jury on corroboration, he should explain what it means, making clear **F5.4** the requirements of credibility, independence and implication (*Fallon* [1993] Crim LR 591). The judge should also indicate the evidence which is and is not capable of being corroboration (*Charles* (1976) 68 Cr App R 334n; *Cullinane* [1984] Crim LR 420; *Webber* [1987] Crim LR 412) and, in the case of evidence which is capable of being corroboration, should explain to the jury that it is for them to decide whether the evidence does in fact constitute corroboration (*Tragen* [1956] Crim LR 332; *McInnes* (1989) 90 Cr App R 99).

CARE WARNINGS

General

In appropriate circumstances the jury should be warned to exercise caution before acting on the **F5.5** evidence of certain types of witness, if unsupported. Whether a warning is given is a matter of judicial discretion dependent on the particular circumstances of the case, and failure to give a warning therefore will not necessarily furnish grounds for a successful appeal. Equally, if a warning is given, the strength of warning and the extent to which the judge should elaborate upon it, also turn on the particular circumstances of the case. The categories of witness that fall to be considered, for the purposes of considering whether to give a care warning, are:

(a) accomplices giving evidence for the prosecution and complainants in sexual cases (which fall to be considered together);
(b) other witnesses whose evidence may be unreliable;
(c) witnesses whose evidence may be tainted by an improper motive;
(d) children; and
(e) patients at a secure hospital.

Accomplices Giving Evidence for the Prosecution and Complainants in Sexual Cases

Position at Common Law   At common law, the jury had to be warned of the danger of acting **F5.6** on the evidence, if not corroborated, of accomplices giving evidence for the prosecution and complainants, whether male or female, in sexual cases. Where a warning was required, it had to be a 'full' warning, comprising:

(a) a warning to the jury that it was dangerous to convict without corroboration but that they could do so if satisfied of the truth of the evidence of the accomplice or complainant;
(b) an explanation of the technical meaning of corroboration (see **F5.3**);
(c) an indication of what evidence was and was not capable of being corroboration; and
(d) an explanation that it was for them to decide whether evidence did in fact constitute corroboration.

Effect of the CJPO 1994, s. 32   Section 32 of the CJPO 1994 removed the requirement **F5.7** for full warnings. There were a number of compelling reasons in favour of such reform. They included the following:

(a) a full warning was required irrespective of the particular circumstances of the case or the credibility of the particular accomplice or complainant;

(b) the highly technical rules relating to the meaning of corroboration had rendered the full warning complex and difficult to understand; and

(c) many sexual offences are committed in circumstances in which it is difficult or impossible to obtain corroboration.

Criminal Justice and Public Order Act 1994, s. 32

(1) Any requirement whereby at a trial on indictment it is obligatory for the court to give the jury a warning about convicting the accused on the uncorroborated evidence of a person merely because that person is—

(a) an alleged accomplice of the accused, or

(b) where the offence charged is a sexual offence, the person in respect of whom it is alleged to have been committed,

is hereby abrogated.

...

(3) Any requirement that—

(a) is applicable at the summary trial of a person for an offence, and

(b) corresponds to the requirement mentioned in subsection (1) above...

is hereby abrogated.

F5.8 The effect of these provisions is to abrogate the requirements whereby a full warning was obligatory. The judge, however, still retains the discretion to warn the jury to exercise caution whenever he considers it appropriate to do so, whether in respect of an accomplice or a complainant or any other witness. This was made clear in *Makanjuola* [1995] 3 All ER 730, the leading authority on s. 32, in which Lord Taylor CJ summarised the relevant principles (at p. 1351).

(1) Section 32(1) abrogated the requirement to give a corroboration direction in respect of an alleged accomplice or a complainant of a sexual offence, simply because a witness falls into one of those categories. (2) It is a matter for the judge's discretion what, if any warning, he considers appropriate in respect of such a witness as indeed in respect of any other witness in whatever type of case. Whether he chooses to give a warning and in what terms will depend on the circumstances of the case, the issues raised and the content and quality of the witness's evidence. (3) In some cases, it may be appropriate for the judge to warn the jury to exercise caution before acting upon the unsupported evidence of a witness. This will not be so simply because the witness is a complainant of a sexual offence nor will it necessarily be so because a witness is alleged to be an accomplice. There will need to be an evidential basis for suggesting that the evidence of the witness may be unreliable. An evidential basis does not include mere suggestion by cross-examining counsel. (4) If any question arises as to whether the judge should give a special warning in respect of a witness, it is desirable that the question be resolved by discussion with counsel in the absence of the jury before final speeches. (5) Where the judge does decide to give some warning in respect of a witness, it will be appropriate to do so as part of the judge's review of the evidence and his comments as to how the jury should evaluate it rather than as a set-piece legal direction. (6) Where some warning is required, it will be for the judge to decide the strength and terms of the warning. It does not have to be invested with the whole florid regime of the old corroboration rules. (7) It follows that we emphatically disagree with the tentative submission [that if a judge does give a warning, he should give a full warning and should tell the jury what corroboration is in the technical sense and identify the evidence capable of being corroborative]. Attempts to re-impose the straitjacket of the old corroboration rules are strongly to be deprecated. (8) Finally, this court will be disinclined to interfere with a trial judge's exercise of his discretion save in a case where that exercise is unreasonable in the *Wednesbury* sense: see *Associated Provincial Picture Houses Ltd v Wednesbury Corporation* [1948] 1 KB 223.

The discretion imparted to trial judges by *Makanjuola* is a wide discretion and, where it is appropriate for the judge to warn the jury to exercise caution, no set form of words is required (*Blasiak* [2010] EWCA Crim 2620, where, in the case of a witness who was an in-patient at a psychiatric unit, it sufficed to draw attention to the central question of her alleged unreliability).

F5.9 Circumstances in which Warning Should be Given As to the circumstances in which it may be appropriate for the judge to give a warning, in *Makanjuola* Lord Taylor said (at p. 1351):

The judge will often consider that no special warning is required at all. Where, however, the witness has been shown to be unreliable, he or she may consider it necessary to urge caution. In a more extreme case, if the witness is shown to have lied, to have made previous false complaints, or to bear the defendant some grudge, a stronger warning may be thought appropriate and the judge may suggest it would be wise to look for some supporting material before acting on the impugned witness's evidence. We stress that these observations are merely illustrative of some, not all, of the factors which the judges may take into account in measuring where a witness stands in the scale of reliability and what response they should make at that level in their directions to the jury.

'**Supporting Material**'   In cases in which, after *Makanjuola*, the trial judge decides to direct   **F5.10**
the jury that 'it would be wise to look for some supporting material' it is incumbent on the judge to identify any 'independent supporting evidence' (*B* [2000] Crim LR 181). It is submitted that such evidence may be furnished by any of the following.

(a) Evidence of an out-of-court confession by the accused.
(b) A damaging admission made by the accused in the course of giving evidence.
(c) Lies told by the accused, whether told in or out of court. In order to constitute 'supporting evidence', however, it is submitted that the lie should meet the criteria formerly employed to determine whether a lie amounted to corroboration in the technical sense, namely that (i) the lie must relate to a material issue, (ii) the motive for the lie must be a realisation of guilt and a fear of the truth, as opposed to a lie told, for example, in an attempt to bolster up a just cause or out of shame or a wish to conceal disgraceful behaviour from the family, and (iii) the lie must be shown to be such by evidence other than that of the witness whose evidence is to be supported, i.e. by admission or by evidence from an independent witness (*Lucas* [1981] QB 720 at p. 724; and see also *Credland v Knowler* (1951) 35 Cr App R 48 and *Dawson v McKenzie* [1908] 45 SLR 473).
(d) Evidence of the silence of the accused, where an accusation is made by someone speaking to him on even terms, admissible at common law to show that he accepts the accusation (see **F19.3** to **F19.8**).
(e) Inferences properly drawn under the CJPO 1994, ss. 34 to 37 (see **F19.9** *et seq.*).
(f) Evidence of refusal to consent to the taking of 'intimate samples' (see **F19.54**).
(g) Evidence of bad character to prove guilt (see **F12.36** *et seq.*).

It is submitted that in sexual cases in which a special warning is properly given in respect of the   **F5.11**
evidence of the complainant, the following evidence would not constitute 'supporting material'.

(a) Evidence of a recent complaint admissible by way of exception to the rule against previous consistent statements (see **F6.33**). Such evidence is not truly 'supportive' in that it emanates from the complainant herself (*Whitehead* [1929] 1 KB 99; see also *AA* [2007] EWCA Crim 1779 at **F6.34**).
(b) Evidence of the complainant's distress. This evidence also emanates from the complainant herself but, it is submitted, could be 'supportive' when the distress was observed shortly after the offence and there was nothing to suggest that it was simulated (*Redpath* (1962) 46 Cr App R 319, *Chauhan* (1981) 73 Cr App R 323 and *Dowley* [1983] Crim LR 168). The weight to be given to evidence of distress varies infinitely and rather than warning juries routinely that little weight should be attached to such evidence, in appropriate cases the judge should alert the jury to the sometimes very real risk that the distress may have been feigned (*Romeo* [2004] 1 Cr App R 418).
(c) Medical evidence, in a case of rape, to show that someone had intercourse with the complainant at a time consistent with her evidence. Such medical evidence, by itself, neither implicates the accused nor proves absence of consent (*James v R* (1970) 55 Cr App R 299; and cf. per Lord Lane CJ in *Hills* (1987) 86 Cr App R 26 at p. 31. See also *Pountney* [1989] Crim LR 216 and *Franklin* [1989] Crim LR 499).

It may well be that there is properly no desire to revive 'the whole florid regime of the old corroboration rules', but it is submitted that in the 'more extreme case' in which a special warning is thought to be desirable, evidence in the foregoing categories cannot fairly be described as evidence supportive of the evidence of the impugned witness.

Other Witnesses whose Evidence May be Unreliable

F5.12 Prior to the implementation of CJPO 1994, s. 32, there were a number of common-law decisions to the effect that a jury should be warned to exercise caution before acting on the evidence of particular types of witness whose evidence might be unreliable for one of a number of reasons. Some of the authorities suggested that the warning was discretionary or desirable as a matter of practice; others suggested that it was sometimes obligatory. In *Muncaster* [1999] Crim LR 409, it was held that all such authorities need to be reconsidered in the light of *Makanjuola* which must be read as applying to all cases in which the evidence of a witness may be suspect because he falls into a particular category. See also *Cundell* [2009] EWCA Crim 2072.

An Accomplice who is a Co-accused

F5.13 An accomplice, being an accused who, in giving evidence in his own defence, incriminates another co-accused, may be regarded as having a purpose of his own to serve. For this reason it was held, prior to the implementation of the CJPO 1994, s. 32, that it was desirable to warn the jury of the danger of acting on his unsupported evidence, but that every case should be looked at in the light of its own facts (*Prater* [1960] 2 QB 464 and *Knowlden* (1983) 77 Cr App R 94; and cf. *Perman* [1995] Crim LR 736, where the evidence incriminated the co-accused in one material respect, but otherwise exonerated him). Where a warning was given, the jury simply had to be told that the witness might have had a purpose of his own to serve (*Cheema* [1994] 1 All ER 639). Following *Makanjuola* [1995] 3 All ER 730, whether a warning is given at all and, if it is, the strength of the warning, continue to be matters of judicial discretion dependent on the particular circumstances of the case (*Muncaster* [1999] Crim LR 409). In *Jones* [2004] 1 Cr App R 60 it was held that in the case of cut-throat defences, even if they are mirror-image cut-throat defences, a warning should normally be considered and given and the judge, in exercising his discretion as to what to say, should at least warn the jury to examine the evidence of each co-accused with care because each has or may have an interest of his own to serve. (Cf. *Burrows* [2000] Crim LR 48 which, according to *Jones*, turned on its own particular facts.) However, failure to give such a warning, where required, will not found a successful appeal if the fact that each of the accused had an axe to grind would have been obvious to the jury (*Petkar* [2004] 1 Cr App R 270). There is a particular need for a warning where one co-accused has refused to answer questions in interview and was therefore able, if he wished, to tailor his defence to the facts in evidence. In many or most cases where a trial judge has to consider what if any warning to give, where co-accused have given evidence against each other, he might consider four points to put to the jury. (1) The jury should consider the case for and against each accused separately. (2) The jury should decide the case on all the evidence, including the evidence of each accused's co-accused. (3) When considering the evidence of a co-accused, the jury should bear in mind that he may have an interest to serve or an axe to grind. (4) The jury should assess the evidence of co-accused in the same way as that of the evidence of any other witness in the case (*Jones* [2004] 1 Cr App R 60).

Witnesses whose Evidence May be Tainted by an Improper Motive

F5.14 At common law, a judge is obliged to advise a jury to proceed with caution where there is material to suggest that a witness's evidence may be tainted by an improper motive, the strength of advice varying according to the facts of the case (*Beck* [1982] 1 All ER 807). Thus where an offender, awaiting sentence, gives evidence for the prosecution in another case, knowing that at the very least he thereby stands a chance of having his sentence reduced, the potential fallibility of his evidence should be put squarely to the jury (*Chan Wai-Keung v R* [1995] 2 All ER 438). See also, in the case of an accused who has entered into an agreement pursuant to the SOCPA 2005, s. 73 (see **E1.13**), *Daniels* [2011] 1 Cr App R 228. *Ashgar* [1995] 1 Cr App R 223 was a murder charge arising out of a fight involving a number of men. Three of the men pleaded guilty to affray and gave evidence against A. The defence case was that they had colluded with others to fabricate a story incriminating A to protect one of their number. It was held that a warning should have been given on the danger of convicting A on the evidence of the three men without some independent supporting evidence.

In *Pringle v The Queen* [2003] UKPC 9, a case of murder which depended in part on the **F5.15** evidence of a cellmate that the accused had confessed to him, the Privy Council held that if there are indications that a cell confession may be tainted by an improper motive — which was thought to be not an exacting test — the judge should draw the jury's attention to these indications and their possible significance. On the facts the judge should have pointed out that the cellmate was an untried prisoner, it was not unknown for persons in his position to wish to ingratiate themselves with the police, that to report a confession was a convenient and obvious way of doing so, and that the jury should therefore be cautious before accepting his evidence. In *Benedetto v The Queen* [2003] 1 WLR 1545 the Privy Council went further and held that evidence from an untried prisoner that a fellow untried prisoner confessed to him that he was guilty of the crime for which he was being held in custody, raises an acute problem which will always call for special attention in view of the danger that it may lead to a miscarriage of justice. It was held that the evidence of prisoner informers is inherently unreliable in view of the personal advantage which such witnesses think they may obtain by providing information to the authorities. Such witnesses, it was said, tend to have no interest whatsoever in the proper course of justice. The prisoner against whom the evidence is given is always at a disadvantage. He is afforded none of the usual protections against the inaccurate recording or invention of words used by him when interviewed by the police and it may be difficult for him to obtain all the information needed to expose fully the informer's bad character. There are two steps which the judge must take, both equally important, first to draw the jury's attention to the indications that may justify the inferences that the prisoner's evidence is tainted and secondly to advise the jury to be cautious before accepting his evidence. The judge must examine the evidence so that he can instruct the jury fully as to where the indications are to be found and as to their significance. However, in *Stone* [2005] EWCA Crim 105, it was held that not every case involving a cell confession requires the detailed directions discussed in *Pringle* and *Benedetto*. The court held as follows.

(a) Cell confessions prompt the most careful consideration by the trial judge, but he is not trammelled by fixed rules. The judge is best placed to decide the strength of any warning and the necessary extent of any accompanying analysis.

(b) In the case of a standard two-line confession, there is generally a need to point out that such confessions are often easy to concoct and difficult to prove and that experience has shown that prisoners may have many motives to lie. Further, if the prison informant has a significant criminal record or history of lying, this should usually be pointed out, together with an explanation that it gives rise to a need for great care, and why.

(c) However, a summing-up should be tailored by the trial judge to the circumstances of the particular case. Where (as in *Stone* itself) an alleged confession, for whatever reason, would not be easy to invent, then it would be absurd to require a judge to tell the jury that cell confessions are easy to concoct. Similarly, where (as in *Stone* itself) the defence has deliberately not cross-examined the informant about the motive of hope of obtaining advantage, the judge is not required to tell the jury that, merely because the informant was a prisoner, there might, intrinsically, have been such a motive.

(d) There are cases where the prisoner has witnessed the acts constituting the offence in which it is appropriate to treat him as an ordinary witness about whose evidence nothing out of the usual needs to be said and, in relation to those cases, there is no suggestion that a potential motive to gain advantage with the authorities will be absent. Furthermore, indications that the prison informant's evidence may be tainted by an improper motive have to be found in the evidence.

(e) Moreover, it is clear from *Muncaster* [1999] Crim LR 409 (see **F5.12**) and the general language used in *Makanjuola* [1995] 3 All ER 730 (see **F5.8**) that obligations to give special warnings arising in cases such as *Beck* have to be looked at in the light of the statutory abrogation in relation to accomplices giving evidence for the prosecution and complainants in sexual cases. It would be absurd to suppose that the rules for cases such as *Beck* have survived the statutory abrogation so as to impose obligations more onerous than those now applicable to the original cases.

A warning may be appropriate in the case of the unsupported evidence of a woman upon whose immoral earnings the accused is charged with having lived, even if she is not an accomplice (*King* (1914) 10 Cr App R 117 and cf. *Hanton* (1985) *The Times*, 14 February 1985) and in the case of a spouse (or, presumably, civil partner) of an accomplice called to give evidence on his or her behalf (*Allen* [1965] 2 QB 295). A warning may also be appropriate in the case of a witness acting out of malevolence or spite, or with some financial or other personal interest in the outcome of the trial, or who is biased or partial for some other reason.

Children

F5.16 There was a time when an accused was not liable to be convicted on the unsworn evidence of a child appearing on behalf of the prosecution unless that evidence was corroborated (CYPA 1933, proviso to s. 38(1)); and when the sworn evidence of a child required a corroboration warning as a matter of law (see, e.g., *Cleal* [1942] 1 All ER 203). The former statutory requirement has been repealed (CJA 1991, s. 101(2)); as to the latter common-law rule, the CJA 1988, s. 34(2), now provides that 'Any requirement whereby at a trial on indictment it is obligatory for the court to give the jury a warning about convicting the accused on the uncorroborated evidence of a child is abrogated'. Despite these statutory reforms, in some cases the evidence of some children may remain unreliable, whether by reason of childish imagination, suggestibility or fallibility of memory. In *Pryce* [1991] Crim LR 379, it was held that it was not necessary to give a direction to treat the evidence of a six-year-old with caution, because in effect that would be to reintroduce an abrogated rule, but, after *Makanjuola* [1995] 3 All ER 730, it is submitted that whether a direction is given, and if so the terms of the direction, are matters of judicial discretion turning on the circumstances of the case (*L* [1999] Crim LR 489; *Barker* [2010] EWCA Crim 4). Circumstances of importance, it is submitted, will include the intelligence of the child and, in the case of unsworn evidence, the extent to which the child understands the duty of speaking the truth.

Patients at a Secure Hospital

F5.17 In *Spencer* [1987] AC 128, nursing staff of a secure hospital were charged with ill-treating patients who had been convicted of crimes and who were suffering from mental disorders. The prosecution case was made up of the evidence of patients who were characterised as being not only mentally unbalanced and of bad character, but also as anti-authoritarian, prone to lie, and possibly with old scores to settle. The House of Lords held that where the only prosecution evidence comes from a witness who, by reason of his mental condition and criminal connection fulfils criteria analogous to those which (at one time) justified a full corroboration warning, the judge should warn the jury that it is dangerous to convict on such evidence if uncorroborated, although the warning need not amount to the 'full' warning (see **F5.6**). Thus use of the words 'danger' or 'dangerous' is not essential to an adequate warning, provided that the jury are made fully aware of the dangers of convicting on such evidence. Similarly, the extent to which the judge should refer to any corroborative material depends on the facts of each case. It is submitted that 'corroborative material', for these purposes, was not intended to denote material which is corroborative in the strict or technical sense (see **F5.3**) and that notwithstanding the analogy drawn with cases which justified a 'full' corroboration warning, the warning given should reflect the circumstances of the particular case (see *Causley* [1999] Crim LR 572). See also *Blasiak* [2010] EWCA Crim 2620, considered at **F5.8**.

SUDDEN UNEXPLAINED INFANT DEATHS

Infant deaths are said to be attributable to Sudden Infant Death Syndrome (SIDS), colloqui- **F5.18**
ally 'cot deaths', where the deaths are unexplained and the cause or causes, although natural,
are, or are as yet, unknown. There is no underlying condition for every SIDS death, but in each
case the mechanism of death is the same, namely apnoea, loss of breath or cessation of breathing. In *Cannings* [2004] 1 All ER 725 the accused was convicted of the murder of two of her
four children, J who had died aged six weeks and M who had died aged 18 weeks. Her eldest
child, G, had also died aged 13 weeks. There was no direct evidence of the crimes alleged. The
Crown's case, which was that the accused had smothered J and M, having previously smothered
G, depended on specialist evidence about the conclusions to be drawn from the history of three
infant deaths and further 'Acute' or 'Apparent Life Threatening Events' in the same family. The
defence case was that the deaths were attributable to SIDS. At the appeal reliance was placed on
fresh expert evidence, a substantial body of research suggesting that infant deaths occurring in
the same family can and do occur naturally, even when they are unexplained. The appeal was
allowed. It was held that the correct approach, where three infant deaths have occurred in the
same family, each apparently unexplained, and for each of which there is no evidence extraneous
to the expert evidence that harm was or must have been inflicted — e.g., indications or admissions of violence, or a pattern of ill-treatment — is to start with the fact that three such deaths
were indeed rare, but to proceed on the basis that, if there is nothing to explain them, in our current state of knowledge they remain unexplained and, although some parents do smother their
infant children, possible natural deaths. Whether there are one, two or even three deaths, the
exclusion of currently known natural causes of infant death does not establish that the death or
deaths resulted from the deliberate infliction of harm. Stressing that in many important respects
we are still at the frontiers of knowledge in relation to unexplained infant deaths, it was further
held, *per curiam*, (at [178]):

> ...for the time being, where a full investigation into two or more sudden unexplained infant deaths
> in the same family is followed by a serious disagreement between reputable experts about the cause
> of death, and a body of such expert opinion concludes that natural causes, whether explained or
> unexplained, cannot be excluded as a reasonable (and not a fanciful) possibility, the prosecution of
> a parent or parents for murder should not be started, or continued, unless there is additional cogent
> evidence, extraneous to the expert evidence, (such as [indications or admissions of violence, or a
> pattern of ill-treatment]) which tends to support the conclusion that the infant, or where there is
> more than one death, one of the infants, was deliberately harmed. In cases like the present, if the
> outcome of the trial depends exclusively or almost exclusively on a serious disagreement between
> distinguished and reputable experts, it will often be unwise, and therefore unsafe, to proceed.

Cannings was distinguished in *Kai-Whitewind* [2005] 2 Cr App R 457, on the basis that it **F5.19**
concerned inferences based upon coincidence or the unlikelihood of two or more infant deaths
in the same family, or one death where another child or other children in the family had suffered unexplained 'Apparent Life Threatening Events'. There was a need for additional cogent
evidence in such a case because there was essentially no evidence beyond the inferences based
upon coincidence which the prosecution experts were prepared to draw but as to which other
reputable experts in the same specialist field took a different view. It did not follow that, whenever there was a conflict between expert witnesses, the case for the prosecution had to fail unless
the conviction was justified by evidence independent of the expert witnesses. In *Kai-Whitewind*
there was a single death, no suggestion that any inference should be drawn against the accused
from any previous incident involving any of her other children, and the evidence about the
child's condition found on the post-mortem examination — including new and old blood in
the lungs consistent with two distinct episodes of upper airway obstruction — was evidence of
fact and precisely the kind of material which was sought but not found in *Cannings*. The dispute
between the experts about the interpretation of the post-mortem findings did not extinguish
the findings themselves and it was therefore for the jury to evaluate the expert evidence, taking

account of the facts found at the post-mortem and bearing in mind the additional prosecution evidence against the accused. For expert evidence generally, see **F10.4** *et seq.*

Cannings was also distinguished in *Hookway* [2011] EWCA Crim 1989 (also considered at **F10.10**), a case involving mixed DNA profiles in which the prosecution did not depend exclusively or almost exclusively on the disputed prosecution evidence, and the dispute between the experts was not whether there was DNA evidence incriminating the appellants, but as to the strength of that evidence.

As to the need for special caution in cases involving 'shaken baby syndrome' in which developing medical science is relevant, see also *Henderson* [2010] 2 Cr App R 185, considered at **F10.43**.

Section F6   Examination-in-chief

INTRODUCTION

Examination-in-chief is the examination of a witness by the party calling him and its object is to **F6.1** elicit from the witness evidence supportive of the party's case. Examination-in-chief must be conducted in accordance with the exclusionary rules of general application, such as those relating to hearsay, opinion and the character of the accused. The court may also ask a witness questions and, in particular, where the accused is not represented, may ask any question necessary in the interests of the accused (CrimPR, r. 38.11(6)); the note to r. 38.11 states that the questions that may be put are in the discretion of the court, subject to the rules of evidence and r. 1.3 (application by the court of the overriding objective). This section concerns five other rules governing examination-in-chief:

(a) the rules requiring the prosecution and defence to call all of their evidence before the close
   of their case; and the rules relating to
(b) leading questions;
(c) refreshing the memory;
(d) previous consistent or self-serving statements; and
(e) impeaching the credit of one's own witness.

For the judicial directions that may be given to advocates on how to examine (and cross-examine) young witnesses, see the Judicial College Bench Checklist: Young Witness Cases, considered at **D14.48**.

RULE REQUIRING PROSECUTION TO CALL ALL THEIR EVIDENCE BEFORE THE CLOSE OF THEIR CASE

General Rule

It is a rule of practice, but not law, that all of the evidence which the prosecution intend to rely **F6.2** on as probative of the guilt of the accused should be called before the close of their case (*Rice* [1963] 1 QB 857). The rule applies not only to the adducing of evidence, but also to matters put in cross-examination of the accused (*Kane* (1977) 65 Cr App R 270). The rule is confined to evidence probative of guilt, and does not extend to evidence going only to the credit of the accused (*Halford* (1978) 67 Cr App R 318).

Some of the exceptions to this rule are covered in other sections of this work: as to evidence admissible in rebuttal under exceptions to the rule of finality of answers to questions on collateral matters, see **F7.42** to **F7.59**; as to evidence in rebuttal of evidence of the good character of the accused, see **F13.23**; and as to evidence, in cases under the PACE 1984, s. 74(3), in rebuttal of defence evidence that the accused was not guilty of the offence of which he stands convicted, see *C* [2011] 1 WLR 1942 at **F11.20**. The three recognised exceptions which call for consideration at this stage are:

(a) evidence not previously available;
(b) failure to call evidence by reason of inadvertence or oversight; and
(c) evidence in rebuttal of matters arising *ex improviso*.

F6.3 Although these three exceptions are well established, some authorities clearly suggest that there is scope for a more generalised discretionary approach to admissibility, having regard to whether the accused will be unfairly prejudiced (as when the defence would have been conducted differently had the evidence in question been adduced as part of the prosecution case). In *Jolly v DPP* [2000] Crim LR 471, a decision relating to summary trial, it was held that although any trial court had to recognise that it was the duty of the prosecution to call its evidence before closing its case, it was 'beyond argument' that there was a general discretion to permit the calling of evidence at a later stage which, in a magistrates' court, extended up to the time when the Bench retired. Before exercising the discretion, the court would look carefully at the interests of justice overall and in particular the risk of any prejudice whatsoever to the defence. The result would be that the discretion would be sparingly exercised, but it was doubtful whether it assisted a court to speak in terms of 'exceptional circumstances'. Each case, it was said, had to be considered on its own facts. See also *Cook v DPP* [2001] Crim LR 321 and *Khatibi v DPP* (2004) 168 JP 361. However, magistrates, after they have retired to consider their verdict, do have a discretion to receive further evidence in 'special circumstances' (*Malcolm v DPP* [2007] 3 All ER 578, following *Webb v Leadbetter* [1966] 2 All ER 114, and holding the decision in *R (Travers) v DPP* (2005) 169 JP 421 to have been wrongly decided). In deciding whether special circumstances exist, the magistrates can consider the nature of the defence approach to litigation and, for example, whether there was an ambush of the prosecution in the defence closing speech, and should have regard to the overriding objective in the CrimPR that criminal cases be dealt with justly (*Malcolm v DPP*).

In the Crown Court, once the jury has retired to consider its verdict, no further evidence may be adduced (*Owen* [1952] QB 362). However, this principle has been relaxed in the case of material put before the jury at the request of the accused because it assists his case (*Hallam* [2007] EWCA Crim 1495; *Khan* [2008] EWCA Crim 1112).

Evidence Not Previously Available

F6.4 The question whether or not evidence available for the first time after the close of the prosecution case should be admitted, is a matter to be determined by the trial judge in his discretion, which should be exercised in such a way and subject to such safeguards as seem to him best suited to achieve justice between the Crown and the defendants, and between the defendants. However, the admission of such evidence will be rare (*Rice* [1963] 1 QB 857, per Winn J; and see also *Kane* (1977) 65 Cr App R 270). The evidence may be admitted even if not strictly of a rebutting character, but the court must be vigilant in the exercise of its discretion, in case injustice is done to the accused, and should consider whether it is desirable to grant a defence application for an adjournment (*Doran* (1972) 56 Cr App R 429). In *Doran* the prosecution were allowed to call two witnesses after the close of their case. The witnesses, of whose existence the prosecution had no prior knowledge, were members of the public, present at the trial, who realised that they could give material evidence. See also *Patel* [1992] Crim LR 739, where the judge gave defence counsel the opportunity to seek an adjournment, take further instructions and call evidence. In *Pilcher* (1974) 60 Cr App R 1, the Court of Appeal, having recognised the general rule and the exception in the case of evidence in rebuttal of matters arising *ex improviso*, i.e. evidence which becomes relevant in circumstances which the prosecution could not have foreseen at the time when they presented their case (see **F6.10**), said (at p. 5):

> We do not say that ... where the matter has not arisen *ex improviso* the judge had no kind of discretion at all, but we are firmly of opinion that in cases where the matter does not arise *ex improviso* the judge's discretion should not be exercised to allow the late introduction of an additional witness called for the prosecution whose evidence was available before the case for the prosecution closed.

As was pointed out in *Scott* (1984) 79 Cr App R 49, however, the judgment in *Pilcher* seems to narrow the circumstances in which evidence can be called in rebuttal in a way which does not agree with *Doran* (1972) 56 Cr App R 429. It is submitted that *Pilcher* should not be treated as restricting either the exception recognised in *Doran* or the exception, considered at **F6.5**, in the case of failure to call evidence of a formal or technical nature by reason of inadvertence or oversight.

Failure to Call Evidence by Reason of Inadvertence or Oversight

Formal, Technical or Uncontentious Evidence   The judge has a discretion to admit evidence **F6.5** of a formal, technical or uncontentious nature which, by reason of inadvertence or oversight, has not been adduced by the prosecution before the close of their case. Many of the cases relate to the failure to prove a statutory instrument by production of a Stationery Office copy. See, e.g., *Palastanga v Solman* [1962] Crim LR 334, a case brought under the Motor Vehicles (Construction and Use) Regulations 1955. See also *Duffin v Markham* (1918) 88 LJ KB 581, *Royal v Prescott-Clarke* [1966] 2 All ER 366 and *Hammond v Wilkinson* (2001) 165 JP 786. Compare *Tyrell v Cole* (1918) 120 LT 156 and *Ashley* (1967) 52 Cr App R 42: the Prison Rules require proof by production of a Queen's Printer's Copy. Similarly, evidence may be admitted to make good a failure to prove that leave of the DPP to bring proceedings has been obtained (see *Price v Humphries* [1958] 2 QB 353, in which a submission of no case having succeeded on the basis of the failure to prove such consent, the Divisional Court, applying *Waller* [1910] 1 KB 364 and allowing the appeal, held that unless the defence object before the close of the prosecution case, the court should act on the assumption that the clerk had fulfilled his duty, on the application for issue of the summons, to check that the appropriate consent had been given). A further example is *McKenna* (1956) 40 Cr App R 65, a charge of exporting articles made wholly or mainly of iron or steel, in which a submission of no case was made on the basis that no evidence had been adduced that the articles in question, which included steamrollers, lorries, traction engines and concrete mixers, were made of iron or steel. The judge recalled a prosecution witness to give such evidence. It was held that in the circumstances the judge had a complete discretion whether to allow a witness to be recalled; the appellate courts would not interfere with the exercise of that discretion unless it had resulted in an injustice. On the facts, there was no injustice: it required no great leap of the imagination to think that the objects in question were made of iron or steel, and even in the absence of the additional evidence, there was a case to answer.

Evidence as to Matters of Substance   In appropriate circumstances the prosecution, after **F6.6** the close of their case, may even be permitted to call evidence relating to a matter of substance. Thus, in *Piggott v Simms* [1973] RTR 15, in which the prosecution, after the close of their case, were given leave to admit in evidence an analyst's certificate, the Divisional Court held that, although this was a failure to adduce a vital part of their prosecution case, the justices had an absolute discretion to allow the evidence to be admitted. Likewise in *Matthews v Morris* [1981] Crim LR 495, it was held that justices had correctly permitted the prosecution to reopen their case to put in evidence a statement, made by the owner of the money allegedly stolen, which, although it had been served on the defence under the CJA 1967, s. 9, was omitted from the prosecution case by reason of simple mistake. According to *Middleton v Rowlett* [1954] 2 All ER 277 the court even has a discretion in the case of evidence relating to the identity of the accused. That was a case of dangerous driving, in which the magistrates had refused to allow the prosecution to reopen their case in order to prove the identity of the driver. Although the Divisional Court described the case as 'borderline', it was held that the magistrates were not bound to exercise their discretion in favour of the prosecution. Cf. *Smith v DPP* [2008] EWHC 771 (Admin), where the prosecution was allowed to *bolster* its case on identification.

In *Francis* [1990] 1 All ER 225, the prosecution called an identification witness to give evidence **F6.7** that at a group identification he had identified the man standing in position number 20 but failed to call any evidence to prove that the man standing at that position was the appellant. The failure was due to a simple misunderstanding between counsel: counsel for the prosecution was under the impression that the name of the person standing at that position was not in issue. After the close of the prosecution case, the trial judge allowed the prosecution to recall the inspector in charge of the identification to say who it was who was standing at position number

20. On appeal, it was held that although the failure was not a mere technicality, but an essential, if minor, link in the chain of identification evidence, the discretion of the judge to admit evidence after the close of the prosecution case is not limited to cases where an issue has arisen *ex improviso* or where what has been omitted is a mere formality. This was one of those rare cases falling outside the two established exceptions and the judge had not erred in the exercise of his discretion. See also, applying *Francis, Jackson* [1996] 2 Cr App R 420.

F6.8   Tendering Evidence After the Start of the Defence Case   In *Munnery* [1992] Crim LR 215, where the judge allowed the prosecution to call a witness after the close of their case but before the defence case had begun, it was held that the proposition in *Francis*, that the discretion should only rarely be exercised outside the two exceptions, could be expanded to include the words 'especially when the evidence is tendered after the case for the defendant has begun'. An example of the discretion being exercised at this late stage is *James v South Glamorgan County Council* (1994) 99 Cr App R 321. In that case, in which there had not been a submission of no case to answer, the prosecution were allowed to reopen their case, after the accused had given his evidence-in-chief, to call their main witness, who had arrived late because of transport difficulties and genuine confusion as to the whereabouts of the court. Evidence may also be called, at this late stage, by the judge himself. In *Bowles* [1992] Crim LR 726, the defence case had begun when the trial judge, in answer to a question from the jury, decided in the interests of justice to admit further evidence himself, rather than have the prosecution reopen its case. It was held that the judge was justified in calling the evidence; the defence had not yet closed their case, the evidence was non-controversial and did not contradict that of the accused (although it did support the prosecution case) and it is 'undesirable that a jury should decide a case on a factual basis which may be false and the truth or falsity of which has been raised by the jury and can easily and readily be resolved without injustice to the accused'. See also *Aitken* (1991) 94 Cr App R 85, where the jury was provided with a written summary of a tape-recorded interview during which the accused had made an admission. The accused said that the admission was made under pressure and was untrue. During the defence closing speech, the jury asked to listen to the tape and, when the speech was concluded and after hearing submissions, the judge allowed them to do so. The appeal was dismissed. Where the judge is satisfied that no injustice will be done to the accused, the admission of further evidence is a matter of discretion for the judge.

F6.9   Late Evidence as to Fundamental Issues   The discretion should not be used to allow the prosecution the opportunity to prove the very matter in issue which it has failed to prove. In *Gainsborough Justices, ex parte Green* (1984) 78 Cr App R 9, the prosecution evidence in support of an allegation of a breach of a community service order revealed no such breach. The justices, rejecting a submission of no case to answer, allowed further evidence to be called to establish the breach. The Divisional Court quashed the conviction.

F6.10   Evidence in Rebuttal of Matters Arising *Ex Improviso*

> There is no doubt that the general rule is that where the Crown begins its case like a plaintiff in a civil suit, they cannot afterwards support their case by calling fresh witnesses, because they are met by certain evidence that contradicts it. They stand or fall by the evidence they have given. They must close their case before the defence begins; but if any matter arises, *ex improviso* which no human ingenuity can foresee, on the part of a defendant in a civil suit, or a prisoner in a criminal case, there seems to me no reason why that matter which so arose *ex improviso* may not be answered by contrary evidence on the part of the Crown. (*Frost* (1839) 4 St Tr NS 85 per Tindal CJ at col. 386.)

Lord Goddard CJ, in *Owen* [1952] 2 QB 362, said of this statement (at p. 367) that it was in 'probably wider language than would be applied at the present day'. Under the modern law, it is for the judge, in the exercise of his discretion, to determine whether the relevance of the evidence in question could *reasonably* have been anticipated (*Scott* (1984) 79 Cr App R 49). If the prosecution can reasonably foresee that certain evidence, available *ab initio*, is relevant to their case, it must be adduced as a part of that case and not to remedy defects in the case after it has been closed (*Day* [1940] 1 All ER 402). In *Day*, a charge of forgery and obtaining money by a forged instrument, the prosecution had in their possession from the start of the proceedings, specimens of the accused's admitted handwriting. The prosecution's case depended on the uncorroborated evidence of an accomplice. After the close of the defence case, the judge allowed the prosecution to call a handwriting expert. Quashing the conviction, the Court of Criminal Appeal held that the judge had wrongly exercised his discretion in admitting the additional evidence, which did not relate to any matter that had arisen *ex improviso* but the possible need for which ought to have been foreseen. *Day* may be contrasted with *Milliken* (1969) 53 Cr App R 330, in which the accused, when giving evidence, for the first time accused certain police officers, some of whom gave evidence that they had seen the accused committing the offence, of a conspiracy to fabricate evidence. The trial judge allowed the prosecution to call evidence in rebuttal, on the basis that such evidence became relevant only when the accused gave evidence, a ruling upheld by the Court of Appeal. (The Court of Appeal also held that the evidence in question was not in any sense probative of the guilt of the accused, since it consisted of no more than denials of the accusations of conspiracy and concoction, but cf. *Busby* (1981) 75 Cr App R 79 and *Mendy* (1976) 64 Cr App R 4, which are considered at **F7.42** and **F7.51**.) See also *Flynn* (1957) 42 Cr App R 15, in which the prosecution were allowed to call evidence in rebuttal of an alibi defence, the details of which became known for the first time when the accused gave evidence; and *Blick* (1966) 50 Cr App R 280.

The *ex improviso* principle requires the prosecution to adduce evidence before the close of its   **F6.11**
case only if it is clearly relevant. Thus, in *Levy* (1966) 50 Cr App R 198, it was held that there was room for the exercise by the judge of his discretion to admit, in rebuttal, evidence in the possession of the prosecution *ab initio*, which was of marginal relevance. The Court of Criminal Appeal said (at p. 202):

> It is quite clear and long established that the judge has a discretion with regard to the admission of evidence in rebuttal; the field in which that discretion can be exercised is limited by the principle that evidence which is clearly relevant — not marginally, minimally or doubtfully relevant, but clearly relevant — to the issues and within the possession of the Crown should be adduced by the prosecution as part of the prosecution's cases and such evidence cannot properly be admitted after evidence for the defence.

Equally, the *ex improviso* principle has to be applied with a recognition that the prosecution are expected to act reasonably to what may be suggested as pre-trial warnings of evidence likely to be given which calls for denial beforehand, and to suggestions put in cross-examination of their witnesses. 'They are not expected to take notice of fanciful and unreal statements no matter from what source they emanate' (*Hutchinson* (1985) 82 Cr App R 51, per Watkins LJ at p. 59). In this case, the accused was convicted of murder. Before the trial he wrote a letter, passed on to the DPP, containing allegations against a journalist. At the trial he alleged that the journalist was the murderer. The Court of Appeal held that the trial judge, at the close of the defence case, had properly given leave to the prosecution to call the journalist to give evidence in rebuttal; although the letter had alerted them to the possibility of what the accused might say in evidence, it contained many other allegations which were so obviously ridiculous and untrue as to justify the prosecution in regarding the whole of it either as a wicked farrago of lying nonsense or the ravings of a deranged mind. It was unreasonable, therefore, to say that the prosecution should have anticipated that anything said in it would be repeated in court.

It seems that the prosecution may rely upon the *ex improviso* principle to adduce evidence not only in rebuttal of defence *evidence*, but also, in appropriate circumstances, in rebuttal of matters unsupported by evidence but arising by implication from the submissions made by counsel for the defence in his closing speech (*O'Hadhmaill* [1996] Crim LR 509).

RULE REQUIRING DEFENCE TO CALL ALL THEIR EVIDENCE BEFORE THE CLOSE OF THEIR CASE

F6.12   A judge may permit an accused to be recalled to deal with matters which have arisen since he gave evidence if he could not reasonably have anticipated them and it appears to be in the interests of justice (*Cook* [2005] EWCA Crim 2011 at [28]). A judge may, as a matter of discretion and in the interests of justice, allow an accused to be called to clarify some feature of his evidence or to address a possible source of misunderstanding or to be given the opportunity to answer new allegations by a co-accused not put to him under cross-examination. However, it is difficult to imagine any situation in which an accused should be permitted to be recalled to advance a new account of facts contradicting his earlier evidence; that would normally constitute an abuse of process (*Ikram* [2008] 2 Cr App R 347).

LEADING QUESTIONS

Leading Questions Generally Impermissible in Chief

F6.13   The general rule is that in examination-in-chief a witness may not be asked leading questions, i.e. questions framed in such a way as to suggest the answer sought or to assume the existence of facts yet to be established. Evidence elicited by such questions is not inadmissible, but the weight to be attached to it may be substantially reduced (*Moor v Moor* [1954] 2 All ER 458; *Wilson* (1913) 9 Cr App R 124). 'Leading' is a relative, not an absolute, term (W.M. Best, *The Principles of the Law of Evidence* (12th edn by S.L. Phipson, 1922), at p. 562); and for this reason strict adherence to the rule is not always desirable or possible. Thus leading questions may be allowed, in the interests of justice, at the discretion of the judge. For example, when a magistrate dies in the course of a case in which a witness has given his evidence, the witness, when recalled before a new magistrate, may be asked whether his deposition represents his evidence (*Ex parte Bottomley* [1909] 2 KB 14, at p. 21). It is virtually impossible to ask a witness to identify a person or object in court without the use of leading questions, and accordingly leading questions of this kind are also allowed (*Watson* (1817) 2 Stark 116, at p. 128). There are two other frequently recurring situations to which the general rule does not apply:

(a) Leading questions may be asked on formal and introductory matters, such as a witness's name, address and occupation; and questions which relate to other relevant facts which are not in dispute, or which are merely introductory to questions about facts which are in dispute, are also generally allowed (*Robinson* (1897) 61 JP 520).

(b) Leading questions may be put to a witness if the party calling him has been given leave to treat him as hostile (see **F6.54**).

REFRESHING THE MEMORY

General

F6.14   At common law, a witness in the course of giving his evidence, may refer to a document in order to refresh his memory provided that the document was made or verified by him either at the time of the event in question or so shortly thereafter that the facts were fresh in his memory (*Simmonds* [1969] 1 QB 685; *Richardson* [1971] 2 QB 484; *Da Silva* [1990] 1 All ER 29 at p. 32). The common-law rule has been relaxed by the CJA 2003, s. 139(1), which substitutes for the requirement of contemporaneity, or that the facts were fresh in the memory, two conditions: (1) that the witness gives evidence that the document records his recollection at the time he made it and (2) that his recollection at that time is likely to have been significantly better than at the time of his oral evidence. Section 139(2), designed to avoid the practical difficulties of refreshing the memory in the witness box from a sound recording, provides for the refreshing of memory from a transcript of a sound recording. The trial judge has a residual discretion to refuse an application under s. 139 even if the statutory conditions are met (*McAfee* [2006] EWCA Crim 2914).

Criminal Justice Act 2003, s. 139

(1) A person giving oral evidence in criminal proceedings about any matter may, at any stage in the course of doing so, refresh his memory of it from a document made or verified by him at an earlier time if—

    (a) he states in his oral evidence that the document records his recollection of the matter at that earlier time, and

    (b) his recollection of the matter is likely to have been significantly better at that time than it is at the time of his oral evidence.

(2) Where—

    (a) a person giving oral evidence in criminal proceedings about any matter has previously given an oral account, of which a sound recording was made, and he states in that evidence that the account represented his recollection of the matter at the time,

    (b) his recollection of the matter is likely to have been significantly better at the time of the previous account than it is at the time of his oral evidence, and

    (c) a transcript has been made of the sound recording,

    he may, at any stage in the course of giving his evidence, refresh his memory of the matter from that transcript.

F6.15 An application to refresh memory will normally be made by counsel, but it is the proper function of the judge, where the interests of justice demand it, to suggest that a witness, including a prosecution witness, refresh his memory from a document (*Tyagi* (1986) *The Times*, 21 July 1986, per Ralph Gibson LJ). Section 139(1) and (2) apply to any person giving oral evidence, including the accused (see, at common law, *Britton* [1987] 2 All ER 412).

Under s. 139(1) and (2), the witness may refresh his memory 'at any stage' in the course of giving his oral evidence. Thus, although a witness refreshing his memory in court will normally do so in examination-in-chief, provided the conditions are met there is nothing wrong in principle in allowing a witness to refresh his memory during re-examination (see, at common law, *Harman* (1984) 148 JP 289 and *Sutton* (1991) 94 Cr App R 70).

Concerning the condition in s. 139(1)(b), ultimately it is a matter for the assessment of the judge, whatever the witness's view of the matter (*Mangena* (2010) 174 JP 67; *Chinn* [2012] 3 All ER 502).

Making or Verification of Document

F6.16 Although under the common-law rule a document includes a tape recording (*Bailey* [2001] EWCA Crim 733), for the purposes of the CJA 2003, s. 139(1), 'document' means anything in which information of any description is recorded, but not including any recording of sounds or moving images (s. 140). Both at common law and under s. 139(1), the document must have been prepared by the witness himself or by another, provided in the latter case that the witness verified the document. For examples of verification, see *Langton* (1876) 2 QBD 296, *Anderson v Whalley* (1852) 3 Car & Kir 54 and *Sekhon* (1987) 85 Cr App R 19. A witness may refresh his memory from his deposition or from a statement to the police taken down by a police officer and then read over by the maker (*Mullins* (1848) 3 Cox CC 528; *Gleed v Stroud* (1962) 26 JCL 161; and *Lau Pak Ngam v R* [1966] Crim LR 443, approved in *Richardson* [1971] 2 QB 484).

F6.17 **Interpreters**   In the case of interpreters, see *Attard* (1958) 43 Cr App R 90: at an interview at which an accused is questioned through an interpreter, in the absence of an independent note made by the interpreter of the questions put and the answers given, the interpreter should initial the interview record so that he may use it to refresh his memory when giving evidence.

F6.18 **Aural or Visual Verification**   It is submitted that under s. 139(1), as at common law, verification can be aural or visual. Despite the *obiter dictum* of Winn J in *Mills* [1962] 3 All ER 298, at p. 1156, that the witness should both *see* and *read* a note made by another, in *Kelsey* (1982) 74 Cr App R 213 the Court of Appeal held that where one person dictates a note to another, hears it read back to him, and confirms its accuracy without reading it himself, the first person may use the note to refresh his memory in court, provided that another witness is called to prove that the note used in court is the same one that was dictated and read back. H, a prosecution witness, refreshed his memory as to the registration number of a car from a note dictated to a police officer. H saw the officer making the note but did not read it himself. The officer read the note back aloud and H confirmed that it was correct. At trial the officer gave evidence that the note used by H was the one that he had made. The Court of Appeal dismissed the appeal on the ground that verification could be aural or visual, the important matter being whether the witness satisfied himself, while the matters were fresh in his mind, that the record was made and that it was accurate. The note in this case, since it was made by a person in the course of a 'profession or other occupation', might be admissible itself as evidence of the facts contained in it under the CJA 2003, s. 117, subject to the discretion to exclude under ss. 117(6) and 126: see **F16.94**. The principle of aural verification, however, continues to assist in cases where the note is not made by someone 'in the course of a trade, business, profession or other occupation, or as the holder of a paid or unpaid office'.

Originals and Copies

F6.19 Under the CJA 2003, s. 139(1), there is no requirement that the document be the first or only document made or verified by the witness recording his recollection of the matters in question. Thus, as in the common-law cases, where the decisions turn in part on the now abandoned requirement of contemporaneity, it would seem that a witness may refresh his memory from a document notwithstanding that it is based on original notes or a tape recording made by him. In *Cheng* (1976) 63 Cr App R 20, an officer prepared his committal statement in March from his original notes, which had been made after the accused's arrest in February. By the time of the trial, some three years later, the original notebook had been lost. The Court of Appeal held that, although the committal statement was a partial, and therefore not an exact, copy of the earlier notes from which it had been prepared, it substantially reproduced the notes and could be used by the officer to refresh his memory. Similarly, in *A-G's Ref (No. 3 of 1979)* (1979) 69 Cr App R 411, the Court of Appeal held that a police officer could refresh his memory from a notebook, compiled within two hours of an interview when the facts were still fresh in his memory, on the basis of earlier brief jottings made at the interview, notwithstanding that at the trial he could neither decipher the jottings nor recollect fully the questions put and answers given. In *Mills* [1962] 3 All ER 298 it was held that a police officer who had heard, and made a tape recording of, a conversation between two accused, could refresh his memory by referring to notes written up with the assistance of the tape recording, which was not itself admitted in evidence.

F6.20 It is submitted that where the original of a document has been lost or destroyed, under s. 139(1), as at common law, a witness may use a copy if it is proved to be an accurate copy either by the witness himself or by some other person. Thus, in *Topham v M'Gregor* (1844) 1 Car & Kir 320, the author of an article, written some 14 years earlier, who had no independent recollection of its contents, was allowed to 'refresh his memory' from a copy of the newspaper in which it appeared, evidence having been given by the editor that the original manuscript had been lost and that the newspaper was an accurate copy. See also *Chisnell* [1992] Crim LR 507, where an officer was allowed to refresh his memory from a statement, made nine months after an interview and compiled on the basis of a contemporaneous note, since the court was satisfied that the note, which had been lost, had been accurately transcribed into the statement.

Present Recollection Revived and Past Recollection Recorded

F6.21 Both the common-law rule and the statutory rules apply not only in the case of 'present recollection revived' (J.H. Wigmore, *Evidence in Trials at Common Law*, vol. 3 (revised by J.H.

Chadbourn, 1970), ch. 28), i.e. where the witness refreshes his memory on sight of the document, but also in the case of 'past recollection recorded' (Wigmore, *loc. cit.*), i.e. where the witness has no independent recollection of the facts in question but testifies as to the accuracy of the document (*Maugham v Hubbard* (1828) 8 B & C 14, *Topham v M'Gregor* (1844) 1 Car & Kir 320 and *Bryant* (1946) 31 Cr App R 146). To say that a witness, in the case of 'past recollection recorded' has refreshed his memory is to create a fiction. It would be preferable in principle to treat the out-of-court statement as hearsay admissible for the truth of its contents but, save in exceptional circumstances, at common law it is what the witness says and not the document which constitutes the evidence in the case (*Maugham v Hubbard*, and see further *Sekhon* (1987) 85 Cr App R 19 and *Virgo* (1978) 67 Cr App R 323, both considered at **F6.22** *et seq.*). However, the common-law position has been reversed by the CJA 2003, s. 120(1), (4) and (6).

Criminal Justice Act 2003, s. 120

(1) This section applies where a person (the witness) is called to give evidence in criminal proceedings.

...

(4) A previous statement by the witness is admissible as evidence of any matter stated of which oral evidence by him would be admissible, if—

    (a) any of the following three conditions is satisfied, and

    (b) while giving evidence the witness indicates that to the best of his belief he made the statement, and to the best of his belief it states the truth.

...

(6) The second condition is that the statement was made by the witness when the matters stated were fresh in his memory but he does not remember them, and cannot reasonably be expected to remember them, well enough to give oral evidence of them in the proceedings.

The following principles relating to s. 120(4) and (6) derive from the decision of the Court of Appeal in *Chinn* [2012] 3 All ER 502. Under s. 120(4), the previous statement does not have to be in a document. Section 120(4) and (6) are not limited to statements about 'routine' matters. If any of the matters set out in s. 120(6) are disputed, the judge must decide the issue. If there is a dispute about whether the witness cannot reasonably be expected to remember the matters stated well enough to give oral evidence of them, the judge must decide the matter objectively, taking all relevant factors into account, including the characteristics of the particular witness, the nature of the particular incident, the circumstances in which it occurred, and what has happened to the witness between the time of the incident and the trial. Where a witness gives evidence that in effect satisfies the conditions set out in s. 120(6), but this is disputed, then in the absence of the jury the witness should be asked why he does not recall the matters in question and can be cross-examined on both the alleged failure of memory and alleged reasons for it. Any further arguments about discretionary exclusion under the PACE 1984, s. 78, should also be addressed at this stage. If the previous statement is ruled admissible, the judge should explain, when he sums up, that the jury can consider the matter because the witness could not reasonably be expected to remember the matter well enough to give oral evidence. No reference to hearsay or the statute is necessary. The judge should direct the jury to consider the reliability of the witness's earlier recollection and should emphasise that it is for them to decide what weight to give to the evidence in the previous statement.

Production for Inspection and Cross-examination

A witness who has used a document in court to refresh his memory must produce it for the inspection of the opposing party, who may wish to cross-examine on its contents (*Beech v Jones* (1848) 5 CB 696; *Sekhon* (1987) 85 Cr App R 19). In the majority of cases, the fact that such cross-examination takes place will not make the record evidence in the case, nor will it be necessary for the jury to inspect the document, and it will be inappropriate for the record to become an exhibit (*Sekhon* at p. 22). However, in five situations the document, at the request of the opposing party, may be shown to the jury:

F6.22

F

Part F Evidence

(a) In *Senat v Senat* [1965] P 172, Sir Jocelyn Simon P said (at p. 177, emphasis added):

> Where a document is used to refresh a witness's memory, cross-examining counsel may inspect that document in order to check it, without making it evidence. Moreover he may cross-examine upon it without making it evidence *provided that* his cross-examination does not go further than the parts which are used for refreshing the memory of the witness.

See also *Gregory v Tavernor* (1833) 6 C & P 280 and *Britton* [1987] 2 All ER 412. If cross-examining counsel does go beyond the parts used by the witness to refresh his memory, the document is put in evidence and the jury are allowed to see the document upon which the cross-examination is based. At common law the document is evidence of the witness's consistency or inconsistency going only to his credit (*Virgo* (1978) 67 Cr App R 323; *Britton* [1987] 2 All ER 412). Under the CJA 2003, s. 120(1) and (3), which do not purport to alter the common-law rule as to the circumstances in which the document may be exhibited (*Pashmfouroush* [2006] EWCA Crim 2330), the document is also admissible as evidence of any matter stated.

Criminal Justice Act 2003, s. 120

(1) This section applies where a person (the witness) is called to give evidence in criminal proceedings.

...

(3) A statement made by the witness in a document—
   (a) which is used by him to refresh his memory while giving evidence,
   (b) on which he is cross-examined, and
   (c) which as a consequence is received in evidence in the proceedings,
   is admissible as evidence of any matter stated of which oral evidence by him would be admissible.

The following principles relating to s. 120(3) were established in *Chinn* [2012] 3 All ER 502. The word 'which' refers back to 'a document'. Section 120(3)(a) contemplates that the document has to be used by the witness to refresh his memory while giving evidence in chief. His oral evidence about the facts of which he has refreshed his memory is admissible oral evidence in the normal way. Under s. 120(3), it is the 'statement' in the document used to refresh memory that also becomes evidence of the matters stated. If the witness fails to refresh his memory, s. 120(3) does not apply; such a situation is covered by s. 120(4) and (6) (see **F6.21**).

F6.23   (b) The jury may inspect a memory-refreshing document if it is necessary to their determination of a point in issue. An example is *Bass* [1953] 1 QB 680. In that case the only evidence against the accused was a confession allegedly made to two police officers who, although denying that they had prepared their notes in collaboration, read identical accounts of the interview with the accused. The trial judge rejected a defence application that the jury be allowed to inspect the notebooks. The Court of Criminal Appeal endorsed the practice of officers collaborating in the preparation of their notes after an interview (in order to ensure that they had a correct version of what was said); but, allowing the appeal, held that the jury should have been allowed to inspect the notebooks because it might have assisted them in their evaluation of the credibility and accuracy of the officers. See also *Sekhon* (1986) 85 Cr App R 19, per Woolf LJ at p. 22: where the nature of the cross-examination involves the suggestion that the witness has subsequently fabricated his evidence, which will usually involve, if not expressly at least by implication, the allegation that the record is concocted, the record may be admissible to rebut this suggestion and, if the nature of the record assists as to this, to show whether or not it is genuine, i.e. whether or not it has the appearance of being a contemporaneous record which has not subsequently been altered.

Although there is no ban on conferring, it may affect the value of an officer's evidence because, however much he may strive to record only what he saw or heard himself, there is a real risk that his recollection will have been 'contaminated' so that he may in good faith incorporate elements derived from other witnesses or subconsciously suppress elements which seem to be inconsistent with their accounts. There is also the risk of deliberate distortion or fabrication.

However, it is important to recognise that an 'uncontaminated' first account will not necessarily be more accurate than an account produced after discussion. Such discussion will often remind an officer of something which he has forgotten or misstated in his first account or help him to make sense of recollections which were confused: 'Memory of any complex event involves elements of reconstruction, and a purist insistence that only "actual" memory is valid would be misconceived' (Underhill J in *R (Saunders) v Independent Police Complaints Commission* [2009] 1 All ER 379 at [11]–[16]).

(c) Where the record is inconsistent with the witness's evidence, it can be admitted as evidence **F6.24** of this inconsistency (*Sekhon* at p. 23). See also the CJA 2003, s. 119(1)(a), at **F6.49**.

(d) It is appropriate for the record to be put before the jury where it is difficult for the jury to follow the cross-examination of the witness who has refreshed his memory without having the record or, in practice, copies of the record, before them (*Sekhon*).

(e) There may be cases where it is convenient to use the record as an *aide-mémoire* as to the witness's evidence where that evidence is long and involved. However, care should be exercised in adopting this course in cases where the evidence, and therefore the record, is bitterly contested, because of the danger that the use of the document for this purpose could result in the jury misunderstanding its status, and lead to their wrongly regarding the document as being evidence in itself (*Sekhon*).

Treatment of Memory-refreshing Documents as Exhibits

Where, as is normally the case, a memory-refreshing document is permitted to go before the **F6.25** jury for the limited purpose of assisting them to evaluate the truth of the evidence given in the witness box, it is of no practical importance whether the document is treated as an exhibit, although in a case involving a large number of documents, it may be appropriate to give each one an exhibit number just to identify the document. The exception is the case in which the document provides, because of its nature, material by which its authenticity can be judged: such material can amount to evidence in the case, but only for the purpose of assessing authenticity (*Sekhon* (1986) 85 Cr App R 19, distinguishing *Fenlon* (1980) 71 Cr App R 307 and *Dillon* (1983) 85 Cr App R 29).

The question whether a memory-refreshing document, admitted under s. 120(3) (see **F6.22**) and produced as an exhibit, should accompany the jury when they retire, is governed by the CJA 2003, s. 122.

Criminal Justice Act 2003, s. 122

(1) This section applies if on a trial before a judge and jury for an offence—
  (a) a statement made in a document is admitted in evidence under section 119 or 120, and
  (b) the document or a copy of it is produced as an exhibit.
(2) The exhibit must not accompany the jury when they retire to consider their verdict unless—
  (a) the court considers it appropriate, or
  (b) all the parties to the proceedings agree that it should accompany the jury.

The reason for the general rule in s. 122 is the risk that the jury will place disproportionate weight on the contents of the document as compared with the oral evidence. It is normally sufficient for the judge to give a reminder in the summing-up of the contents of the statement and anything said by the witness about the document and the circumstances in which it was made. In cases where it is right for the jury to take the document with them, the judge should impress upon them the reason why they are being given the document and the importance of not attaching disproportionate weight to it (*Hulme* [2007] 1 Cr App R 334).

Refreshing Memory out of Court

See **F6.14** for the general rule on refreshing memory set out in the CJA 2003, s. 139. **F6.26**

F6.27 **Prior to Going into the Witness-box**   The conditions on which a witness may refresh his memory while giving evidence in the witness-box do not apply to a witness who refreshes his memory from a statement before going into the witness-box. In *Richardson* [1971] 2 QB 484 the accused was convicted of burglary offences committed 18 months earlier. Before the trial, four prosecution witnesses were shown their police statements, which they had made some weeks after the alleged offences. On appeal it was argued that the evidence of the four witnesses was, in the circumstances, inadmissible. The appeal was dismissed on the ground that there can be no general rule (which, unlike the rule as to what can be done in the witness-box, would be unenforceable) that witnesses may not before trial see the statements which they made at some period reasonably close to the time of the events which are the subject of the trial. See also, however, *Thomas* [1994] Crim LR 745 where, for reasons that are not disclosed, it was held to be undesirable for a child aged eight to be shown her signed police statement before giving evidence. In *Richardson*, Sachs LJ, giving the judgment of the Court of Appeal, made the following observations:

(a) It has been recognised in Home Office Circular 82–1969, *Supplies of Copies of Witnesses' Statements*, issued with the approval of the Lord Chief Justice and the judges of the Queen's Bench Division, that witnesses for the prosecution in criminal cases are normally entitled, if they so request, to copies of any statements taken from them by police officers.

(b) It is the practice, normally, for witnesses for the defence to be allowed to have copies of their statements and to refresh their memories from them before going into the witness-box.

(c) The court agreed with the following two observations of the Supreme Court of Hong Kong in *Lau Pak Ngam v R* [1966] Crim LR 443: 'Testimony in the witness-box becomes more a test of memory than truthfulness if witnesses are deprived of the opportunity of checking their recollection beforehand by reference to statements or notes made at a time closer to the events in question.' 'Refusal of access to statements would tend to create difficulties for honest witnesses but be likely to do little to hamper dishonest witnesses.'

(d) Obviously it would be wrong if several witnesses were handed statements in circumstances which enabled one to compare with another what each had said.

F6.28 Concerning (d), it is incumbent on prosecuting authorities and judges to ensure that witnesses are informed that they should not discuss cases in which they are involved (*Shaw* [2002] EWCA Crim 3004). As a general rule, discussions between witnesses, particularly just before going into court to give evidence, should not take place, nor should statements or proofs of evidence be read to witnesses in each other's presence (*Skinner* (1994) 99 Cr App R 212). Where such discussions have taken place, each case has to be dealt with on its own facts. If it emerges in cross-examination of the witnesses that the discussion may have led to fabrication, the court may take the view that it would be unsafe to leave any of the evidence of the witnesses concerned to the jury, but in other cases it may suffice to direct the jury on the implications which such conduct might have for the reliability of the evidence of the witnesses concerned (*Arif* (1993) *The Times*, 17 June 1993; and see also *Shaw*).

F6.29 **After Going into the Witness-box**   It is unlikely that resort will be had to the common-law authorities on the conditions for refreshing the memory after going into the witness-box, given that, speaking generally, the common-law rules have been relaxed by the CJA 2003 (see **F6.14**). However, the authorities are instructive in making clear that in some cases it may be appropriate for the witness to withdraw from the witness-box and read his statement in peace (per Stuart-Smith LJ in *Da Silva* [1990] 1 All ER 29, at p. 35) and that, in the case of a witness who is dyslexic and cannot read his earlier statement, he may be given the opportunity of adopting it by having counsel read it out in the absence of the jury (*Gordon* [2002] EWCA Crim 1).

F6.30 **Informing the Defence**   If prosecution witnesses have refreshed their memories out of court and before entering the witness-box, it is desirable, but not essential, that the defence should be informed of this (*Worley v Bentley* [1976] 2 All ER 449, affirmed in *Westwell* [1976] 2 All ER 812). (See also, *sed quaere, H* [1992] Crim LR 516, which suggests that child victims of sexual offences should refresh their memory out of court only *with the consent* of the defence.) In some cases the fact that a witness has read his statement out of court may be relevant to the weight which can properly be attached to his evidence, and injustice might be caused to the accused if the jury were left in ignorance of the fact. Accordingly, if the prosecution are aware that statements have been seen by their witnesses, it will be appropriate to inform the defence, although if for any reason this is not done, the omission cannot of itself be a ground for acquittal (*Westwell*).

Cross-examination on Memory-refreshing Document　　If a witness has refreshed his memory **F6.31** out of court and before entering the witness-box, counsel for the other side is entitled not only to inspect the memory-refreshing document, but also to cross-examine the witness upon the relevant matters contained therein. If counsel cross-examines upon material in the document from which the witness has refreshed his memory, the document is not thereby made evidence in the case; but if he cross-examines upon material which has not been referred to by the witness, this entitles the party calling the witness to put the document in evidence so that the tribunal of fact may see the document upon which the cross-examination is based. In this respect, therefore, the rules are the same as those which apply in the case of a witness refreshing his memory in the witness-box (as to which, see **F6.22**). See *Owen v Edwards* (1983) 77 Cr App R 191.

PREVIOUS CONSISTENT (SELF-SERVING) STATEMENTS

General Rule against Previous Consistent Statements

There is a general common-law rule excluding previous consistent or self-serving statements, **F6.32** sometimes referred to as the rule against narrative, to which there is a range of important statutory and common-law exceptions. Under the rule, a witness may not be asked about a previous oral or written statement made by him and consistent with his evidence (*Roberts* [1942] 1 All ER 187; *Larkin* [1943] KB 174; *Oyesiku* (1971) 56 Cr App R 240, at pp. 245–7). Equally, evidence of the previous statement may not be given by any other witness (*Roberts*). The previous statement, which may also be inadmissible as evidence of the facts contained in it under the rule against hearsay, is excluded as evidence of the accused's *consistency*. In *Roberts* [1942] 1 All ER 187, the accused was convicted of the murder of a girl by shooting her. His defence was that the gun went off accidentally when he was trying to make up a quarrel with her. The Court of Criminal Appeal held that evidence that two days after the event the accused had told his father that his defence would be accident had been properly excluded. Such evidence is easily manufactured and of no evidential value. The fact that the accused has said the same thing to someone else on a previous occasion does not confirm his evidence (*Roberts*, at p. 191).

The general rule applies in examination-in-chief, cross-examination and re-examination. Thus the credibility of a witness may not be bolstered by evidence of a previous consistent statement merely because his testimony has been impeached in cross-examination, and this remains the case 'even if the impeachment takes the form of contradiction or inconsistency between the evidence given at the trial and something said by the witness on a former occasion' (*Coll* (1889) 24 LR Ir 522, per Holmes J at p. 541. See also *Weekes* [1988] Crim LR 245; *Beattie* (1989) 89 Cr App R 302 per Lord Lane CJ at pp. 306–7; and *P (GR)* [1998] Crim LR 663). Equally, there is no exception to the general rule to the effect that where counsel cross-examines to show inconsistencies, the witness can be re-examined to show consistency (*Beattie* (1989) 89 Cr App R 302 per Lord Lane CJ at p. 307). However, the court does have a residual discretion, necessary in the interests of justice, to permit re-examination to show consistency, to ensure that as a result of the cross-examination the jury is not positively misled as to the existence of some fact or the terms of an earlier statement (*Ali* [2004] 1 Cr App R 501).

Complaints

At common law, if the complainant, in a case of rape or some other sexual offence, made a **F6.33** voluntary complaint shortly after the alleged offence, the person to whom the complaint was made may give evidence on behalf of the prosecution of the particulars of the complaint, not as evidence of the facts complained of, but to show the consistency of the conduct of the complainant with the complainant's evidence and, in cases where consent is in issue, as tending to negative consent (see generally *Lillyman* [1896] 2 QB 167). The CJA 2003, s. 120(7), has extended this common-law principle to cover a previous statement, whether oral or written, by a person against whom any type of offence has been committed, provided that it is an offence to which the proceedings relate, that the statement consists of a complaint about conduct which would, if proved, constitute the offence, and the complainant, in giving evidence, indicates that to the best of her belief, she made the statement and it states the truth. A statement received under s. 120(7) is admissible as evidence of the matters stated and, provided that the evidence is given by the person to whom the complaint was made (*White v R* [1999] 1 Cr App R 153), also goes to the consistency of the witness. Section 120(7) is much wider than the common-law principle, which is likely to be invoked only rarely. For detailed treatment of the common-law principle, see earlier editions of this work.

F6.34   Criminal Justice Act 2003, s. 120

(1) This section applies where a person (the witness) is called to give evidence in criminal proceedings.

...

(4) A previous statement by the witness is admissible as evidence of any matter stated of which oral evidence by him would be admissible, if—
   (a) any of the following three conditions is satisfied, and
   (b) while giving evidence the witness indicates that to the best of his belief he made the statement, and that to the best of his belief it states the truth.

...

(7) The third condition is that—
   (a) the witness claims to be a person against whom an offence has been committed,
   (b) the offence is one to which the proceedings relate,
   (c) the statement consists of a complaint made by the witness (whether to a person in authority or not) about conduct which would, if proved, constitute the offence or part of the offence,

...

   (e) the complaint was not made as a result of a threat or a promise, and
   (f) before the statement is adduced the witness gives oral evidence in connection with its subject matter.

(8) For the purposes of subsection (7) the fact that the complaint was elicited (for example, by a leading question) is irrelevant unless a threat or a promise was involved.

These provisions, although similar in some respects to the common-law rules, do not codify the law but are freestanding and provide their own criteria (*O* [2006] 2 Cr App R 405; see also *Xhabri* [2006] 1 All ER 776).

Prosecutors assembling the evidence to be called at trial should have s. 120(4)(b) well in mind if it is intended to rely on a previous statement as evidence of the truth of its contents, especially where a video interview is to stand as the witness's evidence in chief (*AA* [2007] EWCA Crim 1779). If the criteria are not met, the complaint may be admissible nonetheless under s. 114 (see **F15** and *Gillooley* [2009] EWCA Crim 671).

As to s. 120(7)(b), an 'offence... to which the proceedings relate' refers to an offence on the indictment and therefore the provisions do not cover a statement made by a person against whom an offence has been committed if that offence is not on the indictment (*Trewin* [2008] EWCA Crim 484, *obiter*).

F6.35   Section 120(7) contains no requirement of 'recency' and therefore allows for the admissibility of a complaint made months or even years after the offence. Furthermore, as at common law (*Lee* (1912) 7 Cr App R 31; *Wilbourne* (1917) 12 Cr App R 280), there is no limitation in the 2003 Act as to the admission of more than one complaint. In *O* it was held that there is no reason to import such a limitation, although the court added that there is obviously a need to restrict evidence of 'complaint upon complaint', which may merely be self-serving. In that case, a second complaint, made to a person different from the person to whom the first complaint was made, was held to have been properly admitted because of its relevance over and above that of the first complaint. Section 120(7)(e) requires that the complaint was not made as a result of a threat or promise, and under s. 120(8), which does not follow the common-law approach, the fact that the complaint was elicited by a leading question, such as 'Did X (naming the accused) assault you?', is irrelevant unless a threat or promise was made. However, a complaint elicited by way of a leading question is bound to affect the weight to be attached to it. Section 120(7)(f) requires that before the statement is introduced in evidence, the witness 'gives oral evidence in connection with its subject matter', words that suggest that this requirement will be met if the complainant gives some evidence in relation to the conduct referred to in her complaint, even if that evidence does not replicate the complaint or is not wholly consistent with it.

In order to reflect (a) the substantive change in the law effected by s. 120 and (b) the fact that the previous statement comes from the same person who makes the accusation in the witness box, the judge should direct the jury that the complaint is, if they are satisfied that it was made, evidence of the truth of what was stated. In deciding what weight it should bear, the jury should have in mind the fact that it comes from the same person who makes the complaint in the witness box and not from some independent source (*AA* [2007] EWCA Crim 1779 at [16]). However, failure to give such a direction will not result in a successful appeal against conviction if there was no risk of the jury treating the complaint as independent evidence because they were directed in such a way that they must have understood that it was only relevant to the truthfulness and reliability of the complainant (*Amrani* (2011) 175 JP 437). See also *H* [2012] 1 Cr App R 413, where defence counsel had not asked for an independence direction, and such a direction was not given, but the trial judge had stressed that there were no independent witnesses to the alleged conduct. Similarly, in the absence of a direction on independence, a conviction will not be quashed where evidence of the complaint was admitted, under the CJA 2003, s. 120, to rebut an allegation of recent fabrication (*AD* [2011] EWCA Crim 1943).

Self-serving Statements Made on Accusation

In *Pearce* (1979) 69 Cr App R 365, at pp. 368 and 370, the Court of Appeal could see no reason   **F6.36** for casting doubt on the well-established practice, on the part of the prosecution, to admit in evidence all unwritten, and most written, statements made by an accused person to the police, whether they contain admissions or whether they contain denials of guilt. If such a statement is wholly adverse to the accused, it may be admitted as evidence of the truth of the facts contained in it under the PACE 1984, s. 76 (see **F17.8**). If it is a mixed statement, i.e. a statement containing both inculpatory and exculpatory parts, such as 'I killed X. If I had not done so, X would certainly have killed me there and then', the whole statement is admissible (see principle 2(b) in *Pearce*, at **F6.38**), and both parts are admitted as evidence of the truth of the facts they contain (see *Duncan* (1981) 73 Cr App R 359, *Hamand* (1985) 82 Cr App R 65, *Sharp* [1988] 1 All ER 65 and generally at **F17.93**). However, if the statement is purely exculpatory or self-serving, it is not admitted as evidence of the facts stated in it; it 'is evidence in the trial because of its vital relevance as showing the reaction of the accused when first taxed with the incriminating facts' (*Storey* (1968) 52 Cr App R 334, per Widgery LJ at pp. 337–8). The police having found cannabis in the accused's flat, she told them that it belonged to a man who had brought it there against her will. The Court of Appeal upheld the trial judge's rejection of a submission of no case to answer, on the ground that the accused's statement was not evidence of the facts stated but only evidence of her reaction, which was insufficient to negative evidence of possession. Likewise, in a case where the accused gives no evidence, there is no duty on the judge to remind the jury of voluntary statements made by the accused to the police in exonerating himself (*Barbery* (1975) 62 Cr App R 248; *Tooke* (1989) 90 Cr App R 417). In *Barbery* Eveleigh J said (at p. 250): 'In *Storey*, Widgery LJ ... pointed out that such a statement, while being admissible for the jury's consideration ... as to the consistency of an accused's defence, was not admissible as evidence of the truth of the contents . . . and it is therefore no part of the judge's duty to put that statement before the jury as being a factor for their consideration in coming to their conclusion'. But contrast *Donaldson* (1976) 64 Cr App R 59 at p. 69; and see also *Squire* [1990] Crim LR 341.

F6.37 **The Principles as Set Out in** *Pearce*   The reference in *Storey* to the reaction of the accused 'when first taxed' must not be read as limiting the principle recognised to statements made on the first encounter with the police (*Pearce* (1979) 69 Cr App R 365). The facts in *Pearce* were as follows. On 6 March the appellant, the manager of a shop, was taxed by his employer's security officer with incriminating facts relating to handling stolen goods, and denied knowledge of them. Two days later he was arrested by the police and made a voluntary statement in the presence of his solicitor. Subsequently, in an interview, he gave certain answers which were relied on by the prosecution. The next day, he made another voluntary statement which was self-serving. The trial judge excluded evidence of all statements made to the police, except those parts of the interview on which the prosecution relied, on the grounds that they were self-serving and therefore inadmissible. On appeal it was argued that the statements had been properly excluded because they were not made when the appellant was first taxed with the incriminating facts on 6 March.

F6.38 Rejecting this argument and quashing the conviction, the Court of Appeal summarised the principles as follows (at p. 369):

(1) A statement which contains an admission is always admissible as a declaration against interest and is evidence of the facts admitted. With this exception a statement made by an accused person is never evidence of the facts in the statement. [It is now clear, however, that the exception encompasses statements which are either wholly or partially adverse to the accused (see *Sharp* [1988] 1 All ER 65 and generally at **F17.93**).]

(2) (a) A statement that is not an admission is admissible to show the attitude of the accused at the time when he made it. This however is not to be limited to a statement made on the first encounter with the police. The reference in *Storey* to the reaction of the accused 'when first taxed' should not be read as circumscribing the limits of admissibility. The longer the time that has elapsed after the first encounter the less the weight which will be attached to the denial. The judge is able to direct the jury about the value of such statements. (b) A statement that is not in itself an admission is admissible if it is made in the same context as an admission, whether in the course of an interview, or in the form of a voluntary statement. It would be unfair to admit only the statements against interest while excluding part of the same interview or series of interviews. It is the duty of the prosecution to present the case fairly to the jury; to exclude answers which are favourable to the accused while admitting those unfavourable would be misleading. (c) The prosecution may wish to draw attention to inconsistent denials. A denial does not become an admission because it is inconsistent with another denial. There must be many cases however where convictions have resulted from such inconsistencies between two denials.

(3) Although in practice most statements are given in evidence even when they are largely self-serving, there may be a rare occasion when an accused produces a carefully prepared written statement to the police, with a view to it being made part of the prosecution evidence. The trial judge would plainly exclude such a statement as inadmissible.

On the facts, the case fell within principles 2(a) and (b). The first statement was relevant to show the attitude of the appellant at the start of the interview: it set the scene, and when it was decided to admit part of the interview, the only fair course was to admit the statement to put the interview in context. The same principle applied to the questions and answers in the interview which were excluded and to the second voluntary statement on the next day. *Pearce* was applied in *McCarthy* (1980) 71 Cr App R 142.

F6.39 Principle 2(a) above cannot be relied upon to admit in evidence a statement which adds no weight to other evidence already before the jury as to the accused's reaction to the suggestion that he had committed an offence. In *Tooke* (1989) 90 Cr App R 417, a case of unlawful wounding, the attack took place at 9 p.m. and shortly thereafter, at the scene, T made an exculpatory statement. At 9.40 p.m., T went voluntarily to a police station and made a witness statement setting out his version. The statement made at the scene was admissible, but not the one made at the station: the latter, although spontaneous, added nothing to the evidence of reaction already supplied by the former.

Principle 2(b) above makes it clear, in the case of a 'mixed statement', that, if the prosecution **F6.40** rely on the parts of the statement unfavourable to the accused, they are obliged to put in evidence the other parts of the statement which are favourable to the accused. However, principle 2(a) is not entirely clear: in the case of a statement which is wholly self-serving, are the prosecution *obliged* to adduce such evidence; and are the defence *entitled* to elicit evidence of such statements in cross-examination of the prosecution witnesses? *McCarthy* (1980) 71 Cr App R 142 supports an affirmative answer. In that case the judge had refused to admit details of an alibi given at a police interview. The Court of Appeal held that the evidence had been *improperly excluded* (although the case against the appellant was strong and the proviso was applied), since it did not come within the exception referred to in *Pearce* (i.e. principle 3). Lawton LJ said (at p. 145):

> One of the best pieces of evidence that an innocent man can produce is his reaction to an accusation of a crime. If he has been told, as the appellant was told, that he was suspected of having committed a particular crime at a particular time and place and he says at once, 'That cannot be right, because I was elsewhere', and gives details of where he was, that is something which the jury can take into account.

Principle 3 is designed to prevent an accused from attempting to take unfair advantage of prin- **F6.41** ciple 2(a). An example is *Newsome* (1980) 71 Cr App R 325. On a charge of rape, it was held that a self-serving statement, dictated by the accused to the police after consultation with, and in the presence of, his solicitor, some 13 hours after the alleged offence and subsequent to several interviews with the police, was inadmissible under principle 3. See also *Thatcher* [1967] 1 WLR 1278 (a statement drafted by counsel on instructions and submitted to the officer in charge of the case for his signature). In *Hutton* (1988) *The Times*, 27 October 1988, the police, in exercise of their right to do so under the PACE 1984, s. 58, delayed access to a solicitor and interviewed the accused three times. He refused to sign the notes of those interviews. After being charged, he was allowed access to his solicitor, in whose presence he dictated to the police a self-serving statement consistent with the evidence he gave at the trial. On appeal, it was argued that the statement should have been admitted, because the police, in exercising their rights under s. 58, had prevented the accused from making known his reaction to the charge. Rejecting the argument, the court held that exercise of the s. 58 right did not affect the question whether the statement could properly be described as a spontaneous reaction, and therefore admissible under principle 2(a), or a carefully prepared draft following consultation, and therefore inadmissible under principle 3. The trial judge had properly concluded that the statement fell outside principle 2(a).

Statements in Rebuttal of Allegations of Recent Fabrication

The previous consistent statement of a witness will not become admissible merely because his **F6.42** evidence is impeached in cross-examination (*Fox v General Medical Council* [1960] 3 All ER 225), even if this takes the form of cross-examination on a previous inconsistent statement (see *Coll* (1889) 24 LR Ir 522 at p. 541 and the other authorities considered at **F6.32**). However, if in cross-examination it is suggested to a witness that his evidence is a recent fabrication, evidence of a previous consistent statement will be admissible in re-examination to negative the suggestion and confirm the witness's credibility (*Y* [1995] Crim LR 155). The principle has no application where a witness is cross-examined on the basis that his account was fabricated from the outset, unless the effect of the cross-examination is in fact to create the impression that he invented his story at a later stage (*Athwal* [2009] 1 WLR 2430). In a trial for a sexual offence in which the previous statement amounts to a complaint, it may be admissible to rebut the allegation of recent fabrication notwithstanding that it is inadmissible as a recent complaint (see *Tyndale* [1999] Crim LR 320 and **F6.33**).

F6.43   In *Oyesiku* (1971) 56 Cr App R 240, Karminski LJ, giving the judgment of the Court of Appeal (at p. 245), approved the following statement of Dixon CJ in *Nominal Defendant v Clements* (1960) 104 CLR 476, at pp. 479–80:

> If the credit of a witness is impugned as to some material fact to which he deposes upon the ground that his account is a late invention or has been lately devised or reconstructed, even though not with conscious dishonesty, that makes admissible a statement to the same effect as the account he gave as a witness if it was made by the witness contemporaneously with the event or at a time sufficiently early to be inconsistent with the suggestion that his account is a late invention or reconstruction. But, inasmuch as the rule forms a definite exception to the general principle excluding statements made out of court and admits a possibly self-serving statement made by the witness, great care is called for in applying it. The judge at the trial must determine for himself upon the conduct of the trial before him whether a case for applying the rule of evidence has arisen and, from the nature of the matter, if there be an appeal, great weight should be given to his opinion by the appellate court. It is evident however that the judge at the trial must exercise care in assuring himself not only that the account given by the witness in his testimony is attacked on the ground of recent invention or reconstruction or that a foundation for such an attack has been laid by the party but also that the contents of the statement are in fact to the like effect as his account given in his evidence and that having regard to the time and circumstances in which it was made it rationally tends to answer the attack.

In *Oyesiku* the conviction was quashed because the trial judge had improperly refused to allow the jury to see the previous statement; by inspection of it, the jury would have been in a better position to assess the extent to which it rebutted the attack made on the witness's testimony. See also *Sekhon* (1987) 85 Cr App R 19, at **F6.22** *et seq*. For earlier authority, see *Benjamin* (1913) 8 Cr App R 146 and *Flanagan v Fahy* [1918] 2 IR 361.

F6.44   Under the CJA 2003, s. 120(1) and (2), a statement by a witness admitted as evidence to rebut a suggestion that his oral evidence has been fabricated will be admissible for the truth of its contents.

Criminal Justice Act 2003, s. 120

(1) This section applies where a person (the witness) is called to give evidence in criminal proceedings.
(2) If a previous statement by the witness is admitted as evidence to rebut a suggestion that his oral evidence has been fabricated, that statement is admissible as evidence of any matter stated of which oral evidence by the witness would be admissible.

Section 120(2) itself does not govern admissibility, which must be considered by reference to the principles which have governed this question in the past (*Trewin* [2008] EWCA Crim 484 at [18] and [20]).

Where hearsay is admissible under s. 120(2), compliance with the requirements of timely formal notice will not normally be possible and it will be for the judge to consider whether it would be fair to exercise the power in the CrimPR, r. 34.5 (see Supplement, **R-269**) to dispense with the requirements (*Athwal* [2009] 1 WLR 2430).

Although s. 120(2) refers to 'fabrication' without the qualification 'recent', the clear intention was to leave the common-law principle intact. However, the principle is not to be confined to a temporal straitjacket. 'Recent' is an elastic description designed to assist in the identification of circumstances in which a previous consistent statement should be admitted where there is a rational basis for its use as a tool for deciding where the truth lies. The touchstone is whether the evidence may fairly assist in that way, and not the length of time (*Athwal*). For example, in *MH* [2012] EWCA Crim 2725, where it was alleged by a father that his son had been coached by his mother to give false evidence against him to stop him from seeing his children and by reason of the financial dispute between him and his wife, evidence of the son's complaints to the mother against the father prior to the breakdown of the marriage was admissible in rebuttal, but not evidence of such complaints made at a time when the father was not permitted to see his children and when he and his wife were in financial dispute.

Evidence of Previous Identification and Description   **F6.45**

> In cases where there has been a considerable lapse of time between the offence and the trial, and where there might be a danger of the witness's recollection of the prisoner's features having become dimmed, no doubt it strengthens the value of the evidence if it can be shown that in the meantime, soon after the commission of the offence, the witness saw and recognised the prisoner. (*Fannon* (1922) 22 SR (NSW) 427, per Ferguson J at pp. 429–30)

It is for reasons of this kind that evidence that a witness identified the accused out of court may be given by the witness himself and by any person who witnessed the identification. In *Christie* [1914] AC 545, a case of indecent assault on a small boy, the boy gave unsworn evidence of the assault and identified the accused, but was not questioned as to a previous identification. The boy's mother and a constable were then allowed to give evidence that, shortly after the offence alleged, they saw the boy approach the accused and identify him by saying, 'That is the man'. The House of Lords, by a majority, held that this evidence had been properly admitted. Viscount Haldane LC (who was of the opinion that this evidence *would have been* admissible if the boy had given evidence of his out-of-court identification) described the evidential value of such evidence as follows (at p. 551): 'Its relevancy is to show that the boy was able to identify at the time and to exclude the idea that the identification of the prisoner in the dock was an afterthought or mistake.' See also *Fowkes* (1856) *The Times*, 8 March 1856, at **F6.48**.

As a general rule, a 'dock identification', i.e. an identification of the accused for the first time in court, is undesirable and should be avoided (*Cartwright* (1914) 10 Cr App R 219); and the usual practice is to elicit evidence of a witness's previous out-of-court identification *before* asking him whether that person is in court. As to dock identifications generally and evidence of previous identification, see **F18**.

Section 120(5) of the CJA 2003, when read in conjunction with s. 120(1) and (4) of the Act, has   **F6.46** extended the common-law principle relating to evidence of *previous identification of the accused* to cover a previous oral or written statement of a witness which *identifies or describes a person, object or place*, provided that the witness, while giving evidence, indicates that to the best of his belief, he made the statement and it states the truth. A statement received under s. 120(5) is admitted as evidence of any matter stated, as well as evidence of the witness's consistency.

Criminal Justice Act 2003, s. 120

(1) This section applies where a person (the witness) is called to give evidence in criminal proceedings.

...

(4) A previous statement by the witness is admissible as evidence of any matter stated of which oral evidence by him would be admissible, if—
   (a) any of the following three conditions is satisfied, and
   (b) while giving evidence the witness indicates that to the best of his belief he made the statement, and that to the best of his belief it states the truth.

(5) The first condition is that the statement identifies or describes a person, object or place.

The following principles relating to s. 120(4) and (5) derive from the decision of the Court of   **F6.47** Appeal in *Chinn* [2012] 3 All ER 502. Under s. 120(4), the previous statement does not have to be in a document. The scope of s. 120(5) stems from its purpose, which is not to introduce an identification or description in a vacuum, which would be of no use, but in the relevant context, because the person, object or place is being identified or described for a particular purpose. Thus, for example, s. 120(5) can be used to admit a statement that it was Mr X who was at the ABC Bar on a certain day at a certain time. However, other parts of the narrative in the witness statement that go beyond such an identification (or description) are not admissible. Where the case turns wholly or partly on identification evidence and the accused has been identified in a statement admitted under s. 120(4) and (5), the judge will have to consider whether some sort of Turnbull direction, in a suitably adapted form, is needed. In certain circumstances, e.g., where the only evidence of identification of an accused is sought to be adduced under s. 120(4) and (5), consideration may be given to discretionary exclusion under the PACE 1984, s. 78. In a suitable case, the judge may also consider whether to exercise the power to stop the case under the CJA 2003, s. 125 (considered at **F16.94**).

Statements Forming Part of *Res Gestae*

F6.48   A previous statement of a witness which was so closely associated in time, place and circumstances with some act or event in issue that it can be said to form a part of the *res gestae*, i.e. the same transaction, is admissible as evidence of consistency to confirm evidence given by the witness to the same effect. Such a statement is also admissible for the truth of its contents (see **F16.55** to **F16.62**). In *Fowkes* (1856) *The Times*, 8 March 1856, the accused, commonly known as 'the butcher', was charged with murder. The victim's son gave evidence that he and a police officer were in a room with his father; that a face appeared at the window through which the fatal shot was then fired; and that he thought the face was that of the accused. He was also allowed to give evidence that on seeing the face, he had shouted, 'There's Butcher'; and the officer, who had not seen the face, was also allowed to give evidence as to this exclamation.

PREVIOUS INCONSISTENT STATEMENTS

F6.49   If a witness in examination-in-chief (or cross-examination) admits making a previous oral or written inconsistent statement, the statement is admissible under the CJA 2003, s. 119, as evidence of any matter stated of which oral evidence by him would be admissible.

Criminal Justice Act 2003, s. 119

> (1) If in criminal proceedings a person gives oral evidence and—
>   (a) he admits making a previous inconsistent statement...
>   the statement is admissible as evidence of any matter stated of which oral evidence by him would be admissible.

UNFAVOURABLE AND HOSTILE WITNESSES

General Rule against Impeaching Credit of Own Witness

F6.50   The general rule is that a party is not entitled to impeach the credit of his own witness by asking questions or adducing evidence concerning such matters as the witness's bad character, previous convictions, bias or previous inconsistent statements. However, the general rule appears to have no application where evidence of a witness's bad character is introduced not to impeach his credit in relation to his testimony, but because it supports some other discrete part of the prosecution case (*Ross* [2007] EWCA Crim 1457). In the case of a witness who is 'unfavourable', i.e. a witness who displays no hostile animus to the party calling him but merely fails to come up to proof or gives evidence unfavourable to that party, the general rule prevails: the only remedy available to the party is to call other witnesses, if available, with a view to proving that which the unfavourable witness failed to establish (*Ewer v Ambrose* (1825) 3 B & C 746). Insofar as this results in two equally credible witnesses directly contradicting each other upon a major fact in issue, it has been said that the party calling them is not entitled to accredit the one and discredit the other; the testimony of both is to be disregarded (*Sumner and Leivesley v John Brown & Co.* (1909) 25 TLR 745, per Hamilton J). However, in *Brent* [1973] Crim LR 295 it was held that this dictum does not apply to criminal proceedings, because of the Crown's duty to call all relevant evidence. In the case of a witness who appears to the judge to be hostile, that is to say not desirous of telling the truth to the court at the instance of the party calling him (Stephen's *Digest of the Law of Evidence* (12th edn, 1936), Article 147), the general rule is modified, but in only two respects:

(a) under the Criminal Procedure Act 1865, s. 3, that party may, by leave of the judge, prove a previous inconsistent statement of the witness (see **F6.54**); and
(b) at common law, the party calling the witness may cross-examine him by asking leading questions (see *Thompson* (1976) 64 Cr App R 96, at **F6.55**).

Calling Witnesses who are Likely to be Hostile

F6.51 The prosecution may call a person as a witness even if he has shown signs that he is likely to be hostile, for example by retracting a statement or by making a second statement prior to the trial. (*Mann* (1972) 56 Cr App R 750). Equally, the fact that a witness has been treated as hostile before the magistrates is not by itself a reason making it improper for the prosecution to call him at the trial and, if necessary, to apply for leave to treat him as hostile again, although each case turns on its own facts (*Vibert* (21 October 1974 unreported)). Nor is it a bar to an accused calling a witness to give evidence against a co-accused and to the witness being treated as hostile that he was expected to resile from what he had previously said; and if his previous inconsistent statement is proved, it will be evidence of the truth of its contents under the CJA 2003, s. 119 (*Osborne* [2010] EWCA Crim 1981, but see also, in the case of a prosecution witness, *Dat* [1998] Crim LR 488, where it was held that the prosecution should cross-examine the witness by degrees so as to limit the damage which might occur as a result of wide-ranging cross-examination on the previous statement; for the CJA 2003, s. 119, see **F6.56**). A *voir dire* before a decision on whether to allow a witness to be treated as hostile is only appropriate in exceptional circumstances because a jury may see the witness apparently giving evidence in one frame of mind and then see a complete turn-around after events which have taken place in their absence (*Khan* [2002] EWCA Crim 945). Similarly, it is only in very exceptional cases that a *voir dire* should be held to decide whether or not a witness who has yet to be called might prove to be hostile (*Olumegbon* [2004] EWCA Crim 2337). However, in cases in which a person indicates that he is no longer in a position to further assist the prosecution or court, or claims to be no longer able to remember anything, it seems that the judge has a discretion to hold a *voir dire* to decide whether to prevent him being called at all (*Honeyghon* [1999] Crim LR 221).

Time at which to Apply to Treat Witness as Hostile

F6.52 The application to treat a witness as hostile should be made when the witness first shows unmistakable signs of hostility (*Pestano* [1981] Crim LR 397). If counsel for the prosecution has a statement directly contradicting one of their witnesses who gives evidence that he is unable to identify the accused, he should at once show the statement to the judge and ask for leave to cross-examine the witness (*Fraser* (1956) 40 Cr App R 160). However, although there may be circumstances where a witness is displaying such an excessive degree of hostility that the only appropriate course is to treat him as hostile, if he gives evidence contrary to an earlier statement (or fails to give the evidence expected) the party calling him and the trial judge should first consider inviting him to refresh his memory from material which it is legitimate to use for that purpose and should not immediately proceed to treat him as hostile (*Maw* [1994] Crim LR 841). In *Powell* [1985] Crim LR 592 it was held that the prosecution, during re-examination, had been properly allowed to treat as hostile a witness who had shown no signs of hostility during examination-in-chief. Although such an application is a little unusual, it is a matter for the judge's discretion (*Powell*). See also *Little* (1883) 15 Cox CC 319.

Role of Judge and Jury

F6.53 The discretion of the judge, however hostile the witness, is absolute (*Rice v Howard* (1886) 16 QBD 681; *Price v Manning* (1889) 42 Ch D 372); and the decision will rarely be open to a successful challenge on appeal (*Manning* [1968] Crim LR 675).

Although the question whether a witness is hostile is for the judge, the jury should not be excluded from the proceedings while the decision is taken. In *Darby* [1989] Crim LR 817, in which an application to treat a witness as hostile was deferred by the judge, who had him questioned further in the absence of the jury before ruling that he was hostile, it was held that the evidence and demeanour of the witness should have been tested in the presence of the jury.

Criminal Procedure Act 1865, s. 3

F6.54
Criminal Procedure Act 1865, s. 3

> A party producing a witness shall not be allowed to impeach his credit by general evidence of bad character, but he may, in case the witness shall, in the opinion of the judge, prove adverse, contradict him by other evidence, or, by leave of the judge, prove that he has made at other times a statement inconsistent with his present testimony; but before such last mentioned proof can be given the circumstances of the supposed statement, sufficient to designate the particular occasion, must be mentioned to the witness, and he must be asked whether or not he has made such statement.

The first part of this section puts on a statutory basis the common-law rule that a party calling a witness is not entitled to impeach his credit by evidence of bad character, i.e. evidence of previous misconduct, convictions, or other evidence designed to show that the witness is not to be believed on oath. The remaining two rules in the section apply to witnesses who, in the opinion of the judge, prove 'adverse', which means 'hostile' and not merely 'unfavourable' (*Greenough v Eccles* (1859) 5 CB NS 786, a decision on the construction of the Common Law Procedure Act 1854, s. 22, which was repealed but re-enacted by s. 3 of the 1865 Act).

The first rule is that a party may 'contradict' a hostile witness, i.e. call other witnesses to prove that which the hostile witness has failed to establish. Although s. 3 suggests that this rule applies only to hostile witnesses, according to Williams and Willes JJ in *Greenough v Eccles*, it has not affected the common-law rule to the same effect in the case of unfavourable witnesses (*Ewer v Ambrose* (1825) 3 B & C 746).

The second rule, which does apply only in the case of a witness who is, in the opinion of the judge, hostile, allows the judge to give leave to prove that the witness has made at other times a statement inconsistent with his present testimony. A witness for the defence who is treated as hostile is in the same position as a hostile prosecution witness, and accordingly is open to cross-examination on a previous inconsistent statement (*Booth* (1981) 74 Cr App R 123). The leave of the judge may be given whether the previous inconsistent statement was oral or written (*Prefas* (1986) 86 Cr App R 111). Cross-examination on the contents of an *Achieving Best Evidence* interview may be permitted notwithstanding an earlier ruling by the judge that it would not be in the interests of justice to permit the interview to be played as the evidence-in-chief of the witness (*Mazekelua* [2011] EWCA Crim 1458). If the witness, when asked, admits that he made the previous statement, this will clearly suffice as proof that he did make it. If the witness does not make such an admission, whether the earlier statement can be used depends on the facts of the particular case. In *Baldwin* [1986] Crim LR 681, where the witness accepted that he had made some parts of a written statement and accepted that the signatures on the statement were his, it was held that this was evidence entitling the judge to conclude that the witness had made the statement, and therefore to rule that cross-examination on it was permissible.

If the nature of the evidence given justifies it, an application may be made to treat as hostile the spouse or civil partner of an accused who is competent but not compellable for the prosecution, and who has waived his or her right to refuse to testify. However, it is desirable that the judge should explain to the spouse or civil partner, in the absence of the jury and before the oath is taken, that if the choice is made to give evidence, he or she may be treated like any other witness (*Pitt* [1983] QB 25). See generally, **F4.14**. However, even if the spouse or civil partner elects not to give evidence, his or her written statement may be admissible under the CJA 2003, s. 114(1)(d) (see **F16.38**).

Hostile Witnesses at Common Law

The Criminal Procedure Act 1865, s. 3, has not destroyed or removed the common-law right **F6.55** of the judge, in the exercise of his discretion, to allow cross-examination of a hostile witness by asking leading questions about a previous statement. In *Thompson* (1976) 64 Cr App R 96 the appellant was convicted of incest with his daughter. She had made a statement to the police implicating her father but, when sworn as a witness at the trial, she refused to give evidence, and leave was given to treat her as hostile. She was asked leading questions, her previous statement was put to her, and she eventually agreed that its contents were true. It was argued, on appeal, that since the girl had initially given no evidence, there was no 'present testimony' with which her previous statement could be said to be inconsistent, and therefore s. 3 did not apply. Lord Parker CJ found it unnecessary to decide whether s. 3 applied to the facts, since the common-law cases prior to the 1865 Act recognised that pressure could be brought to bear upon witnesses who refused to co-operate. Thus, in *Clarke v Saffery* (1824) Ry & M 126, in which there does not appear to have been evidence contradicting the earlier statement, Best CJ said (at p. 126): 'If a witness, by his conduct in the box, shows himself decidedly adverse, it is always in the discretion of the judge to allow a cross-examination'. In *Bastin v Carew* (1824) cited Ry & M 127, Lord Abbott CJ said: '... in each particular case there must be some discretion in the presiding judge as to the mode in which the examination shall be conducted, in order best to answer the purposes of justice'. On this basis, the appeal was dismissed. It is submitted that if the witness in the case had denied making the previous statement and not accepted the truth of its contents, it would not have been open to proof at common law.

Evidential Value of Previous Inconsistent Statement of Hostile Witness

If a hostile witness, on being cross-examined, does not admit the truth of a previous inconsist- **F6.56** ent statement, it is admitted, under the CJA 2003, s. 119, as evidence of the matters stated. However, if, under cross-examination, he admits making the statement and the truth of its contents, the contents become part of his evidence and there is no need to rely on s. 119 (*Gibbons* (2009) 173 JP 260; and see also, prior to the 2003 Act, *Maw* [1994] Crim LR 841).

Criminal Justice Act 2003, s. 119

(1) if in criminal proceedings a person gives oral evidence and—

...

   (b) a previous inconsistent statement made by him is proved by virtue of section 3, 4 or 5 of the Criminal Procedure Act 1865,
   the statement is admissible as evidence of any matter stated of which oral evidence by him would be admissible.

A statement admissible in law under s. 119 may nonetheless fall to be excluded as a matter of discretion pursuant to the PACE 1984, s. 78. If the statement is admitted, it remains open to the defence, at the close of the prosecution case, to submit that there is no case to answer, on the basis that the prosecution evidence is too unreliable (see **D16.54** *et seq.*), or that the judge should exercise the power under the CJA 2003, s. 125 (unconvincing hearsay — see **F16.93**), and either direct the jury to acquit or discharge the jury (*Bennett* [2008] EWCA Crim 248; *Joyce* [2005] EWCA Crim 1785). The observation in *Joyce* that there is no difference between the duty on the judge under s. 125 and under *Galbraith* [1981] 2 All ER 1060 (see **D16.55**) was disapproved in *Riat* [2013] 1 All ER 349 at [28]).

Direction as to Status of Evidence The judge should direct the jury that the previous state- **F6.57** ment is evidence in the case, but not that it is just as much evidence as the witness's evidence in

F

Part F Evidence

court. The judge may also direct the jury that they may consider the statement when deciding upon their verdict if they are sure that it is true or, in the case of a statement exculpatory of the accused, if they conclude that it *may* be true (*Billingham* [2009] 2 Cr App R 341). According to the *Crown Court Bench Book*, the jury may be invited to treat the witness's evidence as completely unreliable and therefore worthless or, on the contrary, to act on the earlier statement if, after careful consideration, they think it right to do so. A similar approach was adopted in *Parvez* [2010] EWCA Crim 3229, where the issue was whether or not the jury were sure that it was fear that had led the witness to retract an earlier statement. It was held that if they were sure, then, subject to caution, they could act upon it, but if they were not, they should not rely upon it.

F6.58   Direction on 'Unreliability'   In *Golder* [1960] 3 All ER 457, Lord Parker CJ said (at pp. 1172–3):

> ...when a witness is shown to have made previous statements inconsistent with the evidence given by that witness at the trial, the jury should...be directed that the evidence given at the trial should be regarded as unreliable.

The dictum in *Golder* was cited with approval in *Oliva* [1965] 3 All ER 116, at pp. 1036–7. However, Lord Parker's dictum was *obiter* and in *Driscoll v The Queen* (1977) 137 CLR 517, at pp. 535–7, the High Court of Australia refused to accept that it was *always* necessary or even appropriate to direct a jury in this way, a view endorsed by the House of Lords in *Governor of Pentonville Prison, ex parte Alves* [1993] AC 284 (at p. 298) and by the Court of Appeal in *Goodway* [1993] 4 All ER 894 (at p. 899). Thus in *Pestano* [1981] Crim LR 397, where the prosecution cross-examined the witness on his deposition, but nonetheless sought to rely upon his evidence insofar as it supported their case, it was held that the evidence was for the jury to consider, subject to a proper warning from the judge as to the weight which could be attached to it. See also *Nelson* [1992] Crim LR 653.

The direction to treat the witness's evidence as 'unreliable' may be inappropriate when a witness gives a rational or convincing explanation for the earlier contradictory statement or gives evidence to the benefit of the accused (*Thomas* [1985] Crim LR 445; *Khan* [2002] EWCA Crim 945). Nonetheless, if a witness has been treated as hostile, it is necessary for the jury to consider whether he should be treated as creditworthy at all, and they should be clearly directed on that point before considering which parts of the evidence are worthy of acceptance and which are to be rejected. It is insufficient to tell the jury to approach the evidence with great caution and reservation. The judge should give a clear warning about the dangers involved in a witness who contradicts himself and should direct them to consider whether they can give any credence to such a witness. It is only if they can, that they may then consider which parts of his evidence they can accept (*Maw* [1994] Crim LR 841). See also *Greene* [2009] EWCA Crim 2282, where it was held that, in all but exceptional cases, once a witness has been treated as hostile, some warning should be given to approach his evidence with caution, even if, in the event, he proves not to be hostile and reverts to his original account; the precise nature of the direction will be dependent upon the particular circumstances of the case.

F6.59   Documents   The question whether a document admitted under s. 119 and produced as an exhibit should accompany the jury when they retire is governed by the CJA 2003, s. 122 (see F6.25). In the absence of some specific feature of the document requiring the jury to be given it, the judge will remind the jury in his summing-up of its contents and anything said by the witness about it and the circumstances in which it was made. If the jury are to be given the document, the judge should not only give the general direction about hostile witnesses, but also impress upon the jury the reason why they are being given the document and the importance of not attaching disproportionate weight to its contents as compared with the oral evidence (*Hulme* [2007] 1 Cr App R 334).

Section F7 Cross-examination and Re-examination

CROSS-EXAMINATION: GENERAL CONSIDERATIONS

Nature and Sequence of Cross-examination

Cross-examination is the questioning of a witness by (a) the opponent of the party calling **F7.1**
him or (b) any other party to the proceedings. Thus, as to the latter, an accused has the right
to cross-examine a co-accused who has chosen to give evidence (and any witnesses called by
the co-accused). This applies not only where the co-accused has given evidence unfavourable
to the accused (*Hadwen* [1902] 1 KB 882; *Paul* [1920] 2 KB 183), but also if the co-accused
has merely given evidence in his own defence (*Hilton* [1972] 1 QB 421, per Fenton Atkinson
LJ at pp. 423–4). Usually cross-examination follows immediately after examination-in-chief,
but witnesses are sometimes merely tendered by the prosecution for cross-examination. Such a
witness is called by the prosecution, sworn, asked no questions in chief other than his name and
address, and then cross-examined by the defence (*Brooke* (1819) 2 Stark 472).

As to the sequence of cross-examination, both prosecution and defence witnesses may be cross-
examined by any co-accused in the order their names appear in the indictment or as directed
by the court (CrimPR, r. 38.11(4)(b) and (c)). A defence witness may be cross-examined by the
prosecution after cross-examination by any co-accused (r. 38.11(c)).

Cross-examination by an Accused in Person

As a general rule, an accused is entitled to cross-examine in person any witness called by the **F7.2**
prosecution. The general rule is subject to a common-law restriction and important statutory
exceptions. Concerning the former, a trial judge is not obliged to give an unrepresented accused
his head to ask whatever questions, at whatever length, he wishes (*Brown* [1998] 2 Cr App R
364). As to the latter, the YJCEA 1999, ss. 34 to 39, protect three categories of witness from
cross-examination by an accused in person. Under the YJCEA 1999, s. 34, no person charged
with a sexual offence as defined in s. 62 of the Act (see **F7.22**) may cross-examine in person the
complainant, either in connection with the offence or in connection with any other offence (of
whatever nature) with which that person is charged in the proceedings; under s. 35, no person
charged with one of a number of specified offences may cross-examine in person a 'protected
witness' either in connection with the offence, or in connection with any other offence (of whatever nature) with which that person is charged in the proceedings; and under s. 36, the court has
a general power, in cases not covered by ss. 34 and 35, to give a direction prohibiting the accused
from cross-examining a witness in person if:

(a) the quality of evidence given by the witness is likely to be diminished by such cross-examination and would be likely to be improved by such a direction; and
(b) it would not be contrary to the interests of justice.

In deciding whether (a) applies in the case of a witness, the court must have regard to the particular matters set out in s. 36(3), including the nature of the questions likely to be asked. The
accused should not be denied the opportunity to make representations in relation to the matters
set out in s. 36(3) (*R (Hillman) v Richmond Magistrates' Court* [2003] EWHC 2580 (Admin)).

F

Part F Evidence

Section 38 provides that, where an accused is prevented from cross-examining a witness in person, the court must invite him to appoint a legal representative; and that if he fails to do so and the court decides that it is in the interests of justice for the witness to be cross-examined by a legal representative appointed to represent the interests of the accused, the court must choose and appoint such a representative, who shall not be responsible to the accused. Under s. 39, where an accused is prevented from cross-examining a witness in person, the judge must give the jury such warning (if any) as he considers necessary to ensure that the accused is not prejudiced by any inference that might be drawn from the fact that such cross-examination has been prevented or by the fact that the cross-examination was carried out by a court-appointed representative.

For the procedural rules relating to the restriction on cross-examination by an accused, see the CrimPR, part 31 (see Supplement, **R-242** *et seq.*).

F7.3   Youth Justice and Criminal Evidence Act 1999, ss. 34 to 39

34. No person charged with a sexual offence may in any criminal proceedings cross-examine in person a witness who is the complainant, either—
    (a) in connection with that offence, or
    (b) in connection with any other offence (of whatever nature) with which that person is charged in the proceedings.

35.—(1) No person charged with an offence to which this section applies may in any criminal proceedings cross-examine in person a protected witness, either—
    (a) in connection with that offence, or
    (b) in connection with any other offence (of whatever nature) with which that person is charged in the proceedings.
(2) For the purposes of subsection (1) a 'protected witness' is a witness who—
    (a) either is the complainant or is alleged to have been a witness to the commission of the offence to which this section applies, and
    (b) either is a child or falls to be cross-examined after giving evidence in chief (whether wholly or in part)—
        (i) by means of a video recording made (for the purposes of section 27) at a time when the witness was a child, or
        (ii) in any other way at any such time.
(3) The offences to which this section applies are—
    (a) any offence under—
    ...
        (iva) any of sections 33 to 36 of the Sexual Offences Act 1956;
        (v)   the Protection of Children Act 1978; or
        (vi) part 1 of the Sexual Offences Act 2003 or any relevant superseded enactment;
    (b) kidnapping, false imprisonment or an offence under section 1 or 2 of the Child Abduction Act 1984;
    (c) any offence under section 1 of the Children and Young Persons Act 1933;
    (d) any offence (not within any of the preceding paragraphs) which involves an assault on, or injury or a threat of injury to, any person.
(3A) In subsection (3)(a)(vi) 'relevant superseded enactment' means—
    (a) any of sections 1 to 32 of the Sexual Offences Act 1956;
    (b) the Indecency with Children Act 1960;
    (c) the Sexual Offences Act 1967;
    (d) section 54 of the Criminal Law Act 1977.
(4) In this section 'child' means—
    (a) where the offence falls within subsection (3)(a), a person under the age of 18; or
    (b) where the offence falls within subsection (3)(b), (c) or (d), a person under the age of 14.
(5) For the purposes of this section 'witness' includes a witness who is charged with an offence in the proceedings.

36.—(1) This section applies where, in a case where neither of sections 34 and 35 operates to prevent an accused in any criminal proceedings from cross-examining a witness in person—
    (a) the prosecutor makes an application for the court to give a direction under this section in relation to the witness, or
    (b) the court of its own motion raises the issue whether such a direction should be given.

(2) If it appears to the court—

   (a) that the quality of evidence given by the witness on cross-examination—

      (i) is likely to be diminished if the cross-examination (or further cross-examination) is conducted by the accused in person, and

      (ii) would be likely to be improved if a direction were given under this section, and

   (b) that it would not be contrary to the interests of justice to give such a direction, the court may give a direction prohibiting the accused from cross-examining (or further cross-examining) the witness in person.

(3) In determining whether subsection (2)(a) applies in the case of a witness the court must have regard, in particular, to—

   (a) any views expressed by the witness as to whether or not the witness is content to be cross-examined by the accused in person;

   (b) the nature of the questions likely to be asked, having regard to the issues in the proceedings and the defence case advanced so far (if any);

   (c) any behaviour on the part of the accused at any stage of the proceedings, both generally and in relation to the witness;

   (d) any relationship (of whatever nature) between the witness and the accused;

   (e) whether any person (other than the accused) is or has at any time been charged in the proceedings with a sexual offence or an offence to which section 35 applies, and (if so) whether section 34 or 35 operates or would have operated to prevent that person from cross-examining the witness in person;

   (f) any direction under section 19 which the court has given, or proposes to give, in relation to the witness.

(4) For the purposes of this section—

   (a) 'witness', in relation to an accused, does not include any other person who is charged with an offence in the proceedings; and

   (b) any reference to the quality of a witness's evidence shall be construed in accordance with section 16(5).

37.—(1) Subject to subsection (2), a direction has binding effect from the time it is made until the witness to whom it applies is discharged.

In this section 'direction' means a direction under section 36.

(2) The court may discharge a direction if it appears to the court to be in the interests of justice to do so, and may do so either—

   (a) on an application made by a party to the proceedings, if there has been a material change of circumstances since the relevant time, or

   (b) of its own motion.

(3) In subsection (2) 'the relevant time' means—

   (a) the time when the direction was given, or

   (b) if a previous application has been made under that subsection, the time when the application (or last application) was made.

(4) [The court must state in open court its reasons for its decision in relation to a direction.]

(5) [Power to make rules of court.]

38.—(1) This section applies where an accused is prevented from cross-examining a witness in person by virtue of section 34, 35 or 36.

(2) Where it appears to the court that this section applies, it must—

   (a) invite the accused to arrange for a legal representative to act for him for the purpose of cross-examining the witness; and

   (b) require the accused to notify the court, by the end of such period as it may specify, whether a legal representative is to act for him for that purpose.

(3) If by the end of the period mentioned in subsection (2)(b) either—

   (a) the accused has notified the court that no legal representative is to act for him for the purpose of cross-examining the witness, or

   (b) no notification has been received by the court and it appears to the court that no legal representative is to so act,

the court must consider whether it is necessary in the interests of justice for the witness to be cross-examined by a legal representative appointed to represent the interests of the accused.

(4) If the court decides that it is necessary in the interests of justice for the witness to be so cross-examined, the court must appoint a qualified legal representative (chosen by the court) to cross-examine the witness in the interests of the accused.

(5) A person so appointed shall not be responsible to the accused.

(6) and (7) [Power to make rules of court.]

(8) For the purposes of this section—

    (a) any reference to cross-examination includes (in a case where a direction is given under section 36 after the accused has begun cross-examining the witness) a reference to further cross-examination; and

    (b) 'qualified legal representative' means a legal representative who has a right of audience (within the meaning of the Courts and Legal Services Act 1990) in relation to the proceedings before the court.

39.—(1) Where on a trial on indictment with a jury an accused is prevented from cross-examining a witness in person by virtue of section 34, 35 or 36, the judge must give the jury such warning (if any) as the judge considers necessary to ensure that the accused is not prejudiced—

    (a) by any inferences that might be drawn from the fact that the accused has been prevented from cross-examining the witness in person;

    (b) where the witness has been cross-examined by a legal representative appointed under section 38(4), by the fact that the cross-examination was carried out by such a legal representative and not by a person acting as the accused's own legal representative.

(2) Subsection (8)(a) of section 38 applies for the purposes of this section as it applies for the purposes of section 38.

Object of Cross-examination

F7.4   The object of cross-examination is:

(a) to elicit from the witness evidence supporting the cross-examining party's version of the facts in issue;

(b) to weaken or cast doubt upon the accuracy of the evidence given by the witness in chief; and

(c) in appropriate circumstances, to impeach the witness's credibility.

Role of the Judge during Cross-examination

F7.5   The court may ask a witness questions and, in particular, where the accused is not represented, ask a witness any question necessary in the interests of the accused (CrimPR, r. 38.11(6)); the note to r. 38.11 states that the questions that may be put are in the discretion of the court, subject to the rules of evidence and r. 1.3 (application by the court of the overriding objective).

In general, when cross-examination is being conducted by competent counsel, a judge should not intervene, save to clarify matters he does not understand or thinks the jury may not understand. If he wishes to ask questions about matters that have not been touched upon, it is generally better to wait until the end of the examination or cross-examination. A judge should not be criticised for occasional transgressions, but there may come a time, depending on the nature and frequency of the interruptions, that the Court of Appeal is of the opinion that defence counsel was so hampered in the way he properly wished to conduct the cross-examination that the judge's conduct amounts to a material irregularity (*Sharp* [1994] QB 261). In rare cases, as when a child complainant becomes truculent during cross-examination and declines to answer any more questions, a judge may take over the questioning, provided that, having unsuccessfully tried to change the witness's mind, he consults with cross-examining counsel as to the questions to be put and gives an appropriate direction to the jury (*Cameron* [2001] EWCA Crim 562). As to the power of the judge to impose time-limits on cross-examination, see F7.15.

Order of Cross-examination

F7.6   If there are two or more accused jointly indicted and separately represented by counsel, the order of cross-examination is the order in which the names of the accused appear on the indictment (*Barber* (1844) 1 Car & Kir 434).

Liability to Cross-examination

F7.7   All witnesses are liable to cross-examination, except:

(a) a witness called merely to produce a document, who is not sworn (*Sumners v Moseley* (1834) 2 CR & M 477) or who is sworn unnecessarily (*Rush v Smith* (1834) 1 Cr M & R 94);

(b) a witness unable to speak as to the matters supposed to be within his knowledge who is called by mistake, provided that the mistake is discovered after the witness has been sworn but before his examination-in-chief (*Wood v Mackinson* (1840) 2 Mood & R 273); and

(c) a witness called by the judge, who may only be cross-examined with the judge's leave, which should be given if the witness is adverse to either party (*Coulson v Disborough* [1894] 2 QB 316; *Cliburn* (1898) 62 JP 232).

The evidence in chief of a witness who dies before cross-examination remains admissible, although little weight may attach to it (*Doolin* (1832) 1 Jebb CC 123). Similarly, if a witness, during cross-examination, becomes incapable through illness of answering any further questions, the trial may continue on the basis of the evidence already given (*Stretton* (1986) 86 Cr App R 7). In *Stretton*, the witness was the victim of sexual offences and the judge gave a carefully worded direction to the jury to acquit if they felt that the absence of cross-examination prevented them from judging fairly her credibility. See also *Wyatt* [1990] Crim LR 343 in which a seven-year-old girl, the victim of an indecent assault, was cross-examined through video link for about 20 minutes. She became visibly distressed and the judge adjourned the case for about 20 minutes. After the adjournment, the girl continued to cry and the judge decided that her evidence should proceed no further, even though counsel for the defence still had one important question to ask. The appeal was dismissed: the judge had not erred in the exercise of his discretion to adjourn for the length of time that he did and had directed the jury fairly on the girl's evidence and left it to them to determine her credibility. *Stretton* and *Wyatt* were both distinguished in *Lawless* (1994) 98 Cr App R 342. In that case the only direct evidence on one important part of the prosecution case was given by a witness who, at the end of his examination-in-chief, suffered a heart attack and was unable to give further evidence. It was held at least doubtful whether any direction to the jury, however strongly expressed, could have overcome the powerful prejudice of his evidence going wholly untested by cross-examination.

Effect of Failure to Cross-examine

In *Wood Green Crown Court, ex parte Taylor* [1995] Crim LR 879, the Divisional Court approved **F7.8** the following principle as stated in the 1995 edition of this work: a party who fails to cross-examine a witness upon a particular matter in respect of which it is proposed to contradict him or impeach his credit by calling other witnesses, tacitly accepts the truth of the witness's evidence in chief on that matter, and will not thereafter be entitled to invite the jury to disbelieve him in that regard. The proper course is to challenge the witness while he is in the witness-box or, at any rate, to make it plain to him at that stage that his evidence is not accepted (*Hart* (1932) 23 Cr App R 202). Thus in *Bircham* [1972] Crim LR 430, counsel for the accused was not permitted to suggest to the jury in his closing speech that the co-accused and a prosecution witness had committed the offence charged, where the allegation had not been put to either in cross-examination.

> ... nothing would be more absolutely unjust than not to cross-examine witnesses upon evidence which they have given, so as to give them notice, and to give them an opportunity of explanation, and an opportunity very often to defend their own character, and, not having given them such an opportunity, to ask the jury afterwards to disbelieve what they have said, although not one question has been directed either to their credit or to the accuracy of the facts they have deposed to. (*Browne v Dunn* (1893) 6 R 67, per Lord Halsbury at pp. 76–7, followed in *Fenlon* (1980) 71 Cr App R 307.)

See also para. 708(g) of the Code of Conduct of the Bar of England and Wales. Evidence to contradict a witness which was not put to him in cross-examination, may be admitted, provided that the witness is then recalled and cross-examination of him reopened in order to put the new evidence to him (*Cannan* [1998] Crim LR 284).

Flexible Rule   The rule under discussion is not hard-and-fast or inflexible. Thus where it is proposed to invite the jury to disbelieve a witness on a particular matter, it will not always be necessary **F7.9**

to put to him explicitly that he is lying, provided that the overall tenor of the cross-examination is designed to show that his account is incapable of belief (*Lovelock* [1997] Crim LR 821). Indeed in some cases it may be that the point upon which the witness is to be impeached is manifest, as when the story he tells is incredible, and it is unnecessary to cross-examine him upon it at all: the most effective cross-examination would be to ask him to leave the box (*Browne v Dunn*, per Lords Herschell LC and Morris). Application of the rule may also be unnecessary in the case of a witness whose evidence is purely corroborative of the evidence of another witness whose evidence-in-chief has already been challenged in cross-examination. It is a sensible practice, however, to secure the assurance of the trial judge, and the agreement of the party calling the witness, that failure to cross-examine in such circumstances will not be taken as a tacit acceptance of the witness's evidence. The rule has also been held to be inapplicable in the case of proceedings in magistrates' courts (*O'Connell v Adams* [1973] RTR 150). This may explain *Wilkinson v DPP* (2003) 167 JP 229, in which the accused was convicted following a summary trial in which the prosecution failed to cross-examine her; it was held that there was nothing to show that the trial was unfair and that the district judge had been entitled to reject her evidence.

F7.10   **Child Witness**   It seems that a party may cross-examine a young child witness upon a particular matter with a view to inviting the jury to disbelieve him in that regard notwithstanding the real possibility that the child will assent to what is suggested simply to please or to bring the questioning to a conclusion, or a speedier conclusion, so that it can be very difficult to tell whether the child is truly changing his account or simply taking the line of least resistance. In the case of such assent on the part of a child appearing for the prosecution, this could lead to a submission of no case to answer, as when the evidence, taken at its highest, is such that no jury could safely be sure of guilt, but not when, as in *W* [2010] EWCA Crim 1926, it was open to the jury to conclude, particularly in the light of the other evidence, that the child was not agreeing in any meaningful way to what was being suggested.

RULES GOVERNING CONDUCT OF CROSS-EXAMINATION

Scope of Cross-examination

F7.11   Questions in cross-examination are not restricted to matters raised in chief, but may relate to any fact in issue (or relevant fact), or to the credibility of the witness. Cross-examination is governed by the following general rules.

Leading Questions

F7.12   A witness under cross-examination may be asked leading questions. This is so even if he appears to be more favourable to the cross-examining party than to the party calling him (*Parkin v Moon* (1836) 7 C & P 408).

Exclusionary Rules of Evidence

F7.13   The exclusionary rules of evidence relating to hearsay, opinion, privilege etc. apply to cross-examination as they apply to examination-in-chief: see, in the case of inadmissible hearsay, *Thomson* [1912] 3 KB 19, *Windass* (1988) 89 Cr App R 258 and *Gray* [1998] Crim LR 570.

In *Treacy* [1944] 2 All ER 229, a charge of murder, it was held that the accused had been cross-examined improperly upon certain inadmissible confessions made on arrest and inconsistent with his evidence. It has been said that the principle established in this case, that an accused cannot be cross-examined by the prosecution in such a way as to reveal that he made an inadmissible confession, also obtains in favour of any co-accused (*Rice* [1963] 1 QB 857, per Winn J at pp. 868–9). However, see also *Rowson* [1986] QB 174 and other authorities considered in **F17.84**.

Power of Judge to Restrain Unnecessary or Improper Questions

The trial judge has a discretion to prevent any questions in cross-examination which, in his opinion, **F7.14** are unnecessary, improper or oppressive. Cross-examination is a powerful weapon entrusted to counsel, and should be conducted with restraint and a measure of courtesy and consideration which a witness is entitled to expect in a court of law (*Mechanical & General Inventions Co. Ltd v Austin* [1935] AC 346, per Lord Sankey LC at pp. 359–60). Thus, it is no part of the duty of counsel for the defence to embark on lengthy cross-examination on matters which are not really in issue (*Kalia* (1974) 60 Cr App R 200). See also *Simmonds* [1969] 1 QB 685 and *Maynard* (1979) 69 Cr App R 309. Likewise, questions should not be in the nature of comment on the facts; comments should be confined to speeches. Nor should questions be framed in such a way as to invite argument rather than elicit evidence on the facts in issue. Thus counsel should avoid questions such as 'I suggest to you that…' and 'Do you ask the jury to believe that…'. Cross-examination should be confined to putting questions of fact. Counsel should not state what somebody else has said or is expected to say. The time for statements such as 'The defendant's recollection is…' or 'The defendant will say…' is the opening speech; such statements should not be made, or put in the form of a question, in cross-examination (*Baldwin* (1925) 18 Cr App R 175, per Lord Hewart CJ at pp. 178–9). The same restrictions apply to questions put by the judge (see *Wilson* [1991] Crim LR 838, where the judge asked the accused 'So this 12-year-old girl has made wicked lies about you?'). See also **F7.16** to **F7.18**.

For the judicial directions that may be given to advocates on how to cross-examine young and vulnerable witnesses, see the Judicial College Bench Checklist: Young Witness Cases, the Advocacy Training Council Report, *Raising the Bar: The handling of vulnerable witnesses, victims and defendants in court*, *E* [2011] EWCA Crim 3028 and *Wills* [2012] 1 Cr App R 16, considered at **D14.48**.

Power of Judge to Impose Time-limits

The court has a general duty to deal with cases efficiently and expeditiously and to manage cases **F7.15** actively to ensure that evidence is presented in the shortest and clearest way, giving any direction appropriate (CrimPR, rr. 1.1(2)(e), 3.2(2)(e) and 3.2(3): see Supplement, **R-1** and **R-9**). As part of its case management powers, the court may limit the duration of any stage of the hearing and the cross-examination of a witness (CrimPR, r. 3.10(b)(ii) and (d)(i)). The following propositions derive from *B* [2005] EWCA Crim 805.

(a) Although the imposition of time-limits for cross-examination (or examination-in-chief) of witnesses should not become a routine feature of trial management, judges are fully entitled, and indeed obliged, to impose reasonable time-limits where counsel indulge in prolix and repetitious questioning.

(b) It is not the duty of counsel to put to a witness every point of an accused's case, however peripheral, or to embark on lengthy cross-examination on matters which are not really in issue. The duty is to discriminate between important and relevant features of a defence case which have to be put to a witness and minor and/or unnecessary matters which do not need to be put.

(c) Entitlement to a fair trial is not inconsistent with proper judicial control over the use of court time and the Court of Appeal will not interfere with a decision made by a judge in this respect unless it is plain that it resulted in unfairness.

In *Ali* [2014] EWCA Crim 140, a case of rape of a girl, it was held that it was properly open to the judge to restrict cross-examination of the girl about a previous false complaint: she had already been cross-examined at considerable length, she was in significant distress and she had admitted that the previous complaint was false, the details in that respect having been reduced to writing and placed before the jury as part of the admission.

Cross-examination as to Credit

'Since the purpose of cross-examination as to credit is to show that the witness ought not to be **F7.16** believed on oath, the matters about which he is questioned must relate to his likely standing after cross-examination with the tribunal which is trying him or listening to his evidence' (*Sweet-Escott* (1971) 55 Cr App R 316 at p. 320; *Hobbs v C. T. Tinling & Co. Ltd* [1929] 2 KB 1 per Sankey LJ at p. 51). Thus he may be cross-examined about his means of knowledge of the facts to which he has testified, his opportunities for observation, his powers of perception, the quality of his memory, mistakes, omissions and inconsistencies in his evidence, and omissions or inconsistencies in previous statements that relate to his likely standing with the jury after cross-examination but which are not 'relative to the subject matter of the indictment' (*Funderburk* [1990] 2 All ER 482). As to quality of memory, there is a risk of 'contamination' or collusion when officers have conferred in the production of statements about events or interviews (*R (Saunders) v Independent Police Complaints Commission* [2009] 1 All ER 379). As to omissions, where an accused is charged with a sexual offence and asserts fabrication on the part of the complainant, he may be cross-examined as to what facts are known to him that might explain why the complainant would make a false accusation against him (*Brook* [2003] 1 WLR 2809). In a sexual case, the defence may seek to undermine the credibility of the complainant by cross-examination on her delay in making her complaint, in which case the judge should direct the jury that, whereas some may complain immediately to the first person seen, others may feel shame and shock and not complain for some time, and that a late complaint is not necessarily a false one (*D* [2008] EWCA Crim 2557 at [9]–[12]). A witness may also be cross-examined about his previous convictions or bias (if, in either case, it is lawful to do so under the rules relating to evidence of bad character in the CJA 2003, part 11, considered below and at **F12** and **F14**), any mental or physical disability affecting his reliability, and any previous statements made by him 'relative to the subject-matter of the indictment' and inconsistent with his testimony; and if the witness denies any of these matters, the cross-examining party is entitled to prove them (see **F7.51** to **F7.59**). Cross-examination designed to impugn a witness's credibility should always comply with the rules contained in the Code of Conduct of the Bar (see **F7.18**).

F7.17 **Bad Character**   Any questions in cross-examination as to a witness's bad character are subject to the rules set out in the CJA 2003, part 11. Section 99 of the Act abolishes the common-law rules governing the admissibility of evidence of 'bad character' in criminal proceedings and the intention appears to be to abolish not only the rules as to the introduction of such evidence in examination-in-chief, but also the rules governing cross-examination about bad character. Thus such cross-examination is permitted only if it comes within one of the specified categories of admissibility set out in s. 100 (non-defendant's bad character — see **F14**) or 101 (defendant's bad character — see **F12**). Evidence of bad character for the purposes of the Act is defined by s. 98 as evidence of, or of a disposition towards, misconduct, other than evidence which 'has to do with the alleged facts of the offence with which the defendant is charged' or 'evidence of misconduct in connection with the investigation or prosecution of that offence'. Section 108 of the 2003 Act imposes an additional restriction in relation to offences committed by the accused when a child (see **F12.98**). There is a further restriction in the YJCEA 1999, s. 41: in the case of sexual offences, except with the leave of the court, no question may be asked in cross-examination about any sexual behaviour of the complainant (see **F7.22** to **F7.41**).

The Code of Conduct of the Bar

F7.18 The Code of Conduct of the Bar of England and Wales also regulates the conduct of cross-examination.

Concerning cross-examination, see in particular para. 708 and paras. 5.10, 5.11, 11.1 and 13.5 of the Written Standards. In *McFaden* (1975) 62 Cr App R 187, the Court of Appeal said that the Bar Council Rules (now superseded by the Code), although they had strong persuasive force, did not bind the courts.

Inspection of and Cross-examination on Documents

F7.19 As to cross-examination of a witness on a previous inconsistent statement, see the Criminal Procedure Act 1865, ss. 4 and 5, at **F7.45**.

In the case of a document used by a witness to refresh his memory, the cross-examining party may inspect the document without thereby making it evidence (*Gregory v Tavernor* (1833) 6 C & P 280; *Senat v Senat* [1965] P 172). (As to the cross-examination of a witness on a document used by him to refresh his memory, see **F6.22**.) However, if a party calls for and inspects a document in the possession of another party which has *not* been used to refresh a witness's memory, the other party may require him to put it in evidence (*Wharam v Routledge* (1805) 5 Esp 235; and *Calvert v Flower* (1836) 7 C & P 386, applied in *Stroud v Stroud (No. 1)* [1963] 3 All ER 539). The rule is obscure: it is unclear whether the document is admitted for the truth of its contents or as evidence of the consistency of the witness. In *Stroud v Stroud (No. 1)* Wrangham J said (at p. 1082): 'the rule itself has never been abrogated, and it may still be of practical importance, for example in criminal proceedings, where there is no discovery.' The Criminal Law Revision Committee recommended abolition of the rule in criminal proceedings, in which it appears never to have been applied (see *Eleventh Report: Evidence (General)* (1972) Cmnd 4991, para. 223).

A document, the contents of which are inadmissible, is not rendered admissible by being put to a witness in cross-examination (*Treacy* [1944] 2 All ER 229). However, in cross-examination counsel may produce to the witness a document containing an inadmissible hearsay statement and ask him, *without reading it aloud*, whether he accepts the contents as true. If the witness does accept the contents as true, they become evidence in the case; but if not, the contents remain inadmissible hearsay (*Gillespie* (1967) 51 Cr App R 172; applied in *Cross* (1990) 91 Cr App R 115). In *Cooper* (1985) 82 Cr App R 74, the Court of Appeal, applying *Gillespie*, held that if the prosecution propose to cross-examine in this way, they should first establish the finding (or creation) of the document as a part of their case, without at that stage indicating the contents of the document to the jury. Similarly, it has been held that it is improper for counsel, when asking a witness to look at a document (the contents of which are inadmissible) and to say whether he still adheres to his answer, to describe to the jury its nature or contents. The proper course is simply to hand the document to the witness, direct him to look at it, and then to ask whether he still adheres to his answer (*Yousry* (1914) 11 Cr App R 13, per Lord Coleridge CJ at p. 18). See also *Tompkins* (1977) 67 Cr App R 181. **F7.20**

In *Hackney* (1982) 74 Cr App R 194, the Court of Appeal considered the growing practice of the defence, during the trial, to call for, and then cross-examine police officers on, records made during the accused's detention at a police station. Noting that entries in such records are often made by a number of police officers, and therefore that any inquiry into the completeness and accuracy of such records would often entail the questioning of many officers, the Court of Appeal said (at p. 198): **F7.21**

> These records, it should be emphasised, do not prove themselves. The prosecution do not have to produce them without some notice which allows proper opportunity of proving and explaining their contents by the evidence of officers who actually made the records. We think that judges should control the use made of such documents with these factors in mind and also ensure that the use of them is strictly confined to an issue in the case (the credibility of a witness, for example) that time spent exploring them is not inordinate and that indiscriminate use of them is not made either by counsel or by a defendant in person. When deciding what use, if any, should be made of such documents, the judge should take account of whether the defence before the trial began, could have given notice to the prosecution for the production of the documents so that proper steps could have been, at the outset of the trial, taken for the production not only of the documents, but also of witnesses able properly to inform the jury about the contents of them.

PROTECTION OF COMPLAINANTS IN PROCEEDINGS FOR SEXUAL OFFENCES

The Restriction

The circumstances in which, in proceedings for sexual offences, evidence may be adduced, or the complainant cross-examined, by or on behalf of the accused, about any sexual behaviour or **F7.22** experience on his or her part involving the accused or any other person, is governed by the YJCEA 1999, ss. 41 to 43. The intention of these provisions is to counter what in Canadian jurisprudence was described as the twin myths, namely 'that unchaste women were more likely to consent to intercourse and in any event were less worthy of belief' — see *Seaboyer* [1991] 2 SCR 577 at 604, 630 per McLachlin J (per Lords Steyn and Hutton in *A (No. 2)* [2002] 1 AC 45 at [27] and [147] respectively). The provisions are also born of a recognition that to allow victims of sexual offences to be harassed unfairly by questions about their previous sexual experiences is unjust to them and bad for society, because if victims are afraid to complain then the guilty may escape justice.

Under s. 41(1), if at a trial a person is charged with a sexual offence (a) no evidence may be adduced and (b) no question may be asked in cross-examination, by or on behalf of any accused at the trial, about any sexual behaviour of the complainant, except with the leave of the court. Section 41 applies to other proceedings as it applies to a trial, including a hearing held between conviction and sentence for the purposes of deciding matters relevant to the court's decision as to how the accused is to be dealt with (s. 42(3)). A 'sexual offence' is widely defined in s. 62 as any offence under the SOA 2003, part 1, or any relevant superseded offence, namely rape or burglary with intent to rape, any offence under SOA 1956, ss. 2 to 12 and ss. 14 to 17, an offence under the Mental Health Act 1959, s. 128, an offence under the Indecency with Children Act 1960, s. 1, and an offence under the Criminal Law Act 1977, s. 54. Under s. 42(1)(c), 'sexual behaviour' means 'any sexual behaviour or other sexual experience, whether or not involving any accused or other person, but excluding (except in section 41(3)(c)(i) and (5)(a)) anything alleged to have taken place as part of the event which is the subject matter of the charge against the accused'. It is submitted that this very wide definition will cover verbal and not merely physical advances of a sexual nature (see, e.g., *Hinds* [1979] Crim LR 111 and *Viola* [1982] 3 All ER 73, both decisions under the Sexual Offences (Amendment) Act 1976). The phrases 'sexual behaviour' and 'other sexual experience' seem to be referring to acts or events of a sexual character, as opposed to the existence of a relationship, acquaintanceship or familiarity (per Lord Clyde in *A (No. 2)* at [128]). The phrases are wide enough to embrace the viewing of pornography or sexually-charged messaging over a live internet connection, and it will also amount to 'sexual behaviour' to answer questions in a sexually explicit quiz (*Ben-Rejab* [2012] 1 WLR 2364). 'Sexual behaviour' it has been said, is a matter of impression and common sense (*Mukadi* [2003] EWCA Crim 3765). However, whether either behaviour or experience is 'sexual' does not depend upon the perception of the complainant, because that would result in many vulnerable people, including children and those with learning difficulties, losing the protection of s. 41. In *P (R)* [2014] 1 Cr App R 401 (28) it was held that, although a question about an abortion may be a way of asking about a complainant's sexual behaviour, questions about the accused's emotional and financial support for the complainant in relation to an abortion performed after the offences, which were relevant as tending to detract from her account that she viewed him with distaste because of the offences, were not questions about sexual behaviour.

F7.23 There is no difference in substance between a question asked of a female complainant about her suggested sexual habits or promiscuity or frequency of casual sexual engagement and questions asked of a male complainant about his suggested homosexuality and casual homosexual encounters. In each case the questions are predicated on the proposition that previous consent is evidence of present consent and fall squarely within the restriction in s. 41(1) (*B* [2007] EWCA Crim 23).

Section 41 applies only to defence evidence and questions. In *Soroya* [2006] EWCA Crim 1884, a rape case in which the issue was consent, the complainant gave evidence of the fact that during the incident she had said to the appellant that she was a virgin in the hope that this might cause him to desist from the assault on her. The prosecution also produced evidence that what she had said was false because she had had sexual intercourse on a previous occasion. On appeal, it was argued that evidence of the complainant's sexual history had been improperly introduced in circumstances which would not have been permitted had the defence sought to adduce it, which infringed the principle of equality of arms between the defence and prosecution and thereby constituted a breach of the right to a fair trial under the ECHR, Article 6. It was further argued that

s. 41 should be construed in such a way as to embrace the prosecution. Dismissing the appeal, it was held that what the complainant had said to the appellant had been relevant and admissible evidence bearing on the issue of consent; that the evidence of previous intercourse exposed the falsity of what she had said; and that no justified complaint could be directed at its admission.

It seems that s. 41(1) will apply in the case of evidence or questions about a complainant's false denial of a previous sexual experience, for example a false assertion that she was a virgin at the time of the alleged rape, whereas earlier on the same day she had had sexual intercourse with someone other than the accused (*S* [2003] All ER (D) 408 (Feb)). The reason is that it is only if the sexual behaviour is established that the denial can be said to be false (*Winter* [2008] EWCA Crim 3 at [25]). On the other hand, normally evidence or questions about a complainant's previous false complaints of sexual assaults or about her failure to complain about the assault which is the subject-matter of the charge when complaining about other sexual assaults, are not 'about any sexual behaviour of the complainant' under s. 41(1). They relate not to her sexual behaviour, but to her past statements or failure to complain. The purpose of the YJCEA 1999 was not to exclude such evidence. However, if the defence wishes to put questions about previous false complaints, there are two hurdles. First, leave is required under the CJA 2003, s. 100(4) (see **F14.16** *et seq.*), because such questioning relates to the bad character of the complainant (*V* [2006] EWCA Crim 1901). However, leave may not be required if the complaint was not a deliberate lie but, say, the product of alcoholism and personality problems and therefore does not fall within the definition of 'bad character' in the CJA 2003, ss. 98 and 112(1) (*Davarifar v R* [2009] EWCA Crim 2294). Secondly, the defence should seek a ruling from the judge that s. 41 does not exclude the questions.

It would be professionally improper to put such questions in order to elicit evidence about past   **F7.24**
sexual behaviour as such under the guise of previous false complaints. In any case the defence must have, and the judge is entitled to seek assurances from the defence that it has, a proper evidential basis for asserting that the previous statement was (a) made and (b) untrue. If not, the questions would not be about lies but about the sexual behaviour of the complainant within s. 41(1) (*T* [2002] 1 All ER 683, applied in *E* [2004] EWCA Crim 1313 and *Abdelrahman* [2005] EWCA Crim 1367). See also *H* [2003] All ER (D) 332 (Jul). The authorities are in some conflict as to when there can be said to be a 'proper evidential basis'. It has been said that it suffices if there is material such that, depending on the answers given by the complainant in cross-examination, the jury could be satisfied that the previous complaint was untrue, or material which is capable of founding an inference that the complaint was untrue (*Garaxo* [2005] EWCA Crim 1170). Similarly, it has been held that a proper evidential basis is 'less than a strong factual foundation for concluding that the previous complaint was false' but does require 'some material from which it could properly be concluded that the complaint was false' (*Murray* [2009] EWCA Crim 618). In other words, the defence must be able to point to material that is capable of supporting — not which must inevitably support — the inference of falsity (*E* [2009] EWCA Crim 2668). However, in *D* [2009] EWCA Crim 2137, where the defence were not permitted to cross-examine the complainant about inconsistencies between her witness statement and other witness statements made at the time, it was held that the earlier authorities are not to be regarded as authorising the use of a trial to investigate the truth or falsity of a previous allegation merely because there is some material which could be used to try and persuade a jury that it was in fact false. When there is evidence of a previous complaint, it seems that a complainant's subsequent failure to co-operate with the police may or may not justify a conclusion that it was untrue, depending on the circumstances (*V* [2006] EWCA Crim 1901; *Garaxo* [2005] EWCA Crim 1170). The mere fact that the police decided that there was insufficient evidence to prosecute does not amount to evidence that the previous accusation was false (*D* [2009] EWCA Crim 2137). Equally, the decision of the CPS not to prosecute is irrelevant — it is for the court to decide whether there is the necessary evidential basis (*Davarifar*). In *A* [2012] EWCA Crim 1273, in which the complainant claimed to have been sexually assaulted on four previous occasions, but there was no evidence to suggest that any of the allegations was false, it was held that the number of allegations alone did not entitle the defence to explore the possibility that they were false.

The principle established in *T* does not extend to cases in which the accused seeks to rely simply on the fact that the complainant made a statement about her previous sexual experience (as when evidence of the fact is said to be relevant to the defence of belief in consent), rather than the truth or falsity of such a statement. Evidence that such a statement was made falls within s. 41(1) (*W* [2004] EWCA Crim 3103).

Lifting the Restriction

F7.25 The court may give leave in relation to any evidence or question only on an application made by or on behalf of the accused (YJCEA 1999, s. 41(2)). The application shall be heard in private and in the absence of the complainant (s. 43(1)). After the application has been determined, the court must state in open court (but in the absence of the jury, if there is one) its reasons for giving or refusing leave and, if leave is given, the extent to which the evidence may be adduced or questions asked (s. 43(2)). The court may not give leave in relation to any evidence or question unless it is satisfied that s. 41(3) or (5) applies (s. 41(2)(a)) and that a refusal 'might have the result of rendering unsafe a conclusion of the jury or (as the case may be) the court on any relevant issue in the case' (s. 41(2)(b)). A 'relevant issue' means any issue falling to be proved by the prosecution or defence in the trial of the accused (s. 42(1)(a)). The test in s. 41(2)(b) must always be met. The test will be satisfied, it is submitted, when to disallow the evidence or question would be to prevent the jurors (or court) from taking into account material which might cause them to come to a different conclusion on a relevant issue. If this is correct, the test in s. 41(2)(b) is not particularly onerous: the judge need only be satisfied that a refusal might lead the jury to a different conclusion, not that such a consequence is probable. However, the judge is unlikely to be so satisfied where there is other evidence before the jury in support of the conclusion advanced by the defence to which the evidence sought to be admitted under s. 41 adds nothing (*Mokrecovas* [2002] 1 Cr App R 226) or which is stronger and more compelling than the evidence sought to be adduced under s. 41 (*Bahador* [2005] EWCA Crim 396). Under s. 41(6), for the purposes of s. 41(3) and (5), the evidence or question must relate to a specific instance or specific instances of alleged sexual behaviour on the part of the complainant as opposed to, for example, evidence or a question to the effect that the complainant was promiscuous or a prostitute. Furthermore, in the case of a prostitute, information contained by way of a list of previous convictions for prostitution is incapable of fulfilling the requirements of s. 41(6); otherwise any encounter could fall under s. 41(6) if it could be assigned a date and time (*White* [2004] EWCA Crim 946, a decision under s. 41(3)(c) and considered at **F7.38**).

F7.26 The operation of s. 41 involves, not the exercise of judicial discretion, but the making of a judgement whether to admit or exclude evidence which is relevant or asserted by the defence to be relevant. If it is relevant, then subject to s. 41(4) (see **F7.27**) and assuming that the criteria for admitting the evidence are established (see **F7.27** to **F7.39**), all the evidence relevant to the issues may be adduced. As part of his control over the case, the judge must ensure that a complainant is not unnecessarily humiliated or cross-examined with inappropriate aggression, or treated otherwise than with proper courtesy, but this does not permit him, by way of a general discretion, to prevent the proper deployment of evidence admissible under s. 41 merely because it comes in a stark, uncompromising form (*F* [2005] 1 WLR 2848, where the evidence included videotapes of the complainant stripping and masturbating). In *T* [2012] EWCA Crim 2358 it was held that the judge has no discretion to exclude evidence admissible under s. 41 and therefore cannot exclude where such evidence has been raised without any advance notice, a matter that goes to the weight to be attached to it.

Section 41(3) and (4): Evidence or a Question Relating to a Relevant Issue

F7.27 Section 41(3) of the YJCEA 1999 is set out at **F7.40**. In s. 41, 'issue of consent' means any issue whether the complainant in fact consented to the conduct constituting the offence with which the accused is charged and accordingly does not include any issue as to the belief of the accused that the complainant so consented (s. 42(1)(b)).

Section 41(4) provides as follows:

(4) For the purposes of subsection (3) no evidence or question shall be regarded as relating to a relevant issue in the case if it appears to the court to be reasonable to assume that the purpose (or main purpose) for which it would be adduced or asked is to establish or elicit material for impugning the credibility of the complainant as a witness.

Section 41(4) applies only where 'the purpose (or main purpose)' for which the evidence is adduced or the question is asked is to impugn the credibility of the complainant. An example is furnished by *Islam* [2012] EWCA Crim 3106. On a charge of rape, the defence being consent, the defence wished to question the complainant about her flirtatious behaviour towards a number of other men in a bar a few hours before the alleged offence, with a view to suggesting that she was 'up for sex'. The trial judge ruled that the questions did not pass the test under s. 41(2) and fell foul of s. 41(4), having as their main purpose the intention of impugning the credibility of the complainant as a witness by reason of her unchaste behaviour. The Court of Appeal upheld the ruling. The questions about the complainant's behaviour and mood in the company of young friends in a bar laid no basis for saying that she would be 'up for sex' with a complete stranger a few hours later. The questioning involved an implied allegation of wanton promiscuity which the broad intention of s. 41 was designed to restrict.

In one sense, any evidence which directly challenges the evidence of a complainant, or seeks to demonstrate a malicious motive, involves an attack on her credibility. However, merely because evidence may impugn the complainant's credibility, it does not follow that the purpose or the main purpose for deploying it is to do so (Judge LJ in *F* [2005] 1 WLR 2848 at [27]). In *Martin* [2004] 2 Cr App R 354, a case of indecent assault involving enforced oral sex, M said that the complainant had fabricated her evidence because he had rejected her advances. The trial judge allowed the defence to question her about his allegation that two days earlier she had pestered him for sex. The Court of Appeal held that the defence should also have been allowed to question her about his allegation that on the earlier occasion she had performed an act of oral sex upon him, after which he had rejected her. It was held that, although one purpose of such questioning would have been to impugn the credibility of the complainant, it would also have gone to the accused's credibility and strengthened the defence case of fabrication, because the jury might have interpreted a rejection after the performance of oral sex as more hurtful than rejection after mere verbal advances. **F7.28**

The application of s. 41(4) gives rise to real difficulties in cases where, as is often the case, the difference between questions going to credit and questions going to the issue barely exists (*Funderburk* [1990] 2 All ER 482 at F7.44). As Lord Hutton said, in the context of issues of consent, in *A (No. 2)* (at [138]): **F7.29**

> Issues of consent and issues of credibility may well run so close to each other as almost to coincide. A very sharp knife may be required to separate what may be admitted from what may not. The purpose of subsection (4) may be taken to be the abolition of the false idea that a history of sexual behaviour in some way was relevant to credit. The recognition of that myth as heresy is to be welcomed. But the subsection may have to be carefully handled in order to secure that the myth remains buried in the past and at the same time secure the availability of evidence of sexual behaviour which is properly admissible as bearing on the issue of consent. [Cf. Lord Hope at [76] and [95].]

Section 41(3)(a): A Relevant Issue Other than Consent

Examples of issues which fall within the YJCEA 1999, s. 41(3)(a), would include (a) the defence of reasonable belief in consent; (b) that the complainant was biased against the accused or had a motive to fabricate the evidence; (c) that there is an alternative explanation for the physical conditions on which the Crown relies to establish that intercourse took place; and (d) especially in the case of young complainants, that the detail of their account must have come from some other sexual activity which provides an explanation for their knowledge of that activity (per Lord Hope in *A (No. 2)* [2002] 1 AC 45 at [79]). However, it seems that the example in (d) above is confined to young complainants. In *M* [2005] EWCA Crim 3376, it was held that **F7.30** an application to cross-examine the 14-year-old complainant about possible sexual intercourse with a boy from school had been properly refused on the basis that, by reason of the complainant's age and the way of children of her age, she could have acquired her knowledge of sexual intercourse through conversations with friends.

F7.31   In cases of rape, when considering the effect of a complainant's past sexual promiscuity upon the accused's belief that the complainant was consenting to intercourse, there is a difference between believing that the complainant is consenting to intercourse, which is relevant, and believing that the complainant will consent, which is not relevant (*Barton* (1987) 85 Cr App R 5, a decision relating to a defence of *mistaken* belief in consent decided under ss. 1(2) and 2 of the Sexual Offences (Amendment) Act 1976). This distinction remains valid in relation to a defence of *reasonable* belief in consent, for the purposes of the YJCEA 1999, s. 41 (*Winter* [2008] EWCA Crim 3 at [28]). Each case, however, turns on its own facts and, in an appropriate case, belief that the accused will consent may be a 'relevant issue in the case' for the purposes of s. 41, as when, without the evidence of the complainant's sexual behaviour, the jury may infer from the other evidence that the accused's intention from the outset was to have intercourse with the complainant with or without her consent (*Gjoni* [2014] EWCA Crim 691).

F7.32   In *T* [2012] EWCA Crim 2358 the defence sought to introduce evidence of a photograph allegedly sent to the accused around Valentine's Day, showing the complainant dressed in a bikini or underwear. It was held that the evidence went to a relevant issue other than consent, because the defence case was that the complainant was interested in him, he was not interested in her, and the motive for her false allegation was her affront at his lack of interest. See also *F* [2005] 1 WLR 2848, a case of alleged childhood sexual abuse, the defence being that the complaints were false and motivated by a desire for revenge after the accused had ended an adult sexual relationship with the complainant, where it was held that evidence relating to the complainant's erotic and sometimes pornographic behaviour in the course of the adult relationship was relevant to the alleged desire for revenge and the critical question whether there had been childhood abuse.

Section 41(3)(b) and (c): An Issue of Consent

F7.33   It is plain from the wording of the YJCEA 1999, s. 41(3)(b) and (c), that in a rape case in which consent is in issue leave cannot be given in relation to any evidence or question about sexual behaviour of the complainant which amounts to nothing more than previous voluntary sexual intercourse with the accused. Section 41(3), in this respect, operates to reverse the decision in *Riley* (1887) 18 QBD 481. However, where the complainant and the accused are married or have cohabited, the tribunal of fact may well infer that there has been such voluntary sexual intercourse, and it is submitted that in these circumstances the trial judge, in the spirit of the new legislative framework, should direct the jury that they should draw no such inference because, without more, previous acts of voluntary sexual intercourse can have no bearing on any relevant issue in the case.

F7.34   **Section 41(3)(b)**   Section 41(3)(b) covers behaviour such as sexual advances made by the complainant towards the accused or others shortly before or after 'the event which is the subject matter of the charge against the accused' and behaviour indicative of consent at the time of 'the event'. The evidence or question must relate to sexual behaviour of the complainant alleged to have taken place at or about the same time as 'the event', but excluding anything alleged to have taken place as part of the event which is the subject-matter of the charge (s. 42(1)(c)). The distinction between sexual behaviour which took place 'at...the same time as the event' and such behaviour which took place 'as part of the event' is far from clear. The phrase 'at or about the same time as the event' introduces an extremely narrow temporal restriction. The use of the words 'or about' provides a degree of elasticity, but cannot be strained to extend the restriction to days, weeks, or months. The explanatory note to the Act prepared by the Home Office states that it is expected that the phrase will generally be interpreted no more widely than 24 hours before or after the offence (*A (No. 2)* [2002] 1 AC 45 at [9], [40], [82] and [132]). An example of the application of s. 41(3)(b) in a rape case would be where it is alleged that the complainant invited the accused to have sexual intercourse with her earlier in the evening (per Lord Steyn in *A (No. 2)* at [40]). See also, *sed quaere*, *Mukadi* [2003] EWCA Crim 3765.

Section 41(3)(c)   Section 41(3)(c) covers any sexual behaviour of the complainant on another   **F7.35**
occasion which is, in any respect, so similar in nature to her sexual behaviour which, according to the defence, took place as part of the event which is the subject-matter of the charge, or
shortly before or after that 'event', that the similarity cannot reasonably be explained as a coincidence. The sexual behaviour could have been with the accused or another and could have taken
place before or after the 'event'. See *T* [2004] 2 Cr App R 551, considered below.

As to the requirement that the similarity cannot reasonably be explained as a coincidence, a   **F7.36**
comparison can be made between s. 41(3)(c) and the concept of similar fact evidence, especially
as formulated by Lord Salmon in *DPP v Boardman* [1975] AC 421 at p. 462. The restriction is
significantly tighter than the test laid down in *DPP v P* [1991] 2 AC 447 (per Lord Hope in *A
(No. 2)* at [83]), but the standard is something short of striking similarity (per Lord Clyde in *A
(No. 2)* [2002] 1 AC 45 at [133]). Lord Clyde said (at [135]):

> It is only a similarity that is required, not an identity. Moreover the words 'in any respect' deserve
> to be stressed. On one view any single factor of similarity might suffice...provided that it is not
> a matter of coincidence. That the behaviour was with the same person, the defendant, must be
> at least a relevant consideration. But if the identity of the defendant was alone sufficient as the
> non-coincidental factor, that would seem to open the way in almost every case for a complete
> enquiry into the whole of the complainant's sexual behaviour with the defendant at least in the
> recent past, and that can hardly have been the intention of the provision. What must be found
> is a similarity in some other or additional respect. Further, the similarity must be such as cannot
> reasonably be explained as coincidence. To my mind that does not necessitate that the similarity
> has to be in some rare or bizarre conduct. So long as the particular factor is of a significance which
> goes beyond the realm of what could reasonably be explained as a coincidence, it should suffice.

An example would be a rape case in which the accused, who says that after consensual intercourse the complainant tried to blackmail him by alleging rape, wishes to cross-examine her
about a previous similar attempt to blackmail him (per Lord Steyn in *A (No. 2)* at [42]). Section
41(3)(c), however, would not cover, in a case where at the time of the alleged offence and before
intercourse kissing or other affectionate behaviour took place, evidence that for a number of
months prior to the date of the alleged offence the accused had had frequent consensual intercourse with the complainant, in each case preceded by affectionate behaviour (per Lord Hutton
in *A (No. 2)* at [159]). In *T* [2004] 2 Cr App R 551, T was convicted of rape, indecent assault
and false imprisonment. The complainant had previously been in a relationship with T. Shortly
after the relationship ended they agreed to meet in a park. They went inside a climbing frame,
where the sexual acts took place. The issue was consent. The trial judge refused leave to cross-
examine on, or adduce evidence of, the fact that three weeks prior to the alleged offences T
and the complainant had had consensual sex in the same climbing frame adopting the same
positions, both standing and the complainant facing away from the accused. He ruled that the
behaviour was insufficiently relevant and that he was constrained by the temporal limitation of
s. 41(3)(c)(ii). Allowing the appeal, it was held that the trial judge should have considered the
matter under s. 41(3)(c)(i), which had no time constraint, and that had he done so he might
have ruled the evidence admissible. (But see *MM* [2011] EWCA Crim 1291, where the similarity test was not met.) As to s. 41(3)(c)(ii), the Court of Appeal observed that, although it contained words which at first sight might appear to contain temporal limitations, it was doubtful
that that was correct when s. 41(3)(c) was construed as a whole.

Decisions on similarity for the purposes of s. 41(3)(c) are sometimes easy but, where that is not
the case, the Court of Appeal will not interfere if the decision reached was open to the judge and
within the margin of judgement open to him (*Harris* [2009] EWCA Crim 434).

Section 41 and the Right to a Fair Trial

F7.37   In *A (No. 2)* [2002] 1 AC 45, the House of Lords held that although prima facie a sexual relationship between an accused and complainant may be relevant to the issue of consent so as to render
its exclusion under s. 41 a contravention of the accused's right to a fair trial under the ECHR,
Article 6, it is possible under the HRA 1998, s. 3, to read s. 41, and in particular s. 41(3)(c),
as subject to the implied provision that evidence or questioning which is required to ensure
a fair trial under Article 6 should not be excluded. In the opinion of Lord Steyn (at [46]), an
opinion shared by all of their lordships, if a trial judge finds it necessary to apply the interpretative obligation under s. 3 to the words of s. 41(3)(c), then he should construe those words by
applying the following test:

> ... due regard always being paid to the importance of seeking to protect the complainant from
> indignity and from humiliating questions, the test of admissibility is whether the evidence (and
> questioning in relation to it) is nevertheless so relevant to the issue of consent that to exclude it
> would endanger the fairness of the trial under [ECHR, Article 6].

According to Lord Steyn (at [31]), as a matter of common sense a prior sexual relationship between
the complainant and the accused may, depending on the circumstances, be relevant to the issue of
consent. Where there has been a recent close and affectionate relationship between the complainant and the accused, it is probable that the evidence will be relevant, not of course to prove consent,
but to her show her specific mindset towards the accused, i.e. her affection for him. On the other
hand, evidence of the kind which the accused in *A (No. 2)* wished to give, namely evidence of no
more than some isolated acts of intercourse, albeit fairly recent, but without the background of an
affectionate relationship, is probably not relevant (Lord Hutton at [151]–[154] and Lord Steyn at
[31]). Moreover, according to Lord Clyde (at [125]), evidence of the complainant's sexual behaviour with men other than the accused should not be accepted as relevant to the question of consent.

F7.38   *A (No. 2)* [2002] 1 AC 45 was followed in *R* [2003] EWCA Crim 2754 but distinguished in
White [2004] EWCA Crim 946 in which W, convicted of rape, said that the complainant had
asked him for money, which he had refused to give, and that after consensual intercourse he
awoke to find her with his wallet. The trial judge refused an application to cross-examine the
complainant on her previous and contemporaneous activities as a prostitute, the fact that she
worked as a prostitute being of no relevance to the issue of consent as it was no part of W's case
that he had offered payment. Dismissing the appeal, it was held that in the present day a prostitute was as entitled as any other to say 'no' and the fact that she was a prostitute did not mean
that she was more likely to say 'yes' to sex. The bare fact that she was a prostitute was irrelevant
to the issue of consent: there had to be something about the specific circumstances that had
probative force and was so similar to the conduct complained of as to be beyond coincidence.

Section 41(5): Evidence or a Question Relating to Evidence Adduced by the Prosecution

F7.39   Section 41(5) applies if the evidence or question:

(a) relates to any evidence adduced by the prosecution about any sexual behaviour of the complainant (including anything alleged to have taken place as part of the event which is the
subject-matter of the charge — see s. 42(1)(c)); and

(b) in the opinion of the court, would go no further than is necessary to enable the evidence
adduced by the prosecution to be rebutted or explained by or on behalf of the accused.

If, for example, the accused denies any sexual activity with the complainant, and she alleges that
he was responsible for her pregnancy, evidence that she had previously attributed her pregnancy
to someone else will be admissible in rebuttal (*F* [2008] EWCA Crim 2859). Similarly, if in a
rape case, the complainant gives evidence that she has only ever had consensual sexual intercourse with her husband, evidence or questions might be permitted about previous consensual
intercourse with the accused or another person before or after the alleged rape. However, it
seems that if the complainant gives evidence of having been in a happy long-term relationship

with her partner at the time of the alleged offence, evidence that she was having an affair with another man will not be admissible by way of explanation or rebuttal (*Winter* [2008] EWCA Crim 3 at [31]). See also *F* [2005] 1 WLR 2848, where the court noted (at [28]) that s. 41(4) applies only for the purposes of s. 41(3) and does not apply for the purposes of s. 41(5).

The phrase 'evidence adduced by the prosecution' in s. 41(5)(a) covers not only the evidence-in-chief of prosecution witnesses and the evidence of defence witnesses under cross- examination by the prosecution, but also the evidence of prosecution witnesses under cross-examination by the defence, provided that it is not deliberately elicited by defence counsel and was potentially damaging to the defence case (*Hamadi* [2007] EWCA Crim 3048). Where evidence is adduced by the prosecution about sexual behaviour of the complainant and they also have material that would enable the evidence to be rebutted, the material should be disclosed to the defence (*A-M* [2013] EWCA Crim 2622).

Statutory Provisions on Protection of Claimants in Sexual Offence Proceedings

Youth Justice and Criminal Evidence Act 1999, ss. 41 to 43   F7.40

41.—(1) If at a trial a person is charged with a sexual offence, then, except with the leave of the court—
  (a) no evidence may be adduced, and
  (b) no question may be asked in cross-examination,
by or on behalf of any accused at the trial, about any sexual behaviour of the complainant.
  (2) The court may give leave in relation to any evidence or question only on an application made by or on behalf of an accused, and may not give such leave unless it is satisfied—
  (a) that subsection (3) or (5) applies, and
  (b) that a refusal of leave might have the result of rendering unsafe a conclusion of the jury or (as the case may be) the court on any relevant issue in the case.
  (3) This subsection applies if the evidence or question relates to a relevant issue in the case and either—
  (a) that issue is not an issue of consent; or
  (b) it is an issue of consent and the sexual behaviour of the complainant to which the evidence or question relates is alleged to have taken place at or about the same time as the event which is the subject matter of the charge against the accused; or
  (c) it is an issue of consent and the sexual behaviour of the complainant to which the evidence or question relates is alleged to have been, in any respect, so similar—
    (i)   to any sexual behaviour of the complainant which (according to evidence adduced or to be adduced by or on behalf of the accused) took place as part of the event which is the subject matter of the charge against the accused, or
    (ii) to any other sexual behaviour of the complainant which (according to such evidence) took place at or about the same time as that event,
that the similarity cannot reasonably be explained as a coincidence.
  (4) For the purposes of subsection (3) no evidence or question shall be regarded as relating to a relevant issue in the case if it appears to the court to be reasonable to assume that the purpose (or main purpose) for which it would be adduced or asked is to establish or elicit material for impugning the credibility of the complainant as a witness.
  (5) This subsection applies if the evidence or question—
  (a) relates to any evidence adduced by the prosecution about any sexual behaviour of the complainant; and
  (b) in the opinion of the court, would go no further than is necessary to enable the evidence adduced by the prosecution to be rebutted or explained by or on behalf of the accused.
  (6) For the purposes of subsections (3) and (5) the evidence or question must relate to a specific instance (or specific instances) of alleged sexual behaviour on the part of the complainant (and accordingly nothing in those subsections is capable of applying in relation to the evidence or question to the extent that it does not so relate).
  (7) Where this section applies in relation to a trial by virtue of the fact that one or more of a number of persons charged in the proceedings is or are charged with a sexual offence—
  (a) it shall cease to apply in relation to the trial if the prosecutor decides not to proceed with the case against that person or those persons in respect of that charge; but

(b) it shall not cease to do so in the event of that person or those persons pleading guilty to, or being convicted of, that charge.

(8) Nothing in this section authorises any evidence to be adduced or any question to be asked which cannot be adduced or asked apart from this section.

42.—(1) In section 41—

(a) 'relevant issue in the case' means any issue falling to be proved by the prosecution or defence in the trial of the accused;

(b) 'issue of consent' means any issue whether the complainant in fact consented to the conduct constituting the offence with which the accused is charged (and accordingly does not include any issue as to the belief of the accused that the complainant so consented);

(c) 'sexual behaviour' means any sexual behaviour or other sexual experience, whether or not involving any accused or other person, but excluding (except in section 41(3)(c)(i) and (5)(a)) anything alleged to have taken place as part of the event which is the subject matter of the charge against the accused; and

(d) subject to any order made under subsection (2), 'sexual offence' shall be construed in accordance with section 62.

(2) [Secretary of State's power to add or remove offences.]

(3) Section 41 applies in relation to the following proceedings as it applies to a trial, namely—

(a) and (b) [repealed],

(c) the hearing of an application under paragraph 2(1) of Schedule 3 to the Crime and Disorder Act 1998 (application to dismiss charge by person sent for trial under section 51 or 51A of that Act),

(d) any hearing held, between conviction and sentencing, for the purpose of determining matters relevant to the court's decision as to how the accused is to be dealt with, and

(e) the hearing of an appeal,

and references (in section 41 or this section) to a person charged with an offence accordingly include a person convicted of an offence.

43.—(1) An application for leave shall be heard in private and in the absence of the complainant. In this section 'leave' means leave under section 41.

(2) Where such an application has been determined, the court must state in open court (but in the absence of the jury, if there is one)—

(a) its reasons for giving, or refusing, leave, and

(b) if it gives leave, the extent to which evidence may be adduced or questions asked in pursuance of the leave,

and, if it is a magistrates' court, must cause those matters to be entered in the register of its proceedings.

(3) [Power to make rules of court.]

Procedure on Applications under s. 41

F7.41   Where an accused wants to introduce evidence or cross-examine a witness about a complainant's sexual behaviour under YJCEA 1999, s. 41, the defence must apply in writing. The CrimPR, part 36, makes provision as to the procedure for making such an application, the time at which such an application should be made and its contents and service (see Supplement, R-276 *et seq.*). Failure to comply with these procedural rules makes it more likely that things will go wrong at the trial, either because the statutory protection given to the complainant will be undermined or because the defence will be prohibited from pursuing a legitimate line of questioning (*Crossland* [2013] EWCA Crim 2313).

RULE OF FINALITY OF ANSWERS TO QUESTIONS ON COLLATERAL MATTERS

General Rule

F7.42   The general rule, based on the desirability of avoiding a multiplicity of essentially irrelevant issues, is that evidence is not admissible to contradict answers given by a witness to questions put in cross-examination which concern collateral matters, i.e. matters which go merely to credit but which are otherwise irrelevant to the issues in the case (*Harris v Tippett* (1811) 2 Camp 637; *Palmer v Trower* (1852) 8 Exch 247). However, insofar as the questions relate to the witness's previous misconduct or disposition towards misconduct, some of the authorities, such as *Edwards* [1991] 2 All ER 266 (see F7.43), must be treated with caution: whether questions should be asked, or evidence adduced, concerning a witness's bad character is now governed by the CJA 2003, ss. 100 and 101 (see F12.15 and F14.6). In *A-G v Hitchcock* (1847) 1 Exch 91, Pollock CB said (at p. 99): 'The test whether a matter is collateral or not is this: if the answer of a witness is a matter which you would be allowed on your own part to prove in evidence — if it have such a connection with the issues that you would be allowed to give it in evidence — then it is a matter on which you may contradict him.' The narrowness and difficulty of this distinction may be illustrated by comparing the decision in *A-G v Hitchcock* with the decisions in *TM* [2004] EWCA Crim 2085 and *Busby* (1981) 75 Cr App R 79. In *A-G v Hitchcock* a maltster was charged with having used a cistern for the making of malt in breach of certain statutory requirements. A prosecution witness, having sworn that the cistern had been used, was asked in cross-examination whether he had not said to one Cook that the Excise officers had offered him £20 to give evidence that the cistern had been used. Upon denial of this allegation, it was held that the defendant was not allowed to call Cook to contradict the witness, because proof that a bribe was offered to the witness and not accepted was irrelevant to the matter in issue. In *TM* certain sexual offences came to light when a private investigator and inquiry agents, being used for the purposes of family proceedings by a man, S, whose wife had been having an affair with M, interviewed the victims of the offences. M denied all the offences and said that S had set out to destroy him and had induced the victims to give evidence against him by offers of financial reward. It was held that M should have been allowed to call a witness to give evidence that she had been approached by the private investigator and when she had refused to give adverse information had been told that S had unlimited funds for the right information. When viewed in isolation, the witness's evidence was collateral, but although 'borderline', it was relevant as showing that the *victims* might have been offered money or been influenced by the offer of money. In *Busby*, a prosecution for burglary and handling, police officers were cross-examined to the effect that they had fabricated statements attributed to the accused and indicative of his guilt, and had threatened W, a potential defence witness, to stop him giving evidence. These allegations were denied. The trial judge ruled that the defence could not call W to give evidence that he had been threatened by the officers, because this would go solely to their credit. Allowing the appeal against conviction, the Court of Appeal held that the trial judge had erred: the evidence was relevant to an issue which had to be tried, because, if true, it showed that the police were prepared to go to improper lengths in order to secure a conviction, which would have supported the defence case that the statements attributed to the accused had been fabricated. See also *Marsh* (1985) 83 Cr App R 165 and cf. *Phillips* (1936) 26 Cr App R 17, at F7.53.

In *Funderburk* [1990] 2 All ER 482, at p. 591, *Busby* was treated as having created a new *exception* to the rule of finality. However, in *Edwards* [1991] 2 All ER 266, it was held that the fact that the police were allegedly prepared to prevent the potential witness from giving evidence, came within the exception of bias (see F7.51); and that if the decision could not be explained on that basis, it was inconsistent with the general rule and inconsistent with the decision in *Harris v Tippett* itself (where the facts were not dissimilar to those in *Busby*). In *Edwards* a number of officers involved in the case had given evidence in other trials, which had resulted in acquittal, in circumstances which tended to cast doubt on their reliability. In the other trials, evidence showed that some interview notes were inaccurate and that others had seemingly been rewritten to include admissions which did not exist in the originals. It was held that:

F7.43

(a) it could be put to the officers in cross-examination that they had given evidence in the previous trials, that in each trial there was an issue as to whether alleged confessions had been fabricated and that each trial had ended in acquittal, because there was a sufficient connection between the evidence given by the officers in those trials and their eventual outcome to entitle such cross-examination on the question of their credibility in the instant case; but

F

(b) if the officers denied such allegations, they could not be proved by evidence in rebuttal, because the questioning would be as to credit alone, a collateral issue, and would not fall within any of the exceptions to the rule of finality.

Whether a particular item of evidence goes to an issue before the court or is merely collateral can be a question of some nicety. It only adds to the difficulty, it is submitted, to suggest that whether the rule of finality applies may turn on whether the matter which the cross-examining party seeks to prove is a single and distinct fact which is easy of proof rather than a broad and complex issue which is difficult of proof (*S* [1992] Crim LR 307). In *Funderburk* the court urged a flexible approach to the rule, on the basis that a general rule designed to serve the interests of justice should not be used to defeat justice by an over-pedantic approach. Henry J observed (at p. 598D), 'The utility of the test may lie in the fact that the answer is an instinctive one based on the prosecutor's and the court's sense of fair play rather than any philosophic or analytic process' (but cf. per Evans LJ in *Neale* [1998] Crim LR 737). Accordingly it has been held that the issue of sufficient relevance is one for the trial judge and that the Court of Appeal will only interfere with a decision to exclude evidence as being insufficiently irrelevant if it is either wrong in principle or plainly wrong as being outside that wide ambit (*Somers* [1999] Crim LR 744).

F7.44   The Court of Appeal in *Funderburk* also agreed with the editors of *Cross on Evidence* (7th edn, 1990, at p. 322) that where the disputed issue is a sexual one between two persons in private, the difference between questions going to credit and questions going to the issue is reduced to vanishing-point because sexual intercourse, whether or not consensual, most often takes place in private and leaves few visible traces of having occurred, so that the evidence is often effectively limited to that of the parties, and much is likely to depend upon the balance of credibility between them. See further at F7.47.

Previous Inconsistent Statements

F7.45   If a witness under cross-examination admits to having made a previous oral or written statement inconsistent with his testimony, no further proof of the statement is required or, it seems, allowed (*P (GR)* [1998] Crim LR 663). However, if the witness denies having made such a statement, and the statement is relevant to an issue in the case, then it may be proved. The statement may be proved even if contained in a letter sent by an accused's solicitor to the CPS suggesting that the accused might plead guilty to a lesser offence, because there is nothing in criminal law akin to without prejudice privilege (*Hayes* [2004] 1 Cr App R 557).

Proof of a previous inconsistent statement is governed by the Criminal Procedure Act 1865, ss. 4 and 5. Section 4 applies to both oral and written statements, but s. 5 applies to written statements only (*Derby Magistrates' Court, ex parte B* [1996] AC 487).

F7.46   Oral and Written Statements under s. 4

Criminal Procedure Act 1865, s. 4

If a witness, upon cross-examination as to a former statement made by him relative to the subject-matter of the indictment or proceeding, and inconsistent with his present testimony, does not distinctly admit that he has made such statement, proof may be given that he did in fact make it; but before such proof can be given the circumstances of the supposed statement, sufficient to designate the particular occasion, must be mentioned to the witness, and he must be asked whether or not he has made such statement.

Section 4 is not confined to previous statements on oath (*Hart* (1957) 42 Cr App R 47, at p. 50; and *O'Neill* [1969] Crim LR 260 — oral statement made to the police). A witness who 'does not distinctly admit' to the making of the previous statement would include, in addition to a witness who denies such a statement, a witness who claims to have no recollection of it, who is equivocal on the subject, or who declines to answer. However, s. 4 does not apply to a party's own hostile witness. Proof of the previous inconsistent statement of a hostile witness requires the leave of the judge under s. 3 of the 1865 Act (see **F6.54**), a requirement which cannot be circumvented by reliance on s. 4 of the Act (*Booth* (1981) 74 Cr App R 123).

'Relative to the Subject-matter'   Whether a statement is 'relative to the subject-matter of the   **F7.47** indictment or proceeding' is a matter within the discretion of the judge (*Bashir* [1969] 3 All ER 692 per Veale J at p. 1306; and *Hart* (1957) 42 Cr App R 47 per Devlin J at p. 50). For the difficulties to which the issue may give rise, see *Funderburk* [1990] 2 All ER 482. F was convicted on three counts of sexual intercourse with a girl of 13. In her evidence, the girl gave evidence of a number of acts of intercourse with F, the description of the first act clearly describing the loss of her virginity. The defence was that the child was lying and in order to explain how so young a child could, if she were lying, have given such detailed and varied accounts of the acts of intercourse, wished to show that she was sexually experienced and had either transposed to F experiences which she had had with others and/or fantasised about experience with F. For this purpose, the defence wished to put to her that she had told a potential defence witness, P, that before the first incident complained of she had had sexual intercourse with two named men. The defence then wished to call P to give evidence of the conversation. The trial judge, applying the test in s. 4 of the 1865 Act, ruled that the complainant's previous inconsistent statement could not be put to her, nor could P be called, because the complainant's virginity was immaterial to the question whether F had had sexual intercourse with her and therefore was not 'relative to the subject-matter of the indictment'. On the question whether the previous inconsistent statement could be put in cross-examination *to challenge the complainant's credibility*, it was held that there was nothing in s. 4 to prevent this, even if, under s. 4, evidence of the making of that statement would not be allowed because it was not relative to the subject-matter of the indictment. The test for allowing cross-examination *as to credit* was that suggested by Lawton J in *Sweet-Escott* (1971) 55 Cr App R 316: how might the matters put to the witness affect his or her standing with the jury after cross-examination (see **F7.16**). Applying that test, the cross-examination should have been allowed since the jury might reasonably have wished to reappraise her evidence about the loss of her virginity and her credibility if they had heard of her previous statements regarding her earlier sexual experiences. On the question whether, if the complainant had been cross-examined about the conversation with P and she had denied making the previous statements, the defence would have been entitled to call P to prove the conversation, it was held that the previous statements were relative to the subject-matter of the indictment and therefore P could have been called to prove them under s. 4. Where the disputed issue is a sexual one between two persons in private, the difference between questions going to credit and questions going to the issue is reduced to vanishing-point. On the way the prosecution had presented the evidence, the challenge to the loss of virginity went far beyond a mere question of the complainant's credibility and was sufficiently closely related to the subject-matter of the indictment for justice to require investigation for the basis of such a challenge. (Cf. *Neale* [1998] Crim LR 737 and also, *sed quaere Gibson* [1993] Crim LR 453.) See also *Nagrecha* [1997] 2 Cr App R 401. N was accused of indecently assaulting the complainant. There were no witnesses. Under cross-examination, the complainant denied that she had made allegations of sexual impropriety against other men. It was held that evidence of the making of the other allegations was admissible because it went to the central issue of whether or not there had been any indecent assault.

Written Statements under s. 5   **F7.48**

Criminal Procedure Act 1865, s. 5

A witness may be cross-examined as to previous statements made by him in writing or reduced into writing relative to the subject matter of the indictment or proceeding, without such writing being shown to him; but if it is intended to contradict such witness by the writing, his attention must, before such contradictory proof can be given, be called to those parts of the writing which are to be used for the purpose of so contradicting him: provided always, that it shall be competent for the judge, at any time during the trial, to require the production of the writing for his inspection, and he may thereupon make such use of it for the purposes of the trial as he may think fit.

F7.49   The first part of s. 5 expressly allows cross-examination on a previous written statement *without* such writing being shown to the witness. However, if counsel proposes to cross-examine in this way, he must have the writing with him, even if he does not intend to *contradict* the witness with it, because under the proviso to s. 5, the judge may require its production for his inspection, and may thereupon make such use of it as he may think fit (*Anderson* (1929) 21 Cr App R 178). If the writing is shown to the witness, this may be done without putting it in evidence. Thus, counsel may hand the document to the witness, direct him to read the relevant part of it to himself, and then ask whether he wishes to adhere to his testimony. If the witness accepts the truth of the former statement, it becomes part of his evidence; if he adheres to his testimony, there is no obligation on the cross-examining party to contradict the witness and put the document in evidence (a course which it may be wise to avoid, especially if the inconsistency relates to some minor matter, and in all other respects the former statement is *consistent* with the witness's evidence). However, if counsel does wish to contradict the witness, he must put the document in evidence by reading out aloud the contradictory statement. The statement may then be inspected to see how far the suggested contradiction exists; whether the absence of a particular statement is explained by the context; and whether the discrepancy is only a minute point so that, taken as a whole, the document is more in the nature of confirmation rather than contradiction (see generally *Riley* (1866) 4 F & F 964 per Channell B; and *Wright* (1866) 4 F & F 967). It is open to the judge to allow the whole of the written statement to go before the jury, because under s. 5 he may 'make such use of it for the purposes of the trial as he may think fit'. For example, he may call attention to other parts of the statement to which no reference has been made (*Birch* (1924) 18 Cr App R 26, per Avory J at p. 28). However, he has a discretion to allow only part of the statement to go before the jury and therefore, in appropriate circumstances, may permit the jury to see only those parts of the statement upon which the cross- examination was based and not all the other parts relating to other unconnected matters (*Beattie* (1989) 89 Cr App R 302).

F7.50   **Criminal Justice Act 2003, s. 119(1)**   Under the CJA 2003, s. 119(1), a previous inconsistent statement that a witness admits to having made, or that is proved by virtue of the Criminal Procedure Act 1865, s. 4 or s. 5, is admissible for the truth of its contents.

Criminal Justice Act 2003, s. 119

(1) If in criminal proceedings a person gives oral evidence and—
    (a) he admits making a previous inconsistent statement or
    (b) a previous inconsistent statement made by him is proved by virtue of section 3, 4 or 5 of the Criminal Procedure Act 1865,
    the statement is admissible as evidence of any matter stated in it of which oral evidence by him would be admissible.

A judge should direct a jury that a statement covered by s. 119(1) is evidence in the case, but not that it is just as much evidence as the witness's testimony, because they may reject a statement in evidence and accord it no weight, if they do not consider it to be true. If the previous statement supports the prosecution case, the jury should be directed that it is evidence that they may consider when deciding upon their verdict if they are sure that it is true; but if the previous statement is exculpatory of the accused, the jury should be directed that they may consider it when deciding upon their verdict, if they conclude that it *may* be true (*Billingham* [2009] 2 Cr App R 431).

Where a previous inconsistent statement is admissible under s. 119 on behalf of the prosecution, it may nonetheless be excluded under the PACE 1984, s. 78 (see, e.g., *Coates* [2008] 1 Cr App R 52).

Bias and Partiality

F7.51   Evidence has always been admissible to contradict a witness's denial of bias or partiality towards one of the parties, and to show that he is prejudicial concerning the case being tried (*Mendy* (1976) 64 Cr App R 4, per Geoffrey Lane LJ at p. 6). For earlier authority, see *Yewin* (1811) cited 2 Camp 638 and *Dunn v Aslett* (1838) 2 Mood & R 122. To the extent that this common-law doctrine allows the introduction of evidence of, or of a disposition towards, misconduct on the part of a witness, it has been abolished by the CJA 2003, s. 99. However, much evidence of bias is likely to remain admissible under the doctrine, because it will fall outside the statutory definition of evidence of bad character in s. 98 of the 2003 Act, which excludes 'evidence of, or of a disposition towards misconduct…which has to do with the alleged facts of the offence with which the defendant is charged, or is evidence of misconduct in connection with the investigation or prosecution of that offence'. If the evidence in question is not admissible on that basis, it is nonetheless likely to be admitted under the CJA, s. 100(1)(b), i.e. as evidence of the bad character of a person other than the accused that has substantial probative value in relation to a matter which is in issue in the proceedings and is of substantial importance in the context of the case as a whole (see **F14**).

In *A-G v Hitchcock* (1847) 1 Exch 91 it was held that although evidence is not admissible to   **F7.52** contradict a witness's denial that he was *offered* a bribe to give false evidence, because this does not show that he is not a fair and credible witness, evidence is admissible to rebut a witness's denial that he *accepted* such a bribe, because that tends to show his partiality. Pollock CB said: 'A witness may be asked how he stands affected towards one of the parties; and if his relation towards them is such as to prejudice his mind, and fill him with sentiments of revenge and other feelings of a similar kind, and if he denies the fact, evidence may be given to show the state of his mind and feelings'.

In *Shaw* (1888) 16 Cox CC 503 it was held that the accused may call evidence to contradict   **F7.53** a prosecution witness who, in cross-examination, denies having threatened to be revenged on the accused following a quarrel with him. See also *Whelan* [1996] Crim LR 423. In *Phillips* (1936) 26 Cr App R 17, a case of incest, the principal prosecution witnesses, the accused's two daughters, were cross-examined on the basis that (a) they had been 'schooled' by their mother into giving false evidence, and (b) they had made admissions that evidence given by them in previous criminal proceedings against their father was false. Both allegations were denied. The trial judge refused to allow the defence to call the woman to whom the admissions were alleged to have been made. Quashing the conviction, the Court of Criminal Appeal held that this evidence should have been admitted because the bias that it would have revealed went to the very foundation of the accused's defence.

In *Mendy* (1976) 64 Cr App R 4, the accused was convicted of assault. At her trial, prospective   **F7.54** witnesses were kept out of court in accordance with the normal practice. While a police officer was giving evidence, a man in the public gallery was seen taking notes. He was later seen discussing the case with the accused's husband, apparently describing the officer's evidence to him. The husband, under cross-examination, denied this incident. The Court of Appeal held that the trial judge had properly allowed the prosecution to call evidence in rebuttal: the husband was prepared to lend himself to a scheme, designed to defeat the purpose of keeping prospective witnesses out of court, to enable him the more convincingly to describe how he, and not his wife, had caused the injuries alleged.

Previous Convictions

If a witness, lawfully cross-examined as to a previous conviction, denies it or refuses to answer,   **F7.55** it may be proved against him under the Criminal Procedure Act 1865, s. 6.

> **Criminal Procedure Act 1865, s. 6**
>
> If, upon a witness being lawfully questioned as to whether he has been convicted of any felony or misdemeanour, he either denies or does not admit the fact, or refuses to answer, it shall be lawful for the cross-examining party to prove such conviction…

Someone other than the accused will only be 'lawfully questioned' as to his previous convictions if the questions are lawful under the CJA 2003, s. 100 (see **F14**), and an accused will only be 'lawfully questioned' as to his previous convictions if the questions are lawful under the CJA 2003, s. 101 (see **F12**). There is an additional restriction in the case of offences committed by the accused when a child (see s. 108 of the 2003 Act, considered at **F12.98**). Under CPD V, para. 35A.2 (see Supplement, **PD–47**), when considering bad character applications under the CJA 2003, regard should always be had to the general principles of the Rehabilitation of Offenders Act 1974. Under the 1974 Act, in civil proceedings cross-examination of any witness about a spent conviction is prohibited unless the judge is satisfied that it is not possible for justice to be done except by admitting the conviction (ss. 4(1) and 7(3): see **D20.49**). Under the precursor to para. 35A.2, no reference was to be made to a spent conviction if that could reasonably be avoided, but according to *Corelli* [2001] EWCA Crim 974, that test did not operate to remove an unfettered statutory entitlement of a co-accused to cross-examine another co-accused on his previous convictions. (The statutory entitlement in that case arose under the Criminal Evidence Act 1898, s. 1(3)(iii); see now the CJA 2003, s. 101(1)(e), considered at **F12.67**).

In *Smallman* [1982] Crim LR 175, prosecuting counsel, without seeking the leave of the judge, referred to the spent conviction of a defence witness when cross-examining him. The judge directed the jury to leave out of account the prejudice resulting from the reference. The Court of Appeal held that counsel's reference to the spent conviction could not be a ground for quashing an otherwise perfectly proper conviction.

F7.56 Two cases where the charge was wounding and the defence was self-defence can usefully be compared. In *Evans* (1992) 156 JP 539, it was held that the judge should have allowed the defence to cross-examine the victim on her previous but spent convictions for dishonesty and violence because, evidentially, there was a head-on collision between the accused and the victim, and the jury were entitled to know of the victim's criminal record. In *Lawrence* [1995] Crim LR 815, the trial judge refused the defence permission to question the victim in detail on his 20 previous spent convictions, the majority of which were for offences of dishonesty, but only allowed questions on four more recent offences of dishonesty. The Court of Appeal held that the effect of the directions is to give the judge a wide discretion and that although it might have exercised the discretion differently and allowed cross-examination on one of the spent convictions, which involved perverting the course of justice, it was impossible to say that the judge had erred in principle. See also *Whelan* [1996] Crim LR 423.

As to proof of previous convictions, see the PACE 1984, s. 73, at **F11.1**. Where a witness who is cross-examined on a conviction accepts the conviction but claims his innocence, the cross-examining party is not entitled to adduce evidence in rebuttal, such as evidence from the victim of the offence on which the witness stands convicted, because such evidence would go solely to credibility (*Irish* [1995] Crim LR 145, applying *Edwards* [1991] 2 All ER 266, considered at **F7.43**).

Medical Evidence of Disability Affecting Reliability

F7.57 Medical evidence is admissible to show that a witness suffers from some disease or defect or abnormality of mind that affects the reliability of his evidence. Such evidence is not confined to a general opinion of the unreliability of the witness but may give all the matters necessary to show, not only the foundation of and reasons for the diagnosis, but also the extent to which the credibility of the witness is affected. (*Toohey v Metropolitan Police Commissioner* [1965] AC 595, per Lord Pearce at p. 609.)

If the defence adduce such evidence, it may be open to the Crown to call an expert in rebuttal, or even (anticipating the defence expert) as part of the prosecution case. It may even be open to the Crown to rebut by expert evidence a case put only in cross-examination that a prosecution witness is unreliable by reason of mental abnormality. Much may depend on the nature of the abnormality and of the cross-examination. But the rebuttal evidence should be restricted to meeting the specific challenge and should not extend to oath-helping: the Crown cannot call a witness of fact and then, without more, call a psychologist or psychiatrist to give reasons why the jury should regard that witness as reliable (*Robinson* [1994] 3 All ER 346; and see also *Beard* [1998] Crim LR 585). As to oath-helping, however, see also *S* [2006] EWCA Crim 2389, which concerned an autistic girl, aged 13, who was the victim of sexual offences. An expert witness was not allowed to comment directly on the veracity of the complainant, but did give evidence that a child such as the complainant would not easily have been able to invent the story she had told. It was held that this evidence had been properly admitted and that *Robinson* could be distinguished because, whereas the expert evidence in that case had related directly to one particular witness, in the instant case the evidence was of general application and it remained for the jury to decide whether the complainant was to be believed as to the particular allegation she had made. See also *Tobin* [2003] EWCA Crim 190.

In *Toohey*, T was charged with others with assaulting M with intent to rob. The defence case **F7.58** was that M had been drinking and that the accused were trying to help him, but that he became hysterical and accused them of assaulting him. The trial judge ruled that the medical evidence of a doctor, who had examined M shortly after the alleged assault, that drink could exacerbate hysteria, and that M was more prone to hysteria than a normal person, was inadmissible. The House of Lords quashed the conviction on the grounds that the evidence was admissible, not only because of its relevance to the facts in issue, but also in order to impeach the credibility of M, *qua* witness. Lord Pearce said (at p. 608):

> If a witness purported to give evidence of something which he believed that he had seen at a distance of 50 yards, it must surely be possible to call the evidence of an oculist to the effect that the witness could not possibly see anything at a greater distance than 20 yards, or the evidence of a surgeon who had removed a cataract from which the witness was suffering at the material time and which would have prevented him from seeing what he thought he saw. So, too, must it be allowable to call medical evidence of mental illness which makes a witness incapable of giving reliable evidence...

See also *Eades* [1972] Crim LR 99, a charge of causing death by dangerous driving. In his first statement to the police, one week after the accident, the accused said that he had not suffered from any concussion but was unable to remember any details of the accident itself (although he could remember incidents before and after the accident). Six weeks later, in a second statement to the police, he said that a few days earlier he had driven past the *locus in quo* and, as a result of a car emerging from a side road into his path, he had suddenly remembered the circumstances of the accident. Nield J ruled that if the accused gave evidence, the prosecution would be entitled to call a psychiatrist, who, although he had not examined the accused, had heard the prosecution evidence, to contradict the accused by evidence that his account as to how he had recovered his memory was not consistent with medical knowledge. Such evidence would be admissible because it would be not only relevant to a fact in issue, but also would tend to impugn the reliability of the accused as a witness.

The principle established in *Toohey*, in accordance with the rules governing the use of expert evidence generally, is applicable only in relation to some physical or mental disability calling for expertise, as opposed to matters affecting reliability upon which the jury are capable of forming their own opinion without expert assistance. Thus, expert evidence is generally inadmissible on the issue of an accused's credibility (*Turner* [1975] QB 834, at p. 842). Compare *Lowery v The Queen* [1974] AC 85, and see generally **F10**. In *Toohey*, Lord Pearce said (at p. 608):

> Human evidence shares the frailties of those who give it. It is subject to many cross-currents such as partiality, prejudice, self-interest and, above all, imagination and inaccuracy. Those are matters with which the jury, helped by cross-examination and common sense, must do their best. But when a witness through physical (in which I include mental) disease or abnormality is not capable of giving a true or reliable account to the jury, it must surely be allowable for medical science to reveal this vital hidden fact to them.

In *MacKenney* [2004] 2 Cr App R 32, the accused were convicted of murder. At their trial, **F7.59** in 1980, they alleged that the chief prosecution witness, an accomplice, had fabricated his evidence. The defence sought to call a psychologist, by whom the witness had refused to be examined. The psychologist had watched the witness as he gave his evidence and was of the opinion that he was a psychopath who was likely to be lying and whose mental state meant that his demeanour and behaviour in giving evidence would not betray the usual indications to the jury as to when he was lying. The trial judge ruled the evidence inadmissible and the convictions were upheld on appeal. In 2001 the Criminal Cases Review Commission referred the convictions to the Court of Appeal. There was fresh evidence, from a forensic psychiatrist, who also had not examined the witness, whose opinion was very similar to that of the psychologist which had been ruled inadmissible at the trial. It was held, adopting the approach to the relevance and admissibility of expert evidence set out in *O'Brien* [2000] Crim LR 676 (considered at **F10.20**), that the evidence of the psychologist would today be admissible. The reference was determined on the fresh evidence, on the basis of which the court concluded that the convictions were unsafe and should be quashed. It was held that the absence of an examination by the expert went to the weight to be attached to the opinion, and not to its admissibility. It was also held that the court must be on its guard against any attempt to detract from the jury's task of finding for themselves what evidence to believe: the court should not allow evidence to be put before the jury which does not allege any medical abnormality as the basis for the evidence of a witness being approached with particular caution.

RE-EXAMINATION

F7.60   After cross-examination, a witness may be re-examined by the party who called him. This applies even in the case of a hostile witness, who may be re-examined on any new matters which arose out of cross-examination (*Wong* [1986] Crim LR 683). Leading questions may not be asked in re-examination. The principal rule of re-examination is that, except with the leave of the judge, questions should be confined to matters, including any new matters, arising out of cross-examination. This rule applies not only in the case of a witness who has been examined in chief, but also in the case of a witness whose name is notionally on the back of the indictment and who was called by the prosecution merely to allow the defence to cross-examine him (*Beezley* (1830) 4 C & P 220). Where a witness under cross-examination gives evidence of part of a conversation with him on some previous occasion, questions may not be asked in re-examination about everything else that was said at the same time, but only about so much as can be in some way connected with the statement as to which he was cross-examined, such as other statements which qualify or explain it in any way (*Prince v Samo* (1838) 7 A & E 627, per Lord Denman CJ, citing Lord Tenterden in *Queen Caroline's Case* (1820) 2 B & B 284, at p. 297).

A witness may refresh his memory in re-examination: see **F6.14**. As to the admissibility of previous consistent statements in re-examination, see **F6.32** *et seq.*

Section F8   Documentary Evidence and Real Evidence

PROOF OF PRIVATE DOCUMENTS

Statements contained in documents are subject to the general rules of evidence on admissibility, **F8.1**
including those relating to relevance, hearsay, opinion and privilege. Two additional requirements, concerning documents on the contents of which a party seeks to rely, are: (a) proof of the
contents and (b) proof of due execution.

Concerning presumptions relating to documents, see **F8.43**. As to stamped documents,
see **F8.44**.

PROOF OF CONTENTS: THE BEST EVIDENCE RULE

The General Rule

At common law, the general rule, often regarded as the only remaining instance of the best **F8.2**
evidence rule, is that a party seeking to rely upon the contents of a document must adduce
primary evidence of those contents, i.e. either the original document in question, a copy of an
enrolled document, or informal admissions made by parties concerning the contents. Thus
if an original document is available in one's hands, one must produce it and one cannot give
secondary evidence by producing a copy (*Kajala v Noble* (1982) 75 Cr App R 149 at p. 152).
A party having a document available in his hands means a party who has the original of the
document with him in court, or could have it in court without any difficulty (*Governor of
Pentonville Prison, ex parte Osman* [1990] 3 All ER 701 at p. 308). The rule, in criminal cases,
is confined to written documents in the strict sense of the term, and has no relevance to tape
recordings and films (*Kajala v Noble* (1982) 75 Cr App R 149). As to the use of tape recordings,
see **F8.53**; as to photographs, video recordings and films, see **F8.58**. The general rule does not
apply if:

(a) it is unnecessary to place reliance upon the contents because the fact or matter in issue,
    although recorded in a document, can be proved by other evidence (see, e.g., *Holy Trinity,
    Kingston-upon-Hull (Inhabitants)* (1827) 7 B & C 611: the fact of a tenancy; *Manwaring*
    (1856) Dears & B 132: proof of a marriage, which may have been registered, by the testi-
    mony of a person who had attended the ceremony; and *Seberg* (1870) LR 1 CCR 264: proof
    by the testimony of eye-witnesses that a ship was British and sailing under the British flag,
    without production of the register of the vessel); or
(b) the document is tendered merely for the purpose of identifying it or establishing the bare
    fact of its existence (*Boyle v Wiseman* (1855) 11 Exch 360, at p. 367 and *Elworthy* (1867)
    LR 1 CCR 103).

To the general rule there are a number of common-law and statutory exceptions, providing for **F8.3**
proof of the contents of documents by secondary evidence. Generally speaking, such secondary
evidence may take the form of a copy, a copy of a copy or oral evidence, and 'there are no degrees
of secondary evidence' (per Lord Abinger CB in *Doe d Gilbert v Ross* (1840) 7 M & W 102).

Thus, an inferior copy may be tendered even if a better copy is available (*Lafone v Griffin* (1909) 25 TLR 308 and *Collins* (1960) 44 Cr App R 170; but contrast *Everingham v Roundell* (1838) 2 Mood & R 138). Likewise, oral evidence of the contents is admissible even if a copy is available (*Brown v Woodman* (1834) 6 C & P 206). The exceptions to the rule that there are no degrees of secondary evidence are the contents of:

(a) a will admitted to probate, which may not be proved by oral evidence if the original or probate copy exists;
(b) judicial documents and bankers' books (see **F8.13**), which are generally proved by office copies and examined copies respectively; and
(c) various public documents (see **F8.13** *et seq.*), which may be proved by oral evidence only if examined, certified, or other copies are unavailable.

F8.4   The law, as set out above, is well established. However, the Court of Appeal in *Springsteen v Masquerade Music Ltd* [2001] EWCA Civ 563 appears to reject the notion that, at common law, there is a general rule accompanied by a number of exceptions, in favour of a more generalised approach whereby the admissibility of secondary evidence of the contents of a document depends upon the weight to be attached to the secondary evidence. Observing 'with confidence' that the best evidence rule had finally expired, the court held that:

(a) Where the party seeking to adduce the secondary evidence could readily produce the document, it might be expected that, absent some special circumstances, the court would decline to admit the secondary evidence on the ground that it was worthless.
(b) At the other extreme, where that party genuinely could not produce the document, it might be expected that, absent some special circumstances, the court would admit the secondary evidence and attach such weight to it as it considered appropriate in the circumstances.
(c) In cases falling between these two extremes, it was for the court to make a judgment as to whether in all the circumstances any weight should be attached to the secondary evidence.
(d) Thus the admissibility of secondary evidence of the contents of documents is entirely dependent on whether or not any weight was to be attached to the evidence, which was a matter for the court to decide.

It remains to be seen whether this new approach will be followed in the civil courts or adopted in the criminal context.

Statutory Provisions

F8.5   The common-law authorities have been affected by the CJA 2003, s. 133, and the PACE 1984, s. 71.

Criminal Justice Act 2003, s. 133

Where a statement in a document is admissible as evidence in criminal proceedings, the statement may be proved by producing either—
(a) the document, or
(b) (whether or not the document exists) a copy of the document or of the material part of it, authenticated in whatever way the court may approve.

A 'statement' for these purposes is any representation of fact or opinion made by a person by whatever means, and includes a representation made in a sketch, photofit or other pictorial form (s. 115(2)); a 'document' means anything in which information of any description is recorded (s. 134(1)); and a 'copy' means anything on to which information recorded in the document has been copied, by whatever means and whether directly or indirectly (s. 134(1)).

Police and Criminal Evidence Act 1984, s. 71

In any proceedings the contents of a document may (whether or not the document is still in existence) be proved by the production of an enlargement of a microfilm copy of that document or of the material part of it, authenticated in such manner as the court may approve.

For the definition of 'proceedings', see s. 72 of the 1984 Act.

Two views are possible with regard to the construction of the CJA 2003, s. 133. On one view, it **F8.6** applies only to hearsay statements contained in documents, and not to the proof of the contents of a document as evidence in their own right. On the other view, it is not confined to the various types of documentary hearsay statement admissible under the 2003 Act itself, but applies to any statement contained in a document and admissible in evidence. Either way, s. 133, which on its wording is permissive rather than mandatory as to the means of proof, must be read subject to:

(a) the exceptions to the general rule at common law, whereby the contents of a document may be proved by secondary evidence which may take the form of *oral* evidence, which is not permitted under s. 133 (*Nazeer* [1998] Crim LR 750); and, it seems
(b) statutory exceptions to the general rule at common law, principally relating to public and judicial documents and bankers' books, which, although they allow for proof of the contents of such documents by copies, require those copies to take a particular form (which is not the case under s. 133).

In the cases to which s. 133 does apply, it remains to be seen in what manner the courts will **F8.7** require copies to be 'authenticated'. (For the difficulties that can arise in the case of some computer printouts of screen images, see *Skinner* [2005] EWCA Crim 1439, a decision under the CJA 1988, s. 27, the statutory precursor to s. 133.) In the normal case, it is submitted, the court will require the same proof as was necessary when relying upon secondary evidence under one of the common-law exceptions to the general rule, namely proof by the evidence of a person with custody or control of the copy (or some other appropriate person) that it is a true copy of the original. In *Collins* (1960) 44 Cr App R 170, the accused was convicted of obtaining money by false pretences, having cashed a cheque on his bank account which he knew to have been closed. When he failed, after notice to do so, to produce a letter sent to him informing him that the account had been closed, secondary evidence of the contents of the letter became admissible. However, the Court of Criminal Appeal held that a copy of a carbon copy of the letter, produced at the trial by a manager of the bank, had been improperly admitted, there having been no proof that it was a true copy of the carbon copy or that it was in the same terms as the original. Compare *Wayte* (1983) 76 Cr App R 110: the mere fact that it is easy to construct a false document by photocopying techniques does not render a photocopy inadmissible; the fact that the document was a photocopy went to its weight and not its admissibility. The Court of Appeal in that case also gave guidance on the procedure to be adopted when it is sought to produce in evidence photocopies:

(a) Documents should not normally be handed to the jury until questions of admissibility have been determined.
(b) Prior warning of the intention to produce such copies should be given to opposing counsel so that they may have the chance to consider their admissibility.
(c) If the accused is unrepresented, the guidance of the court should be sought before the document is put before the jury.
(d) On very rare occasions, it may be necessary to hold a trial within a trial on the question of admissibility, although ultimately the issue of the genuineness of the copies should be left to the jury.

In relation to copies, the information may have been copied from the original either 'directly or indirectly' (CJA 2003, s. 134(1)). Thus there is no obligation to produce the best copy rather than an inferior copy, even if the best copy, or indeed the original document, is still in existence.

At common law, prior to the decision in *Springsteen v Masquerade Music Ltd* [2001] EWCA **F8.8** Civ 563 (see **F8.4**), there were four established categories of exception to the general rule that a party seeking to rely upon the contents of a document must produce primary evidence of those contents. Since the coming into force of the CJA 2003, s. 133, and on the assumption that the second view of the true construction of that section set forth above is correct, it may only be necessary to rely upon such exceptions if, there being no copy of the document in question, it is sought to adduce *oral* evidence of its contents.

Failure to Produce Original after Notice

F8.9 A party seeking to rely upon the contents of a document may prove them by secondary evidence if the original is in the possession or control of the other party to the proceedings who, having been served with a notice to produce it, fails to do so (*Hunter* (1829) 3 C & P 591, where secondary evidence was admitted as to the contents of an allegedly forged deed, the deed itself being in the custody of the accused who, despite notice, refused to produce it). See also *Collins* (1960) 44 Cr App R 170, at **F8.7**. Service of a notice to produce is unnecessary where the requirement to produce the original can be implied, as when the indictment gives sufficient notice of the subject of inquiry: see *Aickles* (1784) 1 Leach 294, where on a charge of theft of a bill of exchange, parol evidence concerning it was given without service of a notice; *Clube* (1857) 3 Jur NS 698 and *Hunt* (1820) 3 B & Ald 566. Compare *Kitson* (1853) Dears CC 187, where, on a charge of setting fire to property with intent to defraud an insurance company, secondary evidence as to the contents of the policy of insurance was held to be inadmissible. See also *Elworthy* (1867) LR 1 CCR 103, where, on a charge of perjury, it being alleged that the accused had falsely sworn that there was no draft of a statutory declaration prepared by him, it was held that, although the prosecution could properly adduce parol evidence that such a draft existed and was in the possession of the accused, secondary evidence of the contents of the draft, and of certain alterations made in it was inadmissible, the Crown having given no notice to the accused to produce the original. Notice to produce is also excused where the opponent of the party seeking to rely on the document admits that it has been lost (*Haworth* (1830) 4 C & P 254).

Stranger's Lawful Refusal to Produce Original

F8.10 If a stranger to the proceedings, having been served with a subpoena *duces tecum, unlawfully* refuses to produce the document in his possession, its contents cannot be proved by secondary evidence, because the stranger is bound to produce it and is punishable for contempt if he refuses to do so (*Llanfaethly (Inhabitants)* (1853) 2 E & B 940). However, the contents may be proved by secondary evidence if the stranger *lawfully* refuses to comply with the subpoena: see *Mills v Oddy* (1834) 6 C & P 728 (a claim to privilege); *Kilgour v Owen* (1889) 88 LT Jo 7 (stranger outside the jurisdiction); and *Nowaz* [1976] 3 All ER 5, where the Pakistani consulate having refused, on the grounds of diplomatic immunity, to produce a photograph and an application for a passport, a police officer who had seen the documents was allowed to give oral evidence of their contents.

Original Lost or Destroyed

F8.11 The contents of a document may be proved by secondary evidence if it can be proved that the original has been destroyed or cannot be found after due search: see *Wayte* (1983) 76 Cr App R 110, where, two letters having been lost, a photocopy of the one and a photocopy of a carbon copy of the other were held to be admissible. The quality of evidence required to show the destruction (or loss and due search) varies according to the nature and value of the document in question (*Brewster v Sewell* (1820) 3 B & Ald 296). See also *Hall* (1872) 12 Cox CC 159.

Production of Original Impossible or Inconvenient

F8.12 The contents of a document may be proved by secondary evidence if production of the original is physically or legally impossible. As to the former, see *Mortimer v M'Callan* (1840) 6 M & W 58, at p. 72 (inscriptions upon tombstones or on a wall); and *Hunt* (1820) 3 B & Ald 566 (inscriptions on flags or banners). As to the latter, see *Owner v Bee Hive Spinning Co. Ltd* [1914]

1 KB 105 (a notice statutorily required to be constantly affixed at a factory or workshop); and *Alivon v Furnival* (1834) 1 Cr M & R 277 (a document in the custody of a foreign court). In addition to the statutory provisions governing the proof of the contents of public documents by secondary evidence, at common law secondary evidence may also be used to prove the contents of such documents if production of the originals would entail a high degree of public inconvenience. In *Mortimer v M'Callan* (1840) 6 M & W 58, Alderson B said (at p. 72):

> The [books of the Bank of England] are not capable of being produced without so much public inconvenience, that the courts have directed them to remain in the Bank, and copies of them to be received in evidence for the purpose for which the books are receivable.

PROOF OF PUBLIC AND JUDICIAL DOCUMENTS

Statutory Provisions of General Application

A large number of statutes provide for the proof of the contents of various public and judicial **F8.13** documents by secondary evidence, which, for these purposes, is usually required to take the form of an examined, certified, office, Queen's Printer's or Stationery Office copy. An examined copy is a copy proved by oral evidence to correspond with the original. A certified copy is a copy signed and certified to be accurate by an official who has custody of the original. An office copy is a copy made in the office of the High Court and authenticated, with the seal of the court, by an officer who has custody of the original and the lawful power to provide copies. Two provisions of general importance are the Evidence Act 1845, s. 1, and the Evidence Act 1851, s. 14.

Under s. 1 of the 1845 Act, where a statute provides for proof of a document by a certified, **F8.14** sealed or stamped copy, the copy, provided it purports to be signed, sealed or stamped, is admissible without any proof of the signature, seal or stamp, as the case may be.

Evidence Act 1845, s. 1

Whenever by any Act now in force or hereafter to be in force any certificate, official or public document, or document or proceeding of any corporation or joint-stock or other company, or any certified copy of any document, by-law, entry in any register or other book, or of any other proceeding, shall be receivable in evidence of any particular in any court of justice, or before any legal tribunal, or either House of Parliament, or any committee of either House, or in any judicial proceeding, the same shall respectively be admitted in evidence, provided they respectively purport to be sealed or impressed with a stamp or sealed and signed, or signed alone, as required, or impressed with a stamp and signed, as directed by the respective Acts made or to be hereafter made, without any proof of the seal or stamp, where a seal or stamp is necessary, or of the signature or of the official character of the person appearing to have signed the same, and without any further proof thereof, in every case in which the original record could have been received in evidence.

Under the Evidence Act 1851, s. 14, if no other statute provides for the proof by means of a **F8.15** copy of the contents of a document of such a public nature that it is admissible in evidence on production from proper custody, the contents of such a document may be proved by a certified or examined copy.

Evidence Act 1851, s. 14

Whenever any book or other document is of such a public nature as to be admissible in evidence on its mere production from the proper custody, and no statute exists which renders its contents provable by means of a copy, any copy thereof or extract therefrom shall be admissible in evidence in any court of justice, or before any person now or hereafter having by law or by consent of parties authority to hear, receive, and examine evidence, provided it be proved to be an examined copy or extract, or provided it purport to be signed and certified as a true copy or extract by the officer to whose custody the original is entrusted, and which officer is hereby required to furnish such certified copy or extract to any person applying at a reasonable time for the same, upon payment of a reasonable sum for the same.

Acts of Parliament and Journals of Either House

F8.16 Private and local and personal Acts of Parliament and Journals of either House may be proved by Queen's Printer's or Stationery Office copies.

Evidence Act 1845, s. 3

All copies of private and local and personal Acts of Parliament not public Acts, if purporting to be printed by the Queen's printers, and all copies of the journals of either House of Parliament, and of royal proclamations, purporting to be printed by the printers to the Crown or by the printers to either House of Parliament, or by any or either of them, shall be admitted as evidence thereof by all courts, judges, justices, and others without any proof being given that such copies were so printed.

Documentary Evidence Act 1882, s. 2

Where any enactment, whether passed before or after [19 June 1882] provides that a copy of any Act of Parliament, proclamation, order, regulation, rule, warrant, circular, list, gazette, or document shall be conclusive evidence, or be evidence, or have any other effect, when purporting to be printed by the Government Printer, or the Queen's Printer, or the Queen's printer for Scotland, or a printer authorised by Her Majesty, or otherwise under Her Majesty's authority, whatever may be the precise expression used, such copy shall also be conclusive evidence, or evidence, or have the said effect (as the case may be) if it purports to be printed under the superintendence or authority of Her Majesty's Stationery Office.

As to public Acts, the Interpretation Act 1978, s. 3, provides that 'Every Act is a public Act to be judicially noticed as such unless the contrary is expressly provided by the Act'. Section 3 applies to all Acts passed after 1850. At common law, judicial notice is taken of earlier enactments, if public. See **F1.6**.

Royal Proclamations and Orders or Regulations Issued by Government

F8.17 These may be proved by Queen's Printer's or Stationery Office copies (see the Documentary Evidence Act 1868, ss. 2 to 6; and the Documentary Evidence Act 1882, s. 2).

Documentary Evidence Act 1868, s. 2

Prima facie evidence of any proclamation, order, or regulation issued before or after the passing of this Act by Her Majesty or by the Privy Council, also of any proclamation, order, or regulation issued before or after the passing of this Act by or under the authority of any such department of the government or officer or office-holder in the Scottish Administration as is mentioned in the first column of the Schedule hereto, may be given in all courts of justice, and in all legal proceedings whatsoever, in all or any of the modes hereinafter mentioned; that is to say:
(1) By the production of a copy of the Gazette purporting to contain such proclamation, order, or regulation.
(2) By the production of a copy of such proclamation, order, or regulation purporting to be printed by the government printer, or, where the question arises in a court in any British colony or possession, of a copy purporting to be printed under the authority of the legislature of such British colony or possession.
(3) By the production, in the case of any proclamation, order, or regulation issued by Her Majesty or by the Privy Council, of a copy or extract purporting to be certified to be true by the Clerk of the Privy Council, or by any one of the lords or others of the Privy Council, and, in the case of any proclamation, order, or regulation issued by or under the authority of any of the said departments or officers or office-holders, by the production of a copy or extract purporting to be certified to be true by the person or persons specified in the second column of the said Schedule in connection with such department or officer or office-holder.
Any copy or extract made in pursuance of this Act may be in print or in writing, or partly in print and partly in writing.
   No proof shall be required of the handwriting or official position of any person certifying, in pursuance of this Act, to the truth of any copy of or extract from any proclamation, order, or regulation.

F8.18 In *Clarke* [1969] 2 QB 91, at p. 97, the Court of Appeal said that the word 'order' in the 1868 Act should be given a wide meaning, covering 'any executive act of government performed by the bringing into existence of a public document for the purpose of giving effect to an Act of Parliament'; and held that the Breath Test (Approval) (No. 1) Order 1968 (printed by HMSO), although not a statutory instrument, was an 'order' within s. 2 of the Act. As to statutory instruments, see further F8.20. An 'order' within s. 2 of the Act also covers a licence issued by the governor of a prison on behalf of the Secretary of State for the Home Office under the CJA 1991, s. 40A (*West Midlands Probation Board v French* [2009] 1 WLR 1715).

Proclamations, Treaties and Other Acts of State of Foreign States or British Colonies, and Judgments etc. of Courts in Foreign States or British Colonies

These may be proved by examined or authenticated copies (see the Evidence Act 1851, s. 7, **F8.19** below; and the Evidence Act 1845, s. 1, at **F8.14**). As to colonial documents, see also the Documentary Evidence Act 1868, s. 3.

Evidence Act 1851, s. 7

All proclamations, treaties, and other acts of State of any foreign State or of any British colony, and all judgments, decrees, orders, and other judicial proceedings of any court of justice in any foreign State or in any British colony, and all affidavits, pleadings, and other legal documents filed or deposited in any such court, may be proved in any court of justice, or before any person having by law or by consent of parties authority to hear, receive, and examine evidence, either by examined copies or by copies authenticated as hereinafter mentioned; that is to say, if the document sought to be proved be a proclamation, treaty, or other act of State, the authenticated copy to be admissible in evidence must purport to be sealed with the seal of the foreign State or British colony to which the original document belongs; and if the document sought to be proved be a judgment, decree, order, or other judicial proceeding of any foreign or colonial court, or an affidavit, pleading, or other legal document filed or deposited in any such court, the authenticated copy to be admissible in evidence must purport either to be sealed with the seal of the foreign or colonial court to which the original document belongs, or, in the event of such court having no seal, to be signed by the judge, or, if there be more than one judge, by any one of the judges of the said court; and such judge shall attach to his signature a statement in writing on the said copy that the court whereof he is a judge has no seal; but if any of the aforesaid authenticated copies shall purport to be sealed or signed as hereinbefore respectively directed, the same shall respectively be admitted in evidence in every case in which the original document could have been received in evidence, without any proof of the seal where a seal is necessary, or of the signature, or of the truth of the statement attached thereto, where such signature and statement are necessary, or of the judicial character of the person appearing to have made such signature and statement.

When s. 7 is used to prove a foreign conviction, it still has to be established that the examined copy relates to the person said to have been convicted. This can be proved by any relevant admissible evidence, including evidence of fingerprints (*Mauricia* [2002] 2 Cr App R 377).

Statutory Instruments

Statutory instruments may be proved by Queen's Printer's or Stationery Office copies (see **F8.20** the Documentary Evidence Act 1868, s. 2, and the Documentary Evidence Act 1882, s. 2). However, where a photocopy from a commercial publication is produced instead, and there is no suggestion of any inaccuracy in the version before the court, the proviso to the Criminal Appeal Act 1968, s. 2, may apply (*Koon Cheung Tang* [1995] Crim LR 813). See also *Ashley* (1967) 52 Cr App R 42 and *Palastanga v Solman* [1962] Crim LR 334 (at **F6.5**), and, as to the proof of the date of issue of statutory instruments, the Statutory Instruments Act 1946, s. 3.

By-laws

By-laws may be proved by certified printed copies. **F8.21**

Local Government Act 1972, s. 238

The production of a printed copy of a by-law purporting to be made by a local authority, the Greater London Authority or an Integrated Transport Authority for an integrated transport area in

England or a combined authority upon which is endorsed a certificate purporting to be signed by the proper officer of the authority stating—
(a) that the by-law was made by the authority;
(b) that the copy is a true copy of the by-law;
(c) that on a specified date the by-law was confirmed by the authority named in the certificate or, as the case may require, was sent to the Secretary of State and has not been disallowed;
(d) the date, if any, fixed by the confirming authority for the coming into operation of the by-law;
shall be prima facie evidence of the facts stated in the certificate, and without proof of the handwriting or official position of any person purporting to sign the certificate.

Colonial and Foreign Laws

F8.22 Colonial statutes may be proved by copies certified by the clerk or other proper officer of the colonial legislative body (the Colonial Laws Validity Act 1865, s. 6), or by copies purporting to be printed by the government printer of that possession (the Evidence (Colonial Statutes) Act 1907, s. 1). Subject to this, and except where ascertained by the British Law Ascertainment Act 1859, colonial and foreign law, including Scots law, even if written, cannot be proved in an English court by production of the documents in which it is recorded, or a copy thereof, but generally requires proof by a suitably qualified expert (*Sussex Peerage Case* (1844) 11 Cl & F 85; *Governor of Brixton Prison, ex parte Shuter* [1960] 2 QB 89). See further, **F10.27**.

Public Records

F8.23 By virtue of the Public Records Act 1958, s. 9, public records in the Public Record Office may be proved by copies which have been examined, certified and sealed or stamped.

Births, Deaths and Marriages

F8.24 An entry in the register of births or deaths may be proved by a certified copy purporting to be sealed or stamped with the seal of the General Register Office, and is admissible evidence of the birth or death to which it relates (see the Births and Deaths Registration Act 1953, s. 34). (As to adopted children, see also the Adoption and Children Act 2002, s. 77(4).) Likewise, proof of the celebration of a marriage or of a civil partnership may be effected by the production of a certified copy of an entry kept at the General Register Office (see the Marriage Act 1949, s. 65(3), and the Civil Partnership (Registration Provisions) Regulations 2005 (SI 2005 No. 3176), reg. 13(4)). In order to prove a birth or death (or the marriage of persons), it is also necessary to adduce some evidence to identify the person in question with the person named in the certified copy (*Bellis* (1911) 6 Cr App R 283). The same applies where it is sought to prove a person's age by production of a birth certificate. Thus, although age may be proved by other means, e.g., by the testimony of someone present at the time of the birth, by inference from appearance or by hearsay declarations as to pedigree (*Cox* [1898] 1 QB 179), if a certificate of birth is produced to prove age, evidence must also be adduced to positively identify the person as the person named in the certificate (*Rogers* (1914) 10 Cr App R 276: proof of the age of the complainant on a charge of unlawful sexual intercourse with a girl under 13). A certified copy of an entry in the register of deaths is prima facie evidence of the fact and date of a death; but information contained in the certificate concerning the cause of death, and based on information supplied by a coroner, is inadmissible as evidence of the cause of death (*Bird v Keep* [1918] 2 KB 692, per Swinfen Eady MR, *obiter*).

Records of marriages, baptisms and burials entered in parish registers may be proved by an examined copy or by a copy certified as a true copy by the incumbent to whose custody the original is entrusted (see the Evidence Act 1851, s. 14, at **F8.15**).

F8.25 **Foreign Records**   Births, deaths and marriages out of England may be proved by entries properly and regularly recorded in foreign registers kept under the sanction of public authority (see *Lyell v Kennedy* (1889) 14 App Cas 437, per Lord Selborne at pp. 448–9, and generally **F16.49**). See also the Registration of Births, Deaths and Marriages (Scotland) Act 1965. Births, deaths and marriages out of England may also be proved by certified copies of registers kept under the local law in any case where the Evidence (Foreign, Dominion and Colonial Documents) Act 1933 has been applied by an Order in Council. As to proof of records kept in an Army Register in respect of an officer or soldier serving overseas, see the Registration of Births, Deaths and Marriages (Army) Act 1879, s. 3. As to returns of births and deaths on ships registered in the UK, and on ships not registered in the UK but calling at a port in the UK, see the Merchant Shipping Act 1995, s. 108, and the Merchant Shipping (Returns of Births and Deaths) Regulations 1979, (SI 1979 No. 1577). As to births, deaths and marriages on Her Majesty's ships at sea and service aircraft, see the Registration of Births, Deaths and Marriages (Special Provisions) Act 1957, s. 2.

Minute-books of Local Authorities

The minutes of the proceedings of local authorities required to be drawn up, entered in a book **F8.26** and signed under the Local Government Act 1972, shall be received in evidence without further proof; and until the contrary is proved, where a minute of such proceedings has been made and signed, the meeting shall be deemed to have been duly convened and held, and all the members present shall be deemed to have been duly qualified (Local Government Act 1972, sch. 12, part VI, para. 41). A document which purports to be a copy of the minutes of the proceedings at a meeting of a local authority (or a committee of a local authority, or a subcommittee of such a committee) or a precursor of a local authority, and which bears a certificate purporting to be signed by the proper officer of the authority and stating that the minutes were signed in accordance with para. 41, shall be evidence in any proceedings of the matters stated in the certificate and of the terms of the minutes in question (Local Government (Miscellaneous Provisions) Act 1976, s. 41(1)).

Professional Lists

Various statutes provide for proof that a person is or is not professionally qualified by produc- **F8.27** tion of a list, register or certificate of a registrar. Thus, any list purporting to be published by authority of the Law Society and to contain the names of solicitors who have obtained practising certificates for the current year shall, until the contrary is proved, be evidence that the persons so named are solicitors holding such certificates (Solicitors Act 1974, s. 18(1)). The absence from any such list of the name of any person shall, until the contrary is proved, be evidence that that person is not qualified to practise as a solicitor under a certificate for the current year, but in the case of any such person an extract from the roll certified as correct by the Society shall be evidence of the facts appearing in the extract. See also the Medical Act 1983, s. 34 (registered medical practitioners); the Nursing and Midwifery Order 2002 (SI 2002 No. 253), reg. 8(3); the Health Professions Order 2002 (SI 2002 No. 254), reg. 8(4); the Dentists Act 1984, s. 14(6); the Pharmacy Order 2010 (SI 2010 No. 231), part 4 (registered pharmacists and pharmacy technicians); and the Veterinary Surgeons Act 1966, ss. 2 and 9.

Documents Relevant to Insolvency

In relation to bankruptcy law, any document purporting to be or to contain any order, direc- **F8.28** tion or certificate issued by the Secretary of State shall be received in evidence and be deemed to be (or contain) that order or certificate or those directions without further proof, unless the contrary is shown; and a certificate signed by the Secretary of State or an officer on his behalf and confirming the making of any order, the issuing of any document or the exercise of any discretion, power or obligation arising or imposed under the Insolvency Act 1986 or the Insolvency Rules 1986 (SI 1986 No. 1925) is conclusive evidence of the matter dealt with in the certificate (Insolvency Rules 1986, r. 12.6). A copy of the Gazette containing any notice required by the Act or the Rules to be gazetted is evidence of any facts stated in the notice; and in the case of an order of the court, notice of which is required to be gazetted, a copy of the Gazette containing the notice may be produced in any proceedings as conclusive evidence that the order was made on the date specified in the notice (Insolvency Rules 1986, r. 12.20).

Company Investigations

F8.29   A copy of any report of inspectors appointed under part XIV of the Companies Act 1985, certified by the Secretary of State to be a true copy, is admissible in any legal proceedings as evidence of the opinion of the inspectors in relation to any matter contained in the report; and a document purporting to be such a certificate shall be received in evidence and deemed to be such a certificate unless the contrary is proved (Companies Act 1985, s. 441).

Proceedings in Civil Courts

F8.30   Under the Civil Procedure Rules 1998, r. 2.6(3), a document purporting to bear the court's seal shall be admissible in evidence without further proof. See also the Senior Courts Act 1981, s. 132: 'Every document purporting to be sealed or stamped with the seal or stamp of the Supreme Court shall be received in evidence in all parts of the UK without further proof'. An official copy of the whole or any part of a will may be obtained under the Senior Courts Act 1981, s. 125, and may be proved under s. 132 of that Act. On a prosecution for perjury (or procuring or suborning the commission of perjury) alleged to have been committed on the trial of any indictment, the fact of that former trial shall be sufficiently proved by a certificate signed by the clerk (or his deputy) of the court where the indictment was tried without proof of the signature (Perjury Act 1911, s. 14).

Proceedings in County Courts

F8.31   Records of county court proceedings may be proved by certified copies.

County Courts Act 1984, s. 12

(2) Any entry in a book or other document required by the said regulations to be kept for the purposes of this section, or a copy of any such entry or document purporting to be signed and certified as a true copy by a judge of the county court, shall at all times without further proof be admitted in any court or place whatsoever as evidence of the entry and of the proceeding referred to by it and of the regularity of that proceeding.

Proceedings in Magistrates' Courts

F8.32   The CrimPR, r. 5.7, provides that the register of a magistrates' court, or an extract from the register certified by the magistrates' court officer as a true extract, shall be admissible in any legal proceedings as evidence of proceedings of the court entered in the register.

Affidavits

F8.33   On a prosecution for perjury in an affidavit, the affidavit itself must be produced and proved (*Rees d Howell and Dalton v Bowen* (1825) M'Cle & Yo 383), unless it can be proved to have been lost or destroyed, in which case secondary evidence is admissible of its contents and the signature of the accused (*Milnes* (1860) 2 F & F 10, and see **F8.11**).

Convictions and Acquittals

F8.34   Provision for the proof of convictions and acquittals is made in the PACE 1984, s. 73. This is dealt with at **F11**.

BANKERS' BOOKS

General

In order to facilitate the proof of matters recorded in bankers' books, the Bankers' Books Evidence **F8.35**
Act 1879 provides for proof of the contents of such books by the production of examined copies.

Bankers' Books Evidence Act 1879, s. 3

Subject to the provisions of this Act, a copy of any entry in a banker's book shall in all legal proceedings be received as prima facie evidence of such entry, and of the matters, transactions, and accounts therein recorded.

The expressions 'bank' and 'banker' are defined by s. 9(1) of the Act to mean a deposit-taker (an expression defined by s. 9(1A)–(1C)) and the National Savings Bank.

'Bankers' books' were originally defined to include ledgers, daybooks, cash books, account books, and all other books used in the ordinary business of the bank. Section 9(2) of the 1879 Act, as substituted by the Banking Act 1979, has now extended that definition. It provides that expressions in the Act relating to 'bankers' books' include 'ledgers, daybooks, cash books, account books and other records used in the ordinary business of the bank, whether those records are in written form or are kept on microfilm, magnetic tape or any other form of mechanical or electronic data retrieval mechanism'. In *Williams v Williams* [1988] QB 161, it was held that paid cheques and paying-in slips retained by a bank after the conclusion of a banking transaction to which they relate are not 'bankers' books', because, even if bundles of such documents can be treated as 'records used in the ordinary business of the bank', the act of adding an individual cheque (paying-in slip) cannot be regarded as the making of an 'entry' in the records. It is submitted that similar reasoning may be used to justify the decision reached in *Dadson* (1983) 77 Cr App R 91 prior to the coming into force of the extended definition, that copies of letters written by a bank and contained in a file of its correspondence, were not 'bankers' books'. The words 'other records used in the ordinary business of the bank' are to be construed *eiusdem generis* with ledgers, daybooks, cash books and account books and therefore do not cover records kept by the bank of conversations between its employees and customers or others or internal memoranda (*Re Howglen Ltd* [2001] 1 All ER 376). In the case of documents falling outside the statutory definition, use may be made, in appropriate circumstances, of the hearsay provisions of the CJA 2003, including s. 133 of that Act (see **F8.5**).

Bankers' Books Evidence Act 1879, ss. 4 to 8 **F8.36**

4. A copy of an entry in a banker's book shall not be received in evidence under this Act unless it be first proved that the book was at the time of the making of the entry one of the ordinary books of the bank, and that the entry was made in the usual and ordinary course of business, and that the book is in the custody or control of the bank.

    Such proof may be given by a partner or officer of the bank, and may be given orally or by an affidavit sworn before any commissioner or person authorised to take affidavits.
5. A copy of an entry in a banker's book shall not be received in evidence under this Act unless it be further proved that the copy has been examined with the original entry and is correct.

    Such proof shall be given by some person who has examined the copy with the original entry, and may be given either orally or by an affidavit sworn before any commissioner or person authorised to take affidavits.
6. A banker or officer of a bank shall not, in any legal proceeding to which the bank is not a party, be compellable to produce any banker's book the contents of which can be proved under this Act, or to appear as a witness to prove the matters, transactions, and accounts therein recorded, unless by order of a judge made for special cause.
7. On the application of any party to a legal proceeding a court or judge may order that such party be at liberty to inspect and take copies of any entries in a banker's book for any of the purposes of such proceedings. An order under this section may be made either with or without

summoning the bank or any other party, and shall be served on the bank three clear days before the same is to be obeyed, unless the court or judge otherwise directs.

8. The costs of any application to a court or judge under or for the purposes of this Act, and the costs of anything done or to be done under an order of a court or judge made under or for the purposes of this Act shall be in the discretion of the court or judge, who may order the same or any part thereof to be paid to any party by the bank, where the same have been occasioned by any default or delay on the part of the bank. Any such order against a bank may be enforced as if the bank was a party to the proceeding.

F8.37 'A court', for the purposes of s. 7, includes justices before whom criminal proceedings are pending (*Kinghorn* [1908] 2 KB 949). An application under s. 7 in criminal proceedings will not be refused on the grounds that it incriminates the party against whom it is made; but it is a serious interference with the liberty of the subject, and the court should be satisfied, before making an order, that the application is more than a mere 'fishing expedition' by considering whether the prosecution have other evidence to support the charge. The court should also limit the period of disclosure of the bank account to a period in time which is strictly relevant to the charge (*Williams v Summerfield* [1972] 2 QB 512). In *Marlborough Street Stipendiary Magistrate, ex parte Simpson* (1980) 70 Cr App R 290, orders under the Act were quashed on the grounds that they were not limited to a defined period in time. See also *Nottingham City Justices, ex parte Lynn* (1984) 79 Cr App R 238, where, on a charge of drug smuggling, an order for the inspection of accounts over a period of three years was reduced to a period of six months, on the ground that there was insufficient evidence to link the accused with offences during most of the three years.

F8.38 **Bank Accounts of a Non-party**   An order may be made to inspect the accounts of a person who is not a party to the proceedings, even if not compellable as a witness. Thus in *Andover Justices, ex parte Rhodes* [1980] Crim LR 644, the Divisional Court upheld an order in respect of the account of the husband of an accused, charged with the theft of money, who had told the police that the money was in her husband's account. However, in criminal cases, such an order should be made only in exceptional circumstances, and where the private interest in keeping a bank account confidential is outweighed by the public interest in assisting a prosecution (*Grossman* (1981) 73 Cr App R 302, at p. 307). In *MacKinnon v Donaldson, Lufkin and Jenrette Securities Corporation* [1986] Ch 482, *Grossman* was applied, although it was acknowledged that the decision in that case had been given *per incuriam* since the proceedings were criminal and, under the Supreme Court Act 1981 (now the Senior Courts Act 1981), s. 18(1)(a), the Court of Appeal had no jurisdiction.

F8.39 **Foreign Banks**   In *MacKinnon v Donaldson, Lufkin and Jenrette Securities Corporation* [1986] Ch 482 it was held that, save in exceptional circumstances, an order should not be made against a foreign bank which is not a party to the proceedings, even if it carries on business within the jurisdiction and is a recognised bank under the Banking Act 1979, to produce documents outside the jurisdiction concerning business transacted outside the jurisdiction, because an order under the 1879 Act is an exercise of sovereign authority to assist in the administration of justice, and foreign banks owe their customers a duty of confidence regulated by the law of the country where the documents are kept.

F8.40 **Procedure**   An application under s. 7 of the 1879 Act may be made *ex parte*, but 'there is much to be said for notice being given' (*Marlborough Street Stipendiary Magistrate, ex parte Simpson* (1980) 70 Cr App R 291, per Widgery LJ at p. 294). See also, in the case of accounts of a person who is not a party to the proceedings, *Grossman* (1981) 73 Cr App R 302, per Oliver LJ at p. 309: either the order should not be made until the person affected has been informed and given an opportunity to be heard, or it should be made in the form of an order *nisi*, allowing a period for that person to show cause why the order should not take effect.

An order under s. 7 of the 1879 Act is not a precondition of adducing evidence under s. 3. The purpose of s. 7 is to enable a banker's books to be inspected and copied despite the duty of confidentiality owed by the banker to the customer, but an order would be unnecessary if, for instance, the customer waived his right to confidentiality and the bank agreed to inspection and copying (*Wheatley v Commissioner of Police of the British Virgin Islands* [2006] 1 WLR 1683, construing the British Virgin Islands Bankers' Books (Evidence) Act 1881).

PROOF OF DUE EXECUTION

The due execution of a document is established by:

F8.41

(a) proof that it was signed by the person by whom it purports to have been signed; and
(b) if attestation is necessary, proof that it was attested.

In the case of public and judicial documents, the statutory provisions which enable their contents to be proved by copies also dispense with the need to prove due execution (see **F8.13** to **F8.34** and **F1.6**). Where a party seeks to rely upon the contents of a private document, due execution may be formally admitted or presumed. A document which is more than 20 years old, produced from proper custody and otherwise free from suspicion, is presumed to have been duly executed. At common law the period was 30 years, but 20 years was substituted by the Evidence Act 1938, s. 4. A document comes from proper custody even if not found in the best and most proper place of deposit, provided that the court is satisfied that the place in which it was found was custody that was reasonable and natural in the circumstances (*Bishop of Meath v Marquess of Winchester* (1836) 3 Bing NC 183, per Tindal CJ). Proof of due execution is also unnecessary if the document in question is in the possession of an opponent who refuses to comply with a notice to produce it (*Cooke v Tanswell* (1818) 8 Taunt 450). Subject to the foregoing, a party seeking to rely on the contents of a private document must prove its due execution.

Proof that a document was signed or written by the person by whom it purports to have been signed or written may be effected in a variety of ways:

F8.42

(a) by the admission of the person in question (*Waldridge v Kennison* (1794) 1 Esp 143);
(b) by the testimony (or admissible hearsay assertion) of the signatory identifying his own signature (hand);
(c) by the testimony (or admissible hearsay assertion) of a person who witnessed the execution of the document;
(d) by the opinion evidence of a person acquainted with the signature or handwriting (*Doe d Mudd v Suckermore* (1836) 5 A & E 703 at p. 705, and *Slaney* (1832) 5 C & P 213); or
(e) by comparison of the document in question with another document which is admitted or proved to have been signed or written by the person in question under the Criminal Procedure Act 1865, s. 8. See further **F10.25**.

Any of these methods of proof may also be used in the case of a private document which, although not required by law to be attested, was in fact attested. Under the Criminal Procedure Act 1865, s. 7: 'It shall not be necessary to prove by the attesting witness any instrument to the validity of which attestation is not requisite, and such instrument may be proved as if there had been no attesting witness thereto'.

Where a document requires attestation to be formally valid, it is not strictly necessary to prove attestation by calling an attesting witness, except in the case of wills and other testamentary documents. Under the Evidence Act 1938, s. 3, 'an instrument to the validity of which attestation is requisite may, instead of being proved by an attesting witness, be proved in the manner in which it might be proved if no attesting witness were alive: Provided that nothing in this section shall apply to the proof of wills and other testamentary documents.' Thus, the attestation of private documents other than testamentary documents may be proved by the testimony of an attesting witness; or by evidence as to the handwriting of the attesting witness; or by other evidence, such as the testimony of a non-attesting witness to the execution.

PRESUMPTIONS CONCERNING DOCUMENTS

F8.43 A document which is more than 20 years old and comes from proper custody is presumed to have been duly executed. It is also presumed that:

(a) a document was made on the date which it bears (*Re Adamson* (1875) LR 3 P & D 253 at p. 256);

(b) a deed was duly sealed (*Re Sandilands* (1871) LR 6 CP 411); and

(c) an alteration or erasure in a deed was made before execution, but that an alteration or erasure in a will was made after execution (*Doe d Tatum v Catomore* (1851) 16 QB 745).

STAMPED DOCUMENTS

F8.44 In criminal proceedings, a document required to be stamped for the purposes of stamp duty is admissible even if not duly stamped (Stamp Act 1891, s. 14).

REAL EVIDENCE

Tangible Objects

F8.45 Real evidence is usually some material object, the existence, condition or value of which is in issue or relevant to an issue, produced in court for inspection by the tribunal of fact. (As to inspection out of court, see **F8.50**.) Little if any weight can attach to real evidence in the absence of accompanying testimony identifying the object and connecting it with the facts in issue. In some cases the tribunal of fact must not draw its own unaided conclusion without the assistance of expert testimony: see, e.g., *Tilley* [1961] 3 All ER 406 and *Hipson* [1969] Crim LR 85 (comparison of handwriting).

There is no rule of law that an object must be produced, or its non-production excused, before oral evidence may be given about it. In *Hocking v Ahlquist Bros Ltd* [1944] KB 120, proceedings against manufacturers of clothing for non-compliance with restrictions relating to the method of manufacture, in which evidence as to the condition of the garments was received from witnesses who had visited the manufacturer's premises, it was held that the magistrate had been wrong to dismiss the information on the basis that the garments were not produced at the trial. See also *Miller v Howe* [1969] 3 All ER 451: it is not necessary for the police to produce the very breath test device used by them on a particular occasion. Non-production, however, may give rise to an inference adverse to the party failing to produce the object in question (*Armory v Delamirie* (1722) 1 Str 505), and may go to the weight of the oral evidence adduced. In *Francis* (1874) LR 2 CCR 128, a trial for attempting to pass off a false ring, at which the ring was not produced but witnesses who had seen it gave evidence as to its falsity, Lord Coleridge CJ said (at p. 133): 'though the production of the article may afford ground for observation more or less weighty, according to the circumstances, it only goes to the weight, not the admissibility of the evidence'.

F8.46 Once an article has become an exhibit, the court has a responsibility, for the purposes of justice, to preserve and retain it until the trial is concluded, or to arrange for its preservation and retention, the usual course being for the court to entrust the exhibits to the police or to the DPP. The duty of the prosecution, if entrusted with exhibits pending trial, is:

(a) to take all proper care to preserve the exhibits safe from loss or damage;

(b) to co-operate with the defence in order to allow them reasonable access to the exhibits for the purpose of inspection and examination; and

(c) to produce the exhibits at the trial (*Lambeth Metropolitan Stipendiary Magistrate, ex parte McComb* [1983] QB 551). See also *Uxbridge Justices, ex parte Sofaer* (1986) 85 Cr App R 367.

Behaviour, Appearance and Demeanour

In addition to material objects, the following may also be regarded as varieties of real evidence: **F8.47**

(a) a person's behaviour, e.g., his misconduct in court for the purposes of contempt of court;
(b) a person's physical appearance, e.g., for the purposes of identification or on the question of the existence or causation of personal injuries;
(c) a person's demeanour or attitude which, in the case of a witness, may be relevant to his credit, the weight to be attached to his evidence, or whether he is to be treated as hostile.

Documents as Real Evidence

Documents on the contents of which a party seeks to rely, whether as evidence of their truth,   **F8.48**
under an exception to the hearsay rule, or as original evidence, are subject to the rules as to
proof of contents and due execution, dealt with at **F8.2** to **F8.44**. These rules, however, have
no application if:

(a) the contents are referred to merely for the purposes of identifying the document in question or establishing the bare fact of its existence (*Boyle v Wiseman* (1855) 11 Exch 360, at pp. 367 *et seq.*); or
(b) the document is tendered as a material object, regardless of its contents, in order to show, e.g., its appearance, that it bears certain fingerprints, that it is made of a particular substance, or that it is in a particular physical condition.

In such cases, a document may be treated as a tangible object to the extent relevant to do so, and
becomes a piece of real evidence.

Statements Produced by Computers and Mechanical Devices

Where a computer or mechanical or other device is used as a calculator, i.e. as a tool which does   **F8.49**
not contribute its own knowledge, but merely performs a sophisticated calculation which could
have been done manually, the printout or other reading is not hearsay but an item of real evidence, the proof and relevance of which depends on the evidence of those using the device, such
as the computer programmer and other experts involved: see **F15.26**. See also the CJA 2003,
s. 129, regarding the admission of representations of fact made otherwise than by a person (see
F15.27).

There is a rebuttable presumption as to the correct functioning of mechanical and other instruments (see **F3.60**). However, in the case of computer printouts, before the judge can decide
whether they are admissible as real evidence or as hearsay pursuant to statute, it is necessary for
appropriate authoritative evidence to be called to describe the function and operation of the
computer (*Cochrane* [1993] Crim LR 48).

Views

The term 'view' is used to describe both an inspection out of court of some material object   **F8.50**
which it is inconvenient or impossible to bring to court (see, e.g., *London General Omnibus Co.
Ltd v Lavell* [1901] 1 Ch 135 (an omnibus)), and an inspection of the *locus in quo*.

A view should not take place after the summing-up: see *Lawrence* [1968] 1 All ER 579, which
was distinguished in *Nixon* [1968] 2 All ER 33, where the inspection was at the express request
of the defence. A view should be attended by the judge, the tribunal of fact, the parties, their
counsel, and the shorthand writer. In the case of magistrates, as a general rule a visit to the *locus
in quo* should take place before the conclusion of the evidence and in the presence of the parties
or their representatives, so as to afford them the opportunity of commenting on any feature of
the locality which has altered since the time of the incident or any feature not previously noticed
by the parties which impresses the magistrates (*Parry v Boyle* (1987) 83 Cr App R 310). The
presence of the accused is important because he may be able to point out some important matter

of which his legal adviser is ignorant or about which the magistrates are making a mistake (*Ely Justices, ex parte Burgess* [1992] Crim LR 888). See also *Gibbons v DPP* (12 December 2000 unreported).

F8.51   In a trial by jury, the judge should be present at a view, whether or not any witness is present for the purposes of a demonstration (*Hunter* [1985] 2 All ER 173). However, if the judge is absent, a conviction will not necessarily be quashed. In *Turay* [2007] EWCA Crim 2821, where the judge, counsel and the accused were not present at the view (at which no evidence was given), the appeal against conviction was dismissed, the appellant being unable to point to any significant or actual disadvantage to the defence or any damage to the trial process itself. A judge attending a view should take precautions to prevent any witnesses who are present from communicating, except by way of demonstration, with the jury (*Martin* (1872) LR 1 CCR 378; *Karamat v The Queen* [1956] AC 256). A witness who has already given evidence at the trial may take part in a view; but witnesses taking part in a view should be recalled to be cross-examined, if desired (*Karamat v The Queen*).

It is improper for one juror to attend a view and report back to the others. In *Gurney* [1976] Crim LR 567 the Court of Appeal held that this contravened the principle that the jury should remain together at all times, and quashed the conviction. If the accused declines to attend a view, he cannot afterwards raise the objection that his absence of itself made the view illegal, though he could object if any evidence were given outside the scope of the view as ordered (*Karamat v The Queen*).

It is critical, before any court embarks upon a view, that there is clarity about precisely what is to happen, who is to stand in what position, what (if any) objects should be placed in what position, and who will do what. None of this should happen at the scene of the view, which should be conducted without discussion (*M v DPP* [2009] 2 Cr App R 181).

Lip-reading

F8.52   An expert lip-reader who, after viewing a CCTV recording of someone speaking, gives opinion evidence as to what was said, is providing assistance to the jury in their interpretation of a variety of real evidence. Such evidence is capable of passing the ordinary tests of relevance and reliability and is therefore potentially admissible. However, it requires a special warning from the judge as to its limitations and the concomitant risk of error, not least because the expert may not be completely accurate (*Luttrell* [2004] 2 Cr App R 520).

Tape Recordings and Transcripts

F8.53   The contents of tape recordings, produced and played over in court, may be admitted as:

(a) evidence of their truth, under an exception to the hearsay rule (see, e.g., *Senat* (1968) 52 Cr App R 282: tape recordings of incriminating conversations obtained by telephone tapping; and *Maqsud Ali* [1966] 1 QB 688); or

(b) a variety of original evidence, e.g., simply to show that the recording was made.

In either event, the voices recorded must be properly identified (*Maqsud Ali*, at p. 701). At common law, it was held that there is no objection to a properly proved transcript of the recording being put before the jury, provided they are guided by what they *hear* (*Maqsud Ali*, at p. 702). See also *Rampling* [1987] Crim LR 823: the transcript, *not in itself evidence*, may be used as a convenience to the jury. However, a tape recording is a 'document' for the purposes of the CJA 2003, s. 133 (CJA 2003, s. 134(1)). Thus, where a statement contained in a tape is admissible as evidence, it may be proved by production of the tape; or (whether or not the original is still in existence) by the production of a copy of the tape, or of the material part of it, authenticated in whatever way the court may approve; and it is immaterial how many removes there are between a copy and the original. A copy, for these purposes, includes a transcript of the sounds embodied in the tape (CJA 2003, s. 134(1)). As to 'authentication', it is submitted that the courts are likely to require the same kind of proof that was necessary in the case of copies at common law before s. 133 came into force, namely a proper explanation as to why the originals are not available, and proof of the complete accuracy of the copies (*Robson* (June 1973 unreported)).

In the case of tape recordings and transcripts of police interviews, s. 133 must be read in conjunction with the Code of Practice on Tape Recording (PACE Code E), together with CPD V, paras. 27C.1 to 27C.16 (see Supplement, **PD-40**). The provisions of PACE Code E must be followed in all areas where interviews with suspects are required to be recorded by virtue of the provisions of an order made under s. 60(1)(b) of the PACE 1984. Under s. 67(11) of the 1984 Act, Code E is admissible in evidence, and if any provision thereof appears to the court to be relevant to any question arising in the proceedings, it shall be taken into account in determining that question.

The Common-law Authorities Section 133 of the CJA 2003 must also be read, it is submit- **F8.54** ted, in conjunction with the common-law authorities before it came into force. At common law, if the prosecution seek to adduce a tape recording in evidence, the judge must be satisfied, in the absence of the jury, that the prosecution have made out a prima facie case of originality and authenticity, by evidence which defines and describes the provenance and history of the tape up to the moment of its production in court. If such evidence appears to remain intact after cross-examination, it is not incumbent on the judge to hear and weigh other evidence which might controvert the prima facie case. The judge is required to be satisfied to the civil standard, on a balance of probabilities, because application of the criminal standard would amount to an usurpation by the judge of the function of the jury (*Robson* [1972] 2 All ER 699, per Shaw J, a ruling upheld by the Court of Appeal (unreported); cf. *Stevenson* [1971] 1 All ER 678). A better approach, it is submitted, also involving no usurpation of the jury function, would be for the judge to decide the issue as if the party seeking to adduce the evidence bore an evidential burden. The question for the judge would then be whether sufficient evidence had been adduced to justify, as a possibility, a finding by the jury, on the issues of originality and genuineness, favourable to the party seeking to admit the tape.

In *Rampling* [1987] Crim LR 823, the Court of Appeal gave the following general guidance **F8.55** upon the use in trials of tape recordings and transcripts of police interviews:

(a) The tape can be produced and proved by the interviewing officer or any other officer present when it was taken.
(b) The officer should have listened to the tape before the trial so that he can, if required, deal with any objections to its authenticity or accuracy.
(c) As to authenticity, he can, if required, prove who spoke the recorded words.
(d) As to accuracy, he can deal with any challenge, e.g., that the recording has been falsified by addition or omission.
(e) The transcript of the recording can be produced by the officer, who, before the trial, should have checked it against the recording for accuracy. The tape recording is the evidence in the case and can be made an exhibit; the transcript, not in itself evidence, may be used as a convenience to the jury (but see now the CJA 2003, s. 133).
(f) Use of the transcript is an administrative matter to be decided in his discretion by the trial judge. In many cases the accused will agree to its use and will not require the tape to be played at all, in which case the transcript will be read out by the officer who produced it; however, the accused is entitled, if he so wishes, to have any part of the tape played to the jury.
(g) If any part of the tape is played, it is for the judge to decide whether the jury should have the transcript, in order to follow the tape, and have it with them when they retire; the use of the transcript is within the judge's discretion and is not dependent on the consent of the parties; a transcript is usually of very considerable value to the jury, but each case has to be decided on its own facts.

F8.56 **Jury's Access to Tape** Where the tape becomes an exhibit (see (e) above), the jury may take it with them when they retire like any other exhibit in the case, and it makes no difference if the tape has already been heard in open court. In most cases, nothing turns on the tone of voice in which an interview was conducted and therefore it will usually be sufficient for the jury to have a transcript, much of which can and should be summarised; but where the tone of voice is all-important, for example when it is alleged that the interviewing officer spoke in a raised voice or in a brusque and intimidating manner, then subject to editing out any inadmissible material, the jury should be given the original tape (*Emmerson* (1991) 92 Cr App R 284). The Court of Appeal, in that case, also gave the following general guidance (at p. 287):

> (1) If the whole of the tape has been played in open court there is no reason why the jury should not have the tape if either side or the jury want it as well as any transcript. It is the tape, after all, which is the evidence. But in order not to waste time the jury should always be directed to the relevant part of the tape. (2) If only part of the tape has been played in open court but the jury have a transcript of the whole tape, then there is no reason why the jury should not have the whole tape. (3) If only part of the tape has been played in open court and the jury have no transcript, then the tape should be edited so as to ensure that the jury do not have anything that has not been given in evidence. (4) We see no advantage, and some disadvantage, in a court being reassembled in order to enable the jury to re-hear a passage of the tape which they have already heard in open court. This would seem to serve no useful purpose and be productive of unnecessary inconvenience.

F8.57 If the tape is not played during the course of a trial but, after retirement, the jury ask to hear it rather than rely on the written transcript, they are entitled to hear it because the tape is the exhibit and the transcript merely a convenient method of presenting it (*Riaz* (1991) 94 Cr App R 339). However, where the prosecution opt not to play the tape but to provide the jury with an agreed transcript and agreed expert comment on it, the jury should not be allowed to conduct their own inquiry as to what is on the tape (*Hagan* [1997] 1 Cr App R 464). If the jury are entitled to hear the tape, although it is a matter of judicial discretion, the better practice is to bring the jury back into open court to hear the tape because of the difficulties which might arise if they are permitted free access to the tape, including the risk that they might hear matters inadvertently left on the tape which they should not hear (*Riaz*). Equally, however, where the jury ask to hear a tape, of which there is an agreed transcript, which does not contain inadmissible passages and which *has* already been played in court, the judge may, in his discretion, permit them to listen to it in the privacy of their retiring room (*Tonge* [1993] Crim LR 876). As to a jury request to hear a tape during or after closing speeches, but before retirement, see *Aitken* (1991) 94 Cr App R 85 at **F6.8**.

Photographs, Video Recordings and Films

F8.58 A photograph may be admitted in evidence to enable a witness to identify a person or thing. In *Tolson* (1864) 4 F & F 103, a case of bigamy, a photograph was produced, which was admitted to be a photograph of the first husband, and a witness was allowed to testify that he had seen the man in the photograph alive after the date of the allegedly bigamous marriage.

A photograph (or film) the relevance of which can be established by the testimony of someone with personal knowledge of the circumstances in which it was taken (or made), may also be admitted to prove the commission of an offence and the identity of the offender. In *Dodson* [1984] 1 WLR 971, it was held that photographs taken at half-second intervals by security cameras installed at a building society office at which an armed robbery had been attempted, were admissible, on the issue of whether an offence had been committed and, if so, who had committed it, even though no witnesses were called to identify the men in the photographs. However, in a case in which the jury is invited to 'identify' the accused in court from a photograph or video recording of the offender committing the offence, they should be warned of the risk of mistaken identity and of the need to exercise particular care in any identification which they make. They must take into account whether the appearance of the accused has changed since the visual recording was made, but a full *Turnbull* direction (*Turnbull* [1977] QB 224: see **F18.9**) is inappropriate because the process of identifying a person from a photograph is a commonplace event and some things are obvious from the photograph itself. Thus they do not need to be told that the photograph is of good quality or poor, nor whether the person is shown in close-up or was distant from the camera etc. (*Blenkinsop* [1995] 1 Cr App R 7, approving *Downey* [1995] 1 Cr App R 547; cf. *Taylor v Chief Constable of Cheshire* [1986] 1 All ER 225, below). However, it seems that a request by them that the accused stand up and turn around, in order that they may be given a better view of him, does not have to be met, at least not by an accused who has elected not to testify (*McNamara* [1996] Crim LR 750).

F8.59 In *Roberts* [1998] Crim LR 682, a police constable made a written statement relating to charges of assault and affray. A video camera had recorded the events in question and the constable later provided a commentary on the video to enable prosecuting counsel to explain to the jury, when viewing it, who was who and where the events took place. The video was then made available to the defence. It was held that it was not wrong in principle that the constable had seen the video. On seeing a video a witness might find that in some respects his recollection had been at fault and might wish to modify earlier evidence. However, nothing should be done which amounted to rehearsing the evidence of a witness or coaching him so as to encourage him to alter the evidence already given. The acid test was whether the procedure adopted was such as to taint the resulting evidence. That was not so in the instant case. The video had been made available to the defence and had been shown to defence witnesses before they gave their evidence, and the constable had been directly challenged on discrepancies between his first statement and his commentary.

F8.60 In *Thomas* [1986] Crim LR 682, a case of reckless driving, a video recording of the route taken by the accused was admitted to remove the need for maps and still photographs, and to convey a more accurate picture of the roads in question. In *The Statue of Liberty* [1968] 2 All ER 195, a civil action concerning a collision between two ships, Sir Jocelyn Simon P, rejecting a submission that a cinematograph film of radar echoes, recorded by a shore radar station, was inadmissible because produced mechanically without human intervention, said (at p. 740): 'If tape recordings are admissible, it seems that a photograph of radar reception is equally admissible — or indeed, any other type of photograph. It would be an absurd distinction that a photograph should be admissible if the camera were operated manually by a photographer, but not if it were operated by a trip or clock mechanism.' Compare *Wood* (1982) 76 Cr App R 23, at **F15.27**.

F8.61 **Admissibility as Hearsay or Real Evidence** Photographs and films are excluded from the definition of a 'statement' for the purposes of the provisions relating to hearsay in the CJA 2003 (see s. 115(2) at **F15.2**) but both would appear to be admissible at common law as a variety of real evidence (see *The Statue of Liberty* [1968] 2 All ER 195, where a film, in effect, contained a statement as to the paths taken by the two ships). Moreover, it has been said that a photograph, together with the sketch and the photofit, is in a class of evidence of its own, to which neither the rule against hearsay nor the rule against previous consistent or self-serving statements applies (*Cook* [1987] QB 417 per Watkins LJ; applied in *Constantinou* (1989) 91 Cr App R 74). However, representations made in a sketch or photofit are covered by the definition of 'statement' in the CJA 2003, s. 115(2). As to evidence of previous identification of the accused by police photographs, see further at **F18**.

F8.62 **Proof of Contents** The contents of photographs and films on which a party seeks to rely may be proved by production of the original; or by production of a copy proved to be an authentic copy; or by the parol evidence of witnesses who have seen the photograph or film. In *Kajala v Noble* (1982) 75 Cr App R 149 Ackner LJ held that the rule, that if an original document is available in a party's hands he must produce it and cannot give secondary evidence of it, was confined to written documents in the strict sense of the term and has no relevance to tapes or films. In *Taylor v Chief Constable of Cheshire* [1986] 1 All ER 225, a video cassette recording, made by a security camera and showing a person in a shop picking up an item and putting it into his jacket, was played to police officers who identified the person as Taylor. The recording, after it had been returned to the shop, was accidentally erased. Evidence by the officers of what they had seen on the video was held to have been properly admitted, on the ground that what they had seen on the video was no different in principle from the evidence of a bystander who had actually witnessed the incident, and the appeal against conviction was dismissed. The Court of Appeal held that the weight and reliability of the evidence had to be assessed carefully and, because identification was in issue, by reference to the guidelines laid down in *Turnbull* [1977] QB 224, which had to be applied in relation to not only the camera, but also the visual display unit or recorded copy and the officers. See also *Constantinou* (1989) 91 Cr App R 74.

F8.63 **Jury Access**   Where a video or film has been shown in court and the jury, after retirement, ask to see it again, they may do so, but it is better if they see it again in open court (*Imran* [1997] Crim LR 754, in which the jury had seen a silent video of an attempted robbery). Cf. *Rawlings* [1995] 1 All ER 580 (video recordings of children's evidence), which is considered at **D14.35**.

F8.64 **PACE Code on Video-recording Interviews**   For the procedures to be followed on video-recording interviews with suspects, see PACE Code F.

Section F9   Public Policy and Privilege

EXCLUSION ON GROUNDS OF PUBLIC POLICY

This section concerns the principles of law governing the non-disclosure of material on the **F9.1**
grounds of public policy and the exclusion of such material from evidence. As to the procedure
on disclosure generally, see **D9**; as to the specific procedure to be followed on an application to
the court that unused material should not be disclosed on such grounds, see **D9.50** *et seq*. Part I
of the CPIA 1996 generally disapplies the common-law rules relating to the prosecution duty
of disclosure, but s. 21(2) of that Act preserves the rules of common law as to whether disclosure
is in the public interest.

General Principles

It is in the public interest to withhold material, the disclosure of which would harm the nation or **F9.2**
the proper functioning of the public service. It is also in the public interest that justice should be
done, and should be publicly seen to be done, by the reception of all relevant evidence. If there is
a conflict between these two interests, whether otherwise admissible evidence should be withheld
in the public interest is a question of balance, to be decided by the courts and not by the executive
(*Conway v Rimmer* [1968] AC 910). If the evidence is excluded, it is said to be withheld by reason
of public interest immunity: see *Lewes Justices, ex parte Secretary of State for the Home Department*
[1973] AC 388, per Lord Reid at p. 400, disapproving use of the expression 'Crown privilege';
but contrast *Science Research Council v Nasse* [1980] AC 1028, per Lord Scarman at p. 1087.
There is no absolute bar to a claim for public interest immunity where the claim, if successful,
would prevent the disclosure of evidence of serious criminal misconduct by officials of the State,
even in the case of torture or cruel, inhuman or degrading treatment, or other war crimes (*R
(Mohamed) v Secretary of State for Foreign and Commonwealth Affairs* [2009] 1 WLR 2653).

In some cases, the relevant minister (or head of department) or the A-G may intervene to claim
immunity. Alternatively, the claim to immunity may be made by the party seeking to withhold
the evidence, either on its own initiative or at the request of the relevant government department (see, e.g., *Burmah Oil Co. Ltd v Bank of England* [1980] AC 1090). If necessary, the judge
himself should raise the issue, because if there is a public interest to be protected, that should
be done regardless of party advantage (*Duncan v Cammell Laird & Co. Ltd* [1942] AC 624, per
Viscount Simon LC at p. 642).

A claim to public interest immunity may be supported by affidavit evidence from the relevant **F9.3**
minister (or head of department), or by a certificate signed by the minister. However, a minister's affidavit or certificate is not final (except, it seems, in cases concerning national security: see *Balfour v Foreign and Commonwealth Office* [1994] 2 All ER 588, considered at **F9.11**).
Although an objection by the Crown to the disclosure of material is entitled to the greatest
weight, the court may ask for clarification or amplification of the objection, and has the power
to inspect documentary evidence privately and to order its production notwithstanding ministerial objection (*Conway v Rimmer* [1968] AC 910). In *Conway v Rimmer*, it was suggested
that certain classes of documents, such as Cabinet papers and Foreign Office despatches, should
never be disclosed, whatever their contents may be (see per Lords Reid and Upjohn at pp. 952
and 993 respectively). Since then, however, the House of Lords has made it clear that the courts

F

Part F: Evidence

should be prepared to evaluate 'class' claims, even in the case of high-level government papers, and in appropriate circumstances, albeit very rarely, to require their disclosure (*Burmah Oil Co. Ltd v Bank of England* [1980] AC 1090, per Lord Keith at p. 1134; *Air Canada v Secretary of State for Trade (No. 2)* [1983] 2 AC 394, per Lord Fraser at p. 432).

F9.4 In December 1996 the Lord Chancellor issued a statement that the division into class and contents claims would no longer be applied, and that in future ministers would focus directly on the damage that disclosure of sensitive documents would cause. Under this approach, ministers claim immunity only when they believe that disclosure of a document will cause real damage or harm to the public interest. Damage will normally have to be in the form of a direct or immediate threat to the safety of an individual or to the nation's economic interests or relations with a foreign state, although in some cases the anticipated damage might be indirect or longer term, such as damage to a regulatory process. In any event the nature of the harm will have to be clearly explained, and ministers will no longer be able to claim immunity for internal advice or national security material merely by pointing to the general nature of the document. It is submitted that non-governmental bodies claiming public interest immunity, although not bound by the Lord Chancellor's statement, should adopt the same approach.

F9.5 Decisions as to what should be withheld from disclosure are for the court and should not be made (without reference to the court) by the prosecution, the police, the DPP or counsel (*Ward* [1993] 2 All ER 577 and, in the case of co-accused, *Adams* [1997] Crim LR 292). The principles are the same whether the proceedings are summary or on indictment, but when, in the case of an either way offence, it is known that a contested issue as to the disclosure of sensitive material is likely to arise, that consideration may sometimes properly found an application by the Crown for trial on indictment (*Bromley Magistrates' Court, ex parte Smith* [1995] 4 All ER 146, distinguishing *DPP, ex parte Warby* [1994] Crim LR 281). The rule established in *Ward* is now reflected in the relevant disclosure provisions of the CPIA 1996. These procedural rules, including the *ex parte* procedure for certain public interest immunity applications and the rules relating to the appointment of a 'special advocate' or 'special counsel', are considered at **D9.50 et seq**. As to immunity claims in summary trials, see also **D9.64**. If, in the course of a public interest immunity hearing (whether on the *voir dire* or otherwise) prosecution witnesses lied to the judge, the prosecution would be likely to be tainted beyond redemption, however strong the evidence against the accused might otherwise be (*Early* [2003] 1 Cr App R 288).

F9.6 In *Keane* [1994] 2 All ER 478 Lord Taylor CJ held that it is for the prosecution to put before the court only those documents which it regards as material but wishes to withhold. It is generally for the prosecution, not the court, to identify the documents and information which are material. However, if, in an exceptional case, the prosecution are in doubt about the materiality of some documents or information, the court may be asked to rule on that issue. When the court is seized of the material, the judge should perform the balancing exercise, balancing the weight of the public interest in non-disclosure against the importance of the documents to the issues of interest to the defence, present and potential, so far as they have been disclosed to him or he can foresee them. However a ruling made prior to the hearing is not necessarily final, because issues may later emerge whereby the public interest in non-disclosure is eclipsed by the accused's need for access (*Bower* [1994] Crim LR 281). The trial judge is under a continuous duty, in the light of the way in which the trial develops, to keep his initial decision under review, and prosecuting counsel must inform himself fully as to the content of any disputed material so as to be in a position to invite the judge to reassess the situation if the previous denial of the material arguably becomes untenable in the light of developments in the trial (*Brown* [1994] 1 WLR 1599 at p. 1608). See also **D9.24**.

F9.7 **Voluntary Disclosure** The CPS may voluntarily disclose to the defence documents which would otherwise be in a class covered by public interest immunity, without referring the matter to the court for a ruling, subject to the safeguard of first seeking the express written approval of the Treasury Solicitor. The CPS should submit to him copies of the documents in question, identify the public interest immunity class into which they fall and indicate the materiality of the documents to the proceedings in which it is proposed to disclose them. The Treasury Solicitor should consult any other relevant government department and satisfy himself that the balance falls clearly in favour of disclosure. He should be more ready to disclose documents likely to assist the defence than those which the CPS wish to disclose with a view to further-ing the interests of the prosecution. Before approving disclosure of documents of a particular class sought to be used by the prosecution, he should consider not only their importance to the prosecution's case, but also the importance of the prosecution itself: it may be preferable to abandon the case rather than damage the integrity of the class claim. He should also maintain a permanent record of all approvals given so that any court ruling on disclosure would know how far immunity for that particular class of documents had been weakened by previous voluntary disclosure (*Horseferry Road Magistrates, ex parte Bennett (No. 2)* [1994] 1 All ER 289).

The Balancing Exercise　　The principle of public interest immunity is applicable to criminal **F9.8** proceedings, but involves a different balancing exercise to that in civil proceedings. The judge will balance the desirability of preserving the public interest in non-disclosure against the inter-ests of justice. Where the interests of justice arise in a criminal case touching and concerning liberty (or conceivably, on occasion, life), the weight to be attached to the interests of justice is plainly very great; it is a matter of whether the interests of justice outweigh the considerations of public interest as spoken to in the certificate of the minister. Any prior disclosure of the informa-tion in question is a matter to be taken into account in the balance. In assessing the interests of justice, the court must ask whether a document to which the certificate relates is material to the proceedings. Its materiality will depend on the purpose for which it is sought to be deployed. In cases concerning the identity of informers or persons who have allowed their premises to be used for police surveillance (see **F9.17**), there have been observations to the effect that the privilege cannot prevail if the evidence is necessary for the prevention of a miscarriage of justice — no bal-ance is called for (*Governor of Brixton Prison, ex parte Osman* [1991] 1 All ER 108). But see also, in cases concerning the identity of informers, *Keane* [1994] 2 All ER 478, per Lord Taylor CJ (at pp. 751–2):

> We prefer to say that the outcome in the instances given by Lord Esher MR [in *Marks v Beyfus* (1890) 25 QBD 494: see **F9.9**] and Mann LJ [in *Ex parte Osman*] results from performing the balancing exercise, not from dispensing with it. If the disputed material may prove the defendant's innocence or avoid a miscarriage of justice, then the balance comes down resoundingly in favour of disclosing it.

In *Clowes* [1992] 3 All ER 440, the accused were charged with theft and fraud following the **F9.9** collapse of two deposit-taking companies owing investors over £115 million. Public interest immunity was claimed in respect of transcripts of confidential interviews conducted by the liquidators of the company in order to establish whether civil claims could be brought. Phillips J held that he did not find very easy the concept of a balancing exercise between the nature of the public interest on the one hand and the degree and potential consequences of the risk of a mis-carriage of justice on the other, but would not readily accept that proportionality between the two is never of relevance. On the facts, it did not seem that the public interest in question should carry greater weight than the public interest in concealing the identity of a police informer (see **F9.14**). Those interviewed inevitably accepted some risk of dissemination of the information they gave and there would be a relatively limited effect on 'the wells of voluntary information'. On the other hand, the accused were charged with grave offences and it was therefore of particu-lar importance that no unnecessary impediment should be put in the way of presenting their defence in the best light. Another significant factor was the complexity of the evidence and the risk of lapse of memory on the part of witnesses.

The Heads of Public Interest Immunity

The heads of public interest immunity which have been recognised by the courts relate to **F9.10** national security, diplomatic relations, international comity, the proper functioning of the public service, informers and information for the detection of crime, judges, jurors and sources of information contained in publications. Each is considered in the following paragraphs.

National Security, Diplomatic Relations and International Comity

F9.11   Documents falling within this category are those most readily protected against disclosure; in the case of national security, it seems that a ministerial certificate will be conclusive (*Balfour v Foreign and Commonwealth Office* [1994] 2 All ER 588). That case concerned material relating to the security and intelligence services. It was held that once there is an actual or potential risk to national security demonstrated by an appropriate ministerial certificate, the court should not exercise its right to inspect. See also *Hennessy v Wright* (1888) 21 QBD 509 (communications between the governor of a colony and the colonial secretary); *Chatterton v Secretary of State for India in Council* [1895] 2 QB 189 (communications between the government and the commander-in-chief of forces overseas); *Asiatic Petroleum Co. Ltd v Anglo Persian Oil Co. Ltd* [1916] 1 KB 822 (information relating to the Persian campaign in the First World War); *M. Isaacs & Sons Ltd v Cook* [1925] 2 KB 391 (diplomatic despatches); *Duncan v Cammell Laird & Co. Ltd* [1942] AC 624 (information on the design of a new submarine); and *Buttes Gas and Oil Co. v Hammer* (*No. 3*) [1981] QB 223 (confidential communications with foreign sovereign states or concerning their interest in international territorial disputes).

Proper Functioning of Public Service

F9.12   Public interest immunity may be claimed for communications to and from ministers and high-level government officials, regarding the formulation of government policy: see, e.g., *Burmah Oil Co. Ltd v Bank of England* [1980] AC 1090 (memoranda of meetings attended by ministers or government officials relating to government policy on economic matters); and *Air Canada v Secretary of State for Trade (No. 2)* [1983] 2 AC 394 (ministerial papers and inter-departmental communications between senior civil servants concerning government policy in relation to the British Airports Authority).

The public also has an interest in the effective working of non-governmental bodies and agencies performing public functions. However, although the categories of public interest are not closed, the courts can only proceed by analogy with interests which have previously been recognised by the authorities: see *D v National Society for the Prevention of Cruelty to Children* [1978] AC 171, per Lords Diplock, Hailsham and Simon at pp. 219, 226 and 240 respectively, applied in *Science Research Council v Nasse* [1980] AC 1028 (in which the House rejected a claim in respect of confidential reports on employees seeking promotion). Examples include *Re D (Infants)* [1970] 1 All ER 1086 (local authorities); *Lewes Justices, ex parte Secretary of State for the Home Department* [1973] AC 388 (the Gaming Board); *D v National Society for the Prevention of Cruelty to Children* [1978] AC 171 (the NSPCC); and *Buckley v Law Society (No. 2)* [1984] 3 All ER 313 (the Law Society).

Police Communications

F9.13   Public interest immunity also attaches to police communications relating to the investigation of crime, such as documents or information upon the strength of which search warrants have been obtained (*Taylor v Anderton* (1986) *The Times*, 21 October 1986). Reports sent by the police to the DPP, even if the prosecution has been completed, have also attracted immunity, on the ground that there should be freedom of communication with the DPP, without fear that such reports may be inspected, analysed or investigated in subsequent civil proceedings (*Evans v Chief Constable of Surrey* [1988] QB 588). Immunity also attaches to international communications between police forces or prosecuting authorities (*Horseferry Road Magistrates' Court, ex parte Bennett (No. 2)* [1994] 1 All ER 289), although in that case the balance favoured disclosure, the documents being relevant to the issue of whether B had been unlawfully returned to the jurisdiction. In appropriate circumstances, immunity may also be claimed for internal police communications other than those relating to the investigation of crime, on the ground that the public has an interest in the proper functioning of the police force (*Conway v Rimmer* [1968] AC 910).

Immunity may also be claimed for police complaints and disciplinary files (*Halford v Sharples* [1992] 3 All ER 624). There is no immunity, however, for written complaints against the police prompting investigations under part IX of the PACE 1984 (*Conerney v Jacklin* [1985] Crim LR 234); and there is no class immunity for statements obtained for the purposes of such investigations, although immunity may be claimed in the case of a particular document by reason of its contents (*Chief Constable of the West Midlands Police, ex parte Wiley* [1995] 1 AC 274, overruling *Neilson v Laugharne* [1981] QB 736 and cases in which it was subsequently applied). However, the working papers and reports prepared by the investigating officers do form a class which is entitled to immunity, and therefore production of such material should be ordered only where the public interest in disclosure of their contents outweighs the public interest in preserving confidentiality (*Taylor v Anderton* [1995] 2 All ER 420).

Public interest immunity does not attach to statements made during the course of a police grievance procedure, initiated by an officer, alleging either racial or sexual discrimination (*Commissioner of Police of the Metropolis v Locker* [1993] 3 All ER 584).

Informers and Information for Detection of Crime

There is a long-established rule of law that in public prosecutions witnesses may not be asked, **F9.14** and should not be allowed to disclose, the names of informers or the nature of the information given (*Hardy* (1794) 24 St Tr 199). In principle, the rule should prevent disclosure of not only the name of the informer, but also any information that will enable him to be identified (*Omar* 2007 ONCA 117 (Court of Appeal for Ontario)). The rule applies to public prosecutions brought by the DPP and bodies authorised by statute to bring public prosecutions. It also applies to police prosecutions, but not to other private prosecutions. The rationale of the rule was explained by Lawton LJ in *Hennessey* (1978) 68 Cr App R 419 (at p. 425): 'The courts appreciate the need to protect the identity of informers, not only for their own safety but to ensure that the supply of information about criminal activities does not dry up.' See also *D v National Society for the Prevention of Cruelty to Children* [1978] AC 171, per Lord Diplock at p. 218. The judge is obliged to apply the rule even if it is not invoked by the party entitled to object to disclosure (*Marks v Beyfus* (1890) 25 QBD 494, per Lord Esher MR at p. 500; *Rankine* [1986] QB 861, per Mann J at p. 867).

However, if a witness called at trial is a participating informant in the very instance with which the trial is concerned, there has to be a very strong countervailing interest for his status not to be revealed (*Patel* [2001] EWCA Crim 2505). In that case, it was not for HM Customs to determine the matter in their own favour without putting their own counsel or the court fully in the picture. As to interception of communications, see **D1.187**.

There is an exception to the common-law rule where the judge is of the opinion that disclosure **F9.15** is necessary to establish the innocence of the accused.

> ...if upon the trial of a prisoner the judge should be of opinion that the disclosure of the name of the informant is necessary or right in order to show the prisoner's innocence, then one public policy is in conflict with another public policy, and that which says that an innocent man is not to be condemned when his innocence can be proved is the policy that must prevail. (*Marks v Beyfus* (1890) 25 QBD 494, per Lord Esher MR at p. 498)

This outcome, however, results from performing the balancing exercise, not from dispensing with it (*Keane* [1994] 2 All ER 478: see **F9.6**). Judges should scrutinise applications for disclosure of details about informants with very great care and should be astute to see whether assertions that knowledge of such details is essential to the running of a defence are justified. In some cases, the informant is an informant and no more; but even when the informant has participated in the events constituting, surrounding or following the crime, the judge must consider whether his role so impinges on an issue of interest to the defence, present or potential, as to make disclosure necessary (*Turner* [1995] 3 All ER 432, per Lord Taylor CJ at p. 268).

It is of the highest importance to public confidence in the administration of justice that, where the interests of justice require an express or implied undertaking of confidence as to the identity of an informant to be broken, unless there is informed consent from the informant, the decision to break it is a decision of the judge. The CPS should therefore apply to the court which should reach its own decision and not simply defer to the view of the prosecutor (*R (VW)) v CPS* [2011] EWHC 2480 (Admin)).

F9.16   In *Agar* [1990] 2 All ER 442, the accused alleged that the police had arranged with an informer to ask the accused to go to the informer's house, where drugs allegedly found on him had been planted by the police. It was held that the disclosure of the identity of the informer was necessary to enable the accused to put forward the tenable defence that he had been set up by the police and the informer acting in concert. Therefore, counsel for the accused should have been permitted to cross-examine police witnesses to elicit the fact that the informer had told the police that the accused was coming to his house. (Compare *Slowcombe* [1991] Crim LR 198, where disclosure of the identity of an informer would have contributed little or nothing to the issue which the jury had to consider, and *Menga* [1998] Crim LR 58.) *Agar* was applied in *Langford* [1990] Crim LR 653. See also *Vaillencourt* [1993] Crim LR 311, *Reilly* [1994] Crim LR 279 and *Baker* [1996] Crim LR 55. It is for the accused to show that there is good reason to expect that disclosure is necessary to show his innocence (*Hennessy* (1978) 68 Cr App R 419, per Lawton LJ, and *Hallett* [1986] Crim LR 462). In *Hennessy*, Lawton LJ said (at p. 426): 'This should normally be done, not in the course of a trial, but in any proceedings which may be started to set aside a subpoena or a witness summons served upon a Crown witness who is alleged to be in possession of, or to have control over, tape recordings, transcripts of such recordings and the like'.

F9.17   **Disclosure Relating to Premises**   The rule also protects the identity of persons who have allowed their premises to be used for police surveillance, and the identity of their premises (*Rankine* [1986] QB 861). If the accused submits that disclosure of the identification of the premises is necessary in order to show his innocence, the judge may nonetheless exclude the evidence, provided that the prosecution have provided a proper evidential basis for such exclusion. In *Johnson* [1988] 1 All ER 121, Watkins LJ gave the following guidance as to the minimum evidential requirements in this regard (at pp. 1385–6):

(a) The police officer in charge of the observations to be conducted, no one of lower rank than a sergeant should usually be acceptable for this purpose, must be able to testify that beforehand he visited all observation places to be used and ascertained the attitude of occupiers of premises, not only to the use to be made of them, but to the possible disclosure thereafter of the use made and facts which could lead to the identification of the premises thereafter and of the occupiers. He may of course in addition inform the court of difficulties, if any, usually encountered in the particular locality of obtaining assistance from the public.

(b) A police officer of no lower rank than a chief inspector must be able to testify that immediately prior to the trial he visited the places used for observations, the results of which it is proposed to give in evidence, and ascertained whether the occupiers are the same as when the observations took place and whether they are or are not, what the attitude of those occupiers is to the possible disclosure of the use previously made of the premises and of facts which could lead at the trial to identification of premises and occupiers.

Such evidence will of course be given in the absence of the jury when the application to exclude the material evidence is made. The judge should explain to the jury, as this judge did, when summing up or at some appropriate time before that, the effect of his ruling to exclude, if he so rules.

F9.18   In *Johnson*, the appellant was convicted of supplying drugs. The only evidence against him was given by police officers, who testified that, while stationed in private premises in a known drug-dealing locality, they had observed him selling drugs. The defence applied to cross-examine the officers on the exact location of the observation posts, in order to test what they could see, having regard to the layout of the street and the objects in it. In the jury's absence the prosecution called evidence as to the difficulty of obtaining assistance from the public, and the desire of the occupiers, who were also occupiers at the time of the offence, that their names and addresses should not be disclosed because they feared for their safety. The judge ruled that the exact location of the premises need not be revealed. The appeal was dismissed: although the conduct of the defence was to some extent affected by the restraints placed on it, this led to no injustice. The jury were well aware of the restraints, and were most carefully directed about the very special care they had to give to any disadvantage they may have brought to the defence. *Johnson* was applied and approved in *Hewitt* (1992) 95 Cr App R 81. See also *Grimes* [1994] Crim LR 213. The guidelines in *Johnson* do not require a threat of violence before protection can be afforded to the occupier of an observation post; it suffices if the occupier is in fear of harassment (*Blake v DPP* (1993) 97 Cr App R 169).

The extension of the rule established in *Rankine* [1986] QB 861 is based on the protection of **F9.19** the owner or occupier of the premises, and not on the identity, *simpliciter*, of the observation post. Thus, where officers have witnessed the commission of an offence as part of a surveillance operation conducted from an unmarked police vehicle, information relating to the surveillance and the colour, make and model of the vehicle should not be withheld (*Brown* (1987) 87 Cr App R 52). However, Hodgson J said (at p. 59):

> We do not rule out the possibility that with the advent of no doubt sophisticated methods of criminal investigation, there may be cases where the public interest immunity may be successfully invoked in criminal proceedings to justify the exclusion of evidence as to police techniques and methods.

Informer's Wish to Disclose Name   A further exception to the common-law rule against **F9.20** disclosure of the name of an informer was established in *Savage v Chief Constable of Hampshire* [1997] 2 All ER 631, in which it was held that a police informer who wishes personally to sacrifice his own anonymity will not be precluded from doing so by a claim of immunity, because in such circumstances the primary justification for the claim (that disclosure would endanger the safety of the informer) disappears. The wishes of the informer, however, are not conclusive, and in appropriate cases may be outweighed by other considerations, as when discovery may assist others involved in crime, hamper police operations, or indicate the state of police inquiries into a particular crime.

Informer Called as a Witness   In *Patel* [2001] EWCA Crim 2505, the Court of Appeal stated **F9.21** that if a witness called at trial is a participating informer in the very instance in which the trial is concerned, there will have to be a very strong countervailing interest for his status not to be revealed. In this case, it was not for HM Customs to determine the matter in their own favour without putting their own counsel or the court fully in the picture. Nor, the court stated, was it for the judge to have to piece together stray pieces of information in order to decide whether an individual was or was not a participating informer.

Judges and Jurors

A judge, including a master of the Supreme Court, cannot be compelled to give evidence of **F9.22** matters of which he became aware relating to, and as a result of, the performance of his judicial functions (as opposed to extraneous matters, such as a crime committed in the face of the court). However, the judge remains competent to give evidence, and if a situation arises where his evidence is vital, the judge should be able to be relied on not to allow his non-compellability to stand in the way of his giving evidence (*Warren v Warren* [1997] QB 488, in which the authorities are reviewed).

A jury's verdict cannot be impeached by the testimony of a juror as to the deliberations of the jury in the jury room (see *Thompson* [1962] 1 All ER 65, considered at **D19.28**, *Roads* [1967] 2

QB 108 and *Lalchan Nanan v The State* [1986] AC 860; and compare *Newton* (1912) 7 Cr App R 214 (a foreman's disclosure in open court that the jury decided the case on an impermissible basis), *Willmont* (1914) 10 Cr App R 173 (proof of misconduct by the officer in charge of the jury or the clerk) and *Hood* [1968] 2 All ER 56 (evidence of a juror as to matters extrinsic to the manner in which the verdict was reached)). When, during the course of a trial, an irregularity relating to the jury has been drawn to the attention of the judge, the judge may question the juror involved, but the inquiry should be directed towards ascertaining whether the juror can remain faithful to the oath and not towards the deliberations of the jury (CPD VI, paras. 39M.3 and 39M.9 (see Supplement, **PD-60**); and see also *Mirza* [2004] 1 AC 1118 and *Smith and Mercieca* [2005] 2 All ER 29, considered at **D19.30** to **D19.32**). After a verdict has been returned, the responsibility for any investigation of any irregularity lies with the Court of Appeal. The Court of Appeal can hear evidence from a juror on a question of alleged jury bias, but the interviewing of a juror on such an issue requires the leave of the Court of Appeal, which will only be granted in rare and exceptional cases (*Adams* [2007] 1 Cr App R 449; and see also **D13.51**).

Sources of Information Contained in Publications

F9.23   Contempt of Court Act 1981, s. 10

> No court may require a person to disclose, nor is any person guilty of contempt of court for refusing to disclose, the source of information contained in a publication for which he is responsible, unless it be established to the satisfaction of the court that disclosure is necessary in the interests of justice or national security or for the prevention of disorder or crime.

Section 10 substitutes for the common-law discretionary protection a rule of law of wide and general application, subject only to the four exceptions specified (*Secretary of State for Defence v Guardian Newspapers Ltd* [1985] AC 339, per Lord Scarman). The section applies to information which has been communicated and received for the purposes of publication, even if it is not 'contained in a publication', because the purpose underlying the statutory protection of sources of information is as much applicable before as after publication (*X Ltd v Morgan-Grampian (Publishers) Ltd* [1991] 1 AC 1, per Lord Bridge of Harwich). It is sufficient, in order to be protected by s. 10, that an order of the court *may*, and not necessarily *will*, result in disclosure of a source of information (*Secretary of State for Defence v Guardian Newspapers Ltd* [1985] AC 339, per Lord Roskill at p. 368). It is a question of fact and not discretion whether an exception applies, and the burden of proof is on the party seeking disclosure (per Lords Diplock and Scarman, at pp. 345 and 364 respectively). Disclosure must be shown to be 'necessary': expediency, however great, will not suffice (per Lord Diplock, at p. 350; *Handmade Films (Productions) Ltd v Express Newspapers plc* [1986] FSR 463). Under s. 10 the judge must first decide whether disclosure is necessary in the interests of justice etc. If he is not so satisfied, he cannot order disclosure; but if he is so satisfied, he must decide whether as a matter of discretion he should order disclosure, which involves weighing the need for disclosure against the need for protection (*John v Express Newspapers plc* [2000] 3 All ER 257).

F9.24   Disclosure 'Necessary in the Interests of Justice'   The word 'justice' in the Contempt of Court Act 1981, s. 10, is not used as the antonym of 'injustice', but in the technical sense of the administration of justice in the course of legal proceedings in a court of law or a tribunal, or a body exercising the judicial powers of the state (*Secretary of State for Defence v Guardian Newspapers Ltd* [1985] AC 339, per Lord Diplock at p. 350). It has since been held that the word should not be so confined (see *X Ltd v Morgan-Grampian (Publishers) Ltd* [1991] 1 AC 1 at **F9.25**). However, in cases where disclosure is sought for the purposes of legal proceedings, in order to decide whether the exception applies, it is essential first to identify and define the issue in the legal proceedings which requires disclosure, and then to decide whether, looking at the nature of that issue and the circumstances of the case, disclosure is necessary (*Maxwell v Pressdram Ltd* [1987] 1 All ER 621, per Kerr LJ at pp. 308–9). The mere fact that the information in question is relevant to the issue is not sufficient: disclosure must be necessary in the interests of justice (*Maxwell v Pressdram Ltd*, per Parker LJ, at p. 310).

In *X Ltd v Morgan-Grampian (Publishers) Ltd* [1991] 1 AC 1, the House of Lords agreed with the **F9.25**
dictum of Lord Diplock in *Secretary of State for Defence v Guardian Newspapers Ltd* [1985] AC 339
that the word 'justice' is not used as the antonym of 'injustice', but held that the word should not
be confined to the technical sense of the administration of justice in the course of legal proceedings in a court of law. It is 'in the interests of justice' that persons should be enabled to exercise
important legal rights and to protect themselves from serious legal wrongs whether or not resort
to proceedings in a court of law will be necessary to obtain these objectives. This construction
emphasises the importance of the balancing exercise. It will not be sufficient, *per se*, for a party
seeking disclosure of a source to show merely that he will be unable without disclosure to exercise
the legal right or avert the threatened legal wrong. The judge must always weigh in the scales the
importance of enabling the ends of justice to be attained in the circumstances of the particular case
on the one hand against the importance of protecting the source on the other. It is only if satisfied
that disclosure in the interests of justice is of such preponderating importance as to override the
statutory privilege against disclosure that the threshold of necessity will be reached. Many factors
will be relevant. Lord Bridge of Harwich gave the following illustrations. If the party seeking disclosure shows that his very livelihood depends on it, the case will be near one end of the spectrum;
but if he merely seeks to protect a minor interest in property, the case will be at or near the other
end of the spectrum. On the other side, one important factor will be the nature of the information obtained: the greater the legitimate public interest in the information, the greater will be the
importance of protecting the source. Another perhaps more significant factor is the manner in
which the information was obtained by the source: if the information was obtained legitimately this
will enhance the importance of protecting the source. Conversely, if the information was obtained
illegally, this will diminish the importance of protecting the source unless this factor is counterbalanced by a clear public interest in publication, as when the source has acted to expose iniquity.

Goodwin v UK (1996) 22 EHRR 123, a decision of the ECtHR, dealt with the same facts as **F9.26**
those which were the subject of the decision in *X Ltd v Morgan-Grampian (Publishers) Ltd*
[1991] 1 AC 1, but under the ECHR, Article 10. The tests applied by the ECtHR and the
House of Lords were substantially the same, but the ECtHR came to a conclusion opposite to
that reached by the House of Lords. The explanation may well be that put forward by Thorpe
LJ in *Camelot Group plc v Centaur Communications Ltd* [1999] QB 124: the making of a value
judgement on competing facts is very close to the exercise of a discretion, and the period of
time between the decisions in London and Strasbourg was six years, a period during which
standards fundamental to the performance of the balancing exercise may change materially.

Effect of ECHR, Article 10   In *Ashworth Hospital Authority v MGN Ltd* [2001] 1 All ER 991, **F9.27**
which concerned the disclosure of confidential medical records to the press, the Court of Appeal
considered the proper approach to s. 10 of the Contempt of Court Act 1981 in the light of the
HRA 1998, s. 3, and the ECHR, Article 10. The court held as follows:

(a) Section 10 sets out to give effect to the general requirements of Article 10 in the narrow
    context of protection of the sources of information of the press. Article 10 permits the right
    of freedom of expression to be circumscribed where necessary in a democratic society to
    achieve a number of specified legitimate aims.
(b) The approach to the interpretation of s. 10 should, insofar as possible (i) equate the specific
    purposes for which disclosure of sources is permitted under s. 10 with 'legitimate aims'
    under Article 10 and (ii) apply the same test of necessity to that applied by the ECtHR when
    considering Article 10.
(c) The wider interpretation of the 'interests of justice' in *X Ltd v Morgan-Grampian (Publishers)
    Ltd* [1991] 1 AC 1 (see **F9.25**) accords more happily with the scheme of Article 10 than the
    interpretation of Lord Diplock in *Secretary of State for Defence v Guardian Newspapers Ltd*
    [1985] AC 339. Thus 'interests of justice' in s. 10 means interests that are justiciable. It is
    difficult to envisage any such interest that would not fall within one or more of the relevant
    'legitimate aims' under Article 10.

F

Part F Evidence

Affirming the decision, the House of Lords ([2002] 1 WLR 2033) accepted the approach of the ECtHR in *Goodwin v UK* (1996) 22 EHRR 123 that, as a matter of general principle, the 'necessity' for any restriction of freedom of expression must be convincingly established and that limits on the confidentiality of journalistic sources call for the most careful scrutiny by the court. It was further held that any restriction of the right to freedom of expression must meet two further requirements: (i) exercise of the disclosure jurisdiction because of Article 10(2) should meet a 'pressing social need' and (ii) the restriction should be proportionate to the legitimate aim which is being pursued.

F9.28   **Material Protected by Legal Professional Privilege**   It will not inevitably be in the interests of justice to order disclosure of the source of information where the nature of that information suggests that the source has seen material protected by legal professional privilege (*Saunders v Punch Ltd* [1998] 1 All ER 234). In the context of such material it has been held that, before ordering disclosure, the minimum requirement is that the person seeking disclosure has explored other means of identifying the source. It cannot be assumed that it will not be possible to find the source of the information by other means; and when weighing the conflicting public interests involved, it is to be remembered that there is no certainty that ordering a journalist to reveal his sources will be any more successful than the use of other means (*John v Express Newspapers plc* [2000] 3 All ER 257).

F9.29   **Disclosure 'Necessary for the Prevention of Crime'**   Concerning the prevention of crime, disclosure will be ordered if shown to be necessary, either for the prevention of crime generally or for the prevention of a particular and identifiable future crime. See *Re an Inquiry under the Company Securities (Insider Dealing) Act* [1988] AC 660. In this case, a journalist who had used confidential price-sensitive information about take-over bids was ordered to disclose his source to inspectors appointed by the Secretary of State to investigate suspected leaks of this kind, on the grounds that they needed the information to expose the leaking of official information and criminal insider trading, and to prevent such behaviour in the future. However, as in the case of the other exceptions, a claim under this head will succeed only if there is clear and specific evidence of 'necessity'. The party seeking disclosure should adduce evidence on matters such as the extent of his inquiries to identify the sources, whether he referred the matter to the police, and whether criminal investigation is the intended or likely outcome (*X v Y* [1988] 2 All ER 648).

CONFIDENTIAL BUT NON-PRIVILEGED RELATIONSHIPS

F9.30   At common law no privilege attaches to communications made in confidence except in the case of:

(a) communications between a client and a legal adviser made for the purpose of the obtaining and giving of legal advice; and

(b) communications between a client or his legal adviser and third parties, the dominant purpose of which was preparation for contemplated or pending litigation (see **F9.49** *et seq.*).

F9.31   Although the courts have an inherent wish to respect the confidences which arise between doctor and patient, bankers and customers etc., if the question to be put to a witness is relevant and necessary in order that justice be done, the witness will be directed to answer (see, e.g., *A-G v Mulholland* [1963] 2 QB 477, per Lord Denning MR at pp. 489–90). Thus, no privilege exists to protect medical records or communications between doctor and patient (*Duchess of Kingston* (1776) 20 St Tr 355; *Gibbons* (1823) 1 C & P 97; *Wheeler v Le Marchant* (1881) 17 Ch D 675, at p. 681; *Hunter v Mann* [1974] QB 767; *McDonald* [1991] Crim LR 122; *Gayle* [1994] Crim LR 679). This remains the case, notwithstanding that the rule is regarded as unsatisfactory and one which the Supreme Court has the power to alter (*D v National Society for the Prevention of Cruelty to Children* [1978] AC 171, per Lord Edmund-Davies at pp. 244–5). But see also *K (TD)* (1993) 97 Cr App R 342 at **F9.32**. In the case of communications between priest and penitent, there is slender authority in favour of the existence of a privilege: see *Hay* (1860) 2 F & F 4 (in which it was stressed that the priest was asked about a fact and not a communication) and the *obiter dictum* of Best CJ in *Broad v Pitt* (1828) 3 C & P 518: 'I, for one, will never compel a clergyman to disclose communications made to him by a prisoner; but if he chooses to disclose them I shall receive them in evidence'. However, most of such authority as there is, is against the existence of any such privilege (*Normanshaw v Normanshaw* (1893) 69 LT 468; *Wheeler v Le Marchant* (1881) 17 Ch D 675, at p. 681; and the authorities cited in Stephen's *Digest of the Law of Evidence* (12th edn, 1936), at p. 220). Similarly, there is no privilege for confidential communications between friends (*Duchess of Kingston's Case* (1776) 20 St Tr 355); or for documents in the possession of an accountant relating to his client's affairs (*Chantrey Martin & Co. v Martin* [1953] 2 QB 286). At common law there is no privilege for journalists who seek to conceal the identities of their sources of information (*A-G v Clough* [1963] 1 QB 773; *A-G v Mulholland* [1963] 2 QB 477). But see now the Contempt of Court Act 1981, s. 10, above. Concerning a court welfare officer's report, the appropriate court may give leave for it to be used in other proceedings if, after evaluating and balancing the need to maintain the confidentiality of the report against the need for its contents to be put in evidence for there to be a fair trial of the action, the court decides that the interests of justice require the confidentiality of the report to be released (*Brown v Matthews* [1990] Ch 662). See also *Elleray* [2003] 2 Cr App R 165: where an offender, during a conversation with a probation officer being held for the purpose of preparing a pre-sentence report, admits to having committed another offence, the prosecution should consider carefully whether it is right to rely on the evidence and should only rely on it if they decide that it is in the public interest to do so. If they do rely on the evidence, the court still has a discretion to exclude it under the PACE 1984, s. 78.

Although at common law no privilege attaches to confidential communications *per se*, in appropriate circumstances a party may be able to rely upon some other head of privilege, such as the privilege which attaches to communications made in the course of matrimonial conciliation (which has also been treated as a limb of public interest immunity: see *D v National Society for the Prevention of Cruelty to Children* [1978] AC 171, per Lords Hailsham and Simon at pp. 226 and 236–7 respectively). Alternatively, a claim to public interest immunity may succeed. Thus an interview with a child victim of a sexual offence, which is conducted on a confidential basis for therapeutic purposes, ought not to be disclosed, unless the interests of justice so require, but where the liberty of the subject is an issue and disclosure might be of assistance to an accused, a claim for disclosure will often be strong (*K (TD)* (1993) 97 Cr App R 342). Similarly immunity may be claimed for confidential documents relating to abortions carried out under the Abortion Act 1967 (*Morrow v DPP* [1994] Crim LR 58). **F9.32**

In the absence of consent to disclosure by a taxpayer, public interest immunity does attach to documents relating to his tax affairs in the hands of the Inland Revenue, because as a matter of public policy the State should not by compulsory powers obtain information from a citizen for one purpose and then use it for another; but no such immunity attaches to documents held by the taxpayer himself, or his agents, relating to his tax affairs (*Lonrho plc v Fayed (No. 4)* [1994] 1 All ER 870). A claim to public interest immunity may also succeed when the person claiming immunity is exercising a statutory function, the effective performance of which would be impaired by disclosure. See, e.g., *Lonrho Ltd v Shell Petroleum Co. Ltd* [1980] 1 WLR 627 (immunity granted in subsequent litigation for evidence given in confidence to the Bingham Inquiry into the operation of sanctions against Rhodesia) and contrast *Re Arrows Ltd (No. 4)* [1995] 2 AC 75. See also *Re Barlow Clowes Gilt Managers Ltd* [1992] Ch 208. The liquidators of a company are under no duty to assist directors of the company in defending criminal charges, by providing them with information given to the liquidators by third parties in circumstances of confidentiality and by assurances, express or implied, that it would be used only for the purpose of the liquidation. The provision of such information would jeopardise the proper and efficient functioning of the process of compulsory liquidation because of the danger that professional men would no longer co-operate with liquidators on a voluntary basis. However, **F9.33**

F

whether the information in question constitutes 'material evidence' for the purposes of a witness summons is a question for the Crown Court (see further *Clowes* [1992] 3 All ER 440 at **F9.9**). It has also been held, in *Umoh* (1986) 84 Cr App R 138, that although no privilege analogous to that between a lawyer and his client can arise to protect confidential communications about the substance of a legal aid application between a prison legal aid officer and a prisoner, such communications should attract public interest immunity, because a prisoner does not have the freedom to go to a solicitor's office, and if he seeks assistance from such an officer he is likely to disclose and discuss matters connected with the alleged offence. It is in the public interest that such discussions, save in exceptional circumstances, should remain confidential, or otherwise prisoners would be reluctant to take advantage of the scheme.

PRIVILEGED RELATIONSHIPS: GENERAL PRINCIPLES

F9.34 Relevant and otherwise admissible evidence may be excluded on the grounds of either the privilege against self-incrimination (see **F9.35** to **F9.48**) or legal professional privilege (see **F9.49** to **F9.72**).

The following principles are of general application:

(a) A person entitled to claim privilege may refuse to answer the question put or disclose the document sought. The judge should not balance the claim to privilege against the importance of the evidence in relation to the trial. But see *Rank Film Distributors Ltd v Video Information Centre* [1982] AC 380, per Lord Fraser at p. 445.
(b) If a person entitled to claim privilege fails to do so or waives his privilege, no other person may object. The privilege is that of the witness, and neither party can take advantage from it. Thus, if a judge improperly rejects a claim to privilege made by a witness who is not a party to the proceedings, no appeal will lie, for there has been no infringement of the rights of the parties. In *Kinglake* (1870) 11 Cox CC 499, where a claim to privilege made by a prosecution witness on the basis that his evidence would tend to incriminate himself was overruled by the judge, it was not open to the accused to object that the witness's evidence had been improperly admitted.
(c) A party seeking to prove a particular matter in relation to which his opponent or a witness claims privilege, is entitled to prove the matter by other evidence, if available (see **F9.71**).
(d) No adverse inferences may be drawn against a party or witness claiming privilege (*Wentworth v Lloyd* (1864) 10 HL Cas 589).

PRIVILEGE AGAINST SELF-INCRIMINATION

Scope of Privilege

F9.35 Under the Criminal Evidence Act 1898, s. 1(2), 'a person charged in criminal proceedings who is called as a witness in the proceedings may be asked any question in cross-examination notwithstanding that it would tend to criminate him as to any offence with which he is charged in the proceedings'. Subject to s. 1(2), no witness is bound to answer questions in court (or to produce documents or things at trial) if to do so would, in the opinion of the judge, have a tendency to expose him to any criminal charge, penalty or forfeiture (of property) which the judge regards as reasonably likely to be preferred or sued for (*Blunt v Park Lane Hotel Ltd* [1942] 2 KB 253, per Goddard LJ at p. 257). The courts may substitute a different protection in place of the privilege when requiring a person to comply with a disclosure order, provided adequate protection is available, as when the prosecuting authorities unequivocally agree not to make use of the information (*AT & T Istel v Tully* [1993] AC 45). An affidavit sworn by a person in compliance with such an order may then be inadmissible against him in any subsequent criminal trial, but the Crown will not necessarily be prevented from using it to demonstrate his inconsistency and thus to impugn his credit (*Martin* [1998] 2 Cr App R 385). Penalties arise mainly under statutes relating to the revenue, and under EC regulations (see, e.g., *Rio Tinto Zinc Corporation v Westinghouse Electric Corporation* [1978] AC 547). 'Additional damages', which may be awarded under statutes for breach of copyright, are not penalties (*Rank Film Distributors Ltd v Video Information Centre* [1982] AC 380, at p. 425). A witness may not claim privilege on the basis that his answer to the question put would expose him to civil liability (Witnesses Act 1806). Nor does the privilege extend to answers which would expose the witness to criminal liability under foreign law (*King of the Two Sicilies v Willcox* (1851) 1 Sim NS 301; *Re Atherton* [1912] 2 KB 251, at p. 255). See also *Arab Monetary Fund v Hashim* [1989] 3 All ER 466. However, this issue may need to be revisited in the light of the ECHR, Article 6, and in the context of extradition proceedings (per Moses LJ in *Khan* [2007] EWCA Crim 2331 at [26]).

Subject to any statutory exceptions (see **F9.40**), an agent, trustee or other fiduciary of a party may claim the privilege in an action brought against him by that party for breach of that duty (*Bishopsgate Investment Management Ltd v Maxwell* [1993] Ch 1).

Requirement of Real and Appreciable Danger

It is dangerous to assess the strength of a claim to privilege by reference to the motive of the person seeking to invoke it; his motive may be mixed or even *mala fides*, but if the answer to the question will expose him to the risk of future prosecution, the privilege must be upheld (see per Moses LJ in *Khan* [2007] EWCA Crim 2331 at [35], approving Kirby P in *Accident Insurance Mutual Holdings Ltd v McFadden* [1993] 31 NSWLR 412). However, if the fact of the witness being in danger be once made to appear, great latitude should be allowed to him in judging for himself the effect of any particular question, for a question which might appear at first sight a very innocent one, may, by affording a link in the chain of evidence, become the means of bringing home an offence to the witness. Subject to this reservation, the court, before acceding to a claim to privilege, should satisfy itself, from the circumstances of the case and the nature of the evidence which the witness is called to give, that there is a reasonable ground to apprehend real and appreciable danger to the witness with reference to the ordinary operation of the law in the ordinary course of things, and not a danger of an imaginary or insubstantial character. See *Boyes* (1861) 1 B & S 311, per Cockburn CJ. In *R (CPS) v Bolton Magistrates' Court* [2004] 2 All ER 848, the Divisional Court, citing with approval the foregoing text, held that it is not sufficient to ascertain that the claim was made on legal advice. The duty of the court is non-delegable: the court cannot simply adopt the conclusion of a solicitor advising the witness, whose conclusion may or may not be correct. In refusing protection, it seems that the court may also take into account the triviality of any charge likely to be brought.

F9.36

In *Rank Film Distributors Ltd v Video Information Centre* [1982] AC 380, a case concerning the application of the privilege to an *Anton Piller* order, Lord Fraser held (at p. 445) that protection should be refused, partly because the likelihood of prosecution under the Copyright Act 1956, s. 21, was too remote, but also because it would be 'unreasonable to allow the possibility of incrimination of such offences to obstruct disclosure of information which would be of much more value to the owners of the infringed copyright than any protection they might obtain from s. 21'. Protection may also be properly refused if the evidence against the witness is already so strong that, if proceedings are to be taken, they will be taken whether or not the witness answers: see, e.g., *Khan v Khan* [1982] 2 All ER 60, where the witness's conduct 'reeked of dishonesty', and evidence as to his use of the proceeds of a stolen cheque did not materially increase the risk of his prosecution for its theft. See also *Khan* [2007] EWCA Crim 2331, where K, having pleaded guilty to an offence, was called as a witness by a co-accused and was found guilty of contempt for refusing to answer questions about matters as to which he had already incriminated himself by his guilty plea.

F9.37

Incrimination Must be of Person Claiming Privilege

In criminal cases, the privilege against self-incrimination is restricted to the person claiming it, and does not extend to questions the answers to which would tend to incriminate a spouse: see

F9.38

Rio Tinto Zinc Corporation v Westinghouse Electric Corporation [1978] AC 547, per Lord Diplock at p. 637, and *Pitt* [1983] QB 25, where the Court of Appeal, in holding that an accused's spouse, if she elects to testify, should be treated like any other witness, surely must have assumed that she cannot then claim privilege against the incrimination of her husband; and contrast *All Saints, Worcester (Inhabitants)* (1817) 6 M & S 194, per Bayley J at p. 201. There is no privilege against incriminating strangers (*Minihane* (1921) 16 Cr App R 38). A company may claim privilege in the same way as an individual (*Triplex Safety Glass Co. Ltd v Lancegaye Safety Glass (1934) Ltd* [1939] 2 KB 395). However, the privilege is that of the company and therefore does not extend to incrimination of its office holders (see *Rio Tinto Zinc Corporation v Westinghouse Electric Corporation* per Lord Diplock at pp. 637–8; *Sociedade Nacional de Combustiveis de Angola UEE v Lundqvist* [1991] 2 QB 310 per Beldam LJ at p. 336; and *Tate Access Floors Inc. v Boswell* [1991] Ch 512).

Necessity of Claiming Privilege

F9.39   A witness may claim the privilege only after he has been sworn and the question put; he is not entitled to refuse to take the oath on the grounds of the privilege (*Boyle v Wiseman* (1855) 1 Exch 647). Although in practice a judge will often warn a witness of his right not to answer a question which might expose him to a criminal charge, in the absence of such a warning, the witness must claim the privilege himself (*Thomas v Newton* (1827) 2 C & P 606). The witness may claim the privilege at any stage of the proceedings, even if he has already answered, without objection, questions which he was not obliged to answer (*Garbett* (1847) 1 Den CC 236). If the witness answers without seeking the protection of the court, his answers may be used in the proceedings in question and in any subsequent criminal proceedings brought against him (*Sloggett* (1856) Dears CC 656; *Coote* (1873) LR 4 PC 599). However, if a judge wrongly denies a witness the protection of privilege, anything the witness is then compelled to say is treated as having been said involuntarily and will be excluded from the subsequent criminal proceedings (*Garbett* (1847) 1 Den CC 236).

Statutory Provisions Requiring Answers to Questions

F9.40   **General**   Various statutes and statutory instruments require specified persons in specified circumstances to answer questions or produce documents or information notwithstanding that compliance may incriminate them. Clear language is required to show that Parliament intended to abrogate the privilege (*R (Malik) v Manchester Crown Court* [2008] 4 All ER 403, where it was held that the Terrorism Act 2000, sch. 5, para. 6 (see **B10.5**) does not oust the privilege). However some provisions abrogate the privilege impliedly, on the grounds that they would otherwise be largely ineffective (see, e.g., *Bank of England v Riley* [1992] Ch 475, *Re London United Investments plc* [1992] Ch 578 and *Bishopsgate Investment Management Ltd v Maxwell* [1993] Ch 1). In deciding as a matter of construction, under English domestic law, whether such a provision does impliedly abrogate the privilege, the court must consider on the one hand the public interest in obtaining the information, and on the other the 'right to silence' to be affected and the strength of the grounds for preserving it, looking at whether the request forms a part of criminal proceedings, and touches on the rules which prohibit interrogation without caution or after charge, or amounts to a potential abuse of investigatory powers which those rules are designed to prevent (*Hertfordshire County Council, ex parte Green Environmental Industries Ltd* [2000] 2 AC 412). As to the further question whether implied abrogation would amount to a violation of the right to a fair trial under the ECHR, Article 6, under the European jurisprudence the impact of Article 6 is confined to the use of answers in evidence at a criminal trial and is not concerned with extra-judicial inquiries: see *Saunders v UK* (1997) 23 EHRR 313 at p. 337 (examination by inspectors appointed by the Secretary of State under the Companies Act 1985), *Hertfordshire County Council, ex parte Green Environmental Industries Ltd* (a local authority request for information under the Environmental Protection Act 1990), *Kearns* [2002] 1 WLR 2815 (a demand by the Official Receiver to see a bankrupt's accounting records) and *Brady* [2004] 3 All ER 520 (a requirement by the Official Receiver for information relating to insolvent companies).

Provisions which expressly abrogate the privilege against self-incrimination, typically go on to prevent the answers from being used against the person who answered the question in criminal proceedings in which he is charged with a specified offence. Some examples follow.

Examples Under the Theft Act 1968, s. 31(1), which requires questions to be answered and **F9.41** orders to be complied with in proceedings for the recovery or administration of any property or dealing with property, notwithstanding that compliance may expose the witness or his spouse or civil partner to a charge for an offence under the Theft Act 1968, the answers may not be used in proceedings for any such offence. Neither the revocation of the privilege nor the restriction on the use of the answers applies to non-Theft Act offences (*Sociedade Nacional de Combustiveis de Angola UEE v Lundqvist* [1991] 3 All ER 283). However, where to answer the question etc. would expose the relevant person to an offence under the Theft Act 1968 and he claims that it would also expose him to a non-Theft Act offence, the test concerning the latter offence is whether to answer the question etc. would create or increase the risk of proceedings for that offence, separate and distinct from its connection with the Theft Act offence. If the answer is no, there is no privilege, but if it is yes, then the privilege subsists in relation to the latter offence (*Renworth v Stephansen* [1996] 3 All ER 244).

Under the Fraud Act 2006, s. 13, which is plainly modelled on s. 31(1), questions are to be answered and orders are to be complied with in proceedings for the recovery or administration of any property etc., notwithstanding that compliance may result in incrimination of an offence under the 2006 Act or a related offence, but the answers may not be used in evidence in proceedings for any such offence. Under s. 13(4), 'related offence' means conspiracy to defraud and any other offence involving any form of fraudulent conduct or purpose, a phrase that covers offering or giving a bribe (*Kensington International Ltd v Republic of Congo* [2008] 1 All ER (Comm) 934) and money laundering under the POCA 2002, s. 328(1) (see **B21.15**) (*JSC BTA Bank v Ablyazov* [2010] 1 WLR 976).

Under the Senior Courts Act 1981, s. 72, the privilege is withdrawn in various proceedings **F9.42** relating to apprehended or actual infringement of rights pertaining to any intellectual property or any apprehended or actual passing off. Section 72(3) provides that answers compelled by reason of such withdrawal of privilege cannot be used in proceedings for certain offences disclosed or for the recovery of certain penalties, liability to which was disclosed.

Under the Children Act 1989, s. 98, in any proceedings in which a court is hearing an application relating to the care, supervision or protection of a child, no one shall be excused from giving evidence on any matter or answering any question put in the course of his giving evidence on the grounds that to do so might incriminate him or his spouse or civil partner of an offence. Under s. 98(2), a statement or admission made in such proceedings shall not be admissible in evidence against the person making it or his spouse or civil partner in proceedings for an offence other than perjury. A 'statement or admission', for these purposes, includes a filed statement of the evidence which a party intends to adduce at the hearing, an oral admission made by a parent to a guardian *ad litem* (*Oxfordshire County Council v P* [1995] Fam 161) and, after the proceedings have started, an oral statement to a social worker carrying out the local authority's duties of investigation in a child protection case (*Cleveland County Council v F* [1995] 2 All ER 236). Both of these decisions, however, have since been doubted (*Re G (A Minor) (Social Worker: Disclosure)* [1996] 2 All ER 65).

Under the CJA 1987, s. 2, the Director of the SFO may require someone under investigation for a **F9.43** suspected offence involving serious or complex fraud, or anyone else, to answer questions etc., but a statement in response to such a requirement may be used against its maker only on a prosecution:

(a) for making a false or misleading statement in purported compliance with a requirement under s. 2, or

(b) for some other offence if, in giving evidence, he makes a statement inconsistent with it, and evidence relating to it is adduced, or a question relating to it is asked, by him or on his behalf.

However, it would appear that a statement previously made by an accused in response to questions under the CJA 1987, s. 2, can be used by a *co-accused*, provided it is relevant to his defence, and if this infringes the accused's right to a fair trial, he should be severed from the indictment (*Wickes* (NLJ, 25 July 2003, p. 1140, unreported)).

Under the Companies Act 1985, officers of a company and others possessing relevant information are required to answer questions put by Board of Trade inspectors investigating suspected fraud in the conduct or management of a company, but under s. 434(5A) and (5B) of the Act, in criminal proceedings in which a person who complied with such a requirement is charged with an offence (other than an offence under the Perjury Act 1911, s. 2 or s. 5), no evidence relating to the answer may be adduced and no question relating to it may be asked by or on behalf of the prosecution unless evidence relating to it is adduced, or a question relating to it is asked, by or on behalf of the person charged. For other similar statutory provisions, see the YJCEA 1999, s. 59 and sch. 3.

F9.44   If a statute revokes the privilege without *any* restriction upon the use that may be made of the answers, the answers will not be treated as having been given involuntarily and may be used in any subsequent criminal proceedings (*Scott* (1856) Dears & B 47). Such use will not invariably amount to a violation of Article 6. In *Brown v Stott* [2003] 1 AC 681, the Privy Council held that at a trial for driving after consuming excess alcohol contrary to the Road Traffic Act 1988, s. 5(1)(a), the introduction of evidence of an admission obtained from the accused under s. 172(2)(a) of the 1988 Act (see C2.12) did not infringe her right to a fair hearing under Article 6. It was held that there was a clear public interest in enforcement of road traffic legislation and that s. 172, properly applied, did not represent a disproportionate response to this serious social problem. *Brown v Stott* was applied in *Mawdesley v Chief Constable of the Cheshire Constabulary* [2004] 1 All ER 58 on a charge of driving in excess of the speed limit. In *O'Halloran v UK* (2007) 47 EHRR 397, it was held that there was no violation of Article 6 in the case of O, a case akin to that of *Mawdesley*, nor in the case of F, a conviction for failing to comply with s. 172. It was held that the privilege against self-incrimination is not an absolute right, being part of the broader right to a fair trial in Article 6. Cases of direct compulsion do not necessarily lead to violation; other factors may be relevant in deciding whether the essence of the privilege against self-incrimination has been violated. Thus in addition to (a) the direct nature of the compulsion (s. 172, for example, provides compulsion in the form of a fine of up to £1,000 and disqualification from driving or three penalty points), account should be taken of (b) the fact that the compulsion was part of a regulatory scheme that fairly imposes obligations on drivers in order to promote safety on roads, (c) the fact the information required is the simple specific and restricted fact of who was driving, (d) that the offence under s. 172 has a defence of due diligence, and (e) that in the case of O, the identity of the driver was only one element of the offence and the speeding still had to be proved. *Brown v Stott* was distinguished in *K (A)* [2010] QB 343, which concerned proceedings for cheating the public revenue; it was held that the use of information about financial resources obtained under threat of imprisonment in matrimonial ancillary relief proceedings would infringe the right to a fair hearing.

F9.45   In *Allen (No. 2)* [2001] 4 All ER 768, a case of cheating the public revenue of tax, the appellant had provided a schedule of assets in compliance with a notice given by an inspector under the Taxes Management Act 1970, s. 20. A person who fails to comply with such a notice is liable to a penalty (s. 98(1) of the 1970 Act). The House of Lords held that since the state, for the purpose of collecting tax, is entitled to require a citizen to inform it of his income and to enforce penalties for failure to do so, the s. 20 notice could not constitute a violation of the right against self- incrimination. Allen's application to the ECtHR was unsuccessful. It was held that the requirement that he declare his assets to the tax authorities did not disclose any issue under

Article 6(1), even though there was a penalty for failure to comply. The charge was one of making a false declaration of assets — it was not an example of forced self-incrimination in relation to some previously committed offence (*Allen v UK* (2002) 35 EHRR CD289; but see also *JB v Switzerland* [2001] Crim LR 748).

Free-standing Material Not Created under Compulsion   In *Saunders v UK* (1997) 23 EHRR **F9.46**
313, according to the judgment of the majority of the court, the right not to incriminate oneself is primarily concerned with respecting the will of an accused to remain silent and, as understood in Convention countries and elsewhere, it does not extend to the use in criminal proceedings of material obtained by compulsion which has an existence independent of the will of the suspect, such as documents acquired pursuant to a warrant, breath, blood and urine samples, and bodily tissue for the purposes of DNA testing. See also *L v UK* [2000] 2 FLR 322 and cf. *Funke v France* (1993) 16 EHRR 297 and *Heaney and McGuinness v Ireland* (2001) 33 EHRR 264. However, such material may not be used if obtained by forced medical intervention constituting inhuman or degrading treatment, contrary to the ECHR, Article 3, and involving a high degree of force in defiance of the will of the accused (*Jalloh v Germany* (2007) 44 EHRR 667). The distinction drawn in *Saunders* was approved in *A-G's Ref (No. 7 of 2000)* [2001] 1 WLR 1879 in which a bankrupt delivered up to the Official Receiver, pursuant to the duty imposed by the Insolvency Act 1986, s. 291, various documents relating to his estate and affairs, including documents relating to his gambling activities. Under s. 291(6), if he had failed to comply with this duty, he would have been in contempt of court and liable to imprisonment. He was subsequently charged with an offence contrary to s. 362(1)(a) of the 1986 Act, namely material contribution to his insolvency by gambling. The Court of Appeal held that use by the prosecution of the documents relating to his gambling activities would not violate his rights under Article 6. Under domestic law, the documents were admissible in law, subject to the discretion to exclude under s. 78. As to the European jurisprudence, the court approved the distinction made in *Saunders* and did so for the reasons advanced by Justice La Forest in *Thomson Newspapers Ltd v Director of Investigation & Research* (1990) 54 CCC 417 (Supreme Court of Canada), namely that, whereas a compelled statement is evidence that simply would not have existed independently of the exercise of the power of compulsion, evidence which exists independently of the compelled statement could have been found by other means and its quality does not depend on its past connection with the compelled statement. Insofar as there was a difference of view between *Funke* and *Saunders*, the court preferred the approach in *Saunders*. The same principle was applied in *Hundal* [2004] 2 Cr App R 307.

C plc v P [2008] Ch 1 concerned intellectual property proceedings in which indecent images of **F9.47** children were found on a computer which was the subject of a search order. The Court of Appeal held that the offending material was not privileged from disclosure to the police. A majority of the court regarded itself as bound by *A-G's Ref (No. 7 of 2000)* to reach this conclusion, on the basis that if, in that case, the privilege did not extend to documents which were independent evidence, the same must apply to things which existed independently of a search order. The case was thought to be no different from one in which counterfeit bags of a particular brand, being the subject of a search order, are found to contain drugs or an illegal weapon. According to the Divisional Court in *R (Malik) v Manchester Crown Court* [2008] 4 All ER 403, until the House of Lords has determined the appeal, judges should treat the privilege as an important relevant factor to be taken into account when exercising discretion in respect of the admissibility of pre-existing documents, the other factors being the degree of benefit of the material to the investigation, the importance of the privilege, the risk of prosecution, the gravity of the offence and the power to exclude evidence under the PACE 1984, s. 78. See also *S* [2009] 1 All ER 716, where it was held that a requirement in a notice under the RIPA 2000, s. 49, for disclosure of a key to data in encrypted files did not infringe the privilege nor contravene the ECHR, Article 6.

Production Orders under PACE 1984, s. 9   In *R (Bright) v Central Criminal Court* [2001] **F9.48** 2 All ER 244, the majority view was that a trial judge, in his discretion, may make production orders under the PACE 1984, s. 9 (see **D1.155**), even though the subject of the order may incriminate himself by handing over the material. If the subject of the order is prosecuted, the trial judge may consider the ECHR, Article 6, and whether to exclude the evidence under the PACE 1984, s. 78.

LEGAL PROFESSIONAL PRIVILEGE

Scope of Privilege

F9.49 A client may, and his legal adviser must (subject to the client's waiver), refuse to give oral evidence or to produce documents relating to two types of confidential communication:

(a) communications between the client and his legal adviser made for the purpose of enabling the client to obtain or the adviser to give legal advice about any matter, whether or not litigation was contemplated at the time (*Greenough v Gaskell* (1833) 1 My & K 98); and
(b) communications between the client or his legal adviser and third parties, the sole or dominant purpose of which was to enable the legal adviser to advise or act in relation to litigation that was pending or in the contemplation of the client (*Waugh v British Railways Board* [1980] AC 521).

The privilege also covers items enclosed with or referred to in such communications and brought into existence (i) in connection with the giving of legal advice or (ii) in connection with or in contemplation of legal proceedings and for the purposes of such proceedings: see *R* [1994] 4 All ER 260 and the PACE 1984, s. 10(1)(c). Section 10, which is considered at **F9.62** and **F9.66**, purports to reflect the position at common law.

F9.50 In *R (Morgan Grenfell & Co Ltd) v Special Commissioner of Income Tax* [2003] 1 AC 563, Lord Hoffmann said (at [7]–[8]):

> Legal professional privilege is a fundamental human right long established in the common law. It is a necessary corollary of the right of any person to obtain skilled advice about the law. Such advice cannot be effectively obtained unless the client is able to put all the facts before the advisor without fear that they may afterwards be disclosed and used to his prejudice.... It has been held by the European Court of Human Rights to be part of the right of privacy guaranteed by [the ECHR] Article 8... the courts will ordinarily construe general words in a statute, although literally capable of having some startling or unreasonable consequence, such as overriding fundamental human rights, as not having been intended to do so. An intention to override such rights must be expressly stated or appear by necessary implication.

In that case, it was held that, on its true construction, the Taxes Management Act 1970, s. 20(1), does not entitle an inspector of taxes to require a tax payer to deliver up material that is subject to legal professional privilege. As to the meaning of 'necessary implication', see further *B v Auckland District Law Society* [2003] 2 AC 736. See also *Robinson* [2002] EWCA Crim 2489, in which it was held, *per curiam*, that use of a clerk in a solicitor's office as an informant was not only a serious breach of an accused's right to communicate confidentially with a legal adviser under the seal of legal professional privilege but, on the face of it, and if encouraged by the police, an infringement by them of the accused's rights. The RIPA 2000 permits covert surveillance of communications between someone in custody and his lawyer, notwithstanding that they are covered by legal professional privilege and despite the statutory right under the PACE 1984, s. 58 (see **D1.55** *et seq.*) to consult a solicitor privately (*McE v Prison Service of Northern Ireland* [2009] 1 AC 908). However, the House of Lords in *McE* was not required to answer the separate question as to what use could be made of information thus obtained.

F9.51 A legal adviser, for the purposes of legal professional privilege, includes, in addition to a solicitor or a barrister, employed advisers (*Alfred Crompton Amusement Machines Ltd v Customs and Excise Commissioners (No. 2)* [1974] AC 405) and overseas advisers (*Re Duncan* [1968] P 306). In Case C-550/07 P *Akzo Nobel Chemicals Ltd v European Commission* [2011] 2 AC 338, which concerned an investigation into alleged infringements of EU anti-trust law, it was held that the privilege did not apply in relation to a corporation's own in-house lawyers, but it was acknowledged that in a minority of the Member States, including the UK, the privilege does cover communications with in-house lawyers, including such communications in the case of investigations by national competition authorities in those Member States. The privilege does not apply, at common law, in relation to any professional other than a solicitor or barrister or appropriately qualified foreign lawyer, and does not apply, therefore, in relation to other professionals with specialist knowledge of the law and who advise on it, such as accountants with the expertise to advise on tax law (*R (Prudential plc) v Special Commissioner of Income Tax* [2013] 2 All ER 247).

Legal Advice Privilege

The privilege, in the case of communications between a client and his legal adviser, is known **F9.52** as 'legal advice privilege'. The law relating to legal advice privilege is in a state of great flux. It is clear that communications must have been made either in the course of that relationship or with a view to its establishment (*Minter v Priest* [1930] AC 558). The privilege extends to instructions given by the client to the solicitor or by the solicitor to the barrister and to counsel's opinion taken by a solicitor (*Bristol Corporation v Cox* (1884) 26 Ch D 678). However, documents emanating from, or prepared by, independent third parties and passed to the lawyer for the purposes of advice are not privileged. In *Three Rivers District Council v Governor and Company of the Bank of England (No. 5)* [2003] QB 1556 it was held that legal advice privilege protects only direct communications between the client and the lawyer and evidence of the content of such communications, and that in the case of a corporate client the privilege covers only communications with those officers or employees expressly designated to act as 'the client'. The privilege will not extend to documents prepared by other employees or ex-employees, even if they were prepared with the dominant purpose of obtaining legal advice, prepared at the lawyer's request, or sent to the lawyer.

The leading authority is *Three Rivers District Council v Governor and Company of the Bank of* **F9.53** *England (No. 6)* [2005] 1 AC 610. The House of Lords held that the policy basis for legal advice privilege is that it is necessary, in a society in which the restraining and controlling framework was built on a belief in the rule of law, that communications between clients and lawyers, whereby the clients are hoping for the assistance of the lawyers' legal skills in the management of their affairs, should be secure against the possibility of any scrutiny from others. Lord Scott accepted as correct the approach of Taylor LJ in *Balabel v Air India* [1988] Ch 317 at pp. 330–1, where he said that for the purpose of attracting legal advice privilege 'legal advice is not confined to telling the client the law; it must include advice as to what should prudently and sensibly be done in the relevant legal context' but that 'to extend privilege without limit to all solicitor and client communications upon matters within the ordinary business of a solicitor and referable to that relationship [would be] too wide'. Lord Scott said that if a solicitor became the client's 'man of business', responsible for advising him on matters such as investment and finance policy and other business matters, the advice might lack a relevant legal context. The judge would have to ask whether it related to the rights, liabilities, obligations or remedies of the client under either private or public law, and, if so, whether the communication fell within the policy underlying the justification for the privilege, the criterion being an objective one.

Joint interest legal professional privilege can arise in two circumstances: first, when two or more legal persons jointly retain the same lawyer; and secondly, when there is no joint retainer but the parties have a joint interest in the subject matter of the communication in issue at the time when it comes into existence. *R (Ford) v Financial Services Authority* [2012] 1 All ER 1238 concerned the second set of circumstances, the issue being whether directors of a company could assert joint legal privilege in respect of advice provided for them by solicitors retained by the company. It was held that, apart from cases in which there is no legal distinction between those claiming joint privilege, an individual claiming joint privilege with others in a communication with a lawyer will need to establish that: he communicated with the lawyer for the purpose of seeking advice in an individual capacity; he made clear to the lawyer that he was seeking legal advice in an individual capacity rather than as a representative of a corporate body; those with whom the joint privilege was claimed knew or ought to have appreciated the legal position; the lawyer knew or ought to have appreciated that he was communicating with the individual in that individual capacity; and the communication with the lawyer was confidential.

F9.54   Legal advice privilege does not cover records of time spent with a client on attendance notes, time sheets or fee records, because they are not communications between client and legal adviser, or records of appointments, because they are not communications made in connection with legal advice (*Manchester Crown Court, ex parte Rogers* [1999] 4 All ER 35). Nor does it cover a lawyer's records of a client's telephone numbers and of the dates when the client telephoned the lawyer (*R (Miller Gardner Solicitors) v Minshull Street Crown Court* [2002] EWHC 3077 (QB)). Equally, the privilege does not cover attendance notes made by a solicitor recording what took place in court or in chambers in the presence of the parties on both sides (*Ainsworth v Wilding* [1900] 2 Ch 315); nor does it cover attendance notes recording meetings between the legal advisers of the parties on both sides (with or without their clients in attendance) or attendance notes recording telephone conversations between the parties, because all such notes are not communications between solicitor and client but merely records setting out what passed publicly between the two parties or their advisers (*Parry v News Group Newspapers Ltd* (1990) 140 NLJ 1719). The privilege attaches to communications between the client and his legal adviser for the purposes of obtaining and giving legal advice, and not to *facts* perceived by the legal adviser in the course of that relationship. Thus a solicitor may generally be compelled to give evidence as to his client's identity (*Studdy v Sanders* (1823) 2 Dow & Ry KB 347). In *R (Howe) v South Durham Magistrates' Court* [2005] RTR 55, it was held that a solicitor present in court when an order had been made disqualifying a person from driving could be compelled in a subsequent prosecution to give evidence as to the identity of that person and to produce attendance notes in relation to the disqualification (with anything in the notes attracting privilege blacked out). Equally, a solicitor may be compelled to give evidence as to his client's handwriting (*Dwyer v Collins* (1852) 7 Exch 639) or mental capacity (*James v Godrich* (1844) 5 Moore PCC 16). See also *Brown v Foster* (1857) 1 H & N 736: a barrister who has seen a book produced at his client's trial may give evidence in subsequent proceedings as to its contents.

Litigation Privilege

F9.55   The privilege, in the case of communications with third parties, is known as 'litigation privilege'. Litigation privilege covers communications between a client or his lawyer and third parties, the sole or dominant purpose of which was to enable the lawyer to advise or act in relation to pending or contemplated litigation. It also attaches to the identity and other details of witnesses intended to be called in adversarial litigation, whether or not their identity is the fruit of legal advice. A party has a legitimate interest in protecting the identity of witnesses he intends to call until a late stage in the litigation. Litigation privilege, like legal professional privilege, is a basic or fundamental right, which may only be intruded upon by force of subordinate legislation if the statute providing the subordinate instrument's *vires* makes it plain that such an authority was intended to be conveyed (*R (Kelly) v Warley Magistrates' Court* [2008] 1 Cr App R 195).

F9.56   **Types of Documents Covered**   The privilege covers documents created by a party for the purpose of instructing the lawyer and obtaining his advice in the conduct of the litigation (*Anderson v Bank of British Columbia* (1876) 2 Ch D 644, per James LJ at p. 656), but not documents obtained by a party or his adviser for the purpose of litigation that were not created for that purpose (*Ventouris v Mountain* [1991] 3 All ER 472). A copy or translation of an unprivileged document in the control of a party does not become privileged merely because the copy or translation was made for the purpose of the litigation (see, in the case of copies, *Dubai Bank Ltd v*

Galadari [1990] Ch 98 and, in the case of translations, *Sumitomo Corporation v Credit Lyonnais Rouse Ltd* [2002] 4 All ER 68). However, privilege will attach to a copy of an unprivileged document if the copy was made for the purpose of litigation and the original is not, and has not at any time been, in the control of the party claiming privilege (*The Palermo* (1883) 9 PD 6 and *Watson v Cammell Laird & Co. (Shipbuilders & Engineers) Ltd* [1959] 2 All ER 757). Privilege will also attach where a solicitor has copied or assembled a selection of third-party documents for the purposes of litigation, if its production will betray the trend of the advice he is giving his client (*Lyell v Kennedy (No. 3)* (1884) 27 Ch D 1), but this principle does not extend to a selection of own client documents, or copies or translations representing the fruits of such a selection, made for the purposes of litigation (*Sumitomo Corporation v Credit Lyonnais Rouse Ltd*, overruling *Dubai Bank Ltd v Galadari (No. 7)* [1992] 4 All ER 68).

Dominant Purpose The dominant purpose for which a document was brought into existence **F9.57** should be ascertained by an objective view of all the evidence, taking into account the intention of not only its author, but also the person or authority under whose direction it was procured (*Guinness Peat Properties Ltd v Fitzroy Robinson Partnership* [1987] 2 All ER 716). However, it should be noted that in *Secretary of State for Trade and Industry v Baker* [1998] Ch 356, Sir Richard Scott V-C doubted the correctness of the decisions in both *Re Highgrade Traders Ltd* and *Guinness Peat Properties Ltd v Fitzroy Robinson Partnership*.

Third Party's Involvement If a client communicates with a lawyer via a third party who is not **F9.58** merely an agent for communication, but someone who also has to make a preliminary decision on whether to refer the matter to the lawyer, no privilege will attach to the information supplied to the third party (*Jones v Great Central Railway Co.* [1910] AC 4).

Death of Client Legal professional privilege survives the death of a client and vests in his **F9.59** or her personal representative or, once administration is complete, the person entitled to the deceased's estate. Such persons, therefore, are entitled to either claim or waive the privilege (*Molloy (Deceased)* [1997] 2 Cr App R 283).

Effect of Rules Governing Disclosure of Expert Evidence

The common-law principles relating to communications with third parties must now be read **F9.60** subject to the CrimPR, part 33 (see **D15.77**, **F10.44** to **F10.48**, and Supplement, **R-256**, where the rules are set out). These rules make provision, subject to exceptions, for the disclosure of expert evidence between the parties to Crown Court and summary trials. Under r. 33.4(2), a party may not introduce expert evidence if he has not complied with the requirement of service of such evidence unless every other party agrees or the court gives permission. The rule does not *compel* disclosure: if an expert's report is unhelpful to the party obtaining it, he need not disclose it to his opponent, and the opponent cannot require him, his solicitor or the expert to give evidence as to the instructions given to the expert or the report he prepared. The expert may, however, be called by the opponent to give evidence of facts he has observed and of his opinion on those facts (*Harmony Shipping Co. SA v Saudi Europe Line Ltd* [1979] 3 All ER 177, applied in *King* [1983] 1 All ER 929), unless his opinion is based on examination of an item which is itself privileged because it was brought into existence for the purpose of obtaining legal advice etc. (*R* [1994] 4 All ER 260, at **F9.63**) or his opinion is inextricably dependent, or based to a material extent, on other privileged material such as communications with an accused (*Davies* (2002) 166 JP 243).

Pre-existing Documents and Items

At common law, a legal adviser (or third party) has no greater privilege than his client. Thus, a **F9.61** document that is not privileged in the hands of the client does not become privileged if given into the custody of a lawyer for the purposes of obtaining legal advice (or if sent by the lawyer to a third party in connection with pending or contemplated litigation). In *Peterborough Justices, ex parte Hicks* [1977] 1 All ER 225, in which the client had sent a forged document to his solicitor for the purposes of obtaining legal advice, a warrant was ordered under the Forgery Act 1913, s. 16, to search the solicitor's premises and seize the document. On an application for certiorari to quash the search warrant, it was held that the document was not privileged in the hands of the solicitor because it would have been open to seizure in the hands of the client. Eveleigh J said (at p. 1374): '. . . it is the privilege of the client . . . the solicitor holds the document in the right of his client and can assert in respect of its seizure no greater authority than the client himself . . . possesses'. In *Frank Truman Export Ltd v Metropolitan Police Commissioner* [1977] QB 952, Swanwick J expressed views to the contrary, but these dicta were doubted in *King* [1983] 1 All ER 929. In *King*, a case of conspiracy to defraud, an expert instructed by the defence was subpoenaed to produce sample handwriting sent to him by the accused's solicitors for examination (although the instructions sent to him and the report he produced were held to be privileged). But see also *R* [1994] 4 All ER 260, discussed at **F9.63**.

F9.62   **PACE 1984, ss. 9 and 10**   The principle established in *Peterborough Justices, ex parte Hicks* [1977] 1 All ER 225 must now be read subject to the provisions of the PACE 1984. Section 9(2)(a) of the 1984 Act repeals previous legislation insofar as it authorised, by the issue of a warrant, searches for, *inter alia*, 'items subject to legal privilege' and 'special procedure material'. Section 8 of the 1984 Act provides for the issue of warrants of entry and search if, *inter alia*, a justice of the peace is satisfied that the material sought does not consist of or include 'items subject to legal privilege' or 'special procedure material'. Unless 'special procedure material' has been voluntarily disclosed by the person who acquired or created it (*Singleton* [1995] 1 Cr App R 431), under s. 9(1), a constable may obtain access to such material for the purposes of a criminal investigation by making an application *inter partes* on notice to a circuit judge. Under s. 14(2), 'special procedure material', includes material, other than items subject to legal privilege, in the possession of a person who acquired or created it in the course of any trade, business, profession etc. and holds it subject to an express or implied undertaking to hold it in confidence. The phrase 'items subject to legal privilege' is defined in s. 10 of the Act, which, it has been held, is intended to reflect the position at common law (see the majority view in *Central Criminal Court, ex parte Francis* [1989] AC 346, at **F9.66**). Thus, for example, as at common law, 'legal privilege' in s. 10 does not embrace all communications between a client and his solicitor and therefore will not necessarily cover such items as a conveyance or other legal document, unless connected to legal advice or legal proceedings (*R (Faisaltex Ltd) v Preston Crown Court* [2009] 1 Cr App R 549).

Police and Criminal Evidence Act 1984, s. 10

(1) Subject to subsection (2) below, in this Act 'items subject to legal privilege' means—
   (a) communications between a professional legal adviser and his client or any person representing his client made in connection with the giving of legal advice to the client;
   (b) communications between a professional legal adviser and his client or any person representing his client or between such an adviser or his client or any such representative and any other person made in connection with or in contemplation of legal proceedings and for the purposes of such proceedings; and
   (c) items enclosed with or referred to in such communications and made—
      (i) in connection with the giving of legal advice; or
      (ii) in connection with or in contemplation of legal proceedings and for the purposes of such proceedings,
   when they are in the possession of a person who is entitled to possession of them.
(2) Items held with the intention of furthering a criminal purpose are not items subject to legal privilege.

F9.63   In *Guildhall Magistrates' Court, ex parte Primlaks Holdings Co. (Panama) Inc.* [1990] 1 QB 261, it was held that loss of legal privilege by virtue of s. 10(2) does not mean that no express or implied undertaking to hold in confidence can exist. A solicitor's correspondence with his client (and its enclosures) will, if not privileged, fall squarely within s. 14. Thus if, on an application under s. 8, a justice cannot be satisfied that there are reasonable grounds for believing that the material sought does not include any items which are, prima facie, subject to legal privilege or any material which is, prima facie, special procedure material, he should refuse the application and leave the applicant to proceed under s. 9 so that the matter can be fully ventilated before a circuit judge, who will consider the matter *inter partes*. Likewise if the police are aware that what they seek includes items which are, prima facie, the subject of legal privilege, they should proceed under s. 9. It was further observed (at pp. 273–4) that documents of a client sent to a professional legal adviser under cover of privileged correspondence for the purpose of obtaining legal advice would not be within s. 10(1)(c) if they were pre-existing documents and were not made in connection with the giving of legal advice or in connection with or in contemplation of legal proceedings and for the purposes of such proceedings; but such pre-existing documents would be, prima facie, within s. 14(2), and therefore it would be open to the police to make an application under s. 9 of the Act in order to have access to them. However, a document forged by a solicitor or supplied to him by a fraudulent client does not constitute special procedure material because, from its nature, it could not have been acquired or created in the course of the profession of a solicitor (*Leeds Magistrates' Court, ex parte Dumbleton* [1993] Crim LR 866).

In *R* [1994] 4 All ER 260 it was held that the word 'made' in s. 10(1)(c) is used in a general sense and is wide enough to include the meaning 'brought into existence'. It was also held that where an item is protected from production under s. 10(1)(c), oral evidence of opinion based upon the item is also inadmissible. A scientist had carried out DNA tests at the request of the defence solicitors on a blood sample provided by the accused. It was held that s. 10(1)(c) applied not only so as to enable the defence to object to the sample being produced in evidence (because the sample was an item brought into existence for the purposes of legal proceedings), but also so as to prevent the prosecution from calling the scientist to give evidence of opinion based on the sample.

Information Helpful in Establishing Innocence

In *Derby Magistrates' Court, ex parte B* [1996] AC 487 the appellant was acquitted of murder.   **F9.64** His step-father was subsequently charged with the murder and at his committal proceedings, the appellant was called as a prosecution witness. Counsel for the defence sought to cross-examine the appellant on certain factual instructions that he had given to his solicitors when he had been charged with the offence. The appellant declined to waive his privilege. The magistrates then issued summonses, directing the appellant and his solicitor to produce documentary evidence of the instructions, on the basis that the public interest that all relevant and admissible evidence should be made available to the defence outweighed the public interest which protected confidential communications between a solicitor and a client. An application for judicial review of the decision was refused, but the House of Lords allowed the appeal. It was held that no exception should be allowed to the absolute and permanent nature of 'legal professional privilege' (a phrase used to refer to the privilege attaching to the solicitor-client relationship and not to all other forms of legal professional privilege: see *Re L (A Minor) (Police Investigation: Privilege)* [1997] AC 16) and therefore, overruling *Barton* [1973] 2 All ER 1192 and *Ataou* [1988] 2 All ER 321, there could be no question of a balancing exercise of the kind performed by the magistrates. A client must be sure that what he tells his lawyer in confidence will never be revealed without his consent. Once any exception to the general rule is allowed, the client's confidence is necessarily lost. Therefore the documents in question, being protected by legal professional privilege, were immune from production. However, Lord Nicholls, who also rejected any question of a balancing exercise, observed that in cases where the client no longer has any interest in maintaining the privilege, the privilege is spent. His lordship preferred to reserve his final view on the point, being of the opinion that the point did not arise since the appellant had a legitimate interest in not disclosing material which might suggest that he had been improperly acquitted, but in a dictum which, it is submitted, has much to commend it, said (at p. 701):

> I would not expect a law, based explicitly on considerations of the public interest, to protect the right of a client when he has no interest in asserting the right and the enforcement of the right would be seriously prejudicial to another in defending a criminal charge or in some other way.

Communications in Furtherance of Crime or Fraud

F9.65   Communications in furtherance of crime or fraud are a well-recognised exception to the principle of legal professional privilege (*Derby Magistrates' Court, ex parte B* [1996] AC 487, per Lord Lloyd at p. 509). In *Cox* (1884) 14 QBD 153 a solicitor was compelled to disclose communications with the accused, in which the accused had sought his advice in drawing up a bill of sale alleged to be fraudulent. Stephen J, delivering the judgment of the Court for Crown Cases Reserved, held that if a client applies to a legal adviser for advice intended to facilitate or to guide the client in the commission of a crime or fraud, the legal adviser being ignorant of the purpose for which his advice is sought, the communication between the two is not privileged. See also *Hayward* (1846) 2 Car & Kir 234 and *Smith* (1915) 11 Cr App R 229. The principle can be relied upon only if there is prima facie evidence that it was the client's intention to obtain advice in furtherance of his criminal or fraudulent purpose (*O'Rourke v Darbishire* [1920] AC 581). Although a court may look at the communications in question — the 'closed material' — to decide whether they came into existence in furtherance of such a purpose (*Governor of Pentonville Prison, ex parte Osman* [1990] 3 All ER 701, at pp. 309–10), as a rule the court should not do so: there must be some exceptional factor of real weight before the court can examine the closed material and the mere fact that the test is not satisfied on the open material is not such a factor (*BBGP Managing General Partner Ltd v Babcock & Brown Global Partners* [2011] Ch 296). In *Minchin* [2013] EWCA Crim 2412, a case of conspiracy to pervert the course of justice relating to an allegedly false alibi, it was held that material in support of the purported alibi held by solicitors was not protected by the privilege because there was 'free-standing and independent' evidence of the conspiracy. The exception does apply if the legal adviser is aware of or is a party to the crime or fraud, but not if he merely volunteers a warning to his client that certain conduct could result in his being prosecuted (*Butler v Board of Trade* [1971] Ch 680). Fraud, for the purposes of the exception, is not limited to the tort of deceit, and includes all forms of fraud and dishonesty, such as fraudulent breach of trust, fraudulent conspiracy, trickery and sham contrivances, but does not cover the tort of inducing a breach of contract (*Crescent Farm (Sidcup) Sports Ltd v Sterling Offices Ltd* [1972] Ch 553, per Goff J at p. 565) or the torts of trespass and conversion (*Dubai Aluminium Co. Ltd v Al Alawi* [1999] 1 All ER 703). 'Fraud', in this context, is used in a relatively wide sense. Thus privilege will not attach to legal advice on how to structure a transaction which has been devised to prejudice the interests of a creditor by putting assets beyond his reach (*Barclays Bank Plc v Eustice* [1995] 4 All ER 511).

The exception is not confined to cases in which solicitors advise on or set up criminal or fraudulent transactions yet to be undertaken, but also covers criminal or fraudulent conduct undertaken for the purposes of acquiring evidence in, or for, litigation. Thus where documents have been generated by, or report on, conduct which constitutes a crime under the data protection legislation, and those documents are relevant to an issue in the proceedings, they will not be protected from disclosure by legal professional privilege (*Dubai Aluminium Co. Ltd v Al Alawi*).

F9.66   There appeared to be no common-law authority prior to the judgments in *Central Criminal Court, ex parte Francis* [1989] AC 346 to the effect that a criminal intent on the part of a stranger to the relationship of a solicitor and client destroys the privilege of the client (see the speech of Lord Oliver, dissenting, in *Ex parte Francis*). Such authority as there was suggested the contrary: see, e.g., *Banque Keyser Ullman SA v Skandia (UK) Insurance Co. Ltd* [1986] 1 Lloyd's Rep 336, in which it was held that the principle of *Cox* (1884) 14 QBD 153 does not extend to the correspondence between a solicitor and the victim of a fraudster. However, the decision of the majority of the House of Lords in *Ex parte Francis* provides persuasive authority that the intention of furthering a criminal purpose may be that of the client, the solicitor or any other person. That case concerned the construction of the PACE 1984, s. 10(2), which provides that: 'Items held with the intention of furthering a criminal purpose are not items subject to legal privilege'. In *Snaresbrook Crown Court, ex parte DPP* [1988] QB 532, it was held, giving these words their natural meaning, that what is relevant is the intention of the person holding the items in question. However, in *Ex parte Francis*, a majority of the House, rejecting this construction, held that s. 10(2) was not intended to restrict the principle of *Cox* (1884) 14 QBD 153 to cases in which the legal adviser has the intention of furthering a criminal purpose, but *reflected the position at common law*, and therefore the intention to which it referred could be that of the person holding the document or any other person. On that basis it was held that no privilege attached to documents relating to the purchase of a property by a client and innocently held by a solicitor, because a third party, a relative of the client, intended them to be used to further his criminal purpose in laundering the proceeds of illegal drug trafficking. See also *R (Hallinan, Blackburn Gittings & Notts) (a firm) v Crown Court at Middlesex Guildhall* [2005] 1 WLR 766, where a draft statement, made pursuant to a specific agreement to pervert the course of justice, was forwarded to the accused's solicitors.

In *Leeds Magistrates' Court, ex parte Dumbleton* [1993] Crim LR 866, a warrant was issued to **F9.67** search for and seize documents held by a solicitor and allegedly forged by him and another. It was held that the documents were not covered by s. 10(1) because the phrase 'made in connection with ... legal proceedings' meant lawfully made, and did not extend to forged documents or copies thereof; in any event the items were held with the intention of furthering a criminal purpose — the word 'held' in s. 10(2) relating to the time at which the documents came into the possession of the person holding them.

Waiver of Privilege

In *Ahmed* [2007] EWCA Crim 2870 the Court of Appeal set out the following principles relat- **F9.68** ing to waiver of legal professional privilege.

(a) Documents may be disclosed for a limited purpose without waiving privilege generally.
(b) However, if a document or communication is disclosed voluntarily, privilege will normally be lost generally and with it the right to withhold production of other documents or communications relating to the same subject-matter, or 'transaction'.
(c) The principle governing the loss of privilege in the transaction generally is one of fairness. It is contrary to the interests of justice to allow a person to disclose a limited range of material relating to a particular matter, perhaps chosen to serve his own interests, whilst depriving the other party to the litigation of the full picture which the remainder of the material relating to that matter would disclose.
(d) However, the importance of legal professional privilege to the proper administration of justice was such that it should be jealously guarded and it followed that courts should not be astute to hold that a litigant had lost the right to claim privilege save to the extent that justice and the right to a fair trial made that necessary. It is necessary to identify the confidential communications which the person chose to disclose and see to what extent fairness demanded that other documents or communications should also be disclosed.

Waiver of Privilege and the Criminal Justice and Public Order Act 1994, s. 34

In *Condron* [1997] 1 WLR 827, the Court of Appeal gave the following guidance relating to **F9.69** legal professional privilege where an accused refuses to answer police questions on the advice of his solicitor. Communications between an accused and his solicitor prior to interviews by the police are subject to the privilege. If an accused gives as a reason for not answering that he has been advised by his solicitor not to do so, that advice does not amount to a waiver of privilege. But if the accused wishes to invite the court not to draw an adverse inference under the CJPO 1994, s. 34 (see **F19.10**), it is necessary to go further and state the basis or reason for the advice. This may well amount to a waiver of privilege so that the accused, or if his solicitor is also called, the solicitor, can be asked whether there were any other reasons for the advice, and the nature of the advice given, so as to explore whether the advice may also have been given for tactical reasons. However, it should be borne in mind that the information which the prosecution seek to draw from failure to mention facts in interview is that they have been subsequently fabricated. It is open to an accused to attempt to rebut this inference by showing that the relevant facts were communicated to a third party, usually the solicitor, at about the time of the interview. This does not involve waiver of privilege if it is the solicitor to whom the fact is communicated.

It is probably desirable that the judge should warn counsel, or the accused, that the privilege may be taken to have been waived if the accused gives evidence of the nature of the advice.

F9.70 If the defence reveal the basis or reason for the solicitor's advice to the accused not to answer police questions, this will amount to a waiver of privilege whether the revelation is made by the accused or by the solicitor acting within the scope of his authority as agent on behalf of the accused, and whether the revelation is made in the course of pre-trial questioning, in evidence before the jury, or in evidence on the *voir dire* which is *not* repeated before the jury (*Bowden* [1999] 4 All ER 582). *Bowden* was followed in *Loizou* [2006] EWCA Crim 1719, where Hooper LJ said (at [84]):

> There is a distinction between *having* to reveal what was said to a solicitor to rebut an allegation of recent fabrication and *volunteering* information about the legal advice... In the former scenario the reason privilege has not been waived is that there is no way of dealing with the allegation other than by revealing what was said. In the latter scenario, while the effect may be to enable an allegation of recent fabrication to be made, this is the consequence of the voluntary provision by or on behalf of the defendant of information which because of its partial nature is misleading.

See also *Seaton* [2011] 1 All ER 932 and see further **F19.26**.

Waiver of Privilege and Use of Secondary Evidence

F9.71 Legal professional privilege prevents the giving of oral evidence or the production of documents by particular persons, namely the client, the legal adviser (or his clerk or agent) or third parties (in the case of protected communications between the client or his legal adviser and such third parties). If a privilege has been waived, because the contents of a privileged communication have become known to any other person, whether by overhearing a privileged conversation or by obtaining the original or a copy of a privileged document, that person may be compelled to give oral evidence in that regard or to produce the document or copy (see, in the case of copies of privileged documents, *Calcraft v Guest* [1898] 1 QB 759 and, in the case of originals, *Waugh v British Railways Board* [1980] AC 521 per Lord Simon at p. 536 and *Governor of Pentonville Prison, ex parte Osman* [1990] 3 All ER 701 at pp. 309–10). This principle applies not only if the privileged communication was disclosed by accident or error on the part of the client or his legal adviser, but also where it was obtained by improper or even criminal means on the part of his opponent (or some third party). But see also *ITC Film Distributors Ltd v Video Exchange Ltd* [1982] Ch 431, which is considered at **F2.17**. In *Tompkins* (1977) 67 Cr App R 181, a note from the accused to his counsel had been found on the floor of the court and handed to prosecuting counsel by a representative of his instructing solicitor. The contents of the note being in flat contradiction to an answer given by the accused in cross-examination, prosecuting counsel handed the note to the accused, and without referring to its contents asked the accused whether he adhered to the answer he had given. The judge ruled that the cross-examination was proper but that no direct reference should be made to the note. The accused then admitted the opposite of what he had said. The Court of Appeal held that counsel had been properly allowed to put questions in cross-examination on the basis of the contents of the note. In *Cottrill* [1997] Crim LR 56, applying *Tompkins*, it was held that a statement made by the accused to his solicitors, and voluntarily sent by them to the prosecution without his knowledge or consent, could be used in cross-examination, if his evidence did not accord with the account given in the statement, subject to the provisions of the PACE 1984, s. 78. See also *Willis* [2004] EWCA Crim 3472; and see further the Code of Conduct of the Bar, Written Standards, paras. 7.1 to 7.3.2, discussed at **D16.8**.

F9.72 In *Butler v Board of Trade* [1971] Ch 680 the plaintiff, who was being prosecuted by the Board of Trade for alleged offences under the Companies Act 1948, sought a declaration that the Board was not entitled to produce in evidence at the criminal trial a copy of a letter from the plaintiff's solicitor to the plaintiff, which had been accidentally included in papers handed over to the Official Receiver. It was held that, although the original letter was privileged, the copy was admissible in the criminal proceedings under the rule in *Calcraft v Guest* [1898] 1 QB 759, the principle established in *Lord Ashburton v Pape* [1913] 2 Ch 469 being inapplicable. Goff J said (at p. 690):

> ... it would not be a right or permissible exercise of the equitable jurisdiction in confidence to make a declaration at the suit of the accused in a public prosecution in effect restraining the Crown from adducing admissible evidence relevant to the crime with which he is charged. It is not necessary for me to decide whether the same result would obtain in the case of a private prosecution, and I expressly leave that point open.

Statements Made in 'Without Prejudice' Negotiations

In *K (A)* [2010] QB 343 the question arose whether a third party, into whose hands had fallen **F9.73** evidence of damaging admissions made in the course of 'without prejudice' negotiations, was entitled to rely on them in subsequent criminal proceedings against the party who made them. It was held that the immediate purpose of the 'without prejudice' rule is to enable parties to negotiate freely without compromising their positions in relation to their current dispute and that, although it may be justifiable to extend the scope of the protection to subsequent proceedings involving either of the parties to the original negotiations, the public interest in preserving confidentiality becomes weaker the more remote the subject-matter of those proceedings becomes from the subject of the original negotiations. Criminal proceedings involve different parties and therefore are necessarily at one remove from the original dispute and the public interest in prosecuting crime is sufficient to outweigh the public interest in the settlement of disputes, but in appropriate circumstances it may be possible to exclude evidence of the admissions under the PACE 1984, s. 78.

Section F10   Opinion Evidence

GENERAL RULE

F10.1   The general rule is that witnesses may only give evidence of facts they personally perceived and not evidence of their opinion, i.e. evidence of inferences drawn from such facts. The assumption that it is possible to distinguish fact from inference is arguably false (see Thayer, *A Preliminary Treatise on Evidence at the Common Law* (1898), at p. 524), but the distinction has given rise to little case law. In *Meads* [1996] Crim LR 519, it was held that evidence of tests showing the speed at which the handwritten notes of disputed interviews had been made, and whether they could have been written in the time claimed by officers, was no more opinion evidence than evidence of the timing of a given journey in order to test an alibi. The inferences to be drawn from such evidence were for the jury. In *Allad* [2014] EWCA Crim 421, it was held that a witness was entitled to explain how VAT carousel frauds operate but should not have expressed an opinion on the issue before the jury, namely whether the accused would have known that they had participated in a fraud.

There are two exceptions to the general rule:

(a) *Non-experts*. A statement of opinion on any matter not calling for expertise, if made by a witness as a way of conveying relevant facts personally perceived by him, is admissible as evidence of what he perceived.

(b) *Experts*. Subject to compliance with the CrimPR, part 33 (expert evidence) (see **D9.69**, **D15.77** and **F10.44**), a statement of opinion on any relevant matter calling for expertise may be made by a witness qualified to give such an expert opinion.

If objection to the admissibility of expert opinion evidence is made, it is for the party proffering the evidence to prove its admissibility (*Atkins* [2010] 1 Cr App R 117, approved in *Reed* [2010] 1 Cr App R 310, where it was said (at [113]) that, unless the admissibility is challenged, the judge will admit the evidence as sufficient safeguards are provided by the rules on pre-trial disclosure: see **F10.44**). An objection to the admissibility of expert opinion evidence will necessarily fail if the witness is not an expert and expresses no expert opinion (see *Foulger* [2012] EWCA Crim 1516, where the witness was not an expert communications data investigator but simply put otherwise relatively complicated telephone data into a more user-friendly format, using charts, maps and summaries).

NON-EXPERT OPINION EVIDENCE

F10.2   A statement of opinion may be given by a witness, on a matter not calling for expertise, as a compendious means of conveying facts perceived by him. Thus an identification witness is not required to give a description of the offender or some other person, leaving it to the tribunal of fact to decide whether that description fits the accused or other person identified, but may express his opinion that the accused (or other person) is the person he saw on the occasion in question. Likewise, a non-expert may give evidence of opinion to identify an object (*Lucas v Williams & Sons* [1892] 2 QB 113: a picture), handwriting with which he is familiar (*Doe d Mudd v Suckermore* (1836) 7 LJ QB 33; *Slaney* (1832) 5 C & P 213; *Rickard* (1918) 13 Cr App R 40) or a voice which he recognises (*Deenik* [1992] Crim LR 578) or with which he is familiar (*Robb* (1991) 93 Cr App R 161; *Flynn* [2008] 2 Cr App R 266 at [14]). Other examples include evidence of a person's age (*Cox* [1898] 1 QB 179) or the general appearance of his state of health, mind or emotion; the speed of a vehicle (see the Road Traffic Regulation Act 1984, s. 89(2)); the state of the weather; and the passage of time. In *Beckett* (1913) 8 Cr App R 204, the value of a plate glass window was established by the evidence of a non-expert. It is submitted, however, that non-expert opinion evidence should not be received on the value of less commonplace objects or objects such as antiques and works of art, the valuation of which calls for expertise. On a charge of driving when unfit through drink, the fitness of the accused to drive is a matter calling for expertise, though a non-expert may give evidence of his impression as to whether the accused had taken drink, provided he describes the facts on the basis of which he formed that impression (*Davies* [1962] 3 All ER 97, applied in *Tagg* [2002] 1 Cr App R 22). See also *Neal* [1962] Crim LR 698. Although scientific evidence is not always required to identify a prohibited drug, police officers' descriptions of a drug must be sufficient to justify the inference that it was the drug alleged (*Hill* (1993) 96 Cr App R 456). The evidence of a non-expert is not admissible in support of an accused's plea of insanity (*Loake* (1911) 7 Cr App R 71, per Lord Alverstone CJ).

In *Davies* [1962] 3 All ER 97, one of the reasons given by Lord Parker CJ as to why the non-expert **F10.3** could not give his opinion on whether the accused, as a result of the drink he had taken, was unfit to drive a car, was that this was 'the very matter which the court itself has to determine'. However, the common-law rule preventing any witness from expressing his opinion on an ultimate issue, i.e. one of the very issues to be determined by the court, appears to be virtually obsolete (see the Criminal Law Revision Committee, *Eleventh Report: Evidence (General)* (1972) Cmnd 4991, para. 270). In *Beckett* (1913) 8 Cr App R 204, the value of the window was the very issue to be decided by the court. As to expert opinion evidence on ultimate issues, see **F10.35**.

EXPERT OPINION EVIDENCE

Competence of Expert Witnesses

Occasionally statute prescribes the qualifications which a person must possess if he is to give **F10.4** expert opinion evidence on a particular matter. For example, a jury shall not acquit on the ground of insanity, except on the evidence of two or more registered medical practitioners, at least one of whom is approved by the Secretary of State as having special experience in the diagnosis or treatment of mental disorder (Criminal Procedure (Insanity and Unfitness to Plead) Act 1991, ss. 1(1) and 2). Subject to provisions of this kind, whether a witness is properly qualified in the subject calling for expertise is a question for the court. In *Clarke* [2013] EWCA Crim 162, for example, a murder trial, it was held that an expert in osteoarticular pathology had the expertise to consider fractures to the ribs as a possible cause of death, but had neither the experience nor expertise to consider other possible causes of death. Courts need to be scrupulous to ensure that evidence proffered as expert evidence is based upon specialised experience, knowledge or study: mere self-certification is insufficient (*Atkins* [2010] 1 Cr App R 117 at [27]). In rare cases it will be necessary to hold a *voir dire* to decide whether a witness should be allowed to give expert evidence, but in the vast majority of cases the judge will be able to make the decision on the basis of written material (*G* [2004] 2 Cr App R 638). If it appears to a judge that a *voir dire* may be helpful to decide whether a witness should be allowed to give expert evidence, he can canvass that point with counsel but, if the defence want to contest the competence of an expert in a *voir dire*, the burden is on them to make such an application to the judge (*Francis* [2013] EWCA Crim 123). If a witness does give expert evidence, the judge has the power, should the need arise, to remove his expert status and limit his evidence to factual matters (*G*).

The expert's competence or skill may stem from formal study or training, experience, or both. **F10.5** In *Oakley* (1979) 70 Cr App R 7 a police officer with qualifications and experience in accident investigation was allowed to give evidence, on a charge of causing death by dangerous driving, as to how an accident occurred. See also *Hodges* [2003] 2 Cr App R 247 and *Ibrahima* [2005] EWCA Crim 1436, considered at **F10.34**. Compare, *sed quaere, Somers* [1963] 3 All ER 808, in which a doctor was allowed to prove the conversion of figures in an analyst's certificate into the amount of alcohol consumed by the accused, although not an expert in such conversion, and to prove the rate of bodily destruction of alcohol, having refreshed his memory from a BMA publication. See also *Inch* (1989) 91 Cr App R 51, in which it was held that a medical orderly with much experience in the treatment of cuts and lacerations was insufficiently qualified to express an opinion as to whether an inch-long cut to the forehead had been caused by a blunt instrument rather than a head-butt. However, in *Francis* [2013] EWCA Crim 123, in contrast, it was held that a doctor who was not a forensic pathologist, but who had spent ten years in emergency medicine and would have dealt with many thousands of cases of lacerations and cuts, had properly been allowed to express an opinion that it was impossible that certain injuries had been caused by a pin and were far more likely to have been caused by a sharp blade. In *Silverlock* [1894] 2 QB 766 a solicitor, who had for ten years studied handwriting and on several occasions compared handwriting professionally, was allowed to give expert evidence that an advertisement was in the handwriting of the accused. Affirming the conviction, Lord Russell CJ said (at p. 771):

> There is no decision which requires that the evidence of a man who is skilled in comparing handwriting, and who has formed a reliable opinion from past experience, should be excluded because his experience has not been gained in the way of his business. It is, however, really unnecessary to consider this point; for it seems... in the present case that the witness was not only *peritus*, but was *peritus* in the way of his business.

F10.6   In *Robb* (1991) 93 Cr App R 161, an experienced phonetician was allowed to give expert opinion evidence that the voice on two different tapes was the voice of the same person, notwithstanding that his technique, which was one of auditory analysis alone, was not generally respected in the field of phonetics because it was not supplemented and verified by acoustic analysis based on physical measurement of resonance and frequency. In *O'Doherty* [2003] 1 Cr App R 77, a decision of the Court of Appeal of Northern Ireland, it was held that as a general rule, subject to exceptions, no prosecution should now be brought based on voice identification given by an expert which was solely confined to auditory analysis — there should always be expert evidence of acoustic analysis, including formant analysis. However, it has since been stated that it is 'neither possible nor desirable' to go as far as the Court of Appeal of Northern Ireland in this respect (*Flynn* [2008] 2 Cr App R 266 at [62]–[63]). The requirement in *O'Doherty* applies to voice identification by an expert, not a lay listener. As to the latter, the key to admissibility is the degree of familiarity of the witness with the voice in question, but it is desirable that an expert should be instructed to give an independent opinion on the validity of the lay listener evidence (*Flynn*).

Conflicts of Interest

F10.7   In *Toth v Jarman* [2006] 4 All ER 1276 it was held that, although a conflict of interest does not automatically disqualify an expert, where the conflict is material or significant the court is likely to decline to act on his evidence or indeed to give permission for his evidence to be adduced. It is therefore important that the party who wishes to call an expert with a potential conflict of interest of any kind — including a financial interest, a personal connection or an obligation (e.g., as a member or officer of some other body) — should disclose the details to the other party and to the court at the earliest possible opportunity. It is for the court and not the parties to decide whether a conflict is material or not. The fact that there is a risk of bias or lack of objectivity that is subliminal, as opposed to conscious, will not prevent an expert from giving his evidence (*Stubbs* [2006] EWCA Crim 2312). However, if there is a relationship between the proposed expert and the party calling him which a reasonable observer might think was capable of affecting the views of the expert so as to make the expert unduly favourable to that party, his evidence should be excluded, however unbiased his conclusions might be, on the grounds of public policy that justice must not only be done but also must be seen to be done (*Liverpool Roman Catholic Archdiocese Trustees Incorporated v Goldberg (No. 2)* [2001] 4 All ER 950).

Matters Calling for Expertise

Expert opinion evidence may only be received on a subject calling for expertise, which a lay **F10.8**
person, such as a magistrate or a juror, could not be expected to possess to a degree sufficient
to understand the evidence given in the case unaided. If the tribunal of fact can form its own
opinion without the assistance of an expert, the matter being within its own experience and
knowledge, expert opinion evidence is inadmissible because it is unnecessary (*Turner* [1975]
QB 834, per Lawton LJ at p. 841, applied in *Loughran* [1999] Crim LR 404). Thus a psychologist or other medical expert will not be permitted to give an opinion on the likely deterioration
of memory of an ordinary witness (*Browning* [1995] Crim LR 227). On the other hand, the
unlikelihood of the coincidence that a number of complainants all suffered from false memory
of sexual assault is a matter calling for expert evidence, being outside the experience of the jury
(*Nicholson* [2012] 2 Cr App R 405 at [35]). In *H (JR) (Childhood Amnesia)* [2006] 1 Cr App
R 195, it was held that, although a witness's ability to remember events will ordinarily be well
within the experience of jurors, in rare cases in which a witness gives evidence of an event, said
to have occurred at an early age, and the evidence is very detailed and contains a number of
extraneous facts, an appropriately qualified expert may give evidence that it should be treated
with caution and may well be unreliable, because recall of events during 'the period of childhood amnesia', which extends to the age of about seven, will be fragmented, disjointed and
idiosyncratic rather than a detailed narrative account. In the absence of such expert evidence,
which is likely to be outside the knowledge and experience of the jury, there is a danger that
the jury may find the detailed account more convincing than they safely should, because detail
normally enhances credibility to the ear of the listener. However, in *S* [2007] 2 All ER 974,
it was held that the ambit of the decision in *H (JR)* should not be widened, and in *Anderson*
[2012] EWCA Crim 1785, the correctness of the decision was doubted in light of criticisms of
the methodology of the expert who had given evidence in the case (see also *H* [2012] 1 Cr App
R 412). In some cases, it seems that jurors may receive assistance on a matter within their own
experience and knowledge if it is provided by someone who has had more time and better facilities to consider that matter than it would be practicable to afford to them (see *Clare* [1995] 2 Cr
App R 333, where an officer who did not know the accused but had viewed a video-recording
about 40 times, examining it in slow motion and rewinding and replaying it as frequently as was
necessary, was permitted to give evidence of identification based on a comparison between the
video images and contemporary photographs of the accused).

The subjects calling for expertise, which are so diverse as to defy comprehensive classification, **F10.9**
include a variety of medical, psychiatric, scientific and technological matters, and questions
relating to standards of professional competence. Specific examples include accident investigation and driver behaviour (*Dudley* [2004] EWCA Crim 3336); age, in the absence of documentary or other reliable evidence (*R (I) v Secretary of State for the Home Department* [2005]
EWHC 1025 (Admin) and *Re N (a child) (residence order)* [2006] EWHC 1189 (Fam)); ballis-
tics; blood tests; breath tests and blood/alcohol levels (sometimes including back-calculations
thereof, i.e. calculation of the amount of alcohol eliminated in the period between driving and
providing a specimen, in order to show that the level was above the prescribed limit at the time
of driving: see *Gumbley v Cunningham* [1989] AC 281); forgeries; handwriting identification
(including the analysis of indented impressions of handwriting, left on one document as a
result of writing on another, and revealed by Electrostatic Detection Apparatus (ESDA): see
Wellington [1991] Crim LR 543); fingerprint identification (see **F18.35**); ear-print identification (*Dallagher* [2003] 1 Cr App R 195 and *Kempster (No. 2)* [2008] 2 Cr App R 256; see
F18.37); voice identification (see **F18.24**); identification by facial mapping (*Stockwell* (1993)
97 Cr App R 260 and *Hookway* [1999] Crim LR 750; see **F18.21**), expert evidence of which may
form the basis of a conviction (*Mitchell* [2005] EWCA Crim 731); facial identification by video
superimposition (*Clarke* [1995] 2 Cr App R 425); 'reverse projection', the technique of super-
imposing one CCTV recording upon another as a means of comparing, e.g., the height of the
individuals shown (*Barnes* [2012] EWCA Crim 1605); genetic fingerprinting (the technique

whereby a human cell taken from a sample of blood, saliva, semen or hair is analysed to reveal a person's DNA or genetic 'fingerprint': see **F18.27**); the physical signs of child sexual abuse (*S* [2012] EWCA Crim 1433); 'shaken baby syndrome' (*Henderson* [2010] 2 Cr App R 185, considered at **F10.43** and **F10.46**); Sudden Infant Death Syndrome (SIDS) *(Cannings* [2004] 1 All ER 725, considered at **F5.18**); insanity; automatism; diminished responsibility; and the competence of a medical practitioner (*Whitehead* (1848) 3 Car & Kir 202: expert opinion evidence as to the state of knowledge and skill of a physician as shown by his treatment of the case in question).

Reliability

F10.10 A jury is entitled to rely on an expert opinion which falls short of scientific certainty. In *Gian* [2009] EWCA Crim 2553, a murder trial, the pathologist described the cause of death as two stab wounds but agreed as a theoretical possibility that the victim could have died from the consumption of cocaine. It was held that the judge had properly refused to withdraw the case from the jury. Such withdrawal was not justified by the mere fact that, as a matter of scientific certainty, it was not possible to rule out a proposition consistent with innocence. Juries are required to consider expert evidence in the context of all other relevant evidence and to make judgements based on realistic and not fanciful possibilities. See also *Bracewell* (1979) 68 Cr App R 44 and *Kai-Whitewind* [2005] 2 Cr App R 457. Similarly, evidence should not be excluded, or withdrawn from the jury, where the prosecution and defence experts disagree, but each states that the other's opinion is valid and tenable. *Hookway* [2011] EWCA Crim 1989 concerned two mixed DNA profiles. In the case of each, the two experts agreed that all of the accused's DNA components were represented. The prosecution expert was of the view that the components were at a higher level compared to the remaining components and therefore suitable for statistical interpretation, a view not shared by the defence expert. Support for both of the conflicting views could be found within the scientific community and each expert thought that the opinion of the other was valid and tenable. It was held that it was open to the jury to consider the expert evidence and to place what they considered to be the appropriate weight on the opinion of either expert. It was also held that, in doing so, they could take account of their conclusions in relation to the other evidence in the case. If, for example, they rejected the account of one of the accused of his innocent presence as being a concocted attempt to explain the possible presence of his DNA, this would support the more incriminating evidence of the prosecution expert.

F10.11 There is a related but separate question: whether an expert's opinion must be reliable in order to be admissible. Under the CrimPR, r. 33.4(h), an expert's report must include such information as the court may need to decide whether the expert's evidence is sufficiently reliable to be admissible as evidence. Under the test for admissibility of expert evidence set out in *Bonython* (1984) 15 ACR 364, regard must be had to (a) whether the subject matter calls for expertise, (b) whether the witness has the requisite expertise and (c) 'whether the subject matter of the opinion forms part of a body or knowledge or experience which is sufficiently organised or recognised to be accepted as a reliable body of knowledge or experience'. This test has been cited with approval within the English jurisdiction but the third element of the test is only rarely applied as a condition of admissibility. An example is *Gilfoyle* [2001] 2 Cr App R 57 (see **F10.21**); and see also *Kwaik* [2013] EWCA Crim 2397, where it was held that an expert analysis based on a computer modelling technique relating to how car collisions can occur was 'insufficiently robust'; the modelling covered about 200 different simulations, but several thousand would need to be carried out for a typical full stochastic analysis. In *Gilfoyle* it was held that the principle in *Frye v United States* 293 F 1013 (1923) — evidence based on a new brand of science or medicine is not admissible until accepted by the scientific community as being able to produce accurate and reliable opinion — accorded with the English approach. But see also *Harris* [2006] 1 Cr App R 55 at **F10.36**. However, the *Frye* test is no longer the governing principle in the USA. In *Daubert v Merrell Dow Pharmaceuticals* 509 US 579 (1993) the Supreme Court held that in federal courts the *Frye* test had been superseded by r. 702 of the Federal Rules of Evidence 1975. Under CPD V, para. 33A.4 see Supplement, **PD-46**), courts are encouraged to take into account, in deciding whether there is a sufficiently reliable scientific basis for expert opinion to be admitted, a range of factors set out para. 33A.5; and under para. 33A.6, courts, in considering reliability, especially the reliability of expert scientific opinion, should be astute to identify potential flaws of the kind listed in para. 33A.6. The following cases were all decided prior to the making of the directions in paras. 33A.1 to 33A.6.

In *Dallagher* [2003] 1 Cr App R 195 ear-print evidence was held to have been properly admitted. **F10.12** The court appeared to accept that the English approach is analogous to that of r. 702 of the Federal Rules of Evidence, and also referred to *Daubert*, yet none of the factors listed in that case, had they been considered, would have supported the case for admission of the expert evidence. (See also *Kempster (No. 2)* [2008] 2 Cr App R 256.) Instead, the court approved a passage from *Cross and Tapper on Evidence* (9th edn, 1999), at p. 523 which, after a reference to *Frye*, states: 'The better, and now more widely accepted, view, is that so long as a field is sufficiently well-established to pass the ordinary test of relevance and reliability, then no enhanced test for admissibility should be applied, but the weight of the evidence should be established by the same adversarial forensic techniques applicable elsewhere.' This passage was also applied in *Luttrell* [2004] 2 Cr App R 520, where the court rejected an argument that lip-reading evidence should not be admitted unless it could be seen to be reliable on the basis that the methods used were sufficiently explained to be tested in cross-examination and so to be verifiable or falsifiable. Cf. *O'Doherty* [2003] 1 Cr App R 77 at **F10.6**. The passage was further endorsed in *Reed* [2010] 1 Cr App R 310, where expert evaluative evidence of the possible ways in which DNA was transferred was held to be admissible notwithstanding that scientific knowledge and research on such transferability is plainly incomplete (see **F18.27**). Similarly, an expert in facial mapping is not confined to identification of the similarities or dissimilarities between the faces compared, but may express a view using expressions ranging from 'lends no support' (to the person in question being the accused) through to 'lends powerful support', notwithstanding that there is no established statistical database by which such expressions could be given numerical values, but it should be made clear to the jury that they are expressions of subjective opinion (*Atkins* [2010] 1 Cr App R 117). *Atkins* was followed in *Dlugosz* [2013] 1 Cr App R 425 (32), where it was held that in cases involving the use of Low Template DNA evidence derived from 'mixed samples', evaluative expert evidence may be admissible in the absence of statistical evidence of the relevant DNA match probability and notwithstanding the inability — which was not the case in *Atkins* — to use a hierarchy or sliding scale of support. (*Dlugosz* is considered more fully at **F18.27**.) In *Nicholson* [2012] 2 Cr App R 405 it was submitted that the jury should not have been permitted to consider the unlikelihood of the coincidence that the complainants were suffering from false memory without providing a statistical probability value for the coincidence. Rejecting the submission, Pitchford LJ said (at [43]): 'It is not the law that a statistical value must be placed upon any coincidence on the unlikelihood of which one of the parties to a criminal trial relies'. See also *T (Footwear mark evidence)* [2011] 1 Cr App R 85, where it was held that although there were no sufficiently reliable data for an expert on footwear marks to express an opinion based on mathematical formulae and likelihood ratios, an expert may nonetheless give an evaluative opinion that a shoe could or could not have made a mark based on factors such as class characteristics (i.e. those resulting from manufacture of the footwear) and identifying characteristics, such as objects attached to the sole and damage caused by cuts.

In *I* [2012] EWCA Crim 1288, where an expert opinion rested upon a hypothesis that could **F10.13** have been tested to ensure its reliability, the Court of Appeal declined to require such testing as a condition of admissibility. It was held that expert opinion evidence based on a test that was clearly reliable when applied in one context could be admitted notwithstanding that it was being applied in a novel context without any evaluation of its efficacy in that context. Cf. *Holdsworth* [2008] EWCA Crim 971, where the Court of Appeal acknowledged the dangers of relying on expert hypotheses with inadequate empirical foundations and observed that special caution was needed where expert evidence was not just relied upon as material supportive of a prosecution but was fundamental to it.

States of Mind

F10.14   **Insanity, Diminished Responsibility and Automatism**   As to the need for expert evidence to prove insanity, see **A3.23, D12.9, D12.16** and **F10.4**. On the issue of diminished responsibility, the Court of Appeal in *Dix* (1981) 74 Cr App R 306, applying a dictum in *Byrne* [1960] 2 QB 396 at p. 402, said (at p. 311): 'while the Homicide Act 1957, s. 2(1) does not in terms require that medical evidence be adduced in support of a defence of diminished responsibility, it makes it a practical necessity if that defence is to begin to run at all'. As to automatism, see *Smith* [1979] 3 All ER 605 where the defence was automatism, by sleepwalking. The Court of Appeal held that the type of automatism in question was not something within the realm of the ordinary juror's experience but a matter on which the jury should not be deprived of expert assistance. See also *Hill v Baxter* [1958] 1 QB 277, at p. 285.

F10.15   **Psychiatric Injury**   Where psychiatric injury is relied on as the basis for an allegation of assault occasioning actual bodily harm, and the matter is not admitted by the defence, the Crown should call expert evidence to prove the injury; in the absence of such evidence the question whether the assault occasioned such injury should not be left to the jury (*Chan-Fook* [1994] 2 All ER 552, applied in *Morris* [1998] 1 Cr App R 386).

F10.16   **Intent**   In appropriate circumstances, expert medical evidence may be admissible on the question of the effect of a medical abnormality upon intent. Thus in *Toner* (1991) 93 Cr App R 382, a physician gave evidence that the accused had been suffering from a minor hypoglycaemic state caused by the ingestion of food after a prolonged fast. It was held that the defence had been improperly prevented from asking the witness what the effect of that minor degree of hypoglycaemia would be on the ability to make judgements or to form specific intents. The Court of Appeal held that there is no distinction between medical evidence relating to hypoglycaemia and its possible effect upon intent, and medical evidence as to the effect of a drug upon intent: both are matters outside the ordinary experience of jurors who cannot bring to bear their own judgement without the assistance of expert evidence. Similarly in *Huckerby* [2004] EWCA Crim 3251, evidence that the accused was suffering from post-traumatic stress disorder, a recognised mental condition with which the jury would not be expected to be familiar, was admissible because it was relevant to an essential issue bearing upon his guilt or innocence, namely whether it had caused him to panic and co-operate with criminals in circumstances in which he would otherwise not have done so. Subject to cases of this kind, however, and except in the case of an accused who comes into the class of mental defective, expert psychiatric evidence is not admissible on the issue of whether the accused did, or did not, have the required *mens rea*. In *Chard* (1971) 56 Cr App R 268 the Court of Appeal held that the judge, in a murder trial, had properly refused a defence application to call a medical witness to give evidence about the accused's intent to kill or do grievous bodily harm because the accused was entirely normal and was not, e.g., suffering from insanity or diminished responsibility. See also *Reynolds* [1989] Crim LR 220 and, in the case of adolescents, *Coles* [1995] 1 Cr App R 157. Similarly, in *Masih* [1986] Crim LR 395, a case of rape in which the accused suffered from no psychiatric illness, but had an intelligence quotient of 72, just above the level of subnormality, on the question of whether he knew the complainant was not consenting, or was reckless as to whether she consented, psychiatric evidence as to his state of mind, intelligence and ability to appreciate the situation was held to be inadmissible. Upholding the ruling, the Court of Appeal held that, generally speaking, if an accused comes into the class of mental defective, with an IQ of 69 or below, then insofar as the defectiveness is relevant to an issue, expert evidence may be admitted, provided that it is confined to an assessment of the accused's IQ and an explanation of any relevant abnormal characteristics (in order to enlighten the jury on a matter that is abnormal and outside their experience). However, if an accused is within the scale of normality, albeit at the lower end, as was the appellant, expert evidence should generally be excluded. See also *Hall* (1987) 86 Cr App R 159 and *Henry* [2006] 1 Cr App R 118.

F10.17   In *Wood* [1990] Crim LR 264, the accused, charged with murder, raised the partial defence under Homicide Act 1957, s. 4, of the unsuccessful execution of a suicide pact. In support of this defence, and relying upon an analogy with diminished responsibility, the defence sought unsuccessfully to introduce psychiatric evidence to the effect that the accused suffered from a personality disorder. Refusing leave to appeal, it was held that whereas the defence of diminished responsibility was founded on the existence of some abnormality of mind, in the case of a suicide pact, once the killing had been proved, the questions for the jury are whether there was such a pact and, if so, whether at the time of the killing the accused was acting in pursuance thereof and had the settled intention of dying in pursuance thereof. That the applicant had a personality which was to some extent abnormal and liable to give way to excesses of behaviour under stress was not something outside the ordinary experience of the average juror.

Provocation and Loss of Control   Psychiatric evidence is inadmissible in order to establish   **F10.18** that the accused was likely to have been provoked. In *Turner* [1975] QB 834 the Court of Appeal upheld the refusal of a trial judge to allow the defence to call a psychiatrist, on the issues of credibility and provocation, to prove that the accused had had a deep emotional relationship with the victim, which was likely to have caused an explosive release of blind rage after her confession of infidelity to him, and that subsequent to the killing he had behaved like someone suffering from profound grief. The court held that these were matters well within ordinary human experience and upon which the jury required no expert assistance. The evidence was not admissible on the issue of provocation, therefore, and the same reasoning prevented its admission on the issue of credibility. *Sed quaere*, whether expert evidence might not be admitted on an issue of provocation, where the accused suffers from some mental abnormality (*Camplin* [1978] AC 705). *Turner* was distinguished in *McDonald* [1991] Crim LR 122. In that case evidence was adduced of an out-of-court statement made by the accused explaining why he had killed the victim, an explanation which was sufficient to lay a foundation for the defence of provocation. Subsequently, in the course of a psychiatric examination, the accused admitted that the explanation was invented. It was held that it was not unfair for the psychiatrist to give evidence of the admission, because it related to a factual matter, not a medical issue.

Duress   In the case of duress, psychiatric evidence may be admissible to show that an accused   **F10.19** was suffering from some mental illness, mental impairment or recognised psychiatric condition, if persons generally suffering from such a condition might be more susceptible to pressure and threats, and thus to assist the jury in deciding whether a reasonable person with such a condition might have been impelled to act as the accused had. Psychiatric evidence is not admissible simply to show that an accused not suffering from such a condition, was especially timid, suggestible or vulnerable to pressure and threats (*Walker* [2003] EWCA Crim 1837).

Concerning the defence of duress by threats, expert evidence is admissible for the purposes of the subjective limb of the test, provided that the mental condition or abnormality in question is outside the knowledge and experience of laymen, but inadmissible for the purposes of the objective limb (*Hegarty* [1994] Crim LR 353; cf. *Horne* [1994] Crim LR 584 and *Hurst* [1995] 1 Cr App R 82).

Reliability or Truth of Confessions   The expert evidence of a psychiatrist or psychologist   **F10.20** is admissible on the issue of the reliability or truth of a confession if it is to the effect that no reliance can be placed on the confession because the accused was suffering from a personality disorder so severe as properly to be categorised as a mental disorder (*Ward* [1993] 2 All ER 577). Admissible evidence from psychiatrists, however, is not confined to evidence of such personality disorders. The test is not whether an abnormality fits into a recognised category such as anti-social personality disorder. That is neither necessary nor sufficient. It is sufficient for the disorder to be of a type which might render a confession or evidence unreliable. However, there must be a very significant deviation from the norm shown, and an independent history, pre-dating the confession or the giving of evidence, which points to or explains the abnormalities. If such evidence is admitted, the jury must be directed that they are not obliged to accept it, but should consider it, if they think it right to do so, as throwing light on the personality of the accused and bringing to their attention aspects of that personality of which they might otherwise have been unaware (*O'Brien* [2000] Crim LR 676, applied in *Smith* [2003] EWCA Crim 927). Psychiatric evidence is not admissible in the case of someone with an histrionic personality disorder characterised by emotional superficiality and impulsive behaviour when under stress, but who does not suffer from mental illness and is not below normal intelligence (*Weightman* (1990) 92 Cr App R 291). However, the expert evidence of a psychologist is admissible to show that a confession made by someone not suffering from any personality or abnormal disorder is likely to be unreliable if it was a 'coerced compliant confession', a phenomenon falling outside the experience of the jury. A coerced compliant confession is one brought about by fatigue, together with an inability to control what is happening, which may induce the individual to experience a growing desire to give up resisting suggestions put to him so that eventually he can take no more and is overwhelmed by the need to achieve the immediate goal of bringing the interrogation to an end (*Blackburn* [2005] 2 Cr App R 440). See also, as to the admissibility of psychiatric evidence on a *voir dire* to determine the admissibility of a confession, **F17.18** and **F17.21**.

F10.21 **Psychological Autopsies** The present academic status of 'psychological autopsies' is not such as to allow them to be admitted as a basis for expert opinion evidence (*Gilfoyle* [2001] 2 Cr App R 57). In *Gilfoyle*, a murder trial in which the only other possible explanation for the death was suicide, the Court of Appeal declined to hear the fresh evidence of a distinguished psychologist who had carried out a 'psychological autopsy' of the deceased, relying upon the dictum of Lord President Cooper in *Davie v Magistrates of Edinburgh* 1953 SC 34 at p. 40 that expert witnesses must furnish the court 'with the necessary scientific criteria for testing the accuracy of their conclusions, so as to enable the judge or jury to form their own independent judgement by the application of these criteria to the facts proved in evidence'. One of the reasons for the decision was that the psychologist's reports identified no criteria by reference to which the court could test the quality of his opinions; there was no database comparing real and questionable suicides and no substantial body of academic writing approving his methodology. Another reason was that English, Canadian and US authority pointed against the admission of the evidence. The principle in *Frye v United States* 293 F 1013 (1923), that evidence based on a developing new brand of science or medicine is not admissible until accepted by the scientific community as being able to provide accurate and reliable opinion, accorded with the English approach. (But see further **F10.11**.)

Credibility

F10.22 Medical evidence is admissible to show that a witness suffers from some disease or defect or abnormality of mind that affects the reliability of his evidence. Such evidence is not confined to a general opinion of the unreliability of the witness but may give all the matters necessary to show, not only the foundation of and reasons for the diagnosis, but also the extent to which the credibility of the witness is affected. (*Toohey v Metropolitan Police Commissioner* [1965] AC 595, per Lord Pearce at p. 609)

See further **F7.57**. In the case of evidence of 'abnormality of mind', the approach set out in *O'Brien* [2000] Crim LR 676 and considered at **F10.20** applies whether the expert evidence that is being considered relates to a witness or an accused. However, especially in the case of a witness, it is important to take into account the importance of the evidence that the witness gives. If it is of little significance to the issues at the trial, the admission of expert evidence is unlikely to be justified (*MacKenney* [2004] 2 Cr App R 32, considered at **F7.59**, at [15]). Subject to the principle of *Toohey v Metropolitan Police Commissioner*, it is only in exceptional cases that psychologists and psychiatrists may be called to prove the probability of the veracity of the accused (*Henry* [2006] 1 Cr App R 118 at [15]) or another witness (*The Queen v Joyce* [2005] NTSC 21, concerning the credibility of a child, and *S* [2006] EWCA Crim 2389). Thus, for example, opinion evidence should not be given as to the truth or otherwise of a complaint of sexual abuse (*C* [2012] EWCA Crim 1478). An example of an exceptional case is *Lowery v The Queen* [1974] AC 85. L and K were charged with an apparently motiveless murder, the circumstances being that one or both of them must have committed the offence. Each blamed the other for the crime. The Privy Council held that the trial judge had properly permitted K to call a psychologist, who had carried out personality tests on both L and K, to show that K's version of events was more probable than that of L, since, compared to K, L's character and disposition were such that he was more likely to have committed the offence. Commenting upon this decision in *Turner* [1975] QB 834, Lawton LJ said (at p. 842):

> In every case what is relevant and admissible depends on the issues raised in that case. In *Lowery v The Queen* the issues were unusual; and the accused to whose disadvantage the psychologist's evidence went had in effect said before it was called that he was not the sort of man to have committed the offence....

> We adjudge *Lowery v The Queen* to have been decided on its special facts. We do not consider that it is an authority for the proposition that in all cases psychologists and psychiatrists can be called to prove the probability of the accused's veracity.

In *Rimmer* [1983] Crim LR 250, the two accused were charged with murder, and each blamed **F10.23** the other. On the basis of a medical report, counsel for B cross-examined R, suggesting to him that he had a history of mental illness and that he had killed the victim in a fit of uncontrollable temper to which he was accustomed. The Court of Appeal upheld the ruling of the trial judge that R was not entitled to call medical evidence to establish that he was not, and never had been, mentally ill. See also *Miller* [1952] 2 All ER 667, *Neale* (1977) 65 Cr App R 304, and *Bracewell* (1978) 68 Cr App R 44.

Expert evidence may be admitted as to the dangers of evidence produced through hypnotherapy. **F10.24** In *Clark* [2006] EWCA Crim 231, A, aged 33 at the time of the trial, gave evidence of sexual offences against her when she was aged 10 to 12. The first time she had spoken of the abuse was during a hypnotherapy session with S shortly before the trial. She said that her subconscious had not previously allowed her to speak of the matter. It was held that A's evidence had been correctly admitted but that the defence should have been allowed to call an expert, not to give his opinion on A's truthfulness, but to criticise S's techniques and to express his opinion about the danger that *if* A's recollection was falsely engendered through the counselling, A would thereafter have regarded it as genuine memory. However, as a matter of principle, evidence produced by the administration of some mechanical, chemical or hypnotic truth test on a witness is inadmissible to show the veracity or otherwise of that witness (*Fennell v Jerome Property Maintenance Ltd* (1986) *The Times*, 26 November 1986). The previous statements of the witness are not only inadmissible hearsay, but insofar as they are consistent with his testimony, inadmissible as evidence of consistency under the rule against previous self-serving statements (see **F6.32** and cf. the CJA 2003, s. 120, at **F6.34**, **F6.44** and **F6.46**).

Handwriting

Handwriting may be identified by a non-expert familiar with the handwriting in question (*Doe* **F10.25** *d Mudd v Suckermore* (1836) 5 A & E 703, and *Slaney* (1832) 5 C & P 213). The witness's knowledge, however, must not have been acquired for the express purpose of qualifying him to testify at the trial (*Crouch* (1850) 4 Cox CC 163). An expert should be called if there is to be a comparison of the 'disputed writing' with specimen handwriting proved or admitted to have been written by the person in question, under the Criminal Procedure Act 1865, s. 8 (*Tilley* [1961] 3 All ER 406; *Harden* [1963] 1 QB 8). Such expert evidence is admissible under s. 8 even if the expert has not seen the original 'disputed writing' (e.g., because it is lost), but has made his comparison with a photocopy of the original (*Lockheed-Arabia v Owen* [1993] QB 806). See further **F8.41**. As to the standard of proof required to establish the genuineness of specimen handwriting, see *Ewing* [1983] QB 1039 and *Angeli* [1979] 3 All ER 950.

Obscenity

In the normal case, the issues of indecency or obscenity should be determined by the jury with- **F10.26** out expert assistance. In *Anderson* [1972] 1 QB 304, Lord Widgery CJ said (at p. 313) that in the ordinary run of the mill cases, the issue 'obscene or no' under the Obscene Publications Act 1959 must be tried without the assistance of expert evidence. His lordship said that *DPP v A and*

BC Chewing Gum Ltd [1968] 1 QB 159 'should be regarded as highly exceptional and confined to its own circumstances, namely, a case where the alleged obscene matter was directed at very young children, and was of itself of a somewhat unusual kind'. In the latter case the accused were charged with publishing for gain obscene battle cards (which were sold together with packets of bubble gum), contrary to the Obscene Publications Act, s. 2(1), and the Obscene Publications Act 1964, s. 1(1). The Divisional Court held that the magistrates had improperly prevented the prosecution from introducing evidence of experts in child psychiatry as to the likely effect of the cards on children. Lord Parker CJ held that, when considering the effect of something on an adult, an adult jury may be able to judge just as well as an adult witness; but when one is dealing with children of different age groups and children from five upwards, any jury, and any justices, need all the help they can get as to the effect on different children. See also *Skirving* [1985] QB 819, a prosecution arising out of the publication of a book entitled *Attention Coke Lovers. Free Base. The Greatest Thing Since Sex*, which contained explanations, instructions and 'recipes' on how to make use of cocaine to maximum effect. The Court of Appeal held that expert evidence on the characteristics of cocaine and the effects of the various methods of ingesting the drug was admissible, because it was outside the experience of the ordinary person, and only when equipped with such information would the jury be in a position to decide whether the publication had a tendency to deprave and corrupt.

Expert opinion evidence is also admissible on questions of a literary, artistic or scientific nature in relation to the defence of 'public good' under the Obscene Publications Act 1959, s. 4 (see s. 4(2)).

Foreign Law

F10.27 Points of foreign law of any jurisdiction other than that of England and Wales are questions of fact to be decided on the evidence by the judge (Administration of Justice Act 1920, s. 15: see also **F1.34**). Thus, if there has been an English decision on a point of foreign law and the same point subsequently arises again, it must be decided on new evidence (*M'Cormick v Garnett* (1854) 5 De GM & G 278). The general rule is that the law of a foreign country, whether written or not, must be proved by the testimony of a competent expert, by the witness statement of such an expert (if admissible), or on the basis of a statement of agreed facts pursuant to the CJA 1967, s. 10 (*Ofori* (1994) 99 Cr App R 223). If the expert witnesses agree on a point of foreign law, the court is not entitled to reject their evidence and to conduct its own research by referring to textbooks and foreign law reports (*Bumper Development Corporation Ltd v Commissioner of Police of the Metropolis* [1991] 4 All ER 638). The expert may refresh his memory from foreign law books, but the law itself is proved by his oral evidence (*Sussex Peerage Case* (1844) 11 Cl & F 85). A witness is competent for these purposes if he is a practitioner in the relevant jurisdiction (*Baron de Bode's Case* (1845) 8 QB 208). There is old authority that a practitioner from the jurisdiction in question should always be called (*Bristow v Sequeville* (1850) 5 Exch 275). However, a witness has been held to be suitably qualified for these purposes if he is:

(a) a former practitioner in the relevant jurisdiction (*Re Duke of Wellington* [1947] Ch 506);
(b) a person qualified to practise in the relevant jurisdiction, even if he has not done so (*Barford v Barford and McLeod* [1918] P 140); or
(c) a person who has acquired the appropriate expertise by academic study (*Brailey v Rhodesia Consolidated Ltd* [1910] 2 Ch 95, reader in Roman-Dutch law to the Council of Legal Education); as an embassy official (*In the Goods of Dost Aly Khan* (1889) 6 PD 6); or in the course of a non-legal business such as banking (*De Beéche v South American Stores (Gath and Chaves) Ltd* [1935] AC 148).

F10.28 Exceptions   There are two exceptions to the general rule:

(a) The Evidence (Colonial Statutes) Act 1907, s. 1, and the Colonial Laws Validity Act 1865, s. 6, provide for proof of colonial statutes etc.; and English courts may construe such statutes without accompanying expert evidence (see the authorities cited in *Jasiewicz v Jasiewicz* [1962] 3 All ER 1017).

(b) The British Law Ascertainment Act 1859 provides that an English court may state a case on a point of foreign law for the opinion of a superior court in another part of Her Majesty's dominions, and that the opinion thus produced is admissible evidence on the point of law in question.

Competence of Witnesses

Determination of the question whether a child is competent to give evidence for the purposes of the YJCEA 1999, s. 54, does not normally require any input from an expert, but a decision as to the competence of a mentally handicapped person, whether adult or child does require appropriate expert medical evidence (see **F4.27**). **F10.29**

Proof of Facts Upon which Expert Opinion Evidence Based

Before a court can assess the value of an opinion it must know the facts upon which it is based. If the expert has been misinformed about the facts or has taken irrelevant facts into consideration or has omitted to consider relevant ones, the opinion is likely to be valueless. In our judgment, counsel calling an expert should in examination-in-chief ask his witness to state the facts upon which his opinion is based. It is wrong to leave the other side to elicit the facts by cross-examination (*Turner* [1975] QB 834 at p. 840). **F10.30**

In some cases, some of the relevant facts upon which the opinion is based can be proved by the expert himself, as when he has examined an exhibit or a fingerprint and therefore has personal or first-hand knowledge of those facts. In other cases, however, the expert will have no personal or first-hand knowledge of the facts, or all of the facts, upon which his opinion is based. For example, in a trial for murder by stabbing, in which the defence is that the victim's injuries were self-inflicted, a medical witness who has not examined the body may be asked whether, assuming that the facts, described by another medical witness who has examined the body, are true, the wound was inflicted by a person other than the deceased (*Mason* (1911) 7 Cr App R 67; and see also *Francis* [2013] EWCA Crim 123). Similarly, an expert may give his expert opinion on the basis of preparatory work, such as scientific tests carried out by assistants. Whether or not the expert has personal knowledge of the facts upon which his opinion is based, those facts must be proved. This may be done by calling the person with personal knowledge of them. However, under the CJA 2003, s. 127, a statement made by such a person for the purposes of either a criminal investigation or criminal proceedings may be admitted without the need to call him, and in evidence given in the proceedings the expert may base his opinion on the statement, unless, on an application by a party to the proceedings, the court orders that application of the section is not in the interests of justice.

Criminal Justice Act 2003, s. 127 **F10.31**

(1) This section applies if—
   (a) a statement has been prepared for the purposes of criminal proceedings,
   (b) the person who prepared the statement had or may reasonably be supposed to have had personal knowledge of the matters stated,
   (c) notice is given under the appropriate rules that another person (the expert) will in evidence given in the proceedings orally or under section 9 of the Criminal Justice Act 1967 base an opinion or inference on the statement, and
   (d) the notice gives the name of the person who prepared the statement and the nature of the matters stated.
(2) In evidence given in the proceedings the expert may base an opinion or inference on the statement.
(3) If evidence based on the statement is given under subsection (2) the statement is to be treated as evidence of what it says.
(4) This section does not apply if the court, on an application by a party to the proceedings, orders that it is not in the interests of justice that it should apply.
(5) The matters to be considered by the court in deciding whether to make an order under subsection (4) include—

(a) the expense of calling as a witness the person who prepared the statement;

(b) whether relevant evidence could be given by that person which could not be given by the expert;

(c) whether that person can reasonably be expected to remember the matters stated well enough to give oral evidence of them.

(6) Subsections (1) to (5) apply to a statement prepared for the purposes of a criminal investigation as they apply to a statement prepared for the purposes of criminal proceedings, and in such a case references to the proceedings are to criminal proceedings arising from the investigation.

F10.32 **Facts Derived from the Use of a Computer**   Where an expert bases his opinion on facts derived from the use of a computer, it seems that there is no obligation to produce the printout (see *Golizadeh* [1995] Crim LR 232, where an expert was allowed to give his opinion that a certain substance was opium on the basis of a printout of a machine used by him to analyse its chemical constituents, the printout itself not having been produced in evidence).

F10.33 **Special Treatment of Hearsay**   An expert is not subject to the rule against hearsay in the same way as a non-expert or a witness of fact. Thus, although an expert cannot prove facts upon which his opinion is based, but of which he has no personal or first-hand knowledge, because that would be an infringement of the hearsay rule, he may rely upon such facts as a part of the process of forming an opinion. However, if there is no direct evidence to establish such facts, the weight to be attached to the opinion of the expert is likely to be minimal. In *Bradshaw* (1985) 82 Cr App R 79, a murder trial, the only issue was that of diminished responsibility. (The burden of proof was on the defence: Homicide Act 1957, s. 2(2).) Counsel for the defence sought guidance from the judge as to how far the doctors would be permitted to give evidence as to what the accused had told them during interviews, how far they could express opinions based upon such statements, and whether the judge would make adverse comment if the accused were not to give evidence. The judge replied that, if the truth of what the accused had said to the doctors was in question, the only appropriate course was for the accused to prove the facts upon which the expert opinion was based, or for those facts to be proved by other evidence. The accused, who had recovered from any abnormality of mind at the date of the trial, gave evidence and was cross-examined. He appealed against conviction on the grounds that the ruling of the judge was erroneous. The appeal was dismissed. Lord Lane CJ said (at p. 83):

> Although as a concession to the defence doctors are sometimes allowed to base their opinions on what the defendant has told them (i.e. hearsay) without those matters being proved by admissible evidence, yet the strict (and correct) view is that expressed at p. 446 of *Cross on Evidence*, 5th ed., in the following terms: 'A doctor may not state what a patient told him about past symptoms as evidence of the existence of those symptoms because that would infringe the rule against hearsay, but he may give evidence of what the patient told him in order to explain the grounds on which he came to a conclusion with regard to the patient's condition'.

> Thus, if the doctor's opinion is based entirely on hearsay and is not supported by direct evidence, the judge will be justified in telling the jury that the defendant's case (if that is so) is based upon a flimsy or non-existent foundation and that they should reach their conclusion bearing that in mind. In proper cases, for example where, as here, the defendant has completely recovered from any abnormality of mind by the time of the trial, there is no reason why the judge should not comment upon the fact that the defendant could have provided the necessary evidence had he wished to do so, the burden of proof being upon him.

F10.34 As a part of the process of forming an opinion, expert witnesses may refer not only to their own research, tests and experiments, but also to works of authority, learned articles, research papers, and other similar material written by others and forming part of the general body of knowledge falling within their field of expertise (see generally *Davie v Magistrates of Edinburgh* 1953 SC 34; *Seyfang v G.D. Searle & Co.* [1973] QB 148, at p. 151; and *H v Schering Chemicals Ltd* [1983] 1 All ER 849). In *Abadom* [1983] 1 All ER 364, on the question of whether fragments of glass embedded in the shoes of the accused had come from a window allegedly broken during a robbery, an expert gave evidence that, based upon his personal analysis of the samples, the glass in the shoes and that from the window bore an identical refractive index; and that, having consulted unpublished statistics compiled by the Home Office Central Research Establishment, which showed that that index occurred in only 4 per cent of all glass samples investigated, in his opinion there was a very strong likelihood that the glass in the shoes came from the window. It was argued, on appeal, that the evidence of the Home Office statistics was inadmissible hearsay, since the expert had no knowledge of the analysis on which the statistics had been based. The appeal was dismissed on the ground that the primary facts, i.e. the refractive indices of the glass samples, had been proved by the expert on the basis of his own analysis; and that once the primary facts upon which an opinion is based have been proved by admissible evidence, an expert is entitled to draw on the work of others as part of the process of arriving at his conclusion, and this involves no breach of the hearsay rule. The Court of Appeal pointed out that part of the experience and expertise of experts lies in their knowledge and evaluation of *unpublished* material; they may draw on such material, provided that they refer to it in their evidence so that the cogency and probative value of their conclusions can be tested and evaluated by reference thereto. See also *Ahmed* [2011] EWCA Crim 184, and compare *Somers* [1963] 3 All ER 808, considered at **F10.5**. *Abadom* was applied in *Hodges* [2003] 2 Cr App R 247, a case of conspiracy to supply heroin in which a very experienced drugs officer gave expert evidence, derived in part from what he had been told by others, including other officers, informants and drug users, as to the usual method of supplying heroin, as to its purchase price, and that 14 grammes of heroin was more than would have been for personal use. Similarly, in *Ibrahima* [2005] EWCA Crim 1436, a case of possession of ecstasy tablets with intent to supply, it was held that a person with no medical or psychological qualifications, but with experience and knowledge of drug use as a deputy director of a drug advice charity, was entitled to give evidence, whether for the prosecution or defence, as to what quantities of ecstasy are consistent with personal use, and as to how users acquire an increasing tolerance of the drug, leading to higher consumption, provided that he gave the categories of his sources of information. However, see also *Edwards* [2001] EWCA Crim 2185, where the issue was whether the ecstasy tablets found in the accused's possession were for personal consumption or for supply. 'Experts', neither of whom had any formal medical or toxicological qualifications, were not permitted to give evidence based on their experience, rather than any academic material such as statistical surveys or reports, as to the personal consumption rates of ecstasy tablet users.

Opinions on Ultimate Issues

In its *Eleventh Report: Evidence (General)* (1972), Cmnd 4991, para. 268, the Criminal Law **F10.35** Revision Committee was of the opinion that the old common-law rule that a witness should not express an opinion on an ultimate issue, i.e. one of the very issues to be determined by the court, probably no longer existed. In practice the rule is largely ignored, or treated as being of only semantic effect, so that an expert *is* allowed to express an opinion on an ultimate issue, provided that the actual words he employs are not noticeably the same as those which will be used when the issue falls to be considered by the court. In *DPP v A and BC Chewing Gum Ltd* [1968] 1 QB 159, Lord Parker CJ said (at p. 164):

> I think it would be wrong to ask the direct question as to whether any particular cards tended to corrupt or deprave, because that final stage was a matter which was entirely for the justices. No doubt, however, in such a case the defence might well put it to the witness that a particular card or cards could not corrupt, and no doubt, whatever the strict position may be, that question coming from the defence would be allowed, if only to give the defence an opportunity of getting an answer 'No' from the expert.
>
> ...I myself would go a little further in that I cannot help feeling that with the advance of science more and more inroads have been made into the old common-law principles. Those who practise in the criminal courts see every day cases of experts being called on the question of diminished responsibility, and although technically the final question 'Do you think he was suffering from diminished responsibility?' is strictly inadmissible, it is allowed time and time again without any objection.

Thus the rule has become 'a matter of form rather than substance' (*Stockwell* (1993) 97 Cr App R 260 at p. 265). For illustrations, see *Mason* (1911) 7 Cr App R 67 (whether wounds were self-inflicted), *Holmes* [1953] 2 All ER 324 (insanity), *Silcott* [1987] Crim LR 765 (the unreliability of a confession), *Hookway* [1999] Crim LR 750 (establishing identity by expert evidence of facial mapping) and *Udenze* [2001] EWCA Crim 1381 (in a rape case, the effects of alcohol on the ability to give informed consent). As to possession of drugs with intent to supply, see *Hodges* [2003] 2 Cr App R 247, considered at **F10.34**; but see also *Jeffries* [1997] Crim LR 819. See also *Atkins* [2010] 1 Cr App R 117.

Duty of Experts

F10.36   In *Harris* [2006] 1 Cr App R 55, it was held that the description of the obligations of an expert witness set out by Creswell J in *National Justice Cia Naviera SA v Prudential Assurance Co Ltd (Ikarian Reefer)* [1993] 2 Lloyd's Rep 68 at p. 81 and the guidance for experts giving evidence involving children provided by Wall J in *In re AB (Child Abuse: Expert Witnesses)* [1995] 1 FLR 181 were both very relevant in criminal proceedings and should be kept well in mind by both prosecution and defence. Some of the factors set out by Creswell J in the former case were summarised in *Harris* (at [271]) as follows:

(1)   Expert evidence presented to the court should be and be seen to be the independent product of the expert uninfluenced as to form or content by the exigencies of litigation.

(2)   An expert witness should provide independent assistance to the court by way of objective unbiased opinion in relation to matters within his expertise. An expert witness in the High Court should never assume the role of the advocate.

(3)   An expert witness should state the facts or assumptions on which his opinion is based. He should not omit to consider material facts which detract from his concluded opinion.

(4)   An expert should make it clear when a particular question or issue falls outside his expertise.

(5)   If an expert's opinion is not properly researched because he considers that insufficient data is available then this must be stated with an indication that the opinion is no more than a provisional one.

(6)   If after exchange of reports, an expert witness changes his view on material matters, such changes of view should be communicated to the other side without delay and when appropriate to the court.

F10.37   In *In re AB (Child Abuse: Expert Witnesses)*, Wall J, referring to cases in which there is a genuine disagreement on a scientific or medical issue or where it is necessary for a party to advance a particular hypothesis to explain a given set of facts, said (at p. 192):

> Where that occurs, the judge [in a criminal case, jury] will have to resolve the issue which is raised. Two points must be made. In my view, the expert who advances such a hypothesis owes a very heavy duty to explain to the court that what he is advancing is a hypothesis, that it is controversial (if it is) and to place before the court all material which contradicts the hypothesis. Secondly, he must make all his material available to the other experts in the case. It is the common experience of the courts that the better the experts the more limited their areas of disagreement, and in the forensic context of a contested case relating to children, the objective of the lawyers and the experts should always be to limit the ambit of disagreement on medical issues to the minimum.

In *Harris* itself it was stressed (at [270]) that developments in scientific thinking should not be kept from the court, simply because they remain at the stage of a hypothesis, but it is of the first importance that the true status of the expert's evidence is frankly indicated to the court. As to limiting the ambit of disagreement, it was further pointed out (at [273]) that the CrimPR, r. 24 (see now the CrimPR, r. 33), and para. 15 of the Plea and Case Management form make provision for experts to come together and, if possible, agree points of agreement or disagreement with a summary of reasons. (See also, endorsing the importance of this provision, *Holdsworth* [2008] EWCA Crim 971.) In cases involving allegations of child abuse, it was said that the judge should be prepared to give directions in respect of expert evidence, taking into account the guidance to which the court had referred.

In *B (T)* [2006] 2 Cr App R 22 it was emphasised that the duties of an expert witness as set out **F10.38** in *The Ikarian Reefer* and *Harris* are owed to the court and override any obligation to the person from whom the expert has received instructions, or by whom the expert is paid. Experts should maintain professional objectivity and impartiality at all times.

The duties of an expert, as set out in *Harris* and *B (T)* have been reinforced by the CrimPR, r. 33.2, which provides that an expert must help the court to achieve the overriding objective by giving objective, unbiased opinion on matters within his expertise, and that this duty over-rides any obligation to the person instructing him or by whom he is paid. This duty includes an obligation (a) to define his area or areas of expertise in his report and when giving evidence, (b) when giving evidence, to draw the court's attention to any question to which the answer would be outside his area or areas of expertise, and (c) to inform all parties and the court if his opinion changes from that contained in a report served as evidence or given in a statement.

For the CrimPR, part 33, see Supplement, **R-256** *et seq.*

In *Cleobury* [2012] EWCA Crim 17 consideration was given to the duty of an expert on appeal. It was held that, where it is in the interests of justice for the Court of Appeal to hear fresh expert evidence (e.g., after the trial there is some new scientific discovery), it is essential that the expert present his report as evidence within his sphere of expertise and not as an advocate's critique of either what happened at the trial or the judge's summing-up.

Content of Expert's Report

In *B (T)* [2006] 2 Cr App R 22 it was held that, in addition to the specific factors referred to in **F10.39** *The Ikarian Reefer* [1993] 2 Lloyd's Rep 68 and *Harris* [2006] 1 Cr App R 55, the following are necessary inclusions in an expert report.

(a) Details of the expert's academic and professional qualifications, experience and accredita-tion relevant to the opinions expressed in the report and the range and extent of the exper-tise and any limitations upon the expertise.
(b) A statement setting out the substance of all the instructions received, with written or oral questions upon which an opinion is sought, the materials provided and considered, and the documents, statements, evidence, information or assumptions which are material to the opinions expressed or upon which those opinions are based.
(c) Information relating to who has carried out measurements, examinations, tests etc., and the methodology used, and whether or not such measurements etc., were carried out under the expert's supervision.
(d) Where there is a range of opinion in the matters dealt with in the report, a summary of the range of opinion and the reasons for the opinion given. In this connection any material facts or matters which detract from the expert's opinions and any points which should fairly be made against any opinions expressed should be set out.
(e) Relevant extracts of literature or any other material which might assist the court.
(f) A statement to the effect that the expert has complied with his or her duty to the court to provide independent assistance by way of objective, unbiased, opinion in relation to matters within his or her expertise, and an acknowledgement that the expert will inform all parties (and, where appropriate, the court) in the event that his or her opinion changes on any mate-rial issues.

Where, on an exchange of experts' reports, matters arise which require a further or supplemen-tary report, the above guidelines should be complied with in that report.

The guidelines on the contents of an expert's report set out in *B(T)* are mirrored, and in some respects amplified, in the CrimPR, r. 33.4 (see Supplement, **R-259**). Under r. 33.4(h), an expert's report must include such information as the court may need to decide whether the expert's opinion is sufficiently reliable to be admissible as evidence.

F10.40   An expert report must be full and transparent, and material such as formulae and statistics should not be excluded because they may confuse the jury; if the court is not aware of the way in which an expert has reached his opinion, it cannot evaluate reliability and decide whether the opinion is admissible (*T (Footwear mark evidence)* [2011] 1 Cr App R 85).

In *Puaca* [2005] EWCA Crim 3001, a murder conviction was quashed because a review of the development and bases of the views and evidence of the Crown's pathologist, who had undertaken the post-mortem examination, established that his conclusions could not safely be relied on. It was held that the duty of all pathologists is to comply from the start with the obligations imposed on expert witnesses; that it is wholly wrong for a pathologist carrying out the first post-mortem at the request of the police or the coroner merely to leave it to the defence to instruct a pathologist to prepare a report setting out contrary arguments; and that there was also a need, in certain cases, to refer to ante-mortem records.

Function and Weight of Expert Evidence

F10.41   The duty of the expert witness is 'to furnish the judge or jury with the necessary scientific criteria for testing the accuracy of their conclusions, so as to enable the judge or jury to form an independent judgement by the application of those criteria to the facts proved in evidence'; and it is a misdirection, therefore, to tell the jury that expert evidence should be accepted if uncontradicted (*Davie v Magistrates of Edinburgh* 1953 SC 34, per Lord President Cooper at p. 40). See also *Lanfear* [1968] 2 QB 77 and *Rivett* (1950) 34 Cr App R 87, in which the Court of Appeal refused to interfere with a conviction despite medical evidence of insanity. Equally, it is incumbent on magistrates to approach the evidence of an expert critically, even if no expert is called on the other side, and to be willing to reject the evidence if it leaves questions unanswered (*DPP v Wynne* (2001) *Independent*, 19 February 2001). When expert evidence is given on an ultimate issue, it should be made clear to the jury that they are not bound by the opinion, and that the issue is for them to decide (*Stockwell* (1993) 97 Cr App R 260 per Lord Taylor CJ), but there is no requirement that such a warning be conveyed in any particular way (*Fitzpatrick* [1999] Crim LR 832).

However, it has also been held that it is wrong to direct a jury that they may disregard scientific evidence when the only such evidence adduced on a particular question dictates one answer and only a scientist is qualified to answer that question (*Anderson v The Queen* [1972] AC 100). See also *Matheson* [1958] 2 All ER 87 and *Bailey* (1961) 66 Cr App R 31, in both of which the Court of Criminal Appeal substituted verdicts of manslaughter. In *Matheson* it was held that where the medical evidence of diminished responsibility is uncontradicted and the jury return a verdict of guilty of murder, if there are facts entitling the jury to reject or differ from the expert opinion, the Court of Appeal will not interfere with the verdict; but if there are no facts or circumstances to displace or throw a doubt on the unchallenged medical evidence, such a verdict would not be a true verdict in accordance with the evidence. On the other hand, in *Walton v The Queen* [1978] AC 788, a conviction for murder was upheld despite uncontradicted medical evidence of diminished responsibility. *Matheson* and *Bailey* were distinguished on the basis of the greater weight and quality of the medical evidence in those cases. *Walton* was followed in *Kiszko* (1978) 68 Cr App R 62. In *Sanders* (1991) 93 Cr App R 245, the Court of Appeal held that two clear principles emerged from the cases, on the issue of diminished responsibility:

(a) if there were no other circumstances to consider, unequivocal, uncontradicted medical evidence favourable to an accused should be accepted by a jury and they should be so directed; and

(b) where there were other circumstances to consider, the medical evidence, though it be unequivocal and uncontradicted, must be assessed in the light of the other circumstances.

F10.42   *Khan* [2010] 1 Cr App R 74, while following the approach adopted in *Sanders*, makes clear that, where the defence of diminished responsibility is raised by the defence and contested by the Crown, it will only be in very exceptional cases that a judge will be entitled to withdraw a charge of murder from the jury at the close of the case. It was held that, in order to do so, the judge would have to be satisfied that the evidence, both medical and factual, was such that no reasonable jury, properly directed, could conclude that the defendant had failed to prove, on a balance of prob-abilities, the ingredients of the defence set out in the Homicide Act 1957, s. 2(1) (see **B1.18**).

In deciding what weight, if any, to attach to the evidence of an expert, the jury are entitled to take into account his qualifications and experience, his credibility, and the extent to which his evidence is based on assumed facts which are or are not established. An opinion will not neces-sarily be intrinsically more persuasive because it is shared by two experts and parties should not be encouraged to expect that public money should be spent on duplicating experts (*Meachen* [2009] EWCA Crim 1701 at [23]).

> On a trial of fitness to plead, save in cases where the unfitness is clear, the court must rigorously examine the evidence of psychiatrists before reaching its conclusion (*Walls* [2011] 2 Cr App R 61).

In cases concerning 'shaken baby syndrome' in which the prosecution is able, by advancing an **F10.43** array of experts, to identify a non-accidental injury and the defence can identify no alternative cause, the temptation to conclude that the prosecution has proved its case must be resisted because in this, as in so many fields of medicine, the evidence may be insufficient to exclude, beyond reasonable doubt, an unknown cause (*Henderson* [2010] 2 Cr App R 185 at [1]). In *Henderson*, the Court of Appeal gave the following general guidance on the content of the summing-up in cases in which the evidence to prove guilt consists only of expert evidence.

(1) There must be a logically justifiable basis for accepting or rejecting the evidence. A logi-cally justifiable conclusion depends upon the structure and quality of the directions in the summing-up.

(2) Before the trial starts, the issues, the expert evidence and the sources upon which the evidence is based, should be clear. Thus the direction of examination-in-chief, cross-examination, submissions and speeches to the jury should be focused.

(3) The judge should generally take the opportunity to discuss the issues of expert evidence before the time comes for counsel to address the jury and thus be in a position carefully to structure his summing-up to those issues.

(4) The judge will be able to identify which evidence goes to the resolution of those issues. He should generally sum up issue by issue, dealing with the opinions and any written sources for them issue by issue, unless there is good reason not to do so. Merely repeating the expert evidence in the order in which it was given serves only to confuse. The jury should be con-fronted with the issues it must decide and the factors they should consider as the basis for judgement, one way or the other. Anyone reading a summing-up composed in that way should be able to understand the route followed by the jury in reaching its verdict.

(5) In cases concerning 'shaken baby syndrome', there are two important features of the content of the summing-up. First, if there is a realistic possibility of an unknown cause, the jury should be reminded of it and instructed that unless the evidence leads them to exclude any such pos-sibility, they cannot convict. Where relevant, they should also be reminded that medical science develops and that which was previously thought unknown may subsequently be recognised and acknowledged. In such cases, they should be reminded that special caution is needed where expert evidence is fundamental to the prosecution. Second, the jury also need directions on how to approach conflicting expert evidence. The jury's conclusion cannot be left merely to general impression, but needs to be directed to the pointers to reliable evidence and the basis for distinguishing between what may be relied upon and that which should be rejected.

(6) The guidance given in *Harris* [2006] 1 Cr App R 55 (see **F10.36**) is of assistance not only to judges, practitioners and experts, but also to juries. If the issue arises, a jury should be asked to judge whether the expert has, in the course of his evidence, assumed the role of an advocate, influenced by the side whose cause he seeks to advance. If it arises, the jury should be asked to judge whether the witness has gone outside his area of expertise. The jury should examine the basis of the opinion. Can the witness point to a recognised, peer- reviewed source of the opinion? Is the clinical experience of the witness up-to-date and equal to the experience of others whose evidence he seeks to contradict? The judge should guide the jury

by identifying those reasons which would justify either accepting or rejecting any conflicting expert opinion on which either side relies.

The requirement, as set out in (5) above, to direct the jury that there is a need for special caution and that they should not overlook the realistic possibility that the cause of death was unknown, does not need to be given in those precise terms, provided that the judge sums the case up in such a way that the jury are left in no doubt that they should not convict unless, giving full weight to the uncertainties in medical science, they are sure that the accused shook the child in the way the Crown alleged (*Arshad* [2012] EWCA Crim 18 at [15]).

Pre-trial Disclosure of Expert Evidence

F10.44 The CrimPR, rr. 33.3 to 33.5 (see Supplement, **R-258** *et seq.*), makes provision for the pre-trial disclosure of expert evidence between the parties to Crown Court and magistrates' court proceedings (see also **D9.69** and **D15.77**).

Rule 33.3(1) requires a party who wants another party to admit as fact a summary of an expert's conclusions to serve the summary on the court officer and on each party from whom the admission is sought. A party on whom such a summary is served must serve a response stating which, if any, of the conclusions are admitted as fact and, where a conclusion is not admitted, what are the disputed issues concerning that conclusion (r. 33.3(2)(a)). The response must be served on the court officer and on the party who served the summary as soon as practicable and in any event no more than 14 days after service of the summary (r. 33.3(2)(b)). Rule 33.3(3)(a) and (b) requires that a party who wants to introduce expert evidence otherwise than as admitted fact must serve a report by the expert which complies with r. 33.4 (see **F10.39**) on the court officer and each other party as soon as practicable and in any event with any application in support of which that party relies on that evidence. The report should be accompanied by notice of anything of which the party serving it is aware which might reasonably be thought capable of detracting substantially from the credibility of the expert (r. 33(3)(c)). Under r. 33(3)(3)(d), if another party so requires, the party wanting to introduce the expert evidence must give that party a copy of, or a reasonable opportunity to inspect, (i) a record of any examination, measurement, test or experiment on which the expert's findings and opinion are based, or that were carried out in the course of reaching those findings and opinion, and (ii) anything on which such examination, measurement etc. was carried out. Unless the parties otherwise agree or the court directs, a party may not (a) introduce expert evidence if he has not complied with r. 33.3(3), or (b) introduce in evidence an expert report if the expert does not give evidence in person (r. 33.3(4)). Under the CrimPR, r. 33.5, a party who serves on another party or on the court a report by an expert must at once inform the expert. The phrase 'expert evidence (whether of fact or opinion)' is sufficiently wide to embrace not only the oral evidence to be given by an expert witness, but also an expert report which it is proposed to adduce under the exception to the hearsay rule contained in the CJA 1988, s. 30(1) (see **F10.49**).

The effect of the CrimPR, rr. 1.2 and 3.3, is that it is incumbent upon both the prosecution and the defence to alert the court and the other side at the earliest practicable moment if they are intending or may be intending to adduce expert evidence. This should be done if possible at a Plea and Case Management Hearing or, if it cannot be done then, as soon as the possibility becomes live. In *Ensor* [2010] 1 Cr App R 255, where service by the defence of an expert report had been so late as to constitute a grave breach of the rules, it was held that the trial judge had properly refused to admit the evidence.

F10.45 The CrimPR do not supplant or detract from the prosecution's general duty of disclosure in respect of scientific evidence, which exists irrespective of any defence request, extends to anything which may arguably assist the defence, and obliges the prosecution to make full and proper inquiries from forensic scientists in order to ascertain whether there is discoverable material. In *Clark* [2003] EWCA Crim 1020, the accused's convictions for the murder of her two infant sons were quashed where a forensic pathologist, in breach of normal practice, had omitted from his autopsy report and had failed to disclose the fact that, in the case of one of the infants, following microbiological examination of certain bodily fluids, a form of bacteria which in some parts of the body can prove lethal had been isolated.

In *Henderson* [2010] 2 Cr App R 185, the Court of Appeal laid down the following general guidance on case management in cases in which the evidence to prove guilt consists only of expert evidence. **F10.46**

(1) Justice in such cases depends upon proper advanced preparation and control of the evidence from the stage of investigation onwards. The evidential picture may change as opinions from experts are obtained by either side.
(2) The problem for the courts is how to manage expert evidence so that a jury may be properly directed in a way which will, so far as possible, ensure that any verdict they reach may be justified on a logical basis. A jury can only approach conflicting expert evidence if it is properly marshalled and controlled before it is presented to them.
(3) The judge who is to hear a case should deal with the pre-trial hearings. It is desirable that the judge has experience of the complex issues and understanding of the medical learning.
(4) Proper and robust pre-trial management is essential in order to identify the real medical issues and avoid unnecessary detail.
(5) Before the trial, the judge should be in a position to identify whether the expert evidence is admissible.
(6) In cases concerning 'shaken baby syndrome', the judge should be familiar with the Kennedy Report on Sudden Unexpected Death in Infancy of September 2004, which recommends a checklist of four matters before expert evidence is admitted: (i) is the expert still in practice? (ii) to what extent is he an expert in the subject to which he testifies? (iii) when did he last see a case in his own clinical practice? and (iv) to what extent is his view widely held?
(7) Generally it will be necessary for the court to direct a meeting of experts so that a statement can be prepared of areas of agreement and disagreement (CrimPR, r. 33.6(2)). The meeting should take place well in advance of the trial and be attended by all significant experts, including the defence experts. A careful and detailed minute should be prepared and signed by all participants. Usually it will be preferable if others, particularly legal representatives, do not attend. The court may be required to exercise its power to exclude evidence from an expert who has not complied with a direction (CrimPR, r. 33.6(4)).
(8) Defence experts are not obliged to reveal a previous report they have made in the case, nor to reveal adverse criticism by judges in the past, but a failure to do so will not avail the defence. A judge may well be able to exercise his powers under the CrimPR to ensure advance disclosure of any such reports or criticism. Failure to do so would be contrary to the overriding objective and expose the expert to cross-examination on those matters. Those acting on behalf of the accused should satisfy themselves that any such previous report or criticism is disclosed. Failure to do so by either side will only cast suspicion upon the cogency of the opinion.

Pre-hearing Discussion of Expert Evidence

Where more than one party wants to introduce expert evidence, the court may direct the experts to discuss the issues and prepare a statement for the court of the matters on which they agree and disagree, giving their reasons; if an expert does not comply with such a direction, his evidence may not be introduced without the leave of the court (CrimPR, r. 33.6: see Supplement, **R-261**). **F10.47**

Single Joint Experts

Where more than one accused wants to introduce expert evidence, the court may direct that the evidence be given by one expert only (CrimPR, r. 33.7(1): see Supplement, **R-262**). Provision is also made for selection of an expert where the co-accused cannot agree who should be the expert (r. 33.7(2)) and for giving instructions and directions to the expert (r. 33.8: see Supplement, **R-263**). **F10.48**

Presentation of Expert and Complicated Evidence

F10.49   Criminal Justice Act 1988, s. 30

(1) An expert report shall be admissible as evidence in criminal proceedings, whether or not the person making it attends to give oral evidence in those proceedings.

(2) If it is proposed that the person making the report shall not give oral evidence, the report shall only be admissible with the leave of the court.

(3) For the purpose of determining whether to give leave the court shall have regard—

(a) to the contents of the report;

(b) to the reasons why it is proposed that the person making the report shall not give oral evidence;

(c) to any risk, having regard in particular to whether it is likely to be possible to controvert statements in the report if the person making it does not attend to give oral evidence in the proceedings, that its admission or exclusion will result in unfairness to the accused or, if there is more than one, to any of them; and

(d) to any other circumstances that appear to the court to be relevant.

(4) An expert report, when admitted, shall be evidence of any fact or opinion of which the person making it could have given oral evidence.

(5) In this section 'expert report' means a written report by a person dealing wholly or mainly with matters on which he is (or would if living be) qualified to give expert evidence.

Section F11   Admissibility of Previous Verdicts

PROOF OF CONVICTIONS AND ACQUITTALS

General

The PACE 1984, s. 73, provides for the proof of convictions and acquittals in the UK by a certificate of conviction or acquittal, together with proof that the person named in the certificate is the person whose conviction or acquittal is in issue. As to the latter issue, although it is for the judge to decide whether there is prima facie evidence fit for the jury's consideration, ultimately it is a question of fact for the jury to decide (*Burns* [2006] 1 WLR 1273; *Lewendon* [2006] 1 WLR 1278).   **F11.1**

Police and Criminal Evidence Act 1984, ss. 73 and 82   **F11.2**

73.—(1)   Where in any proceedings the fact that a person has in the United Kingdom or any other member State been convicted or acquitted of an offence otherwise than by a Service court is admissible in evidence, it may be proved by producing a certificate of conviction or, as the case may be, of acquittal relating to that offence, and proving that the person named in the certificate as having been convicted or acquitted of the offence is the person whose conviction or acquittal of the offence is to be proved.

(2)   For the purposes of this section a certificate of conviction or of acquittal—

  (a)   shall, as regards a conviction or acquittal on indictment, consist of a certificate, signed by the proper officer of the court where the conviction or acquittal took place, giving the substance and effect (omitting the formal parts) of the indictment and of the conviction or acquittal; and

  (b)   shall, as regards a conviction or acquittal on a summary trial, consist of a copy of the conviction or of the dismissal of the information, signed by the clerk of the court where the conviction or acquittal took place or by the clerk of the court, if any, to which a memorandum of the conviction or acquittal was sent; and

  (c)   shall, as regards a conviction or acquittal by a court in a member State (other than the United Kingdom), consist of a certificate, signed by the proper officer of the court where the conviction or acquittal took place, giving details of the offence, of the conviction or acquittal, and of any sentence;

and a document purporting to be a duly signed certificate of conviction or acquittal under this section shall be taken to be such a certificate unless the contrary is proved.

(3)   In subsection (2) above 'proper officer' means—

  (a)   in relation to a magistrates' court in England and Wales, the designated officer for the court; and

  (b)   in relation to any other court in the United Kingdom, the clerk of the court, his deputy or any other person having custody of the court record; and

  (c)   in relation to any court in another member State ('the EU court'), a person who would be the proper officer of the EU court if that court were in the United Kingdom.

(4)   The method of proving a conviction or acquittal authorised by this section shall be in addition to and not to the exclusion of any other authorised manner of proving a conviction or acquittal.

82.—(1)   In this Part of this Act— . . .

'proceedings' means criminal proceedings, including service proceedings and

'Service court' means the Court Martial or the Service Civilian Court.

(1A)   In subsection (1) 'service proceedings' means proceedings before a court (other than a civilian court) in respect of a service offence; and 'service offence' and 'civilian court' here have the same meanings as in the Armed Forces Act 2006

(2)   [Repealed.]

(3) Nothing in this part of this Act shall prejudice any power of a court to exclude evidence (whether by preventing questions from being put or otherwise) at its discretion.

Proof of Identity

F11.3   Concerning the requirement, in the PACE 1984, s. 73(1), of proof that the person named in the certificate is the person whose conviction or acquittal is to be proved, in *Pattison v DPP* [2006] 2 All ER 317 it was held that, where s. 73(1) is relied upon by the prosecution to prove the conviction of an accused, the following general principles could be distilled from the authorities:

(a) The prosecution must prove to the criminal standard that the accused is the person named on the certificate.

(b) This proof may be effected by an admission by or on behalf of the accused, by evidence of fingerprints or by the evidence of someone who was present in court at the time.

(c) However, there is no prescribed means of proof; the matter can be proved by any admissible means.

(d) An example of such means is a match between the personal details of the accused and the personal details recorded on the certificate.

(e) Even if the personal details, such as the name of the accused, are not uncommon, a match will be sufficient for a prima facie case.

(f) In the absence of any evidence contradicting such a prima facie case, the evidence will be sufficient.

(g) The failure of the accused to give any contradictory evidence in rebuttal will be a matter to take into account. If it is proper and fair to do so, and a warning has been given, it can additionally give rise to an adverse inference under the CJPO 1994, s. 35(2) (see **F19.42**).

Similarity in name and date of birth between a certificate and an accused may or may not amount to prima facie evidence of identity. Each case must depend on its own facts and the material which is available. For example, if an accused has an extremely common name and the date of birth on the certificate is not precisely the same as that of the accused, it may well be that it does not constitute prima facie evidence of identity. On the other hand, if the accused has a highly unusual name with many different component parts, it may constitute prima facie evidence of identity without evidence of an identical date of birth (*Burns* [2006] 1 WLR 1273).

Summary Offences, Orders Made by Magistrates and Endorsements

F11.4   To overcome the difficulties, at common law, in seeking to prove the previous convictions of a person convicted of a summary offence, if he does not attend the court, the MCA 1980, s. 104, provides that, if the court is satisfied that, not less than seven days before the hearing, a notice, stating the alleged previous convictions which it is proposed to bring to the attention of the court, has been served on the accused, and the accused is not present before the court, the court may take account of the convictions as if the accused had appeared and admitted them. Endorsements on a driving licence of the particulars of a conviction or disqualification may be produced as prima facie evidence of the matters endorsed (RTOA 1988, ss. 31(1) and 44(1)).

Convictions Overseas

F11.5   For the purposes of extradition proceedings, the fact of a conviction overseas may be proved by a properly certified copy of the court record (see the Extradition Act 1989, sch. 1, para. 12, and *Re Mullin* [1993] Crim LR 390). As to proof of foreign convictions in asset recovery proceedings under the POCA 2002, see *Asset Recovery Agency v Virtosu* [2009] 3 All ER 637 at **F11.9**. The CAJA 2009, s. 144 and sch. 17, para. 13, amend the PACE 1984, s. 73, so as to provide for the proof of previous convictions in other EU Member States (see **F11.1**).

CONVICTIONS AS EVIDENCE OF FACTS ON WHICH BASED

At common law, the convictions of one person were not admissible as evidence of the facts on **F11.6** which they were based at the subsequent trial of another: see *Turner* (1832) 1 Mood CC 347 at p. 349 (one person's conviction for theft inadmissible as evidence of such theft at the trial of another charged with handling the stolen goods); *Hassan* [1970] QB 423 (a woman's convictions for prostitution inadmissible as evidence of such prostitution at the trial of a man charged with living off her immoral earnings); and *Spinks* [1982] 1 All ER 587 (a principal's conviction of wounding inadmissible as evidence of such wounding at the subsequent trial of an alleged accessory). The PACE 1984, s. 74(1), has now reversed the common-law rule, and s. 74(2) has created a persuasive presumption: the person (other than the accused) convicted of an offence shall be taken to have committed that offence unless the contrary is proved. The legal burden is borne by the party against whom the presumption operates; and if borne by the accused, may be discharged by proof on a balance of probabilities (see *Carr-Briant* [1943] KB 607 and generally **F3.54** and **F3.70**). Section 74(3) creates a similar presumption in the case of the previous convictions of *the accused*, provided that evidence is admissible of the fact that the accused has committed the offence in respect of which he has been convicted.

Police and Criminal Evidence Act 1984, ss. 74 and 75   **F11.7**

74.—(1) In any proceedings the fact that a person other than the accused has been convicted of an offence by or before any court in the United Kingdom or any other member State or by a Service court outside the United Kingdom shall be admissible in evidence for the purpose of proving that that person committed that offence, where evidence of his having done so is admissible, whether or not any other evidence of his having committed that offence is given.

(2) In any proceedings in which by virtue of this section a person other than the accused is proved to have been convicted of an offence by or before any court in the United Kingdom or any other member State or by a Service court outside the United Kingdom, he shall be taken to have committed that offence unless the contrary is proved.

(3) In any proceedings where evidence is admissible of the fact that the accused has committed an offence, if the accused is proved to have been convicted of the offence—
(a) by or before any court in the United Kingdom or any other member State; or
(b) by a Service court outside the United Kingdom,
he shall be taken to have committed that offence unless the contrary is proved.

(4) Nothing in this section shall prejudice—
(a) the admissibility in evidence of any conviction which would be admissible apart from this section; or
(b) the operation of any enactment whereby a conviction or a finding of fact in any proceedings is for the purposes of any other proceedings made conclusive evidence of any fact.

75.—(1) Where evidence that a person has been convicted of an offence is admissible by virtue of section 74 above, then without prejudice to the reception of any other admissible evidence for the purpose of identifying the facts on which the conviction was based—
(a) the contents of any document which is admissible as evidence of the conviction; and
(b) the contents of—
(i) the information, complaint, indictment or charge-sheet on which the person in question was convicted, or
(ii) in the case of a conviction of an offence by a court in a member State (other than the United Kingdom), any document produced in relation to the proceedings for that offence which fulfils a purpose similar to any document or documents specified in sub-paragraph (i),
shall be admissible in evidence for that purpose.

(2) Where in any proceedings the contents of any document are admissible in evidence by virtue of subsection (1) above, a copy of that document, or of the material part of it, purporting to be certified or otherwise authenticated by or on behalf of the court or authority having custody of that document shall be admissible in evidence and shall be taken to be a true copy of that document or part unless the contrary is shown.

(3) Nothing in any of the following—
   (a)   section 14 of the Powers of Criminal Courts (Sentencing) Act 2000 (under which a conviction leading to probation or discharge is to be disregarded except as mentioned in that section);
   (aa)   section 187 of the Armed Forces Act 2006 (which makes similar provision in respect of service convictions);
   (b)   section 247 of the Criminal Procedure (Scotland) Act 1995 (which makes similar provision in respect of convictions on indictment in Scotland); and
   (c)   section 8 of the Probation Act (Northern Ireland) 1950 (which corresponds to section [14 of the Powers of Criminal Courts (Sentencing) Act 2000]) or any legislation which is in force in Northern Ireland for the time being and corresponds to that section,
   shall affect the operation of section 74 above; and for the purposes of that section any order made by a court of summary jurisdiction in Scotland under section 228 or section 246(3) of the said Act of 1995 shall be treated as a conviction.
(4) Nothing in section 74 above shall be construed as rendering admissible in any proceedings evidence of any conviction other than a subsisting one.

For the definition of 'proceedings' and 'Service court', see s. 82 at **F11.2**.

A 'subsisting' conviction means either a finding of guilt that has not been quashed on appeal or a formal plea of guilt that has not been withdrawn; whether the accused has been sentenced is irrelevant (*Robertson* [1987] QB 920). An admission of an offence in a police caution is not a conviction and therefore not covered by ss. 74 and 75 but, where evidence of such an admission is admitted, an accused may challenge it, and notice of such a challenge should be given under the CrimPR, r. 35.3(4)(b) (*Olu* [2011] 1 Cr App R 404).

F11.8   It seems that one co-accused may rely upon s. 74(1) to adduce evidence of the convictions of another co-accused, provided that they are relevant to an issue in the proceedings (*Hendrick* [1992] Crim LR 427, where the convictions were held to be irrelevant). It is possible to envisage situations in which a co-accused pleads guilty to a charge even though the evidence is far from conclusive against him, and in such a case it could well be unfair to allow the prosecution to use the conviction as evidence, on that charge, against the remaining accused (*Lee* [1996] Crim LR 825). Where one co-accused pleads guilty towards or at the end of the prosecution case and the prosecution make an application to reopen their case to adduce evidence of the guilty plea under s. 74(1), the plea, if relevant to an issue in the proceedings, is admissible, subject to exercise of the discretion to exclude under s. 78, as when it would be unfair because, had the guilty plea been entered and admitted in evidence at an earlier stage, cross-examination might have been conducted differently (*Chapman* [1991] Crim LR 44).

Foreign Convictions

F11.9   Foreign convictions, apart from convictions by Service courts outside the UK and convictions in other EU Member States, are not covered by the PACE 1984, s. 74, but may be admissible under the bad character provisions of the CJA 2003 (see **F12** and **F14**) and, if admissible, may be proved under the Evidence Act 1851, s. 7 (see **F8.19**) (*Kordasinski* [2007] 1 Cr App R 238). See also *De Oliveira* [2009] EWCA Crim 378.

In civil asset recovery proceedings under the POCA 2002 against a person convicted in a foreign country, a foreign judgment containing a summary of the matters found proved by the court is, for the purposes of s. 241 of the 2002 Act, evidence of the truth of those facts and of such conduct being unlawful under the criminal law of that country (*Asset Recovery Agency v Virtosu* [2009] 3 All ER 637).

Convictions of Persons Other than the Accused

F11.10 **Relevance to an Issue in the Proceedings**   The wording of the PACE 1984, s. 74(1), was amended by the CJA 2003. The words 'that that person committed that offence, where evidence of his having done so is admissible' were substituted for the original words 'where to do so is relevant to any issue in those proceedings'. The amendment is cosmetic, insofar as evidence of the commission of the offence, in order to be 'admissible', must be relevant to an issue in the proceedings, and it is submitted that such of the following cases in which the court had to decide whether the commission of an offence was 'relevant to any issue in proceedings' would be decided in the same way under s. 74(1) as amended.

In *Hasson* [1997] Crim LR 579 the accused were charged with being concerned in the supply of drugs. It was held that the previous drug-related convictions of six men with whom the accused had socialised had been improperly admitted because it was not the Crown case that the accused were supplying them with drugs and there was no evidence to show that meetings with them were related to the offence charged.

In some cases proof of the commission of an offence by a person other than the accused will establish an essential ingredient of the offence with which the accused is charged, and therefore will be clearly relevant to an 'issue in those proceedings'. In *Pigram* [1995] Crim LR 808, in which officers had seen H and P transfer goods from H's van to P's lorry and H and P were jointly charged with handling, it was held that H's guilty plea was admissible against P for the purposes of proving that the goods were stolen.

The phrase 'issue in those proceedings', however, was not confined to an issue which was an **F11.11** essential ingredient of the offence charged. In *Robertson* [1987] QB 920, the Court of Appeal held that the phrase also covered less fundamental issues, e.g. evidential issues arising in the proceedings. The court also rejected the argument that s. 74(1) applies only to the proof of convictions of offences in which the accused on trial did not participate. Robertson was charged with two co-accused with conspiracy to commit burglary. The co-accused pleaded not guilty to the conspiracy but guilty to some 16 burglaries committed during the period of the conspiracy. Evidence of these convictions was held to be admissible, because it could be inferred from the fact that the co-accused had committed these offences that there was a conspiracy between them, and that was the conspiracy to which, the prosecution alleged, Robertson was a party. In *Golder*, the appeal which was heard with and is reported with *Robertson* [1987] QB 920, Golder was charged with a robbery committed at garage H. Two of his co-accused pleaded guilty to that robbery, and also to another robbery committed at garage G. The evidence against Golder consisted primarily of a confession statement, which he alleged to have been fabricated by the police, in which he made reference to both robberies. The evidence of the guilty pleas was held to be admissible: proof of the commission of the offences at both garages was relevant, because it showed that the contents of Golder's confession were in accordance with the facts as they were known and the confession was therefore more likely to be true; and proof of the commission of the offence at garage H was relevant, because robbery at that garage was one of the matters which the prosecution had to prove.

The decision in *Robertson* that the phrase 'issue in those proceedings' should be given a wide **F11.12** interpretation so as to include evidentiary matters, was applied in *Castle* [1989] Crim LR 567. C and others, including F, were charged with robbery. The victim, when seeing C and F at the identification parade, said 'yes' in respect of C and 'possibly' in respect of F. F pleaded guilty. It was held that evidence of the guilty plea was admissible because relevant to the issue of the reliability of the identification of C. The evidence, by confirming that the victim was correct in his 'possible' identification of F, tended to corroborate the correctness of his positive identification of C. See also, *sed quaere, Buckingham* (1994) 99 Cr App R 303: evidence of W's conviction of conspiracy to pervert the course of justice by obtaining, as the accused in a previous trial, false evidence of defence witnesses, was admissible at the trial of those witnesses for doing acts intended to pervert the course of justice because, although it was not probative that any of the witnesses had given false evidence, it established the conspiracy.

The Discretion to Exclude   Where a conviction is admissible under the PACE 1984, s. 74, the **F11.13** Court of Appeal will allow an appeal against a judge's ruling not to exclude it under s. 78 only if no judge could reasonably have made it or it was made on a false basis (*Abdullah* [2010] EWCA Crim 3078, following *Smith* [2007] EWCA Crim 2105).

In *O'Connor* (1987) 85 Cr App R 298, B and O'Connor were jointly charged with having conspired together (and with no one else) to obtain property by deception. At the trial of O'Connor, B's plea of guilty was admitted, together with all the detail contained in the conspiracy count (see the PACE 1984, s. 75(1)(b), at **F11.7**). The Court of Appeal upheld O'Connor's conviction by application of the proviso which then applied, but held that the evidence should have been excluded on the ground that it was impossible realistically to exclude the possibility that the jury might infer from B's admission, and the detail contained in the count, that not only had B conspired with O'Connor, but that the converse had also taken place. Furthermore, it was not open to the defence to challenge or test what had been said by B. The Court concluded that if it was appropriate within the section to admit the conviction, the judge should have excluded it under s. 78, on the basis that it would have had such an adverse effect on the fairness of the proceedings that it ought not to have been admitted. In *Mattison* [1990] Crim LR 117, M was charged in one count with gross indecency with D. In another count, D was charged with gross indecency with M. D pleaded guilty and at M's trial evidence of that plea was admitted. The judge directed the jury that the evidence of D's plea did not mean that M was guilty, but was before them to make the background accurate. Allowing the appeal, it was held that although D's guilty plea was relevant in the proceedings against M, the judge, bearing in mind M's defence, which was one of complete denial, should have exercised the discretion under s. 78 to exclude the evidence. See also *Fedrick* [1990] Crim LR 403 and *Turpin* [1990] Crim LR 514. It seems that evidence of a conviction, which would otherwise be clearly admissible under s. 74, may also be excluded under s. 78 on the basis that it adds little to an already strong case against the accused (*Warner* (1993) 96 Cr App R 324).

F11.14 In *Robertson* [1987] QB 920, counsel for the appellant, relying upon *O'Connor*, submitted that the convictions in that case should also have been excluded under s. 78, because the prosecution, in relying on s. 74, had deprived Robertson of the opportunity to cross-examine the co-accused. The Court of Appeal rejected the argument, distinguishing *O'Connor*. Robertson's name did not appear on any of the burglary counts, and even if the co-accused had given evidence in accordance with their guilty pleas, Robertson's counsel would have been unlikely to cross-examine them (or, if he had done so, he would have seriously prejudiced Robertson). (In this respect, see also *Kempster* [1989] 1 WLR 1125, discussed at **F11.17**.) However, the Court added (at p. 928): 'Section 74 is a provision which should be sparingly used. There will be occasions where, although the evidence may be technically admissible its effect is likely to be so slight that it will be wiser not to adduce it. This is particularly so when there is a danger of a contravention of section 78.' It was further observed that where the evidence is admitted, the judge should be careful to explain to the jury its effect and limitations.

F11.15 In *Turner* [1991] Crim LR 57, T and L, in separate cars, were driving at night down a hill. L overtook T, collided with an oncoming vehicle and killed his (L's) passenger. The prosecution alleged that L and T were racing. L pleaded guilty to causing death by reckless driving. T was tried on the same charge and denied that he was racing. It was held that L's guilty plea was relevant to T's trial because the prosecution case was that L had been the principal and T the secondary party who aided and abetted L. The question was whether the plea should have been excluded under s. 78. Provided that the judge made it clear, as he did, that L's plea did not amount to an admission that he was racing, there was nothing unfair in admitting the evidence. In *Bennett* [1988] Crim LR 686, B was charged with theft. Her co-accused, a supermarket cashier, pleaded guilty to theft, the allegation being that she passed goods to B for less than their true price. Evidence of the guilty plea was admitted against B. The Court of Appeal held that any decision to the contrary would have bewildered the jury. The evidence was adduced to establish that there had been a theft. The issue of whether B had been a party to the theft had been fairly left with the jury, and the judge had properly exercised his discretion under s. 78. See also *Stewart* [1999] Crim LR 746.

Cases of Conspiracy and Joint Enterprise   In *Lunnon* [1988] Crim LR 456, in which there   **F11.16**
were three accused jointly charged with conspiracy, it was held that the guilty plea of one of
them had been properly admitted to prove the existence of the conspiracy: the judge had separated two questions for the jury, namely (a) whether there was a conspiracy and (b) who was
a party to it, and had made it clear that, despite the evidence of the guilty plea, the jury could
acquit the accused. (See also *Garrity* [1994] Crim LR 828; and compare *Humphreys* [1993]
Crim LR 288, where it was held that the evidence should have been excluded under the PACE
1984, s. 78, because there was other prosecution evidence of the conspiracy, and *Abdullah*
[2010] EWCA Crim 3078, where it was held that the evidence may be admissible if the
count of conspiracy against the former co-accused is amended to allege 'with others unknown',
thereby enabling the judge to direct the jury that the conviction does not help in any way as to
whether any of the co-accused is guilty of the conspiracy.) In *Chapman* [1991] Crim LR 44,
C and seven others were charged with conspiracy to obtain by deception. The pleas of guilty
by one of the others to two specific counts of obtaining by deception, being two incidents in
which he was involved with C, were held to be relevant; and since there were others in the
conspiracy, and since the other co-accused did not plead guilty to conspiracy but to specific
obtainings by deception, the evidence of the conviction did not inevitably import the complicity of C. See also *Hunt* [1994] Crim LR 747 and cf. *Curry* [1988] Crim LR 527. The appellant,
Curry, was convicted of conspiracy to obtain property by deception. She was charged with two
others, one of whom, H, had pleaded guilty. The prosecution case was that Curry, with H's
knowledge, had used H's credit card to obtain goods, and that H then intended to report the
card as stolen in order to avoid liability to pay for the goods. The other co-accused, W, had
driven the women to the shops. Evidence of H's guilty plea was admitted to establish the existence of an unlawful agreement to deceive. The Court of Appeal, distinguishing *Lunnon* (1988)
88 Cr App R 71, quashed the conviction on the grounds that the evidence of the guilty plea
clearly implied as a matter of fact that the appellant had been a party to the conspiracy, even
though it did not have that effect as a matter of law, and should have been excluded under s. 78.
Section 74, it was said, should be sparingly used, particularly in relation to joint offences such
as conspiracy and affray. It should not be used where the evidence, expressly or by necessary
inference, suggests the complicity of the accused.

This last observation in *Curry* was reiterated in *Kempster* [1989] 1 WLR 1125, in which the   **F11.17**
Court of Appeal noted that the effect of admitting a conviction as evidence of the complicity of
the accused, is that the prosecution will not have to call the person convicted as a witness and
the defence will be deprived of any opportunity to cross-examine him, in particular as to the
complicity of the accused. Staughton LJ said (at p. 22):

> No doubt such cross-examination may in itself be unlikely in some cases, or else turn out to be a
> disaster, as the Lord Chief Justice put it in *Robertson*. But one cannot always assume that.

Where joint enterprise is relied upon, but it leaves open the question whether the ingredients of
the offence are satisfied in the separate case of each of the accused, the guilty plea of a co-accused
may be admissible. In deciding whether it should be excluded under s. 78, regard should be
had not just to the interests of the accused, but to those of the prosecution and of justice as a
whole, so that, for example, an initial decision to exclude the evidence may be reversed in order
to avoid the jury from being misled by the evidence of the accused (*Tee* [2011] EWCA Crim
462, applying *Stewart* [1995] 1 Cr App R 441). Cf. *Turpin* [1990] Crim LR 514 and *Betterley*
[1994] Crim LR 764 and see also *Marlow* [1997] Crim LR 457.

Purpose of Adducing Evidence   The Court of Appeal in *Kempster* [1989] 1 WLR 1125 also   **F11.18**
stressed that it is important to ascertain the purpose for which evidence under the PACE 1984,
s. 74, is to be adduced before deciding whether it should be excluded under s. 78; and that if the
evidence is admitted, the trial judge should be careful not only to direct the jury about the purpose for which it has been admitted, but also to ensure that counsel do not seek to use it for any
other purpose. In that case, evidence of the guilty pleas of a number of co-accused was admitted

but not the detailed particulars of the offences committed. At the time of the application to admit, it was unclear whether the prosecution were relying on the evidence in order to prove the guilt of the accused or merely to prevent mystification of the jury, and therefore there was no clear and informed decision by the judge about any adverse effect the evidence might have on the fairness of the proceedings. In the event, the jury were encouraged to rely on the evidence for the purpose of proving the guilt of the accused. The convictions were quashed. In *Mahmood* [1997] 1 Cr App R 414, L, KM and NM were charged with rape. The prosecution case was that the complainant was too drunk to have consented. L pleaded guilty. KM and NM admitted intercourse but alleged consent or alternatively belief in consent. It was held that evidence of L's plea should not have been admitted because, without knowing the basis for it, it was not possible to identify any issue to which it was relevant. There was a real danger that the jury would assume it meant that L knew the complainant could not consent by reason of drink (whereas it is possible that he believed she could consent, but knew she was not consenting or was reckless as to whether she was consenting) and conclude therefore that KM and NM must also have known that she could not consent, an approach which would preclude proper consideration of the state of mind of each accused. Cf. *Skinner* [1995] Crim LR 805 and *Girma* [2010] 1 Cr App R (S) 172. See also *Boyson* [1991] Crim LR 274, where the Court of Appeal held, *per curiam*, that it did not approve of the growing practice of allowing evidence to go before a jury which is irrelevant, inadmissible, prejudicial or unfair simply because it is convenient for the jury to have 'the whole picture', and *Hall* [1993] Crim LR 527.

Convictions of Accused

F11.19   It is clear from the wording of the PACE 1984, s. 74(3), that its purpose is not to define or enlarge the circumstances in which evidence of the fact that the accused has committed an offence is admissible, but is simply to assist in the mode of proof of that fact. The evidence, of course, must also be relevant to an issue in the proceedings and, it is submitted, may be relevant either to an essential ingredient of the offence charged or some less fundamental issue arising in the course of the proceedings (*Harris* [2001] Crim LR 227, a decision under the original version of s. 74(3), which contained the words 'in so far as that evidence is relevant to any matter in issue in the proceedings . . .'; and cf. *Robertson* [1987] QB 920, considered at **F11.11**).

There are only three situations, it is submitted, in which reliance may be placed on s. 74(3). The first is where the prosecution seek to prove, as an element of the offence with which the accused is charged, the fact that he committed some other offence in respect of which he has been convicted. Thus when, after a person's conviction of an offence under the OAPA 1861, s. 18, the victim dies from the injuries and that person is charged with murder, the prosecution, in reliance upon s. 74(3), need prove only that death resulted from the injuries; it is for the accused to prove on a balance of probabilities, if he can, that he did not inflict the grievous bodily harm or had no intent to do so (*Clift* [2013] 2 All ER 776, which also makes clear (at [36]), concerning the possibility of exclusion of evidence of the conviction under the PACE 1984, s. 78, that it would be an improper exercise of that discretion to circumvent s. 74(3) 'for no better reason than judicial or academic distaste for it'). The second situation in which reliance may be placed upon s. 74(3) is where the prosecution seek to adduce evidence of the accused's commission of an offence, in respect of which he has been convicted, under the CJA 2003, s. 101 (see **F12.15**). The third situation is where, a conviction having been proved as part of the prosecution case pursuant to statutory provisions such as s. 101 (see **F12.15**) or the Theft Act 1968, s. 27(3)(b) (see **F12.99**), the accused denies having committed the offence in question.

F11.20   In *C* [2011] 1 WLR 1942 the following principles were set out with a view to ensuring that where an accused seeks to rebut the presumption under the PACE 1984, s. 74(3), both sides may adduce relevant evidence without turning the trial into a retrial of the offence in question. The prosecution is not required, merely because the accused denies that he was guilty of the offence, to prove that he was, or to assist him to prove that he was not, or to call witnesses for either purpose. The presumption is that the conviction truthfully reflects that the accused committed the offence. Equally, however, the accused cannot be prevented from seeking to demonstrate that he did not commit the offence and is entitled to adduce evidence that will enable him to prove, whether by cross-examination of prosecution witnesses or calling evidence of his own, that he was not guilty. If the accused does adduce such evidence, it is open to the Crown to call evidence in rebuttal. It is essential that the defence statement identifies all the ingredients of the case which the accused will advance for the purpose of rebutting the presumption. That may enable the prosecution to prepare draft admissions of fact and to collate the necessary prosecution evidence; the bare assertion by the defence that the accused did not commit the offence is inadequate. The trial judge may make whatever decisions are proper for the proper conduct of the trial, but at the very least it is open to him to consider permitting the Crown to postpone its decision whether to call any relevant evidence until after the close of the defence case. See also, in the case of challenging an admission in a police caution, *Olu* [2011] 1 Cr App R 404, considered at **F11.7**.

THE RELEVANCE AND ADMISSIBILITY OF ACQUITTALS

Evidence of an earlier acquittal is generally irrelevant and therefore inadmissible, but an exception exists where a witness's credibility is directly in issue and there is a clear inference from the earlier verdict that the jury in that trial rejected his evidence because they did not believe him (*D* [2007] EWCA Crim 684, which is considered, together with the other authorities, at **F1.17**).   **F11.21**

In *Sambasivam v Public Prosecutor of Malaya Federation* [1950] AC 458, S was charged with two offences (a) carrying a revolver, in respect of which a new trial was ordered, and (b) being in possession of ten rounds of ammunition (six of which were loaded in the revolver), of which he was acquitted. At the new trial, the prosecution relied on a statement allegedly made by S in which he admitted both charges. S was convicted. The Privy Council quashed the conviction on the ground that the judge should have directed the tribunal of fact that the accused had been acquitted of being in possession of ammunition, and that the prosecution were bound to accept that the part of the alleged statement relating to the ammunition must be regarded as untrue. Lord MacDermott said (at p. 479):

> The effect of a verdict of acquittal pronounced by a competent court on a lawful charge and after a lawful trial is not completely stated by saying that the person acquitted cannot be tried again for the same offence. To that it must be added that the verdict is binding and conclusive in all subsequent proceedings between the parties to the adjudication.

In *Hay* (1983) 77 Cr App R 70, H made a written confession to two unconnected charges, one of arson and one of burglary. At his trial for the arson charge, his confession was admitted in edited form, excluding references to the burglary. His defence was one of alibi and he alleged that the police had fabricated his confession. He was acquitted. At his subsequent trial for burglary, the judge refused to allow H to adduce evidence of the previous acquittal and alibi evidence, ruling that both were irrelevant to the charge of burglary. On appeal against conviction, the Court of Appeal, having considered the passage (set out above) from Lord MacDermott's judgment in *Sambasivam*, allowed the appeal. O'Connor LJ said (at p. 75):

> The jury ought to have been told of the acquittal and directed that it was conclusive evidence that the accused was not guilty of arson, and that his confession to that offence was untrue. The jury should have been directed that in deciding the contest between the appellant and the police officers as to the part of the statement referring to the burglary, they should keep in mind that the first part must be regarded as untrue.

The decisions in *Sambasivam* and *Hay* must be read subject to the subsequent authorities on the topic.

F11.22   The decision in *Sambasivam* is not to be regarded as an authority in support of the existence of the doctrine of issue estoppel, which is inapplicable in criminal cases (*DPP v Humphrys* [1977] AC 1: see **D12.29**). An acquittal is not conclusive evidence of innocence and does not establish that all relevant issues were resolved in favour of the accused (*Terry* [2005] QB 996, considered at **F11.23**, and *Colman* [2005] QB 996). In *Z* [2000] 2 AC 483, Z was charged with rape, his defence being consent or mistaken belief in consent. The prosecution wished to adduce evidence of four previous incidents, involving four different women, each of which had resulted in a rape trial at which Z's defence had been consent. Z was convicted in one of the cases, but was acquitted in the other three. The judge ruled that the evidence came within the ambit of the similar fact doctrine, but that the evidence of the three women in respect of whom Z had been acquitted was inadmissible by reason of the statement of Lord MacDermott in *Sambasivam* (as set out at **F11.21**), and that by itself the evidence of the woman in respect of whom Z had been convicted did not establish a sufficiently cogent picture of similar facts to be admitted. The Court of Appeal upheld the decision. The prosecution appealed. The House of Lords allowed the appeal on the following grounds:

(a) It had been right to set aside the conviction in *Sambasivam*, but the proper grounds for doing so were those given by Lord Pearce in *Connelly v DPP* [1964] AC 1254 at pp. 1362 and 1364, namely that a man should not be prosecuted a second time where the two offences were in fact founded on one and the same incident (the carrying of the revolver and the ammunition) and that a man should not be tried for a second offence (carrying the revolver in which some of the ammunition was loaded) which was manifestly inconsistent on the facts with a previous acquittal (acquittal of possession of the ammunition). (See also *Yam* [2010] EWCA Crim 2072 at [10]: *Sambasivam* is best explained as an example of the power to prevent an abuse of the process of the court where a further trial would be unfair or oppressive, which involves a judgement of fairness in the light of the individual facts of the case.)

(b) Provided that an accused is not placed in double jeopardy in the way described by Lord Pearce, evidence which is relevant on a subsequent prosecution is not inadmissible because it shows or tends to show that the accused was, in fact, guilty of an offence of which he had earlier been acquitted. The statement of Lord MacDermott in *Sambasivam* (as set out above) requires to be qualified in this way.

(c) The judgments in *G (an Infant) v Coltart* [1967] 1 All ER 271 should not be followed: a distinction should not be drawn between evidence which shows guilt of an earlier offence of which the accused has been acquitted and evidence which tends to show guilt of such an offence or which appears to relate to one distinct issue rather than the issue of guilt of such an offence.

(d) In the present case, Z would not be placed in double jeopardy and the evidence of the earlier complainants, being relevant and admissible under the similar facts doctrine, should not be inadmissible because it shows that the accused was in fact guilty of the offences of rape of which he had earlier been acquitted.

Evidence of the kind relied on in *Z* is now admissible under the CJA 2003, s. 101(1)(d), whereby evidence of the accused's bad character is admissible 'if it is relevant to an important matter in issue between the defendant and the prosecution', subject to the discretion to exclude it under s. 101(3).

F11.23   In *Terry* [2005] QB 996, it was observed, concerning the passage in the judgment of O'Connor LJ in *Hay* set out above, that it went further than was necessary to correct the judge's decision on relevance and admissibility and was inconsistent with the rationale of the decision in *Z*, because an acquittal is not conclusive evidence of innocence and does not mean that all relevant issues were resolved in favour of the accused. In *Terry*, Auld LJ also observed (at [45]) that the ruling of the House of Lords in *Z* is not restricted to similar fact evidence: the critical questions are whether the evidence in question is admissible, whatever its species, as relevant to an issue in the case, and whether it is fair to admit it.

Section F12   Character Evidence: Evidence of Bad Character of Accused

EVIDENCE OF BAD CHARACTER UNDER THE CRIMINAL JUSTICE ACT 2003

Introduction

The provisions of chapter 1 of part 11 of the CJA 2003 (ss. 98 to 110 and 112), with minor **F12.1** exceptions, codify the law governing the admissibility of evidence of bad character, replacing both the common law and the provisions of the Criminal Evidence Act 1898, s. 1(3), which formerly governed the cross-examination of the accused on matters relating to his bad character. The courts have had much work to do to interpret the new provisions in a coherent way, but the emergence of a shared approach and common understanding throughout the early judgments of the Court of Appeal resolved many of the ambiguities in the drafting. The key decisions are *Hanson* [2005] 1 WLR 3169; *Highton* [2005] 1 WLR 3472; *Edwards* [2006] 1 WLR 1524; *Weir* [2006] 2 All ER 570; *Renda* [2006] 2 All ER 553; and *Lawson* [2007] 1 WLR 1191. In *Campbell* [2007] 1 WLR 2798 (see **F12.23**), the Court of Appeal identified and sought to resolve some further inconsistencies in the text in a radical and controversial fashion.

The bad character provisions should be used in cases where a jury is determining, pursuant to the Criminal Procedure and Insanity Act 1964, s. 4A, whether an accused who is unfit to plead did the act charged against him. Either the CJA 2003 is of direct application or the court should adopt the same rules of evidence as in criminal proceedings (*Creed* [2011] EWCA Crim 144, applying *Chal* [2008] 1 Cr App R 247, a decision in relation to hearsay evidence: see **F15.1**).

The statutory scheme is different from the old law of bad character in many respects. For the **F12.2** purposes of organisation of the materials appearing in this work, the exposition of the statutory principles is most easily dealt with under the categories of admissibility laid down in the CJA 2003, s. 101. For the purposes of comparison, and to assist in the interpretation of some aspect of the new provisions, it may still be helpful to make reference to the 'old' law of character, but subject to the very clear 'health warning' that the new law embodies a different approach to admissibility, which gives effect to Parliament's intention that 'evidence of bad character would be put before juries more frequently than had hitherto been the case' (*Edwards* [2006] 1 WLR 1524) and that this change of intention may render the old authorities of little or no value. Thus:

> The right way to deal with the new law is not first to ask what would have been the position under the old. In saying that, we do not doubt that some, perhaps many, of the familiar considerations of relevance and fairness which confronted courts before the 2003 Act in cases of multiple allegations where they were said to be of a similar kind will continue to confront them dealing with such cases afterwards. Nor do we doubt that the answers may be the same. There has, however, been a sea-change in the law's starting-point (*Chopra* [2007] 1 Cr App R 225).

This observation, though made in the specific context of cases involving multiple allegations (see **F12.58**), is of equal assistance with regard to other cases in which evidence of bad character is in issue. Although the drafting of the CJA 2003 would have admitted of an interpretation preserving far more of the old law, the courts have made sparing reference to previous authorities and have treated the new provisions, in the way that Parliament intended, as a new departure. The rules of the common law are not to be brought back by a restrictive interpretation of the new law (*Bullen* [2008] 2 Cr App R 364).

The relevant rules are now the CrimPR, part 35 (see Supplement, **R-270** *et seq.*).

It should be noted that the CJA 2003, s. 100, makes separate provision for leave to be obtained before introducing evidence of the bad character of a person other than the accused. This matter is dealt with further at **F14**.

Bad Character

F12.3 The CJA 2003, s. 101, provides that evidence of the bad character of an accused is admissible 'if but only if' it falls within a specific statutory permission, or a 'gateway' as the courts commonly say, in s. 101(a)–(g). Other evidence which does not constitute evidence of bad character within the meaning of the Act, but which nevertheless shows the accused in a bad light, may be admitted on normal principles of relevance, subject to the application of the PACE 1984, s. 78 (*Manister*, heard with *Weir* [2006] 2 All ER 570).

Criminal Justice Act 2003, s. 98

References in this Chapter to evidence of a person's 'bad character' are to evidence of, or of a disposition towards, misconduct on his part, other than evidence which—
(a) has to do with the alleged facts of the offence with which the defendant is charged, or
(b) is evidence of misconduct in connection with the investigation or prosecution of that offence.

'Misconduct' means the commission of an offence or other reprehensible behaviour (s. 112(1)). Thus any evidence suggesting guilt of an offence is evidence of misconduct, whether or not the accused has been charged with or convicted of it. The use of evidence of criminal misconduct not resulting in proceedings may require special caution (see **F12.42**). For multiple charges in the same proceedings, see **F12.58**. For acquittals in previous proceedings, see **F12.66**.

F12.4 **Convictions**   Where convictions are relied upon, it is likely that the value of the evidence will depend on the proof of the circumstances of the offence, not merely upon the actual previous conviction and the matters formally established thereby, and such circumstances will require to be properly proved (*Humphris* (2005) 169 JP 441). *Humphris* was approved in *Ainscough* (2006) 170 JP 517, where the giving of evidence by a police officer based on data held on the Police National Computer was held to be an inappropriate way to settle a dispute between prosecution and defence as to the facts of the previous convictions. It was also observed that the remedy suggested in *Humphris* — procuring a statement by, or evidence from, the victim of an allegedly similar offence — would not be appropriate in cases where D had been dealt with on a plea offered on a different factual basis. The court drew attention to the need for caution and to avoid 'satellite issues' about what did, or did not, happen previously. Where the circumstances of the offence are of the essence, there is an obligation on the party relying upon them to be specific (*Hanson* [2005] 1 WLR 1369), and it is good practice for details to be available if required (*Lamaletie* (2008) 172 JP 249). Proof of relevant details may be achieved through records admissible under the CJA 2003, s. 117 (*Hogart* [2007] EWCA Crim 338).

Note that, while it may be convenient to speak and think of 'previous' convictions, offences occurring subsequent to the offence charged may, as under the old law, be admissible (*Adenusi* (2007) 171 JP 169), as may evidence of propensity exhibited after the offence, provided that the propensity is one that might be expected to be continuing. In *Norris* [2013] EWCA Crim 712 evidence tending to show that N harboured racist views was admitted to connect him with a racially motivated murder: although the evidence was gathered 20 months later, it was open to the jury to draw an inference that N's attitudes were not a recent acquisition. A conviction resulting from a plea of guilty during the instant investigation is also a conviction for these purposes (*Andronicou* [2010] EWCA Crim 2232 where the plea was to an old offence, A having avoided prosecution previously by absconding). See also *Turnbull* [2013] EWCA Crim 676, in which the Court of Appeal identified as potentially 'confusing' an observation by the judge that a plea to an offence under the OAPA 1861, s. 20, was relevant to the question whether T intended to cause grievous bodily harm under s. 18. If a reference is to be made to the plea in these commonly occurring circumstances it would appear crucial to balance it with the clearest direction that the intention for the lesser offence does not establish the ulterior intent for the greater crime.

Convictions before a foreign court may be adduced as evidence of bad character under the CJA 2003 (*Kordansinski* [2007] 1 Cr App R 238). The CAJA 2009, s. 144 and sch. 17, para. 1(2), amended the CJA 2003, s. 103 (see **F12.36**), so as to insert new subsections (7) to (11), which provide for the treatment of previous convictions outside England and Wales. The broad effect of the amendments is that the foreign conviction is treated as being admissible if the corresponding offence in England and Wales would be so treated. See *Plaza* [2013] EWCA Crim 501, where a recent Dutch conviction for importing cocaine had 'powerful probative force' in relation to establishing P's involvement in a conspiracy to import cocaine into the UK, and see also *Brooks* [2014] EWCA Crim 562.

As to the proof that a conviction applies to the individual before the court, see *Lewendon* [2006] 1 WLR 1278 and *Burns* [2006] 1 WLR 1273, citing *Pattison v DPP* [2006] 2 All ER 317 with approval.

Reprehensible Behaviour   The definition of bad character differs from that originally proposed by the Law Commission (*Evidence of Bad Character in Criminal Proceedings*, Law Com No. 273 (2001)), which referred to evidence that a person had behaved, or was disposed to behave, in a way that, in the opinion of the court, might be viewed with disapproval by a reasonable person. This was rejected during the Act's passage through Parliament as too vague and potentially too wide, but it is unclear what is gained by the substitution of 'misconduct' defined in terms of 'reprehensible behaviour'.   **F12.5**

In *Renda* [2006] 2 All ER 553, the Court of Appeal noted that the word 'reprehensible' connoted some element of culpability or blameworthiness. In that case, however, the fact that the accused had been found unfit to plead to the incident in question, which involved gratuitous violence, was not such as to extinguish the element of culpability. In the absence of direct evidence to the contrary, the behaviour was reprehensible. Conduct is not necessarily 'reprehensible' under s. 98 simply because it is morally lax, as in the case of *Manister*, one of the appeals heard with *Weir* [2006] 2 All ER 570. In that case it was held wrong to regard the instigation of a sexual relationship by a man in his thirties with a girl of 16 as 'reprehensible'. As it was relevant, the result was that the evidence was admissible (see **F12.3**). In *Fox* [2009] EWCA Crim 653 the Court of Appeal doubted whether the keeping by the accused of a notebook containing his 'dirty thoughts' could fall within the provision, but concluded that in any event its prejudicial effect outweighed its probative value. See also *Kiernan* [2008] EWCA Crim 972, where a husband gave his wife forms to sign in blank and this was not misconduct in absence of 'telling and specific' context; as it was not otherwise relevant, it was rightly excluded. What is reprehensible is to be distinguished from what is irritating, inconvenient or upsetting to another (*Scott* [2009] EWCA Crim 2457, decided under s. 100 (see **F14.3** *et seq.*), in which the complainant in a case of rape and sexual assault had been warned by police to cease her attempts to communicate with a female friend of the accused. In *Edwards* [2006] 1 WLR 1524, the Court of Appeal cautioned against the inclusion in applications to admit evidence under s. 101 of matters which, on proper analysis, did not disclose bad character (in that case the possession of an antique firearm lawfully held by the accused). In *Cambridge* [2011] EWCA Crim 2009 the Court of Appeal regarded as 'quixotic' the suggestion that having being shot could be evidence of bad character but, as the shooting had the characteristics of a difference of opinion between gangs, it might have been preferable to treat it as such.   **F12.6**

F12.7   In *Osbourne* [2007] EWCA Crim 481, the Court of Appeal considered that 'in the context' of a charge of murder, the aggressive, shouting behaviour of one partner towards another over the care of a young child did not constitute reprehensible behaviour. It would, it is submitted, have been preferable to take a more generalised view of what constitutes reprehensible behaviour, and to hold the shouting to be reprehensible but at the same time not relevant to the charge faced by the accused (of murdering a drug dealer). A context-specific test for what is reprehensible will render decision-making unnecessarily complex. Violent rap lyrics written by the accused were regarded as reprehensible behaviour in *Saleem* [2007] EWCA Crim 1766. See as to the now well-established principle of admitting gang membership as evidence of bad character, *Lewis* [2014] EWCA Crim 48 discussed at **F12.49**.

F12.8   **Reputation and Bad Character**   Section 99(2) of the CJA 2003 preserves the option of proving bad character via reputation at common law, linking with the preserved hearsay exception in s. 118(1) (see **F16.48**). The use of evidence of bad reputation in rebuttal is dealt with at **F13.22**.

F12.9   **'Has to do with' Alleged Facts**   Excluded from the definition, and therefore admissible subject to relevance, is evidence of misconduct which 'has to do with the alleged facts' of the offence charged, or which is evidence in connection with the investigation or prosecution of that offence (CJA 2003, s. 98). This loose phrase would seem broad enough to cover, for example, the fact that an offence of rape follows on from an assault that is not made the subject of any separate charge, or where it is followed by the theft of items of clothing from the complainant. Thus, e.g., in *Brand* [2009] EWCA Crim 2878 B was retried for kidnap and rape, the jury having failed to agree. His conviction at the first trial for stealing the handbag of the victim as part of the same incident was admissible under s. 98(a) and was 'plainly relevant evidence'. A difficult line may have to be drawn between evidence of this kind and evidence which falls within the definition of evidence of bad character but is admissible via a specific gateway. In *M* [2006] EWCA Crim 193 the complainant was cross-examined as to why, in the aftermath of an alleged rape, she was passive, made no complaint and got into a car with her alleged attacker. This rendered admissible her account of previous threats to shoot her and her belief that M had a gun. The evidence was thought to 'have to do with' the alleged facts, but if not the court thought it was admissible under gateway (c) as 'explanatory' evidence (see **F12.28**). In drugs cases, 'lifestyle' evidence may be received, as it was at common law, to support an inference that the accused's income must be derived from drugs (*Green* [2009] EWCA Crim 1688). The trial judge was held to have correctly directed the jury to consider whether the standard of living of the accused was explicable only by G being part of one of the conspiracies charged. This would not preclude the use of such evidence to establish guilt via an inference of propensity under gateway (d) in an appropriate case but it is important that the distinction between the two types of evidence is strictly maintained. Thus in *Mohammed* [2013] EWCA Crim 901, a 'deal list' was admitted that referred both to cannabis, which was the subject of the charge, and to cocaine, which was not. It was held that the issue of the admissibility of the references to cocaine should have been considered separately under s. 101(1)(d), while the references to cannabis were 'to do' with the charge and were rightly admitted.

F12.10   In some of the leading authorities the bad character evidence 'has to do' with the index offence because of a temporal connection. In *Machado* (2006) 170 JP 400, decided in relation to s.100 (bad character of non-defendant: see **F14.4**), evidence tending to show the alleged victim of a robbery had taken drugs was held to be within the wording, as providing support for the defence explanation of his sudden collapse (the prosecution having alleged that the accused pushed him over). In *Tirnaveanu* [2007] 4 All ER 301 a broad submission that evidence 'has to do' with the facts if it shows the accused was the person who committed the offences was rejected. The court approved the 'fact-specific' analysis applied in *Machado*, stating that there must be 'some nexus in time' between the offence charged and the evidence of misconduct to be adduced. In *McNeill* (2008) 172 JP 50 the court endorsed as a 'working model' the proposition that evidence falls within the exception if it would either have been admissible at common law 'outside the context of bad character or propensity', or if it related directly to the offence, provided it was reasonably contemporaneous and closely associated with the alleged facts. The evidence admitted consisted of a statement made two days after the alleged offence of making a threat to kill, in which the accused reiterated to a third party her threat to kill the same individual. Where the *actus reus* of the offence continues over time, evidence admitted as having to do with the alleged facts may appertain to any point in the commission of the offence (*Vehicle and Operator Services Agency v Ace Crane and Transport Ltd* [2010] 2 All ER 791). In *Hastings-Cokar* [2014] EWCA Crim 555 the temporal principle was held to extend to the discovery of ammunition discovered as a result of an immediate search of premises consequent upon the finding of the firearm that was the subject of the charge; however, had it been treated as bad character evidence, it would also have been admissible on that ground. An important qualification on *Tirnaveanu* and *McNeill* was added in *Sule* [2013] 1 Cr App R 42 (3), to the effect that a nexus in time is only of importance where the connection is based (as it was in both *Tirnaveanu* and *McNeill*) on additional misconduct which is said to be in effect part of the sequence of events under consideration. Where the bad character evidence 'has to do with' the facts for some other reason (as in *Sule,* the possible provision of a motive for the index offence), such evidence may be admissible despite the absence of a temporal nexus. In *Sule* the evidence that a killing by S was a reprisal as part of a feud between gangs suggested misconduct over a period of months, but was not thereby inadmissible under s. 98. Comments in *Fox* [2009] EWCA Crim 653, to the effect that the words 'has to do with' relate only to the *actus reus* of the offence, were disapproved in *IA* [2013] EWCA Crim 1308, where the correct approach was said to be one of 'direct relevance'. It is submitted that this is the correct approach.

Misconduct in Connection with Investigation or Prosecution   A 'gateway' is not necessary in order to admit evidence relating, say, to the telling of lies in interview or the attempted intimidation of witnesses, as this would appear to be 'misconduct in connection with the investigation or prosecution of the offence', as referred to in the CJA 2003, s. 98(b). That provision is not limited to conduct by the prosecuting authorities (*Apabhai* (2011) 175 JP 292) and comments in *Scott* [2009] EWCA Crim 2457 do not, properly construed, suggest otherwise. In *Apabhai,* evidence of an attempt by a co-accused to blackmail A in relation to the matters under investigation was held to be within the provision. On the facts, it was also the case that the purpose of adducing the evidence was not to demonstrate the co-accused's bad character, but rather to show his motive for incriminating A. The question of purpose would not, however, appear to be relevant to the question of admissibility under s. 98(b). **F12.11**

Bad Character and Cross-examination   Under the CJA 2003, there is no longer a different set of reference points for the definition of bad character evidence according to whether it is to be employed as evidence-in-chief or in cross-examination of the accused. The definition in s. 98 applies for all purposes, as does the qualification that evidence that 'has to do with the alleged facts' of the offence charged or 'is evidence of misconduct in connection with the investigation' is excluded from the definition. Under the Criminal Evidence Act 1898, there was a specific prohibition on the asking of questions of the accused which is not replicated in the CJA 2003, which deals with admissibility of 'evidence' of bad character. However, the evidence that is admissible under s. 101(1)(c)–(g) includes evidence that 'a witness is to be invited to give in cross-examination' (s. 104(2), regarding evidence elicited for the co-accused, and s. 112(1), defining the meaning of 'prosecution evidence' for the purposes of the other provisions). It would appear, therefore, that the putting of a question to which a truthful answer would elicit inadmissible evidence of bad character is normally impermissible — although the matter could have been made clearer. **F12.12**

Previous Allegations as Evidence of Bad Character   It does not appear that the CJA 2003, s. 98, conveys any necessary protection against the revelation of a mere charge (either in the sense of 'charged in court', as in *Stirland v DPP* [1944] AC 315, or in the sense of having been previously suspected) unless the suggestion is that the accused committed the offence with which he was charged, so that the allegation becomes one of the commission of an offence (see F12.3). However, the point made in relation to the previous law in *Maxwell v DPP* [1935] AC 309 continues to hold good: the court should not permit a matter to be raised unless it is demonstrably relevant. The mere making of an allegation will not normally be relevant either **F12.13**

to guilt or to the credibility of the accused as a witness (*Bovell* [2005] 2 Cr App R 401 (decided under s. 100), *Edwards* [2006] 1 WLR 1524). Where it is relevant, it may be admitted where the purpose is not to show bad character (*Hussain* [2008] EWCA Crim 1117).

F12.14   **Evidence of Matters Already before the Jury**   Under the Criminal Evidence Act 1898, s. 1(3), the use of the phrase 'tending to show' matters relating to the accused's bad character was held to import the qualification that matters already before the jury were not covered by the accused's shield (*Jones v DPP* [1962] AC 635). Under the CJA 2003, the prohibition relates to 'evidence of' bad character, and it could be argued that this is a wider prohibition that is not confined to the revelation of previously unmentioned matters. Any additional protection apparently conferred is illusory, however, in that evidence of a relevant matter of the type in issue in *Jones v DPP* (the recycling of a previous alibi) would undoubtedly be rendered admissible by the wide exception in s. 101(1)(d).

The Statutory 'Gateways' — Overview

F12.15   **Criminal Justice Act 2003, s. 101**

(1) In criminal proceedings evidence of the defendant's bad character is admissible if, but only if—
    (a) all parties to the proceedings agree to the evidence being admissible,
    (b) the evidence is adduced by the defendant himself or is given in answer to a question asked by him in cross-examination and intended to elicit it,
    (c) it is important explanatory evidence,
    (d) it is relevant to an important matter in issue between the defendant and the prosecution,
    (e) it has substantial probative value in relation to an important matter in issue between a defendant and a co-defendant,
    (f) it is evidence to correct a false impression given by the defendant, or
    (g) the defendant has made an attack on another person's character.
(2) Sections 102 to 106 contain provision supplementing subsection (1).
(3) The court must not admit evidence under subsection (1)(d) or (g) if, on an application by the defendant to exclude it, it appears to the court that the admission of the evidence would have such an adverse effect on the fairness of the proceedings that the court ought not to admit it.
(4) On an application to exclude evidence under subsection (3) the court must have regard, in particular, to the length of time between the matters to which that evidence relates and the matters which form the subject of the offence charged.

F12.16   Section 101(1)(a) makes it clear that evidence of bad character may be admissible by general consensus of the parties (compare the corresponding provision making hearsay admissible by agreement in the CJA 2003, s. 114(1)(c): see **F15.1** and **F16.6**). Thus, for example, in *Kalu* [2007] EWCA Crim 22 a caution for excessive chastisement was admitted by agreement and relied on by both prosecution and defence: by the defence to support a claim that he had learned his lesson, and by the prosecution as part of an alleged history of cruelty to the children in his care. Evidence admitted 'without demur' by skilled counsel and trial judge may be said to have been admitted by 'tacit' agreement (*Marsh* [2009] EWCA Crim 2696). See also *J (DC)* [2010] 2 Cr App R 8, where it was said that, in the interests of good trial management, the court should be informed of any agreement to admit bad character evidence at the beginning of the trial. Further, the mere fact of agreement, though sufficient to overcome an objection based on bad character (or hearsay: as to which, see **F16.6**) did not justify putting in evidence documents subject to public interest immunity disclosed for the purpose of cross-examination of prosecution witnesses, for which a further order would have been required. Where there are multiple defendants, the gateway clearly requires that the consent of all must be secured, bearing in mind that they may have very different interests (*Ferdinand* [2014] EWCA Crim 1243).

Section 101(1)(b) retains the rule that the accused can elect to tender evidence of his own bad character.

Section 101(1)(c) broadly reflects the common law on 'background' evidence, and is dealt with further at **F12.28**. Section 101(1)(d), however, cuts across much of the thinking of the old law by regarding as admissible evidence that is merely 'relevant' to an important issue between the accused and the prosecution. At common law, the rules on 'similar fact' evidence in particular required a high degree of probative value in order to overcome the prejudicial effect involved in the reception of such evidence (*DPP v P* [1991] 2 AC 447). The CJA 2003 removes this requirement from the test of admissibility, relegating questions of fairness to the court's power to exclude evidence to avoid prejudice (s. 101(3): see **F12.18**). Although it was initially accepted in *Edwards* [2006] 1 Cr App R 31, following *O'Brien v Chief Constable of South Wales Police* [2005] 2 AC 534, that the CJA 2003 continues to set a standard of 'enhanced relevance' for admissibility of prosecution evidence, the subsequent decision of the Court of Appeal on the facts of *Somanathan*, one of the appeals heard with *Weir* [2006] 2 All ER 570, makes it clear that the CJA 2003 'completely reverses the pre-existing general rule' and that the 'pre-existing, one-stage test which balanced probative value against prejudicial effect is obsolete'. *O'Brien*, a civil case, is 'capable of being misunderstood' on the point: in other words, clearly wrong.

The most radical aspect of the change brought about by s. 101(1)(d) in combination with s. 103 **F12.17** is that an accused's propensity becomes a matter towards which relevant prosecution evidence may be directed (see **F12.39** *et seq.*). Section 101(1)(d) has the additional function of admitting evidence to show the untruthfulness of an accused person, and this is dealt with at **F12.44**. Section 101(1)(e) corresponds roughly to the common-law rules permitting a co-accused to adduce evidence of the accused's bad character where it has substantial value in relation to an important issue between them (see **F12.67** *et seq.*). Section 101(1)(f), evidence to correct a false impression, corresponds broadly to the former category of evidence in rebuttal of evidence of good character adduced by an accused (see **F12.85**) and s. 101(1)(g), evidence to meet an attack on another person, is similar to the previous category of evidence to meet a defence case that involves making imputations on the character of another (see **F12.91**).

Inherent in the gateways, and in the provisions of ss. 102 to 106 which explain the key terms therein, is a sense of the separation of the function of evidence going to the issue and that going to credit. This distinction is called into question in *Campbell* [2007] 1 WLR 2798 (see **F12.23**), where the point is made that the pre-Act law was over-dependent on it to the point of contravening common sense; e.g., where evidence of offences of the same type as the offence charged was regarded as relevant only to the credit of the accused as a witness. *Campbell* champions a broader mandate for common sense at the risk of rendering meaningless the impact of the distinction within the CJA 2003 itself.

POWERS OF EXCLUSION

Criminal Justice Act 2003, s. 101   **F12.18**

(3) The court must not admit evidence under subsection (1)(d) or (g) if, on an application by the defendant to exclude it, it appears to the court that the admission of the evidence would have such an adverse effect on the fairness of the proceedings that the court ought not to admit it.

The principal mechanism by which the court can ensure that an accused is not prejudiced by revelations of evidence under s. 101(1)(d) or (g) is the exclusionary power under s. 101(3): that it appears to the court that the admission of the evidence would have such an adverse effect on the fairness of the proceedings that the court ought not to admit it.

The power, it should be noted, comes into play on application by the defence to exclude the evidence rather than on the prosecution application to admit it. The power under s. 101(3) does not appear to be exercisable by the court of its own motion (*Highton* [2005] 1 WLR 3472) but, if necessary (e.g. to protect an unrepresented accused), an application could be prompted by the court.

In *Hanson* [2005] 1 WLR 3169 the Vice-President (Rose LJ) drew attention to the wording 'must not admit', in s. 101(3), with the comment that this was a stronger formula than the one in use in the PACE 1984, s. 78 ('may refuse to allow'). His lordship also expressed the hope that prosecutors would not routinely apply to use evidence of the accused's convictions, but would take into account the particular circumstances of each case. The difference in wording was also noted in *Weir* [2006] 2 All ER 570, but the currently preferred view is to regard the two provisions as being on all fours in that a court has no discretion under s. 78 once the conditions for exclusion are satisfied (*Tirnaveanu* [2007] 4 All ER 301).

F12.19   Section 101(3) cannot be used to restrict any of the other five gateways, which appear to lead directly to admissibility. This raises no issues of difficulty in relation to (a) or (b), where the accused has control over the issue. Nor is the absence of discretion a novelty in relation to (e), where it is the co-accused who is entitled to invoke the exception; as at common law there is no discretion to prevent the co-accused taking advantage of the rule permitting him to adduce evidence of the accused's bad character (*Murdoch v Taylor* [1965] AC 574). In relation to explanatory evidence admitted under s. 101(1)(c), however, and evidence to correct a false impression under s. 101(1)(f), it may be envisaged that there will be cases where the defence will seek to make an argument for exclusion based on unfairness.

As there is no specific provision in chapter 1 of part 11 of the CJA 2003 that excludes the operation of s. 78 of the PACE 1984, it has so far been accepted that it still applies. In *Highton*, a case which did not call directly for the application of s. 78, the inclination of the Court of Appeal was to say that it provided 'an additional protection' to an accused. Judges were encouraged to apply s. 78 pending a definitive ruling to the contrary, so as to avoid any risk of injustice. In considering the appeal of *Somanathan*, one of the appeals heard with *Weir* [2006] 2 All ER 570, the court noted that, of the three provisions relied upon by the prosecution, s. 101(3) applied to two, but not to the third, (i.e. s. 101(1)(f)). The court saw 'no reason to doubt' that s. 78 should be considered where s. 101(1)(f) is relied on, although (as in *Highton*) it did not assist the applicant to do so. See also *O'Dowd* [2009] 2 Cr App R 280. For the position in relation to gateway (c), see *Davis* (2008) 172 JP 358 at **F12.31**.

F12.20   Among the arguments against the application of s. 78 is that chapter 2 of part 11, which deals with hearsay, includes a provision under which the effect of s. 78 is specifically preserved, together with the operation of any other power of the court to exclude evidence at its discretion (s. 126(2)). In favour of its application is that, where the court sees the exclusion of the evidence as necessary in order to ensure a fair trial under the ECHR, Article 6, this should be sufficient to override any inference arising from the structure of the Act that Parliament's intention was to exclude the general operation of s. 78. In *Highton* Lord Woolf noted that s. 78 serves 'a very similar purpose' to Article 6. In *Dixon* [2012] EWCA Crim 2163 the Court of Appeal respectfully agreed with Lord Woolf's observations, and drew particular attention (at [13]) to the 'repeated references to "fairness" ' in the statutory provisions as support for this view.

For discretionary exclusion generally, see **F2.18** *et seq.*

WEIGHT OF CHARACTER EVIDENCE AND JUDICIAL DIRECTION

Introduction

F12.21   The courts in interpreting the provisions have accepted that the CJA 2003 provides a new framework for the wider admissibility of evidence of bad character, making a small but crucial adjustment to the literal wording to ensure that s. 78 of the PACE 1984 can be invoked despite Parliament's apparent intention to restrict its application (see **F12.20**). The key stages are now as set out in *Edwards* [2006] 1 WLR 1524:

(1) The judge determines admissibility under the relevant statutory gateway(s).
(2) Where it is raised, the judge also determines any question of exclusion in respect of prosecution evidence, e.g. under s. 101(3) or 103(3) of the CJA 2003, or s. 78 of the PACE 1984.

(3) Once evidence of bad character is admitted, questions of weight are for the jury, subject to the judge's power to stop the case where the evidence is contaminated (under s. 107 at F12.63) and the judge's direction as to the use to which the evidence may be put.

(4) The direction on the evidence is of paramount importance. If the ground of the trial has shifted since the evidence was admitted, it may be necessary to tell the jury that it is of little weight.

The Court of Appeal also expressed the view that, if evidence of marginal relevance was tendered under s. 101, it was potentially difficult for the judge to deal with in summing-up, and this should be borne in mind by the parties. This reflects observations in the earlier case of *Hanson* [2005] 1 WLR 3169, which was approved in *Edwards*, where the Court of Appeal stated that the purpose of the legislation was 'to assist in the evidence-based conviction of the guilty, without putting those who are not guilty at risk of conviction by prejudice'. As in *Edwards*, much stress was laid on the importance of the direction to the jury, but the hope was also expressed that the prosecution would avoid routine applications wherever an accused has previous convictions, preferring rather to focus on the particular circumstances of each case.

Hanson also outlines the content of a direction on bad character which, though couched in terms of a case involving evidence of propensity, is of more general relevance. A proper direction should: **F12.22**

(1) give the jury a clear warning against the dangers of placing undue reliance on previous convictions;
(2) stress that evidence of bad character cannot be used to bolster a weak case, or to prejudice a jury against the defendant;
(3) emphasise that the jury should not infer guilt from the existence of convictions.

Thus the protection of the accused from prejudice arising from the use of convictions (or it would seem of any other evidence of bad character) under the CJA 2003 depends critically on the ability of the jury to adhere to judicial guidance: under the 'old' law they were prevented from showing prejudice by dint of the evidence being concealed from them. The judicial direction was described in *Eastlake* [2007] EWCA Crim 603 as the 'safety valve' within the new scheme, and in *Isichei* (2006) 170 JP 753 the Court of Appeal noted the dependence of the system on the jury's loyalty to, and understanding of, the judge's directions. In *X* [2012] EWCA Crim 2276 convictions were quashed where a direction had, *inter alia*, failed to warn against placing undue reliance on convictions and that a relevant propensity, if established, would be only one factor to consider. See also *Ellis* [2010] EWCA Crim 163, where the failure to direct the jury not to infer that the accused had been untruthful in the instant case because he had been so on previous occasions was an omission 'of some significance', although not, on the facts, such as to render his conviction unsafe. The decision in *Campbell* [2007] 1 WLR 2798, to the extent that it diminishes the importance of a failure to direct on bad character, weakens this protection (see F12.23); see also *Bullas* [2012] All ER (D) 21 (Nov), where it was held that the jury would have realised (despite the absence of a direction) that evidence of B's homosexual tendencies was admitted simply to rebut his specific denial of the matter, and not to suggest any propensity to commit the sexual assaults on young boys with which he was charged. See also F12.6.

Evidence Once Admitted can be Used for All Relevant Purposes

Of particular difficulty in directions under the pre-Act law was the case where an aspect of the accused's bad character was admissible for a specific purpose and no other. This problem is largely avoided under the CJA 2003 by decisions holding that evidence, once it passes through a gateway, may be used for any purpose for which it is relevant. In *Highton* [2005] 1 WLR 3472 it was held that evidence admitted under the gateway in s. 101(1)(g) of the CJA 2003 (following an attack on another person's character) was not to be used merely as a yardstick by which to measure the credit to be given to the accused's account: 'the use to which [evidence] may be put **F12.23** depends upon the matters to which it is relevant, rather than upon the gateway through which it was admitted'. In *Edwards* [2006] 1 WLR 1524 it was held, following *Highton*, that evidence admitted at the accused's own behest under s. 101(1)(b) could thereafter be used as evidence for any relevant purpose. More crucially, *Highton* was said in *Campbell* [2007] 1 WLR 2798 to apply where evidence of the accused's propensity to violence had been properly admitted under s. 101(1)(d), and the issue was as to its use in relation to his credibility (the converse of the situation in *Highton* itself). The Court of Appeal, while accepting the general guidance in *Hanson* [2005] 1 WLR 3169 (see **F12.21**) stressed the importance of relating the evidence to the facts of the case in a common-sense way, bearing in mind that 'if the jury learn that a defendant has shown a propensity to commit criminal acts they may well at one and the same time conclude that he is guilty and that he is less likely to be telling the truth when he says that he is not'. In *Singh* [2007] EWCA Crim 2140, in which the evidence had been admitted via gateway (g), Hughes LJ stressed that the evidence thus admitted for all purposes was more broadly based than would have been permissible under gateway (d) in relation to evidence probative either of guilt or untruthfulness. A careful direction was also given in *Singh* in 'mitigation of' S's bad character, to the effect that he had pleaded guilty to his past offences. That this is a two-edged sword was shown in *Speed* (2013) 177 JP 649 where S, charged with indecent exposure, had adduced evidence of a range of his convictions under gateway (b), partly in order to show that, at the age of 60, he had no record in respect of any sexual offences. It was held not to be unfair for the trial judge to suggest to the jury that the conduct of the accused in pleading not guilty in the past, when facing charges of which he knew he was guilty, was relevant to his credibility as a witness, even though he had not given evidence in those proceedings and it is far from clear that he had done anything more than put the prosecution to proof of its case.

F12.24   In *Lafayette* [2008] EWCA Crim 3238 the Court of Appeal noted that a conviction which was relevant and admissible under s. 101(1)(g) following an attack on a prosecution witness might not be relevant to any issue of propensity. In such a case, a specific direction to use the evidence in relation to credibility only would be advisable. The decision does not appear to be inconsistent with *Highton* or *Campbell*, which were dealing with evidence which was doubly relevant. In *Williams* [2011] EWCA Crim 2198 W's previous convictions were not relied on as evidence of propensity and, though relevant to credibility under gateway (g), there was a risk that their prejudicial effect would outweigh their probative value in the absence of 'sufficiently strong and clear' directions as to the limited purpose for which they were admissible. No such direction having been given, the Court of Appeal could not be satisfied that the jury had not drawn impermissible inferences from the previous convictions, and W's appeal was allowed. See also *Tollady* [2010] EWCA Crim 2614 in which evidence of her own prior conviction was adduced by T in order to make a point about the hostility of the officer who had arrested her on that occasion. There were similarities in relation to T's aggressive behaviour on both occasions that rendered the conviction relevant in respect of T's criminal propensity. However the Court of Appeal considered (at [26]) that the five-year-old conviction for disorderly behaviour to which T had pleaded guilty, even if technically admissible in relation to T's credibility under *Campbell*, ought not to have been drawn to the jury's attention in the summing-up as having a bearing on that issue.

F12.25   A potentially disturbing aspect of *Campbell* is the suggestion that an omission to direct the jury on the relevance of bad character will, to the extent that the application of the evidence to the facts is simply a matter of common sense, not automatically be treated as a ground of appeal. See also *Saleem* [2007] EWCA Crim 1923, where the Court of Appeal said that 'although the judge could have given the jury more help than he did, we do not consider that his failure to do so rendered the conviction unsafe, as the jury would have appreciated the relevance of the evidence', *Walker* [2007] EWCA Crim 2631, and *Marsh* [2009] EWCA Crim 2696. The courts should not be quick to assume that juries exercise the same 'common sense' as judges in respect of evidence of bad character. Reassuringly, in *O'Dowd* [2009] 2 Cr App R 280, the Court of Appeal affirmed the duty 'save in the simplest of cases' to pull together in a direction the strengths and weaknesses of bad character evidence in a manner tailored to the evidence in the case.

Particular care would appear still to be required if evidence admitted under the gateway in s. 101(1)(c) (explanatory evidence) is capable of being considered relevant to the accused's propensity to commit the offence. In *Davis* (2008) 172 JP 358, the Court considered that the approach in *Campbell* is not 'easily applied' to gateway (c) and suggested a cautious reading of that gateway to prevent the admission of evidence that also shows propensity.

Reasons for Rulings

Criminal Justice Act 2003, s. 110

F12.26

(1) Where the court makes a relevant ruling—
    (a) it must state in open court (but in the absence of the jury, if there is one) its reasons for the ruling;
    (b) if it is a magistrates' court, it must cause the ruling and the reasons for it to be entered in the register of the court's proceedings.
(2) In this section 'relevant ruling' means—
    (a) a ruling on whether an item of evidence is evidence of a person's bad character;
    (b) a ruling on whether an item of such evidence is admissible under section 100 or 101 (including a ruling on an application under section 101(3));
    (c) a ruling under section 107.

Section 107, which codifies the power of the court to stop a case where contaminated evidence of bad character has been admitted, is considered at **F12.63**.

There is a general duty, in the terms described in s. 110, to give reasons for rulings in relation to bad character. When considering the trial judge's stance in *Osbourne*, one of the appeals heard with *Renda* [2006] 2 All ER 553, the Court of Appeal indicated that the mere observation that the jury was entitled to know about character was regarded as an 'over-parsimonious' compliance with s. 110. The point at issue concerned the character of a witness rather than an accused (s. 100: see **F14**) but it is submitted that the principle is the same.

Notice

Section 111 of the CJA 2003 permits rules of court to be made in relation to evidence of bad character to supplement the provisions of the Act. Section 111(2) requires provision to be made for the giving of notice by the prosecution of an intention to adduce evidence of an accused's bad character in chief or to elicit such evidence in cross-examination, and permits the making of rules in respect of the giving of notice by a co-accused. The relevant rules are the CrimPR, part 35 (see Supplement, **R-237** *et seq.*). The rules are applied to all parties wishing to adduce evidence of bad character, and also to an accused's application to exclude bad character evidence: all must be in due form and time limits are set. The accused may waive his entitlement to notice, and the court has power to allow notices to be given in a different form, or at a different time, where to do so is in the interests of justice. Where the rules have not been complied with, the judge's power to exclude evidence should be regarded as a power to prevent unfairness rather than a disciplinary sanction. If unfairness can be cured and the interests of justice require evidence to be admitted then it should not be excluded. But there will be cases where the power can properly be deployed to prevent substantial unfairness that cannot be cured by an adjournment (*Musone* [2007] 1 WLR 2467, decided in relation to the notice provisions for hearsay, but held in *Hassett* [2008] EWCA Crim 1634 to be equally germane to bad character).

F12.27

EXPLANATORY EVIDENCE

Introduction

In the CJA 2003, s. 101(1)(c), special provision is made for the admission of 'explanatory' evidence — evidence without which it would be 'impossible or difficult to understand other evidence in the case' — provided that its value for understanding the case as a whole is substantial. It follows that, where the evidence requires no 'footnote or lexicon' but is readily understandable

F12.28

without evidence of bad character, s. 101(1)(c) does not apply (*Beverley* [2006] EWCA Crim 1287). See also *Davis* (2008) 172 JP 358 (issue of provocation 'entirely comprehensible' without evidence of bad character).

The operation of the statutory provision is not confined to prosecution evidence. Section 101(1)(c) is supplemented by s. 102.

Criminal Justice Act 2003, ss. 101 and 102

101.—(1) In criminal proceedings evidence of the defendant's bad character is admissible if, but only if—

    (a) ...

    (b) ...

    (c) it is important explanatory evidence;

    (d) ...

102. For the purposes of section 101(1)(c) evidence is important explanatory evidence if—

    (a) without it, the court or jury would find it impossible or difficult properly to understand other evidence in the case, and

    (b) its value for understanding the case as a whole is substantial.

F12.29 Where an offence is alleged it may be necessary to give evidence of the background against which the offence is committed, even though to do so will reveal facts showing the accused in a discreditable light. The necessity to admit evidence of this kind, for its explanatory as distinct from its probative value, was well-accepted at common law in a line of authorities that continue to be relevant under the CJA 2003 (*Osbourne* [2007] EWCA Crim 481). The most frequently approved statement of principle was that of Purchas LJ in *Pettman* (2 May 1985 unreported) who said:

> Where it is necessary to place before the jury evidence of part of a continual background of history relevant to the offence charged in the indictment and without the totality of which the account placed before the jury would be incomplete or incomprehensible, then the fact that the whole account involves including evidence establishing the commission of an offence with which the accused is not charged is not of itself a ground for excluding the evidence.

In *Dolan* [2003] 1 Cr App R 281 the court approved the basis for admitting background evidence as explained in the commentary on *Stevens* [1995] Crim LR 649, where it was said that 'it is helpful to have it and difficult for the jury to do their job if events are viewed in total isolation from their history'. That the evidence is helpful is not by itself enough, nor is it sufficient that the jury might wonder about a gap in the evidence that the bad character evidence might fill; to say that the evidence fills out the picture is not the same as saying that the picture is impossible or difficult to see without it (*Lee* (2012) 176 JP 231). See also *C* [2012] EWCA Crim 2034, in which the sexual abuse and domination of the complainant by C during her childhood was necessary to explain why her apparent compliance in a sexual relationship after her sixteenth birthday should not be regarded as indicating consent.

The bad character thus revealed may be incidental to the offence charged, as in *Neale* (1977) 65 Cr App R 304, where the offence charged was arson of a hostel for boys released from Borstal in which N was an inmate, and *Toussaint-Collins* [2009] EWCA Crim 316, where it was inevitably revealed that a letter which was relevant to the proceedings was sent by the accused from prison; or germane to the inquiry into guilt, as in *Hagan* (1873) 12 Cox CC 357, where evidence was given of statements made by the accused showing animosity towards the child he was alleged to have murdered.

Explanatory evidence was carefully scrutinised at common law to ensure that it did not become a backdoor method of smuggling in inadmissible evidence of propensity (see, e.g., *Dolan* and *Underwood* [1999] Crim LR 227). Under the CJA 2003, s. 101(1)(d), relevant evidence of propensity becomes admissible and is likely, subject to an argument about exclusion based on prejudice, to be admitted (for example, in *Golds* [2014] EWCA Crim 748, where evidence of a 'background of violence' in G's relationship with his partner was not strictly necessary in the sense required by gateway (c), but was of sufficient relevance to demonstrate propensity under (d)).

Where evidence tendered as explanatory is also evidence of propensity, particular caution is required in applying gateway (c). That gateway should not be deployed to 'slide in' evidence of propensity under the guise of explanatory evidence where the former would not be admissible, or would be subject to additional safeguards (*Davis* (2008) 172 JP 358, *Saint* [2010] EWCA Crim 1924). Such evidence once admitted may require a particularly careful direction. Thus, for example, in one of the appeals heard with *Edwards* [2006] 1 Cr App R 31, *Chohan*, evidence was admitted to support an identification of C as a robber from a person who recognised him from the many occasions on which she had sold him drugs. The separate functions of this background evidence and other evidence of the accused's record which went to his propensity were rightly maintained in the judge's direction. In *Norris* [2014] EWCA Crim 419 it was the complainant's discovery that N had a recent conviction for sexual offending that had led to her revelation of serious offences against her many years before. As the trial judge had carefully considered the risk of prejudice, and made clear in his direction that the conviction was not evidence of propensity, it was held that the evidence was rightly admitted. It is equally possible that evidence of a previous offence which is closely connected to the crime charged may be admissible propensity evidence without being necessary explanatory evidence (*Gillespie* [2011] EWCA Crim 3152), or that evidence may be admissible via both gateways for different purposes (see *Mortimore* [2013] EWCA Crim 1639, where a previous conviction for child abduction and a subsequent warning notice were evidence of M's *mens rea* on the subsequent occasion under gateway (d) and also, under gateway (c), necessary to explain the context of the relationship between M and the teenage girl he sheltered in his home). See also *Lee* (2012) 176 JP 231, where it was said that evidence admitted under one gateway sometimes becomes admissible on another basis, making it particularly important for the jury to have directions that focus their attention on the use they may make of the evidence.

Where explanatory evidence is admitted, it may be fairest to present it in the form of an agreed **F12.30** statement of facts, for the avoidance of prejudice and to prevent the distraction of the jury (cf. the common law's approach in *Butler* [1999] Crim LR 835) and see *Cundell* [2009] EWCA Crim 2072, where the previous misconduct was admitted by agreement under s. 101(1)(a) (see **F12.16**) but would otherwise have been clearly admissible under gateway (c).

Discretion and s. 101(1)(c)

It should be noted that the court has no explicit statutory discretion to exclude evidence that satis- **F12.31** fies the test in the CJA 2003, s. 101(1)(c). Where the evidence is necessary for the proper exposition of the case, in the sense that it would be 'impossible' for the court to manage without it, this makes sense (cf. *Dolan* [2003] 1 Cr App R 281). If, however, it is merely 'difficult', the court will have to consider whether it should have recourse to the general power of exclusion of prosecution evidence in the PACE 1984, s. 78. The observations of the Court of Appeal in *Highton* [2005] 1 WLR 3472 and subsequent authorities (see **F12.18**) would seem to provide some support for this argument. The common law appears to provide for the application of discretion, in cases such as *M (T)* [2000] 1 All ER 148 and *W* [2003] EWCA Crim 3024. Dicta in *Davis* (2008) 172 JP 358 acknowledge that the role of s. 78 is 'possibly controversial' under the Act. See also *Henderson* [2010] 2 Cr App R 185 and the appeal of *Oyediran*, where explanatory evidence that was critical in relation to the ability of the co-accused (the mother of the deceased baby) to appreciate risk to her child was also potentially prejudicial to O, in that it showed him to be of a violent disposition. The prejudice was said to have been overcome by a clear direction as to the proper use of the evidence.

Evidence of Motive or Intention as Explanatory Evidence   Cases in which the previous deal- **F12.32** ings between the parties are said to show motive or intention sit somewhat uneasily between explanatory evidence and evidence relevant to the issue (CJA 2003, s. 101(1)(d): see **F12.36** *et seq.*). The sort of evidence described below will undoubtedly continue to be received in trials under the CJA 2003, but it may be that the courts will feel more comfortable invoking s. 101(1)(d) in future. This has the advantage that it will not be necessary to explain why it is 'difficult' to understand the evidence without the additional evidence of intention or motive, or to show the 'substantial' value of the evidence in understanding the case as a whole.

A case illustrating the different emphasis of the two provisions is *Beverley* [2006] EWCA Crim 1287, in which previous convictions for possession of small quantities of cannabis were advanced by the prosecution at the trial of the accused for conspiracy to import a kilo of cocaine. B's appeal was allowed on the ground that the jury would not have been 'disabled or disadvantaged' in understanding the case against B in the absence of evidence of the convictions, so that s. 101(1)(c) was 'entirely unavailable'. Section 101(1)(d) was also discounted on the ground that the previous convictions did not establish a relevant propensity, so as to establish guilty knowledge, in light of the differences in the circumstances, and also the age of the convictions (see **F12.39** *et seq.*).

F12.33   At common law it was typically under a broad banner of background evidence that courts admitted, for example, evidence given to show prior assaults by the accused on the victim, or menaces or threats uttered to him (*Bond* [1906] 2 KB 389) and evidence of previous acts or words showing enmity as admissible evidence of motive (*Ball* [1911] AC 47 at p. 68). See also *Williams* (1986) 84 Cr App R 299 and *Fulcher* [1995] 2 Cr App R 251, where the previous non-accidental injuries sustained by the baby that F was alleged to have murdered were held to have been relevant to show not only that the child, being in pain, was more likely to be fractious, but also how F was likely to react to the child crying. In *Giannetto* [1997] 1 Cr App R 1, *Ball* and *Williams* were held to justify the admission of the diary of a deceased woman to show a history of threatening and violent behaviour by G towards her, and to form the basis for an inference that G was more likely to have killed her (although it was recognised that a direction that threats and assaults do not always lead to murder was also required). To the same effect are *Phillips* [2003] 2 Cr App R 528, where the unhappy history of the marriage between P and the woman he was charged with murdering was adduced to show motive, and *Shaw* [2002] EWCA Crim 1997, where the history of dealings between S and the police was adduced to shed light on whether S was more likely to have been the aggressor or the innocent victim of an assault by police officers. *Shaw* is a borderline case of relevance, though it may be significant that S chose to adduce something of the history himself in order to show why he believed he was likely to be attacked. In such circumstances, there was a danger that the jury would be left with a misleading picture. Under the CJA 2003 it would appear that s. 101(1)(d) might well provide an alternative route to admissibility in such cases.

F12.34   In *Sidhu* (1994) 98 Cr App R 59, a video apparently showing S leading the activities of a group of armed rebels in Pakistan was admitted to show his object in participating in a conspiracy to possess explosives in England, which it was alleged was designed to further the interests of the same group. It was held that, provided there was a sufficient nexus in time between S's visit to Pakistan and the offence charged, and provided also that it was necessary to lead the evidence in order to give the jury a complete picture, it was admissible as evidence of a 'continual background of history' relevant to S's part in the conspiracy. As with evidence of motive, such evidence might now be received in the alternative under s. 101(1)(d) on grounds of relevance to the issue.

In *M (T)* [2000] 1 All ER 148, evidence was admitted of the abuse that M and his sister S had suffered at the hands of older members of their family, including instances where M had been forced to abuse his siblings. Without such evidence, the two counts of rape of S could not properly be understood: e.g., the jury would inevitably have wondered why S did not turn to other family members for help. See also *M* [2006] EWCA Crim 193, in which previous threats of violence by M towards the girl he was charged with raping were held admissible, either under the CJA 2003, s. 101(1)(c), or as evidence 'having to do' with the alleged facts (see **F12.9**).

F12.35   In *Sawoniuk* [2000] 2 Cr App R 220, the Court of Appeal upheld the decision of the trial judge to admit evidence that S, charged with four murders in Belarus in 1942, had been a member of a group of policemen involved in a 'search and kill' operation to eliminate Jewish survivors of an earlier massacre. S had claimed not to have been a member but, as the killer was one of the group, it was necessary to the prosecution case to show that he was. Lord Bingham CJ agreed that the evidence was admissible for this purpose, but considered that it could also have been introduced on the broader basis that it was background evidence, as criminal charges 'cannot fairly be judged in a factual vacuum'. Again, the CJA 2003 would seem to provide more than one route for the admissibility of such evidence, and both s. 101(1)(c) and (d) are likely to be canvassed. In terms of outcome, little depends on which of these two routes is chosen (*Tirnaveanu* [2007] 4 All ER 301).

EVIDENCE OF BAD CHARACTER ADDUCED BY PROSECUTION TO PROVE GUILT OR UNTRUTHFULNESS

Criminal Justice Act 2003: Admissibility under s. 101(1)(d)

Criminal Justice Act 2003, s. 101   F12.36

(1) In criminal proceedings evidence of the defendant's bad character is admissible if, but only if—

...

(d) it is relevant to an important matter in issue between the defendant and the prosecution.

The key provision in s. 101(1)(d) is supplemented by s. 103, which fleshes out both the issues to which the provision may apply and the type of evidence that may be rendered admissible thereunder.

Criminal Justice Act 2003, s. 103

(1) For the purposes of section 101(1)(d) the matters in issue between the defendant and the prosecution include—
  (a) the question whether the defendant has a propensity to commit offences of the kind with which he is charged, except where his having such a propensity makes it no more likely that he is guilty of the offence;
  (b) the question whether the defendant has a propensity to be untruthful, except where it is not suggested that the defendant's case is untruthful in any respect.
(2) Where subsection (1)(a) applies, a defendant's propensity to commit offences of the kind with which he is charged may (without prejudice to any other way of doing so) be established by evidence that he has been convicted of—
  (a) an offence of the same description as the one with which he is charged, or
  (b) an offence of the same category as the one with which he is charged.
(3) Subsection (2) does not apply in the case of a particular defendant if the court is satisfied, by reason of the length of time since the conviction or for any other reason, that it would be unjust for it to apply in his case.
(4) For the purposes of subsection (2)—
  (a) two offences are of the same description as each other if the statement of the offence in a written charge or indictment would, in each case, be in the same terms;
  (b) two offences are of the same category as each other if they belong to the same category of offences prescribed for the purposes of this section by an order made by the Secretary of State.
(5) A category prescribed by an order under subsection (4)(b) must consist of offences of the same type.
(6) Only prosecution evidence is admissible under section 101(1)(d).

The CAJA 2009, s. 144 and sch. 17, para. 1(2), amended the CJA 2003, s. 103, so as to insert new subsections (7) to (11), which provide for the treatment of previous convictions outside England and Wales. The broad effect of the amendments is that the foreign conviction is treated as being admissible if the corresponding offence in England and Wales would be so treated.

Relevance to Important Matter   Under the CJA 2003, s. 101(1)(d), the prosecution are   F12.37
required to show that evidence of bad character is relevant to an 'important matter in issue' between prosecution and defence. 'Important matter' means 'a matter of substantial importance in the context of the case as a whole' (s. 112(1)). While the issue must be of substantial importance, however, it is not necessary for the evidence of bad character to be, as it had to be at common law, of substantial probative value. Were it thus, the inclusion in s. 103(1)(a) of

evidence of propensity as a matter in issue between the parties would be of very limited effect (*Chopra* [2007] 1 Cr App R 225; *Wallace* [2008] 1 WLR 572).

The effect, as stated in *Weir* [2006] 2 All ER 570, in relation to the appeal of Somanathan, is that the threshold for admitting an accused's bad character is satisfied if the evidence is merely relevant to an important issue between the prosecution and the defence. Provided the record is so relevant, the court's power to exclude evidence under s. 101(3) is now the focal point of cases where evidence of bad character is tendered under s. 101(1)(d) and objected to by the defence. Where evidence is admitted, the accused's protection from unfairness lies in the direction to be given by the trial judge (see **F12.21**). An appeal court is unlikely to interfere unless the judge's judgement as to the capacity of prior events to establish propensity is plainly wrong or his discretion has been exercised unreasonably in the *Wednesbury* sense (*Hanson* [2005] 1 WLR 3169, applied to the decision of a District Judge in *DPP v Chand* (2007) 171 JP 285).

F12.38 A sea-change in admissibility under the CJA 2003 is that the accused's propensity becomes a potential issue between the defence and prosecution (see **F12.39**). Where, however, the history does not establish a relevant propensity, it may still be the case that the history has relevance to an issue in the case under s. 101(1)(d). In *Beverley* [2006] EWCA Crim 1287, for example, a previous conviction for possession of cannabis was held not to establish a relevant propensity in relation to the importation of cocaine, which is correct. However, it is submitted that it might have had significance in showing that the accused understood perfectly well the 'language' of drugs which he claimed not to know, but this was not explored. Propensity evidence is important under s. 101(1)(d), but it is not the only way of using evidence of bad character. In *Colliard* [2008] EWCA Crim 1175, where a drugs conviction was relevant both to knowledge and propensity, the court took care to distinguish the two in its reasoning. In *Jordan* [2009] EWCA Crim 953, the trial judge purported to admit as relevant to J's propensity his convictions for a firearm offence and a robbery. Holding that the true relevance of these convictions was to rebut J's coincidental presence as an innocent passenger in a car containing all the trappings for an armed robbery, the Court of Appeal rightly stressed that 'matters in issue' are not limited to questions of propensity. See also *Nicholas* [2011] EWCA Crim 1175. Further confirmation of the principle that admitting propensity evidence is only one example of the function of gateway (d) is provided in *O* (2009) 173 JP 616. Rix LJ commented (*obiter*): 'Although it is the example that section 103(1)(a) illustrates and underlines, gateway (d) is more generally concerned with relevance to an important matter in issue between a defendant and the prosecution'. See also *Thomas* [2010] EWCA Crim 148 (previous involvement in robberies using a knife a 'potentially important link' to whether accused knew of presence of knife in the instant case), *Rogers* [2013] EWCA Crim 2406 (convictions for burglary in a particular village rebutting D's claim to be unfamiliar with the area as well as showing propensity) and *Ali* [2010] EWCA Crim 1619 (photographic evidence of the accused's attraction to firearms admissible to confirm disputed identification whether it was evidence of propensity or not). In *McAllister* [2009] 1 Cr App R 129 a careful distinction was said to be required between an argument for admission of bad character evidence dependent on propensity and one dependent on a different form of reasoning, for in the latter the specific safeguards provided by the *Hanson* direction on propensity (see **F12.39**) are inappropriate and misleading. See also *Wallace* [2008] 1 WLR 572.

F12.39 **Propensity as an Issue** Propensity to commit offences 'of the kind charged' is now to be taken to be an issue between the defence and the prosecution except where it makes it no more likely that the accused is guilty (CJA 2003, s. 103(1)(a)), and propensity to untruthfulness is to be so taken unless it is not suggested that the accused's case is untruthful in any respect (s. 103(1)(b)). This appears to be a 'deeming' provision, given that propensity is not an issue in the normal sense so much as a means of proving what is in issue. However 'the fact that section 103(1) seems also to have the effect of potentially including the "question of" propensity among the "matters in issue" should not be overstated to the extent that sight is lost of the need for relevance: the bad character must still be relevant to an "important" issue' (*Bullen* [2008] 2 Cr App R 364).

Where it is so relevant, the test for admissibility imposes no additional hurdle that the matter to which it is directed is supported by other evidence: evidential weakness and insufficiency of evidence may, however, bear on the question of discretionary exclusion (*Bowman* [2014] EWCA Crim 716). See also *Goddard* [2012] EWCA Crim 1756, in which prejudicial evidence of their sexual interest in young boys was admitted at the trial of the two accused, despite the fact that the interest had been clearly admitted, and there was no adequate consideration of the relevance of the evidence to any disputed issue; it was held that the evidence should have been excluded.

The steps which have to be followed by the trial judge in determining the use which may be made of evidence of propensity consisting of convictions under s. 101(1)(d) were spelled out in detail in *Hanson* [2005] 1 WLR 3169. In brief these flow as follows:

(1) Does the history of conviction(s) establish a propensity to commit offences of the kind charged?
(2) If so, does the propensity make it more likely that the defendant committed the crime charged?
(3) Where the convictions are for offences of the same category or description (s. 103(2)) is it unjust to rely on them (s. 103(3))? Where the propensity is proved by other means, as permitted by s. 103(1) and (2), is it unfair under s. 101(3) to admit the evidence?

According to *Hanson*, propensity can be demonstrated by one previous event if sufficiently probative, as, for example, where the behaviour would have been regarded as 'strikingly similar' or otherwise admissible at common law (compare *DPP v P* [1991] 2 AC 447). Other examples given were of an offence of fire-setting, or a single sexual offence (and see *Pickstone*, heard with *Hanson*, and *W* (2009) 173 JP 337, where the offence establishing propensity was committed many years before but was of a similar nature and might well have been 'striking', and *Miller* [2010] EWCA Crim 1578, where the single offence of rape, though not strikingly similar, showed a propensity to abuse power over a young victim). In *Clarke* [2012] EWCA Crim 9 a strikingly similar previous sexual offence would have been enough, by itself, to provide the requisite probative value, although other offences were also admitted. See also *Burdess* [2014] EWCA Crim 270, where the single previous rape was of a strikingly similar nature, and *Balazs* [2014] EWCA Crim 947, where a single rape and related offences of violence and harassment showed a propensity towards using sexual and violent behaviour to control a partner. However it does not follow that a single conviction for rape will inevitably be admissible (see *Bennabbou* [2012] EWCA Crim 1256, where the conviction was old and the circumstances dissimilar, and see to similar effect *Laws-Chapman* [2013] EWCA Crim 1851, where an old conviction for buggery that appeared to have been consensual, and might not have constituted an offence at all under the current law, should not have been admitted to show propensity where the charge concerned violent paedophile behaviour against a non-consenting child in the company of a group of other men). See also *Williams* [2006] EWCA Crim 2052 and *Jackson* [2011] EWCA Crim 1870 (propensity to strangle) and *Turner* [2010] EWCA Crim 2300 (previous offence shared characteristics of ruthless violence applied to a stranger as part of the 'enforcement' activities of a biker gang). In *Cundell* [2009] EWCA Crim 2072, where an offence of solicitation to murder C's wife was alleged to have taken place in prison, and to be in effect an exact repetition of the offence that had led to C's incarceration, the previous conviction was admitted by consent under s. 101(1)(a), but would otherwise have been admissible not merely as explanatory evidence, but as evidence of propensity, and the judge was correct to direct the jury as to its use for the latter purpose. The Court of Appeal found it hard to imagine a case in which the previous conviction could be more relevant. See also *Koc* [2008] EWCA Crim 77, where a single recent conviction for handling heroin was admissible where the defence to a charge of conspiracy involving heroin was that the accused believed he was dealing with counterfeit clothes. Closer to the borderline is *Bowman* [2014] EWCA Crim 716, where a single, somewhat old, conviction for joint possession of a firearm was held admissible in relation to the issue whether B had brought a gun to the scene of a crime or, as he claimed, had wrestled it from an opponent. Much would seem to turn on whether the carrying of firearms constitutes a 'distinctive' feature, the

F12.40

F

Court of Appeal relying on *Burdess*. Contrast *Colliard*, where there were no special features and the court observed that the judge was 'not clearly wrong' to admit the conviction (which was also clearly admissible to show knowledge).

The requirement in *Hanson* to give careful consideration to the probative value of propensity evidence was stressed in *Urushadze* [2008] EWCA Crim 2498, where U's previous convictions for shoplifting were of little value in indicating a propensity towards street robbery. To similar effect is *Kane* [2013] EWCA Crim 1487, where the Court of Appeal was concerned with an 'undifferentiated mass' of bad character evidence and commented forcefully that '[p]oints which are devoid of content as legitimate bad character evidence cannot acquire such a status simply by heaping them together with other points which themselves also have no proper claim to admissibility as bad character evidence under the requirements of the 2003 Act'. Where the probative value of a range of convictions is properly evaluated by the judge, however, there is no reason why they cannot be tendered for their cumulative effect (*Brooks* [2014] EWCA Crim 562: mixture of drugs-related offences including trafficking and false passports). In cases where a jury may have difficulty disentangling the relevance of the evidence, a careful direction will be needed: see *Norris* [2013] EWCA Crim 712, where the judge provided very clear guidance to the jury that propensity evidence pointing to N's racist attitudes was relevant only once they had concluded, in reliance on the scientific evidence in the case, that he had been correctly identified as a participant in a murder: at that point, it was relevant to his own state of mind and his awareness of the intentions of others in the group. The 'force and clarity' of the directions given enabled the Court of Appeal to conclude that the jury would have honoured the restriction thus placed on the use of the evidence. Although a judge is allowed some latitude in making a judgement about relevance, a ruling may be interfered with on appeal where he has 'plainly erred' (*Murphy* [2006] EWCA Crim 3408, in which an old offence of possession of a firearm was considered to provide 'too slender a basis' for an inference about propensity). See also *Beverley* [2006] EWCA Crim 1287 at **F12.38**. In *Leaver* [2006] EWCA Crim 2988, the accused was charged with rape by continuing with intercourse in a violent manner after the complainant had withdrawn her original consent, and with causing her serious injury with intent when she refused to engage in further sexual activity. It was held that a conviction for indecent exposure, which had not been accompanied by circumstances of any violence, did not bear on the questions for the jury, which were whether the accused reasonably believed the complainant was consenting to intercourse, and whether he had intended to do her serious injury. In *Fyle* [2011] EWCA Crim 1213 evidence of a previous wounding with intent by F when 16 and to which he had pleaded guilty was not admissible in relation to the murder by strangulation of a transsexual prostitute; there were few similarities, the probative value of the conviction was slight and its prejudicial effect considerable in a prosecution where the remaining evidence was circumstantial. Contrast *D* [2011] 4 All ER 568, where it was said that the propensity of a person charged with sexual offences against a child to view pornographic images of children, while it did not of itself make it likely that he would act out the activity displayed, might be admissible in support of a child complainant's evidence, on the basis of the unlikelihood of the complainant having by coincidence falsely accused a person with such an unusual propensity. See to similar effect *Latham* [2014] EWCA Crim 207, where the details of the convictions were 'sparse' but still capable of establishing a propensity to have a sexual interest in children.

Such evidence was, however, rightly said to require the making of a very careful judgement with regard to fairness. *D* was considered in *W* [2011] EWCA Crim 2463, a case in which a range of offences were tried together which were very different not only in terms of seriousness but in the fact that some had happened many years before. The Court of Appeal expressed surprise that they were tried together at all but, this having been done, a proper direction on the cross-admissibility of propensity evidence in such circumstances required the careful grouping of counts so that the jury would not be left with the sense that all propensity evidence was equally cross-admissible and that they were being invited to form a judgement on the basis that either 'it did happen or it didn't'. See also *Saint* [2010] EWCA Crim 1924, where the accused's obsession with watching others have sex in a park where the alleged rape took place should have been excluded, either because it was of insufficient relevance (there being no evidence that a voyeur committed the rape) or because its prejudicial effect vastly outweighed its probative value. In *Harris* [2009] EWCA Crim 434, on the other hand, the accused's previous convictions for violence were held to have been rightly admitted at his trial for rape, on the issue of which of the parties had behaved aggressively, and in *Franklin* [2013] EWCA Crim 84 a girl's previous convictions for assault and robbery were held admissible to connect her to a joint enterprise that had violence or the fear of violence as its object. In *Dossett* [2013] EWCA Crim 710 the identification of D as the perpetrator of a street robbery was supported by evidence of a similar 'casual opportunistic public offence' of robbery committed with the same co-defendant, and of an incident involving similar violence in the same neighbourhood but not involving robbery. The Court of Appeal stressed the importance of the factual connections rather than the legal dissimilarities, relying on *Hanson*.

Propensity may cease to be of relevance if the defence departs from the line anticipated at the outset of the trial. In *Bullen* [2008] 2 Cr App R 364, B's long history for offences of violence was relevant to the anticipated defence of self-defence to murder but, when B admitted manslaughter and relied on his intoxication in relation to the murder, the propensity no longer made it more likely that B committed the offence charged. Even if the convictions had some relevance, it would have been unfair to rely on a raft of convictions that did not in themselves throw any light on the sole remaining issue of intention.

According to *Hanson*, the calculation over whether to exclude a conviction under s. 101(3) or 103(3) involves a range of issues, including the similarity between the conviction and the offence charged, bearing in mind that offences may be of the same category or description but factually different. The gravity and age of the offence for which the accused has been convicted are also factors, with particular care being addressed to the use of old convictions which are likely to be prejudicial unless they can clearly be shown to demonstrate continuing propensity. In *Cox* [2014] EWCA Crim 804, a history of incidents stretching back over 20 years was admissible in order to show a propensity to seek out a knife to threaten others when under pressure. A case near the line is *Ullah* [2006] EWCA Crim 2003, in which a single conviction for a somewhat similar offence of obtaining by deception in 1989 was admitted at U's trial for conspiracy to defraud, but see *Turner* where the previous single offence of gang violence was committed in 1993 and yet was clearly admissible. Another cause for concern arises when previous events are disputed, for then the court must be particularly careful to avoid the diversion of the trial into 'satellite' issues not covered by the indictment. See, in addition to *Hanson*, *Lamb* [2006] EWCA Crim 3347. The court should also consider the weight of the other evidence in the case, as it is unlikely to be just to admit convictions where there is very little other evidence. See *DPP v Chand* (2007) 171 JP 285, in which the District Judge's decision to exclude C's conviction for theft by shoplifting on a charge of stealing a charity box was based both on dissimilarity and the weakness of the prosecution case. The Divisional Court regarded this as a conclusion that could not be condemned as perverse. Where it is foreseeable that the evidence of witnesses might not be as anticipated in their witness statements, and there is in consequence a risk that the use of bad character evidence will overshadow the rest of the prosecution case, it may be desirable to delay a ruling on admissibility until the Crown has called its witnesses (*Gyima* [2007] EWCA Crim 429).

F12.41

The facts of *Hanson* itself illustrate the careful scrutiny of conviction evidence to determine the existence and possible value of propensity. H was charged with burglary from a room that, it was contended, he alone had opportunity to enter at the relevant time. His various convictions for offences of dishonesty were all within part 1 of the 'Categories of Offences' Schedule (see F12.45 *et seq*.), but the Court of Appeal nevertheless considered that the judge was obliged to review the relevance to propensity of the individual convictions, as a conviction of the same description or category as the offence charged was not necessarily sufficient in order to show a propensity to commit offences of the kind charged. H's convictions for handling and aggravated vehicle-taking, though of the same 'category' as burglary, were not, without more, such as to demonstrate a propensity to burgle. This does not mean that there must be available full details of a previous offence in order to enable relevance to propensity to be determined; all depends on the facts of a particular case, although it is good practice for details to be available if required (*Lamaletie* (2008) 172 JP 249).

F12.42   Propensity evidence that is not supported by convictions requires particular care. See, e.g., *McKenzie* (2008) 172 JP 377, where evidence of risks taken by a driver on other occasions were used to demonstrate his preparedness to drive dangerously. In *O'Dowd* [2009] 2 Cr App R 280, two of three previous allegations of rape related to events many years before; one had resulted in an acquittal and one in a stay, and all were hotly disputed. The Court of Appeal opined: 'If ever there was a case to illustrate the dangers of satellite litigation through the introduction of bad character evidence, this is it'. Despite the judge's careful handling of the evidence and the similarities between their accounts, the court concluded that he ought to have arrived at a different conclusion as to the fairness of the cumulative effect on the trial of proceeding with all the allegations, given their nature and complexity. Consideration should have been given to directing the Crown to pick the 'best' out of the three allegations. *Hanson* and *McKenzie* were applied in *M* [2010] All ER (D) 196 (Dec). M appealed against convictions for sexually abusing his partner's grandson. The prosecution had relied, as evidence of propensity, on allegations by the victim's sister that she had been sexually abused by M in the same room. Those allegations had previously been brought to trial but resulted in acquittal, the prosecution having offered no evidence. There were various similarities of detail and the evidence was held to have been properly admitted. The danger of 'satellite issues' may be particularly acute with older allegations. Where the evidence of propensity relied upon by the prosecution in a sexual case consisted of statements by non-witnesses of similar (old) offences committed against them, the judge was wrong to treat the application as 'straightforward': the use of hearsay evidence in support of allegations of misconduct requires particular caution (*Z* [2009] 3 All ER 1015, and see as to hearsay **F16.41**).

F12.43   Other examples of the use of propensity evidence to prove guilt appear in the following sections, which are arranged according to the function of the evidence: supporting identification, rebutting a defence etc. The use of propensity evidence is not, however, conditional upon the raising of a defence, and may be admissible where the defence is a complete denial (*Wilkinson* [2006] EWCA Crim 1332). A clear example of the use of propensity evidence to rebut a complete denial occurred in *Montakhab* [2012] EWCA Crim 2012, where M denied putting his hand on the thigh of a young woman on a bus, and it was held that it would have been an 'affront to common sense' to exclude seven offences of sexual assault, six of which had taken place while sitting next to a young woman on a bus.

F12.44   **Propensity to Untruthfulness**   In relation to evidence of propensity to show untruthfulness, *Hanson* [2005] 1 WLR 3169 (see **F12.39**) requires a distinction to be drawn between offences of dishonesty, which may or may not display a propensity to untruthfulness, and evidence which does display such a propensity. The latter category might, for example, include an offence involving lying or making false representations, or the putting forward by the accused of an account in his own defence which can be shown to have been disbelieved. In *Spence* [2010] EWCA Crim 2256 S, a lorry driver, was tried for being knowingly concerned in the fraudulent importation of drugs, and his defence involved a denial of knowledge of the presence of the drugs in his vehicle. Demonstrable lies told by S in relation to previous offences of importing tobacco were held to have been rightly relied upon by the prosecution: the lies were not merely evidence of a general propensity to untruthfulness but were integral to the offences themselves.

Hanson was also applied in *Norris* [2014] EWCA Crim 419, in which N had been guilty of 'previous sustained lying in a court context', including the construction of an admittedly false military history in an attempt to mitigate sentence. The Court of Appeal noted but did not follow the narrower approach to the statute in *Campbell* [2007] 1 WLR 2798, where admissibility was thought to be limited to offences in which lying was an element of a crime of which the accused had been convicted, preferring the broader approach in *Jarvis* [2008] EWCA Crim 488.

It should be noted that, paradoxically, evidence of a non-defendant's previous convictions for offences of this type will be admissible under the CJA 2003 only where the court gives leave to adduce it on the ground that it is of substantial probative value and substantial importance to the case (s. 100: see F14).

Examples of the use of evidence of propensity to show untruthfulness are to be found in the following text in relation to s. 101(1)(d).

Prescribed Categories of Offences to Show Propensity The categories of offences so far pre- **F12.45** scribed using the power under the CJA 2003, s. 103(4)(b) (see F12.36), broadly relate to offences of dishonesty and sexual offences against persons under the age of 16, as contained in the schedule to the Criminal Justice Act 2003 (Categories of Offences) Order 2004 (SI 2004 No. 3346). It should be noted, however, that (under s. 103(1) and (2)) the existence of offences of the same description or category is only one method of proving propensity, so that other relevant evidence may also be relied upon. Thus, for example, a history of separate investigations of the accused for sexual offences against children, which are of probative value in establishing disposition where the investigations had not resulted in prosecution, might be admitted. And in *Weir* [2006] 2 All ER 570, it was permissible to prove a caution for a non-scheduled offence of taking an obscene photograph of a child; the Court of Appeal pointed out that, while the task of deciding the admissibility of offences within the categories is easier, the opening words of s. 103(2) make clear that the categories do not provide the only route to admissibility. See also *Lamb* [2006] EWCA Crim 3347 at F12.41 (propensity to stab). In *Johnson* [2009] 2 Cr App R 101 the Court relied on the breadth of s. 103(2) in order to admit evidence of the non-prescribed offence of conspiracy to burgle. The Court explained that the prescribed categories provide 'permissive and simple ways of establishing propensity. Where they do not apply, propensity may still be established by other means.'

Conversely, the existence of a conviction for a scheduled offence does not, without more, make it admissible: the steps described in *Hanson* [2005] 1 WLR 3169 (see F12.39) to ensure relevance and fairness in admitting propensity evidence must also be gone through.

F12.46

Criminal Justice Act 2003 (Categories of Offences) Order 2004
(SI 2004 No. 3346), schedule

PRESCRIBED CATEGORIES OF OFFENCES

PART I

THEFT CATEGORY

1. An offence under section 1 of the Theft Act 1968 (theft).
2. An offence under section 8 of that Act (robbery).
3. An offence under section 9(1)(a) of that Act (burglary) if it was committed with intent to commit an offence of stealing anything in the building or part of a building in question.
4. An offence under section 9(1)(b) of that Act (burglary) if the offender stole or attempted to steal anything in the building or that part of it.
5. An offence under section 10 of that Act (aggravated burglary) if the offender committed a burglary described in paragraph 3 or 4 of this Part of the Schedule.
6. An offence under section 12 of that Act (taking motor vehicle or other conveyance without authority).
7. An offence under section 12A of that Act (aggravated vehicle-taking).
8. An offence under section 22 of that Act (handling stolen goods).
9. An offence under section 25 of that Act (going equipped for stealing).
10. An offence under section 3 of the Theft Act 1978 (making off without payment).
11. An offence of—
    (a) aiding, abetting, counselling, procuring or inciting the commission of an offence specified in this Part of this Schedule; or
    (b) attempting to commit an offence so specified.

PART 2

SEXUAL OFFENCES (PERSONS UNDER THE AGE OF 16) CATEGORY

1. An offence under section 1 of the Sexual Offences Act 1956 (rape) if it was committed in relation to a person under the age of 16.
2. An offence under section 5 of the Sexual Offences Act 1956 (intercourse with a girl under thirteen).
3. An offence under section 6 of that Act (intercourse with a girl under sixteen).
4. An offence under section 7 of that Act (intercourse with a defective) if it was committed in relation to a person under the age of 16.
5. An offence under section 10 of that Act (incest by a man) if it was committed in relation to a person under the age of 16.
6. An offence under section 11 of that Act (incest by a woman) if it was committed in relation to a person under the age of 16.
7. An offence under section 12 of that Act (buggery) if it was committed in relation to a person under the age of 16.
8. An offence under section 13 of that Act (indecency between men) if it was committed in relation to a person under the age of 16.
9. An offence under section 14 of that Act (indecent assault on a woman) if it was committed in relation to a person under the age of 16.
10. An offence under section 15 of that Act (indecent assault on a man) if it was committed in relation to a person under the age of 16.
11. An offence under section 128 of the Mental Health Act 1959 (sexual intercourse with patients) if it was committed in relation to a person under the age of 16.
12. An offence under section 1 of the Indecency with Children Act 1960 (indecent conduct towards young child).
13. An offence under section 54 of the Criminal Law Act 1977 (inciting a girl under 16 to have incestuous sexual intercourse).
14. An offence under section 3 of the Sexual Offences (Amendment) Act 2000 (abuse of a position of trust) if it was committed in relation to a person under the age of 16.
15. An offence under section 1 of the Sexual Offences Act 2003 (rape) if it was committed in relation to a person under the age of 16.
16. An offence under section 2 of that Act (assault by penetration) if it was committed in relation to a person under the age of 16.
17. An offence under section 3 of that Act (sexual assault) if it was committed in relation to a person under the age of 16.
18. An offence under section 4 of that Act (causing a person to engage in sexual activity without consent) if it was committed in relation to a person under the age of 16.
19. An offence under section 5 of the Sexual Offences Act 2003 (rape of a child under 13).
20. An offence under section 6 of that Act (assault of a child under 13 by penetration).
21. An offence under section 7 of that Act (sexual assault of a child under 13).
22. An offence under section 8 of that Act (causing or inciting a child under 13 to engage in sexual activity).
23. An offence under section 9 of that Act (sexual activity with a child).
24. An offence under section 10 of that Act (causing or inciting a child to engage in sexual activity).
25. An offence under section 14 of that Act if doing it will involve the commission of an offence under sections 9 and 10 of that Act (arranging or facilitating the commission of a child sex offence).
26. An offence under section 16 of that Act (abuse of position of trust: sexual activity with a child) if it was committed in relation to a person under the age of 16.
27. An offence under section 17 of that Act (abuse of position of trust: causing or inciting a child to engage in sexual activity) if it was committed in relation to a person under the age of 16.
28. An offence under section 25 of that Act (sexual activity with a child family member) if it was committed in relation to a person under the age of 16.
29. An offence under section 26 of that Act (inciting a child family member to engage in sexual activity) if it was committed in relation to a person under the age of 16.
30. An offence under section 30 of that Act (sexual activity with a person with a mental disorder impeding choice) if it was committed in relation to a person under the age of 16.

31. An offence under section 31 of that Act (causing or inciting a person with a mental disorder impeding choice to engage in sexual activity) if it was committed in relation to a person under the age of 16.

32. An offence under section 34 of that Act (inducement, threat, or deception to procure activity with a person with a mental disorder) if it was committed in relation to a person under the age of 16.

33. An offence under section 35 of that Act (causing a person with a mental disorder to engage in or agree to engage in sexual activity by inducement, threat or deception) if it was committed in relation to a person under the age of 16.

34. An offence under section 38 of that Act (care workers: sexual activity with a person with a mental disorder) if it was committed in relation to a person under the age of 16.

35. An offence under section 39 of that Act (care workers: causing or inciting sexual activity) if it was committed in relation to a person under the age of 16.

36. An offence of—
    (a) aiding, abetting, counselling, procuring or inciting the commission of an offence specified in this Part of this Schedule; or
    (b) attempting to commit an offence so specified.

Presumption of Commission Created by Conviction   To facilitate the operation of the CJA   **F12.47**
2003, s. 103(4)(b), and the statutory instrument made under it (see **F12.45**), the PACE 1984, s. 74(3), was amended by the CJA 2003 so that proof of conviction for an offence creates a presumption that the accused committed it, even where its relevance is only to show disposition — a function of the use of previous convictions which was formerly excluded (see **F11.19**). The supplementary provisions of the PACE 1984, s. 75 (see **F11.7**) will also apply, so that regard may be had to a range of documents including the indictment in order to determine the facts on which the conviction adduced in support of propensity was based. The CAJA 2009, sch. 17, amends the PACE 1984, s. 75, to extend its effect to convictions in other EU Member States (see **F11.7**).

As to the need to supplement conviction evidence with statements admissible under the hearsay provisions of the CJA 2003 in order to provide evidence of the detail of, for example, the *modus operandi* adopted in relation to previous offences where this is in dispute, see *Humphris* (2005) 169 JP 441, *Ainscough* (2006) 170 JP 517, at **F16.30** and *Hogart* [2007] EWCA Crim 338. No such supplementation is required where there is agreement by the defence as to the relevant circumstances, even if other matters are disputed (*K* [2008] EWCA Crim 3301).

Identifying the Accused by Evidence of Bad Character under the Criminal Justice Act 2003, s. 101(1)(d)

An important function of evidence of bad character at common law was to identify the accused as   **F12.48**
the perpetrator of an offence, whether by demonstrating that the crime bore his 'signature', or by the more prosaic linkage of matters pointing to his involvement (*W (John)* [1998] 2 Cr App R 289, explaining *DPP v P* [1991] 2 AC 447). The connection may be arrived at via an inference from propensity (**F12.39**) or by any other relevant inference drawn under gateway (d) (**F12.37**): the effect is the same, though the process of reasoning is different, and will need to be reflected in the summing up. In *Suleman* [2012] 2 Cr App R 381, for example, evidence of a large number of similar examples of arson affecting S's family were rightly admitted in support of an argument that it would have been an amazing coincidence had S not been the author of all of them. But these fires were not evidence of propensity until the point where the jury had concluded that S was indeed the cause of them all, and should not have been presented as such. In only one count was there the direct evidence of identification that would have supported an inference of propensity that could have been brought to bear on the question of who started the other fires. The dominant direction to the jury, therefore, needed to be grounded in the unlikelihood of coincidence rather than in propensity.

Where a feature is said to be the equivalent of a signature, it is an acknowledgement that it possesses to a very high degree the unusual features associated with 'striking similarity' at common law (*DPP v Boardman* [1975] AC 421; *Smith* (1915) 11 Cr App R 229; *Barrington* [1981] 1 All ER 1132). When such cases arise under the CJA 2003, the evidence of bad character may support the prosecution case to the extent that very little other evidence is required to convince of guilt.

In the old case of *Straffen* [1952] 2 QB 911, the murder of a young girl who was found strangled was considered unusual in that no attempt had been made to assault her sexually or to conceal the body. S came under immediate suspicion because he had previously strangled two other girls, each murder having the same peculiar features, and because he was in the neighbourhood at the time, having just escaped from Broadmoor. Under these circumstances, very little other evidence was required to convict S of the third murder: it bore his 'fingerprints'. See also *Butler* (1986) 84 Cr App R 12 (rapist identified by reference to strikingly similar conduct engaged in, albeit consensually, with his girlfriend) and *Tricoglus* (1976) 65 Cr App R 16, in which the two rapes with which T was charged were sufficiently peculiar to be regarded as the work of the same man, although T's conviction was quashed because further similar fact evidence that had been used to link him with the crimes was inadmissible. Not all 'signature' cases are of a sexual nature. For example, in *Mullen* [1992] Crim LR 735, it was M's distinctive use of a blow-torch to crack glass in order to enter and burgle premises that provided the link between his crimes. In 'signature' cases under the CJA 2003, the normal direction that evidence of bad character should not be the sole or even the main evidence of guilt (see **F12.21**) may be over-cautious.

F12.49   Evidence of misconduct may go to support identification without necessarily amounting to 'signature evidence'. Thus, for example, in *Eastlake* [2007] EWCA Crim 603 two brothers were charged with an offence of street violence. Their propensity (jointly and separately) to commit such offences was admissible to support their disputed identifications, particularly in light of the brothers' defence that they spent the evening together, which strengthened the argument that it would have been a strange coincidence if they had been wrongly identified. See also *Dossett* [2013] EWCA Crim 710, where one of the convictions was for a different offence in similar circumstances and the other for the same offence in slightly different circumstances but in the same area, and with the same co-accused; *Cushing* [2006] EWCA Crim 1221, where the previous offences were for the same crime (burglary) but were factually distinct; and *Brisland* [2008] EWCA Crim 2773, where two thefts were committed by a man posing as an employee to deceive delivery men, and the identification of B from CCTV footage in respect of one offence was capable of linking him to the other crime. In *Smith* [2009] 1 Cr App R 521, 'compelling' evidence that the accused was part of a gang who had shot four men, killing one of them, was supplemented by evidence of his conviction for attempted murder by shooting. This was held to make it more likely that he was a member of a group prepared to use guns. *Smith* was applied to the identification of property as belonging to an accused in *Elliott* (2011) 175 JP 39. Guns and drugs were found in a store cupboard outside S's home. To rebut a suggestion that the items were deposited by others, the prosecution adduced evidence to show that S was a member of a local criminal gang, which was involved in drug crime and the carrying or use of firearms. The Court of Appeal held the evidence 'was plainly capable' of assisting the jury in resolving the disputed issue. Rejecting a subsidiary argument that the evidence should have been rejected as prejudicial because it consisted of a broad treatment of numerous circumstances suggesting gang membership and thus distracted the jury's attention from the key issue, the Court noted (at [31]) that circumstantial evidence of gang membership was likely to be of this sort: 'Violent gangs, which provide no social amenity and exist for criminal purposes, are unlikely to issue membership cards, and so proof of membership will almost inevitably involve the prosecution in putting forward evidence of a number of circumstances from which gang membership could be inferred'. *Smith and Elliott* were applied in *Lewis* [2014] EWCA Crim 48, where it was said to be 'well-established' that evidence of membership of a criminal gang may be admissible under the CJA 2003, s. 101(1)(d). In Lewis the evidence served not only to identify those taking part in a riot, but also to provide evidence of common purpose and to rebut innocent presence. As in *Elliott*, the Court paid careful attention to the risk of prejudice arising from evidence of membership.

Bad character may also be relevant (and therefore admissible) to support identification without any similarity between the past and present offences, as in *Isichei* (2006) 170 JP 753, where the fact that a robber, identified as I, had asked for 'coke' was sufficient to admit I's previous convictions for cocaine-related offences.

The impact of the CJA 2003 on the use of bad character evidence for purposes of identifica- **F12.50**
tion raises particularly difficult issues. It should not be forgotten that the process of detection
of crime may, understandably, focus on the accused's convictions for crimes of a particular
type, nor that these might be highly prejudicial if relied on in the absence of strong supporting evidence of identification. In *H* [2014] EWCA Crim 420 H's image was picked out of an
identification procedure in which it had been included largely because of his criminal record
for the 'unusual combination' of an offence of violence following on from a sexual assault. The
case was otherwise weak, but H was convicted after it was suggested that it would have been an
'enormous coincidence' if a man with H's record had been wrongly identified. Holding the conviction unsafe, the Court of Appeal pointed out that the jury should have been told why H had
become a suspect to enable them to assess the true force of this so-called coincidence. Compare
Randall [2006] EWCA Crim 1413, where a 'fleeting glimpse' identification of a burglar was
supported by evidence of R's propensity to commit that crime, the judge's pithy direction being
that the victim 'had no hesitation in picking [R] out on the video at the identification procedure. She was burgled. She picked out a burglar. Was that pure coincidence?' The risk that it
might not have been 'pure' coincidence, but that an accused person might have found himself
on the parade because of his previous record, is one the jury also needs to be alerted to where
it appears to be relevant. By contrast in *N* [2014] EWCA Crim 506 there was evidence that N
was at the party where an assault occurred, and his DNA was on the broken bottle that had been
used as a weapon. The risk that he had been mistakenly identified by two witnesses was countered by N's previous convictions for street robbery, using the argument from coincidence, and
it was held that this was acceptable provided the jury was directed to avoid an inference based
on propensity. In some cases the fair course might be the admission of such evidence against
the accused coupled with a strong direction about the need to eliminate the possibility that the
offences were the work of others of equally bad character (cf. *Miller* [2003] EWCA Crim 2840).
In *Brima* [2007] 1 Cr App R 316, a man ran up, fatally stabbed the victim in front of several witnesses and ran away. B's defence was that the crime was committed by A, his friend. A positive
identification of B by one of the witnesses was supported by some scientific evidence (though in
some respects this also pointed to A) and by the evidence of A himself. Propensity evidence in
the form of B's two previous convictions for assaults using a knife was held to have been rightly
admitted, although in neither of the previous incidents was a serious injury inflicted. The Court
of Appeal noted that, in light of B's attack on A, B's convictions would in any event have been
brought out under s. 101(1)(g).

Where an eye-witness identifies the accused as responsible for one offence, and it is sought to **F12.51**
support the correctness of the identification by reference to another eye-witness identification
in respect of a separate offence, it was said in *Robinson* [1953] 2 All ER 334 that admissibility
could be justified on the basis that it was a remarkable coincidence that R was separately identified by different witnesses as having been involved in two different robberies. Whether such a
coincidence is remarkable or not must depend on the facts, but the risk of error inherent in fleeting glimpse identifications is not necessarily counteracted by other purported identifications of
the same person. The same logic would point to admissibility under the CJA 2003, but the use
of s. 101(3) to counter the possible unfairness arising from the linkage of two weak identifications would also require to be considered.

Bad Character Evidence Rebutting Defence

A common function that evidence of bad character may be called upon to perform is to show **F12.52**
an event involving an accused person in its true light, rebutting an otherwise plausible innocent
explanation. An example is given in the government's White Paper *Justice for All* (2002) of a
young man found in possession of a car that has been reported stolen. He claims that he has
permission from 'a friend of a friend' to borrow the car, but he has three recent convictions for
taking without consent. The convictions would be relevant to an assessment whether it was
likely that an informal arrangement of the sort testified to by the accused might have come into

being, or that he might have believed that it had, notwithstanding his propensity to take cars without permission when the fancy seized him.

F12.53   In applying the CJA 2003, s. 101(1)(d), in such instances, it is important to remember that a defence may be rebutted via an inference to be drawn from propensity (as in the illustration above) or because the evidence of bad character has a probative value independent of any inference from propensity (see further, as to propensity, **F12.39** *et seq.* and, as to other relevant inferences, **F12.37**).

Many defences that might appear credible if the prosecution is confined to one set of facts may be shown to be unlikely by reference to other instances of misconduct, and common-law examples abound. In *Bond* [1906] 2 KB 389, the prosecution case was that B, a doctor, had operated upon a young woman who was pregnant with his child, with intent to procure her miscarriage. The defence that he was carrying out a lawful medical examination of the girl was held to have been properly rebutted by the evidence of another girl, who claimed that nine months previously B had operated on her when she became pregnant by him, with the intention of terminating her pregnancy, and that he had told her that he had 'put dozens of girls right'. In *Mortimer* (1936) 25 Cr App R 150, M was charged with the murder of a woman cyclist by deliberately driving a motor car at her. To rebut any suggestion that this was a case of manslaughter lacking the element of intention required for murder, evidence was adduced to show that M had, on the evening before the incident, knocked down two other women cyclists in a similar way, that some hours after the incident he had knocked one other woman off her bicycle and that he had attempted to avoid capture by driving his car at police officers who tried to apprehend him. In *Smith* (1915) 11 Cr App R 229, S was charged with the murder of a woman with whom he had been through a ceremony of marriage, and who was found drowned in her bath. Evidence was given that two other women whom S had induced to 'marry' him had met with the same fate. Each death benefited S, who had taken the precaution of insuring the women's lives.

In each of these three common-law examples, the function of the evidence was to put a different complexion on what had occurred; in *Bond* by showing a criminal purpose, in *Mortimer* by showing an intention to cause death or injury, and in *Smith* by showing that the deaths had not occurred through natural causes but through the activities of the accused.

F12.54   A case similar to *Bond* but decided under the CJA 2003 is *Adams* [2006] EWCA Crim 2013, where the defence to possession of a large quantity of a controlled drug was that A intended to use it to commit suicide. Previous offences of supply and attempting to supply were properly admitted to rebut the defence and to indicate criminal intent. As at common law, the use of such evidence is easier to justify where the accused already has considerable explaining to do than where it is the mainstay of the case against him. In *Cambridge* [2011] EWCA Crim 2009 C attempted to dissociate himself from a gun found in a plastic bag, where both the gun and the bag could be scientifically linked to him and evidence of his previous illegal possession of a pellet gun was admitted to rebut his defence of innocent association. In *Akunyili* [2014] EWCA Crim 346 A's defence to a charge of rape was properly rebutted both by the strikingly similar circumstances of an earlier rape conviction and by the almost identical defence he had run in the course of that case. Where there is little other evidence besides the misconduct, the evidence may be susceptible to exclusion under s. 101(3) unless (as in cases like *Smith*) it has such a strong appeal that not much more is needed to enable an inference of guilt to be drawn.

F12.55   Evidence of a propensity to untruthfulness may also (and despite statements in *Campbell* [2007] 1 WLR 2798) be of particular importance for the jury in their assessment of the credibility of a defence. In *Malone* [2006] EWCA Crim 1860, M was charged with the murder of his wife, who had been found dead, and who he claimed had been murdered by members of the criminal fraternity who had also threatened him. The prosecution claimed that he had sought to lay a false trail in relation to the wife's disappearance. Evidence that he had, well before his wife's death, falsified a report, claiming to be from a private investigator who had uncovered evidence of the deceased's secret life, was admitted. The Court of Appeal opined that it was relevant to the issue whether he was telling the truth.

Nature of Defence as Factor Affecting Relevance Evidence that is directed to the proof of some **F12.56** fact that is not in issue cannot be received, not because of the prejudicial effect of such evidence but simply because it is irrelevant. It is apparent, therefore, that the nature of the defence or defences reasonably open to the accused may have a bearing on the purpose that evidence of bad character may serve, which bears on its relevance and therefore on its admissibility. This was true of evidence received at common law and remains crucial under the provisions of the CJA 2003.

Under s. 101(1)(d), the criteria to be applied are relevance to an important matter in issue between prosecution and defence and (where application is made by the defence to exclude) unfairness. However, the nature of the defence relied upon continues to play a major part in determining the relevance, and therefore the admissibility, of evidence of character. Section 103(1) may lend itself to the argument that the accused's propensity is always in issue unless it is clearly irrelevant but it is submitted that it is not an important issue (as required by s. 101(1)(d)) unless the circumstances of the case (which may include the nature of the defence raised) are such as to make it so (see further **F12.39**).

Anticipating Defence to be Raised The reforms to the rule regarding the application of **F12.57** pre-trial disclosure to the defence (see **D9.29**) significantly assist the prosecution in antici-pating the issues at trial to which evidence of bad character may be relevant. Where the exact relevance remains unclear, it is better to delay a ruling until the evidence unfolds. See, e.g., *M* [2006] EWCA Crim 193, where the defence to a charge of rape involved a suggestion, put to the complainant in cross-examination, that she had neglected an opportunity to complain. This rendered admissible an account by the complainant of her belief, based on a previous incident, that the accused had a gun in his possession.

Multiple Charges and Accusations under the Criminal Justice Act 2003, s. 101(1)(d)

Section 112(2) of the CJA 2003 provides that, where an accused faces multiple charges in the **F12.58** same proceedings, the 'bad character' provisions apply as if each was charged in separate proceed-ings: in other words a 'gateway' is required to facilitate cross-admissibility between charges in the same proceedings in exactly the same way as where only one offence is charged. Where an accused faces more than one charge of a similar nature or where evidence of similar allegations is tendered in support of one charge, the evidence of one accuser may be admissible to support the evidence of another. The principles to be applied to cases of this kind do not differ materially from those applicable where evidence of bad character is used to rebut an explanation otherwise open to the accused: indeed, the function of evidence of multiple accusers is often to rebut such an explana-tion. Separate exposition is helpful, however, in order to bring out the special problems of collu-sion that have arisen under this heading, and that will continue to arise now that the governing provisions are those of the CJA 2003. The Act is also constructed in such a way as to anticipate the special problems arising out of contamination of evidence by matters other than collusion.

The underlying principle is that the probative value of multiple accusations may depend in part **F12.59** on their similarity, but also on the unlikely prospect that the same person would find himself falsely accused on different occasions by different and independent individuals. The making of multiple accusations is a coincidence in itself, which has to be taken into account in deciding admissibility. As Lord Cross of Chelsea put it in *DPP v Boardman* [1975] AC 421 (at p. 460):

> ... the point is not whether what the appellant is said to have suggested would be, as coming from a middle-aged active homosexual, in itself particularly unusual but whether it would be unlikely that two youths who were saying untruly that the appellant had made homosexual advances to them would have put such a suggestion into his mouth.

Similarly under the CJA 2003 in *Chopra* [2007] 1 Cr App R 225 where the three young com-plainants each separately alleged that C, a dentist, had squeezed their breasts in the course of treatment, there was a sufficient connection to warrant cross-admissibility: the court noted that it was more likely to be true than if only one of them had said it, and was not persuaded by the argument that there were many more patients of C who had made no such allegation. See also *Wallace* [2008] 1 WLR 572.

F12.60   In directing the jury where evidence is cross-admissible under the provisions of s. 101, it would be over-restrictive to suggest that the jury should first determine that they are satisfied in relation to one of the counts before moving on to use the evidence in relation to that count in dealing with any other. The jury, though obliged to reach a verdict on each count separately, may use admissible evidence in relation to any count, including the evidence of bad character arising from another (*Freeman* [2009] 2 All ER 18, disapproving comments in *S* [2008] EWCA Crim 544). In part the confusion may have arisen because of a perceived need to conclude that the accused has a propensity to commit such an offence (an inference dependent on his having done so on one occasion) before moving to consider another. However, the process of reasoning in cases such as *Chopra* does not depend on reasoning via propensity, but via coincidence, and is holistic rather than sequential (see *McAllister* [2009] 1 Cr App R 129 and **F12.38** for the distinction between propensity and non-propensity cases). *Freeman* was applied in *O'Leary* [2013] EWCA Crim 1371, in which the accused faced two sets of charges relating to the deception of elderly and vulnerable victims, both of whom were suffering from dementia. It was held that the circumstances of the two transactions were admissible in relation to one another on the issue whether the accused acted dishonestly and had targeted the victims because they were vulnerable. Again, the reasoning was holistic rather than sequential. Likewise in *Lyons* [2012] EWCA Crim 659 the stark issue for the jury was whether 11 women had made up sexual allegations against L, a guru at the centre of a group of young, mainly female followers, or his loyal supporters were trying to protect him by denying that anything untoward happened at their meetings. It would have been impossible to take the evidence of each complainant in complete isolation before forming a view as to its truth, and unnecessary as the prosecution's case was of the emergence of a pattern of offending which made L's innocence an unlikely coincidence. It was otherwise in *Norris* [2009] EWCA Crim 2697, where, on the facts, it was necessary for the jury to be sure that the accused, a nurse, had deliberately administered a fatal injection to one patient before using that evidence to assist in their deliberations regarding the deaths of other patients. Where both coincidence and propensity arguments are in play, a particularly careful direction may be required to prevent the jury 'overvaluing the accumulation of inference' (*Nicholson* [2012] 2 Cr App R 405). In that case the defence to sexual assaults allegedly committed on patients recovering from anaesthesia was that their memories were false. The accumulation of complaints provided a strong argument based on the unlikelihood of coincidence, but it was also the case that a relevant propensity of N could be established at the point where the jury were persuaded of his guilt in relation to any one complainant. See also *Rakib* [2012] 1 Cr App R (S) 1, in which the prosecution case was that the jury could be satisfied that R had exposed himself to the complainant in relation to count 1, and could then use their conclusion to support the somewhat weaker evidence on count 2 that he had done so a second time using the same unusual *modus operandi*.

The approach sanctioned at common law stopped short of supporting the conclusion that the mere existence of multiple accusations of similar offences was a *guarantee* of admissibility. As the Court of Appeal previously noted in *Wilmot* (1989) 89 Cr App R 341 (at p. 348), prejudice would result if the jury were to convict on the argument that 'If this many accusations are made, there must be something in each of them'. The risk of prejudice arising in such a case will continue to be the basis of an argument for exclusion under the CJA 2003, s. 101(3) and the court will take into account, among other things, the strength of the other evidence in the case in reaching its decision (see **F12.18**).

F12.61   The protective value of both the common-law rule of exclusion, and the new rule provided by combining s. 101(1)(d) and 101(3) is weakened in cases involving multiple accusations in consequence of the rules about joinder of counts. These permit charges to be tried together where the evidence in relation to one is similar to, though inadmissible in respect of, another (see as to joinder **D11.63** *et seq.*). Where this occurs, the efficacy of the decision to regard evidence of bad character as inadmissible depends entirely on the ability of the jury to follow a direction to disregard the evidence on one count when considering another. As the rule of admissibility at common law became more permissive over time, there were fewer cases in which charges could be joined where the evidence was not also cross-admissible (*Christou* [1997] AC 117: see **D11.85**). Under the CJA 2003, the rules on admissibility will be drawn even closer to the rules on joinder, which operate in respect of two or more charges founded on the same facts or forming part of a series of offences of the same or a similar character. Thus the problem, in cases such as *D* [2004] 1 Cr App R 19 (of directing the jury where evidence is not cross-admissible) or *Carman* [2004] EWCA Crim 540 (where some allegations were cross-admissible, some not), becomes thankfully less likely to arise. See also *W* [2011] EWCA Crim 2463, an appeal involving allegations that were different not only in terms of seriousness but also in that some had been committed many years before. Though the appeal was allowed because of the failure to formulate an appropriate direction on cross-admissibility, it was the view of all the members of the Court of Appeal that they would have ordered severance of the counts. Cases where the evidence in respect of two offences that are properly joined is not cross-admissible will still arise under the CJA 2003, and the 'remedy' will continue to be a direction to the jury not to carry evidence over from one allegation to another.

In *H* [2012] 1 Cr App R 413, a sexual offences case arising out of a trial in 2005, there was no application to bring the gateway in s. 101(1)(d) into effect, though the Court of Appeal was of the view that such an application would, in light of more modern jurisprudence, have succeeded. The trial judge instructed the jury to give separate consideration to the accounts of the complainants (three young boys) but added a rider as to the possibility of the evidence of one child supporting the other when each said he was present when the other was abused. It was held that, where cross-admissibility is not contended for, there is no rule of law requiring a direction not to treat the evidence of one complainant as supportive of the other. Instead the strength and content of the direction should fit the facts of the particular case, which it was held to have done in the instant case.

Risk of Collusion between Witnesses   It is obvious that an apparently strong nexus between accounts of events given by different witnesses does not prove guilt if it can be accounted for by collusion. In *Pepperell* [2009] EWCA Crim 1209, for example, fresh evidence establishing a close connection between complainants who had been treated at trial as virtually independent was determinative of the appeal. For some time, controversy surrounded the question whether evidence which carries a real risk of collusion should be excluded, or should be left to the jury with a suitable warning. In *H* [1995] AC 596, the House of Lords decided that, since the credibility of a witness was a matter for the jury, the risk of collusion should normally go to weight not to admissibility. The judge should therefore approach the question of admissibility on the basis that the similar facts alleged are true, with the possible exception of cases where the evidence of collusion was patent, and subject to the power of the judge to withdraw the issue from the jury where no reasonable jury could find the evidence to be genuine. H was charged with sexual offences against his stepdaughter, A, and his adopted daughter, B. If A's account was true, it was possessed of sufficient probative value to be admissible as similar fact evidence in relation to the offence against B, and to corroborate B's evidence, and vice versa. However, the relationship between the girls was such that they could easily have colluded, and the defence contended that they had deliberately conspired to put together a totally false story. The House of Lords unanimously upheld the decision of the trial judge to leave the evidence to the jury, subject to a warning about the risk of collusion.

F12.62

The common-law rule as to the assumption of truth stated in *H* is substantially replicated in the CJA 2003, s. 109. Cases under the CJA 2003 have proceeded on the basis that *H* remains good law, and this would seem correct (see, e.g., *Somanathan*, heard with *Weir* [2006] 2 All ER 570).

F12.63

F

Criminal Justice Act 2003, s. 109

(1) Subject to subsection (2), a reference in this chapter to the relevance or probative value of evidence is a reference to its relevance or probative value on the assumption that it is true.

(2) In assessing the relevance or probative value of an item of evidence for any purpose of this chapter, a court need not assume that the evidence is true if it appears, on the basis of any material before the court (including any evidence it decides to hear on the matter), that no court or jury could reasonably find it to be true.

Similarly, the common-law rule as to collusion and other forms of contamination is preserved in s. 107.

Criminal Justice Act 2003, s. 107

(1) If on a defendant's trial before a judge and jury for an offence—
   (a) evidence of his bad character has been admitted under any of paragraphs (c) to (g) of section 101(1), and
   (b) the court is satisfied at any time after the close of the case for the prosecution that—
      (i) the evidence is contaminated, and
      (ii) the contamination is such that, considering the importance of the evidence to the case against the defendant, his conviction of the offence would be unsafe,
   the court must either direct the jury to acquit the defendant of the offence or, if it considers that there ought to be a retrial, discharge the jury.

(2) Where—
   (a) a jury is directed under subsection (1) to acquit a defendant of an offence, and
   (b) the circumstances are such that, apart from this subsection, the defendant could if acquitted of that offence be found guilty of another offence,
   the defendant may not be found guilty of that other offence if the court is satisfied as mentioned in subsection (1)(b) in respect of it.

(3) If—
   (a) a jury is required to determine under section 4A(2) of the Criminal Procedure (Insanity) Act 1964 whether a person charged on an indictment with an offence did the act or made the omission charged,
   (b) evidence of the person's bad character has been admitted under any of paragraphs (c) to (g) of section 101(1), and
   (c) the court is satisfied at any time after the close of the case for the prosecution that—
      (i) the evidence is contaminated, and
      (ii) the contamination is such that, considering the importance of the evidence to the case against the person, a finding that he did the act or made the omission would be unsafe,
   the court must either direct the jury to acquit the defendant of the offence or, if it considers that there ought to be a rehearing, discharge the jury.

(4) This section does not prejudice any other power a court may have to direct a jury to acquit a person of an offence or to discharge a jury.

(5) For the purposes of this section a person's evidence is contaminated where—
   (a) as a result of an agreement or understanding between the person and one or more others, or
   (b) as a result of the person being aware of anything alleged by one or more others whose evidence may be, or has been, given in the proceedings,
   the evidence is false or misleading in any respect, or is different from what it would otherwise have been.

F12.64   The common-law principles described above applied not only to cases of deliberate conspiracy between witnesses, but also to those where there is a risk that one witness may unconsciously have been influenced by the account of another witness (*H* and *Ryder* [1994] 2 All ER 859). The same considerations would seem in theory also to be applicable where the risk of falsity arises not from collusion between witnesses, but from what Lord Wilberforce in *DPP v Boardman* [1975] AC 421 (at p. 444) described as 'a process of infection from media or publicity or simply from fashion'. It would appear that the provisions of s. 107(5) cover both the obvious case of deliberate collusion and the more subtle process of unconscious contamination referred to in the common-law authorities. This was accepted in *Lamb* [2007] EWCA Crim 1766, where allegations of sexual activity in breach of trust were made against a schoolteacher by two girls, one of whom had persuaded the other to join with her in making disclosure. The court regarded s. 107 as applicable to 'collusion or innocent contamination', which is persuasive although ultimately the question was not one of admissibility but of whether the judge's direction had done justice to the risk of innocent contamination. In any event, the preservation in s. 107(4) of any other common-law powers the court may have makes it certain that, if some cases of unconscious contamination are not caught by the Act, they are subject to the court's common-law jurisdiction. Note that the statutory provisions apply only to trial on indictment (s. 107(1)). See also *K* [2008] EWCA Crim 3301, where the true question to be resolved was whether the witnesses, who were brothers, were honestly endeavouring to recall events of many years past, or dishonestly dissembling. The judge's decision to focus the jury's attention on the individual counts without directing on cross-admissibility reflected the way in which the case had been run, and a more specific direction on contamination was not called for. In *N (H)* [2011] EWCA Crim 730 it was noted that questions of collusion and contamination may arise on the facts of a case whether or not the jury are invited to treat allegations by different complainants as cross-admissible. Even where the jury are not so invited, there may still be a need to provide them with guidance about the risk of collusion and/or contamination, depending on the circumstances of the case.

In *C* [2006] 3 All ER 689, the Court of Appeal suggested that a trial judge should postpone **F12.65**
a decision on a plausible submission that there has been contamination until the suggested contaminated evidence has been examined at trial. The judge could then 'have well in mind the precise details of the evidence actually given, with such weaknesses and problems as may have emerged'. This is so, though it also puts a premium on the jury's ability to disregard evidence which the judge decides is contaminated.

Acquittals: Special Considerations

On rare occasions the prosecution contends that D has been guilty of past relevant miscon- **F12.66**
duct despite the fact that he has been acquitted by another court in respect of that conduct. Under the CJA 2003, as at common law, the prosecution would be adducing evidence of 'bad character', despite the acquittal, because the contention is that the accused had been guilty of misconduct on the previous occasion, even though no attempt is made to punish him for it (see **F12.13**). The evidence would be admissible if the prosecution could show its relevance to an important issue under s. 101(1)(d) leaving the accused to contend for the exercise of the specific statutory discretion in s. 101(3).

At common law the use of such evidence was at one time thought to be objectionable under the double jeopardy rule, until the decision of the House of Lords in *Z* [2000] 2 AC 483. Z was charged with the rape of C, and his defence was consent. On four separate occasions Z had been tried for the rape of other women, and on three occasions acquitted. The prosecution contended that evidence from all four previous complainants was admissible to rebut the defence put forward in respect of C. It was conceded that the evidence of the four, taken cumulatively, possessed the degree of probative value required for admissibility at common law. The House of Lords held that evidence may be adduced to prove the guilt of the accused in relation to the offence for which he is on trial notwithstanding that it shows that he has committed other offences of which he has been acquitted. Provided that the prosecutor does not seek in any way to punish the accused for the other offences, the double jeopardy rule is not infringed. Under *Z*, it remained open for the judge to exercise discretion to prevent the unfair use of such evidence. The obvious vehicle for exclusion under the Act would be s. 101(3).

In *Smith*, one of the appeals heard with *Edwards* [2006] 1 WLR 1524, the rule in *Z* was applied where the accused had been led to believe that he would not be prosecuted in respect of a particular allegation. This did not prevent the subsequent use of the allegation as evidence of propensity, subject to the application of the court's power to prevent unfair use. See also *Nguyen* [2008] 2 Cr App R 99, where the accused was held to be 'not necessarily worse off' in consequence of the prosecution's decision not to prosecute for lesser offences of violence but to use them as evidence of propensity on a murder charge. In *T (P)* [2013] EWCA Crim 2398, some 30 years had passed since the original acquittals for sexual offences. A challenge based on the fact that there no longer existed relevant material that would have assisted the jury in assessing the reliability of the evidence was dismissed. On the facts, it appears that the portions of the evidence that were significant in the later prosecution (for a series of serious sexual offences together with the murder of one victim) were supported by statements of the accused including what amounted to an admission of one rape. The lapse of time, which might in other circumstances have proved critical, did not appear to provide a genuine impediment to challenging the relevant parts of the evidence of the two complainants.

EVIDENCE OF BAD CHARACTER ADDUCED BY A CO-ACCUSED

Criminal Justice Act 2003: Evidence of Bad Character Going to Matter in Issue Between Co-accused

F12.67   The relevant provision of the Criminal Justice Act 2003 is s. 101(1)(e), which is supplemented by s. 104.

Criminal Justice Act 2003, ss. 101 and 104

101.—(1) In criminal proceedings evidence of the defendant's bad character is admissible if, but only if—

...

(e) it has substantial probative value in relation to an important matter in issue between the defendant and a co-defendant,

...

104.—(1) Evidence which is relevant to the question whether the defendant has a propensity to be untruthful is admissible on that basis under section 101(1)(e) only if the nature or conduct of his defence is such as to undermine the co-defendant's defence.

(2) Only evidence—
(a) which is to be (or has been) adduced by the co-defendant, or
(b) which a witness is to be invited to give (or has given) in cross-examination by the co-defendant,

is admissible under section 101(1)(e).

Section 104(1) is primarily relevant to the cut-throat defence where the evidence of propensity is directed more towards establishing lack of veracity than to the issue of guilt. This is dealt with at **F12.75**. The restriction applied by s. 104(1) does not bite where the evidence of propensity is not directed to untruthfulness but to the issue of commission of the offence. In such cases, s. 101(1)(e) permits propensity evidence to be adduced against an accused by a co-accused whatever the nature of the defence, provided that it is of 'substantial probative value' in relation to an issue between them — though this will frequently occur because one blames the other. Thus in *West* [2006] EWCA Crim 1843, for example, one of the three men accused of the murder of a fourth sought for the first time in giving his evidence to blame W, which created an issue between them which should have allowed W to have recourse to his co-accused's previous convictions for violence. In *De Vos* [2006] EWCA Crim 1688 D's convictions for drugs offences were admissible in relation to his contention that he was an innocent 'mule' duped by his co-accused. In *Land* [2006] EWCA Crim 2856 L, an employee of the CPS, disclosed information to K as a result of which both were charged with offences relating to the administration of justice. L's defence was that he had acted in fear of K, and set about proving K's bad character. Various previous convictions and matters relating to a drugs deal were admitted, but other matters relating, *inter alia*, to the discovery of a sword at K's home were said to have been properly excluded on the grounds that they lacked the necessary 'substantial probative value' in relation to an important issue in the case. The court also endorsed the earlier comment of the court in *Edwards* [2006] 1 WLR 1524 that the trial judge's 'feel' for what is important in the context of the case is most likely to be correct. Where an accused's defence to involvement in a serious assault was that he had punched the complainant in self-defence, and that his co-accused had caused the serious injuries by a subsequent exchange of blows, the trial judge's conclusion that evidence of his co-accused's propensity to violence was not of substantial probative value was reasonable. The co-accused had not sought to implicate the accused, and the issue for the jury was whether the accused had taken part in an unprovoked attack (*Passos-Carr* [2009] EWCA Crim 2018).

Note that there is no discretion to restrain an accused from taking advantage of s. 101(1)(e). **F12.68** Where evidence of propensity satisfies the test for admissibility in s. 101(1)(e) it may be adduced notwithstanding that it is also highly prejudicial: s. 101(3) does not apply (*Musone* [2007] 1 WLR 2467, where the court also considered and dismissed argument based on the ECHR, Article 6, before concluding that 'The only apparent control on the deployment of evidence by one defendant against another is that which is contained in section 101(1)(e)'). See also *Apabhai* (2011) 175 JP 292, pointing out that there is no statutory or residual common-law support for such a discretion, and *Phillips* [2012] 1 Cr App R 332, emphasising that there is no discretion to exclude such evidence on either fairness or 'case management' grounds where the introduction of untried satellite fraud issues on an already complicated prosecution was likely to confuse the jury. The common law followed the same rule: e.g., in *Grant* [2004] EWCA Crim 2910, G was charged with murder and was shown by his co-accused to have a relevant propensity by reference to an incident some months earlier for which he was awaiting trial. G relied on his privilege against self-incrimination in respect of the earlier incident, as he was entitled to do, thereby hampering his challenge to the evidence. Provided, however, that G had the opportunity to give the evidence he wanted and to cross-examine the witnesses called for the co-accused, and the matter was summed up fairly, the court was satisfied that there was no unfairness.

Where a co-accused, by making a late application, puts his co-accused in the position of being unable to deal fairly with the evidence relating to his character (which would otherwise be admissible), the judge may have recourse to his power under the CrimPR to disallow the late application (*Jarvis* [2008] EWCA Crim 488, and cf. *Musone*, where a similar point is made in relation to a late application to adduce hearsay evidence). *Musone* and *Jarvis* were considered in *Ramirez* [2009] EWCA Crim 1721, where it was said that the failure of the judge to consider whether there had been a deliberate manipulation of the rules by the co-accused or his counsel was immaterial where the giving of the evidence, even without proper notice, would not have prevented the fair trial of the appellant. However, the court also stressed that its conclusion was reached on the particular facts of the case, and that in another case the giving of bad character evidence by a co-accused without proper notice might necessitate a retrial and lead to severe sanctions against any legal representative found to have been involved in deliberate manipulation of the rules.

Distinguishing the Criminal Justice Act 2003, s. 101(1)(e), from the Common-law Position

These provisions were intended to reflect the position at common law, described in detail in **F12.69** previous editions of this work. However, the Act was drafted before the decision of the House of Lords in *Randall* [2004] 1 All ER 467. In that case, R and G were jointly charged with the murder of B, who had been assaulted in the street. Both admitted involvement in persuading B to leave the nearby house of R's aunt, but G denied following B into the street, and R admitted only to inflicting minor injuries on B in self-defence. G had a 'formidable record' for offences, including serious offences of violence, and it was R's contention that G was more likely to have killed B. The Court of Appeal held that the trial judge wrongly directed the jury that the record of G was relevant only to the truthfulness of the evidence he gave at trial. Where there was a cut-throat defence the 'imbalance' between the record of offending of the two men tended to support the version of events put forward by R. The only issue before the House of Lords was whether G's propensity to use violence was relevant to the issue whether it was R who committed the assault. Lord Steyn, in an opinion in which the other lords concurred, rejected the argument put forward by the Crown that propensity 'proves nothing' in relation to guilt. The relevance of evidence of propensity was to be determined, like other evidence, by reference to whether 'the evidence is capable of increasing or diminishing the probability of the existence of a fact in issue'.

Lord Steyn approved as 'high authority' for the proposition that evidence of a co-accused's propensity may be relevant the decision of the Privy Council in *Lowery v The Queen* [1974] AC 85. Lord Morris stated that, where the question is which of two men committed a murder, it would be 'unjust to prevent either of them from calling any evidence of probative value which could point to the probability that the perpetrator was the one rather than the other'.

F12.70   The major difference that appears to exist between the common law as described in *Randall*, and the statutory provision of the CJA 2003, s. 101(1)(e), is that bad character evidence adduced under the Act must be of 'substantial probative value in relation to an issue' between the accused, rather than being merely relevant. Contrast s. 101(1)(d), which stipulates relevance as the standard for admissibility of prosecution evidence (see **F12.36**). The explanation for applying a harder test for admissibility in respect of evidence from a co-accused is that the court has no discretion to exclude evidence from an accused person (contrast, in relation to prosecution evidence, s. 101(3), supplemented by the PACE 1984, s. 78, at **F12.18**). It appears from the Explanatory Notes which accompanied the Criminal Justice Bill when it was first introduced to Parliament that the reference to 'substantial' is intended only to exclude evidence of 'marginal or trivial value' rather than to impose any specific requirement with regard to the cogency of the evidence. If this is so, there would appear to be no inconsistency with *Randall*, and cases decided under the authority of *Randall* may be of relevance to the construction of the new provision. It appears to have been so considered in *Musone* [2007] 1 WLR 2467 where, however, the court deliberately refrained from expressing a concluded view as to the meaning of 'substantial' probative value in s. 101(1)(e). In many cases the outcome would be the same whether or not the word 'substantial' requires an enhanced degree of probative value. For example in *Miah* [2011] EWCA Crim 945 the Court of Appeal considered that the conviction of M for robbery did not bear at all upon the issues between M and his co-accused C, who was seeking to show that M was the principal offender and C the compliant follower in a case of murder by arson.

While authorities such *as Apabhai* (2011) 175 JP 292 seem to support the construction that 'substantial' means more than merely trivial, recent authority (rightly, it is submitted) prefers a stronger construction. In *Phillips* [2012] 1 Cr App R 332 Pitchford LJ said that the addition of the word 'substantial' signifies 'an enhancement of the capacity of the evidence to prove or disprove the fact in issue', and that the threshold for admissibility should not be understated (at pp. 348–9). The purpose of the requirement was said to be that the probative strength of the evidence should remove the risk of unfair prejudice. His lordship noted that under the CJA 2003 the bad character of a co-accused was potentially admissible in relation to a multiplicity of issues going beyond what was contemplated in *Randall*, and that the scope for satellite issues has also significantly increased. As an aid to construction, the Court drew attention to the CJA 2003, s. 100(3) (see **F14.10**), which requires the court to have regard to particular factors in reaching an assessment of substantial probative value in relation to the bad character of a non-defendant. It was pointed out that the legal meaning of the term 'substantial' must be the same in both cases, thus suggesting that reference to s. 100(3) might be of value in cases under s. 101(1)(e). *Phillips* was approved in *Turnbull* [2013] EWCA Crim 676, where the Court emphasised the point, also made in that case, that the question of admissibility was 'highly fact-sensitive' and would depend on what other evidence was available on the issue. In *Turnbull* T was able to demonstrate the propensity of the co-accused for violence by cross-examining him about an attack shortly after the offence charged, and this 'dwarfed' the evidence of his old juvenile convictions which the judge had rightly ruled that T could not adduce. *Phillips* was also approved, in relation to s. 100, in *Walsh* [2012] EWCA Crim 2728 (see **F14.6**).

Randall also casts doubt on the correctness of the decision of the Court of Appeal in *Neale*   **F12.71**
(1977) 65 Cr App R 304. On a charge of arson, N claimed that the fire was started by his co-accused, B, and that N was either not there or not participating when the fire was started. In support of this, N sought to adduce evidence that B had a propensity to start fires. However, it was held that B's propensity to start fires on his own did not logically suggest that he had started the fire in question without the help of N. *Neale* was applied in *Knutton* (1993) 97 Cr App R 114, in which K's formidable list of convictions was held to have been of insufficient relevance where the co-accused's defence was alibi. While the relevance of evidence of propensity is clearly to be determined in light of the defence raised, Lord Steyn stated that *Neale* appeared to be a borderline decision, and he questioned what the outcome would have been had N clearly admitted his presence at the scene.

The giving of a standard *Hanson* ([2005] 1 WLR 3159) direction (see **F12.22**) against over-   **F12.72**
valuing propensity evidence was said in *Najib* [2013] EWCA Crim 86 to be likely to confuse the jury where the evidence is adduced by one co-accused against the other, given that a co-accused bears no burden of proof. Nevertheless, it is important to warn against jumping to conclusions based on evidence of bad character. At common law, when evidence of propensity of an accused was adduced by a co-accused but was also relevant to an issue between the Crown and the accused, although the point was not free from controversy the better view was that it was not necessary for a direction to be given to disregard the evidence as between the accused and the Crown. Justice does not require that such a direction be given, and it would needlessly perplex juries. Thus, as Rix LJ said in *B (C)* [2004] 2 Cr App R 570, where propensity is admitted for the sake of a co-defendant's defence, the Crown becomes the beneficiary of that. The same result would appear to follow under the CJA 2003, s. 101(1)(e): although the prosecution cannot take advantage of the gateway, they may be the beneficiary where a co-accused elects to do so. Decisions under the CJA 2003 have not so far considered the weight to be given to common-law authorities. However, the prevailing view is that the CJA 2003 provides a narrower platform for admissibility for evidence by a co-accused but (in a curious twist on the common law) the co-accused might be the beneficiary of the greater latitude afforded to the prosecution. Thus, in *Lambrou* [2005] EWCA Crim 3595, the trial judge, taken by surprise by the commencement of the new provisions, failed to give sufficient consideration to the terms of s. 101(1)(e) as between L and his co-accused, but the conviction admitted in consequence (for an offence of the same kind) could, the court considered, have been admitted at the behest of the prosecution under s. 101(1)(d).

Propensity where Character in Issue

The doctrine of relevance will operate more favourably towards an accused where his co-accused   **F12.73**
sets up his own good character, or at least seeks to assert positive aspects of his character, so as to make him seem less likely than the accused to have committed the offence. This was the case at common law, and would seem also to obtain under the CJA 2003, s. 101(1)(e), where the test of 'substantial probative value in relation to an important matter in issue' will more readily be satisfied where a co-accused has chosen to take this line. Relevant common-law authorities include *Bracewell* (1978) 68 Cr App R 44, where B and L were jointly charged with the murder of an old man in the course of a burglary. B was prevented from adducing evidence-in-chief to show L's violent disposition, on the ground of insufficient relevance, but the position changed when it emerged that L's defence was that he was an experienced burglar of a non-violent type, able to keep a cool head, whereas B was inexperienced, nervous, excitable and probably drunk.

It was held that by raising this defence L had made an issue of his propensity, and that B should at that stage have been allowed to cross-examine him about his violent nature and to call evidence about it if necessary.

F12.74   In *Douglass* (1989) Cr App R 264, D and P were charged with causing death by reckless driving, the charges arising out of an incident in which the prosecution alleged that D was trying to prevent P from overtaking him, and that in vying for position P lost control and collided head-on with an oncoming vehicle. P cross-examined a prosecution witness with a view to showing that P had not drunk alcohol in the two years that the witness had known him. The purpose of this was to invite the jury to contrast P with D, who, according to the prosecution evidence, had been drinking, so as to cast the blame on him. It was held that P had put his character in issue, and that D was wrongly prevented from introducing relevant evidence of P's bad record for motoring offences including drink-driving.

Where one co-accused sought to draw attention to the other's alleged fraudulent conduct on other occasions in order to invite the inference that the other was more likely to have committed the fraud offences charged but the prosecution was happy to regard both as of good character, the giving of both a good character direction and a direction as to how to treat the evidence of bad character tendered by the co-accused required some care, but could not be said to be so confusing as to be prejudicial (*Ferdhaus* [2010] EWCA Crim 220).

Evidence Going to Issue of Untruthfulness between Accused and Co-accused

F12.75   Section 101(1)(e) of the CJA 2003 (see **F12.67**) renders admissible evidence that has 'substantial probative value' in relation to an important matter in issue between the defendant and a co-defendant. 'Important matter' means a matter of substantial importance in the context of the case as a whole' (s. 112(1)). Section 101(1)(e) is supplemented by s. 104, under which limited use may be made of the defendant's propensity to untruthfulness. Note that only defence evidence is admissible under this provision (s. 104(2)).

Criminal Justice Act 2003, s. 104

(1) Evidence which is relevant to the question whether the defendant has a propensity to be untruthful is admissible on that basis under section 101(1)(e) only if the nature or conduct of his defence is such as to undermine the co-defendant's defence.

(2) Only evidence—
    (a) which is to be (or has been) adduced by the co-defendant, or
    (b) which a witness is to be invited to give (or has given) in cross-examination by the co-defendant,
is admissible under section 101(1)(e).

F12.76   The leading case is *Lawson* [2007] 1 WLR 1191. Three young men were alleged to have participated in the manslaughter of a third by pushing him into deep water, where he drowned. The principal offender pleaded guilty, but there was an issue between the two alleged secondary parties, each of whom denied participation, but alleged that the other had made incriminating remarks as to his own intention to push the victim in. Thus both had undermined the defence of the other. The issue of particular difficulty concerned the conviction of L for an offence of violence. This was held not to establish a relevant propensity to offend, but to go instead to credibility, and to have the necessary 'substantial probative value' in relation to that issue. In so deciding, the Court of Appeal rejected the application to s. 101(1)(e) of *Hanson* [2005] 1 WLR 3169 (see **F12.44**), where it was decided that, in relation to s. 101(1)(d), only evidence of direct relevance to veracity, such as a conviction involving lying, is admissible to show untruthfulness. This 'cautious test of admissibility' was held more appropriate to applications by the Crown. An accused should not be so restricted in the evidence of criminal behaviour of a co-accused (or, as it was rendered in *Rosato* [2008] EWCA Crim 1243, 'such a narrow reading would have been well capable of unfairness as between co-defendants'). The court in *Lawson* pointed to the similar outcome in *Osbourne*, an appeal heard with *Renda* [2006] 2 All ER 553, in which a propensity to violence had been admitted on the issue of untruthfulness, and rejected the counterargument based on *M* [2006] EWCA Crim 1126, where such evidence was said not to go to truthfulness, on the ground that the point had not been argued. The distinguishing of *Hanson* is not without difficulty, however, in that both s. 101(1)(d) and (e) deal with an accused having 'a propensity to be untruthful' but it appears that the meaning and content of the propensity is broader in s. 101(1)(e). Where, however, evidence of a propensity not directly suggestive of untruthfulness is admitted under s. 101(1)(d) as being relevant to the guilt of the accused, the effect of *Campbell* [2007] 1 WLR 2798 (see **F12.23**) is that the evidence is admissible for all relevant purposes, including an assessment of his credibility, so that the practical difference between gateways (d) and (e) is reduced.

More consistent with *Hanson* (though the point in *Lawson* was not argued) is *Reid* [2006] EWCA Crim 2900, where the court applied the *Hanson* distinction between untruthfulness and dishonesty in ruling on the co-accused's admissions of offences involving deception. In *Jarvis* [2008] EWCA Crim 488, it was held that there is no warrant for restricting bad character evidence going to a propensity for untruthfulness to evidence of past untruthfulness as a witness: an observation that holds true whether or not *Hanson* applies.

Where the conditions of s. 101(1)(e) are fulfilled, the court has no statutory discretion to **F12.77** restrain the co-accused from adducing relevant evidence of bad character, as s. 101(3) is inapplicable. This mirrors the law as it was laid down both at common law and under the Criminal Evidence Act 1898 (*Murdoch v Taylor* [1965] AC 574, where it was also held that, notwithstanding the absence of discretion, it was still necessary to seek a ruling from the judge as to admissibility before taking advantage of the provision, a point that must still hold good). See also *McGregor* (1992) 95 Cr App R 240. See however **F12.67** as to the judge's powers to disallow a late application by a co-accused where the target of the application would be unable to deal with it effectively.

The restriction of the provision to cases where the 'nature and conduct of the defence is such as to undermine the co-defendant's defence' would seem to import, in relation to evidence of lack of veracity, much of the previous authority in relation to the Criminal Evidence Act 1898, s. 1(3)(iii), where one co-accused's evidence is said to be 'against' another (so as to let in his character only where the effect is to undermine the defence of that other). The phrase 'nature and conduct' also appears in the 1898 Act; the authorities in relation to that expression may also prove of assistance (see **F12.78**).

'Nature and Conduct of Defence'   Where this phrase occurred in the Criminal Evidence Act **F12.78** 1898, in the slightly different context of a defence involving imputations against the prosecution, it was held that answers given in cross-examination were prima facie not to be taken into account in determining the nature or conduct of the defence, as such answers should be taken to form part of the cross-examiner's case (*Jones* (1909) 3 Cr App R 67; *Eidinow* (1932) 23 Cr App R 154). However, answers given in cross-examination which went beyond the scope of the question ran the risk of being held part of the nature and conduct of the defence (*Jones* (1909) 3 Cr App R 67, per Lord Alverstone CJ at p. 69; see also *Courtney* [1995] Crim LR 63). Equally (and more obviously), the accused was exposed to revelations of bad character where his answers in cross-examination did no more than to remove all doubt as to whether the accused was seeking to impugn the character of a prosecution witness (*Selvey v DPP* [1970] AC 304). Where, however, a judge thought that the accused has been trapped into making an imputation by the form of the question put to him, cross-examination on the bad character of the accused was not permitted (*Jones*; *Baldwin* (1925) 18 Cr App R 175). While these authorities cannot be said to be binding on the proper interpretation of s. 104 of the CJA 2003, the use of the same phrase cannot have been accidental.

'Such as to Undermine the Co-defendant's Defence'   The Criminal Evidence Act 1898, **F12.79** s. 1(3)(iii), the forerunner of ss. 101(1)(e) and 104 of the CJA 2003, applied where an accused 'has given evidence against any other person charged in the same proceedings', and authorities dealing with the meaning of the provision may continue to be of relevance. 'Evidence against' meant evidence that supported the prosecution case in a material respect or that undermined the defence of a co-accused (*Murdoch v Taylor* [1965] AC 574, per Lord Donovan at p. 592). His lordship qualified the earlier definition proffered by the Court of Criminal Appeal in *Stannard* [1965] 2 QB 1, in which it was said that the question was whether the evidence 'tended to' support the prosecution case or undermine the defence. This was wrong insofar as it suggested that evidence given by A1 might be evidence against A2 simply because it differed from evidence given by A2.

F12.80   In *Kirkpatrick* [1998] Crim LR 63, it was held that K's defence to indecent assault (which was that he had been intervening to prevent B and another committing the offence) was not undermined by B's defence, which was that he was asleep and took no part in the events. B did not, merely by providing an inconsistent account, undermine K's defence. It is submitted that the decision is correct, even though a jury which believed B's account could not at the same time believe K's. *A fortiori* if the evidence of A1, if believed, would result in the acquittal of A2, even though it is fundamentally inconsistent with the defence put forward by A2. Thus, in *Bruce* [1975] 3 All ER 277, B, M and others were charged with robbery, and convicted of stealing cash from a foreigner. M's defence was that there had been a preconceived plan to rob, but he maintained that he was not a party to it, whereas B claimed that there had been no preconceived plan, and indeed that neither he nor M had received any money from the victim. It was held that the inconsistency between their defences did not entitle counsel for M to cross-examine B on his record, because acceptance of B's evidence would have led to the acquittal of M, not his conviction, and: 'The fact that [B's] evidence undermined [M's] defence by supplying him with another does not make it evidence given against him' (per Stephenson LJ at p. 1259). In a situation where A1 provides an alternative explanation, however, it did not take much to persuade a court that A1 had implicated A2 in the offence. Thus, in *Hatton* (1976) 64 Cr App R 88, Hatton's evidence was found on balance to be against that of Hildon who, together with Hatton and Ripley, was charged with theft of scrap metal. Hatton claimed that all three accused acted in pursuance of a plan to take the scrap, but that their intention was not dishonest, because a relation of Hildon had assured them that he had permission to take it. Hildon, on the other hand, claimed that he had happened by the site while Hatton and Ripley were collecting the metal, and had been persuaded to help on the understanding that they had paid for it. Hatton's evidence was held to support 'a material part of the prosecution case' (i.e. a preconceived plan between the three to collect the scrap), and 'although it provided Hildon with another defence, it not merely undermined his credit but on balance did more to undermine his defence than to undermine the prosecution's case' (per Stephenson LJ at p. 91).

F12.81   It sometimes happens that the only way an accused can assert his innocence is by placing the blame on a co-accused. In this unfortunate situation the shield against cross-examination was lost under the Criminal Evidence Act 1898, and it would appear that in the same situation under the CJA 2003 the defence is inevitably undermined. In *Varley* [1982] 2 All ER 519, V and D were charged with robbery, and D's defence was that he took part in the robbery only because V was present and made threats against D's life. V gave evidence in which he completely denied that he had taken any part in the offence: evidence which clearly undermined D's account, because 'it amounted to saying that not only was [D] telling lies but that [D] would be left as a participant on his own and not acting under duress'. The Court of Appeal summarised the position in the following way (at p. 522):

> Mere denial of participation in a joint venture is not of itself sufficient to rank as evidence against the co-defendant. For the proviso to apply, such denial must lead to the conclusion that if the witness did not participate then it must have been the other who did ... Where the one defendant asserts or in due course would assert one view of the joint venture which is directly contradicted by the other such contradiction may be evidence against the co-defendant.

The same result was reached in *Davis* [1975] 1 All ER 233, in which D, under cross-examination, was driven to accuse O, his co-accused, of stealing a gold cross and chain that had disappeared from a house in circumstances such that either D or O must have taken it. Any denial by D in the circumstances necessarily involved undermining the chance of acquittal of O, and was thus evidence against him. A similar case is *Crawford* [1997] 1 WLR 1329, where the prosecution contended that three women entered a public lavatory and robbed the victim. A's defence was that she had been present, along with C and the third woman, but had taken no part in the robbery. C's defence was that she had left the lavatory by the time the robbery occurred. C's account of events was held to be a 'direct contradiction' of A's so as to undermine A's defence and to permit A to cross-examine C on her previous convictions. In *Hendrick* [1992] Crim LR 427, by contrast, co-accused, F and H, were alleged to have been involved in a joint venture to steal a handbag. F's denial of participation did not lead to the loss of his shield against cross-examination as the innocence of F was not incompatible with the innocence of H.

In *Rigot* [2000] 7 Arch News 2, the Court of Appeal held (contrary to what was said in *Varley*)   **F12.82** that mere denial of participation in a joint venture with the co-accused could be evidence against him where the effect of the denial was merely to suggest that he 'may' have committed the offence, and not that he 'must' have done so. On the facts of the case, however, R's denial was such as to completely undermine the defence advanced by his co-accused, S, who was claiming in effect to have been an innocent dupe of R and his associates in carrying R's drug-laden suitcase into the country. If, as R said, the suitcase was not his and he was a complete innocent, the only explanation S had advanced for her possession of the drugs was necessarily false.

Where evidence undermined a co-accused's defence in the sense described above, it did not matter for the purposes of the Criminal Evidence Act 1898, and should not for the purposes of the CJA 2003, that that the co-accused's defence was already a lost cause, for example because he has effectively admitted his guilt in evidence-in-chief (*Mir* [1989] Crim LR 894).

It was not necessary under the 1898 Act, nor should it be under the CJA 2003, that the evidence of A1 be given with any hostile intent against A2, for 'it is the effect of the evidence upon the minds of the jury which matters, not the state of mind of the person who gives it' (*Murdoch v Taylor* [1965] AC 574, per Lord Donovan at p. 591). Applying this objective test, it is obvious that damaging evidence 'would be just as damaging whether given with regret or whether given with relish' (per Lord Morris, at p. 584).

Where A1 is wrongly denied the opportunity to cross-examine A2 on his convictions in a case where each blames the other for the offence, and both are convicted, it was said in relation to the 1898 Act that it does not follow that A1's conviction is unsafe. The jury must necessarily have disbelieved the evidence 'against' A1 to the extent that they disbelieved the denial of A2 (*Boyce* [2001] EWCA Crim 921).

EVIDENCE OF BAD CHARACTER TO CORRECT FALSE IMPRESSION OR COUNTER ATTACK ON ANOTHER'S CHARACTER

Uses of Bad Character Evidence Contingent on Nature of Defence

The main provisions governing the use of evidence of the accused's bad character to establish the   **F12.83** commission of the offence are the CJA 2003, s. 101(1)(d), where the evidence is to be adduced by the prosecution, and s. 101(1)(e), where the evidence is relied upon by a co-accused. These uses of bad character evidence are dealt with at **F12.36** *et seq*. and **F12.67** respectively. Both

F

subsections (1)(d) and (e) may also permit the use of evidence of bad character to show untruthfulness, though it is doubtful whether those provisions will be of much practical significance in the wake of *Campbell* [2007] 1 WLR 2798 (see **F12.23** and **F12.44**), which permits evidence adduced as relevant to guilt to be taken into account in deciding the credit to be given to the accused's testimony. Given the breadth of s. 101(1)(d) in particular, it may be doubted whether the additional gateways of s. 101(1)(f) and (in particular) s. 101(1)(g) will need to be considered with great frequency in future.

F12.84   The CJA 2003 expressly provides that, in addition to the gateways described above, the accused may also have to meet evidence of bad character designed to correct a false impression he has given (s. 101(1)(f): see **F12.85**), or to repel an attack he has made on the character of another (s. 101(1)(g): see **F12.91**). These methods of deploying bad character evidence are described in the remainder of this section. The first and most obvious difference from the predecessor provision, the Criminal Evidence Act 1898, is that the use of evidence of bad character under the CJA 2003 is not contingent on the decision of the accused to give evidence, as it may be tendered irrespective of whether the accused is called as a witness in the proceedings. This reduces the tactical options open to an accused who wishes to launch an attack upon a prosecution witness or upon a co-accused without exposing his own bad character. It also means that the evidence that is adduced under the provisions, which are considered below, cannot be said, as was frequently the case with evidence adduced under the 1898 Act, to be admissible only in relation to the issue of the credit to be given to the evidence of the accused. Potentially, it is open to a jury to draw on the bad character evidence to prove guilt (see *Highton* [2005] 1 WLR 3472 at **F12.23**). It will be for the courts to decide what use to make of, say, convictions for dishonesty where the accused is charged with a sexual assault, or vice versa, with *Campbell*, decided under s. 101(1)(d), advocating a common-sense approach rather than the old framework of technical distinctions based on the separation of relevance to guilt and credit. The following provisions, already considered, are of equal application to evidence of bad character admitted under the remaining exceptions: s. 107 (stopping the case where evidence contaminated: **F12.63**), s. 109 (assumption of truth in assessment of relevance or probative value: **F12.63**). The provisions of s. 108, regarding the use which can be made of evidence of convictions when the accused was a child, are also of general relevance and are considered at **F12.98**.

Evidence to Correct a False Impression

F12.85   Section 101(1)(f) of the CJA 2003 permits evidence of bad character to be adduced by the prosecution to correct a false impression given by the accused about himself. In *Assani* [2008] EWCA Crim 2563, the Court of Appeal called for closer attention to the provision in s. 105(7) that s. 101(1)(f) admits prosecution evidence only. Applications by one co-accused to adduce evidence of bad character against another fall to be dealt with under s. 101(e).

The provision is supplemented by s. 105, which lays down the circumstances in which the accused is regarded as having given such an impression. Note that evidence admitted under gateway (f) is limited to evidence correcting the false impression (s. 105(6)) so that the general doctrine that evidence, once admitted, is admissible for all purposes to which it is relevant (see **F12.23**), is excluded. The provisions of s. 101(3), which exclude evidence having an adverse effect on the fairness of the proceedings, do not apply to evidence tendered under s. 101(1)(f) (see **F12.18**).

Criminal Justice Act 2003, s. 105

(1)   For the purposes of section 101(1)(f)—

    (a)   the defendant gives a false impression if he is responsible for the making of an express or implied assertion which is apt to give the court or jury a false or misleading impression about the defendant;

    (b)   evidence to correct such an impression is evidence which has probative value in correcting it.

(2) A defendant is treated as being responsible for the making of an assertion if—
   (a) the assertion is made by the defendant in the proceedings (whether or not in evidence given by him),
   (b) the assertion was made by the defendant—
      (i)   on being questioned under caution, before charge, about the offence with which he is charged, or
      (ii) on being charged with the offence or officially informed that he might be prosecuted for it, and evidence of the assertion is given in the proceedings,
   (c) the assertion is made by a witness called by the defendant,
   (d) the assertion is made by any witness in cross-examination in response to a question asked by the defendant that is intended to elicit it, or is likely to do so, or
   (e) the assertion was made by any person out of court, and the defendant adduces evidence of it in the proceedings.
(3) A defendant who would otherwise be treated as responsible for the making of an assertion shall not be so treated if, or to the extent that, he withdraws it or disassociates himself from it.
(4) Where it appears to the court that a defendant, by means of his conduct (other than the giving of evidence) in the proceedings, is seeking to give the court or jury an impression about himself that is false or misleading, the court may if it appears just to do so treat the defendant as being responsible for the making of an assertion which is apt to give that impression.
(5) In subsection (4) 'conduct' includes appearance or dress.
(6) Evidence is admissible under section 101(1)(f) only if it goes no further than is necessary to correct the false impression.
(7) Only prosecution evidence is admissible under section 101(1)(f).

The Law Commission (*Evidence of Bad Character in Criminal Proceedings*, Law Com No. 273, (2001)) recommended that evidence be admissible to correct a false or misleading impression given by the accused, and much of the elaboration of s. 105 follows the pattern set by the Commission. However, the Law Commission's proposal also required the prosecution to satisfy the court that the evidence had 'substantial probative value' in correcting the impression, and that either the evidence was not prejudicial or that, if it was, the interests of justice required it to be admissible (Law Commission draft Bill, cl. 10). None of these safeguards is replicated in s. 101(1)(f) or s. 105: evidence of bad character is admissible provided only that it has 'probative value' in correcting the false impression. This means that the accused is forced back on more slender safeguards: the option to withdraw or dissociate himself from an assertion which would otherwise merit the admission of bad character evidence in rebuttal (s. 105(3)) and the provision that rebuttal evidence is admissible 'only if it goes no further than is necessary to correct the false impression'. The tendency of the courts to permit applications under s. 78 of the PACE 1984 in cases not covered by the specific power of exclusion of evidence of bad character in s. 101(3) of the CJA 2003 is helpful in creating a framework for any further protection the courts may regard as necessary (see **F12.18**).   **F12.86**

The CJA 2003 provisions apply irrespective of whether witnesses are specifically called as to good character, and whether or not the accused elects to give evidence on his own behalf. Evidence admitted under the provision potentially goes towards correcting the false impression in a manner indicative of guilt, not merely of the credit to be given to any testimony the accused gives.   **F12.87**

In *Ullah* [2006] EWCA Crim 2003, U stated in interview that he had never acted dishonestly and that he had been meticulous in his business dealings. The CJA 2003 clarifies the position where the accused, as in *Ullah*, makes misleading assertions during questioning or when charged and these are subsequently given in evidence in the proceedings. These constitute assertions for the purposes of the provision (s. 105(2)(b)) and so they may result in the use of evidence to correct any false impression given, even where the prosecution is responsible for placing the original assertion before the court. In *Ullah* U's previous convictions for deception-related offences were admitted. In such cases, the accused would do well, if he does not stand by the assertion, to disassociate himself from it (s. 105(3)).

In *Renda* [2006] 2 All ER 553, where the issue arose of whether the accused had withdrawn or dissociated himself from a false impression, the Court of Appeal clearly stated that there is a difference between making a positive decision to correct such an impression and being driven in cross-examination to concede its falsity. In the latter case, the accused could derive no benefit from s. 105(3). Nor can an accused expect that answers to questions at interview that are admissible to correct a false impression should be edited out to prevent unfairness: 'if an accused lies in interview and the consequences…are unfortunate, the answer is not to edit out those lies' (*Dixon* [2012] EWCA Crim 2163, where D responded to questions about whether he found children sexually arousing by saying, 'No, it makes me feel sick'. Unknown to the interviewer, D had convictions for sexual assault, including one on a child, which became admissible in consequence).

Examples of False Impression

F12.88   In *Kiernan* [2008] EWCA Crim 972, the accused claimed to have 'paid his debt to society' in relation to an admitted conviction, without mentioning that he had absconded and remained at large. The court observed that he was setting himself up as a reformed character when he was 'nothing of the sort'.

In *Renda* [2006] 2 All ER 553, it was said to be 'most unlikely' to be useful to refer to authorities under the Criminal Evidence Act 1898 in deciding whether an accused has given a 'false impression', which was essentially a question of fact. In that case, where R had clearly misrepresented the nature of his previous employment in an attempt to make himself out to be a man of positive good character, there was indeed little to be gained from such an inquiry. Older decisions, even if only as guides to frequently recurring fact situations, may be of some use, and the leading cases are reproduced for what assistance they might offer in that role.

F12.89   Under the 1898 Act, the shield was not lost where an accused asserted facts relevant to the issue of commission of the offence that incidentally showed him in a good light (*Malindi v The Queen* [1967] AC 439). It was only where he asserted his good character as a separate matter that the shield was down. Under the CJA 2003, the only question is whether he has given a 'false impression' about himself, and it is by no means clear that this leaves the accused the same degree of latitude to present his account of relevant events. Although the statutory definition of 'bad character' is confined to evidence that does not 'have to do with' the facts in issue, there is no corresponding restriction on the meaning of what gives a 'false or misleading impression', though it is submitted that implicitly there must be, for otherwise the judge would have to form a view about the events that are the subject of the charge, and the accused's response to them, in order to decide whether he has given a false impression.

At common law and under the 1898 Act there was doubt as to whether the accused presenting himself as a married man was tantamount to evidence of good character. If the accused is charged with a homosexual offence and chooses to refer to the fact that he has a wife and family (when he has) it would be open to the court to conclude that this is a false impression to the extent that the unspoken but implicit assumption is that he is less likely to have committed the offence charged. This might be sufficient to warrant the admission of evidence of homosexual disposition gleaned from previous convictions. It is also clear that the accused may be held to have given a false impression by means of conduct including dress (s. 105(4) and (5)) but unclear how such a provision permitting rebuttal only to the extent that it is necessary to correct the impression will operate in practice except in the obvious case of a defrocked clergyman (*DS* [1999] Crim LR 911) or its equivalent. Similarly in *Robinson* [2001] EWCA Crim 214 it might be said that an accused who gives evidence waving a Bible is attempting to impress the court with his devotion to the Deity, an impression that might well be false, but only evidence of bad character going directly to the falsity of the impression is admissible in rebuttal.

It would also appear that an accused who adduces evidence of his bad character in order to **F12.90** present himself before the court 'warts and all' may be held to have given a false impression if there are further discreditable revelations to be made. As only prosecution evidence is admissible under s. 101(1)(f), the provision cannot be invoked by a co-accused where one accused is misleadingly trying to present himself, for example, as an experienced burglar with no record for using violence (compare *Bracewell* (1978) 68 Cr App R 44). Such evidence would however appear to be admissible under s. 101(1)(e).

'Attack on Another Person's Character'

The CJA 2003, s. 101(1)(g), permits the prosecution to adduce evidence of bad character to **F12.91** counter an attack on another person. In *Assani* [2008] EWCA Crim 2563, the Court of Appeal drew attention to s. 106(3), which limits the admissibility of bad character evidence under s. 101(1)(g) to prosecution evidence. Applications by one co-accused to adduce evidence of bad character against another fall to be dealt with under s. 101(1)(e) (see **F12.67**). Section 101(1)(g) is supplemented by s. 106, which details the circumstances in which such an attack occurs. An accused may apply to exclude evidence the admission of which under s. 101(1)(g) would have an unfair effect on the fairness of the proceedings (s. 101(3)).

Criminal Justice Act 2003, s. 106

(1) For the purposes of section 101(1)(g) a defendant makes an attack on another person's character if—
    (a) he adduces evidence attacking the other person's character,
    (b) he (or any legal representative appointed under section 38(4) of the Youth Justice and Criminal Evidence Act 1999 to cross-examine a witness in his interests) asks questions in cross-examination that are intended to elicit such evidence, or are likely to do so, or
    (c) evidence is given of an imputation about the other person made by the defendant—
        (i) on being questioned under caution, before charge, about the offence with which he is charged, or
        (ii) on being charged with the offence or officially informed that he might be prosecuted for it.
(2) In subsection (1) 'evidence attacking the other person's character' means evidence to the effect that the other person—
    (a) has committed an offence (whether a different offence from the one with which the defendant is charged or the same one), or
    (b) has behaved, or is disposed to behave, in a reprehensible way; and 'imputation about the other person' means an assertion to that effect.
(3) Only prosecution evidence is admissible under section 101(1)(g).

'Attack'   The CJA 2003, s. 106, uses the word 'imputation', which had specific connotations **F12.92** under the Criminal Evidence Act 1898, s. 1(3)(ii). In the context of the CJA 2003, however, the term is more precisely defined. The accused must either adduce evidence or he (or his representative appointed to cross-examine a witness whom the accused may not cross-examine in person) must ask a question, the effect of which is to suggest that another person has committed an offence or is otherwise of bad character within the meaning of the CJA 2003, s. 98. Thus the old law about what constitutes an imputation is of peripheral relevance, though it might assist as to what is 'reprehensible' behaviour or disposition. In *Lamalatie* (2008) 172 JP 249 the Court of Appeal considered that an allegation that the complainant had started the fight in which he was injured by L would probably be an allegation of 'reprehensible conduct' under the CJA 2003, whatever the position under the old law. In *Matthews* [2013] EWCA Crim 2238 the accused was charged with assault by penetration of a baby left in his care by the mother, R. On the facts, either M or R must have been responsible for the assault. A defence application was made under the CJA 2003, s. 100 (see **F14**) to admit evidence of the mother's bad character, including her substantial record for dishonesty. The prosecution made clear that if the defence pursued the admission of such evidence it would in turn make an application under s. 101(1)(g) to adduce M's own bad character. Although the mere suggestion that the mother caused the injuries would constitute an 'attack' under s. 106, the prosecution may see fit to invoke it only where the defence make an issue of the other person's bad character. Questions asked of the accused on behalf of the prosecution do not trigger the provision (cf. *Jones* (1909) 3 Cr App R 67), although it appears, paradoxically perhaps, that questioning at interview may have this effect (s. 106(1)(c)). Perhaps the authorities under the 1898 Act might be brought to bear on an accused who has been driven into making an attack at interview, given that a frightened or blustering suspect might be particularly likely to overstate his case under interrogation.

F12.93   Evidence of the bad character of a non-defendant is admissible only with the leave of the court under the CJA 2003, s. 100 (see **F14** and *Matthews*). It follows that an 'attack' for the purposes of s. 101(1)(g) based on evidence adduced by the defence will have been preceded by the granting of such leave, and therefore the evidence or question must concern a matter that is important explanatory evidence or is of substantial probative value in relation to an important matter in the case. A gratuitous attack designed merely to blacken the non-defendant's character in an attempt to secure an unmeritorious acquittal will not pass muster under this provision — the 'attack' must be merited. It seems therefore to be unnecessarily punitive to provide that it should (subject to the discretion of the court under s. 101(3): see **F12.97**) be met with apparently unlimited revelations about the accused's own character — revelations that, under the CJA 2003, are admissible for all purposes to which they are relevant (see **F12.23**) — but this appears to be the case.

F12.94   As with s. 101(1)(f) (see **F12.85**), the attack may be made in an out-of-court statement, including an interview in which the accused casts an imputation (s. 106(1)(c)). Again there is no requirement that the evidence of the attack is adduced by the defence, thus in one of the appeals heard with *Renda* [2006] 2 All ER 553 (that of Ball), B was charged with rape and in the course of interview referred to the complainant as 'a slag', criticising her promiscuity in 'very disparaging terms'. His defence at trial was that she was lying and perhaps motivated by a wish for vengeance for past slights. The trial judge's decision to admit evidence of B's bad character on the strength of the specific slights in the interview which had been adduced as part of the prosecution case was supported by the Court of Appeal as a proper exercise of his discretion. Section 106, unlike s. 105 (which supplements s. 101(1)(f)), does not contain a provision permitting the accused to disassociate himself from the imputation. However, the court's discretion to disallow the admission of evidence of bad character could be invoked where the defence does not seek to maintain the attack. In *Nelson* [2006] EWCA Crim 3412, the court questioned the relevance of statements at interview adduced by the prosecution and expressed the view that such evidence should not be adduced simply to provide a basis for gateway (g).

F12.95   **'On Another Person's Character'**   Section 101(1)(g) of the CJA 2003, together with the supplementary provision of s. 106, appears to contemplate an attack on a specific person. It would not therefore be sufficient, where a crime has clearly been committed by someone, for the accused to say that he has not done it and to lay the blame on some unknown individual. Where a specific attack is made, however, it does not matter that the person attacked is not a witness in the case. Thus the problems that arose under the Criminal Evidence Act 1898, s. 1(3), which had to be amended in order to include imputations against the deceased in a homicide case, do not arise in relation to the CJA 2003: an attack on any victim may trigger s. 101(1)(g), as may an attack on any other non-witness. Nor is it necessary, for the same reason, to consider whether a person whose hearsay statement is before the court and who is the subject of an attack by the defence is a 'witness': whether he is or not, the attack still triggers the provision (cf. *Miller* [1997] 2 Cr App R 178). In *Nelson* [2006] EWCA Crim 3412, it was, however, suggested that it would be unusual for evidence of an accused's bad character to be admitted where the only basis for doing so was an attack on a non-witness who is also a non-victim. On the facts of that case, however, the person whose character was attacked was alleged to have been conspiring with a prosecution witness, which provided a proper foundation for gateway (g).

Where the Accused Does Not Testify   Under the Criminal Evidence Act 1898, s. 1(3), the   **F12.96**
accused who made an attack could resist the introduction of his own bad character in retaliation because he was not putting his own character in issue, merely that of the witness. It followed that his bad character was admissible only where specifically permitted by the 1898 Act, i.e. where he gave evidence (*Butterwasser* [1948] 1 KB 4). Under the CJA 2003, however, the accused's bad character may be deployed against him whether he gives evidence or not. This reform was part of the package recommended by the Law Commission, and it is submitted that it is sound in principle. Where the jury have to decide between competing versions of events, the argument that they need to know the character of the person making the attack is as strong where the accused testifies as where he declines to do so.

Discretion   Section 101(3) of the CJA 2003 (see **F12.18**) places the court under a duty to   **F12.97**
exclude evidence where to admit it under s. 101(1)(g) would have such an adverse effect on the fairness of the proceedings that the court ought not to do so. As to the considerations to be taken into account, the view of the Court of Appeal in *Clarke* (2011) 175 JP 281, following a review of the authorities, was that there is no need for the prosecution to demonstrate that evidence of bad character, to be relevant to credibility, demonstrates an underlying propensity to untruthfulness. The purpose of s. 101(1)(g) is identical to the corresponding provision of the Criminal Evidence Act 1898, of which it was said (in *Jenkins* (1945) 31 Cr App R 1) that, where an attack is made, 'it is only fair that the jury should have before them material on which they can form their judgement whether the accused person is any more worthy to be believed than those he has attacked'. The concept is of the general credit of the accused rather than the narrower concept of propensity to untruthfulness arising in relation to s. 101(1)(d) (see **F12.44**). In making their decision, a jury should be permitted recourse to material bearing on the whole of the accused's bad character, not merely those parts that relate specifically to veracity. Defence counsel had relied on the case of *Chrysostomou* [2010] EWCA Crim 1403, in which the Court of Appeal had rejected evidence of texts suggesting C was a drug dealer in relation to an attack by him consisting of an allegation that the complainant of the offence was a user of drugs who owed money to others. *Chrysostomou* appeared to suggest that the test to be applied was that the bad character evidence had to do more than 'blacken the character' of the accused and by doing so to 'dent his credibility generally'. The Court in *Clarke* stated (at [33]) that these observations, if taken to suggest that the bad character evidence should focus more narrowly on credibility, 'do not properly reflect the test which this court has applied when dealing with applications to adduce evidence under paragraph (g)'. However it was important that the evidence adduced should reflect the character of the accused at the time of trial, so that, for example, some old convictions might properly be rejected, particularly those demonstrating propensity to commit the offence charged. See also *Hearne* (2009) 173 JP 97 and *Lamaletie* (2008) 172 JP 249. Note that the evidence in *Chrysostomou* did not involve clear proof of offending: this might be an alternative reason for exercising the discretion against the use of the text evidence concerned.

In *W* [2011] EWCA Crim 472 it was said that authorities on the exercise of discretion under the Criminal Evidence Act 1898 should not be cited in relation to s. 101(3), but the Court of Appeal acknowledged that the matters being relied upon, which were the extent of the allegations against the child complainant and the way in which the questioning of her took place, would as a matter of common sense be relevant to the new provision. Older decisions which might, it is submitted, be pertinent to s. 101(3), if only as guidance, include those applicable to the level of detail that it is legitimate to include about earlier offences when the prime purpose of the evidence adduced by the prosecution is to undermine the credibility of the attack made by the defendant (*McLeod* [1994] 3 All ER 254).

OFFENCES COMMITTED BY ACCUSED WHEN A CHILD

F12.98   **Criminal Justice Act 2003, s. 108**

(1) Section 16(2) and (3) of the Children and Young Persons Act 1963 (offences committed by person under 14 disregarded for purposes of evidence relating to previous convictions) shall cease to have effect.

(2) In proceedings for an offence committed or alleged to have been committed by the defendant when aged 21 or over, evidence of his conviction for an offence when under the age of 14 is not admissible unless—

(a) both of the offences are triable only on indictment, and

(b) the court is satisfied that the interests of justice require the evidence to be admissible.

(2A) and (2B) [Omitted]

(3) Subsection (2) applies in addition to section 101.

Subsections (2A) and (2B), provide for the treatment of previous convictions outside England and Wales. Their broad effect is that a foreign conviction is treated as being admissible if the corresponding offence in England and Wales would be so treated.

The limitation on admissibility of convictions of offences committed by children was introduced at a late stage of the passage through Parliament of the Criminal Justice Bill to mollify strong opposition to the Bill. In *Clark* [2014] EWCA Crim 1053, the Court of Appeal was unable to discern why the provision is geared to defendants under the age of 21 rather than the more natural 18. As C was 19, she was unable to benefit from the provision but thought that in any event 'all judges in this context will be sensitive to an attempt to rely on previous convictions which occurred when the offender was a child'. In the event C's offences exhibited a strong relevant propensity to violence and were rightly admitted. Only where the conviction is for a serious offence (such as rape) and the interests of justice require admissibility should reference be made to offences committed when the accused was a child.

PREVIOUS MISCONDUCT ADMISSIBLE UNDER THE THEFT ACT 1968, s. 27(3)

F12.99   **Theft Act 1968, s. 27**

(3) Where a person is being proceeded against for handling stolen goods (but not for any offence other than handling stolen goods), then at any stage of the proceedings, if evidence has been given of his having or arranging to have in his possession the goods the subject of the charge, or of his undertaking or assisting in, or arranging to undertake or assist in, their retention, removal, disposal or realisation, the following evidence shall be admissible for the purpose of proving that he knew or believed the goods to be stolen goods—

(a) evidence that he has had in his possession, or has undertaken or assisted in the retention, removal, disposal or realisation of, stolen goods from any theft taking place not earlier than 12 months before the offence charged; and

(b) (provided that seven days' notice in writing has been given to him of the intention to prove the conviction) evidence that he has within the five years preceding the date of the offence charged been convicted of theft or of handling stolen goods.

The Theft Act 1968, s. 27(3), applies to all forms of handling (*Ball* [1983] 2 All ER 1089). It can be relied upon by the prosecution only in a case where handling is the only offence involved in the proceedings (*Gardner v New Forest Magistrates' Court* (5 June 1998 unreported)). The provisions of s. 27 are unaffected by the changes made to the admissibility of character evidence at common law by chapter 1 of part 11 of the CJA 2003, although the wider provisions in the CJA for the admissibility of evidence of previous convictions may form an attractive alternative for prosecutors.

F12.100   Section 27 assists only in the proof of guilty knowledge or belief. It may not assist the prosecution where an issue arises as to dishonesty (*Duffas* (1994) 158 JP 224), nor may it be used to prove possession of the goods in question: indeed, the provision cannot be relied upon unless the prosecution have already adduced evidence of the *actus reus* of the handling offence. The mere fact that possession is disputed is not of itself a bar to the use of s. 27 by the prosecution (*List* [1966] 3 All ER 710, per Roskill J, construing the corresponding provision of the Larceny Act 1916). Where, however, the jury will be faced with a number of counts, in some of which possession is in issue and in some of which the issue is guilty knowledge, it was held in *Wilkins* [1975] 2 All ER 734, that 'very great care should be exercised by the judge first of all before he allows evidence of the previous convictions to be given at all or, if he does allow that evidence to be admitted, very great care should be exercised in order to ensure that the jury realise the issues to which those previous convictions are relevant'. *Wilkins* was decided under s. 27(3)(b), but it is submitted that precisely the same considerations apply to evidence adduced under s. 27(3)(a).

Restrictive Construction

It has been the practice of the courts to construe both limbs of the Theft Act 1968, s. 27(3), in   **F12.101** a restrictive way. In *Bradley* (1979) 70 Cr App R 200, the Court of Appeal noted that the section gives the power to introduce evidence that would otherwise not be regarded as relevant, and would therefore be inadmissible, and concluded that it should therefore be construed 'with strict regard to its terms'. In particular, it was held that s. 27(3)(a) does not authorise the giving in evidence of the details of the transaction by which the earlier stolen property had come into the hands of the accused. *Bradley* was applied in *Wood* [1987] 1 WLR 779, in which the Court of Appeal noted a conflict between *Bradley* and the earlier case of *Smith* [1918] 2 KB 415, the decision in *Bradley* being preferred. In *Fowler* (1988) 86 Cr App R 219, *Bradley* was applied to s. 27(3)(b), the court noting that a 'bare recital of conviction is all that is required, and possibly all that it is permissible to provide the jury with'. However, in *Hacker* [1994] 1 All ER 45, it was held by the House of Lords that s. 27(3)(b) must be read together with the PACE 1984, s. 73(2), under which a certificate of conviction of an offence on indictment must give 'the substance and effect (omitting the formal parts) of the indictment and of the conviction'. It followed that where H, who was charged with handling the bodyshell of a car, had a previous conviction for receiving a car, the detail of the subject-matter of the previous conviction, as it appeared on the certificate, was admissible. A similar proposition was advanced with regard to a previous summary conviction. The House of Lords noted that s. 27 had been extensively criticised, but considered that 'not to be able to show what goods had been stolen or handled on a previous occasion might work in some cases to the disadvantage of the defendant himself' (per Lord Slynn at p. 1665).

Discretion

Where evidence is strictly admissible under the Theft Act 1968, s. 27(3), the court has a   **F12.102** power to exclude it at common law or under the PACE 1984, s. 78 (*Hacker* [1994] 1 All ER 45; and see also *Herron* [1967] 1 QB 107, *Smith* (1976) 64 Cr App R 217 and *Perry* [1984] Crim LR 680).

SPENT CONVICTIONS

The Rehabilitation of Offenders Act 1974, s. 4(1), lays down a general rule that a person whose   **F12.103** conviction is 'spent' under the Act is to be treated as a person who has not committed or been charged with or prosecuted for or convicted of or sentenced for the offence or offences which were the subject of that conviction. Section 7(2)(a) excludes criminal proceedings from the operation of this general rule, although the accused is to an extent protected from the use of spent convictions in cross-examination on his record by CPD V, paras. 35A.1 to 35A.3 (see Supplement, **PD-47**, and **D20.49**) which directs the court to have regard to the spirit of the 1974 Act by refusing to allow any mention to be made of a spent conviction, except where it is in the interests of justice to do so. In essence this produces the same test as in civil proceedings that *are* covered by s. 4(1), but in respect of which s. 7(3) provides for evidence of spent convictions to be admitted if justice cannot otherwise be done (*Thomas v Commissioner of Police of the Metropolis* [1997] QB 813, in which careful consideration is given to the relevant criminal authorities). In *Corelli* [2001] EWCA Crim 974 it was held that the effect of s. 7 in combination with the absence of discretion to restrain one accused from cross-examining another on admissible evidence of bad character is that the practice direction which then applied (which was in similar terms to CPD V, paras. 35A.1 to 35A.3) had no application as between co-accused. As the judge has no discretion to restrain a co-accused, it could not be employed to modify the clear words of the 1974 Act. The provisions of the CJA 2003, s. 108 (see **F12.98**), where they apply, constitute an absolute prohibition on the introduction of the criminal record of the accused in respect of offences committed when a child, whether spent or not.

Section F13 Character Evidence: Admissibility of Evidence of Accused's Good Character

INTRODUCTION

History

The practice of permitting an accused person to raise evidence of good character as part of **F13.1** his defence has been described as an anomaly (*Rowton* (1865) Le & Ca 520, per Martin B, at p. 537), and so it is, particularly when viewed in the light of the more restrictive rules restraining the prosecution from introducing evidence of bad character as part of the case against him. Nevertheless, the practice has a long pedigree: early examples are *Turner* (1664) 6 St Tr 565, at p. 613, and *Harris* (1680) 7 St Tr 926, at p. 929. The practice is founded on a notion of indulgence rather than of right: Lord Goddard CJ in *Butterwasser* [1948] KB 4, at p. 6, spoke of a practice, stretching over 200 years, of 'allowing' a prisoner to call evidence of good character.

The questions which arise are as to the purpose for which such evidence may be relied upon; the direction which should be given to a jury; the nature of the evidence which may be adduced in support of a claim to good character, and the kind of evidence which may be adduced in rebuttal by the prosecution or, where relevant, by a co-accused.

The provisions of the CJA 2003 do not affect the entitlement of a person of good character to present himself as such: the Act deals only with the admissibility of evidence of bad character in criminal proceedings. To the extent, however, that the 2003 Act admits more by way of evidence of bad character, some accused may forfeit all or part of the good character direction to which they were previously entitled (*Doncaster* (2008) 172 JP 202: see **F13.15**). Where evidence of bad character may be admitted in rebuttal of an assertion of good character (see **F13.23**), the provisions of the CJA 2003 may come into play.

Purpose of Adducing Evidence of Good Character

The accused was entitled to adduce evidence of his good character long before the law treated **F13.2** him as a competent witness in his own defence (*Vye* [1993] 3 All ER 241 at p. 474). Such evidence was said by Patteson J in *Stannard* (1837) 7 C & P 673 (at pp. 674–5) to point to the improbability of guilt:

> I cannot in principle make any distinction between evidence of facts, and evidence of character: the latter is equally laid before the jury as the former, as being relevant to the question of guilty or not guilty: the object of laying it before the jury is to induce them to believe, from the improbability that a person of good character should have conducted himself as alleged, that there is some mistake or misrepresentation in the evidence on the part of the prosecution, and it is strictly evidence in the case.

When the accused became competent to give evidence, evidence of good character acquired the further function of enhancing his credibility as a witness. Although historically a subsidiary purpose, evidence of good character came to be regarded as 'primarily a matter which goes

F

2625

Part F Evidence

to credibility' (*Bellis* [1966] 1 All ER 552). But good character remained relevant to the issue of guilt, and *Stannard* was approved in *Bryant* [1979] QB 108. The modern tendency is to lay equal emphasis upon both functions of evidence of good character. In *Aziz* [1996] AC 41 Lord Steyn said (at p. 50): 'It has long been recognised that the good character of a defendant is logically relevant to his credibility and to the likelihood that he would commit the offence in question'.

DIRECTIONS

The Need for a Jury Direction

F13.3   In *Aziz* [1996] AC 41, Lord Steyn said that, as evidence of good character is evidence of probative significance, fairness dictates that the judge should direct on it. Failure to give an appropriate direction is likely to be of significance on appeal (*Fulcher* [1995] 2 Cr App R 251), but may not be decisive standing alone if the prosecution case is strong and there are no other successful grounds of appeal (*Balson v The State* [2005] UKPC 2; *Jagdeo Singh v The State of Trinidad and Tobago* [2006] 4 All ER 781; *Maye v The Queen* [2008] UKPC 35; *Brown v The State of Trinidad and Tobago* [2012] 1 WLR 1577 and see *Muirhead v The Queen* [2008] UKPC 40, where the conviction was quashed but their lordships failed to agree about the effect of a failure to direct, standing alone). However, where good character is a crucial aspect of the defence case (e.g., where a drugs 'mule' claims to have been an innocent dupe), an inadequate direction may be decisive (*Moustakim* [2008] EWCA Crim 3096). In a case where the accused bears the onus of proof, and credibility is at the forefront of the case, it is of particular importance that an appropriate direction be given (*Soukala-Cacace* [1999] All ER (D) 1120). Similarly in *D* [2012] 1 Cr App R 448, a case of anal rape turning on the complainant's word against that of the accused, the failure to give the modified direction on propensity (which was all that D was entitled to in respect of his lack of previous convictions for sexual offences) led to the quashing of his conviction. In *Williams* [2012] RTR 240 the failure to give a modified direction, which was all that W was entitled to, was a significant factor in overturning his conviction in a case which depended on his assessment of his speed at the time of an accident which was contradicted by an 'army' of prosecution witnesses. There is, however, no obligation for the trial judge to deal with good character unless the issue has been raised by the defence (*Thompson v R* [1998] AC 811; *Brown v The Queen* [2006] 1 AC 1, where it was noted that a judge would be 'ill-advised' to mention good character unless he had been given information from which he could properly and safely do so). It follows that defence counsel is under an obligation to raise the issue in an appropriate case, so that the accused does not lose the benefit that the direction is designed to confer (*Teeluck v The State of Trinidad and Tobago* [2005] 1 WLR 2421). As with judicial failure to direct, however, counsel's omission will be critical only if good character would have made a difference to the outcome (*Smith v R* [2008] UKPC 34). In the somewhat extreme circumstances of *Gilbert v The Queen* [2006] 1 WLR 2108, in which a bishop was convicted of murdering a teenage girl and his character, if not formally put in issue, was very much in the forefront of the defence case, it was said by Lord Woolf that the judge would have been 'well advised' to clarify the situation before deciding how to direct the jury; nevertheless the omission of a good character direction was not fatal to a conviction based on very substantial evidence.

F13.4   The purpose of the direction is to convey to the jury that they ought to take account of relevant evidence of good character, although it would be going too far to suggest that they are bound to give it any weight. The *Crown Court Bench Book* (March 2010) heralds a move towards the judicial crafting of directions to fit individual cases, and away from, 'specimen directions'. However the specimen direction on good character was never a 'mantra that has to be repeated word for word': the question was always whether the direction, taken as a whole, had conveyed the need to take character appropriately into account (*Starmer* [2010] EWCA Crim 1). An expression such as 'you are entitled to consider' is best avoided as it risks giving the jury the impression that they may choose not to consider the evidence at all (*Miah* [1997] 2 Cr App R 12 and *Moustakim* [2008] EWCA Crim 3096, where the expression 'she is entitled to have it argued on her behalf' was held inadequate). *Moustakim* was considered in *Williams* [2014] EWCA Crim 429, where it was noted that a direction that good character could, rather than should, be taken into account might be appropriate where the accused was not, because of his antecedents, entitled to a 'full' direction but only to a modified one. See also *Lloyd* [2000] 2 Cr App R 355 and *Scranage* [2001] EWCA Crim 1171, where it was held that the failure of the judge to express the direction as an affirmative statement (that character was something to be taken into account) was fatal to the conviction. In *Scranage* the issue was whether S had acted dishonestly in transferring a sum wrongly credited to him by his bank, or whether he had, as he said, been trying to teach the bank a lesson. The evidence of good character was of crucial importance. By contrast, in *Sanchez* [2003] EWCA Crim 735 an incorrect direction to the jury that they might (rather than should) consider the evidence of good character in deciding whether S had taken part in drug-smuggling was not fatal to S's conviction, which was based on overwhelming evidence. And in *Rehman* [2006] EWCA Crim 1900, a direction in which the Court of Appeal detected a degree of 'grudging sloppiness' did not affect the safety of the conviction, as the jury would not have construed it as a licence to leave good character out of their deliberations. Where the essential parts of a direction are given, an appeal is unlikely to succeed even if the direction could helpfully have been fuller, for example by mentioning the accused's distinguished career (*Pershad* [2014] EWCA Crim 692).

Where the offence being tried took place many years before, the good character of the accused **F13.5** in the intervening years may be of particular significance, and should not be underplayed (*Small* [2008] EWCA Crim 2788). *Small* was approved in *GJB v R* [2011] EWCA Crim 867, where reference was made to a 'third limb' of the direction, to the effect that the jury might think that because so long has passed since the alleged historic offences, and the accused has committed no offence in that time, it is less likely that he committed the offences charged. The Court of Appeal recognised that this 'third limb' was no more than an adaptation of the normal propensity direction, but it was an important factor in historic sexual abuse cases where the defence is a straightforward denial, and the accused may have little more than his good name to rely on. *Small* and *GJB v R* were considered in *Enrieu* [2011] All ER (D) 96 (Oct), where the Court once more stressed the importance of an undiluted direction in a case of alleged historic abuse where the accused was a person of hitherto unblemished character.

Direction on Credibility where Accused Testifies

Where an accused testifies, the judge must give a direction as to the relevance of good character **F13.6** to the accused's credibility. In *Berrada* (1989) 91 Cr App R 131, B was convicted of attempted rape. At his trial there was a direct conflict between the evidence of B on the one hand and of the complainant and police witnesses on the other. The trial judge's direction was held to have been defective in that it made no mention of the relevance of evidence of B's previous good character. Waterhouse J said (at p. 134):

> In the judgment of this court, the appellant was entitled to have put to the jury from the judge herself a correct direction about the relevance of his previous good character to his credibility. That is a conventional direction and it is regrettable that it did not appear in the summing-up in this case.

Conventionally, the direction on credibility has become known as the 'first limb' of a character direction, with the 'second limb' consisting of a statement as to the relevance of character to the question whether the accused was likely to have committed the offence. The need for a 'first limb' direction was reaffirmed in *Vye* [1993] 3 All ER 241, where the authorities are reviewed, and *Aziz* [1996] AC 41, in which the House of Lords treats the point as settled by *Vye*. In *Jagdeo Singh v The State of Trinidad and Tobago* [2006] 4 All ER 781 it was held that a 'first limb' direction should not be implied from a direction on the second limb, or be conveyed by a vague phrase such as that good character is a matter to consider 'when you deal with the

Part F Evidence

evidence of the accused'. In that case, the accused was a lawyer of good character, and the key issue related to the veracity of his account of a meeting with a witness whose character was bad. Lord Bingham opined that a jury could not be assumed to have inferred that the accused was a man of probity without a specific direction to that effect, as 'the belief of lawyers in their own probity is not universally shared'.

Direction on Credibility where Accused Does Not Testify

F13.7   In *Vye* [1993] 3 All ER 241, the Court of Appeal further decided that where the accused has not given evidence at trial but relies on admissible exculpatory statements made to the police or others, the judge should direct the jury to have regard to the accused's good character when considering the credibility of those statements. The court thought it 'logical' that such evidence should be taken into account, but drew attention also to the judge's entitlement to make observations about the weight to be given to such exculpatory statements in contrast to evidence on oath (see *Duncan* (1981) 73 Cr App R 359 at **F17.94**, and see generally, as to the point at which statements that are exculpatory become admissible for the defence, **F17.93** *et seq.*). In *Aziz* [1996] AC 41, the House of Lords accepted that this 'clearcut' rule in *Vye* represented the best policy. Where an exculpatory statement was evidence in the case, the credibility of the accused who had given that account was a matter of evidential significance requiring a direction (see also *Woodward* [1996] Crim LR 207, *Garrod* [1997] Crim LR 445 and *Patel* [2010] EWCA Crim 976, where the omission to direct was, on the facts, 'inconsequential').

Vye also decides that, where an accused of good character does not give evidence and has given no pre-trial answers or statements upon which reliance is placed, a 'first limb' direction is not required as no issue as to his credibility arises.

Direction on Propensity

F13.8   The 'second limb' of a character direction deals with the unlikelihood that a person of previous good character would commit the offence charged. In *Vye* [1993] 3 All ER 241, the Court of Appeal was unable to discern any principle or consistent pattern in the earlier authorities as to when a 'second limb' direction should be given and when it need not, and in order to resolve the uncertainty surrounding the issue decided that such a direction should be given in all cases where an accused is of good character, whether he testifies or not. In *Aziz* [1996] AC 41, the House of Lords, while recognising that *Vye* involved a 'policy decision', agreed that the move away from a discretionary system to a settled rule of practice was justified and would reduce the number of appeals.

Vye was applied in *Wren* [1993] Crim LR 952, where it was observed that failure to give a 'second limb' direction might not attract the quashing of a conviction; see also *Anderson* [1995] Crim LR 430. The obligation is, in any event, subject to the judge's entitlement to make observations qualifying the importance of good character, for example by emphasising that it is not in itself a defence and that in some cases the jury may derive limited assistance from the evidence. The example given in *Vye* is where an accused who is charged with murder admits manslaughter, so that the argument that he has never stooped to murder before is countered by the fact that he has never committed manslaughter either. Everything, however, depends on the relevance of the evidence in the circumstances: in *Paria v The State of Trinidad and Tobago* [2003] UKPC 36 the Privy Council pointed out that a defence of provocation might be supported by the argument that a man of good character would have been unlikely to kill unless provoked into a complete loss of self-control (see also *Langton v The State* (Privy Council Appeal No. 35 of 1999 unreported)). In *Fitton* [2001] EWCA Crim 215, the Court of Appeal disagreed with a suggestion that the good character of a nightclub doorman charged with assaulting a customer was less persuasive when the offence was spontaneous: rather the good character of a doorman who is routinely exposed to spontaneous violence may be worth a great deal. More recently, in *Zielinski* [2007] EWCA Crim 704, the Court of Appeal held that a lack of clarity in the second limb of the direction was not fatal where the charge of inflicting grievous bodily harm in a 'road rage' incident involved no more than the reckless use of force: the case was not one in which 'lack of propensity to offend was of such significance as it might have been in many other kinds of alleged offending'.

Where a direction is given about the relevance of good character to guilt it is wrong and unfair **F13.9** to suggest that such evidence comes into play only where the remainder of the evidence leaves the jury in doubt. Evidence of good character is part of the totality of the evidence upon which the jury are to decide whether there is any doubt about guilt (*Handbridge* [1993] Crim LR 287, endorsing the statement of law to this effect in an earlier edition of this work, and see also *Falconer-Atlee* (1973) 58 Cr App R 349 at pp. 357–8). Earlier authorities to the contrary, particularly *Bliss Hill* (1918) 13 Cr App R 125, should, it is submitted, be regarded as wrong on this point.

Where One Accused is of Good Character but Another is Not

The difficulty facing a trial judge in the situation where one accused is of good character but **F13.10** another is not is that by commenting on the good character of the one he may be taken to be highlighting the bad character of the other. Nevertheless the Court of Appeal in *Vye* [1993] 3 All ER 241 held, disapproving of compromise solutions suggested in earlier authorities such as *Gibson* (1991) 93 Cr App R 9, that the accused of good character is entitled to the same direction as if he had stood trial alone. This aspect of *Vye* was applied in *Houlden* (1994) 99 Cr App R 244. The possession of disparate characters is said in *Vye* to be a factor to be considered in deciding whether separate trials are needed, but there is no rule in favour of separate trials in such cases. Where no evidence is put in of the record of the accused with bad character, the judge has a discretion whether to comment about that accused when summing-up (*Shepherd* [1995] Crim LR 153). Where, however, the jury has been told of his previous convictions, the accused is entitled to an appropriate direction as to the use which may be made of them (*Cain* [1994] 2 All ER 398). Where a judge mistakenly attributes convictions to the wrong co-accused counsel should be consulted as to the best way to correct the error (*Purdy* [2007] EWCA Crim 295).

MEANING OF GOOD CHARACTER

Absence of Previous Convictions, Cautions etc. and 'Effective' Good Character

An accused may lay claim to a good character not only where he can adduce positive evidence **F13.11** to that effect, but also where he can truthfully assert that he has no previous convictions (*Aziz* [1996] AC 41). By extension, where a conviction or other evidence detracting from good character is such as to be irrelevant or insignificant in relation to the offence charged, a good character direction is normally given, though the matter is one for the discretion of the judge (*Gray* [2004] 2 Cr App R 498). There is no room in this context for the narrow argument that admission or conviction of offences of dishonesty do not necessarily impinge on the credibility of the accused. While it may not amount to evidence of a propensity to untruthfulness, a dishonest character is relevant to the credibility of evidence (*King* [2012] EWCA Crim 805). Even where a caution in itself is of minor importance, the jury must not be misled by any claim made by the accused, so cautions cannot simply be ignored (*Martin* [2000] 2 Cr App R 42; *Maillett* [2005] EWCA Crim 3159), although it is ultimately a matter of discretion whether the direction is given in whole or (as in *Martin*) in part. As with convictions, the exercise of discretion in relation to a caution becomes necessary where the matter admitted may not be relevant, on a fair view, either to the issue of guilt or credibility or both (*I* [2012] EWCA Crim 2033). Similarly, an accused cannot conceal the fact that he has been found guilty by a foreign court where its findings are not regarded as 'convictions' until confirmed on appeal (*El Delbi* [2003] EWCA

Crim 1767), or that he has admitted some other criminal behaviour (e.g., in *Aziz*, where one of the respondents admitted making a false mortgage application). An accused who sets himself up as of 'exemplary' character cannot complain if the disreputable circumstances of his bankruptcy are made known (*Khan* [2008] 3 All ER 502).

F13.12   In *Hamer* [2011] 1 WLR 528 it was held that the issuing of a penalty notice for disorder (PND) involves neither proof of the commission of a crime nor the admission that a crime has been committed: rather, the PND provides a deterrent to low-level crime in the form of a 'punishment for suspected offending'. As such it places no stain on the good character of an accused and should be kept from a jury when giving a good character direction. By contrast, a caution may provide evidence of an admission of relevant bad character and, where a caution is adduced for this purpose in respect of an accused who is otherwise of good character, the good character direction may be withheld. However, where the accused challenges the caution before the jury, and the jury are told to ignore the caution if not satisfied that the accused committed the offence for which he was cautioned, it would be wrong not to go on to instruct them to treat him, in the event of such a finding, as a man of good character (*Olu* [2011] 1 Cr App R 404).

F13.13   In *Aziz* [1996] AC 41 the House of Lords held that a trial judge has a limited residual discretion to withhold the directions normally given in accordance with *Vye* [1993] 2 All ER 241 where it would 'make no sense' to give them. The principles stated in *Aziz* and subsequent authorities are helpfully distilled in *Gray* [2004] 2 Cr App R 498. Although the Court of Appeal has since rightly applied the caveat that such distillations should not be taken 'as prescribing precisely what a judge is to do', and that the application of underlying principles so as to ensure fairness is of paramount importance (*Payton* [2006] EWCA Crim 1226), it is nevertheless submitted that the following synopsis, based on *Gray*, provides sound guidance:

(1) The primary rule is that a person of previous good character is entitled to a full direction on both limbs of credibility and propensity. Where there are no further facts to complicate the position the direction is mandatory and should be unqualified.

(2) If an accused has a previous conviction, which, because of its age or its nature, may entitle him to be treated as of effective good character, the trial judge has a discretion so to treat him, and if he does so the accused is entitled to a *Vye* direction (see **F13.17**).

(3) Where the previous conviction can only be regarded as irrelevant or of no significance in relation to the offence charged, the discretion ought to be exercised in favour of treating the accused as of good character and entitled to a *Vye* direction. Thus a judge who has decided that an accused is, for the purposes of the trial, of good character must confer the benefit on him of a good character direction (*Payton*).

(4) Where an accused of previous good character, whether absolute or (it was suggested in *Gray*) effective, has been shown at trial to be guilty of criminal conduct, the prima facie rule of practice is to qualify the *Vye* direction rather than to withhold it.

(5) In such a case there remains a narrowly circumscribed residual discretion to withhold a good character direction, in whole or in part, where it would make no sense or would be meaningless or an insult to common sense to do otherwise (*Zoppola-Barraza* [1994] Crim LR 833, and dicta in *Durbin* [1995] 2 Cr App R 84 and *Aziz*; see also *King* [2012] EWCA Crim 805).

(6) Approved examples of the exercise of the residual discretion are not common. *Zoppola-Barraza* is one, as is *Shaw* [2001] 1 WLR 1519, and see *Alkaitis* [2004] EWCA Crim 1072 where, paradoxically, it was said that the withholding of the direction would have been less damaging than the modified direction given. Lord Steyn in *Aziz* appears to have considered that a person of previous good character who is shown beyond reasonable doubt to have been guilty of serious criminal behaviour similar to the offence charged would forfeit his right to any direction (at p. 53) and a similar view was taken in *Doncaster* (2008) 172 JP 202 in relation to the accused's 'persistent, and serious and closely similar and relevant' previous behaviour. On the other hand Lord Taylor's manslaughter/murder example in *Vye* (see **F13.8**), which was cited again in *Durbin*, shows that even in the context of serious crime it may be crucial that a

critical intent separates the admitted criminality from that charged. (In *King* [2012] EWCA Crim 805 it was the credibility limb of the direction that was held to have been properly withheld after the accused admitted serious offences of dishonesty in the course of the trial. See further, as to the withholding of all or part of the direction, **F13.15**.)

(7) A direction should never be misleading. Where therefore an accused has withheld something of his record so that otherwise a trial judge is not in a position to refer to it, the accused may forfeit the more ample, if qualified, direction that the judge might have been able to give (*Martin* [2002] 2 Cr App R 42).

In *Gray*, the accused, aged 18, was charged with murder following an attack on the victim at **F13.14** his place of work by a group of men, one of whom stabbed him to death. G claimed to have been outside the premises when the fatal assault occurred. He had previous convictions for driving with excess alcohol and (because he was under 17) without licence or insurance. These were minor matters that did not impinge on his right to a direction. He also admitted to minor incidents of violence on the occasion of the murder, including punching a man who was trying to restrain one of the other attackers. The Court of Appeal, having 'wavered' on the question, found that a qualified direction would not have been absurd and that the facts fell within principle (4) rather than (5) above. G should have received a normal credibility direction followed by a modified propensity direction pointing out the difference between the intent required for the crime of murder and that admitted by G. See also *DPP v Varlack* [2008] UKPC 56 (defence to murder involved admission of peripheral involvement in drugs trade). Where a trial judge is minded to qualify either or both limbs of a good character direction, it is better to give the conventional direction, followed by the qualification, rather than to modify the direction (*Press* [2013] EWCA Crim 1849, where the credibility direction was qualified in relation to lies told by the accused at interview, and the propensity direction by reference to evidence that the accused had been drinking heavily at the time he claimed to be acting in self-defence).

It is arguable that in formulating principle (3) above there is a risk of confusion between the lack of evidential significance of bad character and the possession of good character. Thus in *Payton* the accused, who had previous cautions and convictions for possession of cannabis, was charged with possession with intent to supply. The record shed no particular light on the issues for the jury — P had never sought to deny possession when accused of it, so his record was of no use to the prosecution either on the matter of guilt or of credibility. Nevertheless for the court to say, as the current authorities do, that such a person is 'of good character' so as to require a positive *Vye* direction may be a step too far.

A full character direction can clearly not be given where the accused's bad character is admissible **F13.15** both as to propensity and credibility under the CJA 2003, for the two directions would pull in opposite ways. Where such an accused has no previous convictions, this might factor into the judge's direction on bad character as a contra-indication (*Doncaster* (2008) 172 JP 202).

In cases where the court is considering the exercise of the residual discretion to withhold a direction under (5) above, it would seem that each limb should be separately considered. In some cases, both limbs may be withheld, as in *Akram* [1995] Crim LR 50, where it was held that revelations about A's use of heroin meant that he should not have been treated as of good character on charges relating to the possession of diamorphine. See also *Young* [2004] EWCA Crim 3520, where the fundamental lies told by the accused rendered a credibility direction absurd, and his unlawful possession of firearms made the propensity direction inappropriate on a charge of murder. The appellant would have been entitled, at best, to a partial and qualified direction. Alternatively, one limb only may be withheld, as in *Martin* [2002] 2 Cr App R 42, where the propensity limb was withheld at M's trial for robbery on the ground of his previous caution for possession of an offensive weapon. See also *Despaigne-Pellon* [2009] EWCA Crim 2580, where the credibility limb should not have been withheld because of a conviction for assault that the jury had been told to disregard.

In *Sanchez* [2003] EWCA Crim 735, it was held that the trial judge had been entitled to with-hold the credibility limb of the direction where S had previously been cautioned for shoplifting, but had never been involved in anything as serious as the cocaine smuggling with which she was charged. Auld LJ said (at [35]):

> As a simple matter of fairness and plain dealing with the jury, a judge may, if circumstances justify it, give only part of the standard good character direction. Whether he does, and, if so, which part he gives, will necessarily turn on the nature and seriousness of the offence, the subject of the formal caution or reprimand and the nature and degree of its similarity to the charge being considered by the jury. A direction only as to credibility may be right, as was considered in the case of *Martin*, or, where as here, the earlier offence may be relevant to the defendant's credibility, a direction only as to lack of propensity may be appropriate.

Wherever the judge is minded to give a direction which is not likely to be anticipated by counsel, submissions on the proposed direction should first be invited (*Aziz* [1996] AC 41).

F13.16   Failure to raise with the judge the nature of the appropriate direction on character was said in *W* [2004] EWCA Crim 3174 to be 'a very considerable pity', as it would have been likely to result in a direction but with a modified credibility limb when in fact (fatally for the conviction) none was given. In *Gonzales* [2004] EWCA Crim 2117, following discussion that left counsel under the impression that a full direction would be given, the trial judge gave a modified direction that had not been canvassed. The Court of Appeal re-emphasised the importance of discussing with counsel any direction that departs from the normal, full direction, although the conviction was upheld. In *D* [2012] 1 Cr App R 448 the appropriate course of action was said to be to warn counsel that the judge was not minded to give the direction as agreed, and to invite further submissions.

F13.17   **Irrelevant and Insignificant Convictions**   Where the accused has previous convictions, it has been seen (see **F13.11**) that he may nevertheless be of 'effective' good character. If the convictions are 'spent' under the Rehabilitation of Offenders Act 1974 (see **F12.103**), he may, with the leave of the court, be put forward as a person of good character (*Nye* (1982) 75 Cr App R 247; *Bailey* [1989] Crim LR 723). Judicial discretion should, so far as possible, be exercised favourably to the accused, but 'the jury must not be misled and no lie must be told to them about this matter' (*Nye*, per Talbot J, at p. 251). It is similarly a matter for the judge's discretion whether, and if so to what extent, an unspent conviction prevents an accused from being treated as of good character; it might well not have that effect, particularly if it is of a different kind from the offence charged (*Timson* [1993] Crim LR 59: drink-driving conviction should have been regarded as irrelevant to charges involving dishonesty; *H* [1994] Crim LR 205: conviction for possessing an offensive weapon irrelevant to charges involving indecent assault on stepdaughter; *Burnham* [1995] Crim LR 491: 'unrelated' offence of criminal damage should have led to a qualified good character direction). Convictions which have been disregarded in this context are frequently of a minor nature in addition to being for unrelated offences. For example, an offence of strict liability, such as driving without insurance, should not be assumed to have been committed knowingly where the effect would be to deprive the accused of a good character direction to which he is otherwise entitled (*Goss* (2003) *The Times*, 27 October 2003). In *Gray* [2004] 2 Cr App R 498 (see **F13.11**), where the discretion to withhold the direction was described as 'narrowly circumscribed', the fact that the previous convictions were for relatively minor driving offences was, when the accused was charged with murder, a reason for regarding him as of 'effective' good character and entitled to the directions.

F13.18   Where old, spent convictions of an accused are regarded as immaterial, he should receive a full good character direction (*S* [2008] All ER (D) 295 (Nov)). By contrast it may be impossible to disregard a conviction, however ancient, if it bears on an issue of character which is before the jury (*Rackham* [1997] 2 Cr App R 222, where R's sexual preference for young girls was in issue and an old conviction for unlawful sexual intercourse with a 13-year-old was properly regarded as preventing R from presenting himself as of good character).

It has already been observed (see **F13.14**) that the decision in *Payton* [2006] EWCA Crim 1226 to disregard convictions for possession of cannabis on a charge of possession with intent may go too far — the fact that convictions do not assist the prosecution to prove their case should not necessarily be regarded as indicating 'good character' on the part of the accused.

In a case where the accused's previous convictions are not of the sort that would debar him from a good character direction, counsel's failure to seek the leave of the court to treat him as of good character may threaten the safety of the conviction (*Kamar* (1999) *The Times*, 14 May 1999).

Effect of Plea of Guilty A difficult question arises where an accused pleads guilty to one   **F13.19** or more of the offences charged at trial. In *Challenger* [1994] Crim LR 202, C was charged with simple possession of cannabis, possession with intent to supply and possession of an offensive weapon, and pleaded guilty to simple possession; a week later he was tried for the two other offences. It was held that the plea meant that C was no longer of good character and that the question of what direction, if any, was appropriate fell to be dealt with in the judge's discretion, taking account of such matters as the nature of the offence and its similarity to the offence charged, and whether the jury would be misled if C was treated as of good character in circumstances where they had not heard about the plea. The judge's decision to give no direction was upheld, despite the presentation of the case by counsel as one where C was of good character apart from the admitted offence. However in *Teasdale* [1993] 4 All ER 290, T, who was charged with causing grievous bodily harm with intent, pleaded guilty to assault occasioning actual bodily harm in respect of the same incident. It was held that T was to be treated as of good character and was entitled to the full direction in *Vye* [1993] 3 All ER 241 (see **F13.6**). In *Challenger* the facts in *Teasdale* were regarded as giving rise to an exception to the general rule applicable wherever a conviction for the offence charged would result in the pleas of guilty being vacated. It is hard to see why this should be so, as the vacation of the plea on the facts in *Teasdale* would not have meant that T had not assaulted the victim and that therefore her character was unblemished: the admitted offence would merely have been swallowed up by proof of the more serious allegation. It is submitted that the same rule should govern all cases involving guilty pleas, and that the approach in *Challenger* is to be preferred.

Other Discreditable Matters An accused who is otherwise of good character may be shown in   **F13.20** a poor light by matters emerging at trial, e.g., the fact that he has lied to the police at interview. In such a case the judge has a discretion to qualify the direction on good character by commenting on matters which may adversely affect the jury's impression of him. The mere fact that the accused faces charges in other criminal proceedings which have yet to be heard should not be regarded as depriving him of his right to a positive direction (*Warden* (6 July 2000 unreported)).

WITNESSES TO CHARACTER

Since the decision in *Rowton* (1865) Le & Ca 520, it has been the rule that witnesses as to char-   **F13.21** acter must testify to the reputation of the accused, and not to specific good acts or individuals' opinions. Lord Cockburn CJ suggested that the true object of the inquiry was in fact the disposition of the accused, but that it was not the practice to inquire into this directly but to arrive at it by 'giving evidence of his general character founded on his general reputation in the neighbourhood in which he lives'. The result was that 'the prisoner cannot give evidence of particular facts, though one fact might weigh more than the opinion of all his friends and neighbours'. Willes J added two further reasons for the exclusion of particular facts: they lack cogency, as even a robber may perform acts of generosity, and they raise issues of which the prosecution have no notice and on which they cannot enter into argument. Although *Rowton* speaks of the accused's reputation within a particular neighbourhood, the concept is capable of an elastic meaning, and it is not uncommon for character witnesses to come from the same workplace as the accused, or the same church or social organisation.

The *Rowton* rule is difficult to apply where character evidence is elicited by the accused in cross-examination of prosecution witnesses, and in cases where evidence of good character is

F

given by the accused himself. Indeed, it may be doubted whether the accused is competent to give evidence of his own reputation. Yet in *Redgrave* (1982) 74 Cr App R 10, it was held that R, charged with importuning for an immoral purpose, was not entitled to raise evidence of his heterosexual disposition to rebut the charge. The effect of *Rowton* was that the accused could 'do no more than say, or call witnesses to prove, that he was not by general repute the kind of young man who would have behaved in the kind of way that the Crown alleged'. The court noted that a practice had grown up, where allegations of homosexual offences were in issue, of allowing an accused to say that he is happily married and enjoys a normal sexual relationship with his wife, but this was regarded as a special indulgence.

F13.22   **Rebuttal of Good Reputation**   Where an accused has raised the issue of his good reputation, whether by calling witnesses or giving evidence on his own behalf, the prosecution may seek to respond by calling witnesses in rebuttal, to whom the rule in *Rowton* (1865) Le & CA 520 also applies. Thus such witnesses may speak only to the bad reputation of the accused, not to specific bad acts done by him. Under the CJA 2003, the rules by which the common law allows evidence of reputation to prove character, good and bad, are specifically preserved (CJA 2003, ss. 99(2) and 118(1)). The preservation of evidence of good reputation was necessary only in so far as such evidence would otherwise have been hearsay (see **F16.54**). The preservation of the rules permitting evidence of bad reputation was also necessitated by the abolition of the common-law rules as to evidence of bad character generally (CJA 2003, s. 99(1)).

F13.23   **Rebuttal of Good Character other than Reputation**   An accused who refers in favourable terms to his own good disposition in order to strengthen his defence may be held to have made an assertion of good character, which the prosecution are entitled to counter if it is untrue. The reason must be that if the court is prepared to indulge the accused by allowing such evidence to be given, it is only right that it should be open to rebuttal if it is misleading.

Under the provisions of the CJA 2003 regarding evidence of bad character, the right of the prosecution to counter the case put forward by the defence is determined by the provisions of the Act. Section 101(1)(f) of the CJA 2003 provides that evidence of the accused's bad character is admissible 'to correct a false impression given' by the accused. The CJA 2003 covers similar ground to the previous common-law rules permitting a misleading assertion of good character to be corrected, although it appears to be wider in important respects. Section 101(1)(f) is considered at **F12.85**.

Section F14   Character Evidence: Evidence of Bad Character of Persons Other than the Accused

INTRODUCTION

F14.1 This section covers the statutory scheme for the introduction of evidence of the bad character of persons other than the accused. Chapter 1 of part 11 (ss. 98 to 113) of the CJA 2003 abolishes the common-law rules (s. 99(1)), amends the Criminal Procedure Act 1865, s. 6, so that cross-examination on the previous convictions of persons other than the accused becomes subject to the new rules on admissibility (s. 331 and sch. 36, para. 79) and all but codifies the law governing the admissibility of evidence of bad character in criminal cases. However, nothing in the scheme under the CJA 2003 affects the exclusion of evidence under either (a) the rule in the Criminal Procedure Act 1865, s. 3, preventing a party from impeaching the credit of his own witness by general evidence of bad character or (b) the YJCEA 1999, s. 41 (see **F7.22** *et seq.*), which restricts evidence and questions about the complainant's sexual history in proceedings for sexual offences (CJA 2003, s. 112(3)). Evidence of spent convictions may also continue to be excluded by virtue of CPD V, paras. 35A.1 to 35A.3 (see Supplement, **PD–47**, and **D20.49**).

Overarching common-law rules that now require to be read subject to the scheme of the CJA 2003 are covered in this edition under the headings of the 'General Rule against Impeaching Credit of Own Witness', considered at **F6.50**, 'Cross-Examination as to Credit' considered at **F7.16** and the 'Rule of Finality of Answers to Questions on Collateral Matters', considered at **F7.42** *et seq.*

Abolition of the Common-law Rules

F14.2 Section 99(1) of the CJA 2003 abolishes 'the common law rules governing the admissibility of evidence of bad character in criminal proceedings'. Although s. 99(1) refers only to the rules governing the admissibility of evidence of bad character and not, in terms, to the common-law rules governing cross-examination about bad character, it is submitted that the intention is to cover both. As to the questioning of witnesses on their bad character in relation to matters covered by the exceptions to the rule of finality of answers to collateral questions, the common-law rules can certainly be said to 'govern' the admissibility of evidence of bad character, because the matters are put to the witness with a view to eliciting such evidence and, if the matters are denied, they can be proved. The common-law rules permitting the questioning of witnesses on their bad character in relation to matters not covered by the exceptions to the rule of finality may also be said to 'govern' the admissibility of evidence of bad character in that they too are questions put with a view to eliciting such evidence, notwithstanding that if the witness denies the matters put, they cannot be proved. This construction is consistent with the procedural requirements for application to adduce or elicit evidence (see **F14.16**).

'Bad Character'

F14.3
Criminal Justice Act 2003, s. 98

References in this Chapter to evidence of a person's 'bad character' are to evidence of, or of a disposition towards, misconduct on his part, other than evidence which—
(a) has to do with the alleged facts of the offence with which the defendant is charged, or
(b) is evidence of misconduct in connection with the investigation or prosecution of that offence.

This wide definition, that generally reflects the common-law concept of bad character, is considered in detail at **F12.3**, as the definition applies equally to evidence of the bad character of an accused. If evidence of bad character does fall within the statutory definition it can be admitted in evidence only if it satisfies the further conditions of admissibility in s. 100 (non-defendant's bad character) or s. 101 (defendant's bad character). Evidence which, though it shows a person in a bad light, is not evidence of bad character within the meaning of the CJA 2003, s. 98, may be given where it is relevant (see **F12.3** *et seq.*, especially *Scott* [2009] EWCA Crim 2457, in which the efforts of a complainant to contact a friend of the accused despite police warnings to desist were regarded as falling short of 'reprehensible' conduct, but were also lacking in relevance and were therefore inadmissible).

Where the inference of bad character is based on the making by a non-defendant of a previous complaint that is alleged to be false, there must be material to provide a proper evidential basis for the inference of falsity (*Withers* [2010] EWCA Crim 3238).

Bad Character 'to do with' the Facts of the Offence or in Connection with its Investigation or Prosecution

F14.4 Section 99(1) of the CJA 2003 abolishes the common-law rules governing admissibility of evidence of bad character as defined by s. 98. It follows that the common-law rules continue to operate insofar as they permit evidence to be adduced which, looking to the wording of s. 98(a), 'has to do with the alleged facts of the offence' or, looking to the wording of s. 98(b), 'is evidence of misconduct in connection with the investigation or prosecution of that offence'. The general meaning of these phrases is considered at **F12.9** to **F12.11**. A case specifically decided in relation to the CJA 2003, s. 100, is *Machado* (2006) 170 JP 400, where evidence tending to show the alleged victim of a robbery had taken drugs was held to be within the words 'has to do with the alleged facts of the offence', as providing support for the defence explanation of his sudden collapse (the prosecution having alleged that the accused pushed him over). An admission of guilt by a co-accused to participation in an offence charged against the accused 'has to do with' the offence charged and is not evidence of the co-accused's bad character (*Smith* [2007] EWCA Crim 2105). Such evidence can, however, be admitted only under the PACE 1984, s.74, which is to be sparingly applied (see **F11.6** *et seq.*).

Section 98(b) of the CJA 2003 would seem apt to cover, for example, evidence that during the investigation the police obtained evidence unlawfully or unfairly (e.g., by fabricating a confession or planting evidence on the accused or in his premises); evidence that during interview the police told lies; and evidence that during the investigation or proceedings the police, or someone on behalf of either the police or accused, had sought to intimidate potential witnesses.

CRIMINAL JUSTICE ACT 2003, s. 100

Background to the Criminal Justice Act 2003, s. 100

F14.5 At common law, a witness other than the accused could be cross-examined, in order to impeach his credibility, about his previous misconduct, e.g., about acts of dishonesty or immorality on his part, about lies he told or false allegations he made, about his drink or drug abuse, and so on. However, insofar as the questions could properly be said to be on collateral matters and the witness denied them, evidence was admissible in rebuttal only exceptionally. The exceptions covered previous convictions, bias and general reputation for untruthfulness (see **F7.42** *et seq.*). Since the purpose of cross-examination as to credit is to show that a witness ought not to be believed on his oath, at common law the matters about which he is questioned must relate to his likely standing after cross-examination with the tribunal which is trying him (per Lawton LJ in *Sweet-Escott* (1971) 55 Cr App R 316, considered at **F7.16**). Despite this important limitation, the Law Commission proposed further restrictions, for three reasons: the power of evidence of bad character to distort the fact-finding process, the need to encourage witnesses to give evidence, and the need for courts 'to control gratuitous and offensive cross-examination of little or no purpose other than to intimidate or embarrass the witness or muddy the waters' ((Law Com No. 273 (2001), para. 9.35).

The views of the Commission are reflected in the terms of the CJA 2003, s. 100.   **F14.6**

Criminal Justice Act 2003, s. 100

(1) In criminal proceedings evidence of the bad character of a person other than the defendant is admissible if and only if—
    (a) it is important explanatory evidence,
    (b) it has substantial probative value in relation to a matter which—
        (i) is a matter in issue in the proceedings, and
        (ii) is of substantial importance in the context of the case as a whole,
    or
    (c) all parties to the proceedings agree to the evidence being admissible.

Although, on its face, s. 100 governs only the admissibility of evidence of bad character and does not, in terms, govern the asking of questions in cross-examination about bad character (cf., in this regard, YJCEA 1999, s. 41), it is submitted that the intention is to cover both. This would be consistent with the interpretation of s. 99(1) of the Act that it abolishes the common-law rules relating not only to the admissibility of evidence of bad character but also to cross-examination of witnesses about bad character (see **F14.2**). Section 100 covers evidence of the bad character of any person other than the accused, whether or not called as a witness, and whether the evidence is to be adduced or elicited by or on behalf of the prosecution, the accused or any co-accused. The use of s. 100 is not limited to evidence going directly to the issue of guilt or innocence: the undermining of a witness's credibility is a legitimate objective of adducing evidence under s. 100 (*Yaxley-Lennon*, one of the appeals heard with *Weir* [2006] 2 All ER 570 at [73]). To decide otherwise, said the Court of Appeal, would mean that there was a significant lacuna in the legislation, creating the potential for unfairness.

In *Phillips* [2012] 1 Cr App R 332, decided under s. 101(1)(e) (evidence of the accused's bad character adduced by co-accused: see **F12.70**), the Court of Appeal noted that both s. 101(1)(e) and s. 100(1) 'have the capacity to change the landscape of a trial' and it was suggested that a strict reading of 'substantial' probative value and 'substantial' importance was required in order to ensure fairness and prevent unnecessary satellite issues. It was suggested (at p. 348) that substantial probative value means 'an enhancement of the capacity of the evidence to prove or disprove the fact in issue'. *Phillips* was applied, in relation to s. 100, in *Walsh* [2012] EWCA Crim 2728. In *Dizaei* [2013] 1 WLR 2257 the Court of Appeal expressed concern (at [37]) that a trial to determine whether the accused had committed an offence could be 'derailed' if a jury became unduly concerned with whether a witness had committed other, separate crimes. In the absence of any discretion under s. 100 to regulate satellite issues generated by the defence, the Court considered that a trial judge's consideration of what was of 'substantial' probative value might legitimately take account of the risk such issues pose to the jury's grasp of the remainder of the evidence. See further **F14.10** and **F14.16**.

Gateways to Admissibility

(a) Important Explanatory Evidence   **F14.7**

Criminal Justice Act 2003, s. 100

(2) For the purposes of subsection (1)(a) evidence is important explanatory evidence if—
    (a) without it, the court or jury would find it impossible or difficult properly to understand other evidence in the case, and
    (b) its value for understanding the case as a whole is substantial.

Section 100(2) covers evidence of, or a disposition towards, misconduct on the part of someone other than the accused without which the account before the court or jury would be incomplete or incoherent. Thus if the matter to which the evidence relates is largely comprehensible without the explanatory evidence, the evidence will be inadmissible. The wording of s. 100(2)(a) is a marginally different formulation of the common-law rule permitting the use of so-called 'background evidence' about the accused, notwithstanding that it reveals his bad character or criminal disposition, where it is part of a continual background or history which is relevant to the offence charged and without the totality of which the account placed before the jury would be incomplete or incomprehensible (per Purchas LJ in *Pettman* (2 May 1985 unreported)). An example, under s. 100(1)(a), given in the Explanatory Notes to the Criminal Justice Bill, is of a case involving the abuse by one person of another over a long period of time. 'For the jury to understand properly the victim's account of the offending and why they [sic] did not seek help from, for example, a parent or other guardian, it might be necessary for evidence to be given of a wider pattern of abuse involving that other person' (para. 360). *Pettman* is considered in relation to s. 101(1)(c) ('explanatory evidence' of defendant's bad character) at **F12.29**. In relation to s. 101(1)(c) it has rightly been held that the phrase 'impossible or difficult to understand' is not satisfied if the evidence is readily understandable without evidence of bad character and the jury requires no 'footnote or lexicon' (*Beverley* [2006] EWCA Crim 1287). The same must be true of s. 100(2)(a).

Explanatory evidence, to be admissible, must also satisfy s. 100(1)(b), i.e. its value for understanding the case as a whole must be 'substantial'. In *Phillips* [2012] 1 Cr App R 332 (see **F12.70**), decided under s. 101(1)(e), it was suggested that a strict reading of 'substantial' was required to prevent unfairness, particularly through the raising of satellite issues.

F14.8   **(b) Evidence of Substantial Probative Value in Relation to Matter in Issue**   Under the CJA 2003, s. 100(1)(b), the probative value of evidence of bad character of a person other than the accused which is tendered in relation to a matter in issue (and of substantial importance) in the proceedings must be 'substantial'. Evidence which might have been admitted at common law under the broader rule in *Sweet-Escott* (1971) 55 Cr App R 316 (see **F14.5**) may be rejected (*Goddard* [2007] EWCA Crim 3134). In *Goddard* the victim of a serious assault, who had identified the accused as one of his attackers, had a range of convictions for minor offences (including crimes of dishonesty), but all were more than three years old. The judge's decision that they were not of substantial probative value in relation to the victim's credibility was upheld. See also *Garnham* [2008] EWCA Crim 266, where reference to common-law authorities was discouraged, and the complainant's substantial record for dishonesty was held to have been properly disregarded where the issue was consent to intercourse, and *Francis* [2013] EWCA Crim 2312, where the old conviction of one complainant for street-fighting and a warning for assault given to another were properly excluded in relation to the issue of whether they were the aggressors in the case. In *Francis*, the Court of Appeal drew attention to the dictum of Hughes LJ in *Braithwaite* [2010] 2 Cr App R 128 (see **F14.12**) that all assessments under s. 100 are highly fact-sensitive. Substantial probative value may be established where, for example, an accused is charged with an offence of violence and claims self-defence, and there is a previous instance of violence by the complainant towards the accused using a weapon. This may be admissible either as explanatory evidence of the accused's state of mind and reason for reacting as he did (see **F14.7**) or to show who was in fact the aggressor under s. 100(1)(b), or indeed as evidence going to the credibility of the complainant (see **F14.9**) (*Riley* [2006] EWCA Crim 2030). Although evidence of propensity is not specifically mentioned, as it is in relation to s. 101 (see **F12.39**), the suggestion that s. 100 could not be used to admit evidence of the propensity of a person other than the accused was dismissed as a 'misconstruction' in *H* (2010) 174 JP 203, where the accused had been improperly hampered in his attempt to prove that the offence charged had been committed by the other person by reference to relevant evidence of that person's propensity.

F14.9   **Credibility as a 'matter in issue'**   A 'matter in issue in the proceedings' covers both issues of disputed fact and issues of credibility (*Yaxley-Lennon*, one of the appeals heard with *Weir* [2006] 2 All ER 570 at [73]). In order to be admissible, the evidence must also be of substantial importance in the context of the case as a whole; evidence which goes only to some minor or trivial issue should not be admitted (see *Simpson* [2010] EWCA Crim 2266, in which S was charged with a rape occurring many years before, and it was said that the complainant's conviction for minor public order offences two years after the rape was not a matter in respect of which leave 'would ever have been given' under the CJA 2003, s. 100). In *Wright* [2014] EWCA Crim 545, W was charged with the rape of C, whose credibility was an important issue. The trial judge was held to have been 'fully justified' in excluding evidence that a police disciplinary tribunal had previously held her not to be a fully credible witness in relation to a complaint that C and others had made. There was no clear indication that C was thought to have lied, and the allegations she had made, some of which were accepted, were of a non-sexual nature. Thus, not only did the evidence fall short of the 'substantial probative value' threshold, it came 'very close to the "anything goes" kind of approach to complainants' that s. 100 was designed to discourage. By contrast, in *Osbourne*, one of the appeals heard with *Renda* [2006] 2 All ER 553, it was held (at [59]) that the conviction of a witness for a serious offence of violence was admissible where without that evidence the jury would have been deprived of 'important evidence of substantial probative value' in relation to his evidence that the complainant had fabricated the robbery which O was alleged to have committed.

In applying the CJA 2003, s. 101(1)(d) (evidence of the defendant's bad character), it has been held that an offence does not display a propensity to untruthfulness within the meaning of s. 103(1)(b) unless it is directly indicative of a propensity to lie, as distinct from a propensity to dishonesty (see *Hanson* [2005] 1 WLR 3169 at **F12.44**). It does not appear, however, that *Hanson* is regarded as establishing a generally applicable meaning of that phrase where it appears elsewhere in the CJA 2003 (see *Lawson* [2007] 1 WLR 1191 at **F12.76**, dealing with s. 101(1)(e) and even in relation to s. 101(1)(d) the courts have tended to marginalise the practical effect of such a distinction (*Campbell* [2007] 1 WLR 2798 at **F12.23**)). Because s. 100 does not specifically limit the court to evidence of 'untruthfulness', it follows that it is up to the judge to decide whether evidence of a non-defendant's bad character should be accorded 'substantial' probative value in relation to an 'important' issue of credibility. The distinction applied in *Hanson* has not found favour in relation to s. 100, the courts preferring the common-law notion that bad character of any sort may have a bearing on credibility. Thus in *Stephenson* [2006] EWCA Crim 2325 it was held (by the same court that decided *Lawson*) that a witness's previous cautions in respect of offences of dishonesty ought to have been admitted to support the defence, and the judge was held to have been wrong to exclude them by applying *Hanson*. *Stephenson* was approved in *Brewster* [2011] 1 WLR 601, where it was said that whether convictions have persuasive value in relation to creditworthiness depends principally on their nature, number and age, but that it was not necessary for the conviction to demonstrate a propensity to untruthfulness. *Brewster* was applied in *South* [2011] EWCA Crim 754, where the Court of Appeal nevertheless went on to hold that the trial judge had failed to make an adequate assessment of the probative value of the many convictions for offences of dishonesty of an alibi witness, and in particular that the judge did not confine himself to admitting only those offences indicative of untruthfulness. *Stephenson* was not cited and it would seem that the decision is overly restrictive.

Matters Relevant to Assessment of Probative Value   Section 100(3) sets out a non-exhaustive list **F14.10** of the factors to which the court must have regard in assessing the probative value of the evidence.

Criminal Justice Act 2003, s. 100

(3) In assessing the probative value of evidence for the purposes of subsection (1)(b) the court must have regard to the following factors (and to any others it considers relevant)—
  (a) the nature and number of the events, or other things, to which the evidence relates;
  (b) when those events or things are alleged to have happened or existed;
  (c) where—
    (i) the evidence is evidence of a person's misconduct, and
    (ii) it is suggested that the evidence has probative value by reason of similarity between that misconduct and other alleged misconduct,
    the nature and extent of the similarities and dissimilarities between each of the alleged instances of misconduct;
  (d) where—
    (i) the evidence is evidence of a person's misconduct,
    (ii) it is suggested that that person is also responsible for the misconduct charged, and
    (iii) the identity of the person responsible for the misconduct charged is disputed,
    the extent to which the evidence shows or tends to show that the same person was responsible each time.

In *Dizaei* [2013] 1 WLR 2257, where it was held that D had been rightly refused leave to adduce evidence of alleged sexual violence by a witness which was unrelated to the relatively minor matter the jury had to try, the Court of Appeal considered that the reference to 'any other' factors the court considers relevant would permit the court to have regard to the proliferation of satellite issues that might arise if a witness was accused of an offence that the jury would have, in effect, to try in order to resolve the case, and that (borrowing from the language of s. 100(2): see **F14.7**) the risk that a jury would find it more difficult properly to understand the case against the accused if their attention was thus divided was relevant to the assessment of probative value. See also **F14.16**.

As to s. 100(3)(a), the more serious the misconduct on the part of a witness, and the greater the number of instances of misconduct on his part, the stronger the likely probative value in relation to the issue of his credibility. As to s. 100(3)(b), evidence of misconduct occurring many years ago is usually likely to have less probative value than more recent misconduct, although very serious misconduct in the past may well have a stronger probative force than recent but comparatively minor misconduct. As to the relevance of the criteria in s. 100 to applications made under the similarly worded s. 101(1)(e), see *Phillips* [2012] 1 Cr App R 332, discussed at **F12.70**.

F14.11   In *Bovell* [2005] 2 Cr App R 401, the Court of Appeal thought it unlikely that the mere making of an allegation against an individual was capable of being evidence within s. 100 but, even if it was, trial judges should be discouraged from entering into inquiries raising 'satellite matters' such as the credibility of the person making the allegation and the reasons why the charge was dropped (citing *Hanson* [2005] 1 WLR 3169). More recently, in *Edwards* [2006] 1 WLR 1524 (a judgment covering four appeals, including that of *Smith*), the Court of Appeal, while specifically approving the aspect of *Bovell* dealing with the need to guard against satellite litigation, questioned whether all allegations could be excluded from the ambit of the statutory scheme for dealing with evidence of bad character. The context in the case of the appellant, Smith, was that previous untried allegations were tendered against him under s. 101 in order to form the basis of an inference of propensity. The distinction drawn by the Court (that *Bovell* applies to allegations against a non-defendant) is surely untenable. The better view is that *Bovell* is dealing with the 'mere making' of an allegation where there is no proof as to its substance, whereas the prosecution case against Smith was that the previous allegations were true and that the evidence, in combination with the evidence of the offences charged, showed that this was so. This is supported by *Miller* [2010] 2 Cr App R 138, where it was said that the purpose of s. 100 is 'to eliminate kite-flying and innuendo against the character of a witness in favour of a concentration upon the real issues in the case'. Unless, therefore, counsel who sought to suggest to a witness that he was guilty of offences with which he had been charged 'was in a position to prove his guilt and intended to prove it', the exercise of cross-examination ought not to have been embarked upon at all. The Court of Appeal added that there might be 'infrequent and limited' instances of cross-examination implicating the witness in bad behaviour which the cross-examiner would be unable to prove, e.g., as to the discrete detail of an admitted conviction or behaviour. Where such an accusation is denied, the jury should be directed that the cross-examiner's case is not advanced by the mere putting of the question. Where the evidence tendered in support of an allegation admissible under s. 100 is hearsay, the court is entitled to take this into account in deciding whether it is of 'substantial probative value' (*Matthews* [2013] EWCA Crim 2238).

F14.12   Section 109 (see **F12.63**) does not require a court, when assessing the probative value of a complaint in the form of an allegation against a witness, to assume that the complaint is true. A complaint is not 'evidence' that the witness did the thing complained of, and s. 109 applies only where such evidence is before the court (*Braithwaite* [2010] 2 Cr App R 128). In *Dizaei* [2013] 1 WLR 2257 the Court of Appeal, in following *Braithwaite*, also pointed out that the bare fact of an allegation, even if assumed to be true, would never be conclusive of the question whether it constitutes evidence of substantial importance, or of substantial probative value. The Court of Appeal in *Braithwaite* also disapproved of the practice proposed by counsel of putting the suggestion to a witness, based on police reports, that he had committed offences other than those for which he had been charged or cautioned (see *Miller* [2010] 2 Cr App R 138 at **F14.11**). However, the Court noted that a penalty notice (the acceptance of which does not necessarily entail an admission) might be capable, depending on the facts, of forming the basis of such questioning. Compare *Hamer* [2011] 1 WLR 528 (see **F13.12**) where the point is made that the mere issuing of a penalty notice involves no stain on the good character of an accused. This is not necessarily inconsistent with the possibility that the notice might properly give rise to such questioning as is sanctioned in *Braithwaite*, but there is a need for care and consistency in developing the principles relating to penalty notices.

Section 100(3)(c) relates to evidence of a person's misconduct the probative value of which   **F14.13** derives from its similarity to other misconduct on his part. Thus, if the accused alleges that a police officer has threatened W, a potential witness for the defence (evidence of which would be admissible under s. 98(b)), and there is evidence that the officer has threatened other potential witnesses for the defence in other cases, then in assessing the probative value of the evidence, the court should have regard to the nature and extent of the similarities and dissimilarities between each of the alleged instances of misconduct.

Section 100(3)(d) relates to evidence which, in cases where the identity of the offender is in dis-   **F14.14** pute, suggests that a person other than the accused is responsible for the offence charged. Such evidence may take the form of evidence of propensity to commit the type of offence charged, provided that it is of substantial probative value (*H* (2010) 174 JP 203). The more striking the nexus between the previous misconduct and the offence charged, the stronger the persuasive value of the evidence. For example (and to make use of an illustration provided by Lord Hailsham in *DPP v Boardman* [1975] AC 421 at p. 454), if the prosecution case in relation to a burglary is that D climbed in through a ground floor window and left a humorous limerick on the walls of the sitting room, evidence that E has previously committed a number of burglaries in the same vicinity, on each occasion having climbed through a ground floor window and having left the same humorous limerick on the walls of the sitting rooms, would be hard to exclude.

(c) **Evidence Admitted by Agreement**   Under the CJA 2003, s. 100(1)(c), evidence of the bad   **F14.15** character of a person other than the accused may be admitted by agreement of 'all parties to the proceedings'. Thus in a case involving more than one defendant, all must agree: see *Ferdinand* [2014] EWCA Crim 1243, decided under the corresponding provision of s. 101 (see **F12.16**). Under s. 100(4), evidence may be admitted under s. 100(1)(c) without the leave of the court.

The Requirement of Leave

Section 100(4) of the CJA 2003 provides that: 'Except where subsection (1)(c) applies, evidence   **F14.16** of the bad character of a person other than the defendant must not be given without the leave of the court'. Evidence admissible under s. 100(1)(a) or (b) must not be adduced without leave. Unfortunately, however, the subsection gives no guidance as to what factors, if any, should be taken into account in deciding whether or not to grant leave, apart from the factors set out in s. 100(2) and (3). It is possible that the difficulty posed where allegations against prosecution witnesses give rise to complex satellite issues (as in *Dizaei* [2013] 1 WLR 2257: see **F14.6** and **F14.10**) might be best considered under this heading, given the absence of any specific discretion to prevent the defence from adducing otherwise admissible evidence. On one reading s. 100(4) also applies to evidence of bad character of complainants admissible under the YJCEA 1999, s. 41 (see **F7.22** *et seq.* and *V* [2006] EWCA Crim 1901, where Crane J acknowledges that both provisions may well be in play, and that 'In many cases s. 41 will be the more formidable obstacle to overcome'). If the leave requirement under s. 100(4) is designed to be additional to the requirements of s. 41, then the issue arises as to what kinds of sexual behaviour on the part of the complainant should be treated as 'bad character' as defined in the CJA 2003. In cases where the defence allege that the complainant has previously made false allegations then, once it appears that there is an evidential basis for suggesting falsity, s. 100 appears to be the dominant provision — the essence of the attack on the complainant is that she is a liar, even if the circumstances also suggest sexual behaviour. A previous complaint of a sexual offence, alleged to be false, was held admissible under s. 100 in *Scott* [2009] EWCA Crim 2457, subject to the laying of the appropriate evidential foundation that the YJCEA 1999, s. 41, is inapplicable. See also *Wright* [2014] EWCA Crim 545, in which s. 100, rather than s. 41, applied to evidence suggesting that the complainant in a sexual case had been a less than credible witness in relation to complaints of misconduct (including some of a sexual nature) against the police. The evidence was inadmissible (see **F14.9**) and s. 100 was described as 'somewhat less prescriptive' than s. 41, albeit, 'and designedly so, prescriptive all the same'. In *Stephenson* [2006] EWCA Crim 2325, where S complained on appeal that he had not been permitted sufficient latitude in relation to the complainant's disturbed background and promiscuity as indicative of the likelihood that she had fabricated the case against S, the Court of Appeal made particular reference to the fact that none of the sexual relationships were alleged to have been falsified, and thereafter confined its observations about s. 100 to the effect of the complainant's cautions for offences of dishonesty (see **F14.9**).

F14.17 Section 111 of the CJA 2003 permits rules of court to be made in relation to evidence of bad character to supplement the provisions of the Act. The relevant rules are contained in the CrimPR, part 35 (see Supplement, **R-270** *et seq.*), with modifications where the proceedings are before the Court of Appeal which are set out in r. 68.7 (see Supplement, **R-524**).

The rules require application to be made to introduce evidence of a non-defendant's bad character and also for cross-examining a witness with a view to eliciting such evidence; they also set time-limits for any party wishing to adduce evidence of a non-defendant's bad character, and also to an application to oppose the use of such evidence.

RELATIONSHIP WITH THE POLICE AND CRIMINAL EVIDENCE ACT 1984, s. 78

F14.18 If the prosecution propose to rely upon evidence admissible under the CJA 2003, s. 100, it will be open to the defence to argue that the evidence should be excluded under the PACE 1984, s. 78, i.e. that having regard to all the circumstances, the admission of the evidence would have such an adverse effect on the fairness of the proceedings that the court ought not to admit it. The potential application of s. 78 to evidence of bad character admissible under the CJA 2003 is considered at **F12.18**.

REASONS FOR RULINGS

F14.19 Under the CJA 2003, s. 110, where the court makes a ruling on whether an item of evidence is evidence of a person's bad character and on whether an item of such evidence is admissible under s. 100, it must state in open court (but in the absence of the jury, if there is one), its reasons for the ruling; and, if it is a magistrates' court, it must cause the ruling and the reasons for it to be entered in the register of the court's proceedings. In *Renda* [2006] 2 All ER 553 (at [60]), the mere observation that the jury was entitled to know about character was regarded as an 'over-parsimonious' compliance with s. 110.

DIRECTIONS TO JURY

F14.20 In *Kelly* [2008] EWCA Crim 1456, the failure of the trial judge to relate a prosecution witness's convictions specifically to his propensity, as distinct from his credibility, was not fatal where there was no danger of the jury missing the significance of the evidence. The Court of Appeal approved a statement from *Campbell* [2007] 1 WLR 2798 (on the CJA 2003, s. 101: see **F12.23**) where it was said that the 'failure to give a direction that is no more than assistance in applying common sense to the evidence should not automatically be treated as a ground of appeal, let alone a reason to allow an appeal'.

Section F15   The Rule Against Hearsay: General Principles

GENERAL

Definition of Hearsay Evidence

Criminal Justice Act 2003, s. 114   **F15.1**

(1) In criminal proceedings a statement not made in oral evidence in the proceedings is admissible
as evidence of any matter stated if, but only if—
(a) any provision of this chapter or any other statutory provision makes it admissible,
(b) any rule of law preserved by section 118 makes it admissible,
(c) all parties to the proceedings agree to it being admissible, or
(d) the court is satisfied that it is in the interests of justice for it to be admissible.

The CJA 2003 applies to trials and other hearings to which the strict rules of evidence apply.
The Act also applies to proceedings under the Criminal Procedure (Insanity) Act 1964, s. 4A,
the purpose of which is to mirror the fact-finding process at a criminal trial (*Chal* [2008] 1 Cr
App R 247). In confiscation proceedings pursuant to the POCA 2002, the hearsay regime in the
CJA 2003 does not apply, but should be used by analogy, borrowing in particular from the fair-
ness provisions in s. 114(1)(d) (see **F16.38**), but bearing in mind the post-conviction context
(*Clipston* [2011] 2 Cr App R (S) 569).

The definition of hearsay in s. 114 of the CJA 2003 has superseded the common-law definition,   **F15.2**
but the two are in many respects similar. Section 114(1) provides that 'a statement not made in
oral evidence in the proceedings is admissible as evidence of any matter stated if, but only if' one
of the exceptional cases applies (for exceptions, see **F16.2**). In a leading common-law authority,
Sharp [1988] 1 All ER 65, Lord Havers stated that the rule was that 'an assertion other than one
made by a person while giving oral evidence in the proceedings is inadmissible as evidence of
any fact asserted'.

The emphasis at common law was on inadmissibility, as hearsay could be admitted only where
an exception to the rule applied. Under the CJA 2003 the rule is reformulated in more positive terms. The essence of hearsay — reliance on a statement made otherwise than while giving evidence to prove the truth of a fact asserted — remains constant. It follows that many
common-law authorities on the scope of the rule will remain valid. The major exception to this
proposition concerns so-called implied assertions (see **F15.17**), some of which are removed
from the scope of the hearsay rule by the restrictive definitions of 'statement' and 'matter stated'
adopted in the CJA 2003.

Criminal Justice Act 2003, s. 115

(1) In this chapter references to a statement or to a matter stated are to be read as follows.
(2) A statement is any representation of fact or opinion made by a person by whatever means; and
it includes a representation made in a sketch, photofit or other pictorial form.
. . .

Hearsay and Conduct   Whereas most hearsay statements are made (whether orally or in writ-   **F15.3**
ing) in words, the CJA 2003, s. 115, confirms that a statement may take any form that enables
a representation of fact to be made. Thus, as at common law, hearsay may also occur in the

Part F Evidence   F

form of conduct. In *Chandrasekera v The King* [1937] AC 220, a woman's throat had been cut, depriving her of the power of speech. She described C as her attacker using sign language, and nodded when asked whether C had caused her injuries. These communications were likened to the language of a deaf person able to converse only by means of a finger alphabet, and the 'conversation' was admitted under an exception to the hearsay rule.

F15.4   **Hearsay and Statements in Other Proceedings**   Under the CJA 2003, s. 114, a statement not made in oral evidence 'in the proceedings' is hearsay. It follows that, as was the case at common law, a statement made on oath in other proceedings is hearsay, and may only be received as evidence of its truth under an exception to the rule (see, e.g., *Berkeley Peerage Case* (1811) 4 Camp 401).

F15.5   **Hearsay and Previous Statements of Witnesses**   The out-of-court statements of witnesses who give evidence in the proceedings may be introduced as evidence of consistency or inconsistency without infringing the hearsay rule. (See as to the circumstances in which statements may be used for this purpose **F6.32** to **F6.47** and **F7.45**.) Such statements are, however, hearsay in relation to the 'matters stated' under the CJA 2003, s. 114(1). At common law there was no general hearsay exception relating to the use of previous statements of witnesses. However, under the CJA 2003, s. 119, a witness's previous inconsistent statement becomes admissible as evidence of the truth of any matter stated by him of which oral evidence by him would be admissible and, under s. 120, evidence of various previous consistent statements likewise may become evidence of the truth of facts stated therein (*Athwal* [2009] 1 WLR 2430, and see generally **F6.36**). The reform of this aspect of the hearsay rule was long overdue. The reasons typically given for the exclusion of hearsay (see **F15.7**) do not apply with the same force to the out-of-court statements of those who subsequently appear as witnesses in the proceedings. In many cases a statement made while events were fresher in the witness's mind might provide evidence of better quality than his subsequent evidence in court.

F15.6   **Proof of the Truth of a Matter Stated**   Evidence is hearsay under the CJA 2003, s. 114(1), only where it is relied upon as 'evidence of any matter stated': in other words, where it is sought to establish the truth of that matter. Thus, where it is sought to establish the registration number of a car involved in an incident, and an eye-witness, A, who has seen the incident, relates the number to B, who has not, it is hearsay for B to tell the court what the number was for the purpose of proving the identity of the car (*McLean* (1967) 52 Cr App R 80; *Jones v Metcalfe* [1967] 3 All ER 205; *Maher v DPP* [2006] EWCA Crim 1271). (Where B makes a note of the number that A verifies, A may give evidence of the number by refreshing his memory from B's note: *Jones v Metcalfe*; *Kelsey* (1982) 74 Cr App R 213. As to refreshing memory, see **F6.14** to **F6.31**.)

Where goods are imported in bags marked 'Produce of Morocco', the marks are hearsay evidence of the country of origin of the goods (*Patel v Comptroller of Customs* [1966] AC 356). The same result follows even where the information is indelibly stamped into the goods (*Comptroller of Customs v Western Lectric Co. Ltd* [1966] AC 367). Similarly, information stamped on to a document is hearsay evidence of the matters stated, e.g., of a date: see *Cook* (1980) 71 Cr App R 205, in which it was assumed that such information was admissible only where there was an applicable exception to the hearsay rule. Compare, however, *Miller v Howe* [1969] 3 All ER 451, in which a police officer was allowed to give evidence identifying a particular device although he had derived his knowledge from the label on the box. A car's vehicle registration document provides only hearsay evidence of its engine number (*Sealby* [1965] 1 All ER 701), as do records compiled in the course of the manufacture of the car (*Myers v DPP* [1965] AC 1001). A person who relates his own date and place of birth necessarily gives hearsay evidence (*Inhabitants of Rishworth* (1842) 2 QB 476, see also *Day* (1841) 9 C & P 722). A party to a conversation that has been conducted through an interpreter infringes the hearsay rule if he seeks to prove what the other party said by relating to the court what the interpreter told him (*Attard* (1958) 43 Cr App R 90). Similarly, where a police officer testifies that a person receiving a commodity alleged to be heroin from the defendant is a 'known heroin user', he is giving hearsay evidence if the basis of his knowledge is information supplied to him by others, including the recipient in question (*Rothwell* (1994) 99 Cr App R 388). In *Horncastle* [2010] 2 AC 373, in a judgment from the Court of Appeal which was affirmed and described as 'complementary' to that of the Supreme Court, Thomas LJ stated that the hearsay rule provides that it is 'ordinarily essential that evidence of the truth of a matter be given in person by a witness who speaks from his own observation or knowledge'.

Rationale of Hearsay Rule

At common law the hearsay rule operated rigidly to exclude evidence — including evidence of **F15.7** undoubted probative value — unless a specific hearsay exception could be brought to bear. The courts had no power to create exceptions to avoid the exclusion of valuable material, as this was the sole prerogative of Parliament (*Myers v DPP* [1965] AC 1001, in which reliable manufacturing records were rejected).

The reforming strategy of the CJA 2003 is to admit hearsay evidence provided that certain safeguards are met: a more inclusionary approach than at common law. The major feature of the new statutory scheme, which enables the court to break free of the mechanical shackles of the common-law rule, is the general 'interests of justice' exception in s. 114(1)(d), under which evidence may be admitted notwithstanding that it does not conform to a specific exception mentioned in s. 114(1)(a) or (b) and the parties are not agreed on its admission under (c). In deciding whether to admit evidence under s. 114(1)(d), the court is directed to consider such matters as the apparent reliability of the maker of the statement, and the amount of difficulty that there may be in challenging the statement so that the evidence will not be admitted if its hearsay nature poses a genuine threat to the interests of justice (see further **F16.38**). To the extent that the courts appear inclined to interpret this new provision widely, the traditional mechanical approach to hearsay has been significantly eroded.

In *Sharp* [1988] 1 All ER 65, Lord Havers said (at p. 11) that the principal reason that led the **F15.8** judges to adopt the hearsay rule was 'the fear that juries might give undue weight to evidence the truth of which could not be tested by cross-examination, and possibly also the risk of an account becoming distorted as it was passed from one person to another'. Similarly, in *Blastland* [1986] AC 41, Lord Bridge of Harwich said (at p. 54): 'The rationale of excluding [hearsay] as inadmissible, rooted as it is in the system of trial by jury, is a recognition of the great difficulty, even more acute for a juror than for a trained judicial mind, of assessing what, if any, weight can properly be given to a statement by a person whom the jury have not seen or heard and which has not been subject to any test of reliability by cross-examination'. The same principles are apparent in the judgment of the Supreme Court in *Horncastle* [2010] 2 AC 373, although Lord Phillips (at [21]) places greater emphasis on reliability:

> There were two principal reasons for excluding hearsay evidence. The first was that it was potentially unreliable. It might even be fabricated by the witness giving evidence of what he alleged he had been told by another. Quite apart from this, the weight to be given to such evidence was less easy to appraise than that of evidence delivered by a witness face to face with the defendant and subject to testing by cross-examination.

While the CJA 2003 provides for the wider admissibility of hearsay evidence, it is not, as the Court of Appeal observed in *Riat* [2013] 1 All ER 349, received as the equivalent of first-hand evidence. Rather, '[i]t is necessarily second-hand and for that reason very often second-best'. Where hearsay evidence is received under the CJA 2003, the safeguards aimed at minimising the dangers identified above include the giving of notice of intention to use hearsay evidence, the provision of special rules to scrutinise the credibility of the maker of the statement (CJA 2003, s. 124: see **F16.92**) and the giving of judicial warnings about hearsay (see **F16.46**).

F

COMMON DEFINITIONAL CHALLENGES

Hearsay Not Rendered Admissible because Tendered by Defence

F15.9   The CJA 2003 creates no special rule of admissibility favouring the defence. In this also, it reflects the common-law tradition. In *Turner* (1975) 61 Cr App R 67, the Court of Appeal rejected an argument that an accused person should be entitled to rely on hearsay evidence to show that a third party who has not been called as a witness has admitted committing the offence charged. The existence of any exception in favour of third-party admissions was also denied, *obiter*, by the House of Lords in *Blastland* [1986] AC 41.

In *Sparks v The Queen* [1964] AC 964, a statement made by a child, who was too young to testify, in which she alleged that she had been attacked by 'a coloured boy', was held inadmissible on behalf of S, a white man. Under the CJA 2003, s. 114(1)(d) (see **F16.38**), evidence of the type rejected in *Sparks* and *Blastland* may in future be admitted where it is in the interests of justice to do so, and the importance of the evidence to the defence will be a factor that the court will consider in deciding where the interests of justice lie (see, e.g., *Prosecution Appeal (No. 2 of 2008)*; *R v Y* [2008] 2 All ER 484). But it remains the case that there is no special hearsay exception for defence evidence.

Statements Tendered for Purpose Other than as Evidence of Facts Asserted

F15.10   The hearsay rule is not infringed where a statement is tendered for some reason other than to establish the matter stated. This proposition is as true under the CJA 2003 as it was at common law: evidence that was not hearsay before the Act remains non-hearsay (original) evidence after it. In *Toussaint-Collins* [2009] EWCA Crim 316, T-C was accused of the murder of G in revenge for the killing of S. For several months, T-C had kept a letter written by a third party, protesting that no-one had avenged S's death. The keeping of the letter provided non-hearsay evidence of T-C's state of mind in relation to G.

Common-law authorities include *Subramaniam v Public Prosecutor* [1956] 1 WLR 965, where S was charged with the capital offence of possession of ammunition. His defence was that he acted under duress. At his trial, he sought to give evidence of threats made to him by certain terrorists who were not called to give evidence, and was prevented from doing so on the ground that such evidence was hearsay. The Privy Council held that this was not the case. The purpose of proving that S had been subjected to threats was not to establish that the threats were true but to show rather that, if they had been believed by S, they might have induced in him an apprehension of instant death if he failed to conform to the terrorists' wishes. The evidence was thus original, non-hearsay evidence, which had been wrongly excluded at trial.

Similar examples may readily be found. In *Davis* [1998] Crim LR 659, D, on being interviewed in connection with theft, failed to reveal facts upon which he afterwards sought to rely in his defence. At trial he wished to give evidence of what his solicitor had said to him prior to the interview, but was prevented from doing so on the grounds that it would infringe the hearsay rule. The Court of Appeal pointed out, correctly, that this was not necessarily the case. It was material for the jury to consider D's reasons for failing to disclose the relevant facts in deciding whether to draw an inference against him under the CJPO 1994, s. 34 (see **F19.10**). If D's purpose in repeating the solicitor's words was simply to show the impact on him of the advice given, the hearsay rule would not have been infringed. It would have been otherwise if D had sought to demonstrate the truth of anything said. See to similar effect *Willis* [1960] 1 All ER 331, *Chapman* [1969] 2 QB 436, and *Woodhouse v Hall* (1980) 72 Cr App R 39. In the latter case, the question to be decided was whether a massage parlour was being run as a brothel. Having defined a brothel as 'an establishment at which two or more women were offering sexual services', the Divisional Court held that it was open to police officers who had attended the premises posing as customers to prove that the women employed there had offered them various sexual services. There was no question of hearsay: the relevant issue was simply whether the offers had been made.

Evidence of State of Mind   A troublesome question at common law was whether the rule **F15.11** is infringed where a statement is used to show the state of mind of the person making it, as distinct from its effect on the person to whom it is made. According to *Blastland* [1986] AC 41 a statement made to a witness by a third party is not hearsay when put in evidence for this purpose. See to similar effect *Gregson* [2003] 2 Cr App R 521: on the question whether the possession of a large quantity of a drug indicated intent to supply, the fact that the accused told his friends at the time that he had been handed vastly more of the drug than he had asked to purchase from his supplier, and was worried about how to dispose of it safely, was admissible to show a contemporaneous state of mind on his part inconsistent with the prosecution case. Evidence of a relevant state of mind was considered to be first-hand hearsay admissible by way of common-law exception to the rule in *Neill v North Antrim Magistrates' Court* [1992] 4 All ER 846, considered further at **F16.17** and **F16.69**, but the preponderance of authority suggests that it is not hearsay in the first place. The inconsistency in the authorities was considered in *Gilfoyle* [1996] 1 Cr App R 302. G was convicted of the murder of his wife, P. Notes written by P in which she expressed an intention to take her own life were admitted to support the defence of suicide. The Court of Appeal considered that evidence of further statements made by P showing that she was not in a suicidal frame of mind, and that she had written the notes in the belief that they were required to help G, a nurse, with a project at work was also admissible. It was said (at p. 321) that 'strictly speaking' such evidence fell outside the hearsay rule, but 'in any event, hearsay evidence to prove the declarant's "state of mind" is an exception to the rule which has been accepted by the common law for many years'. Whether hearsay or not, then, such evidence was clearly admissible at common law.

'Any Matter Stated'   Under the CJA 2003, the statutory definition of hearsay poses the ques- **F15.12** tion whether the statement is tendered as evidence 'of any matter stated'. To the extent that a state of mind is asserted by the speaker, the evidence would appear to be hearsay, which may then be fitted within the preserved common-law exception for *res gestae* in s. 118(1) (see **F16.55**). A statement from which a state of mind may be inferred, on the other hand, may fall outside the definition of 'matter stated' in s. 115(3) and be classified, along with many other 'implied assertions' as original evidence (see **F15.17**).

Illustrations of Non-hearsay Evidence

Further illustrations of the use of statements as non-hearsay evidence which it is submitted **F15.13** will survive the CJA 2003, are an admission of bankruptcy tendered to prove not the truth of the assertion (which was proved by other means), but the maker's knowledge of his insolvency (*Thomas v Connell* (1838) 4 M & W 267); an allegation of forgery made against A tendered to show why A had been arrested (*Perkins v Vaughan* (1842) 4 Man & G 988); a cry of 'murder' by the alleged victim of a rape, tendered to prove lack of consent, and a subsequent request by her for money, tendered to prove the contrary (*Guttridges* (1840) 9 C & P 471). Where negligence by omission is alleged, a promise made by a third party to take action on behalf of D may show why D took no action (*The Douglas* (1882) 7 PD 151). Where D denied knowledge that certain premises were being used as a brothel, an advertisement that he had sought to place, referring to the premises and containing a reference to 'many stunning masseuses', was admissible to show that he did know (*Roberts v DPP* [1994] Crim LR 926).

A statement that is demonstrably false may show a consciousness of guilt (*Mawaz Khan v The Queen* [1967] 1 AC 454; *A-G v Good* (1825) M'Cle & Yo 286; *Binham* [1991] Crim LR 774). Under the CJA 2003, it would seem that a lie cannot be hearsay evidence of a matter that it is not intended to assert (see **F15.17**). In *Minchin* [2013] EWCA Crim 2412 the Court of Appeal accepted that a statement containing the details of an alibi alleged to be false could be tendered by the prosecution without breaching the hearsay rule. 'What mattered was the fact that it was said'.

Upon application of the test described above, it is perfectly possible that evidence may be admissible, original evidence for one purpose, and inadmissible hearsay for another. Such cases require a very careful judicial direction as to the use to which the evidence may properly be put. Where it happens that the evidence is admissible in relation to one count in an indictment but not another, the inadmissibility is relevant to whether the counts should be tried together (*Watson* [1997] Crim LR 680).

Inferences Founded on Statements

F15.14   Where evidence is inadmissible as hearsay, it is not possible to evade the difficulty by adducing evidence from which it can be inferred that the inadmissible statement was made and that it was true. In *Glinski v McIver* [1962] AC 726, Lord Devlin described the 'customary devices' employed where the hearsay rule is sought to be evaded in this way (at pp. 780–1):

> The first consists in not asking what was said in a conversation or written in a document but in asking what the conversation or document was about; it is apparently thought that what would be objectionable if fully exposed is permissible if decently veiled…. The other device is to ask by means of 'Yes' or 'No' questions what was done. (Just answer 'Yes' or 'No': Did you go to see counsel? Do not tell us what he said but as a result of it did you do something? What did you do?) This device is commonly defended on the ground that counsel is asking only about what was done and not about what was said. But in truth what was done is relevant only because from it there can be inferred something about what was said. Such evidence seems to me to be clearly objectionable. If there is nothing in it, it is irrelevant; if there is something in it, what there is in it is inadmissible.

See also *Saunders* [1899] 1 QB 490.

It is submitted that the same criticism can be made of an attempt to draw a circumstantial inference from a hearsay statement in a document. This occurred in *Rice* [1963] 1 QB 857, where the prosecution relied on an airline ticket in the names of 'Rice and Moore', produced by an airline official whose job it was to deal with used tickets, to give rise to a circumstantial inference that R had travelled on the flight in question. Although the Court of Appeal was agreed that the ticket 'must not be treated as speaking its contents for what it might say could only be hearsay', it was held (at p. 872) that 'the production of the ticket from the place where used tickets would properly be kept was a fact from which the jury might infer that probably two people had flown on the particular flight and that it might or might not seem to them by applying their common knowledge of such matters that the passengers bore the surnames that were written on the ticket'. It is submitted, however, that the production of the ticket proved that the traveller was R only if reliance were placed on its 'contents', i.e. on the statement it bore which showed that it had been issued to one Rice. This is supported by the analysis of the House of Lords in *Myers v DPP* [1965] AC 1001, rejecting the argument that it could be inferred from the efficient manner in which records were compiled by the manufacturers of motor vehicles, that what was stated in the records was inherently likely to be true. Lord Morris said (at p. 1027): 'The circumstances referred to show that evidence of the nature now being considered might with advantage be admitted because there would be every expectation that figures would be correctly recorded. This, however, does not change the character of the evidence. It remains hearsay evidence…'

Under the CJA 2003, s. 114(1), it is hard to avoid the conclusion that the statement on the ticket in *Rice* was used as evidence 'of any matter stated'. The broad exception now available for business documents (under s. 117: see **F16.24**) provides a more tenable route to admissibility.

F15.15   A distinction should, however, be drawn between the permissible use of a statement as an original and independent fact, and the impermissible use of it as evidence of the matter stated. In *Lydon* (1986) 85 Cr App R 221 the prosecution were permitted to tender in evidence a piece of paper found near a weapon believed to have been used in a robbery, and bearing ink of a similar kind to that staining the weapon. On the paper, someone had written 'Sean rules' and 'Sean rules 85'. It was held that the words on the paper created an inferential link with L, whose first name was Sean. *Rice* was distinguished, because 'the reference to Sean could be regarded as no more than a statement of fact involving no assertion as to the truth of the contents of the document' (per Woolf LJ at p. 224). *Lydon* was applied in *McIntosh* [1992] Crim LR 651, in which a piece of paper bearing calculations as to the profit and loss made from buying and selling a substance (inferentially a drug) was found on M's premises. The document was not in M's handwriting, but this was immaterial as it was admitted not as evidence of its truth but as purely circumstantial evidence suggesting M's involvement with drug-related offences.

Statements Inextricably Linked to Relevant Acts

Where an issue arises as to the doing of a composite act made up of physical actions and words, **F15.16** the admissibility of the words may be regarded in a different light from the same words standing alone. In *Ratten v The Queen* [1972] AC 378, R was charged with the murder of his wife, and the defence was that she had been shot by accident as R cleaned his gun. The prosecution relied on the evidence of a telephone operator to show that, shortly before she was shot, the victim had telephoned the exchange in a state of hysteria and asked for the police. R denied that any such call had been made. The Privy Council held that, because the making of the call was itself a relevant act, the words used and the state of emotion in which they were spoken were 'relevant and necessary evidence in order to explain and complete the fact of the call being made', and were not hearsay. See also *Blastland* [1986] AC 41, in which it was said (at p. 59) that *Ratten* was authority for the proposition that the admissibility of the telephone call in that case had to be considered as a whole.

Under the CJA 2003, s. 114(1), the position would appear to be that a statement cannot be extricated from the ambit of the hearsay rule merely because it is closely associated with the doing of a relevant act. The association might, however, lead to the admission of the statement as part of the *res gestae* under s. 118 (see **F16.55**) or under other hearsay exceptions considered in **F16**.

HEARSAY AND 'MATTERS STATED'

Criminal Justice Act 2003, s. 115 **F15.17**

(1) In this chapter references to a statement or to a matter stated are to be read as follows.
(2) ...
(3) A matter stated is one to which the chapter applies if (and only if) the purpose, or one of the purposes, of the person making the statement appears to the court to have been—
   (a) to cause another person to believe the matter, or
   (b) to cause another person to act or a machine to operate on the basis that the matter is as stated.

The intended effect of s. 115(3) is to reverse the hearsay aspects of the decision of the House of Lords in *Kearley* [1992] 2 AC 228. K was charged with possession of a controlled drug with intent to supply. The amount found in K's possession being of itself inadequate to warrant an inference of such an intent, the prosecution relied upon evidence that, after K's arrest, a number of telephone calls had been made to his home in which the callers asked for K by his nickname and sought to buy drugs, and that a number of individuals had visited the house and asked to be supplied with drugs. None of these persons was called to give evidence at the trial. The House of Lords, by a majority, held that the hearsay rule precluded the use of the callers' requests as implied assertions by them that K was a supplier of drugs. Lord Bridge stated (at p. 665) that the English authorities were both 'clear and unequivocal' in holding that the hearsay rule applies equally to express and to implied assertions. Lord Ackner (whose preferred view was that the evidence was simply irrelevant in that it proved no more than the state of mind of the callers, which was not in issue) considered that, just as a request for drugs containing an express statement that K was a supplier would clearly have been objectionable as hearsay, so a request containing an implied assertion to the same effect would break the hearsay rule. A non-hearsay purpose for adducing the evidence in *Kearley* was thought by the dissenting minority (Lords

Griffiths and Browne-Wilkinson) to exist in that the conduct of the callers pointed towards the existence of a 'market' for the supply of drugs, but this argument was thought by the majority to be unsound on the basis that the conduct itself was not relevant except as an implied assertion as to the caller's beliefs, which were hearsay.

F15.18   On the facts of *Kearley*, the callers whose requests for drugs were tendered in evidence clearly thought that they were speaking to K. There was thus little danger that, in making their requests, they were seeking to mislead the person to whom they were speaking, or to misrepresent or exaggerate the matter on which the prosecution sought to rely, namely their belief that K was a drug dealer. Under the change in the law brought about by s. 115(3), the 'matter stated' (that K is a dealer) is not one to which the hearsay rule applies unless the person making the request had a purpose either (a) to cause another to believe the matter or (b) to cause another to act as though the matter is as stated. Where the speaker believes that the hearer already knows the matter in question, and is therefore not speaking with either of the hearsay purposes, the evidence is original, non-hearsay evidence under the CJA 2003. (It may, of course, be held to be irrelevant if Lord Ackner's preferred view prevails: s. 115(3) provides only that it is not hearsay.)

In *West Midlands Probation Board v French* [2009] 1 WLR 1715 it was held that where a prisoner is released on licence, the licence is hearsay in consequence of s. 115(3), the purpose of the maker being to cause the prisoner and others to believe the statements in the licence and to act accordingly. However, the purpose of a licence would seem rather to be to lay out the terms on which the prisoner is to be set at liberty; there is no fact the 'truth' of which is in issue.

Matters Not Intended to be Believed or Acted Upon

F15.19   The application of the CJA 2003, s. 115(3) to particular communications has proved difficult in practice. In *Twist* [2011] 3 All ER 1055, a series of conjoined appeals, the Court of Appeal attributed some of the difficulty to the continued use of expressions such as 'implied assertion' that are relics of the common law, and set out a clear three-stage test for ascertaining whether communications are hearsay under the CJA 2003 which is focused on the statutory wording. This analysis was endorsed in *Mateza* [2011] EWCA Crim 2587, where it was said that it was not helpful to look at earlier interpretations of the provision (such as *Leonard* (2009) 173 JP 366: see **F15.21**). The test in *Twist* runs as follows:

(1) Ascertain the matter sought to be proved. Hughes LJ noted that the opening words of s. 114(1) ('admissible as evidence of any matter stated') demonstrate that the CJA 2003, like the common law, is concerned with what it is that a party is seeking to prove. The purpose of the party in adducing a communication has therefore first to be ascertained.

(2) Provided that the matter sought to be proved is a relevant one, the next question is whether there is a statement of that matter in the communication. If not (perhaps because the communication is not a statement at all, but a question such as a request for drugs), no question of hearsay arises.

(3) If the communication does state the matter, was it one of the purposes (not necessarily the only or dominant purpose) that the recipient, or any other person, should believe that matter or that a person should act upon the basis that it is as stated (or, it is submitted, that a machine should operate on that basis)? If yes, it is hearsay; if no, it is not.

F15.20   In the appeal of Twist, the prosecution relied on text messages received by T to establish intent to supply drugs. This was a relevant matter, but the messages, being mere requests for drugs, did not contain any statement that T was a dealer. Even if such a statement could be inferred, the purpose of the senders did not include any intention to cause anyone to believe he was. In the appeal of Boothman, B was charged with conspiracy to supply cannabis and cocaine, and there was considerable traffic in text messages between B, who was advertising a good stock of available drugs, and other persons either placing orders or commenting on issues relating to past supply. Particular objection was taken to the mention of 'lines' in the incoming texts as including statements indicative of the supply of cocaine. But the senders of the texts did not have a purpose to make B believe that he was a supplier of that drug, or to induce him to act upon it as true (as distinct from acting upon it to supply further drugs). The evidence was therefore not hearsay. In the appeal of Tomlinson and Kelly, the matter to be proved was that the accused were in possession of a gun, and the communication in question was a text message to T from a third party seeking the return of a gun. Assuming that the message included, by implication, a suggestion that T had the gun, the sender was not intent on causing T to believe that fact — rather there was a common understanding that such was the case, so again the message was not hearsay. And finally in the appeal of Lowe, L was charged with twice raping his young girlfriend following an argument. The defence was consent, and L claimed that the argument followed the intercourse rather than the other way round. Messages from L to the complainant, apparently apologising for the rape and admitting the sequence of events were held not to be hearsay: though they contained statements of highly relevant matters, L was not seeking to cause the complainant to believe she had been raped: 'if that is what the messages meant, they both knew that'. The statements were also confessions, but nothing turned on that. *Twist* [2011] 3 All ER 1055 was applied in *Khan* [2013] EWCA Crim 2230, where the question was whether one of two parties to a conversation was acquainted with K. The fact that both parties referred to K by his nickname, Bana, suggested that he was well-known to both. No question of hearsay was involved, as there was no purpose on the part of either party to cause the other to believe that he knew 'Bana'.

In all of the appeals heard in *Twist*, it could be said that there was a 'common understanding' **F15.21** between the parties to the communication that rendered it non-hearsay. The same is true of *Elliott* (2011) 175 JP 39, approved in *Twist*, where a letter was written on the basis that both the writer and the recipient supported the same criminal gang, and thereby provided non-hearsay evidence of the recipient's sympathies. See also *MK* (2008) 172 JP 538, *Chrysostomou* [2010] EWCA Crim 1403 and *Bains* [2010] EWCA Crim 873. The case of *Leonard* (2009) 173 JP 366, which has been the subject of some criticism, was defended in *Twist* on the grounds that the prosecution had elected to base their case on the truth of information found in text messages to L about the quality of drugs he had supplied, rather than (as they surely might have done) on the apparent existence of a common understanding about the supply itself.

'Common understanding' is not a necessary feature of all cases saved from the hearsay rule by s. 115(3). In *Isichei* (2006) 170 JP 753 the prosecution wished to prove that a member of a party looking for a nightclub had told his colleagues that he would ring 'Marvin'. The purpose of adducing the evidence was to establish a connection between the accused, whose first name this was, and an individual from the club who subsequently assaulted and robbed two female members of the party. While it could be argued that the caller had, as one of his purposes, the intention of causing the other members of the group to know that he was about to call 'Marvin', it was unlikely that he cared what, if anything, they believed as to the name of his contact. The Court of Appeal noted that the level of semantic analysis required by s. 115(3) was, in the circumstances, both highly artificial and disproportionate to the evidential significance of the call. The Court went on to decide that the call would, even if hearsay, have been admissible under the 'interests of justice' provision in s. 114(1)(d). This provides a sensible 'belt and braces' solution wherever the answer under s. 115(3) is unclear (or not worth the effort of pursuing) and the evidence would, if hearsay, be admissible in any event. However, in *Twist*, Hughes LJ drew attention to the additional complexity involved in admitting evidence by the hearsay route; complexities that need not apply where s. 115(3) accords the evidence non-hearsay status.

In some cases it may be difficult to determine whether a statement is directed at another per- **F15.22** son, and therefore whether it is intended to be believed. In *N* (2007) 171 JP 158 a statement in a complainant's diary regarding her sexual relationship with her uncle would have been hearsay (but admissible for the defence under an exception) had the statement been intended for another, but had it been intended for the writer's sole use it was not hearsay. The Court of Appeal regarded it as 'real or direct evidence outside the hearsay rule'. While it is hard to see how the entry could be real evidence of its truth, the argument that it is evidence of the matter contained in it (though not 'stated' for the purposes of the Act) would seem plausible. The only possible objection to the entry was that it was hearsay, which cannot be sustained under the terms of s. 115(3). See also *Knight* [2007] EWCA Crim 3027 and *Marine Fisheries Agency v Inter Fish Ltd* [2009] EWHC 753 (Admin), where a diary was rightly treated as hearsay in that it appears to have been more in the nature of a record, with some entries being made by a third party.

In *Sukadave Singh* [2006] 1 WLR 1564, the Court of Appeal rejected an argument which would have turned s. 115(3) on its head. By that argument, the provisions of s. 115 qualify only the statutory form of hearsay as described by s. 114; thus, as the rule in *Kearley* [1992] 2 AC 228 subsists only at common law, it remains unaffected. The argument is based on the absence of any express repeal of the common-law hearsay rule. The Court regarded the old rule as effectively abolished by s. 118 (which makes it clear that the only surviving common-law rules are certain preserved exceptions). When read with s. 114, there is no room for any other vestige of common law to remain.

ADMISSIONS BASED ON HEARSAY

F15.23 Where a person admits something, his own knowledge of which is based on hearsay, the admission does not prove the fact. In *Comptroller of Customs v Western Lectric Co. Ltd* [1966] AC 367, it was held that admissions as to the country of origin of goods, which were based on markings on the goods themselves, were inadmissible. Lord Hodson further described such admissions as being of no real value. See also *Surujpaul v The Queen* [1958] 3 All ER 300. The same problem frequently arises in handling cases, where there is a dearth of direct evidence to prove that the goods are stolen. In *Hulbert* (1979) 69 Cr App R 243, H admitted that she bought certain goods at very low prices from unnamed sellers in various public houses, and that, in some cases, the sellers told her that the goods were stolen. It was held that H's admission as to facts within her own knowledge (e.g., the price paid, and the circumstances in which the goods were offered for sale) was admissible evidence that the goods might have been stolen, but that her admission as to what she had been told could not be evidence that the goods were stolen. What she had been told would, however, be admissible to prove the state of her knowledge or belief at the time. See also *Sbarra* (1918) 87 LJ KB 1003, *Korniak* (1982) 76 Cr App R 145 and *Overington* [1978] Crim LR 692; and see **F15.10**.

In cases involving the possession of drugs, the accused's admission that the substance in question was a controlled drug would be inadmissible if based on hearsay, and of limited evidential value if based on his own opinion. In some cases the admissions of experienced drug users have been held to be prima facie evidence of the nature of a substance (*Chatwood* [1980] 1 All ER 467; *Bird v Adams* [1972] Crim LR 174; *Wells* [1976] Crim LR 518). *Mieras v Rees* [1975] Crim LR 224, which appears to be authority to the contrary, is misreported, the charge was one of attempt, where it was accepted that there was no proof as to the nature of the substance (*Chatwood* [1980] 1 All ER 467).

STATEMENTS TENDERED TO PROVE NON-EXISTENCE OF ALLEGED FACTS

F15.24 A difficult question at common law was whether a statement that is hearsay when tendered to prove the truth of a fact asserted in it is equally hearsay when tendered as circumstantial evidence of the non-existence of facts that might have been expected to have been asserted in it if they had been true. The problem arose most acutely with regard to records. In both *Patel* [1981] 3 All ER 94 and *Shone* (1982) 76 Cr App R 72 it was suggested that, provided responsible persons could give evidence of the method of record-keeping, an inference could be drawn about matters not appearing. Thus in *Patel*, which concerned immigration records, evidence as to the method of compilation and custody supported the inference that, if A's name was not recorded, he must be an illegal entrant. Had the CJA 2003, s. 115(3) (see **F15.17**), been applied to the circumstances in *Patel*, it may be argued that, as the purpose of the compiler was not to induce another to believe that A was an illegal entrant, or to cause another to act on the basis that he was, the hearsay rule is not infringed by the use of such records to support circumstantial inferences of a negative nature. Alternatively, to the extent that both the negative and positive use of a record depend on the correctness of the record keeping, negative inferences might be more safely drawn in the same way as positive ones, i.e. within the confines of a hearsay exception. Most records are now admissible under the CJA 2003, s. 117 (see **F16.24**). In *DPP v Leigh* [2010] EWHC 345 (Admin), it was held that the hearsay rule did not apply to evidence, based on records, that the respondent had failed to reply to notices issued pursuant to the RTA 1988, s. 172. The record itself was clearly admissible under the CJA 2003, s. 117, but the Divisional Court preferred the approach in *Patel* and *Shone*.

F15.25

When dealing with 'negative hearsay' otherwise than in the context of records, the common law tended towards a relaxed approach. This, it is submitted, is the best explanation of *Muir* (1983) 79 Cr App R 153. M was charged with theft of a video recorder, hired to him by G Ltd. M's defence was that the video had been taken away by two men who had called at his house. To rebut the suggestion that G Ltd had repossessed the video, S, the district manager of G Ltd, gave evidence that there had been no repossession by the local showroom: a fact within his own knowledge. He was asked in cross-examination about the possibility of repossession by the company's head office, and was allowed to say in response that he had telephoned head office and had been told that they had not ordered the repossession of the video. The Court of Appeal held that, 'in the way in which the evidence came out', it was not hearsay, on the ground that S 'was the best person to give the relevant evidence', including informing the court that a check had been made with head office. This analysis ignores the fact that what S had been told during the check was hearsay. On the facts of the case, the only option open to the prosecution if the rule had been strictly applied would have been to call a further witness from head office, and it may have been that expediency dictated the result. However, the decision was noted to have attracted adverse comment in *Coventry Justices, ex parte Bullard* (1992) 95 Cr App R 175. Under the CJA 2003, s. 114(1)(d) might be deployed if it was in the interests of justice to treat the witness S in *Muir* as an acceptable source of information regarding the possibility of repossession by the company's head office.

MECHANICALLY GENERATED AND COMPUTER GENERATED EVIDENCE

Mechanically Produced Evidence as Hearsay

F15.26

Under the CJA 2003, it is apparent from the definition of 'statement' in s. 115(1) (see **F15.2**) as a representation of fact or opinion *made by a person* that a purely mechanical generation of an image, say, by CCTV is not hearsay. The provision is equally clear that an image generated by human agency such as a representation in a 'sketch, photofit or other pictorial form' is included.

This follows the common law, whereby juries may be allowed to see still photographs taken by a security camera during an armed robbery (*Dodson* [1984] 1 WLR 971), or a video recording of an incident (*Fowden* [1982] Crim LR 588; *Grimer* [1982] Crim LR 674), and they may hear a tape recording of a relevant conversation (*Maqsud Ali* [1966] 1 QB 688). Furthermore, just as a video recording of the commission of an offence is admissible, so also a witness who has seen the recording may give evidence of what he saw, as he is in effect in the same position as a witness with a 'direct view of the action' (*Taylor v Chief Constable of Cheshire* [1986] 1 All ER 225). See also, as to computer-produced evidence, **F15.27**.

In *Cook* [1987] QB 417, the Court of Appeal considered that sketches and photofit likenesses made under the direction of identifying witnesses were analogous to photographs, in that they were not subject to the hearsay rule. The Court distinguished between the production of a sketch

F

Part F Evidence

or photofit, which is not hearsay, and the recital by a witness of the distinguishing features of the person to be identified, which is. There is, however, a difficulty with the analogy preferred by the Court, in that photofit likenesses are compiled at the instigation of a human mind, and are subject to the same dangers as other out-of-court statements. The effect of the CJA 2003, s. 115(1), is to overrule *Cook* and other cases to similar effect such as *Constantinou* (1989) 91 Cr App R 74.

A mechanically generated representation that depends for its accuracy on human input cannot be used in the absence of proof that the input was accurate (see the CJA 2003, s. 129, at F15.28).

Computer Evidence and the Hearsay Rule

F15.27   It follows from the definition of 'statement' in the CJA 2003, s. 115(1) and (2) (see **F15.2**), as a representation 'by a person' that computer evidence may or may not be hearsay. To the extent to which a computer is used merely to perform functions of calculation, no question of hearsay is involved in receiving evidence of what the computer 'said', and in this the 2003 Act follows the common law (*Minors* [1989] 2 All ER 208, per Steyn J at p. 446). The reason, it is submitted, is that the court, when acting on such information, is not being asked to accept the truth of a matter stated by any person. Thus, in *Wood* (1982) 76 Cr App R 23, the prosecution alleged that metal found at W's premises was stolen. Chemists performed tests on samples of the metal, and used a computer as a tool to perform complicated calculations based on the data they had obtained. At trial, the chemists gave evidence of the outcome of the tests, and produced the computer printout to prove the results of the calculations. It was held that the printout was admissible for this purpose and did not constitute hearsay evidence, being instead real evidence analogous to the reaction of litmus paper as evidence of the acidity of a solution. See also *Golizadeh* [1995] Crim LR 232. In the same way, the printout of an Intoximeter that has performed an analysis of specimens of breath is admissible non-hearsay evidence (*Castle v Cross* [1984] 1 All ER 87, where the rule regarding admissibility of computer evidence was said to be the same in this respect as in respect of less sophisticated machines; *Castle v Cross* was affirmed by the House of Lords in *DPP v McKeown* [1997] 1 All ER 737). See *The Statue of Liberty* [1968] 2 All ER 195 (automatic record made by radar set at a shore radio station admissible), and see also the rule as it applies to photographs etc. at **F15.26**.

F15.28   **Printouts and Accuracy**   Where a computer is used to record information that is supplied by a person, the hearsay rule will come into play if it is sought to use a printout from the computer to prove that what the person said was true. Thus, documentary records stored on computer are hearsay (*Minors*), and see *Coventry Justices, ex parte Bullard* (1992) 95 Cr App R 175, in which it was held that the crucial distinction was between 'computer printouts containing information implanted by a human, and printouts containing records produced without human intervention'. Similarly, in *Wood*, it was necessary for the chemists who tested the metal to give evidence of the facts on which the tests were based: the computer printout could not have been used to prove that the information fed into the computer was accurate, only that the calculations performed by the computer itself were correct. The CJA 2003 maintains the same distinction.

Criminal Justice Act 2003, s. 129

(1)   Where a representation of any fact—
   (a)   is made otherwise than by a person, but
   (b)   depends for its accuracy on information supplied (directly or indirectly) by a person, that representation is not admissible in criminal proceedings as evidence of the fact unless it is proved that the information was accurate.

A more difficult problem of classification arose in *Governor of Brixton Prison, ex parte Levin* [1997] AC 741. L was alleged to have initiated unauthorised payment instructions from his computer terminal in Russia, as a result of which the computerised fund transfer service of an American bank was induced to transfer funds from clients' accounts into accounts controlled by L. The transaction occurred automatically upon receipt of the instruction by L, and was duly copied to the American computer's historical records. L objected to the production of printouts showing the transactions on the grounds that they were hearsay, but the House of Lords held that they were not. Lord Woolf said:

> The printouts are tendered to prove the transfers of funds which they record. They do not assert that such transfers took place. They record the transfers themselves, created by the interaction between whoever purported to request the transfers and the computer program in Parsipanny [New Jersey]. The evidential status of the printouts is no different from that of a photocopy of a forged cheque.

In other words the printout proved the thing done because it was the thing done, or at least a copy of the thing done (commentary by Professor Sir John Smith on *Ewing* [1983] Crim LR 472 at p. 473).

Section F16 Exceptions to the Rule Against Hearsay (Excluding Confessions)

INTRODUCTION

Hearsay Exceptions

F16.1 The rule against hearsay, as described in **F15**, has never been an absolute prohibition. However, the various common-law and statutory exceptions to the rule which have grown up over time form a complex network, requiring considerable expertise to interpret. The provisions of the CJA 2003, part II, chapter 2, bring about the codification of the rule and of its most important exceptions, together with a considerable and welcome degree of simplification.

The overall aim is to ensure that, subject to the necessary safeguards, relevant evidence should be admitted where that is in the interests of justice. The provisions of the CJA 2003 constitute a 'crafted code' which, properly applied, is consistent with the right to fair trial accorded by the ECHR, Article 6(3)(d) (*Horncastle* [2010] 2 AC 373: see **F16.33**). The ruling of the Grand Chamber in *Al-Khawaja and Tahery v UK* (2012) 54 EHRR 807 (see **F16.33**) accepts, contrary to previous Strasbourg case law, that the CJA 2003 contains sufficient safeguards against the risk of wrongful conviction. It is convenient to begin with an overview of these provisions before embarking on the detail.

Criminal Justice Act 2003: Statutory Scheme, Notice, and Hearsay Admissible by Agreement

F16.2   Criminal Justice Act 2003, s. 114

(1) In criminal proceedings a statement not made in oral evidence in the proceedings is admissible as evidence of any matter stated if, but only if—
    (a) any provision of this chapter or any other statutory provision makes it admissible,
    (b) any rule of law preserved by section 118 makes it admissible,
    (c) all parties to the proceedings agree to it being admissible, or
    (d) the court is satisfied that it is in the interests of justice for it to be admissible.

See **F15.1** for the proceedings to which s. 114 applies and for elaboration of the definition of hearsay ('a statement not made in oral evidence . . . etc.').

F16.3 **Overview** In order to admit hearsay under the CJA 2003, a party has the options of invoking a statutory rule or a preserved common-law exception, of seeking the agreement of all parties to the use of hearsay, or of persuading the court that the evidence should be received in the interests of justice. The exception for statutory provisions applies to specific hearsay exceptions, and does not, for example, render admissible evidence of an identification at a parade merely because it took place in accordance with the statutory code of practice (*Lynch* [2008] 1 Cr App R 337). The inclusion of the 'interests of justice' exception in s. 114(1)(d) (see **F16.38**) was described by Lord Cooke of

Thorndon in the debates on the Act as the 'great merit' of the whole package of reforms. In effect it modifies the application of the general rule against hearsay — there is no rule against hearsay which it is in the interests of justice to admit — and is thus relevant throughout this section and **F15**.

The principal categories of admissibility dealt with under the new statutory rules concern cases where a witness is unavailable (s. 116: see **F16.8**) and business and other documents (s. 117: see **F16.24**). The preserved common-law rules are contained in s. 118, and concern evidence of public information (see **F16.48**); reputation (see **F16.54**); *res gestae* (see **F16.55**); confessions and admissions (see **F16.72**), common enterprise (see **F16.76**) and expert evidence (see **F16.84**). Sections 119 and 120 respectively make special provision for the previous inconsistent and consistent statements of witnesses in the case, which become more widely admissible as evidence of their truth and not merely of inconsistency or consistency as the case may be (see **F6.32** and **F7.45** respectively, *Chinn* [2012] 3 All ER 502, *Athwal* [2009] 1 WLR 2430, and *MH* [2012] EWCA Crim 2725, where it is made clear that such evidence is admissible hearsay). Supplementary provision is made in s. 121 for the problem of multiple hearsay, as to which there is very little authority at common law (see **F16.90**). Section 122 restricts the circumstances in which a jury may take a copy of a hearsay statement produced as an exhibit into the jury room when considering their verdict. Special provision is made in s. 123 to exclude from the operation of the new statutory exceptions statements by persons who lack competence (see **F16.8**).

Where hearsay evidence is admitted in written form, the CrimPR 2014 provides that either each relevant part of the statement must be read or summarised aloud, or the court and the jury (if there is one) must read the statement and its gist must be summarised aloud.

F16.4 Three related provisions assist in ensuring that the weight of hearsay can be properly assessed, and relied upon only to the extent that it is fair to do so (*Horncastle* [2010] 2 AC 373). They are s. 124 (which provides for the testing of credibility where the maker of a hearsay statement does not attend to testify (see **F16.92**)); s. 125 (power of the Crown Court to stop a case where evidence is unconvincing) and s. 126 (discretion to exclude superfluous evidence: see **F16.93**). The discretion is in addition to the court's existing range of discretions at common law and under the PACE 1984, s. 78.

Special provision is made for the use of copies (s. 133), for the use of transcripts at retrial (s. 131: see **F16.86**) and for removing the power of the court to overrule an objection to the reading of depositions (s. 130).

This section of this work deals with the more important of the various exceptions to the hearsay rule which operate in criminal cases, with the exception of confessions which are dealt with at **F17**. Although the CJA 2003 has significantly simplified the law in this area, it remains the case that the various exceptions overlap: e.g., the first-hand hearsay statement of a deceased victim of violence admissible under the CJA 2003, s. 116, might, if made under the influence of the event itself, also be received under the *res gestae* exception preserved by s. 118(1).

F16.5 **Notice** The CrimPR, part 34, makes provision for the procedure to be followed and other conditions to be fulfilled by a party proposing to tender a hearsay statement in evidence (see Supplement, R-265 *et seq.*). The rules are applicable to all parties wishing to introduce hearsay evidence. The court has a wide power to dispense with the notice requirement altogether, or to allow notice to be given in a different form, or orally; the party entitled to notice may also waive the entitlement. The court is not obliged to give leave to a co-accused who has failed to comply with the notice procedure where to do so might cause incurable unfairness to the prosecution or a fellow defendant (*Musone* [2007] 1 WLR 2467). The rules do not expressly provide that the failure to oppose a notice of hearsay is to be treated as agreement that the evidence may be given in hearsay form for the purposes of the CJA 2003, s. 114(1)(c). Section 132(4) stipulates that the rules may so provide, but in fact they do not. The court would thus appear to have a discretion in the matter.

F

F16.6 **Agreement** The freedom to admit hearsay evidence by agreement is a novel feature of the CJA 2003. There is no definition of 'agreement', but it would appear that failure to object is not necessarily agreement, although agreement may be implied rather than express (*Shah* [2012] EWCA Crim 212) or inferred from circumstances, e.g., where, following disclosure, the accused's legal representative does not demur to the evidence of an absent witness in summary proceedings (*Williams v Vehicle and Operator Services Agency* (2008) 172 JP 328 (Admin)). See also *J (DC)* [2010] 2 Cr App R 8, where it was said that, in the interests of good trial management, the court should be informed of any agreement to admit hearsay evidence at the beginning of the trial. Further, the mere fact of agreement, though sufficient to overcome an objection based on hearsay (or bad character: see **F12.16**), did not justify putting in evidence documents subject to public interest immunity disclosed for the purpose of cross-examination of prosecution witnesses, for which a further order would have been required.

CRIMINAL JUSTICE ACT 2003: UNAVAILABLE WITNESSES; BUSINESS AND OTHER DOCUMENTS AND DISCRETIONARY EXCLUSION

Scope of Criminal Justice Act 2003, ss. 116 and 117: Relationship with Discretionary Exclusion

F16.7 Nothing in the provisions of the CJA 2003, s. 116 or 117, prejudices any power of a court to exclude evidence under the PACE 1984, s. 78 (CJA 2003, s. 126(2)). It follows that courts retain a general exclusionary discretion on grounds of fairness in respect of prosecution evidence in addition to the specific powers conferred by the CJA 2003. In relation to hearsay tendered by the defence, however, the PACE 1984, s. 78, does not apply, leading to concerns that the CJA 2003 will facilitate the manufacture of hearsay evidence for the defence (cf. *James* [2005] 2 Cr App R 71, decided under the 1988 Act, and *Bailey* [2008] EWCA Crim 817). A possible solution may lie in the provision of a new general discretion to exclude in s. 126 (see **F16.93**) but this may be limited to superfluous evidence and not be susceptible to manipulation as a discretion based on fairness.

One function of the application of s. 78 will be to ensure that prosecution evidence is not admitted under s. 116 or 117 that compromises the accused's right to a fair trial, guaranteed by the ECHR, Article 6 (see further **F16.32**).

Unavailable Witnesses

F16.8   *Criminal Justice Act 2003, ss. 116 and 123*

116.—(1) In criminal proceedings a statement not made in oral evidence in the proceedings is admissible as evidence of any matter stated if—
   (a) oral evidence given in the proceedings by the person who made the statement would be admissible as evidence of that matter,
   (b) the person who made the statement (the relevant person) is identified to the court's satisfaction, and
   (c) any of the five conditions mentioned in subsection (2) is satisfied.
   (2) The conditions are—
   (a) that the relevant person is dead;
   (b) that the relevant person is unfit to be a witness because of his bodily or mental condition;
   (c) that the relevant person is outside the United Kingdom and it is not reasonably practicable to secure his attendance;
   (d) that the relevant person cannot be found although such steps as it is reasonably practicable to take to find him have been taken;
   (e) that through fear the relevant person does not give (or does not continue to give) oral evidence in the proceedings, either at all or in connection with the subject matter of the statement, and the court gives leave for the statement to be given in evidence.

(3) For the purposes of subsection (2)(e) 'fear' is to be widely construed and (for example) includes fear of the death or injury of another person or of financial loss.

(4) Leave may be given under subsection (2)(e) only if the court considers that the statement ought to be admitted in the interests of justice, having regard—

  (a) to the statement's contents,

  (b) to any risk that its admission or exclusion will result in unfairness to any party to the proceedings (and in particular to how difficult it will be to challenge the statement if the relevant person does not give oral evidence),

  (c) in appropriate cases, to the fact that a direction under section 19 of the Youth Justice and Criminal Evidence Act 1999 (special measures for the giving of evidence by fearful witnesses etc) could be made in relation to the relevant person, and

  (d) to any other relevant circumstances.

(5) A condition set out in any paragraph of subsection (2) which is in fact satisfied is to be treated as not satisfied if it is shown that the circumstances described in that paragraph are caused—

  (a) by the person in support of whose case it is sought to give the statement in evidence, or

  (b) by a person acting on his behalf,

in order to prevent the relevant person giving oral evidence in the proceedings (whether at all or in connection with the subject matter of the statement).

123.—(1) Nothing in section 116, 119 or 120 makes a statement admissible as evidence if it was made by a person who did not have the required capability at the time when he made the statement.

(2) Nothing in section 117 makes a statement admissible as evidence if any person who, in order for the requirements of section 117(2) to be satisfied, must at any time have supplied or received the information concerned or created or received the document or part concerned—

  (a) did not have the required capability at that time, or

  (b) cannot be identified but cannot reasonably be assumed to have had the required capability at that time.

(3) For the purposes of this section a person has the required capability if he is capable of—

  (a) understanding questions put to him about the matters stated, and

  (b) giving answers to such questions which can be understood.

(4) Where by reason of this section there is an issue as to whether a person had the required capability when he made a statement—

  (a) proceedings held for the determination of the issue must take place in the absence of the jury (if there is one);

  (b) in determining the issue the court may receive expert evidence and evidence from any person to whom the statement in question was made;

  (c) the burden of proof on the issue lies on the party seeking to adduce the statement, and the standard of proof is the balance of probabilities.

F16.9

Section 116 applies only to first-hand hearsay. Where a person makes a statement, but it is not clear whether the statement relates to his own knowledge or to something he has been told, the statement should therefore not be admitted (see *JP* [1999] Crim LR 401, decided under the CJA 1988, s. 23). (Under the CJA 2003, multiple hearsay may be admissible under s. 121 (see **F16.90**). Documents admissible under s. 117 (see **F16.24**) may also contain more than one degree of hearsay.) The requirement that the oral evidence of the person who made the statement would have been admissible as evidence of the matter (s. 116(1)(a)) also serves to ensure that hearsay cannot be received if the evidence would have been inadmissible for some other reason, e.g., that it is evidence of bad character that is not admissible under chapter 1 of part 11 of the CJA 2003 (see **F12** and **F14**).

The person who made the hearsay statement must be identifiable (s. 116(1)(b)) so that those seeking to challenge its credibility must be able to ascertain who made it, and be able where appropriate to invoke s. 124 (see **F16.92**), which is provided by way of a substitute to the right of cross-examination. In *Nkemayang* [2005] EWCA Crim 1937, the Court of Appeal approved of the insistence in the CJA 2003 on strict proof of identity, saying that 'any regime controlling the admissibility of evidence must be alert to the danger of fabricated evidence'. In *Mayers* [2009] 2 All ER 145 the Court of Appeal held that the language of s. 116(1)(b) clearly anticipates the disclosure of the identity of the maker of the statement to the defence; it follows

Part F Evidence

F

that s. 116 cannot be applied to anonymous witnesses. (See, as to preserving anonymity where a witness gives evidence, the CAJA 2009, ss. 86 to 90, at **D14.60**.) In *Ford* [2010] EWCA Crim 2250 an unknown witness to a shooting had stated that he wished to remain anonymous, but had handed the police a note containing the registration number of the getaway car. It was held, following *Mayers*, that the note was inadmissible. A statement by a witness whose identity is unknown might, it is submitted, be received instead under the common law of *res gestae* (see **F16.55**) or under the 'interests of justice' exception in s. 114(1)(d) (see **F16.38**), but it would appear from *Ford* that neither exception can be invoked so as to allow witnesses to choose to provide evidence anonymously, for fear of subverting the statutory scheme in the CAJA 2009.

F16.10   Applications under s. 116 most frequently concern statements in documents, but oral hearsay statements may also be tendered, as may statements made by conduct (for the meaning of 'statement' see s. 115(2) at **F15.2**). In *Musone* [2007] 1 WLR 2467, a man who had been stabbed was asked 'what's happened, mate?' and replied 'Musone's just stabbed me'. The statement was admitted at M's trial for murder under s. 116. By the same token, a gesture or sign language similarly identifying the guilty party could be received.

Section 116(5) prevents a person from being able to rely on a hearsay statement where he has caused the witness's absence precisely so that he can do so. In *Rowley* [2013] 1 WLR 895, the defence was held to be prevented from adducing the record of interview with T, who had been threatened by the accused and had subsequently fled abroad. The threat did not have to be the main or primary cause of the witness's absence, provided it was at least one of the effective causes. To hold otherwise would significantly undermine the policy of the legislation. Further, the provision was not limited to steps taken by the accused after the commencement of proceedings, provided they were done with the intent of preventing the attendance of the witness at the proceedings.

F16.11   **Proof of Unavailability of Maker**   The reasons specified in the CJA 2003, s. 116(2), for not calling the maker of a statement are disjunctive: provided that the party seeking to rely on the statement can establish that one of the reasons exists, it does not matter that other reasons cannot be made out (*Farrand v Galland* [1989] Crim LR 573, decided under the PACE 1984, s. 68). The criminal standard of proof applies to the proof of the conditions of admissibility under s. 116 (see, e.g., *Shabir* [2012] EWCA Crim 2564); this point was established under previous similar legislation in *Minors* [1989] 2 All ER 208 and has not subsequently been doubted. The standard of proof to be achieved by the defence is the ordinary civil standard of proof on a balance of probability (*Mattey* [1995] 2 Cr App R 409).

F16.12   **Unfitness to be a Witness**   Section 116(2)(b) of the CJA 2003 focuses not on the physical act of attending at court, but on the fitness of the witness when there to give evidence, and includes unfitness through any mental condition. The provision is thus satisfied if the witness could be brought to court but there would be no point in doing so. Evidence indicating a medical condition made worse by stress, but not indicating clearly that the witness is unfit, is not sufficient (*McEwan v DPP* (2007) 171 JP 308). It is not necessary to prove mental illness: unfitness caused by the trauma of being the victim of a sexual assault may qualify (*AC* [2014 EWCA Crim 371). Under the previous legislation, which was in similar terms, when a witness was unable to recollect relevant events, and medical evidence established that the cause was a mental disorder giving rise to great anxiety and failure of recall when under stress, the conditions of admissibility were satisfied (*Setz-Dempsey* (1994) 98 Cr App R 23). Other pertinent authorities under the 1988 Act include *Elliott* (2003) *The Times*, 15 May 2003, where it was held that, where the defence can point to proper grounds for wishing to cross-examine a doctor who testifies to the unfitness of a patient, it is right to make an opportunity available for them to do so. The effect of the witness's mental condition at the time the statement was made is, of course, a factor relevant to whether it should be excluded under s. 123 (see **F16.22**). The sudden unfitness of a witness who is hospitalised may be good reason for refusing an adjournment, but not for refusing to consider an application under s. 116 (*CPS v Uxbridge Magistrates* (2007) 171 JP 279). Where a witness becomes unfit during cross-examination then, in deciding whether the trial is in consequence unfair, the trial judge is entitled to bear in mind that a witness's whole evidence could have been received under s. 116 (*Lawless* (2011) 175 JP 93, and see further as to cross-examination F7.7).

Outside the UK and Not Reasonably Practicable to Secure Attendance or Cannot be Found   F16.13
after Reasonable Steps   Wherever possible, the witness should be brought to court: the right of confrontation and the citizen's duty to appear are of equal importance where a witness absents himself (*DT* (2009) 173 JP 425).

In *Castillo* [1996] 1 Cr App R 438 the Court of Appeal held that there were three considerations involved in the issue whether it is reasonably practicable for a witness to attend. The mere fact that it is possible for a witness to come does not answer the question. The court has to consider the importance of the evidence the witness could give, the expense and inconvenience of securing attendance and the weight to be given to the reasons put forward for non-attendance. The court also suggested a consideration of the prejudice to the defence that might arise if prosecution evidence were to be admitted, but this would appear more naturally to be a consideration relevant to the exercise of the court's exclusionary powers: see **F16.32** and the powers referred to at **F16.3**). In *French* (1993) 97 Cr App R 421, it was stressed that, in a case where there was a long history of attempts by the prosecution to secure the attendance of the witness, it was not helpful to ask when, if ever, the witness's attendance might be secured; the matter should be considered as it stood at the date of the application. In *Gyima* [2007] EWCA Crim 429, it was held proper to consider, where the witness was a child, the refusal of his parents to co-operate with the prosecution's efforts to secure attendance as well as the cost of alternative measures. In *Hurst* [1995] 1 Cr App R 82, the words 'reasonably practicable' were said to involve a consideration of the normal steps that would be taken to secure the attendance of a witness, and that cost was a relevant factor. As to the steps it may be reasonably practicable to take, see also *Maloney* [1994] Crim LR 525, *Gonzalez de Orango* [1992] Crim LR 180, and *Holman* [1995] Crim LR 80 (in which Bank of Ireland employees declined to attend the trial without an order of the Irish court and it was held that the statutory conditions were plainly made out). The provision is not intended for use where the prosecution have failed to monitor the witness's availability prior to trial and are then taken by surprise by absence abroad of which they should have been aware (*Bray* (1988) 88 Cr App R 354, decided under the PACE 1984, s. 68). In such cases, the question of what is reasonably practicable must be considered over a longer period than what was practicable on the day of the trial.

In *C & K* [2006] EWCA Crim 197, it was held that the expression 'reasonably practicable' in   F16.14
s. 116(2)(c) was to be judged on the basis of the steps taken, or not taken, to secure the attendance of a witness living abroad who was also a suspect in the case and who had suddenly changed his mind about giving evidence for the prosecution. Issues of admissibility under s. 116 were also inextricably linked to questions of fairness in relation to the court's discretionary powers under the PACE 1984, s. 78 (see **F16.35**) and the CJA 2003, s. 126 (see **F16.93**); in such cases there was likely to be a need to consider, in the interests of fairness, the reason for the change of heart and the viability of alternative modes of giving evidence whereby the witness would be subject to cross-examination. (See also *Radak* [1999] 1 Cr App R 187, decided under the 1988 Act.)

Where facts cannot be agreed, evidence must be called (*DT* (2009) 173 JP 425). In *Case* [1991] Crim LR 192 the only 'evidence' to support the contention that the maker of the statement was out of the country was the statement itself (which was, of course, inadmissible hearsay until proved otherwise), and there was no evidence at all on the issue of whether it would have been practicable to secure the attendance of the maker at the trial. Holding that the statement ought not to have been admitted, the Court of Appeal pointed out that, had the matter been approached properly and with the criminal standard of proof in mind, it was likely that evidence could have been found that would have secured the admissibility of the statement. In *Mattey*

[1995] 2 Cr App R 409, where the statement, which was tendered by the defence, had only to satisfy the condition on a balance of probabilities, it was held inadmissible in part because hearsay was relied on in support of it, but the hearsay may have been admissible evidence of the state of mind of the maker, so that *Case* was distinguishable. In any event, it should be noted that there is no bar to the use of a statement by one witness that is itself admissible to prove the inability of another witness to attend the trial (*Castillo* [1996] 1 Cr App R 438).

F16.15 To tell a judge that a witness cannot be traced carries with it the implication that efforts have been made to trace him. If no such efforts have been made, the judge is being misled (*Shah* [2010] EWCA Crim 2326). In *Coughlan* [1999] 5 Arch News 2, it was said that, where it is suggested that a witness cannot be found after taking all reasonable steps, the importance of the evidence and the cost implications are relevant, although the seriousness of the offence was said not to be relevant. In reality, of course, the resources devoted to tracing witnesses will necessarily take account of the seriousness of the offence. *Coughlan* was considered in *Henry* [2003] EWCA Crim 1296, where D, an associate of the deceased who had made a statement of apparently marginal relevance regarding her murder, had been deported before the trial, leaving a contact address in Jamaica from which he subsequently disappeared. At trial it emerged for the first time that the defence involved a suggestion that D was involved in the murder; however, what constituted 'reasonable steps' had to be assessed in light of the expected importance of D's evidence. In particular, the prosecution could not be expected to attempt to delay the deportation of an overstayer who has provided an overseas address, unless it ought reasonably to have been apparent that he could have given important evidence. Where the notice given to a witness falls short of what the court regards as acceptable, it cannot apply s. 116(2)(d) (*Adams* [2008] 1 Cr App R 430), although in that case, exceptionally, the evidence was admitted under s. 114(1)(d) (see **F16.38**).

F16.16 **Fear**   The terms of the CJA 2003, s. 116(2)(e), do not require that the fear must be attributable to the accused, nor does the ECHR, Article 6 so require (*Horncastle* [2010] 2 AC 373: see the Court of Appeal judgment endorsed and regarded as complementary to the subsequent decision of the Supreme Court). The condition is satisfied where a witness is called to give oral evidence but does not, through fear, cover the relevant matter in the statement (cf. *Ashford Magistrates' Court, ex parte Hilden* [1993] 2 All ER 154 and *Waters* (1997) 161 JP 249). The previous statement of a hostile prosecution witness who is motivated simply by the desire to protect the accused, rather than by fear, remains outside the purview of the section, but may be admissible under the CJA 2003, s. 119 (see **F6.49**) or, as was suggested in *Saunders* [2012] EWCA Crim 1185, s. 114(1)(d) (see **F16.38**). Where fear appears to be only one factor in a witness's refusal to testify, it is necessary to exercise care in evaluating other possible reasons. In *Nelson* [2009] EWCA Crim 1600 the witness was also angry at what she perceived to be the failures of the witness protection system, and anxious about the symptoms of a serious illness and a related medical appointment she had missed because she was forced to attend the court. More should have been done to ascertain the witness's reasons for refusing to testify; the outcome of further investigation might have led the judge to deal differently with her. Section 116(3) makes it clear that fear is to be 'widely construed', and it has been said that courts are now 'ill-advised to seek to test the basis of fear by calling witnesses before them' (*Davies* [2007] 2 All ER 1070). However, the requirement to prove the necessity of relying on the evidence of the absent witness, supported by *Horncastle* and subsequent cases, including *Riat* [2013] 1 All ER 349 and *Shabir* (2013) 177 JP 271, militates towards a close examination of the claim to be in fear. The prevailing view is that the claim should be tested in court if at all possible (*Shabir* at [64]). In any case, the requirement for leave to be obtained requires a close scrutiny of the impact of the fear on the witness, which requires testing in court where possible (see **F16.19**).

F16.17 In *Doherty* (2007) 171 JP 79 a man was injured in a scuffle on a train crowded with football supporters. N, the brother of the injured man, identified the accused as having made an unprovoked attack on the victim, who remembered little of the attack. It was held that leave had properly been given to admit N's statement under s. 116(2)(e), on the strength of further oral and written statements by N that he had received a series of anonymous and implicitly threatening phone calls which appeared to be connected with the trial and in consequence of which he feared for his family's safety. This was sufficient to satisfy the widely drawn 'fear' condition; the question whether the fear was justified was a matter going to the 'interests of justice' test under s. 116(4) (see **F16.19**). Under the previous law, the proof of fear by admissible evidence was a matter which gave rise to difficulty not adverted to in *Doherty*, but it is submitted that the principles remain unchanged. In *Neill v North Antrim Magistrates' Court* [1992] 4 All ER 846, two boys made statements to the police in which they claimed to have witnessed an assault and to have identified one of the perpetrators. However, they did not attend the subsequent committal proceedings, and evidence was given by a police officer that the boys' mothers had told him that the boys were too afraid to attend. The House of Lords held that the statements should not have been received because the evidence of the officer was hearsay, being based on what he had been told by the mothers of the boys and not by the boys themselves. If the boys had communicated their fears to him directly he could have given evidence of what they had told him under the 'long-established law that a person's declaration of his contemporaneous state of mind is admissible to prove the existence of that state of mind', per Lord Mustill at p. 1228 following *Blastland* [1986] AC 41 (see now the CJA 2003, s. 118(1)). However, the point was also made that, even had such evidence been available, a court would be cautious about whether it was in the interests of justice to admit documentary evidence of identification or recognition that formed the principal element in the prosecution's case: a point that might now be made with equal force in relation to the risk of unfairness under s. 116(4) (see **F16.19**).

As to proof of fear by hearsay evidence forming part of the *res gestae*, see **F16.55**. An alternative might be to admit the proof of the witness's fear under the CJA 2003, s. 114(1)(d) ('the interests of justice' exception: see **F16.38**).

F16.18 The evidence of fear must relate to the relevant time. In *McCoy* [1999] All ER (D) 1410, M was charged with 'glassing' B. B failed to attend the trial on the first day. B told a police officer that he had been threatened; although he agreed to attend on the following day, he failed to do so. It was held that there was 'at very least a question mark' whether B's failure to attend on the second day was truly due to fear. To the same effect is *H* [2001] Crim LR 815. The alleged victim of a kidnapping made a statement two months before the trial indicating his fear of reprisals and his intention to abscond, but he in fact remained in the area and was arrested in connection with drugs offences. No evidence of continuing fear was adduced at the trial. Stressing that the fear must be judged at the time of the trial, and that the out-of-date evidence was not by itself sufficient, the Court of Appeal also acknowledged that there might be a 'degree of sensible give and take', for example when a ruling on admissibility was sought in advance of trial to enable counsel for the prosecution to decide how the case should be opened to the jury. Although these are decisions under the CJA 1988, s. 23, they would appear still to be authoritative.

F16.19 **Leave in Fear Cases**   In *Horncastle* [2010] 2 AC 373, in a judgment endorsed and regarded as complementary to the subsequent decision of the Supreme Court, the Court of Appeal stressed that all possible efforts should be made to get the witness to court, bearing in mind the importance of the right to confrontation and that intimidation will only flourish if citizens are readily discouraged from doing their duty. If the circumstances are such that the defence cannot cross-examine the witness to test the relevant matters, it is incumbent on the judge to investigate all possibilities by which the witness might give oral evidence (*Riat* [2013] 1 All ER 349, and *Shabir* (2013) 177 JP 271). See also *Fagan* [2012] EWCA Crim 2248, where it is recognised that a conclusion of intimidation may still be reached without producing the witness in court, and *Claridge* [2013] EWCA Crim 203, where it was said to be a 'counsel to perfection' to expect inquiry to be made of the witness, who was in court, about whether she could be persuaded to testify, but the failure to do so did not threaten the safety of the conviction. Note also *Jabbar* [2013] EWCA Crim 801 and compare *Lawrence* [2014] 1 Cr App R 33 (5), discussed at **F16.42**. Witnesses should never be assured in advance that their evidence will be read (*Horncastle* at [81]). In deciding whether to give leave under the CJA 2003, s. 116(4), to admit the statement of a fearful witness, the court is expressly directed to take into account, along with any other circumstances it regards as relevant, the content of the statement, the risk that its admission or exclusion will result in unfairness having regard to the difficulty of challenging the statement if the relevant person does not give oral evidence, and the possibility that a special measures direction under the YJCEA 1999 (see D14.3) could be made in relation to that person. This last condition directs the court's attention to the possibility that fear may in some cases be assuaged by the application of special measures, e.g., by the use of screens, live-link or video-recorded evidence. These alternatives are preferable to hearsay because the witness is made available to be cross-examined. Thus in *Robinson v Sutton Coldfield Magistrates' Court* [2006] 4 All ER 1029, where the complainant in a case of assault (R's former partner) had begun a new life and did not wish R to be able to trace her, it was necessary for the justices, before receiving her evidence, to consider whether any of the 1999 Act's special measures might meet the case. The possibility that special arrangements could have been made to convey her to court without enabling R to discover where she was living might also have been relevant to the overall question of the interests of justice. In *Doherty* (2007) 171 JP 79 (see **F16.17**), the exercise to be undertaken under s. 116(4) was described as 'not strictly an exercise of discretion but something akin to it', and one which the judge is in the best position to perform. Issues of trial fairness, including an alleged infringement of the ECHR, Article 6(3) (d), can conveniently be subsumed within the s. 116(4) inquiry, but ultimately the issues are the same in fear cases as in other cases of challenge for unfairness based on *Horncastle*: see **F16.33** *et seq.* — many of the leading cases considered there involve fearful witnesses.

F16.20   **Intimidation**   If the reason for the witness's failure to give evidence in person is that he was intimidated by or on behalf of the accused, who then contests the admissibility of the statement for the prosecution, the strong principle that the accused should not profit from his own wrong has been a factor in decisions under the pre-2003 law in relation to the ECHR, Article 6 (*Montgomery* [2002] EWCA Crim 1655; *Harvey* [1998] 10 Arch News 2; *M* [2003] 2 Cr App R 322). In *M* the Court of Appeal considered that to refuse to admit hearsay evidence where an essential or the only witness is kept away by fear would be an intolerable result and would encourage intimidation. On the facts of the case, however, it was wrong, and a breach of Article 6, to admit the hearsay evidence of an essential witness, which was potentially 'completely flawed' and which may have been motivated by the maker's desire to blame M, a person unfit to plead, for an offence in which he was himself implicated. In *Arnold* [2004] EWCA Crim 1293, the Court warned prosecutors that the problems posed by intimidation of witnesses by organised criminals did not provide a licence to prosecutors to resort to proof by hearsay. The note of caution expressed in *Arnold* was endorsed in *Sellick* [2005] 1 WLR 3257. However, the Court in that case felt the need to register an important point which was not fully taken into account in *Arnold*, and took a strong and, it is submitted, welcome line in respect of cases where intimidation is either clearly proved or highly probable. If an accused has been clearly shown to have kept a witness away by fear, he cannot complain that his Article 6(3)(d) right has been infringed, since he is the author of his inability to examine the witness at trial. *Sellick* was approved in *Doherty* (2007) 171 JP 79, decided under the CJA 2003. See also *Boulton* [2007] EWCA Crim 942, where ample evidence of fear was provided by the accused's attempts to 'scupper' the prosecution case by intimidating witnesses, and *Kelly* [2007] EWCA Crim 1715 where the Court endorsed both *Arnold* and the caveat in *Sellick*. Even in cases of clear intimidation, however, it remains important to investigate whether the witness might give oral evidence if brought to court (see *Fagan* [2012] EWCA Crim 2248 and **F16.19**).

Note that, by virtue of the CJA 2003, s. 116(5) (see **F16.8** and **F16.10**), an accused who causes the absence of a witness through fear is also prevented from adducing the witness's statement as hearsay where to do so favours his case and see *Rowley* [2013] 1 WLR 895 at **F16.10**.

F16.21   **Relevance of Availability of Other Evidence**   Where the disputed hearsay evidence is the 'sole or decisive' evidence for the prosecution, the court must pay particular attention to *Horncastle* [2010]

2 AC 373 and the considerations outlined at **F16.33** *et seq*. Authorities such as *Cole* [1990] 2 All ER 108, decided under the CJA 1988, remain relevant: the presence or absence of other evidence enabling the evidence to be challenged is relevant to the calculation of what has been lost to the party deprived of the opportunity to cross-examine. In *Robinson v Sutton Coldfield Magistrates' Court* [2006] 4 All ER 1029, the magistrates were entitled to take account of the unchallenged photographic evidence of the assault, and of a partial admission by R, who further admitted that the complainant was someone who 'does not lie'. Further, although the court cannot require to be told whether the accused intends to give evidence or call witnesses, it is not bound to assess the possibility of challenging the statement upon the basis that the accused will do neither of these things. In *Doherty* (2007) 171 JP 79 the court was influenced not only by the strength of the other evidence of the assault but also by the prospect of witnesses being called who could support the accused's version of events. In some cases, evidence admissible under bad character provisions of the CJA 2003 may provide support for hearsay evidence, as in *O'Leary* [2013] EWCA Crim 1371 (see **F12.60**), where the evidence of elderly fraud victims who suffered from dementia and were unable to testify was cross-admissible and showed that they had been targeted because of their vulnerability.

Competence   A statement by a witness who lacks the competence to testify at the time the **F16.22** statement was made may not be received under the CJA 2003, s. 116 (see s. 123 at **F16.8**). Contrast *D* [2003] QB 90, where a witness suffering from a degenerative mental condition rendering her unfit to give evidence at trial was also probably incompetent to give evidence at the time when her statement was taken. On the question whether the language in s. 23 of the CJA 1988 required she be competent at this point, the Court of Appeal was doubtful that it did, but was confident that the impact of the witness's illness on the admissibility of her statement could be fully and fairly dealt with by the application of the court's exclusionary powers.

Credibility   Section 124 of the CJA 2003 (see **F16.92**) applies in relation to matters bearing **F16.23** on the credibility of the makers of hearsay statements admissible under s. 116.

Business and Other Documents

Criminal Justice Act 2003, s. 117   F16.24

(1) In criminal proceedings a statement contained in a document is admissible as evidence of any matter stated if—
  (a) oral evidence given in the proceedings would be admissible as evidence of that matter,
  (b) the requirements of subsection (2) are satisfied, and
  (c) the requirements of subsection (5) are satisfied, in a case where subsection (4) requires them to be.
(2) The requirements of this subsection are satisfied if—
  (a) the document or the part containing the statement was created or received by a person in the course of a trade, business, profession or other occupation, or as the holder of a paid or unpaid office,
  (b) the person who supplied the information contained in the statement (the relevant person) had or may reasonably be supposed to have had personal knowledge of the matters dealt with, and
  (c) each person (if any) through whom the information was supplied from the relevant person to the person mentioned in paragraph (a) received the information in the course of a trade, business, profession or other occupation, or as the holder of a paid or unpaid office.
(3) The persons mentioned in paragraphs (a) and (b) of subsection (2) may be the same person.
(4) The additional requirements of subsection (5) must be satisfied if the statement—
  (a) was prepared for the purposes of pending or contemplated criminal proceedings, or for a criminal investigation, but
  (b) was not obtained pursuant to a request under section 7 of the Crime (International Co-operation) Act 2003 or an order under paragraph 6 of Schedule 13 to the Criminal Justice Act 1988 (which relate to overseas evidence).
(5) The requirements of this subsection are satisfied if—
  (a) any of the five conditions mentioned in section 116(2) is satisfied (absence of relevant person etc), or

      (b) the relevant person cannot reasonably be expected to have any recollection of the mat-
ters dealt with in the statement (having regard to the length of time since he supplied the
information and all other circumstances).

  (6) A statement is not admissible under this section if the court makes a direction to that effect
under subsection (7).

  (7) The court may make a direction under this subsection if satisfied that the statement's reliability
as evidence for the purpose for which it is tendered is doubtful in view of—

      (a) its contents,

      (b) the source of the information contained in it,

      (c) the way in which or the circumstances in which the information was supplied or
received, or

      (d) the way in which or the circumstances in which the document concerned was created or
received.

Section 117 broadly corresponds to the CJA 1988, s. 24, which it replaces.

F16.25   **Business or Other Documents**   'Business records are made admissible...because, in the
ordinary way, they are compiled by people who are disinterested and, in the ordinary course
of events, such statements are likely to be accurate; they are therefore admissible as evidence
because prima facie they are reliable' (the Court of Appeal in *Horncastle* [2010] 2 AC 373, in a
judgment endorsed and regarded as complementary to the subsequent decision of the Supreme
Court).

Section 117 of the CJA 2003 extends, as did its predecessor (s. 24 of the CJA 1998), to documents created or received by a person in the course of a trade, business, profession or other
occupation, or as the holder of a paid or unpaid office. Section 117 goes further in that it applies
also to parts of documents so created, when the statement in issue is included in that part (for
the meaning of 'statement' see s. 115(2) at **F15.2**) In *Clowes* [1992] 3 All ER 440, decided under
the CJA 1988, s. 24, transcripts of interviews between the liquidators of companies and persons
involved with the companies were held to have been 'received' by the liquidators in the course
of their profession and as holders of the office of liquidator. Documents of a non-commercial
nature such as a National Health Service hospital's records are clearly admissible, as is the transcript of the evidence given by a witness at an earlier trial, which may be admitted at a retrial
even though the court is plainly not a business in any sense (*Lockley* [1995] 2 Cr App R 554).
Similarly, a police custody record was admitted under s. 24 in *Hogan* [1997] Crim LR 349.

Because s. 117, like s. 24 before it, applies only to documentary evidence, the compiler of documents for use in criminal proceedings who leaves out important details of information he has
gathered from others who do not give evidence cannot simply supplement his record with oral
hearsay testimony (*Hinds* [1993] Crim LR 528). Nor can an entry in a record be proved simply
by calling someone who has checked the record (*Motor Depot Ltd and Williams v Kingston upon
Hull City Council* (2013) 177 JP 41), a principle that appears to have been breached in *Grazette
v DPP* [2012] EWHC 3863 (Admin).

F16.26   In *Foxley* [1995] 2 Cr App R 523, the decided under the CJA 1988, s. 24, the documents in
question were copies of credit notes and payments allegedly made by overseas companies to F,
who was accused of receiving them corruptly. They had been obtained by letters of request to
the authorities in the relevant countries. It was objected, *inter alia*, that no evidence was available from the creator as to whether these documents had come into existence in the course of a
business etc., but it was held to be the intention of the statute that the court be allowed to draw
relevant inferences from the documents themselves and from the way in which they had been
placed before the court. Likewise, in *O'Connor* [2010] EWCA Crim 2287, Belgian telephone
records were procured through letters of request, but no accompanying statement as to the
method of compilation was forthcoming. It was held that, to the extent that the documents may
have been statements by a person (rather than non-hearsay mechanically produced evidence)
it was open to the judge to draw inferences that their compilation had been in accordance with
the provisions of the CJA 2003, s. 117. On the face of the documents, it could be inferred that

the compiler had been either an employee of the phone provider or an officer of the Belgian police. Nothing in s. 117 required the production of an explanatory statement, though it may well often be desirable to have one. In *Department of Environment, Food and Rural Affairs v Atkinson* [2002] EWHC 2028 (Admin), the label on a bottle was held to be admissible evidence that it contained a veterinary medicinal product, applying the same inference of reliability from the context. A case that may go too far in this context is *Grazette v DPP*, where an inference was drawn as to the likelihood that the anonymous supplier of information to a Criminal Intelligence Report as to the 'street name' of the accused was correct because the address given for him in the same report was correct.

Personal Knowledge   The 'supplier' of the information (who must have, etc., personal knowledge of the matters dealt with under the CJA 2003, s. 117(2)(b)) may also be the person who 'creates' the document under s. 117(2)(c) (s. 117(3)). Thus, for example, a note made by an operator working for a paging company that messages had been left for a customer would be admissible (as in *Rock* [1994] Crim LR 843, decided under the 1988 Act) as a first-hand hearsay statement. Where such a document is received in evidence under s. 117, it is not necessary, as it is under s. 116 (see **F16.8**), to prove the unavailability of the maker of the statement.   **F16.27**

Section 117 may also be invoked where several degrees of hearsay are involved. Provided each of the persons through whom the information was supplied received it in the course of a trade etc. (s. 117(2)(c)), the facts stated in the document are admissible. See, e.g., *Wellington v DPP* (2007) 171 JP 497 (extract from Police National Computer printout recording previous use of same alias by accused). In *Maher v DPP* (2006) 170 JP 441 a note which had been made (and lost) of a car number plate could not be adduced as second-hand evidence under s. 117 because a relevant passer-on of information had not received it in the course of their trade etc. The evidence was, however, admitted under s. 121(1)(c) as multiple hearsay, on the ground that the value of the evidence, taking into account its apparent reliability, was so high that the interests of justice required admissibility. This apparent incongruity can be explained on the basis that admissibility under s. 117 is 'automatic' (subject to the discretion in s. 117(6) and (7)), hence the need to demonstrate the degree of reliability inherent in the making of a commercial type of record. The ruling in favour of admissibility in *Maher* is based on the determination that the particular record, though not automatically admissible, was (on investigation of its specific properties) sufficiently reliable and important to be received. However, the process by which it was received ought to have included the determination that the passing-on of the information was itself hearsay admissible under s. 114(1)(d) (see **F16.38** and **F16.91**).

A document produced by a computer without any human intervention cannot be said to contain information 'supplied by a person' with 'personal knowledge' (*Pettigrew* (1980) 71 Cr App R 39). However, as such a document is unlikely to constitute hearsay evidence, it will not matter that the conditions of the exception cannot be satisfied (*Wood* (1982) 76 Cr App R 23, considered at **F15.27**).   **F16.28**

The statement is admissible only as evidence of any matter stated of which 'oral evidence given in the proceedings' would be admissible, and this prevents the introduction of evidence that contravenes a rule of admissibility other than the hearsay rule, e.g., the rule against evidence of bad character, or evidence that goes only to credit where the witness's answer is final, as in *Foye* (2013) 177 JP 449. It cannot be a valid objection to the admissibility of evidence under s. 117 that an intermediary through whom the information was supplied could not have given evidence of the fact without contravening the hearsay rule, otherwise s. 117 could not be made to apply to second-hand hearsay, and it is clearly meant to do so (see s. 121 at **F16.90**).

Unavailability of Maker of Statement Prepared for Purposes of Criminal Proceedings or Investigation   It is not generally necessary to show grounds why the supplier of information contained in a statement should not be called before tendering his statement in evidence under the CJA 2003, s. 117. The only exceptions are those statements prepared for the purposes of   **F16.29**

pending or contemplated criminal proceedings, or of a criminal investigation (s. 117(4)(a)), which are not obtained pursuant to a request or order specified in s. 117(4)(b). Here, s. 117(5) applies, and it is necessary to establish either:

(a) one of the reasons for not calling the relevant person that apply in the case of a s. 116 statement (s. 117(5)(a): see **F16.11** *et seq.*); or

(b) that the person cannot reasonably be expected (having regard to the time that has elapsed since he made the statement and to all the circumstances) to have any recollection of the matters dealt with in the statement (s. 117(5)(b)).

In *Minchin* [2013] EWCA Crim 2412 M was charged with conspiracy to pervert the course of justice for providing a false alibi for his son. The Court of Appeal accepted that a solicitor's file note recording a meeting that had taken place with M and his son was inadmissible under s. 117 as it had been prepared for the purposes of criminal proceedings (s. 117(4)) and none of the statutory reasons for not calling the maker applied (s. 117(5)). However, the probative value of the note ultimately led to its admission under s. 114(1)(d) in the interests of justice (see **F16.42**).

F16.30   In *Humphris* (2005) 169 JP 441, an attempt was made to use s. 117 where the prosecution sought to establish the *modus operandi* of previous admissible sexual offences committed by H. The details of the offences were recorded by police officers and other employees all acting under a duty, and the suggestion was that they had the necessary personal knowledge to be the 'relevant person' for the purposes of s. 117(2)(b) and (5). While the court found no difficulty in using s. 117 to establish the fact of conviction, the details of the method used were in each case dependent on information originally supplied by the complainant, who was thus the 'relevant person'. The correct method of proceeding would therefore have been, as it was before the CJA 2003, to take a statement from the complainant. This might, depending on the circumstances, have been admissible under s. 116 (see **F16.8**). See, however, *Ainscough* (2006) 170 JP 517, drawing attention to the fact that a conviction might be complicated by the fact that an accused was sentenced on a different basis as a result of a plea, proffered and accepted by the court at the time. This would affect the fairness of admitting the original complainant's evidence as hearsay and would raise numerous satellite issues about the detail of what occurred (see also **F12.47**).

F16.31   In *Bedi* (1992) 95 Cr App R 21 the 'lost and stolen' reports maintained by a bank in respect of credit cards it had issued were held not to fall within the equivalent provisions of the CJA 1988. An examination of the reports disclosed that they were kept for the proper conduct of the bank's business, not for criminal proceedings. In *Hogan* [1997] Crim LR 349 it was assumed, surely rightly, that a police custody record fell within the equivalent provisions of the 1988 Act, and in *West Midlands Probation Board v French* [2009] 1 WLR 1715 it was held that the licence setting out the conditions of a prisoner's release is not a document prepared for the purposes specified by s. 117(4)(a).

Section 117(5)(b) may apply where a witness is unable to recollect one part of a longer statement but is able to give evidence as to the rest (*Carrington* [1994] Crim LR 438, in which the witness's recollection was supplemented in relation to a car registration number that she had forgotten, in circumstances where she was not entitled to refresh her memory from the statement). See as to the evidence that may satisfy this condition, *Crayden* [1978] 2 All ER 700 at p. 608 (decided under the Criminal Evidence Act 1965) and *Feest* [1987] Crim LR 766 (decided under the PACE 1984).

Section 117(7) allows the court to direct that unreliable 'business' documents be excluded.

Discretionary Exclusion of Statements Admissible under the Criminal Justice Act 2003, ss. 116 and 117

F16.32   Under the CJA 2003, the residual mechanism for exclusion of prosecution evidence that poses a threat to the interests of justice remains the PACE 1984, s. 78, although this is only one of the battery of measures designed to ensure that hearsay does not prejudice a fair trial: hearsay admissible on grounds of fear, for example, has an inbuilt requirement to this effect (see **F16.19**). In *C*

& K [2006] EWCA Crim 197 the Court of Appeal was keen to point out that the satisfaction of (in that case) s. 116 was only 'the first stage in a ruling upon the admissibility of the statement', and in *Horncastle* [2010] 2 AC 373 the Court of Appeal (in a judgment subsequently affirmed and described as 'complementary' to that of the Supreme Court) identified a range of other measures designed to ensure fairness, including the duty to stop a case that, ultimately, proves to be based on unconvincing hearsay (under s. 125: see **F16.93**). The existence of s. 125 does not lead to the conclusion that hearsay should be admitted and a decision on it postponed to the end of the trial: in many cases a ruling will be required in advance of admitting the evidence.

Apart from the possibility of using the CJA 2003, s. 126, to exclude superfluous evidence (see **F16.93**), there is no corresponding mechanism for the exclusion of unfair defence evidence which is otherwise admissible under s. 116 or s. 117 so that, for example, a first-hand hearsay statement by an identifiable individual who has since disappeared and cannot be found is automatically admissible for the defence under s. 116. There is some reason to fear that the automatic admissibility provisions may lead to the fabrication of hearsay evidence, despite the fact that such fabrications (like false alibis) may rebound on their users (*Bailey* [2008] EWCA Crim 817, where counsel argued, unsuccessfully, that a co-accused's reliance on a witness who had fled the country created a 'rogues' charter').

Hearsay, Loss of Right to Cross-examine and Fair Trial Provisions   Fairness-based arguments for   **F16.33** the exclusion of hearsay evidence typically emphasise the loss of the important right to cross-examine the absent witness, and the right of an accused person 'to examine or have examined witnesses against him' under the ECHR, Article 6(3)(d). In *Grant v The State* [2007] 1 AC 1 the Privy Council emphasised that the hearsay rule had always been subject to exceptions which formed inroads on the normal right to cross-examine; the guiding principle in both jurisdictions was that a new exception must not compromise the overall fairness of the proceedings. In the leading case of *Horncastle* [2010] 2 AC 373 the Supreme Court dismissed a specific challenge to the CJA 2003 in *Al-Khawaja and Tahery v UK* (2009) 49 EHRR 1. In that case the ECtHR held that where a conviction is based 'solely or to a decisive degree' on statements made by a person who the accused has had no opportunity to examine or have examined, the rights of the defence are restricted to an extent that is incompatible with Article 6. The Supreme Court in *Horncastle* held that to introduce this qualification would involve rewriting the CJA 2003 to include a provision that Parliament had explicitly rejected. The CJA 2003 sets out a rigorous scheme whereby the credibility and reliability of hearsay evidence can be tested (s. 124: see **F16.92**) and includes an overriding safeguard to stop a case based on unreliable evidence (s. 125: see **F16.94**). The safeguards were both more principled and more practical than the scheme suggested by the ECtHR in *Al-Khawaja*. Subsequently the ruling of the Grand Chamber in *Al-Khawaja and Tahery v UK* (2012) 54 EHRR 807 substantially confirmed the view of the Supreme Court. It was conceded that the statutory framework for admissibility of the evidence of absent witnesses is sufficient, properly applied, to provide for fair trial in such cases. The court must, however, be satisfied that there is a sufficient basis for the absence of the witness, as well as that a fair trial will still be possible despite the absence of the opportunity to cross-examine. The latter condition will be harder to satisfy if the evidence of the absent witness is the sole or decisive evidence against the accused. The Grand Chamber drew attention in particular to the trial judge's power to stop a case based wholly or partly on hearsay where a conviction would be unsafe.

In *Ibrahim* [2012] 4 All ER 225, the Court of Appeal noticed that there are differences in approach between that decision and the decision of the Supreme Court in *Horncastle*. However, the core principle to be deduced is that, where the untested hearsay evidence is 'critical', the question of whether the trial is fair depends on three principal factors: (1) good reason to admit the evidence (i.e. compliance with the CJA 2003); (2) whether the evidence can be shown to be reliable and (3) the extent to which counterbalancing measures exist and have been properly applied: this involves consideration of all the statutory safeguards in the CJA 2003, together with the application of common-law safeguards such as proper directions in the summing-up. In *Riat* [2013] 1 All ER 349 Hughes LJ noted that there seemed to be an element of misunderstanding around the proposition in *Horncastle* that 'sole or decisive' hearsay evidence might be admitted if it was 'demonstrably reliable or its reliability was capable of proper testing and assessment'. There was clearly no rule that evidence had to be independently verified before being put to a jury. Rather, a judge had to ensure that the evidence can safely be held to be reliable, given its strengths and weaknesses, the tools available to the jury for testing it and its importance to the case as a whole. A detailed summary of the relevant principles derived from *Horncastle, Ibrahim* and *Riat* is given in *Shabir* (2013) 177 JP 271. In that case, the evidence of a witness who was in prison and suffering from paranoid schizophrenia with persecutory and paranoid delusions should have been excluded, despite support for parts of his evidence, as it could not be shown that his untested hearsay evidence on the central issue of the identity of S as the gunman was potentially safely reliable. See also *Pedersen* [2013] EWCA Crim 464, in which the statement of the complainant, who was suffering from a mental illness at the time when it was made and had died before the trial, was rightly excluded as to lack of consent in a count relating to rape because there was no evidence by which the conflict between her statement and P's account could properly be resolved. However, further statements by her relevant to the breaching by P of a restraining order were rightly admitted as there was other evidence by which the reliability of her evidence could be assessed. In *T (P)* [2013] EWCA Crim 2398 it was held that the proposition in *Horncastle* regarding the capacity of the jury to assess the reliability of hearsay evidence 'embraces with particular force the evidence of witnesses who had died or who could not be expected to have any present recollection of events described in witness statements made over 30 years previously'. However none of the hearsay evidence in issue in that case was of 'sole or decisive' importance to the success of the prosecution. In *Barney* [2014] EWCA Crim 589, the decisive evidence of a deceased elderly victim identifying B as the perpetrator of a distraction burglary was admitted. The witness's previous descriptions provided a method of testing her reliability, and B's convictions for similar offences provided further support. The leading authorities were also applied in *Harvey* [2014] EWCA Crim 54, in which the evidence of two witnesses who were absent through fear was central to the prosecution, but where there was strong evidence that supported the reliability of their accounts. This included the *res gestae* statement of the two witnesses themselves, made while they were still under the influence of the effect of an armed robbery (for *res gestae*, see **F16.55**) and the extent to which the accounts subsequently given by the two tallied with one another, despite their lack of opportunity to confer immediately after the event. The Court of Appeal also drew attention to the availability for the defence of a significant amount of evidence regarding the bad character of the two witnesses, who had links to the gangland fraternity, that could be deployed in support of a possible alternative explanation for the presence of firearms in the home of one of them, which was also the location for the alleged armed robbery. Frequently cited in recent cases is the summary by Gross LJ in *Friel* [2012] EWCA Crim 2871:

> It is plain to us, therefore, that hearsay of any description is not to be nodded through or adduced as a matter of routine. There is no inflexible rule against admissibility of central (or sole and decisive) hearsay evidence, but, on a spectrum, the more central the hearsay evidence is, the greater the care required. Sometimes hearsay will be inadmissible or even if admissible the trial may need to be halted. But it is also necessary to keep in mind the public interest in securing the conviction of the guilty, as indeed it is always imperative to have regard to the acquittal of the innocent and the avoidance of miscarriages of justice.

F16.34   The effect of the approach of the English courts is well illustrated by the facts of *Horncastle*. The victim of a serious beating gave a statement about how his injuries were incurred which was received following his death from an alcohol-related illness. Although the statement was critical evidence linking the accused to the attack, there was also substantial independent evidence of presence at the scene, the accused had ample opportunity to challenge the victim's credibility, and the judge gave a full and clear direction about the disadvantages of challenging the victim on his memory and other relevant matters. By contrast, in *Ibrahim*, the evidence of W (the deceased victim of an alleged rape), though technically admissible, could not be shown to be reliable given W's heroin addiction, the fact that she had made an admittedly false formal statement to police on a similar matter (the reason for the withdrawal of that complaint being also demonstrably false) and a long and unexplained delay in reporting the rape. The supporting evidence, such as it was, did not overcome the doubts raised about W's reliability, and her evidence should have been excluded either under the PACE 1984, s. 78, or by application of the CJA 2003, s. 125 (see **F16.93**). See also

Riat, Shabir and *Tahery* [2013] EWCA Crim 1053, in which the Court of Appeal, on a reference from the Criminal Cases Review Commission in one of the cases that had been the subject of the application to the Grand Chamber in *Al-Khawaja and Tahery v UK*, held that the trial judge ought not to have admitted the unsupported evidence of a critical witness where the objective factors (his animosity and his previous inconsistency) pointed to unreliability. The bad character of an absent witness is not necessarily a reason for exclusion, even if it provides a basis for an inference of his preparedness to lie, provided that the evidence available to the jury is such that they can properly assess the risk of his having done so (*Adeojo* [2013] EWCA Crim 41, where there was a wealth of other evidence linking the accused with the scene, but the absent witness provided the only direct evidence of identification). See also *Jabbar* [2013] EWCA Crim 801.

The fact that vulnerable witnesses are involved does not absolve domestic courts of their responsibility to ensure there is no breach of Article 6 when allowing witness statements to be read. See *PS v Germany* (2003) 36 EHRR 1139, and *SN v Sweden* (2004) 39 EHRR 304, where the use of special measures was sanctioned provided that the right of the defence to challenge the evidence was also safeguarded. In *J* [2011] EWCA Crim 3021, the statement of a three-year-old boy that he had been beaten by his mother's partner was held to have been rightly admitted under s. 114(1)(d) (see **F16.38**). An important feature of the decision was that the boy's injuries were non-accidental and could only have been caused by J, the boy's mother or his grandmother. As both women gave evidence that it was not them, it could not be said that the child's statement was the 'sole or decisive' evidence against J. In *AC* [2014] EWCA Crim 371, the account of a child victim of rape was presented in hearsay form where she was too traumatised to testify. The tools to test the reliability of her description included the cross-examination of her mother, who had supported her through the disclosure process, and there was supporting evidence of DNA and indecent images of the child on AC's computer.

In the earlier decision of the Court of Appeal in *Cole and Keet* [2007] 1 WLR 2716, Lord Phillips CJ was dealing with two cases of evidence admissible under s. 116 — in *Cole*, statements of the deceased victim of alleged assaults by C and in *Keet* the statement of an elderly victim of alleged fraud, who since making her statement had succumbed to dementia. Turning to s. 114(1)(d), the 'interests of justice' test (see **F16.38**), Lord Phillips transposed the nine criteria for consideration prior to a decision on *admissibility* under that provision (s. 114(2)(a)–(i)) into factors assisting in the decision on *exclusion* under the PACE 1984, s. 78, of evidence otherwise admissible under s. 116 on the grounds that the test in s. 78 was 'unlikely to produce a different result' from that of the 'interests of justice' in s. 114(1)(d). If in every case under s. 116 where unfairness was alleged the courts took to applying the s. 114(2) criteria (with their in-built need to establish that the interests of justice support the evidence going in), the intention behind the 2003 reform of the 'absent witness' provisions would have been substantially defeated. The context of the case was, however, the use of s. 116 in respect of important (possibly 'decisive') evidence. It is submitted that Lord Phillips' transposition should not be regarded as providing a template for all cases, but the s. 114(1)(d) criteria may provide helpful guidance where there is a serious risk that the use of the evidence will deprive the defendant of a fair trial. See also *Pulley* [2008] EWCA Crim 260. The criteria laid down in s. 114(2) were also considered to be relevant to evidence admissible under s. 116 in *Farmborough* [2009] EWCA Crim 2579 (statement by deceased regarding previous violence of accused) and *Gian* [2009] EWCA Crim 2553 (witness claiming deceased had complained of threat by accused). More recently, in *Zejmowicz* [2011] EWCA Crim 1173 it was acknowledged that the judge's consideration of the s. 114(2) factors was 'not strictly necessary', but it appears to have been helpful in dealing with a difficult situation. In that case the prosecution sought to rely on the evidence of two witnesses whose English was not fluent, one present at trial and the other absent, as to allegedly incriminating statements in English made in the presence of both of them by one of the co-accused following a murder. The exchange was caught on CCTV so that the gestures of the co-accused (including punching and kicking) were also before the jury. The witness who gave evidence (the less fluent of the two) was severely undermined in cross-examination, and it was argued that it was for that reason unfair to fill the gap using

F16.35

the evidence of the absent witness. However, it was held that it was right in principle that both accounts should be heard. The absence of the second witness could be dealt with appropriately by a direction stressing the effectiveness of cross-examination in relation to the first.

F16.36   The right to challenge hearsay evidence may be particularly important in cases where the weakness of the evidence is generally acknowledged, as with identification or recognition evidence. Where such evidence is hearsay and constitutes the principal element in the prosecution case, the House of Lords has said that courts will be very reluctant to receive the evidence (*Neill v North Antrim Magistrates' Court* [1992] 4 All ER 846 per Lord Mustill at p. 1229).

Where the prosecutor has delayed proceedings and in consequence a witness is unavailable to testify, the court may exclude the witness's statement on the basis that the prosecution should have proceeded when the witness was available (*French* (1993) 97 Cr App R 421, and see *Radak* [1999] 1 Cr App R 187).

Where the prosecution has read, unopposed, the statement of a witness who is unavailable, the question whether it is permissible for the prosecution to adduce further evidence from the same witness to correct a misleading impression will be decided according to the interests of justice. If the evidence could not have been resisted had it been adduced with the original statement it is likely to be admitted (*Ferdinand* [2014] EWCA Crim 1243).

F16.37   **Fairness and Records**   Where a statement tendered in evidence under the CJA 2003, s. 117, is not a statement prepared for the purpose of criminal proceedings, the absence of any opportunity to cross-examine the maker is likely to be of less importance, even where the statement relied upon is crucial to the case for the prosecution. Thus, in *Schreiber* [1988] Crim LR 112, decided under the Criminal Evidence Act 1965, it was held that customs documents compiled abroad could be given in evidence without calling the maker, even though the documents were the most cogent evidence of fraud by the accused.

CRIMINAL JUSTICE ACT 2003: HEARSAY ADMISSIBLE IN THE INTERESTS OF JUSTICE

F16.38   Criminal Justice Act 2003, s. 114

(1) ... [a] statement not made in oral evidence in the proceedings is admissible as evidence of any matter stated if, but only if—
   ...
   (d) the court is satisfied that it is in the interests of justice for it to be admissible.
(2) In deciding whether a statement not made in oral evidence should be admitted under subsection (1)(d), the court must have regard to the following factors (and to any others it considers relevant)—
   (a) how much probative value the statement has (assuming it to be true) in relation to a matter in issue in the proceedings, or how valuable it is for the understanding of other evidence in the case;
   (b) what other evidence has been, or can be, given on the matter or evidence mentioned in paragraph (a);
   (c) how important the matter or evidence mentioned in paragraph (a) is in the context of the case as a whole;
   (d) the circumstances in which the statement was made;
   (e) how reliable the maker of the statement appears to be;
   (f) how reliable the evidence of the making of the statement appears to be;
   (g) whether oral evidence of the matter stated can be given and, if not, why it cannot;
   (h) the amount of difficulty involved in challenging the statement;
   (i) the extent to which that difficulty would be likely to prejudice the party facing it.

F16.39   Where s. 114(2) directs the court to have regard to certain factors, it does not follow that a judge is bound to reach a conclusion on all of them. Proper investigation of all nine factors would be a lengthy process, which the CJA 2003 does not require. All that is required is the exercise of judgement in the light of the factors specifically identified, together with any others considered by the judge to be relevant (*Taylor* [2006] 2 Cr App R 222). An exercise of judgement will be interfered with on appeal only if it has involved the application of incorrect principles or is outside the band of legitimate decision (*Finch* [2007] 1 WLR 1645; *Musone* [2007] 1 WLR 2467). In considering factors (e) and (f) it is not permissible to reason that the jury may assess matters relating to reliability: the judge is specifically required to make an assessment. Factor (g) requires close attention to be paid to whether there is an alternative to admitting hearsay, including the bringing of an available, though reluctant, witness to court (*Prosecution Appeal (No. 2 of 2008); R v Y* [2008] 2 All ER 484). In assessing potential defence evidence, it is not the interest of the accused that the court is required to consider, it is the interest of arriving at the right conclusion (*Marsh* [2008] EWCA Crim 1816).

Section 114(1)(d) cannot be used as the sole justification to admit multiple hearsay, which can be adduced only to the extent permitted by s. 121 (see **F16.90**). Section 121(1)(c) makes special provision for multiple hearsay to be admissible in the interests of justice (see, e.g., *Musone*).   **F16.40**

A hearing on admissibility under the CJA 2003, s. 114(1)(d), must be conducted on the basis that the material and arguments deployed are available to all concerned parties. Material that had been presented to the judge on an *ex parte* application and was not available to the defence should form no part of the consideration (*Ali* (2008) 172 JP 516).

Relationship with Other Hearsay Exceptions

Exclusionary Rules and Cautious Application of Interests of Justice Exception   The cases indi-   **F16.41** cate that the CJA 2003, s. 114(1)(d), is to be applied with caution. Originally conceived by the Law Commission as a 'safety valve' for the admission of otherwise inadmissible evidence in exceptional circumstances only, there is nothing in the statutory language to indicate that this is how s. 114(1)(d) is to be used (*Sak v CPS* (2008) 172 JP 89, where, however, it was also stated that s. 114 should not be lightly applied). The need for caution in the application of this novel provision was also urged in *Z* [2009] 3 All ER 1015, where the Court of Appeal said it would be 'rare indeed' to admit the hearsay account of a woman who claimed to have been sexually assaulted by the accused when a child, in support of the similar complaint for which the accused was being tried. The hearsay witness was unwilling to relive the trauma of the offences by giving evidence, a ground not recognised by s. 116 (see **F16.8**), and the Court regarded the use of s. 114(1)(d) as an unacceptable means of circumventing the restrictions on hearsay in s. 116. The Court also expressed its concern at the prospect of disputed evidence of bad character being adduced in hearsay form. See, to similar effect, *C* [2010] EWCA Crim 72, where s. 116 was not satisfied in respect of an alleged victim of sexual offences, and her account should not have been presented by her adoptive mother using s. 114(1)(d) instead. A more difficult decision to justify is *Burton* (2011) 175 JP 385, in which the prosecution were permitted to adduce the statement of a 14-year-old complainant that she had been involved in a sexual relationship with B under s. 114(1)(d). Although the circumstances would not have justified the use of s. 116, it may be that the case was exceptional in that the evidence was peripheral, not only in the sense that it was not the 'sole or decisive' evidence, but also that it merely served to confirm J's admissions to the police. However, the dominance of the rule in Z has recently been confirmed in *M* (2011) 175 JP 462 and *Tindle* (2011) 175 JP 462, a case of assault in which the prosecution sought in effect to circumvent their own failure to take 'reasonable steps' to secure the complainant's attendance under s. 116 by tendering the evidence under s. 114(1)(d). It was held, applying Z, that considering, as the court was required to do by s. 114(2)(g), whether oral evidence of the matter could have been given and, if not, why it could not was bound to lead back to the same inquiry as had led to exclusion under s. 116. In *D (E)* (2010) 174 JP 289 it was held that the hearsay statement of a witness which was tendered in order to rebut an allegation of recent fabrication was wrongly admitted where the witness was absent on holiday in circumstances that did not fall within s. 116, and the role of the prosecution in failing to secure the witness's attendance was not properly considered when applying the 'interests of justice' criteria. Pitchford LJ referred to s. 114 in terms of a 'hierarchy' of exceptions; s. 114(1)(d) should not be used to circumvent requirements of other gateways higher up the hierarchy. Hierarchy or no, the terms of s. 114(1)(d) must be strictly adhered to.

F16.42 Where evidence is inadmissible under another hearsay exception for reasons related to the interests of justice, it would be inconsistent to allow s. 114(1)(d) to be invoked to arrive at a different result: see, e.g., *Smith* [2007] EWCA Crim 2105 (plea of guilty technically admissible under the PACE 1984, s. 74, but should have been excluded under s. 78), *McEwan v DPP* (2007) 171 JP 308 (s. 116 inapplicable because of lack of diligence by the prosecutor in securing the necessary proof) and *Warnick* [2013] EWCA Crim 2320 (where the prosecution were unable to demonstrate that the witness was in fear for the purposes of s. 116(1)(e) (see **F16.16**), the same evidence could not be used to admit a statement under s. 114(1)(d) without circumventing the 'fear' provisions). It does not follow that evidence which fails to comply with conditions of another hearsay exception can never be admitted under s. 114(1)(d), as part of its purpose is to fill the gap between other provisions where that is in the interests of justice. Thus in *Adams* (2008) 1 Cr App R 430 a witness had not been given sufficient notice for the court to find that he 'could not be found after taking reasonable steps' (s. 116(2)(d): see **F16.13**), but the evidence was, though technically necessary, uncontentious, and the court allowed proof by hearsay under s. 114(1) (d). In *Sadiq* (2009) 173 JP 471 the Court of Appeal held that the testimony of the alleged victim of a shooting, who had been paralysed and was unable to speak, could be admitted under s. 114(1)(d) at a retrial. The witness had given evidence by means of an alphabet board at the original trial, but had asserted (without giving reasons) his unwillingness to testify at the retrial. However, in *Lawrence* [2014] 1 Cr App R 33 (5) the Court suggested that the reasons for refusal to give evidence at the retrial would have to be considered as carefully as in fear cases under s. 116 (see **F16.19**) before the evidence could be admitted under s. 114(1)(d) and s. 131 (under which s. 114(1)(d) is applicable to retrials: see **F16.86**). In *J* [2011] EWCA Crim 3021, the statement of a three-year-old boy as to the cause of his injuries was held to have been rightly admitted under s. 114(1)(d) in the trial of his mother's partner for cruelty. It is noteworthy that this was not the 'sole or decisive' evidence: the Court stressed that the child's injuries were non-accidental and J had ample opportunity to cross-examine the only other people who could possibly have caused them. See also *MH* [2012] EWCA Crim 2725 (discussed at **F6.44**), where the early disclosures of a very young child were inadmissible under the CJA 2003, s. 120, because he could not confirm that he had made them, but it was held that they could have been received under s. 114(1)(d).

In *Lynch* [2008] 1 Cr App R 337, a statement made by a witness following a positive identification at an identification parade was not sufficiently 'bound up' with the identification to be part of the *res gestae* (see **F16.55**), but was admissible under s. 114(1)(d). In *Gillooley* [2009] EWCA Crim 671, s. 114(1)(d) was employed to admit the first complaints of sexual abuse made by a young man to his mother and his girlfriend. The complaints were made years after the events to which they related, and were inadmissible under s. 120 (see **F6.33**), but were of clear probative value in relation to establishing the way in which the complaint had emerged. In *Taylor* [2006] 2 Cr App R 222, s. 114(1)(d) was invoked in order to plug the common gap in continuity whereby the name of a suspect is supplied by a witness who knows it only because he has been told it by another. See also *Saunders* [2012] EWCA Crim 1185, where s. 114(1)(d) was invoked to admit statements by a witness, B, to two friends that she had seen an offence which in her evidence she had denied having witnessed. B had told her friends that she was too frightened to tell the whole truth, but the provisions governing fearful witnesses (s. 116(2)(e): see **F16.16**) were inapplicable because B had testified on the point. The Court of Appeal said that it would be 'curious' if the previous statements could not be used. A similar authority is *Minchin* [2013] EWCA Crim 2412 where s. 114(1)(d) clearly served the interests of justice in allowing the prosecution to adduce a solicitor's file note of a conversation that proved that there was a conspiracy between the defendants to fabricate an alibi. The note was inadmissible under s. 117 (see **F16.29**) because the defence refused to waive legal privilege in order to allow the solicitor to give oral evidence.

F16.43 Courts are likely to afford rigorous scrutiny to evidence tendered under s. 114(1)(d) that would have been objectionable at common law. In *Prosecution Appeal (No. 2 of 2008); R v Y* [2008] 2 All ER 484 the issue was whether the confession of a third party implicating an accused was capable of being used in evidence against him under s. 114(1)(d), despite a strong common-law rule that the statement could be used only against its maker. The Court of Appeal held that the effect of s. 114(1)(d) was that the evidence was capable of being admitted, there being nothing in s. 118 (which preserves certain common-law rules of admissibility including evidence of confessions and admissions: see **F16.72**) to render such evidence inadmissible under s. 114(1)(d). However, the court also drew attention to the 'rigorous' test to be applied, and the need for particular caution where the prosecution sought to place reliance on a third party's confession in the absence of supporting evidence against an accused. The statement under caution of one co-accused, incriminating another, may similarly be considered for admission under s. 114(1)(d) (*B and S* [2008] EWCA Crim 365), but the provision clearly does not make police interviews routinely admissible in the case of persons other than the interviewee, and *McLean* [2008] 1 Cr App R 155 was said in *R v Y* not to be authority to the contrary. Evidence may have been too readily admissible in *Seton* (2010) 174 JP 241, where the defence was that the murder with which S was charged was committed by P, and the statement of P in a recorded telephone call made from prison in which he expressed his indignation at the assertion was admitted in rebuttal. The Court of Appeal accepted that no attempt had been made to procure the attendance of P, but concluded that, in the light of P's refusal to co-operate with the authorities, it would have been a 'fruitless exercise'. S's assertion against P was made very late in the day, and the court's inference that this was a deliberate ploy may have coloured the decision. It would appear that the reach of s. 114(1)(d) does not extend to the evidence of a witness who wishes to remain anonymous. In *Ford* [2010] EWCA Crim 2250 a note written by such a witness regarding the registration number of a getaway car was held inadmissible. The CAJA 2009, ss. 86 to 90 (see **D14.60**), provide the sole route to admissibility for anonymous witnesses, and that legislation makes no provision for the admissibility of hearsay.

In *L* [2009] 1 WLR 626, the prosecution relied on the out-of-court statement of L's wife, who declined to give evidence on charges against him which included rape of their 20-year-old daughter (as to which she was not compellable). The Court of Appeal held that there was no absolute rule prohibiting the use of s. 114(1)(d), despite the 'paradox' that the evidence that she did not wish to give, and was legally excused from giving, was placed before the jury. The public interest was served by admitting the evidence, taking account of the course of conduct by L which included offences against the same daughter as a child. See also *Horsnell* [2012] EWCA Crim 227.

Section 114 is most likely to be resorted to where evidence is otherwise unlikely to be admissible, but may also provide an alternative argument where it is not clearly so: see *Isichei* (2006) 170 JP 753 (see **F15.21**) and *Xhabri* [2006] 1 All ER 776, where some of the statements by the alleged victim of abduction were also capable of being received under other exceptions (e.g., the extended provision for the reception of evidence of recent complaint in s. 120: see **F6.33**). In the case of first-hand hearsay statements, however, the alternative of admitting the evidence under s. 114(1)(d) was accepted by the court. In *Bains* [2010] EWCA Crim 873 the messages received via mobile telephones in connection with alleged drug dealing were held to be hearsay by application of the decision in *Leonard* (2009) 173 JP 366 (see **F15.21**), though the point was clearly regarded by the Court of Appeal as arguable. In recognising that it was in the interests of justice to admit the messages, the Court noted that, where messages of the kind that drug dealers might be expected to send or receive are in the hands of the prosecution, it is unrealistic to expect the prosecution to call the senders of the messages to prove that what they said was true. See also *Twist* [2011] 3 All ER 1055 at **F15.19**. In the unusual case of *Turner* [2013] 1 Cr App R 327 (25), it was held that s. 114(1)(d) might have been used to admit the evidence of a witness who was unable to testify to matters of a sexual nature owing to acute embarrassment. However, those matters were not in dispute (the issues at trial being consent and her age when the acts took place) and the trial judge was able to circumvent the difficulty by allowing the matters on which the witness was stuck to be put to her and adopted from her previous statement, thus leaving her available for cross-examination in a way that s. 114(1)(d) would not have done.

F16.44

Section 114(1)(d) Benefiting Defence   Section 114(1)(d) may benefit either prosecution or defence, but the question of which party stands to benefit is relevant to the application of the

F16.45

'interests of justice' test (*Prosecution Appeal (No. 2 of 200); R v Y* [2008] 2 All ER 484). A difficult defence case will be that of the third-party confession, which is otherwise inadmissible where the maker is available to be called as a witness but neither side chooses to do so (cf. *Blastland* [1986] AC 41). In the absence of evidence that the statement is unreliable, a difficult decision has to be made balancing the probative value of the statement if true against the reason for not calling the maker. In *Finch* [2007] 1 WLR 1645 the accused sought to rely on a statement made as part of a confession by his erstwhile co-accused, R, who subsequently pleaded guilty. The effect of the plea was that R became a compellable, albeit reluctant, witness for F, and the trial judge's decision that the case was not within s. 114(1)(d) was upheld by the Court of Appeal. Whatever might be the case if R had been unavailable or had demonstrated good reason not to testify, it was said, 'it would not normally be in the interests of justice for evidence which the giver is unprepared to have tested to be put untested before the jury'. An alternative course would have been to invoke the hostile witness provisions of s. 119 (see **F6.50**). See also *Khan* [2009] EWCA Crim 86, in which the statement of a witness unwilling to testify for the defence was held to have been rightly rejected.

WARNING AS TO QUALITY OF HEARSAY

F16.46   As the opportunity to admit evidence under the new statutory exceptions grows, it is of paramount importance that a jury should be made aware of potential weaknesses in hearsay at the point when they come to assess its worth. The *Crown Court Bench Book* (March 2010) heralded a move towards the judicial crafting of directions to fit individual cases, and this may over time affect the weight of previous decisions as to what must be said. This should be borne in mind in interpreting older authorities such as *Grant v The State* [2007] 1 AC 1. In *Grant* the Privy Council considered the elements of a direction on hearsay received under a similar statutory scheme to that under the CJA 2003. It is necessary to remind the jury, however obvious it may be to them, that the statement has not been verified on oath nor the author tested by cross-examination. The judge should point out the specific risks of relying on such evidence and invite the jury to scrutinise the evidence with particular care. Instructing the jury to give the statement such weight as they think fit is proper, but it is not very helpful if there is a risk that the jury, when presented with an apparently plausible statement by a person whose reliability and honesty they have no extraneous reason to doubt, may be inclined to give the statement more weight than the oral evidence they have heard. The jury's attention should be drawn to the context of all the other evidence, and if there are discrepancies between the statement and the evidence of other witnesses, the jury's attention should be specifically drawn to them. While failure to give such directions in respect of prosecution evidence will not necessarily render a trial unfair, it may do so, given the importance of the direction as a safeguard of the interests of the defence.

F16.47   Authorities decided under the statutory schemes that preceded the CJA 2003 also stress the need for the court to assist in the evaluation of the quality of the statement (*Cole* [1990] 2 All ER 108, citing with approval the observations of Lord Griffiths in *Scott v The Queen* [1989] AC 1242). Thus, 'the weight to be attached to the inability to cross-examine and the magnitude of any consequential risk that the admission of the statement will result in unfairness to the accused will depend in part upon the court's assessment of the quality of the evidence shown in the statement'. *Cole* further requires the court to consider whether any potential unfairness may be effectively counterbalanced by a warning to the jury pointing out that the evidence had not been tested by cross-examination and drawing attention to its possible limitations. (In *Cole* the trial judge went even further and commented that the written statement could not possibly have been worth as much as the evidence of other witnesses, but this elaboration was rightly held to be unnecessary in *Greer* [1988] Crim LR 572.) *Cole* was applied in *Kennedy* [1992] Crim LR 64, where the issue was whether K, by fighting with his co-accused, H, was guilty of affray or was acting in self-defence. It was held that a statement by one M, who was the only independent witness to the fight and who had since died, was rightly admitted. It had been contended that M's evidence was flawed in that it was inconsistent with the testimony of both K and H but, as the Court of Appeal rightly pointed out, such inconsistency is not unusual in such cases, and it was sufficient for the trial judge to give the jury a warning of the disadvantages of not having M as a witness in the case. See also *Samuel* [1992] Crim LR 189 and *Kennedy* [1994] Crim LR 50, in which a statement made by W, the victim of an assault (who subsequently died of other causes), was held on balance to have been rightly admitted, notwithstanding that W was very drunk at the time of the incident and that there were important inconsistencies between his version of events and that of other witnesses. However, K's appeal was allowed because the judge had failed to stress these weaknesses when warning the jury how to approach W's statement. Compare *Thompson* [1999] Crim LR 747, in which it was held proper to admit, subject to a warning, the statement of the victim of a robbery notwithstanding that he was awaiting discharge from a hospital to which he had been admitted for drink-related mental problems. It is significant that there was substantial prosecution evidence apart from the victim's statement. In *McCoy* [1999] All ER (D) 1410, the statement of the victim of a serious attack, which provided the main evidence identifying his assailant, was held to have been wrongly received under the CJA 1988, s. 23.

The particular difficulty that arises in giving a warning where the evidence is tendered by the defence was considered in *Abiodun* [2003] EWCA Crim 2167, where a 'mild' direction 'which simply reminded the jury of what in any event would have been obvious to them, i.e. that the witnesses had not been cross-examined', was held not to have impinged on the fairness of the proceedings.

CRIMINAL JUSTICE ACT 2003: PRESERVED COMMON-LAW EXCEPTIONS

Admissibility of Public Documents at Common Law and under the Criminal Justice Act 2003

The CJA 2003, s. 118, makes express provision to save the common law regarding the issue of **F16.48** certain public documents and information.

Criminal Justice Act 2003, s. 118

(1) The following rules of law are preserved.

Public information etc

Any rule of law under which in criminal proceedings—
- (a) published works dealing with matters of a public nature (such as histories, scientific works, dictionaries and maps) are admissible as evidence of facts of a public nature stated in them,
- (b) public documents (such as public registers, and returns made under public authority with respect to matters of public interest) are admissible as evidence of facts stated in them,
- (c) records (such as the records of certain courts, treaties, Crown grants, pardons and commissions) are admissible as evidence of facts stated in them, or
- (d) evidence relating to a person's age or date or place of birth may be given by a person without personal knowledge of the matter.

…

A document compiled by a public officer acting under a public duty to inquire and report facts **F16.49** of public interest, which is maintained in order that interested members of the public may have access to the information contained in it, is admissible at common law by way of exception to the hearsay rule as evidence of the facts stated (*Sturla v Freccia* (1880) 5 App Cas 623). Thus, for example, registers of baptisms, marriages and funerals are public documents, as are surveys of Crown Lands, and university records may prove the granting of degrees (*Collins v Carnegie* (1834) 1 A & E 695). Foreign registers may be public documents if the relevant conditions are satisfied (*Lyell v Kennedy* (1889) 14 App Cas 437; *Sturla v Freccia*). See also the Evidence (Foreign Dominion and Colonial Documents) Act 1933, s. 1 of which confers a power to declare that certain foreign registers are public documents.

One reason for the rule is the presumption that entries in such documents made by public officers are to be relied upon (*Irish Society v Bishop of Derry* (1846) 12 Cl & F 641, per Parke B). However, it is also the case that the rule is based on necessity: were it not for the admissibility of public documents, many facts occurring in the distant past would be incapable of proof.

In modern times the importance of the common-law rule has been overshadowed by various statutes rendering particular documents admissible, and (more importantly) by the CJA 2003, s. 117 (see **F16.24**), under which virtually all of the documents which were receivable under the common-law rule, and many that were not, are admissible. In *West Midlands Probation Board v French* [2009] 1 WLR 1715 it was held that, where a prisoner released on licence was charged with breach of conditions, a copy of the licence could be proved either as a public document under the CJA 2003, s. 118(1)(b), or under s. 117 (see **F16.24**) or under the Documentary Evidence Act 1868, s. 2 (see **F8.17**). It is not clear what hearsay purpose was served by proving the licence: see **F15.18**.

Public Duty

F16.50   The document must have been made in pursuance of what Lord Blackburn termed 'a judicial, or quasi-judicial, duty to inquire' (*Sturla v Freccia* (1880) 5 App Cas 623, at p. 643). The duty must be imposed by virtue of a public office: thus, parish registers of baptisms, marriages and burials are public documents, whereas similar records compiled by other religious groups such as the Quakers are not (*Re Woodward* [1913] 1 Ch 392). Older authority strongly supports the view that the document must be made by the very officer whose duty it is to inquire into the facts, and who would therefore have satisfied himself of the truth of the facts stated (see, e.g., *Sturla v Freccia* and *Daniel v Wilkin* (1852) 7 Exch 429). However, in *Halpin* [1975] QB 907 it was held that the functions of inquirer and recorder could be divided, with the result that the statutory returns of a company kept in the Companies Register were admissible where it appeared that the officer making the return had a duty to inquire, and the Registrar of Companies had the duty to record the results of the inquiry. Geoffrey Lane LJ said (at p. 915): 'The common law should move with the times and should recognise the fact that the official charged with recording matters of public import can no longer in this highly complicated world … have personal knowledge of their accuracy'. The decision has been criticised on the grounds that the House of Lords in *Myers v DPP* [1965] AC 1001 prohibited further judicial extension of the rules admitting hearsay evidence, but, whatever the merits of the criticism, the evidence would now be admissible under the CJA 2003, s. 117 (see **F16.24**).

Where a record is kept by a public officer not for the benefit of others, but simply as a check upon himself, it is not a public document (*Merrick v Wakley* (1838) 8 A & E 170).

Public Matter

F16.51   The subject-matter of the document need not concern the public as a whole. In *Sturla v Freccia* (1880) 5 App Cas 623, Lord Blackburn said (at p. 643):

> I do not think that 'public' … is to be taken in the sense of meaning the whole world. I think an entry in the books of a manor is public in the sense that it concerns all the people interested in the manor. And an entry probably in a corporation book concerning a corporate matter, or something in which all the corporation is concerned, would be 'public' within that sense.

Whether a document deals with a matter of public concern inevitably raises a question of degree, and entries in a corporation's book are not necessarily admissible, despite Lord Blackburn's dictum (see, e.g., *Hill v Manchester & Salford Waterworks Co.* (1833) 5 B & Ad 866). Documents which do not comply with this condition are likely to be admissible under the CJA 1988, s. 24.

Public Reference

F16.52   Documents which are not maintained for the use of such members of the public as may need to refer to them are not admissible under this exception. In *Lilley v Pettit* [1946] KB 401,

P was prosecuted for falsely stating that her husband was the father of her child. It was held that regimental records showing that the husband was a prisoner of war abroad when the child was conceived were inadmissible because they were not intended for the use of the public. See also *Ioannou v Demetriou* [1952] AC 84.

For the same reason, a record which is maintained for a temporary purpose cannot be received under this exception (*Mercer v Denne* [1905] 2 Ch 538; *Heyne v Fischel & Co.* (1913) 30 TLR 190), although there would be no such objection to its reception in evidence under the CJA 2003, s. 117.

Other Registers etc. Admissible by Statute

Some entries in registers are admissible as public documents (see **F16.48**). In many cases, how- **F16.53** ever, statute makes express provision for the admissibility of particular registers. Detailed consideration of such provisions is beyond the scope of this work, and readers are referred to the comprehensive account in chapter 31 of *Phipson on Evidence* (17th edn, 2009).

Note the provisions of the Births and Deaths Registration Act 1953, s. 34. See also the Non-Parochial Registers Act 1840, s. 6, under which certain records and registers deposited in the General Register Office in accordance with that Act are admissible, and the Births and Deaths Registration Act 1858.

An entry in a register showing that a person has died is admissible evidence of the fact and date of death, but not of the cause of death (*Bird v Keep* [1918] 2 KB 692). Where a birth certificate is relied upon to prove some fact contained in it, the evidence may be of no use unless it can be proved that the person named in it is the same individual with whom the court is concerned. This is difficult to establish without breaking the hearsay rule, for the person named cannot himself give evidence that the certificate appertains to him. A person who was present at the birth may establish identity (*Weaver* (1873) LR 2 CCR 85), though such proof may be hard to come by. It is not surprising that, in some cases, hearsay evidence has been admitted: see, e.g., *Bellis* (1911) 6 Cr App R 283, in which the court admitted evidence of inquiries made about the girl whose age was in issue, which had led the inquirer to be satisfied as to her identity.

Evidence of Reputation

The CJA 2003, s. 118(1), makes specific provision for saving the common-law rules admitting **F16.54** evidence of reputation to prove character, and the use of reputation or family tradition to prove or disprove pedigree, the existence of a marriage, any public or general right, or the existence of any person or thing. With the exception of the rules concerning character, which are dealt with at **F13.22**, such evidence is rarely resorted to at common law and is not dealt with in this work.

Note that the preservation of these exceptions in s. 118 operates only to the extent that the common law allows the court to treat such evidence as proving the matter concerned.

Statements Forming Part of *Res Gestae*

The CJA 2003, s. 118(1), makes express provision for saving the common-law rules on *res gestae*. **F16.55**
Criminal Justice Act 2003, s. 118

(1) The following rules of law are preserved.
...
Res gestae
4. Any rule of law under which in criminal proceedings a statement is admissible as evidence of any matter stated if—
   (a) the statement was made by a person so emotionally overpowered by an event that the possibility of concoction or distortion can be disregarded,
   (b) the statement accompanied an act which can be properly evaluated as evidence only if considered in conjunction with the statement, or
   (c) the statement relates to a physical sensation or a mental state (such as intention or emotion).

The statements most commonly received as evidence under the *res gestae* exception are those referred to in (a) and (c). Statements accompanying relevant acts are rarely admitted in criminal cases; the exception is limited to cases where the words spoken are truly 'part and parcel' of an act such as identification (*Lynch* [2008] 1 Cr App R 337, explaining *McCay* [1990] 1 All ER 232). The treatment which follows is confined to the two more frequently occurring varieties of *res gestae*: statements made in response to overpowering events, and statements indicative of contemporaneous sensation or state of mind, including intention and emotion.

Statements in Response to Emotionally Overpowering Events

F16.56 '*Res gestae*' is an inappropriate label for this common-law exception to the hearsay rule, in which admissibility depends on proof of what Lord Ackner in *Andrews* [1987] AC 281 called the 'close and intimate connection' between the exciting events in issue and the making of the statement, the theory being that the spontaneity of the utterance is some guarantee against concoction. The nomenclature has in the past led to confusion and to incorrect decisions, but *Andrews* clarified the law by approving the test for admissibility adopted by the Privy Council in *Ratten v The Queen* [1972] AC 378. In *Mills v The Queen* [1995] 3 All ER 865, the Privy Council praised the changes effected by these decisions, regarding *res gestae* as a modernised exception to the hearsay rule under which the focus was on the probative value of evidence rather than on the question whether it falls within some artificial and rigid category.

F16.57 In *Ratten v The Queen*, Lord Wilberforce described the rule under which spontaneous statements are admitted in the following way (at pp. 389–90):

> A hearsay statement is made either by the victim of an attack or by a bystander — indicating directly or indirectly the identity of the attacker. The admissibility of the statement is then said to depend on whether it was made as part of the *res gestae*. . . . The test should be not the uncertain one, whether the making of the statement should be regarded as part of the event or transaction. This may often be difficult to show. But if the drama, leading up to the climax, has commenced and assumed such intensity and pressure that the utterance can safely be regarded as a true reflection of what was unrolling or actually happening, it ought to be received. The expression '*res gestae*' may conveniently sum up these criteria, but the reality of them must always be kept in mind: it is this that lies behind the best reasoned of the judges' rulings.

Lord Wilberforce's reasoning led him to doubt the correctness of the decision in *Bedingfield* (1879) 14 Cox CC 341, in which the statement of a woman whose throat had been cut a few moments before was rejected, on the ground that it was made after the act to which it related was done. Of this, Lord Wilberforce said (at p. 390) that 'there could hardly be a case where the speaker's words carried more clearly the mark of spontaneity and intense involvement'. In *Andrews* [1987] AC 281, the House of Lords overruled *Bedingfield*, on the ground that it was inconsistent with the true principle as laid down by Lord Wilberforce in *Ratten v The Queen* [1972] AC 378. *Bedingfield* had previously been approved by the Privy Council in *Teper v The Queen* [1952] AC 480. See also *Christie* [1914] AC 545, per Lord Reading, and *Gibson* (1887) 18 QBD 537. These and other statements of the law involving the application of the discredited test must also be regarded as no longer authoritative.

F16.58 In *Andrews* [1987] AC 281, the House of Lords accepted and applied the law as stated in *Ratten v The Queen*. A was charged with the murder by stabbing of M, who was attacked by two men in his own home. Within minutes neighbours called the police, who arrived promptly, whereupon M made a statement identifying his attackers. The trial judge admitted the statement and, in a ruling regarded as 'impeccable' both by the Court of Appeal and the House of Lords, he held that there was no possibility in the circumstances of concoction or fabrication of the identification, and that the injuries sustained by M were of such a nature as to drive out any possibility of his being actuated by malice. He also took account of the fact that M correctly identified the other attacker as O, who had subsequently pleaded guilty to manslaughter. Lord Ackner summarised the position which confronts a trial judge when faced in a criminal case with an application under the *res gestae* doctrine to admit evidence of statements, with a view to establishing the truth of some fact thus narrated. He said (at pp. 300–1):

1. The primary question which the judge must ask himself is — can the possibility of concoction or distortion be disregarded?
2. To answer that question the judge must first consider the circumstances in which the particular statement was made, in order to satisfy himself that the event was so unusual or startling or dramatic as to dominate the thoughts of the victim, so that his utterance was an instinctive reaction to that event, thus giving no real opportunity for reasoned reflection. In such a situation the judge would be entitled to conclude that the involvement or the pressure of the event would exclude the possibility of concoction or distortion, providing that the statement was made in conditions of approximate but not exact contemporaneity.
3. In order for the statement to be sufficiently 'spontaneous' it must be so closely associated with the event which has excited the statement, that it can be fairly stated that the mind of the declarant was still dominated by the event. Thus the judge must be satisfied that the event which provided the trigger mechanism for the statement, was still operative. The fact that the statement was made in answer to a question is but one factor to consider under this heading.
4. Quite apart from the time factor, there may be special features in the case, which relate to the possibility of concoction or distortion. In the instant appeal the defence relied on evidence to support the contention that the deceased had a motive of his own to fabricate or concoct, namely, a malice which resided in him against O'Neill and the appellant because, so he believed, O'Neill had attacked and damaged his house and was accompanied by the appellant, who ran away on a previous occasion. The judge must be satisfied that the circumstances were such that having regard to the special feature of malice, there was no possibility of any concoction or distortion to the advantage of the maker or the disadvantage of the accused.
5. As to the possibility of error in the facts narrated in the statement, if only the ordinary fallibility of human recollection is relied upon, this goes to the weight to be attached to and not the admissibility of the statement and is therefore a matter for the jury. However, here again there may be special features that may give rise to the possibility of error. In the instant case there was evidence that the deceased had drunk to excess, well over double the permitted limit for driving a motor car. Another example would be where the identification was made in circumstances of particular difficulty or where the declarant suffered from defective eyesight. In such circumstances the trial judge must consider whether he can exclude the possibility of error.

Some of the difficulties surrounding identification referred to by Lord Ackner arose and were considered in *Turnbull* (1984) 80 Cr App R 104.

Possibility of Error Prior to the decision in *Andrews*, it had been held, in *Nye* (1977) 66 Cr App R 252, that the possibility of error by the maker of the statement was an 'additional factor to be taken into consideration' when determining admissibility. It is now clear from the extract from the speech of Lord Ackner in *Andrews* set out above, that the risk of error bears on the question of admissibility only in cases having 'special features', e.g., an identification in difficult circumstances or by a person with defective eyesight, or by someone who had been drinking. In *Nye*, one Lucas was driving his car when it was struck from behind by another vehicle in which the accused, N and L, were travelling. One of the accused then got out and punched Lucas in the face, while the other tried to put a stop to the assault. Shortly afterwards, when the police arrived, Lucas spontaneously identified L as the man who had hit him. It was argued that Lucas might have made a mistake as to which of the accused had attacked him. On these facts the Court of Appeal considered that there was no chance of an error, stressing in particular that: 'anyone who has been assaulted usually has good reason for remembering what his assailant's face looks like'. It is therefore unlikely that, applying the test in *Andrews*, special circumstances such as the great stress immediately after a motor accident, will be held to affect the admissibility of evidence. The fact that the maker of the statement had been drinking, though capable of being a 'special feature', does not necessarily lead to exclusion. In *Andrews* the deceased had 'drunk to excess', and in *Edwards* [1992] Crim LR 576 the Divisional Court held that a spontaneous allegation of theft of a wallet made against E by A, who was drunk, was admissible.

F16.59

The possibility of error or concoction on the part of the witness recounting the statement, as opposed to the maker of the statement, is not part of the test for admissibility, though the discretion to exclude such evidence (using the PACE 1984, s. 78) could be brought to bear in an appropriate case (*Saunders* [2012] EWCA Crim 1185).

F16.60   **Offence Must Generate Statement**   The event which generates the statement admitted under the rule stated above must be the commission of the offence in question. This is implicit in both *Ratten v The Queen* and *Andrews*, and is expressly stated by Lord Normand in *Teper v The Queen* [1952] AC 480, who said (at p.488): 'for identification purposes in a criminal trial the event with which the words sought to be proved must be so connected as to form part of the *res gestae*, is the commission of the crime itself, the throwing of the stone, the striking of the blow, the setting fire to the building or whatever the criminal act might be'. A *res gestae* statement will typically have been made by the victim of the offence, or a bystander, but may also, if the conditions of admissibility are satisfied, be made by the accused himself (*Glover* [1991] Crim LR 48).

F16.61   **Statement Not to be Used as Substitute for Available Witness**   In *Andrews* [1987] AC 281, Lord Ackner observed (at p. 302):

> I would, however, strongly deprecate any attempt in criminal prosecutions to use the doctrine as a device to avoid calling, where he is available, the maker of the statement. Thus to deprive the defence of the opportunity to cross-examine him, would not be consistent with the fundamental duty of the prosecution to place all the relevant material facts before the court, so as to ensure that justice is done.

In *A-G's Ref (No. 1 of 2003)* [2003] 2 Cr App R 453, the court observed that *Andrews* was not authority for the proposition that the *res gestae* exception was to be disapplied if better evidence was available. In that case, the prosecution had used the exception, not as a device to avoid calling the victim of an assault to give evidence against the accused, her son, but because she had later made a formal statement claiming to have sustained the injuries accidentally, which the prosecution believed to be untrue. Nevertheless it was held that the trial judge's decision to exclude the *res gestae* statement could be supported on the basis that it was unfair to admit it when it could not be the subject of cross-examination (applying the PACE 1984, s. 78). The prosecution should have been prepared to tender the mother as a witness: it was not an adequate response that the defence might have called her.

F16.62   It does not follow from this rule that the *res gestae* exception has no application where the witness is available to give evidence. In *Shickle* (30 July 1997 unreported), S was charged with murder and evidence was given by her teenage son, A, who had witnessed the event. It was held that A's evidence was properly supplemented by spontaneous statements he made at the time, such as 'Mummy's putting needles in the old boy' and 'Hurry up, we've got to stop Mummy'. Although spontaneous statements are often introduced under this exception because the declarant is dead, or is for some other reason unable to give first-hand evidence, the court could find no reason of principle why the evidence should be withheld when the declarant is available. It was further held that the statement, when admitted, goes not only to the truth of the matter but to the consistency of the maker, on the basis that the greater purpose includes the lesser. It is submitted that the court's approach is entirely correct.

F16.63   **Illustrations of Application of the Rule**   In *Turnbull* (1984) 80 Cr App R 104, a man who had been mortally wounded staggered into a public house. In the minutes before an ambulance arrived, and in the ambulance on the way to hospital, various witnesses thought that they heard the victim state, in answer to the question who had stabbed him, that it was 'Ronnie Tommo'. The deceased had a strong Scottish accent and the prosecution case was that he in fact said 'Turnbull'. The statements were admitted, and it was held to be irrelevant that the deceased went on to mutter other words which the witnesses were unable to understand, for: 'If a man is asked a straight question . . . and he gives an answer . . . the fact that he mumbles something afterwards, or is trying to say something when he loses consciousness cannot make the completeness of what he has just said incomplete so that it cannot be used in evidence' (per O'Connor LJ, at p.111).

In *O'Shea* (24 July 1986 unreported), which was considered in *Andrews* [1987] AC 281, the elderly occupier of a second-floor flat into which O was trying to break, slipped while trying to escape through a window and sustained injuries which eventually resulted in his death. He was found lying where he had fallen an hour or so after the incident, and the statement which he then made, in which he stated the reason for his injuries, was admitted in evidence. By contrast, in *Newport* [1998] Crim LR 581, a telephone call made by N's wife 20 minutes before he inflicted fatal injuries on her, in which she arranged to take sanctuary in a friend's house if she had to flee in a hurry, was held to have been wrongly admitted. On the facts there was an insufficient connection between the incident and the wife's request: the call was not a spontaneous and unconsidered reaction to an immediately impending emergency. In all probability the evidence might have been admitted if restricted to an account of the wife's contemporaneous state of emotion and agitation, either because such evidence is not within the hearsay rule at all or because, if it is, it falls within the exception for statements of contemporaneous feelings (see **F16.67**).

F16.64 In *Tobi v Nicholas* [1988] RTR 343, a collision occurred between a car and a stationary motor coach. Some 20 minutes later the driver of the coach, who had summoned the police, identified T as the driver of the car involved. The coach driver was not called to give evidence at the trial, and the Divisional Court held, applying *Andrews* [1987] AC 281, that there were three reasons why his statement should not have been admitted as part of the *res gestae*:

(1) The event which had occurred was not so unusual or dramatic as to dominate the thoughts of the victim. 'Of course anybody whose vehicle has been damaged is annoyed about it, but there is a world of difference between such an unfortunately commonplace situation and the thoughts of somebody who has been assaulted and stabbed' (per Glidewell LJ, at p. 356).
(2) The statement was not sufficiently contemporaneous with the event.
(3) The *res gestae* doctrine should not be used as a device to avoid calling the maker of the statement where he is available, as the coach driver was, to give evidence.

Where a spontaneous statement includes an element of hearsay in the form of information gleaned from another, the admission of the statement does not of itself warrant the admission of the further element of hearsay. In *Elliott* [2000] Crim LR 51, Y, who had been stabbed, made a statement within minutes in which he said that the man who had attacked him was the same man who previously attacked his brother, and that the name of the man was 'Denrick' (E's first name). Y had been told the name by M, who had witnessed the attack on the brother, and the Court of Appeal held that, once M had given evidence that he had identified E to Y as 'Denrick', there was no hearsay problem involved in admitting the statement of Y in its entirety. While this is true to the extent that it was not necessary to place reliance on that part of Y's statement in which he named E, it would have been better to have stated explicitly that Y's *res gestae* statement could not be evidence of that which he did not know, i.e. the name of his assailant.

F16.65 **Use of Statement Itself to Determine Admissibility**   In *Ratten v The Queen* [1972] AC 378, Lord Wilberforce said (at p. 391) that in principle it would not be right for the involvement of the speaker in the pressure of the drama surrounding the event to be proved only by the statement itself, 'otherwise the statement would be lifting itself into the area of admissibility'. However, it was difficult to imagine a case where there was no other evidence to connect the speaker to the event, and it would not be wrong in principle for the judge to take the statement into account, together with other things, in reaching his decision.

F16.66 **Direction to Jury**   In *Andrews* [1987] AC 281, Lord Ackner said that where a 'spontaneous' statement has been admitted in evidence as part of the *res gestae*, the judge must make it clear to the jury:

(a) that it is for them to decide what was said and to be sure that the witnesses were not mistaken in what they believed had been said to them;

(b) that they must be satisfied that the declarant did not concoct or distort to his advantage or to the disadvantage of the accused the statement relied on, and where there is material to raise the issue, that he was not activated by any malice or ill-will;

(c) where there are special features that bear on the possibility of mistake, then the jury's attention must be invited to those matters.

In *Mills v The Queen* [1995] 3 All ER 865, the Privy Council rejected an argument that a specific direction must always be given as to the risk of mistaken identification by a dying man in a *res gestae* statement. The jury in that case had been adequately directed about the risks of mistaken identification in relation to the evidence of other witnesses, and fairness did not require a repetition.

Statements of Contemporaneous Bodily or Mental Feelings

F16.67 The statements of a person in which he relates his contemporaneous bodily feelings are admissible to prove the feelings, but not their cause. Thus, in *Nicholas* (1846) 2 Car & Kir 246, Pollock CB said (at p. 248):

> If a man says to his surgeon, 'I have a pain in the head', or in such a part of the body, that is evidence; but, if he says to his surgeon, 'I have a wound'; and was to add, 'I met John Thomas, who had a sword, and ran me through the body with it', that would be no evidence against John Thomas.

Similarly, in *Gloster* (1888) 16 Cox CC 471, statements by a woman who was dying from the effects of an illegal operation, naming the person responsible for her bodily condition, were held inadmissible under this exception. Charles J held (at p. 473) that 'the statements must be confined to contemporaneous symptoms, and nothing in the nature of a narrative is admissible as to who caused them, or how they were caused'. *Gloster* was followed in *Thomson* [1912] 3 KB 19, in which the statements of a woman who had recently suffered a miscarriage and who claimed to have operated upon herself were excluded.

F16.68 What is contemporaneous is a question of fact. In *Black* (1922) 16 Cr App R 118, B was convicted of the murder by poisoning of his wife. It was held on appeal that her descriptions of symptoms she had suffered after taking medicine given to her by B were admissible only because they were made in B's presence in such a way as to demand an answer from him. (See, as to statements made in the presence of the accused, **F17.99** *et seq*.) Had the statements been made behind his back it would, per Avory J, have required 'grave consideration whether they could have been admitted', because they concerned her past, rather than her contemporaneous, feelings. However, Salter J in the course of argument said (at p. 119):

> ... 'contemporaneous' cannot be confined to feelings experienced at the actual moment when the patient is speaking; it must include such a statement as 'Yesterday I had a pain after meals'.

In the civil case of *Aveson v Lord Kinnaird* (1805) 6 East 188, statements made by a woman concerning symptoms from which she claimed to have been suffering for some time were admitted, not only to establish her feelings when the statement was made, but also to establish that she had had the same symptoms when seen by a doctor some days previously.

Where a doctor gives expert evidence as to the condition of a patient, he may not give evidence of past symptoms as they have been narrated to him in order to prove that the symptoms existed, although he may be allowed to state what he was told simply in order to explain the conclusion to which he has come. If the existence of past symptoms is in issue, they must be proved by admissible evidence (*Bradshaw* (1985) 82 Cr App R 79).

F16.69 In some cases statements indicating contemporaneous feelings may be admissible as original evidence. In *Conde* (1867) 10 Cox CC 547, evidence was admitted that a child who died from starvation had begged a neighbour to give him bread. Of this request Channell B is reported as having said that 'it was not so much a statement as an act. A complaint of hunger was an act;

although the particulars of the statement might not be receivable, the fact of the complaint was clearly so.' It is also permissible to prove a contemporaneous statement in which the maker claims to be in a particular mental state, such as fear. In *Vincent* (1840) 9 C & P 275, a policeman was allowed to prove statements made by bystanders at a public meeting who claimed that they were frightened by what took place. In *Edwards* (1872) 12 Cox CC 230, E was charged with the murder of his wife, R, and a neighbour testified that a week before R died she came to the neighbour's house bearing a carving knife and a large axe. Quain J allowed the neighbour to state that R had asked her to take care of the implements as 'my husband always threatens me with these and when they're out of the way I feel safer'. In the light of the authorities stated above, it would seem that R's statement should not have been admitted to prove the cause of her fear, but only (if it were relevant to do so) that she was in a state of trepidation when delivering the weapons. Evidence of state of mind may also be used to negate inferences which might otherwise be drawn from conduct. In *Gilfoyle* [1996] 1 Cr App R 302, P died by hanging, leaving suicide notes. Evidence that she was not in a suicidal frame of mind was admissible in order to support the prosecution's contention that P had been tricked by her killer into writing the notes.

In recent times there has been a division of opinion as to whether a statement revealing the maker's state of mind is admissible as non-hearsay evidence from which the state of mind may be inferred (*Blastland* [1986] AC 41; *Kearley* [1992] 2 AC 228) or hearsay admissible under an exception to the rule (*Neill v North Antrim Magistrates' Court* [1992] 4 All ER 846; *Gilfoyle*). Both views are tenable although the preponderance of modern authority favours the former.

Statements of Present Intention

In various criminal cases, statements indicating the present intention of the speaker have been received in evidence, apparently by way of exception to the hearsay rule. In *Buckley* (1873) 13 Cox CC 293, an inspector of police was permitted to narrate a statement made to him by G, a constable, who said that he intended to go that evening to keep watch on B, whom he suspected of theft. G was later found stabbed to death at some distance from B's cottage, and the statement was relied upon as circumstantial evidence that G had carried out his intention, with fatal consequences. No reason was given for the decision to admit the statement, and it may be that the case is best viewed as involving a declaration made by the deceased G in the course of his duty (a common-law exception not preserved by the CJA 2003, s. 118).

F16.70

In *Moghal* (1977) 65 Cr App R 56, M was charged with the murder of R, and his defence was that the crime was committed by S. It was held that a statement made by S six months before, in which S declared her intention to murder R, was admissible. However, statements which S made to the police after R had been killed, in which she described her state of mind and feelings before and at the time of the killing, were rejected as inadmissible hearsay on the ground that 'the condition precedent to the admissibility of such statements is that they should relate to the maker's contemporaneous state of mind or emotion'. What is contemporaneous was said to be a question of degree, but what was said in the course of police investigations occurred far too long after the event to be admitted. Where non-contemporaneous declarations are self-serving, there is an additional reason for excluding them, for such declarations might otherwise be used to construct a fraudulent defence (*Petcherini* (1855) 7 Cox CC 79).

Moghal was doubted by the House of Lords in *Blastland* [1986] AC 41, but only on the ground that the isolated declaration of intention made six months before the murder was insufficiently relevant to be admitted. See also *Wainwright* (1875) 13 Cox CC 171, in which W was charged with the murder of a girl, and the prosecution were not allowed to prove that the victim had announced her intention of going to W's premises on the night she died. Cockburn CJ said that the girl's statement was 'only a statement of intention which might or might not be carried out'.

F16.71 The existence of a hearsay exception for statements of intention seems to have been overlooked in *Thomson* [1912] 3 KB 19, in which the statement of a woman made before she suffered a miscarriage, and in which she declared her intention to operate upon herself, was rejected as inadmissible hearsay. The statement was said not to form part of the *res gestae*, in the sense that it was not a spontaneous statement connected with the operation itself. The possibility that it might be admissible as a declaration of intention does not appear to have been canvassed.

More recently, in *Callender* [1998] Crim LR 337, the Court of Appeal refused to admit statements made by C two weeks before his arrest for conspiring to commit arson, in which he told an acquaintance that his intention was limited to making dummy devices, resembling explosives, which could be used to attract publicity to the cause of animal rights without actually causing damage to property. This mirrored his defence at trial and, if true, was an answer to the charge. C did not give evidence, however, and the court appears to have been concerned that his statement, if admitted, would have permitted C to raise a reasonable doubt about the prosecution case in a manner contrary to the principles of the CJPO 1994, s. 35 (see **F19.42**). But the adverse inferences which the statute permits if an accused fails to testify could still be drawn where his *res gestae* statement is admissible. The reason given for rejection was that the *res gestae* rule was in fact a single principle governed by the decisions in *Andrews* [1987] AC 281 and *Ratten v The Queen* [1972] AC 378 (see **F16.56**). C's statement was thus ruled inadmissible because it was not made in circumstances whereby the possibility of concoction or distortion could be disregarded. It is submitted that this is not the case. The true reason for admitting evidence of a statement revealing the maker's intention or other state of mind, or bodily feelings, is the difficulty of proving the matter by other means. Although C's statement was self-serving, and there was a possibility that he was setting up a defence for himself, it was made when he had no inkling that he was about to be arrested, and might be thought to have had some probative value in relation to his state of mind at the relevant time. Whether it was concocted or not should, under this exception, have been a question for the jury.

Common-law Confessions and Admissions

F16.72 The CJA 2003, s. 118(1), makes express provision for saving the common-law rules on confessions and admissions.

Criminal Justice Act 2003, s. 118

Preservation of certain common law categories of admissibility

(1) The following rules of law are preserved.

...

Confessions etc

5.   Any rule of law relating to the admissibility of confessions or mixed statements in criminal proceedings.

Admissions by agents etc

6.   Any rule of law under which in criminal proceedings—
   (a)   an admission made by an agent of a defendant is admissible against the defendant as evidence of any matter stated, or
   (b)   a statement made by a person to whom a defendant refers a person for information is admissible against the defendant as evidence of any matter stated.

The common law has little part to play in regulating the admissibility of an accused's confession now the CJA 2003 has taken effect. Confessions tendered by the prosecution are currently governed by the PACE 1984, s. 76 (see **F17**). The CJA 2003, s. 128, extends the coverage of s. 76 to confessions adduced by a co-accused (see **F17.27**). The most important of the vestigial rules retained by para. 5 of s. 118(1) is the implied acceptance by the accused of a statement made in his presence (see **F17.99**), which may operate even where the accused is silent in the face of an accusation (see **F19.3**). The latter aspect of the rule was specifically preserved by the CJPO 1994, s. 34(5), and remains of some practical importance despite the statutory inroads on the right to silence made by that Act. To the extent that the admissibility of the self-serving parts of a mixed statement depends on factors not dealt with in the PACE 1984, s. 76, the common law is also preserved by s. 118(1) (see **F17.93**).

Admissions by Agents and Referees

An admission made by the agent of an accused person, such as his legal adviser, may be admissible against him (*Turner* (1975) 61 Cr App R 67). Although at first sight such an admission may appear to be a confession, and thus to be governed by the rules of admissibility in the PACE 1984, s. 76 (see **F17**), it is submitted that this is not the case, for the section applies only to a confession made 'by an accused person', and, by s. 82(1), 'confession' includes any statement adverse to 'the person who made it'. It would seem to follow that vicarious admissions continue to be governed by common-law principles. **F16.73**

A statement made by his agent is admissible against the accused only where it is shown that the statement was made within the scope of the agent's authority. Agency may be inferred from the circumstances: thus, in *Turner* (1975) 61 Cr App R 67, it was held that it is permissible to infer from the fact that a barrister makes an admission in court on behalf of and in the presence of his client, that he was authorised to make it. The strength of the inference depends on the circumstances, however, and in *Evans* [1981] Crim LR 699, it was held that agency was not to be inferred simply from the fact that the admission was made by E's solicitor's clerk.

The strict application of the rule of admissibility may work injustice where there is an issue as to whether the accused intended to make the admission put forward on his behalf, as in *Turner* where counsel later gave evidence that he had exceeded his authority in doing so. The discretion available to the court using the PACE 1984, s. 78 should be considered in such cases. The completion by advocates of pre-trial documentation intended to assist in case management raises particularly sensitive issues. In *R (Firth) v Epping Justices* [2011] 4 All ER 326, the strict rule was applied in pre-trial proceedings to a statement made in what was then a Case Progression Form. As a consequence of *Firth*, defence advocates became cautious about providing information for case management purposes which might then be used as an admission, or in cross-examination of the client. This worked against the 'cards on the table' approach on which good case management is based. In *Newell* [2012] 1 WLR 3142, the Court of Appeal, taking account of guidance issued to prosecutors following *Firth*, held that an advocate completing a PCMH form should be free to help the court with the management of the case by setting out relevant information without the risk of that information being used as a statement admissible against the accused. Provided therefore that the case is conducted in accordance with the letter and spirit of the CrimPR, such information should in the exercise of the court's discretion under s. 78 not be admitted as a statement that can be used against an accused. Only very rarely would it be appropriate not to exercise the discretion. The same rule applies in summary proceedings, except where the information is specifically provided under the part of the relevant documentation relating expressly to admissions or to the acknowledgement that certain matters are not in issue; these will continue to be admissible at trial.

Evidence of agency must, of course, be admissible in its own right. In *Evans* statements made by the solicitor's clerk indicating that he was acting with E's authority were inadmissible to prove agency, being hearsay. *Evans* was distinguished in *Ungvari* [2003] EWCA Crim 2346, where there was ample evidence in the history of trading between two companies to support the inference that the appellant's sister was acting as his agent. **F16.74**

A statement made by a person to whom the accused refers another for information on a particular matter may be evidence against him. Thus, in *Williams v Innes* (1808) 1 Camp 364, an **F16.75** executor referred the plaintiff to a particular individual for information pertaining to the assets of the estate, and it was held that what the referee said was admissible against the executor. Similarly, in *Mallory* (1884) 13 QBD 33, where M told a police officer that his wife would supply a list showing where certain items, suspected of being stolen, were purchased, the list handed over by the wife in M's presence was admissible against him. Coleridge CJ refrained from stating what the outcome would have been had M been absent when the list was handed over, but it is submitted that it would have made no difference.

Statements in Furtherance of Common Enterprise

F16.76   The CJA 2003, s. 118(1), makes express provision for saving the common-law rules on statements in furtherance of a common enterprise.

Criminal Justice Act 2003, s. 118

(1) The following rules of law are preserved.

. . .

Common enterprise

7. Any rule of law under which in criminal proceedings a statement made by a party to a common enterprise is admissible against another party to the enterprise as evidence of any matter stated.

F16.77   **Scope of the Rule**   The rule that the acts and statements of one party to a common purpose may be evidence against another is particularly associated with charges of conspiracy. However, it is not confined to such cases, and applies to other offences where complicity is alleged. Thus, in *Jessop* (1877) 16 Cox CC 204, for example, J was charged with the murder of A, with whom he had entered into a suicide pact to die by taking poison. The plan miscarried and J survived. Field J held that evidence of the purchase of poison by A, being an act done in furtherance of the common purpose, was admissible against J. A more modern illustration is *Jones* [1997] 2 Cr App R 119, in which it was held that the rule applied to a joint enterprise to evade the prohibition on the importation of drugs, despite the fact that no charge of conspiracy was brought.

F16.78   The limits of the doctrine were considered in *Gray* [1995] 2 Cr App R 100. G and others were each convicted of offences relating to insider dealing. Although there was alleged to be a 'network' between them for the passing of information, each allegation related only to an offence committed by one of them alone. The prosecution case consisted mainly of telephone conversations between the defendants, and the judge told the jury that a statement made in the course of such a conversation, though a particular defendant was not party to it, could nevertheless be evidence against that defendant if there was a joint enterprise between them for the unlawful dissemination of 'inside' information and the statement was made in furtherance of that joint enterprise. The Court of Appeal was inclined to the view that this stated the principle too widely: the acts and declarations of a person engaged in a joint enterprise and made in pursuance of that enterprise might be admissible against another, but only where the evidence shows the complicity of that other in a common offence or series of offences. As none of the offences was alleged to have been committed jointly, the rule did not apply. If, contrary to that view, the principle could be stated in the wider form, the prosecution would have to make clear the limits of the alleged agreement in pursuit of which the specific offences were said to have been committed; as this had not been done the appeals were allowed. Thus it appears that the case for a wider principle could still be made. In *Murray* [1997] 2 Cr App R 136, the Court of Appeal adopted the interpretation of *Gray* in the 1996 edition of this work (which is the same as that set out above) and added that that case is authority primarily for the proposition that the common-law exception cannot be extended to cases where individual defendants are charged with a number of separate substantive offences and the terms of a common enterprise are not provided or are ill-defined. An argument, based on dicta in the case, that *Gray* in fact narrows the scope of the common-law exception was rejected. *Murray* was approved in *Williams* [2002] EWCA Crim 2208, where the true rule was considered to be that 'the acts and declarations by

A in furtherance of a sufficiently defined common design are admissible to prove a substantive offence committed alone in pursuance of the same common design, by B'.

The rule permits the actions and declarations of one party, A, to be used in evidence against the **F16.79** other, B, and is thus an exception to the general rule that B is not to be prejudiced by the acts or statements of another, and an exception to the hearsay rule insofar as it may involve reliance on A's statements as evidence of their truth. In *Onyeabor* [2009] EWCA Crim 534 the court regarded as non-hearsay a statement by O's accomplice in furtherance of their joint enterprise, and stated that it was admissible under s. 118(1), rule 7. It is submitted, however, that recourse to s. 118 should not be had unless a hearsay exception is required. As an exception to the hearsay rule, the common enterprise rule defies classification, some writers regarding it as appertaining to the *res gestae* (see *Andrews & Hirst on Criminal Evidence* (4th edn, 2001) at para. 20.26), others as based on implied agency (see *Cross and Tapper on Evidence* (11th edn, 2007) at p. 621), and others as an independent exception, the justification for which is that such evidence must be used if the 'secret' crime of conspiracy is ever to be proved at all (Gilles, *The Law of Criminal Conspiracy* (1981)).

In order for the act or statement of A to be admissible against B, the rule requires:

(1) that the act or statement of A must be in the course and furtherance of the common purpose; and

(2) that independent evidence be adduced of the existence of the conspiracy and the involvement in it of B.

Meaning of Course and Furtherance of Common Purpose   In the leading case of *Blake* **F16.80** (1844) 6 QB 126, B and T were charged with conspiring to avoid payment of duty on imported goods. B, in the course of his employment at the Customs House, certified that the amount of goods imported by T as an agent was less than was in fact the case. T then charged his principal duty on the full amount, recording the charge in his own day book, and split the proceeds with B. It was held that the entry in T's day book was admissible against B, as being evidence of something done in the course of the transaction, but that the counterfoil of the cheque by which B received his share of the proceeds was not, for it was an act done after the common purpose was effected which had nothing to do with the carrying out of the conspiracy. It will be apparent from *Blake* that it may be difficult to distinguish precisely where a transaction begins and ends, and whether acts are done in furtherance of it or not. A clearer case of inadmissibility owing to the termination of the criminal purpose is that of the confession of one conspirator made after his apprehension, which is evidence only against the maker (see, e.g., *Walters* (1979) 69 Cr App R 115, at p. 120). And a more obvious example of a statement which cannot be said to be in furtherance of any criminal purpose occurred in *Steward* [1963] Crim LR 697, where one conspirator simply recited to another the various acts of B which had been done in execution of the common purpose, and the statement was held inadmissible against B. See also *Hardy* (1794) 24 St Tr 199, in which a similar recital by a conspirator of his own past acts was held not to be in furtherance of the conspiracy.

In *Devonport* [1996] 1 Cr App R 221, a statement was admitted which may not, in the strict **F16.81** sense, have furthered the conspiracy. The court was concerned with a document drawn up by D concerning the proposed division of spoils between himself and others involved. This was regarded by Judge J as a document in furtherance of the conspiracy, distinguishing *Blake* on the ground that the document was not a record of distribution after the conspiracy but an indication of the intended or prospective distribution of the proceeds of the conspiracy when it has been fulfilled. Even so, as there was no evidence that the document served any purpose other than D's own convenience, the decision seems to go further than previous authority. So also does *Ilyas* [1996] Crim LR 810, in which a diary was admitted which was a record of the receipt of stolen car parts by some of the parties to the conspiracy. Nothing was made of the argument that the document was a mere record of what had already occurred and not in furtherance of the enterprise. Latham J, however, asserted that it was 'a document created *in the course of, or furtherance*, of the conspiracy' (emphasis added). This would seem to be a new and alternative ground of admissibility, as a document such as the diary can be said to be created in the course of a conspiracy without being in any way in furtherance of it. It would seem that the rule is in the course of being broadened by the courts. See also *Reeves* [1999] 3 Arch News 2, in which an aide-memoire by one conspirator for his own assistance appears to have been regarded as potentially admissible against co-conspirators under this exception, and *Platten* [2006] EWCA Crim 140, where it was said that 'statements made during the conspiracy and as part of the conspiracy, because they are part of making the natural arrangements to carry out the conspiracy, will be admissible'. In *Platten*, the court confined the exclusion of statements which are 'mere narrative' to statements made after the conspiracy is concluded. The Court endorsed the rule of thumb adopted by Kennedy LJ in *Barham* [1997] 2 Cr App R 119 of 'the enterprise in operation'. See also *King* [2012] EWCA Crim 805 (co-conspirator's description of accused as 'the hired muscle' was intended to keep the confidence of a prospective purchaser of drugs and was properly admitted).

Where the hearsay statements of co-conspirators in furtherance of the conspiracy implicate an accused, the trial judge must give a careful direction to the jury that the statements cannot be used to provide the link between that accused and the conspiracy (*Blake* (1993) 97 Cr App R 169).

F16.82   **Requirement of Independent Evidence of Common Purpose**   In *Blake* (1844) 6 QB 126, a case involving conspiracy, Patteson J stated the principle to be that 'you must establish the fact of a conspiracy before you can make the act of one the act of all'. The absence of such independent evidence renders the statement alleged to have been made in furtherance of the conspiracy inadmissible, and it is not possible for the statement itself to provide the evidence of the existence of the conspiracy (see *Jenkins* [2002] EWCA Crim 2475, and commentary by Professor Sir John Smith). This does not mean that such evidence must be brought forward and accepted before the act or statement in question can be proved, for: 'from the nature of this charge [conspiracy] the evidence must necessarily grow up as it proceeds. The acts of the one party must be given in evidence and then the acts of the other, and it may then be shown that those acts fully prove a conspiracy between them' (*Murphy* (1837) 8 C & P 297, per Coleridge J at pp. 302–3). See also *Governor of Pentonville Prison, ex parte Osman* [1990] 3 All ER 701 in which Lloyd LJ said (at p. 316): '... there must always be some evidence other than the hearsay evidence of a fellow conspirator to prove that a particular defendant is party to a conspiracy. Provided there is some other evidence, it does not matter in what order the evidence is adduced.' The principle is thus one of conditional admissibility, in that if, after the evidence has been heard, it transpires that there is no independent evidence of common purpose, the act or statement of A will have to be excluded from the case against B (*Donat* (1985) 82 Cr App R 173. It is submitted that there is no difference in practice between this view and that expressed in *Whittaker* [1914] 3 KB 1283, in which it was said that the act or statement of A, though it may be proved as evidence against him, remains inadmissible against B until the necessary foundation is laid. Insofar as there is a difference, it is submitted that the correct practice is as stated in *Donat*.

F16.83   Failure by the prosecution to satisfy the requirement after evidence of a statement has been admitted *de bene esse* will require a careful direction to the jury, and may require the discharge of the jury and a retrial if the evidence admitted was prejudicial. Where evidence is admitted under the rule it is not necessary for the jury to be directed to convict only if they find evidence against B other than the statement of A. It is for the judge alone to satisfy himself that such evidence exists: if it does, the jury is permitted to look at all the evidence in order to decide guilt (*Barham* [1997] 2 Cr App 119; *King* [2012] EWCA Crim 805). If, however, there is a danger that the jury will rely on the statement by A as primary evidence of B's involvement, 'sweeping away' the other evidence which has led the judge to admit the statement in the first place, the judge should direct the jury as to the shortcomings in the evidence of A, including (if such be the case) the absence of any opportunity to cross-examine A, and the absence of corroborative evidence (*Jones* [1997] 2 Cr App R 119; *Williams* [2002] EWCA Crim 2208). In a case where there was other evidence to connect the accused with the conspiracy, the Court of Appeal did not consider it fatal that the trial judge had failed to warn the jury of the need for caution in convicting on evidence of things said or done by others when the appellant was not present, though it would have been preferable so to warn them (*Sofroniou* [2009] EWCA Crim 1360).

Common-law Admissibility of Body of Expertise

The CJA 2003, s. 118(1), makes express provision for saving the common-law rules allowing an expert to draw on a relevant body of expertise. **F16.84**

Criminal Justice Act 2003, s. 118

(1) The following rules of law are preserved.

. . .

Expert evidence

8. Any rule of law under which in criminal proceedings an expert witness may draw on the body of expertise relevant to his field.

Technically speaking, where an expert draws on the work of others in order to form his opinion, an element of hearsay is necessarily involved. Whether this is objectionable or not depends on the nature of the work referred to. In *Abadom* [1983] 1 All ER 364 (**F10.34**) it was accepted that 'the process of taking account of information stemming from the work of others in the same field is an essential ingredient of the nature of expert evidence', and as such is not subject to the hearsay rule. Where, however, an expert relies on the existence or non-existence of some fact which is basic to the question on which he is asked his opinion, that fact must be proved by admissible evidence. Paragraph 8 of s. 118(1) preserves the effect of *Abadom*. See also, however, s. 127 at **F10.31** which erodes the second part of the rule in *Abadom* by permitting evidence to be given of the preparatory findings on which an expert's opinion is based without the need to call those who made the findings as witnesses in the case.

OTHER STATUTORY EXCEPTIONS

Committal Statements Admissible at Trial

The MCA 1980, ss. 5A to 5F, make far-reaching provision for statements read at committal to be tendered at trial. Under the CPIA 1996, sch. 2, statements and depositions which have been admitted at committal are automatically admissible at trial, except that the court has a discretion to exclude the evidence and a party to the proceedings may object to its admission, although the court has a statutory power to order that the objection be of no effect if it is in the interests of justice so to order. These provisions were repealed upon the coming into force of the CJA 2003, sch. 3 (the abolition of committals: see **D10.1**). The notice provisions of s. 50 were already defunct (*CPS v Gil* [2006] EWHC 1153 (Admin)). **F16.85**

Transcript Admissible at Retrial

Criminal Appeal Act 1968, sch. 2, para. 1 **F16.86**

(1) Evidence given at a retrial must be given orally if it was given orally at the original trial, unless—
   (a) all the parties to the retrial agree otherwise;
   (b) section 116 of the Criminal Justice Act 2003 applies (admissibility of hearsay evidence where a witness is unavailable); or
   (c) the witness is unavailable to give evidence, otherwise than as mentioned in subsection (2) of that section, and section 114(1)(d) of that Act applies (admission of hearsay evidence under residual discretion).

(2) Paragraph 5 of Schedule 3 to the Crime and Disorder Act 1998 (use of depositions) does not apply at a retrial to a deposition read as evidence at the original trial.

The provisions of sch. 2 reaffirm and clarify a wider common-law rule: see *Thompson* [1982] QB 647, in which it was held that the transcript of evidence of a witness might be read out at a retrial upon proof that she was too ill to travel, notwithstanding that the retrial was not ordered by the Court of Appeal under the 1968 Act. Similarly, in *Hall* [1973] 1 QB 496, it was held that a transcript of evidence is admissible at common law at a retrial if the witness has since died, provided it is authenticated in appropriate manner, e.g., by calling the shorthand writer who took the original note.

The terms of the provision, as substituted by the CJA 2003, s. 131, bring the admissibility of evidence at retrial into line with the range of hearsay exceptions in the 2003 Act. In practical terms, the most important change wrought by s. 131 is the incorporation of the provisions of s. 114(1)(d) (see **F16.38**). See *Venn* [2009] EWCA 2541, and *Lawrence* [2014] 1 Cr App R 33 (5), where it was also stressed that the unavailability of the absent witness must relate to the time at, or shortly before the point at which the evidence is required at the retrial.

Video Recordings, Depositions of Child or Young Person and Written Statements Admissible under Criminal Justice Act 1967, s. 9

F16.87   For special measures for assisting witnesses, including children and intimidated witnesses, see **D14.26** *et seq.* For the admission of depositions made by a child or young person under the CYPA 1933, s. 43, see **D14.46**. For the admissibility of written statements under the CJA 1967, s. 9, see **D22.38**.

Statements Admissible under Miscellaneous Statutory Provisions

F16.88   Various statutes make provision for the admission of hearsay statements. The following are the most commonly invoked.

Under the CJA 1988, s. 30 (see **F10.49**), the report of an expert witness on matters of which he would have been competent to give oral evidence is admissible as evidence of the facts and opinions stated therein. This provision applies only to 'written' reports so that the admissibility of, say, a tape-recorded report may be in doubt. Under the CJA 1972, s. 46(1), written statements made in Scotland or Northern Ireland may be admitted as evidence in other criminal proceedings on the same terms as statements made in England and Wales.

Bankers' Books

F16.89   The Bankers' Books Evidence Act 1879, s. 3 (see **F8.35**), was designed to facilitate proof of bankers' records without bringing the original document to court. As the provision is confined to copies, nothing in s. 3 renders the original banker's book admissible: in most cases, however, the original would be admissible under the CJA 2003, s. 117, and a copy would be admissible by virtue of s. 133 of that Act. Before a copy can be given in evidence under s. 3 of the 1879 Act, s. 4 of that Act requires proof to be given that the banker's book was at the time of the relevant entry one of the ordinary books of the bank, that the entry was made in the usual and ordinary course of business, and that the book is in the custody or control of the bank. If the CJA 2003, s. 117, is relied upon, no such conditions need be satisfied. It should also be noted that the 1879 Act confines itself to the various books and records of a bank. In *Dadson* (1983) 77 Cr App R 91, which concerned events which occurred before the 1879 Act was amended to include records, it was held that a file of correspondence was inadmissible under s. 3 as not being a 'book'. The correspondence would now be admissible under the 1879 Act only if it is held to constitute a 'record', whereas the CJA 2003 imposes no such constraint. It was held in *Re*

Howglen Ltd [2001] 1 All ER 376 that a 'record' for this purpose connoted a method by which a bank recorded day-to-day financial transactions: a record of notes of meetings could not be regarded as banker's books within the 1879 Act. A record of a meeting would now be admissible under s. 117 of the 2003 Act.

As to the practice surrounding inspection of bankers' books and their relationship to the best evidence rule, see generally **F8.35**.

CRIMINAL JUSTICE ACT 2003: ADDITIONAL REQUIREMENT FOR THE USE OF MULTIPLE HEARSAY

The CJA 2003, s. 121, stipulates that only limited use can be made of multiple hearsay. This **F16.90** appears to apply whether the hearsay in question is tendered under the new statutory exceptions contained in the Act itself, or under the preserved common-law exceptions, or under other statutory provisions, given that the new rule is negative in form and defines hearsay evidence in the broadest of terms.

Criminal Justice Act 2003, s. 121

(1) A hearsay statement is not admissible to prove the fact that an earlier hearsay statement was made unless—
   (a) either of the statements is admissible under section 117, 119 or 120,
   (b) all parties to the proceedings so agree, or
   (c) the court is satisfied that the value of the evidence in question, taking into account how reliable the statements appear to be, is so high that the interests of justice require the later statement to be admissible for that purpose.
(2) In this section 'hearsay statement' means a statement, not made in oral evidence, that is relied on as evidence of a matter stated in it.

Under this provision, which was revisited during the passage of the Bill through Parliament, **F16.91** multiple hearsay (such as 'A told me that B told him that D shot V') is not admissible even if both the statement by A and the statement by B fit within one or more of the various exceptions to the hearsay rule (e.g., B's statement is a spontaneous statement made as part of the *res gestae*, and A's statement is admissible under s. 116 because A has died since making it). The only exceptions to this principle are where one of the statements is admissible as a business document (see s. 117 at **F16.24**) or a previous statement by a witness in the case, or where the court is so convinced by the value of the evidence that it can invoke the special 'safety valve' in s. 121(1)(c). In *Xhabri* [2006] 1 All ER 776 (considered at **F16.44**), the test in s. 121 was satisfied in relation to a complaint of false imprisonment which was relayed by two friends of the victim to a police officer. The complainant and the officer (though not the two friends) were available for cross-examination. The Court of Appeal considered that both s. 121(1)(a) (admissibility under other provisions) and s. 121(1)(c) (admissibility in the interests of justice) were satisfied. In *Maher v DPP* (2006) 170 JP 441, a note which had been made (and lost) of a car number plate formed the basis of a call to the police in which the number was transmitted. Evidence of the number was received under s. 121(1)(c) although it was inadmissible as a business record under s. 117 (see **F16.27**) on the grounds of reliability. This appears to treat s. 121(c) as an alternative ground of admissibility rather than as a hurdle to be surmounted in respect of otherwise admissible evidence. This process of reasoning was disapproved in *Walker* [2007] EWCA Crim 1698, where it was held to be wrong to 'jump straight' to s. 121 without first locating a hearsay exception for each statement separately. In *Musone* [2007] 1 WLR 2467, s. 121(1)(c) was invoked to admit the narration by a reluctant witness of the victim's dying declaration. First-hand statements by the same witness were admitted under s. 114(1)(d) (see **F16.38**) and the Court of Appeal noted the similarity of the wording of the two 'interests of justice' provisions. The difference is that under s. 121(1)(c) the value of the evidence must be 'so high' that its admission is required. In *Thakrar* [2010] EWCA Crim 1505 the Court approved of the use of s. 121 to admit statements taken in Northern Cyprus from witnesses who claimed to have heard MT confess to three murders and related offences, and to implicate his co-accused KT. The fact that the accounts contained details of the crimes that could only have been known to a participant was held to provide striking evidence of their reliability.

CRIMINAL JUSTICE ACT 2003: EVIDENCE AFFECTING THE CREDIBILITY OF ADMISSIBLE HEARSAY

F16.92   The CJA 2003, s. 124, governs the admissibility of evidence directed towards the discrediting of a hearsay statement where the maker of the statement does not give oral evidence in connection with the subject-matter of the statement. The opposing party is entitled to put in evidence anything which he could have put in if the witness had been present, but in addition, and in order to counterbalance the absence of cross-examination, may also put in material as to which the witness's answers, had he been present, would have been final (*Horncastle* [2010] 2 AC 373, where s. 124 was said to form an essential part of the statutory protection against unfair trial). In *Riat* [2013] 1 All ER 349 Hughes LJ stressed that 'very full' inquiries would be needed, in the case of hearsay evidence that is important to the prosecution, to determine what material might be available to enable the defence to challenge the maker's credibility, and that all relevant material should be disclosed (including material coming to light throughout the trial). A mere check of the Police National Computer would not suffice for this purpose. In *Harvey* [2014] EWCA Crim 54 it was held that the CJA 2003, s. 124, could not be deployed so as to admit bad character evidence to discredit hearsay witnesses where the evidence was of no substantial probative value: the evidence that may be admitted under the section is subject to the same controls as where the witness attends to give evidence, i.e. the provisions of the CJA 2003, s. 100 apply (see **F14.9**).

It does not appear that s. 124 is limited to hearsay statements admissible under the 2003 Act: on the contrary it appears to be of general effect.

The mixture of materials admissible to discredit the maker is similar to that which previously appeared in the CJA 1988, sch. 2. However, the court has wider powers to admit evidence in order to deny or answer the allegation.

Criminal Justice Act 2003, s. 124

(1) This section applies if in criminal proceedings—
   (a) a statement not made in oral evidence in the proceedings is admitted as evidence of a matter stated, and
   (b) the maker of the statement does not give oral evidence in connection with the subject matter of the statement.
(2) In such a case—
   (a) any evidence which (if he had given such evidence) would have been admissible as relevant to his credibility as a witness is so admissible in the proceedings;
   (b) evidence may with the court's leave be given of any matter which (if he had given such evidence) could have been put to him in cross-examination as relevant to his credibility as a witness but of which evidence could not have been adduced by the cross-examining party;
   (c) evidence tending to prove that he made (at whatever time) any other statement inconsistent with the statement admitted as evidence is admissible for the purpose of showing that he contradicted himself.
(3) If as a result of evidence admitted under this section an allegation is made against the maker of a statement, the court may permit a party to lead additional evidence of such description as the court may specify for the purposes of denying or answering the allegation.
(4) In the case of a statement in a document which is admitted as evidence under section 117 each person who, in order for the statement to be admissible, must have supplied or received the information concerned or created or received the document or part concerned is to be treated as the maker of the statement for the purposes of subsections (1) to (3) above.

UNCONVINCING AND SUPERFLUOUS HEARSAY

Under the CJA 2003, s. 125, the Crown Court has a specific power to stop a case where (a) the **F16.93** case depends significantly ('wholly or partly') on a hearsay statement and (b) the evidence is unconvincing to the point where a conviction based on it would be unsafe. The Court of Appeal in *Horncastle* [2010] 2 AC 373, in a judgment endorsed and regarded as complementary to the subsequent decision of the Supreme Court, identified this as part of a set of safeguards forming a 'crafted code' on hearsay that protects the fair trial rights of the accused under the ECHR, Article 6, but added that the provision should not be taken to suggest that hearsay should be admitted, subject to a decision to be taken at the end of the trial. Rather, the provision allows for a proportionate assessment of reliability at the close of the case where there is a legitimate argument that the hearsay is unconvincing but important to the case. In similar circumstances, magistrates are in any event bound to dismiss a case based on such evidence: the object is to prevent a perverse finding by a jury (and by service courts, to which the power also applies: sch. 7, para. 4). In *Ibrahim* [2012] 4 All ER 225 it was said that a judge should have uppermost in his mind the question of whether an untested hearsay statement has been shown to be reliable in light of all the other evidence adduced. If not, and the statement is 'part of the central corpus of evidence without which the case on the relevant count cannot proceed', the statement is 'almost bound to be "unconvincing" such that a conviction based on it will be unsafe'. As to the importance and meaning of 'reliability', see also *Riat* [2013] 1 All ER 349.

In addition, s. 126 confers a power on any court trying a criminal case to exclude hearsay evidence where 'taking account of the danger that to admit it would result in undue waste of time' the case for exclusion outweighs the case for admission. Section 126 operates without prejudice to the common-law power to exclude evidence on the ground that its prejudicial effect outweighs its probative value, or the general discretion to exclude prosecution evidence under the PACE 1984, s. 78. In *Horncastle*, where the Court of Appeal identified s. 126 as providing an essential part of the protection against unfair trial, it was said that the section adds to s. 78 an obligation to regulate 'satellite disputes' arising through the use of hearsay evidence. Note that, unlike the preserved powers, s. 126 can be invoked in respect of evidence tendered by the defence (*Atkinson* [2011] EWCA Crim 1746, where hearsay tendered by one accused, to whose defence it was 'of peripheral help' was held to have been rightly excluded at the behest of his co-accused to whom it was highly prejudicial).

Criminal Justice Act 2003, ss. 125 and 126   **F16.94**

125.—(1) If on a defendant's trial before a judge and jury for an offence the court is satisfied at any time after the close of the case for the prosecution that—

(a) the case against the defendant is based wholly or partly on a statement not made in oral evidence in the proceedings, and

(b) the evidence provided by the statement is so unconvincing that, considering its importance to the case against the defendant, his conviction of the offence would be unsafe,

the court must either direct the jury to acquit the defendant of the offence or, if it considers that there ought to be a retrial, discharge the jury.

(2) Where—

(a) a jury is directed under subsection (1) to acquit a defendant of an offence, and

(b) the circumstances are such that, apart from this subsection, the defendant could if acquitted of that offence be found guilty of another offence,

the defendant may not be found guilty of that other offence if the court is satisfied as mentioned in subsection (1) in respect of it.

(3) If—

(a) a jury is required to determine under section 4A(2) of the Criminal Procedure (Insanity) Act 1964 whether a person charged on an indictment with an offence did the act or made the omission charged, and

(b) the court is satisfied as mentioned in subsection (1) above at any time after the close of the case for the prosecution that—

    (i) the case against the defendant is based wholly or partly on a statement not made in oral evidence in the proceedings, and

    (ii) the evidence provided by the statement is so unconvincing that, considering its importance to the case against the person, a finding that he did the act or made the omission would be unsafe,

the court must either direct the jury to acquit the defendant of the offence or, if it considers that there ought to be a rehearing, discharge the jury.

(4) This section does not prejudice any other power a court may have to direct a jury to acquit a person of an offence or to discharge a jury.

126.(1) In criminal proceedings the court may refuse to admit a statement as evidence of a matter stated if—

(a) the statement was made otherwise than in oral evidence in the proceedings, and

(b) the court is satisfied that the case for excluding the statement, taking account of the danger that to admit it would result in undue waste of time, substantially outweighs the case for admitting it, taking account of the value of the evidence.

(2) Nothing in this chapter prejudices—

(a) any power of a court to exclude evidence under section 78 of the Police and Criminal Evidence Act 1984 (exclusion of unfair evidence), or

(b) any other power of a court to exclude evidence at its discretion (whether by preventing questions from being put or otherwise).

Section F17 The Rule Against Hearsay: Confessions

INTRODUCTION

Definition

Police and Criminal Evidence Act 1984, s. 82

F17.1

(1) In this Part of this Act—
    'confession', includes any statement wholly or partly adverse to the person who made it, whether made to a person in authority or not and whether made in words or otherwise.

The admissibility of confession evidence is governed by provisions to be found in the PACE 1984, part VII, from which the above definition is taken.

At common law, the test for admissibility of confessions was that of voluntariness, and a statement obtained by fear of prejudice or hope of advantage excited or held out by a person in authority was regarded as having been made involuntarily (see, e.g., *Baldry* (1852) 2 Den CC 430, per Baron Parke at p. 444; *Ibrahim v The King* [1914] AC 599; *DPP v Ping Lin* [1976] AC 574). The 1984 Act introduced a new test for admissibility (as to which see **F17.8**) and redefines 'confession'. Section 82(1) makes it clear that the law is no longer concerned with whether the confession was made to a person in authority, such as a police or customs officer, and that the statutory test for admissibility is equally applicable to, for example, an informal admission to a friend or colleague. Dissatisfaction with the common law had been expressed in *Deokinanan v The Queen* [1969] 1 AC 20, in which it was noted that a person who is not in authority may induce an unreliable confession by, for example, offering a bribe. Most confessions will, however, continue to be made to persons in authority such as the police, and the observation made in *Deokinanan v The Queen* that, '[t]he fact that an inducement is made by a person in authority may make it more likely to operate on the accused's mind and lead him to confess', continues to be true.

It should follow from the definition of 'confession' in s. 82(1), and from the provision in s. 76(1) **F17.2** (see **F17.8**) that only a confession made 'by' an accused may be given in evidence 'against him', that where the only proof that the accused made the statement comes from the confession itself it should not be admitted. However, in *Ward* [2001] Crim LR 316, the Court of Appeal held that where a passenger in a car gave W's personal details to a police officer when asked for his own, the statement was admissible as a 'confession' by W, who denied being the passenger. It is submitted that while this is a useful device for admitting a common form of evidence of identification it was not a confession 'by' W unless its truth was assumed. A better approach would be to regard the statement as a form of original evidence, unless this option is now precluded by the hearsay provisions of the CJA 2003, in particular s. 115(3) (see **F15.17**).

The result of a literal application of the definition in *Mawdesley v Chief Constable of Cheshire Constabulary* [2004] 1 All ER 58 was that a statement disclosing the identity of a driver was admissible as a confession if it could be inferred that the accused had written it, even though

Part F Evidence

F

it was unsigned (and therefore inadmissible under the statutory scheme in the Road Traffic Act 1988).

F17.3   Guilty Pleas and Pleas in Mitigation   A plea of guilty is a confession for the purposes of the PACE 1984, s. 82(1), and as such is admissible in evidence provided that the provisions of s. 76(2) are complied with. At common law a plea of guilty was regarded as an admission of fact and was admissible in evidence against an accused who subsequently changed his plea to 'not guilty'. However, it was also stated that such evidence would be likely to be excluded in the discretion of the court or, if admitted, followed by a very careful direction as to the use to which it could be put (*Rimmer* [1972] 1 All ER 604; *Hetherington* [1972] Crim LR 703). A retracted plea of guilty may also, where relevant, be relied upon as a confession by a co-accused under s. 76A (see **F17.28**), to which the court's power of discretionary exclusion does not apply (*Johnson* (2007) 171 JP 574).

An admission made by an accused in other proceedings would similarly constitute a confession for the purposes of the 1984 Act, and could be relied upon provided, as is likely, that it complies with the provisions of s. 76(2) and (which may be more doubtful) that it is not excluded under s. 78. Such evidence would not have been admitted at common law (*McGregor* [1968] 1 QB 371).

A plea in mitigation made by counsel on behalf of a client who has been convicted on his plea of 'not guilty' should not be understood as a confession by the convicted person through his counsel. So to regard mitigation would be both unjust and unrealistic, as it is counsel's duty to accept the verdict and seek to mitigate the consequences (*Wu Chun-Piu v The Queen* [1996] 1 WLR 1113). It is submitted that the same must be true if the convicted person advances his mitigation in person.

Confessions Otherwise than in Words

F17.4   There is no statutory definition of 'statement' for the purposes of part VII of the PACE 1984, but the inclusion in s. 82(1) of the expression 'whether made in words or otherwise' suggests that 'confession' may, in addition to admissions in oral or written form, include conduct such as a nod of acceptance of an accusation or a 'thumbs-up' sign which may be properly regarded as a 'statement' in sign language. In *Li Shu-Ling v The Queen* [1989] AC 270, L, who had previously made a full confession to the police, agreed to take part in a filmed re-enactment of the crime with which he was charged, which was the murder of a woman by strangulation. He gave a running commentary explaining his movements, which he demonstrated on a woman police officer who played the part of the victim. At trial, his account of the killing was entirely different. It was held by the Privy Council (applying common-law principles) that the re-enactment was to be regarded as a confession. Such a film would also constitute a confession under s. 82(1), and may be given in evidence, provided that the conditions of admissibility under the 1984 Act are satisfied. That the conditions of admissibility should be the same for re-enactments or visual demonstrations as for oral or written confessions was confirmed at common law in *Timothy v The State* [2000] 1 WLR 485. Confessions made by two of the accused were excluded following allegations of police misconduct. It was held that the same allegations were relevant to the voluntariness, and therefore to the admissibility, of the conduct of the two in showing the police where they had hidden the murder weapon (see also *Lam Chi Ming v The Queen* [1991] 2 AC 212).

It is submitted that conduct which is not intended to convey guilt, but which may be interpreted as doing so, is not a 'statement' and hence not a confession. Thus, for example, driving away at speed from the scene of an accident is not a confession to which the 1984 Act applies, though evidence of such conduct would be relevant and admissible.

Partly and Wholly Exculpatory Statements

F17.5   A confession may be 'wholly or partly adverse' to the maker, with the result that a so-called 'mixed statement', which is part confession and part exculpation, is a confession for the purposes of the

PACE 1984. (See to the same effect at common law, *Customs and Excise Commissioners v Harz* [1967] 1 AC 760, per Lord Reid at p. 818, and see further as to the use of mixed statements in evidence **F17.93** to **F17.98**.) Whether words amount to at least a partial confession is a question of fact separate and distinct from the question (where this is also in dispute) whether the words in question were spoken at all (*B* [2009] EWCA Crim 2113).

In *Finch* [2007] 1 WLR 1645, the issue was whether the accused could rely on a statement made by R, an erstwhile co-accused, under the PACE 1984, s. 76A (see **F17.28**). The Court of Appeal identified as suitable for full argument the question whether statements made by R in police interviews which went beyond admissions and were exculpatory of F constituted 'confessions' for the purposes of s. 82(1). A simple solution would be to regard the point at which a statement begins and ends as a question of fact.

Where the part of a mixed statement relied upon by the prosecution also forms part of the **F17.6** defence, it may be easier to set aside errors in the manner by which it was obtained. In *Uddin* [2005] EWCA Crim 464, U, who was of very low IQ, was wrongly interviewed without an independent adult. The only admission U made was of his presence at the scene: in all other respects his statement was self-serving, and consistent with his evidence at trial. In holding that the use of the confession did not lead to an unsafe conviction, the Court of Appeal noted that the purpose of the protection of which U had been deprived was to prevent prejudice arising from his failure to do himself justice at interview. As U's admission of presence was an inherent part of the defence, this had not occurred.

A more difficult issue is whether the PACE 1984, s. 82(1), includes a statement which, when **F17.7** made, is purely self-serving, but which becomes 'adverse' to the interests of the accused because of the way in which it is deployed at trial, typically because it is inconsistent with the defence there put forward. In *Sat-Bhambra* (1988) 88 Cr App R 55, the Court of Appeal (*obiter*) considered that a purely exculpatory statement was not a confession, but noted that such a statement might be excluded under the more general power of the court under s. 78 (see **F17.33** to **F17.54**, and *Jelen* (1989) 90 Cr App R 456). *Sat-Bhambra* was approved by the House of Lords in *Hasan* [2005] 2 AC 467, overturning the decision of the Court of Appeal in the same case, reported as *Z* [2003] 1 WLR 1489. It was argued that the definition in s. 82(1) ('"confession" includes any statement wholly or partly adverse') was apt also to 'include' statements that were not adverse when made. According to Lord Steyn, with whom the other members of the House concurred, the word 'includes' was selected simply in order to extend the core meaning of confession to partly adverse statements. The meaning contended for was strained, and also unnecessary, as s. 78 was available to protect an accused where, for example, the police by oppression secured a wholly exculpatory but false statement and then sought to use it 'against' an accused so as to damage his credibility. Although s. 78 is formally couched in the language of discretion and s. 76 in the language of judgment, s. 78 'in truth imports a judgment whether in the light of the statutory criteria of fairness the court ought to admit the evidence'. The House therefore concluded that there was no gap in the procedural safeguards provided by the PACE 1984.

Principles of Admissibility under the Police and Criminal Evidence Act 1984, s. 76

Police and Criminal Evidence Act 1984, s. 76   **F17.8**

(1) In any proceedings a confession made by an accused person may be given in evidence against him insofar as it is relevant to any matter in issue in the proceedings and is not excluded by the court in pursuance of this section.

(2) If, in any proceedings where the prosecution proposes to give in evidence a confession made by an accused person, it is represented to the court that the confession was or may have been obtained—

    (a) by oppression of the person who made it; or

    (b) in consequence of anything said or done which was likely, in the circumstances existing at the time, to render unreliable any confession which might be made by him in consequence thereof, the court shall not allow the confession to be given in evidence against him except insofar as the prosecution proves to the court beyond reasonable doubt that the confession (notwithstanding that it may be true) was not obtained as aforesaid.

(3) In any proceedings where the prosecution proposes to give in evidence a confession made by an accused person, the court may of its own motion require the prosecution, as a condition of allowing it to do so, to prove that the confession was not obtained as mentioned in subsection (2) above.

F17.9   Section 76 appears not to have been intended as a mechanism for regulating the admissibility of a confession made by one co-accused as evidence for another. In *Myers* [1998] AC 124, the House of Lords declined to decide whether s. 76(1) applied to defence evidence, but the CJA 2003, s. 128, added a new s. 76A to the PACE 1984 in order to provide statutory regulation of the admission of the confession of a co-accused (see **F17.28**). For ease of exposition, the position with regard to prosecution evidence will be explained first.

The prosecution do not have to prove the admissibility of a confession upon which they rely unless either (a) the defence 'represents' that it is inadmissible under s. 76(2), or (b) the court of its own motion requires proof of admissibility under s. 76(3). If in either case the prosecution are unable to prove admissibility beyond reasonable doubt, the confession must be excluded, notwithstanding that it may be true: the court has no discretion in the matter (*Paris* (1993) 97 Cr App R 99). In *Beeres v CPS* [2014] EWHC 283 (Admin) it was said that a court should be particularly vigilant to scrutinise a confession that is the sole evidence relied upon by the prosecution. A confession may be excluded in part (cf. s. 76(4) and (6) at **F17.85** *et seq.*). As to procedure, see **F17.62** *et seq.*

A confession which is inadmissible in criminal proceedings in consequence of s. 76 should not be used as the basis for a formal caution (*Metropolitan Police Commissioner, ex parte Thompson* [1997] 1 WLR 1519).

EXCLUSION FOR OPPRESSION: POLICE AND CRIMINAL EVIDENCE ACT 1984, s. 76(2)(a)

Definition of Oppression

F17.10   Police and Criminal Evidence Act 1984, s. 76

(8) In this section 'oppression' includes torture, inhuman or degrading treatment, and the use or threat of violence (whether or not amounting to torture).

The reference to 'torture' may be interpreted in the light of the offence of torture contained in the CJA 1988, s. 134. 'Torture and inhuman or degrading treatment' is also prohibited by the ECHR, Article 3, and reference may be made to case law under Article 3 (see, e.g., *Republic of Ireland v UK* (1978) 2 EHRR 25).

Oppression at Common Law

F17.11   At common law, a confession obtained by oppression was regarded as involuntary and therefore inadmissible (see, e.g., *Callis v Gunn* [1964] 1 QB 495; *Prager* [1972] 1 All ER 1114). 'Oppression' was understood not only to include physical oppression (*Burut v Public Prosecutor* [1995] 2 AC 579, in which the Privy Council held that the manacling and hooding of suspects under interrogation in Brunei was 'plainly oppressive') but carried a wider sense; it was described by Sachs J in *Priestley* (1965) 51 Cr App R 1 at p. 1 as 'something which tends to sap, and has sapped, that free will which must exist before a confession is voluntary'. This, and other common-law definitions of the term, do not, however, provide reliable indications of the meaning of the word in its present statutory context. In *Fulling* [1987] QB 426 the Court of

Appeal held (without referring to the PACE 1984, s. 76(8)) that the 1984 Act does not follow the wording of earlier rules or decisions, nor is it expressed to be a consolidating Act. It is a codifying Act, in the interpretation of which the proper course is to start by ascertaining the natural meaning of the language used, uninfluenced by any considerations derived from the previous state of the law (applying the principles set out by Lord Herschell in *Bank of England v Vagliano Brothers* [1891] AC 107, at pp. 144–5). It was further stated that much of the sort of treatment which would have fallen within the definition of oppression at common law will now fall to be dealt with under the 'reliability' head of exclusion.

Ambit of Oppression

In *Fulling* [1987] QB 426 the prosecution tendered a confession by F in which she admitted her part in an insurance fraud initiated by her boyfriend, D. F claimed that the confession was made in order to secure her release from custody after a police officer had revealed, to F's great distress, not only that D had been unfaithful to her, but also that the 'other woman' was being held in the cell next to F's. On the assumption that these revelations were made, the trial judge ruled that there was no oppression in the sense of 'something above and beyond that which is inherently oppressive in police custody… [importing] some impropriety… actively applied in an improper manner by the police'. The Court of Appeal upheld the ruling of the trial judge. 'Oppression' was to be given its 'ordinary dictionary meaning' of: 'Exercise of authority or power in a burdensome, harsh or wrongful manner; unjust or cruel treatment of subjects, inferiors etc., the imposition of unreasonable or unjust burdens'. **F17.12**

Oppression almost inevitably involves some impropriety on the part of the interrogator (*Fulling* [1987] QB 426 at p. 432). It does not follow that all impropriety necessarily involves oppression; otherwise all wrongful acts, including breaches of the PACE Codes of Practice, could be termed oppressive, which is clearly not so (*Parker* [1995] Crim LR 233; *Re Proulx* [2001] 1 All ER 57). In *Fulling*, the Court of Appeal drew attention to a quotation which exemplifies the meaning of the term: 'There is not a word in our language that expresses more detestable wickedness than oppression'. In *Emmerson* (1991) 92 Cr App R 284, a police officer had given way to impatience during an interview and had raised his voice and used bad language to the accused. The Court of Appeal ruled that to regard such conduct as oppressive would be to give the word a completely false meaning. Unduly hostile questioning may, however, be oppressive: it is a question of degree. In *Paris* (1993) 97 Cr App R 99 a tape recording of an interview with M revealed that he had been 'bullied and hectored'. The Court of Appeal commented that, short of physical violence, it was hard to conceive of a more hostile and intimidating approach by officers to a suspect. The interview was oppressive and M's later confession ought to have been excluded. However, in *L* [1994] Crim LR 839, tactics similar to those employed in *Paris* appear to have been regarded as acceptable provided the reliability of the confession was not compromised. **F17.13**

A degree of impropriety which is insufficient for oppression may serve to support an argument that a confession should be excluded under the PACE 1984, s. 76(2)(b) or s. 78, considered at **F17.17** *et seq.* and **F17.33** *et seq.* respectively. Thus, in *Samuel* [1988] QB 615, the Court of Appeal, while acknowledging the possibility that oppression might be present where access to legal advice is improperly denied, preferred to quash S's conviction by reference to s. 78. Exclusion for oppression is likely to be reserved for those rare cases where an accused has been subjected to misconduct of a deliberate and serious nature, and where the court is anxious to mark its disquiet at the methods employed. An issue which frequently arises in relation to misconduct is the extent to which the use of similar methods by the same officer in relation to other suspects may figure in cross-examination. In relation to oppression, the court's natural reluctance to exclude on this basis may be overcome by the use of such evidence (see, e.g., *Twitchell* [2000] 1 Cr App R 373, in which the Court of Appeal considered that officers alleged **F17.14**

F

to have tortured D could have been cross-examined to 'potentially devastating' effect had the subsequent findings of a court regarding a similar torture by the same officers on another man been available for use in cross-examination).

Repetition of Confession Originally Obtained by Oppression

F17.15   Where a confession made in the course of an interview is excluded on grounds of oppression, it may be necessary to consider whether the effect on the accused was such that the repetition by him of the same information at a later, properly conducted interview ought also to be excluded (*Ismail* [1990] Crim LR 109, in which it was held that to accede to the prosecution's submission that misconduct in earlier interviews could be 'cured' by a properly conducted interview would be to condone flouting of the provisions of the Act and codes designed to protect against false confessions).

Relevance of Character and Attributes of Accused

F17.16   At common law it was held that the nature of oppression varied according to the character and attributes of the accused. Thus, an 'experienced professional criminal' might expect a vigorous interrogation (*Gowan* [1982] Crim LR 821), and in *Dodd* (1981) 74 Cr App 50, O'Connor LJ said (at p. 56) that the trial judge 'was entitled to consider the type of men he was dealing with', all of whom were experienced criminals. O'Connor LJ contrasted the case with that of *Hudson* (1980) 72 Cr App R 163, in which a middle-aged man of previous good character had been subjected to a lengthy, and in certain respects unlawful, interrogation, which was subsequently held to have been oppressive. At the other end of the spectrum, in *Miller* [1986] 3 All ER 119 Watkins LJ said that it might be oppressive to put questions to an accused who is known to be mentally ill so as 'skilfully and deliberately' to induce a delusionary state in him. Despite the rejection in *Fulling* [1987] QB 426 of common-law rulings on oppression, these cases may still be good law, for the Court of Appeal in *Fulling* was concerned to reject the 'artificially wide' common-law definition of oppression, while the above cases appear to proceed on a meaning which is consistent with the ordinary meaning of oppression as adopted in *Fulling*. This view appears to have been confirmed by *Seelig* [1992] 4 All ER 429, in which Henry J, in a ruling described by the Court of Appeal as 'entirely right', took account of the fact that the person being questioned was 'an experienced merchant banker' and 'intelligent and sophisticated', in determining whether he had been questioned in an oppressive way, and in *Smith* [1994] 1 WLR 1396 the Court of Appeal regarded it as relevant that S, who was questioned by a person in authority within a bank, was himself a chairman and managing director of a substantial financial organisation. Similarly in *Paris* (1993) 97 Cr App R 99 (see **F17.13**) the Court, although of the opinion that the bullying and hectoring of M in interview would have been oppressive even with a suspect of normal intelligence, went out of its way to stress that M was on the borderline of mental handicap.

EXCLUSION FOR UNRELIABILITY: POLICE AND CRIMINAL EVIDENCE ACT 1984, s. 76(2)(b)

Unreliability at Common Law

F17.17   At common law, a confession was regarded as involuntary, and therefore inadmissible, if it was obtained by fear of prejudice or hope of advantage held out or excited by a person in authority (*DPP v Ping Lin* [1976] AC 574). The Criminal Law Revision Committee, in its *Eleventh Report: Evidence (General)* (1972) Cmnd 4991, proposed that a confession obtained in consequence of a threat or inducement should not be excluded unless the circumstances were such that any confession made by the accused would be likely to be unreliable. This proposal became the PACE 1984, s. 76(2)(b), though the term 'threat or inducement' was replaced by the wider notion of 'anything said or done'.

Application of Statutory Test

F17.18

The PACE 1984 requires the trial judge to consider a hypothetical question: not whether *this* confession is unreliable, but whether *any* confession which the accused might make in consequence of what was said or done was likely to be rendered unreliable. The purport of this provision was considered in *Re Proulx* [2001] 1 All ER 57, where Mance LJ stated (at [46]):

> The test in s. 76 cannot be satisfied by postulating some entirely different confession. There is also no likelihood that anything said or done would have induced any other confession. The word 'any' must thus, I think, be understood as indicating 'any such' or 'such a' confession as the applicant made. The abstract element involved also reflects the fact that the test is not whether the actual confession was untruthful or inaccurate. It is whether whatever was said or done was, in the circumstances existing as at the time of the confession, *likely* to have rendered such a confession unreliable, whether or not it may be seen subsequently — with hindsight and in the light of all the material available at trial — that it did or did not actually do so.

Thus the court must consider whether what happened was likely in the circumstances to induce *an* unreliable confession to the offence in question, and to ignore any evidence suggesting that the *actual* confession was reliable.

In *Cox* [1991] Crim LR 276, a mentally handicapped accused gave evidence at the *voir dire* in the course of which he admitted one of the offences with which he was charged. The trial judge was held to have wrongly based his decision to admit C's out-of-court confession on the admission by C. The same point was made in *Crampton* (1991) 92 Cr App R 372, where it was said that, if acts are done or words spoken which are likely to induce unreliable confessions, then, whether or not the confession is true, it is inadmissible. Although the judge may not be influenced by evidence that the confession is true in deciding admissibility, he is not precluded from taking into account any other relevant evidence given at trial before the *voir dire* begins which assists him to determine the questions posed by s. 76(2)(b) (*Tyrer* (1989) 90 Cr App R 446 at pp. 449–50). Such evidence must, however, relate to the period before, or at the time when, the confession is made: the judge must 'stop the clock' and consider the issue of reliability at that point in time (a proposition cautiously, but rightly, advanced by Mance LJ in *Re Proulx*).

'Anything Said or Done'   Section 76(2) of the PACE 1984 obliges the judge to consider everything said or done (usually, but not inevitably by the police) and not to confine himself to a narrow analysis analogous to offer and acceptance in the law of contract (*Barry* (1992) 95 Cr App R 384; *Wahab* [2003] 1 Cr App R 232). The use of the phrase 'anything said or done', and the inclusion of all the surrounding circumstances, are indications that the new test follows the common law in acknowledging that a confession may be inadmissible, notwithstanding that the police have not behaved improperly. In *Fulling* [1987] QB 426 the Court of Appeal stated, *obiter*, that it was 'abundantly clear' that a confession may be excluded under s. 76(2)(b) where there is no suspicion of any impropriety. Dicta in *Brine* [1992] Crim LR 123, stating that s. 76(2) is 'primarily concerned' with police misconduct, should not be understood to qualify this statement of principle. See also *Harvey* [1988] Crim LR 241, in which a psychopathically disordered woman of low normal intelligence heard her lover confess to a murder. As this experience may have led her to make a false confession out of a child-like desire to protect her lover, her statement was excluded under s. 76(2)(b). *Harvey* was cited with approval in *Raghip* (1991) *The Times*, 9 December 1991 and in *Wahab*. Such a confession might also be excluded under s. 78 (see **F17.33**). In the rather extreme case of *M* [2000] 8 Arch News 2, it was M's solicitor who, by intervening in the interview in an apparent attempt to secure a confession, rendered the resultant confession unreliable. In *Wahab* the Court of Appeal noted that where the solicitor provides proper legal advice to his client this will not normally be a basis for excluding a confession under s. 76(2). In *Roberts* (2012) 176 JP 33 it was the promise not to involve the police, held out by a shop manager, that gave rise to the inference that anything said in consequence was likely to be unreliable. Nothing in R's subsequent silence (once it became apparent that the police had in fact been summoned) was capable of negating this inference.

F17.19

F

Part F Evidence

F17.20 **Words or Actions of the Accused**   It has been held that a confession cannot be rendered inadmissible under the PACE 1984, s. 76(2)(b), by reason only of something said or done by the accused himself (*Goldenberg* (1988) 88 Cr App R 285). In this case G was interviewed on suspicion of conspiracy to supply controlled drugs. The admissions which he made were alleged by the defence to be (a) an attempt by him to get bail, and (b) tainted by the fact that he was a heroin addict who, having been in custody for some time, would have said or done anything, however false, to gain his release so as to feed his addiction. The Court of Appeal considered that this argument was founded entirely 'on what was said or done by the appellant himself and on his state of mind', and that this was beyond the scope of the provision. The wording of the section, and in particular the words 'in consequence' in s. 76(2)(b), imported a causal link between what was said or done and the subsequent confession.

It followed that the provision was looking to something external to the person making the confession and which was likely to have some effect on him. *Goldenberg* was considered in *Crampton* (1991) 92 Cr App R 372, in which police officers interviewed C, a heroin addict, who it subsequently transpired was suffering from withdrawal symptoms. It was noted that in *Goldenberg* it was G himself who had requested the interview, but this was thought not to provide a ground for distinguishing the case, for it was doubtful whether the requirement for something external to be 'said or done' could be satisfied by the mere holding of an interview with an addict in withdrawal. The words of the statute contemplated some words spoken or acts done by the police which were likely to induce unreliable confessions. In *Walker* [1998] Crim LR 211, the Court of Appeal appears to have considered that the issue of whether W had taken cocaine before confessing had a material bearing on admissibility, but this appears to have been achieved by regarding the impairment of the accused as one of the 'circumstances' referred to in s. 76(2)(b).

F17.21 **'Circumstances'**   The accused's own mental state may be part of the 'circumstances' for the purposes of s. 76(2)(b). In *Re Proulx* [2001] 1 All ER 57, P confessed to a murder to an undercover operative who persuaded him that it was necessary in order to be accepted as a member of a criminal gang anxious to know the truth about his past. Whether this was something likely to induce P to make a false confession was something which could only be determined by an assessment of P (which was easier to make than is usually the case as the confession was video-recorded). It does not matter whether these circumstances were known to the interrogator at the time.

F17.22 In *Everett* [1988] Crim LR 826, E was discovered in a compromising position with a five-year-old boy. On the way to the police station, and while he was there, he admitted indecently assaulting the child. E was a 42-year-old man with a mental age of eight, and was regarded by a medical witness as being in the bottom 2 per cent of the population. The trial judge regarded the medical evidence as irrelevant provided that he was satisfied (as he was) from listening to the tape recording of the police station interview that E's replies were rational and showed understanding of the questions. The Court of Appeal ruled against this approach, and held that the circumstances to be taken into account 'obviously include' the mental condition of a suspect at the time the confession came into being. The test to be applied was an objective one, i.e. not what the police officers thought (if they thought anything) about the mental condition of the suspect, but instead the actual condition of the suspect as subsequently ascertained from a doctor. The confession ought to have been excluded because the prosecution 'most certainly had not' discharged the burden of proving it admissible. Similarly, in *McGovern* (1991) 92 Cr App R 228, it was said that the physical condition and particular vulnerability of M (she was six months pregnant and of limited intelligence), while not being 'anything said or done' to M, were part of the background against which the submission that she had been wrongly denied access to legal advice had to be judged. The combination of circumstances had the far-reaching result that it was appropriate to exclude both the confession made as a direct consequence of the denial of access and a subsequent confession made in the presence of a solicitor which was tarnished as a result of the earlier confession.

F17.23 In *Souter* [1995] Crim LR 729, a confession was held to be inadmissible where it was made by a soldier who was in a state of extreme emotion and distress to an officer who had been sent to calm him down; other relevant factors were that the conversation between the two had an appearance of confidentiality, and the officer had a very partial recollection of the rest of what had been said. The kind of mental condition which may be taken into account under s. 76(2)(b) is not limited to what might be termed 'impairment of intelligence or social functioning', still less to 'mental impairment' (*Walker* [1998] Crim LR 211).

In cases where the mental condition of the accused is a relevant factor, expert evidence is admissible if it demonstrates some form of abnormality relevant to the reliability of a defendant's confession (*O'Brien* [2000] Crim LR 676). In *Ward* (1993) 96 Cr App R 1, it was said that a mental abnormality would have to fall into a recognised category of mental disorder for expert evidence about it to be properly receivable, but in *O'Brien* the Court doubted whether this was so, as the operative consideration was simply whether the abnormality might render the confession unreliable. The Court added that the abnormality would have to be such as to demonstrate a 'very significant deviation from the norm'. Expert evidence might also be crucial to the understanding of whether an accused of low IQ is abnormally suggestible, bearing in mind that such suggestibility might manifest itself at interview without necessarily being apparent to a jury when the accused testifies at trial with the support of counsel and the protection of the judge (*King* [2000] Crim LR 835; *Smith* [2003] EWCA Crim 927). *O'Brien* was further qualified in *Blackburn* [2005] 2 Cr App R 440, where it was said that expert evidence could be received on the question whether a vulnerable individual, after prolonged questioning, might make a false confession, given that the issue is one falling outside the ken of the normal jury. In *Steel* [2003] EWCA Crim 1640, the Court of Appeal reviewed a conviction for murder in 1979 to assess the effect of fresh psychological evidence of suggestibility and vulnerability in interview which drew on techniques that were unavailable at the time of the trial. Unlike in *King*, the defence could not establish that the confession had been improperly obtained. The Court, however, rightly considered that if the new evidence rendered the conviction unsafe it was not necessary to consider whether there had been a breach either of the Judges' Rules (which were in force at the time), or of any more thoroughgoing modern safeguards for the protection of suspects and the avoidance of miscarriages of justice. (As to expert evidence, see also **F10.13**.)

Breach of PACE Codes   It is common for the defence to allege that the 'something said or done' includes a breach by the police of an obligation under the PACE 1984 or the Code of Practice for the Detention, Treatment and Questioning of Persons by Police Officers (PACE Code C). Such a breach will not lead to automatic exclusion of a confession obtained in consequence (*Delaney* (1988) 88 Cr App R 338), though it may, on its own or together with other factors, provide evidence that s. 76(2)(b) has not been complied with. In *Delaney*, D, whose psychological make-up was such that he was likely to feel unusual pressure to escape from interrogation, alleged that he had been induced to confess by a suggestion that the serious indecent assault of which he was suspected was more deserving of treatment than punishment. The interview was not recorded until the following day, in breach of Code C, and the Court of Appeal held that the absence of a reliable record of what occurred 'deprived the court of what was, in all likelihood, the most cogent evidence as to what did indeed happen during those interviews and what did induce the appellant to confess'. The breach was therefore significant, in that, the burden of proof being on the prosecution, the speculation necessarily engendered by the breach was sufficient to tip the scale in favour of the defence. For other cases where confessions were excluded, see, e.g., *Doolan* [1988] Crim LR 747 (failure to caution and to maintain a proper interview record or to show it to D); *Chung* (1991) 92 Cr App R 314 (questioning before allowing access to a solicitor and failure to show note to C or subsequently to his solicitor); *Waters* [1989] Crim LR 62 (improper questioning after charge resulting in ambiguous and potentially unreliable answer); *DPP v Blake* [1989] 1 WLR 432 (the 'spirit of the Code' was broken when a juvenile's estranged father was insisted on by police as the appropriate adult to attend her interview); *Morse* [1991] Crim LR 195 (juvenile's father acting as 'appropriate adult' and subsequently discovered to have low IQ and to be incapable of appreciating the gravity of the situation in which M found himself); *Moss* (1990) 91 Cr App R 371 (suspect of low intelligence

F17.24

interviewed nine times during a lengthy period of detention; access to legal advice improperly denied and no independent person present at interview).

Delaney and *Doolan* serve also to illustrate that 'something said or done' may consist of an omission to fulfil the requirements of the Code, although such an omission might always be described in more positive terms, for example, as interviewing the accused without having cautioned him as the Code requires.

F17.25   **Repetition of Confession Originally Obtained in Breach of PACE Code**   Where a breach of the PACE 1984 or a PACE Code has occurred which renders a confession inadmissible under s. 76(2)(b), it may be necessary to consider whether a repetition of the confession at a subsequent, properly conducted interview is also inadmissible. In *McGovern* (1991) 92 Cr App R 228, a subsequent interview was held inadmissible as it had been tainted by the matters which had led to the exclusion of an earlier interview, namely breaches of s. 58 and the interviewing provisions of Code C. It was further stated that the very fact that admissions were made at an earlier stage was likely to have an effect on the suspect thereafter, with adverse consequences for the admissibility of any repetition of the confession. In *Glaves* [1993] Crim LR 685 the Court of Appeal, whilst denying that there must necessarily be a 'continuing blight' on confessions obtained subsequent to a confession which is excluded under s. 76(2), nevertheless held that the breaches in the case (which included giving C, a juvenile, the impression that he was bound to answer questions) were not cured by a change of police officers and a caution, particularly as C had received no legal advice between the two interviews.

Section 76 and Causation

F17.26   At common law a confession which had been obtained following an inducement was admissible provided the prosecution could establish that the inducement was not the cause of the obtaining (*DPP v Ping Lin* [1976] AC 574, per Lord Hailsham of St Marylebone at p. 601: '...what excludes evidence is a chain of causation resulting from words or conduct on the part of the person in authority...giving rise to a decision by the accused actuated by fear of prejudice or hope of reward'). The PACE 1984, s. 76(2)(a) and (b), import the same causal link by reason of the words '*by* oppression' and '*in consequence of* anything said or done'. It follows that it may be helpful to consider decisions at common law such as *Rennie* [1982] 1 All ER 385, in which Lord Lane CJ held that the judge should avoid any 'refined analysis of the concept of causation' and 'should approach it much as would a jury.... In other words, he should understand the principle and the spirit behind it, and apply his common sense.' See also *Tyrer* (1989) 90 Cr App R 446 and *Barry* (1992) 95 Cr App R 384, in both of which it was accepted that the prosecution may discharge the onus of proof under s. 76(2) by showing that there is no causal link between the confession and things said or done by police officers which might have been conducive to unreliability, and *Crampton* (1991) 92 Cr App R 369 in which *Rennie* was cited in support of the proposition that a confession will not have been caused by anything said or done by an interviewer if a suspect is motivated to confess because he perceives in his own mind that there may be an advantage from doing so. The demeanour of the accused when giving evidence on the *voir dire* may assist the prosecution in showing that he was not affected by threats allegedly made at interview (*Weeks* [1995] Crim LR 52).

CONFESSION TENDERED BY CO-ACCUSED

F17.27   In *Myers* [1998] AC 124, M and Q were charged with murder. Q's defence was that M alone committed the offence, and he sought to rely upon a confession to that effect which M had made. The statement was not relied upon in evidence by the prosecution, in consequence of breaches of the Codes of Practice. However there was no suggestion that the confession was not freely made by M. The House of Lords held that the statement was admissible for Q, although the reasoning behind the decision is somewhat obscure: see previous editions of this work for further discussion. Any such uncertainties have been resolved by the CJA 2003, s. 128. This inserts a new s. 76A which provides that an accused may not give evidence of a co-accused's confession unless the conditions imposed by s. 76A(2) are satisfied. These conditions mirror those imposed on the prosecution except that the burden of proof on the accused is clearly stated to be proof on a balance of probabilities. Note also the provision of s. 128(2), which provides that nothing in the hearsay chapter of the Act makes a confession admissible if it would not be admissible under the PACE 1984, s. 76. This would appear to preclude, for example, the use of an otherwise inadmissible confession as a previous inconsistent statement so as to provide evidence that the confession itself is true (previous inconsistent statements have become generally admissible as proof of the truth of the facts stated under s. 119).

Police and Criminal Evidence Act 1984, s. 76A

F17.28

(1) In any proceedings a confession made by an accused person may be given in evidence for another person charged in the same proceedings (a co-accused) in so far as it is relevant to any matter in issue in the proceedings and is not excluded by the court in pursuance of this section.

(2) If, in any proceedings where a co-accused proposes to give in evidence a confession made by an accused person, it is represented to the court that the confession was or may have been obtained—

    (a) by oppression of the person who made it; or

    (b) in consequence of anything said or done which was likely, in the circumstances existing at the time, to render unreliable any confession which might be made by him in consequence thereof,

the court shall not allow the confession to be given in evidence for the co-accused except in so far as it is proved to the court on the balance of probabilities that the confession (notwithstanding that it may be true) was not so obtained.

(3) Before allowing a confession made by an accused person to be given in evidence for a co-accused in any proceedings, the court may of its own motion require the fact that the confession was not obtained as mentioned in subsection (2) above to be proved in the proceedings on the balance of probabilities.

(4) The fact that a confession is wholly or partly excluded in pursuance of this section shall not affect the admissibility in evidence—

    (a) of any facts discovered as a result of the confession; or

    (b) where the confession is relevant as showing that the accused speaks, writes or expresses himself in a particular way, of so much of the confession as is necessary to show that he does so.

(5) Evidence that a fact to which this subsection applies was discovered as a result of a statement made by an accused person shall not be admissible unless evidence of how it was discovered is given by him or on his behalf.

(6) Subsection (5) above applies—

    (a) to any fact discovered as a result of a confession which is wholly excluded in pursuance of this section; and

    (b) to any fact discovered as a result of a confession which is partly so excluded, if the fact is discovered as a result of the excluded part of the confession.

(7) In this section 'oppression' includes torture, inhuman or degrading treatment, and the use or threat of violence (whether or not amounting to torture).

In *Johnson* (2007) 171 JP 574 the accused had been granted permission to vacate a guilty plea, but at the trial which ensued his co-accused successfully applied to rely on the basis of the plea as a relevant confession under s. 76A. The Court of Appeal commented that it 'understood the frustration of a defendant who is permitted to vacate a guilty plea but not then permitted to enjoy the fruits of vacation by way of a trial unencumbered by the earlier plea'. Section 76A, however, was designed to ensure fairness as between co-accused.

F17.29

Nothing in *Myers* or the CJA 2003, s. 128, changes the rule that an accused person may not rely on the out-of-court confession of a third party to the offence charged (*Blastland* [1986] AC 41: see **F15.8**). *Myers* and s. 128 vary the confession rule only where the maker of the confession is a party to the proceedings. Thus in *Finch* [2007] 1 WLR 1645 the accused was unable to

F

Part F Evidence

rely on a statement, made at interview by R, who subsequently pleaded guilty to his part in the offence, because F and R were not 'charged in the same proceedings'. The Court of Appeal considered the possibility that under the CJA 2003 such evidence might be admitted even where the maker is available to testify under the 'interests of justice' test contained in s. 114(1)(d) (see **F15.7** and **F16.38**), but considered this to be most likely where the maker of the statement was unavailable or had demonstrably good reason not to give evidence. The most appropriate course for F would have been to test the reluctance of R to give evidence, and if R proved hostile to avail himself of the consequent admissibility of R's previous inconsistent statement (under s. 119: see **F6.56**).

THE DISCRETION TO EXCLUDE CONFESSION EVIDENCE

At Common Law

F17.30   The common-law power of a court to exclude evidence in its discretion is considered in general at **F2.1** *et seq*. The following section is concerned only with the application of the discretion to exclude confession evidence.

Police and Criminal Evidence Act 1984, s. 82

(3) Nothing in this Part of this Act shall prejudice any power of a court to exclude evidence (whether by preventing questions from being put or otherwise) at its discretion.

Section 82 applies to part VIII of the 1984 Act, which includes ss. 76 and 78. Prior to the enactment of the Act and the codes of practice made under it, exclusion of confession evidence at common law was recognised in two contexts:

(a) the exclusion of unreliable confessions, the prejudicial effect of which could be said to outweigh their true probative value; and

(b) the exclusion of confession evidence, the admission of which might operate unfairly against the accused.

F17.31   **Exclusion for Unreliability**   In *Miller* [1986] 3 All ER 119 the Court of Appeal acknowledged the existence of a discretion to refuse to admit 'a confession which came from a mind which at the time was possibly irrational and [where] what the defendant said may have been the product of delusions and hallucinations'. In *Isequilla* [1975] 1 All ER 77, the Court accepted the statement that 'it would be in accordance with principle to exclude a confession made by someone whose mental state was such as to render his utterances completely unreliable'. See also *Stewart* (1972) 56 Cr App R 272.

F17.32   **Exclusion for Unfairness**   In *Sang* [1980] AC 402, Lord Diplock said (at p. 437, emphasis added): '*save with regard to admissions and confessions* and generally with regard to evidence obtained from the accused after commission of the offence, he [the trial judge] has no discretion to refuse to admit relevant admissible evidence on the ground that it was obtained by improper or unfair means'. The unfairness discretion was well established at common law with regard to confession evidence. In *Houghton* (1978) 68 Cr App R 197, Lawton LJ held (at p. 206) that evidence 'would operate unfairly against an accused if it had been obtained in an oppressive manner by force or against the wishes of an accused person or by a trick or by conduct of which the Crown ought not to take advantage', and said that trial judges enjoyed a discretion to disallow such evidence. The discretion was recognised to exist, although it was infrequently exercised, with regard to breaches of the Judges' Rules (see, e.g., *Voisin* [1918] 1 KB 531; *Lemsatef* [1977] 2 All ER 835) and where a confession had been extracted following a period of unlawful detention (*Hudson* (1980) 72 Cr App R 163).

The common-law powers, though preserved by the PACE 1984, s. 82(3), are unlikely to be resorted to in practice given the wide ambit of s. 78 (see **F17.33**). The situation in which they are most likely to be used is where a judge becomes aware, after a confession has been admitted in evidence, of circumstances suggesting that it should not have been. Neither s. 76 nor s. 78 applies to this situation (*Sat-Bhambra* (1988) 88 Cr App R 55, discussed in detail at **F17.75**), so the court is thrown back on its common-law powers.

Exclusion under the Police and Criminal Evidence Act 1984, s. 78

F17.33

> **Police and Criminal Evidence Act 1984, s. 78**
>
> (1) In any proceedings the court may refuse to allow evidence on which the prosecution proposes to rely to be given if it appears to the court that, having regard to all the circumstances, including the circumstances in which the evidence was obtained, the admission of the evidence would have such an adverse effect on the fairness of the proceedings that the court ought not to admit it.
>
> (2) Nothing in this section shall prejudice any rule of law requiring a court to exclude evidence.

For the meaning of 'proceedings', see s. 82(1). The power may be used in respect of confession evidence tendered by the prosecution (*Mason* [1988] 3 All ER 481), and numerous instances of its use for this purpose exist. In practice, if not in law, the common-law discretion appears to have been superseded.

The Court of Appeal will not interfere with the exercise of a trial judge's discretion to admit evidence under s. 78 unless satisfied that the decision was perverse (*Dures* [1997] 2 Cr App R 247, applying the general principle stated in *Quinn* [1995] 1 Cr App R 480). It follows that cases in which the discretion is said to have been wrongly exercised are comparatively rare. One example is *Miller* [1998] Crim LR 209, in which the judge adverted to an out-of-date version of the PACE Codes of Practice and thereby reached an incorrect conclusion through failure to note serious breaches of the applicable Code.

Section 78 and the PACE Codes of Practice

Codes of practice issued under the PACE 1984, s. 66, are admissible in evidence in both crimi-   **F17.34** nal and civil proceedings, and any provision of such a code appearing to the court or tribunal conducting the proceedings to be relevant to any question arising in the proceedings, must be taken into account in determining that question by virtue of s. 67(11). Breach of a relevant code provision does not lead to the automatic exclusion of a confession obtained in consequence (see, e.g., *Delaney* (1988) 88 Cr App R 338, where the Court of Appeal heard submissions on ss. 76 and 78, and it was held that '...the mere fact that there has been a breach of the PACE Codes does not of itself mean that evidence has to be rejected'; *Parris* (1988) 89 Cr App R 68 at p. 72, where the same point was made). The question is whether the admission of the evidence would have such an adverse effect on the fairness of the proceedings that the court ought not to admit it. Even a plain and admitted breach, though it is to be deplored, may fail to trigger exclusion if it does not operate in a way prejudicial to the accused (*Canale* [1990] 2 All ER 187). See further **F17.36**. In *Roberts* [1997] 1 Cr App R 217, it was held that breach of a PACE Code C provision designed to protect another suspect could not be prayed in aid by the accused. This was because there was no causal link between the breaches and R's admission. On the facts, however, had the Code been complied with, it might have resulted in a record which would have supported R's contention that the other accused, to whom R subsequently confessed, was acting in the role of police agent in soliciting the confession. It is submitted that the issue is not whether the breach against the other accused caused the confession by R (as plainly it did not) but whether the breach affected the fairness of using R's confession (which it may have done).

Breach of a code of practice is in many cases an important factor in considering whether to   **F17.35** exclude evidence. Where confession evidence is concerned, the code most likely to be involved is Code C, dealing with the detention, treatment and questioning of persons by police officers. Certain of the rights guaranteed by Code C, such as the right of access to legal advice, are also to be found in the body of the 1984 Act itself (see PACE Code C, s. 6, and the PACE 1984, s. 58).

In *Keenan* [1990] 2 QB 54, the Court of Appeal declined to express a view as to whether a court should differentiate between breaches of the Act and of the codes. It is submitted that, whereas the location of such a right in the body of the Act may be an indication of its importance, the principles to be followed when considering the application of s. 78 are no different.

In *Samuel* [1988] QB 615 the Court of Appeal stated that it was undesirable to give any general guidance on the way in which a judge's discretion under s. 78 or under his inherent powers should be exercised, because circumstances may vary infinitely. Without seeking to give any such general guidance, it is submitted that the following considerations have proved to be of importance where s. 78 is concerned.

F17.36   Nature and Extent of Breach   In *Walsh* (1989) 91 Cr App R 161, W was denied access to legal advice, and it was common ground that there had been a breach of the PACE 1984, s. 58 (see **D1.55**). The Court of Appeal observed (at p. 163):

> The main object of section 58 of the Act and indeed of the codes of practice is to achieve fairness — to an accused or suspected person so as, among other things, to preserve and protect his legal rights; but also fairness for the Crown and its officers so that again, among other things, there might be reduced the incidence or effectiveness of unfounded allegations of malpractice.
>
> To our minds it follows that if there are significant and substantial breaches of section 58 or the provisions of the code, then prima facie at least the standards of fairness set by Parliament have not been met. So far as a defendant is concerned, it seems to us also to follow that to admit evidence against him which has been obtained in circumstances where these standards have not been met, cannot but have an adverse effect on the fairness of the proceedings. This does not mean, of course, that in every case of a significant or substantial breach of section 58 or the code of practice the evidence concerned will automatically be excluded. Section 78 does not so provide. The task of the court is not merely to consider whether there would be an adverse effect on the fairness of the proceedings, but such an adverse effect that justice requires the evidence to be excluded.

F17.37   Breach of Right to Legal Advice   In assessing the effect on the fairness of the proceedings of a breach of the PACE 1984, s. 58, it is relevant to note that it has frequently been stressed that the right of access to legal advice is 'fundamental' (see, e.g., *Samuel* [1988] QB 615) and that it is regarded as of great importance in the jurisprudence of the ECtHR (*Murray v UK* (1996) 22 EHRR 29, considered in *Aspinall* [1999] 2 Cr App R 115). In Scotland, *Cadder v HM Advocate* [2010] 1 WLR 2610 is authority for a rule, derived from the ECHR, Article 6, and the ECtHR's decision in *Salduz v Turkey* (2008) 49 EHRR 421 that (save where compelling reasons may exceptionally justify denial of access to a lawyer without unduly prejudicing the defence) the prosecution cannot lead and rely upon evidence of anything said by an accused without the benefit of legal advice during questioning under detention at a police station. In *Ambrose v Harris* [2011] 1 WLR 2435 the Supreme Court considered that it was not necessary to apply the same strict principles to the questioning of a person not yet detained: whether there was a breach of Article 6 in such a case would depend on the circumstances. The authorities under the PACE 1984, s. 78, do not currently reflect the same strict approach to questioning without benefit of legal advice, though Lord Brown in *Ambrose v Harris* noted that the discretionary nature of the statutory power 'sits a little uneasily' with the rule in *Cadder*. Similarly the requirement in *McGowan v B* [2011] 1 WLR 3121 as interpreted in *Saunders* [2012] 2 Cr App R 321, that a waiver of the right to legal advice should be voluntary, informed and unequivocal, may not sit well with cases where the right, for whatever reason, has not been fully presented to the accused. Cases that may ultimately require some reconsideration in light of these authorities include *Alladice* (1988) 87 Cr App R 380, in which A was denied access to legal advice by officers who had genuinely misconstrued the provisions of s. 58. A admitted in evidence that he was able to cope with being interviewed, that he had been given and understood the caution, and that he was aware of his legal rights. However, he had requested legal advice in order to have a check on the conduct of the police during interview. The trial judge found that the interviews were properly conducted, and that the only function of legal advice would have been to remind A of rights of which he was already well aware. On these facts, the Court of Appeal held that there was no obligation to exclude the confession. See also *Dunford* (1990) 91 Cr App R 150, *Oliphant* [1992] Crim LR 40 and, by way of contrast, *Sanusi* [1992] Crim LR 43, in which the failure to inform S, a foreigner, of his right to advice was particularly significant in the light of his lack of familiarity with police procedures and meant that his confession ought to have been excluded. Minor defects in the communication of the right to legal advice that do not bear on the exercise of informed choice by the suspect cannot give rise to unfairness (*Beeres v CPS* [2014] EWHC 283 (Admin)). See also as to waiver **F19.13**.

Breach of Interview Procedures   Breaches of the various provisions of Code C regarding the   **F17.38** procedures to be followed when interviewing suspects have also tended to lead to the exclusion of evidence under the PACE 1984, s. 78, for reasons similar to those stated in *Walsh* (1989) 91 Cr App R 161. In *Keenan* [1990] 2 QB 54, it was said to be desirable that the provisions of Code C which are designed to ensure that interviews are fully recorded and the suspect afforded an opportunity to contest the record be 'strictly complied with', and that the courts would not be slow to exclude evidence obtained following 'substantial breaches' by the interrogator. In *Coelho* [2008] EWCA Crim 627, it was held that the statement in *Keenan* was 'not a matter of rote' so the breach does not automatically result in exclusion. The statement in *Keenan* indicates the way the courts should approach such breaches. In *Coelho*, evidence of a conversation with a police officer in Portuguese should have been excluded because of the attendant risk of mis-understanding. Other provisions which have been held capable of requiring or contributing to the exclusion of evidence are those relating to cautioning, e.g., in *Williams* [2012] EWCA Crim 264 where W was questioned without caution while injured in hospital in circumstances where, viewed objectively, he was already a suspect and not (as the questioning officer thought) simply the victim of an assault by another. Breach of the right to have an appropriate adult present at interview is also likely to trigger exclusion, and in *Aspinall* [1999] 2 Cr App R 115 it was noted that the denial of the right to an appropriate adult might also lead to the failure of the accused to recognise the need for legal advice. A waiver in these circumstances would be worthless. In *Kirk* [1999] 4 All ER 698, the right of the accused to know why he has been arrested and 'at least in general terms the level of the offence in respect of which he is suspected' was held sufficient to warrant the exclusion under s. 78 of a confession to theft of a handbag where the suspect was not warned that he was also under suspicion for the more serious offences of robbery from the same victim and of her manslaughter. It was recognised that the accused might reach a view on such matters as whether to seek legal advice, and what to say in response to questions, in the light of his understanding of the seriousness of the matter under investigation. The Court of Appeal's purposive reading of the PACE 1984 and Code C reflects an approach similar to that of the ECtHR in *Fox, Campbell & Hartley v UK* (1990) 13 EHRR 157 in interpreting the requirement of the ECHR, Article 5(2), that a person arrested be informed promptly of the reasons for his arrest. In similar vein, the Privy Council in *Grant v The State* [2007] 1 AC 1, interpreting the common-law approach to the Judges' Rules in Jamaica, analysed the restrictions on questioning after charge by reference to the increased vulnerability of the accused at that time, and the pressure to speak, before deciding that the essential criterion for admissibility is fairness rather than simply whether the answers were voluntarily given. (As to the content of the provisions of Code C regarding interrogation, see **D1.80** *et seq*.)

The failure of the interrogator to appreciate that he is conducting an 'interview' within the   **F17.39** meaning of that term in Code C by questioning a suspect about his involvement in an offence has proved an important peg on which to hang arguments for exclusion, as such failure frequently leads to a multiplicity of relevant breaches of Code C. The leading authorities are *Absolam* (1988) 88 Cr App R 332 (breaches including failure to caution, to record, and to offer legal advice prior to impromptu questioning by custody officer: confession should have been excluded); *Cox* (1993) 96 Cr App R 464 (informal questioning in C's own home amounting to interview which ought to have taken place only in a police station, inadequate recording and late caution: confession should have been excluded); *Weekes* (1993) 97 Cr App R 222 (inadequate recording and failure to ensure presence of appropriate adult at conversation in police car amounting to interview: confession should have been excluded); *Okafor* (1994) 99 Cr App R 97 (questioning by customs officer during search of O's bag conducted without caution or other incidents of an interview in order not to excite O's suspicion that the drugs in his luggage had been detected: questioning still an interview and confession should have been excluded for breaches); and *Weedersteyn* [1995] 1 Cr App R 405 (W believed he was assisting officers to find drugs importers and was not aware of the significance of his own incriminating statement, taken without caution, until two months later: statement should have been excluded as arising out of an interview not under caution, and because no record was shown to W). The frequent appearance of cases of this type in applications to exclude under s. 78 may in part be accounted for by the difficulty of applying the definition of interview provided by the first revision of Code C which has now been superseded (see *Cox*, in which the authorities are reviewed). The decision in *Miller* [1998] Crim LR 209, in which a confession made in interview without caution was said to have been wrongly admitted, came to appeal only because the judge mistakenly applied the pre-1995 definition. Another example is *Gill* [2003] 4 All ER 681, in which it appears that officers of the Inland Revenue investigating tax fraud did not appreciate that they were required to comply with the code when conducting a 'Hansard' interview. In holding the resultant evidence admissible, the Court of Appeal took account of the fact that the defendants were fully aware that their answers might render them liable to criminal proceedings. By contrast, in *Hawkins* [2005] EWCA Crim 1723, a police officer unfamiliar with health and safety legislation spoke to H about an explosion in which H had been burned and another man killed. H was, at the time, in shock and breathing with the assistance of an oxygen mask, having been given the maximum possible dose of morphine. The officer's failure to realise that H was a suspect rather than a mere witness was immaterial: a view to that effect should have been formed, the interview should not have taken place as it did and the fruits of the interview should have been excluded.

F17.40   **Breaches Not Triggering Exclusion**   Although the provisions regarding the conduct of interviews are of great importance, breaches may nevertheless occur which are insufficiently significant or substantial to trigger the PACE 1984, s. 78. For example, in *Matthews* (1989) 91 Cr App R 43, the decision of the trial judge not to exclude evidence of a confession was upheld where the breach concerned the failure of a police officer to show the suspect a note of a conversation which the suspect had asked to be kept 'off the record'. See also *Courtney* [1995] Crim LR 63 (where the provisions of Code C were 'largely followed'), *RSPCA v Eager* [1995] Crim LR 60 (to similar effect), and *Blackwell* [1995] 2 Cr App R 641 (in which the court's decision that the trial judge was 'perfectly entitled' to admit the evidence was said to be 'highlighted by the technicality of the breaches'. Alternatively, a breach may be more than technical, but in the particular circumstances of the case no unfairness results from admitting the evidence. In *Dunn* (1990) 91 Cr App R 150, the failure of the interviewer to observe the provisions designed to prevent fabrication of the interview record would have been regarded as sufficient to require exclusion but for the fact that D's solicitor's clerk was present during the alleged conversation. It was held that it was legitimate for the trial judge to take account of this factor in exercising his discretion to admit the confession, as the presence of the clerk would have been likely to inhibit fabrication, and provided the accused with a witness as to what was actually said. In *Findlay* [1992] Crim LR 372, two suspects had wrongly been held incommunicado but it was held that the fact that one of them had subsequently had access to a solicitor for half an hour before signing the notes of his interview justified the admission of his confession. In *Ridehalgh v DPP* [2005] RTR 353, it was said that, even if the failure of a police inspector to caution a fellow officer was, on the facts, an error (which it was held not to be), it could not have been unfair to admit the incriminating response, both because the person questioned was himself a police officer and because of his willingness to repeat the same matters shortly afterwards under caution. And in *Rehman* [2006] EWCA Crim 1900 the failure to determine at trial whether there was sufficient evidence on which to caution a traveller in whose bags drugs were found at Customs was not fatal — even if a caution had been required, those stopped and questioned in a Customs check are already aware of the formality of the occasion.

Failure to Establish Breach   Where the defence relies on breaches of PACE Code C in con-   **F17.41** structing a challenge to a confession under the PACE 1984, s. 78, but the court decides that no breach occurred, it follows that it is most unlikely that the discretion will be exercised. For examples, see *Hughes* [1988] Crim LR 519 (provisions regarding interviewing in the absence of a solicitor not infringed), *Maguire* (1989) 90 Cr App R 115 (exchange between police officer and M not an 'interview'), *Menard* (1994) *The Times*, 23 March 1994 (meeting sought by M in order to volunteer information not an 'interview'), *Hughes v DPP* [2010] EWHC 515 (Admin) (informal conversation with potential suspect not 'interview'). Ultimately, however, the question is one of the unfairness of admitting the evidence (*Doncaster* (2008) 172 JP 202, where it was held that tax inspectors were not obliged to administer a caution).

Where the provisions of Code C have changed in the accused's favour since his interrogation, the court may take account of the new provision as the Code reflects what is considered to be fair (*Ward* (1994) 98 Cr App R 337).

Bad Faith   It is not the function of the court to use the PACE 1984, s. 78, to discipline the   **F17.42** police (*Mason* [1988] 3 All ER 481; *Canale* [1990] 2 All ER 187). However, the presence of bad faith where the police have acted in breach of the Act or Code is a factor making it more likely that evidence will be excluded. In *Alladice* (1988) 87 Cr App R 380, the facts of which are stated at F17.37, the Court of Appeal held that there is a distinction to be drawn between cases where the police have acted in bad faith, and cases where the police, albeit in good faith, have fallen foul of s. 58. In the former case, a court would have 'little difficulty in ruling any confession inadmissible under s. 78'. In the latter, the evidence would still fall to be excluded in many cases, so that it behoves the police to use their powers of delaying access to a solicitor only with great circumspection, but it was not possible 'to say in advance what would or would not be fair'. A similar distinction was drawn in *Walsh* (1989) 91 Cr App R 160 where it was said (at p. 163) that 'although bad faith may make substantial or significant that which might not otherwise be so, the contrary does not follow. Breaches which are in themselves significant and substantial are not rendered otherwise by the good faith of the officers concerned.' See also *Samuel* [1988] QB 615, in which a submission was made that, in the absence of impropriety, the discretion should never be exercised to exclude admissible evidence. The Court of Appeal had 'no hesitation in rejecting that submission, although the propriety or otherwise of the way in which the evidence was obtained is something which a court is, in terms, enjoined by the section to take into account'.

Information on which Discretion is to be Exercised

The discretion does not fall to be exercised because the judge of his own motion recognises that a   **F17.43** serious breach such as might trigger exclusion has taken place: if the accused is represented by an advocate who appears competent, and a particular part of the evidence might be the subject of a tactical or strategic plan on the part of the defence, the judge should not take it upon himself to exclude evidence, though he might consider it appropriate to make pertinent inquiry of counsel in the absence of the jury (*Raphaie* [1996] Crim LR 812).

When the defence seek to exclude evidence obtained by or in circumstances alleged to amount   **F17.44** to breaches of the PACE 1984 or a PACE Code, the Court of Appeal in *Keenan* [1990] 2 QB 54 noted that a number of different situations may face the judge:

(a) One or more breaches of a code may be apparent in the custody record itself or from the witness statements.
(b) There may be a prima facie breach which, if objection is taken, must be justified by evidence adduced by the prosecution.
(c) There may be alleged breaches which can probably only be established by the evidence of the accused himself.

Cases under (c) are likely to be rare, and it is likely that in cases under (a) and (b) the judge will have no means of knowing what will ensue after he has made his ruling. If he rules against admissibility, it may be that the accused will exercise his right not to give evidence. To permit the evidence to be given may therefore effectively deprive the accused of a right which he would otherwise have had. If the evidence is admitted, the judge does not know what the response to it may be. The accused may testify that the interview in question never took place at all, or that, though it took place, the questions and answers were fabricated, or that what was said was inaccurately recorded, or he might accept the accuracy of the record. Despite these difficulties, the judge must make his ruling on the information available to him at the time. In *Keenan*, the judge had wrongly assumed that any unfairness which might have been present could be cured by K giving evidence at the trial. Failure to give evidence at the *voir dire* is a different matter, and, in considering whether an accused has been prejudiced by a breach, the judge is entitled to take account of his failure to give evidence at the *voir dire* (*Oni* [1992] Crim LR 183).

F17.45 The record of interview and the contents of the confession itself may assist on the question whether the admission of the evidence would affect the fairness of the proceedings (*Dunford* (1990) 91 Cr App R 150 at p. 155). However, it was also said that it may be necessary to avoid reference to such material in cases where there is a 'root and branch' challenge by the defence to the contents of the statement.

Unfairness Not Arising from Breach of Codes of Practice

F17.46 In various authorities the significance of conduct not amounting to a breach of a code of practice or of the PACE 1984 has been considered, and it is clear that s. 78 may be invoked in such cases, though instances of the exercise of the discretion are rarer. The principles which have developed in relation to confessions apply also to other forms of prosecution evidence, and reference should be made also to **F2.31 to F2.36** . In *Ibrahim* [2009] 4 All ER 208, it was held that a judge's powers under s. 78 to exclude evidence obtained through a 'safety interview' without legal advice under terrorism legislation were sufficient in law; there was no need for a more general principle of exclusion based on public policy.

F17.47 The provisions of Code of Practice C do not apply to conversations between suspects and undercover investigators, unless the undercover pose is deliberately abused as a means of circumventing the code (*Christou* [1992] QB 979; *Bryce* [1992] 4 All ER 569; *Edwards* [1997] Crim LR 348). In deciding whether the code applies the judge should take into account the seriousness of the offence and the potential to put a life at risk (*Rajkuma* [2003] EWCA Crim 1955, where the offence was soliciting to commit murder). Where genuine undercover operations yield evidence, including incriminating statements, the use of subterfuge does not of itself entail a finding of unfairness. Relevant considerations in *Christou* (where undercover police set up as 'shady' jewellers in order to recover stolen property and gather evidence against the thieves and handlers) were that the public interest favoured the operation, that the offences had already been committed and that there was no incitement to crime on the part of the police, and that the suspects had 'applied themselves to the trick' without pressure from the officers. See also *Maclean* [1993] Crim LR 687, a similar operation concerning illegally imported drugs. In *Re Proulx* [2001] 1 All ER 57, an extradition case in which a murder suspect had been induced to confess as a condition of membership of a fictitious criminal gang, Mance LJ (having noted that this was clearly a case where the trick had been applied to P, even though he had willingly fallen in with it) concluded that there would have been 'very considerable difficulty' in upholding a decision to admit such evidence in purely domestic proceedings in the light of decisions such as *Christou, Bryce, Smurthwaite* [1994] 1 All ER 898 (see **F2.37**) and the ruling of Ognall J in *Stagg* (14 September 1994 unreported).

F17.48 **Subterfuge in Interrogation and Non-disclosure** In *Bailey* [1993] 3 All ER 513 subterfuge in the interrogation process was considered. B and S were arrested and charged with robbery, but maintained their right to silence at interview. They were placed together in a bugged police cell, their suspicions being allayed by play-acting on the part of the police, who pretended to be reluctant to leave them alone together. Their resultant incriminating conversation was admitted, and it was held that the fact that B and S could not, under Code of Practice C, properly have been subjected to further questioning did not mean that they had to be protected from the opportunity to speak incriminatingly to one another if they chose to do so. It was acknowledged to appear odd that, alongside the 'rigorously controlled legislative regime' for questioning it should be considered acceptable for 'parallel covert investigations' legitimately to continue, but, provided such stratagems were used only in grave cases and that there was no suggestion of oppression or unreliability, there was nothing unfair about admitting the evidence obtained in consequence.

The Court of Appeal distinguished as improper the subterfuge employed in *Mason* [1988] 3 **F17.49** All ER 481 in which a police officer told deliberate lies to M and to M's solicitor regarding the availability of fingerprint evidence connecting M with the offence of which he was suspected, in order to extract a confession from him. The trial judge admitted the confession, but the Court held that he had failed to take into account one vital factor, 'namely the deceit practised upon the appellant's solicitor. If he had included that in his consideration…he would have been driven to an opposite conclusion.' *Mason* is not, it is submitted, authority for the proposition that lies may safely be told to an accused person provided his legal adviser is not hoodwinked; on the contrary, both aspects of the deception were regarded as equally serious and 'most reprehensible' by the Court of Appeal. The trial judge's failure to take account of the lie told to the solicitor merely provided the ground on which the Court was able to review the exercise of his discretion. *Bailey* was applied in *Roberts* [1997] 1 Cr App R 217, in which R was induced to confess by a fellow suspect, C (with whom he had been placed in a bugged cell), to one robbery with which R had already been charged and to another with which he was subsequently charged. The trial judge's conclusion that C was not a police agent and had not been told what to ask R was regarded as 'unassailable', despite breaches of the Code in relation to C which made it hard to determine what precisely had been said to him (see **F17.34**). On the facts as found, the test was said to be whether the conduct of the police, either wittingly or unwittingly, led to unfairness or injustice, and the judge's decision to admit the evidence was upheld. The only difference between this case and *Bailey* was said to be that the police 'had perhaps a rather firmer basis for their expectations' of a confession than in *Bailey*.

By contrast, in *Allan* [2004] EWCA Crim 2236 the Court of Appeal, following the reasoning **F17.50** of the ECtHR in the same case (*Allan v UK* (2003) 36 EHRR 143) held that evidence should be excluded where, the suspect having decided to exercise his right of silence, the authorities use subterfuge to elicit confessions by using an informer as the 'functional equivalent' of an interrogator. In that case there was evidence that police had coached the informer and instructed him to 'pump' the suspect in the cell they shared while A was awaiting trial for murder. Just as a police officer cannot circumvent the protections of the PACE 1984 and the PACE Codes by adopting an undercover pose (*Christou*), so an informer cannot be used to the same end. As the Court of Appeal rightly states, 'allowing an agent of the state to interrogate a suspect in the circumstances of this case bypasses the many necessary protections developed over the last twenty years'.

The authorities on eavesdropping do not appear to have been adversely affected. In *Mason* **F17.51** [2002] 2 Cr App R 628, M and others were suspected of joint involvement in a series of burglaries and armed robberies, but there was insufficient evidence to do more than arrest individual members of the group for particular offences. Authorisation was obtained for them to be held together in a bugged cell in the hope that they would, in talking to each other, divulge the full extent of the joint enterprise. The resultant recordings were held to have been rightly admitted, following the reasoning in *Bailey*, notwithstanding that there was a clear breach of the ECHR, Article 8, which could not be justified because the surveillance had not taken place according to any publicly accessible legal structure (cf. *PG v UK* (2008) 46 EHRR 1272). Compare *Grant* [2006] QB 60, in which eavesdropping amounting to a deliberate violation of an imprisoned suspect's right to legal professional privilege was held 'so great an affront to the integrity of the justice system' as to render an associated prosecution an abuse of process even if no material is obtained which assists the prosecution. See also *McE v Prison Service of Northern Ireland* [2009] 1 AC 908 at **F9.50**. In *King* [2012] EWCA Crim 805 and in *Plunkett* [2013] 1 WLR

3121 admissions were obtained through covert recording, under the provisions of RIPA 2000, of conversations between suspects awaiting transport in a police vehicle. It was alleged that an unlawful delay had been created in the process of transferring the suspects (in breach of the PACE 1984, s. 30(1A)) to foster the conversations that were recorded. In *King* the Court of Appeal warned against the deliberate flouting of a statutory rule for this purpose, but in neither case was the evidence excluded. In *Plunkett* it was said that any incursion on s. 30(1A) would have been minor in light of the seriousness of the offence and the need to protect the victims of P's crime. Nothing was done 'to call into question the integrity of the criminal justice system'. *Plunkett* was followed in *Khan* [2013] EWCA Crim 2230, where the police had exceeded the authority granted under the RIPA 2000. This resulted in a breach of the appellants' right to privacy but did not, on the facts, impact on the fairness of the trial. The Court of Appeal noted that authorities such as *Bailey* would not be decided any differently today. The breaches were, as in *Plunkett*, of a minor character. More serious breaches are likely to attract the PACE 1984, s. 78, as noted in *Turner* [2013] EWCA Crim 642, the Court of Appeal warned (*obiter*) against covert surveillance which 'significantly' interferes with the accused's legal privilege, so that the 'very integrity' of the administration of justice is undermined. Again, this was contrasted with flaws that are 'minor, short and inconsequential'. See further **F2.41**.

F17.52   In *Farrell* [2004] EWCA Crim 597, the Court of Appeal approved as a 'useful guide' the distinction between active lying intended to induce a confession, and the omission or failure by the police to disclose their whole case in advance of interview. The Court was not prepared to hold that it was necessarily wrong or misleading for the police to hold back some part of their case before interview. In that case there was no attempt to suggest that the case was stronger than it was, and the evidence (which consisted of lies rather than an outright confession, but the relevant principles are the same) was held to have been properly admitted.

F17.53   **Unfairness Arising from Misunderstanding**   Unfairness may arise from misunderstanding as well as from subterfuge. In *Smith* [1994] 1 WLR 1396, S was under the impression that R, the bank manager questioning him, was concerned only to obtain information about the impact of a transaction on the market, and not about S's criminal involvement. Although R was guilty of no impropriety, the Court of Appeal held that S's statements should not have been admitted. In *Hayter v L* [1998] 1 WLR 854 the issue was whether it was an abuse of process for a private prosecution to proceed after an offender had been cautioned by the police (a procedure which necessarily involves an admission of guilt). Holding that it was not, the Divisional Court said that any unfairness arising from the use of the cautioned party's admission in the subsequent proceedings could be met by the s. 78 discretion. As a prerequisite of a caution, a party should be made aware that there is the possibility of a private prosecution, but it might still be thought unfair to permit a confession made in hope of escaping a prosecution to be used in order to found one. Similarly in *De Silva* [2003] 2 Cr App R 74 it was held that telephone conversations participated in by D at the instigation of Customs officers following the discovery of drugs in his suitcase should not be used in evidence against D. The purpose of the exercise was to facilitate the arrest of the callers, so it was part of D's role to behave as though he was guilty, whether he was or not. D's agreement to take part in the exercise followed a 'co-operation interview' with the officers, and it was not the purpose of such interviews to gather or initiate further evidence against the interviewee. In *Elleray* [2003] 2 Cr App R 165 the issue was whether a statement made to a probation officer for the purposes of a pre-sentence report could be used as a confession to a more serious offence (rape) than the one to which E had pleaded guilty and for which he was to be sentenced (indecent assault). It was held that such a case required a careful consideration of the public interest, bearing in mind the need for frankness between a probation officer and offender, and the absence of both caution and access to legal advice. In some cases it might be advisable for the officer to terminate the conversation to allow the offender to seek advice. On balance it was not unfair to admit the evidence.

F17.54   **Unfairness Arising from Physical Condition of the Accused**   The discretion may, it seems, be used in respect of evidence which is unreliable as the result of the physical condition of the suspect, whether or not the interview in which he participates is conducted in breach of the code (see, e.g., *Effik* (1992) 95 Cr App R 427, in which the trial judge, in a ruling endorsed by the Court of Appeal, made it clear that he would have excluded the confession of M, a heroin addict, had it been made at a time when he was suffering acute withdrawal symptoms).

Exclusion of Subsequent Confession

Where a confession is excluded, either under s. 76 or under s. 78, for breach of a code, the question may arise as to whether it would be unfair to admit a subsequent confession which has itself been obtained without breaking the rules. In *Gillard* (1991) 92 Cr App R 61, it was held, upholding the admission of subsequent statements by two accused, that there is no universal rule requiring the exclusion of such a subsequent confession. The question is whether, on the facts of a particular case, there is a sufficient nexus between the circumstances in which the two statements were made to render it unfair to admit the subsequent statement, so that, for example, the accused is still affected by some impropriety which took place during the first, excluded interview. Important considerations are whether the objections leading to the exclusion of the first interview were of a fundamental and continuing nature, and whether the arrangements for the subsequent interview gave the accused a sufficient opportunity to exercise an informed and independent choice as to whether he should repeat or retract what he said, or say nothing (*Neil* [1994] Crim LR 441; *Nelson* [1998] 2 Cr App R 399). See also *Canale* (1990) 91 Cr App R 1, in which a subsequent interview was held to have been tainted by an earlier one in which promises were alleged to have been made; *Y v DPP* [1991] Crim LR 917, in which earlier confessions, despite their spontaneous nature, were excluded because of breaches of the code, but a subsequent, properly conducted interview was held to have been rightly admitted; *Wood* [1994] Crim LR 222, in which a multiplicity of breaches at the first interview of a mentally handicapped suspect tainted a later interview; and *Prouse v DPP* [1999] All ER (D) 748, [1999] 10 Arch News 2, in which the provision of legal advice before the later interview rendered it admissible.   **F17.55**

Confessions by Mentally Handicapped Persons

A confession made by a mentally handicapped person may be admitted in evidence, provided it satisfies the conditions imposed by the PACE 1984, s. 76 (see **F17.8**), and provided also that it is not excluded by the court in the exercise of its discretion to exclude prosecution evidence under s. 78 of the Act. Where such a confession is received in evidence, the provisions of s. 77 come into play and must be complied with.   **F17.56**

Police and Criminal Evidence Act 1984, s. 77

(1) Without prejudice to the general duty of the court at a trial on indictment with a jury to direct the jury on any matter on which it appears to the court appropriate to do so, where at such a trial—
    (a) the case against the accused depends wholly or substantially on a confession by him; and
    (b) the court is satisfied—
        (i) that he is mentally handicapped; and
        (ii) that the confession was not made in the presence of an independent person,
the court shall warn the jury that there is special need for caution before convicting the accused in reliance on the confession, and shall explain that the need arises because of the circumstances mentioned in paragraphs (a) and (b) above.

(2) In any case where at the summary trial of a person for an offence it appears to the court that a warning under subsection (1) above would be required if the trial were on indictment with a jury, the court shall treat the case as one in which there is a special need for caution before convicting the accused on his confession.

(2A) In any case where at the trial on indictment without a jury of a person for an offence it appears to the court that a warning under subsection (1) above would be required if the trial were with a jury, the court shall treat the case as one in which there is a special need for caution before convicting the accused on his confession.

(3) In this section—

'independent person' does not include a police officer or a person employed for, or engaged on, police purposes;

'mentally handicapped' in relation to a person, means that he is in a state of arrested or incomplete development of mind which includes significant impairment of intelligence and social functioning; and

'police purposes' has the meaning assigned to it by section 101(2) of the Police Act 1996.

In its application to Customs and Excise, s. 77(3) is modified to the extent that the definition of 'independent person' includes, in addition to the persons mentioned therein, an officer or any other person acting under the authority of the Commissioners of Customs and Excise (Police and Criminal Evidence Act 1984) (Application to Customs and Excise) Order 1985 (SI 1985 No. 1800)).

There is no need to give a warning in accordance with s. 77 unless the case for the Crown would be 'substantially less strong' without the confession (*Campbell* [1995] Crim LR 157).

F17.57 PACE Code C requires the presence at interview of an 'appropriate adult' when the interviewee is a person at risk by reason, *inter alia*, of mental handicap, unless the interview is conducted on an emergency basis. The concept of an 'appropriate adult' is substantially the same as, though not identical to, the 'independent person' mentioned in s. 77. In particular, a solicitor attending the suspect would be an 'independent person', but would be unlikely to be the 'appropriate adult', who would normally be a relative or someone with experience of caring for the suspect (*Lewis* [1996] Crim LR 260). The warning required by s. 77 serves to draw the magistrates' or jury's attention to the potential unreliability of a confession obtained without this safeguard and should be tailored to any specific evidence of unreliability relating to the accused himself (*Campbell* [1995] Crim LR 157). In *Bailey* [1995] 2 Cr App R 262, it was held to be necessary to give the warning in respect of informal admissions made to members of the public in the absence of an independent third party, but this does not appear to be the mischief at which s. 77 was aimed.

F17.58 In *Lamont* [1989] Crim LR 813, L was convicted of the attempted murder of his baby son. The only evidence of L's intention came from a confession made in an interview at which no independent person was present. Expert defence evidence indicated mental retardation and impairment of intelligence and social functioning, but the trial judge concluded that L was not mentally handicapped and therefore did not warn the jury in accordance with s. 77. Quashing the conviction, the Court of Appeal held that the required direction under s. 77 was an essential ingredient of a fair summing-up, yet the trial judge had neither suggested to nor directed the jury that if they accepted the expert evidence they should exercise the caution called for by the section. The decision of the Court may, however, be open to doubt in part, in that it is the function of the judge, not the jury, to decide whether the accused is mentally handicapped. In establishing whether a defendant is mentally handicapped within the meaning of s. 77(3) it is not appropriate to take figures produced by intelligence tests in one case and to apply them slavishly in another in order to produce a rigid definition: every case has its individual features (*Kenny* [1994] Crim LR 284).

F17.59 **Practical Application of the Rule**   In the present climate of opinion, a confession made by a mentally handicapped person otherwise than in the presence of an independent person would be likely to be excluded at trial under either s. 76 or s. 78 of the 1984 Act. It follows that there will be few cases where a court is called on to follow the procedure laid down in s. 77. In *Moss* (1990) 91 Cr App R 371 it was thought that the section was aimed at two possible cases: (a) where a confession has been properly obtained from a mentally handicapped person in the absence of an independent person in the course of an 'urgent interview' as permitted by Code C; (b) where the interview was in breach of Code C but there was only 'one interview during a comparatively short period of custody'. In *Moss*, confessions obtained in the course of nine interviews over a lengthy period of detention were held to have been wrongly admitted despite the s. 77 direction given by the trial judge: the statements ought to have been excluded under s. 76(2)(b) (see **F17.18**). By contrast, in *Uddin* [2005] EWCA Crim 464, U's appeal failed despite the prosecution's reliance on a confession obtained in the absence of an appropriate adult, and the apparent failure of the judge to give a s. 77 direction (which failure was not noted by the Court of Appeal). The crux of the matter in *Uddin*, however, was that the 'confession' was chiefly composed of self-serving statements. The only element on which the prosecution relied (an admission of presence) was equally an inherent part of the defence case. The Court therefore concluded that the admission of the confession did not threaten the safety of the conviction and would presumably have said the same about the absence of a direction under s. 77. In *Qayyum* [2006] EWCA Crim 1127, the failure of the trial judge to give a formal s. 77 direction following the admission of a confession that, as in *Uddin* was not *per se* damaging to the defence at trial, was held not to render the conviction unsafe, although it was noted that the judge had repeatedly reminded the jury of Q's intellectual shortcomings.

The decision of the Court of Appeal to limit the circumstances in which a case depending on confession evidence of this type should be left to the jury further restricts the ambit of s. 77. In *MacKenzie* (1992) 96 Cr App R 98, the Court of Appeal considered the application of the rule in *Galbraith* [1981] 2 All ER 1060 (see **D16.55**) to the case where the confession of a mentally handicapped person had been admitted at trial, but was unsupported by other evidence. The Court laid down the following rules: **F17.60**

> (1) Where the prosecution case depends wholly upon confessions; (2) the defendant suffers from a significant degree of mental handicap; and (3) the confessions are unconvincing to a point where a jury properly directed could not properly convict upon them, then the judge, assuming that he has not excluded the confessions earlier, should withdraw the case from the jury. The confessions may be unconvincing, for example, because they lack the incriminating details to be expected of a guilty and willing confessor, or because they are inconsistent with other evidence, or because they are otherwise inherently improbable.

M, a mentally handicapped man with a personality disorder, was convicted of two offences of manslaughter and two of arson. The prosecution case in respect of the killings depended entirely on unsupported confessions, whereas the proof of arson, though largely dependent on confessions, was supported by other independent evidence. During questioning M had also confessed to 12 other killings, none of which, in the end, the Crown believed he had committed. At the point in the trial when the confessions to the killings were admitted, it was thought that they contained details which only the killer could have known. On a careful review of the confessions, however, the Court of Appeal considered that the knowledge of the basic circumstances of the killings which they contained were of the sort that would not have been confined to the killer, and that they also contained some striking errors and omissions. Bearing in mind that M's credibility was diminished by his false confessions to other killings, and that he may well have been motivated by a desire to stay in the secure hospital at which he had been detained, the Court was left with at least a lurking doubt as to whether the verdicts of manslaughter were safe and satisfactory. The convictions for arson, however, were allowed to stand. *MacKenzie* was applied in *Wood* [1994] Crim LR 222, in which the only blow which W had confessed to striking was proved by medical evidence not to have caused the death of the victim.

A confession which falls within the first two limbs of the *MacKenzie* test, but which is admitted because it falls outside the third, may require a very careful judicial direction (*Bailey* [1995] 2 Cr App R 262, where it was held that the judge was obliged, in addition to giving the s. 77 warning, to give the jury a 'full and proper statement' of the defendant's case against the confession being accepted by the jury as true). An unusual situation arose in *Hudson* [2007] EWCA Crim 2083, where the Crown's case was that H, who was 'of limited intellectual ability', had been prevailed upon by his family to take more than his share of responsibility for a murder. H's confession   **F17.61** was tendered chiefly to establish, through the falsity of much of its purported detail, H's part in this conspiracy. No attempt was made to exclude the confession, which (with a careful direction from the judge) was correctly left to the jury as the foundation of the case to answer.

DETERMINING THE ADMISSIBILITY OF CONFESSIONS: THE *VOIR DIRE*

F17.62 The general rules regarding the holding of a *voir dire*, or trial within a trial, in order to determine disputed issues regarding preliminary facts on which the admissibility of evidence depends, are dealt with in detail at **D16.41** *et seq.* The principles considered here are those which have particular significance with regard to confessions, or are relevant solely to the reception of confession evidence.

The *Voir Dire* and the Police and Criminal Evidence Act 1984, s. 76

F17.63 At common law, where the admissibility of a confession statement was to be challenged in a trial on indictment, the following practice was followed:

(a) Defending counsel would notify prosecuting counsel that an objection to admissibility was to be raised.
(b) Prosecuting counsel would then refrain from mentioning the statement in his opening to the jury.
(c) At the appropriate time the judge would conduct a trial on the *voir dire* to decide on the admissibility of the statement (*Ajodha v The State* [1982] AC 204).

The PACE 1984, s. 76(2), follows the common law by providing that where the defence represent that a confession on which the prosecution propose to rely was, or may have been, obtained in such a way as to render it inadmissible in evidence, the court shall not allow the confession to be given in evidence except insofar as the prosecution prove to the court beyond reasonable doubt that the confession was not so obtained. Section 76(3) provides in addition that the court may of its own motion require the prosecution, as a condition of allowing them to give a confession in evidence, to prove that it was not obtained in such a way as to render it inadmissible. The *voir dire* therefore remains the correct procedure where objection is taken to the admission of a confession. It enables factual issues to be resolved in the absence of the jury, with the benefit of the accused's evidence should he wish to testify (*Alagaratnam* [2010] EWCA Crim 1506). At common law the *voir dire* was normally held in the absence of the jury only at the request or with the consent of the defence (*Ajodha*, citing *Anderson* (1929) 21 Cr App R 178). However it has now been established that the court may require the jury to withdraw whether the defence consents or not (*Davis* [1990] Crim LR 860, and see also *Hendry* [1988] Crim LR 766).

As to what constitutes a representation for the purposes of s. 76(2), see *Dhorajiwala* [2010] 2 Cr App R 161, where it was said that 'a statement by responsible counsel, upon the basis of documents or proofs of evidence in his possession at the time of speaking' that the confession was or may have been obtained in breach of s. 76 is a 'representation'.

F17.64 In *Liverpool Juvenile Court, ex parte R* [1988] QB 1, it was held that s. 76 requires magistrates conducting a summary trial to hold a *voir dire* to determine admissibility where the defence, before the close of the prosecution case, represent to the court that the confession was obtained in breach of s. 76(2). The decision represents a significant departure from the common law, which regarded the *voir dire* as inappropriate in summary trials (see further as to summary trials, **D22.41**). As magistrates are judges of both fact and law, a ruling that a confession is to be excluded will mean that they have to put the objectionable material out of their minds when considering guilt; this is a task with which it has recently been said 'they are well capable of coping both by training and by disposition' (*Hayter v L* [1998] 1 WLR 854, commenting on the comparable situation which arises after the s. 78 discretion to exclude has been exercised).

According to *Dhorajiwala*, the court's power under s. 76(3) to require the prosecution to prove that the confession was not obtained in breach of s. 76(2) may lead the court to hold a *voir dire* in circumstances where counsel has not requested it. This would seem to be a power that should be sparingly exercised.

Unrepresented Accused   In *Ajodha v The State* [1982] AC 204 Lord Bridge said (at p. 223):   **F17.65**

> Particular difficulties may arise in the trial of an unrepresented defendant, when the judge must, of course, be especially vigilant to ensure a fair trial. No rules can be laid down, but it may be prudent, if the judge has any reason to suppose that the voluntary character of a statement proposed to be put in evidence by the prosecution is likely to be in issue, that he should speak to the defendant before the trial begins and explain his rights in the matter.

The position appears to be unaltered under the 1984 Act, if for 'voluntary character' is read 'admissibility'. The court also enjoys the power under s. 76(3) to put the prosecutor to his proof on the issue of admissibility, and it is submitted that it would generally be appropriate to exercise that power in the case of an unrepresented accused.

Challenging Admissibility at Trial

The position at common law was stated in *Ajodha v The State* [1982] AC 204 by Lord Bridge,   **F17.66** who said (at p. 223):

> Though the case for the defence raises an issue as to the voluntariness of a statement..., defending counsel may for tactical reasons prefer that the evidence bearing on that issue be heard before the jury, with a single cross-examination of the witnesses on both sides, even though this means that the jury hear the impugned statement whether admissible or not. If the defence adopts this tactic, it will be open to defending counsel to submit at the close of the evidence that, if the judge doubts the voluntariness of the statement, he should direct the jury to disregard it, or, if the statement is essential to sustain the prosecution case, direct an acquittal. Even in the absence of such a submission, if the judge himself forms the view that the voluntariness of the statement is in doubt, he should take the like action *proprio motu*.

In *Liverpool Juvenile Court, ex parte R* [1988] QB 1, at p. 10 it was considered that the defence retained this option:

> There remains a discretion open to the defendant as to the stage at which an attack is to be made upon an alleged confession. A trial within a trial will only take place before the close of the prosecution case if it is represented to the court that the confession was, or may have been, obtained by one or other of the processes set out in subparagraph (a) or (b) of section 76(2). If no such representation is made the defendant is at liberty to raise admissibility or weight of the confession at any subsequent stage of the trial.

It may be argued that this view overlooks the power of the court under the PACE 1984,   **F17.67** s. 76(3), to compel the holding of a *voir dire*, apparently irrespective of the defendant's wishes. This power may, however, be intended primarily to enable a court to assist an unrepresented defendant to vindicate his rights, rather than to overrule the wishes of defence counsel where the accused is legally represented. A more fundamental objection to the view taken in *Ex parte R* may be found in *Sat-Bhambra* (1988) 88 Cr App R 55. Certain statements by S had been ruled admissible at the *voir dire*, because there was no evidence to suggest that the statements were likely to be unreliable as a result of the accused's ill health at the time. At the trial, medical evidence was adduced by the defence which came down more strongly in favour of S's contention that he was suffering from hypoglycaemia when he was interviewed. When asked to reconsider his decision on admissibility, the trial judge ruled that the terms of s. 76 prevented him from taking this course. The Court of Appeal agreed, holding (at p. 62):

The words of section 76 are crucial: 'proposes to be given in evidence' and 'shall not allow the confession to be given' are not, in our judgment, appropriate to describe something which has happened in the past. They are directed solely to the situation before the statement goes before the jury. Once the judge has ruled that it should do so, section 76 (and section 78, for the same reasons) ceases to have effect.

The Court went on to consider the powers which the judge may, by virtue of the common law, exercise in this situation, (at p. 62) before concluding: 'If a defendant wishes under section 76 to exclude a confession, the time to make his submission to that effect is before the confession is put in evidence and not afterwards'. It has been noted (see **F17.7**) that the statements in issue in *Sat-Bhambra* were self-serving, and were therefore regarded as not being confessions to which s. 76 applied, as to which, see now *Z* [2003] 1 WLR 1489 at **F17.7**. However, the Court of Appeal was careful to state that its views on that subsidiary matter were *obiter*, so that the *ratio* of the case appears to be that the admissibility of a confession may not be challenged under s. 76 once the confession has been given in evidence. The contrary view, stated by the Divisional Court in *Liverpool Juvenile Court, ex parte R*, was expressed to apply to summary proceedings only, but it is difficult to see why the interpretation of the Act should vary according to the nature of the trial. Thus, the law, whatever the mode of trial, would appear to be as stated in *Sat-Bhambra*. See also *Davis* [1990] Crim LR 860, in which the Court of Appeal inclined to the view (but without deciding the point) that the language of the section anticipated a *voir dire* taking place before the challenged evidence was heard by the jury.

The *Voir Dire* and the Police and Criminal Evidence Act 1984, s. 78

F17.68 Section 78 is set out at **F17.33**. The view taken, *obiter*, by the Court of Appeal in *Sat-Bhambra* (1988) 88 Cr App R 55 was that the wording of the section suggested that defence objections should be made before the confession is given in evidence. The relevant words are 'the court may refuse to allow evidence *on which the prosecution proposes to rely* to be given'. It does not necessarily follow from this that a *voir dire* should always be held; indeed, it has been said that in a summary trial the defence have no right to a *voir dire* simply in order to determine a preliminary issue under s. 78 (*Vel v Chief Constable of North Wales* (1987) 151 JP 510 and see **D22.43**). However, in many cases it will be convenient to investigate the submission in this way, particularly where the defence also challenge the confession under s. 76, and in *Halawa v Federation Against Copyright Theft* [1995] 1 Cr App R 21 it was said, *obiter*, that if, in connection with an application to exclude evidence under s. 78 alone, the accused wished to proceed by way of a trial within a trial, magistrates might find it necessary to proceed in that way in order to allow the accused to give evidence in relation to the evidential issue without prejudicing his right to silence at trial.

In *R* (2000) *Independent*, 10 April 2000, it was held that a ruling in a preparatory hearing regarding s. 78 was a ruling as to admissibility of evidence under the CPIA 1996, s. 31(3) (see **D15.57** to **D15.59**), and that it was subject to appeal to the Court of Appeal. It seems unlikely that s. 31(3) was intended to apply to questions which are not strictly questions of law, although if the application of s. 78 goes to the heart of the proceedings it may be convenient to deal with it as an interlocutory matter.

Disputes as to Making of Confession

F17.69 At common law the *voir dire* was inappropriate in trials on indictment where the defence case was simply that no confession was made (*Ajodha v The State* [1982] AC 204). The Board gave as examples cases where the defence allege that an interview never took place, or that no incriminating answers were given, or, in the case of a written statement, that it is a forgery. The issue of fact whether or not the statement was made by the accused is purely for the jury. In the same case, however, the Privy Council recognised that issues of voluntariness might be intertwined with disputes as to the making of the confession, and that it is a fallacy to suppose that the two grounds of challenge are mutually exclusive. Such a case may arise where the accused claims that he was not the author of a written statement which bears his name, and alleges that his signature at the end of the statement was procured by force or by deception. Such cases required the holding of a *voir dire* to determine the issue of voluntariness at common law, leaving the jury to determine the value and weight of the statement if it is admitted. Issues as to admissibility under the PACE 1984, s. 76, are equally capable of arising in combination with disputes as to the making of the statement, and it is submitted that the principles stated in *Ajodha* continue to represent the law. Where the evidence of a person to whom a disputed confession is alleged to have been made may be tainted by an improper motive (as in the case of a 'cell confession') a specific direction to the jury may be required as to the need for caution (*Pringle v The Queen* [2003] UKPC 9; *Benedetto v The Queen* [2003] 1 WLR 1545; *Lawrence v The Queen* [2014] UKPC 2: see **F5.15**).

Where the defence in a trial on indictment challenge the confession under s. 78, they may ultimately wish to assert at the trial that no confession was made. The issue at the *voir dire* is simply whether the introduction of the confession would have such an adverse effect on the fairness of the proceedings that the court ought not to admit it. It is not the function of the judge to decide whether the confession was made (*Keenan* [1990] 2 QB 54). See, however, *Alladice* (1988) 87 Cr App R 380, in which the trial judge reached such a decision before deciding to admit the statement.

Truth of Confession as Issue on *Voir Dire*

It is not the function of the judge or magistrates at a *voir dire* to determine whether a confession is true, but simply whether it should be admitted. The PACE 1984, s. 76, underlines this limitation by providing that the court shall not allow the confession to be admitted 'except insofar as the prosecution proves beyond reasonable doubt that the confession (notwithstanding that it may be true) was not obtained [in breach of s. 76(2)]'.   **F17.70**

It does not necessarily follow from this that the truth of the statement is irrelevant to the question whether it should be admitted. At common law there was a conflict of authority on the point. In *Hammond* [1941] 3 All ER 318, H was charged with murder. He gave evidence on the *voir dire*, claiming that he had been knocked about and brutally ill-treated in order to induce a confession. It was held that he was properly cross-examined as to whether his confession was true, as it was relevant to the credit to be given to his assertions, on the basis that: 'If a man says, "I was forced to tell the story..." it must be relevant to know whether he was made to tell the truth, or whether he was made to say a number of things which were untrue' (per Humphreys J at p. 321).

In *Wong Kam-ming v The Queen* [1980] AC 247, a majority of the Privy Council disapproved of *Hammond*, and held that it should no longer be followed in Hong Kong. W gave evidence at the *voir dire*, claiming that his confession had been extracted by force. He was cross-examined in detail as to the truth of the statement, which was subsequently excluded. At the trial, prosecuting counsel called evidence to prove that, at the *voir dire*, W had admitted that he was present at the scene of the crime. It was held that the cross-examination was impermissible and that it did not affect the credit of the accused as a witness. Lord Edmund-Davies said (at p. 56): 'If the defendant denies the truth of the confession or some self-incriminating admission contained in it, the question whether his denial is itself true or false cannot be ascertained until after the *voir dire* is over and the defendant's guilt or innocence has been determined by the jury'. If the defendant admits the truth, this tends to show that he is a truthful witness and goes to support his allegations rather than, as *Hammond* supposes, to undermine them. Lord Hailsham of St Marylebone, dissenting on this issue, considered (at p. 262C) that 'the only general limitations on what may be asked or tendered ought to be relevance to the issue to be tried' and concluded that it was not possible 'to say *a priori* that in no circumstances is the truth or falsity of the alleged confession relevant to the question at issue on the *voir dire* or admissible as to credibility of either the prosecution or defence witnesses'. He instanced, *inter alia*, cases in which the   **F17.71** defence argue that, because a confession is demonstrably false, it must have been obtained by improper means. It must then be relevant for the prosecution to cross-examine on the truth of the statement.

It is submitted that Lord Hailsham's dissent in *Wong Kam-ming v The Queen* has logic on its side, but that the view of the majority has a sure foundation in policy, being consistent with the rule under which the accused is protected from the consequences of damaging admissions which further his case at the *voir dire* (see F17.73).

F17.72   Precisely the same questions may fall to be considered under s. 76 or s. 78 of the 1984 Act. Although *Hammond* has never been overruled as far as English courts are concerned, in *Liverpool Juvenile Court, ex parte R* [1988] QB 1 the Divisional Court relied on the authority of *Wong Kam-ming v The Queen* for the proposition that a defendant cannot be asked about the truth of a confession during an inquiry as to its admissibility. It should be noted, however, that:

(a) the judgment in that case expressly confined itself to summary proceedings (where it may be thought particularly important that the justices do not confuse the functions of the *voir dire* and the trial); and, more importantly,

(b) the court was not concerned directly with the question under discussion, but was instead engaged in enumerating the advantages to the defendant of the *voir dire* procedure.

In *Davis* [1990] Crim LR 860 the Court of Appeal referred to *Wong Kam-ming v The Queen* as 'strong persuasive authority' for the view that D could not be cross-examined as to the truth of his confession when giving evidence on the *voir dire*, but the point was not decided as the trial judge's ruling to the contrary had had no bearing upon the outcome of the trial.

Admissibility of Evidence Given on *Voir Dire*

F17.73   In *Wong Kam-ming v The Queen* [1980] AC 247 the Privy Council was unanimously of the opinion that the prosecution could not lead at the trial evidence regarding the testimony given by the defendant at the *voir dire*. Such a rule was necessary (per Lord Hailsham), so that 'the defendant should be able and feel free either by his own testimony or by other means to challenge the voluntary character of the tendered statement'. The rule applies even where the confession is admitted (per Lord Edmund-Davies), because 'it is preferable to maintain a clear distinction between the issue of voluntariness, which is alone relevant to the *voir dire*, and the issue of guilt falling to be decided in the main trial'.

Wong Kam-ming v The Queen was applied in *Brophy* [1982] AC 476. B was tried in Northern Ireland for a large number of offences, including murder, and for being a member of the IRA, a proscribed organisation. At the *voir dire* he succeeded in challenging the admissibility of confessions tendered by the prosecution, on the ground that the statements were extracted from him by extreme misconduct on the part of his interrogators. In support of his case he admitted to membership of the IRA, in order to found an inference that his interrogators would have known of his allegiance and treated him brutally because of it. It was held that the accused's admission, being relevant to the issue at the *voir dire*, was inadmissible for the prosecution at the trial. Furthermore according to Lord Fraser of Tullybelton (at p. 481): 'Where . . . evidence is given at the *voir dire* by an accused person in answer to questions by his counsel, and without objection by counsel for the Crown, his evidence ought . . . to be treated as relevant to the issue at the *voir dire*, unless it is clearly and obviously irrelevant', for example, the accused 'goes out of his way to boast' of his guilt.

Some commentators have argued that the law has altered as a result of the PACE 1984, s. 76, the effect of which is to render such a confession admissible, there being no question of it having been obtained by oppression or in circumstances conducive to unreliability. Even if this is the case, however, the policy behind *Wong Kam-ming v The Queen* and *Brophy* can be preserved and the same result achieved by invoking s. 78 of the 1984 Act to prevent unfairness in the proceedings. It is submitted that the policy is worth preserving, and that the accused would derive no protection from the statutory rules prohibiting the reception of confessions obtained in certain circumstances if the accused could only invoke the rule at the cost of admitting afresh that what he said was true.

Cross-examination on Statements Made on *Voir Dire*

In *Wong Kam-ming v The Queen* [1980] AC 247 W gave evidence at trial and was cross-examined   **F17.74** in detail as to statements made on the *voir dire* which were inconsistent with his testimony. The Privy Council held that where, as in the instant case, the confession had been excluded at the *voir dire*, it was not open to the prosecution to conduct such a cross-examination: 'Once a statement has been excluded... to adopt the words of Humphreys J in *Treacy* [1944] 2 All ER 229, nothing more should be heard of the *voir dire* unless it gives rise to a prosecution for perjury' (per Lord Hailsham at pp. 260–1).

The rule was otherwise where the confession which was the subject of the *voir dire* was admitted in evidence. In such a case (per Lord Hailsham, at p. 261): '... the whole evidence relating to the statement will have to be rehearsed once more... in front of the jury', and '... the statements on oath by the defendant on the *voir dire* as material for cross-examination do not, from the point of view of public policy, stand in any other situation than any other statements made by him, including the statement which has been admitted'.

The reasons of policy underlying the law as stated in *Wong Kam-ming v The Queen* have not altered since the coming into force of the PACE 1984, and it is submitted that the law remains as stated.

CONFESSION ADMISSIBLE AT TRIAL

Reconsidering Admissibility

It has already been noted (see **F17.67**) that in *Sat-Bhambra* (1988) 88 Cr App R 55, the Court   **F17.75** of Appeal held that, once a confession has been ruled admissible on the *voir dire*, the trial judge has no power under the PACE 1984, s. 76 or s. 78, to reconsider his decision if the evidence given at trial convinces him that he was wrong. To this extent the Act reverses the decision in *Watson* [1980] 2 All ER 293, where it was said that the judge had the power to reconsider the question of admissibility of evidence on which he had already ruled, and had the duty to exclude from the jury's consideration evidence which was inadmissible. However, the Court in *Sat-Bhambra* noted that s. 82(3) of the 1984 Act preserved the common-law powers of a court to exclude evidence in its discretion. It followed that the trial judge retained the power, if only under the common law, to take such steps as were necessary to prevent injustice. He might, if he thought that the matter was not capable of remedy by a direction, discharge the jury; he might direct the jury to disregard the statement; or he might by way of direction point out to the jury matters which affect the weight of the confession and leave the matter in their hands. He was not, however, under any obligation to discharge the jury. The change brought about by the Act would seem therefore to be mainly technical, and it is submitted that in any event there is still force in the dictum of the Court of Appeal in *Watson* [1980] 2 All ER 293 that, 'the occasions on which a judge should allow counsel to invite him to reconsider a ruling already made are likely to be extremely rare'.

The problem is perhaps most likely to arise where a decision has been made on the basis that the confession was not obtained pursuant to a breach of the Code of Practice, but it then emerges that a breach may have occurred. In *Hassan* [1995] Crim LR 404, a concession to this effect by a police officer in cross-examination led the trial judge to use his common law powers to reconsider his decision to admit H's confession, although he quite properly did not regard the concession as decisive of whether there had been a breach, and concluded that there had not.

It is also possible to reconsider a decision to exclude a statement. In *Allen* [1992] Crim LR 297 the defence sought to cross-examine a police witness to elicit their version of a conversation, the prosecution version of which had been excluded under s. 78. It was held that the judge had correctly exercised his discretion to admit the prosecution version of what had been said.

Role of Jury

F17.76   Under the PACE 1984 as at common law, the admissibility of the confession is a matter for the judge, and the weight to be given to the confession, once it is admitted, is a matter for the jury. In *Mushtaq* [2005] 3 All ER 1013 the House of Lords confirmed the view of the Court of Appeal in the same case that, as the jury is not a 'public authority' within the meaning of the HRA 1998, s. 6(3), it was not necessary in order to protect the accused from the risk of unfair trial that the jury, independently of the judge, should satisfy themselves as to the admissibility of confession evidence. The traditional division of labour between judge and jury thus survives the HRA 1998.

F17.77   Because the jury are entitled to consider all the circumstances in which a confession is made before deciding whether to act on it, it is the right of counsel for the defence 'to cross-examine again the witnesses who have already given evidence in the absence of the jury; for if he can induce the jury to think that the confession was obtained through some threat or promise, its value will be enormously weakened' (*Murray* [1951] 1 KB 391, decided at common law). The House of Lords in *Mushtaq* confirmed that the jury may be assisted in their function of deciding whether the confession is reliable by hearing the evidence that it was obtained in breach of the PACE 1984, s. 76(2). The House was, however, divided on the issue of the proper direction to be given to a jury in a case where evidence is before them that the confession was obtained by oppression or other improper means (in that case, by alleged threats to exaggerate M's part in the offence if he did not confess). If they conclude that it was so obtained, but is nevertheless reliable, may they act upon it? The traditional direction, given by the trial judge in *Mushtaq*, left the jury free to rely on the confession, if sure that it was true, 'even if it was or may have been made as a result of oppression or other improper circumstances'. A majority of their lordships decided that this direction could not be reconciled with s. 76(2) of the PACE 1984, to the extent that the rejection of an improperly obtained confession is based not solely on its potential unreliability, but on the importance of the defendant's right to avoid self-incrimination (*Lam Chi-ming v The Queen* [1991] AC 212, per Lord Griffiths). To leave the jury with the impression that they could find one or more of these rights to have been improperly infringed, but still rely upon the evidence, would, *per* Lord Roger, have been to contradict the policy:

> The evidence is excluded because, for all the kinds of reasons explained by Lord Griffiths, Parliament considers that it should not play any part in the jury's verdict. It flies in the face of that policy to say that a jury are entitled to rely on a confession even though, as the ultimate arbiters of all matters of fact, they properly consider that it was, or may have been, obtained by oppression or any other improper means.

F17.78   For the same reasons, the majority considered that the traditional direction contained an invitation to act incompatibly with the accused's right against self-incrimination under Article 6(1). The House therefore departed from previous authorities including *Chan Wei Keung v The Queen* [1967] 2 AC 16. Lord Roger, in a speech with which the majority concurred, concluded that the logic of s. 76(2) of the PACE 1984 requires that the jury should be directed that, if they consider that the confession was or may have been obtained by oppression or in consequence of anything that was likely to render it unreliable, they should disregard it. In *Pham* [2008] EWCA Crim 3182 the trial judge, who had not been invited to consider *Mushtaq*, gave a direction which erred by focusing primarily on whether the accused's confessions could be regarded as truthful. However, the Court of Appeal considered that, as the only basis for the accused's contention that the confessions were untrue was an alleged threat to the accused in interview to which the judge also alluded, the overall impression given to the jury was not such as to render the conviction unsafe.

If the jury were to be told that the judge had ruled the confession admissible, it is possible that they might be influenced by the judge's view on admissibility in deciding the issues which are for them to decide. Thus it has been the practice in England, both before and after the PACE 1984, for this information to be withheld from them (*Mitchell v The Queen* [1998] AC 695; *Thompson v The Queen* [1998] AC 811).

If a confession is voluntary, the inference that it is also true follows naturally in most cases. On **F17.79** rare occasions, however, the mental condition of the accused may give rise to doubts as to the reliability of his confession. In such a case, expert medical evidence may be admitted to assist the jury in evaluating the reliability of the confession (*Ward* [1993] 2 All ER 577 (severe personality disorder amounting to mental disorder); *MacKenzie* (1992) 96 Cr App R 98 (mentally handicapped accused also suffering personality disorder: Crown conceded jury entitled to the assistance of expert testimony to evaluate confessions: see also **F17.56**).

Confession Implicating Co-accused

A confession made by an accused person that is admitted in evidence is evidence against him **F17.80** (PACE 1984, s. 76(1)). It is not, at common law, admissible against any other person implicated in it (*Rhodes* (1959) 44 Cr App R 23) unless it is made in the presence of that person and he acknowledges the incriminating parts so as to make them, in effect, his own. The evidence of a co-accused on oath was, by contrast, admissible for all purposes, including the purpose of being evidence against the accused (*Rudd* (1948) 32 Cr App R 138). The common-law rule has been affected by the enactment of the PACE 1984, s. 74 (**F11.6**). Under that provision there is no doubt that the conviction of A is admissible to establish the guilt of A at B's trial, where it is relevant to do so (the most common example being where B is charged with complicity in a crime that the prosecution contends was committed by A, and of which A has been convicted). In *Hayter* [2005] 2 All ER 209, the House of Lords held, by majority, that the rule where A and B are tried for a joint offence is modified as follows. Where the jury are directed first to consider the case against A, which is based on his out-of-court admissions, they may then be told that their finding as to the guilt of A and the role he played may be used as part of the evidence relevant to the guilt of B. In other words their finding of guilt against A, though based on his confession, becomes a building block in the case against B. This differs only marginally from using the confession of A directly (rather than indirectly through a finding of guilt) as evidence against B, but to hold strictly to the common-law rule would be to open a gulf between cases where A and B are jointly tried and cases where A's guilt is established at a separate trial, where s. 74 applies. Some of the older cases, including *Rhodes* itself, would be decided differently today. *Hayter* was distinguished in *Persad v The State of Trinidad and Tobago* [2007] 1 WLR 2379. There, a robbery took place in the course of which one man raped and another man buggered one of the victims. The prosecution sought to establish, by a process of elimination, that B was responsible for the buggery, based on a combination of A's admission of rape, the victim's account that the rapist was not the man who buggered her, and C's admission to robbery as a look-out only. The argument failed principally because C's statement was, as regards the sexual offences, purely exculpatory, so that *Hayter* did not apply; whether, had A and B stood trial alone, A's confession to rape could have been a 'building block' in the case against B when the liability for the sexual offences was not joint was a question left for another time.

The common-law rule that a confession is admissible only against its maker may also be affected **F17.81** by the CJA 2003, s. 114(1)(d) (hearsay admissible in interests of justice: see *Prosecution Appeal (No. 2 of 2008): R v Y* [2008] 2 All ER 484 at **F16.43**) and s. 121 (multiple hearsay admissible in interests of justice). In *Thakrar* [2010] EWCA Crim 1505 a confession to murder admissible against its maker under the multiple hearsay provisions of s. 121 (see **F16.90**) was said also to be admissible against the co-accused (the maker's brother). The confession included details that would have been known only to the murderer and was judged to be highly reliable. The Court of Appeal considered it unlikely that the brother would have been implicated unless he was also guilty. It was also suggested that the statement would have equally been admissible against the brother had he been tried separately. See, however, *Miah* [2011] EWCA Crim 945, in which it appears to have been assumed that pre-trial statements involving confessions made by one accused cannot be admissible against a co-accused.

F17.82   For the circumstances in which a confession may be edited so as to remove incriminating references to a co-accused, see **F17.91**. In exceptional circumstances the existence of a confession by one accused which seriously prejudices another may be grounds for ordering separate trials (*Gunewardene* [1951] 2 KB 600). Joint offences should generally be tried jointly, however, even though this may involve evidence which is inadmissible in respect of a particular accused being given. The fact that there is some risk of prejudice is not enough, though 'if a case is strong enough, if the prejudice is dangerous enough, if the circumstances are particular enough, all rules of this kind must go in the interests of justice' (*Lake* (1976) 64 Cr App R 172, at p. 175).

CONFESSION EXCLUDED AT TRIAL

Effect of Exclusion on Prosecution

F17.83   In *Treacy* [1944] 2 All ER 229, the prosecution had not sought to put in evidence, as part of their case, a statement made by T to a police officer following T's arrest for murder. Instead it was used in cross-examination of T as a previous inconsistent statement. The statement was assumed by the Court of Criminal Appeal to have been inadmissible as part of the prosecution case, and, that being so, it was held that 'nothing more ought to be heard of it, and it is quite a mistake to think that a document can be made admissible in evidence which is otherwise inadmissible simply because it is put to a person in cross-examination'. In *Rice* [1963] 1 QB 857 it was held that the same principle obtains in favour of a co-accused of the maker of the inadmissible statement. The rule prohibits the revelation that the accused has made a statement, 'since evidence of, or revelation of that fact tends in common sense to lend weight to the subsequent evidence'. It does not preclude the use of information derived from the statement as the basis of cross-examination (*Rice*).

Effect of Exclusion on Co-accused

F17.84   A confession which is inadmissible under the PACE 1984, s. 76(2)(b), on behalf of the prosecution may not be relied upon by a co-accused as evidence of its truth at common law. (*Myers* [1998] AC 124: see **F17.27**). It may, however, be put to the maker in cross-examination, in which case the only limitation is relevancy (*Lui Mei Lin v The Queen* [1989] AC 288). It follows that a co-accused cannot be restrained from cross-examining the accused on the content of any previous statement made by him which is relevant, notwithstanding that that statement may have been ruled inadmissible as part of the prosecution case (*Lui Mei Lin v The Queen*, approving *Rowson* [1986] QB 174), or may have been made in circumstances where it could not be used to prove guilt. In *Hinchcliffe* [2002] EWCA Crim 837 the admission by a company director as part of a 'Carecraft' agreement leading to his disqualification was made on the basis that it could not be used in other proceedings, but this was held to be no bar to its use in cross-examination. Where evidence of an otherwise inadmissible previous statement is elicited by a co-accused in cross-examination, the judge should explain to the jury why the statement has previously been excluded and cannot be relied on by the prosecution to prove their case. It should also be remembered that in cross-examination as to credit the cross-examiner is bound by the answers which he receives, and that it is not legitimate to reopen all the circumstances in which the excluded statement was taken. The trial judge should insist that irrelevant material contained in the statement is not referred to, and that such material is, where necessary, excised from any copies which the jury might see (*Lui Mei Lin v The Queen*). Under the CJA 2003, previous inconsistent statements which are admitted in cross-examination are, generally, evidence of the truth of facts stated (s. 119). This does not, however, permit the introduction of a confession which is inadmissible under the PACE 1984, s. 76 (s. 128(2)).

EVIDENCE YIELDED BY INADMISSIBLE CONFESSIONS

Police and Criminal Evidence Act 1984, s. 76

F17.85

(4) The fact that a confession is wholly or partly excluded in pursuance of this section shall not affect the admissibility in evidence—
    (a) of any facts discovered as a result of the confession; or
    (b) where the confession is relevant as showing that the accused speaks, writes or expresses himself in a particular way, of so much of the confession as is necessary to show that he does so.

(5) Evidence that a fact to which this subsection applies was discovered as a result of a statement made by an accused person shall not be admissible unless evidence of how it was discovered is given by him or on his behalf.

(6) Subsection (5) above applies—
    (a) to any fact discovered as a result of a confession which is wholly excluded in pursuance of this section; and
    (b) to any fact discovered as a result of a confession which is partly so excluded, if the fact is discovered as a result of the excluded part of the confession.

Discovery of Facts

The PACE 1984, s. 76(4)(a), follows the common-law rule as stated in *Warickshall* (1783) 1   **F17.86**
Leach 263. W made a full confession to receiving stolen goods, in consequence of which the goods were found concealed in her bed. The confession was ruled inadmissible, but the prosecution were allowed to prove the discovery of the stolen property. It was held that the principle requiring the rejection of certain confessions in evidence 'has no application whatever as to the admission or rejection of facts, whether the knowledge of them be obtained in consequence of an extorted confession, or whether it arises from any other source; for a fact, if it exists at all, must exist invariably in the same manner, whether the confession from which it is derived be in other respects true or false'. In *HM Advocate v P* [2011] 1 WLR 2497, a Scottish case, it was held that there was no absolute rule of human rights law that would require the exclusion of evidence obtained in consequence of confessions or disclosures at an improperly conducted interview. Lord Hope considered that the law as set out in s. 76(4) was consistent with the rights guaranteed by the ECHR, Article 6. The issue in England and Wales in such cases is whether it is fair to admit the evidence discovered as a result of the confession: i.e. the case requires the separate application of s.78.

Some difficulty may arise as to where the 'confession' ends and 'facts discovered as a result of it' begin. At common law, in *Barker* [1941] 2 KB 381 documents delivered up by B as a direct result of an inducement were treated as the equivalent of confession evidence, and excluded accordingly. Section 82(1) of the 1984 Act now provides a definition of 'confession' as including 'any statement wholly or partly adverse to the person who made it . . . whether made in words or otherwise'. Words, documents or conduct which come within this definition and which fall foul of the exclusionary rule in s. 76(2) cannot be treated as 'facts' for the purpose of s. 76(4)(a). Thus, for example, a filmed re-enactment of a murder, in which a defendant is shown disposing of the murder weapon, should be regarded as a confession statement rather than as independent facts (*Lam Chi-ming v The Queen* [1991] 2 AC 212). However, it does not seem entirely satisfactory to regard conduct such as that in *Barker* as the equivalent of a 'statement' by him 'in consequence of anything said or done' under s. 76(2)(b) for the purposes of the 1984 Act, and such evidence would seem to be more correctly considered as admissible evidence of facts which, like all prosecution evidence, may in appropriate circumstances be excluded under s. 78 of the 1984 Act.

Confession Relevant to Show Speech, Writing or Expression

F17.87   Section 76(4)(b) of the 1984 Act embodies a principle stated in argument by Lush J in *Voisin* [1918] 1 KB 531. V was charged with the murder of a woman, part of whose body was found in a parcel together with a handwritten note bearing the legend 'Bladie Belgiam'. V, who had not been cautioned, was asked by the police to write the words 'Bloody Belgian', which he did, misspelling them in precisely the same fashion as the writer of the note. The case did not concern an inadmissible confession, but the principle involved in the reception of the note in evidence was said by Lush J to be that 'it cannot make any difference to the admissibility of handwriting whether it is written voluntarily or under compulsion of threats'. The same point was made (*obiter*) in *Nottle* [2004] EWCA Crim 599. Cars had been damaged by scratching an obscene message to the owner, whose name was Justin, but which the vandal had spelt as 'Jutin'. When asked to write down the same message, N also spelt the name incorrectly. On the assumption that the misspelling constituted a confession, the Court of Appeal found that there had been nothing said or done to render the statement inadmissible under s. 76, but that, even if it had been otherwise, s. 76(4)(b) would have rendered the misspelling admissible. Section 76(4)(b) might also be used, for example, in a case of rape, where a tape-recorded confession is ruled inadmissible, but the voice of the accused can be heard speaking with an unusual speech impediment which was also described by the victim, or with a particular local accent. Care must be taken to avoid prejudice to the accused when adducing such evidence; s. 76(4)(b) permits the prosecution to adduce only 'so much of the confession as is necessary to show' the relevant feature, but even this may in some cases be impossible without the jury becoming aware that a confession has been made. In such cases it will have to be considered whether the risk of prejudice can be overcome by a direction as to the purpose for which the evidence has been adduced, or whether the discretion of the court to exclude prosecution evidence, either under s. 78 of the 1984 Act or at common law, should be exercised. In *Nottle* the Court held that the failure of the police to disclose to N that the name on the car had been spelled 'Jutin' was not a matter which rendered it unfair for the prosecution subsequently to rely on N's identical misspelling.

Linking Facts to Confession

F17.88   At common law there was some controversy as to the extent to which it was permissible to show that certain facts had come to light as the result of an inadmissible confession by the accused. Section 76(5) and (6) of the 1984 Act confirms the view taken in *Warickshall* (1783) 1 Leach 263, and *Berryman* (1854) 6 Cox CC 388 that no such link can be proved. The only exception is where the defence choose to give evidence of how the facts came to be discovered, in which case, presumably, the prosecution may challenge the account given by the defence, even if to do so involves making reference to the excluded statement.

Evidence Yielded by Confession Excluded under s. 78

F17.89   The PACE 1984, s. 76(4), applies only to matters coming to light as a result of a confession excluded under s. 76 itself. Where the confession is excluded in the discretion of the court under s. 78, no statutory rule applies, but the common-law principles suggest that evidence discovered in consequence is admissible.

As to the linking of the discovery with the confession, it may be that a court dealing with an application under s. 78 will not feel compelled to follow the principle laid down in s. 76(5), given that the common law on the point was unclear (see, e.g., *Griffin* (1809) Russ & Ry 151; *Gould* (1840) 9 C & P 364, and the views expressed by a majority of the Criminal Law Revision Committee in its *Eleventh Report: Evidence (General)* (1972) Cmnd 4991, para. 69). It should also be noted that the reasons which led the court to exercise its discretion in respect of the confession may extend also to the subsequently discovered facts, as where an accused discloses information in a confession made after he has been denied access to legal advice by a police officer acting in deliberate and flagrant disregard of s. 58 of the 1984 Act. See also the discussion of *HM Advocate v P* [2011] 1 WLR 2497 at **F17.86**.

Another possibility is that the court will take into account the confirmation of a confession by the discovery of incontrovertible facts in deciding whether to exercise its discretion to exclude the confession statement. Nothing in s. 78 appears to prevent such reasoning, indeed the court is enjoined to have regard to 'all the circumstances' in reaching its conclusion. (Contrast s. 76(2), in which it is clear that the truth of the confession is not a factor to be taken into account in determining admissibility.) The argument is particularly attractive where the defence rely on breach of a provision of a code of practice, the function of which is thought by the court to be to guard against the production of unreliable confession statements, such as the obligation to maintain records of interviews.

EDITING OF CONFESSIONS

Editing at Trial to Protect Accused

Where the confession of an accused person is admitted in evidence against him, the whole confession is admissible, notwithstanding that it includes matter prejudicial to the accused. In *Turner v Underwood* [1948] 2 KB 284 the response of the accused when charged with an offence of indecency was to say 'I have done time for this before', and it was held that the whole confession was admissible in evidence before the magistrates. However, Lord Goddard noted (at p. 286) that: 'It is the practice as a rule in cases which are tried before juries that where the court knows there is something said by a man in his statement which admits a previous conviction, or shows other matter reflecting on his character, the court sees that that is not read out to the jury'.   **F17.90**

Similarly, in *Weaver* [1968] 1 QB 353 Sachs LJ said that a statement by an accused ought to be edited at trial to avoid prejudicing him and to eliminate matters which 'it would be better that the jury should not know'. In *Knight* (1946) 31 Cr App R 52 portions of the accused's confessions which related to other offences which were irrelevant to the offence charged were held to have been improperly received in evidence. Quashing the convictions, Lewis J regarded it as 'contrary to the rules of evidence' to admit what was in effect evidence of the bad character of the accused, who had not put their characters in issue. In some cases the material edited out is irrelevant, in others it has a prejudicial effect exceeding its probative value. See also *Hall* [1971] Crim LR 480. When an agreement has been made that unfairly prejudicial material should be edited before being given to the jury, it is crucial that the proper edited version is put before the jury (see *Gonzales Santana* [2012] EWCA Crim 512, in which a direction to the jury to 'put it out of their minds' did not cure the defect).

When a statement is to be edited in this way, the proper procedure was said in *Weaver* [1968] 1 QB 353 to be that the statement should not be edited until the trial, at which stage, according to Sachs LJ (at p. 358) 'counsel can confer, and the judge can, if necessary, take his part in ensuring that any "editing" is done, if it is done at all, in the right way and to the right degree'.

Where the matter concerned is relevant and admissible in the trial there is no reason to omit it, even if the jury are made aware of other offences (*Evans* [1950] 1 All ER 601).

In *Pearce* (1979) Cr App R 365, it was said that the rule of practice whereby the courts 'admit in evidence all unwritten and most written statements made by an accused person to the police whether they contain admissions or whether they contain denials of guilt', was subject to the limitation that any admission of a previous conviction would be excluded.

Editing at Trial to Protect Co-accused

Where the confession of an accused person is admitted, it is not, as a general rule, admissible in evidence against a co-accused (see **F17.80**). Where an accused has laid blame, perhaps the greater blame, on his co-accused, the risk of prejudice to the co-accused if the whole statement is heard is obvious. The rule, however, is that the prosecution ought to present the accused's   **F17.91** confession as a whole (*Pearce* (1979) 69 Cr App R 365) and the accused could, with good reason, complain if the prosecution picked out certain passages and left out others (*Gunewardene* [1951] 2 KB 600). In *Gunewardene*, G was charged as an accessory to manslaughter arising out of an abortion performed by H, his co-accused. H's confession was read to the jury, including those parts of it which implicated G, the trial judge warning the jury that the statement was not evidence against G. Lord Goddard CJ said (at p. 611) that 'although in many cases counsel do refrain from reading passages which implicate another prisoner and have no real bearing on the case against the prisoner making the statement, we cannot say that anything has been admitted...which was not admissible'.

Gunewardene was applied in *Lobban v The Queen* [1995] 2 All ER 602, where the issue before the Privy Council was whether the exculpatory part of a mixed statement made by L's co-accused, R, which incriminated L in a murder, could be excluded or edited in the exercise of the court's discretion to protect L from prejudice, given that the statement was hearsay and inadmissible as against him. The answer was that it could not; the prosecution had placed reliance upon the mixed statement as against R, and the exculpatory parts were therefore admissible evidence for R (see F17.93). There was no discretion to restrain a co-accused from defending himself by adducing admissible evidence, and nothing to support the suggestion made in earlier cases that the judge had a discretion to edit a confession so as to deprive one defendant of relevant defence evidence in order to minimise injustice to another (see, e.g., *Rogers* [1971] Crim LR 413). This, while a correct application of principle, may remove what has been an attractive option in some cases (see, e.g., the discussion of earlier authorities in *Jefferson* (1994) 99 Cr App R 14 at p. 26), but it would seem still to leave open the possibility of editing out information irrelevant to the co-accused's case, or of editing with the co-accused's consent.

In *Mitchell* [2005] EWCA Crim 3447, the Court of Appeal was concerned with the editing of two sets of statements. In the first, *Lobban* applied because the prosecution were relying on the whole of the interview and the effect of editing out references to the co-accused would have been to leave the jury with an incomplete and unsatisfactory picture of what the maker had said. In the second, *Lobban* did not apply: the references to the co-accused were made, not by the accused himself, but by a police officer putting forward his opinion that the co-accused had committed another crime which was not the subject of any proceedings. That part of the statement could and should have been removed, and the desire of the accused to use it in order to discredit the co-accused was irrelevant.

Pre-trial Editing of Written Statement Made by Suspect

F17.92   Where the prosecution tender written statements in evidence, it will frequently be necessary to edit, *inter alia*, statements which contain inadmissible, irrelevant or prejudicial material. CPD V, paras. 27A.1 to 27A.6 (see Supplement, **PD-38**), recognise that, whereas other written statements may be satisfactorily dealt with by editing, it is preferable in the circumstances identified in para. 27A.4(b), where an interview ranges over more offences than are eventually charged, to prepare a fresh statement. In summary proceedings, there will be a need to prepare fresh statements rather than using the method of striking out or bracketing those parts on which no reliance is to be placed by the prosecution in the proceedings (para. 27A.5).

MIXED STATEMENTS

Admissibility of Mixed Statements

F17.93   The expression 'mixed statement' is used to refer to a statement made by an accused which in part comprises admissions and in part exculpatory or self-serving statements (*Hamand* (1985) 82 Cr App R 65 at p. 67). An example would be 'I admit I hit him, but he was trying to kill me'. A 'partly adverse statement' is a confession by virtue of the PACE 1984, s. 82(1) (see

F17.1), and is admissible as such provided that the requirements of s. 76 are complied with. In *Finch* [2007] 1 WLR 1645, the Court of Appeal identified as suitable for full argument the question whether the presence of an admission in a police interview rendered the entire interview a 'confession'. Whether a particular statement is truly 'mixed' is, it is submitted, a question of fact, and both temporal and contextual separation will be relevant to whether two or more propositions form part of the same statement. It will be a question for the court in each case to determine whether an excuse or explanation so accompanies an admission as to be part of a mixed statement for the purposes of this rule. In *Pearce* (1979) 69 Cr App R 365, the principle was said to be that a statement which is not an admission is admissible if it is made 'in the same context as an admission', and the Court of Appeal accepted that the two parts of the mixed statement may occur at different places in 'the same interview or series of interviews'.

Where an admission is made which is qualified by an explanation or excuse, all the authorities agree that it would be unfair to admit the admission without admitting the explanation (*Sharp* [1988] 1 All ER 65 per Lord Havers at p. 12). In *Jones* (1827) 2 C & P 629, the rule was said to be that 'if a prosecutor uses the declaration of a prisoner, he must take the whole of it together, and cannot select one part and leave another'. In *Pearce* (1979) 69 Cr App R 365, it was said that to exclude answers at interview which are favourable to the accused, while admitting those which are unfavourable, would be misleading, and a breach of duty on the part of the prosecutor, whose obligation is to present the case fairly to the jury. See also *McGregor* [1968] 1 QB 371 and *Duncan* (1981) 73 Cr App R 359, at p. 363.

In many cases, the mixed statement will have been made in the course of questioning of the accused by the police, no distinction being taken in this respect between a written statement and a record of questions and answers at interview (*Polin* [1991] Crim LR 293). It is not, however, a condition of admissibility that the statement was made to a police officer — a point taken by Lord Havers in *Sharp*. Thus, for example, mixed statements have been received which were made by the accused when giving evidence at a previous trial (*McGregor*; *Higgins* (1829) 3 C & P 603).

Under the CJA 2003, s. 118(1), the common-law rules regarding the admissibility of mixed statements are preserved (see **F16.72**).

Evidential Value of Self-serving Parts of Mixed Statements

In *Sharp* [1988] 1 All ER 65, Lord Havers identified two views which had emerged as to the evidential value of the self-serving parts of a mixed statement. The view which the House of Lords accepted is that the whole statement is admissible by way of exception to the hearsay rule, and is thus evidence of the truth of all the facts stated in it. The House expressed approval of the law as stated in *Duncan* (1981) 73 Cr App R 359 by Lord Lane CJ, who said (at p. 365): **F17.94**

> Where a 'mixed' statement is under consideration by the jury in a case where the defendant has not given evidence, it seems to us that the simplest, and, therefore, the method most likely to produce a just result, is for the jury to be told that the whole statement, both the incriminating parts and the excuses or explanations, must be considered by them in deciding where the truth lies. It is, to say the least, not helpful to try to explain to the jury that the exculpatory parts of the statement are something less than evidence of the facts they state.

For examples of earlier decisions to the same effect, see *Clewes* (1830) 4 C & P 221; *McGregor* [1968] 1 QB 371; *Hamand* (1985) 82 Cr App R 65. *Sharp* has been approved by the House of Lords in *Aziz* [1996] AC 41 and by the Privy Council in *Lobban v The Queen* [1995] 2 All ER 602.

The other view which has from time to time been taken, is that the self-serving parts of the statement are not evidence of their truth, but form material which may be of use to the jury in evaluating the admissions. This was said to be the law in, e.g., *Sparrow* [1973] 2 All ER 129 and in *Leung Kam-Kwok v The Queen* (1984) 81 Cr App R 83. The House of Lords in *Sharp* [1988] 1 All ER 65 rejected this 'purist' approach:

(a) because the weight of authority supported the contrary view; and

(b) because common sense suggested that the only way in which a jury could use the self-serving parts of the statement to 'evaluate the facts in the admission' would be if they first reached a conclusion as to the truth of the explanation given by the accused.

The question of the evidential value of a mixed statement arises most acutely in cases where the accused does not testify. In both *Duncan* (1981) 73 Cr App R 359 and *Sharp* [1988] 1 All ER 65 the accused gave no evidence, and the statement of Lord Lane CJ which was approved in *Sharp* concerns the direction to be given to a jury in such a case; indeed it incorporates the right to comment on the failure of the accused to repeat the exculpatory statement on oath (*Downes* (1993) *Independent*, 25 October 1993). Despite this, there is no logical reason why the status of the statement should be any different if the accused testifies.

Weight to be Attached to Self-serving Parts of Mixed Statements

F17.95 In *Sharp* [1988] 1 All ER 65 the House of Lords approved of the following statement of Lord Lane CJ in *Duncan* (1981) 73 Cr App R 359 at p. 365:

> . . . where appropriate, as it usually will be, the judge may, and should, point out that the incriminating parts are likely to be true (otherwise why say them?), whereas the excuses do not have the same weight. Nor is there any reason why, again where appropriate, the judge should not comment in relation to the exculpatory remarks upon the election of the accused not to give evidence.

In *Donaldson* (1976) 64 Cr App R 59 it was said that the jury, when deciding what weight, if any, to give to those parts of the statement which are favourable to an accused who has elected not to give evidence, should take into account that it was not made on oath and has not been tested by cross-examination. See also *McGregor* [1968] 1 QB 371.

Mixed Statements and the Evidential Burden

F17.96 Where the accused bears the evidential burden of establishing a sufficient foundation so that a defence such as self-defence or provocation may be left to the jury, he may rely on the self-serving part of a mixed statement which is admitted in evidence under the principles stated above. In *Hamand* (1985) 82 Cr App R 65, H made a statement to the police in which he admitted that he had struck a man in the face, but claimed that the man had acted in such a way as to lead H to believe that he was about to be attacked. The statement was proved in evidence as part of the prosecution case. The Court of Appeal held that the trial judge had been wrong to rule that H's mixed statement was not evidence of self-defence, thus forcing H to testify in his own defence. In assessing the weight to be given to such a statement where it is not supported by any evidence from the accused himself, the comments of Lord Lane CJ in *Duncan* (1981) 73 Cr App R 359 (see **F17.95**) should be borne in mind.

Prosecution Placing No Reliance on Admission Contained in Mixed Statement

F17.97 The derivation of the rule as stated at **F17.93** and **F17.94** suggests that a mixed statement becomes evidence of the truth of its self-serving parts only where the prosecution elect to rely on it as containing an admission. Some difficulty may arise in cases where the prosecution adduce a mixed statement (by way of discharging their duty under *Pearce* (1979) 69 Cr App R 365 to put statements made to the police before the court (see **F6.36**)) but seek to rely on it only to show the reaction of the accused when taxed with the offence, and not as evidence of its truth. That this may be done is well established (see e.g., *Storey* (1968) 52 Cr App R 334; *Donaldson* (1976) 64 Cr App R 59; *Pearce* (1979) 69 Cr App R 365), and may benefit the prosecution by enabling them to draw attention to any inconsistencies between the explanation advanced in the statement and any defence put forward at trial. It seems unlikely that, in such cases, the self-serving passages become evidence of their truth.

For the same reason, it is submitted, a mixed statement which is not relied on by the prosecution for any purpose ought not to be regarded as admissible evidence for the defence of any excuse or explanation asserted in it. This was accepted by the House of Lords in *Aziz* [1996] AC 41 (at p. 50), where the statement to this effect in the 1995 edition of this work was approved. It should, however, be noted that in *Sharp* [1988] 1 All ER 65 the question certified for decision by the House (as amended by Lord Havers) was: 'Where a statement made to a person out of court by a defendant contains both admissions and self-exculpatory parts do the exculpatory parts constitute evidence of the truth of the facts alleged therein?' The question does not confine itself to cases where the prosecution seek to rely on the admissions contained in the statement. It is submitted, however, in the light of *Aziz*, that the answering of this question in the affirmative by the House of Lords does not provide any warrant for qualifying the law as it is stated above.

In *Garrod* [1997] Crim LR 445, the Court of Appeal considered that a statement was properly regarded as 'mixed' if it contained an admission of fact which was capable of adding some degree of weight to the prosecution case, regardless (apparently) of whether the prosecution were relying on it or not. However the statement in that case was purely exculpatory, whichever test was applied. In *Western v DPP* [1997] 1 Cr App R 474, W appealed against conviction for a public order offence on the grounds that the magistrates had wrongly treated as purely self-serving an interview in which W admitted fighting with the victim but claimed to have acted in self-defence. The prosecution resisted the appeal precisely on the grounds that the interview was not a mixed statement unless the prosecution relied on the admission. The appeal was allowed because there was nothing within the stated case to suggest that the prosecution had *not* relied on the admission: on the contrary the circumstances suggested it was highly likely that they had. *Papworth* [2008] 1 Cr App R 439, applies *Garrod* with the proviso that, as the rule is 'based on fairness to the defendant and simplicity for the jury', the judge should estimate, at the conclusion of all the evidence, the extent to which the prosecution 'place significant reliance on' the incriminating statements. The more significant the reliance, 'the more it is likely that the jury should be told that the parts which explain or excuse those incriminating parts are also evidence in the case' (at [14]). *Papworth* and *Garrod* [1997] Crim LR 445 were applied in *Shirley* [2013] EWCA Crim 1990. The prosecution in that case relied on only very limited admissions (that the accused was known by his middle name of Mark, and that he told people he had served in the army when he had not). As it was open to the judge to conclude that these were not 'significant' statements in the prosecution's case (and both could, it appears, have been proved by other evidence had they been contested), the interview in which S made the concessions could not be viewed, taken as a whole, as a mixed statement. S, who did not testify, was therefore rightly precluded from relying on any self-serving statements made in the same interviews. But it is a misdirection to dismiss as mere evidence of reaction a body of interview evidence the inculpatory parts of which are relied on by the prosecution (*Gijkokaj* [2014] EWCA Crim 386), though in that case the 'obvious' error was held not to amount to material misdirection, given the judge's overall treatment of the defence case. This is not to say that evidence of reaction is necessarily of little value. In *R (Gonzales) v Folkestone Magistrates' Court* (2011) 175 JP 453 it was conceded that the prosecution erred in simply failing to adduce the mixed statement at all, in contravention of the practice approved in *Pearce* (see **F6.36**). The Divisional Court's principal reason for approving the concession was that the prosecution had deprived G of valuable evidence of 'reaction to an accusation' rather than evidence of the truth of the self-serving parts. To the extent that the distinction remains important, it is submitted that this is correct.

F17.98

STATEMENTS IN PRESENCE OF ACCUSED

F17.99 General Rule

> ...the rule of law undoubtedly is that a statement made in the presence of an accused person, even upon an occasion which should be expected reasonably to call for some explanation or denial from him, is not evidence against him of the facts stated save so far as he accepts the statement, so as to make it, in effect, his own. (*Christie* [1914] AC 545, per Lord Atkinson at p. 554)

Under the CJA 2003, s. 118(1), the common-law rules regarding the admissibility of confessions are preserved (see **F16.72**). It is submitted that the rules considered in this section will continue to have effect.

Although it is a salutary rule of practice, there is no rule of law requiring the production, before the content of the statement is given in evidence, of some proof of the accused's acceptance of the statement (*Christie*, modifying the stricter rule suggested by the Court of Criminal Appeal in *Norton* [1910] 2 KB 496). Lord Atkinson considered that the procedure suggested by Pickford J in *Norton* was unobjectionable, provided that it was workable. According to that procedure, in a trial on indictment the judge, where it is possible to do so, decides whether there is any evidence of acknowledgement of the statement. Where acknowledgement cannot be deduced, the fact of a statement having been made in the accused's presence may be given in evidence, but not the contents, and the question asked, what the accused said or did on such a statement being made. If the answer is such that acknowledgement may properly be inferred, the contents of the statement become admissible.

F17.100 If the statement is admitted, the question whether the accused's conduct amounted to an acknowledgement is a question for the jury. If they find that the statement was acknowledged, in whole or in part, then they may take the statement or the relevant part of it into consideration. If they do not so find, they should be directed to disregard the statement altogether (*Norton*). In *Christie*, Lord Atkinson said (at p. 554) that, if the judge is of the view that no evidence has been given on which the jury could reasonably find that the accused had accepted the statement, he should direct the jury to disregard it.

Where the acknowledgement takes the form of a statement by the accused which is wholly or partly adverse to him, he will by virtue of the PACE 1984, s. 82(1), have made a confession for the purposes of part VIII of that Act, and accordingly the conditions of s. 76 must be complied with.

The jury should be given a clear direction as to the inferences to which the accused's conduct may give rise (*Horne* [1990] Crim LR 188; *Chandler* [1976] 1 All ER 585; but see *Black* (1922) 16 Cr App R 118).

Evidence of Acknowledgement

F17.101 In *Christie* [1914] AC 545, Lord Atkinson considered the various ways in which an accused person might accept an accusation put to him (at p. 554):

> He may accept the statement by word or conduct, action or demeanour, and it is the function of the jury which tries the case to determine whether his words, action, conduct or demeanour at the time when the statement was made amounts to an acceptance of it in whole or in part. It by no means follows, I think, that a mere denial by the accused of the facts mentioned in the statement necessarily renders the statement inadmissible, because he may deny his statement in such a manner and under such circumstances as may lead a jury to disbelieve him, and constitute evidence from which an acknowledgement can be inferred.

See also *Norton* [1910] 2 KB 496. In *Christie*, C was charged with indecent assault on a young boy who, shortly after the alleged offence and in the presence of his mother and of a police officer who was on the spot, confronted C with the words 'That is the man,' and gave details of the assault. C replied 'I am innocent'. Although in the form of a denial, the response was regarded as one from which it was open to the jury to draw an inference of acceptance. Lord Moulton said (at p. 559):

> Going back to first principles... the deciding question is whether the evidence of the whole occurrence is relevant or not. If the prisoner admits the charges the evidence is obviously relevant. If he denies it, it may or may not be relevant. For instance, if he is charged with a violent assault and denies that he committed it, that fact might be distinctly relevant if at the trial his defence was that he did commit the act, but that it was in self-defence.

Acceptance by acquiescence was considered sufficient: *O* [2005] EWCA Crim 3082, where the accused stood by, smirking, while his friend explained when asked the reason for an attack that it had been racially motivated.

Where the accused denies the accusation, it must, however, be asked whether the effect on the jury of hearing that an accusation has been made might be to create prejudice on their part which is out of all proportion to the evidential value of the accused's behaviour. If the evidence would have very little or no value, the judge ought to exercise his discretion to exclude it (*Christie*, per Lord Moulton at p. 560).

As to silence in the face of an allegation, see **F19.3** *et seq*.

Accused Confronted with Statement by Co-accused

The principles set out at **F17.99** are of equal application where the accused is confronted with **F17.102** an accusation made by his co-accused. Difficulties may, however, arise if the police show the accused a statement made by a co-accused implicating him, ostensibly to gauge the accused's reaction, but intending also to profit by getting the statement before the court in circumstances where the maker of the statement cannot be called as a witness. The practice was condemned in *Gardner* (1916) 11 Cr App R 265, and, although the Court of Criminal Appeal was not prepared to say that admissions obtained in this way were inadmissible, it appears to have been regarded as within the discretion of the trial judge to exclude statements put to the accused for the purpose of extracting a confession. See also *Taylor* [1978] Crim LR 92, in which it was said that the prejudicial effect of a co-accused's accusation vastly outweighed its probative value as evidence introducing T's reaction, though it does not appear what the reaction of T was alleged to have been. In *Mills* [1947] KB 297 the Court of Criminal Appeal considered that the co-accused's statement ought not to be given in evidence in such circumstances, and the reaction of the accused ought likewise to be excluded unless it could be understood without reference to what the co-accused had said (e.g., where the accused went on to make a full confession).

The practice of the police is now regulated by PACE Code C, para. 16.4 of which provides that, where, after a person has been charged or informed that he may be prosecuted, a police officer wishes to bring to his notice a statement made by, or the content of an interview with, another person, he must give him a true copy of the statement or bring to his attention the content of the interview record whilst doing nothing to invite any reply or comment save to caution him. This should ensure that the only evidence of reaction on which a court is asked to rely will be a voluntary statement under caution. If the co-accused's statement is improperly read, it is likely that the statement will be excluded under the PACE 1984, s. 78, together with the accused's reaction to it, particularly if the latter cannot be made sense of without reference to the statement.

F

Section F18   Evidence of Identification

VISUAL IDENTIFICATION

F18.1   The visual identification of suspects or defendants by witnesses has long been recognised as problematic and potentially unreliable. It is easy for an honest witness to make a mistaken identification, even in some cases where the suspect is well known to him, and some evidence suggests that a confident identification is no more likely to be correct than a cautious or hesitant one. There are several possible reasons for errors of this kind. Some persons may have difficulty in distinguishing between different subjects of only moderately similar appearance, and many witnesses to crimes are able to see the perpetrators only fleetingly, often in stressful circumstances. The risk of mistaken identification may be even greater in cases where the witness is of a different race to the person he identifies, and mistakes may even be caused by a process known as unconscious transference, in which the witness confuses a face he recognises from the scene of the crime (perhaps that of an innocent bystander) with that of the offender. Such problems may then be compounded by the understandable, but often misguided, eagerness of many witnesses to 'help the police' by making a positive identification.

The Criminal Law Revision Committee asserted in its *Eleventh Report: Evidence (General)* (1972), Cmnd 4991, that cases of mistaken identification constituted 'by far the greatest cause of actual or possible wrong convictions'. Much has been done since then to reduce the risks. In particular, three safeguards are now in place. The first can now be found in PACE Code D (see **appendix 1**). The procedures prescribed by Code D are primarily designed to test a witness's ability to identify, under controlled conditions, any suspect he may claim to have seen or recognised on a previous occasion. They also require witnesses to provide the police with descriptions of any offenders etc. they claim to have seen, so that any subsequent identification can be compared with the original description. Failure to comply with Code D procedures must be taken into account by a court and may result in the exclusion of tainted evidence. See **F18.4**.

The other safeguards apply at the trial stage. The Court of Appeal in *Turnbull* [1977] QB 224 (see **F18.9**) prescribed rules to guide judges faced with contested visual identification evidence. These guidelines must also be taken into account by magistrates' courts. Finally, in trials on indictment at least, the prosecution will not invite witnesses to identify the accused for the first time in court: as to this rule against 'dock identification', see **F18.6**.

Identification Evidence and Identification Issues

F18.2   It is important to distinguish between identification evidence and evidence which incriminates by other means. A mere description of the culprit or his clothing is not identification evidence, even if it closely matches the appearance or clothing of the defendant (*Gayle* [1999] 2 Cr App R 130). Nor is it identification evidence where the witness states that the culprit was the driver of a particular vehicle, or the companion of another person, whose own identification is not in dispute (*White* [2000] All ER (D) 602). If there is no identification evidence, the *Turnbull* guidelines do not apply: see for example *M* [2013] EWCA Crim 1311, where the issue was not whether the witness had correctly identified D at the scene but whether D had been an offender or a victim. A witness who has made or who may be able to make an identification should be invited to take part in a Code D identification parade or other identification procedure if the police have a known suspect available (Code D, para. 3.12); but inability to make an identification need not prevent the witness giving other evidence that might incriminate the accused, such as a description of the offence or offender (*George* [2002] EWCA Crim 1923).

If the accuracy of a purported identification (as opposed to the honesty of the accusing witness) is not in issue, then neither the *Turnbull* guidelines nor Code D will need to be considered. In such cases any attempt to apply the *Turnbull* guidelines would merely serve to confuse the jury by focusing their attention on the wrong issue (*Courtnell* [1990] Crim LR 115; *Cape* [1996] 1 Cr App R 191; *Panesar* [2007] EWCA Crim 2510). If, for example, the witness claims to have known the accused well and for many years and to have observed him at close range in conditions of perfect visibility for several minutes, or to have conversed with him in the same room, it is unlikely that any identification issue could arise. **F18.3**

On the other hand, identification issues may sometimes arise, even where the witness claims to have recognised the suspect or accused as someone already well known to him, and they are not necessarily excluded even where the principal line of defence involves an attack on the honesty or truthfulness of the witness. This can be seen in *Conway* (1990) 91 Cr App R 143. Two witnesses claimed to have recognised C as the man responsible for a stabbing and he was arrested. He denied that he knew either of the witnesses and asked to be put on an identification parade, but the police took the view that this was unnecessary, as C was a 'named person'. The Court of Appeal held this to be wrong: identification became an issue as soon as C questioned the witnesses' ability to recognise him, and the identification procedures laid down in Code D should have been followed. By the same token, there would have been an identification issue at trial and the *Turnbull* guidelines would have been applicable.

The general rule, therefore, is that an appropriate *Turnbull* warning should be given, even in cases of alleged recognition. In *Beckford v The Queen* (1993) 97 Cr App R 409, a witness claimed to have recognised B and others as they committed the alleged offence. He knew them well. The defence alleged that his evidence was wilfully false, but the Privy Council nevertheless held that there was also a possibility of genuine mistake. The witness had been 500 feet from the scene of the crime, and the closest he had come to the perpetrators was 120 feet. Mistakes can be made at such distances, even where known acquaintances are involved, and it was held that a *Turnbull* direction should have been given. See also *Bentley* [1991] Crim LR 620, *Bowden* [1993] Crim LR 379, *Giga* [2007] EWCA Crim 345 and *Livingstone v The Queen* [2012] UKPC 36. It does not follow, however, that a Code D identification procedure need be held in such cases, because such a procedure will often be considered to serve no useful purpose in a 'recognition' case (see further **D1.128**).

Dealing at Trial with Breaches of PACE Code D

As with the other codes of practice issued under the PACE 1984, breaches of Code D do not inevitably lead to the exclusion of evidence that may be tainted by the breach (*Khan* [1997] Crim LR 584; *McEvoy* [1997] Crim LR 887; *Selwyn* [2012] EWCA Crim 2968), but it is essential that the trial court or judge determines whether any alleged breaches have occurred, and whether they may have caused any prejudice to the accused (*Grannell* (1989) 90 Cr App R 149; *Ryan* [1992] Crim LR 187; *Quinn* [1995] 1 Cr App R 480; *Hickin* [1996] Crim LR 584). In *Beveridge* (1987) 85 Cr App R 255, the Court of Appeal stated that the determination of such facts can usually be accomplished without the need for a trial within a trial, but this cannot be an absolute rule. The holding of a trial within a trial was not, for example, criticised in *Willoughby* [1999] 2 Cr App R 82. **F18.4**

If it is clear that no prejudice resulted from a breach or failure to observe Code D then there will be no case for excluding the evidence. If, on the other hand, some prejudice may have been caused, it will be necessary to determine, under the PACE 1984, s. 78, whether the adverse effect would be such that justice requires the evidence to be excluded. Cases will, to a large extent, turn on their own facts. A trial court or judge must give reasons for any decision to admit identification evidence obtained in breach of Code D (*Allen* [1995] Crim LR 643).

F18.5 Identification evidence will usually be excluded where important provisions have been flouted. In *Nagah* [1991] Crim LR 55, N's conviction was quashed after evidence had been admitted at his trial of a deliberately staged encounter outside the police station, in which he had been confronted by the identifying witness as he left, after having being told that there was insufficient evidence to charge him. He had previously agreed to stand on an identification parade, but this was never held. See also *Finley* [1993] Crim LR 50, *Gall* (1989) 90 Cr App R 64 and *Deakin* (2013) 177 JP 158.

Failure to observe the requirements of Code D (e.g., by failing to hold any kind of identification procedure where an issue of potential identification arose) may affect other forms of evidence against the accused and a careful direction to the jury may be needed, so that they fully understand the potential for prejudice caused by that breach or failure (*Forbes* [2001] AC 473 at [27]; *Preddie* [2011] EWCA Crim 312; *Gojra* [2010] EWCA Crim 1939). The jury must ordinarily be told 'that an identification procedure enables suspects to put the reliability of an eye-witness's identification to the test, that the suspect has lost the benefit of that safeguard, and that they should take account of that fact in their assessment of the whole case, giving it such weight as they think fit' (*H* [2003] EWCA Crim 174, per Potter LJ; and see also the *Crown Court Bench Book* at p. 111). Failure to comply with Code D may also give rise to issues under the ECHR, notably in cases involving covert videotaping of suspects, which may be open to challenge under Article 8 if not performed in strict accordance with domestic law (*Perry v UK* (2004) 39 EHRR 76).

Dock Identification

F18.6 The term 'dock identification' is best understood as referring to the identification of an accused for the first time during the course of the trial itself (i.e. by a witness who has not previously named him or identified him by means of a Code D identification procedure). Such evidence has long been considered potentially unreliable (*Edwards v The Queen* [2006] UKPC 23), and especially so when a witness who has failed to pick out the accused at an identification parade is then invited to try to identify him in court (*Holland v HM Advocate* [2005] HRLR 25; *Lawrence v The Queen* [2014] UKPC 2), but the dangers otherwise inherent in a dock identification (as defined above) may not be present where the witness says, 'the person whom I have *already* identified to the police as the person who committed the crime is the person who stands in the dock' (*France v The Queen* [2012] UKPC 28).

The A-G and the DPP undertook in 1976 that in cases tried on indictment:

> The [prosecution]...will not invite a witness to identity, who has not previously identified the accused at an identity parade, to make a dock identification unless the witness's attendance at a parade was unnecessary or impracticable, or there are exceptional circumstances.

A judge would ordinarily prohibit any such identification during the course of a trial on indictment (*Fergus* (1993) 98 Cr App R 313), but different considerations may apply in respect of minor summary offences, such as road traffic offences, where the holding of an identity parade or similar Code D procedure may well be impracticable. In *Barnes v Chief Constable of Durham* [1997] 2 Cr App R 505, Popplewell J suggested that the rule of practice that applies to trials on indictment 'has singularly little application to the everyday activities of the magistrates' court'. In *Karia v DPP* (2002) 166 JP 753, Stanley Burnton J adopted a more cautious stance, observing merely that: 'It cannot be sensible to require identity parades to be held in all motoring cases, in circumstances where there is no reason to believe that identity is in issue', but these rulings appear to conflict with *North Yorkshire Trading Standards Department v Williams* (1995) 159 JP 383 in which the Divisional Court rejected the notion that less strict identification rules should apply in respect of summary offences. See further T. Watkin, 'In the Dock — an Overview of Decisions of the High Court on Dock Identifications in the Magistrates' Court' [2003] Crim LR 463 and *Smith v DPP* [2008] EWHC 771 (Admin). Whether dock identification infringes the right to a fair trial under the ECHR, Article 6, depends on all the circumstances of the case. Such a procedure cannot be said to be unfair *per se* (*Holland v HM Advocate* [2005] HRLR 25; *Young v The State* [2008] UKPC 27; *Tido v The Queen* [2012] 1 WLR 115).

There is a danger that a witness may sometimes make a dock identification even where none **F18.7** has been solicited by the prosecution. If that happens (as in *Thomas* [1994] Crim LR 128), it may be necessary for the trial judge to warn the jury against giving it any weight or credence. It would not suffice merely to observe (as did the trial judge in *Thomas*) that an identification of that sort would not ordinarily take place.

There is also a risk, if the accused is not in custody and no identification has previously been arranged, that a witness will identify him as he arrives or waits outside the court. In *Tiplady* (1995) 159 JP 548, the prosecution actually arranged for a group identification in the foyer of the court building as the accused arrived and this evidence was properly admitted at trial. It is unlikely, however, that the circumstances of such an identification would be wholly satisfactory (especially where a considerable time has elapsed since the alleged offence), and it may prove necessary in some cases to exclude such evidence (*Martin* [1994] Crim LR 218, but cf. *Campbell* [1996] Crim LR 500).

Recognition cases, such as *Reid* [1994] Crim LR 442, are different. The Court of Appeal in *Reid* were anxious not to encourage dock identification, but saw no reason to interfere with the trial judge's decision to admit recognition evidence in that case, notwithstanding that no identification parade or group identification had been held. A *Turnbull* direction was still needed, but it was not a case in which the witness's ability to make a leisurely identification was in doubt. See also *Gardner* [2004] EWCA Crim 1639.

Pre-trial Identification: Admissibility

Where a witness can identify the accused at trial, evidence that he has previously identified him **F18.8** under controlled conditions serves to enhance his evidence by demonstrating his consistency. At common law that was all such evidence could ever do. It was admissible by way of exception to the rule against narrative but not as evidence in its own right (*Sealey v The State* [2002] UKPC 52). The CJA 2003 now provides (in s. 120(4) and (5)) that a previous statement by a witness is admissible as evidence of any matter stated of which oral evidence by him would be admissible, if the statement identifies or describes a person, object or place and while giving evidence the witness indicates that to the best of his belief he made the statement, and that to the best of his belief it states the truth. In theory this represents a significant change, but in practice it will usually make little practical difference to the way in which such evidence is perceived by the jury.

In some cases, however, pre-trial identification may be the only such evidence available, and the CJA 2003 may enable the court to rely upon it as admissible hearsay. The witness may, for example, confirm that he made an identification without being able to recall the facts in court, even after attempting to refresh his memory from his original statement (as in *Chinn* [2012] 3 All ER 502); or he may no longer be available to testify (ss. 116 and 117 at **F16.8** *et seq.*); or he may be cross-examined (perhaps as a hostile witness) as to an identification which he now denies or retracts (see s. 119 at **F7.50**; see also **F6.56**). The *Turnbull* guidelines (see **F18.9** *et seq.*) may need to be applied in such cases, perhaps in a suitably adapted form (*Chinn* at [72]–[73]).

The *Turnbull* Guidelines

In response to widespread concern over the problems posed by cases of mistaken identification, **F18.9** the Court of Appeal in *Turnbull* [1977] QB 224 laid down important guidelines for judges in trials that involve disputed identification evidence. The guidelines are also applicable, *mutatis mutandis*, in summary trials and to cases of voice identification or voice recognition (see **F18.24**), and are reproduced (with slight abridgement) below:

> First, whenever the case against an accused depends wholly or substantially on the correctness of one or more identifications of the accused which the defence alleges to be mistaken, the judge should warn the jury of the special need for caution before convicting the accused in reliance on the correctness of the identification or identifications. In addition he should instruct them as to the reason for the need for such a warning and should make some reference to the possibility that a

mistaken witness can be a convincing one and that a number of such witnesses can all be mistaken. Provided this is done in clear terms the judge need not use any particular form of words.

Secondly, the judge should direct the jury to examine closely the circumstances in which the identification by each witness came to be made. How long did the witness have the accused under observation? At what distance? In what light? Was the observation impeded in any way, as for example, by passing traffic or a press of people? Had the witness ever seen the accused before? How often? If only occasionally, had he any special reason for remembering the accused? How long elapsed between the original observation and the subsequent identification to the police? Was there any material discrepancy between the description of the accused given to the police by the witness when first seen by them and his actual appearance? If in any case, whether it is being dealt with summarily or on indictment, the prosecution have reason to believe that there is such a material discrepancy they should supply the accused or his legal advisers with particulars of the description the police were first given. In all cases if the accused asks to be given particulars of such descriptions, the prosecution should supply them. Finally, he should remind the jury of any specific weaknesses which had appeared in the identification evidence.

Recognition may be more reliable than identification of a stranger; but even when the witness is purporting to recognise someone whom he knows, the jury should be reminded that mistakes in recognition of close relatives and friends are sometimes made.

All these matters go to the quality of the identification evidence. If the quality is good and remains good at the close of the accused's case, the danger of a mistaken identification is lessened; but the poorer the quality, the greater the danger.

In our judgment when the quality is good, as for example when the identification is made after a long period of observation, or in satisfactory conditions by a relative, a neighbour, a close friend, a workmate and the like, the jury can safely be left to assess the value of the identifying evidence even though there is no other evidence to support it; provided always, however, that an adequate warning has been given about the special need for caution. Were the Courts to adjudge otherwise, affronts to justice would frequently occur....

When, in the judgment of the trial judge, the quality of the identifying evidence is poor, as for example when it depends solely on a fleeting glance or on a longer observation made in difficult conditions, the situation is very different. The judge should then withdraw the case from the jury and direct an acquittal unless there is other evidence which goes to support the correctness of the identification. This may be corroboration in the sense lawyers use that word; but it need not be so if its effect is to make the jury sure that there has been no mistaken identification....

The trial judge should identify to the jury the evidence which he adjudges is capable of supporting the evidence of identification. If there is any evidence or circumstances which the jury might think was supporting when it did not have this quality, the judge should say so.

Scope of the *Turnbull* Guidelines

F18.10   A *Turnbull* direction need not be provided unless the prosecution case depends wholly or substantially on visual identification (see *McMillan* [2005] EWCA Crim 1774 and **F18.2**), and even where such a direction is necessary no particular form of words need be used (*Mills v The Queen* [1995] 3 All ER 865; *Qadir* [1998] Crim LR 828; *France v The Queen* [2012] UKPC 28). The jury must however be warned that the direction is based on past experience (see the *Crown Court Bench Book*, chapter 7 and *Nash* [2004] EWCA Crim 2696). The absence of an adequate *Turnbull* direction, tailored to the facts of the particular case, and if necessary reiterated in respect of each defendant (*Livingstone v The Queen* [2012] UKPC 36), will usually require a conviction to be quashed as unsafe (*Beckford v The Queen* (1993) 97 Cr App R 409; *Bowden* [1993] Crim LR 379; *Farquharson v The Queen* (1993) 98 Cr App R 398), although it may be condonable if the other evidence is overwhelming (*Freemantle v The Queen* [1994] 3 All ER 225). Where the principal or sole means of defence is a challenge to the credibility of the identifying witness, there may be exceptional cases in which a full *Turnbull* warning is unnecessary or may be given more briefly than in a case where the accuracy of identification is challenged (*Shand v The Queen* [1996] 1 All ER 511; *Giga* [2007] EWCA Crim 345).

F18.11   Paying lip service to the guidelines will not be enough (*Graham* [1994] Crim LR 212), nor will it suffice to give a general warning without reference to any evidence that may support or undermine the identification, or to any circumstances that may have affected the accuracy of the witness's observation (*Reid v The Queen* [1990] 1 AC 363; *Keane* (1977) 65 Cr App R 247). In *H* [2014] EWCA Crim 420, for example, one of the grounds on which D's conviction was quashed was that the trial judge had failed to remind the jury of specific weaknesses which had appeared in the identification evidence on which the prosecution case largely depended. But a judge may properly point out that a mistaken identification (as where a witness has identified a volunteer at a parade) does not necessarily prove that the accused is innocent or that the witness is untrustworthy in other respects, especially if his view of the crime was imperfect (*Trew* [1996] Crim LR 441).

The guidelines may also need to be followed in cases involving the disputed identification of an alleged accomplice (*Bath* (1990) 154 JP 849) and an inadequate direction in respect of the evidence against one accused may render unsafe the conviction of another (*Elliott* (1986) *The Times*, 8 August 1986), although this will depend on the circumstances of the particular case.

The guidelines are not applicable to cases involving the identification of motor vehicles. The reliability of a vehicle identification may however depend, *inter alia*, on the witness having had a satisfactory opportunity to see the vehicle and on his ability to distinguish between one model and another. This should be drawn to the jury's attention (*Browning* (1991) 94 Cr App R 109).

A particularly robust *Turnbull* direction may be needed where for one reason or another the prosecution adduce hearsay evidence of identification in the form of a statement from a witness who is not available to testify at trial (*Vasco* [2012] EWCA Crim 3004).

F18.12 It was held in *Oakwell* [1978] 1 All ER 1223 that the guidelines were 'intended primarily to deal with the ghastly risk run in cases of fleeting encounters' and were not applicable to a case in which the witness may merely have been mistaken as to which person in a well identified group had struck him. In that case the judge had drawn the jury's attention to the possibility that the witness may have been momentarily unsighted, and this was held to be sufficient. *Oakwell* was followed in *Curry* [1983] Crim LR 737 and *Beckles* [1999] Crim LR 148; but in *Bowden* the Court of Appeal held that this principle was applicable only to situations in which the accused's presence at the scene of the crime is admitted. A *Turnbull* warning was accordingly held to have been necessary in *Bowden*, even though a police officer claimed to have had a long and careful look at the offender; see also *B* [2004] EWCA Crim 1481.

It does not follow from *Oakwell* that no *Turnbull* direction would ever be necessary if the accused's presence at the scene is admitted. There will be some circumstances in which it will be appropriate to give such a direction and some in which it will not (contrast *Thornton* [1995] 1 Cr App R 578 with *Slater* [1995] 1 Cr App R 584 and see also *Pattinson* [1996] 1 Cr App R 51).

The applicability of the *Turnbull* guidelines to cases of alleged recognition is discussed at **F18.9**. As the guidelines themselves explain, recognition evidence will often be more reliable than identification of a stranger, but may still be erroneous. Lord Lane CJ elaborated on this point in *Bentley* [1991] Crim LR 620:

> Many people have experienced seeing someone in the street whom they knew, only to discover that they were wrong. The expression, 'I could have sworn it was you' indicated the sort of warning which a judge should give, because that was exactly what a testifying witness did — he swore that it was the person he thought it was. But he may have been mistaken...

Supporting Evidence

F18.13 Evidence capable of supporting a disputed identification may take any admissible form, including D's bad character or previous convictions (*Dossett* [2013] EWCA Crim 710), self-incrimination and other evidence of identification. The judge must identify evidence that is capable of providing such support and warn the jury against reliance on anything that might appear supportive without really having that capability. A prior discussion between judge and counsel is strongly advisable in this context, 'if only so that the judge knows on what points counsel will seek to rely in their speeches to support or undermine the identifications and that counsel will know the judge's view as to whether any particular piece of evidence is capable of having either effect' (*Stanton* [2004] EWCA Crim 490).

Evidence of bad character may need particularly careful handling in this context. In *H*[2014] EWCA Crim 420, D was charged with a sexual offence and the jury were told of his previous convictions for sexual offences, without being told that these were the only reason for him being included in the identification parade in the first place. The jury may thus have supposed it to be an 'enormous coincidence' that the man then identified by the complainant had convictions which bore some similarity to the case before them, but it was in reality no great coincidence. His conviction was quashed.

Where a judge decides that the identification evidence in a given case is of such poor quality that he would not have left the case to the jury in the absence of supporting evidence, there is no obligation on him to warn the jury that they should not convict on the basis of the evidence of identification alone, should they reject the supporting evidence. There might be some cases where, in the light of the evidence that has unfolded, a direction of that kind might be appropriate, but it is not required as a general rule (*Ley* [2007] 1 Cr App R 325).

F18.14 Mutually Supportive Identifications   It is permissible in appropriate cases for two or more disputed identifications of the accused to be treated as mutually supportive (*Weeder* (1980) 71 Cr App R 228; *Shelton* [1981] Crim LR 776) but only if the identifications are 'of a quality that a jury can safely be left to assess' (*Weeder*). It does not matter that both witnesses may have made their identifications from the same spot (*Tyler* (1992) 96 Cr App R 332) and in some cases the identifications may relate to separate incidents (*Barnes* [1995] 2 Cr App R 491). But, even where the evidence identifying D as the perpetrator of one offence is compelling, it cannot rescue a weak identification in respect of another incident unless it is clear that each was committed by the same person (*Younas* [2012] EWCA Crim 2022).

F18.15 Self-incrimination   Disputed identification evidence can clearly be supported by an admissible confession, but careful consideration must be given to cases in which the defendant is alleged to have incriminated himself by lies or false alibis. In *Turnbull* [1977] QB 224, Lord Widgery CJ said (at p. 230):

> Care should be taken by the judge when directing the jury about the support for an identification which may be derived from the fact that they have rejected an alibi. False alibis may be put forward for many reasons; an accused, for example, who has only his own truthful evidence to rely on may stupidly fabricate an alibi and get lying witnesses to support it out of fear that his own evidence will not be enough. Further, alibi witnesses can make genuine mistakes about dates and occasions like any other witnesses can. It is only when the jury is satisfied that the sole reason for the fabrication was to deceive them and there is no other explanation for its being put forward can fabrication provide any support for identification evidence. The jury should be reminded that proving the accused has told lies about where he was at the material time does not by itself prove that he was where the identifying witness says he was.

This guidance remains valid, but the governing principles in relation to self-incrimination by false alibis or other lies, as set out by the Court of Appeal in *Lucas* [1981] QB 720, have now been held applicable in identification cases (*Goodway* [1993] 4 All ER 894). Before such lies can be regarded as supporting an identification, they must accordingly be shown to be deliberate and material; the court or jury must be able to discount any possible innocent motive for the lies and they must be proved to be lies by evidence other than the identification(s) that they are to support.

F18.16 The Accused's Silence   Lord Widgery CJ warned in *Turnbull* [1977] QB 277 that an accused's failure to testify must not be viewed as capable of supporting the evidence against him. This must now be reconsidered in the light of subsequent legislation. Under the CJPO 1994, ss. 34 to 38, the failure of the accused:

(a) to mention facts when questioned or charged which are later relied upon in his defence;
(b) to account for objects in his possession or substances or marks on his body or clothing;

(c) to account for his presence at a particular place; or

(d) to testify at his trial,

may each, in appropriate cases, entitle the court or jury to 'draw such inferences as appear proper'. They do not, in themselves, constitute evidence of guilt and should not be seen as a substitute for satisfactory identification evidence, but the absence of testimony or explanation from the accused may legitimately enable a court or jury to infer, in appropriate cases, that the prosecution evidence is correct and that the accused has no answer to it. See **F19**.

The Quality of the Witness

There is no doubt that some witnesses may be capable of providing more reliable identification **F18.17** evidence than others in the same position. A witness with perfect vision may clearly be expected to do better than a myopic witness who has lost his spectacles. More controversial is the suggestion that police officers may, by virtue of their training, be more observant than ordinary witnesses, or at least better at noting features or details that may be significant. That suggestion was rejected by the Privy Council in *Reid v The Queen* [1990] AC 363, but was subsequently held to be quite proper by the Court of Appeal in *Ramsden* [1991] Crim LR 295, where Lord Lane CJ opined that it would be wrong for a trial judge not to direct the jury as to the potentially greater reliability of police identification. See also *Tyler* (1992) 96 Cr App R 332; *Williams* (1994) *The Times*, 7 October 1994.

Stopping a Trial Based on Inadequate Identification

The *Turnbull* guidelines require the trial judge to direct an acquittal in cases where identification **F18.18** evidence is both deficient and unsupported by sufficient alternative evidence. If necessary, the trial judge should invite the defence to make submissions to that effect (*Fergus* (1993) 98 Cr App R 313). In such cases, the Court of Appeal may quash any conviction, even though the judge's direction on the evidence was otherwise impeccable (see, e.g., *Pope* (1986) 85 Cr App R 201).

In dealing with such cases, a court must not merely apply the principles set out in *Galbraith* [1981] 2 All ER 1060 (see **D16.55** *et seq.*) but must apply what the Court of Appeal in *Richardson* [2012] EWCA Crim 639 referred to as 'an acute combination of *Galbraith* and *Turnbull*'. There is rarely any issue as to whether prosecution witnesses are attempting to tell the truth, but it may still be necessary to decide whether there is sufficient evidence on which a court or jury could properly convict (*Daley v The Queen* [1994] 1 AC 117; *Macmath* [1997] Crim LR 586). Such evidence need not, however, be particularly strong, and a case based on largely unsupported identification evidence may still be left to the jury even though the defence can point to several potential deficiencies in that evidence (*H* [2014] EWCA Crim 420).

In some cases, a witness may have qualified his identification by admitting that he was 'not quite certain', or was only '90 per cent sure'. A defendant cannot properly be convicted on qualified identification evidence alone (*George* [2002] EWCA Crim 1923; *Brown* [2011] EWCA Crim 80). But as with other kinds of weak identification evidence, a qualified identification may have a legitimate role to play alongside other, more reliable, evidence. In *Brown*, for example, the identification was not merely qualified by uncertainty but was weak in a number of other respects, having been made six years after the alleged offence. But the finding of B's fingerprints on documents strewn around the scene of the crime made up for that. The fingerprint evidence was 'devastating' and B had not been able to offer any credible explanation for it.

CCTV, VIDEO AND OTHER IMAGES

The use of photographs or security video footage in police investigations or identification pro- **F18.19** cedures is dealt with at **D1.143**. As to the importance of compliance with the procedures set out by PACE Code D in respect of pre-trial viewing of CCTV and other images, see *Deakin* (2013) 177 JP 158. What follows is concerned with the admissibility and interpretation of visual images offered as evidence at trial.

Photographic and Video Evidence

F18.20 In *A-G's Ref (No. 2 of 2002)* [2003] 1 Cr App R 321, Rose LJ summarised the correct approach
to photographic and video images (at [19]):

> ... there are ... at least four circumstances in which, subject to the judicial discretion to exclude ... and
> subject to appropriate directions in the summing-up, a jury can be invited to conclude that the
> defendant committed the offence on the basis of a photographic image from the scene of the crime:
>
> (i)   where the photographic image is sufficiently clear, the jury can compare it with the defendant
>   sitting in the dock (*Dodson & Williams* (1984) 79 Cr App R 220);
> (ii) where a witness knows the defendant sufficiently well to recognise him as the offender depicted
>   in the photographic image, he can give evidence of this (*Fowden* [1982] Crim LR 588, *Kajala
>   v Noble* (1982) 75 Cr App R 149, *Grimer* [1982] Crim LR 674, *Caldwell* (1994) 99 Cr App R
>   73 and *Blenkinsop* [1995] 1 Cr App R 7); and this may be so even if the photographic image is
>   no longer available for the jury (*Taylor v Chief Constable of Cheshire* (1987) 84 Cr App R 191);
> (iii) where a witness who does not know the defendant spends substantial time viewing and ana-
>   lysing photographic images from the scene, thereby acquiring special knowledge which the
>   jury does not have, he can give evidence of identification based on a comparison between
>   those images and a reasonably contemporary photograph of the defendant, provided that
>   the images and the photograph are available to the jury (*Clare* [1995] 2 Cr App R 333);
> (iv) a suitably qualified expert with facial mapping skills can give opinion evidence of identifica-
>   tion based on a comparison between images from the scene (whether expertly enhanced or
>   not) and a reasonably contemporary photograph of the defendant, provided the images and
>   the photograph are available for the jury (*Stockwell* (1993) 97 Cr App R 260; *Clarke* [1995]
>   2 Cr App R 425; *Hookway* [1999] Crim LR 750).

In the first kind of case, photographs or video recordings (whether originals or copies) may be
shown as real evidence and may provide the court with the equivalent of a direct view of the incident in question. A *Turnbull* direction might be wholly inappropriate in cases where these images
are clear and of high quality (*Najjar* [2014] EWCA Crim 1309) but in most cases the jury must
still be warned of the dangers of mistaken identification, and should be reminded of the need to
exercise great care when attempting to make an identification from photographs or video recordings (*Dodson*; *Blenkinsop*; *Ali* [2008] EWCA Crim 1522). If the accused has subsequently changed
his appearance it may be necessary to provide the jury with a photograph of him that is contemporaneous with the recorded images. As to the use of witness evidence to assist the jury in identifying
the offender from a photograph, see also *West* [2005] EWCA Crim 3034. In many cases, however,
the quality of security images is so poor that juries may need expert assistance. If the jury cannot
view the photo themselves and have to rely on the accuracy of a witness's identification from it,
then a *Turnbull* warning will be required (*Selwyn* [2012] EWCA Crim 2968).

Facial Mapping and Walking Gait Analysis

F18.21 Facial mapping (or photographic comparison) evidence may, in such a case, enhance the value of poor
quality images, but concerns have been expressed as to the proper scope and function of such evidence, particularly where (as in *Hookway* [1999] Crim LR 750) it is not supported by other evidence
incriminating D. Significant facial differences revealed by photographic comparison may prove that
D cannot be the person in the photograph, but where the features appear to match there is no database cataloguing the number of persons with particular facial features or measurements from which
an expert could derive any statistical analysis to explain the significance of such matches. This led the
Court of Appeal to express reservations in *Gray* [2003] EWCA Crim 1001, but in *Gardner* [2004]
EWCA Crim 1639 the Court rejected the suggestion that expert witnesses should be prevented from
expressing opinions as to probabilities based on facial mapping evidence; and in *Ciantar* [2005]
EWCA Crim 3559, it rejected arguments that expert evidence of facial mapping should have been discounted or excluded merely because other experts had expressed doubts as to its quality and sufficiency.

F18.22 The cases on facial mapping were reviewed in *Atkins* [2010] 1 Cr App R 117, where Hughes LJ said (at [31]):

> Where a photographic comparison expert gives evidence, properly based upon study and experi-
> ence, of similarities and/or dissimilarities between a questioned photograph and a known person

(including a defendant) the expert is not disabled either by authority or principle from expressing his conclusion as to the significance of his findings, and … he may do so by use of conventional expressions, arranged in a hierarchy [e.g., 'lends limited support' or 'lends powerful support' but] we think it preferable that the expressions should not be allocated numbers [e.g., a scale of 0–5] lest that run any small risk of leading the jury to think that they represent an established numerical, that is to say measurable, scale. The expressions ought to remain simply what they are, namely forms of words used. They need to be in an ascending order if they are to mean anything at all, and if a relatively firm opinion is to be contrasted with one which is not so firm. They are, however, expressions of subjective opinion, and this must be made crystal clear to the jury charged with evaluating them.

The third of Rose LJ's examples in *A-G's Ref (No. 2 of 2002)* [2003] 1 Cr App R 321 (see **F18.20**) was considered in *Abnett* [2006] EWCA Crim 3320. A police officer, who had spent some time interviewing the appellant and repeatedly viewing CCTV footage of a robbery, together with still images from that film, was permitted to state that he was '100 per cent sure' that one of the robbers pictured was the appellant. He had no specialist training in facial mapping or any other such technique, and (with respect) it is not obvious how or why his repeated viewing of the images would have equipped him to make a significantly more reliable identification than the jury, who had access to the same footage and images. Contrast *Clare* [1995] 2 Cr App R 333, in which the police officer had spent hours analysing footage of crowd violence and was able (*inter alia*) to explain to the jury how the incident in question had developed.

As to the use of 'walking gait analysis' as a method of identification from CCTV video footage, see *Rafiq Mohammed* [2010] EWCA Crim 2696 and *Otway* [2011] EWCA Crim 3. As to the use of 'reverse projection evidence' for the purpose of showing that CCTV images of an offender match the height or build of a defendant, see *Barnes* [2012] EWCA Crim 1605.

Sketches and Photofits

Artist's sketches and composite images or 'photofits' (which now use computer-based E FIT or CD-FIT technology) are fundamentally different from photographs or video in that they depend on the fallible (and potentially mendacious) assertions of the witnesses who help to compile them. An image showing a bald or bearded suspect is manifestly a product of a witness's assertion that the suspect was bald or bearded, and must logically be categorised as a kind of statement, albeit one in visual form. This is now recognised in the CJA 2003, s. 115, which defines a 'statement' for the purpose of the hearsay rule as 'any representation of fact or opinion made by a person by whatever means; and it includes a representation made in a sketch, photofit or other pictorial form'. Such a statement may well be admissible in support of the witness who made it, under the CJA 2003, s. 120, or in the unavoidable absence of that witness, as provided for by s. 116 (see **F18.8**), but it is no longer possible for courts to proceed (as they did before the enactment of the CJA 2003) as if the hearsay rule has nothing to do with it.

F18.23

VOICE IDENTIFICATION

It is generally accepted that the identification of an accused from voice recognition is potentially even more difficult and unreliable than visual identification (especially when the voice is heard only over a telephone) but such evidence may still be taken into account and, where relevant voice recordings exist, expert evidence may then be adduced to help with the identification. See *Roberts* [2000] Crim LR 183, *Chenia* [2003] 2 Cr App R 83, *Davies* [2004] EWCA Crim 2521, *Robinson* [2006] 1 Cr App R 221 and *Flynn* [2008] 2 Cr App R 266.

F18.24

There is no doubt that the *Turnbull* guidelines are applicable in principle to identification by voice recognition, although it may not be necessary to include any specific warning about previous miscarriages of justice (*Phipps v DPP (Jamaica)* [2012] UKPC 24). As to the holding of 'voice identification parades' in the course of police investigations, see *Hersey* [1998] Crim LR 281 and **D1.145**.

F18.25 **Admissibility where No Recording Exists** *Myers* [2010] EWCA Crim 3173 provides an illustration of circumstances in which voice identification may be considered more reliable than usual, even though no recording existed. The identifying witness had been blind for 30 years and had learnt to 'use his ears as his eyes'. He claimed to have recognised the voice of one of two burglars as that of D, his ex-partner's son. Moreover, when the witness called out 'is that you, Daniel?' the other burglar said 'sshh' as if aware that their voices might give them away. There was other circumstantial evidence to support the identification and the conviction was upheld on appeal.

F18.26 **Admissibility where Recording Exists** If there are recordings of the offender's voice, expert evidence may be admissible on the question of whether this matches the voice of the accused. Most phoneticians use acoustic analysis techniques for this purpose, but it was held in *Robb* (1991) 93 Cr App R 161 that an expert who uses only auditory phonetic techniques (a method regarded with suspicion by other experts) may still be competent to testify. In *O'Doherty* [2003] 1 Cr App R 77, the Northern Ireland Court of Appeal ruled auditory phonetic analysis inadequate unless supported by acoustic analysis; but in *Flynn* the Court considered it 'neither possible nor desirable' to go that far. The Court in *Flynn* was however concerned as to the evidential value of non-expert voice identification, by police officers or others, and rejected the idea that by repeated listening to recordings an officer might become an 'expert ad hoc'. It offered this general guidance (at [63]–[64]):

> The increasing use … of lay listener evidence from police officers must … be treated with great caution and great care. Where the prosecution seek to rely on such evidence it is desirable that an expert should be instructed to give an independent opinion on the validity of such evidence. In addition, … great care should be taken by police officers to record the procedures taken by them which form the basis for their evidence. Whether the evidence is sufficiently probative to be admitted will depend very much on the facts of each case.

> It goes without saying that in all cases in which the prosecution rely on voice recognition evidence, whether lay listener, or expert, or both, the judge must give a very careful direction to the jury warning it of the danger of mistakes in such cases.

Flynn was considered in *Tamiz* [2010] EWCA Crim 2638, where covert recordings of incriminating conversations in Arabic, Bengali and Syhleti had been listened to by two translators, each of whom testified that they could identify the same voices in different recordings, although they did not purport to identify the voices as those of any of the appellants. There was no supporting phonetic evidence because there was no expert in phonetics who spoke or understood the languages in question, but the translators had access to many hours of good quality recordings and had already been proved right in their identification of certain other voices. An argument that it had been unfair to admit their evidence was rejected. Fairness, said the Court, involves consideration of the alternatives open to the prosecution. In this case there were none.

The jury should ordinarily be allowed to hear any admissible voice recordings for themselves, so that they may form their own judgement of the opinions expressed (*Bentum* (1989) 153 JP 538; *Flynn*) but should be warned of the dangers of relying on their own untrained ears.

DNA EVIDENCE

F18.27 DNA evidence has been used in criminal trials and investigations in England and Wales for over 20 years. The procedures involved in obtaining and evaluating such evidence have been explained by the Court of Appeal on a number of occasions, but because the science has evolved significantly over the years, some of the earlier accounts must now be read with caution. The basic principles remain unchanged, but modern techniques can now produce more precise matches and enable DNA profiles to be obtained from minute amounts of tissue. This is reflected in the guidance in *Reed* [2010] 1 Cr App R 310 and *Dlugosz* [2013] 1 Cr App R

425 (32), and also in the detailed guidance as to the uses and proper understanding of DNA evidence, techniques and terms that can be found in the Royal Statistical Society's Practitioner Guide No 2: *Assessing the Probative Value of DNA Evidence* (available at www.rss.org.uk/site/cms/contentviewarticle.asp?article=1132).

Low Template DNA   Doubts were at one time expressed as to the reliability of 'low copy number' (or LCN) DNA profiling (an ultra sensitive technique that has the potential to yield a DNA profile from sub-optimal or Low Template DNA samples that are too small to be used in a standard 'Second Generation Multiplex' (or SGM,) profiling test). The use of LCN DNA was temporarily suspended following the Omagh bombing trial (*Hoey* [2007] NICC 49) but a review commissioned by the Forensic Regulator concluded that the process used for obtaining LCN DNA was 'robust and fit for its purpose' and this view was endorsed both in *Reed* and in *Broughton* [2010] EWCA Crim 549. After extensive consideration of expert views, the Court in *Reed* concluded that the underlying science for Low Template DNA analysis is sufficiently reliable to produce profiles, provided the material analysed is above the 'stochastic threshold' of between 100 and 200 picograms. Therefore: **F18.28**

> A challenge to the validity of the method of analysing Low Template DNA by the LCN process should no longer be permitted at trials where the quantity of DNA analysed is above the stochastic threshold of 100–200 picograms in the absence of new scientific evidence. A challenge should only be permitted where new scientific evidence is properly put before the trial court at a Plea and Case Management Hearing (PCMH) or other pre-trial hearing for detailed consideration by the judge.

The Court noted that, under the CrimPR, r. 33.3(1)(f) and (g), an expert witness must identify where there is a range of opinion on the matters dealt with in his report. In such a case, the expert must summarise the scope of opinion and give reasons for his own opinion. If he cannot give his opinion without qualification, he must state the qualification. Under r. 33.6(2), the court has power to direct experts to discuss expert issues in the proceedings and prepare a statement for the court of the matters on which they agree and disagree giving their reasons. The Court of Appeal said (at [131]) that in DNA cases:

(i) It is particularly important to ensure that the obligation under r. 33.3(1)(f) and (g) is followed and also that, where propositions are to be advanced as part of an evaluative opinion…, that each proposition is spelt out with precision in the expert report.

(ii) Expert reports must, after each has been served, be carefully analysed by the parties. Where a disagreement is identified, this must be brought to the attention of the court.

(iii) If the reports are available before the PCMH, this should be done at the PCMH; but if the reports have not been served by all parties at the time of the PCMH (as may often be the case), it is the duty of the Crown and the defence to ensure that the necessary steps are taken to bring the matter back before the judge where a disagreement is identified.

(iv) It will then in the ordinary case be necessary for the judge to exercise his powers under r.33.6 and make an order for the provision of a statement.

(v) We would anticipate, even in such a case, that… much of the science relating to DNA will be common ground. The experts should be able to set out in the statement under r. 33.6 in clear terms for use at the trial the basic science that is agreed, in so far as it is not contained in one of the reports. The experts must then identify with precision what is in dispute — for example, the match probability, the interpretation of the electrophoretograms or the evaluative opinion that is to be given.

(vi) If the order as to the provision of the statement under r. 33.6 is not observed and in the absence of a good reason, then the trial judge should consider carefully whether to exercise the power to refuse permission to the party whose expert is in default to call that expert to give evidence. In many cases, the judge may well exercise that power. A failure to find time for a meeting because of commitments to other matters, a common problem with many experts as was evident in this appeal, is not to be treated as a good reason.

Partial DNA Profiles and Mixed Samples   As to the presentation and evaluation of evidence of partial or incomplete DNA profiles, see *Bates* [2006] EWCA Crim 1395, in which Moore-Bick LJ said (at [30]): **F18.29**

> We can see no reason why partial profile DNA evidence should not be admissible provided that the jury are made aware of its inherent limitations and are given a sufficient explanation to enable them to evaluate it. There may be cases where . . . the judge would consider its probative value to be minimal and decide to exclude the evidence in the exercise of his discretion, but this gives rise to no new question of principle and can be left for decision on a case by case basis.

'Mixed samples' involve DNA material from more than one person. There may be one major profile and one or more minor and incomplete ones. In rape cases, for example, the DNA of the complainant may be mixed with DNA that is alleged to be that of the accused, and perhaps also with traces of DNA from a third person, as is likely where, for example, clothing is examined. Mixed samples may be more difficult to evaluate, particularly where LCN profiling has to be employed. One difficulty is that elements of one incomplete profile may overlap with elements of another and it may be unclear how many individuals have contributed to the DNA material in the sample. See further **F18.32**.

F18.30 **Evaluating DNA Matches** Where a person's DNA profile is found to match that of a crime sample, the significance of that match must be evaluated. It may first be necessary to ascertain the likelihood that the matching profiles do indeed have a common source. The statistical assessment may be conducted by one of two methods. The first expresses the match as a frequency (the 'match probability' or 'random occurrence ratio') which is the familiar 1 in x number (e.g., 1 in a billion). The second, favoured by many scientists, but arguably more difficult for juries to understand, calculates the 'likelihood ratio' (e.g., a given DNA profile is a billion times more likely to be found if it originated from Y as opposed to a person unrelated to Y). In either method, the expert computes the weight of the evidence by comparison with random members of the general population unless instructed differently. If, however, there is a reasonable possibility that a relative (e.g., a brother) is the source, an alternative calculation based on that possibility may need to be put before the jury (*Watters* [2000] EWCA Crim 89).

In *Doheny* [1997] 1 Cr App R 369, the Court of Appeal held that where D's DNA profile is alleged to match that of the crime stain:

> The expert should not be asked his opinion on the likelihood that it was the defendant who left the crime stain, nor when giving evidence should he use terminology which may lead the jury to believe that he is expressing such an opinion . . . . Provided he has the necessary data and statistical expertise, it may be appropriate for him to say how many people with the matching characteristics are likely to be found in the United Kingdom or perhaps in a more limited relevant subgroup such as, for instance, the Caucasian sexually active males in the Manchester area).

This contrasts with some other forensic disciplines (such as facial mapping or handwriting analysis) where experts are sometimes permitted to express personal conclusions regarding identity.

Potential interpretational pitfalls must be avoided. The notorious 'prosecutor's fallacy' typically involves confusing the random occurrence ratio with the probability of innocence. The odds against a randomly selected individual matching a DNA profile obtained from the crime stain might be estimated in a given case at a billion to one but, if the only evidence against D is a match between his DNA profile and that of the crime stain, one cannot possibly conclude from this that the odds against him being innocent are a billion to one. See *Deen* (1994) *The Times*, 10 January 1994 and *Gordon* [1995] 1 Cr App R 290. To draw a simple analogy, it may be that only one person in 1000 wears size 14 shoes, but even if D and the offender each wears size 14 shoes that does not mean there is only one chance in 1000 of D being innocent. There may indeed be other suspects, each of whom wears size 14 shoes.

F18.31 Evidence of DNA profiling will usually be supported or contradicted by other evidence (e.g., alibi evidence or a confession) and its value can be assessed only in conjunction with this other evidence (on which a DNA expert will not be competent to express an opinion). It is for the court or jury to assess the totality of the evidence. As Phillips LJ explained in *Doheny*:

> If one person in a million has a DNA profile which matches that obtained from the crime stain, then the suspect will be 1 of perhaps 26 men in the United Kingdom who share that characteristic. If no fact is known about the defendant, other than that he was in the United Kingdom at the time

of the crime, the DNA evidence tells us no more than that there is statistical probability that he was the criminal of 1 in 26. The significance of the DNA evidence will depend critically upon what else is known about the suspect. If he has a convincing alibi at the other end of England at the time of the crime, it will appear highly improbable that he can have been responsible for the crime, despite his matching DNA profile. If, however, he was near the scene of the crime when it was committed, or has been identified as a suspect because of other evidence which suggests that he may have been responsible for the crime, the DNA evidence becomes very significant.

When evaluating such evidence, juries must be directed to use their common sense and knowledge of the world. They should not (in the absence of special circumstances) be invited to undertake complex Bayesian calculations. Inviting juries to use Bayes' Theorem when much of the evidence cannot be assigned a meaningful statistical value is 'a recipe for confusion, misunderstanding and misjudgment' (*Adams (No. 2)* [1998] 1 Cr App R 377 at p. 384).

Even where there is no dispute as to the source of the DNA sample in question (as where the defence concede that it was left by D), it may not necessarily prove his guilt. The defence may offer an 'innocent explanation' for even the most intimate DNA match (cf. *Powell* [1996] 1 Cr App R 31) and this would need to be disproved before D can be convicted.

In *Ogden* [2013] EWCA Crim 1294, DNA extracted from blood found on a scarf at the scene of a burglary was the only evidence linking D with the crime, but, as the Court of Appeal explained:

> It was not possible to date the DNA. It was therefore possible that another person had carried the scarf to the scene of the burglary, the defendant's DNA already being on it. It was not possible either to say how the DNA came to be on the scarf, whether it was by direct contact with somebody or by airborne droplets. There was no independent evidence that the burglar had cut himself on the window.

A further problem was the scarf itself had been accidentally destroyed and a second blood stain found on it had never been tested. In those circumstances, said the Court, a submission of no case to answer ought to have been accepted. See also *Grant* [2008] EWCA Crim 1890.

Presenting Evidence from Mixed or Incomplete Profiles   The difficulties that may arise when evaluating mixed samples were considered in *Dlugosz* [2013] 1 Cr App R 425 (32). The Court of Appeal considered three conjoined appeals, each of which raised issues as to the evaluation of low template and mixed profile DNA evidence, and as to the way in which such evidence should be presented in court. **F18.32**

In each of the appeals, it was argued that, unless statistical evidence of the relevant DNA match probability could be given, then evaluative opinion ('this lends substantial support' etc.) should not be admitted either, because (so the argument went) the jury would otherwise lack any firm basis on which to evaluate the significance of the evidence given. In the absence of such statistical evidence, expert witnesses should be confined to stating whether the defendant could or could not have contributed to the relevant sample.

The Court rejected this argument, citing *Atkins* [2010] 1 Cr App R 117, *Reed* [2010] 1 Cr App R 310 and *Weller* [2010] EWCA Crim 1085 as authority to the contrary. Nor would the Court accept that an expert should be permitted to provide an evaluative opinion only if he is able to use a hierarchy or sliding scale of support (as in *Atkins*). In determining the admissibility of any expert evidence, a court must always be satisfied that there is a sufficiently reliable scientific basis for the evidence to be admitted; but (at [14] and [28]):

> ... an expert is not bound to express an evaluative opinion by reference to the hierarchy; he can use other phrases. The real significance of the expert's inability to use the hierarchy might be that it is indicative of the lack of a proper basis on which to express an opinion. In our view, it can be no more than that. It is a matter to be taken into account in an assessment of whether there is a sufficiently reliable scientific basis for such an evaluative opinion to be given.....

> ... provided the conclusions from the analysis of a mixed profile are supported by detailed evidence in the form of a report of the experience relied on and the particular features of the mixed profile which make it possible to give an evaluative opinion in the circumstances of the particular case,

such an opinion is, in principle, admissible, even though there is presently no statistical basis to provide a random match probability and the sliding scale cannot be used.

See also *Thomas* [2011] EWCA Crim 1295.

F18.33 **Forensic Examination Record** Experts may use technicians to assist in carrying out their forensic examinations. This must be disclosed either in the body of the expert's statement or in an accompanying exhibit referred to as a Forensic Examination Record (FER). It is essential that admissible evidence is before the court as to each stage of the process by which the DNA profiles were produced and the match obtained. Thus, evidence from an expert who has compared DNA profiles must be supported by admissible evidence as to the primary facts, i.e. the procedures by which those profiles were obtained and the sources of the samples themselves (*Loveridge* [2001] EWCA Crim 734). The CJA 2003, s. 127, may be of assistance here (see **F10.31**).

Use of Improperly Retained DNA Material or Profiles

F18.34 The PACE 1984, s. 63T(2), provides that where fingerprints, DNA profiles, footwear impressions or other samples ought to have been destroyed in accordance with ss. 63D, 63R or 63S of the Act, that material must not thereafter be used:

(a) in evidence against the person to whom the material relates, or
(b) for the purposes of the investigation of any offence.

It follows that the original material is inadmissible as prosecution evidence, but s. 63T(2) does not specifically deal with the admissibility of any fresh specimens or prints that may have been taken from a suspect once he has been identified by unlawfully retained material. Such a case would raise issues similar to those considered by the House of Lords in *A-G's Ref (No. 3 of 1999)* [2001] 2 AC 91, in which it was held that the unlawful retention and use of such material during the investigation did not preclude the admission of fresh samples (or other evidence) taken from D after he had been identified, although such evidence would be subject to possible discretionary exclusion under the PACE 1984, s. 78 (see **F2.28** *et seq.*).

FINGERPRINTS AND BODY OR FOOTWEAR IMPRESSIONS

Fingerprints

F18.35 Fingerprint evidence should be presented by a qualified expert, with appropriate experience in the examination and comparison of such evidence (*Barnes* [2005] EWCA Crim 1158). Police forces do not recognise the competence of those who have obtained their qualifications overseas; but it is for a judge to decide whether a person is a competent expert, not the police (*Smith* [2011] 2 Cr App R 174 at [61]). Properly presented fingerprint evidence may provide sufficient identification, even if unsupported by other evidence, but the accused must be linked to the relevant prints by admissible evidence (*Chappell v DPP* (1988) 89 Cr App R 82). In *Buckley* (1999) 163 JP 561, Rose LJ said:

> Fingerprint evidence, like any other evidence, is admissible ... if it tends to prove the guilt of the accused. It may so tend, even if there are only a few similar ridge characteristics, but it may, in such a case, have little weight. It may be excluded in the exercise of judicial discretion, if its prejudicial effect outweighs its probative value ....

He added that courts or judges would have to consider the experience and expertise of the witness presenting it, the number of similar ridge characteristics identified, the presence of any dissimilar characteristics, the size of the crime print (a given number of matches in a fragment of a print may be more compelling than a similar number in a complete print) and the quality and clarity of that print (including any evidence of injury to the person who left the print, and any smearing or contamination of the print). There is no longer any support for the old '16 point standard'. The latest guidelines on fingerprint analysis emphasise the primacy of subjective evaluation when comparing prints, and do not rely on any particular number of matching characteristics. Where fingerprint experts disagree as to points of similarity, the judge must make it clear that any dissimilarity between the accused's prints and those from the crime scene must suffice to show that he could not have left those prints.

Footprints and Footwear Impressions

A clear dissimilarity between a footprint from a crime scene and one taken from the accused **F18.36** may similarly establish his innocence, but the converse is not true: even if footprints appear to match exactly this can at most place him within a given group of individuals who could have left the crime scene prints.

Much the same is true of footwear impressions. In *T (footwear mark evidence)* [2011] 1 Cr App R 85 the Court of Appeal warned that there was no sufficiently reliable data on which an expert witness could purport to offer any kind of scientific or statistical assessment as to whether footwear impressions had been left by the accused:

> An attempt to assess the degrees of probability where footwear could have made a mark based on figures relating to distribution is inherently unreliable and gives rise to a verisimilitude of mathematical probability based on data where it is not possible to build that data in a way that enables this to be done; none in truth exists…We are satisfied that in the area of footwear evidence, no attempt can realistically be made in the generality of cases to use a formula to calculate the probabilities. The practice has no sound basis….

> An opinion that a shoe 'could have made the mark' is not in our view the same as saying that 'there was moderate [scientific] support for the prosecution case'. The use of the term 'could have made' is a more precise statement of the evidence; it enables a jury better to understand the true nature of the evidence than the more opaque phrase 'moderate scientific support'.

> However there are cases where it would not be right to confine an examiner (where there are solely class characteristics) to opining on whether the mark could or could not have been made. There may be factors that enable him to go further than 'could have made' and express, on the basis of such factors, a more definite evaluative opinion. It would not be appropriate for us to express a view on the factors which would properly enable an examiner to express a more definitive evaluative opinion, but they would certainly include an unusual size or pattern.

> However, it is important to emphasise that the examiner is giving his opinion on the matters within his expertise—namely the footwear, the marks and, if relevant, scenes of crime evidence; it is not his function to evaluate the other evidence in the case.

Ear-prints

Some doubts surround the use of ear-print evidence as a result of its role in the gross miscarriage **F18.37** of justice that occurred in *Dallagher* [2003] 1 Cr App R 12, where following the quashing of D's conviction for murder the ear-print evidence on which he had been convicted was utterly discredited at his retrial. But ear-print evidence may still have its uses. In *Kempster (No. 2)* [2008] 2 Cr App R 19 the Court of Appeal concluded:

> Ear-print comparison is capable of providing information which could identify the person who has left an ear-print on a surface. That is certainly the case where minutiae can be identified and matched. Where the only information comes from the gross features, we do not understand [the experts] to say that no match can ever be made, but there is likely to be less confidence in such a match because of the flexibility of the ear and the uncertainty of the pressure which will have been applied at the relevant time.

> On the basis of the evidence that we have heard, we are of the view that the latter can only be the case where the gross features truly provide a precise match. We have no doubt that evidence of those experienced in comparing ear-prints is capable of being relevant and admissible. The question in each case will be whether it is probative. In the present case…we are struck by the gross similarity of the shape and size of the ear-prints used for the comparison, and by the close similarity of the notch and the nodule on each. This, in our view, establishes that the ear-print at the scene is consistent with having been left by the appellant. But having examined the comparisons of the gross features, it is also apparent to us that they do not provide a precise match. The differences may well be explicable by differences in pressure, or movement, but the extent of the mismatch is such as to lead us to the conclusion that it could not be relied on by itself as justifying a verdict of guilty.

Section F19   Inferences from Silence and the Non-production of Evidence

THE RIGHT TO SILENCE

F19.1 An accused person in a criminal trial has traditionally been accorded a 'right to silence', sometimes termed a privilege against self-incrimination. These concepts are not specifically mentioned in the rights guaranteed by the ECHR, Article 6, but it has been held that they constitute 'generally recognised international standards which lie at the heart of the notion of a fair procedure under Article 6' (*Murray v UK* (1996) 22 EHRR 29; *Saunders v UK* (1997) 23 EHRR 313). Although the right is said in *Murray* not to be an absolute right, the extent to which the provisions of the CJPO 1994, ss. 34 to 38, operate consistently with the right to a fair trial is still a matter of some debate.

Aspects of the right to silence which are recognised in domestic law are that the accused is not a compellable witness at trial (see **F4.10**) and that he is under no general duty to assist the police with their inquiries (*Rice v Connolly* [1966] 2 QB 414). In recent years it has become fashionable to confer statutory powers upon certain individuals charged with the duty of inquiring into various commercial or financial activities by virtue of which a person who refuses to answer their questions incurs a penalty. In *Saunders v UK*, the ECtHR held that the right to a fair trial was contravened where evidence obtained by these methods was used at trial. The YJCEA 1999, s. 59 and sch. 3, respond to the decision in *Saunders v UK* by restricting the use which can be made of evidence obtained under compulsion under a variety of statutory provisions including the Companies Act 1985, s. 434 (the provision in issue in *Saunders v UK*: see **F9.46**). The powers of investigation themselves are not affected: only the use of evidence obtained under them. The effect of the amendments to s. 434 and to other legislation granting similar powers is that, in criminal proceedings, the prosecution will not be able to adduce evidence, or put questions, about the accused's answers to inspectors conducting an investigation using their powers of compulsion unless the evidence is first adduced, or a question asked, by or on behalf of the accused in the proceedings.

F19.2 At common law, the right to silence was supplemented by a further right: no inferences were generally permitted to be drawn from the exercise of the right to silence either by a suspect under investigation or by an accused person at his trial. This right has been substantially eroded by the CJPO 1994, ss. 34 to 38, which specify the circumstances in which adverse inferences may be drawn from the exercise of the primary right. Where the statutory scheme does not apply, the common-law rule still applies (*McGarry* [1999] 3 All ER 805 and **F19.33**). Where the statutory scheme comes into play, the court is under an obligation to ensure that the jury are properly directed regarding the limited inferences which can be drawn (*Condron v UK* (2001) 31 EHRR 1). In *Condron v UK*, the ECtHR accepted that the right to silence could not of itself prevent the accused's silence, in cases which clearly call for an explanation by him, being taken into account in assessing the persuasiveness of the prosecution evidence, but also stressed that a fair procedure (under Article 6) required 'particular caution' on the part of a domestic court before invoking the accused's silence against him. Whether the statutory scheme, as supplemented by the decisions of domestic courts, fulfils this requirement is a matter that is likely to continue to figure in criminal appeals.

OUT-OF-COURT SILENCE AT COMMON LAW

Accused and Accuser on 'even terms'

The conduct of the accused when an accusation is made against him may form the basis of an **F19.3**
inference that he accepts the accusation (see **F17.99**). In the authorities that follow, it was the
silence of the accused which was relied upon as the basis for such an inference. The CJPO 1994,
s. 34(5) (see **F19.10**), makes it clear that insofar as these authorities permit inferences to be
drawn they remain good law. Even if none of the statutory inferences is in play, therefore, the
trial judge needs to have the possibility of a common-law inference in mind before resorting to
the standard direction (in accordance with *McGarry* [1999] 3 All ER 805: see **F19.33**) that no
inference should be drawn.

In *Norton* [1910] 2 KB 496 it was accepted that the silence of the accused 'on an occasion which **F19.4**
demanded an answer' might be conduct from which an inference of acknowledgement might
be drawn. In *Mitchell* (1892) 17 Cox CC 503, Cave J described more fully the circumstances
in which silence in the face of an accusation might be tantamount to an admission of guilt. He
said (at p. 508):

> Now the whole admissibility of statements of this kind rests upon the consideration that if a charge
> is made against a person in that person's presence it is reasonable to expect that he or she will imme-
> diately deny it, and that the absence of such a denial is some evidence of an admission on the part
> of the person charged, and of the truth of the charge. Undoubtedly, when persons are speaking on
> even terms, and a charge is made, and the person charged says nothing, and expresses no indigna-
> tion, and does nothing to repel the charge, that is some evidence to show that he admits the charge
> to be true.

It follows that silence does not constitute an acknowledgement of guilt if the circumstances
are such that a reasonable person would not be expected to counter the allegation. In *Mitchell*
the accusation was made by a woman on her deathbed. M and her solicitor were present to
hear the statement, which was recorded by a magistrate for use at M's trial for manslaughter.
The statement proved to be inadmissible either as a dying declaration or a deposition, and the
prosecution sought instead to admit the accusation as a statement made in M's presence. Cave
J refused the application, holding that it would be 'monstrous' to say that, because M had not
'started up and denied' the charge, she must have accepted it. In all the circumstances, including the woman's condition, the formality of the proceedings, and the presence of a solicitor to
represent M's interests, it was unreasonable to expect any response from M.

Mitchell was approved by the Privy Council in *Parkes v The Queen* [1976] 3 All ER 380. A girl
was stabbed to death, and P was charged with her murder. The girl's mother gave evidence that,
on finding her daughter injured, she immediately accused P, who made no reply. When she
threatened to detain him until the police arrived, he tried to stab her. It was held that P's reactions to the accusations, including his silence, were matters to be taken into account by the jury
in deciding whether P had committed the offence charged. It is not entirely clear whether the
outcome would have been the same had silence alone been relied on as evidence of guilt, for the
Board made a particular point of noting that P's reaction was 'not one of mere silence', but it is
submitted that the difference is that mere silence might be entitled to less weight than silence
coupled with positive conduct, depending on the circumstances.

Where silence may be attributable to a variety of factors it is for the jury to decide what inference **F19.5**
to draw. In *Coll* [2005] EWCA Crim 3675, C was attending to the wounds of the dying victim
when her co-accused allegedly made a remark suggesting that C should offer to be a witness 'so
they can't tell we did it'. The failure of C to react adversely to the use of 'we' rather than 'I' (her
defence being that the co-accused alone was responsible) was held to have been properly left to
the jury, along with C's explanation that she was not listening properly and was in shock. See

also *O* [2005] EWCA Crim 3082, where the accused's acquiescence while his friend gave a racial motive for an attack constituted an admission (see **F17.101**).

Accusations by or in the Presence of Police Officers

F19.6   It is not clear whether the principles stated above apply to accusations by or in the presence of police officers. In *Hall v The Queen* [1971] 1 All ER 322, H was charged jointly with T and G with unlawful possession of drugs. Premises occupied by the three had been searched by the police in H's absence and a quantity of drugs found in a bag which T said belonged to H. Shortly afterwards the police brought H to the premises, where he was told of the allegation made by T. H, who had not been cautioned, said nothing. It was held that the principle that a person is entitled to refrain from answering a question put to him for the purpose of discovering whether he has committed a crime meant that, 'exceptional circumstances' apart, 'silence alone on being informed by a police officer that someone else has made an accusation against him cannot give rise to an inference that the person to whom this information is communicated accepts the truth of the accusation'. The fact that H was not under caution was irrelevant as the 'caution merely serves to remind the accused of a right which he already possesses at common law. The fact that in a particular case he has not been reminded of it is no ground for inferring that his silence was not in exercise of that right, but was an acknowledgement of the truth of the accusation.'

F19.7   The law stated in *Hall* must now be read subject to the CJPO 1994, ss. 34, 36 and 37 (see **F19.10** *et seq.*). Silence in the face of the sort of questioning to which those provisions apply may clearly give rise to specific adverse inferences arising out of the failure to mention facts subsequently relied upon (s. 34) or to account for various matters including the possession of incriminating material and presence at the scene of an offence (ss. 36 and 37); the caution and warnings to be given to suspects makes this clear (PACE Code C, paras. 10.5 and 10.10 and annex C).

The decision in *Hall*, however, would seem still to be authority for the principle that a suspect, whether cautioned or not, should not be regarded as accepting the truth of a charge which he does not deny. In *Chandler* [1976] 3 All ER 105, however, the Court of Appeal expressed reservations about the correctness of the law as stated in *Hall*, regarding it as in conflict with the general rule laid down in *Christie* [1914] AC 545 (see **F17.99**), a criticism reiterated in *Raviraj* (1986) 85 Cr App R 93. The right of a person not to incriminate himself was well accepted, but it 'does not follow that a failure to answer an accusation or question when an answer could reasonably be expected may not provide some evidence in support of an accusation' (*Chandler*, at p. 589). If *Chandler* is right about this, and *Hall* is wrong, the inferences which may be drawn from silence under police questioning may, subject to what is said below, go beyond what is expressly permitted by the 1994 Act. *Chandler* does, however, accept two important limitations: an inference of acceptance cannot be drawn (a) where the parties are not on even terms and (b) where the suspect has been cautioned that he does not have to say anything. The former qualification is supported also by *Parkes v The Queen* [1976] 3 All ER 380 (see **F19.4**). In *Chandler* the presence of C's solicitor at interview was said to entail that the parties were on 'even terms', though the direction by the judge as to the inference that might be drawn was faulty. *Chandler* was applied in *Horne* [1990] Crim LR 188, in which police officers brought about a confrontation between H and a man he was suspected of having wounded. The man, still bleeding from his wounds, accused H of having caused them, and H refrained from making any reply. As in *Chandler*, the jury were not given adequate direction with regard to the use which could be made of the accused's silence.

F19.8   The principles stated above were held in *Collins* [2004] 1 WLR 1705 to be of equal application where a lie is told in the presence and hearing of the accused (in this instance by a co-accused) and the question is whether the accused, by his silence, has adopted the untrue statement as his own. On the facts of the case, where the lie was told in response to a question asked by a police officer and the parties were not on equal terms, there was no evidential basis for an inference other than that C's silence was an exercise by him of his right to silence.

It was accepted in *Chandler* that the drawing of inferences after a suspect has been cautioned that he need say nothing is inappropriate. Since the coming into force of the PACE 1984 and its Codes of Practice, the questioning of a suspect otherwise than under caution which occurred in *Chandler* would rarely be permissible. For this reason the decision has been of limited effect in recent years, but it is arguable that the caution and warnings relating to the inferences which may be drawn under the 1994 Act will, because they put the accused on notice that specific inferences may be drawn, open the door to an argument that wider inferences are also possible, at least where the suspect's legal adviser is also present. However the caution before interview continues to include the words 'You do not have to say anything'. This being so, it is submitted that the appropriate inference from failure to deny an accusation under caution is still that the suspect is relying on his right to silence.

OUT-OF-COURT SILENCE UNDER THE 1994 ACT

Failure to Reveal Facts Afterwards Relied upon in Court

A strong argument for drawing an adverse inference from silence occurs where the accused **F19.9** withholds his defence under interrogation but presents it at trial when it may be too late for it to be countered. At common law it was improper to invite the jury to draw an adverse inference. In *Gilbert* (1977) 66 Cr App R 237, G, who was suspected of murdering a colleague, declined to answer questions put to him under caution, but on the following day proffered a statement which dealt only with his business relationship with the deceased and not with the circumstances surrounding the killing. At trial, G relied on self-defence. The trial judge correctly directed the jury that no inferences could be drawn from G's refusal to answer questions, but went on to suggest that, so far as the statement was concerned, it was 'remarkable' that nothing was said about self-defence. This was held to be misdirection. The authorities (some of which were considered to be in conflict) established that the jury should not be invited to form an adverse opinion against an accused on account of his exercise of the right to silence. Section 34 of the CJPO 1994 addresses this problem.

Criminal Justice and Public Order Act 1994, s. 34   **F19.10**

(1) Where, in any proceedings against a person for an offence, evidence is given that the accused—
   (a) at any time before he was charged with the offence, on being questioned under caution by a constable trying to discover whether or by whom the offence had been committed, failed to mention any fact relied on in his defence in those proceedings; or
   (b) on being charged with the offence or officially informed that he might be prosecuted for it, failed to mention any such fact; or
   (c) at any time after being charged with the offence, on being questioned under section 22 of the Counter-Terrorism Act 2008 (post-charge questioning), failed to mention any such fact,
   being a fact which in the circumstances existing at the time the accused could reasonably have been expected to mention when so questioned, charged or informed, as the case may be, subsection (2) below applies.
(2) Where this subsection applies—
   (a) [repealed];
   (b) a judge, in deciding whether to grant an application made by the accused under paragraph 3 of schedule 2 to the Crime and Disorder Act 1998;
   (c) the court, in determining whether there is a case to answer; and
   (d) the court or jury, in determining whether the accused is guilty of the offence charged, may draw such inferences from the failure as appear proper.
(2A) Where the accused was at an authorised place of detention at the time of the failure, subsections (1) and (2) above do not apply if he had not been allowed an opportunity to consult a solicitor prior to being questioned, charged or informed as mentioned in subsection (1) above.

(3) Subject to any directions by the court, evidence tending to establish the failure may be given before or after evidence tending to establish the fact which the accused is alleged to have failed to mention.

(4) This section applies in relation to questioning by persons (other than constables) charged with the duty of investigating offences or charging offenders as it applies in relation to questioning by constables; and in subsection (1) above 'officially informed' means informed by a constable or any such person.

(5) This section does not—

    (a) prejudice the admissibility in evidence of the silence or other reaction of the accused in the face of anything said in his presence relating to the conduct in respect of which he is charged, in so far as evidence thereof would be admissible apart from this section; or

    (b) preclude the drawing of any inference from any such silence or other reaction of the accused which could properly be drawn apart from this section.

(6) This section does not apply in relation to a failure to mention a fact if the failure occurred before the commencement of this section.

F19.11   The function of s. 34 is to permit the tribunal of fact to draw 'such inferences as appear proper' (s. 34(2)) from the accused's silence, provided that the various conditions set forth in s. 34(1) are made out and any questions of fact arising thereunder are resolved against the accused (*Argent* [1997] 2 Cr App R 27). The provision applies only where a particular fact is advanced by the defence which is suspicious by reason of not being put forward at an early opportunity: s. 34 does not apply simply because the accused has declined to answer questions (*Argent*; *T v DPP* (2007) 171 JP 605; and see **F19.16**). Thus *Gilbert* (1977) 66 Cr App R 237 is reversed to the extent that G's reticence about his defence, and the reasons for it, could now be explored with a view (if no plausible explanation appears) to drawing an inference of guilt. Section 34 is, however, capable of applying to a case in which the accused, though he discloses his defence, fails to mention a particular fact that he thereafter relies upon. In such a case there is a discretion whether to give a warning. In *Abdalla* [2007] EWCA Crim 2495 the accused immediately disclosed his defence of self-defence, but neglected to mention that he believed his victim was armed with a hammer. The decision of the judge to proceed in a 'low key' way without giving a warning was upheld. The Court of Appeal referred with approval to the statement of Hedley J in *Brizzalari* [2004] EWCA Crim 310 that the mischief at which s. 34 is primarily directed is 'the positive defence following a "no comment" interview and/or the "ambush" defence'. Counsel should not complicate trials and summings-up by invoking the section unless the merits of the individual case require it. *Brizzalari* was approved in *Maguire* (2008) 172 JP 417, where the Court discouraged 'anything which over-formalises common sense'. See also *Smith* [2011] EWCA Crim 1098, endorsing, in particular, the point in *Brizzalari* that to give the direction in a case where the accused has put forward no more than a bare denial would be tantamount to directing that guilt may be inferred simply from the exercise of the right to silence, which is not the purpose of s. 34.

F19.12   It is now accepted that the adverse inference which may be drawn under s. 34 includes a general inference of guilt. The specimen direction (*Crown Court Bench Book*, appendix 2) tells the jury that they may take the failure to mention the fact into account as 'some additional support' for the prosecution case.

Decisions of the ECtHR have confirmed that the mere fact that a trial judge leaves a jury with the option of drawing an adverse inference from silence in interview is not incompatible with the requirements of a fair trial. Whether the drawing of adverse inferences infringes the ECHR, Article 6, is a matter to be determined in light of all the circumstances of the case, having regard to the situations where inferences may be drawn, the weight attached to them by the national court, and the degree of compulsion inherent in the situation. Of particular importance are the terms of the judge's direction to the jury on the drawing of adverse inferences (*Condron v UK* (2001) 31 EHRR 1; *Beckles v UK* (2003) 36 EHRR 162).

The domestic cases show that s. 34 has given rise to much more difficulty in directing the jury than s. 35 (failure to testify at trial: see **F19.41**). Although each case requires a direction tailored to its own facts, trial judges should follow closely the specimen direction which was accepted by the ECtHR in *Beckles v UK* (*Chenia* [2003] 2 Cr App R 83). Failure to give a proper direction will not, however, necessarily involve a breach of Article 6, nor render a conviction unsafe (*Chenia*, where earlier authorities are considered). In *Chenia*, the factors which persuaded the court that C had received a fair trial included the strength of the evidence, the fact that his failure to mention relevant facts was not consequent upon legal advice (as to which, see **F19.24**) and the clear and accurate direction given on the failure of C to give evidence in the case.

Access to Legal Advice   Section 34(2A) of the CJPO 1994 was added by the YJCEA 1999, **F19.13** s. 58, to bring the law into line with the judgment of the ECtHR in *Murray v UK* (1996) 22 EHRR 29. The Court considered that even the lawful exercise of a power to delay access to legal advice could, where the accused was at risk of adverse inferences under the statutory scheme, be sufficient to deprive the accused of a fair procedure under Article 6. The accused was faced with a 'fundamental dilemma' at the outset of the investigation, in that his silence might lead to adverse inferences being drawn against him, while breaking his silence might prejudice his defence without necessarily removing the possibility of inferences being drawn against him. The dilemma is resolved by postponing the prospect that inferences will be drawn until the accused has had the opportunity of consulting with a legal adviser. The postponement occurs in exactly the same way whether access to legal advice is delayed lawfully or unlawfully. An 'authorised place of detention' is defined by s. 38(2A) to include police stations and any other place prescribed by order. The caution to be given to a person to whom a restriction on drawing inferences applies is specified by PACE Code C, annex C.

Where an accused person has been offered legal advice but has elected to proceed without it, an issue may arise as to whether there has been an effective waiver for the purposes of drawing inferences. Although the leading case of *McGowan v B* [2011] 1 WLR 3121 is primarily concerned with confessions obtained following waiver, Lord Hamilton also acknowledged the advantage of access to legal advice in deciding whether to respond in interview. In *McGowan* the issue was whether the jurisprudence of the ECtHR supports a rule that the right of access to legal advice during police questioning can be waived only if the accused has received advice from a lawyer as to whether or not he should do so. It was held that it does not. However in *Saunders* [2012] 2 Cr App R 321 the Court of Appeal regarded the speeches in *McGowan* as authority for the proposition that a waiver should be 'voluntary, informed and unequivocal'. In *Saunders*, S was 'particularly well-fitted' to decide whether she wanted legal advice or not: she was intelligent, had previous convictions for fraud, and a law degree. Had she been unintelligent or vulnerable, her waiver might have been called into question.

No Conviction etc. Wholly or Mainly on Silence

Criminal Justice and Public Order Act 1994, s. 38   F19.14

(3) A person shall not have the proceedings against him transferred to the Crown Court for trial, have a case to answer or be convicted of an offence solely on an inference drawn from such a failure or refusal as is mentioned in section 34(2), 35(3), 36(2) or 37(2).

(4) A judge shall not refuse to grant such an application as is mentioned in section 34(2)(b), 36(2) (b) and 37(2)(b) solely on an inference drawn from such a failure as is mentioned in section 34(2), 36(2) or 37(2).

Section 38(3) applies to all four of the provisions of the 1994 Act which operate to permit the drawing of inferences from silence, and s. 38(4) to the three appertaining to out-of-court silence.

F19.15   Where the issue is whether the jury should be at liberty to convict in reliance on an inference drawn under s. 34, it is essential that they be directed that such an inference cannot standing alone prove guilt (*Abdullah* [1999] 3 Arch News 3), though the omission of the direction is not necessarily fatal if the prosecution evidence taken apart from the inference is overwhelming (*Adeyinka* [2014] EWCA Crim 504). A more pressing question is whether the courts should go beyond the rule laid down in s. 38(3) in order to ensure that no conviction is based *mainly* on one or more of the statutory inferences. In *Murray v UK* (1996) 22 EHRR 29, there is a very strong statement that it would be incompatible with the accused's rights to base a conviction 'solely or mainly on the accused's silence or on a refusal to answer questions or to give evidence himself'; see also *Condron v UK* (2001) 31 EHRR 1. To the extent that the statutory scheme does not expressly prevent a conviction founded 'mainly' on silence, therefore, it may be defective. In *Doldur* [2000] Crim LR 178, the Court of Appeal held that there was no need for a judge to direct a jury that, before they could draw an inference under s. 34, they must be satisfied that there was a case to answer. Such a direction has been held to be required in relation to s. 35 (see **F19.49**) where the accused does not testify, but the Court regarded the two cases as distinguishable in that, under s. 35, there was a logical reason for confining the jury to considering whether the prosecution had established a prima facie case as a prerequisite to drawing an inference, whereas under s. 34 the jury would need to have regard to evidence adduced by the defence in order to decide whether s. 34 applied. This is true, but the need to honour *Murray* may well require some further elaboration. The specimen direction made reference to the need for the jury to be satisfied that there is a case to meet, and in *Milford* [2001] Crim LR 330, the Court of Appeal noted that *Doldur*, although based on compelling logic, had failed to address 'the European dimension', and considered that both *Condron* [1997] 1 WLR 827 and *Birchall* [1999] Crim LR 311 were to the contrary (see also **F19.31** as to the *Crown Court Bench Book*). In *Beckles v UK* (2003) 36 EHRR 162, the ECtHR, after considering the above authorities, confirmed that the correct principle was, as stated in *Murray v UK*, that a conviction based solely or mainly on silence or a refusal to answer questions would be incompatible with the right to silence. More recently, in *Chenia* [2003] 2 Cr App R 83, the Court of Appeal confirmed that a direction which omitted reference to the need to consider whether there was a case to answer is 'deficient', but on the facts did not consider it was fatal to a conviction where the existence of a prima facie case is beyond dispute. Further, in *Petkar* [2004] 1 Cr App R 270, it was held that the jury should be told in terms not to convict 'wholly or mainly' on an adverse inference, and that the words 'or mainly' were required to 'buttress' the requirement for proof of a case to answer otherwise than by means of the inference. In *Parchment* [2003] EWCA Crim 2428, it was said that where the case against an accused was weak it was crucial that the limited function of the failure to mention something in interview was clearly spelled out to the jury, and accordingly a conviction for murder was quashed where the appropriate direction had not been given.

Fact Relied On

F19.16   Section 34 of the CJPO 1994 does not apply where the accused makes no attempt to put forward at trial some previously undisclosed fact (e.g., where he simply contends that the prosecution has failed to prove its case). In *Moshaid* [1998] Crim LR 420, M, acting on legal advice, declined to answer any questions. At trial he did not give or call any evidence. It was held that s. 34 did not bite in these circumstances. It goes too far, however, to suggest that s. 34 applies only where the accused gives evidence: a fact relied on may be established by a witness called by the accused, or may be elicited from a prosecution witness (*Bowers* [1988] Crim LR 817). In *Webber* [2004] 1 All ER 770, where the authorities are reviewed by Lord Bingham, it was held that an accused 'relies on' a fact or matter in his defence not only where he gives or adduces evidence of it but also where counsel, acting on his instructions, puts a specific and positive case to prosecution witnesses, as opposed to asking questions intended to probe or test the prosecution case. The effect of specific and positive suggestions from counsel, whether or not accepted, is to plant in the jury's mind the accused's version of events. This may be so even if the witness rejects the suggestion, since the jury may mistrust the witness's evidence. If the judge is in doubt whether counsel is merely testing the prosecution case or putting a positive case, counsel should be asked, in the absence of the jury, to make the position clear. However, the positive case ought to be apparent from the defence statement made in advance of trial. The same reasoning also led the House of Lords to conclude that the adoption by counsel of evidence given by a co-defendant may amount to reliance on the relevant facts or matters. Following *Webber* it has been held that the putting forward by an accused of a possible explanation for his fingerprints being on a car number plate is a 'fact' as broadly construed in that case (*Esimu* (2007) 171 JP 452). See also *King* [2012] EWCA Crim 805, where K's belief in the guilt of one or more named individuals of the crime with which he was charged was a 'fact'.

In *Betts* [2001] 2 Cr App R 257, a bare admission at trial of a part of the prosecution case was held incapable of constituting a 'fact' for the purposes of s. 34. The alternative construction would effectively have removed the accused's right to silence by requiring him to make admissions at interview, an obligation which would have conflicted with the ECHR, Article 6. A direction under s. 34 will rarely, if ever, be appropriate in relation to the failure to mention an admittedly true fact, since the adverse inference under s. 34 is that a matter not mentioned at interview is unlikely to be true (*Webber* [2004] 1 All ER 770; see also *Wheeler* [2008] EWCA Crim 688, *Chivers* [2011] EWCA Crim 1212 and *Zeinden* [2012] EWCA Crim 2489, in which the judge's direction erroneously mixed together a fact subsequently relied on with other, innocuous, facts that did not give rise to any inference).

If the prosecution fail to establish that the accused has failed to mention a fact, the jury should **F19.17** be directed to draw no inference (*B (MT)* [2000] Crim LR 181). Where the judge directs the jury on the basis that s. 34 applies, it is important that the facts relied on should be identified in the course of the direction (*Chenia*; *Lewis* [2003] EWCA Crim 223) and should not be mixed with other, innocuous, facts from which no inference can be drawn (*Zeinden*). In *Lowe* [2007] EWCA Crim 833 the judge was allowed some latitude in a complex case in not having to list all of the facts, as distinct from the parts of the defence case, which were not mentioned. The identification of the specific fact or facts is required by the specimen direction (*Crown Court Bench Book*, appendix 2) which also suggested that any proposed direction should be discussed with counsel before closing speeches. In *B* the Court of Appeal stated:

> In our view it is particularly important that judges should take this course in relation to directions as to the application of section 34. That section is a notorious minefield. Discussion with counsel will reduce the risk of mistakes.

When directing a jury in relation to a group of defendants, it is preferable to avoid a direc- **F19.18** tion that deals with their position compendiously rather than individually. A compendious approach runs the risk that the direction will fail to identify what exactly each defendant has relied on at trial that he did not say earlier (*Miah* [2009] EWCA Crim 2368).

Where the prosecution is able to identify a specific fact relied upon within the meaning of s. 34, it does not necessarily follow that the point should be taken at trial: prosecutors should remember that the twin mischiefs at which the section is aimed are the positive defence following a 'no comment' interview and the 'ambush' defence. Consideration should therefore be given in other cases to whether the withholding of the fact is sufficient to justify the sanction of s. 34, given the weight juries are likely to give to being directed as to adverse inferences (*Brizzalari* [2004] EWCA Crim 310).

Prepared Statements Where the accused at the relevant time gives a prepared statement in **F19.19** which certain facts are set forth, it cannot subsequently be said that he has failed to mention those facts. The aim of s. 34 of the CJPO 1994 was to encourage a suspect to disclose his factual defence, not to sanction inferences from the accused's failure to respond to questions (*Knight* [2004] 1 WLR 340, and see *T v DPP* (2007) 171 JP 605). A prepared statement may, however, be a dangerous device for an innocent accused who later discovers that something significant has been omitted (*Knight* and *Turner* [2004] 1 All ER 1025). In *Turner* it was noted that, as inconsistencies between the prepared statement and the defence at trial do not necessarily amount to reliance on unmentioned facts, the judge must be particularly careful to pinpoint any fact that might properly be the subject of a s. 34 direction. Alternatively, the jury might more appropriately be directed to regard differences between the prepared statement and the accused's evidence as constituting a previous lie rather than as the foundation for a direction under s. 34.

Caution or Charge

F19.20   Inferences before a suspect is charged under the CJPO 1994, s. 34, may not be drawn except 'on being questioned under caution by a constable' (s. 34(1)(a)). If no questions have been put, e.g., because the accused refuses to leave his cell for questioning, the section cannot apply, as the statutory language cannot be ignored (*Johnson* [2005] EWCA Crim 971). It does not, however, follow that a fact can only be 'mentioned' in the form of an answer to a question: in *Ali* [2001] EWCA Crim 863, the accused handed over a prepared statement in which the relevant facts were mentioned and this was sufficient to prevent an inference, although he subsequently declined to answer questions: see also *Knight* [2004] 1 WLR 340. (The reference to 'constable' includes others charged with investigating offences: s. 34(4).)

F19.21   The caution makes clear the risks that attend the failure to mention facts which later form part of the defence. It is set out in Code C, para. 10.5 and runs as follows:

> You do not have to say anything. But it may harm your defence if you do not mention when questioned something which you later rely on in court. Anything you do say may be given in evidence.

Minor deviations from the formula are not a breach of the code as long as the sense is preserved (para. 10.7), and an officer is permitted to paraphrase if it appears that the person with whom he is dealing does not understand what the caution means (Note for Guidance 10D). A suspect who has been arrested should not normally be questioned about his involvement in an offence except in an interview at a police station, and it is envisaged that questioning to which s. 34 applies should occur in the course of such an interview which, being properly recorded, will then allow the court to make reliable deductions about the nature and extent of any silence. Clearly, if the accused alleges that he did mention the relevant fact when questioned, the prosecution will have to prove the contrary before any adverse inference can be drawn. Where it is alleged that a 'significant silence' (i.e. one which appears capable of being used in evidence against the suspect) has occurred before his arrival at a police station, then at the beginning of an interview at the station the interviewing officer should put the matter to the suspect, under caution, and ask him whether he confirms or denies that earlier silence and whether he wishes to add anything (para. 11.4). The consequence of failing to go through this procedure (which applies to evidentially significant statements as it does to silences) must be to increase significantly the likelihood that the evidence in question will be excluded under s. 78 if the suspect denies that the earlier statement was made or that the silence occurred. Furthermore if the suspect is questioned improperly in circumstances prohibited by Code C, e.g., where sufficient evidence for the accused to be charged already exists, s. 34 should not be brought to bear on the suspect's failure to respond (*Pointer* [1997] Crim LR 676; *Gayle* [1999] 2 Cr App R 130). There is a lack of consistency in the authorities on when there is sufficient evidence for this purpose (*McGuinness* [1999] Crim LR 318; *Ioannou* [1999] Crim LR 586; *Odeyemi* [1999] Crim LR 828; *Flynn* [2001] EWCA Crim 1633; *Elliott* [2002] EWCA Crim 931), but no doubt about the principle.

F19.22   The drawing of inferences from the withholding of a fact at the point of charge under s. 34(1)(b) is a distinct process from that under s. 34(1)(a). Where, therefore, no inference could be drawn from silence at interview because the interview itself had been excluded under the PACE 1984, s. 78, it did not follow that an inference could not be drawn from silence at the point of charge as long as there is no unfairness in doing so (*Dervish* [2002] 2 Cr App R 105). In that case D had the opportunity 'in a single sentence' to put the essence of his defence following charge, and the police would thereafter have been precluded from questioning him about it. Since he declined to do so, it was rightly left to the jury to decide whether an inference should be drawn.

Facts which Should Have Been Mentioned

Adverse inferences may be drawn from a fact subsequently relied on in defence only where the fact is one which, in the circumstances existing at the time, the accused could reasonably have been expected to mention (s. 34(1)). If the accused gives evidence, his reason for failing to disclose should be explored (*T v DPP* (2007) 171 JP 605), and any explanation advanced by the accused for non-disclosure must be considered in deciding what inferences, if any, should be drawn (*Webber* [2004] 1 All ER 770, where the House of Lords considered that the jury was 'very much concerned' with the truth or otherwise of an explanation from the accused as, if they accept it as true or possibly so, no adverse inference should be drawn from his failure to mention it). In *Walton* [2013] EWCA Crim 2536 the accused was not asked at any point about his failure to answer questions at interview (where he had tendered a prepared statement). Nor does it appear that he was invited to deal with the question why he had made no previous mention of particular facts later relied on in his defence. Although counsel for the prosecution did not seek a direction on adverse inference, the trial judge elected to give one. The Court of Appeal (at [8]) considered the direction to be both wrong and unfair in the circumstances. '[T]he jury were invited to consider an adverse inference without knowing what if anything the appellant might have had to say about his silence.' Ultimately an adverse inference is appropriate only where the jury concludes that the silence can only sensibly be attributed to the defendant's having no answer, or none that would stand up to questioning (*Condron* [1997] 1 WLR 827; *Betts* [2001] 2 Cr App R 257; *Daly* [2002] 2 Cr App R 201; *Petkar* [2004] 1 Cr App R 270). Similar formulae appear also in *Condron v UK* (2001) 31 EHRR 1, and *Beckles v UK* (2003) 36 EHRR 162). In *Barnes* (4 July 2003 unreported), B's contention was that he thought that he had mentioned the fact in issue during his interview. As this was not advanced as a reason for non-disclosure, it was said that it provided no impediment to the drawing of an adverse inference. While this may be so, if B genuinely believed that he had mentioned the fact, then his state of mind at interview was not that of a guilty person withholding information. It is important that any direction given should reflect this. In *Hilliard* [2004] EWCA Crim 837, H's only chance to mention a fact was when a witness's statement had been read to him in interview. He had not been told that he should correct any statement with which he disagreed. It was held that it would be 'wholly unsafe' to seek to draw an adverse inference since H had never had the opportunity to deal with the matter (which was not central) even if he ought to have identified it as something that was important enough to mention. In *M* [2012] 1 Cr App R 26 the officers interviewing M on suspicion of rape mistakenly attributed a date to the allegation that was some three months after the day on which the complainant, M's babysitter, had said that the offence had occurred. M had responded truthfully that nothing had occurred on the date put to him and 'it was hard to see how in those circumstances he could have been expected to say more'. M subsequently relied on facts relevant to the earlier date (e.g., the fact that his partner had arrived home very shortly after the alleged incident) but these were not facts which he could reasonably have been expected to mention in the context of the original investigation.

The specific references to the accused and to the circumstances indicates that a range of factors may be relevant to what might have been expected to be forthcoming, including age, experience, mental capacity, health, sobriety, tiredness and personality. A restrictive approach would not be appropriate (*Argent* [1997] 2 Cr App R 27).

The failure of the interviewer to disclose relevant information when asked to do so by the accused or his legal adviser is another factor bearing upon the propriety of drawing an inference. If little information is forthcoming a legal adviser may well counsel silence until a better assessment of the case to answer can be made (*Roble* [1997] Crim LR 449).

Legal Advice to Remain Silent   The difficult issue of what use, if any, can be made of a failure to advance facts following legal advice to remain silent has been the subject of numerous decisions, both by domestic courts and Strasbourg. In *Beckles* [2005] 1 All ER 705, Lord Woolf CJ,

F19.23

F19.24

commented that the position in such cases is 'singularly delicate'. On the one hand, the courts not unreasonably seek to avoid having the accused drive a coach and horses through s. 34 by advancing an explanation for silence that is easy to make and difficult to investigate because of legal professional privilege. On the other hand, 'it is of the greatest importance that defendants should be able to be advised by their lawyer without their having to reveal the terms of that advice if they act in accordance with that advice'. Perhaps because of this, the authorities have not all spoken with one voice, although now a consistent theme seems to be emerging. In *Condron* [1997] 1 WLR 827, C and his wife, admitted heroin addicts, were convicted of offences relating to the supply of the drug. At interview both remained silent, on the advice of their solicitor who (despite medical advice to the contrary) considered that their drug withdrawal symptoms rendered them unfit to be interviewed. At trial, the defence relied upon detailed innocent explanations of prosecution evidence which could have been put forward at the time of interview. It was held that the giving of legal advice to remain silent did not of itself preclude the drawing of inferences: all depends on the view the jury takes of the reason advanced by the accused, after having been directed in accordance with the formula (above) that they should consider whether the silence can only sensibly be attributed to the accused having no answer, or none that would stand up to questioning. (Such a direction was said to be 'desirable' in *Condron*, but the ECtHR subsequently considered that fairness required a direction to be given which left the jury in no doubt in this important matter (*Condron v UK* (2001) 31 EHRR 1).) In *Beckles* [2005] 1 All ER 705, the Court of Appeal reviewed a number of post-*Condron* authorities, including the earlier decision of the ECtHR in *Beckles* itself ((2003) 36 EHRR 162). Two strands of authority, one proceeding from *Betts* [2001] 2 Cr App R 257, and the other from *Howell* [2005] 1 Cr App R 1 and *Knight* [2004] 1 WLR 340 had been regarded as in conflict, with *Betts* favouring a subjective test (did the accused genuinely rely on legal advice?) and *Howell* and *Knight* an objective test (did the accused reasonably rely on legal advice?). The Court of Appeal in *Beckles* adopted the reconciliation of the two strands proposed by Auld LJ in *Hoare* [2005] 1 WLR 1804, which accepts that 'genuine reliance by a defendant on his solicitor's advice to remain silent is not in itself enough to preclude adverse comment'. Auld LJ went on:

> It is not the purpose of section 34 to exclude a jury from drawing an adverse inference against a defendant because he genuinely or reasonably believes that, regardless of his guilt or innocence, he is entitled to take advantage of that advice to impede the prosecution case against him. In such a case the advice is not truly the reason for not mentioning the facts. The section 34 inference is concerned with flushing out innocence at an early stage, or supporting other evidence of guilt at a later stage, not simply with whether a guilty defendant is entitled, or genuinely or reasonably believes that he is entitled, to rely on legal rights of which his solicitor has advised him. Legal entitlement is one thing. An accused's reason for exercising it is another. His belief in his entitlement may be genuine, but it does not follow that his reason for exercising it is…

F19.25   In *Hoare*, the defence to producing a Class B drug was that H believed he was involved in the secret production of a cure for cancer. H had given a 'no comment' interview following legal advice, the solicitor apparently having thought that there was insufficient disclosure of the evidence against H at that stage. Under cross-examination, H said that, while he could have given his explanation at the time, he had been stunned and surprised, had not had much sleep, and 'most people would act on the advice of their lawyer'. The true question, however, according to *Hoare*, is not whether H's solicitors rightly or wrongly believed that H was not required to answer the questions, nor whether H genuinely relied on the advice in the sense that he believed he had the right to do so. The true question is whether H remained silent 'not because of that advice but because he had no or no satisfactory explanation to give'. Similarly in *Karapetyan* [2013] EWCA Crim 74, it was not disputed that K had a 'reason' for silence in that his preferred solicitor, who was unable to attend the interview, had advised him to make no comment. However the jury, following a proper direction on the matter, were entitled to conclude that the fact relied on (that K was not a driver who had given false details to a police officer, and that the offender was probably a man to whom K had rented the car) could reasonably have been expected to be mentioned. See also *Essa* [2009] EWCA Crim 43, where the Court of Appeal added the rider that in such cases a court may wish to pause and consider whether a s. 34 direction helps the jury (e.g., where the defence at trial is a simple denial of presence).

Waiver of Privilege and Statements   The accused who wishes to give an account of his reasons for silence following legal advice may find it hard to do so without waiving privilege. While no waiver is involved in a bare assertion that he had been advised to remain silent, little weight in likely to attach to such an assertion unless the reasons for it are before the court (*Condron* [1997] 1 WLR 827; *Robinson* [2003] EWCA Crim 2219). In *Bowden* [1999] 4 All ER 582 a waiver was held to have occurred where B called evidence in his defence of a statement made by his solicitor at interview, namely that he had advised B to remain silent because of the lack of evidence against him. B was held to have been properly cross-examined about the extent to which he had disclosed to the solicitor the facts that subsequently formed the basis of his defence. Lord Bingham CJ stated, *obiter*, that the giving of evidence at a *voir dire* as to the reasons for legal advice for silence would operate as a waiver of privilege at trial even if the evidence was not repeated before the jury: the accused cannot 'have his cake and eat it' where privilege is concerned. The same point is also made, though in less emphatic terms, by the ECtHR in *Condron v UK* (2001) 31 EHRR 1, where it is said that there was no compulsion on C to disclose the advice given, other than the indirect compulsion to provide a convincing explanation for silence, and that because C chose to make the content of the solicitor's advice part of his defence he could not complain that the CJPO 1994 overrode the confidentiality of discussions with his legal adviser. See also *Loizou* [2006] EWCA Crim 1719. In *Hall-Chung* [2007] EWCA Crim 3429 it was held that the issue is not whether the prosecution or the defence adduces the evidence, but whether waiver has in fact occurred. The circumstances of the waiver, and how it is deployed by the Crown, may be relevant to whether it is fair to exclude evidence pursuant to the PACE 1984, s. 78.   **F19.26**

Where the accused's solicitor, following a consultation with his client, makes a statement to the officers conducting the interview with regard to the accused's reasons for silence (in the presence of the accused who says nothing in dissent), the statement may be given in evidence and may form the basis of an adverse inference (*Fitzgerald* [1998] 4 Arch News 2). It would appear that the Court of Appeal had in mind by way of exception to the hearsay rule either the doctrine of admission by an agent, or implied admission by silence where a statement is made in the presence of the accused (see **F16.73** and **F19.3** respectively). In *Bowden* the Court of Appeal expressed a preference for the explanation based on agency, which it is submitted is correct. In this connection it is relevant to note that privilege should not be regarded as waived if the accused merely seeks to demonstrate the fact that he communicated relevant exculpatory facts to his legal adviser prior to the interview (cf. *Wilmot* (1988) 89 Cr App R 341). Nor is it hearsay for the accused to tell the court what advice the solicitor gave him, provided that his purpose in doing so is not to establish the truth of any fact narrated by the solicitor. It is the accused's reason for withholding facts that is in issue so, provided that, for example, he merely wishes to explain the impact upon him of the advice given, there is no hearsay problem (*Davis* [1998] Crim LR 659). In *Hill* [2003] EWCA Crim 1179, H contended that an interview conducted in the presence of a solicitor should have been excluded (and therefore unavailable as the basis for an inference) on the ground that her solicitor was affected by a conflict of interest as the representative of a co-accused. It was held that the proper course would have been to waive privilege and consider the matter fully on a *voir dire*: the court should not be asked to speculate that the solicitor had acted improperly.   **F19.27**

In some cases the reasons for the advice given to the accused may be difficult to explain to a jury without descending into legal complexity, or revealing that the accused is no stranger to the legal process. The point was raised (but not answered) in *Beard* [2002] EWCA Crim 772, where it was considered that there was on the facts no such difficulty in leaving the issue to the jury. Where it is otherwise, it will be necessary to consider whether to exclude evidence relating to the interview on the ground of unfairness.   **F19.28**

A frequent outcome of consultation with a legal adviser is that the accused volunteers a prepared statement which is subsequently relied upon as demonstrating that he has 'mentioned' those facts which form the basis of his defence at trial. If the statement proves incomplete, a particularly careful direction may be required (see **F19.19**) which may be complicated further by the fact that the statement was originally crafted on legal advice.

Direction as to Permissible Inferences

F19.29   Where the fact is one which the accused could reasonably have been expected to mention it will be permissible to draw 'such inferences from the failure as appear proper' (s. 34(2)) in a variety of contexts including the determination of guilt (s. 34(2)(d), and whether there is a case to answer (s. 34(2)(c)), bearing in mind always that an inference drawn under the subsection is not by itself sufficient to sustain either determination (s. 38(3): see **F19.14**). Although the most common inference from failure to reveal facts which are subsequently relied on is that the facts have been invented after the interview, it may equally appear to the jury that the accused had the facts in mind at the time of interview, but was unwilling to expose his account to scrutiny (*Milford* [2001] Crim LR 330). Similarly, the jury may deduce that the accused was faced with a choice between on the one hand silence, and on the other either lying or incriminating himself further with the truth. Again, this is a permissible inference under s. 34 (*Daniel* [1998] 2 Cr App R 373). It follows that, even if it is common ground that an accused spoke to his solicitor about a proposed defence of alibi before any interview took place, his failure to reveal the alibi in interview was still a matter from which inferences could be drawn if the jury were unconvinced by the accused's explanation (*Taylor* [1999] Crim LR 77). Nothing in *Condron* or *Cowan* should be read as indicating that the only adverse inference to be drawn is one of recent fabrication (*Beckles* [1999] Crim LR 148). Where the inference which the prosecution suggests should be drawn is not the standard inference of late fabrication but is less severe, the judge should make this clear when summing-up (*Petkar* [2004] 1 Cr App R 270).

In cases where the accused explains his failure to mention facts on the ground that he was acting on legal advice, but without explaining the reasons behind the advice, the trial judge should be particularly careful to avoid directing the jury in such a way as to indicate that the silence is necessarily a guilty one (*Bresa* [2005] EWCA Crim 1414 and see **F19.24** as to the construction of a possible inference following legal advice).

F19.30   In some cases an inference cannot logically be drawn without first concluding that the accused is guilty, and in such cases, s. 34 has been said to be of no assistance (*Mountford* [1999] Crim LR 575). M, charged with possession of heroin with intent to supply, put forward the defence that the actual dealer was W, the main prosecution witness, while he was merely a customer. M gave as his explanation for failing to reveal this defence at interview his reluctance to expose W to prosecution. The Court of Appeal held that the jury could not properly reject M's reason for not mentioning this fact without first concluding that the fact was untrue: the very issue on which M's guilt turned. In these (somewhat unusual) circumstances the judge should not have left s. 34 to the jury. (See also *Gill* [2001] 1 Cr App R 160, a case on similar facts.) In *Daly* [2002] 2 Cr App R 201, however, the decision in *Mountford* was doubted on the ground that there is nothing in s. 34 which requires that the issue be one which is capable of separate resolution in the case. While this is true, there is much to be said for the view that the judge should steer the jury in the direction of a logical resolution to the issues. However a differently-constituted later court made the same point in *Gowland-Wynn* [2002] 1 Cr App R 569, and it may be that the qualification in *Mountford* is too subtle. In *Chenia* [2003] 2 Cr App R 83, the approach in *Mountford* was said to be appropriate in the 'rare case' only and in *Webber* [2004] 1 All ER 770 the House of Lords (while not specifically overruling *Mountford*) considered that the s. 34 direction was rightly given in that case, which is tantamount to outright rejection. *Webber* was a very different type of case, however, and did not involve the problem of circularity in *Mountford*.

F19.31   **Direction where s. 34 Applicable**   In all cases where the CJPO 1994, s. 34, is to be relied upon, it is submitted that a clear judicial direction will be required as to the nature of the inference that may properly be drawn. Where prosecution counsel had not sought to rely upon s. 34, and had not raised the matter with the accused in cross-examination, the Court of Appeal in *Khan* [1999] 2 Arch News 2 rightly 'deprecated' the decision of the trial judge to direct the jury that they might draw an inference under s. 34 without having raised the matter with counsel. It was held, however, that (as there would have been no basis upon which the judge could have been deterred from giving the direction had the matter been argued) K had suffered no disadvantage. It is submitted that this is a dangerous approach. A trial judge ought not, in fairness, to leave it open to the jury to make use of silence which, because the defence did not expect to have to explain it away, has not been the subject of any comment by the accused or the defence witnesses. If the judge thinks that s. 34 might come into play, the matter should be raised in time for it to be the subject of evidence not speculation. If, on the other hand, there has been no discussion with counsel of the intended direction in circumstances where it is clear to the defence that the prosecution are relying on the accused's failure to mention a specific fact, it is unlikely that the omission will render the trial unfair (*Barnes* (4 July 2003 unreported)). In *Brooks* [2004] EWCA Crim 3021, the direction had been discussed with counsel, who were left with the impression that no direction of the kind that was in due course given would be given. The importance of following and adapting the relevant specimen direction is frequently mentioned in connection with s. 34, and although it need not be slavishly adhered to in every case (*Salami* [2003] EWCA Crim 3831) it affords particularly useful guidance in this difficult area. The *Crown Court Bench Book* (March 2010) heralded a move towards the judicial crafting of directions to fit individual cases and away from 'specimen directions'. However, given the difficulty of directing a jury in relation to s. 34, the formula approved in numerous decisions over time continues to provide the best guide.

A direction may be called for where there is more than one accused. If A has failed to mention   **F19.32** a relevant fact so as to attract a s. 34 direction, it is desirable in the case of co-accused B whose case stands or falls with A's to give a direction not to draw any inference against B. Where more than one accused attracts a s. 34 direction, the judge should avoid dealing with their cases compendiously but should identify what each has said at trial that he did not say earlier (*Miah* [2009] EWCA Crim 2368).

A direction may also be called for in relation to something said by the accused which the prosecution claim both conceals a fact later relied on and constitutes a positive lie. In such a case the facts may require that both a s. 34 direction and a *Lucas* direction (see **F1.21**) should be given; see *Turner* [2004] 1 All ER 1025. However, in *Hackett* [2011] 2 Cr App R 35, the Court of Appeal observed that it is usually unhelpful to give both directions; the judge should select and if necessary adapt the direction more appropriate to the facts and issues in the case, following observations in *Rana* [2007] EWCA Crim 2261. Where separate directions are given, it is important that they should be consistent (*Stanislas* [2004] EWCA Crim 2266). In *Hackett* the issue as to whether H had lied was a subsidiary question: the key issue was whether the explanation he had given at trial was a late invention, it not having been mentioned at interview. A s. 34 direction was called for, but once the jury, following that direction, had concluded that the explanation was false, there was no need for what is in essence the protection of a *Lucas* direction, the function of which is to point out that there might be an innocent reason for lying.

As to the circumstances in which a conviction may be safe notwithstanding the significant misdirection of a jury under s. 34, see *Boyle* [2006] EWCA Crim 2101 and *Lowe* [2007] EWCA Crim 833. In *Adetoro v UK* [2010] ECHR 609 the failure of the judge to direct the jury that they should specifically reject the accused's reason for silence before drawing an inference was not fatal to the fairness of the trial where the jury must, in rejecting the accused's defence, have also rejected his reason for remaining silent.

As to the 'unfair' use of silence, see **F19.40**.

Direction where s. 34 Not Applicable to Accused's Silence   Where the judge concludes   **F19.33** that the requirements of the CJPO 1994, s. 34, have not been met, but the jury have been made aware of the accused's failure to answer questions, it was held in *McGarry* [1999] 3 All ER 805 that a direction should be given to the jury that they should not hold the accused's silence against him. If that were not done, the jury would be left in 'no-man's land' between the common-law rule and the statutory exception, without any guidance as to how to regard the accused's silence. This was qualified in *La Rose* [2003] EWCA Crim 1471, where it was held that the omission of the so-called 'counterweight' direction was not fatal where L had never given any explanation for his conduct and had declined to give evidence at trial, thus attracting a s. 35 direction (see **F19.42**). The *McGarry* direction may also be problematic in that it may do harm by drawing attention to the accused's failure to answer questions, so that the failure to give the direction may be a benefit (*Thomas* [2002] EWCA Crim 1308; *Jama* [2008] EWCA Crim 2861).

Failure to Account for Objects, Substances, Marks and Presence

F19.34   Criminal Justice and Public Order Act 1994, ss. 36 and 37

36.—(1) Where—
  (a) a person is arrested by a constable, and there is—
     (i)   on his person; or
     (ii) in or on his clothing or footwear; or
     (iii) otherwise in his possession; or
     (iv) in any place in which he is at the time of his arrest,
     any object, substance or mark, or there is any mark on any such object; and
  (b) that or another constable investigating the case reasonably believes that the presence of the object, substance or mark may be attributable to the participation of the person arrested in the commission of an offence specified by the constable; and
  (c) the constable informs the person arrested that he so believes, and requests him to account for the presence of the object, substance or mark; and
  (d) the person fails or refuses to do so,
  then if, in any proceedings against the person for the offence so specified, evidence of those matters is given, subsection (2) below applies.
(2) Where this subsection applies—
  (a) [repealed];
  (b) a judge, in deciding whether to grant an application made by the accused under paragraph 3 of schedule 2 to the Crime and Disorder Act 1998;
  (c) the court, in determining whether there is a case to answer; and
  (d) the court or jury, in determining whether the accused is guilty of the offence charged,
  may draw such inferences from the failure or refusal as appear proper.
(3) Subsections (1) and (2) above apply to the condition of clothing or footwear as they apply to a substance or mark thereon.
(4) Subsections (1) and (2) above do not apply unless the accused was told in ordinary language by the constable when making the request mentioned in subsection (1)(c) above what the effect of this section would be if he failed or refused to comply with the request.
(4A) Where the accused was at an authorised place of detention at the time of the failure or refusal, subsections (1) and (2) do not apply if he had not been allowed an opportunity to consult a solicitor prior to the request being made.
(5) This section applies in relation to officers of customs and excise as it applies in relation to constables.
(6) This section does not preclude the drawing of any inference from a failure or refusal of the accused to account for the presence of an object, substance or mark or from the condition of clothing or footwear which could properly be drawn apart from this section.
(7) This section does not apply in relation to a failure or refusal which occurred before the commencement of this section.
37.—(1) Where—
  (a) a person arrested by a constable was found by him at a place at or about the time the offence for which he was arrested is alleged to have been committed; and
  (b) that or another constable investigating the offence reasonably believes that the presence of the person at that place and at that time may be attributable to his participation in the commission of the offence; and

(c) the constable informs the person that he so believes, and requests him to account for that presence; and

(d) the person fails or refuses to do so,

then if, in any proceedings against the person for the offence, evidence of those matters is given, subsection (2) below applies.

(2) Where this subsection applies—

    (a) [repealed];

    (b) a judge, in deciding whether to grant an application made by the accused under paragraph 3 of schedule 2 to the Crime and Disorder Act 1998;

    (c) the court, in determining whether there is a case to answer; and

    (d) the court or jury, in determining whether the accused is guilty of the offence charged,

may draw such inferences from the failure or refusal as appear proper.

(3) Subsections (1) and (2) do not apply unless the accused was told in ordinary language by the constable when making the request mentioned in subsection (1)(c) above what the effect of this section would be if he failed or refused to comply with the request.

(3A) Where the accused was at an authorised place of detention at the time of the failure or refusal, subsection (1) and (2) do not apply if he had not been allowed an opportunity to consult a solicitor prior to the request being made.

(4) This section applies in relation to officers of customs and excise as it applies in relation to constables.

(5) This section does not preclude the drawing of any inference from a failure or refusal of the accused to account for his presence at a place which could properly be drawn apart from this section.

(6) This section does not apply in relation to a failure or refusal which occurred before the commencement of this section.

An 'authorised place of detention' is defined by s. 38(2A) to include police stations and any other place prescribed by order.   **F19.35**

Sections 36 and 37 are based on the Irish Criminal Justice Act 1984. They go further than s. 34, which relates to the weight to be given to D's defence, and amount to positive evidence to support the prosecution case.

Basis for Inference

Neither s. 36 nor s. 37 of the CJPO 1994 permits an inference to be drawn unless four conditions are satisfied: **F19.36**

(a) the accused is arrested;

(b) a constable (not necessarily the arresting officer) reasonably believes that the object, substance or mark, or the presence of the accused at the relevant place, may be attributable to the accused's participation in a crime (in s. 36 an offence 'specified by the constable'; in s. 37 the offence for which he was arrested);

(c) the constable informs the accused of his belief and requests an explanation of the matter in question;

(d) the constable tells the suspect in ordinary language the effect of a failure or refusal to comply with the request.

The four conditions may, on their face, be satisfied where an arrested person is confronted with incriminating circumstances before he is taken to the police station for interview. However, a request for information under the two sections would appear to be a form of questioning, and because an arrested suspect should not normally be questioned about his involvement in an offence except in interview at a police station or other authorised place of detention (PACE Code C, para. 11.1) the tendering in evidence of an unproductive request for information 'on the beat' should be the exception rather than the norm. If such a request is made and is alleged to have yielded a silence from which inferences can properly be drawn, the procedure for putting the silence to the suspect in a subsequent interview at the police station will apply (para. 11.4: see **F19.21**). The 'special warnings' to be given at interview in connection with ss. 36 and 37 are dealt with in PACE Code C, paras. 10.10 and 10.11.

Part F Evidence

F19.37   As with s. 34 (see **F19.10**), only 'proper' inferences may be drawn. The jury must be satisfied that the accused has failed to 'account' for the relevant matter (*Compton* [2002] EWCA
Crim 2835) and that any explanation advanced by the accused should be rejected as implausible before an inference can be said to be proper (see **F19.23**). Clearly the strength of the
inference increases with the suspicious nature of the circumstances, so that if the accused is
arrested when in possession of a car with explosive devices in full view on the back seat, his
failure to give an account is more suggestive of guilt than if he refuses to account for a dirty
mark on his clothing following a fight in which he is alleged to have fallen to the ground.
In some cases a strong inference is proper. In *Connolly* (10 June 1994 unreported), C had
been given an opportunity to account for an incriminating receipt found in his pocket,
and his presence near the scene of the crime, but had maintained complete silence. The
Court of Appeal for Northern Ireland accepted the trial judge's inference, drawn under
provisions equivalent to ss. 36 and 37, that C was determined to sit out interrogation,
assess the strength of the case against him and, if charged, to present a version of his activities unembarrassed by any statements to which he might have committed himself during
interview.

F19.38   Sections 36 and 37 are somewhat restrictively drawn. Section 36 is concerned with the state of
the suspect at the time of his arrest, and not with his state at other relevant times, e.g., when
seen by an eye-witness at the time of the crime. Section 37 is similarly concerned only with
the suspect's location at the time of arrest, and applies only when he was found at the location
of the crime at or about the relevant time. No mention is made of his presence at the scene at
other relevant times: what if he gave the police the slip at the scene and was arrested elsewhere?
If the intention is to build upon already suspicious circumstances by allowing an additional
guilty inference if the accused fails to explain them, it is not clear why the provisions are so
restrictive: a suspected rapist may have inferences drawn for failing to explain away stains on
his trousers, but not for refusing to explain why he is not wearing any (unless he has discarded
them nearby).

F19.39   Section 38(3) (see **F19.14**) provides that an inference drawn under these provisions may, *inter
alia*, form part of the case to answer or contribute to a verdict of guilty, though neither outcome
may be based 'solely' upon such an inference. It is not clear what this means. An inference
drawn under ss. 36 and 37 can never exist 'solely', in the sense of independently of the proof
of the suspicious circumstances for which the accused refuses to account. In some cases, such
circumstances may be sufficient to convict, as in the case of the man arrested with two bombs
on the back seat of his car. The fact that the accused gave no explanation cannot prevent the
circumstances having this effect: on the contrary, it strengthens the inference to be drawn from
them. Perhaps the intention behind the provision is to prompt the judge to tell the jury not to
convict just because the accused has been unhelpful.

It is not clear how frequently these two provisions will function independently of ss. 34 and 35.
If D goes on to present a defence relying on facts he could have mentioned earlier, as in *Connolly*,
it is likely that s. 34 will also apply. If he gives no evidence, then s. 35 (see **F19.42**) may come
into play.

Unfair Use of Pre-trial Silence

F19.40   Failure or refusal to respond to questioning relevant to ss. 34, 36 and 37 seems unlikely to be
regarded as a 'statement', and is thus incapable of being a confession within s. 82 of the PACE
1984 for the purposes of s. 76 of that Act (see **F17.8**). Silence obtained by oppression or in
circumstances conducive to unreliability would not therefore be automatically inadmissible, as
would a confession similarly obtained. It would, however, be subject to exclusion under the discretion conferred by the PACE 1984, s. 78, in respect of all prosecution evidence, to the extent
that it would be unfair to make use of it.

Extensive use has also been made of s. 78 in rejecting confession evidence which, while admissible under s. 76, has been obtained in breach of the 1984 Act or Codes of Practice, or by other unfair means (see F17.30). These authorities would seem to apply also to silence, with the result that, for example, failure to make proper records of an interrogation may lead to exclusion.

FAILURE OF ACCUSED TO TESTIFY

The CJPO 1994 repealed the Criminal Evidence Act 1898, s. 1(b). The 1898 Act provided **F19.41** that the failure of the accused to testify was not to be made the subject of any comment by the prosecution. Comment by the judge was permissible but the scope for it was limited, and it had always to be accompanied by a reminder that the accused was not bound to give evidence and that, while the jury had been deprived of the opportunity of hearing his story tested in cross-examination, they were not to assume that he was guilty because he had not gone into the witness-box (*Bathurst* [1968] 2 QB 99). Stronger comment was permitted where the defence case involved the assertion of facts which were at variance with the prosecution evidence, or additional to it and exculpatory, and which, if true, would have been within the accused's own knowledge (*Martinez-Tobon* [1994] 1 WLR 388).

Failure to Testify following the 1994 Act

Under the CJPO 1994, s. 35, it is submitted that the common-law authorities will continue **F19.42** to provide useful guidance as to the type of case in which the strongest inferences are permissible. (See further F19.45 to F19.52.) A careful direction will be required in all cases where the accused does not testify, in order to make the jury aware of the inferences which may properly be drawn, not least because of the need to comply with the 'fair trial' provisions of the ECHR, Article 6 (*Birchall* [1999] Crim LR 311).

Criminal Justice and Public Order Act 1994, s. 35

(1) At the trial of any person for an offence, subsections (2) and (3) below apply unless—
  (a) the accused's guilt is not in issue; or
  (b) it appears to the court that the physical or mental condition of the accused makes it undesirable for him to give evidence;
  but subsection (2) below does not apply if, at the conclusion of the evidence for the prosecution, his legal representative informs the court that the accused will give evidence or, where he is unrepresented, the court ascertains from him that he will give evidence.
(2) Where this subsection applies, the court shall, at the conclusion of the evidence for the prosecution, satisfy itself (in the case of proceedings on indictment with a jury, in the presence of the jury) that the accused is aware that the stage has been reached at which evidence can be given for the defence and that he can, if he wishes, give evidence and that, if he chooses not to give evidence, or having been sworn, without good cause refuses to answer any question, it will be permissible for the court or jury to draw such inferences as appear proper from his failure to give evidence or his refusal, without good cause, to answer any question.
(3) Where this subsection applies, the court or jury, in determining whether the accused is guilty of the offence charged, may draw such inferences as appear proper from the failure of the accused to give evidence or his refusal, without good cause, to answer any question.
(4) This section does not render the accused compellable to give evidence on his own behalf, and he shall accordingly not be guilty of contempt of court by reason of a failure to do so.
(5) For the purposes of this section a person who, having been sworn, refuses to answer any question shall be taken to do so without good cause unless—
  (a) he is entitled to refuse to answer the question by virtue of any enactment, whenever passed or made, or on the ground of privilege; or
  (b) the court in the exercise of its general discretion excuses him from answering it.
(6) [Repealed.]

(7) This section applies—
  (a) in relation to proceedings on indictment for an offence, only if the person charged with the offence is arraigned on or after the commencement of this section;
  (b) in relation to proceedings in a magistrates' court, only if the time when the court begins to receive evidence in the proceedings falls after the commencement of this section.

F19.43 **Procedure**   CPD VI, paras. 39P.1 to 39P.5 (see Supplement, **PD-62**), provide detailed guidance on the procedure where the accused declines to give evidence. The court's obligation in s. 35(2) to satisfy itself that the accused knows that he can, if he wishes, give evidence is mandatory and cannot be overlooked even where the accused has, by absconding, put himself beyond the reach of the warning (*Gough* [2002] 2 Cr App R 121).

It has long been the recommended practice, and is of great importance in light of s. 35, for counsel to record the decision of the accused not to give evidence, and to sign it and indicate that it was made voluntarily (see **D17.12** and *Bevan* (1994) 98 Cr App R 354 and *Chatroodi* [2001] EWCA Crim 585). The decision is frequently a stressful one for the accused, and where there is a potential issue as to his capacity to make a decision it is of particular importance that the necessary considerations are fully and properly spelled out to him (*Cox* [2013] EWCA Crim 1025). Where it is contended on appeal that the accused was misadvised, or was not in a position to make an informed decision, he must provide the court with a statement setting out the relevant history (*Farooqi* [2014] 1 Cr App R 69 (8)).

F19.44 **Charge of Causing or Allowing a Child or Vulnerable Adult to Die or Suffer Serious Physical Harm**   The DVCVA 2004, ss. 6 and 6A, make special provision for the inferences to be drawn where a person fails to testify when charged with an offence under s. 5 of that Act (causing or allowing child or vulnerable adult to die or suffer serious physical harm: see **B1.73**).

Domestic Violence, Crime and Victims Act 2004, s. 6

(2) Where by virtue of section 35(3) of the Criminal Justice and Public Order Act 1994 a court or jury is permitted, in relation to the section 5 offence, to draw such inferences as appear proper from the defendant's failure to give evidence or refusal to answer a question, the court or jury may also draw such inferences in determining whether he is guilty—
  (a) of murder or manslaughter, or
  (b) of any other offence of which he could lawfully be convicted on the charge of murder or manslaughter,
  even if there would otherwise be no case for him to answer in relation to that offence.

Section 6A makes similar provision in relation to inferences about relevant offences where the accused is charged with allowing a child or vulnerable adult to suffer serious physical harm.

See further **F19.49**.

'Proper' Inferences of Guilt

F19.45 Under the CJPO 1994, s. 35, the 'proper' inferences come about as a result of the failure of the accused to give evidence or his refusal without good cause to answer any question (s. 35(3)). Defendants whose 'physical or mental condition make it undesirable' for them to give evidence are excluded from the operation of the section, together with those whose 'guilt is not in issue' (s. 35(1)). By virtue of s. 35(5), the accused may be excused from answering a particular question on grounds of privilege or statutory entitlement, or in the discretion of the court. Subject to these exceptions, the accused must answer all proper questions or risk the drawing of inferences, and a judge may remind him of his duty in this regard, though he should avoid doing so in an oppressive way (*Ackinclose* [1996] Crim LR 747).

An observation that the accused has, by failing to give evidence, deprived the jury of contradiction or explanation of prosecution evidence can only fairly be made if the uncontradicted evidence concerns a matter about which the accused can confidently be expected to have personal knowledge (*Hamidi* [2010] EWCA Crim 66). In some cases, the evidence of the accused is superfluous (e.g., where the only issue was as to whether agreed facts fell within the offence of keeping a disorderly house: *McManus* [2001] EWCA Crim 2455). In such a case a s. 35 direction is inappropriate and prejudicial. The court is obliged to satisfy itself that defendants who have not indicated that they intend to give evidence understand the consequences of declining to do so (s. 35(2) and (3) and CPD VI, paras. 39P.1 to 39P.5: see Supplement, **PD-62**). CPD VI, paras. 39P.2 and 39P.3 make clear that the burden of explaining the option to testify and the consequences of failing to do so to the defendant rests, in the case of a legally represented defendant, with the legal representative.

Accused with Physical or Mental Limitations The meaning of s. 35(1)(b) of the CJPO **F19.46** 1994 was considered in *Friend* [1997] 2 All ER 1011. F was tried for murder. He had a physical age of 15, a mental age of 9, and an IQ of 63. Expert evidence suggested that, although not suggestible, his powers of comprehension were limited and he might find it difficult to do justice to himself in the witness box. Nevertheless F had given a clear account of his defence at various stages prior to trial. Taking all of these matters into account, the trial judge ruled that F's mental condition did not make it 'undesirable' for him to give evidence, so that his failure to do so led to the jury being directed that they might draw inferences under s. 35(3). The Court of Appeal agreed, noting that it would only be in a rare case that the judge would be called upon to arrive at a decision under s. 35(1)(b); generally an accused who was unable to comprehend proceedings so as to make a proper defence would be unfit to plead, so the issue would not arise (but see *Walls* [2011] 2 Cr App R 61 (see **F10.42**), requiring a rigorous examination of the evidence in fitness to plead cases, which a later court in *Dixon* [2013] 3 All ER 242 suggested might throw up more applications under s. 35(1)(b)). *Friend* also decides that s. 35(1)(b) gave a wide discretion to a trial judge which did not require to be circumscribed by any further judicial test. The trial judge had been right not to base his conclusion on the mental age of F: a person with a mental age of less than 14 did not automatically qualify for the protection of the section. Nor was he bound to determine the issue on the expert evidence alone, but was entitled to take account of the behaviour of F before and after the commission of the offence including the way in which he had put his defence in interview. (The conduct of F at the time of the offence, which was hotly disputed, was rightly not considered by the judge.) The trial judge in *Friend* seems to have been much influenced by the fact that young children regularly appear as witnesses in criminal cases, and that measures can be taken by which they and other vulnerable witnesses can, if their needs are correctly assessed, be protected from unfair or oppressive cross-examination. Thus, as the main reason for questioning the desirability of F testifying was that he might give a poor account of himself unless care were taken to ensure that he understood and had time to respond to questions, the fact that the court itself could respond sensitively to F's needs was a factor militating against the defence argument. The outcome suggests that the discretion will be exercised against the background of an assumption that it is generally desirable for an accused to testify, so that cases in which it can be said to be 'undesirable' will be rare indeed. The possibility of using an intermediary to overcome communication difficulties also weighs in the balance in favour of the giving of evidence (as in *Dixon*).

In *Tabbakh* (2009) 173 JP 201 the trial judge was held entitled to conclude that T's history of **F19.47** self-harm and post-traumatic stress disorder did not render it undesirable for him to give evidence: the risk that he might react in a hostile way to questioning and lose his self-control was one which could be taken into account by the jury, and did not justify a comprehensive failure to testify. In *Ensor* [2010] 1 Cr App R 255 it was held that s. 35(1)(b) requires that the accused's physical or mental condition is such that if he gives evidence it will have a 'significantly adverse effect on him'. However in *Dixon* it was pointed out that the sole issue in *Ensor* related to the adverse effect on E's health, and that there was no warrant for confining s. 35(1)(b) to such cases. In *Dixon* it was held relevant to consider the accused's difficulty in expressing himself and his problems of understanding, which were such that the judge had made an intermediary available to assist him had he testified. Nevertheless these features did not, properly considered, require the judge to find that it was undesirable for D to testify. In *Charisma* (2009) 173 JP 633 an alleged loss of memory of the alleged incident did not amount to a justification for not giving evidence in which the memory loss could have been tested.

Both *Friend* and the later decision in *A* [1997] Crim LR 883 require there to be an evidential basis for a ruling that s. 35(1)(b) applies. A *voir dire* may be required to determine the issue, although the judge is, according to *A*, under no obligation to initiate the procedure if defence counsel does not seek to do so (see also *Anwoir* [2009] 4 All ER 582). In *R (DPP) v Kavanagh* [2005] EWHC 820 (Admin), it was doubted whether, even in summary trial, non-expert evidence (such as that of a family member) as to the mental condition of the accused could be sufficient. In that case K's mother had testified to his history of depression, but even her evidence taken at its highest fell short of disclosing a subsisting condition making it undesirable for him to give evidence. In *Anwoir*, it was held that a judge could revisit a ruling that it was undesirable for an accused to testify. However, it was in that case unfair for the medical evidence rejected by the judge to be withheld from the jury.

F19.48   **Nature of Inference under s. 35**   The adverse inference which it may be proper to draw under s. 35(3) of the CJPO 1994 is that the accused 'is guilty of the offence charged'. As s. 35 does not come into play until after the close of the evidence for the prosecution, it presupposes that a prima facie case has already been established against the accused. In *Murray v DPP* [1994] 1 WLR 1, a decision concerning the equivalent provision in the Criminal Evidence (Northern Ireland) Order 1988 (SI 1988 No. 1987, N.I. 20), M was convicted of attempted murder and possession of a firearm with intent to endanger life. Scientific evidence linked M with a car used in the attack: the situation was one calling for 'confession and avoidance'. M advanced various explanations during interrogation, but gave no evidence at trial, from which failure the trial judge drew a strong adverse inference. The House of Lords considered that the inference was justified. The 1988 Order was intended to change the law and practice and to lay down new rules as to the comments which could be made and inferences which could be drawn. The accused is not compellable to testify, but he must risk the consequences if he does not do so. These consequences are not simply that specific inferences may be drawn from specific facts, but include in a proper case the inference that the accused is guilty. As to what is proper, Lord Slynn said (at p. 11):

> If there is no prima facie case shown by the prosecution there is no case to answer. Equally, if parts of the prosecution case had so little evidential value that they called for no answer, a failure to deal with those specific matters cannot justify an inference of guilt.

> On the other hand, if aspects of the evidence taken alone or in combination with other facts clearly call for an explanation which the accused ought to be in a position to give, if an explanation exists, then a failure to give any explanation may as a matter of common sense allow the drawing of an inference that there is no explanation and that the accused is guilty.

F19.49   **No Conviction Solely on Inference from s. 35**   As with ss. 34, 36 and 37 of the CJPO 1994, the accused cannot be convicted solely on an inference drawn from a failure or refusal (s. 38(3): see **F19.14**). In *Cowan* [1996] QB 373 the Court of Appeal emphasised that the prosecution remains under an obligation to establish a prima facie case before any question of the accused testifying is raised. Their lordships took this to mean not only that the case should be fit to be left to the jury, but also that the judge should make clear to the jury that *they* must be convinced of the existence of a prima facie case before drawing an adverse inference from silence. This may seem to go beyond the strict requirement of the statute, but serves to ensure conformity with the principle in *Murray v UK* (1996) 22 EHRR 29 that the accused should not be convicted 'solely or mainly' on an inference from silence (*Birchall* [1999] Crim LR 311: see also **F19.15**). In a case where there is a compelling case for the accused to answer it has been held that the failure to direct in accordance with this aspect of *Cowan* could not affect the safety of the conviction (*Bromfield* [2002] EWCA Crim 195). In *Whitehead* [2006] EWCA Crim 1486, where the case for the prosecution in a sexual offence depended on the credibility of a complainant who had delayed making a complaint for more than ten years, the Criminal Cases Review Commission referred the case to the Court of Appeal on the basis that the omission to direct the jury that they should first find a case to answer might have led to them using the accused's failure to testify to 'shore up' the deficiencies in the complainant's evidence. The Court of Appeal dismissed this possibility as 'fanciful' in light of the very clear directions that had been given to the jury that they had to be 'sure' the complainant was not lying, and that the accused's silence was not by itself proof of guilt. The Court considered that the direction to the jury to find a prima facie case before considering the implications of the accused's silence 'amplifies and spells out' what is already implicit in the separate injunction that failure to give evidence cannot by itself prove guilt. See also *Hobson* [2013] 1 WLR 3733, in which a specific comment by the trial judge might, taken in isolation, have led the jury to think that they should consider the inference to be drawn from H's failure to give evidence before deciding whether he had a case to answer. Read as a whole, however, the direction would not have created this false impression.

The power to draw an inference under the DVCVA 2004, s. 6(2) or s. 6A(2) (see **F19.44**), in circumstances where there would otherwise be no case to answer constitutes an (as yet untested) exception to the *Murray* principle.

Drawing an Inference: General Rule   In *Cowan* [1996] QB 373, the Court of Appeal rejected   **F19.50**
an argument that s. 35 should be permitted to operate in exceptional cases only. The plain wording of s. 35 indicated that it was not limited to exceptional cases: on the contrary, the exceptional cases were those dealt with in s. 35(1) in which the provisions were *not* to be invoked. However, it was open to a court in any case to which the exceptions in s. 35(1) did not apply to decline to draw an inference from silence, though for a judge to advise a jury against drawing such an inference would require either 'some evidential basis for doing so or some exceptional factors in the case making that a fair course to take'. The Court of Appeal gave no example of the situation in which it would be improper to draw an inference from silence, although it stipulated that an inference could not be drawn unless the jury decides that the silence 'can only sensibly be attributed' to the accused having no answer, or none that would stand up to cross-examination.

Cowan was applied in *Napper* (1997) 161 JP 16. N claimed that the failure of the police to interview him while the frauds with which he was charged were reasonably fresh in his mind should have led the judge to direct the jury to draw no adverse inferences from his silence at trial. It was held that this was not, under *Cowan*, an exceptional case where such a direction would have been justified in the interests of justice. Nothing prevented N from making his own record from which to refresh his memory, and the crucial issues were in any case sufficiently memorable to present him with no difficulty of recollection. More recently in *Becouarn* [2003] EWCA Crim 1154 it was held (on facts similar to those in *Cowan*) that the normal s. 35 direction should be given notwithstanding that B's reason for not testifying was that his criminal record would have been revealed because his defence consisted of an assertion that prosecution witnesses had committed the crime with which he was charged. That practice was endorsed by the House of Lords (*Becouarn* [2005] 1 WLR 2589), although it was not to be an invariable practice having regard to the trial judge's overriding discretion to avoid unfairness by declining to give a direction in a particular case, the decision is effectively superseded by the CJA 2003, s. 101. Under s. 101(1)(g) (see **F12.91**), an accused who has attacked another person's character renders himself liable to the disclosure of his own bad character whether he testifies or not, so that the option of not testifying now entails the likelihood of both disclosure of the record and a s. 35 direction and the dilemma facing the accused in *Becouarn* no longer obtains.

No Inference where Prosecution Case is Weak   It seems from the observations of Lord Slynn   **F19.51**
in *Murray v DPP* [1994] 1 WLR 1 (see **F19.48**) that inferences of guilt should not be drawn from failure to give evidence to contradict a prosecution case of 'little evidential value'. This accords with the position at common law, where it was considered improper for a judge to bolster a weak prosecution case by making comments on an accused's failure to give evidence (*Waugh v The King* [1950] AC 203). However in *RS v DPP* [2013] EWHC 322 (Admin) the Divisional Court rejected an argument that no inferences should be drawn from the failure of a child to testify in a case of robbery of a mobile phone that depended on the correctness of an

identification substantially based on hearsay evidence. It was held that, once it had been decided that there was a case to answer, the failure of the accused to give evidence about relevant matters in his police interview (in the absence of evidence of a reason for his silence) made the drawing of an inference permissible. Lord Slynn's comments in *Murray* were cited in argument but appear not to have affected the outcome.

F19.52 **Strong Inference where Facts Clearly Call for Explanation or are within the Accused's Knowledge**   In *Mutch* [1973] 1 All ER 178, the Court of Appeal identified exceptional cases at common law in which stronger comment was justified. They were those in which an inference could be drawn from uncontested or clearly established facts which point so strongly to guilt as to call for an explanation. *Corrie* (1904) 20 TLR 365 and *Bernard* (1908) 1 Cr App R 218 are cited in *Mutch* as exceptional examples of the kind of case in which such an inference may properly be drawn. So also is *Brigden* [1973] Crim LR 579. The accused gave no evidence, but alleged that the police had planted incriminating evidence on him and cross-examined a prosecution witness on a conviction. It is submitted that such a case would support a strong inference under the CJPO 1994 that the defence was untrue. The same may be said of other cases concerning facts within the accused's own knowledge which were said to justify strong comment at common law in *Martinez-Tobon* [1994] 1 WLR 388 (see **F19.41**).

Burden on Accused

F19.53 A different form of comment was required at common law in cases in which the accused bears the burden of proof, namely 'that he is not bound to go into the witness box, nobody can force him to go into the witness box, but the burden is upon him, and if he does not, he runs the risk of not being able to prove his case' (*Bathurst* [1968] 2 QB 99: see **F19.41**). The same situation under the CJPO 1994 would seem to justify a strong adverse inference if the defence is one which, if true, could be proved by the accused's own evidence (e.g., that his possession of an offensive weapon was lawful: Prevention of Crime Act 1953, s. 1(1), see **B12.138**).

Where diminished responsibility is set up by way of defence, and there are matters about which the accused could give evidence which are relevant to the issue before the jury, inferences may be drawn in the usual way unless the condition of the accused is such as to make it undesirable for him to give evidence within the meaning of s. 35(1)(b) (see **F19.46**). Comments in *Bathurst* [1968] 2 QB 99 that only rarely could an inference be drawn provide no authority for any wider exemption from inferences in such a case (*Barr* [2010] 2 All ER 1004). In some cases, the defence requires no contribution from the accused, in which case no inference can properly be drawn (see **F19.45**).

ACCUSED FAILING TO PROVIDE SAMPLES ETC.

F19.54 At common law, an adverse inference could be drawn from unhelpful conduct other than silence while under interrogation. In *Smith* (1985) 81 Cr App R 286, S was asked in the presence of his solicitor if he was willing to provide a sample of hair. When he asked why, S was told that it was for comparison with hairs found at the scene of the robbery of which he was suspected. He replied 'In that case, no I am not'. It was held that the fact that, at that time, such samples could not lawfully be taken without S's consent did not mean that no inferences could be drawn from his refusal. Leonard J considered that it would be 'contrary to good sense' to prohibit the drawing of inferences and that the case was 'in a wholly different category' from evidence of a failure to answer questions under caution. Nevertheless the court borrowed from the rules regarding silence when it stressed the fact that the presence of S's solicitor rendered the parties 'on even terms' (see **F19.3**). (See also *McVeigh v Beattie* [1988] Fam 69, in which it was held that the refusal of the respondent in affiliation proceedings to submit to a blood test which might have excluded the possibility that he had fathered the child in question could, in the absence of a reasonable explanation, amount to corroboration of the evidence of the complainant.)

The police have wide powers to take biometric samples and impressions, and also footwear impressions, both with and without consent (although 'intimate' samples can only be taken with consent) (see generally D1.104 *et seq*. and the PACE 1984, ss. 61 to 63A). The rule in *Smith* has found statutory expression in s. 62(10), which permits 'such inferences as appear proper' to be drawn 'where the appropriate consent to the taking of an intimate sample from a person was refused without good cause' in a variety of circumstances including the determination of whether the person is guilty of the offence charged.

FAILURE TO CALL WITNESSES OR PROVIDE EVIDENCE

If the accused fails to call a particular person as a witness, then, if appropriate, as when the prosecution had no possible means of knowing that that person had any relevant evidence to give until the accused himself gave evidence at the trial, the judge may direct the jury that they may take into account the fact that the potential witness was not called, but should exercise a degree of care. In particular he should avoid the suggestion that the failure is something of importance where there may be a valid reason for not calling the witness (Megaw LJ in *Gallagher* [1974] 3 All ER 118, affirmed in *Couzens* [1992] Crim LR 822). Comment may also be justified if there is a very strong case for suggesting that an account which an accused is giving has recently been fabricated and where, if it has not, there would be another witness or other witnesses of any description who could substantiate the accused's story if it were true (*Wilmot* (1988) 89 Cr App R 341 per Glidewell LJ at p. 352). However, comment in this area has to be made with circumspection and reserve (*Weller* [1994] Crim LR 856). In *Weller* the Court of Appeal held that it could not envisage any case in which it would be appropriate to make a comment to the effect that if there were any truth in the accused's story, he would have been expected to have called a particular witness. In the somewhat extreme case of *Forsyth* [1997] 2 Cr App R 299, the witness, J, was not one whom the defence might have been expected to call in the light of the issues raised by prosecution or defence at trial, but his absence was the subject of comment by prosecuting counsel in his closing address, and the jury subsequently asked the judge for guidance. It was held that the judge should have made it clear to the jury that they should draw no inference from the absence of J, and that they should decide the case on the evidence and without speculating on what J might have said. See also *Wright* [2000] Crim LR 510, where it was said that comments on the failure to call a particular witness may amount to a reversal of the burden of proof, and *Rodenhurst* (2001) *Independent*, 23 July 2001, where the court approved the trial judge's warning that 'the danger of speculating about a witness's absence is precisely that you may impute some motive that may be entirely wrong'.

Comment on Failure of Spouse or Civil Partner of Accused to Testify

The failure of the spouse or civil partner of the accused to give evidence shall not be made the subject of any comment by the prosecution (PACE 1984, s. 80A). In *Brown* [1983] Crim LR 38, it was held with respect to the forerunner of s. 80A that the wording was mandatory, and that breach of the prohibition would amount to a material irregularity in the course of the trial. However, whether a breach would lead to a conviction being quashed depended upon all the circumstances, and in particular whether the trial judge corrected the breach in his summing-up. In *Dickman* (1910) 5 Cr App R 135, in which counsel inadvertently commented upon the failure of the spouse of the accused to testify but the jury were told to dismiss the comment from their minds, the appeal against conviction was dismissed. Likewise in *Hunter* [1969] Crim LR 262, where a comment was made in breach of the prohibition but the judge, refusing to discharge the jury, warned them about the comment, the conviction was upheld. These cases may be contrasted with *Naudeer* [1984] 3 All ER 1036. N, a man of good character, was convicted of theft. At the trial, counsel for the prosecution suggested that the failure of N's wife to give evidence had deprived the jury of what would probably have been material evidence, and the

F19.55

F19.56

judge failed in his summing-up to give any direction to repair the breach of the prohibition on such comment. The Court of Appeal quashed the conviction on the grounds that the breach was central to the overall justice of the case, particularly since the accused was a man of good character (which he had put before the jury), and the question of his bona fides was central to the offence itself. It was the duty of the judge, depending upon the circumstances of each case, to remedy any breach of the prohibition on such comment in his summing-up.

F19.57 Section 80A of the PACE 1984 does not prevent comment by the judge on the failure of the spouse or civil partner of the accused to testify. In *Naudeer*, Purchas LJ said (at p. 1039) that 'if a judge in the exercise of his discretion decides to comment upon the failure of the accused to call his spouse or to give evidence himself he must, except in exceptional circumstances, do this with a great deal of circumspection'. The same degree of circumspection would also appear to be required in the case of failure to call cohabitees, who are not covered by s. 80(8) (*Weller* [1994] Crim LR 856). In *Whitton* [1998] Crim LR 492, prosecuting counsel commented on the failure of W's husband, who had been present when she allegedly assaulted a neighbour, to give evidence. This clear breach was, however, held to have been subsumed in the summing-up in which the trial judge quite properly elected to make a comment of his own. It was not possible in the circumstances to argue that counsel's comment undermined the safety of W's conviction, though this should clearly not be read as an invitation to counsel to disregard the statutory provision, however strong the case for judicial comment. See also *Marsh* [2008] EWCA Crim 1816, where the comment went uncorrected by the judge, but the conviction was not rendered unsafe.

Appendix 1   Codes of Practice under the Police and Criminal Evidence Act 1984

PACE CODE A

REVISED CODE OF PRACTICE FOR THE EXERCISE BY:

POLICE OFFICERS OF STATUTORY POWERS OF STOP AND SEARCH

POLICE OFFICERS AND POLICE STAFF OF REQUIREMENTS TO RECORD PUBLIC ENCOUNTERS

Commencement—Transitional Arrangements

This code applies to any search by a police officer and the recording of public encounters taking place after 00.00 on 27 October 2013.

1.0 General

1.01 This code of practice must be readily available at all police stations for consultation by police officers, police staff, detained persons and members of the public.

1.02 The notes for guidance included are not provisions of this code, but are guidance to police officers and others about its application and interpretation. Provisions in the annexes to the code are provisions of this code.

1.03 This code governs the exercise by police officers of statutory powers to search a person or a vehicle without first making an arrest. The main stop and search powers to which this code applies are set out in Annex A, but that list should not be regarded as definitive (see *Note 1*). In addition, it covers requirements on police officers and police staff to record encounters not governed by statutory powers. This code does not apply to:

   (a)   the powers of stop and search under:
      (i)   the Aviation Security Act 1982, section 27(2), and
      (ii) the Police and Criminal Evidence Act 1984, section 6(1) (which relates specifically to powers of constables employed by statutory undertakers on the premises of the statutory undertakers);

   (b)   searches carried out for the purposes of examination under Schedule 7 to the Terrorism Act 2000 and to which the Code of Practice issued under paragraph 6 of Schedule 14 to the Terrorism Act 2000 applies.

   (c)   the powers to search persons and vehicles and to stop and search in specified locations to which the Code of Practice issued under section 47AB of the Terrorism Act 2000 applies.

1 Principles governing stop and search

1.1   Powers to stop and search must be used fairly, responsibly, with respect for people being searched and without unlawful discrimination. Under the Equality Act 2010, section 149, when police officers are carrying out their functions, they also have a duty to have due regard to the need to eliminate unlawful discrimination, harassment and victimisation, to advance equality of opportunity between people who share a relevant protected characteristic and people who do not share it, and to take steps to foster good relations between those persons. (See *Notes 1* and *1A*.)

1.2   The intrusion on the liberty of the person stopped or searched must be brief and detention for the purposes of a search must take place at or near the location of the stop.

1.3   If these fundamental principles are not observed the use of powers to stop and search may be drawn into question. Failure to use the powers in the proper manner reduces their effectiveness. Stop and search can play an important role in the detection and prevention of crime, and using the powers fairly makes them more effective.

1.4   The primary purpose of stop and search powers is to enable officers to allay or confirm suspicions about individuals without exercising their power of arrest. Officers may be required to justify the use or authorisation of such powers, in relation both to individual searches and the overall pattern of their activity in this regard, to their supervisory officers or in court. Any misuse of the powers is likely to be harmful to policing and lead to mistrust of the police. Officers must also be able to explain their actions to the member of the public searched. The misuse of these powers can lead to disciplinary action.

1.5   An officer must not search a person, even with his or her consent, where no power to search is applicable. Even where a person is prepared to submit to a search voluntarily, the person must not be searched unless the necessary legal power exists, and the search must be in accordance with the relevant power and the provisions of this Code. The only exception, where an officer does not require a specific power, applies to searches of persons entering sports grounds or other premises carried out with their consent given as a condition of entry.

2   Explanation of powers to stop and search

2.1   This code applies, subject to paragraph 1.03, to powers of stop and search as follows:

(a)   powers which require reasonable grounds for suspicion, before they may be exercised; that articles unlawfully obtained or possessed are being carried;

(b)   authorised under section 60 of the Criminal Justice and Public Order Act 1994, based upon a reasonable belief that incidents involving serious violence may take place or that people are carrying dangerous instruments or offensive weapons within any locality in the police area, or that it is expedient to use the powers to find such instruments or weapons that have been used in incidents of serious violence;

(c)   *Not used.*

(d)   powers to search a person who has not been arrested in the exercise of a power to search premises (see Code B *paragraph 2.4*); and

(e)   the powers in Schedule 5 to the Terrorism Prevention and Investigation Measures (TPIM) Act 2011 to search an individual who has not been arrested, conferred by:

(i)   paragraph 6(2)(a) at the time of serving a TPIM notice;

(ii)   paragraph 8(2)(a) under a search warrant for compliance purposes; and

(iii)   paragraph 10 for public safety purposes.

See *paragraph 2.18A*.

Searches requiring reasonable grounds for suspicion

2.2   Reasonable grounds for suspicion depend on the circumstances in each case. There must be an objective basis for that suspicion based on facts, information, and/or intelligence which are relevant to the likelihood of finding an article of a certain kind. Reasonable suspicion can never be supported on the basis of personal factors. It must rely on intelligence or information about, or some specific behaviour by, the person concerned. For example, unless the police have a description of a suspect, a person's physical appearance (including any of the relevant 'protected characteristics' set out in the Equality Act 2010 (see *paragraph 1.1* and *Note 1A*), or the fact that the person is known to have a previous conviction, cannot be used alone or in combination with each other, or in combination with any other factor, as the reason for searching that person. Reasonable suspicion cannot be based on generalisations or stereotypical images of certain groups or categories of people as more likely to be involved in criminal activity.

2.3   Reasonable suspicion may also exist without specific information or intelligence and on the basis of the behaviour of a person. For example, if an officer encounters someone on the street at night who is obviously trying to hide something, the officer may (depending on the other surrounding circumstances) base such suspicion on the fact that this kind of behaviour is often linked to stolen or prohibited articles being carried.

2.4   However, reasonable suspicion should normally be linked to accurate and current intelligence or information, such as information describing an article being carried, a suspected offender, or a person who has been seen carrying a type of article known to have been stolen recently from premises in the area. Searches based on accurate and current intelligence or information are more likely to be effective. Targeting searches in a particular area at specified crime problems increases their effectiveness and minimises inconvenience to law-abiding members of the public. It also helps in justifying the use of searches both to those who are searched and to the public. This does not however prevent stop and search powers being exercised in other locations where such powers may be exercised and reasonable suspicion exists.

2.5   Searches are more likely to be effective, legitimate, and secure public confidence when reasonable suspicion is based on a range of factors. The overall use of these powers is more likely to be effective when up-to-date and accurate intelligence or information is communicated to officers and they are well-informed about local crime patterns.

2.6   Where there is reliable information or intelligence that members of a group or gang habitually carry knives unlawfully or weapons or controlled drugs, and wear a distinctive item of clothing or other means of identification to indicate their membership of the group or gang, that distinctive item of clothing or other means of identification may provide reasonable grounds to stop and search a person. (See *Note 9*.)

2.7   A police officer may have reasonable grounds to suspect that a person is in innocent possession of a stolen or prohibited article or other item for which the officer is empowered to search. In that case the officer may stop and search the person even though there would be no power of arrest.

2.8   *Not used.*

2.9   An officer who has reasonable grounds for suspicion may detain the person concerned in order to carry out a search. Before carrying out a search the officer may ask questions about the person's behaviour or presence in circumstances which gave rise to the suspicion. As a result of questioning the detained person, the reasonable grounds for suspicion necessary to detain that person may be confirmed or, because of a satisfactory explanation, be eliminated. (See *Notes 2* and *3*.) Questioning may also reveal reasonable grounds to suspect the possession of a different kind of unlawful article from that originally suspected. Reasonable grounds for suspicion however cannot be provided retrospectively by such questioning during a person's detention or by refusal to answer any questions put.

2.10 If, as a result of questioning before a search, or other circumstances which come to the attention of the officer, there cease to be reasonable grounds for suspecting that an article is being carried of a kind for which there is a power to stop and search, no search may take place. (See *Note 3*.) In the absence of any other lawful power to detain, the person is free to leave at will and must be so informed.

2.11 There is no power to stop or detain a person in order to find grounds for a search. Police officers have many encounters with members of the public which do not involve detaining people against their will. If reasonable grounds for suspicion emerge during such an encounter, the officer may search the person, even though no grounds existed when the encounter began. If an officer is detaining someone for the purpose of a search, he or she should inform the person as soon as detention begins.

Searches authorised under section 60 of the Criminal Justice and Public Order Act 1994

2.12 Authority for a constable in uniform to stop and search under section 60 of the Criminal Justice and Public Order Act 1994 may be given if the authorising officer reasonably believes:

   (a)   that incidents involving serious violence may take place in any locality in the officer's police area, and it is expedient to use these powers to prevent their occurrence;

   (b)   that persons are carrying dangerous instruments or offensive weapons without good reason in any locality in the officer's police area; or

   (c)   that an incident involving serious violence has taken place in the officer's police area, a dangerous instrument or offensive weapon used in the incident is being carried by a person in any locality in that police area, and it is expedient to use these powers to find that instrument or weapon.

2.13 An authorisation under section 60 may only be given by an officer of the rank of inspector or above and in writing, or orally if paragraph 2.12(c) applies and it is not practicable to give the authorisation in writing. The authorisation (whether written or oral) must specify the grounds on which it was given, the locality in which the powers may be exercised and the period of time for which they are in force. The period authorised shall be no longer than appears reasonably necessary to prevent, or seek to prevent incidents of serious violence, or to deal with the problem of carrying dangerous instruments or offensive weapons or to find a dangerous instrument or offensive weapon that has been used. It may not exceed 24 hours. An oral authorisation given where paragraph 2.12(c) applies must be recorded in writing as soon as practicable. (See *Notes 10* to *13*.)

2.14 An inspector who gives an authorisation must, as soon as practicable, inform an officer of or above the rank of superintendent. This officer may direct that the authorisation shall be extended for a further 24 hours, if violence or the carrying of dangerous instruments or offensive weapons has occurred, or is suspected to have occurred, and the continued use of the powers is considered necessary to prevent or deal with further such activity or to find a dangerous instrument or offensive weapon used that has been used. That direction must be given in writing unless it is not practicable to do so, in which case it must be recorded in writing as soon as practicable afterwards. (See *Note 12*.)

2.14A The selection of persons and vehicles under section 60 to be stopped and, if appropriate, searched should reflect an objective assessment of the nature of the incident or weapon in question and the individuals and vehicles thought likely to be associated with that incident or those weapons (see *Notes 10* and *11*). The powers must not be used to stop and search persons and vehicles for reasons unconnected with the purpose of the authorisation. When selecting persons and vehicles to be stopped in response to a specific threat or incident, officers must take care not to discriminate unlawfully against anyone on the grounds of any of the protected characteristics set out in the Equality Act 2010. (See *paragraph 1.1.*)

2.14B The driver of a vehicle which is stopped under section 60 and any person who is searched under section 60 are entitled to a written statement to that effect if they apply within twelve months from the day the vehicle was stopped or the person was searched. This statement is a record which states that the vehicle was stopped or (as the case may be) that the person was searched under section 60 and it may form part of the search record or be supplied as a separate record.

Powers to require removal of face coverings

2.15 Section 60AA of the Criminal Justice and Public Order Act 1994 also provides a power to demand the removal of disguises. The officer exercising the power must reasonably believe that someone is wearing an item wholly or mainly for the purpose of concealing identity. There is also a power to seize such items where the officer believes that a person intends to wear them for this purpose. There is no power to stop and search for disguises. An officer may seize any such item which is discovered when exercising a power of search for something else, or which is being carried, and which the officer reasonably believes is intended to be used for concealing anyone's identity. This power can only be used if an authorisation given under section 60 or under section 60AA, is in force. (See *Note 4.*)

2.16 Authority under section 60AA for a constable in uniform to require the removal of disguises and to seize them may be given if the authorising officer reasonably believes that activities may take place in any locality in the officer's police area that are likely to involve the commission of offences and it is expedient to use these powers to prevent or control these activities.

2.17 An authorisation under section 60AA may only be given by an officer of the rank of inspector or above, in writing, specifying the grounds on which it was given, the locality in which the powers may be exercised and the period of time for which they are in force. The period authorised shall be no longer than appears reasonably necessary to prevent, or seek to prevent the commission of offences. It may not exceed 24 hours. (See *Notes 10* to *13.*)

2.18 An inspector who gives an authorisation must, as soon as practicable, inform an officer of or above the rank of superintendent. This officer may direct that the authorisation shall be extended for a further 24 hours, if crimes have been committed, or are suspected to have been committed, and the continued use of the powers is considered necessary to prevent or deal with further such activity. This direction must also be given in writing at the time or as soon as practicable afterwards. (See *Note 12.*)

Searches under Schedule 5 to the Terrorism Prevention and Investigation Measures Act 2011

2.18A Paragraph 3 of Schedule 5 to the TPIM Act 2011 allows a constable to detain an individual to be searched under the following powers:
  (i)   paragraph 6(2)(a) when a TPIM notice is being, or has just been, served on the individual for the purpose of ascertaining whether there is anything on the individual that contravenes measures specified in the notice;
  (ii) paragraph 8(2)(a) in accordance with a warrant to search the individual issued by a justice of the peace in England and Wales, a sheriff in Scotland or a lay magistrate in Northern Ireland who is satisfied that a search is necessary for the purpose of determining whether an individual in respect of whom a TPIM notice is in force is complying with measures specified in the notice (see *paragraph 2.20*); and
  (iii) paragraph 10 to ascertain whether an individual in respect of whom a TPIM notice is in force is in possession of anything that could be used to threaten or harm any person.
  See *paragraph 2.1(e)*.

2.19 The exercise of the powers mentioned in *paragraph 2.18A* does not require the constable to have reasonable grounds to suspect that the individual:
  (a)   has been, or is, contravening any of the measures specified in the TPIM notice; or
  (b)   has on them anything which:
     • in the case of the power in sub-paragraph (i), contravenes measures specified in the TPIM notice;
     • in the case of the power in sub-paragraph (ii) is not complying with measures specified in the TPIM notice; or

- in the case of the power in sub-paragraph (iii), could be used to threaten or harm any person.

2.20 A search of an individual on warrant under the power mentioned in paragraph 2.18A(ii) must [be] carried out within 28 days of the issue of the warrant and:
- the individual may be searched on one occasion only within that period;
- the search must take place at a reasonable hour unless it appears that this would frustrate the purposes of the search.

2.21 *Not used.*

2.22 *Not used.*

2.23 *Not used.*

2.24 *Not used.*

2.24A *Not used.*

2.25 *Not used.*

2.26 The powers under Schedule 5 only allow a constable to conduct a search of an individual only for specified purposes relating to a TPIM notice as set out above. However, anything found may be seized and retained if there are reasonable grounds for believing that it is or it contains evidence of any offence for use at a trial for that offence or to prevent it being concealed, lost, damaged, altered, or destroyed. However, this would not prevent a search being carried out under other search powers if, in the course of exercising these powers, the officer formed reasonable grounds for suspicion.

Powers to search in the exercise of a power to search premises

2.27 The following powers to search premises also authorise the search of a person, not under arrest, who is found on the premises during the course of the search:
- (a) section 139B of the Criminal Justice Act 1988 under which a constable may enter school premises and search the premises and any person on those premises for any bladed or pointed article or offensive weapon;
- (b) under a warrant issued under section 23(3) of the Misuse of Drugs Act 1971 to search premises for drugs or documents but only if the warrant specifically authorises the search of persons found on the premises; and
- (c) under a search warrant or order issued under paragraph 1, 3 or 11 of Schedule 5 to the Terrorism Act 2000 to search premises and any person found there for material likely to be of substantial value to a terrorist investigation.

2.28 Before the power under section 139B of the Criminal Justice Act 1988 may be exercised, the constable must have reasonable grounds to suspect that an offence under section 139A or 139AA of the Criminal Justice Act 1988 (having a bladed or pointed article or offensive weapon on school premises) has been or is being committed. A warrant to search premises and persons found therein may be issued under section 23(3) of the Misuse of Drugs Act 1971 if there are reasonable grounds to suspect that controlled drugs or certain documents are in the possession of a person on the premises.

2.29 The powers in paragraph 2.27 do not require prior specific grounds to suspect that the person to be searched is in possession of an item for which there is an existing power to search. However, it is still necessary to ensure that the selection and treatment of those searched under these powers is based upon objective factors connected with the search of the premises, and not upon personal prejudice.

3 Conduct of searches

3.1 All stops and searches must be carried out with courtesy, consideration and respect for the person concerned. This has a significant impact on public confidence in the police. Every reasonable effort must be made to minimise the embarrassment that a person being searched may experience. (See *Note 4.*)

3.2 The co-operation of the person to be searched must be sought in every case, even if the person initially objects to the search. A forcible search may be made only if it has been established that the person is unwilling to co-operate or resists. Reasonable force may be used as a last resort if necessary to conduct a search or to detain a person or vehicle for the purposes of a search.

3.3 The length of time for which a person or vehicle may be detained must be reasonable and kept to a minimum. Where the exercise of the power requires reasonable suspicion, the thoroughness and extent of a search must depend on what is suspected of being carried, and by whom. If the suspicion relates to a particular article which is seen to be slipped into a person's pocket, then, in the absence of other grounds for suspicion or an opportunity for the article to be moved elsewhere, the search must be confined to that pocket. In the case of a small article which can readily be concealed, such as a drug, and which might be concealed anywhere on the person, a more extensive search may be necessary. In the case of searches mentioned in paragraph 2.1(b) and (d), which do not require reasonable grounds for suspicion, officers may make any reasonable search to look for items for which they are empowered to search. (See *Note 5*.)

3.4   The search must be carried out at or near the place where the person or vehicle was first detained. (See *Note 6*.)

3.5   There is no power to require a person to remove any clothing in public other than an outer coat, jacket or gloves, except under section 60AA of the Criminal Justice and Public Order Act 1994 (which empowers a constable to require a person to remove any item worn to conceal identity). (See *Notes 4* and *6*.) A search in public of a person's clothing which has not been removed must be restricted to superficial examination of outer garments. This does not, however, prevent an officer from placing his or her hand inside the pockets of the outer clothing, or feeling round the inside of collars, socks and shoes if this is reasonably necessary in the circumstances to look for the object of the search or to remove and examine any item reasonably suspected to be the object of the search. For the same reasons, subject to the restrictions on the removal of headgear, a person's hair may also be searched in public. (See *paragraphs 3.1* and *3.3*.)

3.6   Where on reasonable grounds it is considered necessary to conduct a more thorough search (e.g. by requiring a person to take off a T-shirt), this must be done out of public view, for example, in a police van unless paragraph 3.7 applies, or police station if there is one nearby (see *Note 6*.) Any search involving the removal of more than an outer coat, jacket, gloves, headgear or footwear, or any other item concealing identity, may only be made by an officer of the same sex as the person searched and may not be made in the presence of anyone of the opposite sex unless the person being searched specifically requests it. (See Code C *Annex L* and *Notes 4* and *7*.)

3.7   Searches involving exposure of intimate parts of the body must not be conducted as a routine extension of a less thorough search, simply because nothing is found in the course of the initial search. Searches involving exposure of intimate parts of the body may be carried out only at a nearby police station or other nearby location which is out of public view (but not a police vehicle). These searches must be conducted in accordance with paragraph 11 of Annex A to Code C except that an intimate search mentioned in paragraph 11(f) of Annex A to Code C may not be authorised or carried out under any stop and search powers. The other provisions of Code C do not apply to the conduct and recording of searches of persons detained at police stations in the exercise of stop and search powers. (See *Note 7*.)

Steps to be taken prior to a search

3.8   Before any search of a detained person or attended vehicle takes place the officer must take reasonable steps, if not in uniform (see *paragraph 3.9*), to show their warrant card to the person to be searched or in charge of the vehicle to be searched and whether or not in uniform, to give that person the following information:

    (a)   that they are being detained for the purposes of a search;
    (b)   the officer's name (except in the case of enquiries linked to the investigation of terrorism, or otherwise where the officer reasonably believes that giving their name might put them in danger, in which case a warrant or other identification number shall be given) and the name of the police station to which the officer is attached;
    (c)   the legal search power which is being exercised, and
    (d)   a clear explanation of:
        (i)   the object of the search in terms of the article or articles for which there is a power to search; and
        (ii)   in the case of:
            •   the power under section 60 of the Criminal Justice and Public Order Act 1994 (see *paragraph 2.1(b))*, the nature of the power, the authorisation and the fact that it has been given;
            •   the powers under Schedule 5 to the Terrorism Prevention and Investigation Measures Act 2011 (see *paragraph 2.1(e)* and *2.18A*):
                −   the fact that a TPIM notice is in force or, (in the case of paragraph 6(2) (a)) that a TPIM notice is being served;
                −   the nature of the power being exercised.
            For a search under paragraph 8 of Schedule 5, the warrant must be produced and the person provided with a copy of it.
            •   all other powers requiring reasonable suspicion (see *paragraph 2.1(a)*), the grounds for that suspicion.

(e) that they are entitled to a copy of the record of the search if one is made (see *section 4* below) if they ask within 3 months from the date of the search and:

    (i) if they are not arrested and taken to a police station as a result of the search and it is practicable to make the record on the spot, that immediately after the search is completed they will be given, if they request, either:

- a copy of the record, or
- a receipt which explains how they can obtain a copy of the full record or access to an electronic copy of the record, or

    (ii) if they are arrested and taken to a police station as a result of the search, that the record will be made at the station as part of their custody record and they will be given, if they request, a copy of their custody record which includes a record of the search as soon as practicable whilst they are at the station. (See *Note 16.*)

3.9 Stops and searches under the power mentioned in paragraph 2.1(b) may be undertaken only by a constable in uniform.

3.10 The person should also be given information about police powers to stop and search and the individual's rights in these circumstances.

3.11 If the person to be searched, or in charge of a vehicle to be searched, does not appear to understand what is being said, or there is any doubt about the person's ability to understand English, the officer must take reasonable steps to bring information regarding the person's rights and any relevant provisions of this Code to his or her attention. If the person is deaf or cannot understand English and is accompanied by someone, then the officer must try to establish whether that person can interpret or otherwise help the officer to give the required information.

4 Recording requirements

(a) Searches which do not result in an arrest

4.1 When an officer carries out a search in the exercise of any power to which this Code applies and the search does not result in the person searched or person in charge of the vehicle searched being arrested and taken to a police station, a record must be made of it, electronically or on paper, unless there are exceptional circumstances which make this wholly impracticable (e.g. in situations involving public disorder or when the recording officer's presence is urgently required elsewhere). If a record is to be made, the officer carrying out the search must make the record on the spot unless this is not practicable, in which case, the officer must make the record as soon as practicable after the search is completed. (See *Note 16.*)

4.2 If the record is made at the time, the person who has been searched or who is in charge of the vehicle that has been searched must be asked if they want a copy and if they do, they must be given immediately, either:

- a copy of the record, or
- a receipt which explains how they can obtain a copy of the full record or access to an electronic copy of the record

4.2A An officer is not required to provide a copy of the full record or a receipt at the time if they are called to an incident of higher priority. (See *Note 21.*)

(b) Searches which result in an arrest

4.2B If a search in the exercise of any power to which this Code applies results in a person being arrested and taken to a police station, the officer carrying out the search is responsible for ensuring that a record of the search is made as part of their custody record. The custody officer must then ensure that the person is asked if they want a copy of the record and if they do, that they are given a copy as soon as practicable. (See *Note 16.*)

(c) Record of search

4.3 The record of a search must always include the following information:

(a) A note of the self defined ethnicity, and if different, the ethnicity as perceived by the officer making the search, of the person searched or of the person in charge of the vehicle searched (as the case may be) (see *Note 18*);

(b) The date, time and place the person or vehicle was searched (see *Note 6*);

(c) The object of the search in terms of the article or articles for which there is a power to search;

(d) In the case of:

- the power under section 60 of the Criminal Justice and Public Order Act 1994 (see *paragraph 2.1(b)*), the nature of the power, the authorisation and the fact that it has been given (see *Note 17*);

- the powers under Schedule 5 to the Terrorism Prevention and Investigation Measures Act 2011 (see *paragraphs 2.1(e)* and *2.18A*):
    - the fact that a TPIM notice is in force or, (in the case of paragraph 6(2)(a)), that a TPIM notice is being served;
    - the nature of the power, and
    - for a search under paragraph 8, the date the search warrant was issued, the fact that the warrant was produced and a copy of it provided and the warrant must also be endorsed by the constable executing it to state whether anything was found and whether anything was seized, and
- all other powers requiring reasonable suspicion (see *paragraph 2.1(a)*), the grounds for that suspicion.

    (e) subject to paragraph 3.8(b), the identity of the officer carrying out the search. (See *Note 15*.)

4.3A For the purposes of completing the search record, there is no requirement to record the name, address and date of birth of the person searched or the person in charge of a vehicle which is searched and the person is under no obligation to provide this information.

4.4   Nothing in paragraph 4.3 requires the names of police officers to be shown on the search record or any other record required to be made under this code in the case of enquiries linked to the investigation of terrorism or otherwise where an officer reasonably believes that recording names might endanger the officers. In such cases the record must show the officers' warrant or other identification number and duty station.

4.5   A record is required for each person and each vehicle searched. However, if a person is in a vehicle and both are searched, and the object and grounds of the search are the same, only one record need be completed. If more than one person in a vehicle is searched, separate records for each search of a person must be made. If only a vehicle is searched, the self-defined ethnic background of the person in charge of the vehicle must be recorded, unless the vehicle is unattended.

4.6   The record of the grounds for making a search must, briefly but informatively, explain the reason for suspecting the person concerned, by reference to the person's behaviour and/or other circumstances.

4.7   Where officers detain an individual with a view to performing a search, but the need to search is eliminated as a result of questioning the person detained, a search should not be carried out and a record is not required. (See *paragraph 2.10* and *Notes 3* and *22A*.)

4.8   After searching an unattended vehicle, or anything in or on it, an officer must leave a notice in it (or on it, if things on it have been searched without opening it) recording the fact that it has been searched.

4.9   The notice must include the name of the police station to which the officer concerned is attached and state where a copy of the record of the search may be obtained and how (if applicable) an electronic copy may be accessed and where any application for compensation should be directed.

4.10 The vehicle must if practicable be left secure.

4.10A *Not used.*

4.10B *Not used.*

Recording of encounters not governed by statutory powers

4.11 *Not used.*

4.12 There is no national requirement for an officer who requests a person in a public place to account for themselves, i.e. their actions, behaviour, presence in an area or possession of anything, to make any record of the encounter or to give the person a receipt. (See *Notes 22A* and *22B*.)

4.12A *Not used.*

4.13 *Not used.*

4.14 *Not used.*

4.15 *Not used.*

4.16 *Not used.*

4.17 *Not used.*

4.18 *Not used.*

4.19 *Not used.*

4.20 *Not used.*

5 Monitoring and supervising the use of stop and search powers

5.1   Supervising officers must monitor the use of stop and search powers and should consider in particular whether there is any evidence that they are being exercised on the basis of stereotyped images or inappropriate generalisations. Supervising officers should satisfy themselves that the practice of officers under their supervision in stopping, searching and recording is fully in accordance with this Code. Supervisors must also examine whether the records reveal any trends or patterns which give cause for concern, and if so take appropriate action to address this.

5.2 Senior officers with area or force-wide responsibilities must also monitor the broader use of stop and search powers and, where necessary, take action at the relevant level.

5.3 Supervision and monitoring must be supported by the compilation of comprehensive statistical records of stops and searches at force, area and local level. Any apparently disproportionate use of the powers by particular officers or groups of officers or in relation to specific sections of the community should be identified and investigated.

5.4 In order to promote public confidence in the use of the powers, forces in consultation with police and crime commissioners must make arrangements for the records to be scrutinised by representatives of the community, and to explain the use of the powers at a local level. (See *Note 19*.)

Notes for guidance

Officers exercising stop and search powers

1 This Code does not affect the ability of an officer to speak to or question a person in the ordinary course of the officer's duties without detaining the person or exercising any element of compulsion. It is not the purpose of the code to prohibit such encounters between the police and the community with the co-operation of the person concerned and neither does it affect the principle that all citizens have a duty to help police officers to prevent crime and discover offenders. This is a civic rather than a legal duty; but when a police officer is trying to discover whether, or by whom, an offence has been committed he or she may question any person from whom useful information might be obtained, subject to the restrictions imposed by Code C. A person's unwillingness to reply does not alter this entitlement, but in the absence of a power to arrest, or to detain in order to search, the person is free to leave at will and cannot be compelled to remain with the officer.

1A In paragraphs 1.1 and 2.2, 'relevant protected characteristic' includes: age, disability, gender reassignment, pregnancy and maternity, race, religion/belief, sex and sexual orientation.

2 In some circumstances preparatory questioning may be unnecessary, but in general a brief conversation or exchange will be desirable not only as a means of avoiding unsuccessful searches, but to explain the grounds for the stop/search, to gain co-operation and reduce any tension there might be surrounding the stop/search.

3 Where a person is lawfully detained for the purpose of a search, but no search in the event takes place, the detention will not thereby have been rendered unlawful.

4 Many people customarily cover their heads or faces for religious reasons – for example, Muslim women, Sikh men, Sikh or Hindu women, or Rastafarian men or women. A police officer cannot order the removal of a head or face covering except where there is reason to believe that the item is being worn by the individual wholly or mainly for the purpose of disguising identity, not simply because it disguises identity. Where there may be religious sensitivities about ordering the removal of such an item, the officer should permit the item to be removed out of public view. Where practicable, the item should be removed in the presence of an officer of the same sex as the person and out of sight of anyone of the opposite sex (see Code C *Annex L*).

5 A search of a person in public should be completed as soon as possible.

6 A person may be detained under a stop and search power at a place other than where the person was first detained, only if that place, be it a police station or elsewhere, is nearby. Such a place should be located within a reasonable travelling distance using whatever mode of travel (on foot or by car) is appropriate. This applies to all searches under stop and search powers, whether or not they involve the removal of clothing or exposure of intimate parts of the body (see *paragraphs 3.6* and *3.7*) or take place in or out of public view. It means, for example, that a search under the stop and search power in section 23 of the Misuse of Drugs Act 1971 which involves the compulsory removal of more than a person's outer coat, jacket or gloves cannot be carried out unless a place which is both nearby the place they were first detained and out of public view, is available. If a search involves exposure of intimate parts of the body and a police station is not nearby, particular care must be taken to ensure that the location is suitable in that it enables the search to be conducted in accordance with the requirements of paragraph 11 of Annex A to Code C.

7   A search in the street itself should be regarded as being in public for the purposes of paragraphs 3.6 and 3.7 above, even though it may be empty at the time a search begins. Although there is no power to require a person to do so, there is nothing to prevent an officer from asking a person voluntarily to remove more than an outer coat, jacket or gloves in public.

8   *Not used.*

9   Other means of identification might include jewellery, insignias, tattoos or other features which are known to identify members of the particular gang or group.

Authorising officers

10   The powers under section 60 are separate from and additional to the normal stop and search powers which require reasonable grounds to suspect an individual of carrying an offensive weapon (or other article). Their overall purpose is to prevent serious violence and the widespread carrying of weapons which might lead to persons being seriously injured by disarming potential offenders or finding weapons that have been used in circumstances where other powers would not be sufficient. They should not therefore be used to replace or circumvent the normal powers for dealing with routine crime problems. A particular example might be an authorisation to prevent serious violence or the carrying of offensive weapons at a sports event by rival team supporters when the expected general appearance and age range of those likely to be responsible, alone, would not be sufficiently distinctive to support reasonable suspicion (see *paragraph 2.6*). The purpose of the powers under section 60AA is to prevent those involved in intimidatory or violent protests using face coverings to disguise identity.

11   Authorisations under section 60 require a reasonable belief on the part of the authorising officer. This must have an objective basis, for example: intelligence or relevant information such as a history of antagonism and violence between particular groups; previous incidents of violence at, or connected with, particular events or locations; a significant increase in knife-point robberies in a limited area; reports that individuals are regularly carrying weapons in a particular locality; information following an incident in which weapons were used about where the weapons might be found or in the case of section 60AA previous incidents of crimes being committed while wearing face coverings to conceal identity.

12   It is for the authorising officer to determine the period of time during which the powers mentioned in paragraph 2.1(b) may be exercised. The officer should set the minimum period he or she considers necessary to deal with the risk of violence, the carrying of knives or offensive weapons, or to find dangerous instruments or weapons that have been used. A direction to extend the period authorised under the powers mentioned in paragraph 2.1(b) may be given only once. Thereafter further use of the powers requires a new authorisation.

13   It is for the authorising officer to determine the geographical area in which the use of the powers is to be authorised. In doing so the officer may wish to take into account factors such as the nature and venue of the anticipated incident or the incident which has taken place, the number of people who may be in the immediate area of that incident, their access to surrounding areas and the anticipated or actual level of violence. The officer should not set a geographical area which is wider than that he or she believes necessary for the purpose of preventing anticipated violence, the carrying of knives or offensive weapons, or for finding a dangerous instrument or weapon that has been used or, in the case of section 60AA, the prevention of commission of offences. It is particularly important to ensure that constables exercising such powers are fully aware of where they may be used. If the area specified is smaller than the whole force area, the officer giving the authorisation should specify either the streets which form the boundary of the area or a divisional boundary within the force area. If the power is to be used in response to a threat or incident that straddles police force areas, an officer from each of the forces concerned will need to give an authorisation.

14   *Not used.*

Recording

15   Where a stop and search is conducted by more than one officer the identity of all the officers engaged in the search must be recorded on the record. Nothing prevents an officer who is present

but not directly involved in searching from completing the record during the course of the encounter.

16   When the search results in the person searched or in charge of a vehicle which is searched being arrested, the requirement to make the record of the search as part of the person's custody record does not apply if the person is granted 'street bail' after arrest (see section 30A of PACE) to attend a police station and is not taken in custody to the police station An arrested person's entitlement to a copy of the search record which is made as part of their custody record does not affect their entitlement to a copy of their custody record or any other provisions of PACE Code C section 2 (Custody records).

17   It is important for monitoring purposes to specify when authority is given for exercising the stop and search power under section 60 of the Criminal Justice and Public Order Act 1994.

18   Officers should record the self-defined ethnicity of every person stopped according to the categories used in the 2001 census question listed in Annex B. The person should be asked to select one of the five main categories representing broad ethnic groups and then a more specific cultural background from within this group. The ethnic classification should be coded for recording purposes using the coding system in Annex B. An additional 'Not stated' box is available but should not be offered to respondents explicitly. Officers should be aware and explain to members of the public, especially where concerns are raised, that this information is required to obtain a true picture of stop and search activity and to help improve ethnic monitoring, tackle discriminatory practice, and promote effective use of the powers. If the person gives what appears to the officer to be an 'incorrect' answer (e.g. a person who appears to be white states that they are black), the officer should record the response that has been given and then record their own perception of the person's ethnic background by using the PNC classification system. If the 'Not stated' category is used the reason for this must be recorded on the form.

19   Arrangements for public scrutiny of records should take account of the right to confidentiality of those stopped and searched. Anonymised forms and/or statistics generated from records should be the focus of the examinations by members of the public.

20   *Not used.*

21   In situations where it is not practicable to provide a written copy of the record or immediate access to an electronic copy of the record or a receipt of the search at the time (see *paragraph 4.2A* above), the officer should consider giving the person details of the station which they may attend for a copy of the record. A receipt may take the form of a simple business card which includes sufficient information to locate the record should the person ask for copy, for example, the date and place of the search, and a reference number or the name of the officer who carried out the search (unless paragraph 4.4 applies).

22   *Not used.*

22A   Where there are concerns which make it necessary to monitor any local disproportionality, forces have discretion to direct officers to record the self-defined ethnicity of persons they request to account for themselves in a public place or who they detain with a view to searching but do not search. Guidance should be provided locally and efforts made to minimise the bureaucracy involved. Records should be closely monitored and supervised in line with paragraphs 5.1 to 5.4, and forces can suspend or re-instate recording of these encounters as appropriate.

22B   A person who is asked to account for themselves should, if they request, be given information about how they can report their dissatisfaction about how they have been treated.

Definition of offensive weapon

23   'Offensive weapon' is defined as 'any article made or adapted for use for causing injury to the person, or intended by the person having it with him for such use or by someone else'. There are three categories of offensive weapons: those made for causing injury to the person; those adapted for such a purpose; and those not so made or adapted, but carried with the intention of causing injury to the person. A firearm, as defined by section 57 of the Firearms Act 1968, would fall within the definition of offensive weapon if any of the criteria above apply.

24   *Not used.*

25   *Not used.*

Annex A

Summary of Main Stop and Search Powers to which Code A Applies

This table relates to stop and search powers only. Individual statutes below may contain other police powers of entry, search and seizure.

Power	Object of Search	Extent of Search	Where exercisable
Unlawful articles general			
1. Public Stores Act 1875, s. 6	HM Stores stolen or unlawfully obtained	Persons, vehicles and vessels	Anywhere where the constabulary powers are exercisable
2. Firearms Act 1968, s. 47	Firearms	Persons and vehicles	A public place, or anywhere in the case of reasonable suspicion of offences of carrying firearms with criminal intent or trespassing with firearms
3. Misuse of Drugs Act 1971, s. 23	Controlled drugs	Persons and vehicles	Anywhere
4. Customs and Excise Management Act 1979, s. 163	Goods: (a) on which duty has not been paid; (b) being unlawfully removed, imported or exported; (c) otherwise liable to forfeiture to HM Revenue and Customs	Vehicles and vessels only	Anywhere
5. Aviation Security Act 1982, s. 27(1)	Stolen or unlawfully obtained goods	Airport employees and vehicles carrying airport employees or aircraft or any vehicle in a cargo area whether or not carrying an employee	Any designated airport
6. Police and Criminal Evidence Act 1984, s. 1	Stolen goods; articles for use in certain Theft Act offences; offensive weapons, including bladed or sharply-pointed articles (except folding pocket knives with a bladed cutting edge not exceeding 3 inches); prohibited possession of a category 4 (display grade) firework, any person under 18 in possession of an adult firework in a public place.	Persons and vehicles	Where there is public access
	Criminal Damage: Articles made, adapted or intended for use in destroying or damaging property	Persons and vehicles	Where there is public access
7. Sporting Events (Control of Alcohol etc.) Act 1985, s. 7	Intoxicating liquor	Persons, coaches and trains	Designated sports grounds or coaches and trains travelling to or from a designated sporting event.

Power	Object of Search	Extent of Search	Where exercisable
8. Crossbows Act 1987, s. 4	Crossbows or parts of crossbows (except crossbows with a draw weight of less than 1.4 kilograms)	Persons and vehicles	Anywhere except dwellings
9. Criminal Justice Act 1988 s. 139B	Offensive weapons, bladed or sharply pointed article	Persons	School premises
Evidence of game and wildlife offences			
10. Poaching Prevention Act 1862, s. 2	Game or poaching equipment	Persons and vehicles	A public place
11. Deer Act 1991, s. 12	Evidence of offences under the Act	Persons and vehicles	Anywhere except dwellings
12. Conservation of Seals Act 1970, s. 4	Seals or hunting equipment	Vehicles only	Anywhere
13. Protection of Badgers Act 1992, s. 11	Evidence of offences under the Act	Persons and vehicles	Anywhere
14. Wildlife and Countryside Act 1981, s. 19	Evidence of wildlife offences	Persons and vehicles	Anywhere except dwellings
Other			
15. Paragraphs 6 & 8 of Schedule 5 to the Terrorism Prevention and Investigation Measures Act 2011	Anything that contravenes measures specified in a TPIM notice.	Persons in respect of whom a TPIM notice is being served or is in force	Anywhere
16. Paragraph 10 of Schedule 5 to the Terrorism Prevention and Investigation Measures Act 2011	Anything that could be used to threaten or harm any person.	Persons in respect of whom a TPIM notice is in force.	Anywhere
17. *Not used*			
18. Paragraphs 7 and 8 of Schedule 7 to the Terrorism Act 2000	Anything relevant to determining if a person being examined falls within section 40(1)(b)	Persons, vehicles, vessels etc. *(Note: These searches are subject to the Code of Practice issued under paragraph 6 of Schedule 14 to the Terrorism Act 2000)*	Ports and airports
19. Section 60 Criminal Justice and Public Order Act 1994	Offensive weapons or dangerous instruments to prevent incidents of serious violence or to deal with the carrying of such items or find such items which have been used in incidents of serious violence	Persons and vehicles	Anywhere within a locality authorised under subsection (1)

Annex B

Self-Defined Ethnic Classification Categories

[Omitted.]

Annex C

Summary of Powers of Community Support Officers to Search and Seize

The following is a summary of the search and seizure powers that may be exercised by a community support officer (CSO) who has been designated with the relevant powers in accordance with Part 4 of the Police Reform Act 2002.

When exercising any of these powers, a CSO must have regard to any relevant provisions of this Code, including section 3 governing the conduct of searches and the steps to be taken prior to a search.

1. *Not used*

2. Powers to search requiring the consent of the person and seizure

A CSO may detain a person using reasonable force where necessary as set out in Part 1 of Schedule 4 to the Police Reform Act 2002. If the person has been lawfully detained, the CSO may search the person provided that person gives consent to such a search in relation to the following:

Designation	Powers conferred	Object of Search	Extent of Search	Where Exercisable
1. Police Reform Act 2002, Schedule 4, paragraph 7A	(a) Criminal Justice and Police Act 2001, s. 12(2)	(a) Alcohol or a container for alcohol	(a) Persons	(a) Designated public place
	(b) Confiscation of Alcohol (Young Persons) Act 1997, s. 1	(b) Alcohol	(b) Persons under 18 years old	(b) Public place
	(c) Children and Young Persons Act 1933, s. 7(3)	(c) Tobacco or cigarette papers	(c) Persons under 16 years old found smoking	(c) Public place

3. Powers to search not requiring the consent of the person and seizure

A CSO may detain a person using reasonable force where necessary as set out in Part 1 of Schedule 4 to the Police Reform Act 2002. If the person has been lawfully detained, the CSO may search the person without the need for that person's consent in relation to the following:

Designation	Power conferred	Object of Search	Extent of Search	Where Exercisable
Police Reform Act 2002, Schedule 4, paragraph 2A	Police and Criminal Evidence Act 1984, s. 32	(a) Objects that might be used to cause physical injury to the person or the CSO. (b) Items that might be used to assist escape.	Persons made subject to a requirement to wait.	Any place where the requirement to wait has been made

4. Powers to seize without consent

This power applies when drugs are found in the course of any search mentioned above.

Designation	Power conferred	Object of Seizure	Where Exercisable
Police Reform Act 2002, Schedule 4, paragraph 7B	Police Reform Act 2002, Schedule 4, paragraph 7B	Controlled drugs in a person's possession.	Any place where the person is in possession of the drug.

ANNEX D –DELETED.

ANNEX E – DELETED.

ANNEX F ESTABLISHING GENDER OF PERSONS FOR THE PURPOSE OF SEARCHING

See Code C *Annex L*

PACE CODE B

REVISED CODE OF PRACTICE FOR SEARCHES OF PREMISES BY POLICE OFFICERS AND THE SEIZURE OF PROPERTY FOUND BY POLICE OFFICERS ON PERSONS OR PREMISES

Commencement—Transitional Arrangements

This code applies to applications for warrants made after 00.00 on 27 October 2013 and to searches and seizures taking place after 0.00 on 27 October 2013.

1 Introduction

1.1   This Code of Practice deals with police powers to:
- search premises
- seize and retain property found on premises and persons

1.1A These powers may be used to find:
- property and material relating to a crime
- wanted persons
- children who abscond from local authority accommodation where they have been remanded or committed by a court

1.2   A justice of the peace may issue a search warrant granting powers of entry, search and seizure, e.g. warrants to search for stolen property, drugs, firearms and evidence of serious offences. Police also have powers without a search warrant. The main ones provided by the Police and Criminal Evidence Act 1984 (PACE) include powers to search premises:
- to make an arrest
- after an arrest

1.3   The right to privacy and respect for personal property are key principles of the Human Rights Act 1998. Powers of entry, search and seizure should be fully and clearly justified before use because they may significantly interfere with the occupier's privacy. Officers should consider if the necessary objectives can be met by less intrusive means.

1.3A Powers to search and seize must be used fairly, responsibly, with respect for people who occupy premises being searched or are in charge of property being seized and without unlawful discrimination. Under the Equality Act 2010, section 149, when police officers are carrying out their functions, they also have a duty to have due regard to the need to eliminate unlawful discrimination, harassment and victimisation, to advance equality of opportunity between people who share a relevant protected characteristic and people who do not share it, and to take steps to foster good relations between those persons. See *Note 1A*.

1.4   In all cases, police should therefore:
- exercise their powers courteously and with respect for persons and property
- only use reasonable force when this is considered necessary and proportionate to the circumstances

1.5   If the provisions of PACE and this Code are not observed, evidence obtained from a search may be open to question.

Note for Guidance

1A   In paragraph 1.3A, 'relevant protected characteristic' includes: age, disability, gender reassignment, pregnancy and maternity, race, religion/belief, sex and sexual orientation.

2 General

2.1   This Code must be readily available at all police stations for consultation by:
- police officers
- police staff
- detained persons
- members of the public

2.2   The Notes for Guidance included are not provisions of this Code.

2.3   This Code applies to searches of premises:
(a)   by police for the purposes of an investigation into an alleged offence, with the occupier's consent, other than:
- routine scene of crime searches;

- calls to a fire or burglary made by or on behalf of an occupier or searches following the activation of fire or burglar alarms or discovery of insecure premises;
- searches when paragraph 5.4 applies;
- bomb threat calls;

(b) under powers conferred on police officers by PACE, sections 17, 18 and 32;

(c) undertaken in pursuance of search warrants issued to and executed by constables in accordance with PACE, sections 15 and 16 (see *Note 2A*);

(d) subject to paragraph 2.6, under any other power given to police to enter premises with or without a search warrant for any purpose connected with the investigation into an alleged or suspected offence. (See *Note 2B*.)

For the purposes of this Code, 'premises' as defined in PACE, section 23, includes any place, vehicle, vessel, aircraft, hovercraft, tent or movable structure and any offshore installation as defined in the Mineral Workings (Offshore Installations) Act 1971, section 1. (See *Note 2D*.)

2.4 A person who has not been arrested but is searched during a search of premises should be searched in accordance with Code A. (See *Note 2C*.)

2.5 This Code does not apply to the exercise of a statutory power to enter premises or to inspect goods, equipment or procedures if the exercise of that power is not dependent on the existence of grounds for suspecting that an offence may have been committed and the person exercising the power has no reasonable grounds for such suspicion.

2.6 This Code does not affect any directions or requirements of a search warrant, order or other power to search and seize lawfully exercised in England or Wales that any item or evidence seized under that warrant, order or power be handed over to a police force, court, tribunal, or other authority outside England or Wales. For example, warrants and orders issued in Scotland or Northern Ireland (see *Note 2B(f)*) and search warrants and powers provided for in sections 14 to 17 of the Crime (International Co-operation) Act 2003.

2.7 When this Code requires the prior authority or agreement of an officer of at least inspector or superintendent rank, that authority may be given by a sergeant or chief inspector authorised to perform the functions of the higher rank under PACE, section 107.5

2.8 Written records required under this Code not made in the search record shall, unless otherwise specified, be made:

- in the recording officer's pocket book ('pocket book' includes any official report book issued to police officers) or
- on forms provided for the purpose

2.9 Nothing in this Code requires the identity of officers, or anyone accompanying them during a search of premises, to be recorded or disclosed:

(a) in the case of enquiries linked to the investigation of terrorism; or

(b) if officers reasonably believe recording or disclosing their names might put them in danger.

In these cases officers should use warrant or other identification numbers and the name of their police station. Police staff should use any identification number provided to them by the police force. (See *Note 2E*.)

2.10 The 'officer in charge of the search' means the officer assigned specific duties and responsibilities under this Code. Whenever there is a search of premises to which this Code applies one officer must act as the officer in charge of the search. (See *Note 2F*.)

2.11 In this Code:

(a) 'designated person' means a person other than a police officer, designated under the Police Reform Act 2002, Part 4 who has specified powers and duties of police officers conferred or imposed on them. (See *Note 2G*.)

(b) any reference to a police officer includes a designated person acting in the exercise or performance of the powers and duties conferred or imposed on them by their designation.

(c) a person authorised to accompany police officers or designated persons in the execution of a warrant has the same powers as a constable in the execution of the warrant and the search and seizure of anything related to the warrant. These powers must be exercised in the company and under the supervision of a police officer. (See *Note 3C*.)

2.12 If a power conferred on a designated person:

(a) allows reasonable force to be used when exercised by a police officer, a designated person exercising that power has the same entitlement to use force;

(b) includes power to use force to enter any premises, that power is not exercisable by that designated person except:

(i) in the company and under the supervision of a police officer; or

(ii) for the purpose of:
- saving life or limb; or
- preventing serious damage to property.

2.13 Designated persons must have regard to any relevant provisions of the Codes of Practice.

Notes for guidance

2A   PACE sections 15 and 16 apply to all search warrants issued to and executed by constables under any enactment, e.g. search warrants issued by a:

(a) justice of the peace under the:
- Theft Act 1968, section 26 – stolen property;
- Misuse of Drugs Act 1971, section 23 – controlled drugs;
- PACE, section 8 – evidence of an indictable offence;
- Terrorism Act 2000, Schedule 5, paragraph 1;
- Terrorism Prevention and Investigation Measures Act 2011, Schedule 5, paragraph 8(2)(b) search of premises for compliance purposes (see *paragraph 10.1*).

(b) Circuit judge under:
- PACE, Schedule 1;
- Terrorism Act 2000, Schedule 5, paragraph 11.

2B   Examples of the other powers in paragraph 2.3(d) include:

(a) Road Traffic Act 1988, section 6E(1) giving police power to enter premises under section 6E(1) to:
- require a person to provide a specimen of breath; or
- arrest a person following:
  - a positive breath test;
  - failure to provide a specimen of breath;

(b) Transport and Works Act 1992, section 30(4) giving police powers to enter premises mirroring the powers in (a) in relation to specified persons working on transport systems to which the Act applies;

(c) Criminal Justice Act 1988, section 139B giving police power to enter and search school premises for offensive weapons, bladed or pointed articles;

(d) Terrorism Act 2000, Schedule 5, paragraphs 3 and 15 empowering a superintendent in urgent cases to give written authority for police to enter and search premises for the purposes of a terrorist investigation;

(e) Explosives Act 1875, section 73(b) empowering a superintendent to give written authority for police to enter premises, examine and search them for explosives;

(f) search warrants and production orders or the equivalent issued in Scotland or Northern Ireland endorsed under the Summary Jurisdiction (Process) Act 1881 or the Petty Sessions (Ireland) Act 1851 respectively for execution in England and Wales.

(g) Terrorism Prevention and Investigation Measures Act 2011, Schedule 5, paragraphs 5(1), 6(2)(b) and 7(2), searches relating to TPIM notices (see *paragraph 10.1*).

2C   The Criminal Justice Act 1988, section 139B provides that a constable who has reasonable grounds to suspect an offence under the Criminal Justice Act 1988, section 139A or 139AA has or is being committed may enter school premises and search the premises and any persons on the premises for any bladed or pointed article or offensive weapon. Persons may be searched under a warrant issued under the Misuse of Drugs Act 1971, section 23(3) to search premises for drugs or documents only if the warrant specifically authorises the search of persons on the premises. Powers to search premises under certain terrorism provisions also authorise the search of persons on the premises, for example, under paragraphs 1, 2, 11 and 15 of Schedule 5 to the Terrorism Act 2000 and section 52 of the Anti-terrorism, Crime and Security Act 2001.

2D   The Immigration Act 1971, Part III and Schedule 2 gives immigration officers powers to enter and search premises, seize and retain property, with and without a search warrant. These are similar to the powers available to police under search warrants issued by a justice of the peace and without a warrant under PACE, sections 17, 18, 19 and 32 except they only apply to specified offences under the Immigration Act 1971 and immigration control powers. For certain types of investigations and enquiries these powers avoid the need for the Immigration Service to rely on police officers becoming directly involved. When exercising these powers, immigration officers are required by the Immigration and Asylum Act 1999, section 145 to have regard to this Code's corresponding provisions. When immigration officers are dealing with persons or property at police stations, police officers should give appropriate assistance to help them discharge their specific duties and responsibilities.

2E   The purpose of paragraph 2.9(b) is to protect those involved in serious organised crime investigations or arrests of particularly violent suspects when there is reliable information that those arrested or their associates may threaten or cause harm to the officers or anyone accompanying them during a search of premises. In cases of doubt, an officer of inspector rank or above should be consulted.

2F   For the purposes of paragraph 2.10, the officer in charge of the search should normally be the most senior officer present. Some exceptions are:

(a)   a supervising officer who attends or assists at the scene of a premises search may appoint an officer of lower rank as officer in charge of the search if that officer is:
  • more conversant with the facts;
  • a more appropriate officer to be in charge of the search;

(b)   when all officers in a premises search are the same rank. The supervising officer if available, must make sure one of them is appointed officer in charge of the search, otherwise the officers themselves must nominate one of their number as the officer in charge;

(c)   a senior officer assisting in a specialist role. This officer need not be regarded as having a general supervisory role over the conduct of the search or be appointed or expected to act as the officer in charge of the search.

Except in (c), nothing in this Note diminishes the role and responsibilities of a supervisory officer who is present at the search or knows of a search taking place.

2G   An officer of the rank of inspector or above may direct a designated investigating officer not to wear a uniform for the purposes of a specific operation.

3   Search warrants and production orders

(a)   Before making an application

3.1   When information appears to justify an application, the officer must take reasonable steps to check the information is accurate, recent and not provided maliciously or irresponsibly. An application may not be made on the basis of information from an anonymous source if corroboration has not been sought. (See *Note 3A*.)

3.2   The officer shall ascertain as specifically as possible the nature of the articles concerned and their location.

3.3   The officer shall make reasonable enquiries to:
(i)   establish if:
  • anything is known about the likely occupier of the premises and the nature of the premises themselves;
  • the premises have been searched previously and how recently;
(ii)   obtain any other relevant information.

3.4   An application:
(a)   to a justice of the peace for a search warrant or to a Circuit judge for a search warrant or production order under PACE, Schedule 1 must be supported by a signed written authority from an officer of inspector rank or above:
Note: If the case is an urgent application to a justice of the peace and an inspector or above is not readily available, the next most senior officer on duty can give the written authority.
(b)   to a circuit judge under the Terrorism Act 2000, Schedule 5 for:
  • a production order;
  • search warrant; or
  • an order requiring an explanation of material seized or produced under such a warrant or production order, must be supported by a signed written authority from an officer of superintendent rank or above.

3.5   Except in a case of urgency, if there is reason to believe a search might have an adverse effect on relations between the police and the community, the officer in charge shall consult the local police/community liaison officer:
  • before the search; or
  • in urgent cases, as soon as practicable after the search

(b)   Making an application

3.6   A search warrant application must be supported in writing, specifying:
(a)   the enactment under which the application is made (see *Note 2A*);
(b) (i)   whether the warrant is to authorise entry and search of:
    • one set of premises; or

- if the application is under PACE section 8, or Schedule 1, paragraph 12, more than one set of specified premises or all premises occupied or controlled by a specified person, and
  (ii) the premises to be searched;
(c) the object of the search (see *Note 3B*);
(d) the grounds for the application, including, when the purpose of the proposed search is to find evidence of an alleged offence, an indication of how the evidence relates to the investigation;
(da) Where the application is under PACE section 8, or Schedule 1, paragraph 12 for a single warrant to enter and search:
  (i) more than one set of specified premises; the officer must specify each set of premises which it is desired to enter and search;
  (ii) all premises occupied or controlled by a specified person; the officer must specify;
    - as many sets of premises which it is desired to enter and search as it is reasonably practicable to specify;
    - the person who is in occupation or control of those premises and any others which it is desired to search;
    - why it is necessary to search more premises than those which can be specified, and
    - why it is not reasonably practicable to specify all the premises which it is desired to enter and search;
(db) Whether an application under PACE section 8 is for a warrant authorising entry and search on more than one occasion, and if so, the officer must state the grounds for this and whether the desired number of entries authorised is unlimited or a specified maximum;
(e) That there are no reasonable grounds to believe the material to be sought, when making application to a:
  (i) justice of the peace or a Circuit judge consists of or includes items subject to legal privilege;
  (ii) justice of the peace, consists of or includes excluded material or special procedure material; Note: this does not affect the additional powers of seizure in the Criminal Justice and Police Act 2001, Part 2 covered in paragraph 7.7 (see *Note 3B*).
(f) if applicable, a request for the warrant to authorise a person or persons to accompany the officer who executes the warrant. (See *Note 3C*.)
3.7 A search warrant application under PACE, Schedule 1, paragraph 12(a), shall if appropriate indicate why it is believed service of notice of an application for a production order may seriously prejudice the investigation. Applications for search warrants under the Terrorism Act 2000, Schedule 5, paragraph 11 must indicate why a production order would not be appropriate.
3.8 If a search warrant application is refused, a further application may not be made for those premises unless supported by additional grounds.

Notes for guidance

3A The identity of an informant need not be disclosed when making an application, but the officer should be prepared to answer any questions the magistrate or judge may have about:
- the accuracy of previous information from that source, and
- any other related matters
3B The information supporting a search warrant application should be as specific as possible, particularly in relation to the articles or persons being sought and where in the premises it is suspected they may be found. The meaning of 'items subject to legal privilege', 'excluded material' and 'special procedure material' are defined by PACE, sections 10, 11 and 14 respectively.
3C Under PACE, section 16(2), a search warrant may authorise persons other than police officers to accompany the constable who executes the warrant. This includes, e.g. any suitably qualified or skilled person or an expert in a particular field whose presence is needed to help accurately identify the material sought or to advise where certain evidence is most likely to be found and how it should be dealt with. It does not give them any right to force entry, but it gives them the right to be on the premises during the search and to search for or seize property without the occupier's permission.

4 Entry without warrant – particular powers

(a) Making an arrest etc

4.1 The conditions under which an officer may enter and search premises without a warrant are set out in PACE, section 17. It should be noted that this section does not create or confer any powers of arrest. See other powers in *Note 2B(a)*.

(b) Search of premises where arrest takes place or the arrested person was immediately before arrest

4.2 When a person has been arrested for an indictable offence, a police officer has power under PACE, section 32 to search the premises where the person was arrested or where the person was immediately before being arrested.

(c) Search of premises occupied or controlled by the arrested person

4.3 The specific powers to search premises which are occupied or controlled by a person arrested for an indictable offence are set out in PACE, section 18. They may not be exercised, except if section 18(5) applies, unless an officer of inspector rank or above has given written authority. That authority should only be given when the authorising officer is satisfied that the premises are occupied or controlled by the arrested person and that the necessary grounds exist. If possible the authorising officer should record the authority on the Notice of Powers and Rights and, subject to paragraph 2.9, sign the Notice. The record of the grounds for the search and the nature of the evidence sought as required by section 18(7) of the Act should be made in:
   • the custody record if there is one, otherwise
   • the officer's pocket book, or
   • the search record

5 Search with consent

5.1 Subject to paragraph 5.4, if it is proposed to search premises with the consent of a person entitled to grant entry the consent must, if practicable, be given in writing on the Notice of Powers and Rights before the search. The officer must make any necessary enquiries to be satisfied the person is in a position to give such consent. (See *Notes 5A* and *5B.*)

5.2 Before seeking consent the officer in charge of the search shall state the purpose of the proposed search and its extent. This information must be as specific as possible, particularly regarding the articles or persons being sought and the parts of the premises to be searched. The person concerned must be clearly informed they are not obliged to consent, that any consent given can be withdrawn at any time, including before the search starts or while it is underway and anything seized may be produced in evidence. If at the time the person is not suspected of an offence, the officer shall say this when stating the purpose of the search.

5.3 An officer cannot enter and search or continue to search premises under paragraph 5.1 if consent is given under duress or withdrawn before the search is completed.

5.4 It is unnecessary to seek consent under paragraphs 5.1 and 5.2 if this would cause disproportionate inconvenience to the person concerned. (See *Note 5C.*)

Notes for guidance

5A In a lodging house, hostel or similar accommodation, every reasonable effort should be made to obtain the consent of the tenant, lodger or occupier. A search should not be made solely on the basis of the landlord's consent.

5B If the intention is to search premises under the authority of a warrant or a power of entry and search without warrant, and the occupier of the premises co-operates in accordance with paragraph 6.4, there is no need to obtain written consent.

5C Paragraph 5.4 is intended to apply when it is reasonable to assume innocent occupiers would agree to, and expect, police to take the proposed action, e.g. if:
   • a suspect has fled the scene of a crime or to evade arrest and it is necessary quickly to check surrounding gardens and readily accessible places to see if the suspect is hiding, or
   • police have arrested someone in the night after a pursuit and it is necessary to make a brief check of gardens along the pursuit route to see if stolen or incriminating articles have been discarded.

6 Searching premises – general considerations

(a) Time of searches

6.1 Searches made under warrant must be made within three calendar months of the date the warrant is issued or within the period specified in the enactment under which the warrant is issued if this is shorter. Searches must be made at a reasonable hour unless this might frustrate the purpose of the search.

6.2 Searches must be made at a reasonable hour unless this might frustrate the purpose of the search.

6.3 When the extent or complexity of a search mean it is likely to take a long time, the officer in charge of the search may consider using the seize and sift powers referred to in section 7.

6.3A A warrant under PACE, section 8 may authorise entry to and search of premises on more than one occasion if, on the application, the justice of the peace is satisfied that it is necessary to authorise multiple entries in order to achieve the purpose for which the warrant is issued. No premises may be entered or searched on any subsequent occasions without the prior written authority of an officer of the rank of inspector who is not involved in the investigation. All other warrants authorise entry on one occasion only.

6.3B Where a warrant under PACE section 8, or Schedule 1, paragraph 12 authorises entry to and search of all premises occupied or controlled by a specified person, no premises which are not specified in the warrant may be entered and searched without the prior written authority of an officer of the rank of inspector who is not involved in the investigation.

(b) Entry other than with consent

6.4 The officer in charge of the search shall first try to communicate with the occupier, or any other person entitled to grant access to the premises, explain the authority under which entry is sought and ask the occupier to allow entry, unless:
   (i)   the search premises are unoccupied;
   (ii) the occupier and any other person entitled to grant access are absent;
   (iii) there are reasonable grounds for believing that alerting the occupier or any other person entitled to grant access would frustrate the object of the search or endanger officers or other people.

6.5 Unless sub-paragraph 6.4(iii) applies, if the premises are occupied the officer, subject to paragraph 2.9, shall, before the search begins:
   (i)   identify him or herself, show their warrant card (if not in uniform) and state the purpose of, and grounds for, the search, and
   (ii) Identify and introduce any person accompanying the officer on the search (such persons should carry identification for production on request) and briefly describe that person's role in the process.

6.6 Reasonable and proportionate force may be used if necessary to enter premises if the officer in charge of the search is satisfied the premises are those specified in any warrant, or in exercise of the powers described in paragraphs 4.1 to 4.3, and if:
   (i)   the occupier or any other person entitled to grant access has refused entry;
   (ii) it is impossible to communicate with the occupier or any other person entitled to grant access; or
   (iii) any of the provisions of paragraph 6.4 apply.

(c) Notice of Powers and Rights

6.7 If an officer conducts a search to which this Code applies the officer shall, unless it is impracticable to do so, provide the occupier with a copy of a Notice in a standard format:
   (i)   specifying if the search is made under warrant, with consent, or in the exercise of the powers described in paragraphs 4.1 to 4.3. Note: the notice format shall provide for authority or consent to be indicated (see *paragraphs 4.3* and *5.1*);
   (ii) summarising the extent of the powers of search and seizure conferred by PACE and other relevant legislation as appropriate;
   (iii) explaining the rights of the occupier and the owner of the property seized;
   (iv) explaining compensation may be payable in appropriate cases for damages caused entering and searching premises, and giving the address to send a compensation application (see *Note 6A*), and
   (v)   stating this Code is available at any police station.

6.8 If the occupier is:
   • present; copies of the Notice and warrant shall, if practicable, be given to them before the search begins, unless the officer in charge of the search reasonably believes this would frustrate the object of the search or endanger officers or other people;
   • not present; copies of the Notice and warrant shall be left in a prominent place on the premises or appropriate part of the premises and endorsed, subject to paragraph 2.9 with the name of the officer in charge of the search, the date and time of the search
   The warrant shall be endorsed to show this has been done.

(d) Conduct of searches

6.9 Premises may be searched only to the extent necessary to achieve the purpose of the search, having regard to the size and nature of whatever is sought.

6.9A A search may not continue under:
   • a warrant's authority once all the things specified in that warrant have been found;
   • any other power once the object of that search has been achieved.

6.9B No search may continue once the officer in charge of the search is satisfied whatever is being sought is not on the premises (see *Note 6B*). This does not prevent a further search of the same premises if additional grounds come to light supporting a further application for a search warrant or exercise or further exercise of another power. For example, when, as a result of new information, it is believed articles previously not found or additional articles are on the premises.

6.10 Searches must be conducted with due consideration for the property and privacy of the occupier and with no more disturbance than necessary. Reasonable force may be used only when necessary and proportionate because the co-operation of the occupier cannot be obtained or is insufficient for the purpose. (See *Note 6C*.)

6.11 A friend, neighbour or other person must be allowed to witness the search if the occupier wishes unless the officer in charge of the search has reasonable grounds for believing the presence of the person asked for would seriously hinder the investigation or endanger officers or other people. A search need not be unreasonably delayed for this purpose. A record of the action taken should be made on the premises search record including the grounds for refusing the occupier's request.

6.12 A person is not required to be cautioned prior to being asked questions that are solely necessary for the purpose of furthering the proper and effective conduct of a search, see Code C, *paragraph 10.1(c)*. For example, questions to discover the occupier of specified premises, to find a key to open a locked drawer or cupboard or to otherwise seek co-operation during the search or to determine if a particular item is liable to be seized.

6.12A If questioning goes beyond what is necessary for the purpose of the exemption in Code C, the exchange is likely to constitute an interview as defined by Code C, paragraph 11.1A and would require the associated safeguards included in Code C, section 10.

(e) Leaving premises

6.13 If premises have been entered by force, before leaving the officer in charge of the search must make sure they are secure by:
- arranging for the occupier or their agent to be present;
- any other appropriate means.

(f) Searches under PACE Schedule 1 or the Terrorism Act 2000, Schedule 5

6.14 An officer shall be appointed as the officer in charge of the search (see *paragraph 2.10*), in respect of any search made under a warrant issued under PACE Act 1984, Schedule 1 or the Terrorism Act 2000, Schedule 5. They are responsible for making sure the search is conducted with discretion and in a manner that causes the least possible disruption to any business or other activities carried out on the premises.

6.15 Once the officer in charge of the search is satisfied material may not be taken from the premises without their knowledge, they shall ask for the documents or other records concerned. The officer in charge of the search may also ask to see the index to files held on the premises, and the officers conducting the search may inspect any files which, according to the index, appear to contain the material sought. A more extensive search of the premises may be made only if:
- the person responsible for them refuses to:
  - produce the material sought, or
  - allow access to the index.
- it appears the index is:
  - inaccurate, or
  - incomplete.
- for any other reason the officer in charge of the search has reasonable grounds for believing such a search is necessary in order to find the material sought.

Notes for guidance

6A Whether compensation is appropriate depends on the circumstances in each case. Compensation for damage caused when effecting entry is unlikely to be appropriate if the search was lawful, and the force used can be shown to be reasonable, proportionate and necessary to effect entry. If the wrong premises are searched by mistake everything possible should be done at the earliest opportunity to allay any sense of grievance and there should normally be a strong presumption in favour of paying compensation.

6B It is important that, when possible, all those involved in a search are fully briefed about any powers to be exercised and the extent and limits within which it should be conducted.

6C   In all cases the number of officers and other persons involved in executing the warrant should be determined by what is reasonable and necessary according to the particular circumstances.

7 Seizure and retention of property

(a) Seizure

7.1   Subject to paragraph 7.2, an officer who is searching any person or premises under any statutory power or with the consent of the occupier may seize anything:

(a)   covered by a warrant;

(b)   the officer has reasonable grounds for believing is evidence of an offence or has been obtained in consequence of the commission of an offence but only if seizure is necessary to prevent the items being concealed, lost, disposed of, altered, damaged, destroyed or tampered with;

(c)   covered by the powers in the Criminal Justice and Police Act 2001, Part 2 allowing an officer to seize property from persons or premises and retain it for sifting or examination elsewhere.

See *Note 7B.*

7.2   No item may be seized which an officer has reasonable grounds for believing to be subject to legal privilege, as defined in PACE, section 10, other than under the Criminal Justice and Police Act 2001, Part 2.

7.3   Officers must be aware of the provisions in the Criminal Justice and Police Act 2001, section 59, allowing for applications to a judicial authority for the return of property seized and the subsequent duty to secure in section 60. (See *paragraph 7.12(iii)*.)

7.4   An officer may decide it is not appropriate to seize property because of an explanation from the person holding it but may nevertheless have reasonable grounds for believing it was obtained in consequence of an offence by some person. In these circumstances, the officer should identify the property to the holder, inform the holder of their suspicions and explain the holder may be liable to civil or criminal proceedings if they dispose of, alter or destroy the property.

7.5   An officer may arrange to photograph, image or copy, any document or other article they have the power to seize in accordance with paragraph 7.1. This is subject to specific restrictions on the examination, imaging or copying of certain property seized under the Criminal Justice and Police Act 2001, Part 2. An officer must have regard to their statutory obligation to retain an original document or other article only when a photograph or copy is not sufficient.

7.6   If an officer considers information stored in any electronic form and accessible from the premises could be used in evidence, they may require the information to be produced in a form:

• which can be taken away and in which it is visible and legible, or

• from which it can readily be produced in a visible and legible form.

(b) Criminal Justice and Police Act 2001: Specific procedures for seize and sift powers

7.7   The Criminal Justice and Police Act 2001, Part 2 gives officers limited powers to seize property from premises or persons so they can sift or examine it elsewhere. Officers must be careful they only exercise these powers when it is essential and they do not remove any more material than necessary. The removal of large volumes of material, much of which may not ultimately be retainable, may have serious implications for the owners, particularly when they are involved in business or activities such as journalism or the provision of medical services. Officers must carefully consider if removing copies or images of relevant material or data would be a satisfactory alternative to removing originals. When originals are taken, officers must be prepared to facilitate the provision of copies or images for the owners when reasonably practicable. (See *Note 7C.*)

7.8   Property seized under the Criminal Justice and Police Act 2001, sections 50 or 51 must be kept securely and separately from any material seized under other powers. An examination under section 53 to determine which elements may be retained must be carried out at the earliest practicable time, having due regard to the desirability of allowing the person from whom the property was seized, or a person with an interest in the property, an opportunity of being present or represented at the examination.

7.8A All reasonable steps should be taken to accommodate an interested person's request to be present, provided the request is reasonable and subject to the need to prevent harm to, interference with, or unreasonable delay to the investigatory process. If an examination proceeds in the absence of an interested person who asked to attend or their representative, the officer who exercised the relevant seizure power must give that person a written notice of why the examination was carried out in those circumstances. If it is necessary for security reasons or to maintain confidentiality officers may exclude interested persons from decryption or other processes which facilitate the examination but do not form part of it. (See *Note 7D.*)

7.9   It is the responsibility of the officer in charge of the investigation to make sure property is returned in accordance with sections 53 to 55. Material which there is no power to retain must be:
- separated from the rest of the seized property, and
- returned as soon as reasonably practicable after examination of all the seized property.

7.9A   Delay is only warranted if very clear and compelling reasons exist, for example:
- the unavailability of the person to whom the material is to be returned, or
- the need to agree a convenient time to return a large volume of material

7.9B   Legally privileged, excluded or special procedure material which cannot be retained must be returned:
- as soon as reasonably practicable, and
- without waiting for the whole examination.

7.9C   As set out in section 58, material must be returned to the person from whom it was seized, except when it is clear some other person has a better right to it. (See *Note 7E*.)

7.10   When an officer involved in the investigation has reasonable grounds to believe a person with a relevant interest in property seized under section 50 or 51 intends to make an application under section 59 for the return of any legally privileged, special procedure or excluded material, the officer in charge of the investigation should be informed as soon as practicable and the material seized should be kept secure in accordance with section 61. (See *Note 7C*.)

7.11   The officer in charge of the investigation is responsible for making sure property is properly secured. Securing involves making sure the property is not examined, copied, imaged or put to any other use except at the request, or with the consent, of the applicant or in accordance with the directions of the appropriate judicial authority. Any request, consent or directions must be recorded in writing and signed by both the initiator and the officer in charge of the investigation. (See *Notes 7F* and *7G*.)

7.12   When an officer exercises a power of seizure conferred by sections 50 or 51 they shall provide the occupier of the premises or the person from whom the property is being seized with a written notice:
(i)   specifying what has been seized under the powers conferred by that section;
(ii)   specifying the grounds for those powers;
(iii)   setting out the effect of sections 59 to 61 covering the grounds for a person with a relevant interest in seized property to apply to a judicial authority for its return and the duty of officers to secure property in certain circumstances when an application is made, and
(iv)   specifying the name and address of the person to whom:
- notice of an application to the appropriate judicial authority in respect of any of the seized property must be given;
- an application may be made to allow attendance at the initial examination of the property.

7.13   If the occupier is not present but there is someone in charge of the premises, the notice shall be given to them. If no suitable person is available, so the notice will easily be found it should either be:
- left in a prominent place on the premises, or
- attached to the exterior of the premises.

(c) Retention

7.14   Subject to paragraph 7.15, anything seized in accordance with the above provisions may be retained only for as long as is necessary. It may be retained, among other purposes:
(i)   for use as evidence at a trial for an offence;
(ii)   to facilitate the use in any investigation or proceedings of anything to which it is inextricably linked (see *Note 7H*);
(iii)   for forensic examination or other investigation in connection with an offence;
(iv)   in order to establish its lawful owner when there are reasonable grounds for believing it has been stolen or obtained by the commission of an offence.

7.15   Property shall not be retained under paragraph 7.14(i), (ii) or (iii) if a copy or image would be sufficient.

(d) Rights of owners etc

7.16   If property is retained, the person who had custody or control of it immediately before seizure must, on request, be provided with a list or description of the property within a reasonable time.

7.17   That person or their representative must be allowed supervised access to the property to examine it or have it photographed or copied, or must be provided with a photograph or copy, in either case within a reasonable time of any request and at their own expense, unless the officer in charge of an investigation has reasonable grounds for believing this would:

(i)   prejudice the investigation of any offence or criminal proceedings; or

(ii) lead to the commission of an offence by providing access to unlawful material such as pornography;

A record of the grounds shall be made when access is denied.

Notes for guidance

7A   Any person claiming property seized by the police may apply to a magistrates' court under the Police (Property) Act 1897 for its possession and should, if appropriate, be advised of this procedure.

7B   The powers of seizure conferred by PACE, sections 18(2) and 19(3) extend to the seizure of the whole premises when it is physically possible to seize and retain the premises in their totality and practical considerations make seizure desirable. For example, police may remove premises such as tents, vehicles or caravans to a police station for the purpose of preserving evidence.

7C   Officers should consider reaching agreement with owners and/or other interested parties on the procedures for examining a specific set of property, rather than awaiting the judicial authority's determination. Agreement can sometimes give a quicker and more satisfactory route for all concerned and minimise costs and legal complexities.

7D   What constitutes a relevant interest in specific material may depend on the nature of that material and the circumstances in which it is seized. Anyone with a reasonable claim to ownership of the material and anyone entrusted with its safe keeping by the owner should be considered.

7E   Requirements to secure and return property apply equally to all copies, images or other material created because of seizure of the original property.

7F   The mechanics of securing property vary according to the circumstances; 'bagging up', i.e. placing material in sealed bags or containers and strict subsequent control of access is the appropriate procedure in many cases.

7G   When material is seized under the powers of seizure conferred by PACE, the duty to retain it under the Code of Practice issued under the Criminal Procedure and Investigations Act 1996 is subject to the provisions on retention of seized material in PACE, section 22.

7H   Paragraph 7.14 (ii) applies if inextricably linked material is seized under the Criminal Justice and Police Act 2001, sections 50 or 51. Inextricably linked material is material it is not reasonably practicable to separate from other linked material without prejudicing the use of that other material in any investigation or proceedings. For example, it may not be possible to separate items of data held on computer disk without damaging their evidential integrity. Inextricably linked material must not be examined, imaged, copied or used for any purpose other than for proving the source and/or integrity of the linked material.

8 Action after searches

8.1   If premises are searched in circumstances where this Code applies, unless the exceptions in paragraph 2.3(a) apply, on arrival at a police station the officer in charge of the search shall make or have made a record of the search, to include:

(i)   the address of the searched premises;

(ii)   the date, time and duration of the search;

(iii) the authority used for the search:
  • if the search was made in exercise of a statutory power to search premises without warrant, the power which was used for the search:
  • if the search was made under a warrant or with written consent;
    – a copy of the warrant and the written authority to apply for it, see *paragraph 3.4*; or
    – the written consent;
    shall be appended to the record or the record shall show the location of the copy warrant or consent;

(iv)   subject to paragraph 2.9, the names of:
  • the officer(s) in charge of the search;
  • all other officers and authorised persons who conducted the search;

(v)   the names of any people on the premises if they are known;

(vi)   any grounds for refusing the occupier's request to have someone present during the search, see *paragraph 6.11*;

(vii) a list of any articles seized or the location of a list and, if not covered by a warrant, the grounds for their seizure;

(viii) whether force was used, and the reason;
(ix) details of any damage caused during the search, and the circumstances;
(x) if applicable, the reason it was not practicable;
    (a) to give the occupier a copy of the Notice of Powers and Rights, see *paragraph 6.7*;
    (b) before the search to give the occupier a copy of the Notice, see *paragraph 6.8*;
(xi) when the occupier was not present, the place where copies of the Notice of Powers and Rights and search warrant were left on the premises, see *paragraph 6.8*.

8.2 On each occasion when premises are searched under warrant, the warrant authorising the search on that occasion shall be endorsed to show:
    (i) if any articles specified in the warrant were found and the address where found;
    (ii) if any other articles were seized;
    (iii) the date and time it was executed and if present, the name of the occupier or if the occupier is not present the name of the person in charge of the premises;
    (iv) subject to *paragraph 2.9*, the names of the officers who executed it and any authorised persons who accompanied them, and
    (v) if a copy, together with a copy of the Notice of Powers and Rights was:
      • handed to the occupier, or
      • endorsed as required by paragraph 6.8; and left on the premises and where.

8.3 Any warrant shall be returned within three calendar months of its issue or sooner on completion of the search(es) authorised by that warrant, if it was issued by a:
    • justice of the peace, to the designated officer for the local justice area in which the justice was acting when issuing the warrant; or
    • judge, to the appropriate officer of the court concerned,

9 Search registers

9.1 A search register will be maintained at each sub-divisional or equivalent police station. All search records required under paragraph 8.1 shall be made, copied, or referred to in the register. (See *Note 9A*.)

Note for guidance

9A Paragraph 9.1 also applies to search records made by immigration officers. In these cases, a search register must also be maintained at an immigration office. (See also *Note 2D*.)

10 Searches under Schedule 5 to the Terrorism Prevention and Investigation Measures Act 2011

10.1 This Code applies to the powers of constables under Schedule 5 to the Terrorism Prevention and Investigation Measures Act 2011 relating to TPIM notices to enter and search premises subject to the modifications in the following paragraphs.

10.2 In paragraph 2.3(d), the reference to the investigation into an alleged or suspected offence include the enforcement of terrorism prevention and investigation measures which may be imposed on an individual by a TPIM notice in accordance with the Terrorism Prevention and Investigation Measures Act 2011.

10.3 References to the purpose and object of the entry and search of premises, the nature of articles sought and what may be seized and retained include (as appropriate):
    (a) in relation to the power to search without a search warrant in paragraph 5 (for purposes of serving TPIM notice), finding the individual on whom the notice is to be served.
    (b) in relation to the power to search without a search warrant in paragraph 6 (at time of serving TPIM notice), ascertaining whether there is anything in the premises, that contravenes measures specified in the notice. (See *Note 10A*.)
    (c) in relation to the power to search without a search warrant under paragraph 7 (suspected absconding), ascertaining whether a person has absconded or if there is anything on the premises which will assist in the pursuit or arrest of an individual in respect of whom a TPIM notice is force who is reasonably suspected of having absconded.
    (d) in relation to the power to search under a search warrant issued under paragraph 8 (for compliance purposes), determining whether an individual in respect of whom a TPIM notice is in force is complying with measures specified in the notice. (See *Note 10A*.)

Note for guidance

10A Searches of individuals under Schedule 5, paragraphs 6(2)(a) (at time of serving TPIM notice) and 8(2)(a) (for compliance purposes) must be conducted and recorded in accordance with Code A. See Code A *paragraph 2.18A* for details.

PACE CODE C

REVISED CODE OF PRACTICE FOR THE DETENTION, TREATMENT AND QUESTIONING OF PERSONS BY POLICE OFFICERS

Commencement—transitional arrangements

This Code applies to people in police detention after 0.00 on 2 June 2014, notwithstanding that their period of detention may have commenced before that time.

1 General

1.0   The powers and procedures in this Code must be used fairly, responsibly, with respect for the people to whom they apply and without unlawful discrimination. Under the Equality Act 2010, section 149, when police officers are carrying out their functions, they also have a duty to have due regard to the need to eliminate unlawful discrimination, harassment and victimisation, to advance equality of opportunity between people who share a relevant protected characteristic and people who do not share it, and to take steps to foster good relations between those persons. See *Notes 1A* and *1AA*.

1.1   All persons in custody must be dealt with expeditiously, and released as soon as the need for detention no longer applies.

1.1A A custody officer must perform the functions in this Code as soon as practicable. A custody officer will not be in breach of this Code if delay is justifiable and reasonable steps are taken to prevent unnecessary delay. The custody record shall show when a delay has occurred and the reason. See *Note 1H*.

1.2   This Code of Practice must be readily available at all police stations for consultation by:
* police officers;
* police staff;
* detained persons;
* members of the public.

1.3   The provisions of this Code:
* include the *Annexes*
* do not include the *Notes for Guidance*.

1.4   If an officer has any suspicion, or is told in good faith, that a person of any age may be mentally disordered or otherwise mentally vulnerable, in the absence of clear evidence to dispel that suspicion, the person shall be treated as such for the purposes of this Code. See *Note 1G*.

1.5   If anyone appears to be under 17, they shall in the absence of clear evidence that they are older, be treated as a juvenile for the purposes of this Code and any other Code.

1.5A If anyone appears to have attained the age of 17 and to be under the age of 18, they shall in the absence of clear evidence that they are older, be treated as a 17-year-old for the purposes of this and any other Code. The provisions and *Notes for Guidance* which in accordance with *paragraph 1.5* apply to a juvenile and the way they are to be treated shall also apply to them, except as described in sub-paragraphs (a) and (b) below:

(a) The *statutory* provisions in section 38 of PACE (Detention after charge) which apply only to an *arrested juvenile* as defined in section 37(15) of PACE and to which *paragraphs 16.7* and *16.10* and *Note 16D* of this Code relate, shall *not apply* to a person who appears to have attained the age of 17 for the purposes of:
   (i) the grounds to keep them in police detention after charge; and
   (ii) the requirement to transfer a person who has been kept in police detention after charge to local authority accommodation and the power of the local authority to detain them pending appearance at court.

(b) the *statutory* provisions in section 65(1) of PACE (appropriate consent) which require *appropriate consent* for a person who has *not attained the age of 17* to be given by them and their parent or guardian shall not apply to a person who appears to have attained the age of 17 and whose consent alone shall be sufficient.

In this Code, section 65(1) applies to *Annex A paragraphs 2(b)* and *2B* (Intimate searches) and *Annex K paragraphs 1(b) and 3* (X-Ray and ultrasound scan) and in Code D (Identification) to *paragraph 2.12* and *Note 2A* with regards to taking fingerprints, samples, footwear impressions, photographs and evidential searches and examinations.

See Notes 1L and *1M*.

1.6   If a person appears to be blind, seriously visually impaired, deaf, unable to read or speak or has difficulty orally because of a speech impediment, they shall be treated as such for the purposes of this Code in the absence of clear evidence to the contrary.

1.7   'The appropriate adult' means, in the case of a:
    (a)   juvenile:
        (i)   the parent, guardian or, if the juvenile is in the care of a local authority or voluntary organisation, a person representing that authority or organisation (see *Note 1B*);
        (ii)   a social worker of a local authority (see *Note 1C*);
        (iii)   failing these, some other responsible adult aged 18 or over who is not a police officer or employed by the police.
        Note: *Paragraph 1.5A* extends sub-paragraph (a) to the person called to fulfil the role of the appropriate adult for a 17-year-old detainee.
    (b)   person who is mentally disordered or mentally vulnerable: See *Note 1D*.
        (i)   a relative, guardian or other person responsible for their care or custody;
        (ii)   someone experienced in dealing with mentally disordered or mentally vulnerable people but who is not a police officer or employed by the police;
        (ii)   failing these, some other responsible adult aged 18 or over who is not a police officer or employed by the police.

1.8   If this Code requires a person be given certain information, they do not have to be given it if at the time they are incapable of understanding what is said, are violent or may become violent or in urgent need of medical attention, but they must be given it as soon as practicable.

1.9   References to a custody officer include any police officer who for the time being, is performing the functions of a custody officer.

1.9A   When this Code requires the prior authority or agreement of an officer of at least inspector or superintendent rank, that authority may be given by a sergeant or chief inspector authorised to perform the functions of the higher rank under the PACE, section 107.

1.10   Subject to *paragraph 1.12*, this Code applies to people in custody at police stations in England and Wales, whether or not they have been arrested, and to those removed to a police station as a place of safety under the Mental Health Act 1983, sections 135 and 136, as a last resort (see *paragraph 3.16*). *Section 15* applies solely to people in police detention, e.g. those brought to a police station under arrest or arrested at a police station for an offence after going there voluntarily.

1.11   No part of this Code applies to a detained person:
    (a)   to whom PACE Code H applies because:
        •   they are detained following arrest under section 41 of the Terrorism Act 2000 (TACT) and not charged; or
        •   an authorisation has been given under section 22 of the Counter-Terrorism Act 2008 (CTACT) (post-charge questioning of terrorist suspects) to interview them.
    (b)   to whom the Code of Practice issued under paragraph 6 of Schedule 14 to TACT applies because they are detained for examination under Schedule 7 to TACT.

1.12   This Code does not apply to people in custody:
    (i)   arrested by officers under the Criminal Justice and Public Order Act 1994, section 136(2) on warrants issued in Scotland, or arrested or detained without warrant under section 137(2) by officers from a police force in Scotland. In these cases, police powers and duties and the person's rights and entitlements whilst at a police station in England or Wales are the same as those in Scotland;
    (ii)   arrested under the Immigration and Asylum Act 1999, section 142(3) in order to have their fingerprints taken;
    (iii)   whose detention is authorised under Schedules 2 or 3 to the Immigration Act 1971 or section 62 of the Nationality, Immigration and Asylum Act 2002;
    (iv)   who are convicted or remanded prisoners held in police cells on behalf of the Prison Service under the Imprisonment (Temporary Provisions) Act 1980;
    (v)   *Not used*.
    (vi)   detained for searches under stop and search powers except as required by Code A.
    The provisions on conditions of detention and treatment in *sections 8* and *9* must be considered as the minimum standards of treatment for such detainees.

1.13   In this Code:
    (a)   'designated person' means a person other than a police officer, designated under the Police Reform Act 2002, Part 4 who has specified powers and duties of police officers conferred or imposed on them;

(b) reference to a police officer includes a designated person acting in the exercise or performance of the powers and duties conferred or imposed on them by their designation.

(c) where a search or other procedure to which this Code applies may only be carried out or observed by a person of the same sex as the detainee, the gender of the detainee and other parties present should be established and recorded in line with *Annex L* of this Code.

1.14 Designated persons are entitled to use reasonable force as follows:

(a) when exercising a power conferred on them which allows a police officer exercising that power to use reasonable force, a designated person has the same entitlement to use force; and

(b) at other times when carrying out duties conferred or imposed on them that also entitle them to use reasonable force, for example:

- when at a police station carrying out the duty to keep detainees for whom they are responsible under control and to assist any police officer or designated person to keep any detainee under control and to prevent their escape.
- when securing, or assisting any police officer or designated person in securing, the detention of a person at a police station.
- when escorting, or assisting any police officer or designated person in escorting, a detainee within a police station.
- for the purpose of saving life or limb; or
- preventing serious damage to property.

1.15 Nothing in this Code prevents the custody officer, or other officer given custody of the detainee, from allowing police staff who are not designated persons to carry out individual procedures or tasks at the police station if the law allows. However, the officer remains responsible for making sure the procedures and tasks are carried out correctly in accordance with the Codes of Practice (see *Note 3F*). Any such person must be:

(a) a person employed by a police force and under the direction and control of the Chief Officer of that force; or

(b) employed by a person with whom a police force has a contract for the provision of services relating to persons arrested or otherwise in custody.

1.16 Designated persons and other police staff must have regard to any relevant provisions of the Codes of Practice.

1.17 References to pocket books include any official report book issued to police officers or other police staff.

Notes for Guidance

1A Although certain sections of this Code apply specifically to people in custody at police stations, those there voluntarily to assist with an investigation should be treated with no less consideration, e.g. offered refreshments at appropriate times, and enjoy an absolute right to obtain legal advice or communicate with anyone outside the police station.

1AA In paragraph 1.0, 'relevant protected characteristic' includes: age, disability, gender reassignment, pregnancy and maternity, race, religion/belief, sex and sexual orientation.

1B A person, including a parent or guardian, should not be an appropriate adult if they:

- are:
  - suspected of involvement in the offence;
  - the victim;
  - a witness;
  - involved in the investigation.
- received admissions prior to attending to act as the appropriate adult.

Note: If a juvenile's parent is estranged from the juvenile, they should not be asked to act as the appropriate adult if the juvenile expressly and specifically objects to their presence.

Note: *Paragraph 1.5A* applies this Note to 17-year-old detainees.

1C If a juvenile admits an offence to, or in the presence of, a social worker or member of a youth offending team other than during the time that person is acting as the juvenile's appropriate adult, another appropriate adult should be appointed in the interest of fairness.

Note: *Paragraph 1.5A* applies this Note to 17-year-old detainees.

1D In the case of people who are mentally disordered or otherwise mentally vulnerable, it may be more satisfactory if the appropriate adult is someone experienced or trained in their care rather than a relative lacking such qualifications. But if the detainee prefers a relative to a better qualified stranger or objects to a particular person their wishes should, if practicable, be respected.

1E   A detainee should always be given an opportunity, when an appropriate adult is called to the police station, to consult privately with a solicitor in the appropriate adult's absence if they want. An appropriate adult is not subject to legal privilege.

1F   A solicitor or independent custody visitor present at the police station in that capacity may not be the appropriate adult.

1G   'Mentally vulnerable' applies to any detainee who, because of their mental state or capacity, may not understand the significance of what is said, of questions or of their replies. 'Mental disorder' is defined in the Mental Health Act 1983, section 1(2) as 'any disorder or disability of mind'. When the custody officer has any doubt about the mental state or capacity of a detainee, that detainee should be treated as mentally vulnerable and an appropriate adult called.

1H   *Paragraph 1.1A* is intended to cover delays which may occur in processing detainees e.g. if:
   • a large number of suspects are brought into the station simultaneously to be placed in custody;
   • interview rooms are all being used;
   • there are difficulties contacting an appropriate adult, solicitor or interpreter.

1I   The custody officer must remind the appropriate adult and detainee about the right to legal advice and record any reasons for waiving it in accordance with *section 6*.

1J   *Not used.*

1K   This Code does not affect the principle that all citizens have a duty to help police officers to prevent crime and discover offenders. This is a civic rather than a legal duty; but when police officers are trying to discover whether, or by whom, offences have been committed they are entitled to question any person from whom they think useful information can be obtained, subject to the restrictions imposed by this Code. A person's declaration that they are unwilling to reply does not alter this entitlement.

1L   *Paragraph 1.5A* does not amend section 37(15) of PACE which defines the term 'arrested juvenile' for the purposes of sections 34 to 51 of PACE, or provisions in any other enactment which expressly refer and apply to persons under the age of 17. Until amended by Parliament, these statutory provisions alone do not extend to persons who have attained the age of 17.

1M   The purpose of *paragraph 1.5A* is to extend the safeguards for juveniles to 17-year-olds unless this is precluded by any statutory provisions. *Sub-paragraphs 1.5A(a)* and *(b)* identify the provisions of sections 38 and 65 of PACE concerning detention after charge and appropriate consent which for this reason do not extend to 17-year-olds. All other safeguards in this and other Codes are extended and the requirements which are indicated in the relevant provisions and *Notes for Guidance* are as follows:
   (a) under *paragraph 3.13* of this Code, to identify and inform someone responsible for the welfare of a 17-year-old which is in addition to their right in section 5 of this Code not to be held incommunicado;
   (b) under *paragraph 3.14* of this Code to notify a person who has statutory responsibility under a court order to supervise or monitor a 17-year-old;
   (c) under *paragraph 8.8* with regard to cell accommodation and keeping 17-year-old detainees separate from adults;
   (d) to call a person described by *paragraph 1.7(a)* or *Note 17G* in relation to testing for the presence of Class A drugs, to fulfil the role of the appropriate adult for the purposes of this or any other Code to support and assist a 17-year-old:
      (i) by being present when:
         • they are informed of their rights and entitlements and the grounds for their detention (see *paragraphs 3.17* and *3.18*);
         • they are cautioned or given a special warning (see *paragraphs 10.12* and *10.11A*);
         • they are being interviewed in accordance with this Code (see *sections 11* and *12*) or Codes E or F unless *paragraph 11.15* of this Code allows the interview to go ahead without the adult being present;
         • their detention is being reviewed or an extension is being considered (see *paragraphs 15.3(c)* and *15.3C(a)*):
         • they are charged and related action is taken (see *paragraphs 16.1, 16.3, 16.4A* and *16.6*);
         • samples to test for Class A drugs are requested from a person who has not attained the age of 18 (see *paragraph 17.7*);
         • an intimate search is carried out (see *Annex A paragraphs 2A, 2B* and *5*);
         • a strip search is carried out (see *Annex A paragraph 11(c)*);
         • an x-ray or ultrasound scan is carried out (see *Annex K paragraphs 2* and *3*);
         • procedures in Code D involving witness identification, taking fingerprints, samples, footwear impressions and photographs and when evidential searches and examinations are carried out (see *paragraphs 2.14* and *2.15*).

(ii) by allowing:
- the adult to inspect their custody record and to have a copy of their record (see *paragraphs 2.4, 2.4A* and *2.5*);
- a 17-year-old to consult the adult in private (see *paragraph 3.18*);
- the adult to request legal advice on their behalf to advise and assist them (*see paragraphs 3.19, 6.5A* and *11.17*).

2 Custody records

2.1A When a person:
- is brought to a police station under arrest
- is arrested at the police station having attended there voluntarily or
- attends a police station to answer bail

they must be brought before the custody officer as soon as practicable after their arrival at the station or if applicable, following their arrest after attending the police station voluntarily. This applies to both designated and non-designated police stations. A person is deemed to be 'at a police station' for these purposes if they are within the boundary of any building or enclosed yard which forms part of that police station.

2.1 A separate custody record must be opened as soon as practicable for each person brought to a police station under arrest or arrested at the station having gone there voluntarily or attending a police station in answer to street bail. All information recorded under this Code must be recorded as soon as practicable in the custody record unless otherwise specified. Any audio or video recording made in the custody area is not part of the custody record.

2.2 If any action requires the authority of an officer of a specified rank, subject to *paragraph 2.6A*, their name and rank must be noted in the custody record.

2.3 The custody officer is responsible for the custody record's accuracy and completeness and for making sure the record or copy of the record accompanies a detainee if they are transferred to another police station. The record shall show the:
- time and reason for transfer;
- time a person is released from detention.

2.3A If a person is arrested and taken to a police station as a result of a search in the exercise of any stop and search power to which PACE Code A (Stop and search) or the 'search powers code' issued under TACT applies, the officer carrying out the search is responsible for ensuring that the record of that stop and search is made as part of the person's custody record. The custody officer must then ensure that the person is asked if they want a copy of the search record and if they do, that they are given a copy as soon as practicable. The person's entitlement to a copy of the search record which is made as part of their custody record is in addition to, and does not affect, their entitlement to a copy of their custody record or any other provisions of section 2 (Custody records) of this Code. (See Code A *paragraph 4.2B* and the TACT search powers code *paragraph 5.3.5*).

2.4 The detainee's solicitor and appropriate adult must be permitted to inspect the whole of the detainee's custody record as soon as practicable after their arrival at the station and at any other time on request, whilst the person is detained. This includes the following *specific* records relating to the reasons for the detainee's arrest and detention and the offence concerned, to which *paragraph 3.1(b)* refers:

(a) The information about the circumstances and reasons for the detainee's arrest as recorded in the custody record in accordance with *paragraph 4.3* of Code G. This applies to any further offences for which the detainee is arrested whilst in custody;

(b) The record of the grounds for each authorisation to keep the person in custody. The authorisations to which this applies are the same as those described at items *(i)(a)* to *(d)* in the table in *paragraph 2* of *Annex M* of this Code.

Access to the records in *sub-paragraphs (a)* and *(b)* is *in addition* to the requirements in *paragraphs 3.4(b), 11.1A, 15.0, 15.7A(c)* and *16.7A* to make certain documents and materials available and to provide information about the offence and the reasons for arrest and detention.

Access to the custody record for the purposes of this paragraph must be arranged and agreed with the custody officer and may not unreasonably interfere with the custody officer's duties. A record shall be made when access is allowed and whether it includes the records described in *sub-paragraphs (a)* and *(b)* above.

Note: *Paragraph 1.5A* extends this paragraph to the person called to fulfil the role of the appropriate adult for a 17-year-old detainee.

2.4A When a detainee leaves police detention or is taken before a court they, their legal representative or appropriate adult shall be given, on request, a copy of the custody record as soon as practicable. This entitlement lasts for 12 months after release.

Note: *Paragraph 1.5A* extends this paragraph to the person called to fulfil the role of the appropriate adult for a 17-year-old detainee.

2.5 The detainee, appropriate adult or legal representative shall be permitted to inspect the original custody record after the detainee has left police detention provided they give reasonable notice of their request. Any such inspection shall be noted in the custody record.

Note: *Paragraph 1.5A* extends this paragraph to the person called to fulfil the role of the appropriate adult for a 17-year-old detainee.

2.6 Subject to *paragraph 2.6A*, all entries in custody records must be timed and signed by the maker. Records entered on computer shall be timed and contain the operator's identification.

2.6A Nothing in this Code requires the identity of officers or other police staff to be recorded or disclosed:
   (a) *Not used.*
   (b) if the officer or police staff reasonably believe recording or disclosing their name might put them in danger.

In these cases, they shall use their warrant or other identification numbers and the name of their police station. See *Note 2A*.

2.7 The fact and time of any detainee's refusal to sign a custody record, when asked in accordance with this Code, must be recorded.

Notes for Guidance

2A The purpose of *paragraph 2.6A(b)* is to protect those involved in serious organised crime investigations or arrests of particularly violent suspects when there is reliable information that those arrested or their associates may threaten or cause harm to those involved. In cases of doubt, an officer of inspector rank or above should be consulted.

3 Initial action

(a) Detained persons – normal procedure

3.1 When a person is brought to a police station under arrest or arrested at the station having gone there voluntarily, the custody officer must make sure the person is told clearly about:
   (a) the following continuing rights which may be exercised at any stage during the period in custody:
      (i)   their right to consult privately with a solicitor and that free independent legal advice is available as in *section 6*;
      (ii) their right to have someone informed of their arrest as in *section 5*;
      (iii) their right to consult the Codes of Practice (see *Note 3D*) and
      (iv) if applicable, their right to interpretation and translation (see *paragraph 3.12*) and the right to communicate with their High Commission, Embassy or Consulate (see *paragraph 3.12A*).
   (b) their right to be informed about the offence and (as the case may be) any further offences for which they are arrested whilst in custody, and why they have been arrested and detained in accordance with *paragraphs 2.4, 3.4(a)* and *11.1A* of this Code and *paragraph 3.3* of Code G.

3.2 The detainee must also be given a written notice, which contains information:
   (a) setting out:
      (i)   their rights under *paragraph 3.1, paragraph 3.12* and *3.12A*);
      (ii)   the arrangements for obtaining legal advice, see *section 6*;
      (iii) their right to a copy of the custody record as in *paragraph 2.4A*;
      (iv)   their right to remain silent as set out in the caution in the terms prescribed in *section 10*;
      (v)   their right to have access to materials and documents which are essential to effectively challenging the lawfulness of their arrest and detention for any offence and (as the case may be) any further offences for which they are arrested whilst in custody, in accordance with *paragraphs 3.4(b), 15.0, 15.7A(c)* and *16.7A* of this Code;
      (vi)   the maximum period for which they may be kept in police detention without being charged, when detention must be reviewed and when release is required.
      (vii) their right to medical assistance in accordance with *section 9* of this Code
      (viii) their right, if they are prosecuted, to have access to the evidence in the case before their trial in accordance with the Criminal Procedure and Investigations Act 1996, the Attorney General's Guidelines on Disclosure, the common law and the Criminal Procedure Rules.

(b) briefly setting out their other entitlements while in custody, by:
  (i) mentioning:
    – the provisions relating to the conduct of interviews;
    – the circumstances in which an appropriate adult should be available to assist the detainee and their statutory rights to make representations whenever the need for their detention is reviewed.
  (ii) listing the entitlements in this Code, concerning
    – reasonable standards of physical comfort;
    – adequate food and drink;
    – access to toilets and washing facilities, clothing, medical attention, and exercise when practicable.
  See *Note 3A.*

3.2A The detainee must be given an opportunity to read the notice and shall be asked to sign the custody record to acknowledge receipt of the notice. Any refusal to sign must be recorded on the custody record.

3.3 *Not used.*

3.3A An 'easy read' illustrated version should also be provided if they are available (see *Note 3A*).

3.4 (a) The custody officer shall:
- record the offence(s) that the detainee has been arrested for and the reason(s) for the arrest on the custody record. See *paragraph 10.3* and Code G *paragraphs 2.2* and *4.3*;
- note on the custody record any comment the detainee makes in relation to the arresting officer's account but shall not invite comment. If the arresting officer is not physically present when the detainee is brought to a police station, the arresting officer's account must be made available to the custody officer remotely or by a third party on the arresting officer's behalf. If the custody officer authorises a person's detention, subject to *paragraph 1.8*, that officer must record the grounds for detention in the detainee's presence and at the same time, inform them of the grounds. The detainee must be informed of the grounds for their detention before they are questioned about any offence;
- note any comment the detainee makes in respect of the decision to detain them but shall not invite comment;
- not put specific questions to the detainee regarding their involvement in any offence, nor in respect of any comments they may make in response to the arresting officer's account or the decision to place them in detention. Such an exchange is likely to constitute an interview as in *paragraph 11.1A* and require the associated safeguards in *section 11*.

  Note: This *sub-paragraph* also applies to any further offences and grounds for detention which come to light whilst the person is detained.

  See *paragraph 11.13* in respect of unsolicited comments.

(b) Documents and materials which are essential to effectively challenging the lawfulness of the detainee's arrest and detention must be made available to the detainee or their solicitor. Documents and materials will be 'essential' for this purpose if they are capable of undermining the reasons and grounds which make the detainee's arrest and detention *necessary*. The decision about whether particular documents or materials must be made available for the purpose of this requirement therefore rests with the custody officer who determines whether detention is necessary, in consultation with the investigating officer who has the knowledge of the documents and materials in a particular case necessary to inform that decision. A note should be made in the detainee's custody record of the *fact* that documents or materials have been made available under this sub-paragraph and when. The investigating officer should make a separate note of what is made available and how it is made available in a particular case. This sub-paragraph also applies (with modifications) for the purposes of *section 15 (Reviews and extensions of detention)* and *16 (Charging detained persons)*. See *Note 3 ZA* and *paragraphs 15.0* and *16.7A*.

3.5 The custody officer or other custody staff as directed by the custody officer shall:
(a) ask the detainee whether at this time, they:
  (i) would like legal advice, see *paragraph 6.5*;
  (ii) want someone informed of their detention, see *section 5*;
(b) ask the detainee to sign the custody record to confirm their decisions in respect of (*a*);
(c) determine whether the detainee:
  (i) is, or might be, in need of medical treatment or attention, see *section 9*;
  (ii) requires:

- an appropriate adult (see *paragraphs 1.4, 1.5, 1.5A* and *3.15*);
- help to check documentation (see *paragraph 3.20*);
- an interpreter (see *paragraph 3.12* and *Note 13B*).

(d)   record the decision in respect of (*c*).

Where any duties under this paragraph have been carried out by custody staff at the direction of the custody officer, the outcomes shall, as soon as practicable, be reported to the custody officer who retains overall responsibility for the detainee's care and treatment and ensuring that it complies with this Code. See *Note 3F*.

3.6   When these needs are determined, the custody officer is responsible for initiating an assessment to consider whether the detainee is likely to present specific risks to custody staff or themselves. Such assessments should always include a check on the Police National Computer, to be carried out as soon as practicable, to identify any risks highlighted in relation to the detainee. Although such assessments are primarily the custody officer's responsibility, it may be necessary for them to consult and involve others, e.g. the arresting officer or an appropriate healthcare professional, see *paragraph 9.13*. Reasons for delaying the initiation or completion of the assessment must be recorded.

3.7   Chief officers should ensure that arrangements for proper and effective risk assessments required by *paragraph 3.6* are implemented in respect of all detainees at police stations in their area.

3.8   Risk assessments must follow a structured process which clearly defines the categories of risk to be considered and the results must be incorporated in the detainee's custody record. The custody officer is responsible for making sure those responsible for the detainee's custody are appropriately briefed about the risks. If no specific risks are identified by the assessment, that should be noted in the custody record. See *Note 3E* and *paragraph 9.14*.

3.8A   The content of any risk assessment and any analysis of the level of risk relating to the person's detention is not required to be shown or provided to the detainee or any person acting on behalf of the detainee. But information should not be withheld from any person acting on the detainee's behalf, for example, an appropriate adult, solicitor or interpreter, if to do so might put that person at risk.

3.9   The custody officer is responsible for implementing the response to any specific risk assessment, e.g.:
- reducing opportunities for self harm;
- calling an appropriate healthcare professional;
- increasing levels of monitoring or observation;
- reducing the risk to those who come into contact with the detainee.

See *Note 3E*.

3.10   Risk assessment is an ongoing process and assessments must always be subject to review if circumstances change.

3.11   If video cameras are installed in the custody area, notices shall be prominently displayed showing cameras are in use. Any request to have video cameras switched off shall be refused.

(b)   Detained persons – special groups

3.12   If the detainee appears to be someone who does not speak or understand English or who has a hearing or speech impediment, the custody officer must ensure:
(a)   that without delay, an interpreter is called for assistance in the action under *paragraphs 3.1* to *3.5*. If the person appears to have a hearing or speech impediment, the reference to 'interpreter' includes appropriate assistance necessary to comply with *paragraphs 3.1* to *3.5*. See *paragraph 13.1C* if the detainee is in Wales. See *section 13* and *Note 13B*;
(b)   that in addition to the rights set out in *paragraph 3.1(a)(i)* to *(iv)*, the detainee is told clearly about their right to interpretation and translation;
(c)   that the written notice given to the detainee in accordance with *paragraph 3.2* is in a language the detainee understands and includes the right to interpretation and translation together with information about the provisions in *section 13* and *Annex M*, which explain how the right applies (see *Note 3A*); and
(d)   that if the translation of the notice is not available, the information in the notice is given through an interpreter and a written translation provided without undue delay.

3.12A If the detainee is a citizen of an independent Commonwealth country or a national of a foreign country, including the Republic of Ireland, the custody officer must ensure that in addition to the rights set out in *paragraph 3.1(a)(i)* to *(iv)*, they are informed as soon as practicable about their rights of communication with their High Commission, Embassy or Consulate set out in *section 7*. This right must be included in the written notice given to the detainee in accordance with *paragraph 3.2*.

3.13   If the detainee is a juvenile, the custody officer must, if it is practicable, ascertain the identity of a person responsible for their welfare. That person:

- may be:
  - the parent or guardian;
  - if the juvenile is in local authority or voluntary organisation care, or is otherwise being looked after under the Children Act 1989, a person appointed by that authority or organisation to have responsibility for the juvenile's welfare;
  - any other person who has, for the time being, assumed responsibility for the juvenile's welfare.
- must be informed as soon as practicable that the juvenile has been arrested, why they have been arrested and where they are detained. This right is in addition to the juvenile's right in *section 5* not to be held incommunicado. See *Note 3C*.

Note: *Paragraph 1.5A* extends the obligations in this paragraph to 17-year-old detainees.

3.14 If a juvenile is known to be subject to a court order under which a person or organisation is given any degree of statutory responsibility to supervise or otherwise monitor them, reasonable steps must also be taken to notify that person or organisation (the 'responsible officer'). The responsible officer will normally be a member of a Youth Offending Team, except for a curfew order which involves electronic monitoring when the contractor providing the monitoring will normally be the responsible officer.

Note: *Paragraph 1.5A* extends the obligations in this paragraph to 17-year-old detainees.

3.15 If the detainee is a juvenile, mentally disordered or otherwise mentally vulnerable, the custody officer must, as soon as practicable:
- inform the appropriate adult, who in the case of a juvenile may or may not be a person responsible for their welfare, as in *paragraph 3.13*, of:
  - the grounds for their detention;
  - their whereabouts.
- ask the adult to come to the police station to see the detainee.

Note: *Paragraph 1.5A* extends the obligation to call someone to fulfil the role of the appropriate adult to 17-year-old detainees.

3.16 It is imperative that a mentally disordered or otherwise mentally vulnerable person, detained under the Mental Health Act 1983, section 136, be assessed as soon as possible. A police station should only be used as a place of safety as a last resort but if that assessment is to take place at the police station, an approved mental health professional and a registered medical practitioner shall be called to the station as soon as possible to carry it out. See *Note 9D*. The appropriate adult has no role in the assessment process and their presence is not required. Once the detainee has been assessed and suitable arrangements made for their treatment or care, they can no longer be detained under section 136. A detainee must be immediately discharged from detention under section 136 if a registered medical practitioner, having examined them, concludes they are not mentally disordered within the meaning of the Act.

3.17 If the appropriate adult is:
- already at the police station, the provisions of *paragraphs 3.1* to *3.5* must be complied with in the appropriate adult's presence;
- not at the station when these provisions are complied with, they must be complied with again in the presence of the appropriate adult when they arrive,

and a copy of the notice given to the detainee in accordance with *paragraph 3.2*, shall also be given to the appropriate adult.

Note: *Paragraph 1.5A* extends the obligations in this paragraph to 17-year-old detainees.

3.18 The detainee shall be advised that:
- the duties of the appropriate adult include giving advice and assistance;
- they can consult privately with the appropriate adult at any time.

Note: *Paragraph 1.5A* extends the obligations in this paragraph to 17-year-old detainees.

3.19 If the detainee, or appropriate adult on the detainee's behalf, asks for a solicitor to be called to give legal advice, the provisions of *section 6* apply.

Note: *Paragraph 1.5A* extends the obligations in this paragraph to 17-year-old detainees.

3.20 If the detainee is blind, seriously visually impaired or unable to read, the custody officer shall make sure their solicitor, relative, appropriate adult or some other person likely to take an interest in them and not involved in the investigation is available to help check any documentation. When this Code requires written consent or signing the person assisting may be asked to sign instead, if the detainee prefers. This paragraph does not require an appropriate adult to be called solely to assist in checking and signing documentation for a person who is not a juvenile, or mentally disordered or otherwise mentally vulnerable (see *paragraph 3.15* and *Note 13C*).

(c) Persons attending a police station or elsewhere voluntarily

3.21 Anybody attending a police station or other location (see *paragraph 3.22*) voluntarily to assist police with the investigation of an offence may leave at will unless arrested. See *Note 1K*. The person may only be prevented from leaving at will if their arrest on suspicion of committing the offence is necessary in accordance with Code G. See Code G *Note 2G*.

   (a) If during an interview it is decided that their arrest is necessary, they must:
   - be informed at once that they are under arrest and of the grounds and reasons as required by Code G, and
   - be brought before the custody officer at the police station where they are arrested or, as the case may be, at the police station to which they are taken after being arrested elsewhere. The custody officer is then responsible for making sure that a custody record is opened and that they are notified of their rights in the same way as other detainees as required by this Code.

   (b) If they are not arrested but are cautioned as in *section 10*, the person who gives the caution must, at the same time, inform them they are not under arrest, they are not obliged to remain at the station or other location but if they agree to remain, they may obtain free and independent legal advice if they want. They shall also be given a copy of the notice explaining the arrangements for obtaining legal advice and told that the right to legal advice includes the right to speak with a solicitor on the telephone and be asked if they want advice. If advice is requested, the interviewer is responsible for securing its provision without delay by contacting the Defence Solicitor Call Centre. The interviewer must ensure that other provisions of this Code and Codes E and F concerning the conduct and recording of interviews of suspects and the rights and entitlements and safeguards for suspects who have been arrested and detained are followed insofar as they can be applied to suspects who are not under arrest. This includes:
   - informing them of the offence and, as the case may be, any further offences, they are suspected of and the grounds and reasons for that suspicion and their right to be so informed (see *paragraph 3.1(b)*);
   - the caution as required in *section 10*;
   - determining whether they require an appropriate adult and help to check documentation (see *paragraph 3.5(c)(ii)*); and
   - determining whether they require an interpreter and the provision of interpretation and translation services and informing them of that right. See *paragraphs 3.1(a)(iv), 3.5(c)(ii)* and *3.12, Note 6B* and *section 13[,]*

   but does not include any requirement to provide a written notice in addition to that above which concerns the arrangements for obtaining legal advice..

3.22 If the other location mentioned in *paragraph 3.21* is any place or premises for which the interviewer requires the person's informed consent to remain, for example, the person's home, then the references that the person is 'not obliged to remain' and that they 'may leave at will' mean that the person may also withdraw their consent and require the interviewer to leave.

(d) Documentation

3.23 The grounds for a person's detention shall be recorded, in the person's presence if practicable. See *paragraph 1.8*.

3.24 Action taken under *paragraphs 3.12* to *3.20* shall be recorded.

(e) Persons answering street bail

3.25 When a person is answering street bail, the custody officer should link any documentation held in relation to arrest with the custody record. Any further action shall be recorded on the custody record in accordance with *paragraphs 3.23* and *3.24*.

(f) Requirements for suspects to be informed of certain rights

3.26 The provisions of this section identify the information which must be given to suspects who have been cautioned in accordance with *section 10 of this Code* according to whether or not they have been arrested and detained. It includes information required by EU Directive 2012/13 on the right to information in criminal proceedings. If a complaint is made by or on behalf of such a suspect that the information and (as the case may be) access to records and documents has not been provided as required, the matter shall be reported to an inspector to deal with as a complaint for the purposes of *paragraph 9.2*, or *paragraph 12.9* if the challenge is made during an interview. This would include, for example:
   (a) in the case of a detained suspect:
   - not informing them of their rights (see *paragraph 3.1*);

- not giving them a copy of the Notice (see *paragraph 3.2(a)*)
- not providing an opportunity to read the notice (see *paragraph 3.2A*)
- not providing the required information (see *paragraphs 3.2(a), 3.12(b)* and, *3.12A*);
- not allowing access to the custody record (see *paragraph 2.4*);
- not providing a translation of the Notice (see *paragraph 3.12(c)* and *(d)*); and

(b) in the case of a suspect who is not detained:
- not informing them of their rights or providing the required information (see *paragraph 3.21(b)*);

Notes for Guidance

3ZA For the purposes of *paragraphs 3.4(b)* and *15.0*:

(a) Investigating officers are responsible for bringing to the attention of the officer who is respon-sible for authorising the suspect's detention or (as the case may be) continued detention (before or after charge), any documents and materials in their possession or control which appear to undermine the need to keep the suspect in custody. In accordance with Part IV of PACE, this officer will be either the custody officer, the officer reviewing the need for deten-tion before or after charge (PACE, section 40), or the officer considering the need to extend detention without charge from 24 to 36 hours (PACE, section 42) who is then responsible for determining, which, if any, of those documents and materials are capable of undermining the need to detain the suspect and must therefore be made available to the suspect or their solicitor.

(b) the way in which documents and materials are 'made available', is a matter for the investigating officer to determine on a case by case basis and having regard to the nature and volume of the documents and materials involved. For example, they may be made available by supplying a copy or allowing supervised access to view. However, for view only access, it will be necessary to demonstrate that sufficient time is allowed for the suspect and solicitor to view and consider the documents and materials in question.

3A   For access to currently available notices, including 'easy-read' versions, see https://www.gov.uk/notice-of-rights-and-entitlements-a-persons-rights-in-police-detention.

3B   *Not used.*

3C   If the juvenile is in local authority or voluntary organisation care but living with their parents or other adults responsible for their welfare, although there is no legal obligation to inform them, they should normally be contacted, as well as the authority or organisation unless they are suspected of involvement in the offence concerned. Even if the juvenile is not living with their parents, consider-ation should be given to informing them.

3D   The right to consult the Codes of Practice does not entitle the person concerned to delay unreason-ably any necessary investigative or administrative action whilst they do so. Examples of action which need not be delayed unreasonably include:
- procedures requiring the provision of breath, blood or urine specimens under the Road Traffic Act 1988 or the Transport and Works Act 1992;
- searching detainees at the police station;
- taking fingerprints, footwear impressions or non-intimate samples without consent for evidential purposes.

3E   The Detention and Custody Authorised Professional Practice (APP) produced by the College of Policing (see http://www.app.college.police.uk) provides more detailed guidance on risk assessments and identifies key risk areas which should always be considered.

3F   A custody officer or other officer who, in accordance with this Code, allows or directs the carrying out of any task or action relating to a detainee's care, treatment, rights and entitlements to another officer or any police staff must be satisfied that the officer or police staff concerned are suitable, trained and competent to carry out the task or action in question.

4 Detainee's property

(a) Action

4.1 The custody officer is responsible for:
(a) ascertaining what property a detainee:
(i) has with them when they come to the police station, whether on:
- arrest or re-detention on answering to bail;
- commitment to prison custody on the order or sentence of a court;

- lodgement at the police station with a view to their production in court from prison custody;
- transfer from detention at another station or hospital;
- detention under the Mental Health Act 1983, section 135 or 136;
- remand into police custody on the authority of a court.

(ii) might have acquired for an unlawful or harmful purpose while in custody;

(b) the safekeeping of any property taken from a detainee which remains at the police station.

The custody officer may search the detainee or authorise their being searched to the extent they consider necessary, provided a search of intimate parts of the body or involving the removal of more than outer clothing is only made as in *Annex A*. A search may only be carried out by an officer of the same sex as the detainee. See *Note 4A* and *Annex L*.

4.2   Detainees may retain clothing and personal effects at their own risk unless the custody officer considers they may use them to cause harm to themselves or others, interfere with evidence, damage property, effect an escape or they are needed as evidence. In this event the custody officer may withhold such articles as they consider necessary and must tell the detainee why.

4.3   Personal effects are those items a detainee may lawfully need, use or refer to while in detention but do not include cash and other items of value.

(b) Documentation

4.4   It is a matter for the custody officer to determine whether a record should be made of the property a detained person has with him or had taken from him on arrest. Any record made is not required to be kept as part of the custody record but the custody record should be noted as to where such a record exists. Whenever a record is made the detainee shall be allowed to check and sign the record of property as correct. Any refusal to sign shall be recorded.

4.5   If a detainee is not allowed to keep any article of clothing or personal effects, the reason must be recorded.

Notes for Guidance

4A   PACE, Section 54(1) and *paragraph 4.1* require a detainee to be searched when it is clear the custody officer will have continuing duties in relation to that detainee or when that detainee's behaviour or offence makes an inventory appropriate. They do not require every detainee to be searched, e.g. if it is clear a person will only be detained for a short period and is not to be placed in a cell, the custody officer may decide not to search them. In such a case the custody record will be endorsed 'not searched', *paragraph 4.4* will not apply, and the detainee will be invited to sign the entry. If the detainee refuses, the custody officer will be obliged to ascertain what property they have in accordance with *paragraph 4.1*.

4B   *Paragraph 4.4* does not require the custody officer to record on the custody record property in the detainee's possession on arrest if, by virtue of its nature, quantity or size, it is not practicable to remove it to the police station.

4C   *Paragraph 4.4* does not require items of clothing worn by the person to be recorded unless withheld by the custody officer as in *paragraph 4.2*.

5   Right not to be held incommunicado

(a) Action

5.1   Subject to *paragraph 5.7B*, any person arrested and held in custody at a police station or other premises may, on request, have one person known to them or likely to take an interest in their welfare informed at public expense of their whereabouts as soon as practicable. If the person cannot be contacted the detainee may choose up to two alternatives. If they cannot be contacted, the person in charge of detention or the investigation has discretion to allow further attempts until the information has been conveyed. See *Notes 5C* and *5D*.

5.2   The exercise of the above right in respect of each person nominated may be delayed only in accordance with *Annex B*.

5.3   The above right may be exercised each time a detainee is taken to another police station.

5.4   If the detainee agrees, they may at the custody officer's discretion, receive visits from friends, family or others likely to take an interest in their welfare, or in whose welfare the detainee has an interest. See *Note 5B*.

5.5   If a friend, relative or person with an interest in the detainee's welfare enquires about their whereabouts, this information shall be given if the suspect agrees and *Annex B* does not apply. See *Note 5D*.

5.6   The detainee shall be given writing materials, on request, and allowed to telephone one person for a reasonable time, see *Notes 5A* and *5E*. Either or both of these privileges may be denied or delayed if an officer of inspector rank or above considers sending a letter or making a telephone call may result in any of the consequences in:

(a) *Annex B paragraphs 1* and *2* and the person is detained in connection with an indictable offence;

(b) *Not used.*

Nothing in this paragraph permits the restriction or denial of the rights in *paragraphs 5.1 and 6.1.*

5.7 Before any letter or message is sent, or telephone call made, the detainee shall be informed that what they say in any letter, call or message (other than in a communication to a solicitor) may be read or listened to and may be given in evidence. A telephone call may be terminated if it is being abused. The costs can be at public expense at the custody officer's discretion.

5.7A Any delay or denial of the rights in this section should be proportionate and should last no longer than necessary.

5.7B In the case of a person in police custody for specific purposes and periods in accordance with a direction under the Crime (Sentences) Act 1997, Schedule 1 (productions from prison etc.), the exercise of the rights in this section shall be subject to any additional conditions specified in the direction for the purpose of regulating the detainee's contact and communication with others whilst in police custody. See *Note 5F.*

(b) Documentation

5.8 A record must be kept of any:

(a) request made under this section and the action taken;

(b) letters, messages or telephone calls made or received or visit received;

(c) refusal by the detainee to have information about them given to an outside enquirer. The detainee must be asked to countersign the record accordingly and any refusal recorded.

Notes for Guidance

5A A person may request an interpreter to interpret a telephone call or translate a letter.

5B At the custody officer's discretion and subject to the detainee's consent, visits should be allowed when possible, subject to having sufficient personnel to supervise a visit and any possible hindrance to the investigation.

5C If the detainee does not know anyone to contact for advice or support or cannot contact a friend or relative, the custody officer should bear in mind any local voluntary bodies or other organisations who might be able to help. *Paragraph 6.1* applies if legal advice is required.

5D In some circumstances it may not be appropriate to use the telephone to disclose information under *paragraphs 5.1* and *5.5.*

5E The telephone call at *paragraph 5.6* is in addition to any communication under *paragraphs 5.1* and *6.1.*

5F Prison Service Instruction 26/2012 (Production of Prisoners at the Request of Warranted Law Enforcement Agencies) provides detailed guidance and instructions for police officers and Governors and Directors of Prisons regarding applications for prisoners to be transferred to police custody and their safe custody and treatment while in police custody.

6 Right to legal advice

(a) Action

6.1 Unless *Annex B* applies, all detainees must be informed that they may at any time consult and communicate privately with a solicitor, whether in person, in writing or by telephone, and that free independent legal advice is available. See *paragraph 3.1, Notes 1I, 6B and 6J.*

6.2 *Not used.*

6.3 A poster advertising the right to legal advice must be prominently displayed in the charging area of every police station. See *Note 6H.*

6.4 No police officer should, at any time, do or say anything with the intention of dissuading any person who is entitled to legal advice in accordance with this Code, whether or not they have been arrested and are detained, from obtaining legal advice. See *Note 6ZA.*

6.5 The exercise of the right of access to legal advice may be delayed only as in *Annex B.* Whenever legal advice is requested, and unless *Annex B* applies, the custody officer must act without delay to secure the provision of such advice. If the detainee has the right to speak to a solicitor in person but declines to exercise the right the officer should point out that the right includes the right to speak with a solicitor on the telephone. If the detainee continues to waive this right, or a detainee whose right to free legal advice is limited to telephone advice from the Criminal Defence Service (CDS) Direct (see *Note 6B*) declines to exercise that right, the officer should ask them why and any reasons should be recorded on the custody record or the interview record as appropriate. Reminders of the right to legal advice must be given as in *paragraphs 3.5, 11.2, 15.4, 16.4, 16.5, 2B of Annex A, 3 of Annex K* and *5 of Annex M* of this Code and Code D, *paragraphs 3.17(ii)* and *6.3*. Once it is clear a detainee does not want to speak to a solicitor in person or by telephone they should cease to be asked their reasons. See *Note 6K*.

6.5A In the case of a person who is a juvenile or is mentally disordered or otherwise mentally vulnerable, an appropriate adult should consider whether legal advice from a solicitor is required. If the person indicates that they do not want legal advice, the appropriate adult has the right to ask for a solicitor to attend if this would be in the best interests of the person. However, the person cannot be forced to see the solicitor if they are adamant that they do not wish to do so.

Note: *Paragraph 1.5A* applies this paragraph to 17-year-old detainees.

6.6 A detainee who wants legal advice may not be interviewed or continue to be interviewed until they have received such advice unless:

(a) *Annex B* applies, when the restriction on drawing adverse inferences from silence in *Annex C* will apply because the detainee is not allowed an opportunity to consult a solicitor; or

(b) an officer of superintendent rank or above has reasonable grounds for believing that:

  (i) the consequent delay might:
  - lead to interference with, or harm to, evidence connected with an offence;
  - lead to interference with, or physical harm to, other people;
  - lead to serious loss of, or damage to, property;
  - lead to alerting other people suspected of having committed an offence but not yet arrested for it;
  - hinder the recovery of property obtained in consequence of the commission of an offence.

  See *Note 6A*

  (ii) when a solicitor, including a duty solicitor, has been contacted and has agreed to attend, awaiting their arrival would cause unreasonable delay to the process of investigation.

  Note: In these cases the restriction on drawing adverse inferences from silence in *Annex C* will apply because the detainee is not allowed an opportunity to consult a solicitor.

(c) the solicitor the detainee has nominated or selected from a list:

  (i) cannot be contacted;
  (ii) has previously indicated they do not wish to be contacted; or
  (iii) having been contacted, has declined to attend; and
  - the detainee has been advised of the Duty Solicitor Scheme but has declined to ask for the duty solicitor;
  - in these circumstances the interview may be started or continued without further delay provided an officer of inspector rank or above has agreed to the interview proceeding.

  Note: The restriction on drawing adverse inferences from silence in *Annex C* will not apply because the detainee is allowed an opportunity to consult the duty solicitor;

(d) the detainee changes their mind about wanting legal advice or (as the case may be) about wanting a solicitor present at the interview and states that they no longer wish to speak to a solicitor. In these circumstances, the interview may be started or continued without delay provided that:

  (i) an officer of inspector rank or above:
  - speaks to the detainee to enquire about the reasons for their change of mind (see *Note 6K*), and
  - makes, or directs the making of, reasonable efforts to ascertain the solicitor's expected time of arrival and to inform the solicitor that the suspect has stated that they wish to change their mind and the reason (if given);

  (ii) the detainee's reason for their change of mind (if given) and the outcome of the action in (i) are recorded in the custody record;

  (iii) the detainee, after being informed of the outcome of the action in (i) above, confirms in writing that they want the interview to proceed without speaking or further speaking to a solicitor or (as the case may be) without a solicitor being present and do not wish to wait for a solicitor by signing an entry to this effect in the custody record;

  (iv) an officer of inspector rank or above is satisfied that it is proper for the interview to proceed in these circumstances and:
  - gives authority in writing for the interview to proceed and, if the authority is not recorded in the custody record, the officer must ensure that the custody record shows the date and time of the authority and where it is recorded, and

- takes, or directs the taking of, reasonable steps to inform the solicitor that the authority has been given and the time when the interview is expected to commence and records or causes to be recorded, the outcome of this action in the custody record.

(v) When the interview starts and the interviewer reminds the suspect of their right to legal advice (see *paragraph 11.2*, Code E *paragraph 4.5* and Code F *paragraph 4.5*), the interviewer shall then ensure that the following is recorded in the written interview record or the interview record made in accordance with Code E or F:

  - confirmation that the detainee has changed their mind about wanting legal advice or (as the case may be) about wanting a solicitor present and the reasons for it if given;
  - the fact that authority for the interview to proceed has been given and, subject to *paragraph 2.6A*, the name of the authorising officer;
  - that if the solicitor arrives at the station before the interview is completed, the detainee will be so informed without delay and *a break will be taken* to allow them to speak to the solicitor if they wish, unless *paragraph 6.6(a)* applies, and
  - that at any time during the interview, the detainee may again ask for legal advice and that if they do, a break will be taken to allow them to speak to the solicitor, unless paragraph *6.6(a), (b),* or *(c)* applies.

Note: In these circumstances, the restriction on drawing adverse inferences from silence in *Annex C* will not apply because the detainee is allowed an opportunity to consult a solicitor if they wish.

6.7   If *paragraph 6.6(a)* applies, where the reason for authorising the delay ceases to apply, there may be no further delay in permitting the exercise of the right in the absence of a further authorisation unless *paragraph 6.6(b), (c)* or *(d)* applies. If *paragraph 6.6(b)(i)* applies, once sufficient information has been obtained to avert the risk, questioning must cease until the detainee has received legal advice unless *paragraph 6.6(a), (b)(ii), (c)* or *(d)* applies.

6.8   A detainee who has been permitted to consult a solicitor shall be entitled on request to have the solicitor present when they are interviewed unless one of the exceptions in *paragraph 6.6* applies.

6.9   The solicitor may only be required to leave the interview if their conduct is such that the interviewer is unable properly to put questions to the suspect. See *Notes 6D* and *6E*.

6.10 If the interviewer considers a solicitor is acting in such a way, they will stop the interview and consult an officer not below superintendent rank, if one is readily available, and otherwise an officer not below inspector rank not connected with the investigation. After speaking to the solicitor, the officer consulted will decide if the interview should continue in the presence of that solicitor. If they decide it should not, the suspect will be given the opportunity to consult another solicitor before the interview continues and that solicitor given an opportunity to be present at the interview. See *Note 6E*.

6.11 The removal of a solicitor from an interview is a serious step and, if it occurs, the officer of superintendent rank or above who took the decision will consider if the incident should be reported to the Solicitors Regulatory Authority. If the decision to remove the solicitor has been taken by an officer below superintendent rank, the facts must be reported to an officer of superintendent rank or above, who will similarly consider whether a report to the Solicitors Regulatory Authority would be appropriate. When the solicitor concerned is a duty solicitor, the report should be both to the Solicitors Regulatory Authority and to the Legal Aid Agency.

6.12 'Solicitor' in this Code means:

  - a solicitor who holds a current practising certificate;
  - an accredited or probationary representative included on the register of representatives maintained by the Legal Aid Agency.

6.12A An accredited or probationary representative sent to provide advice by, and on behalf of, a solicitor shall be admitted to the police station for this purpose unless an officer of inspector rank or above considers such a visit will hinder the investigation and directs otherwise. Hindering the investigation does not include giving proper legal advice to a detainee as in *Note 6D*. Once admitted to the police station, *paragraphs 6.6* to *6.10* apply.

6.13 In exercising their discretion under *paragraph 6.12A*, the officer should take into account in particular:

  - whether:
    - the identity and status of an accredited or probationary representative have been satisfactorily established;
    - they are of suitable character to provide legal advice, e.g. a person with a criminal record is unlikely to be suitable unless the conviction was for a minor offence and not recent.

- any other matters in any written letter of authorisation provided by the solicitor on whose behalf the person is attending the police station. See *Note 6F*.

6.14 If the inspector refuses access to an accredited or probationary representative or a decision is taken that such a person should not be permitted to remain at an interview, the inspector must notify the solicitor on whose behalf the representative was acting and give them an opportunity to make alternative arrangements. The detainee must be informed and the custody record noted.

6.15 If a solicitor arrives at the station to see a particular person, that person must, unless *Annex B* applies, be so informed whether or not they are being interviewed and asked if they would like to see the solicitor. This applies even if the detainee has declined legal advice or, having requested it, subsequently agreed to be interviewed without receiving advice. The solicitor's attendance and the detainee's decision must be noted in the custody record.

(b) Documentation

6.16 Any request for legal advice and the action taken shall be recorded.

6.17 A record shall be made in the interview record if a detainee asks for legal advice and an interview is begun either in the absence of a solicitor or their representative, or they have been required to leave an interview.

Notes for Guidance

6ZA No police officer or police staff shall indicate to any suspect, except to answer a direct question, that the period for which they are liable to be detained, or if not detained, the time taken to complete the interview, might be reduced:
- if they do not ask for legal advice or do not want a solicitor present when they are interviewed; or
- if they have asked for legal advice or (as the case may be) asked for a solicitor to be present when they are interviewed but change their mind and agree to be interviewed without waiting for a solicitor.

6A In considering if *paragraph 6.6(b)* applies, the officer should, if practicable, ask the solicitor for an estimate of how long it will take to come to the station and relate this to the time detention is permitted, the time of day (i.e. whether the rest period under *paragraph 12.2* is imminent) and the requirements of other investigations. If the solicitor is on their way or is to set off immediately, it will not normally be appropriate to begin an interview before they arrive. If it appears necessary to begin an interview before the solicitor's arrival, they should be given an indication of how long the police would be able to wait before *6.6(b)* applies so there is an opportunity to make arrangements for someone else to provide legal advice.

6B A detainee has a right to free legal advice and to be represented by a solicitor. This Note for Guidance explains the arrangements which enable detainees to obtain legal advice. An outline of these arrangements is also included in the Notice of Rights and Entitlements given to detainees in accordance with *paragraph 3.2*. The arrangements also apply, with appropriate modifications, to persons attending a police station or other location voluntarily who are cautioned prior to being interviewed. See *paragraph 3.21*.

When a detainee asks for free legal advice, the Defence Solicitor Call Centre (DSCC) must be informed of the request.

Free legal advice will be limited to telephone advice provided by CDS Direct if a detainee is:
- detained for a non-imprisonable offence;
- arrested on a bench warrant for failing to appear and being held for production at court (except where the solicitor has clear documentary evidence available that would result in the client being released from custody);
- arrested for drink driving (driving/in charge with excess alcohol, failing to provide a specimen, driving/in charge whilst unfit through drink), or
- detained in relation to breach of police or court bail conditions

unless one or more exceptions apply, in which case the DSCC should arrange for advice to be given by a solicitor at the police station, for example:
- the police want to interview the detainee or carry out an eye-witness identification procedure;
- the detainee needs an appropriate adult;
- the detainee is unable to communicate over the telephone;
- the detainee alleges serious misconduct by the police;
- the investigation includes another offence not included in the list,
- the solicitor to be assigned is already at the police station.

When free advice is not limited to telephone advice, a detainee can ask for free advice from a solicitor they know or if they do not know a solicitor or the solicitor they know cannot be contacted, from the duty solicitor.

To arrange free legal advice, the police should telephone the DSCC. The call centre will decide whether legal advice should be limited to telephone advice from CDS Direct, or whether a solicitor known to the detainee or the duty solicitor should speak to the detainee.

When a detainee wants to pay for legal advice themselves:

- the DSCC will contact a solicitor of their choice on their behalf;
- they may, when free advice is only available by telephone from CDS Direct, still speak to a solicitor of their choice on the telephone for advice, but the solicitor would not be paid by legal aid and may ask the person to pay for the advice;
- they should be given an opportunity to consult a specific solicitor or another solicitor from that solicitor's firm. If this solicitor is not available, they may choose up to two alternatives. If these alternatives are not available, the custody officer has discretion to allow further attempts until a solicitor has been contacted and agreed to provide advice;
- they are entitled to a private consultation with their chosen solicitor on the telephone or the solicitor may decide to come to the police station;
- If their chosen solicitor cannot be contacted, the DSCC may still be called to arrange free legal advice.

Apart from carrying out duties necessary to implement these arrangements, an officer must not advise the suspect about any particular firm of solicitors.

6B1 *Not used.*

6B2 *Not used.*

6C *Not used.*

6D The solicitor's only role in the police station is to protect and advance the legal rights of their client. On occasions this may require the solicitor to give advice which has the effect of the client avoiding giving evidence which strengthens a prosecution case. The solicitor may intervene in order to seek clarification, challenge an improper question to their client or the manner in which it is put, advise their client not to reply to particular questions, or if they wish to give their client further legal advice. *Paragraph 6.9* only applies if the solicitor's approach or conduct prevents or unreasonably obstructs proper questions being put to the suspect or the suspect's response being recorded. Examples of unacceptable conduct include answering questions on a suspect's behalf or providing written replies for the suspect to quote.

6E An officer who takes the decision to exclude a solicitor must be in a position to satisfy the court the decision was properly made. In order to do this they may need to witness what is happening.

6F If an officer of at least inspector rank considers a particular solicitor or firm of solicitors is persistently sending probationary representatives who are unsuited to provide legal advice, they should inform an officer of at least superintendent rank, who may wish to take the matter up with the Solicitors Regulation Authority.

6G Subject to the constraints of *Annex B*, a solicitor may advise more than one client in an investigation if they wish. Any question of a conflict of interest is for the solicitor under their professional code of conduct. If, however, waiting for a solicitor to give advice to one client may lead to unreasonable delay to the interview with another, the provisions of *paragraph 6.6(b)* may apply.

6H In addition to a poster in English, a poster or posters containing translations into Welsh, the main minority ethnic languages and the principal European languages should be displayed wherever they are likely to be helpful and it is practicable to do so.

6I *Not used.*

6J Whenever a detainee exercises their right to legal advice by consulting or communicating with a solicitor, they must be allowed to do so in private. This right to consult or communicate in private is fundamental. If the requirement for privacy is compromised because what is said or written by the detainee or solicitor for the purpose of giving and receiving legal advice is overheard, listened to, or read by others without the informed consent of the detainee, the right will effectively have been denied. When a detainee speaks to a solicitor on the telephone, they should be allowed to do so in private unless this is impractical because of the design and layout of the custody area or the location of telephones. However, the normal expectation should be that facilities will be available, unless they are being used, at all police stations to enable detainees to speak in private to a solicitor either face to face or over the telephone.

6K A detainee is not obliged to give reasons for declining legal advice and should not be pressed to do so.

7 Citizens of independent Commonwealth countries or foreign nationals

(a) Action

7.1 A detainee who is a citizen of an independent Commonwealth country or a national of a foreign country, including the Republic of Ireland, has the right, upon request, to communicate at any time with the appropriate High Commission, Embassy or Consulate. That detainee must be informed as soon as practicable of this right and asked if they want to have their High Commission, Embassy or Consulate told of their whereabouts and the grounds for their detention. Such a request should be acted upon as soon as practicable. See *Note 7A*.

7.2   A detainee who is a citizen of a country with which a bilateral consular convention or agreement is in force requiring notification of arrest must also be informed that subject to *paragraph 7.4*, notification of their arrest will be sent to the appropriate High Commission, Embassy or Consulate as soon as practicable, whether or not they request it. A list of the countries to which this requirement currently applies and contact details for the relevant High Commissions, Embassies and Consulates can be obtained from the Consular Directorate of the Foreign and Commonwealth Office (FCO) as follows:

- from the FCO web pages:
  - https://gov.uk/government/publications/table-of-consular-conventions-and-mandatory-notification-obligations, and
  - https://www.gov.uk/government/publications/foreign-embassies-in-the-uk
- by telephone to 020 7008 3100,
- by email to fcocorrespondence@fco.gov.uk.
- by letter to the Foreign and Commonwealth Office, King Charles Street, London, SW1A 2AH.

7.3   Consular officers may, if the detainee agrees, visit one of their nationals in police detention to talk to them and, if required, to arrange for legal advice. Such visits shall take place out of the hearing of a police officer.

7.4   Notwithstanding the provisions of consular conventions, if the detainee claims that they are a refugee or have applied or intend to apply for asylum, the custody officer must ensure that UK Visas and Immigration (UKVI) (formerly the UK Border Agency) is informed as soon as practicable of the claim. UKVI will then determine whether compliance with relevant international obligations requires notification of the arrest to be sent and will inform the custody officer as to what action police need to take.

(b) Documentation

7.5   A record shall be made:
- when a detainee is informed of their rights under this section and of any requirement in paragraph 7.2;
- of any communications with a High Commission, Embassy or Consulate, and
- of any communications with UKVI about a detainee's claim to be a refugee or to be seeking asylum and the resulting action taken by police.

Notes for Guidance

7A   The exercise of the rights in this section may not be interfered with even though *Annex B* applies.

8 Conditions of detention

(a) Action

8.1   So far as it is practicable, not more than one detainee should be detained in each cell. See *Note 8C*.

8.2   Cells in use must be adequately heated, cleaned and ventilated. They must be adequately lit, subject to such dimming as is compatible with safety and security to allow people detained overnight to sleep. No additional restraints shall be used within a locked cell unless absolutely necessary and then only restraint equipment, approved for use in that force by the chief officer, which is reasonable and necessary in the circumstances having regard to the detainee's demeanour and with a view to ensuring their safety and the safety of others. If a detainee is deaf, mentally disordered or otherwise mentally vulnerable, particular care must be taken when deciding whether to use any form of approved restraints.

8.3   Blankets, mattresses, pillows and other bedding supplied shall be of a reasonable standard and in a clean and sanitary condition. See *Note 8A*.

8.4   Access to toilet and washing facilities must be provided.

8.5   If it is necessary to remove a detainee's clothes for the purposes of investigation, for hygiene, health reasons or cleaning, replacement clothing of a reasonable standard of comfort and cleanliness shall be provided. A detainee may not be interviewed unless adequate clothing has been offered.

8.6   At least two light meals and one main meal should be offered in any 24-hour period. See *Note 8B*. Drinks should be provided at meal times and upon reasonable request between meals. Whenever necessary, advice shall be sought from the appropriate healthcare professional, see *Note 9A*, on medical and dietary matters. As far as practicable, meals provided shall offer a varied diet and meet any specific dietary needs or religious beliefs the detainee may have. The detainee may, at the custody officer's discretion, have meals supplied by their family or friends at their expense. See *Note 8A*.

8.7   Brief outdoor exercise shall be offered daily if practicable.

8.8   A juvenile shall not be placed in a police cell unless no other secure accommodation is available and the custody officer considers it is not practicable to supervise them if they are not placed in a cell or that a cell provides more comfortable accommodation than other secure accommodation in the station. A juvenile may not be placed in a cell with a detained adult.

Note: *Paragraph 1.5A* extends these requirements to 17-year-old detainees.

(b) Documentation

8.9   A record must be kept of replacement clothing and meals offered.

8.10 If a juvenile is placed in a cell, the reason must be recorded.

Note: *Paragraph 1.5A* extends this requirement to 17-year-old detainees.

8.11 The use of any restraints on a detainee whilst in a cell, the reasons for it and, if appropriate, the arrangements for enhanced supervision of the detainee whilst so restrained, shall be recorded. See *paragraph 3.9.*

Notes for Guidance

8A   The provisions in *paragraph 8.3* and *8.6* respectively are of particular importance in the case of a person likely to be detained for an extended period. In deciding whether to allow meals to be supplied by family or friends, the custody officer is entitled to take account of the risk of items being concealed in any food or package and the officer's duties and responsibilities under food handling legislation.

8B   Meals should, so far as practicable, be offered at recognised meal times, or at other times that take account of when the detainee last had a meal.

8C   The Detention and Custody Authorised Professional Practice (APP) produced by the College of Policing (see http://www.app.college.police.uk) provides more detailed guidance on matters concerning detainee healthcare and treatment and associated forensic issues which should be read in conjunction with sections 8 and 9 of this Code.

9   Care and treatment of detained persons

(a) General

9.1   Nothing in this section prevents the police from calling an appropriate healthcare professional to examine a detainee for the purposes of obtaining evidence relating to any offence in which the detainee is suspected of being involved. See *Notes 9A* and *8C*.

9.2   If a complaint is made by, or on behalf of, a detainee about their treatment since their arrest, or it comes to notice that a detainee may have been treated improperly, a report must be made as soon as practicable to an officer of inspector rank or above not connected with the investigation. If the matter concerns a possible assault or the possibility of the unnecessary or unreasonable use of force, an appropriate healthcare professional must also be called as soon as practicable.

9.3   Detainees should be visited at least every hour. If no reasonably foreseeable risk was identified in a risk assessment, see *paragraphs 3.6 – 3.10*, there is no need to wake a sleeping detainee. Those suspected of being under the influence of drink or drugs or both or of having swallowed drugs, see *Note 9CA*, or whose level of consciousness causes concern must, subject to any clinical directions given by the appropriate healthcare professional, see *paragraph 9.13*:
- be visited and roused at least every half hour;
- have their condition assessed as in *Annex H*;
- and clinical treatment arranged if appropriate.

See *Notes 9B, 9C* and *9H*

9.4   When arrangements are made to secure clinical attention for a detainee, the custody officer must make sure all relevant information which might assist in the treatment of the detainee's condition is made available to the responsible healthcare professional. This applies whether or not the healthcare professional asks for such information. Any officer or police staff with relevant information must inform the custody officer as soon as practicable.

(b) Clinical treatment and attention

9.5   The custody officer must make sure a detainee receives appropriate clinical attention as soon as reasonably practicable if the person:
(a)   appears to be suffering from physical illness; or
(b)   is injured; or

(c) appears to be suffering from a mental disorder; or

(d) appears to need clinical attention.

9.5A This applies even if the detainee makes no request for clinical attention and whether or not they have already received clinical attention elsewhere. If the need for attention appears urgent, e.g. when indicated as in *Annex H*, the nearest available healthcare professional or an ambulance must be called immediately.

9.5B The custody officer must also consider the need for clinical attention as set out in *Note 9C* in relation to those suffering the effects of alcohol or drugs.

9.6 *Paragraph 9.5* is not meant to prevent or delay the transfer to a hospital if necessary of a person detained under the Mental Health Act 1983, section 136. See *Note 9D*. When an assessment under that Act is to take place at a police station, see *paragraph 3.16*, the custody officer must consider whether an appropriate healthcare professional should be called to conduct an initial clinical check on the detainee. This applies particularly when there is likely to be any significant delay in the arrival of a suitably qualified medical practitioner.

9.7 If it appears to the custody officer, or they are told, that a person brought to a station under arrest may be suffering from an infectious disease or condition, the custody officer must take reasonable steps to safeguard the health of the detainee and others at the station. In deciding what action to take, advice must be sought from an appropriate healthcare professional. See *Note 9E*. The custody officer has discretion to isolate the person and their property until clinical directions have been obtained.

9.8 If a detainee requests a clinical examination, an appropriate healthcare professional must be called as soon as practicable to assess the detainee's clinical needs. If a safe and appropriate care plan cannot be provided, the appropriate healthcare professional's advice must be sought. The detainee may also be examined by a medical practitioner of their choice at their expense.

9.9 If a detainee is required to take or apply any medication in compliance with clinical directions prescribed before their detention, the custody officer must consult the appropriate healthcare professional before the use of the medication. Subject to the restrictions in *paragraph 9.10*, the custody officer is responsible for the safekeeping of any medication and for making sure the detainee is given the opportunity to take or apply prescribed or approved medication. Any such consultation and its outcome shall be noted in the custody record.

9.10 No police officer may administer or supervise the self-administration of medically prescribed controlled drugs of the types and forms listed in the Misuse of Drugs Regulations 2001, Schedule 2 or 3. A detainee may only self-administer such drugs under the personal supervision of the registered medical practitioner authorising their use or other appropriate healthcare professional. The custody officer may supervise the self-administration of, or authorise other custody staff to supervise the self-administration of, drugs listed in Schedule 4 or 5 if the officer has consulted the appropriate healthcare professional authorising their use and both are satisfied self-administration will not expose the detainee, police officers or anyone else to the risk of harm or injury.

9.11 When appropriate healthcare professionals administer drugs or authorise the use of other medications, supervise their self-administration or consult with the custody officer about allowing self-administration of drugs listed in Schedule 4 or 5, it must be within current medicines legislation and the scope of practice as determined by their relevant statutory regulatory body.

9.12 If a detainee has in their possession, or claims to need, medication relating to a heart condition, diabetes, epilepsy or a condition of comparable potential seriousness then, even though *paragraph 9.5* may not apply, the advice of the appropriate healthcare professional must be obtained.

9.13 Whenever the appropriate healthcare professional is called in accordance with this section to examine or treat a detainee, the custody officer shall ask for their opinion about:

• any risks or problems which police need to take into account when making decisions about the detainee's continued detention;

• when to carry out an interview if applicable; and

• the need for safeguards.

9.14 When clinical directions are given by the appropriate healthcare professional, whether orally or in writing, and the custody officer has any doubts or is in any way uncertain about any aspect of the directions, the custody officer shall ask for clarification. It is particularly important that directions concerning the frequency of visits are clear, precise and capable of being implemented. See *Note 9F*.

(c) Documentation

9.15 A record must be made in the custody record of:

(a) the arrangements made for an examination by an appropriate healthcare professional under *paragraph 9.2* and of any complaint reported under that paragraph together with any relevant remarks by the custody officer;

(b) any arrangements made in accordance with *paragraph 9.5*;

(c) any request for a clinical examination under *paragraph 9.8* and any arrangements made in response;

(d) the injury, ailment, condition or other reason which made it necessary to make the arrangements in (a) to (c); See *Note 9G*.

(e) any clinical directions and advice, including any further clarifications, given to police by a healthcare professional concerning the care and treatment of the detainee in connection with any of the arrangements made in (a) to (c); See *Notes 9E and 9F*.

(f) if applicable, the responses received when attempting to rouse a person using the procedure in *Annex H*. See *Note 9H*.

9.16 If a healthcare professional does not record their clinical findings in the custody record, the record must show where they are recorded. See *Note 9G*. However, information which is necessary to custody staff to ensure the effective ongoing care and well being of the detainee must be recorded openly in the custody record, see *paragraph 3.8* and *Annex G, paragraph 7*.

9.17 Subject to the requirements of *Section 4*, the custody record shall include:
- a record of all medication a detainee has in their possession on arrival at the police station;
- a note of any such medication they claim to need but do not have with them.

Notes for Guidance

9A A 'healthcare professional' means a clinically qualified person working within the scope of practice as determined by their relevant statutory regulatory body. Whether a healthcare professional is 'appropriate' depends on the circumstances of the duties they carry out at the time.

9B Whenever possible juveniles and mentally vulnerable detainees should be visited more frequently. Note: *Paragraph 1.5A* extends this Note to 17-year-old detainees.

9C A detainee who appears drunk or behaves abnormally may be suffering from illness, the effects of drugs or may have sustained injury, particularly a head injury which is not apparent. A detainee needing or dependent on certain drugs, including alcohol, may experience harmful effects within a short time of being deprived of their supply. In these circumstances, when there is any doubt, police should always act urgently to call an appropriate healthcare professional or an ambulance. *Paragraph 9.5* does not apply to minor ailments or injuries which do not need attention. However, all such ailments or injuries must be recorded in the custody record and any doubt must be resolved in favour of calling the appropriate healthcare professional.

9CA *Paragraph 9.3* would apply to a person in police custody by order of a magistrates' court under the Criminal Justice Act 1988, section 152 (as amended by the Drugs Act 2005, section 8) to facilitate the recovery of evidence after being charged with drug possession or drug trafficking and suspected of having swallowed drugs. In the case of the healthcare needs of a person who has swallowed drugs, the custody officer, subject to any clinical directions, should consider the necessity for rousing every half hour. This does not negate the need for regular visiting of the suspect in the cell.

9D Whenever practicable, arrangements should be made for persons detained for assessment under the Mental Health Act 1983, section 136 to be taken to a hospital. Chapter 10 of the Mental Health Act 1983 Code of Practice (as revised) provides more detailed guidance about arranging assessments under section 136 and transferring detainees from police stations to other places of safety.

9E It is important to respect a person's right to privacy and information about their health must be kept confidential and only disclosed with their consent or in accordance with clinical advice when it is necessary to protect the detainee's health or that of others who come into contact with them.

9F The custody officer should always seek to clarify directions that the detainee requires constant observation or supervision and should ask the appropriate healthcare professional to explain precisely what action needs to be taken to implement such directions.

9G *Paragraphs 9.15* and *9.16* do not require any information about the cause of any injury, ailment or condition to be recorded on the custody record if it appears capable of providing evidence of an offence.

9H The purpose of recording a person's responses when attempting to rouse them using the procedure in *Annex H* is to enable any change in the individual's consciousness level to be noted and clinical treatment arranged if appropriate.

10 Cautions

(a) When a caution must be given

10.1 A person whom there are grounds to suspect of an offence, see *Note 10A*, must be cautioned before any questions about an offence, or further questions if the answers provide the grounds for suspicion, are put to them if either the suspect's answers or silence, (i.e. failure or refusal to answer or answer satisfactorily) may be given in evidence to a court in a prosecution. A person need not be cautioned if questions are for other necessary purposes, e.g.:

(a)   solely to establish their identity or ownership of any vehicle;

(b)   to obtain information in accordance with any relevant statutory requirement, see *paragraph 10.9*;

(c)   in furtherance of the proper and effective conduct of a search, e.g. to determine the need to search in the exercise of powers of stop and search or to seek co-operation while carrying out a search; or

(d)   to seek verification of a written record as in *paragraph 11.13*.

(e)   *Not used.*

10.2 Whenever a person not under arrest is initially cautioned, or reminded they are under caution, that person must at the same time be told they are not under arrest and informed of the provisions of *paragraph 3.21* which explain how they may obtain legal advice according to whether they are at a police station or elsewhere. See *Note 10C*.

10.3 A person who is arrested, or further arrested, must be informed at the time if practicable or, if not, as soon as it becomes practicable thereafter, that they are under arrest and of the grounds and reasons for their arrest, see *paragraph 3.4, Note 10B* and Code G, *paragraphs 2.2* and *4.3*.

10.4 As required by Code G, *section 3*, a person who is arrested, or further arrested, must also be cautioned unless:

(a)   it is impracticable to do so by reason of their condition or behaviour at the time;

(b)   they have already been cautioned immediately prior to arrest as in *paragraph 10.1*.

(b)   Terms of the cautions

10.5 The caution which must be given on:

(a)   arrest; or

(b)   all other occasions before a person is charged or informed they may be prosecuted; see *section 16*,

should, unless the restriction on drawing adverse inferences from silence applies, see *Annex C*, be in the following terms:

'You do not have to say anything. But it may harm your defence if you do not mention when questioned something which you later rely on in Court. Anything you do say may be given in evidence.'

Where the use of the Welsh Language is appropriate, a constable may provide the caution directly in Welsh in the following terms:

'Does dim rhaid i chi ddweud dim byd. Ond gall niweidio eich amddiffyniad os na fyddwch chi'n sôn, wrth gael eich holi, am rywbeth y byddwch chi'n dibynnu arno nes ymlaen yn y Llys. Gall unrhyw beth yr ydych yn ei ddweud gael ei roi fel tystiolaeth.'

See *Note 10G*

10.6 *Annex C, paragraph 2* sets out the alternative terms of the caution to be used when the restriction on drawing adverse inferences from silence applies.

10.7 Minor deviations from the words of any caution given in accordance with this Code do not constitute a breach of this Code, provided the sense of the relevant caution is preserved. See *Note 10D*.

10.8 After any break in questioning under caution, the person being questioned must be made aware they remain under caution. If there is any doubt the relevant caution should be given again in full when the interview resumes. See *Note 10E*.

10.9 When, despite being cautioned, a person fails to co-operate or to answer particular questions which may affect their immediate treatment, the person should be informed of any relevant consequences and that those consequences are not affected by the caution. Examples are when a person's refusal to provide:

•   their name and address when charged may make them liable to detention;

•   particulars and information in accordance with a statutory requirement, e.g. under the Road Traffic Act 1988, may amount to an offence or may make the person liable to a further arrest.

(c)   Special warnings under the Criminal Justice and Public Order Act 1994, sections 36 and 37

10.10 When a suspect interviewed at a police station or authorised place of detention after arrest fails or refuses to answer certain questions, or to answer satisfactorily, after due warning, see *Note 10F*, a court or jury may draw such inferences as appear proper under the Criminal Justice and Public Order Act 1994, sections 36 and 37. Such inferences may only be drawn when:

(a) the restriction on drawing adverse inferences from silence, see *Annex C*, does not apply; and

(b) the suspect is arrested by a constable and fails or refuses to account for any objects, marks or substances, or marks on such objects found:
- on their person;
- in or on their clothing or footwear;
- otherwise in their possession; or
- in the place they were arrested;

(c) the arrested suspect was found by a constable at a place at or about the time the offence for which that officer has arrested them is alleged to have been committed, and the suspect fails or refuses to account for their presence there.

When the restriction on drawing adverse inferences from silence applies, the suspect may still be asked to account for any of the matters in (*b*) or (*c*) but the special warning described *in paragraph 10.11* will not apply and must not be given.

10.11 For an inference to be drawn when a suspect fails or refuses to answer a question about one of these matters or to answer it satisfactorily, the suspect must first be told in ordinary language:

(a) what offence is being investigated;

(b) what fact they are being asked to account for;

(c) this fact may be due to them taking part in the commission of the offence;

(d) a court may draw a proper inference if they fail or refuse to account for this fact; and

(e) a record is being made of the interview and it may be given in evidence if they are brought to trial.

(d) Juveniles and persons who are mentally disordered or otherwise mentally vulnerable

10.11A The information required in *paragraph 10.11* must not be given to a suspect who is a juvenile or who is mentally disordered or otherwise mentally vulnerable unless the appropriate adult is present.

10.12 If a juvenile or a person who is mentally disordered or otherwise mentally vulnerable is cautioned in the absence of the appropriate adult, the caution must be repeated in the adult's presence.

10.12A *Paragraph 1.5A* extends the requirements in *paragraphs 10.11A* and *10.12* to 17-year-old detainees.

(e) Documentation

10.13 A record shall be made when a caution is given under this section, either in the interviewer's pocket book or in the interview record.

Notes for Guidance

10A There must be some reasonable, objective grounds for the suspicion, based on known facts or information which are relevant to the likelihood the offence has been committed and the person to be questioned committed it.

10B An arrested person must be given sufficient information to enable them to understand that they have been deprived of their liberty and the reason they have been arrested, e.g. when a person is arrested on suspicion of committing an offence they must be informed of the suspected offence's nature, when and where it was committed. The suspect must also be informed of the reason or reasons why the arrest is considered necessary. Vague or technical language should be avoided.

10C The restriction on drawing inferences from silence, see *Annex C, paragraph 1*, does not apply to a person who has not been detained and who therefore cannot be prevented from seeking legal advice if they want, see *paragraph 3.21*.

10D If it appears a person does not understand the caution, the person giving it should explain it in their own words.

10E It may be necessary to show to the court that nothing occurred during an interview break or between interviews which influenced the suspect's recorded evidence. After a break in an interview or at the beginning of a subsequent interview, the interviewing officer should summarise the reason for the break and confirm this with the suspect.

10F The Criminal Justice and Public Order Act 1994, sections 36 and 37 apply only to suspects who have been arrested by a constable or an officer of Revenue and Customs and are given the relevant warning by the police or Revenue and Customs officer who made the arrest or who is investigating the offence. They do not apply to any interviews with suspects who have not been arrested.

10G Nothing in this Code requires a caution to be given or repeated when informing a person not under arrest they may be prosecuted for an offence. However, a court will not be able to draw any inferences under the Criminal Justice and Public Order Act 1994, section 34, if the person was not cautioned.

11 Interviews – general

(a) Action

11.1A An interview is the questioning of a person regarding their involvement or suspected involvement in a criminal offence or offences which, under paragraph 10.1, must be carried out under caution. Before a person is interviewed, and, if they are represented, their solicitor must be given sufficient information to enable them to understand the nature of any such offence, and why they are suspected of committing it (see *paragraphs 3.4(a)* and *10.3*), in order to allow for the effective exercise of the rights of the defence. However, whilst the information must always be sufficient for the person to understand the nature of any offence (see *Note 11ZA*), this does not require the disclosure of details at a time which might prejudice the criminal investigation. The decision about what needs to be disclosed for the purpose of this requirement therefore rests with the investigating officer who has sufficient knowledge of the case to make that decision. The officer who discloses the information shall make a record of the information disclosed and when it was disclosed. This record may be made in the interview record, in the officer's pocket book or other form provided for this purpose. Procedures under the Road Traffic Act 1988, section 7 or the Transport and Works Act 1992, section 31 do not constitute interviewing for the purpose of this Code.

11.1 Following a decision to arrest a suspect, they must not be interviewed about the relevant offence except at a police station or other authorised place of detention, unless the consequent delay would be likely to:

(a) lead to:
   - interference with, or harm to, evidence connected with an offence;
   - interference with, or physical harm to, other people; or
   - serious loss of, or damage to, property;

(b) lead to alerting other people suspected of committing an offence but not yet arrested for it; or

(c) hinder the recovery of property obtained in consequence of the commission of an offence.

Interviewing in any of these circumstances shall cease once the relevant risk has been averted or the necessary questions have been put in order to attempt to avert that risk.

11.2 Immediately prior to the commencement or re-commencement of any interview at a police station or other authorised place of detention, the interviewer should remind the suspect of their entitlement to free legal advice and that the interview can be delayed for legal advice to be obtained, unless one of the exceptions in *paragraph 6.6* applies. It is the interviewer's responsibility to make sure all reminders are recorded in the interview record.

11.3 *Not used.*

11.4 At the beginning of an interview the interviewer, after cautioning the suspect, see *section 10*, shall put to them any significant statement or silence which occurred in the presence and hearing of a police officer or other police staff before the start of the interview and which have not been put to the suspect in the course of a previous interview. See *Note 11A*. The interviewer shall ask the suspect whether they confirm or deny that earlier statement or silence and if they want to add anything.

11.4A A significant statement is one which appears capable of being used in evidence against the suspect, in particular a direct admission of guilt. A significant silence is a failure or refusal to answer a question or answer satisfactorily when under caution, which might, allowing for the restriction on drawing adverse inferences from silence, see *Annex C*, give rise to an inference under the Criminal Justice and Public Order Act 1994, Part III.

11.5 No interviewer may try to obtain answers or elicit a statement by the use of oppression. Except as in *paragraph 10.9*, no interviewer shall indicate, except to answer a direct question, what action will be taken by the police if the person being questioned answers questions, makes a statement or refuses to do either. If the person asks directly what action will be taken if they answer questions, make a statement or refuse to do either, the interviewer may inform them what action the police propose to take provided that action is itself proper and warranted.

11.6 The interview or further interview of a person about an offence with which that person has not been charged or for which they have not been informed they may be prosecuted, must cease when:

(a) the officer in charge of the investigation is satisfied all the questions they consider relevant to obtaining accurate and reliable information about the offence have been put to the suspect, this includes allowing the suspect an opportunity to give an innocent explanation and asking questions to test if the explanation is accurate and reliable, e.g. to clear up ambiguities or clarify what the suspect said;

(b) the officer in charge of the investigation has taken account of any other available evidence; and

(c) the officer in charge of the investigation, or in the case of a detained suspect, the custody officer, see *paragraph 16.1*, reasonably believes there is sufficient evidence to provide a realistic prospect of conviction for that offence. See *Note 11B*.

This paragraph does not prevent officers in revenue cases or acting under the confiscation provisions of the Criminal Justice Act 1988 or the Drug Trafficking Act 1994 from inviting suspects to complete a formal question and answer record after the interview is concluded.

(b) Interview records

11.7 (a) An accurate record must be made of each interview, whether or not the interview takes place at a police station.

(b) The record must state the place of interview, the time it begins and ends, any interview breaks and, subject to *paragraph 2.6A*, the names of all those present; and must be made on the forms provided for this purpose or in the interviewer's pocket book or in accordance with Codes of Practice E or F.

(c) Any written record must be made and completed during the interview, unless this would not be practicable or would interfere with the conduct of the interview, and must constitute either a verbatim record of what has been said or, failing this, an account of the interview which adequately and accurately summarises it.

11.8 If a written record is not made during the interview it must be made as soon as practicable after its completion.

11.9 Written interview records must be timed and signed by the maker.

11.10 If a written record is not completed during the interview the reason must be recorded in the interview record.

11.11 Unless it is impracticable, the person interviewed shall be given the opportunity to read the interview record and to sign it as correct or to indicate how they consider it inaccurate. If the person interviewed cannot read or refuses to read the record or sign it, the senior interviewer present shall read it to them and ask whether they would like to sign it as correct or make their mark or to indicate how they consider it inaccurate. The interviewer shall certify on the interview record itself what has occurred. See *Note 11E*.

11.12 If the appropriate adult or the person's solicitor is present during the interview, they should also be given an opportunity to read and sign the interview record or any written statement taken down during the interview.

Note: *Paragraph 1.5A* extends the requirement in this paragraph to interviews of 17-year-old suspects.

11.13 A written record shall be made of any comments made by a suspect, including unsolicited comments, which are outside the context of an interview but which might be relevant to the offence. Any such record must be timed and signed by the maker. When practicable the suspect shall be given the opportunity to read that record and to sign it as correct or to indicate how they consider it inaccurate. See *Note 11E*.

11.14 Any refusal by a person to sign an interview record when asked in accordance with this Code must itself be recorded.

(c) Juveniles and mentally disordered or otherwise mentally vulnerable people

11.15 A juvenile or person who is mentally disordered or otherwise mentally vulnerable must not be interviewed regarding their involvement or suspected involvement in a criminal offence or offences, or asked to provide or sign a written statement under caution or record of interview, in the absence of the appropriate adult unless *paragraphs 11.1* or *11.18 to 11.20* apply. See *Note 11C*.

Note: *Paragraph 1.5A* extends the requirement in this paragraph to 17-year-old suspects.

11.16 Juveniles may only be interviewed at their place of education in exceptional circumstances and only when the principal or their nominee agrees. Every effort should be made to notify the parent(s) or other person responsible for the juvenile's welfare and the appropriate adult, if this is a different person, that the police want to interview the juvenile and reasonable time should be allowed to enable the appropriate adult to be present at the interview. If awaiting the appropriate adult would cause unreasonable delay, and unless the juvenile is suspected of an offence against the educational establishment, the principal or their nominee can act as the appropriate adult for the purposes of the interview.

Note: *Paragraph 1.5A* extends the requirement in this paragraph to 17-year-old suspects.

11.17 If an appropriate adult is present at an interview, they shall be informed:
- that they are not expected to act simply as an observer; and
- that the purpose of their presence is to:
  - advise the person being interviewed;

- observe whether the interview is being conducted properly and fairly; and
- facilitate communication with the person being interviewed.

(d) Vulnerable suspects – urgent interviews at police stations

11.18 The following interviews may take place only if an officer of superintendent rank or above considers delaying the interview will lead to the consequences in *paragraph 11.1(a) to (c)*, and is satisfied the interview would not significantly harm the person's physical or mental state (see *Annex G*):

(a) an interview of a juvenile or person who is mentally disordered or otherwise mentally vulnerable without the appropriate adult being present;

Note: *Paragraph 1.5A* extends this requirement to 17-year-old detainees.

(b) an interview of anyone other than in (a) who appears unable to:
   • appreciate the significance of questions and their answers; or
   • understand what is happening because of the effects of drink, drugs or any illness, ailment or condition;

(c) an interview, without an interpreter being present, of a person whom the custody officer has determined requires an interpreter (see *paragraphs 3.5(c)(ii)* and *3.12*) which is carried out by an interviewer speaking the suspect's own language or (as the case may be) otherwise establishing effective communication which is sufficient to enable the necessary questions to be asked and answered in order to avert the consequences. See *paragraphs 13.2* and *13.5*.

11.19 These interviews may not continue once sufficient information has been obtained to avert the consequences in *paragraph 11.1(a) to (c)*.

11.20 A record shall be made of the grounds for any decision to interview a person under *paragraph 11.18*.

Notes for Guidance

11ZA The requirement in *paragraph 11.1A* for a suspect to be given sufficient information about the offence applies prior to the interview and whether or not they are legally represented. What is sufficient will depend on the circumstances of the case, but it should normally include, as a minimum, a description of the facts relating to the suspected offence that are known to the officer, including the time and place in question. This aims to avoid suspects being confused or unclear about what they are supposed to have done and to help an innocent suspect to clear the matter up more quickly.

11A *Paragraph 11.4* does not prevent the interviewer from putting significant statements and silences to a suspect again at a later stage or a further interview.

11B The Criminal Procedure and Investigations Act 1996 Code of Practice, paragraph 3.5 states 'In conducting an investigation, the investigator should pursue all reasonable lines of enquiry, whether these point towards or away from the suspect. What is reasonable will depend on the particular circumstances.' Interviewers should keep this in mind when deciding what questions to ask in an interview.

11C Although juveniles or people who are mentally disordered or otherwise mentally vulnerable are often capable of providing reliable evidence, they may, without knowing or wishing to do so, be particularly prone in certain circumstances to provide information that may be unreliable, misleading or self-incriminating. Special care should always be taken when questioning such a person, and the appropriate adult should be involved if there is any doubt about a person's age, mental state or capacity. Because of the risk of unreliable evidence it is also important to obtain corroboration of any facts admitted whenever possible.
Paragraph 1.5A extends this Note to 17-year-old suspects.

11D Juveniles should not be arrested at their place of education unless this is unavoidable. When a juvenile is arrested at their place of education, the principal or their nominee must be informed. *Paragraph 1.5A* extends this Note to 17-year-old suspects.

11E Significant statements described in *paragraph 11.4* will always be relevant to the offence and must be recorded. When a suspect agrees to read records of interviews and other comments and sign them as correct, they should be asked to endorse the record with, e.g. 'I agree that this is a correct record of what was said' and add their signature. If the suspect does not agree with the record, the interviewer should record the details of any disagreement and ask the suspect to read these details and sign them to the effect that they accurately reflect their disagreement. Any refusal to sign should be recorded.

12 Interviews in police stations

(a) Action

12.1 If a police officer wants to interview or conduct enquiries which require the presence of a detainee, the custody officer is responsible for deciding whether to deliver the detainee into the officer's custody. An investigating officer who is given custody of a detainee takes over responsibility for the detainee's care and safe custody for the purposes of this Code until they return the detainee to the custody officer when they must report the manner in which they complied with the Code whilst having custody of the detainee.

12.2 Except as below, in any period of 24 hours a detainee must be allowed a continuous period of at least 8 hours for rest, free from questioning, travel or any interruption in connection with the investigation concerned. This period should normally be at night or other appropriate time which takes account of when the detainee last slept or rested. If a detainee is arrested at a police station after going there voluntarily, the period of 24 hours runs from the time of their arrest and not the time of arrival at the police station. The period may not be interrupted or delayed, except:

   (a) when there are reasonable grounds for believing not delaying or interrupting the period would:

      (i) involve a risk of harm to people or serious loss of, or damage to, property;

      (ii) delay unnecessarily the person's release from custody; or

      (iii) otherwise prejudice the outcome of the investigation;

   (b) at the request of the detainee, their appropriate adult or legal representative;

   (c) when a delay or interruption is necessary in order to:

      (i) comply with the legal obligations and duties arising under *section 15*; or

      (ii) to take action required under *section 9* or in accordance with medical advice.

If the period is interrupted in accordance with (*a*), a fresh period must be allowed. Interruptions under (*b*) and (*c*) do not require a fresh period to be allowed.

12.3 Before a detainee is interviewed the custody officer, in consultation with the officer in charge of the investigation and appropriate healthcare professionals as necessary, shall assess whether the detainee is fit enough to be interviewed. This means determining and considering the risks to the detainee's physical and mental state if the interview took place and determining what safeguards are needed to allow the interview to take place. See *Annex G*. The custody officer shall not allow a detainee to be interviewed if the custody officer considers it would cause significant harm to the detainee's physical or mental state. Vulnerable suspects listed at *paragraph 11.18* shall be treated as always being at some risk during an interview and these persons may not be interviewed except in accordance with *paragraphs 11.18* to *11.20*.

12.4 As far as practicable interviews shall take place in interview rooms which are adequately heated, lit and ventilated.

12.5 A suspect whose detention without charge has been authorised under PACE because the detention is necessary for an interview to obtain evidence of the offence for which they have been arrested may choose not to answer questions but police do not require the suspect's consent or agreement to interview them for this purpose. If a suspect takes steps to prevent themselves being questioned or further questioned, e.g. by refusing to leave their cell to go to a suitable interview room or by trying to leave the interview room, they shall be advised their consent or agreement to interview is not required. The suspect shall be cautioned as in *section 10*, and informed if they fail or refuse to co-operate, the interview may take place in the cell and that their failure or refusal to co-operate may be given in evidence. The suspect shall then be invited to co-operate and go into the interview room.

12.6 People being questioned or making statements shall not be required to stand.

12.7 Before the interview commences each interviewer shall, subject to *paragraph 2.6A*, identify themselves and any other persons present to the interviewee.

12.8 Breaks from interviewing should be made at recognised meal times or at other times that take account of when an interviewee last had a meal. Short refreshment breaks shall be provided at approximately two hour intervals, subject to the interviewer's discretion to delay a break if there are reasonable grounds for believing it would:

   (i) involve a:

      • risk of harm to people;

      • serious loss of, or damage to, property;

   (ii) unnecessarily delay the detainee's release; or

   (iii) otherwise prejudice the outcome of the investigation.

See *Note 12B*

12.9 If during the interview a complaint is made by or on behalf of the interviewee concerning the provisions of any of the Codes, or it comes to the interviewer's notice that the interviewee may have been treated improperly, the interviewer should:
(i)   record the matter in the interview record; and
(ii) inform the custody officer, who is then responsible for dealing with it as in *section 9*.

(b) Documentation

12.10 A record must be made of the:
  • time a detainee is not in the custody of the custody officer, and why
  • reason for any refusal to deliver the detainee out of that custody.

12.11 A record shall be made of:
(a) the reasons it was not practicable to use an interview room; and
(b) any action taken as in *paragraph 12.5.*
The record shall be made on the custody record or in the interview record for action taken whilst an interview record is being kept, with a brief reference to this effect in the custody record.

12.12 Any decision to delay a break in an interview must be recorded, with reasons, in the interview record.

12.13 All written statements made at police stations under caution shall be written on forms provided for the purpose.

12.14 All written statements made under caution shall be taken in accordance with *Annex D*. Before a person makes a written statement under caution at a police station, they shall be reminded about the right to legal advice. See *Note 12A*.

Notes for Guidance

12A It is not normally necessary to ask for a written statement if the interview was recorded in writing and the record signed in accordance with *paragraph 11.11* or audibly or visually recorded in accordance with Code E or F. Statements under caution should normally be taken in these circumstances only at the person's express wish. A person may however be asked if they want to make such a statement.

12B Meal breaks should normally last at least 45 minutes and shorter breaks after two hours should last at least 15 minutes. If the interviewer delays a break in accordance with *paragraph 12.8* and prolongs the interview, a longer break should be provided. If there is a short interview and another short interview is contemplated, the length of the break may be reduced if there are reasonable grounds to believe this is necessary to avoid any of the consequences in *paragraph 12.8(i)* to *(iii)*.

13 Interpreters

(a) General

13.1 Chief officers are responsible for making arrangements to provide appropriately qualified independent persons to act as interpreters and to provide translations of essential documents for:
(a) detained suspects who, in accordance with *paragraph 3.5(c)(ii)*, the custody officer has determined require an interpreter, and
(b) suspects who are not under arrest but are cautioned as in *section 10* who, in accordance with *paragraph 3.21*, the interviewer has determined require an interpreter. In these cases, the responsibilities of the custody officer are, if appropriate, assigned to the interviewer. An interviewer who has any doubts about whether an interpreter is required or about how the provisions of this section should be applied to a suspect who is not under arrest should seek advice from an officer of the rank of sergeant or above.
If the suspect has a hearing or speech impediment, references to 'interpreter' and 'interpretation' in this Code include appropriate assistance necessary to establish effective communication with that person. See *paragraph 13.1C* below if the person is in Wales.

13.1A The arrangements *must* comply with the minimum requirements set out in Directive 2010/64/EU of the European Parliament and of the Council of 20 October 2010 on the right to interpretation and translation in criminal proceedings (see *Note 13A*). The provisions *of this* Code implement the requirements for those to whom this Code applies. These requirements include the following:
  • That the arrangements made and the quality of interpretation and translation provided shall be sufficient to *'safeguard the fairness of the proceedings, in particular by ensuring that suspected or accused persons have knowledge of the cases against them and are able to exercise their right of defence'.*
    This term which is used by the Directive means that the suspect must be able to understand their position and be able to communicate effectively with police officers, interviewers, solicitors and appropriate adults as provided for by this and any other Code in the same way as a suspect who

can speak and understand English and who does not have a hearing or speech impediment and who would therefore not require an interpreter.

- The provision of a written translation of all documents considered essential for the person to exercise their right of defence and to '*safeguard the fairness of the proceedings*' as described above. For the purposes of this Code, this includes any decision to authorise a person to be detained and details of any offence(s) with which the person has been charged or for which they have been told they may be prosecuted, see *Annex M*.
- Procedures to help determine:
  - whether a suspect can speak and understand English and needs the assistance of an interpreter, see *paragraph 13.1* and *Notes 13B* and *13C*; and
  - whether another interpreter should be called or another translation should be provided when a suspect complains about the quality of either or both, see *paragraphs 13.10A* and *13.10C*.

13.1B All reasonable attempts should be made to make the suspect understand that interpretation and translation will be provided at public expense.

13.1C With regard to persons in Wales, nothing in this or any other Code affects the application of the Welsh Language Schemes produced by police and crime commissioners in Wales in accordance with the Welsh Language Act 1993. See *paragraphs 3.12* and *13.1*.

(b) Interviewing suspects – foreign languages

13.2 Unless *paragraphs 11.1* or *11.18(c)* apply, a suspect who for the purposes of this Code requires an interpreter because they do not appear to speak or understand English (see *paragraphs 3.5(c)(ii)* and *3.12*) must not be interviewed in the absence of a person capable of interpreting.

13.2A An interpreter should also be called if a juvenile is interviewed and their parent or guardian, present as the appropriate adult, does not appear to speak or understand English, unless the interview is urgent and *paragraphs 11.1* or *11.18(c)* apply.

Note: *Paragraph 1.5A* extends the requirement in this paragraph to interviews of 17-year-old suspects.

13.3 When a written record of the interview is made (see *paragraph 11.7*), the interviewer shall make sure the interpreter makes a note of the interview at the time in the person's language for use in the event of the interpreter being called to give evidence, and certifies its accuracy. The interviewer should allow sufficient time for the interpreter to note each question and answer after each is put, given and interpreted. The person should be allowed to read the record or have it read to them and sign it as correct or indicate the respects in which they consider it inaccurate. If an audio or visual record of the interview is made, the arrangements in Code E or F shall apply.

13.4 In the case of a person making a statement under caution to a police officer or other police staff other than in English:
  - (a) the interpreter shall record the statement in the language it is made;
  - (b) the person shall be invited to sign it;
  - (c) an official English translation shall be made in due course.

(c) Interviewing suspects who have a hearing or speech impediment

13.5 Unless *paragraphs 11.1* or *11.18(c)* (urgent interviews) apply, a suspect who for the purposes of this Code requires an interpreter or other appropriate assistance to enable effective communication with them because they appear to have a hearing or speech impediment (see *paragraphs 3.5(c)(ii)* and *3.12*) must not be interviewed in the absence of an independent person capable of interpreting or without that assistance.

13.6 An interpreter should also be called if a juvenile is interviewed and their parent or guardian, present as the appropriate adult, appears to have a hearing or speech impediment, unless the interview is urgent and *paragraphs 11.1* or *11.18(c)* apply.

Note: *Paragraph 1.5A* extends the requirement in this paragraph to interviews of 17-year-old suspects.

13.7 The interviewer shall make sure the interpreter is allowed to read the interview record and certify its accuracy in the event of the interpreter being called to give evidence. If the interview is audibly recorded or visually recorded, the arrangements in Code E or F apply.

(d) Additional rules for detained persons

13.8 *Not used.*

13.9 If *paragraph 6.1* applies and the detainee cannot communicate with the solicitor because of language, hearing or speech difficulties, an interpreter must be called. A police officer or any other police staff may not be used for this purpose.

13.10 After the custody officer has determined that a detainee requires an interpreter (see *paragraph 3.5(c)(ii)*) and following the initial action in *paragraphs 3.1* to *3.5*, arrangements must also be made for an interpreter to:

- explain the grounds and reasons for any authorisation for their *continued* detention, before or after charge and any information about the authorisation given to them by the authorising officer and which is recorded in the custody record. See *paragraphs 15.3, 15.4* and *15.16(a)* and (*b*);
- be present at the magistrates' court for the hearing of an application for a warrant of further detention or any extension or further extension of such warrant to explain any grounds and reasons for the application and any information about the authorisation of their further detention given to them by the court (see PACE, sections 43 and 44 and *paragraphs 15.2* and *15.16(c)*), and
- explain any offence with which the detainee is charged or for which they are informed they may be prosecuted and any other information about the offence given to them by or on behalf of the custody officer, see *paragraphs 16.1* and *16.3*.

13.10A If a detainee complains that they are not satisfied with the quality of interpretation, the custody officer or (as the case may be) the interviewer, is responsible for deciding whether a different interpreter should be called in accordance with the procedures set out in the arrangements made by the chief officer, see *paragraph 13.1A*.

(e) Translations of essential documents

13.10B Written translations, oral translations and oral summaries of essential documents in a language the detainee understands shall be provided in accordance with *Annex M* (Translations of documents and records).

13.10C If a detainee complains that they are not satisfied with the quality of the translation, the custody officer or (as the case may be) the interviewer, is responsible for deciding whether a further translation should be provided in accordance with the procedures set out in the arrangements made by the chief officer, see *paragraph 13.1A*.

(f) Decisions not to provide interpretation and translation.

13.10D If a suspect challenges a decision:

- made by the custody officer or (as the case may be) by the interviewer, in accordance with this Code (see *paragraphs 3.5(c)(ii)* and *3.21*) that they do not require an interpreter; or
- made in accordance with *paragraphs 13.10A, 13.10B* or *13.10C* not to provide a different interpreter or another translation or not to translate a requested document, the matter shall be reported to an inspector to deal with as a complaint for the purposes of *paragraph 9.2* or *paragraph 12.9* if the challenge is made during an interview.

(g) Documentation

13.11 The following must be recorded in the custody record or, as applicable, the interview record:

(a) Action taken to call an interpreter;
(b) Action taken when a detainee is not satisfied about the standard of interpretation or translation provided, see *paragraphs 13.10A* and *13.10C*;
(c) When an urgent interview is carried out in accordance with *paragraph 13.2* or *13.5* in the absence of an interpreter;
(d) When a detainee has been assisted by an interpreter for the purpose of providing or being given information or being interviewed;
(e) Action taken in accordance with *Annex M* when:

- a written translation of an essential document is provided;
- an oral translation or oral summary of an essential document is provided instead of a written translation and the authorising officer's reason(s) why this would not prejudice the fairness of the proceedings (see *Annex M, paragraph 3*);
- a suspect waives their right to a translation of an essential document (see *Annex M, paragraph 4*);
- when representations that a document which is not included in the table is essential and that a translation should be provided are refused and the reason for the refusal (see *Annex M, paragraph 8*).

Notes for Guidance

13A Chief officers have discretion when determining the individuals or organisations they use to provide interpretation and translation services for their forces provided that these services are compatible with the requirements of the Directive. One example which chief officers may wish to consider is the Ministry of Justice Framework Agreement for interpretation and translation services.

13B A procedure for determining whether a person needs an interpreter might involve a telephone interpreter service or using cue cards or similar visual aids which enable the detainee to indicate their ability to speak and understand English and their preferred language. This could be confirmed through an interpreter who could also assess the extent to which the person can speak and understand English.

13C There should also be a procedure for determining whether a suspect who requires an interpreter requires assistance in accordance with *paragraph 3.20* to help them check and if applicable, sign any documentation.

14 Questioning – special restrictions

14.1 If a person is arrested by one police force on behalf of another and the lawful period of detention in respect of that offence has not yet commenced in accordance with PACE, section 41, no questions may be put to them about the offence while they are in transit between the forces except to clarify any voluntary statement they make.

14.2 If a person is in police detention at a hospital, they may not be questioned without the agreement of a responsible doctor. See *Note 14A*.

Notes for Guidance

14A If questioning takes place at a hospital under *paragraph 14.2*, or on the way to or from a hospital, the period of questioning concerned counts towards the total period of detention permitted.

15 Reviews and extensions of detention

(a) Persons detained under PACE

15.0 The requirement in *paragraph 3.4(b)* that documents and materials essential to challenging the lawfulness of the detainee's arrest and detention must be made available to the detainee or their solicitor, applies for the purposes of this section as follows:

(a) The officer reviewing the need for detention without charge (*PACE, section 40*), or (as the case may be) the officer considering the need to extend detention without charge from 24 to 36 hours (*PACE, section 42*), is responsible, in consultation with the investigating officer, for deciding which documents and materials are essential and must be made available.

(b) When *paragraph 15.7A* applies (application for a warrant of further detention or extension of such a warrant), the officer making the application is responsible for deciding which documents and materials are essential and must be made available *before* the hearing. See *Note 3ZA*.

15.1 The review officer is responsible under PACE, section 40 for periodically determining if a person's detention, before or after charge, continues to be necessary. This requirement continues throughout the detention period and, except as in *paragraph 15.10*, the review officer must be present at the police station holding the detainee. See *Notes 15A* and *15B*.

15.2 Under PACE, section 42, an officer of superintendent rank or above who is responsible for the station holding the detainee may give authority any time after the second review to extend the maximum period the person may be detained without charge by up to 12 hours. Further detention without charge may be authorised only by a magistrates' court in accordance with PACE, sections 43 and 44. See *Notes 15C, 15D* and *15E*.

15.2A An authorisation under section 42(1) of PACE extends the maximum period of detention permitted before charge for indictable offences from 24 hours to 36 hours. Detaining a juvenile or mentally vulnerable person for longer than 24 hours will be dependent on the circumstances of the case and with regard to the person's:

(a) special vulnerability;

(b) the legal obligation to provide an opportunity for representations to be made prior to a decision about extending detention;

(c) the need to consult and consider the views of any appropriate adult; and

(d) any alternatives to police custody.

Note: *Paragraph 1.5A* extends sub-paragraph (c) to 17-year-old detainees.

15.3 Before deciding whether to authorise continued detention the officer responsible under *paragraph 15.1* or *15.2* shall give an opportunity to make representations about the detention to:

(a) the detainee, unless in the case of a review as in *paragraph 15.1*, the detainee is asleep;

(b) the detainee's solicitor if available at the time; and

(c) the appropriate adult if available at the time.

Note: *Paragraph 1.5A* extends the requirement in sub-paragraph (c) to 17-year-old detainees. See *Note 15CA*

15.3A Other people having an interest in the detainee's welfare may also make representations at the authorising officer's discretion.

15.3B Subject to *paragraph 15.10*, the representations may be made orally in person or by telephone or in writing. The authorising officer may, however, refuse to hear oral representations from the detainee if the officer considers them unfit to make representations because of their condition or behaviour. See *Note 15C*.

15.3C The decision on whether the review takes place in person or by telephone or by video conferencing (see *Note 15G*) is a matter for the review officer. In determining the form the review may take, the review officer must always take full account of the needs of the person in custody. The benefits of carrying out a review in person should always be considered, based on the individual circumstances of each case with specific additional consideration if the person is:

(a) a juvenile (and the age of the juvenile); or
   Note: *Paragraph 1.5A* extends this sub-paragraph to 17-year-old detainees.
(b) suspected of being mentally vulnerable; or
(c) in need of medical attention for other than routine minor ailments; or
(d) subject to presentational or community issues around their detention.

15.4 Before conducting a review or determining whether to extend the maximum period of detention without charge, the officer responsible must make sure the detainee is reminded of their entitlement to free legal advice, see *paragraph 6.5*, unless in the case of a review the person is asleep.

15.5 If, after considering any representations, the review officer under *paragraph 15.1* decides to keep the detainee in detention or the superintendent under *paragraph 15.2* extends the maximum period for which they may be detained without charge, then any comment made by the detainee shall be recorded. If applicable, the officer shall be informed of the comment as soon as practicable. See also *paragraphs 11.4* and *11.13*.

15.6 No officer shall put specific questions to the detainee:
   • regarding their involvement in any offence; or
   • in respect of any comments they may make:
      – when given the opportunity to make representations; or
      – in response to a decision to keep them in detention or extend the maximum period of detention.

Such an exchange could constitute an interview as in *paragraph 11.1A* and would be subject to the associated safeguards in *section 11* and, in respect of a person who has been charged, *paragraph 16.5*. See also *paragraph 11.13*.

15.7 A detainee who is asleep at a review, see *paragraph 15.1*, and whose continued detention is authorised must be informed about the decision and reason as soon as practicable after waking.

15.7A When an application is made to a magistrates' court under PACE, section 43 for a warrant of further detention to extend detention without charge of a person arrested for an *indictable offence*, or under section 44, to extend or further extend that warrant, the detainee:
(a) must be brought to court for the hearing of the application;
(b) is entitled to be legally represented if they wish, in which case, *Annex B* cannot apply; and
(c) must be given a copy of the information which supports the application and states:
      (i) the nature of the offence for which the person to whom the application relates has been arrested;
      (ii) the general nature of the evidence on which the person was arrested;
      (iii) what inquiries about the offence have been made and what further inquiries are proposed;
      (iv) the reasons for believing continued detention is necessary for the purposes of the further inquiries;

Note: A warrant of further detention can only be issued or extended if the court has reasonable grounds for believing that the person's further detention is necessary for the purpose of obtaining evidence of an indictable offence for which the person has been arrested and that the investigation is being conducted diligently and expeditiously.
See *paragraph 15.0(b)*

15.8 *Not used.*

(b) Review of detention by telephone and video conferencing facilities

15.9 PACE, section 40A provides that the officer responsible under section 40 for reviewing the detention of a person who has not been charged, need not attend the police station holding the detainee and may carry out the review by telephone.

15.9A PACE, section 45A(2) provides that the officer responsible under section 40 for reviewing the detention of a person who has not been charged, need not attend the police station holding the detainee and may carry out the review by video conferencing facilities. See *Note 15G*.

15.9B A telephone review is not permitted where facilities for review by video conferencing exist and it is practicable to use them.

15.9C The review officer can decide at any stage that a telephone review or review by video conferencing should be terminated and that the review will be conducted in person. The reasons for doing so should be noted in the custody record.

See *Note 15F.*

15.10 When a review is carried out by telephone or by video conferencing facilities, an officer at the station holding the detainee shall be required by the review officer to fulfil that officer's obligations under PACE section 40 and this Code by:

    (a) making any record connected with the review in the detainee's custody record;

    (b) if applicable, making the record in (*a*) in the presence of the detainee; and

    (c) for a review by telephone, giving the detainee information about the review.

15.11 When a review is carried out by telephone or by video conferencing facilities, the requirement in *paragraph 15.3* will be satisfied:

    (a) if facilities exist for the immediate transmission of written representations to the review officer, e.g. fax or email message, by allowing those who are given the opportunity to make representations, to make their representations:

        (i) orally by telephone or (as the case may be) by means of the video conferencing facilities; or

        (ii) in writing using the facilities for the immediate transmission of written representations; and

    (b) in all other cases, by allowing those who are given the opportunity to make representations, to make their representations orally by telephone or by means of the video conferencing facilities.

(c) Documentation

15.12 It is the officer's responsibility to make sure all reminders given under *paragraph 15.4* are noted in the custody record.

15.13 The grounds for, and extent of, any delay in conducting a review shall be recorded.

15.14 When a review is carried out by telephone or video conferencing facilities, a record shall be made of:

    (a) the reason the review officer did not attend the station holding the detainee;

    (b) the place the review officer was;

    (c) the method representations, oral or written, were made to the review officer, see *paragraph 15.11.*

15.15 Any written representations shall be retained.

15.16 A record shall be made as soon as practicable of:

    (a) the outcome of each review of detention before or after charge, and if *paragraph 15.7* applies, of when the person was informed and by whom;

    (b) the outcome of any determination under PACE, section 42 by a superintendent whether to extend the maximum period of detention without charge beyond 24 hours from the relevant time. If an authorisation is given, the record shall state the number of hours and minutes by which the detention period is extended or further extended.

    (c) the outcome of each application under PACE, section 43, for a warrant of further detention or under section 44, for an extension or further extension of that warrant. If a warrant for further detention is granted under section 43 or extended or further extended under 44, the record shall state the detention period authorised by the warrant and the date and time it was granted or (as the case may be) the period by which the warrant is extended or further extended.

    Note: Any period during which a person is released on bail does not count towards the maximum period of detention without charge allowed under PACE, sections 41 to 44.

Notes for Guidance

15A Review officer for the purposes of:

    • PACE, sections 40, 40A and 45A means, in the case of a person arrested but not charged, an officer of at least inspector rank not directly involved in the investigation and, if a person has been arrested and charged, the custody officer.

15B The detention of persons in police custody not subject to the statutory review requirement in *paragraph 15.1* should still be reviewed periodically as a matter of good practice. Such reviews can be carried out by an officer of the rank of sergeant or above. The purpose of such reviews is to check the particular power under which a detainee is held continues to apply, any associated conditions are complied with and to make sure appropriate action is taken to deal with any changes. This includes the detainee's prompt release when the power no longer applies, or their transfer if the power requires the detainee be taken elsewhere as soon as the necessary arrangements are made. Examples include persons:

(a) arrested on warrant because they failed to answer bail to appear at court;

(b) arrested under the Bail Act 1976, section 7(3) for breaching a condition of bail granted after charge;

(c) in police custody for specific purposes and periods under the Crime (Sentences) Act 1997, Schedule 1;

(d) convicted, or remand prisoners, held in police stations on behalf of the Prison Service under the Imprisonment (Temporary Provisions) Act 1980, section 6;

(e) being detained to prevent them causing a breach of the peace;

(f) detained at police stations on behalf of Immigration Enforcement (formerly the UK Immigration Service);

(g) detained by order of a magistrates' court under the Criminal Justice Act 1988, section 152 (as amended by the Drugs Act 2005, section 8) to facilitate the recovery of evidence after being charged with drug possession or drug trafficking and suspected of having swallowed drugs.

The detention of persons remanded into police detention by order of a court under the Magistrates' Courts Act 1980, section 128 is subject to a statutory requirement to review that detention. This is to make sure the detainee is taken back to court no later than the end of the period authorised by the court or when the need for their detention by police ceases, whichever is the sooner.

15C In the case of a review of detention, but not an extension, the detainee need not be woken for the review. However, if the detainee is likely to be asleep, e.g. during a period of rest allowed as in *paragraph 12.2*, at the latest time a review or authorisation to extend detention may take place, the officer should, if the legal obligations and time constraints permit, bring forward the procedure to allow the detainee to make representations. A detainee not asleep during the review must be present when the grounds for their continued detention are recorded and must at the same time be informed of those grounds unless the review officer considers the person is incapable of understanding what is said, violent or likely to become violent or in urgent need of medical attention.

15CA In *paragraph 15.3(b)* and *(c)*, 'available' includes being contactable in time to enable them to make representations remotely by telephone or other electronic means or in person by attending the station. Reasonable efforts should therefore be made to give the solicitor and appropriate adult sufficient notice of the time the decision is expected to be made so that they can make themselves available.

15D An application to a Magistrates' Court under PACE, sections 43 or 44 for a warrant of further detention or its extension should be made between 10am and 9pm, and if possible during normal court hours. It will not usually be practicable to arrange for a court to sit specially outside the hours of 10am to 9pm. If it appears a special sitting may be needed outside normal court hours but between 10am and 9pm, the clerk to the justices should be given notice and informed of this possibility, while the court is sitting if possible.

15E In *paragraph 15.2*, the officer responsible for the station holding the detainee includes a superintendent or above who, in accordance with their force operational policy or police regulations, is given that responsibility on a temporary basis whilst the appointed long-term holder is off duty or otherwise unavailable.

15F The provisions of PACE, section 40A allowing telephone reviews do not apply to reviews of detention after charge by the custody officer. When video conferencing is not required, they allow the use of a telephone to carry out a review of detention before charge. The procedure under PACE, section 42 must be done in person.

15G Video conferencing facilities means any facilities (whether a live television link or other facilities) by means of which the review can be carried out with the review officer, the detainee concerned and the detainee's solicitor all being able to both see and to hear each other. The use of video conferencing facilities for decisions about detention under section 45A of PACE is subject to regulations made by the Secretary of State being in force.

16 Charging detained persons

(a) Action

16.1 When the officer in charge of the investigation reasonably believes there is sufficient evidence to provide a realistic prospect of conviction for the offence (see *paragraph 11.6*), they shall without delay, and subject to the following qualification, inform the custody officer who will be responsible for considering whether the detainee should be charged. See *Notes 11B* and *16A*. When a person is detained in respect of more than one offence it is permissible to delay informing the custody officer until the above conditions are satisfied in respect of all the offences, but see *paragraph 11.6*. If the detainee is a juvenile, mentally disordered or otherwise mentally vulnerable, any resulting action shall be taken in the presence of the appropriate adult if they are present at the time.

Note: *Paragraph 1.5A* requires someone to fulfil the role of the appropriate adult to be present when the action applies to a 17-year-old detainee.

See *Notes 16B* and *16C*.

16.1A Where guidance issued by the Director of Public Prosecutions under PACE, section 37A is in force the custody officer must comply with that Guidance in deciding how to act in dealing with the detainee. See *Notes 16AA* and *16AB*.

16.1B Where in compliance with the DPP's Guidance the custody officer decides that the case should be immediately referred to the CPS to make the charging decision, consultation should take place with a Crown Prosecutor as soon as is reasonably practicable. Where the Crown Prosecutor is unable to make the charging decision on the information available at that time, the detainee may be released without charge and on bail (with conditions if necessary) under section 37(7)(a). In such circumstances, the detainee should be informed that they are being released to enable the Director of Public Prosecutions to make a decision under section 37B.

16.2 When a detainee is charged with or informed they may be prosecuted for an offence, see *Note 16B*, they shall, unless the restriction on drawing adverse inferences from silence applies, see *Annex C*, be cautioned as follows:

'*You do not have to say anything. But it may harm your defence if you do not mention now something which you later rely on in court. Anything you do say may be given in evidence.*'

Where the use of the Welsh Language is appropriate, a constable may provide the caution directly in Welsh in the following terms:

'*Does dim rhaid i chi ddweud dim byd. Ond gall niweidio eich amddiffyniad os na fyddwch chi'n sôn, yn awr, am rywbeth y byddwch chi'n dibynnu arno nes ymlaen yn y llys. Gall unrhyw beth yr ydych yn ei ddweud gael ei roi fel tystiolaeth.*'

Annex C, paragraph 2 sets out the alternative terms of the caution to be used when the restriction on drawing adverse inferences from silence applies.

16.3 When a detainee is charged they shall be given a written notice showing particulars of the offence and, subject to *paragraph 2.6A*, the officer's name and the case reference number. As far as possible the particulars of the charge shall be stated in simple terms, but they shall also show the precise offence in law with which the detainee is charged. The notice shall begin:

'*You are charged with the offence(s) shown below.*' Followed by the caution.

If the detainee is a juvenile, mentally disordered or otherwise mentally vulnerable, a copy of the notice should also be given to the appropriate adult.

Note: *Paragraph 1.5A* provides that a copy of the notice should be given to the person called to fulfil the role of the appropriate adult when a 17-year-old detainee is charged.

16.4 If, after a detainee has been charged with or informed they may be prosecuted for an offence, an officer wants to tell them about any written statement or interview with another person relating to such an offence, the detainee shall either be handed a true copy of the written statement or the content of the interview record brought to their attention. Nothing shall be done to invite any reply or comment except to:

(a) caution the detainee, '*You do not have to say anything, but anything you do say may be given in evidence.*';

Where the use of the Welsh Language is appropriate, caution the detainee in the following terms:

'*Does dim rhaid i chi ddweud dim byd, ond gall unrhyw beth yr ydych yn ei ddweud gael ei roi fel tystiolaeth.*'

and

(b) remind the detainee about their right to legal advice.

16.4A If the detainee:

• cannot read, the document may be read to them;

• is a juvenile, mentally disordered or otherwise mentally vulnerable, the appropriate adult shall also be given a copy, or the interview record shall be brought to their attention.

Note: *Paragraph 1.5A* requires a copy of the record to be given to, or brought to the attention of, the person called to fulfil the role of the appropriate adult for a 17-year-old detainee.

16.5 A detainee may not be interviewed about an offence after they have been charged with, or informed they may be prosecuted for it, unless the interview is necessary:
- to prevent or minimise harm or loss to some other person, or the public
- to clear up an ambiguity in a previous answer or statement
- in the interests of justice for the detainee to have put to them, and have an opportunity to comment on, information concerning the offence which has come to light since they were charged or informed they might be prosecuted

Before any such interview, the interviewer shall:

(a) caution the detainee, '*You do not have to say anything, but anything you do say may be given in evidence.*'

Where the use of the Welsh Language is appropriate, the interviewer shall caution the detainee: '*Does dim rhaid i chi ddweud dim byd, ond gall unrhyw beth yr ydych yn ei ddweud gael ei roi fel tystiolaeth.*'

(b) remind the detainee about their right to legal advice.

See *Note 16B*

16.6 The provisions of *paragraphs 16.2* to *16.5* must be complied with in the appropriate adult's presence if they are already at the police station. If they are not at the police station then these provisions must be complied with again in their presence when they arrive unless the detainee has been released. See *Note 16C*.

Note: *Paragraph 1.5A* extends the requirement in this paragraph to 17-year-old detainees.

16.7 When a juvenile is charged with an offence and the custody officer authorises their continued detention after charge, the custody officer must make arrangements for the juvenile to be taken into the care of a local authority to be detained pending appearance in court unless the custody officer certifies in accordance with PACE, section 38(6), that:

(a) for any juvenile; it is impracticable to do so; or,

(b) in the case of a juvenile of at least 12 years old, no secure accommodation is available and other accommodation would not be adequate to protect the public from serious harm from that juvenile. See *Note 16D*.

Note: The 16 year old maximum age limit for transfer to local authority accommodation, the power of the local authority to detain the person transferred and take over responsibility for that person from the police are determined by section 38 of PACE. For this reason, this paragraph and *Note 16D* do not apply to detainees who appear to have attained the age of 17, see *paragraph 1.5A(a)*.

16.7A The requirement in *paragraph 3.4(b)* that documents and materials essential to effectively challenging the lawfulness of the detainee's arrest and detention must be made available to the detainee and, if they are represented, their solicitor, applies for the purposes of this section and a person's detention after charge. This means that the custody officer making the bail decision (PACE, section 38) or reviewing the need for detention after charge (PACE, section 40), is responsible for determining what, if any, documents or materials are essential and must be made available to the detainee or their solicitor. See *Note 3ZA*.

(b) Documentation

16.8 A record shall be made of anything a detainee says when charged.

16.9 Any questions put in an interview after charge and answers given relating to the offence shall be recorded in full during the interview on forms for that purpose and the record signed by the detainee or, if they refuse, by the interviewer and any third parties present. If the questions are audibly recorded or visually recorded the arrangements in Code E or F apply.

16.10 If arrangements for a juvenile's transfer into local authority care as in *paragraph 16.7* are not made, the custody officer must record the reasons in a certificate which must be produced before the court with the juvenile. See *Note 16D*.

Notes for Guidance

16A The custody officer must take into account alternatives to prosecution under the Crime and Disorder Act 1998 applicable to persons under 18, and in national guidance on the cautioning of offenders applicable to persons aged 18 and over.

16AA When a person is arrested under the provisions of the Criminal Justice Act 2003 which allow a person to be re-tried after being acquitted of a serious offence which is a qualifying offence specified in Schedule 5 to that Act and not precluded from further prosecution by virtue of section 75(3) of that Act the detention provisions of PACE are modified and make an officer of the rank of superintendent or above who has not been directly involved in the investigation responsible for determining whether the evidence is sufficient to charge.

16AB Where Guidance issued by the Director of Public Prosecutions under section 37B is in force, a custody officer who determines in accordance with that Guidance that there is sufficient evidence to charge the detainee, may detain that person for no longer than is reasonably necessary to decide how that person is to be dealt with under PACE, section 37(7)(a) to (d), including, where appropriate, consultation with the Duty Prosecutor. The period is subject to the maximum period of detention before charge determined by PACE, sections 41 to 44. Where in accordance with the Guidance the case is referred to the CPS for decision, the custody officer should ensure that an officer involved in the investigation sends to the CPS such information as is specified in the Guidance.

16B The giving of a warning or the service of the Notice of Intended Prosecution required by the Road Traffic Offenders Act 1988, section 1 does not amount to informing a detainee they may be prosecuted for an offence and so does not preclude further questioning in relation to that offence.

16C There is no power under PACE to detain a person and delay action under *paragraphs 16.2* to *16.5* solely to await the arrival of the appropriate adult. Reasonable efforts should therefore be made to give the appropriate adult sufficient notice of the time the decision (charge etc.) is to be implemented so that they can be present. If the appropriate adult is not, or cannot be, present at that time, the detainee should be released on bail to return for the decision to be implemented when the adult is present, unless the custody officer determines that the absence of the appropriate adult makes the detainee unsuitable for bail for this purpose. After charge, bail cannot be refused, or release on bail delayed, simply because an appropriate adult is not available, unless the absence of that adult provides the custody officer with the necessary grounds to authorise detention after charge under PACE, section 38.

16D Except as in *paragraph 16.7*, neither a juvenile's behaviour nor the nature of the offence provides grounds for the custody officer to decide it is impracticable to arrange the juvenile's transfer to local authority care. Impracticability concerns the transport and travel requirements and the lack of secure accommodation which is provided for the purposes of restricting liberty does not make it impracticable to transfer the juvenile. The availability of secure accommodation is only a factor in relation to a juvenile aged 12 or over when other local authority accommodation would not be adequate to protect the public from serious harm from them. The obligation to transfer a juvenile to local authority accommodation applies as much to a juvenile charged during the daytime as to a juvenile to be held overnight, subject to a requirement to bring the juvenile before a court under PACE, section 46.
This Note does not apply to 17-year-old detainees (see *paragraph 16.7*).

17 Testing persons for the presence of specified Class A drugs

(a) Action

17.1 This section of Code C applies only in selected police stations in police areas where the provisions for drug testing under section 63B of PACE (as amended by section 5 of the Criminal Justice Act 2003 and section 7 of the Drugs Act 2005) are in force and in respect of which the Secretary of State has given a notification to the relevant chief officer of police that arrangements for the taking of samples have been made. Such a notification will cover either a police area as a whole or particular stations within a police area. The notification indicates whether the testing applies to those arrested or charged or under the age of 18 as the case may be and testing can only take place in respect of the persons so indicated in the notification. Testing cannot be carried out unless the relevant notification has been given and has not been withdrawn. See *Note 17F*.

17.2 A sample of urine or a non-intimate sample may be taken from a person in police detention for the purpose of ascertaining whether they have any specified Class A drug in their body only where they have been brought before the custody officer and:
(a) either the arrest condition, see *paragraph 17.3,* or the charge condition, see *paragraph 17.4* is met;
(b) the age condition see *paragraph 17.5,* is met;
(c) the notification condition is met in relation to the arrest condition, the charge condition, or the age condition, as the case may be. (Testing on charge and/or arrest must be specifically provided for in the notification for the power to apply. In addition, the fact that testing of under 18s is authorised must be expressly provided for in the notification before the power to test such persons applies.). See *paragraph 17.1*; and
(d) a police officer has requested the person concerned to give the sample (the request condition).

17.3 The arrest condition is met where the detainee:
(a) has been arrested for a trigger offence, see *Note 17E,* but not charged with that offence; or
(b) has been arrested for any other offence but not charged with that offence and a police officer of inspector rank or above, who has reasonable grounds for suspecting that their misuse of any specified Class A drug caused or contributed to the offence, has authorised the sample to be taken.

17.4 The charge condition is met where the detainee:
  (a) has been charged with a trigger offence, or
  (b) has been charged with any other offence and a police officer of inspector rank or above, who has reasonable grounds for suspecting that the detainee's misuse of any specified Class A drug caused or contributed to the offence, has authorised the sample to be taken.

17.5 The age condition is met where:
  (a) in the case of a detainee who has been arrested but not charged as in *paragraph 17.3*, they are aged 18 or over;
  (b) in the case of a detainee who has been charged as in *paragraph 17.4*, they are aged 14 or over.

17.6 Before requesting a sample from the person concerned, an officer must:
  (a) inform them that the purpose of taking the sample is for drug testing under PACE. This is to ascertain whether they have a specified Class A drug present in their body;
  (b) warn them that if, when so requested, they fail without good cause to provide a sample they may be liable to prosecution;
  (c) where the taking of the sample has been authorised by an inspector or above in accordance with *paragraph 17.3(b)* or *17.4(b)* above, inform them that the authorisation has been given and the grounds for giving it;
  (d) remind them of the following rights, which may be exercised at any stage during the period in custody:
    (i)   the right to have someone informed of their arrest [see *section 5*];
    (ii) the right to consult privately with a solicitor and that free independent legal advice is available [see *section 6*]; and
    (iii) the right to consult these Codes of Practice [see *section 3*].

17.7 In the case of a person who has not attained the age of 17 —
  (a) the making of the request for a sample under *paragraph 17.2(d)* above;
  (b) the giving of the warning and the information under *paragraph 17.6* above; and
  (c) the taking of the sample,
  may not take place except in the presence of an appropriate adult. See *Note 17G*.
  Note: *Paragraph 1.5A* requires someone to fulfil the role of the appropriate adult to be present if the person to be tested appears to be under the age of 18.

17.8 Authorisation by an officer of the rank of inspector or above within *paragraph 17.3(b)* or *17.4(b)* may be given orally or in writing but, if it is given orally, it must be confirmed in writing as soon as practicable.

17.9 If a sample is taken from a detainee who has been arrested for an offence but not charged with that offence as in *paragraph 17.3*, no further sample may be taken during the same continuous period of detention. If during that same period the charge condition is also met in respect of that detainee, the sample which has been taken shall be treated as being taken by virtue of the charge condition, see *paragraph 17.4*, being met.

17.10 A detainee from whom a sample may be taken may be detained for up to six hours from the time of charge if the custody officer reasonably believes the detention is necessary to enable a sample to be taken. Where the arrest condition is met, a detainee whom the custody officer has decided to release on bail without charge may continue to be detained, but not beyond 24 hours from the relevant time (as defined in section 41(2) of PACE), to enable a sample to be taken.

17.11 A detainee in respect of whom the arrest condition is met, but not the charge condition, see *paragraphs 17.3* and *17.4*, and whose release would be required before a sample can be taken had they not continued to be detained as a result of being arrested for a further offence which does not satisfy the arrest condition, may have a sample taken at any time within 24 hours after the arrest for the offence that satisfies the arrest condition.

(b) Documentation

17.12 The following must be recorded in the custody record:
  (a) if a sample is taken following authorisation by an officer of the rank of inspector or above, the authorisation and the grounds for suspicion;
  (b) the giving of a warning of the consequences of failure to provide a sample;
  (c) the time at which the sample was given; and
  (d) the time of charge or, where the arrest condition is being relied upon, the time of arrest and, where applicable, the fact that a sample taken after arrest but before charge is to be treated as being taken by virtue of the charge condition, where that is met in the same period of continuous detention. See *paragraph 17.9*.

(c) General

17.13 A sample may only be taken by a prescribed person. See *Note 17C.*

17.14 Force may not be used to take any sample for the purpose of drug testing.

17.15 The terms 'Class A drug' and 'misuse' have the same meanings as in the Misuse of Drugs Act 1971. 'Specified' (in relation to a Class A drug) and 'trigger offence' have the same meanings as in Part III of the Criminal Justice and Court Services Act 2000.

17.16 Any sample taken:
- (a) may not be used for any purpose other than to ascertain whether the person concerned has a specified Class A drug present in his body; and
- (b) can be disposed of as clinical waste unless it is to be sent for further analysis in cases where the test result is disputed at the point when the result is known, including on the basis that medication has been taken, or for quality assurance purposes.

(d) Assessment of misuse of drugs

17.17 Under the provisions of Part 3 of the Drugs Act 2005, where a detainee has tested positive for a specified Class A drug under section 63B of PACE a police officer may, at any time before the person's release from the police station, impose a requirement on the detainee to attend an initial assessment of their drug misuse by a suitably qualified person and to remain for its duration. Where such a requirement is imposed, the officer must, at the same time, impose a second requirement on the detainee to attend and remain for a follow-up assessment. The officer must inform the detainee that the second requirement will cease to have effect if, at the initial assessment they are informed that a follow-up assessment is not necessary. These requirements may only be imposed on a person if:
- (a) they have reached the age of 18
- (b) notification has been given by the Secretary of State to the relevant chief officer of police that arrangements for conducting initial and follow-up assessments have been made for those from whom samples for testing have been taken at the police station where the detainee is in custody.

17.18 When imposing a requirement to attend an initial assessment and a follow-up assessment the police officer must:
- (a) inform the person of the time and place at which the initial assessment is to take place;
- (b) explain that this information will be confirmed in writing; and
- (c) warn the person that they may be liable to prosecution if they fail without good cause to attend the initial assessment and remain for its duration and if they fail to attend the follow-up assessment and remain for its duration (if so required).

17.19 Where a police officer has imposed a requirement to attend an initial assessment and a follow-up assessment in accordance with *paragraph 17.17*, he must, before the person is released from detention, give the person notice in writing which:
- (a) confirms their requirement to attend and remain for the duration of the assessments; and
- (b) confirms the information and repeats the warning referred to in *paragraph 17.18*.

17.20 The following must be recorded in the custody record:
- (a) that the requirement to attend an initial assessment and a follow-up assessment has been imposed; and
- (b) the information, explanation, warning and notice given in accordance with *paragraphs 17.17* and *17.19*.

17.21 Where a notice is given in accordance with *paragraph 17.19*, a police officer can give the person a further notice in writing which informs the person of any change to the time or place at which the initial assessment is to take place and which repeats the warning referred to in *paragraph 17.18(c)*.

17.22 Part 3 of the Drugs Act 2005 also requires police officers to have regard to any guidance issued by the Secretary of State in respect of the assessment provisions.

Notes for Guidance

17A When warning a person who is asked to provide a urine or non-intimate sample in accordance with *paragraph 17.6(b)*, the following form of words may be used:
  '*You do not have to provide a sample, but I must warn you that if you fail or refuse without good cause to do so, you will commit an offence for which you may be imprisoned, or fined, or both*'.
  Where the Welsh language is appropriate, the following form of words may be used:
  '*Does dim rhaid i chi roi sampl, ond mae'n rhaid i mi eich rhybuddio y byddwch chi'n cyflawni trosedd os byddwch chi'n methu neu yn gwrthod gwneud hynny heb reswm da, ac y gellir, oherwydd hynny, eich carcharu, eich dirwyo, neu'r ddau.*'

17B A sample has to be sufficient and suitable. A sufficient sample is sufficient in quantity and quality to enable drug-testing analysis to take place. A suitable sample is one which by its nature, is suitable for a particular form of drug analysis.

17C A prescribed person in *paragraph 17.13* is one who is prescribed in regulations made by the Secretary of State under section 63B(6) of the Police and Criminal Evidence Act 1984. [The regulations are currently contained in regulation SI 2001 No. 2645, the Police and Criminal Evidence Act 1984 (Drug Testing Persons in Police Detention) (Prescribed Persons) Regulations 2001.]

17D Samples, and the information derived from them, may not be subsequently used in the investigation of any offence or in evidence against the persons from whom they were taken.

17E Trigger offences are:

1.   Offences under the following provisions of the Theft Act 1968:

section 1	(theft)
section 8	(robbery)
section 9	(burglary)
section 10	(aggravated burglary)
section 12	(taking a motor vehicle or other conveyance without authority)
section 12A	(aggravated vehicle-taking)
section 22	(handling stolen goods)
section 25	(going equipped for stealing etc.)

2.   Offences under the following provisions of the Misuse of Drugs Act 1971, if committed in respect of a specified Class A drug:

section 4	(restriction on production and supply of controlled drugs)
section 5(2)	(possession of a controlled drug)
section 5(3)	(possession of a controlled drug with intent to supply)

3.   Offences under the following provisions of the Fraud Act 2006:

section 1	(fraud)
section 6	(possession etc. of articles for use in frauds)
section 7	(making or supplying articles for use in frauds)

3A. An offence under section 1(1) of the Criminal Attempts Act 1981 if committed in respect of an offence under[:]

(a) any of the following provisions of the Theft Act 1968:

section 1	(theft)
section 8	(robbery)
section 9	(burglary)
section 22	(handling stolen goods)

(b) section 1 of the Fraud Act 2006 (fraud)

4.   Offences under the following provisions of the Vagrancy Act 1824:

section 3	(begging)
section 4	(persistent begging)

17F The power to take samples is subject to notification by the Secretary of State that appropriate arrangements for the taking of samples have been made for the police area as a whole or for the particular police station concerned for whichever of the following is specified in the notification:

(a) persons in respect of whom the arrest condition is met;

(b) persons in respect of whom the charge condition is met;

(c) persons who have not attained the age of 18.

Note: Notification is treated as having been given for the purposes of the charge condition in relation to a police area, if testing (on charge) under section 63B(2) of PACE was in force immediately before section 7 of the Drugs Act 2005 was brought into force; and for the purposes of the age condition, in relation to a police area or police station, if immediately before that day, notification that arrangements had been made for the taking of samples from persons under the age of 18 (those aged 14–17) had been given and had not been withdrawn.

17G Appropriate adult in *paragraph 17.7* means the person's –

(a) parent or guardian or, if they are in the care of a local authority or voluntary organisation, a person representing that authority or organisation; or

(b) a social worker of a local authority; or

(c) if no person falling within (a) or (b) above is available, any responsible person aged 18 or over who is not a police officer or a person employed by the police.

Note: *Paragraph 1.5A* extends this Note to the person called to fulfil the role of the appropriate adult for a 17-year-old detainee for the purposes of *paragraph 17.7*.

Annex A

Intimate and Strip Searches

A Intimate search

1. An intimate search consists of the physical examination of a person's body orifices other than the mouth. The intrusive nature of such searches means the actual and potential risks associated with intimate searches must never be underestimated.

(a) Action

2. Body orifices other than the mouth may be searched only:
   (a) if authorised by an officer of inspector rank or above who has reasonable grounds for believing that the person may have concealed on themselves:
      (i) anything which they could and might use to cause physical injury to themselves or others at the station; or
      (ii) a Class A drug which they intended to supply to another or to export;
      and the officer has reasonable grounds for believing that an intimate search is the only means of removing those items; and
   (b) if the search is under *paragraph 2(a)(ii)* (a drug offence search), the detainee's appropriate consent has been given in writing.

2A. Before the search begins, a police officer or designated detention officer, must tell the detainee:
   (a) that the authority to carry out the search has been given;
   (b) the grounds for giving the authorisation and for believing that the article cannot be removed without an intimate search.

   Note: *Paragraph 1.5A* of this Code requires someone to fulfil the role of the appropriate adult to be present when a 17-year-old is told about the authority and grounds for an intimate search.

2B. Before a detainee is asked to give appropriate consent to a search under *paragraph 2(a) (ii)* (a drug offence search) they must be warned that if they refuse without good cause their refusal may harm their case if it comes to trial, see *Note A6*. This warning may be given by a police officer or member of police staff. In the case of juveniles, mentally vulnerable or mentally disordered suspects, the seeking and giving of consent must take place in the presence of the appropriate adult. A juvenile's consent is only valid if their parent's or guardian's consent is also obtained unless the juvenile is under 14, when their parent's or guardian's consent is sufficient in its own right. A detainee who is not legally represented must be reminded of their entitlement to have free legal advice, see Code C, *paragraph 6.5*, and the reminder noted in the custody record.

   Note: *Paragraph 1.5A* of this Code requires someone to fulfil the role of the appropriate adult to be present when the warning is given to a 17-year-old and their consent to a drug offence search is sought and given but the consent of their parent or guardian is not required.

3. An intimate search may only be carried out by a registered medical practitioner or registered nurse, unless an officer of at least inspector rank considers this is not practicable and the search is to take place under *paragraph 2(a)(i)*, in which case a police officer may carry out the search. See *Notes A1 to A5*.

3A. Any proposal for a search under *paragraph 2(a)(i)* to be carried out by someone other than a registered medical practitioner or registered nurse must only be considered as a last resort and when the authorising officer is satisfied the risks associated with allowing the item to remain with the detainee outweigh the risks associated with removing it. See *Notes A1 to A5*.

4. An intimate search under:
   • *paragraph 2(a)(i)* may take place only at a hospital, surgery, other medical premises or police station;
   • *paragraph 2(a)(ii)* may take place only at a hospital, surgery or other medical premises and must be carried out by a registered medical practitioner or a registered nurse.

5. An intimate search at a police station of a juvenile or mentally disordered or otherwise mentally vulnerable person may take place only in the presence of an appropriate adult of the same sex (see *Annex L*), unless the detainee specifically requests a particular adult of the opposite sex who is readily available. In the case of a juvenile, the search may take place in the absence of the appropriate adult only if the juvenile signifies in the presence of the appropriate adult they do not want the adult present during the search and the adult agrees. A record shall be made of the juvenile's decision and signed by the appropriate adult.

   Note: *Paragraph 1.5A* of this Code extends the requirement in this paragraph to an intimate search of a 17-year-old.

6.   When an intimate search under *paragraph 2(a)(i)* is carried out by a police officer, the officer must be of the same sex as the detainee (see *Annex L*). A minimum of two people, other than the detainee, must be present during the search. Subject to *paragraph 5*, no person of the opposite sex who is not a medical practitioner or nurse shall be present, nor shall anyone whose presence is unnecessary. The search shall be conducted with proper regard to the sensitivity and vulnerability of the detainee.

(b) Documentation

7.   In the case of an intimate search, the following shall be recorded as soon as practicable in the detainee's custody record:
  (a)   for searches under *paragraphs 2(a)(i)* and *(ii)*;
    • the authorisation to carry out the search;
    • the grounds for giving the authorisation;
    • the grounds for believing the article could not be removed without an intimate search;
    • which parts of the detainee's body were searched;
    • who carried out the search;
    • who was present;
    • the result.
  (b)   for searches under *paragraph 2(a)(ii)*:
    • the giving of the warning required by *paragraph 2B*;
    • the fact that the appropriate consent was given or (as the case may be) refused, and if refused, the reason given for the refusal (if any).

8.   If an intimate search is carried out by a police officer, the reason why it was impracticable for a registered medical practitioner or registered nurse to conduct it must be recorded.

B Strip search

9.   A strip search is a search involving the removal of more than outer clothing. In this Code, outer clothing includes shoes and socks.

(a) Action

10. A strip search may take place only if it is considered necessary to remove an article which a detainee would not be allowed to keep and the officer reasonably considers the detainee might have concealed such an article. Strip searches shall not be routinely carried out if there is no reason to consider that articles are concealed.

The conduct of strip searches

11. When strip searches are conducted:
  (a)   a police officer carrying out a strip search must be the same sex as the detainee (see *Annex L*);
  (b)   the search shall take place in an area where the detainee cannot be seen by anyone who does not need to be present, nor by a member of the opposite sex (see *Annex L*) except an appropriate adult who has been specifically requested by the detainee;
  (c)   except in cases of urgency, where there is risk of serious harm to the detainee or to others, whenever a strip search involves exposure of intimate body parts, there must be at least two people present other than the detainee, and if the search is of a juvenile or mentally disordered or otherwise mentally vulnerable person, one of the people must be the appropriate adult. Except in urgent cases as above, a search of a juvenile may take place in the absence of the appropriate adult only if the juvenile signifies in the presence of the appropriate adult that they do not want the adult to be present during the search and the adult agrees. A record shall be made of the juvenile's decision and signed by the appropriate adult. The presence of more than two people, other than an appropriate adult, shall be permitted only in the most exceptional circumstances;
    Note: *Paragraph 1.5A* of this Code extends the requirement in this sub-paragraph to a strip search of a 17-year-old.
  (d)   the search shall be conducted with proper regard to the sensitivity and vulnerability of the detainee in these circumstances and every reasonable effort shall be made to secure the detainee's co-operation and minimise embarrassment. Detainees who are searched shall not normally be required to remove all their clothes at the same time, e.g. a person should be allowed to remove clothing above the waist and redress before removing further clothing;

(e) if necessary to assist the search, the detainee may be required to hold their arms in the air or to stand with their legs apart and bend forward so a visual examination may be made of the genital and anal areas provided no physical contact is made with any body orifice;

(f) if articles are found, the detainee shall be asked to hand them over. If articles are found within any body orifice other than the mouth, and the detainee refuses to hand them over, their removal would constitute an intimate search, which must be carried out as in Part A;

(g) a strip search shall be conducted as quickly as possible, and the detainee allowed to dress as soon as the procedure is complete.

(b) Documentation

12. A record shall be made on the custody record of a strip search including the reason it was considered necessary, those present and any result.

Notes for Guidance

A1 Before authorising any intimate search, the authorising officer must make every reasonable effort to persuade the detainee to hand the article over without a search. If the detainee agrees, a registered medical practitioner or registered nurse should whenever possible be asked to assess the risks involved and, if necessary, attend to assist the detainee.

A2 If the detainee does not agree to hand the article over without a search, the authorising officer must carefully review all the relevant factors before authorising an intimate search. In particular, the officer must consider whether the grounds for believing an article may be concealed are reasonable.

A3 If authority is given for a search under *paragraph 2(a)(i)*, a registered medical practitioner or registered nurse shall be consulted whenever possible. The presumption should be that the search will be conducted by the registered medical practitioner or registered nurse and the authorising officer must make every reasonable effort to persuade the detainee to allow the medical practitioner or nurse to conduct the search.

A4 A constable should only be authorised to carry out a search as a last resort and when all other approaches have failed. In these circumstances, the authorising officer must be satisfied the detainee might use the article for one or more of the purposes in *paragraph 2(a)(i)* and the physical injury likely to be caused is sufficiently severe to justify authorising a constable to carry out the search.

A5 If an officer has any doubts whether to authorise an intimate search by a constable, the officer should seek advice from an officer of superintendent rank or above.

A6 In warning a detainee who is asked to consent to an intimate drug offence search, as in *paragraph 2B*, the following form of words may be used:

> *'You do not have to allow yourself to be searched, but I must warn you that if you refuse without good cause, your refusal may harm your case if it comes to trial.'*

Where the use of the Welsh Language is appropriate, the following form of words may be used:

> *'Nid oes rhaid i chi roi caniatâd i gael eich archwilio, ond mae'n rhaid i mi eich rhybuddio os gwrthodwch heb reswm da, y gallai eich penderfyniad i wrthod wneud niwed i'ch achos pe bai'n dod gerbron llys.'*

ANNEX B

DELAY IN NOTIFYING ARREST OR ALLOWING ACCESS TO LEGAL ADVICE

A Persons detained under PACE

1. The exercise of the rights in *Section 5* or *Section 6,* or both, may be delayed if the person is in police detention, as in PACE, section 118(2), in connection with an indictable offence, has not yet been charged with an offence and an officer of superintendent rank or above, or inspector rank or above only for the rights in *Section 5*, has reasonable grounds for believing their exercise will:

(i) lead to:
  • interference with, or harm to, evidence connected with an indictable offence; or
  • interference with, or physical harm to, other people; or
(ii) lead to alerting other people suspected of having committed an indictable offence but not yet arrested for it; or
(iii) hinder the recovery of property obtained in consequence of the commission of such an offence.

2. These rights may also be delayed if the officer has reasonable grounds to believe that:

(i) the person detained for an indictable offence has benefited from their criminal conduct (decided in accordance with Part 2 of the Proceeds of Crime Act 2002); and
(ii) the recovery of the value of the property constituting that benefit will be hindered by the exercise of either right.

3.   Authority to delay a detainee's right to consult privately with a solicitor may be given only if the authorising officer has reasonable grounds to believe the solicitor the detainee wants to consult will, inadvertently or otherwise, pass on a message from the detainee or act in some other way which will have any of the consequences specified under *paragraphs 1* or *2*. In these circumstances, the detainee must be allowed to choose another solicitor. See *Note B3*.

4.   If the detainee wishes to see a solicitor, access to that solicitor may not be delayed on the grounds they might advise the detainee not to answer questions or the solicitor was initially asked to attend the police station by someone else. In the latter case, the detainee must be told the solicitor has come to the police station at another person's request, and must be asked to sign the custody record to signify whether they want to see the solicitor.

5.   The fact the grounds for delaying notification of arrest may be satisfied does not automatically mean the grounds for delaying access to legal advice will also be satisfied.

6.   These rights may be delayed only for as long as grounds exist and in no case beyond 36 hours after the relevant time as in PACE, section 41. If the grounds cease to apply within this time, the detainee must, as soon as practicable, be asked if they want to exercise either right, the custody record must be noted accordingly, and action taken in accordance with the relevant section of the Code.

7.   A detained person must be permitted to consult a solicitor for a reasonable time before any court hearing.

B *Not used*

C Documentation

13.   The grounds for action under this Annex shall be recorded and the detainee informed of them as soon as practicable.

14.   Any reply given by a detainee under *paragraphs 6*...must be recorded and the detainee asked to endorse the record in relation to whether they want to receive legal advice at this point.

D Cautions and special warnings

15.   When a suspect detained at a police station is interviewed during any period for which access to legal advice has been delayed under this Annex, the court or jury may not draw adverse inferences from their silence.

Notes for Guidance

B1   Even if Annex B applies in the case of a juvenile, or a person who is mentally disordered or otherwise mentally vulnerable, action to inform the appropriate adult and the person responsible for a juvenile's welfare, if that is a different person, must nevertheless be taken as in *paragraph 3.13* and *3.15*.
       Note: *Paragraph 1.5A* of this Code extends this Note to 17-year-old detainees.

B2   In the case of Commonwealth citizens and foreign nationals, see *Note 7A*.

B3   A decision to delay access to a specific solicitor is likely to be a rare occurrence and only when it can be shown the suspect is capable of misleading that particular solicitor and there is more than a substantial risk that the suspect will succeed in causing information to be conveyed which will lead to one or more of the specified consequences.

Annex C

Restriction on Drawing Adverse Inferences from Silence and Terms of the Caution when the Restriction Applies

(a) The restriction on drawing adverse inferences from silence

1.   The Criminal Justice and Public Order Act 1994, sections 34, 36 and 37 as amended by the Youth Justice and Criminal Evidence Act 1999, section 58 describe the conditions under which adverse inferences may be drawn from a person's failure or refusal to say anything about their involvement in the offence when interviewed, after being charged or informed they may be prosecuted. These provisions are subject to an overriding restriction on the ability of a court or jury to draw adverse inferences from a person's silence. This restriction applies:
       (a) to any detainee at a police station, see *Note 10C* who, before being interviewed, see *section 11* or being charged or informed they may be prosecuted, see *section 16*, has:
             (i)   asked for legal advice, see *section 6, paragraph 6.1*;
             (ii)   not been allowed an opportunity to consult a solicitor, including the duty solicitor, as in this Code; and
             (iii) not changed their mind about wanting legal advice, see *section 6, paragraph 6.6(d)*.

Note the condition in (ii) will:
- – apply when a detainee who has asked for legal advice is interviewed before speaking to a solicitor as in *section 6, paragraph 6.6(a) or (b)*;
- – not apply if the detained person declines to ask for the duty solicitor, see *section 6, paragraphs 6.6(c) and (d)*.

(b) to any person charged with, or informed they may be prosecuted for, an offence who:
- (i) has had brought to their notice a written statement made by another person or the content of an interview with another person which relates to that offence, see *section 16, paragraph 16.4*;
- (ii) is interviewed about that offence, see *section 16, paragraph 16.5*; or
- (iii) makes a written statement about that offence, see *Annex D paragraphs 4 and 9*.

(b) Terms of the caution when the restriction applies

2.   When a requirement to caution arises at a time when the restriction on drawing adverse inferences from silence applies, the caution shall be:

> '*You do not have to say anything, but anything you do say may be given in evidence.*'

Where the use of the Welsh Language is appropriate, the caution may be used directly in Welsh in the following terms:

> '*Does dim rhaid i chi ddweud dim byd, ond gall unrhyw beth yr ydych chi'n ei ddweud gael ei roi fel tystiolaeth.*'

3.   Whenever the restriction either begins to apply or ceases to apply after a caution has already been given, the person shall be re-cautioned in the appropriate terms. The changed position on drawing inferences and that the previous caution no longer applies shall also be explained to the detainee in ordinary language. See *Note C2*.

Notes for Guidance

C1   The restriction on drawing inferences from silence does not apply to a person who has not been detained and who therefore cannot be prevented from seeking legal advice if they want to, see *paragraphs 10.2 and 3.21*.

C2   The following is suggested as a framework to help explain changes in the position on drawing adverse inferences if the restriction on drawing adverse inferences from silence:
- (a) begins to apply:
  > 'The caution you were previously given no longer applies. This is because after that caution:
  - (i) you asked to speak to a solicitor but have not yet been allowed an opportunity to speak to a solicitor. See *paragraph 1(a)*; or
  - (ii) you have been charged with/informed you may be prosecuted. See *paragraph 1(b)*.
    This means that from now on, adverse inferences cannot be drawn at court and your defence will not be harmed just because you choose to say nothing. Please listen carefully to the caution I am about to give you because it will apply from now on. You will see that it does not say anything about your defence being harmed.'
- (b) ceases to apply before or at the time the person is charged or informed they may be prosecuted, see *paragraph 1(a)*;
  > 'The caution you were previously given no longer applies. This is because after that caution you have been allowed an opportunity to speak to a solicitor. Please listen carefully to the caution I am about to give you because it will apply from now on. It explains how your defence at court may be affected if you choose to say nothing.'

ANNEX D

WRITTEN STATEMENTS UNDER CAUTION

(a) Written by a person under caution

1.   A person shall always be invited to write down what they want to say.

2.   A person who has not been charged with, or informed they may be prosecuted for, any offence to which the statement they want to write relates, shall:
- (a) unless the statement is made at a time when the restriction on drawing adverse inferences from silence applies, see Annex C, be asked to write out and sign the following before writing what they want to say:
  > '*I make this statement of my own free will. I understand that I do not have to say anything but that it may harm my defence if I do not mention when questioned something which I later rely on in court. This statement may be given in evidence.*';

(b) if the statement is made at a time when the restriction on drawing adverse inferences from silence applies, be asked to write out and sign the following before writing what they want to say;

> '*I make this statement of my own free will. I understand that I do not have to say anything. This statement may be given in evidence.*'

3. When a person, on the occasion of being charged with or informed they may be prosecuted for any offence, asks to make a statement which relates to any such offence and wants to write it they shall:

(a) unless the restriction on drawing adverse inferences from silence, see *Annex C*, applied when they were so charged or informed they may be prosecuted, be asked to write out and sign the following before writing what they want to say:

> '*I make this statement of my own free will. I understand that I do not have to say anything but that it may harm my defence if I do not mention when questioned something which I later rely on in court. This statement may be given in evidence.*';

(b) if the restriction on drawing adverse inferences from silence applied when they were so charged or informed they may be prosecuted, be asked to write out and sign the following before writing what they want to say:

> '*I make this statement of my own free will. I understand that I do not have to say anything. This statement may be given in evidence.*'

4. When a person who has already been charged with or informed they may be prosecuted for any offence asks to make a statement which relates to any such offence and wants to write it, they shall be asked to write out and sign the following before writing what they want to say:

> '*I make this statement of my own free will. I understand that I do not have to say anything. This statement may be given in evidence.*';

5. Any person writing their own statement shall be allowed to do so without any prompting except a police officer or other police staff may indicate to them which matters are material or question any ambiguity in the statement.

(b) Written by a police officer or other police staff

6. If a person says they would like someone to write the statement for them, a police officer, or other police staff shall write the statement.

7. If the person has not been charged with, or informed they may be prosecuted for, any offence to which the statement they want to make relates they shall, before starting, be asked to sign, or make their mark, to the following:

(a) unless the statement is made at a time when the restriction on drawing adverse inferences from silence applies, see *Annex C*:

> '*I,..........................., wish to make a statement. I want someone to write down what I say. I understand that I do not have to say anything but that it may harm my defence if I do not mention when questioned something which I later rely on in court. This statement may be given in evidence.*';

(b) if the statement is made at a time when the restriction on drawing adverse inferences from silence applies:

> '*I,..........................., wish to make a statement. I want someone to write down what I say. I understand that I do not have to say anything. This statement may be given in evidence.*'

8. If, on the occasion of being charged with or informed they may be prosecuted for any offence, the person asks to make a statement which relates to any such offence they shall before starting be asked to sign, or make their mark to, the following:

(a) unless the restriction on drawing adverse inferences from silence applied, see *Annex C*, when they were so charged or informed they may be prosecuted:

> '*I,..........................., wish to make a statement. I want someone to write down what I say. I understand that I do not have to say anything but that it may harm my defence if I do not mention when questioned something which I later rely on in court. This statement may be given in evidence.*';

(b) if the restriction on drawing adverse inferences from silence applied when they were so charged or informed they may be prosecuted:

> '*I,..........................., wish to make a statement. I want someone to write down what I say. I understand that I do not have to say anything. This statement may be given in evidence.*'

9. If, having already been charged with or informed they may be prosecuted for any offence, a person asks to make a statement which relates to any such offence they shall before starting, be asked to sign, or make their mark to:

> 'I,............................, wish to make a statement. I want someone to write down what I say. I understand that I do not have to say anything. This statement may be given in evidence.'

10. The person writing the statement must take down the exact words spoken by the person making it and must not edit or paraphrase it. Any questions that are necessary, e.g. to make it more intelligible, and the answers given must be recorded at the same time on the statement form.

11. When the writing of a statement is finished the person making it shall be asked to read it and to make any corrections, alterations or additions they want. When they have finished reading they shall be asked to write and sign or make their mark on the following certificate at the end of the statement:

> 'I have read the above statement, and I have been able to correct, alter or add anything I wish. This statement is true. I have made it of my own free will.'

12. If the person making the statement cannot read, or refuses to read it, or to write the above mentioned certificate at the end of it or to sign it, the person taking the statement shall read it to them and ask them if they would like to correct, alter or add anything and to put their signature or make their mark at the end. The person taking the statement shall certify on the statement itself what has occurred.

Annex E

Summary of Provisions Relating to Mentally Disordered and Otherwise Mentally Vulnerable People

1. If an officer has any suspicion, or is told in good faith, that a person of any age may be mentally disordered or otherwise mentally vulnerable, or mentally incapable of understanding the significance of questions or their replies that person shall be treated as mentally disordered or otherwise mentally vulnerable for the purposes of this Code. See *paragraph 1.4* and *Note E4*.

2. In the case of a person who is mentally disordered or otherwise mentally vulnerable, 'the appropriate adult' means:
    (a) a relative, guardian or other person responsible for their care or custody;
    (b) someone experienced in dealing with mentally disordered or mentally vulnerable people but who is not a police officer or employed by the police;
    (c) failing these, some other responsible adult aged 18 or over who is not a police officer or employed by the police.
    See *paragraph 1.7(b)* and *Note 1D*.

3. If the custody officer authorises the detention of a person who is mentally vulnerable or appears to be suffering from a mental disorder, the custody officer must as soon as practicable inform the appropriate adult of the grounds for detention and the person's whereabouts, and ask the adult to come to the police station to see them. If the appropriate adult:
    • is already at the station when information is given as in *paragraphs 3.1* to *3.5* the information must be given in their presence;
    • is not at the station when the provisions of *paragraphs 3.1* to *3.5* are complied with these provisions must be complied with again in their presence once they arrive.
    See *paragraphs 3.15* to *3.17*.

4. If the appropriate adult, having been informed of the right to legal advice, considers legal advice should be taken, the provisions of *section 6* apply as if the mentally disordered or otherwise mentally vulnerable person had requested access to legal advice. See *paragraph 3.19* and *Note E1*.

5. The custody officer must make sure a person receives appropriate clinical attention as soon as reasonably practicable if the person appears to be suffering from a mental disorder or in urgent cases immediately call the nearest appropriate healthcare professional or an ambulance. It is not intended these provisions delay the transfer of a detainee to a place of safety under the Mental Health Act 1983, section 136 if that is applicable. If an assessment under that Act is to take place at a police station, the custody officer must consider whether an appropriate healthcare professional should be called to conduct an initial clinical check on the detainee. See *paragraphs 9.5* and *9.6*.

6. It is imperative a mentally disordered or otherwise mentally vulnerable person detained under the Mental Health Act 1983, section 136 be assessed as soon as possible. A police station should only be used as a place of safety as a last resort but if that assessment is to take place at the police station, an approved social worker and registered medical practitioner shall be called to the station as soon as possible to carry it out. Once the detainee has been assessed and suitable arrangements been made

for their treatment or care, they can no longer be detained under section 136. A detainee should be immediately discharged from detention if a registered medical practitioner having examined them, concludes they are not mentally disordered within the meaning of the Act. See *paragraph 3.16*.

7. If a mentally disordered or otherwise mentally vulnerable person is cautioned in the absence of the appropriate adult, the caution must be repeated in the appropriate adult's presence. See *paragraph 10.12*.

8. A mentally disordered or otherwise mentally vulnerable person must not be interviewed or asked to provide or sign a written statement in the absence of the appropriate adult unless the provisions of *paragraphs 11.1* or *11.18 to 11.20* apply. Questioning in these circumstances may not continue in the absence of the appropriate adult once sufficient information to avert the risk has been obtained. A record shall be made of the grounds for any decision to begin an interview in these circumstances. See *paragraphs 11.1, 11.15* and *11.18 to 11.20*.

9. If the appropriate adult is present at an interview, they shall be informed they are not expected to act simply as an observer and the purposes of their presence are to:
    - advise the interviewee;
    - observe whether or not the interview is being conducted properly and fairly;
    - facilitate communication with the interviewee.

    See *paragraph 11.17*.

10. If the detention of a mentally disordered or otherwise mentally vulnerable person is reviewed by a review officer or a superintendent, the appropriate adult must, if available at the time, be given an opportunity to make representations to the officer about the need for continuing detention. See *paragraph 15.3*.

11. If the custody officer charges a mentally disordered or otherwise mentally vulnerable person with an offence or takes such other action as is appropriate when there is sufficient evidence for a prosecution this must be carried out in the presence of the appropriate adult if they are at the police station. A copy of the written notice embodying any charge must also be given to the appropriate adult. See *paragraphs 16.1 to 16.4A*

12. An intimate or strip search of a mentally disordered or otherwise mentally vulnerable person may take place only in the presence of the appropriate adult of the same sex, unless the detainee specifically requests the presence of a particular adult of the opposite sex. A strip search may take place in the absence of an appropriate adult only in cases of urgency when there is a risk of serious harm to the detainee or others. See *Annex A, paragraphs 5* and *11(c)*.

13. Particular care must be taken when deciding whether to use any form of approved restraints on a mentally disordered or otherwise mentally vulnerable person in a locked cell. See *paragraph 8.2*.

Notes for Guidance

E1 The purpose of the provision at *paragraph 3.19* is to protect the rights of a mentally disordered or otherwise mentally vulnerable detained person who does not understand the significance of what is said to them. If the detained person wants to exercise the right to legal advice, the appropriate action should be taken and not delayed until the appropriate adult arrives. A mentally disordered or otherwise mentally vulnerable detained person should always be given an opportunity, when an appropriate adult is called to the police station, to consult privately with a solicitor in the absence of the appropriate adult if they want.

E2 Although people who are mentally disordered or otherwise mentally vulnerable are often capable of providing reliable evidence, they may, without knowing or wanting to do so, be particularly prone in certain circumstances to provide information that may be unreliable, misleading or self-incriminating. Special care should always be taken when questioning such a person, and the appropriate adult should be involved if there is any doubt about a person's mental state or capacity. Because of the risk of unreliable evidence, it is important to obtain corroboration of any facts admitted whenever possible.

E3 Because of the risks referred to in *Note E2*, which the presence of the appropriate adult is intended to minimise, officers of superintendent rank or above should exercise their discretion to authorise the commencement of an interview in the appropriate adult's absence only in exceptional cases, if it is necessary to avert an immediate risk of serious harm. See *paragraphs 11.1, 11.18 to 11.20*.

E4 There is no requirement for an appropriate adult to be present if a person is detained under section 136 of the Mental Health Act 1983 for assessment.

ANNEX F
Not Used

ANNEX G

FITNESS TO BE INTERVIEWED

1. This Annex contains general guidance to help police officers and healthcare professionals assess whether a detainee might be at risk in an interview.

2. A detainee may be at risk in a interview if it is considered that:
    (a) conducting the interview could significantly harm the detainee's physical or mental state;
    (b) anything the detainee says in the interview about their involvement or suspected involvement in the offence about which they are being interviewed might be considered unreliable in subsequent court proceedings because of their physical or mental state.
3. In assessing whether the detainee should be interviewed, the following must be considered:
    (a) how the detainee's physical or mental state might affect their ability to understand the nature and purpose of the interview, to comprehend what is being asked and to appreciate the significance of any answers given and make rational decisions about whether they want to say anything;
    (b) the extent to which the detainee's replies may be affected by their physical or mental condition rather than representing a rational and accurate explanation of their involvement in the offence;
    (c) how the nature of the interview, which could include particularly probing questions, might affect the detainee.
4. It is essential healthcare professionals who are consulted consider the functional ability of the detainee rather than simply relying on a medical diagnosis, e.g. it is possible for a person with severe mental illness to be fit for interview.
5. Healthcare professionals should advise on the need for an appropriate adult to be present, whether reassessment of the person's fitness for interview may be necessary if the interview lasts beyond a specified time, and whether a further specialist opinion may be required.
6. When healthcare professionals identify risks they should be asked to quantify the risks. They should inform the custody officer:
    • whether the person's condition:
        – is likely to improve;
        – will require or be amenable to treatment; and
    • indicate how long it may take for such improvement to take effect.
7. The role of the healthcare professional is to consider the risks and advise the custody officer of the outcome of that consideration. The healthcare professional's determination and any advice or recommendations should be made in writing and form part of the custody record.
8. Once the healthcare professional has provided that information, it is a matter for the custody officer to decide whether or not to allow the interview to go ahead and if the interview is to proceed, to determine what safeguards are needed. Nothing prevents safeguards being provided in addition to those required under the Code. An example might be to have an appropriate healthcare professional present during the interview, in addition to an appropriate adult, in order constantly to monitor the person's condition and how it is being affected by the interview.

Annex H
Detained Person: Observation List

[Omitted.]

Annex I

Not used

Annex J

Not used

Annex K

X-Rays and Ultrasound Scans

(a) Action

1. PACE, section 55A allows a person who has been arrested and is in police detention to have an X-ray taken of them or an ultrasound scan to be carried out on them (or both) if:
    (a) authorised by an officer of inspector rank or above who has reasonable grounds for believing that the detainee:
        (i) may have swallowed a Class A drug; and
        (ii) was in possession of that Class A drug with the intention of supplying it to another or to export; and
    (b) the detainee's appropriate consent has been given in writing.

2.   Before an x-ray is taken or an ultrasound scan carried out, a police officer or designated detention officer must tell the detainee:-
     (a)   that the authority has been given; and
     (b)   the grounds for giving the authorisation.
     Note: *Paragraph 1.5A* in this Code requires someone to fulfil the role of the appropriate adult to be present when a 17-year-old is told about the authority and grounds for an x-ray and ultra sound scan.

3.   Before a detainee is asked to give appropriate consent to an x-ray or an ultrasound scan, they must be warned that if they refuse without good cause their refusal may harm their case if it comes to trial, see *Notes K1* and *K2*. This warning may be given by a police officer or member of police staff. In the case of juveniles, mentally vulnerable or mentally disordered suspects the seeking and giving of consent must take place in the presence of the appropriate adult. A juvenile's consent is only valid if their parent's or guardian's consent is also obtained unless the juvenile is under 14, when their parent's or guardian's consent is sufficient in its own right. A detainee who is not legally represented must be reminded of their entitlement to have free legal advice, see Code C, *paragraph 6.5*, and the reminder noted in the custody record.
     Note: *Paragraph 1.5A* in this Code requires someone to fulfil the role of the appropriate adult to be present when the warning is given to a 17-year-old and their consent to an x-ray or ultra sound scan is sought and given but the consent of their parent or guardian is not required.

4.   An x-ray may be taken, or an ultrasound scan may be carried out, only by a registered medical practitioner or registered nurse, and only at a hospital, surgery or other medical premises.

(b)   Documentation

5.   The following shall be recorded as soon as practicable in the detainee's custody record:
     (a)   the authorisation to take the x-ray or carry out the ultrasound scan (or both);
     (b)   the grounds for giving the authorisation;
     (c)   the giving of the warning required by *paragraph 3*; and
     (d)   the fact that the appropriate consent was given or (as the case may be) refused, and if refused, the reason given for the refusal (if any); and
     (e)   if an x-ray is taken or an ultrasound scan carried out:
           • where it was taken or carried out;
           • who took it or carried it out;
           • who was present;
           • the result.

6.   *Not used.*

Notes for Guidance

K1   If authority is given for an x-ray to be taken or an ultrasound scan to be carried out (or both), consideration should be given to asking a registered medical practitioner or registered nurse to explain to the detainee what is involved and to allay any concerns the detainee might have about the effect which taking an x-ray or carrying out an ultrasound scan might have on them. If appropriate consent is not given, evidence of the explanation may, if the case comes to trial, be relevant to determining whether the detainee had a good cause for refusing.

K2   In warning a detainee who is asked to consent to an X-ray being taken or an ultrasound scan being carried out (or both), as in *paragraph 3*, the following form of words may be used:

 '*You do not have to allow an x-ray of you to be taken or an ultrasound scan to be carried out on you, but I must warn you that if you refuse without good cause, your refusal may harm your case if it comes to trial.*'

Where the use of the Welsh Language is appropriate, the following form of words may be provided in Welsh:

 '*Does dim rhaid i chi ganiatáu cymryd sgan uwchsain neu belydr-x (neu'r ddau) arnoch, ond mae'n rhaid i mi eich rhybuddio os byddwch chi'n gwrthod gwneud hynny heb reswm da, fe allai hynny niweidio eich achos pe bai'n dod gerbron llys.*'

Annex L

Establishing Gender of Persons for the Purpose of Searching

1.   Certain provisions of this and other PACE Codes explicitly state that searches and other procedures may only be carried out by, or in the presence of, persons of the same sex as the person subject to the search or other procedure. See *Note L1*.

2. All searches and procedures must be carried out with courtesy, consideration and respect for the person concerned. Police officers should show particular sensitivity when dealing with transgender individuals (including transsexual persons) and transvestite persons (see *Notes L2, L3* and *L4*).

(a) Consideration

3. In law, the gender (and accordingly the sex) of an individual is their gender as registered at birth unless they have been issued with a Gender Recognition Certificate (GRC) under the Gender Recognition Act 2004 (GRA), in which case the person's gender is their acquired gender. This means that if the acquired gender is the male gender, the person's sex becomes that of a man and, if it is the female gender, the person's sex becomes that of a woman and they must be treated as their acquired gender.

4. When establishing whether the person concerned should be treated as being male or female for the purposes of these searches and procedures, the following approach which is designed to minimise embarrassment and secure the person's co-operation should be followed:
    (a)   The person must not be asked whether they have a GRC (see *paragraph 8*);
    (b)   If there is no doubt as to whether the person concerned should be treated as being male or female, they should be dealt with as being of that sex.
    (c)   If at any time (including during the search or carrying out the procedure) there is doubt as to whether the person should be treated, or continue to be treated, as being male or female:
        (i)   the person should be asked what gender they consider themselves to be. If they express a preference to be dealt with as a particular gender, they should be asked to indicate and confirm their preference by signing the custody record or, if a custody record has not been opened, the search record or the officer's notebook. Subject to (ii) below, the person should be treated according to their preference;
        (ii) if there are grounds to doubt that the preference in (i) accurately reflects the person's predominant lifestyle, for example, if they ask to be treated as a woman but documents and other information make it clear that they live predominantly as a man, or vice versa, they should be treated according to what appears to be their predominant lifestyle and not their stated preference;
        (iii) If the person is unwilling to express a preference as in (i) above, efforts should be made to determine their predominant lifestyle and they should be treated as such. For example, if they appear to live predominantly as a woman, they should be treated as being female; or
        (iv) if none of the above apply, the person should be dealt with according to what reasonably appears to have been their sex as registered at birth.

5. Once a decision has been made about which gender an individual is to be treated as, each officer responsible for the search or procedure should where possible be advised before the search or procedure starts of any doubts as to the person's gender and the person informed that the doubts have been disclosed. This is important so as to maintain the dignity of the person and any officers concerned.

(b) Documentation

6. The person's gender as established under *paragraph 4(c)(i)* to *(iv)* above must be recorded in the person's custody record or, if a custody record has not been opened, on the search record or in the officer's notebook.

7. Where the person elects which gender they consider themselves to be under *paragraph [4(c)(i)]* but, following [*4(c)(ii)*] is not treated in accordance with their preference, the reason must be recorded in the search record, in the officer's notebook or, if applicable, in the person's custody record.

(c) Disclosure of information

8. Section 22 of the GRA defines any information relating to a person's application for a GRC or to a successful applicant's gender before it became their acquired gender as 'protected information'. Nothing in this Annex is to be read as authorising or permitting any police officer or any police staff who has acquired such information when acting in their official capacity to disclose that information to any other person in contravention of the GRA. Disclosure includes making a record of 'protected information' which is read by others.

Notes for Guidance

L1   Provisions to which *paragraph 1* applies include:
    • In Code C; *paragraph 4.1* and *Annex A paragraphs 5, 6,* and *11* (searches, strip and intimate searches of detainees under sections 54 and 55 of PACE);
    • In Code A; *paragraphs 2.8* and *3.6* and *Note 4*;

- In Code D; *paragraph 5.5* and *Note 5F* (searches, examinations and photographing of detainees under section 54A of PACE) and paragraph 6.9 (taking samples);
- In Code H; *paragraph 4.1* and *Annex A*; *paragraphs 6, 7* and *12* (searches, strip and intimate searches under sections 54 and 55 of PACE of persons arrested under section 41 of the Terrorism Act 2000).

L2   While there is no agreed definition of transgender (or trans), it is generally used as an umbrella term to describe people whose gender identity (self-identification as being a woman, man, neither or both) differs from the sex they were registered as at birth. The term includes, but is not limited to, transsexual people.

L3   Transsexual means a person who is proposing to undergo, is undergoing or has undergone a process (or part of a process) for the purpose of gender reassignment, which is a protected characteristic under the Equality Act 2010 (see *paragraph 1.0*), by changing physiological or other attributes of their sex. This includes aspects of gender such as dress and title. It would apply to a woman making the transition to being a man and a man making the transition to being a woman, as well as to a person who has only just started out on the process of gender reassignment and to a person who has completed the process. Both would share the characteristic of gender reassignment with each having the characteristics of one sex, but with certain characteristics of the other sex.

L4   Transvestite means a person of one gender who dresses in the clothes of a person of the opposite gender. However, a transvestite does not live permanently in the gender opposite to their birth sex.

L5   Chief officers are responsible for providing corresponding operational guidance and instructions for the deployment of transgender officers and staff under their direction and control to duties which involve carrying out, or being present at, any of the searches and procedures described in *paragraph 1*. The guidance and instructions must comply with the Equality Act 2010 and should therefore complement the approach in this Annex.

Annex M

Documents and Records to te Translated

1.   For the purposes of Directive 2010/64/EU of the European Parliament and of the Council of 20 October 2010 and this Code, essential documents comprise records required to be made in accordance with this Code which are relevant to decisions to deprive a person of their liberty, to any charge and to any record considered necessary to enable a detainee to defend themselves in criminal proceedings and to safeguard the fairness of the proceedings. Passages of essential documents which are not relevant need not be translated. See *Note M1*

2.   The table below lists the documents considered essential for the purposes of this Code and when (subject to *paragraphs 3* to *7*) written translations must be created and provided.

Table of essential documents:

	Essential Documents for the Purposes of this Code	When Translation to be Created	When Translation to be Provided
(i)	The grounds for each of the following authorisations to keep the person in custody as they are described and referred to in the custody record: (a) Authorisation for detention before and after charge given by the custody officer and by the review officer, see Code C *paragraphs 3.4* and *15.16(a)*. (b) Authorisation to extend detention without charge beyond 24 hours given by a superintendent, see Code C *paragraph 15.16(b)*. (c) A warrant of further detention issued by a magistrates' court and any extension(s) of the warrant, see Code C *paragraph 15.16(c)*. (d) An authority to detain in accordance with the directions in a warrant of arrest issued in connection with criminal proceedings including the court issuing the warrant.	As soon as practicable after each authorisation has been recorded in the custody record.	As soon as practicable after the translation has been created, whilst the person is detained or after they have been released (see *Note M3*).

	Essential Documents for the Purposes of this Code	When Translation to be Created	When Translation to be Provided
(ii)	Written notice showing particulars of the offence charged required by Code C *paragraph 16.3* or the offence for which the suspect has been told they may be prosecuted.	As soon as practicable after the person has been charged or reported.	
(iii)	Written interview records: Code C11.11, 13.3, 13.4 & Code E4.7 Written statement under caution: Code C *Annex D*.	To be created contemporaneously by the interpreter for the person to check and sign.	As soon as practicable after the person has been charged or told they may be prosecuted.

3. The custody officer may authorise an oral translation or oral summary of documents (i) to (ii) in the table (but not (iii)) to be provided (through an interpreter) instead of a written translation. Such an oral translation or summary may only be provided if it would not prejudice the fairness of the proceedings by in any way adversely affecting or otherwise undermining or limiting the ability of the suspect in question to understand their position and to communicate effectively with police officers, interviewers, solicitors and appropriate adults with regard to their detention and the investigation of the offence in question and to defend themselves in the event of criminal proceedings. The quantity and complexity of the information in the document should always be considered and specific additional consideration given if the suspect is mentally disordered or otherwise mentally vulnerable or is a juvenile or a 17-year-old (see Code C *paragraph 1.5A*). The reason for the decision must be recorded (see *paragraph 13.11(e)*)

4. Subject to *paragraphs 5* to *7* below, a suspect may waive their right to a written translation of the essential documents described in the table but only if they do so voluntarily after receiving legal advice or having full knowledge of the consequences and give their unconditional and fully informed consent in writing (see *paragraph 9*).

5. The suspect may be asked if they wish to waive their right to a written translation and before giving their consent, they must be reminded of their right to legal advice and asked whether they wish to speak to a solicitor.

6. No police officer or police staff should do or say anything with the intention of persuading a suspect who is entitled to a written translation of an essential document to waive that right. See *Notes M2* and *M3*.

7. For the purpose of the waiver:
    (a) the consent of a person who is mentally disordered or otherwise mentally vulnerable person is only valid if the information about the circumstances under which they can waive the right and the reminder about their right to legal advice mentioned in *paragraphs 3* to *5* and their consent is given in the presence of the appropriate adult.
        Note: *Paragraph 1.5A* in Code C requires someone to fulfil the role of the appropriate adult to be present when a 17-year-old is given the information and reminder mentioned in *sub-paragraph (a)* above and gives their consent to waive their right. The consent of their parent or guardian is not required.
    (b) the consent of a juvenile is only valid if their parent's or guardian's consent is also obtained unless the juvenile is under 14, when their parent's or guardian's consent is sufficient in its own right and the information and reminder mentioned in *sub-paragraph (a)* above and their consent is also given in the presence of the appropriate adult (who may or may not be a parent or guardian).

8. The detainee, their solicitor or appropriate adult may make representations to the custody officer that a document which is not included in the table is essential and that a translation should be provided. The request may be refused if the officer is satisfied that the translation requested is not essential for the purposes described in *paragraph 1* above.

9. If the custody officer has any doubts about
    • providing an oral translation or summary of an essential document instead of a written translation (see *paragraph 3*);
    • whether the suspect fully understands the consequences of waiving their right to a written translation of an essential document (see *paragraph 4*), or
    • about refusing to provide a translation of a requested document (see *paragraph 7*),
    the officer should seek advice from an inspector or above.

Documentation

10. Action taken in accordance with this Annex shall be recorded in the detainee's custody record or interview record as appropriate (see Code C *paragraph 13.11(e)*).

Notes for Guidance

M1 It is not necessary to disclose information in any translation which is capable of undermining or otherwise adversely affecting any investigative processes, for example, by enabling the suspect to fabricate an innocent explanation or to conceal lies from the interviewer.

M2 No police officer or police staff shall indicate to any suspect, except to answer a direct question, whether the period for which they are liable to be detained or if not detained, the time taken to complete the interview, might be reduced:
   • if they do not ask for legal advice before deciding whether they wish to waive their right to a written translation of an essential document; or
   • if they decide to waive their right to a written translation of an essential document.

M3 There is no power under PACE to detain a person or to delay their release solely to create and provide a written translation of any essential document.

PACE CODE D

CODE OF PRACTICE FOR THE IDENTIFICATION OF PERSONS BY POLICE OFFICERS

Commencement—Transitional Arrangements

This code has effect in relation to any identification procedure carried out after midnight on 06 March 2011.

1 Introduction

1.1 This Code of Practice concerns the principal methods used by police to identify people in connection with the investigation of offences and the keeping of accurate and reliable criminal records. The powers and procedures in this code must be used fairly, responsibly, with respect for the people to whom they apply and without unlawful discrimination. The Equality Act 2010 makes it unlawful for police officers to discriminate against, harass or victimise any person on the grounds of the 'protected characteristics' of age, disability, gender reassignment, race, religion or belief, sex and sexual orientation, marriage and civil partnership, pregnancy and maternity when using their powers. When police forces are carrying out their functions they also have a duty to have regard to the need to eliminate unlawful discrimination, harassment and victimisation and to take steps to foster good relations.

1.2 In this code, identification by an eye-witness arises when a witness who has seen the offender committing the crime and is given an opportunity to identify a person suspected of involvement in the offence in a video identification, identification parade or similar procedure. These eye-witness identification procedures (see Part A of section 3 below) are designed to:
   • test the witness' ability to identify the suspect as the person they saw on a previous occasion
   • provide safeguards against mistaken identification.
   While this Code concentrates on visual identification procedures, it does not preclude the police making use of aural identification procedures such as a 'voice identification parade', where they judge that appropriate.

1.2A In this code, separate provisions in Part B of section 3 below apply when any person, including a police officer, is asked if they recognise anyone they see in an image as being someone they know and to test their claim that they recognise that person as someone who is known to them. Except where stated, these separate provisions are not subject to the eye-witnesses identification procedures described in paragraph 1.2.

1.3 Identification by fingerprints applies when a person's fingerprints are taken to:
   • compare with fingerprints found at the scene of a crime
   • check and prove convictions
   • help to ascertain a person's identity.

1.3A Identification using footwear impressions applies when a person's footwear impressions are taken to compare with impressions found at the scene of a crime.

1.4   Identification by body samples and impressions includes taking samples such as blood or hair to generate a DNA profile for comparison with material obtained from the scene of a crime, or a victim.

1.5   Taking photographs of arrested people applies to recording and checking identity and locating and tracing persons who:
- are wanted for offences
- fail to answer their bail.

1.6   Another method of identification involves searching and examining detained suspects to find, e.g., marks such as tattoos or scars which may help establish their identity or whether they have been involved in committing an offence.

1.7   The provisions of the Police and Criminal Evidence Act 1984 (PACE) and this Code are designed to make sure fingerprints, samples, impressions and photographs are taken, used and retained, and identification procedures carried out, only when justified and necessary for preventing, detecting or investigating crime. If these provisions are not observed, the application of the relevant procedures in particular cases may be open to question.

2 General

2.1   This Code must be readily available at all police stations for consultation by:
- police officers and police staff
- detained persons
- members of the public

2.2   The provisions of this Code:
- include the Annexes
- do not include the Notes for guidance.

2.3   Code C, paragraph 1.4, regarding a person who may be mentally disordered or otherwise mentally vulnerable and the Notes for guidance applicable to those provisions apply to this Code.

2.4   Code C, paragraph 1.5, regarding a person who appears to be under the age of 17 applies to this Code.

2.5   Code C, paragraph 1.6, regarding a person who appears to be blind, seriously visually impaired, deaf, unable to read or speak or has difficulty communicating orally because of a speech impediment applies to this Code.

2.6   In this Code:
- 'appropriate adult' means the same as in Code C, paragraph 1.7
- 'solicitor' means the same as in Code C, paragraph 6.12

and the *Notes for guidance* applicable to those provisions apply to this Code.
- where a search or other procedure under this code may only be carried out or observed by a person of the same sex as the person to whom the search or procedure applies, the gender of the detainee and other persons present should be established and recorded in line with Annex F of Code A.

2.7   References to custody officers include those performing the functions of custody officer, see paragraph 1.9 of Code C.

2.8   When a record of any action requiring the authority of an officer of a specified rank is made under this Code, subject to paragraph 2.18, the officer's name and rank must be recorded.

2.9   When this Code requires the prior authority or agreement of an officer of at least inspector or superintendent rank, that authority may be given by a sergeant or chief inspector who has been authorised to perform the functions of the higher rank under PACE, section 107.

2.10 Subject to paragraph 2.18, all records must be timed and signed by the maker.

2.11 Records must be made in the custody record, unless otherwise specified. References to 'pocket book' include any official report book issued to police officers or police staff.

2.12 If any procedure in this Code requires a person's consent, the consent of a:
- mentally disordered or otherwise mentally vulnerable person is only valid if given in the presence of the appropriate adult
- juvenile is only valid if their parent's or guardian's consent is also obtained unless the juvenile is under 14, when their parent's or guardian's consent is sufficient in its own right. If the only obstacle to an identification procedure in section 3 is that a juvenile's parent or guardian refuses consent or reasonable efforts to obtain it have failed, the identification officer may apply the provisions of paragraph 3.21. See Note 2A

2.13 If a person is blind, seriously visually impaired or unable to read, the custody officer or identification officer shall make sure their solicitor, relative, appropriate adult or some other person likely to take an interest in them and not involved in the investigation is available to help check any documentation. When this Code requires written consent or signing, the person assisting may be asked to sign instead, if the detainee prefers. This paragraph does not require an appropriate adult to be called solely to assist in checking and signing documentation for a person who is not a juvenile, or mentally disordered or otherwise mentally vulnerable (see Note 2B and Code C paragraph 3.15).

2.14 If any procedure in this Code requires information to be given to or sought from a suspect, it must be given or sought in the appropriate adult's presence if the suspect is mentally disordered, otherwise mentally vulnerable or a juvenile. If the appropriate adult is not present when the information is first given or sought, the procedure must be repeated in the presence of the appropriate adult when they arrive. If the suspect appears deaf or there is doubt about their hearing or speaking ability or ability to understand English, and effective communication cannot be established, the information must be given or sought through an interpreter.

2.15 Any procedure in this Code involving the participation of a suspect who is mentally disordered, otherwise mentally vulnerable or a juvenile must take place in the presence of the appropriate adult. See Code C paragraph 1.4.

2.15A Any procedure in this Code involving the participation of a witness who is or appears to be mentally disordered, otherwise mentally vulnerable or a juvenile should take place in the presence of a pre-trial support person unless the witness states that they do not want a support person to be present. A support person must not be allowed to prompt any identification of a suspect by a witness. See Note 2AB.

2.16 References to:
- 'taking a photograph', include the use of any process to produce a single, still or moving, visual image
- 'photographing a person', should be construed accordingly
- 'photographs', 'films', 'negatives' and 'copies' include relevant visual images recorded, stored, or reproduced through any medium
- 'destruction' includes the deletion of computer data relating to such images or making access to that data impossible

2.17 Except as described, nothing in this Code affects the powers and procedures:
(i) for requiring and taking samples of breath, blood and urine in relation to driving offences, etc, when under the influence of drink, drugs or excess alcohol under the:
- Road Traffic Act 1988, sections 4 to 11
- Road Traffic Offenders Act 1988, sections 15 and 16
- Transport and Works Act 1992, sections 26 to 38;
(ii) under the Immigration Act 1971, Schedule 2, paragraph 18, for taking photographs and fingerprints from persons detained under that Act, Schedule 2, paragraph 16 (Administrative Controls as to Control on Entry etc.); for taking fingerprints in accordance with the Immigration and Asylum Act 1999; sections 141 and 142(3), or other methods for collecting information about a person's external physical characteristics provided for by regulations made under that Act, section 144;
(iii) under the Terrorism Act 2000, Schedule 8, for taking photographs, fingerprints, skin impressions, body samples or impressions from people:
- arrested under that Act, section 41,
- detained for the purposes of examination under that Act, Schedule 7, and to whom the Code of Practice issued under that Act, Schedule 14, paragraph 6, applies ('the terrorism provisions') See Note 2C;
(iv) for taking photographs, fingerprints, skin impressions, body samples or impressions from people who have been:
- arrested on warrants issued in Scotland, by officers exercising powers under the Criminal Justice and Public Order Act 1994, section 136(2)
- arrested or detained without warrant by officers from a police force in Scotland exercising their powers of arrest or detention under the Criminal Justice and Public Order Act 1994, section 137(2), (Cross Border powers of arrest etc.).

Note: In these cases, police powers and duties and the person's rights and entitlements whilst at a police station in England and Wales are the same as if the person had been arrested in Scotland by a Scottish police officer.

2.18 Nothing in this Code requires the identity of officers or police staff to be recorded or disclosed:
(a) in the case of enquiries linked to the investigation of terrorism;
(b) if the officers or police staff reasonably believe recording or disclosing their names might put them in danger.

In these cases, they shall use warrant or other identification numbers and the name of their police station. See Note 2D

2.19 In this Code:
  (a) 'designated person' means a person other than a police officer, designated under the Police Reform Act 2002, Part 4, who has specified powers and duties of police officers conferred or imposed on them;
  (b) any reference to a police officer includes a designated person acting in the exercise or performance of the powers and duties conferred or imposed on them by their designation.

2.20 If a power conferred on a designated person:
  (a) allows reasonable force to be used when exercised by a police officer, a designated person exercising that power has the same entitlement to use force;
  (b) includes power to use force to enter any premises, that power is not exercisable by that designated person except:
    (i)   in the company, and under the supervision, of a police officer; or
    (ii) for the purpose of:
      • saving life or limb; or
      • preventing serious damage to property.

2.21 Nothing in this Code prevents the custody officer, or other officer given custody of the detainee, from allowing police staff who are not designated persons to carry out individual procedures or tasks at the police station if the law allows. However, the officer remains responsible for making sure the procedures and tasks are carried out correctly in accordance with the Codes of Practice. Any such person must be:
  (a) a person employed by a police authority maintaining a police force and under the control and direction of the Chief Officer of that force;
  (b) employed by a person with whom a police authority has a contract for the provision of services relating to persons arrested or otherwise in custody.

2.22 Designated persons and other police staff must have regard to any relevant provisions of the Codes of Practice.

Notes for Guidance

2A For the purposes of paragraph 2.12, the consent required from a parent or guardian may, for a juvenile in the care of a local authority or voluntary organisation, be given by that authority or organisation. In the case of a juvenile, nothing in paragraph 2.12 requires the parent, guardian or representative of a local authority or voluntary organisation to be present to give their consent, unless they are acting as the appropriate adult under paragraphs 2.14 or 2.15. However, it is important that a parent or guardian not present is fully informed before being asked to consent. They must be given the same information about the procedure and the juvenile's suspected involvement in the offence as the juvenile and appropriate adult. The parent or guardian must also be allowed to speak to the juvenile and the appropriate adult if they wish. Provided the consent is fully informed and is not withdrawn, it may be obtained at any time before the procedure takes place.

2AB The Youth Justice and Criminal Evidence Act 1999 guidance 'Achieving Best Evidence in Criminal Proceedings' indicates that a pre-trial support person should accompany a vulnerable witness during any identification procedure unless the witness states that they do not want a support person to be present. It states that this support person should not be (or not be likely to be) a witness in the investigation.

2B People who are seriously visually impaired or unable to read may be unwilling to sign police documents. The alternative, i.e. their representative signing on their behalf, seeks to protect the interests of both police and suspects.

2C Photographs, fingerprints, samples and impressions may be taken from a person detained under the terrorism provisions to help determine whether they are, or have been, involved in terrorism, as well as when there are reasonable grounds for suspecting their involvement in a particular offence.

2D The purpose of paragraph 2.18(b) is to protect those involved in serious organised crime investigations or arrests of particularly violent suspects when there is reliable information that those arrested or their associates may threaten or cause harm to the officers. In cases of doubt, an officer of inspector rank or above should be consulted.

3 Identification and recognition of suspects

(A) *Identification of a suspect by an eye-witness*

3.0 This part applies when an eye-witness has seen the offender committing the crime or in any other circumstances which tend to prove or disprove the involvement of the person they saw in the crime, for example, close to the scene of the crime, immediately before or immediately after it was committed. It sets out the procedures to be used to test the ability of that eye-witness to identify a person suspected of involvement in the offence as the person they saw on the previous occasion. Except where stated, this part does not apply to the procedures described in Part B and Note 3AA.

3.1   A record shall be made of the suspect's description as first given by a potential witness. This record must:

    (a)   be made and kept in a form which enables details of that description to be accurately produced from it, in a visible and legible form, which can be given to the suspect or the suspect's solicitor in accordance with this Code; and

    (b)   unless otherwise specified, be made before the witness takes part in any identification procedures under paragraphs 3.5 to 3.10, 3.21 or 3.23.

A copy of the record shall where practicable, be given to the suspect or their solicitor before any procedures under paragraphs 3.5 to 3.10, 3.21 or 3.23 are carried out. See Note 3E

(a) Cases when the suspect's identity is not known

3.2   In cases when the suspect's identity is not known, a witness may be taken to a particular neighbourhood or place to see whether they can identify the person they saw on a previous occasion. Although the number, age, sex, race, general description and style of clothing of other people present at the location and the way in which any identification is made cannot be controlled, the principles applicable to the formal procedures under paragraphs 3.5 to 3.10 shall be followed as far as practicable. For example:

    (a)   where it is practicable to do so, a record should be made of the witness' description of the suspect, as in paragraph 3.1(a), before asking the witness to make an identification;

    (b)   care must be taken not to direct the witness' attention to any individual unless, taking into account all the circumstances, this cannot be avoided. However, this does not prevent a witness being asked to look carefully at the people around at the time or to look towards a group or in a particular direction, if this appears necessary to make sure that the witness does not overlook a possible suspect simply because the witness is looking in the opposite direction and also to enable the witness to make comparisons between any suspect and others who are in the area; See Note 3F

    (c)   where there is more than one witness, every effort should be made to keep them separate and witnesses should be taken to see whether they can identify a person independently;

    (d)   once there is sufficient information to justify the arrest of a particular individual for suspected involvement in the offence, e.g., after a witness makes a positive identification, the provisions set out from paragraph 3.4 onwards shall apply for any other witnesses in relation to that individual;

    (e)   the officer or police staff accompanying the witness must record, in their pocket book, the action taken as soon as, and in as much detail, as possible. The record should include: the date, time and place of the relevant occasion the witness claims to have previously seen the suspect; where any identification was made; how it was made and the conditions at the time (e.g., the distance the witness was from the suspect, the weather and light); if the witness's attention was drawn to the suspect; the reason for this; and anything said by the witness or the suspect about the identification or the conduct of the procedure.

3.3   A witness must not be shown photographs, computerised or artist's composite likenesses or similar likenesses or pictures (including 'E-fit' images) if the identity of the suspect is known to the police and the suspect is available to take part in a video identification, an identification parade or a group identification. If the suspect's identity is not known, the showing of such images to a witness to obtain identification evidence must be done in accordance with Annex E.

(b) Cases when the suspect is known and available

3.4   If the suspect's identity is known to the police and they are available, the identification procedures set out in paragraphs 3.5 to 3.10 may be used. References in this section to a suspect being 'known' mean there is sufficient information known to the police to justify the arrest of a particular person for suspected involvement in the offence. A suspect being 'available' means they are immediately available or will be within a reasonably short time and willing to take an effective part in at least one of the following which it is practicable to arrange:

    •   video identification;

    •   identification parade; or

    •   group identification.

Video identification

3.5   A 'video identification' is when the witness is shown moving images of a known suspect, together with similar images of others who resemble the suspect. Moving images must be used unless:

    •   the suspect is known but not available (see paragraph 3.21 of this Code); or

- in accordance with paragraph 2A of Annex A of this Code, the identification officer does not consider that replication of a physical feature can be achieved or that it is not possible to conceal the location of the feature on the image of the suspect.

The identification officer may then decide to make use of video identification but using still images.

3.6   Video identifications must be carried out in accordance with Annex A.

Identification parade

3.7   An 'identification parade' is when the witness sees the suspect in a line of others who resemble the suspect.

3.8   Identification parades must be carried out in accordance with Annex B.

Group identification

3.9   A 'group identification' is when the witness sees the suspect in an informal group of people.

3.10   Group identifications must be carried out in accordance with Annex C.

Arranging eye-witness identification procedures

3.11   Except for the provisions in paragraph 3.19, the arrangements for, and conduct of, the identification procedures in paragraphs 3.5 to 3.10 and circumstances in which an identification procedure must be held shall be the responsibility of an officer not below inspector rank who is not involved with the investigation, 'the identification officer'. Unless otherwise specified, the identification officer may allow another officer or police staff, see paragraph 2.21, to make arrangements for, and conduct, any of these identification procedures. In delegating these procedures, the identification officer must be able to supervise effectively and either intervene or be contacted for advice. No officer or any other person involved with the investigation of the case against the suspect, beyond the extent required by these procedures, may take any part in these procedures or act as the identification officer. This does not prevent the identification officer from consulting the officer in charge of the investigation to determine which procedure to use. When an identification procedure is required, in the interest of fairness to suspects and witnesses, it must be held as soon as practicable.

Circumstances in which an eye-witness identification procedure must be held

3.12   Whenever:
   (i)   an eye witness has identified a suspect or purported to have identified them prior to any identification procedure set out in paragraphs 3.5 to 3.10 having been held; or
   (ii) there is a witness available who expresses an ability to identify the suspect, or where there is a reasonable chance of the witness being able to do so, and they have not been given an opportunity to identify the suspect in any of the procedures set out in paragraphs 3.5 to 3.10, and the suspect disputes being the person the witness claims to have seen, an identification procedure shall be held unless it is not practicable or it would serve no useful purpose in proving or disproving whether the suspect was involved in committing the offence, for example:
      - where the suspect admits being at the scene of the crime and gives an account of what took place and the eye-witness does not see anything which contradicts that.
      - when it is not disputed that the suspect is already known to the witness who claims to have recognised them when seeing them commit the crime.

3.13   An eye-witness identification procedure may also be held if the officer in charge of the investigation considers it would be useful.

Selecting an eye-witness identification procedure

3.14   If, because of paragraph 3.12, an identification procedure is to be held, the suspect shall initially be offered a video identification unless:
   (a)   a video identification is not practicable; or
   (b)   an identification parade is both practicable and more suitable than a video identification; or
   (c)   paragraph 3.16 applies.

The identification officer and the officer in charge of the investigation shall consult each other to determine which option is to be offered. An identification parade may not be practicable because of factors relating to the witnesses, such as their number, state of health, availability and travelling requirements. A video identification would normally be more suitable if it could be arranged and completed sooner than an identification parade. Before an option is offered the suspect must also be reminded of their entitlement to have free legal advice, see Code C, paragraph 6.5.

3.15   A suspect who refuses the identification procedure first offered shall be asked to state their reason for refusing and may get advice from their solicitor and/or if present, their appropriate adult. The suspect, solicitor and/or appropriate adult shall be allowed to make representations about why another procedure should be used. A record should be made of the reasons for refusal and any representations made. After considering any reasons given, and representations made, the identification officer shall, if appropriate, arrange for the suspect to be offered an alternative which the officer considers suitable and practicable. If the officer decides it is not suitable and practicable to offer an alternative identification procedure, the reasons for that decision shall be recorded.

3.16 A group identification may initially be offered if the officer in charge of the investigation considers it is more suitable than a video identification or an identification parade and the identification officer considers it practicable to arrange.

Notice to suspect

3.17 Unless paragraph 3.20 applies, before a video identification, an identification parade or group identification is arranged, the following shall be explained to the suspect:
   (i)   the purposes of the video identification, identification parade or group identification;
   (ii)   their entitlement to free legal advice; see Code C, paragraph 6.5;
   (iii)   the procedures for holding it, including their right to have a solicitor or friend present;
   (iv)   that they do not have to consent to or co-operate in a video identification, identification parade or group identification;
   (v)   that if they do not consent to, and co-operate in, a video identification, identification parade or group identification, their refusal may be given in evidence in any subsequent trial and police may proceed covertly without their consent or make other arrangements to test whether a witness can identify them, see paragraph 3.21;
   (vi)   whether, for the purposes of the video identification procedure, images of them have previously been obtained, see paragraph 3.20, and if so, that they may co-operate in providing further, suitable images to be used instead;
   (vii)   if appropriate, the special arrangements for juveniles;
   (viii)   if appropriate, the special arrangements for mentally disordered or otherwise mentally vulnerable people;
   (ix)   that if they significantly alter their appearance between being offered an identification procedure and any attempt to hold an identification procedure, this may be given in evidence if the case comes to trial, and the identification officer may then consider other forms of identification, see paragraph 3.21 and Note 3C;
   (x)   that a moving image or photograph may be taken of them when they attend for any identification procedure;
   (xi)   whether, before their identity became known, the witness was shown photographs, a computerised or artist's composite likeness or similar likeness or image by the police, see Note 3B;
   (xii)   that if they change their appearance before an identification parade, it may not be practicable to arrange one on the day or subsequently and, because of the appearance change, the identification officer may consider alternative methods of identification, see Note 3C;
   (xiii)   that they or their solicitor will be provided with details of the description of the suspect as first given by any witnesses who are to attend the video identification, identification parade, group identification or confrontation, see paragraph 3.1.

3.18 This information must also be recorded in a written notice handed to the suspect. The suspect must be given a reasonable opportunity to read the notice, after which, they should be asked to sign a second copy to indicate if they are willing to co-operate with the making of a video or take part in the identification parade or group identification. The signed copy shall be retained by the identification officer.

3.19 The duties of the identification officer under paragraphs 3.17 and 3.18 may be performed by the custody officer or other officer not involved in the investigation if:
   (a) it is proposed to release the suspect in order that an identification procedure can be arranged and carried out and an inspector is not available to act as the identification officer, see paragraph 3.11, before the suspect leaves the station; or
   (b) it is proposed to keep the suspect in police detention whilst the procedure is arranged and carried out and waiting for an inspector to act as the identification officer, see paragraph 3.11, would cause unreasonable delay to the investigation.
   The officer concerned shall inform the identification officer of the action taken and give them the signed copy of the notice. See Note 3C

3.20 If the identification officer and officer in charge of the investigation suspect, on reasonable grounds that if the suspect was given the information and notice as in paragraphs 3.17 and 3.18, they would then take steps to avoid being seen by a witness in any identification procedure, the identification officer may arrange for images of the suspect suitable for use in a video identification procedure to be obtained before giving the information and notice. If suspect's images are obtained in these circumstances, the suspect may, for the purposes of a video identification procedure, co-operate in providing new images which if suitable, would be used instead, see paragraph 3.17(vi).

(c) Cases when the suspect is known but not available

3.21 When a known suspect is not available or has ceased to be available, see paragraph 3.4, the identification officer may make arrangements for a video identification (see Annex A). If necessary, the identification officer may follow the video identification procedures but using still images. Any suitable moving or still images may be used and these may be obtained covertly if necessary. Alternatively, the identification officer may make arrangements for a group identification. See Note 3D. These provisions may also be applied to juveniles where the consent of their parent or guardian is either refused or reasonable efforts to obtain that consent have failed. (see paragraph 2.12).

3.22 Any covert activity should be strictly limited to that necessary to test the ability of the witness to identify the suspect.

3.23 The identification officer may arrange for the suspect to be confronted by the witness if none of the options referred to in paragraphs 3.5 to 3.10 or 3.21 are practicable. A 'confrontation' is when the suspect is directly confronted by the witness. A confrontation does not require the suspect's consent. Confrontations must be carried out in accordance with Annex D.

3.24 Requirements for information to be given to, or sought from, a suspect or for the suspect to be given an opportunity to view images before they are shown to a witness, do not apply if the suspect's lack of co-operation prevents the necessary action.

(d) Documentation

3.25 A record shall be made of the video identification, identification parade, group identification or confrontation on forms provided for the purpose.

3.26 If the identification officer considers it is not practicable to hold a video identification or identification parade requested by the suspect, the reasons shall be recorded and explained to the suspect.

3.27 A record shall be made of a person's failure or refusal to co-operate in a video identification, identification parade or group identification and, if applicable, of the grounds for obtaining images in accordance with paragraph 3.20.

(e) Showing films and photographs of incidents and information released to the media

3.28 Nothing in this Code inhibits showing films, photographs or other images to the public through the national or local media, or to police officers for the purposes of recognition and tracing suspects. However, when such material is shown to obtain evidence of recognition, the procedures in Part B will apply. See Note 3AA.

3.29 When a broadcast or publication is made, see paragraph 3.28, a copy of the relevant material released to the media for the purposes of recognising or tracing the suspect, shall be kept. The suspect or their solicitor shall be allowed to view such material before any eye-witness identification procedures under paragraphs 3.5 to 3.10, 3.21 or 3.23 of Part A are carried out, provided it is practicable and would not unreasonably delay the investigation. Each eye-witness involved in the procedure shall be asked, after they have taken part, whether they have seen any film, photograph or image relating to the offence or any description of the suspect which has been broadcast or published in any national or local media or on any social networking site and if they have, they should be asked to give details of the circumstances, such as the date and place as relevant. Their replies shall be recorded. This paragraph does not affect any separate requirement under the Criminal Procedure and Investigations Act 1996 to retain material in connection with criminal investigations.

(f) Destruction and retention of photographs taken or used in eye-witness identification procedures

3.30 PACE, section 64A, see paragraph 5.12, provides powers to take photographs of suspects and allows these photographs to be used or disclosed only for purposes related to the prevention or detection of crime, the investigation of offences or the conduct of prosecutions by, or on behalf of, police or other law enforcement and prosecuting authorities inside and outside the United Kingdom or the enforcement of a sentence. After being so used or disclosed, they may be retained but can only be used or disclosed for the same purposes.

3.31 Subject to paragraph 3.33, the photographs (and all negatives and copies), of suspects not taken in accordance with the provisions in paragraph 5.12 which are taken for the purposes of, or in connection with, the identification procedures in paragraphs 3.5 to 3.10, 3.21 or 3.23 must be destroyed unless the suspect:
   (a) is charged with, or informed they may be prosecuted for, a recordable offence;
   (b) is prosecuted for a recordable offence;

    (c) is cautioned for a recordable offence or given a warning or reprimand in accordance with the Crime and Disorder Act 1998 for a recordable offence; or

    (d) gives informed consent, in writing, for the photograph or images to be retained for purposes described in paragraph 3.30.

3.32 When paragraph 3.31 requires the destruction of any photograph, the person must be given an opportunity to witness the destruction or to have a certificate confirming the destruction if they request one within five days of being informed that the destruction is required.

3.33 Nothing in paragraph 3.31 affects any separate requirement under the Criminal Procedure and Investigations Act 1996 to retain material in connection with criminal investigations.

(B) *Evidence of recognition by showing films, photographs and other images*

3.34 This Part of this section applies when, for the purposes of obtaining evidence of recognition, any person, including a police officer:

    (a) views the image of an individual in a film, photograph or any other visual medium; and

    (b) is asked whether they recognise that individual as someone who is known to them. See Notes 3AA and 3G

3.35 The films, photographs and other images shall be shown on an individual basis to avoid any possibility of collusion and to provide safeguards against mistaken recognition (see Note 3G), the showing shall as far as possible follow the principles for video identification if the suspect is known, see Annex A, or identification by photographs if the suspect is not known, see Annex E.

3.36 A record of the circumstances and conditions under which the person is given an opportunity to recognise the individual must be made and the record must include:

    (a) Whether the person knew or was given information concerning the name or identity of any suspect.

    (b) What the person has been told before the viewing about the offence, the person(s) depicted in the images or the offender and by whom.

    (c) How and by whom the witness was asked to view the image or look at the individual.

    (d) Whether the viewing was alone or with others and if with others, the reason for it.

    (e) The arrangements under which the person viewed the film or saw the individual and by whom those arrangements were made.

    (f) Whether the viewing of any images was arranged as part of a mass circulation to police and the public or for selected persons.

    (g) The date time and place images were viewed or further viewed or the individual was seen.

    (h) The times between which the images were viewed or the individual was seen.

    (i) How the viewing of images or sighting of the individual was controlled and by whom.

    (j) Whether the person was familiar with the location shown in any images or the place where they saw the individual and if so, why.

    (k) Whether or not on this occasion, the person claims to recognise any image shown, or any individual seen, as being someone known to them, and if they do:

        (i)   the reason

        (ii) the words of recognition

        (iii) any expressions of doubt

        (iv) what features of the image or the individual triggered the recognition.

3.37 The record under paragraph 3.36 may be made by:

- the person who views the image or sees the individual and makes the recognition.
- the officer or police staff in charge of showing the images to the person or in charge of the conditions under which the person sees the individual.

Notes for Guidance

3AA The eye-witness identification procedures in Part A should not be used to test whether a witness can recognise a person as someone they know and would be able to give evidence of recognition along the lines that 'On (describe date, time location) I saw an image of an individual who I recognised as AB.' In these cases, the procedures in Part B shall apply.

3A Except for the provisions of Annex E, paragraph 1, a police officer who is a witness for the purposes of this part of the Code is subject to the same principles and procedures as a civilian witness.

3B When a witness attending an identification procedure has previously been shown photographs, or been shown or provided with computerised or artist's composite likenesses, or similar likenesses or pictures, it is the officer in charge of the investigation's responsibility to make the identification officer aware of this.

3C The purpose of paragraph 3.19 is to avoid or reduce delay in arranging identification procedures by enabling the required information and warnings, see sub-paragraphs 3.17(ix) and 3.17(xii), to be given at the earliest opportunity.

3D   Paragraph 3.21 would apply when a known suspect deliberately makes themselves 'unavailable' in order to delay or frustrate arrangements for obtaining identification evidence. It also applies when a suspect refuses or fails to take part in a video identification, an identification parade or a group identification, or refuses or fails to take part in the only practicable options from that list. It enables any suitable images of the suspect, moving or still, which are available or can be obtained, to be used in an identification procedure. Examples include images from custody and other CCTV systems and from visually recorded interview records, see Code F Note for Guidance 2D.

3E   When it is proposed to show photographs to a witness in accordance with Annex E, it is the responsibility of the officer in charge of the investigation to confirm to the officer responsible for supervising and directing the showing, that the first description of the suspect given by that witness has been recorded. If this description has not been recorded, the procedure under Annex E must be postponed. See Annex E paragraph 2

3F   The admissibility and value of identification evidence obtained when carrying out the procedure under paragraph 3.2 may be compromised if:
(a)   before a person is identified, the witness' attention is specifically drawn to that person; or
(b)   the suspect's identity becomes known before the procedure.

3G   The admissibility and value of evidence of recognition obtained when carrying out the procedures in Part B may be compromised if before the person is recognised, the witness who has claimed to know them is given or is made, or becomes aware of, information about the person which was not previously known to them personally but which they have purported to rely on to support their claim that the person is in fact known to them.

4   Identification by fingerprints and footwear impressions

(A)   *Taking fingerprints in connection with a criminal investigation*

(a)   General

4.1   References to 'fingerprints' means any record, produced by any method, of the skin pattern and other physical characteristics or features of a person's:
(i)   fingers; or
(ii)   palms.

(b)   Action

4.2   A person's fingerprints may be taken in connection with the investigation of an offence only with their consent or if paragraph 4.3 applies. If the person is at a police station consent must be in writing.

4.3   PACE, section 61, provides powers to take fingerprints without consent from any person over the age of ten years:
(a)   under section 61(3), from a person detained at a police station in consequence of being arrested for a recordable offence, see Note 4A, if they have not had their fingerprints taken in the course of the investigation of the offence unless those previously taken fingerprints are not a complete set or some or all of those fingerprints are not of sufficient quality to allow satisfactory analysis, comparison or matching.
(b)   under section 61(4), from a person detained at a police station who has been charged with a recordable offence, see Note 4A, or informed they will be reported for such an offence if they have not had their fingerprints taken in the course of the investigation of the offence unless those previously taken fingerprints are not a complete set or some or all of those fingerprints are not of sufficient quality to allow satisfactory analysis, comparison or matching.
(c)   under section 61(4A), from a person who has been bailed to appear at a court or police station if the person:
(i)   has answered to bail for a person whose fingerprints were taken previously and there are reasonable grounds for believing they are not the same person; or
(ii)   who has answered to bail claims to be a different person from a person whose fingerprints were previously taken;
and in either case, the court or an officer of inspector rank or above, authorises the fingerprints to be taken at the court or police station (an inspector's authority may be given in writing or orally and confirmed in writing, as soon as practicable);
(ca)   under section 61(5A) from a person who has been arrested for a recordable offence and released if the person:
(i)   is on bail and has not had their fingerprints taken in the course of the investigation of the offence, or;

    (ii) has had their fingerprints taken in the course of the investigation of the offence, but they do not constitute a complete set or some, or all, of the fingerprints are not of sufficient quality to allow satisfactory analysis, comparison or matching.

(cb) under section 61(5B) from a person not detained at a police station who has been charged with a recordable offence or informed they will be reported for such an offence if they have not had their fingerprints taken in the course of the investigation or their fingerprints have been taken in the course of the investigation of the offence, but they do not constitute a complete set or some, or all, of the fingerprints are not of sufficient quality to allow satisfactory analysis, comparison or matching.

(d) under section 61(6), from a person who has been:

    (i) convicted of a recordable offence;

    (ii) given a caution in respect of a recordable offence which, at the time of the caution, the person admitted; or

    (iii) warned or reprimanded under the Crime and Disorder Act 1998, section 65, for a recordable offence, if, since their conviction, caution, warning or reprimand their fingerprints have not been taken or their fingerprints which have been taken since then do not constitute a complete set or some, or all, of the fingerprints are not of sufficient quality to allow satisfactory analysis, comparison or matching, and in either case, an officer of inspector rank or above, is satisfied that taking the fingerprints is necessary to assist in the prevention or detection of crime and authorises the taking;

(e) under section 61(6A) from a person a constable reasonably suspects is committing or attempting to commit, or has committed or attempted to commit, any offence if either:

- the person's name is unknown and cannot be readily ascertained by the constable; or
- the constable has reasonable grounds for doubting whether a name given by the person is their real name.

Note: fingerprints taken under this power are not regarded as having been taken in the course of the investigation of an offence. [See Note 4C]

(f) under section 61(6D) from a person who has been convicted outside England and Wales of an offence which if committed in England and Wales would be a qualifying offence as defined by PACE, section 65A (see Note 4AB) if:

    (i) the person's fingerprints have not been taken previously under this power or their fingerprints have been so taken on a previous occasion but they do not constitute a complete set or some, or all, of the fingerprints are not of sufficient quality to allow satisfactory analysis, comparison or matching; and

    (ii) a police officer of inspector rank or above is satisfied that taking fingerprints is necessary to assist in the prevention or detection of crime and authorises them to be taken.

4.4 PACE, section 63A(4) and Schedule 2A provide powers to:

(a) make a requirement (in accordance with Annex G) for a person to attend a police station to have their fingerprints taken in the exercise of certain powers in paragraph 4.3 above when that power applies at the time the fingerprints would be taken in accordance with the requirement. Those powers are:

    (i) section 61(5A)—Persons arrested for a recordable offence and released, see paragraph 4.3(ca): The requirement may not be made more than six months from the day the investigating officer was informed that the fingerprints previously taken were incomplete or below standard.

    (ii) section 61(5B)—Persons charged etc. with a recordable offence, see paragraph 4.3(cb): The requirement may not be made more than six months from:

- the day the person was charged or reported if fingerprints have not been taken since then; or
- the day the investigating officer was informed that the fingerprints previously taken were incomplete or below standard.

    (iii) section 61(6)—Person convicted, cautioned, warned or reprimanded for a recordable offence in England and Wales, see paragraph 4.3(d): Where the offence for which the person was convicted etc. is also a qualifying offence (see Note 4AB), there is no time limit for the exercise of this power. Where the conviction etc. is for a recordable offence which is not a qualifying offence, the requirement may not be made more than two years from:

- the day the person was convicted, cautioned, warned or reprimanded, or the day Schedule 2A comes into force (if later), if fingerprints have not been taken since then; or

- the day an officer from the force investigating the offence was informed that the finger-prints previously taken were incomplete or below standard or the day Schedule 2A comes into force (if later).

    (iv) section 61(6D)—A person who has been convicted of a qualifying offence (see Note 4AB) outside England and Wales, see paragraph [4.3(f)]: There is no time limit for making the requirement.

    Note: A person who has had their fingerprints taken under any of the powers in section 61 mentioned in paragraph 4.3 on two occasions in relation to any offence may not be required under Schedule 2A to attend a police station for their fingerprints to be taken again under section 61 in relation to that offence, unless authorised by an officer of inspector rank or above. The fact of the authorisation and the reasons for giving it must be recorded as soon as practicable.

  (b) arrest, without warrant, a person who fails to comply with the requirement.

4.5   A person's fingerprints may be taken, as above, electronically.

4.6   Reasonable force may be used, if necessary, to take a person's fingerprints without their consent under the powers as in paragraphs 4.3 and 4.4.

4.7   Before any fingerprints are taken:

  (a) without consent under any power mentioned in paragraphs 4.3 and 4.4 above, the person must be informed of:

    (i) the reason their fingerprints are to be taken;

    (ii) the power under which they are to be taken; and

    (iii) the fact that the relevant authority has been given if any power mentioned in paragraph 4.3(c), (d) or (f) applies

  (b) with or without consent at a police station or elsewhere, the person must be informed:

    (i) that their fingerprints may be subject of a speculative search against other fingerprints, see Note 4B; and

    (ii) that their fingerprints may be retained in accordance with Annex F, Part (a) unless they were taken under the power mentioned in paragraph 4.3(e) when they must be destroyed after they have being checked (See Note 4C).

(c) Documentation

4.8A A record must be made as soon as practicable after the fingerprints are taken, of:

- the matters in paragraph 4.7(a)(i) to (iii) and the fact that the person has been informed of those matters; and
- the fact that the person has been informed of the matters in paragraph 4.7(b) (i) and (ii).

The record must be made in the person's custody record if they are detained at a police station when the fingerprints are taken.

4.8   If force is used, a record shall be made of the circumstances and those present.

4.9   Not used

(B) *Taking fingerprints in connection with immigration enquiries*
Action

4.10 A person's fingerprints may be taken and retained for the purposes of immigration law enforcement and control in accordance with powers and procedures other than under PACE and for which the UK Border Agency (not the police) are responsible. Details of these powers and procedures which are under the Immigration Act 1971, Schedule 2 and Immigration and Asylum Act 1999, section 141, including modifications to the PACE Codes of Practice are contained in Chapter 24 of the Operational Instructions and Guidance manual which is published by the UK Border Agency (See Note 4D).

4.11 to 4.15 Not used

(C) *Taking footwear impressions in connection with a criminal investigation*

(a) Action

4.16 Impressions of a person's footwear may be taken in connection with the investigation of an offence only with their consent or if paragraph 4.17 applies. If the person is at a police station consent must be in writing.

4.17 PACE, section 61A, provides power for a police officer to take footwear impressions without consent from any person over the age of ten years who is detained at a police station:

  (a) in consequence of being arrested for a recordable offence, see Note 4A; or if the detainee has been charged with a recordable offence, or informed they will be reported for such an offence; and

  (b) the detainee has not had an impression of their footwear taken in the course of the investigation of the offence unless the previously taken impression is not complete or is not of sufficient quality to allow satisfactory analysis, comparison or matching (whether in the case in question or generally).

4.18 Reasonable force may be used, if necessary, to take a footwear impression from a detainee without consent under the power in paragraph 4.17.

4.19 Before any footwear impression is taken with, or without, consent as above, the person must be informed:

(a) of the reason the impression is to be taken;

(b) that the impression may be retained and may be subject of a speculative search against other impressions, see Note 4B, unless destruction of the impression is required in accordance with Annex F, Part (a); and

(c) that if their footwear impressions are required to be destroyed, they may witness their destruction as provided for in Annex F, Part (a).

(b) Documentation

4.20 A record must be made as soon as possible, of the reason for taking a person's footwear impressions without consent. If force is used, a record shall be made of the circumstances and those present.

4.21 A record shall be made when a person has been informed under the terms of paragraph 4.19(b), of the possibility that their footwear impressions may be subject of a speculative search.

Notes for Guidance

4A References to 'recordable offences' in this Code relate to those offences for which convictions, cautions, reprimands and warnings may be recorded in national police records. See PACE, section 27(4). The recordable offences current at the time when this Code was prepared, are any offences which carry a sentence of imprisonment on conviction (irrespective of the period, or the age of the offender or actual sentence passed) as well as the non-imprisonable offences under the Vagrancy Act 1824 sections 3 and 4 (begging and persistent begging), the Street Offences Act 1959, section 1 (loitering or soliciting for purposes of prostitution), the Road Traffic Act 1988, section 25 (tampering with motor vehicles), the Criminal Justice and Public Order Act 1994, section 167 (touting for hire car services) and others listed in the National Police Records (Recordable Offences) Regulations 2000 as amended.

4AB A qualifying offence is one of the offences specified in PACE, section 65A. These indictable offences which concern the use or threat of violence or unlawful force against persons, sexual offences and offences against children include, for example, murder, manslaughter, false imprisonment, kidnapping and other offences such as:

• sections 4, 16, 18, 20 to 24 or 47 of the Offences Against the Person Act 1861;

• sections 16 to 18 of the Firearms Act 1968;

• sections 9 or 10 of the Theft Act 1968 or under section 12A of that Act involving an accident which caused a person's death;

• section 1 of the Criminal Damage Act 1971 required to be charged as arson;

• section 1 of the Protection of Children Act 1978 and;

• sections 1 to 19, 25, 26, 30 to 41, 47 to 50, 52, 53, 57 to 59, 61 to 67, 69 and 70 of the Sexual Offences Act 2003.

4B Fingerprints, footwear impressions or a DNA sample (and the information derived from it) taken from a person arrested on suspicion of being involved in a recordable offence, or charged with such an offence, or informed they will be reported for such an offence, may be subject of a speculative search. This means the fingerprints, footwear impressions or DNA sample may be checked against other fingerprints, footwear impressions and DNA records held by, or on behalf of, the police and other law enforcement authorities in, or outside, the UK, or held in connection with, or as a result of, an investigation of an offence inside or outside the UK. Fingerprints, footwear impressions and samples taken from a person suspected of committing a recordable offence but not arrested, charged or informed they will be reported for it, may be subject to a speculative search only if the person consents in writing. The following is an example of a basic form of words:

'I consent to my fingerprints, footwear impressions and DNA sample and information derived from it being retained and used only for purposes related to the prevention and detection of a crime, the investigation of an offence or the conduct of a prosecution either nationally or internationally. I understand that my fingerprints, footwear impressions or DNA sample may be checked against other fingerprint, footwear impressions and DNA records held by or on behalf of relevant law enforcement authorities, either nationally or internationally. I understand that once I have given my consent for my fingerprints, footwear impressions or DNA sample to be retained and used I cannot withdraw this consent.'

See Annex F regarding the retention and use of fingerprints and footwear impressions taken with consent for elimination purposes.

4C The power under section 61(6A) of PACE described in paragraph 4.3(e) allows fingerprints of a suspect who has not been arrested to be taken in connection with any offence (whether recordable or not) using a mobile device and then checked on the street against the database containing the national fingerprint collection. Fingerprints taken under this power cannot be retained after they have been checked. The results may make an arrest for the suspected offence based on the name condition unnecessary (See Code G paragraph 2.9(a)) and enable the offence to be disposed of without arrest, for example, by summons/charging by post, penalty notice or words of advice. If arrest for a non-recordable offence is necessary for any other reasons, this power may also be exercised at the station. Before the power is exercised, the officer should:
- inform the person of the nature of the suspected offence and why they are suspected of committing it.
- give them a reasonable opportunity to establish their real name before deciding that their name is unknown and cannot be readily ascertained or that there are reasonable grounds to doubt that a name they have given is their real name.
- as applicable, inform the person of the reason why their name is not known and cannot be readily ascertained or of the grounds for doubting that a name they have given is their real name, including, for example, the reason why a particular document the person has produced to verify their real name, is not sufficient.

4D Powers to take fingerprints without consent for immigration purposes are given to police and immigration officers under the:
(a) Immigration Act 1971, Schedule 2, paragraph 18(2), when it is reasonably necessary for the purposes of identifying a person detained under the Immigration Act 1971, Schedule 2, paragraph 16 (Detention of person liable to examination or removal), and
(b) Immigration and Asylum Act 1999, section 141(7) when a person:
- fails without reasonable excuse to produce, on arrival, a valid passport with a photograph or some other document satisfactorily establishing their identity and nationality;
- is refused entry to the UK but is temporarily admitted if an immigration officer reasonably suspects the person might break a residence or reporting condition;
- is subject to directions for removal from the UK;
- has been arrested under the Immigration Act 1971, Schedule 2, paragraph 17;
- has made a claim for asylum
- is a dependant of any of the above.

The Immigration and Asylum Act 1999, section 142(3), also gives police and immigration officers power to arrest without warrant, a person who fails to comply with a requirement imposed by the Secretary of State to attend a specified place for fingerprinting.

5 Examinations to establish identity and the taking of photographs
(A) *Detainees at police stations*
(a) *Searching or examination of detainees at police stations*

5.1 PACE, section 54A(1), allows a detainee at a police station to be searched or examined or both, to establish:
(a) whether they have any marks, features or injuries that would tend to identify them as a person involved in the commission of an offence and to photograph any identifying marks, see paragraph 5.5; or
(b) their identity, see Note 5A.
A person detained at a police station to be searched under a stop and search power, see Code A, is not a detainee for the purposes of these powers.

5.2 A search and/or examination to find marks under section 54A (1) (a) may be carried out without the detainee's consent, see paragraph 2.12, only if authorised by an officer of at least inspector rank when consent has been withheld or it is not practicable to obtain consent, see Note 5D.

5.3 A search or examination to establish a suspect's identity under section 54A (1) (b) may be carried out without the detainee's consent, see paragraph 2.12, only if authorised by an officer of at least inspector rank when the detainee has refused to identify themselves or the authorising officer has reasonable grounds for suspecting the person is not who they claim to be.

5.4 Any marks that assist in establishing the detainee's identity, or their identification as a person involved in the commission of an offence, are identifying marks. Such marks may be photographed with the detainee's consent, see paragraph 2.12; or without their consent if it is withheld or it is not practicable to obtain it, see Note 5D.

5.5   A detainee may only be searched, examined and photographed under section 54A, by a police officer of the same sex.

5.6   Any photographs of identifying marks, taken under section 54A, may be used or disclosed only for purposes related to the prevention or detection of crime, the investigation of offences or the conduct of prosecutions by, or on behalf of, police or other law enforcement and prosecuting authorities inside, and outside, the UK. After being so used or disclosed, the photograph may be retained but must not be used or disclosed except for these purposes, see Note 5B.

5.7   The powers, as in paragraph 5.1, do not affect any separate requirement under the Criminal Procedure and Investigations Act 1996 to retain material in connection with criminal investigations.

5.8   Authority for the search and/or examination for the purposes of paragraphs 5.2 and 5.3 may be given orally or in writing. If given orally, the authorising officer must confirm it in writing as soon as practicable. A separate authority is required for each purpose which applies.

5.9   If it is established a person is unwilling to co-operate sufficiently to enable a search and/or examination to take place or a suitable photograph to be taken, an officer may use reasonable force to:
   (a)   search and/or examine a detainee without their consent; and
   (b)   photograph any identifying marks without their consent.

5.10   The thoroughness and extent of any search or examination carried out in accordance with the powers in section 54A must be no more than the officer considers necessary to achieve the required purpose. Any search or examination which involves the removal of more than the person's outer clothing shall be conducted in accordance with Code C, Annex A, paragraph 11.

5.11   An intimate search may not be carried out under the powers in section 54A.

(b)   Photographing detainees at police stations and other persons elsewhere than at a police station

5.12   Under PACE, section 64A, an officer may photograph:
   (a)   any person whilst they are detained at a police station; and
   (b)   any person who is elsewhere than at a police station and who has been:
       (i)   arrested by a constable for an offence;
       (ii)   taken into custody by a constable after being arrested for an offence by a person other than a constable;
       (iii)   made subject to a requirement to wait with a community support officer under paragraph 2(3) or (3B) of Schedule 4 to the Police Reform Act 2002;
       (iv)   given a direction by a constable under section 27 of the Violent Crime Reduction Act 2006;
       (v)   given a penalty notice by a constable in uniform under Chapter 1 of Part 1 of the Criminal Justice and Police Act 2001, a penalty notice by a constable under section 444A of the Education Act 1996, or a fixed penalty notice by a constable in uniform under section 54 of the Road Traffic Offenders Act 1988;
       (vi)   given a notice in relation to a relevant fixed penalty offence (within the meaning of paragraph 1 of Schedule 4 to the Police Reform Act 2002) by a community support officer by virtue of a designation applying that paragraph to him;
       (vii)   given a notice in relation to a relevant fixed penalty offence (within the meaning of paragraph 1 of Schedule 5 to the Police Reform Act 2002) by an accredited person by virtue of accreditation specifying that that paragraph applies to him; or
       (viii) given a direction to leave and not return to a specified location for up to 48 hours by a police constable (under section 27 of the Violent Crime Reduction Act 2006).

5.12A Photographs taken under PACE, section 64A:
   (a)   may be taken with the person's consent, or without their consent if consent is withheld or it is not practicable to obtain their consent, see Note 5E; and
   (b)   may be used or disclosed only for purposes related to the prevention or detection of crime, the investigation of offences or the conduct of prosecutions by, or on behalf of, police or other law enforcement and prosecuting authorities inside and outside the United Kingdom or the enforcement of any sentence or order made by a court when dealing with an offence. After being so used or disclosed, they may be retained but can only be used or disclosed for the same purposes. See Note 5B.

5.13   The officer proposing to take a detainee's photograph may, for this purpose, require the person to remove any item or substance worn on, or over, all, or any part of, their head or face. If they do not comply with such a requirement, the officer may remove the item or substance.

5.14   If it is established the detainee is unwilling to co-operate sufficiently to enable a suitable photograph to be taken and it is not reasonably practicable to take the photograph covertly, an officer may use reasonable force, see Note 5F.

(a) to take their photograph without their consent; and

(b) for the purpose of taking the photograph, remove any item or substance worn on, or over, all, or any part of, the person's head or face which they have failed to remove when asked.

5.15 For the purposes of this Code, a photograph may be obtained without the person's consent by making a copy of an image of them taken at any time on a camera system installed anywhere in the police station.

(c) Information to be given

5.16 When a person is searched, examined or photographed under the provisions as in paragraph 5.1 and 5.12, or their photograph obtained as in paragraph 5.15, they must be informed of the:

(a) purpose of the search, examination or photograph;

(b) grounds on which the relevant authority, if applicable, has been given; and

(c) purposes for which the photograph may be used, disclosed or retained.

This information must be given before the search or examination commences or the photograph is taken, except if the photograph is:

(i) to be taken covertly;

(ii) obtained as in paragraph 5.15, in which case the person must be informed as soon as practicable after the photograph is taken or obtained.

(d) Documentation

5.17 A record must be made when a detainee is searched, examined, or a photograph of the person, or any identifying marks found on them, are taken. The record must include the:

(a) identity, subject to paragraph 2.18, of the officer carrying out the search, examination or taking the photograph;

(b) purpose of the search, examination or photograph and the outcome;

(c) detainee's consent to the search, examination or photograph, or the reason the person was searched, examined or photographed without consent;

(d) giving of any authority as in paragraphs 5.2 and 5.3, the grounds for giving it and the authorising officer.

5.18 If force is used when searching, examining or taking a photograph in accordance with this section, a record shall be made of the circumstances and those present.

(B) *Persons at police stations not detained*

5.19 When there are reasonable grounds for suspecting the involvement of a person in a criminal offence, but that person is at a police station voluntarily and not detained, the provisions of paragraphs 5.1 to 5.18 should apply, subject to the modifications in the following paragraphs.

5.20 References to the 'person being detained' and to the powers mentioned in paragraph 5.1 which apply only to detainees at police stations shall be omitted.

5.21 Force may not be used to:

(a) search and/or examine the person to:

(i) discover whether they have any marks that would tend to identify them as a person involved in the commission of an offence; or

(ii) establish their identity, see Note 5A;

(b) take photographs of any identifying marks, see paragraph 5.4; or

(c) take a photograph of the person.

5.22 Subject to paragraph 5.24, the photographs of persons or of their identifying marks which are not taken in accordance with the provisions mentioned in paragraphs 5.1 or 5.12, must be destroyed (together with any negatives and copies) unless the person:

(a) is charged with, or informed they may be prosecuted for, a recordable offence;

(b) is prosecuted for a recordable offence;

(c) is cautioned for a recordable offence or given a warning or reprimand in accordance with the Crime and Disorder Act 1998 for a recordable offence; or

(d) gives informed consent, in writing, for the photograph or image to be retained as in paragraph 5.6.

5.23 When paragraph 5.22 requires the destruction of any photograph, the person must be given an opportunity to witness the destruction or to have a certificate confirming the destruction provided they so request the certificate within five days of being informed the destruction is required.

5.24 Nothing in paragraph 5.22 affects any separate requirement under the Criminal Procedure and Investigations Act 1996 to retain material in connection with criminal investigations.

Notes for Guidance

5A   The conditions under which fingerprints may be taken to assist in establishing a person's identity, are described in Section 4.

5B   Examples of purposes related to the prevention or detection of crime, the investigation of offences or the conduct of prosecutions include:

(a)   checking the photograph against other photographs held in records or in connection with, or as a result of, an investigation of an offence to establish whether the person is liable to arrest for other offences;

(b)   when the person is arrested at the same time as other people, or at a time when it is likely that other people will be arrested, using the photograph to help establish who was arrested, at what time and where;

(c)   when the real identity of the person is not known and cannot be readily ascertained or there are reasonable grounds for doubting a name and other personal details given by the person, are their real name and personal details. In these circumstances, using or disclosing the photograph to help to establish or verify their real identity or determine whether they are liable to arrest for some other offence, e.g. by checking it against other photographs held in records or in connection with, or as a result of, an investigation of an offence;

(d)   when it appears any identification procedure in section 3 may need to be arranged for which the person's photograph would assist;

(e)   when the person's release without charge may be required, and if the release is:

(i)   on bail to appear at a police station, using the photograph to help verify the person's identity when they answer their bail and if the person does not answer their bail, to assist in arresting them; or

(ii)   without bail, using the photograph to help verify their identity or assist in locating them for the purposes of serving them with a summons to appear at court in criminal proceedings;

(f)   when the person has answered to bail at a police station and there are reasonable grounds for doubting they are the person who was previously granted bail, using the photograph to help establish or verify their identity;

(g)   when the person arrested on a warrant claims to be a different person from the person named on the warrant and a photograph would help to confirm or disprove their claim;

(h)   when the person has been charged with, reported for, or convicted of, a recordable offence and their photograph is not already on record as a result of (a) to (f) or their photograph is on record but their appearance has changed since it was taken and the person has not yet been released or brought before a court.

5C   There is no power to arrest a person convicted of a recordable offence solely to take their photograph. The power to take photographs in this section applies only where the person is in custody as a result of the exercise of another power, e.g. arrest for fingerprinting under PACE, section 27.

5D   Examples of when it would not be practicable to obtain a detainee's consent, see paragraph 2.12, to a search, examination or the taking of a photograph of an identifying mark include:

(a)   when the person is drunk or otherwise unfit to give consent;

(b)   when there are reasonable grounds to suspect that if the person became aware a search or examination was to take place or an identifying mark was to be photographed, they would take steps to prevent this happening, e.g. by violently resisting, covering or concealing the mark etc. and it would not otherwise be possible to carry out the search or examination or to photograph any identifying mark;

(c)   in the case of a juvenile, if the parent or guardian cannot be contacted in sufficient time to allow the search or examination to be carried out or the photograph to be taken.

5E   Examples of when it would not be practicable to obtain the person's consent, see paragraph 2.12, to a photograph being taken include:

(a)   when the person is drunk or otherwise unfit to give consent;

(b)   when there are reasonable grounds to suspect that if the person became aware a photograph, suitable to be used or disclosed for the use and disclosure described in paragraph 5.6, was to be taken, they would take steps to prevent it being taken, e.g. by violently resisting, covering or distorting their face etc., and it would not otherwise be possible to take a suitable photograph;

(c)   when, in order to obtain a suitable photograph, it is necessary to take it covertly; and

(d)   in the case of a juvenile, if the parent or guardian cannot be contacted in sufficient time to allow the photograph to be taken.

5F   The use of reasonable force to take the photograph of a suspect elsewhere than at a police station must be carefully considered. In order to obtain a suspect's consent and co-operation to remove an item of religious headwear to take their photograph, a constable should consider whether in the circumstances of the situation the removal of the headwear and the taking of the photograph should be by an officer of the same sex as the person. It would be appropriate for these actions to be conducted out of public view.

6 Identification by body samples and impressions

(A) *General*

6.1 References to:
- (a) an 'intimate sample' mean a dental impression or sample of blood, semen or any other tissue fluid, urine, or pubic hair, or a swab taken from any part of a person's genitals or from a person's body orifice other than the mouth;
- (b) a 'non-intimate sample' means:
  - (i) a sample of hair, other than pubic hair, which includes hair plucked with the root, see Note 6A;
  - (ii) a sample taken from a nail or from under a nail;
  - (iii) a swab taken from any part of a person's body other than a part from which a swab taken would be an intimate sample;
  - (iv) saliva;
  - (v) a skin impression which means any record, other than a fingerprint, which is a record, in any form and produced by any method, of the skin pattern and other physical characteristics or features of the whole, or any part of, a person's foot or of any other part of their body.

(B) *Action*

(a) Intimate samples

6.2 PACE, section 62, provides that intimate samples may be taken under:
- (a) section 62(1), from a person in police detention only:
  - (i) if a police officer of inspector rank or above has reasonable grounds to believe such an impression or sample will tend to confirm or disprove the suspect's involvement in a recordable offence, see Note 4A, and gives authorisation for a sample to be taken; and
  - (ii) with the suspect's written consent;
- (b) section 62(1A), from a person not in police detention but from whom two or more non-intimate samples have been taken in the course of an investigation of an offence and the samples, though suitable, have proved insufficient if:
  - (i) a police officer of inspector rank or above authorises it to be taken; and
  - (ii) the person concerned gives their written consent. See Notes 6B and 6C
- (c) section 62(2A), from a person convicted outside England and Wales of an offence which if committed in England and Wales would be [a] qualifying offence as defined by PACE, section 65A (see Note 4AB) from whom two or more non-intimate samples taken under section 63(3E) (see paragraph [6.6(g)]) have proved insufficient if:
  - (i) a police officer of inspector rank or above is satisfied that taking the sample is necessary to assist in the prevention or detection of crime and authorises it to be taken; and
  - (ii) the person concerned gives their written consent.

6.2A PACE, section 63A(4) and Schedule 2A provide powers to:
- (a) make a requirement (in accordance with Annex G) for a person to attend a police station to have an intimate sample taken in the exercise of one of the following powers in paragraph 6.2 when that power applies at the time the sample is to be taken in accordance with the requirement or after the person's arrest if they fail to comply with the requirement:
  - (i) section 62(1A)—Persons from whom two or more non-intimate samples have been taken and proved to be insufficient, see paragraph 6.2(b): There is no time limit for making the requirement.
  - (ii) section 62(2A)—Persons convicted outside England and Wales from whom two or more non-intimate samples taken under section 63(3E) (see paragraph [6.6(g)] have proved insufficient, see paragraph 6.2(c): There is no time limit for making the requirement.

6.3 Before a suspect is asked to provide an intimate sample, they must be:
- (a) informed:
  - (i) of the reason, including the nature of the suspected offence (except if taken under paragraph 6.2(c) from a person convicted outside England and Wales.
  - (ii) that authorisation has been given and the provisions under which given;
  - (iii) that a sample taken at a police station may be subject of a speculative search;

(b) warned that if they refuse without good cause their refusal may harm their case if it comes to trial, see Note 6D. If the suspect is in police detention and not legally represented, they must also be reminded of their entitlement to have free legal advice, see Code C, paragraph 6.5, and the reminder noted in the custody record. If paragraph 6.2(b) applies and the person is attending a station voluntarily, their entitlement to free legal advice as in Code C, paragraph 3.21 shall be explained to them.

6.4 Dental impressions may only be taken by a registered dentist. Other intimate samples, except for samples of urine, may only be taken by a registered medical practitioner or registered nurse or registered paramedic.

(b) Non-intimate samples

6.5 A non-intimate sample may be taken from a detainee only with their written consent or if paragraph 6.6 applies.

6.6 a non-intimate sample may be taken from a person without the appropriate consent in the following circumstances:

(a) under section 63(2A) from a person who is in police detention as a consequence of being arrested for a recordable offence and who has not had a non-intimate sample of the same type and from the same part of the body taken in the course of the investigation of the offence by the police or they have had such a sample taken but it proved insufficient.

(b) Under section 63(3) from a person who is being held in custody by the police on the authority of a court if an officer of at least the rank of inspector authorises it to be taken. An authorisation may be given:

(i) if the authorising officer has reasonable grounds for suspecting the person of involvement in a recordable offence and for believing that the sample will tend to confirm or disprove that involvement, and

(ii) in writing or orally and confirmed in writing, as soon as practicable; but an authorisation may not be given to take from the same part of the body a further non-intimate sample consisting of a skin impression unless the previously taken impression proved insufficient

(c) under section 63(3ZA) from a person who has been arrested for a recordable offence and released if the person:

(i) is on bail and has not had a sample of the same type and from the same part of the body taken in the course of the investigation of the offence, or;

(ii) has had such a sample taken in the course of the investigation of the offence, but it proved unsuitable or insufficient.

(d) under section 63(3A), from a person (whether or not in police detention or held in custody by the police on the authority of a court) who has been charged with a recordable offence or informed they will be reported for such an offence if the person:

(i) has not had a non-intimate sample taken from them in the course of the investigation of the offence;

(ii) has had a sample so taken, but it proved unsuitable or insufficient, see Note 6B; or

(iii) has had a sample taken in the course of the investigation of the offence and the sample has been destroyed and in proceedings relating to that offence there is a dispute as to whether a DNA profile relevant to the proceedings was derived from the destroyed sample.

(e) under section 63(3B), from a person who has been:

(i) convicted of a recordable offence;

(ii) given a caution in respect of a recordable offence which, at the time of the caution, the person admitted; or

(iii) warned or reprimanded under the Crime and Disorder Act 1998, section 65, for a recordable offence, if, since their conviction, caution, warning or reprimand a non-intimate sample has not been taken from them or a sample which has been taken since then has proved to be unsuitable or insufficient and in either case, an officer of inspector rank or above, is satisfied that taking the fingerprints is necessary to assist in the prevention or detection of crime and authorises the taking;

(f) under section 63(3C) from a person to whom section 2 of the Criminal Evidence (Amendment) Act 1997 applies (persons detained following acquittal on grounds of insanity or finding of unfitness to plead).

(g) under section 63(3E) from a person who has been convicted outside England and Wales of an offence which if committed in England and Wales would be a qualifying offence as defined by PACE, section 65A (see Note 4AB) if:

(i) a non-intimate sample has not been taken previously under this power or unless a sample was so taken but was unsuitable or insufficient; and

(ii) a police officer of inspector rank or above is satisfied that taking a sample is necessary to assist in the prevention or detection of crime and authorises it to be taken.

6.6A PACE, section 63A(4) and Schedule 2A provide powers to:

(a) make a requirement (in accordance with Annex G) for a person to attend a police station to have a non-intimate sample taken in the exercise of one of the following powers in paragraph 6.6 when that power applies at the time the sample would be taken in accordance with the requirement:

  (i) section 63(3ZA) — Persons arrested for a recordable offence and released, see paragraph 6.6(c): The requirement may not be made more than six months from the day the investigating officer was informed that the sample previously taken was unsuitable or insufficient.

  (ii) section 63(3A) — Persons charged etc. with a recordable offence, see paragraph 6.6(d): The requirement may not be made more than six months from:
  - the day the person was charged or reported if a sample has not been taken since then; or
  - the day the investigating officer was informed that the sample previously taken was unsuitable or insufficient.

  (iii) section 63(3B) — Person convicted, cautioned, warned or reprimanded for a recordable offence in England and Wales, see paragraph 6.6(e):
  Where the offence for which the person was convicted etc. is also a qualifying offence (see Note 4AB), there is no time limit for the exercise of this power. Where the conviction etc. was for a recordable offence that is not a qualifying offence, the requirement may not be made more than two years from:
  - the day the person was convicted, cautioned, warned or reprimanded, or the day Schedule 2A comes into force (if later), if a sample has not been taken since then; or
  - the day an officer from the force investigating the offence was informed that the sample previously taken was unsuitable or insufficient or the day Schedule 2A comes into force (if later).

  (iv) section 63(3E) — A person who has been convicted of [a] qualifying offence (see Note 4AB) outside England and Wales, see paragraph [6.6(g)]: There is no time limit for making the requirement.

  Note: A person who has had a non-intimate sample taken under any of the powers in section 63 mentioned in paragraph 6.6 on two occasions in relation to any offence may not be required under Schedule 2A to attend a police station for a sample to be taken again under section 63 in relation to that offence, unless authorised by an officer of inspector rank or above. The fact of the authorisation and the reasons for giving it must be recorded as soon as practicable.

(b) arrest, without warrant, a person who fails to comply with the requirement.

6.7 Reasonable force may be used, if necessary, to take a non-intimate sample from a person without their consent under the powers mentioned in paragraph 6.6.

6.8 Before any non-intimate sample is taken:

(a) without consent under any power mentioned in paragraphs 6.6 and 6.6A, the person must be informed of:
  (i) the reason for taking the sample;
  (ii) the power under which the sample is to be taken;
  (iii) the fact that the relevant authority has been given if any power mentioned in paragraph 6.6(b), (e) or [(g)] applies;

(b) with or without consent at a police station or elsewhere, the person must be informed:
  (i) that their sample or information derived from it may be subject of a speculative search against other samples and information derived from them, see Note 6E and
  (ii) that their sample and the information derived from it may be retained in accordance with Annex F, Part (a).

(c) Removal of clothing

6.9 When clothing needs to be removed in circumstances likely to cause embarrassment to the person, no person of the opposite sex who is not a registered medical practitioner or registered health care professional shall be present, (unless in the case of a juvenile, mentally disordered or mentally vulnerable person, that person specifically requests the presence of an appropriate adult of the opposite sex who is readily available) nor shall anyone whose presence is unnecessary. However, in the case of a juvenile, this is subject to the overriding proviso that such a removal of clothing may take place in the absence of the appropriate adult only if the juvenile signifies in their presence, that they prefer the adult's absence and they agree.

[(d)] Documentation

6.10 A record must be made as soon as practicable after the sample is taken of:
- The matters in paragraph 6.8(a)(i) to (iii) and the fact that the person has been informed of those matters; and
- The fact that the person has been informed of the matters in paragraph 6.8(b) (i) and (ii).

6.10A If force is used, a record shall be made of the circumstances and those present.

6.11 A record must be made of a warning given as required by paragraph 6.3.

6.12 *Not used*

Notes for Guidance

6A When hair samples are taken for the purpose of DNA analysis (rather than for other purposes such as making a visual match), the suspect should be permitted a reasonable choice as to what part of the body the hairs are taken from. When hairs are plucked, they should be plucked individually, unless the suspect prefers otherwise and no more should be plucked than the person taking them reasonably considers necessary for a sufficient sample.

6B (a) An insufficient sample is one which is not sufficient either in quantity or quality to provide information for a particular form of analysis, such as DNA analysis. A sample may also be insufficient if enough information cannot be obtained from it by analysis because of loss, destruction, damage or contamination of the sample or as a result of an earlier, unsuccessful attempt at analysis.

(b) An unsuitable sample is one which, by its nature, is not suitable for a particular form of analysis.

6C Nothing in paragraph 6.2 prevents intimate samples being taken for elimination purposes with the consent of the person concerned but the provisions of paragraph 2.12 relating to the role of the appropriate adult, should be applied. Paragraph 6.2(b) does not, however, apply where the non-intimate samples were previously taken under the Terrorism Act 2000, Schedule 8, paragraph 10.

6D In warning a person who is asked to provide an intimate sample as in paragraph 6.3, the following form of words may be used:

'You do not have to provide this sample/allow this swab or impression to be taken, but I must warn you that if you refuse without good cause, your refusal may harm your case if it comes to trial.'

6E Fingerprints or a DNA sample and the information derived from it taken from a person arrested on suspicion of being involved in a recordable offence, or charged with such an offence, or informed they will be reported for such an offence, may be subject of a speculative search. This means they may be checked against other fingerprints and DNA records held by, or on behalf of, the police and other law enforcement authorities in or outside the UK or held in connection with, or as a result of, an investigation of an offence inside or outside the UK. Fingerprints and samples taken from any other person, e.g. a person suspected of committing a recordable offence but who has not been arrested, charged or informed they will be reported for it, may be subject to a speculative search only if the person consents in writing to their fingerprints being subject of such a search. The following is an example of a basic form of words:

'I consent to my fingerprints/DNA sample and information derived from it being retained and used only for purposes related to the prevention and detection of a crime, the investigation of an offence or the conduct of a prosecution either nationally or internationally. I understand that this sample may be checked against other fingerprint/DNA records held by or on behalf of relevant law enforcement authorities, either nationally or internationally. I understand that once I have given my consent for the sample to be retained and used I cannot withdraw this consent.'

See Annex F regarding the retention and use of fingerprints and samples taken with consent for elimination purposes.

6F Samples of urine and non-intimate samples taken in accordance with sections 63B and 63C of PACE may not be used for identification purposes in accordance with this Code. See Code C note for guidance 17D.

Annex A

Video Identification

(a) General

1. The arrangements for obtaining and ensuring the availability of a suitable set of images to be used in a video identification must be the responsibility of an identification officer, who has no direct involvement with the case.

2.   The set of images must include the suspect and at least eight other people who, so far as possible, resemble the suspect in age, general appearance and position in life. Only one suspect shall appear in any set unless there are two suspects of roughly similar appearance, in which case they may be shown together with at least twelve other people.

2A   If the suspect has an unusual physical feature, e.g., a facial scar, tattoo or distinctive hairstyle or hair colour which does not appear on the images of the other people that are available to be used, steps may be taken to:

(a)   conceal the location of the feature on the images of the suspect and the other people; or

(b)   replicate that feature on the images of the other people. For these purposes, the feature may be concealed or replicated electronically or by any other method which it is practicable to use to ensure that the images of the suspect and other people resemble each other. The identification officer has discretion to choose whether to conceal or replicate the feature and the method to be used. If an unusual physical feature has been described by the witness, the identification officer should, if practicable, have that feature replicated. If it has not been described, concealment may be more appropriate.

2B   If the identification officer decides that a feature should be concealed or replicated, the reason for the decision and whether the feature was concealed or replicated in the images shown to any witness shall be recorded.

2C   If the witness requests to view an image where an unusual physical feature has been concealed or replicated without the feature being concealed or replicated, the witness may be allowed to do so.

3.   The images used to conduct a video identification shall, as far as possible, show the suspect and other people in the same positions or carrying out the same sequence of movements. They shall also show the suspect and other people under identical conditions unless the identification officer reasonably believes:

(a)   because of the suspect's failure or refusal to co-operate or other reasons, it is not practicable for the conditions to be identical; and

(b)   any difference in the conditions would not direct a witness' attention to any individual image.

4.   The reasons identical conditions are not practicable shall be recorded on forms provided for the purpose.

5.   Provision must be made for each person shown to be identified by number.

6.   If police officers are shown, any numerals or other identifying badges must be concealed. If a prison inmate is shown, either as a suspect or not, then either all, or none of, the people shown should be in prison clothing.

7.   The suspect or their solicitor, friend, or appropriate adult must be given a reasonable opportunity to see the complete set of images before it is shown to any witness. If the suspect has a reasonable objection to the set of images or any of the participants, the suspect shall be asked to state the reasons for the objection. Steps shall, if practicable, be taken to remove the grounds for objection. If this is not practicable, the suspect and/or their representative shall be told why their objections cannot be met and the objection, the reason given for it and why it cannot be met shall be recorded on forms provided for the purpose.

8.   Before the images are shown in accordance with paragraph 7, the suspect or their solicitor shall be provided with details of the first description of the suspect by any witnesses who are to attend the video identification. When a broadcast or publication is made, as in paragraph 3.28, the suspect or their solicitor must also be allowed to view any material released to the media by the police for the purpose of recognising or tracing the suspect, provided it is practicable and would not unreasonably delay the investigation.

9.   The suspect's solicitor, if practicable, shall be given reasonable notification of the time and place the video identification is to be conducted so a representative may attend on behalf of the suspect. The suspect may not be present when the images are shown to the witness(es). In the absence of the suspect's solicitor, the viewing itself shall be recorded on video. No unauthorised people may be present.

(b) Conducting the video identification

10.   The identification officer is responsible for making the appropriate arrangements to make sure, before they see the set of images, witnesses are not able to communicate with each other about the case, see any of the images which are to be shown, see, or be reminded of, any photograph or description of the suspect or be given any other indication as to the suspect's identity, or overhear a witness who has already seen the material. There must be no discussion with the witness about the composition of the set of images and they must not be told whether a previous witness has made any identification.

11. Only one witness may see the set of images at a time. Immediately before the images are shown, the witness shall be told that the person they saw on a specified earlier occasion may, or may not, appear in the images they are shown and that if they cannot make a positive identification, they should say so. The witness shall be advised that at any point, they may ask to see a particular part of the set of images or to have a particular image frozen for them to study. Furthermore, it should be pointed out to the witness that there is no limit on how many times they can view the whole set of images or any part of them. However, they should be asked not to make any decision as to whether the person they saw is on the set of images until they have seen the whole set at least twice.

12. Once the witness has seen the whole set of images at least twice and has indicated that they do not want to view the images, or any part of them, again, the witness shall be asked to say whether the individual they saw in person on a specified earlier occasion has been shown and, if so, to identify them by number of the image. The witness will then be shown that image to confirm the identification, see paragraph 17.

13. Care must be taken not to direct the witness' attention to any one individual image or give any indication of the suspect's identity. Where a witness has previously made an identification by photographs, or a computerised or artist's composite or similar likeness, the witness must not be reminded of such a photograph or composite likeness once a suspect is available for identification by other means in accordance with this Code. Nor must the witness be reminded of any description of the suspect.

14. After the procedure, each witness shall be asked whether they have seen any broadcast or published films or photographs, or any descriptions of suspects relating to the offence and their reply shall be recorded.

(c) Image security and destruction

15. Arrangements shall be made for all relevant material containing sets of images used for specific identification procedures to be kept securely and their movements accounted for. In particular, no-one involved in the investigation shall be permitted to view the material prior to it being shown to any witness.

16. As appropriate, paragraph 3.30 or 3.31 applies to the destruction or retention of relevant sets of images.

(d) Documentation

17. A record must be made of all those participating in, or seeing, the set of images whose names are known to the police.

18. A record of the conduct of the video identification must be made on forms provided for the purpose. This shall include anything said by the witness about any identifications or the conduct of the procedure and any reasons it was not practicable to comply with any of the provisions of this Code governing the conduct of video identifications.

Annex B

Identification Parades

(a) General

1. A suspect must be given a reasonable opportunity to have a solicitor or friend present, and the suspect shall be asked to indicate on a second copy of the notice whether or not they wish to do so.

2. An identification parade may take place either in a normal room or one equipped with a screen permitting witnesses to see members of the identification parade without being seen. The procedures for the composition and conduct of the identification parade are the same in both cases, subject to paragraph 8 (except that an identification parade involving a screen may take place only when the suspect's solicitor, friend or appropriate adult is present or the identification parade is recorded on video).

3. Before the identification parade takes place, the suspect or their solicitor shall be provided with details of the first description of the suspect by any witnesses who are attending the identification parade. When a broadcast or publication is made as in paragraph 3.28, the suspect or their solicitor should also be allowed to view any material released to the media by the police for the purpose of recognising or tracing the suspect, provided it is practicable to do so and would not unreasonably delay the investigation.

(b) Identification parades involving prison inmates

4. If a prison inmate is required for identification, and there are no security problems about the person leaving the establishment, they may be asked to participate in an identification parade or video identification.

5.   An identification parade may be held in a Prison Department establishment but shall be conducted, as far as practicable under normal identification parade rules. Members of the public shall make up the identification parade unless there are serious security, or control, objections to their admission to the establishment. In such cases, or if a group or video identification is arranged within the establishment, other inmates may participate. If an inmate is the suspect, they are not required to wear prison clothing for the identification parade unless the other people taking part are other inmates in similar clothing, or are members of the public who are prepared to wear prison clothing for the occasion.

(c) Conduct of the identification parade

6.   Immediately before the identification parade, the suspect must be reminded of the procedures governing its conduct and cautioned in the terms of Code C, paragraphs 10.5 or 10.6, as appropriate.

7.   All unauthorised people must be excluded from the place where the identification parade is held.

8.   Once the identification parade has been formed, everything afterwards, in respect of it, shall take place in the presence and hearing of the suspect and any interpreter, solicitor, friend or appropriate adult who is present (unless the identification parade involves a screen, in which case everything said to, or by, any witness at the place where the identification parade is held, must be said in the hearing and presence of the suspect's solicitor, friend or appropriate adult or be recorded on video).

9.   The identification parade shall consist of at least eight people (in addition to the suspect) who, so far as possible, resemble the suspect in age, height, general appearance and position in life. Only one suspect shall be included in an identification parade unless there are two suspects of roughly similar appearance, in which case they may be paraded together with at least twelve other people. In no circumstances shall more than two suspects be included in one identification parade and where there are separate identification parades, they shall be made up of different people.

10.   If the suspect has an unusual physical feature, e.g., a facial scar, tattoo or distinctive hairstyle or hair colour which cannot be replicated on other members of the identification parade, steps may be taken to conceal the location of that feature on the suspect and the other members of the identification parade if the suspect and their solicitor, or appropriate adult, agree. For example, by use of a plaster or a hat, so that all members of the identification parade resemble each other in general appearance.

11.   When all members of a similar group are possible suspects, separate identification parades shall be held for each unless there are two suspects of similar appearance when they may appear on the same identification parade with at least twelve other members of the group who are not suspects. When police officers in uniform form an identification parade any numerals or other identifying badges shall be concealed.

12.   When the suspect is brought to the place where the identification parade is to be held, they shall be asked if they have any objection to the arrangements for the identification parade or to any of the other participants in it and to state the reasons for the objection. The suspect may obtain advice from their solicitor or friend, if present, before the identification parade proceeds. If the suspect has a reasonable objection to the arrangements or any of the participants, steps shall, if practicable, be taken to remove the grounds for objection. When it is not practicable to do so, the suspect shall be told why their objections cannot be met and the objection, the reason given for it and why it cannot be met, shall be recorded on forms provided for the purpose.

13.   The suspect may select their own position in the line, but may not otherwise interfere with the order of the people forming the line. When there is more than one witness, the suspect must be told, after each witness has left the room, that they can, if they wish, change position in the line. Each position in the line must be clearly numbered, whether by means of a number laid on the floor in front of each identification parade member or by other means.

14.   Appropriate arrangements must be made to make sure, before witnesses attend the identification parade, they are not able to:
    (i)   communicate with each other about the case or overhear a witness who has already seen the identification parade;
    (ii)   see any member of the identification parade;
    (iii)   see, or be reminded of, any photograph or description of the suspect or be given any other indication as to the suspect's identity; or
    (iv)   see the suspect before or after the identification parade.

15.   The person conducting a witness to an identification parade must not discuss with them the composition of the identification parade and, in particular, must not disclose whether a previous witness has made any identification.

16.   Witnesses shall be brought in one at a time. Immediately before the witness inspects the identification parade, they shall be told the person they saw on a specified earlier occasion may, or may not, be present and if they cannot make a positive identification, they should say so. The witness must also

be told they should not make any decision about whether the person they saw is on the identification parade until they have looked at each member at least twice.

17.   When the officer or police staff (see paragraph 3.11) conducting the identification procedure is satisfied the witness has properly looked at each member of the identification parade, they shall ask the witness whether the person they saw on a specified earlier occasion is on the identification parade and, if so, to indicate the number of the person concerned, see paragraph 28.

18.   If the witness wishes to hear any identification parade member speak, adopt any specified posture or move, they shall first be asked whether they can identify any person(s) on the identification parade on the basis of appearance only. When the request is to hear members of the identification parade speak, the witness shall be reminded that the participants in the identification parade have been chosen on the basis of physical appearance only. Members of the identification parade may then be asked to comply with the witness' request to hear them speak, see them move or adopt any specified posture.

19.   If the witness requests that the person they have indicated remove anything used for the purposes of paragraph 10 to conceal the location of an unusual physical feature, that person may be asked to remove it.

20.   If the witness makes an identification after the identification parade has ended, the suspect and, if present, their solicitor, interpreter or friend shall be informed. When this occurs, consideration should be given to allowing the witness a second opportunity to identify the suspect.

21.   After the procedure, each witness shall be asked whether they have seen any broadcast or published films or photographs or any descriptions of suspects relating to the offence and their reply shall be recorded.

22.   When the last witness has left, the suspect shall be asked whether they wish to make any comments on the conduct of the identification parade.

(d) Documentation

23.   A video recording must normally be taken of the identification parade. If that is impracticable, a colour photograph must be taken. A copy of the video recording or photograph shall be supplied, on request, to the suspect or their solicitor within a reasonable time.

24.   As appropriate, paragraph 3.30 or 3.31, should apply to any photograph or video taken as in paragraph 23.

25.   If any person is asked to leave an identification parade because they are interfering with its conduct, the circumstances shall be recorded.

26.   A record must be made of all those present at an identification parade whose names are known to the police.

27.   If prison inmates make up an identification parade, the circumstances must be recorded.

28.   A record of the conduct of any identification parade must be made on forms provided for the purpose. This shall include anything said by the witness or the suspect about any identifications or the conduct of the procedure, and any reasons it was not practicable to comply with any of this Code's provisions.

Annex C

Group Identification

(a) General

1.   The purpose of this Annex is to make sure, as far as possible, group identifications follow the principles and procedures for identification parades so the conditions are fair to the suspect in the way they test the witness' ability to make an identification.

2.   Group identifications may take place either with the suspect's consent and cooperation or covertly without their consent.

3.   The location of the group identification is a matter for the identification officer, although the officer may take into account any representations made by the suspect, appropriate adult, their solicitor or friend.

4.   The place where the group identification is held should be one where other people are either passing by or waiting around informally, in groups such that the suspect is able to join them and be capable of being seen by the witness at the same time as others in the group. For example people leaving an escalator, pedestrians walking through a shopping centre, passengers on railway and bus stations, waiting in queues or groups or where people are standing or sitting in groups in other public places.

5.   If the group identification is to be held covertly, the choice of locations will be limited by the places where the suspect can be found and the number of other people present at that time. In these cases,

suitable locations might be along regular routes travelled by the suspect, including buses or trains or public places frequented by the suspect.

6.   Although the number, age, sex, race and general description and style of clothing of other people present at the location cannot be controlled by the identification officer, in selecting the location the officer must consider the general appearance and numbers of people likely to be present. In particular, the officer must reasonably expect that over the period the witness observes the group, they will be able to see, from time to time, a number of others whose appearance is broadly similar to that of the suspect.

7.   A group identification need not be held if the identification officer believes, because of the unusual appearance of the suspect, none of the locations it would be practicable to use, satisfy the requirements of paragraph 6 necessary to make the identification fair.

8.   Immediately after a group identification procedure has taken place (with or without the suspect's consent), a colour photograph or video should be taken of the general scene, if practicable, to give a general impression of the scene and the number of people present. Alternatively, if it is practicable, the group identification may be video recorded.

9.   If it is not practicable to take the photograph or video in accordance with paragraph 8, a photograph or film of the scene should be taken later at a time determined by the identification officer if the officer considers it practicable to do so.

10.   An identification carried out in accordance with this Code remains a group identification even though, at the time of being seen by the witness, the suspect was on their own rather than in a group.

11.   Before the group identification takes place, the suspect or their solicitor shall be provided with details of the first description of the suspect by any witnesses who are to attend the identification. When a broadcast or publication is made, as in paragraph 3.28, the suspect or their solicitor should also be allowed to view any material released by the police to the media for the purposes of recognising or tracing the suspect, provided that it is practicable and would not unreasonably delay the investigation.

12.   After the procedure, each witness shall be asked whether they have seen any broadcast or published films or photographs or any descriptions of suspects relating to the offence and their reply recorded.

(b) Identification with the consent of the suspect

13.   A suspect must be given a reasonable opportunity to have a solicitor or friend present. They shall be asked to indicate on a second copy of the notice whether or not they wish to do so.

14.   The witness, the person carrying out the procedure and the suspect's solicitor, appropriate adult, friend or any interpreter for the witness, may be concealed from the sight of the individuals in the group they are observing, if the person carrying out the procedure considers this assists the conduct of the identification.

15.   The person conducting a witness to a group identification must not discuss with them the forthcoming group identification and, in particular, must not disclose whether a previous witness has made any identification.

16.   Anything said to, or by, the witness during the procedure about the identification should be said in the presence and hearing of those present at the procedure.

17.   Appropriate arrangements must be made to make sure, before witnesses attend the group identification, they are not able to:
   (i)   communicate with each other about the case or overhear a witness who has already been given an opportunity to see the suspect in the group;
   (ii)   see the suspect; or
   (iii)   see, or be reminded of, any photographs or description of the suspect or be given any other indication of the suspect's identity.

18.   Witnesses shall be brought one at a time to the place where they are to observe the group. Immediately before the witness is asked to look at the group, the person conducting the procedure shall tell them that the person they saw may, or may not, be in the group and that if they cannot make a positive identification, they should say so. The witness shall be asked to observe the group in which the suspect is to appear. The way in which the witness should do this will depend on whether the group is moving or stationary.

Moving group

19.   When the group in which the suspect is to appear is moving, e.g. leaving an escalator, the provisions of paragraphs 20 to 24 should be followed.

20.   If two or more suspects consent to a group identification, each should be the subject of separate identification procedures. These may be conducted consecutively on the same occasion.

21. The person conducting the procedure shall tell the witness to observe the group and ask them to point out any person they think they saw on the specified earlier occasion.

22. Once the witness has been informed as in paragraph 21 the suspect should be allowed to take whatever position in the group they wish.

23. When the witness points out a person as in paragraph 21 they shall, if practicable, be asked to take a closer look at the person to confirm the identification. If this is not practicable, or they cannot confirm the identification, they shall be asked how sure they are that the person they have indicated is the relevant person.

24. The witness should continue to observe the group for the period which the person conducting the procedure reasonably believes is necessary in the circumstances for them to be able to make comparisons between the suspect and other individuals of broadly similar appearance to the suspect as in paragraph 6.

Stationary groups

25. When the group in which the suspect is to appear is stationary, e.g. people waiting in a queue, the provisions of paragraphs 26 to 29 should be followed.

26. If two or more suspects consent to a group identification, each should be subject to separate identification procedures unless they are of broadly similar appearance when they may appear in the same group. When separate group identifications are held, the groups must be made up of different people.

27. The suspect may take whatever position in the group they wish. If there is more than one witness, the suspect must be told, out of the sight and hearing of any witness, that they can, if they wish, change their position in the group.

28. The witness shall be asked to pass along, or amongst, the group and to look at each person in the group at least twice, taking as much care and time as possible according to the circumstances, before making an identification. Once the witness has done this, they shall be asked whether the person they saw on the specified earlier occasion is in the group and to indicate any such person by whatever means the person conducting the procedure considers appropriate in the circumstances. If this is not practicable, the witness shall be asked to point out any person they think they saw on the earlier occasion.

29. When the witness makes an indication as in paragraph 28, arrangements shall be made, if practicable, for the witness to take a closer look at the person to confirm the identification. If this is not practicable, or the witness is unable to confirm the identification, they shall be asked how sure they are that the person they have indicated is the relevant person.

All cases

30. If the suspect unreasonably delays joining the group, or having joined the group, deliberately conceals themselves from the sight of the witness, this may be treated as a refusal to co-operate in a group identification.

31. If the witness identifies a person other than the suspect, that person should be informed what has happened and asked if they are prepared to give their name and address. There is no obligation upon any member of the public to give these details. There shall be no duty to record any details of any other member of the public present in the group or at the place where the procedure is conducted.

32. When the group identification has been completed, the suspect shall be asked whether they wish to make any comments on the conduct of the procedure.

33. If the suspect has not been previously informed, they shall be told of any identifications made by the witnesses.

(c) Identification without the suspect's consent

34. Group identifications held covertly without the suspect's consent should, as far as practicable, follow the rules for conduct of group identification by consent.

35. A suspect has no right to have a solicitor, appropriate adult or friend present as the identification will take place without the knowledge of the suspect.

36. Any number of suspects may be identified at the same time.

(d) Identifications in police stations

37. Group identifications should only take place in police stations for reasons of safety, security or because it is not practicable to hold them elsewhere.

38. The group identification may take place either in a room equipped with a screen permitting witnesses to see members of the group without being seen, or anywhere else in the police station that the identification officer considers appropriate.

39.   Any of the additional safeguards applicable to identification parades should be followed if the identification officer considers it is practicable to do so in the circumstances.

(e) Identifications involving prison inmates

40.   A group identification involving a prison inmate may only be arranged in the prison or at a police station.

41.   When a group identification takes place involving a prison inmate, whether in a prison or in a police
station, the arrangements should follow those in paragraphs 37 to 39. If a group identification takes place
within a prison, other inmates may participate. If an inmate is the suspect, they do not have to wear
prison clothing for the group identification unless the other participants are wearing the same clothing.

(f) Documentation

42.   When a photograph or video is taken as in paragraph 8 or 9, a copy of the photograph or video
shall be supplied on request to the suspect or their solicitor within a reasonable time.

43.   Paragraph 3.30 or 3.31, as appropriate, shall apply when the photograph or film taken in accordance
with paragraph 8 or 9 includes the suspect.

44.   A record of the conduct of any group identification must be made on forms provided for the purpose.
This shall include anything said by the witness or suspect about any identifications or the conduct of
the procedure and any reasons why it was not practicable to comply with any of the provisions of this
Code governing the conduct of group identifications.

Annex D

Confrontation by a Witness

1.   Before the confrontation takes place, the witness must be told that the person they saw may, or may
not, be the person they are to confront and that if they are not that person, then the witness should
say so.

2.   Before the confrontation takes place the suspect or their solicitor shall be provided with details of the
first description of the suspect given by any witness who is to attend. When a broadcast or publication is made, as in paragraph 3.28, the suspect or their solicitor should also be allowed to view any
material released to the media for the purposes of recognising or tracing the suspect, provided it is
practicable to do so and would not unreasonably delay the investigation.

3.   Force may not be used to make the suspect's face visible to the witness.

4.   Confrontation must take place in the presence of the suspect's solicitor, interpreter or friend unless
this would cause unreasonable delay.

5.   The suspect shall be confronted independently by each witness, who shall be asked 'Is this the person?'. If the witness identifies the person but is unable to confirm the identification, they shall be
asked how sure they are that the person is the one they saw on the earlier occasion.

6.   The confrontation should normally take place in the police station, either in a normal room or one
equipped with a screen permitting a witness to see the suspect without being seen. In both cases, the
procedures are the same except that a room equipped with a screen may be used only when the suspect's solicitor, friend or appropriate adult is present or the confrontation is recorded on video.

7.   After the procedure, each witness shall be asked whether they have seen any broadcast or published
films or photographs or any descriptions of suspects relating to the offence and their reply shall be
recorded.

Annex E

Showing Photographs

(a) Action

1.   An officer of sergeant rank or above shall be responsible for supervising and directing the showing of photographs. The actual showing may be done by another officer or police staff, see
paragraph 3.11.

2.   The supervising officer must confirm the first description of the suspect given by the witness has been
recorded before they are shown the photographs. If the supervising officer is unable to confirm the
description has been recorded they shall postpone showing the photographs.

3.   Only one witness shall be shown photographs at any one time. Each witness shall be given as much
privacy as practicable and shall not be allowed to communicate with any other witness in the case.

4.   The witness shall be shown not less than twelve photographs at a time, which shall, as far as possible,
all be of a similar type.

5.   When the witness is shown the photographs, they shall be told the photograph of the person they saw
may, or may not, be amongst them and if they cannot make a positive identification, they should say

so. The witness shall also be told they should not make a decision until they have viewed at least twelve photographs. The witness shall not be prompted or guided in any way but shall be left to make any selection without help.

6.   If a witness makes a positive identification from photographs, unless the person identified is otherwise eliminated from enquiries or is not available, other witnesses shall not be shown photographs. But both they, and the witness who has made the identification, shall be asked to attend a video identification, an identification parade or group identification unless there is no dispute about the suspect's identification.

7.   If the witness makes a selection but is unable to confirm the identification, the person showing the photographs shall ask them how sure they are that the photograph they have indicated is the person they saw on the specified earlier occasion.

8.   When the use of a computerised or artist's composite or similar likeness has led to there being a known suspect who can be asked to participate in a video identification, appear on an identification parade or participate in a group identification, that likeness shall not be shown to other potential witnesses.

9.   When a witness attending a video identification, an identification parade or group identification has previously been shown photographs or computerised or artist's composite or similar likeness (and it is the responsibility of the officer in charge of investigation to make the identification officer aware that this is the case), the suspect and their solicitor must be informed of this fact before the identification procedure takes place.

10.   None of the photographs shown shall be destroyed, whether or not an identification is made, since they may be required for production in court. The photographs shall be numbered and a separate photograph taken of the frame or part of the album from which the witness made an identification as an aid to reconstituting it.

(b) Documentation

11.   Whether or not an identification is made, a record shall be kept of the showing of photographs on forms provided for the purpose. This shall include anything said by the witness about any identification or the conduct of the procedure, any reasons it was not practicable to comply with any of the provisions of this Code governing the showing of photographs and the name and rank of the supervising officer.

12.   The supervising officer shall inspect and sign the record as soon as practicable.

Annex F

Fingerprints, Footwear Impressions and Samples—Destruction and Speculative Searches

(a) Fingerprints, footwear impressions and samples taken in connection with a criminal investigation from a person suspected of committing the offence under investigation

1.   The retention and destruction of fingerprints, footwear impressions and samples taken in connection with a criminal investigation from a person suspected of committing the offence under investigation is subject to PACE, section 64.

(b) Fingerprints, footwear impressions and samples taken in connection with a criminal investigation from a person not suspected of committing the offence under investigation

2.   When fingerprints, footwear impressions or DNA samples are taken from a person in connection with an investigation and the person is not suspected of having committed the offence, see Note F1, they must be destroyed as soon as they have fulfilled the purpose for which they were taken unless:

  (a)   they were taken for the purposes of an investigation of an offence for which a person has been convicted; and

  (b)   fingerprints, footwear impressions or samples were also taken from the convicted person for the purposes of that investigation.

      However, subject to paragraph 2, the fingerprints, footwear impressions and samples, and the information derived from samples, may not be used in the investigation of any offence or in evidence against the person who is, or would be, entitled to the destruction of the fingerprints, footwear impressions and samples, see Note F2.

3.   The requirement to destroy fingerprints, footwear impressions and DNA samples, and information derived from samples, and restrictions on their retention and use in paragraph 1 do not apply if the person gives their written consent for their fingerprints, footwear impressions or sample to be retained and used after they have fulfilled the purpose for which they were taken, see Note F1.

4. When a person's fingerprints, footwear impressions or sample are to be destroyed:
    (a) any copies of the fingerprints and footwear impressions must also be destroyed;
    (b) the person may witness the destruction of their fingerprints, footwear impressions or copies if they ask to do so within five days of being informed destruction is required;
    (c) access to relevant computer fingerprint data shall be made impossible as soon as it is practicable to do so and the person shall be given a certificate to this effect within three months of asking; and
    (d) neither the fingerprints, footwear impressions, the sample, or any information derived from the sample, may be used in the investigation of any offence or in evidence against the person who is, or would be, entitled to its destruction.

5. Fingerprints, footwear impressions or samples, and the information derived from samples, taken in connection with the investigation of an offence which are not required to be destroyed, may be retained after they have fulfilled the purposes for which they were taken but may be used only for purposes related to the prevention or detection of crime, the investigation of an offence or the conduct of a prosecution in, as well as outside, the UK and may also be subject to a speculative search. This includes checking them against other fingerprints, footwear impressions and DNA records held by, or on behalf of, the police and other law enforcement authorities in, as well as outside, the UK.

[(c)] Fingerprints taken in connection with Immigration Service enquiries
6. See paragraph 4.10.

Notes for Guidance

F1 Fingerprints, footwear impressions and samples given voluntarily for the purposes of elimination play an important part in many police investigations. It is, therefore, important to make sure innocent volunteers are not deterred from participating and their consent to their fingerprints, footwear impressions and DNA being used for the purposes of a specific investigation is fully informed and voluntary. If the police or volunteer seek to have the fingerprints, footwear impressions or samples retained for use after the specific investigation ends, it is important the volunteer's consent to this is also fully informed and voluntary.
Examples of consent for:
*   DNA/fingerprints/footwear impressions—to be used only for the purposes of a specific investigation;
*   DNA/fingerprints/footwear impressions—to be used in the specific investigation and retained by the police for future use.
To minimise the risk of confusion, each consent should be physically separate and the volunteer should be asked to sign each consent.
    (a) DNA:
        (i) DNA sample taken for the purposes of elimination or as part of an intelligence led screening and to be used only for the purposes of that investigation and destroyed afterwards:

        'I consent to my DNA/mouth swab being taken for forensic analysis. I understand that the sample will be destroyed at the end of the case and that my profile will only be compared to the crime stain profile from this enquiry. I have been advised that the person taking the sample may be required to give evidence and/or provide a written statement to the police in relation to the taking of it'.

        (ii) DNA sample to be retained on the National DNA database and used in the future:

        'I consent to my DNA sample and information derived from it being retained and used only for purposes related to the prevention and detection of a crime, the investigation of an offence or the conduct of a prosecution either nationally or internationally.'

        'I understand that this sample may be checked against other DNA records held by, or on behalf of, relevant law enforcement authorities, either nationally or internationally'.

        'I understand that once I have given my consent for the sample to be retained and used I cannot withdraw this consent.'

    (b) Fingerprints:
        (i) Fingerprints taken for the purposes of elimination or as part of an intelligence led screening and to be used only for the purposes of that investigation and destroyed afterwards:

        'I consent to my fingerprints being taken for elimination purposes. I understand that the fingerprints will be destroyed at the end of the case and that my fingerprints will only be

compared to the fingerprints from this enquiry. I have been advised that the person taking the fingerprints may be required to give evidence and/or provide a written statement
to the police in relation to the taking of it.'

(ii) Fingerprints to be retained for future use:

'I consent to my fingerprints being retained and used only for purposes related to the
prevention and detection of a crime, the investigation of an offence or the conduct of a
prosecution either nationally or internationally'.

'I understand that my fingerprints may be checked against other records held by, or on
behalf of, relevant law enforcement authorities, either nationally or internationally.'

'I understand that once I have given my consent for my fingerprints to be retained and
used I cannot withdraw this consent.'

(c) Footwear impressions:
(i) Footwear impressions taken for the purposes of elimination or as part of an intelligence-led
screening and to be used only for the purposes of that investigation and destroyed afterwards:

'I consent to my footwear impressions being taken for elimination purposes. I understand that the footwear impressions will be destroyed at the end of the case and that my
footwear impressions will only be compared to the footwear impressions from this
enquiry. I have been advised that the person taking the footwear impressions may be
required to give evidence and/or provide a written statement to the police in relation to
the taking of it.'

(ii) Footwear impressions to be retained for future use:

'I consent to my footwear impressions being retained and used only for purposes related
to the prevention and detection of a crime, the investigation of an offence or the conduct
of a prosecution, either nationally or internationally'.

'I understand that my footwear impressions may be checked against other records held by,
or on behalf of, relevant law enforcement authorities, either nationally or internationally.'

'I understand that once I have given my consent for my footwear impressions to be
retained and used I cannot withdraw this consent.'

F2   The provisions for the retention of fingerprints, footwear impressions and samples in paragraph 1
allow for all fingerprints, footwear impressions and samples in a case to be available for any subsequent miscarriage of justice investigation.

ANNEX G

REQUIREMENT FOR A PERSON TO ATTEND A POLICE STATION FOR FINGERPRINTS AND SAMPLES

1.   A requirement under Schedule 2A for a person to attend a police station to have fingerprints or
samples taken:
(a) must give the person a period of at least seven days within which to attend the police station; and
(b) may direct them to attend at a specified time of day or between specified times of day.
2.   When specifying the period and times of attendance, the officer making the requirements must
consider whether the fingerprints or samples could reasonably be taken at a time when the person is
required to attend the police station for any other reason. See Note G1.
3.   An officer of the rank of inspector or above may authorise a period shorter than 7 days if there is an
urgent need for [a] person's fingerprints or sample for the purposes of the investigation of an offence.
The fact of the authorisation and the reasons for giving it must be recorded as soon as practicable.
4.   The constable making a requirement and the person to whom it applies may agree to vary it so as to
specify any period within which, or date or time at which, the person is to attend. However, variation
shall not have effect for the purposes of enforcement, unless it is confirmed by the constable in writing.

Notes for Guidance

G1   The specified period within which the person is to attend need not fall within the period allowed (if
applicable) for making the requirement.

G2 To justify the arrest without warrant of a person who fails to comply with a requirement, (see paragraph 4.4(b) above), the officer making the requirement, or confirming a variation, should be prepared to explain how, when and where the requirement was made or the variation was confirmed and what steps were taken to ensure the person understood what to do and the consequences of not complying with the requirement.

PACE CODE E

CODE OF PRACTICE ON AUDIO RECORDING INTERVIEWS WITH SUSPECTS

[Omitted: see **D1.90**. The full text of Code E is freely available at www.gov.uk/government/uploads/system/uploads/attachment_data/file/306658/2013_PACE_Code_E.pdf.]

PACE CODE F

CODE OF PRACTICE ON VISUAL RECORDING WITH SOUND OF INTERVIEWS WITH SUSPECTS

[Omitted: see **D1.90**. The full text of Code F is freely available at www.gov.uk/government/uploads/system/uploads/attachment_data/file/306661/2013_PACE_Code_F.pdf.]

PACE CODE G

CODE OF PRACTICE FOR THE STATUTORY POWER OF ARREST BY POLICE OFFICERS

Commencement — Transitional Arrangements This Code applies to any arrest made by a police officer after midnight on 12 November 2012.

1. Introduction

1.1 This Code of Practice deals with the statutory power of police to arrest a person who is involved, or suspected of being involved, in a criminal offence. The power of arrest must be used fairly, responsibly, with respect for people suspected of committing offences and without unlawful discrimination. The Equality Act 2010 makes it unlawful for police officers to discriminate against, harass or victimise any person on the grounds of the 'protected characteristics' of age, disability, gender reassignment, race, religion or belief, sex and sexual orientation, marriage and civil partnership, pregnancy and maternity when using their powers. When police forces are carrying out their functions they also have a duty to have regard to the need to eliminate unlawful discrimination, harassment and victimisation and to take steps to foster good relations.

1.2 The exercise of the power of arrest represents an obvious and significant interference with the Right to liberty and security under Article 5 of the European Convention on Human Rights set out in Part I of Schedule 1 to the Human Rights Act 1998.

1.3 The use of the power must be fully justified and officers exercising the power should consider if the necessary objectives can be met by other, less intrusive means. Absence of justification for exercising the power of arrest may lead to challenges should the case proceed to court. It could also lead to civil claims against police for unlawful arrest and false imprisonment. When the power of arrest is exercised it is essential that it is exercised in a non-discriminatory and proportionate manner which is compatible with the Right to liberty under Article 5. See *Note 1B*.

1.4 Section 24 of the Police and Criminal Evidence Act 1984 (as substituted by section 110 of the Serious Organised Crime and Police Act 2005) provides the statutory power for a constable to arrest without warrant for all offences. If the provisions of the Act and this Code are not observed, both the arrest and the conduct of any subsequent investigation may be open to question.

1.5   This Code of Practice must be readily available at all police stations for consultation by police officers and police staff, detained persons and members of the public.

1.6   The notes for guidance are not provisions of this code.

2. Elements of arrest under section 24 PACE

2.1   A lawful arrest requires two elements:

A person's involvement or suspected involvement or attempted involvement in the commission of a criminal offence;

AND

Reasonable grounds for *believing* that the person's arrest is necessary.

- both elements must be satisfied, and
- it can never be necessary to arrest a person unless there are reasonable grounds to suspect them of committing an offence.

2.2   The arrested person must be informed that they have been arrested, even if this fact is obvious, and of the relevant circumstances of the arrest in relation to both the above elements. The custody officer must be informed of these matters on arrival at the police station. See *paragraphs 2.9, 3.3 and Note 3 and Code C paragraph 3.4.*

(a) Involvement in the commission of an offence'

2.3   A constable may arrest without warrant in relation to any offence (see *Notes 1 and 1A*) anyone:
- who is about to commit an offence or is in the act of committing an offence;
- whom the officer has reasonable grounds for suspecting is about to commit an offence or to be committing an offence;
- whom the officer has reasonable grounds to suspect of being guilty of an offence which he or she has reasonable grounds for suspecting has been committed;
- anyone who is guilty of an offence which has been committed or anyone whom the officer has reasonable grounds for suspecting to be guilty of that offence.

2.3A There must be some reasonable, objective grounds for the suspicion, based on known facts and information which are relevant to the likelihood the offence has been committed and the person liable to arrest committed it. See *Notes 2 and 2A.*

(b) Necessity criteria

2.4   The power of arrest is only exercisable if the constable has reasonable grounds for *believing* that it is necessary to arrest the person. The statutory criteria for what may constitute necessity are set out in paragraph 2.9 and it remains an operational decision at the discretion of the constable to decide:
- which one or more of the necessity criteria (if any) applies to the individual; and
- if any of the criteria do apply, whether to arrest, grant street bail after arrest, report for summons or for charging by post, issue a penalty notice or take any other action that is open to the officer.

2.5   In applying the criteria, the arresting officer has to be satisfied that at least one of the reasons supporting the need for arrest is satisfied.

2.6   Extending the power of arrest to all offences provides a constable with the ability to use that power to deal with any situation. However applying the necessity criteria requires the constable to examine and justify the reason or reasons why a person needs to be arrested or (as the case may be) further arrested, for an offence for the custody officer to decide whether to authorise their detention for that offence. See *Note 2C*

2.7   The criteria in paragraph 2.9 below which are set out in section 24 of PACE as substituted by section 110 of the Serious Organised Crime and Police Act 2005 are exhaustive. However, the circumstances that may satisfy those criteria remain a matter for the operational discretion of individual officers. Some examples are given to illustrate what those circumstances might be and what officers might consider when deciding whether arrest is necessary.

2.8   In considering the individual circumstances, the constable must take into account the situation of the victim, the nature of the offence, the circumstances of the suspect and the needs of the investigative process.

2.9   When it is practicable to tell a person why their arrest is necessary (as required by paragraphs 2.2, 3.3 and *Note 3*), the constable should outline the facts, information and other circumstances which provide the grounds for believing that their arrest is necessary and which the officer considers satisfy one or more of the statutory criteria in sub-paragraphs (a) to (f), namely:
- (a) to enable the name of the person in question to be ascertained (in the case where the constable does not know, and cannot readily ascertain, the person's name, or has reasonable grounds for doubting whether a name given by the person as his name is his real name):

An officer might decide that a person's name cannot be readily ascertained if they fail or refuse to give it when asked, particularly after being warned that failure or refusal is likely to make their arrest necessary (see *Note 2D*). Grounds to doubt a name given may arise if the person appears reluctant or hesitant when asked to give their name or to verify the name they have given.

Where mobile fingerprinting is available and the suspect's name cannot be ascertained or is doubted, the officer should consider using the power under section 61(6A) of PACE (see *Code D paragraph 4.3(e)*) to take and check the fingerprints of a suspect as this may avoid the need to arrest solely to enable their name to be ascertained.

(b) correspondingly as regards the person's address:

An officer might decide that a person's address cannot be readily ascertained if they fail or refuse to give it when asked, particularly after being warned that such a failure or refusal is likely to make their arrest necessary. See *Note 2D*. Grounds to doubt an address given may arise if the person appears reluctant or hesitant when asked to give their address or is unable to provide verifiable details of the locality they claim to live in.

When considering reporting to consider summons or charging by post as alternatives to arrest, an address would be satisfactory if the person will be at it for a sufficiently long period for it to be possible to serve them with the summons or requisition and charge; or, that some other person at that address specified by the person will accept service on their behalf. When considering issuing a penalty notice, the address should be one where the person will be in the event of enforcement action if the person does not pay the penalty or is convicted and fined after a court hearing.

(c) to prevent the person in question:

   (i)   causing physical injury to himself or any other person;

          This might apply where the suspect has already used or threatened violence against others and it is thought likely that they may assault others if they are not arrested. See *Note 2D*

   (ii)   suffering physical injury;

          This might apply where the suspect's behaviour and actions are believed likely to provoke, or have provoked, others to want to assault the suspect unless the suspect is arrested for their own protection. See *Note 2D*

   (iii) causing loss or damage to property;

          This might apply where the suspect is a known persistent offender with a history of serial offending against property (theft and criminal damage) and it is thought likely that they may continue offending if they are not arrested.

   (iv)   committing an offence against public decency (only applies where members of the public going about their normal business cannot reasonably be expected to avoid the person in question);

          This might apply when an offence against public decency is being committed in a place to which the public have access and is likely to be repeated in that or some other public place at a time when the public are likely to encounter the suspect. See *Note 2D*

   (v)   causing an unlawful obstruction of the highway;

          This might apply to any offence where its commission causes an unlawful obstruction which it is believed may continue or be repeated if the person is not arrested, particularly if the person has been warned that they are causing an obstruction. See *Note 2D*

(d) to protect a child or other vulnerable person from the person in question.

This might apply when the health (physical or mental) or welfare of a child or vulnerable person is likely to be harmed or is at risk of being harmed, if the person is not arrested in cases where it is not practicable and appropriate to make alternative arrangements to prevent the suspect from having any harmful or potentially harmful contact with the child or vulnerable person.

(e) to allow the prompt and effective investigation of the offence or of the conduct of the person in question. See *Note 2E*

This may arise when it is thought likely that unless the person is arrested and then either taken in custody to the police station or granted 'street bail' to attend the station later, see *Note 2J*, further action considered necessary to properly investigate their involvement in the offence would be frustrated, unreasonably delayed or otherwise hindered and therefore be impracticable. Examples of such actions include:

   (i)   *interviewing the suspect* on occasions when the person's voluntary attendance is not considered to be a practicable alternative to arrest, because for example:

          • it is thought unlikely that the person would attend the police station voluntarily to be interviewed.

- it is necessary to interview the suspect about the outcome of other investigative action for which their arrest is necessary, see (ii) to (v) below.
- arrest would enable the special warning to be given in accordance with Code C paragraphs 10.10 and 10.11 when the suspect is found:
  — in possession of incriminating objects, or at a place where such objects are found;
  — at or near the scene of the crime at or about the time it was committed.
- the person has made false statements and/or presented false evidence;
- it is thought likely that the person:
  — may steal or destroy evidence;
  — may collude or make contact with, co-suspects or conspirators;
  — may intimidate or threaten or make contact with, witnesses.

See *Notes 2F and 2G*

(ii) when considering arrest in connection with the investigation of an *indictable offence* (see *Note 6*), there is a need:
- to enter and search without a search warrant any premises occupied or controlled by the arrested person or where the person was when arrested or immediately before arrest;
- to prevent the arrested person from having contact with others;
- to detain the arrested person for more than 24 hours before charge.

(iii) when considering arrest in connection with any *recordable offence* and it is necessary to secure or preserve evidence of that offence by taking fingerprints, footwear impressions or samples from the suspect for evidential comparison or matching with other material relating to that offence, for example, from the crime scene. See *Note 2H*

(iv) when considering arrest in connection with any offence and it is necessary to search, examine or photograph the person to obtain evidence. See *Note 2H*

(v) when considering arrest in connection with an offence to which the statutory Class A drug testing requirements in Code C section 17 apply, to enable testing when it is thought that drug misuse might have caused or contributed to the offence. See *Note 2I*.

(f) to prevent any prosecution for the offence from being hindered by the disappearance of the person in question.

This may arise when it is thought that:
- if the person is not arrested they are unlikely to attend court if they are prosecuted;
- the address given is not a satisfactory address for service of a summons or a written charge and requisition to appear at court because the person will not be at it for a sufficiently long period for the summons or charge and requisition to be served and no other person at that specified address will accept service on their behalf.

3. Information to be given on arrest

(a) Cautions —when a caution must be given

3.1 Code C paragraphs 10.1 and 10.2 set out the requirement for a person whom there are grounds to suspect of an offence (see *Note 2*) to be cautioned before being questioned or further questioned about an offence.

3.2 *Not used.*

3.3 A person who is arrested, or further arrested, must be informed at the time if practicable, or if not, as soon as it becomes practicable thereafter, that they are under arrest and of the grounds and reasons for their arrest, see paragraphs 2.2 and *Note 3*.

3.4 A person who is arrested, or further arrested, must be cautioned unless:
(a) it is impracticable to do so by reason of their condition or behaviour at the time;
(b) they have already been cautioned immediately prior to arrest as in *paragraph 3.1*.

(b) Terms of the caution (Taken from Code C section 10)

3.5 The caution, which must be given on arrest, should be in the following terms:

'You do not have to say anything. But it may harm your defence if you do not mention when questioned something which you later rely on in Court. Anything you do say may be given in evidence.'

Where the use of the Welsh Language is appropriate, a constable may provide the caution directly in Welsh in the following terms:

'Does dim rhaid i chi ddweud dim byd. Ond gall niweidio eich amddiffyniad os na fyddwch chi"n sôn, wrth gael eich holi, am rywbeth y byddwch chi"n dibynnu arno nes ymlaen yn y Llys. Gall unrhyw beth yr ydych yn ei ddweud gael ei roi fel tystiolaeth.'

See *Note 5*

3.6   Minor deviations from the words of any caution given in accordance with this Code do not constitute a breach of this Code, provided the sense of the relevant caution is preserved. See *Note 6*

3.7   *Not used.*

4. Records of arrest

(a) General

4.1   The arresting officer is required to record in his pocket book or by other methods used for recording information:
  - the nature and circumstances of the offence leading to the arrest;
  - the reason or reasons why arrest was necessary;
  - the giving of the caution; and
  - anything said by the person at the time of arrest.

4.2   Such a record should be made at the time of the arrest unless impracticable to do so. If not made at that time, the record should then be completed as soon as possible thereafter.

4.3   On arrival at the police station or after being first arrested at the police station, the arrested person must be brought before the custody officer as soon as practicable and a custody record must be opened in accordance with section 2 of Code C. The information given by the arresting officer on the circumstances and reason or reasons for arrest shall be recorded as part of the custody record. Alternatively, a copy of the record made by the officer in accordance with paragraph 4.1 above shall be attached as part of the custody record. See *paragraph 2.2* and *Code C paragraphs 3.4 and 10.3.*

4.4   The custody record will serve as a record of the arrest. Copies of the custody record will be provided in accordance with paragraphs 2.4 and 2.4A of Code C and access for inspection of the original record in accordance with paragraph 2.5 of Code C.

(b) Interviews and arrests

4.5   Records of interview, significant statements or silences will be treated in the same way as set out in sections 10 and 11 of Code C and in Codes E and F (audio and visual recording of interviews).

Notes for Guidance

1   For the purposes of this Code, 'offence' means any statutory or common law offence for which a person may be tried by a magistrates' court or the Crown court and punished if convicted. Statutory offences include assault, rape, criminal damage, theft, robbery, burglary, fraud, possession of controlled drugs and offences under road traffic, liquor licensing, gambling and immigration legislation and local government byelaws. Common law offences include murder, manslaughter, kidnapping, false imprisonment, perverting the course of justice and escape from lawful custody.

1A   This code does not apply to powers of arrest conferred on constables under any arrest warrant, for example, a warrant issued under the Magistrates' Courts Act 1980, sections 1 or 13, or the Bail Act 1976, section 7(1), or to the powers of constables to arrest without warrant other than under section 24 of PACE for an offence. These other powers to arrest without warrant do not depend on the arrested person committing any specific offence and include:
  - PACE, section 46A, arrest of person who fails to answer police bail to attend police station or is suspected of breaching any condition of that bail for the custody officer to decide whether they should be kept in police detention which applies whether or not the person commits an offence under section 6 of the Bail Act 1976 (e.g. failing without reasonable cause to surrender to custody);
  - Bail Act 1976, section 7(3), arrest of person bailed to attend court who is suspected of breaching, or is believed likely to breach, any condition of bail to take them to court for bail to be re-considered;
  - Children & Young Persons Act 1969, section 32(1A) (absconding) —arrest to return the person to the place where they are required to reside;
  - Immigration Act 1971, Schedule 2 to arrest a person liable to examination to determine their right to remain in the UK;
  - Mental Health Act 1983, section 136 to remove person suffering from mental disorder to place of safety for assessment;
  - Prison Act 1952, section 49, arrest to return person unlawfully at large to the prison etc. where they are liable to be detained;
  - Road Traffic Act 1988, section 6D arrest of driver following the outcome of a preliminary roadside test requirement to enable the driver to be required to provide an evidential sample;
  - Common law power to stop or prevent a Breach of the Peace — after arrest a person aged 18 or over may be brought before a justice of the peace court to show cause why they should not be bound over to keep the peace — not criminal proceedings.

1B   Juveniles should not be arrested at their place of education unless this is unavoidable. When a juvenile is arrested at their place of education, the principal or their nominee must be informed. (From Code C Note 11D)

2   Facts and information relevant to a person's suspected involvement in an offence should not be confined to those which tend to indicate the person has committed or attempted to commit the offence. Before making a decision to arrest, a constable should take account of any facts and information that are available, including claims of innocence made by the person, that might dispel the suspicion.

2A   Particular examples of facts and information which might point to a person's innocence and may tend to dispel suspicion include those which relate to the statutory defence provided by the Criminal Law Act 1967, section 3(1) which allows the use of reasonable force in the prevention of crime or making an arrest and the common law of self-defence. This may be relevant when a person appears, or claims, to have been acting reasonably in defence of themselves or others or to prevent their property or the property of others from being stolen, destroyed or damaged, particularly if the offence alleged is based on the use of unlawful force, e.g. a criminal assault. When investigating allegations involving the use of force by school staff, the power given to all school staff under the Education and Inspections Act 2006, section 93, to use reasonable force to prevent their pupils from committing any offence, injuring persons, damaging property or prejudicing the maintenance of good order and discipline may be similarly relevant. The Association of Chief Police Officers and the Crown Prosecution Service have published joint guidance to help the public understand the meaning of reasonable force and what to expect from the police and CPS in cases which involve claims of self defence. Separate advice for school staff on their powers to use reasonable force is available from the Department for Education

2B   If a constable who is dealing with an allegation of crime and considering the need to arrest becomes an investigator for the purposes of the Code of Practice under the Criminal Procedure and Investigations Act 1996, the officer should, in accordance with paragraph 3.5 of that Code, 'pursue all reasonable lines of inquiry, whether these point towards or away from the suspect. What is reasonable in each case will depend on the particular circumstances.'

2C   For a constable to have reasonable grounds for believing it necessary to arrest, he or she is not required to be satisfied that there is no viable alternative to arrest. However, it does mean that in all cases, the officer should consider that arrest is the practical, sensible and proportionate option in all the circumstances at the time the decision is made. This applies equally to a person in police detention after being arrested for an offence who is suspected of involvement in a further offence and the necessity to arrest them for that further offence is being considered.

2D   Although a warning is not expressly required, officers should if practicable, consider whether a warning which points out their offending behaviour, and explains why, if they do not stop, the resulting consequences may make their arrest necessary. Such a warning might:
   • if heeded, avoid the need to arrest, or
   • if it is ignored, support the need to arrest and also help prove the mental element of certain offences, for example, the person's intent or awareness, or help to rebut a defence that they were acting reasonably.
   A person who is warned that they may be liable to arrest if their real name and address cannot be ascertained, should be given a reasonable opportunity to establish their real name and address before deciding that either or both are unknown and cannot be readily ascertained or that there are reasonable grounds to doubt that a name and address they have given is their real name and address. They should be told why their name is not known and cannot be readily ascertained and (as the case may be) of the grounds for doubting that a name and address they have given is their real name and address, including, for example, the reason why a particular document the person has produced to verify their real name and/or address, is not sufficient.

2E   The meaning of 'prompt' should be considered on a case by case basis taking account of all the circumstances. It indicates that the progress of the investigation should not be delayed to the extent that it would adversely affect the effectiveness of the investigation. The arresting officer also has discretion to release the arrested person on 'street bail' as an alternative to taking the person directly to the station. See Note 2J.

2F   An officer who believes that it is necessary to interview the person suspected of committing the offence must then consider whether their arrest is necessary in order to carry out the interview. The officer is not required to interrogate the suspect to determine whether they will attend a police station voluntarily to be interviewed but they must consider whether the suspect's voluntary attendance is a practicable alternative for carrying out the interview. If it is, then arrest would not be necessary. Conversely, an officer who considers this option but is not satisfied that it is a practicable alternative, may have reasonable grounds for deciding that the arrest is necessary at the outset 'on the street'. Without such considerations, the officer would not be able to establish that arrest was necessary in order to interview.

Circumstances which suggest that a person's arrest 'on the street' would not be necessary to interview them might be where the officer:

- is satisfied as to their identity and address and that they will attend the police station voluntarily to be interviewed, either immediately or by arrangement at a future date and time; and
- is not aware of any other circumstances which indicate that voluntary attendance would not be a practicable alternative. See paragraph 2.9(e)(i) to (v).

When making arrangements for the person's voluntary attendance, the officer should tell the person:

- that to properly investigate their suspected involvement in the offence they must be interviewed under caution at the police station, but in the circumstances their arrest for this purpose will not be necessary if they attend the police station voluntarily to be interviewed;
- that if they attend voluntarily, they will be entitled to free legal advice before, and to have a solicitor present at, the interview;
- that the date and time of the interview will take account of their circumstances and the needs of the investigation; and
- that if they do not agree to attend voluntarily at a time which meets the needs of the investigation, or having so agreed, fail to attend, or having attended, fail to remain for the interview to be completed, their arrest will be necessary to enable them to be interviewed.

2G   When the person attends the police station voluntarily for interview by arrangement as in Note 2F above, their arrest on arrival at the station prior to interview would only be justified if:

- new information coming to light after the arrangements were made indicates that from that time, voluntary attendance ceased to be a practicable alternative and the person's arrest became necessary; and
- it was not reasonably practicable for the person to be arrested before they attended the station.

If a person who attends the police station voluntarily to be interviewed decides to leave before the interview is complete, the police would at that point be entitled to consider whether their arrest was necessary to carry out the interview. The possibility that the person might decide to leave during the interview is therefore not a valid reason for arresting them before the interview has commenced. See Code C paragraph 3.21.

2H   The necessity criteria do not permit arrest solely to enable the routine taking, checking (speculative searching) and retention of fingerprints, samples, footwear impressions and photographs when there are no prior grounds to believe that checking and comparing the fingerprints etc. or taking a photograph would provide relevant evidence of the person's involvement in the offence concerned or would help to ascertain or verify their real identity.

2I   The necessity criteria do not permit arrest for an offence solely because it happens to be one of the statutory drug testing 'trigger offences' (see Code C Note 17E) when there is no suspicion that Class A drug misuse might have caused or contributed to the offence.

2J   Having determined that the necessity criteria have been met and having made the arrest, the officer can then consider the use of street bail on the basis of the effective and efficient progress of the investigation of the offence in question. It gives the officer discretion to compel the person to attend a police station at a date/time that best suits the overall needs of the particular investigation. Its use is not confined to dealing with child care issues or allowing officers to attend to more urgent operational duties and granting street bail does not retrospectively negate the need to arrest.

3   An arrested person must be given sufficient information to enable them to understand they have been deprived of their liberty and the reason they have been arrested, as soon as practicable after the arrest, e.g. when a person is arrested on suspicion of committing an offence they must be informed of the nature of the suspected offence and when and where it was committed. The suspect must also be informed of the reason or reasons why arrest is considered necessary. Vague or technical language should be avoided. When explaining why one or more of the arrest criteria apply, it is not necessary to disclose any specific details that might undermine or otherwise adversely affect any investigative processes. An example might be the conduct of a formal interview when prior disclosure of such details might give the suspect an opportunity to fabricate an innocent explanation or to otherwise conceal lies from the interviewer.

4   Nothing in this Code requires a caution to be given or repeated when informing a person not under arrest they may be prosecuted for an offence. However, a court will not be able to draw any inferences under the Criminal Justice and Public Order Act 1994, section 34, if the person was not cautioned.

5   If it appears a person does not understand the caution, the person giving it should explain it in their own words.

6   Certain powers available as the result of an arrest — for example, entry and search of premises, detention without charge beyond 24 hours, holding a person incommunicado and delaying access to legal advice — only apply in respect of indictable offences and are subject to the specific requirements on authorisation as set out in PACE and the relevant Code of Practice.

PACE CODE H

CODE OF PRACTICE IN CONNECTION WITH THE DETENTION, TREATMENT AND QUESTIONING BY POLICE OFFICERS OF PERSONS UNDER SECTION 41 OF, AND SCHEDULE 8 TO, THE TERRORISM ACT 2000

Code H applies to people in police detention following their arrest under the Terrorism Act 2000, s. 41; it took effect from midnight on 2 June 2014 notwithstanding that the person may have been arrested before that time.

Code H is not reproduced. The full text of Code H is freely available at www.gov.uk/government/uploads/system/uploads/attachment_data/file/306664/2013_PACE_Code_H.pdf.

Appendix 2   Attorney-General's Guidelines

EXERCISE BY THE CROWN OF ITS RIGHT OF STAND BY

1.   Although the law has long recognised the right of the Crown to exclude a member of a jury panel from sitting as a juror by the exercise in open court of the right to request a stand by or, if necessary, by challenge for cause, it has been customary for those instructed to prosecute on behalf of the Crown to assert that right only sparingly and in exceptional circumstances. It is generally accepted that the prosecution should not use its right in order to influence the overall composition of a jury or with a view to tactical advantage.

2.   The approach outlined above is founded on the principles that:
   a.   the members of a jury should be selected at random from the panel subject to any rule of law as to right of challenge by the defence, and
   b.   the Juries Act 1974 identifies those classes of persons who alone are disqualified from or ineligible for service on a jury. No other class of person may be treated as disqualified or ineligible.

3.   The enactment by Parliament of s. 118 of the Criminal Justice Act 1988 abolishing the right of defendants to remove jurors by means of peremptory challenge makes it appropriate that the Crown should assert its right to stand by only on the basis of clearly defined and restrictive criteria. Derogation from the principle that members of a jury should be selected at random should be permitted only where it is essential.

4.   Primary responsibility for ensuring that an individual does not serve on a jury if he is not competent to discharge properly the duties of a juror rests with the appropriate court officer and, ultimately the trial judge. Current legislation provides, in ss. 9 to s.10 of the Juries Act 1974, fairly wide discretion to excuse, defer or discharge jurors.

5.   The circumstances in which it would be proper for the Crown to exercise its right to stand by a member of a jury panel are:
   a.   where a jury check authorised in accordance with the Attorney-General's Guidelines on Jury Checks reveals information justifying exercise of the right to stand by in accordance with para.11 of the guidelines below [under **Jury Checks**] and the Attorney-General personally authorises the exercise of the right to stand by; or
   b.   where a person is about to be sworn as a juror who is manifestly unsuitable and the defence agree that, accordingly, the exercise by the prosecution of the right to stand by would be appropriate. An example of the sort of exceptional circumstances which might justify stand by is where it becomes apparent that, despite the provisions mentioned in para. 4 above, a juror selected for service to try a complex case is in fact illiterate.

JURY CHECKS

1.   The principles which are generally to be observed are:
   a.   that members of a jury should be selected at random from the panel,
   b.   the Juries Act 1974 identifies those classes of persons who alone are either disqualified from or ineligible for service on a jury; no other class of person may be treated as disqualified or ineligible,
   c.   the correct way for the Crown to seek to exclude a member of the panel from sitting as a juror is by the exercise in open court of the right to request a stand by or, if necessary, to challenge for cause.

2.   Parliament has provided safeguards against jurors who may be corrupt or biased. In addition to the provision for majority verdicts, there is the sanction of a criminal offence for a disqualified person to serve on a jury. The omission of a disqualified person from the panel is a matter for court officials—they will check criminal records for the purpose of ascertaining whether or not a potential juror is a disqualified person.

3.   There are, however, certain exceptional types of case of public importance for which the provisions as to majority verdicts and the disqualification of jurors may not be sufficient to ensure the proper administration of justice. In such cases it is in the interests of both justice and the public that there should be further safeguards against the possibility of bias and in such cases checks which go beyond the investigation of criminal records may be necessary.

4.   These classes of case may be defined broadly as (a) cases in which national security is involved and part of the evidence is likely to be heard in camera, and (b) security and terrorist cases in which a juror's extreme beliefs could prevent a fair trial.

5.   The particular aspects of these cases which may make it desirable to seek extra precautions are:
      a.   in security cases a danger that a juror, either voluntarily or under pressure, may make an improper use of evidence which, because of its sensitivity, has been given in camera,
      b.   in both security and terrorist cases the danger that a juror's personal beliefs are so biased as to go beyond normally reflecting the broad spectrum of views and interests in the community to reflect the extreme views of sectarian interest or pressure group to a degree which might interfere with his fair assessment of the facts of the case or lead him to exert improper pressure on his fellow jurors.

6.   In order to ascertain whether in exceptional circumstances of the above nature either of these factors might seriously influence a potential juror's impartial performance of his duties or his respecting the secrecy of evidence given in camera, it may be necessary to conduct a limited investigation of the panel. In general, such further investigation beyond one of criminal records made for disqualifications may only be made with the records of the police. However, a check may, additionally be made against the records of the Security Service. No checks other than on these sources and no general inquiries are to be made save to the limited extent that they may be needed to confirm the identity of a juror about whom the initial check has raised serious doubts.

7.   No further investigation, as described in para. 6 above, should be made save with the personal authority of the Attorney-General on the application of the Director of Public Prosecutions and such checks are hereafter referred to as 'authorised checks'. When a chief officer of police or the prosecutor has reason to believe that it is likely that an authorised check may be desirable and proper in accordance with these guidelines, he should refer the matter to the Director of Public Prosecutions. In those cases in which the Director of Public Prosecutions believes authorised checks are both proportionate and necessary, the Director will make an application to the Attorney-General.

8.   The Director of Public Prosecutions will provide the Attorney-General with all relevant information in support of the requested authorised checks. The Attorney-General will consider personally the request and, if appropriate, authorise the check.

9.   The result of any authorised check will be sent to the Director of Public Prosecutions. The Director will then decide, having regard to the matters set out in para. 5 above, what information ought to be brought to the attention of prosecuting counsel. The Director will also provide the Attorney-General with the result of the authorised check.

10. Although the right of stand by and the decision to authorise checks are wholly within the discretion of the Attorney-General, when the Attorney-General has agreed to an authorised check being conducted, the Director of Public Prosecutions will write to the Presiding Judge for the area to advise him that this is being done.

11. No right of stand by should be exercised by counsel for the Crown on the basis of information obtained as a result of an authorised check save with the personal authority of the Attorney-General and unless the information is such as, having regard to the facts of the case and the offences charged, to afford strong reason for believing that a particular juror might be a security risk, be susceptible to improper approaches or be influenced in arriving at a verdict for the reasons given above.

12. Information revealed in the course of an authorised check must be considered in line with the normal rules on disclosure.

13. A record is to be kept by the Director of Public Prosecutions of the use made by counsel of the information passed to him and of the jurors stood by or challenged by the parties to the proceedings. A copy of this record is to be forwarded to the Attorney-General for the sole purpose of enabling him to monitor the operation of these guidelines.

14. No use of the information obtained as a result of an authorised check is to be made except as may be necessary in direct relation to or arising out of the trial for which the check was authorised. The information may, however, be used for the prevention of crime or as evidence in a future criminal prosecution, save that material obtained from the Security Service may only be used in those circumstances with the authority of the Security Service.

ACCEPTANCE OF PLEAS AND THE PROSECUTOR'S ROLE IN THE SENTENCING EXERCISE

A: Foreword

A1. Prosecutors have an important role in protecting the victim's interests in the criminal justice process, not least in the acceptance of pleas and the sentencing exercise. The basis of plea, particularly in a case that is not contested, is the vehicle through which the victim's voice is heard. Factual inaccuracies in pleas in mitigation cause distress and offence to victims, the families of victims and witnesses. This can take many forms but may be most acutely felt when the victim is dead and the family hears inaccurate assertions about the victim's character or lifestyle. Prosecution advocates are reminded that they are required to adhere to the standards set out in the Victim's Charter, which places the needs of the victim at the heart of the criminal justice process, and that they are subject to a similar obligation in respect of the Code of Practice for Victims of Crime.

A2. The principle of fairness is central to the administration of justice. The implementation of Human Rights Act 1998 in October 2000 incorporated into domestic law the principle of fairness to the accused articulated in the European Convention on Human Rights. Accuracy and reasonableness of plea plays an important part in ensuring fairness both to the accused and to the victim.

A3. The Attorney General's Guidelines on the Acceptance of Pleas issued on December 7, 2000 highlighted the importance of transparency in the conduct of justice. The basis of plea agreed by the parties in a criminal trial is central to the sentencing process. An illogical or unsupported basis of plea can lead to an unduly lenient sentence being passed, and has a consequential effect where consideration arises as to whether to refer the sentence to the Court of Appeal under section 36 of the Criminal Justice Act 1988.

A4. These Guidelines, which replace the Guidelines issued in October 2005, give guidance on how prosecutors should meet these objectives of protection of victims' interests and of securing fairness and transparency in the process. They take into account paragraphs IV.45.4 and following of the Consolidated Criminal Practice Direction, amended May 2009 and the guidance issued by the Court of Appeal (Criminal) Division in *R v Beswick* [1996] 1 Cr App R 343, *R v Tolera* [1999] 1 Cr App R 25 and *R v Underwood* [2005] 1 Cr App R 178. They complement the Bar Council Guidance on Written Standards for the Conduct of Professional Work issued with the 7th edition of the Code of Conduct for the Bar of England and Wales and the Law Society's Professional Conduct Rules. When considering the acceptance of a guilty plea prosecution advocates are also reminded of the need to apply 'The Farquharson Guidelines on The Role and Responsibilities of the Prosecution Advocate'.

A5. The Guidelines should be followed by all prosecutors and those persons designated under section 7 of the Prosecution of Offences Act 1985 (designated caseworkers) and apply to prosecutions conducted in England and Wales.

B: General Principles

B1. Justice in this jurisdiction, save in the most exceptional circumstances, is conducted in public. This includes the acceptance of pleas by the prosecution and sentencing.

B2. The Code for Crown Prosecutors governs the prosecutor's decision-making prior to the commencement of the trial hearing and sets out the circumstances in which pleas to a reduced number of charges, or less serious charges, can be accepted.

B3. When a case is listed for trial and the prosecution form the view that the appropriate course is to accept a plea before the proceedings commence or continue, or to offer no evidence on the indictment or any part of it, the prosecution should whenever practicable speak to the victim or the victim's family, so that the position can be explained. The views of the victim or the family may assist in informing the prosecutor's decision as to whether it is the public interest, as defined by the Code for Crown Prosecutors, to accept or reject the plea. The victim or victim's family should then be kept informed and decisions explained once they are made at court.

B4. The appropriate disposal of a criminal case after conviction is as much a part of the criminal justice process as the trial of guilt or innocence. The prosecution advocate represents the public interest, and should be ready to assist the court to reach its decision as to the appropriate sentence. This will include drawing the court's attention to:
- any victim personal statement or other information available to the prosecution advocate as to the impact of the offence on the victim;
- where appropriate, to any evidence of the impact of the offending on a community;
- any statutory provisions relevant to the offender and the offences under consideration;
- any relevant sentencing guidelines and guideline cases; and
- the aggravating and mitigating factors of the offence under consideration.

B5. The prosecution advocate may also offer assistance to the court by making submissions, in the light of all these factors, as to the appropriate sentencing range. In all cases, it is the prosecution advocate's duty to apply for appropriate ancillary orders, such as anti-social behaviour orders and confiscation orders. When considering which ancillary orders to apply for, prosecution advocates must always have regard to the victim's needs, including the question of his or her future protection.

C: The Basis of Plea

C1. The basis of a guilty plea must not be agreed on a misleading or untrue set of facts and must take proper account of the victim's interests. An illogical or insupportable basis of plea will inevitably result in the imposition of an inappropriate sentence and is capable of damaging public confidence in the criminal justice system. In cases involving multiple defendants the bases of plea for each defendant must be factually consistent with each other.

C2. When the defendant indicates an acceptable plea, the defence advocate should reduce the basis of the plea to writing. This must be done in all cases save for those in which the defendant has indicated that the guilty plea has been or will be tendered on the basis of the prosecution case.

C3. The written basis of plea must be considered with great care, taking account of the position of any other relevant defendant where appropriate. The prosecution should not lend itself to any agreement whereby a case is presented to the sentencing judge on a misleading or untrue set of facts or on a basis that is detrimental to the victim's interests. There will be cases where a defendant seeks to mitigate on the basis of assertions of fact which are outside the scope of the prosecution's knowledge. A typical example concerns the defendant's state of mind. If a defendant wishes to be sentenced on this basis, the prosecution advocate should invite the judge not to accept the defendant's version unless he or she gives evidence on oath to be tested in cross-examination. Paragraph IV.45.14 of the Consolidated Criminal Practice Direction states that in such circumstances the defence advocate should be prepared to call the defendant and, if the defendant is not willing to testify, subject to any explanation that may be given, the judge may draw such inferences as appear appropriate.

C4. The prosecution advocate should show the prosecuting authority any written record relating to the plea and agree with them the basis on which the case will be opened to the court. If, as may well be the case, the basis of plea differs in its implications for sentencing or the making of ancillary orders from the case originally outlined by the prosecution, the prosecution advocate must ensure that such differences are accurately reflected in the written record prior to showing it to the prosecuting authority.

C5. It is the responsibility of the prosecution advocate thereafter to ensure that the defence advocate is aware of the basis on which the plea is accepted by the prosecution and the way in which the prosecution case will be opened to the court.

C6. In all cases where it is likely to assist the court where the sentencing issues are complex or unfamiliar the prosecution must add to the written outline of the case which is served upon the court a summary of the key considerations. This should take the form of very brief notes on:
- any relevant statutory limitations
- the names of any relevant sentencing authorities or guidelines
- the scope for any ancillary orders (e.g. concerning anti-social behaviour, confiscation or deportation will need to be considered).
- The outline should also include the age of the defendant and information regarding any outstanding offences.

C7. It remains open to the prosecutor to provide further written information (for example to supplement and update the analysis at later stages of the case) where he or she thought that likely to assist the court, or if the judge requests it.

C8. When the prosecution advocate has agreed the written basis of plea submitted by the defence advocate, he or she should endorse the document accordingly. If the prosecution advocate takes issue with all or part of the written basis of plea, the procedure set out in the Consolidated Criminal Practice Direction (and in Part 37.10(5) of the Criminal Procedure Rules) should be followed. The defendant's basis of plea must be set out in writing identifying what is in dispute; the court may invite the parties to make representations about whether the dispute is material to sentence; and if the court decides that it is a material dispute, the court will invite further representations or evidence as it may require and decide the dispute in accordance with the principles set out in *R v Newton* 77 Cr App R13, CA. The signed original document setting out the disputed factual matters should be made available to the trial judge and thereafter lodged with the court papers, as it will form part of the record of the hearing.

C9. Where the basis of plea cannot be agreed and the discrepancy between the two accounts is such as to have a potentially significant effect on the level of sentence, it is the duty of the defence advocate so to inform the court before the sentencing process begins. There remains an overriding duty on the prosecution advocate to ensure that the sentencing judge is made aware of the discrepancy and of the consideration which must be given to holding a *Newton* hearing to resolve the issue. The court should be told where a derogatory reference to a victim, witness or third party is not accepted, even though there may be no effect on sentence.

C10. As emphasised in paragraph IV.45.10 of the Consolidated Criminal Practice Direction, whenever an agreement as to the basis of plea is made between the prosecution and defence, any such agreement will be subject to the approval of the trial judge, who may of his or her own motion disregard the agreement and direct that a *Newton* hearing should be held to determine the proper basis on which sentence should be passed.

C11. Where a defendant declines to admit an offence that he or she previously indicated should be taken into consideration, the prosecution advocate should indicate to the defence advocate and the court that, subject to further review, the offence may now form the basis of a new prosecution.

D: Sentence Indications

D1. Only in the Crown Court may sentence indications be sought. Advocates there are reminded that indications as to sentence should not be sought from the trial judge unless issues between the prosecution and defence have been addressed and resolved. Therefore, in difficult or complicated cases, no less than seven days notice in writing of an intention to seek an indication should normally be given to the prosecution and the court. When deciding whether the circumstances of a case require such notice to be given, defence advocates are reminded that prosecutors should not agree a basis of plea unless and until the necessary consultation has taken place first with the victim and/or the victim's family and second, in the case of an independent prosecution advocate, with the prosecuting authority.

D2. If there is no final agreement about the plea to the indictment, or the basis of plea, and the defence nevertheless proceeds to seek an indication of sentence, which the judge appears minded to give, the prosecution advocate should remind him or her of the guidance given in *R v Goodyear (Karl)* [2005] EWCA 888 that normally speaking an indication of sentence should not be given until the basis of the plea has been agreed or the judge has concluded that he or she can properly deal with the case without the need for a trial of the issue.

D3. If an indication is sought, the prosecution advocate should normally enquire whether the judge is in possession of or has access to all the evidence relied on by the prosecution, including any victim personal statement, as well as any information about relevant previous convictions recorded against the defendant.

D4. Before the judge gives the indication, the prosecution advocate should draw the judge's attention to any minimum or mandatory statutory sentencing requirements. Where the prosecution advocate would be expected to offer the judge assistance with relevant guideline cases or the views of the Sentencing Guidelines Council, he or she should invite the judge to allow them to do so. Where it applies, the prosecution advocate should remind the judge that the position of the Attorney General to refer any sentencing decision as unduly lenient is unaffected. In any event, the prosecution advocate should not say anything which may create the impression that the sentence indication has the support or approval of the Crown.

E: Pleas In Mitigation

E1. The prosecution advocate must challenge any assertion by the defence in mitigation which is derogatory to a person's character, (for instance, because it suggests that his or her conduct is or has been criminal, immoral or improper) and which is either false or irrelevant to proper sentencing considerations. If the defence advocate persists in that assertion, the prosecution advocate should invite the court to consider holding a *Newton* hearing to determine the issue.

E2. The defence advocate must not submit in mitigation anything that is derogatory to a person's character without giving advance notice in writing so as to afford the prosecution advocate the opportunity to consider their position under paragraph E1. When the prosecution advocate is so notified they must take all reasonable steps to establish whether the assertions are true. Reasonable steps will include seeking the views of the victim. This will involve seeking the views of the victim's family if the victim is deceased, and the victim's parents or legal guardian where the victim is a child. Reasonable steps may also include seeking the views of the police or other law enforcement authority, as appropriate. An assertion which is derogatory to a person's character will rarely amount to mitigation unless it has a causal connection to the circumstances of the offence or is otherwise relevant to proper sentencing considerations.

E3. Where notice has not been given in accordance with paragraph E2, the prosecution advocate must not acquiesce in permitting mitigation which is derogatory to a person's character. In such circumstances, the prosecution advocate should draw the attention of the court to the failure to give advance notice and seek time, and if necessary, an adjournment to investigate the assertion in the same way as if proper notice had been given. Where, in the opinion of the prosecution advocate, there are substantial grounds for believing that such an assertion is false or irrelevant to sentence, he or she should inform the court of their opinion and invite the court to consider making an order under section 58(8) of the Criminal Procedure and Investigations Act 1996, preventing publication of the assertion.

E4. Where the prosecution advocate considers that the assertion is, if true, relevant to sentence, or the court has so indicated, he or she should seek time, and if necessary an adjournment, to establish whether the assertion is true. If the matter cannot be resolved to the satisfaction of the parties, the prosecution advocate should invite the court to consider holding a *Newton* hearing to determine the issue.

GUIDANCE ON THE USE OF THE COMMON LAW OFFENCE OF CONSPIRACY TO DEFRAUD

Summary

1. This guidance concerns the issues which the Attorney General asks prosecuting authorities in England and Wales to consider before using the common law offence of conspiracy to defraud, in the light of the implementation of the Fraud Act 2006. It may be supplemented by Departmental-specific guidance issued by individual Directors of the prosecuting authorities.

Background

2. When the Fraud Act 2006 comes into force on 15 January 2007, the prosecution will be able to use modern and flexible statutory offences of fraud. The 2006 Act replaces the deception offences contained in the Theft Acts 1968–1996 with a general offence of fraud that can be committed in three ways:
    *   fraud by false representation;
    *   fraud by failing to disclose information; and
    *   fraud by abuse of position.
    It also introduces other offences which can be used in particular circumstances, notably:
    *   new offences to tackle the possession and supply of articles for use in fraud; and
    *   a new offence of fraudulent trading applicable to sole traders and other businesses not caught by the existing offence in section 458 of the Companies Act 1985.

3. The new offences are designed to catch behaviour that previously fell through gaps in the Theft Acts and could only be prosecuted as conspiracy to defraud. Indeed the Act is based on a Law Commission report (Cm 5560) which also recommended the abolition of the common law offence of conspiracy to defraud. The argument is that the offence is unfairly uncertain, and wide enough to have the potential to catch behaviour that should not be criminal. Furthermore it can seem anomalous that what is legal if performed by one person should be criminal if performed by many.

4. However, consultations showed a widespread view in favour of retention of common law conspiracy to defraud, and the Government decided to retain it for the meantime, but accepted the case for considering repeal in the longer term. Whether there is a continuing need for retention of the common law offence is one of the issues that will be addressed in the Home Office review of the operation of the Fraud Act 2006, which will take place 3 years after its implementation.

5. In 2003, 14,928 defendants were proceeded against in England and Wales for crimes of fraud; 1018 of these were charged with the common law crime of conspiracy to defraud of which 44% were found guilty (compared with 71% for the statutory fraud offences). The expectation now is that the common law offence will be used to a significantly lesser extent once the Fraud Act 2006 has come into force.

Issues to be considered in using the common law offence

6. In selecting charges in fraud cases, the prosecutor should first consider:
    *   whether the behaviour could be prosecuted under statute—whether under the Fraud Act 2006 or another Act or as a statutory conspiracy; and
    *   whether the available statutory charges adequately reflect the gravity of the offence.

7. Statutory conspiracy to commit a substantive offence should be charged if the alleged agreement satisfies the definition in section 1 of the Criminal Law Act 1977, provided that there is no wider dishonest objective that would be important to the presentation of the prosecution case in reflecting the gravity of the case.

8. Section 12 of the Criminal Justice Act 1987 provides that common law conspiracy to defraud may be charged even if the conduct agreed upon will involve the commission of a statutory offence. However, Lord Bingham said in *R v Rimmington* and *R v Goldstein* [(2005) UKHL 63]:
    'I would not go to the length of holding that conduct may never be lawfully prosecuted as a generally-expressed common law crime where it falls within the terms of a specific statutory provi-

sion, *but good practice and respect for the primacy of statute do in my judgment require that conduct falling within the terms of a specific statutory provision should be prosecuted under that provision unless there is good reason for doing otherwise.*'

9. In the Attorney General's view the common law charge may still be appropriate in the type of cases set out in paragraphs 12–15, but in order to understand the circumstances under which conspiracy to defraud is used *prosecutors should make a record of the reasons for preferring that charge.*

Records of decisions

10. Where a charge of common law conspiracy to defraud is proposed the case lawyer must consider and set out in writing in the review note:
    * how much such a charge will add to the amount of evidence likely to be called both by the prosecution and the defence; and
    * the justification for using the charge, and why specific statutory offences are inadequate or otherwise inappropriate.
    * Thereafter, and before charge, the use of this charge should be specifically approved by a supervising lawyer experienced in fraud cases. Equivalent procedures to ensure proper consideration of the charge and recording of the decision should be applied by all prosecuting authorities in their case review processes.

11. Information from these records will be collected retrospectively for the review to be conducted in 3 years. It will enable the identification of where and why the common law offence has been used. It could then also form the basis for any future work on whether, and if so how, to replace the common law or whether it can simply and safely be repealed. It is expected that in 3 years the Government will be able to review the situation in the light of the practical operation not only of the new fraud offences, but of other relevant changes. These include the Lord Chief Justice's protocol on the control and management of heavy fraud cases, and the sample count provisions in the Domestic Violence, Crime and Victims Act 2004. Any actual or proposed changes to the law on assisting and encouraging crime in the light of the Law Commission's study of that issue [Cm 6878, published in July 2006] will also be taken into account.

A Conduct that can more effectively be prosecuted as conspiracy to defraud

12. There may be cases where the interests of justice can only be served by presenting to a court an overall picture which cannot be achieved by charging a series of substantive offences or statutory conspiracies. Typically, such cases will involve some, but not necessarily all of the following:
    * evidence of several significant but different kinds of criminality;
    * several jurisdictions;
    * different types of victims, e.g. individuals, banks, web site administrators, credit card companies;
    * organised crime networks.

13. The proper presentation of such cases as statutory conspiracies could lead to:
    * large numbers of separate counts to reflect the different conspiracies;
    * severed trials for single or discrete groups of conspiracies;
    * evidence in one severed trial being deemed inadmissible in another.

14. If so, the consequences might be that no one court would receive a cohesive picture of the whole case which would allow sentencing on a proper basis. In contrast a single count of common law conspiracy to defraud might, in such circumstances, reflect the nature and extent of criminal conduct in a way that prosecuting the underlying statutory offences or conspiracies would fail to achieve.

B Conduct that can only be prosecuted as conspiracy to defraud

15. Examples of such conduct might include but are not restricted to agreements to the following courses of action:
    * The dishonest obtaining of land and other property which cannot be stolen such as intellectual property not protected by the Copyright, Designs and Patents Act 1988 and the Trademarks Act 1994, and other confidential information. The Fraud Act will bite where there is intent to make a gain or cause a loss through false representation, failure to disclose information where there is a legal obligation to do so, or the abuse of position;
    * Dishonestly infringing another's right; for example the dishonest exploitation of another's patent in the absence of a legal duty to disclose information about its existence;
    * Where it is intended that the final offence be committed by someone outside the conspiracy; and
    * Cases where the accused cannot be proved to have had the necessary degree of knowledge of the substantive offence to be perpetrated;

SECTION 18 RIPA: PROSECUTORS INTERCEPT GUIDELINES

1.   These guidelines concern the approach to be taken by prosecutors in applying section 18 of the Regulation of Investigatory Powers Act (RIPA) in England and Wales.

Background

2.   It has been long-standing Government policy that the fact that interception of communications has taken place in any particular case should remain secret and not be disclosed to the subject. This is because of the need to protect the continuing value of interception as a vital means of gathering intelligence about serious crime and activities which threaten national security. The Government judges that if the use of the technique in particular cases were to be confirmed, the value of the technique would be diminished because targets would either know, or could deduce, when their communications might be intercepted and so could take avoiding action by using other, more secure means of communication.

3.   In the context of legal proceedings, the policy that the fact of interception should remain secret is implemented by section 17 of RIPA. Section 17 provides that no evidence shall be adduced, question asked, assertion or disclosure made or other thing done in, for the purposes of, or in connection with, any legal proceedings which discloses the contents of a communication which has been obtained following the issue of an interception warrant or a warrant under the Interception of Communications Act 1985, or any related communications data ('protected information'), or tends to suggest that certain events have occurred.

4.   The effect of section 17 is that the fact of interception of the subject's communications and the product of that interception cannot be relied upon or referred to by either party to the proceedings. This is given further effect by sections 3(7), 7(6), 7A(9) and 9(9) of the Criminal Procedure and Investigations Act 1996 (as amended). This protects the continuing value of interception whilst also creating a 'level playing-field', in that neither side can gain any advantage from the interception. In the context of criminal proceedings, this means that the defendant cannot be prejudiced by the existence in the hands of the prosecution of intercept material which is adverse to his interests.

Detailed Analysis

First Stage: action to be taken by the prosecutor

5.   Section 18(7)(a) of RIPA provides:
'Nothing in section 17(1) shall prohibit any such disclosure of any information that continues to be available for disclosure as is confined to...a disclosure to a person conducting a criminal prosecution for the purpose only of enabling that person to determine what is required of him by his duty to secure the fairness of the prosecution'.
If protected information is disclosed to a prosecutor, as permitted by section 18(7)(a), the first step that should be taken by the prosecutor is to review any information regarding an interception that remains extant at the time that he or she has conduct of the case.[1] In reviewing it, the prosecutor should seek to identify any information whose existence, if no action was taken by the Crown, might result in unfairness. Experience suggests that the most likely example of such potential unfairness is where the evidence in the case is such that the jury may draw an inference which intercept shows to be wrong, and to leave this uncorrected will result in the defence being disadvantaged.

6.   If in the view of the prosecutor to take no action would render the proceedings unfair, the prosecutor should, first consulting with the relevant prosecution agency, take such steps as are available to him or her to secure the fairness of the proceedings provided these steps do not contravene section 18(10). In the example given above, such steps could include:

(i)   putting the prosecution case in such a way that the misleading inference is not drawn by the jury; or
(ii)   not relying upon the evidence which makes the information relevant; or

---

[1]   Section 15(1) of RIPA provides that it is the duty of the Secretary of State to ensure that arrangements are in place to ensure that (amongst other matters) intercept material is retained by the intercepting agencies only for as long as is necessary for any of the authorised purposes. The authorised purposes include retention which:
'is necessary to ensure that a person conducting a criminal prosecution has the information he needs to determine what is required of him by his duty to secure the fairness of the prosecution'. (section 15(4)(d))

(iii) discontinuing that part of the prosecution case in relation to which the protected information is relevant, by amending a charge or count on the indictment or offering no evidence on such a charge or count; or

(iv) making an admission of fact.[2]

There is no requirement for the prosecutor to notify the judge of the action that he or she has taken or proposes to take. Such a course should only be taken by the prosecutor if he considers it essential in the interests of justice to do so (see below).

Second Stage: disclosure to the judge

7.   There may be some cases (although these are likely to be rare) where the prosecutor considers that he cannot secure the fairness of the proceedings without assistance from the relevant judge. In recognition of this, section 18(7)(b) of RIPA provides that in certain limited circumstances, the prosecutor may invite the judge to order a disclosure of the protected information to him.

8.   If the prosecutor considers that he requires the assistance of the trial judge to ensure the fairness of the proceedings, or he is in doubt as to whether the result of taking the steps outlined at para 6 above would ensure fairness, he must apply to see the judge *ex parte*. Under section 18(8), a judge shall not order a disclosure to him except where he is satisfied that the exceptional circumstances of the case make that disclosure essential in the interests of justice. Before the judge is in a position to order such disclosure the prosecutor will need to impart to the judge such information, but only such information, as is necessary to demonstrate that exceptional circumstances mean that the prosecutor acting alone cannot secure the fairness of the proceedings. Experience suggests that exceptional circumstances in the course of a trial justifying disclosure to a judge arise only in the following two situations:

(1) where the judge's assistance is necessary to ensure the fairness of the trial

This situation may arise in the example given at paragraph 5 above, where there is a risk that the jury might draw an inference from certain facts, which protected information shows would be the wrong inference, and the prosecutor is unable to ensure that the jury will not draw this inference by his actions alone. The purpose in informing the judge is so that the judge will then be in a position to ensure fairness by:

(i)   summing up in a way which will ensure that the wrong inference is not drawn; or

(ii)   giving appropriate directions to the jury; or

(iii) requiring the Crown to make an admission of fact which the judge thinks *essential in the interests of justice* if he is of the opinion that *exceptional circumstances* require him to make such a direction (section 18(9)). However, such a direction **must not** authorise or require anything to be done which discloses any of the contents of an intercepted communication or related data or tends to suggest that anything falling within section 17(2) has or may have occurred or be going to occur (section 18(10)). Situations where an admission of fact is required are likely to be rare. The judge must be of the view that proceedings could not be continued unless an admission of fact is made (and the conditions in section 18(9) are satisfied). There may be other ways in which it is possible for a judge to ensure fairness, such as those outlined at (i) and (ii) above.

In practice, no question of taking the action at (i)–(iii) arises if the protected information is already contained in a separate document in another form that has been or can be disclosed without contravening section 17(1), and this disclosure will secure the fairness of the proceedings.

(2) where the judge requires knowledge of the protected material for some other purpose

This situation may arise where, usually in the context of a PII application, the true significance of, or duty of disclosure in relation to, other material being considered for disclosure by a judge, cannot be appraised by the judge without reference to protected information. Disclosure to the judge of the protected information without more may be sufficient to enable him to appraise the material, but once he has seen the protected information the judge may also conclude that the conditions in section 18(9) are satisfied so that an admission of fact by the Crown is required in addition to or instead of disclosure of the non-protected material.

Another example is a case where protected information underlies operational decisions which are likely to be the subject of cross-examination and it is necessary to inform the judge of the existence of

---

[2] This is acceptable as long as to do so would not contravene section 17 i.e. reveal the existence of an interception warrant. Prosecutors must bear in mind that such a breach might conceivably occur not only from the factual content of the admission, but also from the circumstances in which it is made.

the protected information to enable him to deal with the issue when the questions are first posed in a way which ensures section 17(1) is not contravened.

What if the actions of the prosecutor and/or the judge cannot ensure the fairness of the proceedings?

9. There may be very rare cases in which no action taken by the prosecutor and/or judge can prevent the continuation of the proceedings being unfair, e.g. where the requirements of fairness could only be met if the Crown were to make an admission, but it cannot do so without contravening section 18(10). In that situation the prosecutor will have no option but to offer no evidence on the charge in question, or to discontinue the proceedings in their entirety.

Responding to questions about interception

10. Prosecutors are sometimes placed in a situation in which they are asked by the court or by the defence whether interception has taken place or whether protected information exists. Whether or not interception has taken place or protected information exists, an answer in the following terms, or similar should be given:

> 'I am not in a position to answer that, but I am aware of sections 17 and 18 of the Regulation of Investigatory Powers Act 2000 and the Attorney General's Guidelines on the Disclosure of Information in Exceptional Circumstances under section 18'.

In a case where interception has taken place or protected information exists, an answer in these terms will avoid a breach of the prohibition in section 17 while providing assurance that the prosecutor is aware of his obligations.

11. For the avoidance of doubt, any notification or disclosure of information to the judge in accordance with paragraphs 7–10 must be *ex parte*. It will never be appropriate for prosecutors to volunteer, either *inter partes* or to the Court *ex parte*, that interception has taken place or that protected information exists, save in accordance with section 18 as elaborated in these Guidelines.

Further Assistance

12. Should a prosecutor be unsure as to the application of these guidelines in any particular case, further guidance should be sought from those instructing him or her. In those cases where a prosecutor has been instructed by the Crown Prosecution Service, the relevant CPS prosecutor must seek appropriate guidance from Casework Directorate, CPS Headquarters, Ludgate Hill.

THE PROSECUTOR'S ROLE IN APPLICATIONS FOR WITNESS ANONYMITY ORDERS...

A Foreword

A1. Every defendant has a right to a fair trial. An important aspect of a fair trial is the right of the defendant to be confronted by, and to challenge, those who accuse him or her.

A2. Making an application for a witness anonymity order is therefore a serious step, to be taken by the prosecutor only where there are genuine grounds to believe that the court would not otherwise hear evidence that should be available to it in the interests of justice; that other measures falling short of anonymity would not be sufficient; and that the defendant will have a fair trial if the order is made.

A3. Anonymous witness testimony is not necessarily incompatible with Article 6, even when it is the sole or decisive evidence against the accused. But whether the measures used to allow a witness to give evidence anonymously in any particular case would make the trial unfair has to be evaluated with care on the facts of each case.

A4. When assessing whether and in what terms to make an application for a witness anonymity order, prosecutors have overriding duties to be fair, independent and objective. These guidelines set out the overarching principles by which a prosecutor should consider, and if appropriate apply for, a witness anonymity order in accordance with the considerations set out in the Criminal Evidence (Witness Anonymity) Act 2008.

B The Prosecutor's Duties

B1. The effect of a witness anonymity order is to prevent the defendant from knowing the identity of a witness. Without this information the defendant's ability to investigate and challenge the accuracy or credibility of the witness's evidence may be limited.

B2. When considering whether to make a witness anonymity order the court will consider to what extent the defendant needs to know the identity of the witness in order to challenge the witness's evidence effectively. This question will often be central to the question of whether, having regard to all the circumstances, the witness anonymity order sought would be consistent with a fair trial.

B3. The prosecutor's role is:
  - To act with scrupulous fairness.
  - To examine with care, and probe where appropriate, the material provided in support of the application and the evidential basis for it. Prosecutors should in particular objectively assess any statement made by the witness or witnesses in question and the grounds on which it is based.
  - To be satisfied before making the application that, viewed objectively, it can properly be said that the order is necessary and in the interests of justice and that the defendant can receive a fair trial.
  - To put before the court all material that is relevant to the application. Courts will rely to a significant extent upon the prosecutor and the investigator to provide relevant material. Material will be relevant if the prosecutor relies upon it to support the application, or if it may tend to undermine or qualify the justification for making the order at all, or for making it in the form sought by the prosecutor. Material is particularly relevant if credibility is or may be in issue, for example if there is a known link between the witness and the defendant or a co-accused.
  - To disclose as much relevant material to the defence as possible without identifying the witness, including material that may tend to cast doubt on the credibility, reliability or accuracy of the witness's evidence.

B4. The role of the prosecutor as an independent and impartial minister of justice is of paramount importance. Applications should only be authorised by prosecutors at an appropriately senior level within the prosecuting authority.

B5. The interests of justice include the interests of the victim or victims, the interests of the witness or witnesses, the interests of the defendant and any co-defendants and the wider public interest.

B6. Prosecutors should take all necessary and reasonable steps consistent with a fair trial and the interests of justice to ensure the safety of a witness or the avoidance of real harm to the public interest or the protection of property.

C Applications by Defendants

C1. The Act permits a defendant (as well as a prosecutor) to apply for a Witness Anonymity Order. Prosecutors should respond to such applications independently and objectively. Prosecutors should examine critically, but fairly, the basis for any application and any material put forward in support of any application.

C2. The prosecutor should provide the court with all material within the prosecutor's possession or control that is relevant to the defendant's application.

D Appointment and Role of Special Counsel in Applications for Witness Anonymity

D1. The Act makes no statutory provision for the appointment of Special Counsel.

D2. A criminal court may invite the Attorney General to appoint Special Counsel.[3] However, in line with authority, such an appointment:
  - Should be regarded as '…exceptional, never automatic, a course of last and never first resort.' *R v H* and *R v C* [2004] UKHL 3. The need for Special Counsel has to be shown.
  - The court will take account of the seriousness of the issue that the court has to determine in the particular case. Whether credibility is at issue is likely to be an important consideration. The court will also need to consider the extent to which Special Counsel could further the defendant's case.
  - The court itself can be expected to perform a role of testing and probing the case which is presented on the application. When coupled with the prosecutor's duty to put all relevant material before the court, this may often be sufficient to enable a fair and informed decision to be reached without the need to appoint Special Counsel.

D3. Where appointed, the role of Special Counsel is to make representations on behalf of the accused in any closed proceedings.

D4. The Attorney General will consider each invitation to appoint Special Counsel on its merits, having regard to all the relevant circumstances of the case. In particular, in this context, to the basis of the application, whether it is opposed, the basis upon which it is opposed and the particular considerations that the court wishes Special Counsel to address.

D5. A prosecutor making an application for a witness anonymity order should always be prepared to assist the court to consider whether the circumstances are such that exceptionally the appointment of Special Counsel may be called for. When appropriate a prosecutor should draw to the attention of the

---

[3] Most recently, *Shiv Malik and Manchester Crown Court and Chief Constable of Greater Manchester Police, Constable and Robinson Ltd and Attorney General as interested parties* [2008] EWHC 1362 (Admin).

court any aspect of an application for a witness anonymity order or any aspect of the case that may, viewed objectively, call for the appointment of Special Counsel.

D6. When a court decides to invite the Attorney General to appoint Special Counsel the prosecutor should (regardless of any steps taken by the court or any defendant) ensure that the Attorney General's Office is promptly notified; and assist in ensuring that the Attorney General receives all the information needed to take a decision.

D7. Where Special Counsel is appointed, he or she will initially be provided by the prosecutor with any open material made available to the accused regarding the application (and any other open material requested by Special Counsel). Special Counsel may then seek instructions from the defendant and his legal representatives. Only then will Special Counsel be provided by the prosecutor with the closed or un-redacted material provided to the court.

PLEA DISCUSSIONS IN CASES OF SERIOUS OR COMPLEX FRAUD

A Foreword

A1. These Guidelines set out a process by which a prosecutor may discuss an allegation of serious or complex fraud with a person who he or she is prosecuting or expects to prosecute, or with that person's legal representative. They come into force on the 5th day of May 2009 and apply to plea discussions initiated on or after that date.

A2. The Guidelines will be followed by all prosecutors in England and Wales when conducting plea discussions in cases of serious or complex fraud. For the purposes of the Guidelines, fraud means any financial, fiscal or commercial misconduct or corruption which is contrary to the criminal law. Fraud may be serious or complex if at least two of the following factors are present:

- The amount obtained or intended to be obtained is alleged to exceed £500,000;
- There is a significant international dimension;
- The case requires specialised knowledge of financial, commercial, fiscal or regulatory matters such as the operation of markets, banking systems, trusts or tax regimes;
- The case involves allegations of fraudulent activity against numerous victims;
- The case involves an allegation of substantial and significant fraud on a public body;
- The case is likely to be of widespread public concern;
- The alleged misconduct endangered the economic well-being of the United Kingdom, for example by undermining confidence in financial markets.

Taking account of these matters, it is for the prosecutor to decide whether or not a case is one of fraud, and whether or not it is serious or complex.

A3. The decision whether a person should be charged with a criminal offence rests with the prosecutor. In selecting the appropriate charge or charges, the prosecutor applies principles set out in the Code for Crown Prosecutors ('the Code'). Charges should reflect the seriousness and extent of the offending, give the court adequate sentencing powers and enable the case to be presented in a clear and simple way. The Code also states that prosecutors should not go ahead with more charges to encourage a defendant to plead guilty to a few; equally, prosecutors should not charge a more serious offence to encourage a defendant to plead to a less serious one.

A4. Once proceedings are instituted, the accused may plead guilty to all of the charges selected. If the defendant will plead guilty to some, but not all, of the charges or to a different, possibly less serious charge, the Code states that a prosecutor is entitled to accept such pleas if he or she assesses that the court could still pass an adequate sentence. In taking these decisions the prosecutor also applies the Attorney General's Guidelines on the Acceptance of Pleas and the Prosecutor's Role in the Sentencing Exercise ('the Acceptance of Pleas Guidelines').

A5. The purpose of plea discussions is to narrow the issues in the case with a view to reaching a just outcome at the earliest possible time, including the possibility of reaching an agreement about acceptable pleas of guilty and preparing a joint submission as to sentence.

A6. The potential benefits of plea discussions are that:

- Early resolution of the case may reduce the anxiety and uncertainty for victims and witnesses, and provide earlier clarity for accused persons who admit their guilt (subject to the court's power to reject the agreement);
- The issues in dispute may be narrowed so that even if the case proceeds to trial, it can be managed more efficiently in accordance with Rule 3.2 of the Criminal Procedure Rules 2005. If pleas are agreed, litigation can be kept to a minimum.

A7. Where plea discussions take place prior to the commencement of proceedings, the charges brought by the prosecutor will reflect those agreed, rather than those that the prosecutor would necessarily have preferred if no agreement had been reached. Also, any criminal investigation may not be complete when these discussions take place. For these reasons it is important that the procedures followed should command public and judicial confidence; that any agreement reached is reasonable, fair and just; that there are safeguards to ensure that defendants are not under improper pressure to make admissions; and that there are proper records of discussions that have taken place.

A8. The Guidelines are not intended to prevent or discourage existing practices by which prosecutors and prosecuting advocates discuss cases with defence legal representatives after charge, in order to narrow the issues or to agree a basis of plea. Neither do they affect the existing practice of judicial sentence indications at the plea and case management hearing or later in accordance with the guidance in *R v Goodyear (Karl)* [2005] EWCA 888 (see also the Acceptance of Pleas Guidelines). They complement, and do not detract from or replace, the Code and the Acceptance of Pleas Guidelines, or any other relevant guidance such as the Prosecutor's Pledge, the Victim's Charter and the Code of Practice for Victims of Crime.

A9. Where a plea agreement is reached, it remains entirely a matter for the court to decide how to deal with the case.

B General Principles

B1. In conducting plea discussions and presenting a plea agreement to the court, the prosecutor must act openly, fairly and in the interests of justice.

B2. Acting in the interests of justice means ensuring that the plea agreement reflects the seriousness and extent of the offending, gives the court adequate sentencing powers, and enables the court, the public and the victims to have confidence in the outcome. The prosecutor must consider carefully the impact of a proposed plea or basis of plea on the community and the victim, and on the prospects of successfully prosecuting any other person implicated in the offending. The prosecutor must not agree to a reduced basis of plea which is misleading, untrue or illogical.

B3. Acting fairly means respecting the rights of the defendant and of any other person who is being or may be prosecuted in relation to the offending. The prosecutor must not put improper pressure on a defendant in the course of plea discussions, for example by exaggerating the strength of the case in order to persuade the defendant to plead guilty, or to plead guilty on a particular basis.

B4. Acting openly means being transparent with the defendant, the victim and the court. The prosecutor must:

- Ensure that a full and accurate record of the plea discussions is prepared and retained;
- Ensure that the defendant has sufficient information to enable him or her to play an informed part in the plea discussions;
- Communicate with the victim before accepting a reduced basis of plea, wherever it is practicable to do so, so that the position can be explained; and
- Ensure that the plea agreement placed before the court fully and fairly reflects the matters agreed. The prosecutor must not agree additional matters with the defendant which are not recorded in the plea agreement and made known to the court.

C Initiating Plea Discussions

When and with whom discussions should be initiated and conducted

C1. Where he or she believes it advantageous to do so, the prosecutor may initiate plea discussions with any person who is being prosecuted or investigated with a view to prosecution in connection with a serious or complex fraud, and who is legally represented. The prosecutor will not initiate plea discussions with a defendant who is not legally represented. If the prosecutor receives an approach from such a defendant, he or she may enter into discussions if satisfied that it is appropriate to do so.

C2. Where proceedings have not yet been instituted, the prosecutor should not initiate plea discussions until he or she and the investigating officer are satisfied that the suspect's criminality is known. This will not usually be the case until after the suspect has been interviewed under caution.

C3. The prosecutor should be alert to any attempt by the defendant to use plea discussions as a means of delaying the investigation or prosecution, and should not initiate or continue discussions where the defendant's commitment to the process is in doubt. The prosecutor should ensure that the position is preserved during plea discussions by, for example, restraining assets in anticipation of the making of a confiscation order. Where a defendant declines to take part in plea discussions, the prosecutor should not make a second approach unless there is a material change in circumstances.

Invitation letter

C4. In order to initiate the plea discussions, the prosecutor will send the defendant's representatives a letter which:
- Asks whether the defence wish to enter into discussions in accordance with these Guidelines; and
- Sets a deadline for a response from the defence.

Terms and conditions letter

C5. Where the defence agree to engage in plea discussions, the prosecutor should send them a letter setting out the way in which the discussions will be conducted. This letter should deal with:
- The confidentiality of information provided by the prosecutor and defendant in the course of the plea discussions;
- The use which may be made by the prosecutor of information provided by the defendant; and
- The practical means by which the discussions will be conducted.

Confidentiality and use of information

C6. In relation to confidentiality, the prosecutor will indicate that he or she intends to provide an undertaking to the effect that the fact that the defendant has taken part in the plea discussions, and any information provided by the defence in the course of the plea discussions will be treated as confidential and will not be disclosed to any other party other than for the purposes of the plea discussions and plea agreement (applying these Guidelines), or as required by law. The undertaking will make it clear that the law in relation to the disclosure of unused material may require the prosecutor to provide information about the plea discussions to another defendant in criminal proceedings.

C7. The prosecutor will require the defendant's legal representative to provide an undertaking to the effect that information provided by the prosecutor in the course of the plea discussions will be treated as confidential and will not be disclosed to any other party, other than for the purposes of the plea discussion and plea agreement or as required by law.

C8. In relation to the use of information, the prosecutor will indicate that he or she intends to undertake not to rely upon the fact that the defendant has taken part in the plea discussions, or any information provided by the defendant in the course of the discussions, as evidence in any prosecution of that defendant for the offences under investigation, should the discussions fail. However, this undertaking will make it clear that the prosecutor is not prevented from:
- Relying upon a concluded and signed plea agreement as confession evidence or as admissions;
- Relying upon any evidence obtained from enquiries made as a result of the provision of information by the defendant;
- Relying upon information provided by the defendant as evidence against him or her in any prosecution for an offence other than the fraud which is the subject of the plea discussion and any offence which is consequent upon it, such as money laundering; and
- Relying upon information provided by the defendant in a prosecution of any other person for any offence (so far as the rules of evidence allow).

C9. In exceptional circumstances the prosecutor may agree to different terms regarding the confidentiality and use of information. However, the prosecutor must not surrender the ability to rely upon a concluded and signed plea agreement as evidence against the defendant. The prosecutor may reserve the right to bring other charges (additional to those to which the defendant has indicated a willingness to plead guilty) in specific circumstances, for example if substantial new information comes to light at a later stage, the plea agreement is rejected by the court, or the defendant fails to honour the agreement.

C10. Until the issues of confidentiality and use of information have been agreed to the satisfaction of both parties, and the agreement reflected in signed undertakings, the prosecutor must not continue with the substantive plea discussions.

D   Conducting Plea Discussions

Statement of case

D1. Where plea discussions take place prior to proceedings being instituted, the prosecutor will provide a statement of case to the defence. This is a written summary of the nature of the allegation against the suspect and the evidence which has been obtained, or is expected to be obtained, to support it. The statement of case should include a list of the proposed charges. Material in support of the statement of case may also be provided, whether or not in the form of admissible evidence. However, the prosecutor is not obliged to reveal to the suspect all of the information or evidence supporting his case, provided that this does not mislead the suspect to his or her prejudice.

D2. Where plea discussions are initiated after proceedings have been commenced, but before the prosecutor has provided the defence with a case summary or opening note, the prosecutor may provide a statement of case to assist the defendant in understanding the evidence and identifying the issues.

Unused material

D3. These Guidelines do not affect the prosecutor's existing duties in relation to the disclosure of unused material. Where plea discussions take place prior to the institution of proceedings, the prosecutor should ensure that the suspect is not misled as to the strength of the prosecution case. It will not usually be necessary to provide copies of unused material in order to do this.

Conducting and recording the discussions

D4. Having provided the defence with the statement of case and supporting material, the parties will then be in a position to conduct the plea discussion proper. Whether this is done by correspondence, by face-to-face meetings or by a combination of the two is a matter for the parties to decide in the individual case.

D5. It is essential that a full written record is kept of every key action and event in the discussion process, including details of every offer or concession made by each party, and the reasons for every decision taken by the prosecutor. Meetings between the parties should be minuted and the minutes agreed and signed. Particular care should be taken where the defendant is not legally represented. The prosecutor should only meet with a defendant who is not legally represented if the defendant agrees to the meeting being recorded, or to the presence of an independent third party.

Queen's Evidence

D6. If the defendant offers at any stage to provide information, or to give evidence about the criminal activities of others, any such offer will be dealt with in accordance with sections 71 to 75 of the Serious Organised Crime and Police Act 2005 ('SOCPA'), the judgment of the Court of Appeal in *R v P*, *R v Blackburn* [2007] EWCA Crim 2290 and the guidance agreed and issued by the Director of Public Prosecutions, the Director of the Serious Fraud Office and the Director of Revenue and Customs Prosecutions.

Discussion of pleas

D7. In deciding whether or not to accept an offer by the defendant to plead guilty, the prosecutor will follow sections 7 and 10 of the Code relating to the selection of charges and the acceptance of guilty pleas. The prosecutor should ensure that:
- The charges reflect the seriousness and extent of the offending;
- They give the court adequate powers to sentence and impose appropriate post-conviction orders;
- They enable the case to be presented in a clear and simple way (bearing in mind that many cases of fraud are necessarily complex);
- The basis of plea enables the court to pass a sentence that matches the seriousness of the offending, particularly if there are aggravating features;
- The interests of the victim, and where possible any views expressed by the victim, are taken into account when deciding whether it is in the public interest to accept the plea; and
- The investigating officer is fully appraised of developments in the plea discussions and his or her views are taken into account.

D8. In reaching an agreement on pleas, the parties should resolve any factual issues necessary to allow the court to sentence the defendant on a clear, fair and accurate basis. Before agreeing to proposed pleas, the prosecutor should satisfy him or herself that the Full Code Test as set out in the Code will be made out in respect of each charge. In considering whether the evidential stage of the test will be met, the prosecutor should assume that the offender will sign a plea agreement amounting to an admission to the charge.

Discussion of sentence

D9. Where agreement is reached as to pleas, the parties should discuss the appropriate sentence with a view to presenting a joint written submission to the court. This document should list the aggravating and mitigating features arising from the agreed facts, set out any personal mitigation available to the defendant, and refer to any relevant sentencing guidelines or authorities. In the light of all of these factors, it should make submissions as to the applicable sentencing range in the relevant guideline. The prosecutor must ensure that the submissions are realistic, taking full account of all relevant material and considerations.

D10.   The prosecutor should bear in mind all of the powers of the court, and seek to include in the joint submission any relevant ancillary orders. It is particularly desirable that measures should be included that achieve redress for victims (such as compensation orders) and protection for the public (such as directors' disqualification orders, serious crime prevention orders or financial reporting orders).

D11.   Due regard should be had to the court's asset recovery powers and the desirability of using these powers both as a deterrent to others and as a means of preventing the defendant from benefiting from the proceeds of crime or funding future offending. The Proceeds of Crime Act 2002 requires the Crown Court to proceed to the making of a confiscation order against a convicted defendant who has benefited from his criminal conduct where the prosecutor asks the court to do so, or the court believes that it is appropriate to do so. Fraud is an acquisitive crime, and the expectation in a fraud case should be that a confiscation order will be sought by the prosecutor reflecting the full benefit to the defendant. However, in doing so it is open to the prosecutor to take a realistic view of the likely approach of the court to the determination of any points in dispute (such as the interest of a third party in any property).

D12.   In the course of the plea discussions the prosecutor must make it clear to the defence that the joint submission as to sentence (including confiscation) is not binding on the court.

Liaison with another prosecutor or regulator

D13.   The prosecutor may become aware that another prosecuting authority or regulatory body (either in England and Wales or elsewhere) has an interest in the defendant. The prosecutor should liaise with the other agency, in accordance with the Prosecutors' Convention and any other relevant agreement or guidance. The other agency may wish to take part in the plea discussions, or they may authorise the prosecutor to discuss with the defendant the matters which they are interested in, with a view to resolving all matters in one plea agreement. The prosecutor should warn the defendant that a plea agreement will not bind any other agency which is not a party to it.

E   The Written Plea Agreement

E1.   All matters agreed between the prosecutor and the defence must be reduced to writing as a plea agreement and signed by both parties. The plea agreement will include:
   • A list of the charges;
   • A statement of the facts; and
   • A declaration, signed by the defendant personally, to the effect that he or she accepts the stated facts and admits he or she is guilty of the agreed charges.

E2.   Any agreement under the SOCPA regarding the giving of assistance to the prosecutor by the defendant should be in a separate document accompanying the plea agreement.

E3.   Once a plea agreement is signed in a case where proceedings have not yet been commenced, the prosecutor will review the case in accordance with the Code and, assuming the evidential stage of the Full Code Test is satisfied on the basis of the signed plea agreement and the other available evidence, will arrange for proceedings to be instituted by summons or charge.

E4.   In advance of the defendant's first appearance in the Crown Court, the prosecutor should send the court sufficient material to allow the judge to understand the facts of the case and the history of the plea discussions, to assess whether the plea agreement is fair and in the interests of justice, and to decide the appropriate sentence. This will include:
   • The signed plea agreement;
   • A joint submission as to sentence and sentencing considerations;
   • Any relevant sentencing guidelines or authorities;
   • All of the material provided by the prosecution to the defendant in the course of the plea discussions;
   • Any material provided by the defendant to the prosecution, such as documents relating to personal mitigation; and
   • The minutes of any meetings between the parties and any correspondence generated in the plea discussions.

E5.   It will then be for the court to decide how to deal with the plea agreement. In particular, the court retains an absolute discretion as to whether or not it sentences in accordance with the joint submission from the parties.

F   Failure of Plea Discussions

F1.   There are several circumstances in which plea discussions may result in an outcome other than the defendant pleading guilty in accordance with a plea agreement. The prosecutor or the defendant may break off the discussions. They may be unable to reach an agreement. They may reach an agreement, but intervening events may lead the prosecutor to decide that proceedings should not be instituted. Proceedings may be instituted but the court may reject the plea agreement. The defendant may decline to plead guilty in accordance with the plea agreement, either as a result of a sentence indication given under the procedure set out in *R v Goodyear*, or for some other reason.

F2. If any of these situations arises, the prosecutor may wish for further enquiries to be made with a view to bringing or completing proceedings against the defendant. If proceedings have already been instituted, the prosecutor will use the appropriate means to delay them — either discontinuing under section 23 or 23A of the Prosecution of Offences Act 1985 or (if the indictment has already been preferred) applying for an adjournment or stay of the proceedings. The prosecutor and the defendant's representatives will continue to be bound by the preliminary undertakings made in relation to the confidentiality and use of information provided in the course of the plea discussions.

F3. Where plea discussions have broken down for any reason, it will be rare that the prosecutor will wish to re-open them, but he or she may do so if there is a material change in circumstances which warrants it.

DISCLOSURE

The Attorney-General's Guidelines on Disclosure of Information in Criminal Proceedings are reproduced in **appendix 4**.

Appendix 3   The Code for Crown Prosecutors

1 Introduction

1.1 The Code for Crown Prosecutors (the Code) is issued by the Director of Public Prosecutions (DPP) under section 10 of the Prosecution of Offences Act 1985. This is the seventh edition of the Code and replaces all earlier versions.

1.2 The DPP is the head of the Crown Prosecution Service (CPS), which is the principal public prosecution service for England and Wales. The DPP operates independently, under the superintendence of the Attorney General who is accountable to Parliament for the work of the CPS.

1.3 The Code gives guidance to prosecutors on the general principles to be applied when making decisions about prosecutions. The Code is issued primarily for prosecutors in the CPS, but other prosecutors follow the Code either through convention or because they are required to do so by law.

1.4 In this Code, the term 'suspect' is used to describe a person who is not yet the subject of formal criminal proceedings; the term 'defendant' is used to describe a person who has been charged or summonsed; and the term 'offender' is used to describe a person who has admitted his or her guilt to a police officer or other investigator or prosecutor, or who has been found guilty in a court of law.

2 General Principles

2.1 The decision to prosecute or to recommend an out-of- court disposal is a serious step that affects suspects, victims, witnesses and the public at large and must be undertaken with the utmost care.

2.2 It is the duty of prosecutors to make sure that the right person is prosecuted for the right offence and to bring offenders to justice wherever possible. Casework decisions taken fairly, impartially and with integrity help to secure justice for victims, witnesses, defendants and the public. Prosecutors must ensure that the law is properly applied; that relevant evidence is put before the court; and that obligations of disclosure are complied with.

2.3 Although each case must be considered on its own facts and on its own merits, there are general principles that apply in every case.

2.4 Prosecutors must be fair, independent and objective. They must not let any personal views about the ethnic or national origin, gender, disability, age, religion or belief, political views, sexual orientation, or gender identity of the suspect, victim or any witness influence their decisions. Neither must prosecutors be affected by improper or undue pressure from any source. Prosecutors must always act in the interests of justice and not solely for the purpose of obtaining a conviction.

2.5 The CPS is a public authority for the purposes of current, relevant equality legislation. Prosecutors are bound by the duties set out in this legislation.

2.6 Prosecutors must apply the principles of the European Convention on Human Rights, in accordance with the Human Rights Act 1998, at each stage of a case. Prosecutors must also comply with any guidelines issued by the Attorney General; with the Criminal Procedure Rules currently in force; and have regard to the obligations arising from international conventions. They must follow the policies and guidance of the CPS issued on behalf of the DPP and available for the public to view on the CPS website.

3 The Decision Whether to Prosecute

3.1 In more serious or complex cases, prosecutors decide whether a person should be charged with a criminal offence and, if so, what that offence should be. They make their decisions in accordance with this Code and the DPP's Guidance on Charging. The police apply the same principles in deciding whether to start criminal proceedings against a person in those cases for which they are responsible.

3.2 The police and other investigators are responsible for conducting enquiries into any alleged crime and for deciding how to deploy their resources. This includes decisions to start or continue an investigation and on the scope of the investigation. Prosecutors often advise the police and other investigators about possible lines of inquiry and evidential requirements, and assist with pre-charge procedures. In large scale investigations the prosecutor may be asked to advise on the overall investigation strategy, including decisions to refine or narrow the scope of the criminal conduct and the number of suspects under investigation. This is to assist the police and other investigators to complete the investigation within a reasonable period of time and to build the most effective prosecution case. However, prosecutors cannot direct the police or other investigators.

3.3 Prosecutors should identify and, where possible, seek to rectify evidential weaknesses, but, subject to the Threshold Test (see section 5), they should swiftly stop cases which do not meet the evidential stage of the Full Code Test (see section 4) and which cannot be strengthened by further investigation, or where the public interest clearly does not require a prosecution (see section 4). Although prosecutors primarily consider the evidence and information supplied by the police and other investigators, the suspect or those acting on his or her behalf may also submit evidence or information to the prosecutor via the police or other investigators, prior to charge, to help inform the prosecutor's decision.

3.4 Prosecutors must only start or continue a prosecution when the case has passed both stages of the Full Code Test (see section 4). The exception is when the Threshold Test (see section 5) may be applied where it is proposed to apply to the court to keep the suspect in custody after charge, and the evidence required to apply the Full Code Test is not yet available.

3.5 Prosecutors should not start or continue a prosecution which would be regarded by the courts as oppressive or unfair and an abuse of the court's process.

3.6 Prosecutors review every case they receive from the police or other investigators. Review is a continuing process and prosecutors must take account of any change in circumstances that occurs as the case develops, including what becomes known of the defence case. Wherever possible, they should talk to the investigator when thinking about changing the charges or stopping the case. Prosecutors and investigators work closely together, but the final responsibility for the decision whether or not a case should go ahead rests with the CPS.

3.7 Parliament has decided that a limited number of offences should only be taken to court with the agreement of the DPP. These are called consent cases. In such cases the DPP, or prosecutors acting on his or her behalf, apply the Code in deciding whether to give consent to a prosecution. There are also certain offences that should only be taken to court with the consent of the Attorney General. Prosecutors must follow current guidance when referring any such cases to the Attorney General. Additionally, the Attorney General will be kept informed of certain cases as part of his or her superintendence of the CPS and accountability to Parliament for its actions.

4   The Full Code Test

4.1 The Full Code Test has two stages: (i) the evidential stage; followed by (ii) the public interest stage.

4.2 In most cases, prosecutors should only decide whether to prosecute after the investigation has been completed and after all the available evidence has been reviewed. However there will be cases where it is clear, prior to the collection and consideration of all the likely evidence, that the public interest does not require a prosecution. In these instances, prosecutors may decide that the case should not proceed further.

4.3 Prosecutors should only take such a decision when they are satisfied that the broad extent of the criminality has been determined and that they are able to make a fully informed assessment of the public interest. If prosecutors do not have sufficient information to take such a decision, the investigation should proceed and a decision taken later in accordance with the Full Code Test set out in this section.

The Evidential Stage

4.4 Prosecutors must be satisfied that there is sufficient evidence to provide a realistic prospect of conviction against each suspect on each charge. They must consider what the defence case may be, and how it is likely to affect the prospects of conviction. A case which does not pass the evidential stage must not proceed, no matter how serious or sensitive it may be.

4.5 The finding that there is a realistic prospect of conviction is based on the prosecutor's objective assessment of the evidence, including the impact of any defence and any other information that the suspect has put forward or on which he or she might rely. It means that an objective, impartial and reasonable jury or bench of magistrates or judge hearing a case alone, properly directed and acting in accordance with the law, is more likely than not to convict the defendant of the charge alleged. This is a different test from the one that the criminal courts themselves must apply. A court may only convict if it is sure that the defendant is guilty.

4.6 When deciding whether there is sufficient evidence to prosecute, prosecutors should ask themselves the following:

Can the evidence be used in court?

Prosecutors should consider whether there is any question over the admissibility of certain evidence. In doing so, prosecutors should assess:

a)   the likelihood of that evidence being held as inadmissible by the court; and
b)   the importance of that evidence in relation to the evidence as a whole.

Is the evidence reliable?

Prosecutors should consider whether there are any reasons to question the reliability of the evidence, including its accuracy or integrity.

Is the evidence credible?

Prosecutors should consider whether there are any reasons to doubt the credibility of the evidence.

The Public Interest Stage

4.7   In every case where there is sufficient evidence to justify a prosecution, prosecutors must go on to consider whether a prosecution is required in the public interest.

4.8   It has never been the rule that a prosecution will automatically take place once the evidential stage is met. A prosecution will usually take place unless the prosecutor is satisfied that there are public interest factors tending against prosecution which outweigh those tending in favour. In some cases the prosecutor may be satisfied that the public interest can be properly served by offering the offender the opportunity to have the matter dealt with by an out-of-court disposal rather than bringing a prosecution.

4.9   When deciding the public interest, prosecutors should consider each of the questions set out below in paragraphs 4.12 a) to g) so as to identify and determine the relevant public interest factors tending for and against prosecution. These factors, together with any public interest factors set out in relevant guidance or policy issued by the DPP, should enable prosecutors to form an overall assessment of the public interest.

4.10   The explanatory text below each question in paragraphs 4.12 a) to g) provides guidance to prosecutors when addressing each particular question and determining whether it identifies public interest factors for or against prosecution. The questions identified are not exhaustive, and not all the questions may be relevant in every case. The weight to be attached to each of the questions, and the factors identified, will also vary according to the facts and merits of each case.

4.11   It is quite possible that one public interest factor alone may outweigh a number of other factors which tend in the opposite direction. Although there may be public interest factors tending against prosecution in a particular case, prosecutors should consider whether nonetheless a prosecution should go ahead and those factors put to the court for consideration when sentence is passed.

4.12   Prosecutors should consider each of the following questions:

a)   *How serious is the offence committed?*

The more serious the offence, the more likely it is that a prosecution is required.

When deciding the level of seriousness of the offence committed, prosecutors should include amongst the factors for consideration the suspect's culpability and the harm to the victim by asking themselves the questions at b) and c).

b)   *What is the level of culpability of the suspect?*

The greater the suspect's level of culpability, the more likely it is that a prosecution is required.

Culpability is likely to be determined by the suspect's level of involvement; the extent to which the offending was premeditated and/or planned; whether they have previous criminal convictions and/or out-of-court disposals and any offending whilst on bail or whilst subject to a court order; whether the offending was or is likely to be continued, repeated or escalated; and the suspect's age or maturity (see paragraph d) below for suspects under 18).

Prosecutors should also have regard when considering culpability as to whether the suspect is, or was at the time of the offence, suffering from any significant mental or physical ill health as in some circumstances this may mean that it is less likely that a prosecution is required. However, prosecutors will also need to consider how serious the offence was, whether it is likely to be repeated and the need to safeguard the public or those providing care to such persons.

c)   *What are the circumstances of and the harm caused to the victim?*

The circumstances of the victim are highly relevant. The greater the vulnerability of the victim, the more likely it is that a prosecution is required. This includes where a position of trust or authority exists between the suspect and victim.

A prosecution is also more likely if the offence has been committed against a victim who was at the time a person serving the public.

Prosecutors must also have regard to whether the offence was motivated by any form of discrimination against the victim's ethnic or national origin, gender, disability, age, religion or belief, sexual orientation or gender identity; or the suspect demonstrated hostility towards the victim based on any of those characteristics. The presence of any such motivation or hostility will mean that it is more likely that prosecution is required.

In deciding whether a prosecution is required in the public interest, prosecutors should take into account the views expressed by the victim about the impact that the offence has had. In appropriate cases, this may also include the views of the victim's family.

Prosecutors also need to consider if a prosecution is likely to have an adverse effect on the victim's physical or mental health, always bearing in mind the seriousness of the offence. If there is evidence that prosecution is likely to have an adverse impact on the victim's health it may make a prosecution less likely, taking into account the victim's views.

However, the CPS does not act for victims or their families in the same way as solicitors act for their clients, and prosecutors must form an overall view of the public interest.

d) *Was the suspect under the age of 18 at the time of the offence?*

The criminal justice system treats children and young people differently from adults and significant weight must be attached to the age of the suspect if they are a child or young person under 18. The best interests and welfare of the child or young person must be considered including whether a prosecution is likely to have an adverse impact on his or her future prospects that is disproportionate to the seriousness of the offending. Prosecutors must have regard to the principal aim of the youth justice system which is to prevent offending by children and young people. Prosecutors must also have regard to the obligations arising under the United Nations 1989 Convention on the Rights of the Child.

As a starting point, the younger the suspect, the less likely it is that a prosecution is required.

However, there may be circumstances which mean that notwithstanding the fact that the suspect is under 18, a prosecution is in the public interest. These include where the offence committed is serious, where the suspect's past record suggests that there are no suitable alternatives to prosecution, or where the absence of an admission means that out-of-court disposals which might have addressed the offending behaviour are not available.

e) *What is the impact on the community?*

The greater the impact of the offending on the community, the more likely it is that a prosecution is required. In considering this question, prosecutors should have regard to how community is an inclusive term and is not restricted to communities defined by location.

f) *Is prosecution a proportionate response?*

Prosecutors should also consider whether prosecution is proportionate to the likely outcome, and in so doing the following may be relevant to the case under consideration:

- The cost to the CPS and the wider criminal justice system, especially where it could be regarded as excessive when weighed against any likely penalty. (Prosecutors should not decide the public interest on the basis of this factor alone. It is essential that regard is also given to the public interest factors identified when considering the other questions in paragraphs 4.12 a) to g), but cost is a relevant factor when making an overall assessment of the public interest.)
- Cases should be capable of being prosecuted in a way that is consistent with principles of effective case management. For example, in a case involving multiple suspects, prosecution might be reserved for the main participants in order to avoid excessively long and complex proceedings.

g) *Do sources of information require protecting?*

In cases where public interest immunity does not apply, special care should be taken when proceeding with a prosecution where details may need to be made public that could harm sources of information, international relations or national security. It is essential that such cases are kept under continuing review.

5 The Threshold Test

5.1   The Threshold Test may only be applied where the suspect presents a substantial bail risk and not all the evidence is available at the time when he or she must be released from custody unless charged.

When the Threshold Test may be applied

5.2   Prosecutors must determine whether the following conditions are met:
    a)   there is insufficient evidence currently available to apply the evidential stage of the Full Code Test; and

    b)   there are reasonable grounds for believing that further evidence will become available within a reasonable period; and

    c)   the seriousness or the circumstances of the case justifies the making of an immediate charging decision; and

    d)   there are continuing substantial grounds to object to bail in accordance with the Bail Act 1976 and in all the circumstances of the case it is proper to do so.

5.3   Where any of the above conditions is not met, the Threshold Test cannot be applied and the suspect cannot be charged. The custody officer must determine whether the person may continue to be detained or be released on bail, with or without conditions.

5.4   There are two parts to the evidential consideration of the Threshold Test.

The first part of the Threshold Test – is there reasonable suspicion?

5.5   Prosecutors must be satisfied that there is at least a reasonable suspicion that the person to be charged has committed the offence.

5.6   In determining this, prosecutors must consider the evidence then available. This may take the form of witness statements, material or other information, provided the prosecutor is satisfied that:

    a)   it is relevant; and

    b)   it is capable of being put into an admissible format for presentation in court; and

    c)   it would be used in the case.

5.7   If satisfied on this the prosecutor should then consider the second part of the Threshold Test.

The second part of the Threshold Test – can further evidence be gathered to provide a realistic prospect of conviction?

5.8   Prosecutors must be satisfied that there are reasonable grounds for believing that the continuing investigation will provide further evidence, within a reasonable period of time, so that all the evidence together is capable of establishing a realistic prospect of conviction in accordance with the Full Code Test.

5.9   The further evidence must be identifiable and not merely speculative.

5.10 In reaching this decision prosecutors must consider:

    a)   the nature, extent and admissibility of any likely further evidence and the impact it will have on the case;

    b)   the charges that all the evidence will support;

    c)   the reasons why the evidence is not already available;

    d)   the time required to obtain the further evidence and whether any consequential delay is reasonable in all the circumstances.

5.11 If both parts of the Threshold Test are satisfied, prosecutors must apply the public interest stage of the Full Code Test based on the information available at that time.

Reviewing the Threshold Test

5.12 A decision to charge under the Threshold Test must be kept under review. The evidence must be regularly assessed to ensure that the charge is still appropriate and that continued objection to bail is justified. The Full Code Test must be applied as soon as is reasonably practicable and in any event before the expiry of any applicable custody time limit.

6 Selection of Charges

6.1   Prosecutors should select charges which:

    a) reflect the seriousness and extent of the offending supported by the evidence;

    b) give the court adequate powers to sentence and impose appropriate post-conviction orders; and

    c) enable the case to be presented in a clear and simple way.

6.2   This means that prosecutors may not always choose or continue with the most serious charge where there is a choice.

6.3   Prosecutors should never go ahead with more charges than are necessary just to encourage a defendant to plead guilty to a few. In the same way, they should never go ahead with a more serious charge just to encourage a defendant to plead guilty to a less serious one.

6.4   Prosecutors should not change the charge simply because of the decision made by the court or the defendant about where the case will be heard.

6.5   Prosecutors must take account of any relevant change in circumstances as the case progresses after charge.

7 Out-of-Court Disposals

7.1 An out-of-court disposal may take the place of a prosecution in court if it is an appropriate response to the offender and/or the seriousness and consequences of the offending.

7.2 Prosecutors must follow any relevant guidance when asked to advise on or authorise a simple caution, a conditional caution, any appropriate regulatory proceedings, a punitive or civil penalty, or other disposal. They should ensure that the appropriate evidential standard for the specific out-of-court disposal is met including, where required, a clear admission of guilt, and that the public interest would be properly served by such a disposal.

8 Mode of Trial

8.1 Prosecutors must have regard to the current guidelines on sentencing and allocation when making submissions to the magistrates' court about where the defendant should be tried.

8.2 Speed must never be the only reason for asking for a case to stay in the magistrates' court. But prosecutors should consider the effect of any likely delay if a case is sent to the Crown Court, and the possible effect on any victim or witness if the case is delayed.

Venue for trial in cases involving youths

8.3 Prosecutors must bear in mind that youths should be tried in the youth court wherever possible. It is the court which is best designed to meet their specific needs. A trial of a youth in the Crown Court should be reserved for the most serious cases or where the interests of justice require a youth to be jointly tried with an adult.

9 Accepting Guilty Pleas

9.1 Defendants may want to plead guilty to some, but not all, of the charges. Alternatively, they may want to plead guilty to a different, possibly less serious, charge because they are admitting only part of the crime.

9.2 Prosecutors should only accept the defendant's plea if they think the court is able to pass a sentence that matches the seriousness of the offending, particularly where there are aggravating features. Prosecutors must never accept a guilty plea just because it is convenient.

9.3 In considering whether the pleas offered are acceptable, prosecutors should ensure that the interests and, where possible, the views of the victim, or in appropriate cases the views of the victim's family, are taken into account when deciding whether it is in the public interest to accept the plea. However, the decision rests with the prosecutor.

9.4 It must be made clear to the court on what basis any plea is advanced and accepted. In cases where a defendant pleads guilty to the charges but on the basis of facts that are different from the prosecution case, and where this may significantly affect sentence, the court should be invited to hear evidence to determine what happened, and then sentence on that basis.

9.5 Where a defendant has previously indicated that he or she will ask the court to take an offence into consideration when sentencing, but then declines to admit that offence at court, prosecutors will consider whether a prosecution is required for that offence. Prosecutors should explain to the defence advocate and the court that the prosecution of that offence may be subject to further review, in consultation with the police or other investigators wherever possible.

9.6 Particular care must be taken when considering pleas which would enable the defendant to avoid the imposition of a mandatory minimum sentence. When pleas are offered, prosecutors must also bear in mind the fact that ancillary orders can be made with some offences but not with others.

10 Reconsidering a Prosecution Decision

10.1 People should be able to rely on decisions taken by the CPS. Normally, if the CPS tells a suspect or defendant that there will not be a prosecution, or that the prosecution has been stopped, the case will not start again. But occasionally there are reasons why the CPS will overturn a decision not to prosecute or to deal with the case by way of an out-of-court disposal or when it will restart the prosecution, particularly if the case is serious.

10.2 These reasons include:

a) cases where a new look at the original decision shows that it was wrong and, in order to maintain confidence in the criminal justice system, a prosecution should be brought despite the earlier decision;

b) cases which are stopped so that more evidence which is likely to become available in the fairly near future can be collected and prepared. In these cases, the prosecutor will tell the defendant that the prosecution may well start again;

c) cases which are stopped because of a lack of evidence but where more significant evidence is discovered later; and

d) cases involving a death in which a review following the findings of an inquest concludes that a prosecution should be brought, notwithstanding any earlier decision not to prosecute.

Appendix 4   Disclosure

ATTORNEY-GENERAL'S GUIDELINES ON DISCLOSURE FOR INVESTIGATORS, PROSECUTORS AND DEFENCE PRACTITIONERS

December 2013

Foreword

[Omitted.]

Introduction

These Guidelines are issued by the Attorney General for investigators, prosecutors and defence practitioners on the application of the disclosure regime contained in the Criminal Procedure and Investigations Act 1996 ('CPIA'). The Guidelines emphasise the importance of prosecution-led disclosure and the importance of applying the CPIA regime in a 'thinking manner', tailored, where appropriate, to the type of investigation or prosecution in question.

The Guidelines do not contain the detail of the disclosure regime; they outline the high level principles which should be followed when the disclosure regime is applied.

These Guidelines replace the existing Attorney General's Guidelines on Disclosure issued in 2005 and the Supplementary Guidelines on Digital Material issued in 2011, which is an annex to the general guidelines.

The Guidelines are intended to operate alongside the Judicial Protocol on the Disclosure of Unused Material in Criminal Cases. They are not designed to be an unequivocal statement of the law at any one time, nor are they a substitute for a thorough understanding of the relevant legislation, codes of practice, case law and procedure.

…

The Importance of Disclosure

1. The statutory framework for criminal investigations and disclosure is contained in the Criminal Procedure and Investigations Act 1996 (the CPIA) and the CPIA Code of Practice. The CPIA aims to ensure that criminal investigations are conducted in a fair, objective and thorough manner, and requires prosecutors to disclose to the defence material which has not previously been disclosed to the accused and which might reasonably be considered capable of undermining the case for the prosecution against the accused or of assisting the case for the accused. The CPIA requires a timely dialogue between the prosecution, defence and the court to enable the prosecution properly to identify such material.

2. Every accused person has a right to a fair trial, a right long embodied in our law and guaranteed by Article 6 of the European Convention on Human Rights (ECHR). A fair trial is the proper object and expectation of all participants in the trial process. Fair disclosure to the accused is an inseparable part of a fair trial. A fair trial should not require consideration of irrelevant material and should not involve spurious applications or arguments which serve to divert the trial process from examining the real issues before the court.

3. Properly applied, the CPIA should ensure that material is not disclosed which overburdens the participants in the trial process, diverts attention from the relevant issues, leads to unjustifiable delay, and is wasteful of resources. Consideration of disclosure issues should be an integral part of a good investigation and not something that exists separately.

Disclosure: general principles

4. Disclosure refers to providing the defence with copies of, or access to, any prosecution material which might reasonably be considered capable of undermining the case for the prosecution against the accused, or of assisting the case for the accused, and which has not previously been disclosed (section 3 CPIA).

5. Prosecutors will only be expected to anticipate what material might undermine their case or strengthen the defence in the light of information available at the time of the disclosure decision, and they may take into account information revealed during questioning.

6. In deciding whether material satisfies the disclosure test, consideration should be given amongst other things to:
   (a) the use that might be made of it in cross-examination;
   (b) its capacity to support submissions that could lead to:
       (i)   the exclusion of evidence;
       (ii) a stay of proceedings, where the material is required to allow a proper application to be made;
       (iii) a court or tribunal finding that any public authority had acted incompatibly with the accused's rights under the ECHR;
   (c) its capacity to suggest an explanation or partial explanation of the accused's actions;
   (d) the capacity of the material to have a bearing on scientific or medical evidence in the case.

7. It should also be borne in mind that while items of material viewed in isolation may not be reasonably considered to be capable of undermining the prosecution case or assisting the accused, several items together can have that effect.

8. Material relating to the accused's mental or physical health, intellectual capacity, or to any ill treatment which the accused may have suffered when in the investigator's custody is likely to fall within the test for disclosure set out in paragraph 4 above.

9. Disclosure must not be an open-ended trawl of unused material. A critical element to fair and proper disclosure is that the defence play their role to ensure that the prosecution are directed to material which might reasonably be considered capable of undermining the prosecution case or assisting the case for the accused. This process is key to ensuring prosecutors make informed determinations about disclosure of unused material. The defence statement is important in identifying the issues in the case and why it is suggested that the material meets the test for disclosure.

10. Disclosure should be conducted in a thinking manner and never be reduced to a box-ticking exercise[1]; at all stages of the process, there should be consideration of **why** the CPIA disclosure regime requires a particular course of action and what should be done to achieve that aim.

11. There will always be a number of participants in prosecutions and investigations: senior investigation officers, disclosure officers, investigation officers, reviewing prosecutors, leading counsel, junior counsel, and sometimes disclosure counsel. Communication within the 'prosecution team' is vital to ensure that all matters which could have a bearing on disclosure issues are given sufficient attention by the right person. This is especially so given many reviewing lawyers will be unable to sit behind the trial advocate throughout the trial. In practice, this is likely to mean that a full log of disclosure decisions (with reasons) must be kept on the file and made available as appropriate to the prosecution team.

12. The role of the reviewing lawyer will be central to ensuring all members of the prosecution team are aware of, and carry out, their duties and role(s). Where this involves counsel or more than one reviewing lawyer, this should be done by giving clear written instructions and record keeping.

13. The centrality of the reviewing lawyer does not mean that he or she has to do all the work personally; on the contrary, it will often mean effective delegation. Where the conduct of a prosecution is assigned to more than one prosecutor, steps must be taken to ensure that all involved in the case properly record their decisions. Subsequent prosecutors must be able to see and understand previous disclosure decisions before carrying out their continuous review function.

14. Investigators must always be alive to the potential need to reveal and prosecutors to the potential need to disclose material, in the interests of justice and fairness in the particular circumstances of any case, after the commencement of proceedings but before their duty arises under the Act. For instance, disclosure ought to be made of significant information that might affect a bail decision. This is likely to depend on what the defence chooses to reveal at that stage.

Investigators and Disclosure Officers

15. Investigators and disclosure officers must be fair and objective and must work together with prosecutors to ensure that disclosure obligations are met. Investigators and disclosure officers should be familiar with the CPIA Code of Practice, in particular their obligations to **retain** and **record** relevant material, to **review** it and to **reveal** it to the prosecutor.

16. Whether a case is a summary only matter or a long and complex trial on indictment, it is important that investigators and disclosure officers should approach their duties in a 'thinking manner' and not as a box ticking exercise. Where necessary, the reviewing lawyer should be consulted. It is important that investigators and disclosure officers are deployed on cases which are commensurate with their training, skills and experience. The conduct of an investigation provides the foundation for the entire

---

[1] *R v Olu, Wilson and Brooks* [2010] EWCA Crim 2975 at paragraph 42

case, and may even impact the conduct of linked cases. It is vital that there is always consideration of disclosure matters at the outset of an investigation, regardless of its size.

17. A fair investigation involves the pursuit of material following all reasonable lines of enquiry, whether they point towards or away from the suspect. What is 'reasonable' will depend on the context of the case. A fair investigation does not mean an endless investigation: investigators and disclosure officers must give thought to defining, and thereby limiting, the scope of their investigations, seeking the guidance of the prosecutor where appropriate

18. Where there are a number of disclosure officers assigned to a case, there should be a lead disclosure officer who is the focus for enquiries and whose responsibility it is to ensure that the investigator's disclosure obligations are complied with. Where appropriate, regular case conferences and other meetings should be held to ensure prosecutors are apprised of all relevant developments in investigations. Full records should be kept of such meetings.

19. The CPIA Code of Practice encourages investigators and disclosure officers to seek advice from prosecutors about whether any particular item of material may be relevant to the investigation, and if so, how. Investigators and disclosure officers should record key decisions taken on these matters and be prepared to account for their actions later. An identical approach is not called for in each and every case.

20. Investigators are to approach their task seeking to establish what actually happened. They are to be fair and objective.

21. Disclosure officers (or their deputies) must inspect, view, listen to or search all relevant material that has been retained by the investigator and the disclosure officer must provide a personal declaration to the effect that this task has been undertaken. In some cases, a detailed examination of all material seized may be required. In others, however, a detailed examination of every item of material seized would be virtually impossible: see the **Annex**.

22. Prosecutors only have knowledge of matters which are revealed to them by investigators and disclosure officers, and the schedules are the written means by which that revelation takes place. Whatever the approach taken by investigators or disclosure officers to examining the material gathered or generated in the course of an investigation, it is crucial that disclosure officers record their reasons for a particular approach in writing.

23. In meeting the obligations in paragraph 6.9 and 8.1 of the Code, schedules must be completed in a form which not only reveals sufficient information to the prosecutor, but which demonstrates a transparent and thinking approach to the disclosure exercise, to command the confidence of the defence and the court. Descriptions on non-sensitive schedules must be clear and accurate, and must contain sufficient detail to enable the prosecutor to make an informed decision on disclosure. The use of abbreviations and acronyms can be problematic and lead to difficulties in appreciating the significance of the material.

24. Sensitive schedules must contain sufficiently clear descriptions to enable the prosecutor to make an informed decision as to whether or not the material itself should be viewed, to the extent possible without compromising the confidentiality of the information.

25. It may become apparent to an investigator that some material obtained in the course of an investigation, either because it was considered to be potentially relevant, or because it was inextricably linked to material that was relevant, is, in fact, incapable of impact. It is not necessary to retain such material, although the investigator should err on the side of caution in reaching that conclusion and should be particularly mindful of the fact that some investigations continue over some time and that what is incapable of impact may change over time. The advice of the prosecutor should be sought where appropriate.

26. Disclosure officers must specifically draw material to the attention of the prosecutor for consideration where they have any doubt as to whether it might reasonably be considered capable of undermining the prosecution case or of assisting the case for the accused.

27. Disclosure officers must seek the advice and assistance of prosecutors when in doubt as to their responsibility as early as possible. They must deal expeditiously with requests by the prosecutor for further information on material, which may lead to disclosure.

Prosecutors

28. Prosecutors are responsible for making proper disclosure in consultation with the disclosure officer. The duty of disclosure is a continuing one and disclosure should be kept under review. In addition, prosecutors should ensure that advocates in court are properly instructed as to disclosure issues. Prosecutors must also be alert to the need to provide advice to, and where necessary probe actions taken by, disclosure officers to ensure that disclosure obligations are met. There should be no aspects of an investigation about which prosecutors are unable to ask probing questions.

29. Prosecutors must review schedules prepared by disclosure officers thoroughly and must be alert to the possibility that relevant material may exist which has not been revealed to them or material included which should not have been. If no schedules have been provided, or there are apparent omissions from the schedules, or documents or other items are inadequately described or are unclear, the prosecutor must at once take action to obtain properly completed schedules. Likewise schedules should be returned for amendment if irrelevant items are included. If prosecutors remain dissatisfied with the quality or content of the schedules they must raise the matter with a senior investigator to resolve the matter satisfactorily.

30. Where prosecutors have reason to believe that the disclosure officer has not discharged the obligation in paragraph 21 to inspect, view, listen to or search relevant material, they must at once raise the matter with the disclosure officer and request that it be done. Where appropriate the matter should be raised with the officer in the case or a senior officer.

31. Prosecutors should copy the defence statement to the disclosure officer and investigator as soon as reasonably practicable and prosecutors should advise the investigator if, in their view, reasonable and relevant lines of further enquiry should be pursued. If the defence statement does point to other reasonable lines of enquiry, further investigation is required and evidence obtained as a result of these enquiries may be used as part of the prosecution case or to rebut the defence.

32. It is vital that prosecutors consider defence statements thoroughly. Prosecutors cannot comment upon, or invite inferences to be drawn from, failures in defence disclosure otherwise than in accordance with section 11 of the CPIA. Prosecutors may cross-examine the accused on differences between the defence case put at trial and that set out in his or her defence statement. In doing so, it may be appropriate to apply to the judge under section 6E of the CPIA for copies of the statement to be given to a jury, edited if necessary to remove inadmissible material. Prosecutors should examine the defence statement to see whether it points to other lines of enquiry.

33. Prosecutors should challenge the lack of, or inadequate, defence statements in writing, copying the document to the court and the defence and seeking directions from the court to require the provision of an adequate statement from the defence.

34. If the material does not fulfil the disclosure test there is no requirement to disclose it. For this purpose, the parties' respective cases should not be restrictively analysed but must be carefully analysed to ascertain the specific facts the prosecution seek to establish and the specific grounds on which the charges are resisted.

Prosecution advocates

35. Prosecution advocates should ensure that all material which ought to be disclosed under the Act is disclosed to the defence. However, prosecution advocates cannot be expected to disclose material if they are not aware of its existence. As far as is possible, prosecution advocates must place themselves in a fully informed position to enable them to make decisions on disclosure.

36. Upon receipt of instructions, prosecution advocates should consider as a priority all the information provided regarding disclosure of material. Prosecution advocates should consider, in every case, whether they can be satisfied that they are in possession of all relevant documentation and that they have been fully instructed regarding disclosure matters. If as a result the advocate considers that further information or action is required, written advice should promptly be provided setting out the aspects that need clarification or action.

37. The prosecution advocate must keep decisions regarding disclosure under review until the conclusion of the trial, whenever possible in consultation with the reviewing prosecutor. The prosecution advocate must in every case specifically consider whether he or she can satisfactorily discharge the duty of continuing review on the basis of the material supplied already, or whether it is necessary to inspect further material or to reconsider material already inspected. Prosecution advocates must not abrogate their responsibility under the CPIA by disclosing material which does not pass the test for disclosure, set out in paragraph 4, above.

38. There remains no basis in practice or law for counsel to counsel disclosure.

Defence

39. Defence engagement must be early and meaningful for the CPIA regime to function as intended. Defence statements are an integral part of this and are intended to help focus the attention of the prosecutor, court and co-defendants on the relevant issues in order to identify exculpatory unused material. Defence statements should be drafted in accordance with the relevant provisions of the CPIA.

40. Defence requests for further disclosure should ordinarily only be answered by the prosecution if the request is relevant to and directed to an issue identified in the defence statement. If it is not, then a

further or amended defence statement should be sought by the prosecutor and obtained before considering the request for further disclosure.

41. In some cases that involve extensive unused material that is within the knowledge of a defendant, the defence will be expected to provide the prosecution and the court with assistance in identifying material which is suggested to pass the test for disclosure.

42. The prosecution's continuing duty to keep disclosure under review is crucial, and particular attention must be paid to understanding the significance of developments in the case on the unused material and earlier disclosure decisions. Meaningful defence engagement will help the prosecution to keep disclosure under review. The continuing duty of review for prosecutors is less likely to require the disclosure of further material to the defence if the defence have clarified and articulated their case, as required by the CPIA.

43. In the magistrates' courts, where the provision of a defence statement is not mandatory, early identification of the material issues by the defence, whether through a defence statement, case management form or otherwise, will help the prosecution to focus its preparation of the case and allow any defence disclosure queries to be dealt with promptly and accurately.

Magistrates' Courts (including the Youth Court)

44. The majority of criminal cases are heard in the magistrates' court. The requirement for the prosecution to provide initial disclosure only arises after a not guilty plea has been entered but prosecutors should be alert to the possibility that material may exist which should be disclosed to the defendant prior to the CPIA requirements applying to the case[2].

45. Where a not guilty plea is entered in the magistrates' court, prosecutors should ensure that any issues of dispute which are raised are noted on the file. They should also seek to obtain a copy of any Magistrates' Court Trial Preparation Form. Consideration of the issues raised in court and on the Trial Preparation Form will assist in deciding what material undermines the prosecution case or assists the defendant.

46. Where a matter is set down for trial in the magistrates' court, prosecutors should ensure that the investigator is requested to supply any outstanding disclosure schedules as a matter of urgency. Prosecutors should serve initial disclosure in sufficient time to ensure that the trial date is effective.

47. There is no requirement for a defence statement to be served in the magistrates' court but it should be noted that if none is given the court has no power to hear an application for further prosecution disclosure under section 8 of the CPIA and the Criminal Procedure Rules.

Cases in the Crown Court

48. The exponential increase in the use of technology in society means that many routine Crown Court cases are increasingly likely to have to engage with digital material of some form. It is not only in large and complex cases that there may be large quantities of such material. Where such investigations involve digital material, it will be virtually impossible for investigators (or prosecutors) to examine every item of such material individually and there should be no expectation that such material will be so examined. Having consulted with the prosecution as appropriate, disclosure officers should determine what their approach should be to the examination of the material. Investigators or disclosure officers should decide how best to pursue a reasonable line of enquiry in relation to the relevant digital material, and ensure that the extent and manner of the examination are commensurate with the issues in the case.

49. Consideration should be given to any local or national agreements in relation to disclosure in 'Early Guilty Plea Scheme' cases.

Large and complex cases in the Crown Court

50. The particular challenges presented by large and complex criminal prosecutions require an approach to disclosure which is specifically tailored to the needs of such cases. In these cases more than any other is the need for careful thought to be given to prosecution-led disclosure matters from the very earliest stage. It is essential that the prosecution takes a grip on the case and its disclosure requirements from the very outset of the investigation, which must continue throughout all aspects of the case preparation.

Disclosure Management Documents

51. Accordingly, investigations and prosecutions of large and complex cases should be carefully defined and accompanied by a clear investigation and prosecution strategy. The approach to disclosure in such cases should be outlined in a document which should be served on the defence and the court at

---

[2] See for example *R v DPP ex parte Lee* [1999] 2 All ER 737

an early stage. Such documents, sometimes known as Disclosure Management Documents, will require careful preparation and presentation, tailored to the individual case. They may include:

(a) Where prosecutors and investigators operate in an integrated office, an explanation as to how the disclosure responsibilities have been managed;

(b) A brief summary of the prosecution case and a statement outlining how the prosecutor's general approach will comply with the CPIA regime, these Guidelines and the Judicial Protocol on the Disclosure of Unused Material in Criminal Cases;

(c) The prosecutor's understanding of the defence case, including information revealed during interview;

(d) An outline of the prosecution's general approach to disclosure, which may include detail relating to:

  (i) Digital material: explaining the method and extent of examination, in accordance with the **Annex** to these Guidelines;

  (ii) Video footage;

  (iii) Linked investigations: explaining the nexus between investigations, any memoranda of understanding or disclosure agreements between investigators;

  (iv) Third party and foreign material, including steps taken to obtain the material;

  (v) Reasonable lines of enquiry: a summary of the lines pursued, particularly those that point away from the suspect, or which may assist the defence;

  (vi) Credibility of a witness: confirmation that witness checks, including those of professional witnesses have, or will be, carried out.

52. Thereafter the prosecution should follow the Disclosure Management Document. They are living documents and should be amended in light of developments in the case; they should be kept up to date as the case progresses. Their use will assist the court in its own case management and will enable the defence to engage from an early stage with the prosecution's proposed approach to disclosure.

Material not held by the prosecution

Involvement of other agencies: material held by other Government departments and third parties

53. Where it appears to an investigator, disclosure officer or prosecutor that a Government department or other Crown body has material that may be relevant to an issue in the case, reasonable steps should be taken to identify and consider such material. Although what is reasonable will vary from case to case, the prosecution should inform the department or other body of the nature of its case and of relevant issues in the case in respect of which the department or body might possess material, and ask whether it has any such material.

54. It should be remembered that investigators, disclosure officers and prosecutors cannot be regarded to be in constructive possession of material held by Government departments or Crown bodies simply by virtue of their status as Government departments or Crown bodies.

55. Where, after reasonable steps have been taken to secure access to such material, access is denied, the investigator, disclosure officer or prosecutor should consider what if any further steps might be taken to obtain the material or inform the defence. The final decision on any further steps will be for the prosecutor.

Third party material: other domestic bodies

56. There may be cases where the investigator, disclosure officer or prosecutor believes that a third party (for example, a local authority, a social services department, a hospital, a doctor, a school, a provider of forensic services) has material or information which might be relevant to the prosecution case. In such cases, investigators, disclosure officers and prosecutors should take reasonable steps to identify, secure and consider material held by any third party where it appears to the investigator, disclosure officer or prosecutor that (a) such material exists and (b) that it may be relevant to an issue in the case.

57. If the investigator, disclosure officer or prosecutor seeks access to the material or information but the third party declines or refuses to allow access to it, the matter should not be left. If despite any reasons offered by the third party it is still believed that it is reasonable to seek production of the material or information, and the requirements of section 2 of the Criminal Procedure (Attendance of Witnesses) Act 1965 or as appropriate section 97 of the Magistrates' Courts Act 1980 are satisfied (or any other relevant power), then the prosecutor or investigator should apply for a witness summons causing a representative of the third party to produce the material to the court.

58. Sometimes, for example through multi-agency working arrangements, investigators, disclosure officers or prosecutors may become aware of the content or nature of material held by a third party. Consultation with the relevant third party must always take place before disclosure is made; there

may be public interest reasons to apply to the Court for an order for non-disclosure in the public interest, in accordance with the procedure outlined in paragraph 65 and following.

International matters

59. The obligations under the CPIA Code to pursue all reasonable lines of enquiry apply to material held overseas.

60. Where it appears that there is relevant material, the prosecutor must take reasonable steps to obtain it, either informally or making use of the powers contained in the Crime (International Co-operation) Act 2003 and any EU and international conventions. See CPS Guidance 'Obtaining Evidence and Information from Abroad'.

61. There may be cases where a foreign state or a foreign court refuses to make the material available to the investigator or prosecutor. There may be other cases where the foreign state, though willing to show the material to investigators, will not allow the material to be copied or otherwise made available and the courts of the foreign state will not order its provision.

62. It is for these reasons that there is no absolute duty on the prosecutor to disclose relevant material held overseas by entities not subject to the jurisdiction of the courts in England and Wales. However consideration should be given to whether the type of material believed to be held can be provided to the defence.

63. The obligation on the investigator and prosecutor under the CPIA is to take reasonable steps. Where investigators are allowed to examine files of a foreign state but are not allowed to take copies or notes or list the documents held, there is no breach by the prosecution in its duty of disclosure by reason of its failure to obtain such material, provided reasonable steps have been taken to try and obtain the material. Prosecutors have a margin of consideration as to what steps are appropriate in the particular case but prosecutors must be alive to their duties and there may be some circumstances where these duties cannot be met. Whether the prosecutor has taken reasonable steps is for the court to determine in each case if the matter is raised.

64. In these circumstances it is important that the position is clearly set out in writing so that the court and the defence know what the position is. Investigators and prosecutors must record and explain the situation and set out, insofar as they are permitted by the foreign state, such information as they can and the steps they have taken.

Applications for non-disclosure in the public interest

65. The CPIA allows prosecutors to apply to the court for an order to withhold material which would otherwise fall to be disclosed if disclosure would give rise to a real risk of serious prejudice to an important public interest. Before making such an application, prosecutors should aim to disclose as much of the material as they properly can (for example, by giving the defence redacted or edited copies or summaries). Neutral material or material damaging to the defendant need not be disclosed and there is no need to bring it to the attention of the court. Only in truly borderline cases should the prosecution seek a judicial ruling on whether material in its possession should be disclosed.

66. Prior to the hearing, the prosecutor and the prosecution advocate must examine all material which is the subject matter of the application and make any necessary enquiries of the investigator. The investigator must be frank with the prosecutor about the full extent of the sensitive material. Prior to or at the hearing, the court must be provided with full and accurate information about the material

67. The prosecutor (or representative) and/or investigator should attend such applications. Section 16 of the CPIA allows a person claiming to have an interest in the sensitive material to apply to the court for the opportunity to be heard at the application.

68. The principles set out at paragraph 36 of *R v H & C* [2004] 2 Cr. App. R. 10 [2004] UKHL 3 should be applied rigorously, firstly by the prosecutor and then by the court considering the material. It is essential that these principles are scrupulously adhered to, to ensure that the procedure for examination of material in the absence of the accused is compliant with Article 6.

69. If prosecutors conclude that a fair trial cannot take place because material which satisfies the test for disclosure cannot be disclosed, and that this cannot be remedied by the above procedure; how the case is presented; or by any other means, they should not continue with the case.

Other disclosure

70. Disclosure of any material that is made outside the ambit of CPIA will attract confidentiality by virtue of *Taylor v SFO* [1999] 2 AC 177.

Material relevant to sentence

71. In all cases the prosecutor must consider disclosing in the interests of justice any material which is relevant to sentence (e.g. information which might mitigate the seriousness of the offence or assist the accused to lay blame in part upon a co-accused or another person).

Post-conviction

72. Where, after the conclusion of the proceedings, material comes to light, that might cast doubt upon the safety of the conviction, the prosecutor must consider disclosure of such material.

Applicability of these Guidelines

73. These Guidelines shall have immediate effect.

ANNEX: ATTORNEY-GENERAL'S GUIDELINES ON DISCLOSURE: SUPPLEMENTARY GUIDELINES ON DIGITALLY STORED MATERIAL (2011)

A1. The Guidelines are intended to supplement the Attorney General's Guidelines on Disclosure.

A2. As a result of the number of cases now involving digitally stored material and the scale of the digital material that may be involved, more detailed guidance is considered to be needed. The objective of these Guidelines is to set out how material satisfying the tests for disclosure can best be identified and disclosed to the defence without imposing unrealistic or disproportionate demands on the investigator and prosecutor.

A3. The approach set out in these Guidelines is in line with existing best practice, in that:

   a. Investigating and prosecuting agencies, especially in large and complex cases, will apply their respective case management and disclosure strategies and policies and be transparent with the defence and the courts about how the prosecution has approached complying with its disclosure obligations in the context of the individual case; and

   b. The defence will be expected to play their part in defining the real issues in the case. In this context, the defence will be invited to participate in defining the scope of the reasonable searches that may be made of digitally stored material by the investigator to identify material that might reasonably be expected to undermine the prosecution case or assist the defence.

A4. Only if this approach is followed can the courts be in a position to use their case management powers effectively and to determine applications for disclosure fairly.

A5. The Attorney General's Guidelines are not detailed operational guidelines. They are intended to set out a common approach to be adopted in the context of digitally stored material.

Types of digital material

A6. Digital material falls into two categories: the first category is material which is created natively within an electronic environment (e.g. email, office files, system files, digital photographs, audio etc.); the second category is material which has been digitised from an analogue form (e.g. scanned copy of a document, scanned photograph, a faxed document). Irrespective of the way in which technology changes, the categorisation of digital material will remain the same.

A7. Digital material is usually held on one of the three types of media. Optical media (e.g. CD, DVD, Blu-ray) and Solid-State media (e.g. removable memory cards, solid state music players or mobile devices etc.) cater for usually lower volume storage. Magnetic media (e.g. disk drives and back up tapes) usually cater for the high volume storage.

General principles for investigators

A8. The general principles[1] to be followed by investigators in handling and examining digital material are:

   a. No action taken by investigators or their agents should change data held on a computer or storage media which may subsequently be relied upon in court;

   b. In circumstances where a person finds it necessary to access original data held on computer or storage media, that person must be competent to do so and be able to give evidence explaining the relevance and implications of their actions;

   c. An audit trail or other record of all processes applied to computer-based electronic evidence should be created and preserved. An independent third party should be able to examine those processes (see further the section headed Record keeping and Scheduling below); and

   d. The person in charge of the investigation has overall responsibility for ensuring that the law and these principles are followed.

---

[1] Based on: Association of Chief Police Officers: Good Practice Guide for Computer Based Electronic Evidence version 0.1.4.

A9. Where an investigator has reasonable grounds for believing that digital material may contain material subject to legal professional privilege, very strong legal constraints apply. No digital material may be seized which an investigator has reasonable grounds for believing to be subject to legal privilege, other than where the provisions of the Criminal Justice and Police Act 2001 apply. Strict controls need to be applied where privileged material is seized. See the more detailed section on Legal Professional Privilege starting at paragraph A28 below.

Seizure, relevance and retention

A10. The legal obligations are to be found in a combination of the Police and Criminal Evidence Act 1984 (PACE), the Criminal Justice and Police Act 2001 (CJPA 2001) and the Criminal Procedure and Investigations Act 1996 (the CPIA 1996).

A11. These Guidelines also apply to digital material seized or imaged under other statutory provisions. For example, the Serious Fraud Office has distinct powers of seizure under warrant obtained under section 2(4) of the Criminal Justice Act 1987. In cases concerning indecent images of children and obscene material, special provisions apply to the handling, storage and copying of such material. Practitioners should refer to specific guidance on the application of those provisions.

Seizure

A12. Before searching a suspect's premises where digital evidence is likely to be found, consideration must be given to what sort of evidence is likely to be found and in what volume, whether it is likely to be possible to view and copy, if relevant, the material at the location (it is not uncommon with the advent of cloud computing for digital material to be hosted by a third party) and to what should be seized. Business and commercial premises will often have very substantial amounts of digital material stored on computers and other media. Investigators will need to consider the practicalities of seizing computer hard drives and other media, the effect this may have on the business and, where it is not feasible to obtain an image of digital material, the likely timescale for returning seized items.

A13. In deciding whether to seize and retain digital material it is important that the investigator either complies with the procedure under the relevant statutory authority, relying either on statutory powers or a search warrant, or obtains the owner's consent. In particular, investigators need to be aware of the strong constraints applying to legally privileged material.

A14. A computer hard drive or single item of media, such as a back up tape, is a single storage entity. This means that if any digital material found on the hard drive or other media can lawfully be seized the computer hard drive or single item of media may, if appropriate, be seized or imaged. In some circumstances investigators may wish to image specific folders, files or categories of data where it is feasible to do so without seizing the hard drive or other media, or instead of taking an image of all data on the hard drive or other media. In practice, the configuration of most systems means that data may be contained across a number of hard drives and more than one hard drive or item of media may be required in order to access the information sought.

A15. Digital material must not be seized if an investigator has reasonable grounds for believing it is subject to legal professional privilege, *other than where* sections 50 or 51 of the Criminal Justice and Police Act 2001 apply. If such material is seized it must be isolated from other seized material and any other investigation material in the possession of the investigating authority.

The Police and Criminal Evidence Act 1984

A16. PACE 1984 provides powers to seize and retain anything for which the search has been authorised or after arrest, other than items attracting legal professional privilege.[2] In addition, there is a general power to seize anything which is on the premises if there are reasonable grounds to believe that it has been obtained in the commission of an offence, or that it is evidence and that it is necessary to seize it to prevent it being concealed, lost, altered or destroyed.[3] There is another related power to require information which is stored in any electronic form and is accessible from the premises to be produced in a form in which it can be taken away and in which it is visible and legible or from which it can readily be produced in a visible and legible form.[4]

A17. An image (a forensically sound copy) of the digital material may be taken at the location of the search. Where the investigator makes an image of the digital material at the location, the original need not be seized. Alternatively, when originals are taken, investigators must be prepared to copy

---

[2] By warrant under section 8 and Schedule 1 and section 18 of PACE.
[3] Section 19 of PACE.
[4] Section 20 of PACE.

or image the material for the owners when reasonably practicable in accordance with PACE 1984 Code B 7.17.

A18. Where it is not possible or reasonably practicable to image the computer or hard drive, it will need to be removed from the location or premises for examination elsewhere. This allows the investigator to seize and sift material for the purpose of identifying that which meets the tests for retention in accordance with the 1984 PACE.[5]

The Criminal Justice and Police Act 2001

A19. The additional powers of seizure in sections 50 and 51 of the CJPA 2001 only extend the scope of existing powers of search and seizure under the PACE and other specified statutory authorities[6] where the relevant conditions and circumstances apply.

A20. Investigators must be careful only to exercise powers under the CJPA when it is necessary and not to remove any more material than is justified. The removal of large volumes of material, much of which may not ultimately be retainable, may have serious consequences for the owner of the material, particularly when they are involved in business or other commercial activities.

A21. A written notice must be given to the occupier of the premises where items are seized under sections 50 and 51.[7]

A22. Until material seized under the CJPA 2001 has been examined, it must be kept securely and separately from any material seized under other powers. Any such material must be examined as soon as reasonably practicable to determine which elements may be retained and which should be returned. Regard must be had to the desirability of allowing the person from whom the property was seized—or a person with an interest in the property—an opportunity of being present or represented at the examination.

Retention

A23. Where material is seized under the powers conferred by PACE the duty to retain it under the Code of Practice issued under the CPIA is subject to the provisions on retention under section 22 of PACE. Material seized under sections 50 and 51 of the CJPA 2001 may be retained or returned in accordance with sections 53–58 of that Act.

A24. Retention is limited to evidence and relevant material (as defined in the Code of Practice issued under the CPIA). Where either evidence or relevant material is inextricably linked to non-relevant material which is not reasonably practicable to separate, that material can also be retained. Inextricably linked material is material that is not reasonably practicable to separate from other linked material without prejudicing the use of that other material in any investigation or proceedings.

A25. However, inextricably linked material must not be examined, imaged, copied or used for any purpose other than for providing the source of or the integrity of the linked material.

A26. There are four categories of material that may be retained:
   a. Material that is evidence or potential evidence in the case. Where material is retained for evidential purposes there will be a strong argument that the whole thing (or an authenticated image or copy) should be retained for the purpose of proving provenance and continuity;
   b. Where evidential material has been retained, inextricably linked non-relevant material which is not reasonably practicable to separate can also be retained (PACE Code B paragraph 7);
   c. An investigator should retain material that is relevant to the investigation and required to be scheduled as unused material. This is broader than but includes the duty to retain material which may satisfy the test for prosecution disclosure. The general duty to retain relevant material is set out in the CPIA Code at paragraph 5; or,
   d. Material which is inextricably linked to relevant unused material which of itself may not be relevant material. Such material should be retained (PACE Code B paragraph 7).

A27. The balance of any digital material should be returned in accordance with sections 53–55 of the CJPA 2001 if seized under that Act.

Legal Professional Privilege (LPP)

A28. No digital material may be seized which an investigator has reasonable grounds for believing to be subject to LLP, other than under the additional powers of seizure in the CJPA 2001.

---

[5] Special provisions exist for the investigations conducted by Her Majesty's Revenue and Customs in the application of their powers under PACE—see section 114(2)(b)—and the CJPA 2001.
[6] Schedule 1 of the CJPA 2001.
[7] Section 52 of the CJPA 2001.

A29. The CJPA 2001 enables an investigator to seize relevant items which contain LPP material where it is not reasonably practicable on the search premises to separate LPP material from non-LPP material.

A30. Where LPP material or material suspected of containing LPP is seized it must be isolated from the other material which has been seized in the investigation. The mechanics of securing property vary according to the circumstances; 'bagging up', i.e. placing materials in sealed bags or containers, and strict subsequent control of access, is the appropriate procedure in many cases.

A31. Where material has been identified as potentially containing LPP it must be reviewed by a lawyer independent of the prosecuting authority. No member of the investigative or prosecution team involved in either the current investigation or, if the LPP material relates to other criminal proceedings, in those proceedings should have sight of or access to the LPP material.

A32. If the material is voluminous, search terms or other filters may have to be used to identify the LPP material. If so this will also have to be done by someone independent and not connected with the investigation.

A33. It is essential that anyone dealing with LPP material maintains proper records showing the way in which the material has been handled and those who have had access to it as well as decisions taken in relation to that material.

A34. LPP material can only be retained in specific circumstances in accordance with section 54 of the CJPA 2001 i.e. where the property which comprises the LPP material has been lawfully seized and it is not reasonably practicable for the item to be separated from the rest of the property without prejudicing the use of the rest of the property. LPP material which cannot be retained must be returned as soon as practicable after the seizure without waiting for the whole examination of the seized material.

Excluded and special procedure material

A35. Similar principles to those that apply to LPP material apply to excluded or special procedure material, as set out in section 55 of the CJPA 2001.[8]

Encryption

A36. Part III of the Regulation of Investigatory Powers Act 2000 (RIPA) and the Investigation of Protected Electronic Information Code of Practice govern encryption. See the CPS's Guidance RIPA Part III.

A37. RIPA enables specified law enforcement agencies to compel individuals or companies to provide passwords or encryption keys for the purpose of rendering protected material readable. Failure to comply with RIPA Part III orders is a criminal offence. The Code of Practice provides guidance when exercising powers under RIPA, to require disclosure of protected electronic data in an intelligible form or to acquire the means by which protected electronic data may be accessed or put in an intelligible form.

Sifting/examination

A38. In complying with its duty of disclosure, the prosecution should follow the procedure as outlined below.

A39. Where digital material is examined, the extent and manner of inspecting, viewing or listening will depend on the nature of the material and its form.

A40. It is important for investigators and prosecutors to remember that the duty under the CPIA Code of Practice is to 'pursue all reasonable lines of enquiry including those that point away from the suspect'. Lines of enquiry, of whatever kind, should be pursued only if they are reasonable in the context of the individual case. It is not the duty of the prosecution to comb through all the material in its possession—e.g. every word or byte of computer material—on the look out for anything which might conceivably or speculatively assist the defence. The duty of the prosecution is to disclose material which might reasonably be considered capable of undermining its case or assisting the case for the accused which they become aware of, or to which their attention is drawn.

A41. In some cases the sift may be conducted by an investigator/disclosure officer manually assessing the content of the computer or other digital material from its directory and determining which files are relevant and should be retained for evidence or unused material.

A42. In other cases such an approach may not be feasible. Where there is an enormous volume of material it is perfectly proper for the investigator/disclosure officer to search it by sample, key words, or other appropriate search tools or analytical techniques to locate relevant passages, phrases and identifiers.

---

[8] Special provision exists for investigations conducted by Her Majesty's Revenue and Customs in the application of the powers under PACE—see section 114(2)(b)—and the CJPA 2001.

A43. In cases involving very large quantities of data, the person in charge of the investigation will develop a strategy setting out how the material should be analysed or searched to identify categories of data. Where search tools are used to examine digital material it will usually be appropriate to provide the accused and his or her legal representative with a copy of reasonable search terms used, or to be used, and invite them to suggest any further reasonable search terms. If search terms are suggested which the investigator or prosecutor believes will not be productive—for example because of the use of common words that are likely to identify a mass of irrelevant material, the investigator or prosecutor is entitled to open a dialogue with the defence representative with a view to agreeing sensible refinements. The purpose of this dialogue is to ensure that reasonable and proportionate searches can be carried out.

A44. It may be necessary to carry out sampling and searches on more than one occasion, especially as there is a duty on the prosecutor to keep duties of disclosure under review. To comply with this duty it may be appropriate (and should be considered) where further evidence or unused material is obtained in the course of the investigation; the defence statement is served on the prosecutor; the defendant makes an application under section 8 of the CPIA for disclosure; or the defendant requests that further sampling or searches be carried out (provided it is a reasonable line of enquiry).

Record keeping

A45. A record or log must be made of all digital material seized or imaged and subsequently retained as relevant to the investigation.

A46. In cases involving very large quantities of data where the person in charge of the investigation has developed a strategy setting out how the material should be analysed or searched to identify categories of data, a record should be made of the strategy and the analytical techniques used to search the data. The record should include details of the person who has carried out the process and the date and time it was carried out. In such cases the strategy should record the reasons why certain categories have been searched for (such as names, companies, dates etc.).

A47. In any case it is important that any searching or analytical processing of digital material, as well as the data identified by that process, is properly recorded. *So far as practicable*, what is required is a record of the terms of the searches or processing that has been carried out. This means that in principle the following details may be recorded:

a. A record of all searches carried out, including the date of each search and the person(s) who conducted it;

b. A record of all search words or terms used on each search. However where it is impracticable to record each word or terms (such as where Boolean searches or search strings or conceptual searches are used) it will usually be sufficient to record each broad category of search;

c. A log of the key judgements made while refining the search strategy in the light of what is found, or deciding not to carry out further searches; and,

d. Where material relating to a 'hit' is not examined, the decision not to examine should be explained in the record of examination or in a statement. For instance, a large number of 'hits' may be obtained in relation to a particular search word or term, but material relating to the 'hits' is not examined because they do not appear to be relevant to the investigation. Any subsequent refinement of the search terms and further hits should also be noted and explained as above.

A48. Just as it is not necessary for the investigator or prosecutor to produce records of every search made of hard copy material, it is not necessary to produce records of what may be many hundreds of searches or analyses that have been carried out on digitally stored material, simply to demonstrate that these have been done. It should be sufficient for the prosecution to explain how the disclosure exercise has been approached and to give the accused or suspect's legal representative an opportunity to participate in defining the reasonable searches to be made, as described in the section on sifting/examination.

Scheduling

A49. The disclosure officer should ensure that scheduling of relevant material is carried out in accordance with the CPIA Code of Practice. This requires each item of unused material to be listed separately on the unused material schedule and numbered consecutively. The description of each item should make clear the nature of the item and should contain sufficient detail to enable the prosecutor to decide whether he needs to inspect the material before deciding whether or not it should be disclosed (see paragraph A24).

A50. In some enquiries it may not be practicable to list each item of material separately. If so, these may be listed in a block and described by quantity and generic title. Even if the material is listed in a block, the search terms used and any items of material which might satisfy the disclosure test are listed and described separately. In practical terms this will mean, where appropriate, cross referencing the schedules to your disclosure management document.

A51. The remainder of any computer hard drive/media containing material which is not responsive to search terms or other analytical technique or not identified by any 'hits', and material identified by 'hits' but not examined, is unused material and should be recorded (if appropriate by a generic description) and retained.

A52. Where continuation sheets of the unused material schedule are used, or additional schedules are sent subsequently, the item numbering must be, where possible, sequential to all other items on earlier schedules.

Third party material

A53. Third party material is material held by a person, organisation, or government department other than the investigator and prosecutor within the UK or outside the UK.

Within the UK

A54. The CPIA Code and the AG's Guidelines makes clear the obligation on the prosecution to pursue all reasonable lines of enquiry in relation to material held by third parties within the UK.

A55. If as a result of the duty to pursue all reasonable lines of enquiry, the investigator or prosecutor obtains or receives the material from the third party, then it must be dealt with in accordance with the CPIA i.e. the prosecutor must disclose material if it meets the disclosure tests, subject to any public interest immunity claim. The person who has an interest in the material (the third party) may make representations to the court concerning public interest immunity (see section 16 of the CPIA 1996).

A56. Material not in the possession of an investigator or prosecutor falls outside the CPIA. In such cases the Attorney General Guidelines on Disclosure prescribe the approach to be taken to disclosure of material held by third parties as does the judicial disclosure protocol.

JUDICIAL PROTOCOL ON THE DISCLOSURE OF UNUSED MATERIAL IN CRIMINAL CASES

Introduction

This protocol is prescribed for use by CPD IV Disclosure 22A: Disclosure of Unused Material. It is applicable in all the criminal courts of England and Wales, including the Crown Court, the Court Martial[1] and the magistrates' courts. It replaces the previous judicial document 'Disclosure: a Protocol for the Control and Management of Unused Material in the Crown Court'[2] and it also replaces section 4 'Disclosure' of the Lord Chief Justice's Protocol on the Control and Management of Heavy Fraud and Other Complex Criminal Cases, dated 22 March 2005.[3]

This protocol is intended to provide a central source of guidance for the judiciary, although that produced by the Attorney General also requires attention.

In summary, this judicial protocol sets out the principles to be applied to, and the importance of, disclosure; the expectations of the court and its role in disclosure, in particular in relation to case management; and the consequences if there is a failure by the prosecution or defence to comply with their obligations.

...

The importance of disclosure for fair trials

1. Disclosure remains one of the most important – as well as one of the most misunderstood and abused – of the procedures relating to criminal trials. Lord Justice Gross' review has re-emphasised the need for all those involved to understand the statutory requirements and to undertake their roles with rigour, in a timely manner.

---

[1] The timetables given here may vary in the Court Martial and reference should be made to the Criminal Procedure and Investigations Act 1996 (Application to the Armed Forces) Order 2009 and to any practice note issued by the Judge Advocate General.

[2] The previous judicial protocol was endorsed by the Court of Appeal in *R v K* [2006] EWCA Crim 724; [2006] 2 All ER 552 (Note); [2006] Crim LR 1012.

[3] This protocol also replaces the Protocol for the Provision of Advance Information, Prosecution Evidence and Disclosure of Unused Material in the Magistrates' Courts, dated 12 May 2006, which was adopted as part of the Stop Delaying Justice initiative.

2. The House of Lords stated in *R v H and C* [2004] UKHL 3; [2004] 2 AC 134; [2004] 2 Cr App R 10:

    > Fairness ordinarily requires that any material held by the prosecution which weakens its case or strengthens that of the defendant, if not relied on as part of its formal case against the defendant, should be disclosed to the defence. Bitter experience has shown that miscarriages of justice may occur where such material is withheld from disclosure. The golden rule is that full disclosure of such material should be made. ([2004] 2 AC 134, at 147)

    The Criminal Cases Review Commission has recently noted that failure to disclose material to the defence to which they were entitled remains the biggest single cause of miscarriages of justice.

3. However, it is also essential that the trial process is not overburdened or diverted by erroneous and inappropriate disclosure of unused prosecution material or by misconceived applications. Although the drafters of the Criminal Procedure and Investigations Act 1996 ('CPIA 1996') cannot have anticipated the vast increase in the amount of electronic material that has been generated in recent years, nevertheless the principles of that Act still hold true. Applications by the parties or decisions by judges based on misconceptions of the law or a general laxity of approach (however well-intentioned) which result in an improper application of the disclosure regime have, time and again, proved unnecessarily costly and have obstructed justice. As Lord Justice Gross noted, the burden of disclosure must not be allowed to render the prosecution of cases impracticable.

4. The overarching principle is that unused prosecution material will fall to be disclosed if, and only if, it satisfies the test for disclosure applicable to the proceedings in question, subject to any overriding public interest considerations. The test for disclosure will depend on the date the criminal investigation in question commenced, as this will determine whether the common law disclosure regime applies, or either of the two disclosure regimes under the CPIA 1996.

5. The test for disclosure under section 3 of the CPIA 1996 as amended will be applicable in nearly every case and all those involved in the process will need to be familiar with it. Material fulfils the test if – but only if – it 'might reasonably be considered capable of undermining the case for the prosecution ... or of assisting the case for the accused.'

6. The disclosure process must be led by the prosecution so as to trigger comprehensive defence engagement, supported by robust judicial case management. Active participation by the court in the disclosure process is a critical means of ensuring that delays and adjournments are avoided, given failures by the parties to comply with their obligations may disrupt and (in some cases) frustrate the course of justice.

Disclosure of unused material in criminal cases

7. The court should keep the timetable for prosecution and defence disclosure under review from the first hearing. Judges should as a matter of course ask the parties to identify the issues in the case, and invite the parties to indicate whether further disclosure is sought, and on what topics. For example, it is not enough for the judge to rely on the content of the PCMH form. Proper completion of the disclosure process is a vital part of case preparation, and it may well affect the progress of the case. The court will expect disclosure to have been considered from the outset; the prosecution and defence advocates need to be aware of any potential problems and substantive difficulties should be explained to the judge; and the parties should propose a sensible timetable. Realism is preferable to optimistic but unachievable deadlines which may dislocate the court schedule and imperil the date of trial. It follows that judges should not impose deadlines for service of the case papers or disclosure until they are confident that the prosecution advocate has taken instructions from the individuals who are best placed to evaluate the work to be undertaken.

8. The advocates – both prosecution and defence – must be kept fully informed throughout the course of the proceedings as to any difficulties which may prevent them from complying with their disclosure obligations. When problems arise or come to light after directions have been given, the advocates should notify the court and the other party (or parties) immediately rather than waiting until the date set by the court for the service of the material is imminent or has passed, and they must provide the court with a suggested timetable in order to resolve the problem. The progress of the disclosure process should be reviewed at every hearing. There remains no basis in practice or law for Counsel to Counsel disclosure.

9. If there is a preliminary hearing the judge should seize the opportunity to impose an early timetable for disclosure and to identify any likely problems including as regards third party material and material that will require an application to the Family Court. In an appropriate case the court should consider holding a Joint Criminal/Care Directions Hearing. See Material held by Third Parties, from paragraph 44 below.

10. For the PCMH to be effective, the defence must have a proper opportunity to review the case papers and consider initial disclosure, with a view to preparing a properly completed defence statement which will inform the judge's conduct of the PCMH, and inform the prosecution of the matters required by sections 5, 6A and 6C of the CPIA. As the Court of Appeal noted in *R v Newell* [2012] EWCA Crim 650; [2012] 2 Cr App R 10, 'a typed defence statement must be provided before the PCMH. If there is no defence statement by the time of the PCMH, then a judge will usually require the trial advocate to see that such a statement is provided and not proceed with the PCMH until that is done. In the ordinary case the trial advocate will be required to do that at the court and the PCMH resumed later in the day to avoid delay'. There may be some instances when there will be a well-founded defence application to extend the 28-day time limit for serving a proper defence statement. In a proper case (but never routinely), it may be appropriate to put the PCMH back by a week or more, to enable an appropriate defence statement to be filed.

11. The defence statement can be admitted into evidence under section 6E(4) of the CPIA 1996. However, information included on the PCMH form (which is primarily an administrative form) will not usually be admitted in evidence when the defence advocate has complied with the letter and the spirit of the Criminal Procedure Rules.[4] Introducing the PCMH form (or part of it) during the trial is likely to be an exceptional event. The status of the trial preparation form in the magistrates' court is somewhat different, as discussed below.

12. The court should not extend time lightly or as a matter of course. If an extension is sought, it ought to be accompanied by an appropriate explanation. For instance, it is not sufficient for the prosecutor merely to say that the investigator has delivered the papers late: the underlying reasons are to be provided to the court. The same applies if the defence statement is delayed. Whichever party is at fault, realistic proposals for service are to be set out.

13. Judges should not allow the prosecution to avoid their statutory responsibility for reviewing the unused material by the expedient of permitting the defence to have access to (or providing the defence with copies of) the material listed in the schedules of non-sensitive unused prosecution material irrespective of whether it satisfies, wholly or in part, the relevant test for disclosure. Additionally, it is for the prosecutor to decide on the manner of disclosure, and it does not have to mirror the form in which the information was originally recorded. Rose LJ gave guidance on case management issues in this context in *R v CPS* (Interlocutory Application under sections 35/36 CPIA) [2005] EWCA Crim 2342. Allowing the defence to inspect items that fulfil the disclosure test is also a valid means of providing disclosure.

14. The larger and more complex the case, the more important it is for the prosecution to adhere to the overarching principle and ensure that sufficient prosecution attention and resources are allocated to the task. Handing the defendant the 'keys to the warehouse' has been the cause of many gross abuses in the past, resulting in considerable expenditure by the defence without any material benefit to the course of justice. The circumstances relating to large and complex cases are outlined below.

15. The court will require the defence to engage and assist in the early identification of the real issues in the case and, particularly in the larger and more complex cases, to contribute to the search terms to be used for, and the parameters of, the review of any electronically held material (which can be very considerable). Any defence criticisms of the prosecution approach to disclosure should be timely and reasoned; there is no place for disclosure 'ambushes' or for late or uninformative defence statements. Admissions should be used so far as possible to narrow the real issues in dispute.

16. A constructive approach to disclosure is a necessary part of professional best practice, for the defence and prosecution. This does not undermine the defendant's legitimate interests, it accords with his or her obligations under the Rules and it ensures that all the relevant material is provided. Delays and failures by the prosecution and the defence are equally damaging to a timely, fair and efficient trial, and judges should be vigilant in preventing and addressing abuses. Accordingly, whenever there are potential failings by either the defence or the prosecution, judges, in exercising appropriate oversight of disclosure, should carefully investigate the suggested default and give timely directions.

17. In the Crown Court, the defence statement is to be served within 28 days of the date when the prosecution complies with its duty of initial disclosure (or purports to do so) and whenever section 5(5) of the CPIA applies to the proceedings, and the defence statement must comply with section 6A of the CPIA. Service of the defence statement is a most important stage in the disclosure process, and timely service is necessary to facilitate proper consideration of the disclosure issues well in advance of the trial date. Judges expect a defence statement to contain a clear and detailed exposition of the issues of fact and law. Defence statements that merely rehearse the suggestion that the defendant is innocent do not comply with the requirements of the CPIA.

---

[4] *R v Newell* [2012] EWCA Crim 650; [2012] 2 Cr App R 10.

18. The prosecutor should consider the defence statement carefully and promptly provide a copy to the disclosure officer, to assist the prosecution in its continuing disclosure obligations. The court expects the Crown to identify any suggested deficiencies in the defence statement, and to draw these to the attention of the defence and the court; in particular in large and complex cases, it will assist the court if this is in writing. Although the prosecution's ability to request, and the court's jurisdiction to give, an adverse inference direction under section 11 of CPIA is not contingent on the prosecution having earlier identified any suggested deficiencies, nevertheless the prosecutor must provide a timely written explanation of its position.

19. Judges should examine the defence statement with care to ensure that it complies with the formalities required by the CPIA. As stated in *R v H and C* (supra) (paragraph 35):

> If material does not weaken the prosecution case or strengthen that of the defendant, there is no requirement to disclose it. For this purpose the parties' respective cases should not be restrictively analysed. But they must be carefully analysed, to ascertain the specific facts the prosecution seek to establish and the specific grounds on which the charges are resisted. The trial process is not well served if the defence are permitted to make general and unspecified allegations and then seek far-reaching disclosure in the hope that material may turn up to make them good. Neutral material or material damaging to the defendant need not be disclosed and should not be brought to the attention of the court.

20. If no defence statement – or an inadequate defence statement – is served within the relevant time limits, the judge should investigate the position. At every PCMH where there is no defence statement, including those where an extension has been given, or the time for filing has not yet expired, the defence should be warned in appropriate terms that pursuant to section 6E(2) of the CPIA an adverse inference may be drawn during the trial, and this result is likely if there is no justification for the deficiency. The fact that a warning has been given should be noted.

21. An adverse inference may be drawn under section 11 of the CPIA if the accused fails to discharge his or her disclosure obligations. Whenever the amended CPIA regime applies, the prosecution may comment on any failure in defence disclosure (except where the failure relates to a point of law) without leave of the court, but counsel should use a measure of judgment as to whether it is wise to embark on cross-examination about such a failure.[5] If the accused is cross-examined about discrepancies between his evidence and his defence statement, or if adverse comment is made, the judge must give appropriate guidance to the jury.[6]

22. In order to secure a fair trial, it is vital that the prosecution is mindful of its continuing duty of disclosure. Once the defence statement has been received, the Crown must review disclosure in the light of the issues identified in the defence statement. In cases of complexity, the following steps are then likely to be necessary:
   (i)   Service by the prosecution of any further material due to the defence following receipt of the defence statement.
   (ii) Any defence request to the prosecution for service of additional specific items. As discussed below, these requests must be justified by reference to the defence statement and they should be submitted on the section 8 form.
   (iii) Prosecution response to the defence request.
   (iv) If the defence considers that disclosable items are still outstanding, a section 8 application should be made using the appropriate form.

23. It follows that all requests by the defence to the prosecution for disclosure should be made on the section 8 application form, even if no hearing is sought in the first instance. Discussion and co-operation between the parties outside of court is encouraged in order to ensure that the court is only asked to issue a ruling when strictly necessary. However, use of the section 8 form will ensure that focussed requests are clearly set out in one place.

24. The judge should set a date as part of the timetabling exercise by which any application under section 8 is to be made, if this appears to be a likely eventuality.

25. The Court will require the section 8 application to be served on the prosecution well in advance of the hearing – indeed, prior to requesting the hearing – to enable the Crown to identify and serve any items that meet the test for disclosure.

26. Service of a defence statement is an essential precondition for an application under section 8, and applications should not be heard or directions for disclosure issued in the absence of a properly completed statement (see Part 22 of the Criminal Procedure Rules). In particular, blanket orders in this

---

[5] *R v Essa* [2009] EWCA Crim 43, paragraph 22.
[6] *R v Hanyes* [2011] EWCA Crim 3281.

context are inconsistent with the statutory framework for disclosure laid down by the CPIA and the decision of the House of Lords in *R v H and C* (supra). It follows that defence requests for disclosure of particular pieces of unused prosecution material which are not referable to any issue in the case identified in the defence statement should be rejected.

27. Judges must ensure that defendants are not prejudiced on account of the failures of their lawyers, and, when necessary, the professions should be reminded that if justice is to be done, and if disclosure is to be dealt with fairly in accordance with the law, a full and careful defence statement and a reasoned approach to section 8 applications are essential. In exploring the adequacy of the defence statement, a judge should always ask what the issues are and upon what matters of fact the defendant intends to rely[7] and on what matters of fact the defendant takes issue.

Listing

28. Sufficient time is necessary for the judge properly to undertake the PCMH, and this is a paramount consideration when listing cases. Unless the court is able to sit early, judges who are part heard on trials are probably not best placed to conduct PCMHs.

29. Cases that raise particularly difficult issues of disclosure should be referred to the Resident Judge for directions (unless a trial judge has been allocated) and, for trials of real complexity, the trial judge should be identified at an early stage, prior to the PCMH if possible. Listing officers, working in consultation with the Resident Judge and, if allocated, the trial judge, should ensure that sufficient time is allowed for judges to prepare and deal with prosecution and defence applications relating to disclosure, particularly in the more complex cases.

Magistrates' Courts (including the Youth Court)

30. The principles relating to disclosure apply equally in the magistrates' courts. It follows that whilst disclosure of unused material in compliance with the statutory test is undoubtedly essential in order to achieve justice, it is critical that summary trials are not delayed or made over-complicated by mis-conceived applications for, or inappropriate disclosure of, prosecution material.

31. Magistrates will rely on their legal advisers for guidance, and the latter should draw the attention of the parties and the court to the statutory provisions and the applicable case law. Cases raising disclo-sure issues of particular complexity should be referred to a District Judge (Magistrates' Courts), if available.

32. Although service of a defence statement is voluntary for summary trials (section 6 CPIA), the defen-dant cannot make an application for specific disclosure under section 8 CPIA, and the court cannot make any orders in this regard, unless a proper defence statement has been provided. It follows that although providing a defence statement is not mandatory, it remains a critical stage in the disclosure process. If disclosure issues are to be raised by the defence, a defence statement must be served well in advance of the trial date. Any section 8 application must be made in strict compliance with the Rules.

33. The case-management forms used in the magistrates' courts fulfil some of the functions of a defence statement, and the prosecution must take into account the information provided as to the defence case when conducting its on-going review of unused material. As the Court of Appeal noted in *R v Newell* (supra), admissions can be made in the Trial Preparation Form and the defence is able to iden-tify the matters that are not in issue. Admissions made in these circumstances may be admissible during the trial. However, other information on the form that does not come within the section relating to admissions should be treated in the same way as the contents of a PCMH form in the Crown Court and it should not generally be introduced as part of the evidence at trial. However, the contents of the Trial Preparation Form do not replace the need to serve a defence statement if the defendant seeks to apply for disclosure under section 8 CPIA.

34. The standard directions require that any defence statement is to be served within 14 days of the date upon which the prosecution has complied with, or purported to comply with, the duty to provide initial disclosure. There may be some instances when there will be a well-founded defence application to extend the 14-day time limit for serving the defence statement. These applications must be made in accordance with the Criminal Procedure Rules, in writing and before the time limit expires.

35. Although CCTV footage frequently causes difficulties, it is to be treated as any other category of unused material and it should only be disclosed if the material meets the appropriate test for disclo-sure under the CPIA. The defence should either be provided with copies of the sections of the CCTV or afforded an opportunity to view them. If the prosecution refuses to disclose CCTV material that the defence considers to be discloseable, the courts should not make standard or general directions

---

7 *R v Rochford* [2010] EWCA Crim 1928; [2011] 1 Cr App R 11.

requiring the prosecutor to disclose material of this kind in the absence of an application under section 8. When potentially relevant CCTV footage is not in the possession of the police, the guidance in relation to third party material will apply, although the police remain under a duty to pursue all reasonable lines of inquiry, including those leading away from a suspect, whether or not defence requests are made.

36. The previous convictions of witnesses and any disciplinary findings against officers in the case are frequently discloseable and care should be taken to disclose them as appropriate. Documents such as crime reports or records of emergency calls should not be provided on a routine basis, for instance as part of a bundle of disclosed documents, irrespective of whether the material satisfies the appropriate test for disclosure. Defence advocates should not request this material in standard or routine correspondence, and instead focussed consideration should be given to the circumstances of the particular case. Unjustified requests for disclosure of material of this kind are routinely made, frequently leading to unnecessary delays and adjournments. The prosecution should always consider whether the request is properly made out.

37. The supervisory role of the courts is critical in this context, and magistrates must guard against granting unnecessary adjournments and issuing unjustified directions.

Large and complex cases in the Crown Court

38. Disclosure is a particular problem with the larger and more complex cases, which require a scrupulous approach by the parties and robust case management by the judiciary. If possible, the trial judge should be identified at the outset.

39. The legal representatives need to fulfil their duties in this context with care and efficiency; they should co-operate with the other party (or parties) and the court; and the judge and the other party (or parties) are to be informed of any difficulties, as soon as they arise. The court should be provided with an up-to date timetable for disclosure whenever there are material changes in this regard. A disclosure-management document, or similar, prepared by the prosecution will be of particular assistance to the court in large and complex cases.

40. Judges should be prepared to give early guidance as to the prosecution's approach to disclosure, thereby ensuring early engagement by the defence.

41. Cases of this nature frequently include large volumes of digitally stored material. The Attorney General's 2011 guidance is of particular relevance and assistance in this context: https://www.gov.uk/government/uploads/system/uploads/attachment_data/file/16239/Attorney_General_s_guidelines_on_disclosure_2011.pdf.

42. Applications for witness anonymity orders require particular attention; as the Court of Appeal noted in *R v Mayers and Others* [2008] EWCA Crim 2989; [2009] 1 Cr App R 30, in making such an application, the prosecution's obligations of disclosure 'go much further than the ordinary duties of disclosure'.

43. If the judge considers that there are reasonable grounds to doubt the good faith of the investigation, he or she will be concerned to see that there has been independent and effective appraisal of the documents contained in the disclosure schedule and that its contents are adequate. In appropriate cases where this issue has arisen and there are grounds which show there is a real issue, consideration should be given to receiving evidence on oath from the senior investigating officer at an early case management hearing.

Material held by Third Parties

44. Where material is held by a third party such as a local authority, a social services department, hospital or business, the investigators and the prosecution may need to make enquiries of the third party, with a view to inspecting the material and assessing whether the relevant test for disclosure is met and determining whether any or all of the material should be retained, recorded and, in due course, disclosed to the accused. If access by the prosecution is granted, the investigators and the prosecution will need to establish whether the custodian of the material intends to raise PII issues, as a result of which the material may have to be placed before the court for a decision. This does not obviate the need for the defence to conduct its own enquiries as appropriate. Speculative enquiries without any proper basis in relation to third party material – whether by the prosecution or the defence – are to be discouraged, and, in appropriate cases, the court will consider making an order for costs where an application is clearly unmeritorious and misconceived.

45. The 2013 Protocol and Good Practice Model on Disclosure of Information in Cases of Alleged Child Abuse and Linked Criminal and Care Directions Hearings has recently been published. It provides a framework and timetable for the police and CPS to obtain discloseable material from local authorities, and for applications to be made to the Family Court. It is applicable to all cases of alleged child

abuse where the child is aged 17 years or under. It is not binding on local authorities, but it does represent best practice and therefore should be consulted in all such cases. Delays in obtaining this type of material have led to unacceptable delays to trials involving particularly vulnerable witnesses and every effort must be made to ensure that all discloseable material is identified at an early stage so that any necessary applications can be made and the defence receive material to which they are entitled in good time.

46. There is no specific procedure for disclosure of material held by third parties in criminal proceedings, although the procedure established under section 2 of the Criminal Procedure (Attendance of Witnesses) Act 1965 or section 97 of the Magistrates' Courts Act 1980 is often used for this purpose. Where the third party in question declines to allow inspection of the material, or requires the prosecution to obtain an order before providing copies, the prosecutor will need to consider whether it is appropriate to obtain a witness summons under either section 2 of the Criminal Procedure (Attendance of Witnesses) Act 1965 or section 97 of the Magistrates' Court Act 1980. Part 28 of the Criminal Procedure Rules and paragraphs 3.5 and 3.6 of the Code of Practice under the CPIA 1996 should be followed.

47. Applications for third party disclosure must identify the documents that are sought and provide full details of why they are discloseable. This is particularly relevant when access is sought to the medical records of those who allege they are victims of crime. It should be appreciated that a duty to assert confidentiality may arise when a third party receives a request for disclosure, or the right to privacy may be claimed under article 8 of the ECHR (see in particular Crim PR Part 28.6). Victims do not waive the confidentiality of their medical records, or their right to privacy under article 8 of the ECHR, by making a complaint against the accused. The court, as a public authority, must ensure that any interference with the right to privacy under article 8 is in accordance with the law, and is necessary in pursuit of a legitimate public interest. General and unspecified requests to trawl through such records should be refused. Confidentiality rests with the subject of the material, not with the authority holding it. The subject is entitled to service of the application and has the right to make representations: Criminal Procedure Rule 22.3 and *R (on the application of B) v Stafford Combined Court* [2006] EWHC 1645 (Admin); [2006] 2 Cr App R 34. The 2013 Protocol and Good Practice Model at paragraph 13 should be followed. It is likely that the judge will need to issue directions when issues of this kind are raised (e.g. whether enquiries with the third party are likely to be appropriate; who is to make the request; what material is to be sought, and from whom; and a timetable should be set).

48. The judge should consider whether to take any steps if a third party fails, or refuses, to comply with a request for disclosure, including suggesting that either of the parties pursue the request and, if necessary, make an application for a witness summons. In these circumstances, the court will need to set an appropriate timetable for compliance with Part 28 of the Rules. Any failure to comply with the timetable must immediately be referred back to the court for further directions, although a hearing will not always be necessary. Generally, it may be appropriate for the defence to pursue requests of this kind when the prosecution, for good reason, decline to do so and the court will need to ensure that this procedure does not delay the trial.

49. There are very limited circumstances in which information relating to Family Court proceedings (e.g. where there have been care proceedings in relation to a child who has complained to the police of mistreatment) may be communicated without a court order: see the Family Procedure Rules 12.73. Reference should be made to the 2013 Protocol and Good Practice Model. In most circumstances, a court order will be required and paragraph 11 of the Protocol which sets out how an application should be made should be followed.

Other Government Departments

50. Material held by other government departments or other Crown agencies will not be prosecution material for the purposes of section 3(2) or section 8(4) of the CPIA if it has not been inspected, recorded and retained during the course of the relevant criminal investigation. The CPIA Code of Practice and the Attorney General's Guidelines on Disclosure, however, impose a duty upon the investigators and the prosecution to pursue all reasonable lines of inquiry and that may involve seeking disclosure from the relevant body.

International matters

51. The obligations of the Crown in relation to relevant third-party material held overseas are as set out in *R v Flook* [2009] EWCA Crim 682; [2010] 1 Cr App R 30: the Crown must pursue reasonable lines of enquiry and if it appears there is relevant material, all reasonable steps must be taken to obtain it, whether formally or otherwise. To a great extent, the success of these enquiries will depend on the laws of the country where the material is held and the facts of the individual case. It needs to be recognised that when the material is held in a country outside of the European Union, the power of the

Crown and the courts of England and Wales to obtain third-party material may well be limited. If informal requests are unsuccessful, the avenues are limited to the Crime (International Co-operation) Act 2003 and any applicable international conventions. It cannot, in any sense, be guaranteed that a request to a foreign government, court or body will produce the material sought. Additionally, some foreign authorities may be prepared to show the material in question to the investigating officers, whilst refusing to allow the material to be copied or otherwise made available.

52. As the Court of Appeal observed in *R v Khyam* [2008] EWCA Crim 1612; [2009] 1 Cr App R (S) 77:

> The prosecuting authorities in this jurisdiction simply cannot compel authorities in a foreign country to acknowledge, let alone comply with, our disclosure principles. ([2008] EWCA Crim 1612, at paragraph 37)

The obligation is therefore to take reasonable steps. Whether the Crown has complied with that obligation is for the courts to judge in each case.

53. It is, therefore, important that the prosecution sets out the position clearly in writing, including any inability to inspect or retrieve any material that potentially ought to be disclosed, along with the steps that have been taken.

Applications for Non-Disclosure in the Public Interest

54. Applications in this context, whenever possible, should be considered by the trial judge. The House of Lords in *R v H and C* (supra) has provided useful guidance as to the proper approach to be applied (paragraph 36):

> When any issue of derogation from the golden rule of full disclosure comes before it, the court must address a series of questions:
>
> (1) What is the material which the prosecution seek to withhold? This must be considered by the court in detail.
>
> (2) Is the material such as may weaken the prosecution case or strengthen that of the defence? If No, disclosure should not be ordered. If Yes, full disclosure should (subject to (3), (4) and (5) below) be ordered.
>
> (3) Is there a real risk of serious prejudice to an important public interest (and, if so, what) if full disclosure of the material is ordered? If No, full disclosure should be ordered.
>
> (4) If the answer to (2) and (3) is Yes, can the defendant's interest be protected without disclosure or disclosure be ordered to an extent or in a way which will give adequate protection to the public interest in question and also afford adequate protection to the interests of the defence? This question requires the court to consider, with specific reference to the material which the prosecution seek to withhold and the facts of the case and the defence as disclosed, whether the prosecution should formally admit what the defence seek to establish or whether disclosure short of full disclosure may be ordered. This may be done in appropriate cases by the preparation of summaries or extracts of evidence, or the provision of documents in an edited or anonymised form, provided the documents supplied are in each instance approved by the judge. In appropriate cases the appointment of special counsel may be a necessary step to ensure that the contentions of the prosecution are tested and the interests of the defendant protected (see para 22 above). In cases of exceptional difficulty the court may require the appointment of special counsel to ensure a correct answer to questions (2) and (3) as well as (4).
>
> (5) Do the measures proposed in answer to (4) represent the minimum derogation necessary to protect the public interest in question? If No, the court should order such greater disclosure as will represent the minimum derogation from the golden rule of full disclosure.
>
> (6) If limited disclosure is ordered pursuant to (4) or (5), may the effect be to render the trial process, viewed as a whole, unfair to the defendant? If Yes, then fuller disclosure should be ordered even if this leads or may lead the prosecution to discontinue the proceedings so as to avoid having to make disclosure.
>
> (7) If the answer to (6) when first given is No, does that remain the correct answer as the trial unfolds, evidence is adduced and the defence advanced?
>
> It is important that the answer to (6) should not be treated as a final, once-and-for-all, answer but as a provisional answer which the court must keep under review. ([2004] 2 AC 134, at 155–156)

55. In this context, the following matters are to be emphasised:

(a) The procedure for making applications to the court is set out in the Criminal Procedure Rules, Part 22;

(b) When the PII application is a Type 1 or Type 2 application, proper notice to the defence is necessary to enable the accused to make focused submissions to the court and the notice should be as specific as the nature of the material allows. It is appreciated that in some cases only the generic nature of the material can be identified. In some wholly exceptional cases (Type 3 cases) it may be justified to give no notice at all. The judge should always ask the prosecution to justify the form of notice (or the decision to give no notice at all).

(c)   The prosecution should be alert to the possibility of disclosing a statement in a redacted form by, for example, simply removing personal details. This may obviate the need for a PII application, unless the redacted material satisfies the test for disclosure.

(d)   Except when the material is very short (for instance only a few sheets), or for reasons of sensitivity, the prosecution should supply securely sealed copies to the judge in advance, together with a short statement explaining the relevance of each document, how it satisfies the disclosure test and why it is suggested that disclosure would result in a real risk of serious prejudice to an important public interest; in undertaking this task, the use of merely formulaic expressions is to be discouraged. In any case of complexity a schedule of the material should be provided, identifying the particular objection to disclosure in relation to each item, and leaving a space for the judge's decision.

(e)   The application, even if held in private or in secret, should be recorded. The judge should give some short statement of reasons; this is often best done document by document as the hearing proceeds.

(f)   The recording, copies of the judge's orders (and any copies of the material retained by the court) should be clearly identified, securely sealed and kept in the court building in a safe or locked cabinet consistent with its security classification, and there should be a proper register of the contents. Arrangements should be made for the return of the material to the prosecution once the case is concluded and the time for an appeal has elapsed.

Conclusion

56.   Historically, disclosure was viewed essentially as being a matter to be resolved between the parties, and the court only became engaged if a particular issue or complaint was raised. That perception is now wholly out of date. The regime established under the Criminal Justice Act 2003 and the Criminal Procedure Rules gives judges the power – indeed, it imposes a duty on the judiciary – actively to manage disclosure in every case. The efficient, effective and timely resolution of these issues is a critical element in meeting the overriding objective of the Criminal Procedure Rules of dealing with cases justly.

NEW PROTOCOL IN CHILD ABUSE CASES

In October 2013, the '2013 Protocol and Good Practice Model: Disclosure of information in cases of alleged child abuse and linked criminal and care directions' was issued, having effect from 1 January 2014. It is of special importance where concurrent criminal care proceedings are taking place. It can be accessed at www.judiciary.gov.uk/publications/protocol-good-practice-model-2013/.

Index

Index

Index

Burden of proof (*Cont.*)
driving without insurance F3.13
driving without licence F3.13
fitness to plead D12.6
insanity defence A3.23, F3.1, F3.8
liquor without a licence,
selling F3.15
negligence A2.16
practicality of making workplace
safe F3.14
standard of proof directions
F3.54
too onerous a duty F3.14
admissibility of evidence F3.55
automatism A1.12, F3.43
corruption F3.54
diminished responsibility B1.18,
F3.8, F3.9
driving while disqualified F3.23
driving without insurance F3.13
driving without licence F3.13
drunkenness F3.44
duress F3.42
eviction, protection from F3.28
evidential burden F3.1, F3.3
alibi F3.45
discharge decided by judge F3.1,
F3.3
drunkenness F3.44
duress F3.42
general rule F3.37–F3.47
jury, issue left to F3.40
mistaken belief in consent F3.46
mixed statements F17.96
non-insane automatism F3.43
provocation F3.38–F3.40
self control, loss of F3.38–F3.40
self-defence F3.41
statutory defences F3.47
facts in issue F1.1
fair hearing, right to a A7.88, F3.3
fitness to plead D12.6
highway, deposits on F3.13
hip-flask defence F3.22
homicide F3.29
Human Rights Act 1998 B1.18,
F3.13
imitation firearms F3.35
insanity defence A3.23, F3.1, F3.8
judge's summing-up and D18.27
juror challenging D13.31
legal burden F3.1, F3.2
borne by accused F3.5, F3.54
borne by prosecution F3.4
corruption F3.54
Criminal Justice Act 1988 F3.21
discharge F3.2
DPP v Barker F3.23
driving while disqualified F3.23
driving without insurance F3.13
driving without licence F3.13
drugs F3.19–F3.20

Drummond F3.22
Edwards F3.15
eviction, protection from F3.28
express statutory exceptions
F3.9–F3.10, F3.54
general rule F3.6–F3.17
highway, deposits on F3.13
hip-flask defence F3.22
homicide F3.29
Human Rights Act 1998 B1.18,
F3.11, F3.13
Hunt F3.16–F3.17
implied statutory exceptions
F3.11–F3.17
driving without insurance
F3.13
driving without licence F3.13
human rights F3.11
liquor without a licence,
selling F3.15
negative averments F3.7, F3.15
practicality of making workplace
safe F3.14
summary trials F3.12
trials on indictment F3.11,
F3.15
insolvency F3.26–F3.27
intimidation F3.30
Johnstone F3.24
L v DPP F3.21
Lambert F3.19–F3.20, F3.36
liquor without a licence,
selling F3.15
Makuwa F3.34
misuse of drugs F3.19–F3.20
negativing presumptions F3.70
negligence A2.16
Nimmo v Alexander Cowans F3.14
regulatory offences F3.36
road traffic offences F3.32
Sheldrake v DPP F3.31–F3.33
standard of proof required F3.2
summary trials F3.12
terrorism F3.33
trade marks F3.24
legitimacy, disproving F3.74
mistaken belief in consent F3.46
mixed statements F17.96
negative averments F3.7, F3.15
negligence A2.16
Newton hearings D20.13, D20.23
offensive weapon possession
and B12.156
presumptions *see* Presumptions
provocation F3.38–F3.40
regulatory offences F3.36
road traffic offences F3.13, F3.23,
F3.32
reverse burden F3.18, F3.36
standard of proof required F3.2
summary trials F3.12
terrorism F3.33

trade marks F3.24
Williams F3.35
Burglary
aggravated burglary *see* Aggravated
burglary
aggravating factors B4.81–B4.82
alternative verdicts B4.79, B4.100
building, meaning of B4.84–B4.85
custodial sentences E5.4–E5.7
definition B4.75
distraction burglary B4.81
domestic burglary B4.80–B4.81,
E5.4–E5.7
dwelling, meaning of B4.84–B4.85
elements common to Theft Act 1968
s. 9(1)(a) and (b) B4.83
entry, meaning of B4.86
explosives, definition of B4.102,
B4.105
firearms, definition of B4.102, B4.103
force by householders, use of A3.56,
A3.64
grievous bodily harm proof B4.91,
B4.95
imitation firearms B4.102, B4.103
indictment B4.78
inhabited vehicles B4.84–B4.85
inhabited vessels B4.84–B4.85
intent, with
conditional intent B4.94
grievous bodily harm, to
inflict B4.91
proof of intent B4.89–B4.94
rape B4.93
stealing B4.90
unlawful damage B4.92
mitigating factors B4.80–B4.82
occupied and unoccupied
houses B4.81
offensive weapons, definition
of B4.102, B4.104
place part of offence D11.55
procedure B4.76–B4.77
professional burglars B4.81–B4.82
ram-raiding B4.82
recent possession doctrine F3.65,
F3.66
records of offender B4.80–B4.82
related offences B4.96
sentencing guidelines B4.80–B4.82
seriousness B4.80–B4.82
standard domestic burglary B4.81
stealing, proof B4.95
trespasser, meaning of entering as
a B4.87–B4.88
vagrancy B4.96
vehicles B4.84–B4.85
vessels B4.84–B4.85
Burial records F16.48–F16.49,
F16.50, F16.52
Business documents, hearsay *see* Hearsay,
business or official documents

Index

Useful References